KU-746-673

CARDIFF
CAERDYDD

ACC. No: 02856372

ASLIB DIRECTORY OF INFORMATION SOURCES IN THE UNITED KINGDOM

DIRECTORY OF INFORMATION SOURCES IN THE UNITED KINGDOM

17th EDITION

LONDON AND NEW YORK

17th edition published 2013
by Routledge
2 Park Square, Milton Park, Abingdon, Oxon, OX14 4RN

Simultaneously published in the USA and Canada by Routledge
711 Third Avenue, New York, NY10017

Routledge is an imprint of the Taylor & Francis Group, an Informa business

First published 1928

ISBN 978-1-85743-664-8
ISSN 1743-8616

Editorial Director: Paul Kelly

Typeset in 8pt Palatino
by AMA DataSet Limited, Preston

Printed and bound in Great Britain by
TJ International Ltd, Padstow, Cornwall

FOREWORD

The 17th edition of the ASLIB DIRECTORY OF INFORMATION SOURCES IN THE UNITED KINGDOM offers the reader a wealth of information sources on a potentially limitless range of topics. The pursuers both of great learning and of niche interests, the great collections, the charitable organisations, the statutory bodies and the campaigning groups are there. As well as an introductory profile of the organisation (when it was founded, sometimes what it used to be called, the purpose it exists for and the subject area which it covers), readers will discover where, when and how they might further their initial enquiry.

The information in the directory can be used in a variety of ways. Where a named institution is sought, the Main Directory offers entries listed alphabetically, by the name of the organisation, while the list of Abbreviations and Acronyms, which follows the Main Directory, can provide a full name for a puzzling acronym. Within these covers the reader will discover not only many organisations which they would fully expect to find here, but also many they would never have imagined the existence of, until they had the need to consult it.

However, the reader who is seeking a source of information on a specific topic may prefer to turn first to the extensive Subject Index which forms the final section of the book. Organisations are grouped there by subject and, in the case of broad topics, under sub-headings.

Most of the information that appears in this directory has been provided by the organisations concerned and we are very grateful to those individuals who have given their time to check and update their entry for the new edition.

January 2013

CONTENTS

Main Directory

1 STOP DATA LIMITED

1 Stop Data House, 46 High Street, Ewell, Surrey, KT17 1RW

Tel: 020 8786 9111
Fax: 020 8786 9115
E-mail: info@1stopdata.com

Enquiries to: Managing Director
Direct e-mail: info@1stopdata.com

Founded: 2001; formerly called Graham and Trotman; formerly called Gale Direct (part of the Gale Group) (year of change 2001); incorporates the former Graham & Whiteside Limited (year of change 2001)

Organisation type and purpose: Service industry, publishing house.
Business and professional information supplier.

Subject coverage: Business, professional, academic.

Publications: Printed, and electronic and video

Publications list: Available in print

Access to staff: Contact by letter, by telephone, by fax, by e-mail and via website
Hours: Mon to Fri, 0900 to 1700

100 BLACK MEN OF LONDON

The Bridge, 12–16 Clerkenwell Road, London, EC1M 5PQ

Tel: 0870 121 4100
E-mail: info@100bmol.org.uk
Website: www.100bmol.org.uk

Founded: 2001

Organisation type and purpose: A non-profit organisation formed by a group of African–Caribbean men who aim to help the youth of their community to achieve their full potential, supported by programmes with an emphasis on mentoring, education, economic development and health and wellbeing.

Links with: 100 Black Men of America Inc.; website: http://www.100blackmen.org

14CHRONO CENTRE

Formal name: The Chrono Centre for Climate, the Environment, and Chronology

Archaeology & Palaeoecology Building, Queen's University of Belfast, Belfast, BT7 1NN

Tel: 028 9097 3974
E-mail: s.hoper@qub.ac.uk
Website: www.chrono.qub.ac.uk

Enquiries to: Laboratory Supervisor

Founded: 1970

Organisation type and purpose: University department or institute.

Subject coverage: past and present climate, environment and societal change

Access to staff: Contact by letter, by telephone and by e-mail
Hours: Mon to Fri, 0915 to 1315

174 TRUST

Duncairn Complex, Duncairn Avenue, Belfast, BT14 6BP, Northern Ireland

Tel: 028 9074 7114
E-mail: reception@174trust.org
Website: www.174trust.org

Founded: 1982

Organisation type and purpose: Registered charity (charity number: XN62669A/AR)
To effect change in North Belfast by social action and community development so that North Belfast would become a place of co-operation, prosperity and hope.

Subject coverage: The 174 Trust is a non-denominational Christian organisation that facilitates a variety of essential community projects in North Belfast. Located in the New Lodge community, the Trust offers opportunities and assistance to people of all ages. The 174 Trust is committed to a process of community development based on building relationships with local people, working together to identify and meet local needs.

Publications: Electronic and video
Order electronic and video publications from: Download from website

Publications list: Available online

Access to staff: Contact by letter and via website

1745 ASSOCIATION

Ferry Cottage, Corran, Ardgour, Fort William, Inverness-shire, PH33 7AA

Tel: 01855 841306
E-mail: c.aikman@btinternet.com
Website: www.1745association.org.uk

Enquiries to: Honorary Secretary

Founded: 1946

Organisation type and purpose: Membership association (membership is by subscription), present number of members: 300, voluntary organisation.

Subject coverage: History of the whole Jacobite Movement from 1688 to 1788, particularly with reference to Scotland; the Risings of 1715 and 1745 and their aftermath.

Publications: Printed

Access to staff: Contact by letter and by telephone
Hours: Mon to Fri, 0900 to 1700

2ND AIR DIVISION MEMORIAL LIBRARY (USAAF)

The Forum, Millennium Plain, Norwich, Norfolk, NR2 1AW

Tel: 01603 774747
Fax: 01603 774749
E-mail: 2admemorial.lib@norfolk.gov.uk
Website: www.2ndair.org.uk

Organisation type and purpose: Library administered by the Board of Governors of the 2nd Air Division Memorial Trust, a UK registered charity, working in consultation with Norfolk County Council Library Authority and the Executive Committee of the 2nd Air Division Association.

Subject coverage: Books, periodicals and film on all aspects of American history, culture and life, and specialised material about the Second World War in the air and about the special relationship between the peoples of the UK (particularly East Anglia) and the USA. The Library does not hold any official military personnel records.

Collection: Archive collection deposited with Norfolk Record Office

Library catalogue: All or part available online

Access to staff: Contact by letter, by telephone, by fax, by e-mail and in person
Hours: Mon to Sat, 0900 to 1700

Access to building: Mon to Sat, 0900 to 1700; closed on bank holidays

3M UNITED KINGDOM PLC (3M)

3M United Kingdom PLC, 3M Centre, Cain Road, Bracknell, RG12 8HT

Tel: 01344 858000
Fax: 01344 858278
Website: www.3M.com

Enquiries to: Business Intelligence Manager
Direct tel: 08705 360036

Founded: 1902

Organisation type and purpose: Manufacturing Industry

Subject coverage: Manufacture and marketing of adhesives, adhesive tape, medical products, coated abrasives, reflective products, electrical products, fluorochemicals, reinforced plastics, static eliminators, film cleaners, traffic control, and decorative and recreational products.

Part of: Minnesota Mining and Manufacturing Company; USA

4CHILDREN

City Reach, 5 Greenwich View Place, London, E14 9NN

Tel: 020 7512 2112
Fax: 020 7512 2010
E-mail: info@4Children.org.uk
Website: www.4Children.org.uk

History of institution: re-launched (year of change 2004)

Organisation type and purpose: A national charity (registered charity number 288285) all about children and families.

Subject coverage: Works with government, local authorities, children's service providers, and children and parents to ensure joined-up support for all children and young people aged 0–19 in their local community.
4Children is at the forefront of delivery and supporting innovative children's services, ensuring that all children and families get the support they need in their community, from children's centres to extended schools, childcare to play provision, parenting support to support for young people.
Provides information and support to parents through its dedicated Information Helpline and publications. Also works with employers to highlight the many ways that they can help parents to balance work and family responsibilities.

continued overleaf

Offers authoritative advice and strategic support to help turn policy into practice working with government departments such as the Treasury, Department for Children, Schools and Families, and Department of Health. The organisation has also supported over 100 local authorities to deliver childcare and develop children's and young people's plans, etc.

Information services: Helpline: 020 7512 2100

Library catalogue: All or part available online

Publications: Electronic and video
Order electronic and video publications from: 4Children by post, telephone, fax, or e-mail

Publications list: Available online

Access to staff: Contact by letter, by telephone, by fax and by e-mail

AAA-NORCAP

Formal name: Adults Affected by Adoption-NORCAP

112 Church Road, Wheatley, Oxfordshire, OX33 1LU

Tel: 01865 875000
Fax: 01865 875686
E-mail: enquiries@norcap.org
Website: www.adultsaffectedbyadoption-norcap.org.uk

Founded: 1982

Organisation type and purpose: Adoption support agency (Ofsted reg. no. 67018), registered charity (charity number 1063428).

Subject coverage: Advice on searching for those within the adoption triangle. Research service and intermediary service.

Collection: Microfiche of births, marriages and deaths for England and Wales 1904–1999

Publications: Printed
Order printed publications from: AAA-NORCAP

Access to staff: Contact by letter, by telephone, by fax, by e-mail and via website. Appointment necessary.
Hours: Mon to Fri, 0930 to 1300 and 1330 to 1600

Access to building: Prior appointment required

Access for disabled people: Level entry, access to all public areas

ABBEYFIELD SOCIETY (Abbeyfield)

53 Victoria Street, St Albans, Hertfordshire, AL1 3UW

Tel: 01727 857536
Fax: 01727 846168
E-mail: post@abbeyfield.com
Website: www.abbeyfield.com

Enquiries to: Public Relations
Direct tel: 01727 734091
Direct e-mail: j.burder@abbeyfield.com

Founded: 1956

Organisation type and purpose: To provide housing and innovative services for older people across the UK in 750 sheltered houses and 80 care homes.

Subject coverage: Legal and financial information for starting and running Abbeyfield societies and houses, including housing for older and frail older people.

Collection: Books, journal articles, photographs

Trade and statistical information: The Abbeyfield Profile (latest statistics)

Library catalogue: All or part available in-house

Publications: Printed

Publications list: Available in print

Access to staff: Contact by letter, by telephone, by fax, by e-mail and via website. Appointment necessary. All charged.
Hours: Mon to Fri, 0900 to 1700

Access to building: No prior appointment required

Access for disabled people: Yes

ABC-CLIO

PO Box 1437, Oxford, OX4 9AZ

Tel: 01844 238448
E-mail: salesinternational@abc-clio.com
Website: www.abc-clio.com/international

Enquiries to: International Sales Director

Founded: 1955; formerly called Clio Press Limited

Organisation type and purpose: Publishing house.

Subject coverage: Own publications of general reference in history (World and US) humanities, language arts, library professional development, and general interest.

Library catalogue: All or part available online

Publications: Printed, and electronic and video

Publications list: Available online and in print

Access to staff: Contact by letter, by telephone, by fax, by e-mail and via website
Hours: Mon to Fri, 0900 to 1700

Parent body: ABC-CLIO Inc; 130 Cremona Drive, Suite C, Santa Barbara, CA 93117, USA; tel: +1 805 968 1911; website: www.abc-clio.com

ABERDEEN & GRAMPIAN CHAMBER OF COMMERCE (AGCC)

The Hub, Exploration Drive, Aberdeen Energy Park, Aberdeen, AB23 8GX

Tel: 01224 343900
Fax: 01224 343943
E-mail: info@agcc.co.uk
Website: www.agcc.co.uk

Enquiries to: Policy and Communications Manager
Direct tel: 01224 343913
Direct e-mail: kate.yuill@agcc.co.uk

Founded: 1877; formerly called Aberdeen Chamber of Commerce (year of change 2001)

Organisation type and purpose: Membership association (membership is by subscription), present number of members: 1200.

Trade and statistical information: Aberdeen & Grampian Chamber of Commerce Oil and Survey Series
North-east Third Sector Survey 2012
North-east Energy Sector Survey 2011
North-east Tourism Sector Survey 2011
North-east Food & Drink Sector Survey 2011
British Chambers of Commerce Workforce Survey 2011 – AGCC Report

Publications: Printed

Publications list: Available online

Access to staff: Contact by letter, by telephone, by fax, by e-mail, in person and via website. Appointment necessary.
Hours: Mon to Fri, 0900 to 1700

Access to building: Link for directions: www.agcc.co.uk/contact-us

ABERDEEN AND NORTH EAST SCOTLAND FAMILY HISTORY SOCIETY (ANESFHS)

The Family History Research Centre, 158–164 King Street, Aberdeen, AB24 5BD

Tel: 01224 646323
Fax: 01224 639096
E-mail: enquiries@anesfhs.org.uk
Website: www.anesfhs.org.uk

Founded: 1978

Organisation type and purpose: Membership association (membership is by subscription), present number of members: 5,000, voluntary organisation, registered charity (charity number SCO 12478).

Subject coverage: Genealogy relating to the North East of Scotland, census, parish register information for North East parishes, family history.

Collection: Reference library of books on local and family history
Collection of ancestor charts submitted by members
Historical maps of the area
Parish information
Microfiche of major indexes e.g. All Scotlands OPRs, All Scottish census 1841–1901, IGI, General Register House, Scottish Record Office, BMD for England from 1837, local newspapers
1881 Census (CD-ROM)
Members' research interests
Deryk Cameron Memorial Collection: OPRs and Census (microfilm) for Shetland

Library catalogue: All or part available in-house

Publications: Printed

Publications list: Available online and in print

Access to staff: Contact by letter, by telephone, by e-mail, in person and via website. Non-members charged.
Hours: Mon to Fri, 1000 to 1600; Tue, 1800 to 2100; Sat, 1000 to 1300
Special comments: closed on Local Holidays

Access for disabled people: At no. 160 entrance

Member organisation of: Aberdeen and Grampian Tourist Board; Exchange House, 26–28 Exchange Street, Aberdeen, AB11 6PH; tel: 01224 288828; fax: 01224 288838; e-mail: aberdeen.information@visitscotland.com; website: www.visitscotland.com
Scottish Association of Family History Societies; website: www.safhs.org.uk

ABERDEEN ANGUS CATTLE SOCIETY

Pedigree House, 6 King's Place, Perth, Tayside, PH2 8AD

Tel: 01738 622477
Fax: 01738 636436
E-mail: info@aberdeen-angus.co.uk
Website: www.aberdeen-angus.com

Enquiries to: Chief Executive

Founded: 1879

Organisation type and purpose: Breed Society.

Subject coverage: Pedigree Aberdeen Angus cattle.

Publications: Printed

Access to staff: Contact by telephone, by e-mail and via website
Hours: Mon to Fri, 0900 to 1700

ABERDEEN CITY AND ABERDEENSHIRE ARCHIVES

The Town House, Broad Street, Aberdeen, AB10 1AQ

Tel: 01224 522513 or 01224 481775.
Fax: 01224 522310
E-mail: archives@aberdeencity.gov.uk
Website: www.aberdeencity.gov.uk/archives

Enquiries to: Duty Archivist

Founded: 1980

Organisation type and purpose: Local authority archives service for Aberdeen City and Aberdeenshire Councils.

Subject coverage: Aberdeen City and Aberdeenshire Archives exists to collect and preserve historical records relating to the City of Aberdeen and its locality and to secure significant modern records for future generations.

Information services: Reference library, photocopying/scanning available, e-mail, telephone & postal enquiries, research service, microfilm reader/printer, internet access, laptop facilities, digital photography allowed.

Collection: Aberdeen holds the finest and most complete collection of medieval and early modern burgh records in Scotland, with council minutes dating back to 1398. Also available are various Aberdeenshire burgh records, school records, valuation rolls, poor relief records, electoral registers, and many more.

Non-library collection catalogue: All or part available online and in-house

Library catalogue: All or part available in-house

Publications: Printed, and microform publications

Access to staff: Contact by letter, by telephone, by fax, by e-mail, in person and via website. Appointment necessary.
Hours: Old Aberdeen House: Mon to Wed, 0930 to 1300 and 1400 to 1630
The Town House: Wed to Fri, 0930 to 1630
Special comments: Researchers by prior appointment.

Access to building: Old Aberdeen House is served by a car park. The Town House is served by fee-paying city centre car parks.
Hours: Old Aberdeen House Archive: Mon to Wed, 0930 to 1300 and 1400 to 1630
The Town House Archive: Wed to Fri, 0930 to 1630
Special comments: A visitor badge will be provided by front desk staff.

Access for disabled people: Old Aberdeen House has wheelchair access on the ground floor, but no accessible toilet facilities. The Town House may be inaccessible to larger wheelchairs, but alternative arrangements can be made. Accessible toilet facilities are available.
Hours: Access is available during normal opening hours.

Also at: Aberdeen City and Aberdeenshire Archives – Old Aberdeen House Branch; Old Aberdeen House, Dunbar Street, Aberdeen, AB24 3UJ; tel: 01224 481775; fax: 01224 495830; e-mail: archives@aberdeencity.gov.uk; website: www.aberdeencity.gov.uk/archives

ABERDEEN CITY LIBRARY AND INFORMATION SERVICES (ACL)

Central Library, Rosemount Viaduct, Aberdeen, AB25 1GW

Tel: 01224 522000
Fax: 01224 636811
E-mail: webmonitor@aberdeencity.gov.uk
Website: www.aberdeencity.gov.uk/libraries

Enquiries to: Information Librarian
Direct tel: 01224 652502
Direct fax: 01224 641985
Direct e-mail: informationcentre@aberdeencity.gov.uk

Founded: 1887; formerly called Aberdeen Arts & Recreation Division – Library Services

Organisation type and purpose: Public library.
Business and Technical Dept.

Subject coverage: Public library service covering all subjects including audio-visual lending service. Scottish history, genealogy and tartans.
Specialist business service provides company product information, technical standards, patents and trademarks, and reference and lending services covering all aspects of business management, science and technology.

Collection: British and other technical standards
British, European and US Patents
Cosmo Mitchell Collection on dancing
Collection of company and product directories
George Washington Wilson Collection of photographs
Health and safety data on CD-ROM
Oil and gas collection
Statistics and market research
Walker Collection of music
Patents and Trade Marks

Trade and statistical information: Data on oil and gas explorations including technical standards.
Patent information centre for north of Scotland.
Company and product information relating to UK, Europe, and USA

Library catalogue: All or part available online and in-house

Publications: Electronic and video

Access to staff: Contact by letter, by telephone, by fax, by e-mail and in person. Appointment necessary.
Hours: Mon and Wed, 0900 to 2000; Tue, Thu, Fri and Sat, 0900 to 1700

ABERDEEN COLLEGE

Gallowgate, Aberdeen, AB25 1BN

Tel: 01224 612000 ext 2138
Fax: 01224 612001
E-mail: gallowlib@abcol.ac.uk
Website: www.abcol.ac.uk/library

Enquiries to: Librarian
Direct tel: 01224 612138
Direct e-mail: kapp@abcol.ac.uk

Founded: 1992; formerly called Aberdeen College of Commerce, Aberdeen College of Further Education, Aberdeen Technical College (year of change 1992)

Organisation type and purpose: College of further education.

Subject coverage: Business and commercial, technical, at further education level.
Art, social sciences, catering. Vocational qualifications are available at the College for a wide range of occupations including automotive, hairdressing, professional cookery and construction.

Library catalogue: All or part available in-house

Access to staff: Contact by telephone and by e-mail
Hours: Mon to Thu, 0830 to 2130; Fri, 0830 to 1700; Sat, Sun, 0900 to 1700

Access for disabled people: Parking provided, ramped entry, toilet facilities

ABERDEEN INTERNATIONAL YOUTH FESTIVAL (AIYF)

Custom House, 35 Regent Quay, Aberdeen, AB11 6JR

Tel: 01224 213800
Fax: 01224 213833
E-mail: info@aiyf.org
Website: www.aiyf.org

Enquiries to: Artistic Director
Direct e-mail: stewart@aiyf.org
Other contacts: General Manager

Founded: 1973

continued overleaf

Organisation type and purpose: Registered charity (charity number SCO 14935), suitable for ages: 12 to 25.
Annual international youth arts festival welcoming youth orchestras, choirs, jazz, dance and theatre groups from around the world to take part in a non-competitive festival. Up to 1,000 young participants up to the age of 25 reside at the University, give public performances and experience different cultures and art forms.

Subject coverage: Youth orchestras, choirs, jazz and wind bands, all forms of youth dance groups and theatre companies worldwide. Education: ballet summer school plus Scottish traditional music summer school and opera project.

Publications list: Available online and in print

Access to staff: Contact by letter, by telephone, by fax, by e-mail and via website
Hours: Mon to Fri, 0900 to 1700

Access to building: *Hours:* Mon to Fri, 0900 to 1700

ABERDEENSHIRE LIBRARIES

Meldrum Meg Way, Oldmeldrum, Inverurie, Aberdeenshire, AB51 0GN

Tel: 01651 872707
Fax: 01651 872142
E-mail: alis@aberdeenshire.gov.uk
Website: www.aberdeenshire.gov.uk/libraries

Enquiries to: Principal Libraries Officer

Founded: 1996; formerly called Aberdeenshire Library and Information Service

Organisation type and purpose: Public library, school library service, covers the area of Aberdeenshire.

Subject coverage: Local history, community information, leisure, educational and cultural, open learning through links with colleges.

Information services: Public enquiry service.

Education services: Library service to schools.

Collection: George MacDonald Collection (manuscripts and books)
Strichen Local History Collection (estate papers)

Library catalogue: All or part available online

Publications: Printed, and electronic and video

Access to staff: Contact by letter, by telephone, by fax, by e-mail, in person and via website
Hours: Headquarters: Mon to Fri, 0900 to 1700; Sat, 0900 to 1630.
Special comments: Opening hours in branches vary.

Constituent part of: Education, Learning and Leisure Service of Aberdeenshire Council

ABERDEENSHIRE MUSEUMS SERVICE

Station Road, Mintlaw, Peterhead, Aberdeenshire, AB42 5EE

Tel: 01771 622807
Fax: 01771 623558
E-mail: museums@aberdeenshire.gov.uk
Website: www.aberdeenshire.gov.uk/museums

Enquiries to: Curatorial Officer, Documentation and Conservation
Direct e-mail: david.bertie@aberdeenshire.gov.uk
Other contacts: Principal Museums & Heritage Officer

Founded: 1996; created by the merger of North East of Scotland Agricultural Heritage Centre (NESAHC), North East of Scotland Museums Service (NESMS) (year of change 1996)

Organisation type and purpose: Local government body, operates 12 museums and visitor centres across Aberdeenshire.

Subject coverage: North-east Scotland local history, geology, archaeology, natural history, fishing, shipping and whaling, Banff silver, numismatics, details of museums in the north-east of Scotland.

Collection: Large photograph collection relating to the north-east of Scotland
Peterhead Port Books
Some Peterhead whaling journals, mid-19th century
Some fishing boat records on microfilm
Some Peterhead business records, including Crosse & Blackwell and Cleveland Twist Drill
Some rural trade and farming business records
George Macdonald and Troup Family Archive

Non-library collection catalogue: All or part available online

Publications: Printed

Access to staff: Contact by letter, by telephone, by fax and by e-mail. Appointment necessary.
Hours: HQ building, Mintlaw: Mon to Fri, 0900 to 1630.

Access to building: *Hours:* HQ building, Mintlaw: Mon to Fri, 0900 to 1630; also second Saturday of month, 0900 to 1300.

Access for disabled people: *Hours:* HQ building, Mintlaw: Mon to Fri, 0900 to 1630; also second Saturday of month, 0900 to 1300.

Parent body: Aberdeenshire Council; website: www.aberdeenshire.gov.uk

ABERTAY HISTORICAL SOCIETY

c/o Alder Archaeology, 55 South Methven Street, Perth, PH1 5NX

Tel: 01738 622393
Fax: 01738 631626
E-mail: csmith@alderarchaeology.co.uk
Website: www.abertay.org.uk

Enquiries to: Honorary Sales Secretary

Founded: 1947

Organisation type and purpose: Membership association (membership is by subscription), present number of members: 150, voluntary organisation, registered charity (number SC008207).

Subject coverage: History of Dundee, Tayside and Fife.

Library catalogue: All or part available online and in print

Publications: Printed
Order printed publications from: The Sales Secretary; e-mail: csmith@alderarchaeology.co.uk

Publications list: Available online and in print

Access to staff: Contact by letter, by telephone, by fax, by e-mail and via website
Hours: Mon to Fri, 0900 to 1700

ABERYSTWYTH LIBRARY

Corporation Street, Aberystwyth, Ceredigion, SY23 2BU

Tel: 01970 633703
Fax: 01970 625059
E-mail: llyfrgell.library@ceredigion.gov.uk
Website: www.ceredigion.gov.uk/libraries

Enquiries to: Librarian
Direct tel: 01970 633713
Direct e-mail: williamh@ceredigion.gov.uk

Organisation type and purpose: Public library.

Subject coverage: Welsh local history (Ceredigion); Welsh language publications; Welsh literature.

Collection: Local history

Library catalogue: All or part available online and in-house

Access to staff: Contact by letter, by telephone, by fax, by e-mail and in person
Hours: Mon to Fri, 0900 to 1700

Access to building: No access other than to staff

Also at: Ceredigion County Council; Bibliographical Department

Branch libraries: Aberaeron Library; County Hall, Aberaeron, Ceredigion, SA46 0AT; tel: 01545 570382; e-mail: aeronllb@ceredigion.gov.uk; Cardigan Library; Cardigan, Ceredigion, SA43 1JL; tel: 01239 612578; fax: 01239 612285; e-mail: teifillb@ceredigion.gov.uk; Lampeter Library; Market Street, Lampeter, Ceredigion, SA48 7DR; tel: 01570 423606; e-mail: pedrllb@ceredigion.gov.uk; Llandysul Library; Llandysul, Ceredigion, SA44 4QS; tel: 01559 362899; e-mail: tysulllb@ceredigion.gov.uk; New Quay Library; Church Street, New Quay, Ceredigion; Tregaron Library; Secondary School, Tregaron, Ceredigion, SY25 6HG; tel: 01974 298009; e-mail: caronllb@ceredigion.gov.uk

ABERYSTWYTH UNIVERSITY – HUGH OWEN LIBRARY

Penglais, Aberystwyth, Ceredigion, SY23 3DZ

Tel: 01970 622400
Fax: 01970 622404

E-mail: is@aber.ac.uk
Website: primo.aber.ac.uk
Website: www.aber.ac.uk

Enquiries to: Director of Information Services

Founded: 1872; formerly called University College of Wales, Aberystwyth (year of change 1994)

Organisation type and purpose: University library.

Subject coverage: Accounting and business studies, economics, applied plant biology, genetics and plant breeding, botany, zoology, physical geography including meteorology, biochemistry, biometry, biology, microbiology, cell and immune biology, physics, mathematics, computer science, business studies, theatre, film and television studies, sports science, English and American literature, European literature/languages (French, Spanish, Italian, German), classical studies, history, visual art, social sciences, education, agriculture and agricultural botany and biochemistry, agricultural economics, law, Celtic studies, Welsh, Irish, Breton, Gaelic, Cornish and Manx, politics, international politics, library and information studies.

Collection: 18th- and 19th-century Legal Texts (microfiche Inter Documentation Zug)
Archive of British Master Potters
British Official Publications and Statistical Collection
British Sessional Papers 1801–1930 (Readex microprint)
British Society of Rheology Collection
Canadian Official Publications. Selective Depository 1979–
Celtic Collection
David De Lloyd papers (original compositions and material on Welsh folksongs)
Diplomatic documents
Duff Collection of pamphlets on classical studies
Early American Imprints from 1639 to 1800 (Readex Microprint)
English Legal Sources (microfiche Inter Documentation Zug)
Gregynog Press Collection
George Powell Collection
J C Hotten publications. (Victorian publisher 1856–1873)
J O Francis archive (prompt copies, etc. of his plays)
Learning materials for Welsh Language schools
Lily Newton papers on water pollution
Richard Ellis papers (relating to Edward Lhuyd)
Rudler Collection of 19th-century geological pamphlets
T F Roberts MSS (UCW during his Principalship, 1891–1919)
Thomas Webster Letters (19th-century British geologists)
Three Centuries of Drama: English section 1500–1800 (Readex Microprint) UN and League of Nations publications
David Davies Memorial Library (international politics)

Trade and statistical information: Statistics Collection, official publications, European documentation, Celtic collection

Non-library collection catalogue: All or part available online and in-house

Library catalogue: All or part available online

Publications: Printed

Access to staff: Contact by letter and by telephone. Appointment necessary. Access for members only. Letter of introduction required.
Special comments: Until 19.30 only during term time.

Access to building: *Hours:* Term time: Mon to Thu, 0830 to 0000; Fri 0830 to 2130; Sat and Sun, 1000 to 1800
Vacations: Mon to Fri, 0830 to 1730

Access for disabled people: *Hours:* Term time: Mon to Fri, 0900 to 2200; Sat, 1200 to 1800; Sun, 1200 to 1800
Vacations: Mon to Fri, 0900 to 1730

Constituent institution of the: University of Wales

ABERYSTWYTH UNIVERSITY – THOMAS PARRY LIBRARY

Llanbadarn Fawr, Aberystwyth, Ceredigion, SY23 3AS

Tel: 01970 622417
Fax: 01970 621868
E-mail: parrylib@aber.ac.uk
Website: edina.ac.uk/landlifeleisure
Website: www.irs.aber.ac.uk

Enquiries to: Site Librarian
Direct e-mail: eet@aber.ac.uk
Other contacts: Rural Studies Librarian for agricultural and rural studies enquiries.

Founded: 1996; formerly called Welsh Institute of Rural Studies Library Aberystwyth; formerly called Information and Library Studies Library, University of Wales Aberystwyth (year of change 1991)

Subject coverage: Librarianship; information science; Welsh librarianship; African librarianship; archives and records management; library buildings, planning; children's literature; physical and historical bibliography; publishing, printing and book trade.
Agriculture as practised in the UK (animal production; crop production; farm management; farm mechanisation); forestry; organic husbandry; rural planning; countryside management and conservation; tourism; equine studies.

Collection: Appleton Collection (Victorian colour printing and publishers binding)
Bibliographical collection (private presses and fine printing)
Children's Collection including Horton Collection of early children's books and ephemera
Library literature (library annual reports and guides)
Press cuttings (librarianship and related subjects)
Simon Collection (Curwen Press and related material)
Welsh Studies Collection
Whittinghams Collection (Chiswick Press)
Agricultural and countryside grant information
Agricultural press notices
Countryside management press notices

Non-library collection catalogue: All or part available in-house

Library catalogue: All or part available online

Publications: Electronic and video

Access to staff: Contact by letter, by telephone, by fax and by e-mail. Appointment necessary.
Hours: Term time: Mon to Thu, 0900 to 2100; Fri, 0900 to 1930; Sat, 1200 to 1800
Vacations: Mon to Fri, 0900 to 1730

Access for disabled people: Ramped entry

Parent body: University of Wales Aberystwyth; Directorate of Information Services

ABILITYNET

PO Box 94, Warwick, CV34 5WS

Tel: 01926 312847/0800 269545
Fax: 01926 407425
E-mail: enquiries@abilitynet.org.uk
Website: www.abilitynet.org.uk

Enquiries to: Information Officer

History of institution: formerly called Foundation for Communication for the Disabled, The Computability Centre

Organisation type and purpose: Registered charity (charity number 1067673), consultancy.
Providing information on making computers accessible for people with disabilities.

Subject coverage: Computer access for people with disabilities.

Publications: Printed

Access to staff: Contact by letter, by telephone, by fax, by e-mail, in person and via website
Hours: Mon to Fri, 0900 to 1700

ABINGDON AND WITNEY COLLEGE

Witney Campus, Library and Resource Centre, Holloway Road, Witney, Oxfordshire, OX28 6NE

Tel: 01993 208010
Fax: 01993 703464
E-mail: enquiries@abingdon-witney.ac.uk
Website: www.abingdon-witney.ac.uk

Enquiries to: Librarian

History of institution: formerly called West Oxfordshire College Learning Resources Centre

Organisation type and purpose: Suitable for ages: 16+.
College of further education.

Subject coverage: General further education; stud and stable husbandry; racing industry; Advance Business Solution – Milton Park; Skills Centre at Avenue One – Witney.

Collection: Thoroughbred horse management

Non-library collection catalogue: All or part available in-house

Library catalogue: All or part available in-house

continued overleaf

Access to staff: Contact by letter, by telephone, by fax and in person
Hours: Mon, Tue, Thu, 0830 to 1900; Wed, 0830 to 1700; Fri, 0830 to 1630
Special comments: Non-students, reference only.

Access for disabled people: Parking provided, ramped entry, toilet facilities

Member organisation of: COLRIC; Open University Study Centre

ABORTION RIGHTS

18 Ashwin Street, London, E8 3DL

Tel: 020 7923 9792
E-mail: choice@abortionrights.org.uk
Website: www.abortionrights.org.uk

Enquiries to: Administrator

Founded: 2003; created by the merger of National Abortion Campaign (NAC) and Abortion Law Reform Association (ALRA)

Organisation type and purpose: National organisation, membership association (membership is by subscription), voluntary organisation.
Campaigning for equal access to safe, free abortion on request.

Subject coverage: Abortion in the UK and worldwide; contraception; new reproductive technology; no counselling.

Publications: Printed

Access to staff: Contact by letter, by telephone, by e-mail and via website. Appointment necessary.
Hours: Varies each week

Links with: Voice for Choice; e-mail: vfc@vfc.org.uk; website: www.vfc.org.uk

ABP – PORT OF IPSWICH

Old Custom House, Key Street, Ipswich, Suffolk, IP4 1BY

Tel: 01473 231010
Fax: 01473 230914
E-mail: ipswich@abports.co.uk
Website: www.ABPorts.co.uk

Enquiries to: Sales Manager
Direct fax: 01473 225364

Founded: 1997; formerly called Port of Ipswich; formerly called Ipswich Port Authority (year of change 1997)

Organisation type and purpose: Service industry.

Subject coverage: Port facilities and operation; discharge and loading of containers, roll-on/roll-off, general cargo, bulk solid and bulk liquid vessels.

Publications: Printed

Parent body: Associated British Ports (ABP)

ABP MARINE ENVIRONMENTAL RESEARCH (ABP Research)

Suite B, Waterside House, Town Quay, Southampton, S014 2AQ

Tel: 023 80711 840
Fax: 023 80711 841
E-mail: enquiries@abpmer.co.uk
Website: www.abpmer.co.uk

Enquiries to: Technical Marketing Manager
Other contacts: Library and Information Services

Founded: 1950; formerly called British Transport Docks Board (year of change 1983); formerly called ABP Research and Consultancy Limited (year of change 2002)

Organisation type and purpose: Consultancy, research organisation.
Specialists in water environment consultancy.

Subject coverage: Dock and harbour engineering; rivers, estuaries and coastal research; maritime hydraulics and structures; hydrographic surveying and dredging research; port operations and management.

Collection: Comprehensive library covering all aspects of water environment science and hydraulics research inclusive of over 400 reports and technical guidance notes

Publications: Printed, and electronic and video

Access to staff: Contact by telephone, by fax, by e-mail and via website
Hours: Mon to Fri, 0900 to 1700
Special comments: Library searches will be charged at commercial rates, available on application.

Parent body: Associated British Ports Holdings plc; 150 Holborn, London, EC1N 2LR; tel: 020 7430 1177; fax: 020 7430 1384

AC OWNERS' CLUB LIMITED (ACOC)

Thatch End, Godmanstone, Dorset, DT2 7AQ

Tel: 01300 342058
Fax: 01799 522513
E-mail: rish.morpeth@virgin.net
Website: www.racecar.co.uk/acoc

Enquiries to: Membership Secretary

Founded: 1949

Organisation type and purpose: Membership association (membership is by subscription), present number of members: 700.

Subject coverage: The AC motor car.

Collection: The Club Library contains: documents, publications, etc., concerning AC cars from the early years of the 20th century to date

Library catalogue: All or part available in-house

Publications: Printed

Access to staff: Contact by letter, by telephone and by e-mail
Hours: Mon to Sat, 0900 to 2000

ACADEMY OF ANCIENT MUSIC (AAM)

11b King's Parade, Cambridge, CB2 1SJ

Tel: 01223 301509
E-mail: info@aam.co.uk
Website: www.aam.co.uk

Enquiries to: Concerts & Administration Manager
Direct e-mail: s.martin@aam.co.uk

Founded: 1973

Organisation type and purpose: Registered charity (charity number 1085485).
Period instrument orchestra.

Subject coverage: Performance of classical and baroque music.

Publications: Electronic and video
Order electronic and video publications from: Record shops

Access to staff: Contact by e-mail
Hours: Mon to Fri, 0900 to 1730

ACADEMY OF EXECUTIVES AND ADMINISTRATORS (AEA)

Warwick Corner, 42 Warwick Road, Kenilworth, Warwickshire, CV8 1HE

Tel: 01926 259342
E-mail: info@academyofexecutivesandadministrators.org.uk
Website: www.academyofexecutivesandadministrators.org.uk

Enquiries to: Executive Administrator

Founded: 2002

Organisation type and purpose: Professional body (membership is by subscription, qualification), range of professional diploma courses available.

Publications: Electronic and video

Access to staff: Contact by letter, by telephone, by e-mail and via website

Links with: Faculty of Professional Business and Technical Management; website: www.pbtm.org.uk
Institute of Management Specialists; website: www.instituteofmanagementspecialists.org.uk
Institute of Manufacturing; website: www.instituteofmanufacturing.org.uk
The Academy of Multi-Skills; website: www.academyofmultiskills.org.uk

ACADEMY OF EXPERTS (TAE)

3 Gray's Inn Square, Gray's Inn, London, WC1R 5AH

Tel: 020 7430 0333
Fax: 020 7430 0666
E-mail: admin@academy-experts.org
Website: www.academy-experts.org

Enquiries to: Chief Executive

Founded: 1987

Organisation type and purpose: Professional body (membership is by qualification), consultancy.

Subject coverage: All matters pertaining to experts, especially in contentious matters. Accreditation of practising experts and qualified dispute resolvers. Matters involving alternative dispute resolution (ADR) including training, accreditation and appointments. Cost-efficient dispute resolution, provision of standards for experts, mediators and others.

Collection: Directory of Experts
Register of Qualified Dispute Resolvers

Publications: Printed
Order printed publications from: Website

Access to staff: Contact by letter and by e-mail
Hours: Mon to Fri, 0900 to 1700

Access to building: Prior appointment required

ACADEMY OF MULTI-SKILLS (AMS)

219 Bow Road, London, E3 2SJ

Tel: 0709 201 2910
E-mail: info@academyofmultiskills.org.uk
Website: www.academyofmultiskills.org.uk

Founded: 1995

Organisation type and purpose:
International organisation, professional body (membership is by qualification), training organisation, range of professional diploma courses available.
For all groups and types of people who are multi-skilled. The multi-skilled should register with the academy.

Subject coverage: The principal aim of the Academy is to bring together and help people who have multi-skilled potential, those who wish to lift themselves to higher positions in life by perfecting and securing recognition for their skills. Most people possess more potential than they realise, are already multi-skilled, or have never had their hidden multi-skills recognised. The Academy can help to support and expand their careers.

Access to staff: Contact by letter, by telephone, by e-mail and via website

Links with: Academy of Executives and Administrators (AEA); website: www.academyofexecutivesandadministrators.org.uk
Faculty of Professional Business and Technical Management (FPBTM); website: www.pbtm.org.uk
Institute of Management Specialists (IMS); website: www.instituteofmanagementspecialists.org.uk
The Institute of Manufacturing (IManf); website: www.instituteofmanufacturing.org.uk

ACAS

Formal name: Advisory, Conciliation and Arbitration Service

Information Centre, 22nd Floor, Euston Tower, 286 Euston Road, London, NW1 3JJ

Tel: 08457 38 37 36
E-mail: library@acas.org.uk
Website: www.acas.org.uk

Enquiries to: Senior Information Manager

Founded: 1974

Organisation type and purpose: Statutory body.

Subject coverage: Industrial relations, industrial arbitration and conciliation, trade unions, employee involvement, organisational behaviour, employment law, quality of working life, total quality management, stress, personnel management, management of change.

Information services: Helpline 08457 47 47 47 (Mon to Fri, 0800 to 2000; Sat, 0900 to 1300)

Publications: Printed
Order printed publications from: ACAS Publications, PO Box 235, Hayes, Middlesex, UB3 1HF; tel: 0870 242 9090; fax: 020 8867 3225; e-mail: acas@eclogistics.co.uk

Publications list: Available online and in print

Access to staff: Contact via website. Appointment necessary.
Hours: Mon to Fri, 0900 to 1700

Branches: 11 regional centres

ACCOUNTS COMMISSION FOR SCOTLAND

110 George Street, Edinburgh, EH2 4LH

Tel: 0845 146 1010
E-mail: info@audit-scotland.gov.uk
Website: www.audit-scotland.gov.uk
Website: www.accounts-commission.gov.uk

Enquiries to: Secretary and Business Manager
Direct tel: 0131 625 1809
Other contacts: Audit Scotland Reception; Publications Coordinator

Founded: 1975

Organisation type and purpose: Statutory body.

Subject coverage: The performance of Scottish councils, and police and fire authorities. Audit and value for money review in local government in Scotland.

Library catalogue: All or part available online

Publications: Printed
Order printed publications from: http://www.audit-scotland.gov.uk

Publications list: Available online

Access to staff: Contact by letter, by telephone and by e-mail
Hours: Mon to Fri, 0900 to 1700

ACCRINGTON CENTRAL LIBRARY

St James' Street, Accrington, Lancashire, BB5 1NQ

Tel: 01254 872385
Fax: 01254 301066
E-mail: accrington.library@lancashire.gov.uk
Website: www.lancashire.gov.uk/libraries

Enquiries to: Reference Librarian
Direct tel: 01254 306905

Founded: 1908; formerly called Hyndburn Central Library (year of change 1994)

Organisation type and purpose: Public library.

Subject coverage: Local history of the Hyndburn District of Lancashire, and the county of Lancashire; history of the Accrington Pals (11th Service Battalion, East Lancashire Regiment) in World War I and generally; World War I collection (includes war graves, memorial registers and official histories).

Collection: Commonwealth War Graves Commission Registers for World War I
Richard Broughton collection of books on local history
William Ashworth collection
Accrington and District Historical Association collection
Dowling collection (cinema posters and newspaper cuttings albums concerning the former Accrington Arts Club)
William Turner collection (Accrington Pals)
Lancashire Authors' Association collection

Trade and statistical information: Small area statistics for Hyndburn district of Lancashire. Census figures for Lancashire. General statistics, eg: Annual Abstract of statistics

Non-library collection catalogue: All or part available online

Library catalogue: All or part available online

Publications: Printed

Access to staff: Contact by letter, by telephone, by fax, by e-mail and in person
Hours: Mon and Tue, 0930 to 1930; Wed, 0930 to 1230; Thu and Fri, 0930 to 1700; Sat, 0930 to 1600

Part of: Lancashire County Library & Information Service

ACE CREDIT UNION SERVICES (NFCU)

ACE Credit Union Services, 185 – 189 Shields Road, Byker, Newcastle-Upon-Tyne, NE6 1DP

Tel: 0191 276 3737
Fax: 0191 259 1884

Enquiries to: Chairman
Other contacts: National Co-ordinator

Founded: 1964; formerly called National Federation of Credit Unions

Organisation type and purpose: Advisory body.

Subject coverage: Information, technical advice and training in the registering and operating of credit unions for communities, organisations and employees.

Publications: Printed, and electronic and video

Publications list: Available in print

Access to staff: Contact by letter, by telephone and by fax. Appointment necessary.
Hours: Mon to Fri, 0900 to 1700

ACE STUDY TOURS

Babraham, Cambridge, CB2 4AP

Tel: 01223 835055
Fax: 01223 837394
E-mail: ace@aceculturaltours.co.uk
Website: www.aceculturaltours.co.uk

Enquiries to: Secretary

Founded: 1958; formerly called Association for Cultural Exchange; please select ACE Study Tours

Organisation type and purpose: Service industry.

continued overleaf

Tour operator for educational study tours and courses in England, Europe and worldwide.

Subject coverage: International adult education.

Publications: Printed

Access to staff: Contact by letter, by telephone, by fax and by e-mail
Hours: Mon to Fri, 0900 to 1700

ACEVO

Formal name: Association of Chief Executives of Voluntary Organisations

1 New Oxford Street, London, WC1A 1NU

Tel: 020 7280 4960
Fax: 020 7280 4989
E-mail: info@acevo.org.uk
Website: www.acevo.org.uk

Enquiries to: Receptionist/Publications Officer
Direct e-mail: membership@acevo.org.uk
Other contacts: Head of Policy & Communications for press and policy.

Founded: 1987; formerly called Association of Chief Executives of National Voluntary Organisations (ACENVO)

Organisation type and purpose: Professional body, present number of members: c. 1,800, voluntary organisation, training organisation.
Networking organisation.

Subject coverage: All matters relating to chief executives of voluntary organisations, training, education, legal advice, support, mentoring, twinning, fundraising, helpline.

Library catalogue: All or part available online

Publications: Printed

Publications list: Available online and in print

Access to staff: Contact by letter, by telephone, by fax, by e-mail and via website
Hours: Mon to Fri, 0900 to 1700

ACPPLD

Formal name: Association of Chartered Physiotherapists for People with Learning Disabilities

CIG Liaison Officer, Chartered Society of Physiotherapy, 14 Bedford Row, London, WC1R 4ED

Tel: 020 7306 6611
Website: www.acppld.org.uk

Enquiries to: Chairperson
Direct e-mail: jenny.tinkler@TEWV.nhs.uk

Organisation type and purpose: Professional body (membership is by subscription), present number of members: 250.

Subject coverage: Physiotherapy for people with learning disabilities.

Access to staff: Contact by letter, by telephone and via website. Appointment necessary.
Hours: Mon to Fri, 0900 to 1700

Clinical interest group within the: Chartered Society of Physiotherapy

ACT

Formal name: Association for Children's Palliative Care

Brunswick Court, Brunswick Square, Bristol, BS2 8PE

Tel: 0117 916 6422
Fax: 0117 916 6430
E-mail: info@act.org.uk
Website: www.act.org.uk

Enquiries to: Information and Administration Officer

Founded: 1993

Subject coverage: ACT (Association for Children's Palliative Care) aims to provide information on support services available for families whose children have life-threatening or terminal conditions, regardless of the particular disease involved. It is involved in consultation and contact between service providers and campaigns to encourage the development of children's palliative care services.

Information services: Helpline (tel: 0845 108 2201).

Trade and statistical information: National information service on support services available for families with a child/children with life-limiting or life-threatening conditions

Library catalogue: All or part available online and in-house

Publications: Printed

Publications list: Available online and in print

Access to staff: Contact by letter, by telephone, by fax, by e-mail and via website. Appointment necessary.
Hours: Access to Families/Health Professionals: Mon to Fri, 0900 to 1700

Access to building: Prior appointment required

ACTION AGAINST ALLERGY (AAA)

PO Box 278, Twickenham, Middlesex, TW1 4QQ

Tel: 020 8892 2711/4949
E-mail: aaa@actionagainstallergy.freeserve.co.uk
Website: www.actionagainstallergy.co.uk

Enquiries to: Executive Director

Founded: 1978

Organisation type and purpose: Registered charity (charity number 276637), patient support organisation.
Provides information about allergic illness and related conditions to patients and professionals in the health care field.

Subject coverage: Allergies, allergy-related illness.

Information services: Find-a-Doctor service; wide range of information leaflets concerning allergic illness

Education services: Occasional workshops for parents and professionals

Collection: Information leaflets list available on request with sae

Various papers on different aspects of allergic illness

Publications: Printed
Order printed publications from: Postal address or online.

Publications list: Available online and in print

Access to staff: Contact by letter, by telephone, by e-mail and via website
Hours: Mon to Fri, 0930 to 1700

Access to building: No access other than to staff

ACTION ASTHMA

Allen & Hanburys Limited, Department G, Freepost DR83, Ashford, Kent, TN24 0YX

Tel: 020 8990 3011

Organisation type and purpose: Providing support to asthma sufferers of all ages

Subject coverage: Asthma

Access to staff: Contact by letter
Hours: Mon to Fri, 0900 to 1700

Access to building: No access other than to staff

Access for disabled people: Access to all public areas

Other address: Allen & Hanburys Limited; Stockley Park West, Uxbridge, UB11 1BT; tel: 0181 990 9888; fax: 0181 990 4375

ACTION FOR BLIND PEOPLE

Information & Advice Centre, 14–16 Verney Road, London, SE16 3DZ

Tel: 020 7635 4800; National Freephone Helpline 0303 123 9999
Fax: 020 7635 4900
E-mail: info@actionforblindpeople.org.uk
Website: www.actionforblindpeople.org.uk

Enquiries to: Information Officer

Founded: 1857

Organisation type and purpose: Voluntary organisation, registered charity (charity number 205913).
To provide services for visually impaired people.

Subject coverage: Visual impairment: service provision, general awareness, aids and equipment, accommodation and residential care, leisure and holidays, education, employment and training, welfare rights and grants.

Library catalogue: All or part available in-house

Publications: Printed, and electronic and video

Publications list: Available online and in print

Access to staff: Contact by letter, by telephone, by fax, by e-mail and via website. Appointment necessary.
Hours: Mon to Fri, 0900 to 1700

Access for disabled people: Ramped entry, toilet facilities

ACTION FOR KIDS, CHARITABLE TRUST (AFK)

Ability House, 15A Tottenham Lane, Hornsey, London, N8 9DJ

Tel: 020 8347 8111; minicom no. 020 8347 3486
Fax: 020 8347 3482
E-mail: info@actionforkids.org
Website: www.actionforkids.org

Enquiries to: Information Officer

Founded: 1992

Organisation type and purpose: Registered charity (charity number 1068841).
Provides grants for the provision of mobility aid, provides work experience programmes for disabled young people, assists children and young people suffering physical and mental disability to lead full and independent lives.

Subject coverage: The relief of physical and mental disability – through independence, created by the provision of mobility aids that are not available on the NHS and by supported-into-work learning programmes, both in-house and via outreach, for disabled young people. Equipment provided for those up to age 21; work-related training for those up to age 26.

Publications: Printed, and electronic and video

Access to staff: Contact by letter, by telephone, by fax, by e-mail and via website. Appointment necessary.
Hours: Mon to Fri, 0900 to 1730

Access to building: *Hours:* Mon to Fri, 0900 to 1730

Access for disabled people: Full disabled access and facilities: parking provided, access to all public areas

ACTION FOR ME (AfME)

Formal name: Action for Myalgic Encephalomyelitis

Third Floor, Canningford House, 38 Victoria Street, Bristol, BS1 6BY

Tel: 0845 123 2314 and 0117 927 9551
Fax: 0117 9279552
E-mail: admin@actionforme.org.uk
Website: www.afme.org.uk

Enquiries to: Administrator
Direct e-mail: admin@actionforme.org.uk

Founded: 1987; formerly called ME Action

Organisation type and purpose: National organisation, membership association (membership is by subscription), present number of members: 8,000+, voluntary organisation, registered charity (charity number 1036419).
Over 150 local support groups.
Provides information and support to people with ME and campaigns to government and the medical profession for better understanding and treatment.

Subject coverage: Information on myalgic encephalomyelitis (ME), chronic fatigue syndrome, and post-viral fatigue syndrome.

Library catalogue: All or part available in-house and in print

Publications: Printed
Order printed publications from: Third Floor, Canningford House, 38 Victoria Street, Bristol, BS1

Publications list: Available in print

Access to staff: Contact by letter, by telephone and by e-mail
Hours: Mon to Fri, 0930 to 1700
Special comments: Please telephone initially

Access to building: No access other than to staff

Also at: Action for ME; 73 Watling Street, London, EC4M 9BL; tel: 020 7329 2299; fax: 020 7329 3600; e-mail: london@afme.org.uk

ACTION FOR SOUTHERN AFRICA (ACTSA)

28 Penton Street, London, N1 9SA

Tel: 020 7833 3133
Fax: 020 7837 3001
E-mail: actsa@actsa.org
Website: www.actsa.org

Enquiries to: Office Manager

Founded: 1994; formerly called Anti-Apartheid Movement

Organisation type and purpose: Membership association (membership is by subscription), voluntary organisation. Lobbying support of Southern Africa, campaigning for peace, democracy and development in Southern Africa.

Subject coverage: Peace, democracy and development in Southern Africa, South Africa, Lesotho, Swaziland, Botswana, Namibia, Angola, Zambia, Zimbabwe, Mozambique, Malawi, Tanzania, Mauritius, Democratic Republic of Congo, Seychelles.

Publications: Printed

Publications list: Available online

Access to staff: Contact by letter, by telephone, by fax, by e-mail and via website
Hours: Mon to Fri, 0930 to 1730

Access to building: Prior appointment required

ACTION ON ELDER ABUSE (AEA)

Action on Elder Abuse, PO Box 60001, London, SW16 9BY

Tel: 020 8835 9280
Fax: 020 8696 9328
E-mail: enquiries@elderabuse.org.uk
Website: www.elderabuse.org.uk

Founded: 1993

Organisation type and purpose: International organisation, membership association (membership is by subscription), present number of members: 550, voluntary organisation, registered charity (charity number 1048397).
To prevent the abuse of older people by raising awareness, encouraging education and research, and collecting and disseminating information.

Subject coverage: The abuse of older people by someone in any relationship of trust at home or in care settings.

Information services: Helpline confidential freephone: 080 8808 8141

Non-library collection catalogue: All or part available in-house

Library catalogue: All or part available in-house

Publications: Printed

Publications list: Available online and in print

Access to staff: Contact by letter, by telephone, by fax, by e-mail and via website
Hours: Mon to Fri, 0900 to 1700

ACTION ON PRE-ECLAMPSIA (APEC)

Formal name: Action on Pre-eclampsia

105 High Street, Evesham, Worcs, WR11 4EB

Tel: 01386 761848 (Administration), 020 8427 4217 (Helpline)
E-mail: info@apec.org.uk
Website: www.apec.org.uk

Enquiries to: Chief Executive

Founded: 1991

Organisation type and purpose: Membership association (membership is by subscription), present number of members: 1000, voluntary organisation, registered charity (charity number 1013557).
To prevent or ease suffering from pre-eclampsia by means of enhanced public awareness, increased professional knowledge and skill, and the provision of immediate and continuing support for affected families.

Subject coverage: Pre-eclampsia.

Publications: Printed
Order printed publications from: Can be downloaded from our website or ordered at the above address/telephone number.

Publications list: Available online

Access to staff: Contact by letter, by telephone, by e-mail and via website
Hours: Mon to Fri, 0900 to 1700

Access to building: None

ACTION ON SMOKING AND HEALTH (ASH)

First Floor, 144–145 Shoreditch High Street, London, E1 6JE

Tel: 020 7739 5902
Fax: 0207 729 4732
E-mail: enquiries@ash.org.uk
Website: www.ash.org.uk

Enquiries to: Research Manager

Founded: 1971

Organisation type and purpose: National organisation, voluntary organisation, registered charity (charity number 262067).

Subject coverage: Smoking and its effect on health, tobacco industry, tobacco control activities, statistics on tobacco and smoking, covering the UK and other countries.

Publications: Printed, and electronic and video
Order printed publications from: Online shop on ASH website

continued overleaf

Publications list: Available online and in print

Access to staff: Contact by letter, by telephone, by e-mail and via website
Hours: Mon to Fri, 0900 to 1700
Special comments: No public access to office.

Access to building: No access other than to staff

ACTION WITH COMMUNITIES IN RURAL KENT

15 Manor Road, Folkestone, Kent, CT20 2AH

Tel: 01303 850816
Fax: 01303 850244
E-mail: info@ruralkent.org.uk
Website: www.ruralkent.org.uk

Enquiries to: Director

Founded: 1923

Organisation type and purpose: Membership association (membership is by subscription), present number of members: 400, registered charity (charity number 212796).

Subject coverage: All rural issues.

Publications: Printed

Publications list: Available in print

Access to staff: Contact by letter, by telephone, by fax and by e-mail
Hours: Mon to Fri, 0900 to 1700

Access to building: Prior appointment required

ACTIONAID SCHOOLS

Schools Department, ActionAid, Chataway House, Leach Road, Chard, Somerset TA20 1FR

Tel: 01460 238000
Fax: 01460 67191
E-mail: schools@actionaid.org.uk
Website: www.actionaid.org.uk/schools

Founded: 1972

Organisation type and purpose: ActionAid is an international non-governmental organisation (NGO) that works with and supports the poorest and most vulnerable people around the world.

Subject coverage: The schools team produces award-winning teaching materials, talks and workshops for learners aged 5–19 which explore the links between people and places all over the world.

Publications: Printed, and electronic and video
Order printed publications from: www.actionaid.org.uk/schools-shop
Order electronic and video publications from: www.actionaid.org.uk/schools-shop

Publications list: Available online

Access to staff: Contact by letter, by telephone, by fax, by e-mail and via website
Hours: Mon to Fri, 0900 to 1700

Headquarters address: ActionAid International Head office; Postnet Suite 248, Private Bag X31, Saxonwold 2132, Johannesburg, South Africa; tel: +27 11 7314500; fax: +27 11 8808082; e-mail: mail.jhb@actionaid.org; website: www.actionaid.org

Parent body: ActionAid UK; 33–39 Bowling Green Lane, London, EC1R 0BJ; tel: 020 3122 0561; fax: 020 7278 5667; e-mail: mail@actionaid.org; website: www.actionaid.org.uk

ACTORS' BENEVOLENT FUND

6 Adam Street, London, WC2N 6AD

Tel: 020 7836 6378
Fax: 020 7836 8978
E-mail: office@abf.org.uk
Website: www.actorsbenevolentfund.co.uk

Enquiries to: General Secretary
Other contacts: Assistant General Secretary

Founded: 1882

Organisation type and purpose: Registered charity (charity number 206524), members are all actors (membership is by subscription).
To care for actors and theatrical stage managers unable to work because of poor health, an accident or old age.

Subject coverage: Provides one-off or long-term financial aid and support and help in claiming benefits.

Publications: Printed
Order printed publications from: Website

Access to staff: Contact by letter, by telephone, by fax and by e-mail

Member organisation of: Combined Theatrical Charities

ACUMEDIC CENTRE FOR CHINESE MEDICINE

1 Wyle Cop, Shrewsbury, Shropshire, SY1 1UT

Tel: 01743 236100
Fax: 01743 236100

Enquiries to: Manager

Founded: 1989; formerly called Acumedic Ltd

Organisation type and purpose: Service industry.

Subject coverage: AcuMedic Ltd – The Comprehensive Organisation for Acupuncture & Chinese Herbal Medicine Resources. We offer Courses, Clinics, Health Advice and an Online Shop with TCM supplies, Herb Shop, Book Shop, Acupuncture Needles and more

Access to staff: Contact by telephone
Hours: Mon to Sat, 0900 to 1800, Sun, 0900 to 1800

Affiliated to: Acumedic; 17 Carlisle Road, Colindale, London, NW9 0HD

Parent body: Acumedic Centre; 101 Camden High Street, London, NW1 7JN; tel: 020 7388 6704; fax: 020 7387 5766; e-mail: infon@acumedic.com

ADAM SMITH COLLEGE

Library, St Brycedale Avenue, Kirkcaldy, Fife, KY1 1EX

Tel: 01592 223411
Fax: 01592 640225
E-mail: library@adamsmith.ac.uk
Website: www.adamsmithcollege.ac.uk

Enquiries to: Learner Resources Manager

History of institution: created by the merger of Fife College of Further and Higher Education, and Glenrothes College (year of change 2005)

Organisation type and purpose: College of further and higher education.

Subject coverage: General.

Non-library collection catalogue: All or part available in-house

Library catalogue: All or part available online

Access to staff: Contact by telephone, by e-mail and in person
Hours: Mon to Thu, 0850 to 2100; Fri, 0850 to 1620; Sat, 0900 to 1200

ADAM SMITH LIBRARY

University of Glasgow, 40 Bute Gardens, Glasgow, G12 8RT

Tel: 0141 330 5648
E-mail: adamsmith@lib.gla.ac.uk

Enquiries to: Adam Smith Librarian
Direct e-mail: k.ross@lib.gla.ac.uk

Founded: 1968

Organisation type and purpose: University library.
Library of the Faculty of Law, Business & Social Sciences.

Subject coverage: Anthropology, economics, politics, psychology, sociology, town and regional planning.

Non-library collection catalogue: All or part available online and in-house

Library catalogue: All or part available online and in-house

Access to staff: Contact by letter, by telephone and by e-mail. Appointment necessary.
Hours: Term time: Mon, Wed, Thu, Fri, 0900 to 1700, Tue, 0900 to 2100
Vacations: Mon to Fri, 0900 to 1700

Access for disabled people: Parking provided, ramped entry

ADAMSON PUBLISHING

8 The Moorings, Norwich, NR3 3AX

Tel: 01603 623336
Fax: 01603 624767
E-mail: sales@adamsonbooks.com
Website: www.adamsonbooks.com

Enquiries to: Managing Director

Founded: 1984; formerly called Adamson Books (year of change 2003)

Organisation type and purpose: Publishing house.

Subject coverage: Information for school governors, headteachers and teaching assistants.

Information services: Clerkwise, Governordoc

Non-library collection catalogue: All or part available online and in print

Library catalogue: All or part available online

Publications: Printed
Order printed publications from: Marston Book Services
Order electronic and video publications from: Adamson Publishing

Publications list: Available online

Access to staff: Contact by letter, by telephone, by fax and by e-mail
Hours: Mon to Fri, 0900 to 1700

Access to building: No access other than to staff

ADAS UK LIMITED (ADAS)

Woodthorne Wergs Road, Wolverhampton, West Midlands, WV6 8TQ

Tel: 01902 754190
Fax: 01902 743602
E-mail: mark.talbot@adas.co.uk
Website: www.globalfarmers.com
Website: www.adas.co.uk
Website: www.rbnet.co.uk

Enquiries to: Facilities
Direct tel: 01902 693483
Direct fax: 01902 693438
Direct e-mail: mark.talbot@adas.co.uk

Founded: 1997; formerly called ADAS Executive Agency from 1992 to 1997; formerly called MAFF (year of change 1992)

Organisation type and purpose: Architectural and environmental consultancy.

Subject coverage: Land-based industries, agricultural and environment-related subjects, food.

Publications: Printed

Access to staff: Contact by letter, by telephone, by fax and by e-mail. Appointment necessary. All charged.
Hours: Mon to Fri, 0830 to 1700

Access to building: *Hours:* Mon to Fri, 0830 to 1700 (by invitation only)

Access for disabled people: Mon to Fri, 0830 to 1700
Hours: Phone before visit

ADDACTION

67–69 Cowcross Street, London, EC1M 6PU

Tel: 020 7251 5860
Fax: 020 7251 5890
E-mail: info@addaction.org.uk
Website: www.addaction.org.uk

Enquiries to: Administrator
Other contacts: Press Office (for media enquiries)

Founded: 1967; formerly called Association for Prevention of Addiction (APA) (year of change 1997)

Organisation type and purpose: Registered charity (charity number 1001957).
Addaction provides drug and alcohol treatment services at over 70 projects throughout the country.
To solve drug and alcohol problems and to campaign for innovative approaches to solving drug and alcohol problems.

Subject coverage: Drug and alcohol addiction and misuse.

Non-library collection catalogue: All or part available online

Publications: Printed

Publications list: Available online

Access to staff: Contact by letter, by telephone, by fax and by e-mail
Hours: Mon to Fri, 0900 to 1700

Founder member of: Alcohol Concern; SCODA

ADFAM

Formal name: National Charity for Families and Friends of Drug Users

25 Corsham Street, London, N1 6DR

Tel: 020 7553 7640
Fax: 020 7253 7991
E-mail: admin@adfam.org.uk
Website: www.adfam.org.uk

Enquiries to: Policy and Communications Coordinator
Direct tel: 020 7553 7640
Direct e-mail: admin@adfam.org.uk

Founded: 1984

Organisation type and purpose: Voluntary organisation, registered charity (charity number 1067428), training organisation.
A national organisation working with families affected by drugs and alcohol and a leading agency in substance-related family work; provides a range of publications and resources for families about substances and criminal justice and operates an online message board and searchable database of local support groups that helps families hear about and talk to people who understand their situation; runs a range of training programmes on substances and family support; consultancy; direct support services at London prisons for families of prisoners with drug problems.

Subject coverage: Families and drug use, family dynamics, effects of drug use on the family, training in family support skills, setting up family support groups, drug education for parents, help for families of drug-using prisoners.

Publications: Printed, and electronic and video
Order electronic and video publications from: http://www.adfam.org.uk

Publications list: Available online and in print

Access to staff: Contact by letter, by telephone, by fax and by e-mail
Hours: Mon to Fri, 0900 to 1700
Special comments: Donations welcomed for provision of information.

ADHESIVE TAPE MANUFACTURERS ASSOCIATION (ATMA)

Sussex House, 8–10 Homesdale Road, Bromley, Kent, BR2 9LZ

Tel: 020 8464 0131
Fax: 020 8464 6018
E-mail: tradeassn@craneandpartners.com
Website: www.atmaadhesivetapes.com/

Enquiries to: Secretary

Organisation type and purpose: Trade association.

Subject coverage: Pressure-sensitive tapes, technical aspects and applications of adhesive tapes.

Publications list: Available in print

Affiliated to: European association (AFERA)

ADOPTION UK

46 The Green, South Bar Street, Banbury, Oxfordshire, OX16 9AB

Tel: 01295 752240
Fax: 01295 752241
E-mail: admin@adoptionuk.org.uk
Website: www.adoptionuk.org

Enquiries to: Helpline Adviser

Founded: 1970–71; formerly called Parent to Parent Information on Adoption Services (PPIAS) (year of change 1999)

Organisation type and purpose: Membership organisation for prospective adopters and adoptive parents, present number of members: over 4,500, registered charity (charity number 326654).
Membership subscription £20–£40 per annum. To provide information, advice, support, and training.

Subject coverage: Adoption for children (permanent family placement), especially for those who are racially mixed, who have a physical or mental disability or who are older than the usual age for adoption; support and information service for prospective and existing adoptive families.

Collection: Adoptive families willing to speak to members about any given experience (adoption)

Non-library collection catalogue: All or part available in-house

Library catalogue: All or part available in print

Publications: Printed, and electronic and video

Publications list: Available online and in print

Access to staff: Contact by letter, by telephone, by fax, by e-mail, in person and via website. Appointment necessary. Access for members only.
Hours: Mon to Fri, 0900 to 1700 office; Mon to Fri, 1000 to 1600 helpline
Special comments: Helpline Telephone is answered in person during office hours and by answerphone at all other times.

Access for disabled people: Access to all public areas, toilet facilities

Links with: all adoption agencies and local authorities in the UK

ADULT RESIDENTIAL COLLEGES ASSOCIATION (ARCA)

6 Bath Road, Felixstowe, Suffolk, IP11 7JW

continued overleaf

Tel: 01394 278161
Fax: 01394 271083
E-mail: arcasec@aol.com
Website: www.arca.uk.net

Enquiries to: Honorary Secretary

Founded: 1983

Organisation type and purpose: Membership association (membership is by subscription, qualification), present number of members: 30, institutions, voluntary organisation, suitable for ages: adults.
To promote residential short-term liberal adult education for the benefit of the general public.

Subject coverage: First stop call to member colleges for public enquiries.

Access to staff: Contact by letter, by telephone, by fax and by e-mail
Hours: Mon to Fri, 0900 to 1700

ADVANTAGE AUSTRIA – THE AUSTRIAN TRADE COMMISSION

Formal name: Austrian Embassy – Commercial Section

45 Princes Gate (on Exhibition Road)
London, SW7 2QA

Tel: 020 7584 4411
Fax: 020 7584 7946
E-mail: london@advantageaustria.org
Website: www.advantageaustria.org/uk

Enquiries to: Information Officer

Organisation type and purpose: Official Austrian Foreign Trade Promotion Organisation and the largest provider of services in the area of Austrian foreign trade.

Subject coverage: The gateway to Austria for UK and international companies looking for world-class suppliers! For over 65 years we have been the official representative of Austrian business in the UK, providing Austrian companies with the knowledge, advice and practical support they need to establish trade and investment links with the UK, and UK companies with information about Austria as a business partner and location.

Publications: Printed, and electronic and video
Order printed publications from: e-mail: london@advantageaustria.org
Order electronic and video publications from: e-mail: london@advantageaustria.org

Access to staff: Contact by letter, by telephone, by fax, by e-mail and via website
Hours: Mon to Fri, 0830 to 1700

Access to building: *Hours:* Mon to Fri, 0830 to 1700

ADVERTISING ASSOCIATION (AA)

7th Floor North, Artillery House, 11–19 Artillery Row, London, SW1P 1RT

Tel: 020 7340 1100
Fax: 020 7222 1504
E-mail: aa@adassoc.org.uk
Website: www.adassoc.org.uk/inform/content.html

Founded: 1926

Organisation type and purpose: The Advertising Association is a federation of trade bodies and organisations representing the advertising and promotional marketing industries, including advertisers, agencies, the media and support services in the UK.

Subject coverage: Advertising, marketing, public relations, communications, sales promotion, the media.

Library catalogue: All or part available in-house

Publications: Printed, and electronic and video

Publications list: Available online and in print

Access to staff: Contact by letter, by telephone, by e-mail and via website. Appointment necessary.
Special comments: See AA website for details.

Members: Cinema Advertising Association (CAA); Communication Advertising and Marketing Education Foundation (CAM); Data Publishers Association (DPA); Direct Marketing Association (UK) Limited (DMA); Direct Selling Association (DSA); Incorporated Society of British Advertisers (ISBA); Institute of Practitioners in Advertising (IPA); Institute of Sales Promotion (ISP); Interactive Advertising Bureau (UK) (IAB); Internet Advertising Association – UK Chapter (IAA UK Chapter); ITV plc (ITV); Mail Order Traders' Association (MOTA); Market Research Society (MRS); Marketing Communication Consultants Association; Newspaper Publishers Association Limited (NPA); Newspaper Society (NS); Outdoor Advertising Association of Great Britain Limited (OAA); Periodical Publishers Association (PPA); Point of Purchase Advertising International (POPAI); Radio Centre; Royal Mail (RM); Satellite and Cable Broadcasters' Group (SCBG); Scottish Newspaper Publishers Association (SNPA)

ADVERTISING STANDARDS AUTHORITY (ASA)

Mid City Place, 71 High Holborn, London, WC1V 6QT

Tel: 020 7492 2222
Fax: 020 7242 3696
E-mail: enquiries@asa.org.uk
Website: www.asa.org.uk

Enquiries to: Enquiries Team

Founded: 1962

Organisation type and purpose: Advisory body, professional body, trade association. Regulates UK advertising.

Subject coverage: Pre-publication advice on interpretation of the advertising codes available for advertisers, agencies and the media for all non-broadcast ads.

Collection: Various research and briefing notes

Trade and statistical information: Data on the number and nature of complaints about advertising

Publications: Printed

Access to staff: Contact by letter, by telephone, by fax, by e-mail and via website
Hours: Mon to Fri, 0900 to 1730

Access to building: No access other than to staff

Access for disabled people: Ramped entry

Links with: Committee of Advertising Practice; Mid City Place, 71 High Holborn, London, WC1V 6QT; tel: 020 7492 2222; fax: 020 7242 3696; e-mail: advice@cap.org.uk; website: http://www.cap.org.uk
European Advertising Standards Alliance; website: http://www.easa-alliance.org

ADVICE SERVICE CAPABILITY SCOTLAND

11 Ellersly Road, Edinburgh, EH12 6HY

Tel: 0131 313 5510
Fax: 0131 346 7864
E-mail: advice@capability-scotland.org.uk
Website: www.capability-scotland.org.uk

Enquiries to: Advice Worker

Founded: 1946

Organisation type and purpose: A national disability information and advice service, specialising in information on cerebral palsy.

Subject coverage: Information on a range of disability issues including cerebral palsy.

Collection: A small lending library with resources about cerebral palsy and children's books about disability

Library catalogue: All or part available online

Publications list: Available online and in print

Access to staff: Contact by letter, by telephone, by fax, by e-mail and in person
Hours: Mon to Fri, 0900 to 1300

Access for disabled people: Parking provided, ramped entry, changing places, toilet facilities.

ADVISORY CENTRE FOR EDUCATION (ACE)

United House, North Road, London, N7 9DP

Tel: 020 7697 1140 (Business line only)
E-mail: enquiries@ace-ed.org.uk
Website: www.ace-ed.org.uk

Founded: 1960

Organisation type and purpose: National organisation (membership is by subscription), voluntary organisation, registered charity (charity number 313142), publishing house.
Advises on parents' rights in education. Independent national education advice service for parents.

Subject coverage: Education in the statutory school years 5 to 16, guidance for parents, special education, exclusion from school, education law, governors' duties, choosing a school. Advice available for England and Wales only.

Collection: Education 5–16 books, pamphlets, cuttings.

Non-library collection catalogue: All or part available in-house

Publications: Printed

Publications list: Available online and in print

Access to staff: Contact by telephone
Hours: Free telephone advice line, Mon to Fri, 1400 to 1700; tel: 0808 800 5793
Special comments: Advice is given by telephone only. Internet Web pages also provide downloadable information.

Access to building: No access other than to staff

ADVISORY COMMITTEE ON PROTECTION OF THE SEA (ACOPS)

11 Dartmouth Street, London, SW1H 9BN

Tel: 020 7799 3033
Fax: 020 7799 2933
E-mail: acopsorg@netcomuk.co.uk
Website: www.acops.org

Enquiries to: Programme Officer

Founded: 1952

Organisation type and purpose: Advisory body, registered charity.
Non-Governmental Organisation.

Subject coverage: Protection of the marine environment.

Publications: Printed

Access to staff: Contact by letter, by telephone, by fax and by e-mail
Hours: Mon to Fri, 0900 to 1700

ADVISORY SERVICE FOR SQUATTERS (ASS)

Angel Alley, 84B Whitechapel High St, London, E1 7QX

Tel: 020 3216 0099
Fax: 020 3216 0098
E-mail: advice@squat.freeserve.co.uk
Website: www.squatter.org.uk

Enquiries to: Information Officer

Founded: 1975

Organisation type and purpose: Advisory body, voluntary organisation.

Subject coverage: Squatting history, housing struggles, surveys of squatters and their lifestyles (1970), law relating to squatting, practical and legal advice to squatters and homeless persons.

Collection: Books, photographs, some files on family squatting associations
Documents, relating to squatting in Europe, mainly Holland, France and Germany
Late 1970s bibliography of articles on squatting

Trade and statistical information: Files on squatting in Europe and the world

Publications: Printed

Access to staff: Contact by letter, by telephone, by fax, by e-mail, in person and via website
Hours: Mon to Fri, 1400 to 1800

Links with: COHRE; Hauikstraat 38 bis, Utrecht, 3514 TR, Netherlands; Droit au Logement; 3 bis rue de Vaucouleurs, 75011 Paris, France

ADVOCACY RESOURCE EXCHANGE (ARX)

Unit 3, 60 Duke Street, Liverpool, L1 5AA

Tel: 0151 734 3047
E-mail: chris@advocacyresource.net
Website: www.leevalley.co.uk/cait
Website: www.citizenadvocacy.org.uk

Enquiries to: Information Officer

Founded: 1988; formerly called Citizen Advocacy Information & Training (CAIT); formerly called Advocacy Alliance; formerly called National Citizen Advocacy (year of change 1994)

Organisation type and purpose: Voluntary organisation, registered charity (charity number 1035082), training organisation.
CAIT supports the development of local citizen advocacy schemes, through the provision of information, training and networking.
The support of people disadvantaged through age, mental or physical health, or learning difficulties.

Subject coverage: Citizen advocacy.

Collection: Collection of policies, publicity material and training programmes used by local citizen advocacy schemes
Small library of books and articles on citizen advocacy

Publications: Printed

Publications list: Available online and in print

Access to staff: Contact by letter, by telephone, by fax and via website.
Appointment necessary.
Hours: Mon to Fri, 0900 to 1700

Access to building: No prior appointment required

Access for disabled people: Parking provided, access to all public areas, toilet facilities

Funded by: London Boroughs Grants Committee

Has: some 200 schemes in the UK

ADVOCATES FOR ANIMALS

10 Queensferry Street, Edinburgh, EH2 4PG

Tel: 0131 225 6039
Fax: 0131 220 6377
E-mail: info@advocatesforanimals.org
Website: www.onekind.org

Founded: 1912; formerly called Scottish Society for the Prevention of Vivisection (year of change 1990)

Organisation type and purpose: A leading animal protection charity inspiring a movement of people who care about animals.

Subject coverage: Achieving better animal welfare in the UK and beyond through positive OneKind public awareness and political influence campaigns, animal investigations and education.

Collection: Photographic archive
Video loan library

Trade and statistical information: Data on the use and abuse of animals in the United Kingdom and abroad

Publications: Printed

Access to staff: Contact by letter, by telephone, by fax, by e-mail and via website.
Appointment necessary.
Hours: Mon to Fri, 0900 to 1700

Links with: St Andrew Animal Fund; 10 Queensferry Street, Edinburgh, EH2 4PG; tel: 0131 225 2116; fax: 0131 220 6377

ADVOCATES LIBRARY

Faculty of Advocates, Parliament House, Edinburgh, EH1 1RF

Tel: 0131 260 5683
Fax: 0131 260 5663
E-mail: inqdesk@advocates.org.uk
Website: www.advocates.org.uk/library/index.html

Enquiries to: Reader Services Librarian

Founded: 1689

Organisation type and purpose: Professional body (membership is by qualification), present number of members: 460.
The Advocates Library is a private library servicing members of the Scottish bar.
Legal deposit law materials for Scotland.

Subject coverage: Law, jurisprudence, Roman law and civil law.

Collection: Materials from other common law and Commonwealth jurisdictions, Roman, canon and civil law
Roman-Dutch collection
Session Papers (printed pleadings)

Non-library collection catalogue: All or part available online

Library catalogue: All or part available online

Access to staff: Contact by letter, by telephone, by fax, by e-mail and via website.
Access for members only.
Hours: Mon to Fri, 0900 to 1700
Special comments: Private library, stock made available to public via NLS

Access to building: Prior appointment required

AEA TECHNOLOGY ENVIRONMENT

AEA, The Gemini Building, Fermi Avenue, Harwell, Didcot, OX11 0QR

Tel: 0870 190 1900
Fax: 0870 190 6318
E-mail: enquiry@aeat.co.uk
Website: www.aeat-env.com

Enquiries to: Information Officer

Founded: April 1994; formerly called National Environmental Technology Centre; formerly called Environmental Safety Centre, Warren Spring Laboratory (year of change 1994)

Organisation type and purpose: Environmental consultancy.

Subject coverage: Air pollution, marine pollution, industrial effluent, waste management, recycling, cleaner technology, contaminated land, biotechnology, project hubs, future energy solutions,

continued overleaf

environmental and risk consultancy, chemical emergency response, environmental policy and climate change.

Publications list: Available online and in print

Access to staff: Contact by letter, by telephone, by fax, by e-mail and via website
Hours: Mon to Fri, 0900 to 1700

Registered office: AEA Technology plc; 329 Harwell, Didcot, Oxfordshire, OX11 0QJ

AERO INDEX LIMITED

39 Waylands Mead, The Knoll, Beckenham, Kent, BR3 5XT

Tel: 020 8650 3973
Website: www.aeroindex.com

Enquiries to: Managing Director
Direct e-mail: jr@aeroindex.freeserve.co.uk

Founded: 1993

Organisation type and purpose: Publishing house.

Subject coverage: World aerospace industry.

Publications: Printed

Access to staff: Contact by fax
Hours: Mon to Fri, 0900 to 1700

AEROPLANE COLLECTION LIMITED (TAC)

46 Sylvan Avenue, Timperley, Altrincham, Cheshire WA15 6AB

Tel: 0161 969 2697
E-mail: d.arkle@ntlworld.com

Enquiries to: Secretary

Founded: 1962; formerly called Northern Aircraft Preservation Society

Organisation type and purpose: Registered charity.
Preservation of aviation-related artefacts.

Subject coverage: Aircraft and aero engine preservation, historical aviation research.

Collection: Very detailed collections of books, pictures, photographs and some drawings, all relating to aviation

Access to staff: Contact by letter, by e-mail and in person
Hours: Mon to Fri, daytime

AETHELFLAED

1 Auckland Road, London, SW11 1EW

Tel: 020 7924 5868

Enquiries to: Honorary Treasurer

Founded: 1999

Organisation type and purpose: Learned society (membership is by subscription), present number of members: 23, voluntary organisation, research organisation.
To encourage research and awareness concerning Aethelflaed, Lady of the Mercians, daughter of Alfred The Great.

Subject coverage: Anglo-Saxon England, Aethelflaed, Lady of the Mercians, Old English, Alfred The Great.

Publications: Printed

Access to staff: Contact by letter
Hours: Mon to Fri, 0900 to 1700

AETHERIUS SOCIETY

Formal name: The Aetherius Society

757 Fulham Road, London, SW6 5UU

Tel: 020 7736 4187; 020 7731 1094
Fax: 020 7731 1067
E-mail: info@aetherius.co.uk
Website: www.aetherius.org

Founded: 1955

Organisation type and purpose: International organisation, membership association, voluntary organisation, training organisation, publishing house.
Religious and educational organisation.
Service to humanity.

Subject coverage: UFOs, cosmic contacts and life on other planets, aspects of metaphysics, new age thought, use of prayer, spiritual healing, self-development, psychic development, yoga, enlightenment and spiritual ecology.

Education services: Workshops and lectures.

Publications: Printed, and electronic and video
Order printed publications from: Postal address
Order electronic and video publications from: Postal address

Publications list: Available online and in print

Access to staff: Contact by letter, by telephone, by fax, by e-mail, in person and via website. Appointment necessary.
Hours: Mon to Fri, 0900 to 2100; weekends, variable hours

Also at: The Aetherius Society; Northern UK Branch, 350 Sheffield Road, Birdwell, Barnsley, South Yorkshire, S70 5TU; tel: 01226 744659; The Inner Potential Centre; 36 Kelvedon Road, London, SW6 5BW; tel: 020 7736 4187; e-mail: info@innerpotential.org

Branches: 2 branches and 10 groups in UK

AFASIC

1st Floor, 20 Bowling Green Lane, London, EC1R 0BD

Tel: 020 7490 9410 (admin); 0845 355 5577 (helpline)
Fax: 020 7251 2834
E-mail: info@afasic.org.uk
Website: www.afasic.org.uk

Enquiries to: Information Officer
Other contacts: Helpline Manager (for individual support for parents seeking help)

Founded: 1968; formerly called Association for All Speech Impaired Children

Organisation type and purpose: Membership association (membership is by subscription), voluntary organisation, registered charity (charity number 1045617).
Afasic is the UK charity representing children and young adults with speech, language and communication impairments, working for their inclusion in society and supporting their parents and carers.

Subject coverage: Speech and language difficulties. Speech and language impairments in children and young people; special educational facilities; speech and language therapy; advice to parents; training days.

Publications: Printed

Publications list: Available online and in print

Access to staff: Contact by letter, by telephone, by fax, by e-mail and via website
Hours: Office: Mon to Thu, 0900 to 1700; Fri, 0900 to 1600
Helpline: Mon to Fri, 1030 to 1430

Access to building: Prior appointment required

Also at: Afasic Cymru; Titan House, Cardiff Bay Business Centre, Lewis Road, Cardiff, CF24 5BS; tel: 029 2046 5854; e-mail: jeannette@afasiccymru.org.uk; Afasic Scotland; 1 Prospect 3, Gemini Crescent, Dundee Technology Park, Dundee, DD2 1TY; tel: 01382 561891; fax: 01382 568391; e-mail: admin@afasicscotland.org.uk

AFFINITY

The Old Bank House, 17 Malpas Road, Newport, NP20 5PA

Tel: 01633 893925
E-mail: office@affinity.org.uk
Website: affinity.org.uk/

Enquiries to: Director

Founded: 1952

Organisation type and purpose: Membership association, registered charity (charity number 258924).
Council of Churches; consultancy service.

Subject coverage: Evangelical Christianity, especially the co-ordination of churches outside the Ecumenical Movement.

Publications: Printed

Access to staff: Contact by letter, by telephone and by e-mail. Appointment necessary.

AFGHAN ACADEMY IN UK

14 Sinclair House, The Avenue, London, W13 8AG

Tel: 020 8579 8436/ 020 8991 2796
Fax: 020 8579 8436
E-mail: afghanacademy@gmail.com

Enquiries to: Director
Other contacts: Co-ordinator for reports and works of the other committees within Afghan Academy.

Founded: 1991; formerly called Afghan Link Association (year of change 1991); formerly called Afghanistan, Centre for Research and Development of Thoughts (year of change 1995); formerly called Afghan Academy (year of change 1997)

Organisation type and purpose: Membership association (membership is by subscription), voluntary organisation.
Cultural and welfare.

Afghan Academy provides educational, cultural and welfare services to the Afghan Community. It promotes art and artistic activities among Afghans and works to present Afghan art and culture.

Subject coverage: Afghanistan; Afghan refugees in UK; Afghanistan's cultural heritage; Afghan societies in and outside Afghanistan.

Collection: Publications in Persian/Pushto languages

Publications: Printed, and electronic and video

Publications list: Available online and in print

Access to staff: Contact by letter, by telephone and by fax. Appointment necessary.
Hours: Mon, Tue, Thu, Fri, 1000 to 1500, 24-hour emergency telephone and fax

Access to building: Prior appointment required

AFRICA CENTRE

38 King Street, London, WC2E 8IT

Tel: 020 7836 1973
Fax: 020 7836 1975
Website: www.africacentre.org.uk

Organisation type and purpose: The Centre seeks to project a positive face of Africa in London, providing a focal point for all forms of cultural and social activities related to Africa through meetings, talks, visual arts exhibitions, cinema, literature and the performing arts.

Subject coverage: Contemporary African culture and creativity.

AFRICAN BIRD CLUB (ABC)

c/o Birdlife International, Wellbrook Court, Girton Road, Cambridge, CB3 0NA

E-mail: secretary@africanbirdclub.org
Website: www.africanbirdclub.org

Enquiries to: Secretary
Direct e-mail: chairman@africanbirdclub.org
Other contacts: Chairman

Founded: 1994

Organisation type and purpose: Membership association (membership is by subscription), present number of members: 1,200, registered charity (charity number 1053920).
To promote African ornithology.

Subject coverage: African ornithology and all activities related to the study and conservation of African birds.

Publications: Printed

Access to staff: Contact by letter, by e-mail and via website
Hours: Mon to Fri, 0900 to 1700

AFRICAN STUDIES ASSOCIATION OF THE UNITED KINGDOM (ASAUK)

36 Gordon Square, London, WC1H 0PD

Tel: 020 3073 8335
Fax: 020 3073 8340
E-mail: asa@soas.ac.uk
Website: www.asauk.net/

Enquiries to: Assistant Honorary Secretary
Direct e-mail: secretary@asauk.net

Founded: 1963

Organisation type and purpose: Learned society.

Subject coverage: Symposia and conferences on topics of current importance in Africa.

Publications: Printed

Access to staff: Contact by letter, by telephone and by e-mail
Hours: Mon to Fri, 0930 to 1630

Affiliated to: Royal African Society; At the same address as above.

AFTAID

Formal name: AFTAID – Aid for the Aged in Distress

Epworth House, 25 City Road, London, EC1Y 1AA

Tel: 0870 803 1950
Fax: 0870 803 2128
E-mail: info@aftaid.org.uk
Website: www.aftaid.org.uk

Founded: 1982; created by the merger of Aid for the Aged and Aged in Distress; formerly called Aid for the Aged

Organisation type and purpose: Registered charity (number 299276), voluntary organisation.
Offers direct financial assistance in the form of grants, often in emergency situations and covering a wide range of issues that are not being addressed elsewhere.
Applications are welcomed from the social services, other charities and caring bodies as well as families and the individuals themselves.

Subject coverage: A relatively small charitable organisation that is near unique. For instance, help with winter heating comes in many forms, but if old radiators burst and an elderly couple can't pay for replacements, they lose their central heating. There are no official channels to explore for direct action to replace a useless radiator, but there is AFTAID.

Access to staff: Contact by letter, by telephone, by fax, by e-mail and via website

AGCAS

Formal name: Association of Graduate Careers Advisory Services

AGCAS Administration Office, Millennium House, 30 Junction Road, Sheffield, S11 8XB

Tel: 0114 251 5750
Fax: 0114 251 5751
Website: www.agcas.org.uk

Enquiries to: Chief Executive
Direct e-mail: margaret.dane@agcas.org.uk

Organisation type and purpose: A registered charity in England and Wales (number 1078508) and Scotland (number SC038805), the professional association for higher education (HE) careers practitioners, using the expertise and resources of its membership for the collective benefit of its members, HE careers services, their clients and customers, and the sector overall. Has influence with government, employers, professional bodies, the academic community and the guidance community.

Subject coverage: Graduate careers advice.

Information services: AGCAS e-mail discussion lists provide instant virtual access to over 2,000 careers professionals, based mostly in the UK but also in the Republic of Ireland and world-wide; members use these lists to participate in general or targeted discussions.

Special visitor services: Professional conferences and events across the UK.

Education services: Professional training courses are delivered online and through residential courses.

Publications: Printed, and electronic and video

Access to staff: Contact by letter, by telephone, by fax and by e-mail

AGE CONCERN ENGLAND (ACE)

Astral House, 1268 London Road, London, SW16 4ER

Tel: 020 8765 7200, 020 8679 2832 (Minicom, text phone)
Fax: 020 8765 7211
E-mail: ace@ace.org.uk
Website: www.ageconcern.org.uk

Enquiries to: Library Resources Manager

History of institution: formerly called National Council on Ageing

Organisation type and purpose: Registered charity (charity number 261794).
Hub of a network of about 1,400 Age Concern organisations that provide services on a local basis.
National charity that aims to promote the well-being of all older people, and involve them in all aspects of society.

Subject coverage: All aspects of the welfare of older people including: housing, health and social services, income maintenance, welfare rights, heating, transport and consumer affairs.

Collection: Library of books, journals and a large amount of grey material

Library catalogue: All or part available in-house

Publications: Printed

Publications list: Available in print

Access to staff: Contact by letter, by telephone, by fax, by e-mail and via website. Appointment necessary.
Hours: Mon to Fri, 0930 to 1700
Special comments: Reference only.

Access to building: Prior appointment required

Access for disabled people: Ramped entry, toilet facilities

AGE CONCERN LONDON (ACL)

21 St George's Road, London, SE1 6ES

Tel: 020 7820 6770

continued overleaf

Fax: 020 7820 1063
E-mail: general@aclondon.org.uk
Website: www.ageconcern.org.uk

Enquiries to: Communication Officer
Direct e-mail: pwoodward@aclondon.org.uk

Founded: 1966; formerly called Greater London Conference on Old People's Welfare

Organisation type and purpose: Voluntary organisation, registered charity (charity number 249335), research organisation.
Working across the capital to improve the quality of life for older people and to enhance their status and influence.

Subject coverage: Referral to local Age Concern organisations in the London boroughs. Details available via website or by calling National Age Concern Information Line 0800 009966. Also available in phone book.

Publications: Printed
Order printed publications from: Publications Administrator, Age Concern London
e-mail: vduncan@aclondon.org.uk

Publications list: Available online and in print

Access to staff: Contact by letter, by telephone, by fax, by e-mail and via website
Hours: Mon to Fri, 0930 to 1700
Telephone answered: Mon to Fri, 1100 to 1200 and 1500 to 1600
Answerphone at all other times
Special comments: Building not accessible.

Links with: Age Concern organisations in London

AGE CONCERN SCOTLAND

113 Rose Street, Edinburgh, EH2 3DT

Tel: 0131 220 3345
Fax: 0131 220 2779
E-mail: enquiries@acscot.org.uk

Enquiries to: Information Officer
Direct tel: 0131 625 9331
Direct e-mail: pamela.stewart@acscot.org.uk

Founded: 1943; formerly called Scottish Old People's Welfare Council (year of change 1974)

Organisation type and purpose:
Membership association (membership is by subscription), present number of members: 512, voluntary organisation, training organisation, consultancy, research organisation.
To promote the interests of older people in Scotland.

Subject coverage: Housing; residential accommodation; welfare rights; health; income maintenance; day services; needs of older people and those who work with them or care for them; voluntary services; ageing; statutory services; community care; insurance services.

Library catalogue: All or part available in-house

Publications: Printed, and electronic and video

Publications list: Available in print

Access to staff: Contact by letter, by telephone, by fax and by e-mail. Appointment necessary.
Hours: Mon to Fri, 0900 to 1700

Access to building: Prior appointment required
Hours: Mon to Fri, 0900 to 1700

Access for disabled people: Toilet facilities
Special comments: Chairlift entry

AGE ENDEAVOUR FELLOWSHIP

Registered Office, The Old Well House, 130 Holland Park Avenue, London, W11 4VE

Enquiries to: Chairman

History of institution: formerly called Employment Fellowship

Organisation type and purpose: Registered charity.

Subject coverage: Funding of elderly and respite care.

AGE NI

3 Lower Crescent, Belfast, Northern Ireland, BT7 1NR

Tel: 028 9024 5729
Fax: 028 9023 5497
E-mail: info@ageni.org
Website: www.ageni.org

Direct e-mail: info@ageni.org

History of institution: formerly called Age Concern Northern Ireland and Help the Aged NI (year of change 2009)

Organisation type and purpose: Voluntary organisation.
To enhance and improve the lives of older people, to create a powerful voice for older people.

Subject coverage: In Northern Ireland, there are more people over the age of 50 than under the age of 19 and, in the next 20 years, the number of people over 50 will increase by more than 30%. This carries significant consequences for the fabric of the community. It affects planning for the way of life: education systems, health and social care, work life, family life. Policy decisions taken today will influence how current teenagers live in the next 30 years and beyond. It is important that this message is delivered and acted upon now. Age NI exists to make people think differently about what it means to get older, because age affects everyone in many different ways.

Information services: Advice and advocacy.

Publications: Printed

Access to staff: Contact by letter, by telephone, by fax, by e-mail and via website
Hours: Mon to Fri, 0900 to 1700
Special comments: Advice and advocacy freephone no. 0808 808 7575; Lines are open 8am to 7pm, 7 days a week, all year round

AGECARE – THE ROYAL SURGICAL AID SOCIETY

Formal name: Royal Surgical Aid Society

47 Great Russell Street, London, WC1B 3PB

Tel: 020 7637 4577
Fax: 020 7323 6878
E-mail: enquiries@agecare.org.uk
Website: www.agecare.org.uk

Enquiries to: Chief Executive

Founded: 1862; formerly called RSAS AgeCare

Organisation type and purpose: Registered charity (charity number 216613).
Service provider and facilitator.

Subject coverage: Improvement of the care and well-being of older people, who are physically frail or suffering from dementias, through continuous development of good practice in the Society's own homes, seeking pre-eminence in training, supporting research, promoting awards for excellence and contributing to the exchange of knowledge.

Publications: Printed

Access to staff: Contact by letter, by fax and by e-mail
Hours: Mon to Fri, 0900 to 1700

Homes for the elderly in: Crowborough, Droitwich, Sevenoaks and Shepperton

AGRICULTURAL ECONOMICS SOCIETY (AES)

Holtwood, Red Lion Street, Cropredy, Banbury, Oxon, OX17 1PD

Tel: 01295 750182
E-mail: secretariat@aes.ac.uk
Website: www.aes.ac.uk

Enquiries to: Administrator

Founded: 1926

Organisation type and purpose: Learned society (membership is by subscription), present number of members: c. 900.

Subject coverage: Agricultural economics.

Publications: Printed

Access to staff: Contact by letter, by telephone and by e-mail
Hours: Mon to Fri, 0900 to 1700

AGRICULTURAL ENGINEERS ASSOCIATION (AEA)

Samuelson House, 62 Forder Way, Hampton, Peterborough, PE7 8JB

Tel: 0845 6448748
Fax: 01733 314767
E-mail: ab@aea.uk.com
Website: www.aea.uk.com
Website: www.ope-groundscare.co.uk
Website: www.aea-farm-machinery.co.uk

Enquiries to: Director General

Founded: 1875

Organisation type and purpose: Trade association. To provide a service to agricultural machinery manufacturers and outdoor power turfcare, landscape, forestry and leisure industries.

Subject coverage: European and national technical legislation and regulations relating to agriculture and outdoor power vehicles, agricultural tractors, machinery and equipment, including construction and use, health and safety, standards, type approval, vehicle licensing and environmental issues, economics, statistics, technical and legal aspects.

Trade and statistical information: Data on UK and European markets for agricultural machinery and tractors, economics, statistics, overseas export technical; legal; standards; related to industries (agricultural machinery manufacturers and outdoor power turfcare), landscape, forestry and leisure industries and sole importers

Publications: Printed

Access to staff: Contact by letter, by telephone, by fax, by e-mail and via website. Non-members charged.
Hours: Mon to Fri, 0900 to 1700
Special comments: Directory of members on web page.

Access for disabled people: Parking provided, toilet facilities

AGRICULTURAL INDUSTRIES CONFEDERATION (AIC)

Confederation House, East of England Showground, Peterborough, PE2 6XE

Tel: 01733 385230
Fax: 01733 385270
E-mail: enquiries@agindustries.org.uk
Website: www.agindustries.org.uk/

Direct e-mail: paul.rooke@agindustries.org.uk

Founded: 2003; created by the merger of the Fertiliser Manufacturers Association (1875) and the UK Agricultural Supply Trade Association (1917)

Organisation type and purpose: Trade association (membership is by election or invitation), present number of members: 34. To represent its membership to government and to co-operate with other organisations with shared interests. To promote an understanding of the issues relating to plant nutrients.

Subject coverage: Fertilisers: production, storage, transport, safety, statistics, use and environmental effects.

Trade and statistical information: Summary of fertiliser use in the UK, including historical data

Publications: Printed

Publications list: Available in print

Access to staff: Contact by letter
Hours: Fri, 0900 to 1600

Access to building: No prior appointment required

Links with: European Fertilizer Manufacturers Association; tel: + 322 675 3550; fax: + 322 675 3961; e-mail: main@efma .be; International Fertilizer Industry Association; tel: 00 33 1 539 30500; fax: 00 33 1 539 30547; e-mail: ifa@fertilizer.org

AHMADIYYA MUSLIM ASSOCIATION (UK) (AMA (UK))

The London Mosque, 16 Gressenhall Road, London, SW18 5QL

Tel: 020 8875 4321
Fax: 020 8874 4779
Website: www.al-islam.org

Enquiries to: National Secretary, Publications
Direct tel: 01438 231311; 07974 202225
Direct fax: 01438 231311
Direct e-mail: arshadahmedi@hotmail.com

Founded: 1889; formerly called Jamaat Ahmadiyya, London Mosque

Organisation type and purpose: International organisation, present number of members: over 200m. worldwide, registered charity (charity number 299081). Religious Community.

Subject coverage: Philosophy and teachings of Islam, correct interpretation of the Holy Qur'an and sayings of the Holy Prophet of Islam, facility in many Western and Eastern European languages.

Collection: Approximately 1,000 books on Islam and related subjects in English, Arabic and Urdu
Past editions of the Muslim Herald
Translation and Exegesis of the Qur'an in various European and Eastern languages

Publications: Printed
Order printed publications from: Secretary, Publications, at the same address; e-mail: ishaatuk@aol.com

Publications list: Available in print

Access to staff: Contact by letter, by telephone and by fax. Appointment necessary.
Hours: Mon to Fri, 1030 to 1930; calls may remain unattended during prayers
Special comments: Library and consulting facility available by prior arrangement.

Access to building: No prior appointment required

Constituent bodies: Lajna Imaullah (UK); at the same address; Majlis Ansarullah (UK); at the same address; tel: 020 8687 7845; Majlis Khuddamul Ahmadiyya (UK); at the same address; tel: 020 8687 7904

AHMED IQBAL ULLAH RACE RELATIONS RESOURCE CENTRE

Ground Floor, Devonshire House, Precinct Centre, Oxford Road, Manchester, M13 9PL

Tel: 0161 275 2920
E-mail: rrarchive@manchester.ac.uk
Website: www.racearchive.org.uk

Founded: 1999

Organisation type and purpose: Resource centre founded to combat racist ideas about black people.

Subject coverage: Books, periodical articles, cuttings, video and audio tapes and ephemeral material on key themes of history, politics, culture and identity, women, education and employment, housing, immigration, social services, and criminal justice; also an expanding local history section focused on the history of Manchester's African, Asian and Caribbean communities.

Access to building: *Hours:* Mon to Fri, 0930 to 1630
Special comments: Appointment requested for group visits.

AIIC (UNITED KINGDOM AND IRELAND REGION) (AIIC)

Formal name: International Association of Conference Interpreters (Association Internationale des Interprètes de Conférence)

12 Vicars Road, London, NW5 4NL

Tel: 020 7284 3112
Fax: 020 7284 0240
E-mail: info@aiic.net
Website: www.aiic.net

Enquiries to: Administrator

History of institution: formerly called AIIC (British Isles Region) (year of change 1999)

Organisation type and purpose: International organisation, professional body, service industry, consultancy. Promotes high standards for conference interpreters.

Subject coverage: Interpreting, especially conference interpreting, including: training, research, qualifications, requirements, practice.

Collection: Bibliography of publications Research in the field of interpreting

Access to staff: Contact by letter, by telephone, by fax, by e-mail and via website. Appointment necessary.
Hours: Mon to Fri, 0900 to 1700

Parent body: AIIC; 10 Avenue de Sécheron, Geneva, CH-1202, Switzerland; tel: +41 22 908 1540; fax: +41 22 732 4151; e-mail: info@ aiic.net

AIM25: ARCHIVES IN LONDON AND THE M25 AREA

c/o Director of Archive Services, King's College London, Strand, London, WC2R 2LS

E-mail: aim25@ulcc.ac.uk
Website: www.aim25.ac.uk

Enquiries to: Project Director
Direct tel: 020 7848 2187
Direct e-mail: aim25@ulcc.ac.uk

Organisation type and purpose: To provide electronic access to collection level descriptions of the archives of over ninety higher education institutions and learned societies within the greater London area.

Subject coverage: Social sciences, military history, teaching, medicine, overseas development, vocational history, history of higher education, biography, literary history.

Non-library collection catalogue: All or part available online

Access to staff: Contact by letter, by telephone, by e-mail and via website

AIR DESPATCH ASSOCIATION

E-mail: via website
Website: www.air-despatch.co.uk

Enquiries to: Hon. Secretary
Direct e-mail: hmebmp@aol.com
Other contacts: Membership Officer

continued overleaf

Organisation type and purpose: Veterans' association, open to service personnel of all ranks who have been on the strength of an Air Despatch unit of the British Army (membership is by subscription).

Subject coverage: Air Despatchers served world-wide on training, operations and famine relief duties.

Publications: Printed, and electronic and video
Order electronic and video publications from: Download from website

Access to staff: Contact via website

AIR LEAGUE

Broadway House, Tothill Street, London, SW1H 9NS

Tel: 020 7222 8463
E-mail: via website
Website: www.airleague.co.uk

Founded: 1909

Organisation type and purpose: Registered charity, membership association (membership is by subscription).
To generate national understanding of the importance to the UK of aviation and aerospace, and to excite the interest of young people in these areas by helping them to become involved.

Subject coverage: Helping young people by providing careers and support by way of flying and engineering scholarships and bursaries.

Publications: Electronic and video
Order electronic and video publications from: Download from website

Access to staff: Contact by letter, by telephone and via website

AIRCRAFT RESEARCH ASSOCIATION LIMITED (ARA)

Manton Lane, Bedford, MK41 7PF

Tel: 01234 350681
Fax: 01234 328584
E-mail: ara@ara.co.uk
Website: www.ara.co.uk
Enquiries to: Librarian
Direct e-mail: krentle@ara.co.uk

Founded: 1954

Organisation type and purpose: Research organisation.
Association of major companies.

Subject coverage: Aerodynamics, wind tunnel testing, mathematical modelling, analysis and computing code generation, model design and manufacture.

Library catalogue: All or part available in-house

Access to staff: Contact by letter, by telephone, by fax and by e-mail
Hours: Mon to Fri, 0800 to 1600

AIRFIELDS OF BRITAIN CONSERVATION TRUST (ABCT)

PO Box 26319, Glasgow, G76 6AH

Website: www.abct.org.uk

Founded: 2006

Organisation type and purpose: Registered charity (charity number 1112829).
A recently established charity, Airfields of Britain Conservation Trust is designed to acknowledge the enormous and unique contribution airfields have made in numerous spheres since 1909. A memorial is intended to be erected at each known disused airfield site in Britain in order to provide a permanent reminder for future generations. Historical information will be made publicly available and facilities provided to allow new factual details to be collated. Education advice and support will also be offered in practical ways to assist young people who display clear enthusiasm about Britain's airfields or aviation in general for potential future careers in these areas.

Subject coverage: Establishing memorials and mobilising communities to preserve local airfields.

Publications: Electronic and video
Order electronic and video publications from: Register via website

Access to staff: Contact by letter and via website

AIRSHIP ASSOCIATION LIMITED

E-mail: treasurer@airship-association.org
Website: www.airship-association.org

Enquiries to: The Treasurer

Founded: 1972

Organisation type and purpose: Professional body.
To promote the use of airships for surveillance, load-carrying, advertising and scientific purposes.

Subject coverage: Design, construction and operation of all types of modern airships; provision of information about airship designers and manufacturers, aeronautical engineers.

Information services: e-mail: info@airship-association.org

Publications: Printed

Access to staff: Contact by e-mail and via website. Non-members charged.
Hours: Mon to Fri, 0900 to 1700

AL-ANON FAMILY GROUPS UK AND EIRE AND ALATEEN

61 Great Dover Street, London, SE1 4YF

Tel: 020 7403 0888
Fax: 020 7378 9910
E-mail: enquiries@al-anonuk.org.uk
Website: www.al-anonuk.org.uk

Enquiries to: Public Information Secretary
Direct tel: 020 7407 0215
Other contacts: General Secretary

Founded: 1951

Organisation type and purpose: International organisation, membership association (membership is by qualification), voluntary organisation, registered charity.
Al-Anon is active worldwide and offers understanding and support for families and friends of problem drinkers, whether the alcoholic is still drinking or not. Alateen, a part of Al-Anon, is for young people aged 12 to 17 who have been affected by someone else's drinking, usually that of a parent.

Subject coverage: Alcoholics, alcoholism, and its effects on family and friends.

Information services: Confidential helpline

Publications: Printed
Order printed publications from: Contact literature sales: literature@al-anonuk.org.uk

Publications list: Available online and in print

Access to staff: Contact by letter, by telephone, by fax, by e-mail and via website
Hours: Mon to Fri, 1000 to 1600
Confidential Helpline 020 7403 0888: daily, 1000 to 2200

Constituent bodies: Almost 1000 self-help groups meet in UK and Eire, and 30,000 worldwide

ALBANY TRUST

239a Balham High Road, London, SW17 7BE

Tel: 020 8767 1827
E-mail: info@albanytrust.org
Website: www.albanytrust.org.uk/

Enquiries to: Administrator

Founded: 1958

Organisation type and purpose: Learned society, registered charity (charity number 233564).
Counselling and psychotherapy service.

Subject coverage: Relationships, personal and sexual counselling.

Access to staff: Contact by telephone
Hours: Mon to Fri, 0900 to 1700

Incorporates the: Sexual Law Reform Society

ALBINISM FELLOWSHIP

PO Box 77, Burnley, Lancashire, BB11 5GN

Tel: 01282 771900
E-mail: info@albinism.org.uk
Website: www.albinism.org.uk

Founded: 1979; formerly called Albino Fellowship (year of change 1990)

Organisation type and purpose: National organisation for UK & Ireland. Membership association (membership is by subscription), present number of members: 450, voluntary organisation, registered charity (charity number SCO 09443).
Aims to provide information, advice and support to people with albinism, their families and the professionals working with them.

Subject coverage: Albinism.

Publications: Printed
Order printed publications from: Via website or fellowship address

Publications list: Available online

Access to staff: Contact by letter, by telephone, by e-mail and via website
Hours: Answerphone

ALBION VEHICLE PRESERVATION TRUST (AVPT)

18 Netherdale Drive, Paisley, Renfrewshire, PA1 3DA

E-mail: albionregister@yahoo.co.uk
Website: www.albion-trust.org.uk

Organisation type and purpose:
Preservation trust (Scottish charity no. SC028791) maintaining a 1950 Albion Valiant heavy coach and a 1967 Viking coach. Keeps a register of more than 1,000 surviving Albion vehicles worldwide.

Subject coverage: Albion vehicles.

Links with: Biggar Albion Foundation; The Albion Club, 9 Edinburgh Road, Biggar, Lanarkshire, ML12 6AX

ALCOHOL CONCERN

Suite B5, West Wing, New City Cloisters, 196 Old Street, London, EC1V 9FR

Tel: 020 7566 9800
E-mail: contact@alcoholconcern.org.uk
Website: www.alcoholconcern.org.uk

Founded: 1984

Organisation type and purpose: Voluntary organisation, registered charity (charity number 291705).
To raise public awareness of the problems of alcohol abuse; to improve services for problem drinkers and to promote preventive action. National charity on alcohol misuse. Works to reduce the incidence and costs of alcohol-related harm and to increase the range and quality of services available to people with alcohol-related problems. Provides information and encourages debate on the wide range of public policy issues affected by alcohol, including public health, housing, children and families, crime and licensing. Supports specialist and non-specialist service providers helping to tackle alcohol problems at a local level, whilst also working to influence national alcohol policy.

Subject coverage: Alcohol use and misuse, treatment, health and social effects, policies.

Information services: Factsheets, leaflets and reports on alcohol.

Publications: Printed

Publications list: Available online

Access to staff: Contact by letter, by telephone, by e-mail and via website. Appointment necessary.

Access to building: Office is not open to the public
Hours: Mon to Fri, 0930 to 1630

ALCOHOL FOCUS SCOTLAND (AFS)

2nd Floor, 166 Buchanan Street, Glasgow, G1 2LW

Tel: 0141 572 6700
Fax: 0141 333 1606
E-mail: enquiries@alcohol-focus-scotland.org.uk
Website: www.alcohol-focus-scotland.org.uk

Enquiries to: Chief Executive

Founded: 1973; formerly called Scottish Council on Alcohol

Organisation type and purpose: Scotland's national charity working to reduce the harm caused by alcohol.

Publications list: Available online and in print

Access to staff: Contact by letter, by telephone, by fax, by e-mail and via website. Appointment necessary.

ALCOHOLICS ANONYMOUS (AA)

PO Box 1, 10 Toft Green, York, YO1 7NJ

Tel: 01904 644026
Fax: 01904 629091
E-mail: help@alcoholics-anonymous.org.uk.
Website: www.alcoholics-anonymous.org.uk

Enquiries to: General Secretary

Founded: 1935

Organisation type and purpose:
International organisation, voluntary organisation, registered charity (charity number 226745).

Subject coverage: Alcoholism, recovery from alcoholism.

Publications: Printed, and electronic and video

Publications list: Available in print

Access to staff: Contact by letter, by telephone and by fax
Hours: Mon to Thu, 0900 to 1700; Fri, 0900 to 1630

Also at: Northern Service Office (Scotland); tel: 0141 226 2214; Southern Service Office (London); tel: 020 7833 0022

ALEXANDER STUDIO

Danceworks, 16 Balderton Street, London, W1K 6TN

Tel: 020 7629 1808

Enquiries to: Managers

Organisation type and purpose:
Professional body.

Subject coverage: Stress management, psychophysical health, poise and grace for performing artists, relief from muscular aches and pains.

Publications: Electronic and video

All teachers are members of the: Society of Teachers of the Alexander Technique (STAT)

ALFA LAVAL LIMITED (A-L; Alfa)

7 Doman Road, Camberley, Surrey, GU15 3DN

Tel: 01276 63383
Fax: 01276 685035
E-mail: general.uk@alfalaval.com
Website: www.alfalaval.com

Enquiries to: Public Relations Manager
Direct tel: 01276 413632
Direct fax: 01276 413524
Direct e-mail: peter.rose@alfalaval.com

Founded: 1923; formerly called Alfa-Laval Flow Ltd, Alfa-Laval Separation Ltd, Alfa-Laval Sharples Ltd, Alfa-Laval Thermal Ltd

Organisation type and purpose:
Manufacturing industry.

Subject coverage: Heat transfer technology, sanitary pumps, valves and fittings.

Access to staff: Contact by letter, by telephone, by fax, by e-mail and via website
Hours: Mon to Fri, 0900 to 1700

Access for disabled people: Level entry, toilet facilities

Other addresses: Alfa Laval Limited; 8H May Brook Road, Sutton Coldfield, West Midlands, B76 1AL; tel: 0121 351 3131; fax: 0121 351 7888; Alfa Laval Limited; Office 5 – 9th Floor, Salveson Tower, Blaikies Quay, Aberdeen, AB11 5PW; tel: 01224 424300; fax: 01224 424315

ALFA ROMEO 1900 REGISTER

Mariners, 14 Lower Station Road, Billingshurst, West Sussex, RH14 9SX

E-mail: ar.01177@yahoo.co.uk
Website: www.ar1900reg.org

Enquiries to: Factotum

Founded: 1977

Organisation type and purpose:
International organisation, membership association (membership is by qualification), present number of members: 500.
Register – The register lists cars rather than owners, i.e. cars with owners, not owners with cars.
To record all Alfa Romeo 6C2300, 6C2500 and 1900 still extant and to provide information on these models.

Subject coverage: The Register of Alfa Romeo 6C2300, 6C2500 and 1900 also tries to assist on other uncommon post-war Alfa Romeos, including brochure information.

Publications: Printed

Access to staff: Contact by letter and by telephone

Also at: North American Register; 302 Brown Thrush Road, Savannah, Georgia, 31419, USA

ALFA ROMEO GIULIA 105 REGISTER

144 Sussex Way, Barnet, Hertfordshire, EN4 0BG

Tel: 020 8351 8565

Enquiries to: Secretary

Organisation type and purpose:
Membership association.

Subject coverage: Alfa Romeo Giulia 105 cars.

Access to staff: Contact by letter, by telephone and by fax. Appointment necessary.
Hours: Mon to Fri, 0900 to 1700

Parent body: Alfa Romeo Owners' Club

ALL ENGLAND LAWN TENNIS & CROQUET CLUB

Church Road, Wimbledon, London, SW19 5AE

Tel: 020 8944 1066
Fax: 020 9947 8752
Website: www.wimbledon.org

Enquiries to: Club Secretary
Direct tel: 020 8971 2252
Other contacts: Curator for Wimbledon Lawn Tennis Museum.

Founded: 1868

Organisation type and purpose: Membership association (membership is by election or invitation), present number of members: 375 plus honorary members. Private tennis club.

Subject coverage: Lawn tennis and croquet.

Access to staff: Contact by letter, by telephone and by fax. Appointment necessary.
Hours: Mon to Fri, 0900 to 1700

ALL ENGLAND NETBALL ASSOCIATION LIMITED (AENA Ltd)

Netball House, 9 Paynes Park, Hitchin, Hertfordshire, SG5 1EH

Tel: 01462 442344
Fax: 01462 442343
E-mail: info@englandnetball.co.uk
Website: www.englandnetball.co.uk

Enquiries to: Communications Officer
Direct e-mail: siobhana@aena.co.uk

Founded: 1926; merged with English Schools Netball Association (year of change 1994)

Organisation type and purpose: National organisation, membership association (membership is by subscription, election or invitation), present number of members: 55,000 individual members.
Governing body of netball in England.

Subject coverage: International, national, regional, county and club netball; development, performance, disability, coaching, umpiring, awards.

Collection: Archives and photographs

Publications: Printed, and electronic and video
Order printed publications from: The Sports Motive
fax: 01926 888832

Publications list: Available in print

Access to staff: Contact by letter, by e-mail and via website
Hours: Mon to Fri, 0900 to 1700

Member of: International Federation of Netball Associations; tel: 0121 446 4451; fax: 0121 446 5857; e-mail: ifna@btinternet.com

ALL NATIONS CHRISTIAN COLLEGE (ANCC)

Easneye, Ware, Hertfordshire, SG12 8LX

Tel: 01920 461243
Fax: 01920 462997
E-mail: library@allnations.ac.uk
Website: www.allnations.ac.uk

Enquiries to: Librarian
Direct tel: 01920 443504
Direct e-mail: k.wiseman@allnations.ac.uk

Founded: 1971; created by the merger of All Nations Missionary College, Mount Hermon Missionary Training College, Ridgelands Bible College (year of change 1971); formerly called All Nations Bible College (year of change 1962)

Organisation type and purpose: Training institution for Christian mission.

Subject coverage: Christianity, theology, missiology, anthropology, world religions, intercultural studies.

Information services: Library and information services.

Special visitor services: Open to external members – please contact the Librarian for information.

Education services: Library and information facilities for All Nations Christian College students and staff.

Collection: Archives of constituent colleges

Non-library collection catalogue: All or part available in print

Library catalogue: All or part available online and in-house

Access to staff: Contact by letter, by telephone, by fax, by e-mail, in person and via website. Appointment necessary. Letter of introduction required. Non-members charged.
Hours: Mon to Fri, 0930 to 1700
Special comments: External library membership restricted to church leaders, mission leaders, and theological students.

Access for disabled people: Ramped entry, access to all public areas, toilet facilities

ALL WHEEL DRIVE CLUB (AWDC)

Registered Office: c/o Vallance Lodge & Co, Units 082–086, 555 White Hart Lane, London, N17 7RN

E-mail: secretary@awdc.co.uk
Website: www.awdc.co.uk

Enquiries to: Membership Administrator
Direct tel: 01825 731875

Founded: 1968

Organisation type and purpose: National organisation, membership association (membership is by subscription), present number of members: 2600, voluntary organisation.
Organisation of off-road motorsport events and other activities for 4x4 vehicles.

Subject coverage: Off-road motor sport, its environmental impact, guidance for landowners, unsurfaced vehicular rights of way, their existence and usage. Recreational use of cross-country motorised vehicles.

Access to staff: Contact by letter and by e-mail
Hours: Mon to Fri, 0900 to 1700

Affiliated to: Motor Sports Association

Has: branches throughout the country

ALLARD OWNERS CLUB

1 Brooklyn Court, Woking, Surrey, GU22 7TQ

Tel: 01483 773428
Fax: 01483 773428
E-mail: michellewilson@compuserve.com
Website: www.allardownersclub.org

Enquiries to: Secretary

Founded: 1951

Organisation type and purpose: Membership association.

Subject coverage: Allard cars.

Publications: Printed

Access to staff: Contact by letter
Hours: Mon to Fri, 0900 to 1700

Access to building: No access other than to staff

ALLEGRO CLUB INTERNATIONAL

General Enquiries, Allegro Club International, 11 Russell Court, Hopton Road, London, SW16 2ER

E-mail: enquiries@allegroclubint.org.uk
Website: www.allegroclubint.org.uk

Enquiries to: Membership Secretary
Direct e-mail: ian.sc@dial.pipex.com

Founded: 1990

Organisation type and purpose: Membership association.
Car owners club.

Subject coverage: Providing parts for Allegro cars, helping those who wish to buy or sell such cars, organising gatherings, pooling information for owners, gathering history of Allegro cars. The club has an archive of Allegro-related material.

Publications: Printed

Access to staff: Contact by letter. Access for members only.
Hours: Mon to Fri, 0900 to 1700

Access to building: No access other than to staff

ALLERGY UK

Planwell House, LEFA Business Park, Edgington Way, Sidcup, DA14 5BH

Tel: 01322 619898
Fax: 01322 470330
E-mail: info@allergyuk.org
Website: www.allergyuk.org
Website: www.allergyfoundation.com

Enquiries to: Membership Enquiries
Direct e-mail: raegan@allergyuk.org
Other contacts: Chairman

Founded: 1991; formerly called British Allergy Foundation (BAF) (year of change 2001)

Organisation type and purpose: A national medical charity providing information and support to people with allergies, intolerances and sensitivites (charity number 1003726).
To raise awareness of allergy, provide information for sufferers and raise funds for research.

Subject coverage: All allergy-related disorders, including: respiratory (nose and lungs), dermatological, eye disorders, food-related problems, venom allergy, drug allergy, occupational allergic diseases.

Collection: Data on prevalence of allergic disorders

Publications: Printed

Publications list: Available in print

Access to staff: Contact by letter, by telephone, by fax, by e-mail, in person and via website. Appointment necessary.
Hours: Mon to Fri, 0900 to 1700
Special comments: Helpline: Mon to Fri, 0900 to 1700, tel: 01322 619898

Affiliated to: British Society for Allergy and Clinical Immunology; tel: 020 8398 9240; fax: 020 8398 2766; e-mail: s.duff@co.puserve .com

Has: Local support groups at various UK locations (contact via main office)

Member of: European Federation of Asthma & Allergy Associations (EFA)

ALLIANCE OF LITERARY SOCIETIES (ALS)

59 Bryony Road, Selly Oak, Birmingham, B29 4BY

Tel: 0121 475 1805
E-mail: l.j.curry@bham.ac.uk
Website: www.allianceofliterarysocieties.org .uk

Enquiries to: Membership Secretary
Direct e-mail: johnshorland@aol.com

Founded: 1973

Organisation type and purpose:
Membership association (membership is by subscription), present number of members: 115, suitable for ages: 10+.
Uniting literary societies. Provides mutual help and advice on the running of societies, funding, etc., and encourages working together to save threatened places of literary significance.

Subject coverage: Addresses of member societies; literary enquiries; literary society, etc.

Publications: Printed

Access to staff: Contact by letter, by e-mail and via website

ALPINE CLUB LIBRARY

55 Charlotte Road, London, EC2A 3QF

Tel: 020 7613 0745
Fax: 020 7613 0755
E-mail: library@alpine-club.org.uk
Website: www.alpine-club.org.uk

Enquiries to: Librarian
Other contacts: Archivist; Photo Librarian

Founded: 1857

Organisation type and purpose:
Membership association (membership is by subscription), registered charity (charity number 313051).
Mountaineering club.
Caters specifically for those who climb in the Alps and the Greater Ranges of the world.

Subject coverage: Historical and current information on mountaineering and mountain ranges worldwide including Himalayan database, ski mountaineering, walking, high altitude medicine and climbing equipment.

Collection: Alpine Club Records
The library has one of the most comprehensive collections of mountaineering literature in the world including journals, early books, photographs, manuscripts, newspaper cuttings from 1891, diaries and correspondence, guide books and reports
Expedition Reports
Records of the former Ladies' Alpine Club

Non-library collection catalogue: All or part available in print

Library catalogue: All or part available in-house

Publications: Printed

Access to staff: Contact by letter, by telephone, by fax and by e-mail. Appointment necessary. Non-members charged.
Hours: Tue, Wed, 1000 to 1700

Access for disabled people: *Special comments:* Library on first floor, no lift.

Affiliated to: British Mountaineering Council; 177–179 Burton Road, Manchester, M20 2BB; tel: 0870 010 4878; fax: 0161 445 4500; e-mail: info@thebmc.co.uk

Parent body: Alpine Club; at the same address

ALPINE GARDEN SOCIETY (AGS)

AGS Centre, Avon Bank, Pershore, Worcestershire, WR10 3JP

Tel: 01386 554790
Fax: 01386 554801
E-mail: ags@alpinegardensociety.net
Website: www.alpinegardensociety.org

Enquiries to: Director and Secretary to the Society

Founded: 1929

Organisation type and purpose:
International organisation, membership association (membership is by subscription), present number of members: 13,850, voluntary organisation, registered charity (charity number 207478), suitable for ages: all.
Specialist horticultural plant society.
To disseminate knowledge of alpine and rock garden plants – alpines is a generic term to encompass small hardy plants, including perennials, bulbs, ferns, dwarf conifers, etc.

Subject coverage: Horticultural, with specialist knowledge of the cultivation of alpines and rock plants, small hardy plants, including perennials, bulbs, ferns, dwarf conifers etc. Locations: where to travel in the world to find alpine specimens.
Conservation: the Society encourages conservation and discourages indiscriminate collecting.

Collection: Specialist Library – reference books
Slide Library – hire/loan service

Non-library collection catalogue: All or part available in-house

Library catalogue: All or part available in-house

Publications: Printed, and electronic and video

Publications list: Available online and in print

Access to staff: Contact by letter, by telephone, by fax, by e-mail, in person and via website. Appointment necessary.
Hours: Mon to Thu, 0900 to 1730; Fri, 0900 to 1700

Access for disabled people: Parking provided, ramped entry, toilet facilities

Has: 60 local groups

Seed Distribution Limited: Alpine Garden Society; 11 Boston Close, Culcheth, Warrington, WA3 4LW

ALUMINIUM FEDERATION (ALFED)

Formal name: Aluminium Federation Limited

National Metalforming Centre, 47 Birmingham Road, West Bromwich, West Midlands, B70 6PY

Tel: 0121 601 6363
Fax: 0870 183 9714
E-mail: alfed@alfed.org.uk
Website: www.alfed.org.uk

Enquiries to: Librarian
Direct tel: 0121 601 6746
Other contacts: Technical Executive

Founded: 1963; formerly called Aluminium Development Association

Organisation type and purpose: Trade association (membership is by subscription), present number of members: 200.
Information centre.

Subject coverage: Technical and commercial information on aluminium and its alloys, extrusion, coating, anodising, rolling.

Collection: Library with largest collection in the world on aluminium; full range of traditional library services

Non-library collection catalogue: All or part available online

Library catalogue: All or part available in-house

Publications: Printed

Publications list: Available online and in print

Access to staff: Contact by letter, by telephone, by fax, by e-mail and via website
Hours: Mon to Fri, 0900 to 1700
Special comments: Members and bona fide students only.

Member organisations: Aluminium Alloys Recycling and Melting Association (AARMA); at the same address; Aluminium Extruders Association (AEA); at the same address; Aluminium Finishing Association (AFA); at the same address; Aluminium Primary Producers Association (APPA); at the same address; Aluminium Rolled Products Manufacturers Association (ARPMA); at the same address; Aluminium Stockholders Association (ASA); at the same

continued overleaf

address; tel: 0121 601 6716; fax: 0121 601 6375; Diecasting Society (DCS); at the same address; European Aluminium Particulate Association; at the same address

ALUMINIUM PACKAGING RECYCLING ORGANISATION (ALUPRO)

1 Brockhill Court, Brockhill Lane, Redditch, Worcestershire, B97 6RB

Tel: 01527 597757
Fax: 01527 594140
E-mail: info@alupro.org.uk
Website: www.alupro.org.uk

Enquiries to: Communications Director

Founded: 1994; formerly called Aluminium Can Recycling Association (ACRA), Aluminium Foil Recycling Campaign (AFRC) (year of change 1999)

Organisation type and purpose:
Membership association.
Promotes collection of aluminium packaging through all routes: local authority collection and kerbside systems, 'cash for cans' recycling centres.

Subject coverage: Viable collection opportunities for aluminium, recycling technology, foil in energy from waste plants. Packaging waste legislation.

Publications: Printed

Access to staff: Contact by letter, by telephone, by fax, by e-mail and via website
Hours: Mon to Fri, 0900 to 1700

ALVIS OWNER CLUB

4 Field Lane, Normanby-By-Spital, Market Rasen, Lincolnshire, LN8 2HB

Tel: 01673 878148
E-mail: gensec@alvisoc.org
Website: www.alvisoc.org

Enquiries to: General Secretary
Founded: 1951

Organisation type and purpose:
Membership association (membership is by subscription).

Subject coverage: Technical information, historic information, help and advice on matters concerning the use and restoration of Alvis vehicles.

Publications: Printed

Access to staff: Contact by e-mail and via website. Appointment necessary.
Hours: Mon to Fri, 0900 to 1700

ALVIS REGISTER

The Vinery, Wanborough Hill, Wanborough, Guildford, Surrey, GU3 2JR

Tel: 01483 810308
Fax: 01483 810308
E-mail: enquiries@alvisregister.co.uk

Enquiries to: Registrar
Direct e-mail: joining@alvisregister.com

Founded: 1948

Organisation type and purpose:
Membership association (membership is by subscription), present number of members: 520.

Subject coverage: Alvis cars.

Access to staff: Contact by letter and by telephone
Hours: Mon to Fri, 0900 to 1700

ALZHEIMER SCOTLAND

Formal name: Alzheimer Scotland – Action on Dementia

22 Drumsheugh Gardens, Edinburgh, EH3 7RN

Tel: 0131 243 1453
Fax: 0131 225 3287
E-mail: alzheimer@alzscot.org
Website: www.alzscot.org

Enquiries to: Information Manager
Direct e-mail: mthom@alzscot.org

Founded: 1994

Organisation type and purpose:
Membership association, voluntary organisation, registered charity (charity number SC022315). Provision and promotion of services for people with dementia and their carers. Has a network of branches and services across Scotland; for information contact the National Office.

Subject coverage: Information relating to statistics on numbers of people in Scotland with dementia. Range of services offered in Scotland. Information on all aspects of dementia and on government policy.

Publications: Printed

Publications list: Available online and in print

Access to staff: Contact by letter, by telephone, by fax, by e-mail and via website. Appointment necessary.
Hours: 24-hour Dementia Helpline 0808 808 3000

ALZHEIMER'S RESEARCH TRUST

The Stables, Station Road, Great Shelford, Cambridge, CB22 5LR

Tel: 01223 843899
Fax: 01223 843325
E-mail: enquiries@alzheimers-research.org.uk
Website: www.alzheimers-research.org.uk

Founded: 1992

Organisation type and purpose: A registered charity (number 1077089).
A leading research charity for dementia, dedicated to funding scientific studies to find ways to treat, cure or prevent Alzheimer's disease, vascular dementia, Lewy Body disease and fronto-temporal dementia.

Subject coverage: Funds vital research and provides free information on dementia and the progress being made by research.

Publications: Printed, and electronic and video
Order printed publications from: tel: 01223 843899; e-mail: enquiries@alzheimers-research.org.uk
Order electronic and video publications from: via website

Publications list: Available online

Access to staff: Contact by letter, by telephone, by fax, by e-mail and via website

ALZHEIMER'S SOCIETY (AS)

Devon House, 58 St Katharine's Way, London, E1W 1LB

Tel: 020 7423 3500
Fax: 020 7423 3501
E-mail: info@alzheimers.org.uk
Website: www.alzheimers.org.uk

Enquiries to: Director of Information and Education
Direct e-mail: enquiries@alzheimers.org.uk

Founded: 1979; formerly called Alzheimer's Disease Society (ADS) (year of change 1999)

Organisation type and purpose: National organisation, membership association (membership is by subscription), present number of members: 25,000, voluntary organisation, registered charity (charity number 296645), research organisation. Serves England, Wales and Northern Ireland.
To provide care for people with Alzheimer's disease and other forms of dementia and research into the condition.
To provide support for their carers and families.

Subject coverage: Dementia and dementia care.

Collection: Dementia Knowledge Centre with over 12,500 items including books, articles, dvds and videos

Library catalogue: All or part available in-house

Publications: Printed, and electronic and video

Publications list: Available online and in print

Access to staff: Contact by letter, by telephone, by fax, by e-mail, in person and via website. Appointment necessary. Non-members charged.
Hours: Mon to Fri, 0900 to 1700

Access to building: No access other than to staff
Hours: Mon to Fri, 0900 to 1700

Access for disabled people: Toilet facilities

AMATEUR BOXING ASSOCIATION OF ENGLAND LIMITED (ABA)

Crystal Palace, National Sports Centre, London, SE19 2BB

Tel: 020 8778 0251
Fax: 020 8778 9324
Website: www.amateurboxingassociation.co.uk

Enquiries to: Secretary
Direct e-mail: hannah.mclafferty@abae.org.uk

Founded: 1993; formerly called Amateur Boxing Association

Organisation type and purpose: Membership association (membership is by election or invitation), voluntary organisation, training organisation. Governing body of amateur boxing in England.

Subject coverage: History of boxing, coaching, officials, membership.

Collection: Literature on the Association

Publications: Printed

Access to staff: Contact by letter. Appointment necessary.
Hours: Mon to Fri, 0900 to 1600

Affiliated to: European Boxing Association (EABA); International Amateur Boxing Association (AIBA)

AMATEUR FOOTBALL ALLIANCE (AFA)

Unit 3, 7 Wenlock Road, London, N1 7SL

Tel: 020 8733 2613
Fax: 020 7250 1338
E-mail: info@amateur-fa.com
Website: www.amateur-fa.org

Enquiries to: General Secretary

Founded: 1907

Organisation type and purpose: Membership association (membership is by election or invitation, subscription, qualification), present number of members: 320 affiliated clubs, 340 affiliated referees. Regional governing body for association football.

Subject coverage: Recreational amateur football.

Publications: Printed

Access to staff: Contact by letter, by telephone, by fax, by e-mail and via website
Hours: Mon to Fri, 0915 to 1645

Parent body: The Football Association

AMATEUR SWIMMING ASSOCIATION (ASA)

Harold Fern House, Derby Square, Loughborough, Leicestershire, LE11 5AL

Tel: 01509 618700
Fax: 01509 618701
E-mail: customerservices@swimming.org
Website: www.leicestershireasa.org/

Enquiries to: Customer Services Manager

Founded: 1869

Organisation type and purpose: Governing body of swimming.

Subject coverage: Swimming; diving; water polo; synchronised swimming; competitive swimming; examinations and awards; education and teaching; student research; swimming for people with a disability; aquatic exercise.

Publications: Printed, and electronic and video
Order printed publications from: ASA Merchandising Ltd
Unit 1, Kingfisher Enterprise Park, 50 Arthur Street, Redditch, Worcestershire, B98 8LG, tel: 0800 220292, fax: 01527 514277, e-mail: sales@asa-awards.co.uk

Publications list: Available in print

Access to staff: Contact by letter, by telephone, by fax and by e-mail
Hours: Mon to Fri, 0900 to 1700

Houses the: Institute of Swimming Teachers and Coaches

Member of: Central Council of Physical Recreation; Sports Council

AMATEUR SWIMMING ASSOCIATION, WATER POLO COMMITTEE

177 Urmston Lane, Stretford, Manchester, M32 9EH

Tel: 0161 866 8588
Fax: 0161 865 6041
E-mail: juliemikepolo@supanet.com

Enquiries to: Committee Administrator

Organisation type and purpose: Membership association.

Subject coverage: Water polo.

Access to staff: Contact by letter, by telephone, by fax and by e-mail
Hours: Sun to Sat, 0900 to 2000

Access to building: No access other than to staff

Connections with: Amateur Swimming Association; Harold Fern House, Derby Square, Loughborough, LE11 5AL; tel: 01509 618700; fax: 01509 618701

AMBER FOUNDATION

Shurnhold Trading Estate, Melksham, Wiltshire, SN12 8DE

Tel: 01225 792622
Fax: 01225 792629
Website: www.amber-web.org

Enquiries to: Chief Executive
Direct tel: 01594 837934 (Chief Exec.); 02380 276531 (PR and Fundraising Director)
Direct fax: 01594 837934
Other contacts: PR and Fundraising Director

Founded: 1995

Organisation type and purpose: Registered charity (charity number 1051388) for young unemployed people, who are often also homeless.
To help reduce the level of unemployment within the 18–30 age group, working with ex-offenders, ex-drug users, alcoholics, those who have lost their motivation and self-esteem and those who just need a leg up to move forward, by giving them time and space in a residential environment to rebuild their lives and build their self confidence and self esteem so they are motivated to seek employment. Amber works with the individual, giving them the required confidence and practical skills that they are lacking. Its long-term plan is to expand further and open centres in other areas of the country.

Subject coverage: Runs three residential centres providing temporary 24-hour care and support, offers accredited training courses, including adult literacy and numeracy, and tenancy and housing-related issues. Broader, transferable skills are developed in personal development and team work and leadership courses that involve personal fitness and a wide range of outdoor activities. The charity's Practical Housing Units are also being used by prisons, housing societies, charities for the homeless and other large and small organisations.

Education services: PHUs: 10 modules, accredited by AQA; a complete package of staff training and programme supervision, student learning materials/resources, and registration, verification and certification of achieved PHUs.

Publications: Printed, and electronic and video
Order printed publications from: Report and Accounts, e-mail: sue.condie@amberweb.org
Newsletter, tel: 02380 276531; or order via website
Order electronic and video publications from: available on website

Access to staff: Contact by letter, by telephone, by fax, by e-mail and via website

Also at: Ashley Court Residential Centre; Chawleigh, nr Chulmleigh, Devon, EX18 7EX; tel: 01769 581011; fax: 01769 581379; Bythesea Lodge Residential Centre; Bythesea Road, Trowbridge, Wiltshire, BA14 8HR; tel: 01225 759900; fax: 01225 759909; Farm Place Residential Centre; Stane Street, Ockley, Dorking, Surrey, RH5 5NG; tel: 01306 627927; fax: 01306 627426

AMBER VALLEY BOROUGH COUNCIL (AVBC)

Amber Valley Borough Council, Town Hall, Market Place, Ripley, DE5 3BT

Tel: 01773 570222, 01773 841490 (Minicom)
E-mail: enquiry@ambervalley.gov.uk
Website: www.ambervalley.gov.uk

Enquiries to: Chief Executive

Organisation type and purpose: Local government body (membership is by election or invitation), present number of members: 45.

Subject coverage: Local government issues.

Publications: Printed

Access to staff: Contact by letter, by telephone, by fax, by e-mail and in person. Appointment necessary.
Hours: Mon to Fri, 0900 to 1630, Wed, 1000 to 1630

Access for disabled people: Parking provided, toilet facilities

AMBLESS

Shalom House, Lower Celtic Park, Enniskillen, Co Fermanagh, BT74 6HP

Tel: 028 6632 0320
Fax: 028 6632 0320

Enquiries to: Secretary
Other contacts: Chief Executive

Founded: 1984; formerly called I Am Blessed Ministries (year of change 1990); incorporates the former DAP, Disasters, Accidents Involving People (year of change 1996)

continued overleaf

Organisation type and purpose: Non-profit-making organisation. Ambless is a national charity with a Christian ethos, that works to alleviate distress, suffering, heartache, grief, loneliness and trauma that accidents can cause. The services provided are confidential and discreet and are available to patients, their families and carers. Ambless relies entirely on the free-will support of the general public. Operates the 24-hour Ambless Accident Supportline (028 6632 0321 – tel, fax, SMS text and voicemail) and Ambless Care Car (tel 07920 793456).

Subject coverage: Professional counselling, befriending, information and advice and practical support for people who have suffered an accident, and for their families and carers.

Collection: I am Blessed (newsletter)
Our Companion (newsletter)

Publications: Printed

Access to staff: Contact by letter, by telephone, by fax and in person. Appointment necessary.
Hours: Mon to Sat, 1000 to 2200, 24 hour helplines

Access for disabled people: Parking provided

AMBULANCE SERVICE INSTITUTE (ASI)

2 Appletree Close, Oakley, Basingstoke, Hampshire, RG23 7HL

Fax: 01256 782650
E-mail: ambservinst.uk@virgin.net
Website: www.asi-international.com

Enquiries to: Honorary Secretary

Founded: 1976; formerly called Institute of Ambulance Officers, Institute of Certified Ambulance Personnel, National Institute of Ambulance Instructors

Organisation type and purpose: International organisation, professional body, registered charity, training organisation.

Subject coverage: Ambulance Service organisation, administration and operation; training and qualifying examinations.

Publications: Printed

Publications list: Available online

Access to staff: Contact by letter, by fax, by e-mail and via website
Hours: Mon to Fri, 0900 to 1700

AMBULANCE SERVICE NETWORK

The NHS Confederation, 3rd Floor, 29 Bressenden Place, London, SW1E 5DD

Tel: 020 7074 3200
E-mail: liz.kendall@nhsconfed.org
Website: www.nhsconfed.org/ambulance-trusts/index.cfm

Enquiries to: Information Officer

Founded: 1994; created by the merger of the Ambulance Service Association (ASA) and the NHS Confederation (NHSC); formerly called Association of Chief Ambulance Officers (ACAO) (year of change 1994)

Organisation type and purpose: National organisation, trade association (membership is by qualification), present number of members: 39 Corporate members.
Corporate membership for NHS Ambulance Services.

Subject coverage: NHS Ambulance Services.

Trade and statistical information: Data on Ambulance personnel, finance and operations

Publications: Printed
Order printed publications from: Administrative Assistant, Ambulance Service Association
As main address

Access to staff: Contact by letter
Hours: Mon to Fri, 0900 to 1730

Access to building: Prior appointment required

Access for disabled people: Parking provided, ramped entry, access to all public areas, toilet facilities

AMERICAN AUTO CLUB UK (AAC UK)

2 Cumbers Cottage, Sandy Lane, Hanmer, Whitchurch, Shropshire, SY13 3DL

Tel: 01948 830754
Fax: 01948 830754
E-mail: secaacuk@aol.com
Website: www.american-auto-club.co.uk

Enquiries to: Chief Executive Officer
Other contacts: Membership Secretary, President

Founded: 1981

Organisation type and purpose: International organisation, membership association (membership is by subscription), present number of members: 2600.
To expand interest and ownership of American automobiles in the UK.

Subject coverage: Technical information on American automobiles, registrations, valuations for insurance purposes, location of parts. Recognised by DVLA for providing vehicle data to obtain year-related registrations. There are 47 area representatives covering the United Kingdom and the United States to locate spares etc.

Collection: Collection of books relating to production and data of American cars, trucks and motor cycles

Publications: Printed

Access to staff: Contact by letter, by telephone, by fax and by e-mail
Hours: Mon to Fri, 0900 to 1700

Access to building: No access other than to staff

AMERICAN CHURCH IN LONDON (ACL)

Whitefield Memorial Church, Tottenham Court Road, London, W1T 4TD

Tel: 020 7580 2791
Fax: 020 7580 5013
E-mail: info@amchurch.co.uk
Website: www.amchurch.co.uk

Enquiries to: Secretary
Direct e-mail: churchsecretary@amchurch.co.uk
Other contacts: (1) Senior Pastor; (2) Associate Pastor; (3) Church Secretary

Organisation type and purpose: Church.

Access to staff: Contact by telephone, by fax, by e-mail and via website
Hours: Mon to Fri, 0900 to 1700

Member organisation of: The United Reform Church (URC)

AMERICAN EMBASSY

Formal name: Embassy of The United States of America

Information Resource Centre, American Embassy, 24 Grosvenor Square, London, W1A 1AE

Tel: 020 7894 0925 (1000 to 1200)
E-mail: reflond@state.gov
Website: london.usembassy.gov

Enquiries to: Resource Centre Director
Direct tel: 020 7499 5684

Organisation type and purpose: National government body.
Embassy unit.
To respond to enquiries about the US from journalists, media researchers, academics, libraries, members of parliament, government departments.

Subject coverage: United States government, politics, legislation, society, current affairs.

Collection: Approximately 30 US journal subscriptions in appropriate subject areas (news, current affairs, politics etc)
Approximately 2,000 books
CIS (Congressional Information Service) microfiche collection (1976–2000)
Selected US Government reports and documents

Trade and statistical information: Only basic economic and trade-related statistical data on the US.
Market survey-type information is not held

Library catalogue: All or part available in print

Access to staff: Contact by letter, by telephone and by e-mail. Appointment necessary.
Hours: Mon to Fri, 0900 to 1700

Access to building: Prior appointment essential

Parent body: Department of State; Washington DC, 20520, United States of America; website: http://www.state.gov

AMERICAN TECHNICAL PUBLISHERS LIMITED (ATP)

IHS, Willoughby Road, Bracknell, Berkshire, RG12 8FB

Tel: 01344 328039
Fax: 01344 328005 emeastore@ihs.com
E-mail: emeastore@ihs.com
Website: www.ameritech.co.uk/
Website: www.ihsatp.com/

Enquiries to: Managing Director

Founded: 1980

Organisation type and purpose: Distributor of standards and technical information.

Subject coverage: Providers of technical standards and books of USA engineering societies and publishers.

Publications: Printed, and electronic and video

Access to staff: Contact by letter, by telephone, by fax, by e-mail and via website
Hours: Mon to Fri, 0800 to 1730

AMERICAN UNIVERSITY IN LONDON

97–101 Seven Sisters Road, London, N7 7QP

Tel: 020 7263 2986
Fax: 020 7281 2815
E-mail: grad@aul.edu
Website: www.aul.edu

Enquiries to: Registrar
Direct e-mail: aul@ukbusiness.com or inf@aul.edu

Founded: 1986

Organisation type and purpose: University department or institute.

Non-library collection catalogue: All or part available online

Library catalogue: All or part available in-house

Access to staff: Contact by letter, by telephone, by fax, by e-mail and in person. Appointment necessary.
Hours: Mon to Fri, 0900 to 1700

Access to building: No prior appointment required

AMIIS

Formal name: Advocacy, Mediation and Independent Investigation Service

Astolat, Coniers Way, Guildford, Surrey, GU4 7HL

Tel: 01483 531308
Fax: 01483 301072
E-mail: mediation@amiis.com
Website: www.amiis.com

Enquiries to: Head of Service
Direct e-mail: david@amiis.com

Organisation type and purpose: Membership association (membership is by election or invitation), voluntary organisation.
Resolving problems/complaints for social service users and carers in Surrey.

Subject coverage: Social service users and carers.

Access to staff: Contact by letter, by telephone, by fax, by e-mail and in person
Hours: Mon to Fri, 0900 to 1700

Access for disabled people: Parking provided
Special comments: Access via separate door and lift. Please telephone to make arrangements.

AMNESTY INTERNATIONAL (AI)

Peter Benenson House, 1 Easton Street, London, WC1X 0DW

Tel: 020 7413 5500
Fax: 020 7956 1157
E-mail: via website
Website: www.amnesty.org/en/library
Website: www.amnesty.org.uk/news/index.html
Website: www.amnesty.org.uk/amnesty/index.html
Website: www.amnesty.org.uk/support/index.html
Website: www.amnesty.org.uk/action/index.html

Enquiries to: Information Officer
Direct e-mail: press@amnesty.org

Founded: 1961

Organisation type and purpose: International organisation, membership association (membership is by subscription), voluntary organisation.
Human rights campaigning.
Seeks release of prisoners of conscience; against death penalty, torture, political killings and disappearances; for fair trials for political prisoners.

Subject coverage: Human rights violations worldwide.

Collection: Collection of recent AI reports on human rights issues

Library catalogue: All or part available online

Publications: Printed, and electronic and video, and microform publications
Order printed publications from: Marketing and Supply Team, at postal address

Publications list: Available online and in print

Access to staff: Contact by letter, by telephone, by fax, by e-mail and via website
Hours: Mon to Fri, 1000 to 1800

Access to building: No prior appointment required

AMR

PO Box 8715, London, SE23 3ZB

Tel: 020 8699 1887
E-mail: amr.org@btinternet.com
Website: www.amr.org.uk

Enquiries to: Executive Officer

Founded: 1989

Organisation type and purpose: Membership association (membership is by subscription), present number of members: 35, voluntary organisation, registered charity (charity number 1069744).
Generation, application and dissemination of knowledge within and between families.

Subject coverage: Islam/Muslims. Annual reunion to build inter-generational communication and understanding.

Information services: Building engaged Islamic personalities and characters through inter-generational family-based education, training and social interaction within a safe and enjoyable environment. Information dissemination and sharing through The Muslim News Network (MNN)

Publications: Printed, and electronic and video
Order printed publications from: AMR as above

Publications list: Available online and in print

Access to staff: Contact by letter, by telephone and by e-mail
Hours: Any day of the week – via answering machine message or e-mail

Access to building: No access other than to staff

Affiliated to: Muslim Council of Britain (MCB); PO Box 52, Wembley, HA9 0XW; tel: 020 8903 9024

AMSPAR LIMITED

Formal name: Association of Medical Secretaries, Practice Managers, Administrators and Receptionists Limited

Tavistock House North, Tavistock Square, London, WC1H 9LN

Tel: 020 7387 6005
Fax: 020 7388 2648
E-mail: info@amspar.co.uk
Website: www.amspar.com

Enquiries to: Membership Secretary

Founded: 1964

Organisation type and purpose: Professional body (membership is by subscription, qualification, election or invitation), present number of members: 4,000, registered charity (charity number 313310), suitable for ages: 16+.
National registered awarding body for professional qualifications.

Subject coverage: Professional qualifications for General Practice Managers, medical secretaries, medical receptionists, delivered via a network of approved centres and colleges throughout the United Kingdom.

Publications: Printed

Access to staff: Contact by letter, by telephone, by fax and by e-mail. Appointment necessary.
Hours: Mon to Fri, 0930 to 1730

ANAESTHETIC RESEARCH SOCIETY (ARS)

University Department of Anaesthesia and Intensive Care, Queen's Medical Centre, Nottingham, NG7 2UH

Tel: 0115 823 1002
Fax: 0115 970 0739
Website: www.ars.ac.uk

Enquiries to: Honorary Secretary
Direct e-mail: jonathan.hardman@nottingham.ac.uk

Founded: 1958

Organisation type and purpose: Learned society.
Presentation and publication of ongoing research in anaesthesia and related subjects.

Subject coverage: Anaesthesia; intensive care; acute and chronic pain relief.

Collection: Abstracts published twice a year in the British Journal of Anaesthesia

continued overleaf

Publications: Printed

Access to staff: Contact by letter, by fax, by e-mail and via website
Hours: Mon to Fri, 0900 to 1700

ANAPHYLAXIS CAMPAIGN

PO Box 275, Farnborough, Hampshire, GU14 6SX

Tel: 01252 542029 (Helpline); 01252 546100 (Administration)
Fax: 01252 377140
E-mail: info@anaphylaxis.org.uk
Website: www.anaphylaxis.org.uk

Founded: 1994

Organisation type and purpose:
Membership association (membership is by subscription), present number of members: 6,800, registered charity (charity number 1085527).
Offers support and guidance to those with life-threatening allergies, raises awareness in the food industry, medical profession, etc., promotes research.

Subject coverage: Anaphylaxis, allergic reactions.

Publications: Printed, and electronic and video

Access to staff: Contact by letter, by telephone, by fax, by e-mail and via website
Hours: Mon to Fri, 0900 to 1700
Special comments: Answerphone outside office hours; membership queries to PO Box address.

Also at: Anaphylaxis Campaign Office; 1 Alexandra Road, Farnborough, Hampshire, GU14 6BU; tel: 01252 542029; fax: 01252 377140; e-mail: info@anaphylaxis.org.uk

ANATOMICAL SOCIETY OF GREAT BRITAIN AND IRELAND (ASGBI)

Department Of Anatomy, Windle Building, University College, Cork

Tel: +353 (0)21 490–2246/2238
Fax: +353 (0)21 427–3518
E-mail: m.dorgan@ucc.ie
Website: www.blackwell-science.com
Website: www.journals.cup.org

Enquiries to: Honorary Secretary
Other contacts: Membership Secretary for membership queries, Treasurer for financial queries.

Founded: 1887

Organisation type and purpose: Learned society.

Subject coverage: Gross anatomy, anthropology, histology, cell biology, developmental biology, pathological anatomy, biomechanics and related topics.

Collection: Human embryology database

Publications: Printed
Order printed publications from: Blackwell Science Limited
Osney Mead, Oxford, OX2 0EL, tel: 01865 206206, fax: 01865 721205

Access to staff: Contact by letter, by e-mail and via website
Hours: Mon and Fri, 0915 to 1600, Tue to Thu, 0915 to 1700

ANCIENT AND HONOURABLE GUILD OF TOWN CRIERS (AHGTC)

Formal name: The Ancient and Honourable Guild of Town Criers

10 Weston Road, Guildford, Surrey, GU2 8AS

Tel: 01483 532796
E-mail: secretary@ahgtc.org.uk
Website: www.ahgtc.org.uk

Enquiries to: Secretary
Other contacts: Membership Secretary (for appointment of new Town Criers, new members)

Founded: 1978

Organisation type and purpose:
International organisation, membership association.

Subject coverage: Town crying for local authorities and commercial interests, non-political. Town crying competitions, information, history and organisation; charters the World Town Criers Championship, the European Towncriers Championship.

Publications: Printed

Access to staff: Contact by letter, by telephone, by fax, by e-mail and via website
Hours: Mon to Fri, 0900 to 2200

Access to building: No access other than to staff

Constituent bodies: World Town Criers Championships Limited; at the same address

ANCIENT MONUMENTS SOCIETY (AMS)

St Ann's Vestry Hall, 2 Church Entry, London, EC4V 5HB

Tel: 020 7236 3934
E-mail: office@ancientmonumentssociety.org.uk
Website: www.ancientmonumentssociety.org.uk

Enquiries to: Secretary

Founded: 1924

Organisation type and purpose: National organisation, learned society (membership is by subscription), present number of members: 2,000, voluntary organisation, registered charity (charity number 209605).
Study and conservation of ancient monuments, historic buildings of all ages and fine old craftsmanship.

Subject coverage: Historic buildings of all ages and types, their dating, conservation and care, new uses; planning law as it relates to them; sources of money for their restoration.

Library catalogue: All or part available in-house

Publications: Printed

Publications list: Available in print

Access to staff: Contact by letter, by telephone and by e-mail
Hours: Mon to Fri, 0900 to 1700

Access to building: No access other than to staff

Links with: Friends of Friendless Churches

ANDREA ADAMS CONSULTANCY

Enterprise House, 7 Coventry Road, Coleshill, Warwickshire, B46 3BB

Tel: 0845 124 9644
Website: www.andreaadamsconsultancy.com

Enquiries to: Office Manager

Founded: 1997

Organisation type and purpose: The Andrea Adams Consultancy provides employers with solution focused training and advice to help them effectively manage the diverse and complex problems caused by bullying and harassment in the workplace.

Subject coverage: Workplace bullying/harassment

Trade and statistical information: Statistical information on workplace bullying and rates of occurrence

Publications: Printed

Publications list: Available in print

Access to staff: Contact by letter, by telephone, by fax, by e-mail and via website
Hours: Mon to Fri, 0900 to 1700
Special comments: No visitors.

Access to building: No access other than to staff

ANGELA THIRKELL SOCIETY

54 Belmont Park, London, SE13 5BN

Tel: 020 8244 9339
E-mail: penny.aldred@ntlworld.com
Website: www.angelathirkellsociety.com

Enquiries to: Secretary

Founded: 1980

Organisation type and purpose:
Membership association.
Literary society.

Subject coverage: Life and works of Angela Thirkell and her family.

Publications: Printed

Publications list: Available in print

Access to staff: Contact by letter, by telephone and by e-mail
Hours: Mon to Fri, 0900 to 1700

Links with: Alliance of Literary Societies (ALS); e-mail: l.j.curry@bham.ac.uk; website: http://www.allianceofliterarysocieties.org.uk

ANGLESEY ANTIQUARIAN SOCIETY AND FIELD CLUB (AAS)

Llangefni Library, Education and Leisure Department, Isle of Anglesey County Council, Lôn y Felin, Llangefni, Anglesey, LL77 7RT

Tel: 01248 752092

Fax: 01248 750197
E-mail: mail@hanesmon.org.uk
Website: www.hanesmon.btinternet.co.uk

Enquiries to: Honorary Librarian and Curator
Other contacts: Honorary General Secretary for general information regarding the Society.

Founded: 1911

Organisation type and purpose: Learned society, registered charity (charity number 507837).

Subject coverage: Anglesey; its history, antiquities, archaeology, natural science, geology and literature.

Collection: Collection of printed materials, manuscripts and artefacts pertaining to Anglesey
Lucy Williams, Holyhead Collection
Transactions and Proceedings of various historical and antiquarian societies
William Williams, Pentraeth (1839–1915) Collection

Non-library collection catalogue: All or part available in-house

Publications: Printed
Order printed publications from: Publications Officer, Anglesey Antiquarian Society and Field Club
Bryn Eglwys, Llanddyfnan, Llangefni, Anglesey, LL75 8UL, tel: 01248 450310

Publications list: Available online

Access to staff: Contact by letter, by telephone and by fax. Appointment necessary.
Hours: Mon to Fri, 0900 to 1700

Access for disabled people: Parking provided, level entry, toilet facilities
Special comments: Lift available.

ANGLESEY ARCHIVES SERVICE

Formal name: Gwasanath Archifau Ynys Mon / Anglesey Archives Service

Shire Hall, Glanhwfa Road, Llangefni, Anglesey, LL77 7TW

Tel: 01248 752080
Fax: 01248 751289
E-mail: archifau@anglesey.gov.uk
Website: www.ynysmon.gov.uk

Enquiries to: Archivist

Founded: 1974; formerly called Llangefni Area Record Office of Gwynedd Archives and Museums Service (year of change 1996)

Organisation type and purpose: Local government body.
Record Office.

Subject coverage: Usual holdings of a county record office including parish records, quarter sessions records, poor law unions, local authorities, family and business collections.

Non-library collection catalogue: All or part available in-house

Access to staff: Contact by letter, by telephone, by fax, by e-mail and in person
Hours: Mon, Wed, Thu, Fri, 0900 to 1645; Tue, 1400 to 1645 (1400 to 1845 every 2nd and 4th Tue)
Special comments: Member of the County Archives Research Network; tickets issued on day of visit with suitable identification.

Access to building: No prior appointment required
Hours: Mon, Wed, Thu, Fri, 0915 to 1645; Tue, 1400 to 1645 (1400 to 1845 every 2nd and 4th Tue)
Special comments: Closed: first full week in Nov; St David's day. No prior appointment required except for microform.

Access for disabled people: Toilet facilities
Hours: Mon, Wed, Thu, Fri, 0915 to 1645; Tue, 1400 to 1645 (1400 to 1845 every 2nd and 4th Tue)
Special comments: Stairlift, with prior arrangement access to a ground floor room can be arranged.

ANGLIA RUSKIN UNIVERSITY (ARU)

University Library, Queen's Building, Rivermead Campus, Bishop Hall Lane, Chelmsford, Essex, CM1 1SQ

Tel: 01245 683757
Fax: 01245 683149
E-mail: firstname.lastname@anglia.ac.uk
Website: www.libweb.anglia.ac.uk

Enquiries to: University Librarian

History of institution: formerly called Cambridge College of Arts & Technology, Essex Institute, Chelmer Institute of Higher Education, Anglia Polytechnic University

Organisation type and purpose: University library.

Subject coverage: Law, business, management, telecommunications, languages, built environment, computing, education, nurse education, social welfare, humanities, technology, science, art, design, music, social science, English, women's studies, forensic science, chemistry, communications and media, history, optometry, psychology, politics.

Collection: French Resistance Archive (Cambridge)

Library catalogue: All or part available online

Publications: Printed
Order printed publications from: Acquisitions, University Library, Queen's Building, Rivermead Campus, Bishop Hall Lane, Chelmsford, Essex, CM1 1SQ

Access to staff: Contact by letter, by telephone, by e-mail, in person and via website
Hours: Mon to Thu, 0830 to 2050, Fri, 0830 to 1650, Sat, 1000 to 1650
Check website for vacation period details
Special comments: Appropriate identification should be carried.

Access for disabled people: Parking provided, level entry, toilet facilities

Also at: Anglia Ruskin University; University Library, Cambridge Road Campus, East Road, Cambridge, CB1 1PT; tel: 01223 698301

ANGLIA SUPPORT PARTNERSHIP (ASP)

Kingfisher House, Hinchingbrooke Business Park, Huntingdon, Cambridgeshire, PE29 6FH

Tel: 01480 398500
Fax: 01480 398501
E-mail: asplibrary@asp.nhs.uk
Website: www.asp.nhs.uk

Enquiries to: Head of Knowledge Services
Direct tel: 01480 398622
Direct e-mail: hilary.jackson@cambs-ha.nhs.uk

Founded: 1999; formerly called Cambridge and Huntingdon Health Authority, Cambridge Health Authority, Cambridgeshire Family Health Services Authority, Huntingdon Health Authority, North West Anglia Health Authority, Cambridgeshire Health Authority

Organisation type and purpose: Shared Services Organisation

Subject coverage: Health management, evidence-based health care, public health, social care.

Library catalogue: All or part available online

Access to staff: Appointment necessary.
Hours: Mon to Fri, 0900 to 1700

Access to building: No prior appointment required

Access for disabled people: Access to all public areas

ANGLICAN SOCIETY FOR THE WELFARE OF ANIMALS (ASWA)

PO Box 7193, Hound Green, Hook, Hampshire, RG27 8GT

Tel: 01252 843093
Fax: 01252 843093
E-mail: angsocwelanimals@aol.com
Website: www.aswa.org.uk

Enquiries to: Honorary Secretary

Founded: 1970

Organisation type and purpose: Membership association, registered charity (charity number 1087270).
An Anglican, Christian animal welfare organisation.

Subject coverage: Animal welfare, religious, educational, aiming to raise awareness of animal welfare issues amongst clergy and Christians.

Publications: Printed

Publications list: Available in print

Access to staff: Contact by letter, by telephone, by fax, by e-mail and via website. Appointment necessary.
Hours: Mon to Fri, 0900 to 1700

Access to building: Prior appointment required

ANGLING TRUST

Eastwood House, 6 Rainbow Street, Leominster, Herefordshire, HR6 8DQ

Tel: 0844 770 0616
Fax: 0115 906 1251

continued overleaf

E-mail: admin@anglingtrust.net
Website: www.anglingtrust.net/fl/mapping/map.asp

Founded: 2009; created by the merger of six angling and conservation organisations

Organisation type and purpose: Single governing and representative body for all game, coarse and sea anglers and angling in England, membership association (membership is by subscription).

Subject coverage: Lobbies government, campaigns on environmental and angling issues and runs national and international competitions; fights pollution, commercial over-fishing at sea, over-abstraction, poaching, unlawful navigation, local bans and a host of other threats to angling.

Access to staff: Contact by letter, by telephone, by fax and by e-mail

Development arm: Angling Development Board (ADB)

Legal arm: Fish Legal; website: http://www.fishlegal.net/landing.asp?section=158§ionTitle=Fish+Legal

ANGLO ARGENTINE SOCIETY (AAS)

2 Belgrave Square, London, SW1X 8PJ

Tel: 020 7235 9505
Fax: 020 7235 9505
E-mail: angloargentinesociety@hotmail.co.uk

Enquiries to: Secretary

Founded: 1948

Organisation type and purpose: International organisation, membership association (membership is by subscription), present number of members: 1,100, registered charity (charity number 208002).
To develop relationships between Argentina and the United Kingdom.

Subject coverage: Anglo-Argentine relations.

Access to staff: Contact by letter, by telephone, by fax, by e-mail and in person
Hours: Mon, Wed and Thu, 1330 to 1730

ANGLO BRAZILIAN SOCIETY

32 Green Street, London, W1K 7AU

Tel: 020 7493 8493
Fax: 020 7493 8493
E-mail: anglo@braziliansociety.freeserve.co.uk

Enquiries to: General Secretary

Founded: 1943

Organisation type and purpose: Membership association (membership is by subscription), registered charity.
To promote close and friendly relations between Brazil and the UK.

Subject coverage: Brazil: its people, intellectual, artistic and cultural life.

Collection: Library of Brazilian books

Access to staff: Contact by letter, by telephone and by e-mail
Hours: Tue, Wed, Thu, 1000 to 1600

Member of: Hispanic and Luso-Brazilian Council; 2 Belgrave Square, London, SW1X 8PJ

ANGLO EUROPEAN COLLEGE OF CHIROPRACTIC (AECC)

13–15 Parkwood Road, Bournemouth, BH5 2DF

Tel: 01202 436200
Fax: 01202 436312
E-mail: library@aecc.ac.uk
Website: www.aecc.ac.uk

Enquiries to: Librarian
Direct tel: 01202 436307
Direct fax: 01202 436308
Direct e-mail: doneill@aecc.ac.uk

Founded: 1965

Organisation type and purpose: University department or institute.

Subject coverage: Chiropractic.

Library catalogue: All or part available in-house

Access to staff: Contact by letter, by telephone, by fax, by e-mail and via website. Appointment necessary. Non-members charged.
Hours: Mon to Fri, 0900 to 1700

Access to building: Prior appointment required

Access for disabled people: Parking provided, ramped entry, level entry

ANGLO JEWISH ASSOCIATION (AJA)

Anglo Jewish Association, Suite 21, 58 Acacia Road, London, NW8 6AG

Tel: 020 7449 0909
E-mail: info@anglojewish.org.uk
Website: www.anglojewish.co.uk

Founded: 1871

Organisation type and purpose: Voluntary organisation, registered charity (charity number 256946), suitable for ages: undergraduates and postgraduate students at university.

Subject coverage: Jewish affairs, grants and loans for higher education.

Collection: Archives since 1871 (held at Southampton University)

Access to staff: Contact by letter, by telephone and by fax
Hours: Mon to Thu, 0900 to 1500

Affiliated to: Consultative Council of Jewish Organisations (UN)

ANGLO NORSE SOCIETY

25 Belgrave Square, London, SW1X 8QD

Tel: 020 7235 9529
E-mail: Secretariat @ anglo-norse.org.uk
Website: www.anglo-norse.org.uk/

Enquiries to: Honorary Secretary

Organisation type and purpose: Membership association (membership is by subscription), present number of members: 500, registered charity (charity number 263933).
A society promoting understanding between Britain and Norway.

Subject coverage: Encouraging exchanges of an artistic, social, literary and scientific nature. Teaching of Norwegian in UK.

Publications: Printed

Access to staff: Contact by letter and by telephone
Hours: Tue and Thu only, 1100 to 1600

ANGLO SCOTTISH FAMILY HISTORY SOCIETY

c/o Manchester & Lancashire FHS, Clayton House, 59 Piccadilly, Manchester, M21 2AQ

Tel: 0161 236 9750
Fax: 0161 237 3812
E-mail: office@mlfhs.org.uk
Website: www.mlfhs.org.uk

Enquiries to: General Secretary

Founded: 1964

Organisation type and purpose: Membership association (membership is by subscription), present number of members: c. 4500, registered charity (charity number 515599 (M&LFHS)).
Promotion of family history research.

Subject coverage: Genealogy.

Collection: Extensive collection of genealogical material

Non-library collection catalogue: All or part available in-house

Library catalogue: All or part available in-house

Publications: Printed, and electronic and video, and microform publications

Publications list: Available online and in print

Access to staff: Contact by letter, by telephone, by fax, by e-mail, in person and via website
Hours: Mon, Fri, 1015 to 1300; Tue, Thu, 1015 to 1600

Parent body: Manchester & Lancashire FHS (M&LFHS); At the same address

ANGLO THAI SOCIETY

Southwood, 62a Dore Road, Sheffield, S17 3NE

E-mail: trevorknox@onetell.com

Enquiries to: Secretary

Organisation type and purpose: Voluntary organisation.

Subject coverage: Relations between Thailand and Great Britain; history, culture, economy, national institutions and external relations of Thailand.

Access to staff: Contact by letter
Hours: Mon to Fri, 0900 to 1700

ANGLO TURKISH SOCIETY

43 Montrose Place, London, SW1X 7DU

Tel: 020 7235 8148 or 01420 562506
Fax: 01420 562506

Enquiries to: General Secretary
Direct tel: 01420 562506

Founded: 1953

Organisation type and purpose:
Membership association (membership is by subscription), voluntary organisation, registered charity (charity number 278727).

Subject coverage: Cultural and social Anglo-Turkish links.

Access to staff: Contact by letter
Hours: Mon to Fri, 0900 to 1700

ANGLO-AUSTRIAN MUSIC SOCIETY (AAMS)

158 Rosendale Road, London, SE21 8LG

Tel: 020 8761 0444
Fax: 020 8766 6151
E-mail: info@aams.org.uk
Website: www.aams.org.uk

Enquiries to: General Secretary

Founded: 1942

Organisation type and purpose: Cultural Society. Registered Charity (charity number: 219021).
The Richard Tauber Prize for singers.

Access to staff: Contact by letter, by fax and by e-mail
Hours: Mon to Fri, 0900 to 1700

ANGLO-HELLENIC LEAGUE (AHL)

16–18 Paddington Street, London, W1U 5AS

Tel: 020 7486 9410
Fax: 020 7486 4254
E-mail: anglohellenic.league@virgin.net

Enquiries to: Administrator

Founded: 1913

Organisation type and purpose:
Membership association (membership is by subscription), present number of members: 710, registered charity (charity number 278892).
To strengthen the ties between Great Britain and Greece, and promote social and cultural relations between the peoples of the two countries.

Subject coverage: Great Britain and Greece relationships.

Publications: Printed

Access to staff: Contact by letter and by telephone
Special comments: Closed during August.

ANGLO-ISRAEL ASSOCIATION (AIA)

PO Box 47819, London, NW11 7WD

Tel: 020 8458 1284
Fax: 020 8458 3484
E-mail: info@angloisraelassociation.com
Website: www.angloisraelassociation.com

Enquiries to: Executive Director

Founded: 1949

Organisation type and purpose:
Membership association (membership is by subscription), present number of members: 250, voluntary organisation, registered charity (charity number 313523).
Friendship organisation promoting Anglo-Israeli relations in the UK.

Subject coverage: Israel and its place in the Middle East, Israeli life, scholarships.

Publications: Printed

Publications list: Available in print

Access to staff: Contact by letter, by telephone, by fax, by e-mail and via website. Appointment necessary.
Hours: Mon to Thu, 1000 to 1630

Access to building: No access other than to staff.

Links with: Israel, Britain and the Commonwealth Association; Tel-Aviv, Israel

ANGLO-NORMAN TEXT SOCIETY (ANTS)

School of Languages, Birkbeck College, Malet Street, London, WC1E 7HX

E-mail: i.short@bbk.ac.uk
Website: www.bbk.ac.uk/ants

Enquiries to: Honorary Secretary

Founded: 1938

Organisation type and purpose: Learned society, research organisation, publishing house.

Subject coverage: Anglo-Norman language and literature; mediaeval French language and literature; publication of texts of historical, legal, linguistic and literary value.

Publications: Printed

Publications list: Available online and in print

Access to staff: Contact by letter, by e-mail and via website

ANGUS ARCHIVES

Hunter Library, Restenneth Priory, Forfar, DD8 2SZ

Tel: 01307 468644
E-mail: angus.archive@angus.gov.uk
Website: www.angus.gov.uk/history/archives

Enquiries to: Archivist

Founded: 1989; formerly called Angus Local Studies Centre

Organisation type and purpose: Local government body.

Subject coverage: Burgh and county history, village history, family history, Angus people, archives of Angus.

Collection: Over 800 sets of manuscript collections comprising papers belonging to individuals, businesses and societies in Angus, Arbroath, Brechin, Carnoustie, Edzell, Ferryden, Forfar, Kirriemuir, Montrose and Newtyle. These include:
Antiquities of Forfarshire, 19th century
Poems of Betty Stuart, Kinnaird Castle, 1911
Arbroath Ladies Clothing Society, 1840–1927
Papers of William Dorward, mariner in Arbroath, 1803–1871
Royal Naval Lifeboat Institute, Arbroath Branch, 1854–1983
Brechin Dispensary 1823–1870
Papers of Frederick A Ferguson, Town Clerk of Brechin, 1925–1959
Brechin Guildry papers, 1628-c.1900
Caledonian Railway – Carnoustie Station Lavatory charges, 1920–1974
Carnoustie Townswomen's Guild, 1964–1984
Papers concerning Rev Robert Inglis and Inglis Memorial Hall, 1837–1903
Forfar Baptist Church, 1872–1926
Forfar Tract Society, 1858–1940
Correspondence of J M Barrie, Kirriemuir, 1844–1892
Monifieth Scouts minute book, 1950–1969
Montrose Trades Library, 1855–1904
George Fairweather, Funeral Director, Baltic Street, Montrose, 1911–1971
Correspondence of George Paton, merchant in Montrose, 1762–1766
Newtyle Collection of William Murdoch Duncan, 1970s

Non-library collection catalogue: All or part available online, in-house and in print

Library catalogue: All or part available online and in-house

Publications: Printed, and electronic and video

Access to staff: Contact by letter, by telephone, by e-mail, in person and via website. Appointment necessary.
Hours: Mon to Fri, 1000 to 1600

Access to building: *Hours:* Mon to Fri, 1000 to 1600

ANGUS COUNCIL

Angus House, Orchardbank Business Park, Forfar, DD8 1AX

Tel: 08452 777 778
Fax: 01307 466183
E-mail: cultural@angus.gov.uk
Website: www.angus.gov.uk

Enquiries to: Senior Cultural Services Manager
Other contacts: Libraries Manager

Founded: 1996; formerly a part of Angus District Council; formerly a part of Tayside Regional Council; formerly a part of Dundee City Council (year of change 1996)

Organisation type and purpose: Local government body.
Public library, archives, art galleries and exhibition, museum, education resources service, halls and theatre.
The Libraries and Museums Service is a major community facility within Angus whose purpose is to give unbiased access to information.

Subject coverage: General, Scottish and local history.

Collection: John C. Ewing, Forfar Library (Scottish Material)
Montrose Library (original Montrose Subscription Library)
R. W. Inglis Free Library, Edzell
On microfiche and available for consultation are the following:
British Standards
Census and Parish Records

continued overleaf

Evaluation Volumes
International Genealogical Index
Local Newspapers

Library catalogue: All or part available online and in-house

Publications list: Available in print

Access to staff: Contact by letter, by telephone, by fax, by e-mail and in person
Hours: Mon to Fri, 0900 to 1700

Links with: Chartered Institute of Library and Information Professionals (CILIP); Chartered Institute of Library and Information Professionals, Scotland (CILIPS); Scottish Museums Council; SLIC

ANIMAL CONCERN

PO Box 5178, Dumbarton, Strathclyde, G82 5YJ

Tel: 01389 841639
Fax: 0870 7060327
E-mail: animals@jfrobins.force9.co.uk
Website: www.animalconcern.org

Enquiries to: Campaigns Consultant
Direct tel: 07721 605521
Direct fax: 08707060327
Direct e-mail: animals@jfrobins.force9.co.uk

Founded: 1876; formerly called Scottish Anti-Vivisection Society (SAVS), Animal Concern (Scotland) (year of change 1988)

Organisation type and purpose: Membership association (membership is by subscription), present number of members: c. 250, voluntary organisation, suitable for all ages.
Pressure group.
The elimination of animal exploitation.

Subject coverage: All animal rights and welfare issues.

Collection: Phyllis Walker Memorial Collection of Animal Welfare Literature, Mitchell Library, Glasgow

Publications: Printed
Order printed publications from: Office at above address

Access to staff: Contact by letter, by telephone, by fax, by e-mail and via website. Appointment necessary.
Hours: 24-hour access

Access to building: No access other than to staff

ANIMAL HEALTH TRUST (AHT)

Lanwades Park, Kentford, Newmarket, Suffolk, CB8 7UU

Tel: 01638 751000
Fax: 01638 750410
E-mail: info@aht.org.uk
Website: www.aht.org.uk

Enquiries to: Librarian
Direct e-mail: library@aht.org.uk

Founded: 1947

Organisation type and purpose: Registered charity (charity number 209642), research organisation.
The advancement of veterinary science.

Subject coverage: Veterinary science includes cancer, skin diseases, eye problems, genetics, haematology, immunology, clinical chemistry, microbiology, mycology, pathology, radiography, surgery and epidemiology.

Non-library collection catalogue: All or part available in-house

Library catalogue: All or part available in-house

Publications: Printed

Publications list: Available online

Access to staff: Contact by letter, by telephone, by fax and by e-mail. Appointment necessary.
Hours: Mon to Thu, 0900 to 1200

Access to building: Prior appointment required

ANIMALS' REFUGE

Formal name: The National Equine (and Smaller Animals) Defence League

Oak Tree Farm, Wetheral Shields, Carlisle, CA4 8JA

Tel: 01228 560082
Fax: 01228 560985
E-mail: heatherm@animalrefuge.co.uk
Website: www.animalrefuge.co.uk

Enquiries to: Director

Founded: 1909; formerly called National Equine Defence League

Organisation type and purpose: Registered charity (number 280700).
An animal refuge and rehoming service. The League works to protect all kinds of animals through its Animals' Refuge near Carlisle.

Subject coverage: Provides a home to horses, donkeys, sheep, cattle and goats, and provides a temporary haven for dogs, cats and other small pets awaiting new homes through the League's Adoption Programme.

Special visitor services: School visits, talks, tours, events, dog warden service.

Access to staff: Contact by letter, by telephone and by e-mail

Access to building: *Hours:* Refuge: Sun to Mon, 0930 to 1600
Kennels: Sun to Mon, 1300 to 1600

ANNE FRANK TRUST UK (AFTUK)

Star House, 104–108 Grafton Road, London, NW5 4BA

Tel: 020 7284 5858
Fax: 020 7428 2601
E-mail: info@annefrank.org.uk
Website: www.annefrank.org.uk

Enquiries to: Executive Director
Other contacts: Administrator

Founded: 1990; formerly called Anne Frank Educational Trust (AFETUK)

Organisation type and purpose: Membership association (membership is by subscription), registered charity (charity number 1003279), suitable for ages: all.

Subject coverage: Holocaust education, anti-racism education, citizenship education.

Publications: Printed, and electronic and video

Publications list: Available online and in print

Access to staff: Contact by letter, by telephone, by fax and by e-mail
Hours: Mon to Fri, 0900 to 1700

Access to building: No access other than to staff
Hours: Mon to Fri, 0930 to 1630

ANNUITY BUREAU, THE

The Tower, 11 York Road, London, SE1 7NX

Tel: 020 7902 2300
Fax: 020 7621 1888
E-mail: legalandcosec@aforbes.co.uk
Website: www.annuity-bureau.co.uk

Enquiries to: Head of Marketing
Direct tel: 020 7902 2328
Direct fax: 020 7902 0388
Direct e-mail: david@bureauxltd.co.uk

Founded: 1991

Organisation type and purpose: Service industry.

Subject coverage: Financial service and advice at retirement.

Publications: Printed

Publications list: Available online and in print

Access to staff: Contact by letter, by telephone, by fax, by e-mail and via website
Hours: Mon to Fri, 0900 to 1700

Access for disabled people: Parking provided, ramped entry

Northern Region Branch: Annuity Bureau; Sunhill Laithe, Sunhill, Fleets Lane, Rystone, Skipton, BD23 6NA; tel: 01756 731 900; fax: 01756 730 443

ANTHROPOLOGY LIBRARY

British Museum Department of Ethnography, 6 Burlington Gardens, London, W1S 3EX

Tel: 020 7323 8031
Fax: 020 7323 8013
Website: www.thebritishmuseum.ac.uk
Website: lucy.ukc.ac.uk/AIO.html

Enquiries to: Senior Librarian
Other contacts: Reading Room Supervisor for Reading Room enquiries, appointments, bibliographical information etc.

History of institution: formerly called British Museum Ethnography Library, Museum of Mankind Library (year of change 2001)

Organisation type and purpose: National government body, museum.
The Anthropology Library is a major anthropological collection with its origins in the nineteenth century. It incorporates the former library of the Royal Anthropological Institute (RAI).

Subject coverage: Its scope is worldwide and covers every aspect of anthropology: cultural anthropology, archaeology, some biological anthropology, linguistics, and related fields such as history, sociology and description and travel.

Material culture, ethnography, tribal art and anthropology of indigenous African, American, Asian, Oceanic and some European societies. Archaeology of the New World.

Collection: Incorporates former library of the Royal Anthropological Institute
The library includes the Henry Christy and the Sir Eric Thompson collections and a significant Pictorial Collection
The collection contains around 120,000 books and pamphlets and 4000 journal titles (of which 1450 are current)

Library catalogue: All or part available online

Access to staff: Contact by letter, by telephone and by fax. Appointment necessary.
Hours: Mon to Fri, 0900 to 1700
Special comments: Visitors by prior appointment except Fellows and Junior Fellows of the RAI.
Fellows and Junior Fellows of the RAI can borrow items donated by the RAI.
Other visitors and researchers may have access, by appointment, for reference purposes only.

Departmental library of the: British Museum; currently housed in the former Museum of Mankind; tel: 020 7323 8031; fax: 020 7323 8013; e-mail: ethnography@thebritishmuseum.ac.uk

ANTHROPOSOPHICAL SOCIETY IN GREAT BRITAIN (AS IN GB)

Rudolf Steiner House, 35 Park Road, London, NW1 6XT

Tel: 020 7723 4400
Fax: 020 7724 4364
E-mail: rsh-office@anth.org.uk
Website: www.anth.org.uk

Enquiries to: Librarian
Direct tel: 020 7224 8398
Direct fax: 020 7224 8398
Direct e-mail: rsh-library@anth.org.uk
Other contacts: Executive Secretary

Founded: 1923

Organisation type and purpose:
International organisation, learned society, registered charity (charity number 220480).

Subject coverage: Anthroposophy (science of the spirit and the spiritual world); every field of art, science, religion, philosophy and social life from that aspect, including education, special needs education, medicine, agriculture and social sciences.

Collection: Art prints, photographs, archive material, eg: letters, journals
Books and MSS relating to Rudolf Steiner (1861–1925) and his work

Library catalogue: All or part available in-house

Publications: Printed, and electronic and video

Access to staff: Contact by letter, by telephone, by fax, by e-mail and in person
Hours: Office: 1030 to 1800
Bookshop: Mon to Fri, 1030 to 1400 and 1500 to 1800; Sat, 1030 to 1400 and 1500 to 1700
Library: Tue to Thu, 1100 to 1300 and 1400 to 1700 (Tue, 1930 term time); Fri, 1300 to 1800; Sat, 1200 to 1700

Associated with: Anthroposophical Medical Association; tel: 01299 861561; fax: 01299 861375; Association of Camphill Communities; tel: 01653 694197; fax: 01653 600001; e-mail: info@camphill.org.uk; Bio-Dynamic Agricultural Association; tel: 01453 759501; Committee for Steiner Special Education; Emerson College (Forest Row); tel: 01342 822238; fax: 01342 826055; e-mail: mail@emerson.org.uk; Peredur Centre for the Arts (Schools) of Eurhythmy and Speech Formation (East Grinstead); Rudolf Steiner Press; Steiner Waldorf Schools Fellowship; tel: 01342 822115; fax: 01342 826004; e-mail: mail@waldorf.compulink.co.uk; Tobias School of Art (East Grinstead); tel: 01342 313655; fax: 01342 313655; Triodos Bank (Bristol), and others; tel: 0117 973 9339; fax: 0117 973 9303

ANTI-SLAVERY INTERNATIONAL

Thomas Clarkson House, The Stableyard, Broomgrove Road, London, SW9 9TL

Tel: 020 7501 8920
Fax: 020 7738 4110
E-mail: info@antislavery.org
Website: www.antislavery.org
Website: www.antislavery.org/breakingthesilence
Website: www.recoveredhistories.org

Enquiries to: Librarian
Direct tel: 020 7501 8939
Direct e-mail: j.howarth@antislavery.org

Founded: 1839

Organisation type and purpose: Registered charity (charity number 1049160), research organisation.

Subject coverage: Modern forms of slavery, child labour, child prostitution, indigenous peoples, domestic workers, child domestic workers, history of slavery, female genital mutilation, servile marriage, bonded labour, descent-based slavery, migrant labour, forced prostitution, codes of conduct, trafficking of people, Transatlantic Slave Trade, abolition, forced labour and the supply chain.

Collection: A collection of eighteenth- and nineteenth-century tracts on slavery including Transatlantic Slavery
Binns Collection and supplementary historical and slavery collection (also in microfilm)
Books, documents and research papers on modern forms of slavery
Collection of ILO publications on slavery
Collection of United Nations publications on slavery
Large collection of literature on child labour, bonded labour and trafficking.
Slides and photography relevant to exploited labour including Congo atrocities c. 1900

Non-library collection catalogue: All or part available in-house

Library catalogue: All or part available in-house

Publications: Printed, and electronic and video, and microform publications
Order printed publications from: Publications Officer
tel: 020 7501 8922, fax: 020 7738 4110, e-mail: b.shand@antislavery.org

Publications list: Available online and in print

Access to staff: Contact by letter, by telephone, by e-mail and via website. Appointment necessary.
Hours: Mon to Fri, 1000 to 1700

Access to building: *Hours:* Mon to Fri, 1000 to 1700 by appointment

Member of: End Child Prostitution, Pornography and Trafficking (ECPAT, Ethical Trading Initiative (ETI); Grosvenor Gardens House, 35–37 Grosvenor Gardens, London, SW1W 0BS; tel: 020 7233 9887; fax: 020 7233 9869; e-mail: info@ecpat.org.uk; website: www.ecpat.org.uk

ANTIGUA AND BARBUDA TOURIST OFFICE

2nd Floor, 45 Crawford Place, London, W1H 4LP

Tel: 020 7258 0070
Fax: 020 7258 3826
E-mail: tourisminfo@antigua-barbuda.com
Website: www.antigua-barbuda.com

Enquiries to: Director of Tourism

Organisation type and purpose: To promote Antigua and Barbuda's tourist industry.

Subject coverage: History of the islands, tourism including: weddings and honeymoons, water sports, sightseeing, golf, tennis, maps, sailing, special events, meetings and incentives, family holidays.

Trade and statistical information: Tourism statistics

Publications: Printed, and electronic and video

Access to staff: Contact by letter, by telephone, by fax, by e-mail, in person and via website
Hours: Mon to Fri, 0930 to 1500
Special comments: Contact by telephone is from 0900 to 1700.

Links with: Ministry of Tourism, Culture and Environment

ANTIQUARIAN BOOKSELLERS ASSOCIATION (ABA)

Sackville House, 40 Piccadilly, London, W1J 0DR

Tel: 020 7439 3118
Fax: 020 7439 3119
E-mail: admin@aba.org.uk
Website: www.aba.org.uk

Enquiries to: Administrator

Founded: 1906

Organisation type and purpose: Trade association.

Publications: Printed

Access to staff: Contact by letter, by telephone, by fax and by e-mail
Hours: Mon to Fri, 0930 to 1730

continued overleaf

Access to building: No access other than to staff

Affiliated to: International League of Antiquarian Booksellers; website: http://www.ilab.org

ANTIQUARIAN HOROLOGICAL SOCIETY (AHS)

New House, High Street, Ticehurst, Wadhurst, East Sussex, TN5 7AL

Tel: 01580 200155
Fax: 01580 201323
E-mail: secretary@ahsoc.org
Website: www.ahsoc.demon.co.uk

Enquiries to: Administrator

Founded: 1953

Organisation type and purpose: Learned society, registered charity (charity number 260925).
Practises and promotes the study of antiquarian horology and allied disciplines in 13 countries.

Subject coverage: Promotes the study of clocks and watches, and the history of time measurement in all its forms.

Collection: Library is housed at the Guildhall Library, London

Publications: Printed

Publications list: Available online and in print

Access to staff: Contact by letter, by telephone, by fax and by e-mail
Hours: Mon to Fri, 0900 to 1700

ANTIQUE COLLECTORS' CLUB (ACC)

Sandy Lane, Old Martlesham, Woodbridge, Suffolk, IP12 4SD

Tel: 01394 389950
Fax: 01394 389999
E-mail: sales@antique-acc.com
Website: www.antiquecollectorsclub.com

Enquiries to: Marketing Director
Direct tel: 01394 389966
Direct e-mail: sarah.smye@antique-acc.com

Founded: 1966

Organisation type and purpose: Publishing house.

Subject coverage: Art, antiques, architecture, design, fashion, gardens and gardening.

Publications: Printed

Publications list: Available online and in print

Access to staff: Contact by letter, by telephone, by fax, by e-mail and in person
Hours: Mon to Fri, 0900 to 1700

ANTRIM COURT SERVICE

30 Castle Way, Antrim, BT41 4AQ

Tel: 028 94 462661
Fax: 028 94 463301
E-mail: antrimcourthouse@courtsni.gov.uk

Enquiries to: The Clerk of Petty Sessions

History of institution: formerly called Northern Ireland Court Service

Organisation type and purpose: National government body.

Access to staff: *Hours:* 0930 to 1630

Access for disabled people: Parking provided, access to all public areas, toilet facilities

ANXIETY UK

Zion CRC, 339 Stretford Road, Hulme, Manchester, M15 4ZY

Tel: 0844 477 5774
Fax: 0161 226 7727
E-mail: info@anxietyuk.org.uk
Website: www.anxietyuk.org.uk

Enquiries to: Chief Executive

Founded: 1970; formerly called National Phobics Society

Organisation type and purpose: Registered charity, voluntary organisation (charity number 1113403).

Subject coverage: Anxiety disorders, of which there are over 400 classifications, and specific help for those suffering from anxiety disorders, i.e. phobias, agoraphobia, obsessional and compulsive disorders; depression; help for people with tranquillisers – withdrawal and/or addiction; panic attacks; Body Dysmorphic Disorder; social phobia; Generalised Anxiety Disorder (GAD).

Publications: Printed

Publications list: Available online and in print

Access to staff: Contact by letter, by telephone, by fax, by e-mail, in person and via website. Appointment necessary. Access for members only. Non-members charged.
Hours: Mon to Fri, 0930 to 2100; message service outside office hours
Special comments: When corresponding by letter, please enclose an sae.

Access for disabled people: Access to all public areas

APEX TRUST

Formal name: Apex Charitable Trust Limited

7th Floor, 3 London Wall Buildings, London Wall, London, EC2M 5PD

Tel: 020 7638 5931
Fax: 020 7638 5977
E-mail: jobcheck@apextrust.com or info@apextrust.com
Website: www.apextrust.com

Enquiries to: Chief Executive

Founded: 1965

Organisation type and purpose: National organisation, registered charity (charity number 284736).
The Trust aims to reduce overall crime in society by the appropriate employment of people with a criminal record; by operating 28 projects in prisons and the community giving direct advice to ex-offenders; by raising this issue with employers; and by working with other statutory and voluntary organisations in raising this issue.

Subject coverage: Employment of ex-offenders; placing techniques; social skills training; careers advice; training in probation and after-care service, social services and prison service; attitudes and policies of professional bodies; unemployment and crime.

Collection: No library or collections

Publications: Printed

Publications list: Available online and in print

Access to staff: Contact by letter, by telephone, by fax, by e-mail and via website. Appointment necessary.
Hours: Mon to Fri, 1000 to 1800

Access to building: Prior appointment required
Hours: Mon to Fri, 1000 to 1800

APOSTROPHE PROTECTION SOCIETY (APS)

23 Vauxhall Road, Boston, Lincolnshire, PE21 0JB

Tel: 01205 350056
E-mail: chairman@apostrophe.org.uk

Enquiries to: Chairman

Founded: 2001

Organisation type and purpose: Voluntary organisation.
To urge the correct use of the apostrophe and to give advice.

Subject coverage: Correct use of the apostrophe.

Access to staff: Contact by letter and by e-mail
Hours: Mon to Fri, 0900 to 1700

APPLIED ARTS SCOTLAND

ECA, School of Design and Applied Arts, Hunter Building, Lauriston Place, Edinburgh, EH3 9DF

Tel: 0131 221 6143
E-mail: office@appliedartsscotland.org.uk

Enquiries to: Administrator
Other contacts: Convenor for policy matters.

Founded: 1992; formerly called Association for Applied Arts (AAS) (year of change 2000)

Organisation type and purpose: Membership association (membership is by subscription), present number of members: 300, voluntary organisation, registered charity (charity number SCO 22604).
To promote contemporary applied arts produced in Scotland.

Subject coverage: Applied Arts Scotland holds a commissioning register of slides and information from around 300 makers in Scotland. They offer a commissioning service to public and private companies, galleries, retail outlets etc.

Publications: Printed

Publications list: Available in print

Access to staff: Contact by letter, by telephone and by e-mail. Access for members only. Non-members charged.
Hours: Mon, 0930 to 1730

Access to building: No prior appointment required
Special comments: Commissioning register.

ARAB HORSE SOCIETY (AHS)

Windsor House, The Square, Ramsbury, Marlborough, Wiltshire, SN8 2PE

Tel: 01672 520782
Fax: 01672 520880

Enquiries to: Honorary Secretary
Direct tel: 01323 811385
Direct fax: 01323 811533
Direct e-mail: jean-mary.crozier@virgin.net

Founded: 1918

Organisation type and purpose:
Membership association (membership is by subscription), present number of members: 3950, registered charity (charity number 213366).
Breeding of Arabian horse and its derivatives, horse shows, amateur flat racing.

Subject coverage: Stud book and race records for Arab, Anglo-Arab and part bred Arab horses.

Collection: Library mainly on breed stud books from 1918 when the Society was founded

Trade and statistical information: World data on Arab horse registration

Publications: Printed

Access to staff: Contact by letter, by telephone, by fax, by e-mail and in person
Hours: Mon to Fri, 0900 to 1700

Access to building: No prior appointment required

Affiliated to: British Horse Society; ECAHO; WAHO

ARAB WORLD DOCUMENTATION UNIT (AWDU)

IAIS Building, Exeter University, Stocker Road, Exeter, Devon, EX4 4ND

Tel: 01392 264041
Fax: 01392 264035
E-mail: awdu@exeter.ac.uk
Website: www.library.ex.ac.uk/awdu/bombaydiaries.htm
Website: www.library.ex.ac.uk/awdu
Website: www.library.ex.ac.uk/awdu/KeyTitlesList.html
Website: lib.exeter.ac.uk

Enquiries to: AWDU Librarian
Direct tel: 01392 264051
Direct e-mail: j.p.c.auchterlonie@exeter.ac.uk
Other contacts: Library Assistant (AWDU)

Founded: 1979; formerly called Centre for Arab Gulf Studies Documentation Unit (CAGS) (year of change 2001)

Organisation type and purpose: University library, research organisation.
Reference and research library; documentation unit.
To further the study of the Gulf and Arabian Peninsula region, Arab countries and other Middle East topics.

Subject coverage: Arab Countries, especially Arabian Peninsula and Gulf region; current documentation (often including back-runs to the mid-20th century) with emphasis on statistical material, economic reports, development plans, etc. from governments and official sources including international organisations, commercial sources such as banks, monetary agencies, commerce and industry, and academic and political sources and news media. History of the region, 16th to 20th century, including published, microform and photocopied archives.
Middle East studies: especially economic, political and sociological. Palestine and the Arab–Israeli Conflict.
International petroleum studies.

Collection: Archives held as photocopies or films:
Bombay Archives 1780–1830 (15,000 pages selected for relevance to the Gulf, Red Sea and Arabian Peninsula region, with typed transcripts and detailed index (this collection is unique, being the only copy in Europe)
Some Portuguese archives of the region 1560–1752
French consular correspondence on Muscat 1783–1810
Relevant selections from the National Archives of USA, National Archives of India, UK Foreign Office and India Office records 1800–1959
Microfiche edition Palestine: the British Mandate
Published books from Archive Editions of the region
A substantial library on Palestine, Israel and the Arab–Israeli conflict, including governmental, international, commercial, academic and political publications, plus unpublished and archival materials and research documentation, e.g. papers on Arrabeh 1850–1950
Press cuttings: classified microfiche collection on the Middle East 1957–82
CAABU collection of press cuttings on the Arab World 1968–2001
BBC Summary of World Broadasts for the Middle East in hard copy or microfiche, 1955–2001
Videos and DVDs of Arab feature films (mainly Egyptian), Iranian feature films and some documentaries on the Middle East
Large collection of modern maps on the Middle East

Trade and statistical information: Trade information for countries of the region and regional trade (Middle East).
Statistical information, on every aspect of the countries and the Middle East region.
Primary countries covered: Bahrain, Iraq, Kuwait, Oman, Saudi Arabia, UAE, Yemen, Iran, Palestine, Israel, (also Lebanon, Jordan, Syria and Egypt)

Non-library collection catalogue: All or part available online

Library catalogue: All or part available online

Access to staff: Contact by letter, by telephone, by fax, by e-mail, in person and via website
Hours: Mon to Fri, 1000 to 1600
Special comments: A prior appointment for visitors is essential.

Access for disabled people: Parking provided, level entry, toilet facilities

Parent body: Exeter University Library; Stocker Road, Exeter, EX4 4PT; tel: 01392 264051; fax: 01392 263871; website: http://as.exeter.ac.uk/library

ARBORICULTURAL ASSOCIATION (AA)

Formal name: Arboricultural Association Ltd

The Malthouse, Stroud Green, Standish, Stonehouse, Gloucestershire, GL10 3DL

Tel: 01242 522152
Fax: 01242 577766
E-mail: admin@trees.org.uk
Website: www.trees.org.uk

Enquiries to: Director

Founded: 1964; incorporates the former Association of British Tree Surgeons and Arborists (year of change 1974)

Organisation type and purpose: National organisation, professional body, membership association (membership is by subscription), present number of members: 2300, registered charity.
To advance the science of arboriculture for the public benefit.

Subject coverage: Production, selection, planning and maintenance of ornamental trees, shrubs and amenity woodlands; tree surveys, inspection, pathology; legal matters.

Non-library collection catalogue: All or part available online

Publications: Printed
Order printed publications from: Postal address

Publications list: Available online and in print

Access to staff: Contact by letter, by telephone, by fax, by e-mail and via website
Hours: Mon to Fri, 0900 to 1700

Access to building: No prior appointment required

Access for disabled people: Parking provided

Member organisation of: Society for the Environment; Denham House, 120 Long Street, Atherstone, Warwickshire, CV9 1AF; tel: 0845 337 2951; fax: 01827 718232; e-mail: enquiries@socenv.org.uk; website: www.socenv.org.uk

ARC

Formal name: Association for Real Change

ARC House, Marsden Street, Chesterfield, Derbyshire, S40 1JY

Tel: 01246 555043
Fax: 01246 555045
E-mail: contact.us@arcuk.org.uk
Website: www.arcuk.org.uk

Enquiries to: Chief Executive

Founded: 1976; formerly called Association of Residential Communities

Organisation type and purpose:
Professional body (membership is by subscription), present number of members: 300 organisations, voluntary organisation, registered charity (charity number 285575), training organisation, publishing house.

continued overleaf

Subject coverage: Learning disability (mental handicap), social care, vocational training in health and social care, management, sexual abuse.

Non-library collection catalogue: All or part available in-house and in print

Publications list: Available online

Access to staff: Contact by letter, by telephone, by fax, by e-mail and via website. Appointment necessary.
Hours: Mon to Fri, 0900 to 1700

Access to building: No prior appointment required
Hours: Mon to Fri, 0900 to 1700
Special comments: Library, members only.

Also at: ARC Cymru; Unit 3A, MENTEC, Deiniol Road, Bangor, LL57 2UP; tel: 01248 361990; ARC Northern Ireland; 43 Marsden Gardens, Cave Hill, Belfast, BT15 5AL; tel: 028 9022 9020; fax: 028 9020 9300; e-mail: arc .ni@arcuk.org.uk; ARC Scotland; Unit 13, Hardengreen Business Centre, Eskbank, Dalkeith, Midlothian, EH22 3NX; tel: 0131 663 4444; fax: 0131 663 5522; e-mail: arc .scotland@arcuk.org.uk; ARC Training Consortium; ARC House, Marsden Street, Chesterfield, Derbyshire, S40 1JY; tel: 01246 564970; fax: 01246 55504; e-mail: consortium@arcuk.org.uk

ARC ANTENATAL RESULTS & CHOICES (ARC)

345 City Road, London, EC1V 1LR

Tel: 0207 713 7356
E-mail: info@arc-uk.org
Website: www.arc.uk.org

Enquiries to: Director

Founded: 1988; formerly called Support Around Termination for Abnormality (SATFA) (year of change 1998)

Organisation type and purpose:
Membership association, present number of members: 1,600, voluntary organisation, registered charity (charity number: 299770).

Subject coverage: Helping parents through antenatal testing, decision-making, offering continued support to parents whatever decision they make about the future of the pregnancy, training of health care professionals to provide appropriate services.

Publications: Printed

Publications list: Available online and in print

Access to staff: Contact by letter, by telephone, by fax, by e-mail and in person. Appointment necessary.
Hours: Mon to Fri, 1000 to 1730

ARCHAEOLOGY SCOTLAND (CSA)

Formal name: Council for Scottish Archaeology

Causewayside House, 160 Causewayside, Edinburgh, EH9 1PR

Tel: 0131 668 4189
Fax: 0131 668 4275
E-mail: info@scottisharchaeology.org.uk
Website: www.scottisharchaeology.org.uk

Enquiries to: Director
Other contacts: Assistant Director for co-ordinator of Young Archaeologists' Club Scottish network

Founded: 1944; formerly called The Council for British Archaeology Scotland (CBA Scotland)

Organisation type and purpose: National organisation, membership association (membership is by subscription), present number of members: c. 900, voluntary organisation, registered charity (charity no. SCO 001723), suitable for ages: 8 to 16.
To promote informed opinion concerning the conservation of Scotland's archaeological heritage.

Subject coverage: Archaeology, including education, careers, excavations, sources of information on sites, cultural resource management and integrated environmental approaches, who to contact in other bodies etc.

Collection: Inventory of the Scottish Church Heritage – A database of all sites in Scotland and how to access further details

Publications: Printed

Publications list: Available in print

Access to staff: Contact by letter, by telephone and by fax. Appointment necessary.
Hours: Mon to Fri, 0900 to 1700

Sister body of the: Council for British Archaeology

ARCHDEACON SHARP LIBRARY

The College, Durham, DH1 3EH

Tel: 0191 386 2489
Fax: 0191 386 4267 (Durham Chapter Office)
E-mail: library@durhamcathedral.co.uk

Enquiries to: Head of Collections

Organisation type and purpose: Theological library.
A library of modern theology in English.

Subject coverage: Theology : 20th century printed theology in English.

Non-library collection catalogue: All or part available online

Library catalogue: All or part available online

Access to staff: Contact by letter, by telephone, by e-mail and in person
Hours: Mon to Fri, 0930 to 1645
Special comments: Closed Bank holidays and Christmas to New year, any exceptional closures will be on the Cathedral website.

Parent body: Trustees of Lord Crewe's Charities; c/o Chapter Clerk, Durham Cathedral, The College, Durham, DH1 3EH; tel: 0191 386 4266; fax: 0191 386 4267

ARCHERY GB

Lilleshall National Sports & Conferencing Centre, Newport, Shropshire, TF10 9AT

Tel: 01952 677888
Fax: 01952 606019
E-mail: enquiries@archerygb.org
Website: www.archerygb.org

Enquiries to: Enquiries Officer

Founded: 1861; Grand National Archery Society (year of change 2008)

Organisation type and purpose:
Membership association (membership is by subscription), present number of members: 33,000.
Governing body for the sport of archery in the United Kingdom.

Subject coverage: Target archery; field archery; clout and flight shooting; coaching

Publications: Printed, and electronic and video

Access to staff: Contact by letter, by telephone, by fax and by e-mail
Hours: Mon to Fri, 0900 to 1700

Member organisation of: British Olympic Association; tel: 020 8871 2677; fax: 020 8871 9104; World Archery (FITA); tel: + 4121 614 3050

ARCHIFDY CEREDIGION ARCHIVES

Town Hall, Queen's Square, Aberystwyth, Ceredigion, SY23 2EB

Tel: 01970 633697/8
E-mail: archives@ceredigion.gov.uk
Website: www.archifdy-ceredigion.org.uk

Enquiries to: Archivist

Founded: 1974; formerly called Dyfed Archives; formerly called Cardiganshire Record Office (year of change 1996)

Organisation type and purpose: Local government body.

Subject coverage: Historical information, often in manuscript form, concerning the County of Ceredigion, formerly Cardiganshire.

Access to staff: Contact by letter, by telephone, by e-mail and in person
Hours: Mon, 1000 to 1800, Tue and Wed, 1000 to 1700, Thu and Fri, 1000 to 1600

Access to building: Via library
Hours: Building opens at 0930

Access for disabled people: Toilet facilities and lift

ARCHIFDY MEIRIONNYDD ARCHIVES

Ffordd y Bala, Dolgellau, Gwynedd, LL40 2YF

Tel: 01341 424681/424682
Fax: 01341 424683
E-mail: archives.dolgellau@gwynedd.gov.uk
Website: www.gwynedd.gov.uk/Archives

Enquiries to: Area Archivist

Organisation type and purpose: Local government body.

Subject coverage: Local history.

Non-library collection catalogue: All or part available online and in-house

Library catalogue: All or part available in-house

Access to staff: Contact by letter, by telephone, by fax, by e-mail and in person

Hours: Mon, Thurs, Fri open 0930 to 1700, Tues, Wed and weekends closed
Special comments: Closed first full week in November.

ARCHITECTS REGISTRATION BOARD (ARB)

8 Weymouth Street, London, W1W 5BU

Tel: 020 7580 5861
Fax: 020 7436 5269
E-mail: info@arb.org.uk
Website: www.arb.org.uk

Enquiries to: HR and Communications Coordinator
Direct e-mail: suey@arb.org.uk

Founded: 1997; formerly called Architects Registration Council of the United Kingdom (ARCUK) (year of change 1997)

Organisation type and purpose: Statutory body.
UK statutory regulator of the architects' profession.

Publications: Printed

Publications list: Available online

Access to staff: Contact by letter, by telephone, by fax and by e-mail
Hours: Mon to Fri, 0900 to 1700

Access for disabled people: Entrance lift, toilet facilities

ARCHITECTURAL AND SPECIALIST DOOR MANUFACTURERS ASSOCIATION (ASDMA)

3 Coates Lane, High Wycombe, Buckinghamshire, HP13 5EY

Tel: 01494 447370
E-mail: specialdoors@gmail.com
Website: www.asdma.com

Enquiries to: General Secretary

Founded: 1989

Organisation type and purpose: Trade association (membership is by qualification, election or invitation), present number of members: 14 full, 7 associate, 2 sponsoring.
To promote the use of and correct fitting of specialist timber doorsets, through the adoption of quality and BS Standards, and fair conditions of contract.

Subject coverage: Specialist timber doors, particularly fire, smoke, security and sound-attenuating.

Publications: Printed

Access to staff: Contact by letter, by telephone and by e-mail
Hours: Mon to Fri, 0900 to 1700

ARCHITECTURAL ASSOCIATION (AA)

34–36 Bedford Square, London, WC1B 3ES

Tel: 020 7887 4035
Fax: 020 7414 0782
E-mail: hsklar@aaschool.ac.uk
Website: www.aaschool.ac.uk

Enquiries to: Librarian
Direct tel: 020 7887 4035
Direct e-mail: hsklar@aaschool.ac.uk
Other contacts: Deputy Librarian; Archivist

Founded: 1847

Organisation type and purpose: Professional body, membership association (membership is by subscription).
School of architecture.

Subject coverage: Architecture, building, planning, landscape design.

Collection: AA Archives
Early works on architecture
History of the Association
Material on the Architectural Association from 1847 onwards
Material on the Modern Movement
Rare and early works on architecture

Non-library collection catalogue: All or part available online

Library catalogue: All or part available online

Publications: Printed
Order printed publications from: Publications, Architectural Association

Publications list: Available online and in print

Access to staff: Access for members only. Non-members charged.
Hours: Term time: Mon to Fri, 1000 to 2100; Sat, 1100 to 1700
Vacations: 1000 to 1800
Special comments: Closed August to mid-September.

Constituent bodies: AA Photo Library

ARCHITECTURAL CLADDING ASSOCIATION (ACA)

Architectural Cladding Association, 4th Floor, 60 Charles Street, Leicester, LE1 1FB

Tel: 0116 253 6161
Fax: 0116 251 4568
E-mail: aca@britishprecast.org
Website: www.britishprecast.org

Enquiries to: Secretary

Organisation type and purpose: Trade association.

Subject coverage: Precast concrete architectural cladding.

Publications: Printed

Access to staff: Contact by letter, by telephone, by fax and by e-mail
Hours: Mon to Fri, 0900 to 1700

Product association of the: British Precast Concrete Federation

ARCHITECTURAL GLAZING SERVICES (AGS)

PO Box 2210, London, W1A 1WF

Tel: 0800 028 3708
Fax: 020 7535 5676
E-mail: info@cobaltco.co.uk
Website: www.vanceva.com

Enquiries to: Information Officer
Direct tel: 020 7535 5678
Direct e-mail: wendy@cobaltco.co.uk

Founded: October 2001; incorporated Laminated Glass Information Centre (formed in 1990) (LGIC), date of change, October 2001

Organisation type and purpose: Private venture information centre, sponsored by Solutia SA/NV.
To offer advice to architects, specifiers, trade and industry, media and general public.

Subject coverage: Safety, security, acoustic, solar-resistant laminated glass, also coloured and patterned laminated glass, laminated glass. Available in automotive and architectural sectors.

Publications: Printed, and electronic and video

Publications list: Available in print

Access to staff: Contact by letter, by telephone, by fax and by e-mail
Hours: Mon to Fri, 0900 to 1700

Access to building: No access other than to staff

ARCHITECTURAL HERITAGE FUND (AHF)

Alhambra House, 27–31 Charing Cross Road, London, WC2H 0AU

Tel: 020 7925 0199
Fax: 020 7930 0295
E-mail: ahf@ahfund.org.uk
Website: www.ahfund.org.uk

Founded: 1976

Organisation type and purpose: Registered charity (number 266780).
To promote the conservation of historic buildings in the United Kingdom for beneficial new use by providing advice, information and financial assistance in the form of grants and low-interest working capital loans for projects undertaken by building preservation trusts and other suitable charities. The AHF cannot assist private individuals.

Subject coverage: The permanent preservation of buildings that are listed, scheduled or in a conservation area and of acknowledged historic merit. Projects must involve a change either in the ownership of a property or its use.

Collection: Back issues of own publications

Publications: Printed, and electronic and video

Publications list: Available in print

Access to staff: Contact by letter, by telephone, by fax and by e-mail. Appointment necessary.
Hours: Mon to Fri, 0900 to 1700

Access to building: Mon to Fri, 0900 to 1700

Links with: UK Association of Preservation Trusts (APT); Alhambra House, 27–31 Charing Cross Road, London, WC2H 0AU; tel: 020 7930 1629; fax: 020 7930 0295; e-mail: apt@ahfund.org.uk; website: http://www.ukapt.org.uk

ARCHITECTURAL HERITAGE SOCIETY OF SCOTLAND (AHSS)

The Glasite Meeting House, 33 Barony Street, Edinburgh, EH3 6NX

Tel: 0131 557 0019
E-mail: nationaloffice@ahss.org.uk
Website: www.ahss.org.uk

History of institution: formerly called Scottish Georgian Society

Organisation type and purpose: Learned society (membership is by subscription), present number of members: 1,000, voluntary organisation, registered charity (charity number SCO 07554) and registered as a company limited by guarantee (SC356726).
The Society exists to promote the study and protection of Scottish architecture.

Subject coverage: Architectural conservation and history, planning for listed buildings, protection of the built environment, heritage.

Publications: Printed

Access to staff: Contact by letter, by telephone, by e-mail and via website
Hours: Mon to Fri, 0900 to 1700

ARCHITECTURE AND SURVEYING INSTITUTE (ASI)

St Mary House, 15 St Mary Street, Chippenham, Wiltshire, SN15 3WD

Tel: 01249 444505
Fax: 01249 443602
E-mail: mail@asi.org.uk
Website: www.asi.org.uk

Enquiries to: Chief Executive

Founded: 1926; amalgated with the Guild of Incorporated Surveyors (GIS), date of change, October 1999; formerly called Architects and Surveyors Institute (ASI), Construction Surveyors Institute (CSI), Faculty of Architects and Surveyors (FAS)

Organisation type and purpose:
International organisation, professional body (membership is by subscription, qualification), present number of members: 5500, service industry, suitable for ages: all.
To promote and extend the practice, knowledge and study of architecture and surveying.

Subject coverage: Architecture, surveying, building contracts and associated documentation, careers, examinations.

Publications: Printed
Order printed publications from: ASI Services Limited, St Mary House, 15 St Mary Street, Chippenham, Wiltshire, SN15 3JN, tel: 01249 658262, fax: 01249 443602, e-mail: asinst@aol.com

Publications list: Available in print

Access to staff: Contact by letter, by telephone, by fax and by e-mail.
Appointment necessary.
Hours: Mon to Fri, 0930 to 1600

Member of: Construction Industry Council; Construction Industry Standing Conference; European Group of Surveyors

Subsidiary body: ASI Services Limited

ARCHITECTURE FOUNDATION

The Architecture Foundation, Ground Floor East, 136 – 148 Tooley Street, London, SE1 2TU

Tel: +44 (0)20 7084 6767
Fax: +44 (0)20 7407 9780
E-mail: mail@architecturefoundation.org.uk
Website: www.architecturefoundation.org.uk

Enquiries to: Press and PR Co-ordinator
Direct e-mail: claire@architecturefoundation.org.uk

Founded: 1991

Organisation type and purpose:
Membership association (membership is by subscription), present number of members: 150, voluntary organisation, registered charity (charity number 1006361), suitable for ages: all, research organisation.

Access to staff: Contact by letter, by telephone, by e-mail and via website.
Appointment necessary.
Hours: Tue to Sun, 1200 to 1800

Access for disabled people: Ramped entry, toilet facilities

ARCHITECTURE+DESIGN SCOTLAND (A+DS)

Bakehouse Close, 146 Canongate, Edinburgh, EH8 8DD

Tel: 0131 556 6699
Fax: 0131 556 6633
E-mail: info@ads.org.uk
Website: www.ads.org.uk/

Founded: 1927

Organisation type and purpose: To promote good architecture, design and planning in Scotland's built environment.

Subject coverage: Planning, design of building, urban environment, architecture, all aspects of planning and design of the environment.

Non-library collection catalogue: All or part available online

Library catalogue: All or part available online

Access to staff: Contact by letter, by fax and by e-mail
Hours: Mon to Fri, 0900 to 1700

Access for disabled people: Level entry, toilet facilities
Special comments: Ground floor only.

Sponsoring department: Scottish Executive Education Department (SEED)

ARCHIVE OF ART AND DESIGN (AAD)

Word and Image Department, Victoria and Albert Museum, 23 Blythe Road, London, W14 0QX

Tel: 020 7602 7493
Fax: 020 7602 0980
E-mail: archive@vam.ac.uk
Website: www.vam.ac.uk/resources/archives

Enquiries to: Archivist

Founded: 1978

Organisation type and purpose: Museum.
Archive collection of principally 20th-century archives of designers, design associations and companies involved in the design process.

Subject coverage: British design, design, graphic design, product design, illustration, textiles, fashion, ephemera.

Collection: Over 250 archives, including:
Krazy Kat Arkive of 20th-century popular culture
Papers of individual designers, craftspeople and artists
Heal & Son Ltd, bedding and furniture manufacturers and retailers
Edward Barnard & Sons Ltd, silversmiths
Art and Crafts Exhibition Society
John French, fashion photographer
Eileen Gray, interior and furniture designer and architect
Ambassador, the British export magazine for textiles and fashion

Non-library collection catalogue: All or part available online and in-house

Library catalogue: All or part available online

Publications: Printed
Order printed publications from: Fitzroy Dearborn Publishers, 310 Regent Street, London, W1B 3AX
Publications Department, V & A Museum, South Kensington, SW7 2RL; tel. 020 7942 2000

Publications list: Available in print

Access to staff: Contact by letter, by telephone, by fax and by e-mail.
Appointment necessary.
Hours: 1000 to 1745 daily, Fri 1000 to 2200

Access to building: Prior appointment required
Hours: Tue to Fri, 1000 to 1630
Special comments: Reference only.

Constituent part of: Victoria and Albert Museum's Word and Image Department

Links with: Artists' Papers Register; website: http://www.apr.ac.uk
National Register of Archives

ARCHIVES AND RECORDS ASSOCIATION (ARA)

Prioryfield House, 20 Canon Street, Taunton, Somerset, TA1 1SW

Tel: 01823 327030
Fax: 01823 271719
E-mail: ara@archives.org.uk
Website: www.archives.org.uk

Founded: 1947; created by the merger of National Council on Archives, Society of Archivists, and Association of Chief Archivists in Local Government (year of change 2010)

Organisation type and purpose: Principal professional body for archivists, archive conservators and records managers in the United Kingdom and Ireland.
To promote the care and preservation of archives and the better administration of archive repositories; to advance the training of its members; and to encourage relevant research and publication.

Subject coverage: Archives, records management, archives conservation.

Publications list: Available online and in print

Access to staff: Contact by letter, by telephone, by fax, by e-mail and via website. Appointment necessary.
Hours: Mon to Fri, 0830 to 1630

Member organisation of: International Council on Archives

ARCHIVES AND SPECIAL COLLECTIONS, ANDERSONIAN LIBRARY, UNIVERSITY OF STRATHCLYDE

Andersonian Library, Curran Building, 101 St James Road, Glasgow, G4 0NS

Tel: 0141 548 2497
E-mail: archives@strath.ac.uk
Website: www.strath.ac.uk/archives

Enquiries to: University Archivist

Founded: 1796

Organisation type and purpose: University department or institute.

Subject coverage: Official records of the University of Strathclyde and its antecedents, plus deposited collections.

Collection: Institutional archives of the University of Strathclyde and its antecedent institutions back to 1796
Institutional archives of Jordanhill College and its antecedent institutions back to 1828
Other, deposited, archival collections, such as Patrick Geddes Papers

Non-library collection catalogue: All or part available online and in-house

Publications: Printed
Order printed publications from: University Archivist

Access to staff: Contact by letter, by telephone, by e-mail, in person and via website
Hours: Mon to Fri, 0900 to 1700

Access to building: *Hours:* Mon to Fri, 0900 to 1700

Access for disabled people: Lift

ARG EUROPE LIMITED

Unit 2, 58a Alexandra Road, Ponders End, Enfield, Middlesex, EN3 7EH

Tel: 020 8804 8008
Fax: 020 8805 7600
E-mail: enquiries@arggroup.org
Website: www.asbestos-removal.co.uk

Enquiries to: Managing Director

Founded: 1984; formerly called Asbestos Removal (Groves) Limited (year of change 1997)

Organisation type and purpose: Service industry.
Asbestos removal, asbestos surveys.

Subject coverage: Asbestos in buildings, advice on treatment, removal and identification. Asbestos surveys.

Non-library collection catalogue: All or part available in-house

Library catalogue: All or part available in-house

Access to staff: Contact by letter, by e-mail and via website
Hours: Mon to Fri, 0900 to 1700

Access to building: No access other than to staff

ARGYLL & BUTE COUNCIL

Kilmory, Lochgilphead, Argyll, PA31 8RT

Tel: 01546 602127
Fax: 01546 604138
Website: www.argyll-bute.gov.uk

Founded: 1996

Organisation type and purpose: Local government body.

Subject coverage: Argyll and Bute Council, services and amenities, corporate services, education, environmental services, finance, housing, legal services, personnel services, planning development and tourism, property and technical services, roads and transportation, social services, council tax and other payments, registration of births, deaths and marriages.

Publications: Printed

Access to staff: Contact by letter, by telephone and by fax. Appointment necessary.
Hours: Mon to Fri, 0900 to 1700

ARGYLL & BUTE COUNCIL LIBRARY AND INFORMATION SERVICE

Sandbank Business Park, Highland Avenue, Sandbank, Dunoon, Argyll, PA23 8QZ

Tel: 01369 703214
Fax: 01369 705797
E-mail: libraryhq@argyll-bute.gov.uk
Website: www.argyll-bute.gov.uk

Enquiries to: Culture and Libraries Manager
Other contacts: Head of Community Regeneration (for overall responsibility for libraries, museums and arts)

Founded: 1996; incorporates the former Argyll and Bute District Library, Helensburgh and Lomond Area of Dumbarton District Library (year of change 1996)

Organisation type and purpose: Public library.

Subject coverage: Local studies for Argyll and Bute.

Collection: MacGrory Collection (photographs of Campbeltown and Kintyre, 1890 to 1910)
Robertson Collection (local history)

Non-library collection catalogue: All or part available in-house

Library catalogue: All or part available online

Publications: Printed

Access to staff: Contact by letter, by telephone, by fax, by e-mail and in person. Appointment necessary.
Hours: Mon to Fri, 0900 to 1700

Access for disabled people: *Hours:* Mon to Fri, 0900 to 1700

Parent body: Argyll and Bute Council; Kilmory, Lochgilphead, Argyll, PA31 8RT; tel: 01546 602127; fax: 01546 604138; website: http://www.argyll-bute.gov.uk

ARGYLL, THE ISLES, LOCH LOMOND, STIRLING & TROSSACHS TOURIST BOARD (AILLSTTB)

Old Town Jail, St John Street, Stirling, FK8 1EA

Tel: 01786 445222
Fax: 01786 471301
Website: www.scottish-heartlands.org

Enquiries to: Chief Executive

Founded: 1996; formerly called Bute & Cowal Tourist Board, Forth Valley Tourist Board, Loch Lomond, Stirling & Trossachs Tourist Board, West Highlands & Islands of Argyll Tourist Board (year of change 1996)

Organisation type and purpose: Statutory body, membership association (membership is by subscription).
To promote the area through marketing and visitor services activities at home and abroad.

Subject coverage: Advice to members on marketing, business planning and development.
Accommodation bookings through local and national schemes, promotion through the Board's publications e.g. accommodation guide.

Collection: Slide library available for hire

Publications: Printed

Publications list: Available in print

Access to staff: Contact by letter, by telephone, by fax and by e-mail
Hours: Mon to Fri, 0900 to 1700

Access to building: No prior appointment required

Tourist Information Centres: Aberfoyle (April to October); Main Street, Aberfoyle; tel: 01877 382352; Alva (all year); Mill Trail Visitor Centre, West Stirling Street, Alva; tel: 01259 769696; Ardgartan (April to October); Glen Croe, Ardgartan; tel: 01301 702432; Balloch (April to October); Balloch Road, Balloch; tel: 01389 753533; Bo'ness (April to September); Car Park, Seaview Place, Bo'ness; tel: 01506 826626; Bowmore (all year); The Square, Bowmore, Isle of Islay; tel: 01496 810254; Callander (March to December and weekends only during January and February); Rob Roy & Trossachs Visitor Centre, Ancaster Square, Callander; tel: 01877 330342; Campbeltown (all year); MacKinnon House, The Pier, Campbeltown; tel: 01586 552056; Craignure (all year); The Pier, Isle of Mull; tel: 01680 812377; Drymen (May to September); Drymen Library, The Square, Drymen; tel: 01306 660068; Dumbarton (all year); Milton, A82 Northbound; tel: 01389 742306; Dunblane (May to September); Stirling Road, Dunblane; tel: 01786 824428; Dunoon (all year); 7 Alexandra Parade, Dunoon; tel: 01369 703785; Falkirk (all year); 2–4 Glebe Street, Falkirk; tel: 01324 620244; Helensburgh (April to October); Clock

continued overleaf

Tower, The Pier, Helensburgh; tel: 01436 672642; Inveraray (all year); Front Street, Inveraray; tel: 01499 302063; Killin (March to November); Breadalbane Folklore Centre, Falls of Dochart, Killin; tel: 01567 820254; Lochgilphead (April to October); Lochnell Street, Lochgilphead; tel: 01546 602344; Oban (all year); Argyll Square; tel: 01631 563122; Rothesay (all year); Isle of Bute; tel: 01700 502151; Stirling (all year); Royal Burgh of Stirling, Visitor Centre, Castle Esplanade; tel: 01786 479901; Stirling (all year); 41 Dumbarton Road, Stirling; tel: 01786 475019; Stirling (April to October); M9/M80 Junction 9, Motorway Service Area, Stirling; tel: 01786 814111; Tarbet (Loch Fyne) (April to October); Harbour Street, Tarbet (Loch Fyne); tel: 01880 820429; Tarbet (Loch Lomond) (April to October); Main Street, Tarbet (Loch Lomond); tel: 01301 702260; Tobermory (April to October); The Pier, Tobermory, Isle of Mull; tel: 01688 302182; Tyndrum (April to October); Main Street, Tyndrum; tel: 01838 400246

ARIC

Formal name: aric

Department of Environmental and Geographical Sciences, Manchester Metropolitan University, Chester Street, Manchester, M1 5GD

Tel: 0161 247 1593
Fax: 0161 247 6332
E-mail: aric@mmu.ac.uk
Website: www.doc.mmu.ac.uk/aric/

Enquiries to: Information Officer
Other contacts: All enquiries to the Information Officer

Founded: 1984; formerly called Acid Rain Information Centre (ARIC) (year of change 1991); formerly called Atmospheric Research and Information Centre (ARIC) (year of change 1999)

Organisation type and purpose:
Consultancy, research organisation.
Information centre.
To provide world class research and education in atmospheric and sustainability issues to encourage responsible development.

Subject coverage: Air quality issues, acid rain, greenhouse effect, ozone depletion, transport, waste, sustainability, energy efficiency.

Collection: Many reference books on acidification, global climate change and urban air quality

Library catalogue: All or part available in-house

Publications: Printed, and electronic and video

Publications list: Available in print

Access to staff: Contact by letter, by telephone, by fax, by e-mail and via website. Appointment necessary.
Hours: Mon to Fri, 0900 to 1700

Supported by: Department for Environment, Food and Rural Affairs (DEFRA)

ARMAGH PUBLIC LIBRARY

Abbey Street, Armagh, BT61 7DY

Tel: 028 3752 3142
Fax: 028 3752 4177
E-mail: admin@armaghpubliclibrary.co.uk

Enquiries to: Assistant Keeper
Other contacts: Administration Officer for access to cataloguing of collection.

Founded: 1771

Organisation type and purpose: Registered charity, museum, public library, historic building, house or site, research organisation.

Collection: 17th and 18th century books on theology, philosophy, classic and modern literature, voyages and travels, history, medicine, law
Medieval and 17th and 18th century manuscripts
Engravings by Piranesi, Hogarth and Bartolozzi

Library catalogue: All or part available online

Access to staff: Contact by letter, by telephone and by e-mail. Appointment necessary.
Hours: Mon to Fri, 1000 to 1300 and 1400 to 1600
Special comments: Other times by prior arrangement.

Access to building: No prior appointment required

Access for disabled people: Ramped entry
Special comments: Chairlift to library.

ARMENIAN GENERAL BENEVOLENT UNION (LONDON) (AGBU)

25 Cheniston Gardens, London, W8 6TG

E-mail: arline.medazoumian@agbu.org.uk
Website: www.agbu.org.uk

Enquiries to: Honorary Secretary
Direct e-mail: arline.medazoumian@agbu.org.uk

Founded: 1910

Organisation type and purpose: To support the educational, cultural and social life of the UK Armenian community and promote Armenian culture and heritage within the UK.

Publications: Printed

Access to staff: Contact by letter and by e-mail

Branch of: Armenian General Benevolent Union (AGBU); 55 East 59th Street, New York, NY 10022–1112, USA; tel: (212) 319–6383; fax: (212) 319–6507; e-mail: agbuwb@agbu.org; website: http://www.agbu.org

ARMITT MUSEUM AND LIBRARY

Rydal Road, Ambleside, Cumbria, LA22 9BL

Tel: 01539 431212
Fax: 01539 431313
E-mail: info@armitt.com
Website: www.armitt.com

Founded: 1909

Organisation type and purpose: Art, literature and artefacts relating to the Lake District and its famous inhabitants.

Subject coverage: Art, archaeology, archives, books, geology, photography and local history of the Lake District.

Collection: Library of 10,000 items relating to the Lake District
Archives (manuscripts, letters, folk songs, local account books, Poor Law records and deeds)
Newspapers and parish magazines
Beatrix Potter illustrations

Library catalogue: All or part available in-house

Access to staff: Contact by letter, by telephone, by e-mail and via website. Appointment necessary.

Access to building: *Hours:* Museum: Mon to Sat, 1000 to 1700 (last admission, 1630)
Library: Mon to Fri, 1000 to 1600

ARMY RECORDS SOCIETY (ARS)

Heritage House, PO Box 21, Baldock, Hertfordshire, SG7 5SH

Tel: 01462 896688
Fax: 01462 896677
E-mail: ars@hall-mccartney.co.uk
Website: www.armyrecordssociety.org.uk

Founded: 1985

Organisation type and purpose: Learned society (membership is by subscription).
National organisation for publishing volumes of historical documents relating to history of the British Army.

Subject coverage: British army history (by publications).

Publications: Printed
Order printed publications from: Pub Army Records Society, Heritage House, PO Box 21, Baldock, Hertfordshire, SG7 5SHI tel: 01462 896688; fax: 01462 896677; e-mail: ars@hallmccartney.co.uk

Publications list: Available online and in print

Access to staff: Contact by letter and via website

Membership Administrators: Hall McCartney Limited; Heritage House, PO Box 21, Baldock, Hertfordshire, SG7 5SH; tel: 01462 896688; fax: 01462 896677; e-mail: ars@hall-mccartney.co.uk

AROMATHERAPY COUNCIL (AOC)

PO Box 6522, Desborough, Kettering, Northamptonshire, NN14 2YX

Tel: 0870 7743477
E-mail: info@aromatherapycouncil.co.uk
Website: www.aromatherapycouncil.co.uk

Enquiries to: Secretary
Direct e-mail: publications@aromatherapycouncil.co.uk

Founded: 1991; formerly called Aromatherapy Organisations Council (AOC); formerly called Aromatherapy Consortium (year of change 2006)

Organisation type and purpose: Regulatory authority.

Subject coverage: Aromatherapy.

Publications list: Available online

Access to staff: Contact by letter, by telephone and by e-mail

Access to building: No access other than to staff

AROMATHERAPY TRADE COUNCIL (ATC)

PO Box 219, Market Rasen, LN8 9BR

Tel: 01673 844672
E-mail: info@a-t-c.org.uk
Website: www.a-t-c.org.uk

Enquiries to: Administrator

Founded: 1992

Organisation type and purpose: Trade association for the specialist aromatherapy essential oil trade.

Subject coverage: The regulation and responsible marketing of essential oils and aromatherapy products.

Trade and statistical information: Data on responsible marketing of essential oils. Guidelines on the regulation of essential oils and aromatherapy products.

Publications: Printed

Access to staff: Contact by letter, by telephone, by fax, by e-mail and via website
Hours: Mon to Fri, 0900 to 1700

ARON VECHT AND ASSOCIATES

95 Corringham Road, London, NW11 7DL

Tel: 020 8316 8429
Fax: 020 8316 8405
E-mail: phosphors@vecht.com
Website: www.aronvechtandassociates.com
Website: www.vecht.com

Enquiries to: Principal
Direct tel: 020 8455 4361
Direct fax: 020 8201 9555
Direct e-mail: phosphor@vecht.com

Founded: 1987; formerly called Phosphor Consultants (year of change 1987)

Organisation type and purpose: International organisation, consultancy, research organisation.

Subject coverage: Materials science, semiconductors, phosphors, displays and thin films, as well as ultra-pure chemicals used in the electronics industry, assessment of new technologies in these areas for investment and marketing. Specific areas of expertise include: chemical vapour deposition of thin films, electro-luminescence, liquid crystals and cathode ray phosphors.

Publications: Printed, and electronic and video

Publications list: Available in print

Access to staff: Contact by letter, by telephone, by fax, by e-mail and via website
Hours: Mon to Fri, 0900 to 2400

ART AND ARCHITECTURE SOCIETY (A&A)

70 Cowcross Street, London, EC1M 6EJ

Tel: 020 7733 2436
Fax: 020 7733 2436
E-mail: a&a@tsib.demon.co.uk
Website: www.artandarchitecture.co.uk

Enquiries to: Honorary Secretary

Founded: 1982

Organisation type and purpose: Learned society (membership is by subscription), present number of members: c 400, voluntary organisation.
Furthering artistic collaboration between those creating the built environment.

Subject coverage: Public art, art works, commissions, policy, environmental art, urban design, artists and craftsmen working on architectural commissions, sculpture parks.

Publications: Printed

Access to staff: Contact by letter, by telephone, by fax, by e-mail and via website
Hours: Mon to Fri, 0900 to 1700

ART DIRECTORS & TRIP PHOTO LIBRARY

57 Burdon Lane, Cheam, Surrey, SM2 7BY

Tel: 020 8642 3593
Fax: 020 8395 7230
E-mail: images@artdirectors.co.uk
Website: www.artdirectors.co.uk

Enquiries to: Manager

Organisation type and purpose: Commercial image library.

Subject coverage: Photography, usage of colour pictures for printing, brochures, advertising, audiovisuals, etc. Areas covered: worldwide geography, lifestyle, business and economy, nature and ecology, landscapes, holiday travel, religion and backgrounds.

Non-library collection catalogue: All or part available online

Library catalogue: All or part available online

Access to staff: Contact by letter, by telephone, by fax and by e-mail. Appointment necessary.
Hours: Mon to Fri, 0900 to 1800

ART FUND (NACF)

Formal name: National Art Collections Fund

Millais House, 7 Cromwell Place, London, SW7 2JN

Tel: 020 7225 4800
Fax: 020 7225 4848
E-mail: info@artfund.org
Website: www.artfund.org

Enquiries to: Communications Department
Direct fax: 020 7225 4808/4848

Founded: 1903

Organisation type and purpose: National organisation, membership association (membership is by subscription), present number of members: 80,000, registered charity (charity number 209174). Art charity giving to museums and galleries across the country for the purchase of works of art. The Art Fund is entirely self-funded, raising the money from membership subscriptions, donations and legacies. It also campaigns on behalf of museums and galleries, particularly on issues such as free admission to national collections and funding for acquisitions.

Subject coverage: Art current affairs, art history, bequests, grants.

Non-library collection catalogue: All or part available online

Publications: Printed

Access to staff: Contact by letter, by telephone, by fax, by e-mail and via website
Hours: Mon to Fri, 0930 to 1730

ART LIBRARIES SOCIETY OF THE UK AND IRELAND (ARLIS/UK & Ireland)

Word and Image Department, Victoria and Albert Museum, South Kensington, London, SW7 2RL

Tel: 020 7942 2317
Fax: 020 7942 2394
E-mail: arlis@vam.ac.uk
Website: www.arlis.org.uk

Enquiries to: Business Manager

Founded: 1969

Organisation type and purpose: International organisation, professional body, registered charity (charity number 1048642).
Corporate voice of art and design libraries in the UK and Ireland, making their views known to the appropriate professional and educational bodies.

Subject coverage: Art, architecture and design librarianship.

Publications: Printed

Publications list: Available online and in print

Access to staff: Contact by letter, by telephone, by fax, by e-mail, in person and via website. Appointment necessary.
Hours: Mon to Fri, 1000 to 1700

ARTHRITIC ASSOCIATION

One Upperton Gardens, Eastbourne, East Sussex, BN21 2AA

Tel: 01323 416550
Fax: 01323 639793
E-mail: info@arthriticassociation.org.uk
Website: www.arthriticassociation.org.uk

Direct e-mail: info@arthriticassociation.org.uk

Founded: 1942

Organisation type and purpose: Membership association (membership is by subscription), present number of members: 4000, registered charity (charity number 292569).
To relieve the suffering from arthritis and allied illnesses using complementary techniques.

Subject coverage: Arthritis and allied illnesses.

continued overleaf

Non-library collection catalogue: All or part available in-house

Publications: Printed, and electronic and video

Access to staff: Contact by letter, by telephone, by fax, by e-mail and via website. Appointment necessary.
Hours: Mon to Fri, 1000 to 1300 and 1400 to 1600

ARTHRITIS CARE

18 Stephenson Way, London, NW1 2HD

Tel: 0808 800 4050 (answerphone helpline)
Fax: 020 7380 6505
E-mail: helpline@arthritiscare.org.uk
Website: www.arthritiscare.org.uk

Enquiries to: Information Manager
Direct tel: 020 7380 6577
Direct e-mail: info@arthritiscare.org.uk

Founded: 1947; formerly called British Rheumatism Association (year of change 1980)

Organisation type and purpose: Membership association (membership is by subscription), present number of members: 44,000, voluntary organisation, registered charity (charity number 206563).
National voluntary organisation with over 580 branches.

Subject coverage: Health and well-being of people with arthritis, exercise, self-management, aids and equipment, and holidays.

Trade and statistical information: Statistics on impact of arthritis

Library catalogue: All or part available in-house

Publications: Printed, and electronic and video

Publications list: Available in print

Access to staff: Contact by letter, by telephone, by fax, by e-mail and via website. Appointment necessary.
Hours: Mon to Fri, 0900 to 1700
Special comments: Helpline hours are 1000 to 1600

Access to building: Prior appointment required

Access for disabled people: Toilet facilities

ARTHRITIS RESEARCH CAMPAIGN EPIDEMIOLOGY UNIT (ARC Unit)

School of Epidemiology and Health Sciences, Stopford Building, University of Manchester, Oxford Road, Manchester, M13 9PT

Tel: 0161 275 3235
Fax: 0161 275 5043
E-mail: arcstaff@fs1.ser.man.ac.uk
Website: www.arc.org.uk
Website: www.arc.man.ac.uk

Enquiries to: Information Officer

Founded: 1954; formerly called Arthritis and Rheumatism Council

Organisation type and purpose: Registered charity (charity number 207711), university department or institute, research organisation.
Research into the epidemiology of the rheumatic diseases.

Subject coverage: Epidemiology of rheumatic diseases i.e. incidence and prevalence data on rheumatic diseases.

Collection: Rheumatic disease journals

Publications: Printed, and electronic and video
Order printed publications from: ARC Trading Ltd
Brunel Drive, Northern Road Industrial Estate, Newark, Nottinghamshire, NG24 2DE

Publications list: Available in print

Access to staff: Contact by letter, by telephone, by fax, by e-mail and via website. Appointment necessary. Non-members charged.
Hours: Mon to Fri, 0800 to 1600

Parent body: Arthritis Research Campaign; Copeman House, St Mary's Court, Chesterfield, Derbyshire, S41 7TD; tel: 01246 558033; fax: 01246 558007

ARTIFICIAL INTELLIGENCE APPLICATIONS INSTITUTE (AIAI)

University of Edinburgh, 80 South Bridge, Edinburgh, EH1 1HN

Tel: 0131 650 2732
Fax: 0131 650 6513
E-mail: a.tate@ed.ac.uk
Website: www.aiai.ed.ac.uk/

Enquiries to: Commercial Director
Other contacts: Training Secretary; Publications Secretary

Founded: 1984

Organisation type and purpose: University department or institute, consultancy, research organisation.
Technology transfer.

Subject coverage: Artificial intelligence, knowledge-based systems, modelling, methods, planning, scheduling, information management, process management, intelligent workflow.

Collection: Edinburgh AI Library
Exchange arrangements with international AI Research centres has led to a collection of over 15,000 AI research papers

Publications: Printed, and electronic and video

Publications list: Available online

Access to staff: Contact by letter, by telephone, by fax, by e-mail and via website. Appointment necessary.
Hours: Mon to Fri, 0900 to 1700

Parent body: University of Edinburgh; tel: 0131 650 1000; fax: 0131 650 2147; e-mail: communications.office@ed.ac.uk

ARTS AND BUSINESS (A&B)

Nutmeg House, 60 Gainsford Street, Butlers Wharf, London, SE1 2NY

Tel: 020 7378 8143
Fax: 020 7407 7527
E-mail: head.office@AandB.org.uk
Website: www.aandb.org.uk

Enquiries to: Information Officer

Founded: 1975; formed from Association for Business Sponsorship of the Arts (ABSA) (year of change 2000)

Organisation type and purpose: National organisation, membership association, service industry, registered charity (charity number 274040), consultancy.
To help business people support the arts and the arts to inspire business people, because good business and great art enrich society.

Subject coverage: Arts sponsorship advice to businesses and arts organisations, tax advice, evaluation, research, consultancy, arts funding, the Board Bank, Skills Bank and mentoring placements. Corporate art collections and creative and development training.

Trade and statistical information: Business Investment (of the arts) figures since 1990
Archive surveys

Library catalogue: All or part available in-house

Publications: Printed

Publications list: Available online and in print

Access to staff: Contact by letter, by telephone, by fax, by e-mail and via website. Appointment necessary.
Hours: Mon to Fri, 0930 to 1730

Access to building: Prior appointment required
Hours: Thu, Fri, 0930 to 1730

Arts & Business Offices and Staff: Arts & Business Cymru/Wales; 16 Museum Place, Cardiff, CF10 3BH; tel: 029 2030 3023; fax: 029 2030 3024; e-mail: cymru@AandB.org.uk; Arts & Business East; 67 Regent Street, Cambridge, CB2 1AB; tel: 01223 321421; fax: 01223 365536; e-mail: east@AandB.org.uk; Arts & Business East Midlands; Carlton Studios, Lenton Lane, Nottingham, NG7 2NA; tel: 0115 964 5648; fax: 0115 964 5488; e-mail: nottingham@AandB.org.uk; Arts & Business North West; 127–129 Portland Buildings, Portland Street, Manchester, M1 4PZ; tel: 0161 236 2058; fax: 0161 236 2068; e-mail: north.west@AandB.org.uk; Arts & Business Northern Ireland; 53 Malone Road, Belfast, BT9 6RY; tel: 028 9066 4736; fax: 028 9066 4500; e-mail: northern.ireland@AandB.org.uk; Arts & Business Scotland; 6 Randolph Crescent, Edinburgh, EH3 7TH; tel: 0131 220 2499; fax: 0131 220 2296; e-mail: scotland@AandB.org.uk; Arts & Business South East, Brighton Office; 4 Frederick Terrace, Frederick Place, Brighton, East Sussex, BN1 1AX; tel: 01273 738333; fax: 01273 738666; e-mail: south.east@AandB.org.uk; Arts & Business South East, Eastleigh Office; The Point Dance and Arts Centre, Leigh Road, Eastleigh, Hampshire, SO50 9DE; tel: 023 8061 9172; fax: 023 8061 9173; e-mail: south.east@AandB.org.uk; Arts & Business South West; 61 Park Street, Bristol, BS1 5NU; tel: 0117 929 0522; fax: 0117 929 1756; e-mail: south.west@AandB.org.uk; Arts & Business South West, Exeter Office; Civic Centre, Paris Street, Exeter, Devon, EX1 1JJ; tel: 01392 434272; Arts & Business West Midlands; Suite 16–18, 21 Bennetts Hill, Birmingham, B2 5QP; tel: 0121 248 1200; fax: 0121 248 1202; e-mail: midlands@AandB.org.uk; Arts & Business Yorkshire;

Dean Clough, Halifax, West Yorkshire, HX3 5AX; tel: 01422 367860; fax: 01422 363254; e-mail: yorkshire@AandB.org.uk; Cumbria; Arts & Business North West, Community Foundation, Unit 6B, Lakeland Business Park, Cockermouth, Cumbria, CA13 0QT; tel: 01900 829376; e-mail: elaine/wise@AandB.org.uk; Highlands and Islands Office; Suites 4/5 – 4th Floor, Ballantyne House, 84 Academy Street, Inverness, IV1 1LU; tel: 01463 720886; fax: 01463 720895; e-mail: inverness@AandB.org.uk; North Wales Office; 1–2 Chapel Street, Llandudno, LL30 2SY; tel: 01492 574003; e-mail: lorraine.hopkins@AandB.org.uk; North Wales Office; Room 40, The Town Hall, Lloyd Street, Llandudno, LL30 2UP; tel: 01492 574003; e-mail: lorraine.hopkins@AandB.org.uk; The Sponsors Club for Arts & Business; Cale Cross House, 156 Pilgrim Street, Newcastle upon Tyne, NE1 6SU; tel: 0191 222 0945; fax: 0191 230 0689; e-mail: northern@AandB.org.uk

Member of: Comité Européen pour le Rapprochement de la Culture (CEREC); c/ Tuset 8, 1°, 2°, Barcelona, 08006, Spain; tel: 00 34 93 237 2682; fax: 00 34 93 237 22 84; e-mail: contact@cerec.org

ARTS AND HUMANITIES RESEARCH COUNCIL (AHRC)

Polaris House, North Star Avenue, Swindon, SN2 1FL

Tel: 01793 416000
Fax: 01793 416001
Website: www.ahrc.ac.uk

Founded: 1998; formerly called Arts and Humanities Research Board (year of change 2005)

Organisation type and purpose: Supports world-class research and postgraduate study that furthers understanding of human culture and creativity: from ancient history and heritage science to modern dance and digital content.

Access to staff: Contact by letter, by telephone, by fax, by e-mail and via website

ARTS AND MINDS

Formal name: Cambridgeshire and Peterborough Foundation for the Arts and Mental Health

47–51 Norfolk St, Cambridge, CB1 2LD

Tel: 07758 334660
E-mail: info@artsandminds.org.uk
Website: www.artsandminds.org.uk

Enquiries to: Executive Director
Direct tel: 07545 641810
Direct e-mail: gavin.clayton@artsandminds.org.uk
Other contacts: Admin and Finance Officer

History of institution: incorporates the former portfolio of the Millennium Arts Project established under the auspices of the Friends of Fulbourn Hospital and the Community

Organisation type and purpose: Registered charity (charity number 273281).
To promote and support access to all forms of the arts for mental health service users, learning-disabled people and offenders, many of whom have mental health issues and some of whom have learning disabilities.

Subject coverage: Co-ordinates current arts activities; stimulates provision where access to participation in the arts is weak; provides a forum for the discussion of arts and mental health issues, particularly those affecting the relationship between the statutory and voluntary sectors; raises funds for the arts and mental health activities from statutory and charitable sources, commercial sponsorship, and the sale of works of art produced by participants; commissions providers to offer arts and mental health activities; trains artists participating in activities sponsored by the Foundation; collaborates with other arts and mental health organizations in Cambridgeshire; disseminates information about the arts and mental health.

Special visitor services: Holds an annual Autumn Event seminar.

Access to staff: Contact by letter, by telephone, by fax and by e-mail

Links with: About 20 mental health charities and other charities and organisations

ARTS COUNCIL ENGLAND, LONDON

2 Pear Tree Court, London, EC1R 0DS

Tel: 020 7608 6100, 020 7608 4101/0845 300 6200 (Minicom)
Fax: 020 7608 4100
E-mail: firstname.surname@artscouncil.org.uk
Website: www.artscouncil.org.uk/regions

Enquiries to: Administrator
Other contacts: Publishing Administrator

Organisation type and purpose: Registered charity (charity number 1036733).
London Arts Board is the arts funding and development agency for the capital.

Publications: Printed

Publications list: Available online and in print

Access to staff: Contact by letter, by telephone, by fax and by e-mail
Hours: Mon to Fri, 0900 to 1700
Special comments: Access to staff also by textphone.

ARTS COUNCIL ENGLAND, SOUTH EAST

Sovereign House, Church Street, Brighton, BN1 1RA

Tel: 0845 300 6200
Fax: 0870 242 1257 0845 300 6200
E-mail: enquiries@artscouncil.org.uk
Website: www.artscouncil.org.uk/regions/

Enquiries to: Press Officer
Direct tel: 01273 763053
Direct e-mail: chloe.barker@artscouncil.org.uk

Founded: 1992; formerly called Southern & South East Arts

Organisation type and purpose: Advisory body, registered charity.
Arts funding body, range of information sheets, website, annual review, bi-monthly newsletter.
Regional Arts Development.

Subject coverage: All areas of arts funding for professional artists and art organisations, arts grants, local authority contacts, venues and promoters and National Lottery applications.

Collection: South East Arts Visual Art and Craft Collection (catalogue available)

Trade and statistical information: Arts research data (available to clients only). Local authority contacts, press contacts

Publications: Printed

Publications list: Available in print

Access to staff: Contact by letter, by telephone, by fax, by e-mail and via website
Hours: Mon to Thu, 0900 to 1730; Fri, 0900 to 1700

Access to building: Prior appointment required
Hours: As above

Access for disabled people: Ramped entry
Special comments: Third floor, lifts available.

Also at: Southern & South East Arts; Union House, Eridge Road, Tunbridge Wells, Kent, TN4 8HF; tel: 01892 507200; fax: 0870 2421259; e-mail: infotw@ssea.co.uk

Parent body: Arts Council of England; 14 Great Peter Street, London, SW1P 3NQ; tel: 020 7333 0100; text phone: 020 7973 6564; fax: 020 7973 6590; e-mail: enquiries@artscouncil.org.uk; website: http//www.artscouncil.org.uk

ARTS COUNCIL OF ENGLAND (ACE)

Library, 14 Great Peter Street, London, SW1P 3NQ

Tel: 020 7333 0100, 020 7973 6564 (Minicom)
Fax: 020 7973 6590
E-mail: enquiries@artscouncil.org.uk
Website: www.artscouncil.org.uk

Enquiries to: Information Officer
Direct tel: 020 7973 6517

Founded: 1945; formerly called Arts Council of Great Britain (year of change 1994)

Organisation type and purpose: National government body.
Non-Departmental Public Body (NDPB)
Government grant-aided institution, incorporated under Royal Charter, national body for funding and development of the arts.
To develop and improve knowledge, understanding and practice of the arts; increase the accessibility of the arts; advise and co-operate with government, local authorities and other bodies.

Subject coverage: Cultural policy, marketing, management, economy and financing of the arts, fundraising and sponsorship.

Collection: Market research reports on the arts

Trade and statistical information: Data on the level of central government funding of the arts

continued overleaf

Publications: Printed
Order printed publications from: Marston Book Services
PO Box 269, Abingdon, Oxfordshire, OX14 4YN, tel: 01235 465500, fax: 01235 465555

Publications list: Available online

Access to staff: Contact by letter, by telephone, by fax and via website
Hours: Mon to Fri, 1000 to 1300 and 1400 to 1700
Special comments: Due to limited space, priority is given to artist and art administrator groups, for other categories it is a library of last resort.

Access to building: Prior appointment required

Regional Arts Boards: East England Arts Area covered: Bedfordshire, Cambridgeshire, Essex, Hertfordshire, Norfolk, Suffolk, Lincolnshire; unitary authority of Luton; Eden House, 48–49 Bateman Street, Cambridge, CB2 1LR; tel: 01223 454400; fax: 01223 248075; **East Midlands Arts Board** Area covered: Derbyshire (excluding High Peak District), Leicestershire, Northamptonshire, Nottinghamshire; unitary authorities of Derby, Leicester, Rutland; Mountfields House, Epinal Way, Loughborough, Leicestershire, LE11 0QE; tel: 01509 218292; fax: 01509 262214; **London Arts Board** Area covered: The area of the 32 London Boroughs and the City of London; Elme House, 133 Long Acre, Covent Garden, London, WC2E 9AF; tel: 020 7240 1313; fax: 020 7240 4580; **North West Arts** Area covered: Lancashire, Cheshire, Merseyside, Greater Manchester and High Peak Districts of Derbyshire; Manchester House, 22 Bridge Street, Manchester, M3 3AB; tel: 0161 834 6644; fax: 0161 834 6969; **Northern Arts** Area covered: Cumbria, Durham, Northumberland; unitary authorities of Darlington, Hartlepool, Middlesbrough, Redcar & Cleveland, Stockton; metropolitan districts of Newcastle, Gateshead, North Tyneside, Sunderland & South Tyneside; 9–10 Osborne Terrace, Jesmond, Newcastle upon Tyne, NE2 1NZ; tel: 0191 281 6334; fax: 0191 281 3276; **South East Arts Board** Area covered: Kent, Surrey, East and West Sussex, unitary authority of Brighton and Hove; 10 Mount Ephraim, Tunbridge Wells, Kent, TN4 8AS; tel: 01892 515210; fax: 01892 549383; **South West Arts** Area covered: Cornwall, Devon, Dorset (except districts of Bournemouth, Christchurch & Poole), Gloucestershire and Somerset; unitary authorities of Bristol, Bath and North East Somerset, South Gloucestershire, North Somerset; Bradninch Place, Gandy Street, Exeter, EX4 3LS; tel: 01392 218188; fax: 01392 413554; **Southern Arts Board** Area covered: Berkshire, Buckinghamshire. Hampshire, Isle of Wight. Oxfordshire, Wiltshire; unitary authorities of Bournemouth, Milton Keynes, Poole, Southampton, Swindon; 13 St Clement Street, Winchester, Hampshire, SO23 9DQ; tel: 01962 855099; fax: 01962 861186; **West Midlands Arts Board** Area covered: Hereford & Worcester, Shropshire, Staffordshire, Warwickshire; metropolitan districts of Birmingham, Coventry, Dudley, Sandwell, Solihull, Walsall, Wolverhampton; unitary authority of Stoke-on-Trent; 82 Granville Street, Birmingham, B1 2LH; tel: 0121 631 3121; fax: 0121 643 7239; **Yorkshire & Humberside Arts Board** Area covered: North Yorks; unitary authorities of York, Hull, East Riding, North Lincs; metropolitan districts of Barnsley, Bradford, Calderdale, Doncaster, Kirklees, Leeds, Rotherham, Sheffield, Wakefield; 21 Bond Street, Dewsbury, West Yorkshire, WF13 1AX; tel: 01924 455555; fax: 01924 466 522

ARTS COUNCIL OF ENGLAND (NORTHERN ARTS)

Central Square, Forth Street, Newcastle upon Tyne, NE1 3PJ

Tel: 0845 300 6200
Fax: 0191 230 1020
Website: www.arts.org.uk/directory/regions/northern

Enquiries to: Communications Officer
Direct e-mail: kathryn.goodfellow@artscouncil.org.uk

History of institution: formerly called Northern Arts

Organisation type and purpose: Local government body, advisory body, professional body (membership is by subscription), registered charity (charity number 517711), training organisation, consultancy, research organisation.
Art funding body.
Regional arts board responsible for almost all national and regional arts funding in the North.

Subject coverage: Music, drama, performing arts, visual arts, crafts, literature, film, photography, video, community arts, arts funding and organisation, Millennium Fund and lottery.

Collection: Fundraising library
Slide library (artists index)

Library catalogue: All or part available in-house and in print

Publications: Printed

Access to staff: Contact by letter, by telephone, by fax, by e-mail and via website. Appointment necessary.
Hours: Mon to Fri, 0900 to 1700
Special comments: First floor access only; stairs above, not accessible by lift.

Access to building: No prior appointment required

ARTS COUNCIL OF WALES

Bute Place, Cardiff, CF10 5AL

Tel: 0845 8734 900, 07797800504 (SMS, messages charged at caller's standard network rate only)
Fax: 029 2022 1447
E-mail: funding@artswales.org.uk
Website: www.artswales.org.uk

Enquiries to: Information Adviser

Founded: 1994; formerly called Welsh Arts Council (year of change 1994)

Organisation type and purpose: National government body, advisory body, statutory body (membership is by election or invitation), present number of members: 18 members on ACW's Council, 150+ on panels and committees, registered charity (charity number 1034245).
Distributes National Assembly for Wales and National Lottery funds for the arts in Wales.

Subject coverage: Development of all art forms in Wales, funding for arts activities from National Assembly for Wales and National Lottery sources.

Library catalogue: All or part available online and in print

Order printed publications from: see list of current publications online: www.artswales.org.uk/what-we-do/publications

Publications list: Available online and in print

Access to staff: Contact by letter, by telephone, by fax, by e-mail and via website
Hours: All offices: Mon to Fri, 0900 to 1700

Other addresses: Arts Council of Wales; 36 Prince's Drive, Colwyn Bay, LL29 8LA; tel: 01492 533440, 07797800504 (SMS, messages charged at caller's standard network rate only); fax: 01492 533677; e-mail: funding@artswales.org.uk; website: www.artswales.org.uk
Arts Council of Wales; 6 Gardd Llydaw, Jackson's Lane, Carmarthen, SA31 1QD; tel: 01267 234248, 07797800504 (SMS, messages charged at caller's standard network rate only); fax: 01267 233084; e-mail: funding@artswales.org.uk; website: www.artswales.org.uk

ARUN DISTRICT COUNCIL

Arun Civic Centre, Maltravers Road, Littlehampton, West Sussex, BN17 5LF

Tel: 01903 737500, 01903 732765 (Minicom)
Fax: 01903 730442
Website: www.arun.gov.uk

Enquiries to: Public Relations Manager

Founded: 1974

Organisation type and purpose: Local government body.

Subject coverage: Tourism, strategy co-ordination, consultation processes, customer care.

Publications: Printed
Order printed publications from: Head, Strategy Unit
at the same address, e-mail: strategy.unit@arun.gov.uk

Access to staff: Contact by letter, by telephone, by fax and by e-mail. Appointment necessary.
Hours: Mon to Thu, 0845 to 1715; Fri, 0845 to 1645

ASBESTOS CONTROL AND ABATEMENT DIVISION (ACAD)

Tica House, Allington Way, Yarm Road Business Park, Darlington, Co Durham, D21 4QB

Tel: 01325 466704
Fax: 01325 487691
E-mail: enquiries@tica-acad.co.uk
Website: www.tica-acad.co.uk

Enquiries to: Operations Manager

Other contacts: ACAD Training Co-ordinator for training enquiries.

Founded: 1994; formed from Insulation and Environmental Training Association (IETA), Insulation and Environmental Training Trust Limited (IETTL)

Organisation type and purpose: Advisory body, trade association (membership is by subscription), present number of members: 117 members, 39 associate members, service industry, training organisation, consultancy, research organisation.

Subject coverage: Safe removal of asbestos using latest technology, technical, health and safety advice, training courses. National Vocational Qualifications (NVQs).

Trade and statistical information: Data on health and safety matters relating to asbestos products, removal and waste handling, for the United Kingdom, Europe and some international information

Publications: Printed

Publications list: Available in print

Access to staff: Contact by letter, by telephone, by fax, by e-mail, in person and via website. Appointment necessary. Non-members charged.
Hours: Mon to Fri, 0900 to 1700

Access to building: Prior appointment required

Access for disabled people: Parking provided

Parent body: Thermal Insulation Contractors Association (TICA)

ASCEND

Formal name: Ascend Worldwide

Cardinal Point, Newall Road, Heathrow Airport, Hounslow, Middlesex, TW6 2AS

Tel: 020 8564 6700
Fax: 020 8897 0300
E-mail: info@ascendworldwide.com
Website: www.ascendworldwide.com
Website: https://online.ascendworldwide.com//Login/PortalLogin.aspx
Website: www.ascendv1.com
Website: www.ascendspacetrak.com/Home/Login.aspx

Direct e-mail: uk@ascendworldwide.com

Founded: 1964; formerly a part of Airclaims Limited (year of change 2006)

Organisation type and purpose: International organisation, service industry, consultancy, publishing house.
Aviation Loss Adjuster and Information Provider.

Subject coverage: Commercial aviation, including airline fleets, aircraft, current and future values, accidents, information on communications satellites and launchers (ie commercial astronautics).

Non-library collection catalogue: All or part available in-house

Library catalogue: All or part available in-house

Publications: Printed, and electronic and video

Publications list: Available online and in print

Access to staff: Contact by letter, by telephone, by fax, by e-mail, in person and via website
Hours: Mon to Fri, 0900 to 1700

Headquarters address: Ascend Asia; 35/F Central Plaza, 18 Harbour Road, Wanchai, Hong Kong; tel: +852 2813 6366; fax: +652 2813 6357; e-mail: asia@ascendworldwide.com; website: http://www.ascendworldwide.com
Ascend USA; 380 Lexington Avenue, 17th Floor, New York, NY 10168, USA; tel: +1 212 551 1118; fax: +1 212 551 1001; e-mail: usa@ascendworldwide.com; website: http://www.ascendworldwide.com

ASHFIELD DISTRICT COUNCIL

Council Offices, Urban Road, Kirkby-in-Ashfield, Nottinghamshire, NG17 8DA

Tel: 01623 450000
Fax: 01623 457590
E-mail: info@ashfield-dc.gov.uk
Website: www.ashfield-dc.gov.uk

Enquiries to: Chief Executive

Founded: 1974

Organisation type and purpose: Local government body.

Subject coverage: Local government services.

Access for disabled people: Parking provided, toilet facilities
Special comments: Audio Loop System.

ASHFORD BOROUGH COUNCIL (ABC)

Civic Centre, Tannery Lane, Ashford, Kent, TN23 1PL

Tel: 01233 637311, 01233 637311 (Minicom)
Fax: 01233 645654
E-mail: media@ashford.gov.uk
Website: www.ashford.gov.uk

Enquiries to: Chief Executive
Direct e-mail: john.bunnett@ashford.gov.uk
Other contacts: Marketing and Communications Manager for press issues and general publicity.

Organisation type and purpose: Local government body.

Subject coverage: Local government services.

Publications: Printed, and electronic and video

Access to staff: Contact by letter and by e-mail. Appointment necessary.
Hours: Mon to Fri, 0900 to 1700

ASHFORD LIBRARY

Ashford Gateway Plus, Church Road, Ashford, Kent, TN23 1AS

Tel: 08458 247200
Fax: 01233 620295
E-mail: ashfordlibrary@kent.gov.uk
Website: www.kent.gov.uk/libs

Enquiries to: Customer Service Development Librarian
Direct tel: 08458 247200
Direct fax: 01233 620295
Direct e-mail: ashfordlibrary@kent.gov.uk

Organisation type and purpose: Public library.

Subject coverage: General, local railways, local studies.

Collection: Local Railway Collection
Local studies

Library catalogue: All or part available online

Access to staff: Contact by letter, by telephone, by fax, by e-mail, in person and via website
Hours: Mon to Thu, 0900 to 2000; Fri and Sat, 0900 to 1800

Access to building: *Hours:* Mon to Thu, 0900 to 2000; Fri and Sat, 0900 to 1800

Access for disabled people: Fully accessible
Hours: Mon to Thu, 0900 to 2000; Fri and Sat, 0900 to 1800

ASIA HOUSE

63 New Cavendish Street, London, W1G 7LP

Tel: 020 7307 5454
Fax: 020 7307 5459
E-mail: enquiries@asiahouse.co.uk
Website: www.asiahouse.org

Founded: 1996

Organisation type and purpose: A non-profit, non-political organisation serving as a focal point for the development of understanding of business, and of diplomatic and cultural interaction, between Asia and Britain. Runs a programme of events for the public.

Subject coverage: The organisation's geographical scope extends west–east from Iran to Japan and north–south from the central Asian republics to Indonesia

Access to building: *Hours:* Mon to Fri, 0900 to 1900; Sat (only when there is an exhibition in the gallery), 1000 to 1800

ASIAN ART IN LONDON (AAL)

Asian Art in London, 20 Rutland Gate, London, SW7 1BD

Tel: 020 7499 2215
Fax: 020 7499 2216
E-mail: info@asianartinlondon.com
Website: www.asianartinlondon.com

Enquiries to: Project Manager

Founded: 1998

Organisation type and purpose: Membership association (membership is by subscription), present number of members: 40–50.
Annual event.
AAL is an annual event that promotes private dealers, auction houses, societies, academic institutions and museums that deal in and provide Asian Art.

Subject coverage: Chinese, Japanese, Islamic and Middle Eastern, Indian, South East Asian, Himalayan and Tibetan, Korean art, antique and contemporary art.

continued overleaf

Non-library collection catalogue: All or part available in-house

Publications: Printed

Access to staff: Contact by letter, by telephone, by fax, by e-mail, in person and via website. Appointment necessary.
Hours: Mon to Fri, 0900 to 1800

Access to building: Prior appointment required
Hours: Mon to Fri, 0900 to 1800

ASIAN FAMILY COUNSELLING SERVICE (AFCS)

Suite 51, The Lodge, Windmill Place, 24 Windmill Lane, Southall, Middlesex, UB2 4NJ

Tel: 020 8571 3933; 020 8813 9714
Fax: 020 8571 3933
E-mail: afcs@btconnect.com
Website: www.asianfamilycounselling.org

Enquiries to: Administrator

Founded: 1985

Organisation type and purpose: Voluntary organisation, registered charity (charity number 517595), training organisation, consultancy.

Subject coverage: Marital and family counselling service.

Access to staff: Contact by letter, by telephone, by fax and by e-mail. Appointment necessary. All charged.
Hours: Mon to Fri, 1000 to 1600

Access for disabled people: Wheelchair access not available.

ASIAN STUDIES CENTRE (ASC)

St Antony's College, Woodstock Road, Oxford, OX2 6JF

Tel: 01865 274559
Fax: 01865 274559
E-mail: asian@sant.ox.ac.uk
Website: www.sant.ox.ac.uk/asian

Enquiries to: Secretary

Founded: 1982; formerly called Far East Centre (year of change 1982)

Organisation type and purpose: Research organisation.
A scholarly Centre for Asian Studies within St Antony's College conducting seminars and special talks on Asia; funded by endowment at St Antony's College.

Subject coverage: History; anthropology; international relations; politics; economics; Asia, with special reference to Japan, Korea, China (including Hong Kong, Taiwan and Tibet), India and Southeast Asia.

Collection: A collection of c. 4,000 books and periodicals; access restricted to members of St Antony's College
The Asian Studies Collection is held in the St Antony's College Library (books primarily related to international relations in Asia)

Access to staff: Contact by letter, by telephone, by fax, by e-mail, in person and via website. Appointment necessary.
Hours: Mon, Tue, Thu, Fri, 0930 to 1600

ASIAN WOMEN'S RESOURCE CENTRE (AWRC)

108 Craven Park, London, NW10 8QE

Tel: 020 8961 6549
Fax: 020 8838 1823
E-mail: asianwomencentre@aol.com
Website: www.asianwomencentre.org.uk

Enquiries to: Director
Direct tel: 020 8961 5701

Founded: 1980

Organisation type and purpose: Voluntary organisation, registered charity (charity number 1049058).
Advice centre.

Subject coverage: Educational and social resources for Asian women living in England.

Publications: Printed

Access to staff: Contact by letter, by telephone, by fax, by e-mail, in person and via website. Appointment necessary.
Hours: Mon to Fri, 1000 to 1700

Access for disabled people: Ramped entry

ASKHAM BRYAN COLLEGE

Askham Bryan, York, YO23 3FR

Tel: 01904 772277
Fax: 01904 772288
E-mail: enquiries@askham-bryan.ac.uk
Website: www.askham-bryan.ac.uk

Enquiries to: Learning Resources Manager
Direct tel: 01904 772234
Direct e-mail: lrc@askham-bryan.ac.uk

Founded: 1948

Organisation type and purpose: College of further and higher education – land based.

Subject coverage: Agriculture, Adventure, Animal Management, Butchery, Social Care, Childcare, Countryside, Engineering, Environment, Equine, Floristry, Forensic Sciences, Forestry and Arboriculture, Hair and Beauty, Horticulture, Rural Construction, Veterinary Nursing

Library catalogue: All or part available in-house

Publications: Printed
Order printed publications from: Rural Business Research Unit, Askham Bryan College
tel: 01904 772218; fax: 01904 700129; e-mail: ml@askham-bryan.ac.uk

Access to staff: Contact by letter, by telephone, by e-mail and via website. Access for members only.
Hours: Term Time: Mon to Thurs, 0845 to 2030; Fri, 0845 to 1700; Sun, 1245 to 1730
Vacations: Mon to Fri, 0900 to 1700

Access for disabled people: Parking provided, ramped entry, power-assisted front door, disabled toilet, lift access to first floor, accessible shelving

Affiliated to: Harper Adams University College

Also at: Askham Bryan College; Bedale Centre, Benkhill Drive, Bedale, Yorkshire, DL8 2EA; tel: 01677 422344; Askham Bryan College; Guisborough Centre, Avenue Place, Redcar Road, Guisborough, Cleveland, TS14 6AX; tel: 01287 633870; Askham Bryan College; Harrogate Centre, Great Yorkshire Showground, Harrogate, North Yorkshire, HG2 8BW; tel: 01423 546199; Askham Bryan College; Thirsk Rural Business Centre, Blakey Lane, Thirsk, YO7 3AB; tel: 01845 574928; Newton Rigg College; Penrith, Cumbria, CA11 0AH; tel: 01768 893400; e-mail: enquiries@newtonrigg.ac.uk

In partnership with: Wakefield College, Scarborough Sixth Form College, Bradford College

ASLIB PROFESSIONAL RECRUITMENT LIMITED (APR)

Howard House, Wagon Lane, Bingley, BD16 1WA

Tel: 01274 777700
Fax: 01274 785201
E-mail: recruit@aslib.com
Website: www.aslib.com

Enquiries to: Manager
Other contacts: Recruitment Consultant

Organisation type and purpose: Library and Information Recruitment Specialists.

Subject coverage: Recruitment of both temporary and permanent library and information staff for placement in all sectors.

Publications: Printed

Access to staff: Contact by letter, by telephone, by fax, by e-mail and via website. Appointment necessary.
Hours: Mon to Fri, 0915 to 1715

Wholly owned subsidiary of: Aslib

ASLIB, THE ASSOCIATION FOR INFORMATION MANAGEMENT

Howard House, Wagon Lane, Bingley, BD16 1WA

Tel: 01274 785248
Fax: 01274 785200
E-mail: hshukla@aslib.com
Website: www.aslib.com
Website: www.managinginformation.com

Enquiries to: Relationship Manager
Direct e-mail: hshukla@aslib.com

Founded: 1924

Organisation type and purpose:
International organisation, membership association (membership is by subscription), members in some 70 countries.
Aslib actively promotes best practice in the management of information resources. It lobbies on all aspects of the management of, and legislation concerning, information at local, national and international levels.
Publishes Managing Information (10 times a year).

Subject coverage: Information management, information science, librarianship, applications of information technology, automation of information and library services, online information retrieval, information sources, records management, CD-ROM, thesaurus and database construction, data protection, intellectual property, information governance.

Order printed publications from: Aslib corporate members receive discounts on titles published by Emerald and Taylor & Francis

Publications list: Available online and in print

Access to staff: Contact by letter, by telephone, by fax, by e-mail and via website. Appointment necessary. Non-members charged.
Hours: Mon to Fri, 0915 to 1715

Member of: European Council of Information Associations (ECIA)

ASPARAGUS GROWERS' ASSOCIATION

BGA House, Nottingham Road, Louth, Lincolnshire, LN11 0WB

Tel: 01507 353789
Fax: 01507 600689
E-mail: jayne.dyas@britishgrowers.org
Website: www.british-asparagus.co.uk

Enquiries to: Membership Secretary

Founded: 1984

Organisation type and purpose: National organisation, trade association.

Access to staff: Contact by letter, by telephone, by fax and by e-mail
Hours: Mon to Fri, 0900 to 1700

ASSIST UK

Formal name: Assist UK Independence

Red Bank House, 4 St Chads street, Manchester, M8 8QA

Tel: 0161 832 9757
E-mail: general.info@assist-uk.org
Website: www.assist-uk.org

Enquiries to: Chief Executive
Other contacts: Communications Officer

Founded: 1985; formerly called Disabled Living Centres Council (DLCC) (year of change 2005)

Organisation type and purpose: A membership organisation leading a network of Disability and Independent Living Centres and services.
The central point for local experience to feed national learning and support local delivery, ensuring that advice and product and service support is available free and impartially at the point of client contact.

Subject coverage: Creating a Disabled Living Centre, providing contact with Disabled Living Centres, working with other organisations to provide access to their services for disabled living.

Publications: Printed, and electronic and video

Publications list: Available online and in print

Access to staff: Contact by letter, by telephone, by e-mail and via website. Appointment necessary.
Hours: Mon to Fri, 0900 to 1630

Access to building: Prior appointment required.

Access for disabled people: Parking provided, level entry, access to all public areas, toilet facilities.

Member organisations: 41 Disabled / Independent Living Centres

ASSOCIATED BRITISH PORTS HOLDINGS PLC (ABPH)

150 Holborn, London, EC1N 2LR

Tel: 020 7430 1177
Fax: 020 7430 1384
E-mail: pr@abports.co.uk
Website: www.abports.co.uk

Enquiries to: Corporate Communications Manager
Direct e-mail: mcollins@abports.co.uk

Founded: 1983; formerly called British Transport Docks Board (year of change 1983)

Organisation type and purpose: Service industry.
Ports, transport and property company. Ports owner and operator; subsidiaries include property, ferry, transport services, auto-processing terminals, computer and research companies, and dredging division.

Subject coverage: Transport, the port industry, property development and investment, shipping, auto-processing, research, computing, dredging.

Publications: Printed

Access to staff: Contact by letter, by telephone and by fax
Hours: Mon to Fri, 0830 to 1800

ASSOCIATION FOR ARCHERY IN SCHOOLS (AAS)

Bloxham School, Banbury, Oxfordshire, OX15 4PE

Tel: 01295 721463
Fax: 01295 721463
Website: www.aasinfo.demon.co.uk

Enquiries to: Secretary
Direct tel: 01295 724338
Direct e-mail: cfe@blockhamschool.com

Founded: 1963

Organisation type and purpose: Membership association (membership is by subscription), voluntary organisation, suitable for ages: Under 18.
Promotion of Archery in schools and colleges.

Subject coverage: Archery achievement (a Badge Scheme); formation of archery clubs; equipment; coaching; tournaments.

Publications: Printed

Access to staff: Contact by letter, by telephone, by fax, by e-mail and via website
Hours: Answerphone/Fax during working day; personal contact late night, 2300 to 0200

Affiliated to: Fédération Internationale de Tir à l'Arc (FITA); Grand National Archery Society (GNAS); National Council for School Sports (NCSS)

ASSOCIATION FOR ASTRONOMY EDUCATION (AAE)

Formal name: Association for Astronomy Education

Royal Astronomical Society, Burlington House, Piccadilly, London, W1J 0BQ

Website: www.aae.org.uk

Enquiries to: Secretary
Direct e-mail: secretary@aae.org.uk

Founded: 1981

Organisation type and purpose: Membership association (membership is by subscription), present number of members: 120, registered charity (charity number 1046041).
To promote astronomy education at all levels and to support teachers through training, information and resources.

Subject coverage: Astronomy education.

Publications: Printed
Order printed publications from: ASE Publications
College Lane, Hatfield, Hertfordshire, AL10 9AA, tel: 01707 283000

Access to staff: Contact by letter, by e-mail and via website
Hours: Mon to Fri, 0900 to 1700

ASSOCIATION FOR BETTER LIVING AND EDUCATION (ABLE)

Saint Hill Manor, East Grinstead, West Sussex, RH19 4JY

Tel: 01342 301902
Fax: 01342 327539
E-mail: ableuk@able.org
Website: www.able.org

Enquiries to: Executive Director

Founded: 1985

Organisation type and purpose: Membership association, voluntary organisation.
To work in the field of eradicating drug abuse, crime, illiteracy and forwarding a non-religious moral code.

Publications: Printed

Access to staff: Contact by letter, by telephone and by fax
Hours: Mon to Sat, 1000 to 2200

ASSOCIATION FOR CAREERS EDUCATION AND GUIDANCE (ACEG)

Tel: 01295 720809
Fax: 01295 720809
E-mail: info@aceg.org.uk
Website: www.aceg.org.uk

Enquiries to: General Secretary

Founded: 1969; formerly called National Association of Careers Teachers (year of change 1974); formerly called National Association of Careers & Guidance Teachers (year of change 2006)

Organisation type and purpose: Membership association with over 1,600 members, the professional subject association for careers education and guidance (CEG) in schools and colleges in England and Wales. Members are careers

continued overleaf

practitioners in schools and colleges and those working in Connexions partnerships and local authorities who support these practitioners.
Committed to promoting the highest standards in CEG for all young people through excellence and innovation in careers work; campaigns on appropriate matters.

Subject coverage: Careers and education guidance in schools and colleges in England and Wales.

Publications: Printed

Publications list: Available online

Access to staff: Contact by telephone, by fax and by e-mail

ASSOCIATION FOR CERAMIC TRAINING & DEVELOPMENT (ACTD)

St James House, Webberley Lane, Stoke-on-Trent, Staffordshire, ST3 1RJ

Tel: 01782 597016
Fax: 01782 597015
E-mail: actd@actd.co.uk

Enquiries to: Director

Founded: 1993

Organisation type and purpose: National training organisation.

Non-library collection catalogue: All or part available in-house

Library catalogue: All or part available in-house

Access to staff: Contact by letter
Hours: Mon to Fri, 0900 to 1700

ASSOCIATION FOR CLINICAL BIOCHEMISTRY (ACB)

130–132 Tooley Street, London, SE1 2TU

Tel: 020 7403 8001
Fax: 020 7403 8006
E-mail: enquiries@acb.org.uk
Website: www.acb.org.uk

Enquiries to: Administrator

Founded: 1953

Organisation type and purpose: Professional body, trade union, present number of members: 2,200.

Subject coverage: Clinical biochemistry, chemical pathology, biochemical medicine, clinical chemistry, clinical sciences.

Collection: Archives of the Association

Non-library collection catalogue: All or part available in-house

Library catalogue: All or part available online

Publications: Printed, and electronic and video

Publications list: Available online and in print

Access to staff: Contact by letter, by fax and by e-mail
Hours: Mon to Fri, 0900 to 1700

Access for disabled people: Ramped entry, access to all public areas, toilet facilities

Associated, for professional matters, with the: Association of Clinical Cytogeneticists (ACC); Association of Clinical Microbiologists (ACM)

Linked, for scientific and educational matters, with the: International Federation of Clinical Chemistry and Laboratory Medicine (IFCC)

ASSOCIATION FOR COACHING (AC)

Golden Cross House, 8 Duncannon Street, London, WC2N 4JF

Tel: 08456531050
E-mail: enquiries@associationforcoaching.com
Website: www.associationforcoaching.com

Enquiries to: Chairman
Direct tel: 07884 434547
Direct e-mail: ktulpa@associationforcoaching.com

Founded: 2002

Organisation type and purpose: National organisation, advisory body, professional body (membership is by qualification, election or invitation).

Subject coverage: Advancing education and best practice in coaching; executive, business, performance, private.

Access to staff: Contact by telephone, by fax, by e-mail, in person and via website
Hours: Mon to Fri, 0900 to 1700

ASSOCIATION FOR CONTINENCE ADVICE (ACA)

Association for Continence Advice, Drumcross Hall, Bathgate, West Lothian, EH48 4JT

Tel: 01506 811077
Fax: 01506 811477
E-mail: aca@fitwise.co.uk
Website: www.fitwise.co.uk

Enquiries to: Membership Secretary; Administration Officer
Direct e-mail: katie@fitwise.co.uk

Founded: 1980

Organisation type and purpose: International organisation, advisory body, membership association (membership is by subscription), present number of members: 491, voluntary organisation, registered charity, training organisation, consultancy.
Membership organisation for healthcare professionals working with people with bladder and bowel dysfunction.

Publications: Printed

Access to staff: Contact by letter, by telephone, by fax, by e-mail and via website
Hours: Mon to Fri, 0900 to 1700

Access to building: *Hours:* Mon to Fri, 0900 to 1700

Access for disabled people: via delivery area

Branches: Has 10 regional branches

ASSOCIATION FOR EDUCATION WELFARE MANAGEMENT (AEWM)

1 The Boundary, Bradford, West Yorkshire, BD8 0BQ

Tel: 01924 305519 (daytime), 01274 542295 (evening)
Fax: 01924 305646

Enquiries to: General Secretary
Direct e-mail: frances.molloy@ed.lancscc.gov.uk
Other contacts: Assistant Secretary (publicity)

Founded: 1917

Organisation type and purpose: National organisation, professional body (membership is by subscription), present number of members: 150.
Promotes good practice and provides professional support, responds to government initiatives.

Subject coverage: Education welfare management.

Access to staff: Contact by letter and by e-mail
Hours: Mon to Fri, 0900 to 1700

ASSOCIATION FOR GROUP AND INDIVIDUAL PSYCHOTHERAPY (AGIP)

1 Fairbridge Road, London, N19 3EW

Tel: 020 7272 7013
Fax: 020 7272 6945
E-mail: office@agip.org.uk
Website: www.agip.org.uk

Enquiries to: Administrator

Founded: 1974

Organisation type and purpose: Registered charity (charity number 1083030), training organisation.
Provision of services in psychotherapy.

Subject coverage: Psychoanalytic psychotherapy, training, clinical and supervision services.

Special visitor services: Low-fee psychotherapy clinic.

Education services: Education and training in psychotherapy.

Services for disabled people: By arrangement.

Access to staff: Contact by letter, by telephone, by fax, by e-mail and via website
Hours: Mon to Fri, 0900 to 1230

Member of: United Kingdom Council for Psychotherapy

ASSOCIATION FOR HUMANISTIC PSYCHOLOGY IN BRITAIN (AHPB)

BM Box 3582, London, WC1N 3XX

Tel: 08457 078506
E-mail: admin@ahpb.org
Website: www.ahpb.org.uk

Enquiries to: Administrator

Founded: 1969

Organisation type and purpose: Professional body, voluntary organisation, registered charity (charity number 290548).

Subject coverage: Humanistic psychology; counselling and psychotherapy; training.

Publications: Printed, and electronic and video
Order printed publications from: admin@ahpb.org.uk

Access to staff: Contact by letter, by telephone, by e-mail and via website
Hours: 24-hour answering machine.

ASSOCIATION FOR INDUSTRIAL ARCHAEOLOGY (AIA)

David de Haan & Anne Sutherland, AIA Liaison Office, The Ironbridge Institute, Ironbridge Gorge Museum, Coalbrookdale, Telford, TF8 7DX

Tel: 01740 656280
E-mail: aia-enquiries@contacts.bham.ac.uk

Enquiries to: Secretary
Other contacts: Correspondence Secretary

Founded: 1973

Organisation type and purpose: Advisory body, learned society (membership is by subscription), voluntary organisation, research organisation, publishing house.

Subject coverage: Industrial archaeology; conservation; preservation.

Education services: Group education facilities, resources for Further or Higher Education.

Publications: Printed
Order printed publications from: Sales Officer Barn Cottage, Bridge Street, Bridgnorth, Shropshire, WV15 6AF, tel: 01746 765159

Publications list: Available in print

Access to staff: Contact by letter, by telephone and by fax
Hours: Mon to Fri, 0900 to 1700

Access to building: No prior appointment required

Also at: AIA Liaison Officer; School of Archaeological Studies, University of Leicester, University Road, Leicester, LE1 7RH; tel: 0116 252 5337; fax: 0116 252 5005; e-mail: aia@le.ac.uk

Links with: Ironbridge Gorge Museum Trust; tel: 01952 433522

ASSOCIATION FOR LANGUAGE LEARNING (ALL)

University of Leicester, University Road, Leicester, LE1 7RH

Tel: 0116 229 7600
E-mail: info@all-languages.org.uk
Website: www.all-languages.org.uk

Enquiries to: Director

Founded: 1990

Organisation type and purpose:
Professional body, membership association (membership is by subscription), present number of members: 4800, registered charity (charity number 1001826).
Support for teachers of all modern foreign languages in all sectors of education.

Subject coverage: Modern foreign language teaching and learning at all levels of education from primary to university, adult education and training, Asian languages, French, German, Italian, Portuguese, Russian, Spanish teaching in schools and universities, teaching materials and sources of auxiliary teaching materials.

Publications: Printed

Publications list: Available in print

Access to staff: Contact by letter, by telephone, by fax, by e-mail, in person and via website
Hours: Mon to Fri, 0900 to 1700

Affiliated to: Fédération Internationale de Professeurs de Français (FIPF); Fédération Internationale de Professeurs de Langues Vivantes (FIPLV); IDV; MAPRYAL

ASSOCIATION FOR LATIN LITURGY (ALL)

47 Western Park Road, Leicester, LE3 6HQ

Tel: 0116 285 6158
E-mail: enquiries@latin-liturgy.org
Website: www.latin-liturgy.org

Enquiries to: Chairman
Direct e-mail: enquiries@latin-liturgy.org

Founded: 1969

Organisation type and purpose: Learned society, membership association (membership is by subscription), present number of members: 300.
Religious (Roman Catholic). Shares aims with the Latin Liturgy Assoc. (USA), the Vereniging voor Latijnse Liturgie (Netherlands) and Pro Liturgia (France). There is a formal Federation of the three European associations.
To promote understanding of the value of the Catholic liturgy and its music in Latin, and in a practical way to encourage its use.

Subject coverage: The Latin liturgy of the Roman Catholic Church and its associated music in the past and at the present day. The teaching of ecclesiastical Latin. Advice on printed texts connected with the above.

Publications: Printed, and electronic and video
Order printed publications from: Publications Manager, 47 Western Park Road, Leicester, LE3 6HQ; e-mail: sales@latin-liturgy.org.uk
Order electronic and video publications from: Publications Manager, 47 Western Park Road, Leicester, LE3 6HQ; e-mail: sales@latin-liturgy.org.uk

Publications list: Available online and in print

Access to staff: Contact by letter, by e-mail and via website
Hours: Mon to Fri, 0900 to 1700

ASSOCIATION FOR LEARNING TECHNOLOGY (ALT)

Gipsy Lane, Headington, Oxford, OX3 0BP

Tel: 01865 484125
Fax: 01865 484165
E-mail: admin@alt.ac.uk
Website: www.alt.ac.uk

Enquiries to: Director of Development
Other contacts: Administrator for membership enquiries or conference booking information.

Founded: 1993

Organisation type and purpose: Learned society (membership is by subscription), present number of members: 700, registered charity (charity number 1063519).

Subject coverage: Innovative teaching and learning in further and higher education, application of learning technology, interchange and representation of the membership.

Publications: Printed, and electronic and video

Publications list: Available in print

Access to staff: Contact by letter, by telephone, by fax, by e-mail and via website
Hours: Mon to Fri, 0900 to 1700

Access to building: No access other than to staff

ASSOCIATION FOR LOW COUNTRIES STUDIES (ALCS)

Department of Germanic Studies, University of Sheffield, Jessop West, 1 Upper Hanover Street, Sheffield, S3 7RA

Tel: 0114 222 4396
Fax: 0114 222 2160
E-mail: alcs@sheffield.ac.uk
Website: alcs.group.shef.ac.uk

Enquiries to: Administrator

Founded: 1995

Organisation type and purpose: Learned society (membership is by subscription).
To promote the scholarly study of the language, culture, history and society of the Low Countries; to encourage research in Low Countries Studies; to increase public awareness of the Low Countries, especially the Dutch Language, and Dutch and Flemish culture, history and society; to represent the interests of Low Countries Studies in higher education at national and international level.

Subject coverage: Study of language, literature, history, art, politics, geography and culture of the Low Countries, i.e. the Netherlands and Belgium (particularly Flanders).

Publications: Printed
Order printed publications from: http://alcs.group.shef.ac.uk/aboutus/subscription.htm

Publications list: Available online

Links with: University Council for Modern Languages in Higher Education (UCML)

ASSOCIATION FOR MANAGEMENT EDUCATION AND DEVELOPMENT (AMED)

1st Floor, 62 Paul Street, London, EC2A 4NA

Tel: 020 7613 4121
Fax: 01923 859999
E-mail: ahatherill@aol.com
Website: www.amed.org.uk
Website: www.amed.co.uk

Enquiries to: Membership Secretary
Direct tel: 01923 859999
Direct e-mail: allyson@management.org.uk
Other contacts: Office Manager

Founded: 1978

continued overleaf

Organisation type and purpose:
Membership association (membership is by subscription), present number of members: 1,200.
For the development and propagation of management, organisational learning and education.

Subject coverage: Learning, knowledge management, change management, board and director development, organisation developments, management development, management consultancy.

Library catalogue: All or part available online

Publications: Printed, and electronic and video
Order printed publications from: AMED
The Gardeners Cottage, Shenley Park, Radlett Lane, Shenley, WD7 9DW

Publications list: Available in print

Access to staff: Contact by letter, by telephone, by fax, by e-mail and via website
Hours: Mon to Fri, 0900 to 1700

ASSOCIATION FOR MEDICAL OSTEOPATHY

8–10 Boston Place, London, NW1 6QH

Tel: 020 7262 5250
Fax: 020 7723 7492

Enquiries to: Honorary Secretary
Other contacts: Membership Secretary

Founded: 1911; formerly called Association of Medical Osteopaths, British Osteopathic Association (BOA), London College of Osteopathic Medicine

Organisation type and purpose:
Professional body (membership is by qualification), present number of members: 120.
Medically qualified osteopaths trained at the London College of Osteopathic Medicine.

Subject coverage: Osteopathic medicine; UK sources of treatment.

Library catalogue: All or part available in-house

Publications: Printed

Access to staff: Contact by letter, by telephone and by fax. Access for members only.
Hours: Mon to Fri, 0930 to 1700

Access to building: No access other than to staff

Access for disabled people: Level entry, toilet facilities

At the same address is the: Osteopathic Association Clinic; tel: 020 7262 1128; fax: 020 7723 7492

Close links with: Osteopathic Trusts Limited; tel: 020 7262 5250; fax: 020 7723 7492

ASSOCIATION FOR PALLIATIVE MEDICINE OF GREAT BRITAIN AND IRELAND (APM)

76 Botley Road, Park Gate, Southampton, SO31 1BA

Tel: 01489 565665
E-mail: sabine.tuck@apmonline.org
Website: www.apmonline.org

Enquiries to: Administrator

Founded: 1985

Organisation type and purpose:
Professional body, membership association (membership is by subscription, qualification), present number of members: 1,050, registered charity (charity number 1053572).

Subject coverage: Palliative Medicine

Publications: Printed

Access to staff: Contact by letter, by telephone and by e-mail
Hours: Mon to Fri

ASSOCIATION FOR PASTORAL CARE OF THE MENTALLY ILL (APCMH)

Cornerstone House, 14 Willis Road, Croydon, Surrey, CR0 2XX

Tel: 020 8665 6718
Fax: 020 8665 1972
E-mail: apcmh@croydononline.org

Enquiries to: Development Officer

Founded: 1984

Organisation type and purpose: Voluntary organisation.

Subject coverage: Mental health especially spirituality and mental health promotion.

Publications: Printed

Access to staff: Contact by letter, by telephone, by fax and by e-mail
Hours: Mon, Wed, Fri, 0830 to 1530

Access to building: No access other than to staff

National Office: APCMH; c/o Marylebone Park Church, Marylebone Road, London, NW1 5LT; tel: 01483 538936

ASSOCIATION FOR PERIOPERATIVE PRACTICE (AFPP)

Daisy Ayris House, 6 Grove Park Court, Harrogate, North Yorkshire, HG1 4DP

Tel: 01423 508079
Fax: 01423 531613
E-mail: hq@afpp.org.uk
Website: www.afpp.org.uk

Enquiries to: Chairman

Founded: 1964; formerly called National Association of Theatre Nurses (year of change 2005)

Organisation type and purpose: Advisory body, membership association (membership is by subscription), training organisation.

Subject coverage: Operating theatre nursing (all surgical specialisations); theatre technique; staffing of operating theatres; non-nursing staff in theatres; planning; patient care; anaesthetic room nursing; recovery room nursing; legal implications of patients' safety and accidents; sterilisation.

Collection: Journals on nursing (national)
Journals on perioperative nursing (national and international)
Books on theatre nursing and related topics

Publications: Printed
Order printed publications from: AFPP directly or website

Publications list: Available online and in print

Access to staff: Contact by letter, by telephone, by fax, by e-mail and via website
Hours: Mon to Fri, 0830 to 1630

ASSOCIATION FOR PHYSICAL EDUCATION (AFPE)

Building 25, London Road, Reading, Berkshire, RG1 5AQ

Tel: 0118 378 6240
Fax: 0118 378 6242
E-mail: enquiries@afpe.org.uk
Website: www.afpe.org.uk

Enquiries to: Chief Executive

Founded: 2006

Organisation type and purpose:
Professional body (membership is by subscription), registered charity (charity number 1114673), research organisation.

Subject coverage: Physical education, continuing professional development, health and fitness education.

Collection: PEA Archives in the Library, Sheffield University

Publications: Printed

Publications list: Available in print

Access to staff: Contact by letter, by telephone, by fax, by e-mail and via website. Appointment necessary.
Hours: Mon to Fri, 0900 to 1700

Access to building: Prior appointment required

Access for disabled people: Parking provided

ASSOCIATION FOR POST NATAL ILLNESS (APNI)

145 Dawes Road, Fulham, London, SW6 7EB

Tel: 020 7386 0868
Fax: 020 7386 8885
E-mail: info@apni.org
Website: www.apni.org

Enquiries to: Information Officer

Founded: 1979

Organisation type and purpose:
Membership association, present number of members: 1,800, voluntary organisation, registered charity (charity number 280510).
Provides information and support to mothers suffering from postnatal depression, information for health professionals, supports research into postnatal illness.

Subject coverage: The management and treatment of postnatal illness.

Publications: Printed

Publications list: Available in print

Access to staff: Contact by letter, by telephone, by fax, by e-mail and via website
Hours: Mon to Fri, 1000 to 1400

ASSOCIATION FOR PROJECT MANAGEMENT (APM)

150 West Wycombe Road, High Wycombe, Buckinghamshire, HP12 3AE

Tel: 0845 458 1944
Fax: 01494 528937
E-mail: info@apm.org.uk
Website: www.apm.org.uk

Enquiries to: Chief Executive
Other contacts: Head of Professional Development; Head of Membership; Head of Marketing

Founded: 1972; formerly called Association of Project Managers (year of change 1997)

Organisation type and purpose: National organisation, professional body (membership is by subscription), present number of members: 17,000, registered charity (charity number 290927).
Promotion of the professions of Project Management both in the UK and internationally and the development of the art and science of project management.

Subject coverage: Project management across all sectors of business and industry.

Publications: Printed, and electronic and video
Order printed publications from: Turpin Distribution: 01767 604951
Order electronic and video publications from: Turpin Distribution: 01767 604951

Access to staff: Contact by letter, by telephone, by fax and by e-mail
Hours: Mon to Fri, 0900 to 1700

Access to building: *Hours:* Mon to Fri, 0900 to 1700

Access for disabled people: Parking provided, level entry
Hours: Mon to Fri, 0900 to 1700

Affiliated to: International Project Management Association (IPMA); Service Secretariat, PO Box 30, Monmouth, NP5 4YZ; tel: 01594 531007; fax: 01594 531008; e-mail: ipma@btinternet.com; website: http://www.ipma.co.uk

ASSOCIATION FOR PUBLIC SERVICE EXCELLENCE (APSE)

2nd floor Washbrook House, Lancastrian Office Centre, Talbot Road, Old Trafford, Manchester, M32 0FP

Tel: 0161 772 1810
Fax: 0161 772 1811
E-mail: enquiries@apse.org.uk
Website: www.apse.org.uk

Enquiries to: Secretariat
Other contacts: Principal Advisor for publications, press releases, briefing notes

Founded: 1981; formerly called Association of Direct Labour Organisations (ADLO) (year of change 2000)

Organisation type and purpose: Local government body, advisory body, professional body (membership is by subscription), present number of members: 270, training organisation, consultancy, research organisation.
To consult, develop, promote and advise on best practice in the delivery of public services.

Subject coverage: Public sector contracting, service delivery issues such as quality, structures, etc, best value, PFI, TUPE, housing stock transfers, best value consultancy, local government benchmarking.

Collection: Small library and resource unit

Trade and statistical information: Data on local government direct service provision

Non-library collection catalogue: All or part available online

Library catalogue: All or part available online

Publications: Printed
Order printed publications from: e-mail: enquiries@apse.org.uk

Publications list: Available online and in print

Access to staff: Contact by letter, by telephone, by fax, by e-mail and via website. Appointment necessary. Access for members only. Non-members charged.
Hours: Mon to Fri, 0900 to 1700

Access to building: No access other than to staff

Access for disabled people: Access to all public areas

Also at: Association for Public Service Excellence (Scottish APSE); Brandon House Business Centre, Unit 18–20, 23–25 Brandon Street, Hamilton, ML3 8DA; tel: 01698 459051; fax: 01698 200316; e-mail: enquiries@apse.org.uk

ASSOCIATION FOR RATIONAL EMOTIVE BEHAVIOUR THERAPY

PO Box 39207, London, SE3 7XH

Tel: 020 8293 4334
Fax: 020 8293 4114
E-mail: rebtadmin@managingstress.com
Website: rebt.bizland.com

Enquiries to: Honorary Secretary
Other contacts: Membership Secretary

Founded: 1993; formerly called Association for Rational Emotive Behaviour Therapists (year of change 2002)

Organisation type and purpose: Professional body (membership is by subscription, qualification), present number of members: 85.
To promote the art and science of rational emotive behaviour therapy.

Non-library collection catalogue: All or part available online

Publications: Printed, and electronic and video

Access to staff: Contact by letter, by telephone, by e-mail and via website
Hours: Mon to Fri, 1000 to 1700

ASSOCIATION FOR ROAD TRAFFIC SAFETY AND MANAGEMENT (ARTSM)

ARTSM Shepstone, Holmesdale Road, South Nutfield, Surrey, RH1 4JE

Tel: 01737 823360
Fax: 020 8977 8339
Website: www.artsm.org.uk

Enquiries to: General Secretary
Direct e-mail: philip.crickmay@artsm.org.uk

Founded: 1933; formerly called Association of Road Traffic Sign Makers (ARTSM) (year of change 1995)

Organisation type and purpose: Trade association (membership is by subscription, qualification), present number of members: 41.

Subject coverage: Transport, road safety, pedestrian safety, road traffic signs, permanent and portable variable message signs, portable traffic signals, sign luminaires, street lighting, street name plates, traffic cones and lamps, sign erection, sign design-computer systems, vehicle detection and control.

Publications: Printed

Access to staff: Contact by letter, by telephone, by fax, by e-mail and via website. Appointment necessary.
Hours: Mon, Tue, Thu, 0900 to 1700

ASSOCIATION FOR SCIENCE EDUCATION (ASE)

College Lane, Hatfield, Hertfordshire, AL10 9AA

Tel: 01707 283000
Fax: 01707 266532
E-mail: info@ase.org.uk
Website: www.ase.org.uk

Enquiries to: Chief Executive
Other contacts: Executive Director (Professional and Curriculum Innovation) – bookselling operations; Co-ordinator Journals – magazines

Founded: 1901

Organisation type and purpose: Professional body (membership is by subscription), present number of members: 15,000, registered charity (charity number 313123), suitable for ages: 3 to 19, publishing house.
Educational organisation.

Subject coverage: Primary, secondary and further education science education, study for its improvement, school safety issues.

Publications: Printed, and electronic and video

Publications list: Available online and in print

Access to staff: Contact by letter, by telephone, by fax, by e-mail and via website. Appointment necessary.
Hours: Mon to Fri, 0900 to 1700

Links with: 40 International Science Teacher Education Associations

ASSOCIATION FOR SCOTTISH LITERARY STUDIES (ASLS)

Scottish Literature, 7 University Gardens, University of Glasgow, Glasgow, G12 8QH

Tel: 0141 330 5309
Fax: 0141 330 5309
E-mail: office@asls.org.uk
Website: www.asls.org.uk

Enquiries to: Director

Founded: 1970

continued overleaf

Organisation type and purpose:
International organisation, membership association (membership is by subscription), present number of members: 600, registered charity (charity number SC006535), publishing house.
ASLS is an educational charity promoting the languages and literature of Scotland, from the study of classic texts to encouraging contemporary talent.

Subject coverage: Languages and literature of Scotland.

Publications: Printed, and electronic and video

Publications list: Available online and in print

Access to staff: Contact by letter, by telephone, by fax, by e-mail and via website
Hours: Mon to Fri, 0900 to 1700

ASSOCIATION FOR SHARED PARENTING (A.S.P.)

PO Box 2000, Dudley, West Midlands, DY1 1YZ

Tel: 01789 751157
Fax: 01789 751081
Website: www.sharedparenting.org.uk
Website: www.sharedparenting.f9.co.uk/

Enquiries to: Honorary Secretary
Direct e-mail: owner@sharedparenting.org.uk

Founded: 1993; formerly called Families Need Fathers (West Midlands Branch) (FNF) (year of change 1993)

Organisation type and purpose:
Membership association (membership is by subscription), present number of members: 80, voluntary organisation, registered charity (charity number 1042874).
To promote the right of children to have sufficient contact with both parents after separation or divorce.

Subject coverage: The Children Act 1989, parental responsibility, family court procedures, divorce and children, maintaining contact with children after separation or divorce, how to manage your solicitor, use of child contact centre.

Publications: Printed

Access to staff: Contact by letter and by telephone
Hours: Daily, 0800 to 2200

Other branches in: Leicestershire; tel: 0116 254 8453

ASSOCIATION FOR SPECIALIST FIRE PROTECTION (ASFP)

Kingsley House, Ganders Business Park, Kingsley, Bordon, Hampshire, GU35 9LU

Tel: 01420 471612
Fax: 01420 471611
E-mail: info@asfp.org.uk
Website: www.asfp.org.uk

Direct e-mail: info@asfp.org.uk

Founded: 1975

Organisation type and purpose: Trade association, present number of members: 64.
Represents UK manufacturers, distributors, contractors, consultants, testing houses and others involved in passive fire protection products and services. Produces a wide range of relevant publications.

Subject coverage: Passive fire protection products and services.

Information services: Technical information on passive fire protection is provided by ASFP Technical Officer.

Library catalogue: All or part available online

Publications: Printed

Publications list: Available online and in print

Access to staff: Contact by letter, by telephone, by fax, by e-mail and via website
Hours: Mon to Fri, 0900 to 1700

ASSOCIATION FOR SPINA BIFIDA AND HYDROCEPHALUS (ASBAH)

ASBAH House, 42 Park Road, Peterborough, Cambridgeshire, PE1 2UQ

Tel: 01733 555988
Fax: 01733 555985
E-mail: helpline@asbah.org
Website: www.asbah.org

Enquiries to: Helpline and Information Service
Direct tel: 0845 450 7755
Direct e-mail: briand@asbah.org

Founded: 1966

Organisation type and purpose: Voluntary organisation, registered charity (charity number 249338).
40 affiliated local associations in UK.
Provides information, advice and support to families/individuals with spina bifida and/or hydrocephalus.

Subject coverage: Spina bifida, hydrocephalus, (antenatal testing, welfare and help as to benefit entitlement, education, mobility, continence, training and employment, aids and appliances in relation to spina bifida or hydrocephalus only).

Publications: Printed

Publications list: Available online and in print

Access to staff: Contact by letter, by telephone, by fax, by e-mail and via website
Hours: Mon to Fri, 0900 to 1700. Helpline: Mon to Fri, 1000 to 1600

ASSOCIATION FOR THE CONSERVATION OF ENERGY (ACE)

Westgate House, Prebend Street, London, N1 8PT

Tel: 020 7359 8000
Fax: 020 7359 0863
E-mail: info@ukace.org
Website: members.aol.com/aceuk/home.htm
Website: www.ukace.org

Enquiries to: Office Manager
Other contacts: Research Director for research function.

Founded: 1981

Organisation type and purpose:
Membership association (membership is by subscription, election or invitation), present number of members: 18, research organisation.
Campaigning organisation.
To increase investment in energy conservation.

Subject coverage: Energy conservation (policy rather than product related), greenhouse effect, CO2 emissions, fuel poverty.

Collection: Material on energy conservation policy

Publications list: Available in print

Access to staff: Contact by letter, by telephone, by fax, by e-mail and via website
Hours: Mon to Fri, 0930 to 1730
Special comments: Strictly no personal callers.

Links with: British Energy Efficiency Federation

ASSOCIATION FOR UNIVERSITY AND COLLEGE COUNSELLING (AUCC)

British Association for Counselling and Psychotherapy, 15 St John's Business Park, Lutterworth, Leicestershire, LE17 4HB

Tel: 01455 883300; minicom no. 01455 0307
Fax: 01455 550243
E-mail: bacp@bacp.co.uk
Website: www.bacp.co.uk
Website: www.counselling.co.uk

Enquiries to: Administrator

Founded: 1971; formerly called Association of Student Counsellors (year of change 1997)

Organisation type and purpose: Voluntary organisation.
To promote counselling in institutions of post-compulsory education.

Subject coverage: Provision of counselling services in post-compulsory education, practice of student counselling, careers counselling, training and professional development of members, advisory service to members for their institutional provision, appropriate conditions of service for counsellors in institutions.

Trade and statistical information: Statistical survey of institutions (available to contributing members only)

Publications: Printed

Publications list: Available online and in print

Access to staff: Contact by letter, by telephone, by fax, by e-mail and via website. Appointment necessary.
Hours: Mon to Fri, 0900 to 1700

Access to building: Prior appointment required
Hours: Mon to Fri, 0900 to 1700

Access for disabled people: Parking provided, ramped entry, toilet facilities

Constituent part of: British Association for Counselling and Psychotherapy

ASSOCIATION OF ACCOUNTING TECHNICIANS (AAT)

AAT, 140 Aldersgate Street, London, EC1A 4HY

Tel: 020 7837 8600
Fax: 020 7837 6970
E-mail: info@aat.org.uk
Website: www.aat.org.uk

Enquiries to: Communications Manager
Direct tel: 020 7415 7670
Direct fax: 020 7415 7699
Direct e-mail: kate.martin@aat.org.uk

Founded: 1980

Organisation type and purpose:
International organisation, professional body (membership is by subscription, qualification), present number of members: 105,000, registered charity (charity number 1050724), suitable for ages: 16+.
The Association of Accounting Technicians is the only dedicated professional body approved to award National Vocational Qualifications (NVQs) and Scottish Vocational Qualifications (SVQs) in Accounting.
The Association was established in 1980 to provide a recognised qualification body for Accounting Technicians.

Subject coverage: Training as an Accounting Technician – NVQs/SVQs in Accounting AAT Qualifications. Membership of the AAT and Continuing Professional Development.

Publications: Printed

Publications list: Available online and in print

Access to staff: Contact by letter, by telephone, by fax, by e-mail, in person and via website. Appointment necessary.
Hours: Mon to Fri, 0900 to 1700

ASSOCIATION OF AMERICAN DANCING (AAD)

Aspenshaw Hall, Thornsett, High Peak, Derbyshire, SK22 1AU

Tel: 01663 744986
E-mail: email@a-a-d.wanadoo.co.uk
Website: www.the-aad.org.uk

Enquiries to: Director

Founded: 1936

Organisation type and purpose:
Professional body, membership association (membership is by qualification), training organisation.
Examination and teaching body in dance disciplines.

Subject coverage: Most dance forms, particularly ballet, mime, tap, acrobatic and modern stage dancing.

Library catalogue: All or part available in-house

Publications: Printed, and electronic and video
Order printed publications from: General Secretary, Association of American Dancing

Publications list: Available in print

Access to staff: Contact by letter, by telephone, by e-mail and via website. Appointment necessary.
Hours: Mon to Fri, 1000 to 1700

Access to building: *Hours:* Mon to Fri, 1000 to 1700

Access for disabled people: *Hours:* Mon to Fri, 1000 to 1700

Affiliated to: Council for Dance Education and Training (UK); London

ASSOCIATION OF APPLIED BIOLOGISTS (AAB)

c/o Warwick HRI, Wellesbourne, Warwickshire, CV35 9EF

Tel: 02476 575195
Fax: 01789 470234
E-mail: rebecca@aab.org.uk
Website: www.aab.org.uk

Enquiries to: Executive Officer

Founded: 1904

Organisation type and purpose:
International organisation, learned society (membership is by election or invitation), present number of members: 800, registered charity (charity number 275655), training organisation, publishing house.

Subject coverage: Plant breeding, pathology, physiology, virology, entomology, nematology, host plant resistance to diseases and pests, plant microbial interactions, bio-control, crop physiology, weeds and crop agronomy, post-harvest biology, pesticide application.

Publications: Printed, and electronic and video

Publications list: Available online and in print

Access to staff: Contact by letter, by telephone, by fax and via website. Appointment necessary.
Hours: Mon to Fri, 0900 to 1700

Access to building: Prior appointment required

Access for disabled people: Parking provided, toilet facilities

Affiliated to: Institute of Biology

ASSOCIATION OF ART & ANTIQUES DEALERS (LAPADA)

Formal name: The Association of Art & Antiques Dealers

535 Kings Road, London, SW10 0SZ

Tel: 020 7823 3511
Fax: 020 7823 3522
E-mail: lapada@lapada.org
Website: www.lapada.org

Enquiries to: Chief Executive

Founded: 1974; formerly called London and Provincial Antique Dealers Association (LAPADA)

Organisation type and purpose: Trade association (membership is by qualification), present number of members: 600.

Subject coverage: Trade in art and antiques.

Publications list: Available online and in print

Access to staff: Contact by letter, by telephone, by fax, by e-mail and via website
Hours: Mon to Fri, 0900 to 1700

Member organisation of: Confédération Internationale des Négociants en Oeuvres d'Art (CINOA)

ASSOCIATION OF ART HISTORIANS (AAH)

Cowcross Court, 70 Cowcross Street, London, EC1M 6EJ

Tel: 020 7490 3211
E-mail: admin@aah.org.uk
Website: www.aah.org.uk

Enquiries to: Administrator

Founded: 1974

Organisation type and purpose:
Membership association.

Subject coverage: Art history, art, design, architecture, photography, film and media, museum studies, conservation, cultural studies.

Publications: Printed, and electronic and video
Order printed publications from: Wiley -Blackwell Publishing

Publications list: Available online

Access to staff: Contact by letter, by telephone, by fax, by e-mail and via website
Hours: Mon to Fri, 0930 to 1730

Links with: College Art Association (CAA); USA; Scottish Society of Art Historians (SSAH)

ASSOCIATION OF AUTHORS' AGENTS (AAA)

President, Peter Straus c/o Rogers, Coleridge & White Ltd, 20 Powis Mews, London, W11 1JN

Tel: 020 7221 3717
E-mail: peters@rcwlitagency.com
Website: www.agentsassoc.co.uk
Website: www.writersservices.com

Organisation type and purpose: A voluntary body and membership organisation for literary agents.
To provide a forum for member agencies to discuss industry matters, to uphold a code of good practice, and to provide a vehicle for representing the interests of agents and authors.

Subject coverage: Literary agents and their work. Members have each practised as literary agents for a period of three years or more, are based in the UK, have a list of clients who are actively engaged in writing, and abide by a code of practice as detailed on the website.

Access to staff: Contact by letter, by telephone and by e-mail

Also at: Secretary, Olivia Guest; c/o Jonathan Clowes Ltd. 10 Iron Bridge House, Bridge Approach, London, NW1 8 BD; tel: 020 7722 7674; e-mail: olivia@ jonathanclowes.co.uk

ASSOCIATION OF BAKERY INGREDIENT MANUFACTURERS (abim)

4a Torphichen Street, Edinburgh, EH3 8JQ

continued overleaf

Tel: 0131 229 9415
Fax: 0131 229 9407
E-mail: abim@abim.org.uk
Website: www.abim.org.uk

Enquiries to: Executive Secretary

Founded: 1917; formerly called Bakery Allied Traders' Association (BATA) (year of change 1999)

Organisation type and purpose: Trade association (membership is by subscription). Acts as lobbying organisation for trade sector.

Subject coverage: Bakery ingredients.

Publications: Printed

Publications list: Available online

Access to staff: Contact by letter, by telephone, by fax, by e-mail and via website. Appointment necessary. Access for members only.
Hours: Mon to Fri, 0900 to 1700

Access to building: Prior appointment required

Member of: FEDIMA; FMBRA; Food and Drink Federation; UKBICC

ASSOCIATION OF BLIND PIANO TUNERS (ABPT)

31 Wyre Crescent, Lynwood, Darwen, Lancashire, BB3 0JG

Tel: 0844 736 1976
E-mail: abpt@uk-piano.org
Website: www.uk-piano.org

Enquiries to: Secretary

Organisation type and purpose: A registered charity (number 294885).
To serve the professional and particular needs of its members and other blind and partially sighted piano tuners throughout the world; to continue as the leading authority and association for blind or partially sighted piano tuners, insisting that only those professionally trained, examined, and qualified are accepted into membership, ensuring that the public knows that an ABPT member will offer skilled, professional, and reliable service.

Subject coverage: Pianos and piano tuning.

Education services: Offers ongoing training to piano tuners who wish to acquire extra levels of ability.

Access to staff: Contact by letter, by telephone and by e-mail

ASSOCIATION OF BREASTFEEDING MOTHERS (ABM)

PO Box 207, Bridgwater, Somerset, TA6 7YT

Tel: 08444 122948 (admin)
E-mail: info@abm.me.uk
Website: www.abm.me.uk

Enquiries to: Helpline
Direct tel: 08444 122949

Founded: 1979

Organisation type and purpose: Membership association (membership is by subscription), registered charity (charity number 280537).
Promotion of breastfeeding and provision of counselling for mothers with breastfeeding problems, training breastfeeding counsellors.

Subject coverage: Support and information on breastfeeding for mothers and health professionals; counsellor training available.

Information services: Breastfeeding helpline

Publications: Printed

Publications list: Available online and in print

Access to staff: Contact by letter, by telephone, by e-mail and via website
Hours: Daily, 0930 to 2230

ASSOCIATION OF BRITISH & IRISH WILD ANIMAL KEEPERS (ABWAK)

Twycross Zoo, Burton Road, Atherstone, Warwickshire, CV9 3PX

Tel: 01827 880250
Fax: 01827 880700
E-mail: amy.hulse@twycrosszoo.org
Website: www.abwak.co.uk

Enquiries to: Honorary Secretary
Direct fax: 01827 881049

Founded: 1974

Organisation type and purpose: Professional body.

Subject coverage: Animal husbandry and zoos.

Publications: Printed
Order printed publications from: Publications Officer, Leeds Castle, Maidstone, Kent, ME17 1PL

Publications list: Available in print

Access to staff: Contact by letter, by e-mail and via website
Hours: Mon to Fri, 0900 to 1700

ASSOCIATION OF BRITISH CERTIFICATION BODIES LIMITED (ABCB)

Sandover Centre, 129A Whitehorse Hill, Chislehurst, Kent, BR7 6DQ

Tel: 020 8295 1128
Fax: 020 8467 8095
E-mail: tinman@abcb.org.uk
Website: www.abcb.org.uk/

Enquiries to: Chief Executive
Direct tel: 01525 630679
Direct e-mail: trevor.nash@abcb.org.uk

Founded: 1984

Organisation type and purpose: National organisation, trade association (membership is by subscription, qualification), present number of members: 25.
To promote ABCB as the UK's centre of excellence for product, quality management and environmental certification for the benefit of its members.

Trade and statistical information: List of members

Publications: Printed

Access to staff: Contact by letter, by telephone, by fax and by e-mail
Hours: Mon to Fri, 0900 to 1700

ASSOCIATION OF BRITISH CHORAL DIRECTORS (abcd)

15 Granville Way, Sherborne, Dorset, DT9 4AS

Tel: 01935 389482
E-mail: rachel.greaves@abcd.org.uk
Website: www.abcd.org.uk

Enquiries to: General Secretary
Other contacts: Head of Training and Events

Founded: 1986

Organisation type and purpose: A registered charity (number 1085226), membership association (membership is by subscription and is open to individuals and organisations employed or involved in music), current number of members: over 700 individual members and 55 associate and corporate members.
A forum for conductors of choral music in the United Kingdom.
To promote, improve and maintain the education, training and development of choral directors with a view to improving standards in all sectors of choral activity.

Subject coverage: Choral music and directors of choral music.

Education services: Regional and national training courses and conventions.

Publications: Printed

Access to staff: Contact by letter, by telephone, by e-mail and via website

ASSOCIATION OF BRITISH CORRESPONDENCE COLLEGES (ABCC)

PO Box 17926, London, SW19 3WB

Tel: 020 8544 9559
E-mail: info@homestudy.org.uk
Website: www.homestudy.org.uk

Enquiries to: Secretary

Founded: 1955

Organisation type and purpose: Trade association (membership is by qualification), present number of members: 22.

Subject coverage: Distance education; academic, professional, commercial and technical courses.

Access to staff: Contact by letter, by telephone, by e-mail and via website
Hours: Mon to Fri, 1430 to 1800 (variable)

ASSOCIATION OF BRITISH CYCLING COACHES (ABCC)

Association of British Cycle Coaches, The Barn, Cove Road, Silverdale, Lancashire, LA5 0SQ

Tel: 01406 370744
Fax: 01406 373150
E-mail: info@abcc.co.uk
Website: www.abcc.co.uk

Enquiries to: Administrator

Founded: before 1970; formerly called British Cycling Coaches Association (BCCA) (year of change c.1990)

Organisation type and purpose: Membership association (membership is by qualification), present number of members: 702, voluntary organisation, training organisation.
To educate, qualify and maintain a register of cycling coaches.

Subject coverage: Cycling coaching.

Publications: Printed, and electronic and video
Order electronic and video publications from: Administrator

Access to staff: Contact by letter, by telephone, by fax, by e-mail and via website
Hours: Mon to Fri, 0900 to 1700

ASSOCIATION OF BRITISH DISPENSING OPTICIANS (ABDO)

ABDO College, Godmersham Park, Godmersham, Canterbury, Kent, CT4 7DT

Tel: 01227 738829
Fax: 01227 733900
E-mail: general@abdolondon.org.uk
Website: www.abdo.org.uk

Enquiries to: Reception
Direct tel: 01227 733905
Other contacts: Head of Distance Learning Department (for education matters)

Founded: 1989; formerly called Association of Dispensing Opticians

Organisation type and purpose: Professional body (membership is by subscription, qualification), present number of members: 6,400, training organisation.

Subject coverage: Optics and opticians.

Publications: Printed
Order printed publications from: ABDO College Bookshop

Publications list: Available online and in print

Access to staff: Contact by letter, by telephone, by fax and via website. Appointment necessary. Access for members only.
Hours: Mon to Fri, 0900 to 1700

Access for disabled people: Parking provided, ramped entry, toilet facilities

ASSOCIATION OF BRITISH HEALTHCARE INDUSTRIES (ABHI)

111 Westminster Bridge Road, London, SE1 7HR

Tel: 020 7960 4360
Fax: 020 7960 4361
E-mail: enquiries@abhi.org.uk
Website: www.abhi.org.uk

Founded: 1988; created by the merger of British Health Care Export Council (BHEC) and British Health Care Trade and Industry Confederation (BHTIC) (year of change 1988)

Organisation type and purpose: Trade association (membership is by subscription, qualification), present number of members: 200.
To promote medical technology and systems for better health care and to be a facilitator of industry growth and health-care development by supporting the industry.

Subject coverage: The medical devices industry, technical and regulatory affairs, NHS, overseas trade.

Publications: Printed

Publications list: Available online

Access to staff: Contact by letter, by telephone, by fax, by e-mail and via website. Appointment necessary.
Hours: Mon to Fri, 0900 to 1700

Access to building: No prior appointment required
Hours: Mon to Fri, 0900 to 1700
Special comments: Members can use the library.

Access for disabled people: Access to all public areas

ASSOCIATION OF BRITISH INSURERS (ABI)

51 Gresham Street, London, EC2V 7HQ

Tel: 020 7600 3333
Fax: 020 7696 8999
E-mail: info@abi.org.uk
Website: www.abi.org.uk

Enquiries to: Consumer Support Adviser
Direct tel: 020 7216 7416

Founded: 1985; formerly called British Insurance Association, Fire Offices Committee, Life Offices Association

Organisation type and purpose: Trade association (membership is by subscription, qualification).

Subject coverage: UK insurance industry, EC insurance sector, statistics.

Publications: Printed
Order printed publications from: Download from website or ring 020 7216 7617 after consulting website publications list

Publications list: Available online

Access to staff: Contact by letter, by telephone, by fax, by e-mail and via website. Access for members only.
Hours: Mon to Fri, 0900 to 1300 and 1400 to 1700

ASSOCIATION OF BRITISH INTRODUCTION AGENCIES (ABIA)

Suite 109, 315 Chiswick High Rd, London, W4 4HH

Tel: 020 8742 0386
Website: www.abia.org.uk

Enquiries to: Press Officer
Direct tel: 07530 415 388
Direct e-mail: press@abia.org.uk

Founded: 1981

Organisation type and purpose: Trade association, membership association (membership is by qualification), present number of members: 30, research organisation.
To monitor, regulate and disseminate information regarding the industry, enforcing the code of conduct supported by the Office of Fair Trading.

Subject coverage: Introduction agencies, including marriage bureaux and introduction and dating agencies.

Trade and statistical information: Available upon request

Publications: Printed

Access to staff: Contact by letter, by fax, by e-mail and via website
Hours: Telephone between 0930 to 1700
Special comments: No visitors.

ASSOCIATION OF BRITISH INVESTIGATORS (ABI)

295 – 297 Church Street, Blackpool, Lancashire FY1 3PJ

Tel: 01253 297 502
E-mail: info@theabi.org.uk
Website: www.theabi.org.uk

Enquiries to: Company Secretary
Other contacts: President for Administrative Head of organisation.

Founded: 1913

Organisation type and purpose: International organisation, trade association (membership is by qualification), present number of members: 400.
Association for private investigators. Representation and training.

Subject coverage: Any legally obtainable information about individuals, corporations, associations, trusts etc worldwide.

Publications: Printed

Access to staff: Contact by letter, by telephone, by fax and by e-mail
Hours: Mon to Fri, 0900 to 1700

ASSOCIATION OF BRITISH ORCHESTRAS (ABO)

32 Rose Street, London, WC2E 9ET

Tel: 020 7557 6770
Fax: 020 7557 6799
E-mail: info@abo.org.uk
Website: www.abo.org.uk

Enquiries to: Director
Direct e-mail: mark@abo.org.uk

Founded: 1947

Organisation type and purpose: The ABO exists to support, develop and advance the interests and activities of the orchestral profession in the UK.
The ABO's key activities centre around Advocacy, Services, Information and Learning and are delivered through conferences, seminars, negotiations, training opportunities, education initiatives and representation.
Full membership is open to professional orchestras that have been in existence for more than two years and have given at least 24 performances. Associate, Corporate and Individual membership is also available.

Subject coverage: Professional orchestras in the UK.

continued overleaf

Library catalogue: All or part available online

Publications: Printed

Publications list: Available online and in print

Access to staff: Contact by letter, by telephone, by fax, by e-mail and via website. Appointment necessary.
Hours: Mon to Fri, 0930 to 1730

Access to building: Prior appointment required

ASSOCIATION OF BRITISH PEWTER CRAFTSMEN (ABPC)

Unit 10, Edmund Road Business Centre135 Edmund Road, Sheffield, S2 4ED

Tel: 0114 252 7550
Fax: 0114 252 7555
E-mail: enquiries@abpcltd.co.uk
Website: www.britishpewter.co.uk/

Enquiries to: Secretary

Organisation type and purpose: Trade association.

Subject coverage: Manufacture of articles of pewter.

Collection: Collections at Pewter Hall, Oat Lane, London

Publications: Printed

Access to staff: Contact by letter, by telephone and by fax
Hours: Mon to Fri, 0900 to 1700

ASSOCIATION OF BRITISH PHILATELIC SOCIETIES LIMITED (ABPS)

c/o Royal Philatelic Society, 41 Devonshire Place, London, W1G 6JY

E-mail: secretary@abps.org.uk
Website: www.abps.org.uk

Enquiries to: Chairman
Direct e-mail: chair@abps.org.uk

Founded: 1994; formerly called British Philatelic Federation (BPF) (year of change 1994)

Organisation type and purpose: National UK organisation and membership association (membership by subscription), present number of members: 15,000 mainly through 19 area federations and over 300 local and specialist stamp, postal history and post card collecting clubs and societies Federation of Stamp collectors, societies, etc.

Subject coverage: Philately generally, stamp collecting, postal history including postcards.

Publications: Printed

Publications list: Available online and in print

Access to staff: Contact by letter, by e-mail and via website. Appointment necessary.
Hours: Mon to Fri, 0900 to 1700

Affiliated to: Fédération Internationale de Philatélie (FIP); Federation of European Philatelic Federations (FEPA)

ASSOCIATION OF BRITISH PICTURE RESTORERS (ABPR)

Formal name: The Association of British Picture Restorers

PO Box 258, Norwich, NR13 4WY

Tel: 01603 516237
Fax: 01603 510985
E-mail: office@bapcr.org.uk
Website: www.bapcr.org.uk/

Enquiries to: Secretary

Founded: 1943

Organisation type and purpose: Professional body.

Subject coverage: Restoration and conservation of oil paintings; professional training.

Publications: Printed

Access to staff: Contact by letter, by telephone, by fax and by e-mail
Hours: Mon to Fri, 0930 to 1730

Affiliated to: IIC; IPC; SSCR

ASSOCIATION OF BRITISH RIDING SCHOOLS (ABRS)

Queen's Chambers, 38–40 Queen Street, Penzance, Cornwall, TR18 4BH

Tel: 01736 369440
Fax: 01736 351390
E-mail: office@abrs-info.org
Website: www.abrs-info.org

Enquiries to: General Secretary

Founded: 1954

Organisation type and purpose: National organisation, advisory body, professional body (membership is by subscription), voluntary organisation, training organisation.
Professional association for proprietors, managers and staff of riding establishments.

Subject coverage: Standards of instruction; horsemastership, welfare of horses and ponies in riding establishments, problems of riding establishments.

Publications: Printed
Order printed publications from: ABRS

Publications list: Available online and in print

Access to staff: Contact by letter, by telephone, by fax and by e-mail
Hours: Mon to Fri, 0930 to 1730

Member organisation of: British Equestrian Federation (BEF); British Equestrian Trade Association (BETA); Central Council of Physical Recreation (CCPR); SEA; SSA

ASSOCIATION OF BRITISH THEATRE TECHNICIANS (ABTT)

55 Farringdon Road, London, EC1M 3JB

Tel: 020 7242 9200
Fax: 020 7242 9303
E-mail: office@abtt.org.uk
Website: www.abtt.org.uk

Enquiries to: Administrator

Founded: 1961

Organisation type and purpose: Membership association (membership is by subscription), voluntary organisation, registered charity, training organisation.

Subject coverage: Technical aspects of theatre; design and planning of theatre buildings; training and careers in the technical theatre.

Library catalogue: All or part available in-house

Publications: Printed

Publications list: Available online and in print

Access to staff: Contact by letter, by telephone, by fax and by e-mail
Hours: Mon to Fri, 1000 to 1700

Affiliated to and at the same address as: Society of British Theatre Designers

ASSOCIATION OF BRITISH THEOLOGICAL AND PHILOSOPHICAL LIBRARIES (ABTAPL)

Website: www.newman.ac.uk/abtapl/index.html
Website: www.le.ac.uk/abtapl/

Enquiries to: Honorary Secretary
Other contacts: Chairman

Founded: 1954

Organisation type and purpose: National organisation, professional body (membership is by subscription), present number of members: 200.

Subject coverage: Theology, religious studies, philosophy, librarianship.

Publications: Printed

Access to staff: Contact by letter, by fax and by e-mail
Hours: Mon to Fri, 0900 to 1700
Special comments: Voluntary organisation, no paid staff.

Links with: American Theological Libraries Association; Conseil International des Associations des Bibliothèques de Théologie; Library Association

ASSOCIATION OF BRITISH TRAVEL AGENTS (ABTA)

ABTA Ltd, 30 Park Street, London SE1 9EQ

Tel: 020 7637 2444
Fax: 020 7637 0713
E-mail: abta@abta.co.uk
Website: www.abta.com

Enquiries to: Information Officer
Direct tel: 0901 201 5050 (charged at 50p per min)
Direct fax: 020 7307 1992
Other contacts: Policy and Research Executive for research.

Founded: 1950

Organisation type and purpose: Trade association.

Subject coverage: Travel destinations, travel advice, details of ABTA members.

Publications: Printed, and electronic and video
Order printed publications from: ABTA Magazine, Absolute Publishing
197–199 City Road, London, EC1V 1JN

Access to staff: Contact by telephone. All charged.
Hours: Mon to Fri, 0830 to 1800

Access for disabled people: Ramped entry, toilet facilities

Subsidiary body: ABTA National Training Board; Waterloo House, 11–17 Chertsey Road, Woking, Surrey; tel: 01483 727321; fax: 01483 756698

ASSOCIATION OF BROADCASTING DOCTORS (ABD)

PO Box 15, Sindalthorpe House, Ely, Cambridgeshire, CB7 4SG

Tel: 01353 688456 or 688588
Fax: 01353 688451
E-mail: info@abdoctors.com
Website: www.broadcasting-doctor.org

Enquiries to: Director
Other contacts: Administrator

Founded: 1988

Organisation type and purpose: Professional body (membership is by election or invitation), present number of members: 755, voluntary organisation, training organisation, consultancy.
Support for clinicians who also broadcast.

Subject coverage: Medical broadcasting, all medical specialities. The provision of medical practitioners and specialists as contributors to radio and television, and of producers and journal editors.

Collection: Library of written and recorded material

Publications: Printed, and electronic and video

Access to staff: Contact by letter, by telephone, by fax, by e-mail and via website
Hours: 0600 to 1900, seven days a week

Administered by: Soundplan Broadcasting Services Limited; at the same address

ASSOCIATION OF BROKERS & YACHT AGENTS (ABYA)

The Glass Works, Penns Road, Petersfield, Hants, GU32 2EW

Tel: 01730 710425
Fax: 01730 710423
E-mail: info@ybdsa.co.uk
Website: www.abya.co.uk

Enquiries to: Chief Executive
Direct e-mail: info@ybdsa.co.uk
Other contacts: Tonnage Measurers

Founded: 1912

Organisation type and purpose: National organisation, professional body (membership is by qualification, election or invitation), present number of members: 150.
Training and maintaining of standards, support of yacht brokers.

Subject coverage: Brokerage of yachts and small craft; training; tonnage measurement as required for registration by the Department of Trade; certification under the MCA Small Commercial Vessel Code; registration and its benefits; codes of practice; forms of contract.

Library catalogue: All or part available in-house

Publications: Printed

Publications list: Available online and in print

Access to staff: Contact by letter, by telephone, by fax, by e-mail, in person and via website. Appointment necessary.
Hours: Mon to Fri, 0900 to 1700

Access to building: Prior appointment required

Access for disabled people: Parking provided

Parent body: Yacht Brokers Designers & Surveyors Association (YBDSA)

Sister bodies: Professional Charter Association (PCA); Yacht Designers and Surveyors Association (YDSA)

ASSOCIATION OF BUILDING COMPONENT MANUFACTURERS LIMITED (ABCM)

Clark House, 3 Brassey Drive, Aylesford, Kent, ME20 7QL

Tel: 01622 715577
Fax: 08700 54 39 15
Website: www.building-components.org

Enquiries to: Director

Founded: 1965

Organisation type and purpose: Trade association (membership is by subscription).

Access to staff: Contact by letter, by telephone, by fax, by e-mail and via website
Hours: Mon to Fri, 0900 to 1700

ASSOCIATION OF BUILDING ENGINEERS (ABE)

Lutyens House, Billing Brook Road, Weston Favell, Northampton, NN3 8NW

Tel: 01604 404121
Fax: 01604 784220
E-mail: building.engineers@abe.org.uk
Website: www.abe.org.uk

Enquiries to: Marketing & Events Manager
Direct e-mail: info@abe.org.uk
Other contacts: Editor ABE Journal

Founded: 1925; formerly called Incorporated Association of Architects and Surveyors (IAAS) (year of change 1993); incorporates the former Institute of Maintenance and Building Management (IMBM) (year of change 2008)

Organisation type and purpose: Professional body.
To specialise in the technology of building.

Subject coverage: Building surveying and construction in general, architecture, technology of building, town planning, valuation, estate management.

Education services: Provision of relevant training courses to those specialising in the technology of building. For details on all courses / to access the prospectus, see: http://www.abe.org.uk.

Publications: Printed

Access to staff: Contact by letter, by telephone, by fax, by e-mail and via website. Appointment necessary. Non-members charged.
Hours: Mon to Fri, 0900 to 1700

Access to building: *Hours:* Mon to Fri, 0900 to 1700

Member organisation of: Construction Industry Council; Construction Industry Standing Conference; L'Association d'experts européens du bâtiment et de la construction

ASSOCIATION OF BUSINESS RECOVERY PROFESSIONALS (R3)

8th Floor, 120 Aldersgate Street, London, EC1A 4JQ

Tel: 020 7566 4200
Fax: 020 7566 4224
E-mail: association@r3.org.uk
Website: www.r3.org.uk

Enquiries to: Chief Executive Officer
Direct tel: 020 7566 4219

Founded: 1990

Organisation type and purpose: National organisation, professional body, trade association, membership association (membership is by subscription), present number of members: 4,000.
A strong voice for all those who work with underperforming businesses and people in financial difficulty.

Subject coverage: Business recovery, rescue and renewal, including insolvency.

Publications: Printed, and electronic and video
Order printed publications from: http://www.r3.org.uk

Publications list: Available online and in print

Access to staff: Contact by letter, by telephone, by fax and by e-mail
Hours: Mon to Fri, 0900 to 1700

Access to building: Prior appointment required

Access for disabled people: Access to all public areas, toilet facilities

ASSOCIATION OF CATERING EXCELLENCE (ACE)

Bourne House, Horsell Park, Woking, Surrey, GU21 4LY

Tel: 01483 765111
Fax: 01483 751991
E-mail: admin@acegb.org
Website: www.acegb.org

Enquiries to: Administrator

Founded: 1948

Organisation type and purpose: Professional body (membership is by subscription, qualification), service industry.

continued overleaf

Subject coverage: Contract catering and all subjects allied to staff catering.

Access to staff: Contact by letter, by telephone, by fax and by e-mail. Non-members charged.
Hours: Mon to Fri, 0900 to 1700

ASSOCIATION OF CEREAL FOOD MANUFACTURERS (ACFM)

6 Catherine Street, London, WC2B 5JJ

Tel: 020 7836 2460
Fax: 020 7836 0580

Enquiries to: Executive Secretary

Organisation type and purpose: Trade association.
Lobbying organisation.

Subject coverage: Breakfast cereal products and related legislation.

Access to staff: Appointment necessary. Access for members only.
Hours: Mon to Fri, 0900 to 1700

Affiliated to: CEEREAL; Rond Point, Schuman 9 bte 11, Brussels, B-1040, Belgium

Umbrella organisation: Food and Drink Federation; 6 Catherine Street, London, WC2B 5JJ

ASSOCIATION OF CERTIFIED FRAUD EXAMINERS (UK) (ACFE(UK))

78 York Street, London, W1U 1DP

Tel: 0207 692 1888
E-mail: info@acfeuk.co.uk
Website: www.acfeuk.co.uk

Enquiries to: Executive Secretary

Founded: 1993

Organisation type and purpose: Membership association (membership is by subscription, qualification), present number of members: 500.
UK Chapter.

Publications: Printed, and electronic and video

Publications list: Available online and in print

Access to staff: Contact by letter, by telephone, by fax and by e-mail. Appointment necessary.
Hours: Mon to Fri, 0900 to 1700

Headquarters: ACFE; The Gregor Building, 716 West Avenue, Austin, Texas, 78701, USA

ASSOCIATION OF CHARITABLE FOUNDATIONS (ACF)

Central House, 14 Upper Woburn Place, London, WC1H 0AE

Tel: 020 7255 4499
Fax: 020 7255 4496
E-mail: acf@acf.org.uk
Website: www.acf.org.uk

Enquiries to: Chief Executive

Founded: 1989

Organisation type and purpose: Membership association (membership is by subscription), voluntary organisation, registered charity (charity number 1105412). Membership body for more than 300 charitable grant-making trusts and foundations.

Subject coverage: Philanthropy, charitable grant-making, relevant aspects of charity and investment law.

Publications: Printed

Publications list: Available online

Access to staff: Contact by letter, by e-mail and via website. Appointment necessary.
Hours: Mon to Fri, 0930 to 1730

ASSOCIATION OF CHARITY ORGANISATIONS (ACO)

Central House, 14 Upper Woburn Place, London WC1H 0NN

Tel: 020 7255 4480
Fax: 020 7255 4496
E-mail: info@aco.uk.net

Enquiries to: Chief Executive
Other contacts: Administrative Officer; Helpline Co-ordinator (for queries relating to grants from a member charity).

Founded: 1946; incorporates the former Occupational Benevolent Funds Alliance (OBFA)

Organisation type and purpose: Professional body, membership association (membership is by subscription), present number of members: over 200 charities, registered charity (charity number 1118605).

Subject coverage: Charities; benevolent funds, residential and nursing home care of older people in the voluntary sector; effects of legislation, interest of members.

Collection: ACO holds details of a large number of grant-making charities which might help individuals in need (not projects)

Trade and statistical information: Database of member funds

Access to staff: Contact by letter, by telephone, by fax and by e-mail. Appointment necessary.
Hours: Mon to Fri, 1000 to 1600

ASSOCIATION OF CHARTERED CERTIFIED ACCOUNTANTS (ACCA)

29 Lincoln's Inn Fields, London, WC2A 3EE

Tel: 020 7059 5000
Fax: 020 7059 5050
E-mail: info@accaglobal.com
Website: www.accaglobal.com

Direct tel: 0044 141 582 2000 (ACCA Connect for admin queries)

Founded: 1904; created by the merger of London Association of Accountants and (Scottish-based) Corporation of Accountants (year of change 1939); created by the merger of Association of Certified and Corporate Accountants (ACCA) and Institution of Certified Public Accountants (year of change 1941); formerly called London Association of Accountants (year of change 1933); formerly called London Association of Certified Accountants (year of change 1939); formerly called Association of Certified and Corporate Accountants (ACCA) (year of change 1971); formerly called Association of Certified Accountants (year of change 1984); formerly called Chartered Association of Certified Accountants (year of change 1996)

Organisation type and purpose: The global body for professional accountants employed in industry, financial services, the public sector, or in public practice, current number of members: 140,000 members and 404,000 students.

Subject coverage: Supports members and students throughout their careers, providing services through a network of 83 offices and active centres world-wide.

Collection: Online technical library

Publications: Electronic and video
Order electronic and video publications from: Download from website

Publications list: Available online

Access to staff: Contact by letter, by telephone, by fax and by e-mail

ASSOCIATION OF CHARTERED PHYSIOTHERAPISTS IN INDEPENDENT HEALTHCARE (ACPIHC)

14 Bedford Row, London, WC1R 4ED

Tel: 020 7306 6666

Enquiries to: Chair
Direct tel: 020 7908 3742
Direct e-mail: annie.karim@hcahealthcare.co.uk

History of institution: formerly called Association of Chartered Physiotherapists in Independent Hospitals & Charities (ACPIH)

Organisation type and purpose: National organisation, advisory body, professional body.
To assist Chartered Physiotherapists working in independent hospitals and give information about physiotherapy within independent hospitals.

Subject coverage: Physiotherapy in independent hospitals or charities.

Publications: Printed

Access to staff: Contact by letter, by telephone and by e-mail
Hours: Mon to Fri, 0900 to 1700

Group within the: Chartered Society of Physiotherapy

ASSOCIATION OF CHARTERED PHYSIOTHERAPISTS IN MANAGEMENT (ACPM)

14 Bedford Row, London, WC1R 4ED

Tel: 020 7306 6666
Fax: 020 7306 6611

Enquiries to: Honorary Secretary
Other contacts: Chairman

Founded: 1944; formerly called Association of District and Superintendent Chartered Physiotherapists (ADSCP)

Organisation type and purpose: Professional body.

Subject coverage: Physiotherapy.

Publications: Printed

Access to staff: Contact by letter, by telephone and by fax
Hours: Mon to Fri, 0900 to 1700

Group within the: Chartered Society of Physiotherapy

ASSOCIATION OF CHARTERED PHYSIOTHERAPISTS IN OCCUPATIONAL HEALTH AND ERGONOMICS (ACPOHE)

c/o Chartered Society of Physiotherapy, 14 Bedford Row, London, WC1R 4ED

Tel: 020 7242 1941
Website: www.acpohe.org.uk

Enquiries to: Chairman
Direct tel: 01284 748200
Direct e-mail: nicola.hunter@buryphysio.co.uk; jan.vickery@milligan-and-hill.co.uk
Other contacts: Membership Secretary

Founded: 1948; formerly called Association of Chartered Physiotherapists in Occupational Health (ACPOH)

Organisation type and purpose: National organisation, professional body (membership is by subscription, qualification), present number of members: 550.
Occupational interest group of the Chartered Society of Physiotherapy.

Subject coverage: Occupational health physiotherapy, ergonomics, education and training, health promotion and fitness in the workplace, work hardening and conditioning, functional capacity evaluation, pre-employment screening, health and safety (risk assessment and risk management), moving and handling, workplace design, rehabilitation.

Publications: Printed

Access to staff: Contact by letter, by telephone, by e-mail and via website
Hours: Mon to Fri, 0900 to 1700

Constituent part of: Chartered Society of Physiotherapy; as above

ASSOCIATION OF CHARTERED PHYSIOTHERAPISTS IN RESPIRATORY CARE (ACPRC)

School of Health and Population Sciences, 52 Pritchatts Road, University of Birmingham, Edgbaston, Birmingham, B15 2TT

Tel: 0121 415 8606
E-mail: c.r.liles@bham.ac.uk

Organisation type and purpose: Membership association (membership is by subscription), present number of members: over 500.

Subject coverage: Respiratory diseases, cardiorespiratory physiotherapy, education, research, audit, management, physiotherapy techniques.

Publications: Printed

Access to staff: Contact by letter, by telephone and by fax
Hours: Mon to Fri, 0900 to 1700

Special Interest Group within the: Chartered Society of Physiotherapy; tel: 020 7306 6666; fax: 020 7306 6611

ASSOCIATION OF CHARTERED PHYSIOTHERAPISTS IN WOMEN'S HEALTH (ACPWH)

14 Bedford Row, London, WC1R 4ED

Tel: 020 7306 6666

Enquiries to: Secretary
Direct e-mail: juliabraytq@hotmail.com
Other contacts: Chairman for when Secretary is unavailable.

Founded: 1948; formerly called Association of Chartered Physiotherapists in Obstetrics and Gynaecology (year of change 1993)

Organisation type and purpose: National organisation, professional body (membership is by subscription), present number of members: 700.

Subject coverage: Physiotherapy in obstetrics and gynaecology; antenatal education and advice; postnatal education advice and exercise, female and male bladder and bowel dysfunction; musculoskeletal problems relating to pregnancy or gynaecological in nature, particularly pelvic floor weakness.

Publications: Printed

Publications list: Available in print

Access to staff: Contact by letter and by e-mail

Group within the: Chartered Society of Physiotherapy; at the same address; tel: 020 7306 6666

ASSOCIATION OF CHARTERED PHYSIOTHERAPISTS INTERESTED IN NEUROLOGY (ACPIN)

c/o Therapy Services, National Hospital for Neurology and Neurosurgery, Queen Square, London, WC1N 3BG

E-mail: anne.rodger@hotmail.co.uk
Website: www.acpin.net/

Enquiries to: Secretary

Organisation type and purpose: Professional body.

Subject coverage: Physiotherapy; neurology.

Publications: Printed

Access to staff: Contact by letter, by e-mail and via website
Hours: Mon to Fri, 0900 to 1700

Access to building: None

Professional Network of the: Chartered Society of Physiotherapy

ASSOCIATION OF CHIEF POLICE OFFICERS OF ENGLAND, WALES AND NORTHERN IRELAND (ACPO)

1st Floor, 10 Victoria Street, London, SW1H 0NN

Tel: 020 7084 8950
E-mail: info@acpo.pnn.police.uk
Website: www.acpo.police.uk

Organisation type and purpose: A voluntary association of chief officers (membership is by subscription) open to police officers who hold the rank of Chief Constable, Deputy Chief Constable, or Assistant Chief Constable, or their equivalents, in the 44 forces of England, Wales and Northern Ireland, national police agencies and certain other forces in the UK, the Isle of Man and the Channel Islands, and certain senior non-police staff, current number of members: 349.
ACPO is not a staff association and works on behalf of the Service, rather than its own members.
Works in the public interest and, in equal and active partnership with government and the Association of Police Authorities, leads and co-ordinates the direction and development of the police service in England, Wales and Northern Ireland. In times of national need ACPO – on behalf of all chief officers – coordinates the strategic policing response.

Subject coverage: Police service in England, Wales and Northern Ireland.

Publications: Electronic and video
Order electronic and video publications from: Download from website

Publications list: Available online

Access to staff: Contact by letter, by telephone, by e-mail and via website

Links with: ACPO Criminal Records Office (ACRO); website: http://www.acro.police.uk/police_certificates.aspx
ACPO Vehicle Crime Intelligence Service (AVCIS); e-mail: http://www.acpo.police.uk/NationalPolicing/ACPOVehicleCrimeIntelligenceService/Default.aspx; National Ballistics Intelligence Service (NABIS); website: http://www.nabis.police.uk/home.asp
National Coordinator Domestic Extremism (NCDE); website: http://www.acpo.police.uk/NationalPolicing/NationalDomesticExtremismUnit/AboutNDEU.aspx

ASSOCIATION OF CHRISTIAN COMMUNITIES AND NETWORKS (NACCAN)

Community House, Eton Road, Newport, Gwent, NP19 0BL

Tel: 01633 265486
E-mail: moderator@naccan.freeserve.com.uk

Enquiries to: Moderator

Founded: 1971; formerly called National Association of Christian Communities and Networks (year of change 1999)

Organisation type and purpose: International organisation, membership association (membership is by subscription), present number of members: 286, voluntary organisation, registered charity (charity number 283972), training organisation.
Links together Networks, Groups, Communities and individuals from a wide variety of Christian traditions committed to living out the implications of what Christian Community means.

continued overleaf

Subject coverage: Linking, informing, affirming Christian communities and networks in Britain, particularly those taking new initiatives in the local scene, with some contacts overseas also.

Trade and statistical information: Information provided on communities and networks in membership

Publications: Printed

Access to staff: Contact by letter, by telephone and by e-mail. Appointment necessary.
Hours: Mon, Thu, 1000 to 1600; Tue, Wed, and Fri, 0900 to 1700. Ansaphone 24 hours

Affiliated to: CCBI; CYTUN

ASSOCIATION OF CHRISTIAN COUNSELLORS (ACC)

29 Momus Boulevard, Coventry, Warwickshire, CV2 5NA

Tel: 0845 124 9569
Fax: 0845 124 9571
E-mail: office@acc-uk.org
Website: www.acc-uk.org

Enquiries to: Chief Executive
Direct e-mail: ceo@acc-uk.org

Founded: 1992

Organisation type and purpose: Professional body, registered charity (charity number 1018559).

Subject coverage: Christian counselling, training in Christian counselling, accreditation for Christian counsellors, affiliation for Christian Counselling agencies, referrals for those requiring Christian counselling.

Publications: Printed, and electronic and video

Access to staff: Contact by letter, by telephone, by fax, by e-mail, in person and via website
Hours: Mon to Fri, 0900 to 1700

Access to building: No prior appointment required

ASSOCIATION OF CIRCUS PROPRIETORS OF GREAT BRITAIN (ACP)

PO Box 131, Blackburn, Lancashire, BB1 9GJ

Tel: 01254 814789
Fax: 01254 814789
E-mail: malcolmclay@talk21.com
Website: www.circus-uk.co.uk

Enquiries to: Secretary
Direct e-mail: malcolm@circus-uk.co.uk

Founded: 1932

Organisation type and purpose: Advisory body, trade association (membership is by election or invitation), present number of members: 14.
To monitor the circus industry in the UK and to advise on standards of animal welfare, and the training and keeping of performing animals.

Subject coverage: Circus training and career opportunities in the circus; the welfare of performing animals and the ethics of animal training. Acts as the consultative body for Government and other authorities on legislation or other proposals affecting the circus industry.

Publications: Printed

Access to staff: Contact by letter, by telephone, by fax, by e-mail, in person and via website. Appointment necessary.
Hours: Mon to Fri, 0900 to 1700

Member organisation of: Variety and Entertainments Council (VAEC)

ASSOCIATION OF CLINICAL PATHOLOGISTS (ACP)

189 Dyke Road, Hove, East Sussex, BN3 1TL

Tel: 01273 775700
Fax: 01273 773303
E-mail: info@pathologists.org.uk
Website: www.pathologists.org.uk

Enquiries to: General Administrator

Founded: 1927

Organisation type and purpose: International organisation, learned society, professional body (membership is by election or invitation), registered charity (charity number 209555).

Subject coverage: Clinical pathology.

Publications: Printed

Access to staff: Contact by letter, by telephone, by fax, by e-mail and via website. Appointment necessary. Access for members only.
Hours: Mon to Fri, 0900 to 1700

ASSOCIATION OF COLLEGES (AoC)

2–5 Stedham Place, London, WC1A 1HU

Tel: 020 7034 9900
Fax: 020 7034 9950
E-mail: enquiries@aoc.co.uk
Website: www.aoc.co.uk

Enquiries to: Director of Communications

Founded: 1997; formerly called Association for Colleges (AfC), Colleges' Employers Forum (CEF) (year of change 1996)

Organisation type and purpose: Membership association (membership is by subscription), present number of members: 450, service industry, suitable for ages: 16+. Colleges of further education.
Representation of the interests of further education colleges, sixth form colleges, tertiary and specialist colleges throughout the UK by lobbying, member consultations, conferences and seminars and research.

Subject coverage: Further education, 16–19 year-olds' education, sixth form colleges, general further education and specialist colleges, adult education, lifelong learning, training.

Collection: The Association holds a historical library of information

Library catalogue: All or part available online

Publications: Printed

Publications list: Available online and in print

Access to staff: Contact by letter, by telephone, by fax, by e-mail and via website. Appointment necessary.
Hours: Mon to Fri, 0830 to 1700

ASSOCIATION OF COMMONWEALTH ARCHIVISTS AND RECORD MANAGERS (ACARM)

c/o IRMT, 4th Floor, 7 Hatton Garden, London, EC1N 8AD

Tel: 020 7831 4101
E-mail: newsletter@acarm.org
Website: www.acarm.org

Enquiries to: Membership Secretary
Direct fax: 020 7831 6303

Founded: 1984

Organisation type and purpose: Individual and institutional membership organisation (membership by subscription).
ACARM seeks to promote professional development and the sharing of solutions to the problems of managing records and archives (in paper and electronic formats) throughout the Commonwealth.

Publications: Printed

Access to staff: Contact by letter, by telephone, by e-mail and via website

ASSOCIATION OF COMMONWEALTH UNIVERSITIES (ACU)

Woburn House, 20–24 Tavistock Square, London, WC1H 9HF

Tel: +44 (0) 207 380 6700
Fax: +44 (0) 207387 2655
E-mail: info@acu.ac.uk
Website: www.acu.ac.uk
Website: www.csfp-online.org
Website: www.obhe.ac.uk

Enquiries to: Secretary General

Founded: 1913

Organisation type and purpose: International organisation, membership association (membership is by subscription), present number of members: 487 universities, registered charity (charity number 314137).
Voluntary association of universities which aims to strengthen through international co-operation and understanding its 487 members in 35 Commonwealth countries or regions including the UK.

Subject coverage: Commonwealth-wide university / higher education information; administers several scholarship and fellowship schemes; advertises academic, administrative and technical job vacancies at HE institutions in the Commonwealth. Hosts Policy and Research Unit. Hosts the Observatory on Borderless Higher Education (OBHE).

Collection: 18,500 volume reference library

Publications: Printed

Publications list: Available online and in print

Access to staff: Contact by letter, by telephone, by e-mail and via website. Appointment necessary.

Hours: Mon to Fri, 0930 to 1730

Access to building: No prior appointment required
Hours: Library: Mon to Fri, 1000 to 1300 and 1400 to 1700

Formal consultative relations with: UNESCO

Works closely with: Commonwealth Secretariat

ASSOCIATION OF COMMUNITY HEALTH COUNCILS FOR ENGLAND AND WALES (ACHCEW)

Tel: 020 7609 8405
Fax: 020 7700 1152
E-mail: mailbox@achcew.org.uk
Website: www.achcew.org.uk

Enquiries to: Director

Founded: 1977

Organisation type and purpose: Membership association.
Providing forum, support and research facilities.

Subject coverage: Community Health Councils: constitution, research and activities, representation of the patient/consumer in primary and institutional health care services, NHS complaints procedures.

Collection: Library of Reports published by individual Community Health Councils

Publications: Printed

Publications list: Available in print

Access to staff: Appointment necessary.
Hours: Mon to Fri, 0900 to 1700
Special comments: No disabled access.

ASSOCIATION OF COMMUNITY WORKERS (ACW)

Stephenson Buildings, Elswick Road, Newcastle upon Tyne, NE4 6SQ

Tel: 0191 272 4341
E-mail: lesleyleach@acw1.fsbusiness.co.uk

Enquiries to: Information Officer

Founded: 1969

Organisation type and purpose: Membership association (membership is by subscription), voluntary organisation.

Subject coverage: Community work, organisation and practice, collective action, policies and activities.

Publications: Printed

Publications list: Available in print

ASSOCIATION OF CONSULTANT ARCHITECTS LTD (ACA)

60 Godwin Road, Bromley, Kent, BR2 9LQ

Tel: 020 8466 9079
Fax: 020 8466 9079
E-mail: office@acarchitects.co.uk
Website: www.acarchitects.co.uk

Enquiries to: Secretary-General

Founded: 1975

Organisation type and purpose: Membership association (membership is by qualification, subscription), present number of members: 600.
Represents the interests of architects in private practice.

Subject coverage: Architectural practices and practice.

Trade and statistical information: Data on specialist services provided by member architectural practices

Library catalogue: All or part available online

Publications: Printed

Publications list: Available online and in print

Access to staff: Contact by letter, by telephone, by fax, by e-mail and via website
Hours: Mon to Fri, 0900 to 1730

ASSOCIATION OF CONSULTING ACTUARIES (ACA)

St Clement's House, 27–28 Clement's Lane, London, EC4N 7AE

Tel: 020 3207 9380
Fax: 020 3207 9134
E-mail: acahelp@aca.org.uk

Enquiries to: Honorary Secretary

Founded: 1952

Organisation type and purpose: Trade association (membership is by subscription, qualification), present number of members: 1,000.
Association of Fellows of the Institute or Faculty of Actuaries engaged in consulting work.

Subject coverage: Consultancy in retirement benefits and pension arrangements, sickness and hospital benefit schemes, investment policy, financial planning of funds, operational research and other statistical applications, mergers, life and general insurance, damages and divorce settlements.

Publications: Printed

Publications list: Available online and in print

Access to staff: Contact by letter, by telephone, by fax, by e-mail and via website
Hours: Mon to Fri, 0900 to 1700

Access to building: Prior appointment required

ASSOCIATION OF CONSULTING SCIENTISTS LIMITED (ACS)

5 Willow Heights, Cradley Heath, West Midlands, B64 7PL

Tel: 0121 602 3515
E-mail: secretary@consultingscientists.co.uk
Website: www.consultingscientists.com

Enquiries to: Secretary
Direct e-mail: sg@sgconsult.co.uk

Founded: 1958

Organisation type and purpose: Advisory body, professional body (membership is by election or invitation), present number of members: 17, consultancy, research organisation.
The Association provides a forum for all member scientists practising as consultants.

Subject coverage: Consulting activities – expert witnesses, health and safety, environmental, microbiological testing, laboratory testing.

Access to staff: Contact by letter, by telephone, by e-mail and via website
Hours: Variable

ASSOCIATION OF CONTACT LENS MANUFACTURERS (ACLM)

PO Box 735, Devizes, Wiltshire, SN10 3TQ

Tel: 01380 860418
Fax: 01380 860863
E-mail: secgen@aclm.org.uk
Website: www.aclm.org.uk

Enquiries to: Secretary General

Founded: 1962

Organisation type and purpose: National organisation, trade association (membership is by subscription, election or invitation), present number of members: 18, manufacturing industry.
Members represent the overwhelming part of the UK market.
To promote and increase the wearing of contact lenses.

Subject coverage: Contact lenses, contact lens care products, contact lens materials.

Non-library collection catalogue: All or part available online and in print

Publications: Printed

Publications list: Available online

Access to staff: Contact by letter, by telephone, by fax, by e-mail and via website
Hours: Mon to Fri, 0900 to 1700

ASSOCIATION OF CORPORATE TREASURERS (ACT)

51 Moorgate, London, EC2R 6BH

Tel: 020 7847 2540
Fax: 020 7374 8744
E-mail: enquiries@treasurers.org
Website: www.treasurers.org

Enquiries to: Head of Marketing & Communications
Direct tel: 020 7847 2547
Direct e-mail: snewell@treasurers.org
Other contacts: Chief Executive (for enquiries relating to the ACT or treasury profession)

Founded: 1979

Organisation type and purpose: Professional body (membership is by qualification).

Subject coverage: Treasury, risk management, corporate finance

Education services: Provider of treasury qualifications

Library catalogue: All or part available in-house

Publications: Printed, and electronic and video
Order printed publications from: http://www.global-investor.com

Publications list: Available online

continued overleaf

Access to staff: Contact by letter, by telephone, by fax and by e-mail
Hours: Mon to Fri, 0900 to 1700

Access to building: No prior appointment required

Access for disabled people: Level entry, access to all public areas, toilet facilities

ASSOCIATION OF COST ENGINEERS (ACostE)

Administration Office, Lea House, 5 Middlewich Road, Sandbach, Cheshire, CW11 1XL

Tel: 01270 764798
Fax: 01270 766180
E-mail: enquiries@acoste.org.uk; info@acoste.org.uk
Website: www.acoste.org.uk

Organisation type and purpose: A professional association for cost engineers, an international organisation with members from many countries around the world. Plays a key role in setting standards and in recognition of cost engineers and project control professionals.
Subject coverage: Prediction, planning and control of the true cost of projects have become key functions in many organisations. ACostE can take a key role in understanding why spending on major projects often significantly exceeds the initial cost estimate. Introduction of good practice and standards in project control is necessary for success.

Library catalogue: All or part available online

Publications: Printed, and electronic and video
Order printed publications from: Journal: website
Books: Merchandise Department, The Association of Cost Engineers, Administration Office, Lea House, 5 Middlewich Road, Sandbach, Cheshire, CW11 1XL; tel: 01270 764798
Order electronic and video publications from: Download from website

Publications list: Available online

Access to staff: Contact by letter, by telephone, by fax and by e-mail
Hours: Mon to Fri, 0900 to 1600
Special comments: Out of these hours there is an answering service.

ASSOCIATION OF COSTS LAWYERS (ACL)

Church Cottage, Church Lane, Stuston, Diss, Norfolk, IP21 4AG

Tel: 01379 741404
Fax: 01379 742702
E-mail: enquiries@alcd.org.uk
Website: www.costslawyer.co.uk

Enquiries to: Administrator

Founded: 1977

Organisation type and purpose: Professional body (membership is by qualification), present number of members: 850.
Membership subscription is required.
Csots Lawyers are qualified and regulated specialists in the law who operate by advising upon and applying laws and directions that relate to the evaluation and recovery of solicitors' fees.

Publications: Printed

Publications list: Available in print

Access to staff: Contact by letter, by telephone, by e-mail and via website
Hours: Mon to Fri, 0900 to 1700

ASSOCIATION OF CRICKET STATISTICIANS AND HISTORIANS (ACS)

Archives Department, Glamorgan Cricket, Sophia Gardens, Cardiff, CF11 9XR

Tel: 0115 945 5407
E-mail: office@acscricket.com
Website: acscricket.com

Enquiries to: Secretary

Founded: 1973; formerly called Association of Cricket Statisticians (year of change 1994)

Organisation type and purpose: International organisation, learned society (membership is by subscription), present number of members: 1,300, voluntary organisation, suitable for ages: all, research organisation, publishing house.
To research and publish all aspects of cricket history and statistical record.

Subject coverage: Cricket and cricketers at all levels throughout the world, both historical and contemporary.

Publications: Printed

Access to staff: Contact by letter, by telephone, by fax and in person

Access for disabled people: Level access, ground floor, direct access to street, wide door

ASSOCIATION OF DENTAL IMPLANTOLOGY (ADI)

98 South Worple Way, London, SW14 8ND

Tel: 020 8487 5555
Fax: 020 8487 5566
E-mail: via website
Website: www.adi.org.uk

Founded: 1987

Organisation type and purpose: A registered charity (number 800238), representative body (but not a governing body) of implant dentistry in the United Kingdom encompassing clinicians, consultants, oral surgeons, technicians, hygienists, nurses and individuals from the healthcare sector. Membership is by subscription and is open to all who hold an interest in dental implants; has over 1,700 active members drawn from every UK county plus several countries abroad.
Dedicated to providing on-going postgraduate education to the dental profession in order to extend awareness of dental implant treatment as an option for improving patient oral health and to improving the standards of implant dentistry by providing continuing education and encouraging scientific research.

Subject coverage: A broad-based association of general dentists, oral and maxillofacial surgeons, periodontists, prosthodontists, orthodontists, laboratory technicians, auxiliaries, post-graduate dental students and manufacturer representatives.

Access to staff: Contact by letter, by telephone, by fax and via website

ASSOCIATION OF DIRECTORS OF ADULT SOCIAL SERVICES (ADASS)

Association of Directors of Adult Social Services, Local Government House, Smith Square, London SW1P 3HZ

Tel: 020 7072 7433
Fax: 020 7863 9133
E-mail: team@adass.org.uk
Website: www.adass.org.uk/

Enquiries to: Honorary Secretary

Organisation type and purpose: Local government body, professional body.

Subject coverage: Social services.

Publications list: Available in print

Access to staff: Contact by letter, by telephone, by fax and by e-mail
Hours: Mon to Fri, 0900 to 1700

ASSOCIATION OF DISABLED PROFESSIONALS (ADP)

BCM ADP, London, WC1N 3XX

Tel: 01204 431638
Fax: 01204 431638
E-mail: info@adp.org.uk
Website: www.adp.org.uk
Website: www.disabled-entrepreneurs.net

Enquiries to: Volunteer Advisor

Founded: 1971

Organisation type and purpose: Voluntary organisation, registered as a charitable company limited by guarantee (company number 6390586; charity number 1121706).

Subject coverage: Education, training and employment opportunities for disabled people, career prospects. Also provides support to disabled people in self-employment.

Publications: Printed
Order electronic and video publications from: info@adp.org.uk

Access to staff: Contact by letter, by telephone, by fax, by e-mail and via website
Hours: 24-hour answerphone

Also at: Association of Disabled Professionals; Beechers Brook, 16 Aintree Drive, Waterlooville, Hampshire, PO7 8NG

ASSOCIATION OF DOMESTIC MANAGEMENT (ADM)

3 Hagg Bank Cottages, Wylam, Northumberland, NE41 8JT

Tel: 01661 853097
Fax: 01661 853097
E-mail: adm@adom.demon.co.uk
Website: www.adom.demon.co.uk

Enquiries to: Business Manager

Founded: 1974

Organisation type and purpose: Professional body.

Subject coverage: Facilities management.

Publications: Printed

Publications list: Available in print

Access to staff: Contact by letter, by telephone, by fax, by e-mail and via website. Appointment necessary.
Hours: Tue, Thu and Fri, 0830 to 1515

Access to building: No access other than to staff

Founder member of: ADM Conference & Exhibition Ltd; British Cleaning Council

Has links with: CAMRASO; Hefma; NHS Estates; The Knowledge Centre

ASSOCIATION OF DRAINAGE AUTHORITIES (ADA)

6 Electric Parade, Surbiton, Surrey, KT6 5NT

Tel: 020 8399 7350
Fax: 020 8399 1650
E-mail: admin@ada.org.uk
Website: www.ada.org.uk/

Enquiries to: Chief Executive

Founded: 1937

Organisation type and purpose: Advisory body, membership association.

Subject coverage: Flood risk-management, lowland drainage, water level management.

Publications: Printed

Access to staff: Contact by letter, by telephone and by e-mail
Hours: Mon to Fri, 0900 to 1700

ASSOCIATION OF DRUM MANUFACTURERS (ADM)

St John's House, 4 London Road, Crowborough, East Sussex, TN6 2TT

Tel: 01892 654414
Fax: 01892 654981
E-mail: info@theipa.co.uk
Website: www.the-adm.co.uk

Enquiries to: Secretary

Founded: 1896

Organisation type and purpose: Trade association, present number of members: 15.

Subject coverage: Drum manufacturing.

Access to staff: Contact by letter
Hours: Mon to Fri, 0900 to 1700

ASSOCIATION OF EASTERN MOTOR CLUBS (AEMC)

9 Dales Court, Dales Road, Ipswich, IP1 4JR

Tel: 01473 463444
Fax: 01473 463444
Website: www.aemc.co.uk

Enquiries to: Honorary Secretary

Founded: 1950

Organisation type and purpose: Membership association (membership is by qualification), voluntary organisation.

Subject coverage: Motor car sports in East Anglia for amateur enthusiasts.

Access to staff: Contact by letter, by telephone and by fax
Hours: Mon to Fri, 0900 to 1700

Recognised by the: Motor Sports Association (MSA); Riverside Park, Colnbrook, Slough, SL3 0HG; tel: 01753 765000; fax: 01753 682938; website: http://www.msauk.org

ASSOCIATION OF ELECTORAL ADMINISTRATORS (AEA)

PO Box 201, South Eastern, Liverpool, L16 5HH

Tel: 0151 281 8246
Fax: 0151 281 8246
E-mail: gina.armstrong@aea-elections.co.uk
Website: www.aea-elections.co.uk

Enquiries to: Executive Director (Resources)

Founded: 1987

Organisation type and purpose: Advisory body, professional body (membership is by subscription), present number of members: 1,000, training organisation, consultancy.
To offer impartial and professional advice on electoral arrangements and the democratic process at central and local government. Ballot services organisation providing services to the NHS, private organisations and charitable institutions.

Subject coverage: Elections, electoral processes, electoral registration, training.

Collection: Basic practice publications
Archival records of Association business

Publications: Printed

Access to staff: Contact by letter, by telephone, by fax, by e-mail and via website
Hours: Mon to Fri, 0900 to 1700

ASSOCIATION OF ELECTRICITY PRODUCERS (AEP)

Charles House, 5–11 Regent Street, London, SW1Y 4LR

Tel: 020 7930 9390
Fax: 020 7930 9391
E-mail: enquiries@aepuk.com
Website: www.energy-uk.org.uk

Enquiries to: Chief Executive
Direct tel: 020 7747 2931
Direct e-mail: rhunter@aepuk.com

Founded: 1987

Organisation type and purpose: Trade association (membership is by subscription), present number of members: 100, service industry.

Subject coverage: Electricity generation, competition in electricity production, liberalised electricity markets, renewable energy.

Publications list: Available in print

Access to staff: Contact by letter, by telephone, by fax and by e-mail. Appointment necessary.
Hours: Mon to Fri, 0900 to 1700

ASSOCIATION OF EUROPEAN BRAND OWNERS (MARQUES)

MARQUES Ltd, Unit Q, Troon Way Business Centre, Humberstone Lane, Thurmaston, Leicester, LE4 9HA

Tel: 0116 274 7355
Fax: 0116 274 7365
E-mail: info@marques.org
Website: www.marques.org

Enquiries to: Secretary General

Founded: 1987; formerly called Association of European Trade Mark Proprietors (year of change 1997)

Organisation type and purpose: International organisation, trade association (membership is by subscription).

Subject coverage: Brand names, trade mark protection.

Access to staff: Contact by letter, by telephone, by fax, by e-mail and via website
Hours: Mon to Fri, 0900 to 1700

ASSOCIATION OF EVENT ORGANISERS LIMITED (AEO)

119 High Street, Berkhamsted, Hertfordshire, HP4 2DJ

Tel: 01442 285810
Fax: 01442 875551
E-mail: info@aeo.org.uk
Website: www.aeo.org.uk

Enquiries to: Director General
Other contacts: Commercial Manager for administration, membership, exhibition enquiries.

Founded: 1930; formerly called Association of Exhibition Organisers Ltd (year of change 2006)

Organisation type and purpose: Trade association.

Subject coverage: Exhibitions and events world-wide, when, where and who; career information for exhibition organisers.

Publications: Printed, and electronic and video

Access to staff: Contact by letter, by telephone, by fax, by e-mail and via website. Appointment necessary.
Hours: Mon to Fri, 0900 to 1700

Member organisation of: Union des Foires Internationales (UFI); 35 bis rue Jouffroy d'Abbans 5F, Paris 75017, France

ASSOCIATION OF FLIGHT ATTENDANTS (AFA)

AFA Council 07, United Airlines Cargo Centre, Shoreham Road East, Heathrow Airport, Hounslow, Middlesex, TW6 3UA

Tel: 020 8276 6723
Fax: 020 8276 6706
E-mail: afalhr@unitedafa.org
Website: www.afalhr.org.uk

Enquiries to: General Secretary

Organisation type and purpose: International organisation, trade union (membership is by qualification), present number of members: 800.

continued overleaf

Subject coverage: Airline safety and security, cabin crew issues.

Access to staff: Contact by letter, by telephone, by fax, by e-mail, in person and via website
Hours: Mon to Fri, 0900 to 1700

Access to building: Prior appointment required

Access for disabled people: Parking provided, access to all public areas, toilet facilities

ASSOCIATION OF FRIENDLY SOCIETIES (AFS)

Denzell House, Denzell Gardens, Dunham Road, Bowden, Cheshire, WA14 4QE

Tel: 0161 952 5051
Fax: 0161 929 5163
E-mail: enquiries@shepherdsfriendly.co.uk
Website: www.afs.org.uk

Enquiries to: Administrator

Founded: 1995; formed by the merger of Association of Collecting Friendly Societies and other existing organisations of Friendly Societies, National Conference of Friendly Societies

Organisation type and purpose: Trade association.

Subject coverage: Matters relating to member societies and the Friendly Society Movement, particularly information on legislation and regulation applying to them, financial services and welfare state reform.

Publications: Printed

Access to staff: Contact by letter, by telephone, by fax and by e-mail. Appointment necessary.
Hours: Mon to Fri, 0900 to 1700

Access to building: Prior appointment required

ASSOCIATION OF GENEALOGISTS AND RESEARCHERS IN ARCHIVES (AGRA)

29 Badgers Close, Horsham, West Sussex, RH12 5RU

E-mail: agra@agra.org.uk
Website: www.agra.org.uk

Enquiries to: Secretary

Founded: 1968

Organisation type and purpose: National organisation, professional body (membership is by subscription, qualification), present number of members: 100, consultancy, research organisation.

Subject coverage: Family history, family trees, locating missing relatives, translations, surname studies, manorial records, histories of properties, palaeography, census and probate research, baptism and marriage indexes, army and navy records.

Publications: Printed

Access to staff: Contact by letter, by e-mail and via website
Hours: Mon to Fri, 0900 to 1700

ASSOCIATION OF GEOTECHNICAL AND GEOENVIRONMENTAL SPECIALISTS (AGS)

Forum Court, 83 Copers Cope Road, Beckenham, Kent, BR3 1NR

Tel: 020 8658 8212
Fax: 020 8663 0949
E-mail: ags@ags.org.uk
Website: www.ags.org.uk

Enquiries to: Administrator

Founded: 1990

Organisation type and purpose: Trade association.

Subject coverage: Geotechnics e.g. foundations (design and construction), site investigation, laboratory testing, geoenvironment testing, remediation, monitoring, geotechnical design, geoenvironmentalism.

Publications: Printed

Access to staff: Contact by letter, by telephone, by fax and by e-mail
Hours: Mon to Fri, 0900 to 1700

Members of: Ground Forum

ASSOCIATION OF GOLF WRITERS (AGW)

1 Pilgrims Bungalow, Mulberry Hill, Chilham, Kent, CT4 8AH

Tel: 01227 732496
Fax: 01227 732496
E-mail: enquiries@agwgolf.org
Website: www.agwgolf.org

Enquiries to: Administrator
Other contacts: Honorary Secretary

Founded: 1938

Organisation type and purpose: Membership association.

Subject coverage: Golf; sports writing.

Publications: Printed

Access to staff: Contact by letter, by telephone, by fax and by e-mail
Hours: Mon to Fri, 0900 to 1700

ASSOCIATION OF GRACE BAPTIST CHURCHES (SE) (AGBC(SE))

7 Arlington Way, London, EC1R 1XA

Tel: 020 7278 1200
Fax: 020 7278 3598
E-mail: assoc@agbcse.org.uk
Website: www.agbcse.org.uk

Enquiries to: Association Secretary
Other contacts: Company Secretary for finance and legal.

Founded: 1871

Organisation type and purpose: Registered charity (charity number 276352).
To promote the unity and prosperity of associated churches and devise and employ means for the furtherance of the Gospel in London, Berkshire, Buckinghamshire, Essex, Hampshire, Hertfordshire, Kent, Oxfordshire, Surrey and Sussex.

Access to staff: Contact by letter, by telephone, by fax and by e-mail
Hours: Mon to Fri, 0900 to 1700

Access to building: Prior appointment required

Access for disabled people: Ramped entry

ASSOCIATION OF GRADUATE RECRUITERS (AGR)

The Innovation Centre, Warwick Technology Park, Gallows Hill, Warwick, CV34 6UW

Tel: 01926 623236
Fax: 01926 623237
E-mail: info@agr.org.uk
Website: www.agr.org.uk

Enquiries to: Chief Executive

Founded: 1968

Organisation type and purpose: Professional body.

Subject coverage: Graduate recruitment from the employer's viewpoint.

Trade and statistical information: Graduate vacancies and salaries information

Publications: Printed

Publications list: Available online and in print

Access to staff: Contact by letter, by telephone, by fax, by e-mail and via website
Hours: Mon to Fri, 0900 to 1700

Access for disabled people: Parking provided, access to all public areas, toilet facilities

ASSOCIATION OF HEAD TEACHERS AND DEPUTES IN SCOTLAND (AHDS)

PO Box 18532, Inverurie, AB51 0WS

Tel: 0845 260 7560
E-mail: info@ahds.org.uk
Website: www.ahds.org.uk

Enquiries to: General Secretary

Founded: 1975

Organisation type and purpose: Trade union

Subject coverage: Trade Union support for headteachers and deputes from Scotland's nursery, primary and special schools

Access to staff: Contact by letter, by telephone, by e-mail, in person and via website. Appointment necessary.
Hours: Mon to Fri, 0900 to 1700

ASSOCIATION OF ILLUSTRATORS (AOI)

The Association of Illustrators, 2nd Floor, Back Building, 150 Curtain Road, London, EC2A 3AT

Tel: 020 7613 4328
Fax: 020 7613 4417
E-mail: info@theaoi.com
Website: www.aoisupplement.co.uk

Enquiries to: Membership Secretary

Founded: 1974

Organisation type and purpose: Trade association (membership is by subscription).

Subject coverage: Illustration and illustrators; ethics, copyright law, fees and standard practice.

Publications: Printed

Access to staff: Contact by telephone, by fax and by e-mail. Appointment necessary.
Hours: Mon to Fri, 0900 to 1700

Within the: Joint Ethics Committee for the Visual Arts

ASSOCIATION OF INDEPENDENT COMPUTER SPECIALISTS (AICS)

Honeyhill, Bismore, Eastcombe, Stroud, Gloucestershire, GL6 7DG

Tel: 01452 770060
E-mail: honsec@aics.org.uk
Website: www.aics.org.uk

Enquiries to: Honorary Secretary

Founded: 1972

Organisation type and purpose: Trade association for individuals and independent firms whose main business is the supply of computer-related services, including consultancy.

Publications: Printed, and electronic and video

Access to staff: Contact by letter, by telephone, by e-mail and via website
Hours: Mon to Fri, 0930 to 1730

Access to building: No access other than to staff

ASSOCIATION OF INDEPENDENT LIBRARIES (AIL)

The Leeds Library, 18 Commercial Street, Leeds, West Yorkshire, LS1 6AL

Tel: 0113 245 3071
E-mail: enquiries@leedslibrary.co.uk

Enquiries to: Honorary Secretary
Direct tel: 01473 253992

Founded: 1989

Organisation type and purpose: National organisation.
To promote an interest in libraries, reading, literature generally and in the many and varied special collections.

Access to staff: Contact by letter and by telephone. Appointment necessary.
Hours: Mon to Fri, 0900 to 1700

ASSOCIATION OF INDEPENDENT MUSEUMS (AIM)

63 Wiston Avenue, Worthing, West Sussex, BN14 7PX

Tel: 01903 201370
E-mail: aimadmin@aim-museums.co.uk
Website: www.aim-museums.co.uk

Founded: 1977

Organisation type and purpose: Professional body, trade association (membership is by subscription), present number of members: 900, voluntary organisation.
National museum association for those institutions not directly administered by central or local government.

Subject coverage: Museum development; management; administration; fundraising; marketing; display; publications, particularly for the independent sector.

Publications: Printed

Access to staff: Contact by letter, by telephone and by e-mail
Hours: Mon to Fri, 0900 to 1700

ASSOCIATION OF INDEPENDENT PSYCHOTHERAPISTS (AIP)

22 Linden Road, London, N10 3DH

Tel: 020 7700 1911
E-mail: info@aip.org.uk
Website: www.aip.org.uk

Founded: 1988

Organisation type and purpose: Professional body (membership is by election or invitation), voluntary organisation, training organisation, consultancy.

Subject coverage: Psychotherapy.

Information services: Psychotherapy referral service, e-mail: referrals@aip.org.uk

Education services: Psychotherapy training; e-mail training@aip.org.uk

Access to staff: Contact by letter, by telephone and by e-mail
Hours: Mon to Fri, 0900 to 1700

Also at: Association of Independent Psychotherapists; 8 Victoria Mansions, 135 Holloway Road, London, N7 8LZ

ASSOCIATION OF INDEPENDENT TOUR OPERATORS LIMITED (AITO)

133a St Margaret's Road, Twickenham, Middlesex, TW1 1RG

Tel: 020 8744 9280
Fax: 020 8744 3187
E-mail: info@aito.com
Website: www.aito.co.uk

Enquiries to: Chairman

Founded: 1976

Organisation type and purpose: Trade association (membership is by subscription), present number of members: 157.

Subject coverage: Overseas tour operations.

Publications: Printed

Publications list: Available online and in print

Access to staff: Contact by letter, by telephone, by fax and by e-mail
Hours: Mon to Thu, 0900 to 1730; Fri, 0900 to 1700

ASSOCIATION OF INTERIOR SPECIALISTS LIMITED (AIS)

Olton Bridge, 245 Warwick Road, Solihull, West Midlands, B92 7AH

Tel: 0121 707 0077
Fax: 0121 706 1949
E-mail: info@ais-interiors.org.uk
Website: www.ais-interiors.org.uk

Enquiries to: Chief Executive

Founded: 1998; formed by the merger of Partitioning & Interiors Association Limited (PIA), Suspended Ceilings and Interiors Association Limited (SCIA) (year of change 1998)

Organisation type and purpose: A single source serving the interiors fit-out industry, the AIS is a trade association that represents some 466 companies involved in the manufacture, supply and installation of all aspects of interior fit-outs and refurbishments, with particular emphasis on ceilings and partitions. Its members operate in retail and commercial offices, the public sector, banks and building societies, hotels and leisure, airports and hospitals.

Subject coverage: All aspects of interior fit-out, including industrial and commercial partitioning, operable walls, suspended ceilings, drylining, access flooring. Manufacture, supply and installation.

Publications: Printed

Access to staff: Contact by letter, by telephone, by fax, by e-mail and via website
Hours: Mon to Fri, 0900 to 1700

Access to building: No prior appointment required

Members of: National Specialist Contractors Council (NSCC); Construction House, 54–56 Leonard Street, London, EC2A 4JX; tel: 020 7608 5090; fax: 020 7608 5081

ASSOCIATION OF INTERNATIONAL ACCOUNTANTS (AIA)

AIA Head Office, Staithes 3, The Watermark, Metro Riverside, Newcastle upon Tyne, NE11 9SN

Tel: 0191 493 0277
Fax: 0191 493 0278
E-mail: aia@aiaworldwide.com
Website: www.aiaworldwide.com/

Enquiries to: Membership Services
Direct e-mail: membership.services@aiaworldwide.com

Founded: 1928

Organisation type and purpose: International organisation, professional body (membership is by qualification). Accounting body.
Under the Companies Act 1989 the AIA Accountancy qualification is a recognised professional qualification for company auditors in the United Kingdom.

Subject coverage: Financial and management accountancy, investigations, auditing, management consultancy, taxation.

Publications: Printed

Publications list: Available online

Access to staff: Contact by letter, by telephone, by fax, by e-mail and via website
Hours: Mon to Fri, 0900 to 1700

Access to building: No access other than to staff

Access for disabled people: Parking provided

continued overleaf

Affiliated to: Asociación Española de Expertos Contables y Fiscales; European Accounting Association (EAA); International Association for Accounting and Research (IAAER); International Institute of Accountants (New Zealand)

Other addresses: AIA Hong Kong Branch; Room 1003, 10F Emperor Group Centre, 288 Hennessy Road, Wanchai, Hong Kong; tel: 00 852 2845 4982; fax: 00 852 2845 7495; e-mail: aiahkbr@netvigator.com; Persatuan Alumni Akauntan – Cawangan Malaysia; Suite 20–10, Level 20, Wisma Uoa II, 21 Jalan, Pinang, 50450 Kuala Lumpur, Malaysia; tel: 00 60 3 2166 3020; fax: 00 60 3 2166 4020; e-mail: paaicm@tm.net.my

ASSOCIATION OF JEWISH REFUGEES IN GREAT BRITAIN (AJR)

Jubilee House, Merrion Avenue, Stanmore, Middlesex, HA7 4RL

Tel: 020 8385 3070
Fax: 020 8385 3080
E-mail: enquiries@ajr.org.uk
Website: www.ajr.org.uk

Enquiries to: Administrator
Direct e-mail: susie@ajr.org.uk

Founded: 1941

Organisation type and purpose: Membership association, present number of members: 3,500, voluntary organisation, registered charity (charity number 211239). Representation and welfare for Jewish refugees from Nazi persecution, and their families.

Subject coverage: Matters pertaining to former Jewish refugees from Nazi persecution in fields of restitution, compensation, social welfare, old age homes, accommodation, historical and political matters.

Publications: Printed

Access to staff: Contact by letter, by telephone, by fax, by e-mail and via website
Hours: Mon to Thu, 0930 to 1700; Fri, 0930 to 1330

Access to building: No prior appointment required

Access for disabled people: Toilet facilities

Affiliated to: AJR Charitable Trust; at the same address

Also: Association of Jewish Refugees Day Centre; 15 Cleve Road, London, NW6 3RL; tel: 020 7328 0208

ASSOCIATION OF KI AIKIDO (AKA)

17 Langland Gardens, London, NW3 6QE

Tel: 020 7435 1330
E-mail: ki@footloosefilms.com
Website: www.happyaikido.com

Direct e-mail: happyaikido@happyaikido.com

Founded: 1987

Organisation type and purpose: Training organisation.
Training in martial art of Aikido, self-defence and calmness under pressure in daily life.

Subject coverage: Martial art of Ki Aikido.

Access to staff: Contact by telephone and by e-mail. Appointment necessary.
Hours: Mon and Wed, 1930 to 2130

Access to building: Prior appointment required

Access for disabled people: *Hours:* Mon, 19:30–21:30; Wed, 19:30–21:30

ASSOCIATION OF LANDSCAPE CONTRACTORS OF IRELAND (NORTHERN REGION) (ALCI)

22 Summerhill Park, Bangor, BT20 5QQ

Tel: 028 9127 2823
Fax: 028 9127 2823
E-mail: secretary@alci.org.uk

Enquiries to: Secretary

Founded: 1971

Organisation type and purpose: Trade association.
Representation of the landscape contracting industry in Ireland.

Subject coverage: Training needs and educational matter relating to the landscaping industry, including contract procedures, standards of quality and workmanship, and management.

Publications: Printed

Access to staff: Contact by letter, by telephone, by fax and by e-mail. Appointment necessary.
Hours: Mon to Fri, 0900 to 1700

Access to building: Prior appointment required

Works closely with: British Association of Landscape Industries; Institute of Groundsmen

ASSOCIATION OF LASER USERS (AILU)

100 Ock Street, Abingdon, Oxfordshire, OX14 5DH

Tel: 01235 539595
Fax: 01235 550499
E-mail: admin@ailu.org.uk
Website: www.ailu.org.uk

Enquiries to: Executive Secretary

Founded: 1995

Organisation type and purpose: Professional body, membership association (membership is by subscription), present number of members: 350, manufacturing industry.
To disseminate information and aid networking.

Subject coverage: Laser use in industry. Manufacturers and supplies of laser and laser-related equipment and services. Laser applications topics, including materials processing and measurement.

Trade and statistical information: Centres for UK laser activity

Publications: Printed

Access to staff: Contact by letter, by telephone, by fax, by e-mail and via website
Hours: Mon to Fri, 0900 to 1700

ASSOCIATION OF LAW TEACHERS (ALT)

City Law School, 4 Gray's Inn Place, London, WC1R 5DX

Tel: 020 7404 5787, ext 368
E-mail: amanda.fancourt.1@city.ac.uk

Enquiries to: Honorary Secretary

Founded: 1965

Organisation type and purpose: Professional body (membership is by subscription), present number of members: 500, research organisation.

Subject coverage: Legal education, academic law.

Publications: Printed
Order printed publications from: Nigel Duncan (Editor The Law Teacher), City Law School, 4 Gray's Inn Place, London, WC1R 5DX

Access to staff: Contact by letter, by telephone, by fax and by e-mail
Hours: Mon to Fri, 0900 to 1700

ASSOCIATION OF LEADING VISITOR ATTRACTIONS (ALVA)

4 Westminster Palace Gardens, Artillery Row, London, SW1P 1RL

Tel: 020 7222 1728
Fax: 020 7222 1729
E-mail: email@alva.org.uk
Website: www.alva.org.uk

Enquiries to: Information Officer

Founded: 1989

Organisation type and purpose: Trade association.

Access to staff: Contact by letter, by telephone, by fax, by e-mail, in person and via website. Appointment necessary.
Hours: Mon to Fri, 0900 to 1700

Access to building: Prior appointment required

ASSOCIATION OF LEARNED AND PROFESSIONAL SOCIETY PUBLISHERS (ALPSP)

1 Abbey Cottages, The Green, Sutton Courtenay, Oxfordshire, OX14 4AF

Tel: 01235 847776
Fax: 0870 706 0332
E-mail: ian.russell@alpsp.org
Website: www.alpsp.org

Enquiries to: Chief Executive
Direct tel: 01442 828928

Founded: 1972

Organisation type and purpose: ALPSP is the international association for the community of scholarly and professional publishers and those who work with them. Membership is open to organizations working in research-based publishing or a related industry. ALPSP advocates best practice, carries out research and other projects, monitors national and international issues, represents members' interests to the wider world and provides an extensive professional development programme. The Association provides co-operative services such as the ALPSP Learned Journals Collection and the ALPSP e-books Collection.

Subject coverage: Scholarly journal and book publishing; learned and professional society publishing; not-for-profit publishing (e.g. learned societies, university presses, non-governmental organisations etc.).

Publications: Printed, and electronic and video
Order printed publications from: Ian Hunter, Finance and Admin Manager, 51 Middletons Road, Yaxley, Peterborough, Cambridgeshire, PE7 3NU; e-mail: admin@alpsp.org; tel: 0173 324 7178

Publications list: Available online

Access to staff: Contact by letter, by telephone, by fax, by e-mail, in person and via website. Appointment necessary.
Hours: Mon to Fri, 0900 to 1700

Links with: Copyright Licensing Agency; Publishers Licensing Society; Publishing Skills Group

ASSOCIATION OF LIBERAL DEMOCRAT COUNCILLORS (ALDC)

Birchcliffe Centre, Birchcliffe, Hebden Bridge, West Yorkshire, HX7 8DG

Tel: 01422 843785
Fax: 01422 843036
E-mail: info@aldc.org
Website: www.aldc.org

Enquiries to: Information Officer

Organisation type and purpose: Membership association (membership is by subscription).

Access to staff: Contact by letter, by telephone, by fax, by e-mail and via website. Access for members only.
Hours: Mon to Fri, 0900 to 1700

ASSOCIATION OF LICENSED MULTIPLE RETAILERS (ALMR)

9B Walpole Court, Ealing Studios, London, W5 5ED

Tel: 020 8579 2080
Fax: 020 8579 7579
E-mail: info@almr.org.uk
Website: www.almr.org.uk

Organisation type and purpose: A network of entrepreneurial retailers and industry suppliers that champions the smaller independent companies that own and operate pubs, bars and restaurants in the UK.

Subject coverage: Core membership is the smaller independent company that operates managed pubs and bars at every level in the market, many of which also have a bias towards food, entertainment and sports. They may be either leasehold or freehold or other ownership basis. The ALMR's title assumes 'multiple' sites, but 2 is an acceptable threshold.

Publications: Electronic and video
Order electronic and video publications from: Download from website

Publications list: Available online

Access to staff: Contact by letter, by telephone, by fax and by e-mail

ASSOCIATION OF LLOYD'S MEMBERS (ALM)

100 Fenchurch Street, London, EC3M 5LG

Tel: 0207 488 0033
Fax: 020 7488 7555
E-mail: mail@alm.ltd.uk
Website: www.alm.ltd.uk

Enquiries to: Consultant
Direct e-mail: edward.vale@alm.ltd.uk; linda.evans@alm.ltd.uk
Other contacts: Senior Administrator / Membership Enquiries

Founded: c. 1984

Organisation type and purpose: Represents private capital at Lloyd's insurance market, membership is by subscription.
To represent and advance members' interests whether they participate on an unlimited or a limited liability basis, either alone or in group vehicles.

Subject coverage: Private underwriters at Lloyd's.

Publications: Printed

Publications list: Available online

Access to staff: Contact by letter, by telephone, by fax and by e-mail

ASSOCIATION OF LONDON CHIEF LIBRARIANS (ALCL)

c/o London Libraries Development Agency, 6 Charing Cross Road, London, WC2H 0HF

Tel: 020 7641 5266
Fax: 020 7641 5266

Enquiries to: Honorary Secretary
Other contacts: President

Founded: 1965

Organisation type and purpose: Local government body, professional body, public library.

Subject coverage: London public libraries.

Access to staff: Contact by letter, by telephone, by fax and by e-mail
Hours: Mon to Fri, 0900 to 1700

ASSOCIATION OF LONDON GOVERNMENT (ALG)

59½ Southwark Street, London, NW6 7NE

Tel: 020 7934 9999
Fax: 020 7934 9991
E-mail: info@alg.gov.uk

Enquiries to: Press and Publications Manager

Founded: 2000; formerly called London Borough Grants Committee (LBGC) (year of change 1997); formerly called London Boroughs Grants Unit (LBGU) (year of change 2000)

Organisation type and purpose: Local government body.
Grant-making body, as defined by Section 48 of the Local Government Act 1985.
To distribute grants to voluntary organisations on a London-wide basis.

Subject coverage: Strategic funding of the voluntary sector in London, grant applications and monitoring processes; funding initiatives; the LBG and London Boroughs Grant Committee; advice and guidance for voluntary organisations; funding sources and other information.

Publications: Printed

Publications list: Available in print

Access to staff: Contact by letter, by telephone, by fax, by e-mail, in person and via website
Hours: Mon to Fri, 0915 to 1715

Access for disabled people: Parking provided, ramped entry, access to all public areas, toilet facilities

ASSOCIATION OF MANUFACTURERS OF POWER GENERATING SYSTEMS (AMPS)

Samuelson House, 62 Forder Way, Hampton, Peterborough, PE7 8JB

Tel: 0845 644 8748
Fax: 01733 314767
E-mail: ab@amps.org.uk
Website: www.amps.org.uk

Enquiries to: Director General

Founded: 1977

Organisation type and purpose: Trade association (membership is by subscription).
The international promotion of the UK power generation systems industry.

Subject coverage: Promotion of the interests and sales of the United Kingdom's manufacturers of diesel and gas driven electrical generating systems worldwide. By representation on British, European and International Standards Committees, EUROPGEN and other bodies, to speak with one voice on all issues of technical standards, legislation and commercial policy that affect members' interests. To help members maintain the highest technical standards, quality and customer support.

Trade and statistical information: Data on worldwide market for diesel and gas turbine electrical power generating systems – volume and value

Publications: Printed, and electronic and video

Publications list: Available in print

Access to staff: Contact by letter, by telephone, by fax and by e-mail
Hours: Mon to Fri, 0830 to 1700

Member of: British Electrotechnical and Allied Manufacturers' Association (BEAMA); Electrical Generating System Association, USA (EGSA); Electricity Supply Association of Australia Limited (ESSA); European Generating Set Association (EUROPGEN); Institution of Diesel and Gas Turbine Engineers (IDGTE)

ASSOCIATION OF MBAS

Formal name: Association of Masters in Business Administration

25 Hosier Lane, London, EC1A 9LQ

Tel: 020 7246 2686

continued overleaf

Fax: 020 7246 2687
E-mail: info@mbaworld.com
Website: www.mbaworld.com

Enquiries to: Company Secretary
Direct e-mail: p.north@mbaworld.com
Other contacts: Membership Secretary

Founded: 1967; formerly called Business Graduates Association (BGA) (year of change 1987)

Organisation type and purpose:
Professional body, membership association (membership is by subscription, qualification), present number of members: 9,000, registered charity (charity number 313412), suitable for ages: 24+.
To promote and improve management standards.

Subject coverage: MBA courses worldwide, accreditation of MBA courses, funding for MBA courses.

Trade and statistical information: Data on the number of MBA courses available and the numbers of students graduating each year.
Salary and careers data of MBAs

Publications: Printed

Access to staff: Contact by letter, by telephone, by fax, by e-mail, in person and via website. Appointment necessary.
Hours: Mon to Fri, 0900 to 1700

ASSOCIATION OF MEDICAL RESEARCH CHARITIES (AMRC)

Charles Darwin House, 12 Roger Street, London, WC1N 2JU

Tel: 020 7685 2620
Fax: 020 7685 2621
E-mail: info@amrc.org.uk
Website: www.amrc.org.uk

Enquiries to: Chief Executive

Founded: 1987

Organisation type and purpose:
Membership association of charities that fund medical research in the UK.
Membership is by application.
Members must use peer review, have a research strategy in place, and sign up to AMRC position statements in order to qualify for membership.
Present number of members: 114.
Registered charity (charity no. 296772), company limited by guarantee (company no. 2107400).
Aims to further medical research in the UK generally; in particular to further effectiveness of those charities in which a principal activity is medical research.

Subject coverage: Advice and guidance on best practice in medical research.
Information on the contribution of charities to UK medical research.

Trade and statistical information: Data on the funding of medical research charities, including distribution and types of funds

Publications: Electronic and video

Access to staff: Contact by letter, by telephone, by fax, by e-mail and via website. Appointment necessary.
Hours: Mon to Fri, 0930 to 1730

Access to building: Prior appointment required

Access for disabled people: Toilet facilities

ASSOCIATION OF MOTOR RACING CIRCUIT OWNERS LTD (AMRCO Ltd)

BARC, Thruxton Circuit, Andover, Hampshire, SP11 8PN

Tel: 01264 882200
Fax: 01264 882233
E-mail: amrco@barc.net
Website: www.motorsportsuk.co.uk

Enquiries to: Honorary Secretary

Founded: 1962

Organisation type and purpose: Trade association, membership association (membership is by subscription, qualification), present number of members: 18.
To represent the interests of UK motor sport circuit owners.

Subject coverage: Motor sport organisation and race circuit management. Circuits include: Anglesey, Brands Hatch, Cadwell Park, Castle Combe, Croft, Donington Park, Goodwood, Kirkistown, Knockhill, Lydden Hill, Mallory Park, Mondello Park, Oulton Park, Pembrey, Rockingham, Silverstone, Snetterton and Thruxton.

Access to staff: Contact by letter
Hours: Mon to Fri, 0900 to 1700

ASSOCIATION OF MUSLIM SCHOOLS (AMS)

AMS UK, PO BOX 14109, Birmingham, B6 9BN

Tel: 0844 482 0407
E-mail: ams@webstar.co.uk

Enquiries to: Director

Founded: 1992

Organisation type and purpose:
Membership association (membership is by subscription), present number of members: 52 schools, training organisation, consultancy.
Members are full-time Muslim schools.
To enhance the development of Muslim schools.

Subject coverage: Muslim schools, Islamic education, general education, Islam.

Publications: Printed

Access to staff: Contact by letter, by telephone and by fax
Hours: Mon to Fri, 0900 to 1700

Connections with: Association of Muslim Schools; PO Box 537, Lenasia, 1820, South Africa

ASSOCIATION OF NATIONAL TOURIST OFFICE REPRESENTATIVES (ANTOR)

ANTOR Executive Secretary, 39 Pennington Close, Colden Common, Winchester, Hampshire, SO21 1UR

Tel: 0870 241 9084
Fax: 01962 711239
E-mail: esther@antor.com
Website: www.antor.com

Founded: 1952

Organisation type and purpose:
International organisation, professional body (membership is by subscription, election or invitation), present number of members: over 90 National Tourist Office members, voluntary organisation.

Subject coverage: Tourism in each member country, tourist planning facilities.

Access to staff: Contact by letter, by telephone, by e-mail and via website. Appointment necessary.
Hours: Telephone has an answering machine

ASSOCIATION OF NATURAL BURIAL GROUNDS (ANBG)

The Natural Death Centre, In the Hill House, Watley Lane, Twyford, Winchester, SO21 1QX

Tel: 01962 712 690
E-mail: contact@naturaldeath.org.uk
Website: www.naturaldeath.org.uk

Enquiries to: Manager

Founded: 1994

Organisation type and purpose: Registered charity.

Subject coverage: Association for the 240+ green burial grounds (and 50 more at planning stage) where body is buried with a tree planted instead of a headstone; legal, ecological, and other issues pertaining to such a burial method.

Trade and statistical information: Details of sites run by councils, farmers and wildlife trusts

Publications: Printed

Access to staff: Contact by letter, by telephone, by e-mail and via website
Hours: Mon to Fri, 1100 to 1400

Links with: Natural Death Centre charity; at the same address; website: http://www.naturaldeath.org.uk

ASSOCIATION OF NEWSPAPER AND MAGAZINE WHOLESALERS (ANMW)

c/o Smiths News Ltd, Wakefield House, Aspect Park, Pipers Way, Swindon, SN3 1RF

Tel: 0845 1213210
E-mail: enquiries@anmw.co.uk
Website: www.anmw.co.uk

Enquiries to: Chairman
Direct e-mail: howard.birch@smithsnews.co.uk

Founded: 1904

Organisation type and purpose: Trade association.

Subject coverage: Wholesaling of newspapers and magazines within the United Kingdom.

Access to staff: Contact by letter, by telephone, by fax and by e-mail
Hours: Mon to Fri, 0900 to 1700

ASSOCIATION OF NOISE CONSULTANTS (ANC)

The Old Pump House, 1a Stonecross, St Albans, Hertfordshire, AL1 4AA

Tel: 020 8253 4518
E-mail: info@theanc.co.uk
Website: www.association-of-noise-consultants.co.uk

Enquiries to: Manager

Founded: 1973

Organisation type and purpose:
Professional body, present number of members: 115 corporate members.

Subject coverage: To help potential clients identify the services of consultancy advice in the fields of noise and vibration.

Non-library collection catalogue: All or part available online

Publications: Printed

Publications list: Available online

Access to staff: Contact by telephone and by e-mail
Hours: Mon to Fri, 0900 to 1700

Access to building: No access other than to staff

ASSOCIATION OF NORTHUMBERLAND LOCAL HISTORY SOCIETIES (ANLHS)

c/o 11 Beverley Terrace, Cullercoats, North Shields, Tyne & Wear, NE30 4NT

E-mail: mail@anlhs.org.uk
Website: www.anlhs.org.uk

Enquiries to: Secretary

Founded: 1966; formerly called Northumberland Local History Society (year of change 1979)

Organisation type and purpose:
Membership association (membership is by subscription), present number of members: 130 individual, 53 societies, voluntary organisation, registered charity (charity number 251179).
Umbrella organisation supporting affiliated local history societies in Northumberland and Newcastle. Annual research project, lectures and meetings.

Subject coverage: History of the geographic county of Northumberland (including Tyne and Wear and North Tyneside), excluding family history.

Collection: At Northumberland Collection Service:
War Memorials Index of Northumberland
Shops and Businesses of Northumberland

Publications: Printed
Order printed publications from: The Secretary

Publications list: Available online

Access to staff: Contact by letter, by e-mail and via website

Affiliated to: British Association for Local History

ASSOCIATION OF NURSES IN SUBSTANCE ABUSE (ANSA)

37 Star Street, Ware, Hertfordshire, SG12 7AA

Tel: 0870 241 3503
Fax: 0192 0462 730
E-mail: info@ansauk.org
Website: www.ansa.uk.net

Enquiries to: Chairman

Founded: 1983

Organisation type and purpose:
Membership association (membership is by subscription).
Membership organisation for nurses and other allied professions working in the field of substance misuse or with an interest in this area of work.

Subject coverage: All aspects of substance misuse, its effects and treatment.

Publications: Printed

Publications list: Available in print

Access to staff: Contact by letter, by telephone, by e-mail and via website

ASSOCIATION OF OPTOMETRISTS (AOP)

2 Woodbridge Street, London, EC1R 0DG

Tel: 020 7549 2000
Fax: 020 7251 8315
E-mail: postbox@aop.org.uk
Website: www.aop.org.uk

Enquiries to: Chief Executive

Founded: 1946; formerly called Association of Optical Practitioners (AOP) (year of change 1987)

Organisation type and purpose:
Professional body (membership is by subscription), present number of members: 9000.

Subject coverage: Optometry, including eye care and protection in industry, DIY, drivers' vision, sports vision, eye care for the elderly, children, road safety.

Publications: Printed
Order printed publications from: Editor, Optometry Today
Victoria House, 178–180 Fleet Road, Fleet, Hampshire, GU13 8DA, tel: 01252 816266, fax: 01252 816176, e-mail: info@optometry.co.uk

Access to staff: Contact by letter, by telephone, by fax, by e-mail and via website. Appointment necessary.
Hours: Mon to Fri, 0830 to 1730

Access to building: Prior appointment required

Houses the: Optical Functional Whitley Council; Optometric Fees Review Committee

ASSOCIATION OF PAEDIATRIC CHARTERED PHYSIOTHERAPISTS (APCP)

APCP, PO Box 610, Huntingdon, PE29 9FJ

Tel: 0131 339 7555
Fax: 0131 476 3388
E-mail: va@apcp.org.uk
Website: apcp.org.uk/

Enquiries to: Secretary
Other contacts: Chairman

Founded: 1973

Organisation type and purpose: Advisory body, professional body.

Subject coverage: Physiotherapy treatment for children in areas of speciality i.e. respiratory care, neuro-developmental, cerebral palsy, learning disability, dyspraxia, orthopaedic, neonatal care.

Publications list: Available in print

Access to staff: Contact by letter, by telephone, by fax and by e-mail
Hours: Mon to Fri, 0900 to 1700

Parent body: Chartered Society of Physiotherapy; tel: 020 7306 6666

ASSOCIATION OF PERSONAL INJURY LAWYERS (APIL)

11 Castle Quay, Nottingham, NG7 1FW

Tel: 0115 958 0585
Fax: 0115 958 0885
E-mail: via website
Website: www.apil.org.uk

Founded: 1990

Organisation type and purpose: A not-for-profit organisation that exists to help its 4,700 members fight for the rights of injured people, a trusted organisation in the promotion, encouragement and development of expertise in personal injury law.
To promote full and just compensation for all types of personal injury; to promote and develop expertise in the practice of personal injury law; to promote wider redress for personal injury in the legal system; to campaign for improvements in personal injury law; to promote safety standards and alert the public to hazards; to provide a communication network for its members.

Subject coverage: Personal injury, personal injury law.

Publications: Electronic and video
Order electronic and video publications from: Download from website

Publications list: Available online

Access to staff: Contact by letter, by telephone, by fax and by e-mail

ASSOCIATION OF PHOTOGRAPHERS LIMITED (AOP)

81 Leonard Street, London, EC2A 4QS

Tel: 020 7739 6669
Fax: 020 7739 8707
E-mail: general@aophoto.co.uk
Website: www.aophoto.co.uk

Enquiries to: Membership Secretary
Other contacts: Chief Executive

Founded: 1968; formerly called Association of Fashion, Advertising and Editorial Photographers (AFAEP)

continued overleaf

Organisation type and purpose: Trade association (membership is by subscription, election or invitation), present number of members: 1900.
To support and promote the interests of photographers in the areas of fashion, editorial and advertising photography.

Subject coverage: Copyright, standards and ethics, education.

Collection: Careers Information
Photographic Reference Books

Publications: Printed, and electronic and video
Order printed publications from: Ventura BHP The Plant Shop, Lenham Road, Kingswood, Maidstone, Kent, ME17 1LZ, tel: 01622 844417, fax: 01622 844418

Access to staff: Access for members only.
Hours: Mon to Fri, 0930 to 1800

Access for disabled people: Level entry

ASSOCIATION OF PHYSICAL & NATURAL THERAPISTS (APNT)

27 Old Gloucester Street, London, WC1N 3XX

Tel: 07966 181 588
E-mail: apntsource@lineone.net
Website: www.apnt.org.uk

Enquiries to: General Secretary

Founded: 1986

Organisation type and purpose: National organisation, membership association (membership is by subscription), training organisation.

Access to staff: Contact by telephone and by e-mail
Hours: Mon to Fri, 0900 to 1700

Member of: Aromatherapy Organisations Council; British Complementary Medicine Association

ASSOCIATION OF PIONEER MOTOR CYCLISTS (APMC)

Heather Bank, May Close, Liphook Road, Headley, Bordon, Hampshire, GU35 8LR

Tel: 01428 712666

Enquiries to: Honorary Secretary
Direct e-mail: john@barraclough40.freeserve.co.uk
Other contacts: News Editor

Organisation type and purpose: International organisation, membership association.
All members have held motorcycle driving licences for 50 years for Pioneer Status and 40 years for Companion Member.
For motorcyclists to combine knowledge and meet socially during the year.

Subject coverage: History of motor cycles and motorcycling.

Collection: Available only to members on application
Large collection of books, bound volumes of periodicals and other ephemera relating to the history of motor cycles and motorcycling (personal property of the present secretary)

Publications: Printed

Access to staff: Contact by letter and by telephone. Letter of introduction required.
Hours: Mon to Fri, 0900 to 1700

ASSOCIATION OF PLAY INDUSTRIES (API)

Federation House, National Agricultural Centre, Stoneleigh Park, Warwickshire, CV8 2RF

Tel: 024 7641 4999
Fax: 024 7641 4990
E-mail: api@api-play.org
Website: www.api-play.org

Enquiries to: Association Manager
Direct tel: 024 7641 4999 ext 208

Founded: 1984

Organisation type and purpose: Trade association (membership is by subscription), present number of members: 60.

Subject coverage: Manufacturers and suppliers of play equipment and impact-absorbing surfaces.

Publications: Printed

Access to staff: Contact by letter, by telephone, by fax and by e-mail
Hours: Mon to Fri, 0900 to 1700

Member of: Federation of European Play Industries (FEPI)

Part of: The Federation of Sports and Play Associations

Subsidiary body: Constructors Section; Indoor Play Section; Outdoor Play Section; Surfacing Section

ASSOCIATION OF PLEASURE CRAFT OPERATORS / CANAL BOATBUILDERS ASSOCIATION (APCO/CBA)

Marine House, Thorpe Lea Road, Egham, Surrey, TW20 8BF

Tel: 01784 223603
Fax: 01784 475899
E-mail: apco@britishmarine.co.uk
Website: www.britishmarine.co.uk
Website: www.apco.org.uk/

Enquiries to: Administrator
Direct e-mail: info@apco.org.uk

Founded: 1954

Organisation type and purpose: Trade association.
Operation of hireboats, passenger, hotel boats and all business involved in the inland waterways of England & Wales, including boat building and maintenance.

Subject coverage: Information about boating holidays on the inland waterways of England and Wales and other businesses on the inland waterways. General information about the Association's aims.

Publications: Printed

Access to staff: Contact by letter, by telephone and by fax
Hours: Mon to Fri, 0900 to 1600

Group Associations of the: British Marine Federation (BMF); tel: 01784 473377; fax: 01784 439678; e-mail: info@britishmarine.co.uk

ASSOCIATION OF PLUMBING AND HEATING CONTRACTORS (APHC)

12 The Pavilions, Cranmore Drive, Solihull, B90 4SB

Tel: 0121 711 5030
Fax: 0121 705 7871
E-mail: info@aphc.co.uk
Website: www.licensedplumber.co.uk

Enquiries to: National Director
Direct e-mail: members@aphc.co.uk
Other contacts: Commercial Director (for membership, PR, publications, database information, business development and marketing)

Founded: 1925; formerly called National Association of Plumbing and Domestic Engineers; formerly called National Association of Plumbing Heating and Mechanical Services Contractors (year of change 1997)

Organisation type and purpose: Trade association, consultancy.

Subject coverage: Plumbing, heating, air conditioning, sprinkler systems, building dynamics and building maintenance services.
Training (BPEC certification), modern apprenticeships, training grants to employers, trainee placement (BSI Training Limited).

Collection: Archive of trade association journals relating to plumbing

Trade and statistical information: List of member firms including sole traders

Publications: Printed, and electronic and video

Access to staff: Contact by letter, by telephone, by fax, by e-mail and via website. Appointment necessary. Non-members charged.
Hours: Mon to Fri, 0900 to 1700

Affiliated to: British Plumbing Employers Council (BPEC); British Plumbing Employers Council Certification Limited (BPEC); Joint Industry Board (JIB); Union Internationale de la Couverte et Plomberie (UICP); 9 rue la Pérouse, 75784 Paris Cedex 16, France

ASSOCIATION OF POLICY MARKET MAKERS (APMM)

Holywell Centre, 1 Phipp Street, London, EC2A 4PS

Tel: 020 7739 3949
Fax: 020 7613 2990
E-mail: enquiries@apmm.org
Website: www.apmm.org

Enquiries to: Executive Director

Founded: 1992

Organisation type and purpose: Trade association (membership is by subscription), present number of members: 8 companies.
To establish and maintain an orderly market in Traded Endowment Policies (TEPs). To provide objective information. To act as a focus and a voice for the market.

Publications: Printed

Access to staff: Contact by letter, by telephone, by fax, by e-mail and via website
Hours: Mon to Fri, 0830 to 1745

ASSOCIATION OF PORT HEALTH AUTHORITIES (APHA)

3rd Floor, Walbrook Wharf, 78–83 Upper Thames Street, London, EC4R 3TD

Tel: 0870 744 4505
Fax: 0870 838 1155
E-mail: office@porthealth.co.uk
Website: htp://www.porthealth.co.uk

Enquiries to: Executive Secretary

Founded: 1899

Organisation type and purpose:
Membership association (membership is by subscription).
Health control of ships, aircraft and imported food control.

Subject coverage: EU and UK law relating to public health, food control and pollution; environmental health relating to ships, and aircraft, fish and shellfish production.

Collection: Minutes and Papers from 1898 to date

Publications: Printed, and electronic and video
Order printed publications from: e-mail: office@porthealth.co.uk
Order electronic and video publications from: website: http://www.porthealth.co.uk

Publications list: Available online

Access to staff: Contact by letter, by telephone, by fax and by e-mail.
Appointment necessary.
Hours: Mon to Fri, 0900 to 1700

Access to building: By appointment

ASSOCIATION OF PRACTISING ACCOUNTANTS (APA)

The Association of Practising Accountants, 105 St Peters Street, St Albans, Hertfordshire, AL1 3EJ

Tel: 01727 896087
Fax: 01727 896026
E-mail: info@apa-uk.co.uk
Website: www.apa-uk.co.uk

Enquiries to: Secretary
Direct tel: 01727 896087
Direct fax: 01727 896026
Direct e-mail: jmellish@kingstonsmith.co.uk

Founded: 1988

Organisation type and purpose:
Membership Association (membership is by election or invitation).

Subject coverage: Accountancy.

Publications: Printed
Order printed publications from: website: http://www.apa-uk.co.uk

Access to staff: Contact by letter, by e-mail and via website
Hours: Mon to Fri, 0900 to 1700

ASSOCIATION OF PRINTING MACHINERY IMPORTERS (APMI)

65 Hazlewell Road, London, SW15 6UT

Tel: 020 8780 2966
Fax: 020 8780 2864

Enquiries to: Secretary

Founded: 1959

Organisation type and purpose: Trade association (membership is by election or invitation), present number of members: 39.

Subject coverage: Printing machinery and equipment imported into the United Kingdom.

Publications: Printed

Access to staff: Contact by letter, by telephone and by fax
Hours: Mon to Fri, 0900 to 1700

ASSOCIATION OF PRIVATE CLIENT INVESTMENT MANAGERS AND STOCKBROKERS (APCIMS)

22 City Road, Finsbury Square, London, EC1Y 2AJ

Tel: 020 7448 7100
Fax: 020 7638 4636
E-mail: info@apcims.co.uk
Website: www.apcims.co.uk

Enquiries to: Head of Information
Direct e-mail: jasonb@apcims.co.uk

Founded: 1990

Organisation type and purpose: Trade association.

Subject coverage: Investment and stockbroking for private individuals.

Publications: Printed

Access to staff: Contact by letter, by telephone, by fax, by e-mail and via website
Hours: Mon to Fri, 0900 to 1730

Access to building: No access other than to staff

ASSOCIATION OF PROFESSIONAL LANDSCAPERS (APL)

19 High Street, Theale, Reading, Berkshire, RG7 5AH

Tel: 0118 9303132
Fax: 0118 9303453
E-mail: apl@the-hta.org.uk

Enquiries to: Administrator
Other contacts: Publicity Officer for PR & Publicity.

Founded: 1994

Organisation type and purpose: Trade association (membership is by subscription), present number of members: 114.

Subject coverage: Landscape gardening.

Access to staff: Contact by letter, by telephone, by fax, by e-mail and via website

Specialist group within: Horticultural Trades Association (HTA); 19 High Street, Theale, Reading, Berkshire, RG7 5AH; tel: 01189 303132; fax: 01189 323453; e-mail: info@the-hta.org.uk

ASSOCIATION OF PROFESSIONAL MUSIC THERAPISTS (APMT)

2nd Floor, 24–27 White Lion Street, London, N1 9PD

Tel: 020 7837 6100
Fax: 020 7837 6142
E-mail: info@bamt.org
Website: www.apmt.org

Enquiries to: Administrator

Founded: 1976

Organisation type and purpose:
Professional body (membership is by qualification), present number of members: 600.
To maintain high standards of practice and training. To assist music therapists in development and all matters pertaining to their profession.

Subject coverage: Music therapy; learning difficulties; mental health disabilities; autism; special needs; career literature.

Publications: Printed

Publications list: Available online and in print

Access to staff: Contact by letter, by telephone, by fax and by e-mail
Hours: Mon to Fri, 0930 to 1530

Links with: British Society for Music Therapy; 2nd Floor, 24–27 White Lion Street, London, N1 9PD; tel: 020 7837 6100; fax: 020 7837 6142; e-mail: info@bsmt.org

ASSOCIATION OF PROFESSIONAL RECORDING SERVICES LIMITED (APRS)

PO Box 22, Totnes, Devon, TQ9 7YZ

Tel: 01803 868600
Fax: 01803 868444
E-mail: info@aprs.co.uk
Website: www.aprs.co.uk

Enquiries to: Executive Director
Other contacts: Administration (for Head Office)

Founded: 1947; formerly called Association of Professional Recording Studios

Organisation type and purpose:
International organisation, trade association (membership is by subscription, qualification), present number of members: 200.
Membership is by subsciption for individuals and by qualification for companies.
Furthering standards and needs of companies and individuals in audio-related industries.

Subject coverage: Professional sound recording and related technology.

Publications: Printed

Access to staff: Contact by letter, by telephone, by fax, by e-mail and via website.
Appointment necessary.
Hours: Mon to Fri, 0900 to 1700

Links with: Music Producers Guild (MPG)

ASSOCIATION OF PROFESSIONAL TOURIST GUIDES (APTG)

128 Theobald's Road, London, WC1X 8TN

continued overleaf

Tel: 020 7611 2545
E-mail: aptg@aptg.org.uk
Website: www.guidelondon.org.uk

Enquiries to: Administrator

Founded: 1989

Organisation type and purpose:
Professional body (membership is by qualification), present number of members: 500.
Membership association for Blue Badge Tourist Guides.

Subject coverage: Tourism issues.

Publications: Printed

Publications list: Available in print

Access to staff: Contact by letter, by telephone and by e-mail
Hours: Mon to Fri, 1000 to 1530

Access to building: No access other than to staff

ASSOCIATION OF PROFESSIONAL VIDEOMAKERS (APV)

Ambler House, Helpringham, Lincolnshire, NG34 0RB

Tel: 01529 421717
Fax: 01529 421742
E-mail: jan@videomakers.com
Website: www.apv.org.uk

Enquiries to: Information Officer

Founded: 1995

Organisation type and purpose:
Membership association (membership is by subscription), present number of members: 500.

Subject coverage: Video production and associated trades, skills.

Access to staff: Contact by letter, by telephone, by fax and by e-mail
Hours: Mon to Fri, 0900 to 1700

ASSOCIATION OF RADICAL MIDWIVES (ARM)

16 Wytham Street, Oxford, OX1 4SU

Tel: 01865 248159
E-mail: sarahmontagu@gmail.com
Website: www.midwifery.org.uk

Enquiries to: Secretary

Founded: 1976

Subject coverage: Midwifery, maternity care, childbirth, breastfeeding, post-natal care.

Publications: Printed

Publications list: Available online

Access to staff: Contact by letter, by telephone and by e-mail
Hours: Mon to Fri, 0900 to 1700

ASSOCIATION OF REFLEXOLOGISTS (UK) (AoR)

5 Fore Street, Taunton, TA1 1HX

Tel: 01823 351010
Fax: 01823 336646
E-mail: info@aor.org.uk
Website: www.aor.org.uk

Enquiries to: Executive Director
Direct tel: 01278 733393
Direct fax: 01278 733665
Direct e-mail: aoreo@reflexology.org
Other contacts: Chairman for policy.

Founded: 1984

Organisation type and purpose:
Professional body, membership association (membership is by qualification).
Awarding Body for Practitioner Qualification in Reflexology.
Accrediting Body for Practitioner Courses in Reflexology.

Subject coverage: Reflexology, complementary therapies, integrated health.

Trade and statistical information:
Information on courses, reflexology organisations worldwide, training standards, career opportunities

Publications: Printed

Publications list: Available in print

Access to staff: Contact by letter, by telephone, by fax and by e-mail
Hours: Mon to Fri, 0900 to 1700

Member of: International Council of Reflexologists; Reflexology in Europe Network

Other departments at: AoR Administration; Katepwa House, Ashfield Park Avenue, Ross-on-Wye, Herefordshire, HR9 5AX; tel: 01989 567667; fax: 01989 567676; e-mail: aor@assocmanagement.co.uk; AoR Training and Education; 19 Benson Road, Henfield, West Sussex, BN5 9HY; tel: 01273 492385; fax: 01273 495920; e-mail: aor@reflexology.org

ASSOCIATION OF RELOCATION AGENTS (ARA)

PO Box 189, Diss, Norfolk, IP22 1PE

Tel: 08700 737475
Fax: 08700 718719
E-mail: arp.relocation@gmail.com
Website: www.relocationagents.com

Enquiries to: Chief Executive

Founded: 1986

Organisation type and purpose: Trade association.

Subject coverage: Relocation services, setting up relocation agencies, relocation industry.

Publications: Printed

Access to staff: Contact by letter, by telephone, by fax, by e-mail and via website
Hours: Mon to Fri, 0900 to 1700

ASSOCIATION OF RESEARCHERS IN MEDICINE & SCIENCE (ARMS)

c/o Henry Wellcome, LINE, Dorothy Hodgkin Building, Whitson Street, University of Bristol, Bristol, BS1 3NY.

Tel: 0117 331 3050
Fax: 0117 331 3049
E-mail: david.jessop@bris.ac.uk
Website: www.hop.man.ac.uk/arms/arms.html

Enquiries to: Chairman
Direct tel: 07973 675422

Founded: 1978

Organisation type and purpose: Voluntary organisation, research organisation.

Subject coverage: Medical and scientific research, contract research, science policy, conditions of employment etc.

Publications: Printed

Access to staff: Contact by letter, by fax, by e-mail and via website
Hours: Mon to Fri, 0900 to 1700

ASSOCIATION OF RESIDENTIAL LETTING AGENTS (ARLA)

Arbon House, 6 Tournament Court, Edgehill Drive, Warwick, CV34 6LG

Tel: 0845 250 6001
E-mail: info@arla.co.uk
Website: www.arla.co.uk

Enquiries to: Administrator

Founded: 1981

Organisation type and purpose: Trade association (membership is by subscription).
National professional and regulatory body for agents specialising in residential letting and management.

Subject coverage: Private sector residential rental property; law and property; management and administration.

Publications: Printed

Access to staff: Contact by letter, by telephone, by fax and by e-mail
Hours: Mon to Fri, 0900 to 1730

Access to building: No access other than to staff

ASSOCIATION OF RESIDENTIAL MANAGING AGENTS LTD (ARMA)

178 Battersea Park Road, London, SW11 4ND

Tel: 020 7978 2607
Fax: 020 7498 6153
E-mail: info@arma.org.uk
Website: www.arma.org.uk

Enquiries to: Secretary

Founded: 1991

Organisation type and purpose: Trade association (membership is by subscription), present number of members: 200+, service industry.
Trade association representing managers of residential leasehold blocks of flats in England and Wales.

Subject coverage: Matters relating to block management of residential property.

Publications: Printed

Publications list: Available online

Access to staff: Contact by letter, by fax, by e-mail and via website
Hours: Mon to Fri, 0900 to 1700

Access to building: No access other than to staff

ASSOCIATION OF SCHOOL AND COLLEGE LEADERS (ASCL)

130 Regent Road, Leicester, LE1 7PG

Tel: 0116 299 1122
Fax: 0116 299 1123
Website: www.ascl.org.uk

Founded: 1977

Organisation type and purpose: Professional body, trade union. Represents more than 14,000 senior leaders in secondary schools and colleges.

Subject coverage: Secondary and further education.

Publications: Printed

Publications list: Available in print

Access to staff: Contact by letter, by telephone and by fax
Hours: Mon to Fri, 0900 to 1700

ASSOCIATION OF SCOTTISH VISITOR ATTRACTIONS (ASVA)

Epic House, 28–32 Cadogan Street, Glasgow G2 7LP

Tel: 0141 229 0923
E-mail: info@asva.co.uk
Website: www.asva.co.uk

Enquiries to: Administrator

Founded: 1989

Organisation type and purpose: Trade association (membership is by subscription), present number of members: 500.

Subject coverage: All aspects of visitor attraction in Scotland, development, operations and marketing.

Publications list: Available in print

Access to staff: Contact by letter and by e-mail
Hours: Mon to Fri, 0900 to 1700

ASSOCIATION OF SEA TRAINING ORGANISATIONS (ASTO)

Unit 10, North Meadow, Royal Clarence Yard, Gosport, Hampshire, PO12 1BP

Tel: 023 9250 3222
Fax: 023 9250 3222
E-mail: office@asto.org.uk
Website: www.asto.org.uk

Enquiries to: Business Manager

Founded: 1971

Organisation type and purpose: Membership association (membership is by election or invitation), registered charity, training organisation.

Subject coverage: Sail training for young people and adults, able-bodied or disabled, personal development for young people.

Publications: Printed

Access to staff: Contact by letter, by telephone and by fax
Hours: Mon to Fri, 0900 to 1700

Supported by: Royal Yachting Association

ASSOCIATION OF SHOW AND AGRICULTURAL ORGANISATIONS (ASAO)

PO Box 1201, Wincanton, Somerset, BA9 8YD

Tel: 01749 814086
Fax: 01749 812655
E-mail: asaosecretary@asao.co.uk
Website: www.asao.co.uk

Enquiries to: Secretary
Direct e-mail: paul.hooper@bathandwest.co.uk

Founded: 1923

Organisation type and purpose: National organisation, trade association (membership is by subscription), present number of members: 187, voluntary organisation, registered charity (charity number 1023932).

Subject coverage: Organisation of agricultural and similar shows.

Publications list: Available in print

Access to staff: Appointment necessary.
Hours: Mon to Fri, 0900 to 1700

ASSOCIATION OF SINGER CAR OWNERS (ASCO)

39 Oakfield, Rickmansworth, Hertfordshire, WD3 8LR

Tel: 01923 778575
Website: www.asco.org.uk

Enquiries to: General Secretary

Founded: 1976

Organisation type and purpose: Membership association (membership is by subscription), present number of members: 200.

Subject coverage: Restoration, technical advice, source materials on all aspects of Singer cars.

Publications: Printed

Access to staff: Contact by letter and by telephone
Hours: Mon to Sun, 1000 to 1900

ASSOCIATION OF SOCIAL ANTHROPOLOGISTS OF THE COMMONWEALTH (ASA)

50 Fitzroy Street, London, W1T 5BT

E-mail: admin@theasa.org
Website: www.theasa.org

Enquiries to: Administrator

Organisation type and purpose: Professional body (membership is referenced).

Subject coverage: Social anthropology and its various sub-fields.

Publications: Printed, and electronic and video

Publications list: Available online

Access to staff: Contact by letter and by e-mail
Hours: Mon to Fri, 0900 to 1700
Special comments: Office is remote so best access is via e-mail.

Links with: Association of Learned Societies in the Social Sciences

ASSOCIATION OF STAINLESS FASTENER DISTRIBUTORS (ASFAD)

Ikon Trading Estate, Droitwich Road, Hartlebury, DY10 4EU

E-mail: info@bafd.org
Website: www.bafd.org

Enquiries to: General Secretary

Founded: 1984

Organisation type and purpose: Trade association (membership is by qualification, election or invitation).

Subject coverage: Sources of supply of stainless fasteners and distribution.

Access to staff: Contact by letter, by telephone, by fax and by e-mail. Access for members only.
Hours: Mon to Fri, 0900 to 1700

Members of: European Fastener Distributors Association (EFDA); Germany

Parent body: British Association of Fastener Distributors (BAFD); at the same address

ASSOCIATION OF SUPERVISORS OF MIDWIVES (ASM)

West Yorkshire Health Authority, Bleneim House West One, Duncombe Street, Leeds, West Yorkshire, LS14PL

Tel: 0113 295 2094
Fax: 0113 295 2222
E-mail: jean.duerden@westyorks.nhs.uk

Enquiries to: Honorary Secretary

Founded: 1910

Subject coverage: Supervision of midwives.

Publications: Printed

Access to staff: Contact by letter, by telephone, by fax and by e-mail
Hours: Mon to Fri, 0900 to 1700

ASSOCIATION OF SUPPLIERS TO THE BRITISH CLOTHING INDUSTRY (ASBCI)

Unit 5, 25 Square Road, Halifax, West Yorkshire, HX1 1QG

Tel: 01422 354666
Fax: 01422 381184
E-mail: info@asbci.co.uk
Website: www.asbci.co.uk

Founded: 1992; incorporates the former British Interlining Manufacturers' Association

Organisation type and purpose: Represents and provides technical support to members in all the key sectors connected with supplying the British clothing industry; has over 100 members.

Subject coverage: Fibres, fabrics, linings, interlinings, adhesives, dyers, sewing threads, buttons, zips, trims, sleeve head rolls, shoulder pads, machinery, presses, waistbands, garment processors, clothing consultants, clothing manufacturers, retailers, dry cleaners, launderers, domestic

continued overleaf

detergent manufacturers, chemical suppliers, computer suppliers to the clothing industry, textile testing houses, research organisations, textile universities, and training bodies.

Publications: Printed, and electronic and video
Order electronic and video publications from: Download from website

Publications list: Available online

Access to staff: Contact by letter, by telephone, by fax and by e-mail

ASSOCIATION OF SURGEONS OF GREAT BRITAIN AND IRELAND (ASGBI)

The Royal College of Surgeons, 35–43 Lincoln's Inn Fields, London, WC2A 3PN

Tel: 020 7973 0300
Fax: 020 7430 9235
E-mail: admin@asgbi.org.uk
Website: www.asgbi.org.uk

Enquiries to: Chief Executive
Direct tel: 020 7973 0304
Direct e-mail: admin@asgbi.org.uk

Founded: 1920

Organisation type and purpose:
Professional body, membership association (membership is by subscription, election or invitation), present number of members: 1,100, registered charity (charity number 1068016).
The advancement of the science and art of surgery.

Subject coverage: General surgery and the specialities thereof: upper and lower GI, vascular, endocrine, transplant, breast, laparascopic surgery.

Access to staff: Contact by letter, by telephone, by fax, by e-mail, in person and via website
Hours: Mon to Fri, 0900 to 1700

ASSOCIATION OF TANK AND CISTERN MANUFACTURERS (ATCM)

22 Grange Park, St Arvans, Chepstow, Monmouthshire, NP16 6EA

Tel: 01291 623634
E-mail: imcc@atcmtanks.org.uk
Website: www.atcmtanks.org.uk

Enquiries to: Chairman
Other contacts: Secretary

Founded: 1969; formerly called Plastic Tanks and Cisterns Manufacturers' Association (year of change 1992)

Organisation type and purpose: Trade association (membership is by subscription), present number of members: 16, manufacturing industry.
The ATCM is a group of like-minded manufacturers who co-operate and promote with common interest the manufacture of tanks and cistern products conforming to highest possible standards of quality.
Co-operation between members in technical matters, standard production in UK and Europe, and action on behalf of members when making representations to government and regulatory authorities.

Subject coverage: Manufacture and installation of tanks and cisterns for the storage of water, oil or chemical products.

Information services: Technical papers posted on the ATCM web site avilable for download.

Non-library collection catalogue: All or part available online

Library catalogue: All or part available online

Access to staff: Contact by letter, by telephone, by e-mail and via website
Hours: Mon to Fri, 0900 to 1700

Member organisation of: Chartered Institute of Plumbing and Heating Engineering

ASSOCIATION OF TAXATION TECHNICIANS (ATT)

First Floor, Artillery House, 11–19 Artillery Row, London, SW1P 1RT

Tel: 020 7235 2544
Fax: 020 7235 2562
E-mail: info@att.org.uk
Website: www.att.org.uk

Enquiries to: Head of Education Department

Founded: 1989

Organisation type and purpose:
Professional body, registered charity (charity number 803480), training organisation.

Subject coverage: Taxation.

Collection: Tax Library located at King's College, London (members only)

Publications: Printed

Access to staff: Contact by letter, by telephone, by fax, by e-mail and via website
Hours: Mon to Fri, 0900 to 1700

Access to building: No access other than to staff

Associated with: Chartered Institute of Taxation; 12 Upper Belgrave Street, London, SW1X 8BB; tel: 020 7235 9381; fax: 020 7235 2562; e-mail: post@ciot.org.uk

ASSOCIATION OF TEACHERS OF MATHEMATICS (ATM)

Unit 7, Prime Industrial Park, Shaftesbury Street, Derby, DE23 8YB

Tel: 01332 346599
Fax: 01332 204357
E-mail: admin@atm.org.uk
Website: www.atm.org.uk

Enquiries to: Administrative Officer

Founded: 1952

Organisation type and purpose:
International organisation, membership association (membership is by subscription), present number of members: 3000, registered charity (charity number 293125).
Mathematics Association.

Subject coverage: Mathematics education at primary, secondary and tertiary levels.

Publications: Printed
Order printed publications from: www.atm.org.uk

Publications list: Available online and in print

Access to staff: Contact by letter, by telephone, by fax, by e-mail and via website
Hours: Mon to Fri, 0900 to 1630

ASSOCIATION OF TECHNICAL LIGHTING AND ACCESS SPECIALISTS (ATLAS)

6–8 Bonhill Street, London, EC2A 4BX

Tel: 0844 249 0026
Fax: 0844 249 0027
E-mail: info@atlas.org.uk
Website: www.atlas.org.uk

Enquiries to: Secretariat
Direct tel: 0844 249 0026
Direct fax: 0822 249 0027
Direct e-mail: info@atlas.org.uk

Founded: 1946; formerly called National Federation of Master Steeplejacks and Lightning Conductor Engineers (NFMS&LCE) (year of change 2003)

Organisation type and purpose: Trade association

Subject coverage: Steeplejacking and lightning conductor engineering

Access to staff: Contact by letter, by telephone, by fax, by e-mail and via website
Hours: 0900 to 1700

Member organisation of: National Specialist Contractors Council; 6–8 Bonhill Street; tel: 0844 249 5351; fax: 0844 249 5352; e-mail: enquiries@nscc.org.uk; website: www.nscc.org.uk

ASSOCIATION OF THE BRITISH PHARMACEUTICAL INDUSTRY (ABPI)

7th floor, Southside, 105 Victoria Street, London, SW1E 6QT

Tel: 0870 890 4333
Fax: 020 7747 1447
E-mail: abpi@abpi.org.uk
Website: www.abpi.org.uk

Enquiries to: Information Officer
Direct e-mail: ccoomber@abpi.org.uk
Other contacts: Information Services Executive

Founded: 1929

Organisation type and purpose: Trade association.
Represents the pharmaceutical industry operating in the UK in a way that assures patients access to the best available medicines, creates a favourable political, economic and regulatory environment, encourages innovative research and development, and affords fair commercial returns.

Subject coverage: General information on the UK pharmaceutical industry, careers, education and training.

Library catalogue: All or part available in-house

Publications: Printed
Order printed publications from: abpi@edist.co.uk

Publications list: Available online

Access to staff: Contact by letter, by telephone, by fax, by e-mail and via website. Access for members only.
Hours: Mon to Fri, 0830 to 1630
Special comments: Priority given to members.

Access to building: No access other than to staff
Special comments: Members only.

Also at: ABPI Cymru Wales; 2 Caspian Point, Pierhead Street, Cardiff Bay, CF10 4DQ; tel: 0870 890 4333; fax: 029 2045 4298; e-mail: wales@abpi.org.uk; ABPI Northern Ireland; 224 Lisburn Road, Belfast, BT9 6GE; tel: 029 2045 4297; ABPI Scotland; Third Floor East, Crichton House, 4 Crichton's Close, Canongate, Edinburgh, EH8 8DT; tel: 0870 890 4333; fax: 0131 523 0491

Associated with: Office of Health Economics; tel: 020 7747 8850; fax: 020 7747 8851; e-mail: ohegeneral@ohe.org; website: http://www.ohe.org

Member organisation of: European Federation of Pharmaceutical Industry's Associations (EFPIA); Brussels; tel: +32 2 6262555; fax: +32 2 6262566; International Federation of Pharmaceutical Manufacturers' Associations (IFPMA); Geneva; tel: +41 22 338 32 00; fax: +41 22 338 32 99

ASSOCIATION OF TOWN CENTRE MANAGEMENT (ATCM)

Queen Anne's Gate, Westminster, London, SW1H 9BT

Tel: 020 7222 0120; 0300 330 0980
E-mail: office@atcm.org
Website: www.atcm.org

Organisation type and purpose: Europe's largest membership organisation dedicated to helping town and city centres realise their natural roles both as prosperous locations for business and investment, and as focal points for vibrant, inclusive communities. Members are primarily public private partnerships from across the UK as well as both public and private sector stakeholders. ATCM works with all those interested in promoting the vitality and viability of town and city centres, in the UK and further afield and has 4 principal areas of work: places, people, partnerships and policy.

Subject coverage: Has an extensive knowledge bank of good practice initiatives in town and city centres that have made a difference to that centre, and these are accessible to members on line, through publications and through the events programme. Runs training programmes in both personal and technical skills for those engaged in the management of centres and, in partnership with universities and others, offers access to academic and vocational qualifications. Supports partnership creation, development and review through a wide range of programmes that can involve large or small groups and through various publications and works closely with policy makers to ensure that the critical role that town and city centres play in society is never underestimated.

Publications: Printed

Publications list: Available online

Access to staff: Contact by letter, by telephone and by e-mail

ASSOCIATION OF TRANSLATION COMPANIES LIMITED (ATC)

Association of Translation Companies, Unit 24, Level 6 North, New England House, New England Street, Brighton, BN1 4GH

Tel: 01273 676777
Fax: 08450 582590
E-mail: admin@atc.org.uk
Website: www.atc.org.uk

Enquiries to: General Secretary

Founded: 1976

Organisation type and purpose: Professional body, trade association (membership is by subscription, qualification), present number of members: 85.
To provide the use of professionally produced translations by commerce and industry and to regulate translation companies who are members.

Subject coverage: Information on the sourcing of translation, matching language and specialist subject matter.

Collection: Libraries, of some members, on unusual subjects, of specialist technical and other glossaries, of translations of foreign technical standards

Trade and statistical information: The ATC conducts regular surveys of the translation profession, some of the results may be purchased by interested parties

Publications: Printed

Access to staff: Contact by letter, by telephone, by fax, by e-mail and via website. Appointment necessary.
Hours: Mon to Fri, 0900 to 1700

ASSOCIATION OF TUTORS (AOT)

Doddridge Centre, 109 St James Road, Northampton, NN5 5LD

Tel: 01604 586384
Website: www.tutor.co.uk

Enquiries to: Secretary
Direct tel: 01491 638685
Direct e-mail: hilarychampion@aot.org.uk

Founded: 1958

Organisation type and purpose: Professional body (membership is by election or invitation).

Subject coverage: All aspects of tutoring.

Access to staff: Contact by letter
Hours: Mon to Fri, 0900 to 1700

ASSOCIATION OF UNIVERSITY ADMINISTRATORS (AUA)

AUA National Office, University of Manchester, Oxford Road, Manchester, M13 9PL

Tel: 0161 275 2063
Fax: 0161 275 2036
E-mail: aua@manchester.ac.uk
Website: www.aua.ac.uk

Founded: 1961; created by the merger of Association of Polytechnic Administrators (APA) and the Conference of University Administrators (CUA); formerly called Meeting of University Academic Administrative Staff

Organisation type and purpose: Professional association.
To advance and assist in the advancement of education by fostering sound methods of leadership, management and administration in further and higher education by education, training, and other means; to advance and promote the professional development of all who work in professional services roles in higher education and to be an authoritative advocate and champion for the sector. Has over 4,000 members in the UK and world-wide associated with 150 branches based in universities, higher education colleges and HE-related bodies.

Subject coverage: Professional services roles in higher education.

Education services: Offers post-graduate certificate and continuing professional development framework.

Publications: Printed, and electronic and video
Order printed publications from: Available to members
Order electronic and video publications from: Available to members

Access to staff: Contact by letter, by telephone, by fax and by e-mail

ASSOCIATION OF UNIVERSITY CHIEF SECURITY OFFICERS (AUCSO)

E-mail: aucsec@aim.com
Website: www.aucso.org.uk

Enquiries to: Secretary

Founded: 1984

Organisation type and purpose: A forum for security professionals charged with responsibility for the provision and management of security services and personal safety in universities, colleges and institutions of learning within the UK, Ireland and Europe. Currently, 123 universities and HE colleges or institutions are members.
To promote a common purpose in the application of law enforcement policies and security programmes, as it applies to the security and personal safety of staff and students on campus; to exchange experiences and promote partnership working among members, the police service and other agencies to identify trends in crime and disorder and to identify or share solutions; to identify and promote excellence, professionalism and raise standards in security services and to encourage the development of strategic planning and common policies to complement teaching, learning and research; to establish areas of expertise among members, share information and good practices; to consider and debate new and existing legislation, government directives and areas of potential risk, identifying solutions and future needs, and to liaise on these matters with government or other

continued overleaf

organisations; to identify and encourage the professional training, development and career paths for all members; to promote interest, discussion, consultation, formulation of ideas and policy; to promote the activities of the Association and its members regionally, nationally and internationally.

Subject coverage: Exchange of knowledge and keeping up to date with crime trends, legislation and other information related to security services. Members can provide advice to each other either by the e-mail list, by arranging visits, or at regional meetings. They are also invited to attend and address the annual conference held at different universities within the UK and Ireland each spring.

Access to staff: Contact by e-mail

ASSOCIATION OF VETERINARY TEACHERS AND RESEARCH WORKERS (AVTRW)

Department of Agriculture for Northern Ireland, Veterinary Sciences Division, Stoney Road, Stormont, Belfast, BT4 3SD

Tel: 02890 525606
Fax: 02890 525754
E-mail: john.mcevoy@dardni.gov.uk
Website: www.avtrw.org.uk

Enquiries to: Honorary Secretary
Other contacts: Affiliated to British Veterinary Association

Founded: 1946

Organisation type and purpose: International organisation, professional body (membership is by subscription), present number of members: 850.

Subject coverage: Veterinary teaching and research.

Publications: Printed
Order printed publications from: UFAW
8 Hamilton Close, Potters Bar, Hertfordshire, EN6 3QD

Access to staff: Contact by letter, by telephone, by fax and by e-mail
Hours: Mon to Fri, 0900 to 1700

Affiliated to: British Veterinary Association; tel: 020 7636 6541; fax: 020 7436 2970; e-mail: bvahq@bva.co.uk

ASSOCIATION OF WHEELCHAIR CHILDREN (AWC)

6 Woodman Parade, North Woolwich, London, E16 2LL

Tel: 0844 544 1050
Fax: 0844 544 1055
E-mail: headoffice@wheelchairchildren.org.uk
Website: www.wheelchairchildren.org.uk

Enquiries to: Fundraising Co-ordinator
Direct tel: 0870 121 0053
Direct fax: 0870 121 0051

Founded: 1990

Organisation type and purpose: Registered charity (charity number 1057894).
To provide expert training and advice for wheelchair-using children throughout the UK, to help them become more independently mobile, both in the home and out of doors.

Subject coverage: Information, support and training for children in wheelchairs throughout the UK.

Publications: Printed

Access to staff: Contact by letter, by telephone, by fax, by e-mail, in person and via website
Hours: Mon to Fri, 0900 to 1700
Special comments: First floor office.

National Headquarters at: Association of Wheelchair Children; 6 Woodman Parade, North Woolwich, London, E16 2LL; tel: 0870 121 0050; fax: 0870 121 0051; e-mail: hq@awc.btinternet.com

ASSOCIATION OF WOMEN BARRISTERS (AWB)

Administrator, General Council of The Bar, 2–3 Cursitor Street, London, EC4A 1NE

Tel: 020 7242 1289
Fax: 020 7242 1107
E-mail: jbradley@barcouncil.org.uk
Website: www.womenbarristers.co.uk

Enquiries to: Chairwoman
Direct e-mail: alcqc@hotmail.com
Other contacts: Administrator for contact details.

Founded: 1991

Organisation type and purpose: National organisation, membership association (membership is by subscription), present number of members: c. 500.

Subject coverage: Women barristers.

Publications: Electronic and video
Order printed publications from: Administrator

Publications list: Available online

Access to staff: Contact by letter, by telephone, by e-mail and via website
Hours: Mon to Fri, 0900 to 1700
Special comments: Personal visits not recommended to Administrator's office.

ASSOCIATION OF YOUNG PEOPLE WITH ME (AYME)

10 Vermont Place, Tongwell, Milton Keynes, MK15 8JA

Tel: 08451 232389
E-mail: info@ayme.org.uk
Website: www.ayme.org.uk

Enquiries to: CEO

Founded: 1995

Organisation type and purpose: National organisation, membership association (membership is by qualification), present number of members: 3,500, registered charity (charity number 1082059).

Subject coverage: Advice and information for young people with ME / CFS aged 0 to 25 years and their families.

Publications: Printed

Publications list: Available online and in print

Access to staff: Contact by letter, by telephone, by fax, by e-mail, in person and via website
Hours: Mon to Fri, 1000 to 1400

Access to building: No prior appointment required
Hours: Mon to Fri, 1000 to 1400

Access for disabled people: Parking provided, toilet facilities

ASTA BEAB CERTIFICATION SERVICES

Intertek House, Cleeve Road, Leatherhead, Surrey, KT22 7SB

Tel: 01372 370900
Fax: 01372 370999
E-mail: info@beab.co.uk
Website: www.uk.intertek-etlsemko.com/

Enquiries to: Administrative Officer

Founded: 2004; created by the merger of the Association of Short-circuit Testing Authorities (ASTA) and the British Electrotechnical Approvals Board (BEAB)

Organisation type and purpose: Trade association.

Subject coverage: Safeguarding and protection of the public by testing and approving electrical appliances and electrotechnical equipment to British Standards.

Publications: Printed

Publications list: Available online and in print

Access to staff: Contact by letter, by telephone, by fax, by e-mail and via website. Appointment necessary.
Hours: Mon to Thu, 0900 to 1700; Fri, 0900 to 1630

Constituent part of: Intertek Testing Services (ITS)

ASTHMA UK

Summit House, 70 Wilson Street, London, EC2A 2DB

Tel: 020 7786 4900
Fax: 020 7256 6075
E-mail: info@asthma.org.uk
Website: www.asthma.org.uk

Enquiries to: Supporter Care Team
Direct tel: 0800 121 62 55
Direct fax: 020 7256 6075
Direct e-mail: info@asthma.org.uk

Founded: 1927

Organisation type and purpose: Membership association (membership is by subscription), voluntary organisation, registered charity (charity number 802364). Provides information, advice and support to people with asthma and their carers; provides funding for research into asthma and related allergies.

Subject coverage: Asthma, medication, anyone involved, e.g. people with asthma, family, health professionals.

Publications: Printed, and electronic and video
Order printed publications from: Website

Publications list: Available online and in print

Access to staff: Contact by letter, by telephone, by fax and by e-mail
Hours: Helpline only: 0900 to 1900

Access to building: No access other than to staff

Also at: Asthma UK Cymru; 3rd floor, Eastgate House, 35–43 Newport Road, Cardiff, CF24 0AB; tel: 029 2043 5400; Asthma UK Northern Ireland; Ground floor, Unit 2, College House, City Link Business Park, Durham Street, Belfast, BT12 4HQ; tel: 0800 151 3035; Asthma UK Scotland; 4 Queen Street, Edinburgh, EH2 1JE; tel: 0131 226 2544; fax: 0131 226 2401

ASTON MARTIN OWNERS CLUB LIMITED (AMOC)

Drayton St Leonard, Wallingford, Oxfordshire, OX10 7BG

Tel: 01865 400400
Fax: 01865 400200
E-mail: hqstaff@amoc.org
Website: www.amoc.org

Enquiries to: Secretary
Direct tel: 01865 891831
Direct e-mail: secretary@amoc.org

Founded: 1935

Organisation type and purpose:
International organisation, membership association (membership is by subscription), present number of members: 5,000.
To provide for the needs and interests of owners of Aston Martin cars.

Subject coverage: Aston Martin history, technical information.

Collection: Large archive of material relating to Aston Martins including: drawings for pre-war cars; racing history; brochures; etc

Publications: Printed

Access to staff: Contact by letter, by telephone, by fax, by e-mail and via website. Appointment necessary. Non-members charged.
Hours: Mon to Fri, 0900 to 1700

Access to building: *Special comments:* Wed afternoon, open to public

ASTON UNIVERSITY, LIBRARY & INFORMATION SERVICES

Library & Information Services, Aston Triangle, Birmingham, B4 7ET

Tel: 0121 204 3000
Fax: 0121 204 4530
E-mail: library@aston.ac.uk
Website: library.aston.ac.uk
Website: www.aston.ac.uk/lis/general.htm
Website: www.aston.ac.uk/lis/

Enquiries to: Enquiries
Direct tel: 0121 204 4525

Founded: 1895

Organisation type and purpose: University Library.

Subject coverage: Applied psychology, environmental health, ophthalmic optics, sociology and social history, political and economics studies, environmental planning and design, biological sciences, chemistry and chemical engineering, computer studies, electrical and electronic engineering, languages and linguistics, management, mathematics, mechanical engineering, pharmacy and pharmacology, production technology, international business and company information.

Library catalogue: All or part available online

Publications: Printed

Access to staff: Contact by e-mail and via website. Access for members only.
Hours: Term time: service hours; Mon, Tue, Thu, 0900 to 1800; Wed, 1000 to 1800; Fri, 0900 to 1700; Sat, 1000 to 1300; reference hours are longer
Vacations: Mon to Fri, 0900 to 1700
For full details – see website at http://www.aston.ac.uk/lis
Special comments: An access control system is in use, for details see website at http://www.aston.ac.uk/lis
Non-members of the university can use printed resources only.

ASTRA ZENECA UK LIMITED

Brixham Environmental Laboratory, Freshwater Quarry, Brixham, Devon, TQ5 8BA

Tel: 01803 882882
Fax: 01803 882974
Website: www.brixham.astrazeneca.com

Enquiries to: Marketing Officer
Direct e-mail: neil.mccrae@astrazeneca.com

History of institution: formerly called ICI Brixham Laboratory; formerly called ICI Group Environmental Laboratory (year of change 1993); formerly called Brixham Environmental Laboratory, Zeneca (year of change 2000)

Organisation type and purpose: Research organisation.
Company Laboratory of Zeneca Limited providing a service to Zeneca business and external clients.

Subject coverage: Ecology, effluents, environment and environmental sciences, estuaries, marine sciences, mathematics, oceanography, hydrology, waste treatment, toxicology, environmental assessment, groundwater monitoring.

Collection: Ray Society publications

Non-library collection catalogue: All or part available online

Library catalogue: All or part available in-house

Publications: Printed

Publications list: Available online

Access to staff: Contact by letter, by telephone, by fax, by e-mail and via website. All charged.
Hours: Mon to Fri, 0900 to 1700

ASTROLOGICAL ASSOCIATION, THE (AA)

BCM 450, London, WC1N 3XX

Tel: 0208 625 0098
E-mail: office@astrologicalassociation.com
Website: www.astrologicalassociation.com

Enquiries to: Media Enquiries
Direct e-mail: media@astrologicalassociation.com

Founded: 1958

Organisation type and purpose:
International organisation, membership association (membership is by subscription), present number of members: 1600, voluntary organisation, suitable for ages: all.
To give out information on astrology. To inform members of current trends and developments. A forum for the exchange of astrological research.

Subject coverage: Astrology, history of astrology, historical studies, research practice, data collection of natal data on famous and infamous.

Publications: Printed, and electronic and video

Access to staff: Contact by letter, by telephone, by fax, by e-mail and via website. Non-members charged.
Hours: Mon, Tue, Wed, Fri, 1100 to 1700; closed Thu

ASUCPLUS (ASUC)

Kingsley House, Ganders Business Park, Kingsley, Bordon, Hampshire, GU35 9LU

Tel: 01420 471613
Fax: 01420 471611
E-mail: admin@asuc.org.uk
Website: www.asuc.org.uk

Enquiries to: Secretary

Founded: 1992

Organisation type and purpose: Trade association, present number of members: 21.
Members are specialists in subsidence repair techniques and engineered foundation solutions, including new-build foundations and basement development.

Subject coverage: Subsidence repair, foundations.

Access to staff: Contact by letter, by telephone, by fax, by e-mail and via website
Hours: Mon to Fri, 0900 to 1700

ATAXIA UK

Lincoln House, Kennington Business Park, 1–3 Brixton Road, London, SW9 6DE

Tel: 020 7582 1444
Fax: 020 7582 9444
E-mail: office@ataxia.org.uk
Website: www.ataxia.org.uk

Enquiries to: Administrator
Direct e-mail: cmcgowan@ataxia.org.uk

Founded: 1964; formerly called Friedreich's Ataxia Group (FAG) (year of change 2001)

Organisation type and purpose: Registered charity (charity number 102391).
Helpline, limited welfare grants for those who have ataxia, local branches, contacts and meetings.
To raise money for research into ataxias and to provide information, advice and support to sufferers and their families, carers, professionals, and the general public.

continued overleaf

Subject coverage: Ataxias, Friedreich's, Cerebellar and other diseases of the nervous system, beginning in childhood or early adulthood, research projects funded by the Group, management and care of sufferers.

Publications: Printed, and electronic and video

Publications list: Available online and in print

Access to staff: Contact by letter, by telephone, by fax, by e-mail and via website
Hours: Mon to Fri, 0900 to 1700
Special comments: Answerphone available out of office hours.

Branches: 40 local branches throughout the UK

ATHENAEUM LIVERPOOL

The Athenaeum, Church Alley, Liverpool, L1 3DD

Tel: 0151 709 7770
Fax: 0151 709 0418
E-mail: library@theathenaeum.org.uk
Website: www.theathenaeum.org.uk

Enquiries to: Librarian

Founded: 1797

Organisation type and purpose: Membership association (membership is by subscription, election or invitation), present number of members: 543.

Subject coverage: General collection: Merseyside, Lancashire and Cheshire, including maps, views, playbills. Genealogy, 19th-century economic pamphlets, 18th-century individual plays, natural history.

Collection: 18th-century plays
Blanco White and South American Collection
Eshelby Collection
Genealogy
Jackson pamphlets
Liverpool playbills
Robert Gladstone pamphlets and 17th-century law
Roscoe Collection
Teignmouth Bibles
Topography
Yorkshire history

Non-library collection catalogue: All or part available in-house and in print

Library catalogue: All or part available in-house

Publications: Printed, and microform publications

Access to staff: Contact by letter, by telephone, by fax, by e-mail, in person and via website. Appointment necessary. Letter of introduction required.
Hours: Members: 0900 to 1600; others: Tue to Thu, 1300 to 1600

ATLANTIC SALMON TRUST LIMITED (AST)

Suite 3/11, King James VI Business Centre, Friarton Road, Perth, PH2 8DG

Tel: 01738 472032
E-mail: director@atlanticsalmontrust.org
Website: www.atlanticsalmontrust.org

Enquiries to: Trust Administrator
Direct e-mail: marjorie@atlanticsalmontrust.org

Founded: 1967; formed from Atlantic Salmon Research Trust (ASRT) (year of change 1980)

Organisation type and purpose: Voluntary organisation.
Conservation and enhancement of stocks of wild Atlantic salmon and sea trout.

Subject coverage: Wild Atlantic salmon and sea trout management and conservation.

Publications: Printed

Publications list: Available in print

Access to staff: Contact by letter, by telephone, by fax and by e-mail. Appointment necessary.
Hours: Mon to Fri, 0830 to 1630

Associated with: Association Internationale de Défense du Saumon Atlantique (France); International Atlantic Salmon Foundation (Canada); tel: 00 1 506 529 4581; fax: 00 1 506 529 4438

ATOMIC WEAPONS ESTABLISHMENT (AWE)

Aldermaston, Reading, Berkshire, RG7 4PR

Tel: 0118 981 4111
Fax: 0118 981 5320
E-mail: enquiries@awe.co.uk
Website: www.awe.co.uk

Enquiries to: Librarian
Direct tel: 0118 982 5722
Direct e-mail: library@awe.co.uk

History of institution: formerly called Atomic Weapons Research Establishment (AWRE)

Organisation type and purpose: Research organisation.

Subject coverage: Science, technology and engineering supporting the Company's programme.

Library catalogue: All or part available in-house

Access to staff: Contact by telephone and by e-mail. Appointment necessary.
Hours: Mon to Fri, 0830 to 1600

Access to building: Prior appointment required

Access for disabled people: Parking provided, ramped entry

ATTEND

The King's Fund, 11–13 Cavendish Square, London, W1G 0AN

Tel: 0845 4500285
Fax: 0207 307 2571
E-mail: info@attend.org.uk
Website: www.attend.org.uk

Enquiries to: Chief Executive
Other contacts: Communications Officer (for general external enquiries)

Founded: 1949; formerly called National Association of Hospital and Community Friends (year of change 2006)

Organisation type and purpose: National organisation, membership association (membership is by subscription), present number of members: 700, voluntary organisation, registered charity (charity number 5713403).

Subject coverage: Volunteering in the health sector. Legal, financial and general advice relating to running Friends' charities in hospital or the community.

Information services: Information and advice to members on volunteer-related issues.

Education services: Attend Academy provides accredited qualifications in volunteer management and courses in volunteer-related issues.

Services for disabled people: Attend ABI supports people with Acquired Brain Injury back into work, volunteering or education.

Collection: Archive information available relating to the history of the National Association of Hospital and Community Friends

Non-library collection catalogue: All or part available in-house

Publications: Printed

Publications list: Available online and in print

Access to staff: Contact by letter, by telephone, by fax, by e-mail, in person and via website. Appointment necessary.
Hours: Mon to Fri, 0900 to 1700

Access to building: Prior appointment required

Access for disabled people: Parking provided, ramped entry, access to all public areas, toilet facilities

Member organisations: 700 independent affiliated health and social care charities across the UK

AUDAX UNITED KINGDOM (AUK)

8 Nap View, Awliscombe, Honiton, Devon, EX14 3PL

Tel: 01404 46588 (day)
Fax: 01404 46501
E-mail: ian@audax.uk.net
Website: www.audax.uk.net/cal/
Website: www.audax.uk.net/faq.htm
Website: www.audax.uk.net

Enquiries to: Honorary Secretary

Founded: 1976

Organisation type and purpose: National organisation, membership association (membership is by subscription), present number of members: 3,800.
Produces calendars of, validates and keeps records of long-distance cycle rides registered as Brevets de Randonneurs.

Subject coverage: Calendar of Brevets de Randonneurs cycling events in the UK; links to international events and cycling-related information.

Collection: Results of successful Brevets de Randonneurs cycle rides in the UK from 1987

Trade and statistical information: 365 events of between 50 and 1,400 km calendared in 2001, in the UK, with 14,000 successful riders

Non-library collection catalogue: All or part available in-house

Publications: Printed
Order printed publications from: Audax United Kingdom
10 Huntingdon Drive, The Park, Nottingham, NG7 1BW, e-mail: young@lineone.net

Access to staff: Contact by letter, by telephone, by fax, by e-mail and via website
Hours: Mon to Fri, 0900 to 1700

Affiliated with: The Cyclist Touring Club

Associated with: Audax Club Parisien

Member of: Les Randonneurs Mondiaux

AUDIO ENGINEERING SOCIETY LTD (AES)

PO Box 645, Slough, SL1 8BJ

Tel: 01628 663725
E-mail: uk@aes.org
Website: www.aes.org

Enquiries to: Administrator

Founded: 1970

Organisation type and purpose:
International organisation, professional body.

Subject coverage: Audio engineering.

Collection: Society's Publications

Library catalogue: All or part available online

Publications: Printed

Publications list: Available online and in print

Access to staff: Contact by telephone and by e-mail
Hours: Mon to Fri, 0900 to 1700

Access to building: No access other than to staff

Affiliated to: Audio Engineering Society Inc; 60 East 42nd Street, New York, NY, 10165, USA; tel: +1 212 661 8528; fax: +1 212 682 0477; e-mail: hq@aes.org

AUDIO VISUAL ASSOCIATION (AVA)

156 High Street, Bushey, Watford, Hertfordshire, WD23 3HF

Tel: 020 8950 5959
Fax: 020 8950 7560

Enquiries to: Chairman

Founded: 1977

Organisation type and purpose:
Membership association.
To represent professionals involved in audiovisual, video and multimedia.

Subject coverage: Professional audiovisual up to broadcast standard including multimedia.

Access to staff: Contact by letter and by telephone
Hours: Mon to Fri, 0900 to 1700

Specialist interest group of the: British Institute of Professional Photography

AUDIT COMMISSION

1st Floor, Millbank Tower, Millbank, London, SW1P 4HQ

Tel: 0844 798 1212
Fax: 0844 798 2945
E-mail: audit-commission@audit-commission.gov.uk
Website: www.audit-commission.gov.uk

Enquiries to: Public enquiries team
Direct tel: 0844 798 3131
Direct e-mail: public-enquiries@audit-commission.gov.uk

Founded: 1982

Organisation type and purpose: Statutory body.

Subject coverage: Local government and health service.

Order printed publications from: Audit Commission, PO Box 3570, Dorcan Three Hundred, Murdock Road, Dorcan, Swindon, SN3 9AR.; tel: 0800 50 20 30; e-mail: ac-orders@audit-commission.gov.uk

Publications list: Available online

Access to staff: Contact by letter, by telephone, by fax, by e-mail and via website. Appointment necessary.
Hours: Mon to Fri, 0900 to 1700

AUSTIN 3 LITRE OWNERS' CLUB

78 Croft Street, Ipswich, Suffolk, IP2 8EF

Tel: 01473 684867
E-mail: n.kidby@virgin.net

Enquiries to: Secretary

Organisation type and purpose:
International organisation, membership association (membership is by subscription), present number of members: 45.
To provide a service to owners of 1967–1971 Austin 3 litre cars, provide bimonthly newsletter and a spares service.

Subject coverage: All mechanical information on Austin 3 litres, details of part numbers for spares, history of Austin 3 litres.

Collection: Selected archive material i.e. road tests, period advertisements, magazine articles

Publications: Printed

Access to staff: Contact by letter, by telephone and by fax. Appointment necessary.
Hours: Mon to Fri, 0900 to 2100

AUSTIN A40 FARINA CLUB

2 Ivy Cottages, Fullers Vale, Headley Down, Bordon, Hampshire, GU35 8NR

E-mail: thinton@surrart.ac.uk
Website: www.a40farinaclub.org

Enquiries to: Events and Publicity Officer
Direct tel: 01628 673472
Direct e-mail: the.minters@btopenworld.com

Founded: 1979

Organisation type and purpose:
Membership association.
Actively pursuing the recognition of the A40 in its true light and seeking to ensure its continuing place in the history of British motor cars.

Subject coverage: All aspects of the Austin A40 Farina MkI and MkII (1958–1967), including history, information, owners' register, technical advice.

Collection: Archives, books and magazines on the A40

Publications: Printed

Access to staff: Contact by letter, by e-mail and via website
Hours: Mon to Fri, 1800 to 2200; Sat, Sun, any reasonable time

Other addresses: Austin A40 Farina Club; 26 Wootton Way, Maidenhead, Berkshire, SL6 4QU; tel: 01628 673472; e-mail: the.minters@btopenworld.com; Austin A40 Farina Club; 75 Tennal Road, Harbourne, Birmingham, B32 2JB; Events & Publicity Officer; Membership Secretary

AUSTIN BIG SEVEN REGISTER

101 Derby Road, Chellaston, Derby, DE73 5SB

Enquiries to: Registrar

Founded: 1969

Organisation type and purpose:
Membership association.
Car club for 1937–39 Austin Big Seven.
To register all cars of this marque which have survived and are being restored or used.

Subject coverage: Technical information, advice and information, spares advice.

Collection: Books, documents, technical information, relating to 1937–39 Austin Big Sevens

Publications: Printed

Access to staff: Contact by letter and by telephone
Hours: Mon to Sat, 1800 to 2000

Member organisation of: Austin Seven Clubs Association; Federation of Austin Clubs, Registers and Associations; e-mail: austinfederation@aol.com; Federation of British Historic Motor Vehicle Clubs

AUSTIN CAMBRIDGE/ WESTMINSTER CAR CLUB (ACWCC)

26 Railton Jones Close, Stoke Gifford, South Gloucestershire, BS34 8BF

Tel: 0117 9314881
E-mail: acwcc@blueyonder.co.uk
Website: www.acwcc.org

Enquiries to: Information Officer

Founded: 1980

Organisation type and purpose:
International organisation, membership association (membership is by subscription), present number of members: 120.

continued overleaf

Subject coverage: Austin Cambridge 1954–69, Morris Oxford 1959–71, MG Magnette 1959–68, Riley 1959–69, Wolseley 1959–71, Austin Westminster 1954–68, 3L Austin 1968–71; spares, stockists, advice.

Publications: Printed

Access to staff: Contact by letter, by telephone and by e-mail
Hours: Mon to Fri, 0900 to 2100

AUSTIN MAXI CLUB

Formal name: Austin Maxi Owners Club

27 Queen Street, Bardney, Lincolnshire, LN3 5XF

Tel: 01526 398377
Fax: 01526 398377
Website: www.austinmaxiclub.org

Enquiries to: Membership Secretary

Founded: 1989

Organisation type and purpose: Membership association.

Subject coverage: Austin Maxi, its continuation of use, availability of spares.

Access to staff: Contact by letter
Hours: Mon to Fri, 0900 to 1700

AUSTRALASIAN PLANT SOCIETY (APS)

1 Iffin Cottages, Iffin Lane, Canterbury, Kent, CT4 7BE

Tel: 01227 780038
E-mail: secretary@anzplantsoc.org.uk
Website: www.anzplantsoc.org.uk

Enquiries to: Honorary Secretary
Direct e-mail: membership@anzplantsoc.org.uk

Founded: 1988; formerly called Australian Plant Society (year of change 1992)

Organisation type and purpose: National organisation (membership is by subscription), present number of members: 150.

Subject coverage: Details about wild plants of Australia and New Zealand.

Collection: Colour slides
Books about Antipodean plants

Non-library collection catalogue: All or part available in-house

Publications: Printed

Access to staff: Contact by letter, by telephone and by e-mail
Hours: Daily, 0900 to 1700

AUSTRALIA'S NORTHERN TERRITORY TOURIST COMMISSION (NTTC)

1st Floor, Beaumont House, Lambton Road, London, SW20 0LW

Tel: 020 8944 2992
Fax: 020 8944 2993

Enquiries to: Manager
Direct e-mail: fburrows@tourismnt.australia.com

Organisation type and purpose: Marketing office for Australia's Northern Territory.

Subject coverage: Holiday information for Australia's Northern Territory.

Publications: Printed, and electronic and video

Access to staff: Contact by letter, by telephone, by fax and by e-mail
Hours: Mon to Fri, 0900 to 1700
Special comments: Office not open to the general public.

Parent body: Northern Territory Tourist Commission; PO Box 1155, Darwin, NT 0801, Australia

AUSTRALIAN BUSINESS

Swire House, 59 Buckingham Gate, London, SW1E 6AJ

Tel: 0870 8900720
Fax: 020 7379 0721
E-mail: enquiries@australianbusiness.co.uk
Website: www.australianbusiness.co.uk

Enquiries to: Director

Organisation type and purpose: Membership association.

Subject coverage: Trade between Australia and New Zealand, and the UK.

Access to staff: Contact by fax and by e-mail. Non-members charged.
Hours: Mon to Fri, 0900 to 1700

AUSTRIAN CULTURAL FORUM (ACF)

28 Rutland Gate, London, SW7 1PQ

Tel: 020 7225 7300
Fax: 020 7225 0470
E-mail: office@acflondon.org
Website: www.acflondon.org

Enquiries to: Librarian
Direct e-mail: librarian@acflondon.org

Founded: 1956; formerly called Austrian Cultural Institute (ACI) (year of change 2001)

Organisation type and purpose: National government body.
Cultural affairs body.

Subject coverage: Cultural aspects of Austrian life.

Collection: Austrian studies

Non-library collection catalogue: All or part available in-house

Library catalogue: All or part available online

Publications: Printed

Access to staff: Contact by letter, by telephone and by e-mail. Appointment necessary.
Hours: Mon to Thu, 1430 to 1630 (library)

Access to building: via Rutland Gate
Hours: Mon to Thu, 1430 to 1630 (library)

Constituent part of: Austrian Embassy

AUSTRIAN EMBASSY

18 Belgrave Mews West, London, SW1X 8HU

Tel: 020 7344 3250
Fax: 020 7344 0292
E-mail: embassy@austria.org.uk
Website: www.austria.org.uk

Enquiries to: Information Officer
Other contacts: Consul General for consular matters.

Organisation type and purpose: Embassy and Consulate.

Subject coverage: General information on Austria, consular service, assistance to Austrian citizens living in the UK.

Collection: Information material (booklets, pamphlets etc.) available by letter or fax to the Information Officer

Library catalogue: All or part available in-house

Publications: Electronic and video

Access to staff: Contact by letter, by telephone, by fax, by e-mail, in person and via website. Appointment necessary.
Hours: Consulate: Mon to Fri, 0900 to 1200

Connections with: Austrian Cultural Forum; 28 Rutland Gate, London, SW7 1PQ; tel: 020 7584 8653; fax: 020 7225 0470; e-mail: culture@austria.org.uk; Austrian Trade Commission; 45 Princes Gate, Exhibition Road, London, SW7 2QA; tel: 020 7584 4411; fax: 020 7584 2565; e-mail: london@wko.at

Parent body: Austrian Federal Ministry of Foreign Affairs; Ballhausplatz 2, Wien, A-1014, Austria; tel: + 43 1 53115; website: http://www.bmaa.gv.at

AUTHORS' LICENSING & COLLECTING SOCIETY LIMITED (ALCS)

The Writers' House, 13 Haydon Street, London, EC3N 1DB

Tel: 020 7264 5700
Fax: 020 7264 5755
E-mail: alcs@alcs.co.uk
Website: www.alcs.co.uk

Enquiries to: Communications Manager

Founded: 1977

Organisation type and purpose: International organisation, membership association, present number of members: 18,000 full members, 35,000 associate members.
British collecting society for all writers. Ensures hard-to-collect revenues due to authors are efficiently collected and speedily distributed. Campaigns to raise awareness of copyright issues and authors' rights among writers.

Subject coverage: Database of film, broadcasting and literary information containing information on British writers and film and television works including foreign episode titles, details of daily programming in the United Kingdom and several other European Countries that relate to writers' works. Also a database of books holding details of works photocopied since licensing introduced in 1984. Information on literary estates and literary agents.

Publications: Printed

Access to staff: Contact by letter, by telephone, by fax, by e-mail and via website. Appointment necessary.
Hours: Mon to Fri, 0930 to 1750

Affiliations with: NUJ and other writers' organisations; Society of Authors; Writers Guild of Great Britain

Constituent member of: Copyright Licensing Agency (CLA); Educational Recording Agency (ERA)

Lead partner in: BCC; CISAC; EU Imprimatur Project; European Writers' Congress; IFRRO

AUTISM INDEPENDENT UK (SFTAH)

199–203 Blandford Avenue, Kettering, Northamptonshire, NN16 9AT

Tel: 01536 523274
Fax: 01536 523274
E-mail: autism@autismuk.com
Website: www.autismuk.com

Enquiries to: Chief Executive
Direct e-mail: keithlovett@ntlworld.com

Founded: 1987; formerly called Society for the Autistically Handicapped

Organisation type and purpose: National organisation, voluntary organisation, registered charity (charity number 803003), training organisation.

Subject coverage: Specialised information: autism, Asperger's Syndrome, education, care and treatment, training, statementing.

Library catalogue: All or part available online and in print

Publications: Printed

Publications list: Available online

Access to staff: Contact by letter, by telephone, by fax, by e-mail, in person and via website. Appointment necessary.
Hours: Every day, 0900 to 1700, answerphone at other times
Special comments: Appointments necessary for reference library.

Access to building: Prior appointment required

Access for disabled people: *Special comments:* One step

AUTO-CYCLE UNION (ACU)

ACU House, Wood Street, Rugby, CV21 2YX

Tel: 01788 566400
Fax: 01788 573585
E-mail: admin@acu.org.uk
Website: www.acu.org.uk

Enquiries to: General Secretary
Direct e-mail: gary@acu.org.uk

Founded: 1903; formerly called Auto-Cycle Club (year of change 1907)

Organisation type and purpose: The Governing Body for motorcycle sport throughout Britain.
To provide all participants in motorcycle sport with enjoyable, safe and competitive days of sporting action. Has over 630 clubs divided into 20 centres.

Subject coverage: The sport of motorcycling at all levels.

Publications: Electronic and video
Order electronic and video publications from: website

Access to staff: Contact by letter, by telephone, by fax and by e-mail

Member organisation of: Fédération Internationale de Motorcyclisme (FIM)

AUTOMATIC DOOR SUPPLIERS ASSOCIATION LIMITED (ADSA)

411 Limpsfield Road, Warlingham, Surrey, CR6 9HA

Tel: 01883 624961
Fax: 01883 626841
E-mail: admin@adsa.org.uk
Website: www.adsa.org.uk

Enquiries to: Office Manager

Founded: 1985

Organisation type and purpose: Trade association, consultancy.

Subject coverage: Supply/installation of automatic doors and the safety aspects of these.

Publications: Printed

Access to staff: Contact by letter, by telephone, by fax, by e-mail, in person and via website
Hours: Mon to Fri, 0900 to 1700

AUTOMATIC VENDING ASSOCIATION (AVA)

1 Villiers Court, 40 Upper Mulgrave Road, Cheam, Surrey, SM2 7AJ

Tel: 020 8661 1112
Fax: 020 8661 2224
Website: www.ava-vending.co.uk

Enquiries to: Director
Direct e-mail: janette@ava-vending.co.uk

Founded: 1929; formerly called Automatic Vending Association of Britain (AVAB) (year of change 2000)

Organisation type and purpose: Trade association.

Subject coverage: Availability and suitability of automatic vending machines systems for catering or retailing services, UK vending market, explaining refreshment vending.

Trade and statistical information: Size of the installed vending machine base and the products being sold through it, available as the AVA Census

Publications: Electronic and video

Publications list: Available online

Access to staff: Contact by letter, by telephone, by fax, by e-mail and via website
Hours: Mon to Fri, 0900 to 1700

Access for disabled people: Parking provided, level entry, toilet facilities

AUTOMOBILE ASSOCIATION (AA)

AA Press Office, Fanum House, Basing View, Basingstoke, RG21 4EA

Tel: 01256 495969
E-mail: press.office@theaa.com
Website: www.theaa.com

Enquiries to: Press Officer

Founded: 1905

Organisation type and purpose: Service industry.

Subject coverage: Motoring developments (non-commercial): technical, statistical, legislative, environmental and related transport and travel.

Collection: Archives of the Association from 1905

Access to staff: Contact by letter, by telephone and by e-mail
Hours: Mon to Fri, 0900 to 1700

AUTOMOTIVE DISTRIBUTION FEDERATION (ADF)

68 Coleshill Road, Hodge Hill, Birmingham, B36 8AB

Tel: 0121 784 3535
Fax: 0121 784 4411
E-mail: admin@adf.org.uk

Enquiries to: Secretary

Founded: 1930; formerly called Motor Factors Association (MFA) (year of change 1990)

Organisation type and purpose: Trade association (membership is by subscription), present number of members: 340 companies.
The Automotive Distribution Federation represents the opinions of manufacturers, importers and wholesale distributors (motor factors) of vehicle parts and accessories.

Subject coverage: Manufacturers, importers and wholesale distributors (motor factors) of vehicle parts and accessories.

Publications: Printed

Access to staff: Contact by letter, by telephone, by fax, by e-mail and via website. Appointment necessary.
Hours: Fri, 0900 to 1630

AUTOVIA CAR CLUB

43 Tilbury Road, Tilbury Juxta Clare, Halstead, Essex, CO9 4JJ

Tel: 01787 237676
E-mail: glthomas@gotadsl.co.uk

Enquiries to: Secretary

Founded: 1990

Organisation type and purpose: National organisation.

Subject coverage: Riley Autovia cars.

Access to staff: Contact by letter and by telephone
Hours: Mon to Fri, 0900 to 1700

AVERT

4 Brighton Road, Horsham, West Sussex, RH13 5BA

Tel: 01403 210202
Fax: 01403 211001
E-mail: info@avert.org
Website: www.avert.org

Enquiries to: Information Officer

Founded: 1986; formerly called Aids Education and Research Trust

Organisation type and purpose: Registered charity (charity number 1074849).

continued overleaf

To combat HIV and AIDS world-wide.

Subject coverage: HIV and AIDS information.

Collection: Reference library

Trade and statistical information: Statistics on epidemiology of HIV and AIDS in United Kingdom especially

Publications: Printed

Publications list: Available online and in print

Access to staff: Contact by letter, by telephone, by fax, by e-mail and via website
Hours: Mon to Fri, 0900 to 1700

Access to building: Prior appointment required
Hours: Mon to Fri, 0900 to 1700

Access for disabled people: Parking provided, ramped entry, level entry, access to all public areas, toilet facilities

AVIATION ENVIRONMENT FEDERATION (AEF)

Broken Wharf House, 2 Broken Wharf, London, EC4V 3DT

Tel: 020 7248 2223
Fax: 020 7329 8160
E-mail: info@aef.org.uk
Website: www.aef.org.uk
Website: www.aef.org.uk/publications.htm

Enquiries to: Information Officer

Founded: 1975; formerly called Airfields Environment Federation (year of change 1993)

Organisation type and purpose: National organisation, membership association (membership is by subscription), present number of members: 110, voluntary organisation, consultancy, research organisation.
Addresses all the environmental impacts of aircraft and aerodrome operations.

Subject coverage: Environmental and amenity effects and impacts of aviation.

Collection: Environmental statements
Industry and government reports
Papers, journals
Planning inquiry documents

Trade and statistical information: World data on the environmental performance of the aviation industry

Publications: Printed

Publications list: Available online and in print

Access to staff: Contact by letter, by telephone, by fax, by e-mail and via website. Appointment necessary. Non-members charged.
Hours: Mon to Fri, 0930 to 1630

Access to building: Prior appointment required

Co-ordinator of: Green Skies; tel: 020 7248 2223; e-mail: info@greenskies.org

Member organisation of: European Environment Bureau; Brussels, Belgium

AVON LOCAL HISTORY AND ARCHAEOLOGY (ALHA)

5 Parrys Grove, Bristol, BS9 1TT

Tel: 0117 968 4979
Fax: 0117 968 4979
E-mail: wm.evans@btopenworld.com
Website: www.avonlocalhistandarch.co.uk

Founded: 1976

Organisation type and purpose: Umbrella organisation for local groups and societies. County local history liaison.
Promotion of local history in the region and a co-ordinating forum.

Subject coverage: Local history and archaeology in Avon (Bristol and Bath) area; especially contacts and club collections.

Publications: Printed
Order printed publications from: mikeleigh@blueyonder.co.uk

Publications list: Available in print

Access to staff: Contact by letter, by telephone, by fax and by e-mail

Links with: some 80 affiliated groups and societies

AVON PARK INTERNATIONAL RACING ASSOCIATION (APIRA)

The Annex, Half Moon Farm, Rushall, Diss, Norfolk, IP21 4QD

Tel: 01379 740100
Fax: 01379 740100
E-mail: enquiries@shakespearecountyraceway.co.uk
Website: www.shakespearecountyraceway.com

Enquiries to: General Secretary
Direct fax: 01789 252030
Direct e-mail: wendy@shakespearecountyraceway.org.uk
Other contacts: Events Information and Race-Meetings Secretary; Membership Secretary

Founded: 1990; formerly called NDRC-NDRA

Organisation type and purpose: International organisation, membership association (membership is by subscription), present number of members: 350
Motor sports racing organisation for drag racing.

Subject coverage: Drag car racing covered by the Motorsport Association and the Auto Cycle Union.

Publications: Printed
Order printed publications from: LA Performance Services
60 Berry Road, Paignton, Devon, TQ3 3QJ, tel: 01803 554308, e-mail: la.racing@virgin.net

Publications list: Available online

Access to staff: Contact by letter, by telephone, by fax, by e-mail, in person and via website. Letter of introduction required.
Hours: Mon to Fri, 0900 to 1700

Access to building: No prior appointment required
Hours: Racing commences 1000 to 1800

Access for disabled people: Parking provided, level entry, access to all public areas, toilet facilities
Special comments: Viewing ramp for disabled wheelchair persons and their carers.

Affiliated to: Auto Cycle Union; ACU House, Wood Street, Rugby, Warwickshire, CV21 2YX; tel: 01788 566400; fax: 01788 573585; website: http://www.acu.org.uk
The Motor Sports Association (MSA); Motor Sports House, Riverside Park, Colnbrook, Slough, Berkshire, SL3 0HG; tel: 01753 681736; fax: 01753 682936; website: http://www.msauk.org

Track Owner: Avon Park International Racing Association; Airfield House, Long Marston, Stratford Upon Avon, Warwickshire, CV37 8LL; tel: 01789 414119; fax: 01789 262030; website: http://www.shakespearecountyraceway.org.uk

AWDURDOD PARC CENEDLAETHOL ERYRI / SNOWDONIA NATIONAL PARK AUTHORITY (APCE / SNPA)

Swyddfa'r Parc Cenedlaethol, Penrhyndeudraeth, Gwynedd, LL48 6LF

Tel: 01766 770274
Fax: 01766 771211
E-mail: parc@eryri-npa.gov.uk
Website: www.eryri-npa.gov.uk

Founded: 1951

Organisation type and purpose: Local government body.

Subject coverage: Farming; woodland management; ecology; planning; visitor services; conservation; demography; education; agriculture.

Publications: Printed, and microform publications

Access to staff: Contact by letter, by telephone, by fax, by e-mail and via website
Hours: Mon to Fri, 0900 to 1700

Access for disabled people: Parking provided, level entry, toilet facilities

AXISWEB

Formal name: Axis – the online resource for contemporary art

Studio 17/18, 46 The Calls, Leeds, LS2 7EY

Tel: 0113 2429830
E-mail: info@axisweb.org
Website: www.axisweb.org

Enquiries to: Projects Coordinator
Direct e-mail: ruth@axisweb.org

Founded: 1991; formerly called Axis – visual arts information service

Organisation type and purpose: Registered charity (charity number 10022841); online directory of UK contemporary visual artists and curators; contemporary art information service. Axis is a contemporary visual arts service that provides information about professional artists and curators living/working in the UK to a national and international audience.

Subject coverage: Directory of artists and curators, visual arts information service; featured artists, news and commentary about UK contemporary art.

Trade and statistical information: Online directory of UK contemporary visual artists and curators

Non-library collection catalogue: All or part available online

Access to staff: Contact by letter, by telephone, by fax, by e-mail, in person and via website. Appointment necessary.
Hours: Mon to Fri, 0900 to 1700

Access to building: *Hours:* Mon to Fri, 0900 to 1700

Access for disabled people: Mon to Fri, 0900 to 1700
Hours: Mon to Fri, 0900 to 1700

Funded by: Arts Council England; website: http://www.artscouncil.org.uk
The Arts Council of Wales; website: http://www.artswales.org.uk

AXREM

Formal name: Association of Healthcare Technology Providers for Imaging, Radiotherapy and Care

Broadwall House, 21 Broadwall, London, SE1 9PL

Tel: 020 7207 9660
Fax: 020 7642 8096
E-mail: peter.lawson@axrem.org.uk
Website: www.axrem.org.uk/

Enquiries to: Director

Organisation type and purpose: Trade association.

Subject coverage: Commerce and technology of the medical diagnostic imaging and radio-therapy equipment.

AYRSHIRE CATTLE SOCIETY OF GREAT BRITAIN AND IRELAND

17 Barns Street, Ayr, Scotland, KA7 1XB

Tel: 01292 267123
Fax: 01292 611973
E-mail: society@ayrshirescs.org
Website: www.ayrshirescs.org

Enquiries to: General Manager

Founded: 1877

Organisation type and purpose:
International organisation, advisory body, membership association (membership is by subscription), present number of members: 1,000, registered charity (charity number SC007015).
Breed Society.

Subject coverage: Ayrshire cattle breeding and pedigrees; production records; linear type evaluations; AI use with Ayrshire cattle; livestock pedigree record systems.

Collection: Books, microfilm and tape journals since 1923
Herd books since 1877

Publications: Printed

Access to staff: Contact by letter, by telephone, by fax, by e-mail and via website. Appointment necessary.
Hours: Mon to Fri, 0900 to 1700

Affiliated to: World Federation of Ayrshire Breed Societies

A|D|S GROUP LTD (A|D|S)

Salamanca Square, 9 Albert Embankment, London, SE1 7SP

Tel: 0207 091 4500
Fax: 0207 091 4545
E-mail: enquiries@adsgroup.org.uk
Website: www.adsgroup.org.uk

Enquiries to: Director – Overseas and Exports
Direct tel: 01428 602622
Direct fax: 01428 602628
Direct e-mail: b.salzmann@the-dma.org.uk

History of institution: created by the merger of Association of Police and Public Security Suppliers (APPSS), the Defence Manufacturers Association (DMA) and the Society of British Aerospace Companies (SBAC)

Organisation type and purpose: The trade organisation advancing UK aeroSpace, defence and security industries, with Farnborough International Limited as a wholly-owned subsidiary. A|D|S also encompasses the British Aviation Group (BAG).

Collection: Deso publications
A|D|S publications
Exhibition catalogues
Foreign industry directories
Many Jane's books
Several defence periodicals
Library of Information maintained

Trade and statistical information: Some data on the UK defence industry and export markets

Library catalogue: All or part available in-house

Publications: Printed

Publications list: Available in print

Access to staff: Contact by letter, by telephone, by fax, by e-mail and via website. Appointment necessary.
Hours: Mon to Fri, 0900 to 1730

Access to building: No prior appointment required

BACH CHOIR, THE

The Bach Choir, PO Box 61756, London SW1H 0UZ

Tel: 020 8742 3661
Fax: 020 8742 3661
E-mail: genman@thebachchoir.org.uk
Website: www.thebachchoir.org.uk

Enquiries to: General Manager
Direct e-mail: pr@thebachchoir.org.uk

Founded: 1876

Organisation type and purpose:
Membership association (membership is by subscription, qualification), present number of members: 250, registered charity (charity number 238287).
Choral Society.

Subject coverage: The performance of choral music.

Access to staff: Contact by letter, by telephone, by fax and by e-mail. Appointment necessary. Letter of introduction required.
Hours: Mon to Fri, 0900 to 1700

BACKCARE

16 Elmtree Road, Teddington, Middlesex, TW11 8ST

Tel: 020 8977 5474, 0845 130 2704 (Helpline)
Fax: 020 8943 5318
E-mail: info@backcare.org.uk
Website: www.backcare.org.uk

Enquiries to: Communications Manager

Founded: 1968; formerly called Back Pain Association (BPA); formerly called National Back Pain Association (NBPA) (year of change 1999)

Organisation type and purpose: Advisory body, membership association, voluntary organisation, registered charity (charity number 256751).
Charity dedicated to educating people on how to avoid preventable back pain, and supporting those living with back pain.
Research.

Subject coverage: Back pain, encouragement of research into causes and treatment, prevention of damage by proper use of the body, formation of branches to inform and aid people with back pain.

Publications: Printed, and electronic and video

Publications list: Available online and in print

Access to staff: Contact by letter, by telephone, by fax, by e-mail and via website
Hours: Mon to Fri, 0900 to 1700

BACKPACKERS CLUB

49 Lyndhurst Road, Exmouth, Devon, EX8 3DS

Tel: 01395 265159
E-mail: wjbeed@genie.co.uk
Website: www.catan.demon.co.uk/backpack/

Enquiries to: General Secretary

Founded: 1972

Organisation type and purpose: National organisation, membership association (membership is by subscription).
Leisure, camping club.

Subject coverage: Specialist organisation for lightweight camping, catering for walkers, cyclists and canoeists (national/international).

Collection: Extensive Club Library of camping books and walking guides

Library catalogue: All or part available in-house

Publications: Printed, and electronic and video

Access to staff: Contact by letter and by telephone
Hours: Mon to Fri, 0900 to 1700 and answerphone

BACTA

Formal name: British Amusement Catering Trades Association

134–136 Buckingham Palace Road, London, SW1W 9SA

Tel: 020 7730 6444
Fax: 020 7730 8103
E-mail: info@bacta.org.uk

Enquiries to: Public Relations Manager
Direct tel: 020 7841 3234

Founded: 1974

Organisation type and purpose: Trade association.
Represents Britain's pay-to-play leisure machines industry.

Subject coverage: Manufacture and operation of coin-operated leisure machines.

Trade and statistical information: Data on pay-to-play leisure machines

Publications: Printed

Access to staff: Contact by letter, by telephone, by fax and by e-mail
Hours: Mon to Fri, 0900 to 1700

Access to building: No prior appointment required

Links with: Euromat; National Amusements Council

BACUP NATURAL HISTORY SOCIETY (BACUP 'NAT')

24 Yorkshire Street, Bacup, Lancashire, OL13 8AE

E-mail: bacupnatural@gmail.com

Enquiries to: General Secretary
Direct tel: 01706 873042
Other contacts: Museum Curator, tel: 01706 873961

Founded: 1878

Organisation type and purpose: Learned society (membership is by subscription), present number of members: 70, voluntary organisation, registered charity, museum.

Subject coverage: Natural history – flora, fauna, fossils, local history and domestic bygones.

Collection: Library of over 2,000 books
Copies of Bacup newspapers from 1863
Some 4,000 photographs of old Bacup and its mills, houses, farms, churches, public houses etc

Non-library collection catalogue: All or part available in-house

Library catalogue: All or part available in-house

Access to staff: Contact by letter and in person
Hours: Mon to Fri, 0900 to 1700

Has a section: Bacup Camera Club; at the same address

BADMINTON ENGLAND

Formal name: Badminton Association of England Ltd

National Badminton Centre, Bradwell Road, Loughton Lodge, Milton Keynes, Buckinghamshire, MK8 9LA

Tel: 01908 268400
Fax: 01908 268412
E-mail: enquiries@badmintonengland.co.uk
Website: www.badmintonengland.co.uk

Other contacts: Press Officer

Founded: 1893

Organisation type and purpose:
Professional body.
Governing body of the sport of badminton in England.

Subject coverage: Badminton: rules-regulations, courts, lighting, playing facilities, shuttles, coaching, events, championships, players, general information.

Collection: A number of historic books on badminton

Publications: Printed, and electronic and video

Publications list: Available online and in print

Access to staff: Contact by letter, by telephone, by fax, by e-mail and in person. Appointment necessary.
Hours: Mon to Thu, 0900 to 1700; Fri, 0900 to 1530

Affiliated to: British Olympic Association; Central Council of Physical Recreation; Commonwealth Games Council; European Badminton Union; tel: + 49 2151 503020; fax: + 49 2151 503111; e-mail: ebu.gen.sec@t-online.de; International Badminton Federation; tel: 00603 92837 155; e-mail: info@intbadfed.org; Sport England

BADMINTONSCOTLAND

Formal name: Scottish Badminton Union Ltd

The Cockburn Centre, 40 Bogmoor Place, Glasgow, G51 4TQ

Tel: 0141 445 1218
Fax: 0141 425 1218
E-mail: enquiries@badmintonscotland.org.uk
Website: www.badmintonscotland.org.uk

Founded: 1911

Organisation type and purpose: Governing body of the sport of badminton in Scotland.

Publications: Printed

Access to staff: Contact by letter, by telephone, by e-mail and via website
Hours: Mon to Fri, 0900 to 1700

Access to building: Prior appointment required

BAE SYSTEMS

Eastwood House , Glebe Road Chelmsford, Essex, CM1 1QW United Kingdom

Tel: +44 (0) 1245 702702
Fax: +44 (0) 1245 702700
E-mail: arthur.jones@baesystems.com

Enquiries to: Senior Information Officer
Direct tel: 01245 242394
Direct e-mail: baddow.library@baesystems.com

History of institution: formerly called GEC Marconi Research Centre, Marconi Research Centre

Organisation type and purpose: Manufacturing industry, research organisation.

Subject coverage: Electronics, communications, radar, avionics, antennas, microwave research, remote sensing, radio propagation.

Library catalogue: All or part available in-house

Access to staff: Contact by letter, by telephone, by fax and by e-mail
Hours: Mon to Fri, 0900 to 1600

Access to building: Prior appointment required

BALINT SOCIETY

Tollgate Health Centre, 220 Tollgate Road, London, E6 5JS

Tel: 020 7439 9399
Fax: 020 7473 9388
E-mail: david.watt7@nhs.net
Website: www.balint.co.uk

Enquiries to: Honorary Secretary

Founded: 1969

Organisation type and purpose: Learned society, professional body, registered charity, training organisation, research organisation.

Subject coverage: Research and education on the doctor-patient relationship.

Collection: Balint Archives

Publications: Printed

Access to staff: Contact by letter, by telephone, by fax and by e-mail
Hours: Mon to Fri, 0900 to 1700

Links with: International Balint Federation; e-mail: info@balintinternational.com; website: http://www.balintinternational.com/

BALLIOL COLLEGE LIBRARY

Balliol College, Oxford, OX1 3BJ

Tel: 01865 277709
Fax: 01865 277803
E-mail: library@balliol.ox.ac.uk
Website: www.balliol.ox.ac.uk/library

Enquiries to: Librarian
Direct tel: 01865 277770

Founded: 1263

Organisation type and purpose: College of University of Oxford

Subject coverage: Information relating to collections.

Collection: Archives
Early printed books
Mediaeval manuscripts
Modern manuscripts
Special collections relating to history of Balliol and to former members

Non-library collection catalogue: All or part available online, in-house and in print

Library catalogue: All or part available online and in-house

Publications: Printed, and microform publications

Access to staff: Contact by letter, by e-mail and via website. Appointment necessary.
Hours: Mon to Fri, 0900 to 1700

BALTIC EXCHANGE

38 St Mary Axe, London, EC3A 8BH

Tel: 020 7623 5501
Fax: 020 7369 1622
E-mail: enquiries@balticexchange.com
Website: www.balticexchange.com

Enquiries to: Chief Executive
Other contacts: Development Manager for membership, marketing, press and PR.

Founded: 1900

Organisation type and purpose:
International organisation, professional body, trade association, membership association (membership is by subscription), present number of members: 700 corporate. Shipping Exchange.
To match bulk ships and bulk cargoes, and to buy and sell bulk vessels.

Subject coverage: Shipping, including chartering, freight rates, sale and purchase of ships.

Trade and statistical information: Four daily bulk shipping indices and daily market reports

Publications: Printed

Access to staff: Contact by letter, by telephone, by fax, by e-mail and via website. Appointment necessary.
Hours: Mon to Fri, 0900 to 1700

BANGOR UNIVERSITY – ARCHIVES DEPARTMENT

College Road, Bangor, Gwynedd, LL57 2DG

Tel: 01248 382966
Fax: 01248 382979
E-mail: e.w.thomas@bangor.ac.uk
Website: www.archiveshub.ac.uk
Website: www.bangor.ac.uk/is/library/archives.html

Enquiries to: Archivist

Founded: 1884

Organisation type and purpose: University library.
Archives Department within University Library.

Subject coverage: University of Wales, Bangor; North Wales – history, people, topography; estate and family papers from counties of Anglesey, Caernarfon, Flint, Denbigh and Merioneth. Subject areas include: literary, historical and antiquarian manuscripts; industrial and business enterprises records e.g. mines and quarries; records of religious and educational bodies; records of ownership of land and property; personal and family archives; farming and agricultural records; records of a political nature; genealogical records; records of plantations in Jamaica and the West Indies; hunting records.

Non-library collection catalogue: All or part available in-house

Library catalogue: All or part available online

Access to staff: Contact by letter, by telephone, by fax, by e-mail and in person
Hours: Mon to Fri, 0900 to 1300 and 1400 to 1700

BANGOR UNIVERSITY – LIBRARY AND ARCHIVE SERVICE (PBU)

College Road, Bangor, Gwynedd, LL57 2DG

Tel: 01248 382981
Fax: 01248 382979
E-mail: library@bangor.ac.uk
Website: www.bangor.ac.uk/library

Enquiries to: University Librarian
Direct tel: 01248 383772
Direct fax: 01248 382979
Direct e-mail: isse04@bangor.ac.uk
Other contacts: Library Administrator

History of institution: formerly called Bangor University College of North Wales Library (year of change 1997)

Organisation type and purpose: University library service

Subject coverage: Accountancy, banking, finance, administration and social policy, environmental planning, leisure and tourism, communication and media studies; agriculture and forest studies, biological sciences, chemistry; education, ITT – primary and secondary; electronic engineering and computing systems; English and linguistics; health and physical education; health and midwifery, radiography; history, Welsh history, archaeology; mathematics; modern languages (French, German, Spanish, Russian, Italian); music; ocean studies; psychology; sociology, social policy, criminology; theology and religious studies; Welsh and Celtic language, literature and traditions.

Collection: Archive of Welsh Music
Bangor Cathedral Library (on deposit)
Frank Brangwyn Collection
G S Evans Collection of botanical materials
Local (North Wales) estate records
Welsh material (particularly historical, religious, literary; printed and manuscript)

Non-library collection catalogue: All or part available in-house

Library catalogue: All or part available online

Access to staff: Contact by letter, by telephone, by fax, by e-mail, in person and via website
Hours: Hours vary from library to library, please phone or see web pages

Access to building: No prior appointment required

Other addresses: Deinol Library; Adeilad Deiniol, Deiniol Road, Bangor, Gwynedd, LL57 2UX; tel: 01248 382963; fax: 01248 383826; e-mail: library@bangor.ac.uk; Fron Heulog Library (School of Healthcare Sciences); Ffriddoedd Road, Bangor, Gwynedd, LL57 2EF; tel: 01248 383131; e-mail: library@bangor.ac.uk; Normal Library; Ffordd Caergybi, Bangor, Gwynedd, LL57 2PX; tel: 01248 383048; fax: 01248 383976; e-mail: library@bangor.ac.uk; Wrexham Maelor Library (School of Healthcare Sciences); School of Healthcare Sciences, Archimedes Centre, Technology Park, Wrexham, Clwyd, LL13 7YP; tel: 01978 316370; fax: 01978 311154; e-mail: library@bangor.ac.uk

BANK OF ENGLAND

Information Centre, Threadneedle Street, London, EC2R 8AH

Tel: 020 7601 4715
Fax: 020 7601 4356
E-mail: informationcentre@bankofengland.co.uk
Website: www.bankofengland.co.uk

Enquiries to: Information Centre Manager

Founded: 1694

Organisation type and purpose: Central bank.

Subject coverage: UK and overseas banking and financial economics, history of British banking, banking and monetary statistical data, central banking.

Collection: 19th-century government reports on banking and finance
Acts of Parliament from 1693
Collections include United Kingdom 17th- to 19th-century economic tracts
Sets include:
The Course of the Exchange (Castaing, Shergold, Lutyens and Wetenhall) from 1698 to 1898

Library catalogue: All or part available in-house

Publications: Printed, and electronic and video
Order printed publications from: Publications Group, Bank of England, Threadneedle Street, London, EC2R 8AH; tel: 020 7601 4886

Publications list: Available online

Access to staff: Appointment necessary.
Hours: Mon to Fri, 0900 to 1730

BANKRUPTCY ASSOCIATION

4 Johnson Close, Abraham Heights, Lancaster, LA1 5EU

Tel: 01539 469474
E-mail: mcqueen314@btinternet.com
Website: www.theba.org.uk

Enquiries to: Founder

Founded: 1983; formerly called Association of Bankrupts (year of change 1991); formerly called Bankruptcy Association of Great Britain and Ireland (year of change 2000)

Organisation type and purpose:
Membership association (membership is by subscription).
To provide advice and support to those who experience bankruptcy and its long-term effects.

Subject coverage: Insolvency in general, but particularly personal bankruptcy, debt, liquidation and reform of insolvency law.

Publications: Printed

Publications list: Available online and in print

continued overleaf

Access to staff: Contact by letter, by telephone, by e-mail and via website. Appointment necessary. Access for members only.
Special comments: Helpline for general enquiries: Mon to Fri, 1230 to 1700

BAPC (BAPC)

Formal name: Britsih Association for Print & Communication

Catalyst House, 720 Centennial Road, Centennial Park, Elstree, Herts, WD6 3SY

Tel: 020 8736 5862
Fax: 020 8736 5889
E-mail: info@bapc.co.uk
Website: www.bapc.co.uk

Enquiries to: Executive Director
Other contacts: Chairman for public relations

Founded: 1978

Organisation type and purpose: National organisation, trade association (membership is by subscription, qualification).

Subject coverage: Trade association within the print sector, providing its members with a wide range of facilities and benefits to help printers survive and succeed, including free legal advice, marketing support, technical assistance, product assessment, seminars, conferences, magazines and newsletters, tailored insurance and credit-check scheme, health, safety and employment hotline, arbitration, mentoring and distance-learning schemes.

Access to staff: Contact by letter, by telephone, by e-mail and via website
Hours: Mon to Fri, 0900 to 1700

Access to building: Prior appointment required

BAPTIST HISTORICAL SOCIETY (BHS)

Baptist House, PO Box 44, 129 Broadway, Didcot, Oxfordshire, OX11 8RT

Tel: 01235 517700
Fax: 01235 517715
E-mail: stephen.bhs@dsl.pipex.com
Website: www.baptisthistory.org.uk

Enquiries to: Honorary Secretary

Founded: 1908

Organisation type and purpose: Learned society (membership is by subscription), present number of members: 550, registered charity (charity number 271367).
Study and recording of Baptist Church history and theology.

Subject coverage: Baptist Church history and theology, including original church records and published bibliographies.

Publications: Printed

Publications list: Available online and in print

Access to staff: Contact by letter, by e-mail and via website
Hours: Mon to Fri, 0900 to 1700

Also at: Angus Library; Regents Park College, Oxford, OX1 2LB; tel: 01865 288120; e-mail: angus.library@regents.ox.ac.uk; Honorary Secretary; Baptist Historical Society, 60 Strathmore Avenue, Hitchin, Hertfordshire, SG5 1ST; tel: 01462 431816; e-mail: stephen.bhs@dsl.pipex.com

BAPTIST UNION OF SCOTLAND

48 Speirs Wharf, Glasgow, G4 9TH

Tel: 0141 423 6169
Fax: 0141 424 1422
E-mail: admin@scottishbaptist.org.uk
Website: www.scottishbaptist.org.uk

Enquiries to: General Director

Founded: 1869

Organisation type and purpose: Voluntary organisation, registered charity (charity number SC004960).
Church organisation.

Subject coverage: Baptist Church life and organisation; current ministerial conditions and persons; denominational budget, policies, programmes and development.

Trade and statistical information: Statistics of Baptist Churches in Scotland

Publications: Printed

Publications list: Available in print

Access to staff: Contact by letter, by telephone, by fax and by e-mail. Appointment necessary.
Hours: Variable

Access to building: *Hours:* Mon to Thu, 0900 to 1600; Fri, 0900 to 1200
Special comments: Closed weekends and public holidays.

Access for disabled people: *Hours:* Mon to Thu, 0900 to 1600; Fri, 0900 to 1200
Special comments: Closed weekends and public holidays

Affiliated to: Baptist World Alliance;; European Baptist Federation; Evangelical Alliance; Fellowship of Baptists in Britain and Ireland

BAR ASSOCIATION FOR COMMERCE, FINANCE AND INDUSTRY (BACFI)

PO Box 4352, Edlesborough, Dunstable, Bedfordshire, LU6 9EF

Tel: 01525 222244
E-mail: secretary@bacfi.org
Website: www.bacfi.org

Enquiries to: Secretary

Founded: 1965; created by the merger of BACFI and Employed & Non Practising Bar Association (ENPBA) (year of change 2004)

Organisation type and purpose: Membership association (membership is by subscription).

Subject coverage: Professional interests of barristers working in-house or outside chambers. It runs training seminars and provides networking events for members and represents their views on the Bar Council and with the Bar Standards Board.

Collection: Archive of BACFI responses to Bar Council and Bar Standards Board consultations and Professional Issues information on http://www.bacfi.org

Access to staff: Contact by letter, by telephone, by e-mail and via website

BARBICAN LIBRARY

Barbican Centre, Silk Street, London, EC2Y 8DS

Tel: 020 7638 0569
Fax: 020 7638 2249
E-mail: barbicanlib@cityoflondon.gov.uk
Website: www.cityoflondon.gov.uk/barbicanlibrary

Enquiries to: Librarian

Founded: 1982

Organisation type and purpose: Local government body, public library.

Subject coverage: General lending library collection with strengths in London history, fine and performing arts, including art history, painting, sculpture, ceramics, photography, cinema, film and theatre, music and finance.

Services for disabled people: CCTV magnifier, large and trackerball keyboards, induction loops, Jaws and ZoomText available on some PCs

Collection: Crime fiction collection
Libraries of the Gilbert and Sullivan Society
Music preserved archive studio of live performance recordings (audio and video) not available commercially, includes interviews with artists.
The Society of Technical Analysts.

Non-library collection catalogue: All or part available online and in-house

Library catalogue: All or part available online and in-house

Access to staff: Contact by letter, by telephone, by fax, by e-mail, in person and via website. Appointment necessary.
Hours: Mon and Wed, 0930 to 1730; Tue and Thu, 0930 to 1930; Fri, 0930 to 1400; Sat, 0930 to 1600

Access to building: No prior appointment required

Access for disabled people: Parking provided, level entry, access to all public areas.
Special comments: Internal lift to Music Library.

Branch libraries: City of London: Culture, Heritage and Libraries; Guildhall Library, Aldermanbury, London; tel: 020 7382 1852

Parent body: City of London; tel: 020 7332 1852

BARBOUR ENVIRONMENT, HEALTH & SAFETY

Building B, Kingswood, Kings Ride, Ascot, Berkshire, SL5 8AJ

Tel: 0845 300 0241
Fax: 01344 899 332
E-mail: enquiries@barbourehs.com
Website: www.barbour-ehs.com

Enquiries to: Marketing Manager
Direct tel: 01344 899240

Founded: 1947

Organisation type and purpose: Publishing house.

Information providers.

Subject coverage: A leading UK supplier of specialist information services to professionals working in the health, safety and environment sectors. Its services are used across a variety of commercial and public organisations in the UK and Ireland and are designed to help improve decision making, understanding of complex information areas, reduction of risks and management of projects.

Information services: Barbour Environment, Health & Safety Online Information Service

Non-library collection catalogue: All or part available online

Library catalogue: All or part available online and in print

Access to staff: Contact by letter, by telephone, by fax, by e-mail and via website
Hours: Mon to Fri, 0900 to 1700

Access to building: *Hours:* Mon to Fri, 0900 to 1700

Access for disabled people: Accessible
Hours: Mon to Fri, 0900 to 1700

Branch of: United Business Media Plc; website: http://www.ubm.com

Links with: Barbour ABI; The Chapter House, Hinderton Hall Estate, Neston, Cheshire, CH64 7UX; tel: 0151 353 3500; fax: 0151 353 3501; e-mail: info@barbour-abi.com; website: http://www.barbour-abi.com

BAREMA

Formal name: Trade Association for Anaesthetic & Respiratory Equipment

The Stables, Sugworth Lane, Radley, Oxon, OX14 2HX

Tel: 01865 736393
Fax: 01865 736393
E-mail: barema@btinternet.com
Website: barema.org.uk

Enquiries to: Secretary

Organisation type and purpose: Trade association for anaesthetic & respiratory equipment.
To promote co-operation between registered companies engaged in the manufacture, distribution and servicing of anaesthetic and respiratory equipment and generally to further the individual and collective interests of these companies; to encourage and expand the use of safe and effective products in health care markets; to create an environment whereby the innovation of technically advanced products can be developed; to work in partnership with health care professionals to influence the regulatory environment by providing responsible input; to strive to improve patient safety, through active participation in the preparation and promotion of Technical Safety Standards and procedures for anaesthetic, respiratory and associated devices; to maintain an ongoing, close relationship with the medical profession through mutual participation in matters leading to enhancement of the knowledge base of all and consequent improvement of devices, procedures and in patient health and safety.

Access to staff: Contact by letter, by telephone, by fax and by e-mail

BARING FOUNDATION

60 London Wall, London, EC2M 5TQ

Tel: 020 7767 1348
Fax: 020 7767 7121
E-mail: baring.foundation@uk.ing.com
Website: www.baringfoundation.org.uk

Enquiries to: Administration Officer

Founded: 1969

Organisation type and purpose: Registered charity (charity number 258583).
Grant-making charity.

Subject coverage: Three grant programmes: Strengthening the Voluntary Sector Independence programme; Arts programme; International Development programme

Publications: Printed

Publications list: Available online and in print

Access to staff: Contact by letter, by telephone, by fax, by e-mail and via website
Hours: Mon to Fri, 0900 to 1700

Access for disabled people: Access to all public areas, toilet facilities

BARKING AND DAGENHAM ADULT & COMMUNITY SERVICES DEPARTMENT

Central Library, Barking, Essex, IG11 8DQ

Tel: 020 8724 8723
Fax: 020 8724 8733
E-mail: reference@lbbd.gov.uk
Website: www.lbbd.gov.uk/4-libraries/lib-menu.html

Enquiries to: Librarian

Founded: 1888

Organisation type and purpose: Local government body, public library.

Subject coverage: Printing, journalism, publishing and newspapers, local history. Fiction (Joint Fiction Reserve) B-BAI.

Collection: Fanshawe manuscripts and portraits

Non-library collection catalogue: All or part available online and in-house

Library catalogue: All or part available online and in-house

Publications list: Available online and in print

Access to staff: Contact by letter, by telephone, by fax, by e-mail, in person and via website. Appointment necessary.
Hours: Barking Library: Mon to Thu, 0900 to 2130; Fri, 0900 to 1900; Sat, 0900 to 1700; Sun, 1000 to 1600

Access to building: No prior appointment required

Access for disabled people: Access to all public areas

Also at: Local History Collection housed at Local Studies Centre, Valence House Museum; Becontree Avenue, Dagenham, Essex, RM8 3HT; tel: 020 8270 6896; Valence Library; Becontree Avenue, Dagenham, Essex, RM8 3HT; tel: 020 8270 6896

Parent body: London Borough of Barking and Dagenham

BARNABAS TRUST

Freepost TN2186, Tonbridge, Kent, TN11 9BR

Tel: 01732 366766
Fax: 01732 366767
E-mail: headoffice@barnabas.org.uk
Website: www.barnabas.org.uk

Enquiries to: Chief Executive

Founded: 1978; formerly called Belgrave Trust (year of change 1978)

Organisation type and purpose: Registered charity (charity number 276346).

Subject coverage: Holiday centres for groups of young people including church, secular and school.

Access to staff: Contact by letter, by telephone, by fax, by e-mail and via website. Appointment necessary.
Hours: Mon to Fri, 0900 to 1700

BARNARDO'S

Tanners Lane, Barkingside, Ilford, Essex, IG6 1QG

Tel: 020 8550 8822
Fax: 020 8551 6870
Website: www.barnardos.co.uk

Enquiries to: Information Officer
Direct tel: 020 8498 7556
Direct e-mail: barninfo@compuserve.com
Other contacts: Librarian

Founded: 1867; formerly called Dr Barnardo's (year of change 1988)

Organisation type and purpose: Voluntary organisation, registered charity (charity number 216250).
Child care organisation.
To help the most vulnerable children and young people transform their lives and fulfil their potential.

Subject coverage: Social welfare policy and practice. Child care, social services with families, neighbourhoods and communities.

Collection: Archives, dating from 1860s (held by Liverpool University, restricted access)
Films, dating from 1920s
History of Barnardo's
Photographs, dating from 1874 (estimated 500,000)

Publications: Printed, and electronic and video
Order printed publications from: Child Care Publications
Barnardo's Trading Estate, Paycocke Road, Basildon, Essex, SS14 3DR, tel: 01268 520224, fax: 01268 284804

Publications list: Available in print

Access to staff: Appointment necessary.
Hours: Mon to Fri, 0930 to 1630

Access for disabled people: Parking provided, level entry, toilet facilities

BARNET AND DISTRICT LOCAL HISTORY SOCIETY

Barnet Museum, 31 Wood Street, Barnet, Hertfordshire, EN5 4BE

Tel: 020 8440 8066
E-mail: enquiries@barnetmuseum.co.uk
Website: www.barnetmuseum.co.uk

Enquiries to: Honorary Secretary

Founded: 1927

Organisation type and purpose: Learned society, voluntary organisation, museum.

Subject coverage: Local history of Barnet and District, historical and archaeological records.

Collection: Books, documents, maps, costumes, exhibitions and artefacts relating to history of Barnet

Library catalogue: All or part available in-house

Publications: Printed

Publications list: Available in print

Access to staff: Contact by letter and in person
Hours: Tue, Wed, Thu, 1430 to 1630; Sat, 1030 to 1230 and 1400 to 1600
Special comments: Donations appreciated

Affiliated to: Hertfordshire Association for Local History; London and Middlesex Archaeological Society

BARNET LIBRARIES, MUSEUMS AND LOCAL STUDIES

Building 4, North London Business Park, Oakleigh Road South, London, N11 1NP

Tel: 020 8359 2000
Fax: 020 8359 4156
E-mail: hendon.library@barnet.gov.uk
Website: www.barnet.gov.uk/libraries
Website: www.libraries.barnet.gov.uk

Enquiries to: Reference Librarian, Hendon Library
Direct tel: 020 8359 2628
Direct fax: 020 8359 2885
Direct e-mail: hendon.library@barnet.gov.uk
Other contacts: Information and Heritage Manager for borough-wide reference and information services.

Founded: 1965

Organisation type and purpose: Local government body, public library.

Subject coverage: General, local studies.

Collection: Local history including the C O Banks Collection on Finchley

Non-library collection catalogue: All or part available online

Library catalogue: All or part available in-house

Publications: Printed

Publications list: Available in print

Access to staff: Contact by letter, by telephone, by fax, by e-mail and via website. Appointment necessary.
Hours: Mon to Fri, 0900 to 1700

BARNET LOCAL STUDIES & ARCHIVES CENTRE

Formal name: London Borough of Barnet Local Studies and Archives Centre

Hendon Library (first floor), The Burroughs, London NW4 4BQ

Tel: 020 8359 3960
E-mail: library.archives@barnet.gov.uk
Website: www.barnet.gov.uk/archives

Enquiries to: Local Studies Manager
Other contacts: Heritage Officer; Local Studies Assistant

Founded: 1974

Organisation type and purpose: Local government body.

Subject coverage: Local history.

Information services: Public computers with internet access.

Special visitor services: Arranged individually.

Education services: Relevant work undertaken with local primary, secondary and further education establishments.

Services for disabled people: Disabled access to all public facilities.

Collection: Local reference collections
Local archive/MSS collections
Photographic and maps collections

Non-library collection catalogue: All or part available online and in-house

Library catalogue: All or part available online and in-house

Access to staff: Contact by letter, by telephone, by e-mail and in person. Appointment necessary.
Hours: Tue, Wed, Fri, 0930 to 1630; Thu, 1300 to 1900; first and third Sat of each month, 0930 to 1630

Access to building: Prior appointment required
Special comments: Fully accessible, sited on ground floor.

Access for disabled people: Low level ramp to entry; all public areas on ground floor and accessible

BARNETT RESEARCH CENTRE AT TOYNBEE HALL

Formal name: Toynbee Hall

28 Commercial Street, London, E1 6LS

Tel: 020 7392 2939
Fax: 020 7377 5964
E-mail: info@toynbeehall.org.uk
Website: www.toynbeehall.org.uk

Enquiries to: Librarian/Archivist
Direct tel: 020 7392 2939
Direct e-mail: barnettresearchcentre@toynbeehall.org.uk

Founded: 1884

Organisation type and purpose: Voluntary organisation.

Collection: Specialist library on the history of social policy and welfare, archives of Toynbee Hall

Non-library collection catalogue: All or part available online and in-house

Library catalogue: All or part available in-house

Publications: Printed, and electronic and video

Access to staff: Contact by letter, by telephone, by e-mail, in person and via website. Appointment necessary.
Hours: Tue to Thu, 0930 to 1630

Access to building: No appointment required, but we welcome enquiries in advance of visits

BARNSLEY ARCHIVE AND LOCAL STUDIES DEPARTMENT

Central Library, Shambles Street, Barnsley, South Yorkshire, S70 2JF

Tel: 01226 773950
Fax: 01226 773955
E-mail: archives@barnsley.gov.uk
Website: www.barnsley.gov.uk/archives

Enquiries to: Archives and Local Studies Officer
Other contacts: Local Studies Librarian (for local studies enquiries)

Organisation type and purpose: Local government body.

Subject coverage: Relating to Barnsley Metropolitan Borough Council.

Collection: Census enumeration returns (microfilm or microfiche)
IGI for northern counties of England and Ireland
GRO Index for births, marriages and deaths
Local newspapers (mainly on microfilm)
Local publications such as annual reports and newsletters of organisations, church magazines, council minutes
Parish register copies (printed or microfilm)
Deeds, wills, estate papers
Local photographs and maps

Non-library collection catalogue: All or part available online, in-house and in print

Library catalogue: All or part available in-house

Publications: Printed

Publications list: Available online and in print

Access to staff: Contact by letter, by telephone, by fax, by e-mail, in person and via website

Access to building: *Hours:* Mon, 0930 to 1300 and 1400 to 1700; Tue, Thu and Fri, 0930 to 1300 and 1400 to 1730; Wed, 0930 to 1300 and 1400 to 1800; Sat, 0930 to 1300

BARNSLEY CHAMBER OF COMMERCE AND INDUSTRY (BCCI)

Business Innovation Centre, Innovation Way, Wilthorpe, Barnsley, South Yorkshire, S75 1JL

Tel: 01226 217770
Fax: 01226 215729
E-mail: info@barnsleychamber.co.uk

Enquiries to: Chief Executive

Founded: 1882

Organisation type and purpose: Membership association (membership is by subscription), present number of members: 800, service industry.
Chamber of Commerce.

Subject coverage: Policy, representation, export service, debt recovery, general business advice.

Trade and statistical information: Trade surveys

Publications list: Available in print

Access to staff: Contact by letter, by telephone, by fax, by e-mail and in person
Hours: Mon to Fri, 0900 to 1700

Access for disabled people: Parking provided, ramped entry, level entry, toilet facilities

BARNSLEY METROPOLITAN BOROUGH COUNCIL

Town Hall, Barnsley, South Yorkshire, S70 2TA

Tel: 01226 770770
Fax: 01226 773099
E-mail: townhall@barnsley.gov.uk
Website: www.barnsley.gov.uk

Enquiries to: Chief Executive

Founded: 1974

Organisation type and purpose: Local government body.

Subject coverage: Local government services provided to 227,000 citizens covering education, housing, social services, planning, highways, economic development and training.
Order printed publications from: Public Relations officer
at the same address, tel: 01226 773400, fax: 01226 773399

Access to staff: Contact by letter, by telephone, by fax, by e-mail, in person and via website
Hours: Mon to Fri, 0900 to 1700

Access for disabled people: Ramped entry

BARNSLEY METROPOLITAN BOROUGH LIBRARY SERVICES

Reference and Information team, First Floor, Central Library, Shambles Street, Barnsley, South Yorkshire, S70 2JF

Tel: 01226 773933 or 773934
Fax: 01226 773955
E-mail: barnsleylibraryenquiries@barnsley.gov.uk
Website: www.barnsley.gov.uk/libraries

Enquiries to: Chief Librarian
Direct tel: 01226 773926

Organisation type and purpose: Public library.

Subject coverage: General lending and information; multimedia; local studies and archives (historical and other information on the Barnsley Metropolitan District).

Collection: Barnsley Archive Collection
Barnsley Local History Collection
Dransfield Collection (local history of Penistone)

Library catalogue: All or part available online

Access to staff: Contact by letter, by telephone, by fax, by e-mail, in person and via website
Hours: Mon and Wed, 0930 to 1900; Tues, Thurs and Fri, 0930 to 1730; Sat, 0930 to 1600 for Central Library
Special comments: Hours for specific departments vary.

Access for disabled people: Level entry, access to all public areas, toilet facilities

Parent body: Barnsley Metropolitan Borough Council

BARWICK-IN-ELMET HISTORICAL SOCIETY

G. Thornton (Chairman), 8 Richmondfield Lane, Barwick-in-Elmet, Leeds, LS15 4EZ

Website: www.barwickinelmethistoricalsociety.com

Enquiries to: Secretary
Direct tel: 01132 867341
Direct e-mail: gday63@googlemail.com

Founded: 1984

Organisation type and purpose: Membership assocation, current mems: over 55.
To record, research and publish on the history of this Yorkshire parish.

Collection: The society has a resource centre in Barwick-in-Elmet containing a wide range of documents and photographs, mostly secondary copies.

Non-library collection catalogue: All or part available in-house

Publications: Printed
Order printed publications from: e-mail: editor.barwicker@googlemail.com

Publications list: Available online

Access to staff: Contact by letter, by telephone, by e-mail and via website

BASEC

Formal name: British Approvals Service for Cables

Presley House, Presley Way, Crownhill, Milton Keynes, Buckinghamshire, MK8 0ES

Tel: 01908 267300
Fax: 01908 267255
E-mail: mail@basec.org.uk
Website: www.basec.org.uk
Website: www.env-basec.org.uk

Enquiries to: Chief Executive

Founded: 1971; formerly called British Approvals Service for Electric Cables (BASEC)

Organisation type and purpose: Service industry.
Certification Body.

Subject coverage: ISO 9000 certification, cable, ancillary product, instruments, installation, rod rolling, stockists; quality certification; product certification for cables; UK cable market certificate holders; new product assessment (cables). Environmental certification to ISO 14001 and/or EMAS. Certification of Health and Safety management systems to OHSAS 18001.

Collection: Worldwide ISO 9000 cable manufacturers listings

Publications: Printed

Access to staff: Contact by letter, by telephone, by fax, by e-mail and via website
Hours: Mon to Thu, 0900 to 1700; Fri, 0900 to 1300

BASIC SKILLS AGENCY AT NIACE (BSA at NIACE)

21 DeMontfort Street, Leicester, LE1 7GE

Tel: 0116 204 4200
Fax: 0116 285 4514
E-mail: enquiries@niace.org.uk
Website: archive.basic-skills.co.uk/aboutus

Enquiries to: Information Officer
Other contacts: Director (Literacy, Language and Numeracy & Workplace)

Founded: 1975; formerly called ALBSU; formerly called Basic Skills Agency (year of change 2008)

Organisation type and purpose: The BSA became an independent charity with government support in 1990. The Agency's work was critical for developing a strategy for literacy, language and numeracy and a range of work in the schools sector. In the light of changing circumstances the BSA's board sought an effective partner to take forward its work with adults and young people. Following competition, NIACE, working with Tribal, was successful in offering a way forward. The BSA's work in Wales will be assimilated into the Welsh Assembly Government in line with Welsh Assembly policy.

Subject coverage: Basic literacy (including English for speakers of other languages, ESOL), numeracy and related basic skills.

Trade and statistical information: Data on the scale of need in England and Wales

Publications: Printed, and electronic and video
Order printed publications from: Basic Skills Agency
Prolog-UK, PO Box 5050, Sherwood Park, Annesly, Nottingham, NG15 0DL

Publications list: Available online and in print

Access to staff: Contact by letter, by telephone, by fax, by e-mail and via website
Hours: Mon to Fri, 0900 to 1730

Constituent part of: NIACE; website: http://www.niace.org.uk

Links with: Basic Skills Cymru; website: http://www.basic-skills-wales.org/bsastrategy/en/home/index.cfm
Tribal; website: http://www.tribalgroup.co.uk

BASILDON DISTRICT COUNCIL

The Basildon Centre, St Martin's Square, Basildon, Essex, SS14 1DL

Tel: 01268 533333
Fax: 01268 294350
Website: www.basildondistrict.com

continued overleaf

Enquiries to: Public Relations Manager
Direct tel: 01268 294157
Direct fax: 01268 294148
Direct e-mail: marketingcommunications@basildon.gov.uk

Organisation type and purpose: Local government body.

Subject coverage: Detailed information about Basildon Council services and policies. General information about Basildon. The District Council is responsible for providing a wide range of services in a thriving district of 165,000 people. It is helping lead a significant set of partnerships to regenerate the area, the most important examples being: Community Safety , Thames Gateway, South Essex, and Gardener's Lane South.

Publications: Printed

Access to staff: Contact by letter, by telephone, by fax and by e-mail
Hours: Mon to Fri, 0900 to 1715

BASINGSTOKE AND DEANE BOROUGH COUNCIL

Civic Offices, London Road, Basingstoke, Hampshire, RG21 4AH

Tel: 01256 844844
Fax: 01256 844200
E-mail: customer.service@basingstoke.gov.uk
Website: www.basingstoke.gov.uk

Enquiries to: Head of Corporate Communications
Direct tel: 01256 845485
Direct e-mail: m.reid@basingstoke.gov.uk

Founded: 1974

Organisation type and purpose: Local government body.

Subject coverage: Local government including: environmental health, leisure, events, housing needs, planning, development, local plans, policy and committees, business development.

Publications: Printed

Access to staff: Contact by letter, by telephone, by fax, by e-mail, in person and via website
Hours: Mon to Thu, 0830 to 1700; Fri, 0830 to 1630

Access for disabled people: Parking provided, ramped entry, level entry, toilet facilities

BASINGSTOKE COLLEGE OF TECHNOLOGY (BCOT)

Worting Road, Basingstoke, Hampshire, RG21 8TN

Tel: 01256 354141
Fax: 01256 306444
E-mail: information@bcot.ac.uk
Website: www.bcot.ac.uk

Enquiries to: Learning Resources Manager
Direct tel: 01256 306383
Direct e-mail: learning.resources@bcot.ac.uk

Organisation type and purpose: College of further education.

Subject coverage: General library to support GCSE, A-levels, NVQs, BTEC, some HND and HNC; engineering; building; business studies.

Library catalogue: All or part available online

Access to staff: Contact by letter, by telephone, by fax, by e-mail and in person
Hours: Term time: Mon, 0830 to 1700; Tue to Thu, 0830 to 1900; Fri, 0830 to 1630; Sat closed
Vacations: Mon to Fri, 0845 to 1700; Sat closed
Special comments: Visitors need to make an appointment in advance for security arrangements.

Links with: University of Portsmouth; Winston Churchill Avenue, Portsmouth, Hampshire, PO1 2UP; University of Winchester

BASKETMAKERS' ASSOCIATION

64 Lakes Lane, Newport Pagnell, Milton Keynes, MK16 8HR

Tel: 0845 201 1936
E-mail: honsec@basketassoc.org
Website: www.basketassoc.org

Founded: 1975

Organisation type and purpose: Membership association (membership is by subscription), present number of members: 1,000–1,200.
To promote the craft of basketmaking and chair seating.

Subject coverage: All forms of basketry; willow work, cane work, rush work, coil work; hedgerow basketry; chair seating; straw work; growth and preparation of materials; history, tools, books and equipment, courses list nationwide (send large sae to publications sales).

Publications: Printed, and electronic and video
Order printed publications from: Sales, Basketmakers Association
216 Walton Road, East Molesey, Surrey, KT8 0HR

Access to staff: Contact by letter, by telephone, by fax and by e-mail
Hours: Mon to Fri, 0900 to 1700

BAT CONSERVATION TRUST (BCT)

250 Kennington Lane, London, SE11 5RD

Tel: 0845 1300 228
Fax: 020 78207198
E-mail: enquiries@bats.org.uk
Website: www.bats.org.uk

Enquiries to: Helpline

Founded: 1991

Organisation type and purpose: National organisation, membership association (membership is by subscription), present number of members: 4,000, voluntary organisation, registered charity (charity number 1012361), training organisation, consultancy, research organisation.
BCT is the UK organisation solely devoted to the conservation of bats and their habitats through: conservation projects, research, supporting and educating people who find bats in their property, and encouraging appreciation of these animals.

Subject coverage: Biology and conservation of bats.

Library catalogue: All or part available in-house

Publications: Printed

Publications list: Available in print

Access to staff: Contact by letter, by telephone, by fax, by e-mail and via website
Hours: Mon to Fri, 0900 to 1730

Umbrella group for:: over 90 voluntary bat groups in the UK

BATH AND NORTH EAST SOMERSET COUNCIL (B&NES)

Formal name: Bath and North East Somerset

Riverside, Temple Street, Keynsham, Somerset, BS31 1CA

Tel: 01225 39 40 41
Fax: 01225 47 78 09
E-mail: communications_marketing@bathnes.gov.uk
Website: www.bathnes.gov.uk

Enquiries to: Information and Publications Officer
Direct tel: 01225 477413
Direct fax: 01225 477499
Other contacts: Communications & Marketing Manager

Founded: 1996; formed from Avon County Council, Bath City Council, Wansdyke District Council (year of change 1996)

Organisation type and purpose: Local government body.
Local authority.
To provide local services.

Subject coverage: Education, environmental health, economic development, housing, libraries, planning, roads, social services and many others.

Publications: Printed
Order printed publications from: Information and Publicity Officer, Bath and North East Somerset Council
Guildhall, High Street, Bath, Somerset, BA1 5AW, e-mail: juliet_williams@bathnes.gov.uk

Access to staff: Contact by letter, by telephone, by fax, by e-mail and in person. Appointment necessary.
Hours: Mon to Thu, 0830 to 1700; Fri, 0830 to 1630

Access for disabled people: Parking provided

Other addresses: Guildhall; High Street, Bath, BA1 5AW; tel: 01225 477000; The Hollies; Midsomer, Wotton, BA3 2OP

BATH AND NORTH EAST SOMERSET RECORD OFFICE

Guildhall, High Street, Bath, BA1 5AW

Tel: 01225 477421
Fax: 01225 477439
E-mail: archives@bathnes.gov.uk
Website: www.batharchives.co.uk

Enquiries to: Archivist

History of institution: formerly called Bath City Record Office (year of change 1996)

Organisation type and purpose: Local government body.
Record office.

Subject coverage: History of Bath and district.

Collection: Official records of the City of Bath from the 12th century
Records of local businesses, families and organisations
Collections of photographs, maps and plans

Non-library collection catalogue: All or part available online and in-house

Access to staff: Contact by letter, by telephone, by fax, by e-mail and in person
Hours: Tue to Thu, 0900 to 1300 and 1400 to 1700; Fri, 0900 to 1300 and 1400 to 1630

Access for disabled people: By prior arrangement

BATH PRESERVATION TRUST (BPT)

No 1 Royal Crescent, Bath, BA1 2LR

Tel: 01225 338727
Fax: 01225 481850
E-mail: admin@bptrust.org.uk
Website: www.bath-preservation-trust.org.uk

Enquiries to: Administrator
Other contacts: Director

Founded: 1934

Organisation type and purpose: Membership association (membership is by subscription), present number of members: 1070, registered charity (charity number 203048).
Buildings preservation trust.

Subject coverage: The trust exists to preserve the historic character and amenities of Bath.

Publications: Printed

Access to staff: Contact by letter
Hours: Mon to Fri, 0900 to 1700

Access to building: Prior appointment required

BATH ROYAL LITERARY AND SCIENTIFIC INSTITUTION

16–18 Queen Square, Bath, Somerset, BA1 2HN

Tel: 01225 312084
Fax: 01225 442460
E-mail: admin@brlsi.org
Website: www.brlsi.org

Enquiries to: Administrator

Founded: 1824

Organisation type and purpose: Membership organisation (membership by donation/subscription).
Research institution, museum and library.

Subject coverage: Literature, geology, natural history, archaeology, fine art, photography, social history and local history of Bath.

Collection: Library:
Rev. Leonard Jenyns Collection (science and natural history)
Christopher Edmund Broome Collection (botany, especially the lower plants, fungi and algae)
Parliamentary Collection
Libraries of the Bath Natural History and Antiquarian Field Club and the Bath District of the Somerset Archaeological and Natural History Society
Geology:
Moore Collection (32 Plesiosaurs and Ichthyosaurs)
William Lonsdale Collection (rocks and fossils)
Natural history:
Jenyns Herbarium of British Plants (3,000 specimens)
Broome Herbarium (6,600 British and European specimens)
Shell Collection (17,000 specimens)
Other collections for archaeology, social history, fine art, photography and archives

Non-library collection catalogue: All or part available online and in-house

Access to staff: Contact by letter, by telephone, by fax, by e-mail and via website

BATH SPA UNIVERSITY

Library, Newton Park, Bath, BA2 9BN

Tel: 01225 875490
Fax: 01225 875493
Website: www.bathspa.ac.uk/services/library/

Enquiries to: Head of Library and Information Services

History of institution: created by the merger of Bath College of Education (Home Economics), Newton Park College and Bath Academy of Art

Organisation type and purpose: The university is an accredited institution for the award of its own degrees up to taught Masters level.

Subject coverage: Education (primary and secondary), English, history, study of religions, environmental biology, geography, creative arts, fine art, ceramics, graphic design, social sciences, psychology, food management, music, visual culture, health studies, business studies, dance.

Library catalogue: All or part available online

Access to staff: Contact by letter and by telephone. Appointment necessary. Non-members charged.
Hours: Mon to Fri, 0900 to 1700

Access for disabled people: Level entry via ramp, lifts

Library is part of the: UK Libraries Plus

BATHROOM MANUFACTURERS ASSOCIATION (BMA)

The Bathroom Manufacturers Association, Innovation Centre 1, Keele University Science & Business Park, Newcastle-under-Lyme, ST5 5NB

Tel: 01782 631619
Fax: 01782 630155
E-mail: info@bathroom-association.org.uk
Website: www.bathroom-association.org.uk

Enquiries to: CEO

History of institution: formerly called Council of British Ceramic Sanitaryware Manufacturers (CBCSM) (year of change 1987); formerly called British Bathroom Council (BBC) (year of change 1999); formerly called Bathroom Association (BA) (year of change 2001)

Organisation type and purpose: Trade association.

Subject coverage: Information on bathroom products sold in the UK, including sanitaryware, baths, taps and showers, and bathroom refurbishment.

Collection: Factsheets on bathroom refurbishment

Publications: Printed

Access to staff: Contact by letter, by fax, by e-mail and via website
Hours: Mon to Fri, 0900 to 1700

BATTERSEA DOGS & CATS HOME

4 Battersea Park Road, London, SW8 4AA

Tel: 020 7622 3626
Fax: 020 7622 6451
E-mail: info@battersea.org.uk
Website: www.battersea.org.uk

Founded: 1860; formerly called The Temporary Home for Lost & Starving Dogs; formerly called The Dogs Home Battersea; formerly called Battersea Dogs Home (year of change 2005)

Organisation type and purpose: Registered charity (charity number 206394).
Animal rescue and rehoming.

Subject coverage: Practical problems, help to owners of lost dogs and cats, rehoming of animals, advice on pet ownership and behavioural problems.

Publications: Printed

Publications list: Available in print

Access to staff: Contact by letter, by telephone, by fax, by e-mail, in person and via website. Appointment necessary. All charged.
Hours: Office hours

Access to building: at postal address
Hours: 24 hours, for stray dogs and cats only

Also at: Battersea Dogs & Cats Home; Crowhurst Lane, Ash, Kent; tel: 01474 874994; Battersea Dogs & Cats Home; Priest Hill, Old Windsor, Berkshire, SL4 2JN; tel: 01784 432989

Member organisation of: Association of Dogs and Cats Homes

BATTERY VEHICLE SOCIETY (BVS)

21 Hartley Road, Chorlton-cum-Hardy, MANCHESTER, M21 9NG

Tel: 0845 094 2173
E-mail: contact@batteryvehiclesociety.org.uk
Website: www.batteryvehiclesociety.org.uk

Enquiries to: Enquiries Officer
Other contacts: Secretary

Founded: 1973

continued overleaf

Organisation type and purpose: Learned society (membership is by subscription), present number of members: 350, voluntary organisation, research organisation.

Subject coverage: Battery, hybrid and solar electric traction: technical, commercial, recreational and historic aspects.

Collection: Books, periodicals, brochures, drawings, diagrams, photographs

Trade and statistical information: Data on the availability of battery-electric cars and light commercials, and parts thereof

Publications: Printed

Access to staff: Contact by letter, by telephone and by e-mail
Hours: Mon to Fri, 0800 to 2100

Affiliated to: Royal Automobile Club; Transport Trust

BBC CYMRU WALES (BBC)

Research & Archives, Ty Oldfield – MO28, Llandaff, Cardiff, CF5 2YQ

Tel: 029 2032 3309
Fax: 029 2032 2798
E-mail: edith.hughes@bbc.co.uk
Website: www.bbc.wales.com

Enquiries to: Manager Research & Archives

Founded: 1928

Organisation type and purpose: National broadcaster.

Subject coverage: TV film and videotape, radio productions, film transfer servcice (fee payable).

Collection: Film and TV archive
News cuttings
Radio Times – 1928 to present
Sound archive
Stills collection

Publications: Electronic and video

Access to staff: Contact by letter, by telephone, by fax and by e-mail. Appointment necessary.
Hours: Mon to Fri, 0930 to 1730

BBC HAYMARKET EXHIBITIONS LIMITED

2–14 Shortlands, London, W6 8DJ

Tel: 020 8267 8300
Fax: 020 8267 8350
Website: www.haymarketgroup.com

Enquiries to: Operations Director

Organisation type and purpose: Exhibition organisers.

Subject coverage: Organisation of consumer exhibitions.

Access to staff: Contact by letter
Hours: Mon to Fri, 0930 to 1730

Connections with: Haymarket Exhibitions Limited; At the same address

BBC INFORMATION AND ARCHIVE (BBC I&A)

Formal name: British Broadcasting Corporation

BC3 D4 Broadcast Centre, Media Village, 201 Wood Lane, London, W12 7TP

Tel: 020 8008 2288
Fax: 020 8936 9002
E-mail: research.gateway@bbc.co.uk
Website: www.bbc.co.uk/archive

Founded: 1932

Organisation type and purpose: Media. National broadcaster.

Access to staff: Contact by telephone, by fax and by e-mail. All charged.
Hours: Mon to Fri, 0930 to 1730

BBC MONITORING (BBC)

Caversham Park, Reading, Berkshire, RG4 8TZ

Tel: 0118 948 6289
Fax: 0118 946 3823
E-mail: marketing@mon.bbc.co.uk
Website: www.monitor.bbc.co.uk

Enquiries to: Business Development and Customer Relations

Founded: 1939

Organisation type and purpose: International organisation, publishing house.
Foreign Affairs news service compiled from international news media monitoring.

Subject coverage: Continually updated political and economic news from more than 140 countries. Coverage includes government policy, international relations, security issues, globalisation, energy, trade, investment and human rights.

Publications: Printed, and electronic and video, and microform publications

Publications list: Available online

Access to staff: Contact by letter, by telephone, by fax, by e-mail and via website. All charged.
Hours: Open 24 hours; main office 0900 to 1730

Access to building: No access other than to staff

Links with: BBC World Service, BBC

BBC SCOTLAND

40 Pacific Quay, Glasgow, G51 1DA

Tel: 0141 422 6000
E-mail: enquiries.scot@bbc.co.uk
Website: www.bbc.co.uk/scotland/

Enquiries to: Organiser, Library Services

Organisation type and purpose: National government body.
Broadcasting organisation.

Subject coverage: Information relevant to BBC Scotland broadcast output, Scotland and related topics form the basis of all collections.

Collection: BBC Scotland radio broadcasts from 1949 onwards (tape and disc)
BBC Scotland TV broadcasts from 1952 onwards (film and tape)
Scottish press cuttings from 1968 onwards (microform)

Access to staff: Contact by letter and by fax. All charged.
Hours: Mon to Fri, 0900 to 1700

Access to building: No access other than to staff

Access for disabled people: Parking provided, level entry, toilet facilities
Special comments: Access to most areas

Also at the same address:: BBC Radio Scotland, BBC Alba, Radio nan Gaidheal

BBC WRITTEN ARCHIVES CENTRE (BBC)

Formal name: British Broadcasting Corporation

Peppard Road, Caversham Park, Reading, Berkshire, RG4 8TZ

Tel: 0118 948 6281
Fax: 0118 946 1145
E-mail: heritage@bbc.co.uk
Website: www.bbc.co.uk/historyofthebbc/contacts/wac.shtml
Website: www.bbc.co.uk/aboutthebbc

Founded: 1922

Organisation type and purpose: International organisation.
Broadcasting organisation.

Subject coverage: Correspondence, minutes of meetings, news bulletins, scripts, press cuttings and other detailed information relating to the whole of the BBC's output, regional and national, at home and overseas; papers relating to the history and development of the BBC, including technical development, from 1922, constitute a major source for 20th-century social and political history, biography, music, drama and the arts in the 20th century, as well as broadcasting itself.

Collection: Collection of press cuttings on all aspects of broadcasting (1922–mid 1960s)
Complete sets of Radio Times from 1923
The Listener and all BBC Schools publications

Non-library collection catalogue: All or part available in-house

Library catalogue: All or part available in-house

Order printed publications from: BBC Worldwide Ltd, Media Centre, 201 Wood Lane, London, W12 7TQ; tel: 020 8433 2000

Access to staff: Contact by letter, by telephone, by fax, by e-mail and via website. Appointment necessary.
Hours: Mon to Fri, 0930 to 1730
Special comments: No loans.

Access to building: Prior appointment required
Hours: Wed to Fri, 0945 to 1700

Access for disabled people: Parking provided, access to all public areas, toilet facilities

BBC YOUNG MUSICIAN OF THE YEAR

Room 3223, White City, 201 Wood Lane, London, W12 7TS

Tel: 020 8752 4212
Fax: 020 8752 4050
E-mail: young.musician@bbc.co.uk
Website: www.bbc.co.uk/youngmusician

Enquiries to: Artistic Administrator

Founded: 1978

Organisation type and purpose: National organisation.
Music competition.

Subject coverage: Competition for young classical musicians.

Access to staff: Contact by letter, by telephone, by fax, by e-mail and via website
Hours: Mon to Fri, 0900 to 1700

BEAFORD ARTS

Beaford Arts, Greenwarren House, Beaford, Winkleigh, EX19 8LU

Tel: 01805 603201
Fax: 01805 603202
E-mail: info@beaford-arts.org.uk
Website: www.beaford-arts.co.uk

Enquiries to: Director
Direct tel: 01805 603734

Founded: 1972; formerly called Beaford Archive, Beaford Photographic Archive

Organisation type and purpose: Registered charity (charity number 279784).
Photographic Archive.

Subject coverage: Old North Devon from 1850 to present day, including all aspects of life from domestic to industrial and from childhood to old age; images of farming, transport, leisure, costume, trades and crafts, landscapes and streetscapes.

Collection: The Old Archive of 9,000 negatives and prints of images taken from the 1850s until World War II and after
The New Archive, the lifetime's study of North Devon by James Ravilious, 8,300 negatives and prints
Contemporary collection currently 4,000 negatives and prints

Publications: Printed

Access to staff: Contact by letter, by telephone, by fax and by e-mail.
Appointment necessary.
Hours: Mon to Fri, 0900 to 1800

Access to building: Prior appointment required
Hours: Telephone for information on access to library and archive.

Access for disabled people: Toilet facilities
Special comments: Wheelchair access to archive

BEAT

Formal name: Eating Disorders Association

Wensum House, 103 Prince of Wales Road, Norwich, Norfolk, NR1 1DW

Tel: 0300 123 3355
Fax: 01603 664915
E-mail: info@b-eat.co.uk
Website: www.b-eat.co.uk

Enquiries to: Press Officer
Direct e-mail: media@b-eat.co.uk

Founded: 1989; incorporates the former Anorexic Aid, Anorexic Family Aid, Eating Disorders Association.

Organisation type and purpose: Beat is the UK's leading nationwide charity supporting people affected by eating disorders and campaigning on their behalf.

Subject coverage: Beat provides helplines for adults and young people, a UK wide network of self help and support groups and online support including information, message boards and live chat. We also provide expert knowledge, education and training to health and social care professionals and support and encourage research into eating disorders.

Publications: Printed

Publications list: Available online

Access to staff: Contact by telephone, by fax, by e-mail and via website
Hours: Administration only: 0900 to 1700
Special comments: Youth Helpline: Mon to Fri, 1630 to 2030; Sat 1300 to 1630; tel. 0845 634 7650
Adult Helpline: Mon to Fri, 1030 to 2030; Sat 1300 to 1630; tel. 0845 634 1414.

BEATSON INSTITUTE FOR CANCER RESEARCH

Garscube Estate, Switchback Road, Bearsden, Glasgow, G61 1BD

Tel: 0141 330 3953
Fax: 0141 942 6521
E-mail: library@beatson.gla.ac.uk
Website: www.beatson.gla.ac.uk

Enquiries to: Scientific Administrator
Direct tel: 0141 330 8722

Founded: 1912; formerly called CRC Beatson Laboratories; formerly called Beatson Institute for Cancer Research (year of change 1967)

Organisation type and purpose: Research organisation.

Subject coverage: Molecular biology, cell biology, molecular pathology, cancer research, proteomics, pharmacology, medical oncology, radiation oncology.

Collection: Historical collection relating to Sir George Beatson and the founding of the Royal Glasgow Cancer Hospital

Non-library collection catalogue: All or part available in-house

Library catalogue: All or part available in-house

Publications: Printed

Publications list: Available in print

Access to staff: Contact by letter, by telephone, by fax and by e-mail.
Appointment necessary.

Access to building: Prior appointment required

Access for disabled people: Parking provided, level entry, toilet facilities

Links with: University of Glasgow

BEAULIEU ARCHIVES

John Montagu Building, Beaulieu, Brockenhurst, Hampshire, SO42 7ZN

Tel: 01590 612345
Fax: 01590 612624
E-mail: info@beaulieu.co.uk
Website: www.beaulieu.co.uk

Enquiries to: Archivist

Founded: 1952

Organisation type and purpose: Museum.
Montagu family & Beaulieu estate private archives.
Private estate and leisure destination.

Subject coverage: Family of Lords Montagu of Beaulieu, Beaulieu Estate and Parish, Buckler's Hard 18th-century shipbuilding village, Beaulieu Abbey. Ditton Park Estate, Slough, Buckinghamshire.

Collection: Beaulieu History
Archive of the Montagu family

Non-library collection catalogue: All or part available in-house

Publications: Printed
Order printed publications from: Shops Manager, Beaulieu Enterprises Limited
John Montagu Building, Beaulieu, Brockenhurst, Hampshire, SO42 7ZN, tel: 01590 614639, fax: 01590 612624, e-mail: info@beaulieu.co.uk

Access to staff: Contact by letter, by telephone, by fax, by e-mail and via website.
Appointment necessary.
Hours: Mon to Fri, 1000 to 1500

Access for disabled people: Parking provided, ramped entry, toilet facilities
Special comments: Access to Archives by ramped entry and lift.

BEAUMONT SPECIALIST FABRICATIONS LIMITED

Catalina House, Rue de la Carriere, Les Banques St Sampson, Guernsey, GY2 4BG

Tel: +44 (0)1481 243 257
Fax: 01747 861076
E-mail: mib@beaumont-chimneys.co.uk
Website: www.beaumont-chimneys.co.uk

Enquiries to: Director

Founded: 2001; formerly called Beaumont Chimneys (year of change 1949); formerly called F E Beaumont Limited (year of change 2001)

Organisation type and purpose: Manufacturing industry.
Design, manufacturing, installation, inspection and maintenance of steel chimneys and associated items.

Subject coverage: Steel chimneys, flue liners, flue ducting, aerodynamic stabiliser vanes, counterbalance dampers.

Publications: Printed

Access to staff: Contact by letter, by telephone and by fax
Hours: Mon to Thu, 0845 to 1700; Fri, 0845 to 1600

BEAVERBROOK FOUNDATION

Third Floor, 11/12 Dover Street, London, W1S 4LJ

continued overleaf

Tel: 020 7042 9435
E-mail: jane@beaverbrookfoundation.org
Website: www.beaverbrookfoundation.org

Enquiries to: Secretary

Organisation type and purpose: Registered charity.

Access to staff: Contact by letter
Hours: Mon to Fri, 0900 to 1700

BEDFORD CENTRAL LIBRARY

Harpur Street, Bedford, MK40 1PG

Tel: 01234 718178, 01234 718168 (Reference Library)
Fax: 01234 342163
E-mail: centralp@bedford.gov.uk
Website: www.bedford.gov.uk

Enquiries to: The Library Manager
Direct e-mail: bedfordshirelibraries@bedford.gov.uk.

Organisation type and purpose: Local government body, public library.

Subject coverage: Local community information, business information, local studies, family history, John Bunyan.

Collection: Bedford Old Library
Bedfordshire Local Studies Library
Fowler Collection
Frank Mott Harrison Collection (John Bunyan)
George Offor Collection
General Registrar's Index to Births, Marriages and Deaths, including the overseas index (microfiche)
Mark Rutherford Collection 1837–2002

Non-library collection catalogue: All or part available online

Library catalogue: All or part available online

Access to staff: Contact by letter, by telephone, by fax, by e-mail, in person and via website
Hours: Mon, Tue, Wed, Fri, 0900 to 1800; Thu, 0900 to 1300; Sat, 0900 to 1700

Access for disabled people: Lift, wide doors, toilet facilities

Parent body: Bedford Borough Council

BEDFORD COLLEGE

Cauldwell Street, Bedford, MK42 9AH

Tel: 01234 291000, 01234 291320 (Learning Resources Centre)
Fax: 01234 342674
E-mail: learningresources@bedford.ac.uk
Website: www.bedford.ac.uk

Enquiries to: Learning Resources Service Manager
Direct tel: 01234 291320
Direct e-mail: hcjones@bedford.ac.uk

Founded: 1993; created by the merger of Shuttleworth College (formerly part of Writtle College) and Bedford College (year of change 2009)

Organisation type and purpose: Suitable for ages: 14+.

Subject coverage: Engineering (mechanical, electrical, electronic, motor vehicle, aeronautical engineering), construction, business studies, art and design, English as a foreign language, leisure, sport, tourism, catering, computing, performing arts, health, social and child care, hair, beauty and holistic therapies, agriculture, animal care, equine studies, horticulture, land management.

Non-library collection catalogue: All or part available in-house

Library catalogue: All or part available online

Access to staff: Contact by letter, by telephone, by e-mail and via website. Appointment necessary.
Hours: Term time: Mon to Thu, 0830 to 1830; Fri, 0830 to 1630
Vacations: Mon to Fri, 1000 to 1600
Special comments: Closed on some Fridays in vacation until mid-August. Please ring for details.

Access for disabled people: Access to all public areas, toilet facilities, parking provided, ramped entry

BEDFORDSHIRE AND LUTON ARCHIVES AND RECORDS SERVICE (BLARS)

Riverside Building, Borough Hall, Cauldwell Street, Bedford, MK42 9AP

Tel: 01234 228833/4, 01234 228777
Fax: 01234 228854
E-mail: archive@bedford.gov.uk
Website: www.bedford.gov.uk/archive

Enquiries to: Archivist
Other contacts: Ops Manager (Customer Services & Outreach)

Founded: 1913; formerly called Bedfordshire Record Office (year of change 1997)

Organisation type and purpose: Local government body; archive repository.
The Service collects and preserves a comprehensive and evolving archive illustrating all aspects of Bedfordshire life and history, including contemporary records of archival value; facilitates public and community access to the records; and promotes their use for business, education, cultural and recreational purposes.

Subject coverage: Bedfordshire history – all aspects; documents recording or illustrating: the topography, ownership, occupations and use of land in Bedfordshire; human activity in Bedfordshire, e.g. the social, economic, religious, cultural, political, administrative life and history of the county's inhabitants, communities, organisations and government at all levels.

Information services: Advice on holdings is free; there is a charge for research.

Education services: Limited: small groups can be catered for on site; talks offered to local societies.

Services for disabled people: See website for advice. Hearing loop and adjustable chairs on site

Collection: Unique archive material from a variety of sources. Major holdings include quarter sessions archives, county council, district and parish council archives, Bedford estate papers, Lucas (Wrest Park) collection, Whitbread Family papers, Bedford archdeaconry records, ecclesiastical parish records, Pym Family papers and estate archives, and records from Orlebar estate, Methodist Church, Beds and Herts Regiment, Poor Law unions and London Brick Company

Non-library collection catalogue: All or part available online

Library catalogue: All or part available online

Publications: Printed, and electronic and video, and microform publications
Order printed publications from: Archive
Order microform publications from: archive@bedford.gov.uk

Publications list: Available online

Access to staff: Contact by letter, by telephone, by fax, by e-mail, in person and via website
Hours: Mon, 0900 to 1900; Tue, Wed and Fri, 0900 to 1700
Closed Thu and weekends

Access to building: same as opening hours
Hours: As access to staff

Access for disabled people: Access to all public areas
Hours: As standard opening hours
Special comments: Access possible, please contact the service in advance. Guidance on website.

Parent body: Bedford Borough Council; Borough Hall, Bedford, MK42 9AP; tel: 01234 267422; fax: 01234 221606; e-mail: centralp@bedford.gov.uk; website: http://www.bedford.gov.uk

BEDFORDSHIRE FAMILY HISTORY SOCIETY

PO Box 214, Bedford, MK42 9RX

E-mail: bfhs@bfhs.org.uk
Website: www.bfhs.org.uk

Enquiries to: Honorary Secretary

Founded: 1977

Organisation type and purpose:
Membership association (membership is by subscription), present number of members: 1,000, registered charity (charity number 281677).
To bring together those interested in family history, genealogy and heraldry, primarily in Bedfordshire.

Publications: Printed, and electronic and video, and microform publications
Order printed publications from: bookstall@bfhs.org.uk
Order microform publications from: parishsales@bfhs.org.uk
Order electronic and video publications from: parishsales@bfhs.or.uk

Publications list: Available online and in print

Access to staff: Contact by letter, by e-mail and via website
Hours: Mon to Fri, 0900 to 1700

BEDFORDSHIRE HISTORICAL RECORD SOCIETY (BHRS)

48 St Augustine's Road, Bedford, MK40 2ND

Tel: 01234 309548
E-mail: rsmart@ntlworld.com
Website: www.bedfordshirehrs.org.uk

Enquiries to: Honorary Secretary

Founded: 1913

Organisation type and purpose: Learned society (membership is by subscription), present number of members: 250, registered charity (charity number 1098629).
Record publishing society (historical source materials for Bedfordshire).
Publication of materials for the history of Bedfordshire.

Subject coverage: Bedfordshire local history, archival sources.

Collection: The Fowler Library (owned by BHRS but housed by the University of Northampton)

Non-library collection catalogue: All or part available online and in print

Publications: Printed, and microform publications

Publications list: Available online and in print

Access to staff: Contact by letter, by telephone, by e-mail and via website
Hours: Mon to Fri, 0900 to 1700

BEES FOR DEVELOPMENT (BfD)

1 Agincourt Street, Monmouth, NP25 3DZ

Tel: 01600 714848
E-mail: info@beesfordevelopment.org
Website: www.beesfordevelopment.org

Enquiries to: Director

Founded: 1993

Organisation type and purpose: International organisation, training organisation, consultancy.

Subject coverage: Beekeeping in developing countries.

Library catalogue: All or part available in-house

Access to staff: Contact by letter, by telephone, by fax, by e-mail and via website. Appointment necessary.
Hours: Mon to Fri, 0900 to 1700
Special comments: Strictly by prior appointment.

Access to building: Prior appointment required

BELARUS EMBASSY

Formal name: The Embassy of the Republic of Belarus

6 Kensington Court, London, W8 5DL

Tel: 020 7937 3288
Fax: 020 7361 0005
E-mail: uk.london@mfa.gov.by
Website: www.uk.belembassy.org

Enquiries to: Ambassador

Organisation type and purpose: National government body.
Embassy.

Subject coverage: Belarus and Belarusian governmental matters, economy and trade.

Trade and statistical information: Belarusian market

Access to staff: Contact by letter, by telephone, by fax and by e-mail
Hours: Mon to Fri, 0900 to 1800

Access to building: No access other than to staff

BELFAST AND LISBURN WOMEN'S AID

Support & Resource Centre, 30 Adelaide Park, Belfast, BT9 6FY

Tel: 028 9066 6049; 24-hour helpline: 0800 9171 414
E-mail: admin@belfastwomensaid.org.uk
Website: www.belfastwomensaid.org.uk

Organisation type and purpose: Registered charity.
Provides confidential support, information and emergency accommodation for women and children affected by domestic violence. To provide temporary refuge for women and their children suffering mental, physical or sexual abuse within the home; to offer support and advice to any woman who asks for it, whether or not she is living in a refuge, and to offer supportive aftercare to women leaving the refuge; to encourage the woman to take control of her own future, whether this involves returning home or beginning an independent life; to recognise and care for the needs of the children involved; to educate and inform the public, the media, the courts and statutory and voluntary agencies, always mindful of the fact that abused women are a direct result of the general position of women in our society.

Subject coverage: Women's Aid's 3 refuges – in Belfast and in Lisburn, its outreach work, personal development training, awareness-raising for statutory and voluntary agencies, young people's projects, and inter-agency work.

Education services: Awareness-raising training for statutory and voluntary agencies. Links with schools and youth clubs throughout Belfast and Lisburn to promote healthy and non-abusive relationships.

Publications: Printed, and electronic and video
Order printed publications from: Above address
Order electronic and video publications from: Download from website

Access to staff: Contact by letter, by telephone, by e-mail and in person

Access to building: *Hours:* 0900 to 1730

BELFAST CARERS' CENTRE

Belfast Carers' Centre, The Mount, 2 Woodstock Link, Belfast, BT6 8DD

Tel: 028 9073 0173
Fax: 028 9073 0199
E-mail: info@carerscentre.org
Website: www.carerscentre.org

Enquiries to: Manager
Direct e-mail: r.devlin@carerscentre.org

Founded: 2002; formerly called Princess Royal Trust Limited

Organisation type and purpose: Registered charity.

Subject coverage: Information and support for carers. Registered charity number XR27404

Collection: Range of information material pertinent to carers.

Publications list: Available online and in print

Access to staff: Contact by letter, by telephone, by fax, by e-mail and via website. Appointment necessary.
Hours: Mon to Fri, 0900 to 1700

Access to building: No prior appointment required
Hours: Mon to Fri, 0900 to 1700

BELFAST CITY COUNCIL

Chief Executive's Department, Belfast City Hall, Belfast, BT1 5GS

Tel: 028 9032 0202, 028 9027 0405 (Minicom)
Fax: 028 9027 0325
E-mail: generalenquiries@belfastcity.gov.uk
Website: www.belfastcity.gov.uk/

Enquiries to: Director
Direct e-mail: shawa@belfastcity.co.uk
Other contacts: Head of Capital Works, Tourism Manager, Events Manager, Culture and Arts Manager,

Organisation type and purpose: Local government body.

Subject coverage: Economic development, arts, tourism development and events in Belfast.

Publications: Printed

Access to staff: Contact by letter, by telephone, by fax and by e-mail. Appointment necessary.
Hours: Mon to Fri, 0900 to 1700

Access to building: Prior appointment required

Connections with: Belfast First Stop Business Shop (First Stop Shop); tel: 028 9027 8399; Belfast Visitor & Convention Bureau (BVCB); tel: 028 9023 9026; Investment Belfast Limited (IBL); tel: 028 9031 136

BELFAST INSTITUTE OF FURTHER AND HIGHER EDUCATION (BIFHE)

Gerald Moag Campus, Millfield, Belfast, BT1 1HS

E-mail: Admissions@belfastmet.ac.uk
Website: www.belfastinstitute.ac.uk

Enquiries to: Information Officer
Direct e-mail: information_services@belfastinstitute.ac.uk
Other contacts: Director

Founded: 1991; formerly called College of Business Studies, College of Technology, Rupert Stanley College

Subject coverage: Education and training at all levels in all subjects except mining, agriculture and marine technology.

Publications: Printed

continued overleaf

Access to staff: Contact by letter, by telephone, by fax, by e-mail and in person
Hours: Mon to Thu, 0900 to 1700; Fri, 0900 to 1600

BELFAST PUBLIC LIBRARIES

Royal Avenue, Belfast, BT1 1EA

Tel: 028 9050 9150
Fax: 028 9033 2819
E-mail: info@libraries.belfast-elb.gov.uk

Enquiries to: Chief Librarian
Direct e-mail: outreach.belb@librariesni.org.uk

Founded: 1888; formerly called Belfast City Libraries

Organisation type and purpose: Local government body, public library.

Subject coverage: Departmentalised as follows:
General Reference Library; social sciences, philosophy, religion, history, arts, literature, science, medicine, law
Local History Library; local studies and Irish material
Music Library; music, records, cassettes, CDs, scores
Business Library; business information
Electronic Information Services; internet access, CD-ROM, on-line searching, software application, e-mail.

Collection: Belfast Theatre Posters
Early Belfast printed books
F J Bigger Collection
Grainger, Moore, Riddell and Horner Collections
Irish and Belfast Newspapers from 1761
Irish folksong and music records
Irish history, archaeology and antiquarian material
J S Crone Collection
UN Depository Library

Publications: Printed

Access to staff: Contact by letter, by telephone, by fax, by e-mail and in person
Hours: Mon, Thu, 0900 to 2000; Tue, Wed, Fri, 0900 to 1730; Sat, 0900 to 1300

Access for disabled people: Level entry, access to all public areas, toilet facilities

BELGIAN EMBASSY

103 Eaton Square, London, SW1W 9AB

Tel: 020 7470 3700
Fax: 020 7259 6213
E-mail: info@belgium-embassy.co.uk
Website: belgium.fgov.be
Website: www.belgium.fgov.be
Website: www.belgium-embassy.co.uk

Enquiries to: Information Officer

Organisation type and purpose: Diplomatic mission.

Subject coverage: General (politics, media, monarchy, etc), culture, economics, working and living in Belgium, visas and passports.

Publications: Printed

Heads or is associated with the: Anglo-Belgian Club; 60 Knightsbridge, London, SW1X 7LF; tel: 020 7235 2121; fax: 020 7243 9470; Belgian Consulates; Belgian Tourist Office Brussels-Ardennes; 217 Marsh Wall, London, E14 9FJ; tel: 020 7531 0390; fax: 020 7531 0393; e-mail: info@belgium-tourism.net; Belgo-Luxembourg Chamber of Commerce; Riverside House, 27–29 Vauxhall Grove, London, SW8 1SY; tel: 020 7820 7839; fax: 020 7793 1628; Tourism Flanders-Brussels; 31 Pepper Street, London, E14 9RW; tel: 020 7867 0311; fax: 020 7458 0045; e-mail: info@flanders-tourism.org

BELIZE HIGH COMMISSION

Third Floor, 45 Crawford Place, London, W1H 4LP

Tel: 020 7723 3603
Fax: 020 7723 9637
E-mail: bzhc-lon@btconnect.com
Website: www.belizehighcommission.com

Enquiries to: High Commissioner
Other contacts: The First Secretary for Consular and Administrative Affairs

Organisation type and purpose: National government body.
Diplomatic mission of the government of Belize.

Subject coverage: Belize: economics, tourism, politics, investment, trade, social structure, citizenship and visas.

Publications: Printed

Access to staff: Contact by letter, by telephone, by fax and by e-mail. Appointment necessary.
Hours: Mon to Fri, 1000 to 1800

Access to building: Prior appointment required
Hours: Consular Hours: Mon to Wed, 1000 to 1300

BELL COLLEGE TECHNICAL INFORMATION SERVICE (BECTIS)

Bell College of Technology, Almada Street, Hamilton, South Lanarkshire, ML3 0JB

Tel: 01698 285658
Fax: 01698 286856
Website: www.bell.ac.uk

Enquiries to: Information Officer

Organisation type and purpose: Commercial information service.
To make the resources of Bell College Library available to the industrial community.

Subject coverage: Industrial, commercial and public authorities information, technical and managerial subjects, British Standards.

Publications: Printed

Access to staff: Contact by letter, by telephone, by fax, by e-mail and in person
Hours: Mon to Fri, 0830 to 1630

Access to building: No access other than to staff
Hours: Term time: Mon to Thu, 0830 to 2100; Fri, 0830 to 1630; Sat 0900 to 1300

BENESH INSTITUTE

36 Battersea Square, London, SW11 3RA

Tel: 020 7326 8031
Fax: 020 7924 3129
E-mail: beneshinstitute@rad.org.uk
Website: www.benesh.org

Enquiries to: Director

Founded: 1962; formerly called Institute of Choreology

Organisation type and purpose: Professional body (membership is by subscription), registered charity (charity number 312826), suitable for ages: 16+.
Education and research institute in movement notation.

Subject coverage: Benesh Movement Notation, anthropology, choreography, computer research, dance techniques, dance repertoire, ethnic dance, physiotherapy.

Collection: Choreographic scores in Benesh Movement Notation

Library catalogue: All or part available online

Publications: Printed, and electronic and video
Order printed publications from: http://www.radenterprises.co.uk
Order electronic and video publications from: http://www.radenterprises.co.uk

Publications list: Available online

Access to staff: Contact by letter, by telephone, by fax and by e-mail. Appointment necessary. Non-members charged.
Hours: Mon to Thu, 1000 to 1800; Fri, 1000 to 1730

Access to building: Prior appointment required
Hours: Mon to Thu, 1000 to 1800; Fri, 1000 to 1730

Access for disabled people: Ramped entry, toilet facilities
Special comments: Wheelchair access to first two floors.

Links with: The Royal Academy of Dance; at the same address; tel: 020 7326 8000; fax: 020 7924 3129; e-mail: info@rad.org.uk; website: http://www.rad.org.uk

BERKELEY ENTHUSIASTS CLUB

41 Gorsewood Road, St Johns, Woking, Surrey, GU21 1UZ

Tel: 01483 475330
E-mail: BECMembership@gmail.com

Enquiries to: Secretary

Founded: 1963

Organisation type and purpose: Membership association (membership is by subscription), present number of members: 300, voluntary organisation.

Subject coverage: Preservation of all types of 3- and 4-wheeled Berkeley sports cars, sources of cars, parts, technical advice.

Publications: Printed

Access to staff: Contact by letter
Hours: Mon to Fri, 0900 to 1700

BERKSHIRE ARCHAEOLOGICAL SOCIETY (BAS)

43 Laburnham Road, Maidenhead, Berkshire, SL6 4DE

Tel: 01628 631225

Website: www.berksarch.co.uk/

Enquiries to: Honorary Secretary

Founded: 1871

Organisation type and purpose: Learned society.

Subject coverage: Berkshire archaeology and history.

Collection: Library of rare books on Berkshire
Pre-1998 archaeological periodicals from UK mostly, some from elsewhere, for sale from October 1998, please apply for catalogue

Publications: Printed

Access to staff: Contact by letter
Hours: Mon to Fri, 0900 to 1700
Special comments: International reply coupon requested if outside UK.

Member of: Council for British Archaeology

Practical Arm: Berkshire Field Research Group

BERKSHIRE LOCAL HISTORY ASSOCIATION (BLHA)

1 Priest Hill, Caversham, Reading, RG4 7RZ

Tel: 0118 948 3354
E-mail: chairman@blha.org.uk
Website: www.blha.org.uk

Enquiries to: Chairman
Other contacts: Newsletter Editor

Founded: 1976

Organisation type and purpose:
Membership association (membership is by subscription), present number of members: 40 corporate bodies, 80 individuals and voluntary organisations.
Our object is to encourage interest in local history in the county, both before and after the 1974 boundary changes. This includes visits, day schools, training workshops, opportunities for research, loans, awards and prizes for research and publication.

Subject coverage: All aspects of the history of Berkshire, its towns, parishes, people, landscape, etc.

Publications: Printed

Access to staff: Contact by letter, by telephone and by e-mail
Hours: Mon to Fri, 0900 to 1700

Affiliated to: British Association for Local History

Members include: Berkshire Archaeological Society; tel: 01628 631225; website: berksarch.co.uk
Berkshire Family History Society; tel: 0118 984 3995; website: www.berksfhs.co.uk
Berkshire Industrial Archaeology Group; tel: 0118 978 5234; website: www.biag.org.uk
Berkshire Record Office; tel: 0118 901 5132; fax: 0118 901 5131; e-mail: arch@reading.gov .uk; many local history and historical societies in the county; Reading Borough Libraries; website: www.readinglibraries .org.uk

Other addresses: Berkshire Local History Association; 18 Foster Road, Abingdon, Oxfordshire, OX14 1YN

BERKSHIRE RECORD OFFICE

9 Coley Avenue, Reading, Berkshire, RG1 6AF

Tel: 0118 937 5132
Fax: 0118 937 5131
E-mail: arch@reading.gov.uk
Website: www.berkshirerecordoffice.org.uk

Enquiries to: County Archivist

Founded: 1948

Organisation type and purpose: Local government body.

Subject coverage: Family and local history relating to Berkshire (including area now in Oxfordshire).

Collection: Business archives, charity archives, church archives, estate and family archives, local government archives, hospital archives, court archives

Non-library collection catalogue: All or part available online and in-house

Publications: Electronic and video

Access to staff: Contact by letter, by telephone, by fax, by e-mail, in person and via website
Hours: Mon, telephone only; Tue and Wed, 0900 to 1700; Thu, 0900 to 2100; Fri, 0900 to 1630
Special comments: Closed for two weeks' stocktaking, usually last week in November and first week in December.

Access for disabled people: Parking provided, level entry, access to all public areas, toilet facilities

Parent body: Bracknell Forest Council; Reading Borough Council; Royal Borough of Windsor and Maidenhead; Slough Borough Council; West Berkshire Council; Wokingham Borough Council

BERKSHIRE, BUCKINGHAMSHIRE AND OXFORDSHIRE WILDLIFE TRUST (BBOWT)

The Lodge, 1 Armstrong Road, Littlemore, Oxford, OX4 4XT

Tel: 01865 775476
Fax: 01865 711301
E-mail: info@bbowt.org.uk
Website: www.bbowt.org.uk

Enquiries to: Information Officer
Direct e-mail: wildinfo@bbowt.org.uk

Founded: 1961; formerly called Berkshire, Buckinghamshire and Oxfordshire Naturalists' Trust (BBONT) (year of change 1999)

Organisation type and purpose: Voluntary organisation, registered charity (charity number 204330).
Environmental, conservation, wildlife organisation.

Subject coverage: All aspects of wildlife in Berkshire, Buckinghamshire and Oxfordshire.

Collection: Guides to nature reserves in these three counties

Publications: Printed

Access to staff: Contact by letter, by telephone, by fax, by e-mail and via website. Appointment necessary.
Hours: Mon to Fri, 0900 to 1700

Parent body: Wildlife Trusts; UK Office, The Kiln, Waterside, Mather Road, Newark, Notts, NG24 1NT; tel: 0870 036 7711; fax: 0870 036 0101; e-mail: enquiry@ wildlifetrusts.org

BERLIOZ SOCIETY

450b Lea Bridge Road, London, E10 7DY

Tel: 020 8539 9122
E-mail: sqing@btinternet.com
Website: www.theberliozsociety.org.uk

Enquiries to: Honorary Secretary

Founded: 1952

Organisation type and purpose:
Membership association (membership is by subscription), present number of members: 240.

Subject coverage: Music of Berlioz, life of Berlioz, performances of Berlioz' work, Berlioz' writing.

Non-library collection catalogue: All or part available in-house

Library catalogue: All or part available in-house

Publications: Printed
Order printed publications from: Bulletin, Berlioz Society, 450b Lea Bridge Road, London, E10 7DY

Access to staff: Contact by letter, by telephone, by e-mail and via website

Access to building: No access other than to staff

BERMUDA TOURISM

26 York Street, London, W1U 6PZ

Tel: 0207 096 4246
Fax: 0207 096 0509
E-mail: ukeurope@bermudatourism.com

Enquiries to: Manager
Other contacts: Sales Administration Co-ordinator

Founded: 1985; formerly called Bermuda Tourism BCB Limited

Organisation type and purpose: National Tourist Office.

Subject coverage: Bermuda, tourism and travel.

Publications: Printed

Access to staff: Contact by e-mail
Hours: Mon to Fri, 0900 to 1700

Access to building: No access other than to staff

BERTRAND RUSSELL PEACE FOUNDATION LIMITED (BRPF)

Russell House, Bulwell Lane, Nottingham, NG6 0BT

Tel: 0115 978 4504
Fax: 0115 942 0433
E-mail: elfeuro@compuserve.com
Website: www.russfound.org
Website: www.spokesmanbooks.com

Enquiries to: Secretary
Direct tel: 0115 970 8318

continued overleaf

Direct e-mail: julia@brpf.demon.co.uk

Founded: 1963

Organisation type and purpose:
International organisation (membership is by election or invitation), research organisation, publishing house.
To investigate the causes of international and social conflict and to work for peace and disarmament.

Subject coverage: International relations, politics, economics, civil liberties.

Publications: Printed
Order printed publications from: http://www.spokesmanbooks.com

Publications list: Available online and in print

Access to staff: Contact by letter, by telephone, by fax, by e-mail and via website
Hours: Mon to Fri, 0900 to 1700

Access to building: Prior appointment required

BERWICK-UPON-TWEED RECORD OFFICE

Council Offices, Wallace Green, Berwick-upon-Tweed, Northumberland, TD15 1ED

Tel: 01289 301865
Fax: 01289 330540
E-mail: berwickarchives@woodhorn.org.uk
Website: www.experiencewoodhorn.com/berwick-record

Enquiries to: Archivist

Founded: 1980

Organisation type and purpose: Local government body.
Record office.

Subject coverage: Local and family history of North Northumberland including Berwick-upon-Tweed.

Collection: Berwick Borough Archives, 16th to 20th centuries
Berwick Salmon Fisheries company records
Ford and Etal Estate records
IGI (England, Scotland and Ireland, microfiche)
North Northumberland census returns, 1841 to 1901 (microfilm)
North Northumberland parish registers (microfilm)
GRO Birth, Marriage and Death Indexes, 1837 to 1955 (microfiche)

Non-library collection catalogue: All or part available in-house

Publications: Printed, and microform publications

Publications list: Available online and in print

Access to staff: Contact by letter, by telephone, by fax, by e-mail and in person
Hours: Only Wed & Thu, 0930 to 1300 and 1400 to 1700

Access for disabled people: Level entry, toilet facilities

Parent body: Woodhorn Trust; Woodhorn, QEII Country Park, Ashington, Northumberland, NE63 9YF; tel: 01670 528080; website: htttp://www.experiencewoodhorn.com

BEVIN BOYS ASSOCIATION (BBA)

23 Great Cranford Street, Poundbury, Dorchester, Dorset, DT1 3SQ

Tel: 01305 261269

Enquiries to: Archivist / Public Relations
Direct tel: 01305 261269
Other contacts: Vice President / National Chairman

Founded: 1989

Organisation type and purpose: Voluntary organisation.
To encourage comradeship, and organise reunions and events throughout the UK for all ex-Bevin Boys who worked in the coal mines to serve their National Service in lieu of service in the Forces during WWII. Bevin Boys were so named after Ernest Bevin the wartime Minister of Labour and National Service.

Publications: Printed

Access to staff: Contact by letter and by telephone
Hours: Mon to Fri, 0900 to 1700

BEXLEY LIBRARY SERVICE

Central Library, Townley Road, Bexleyheath, Kent, DA6 7HJ

Tel: 020 8303 7777 ext. 3450
Fax: 020 8304 7058
E-mail: centrallibrary@bexley.gov.uk
Website: www.bexley.gov.uk

Enquiries to: Library Manager

Organisation type and purpose: Local government body, public library.

Subject coverage: General.

Collection: Government publications

Non-library collection catalogue: All or part available online

Library catalogue: All or part available online

Access to staff: Contact by letter, by telephone, by fax, by e-mail and in person
Hours: Mon, Tue, Wed, Fri, 0930 to 1730; Thu 0930 to 2000; Sat, 0930 to 1700; Sun, 1000 to 1400

Branch of: South East Area Libraries Information Co-operative (SEAL)

BEXLEY LOCAL STUDIES AND ARCHIVE CENTRE

Central Library, Townley Road, Bexleyheath, Kent, DA6 7HJ

Tel: 020 3045 3369
Fax: 020 8304 7058
E-mail: archives@bexley.gov.uk
Website: www.bexley.gov.uk/archives

Enquiries to: Local Studies Manager
Other contacts: Archivist (for archive collection enquiries)

Founded: 1972; formerly called Bexley Local Studies Society

Organisation type and purpose: Public library, Diocesan Record Office for Rochester and Southwark, Local Authority Record Office for Bexley

Subject coverage: Historical information for area now covered by London Borough of Bexley.

Non-library collection catalogue: All or part available online and in-house

Library catalogue: All or part available online and in-house

Publications: Printed, and electronic and video, and microform publications

Publications list: Available online

Access to staff: Contact by letter, by telephone, by fax, by e-mail, in person and via website
Hours: Mon to Wed, 1000 to 1730; Thu, 1000 to 1900; Fri, 1000 to 1300; Sat, 1000 to 1700

Access for disabled people: Access to all public areas, toilet facilities

Parent body: London Borough of Bexley; Civic Offices, Bexleyheath, Broadway, Kent, DA6 7LB; tel: 020 8303 7777; website: http://www.bexley.gov.uk

BFI NATIONAL ARCHIVE

Formal name: British Film Institute

Curatorial Unit, 21 Stephen Street, London, W1T 1LN

Tel: 020 7255 1444
Fax: 020 7580 7503
E-mail: information.unit@bfi.org.uk
Website: www.bfi.org.uk/national archive
Website: www.bfi.org.uk

Founded: 1935

Organisation type and purpose: National government body.
Cultural organisation.

Subject coverage: Art and history of the cinema and of television, the documentary record of the 20th century. Films, video and TV programmes produced, shown, distributed or transmitted in the UK; preservation and restoration; cataloguing of film and TV material.

Collection: The Archive holds approximately 450,000 titles dating from 1895 to the present day
The Collection comprises features and short films, animation, documentaries, newsreels, television programmes, amateur films and videos

Non-library collection catalogue: All or part available online and in-house

Publications: Printed

Access to staff: Contact by letter, by telephone, by fax, by e-mail and in person
Hours: Mon to Fri, 1000 to 1730

Access to building: Appointment required

BFI – Imax Cinema: 1 Charlie Chaplin Walk, South Bank, Waterloo, London, SE1 8XR; tel: 020 7902 1234

Founder member of: International Federation of Film Archives

BFMS

Formal name: British False Memory Society

Bradford on Avon, Wiltshire, BA15 1NF

Tel: 01225 868682

Fax: 01225 862251
E-mail: bfms@bfms.org.uk
Website: www.bfms.org.uk

Enquiries to: Administrator
Direct e-mail: bfms@bfms.org.uk

Founded: 1993; formerly called ACAP, British False Memory Society

Organisation type and purpose: Registered charity (charity number 1040683).
Formed in 1993 to raise awareness of dangers of 'recovered memory therapy', which has given rise to an epidemic of decades-delayed, uncorroborated allegations against parents of childhood sexual abuse. Comprehensive archive on damage to patients and families as a result of false allegations influenced by therapy and associated beliefs; legal implications of 'recovered memory' and unreliable allegations in the criminal and civil courts, with case histories and contacts.

Subject coverage: False memory/recovered memory including legal implications.

Collection: Books, videos, audio cassettes, academic papers and newspaper, journal and magazine cuttings

Non-library collection catalogue: All or part available in-house

Library catalogue: All or part available in-house

Publications: Printed, and electronic and video

Access to staff: Contact by letter, by telephone, by fax, by e-mail and via website. Appointment necessary. Access for members only.
Hours: Mon to Thu, 0915 to 1700
Special comments: Lift serves the first two flights of stairs, but not the third flight of stairs.

Access to building: *Hours:* Mon to Thurs, 0915 to 1700

Access for disabled people: Ramped entry
Special comments: Lift to 1st floor only.

BFWG CHARITABLE FOUNDATION

Formal name: FfWG

20 Fern Road, Storrington, Pulborough, West Sussex, RH20 4LW

Tel: 01903 746723
Fax: 01903 746723
E-mail: valconsidine@btinternet.com
Website: www.ffwg.org.uk

Enquiries to: Company Secretary
Direct e-mail: jean.c@blueyonder.co.uk (re grants)
Other contacts: Grants Administrator (for details relating to grant applications)

Founded: 1925; formerly called Crosby Hall (year of change 1993)

Organisation type and purpose: Registered charity (charity number 312903).
Grant awarding charity.
Grants to help women graduates with their living expenses while registered for study or research at an approved institution of higher education in Great Britain.

Access to staff: Contact by letter, by telephone, by fax, by e-mail, in person and via website. Appointment necessary.
Hours: Mon to Fri, 0900 to 1645

Member organisation of: International Federation of University Women (IFUW); 8 rue de l'Ancien Port, 1201, Geneva, Switzerland; tel: +41 22 731 1280; fax: +41 22 738 0440; e-mail: ifuw@ifuw.org; University Women of Europe (UWE)

Parent body: British Federation of Women Graduates (BFWG); 4 Mandeville Courtyard, 142 Battersea Park Road, London, SW11 4NB; tel: 020 7498 8037; fax: 020 7498 8037; e-mail: bfwg@bfwg.demon.co.uk

BG GROUP PLC

Information Centre, 100 Thames Valley Park Drive, Reading, Berkshire, RG6 1PT

Tel: +44 (0) 118 935 3222
Fax: +44 (0) 118 935 3484
E-mail: padraig.cronin@bg-group.com

Enquiries to: Commercial Intelligence Manager
Other contacts: Information Analyst

History of institution: formerly called British Gas (year of change 1997); formerly called BG plc (year of change 1999)

Organisation type and purpose:
International organisation, industrial commercial company.
Gas exploration and production, overseas gas-related ventures.

Subject coverage: Oil/gas exploration and production, LNG, power generation, gas transmission and distribution.

Library catalogue: All or part available in-house

Access to staff: Contact by letter, by telephone and by fax
Hours: Mon to Fri, 0900 to 1700

Access to building: Prior appointment required

Access for disabled people: Parking provided, access to all public areas

BHF GROUP

225 Bristol Road, Edgbaston, Birmingham, B5 7UB

Tel: 0121 446 6688 or 01295 713333
Fax: 01295 711665
E-mail: info@bira.co.uk
Website: www.bira.co.uk

Enquiries to: Information Officer

Founded: 1899

Organisation type and purpose: Trade association.
Trade Federation.
Represents more than 4,000 primary retail outlets in hardware, ironmongery, DIY, building supplies and agricultural machinery.

Subject coverage: Finance clearing house, merchandising company, insurance, inter-firm comparison, computer systems, information service, training, shop design, direct mail.

Publications: Printed

Access to staff: Contact by letter and by e-mail. Access for members only.
Hours: Mon to Fri, 0900 to 1700

Links with: British Retail Consortium; DTI De-Regulation Task Force; Eurocommerce Limited; International Hardware Association; Rainy Day Trust

BHR GROUP

Formal name: A trading name of VirtualPiE Ltd

The Fluid Engineering Centre, Cranfield, Bedfordshire, MK43 0AJ

Tel: 07785 621694
Fax: 01234 750074
E-mail: contactus@bhrgroup.com
Website: www.bhrgroup.com
Enquiries to: Manager – Information Service
Direct tel: 07785 621694
Direct e-mail: nguy@bhrgroup.co.uk

Founded: 1947

Organisation type and purpose:
Consultancy, research organisation.
Independent technology organisation.

Subject coverage: Fluid dynamics and process engineering, more specifically: pumps and other fluid machines, fluid power, tribology, abrasive waterjet and plain water jet cutting and cleaning technology, fluid sealing and containment integrity, multiphase flow, pipeline technology; flow in pipes, cavitation, flow measurement and control, hydraulic transport of solid materials in pipelines, open channel flow, civil engineering, hydraulic structures (dams, spillways, flood defences, cooling systems, etc.), fluid effects on structures, industrial aerodynamics, biotechnology; process technology, process intensification, fluid control, valves, oil and gas production improvement, oil and gas transport, water and waste water treatment, water supply modelling software systems, knowledge-based software tools for water resource allocation planning, biodiesel production; knowhow for reduction of emissions, computational fluid dynamics (CFD), pipeline pigging and pipe protection, mixing – batch and inline, filtration and separation.

Non-library collection catalogue: All or part available online and in-house

Library catalogue: All or part available in-house

Publications list: Available online

Access to staff: Contact by letter, by telephone, by fax, by e-mail, in person and via website
Hours: Mon to Wed, 0900 to 1700
Special comments: Charges, either by subscription or one-off, for certain services; details on request.

Access to building: By arrangement

BIAB ONLINE – BRITISH AND IRISH ARCHAEOLOGICAL BIBLIOGRAPHY (biab online)

St Mary's House, 66 Bootham, York, YO30 7BZ

continued overleaf

Tel: 01904 671417
Fax: 020 7969 5300 (shared)
E-mail: info@biab.ac.uk
Website: www.biab.ac.uk

Enquiries to: Chief Bibliographer & Editor

Founded: 1968; formerly called British Archaeological Abstracts (year of change 1991); formerly called British Archaeological Bibliography (year of change 1997)

Organisation type and purpose: Research organisation.
biab online is a service provided by the Council for British Archaeology (CBA) with the support of funding from English Heritage, Society of Antiquaries of London, Cadw, the Heritage Council of the Republic of Ireland, RCAHMW, RCAHMS, Historic Scotland, Society of Antiquaries of Scotland, Archaeology Scotland, and the Northern Ireland Environment Agency. It provides the abstracts and indexing service for British and Irish Archaeology and is now available online at http://www.biab.ac.uk.
To compile and publish a comprehensive bibliography for the archaeology of Great Britain and Ireland.

Subject coverage: Archaeology of Great Britain and Republic of Ireland; publications relating to the archaeology of Great Britain and Ireland.

Collection: Electronic data on archaeology bibliography from 1695 to 1980, citations only; 1967 to present, citations and abstracts

Publications: Electronic and video

Access to staff: Contact by letter, by telephone, by fax and by e-mail. Appointment necessary.
Hours: Mon to Fri, 1000 to 1730
Special comments: Staff are part-time – e-mailing ahead is recommended

Links with: Council for British Archaeology (CBA); St Mary's House, 66 Bootham, York, YO30 7BZ; tel: 01904 671 417; fax: 01904 671 384; website: http://www.britarch.ac.uk

BIBIC

Formal name: British Institute for Brain Injured Children

Knowle Hall, Bridgwater, Somerset, TA7 8PJ

Tel: 01278 684060
E-mail: info@bibic.org.uk
Website: www.bibic.org.uk

Founded: 1972

Organisation type and purpose: National organisation, voluntary organisation, registered charity (charity number 1057635). Caters for children from the age of 6 months to 18 years. BIBIC exists to maximise the potential of children with conditions affecting their social, sensory communication, motor and learning abilities.

Subject coverage: BIBIC's home-based therapy helps rehabilitate children variously diagnosed as having autism, autistic tendencies, brain damage, brain injury, cerebral palsy, developmental delay, Downs syndrome, dyslexia, epilepsy, hydrocephalus, learning difficulties, learning disability, microcephalus, dyspraxia, attention deficit hyperactivity disorders (ADHD). It draws not only on sensory-motor techniques but also incorporates aspects derived from speech therapy, physiotherapy and occupational therapy in a medically overseen environment.

Access to staff: Contact by letter, by telephone, by e-mail and via website. Appointment necessary.
Hours: Mon to Fri, 0900 to 1700

Access for disabled people: Parking provided, ramped entry, toilet facilities, lift
Special comments: Access to most public areas

BIBLE SOCIETY (BFBS)

Formal name: British & Foreign Bible Society

Contact Centre, Stonehill Green, Westlea, Swindon, Wiltshire, SN5 7DG

Tel: 01793 418100
Fax: 01793 418118
E-mail: contactus@biblesociety.org.uk
Website: www.biblesociety.org.uk

Enquiries to: Contact Centre
Direct tel: 01793 418222

Founded: 1804

Organisation type and purpose: Registered charity (charity number 232759).
Helping church people to own, use, value and share the Bible.

Subject coverage: Bible translation and distribution of the scriptures throughout the world, printing history, linguistics, church growth, mission, bible commentaries, social and religious trends, research reports relating to these.

Collection: Catalogue of manuscripts
Historical catalogue of printed Bibles with sectional revisions for African, English, Indian and Chinese scriptures
Scriptures Library and Archive (28,000 volumes in more than 2,000 languages) now housed in Cambridge University Library, access via Contact Centre, Swindon

Publications: Printed, and electronic and video
Order printed publications from: website: http://www.bibleresources.org.uk

Publications list: Available online

Access to staff: Contact by letter, by fax and by e-mail. Appointment necessary.
Hours: Mon to Fri, 0900 to 1700

Access for disabled people: Parking provided, ramped entry, access to all public areas, toilet facilities

Founder member of: United Bible Society – a fellowship of national bible societies around the world (UBS)

BIBLE TEXT PUBLICITY MISSION

PO Box 2677, Romford, Essex, RM7 8XF

Tel: 01708 733293
E-mail: ceochelmsford@btpm.org.uk
Website: www.btpm.org.uk

Organisation type and purpose: A Christian Mission committed to proclaiming the contents of the Bible on posters in public places.

Subject coverage: Posters and/or cards in railway stations, tube stations, Buses and HM Prisons.

Information services: Tel. for discussion of any issues arising from the posters, or for help and guidance.

Access to staff: Contact by letter, by telephone and by e-mail

Member organisation of: Evangelical Alliance

BIBLIOGRAPHICAL SOCIETY

Formal name: The Bibliographical Society

c/o Institute of English Studies, Room 306, Senate House, Malet Street, London, WC1E 7HU

E-mail: secretary@bibsoc.org.uk
Website: www.bibsoc.org.uk

Enquiries to: Honorary Secretary

Founded: 1892

Organisation type and purpose: Learned society.
Membership organisation (membership by subscription)
To promote and encourage study and research in the fields of: historical, analytical, descriptive and textual bibliography, and the history of printing, publishing, bookselling, bookbinding and collecting.
To hold meetings at which papers are read and discussed. To print and publish a journal and books concerned with bibliography.
To maintain a bibliographical library.
To support bibliographical research by awarding grants and bursaries.

Collection: Society's library is housed at Senate House, University of London. The catalogue for the library is now available electronically, via the catalogue of the School of Advanced Study at the University of London (go to http://catalogue.ulrls.lon.ac.uk/ and select Bibliographical Society from the options).

Library catalogue: All or part available online

Publications list: Available online

Access to staff: Contact by letter and by e-mail

BIBRA TOXICOLOGY ADVICE & CONSULTING LTD

Westmead House, 123 Westmead Road, Sutton, Surrey, SM1 4JH

Tel: 020 8722 4701
Fax: 020 8722 4706
E-mail: info@bibratoxadvice.co.uk
Website: www.bibra-information.co.uk/

Enquiries to: Information Officer
Other contacts: Sales Manager

Founded: 1960; created by the merger of BIBRA Information Services Ltd and Toxicology Advice & Consulting Ltd (year of change 2007); formerly called TNO BIBRA International Limited

Organisation type and purpose: Consultancy, research organisation.
Independent research and advice on the health effects of chemicals.

Subject coverage: Chemical toxicology and ecotoxicology and safety in use, including industrial chemicals, food additives, food contaminants such as packaging migrants, pesticides, feed additives and other agricultural chemicals, cosmetics and toiletry components, dry excipients, surgical products, tobacco additives and air and water pollutants, international legislation on the foregoing subjects, need for and design of toxicological tests on specific materials.

Collection: Unique collection of over 400,000 specially selected up-to-date research papers, reports, expert comment, and legislative material relating to the health effects of chemicals

Publications: Printed

Access to staff: Contact by letter, by telephone, by fax and by e-mail
Hours: Mon to Fri, 0900 to 1715

Parent body: TNO Nutrition and Food Research Institute; Utrechtseweg 48, PO Box 360, Zeist, Netherlands; tel: +31 3 694 4754; fax: +31 3 695 7928; e-mail: infodesk@tno.nl

BICYCLE ASSOCIATION OF GREAT BRITAIN LIMITED (BA)

The Bicycle Association, 3 The Quadrant, COVENTRY, CV1 2DY

Tel: +44 (0) 2476 553838
Fax: +44 (0) 2476 553838
E-mail: office@ba-gb.com

Enquiries to: Secretary

Organisation type and purpose: Trade association.

Subject coverage: British bicycle industry, manufacture, statistics, imports, accessories.

Trade and statistical information: UK market for bicycles

Order printed publications from: Secretary

Publications list: Available in print

Access to staff: Contact by letter and by telephone
Hours: Mon to Fri, 0900 to 1700

Access to building: No access other than to staff

BIGGAR ALBION FOUNDATION

The Albion Archive, 9 Edinburgh Road, Biggar, Lanarkshire, ML12 6AX

Tel: 01899 221497
E-mail: info@albionarch.co.uk
Website: www.albion-trust.org.uk

Enquiries to: Secretary

Founded: 1999

Organisation type and purpose: Foundation responsible for the Albion Club (membership is open to all those interested in Albion vehicles), the Albion Archive, the Biggar Rally and the Albion museum.

Subject coverage: Albion vehicles (1899–1976).

Information services: Identification of Albion lorries/vehicles for DVLA.

Special visitor services: Archive.

Collection: Albion archive of material relating to Albion commercial vehicles

Publications: Printed

Links with: Albion Vehicle Preservation Trust; 18 Netherdale Drive, Paisley, Renfrewshire, PA1 3DA

BILLINGS NATURAL FAMILY PLANNING CENTRE (The BOM Trust)

The Basement, 58b Vauxhall Grove, London, SW8 1TB

Tel: 020 7793 0026
Fax: 020 7793 0026

Enquiries to: Director General
Other contacts: Secretary for book and literature orders.

Founded: 1987; formerly called Billings Family Life Centre, Billings Natural Family Planning Centre

Organisation type and purpose: International organisation, national organisation, professional body (membership is by qualification, election or invitation), voluntary organisation, registered charity (charity number 10077245), suitable for ages: 12 to 22, training organisation, consultancy.

Subject coverage: Literature, teaching and teacher training in the Billings Ovulation Method providing a means of natural family planning for the achievement or avoidance of pregnancy. Teacher training and education courses in human sexuality which, while addressing all aspects of the human person including fertility, teach chastity.

Access to staff: Contact by letter, by telephone and by fax. Appointment necessary.
Hours: Mon, Tue, Wed, Fri, 1000 to 1800
Special comments: Evening and weekend appointments.
Charges made to all users (with exceptions). May close during state school holidays.

Access to building: Prior appointment required
Hours: Mon to Fri, 1000 to 1700; plus some evenings and Sats
Special comments: Closed on some evenings, some weekends and some school holidays.

Affiliated with the: World Organisation of Ovulation Method Billings (WOOMB)

Other addresses: Billings NFP Centre (Hours: Tue and Thu, 0930 to 1230); Margaret House, 132 Huntley Street, Aberdeen, AB10 1SU; tel: 01224 643300; e-mail: mariesandison@hotmail.com

Parent body: Billings Family Life Centre (WOOMB); 27 Alexandra Parade, North Fitzroy, 3068, Australia; tel: + 61 3 948 1722 / 1 800 336 860; fax: + 61 3 9482 4208; e-mail: billings@ozemail.com.au; website: http://www.woomb.org

BINGO ASSOCIATION, THE

Lexham House, 75 High Street North, Dunstable, Bedfordshire, LU6 1JF

Tel: 01582 860921
Fax: 01582 860925
E-mail: info@bingo-association.co.uk
Website: www.bingo-association.co.uk

Enquiries to: Chief Executive
Other contacts: Administration Manager for centre of activity.

Founded: 1985; formerly called Bingo Association of Great Britain (year of change 1998)

Organisation type and purpose: Trade association (membership is by qualification, election or invitation), present number of members: 125.

Subject coverage: Licensed bingo in Great Britain; Gaming Act 1968 and the law appertaining to licensed bingo, where, how and when you can play; history of bingo.

Publications: Printed

Access to staff: Contact by letter, by telephone, by fax, by e-mail, in person and via website. Appointment necessary.
Hours: Mon to Fri, 0900 to 1700

BIO INDUSTRY ASSOCIATION SCOTLAND (BIA Scotland)

Centre House, Midlothian Innovation Centre, Pentlandfield, Roslin, Midlothian, EH25 9RE

Tel: 0131 440 6161
Fax: 0131 440 2871
Website: www.bioindustry.org

Enquiries to: Director
Direct e-mail: sjohnstone@bioindustry.org

Founded: 2001; formerly called Scottish Biomedical Association (SbA) (year of change 2001)

Organisation type and purpose: Trade association.

Subject coverage: All aspects associated with the promotion of the healthcare industry, biomedical and biotechnology sectors in Scotland.

Publications: Printed, and electronic and video
Order printed publications from: Bio Industry Association
14/15 Belgrave Square, London, SW1X 8PS, tel: 020 7565 7192, fax: 020 7565 7191, e-mail: rgrant@bioindustry.org

Publications list: Available in print

Access to staff: Contact by letter, by telephone, by fax and by e-mail. Appointment necessary.
Hours: Mon to Fri, 0900 to 1700

Parent body: BIA; 14–15 Belgrave Square, London, SW1X 8PS; tel: 020 7565 7190; fax: 020 7565 7191

BIOCHEMICAL SOCIETY

Third Floor, Eagle House, 16 Procter Street, London, WC1V 6NX

Tel: 020 7280 4100
Fax: 020 7280 4170
E-mail: genadmin@biochemistry.org
Website: www.biochemistry.org
Website: www.portlandpress.com

Enquiries to: Membership Secretary
Direct e-mail: membership@biochemistry.org

Founded: 1911

continued overleaf

Organisation type and purpose: National organisation, learned society (membership is by election or invitation), present number of members: 7200, registered charity (charity number 253894), publishing house.

Subject coverage: Biochemistry, biotechnology, biomolecular sciences, molecular biology, genetics, cell biology.

Collection: Contact Archivist at: genadmin@biochemistry.org

Publications: Printed
Order printed publications from: Portland Press, Commerce Way, Colchester, Essex, CO2 8HP; tel: 01206 796351; fax: 01206 799331; e-mail: sales@portland-services.com

Publications list: Available online and in print

Access to staff: Contact by letter, by telephone, by fax, by e-mail and via website
Hours: Mon to Fri, 0900 to 1700

Links with: Portland Press; tel: 020 7580 5530; fax: 020 7323 1136; e-mail: editorial@portlandpress.com

Members of: Association of Learned and Professional Society Publishers; Federation of European Biochemical Societies; International Union of Biochemistry and Molecular Biology

Other address: Biochemical Society; Commerce Way, Colchester, Essex, CO2 8HP; tel: 01206 796351; fax: 01206 799331; e-mail: membership@biochemistry.org

BIOINDUSTRY ASSOCIATION (BIA)

14–15 Belgrave Square, London, SW1X 8PS

Tel: 020 7565 7190
Fax: 020 7565 7191
E-mail: admin@bioindustry.org
Website: www.bioindustry.org

Organisation type and purpose: The trade association for innovative enterprises in the UK's bioscience sector.
To promote the human health benefits of new bioscience technologies, encouraging the commercial success of the bioscience industry by focusing on emerging enterprise and the related interests of companies with whom such enterprise trades.
Supports member interests by lobbying government and parliament in the UK and Brussels, providing high quality information and business services, and attracting investment from both private and government sources.

Subject coverage: The Association defines bioscience companies as those that are developing products or services that are derived from the study of living systems, or use living systems in their research, development and/or manufacturing activities. Such companies will typically be working in the fields of human or animal healthcare, including: diagnostics; therapeutics; vaccines and nutrition; environmental protection or remediation; or will be companies providing technical or commercial services to such companies.

Publications: Electronic and video
Order electronic and video publications from: Download from website

Publications list: Available online

Access to staff: Contact by letter, by telephone, by fax and by e-mail

BIOMEDICAL RESEARCH EDUCATION TRUST (BRET)

25 Shaftesbury Avenue, London, W1D 7EG

Tel: 020 7287 2595
Fax: 020 7287 2595
E-mail: t.g@bret.org.uk
Website: www.bret.org.uk

Enquiries to: Director
Direct e-mail: ted@tgriffiths.net

Founded: 1988

Organisation type and purpose: Service industry, registered charity (charity number 292366), training organisation.
Information for schools and other interested groups about why animals are used for medical research.

Subject coverage: Animal welfare, information for schools, biomedical research.

Publications: Printed, and electronic and video

Access to staff: Contact by letter, by telephone, by fax, by e-mail and via website
Hours: Mon to Fri, 0900 to 1700

Parent body: Research Defence Society

BIOSS INTERNATIONAL (BIOSS)

33 St. James's Square, London SW1Y 4JS

Tel: +44 (0) 20 7661 9387
Fax: +44 (0) 20 7661 9400
E-mail: info@biosseurope.com
Website: www.bioss.com

Enquiries to: Secretary General
Other contacts: Secretary & Registrar (Finance and Legal)

Founded: 1968; formerly called Bioss International Ltd; formerly called Brunel Institute of Organisation and Social Studies (year of change 2001)

Organisation type and purpose: International organisation, advisory body, membership association (membership is by qualification, election or invitation), present number of members: over 200, registered charity (charity number 1016381).

Subject coverage: Social policy, social organisation, social relationships, social institutions, social stratification and mobility, individual behaviour and capacity, education, church and the community, youth in society.
Career path appreciation, mapping and appraisal. The use and management of strategic information and the management of change and Organisation Mapping.

Publications: Printed

Access to staff: Contact by letter, by telephone, by fax, by e-mail and via website. Appointment necessary.
Hours: Mon to Fri, 0900 to 1700

Other officers worldwide: BIOSS International; Information at same address

BIOTECHNOLOGY AND BIOLOGICAL SCIENCES RESEARCH COUNCIL (BBSRC)

Polaris House, North Star Avenue, Swindon, Wiltshire, SN2 1UH

Tel: 01793 413200
Fax: 01793 413201
E-mail: press.office@bbsrc.ac.uk
Website: www.bbsrc.ac.uk

History of institution: formerly called AFRC, Science and Engineering Research Council (year of change 1994)

Organisation type and purpose: Research organisation.

Subject coverage: Agriculture, food, biotechnology, pharmaceutical, chemical and healthcare industries.

Publications: Printed, and electronic and video

Access to staff: Contact by e-mail. Appointment necessary.
Hours: Mon to Fri, 0900 to 1700

BIPOLAR UK

11 Belgrave Road, London, SW1V 1RB

Tel: 020 7931 6480
Fax: 020 7931 6481
E-mail: info@bipolaruk.org.uk
Website: www.bipolaruk.org.uk

Enquiries to: Administrator
Direct tel: 020 7931 6480

Founded: 1984

Organisation type and purpose: Bipolar UK is the national charity dedicated to supporting individuals with the much misunderstood and devastating condition of bipolar, their families and carers.

We provide a range of services to enable people affected by bipolar and associated illnesses to take control of their lives. Each year we reach out and support over 65,000 individuals through our services and information/advice publications. We also work in partnership with research organisations and campaign for new developments to tackle key issues.

Our services encompass a national network of self help groups, self management training courses, a mentoring scheme working with hospitals and psychiatric units, members services incorporating a dedicated Helpline, a youth service, workplace training and our vibrant e Community, a web-based discussion forum for individuals affected by bipolar to share their views and experiences.

Subject coverage: Mental health, manic depression, self-help group support, drug treatment, self-management.

Non-library collection catalogue: All or part available online and in print

Library catalogue: All or part available online

Publications: Printed

Publications list: Available in print

Access to staff: Contact by letter, by

telephone, by fax, by e-mail and via website
Hours: Mon to Fri, 0900 to 1700

BIRDLIFE INTERNATIONAL

Wellbrook Court, Girton Road, Cambridge, CB3 0NA

Tel: 01223 277318
Fax: 01223 277200
E-mail: birdlife@birdlife.org
Website: www.birdlife.org

Enquiries to: Communications Manager
Direct tel: 01223 279813
Direct e-mail: martin.fowlie@birdlife.org.uk
Other contacts: Information Scientist & Librarian

Founded: 1922; formerly called International Council for Bird Preservation (year of change 1993)

Organisation type and purpose: International organisation (membership is by subscription), registered charity (charity number 1042125), research organisation. Carries out field projects, research and advocacy relating to threatened bird species and their habitats.

Subject coverage: Status of bird species throughout the world especially all endangered species; conservation problems and priorities concerning threatened bird species and their habitats.

Collection: Library and reprint collection relating to threatened birds

Trade and statistical information: World data on threatened bird species

Library catalogue: All or part available in-house

Publications: Printed
Order printed publications from: For books only: NHBS Limited, 2–3 Wills Road, Totnes, Devon, tel: 01803 865913, fax: 01803 865280, e-mail: sales@nhbs.co.uk
For Threatened Birds of the World: Lynx Edicions, Passeig de Gràcia, Barcelona, 12 E-08007, Spain, tel: +34 93 301 07 77, fax: +34 93 302 1475, e-mail: lynx@hbw.com

Access to staff: Contact by letter, by telephone, by fax, by e-mail and via website
Hours: Mon to Fri, 0900 to 1700

Access to building: By prior appopintment only
Hours: Mon to Fri, 0900 to 1700

Access for disabled people: Toilet facilities

Partnership of: National conservation organisations worldwide, present in more than 100 countries or territories

BIRKBECK COLLEGE LIBRARY

Library, Malet Street, London, WC1E 7HX

Tel: 020 7631 6063
Fax: 020 7631 6066
E-mail: library-help@bbk.ac.uk
Website: www.bbk.ac.uk/lib

Enquiries to: Librarian
Direct tel: 020 7631 6250
Direct e-mail: p.payne@bbk.ac.uk

Founded: 1823

Organisation type and purpose: University library.

Subject coverage: Applied linguistics, economics, English, film studies, French, geography, German, history, history of art, philosophy, politics, psychology, occupational psychology, sociology, Spanish, chemistry, botany, zoology, statistics, computer science, crystallography, geology, law, management and business studies.

Library catalogue: All or part available online

Publications: Printed

Access to staff: Contact by letter, by telephone, by fax, by e-mail and via website. Non-members charged.
Hours: Term time: Mon to Fri, 1000 to 2215; Sat, 1000 to 1745; Sun, 1000 to 1745
Vacations: times vary, check website

Access to building: *Hours:* Term time: Mon to Sun, 0830 to 2345
Vacations: times vary, check website

Parent body: University of London

BIRMINGHAM AND DISTRICT BUTCHERS ASSOCIATION (BBA)

Office 6, Centre Block, Wholesale Market Precinct, Pershore St, Birmingham, B5 6UL

Tel: 0121 622 4900

Enquiries to: Secretary

Founded: 1878

Organisation type and purpose: Trade association.

Subject coverage: All aspects relating to the running of a retail butcher's shop, including current legislation and consumer opinion on a daily basis.

Access to staff: Contact by letter and by telephone
Hours: Mon to Fri, 0900 to 1300, with 24-hour answering service

BIRMINGHAM AND MIDLAND INSTITUTE (BMI)

9 Margaret Street, Birmingham, B3 3BS

Tel: 0121 236 3591
Fax: 0121 212 4577
E-mail: admin@bmi.org.uk
Website: www.bmi.org.uk

Enquiries to: Administrator

Founded: 1854; incorporates the former Birmingham Library (founded 1779) (year of change 1955)

Organisation type and purpose: Learned society (membership is by subscription), present number of members: 300, registered charity (charity number 522852).
Founded by Act of Parliament in 1854 for the Diffusion and Advancement of Science, Literature and Art amongst all Classes of Persons resident in Birmingham and the Midland Counties.

Subject coverage: Science, literature and art.

Collection: 18th-century volumes
19th- and 20th-century volumes on history, literature, natural history, science, travel, biography, autobiography, poetry
Late 19th- and early 20th-century fiction
Classical music books, records, CDs

Non-library collection catalogue: All or part available in-house

Library catalogue: All or part available in-house and in print

Publications: Printed

Access to staff: Contact by letter, by telephone, by fax, by e-mail and in person. Appointment necessary. Non-members charged.
Hours: Mon to Fri, 0900 to 1800

Access to building: Prior appointment required
Hours: Library: Mon to Fri, 1000 to 1800
Special comments: Members only. Charge for non-members research. Reference only for non-members.

Access for disabled people: Ramped entry
Hours: As above

BIRMINGHAM ARCHIVES AND HERITAGE

Birmingham Central Library, Chamberlain Square, Birmingham, B3 3HQ

Tel: 0121 303 4549
Fax: 0121 464 1176
E-mail: archives.heritage@birmingham.gov.uk
Website: www.birmingham.gov.uk/archivesandheritage

Organisation type and purpose: Local government body; public library; archives; records office. To collect, preserve and make available for research archival collections, printed reference material, maps and family history sources relating to the City of Birmingham, 12th to 21st centuries.

Subject coverage: Sources for local and family history in the Birmingham area.

Collection: Original archive materials, including local authority records, church records, business records, estate and family records, public records (e.g. courts, hospitals, coroners), maps and photographs, and printed reference books.

Non-library collection catalogue: All or part available online and in-house

Library catalogue: All or part available online and in-house

Access to staff: Contact by letter, by telephone, by fax, by e-mail, in person and via website
Hours: Open-access research area for published and printed material, microfiche and microfilm collections, Mon to Fri, 0900 to 2000 (except bank holidays); Sat, 0900 to 1700. Archives searchroom area for original documents, archive collections, photographs, rare and fragile material, Tue, Wed, Fri and Sat, 1000 to 1700; Thu, 1000 to 2000
Special comments: Official proof of identity is required for viewing archive material, photographs and any other material served in the archives searchroom area

BIRMINGHAM ASSOCIATION OF YOUTH CLUBS (BAYC)

Hilda Simister House, 581 Pershore Road, Selly Park, Birmingham, B29 7EL

Tel: 0845 241 0923

continued overleaf

Fax: 0845 241 0924
E-mail: info@bayc.org

Enquiries to: Chief Executive
Other contacts: Principal Development Officer for affiliations and support services.

Founded: 1898

Organisation type and purpose: Membership association, voluntary organisation, registered charity (charity number 1090789).
Youth Club Association.
Servicing agency for mixed youth groups in Birmingham and the Black Country.

Subject coverage: Good practice in youth work; networks and contacts; volunteering opportunities for young people; project design and development; curriculum development; specialist work with young women and young men; accreditator of young people's voluntary activity, capacity building for youth groups.

Collection: Resources on work with girls and young women, boys and young men, youth work policy and practice, residential centres and projects, action research with young people, involving disabled young people as volunteers

Trade and statistical information: Profile of youth groups in Birmingham and surrounding areas

Publications: Printed

Access to staff: Contact by letter, by telephone, by fax and by e-mail. Appointment necessary.
Hours: Mon to Fri, 0915 to 1800

Access for disabled people: Parking provided, ramped entry

Affiliated to: UK Youth; 2nd Floor, Kirby House, 20–24 Kirby Street, London, EC1N 8TS; tel: 020 7242 4045; fax: 020 7242 4125; e-mail: info@ukyouth.org

BIRMINGHAM AUTOMOTIVE SAFETY CENTRE (BASC)

School of Engineering (Mechanical and Manufacturing Engineering), University of Birmingham, Edgbaston, Birmingham, B15 2TT

Tel: 0121 414 5156
Fax: 0121 414 4180
Website: barc.bham.ac.uk

Enquiries to: Manager
Direct tel: 0121 414 7384
Direct e-mail: a.m.hassan@bham.ac.uk

Founded: 1970; formerly called Accident Research Centre; formerly called Accident Research Unit (year of change 1999)

Organisation type and purpose: University department or institute, training organisation, consultancy, research organisation.

Subject coverage: Injuries and vehicle design, accident causation, transport, safety, product liability.

Access to staff: Contact by letter, by telephone, by fax, by e-mail and via website. Appointment necessary.
Hours: Mon to Fri, 0900 to 1700

BIRMINGHAM BIBLIOGRAPHICAL SOCIETY

c/o Information Services, The University of Birmingham, Edgbaston, Birmingham, B15 2TT

Tel: 0121 414 3132

Enquiries to: Honorary Secretary
Direct e-mail: j.hinks@bham.ac.uk

Organisation type and purpose: Learned society.

Subject coverage: Bibliographical and allied subjects, printing, booktrade etc; West Midlands Bibliography; local history of the book trade. On-going research project on the West Midlands book trade.

Publications: Printed

Access to staff: Contact by e-mail
Hours: Mon to Fri, 0900 to 1700

BIRMINGHAM BOTANICAL GARDENS AND GLASSHOUSES (BBHS)

Westbourne Road, Edgbaston, Birmingham, B15 3TR

Tel: 0121 454 1860
Fax: 0121 454 7835
E-mail: admin@ birminghambotanicalgardens.org.uk
Website: www .birminghambotanicalgardens.org.uk

Enquiries to: Chief Executive
Other contacts: Plant Collections Manager (for scientific and educational enquiries)

Founded: 1832; also known as Birmingham Botanical and Horticultural Society Limited

Organisation type and purpose: Membership association (membership is by subscription), present number of members: 5,000, registered charity (charity number 528981), suitable for all ages.
The Company, which is limited by guarantee, is an educational charity the aims of which are: to further public education in botany, horticulture and zoology, and provide facilities for research; to maintain and operate the Birmingham Botanical Gardens and Glasshouses for the above purpose, and for the recreation of the public.

Subject coverage: Horticulture, history of Birmingham Botanical Gardens.

Collection: 7,000 plants

Non-library collection catalogue: All or part available in-house and in print

Library catalogue: All or part available in-house and in print

Publications: Printed, and electronic and video

Publications list: Available online

Access to staff: Contact by letter, by telephone, by fax, by e-mail and via website. Appointment necessary.
Hours: Mon to Fri, 0900 to 1700 (variable according to season)

Access for disabled people: Parking provided, ramped entry, access to all public areas, toilet facilities

BIRMINGHAM BOYS AND GIRLS UNION (BBGU)

Woodlands Camp, Bournevale, Walsall, West Midlands, WS9 0SH

Tel: 0121 353 7329
Fax: 0121 353 7329

Enquiries to: Warden

Founded: 1906

Organisation type and purpose: Registered charity (charity number 522487), suitable for ages: 7+.
Residential outdoor activity centre giving priority to disadvantaged and handicapped groups.

Subject coverage: Outdoor education; animal sanctuary; environmental.

Publications: Printed

Access to staff: Contact by letter, by telephone and in person. Appointment necessary.
Hours: Mon to Fri, 0900 to 1700

Access for disabled people: Parking provided, ramped entry, toilet facilities

BIRMINGHAM BURNS CENTRE

Selly Oak Hospital, Raddlebarn Road, Birmingham, B29 6JD

Tel: 0121 627 1627
Fax: 0121 627 8782
E-mail: Communications@uhb.nhs.uk

Enquiries to: Clinical Lead in Burns
Direct tel: 0121 627 8784
Direct e-mail: remopapini@doctors.org.uk
Other contacts: Burns & Plastic Surgery Co-ordinator for clinical service lead in burns.

Founded: 1944; formed from Birmingham Accident Hospital, date of change, October 1995; formerly called West Midlands Regional Burns Unit (year of change 1993)

Organisation type and purpose: Hospital.
Hospital department specialising in care of burn victims.

Subject coverage: Care of burns, epidemiology, pathology, acute care, aftercare and rehabilitation, aspects of clinical use of cultured skin and skin substitutes.

Access to staff: Contact by letter, by telephone, by fax and by e-mail. Appointment necessary.
Hours: 24 hours

Access for disabled people: Toilet facilities

Part of: National Health Service

BIRMINGHAM CHAMBER OF COMMERCE AND INDUSTRY (BCI)

75 Harborne Road, Edgbaston, Birmingham, B15 3DH

Tel: 0121 454 6171, 0845 606 2666 (Minicom)
Fax: 0121 455 8670
E-mail: info@birminghamchamber.org.uk
Website: www.bci.org.uk

Enquiries to: Information Officer

Founded: 1813

Organisation type and purpose: Trade association, membership association (membership is by subscription).

Subject coverage: Business information, export documentation, export advice and trade missions, business management and policy.

Collection: Business directories and databases
British Standards

Publications: Printed

Access to staff: Contact by letter, by telephone, by fax, by e-mail, in person and via website. Non-members charged.
Hours: Mon to Fri, 0900 to 1700

Access for disabled people: Parking provided, ramped entry, access to all public areas, toilet facilities

Member of: Association of British Chambers of Commerce

Partner in: Birmingham Economic Development Partnership; Business Link Birmingham

BIRMINGHAM CHINESE SOCIETY

11 Allcock Street, Birmingham, B9 4DY

Tel: 0121 773 0099 / 0870 2030100
Fax: 0121 772 6288
E-mail: icbcs88@yahoo.co.uk
Website: www.birminghamchinesesociety.co.uk/

Enquiries to: Manager

Founded: 1988

Organisation type and purpose: Voluntary organisation, registered charity (charity number 1049035), training organisation. Umbrella organisation.

Subject coverage: Information and advice centre, employment, business; training, ESOL, IT, Chinese input, basic food hygiene course, intermediate food hygiene course, first aid, home maintenance course; health, mental health, men and women; business offering advice to local Chinese businesses; translation and interpreting service, Cantonese, Mandarin, Haka, Vietnamese to English.

Access to staff: Contact by letter, by telephone, by fax, by e-mail, in person and via website. Appointment necessary.
Hours: Mon to Fri, 1000 to 1700

BIRMINGHAM CITY UNIVERSITY

Kenrick Library, Perry Barr, Birmingham, B42 2SU

Tel: 0121 331 5000 (main switchboard)
Fax: 0121 356 2875
Website: library.bcu.ac.uk

Enquiries to: Director of Library and Learning Resources
Direct tel: 0121 331 6300
Direct e-mail: judith.andrews@bcu.ac.uk

Organisation type and purpose: University library.

Subject coverage: Construction technology, quantity surveying, computer studies, architecture, economics, management, communications studies, English, nursing, midwifery and community health, law, sociology, social work, accounting, finance, speech therapy, town planning, landscape architecture, housing, government, banking, fine art, art education, fashion and textiles, foundation and community studies, jewellery, silversmithing and horology, three-dimensional design, visual communication, education, music, psychology, media, electrical engineering, mechanical engineering, acting, drama.

Collection: Birmingham Flute Society Library
Royal College of Organists Library
Early Printed Music Collection (pre- c.1850)
Material samples from late 19th century to mid-20th century
Piranesi engravings (15 vols)

Library catalogue: All or part available online

Publications list: Available online and in print

Access to staff: Contact by letter, by telephone, by fax, by e-mail, in person and via website. Appointment necessary.
Hours: Mon to Fri, 0900 to 1700

Access to building: No prior appointment required. Kenrick Library has controlled access and identification is required.

BIRMINGHAM CIVIL JUSTICE CENTRE

Formal name: Ministry of Justice, Midlands Region Judicial and Court Library Service

The Library, The Priory Courts, 33 Bull Street, Birmingham, B4 6DS

Tel: 0121 681 3446
Fax: 0121 681 3444
E-mail: mike.troon@justice.gsi.gov.uk; joanne.jarvie@justice.gsi.gov.uk

Organisation type and purpose: National government body, Ministry of Justice (MoJ) Regional Library Service.
To provide a legal information service for judiciary and MoJ staff throughout the Midlands Region (including all court libraries).

Subject coverage: Law reports, public general acts and measures, statutory instruments, legal books and periodicals.

Library catalogue: All or part available in-house

Access to staff: Appointment necessary.
Hours: Mon to Fri, 0830 to 1530
Special comments: The Priory Courts Library is primarily for the use of the judiciary and staff of the Ministry of Justice in the Midlands Region.

Access to building: Prior appointment required

BIRMINGHAM EARLY MUSIC FESTIVAL LTD (BEMF)

PO Box 15747, Birmingham, B132 9FY

Tel: 07745 887326
Fax: 0121 427 1511
E-mail: info@bemf.net
Website: www.bemf.net

Enquiries to: Administrator

Founded: 1992

Organisation type and purpose: Registered charity (charity number 1039399).
Runs annual festival of early music.

Subject coverage: Early music.

Access to staff: Contact by letter, by telephone, by e-mail and via website
Hours: Mon to Fri, 0900 to 1700

Access to building: No access other than to staff

BIRMINGHAM ECONOMIC STRATEGY

Birmingham City Council, Victoria Square, Birmingham, B1 1BB

Tel: 0121 303 3719
Fax: 0121 303 3076
E-mail: contact@birmingham.gov.uk
Website: www.birmingham.gov.uk/birminghameconomy

Enquiries to: Information Service
Other contacts: Business Centre Manager (for major projects, strategies, analysis)

Founded: 1994

Organisation type and purpose: Local government body, research organisation.
Source of information and analysis on the operation of the Birmingham economy and labour market.

Subject coverage: The Birmingham economy and labour market.

Collection: Wide variety of reports and information on the Birmingham economy

Trade and statistical information: Data on the Birmingham economy, economic forecasts, volume of investment, employment (occupation, sector), unemployment, impact & evaluation studies

Access to staff: Contact by letter, by telephone, by fax, by e-mail and via website. Appointment necessary.
Hours: Mon to Fri, 0900 to 1700
Special comments: Charges made for some services.

Access for disabled people: Level entry, access to all public areas

Affiliated to: Birmingham Economic Development Partnership Limited

Parent body: Birmingham City Council

BIRMINGHAM FOCUS ON BLINDNESS (Birmingham Focus)

48–62 Woodville Road, Harborne, Birmingham, B17 9AT

Tel: 0121 478 5200; 0121 478 5222 (helpline)
Fax: 0121 478 5280
E-mail: info@birminghamfocus.org.uk
Website: www.birminghamfocus.org.uk

Enquiries to: Chief Executive
Direct tel: 0121 478 5201
Direct e-mail: rob@birminghamfocus.org.uk
Other contacts: Marketing Manager

Founded: 1846; formerly a part of Birmingham Royal Institution for the Blind (BRIB) (year of change 1997); formerly called BRIB – Working with Blind People (year of change 1998)

continued overleaf

Organisation type and purpose: Registered charity (charity number 1065745).
Welfare organisation.

Subject coverage: Welfare of blind and partially sighted people in Birmingham, training and development, low vision assessment, rehabilitation and aids, blindness with multiple disabilities.

Publications: Printed, and electronic and video

Access to staff: Contact by letter, by telephone, by fax, by e-mail, in person and via website. Appointment necessary.
Hours: Mon to Fri, 0900 to 1700

Member organisation of: National Association of Local Societies for Visually Impaired (NALSVI); Queen Alexandra College

BIRMINGHAM LAW SOCIETY

Birmingham Law Society, Cornwall Buildings, 45–51 Newhall Street, Birmingham, B3 3QR

Tel: 0121 222 4190
Fax: 0121 222 4197
E-mail: info@birminghamlawsociety.co.uk
Website: www.birminghamlawsociety.co.uk

Founded: 1818

Organisation type and purpose: Professional body (membership is by subscription).

Subject coverage: Law.

Library catalogue: All or part available in-house

Access to staff: Contact by letter, by telephone, by fax and by e-mail. Appointment necessary. Access for members only.
Hours: Mon to Fri, 0900 to 1700

Access to building: Prior appointment required

BIRMINGHAM LIBRARIES (BLS)

Central Library, Chamberlain Square, Birmingham, B3 3HQ

Tel: 0121 303 4511, 0121 235 4511 (Minicom)
Fax: 0121 233 4458
E-mail: centrallibrary@birmingham.gov.uk
Website: www.birmingham.gov.uk/libraries

Enquiries to: Librarian
Direct tel: 0121 303 4220
Direct e-mail: centrallibrary@birmingham.gov.uk
Other contacts: Information Officer for fee-based business information service.

Founded: 1866; formerly called Birmingham Public Libraries (BPL); formerly called Birmingham Library Services (BLS) (year of change 2001)

Organisation type and purpose: Public library.

Subject coverage: Local studies and history; Birmingham information, history, geography, maps, genealogy, photographs; science, technology management, environment, engineering, motor manuals, information technology, building, manufacturing, general and production management; social sciences, politics, economics, law, education (including open learning, school governor information), community information, health information, philosophy, religion, transport; arts, languages and literature; fine and performing arts, music, scores, sets of vocal scores, sound recordings; business information, telephone and trade directories, company information, annual reports, statistics, market research reports, marketing, company histories; archives.

Collection: Archives (of Birmingham)
Baskerville Collection
Boulton and Watt and Priestley collections
British Standards
Early and fine printing
Francis Bedford Collection of photographs
Francis Frith Collection of photographs
Kings Norton and Sheldon Parochial libraries
Local history of Birmingham and surrounding counties
Marston Rudland Collection of engraved portraits
Milton, Johnson, Cervantes, War poetry collections
National organ archive
Official publications
Parker Collection of early children's books and games
Patents (British, European, US and PCT)
Railway collection
Shakespeare
Stone Collection of Victorian and Edwardian photographs
Trade union collection
UN depository library

Non-library collection catalogue: All or part available in-house

Library catalogue: All or part available online

Publications: Printed, and electronic and video
Order printed publications from: Room Bookings and Sales, Birmingham Library Services
tel: 0121 303 2868

Publications list: Available in print

Access to staff: Contact by letter, by telephone, by fax, by e-mail, in person and via website
Hours: Mon, Tue, Thu, Fri, 0900 to 2000; Sat, 0900 to 1700
Special comments: Archives section has restricted opening hours, closing at 1700 each day and all day Wednesday.

Houses the: Diocesan Record Office; Information Direct

Member of: UK Patents Information Network

Parent body: Birmingham City Council

BIRMINGHAM LOCAL MEDICAL COMMITTEE

36 Harborne Road, Edgbaston, Birmingham, B15 3AF

Tel: 0121 454 5008
Fax: 0121 455 0758
Website: www.blmc.co.uk

Enquiries to: Executive Secretary / Business manager
Other contacts: Doctors

Founded: 1911

Organisation type and purpose: Professional body.

Subject coverage: Advice on range of medical and medico/legal matters to GPs.

Access to staff: Contact by letter and by fax
Hours: Mon to Fri, 1030 to 1530

Access to building: Appointment required

Access for disabled people: Parking provided, ramped entry

BIRMINGHAM ROYAL BALLET (BRB)

Thorp Street, Birmingham, B5 4AU

Tel: 0121 245 3500
Fax: 0121 245 3570
E-mail: info@brb.org.uk
Website: www.brb.org.uk

Enquiries to: Communications Director
Direct e-mail: keithlongmore@brb.org.uk

Founded: 1990; formed from Sadler's Wells Royal Ballet (SWRB) (year of change 1989)

Organisation type and purpose: Ballet company.

Subject coverage: Information concerning Birmingham Royal Ballet and its history.

Collection: Cast lists, photographs, programmes

Trade and statistical information: Casting, performance dates

Non-library collection catalogue: All or part available in-house

Library catalogue: All or part available in-house

Publications: Electronic and video

Access to staff: Contact by letter and by e-mail
Hours: Mon to Fri, 0900 to 1700

Access to building: Prior appointment required
Hours: Mon to Fri, 0930 to 1730

Access for disabled people: Level entry

BIRMINGHAM SCHOOL OF ACTING (BSA)

Level 0 – Millennium Point, Curzon Street, Birmingham, B4 7XG

Tel: 0121 331 7220
Fax: 0121 331 7221
E-mail: info@bsa.bcu.ac.uk
Website: www.bsa.bcu.ac.uk

Enquiries to: Director
Direct tel: 0121 331 7224
Direct e-mail: stephen.simms@bcu.ac.uk
Other contacts: Registrar, Admissions Manager, Marketing Manager

Founded: 1936; formerly called Birmingham School of Speech and Drama; formerly called Birmingham School of Speech Training & Dramatic Art Ltd

Organisation type and purpose: Birmingham School of Acting is a small specialist institution offering full-time higher education courses at undergraduate and postgraduate level and part-time and summer school courses for adults, young people and children. Birmingham School of Acting is a faculty of Birmingham City University and its acting courses are accredited by the National Council for Drama Training (NCDT).

Subject coverage: Acting technique, extending natural talent for the professional theatre, dance, fencing and stage fighting, stage management, radio technique, voice production and speech training, relaxation and stress management.

Collection: Drama and play collection

Library catalogue: All or part available in-house

Publications: Printed, and electronic and video

Publications list: Available in print

Access to staff: Contact by letter, by telephone, by fax, by e-mail and via website. Appointment necessary.
Hours: Mon to Fri, 0900 to 1700

Access for disabled people: All levels entry, toilet facilities

BISCUIT, CAKE, CHOCOLATE & CONFECTIONERY ASSOCIATION (BCCCA)

6 Catherine Street, London, WC2B 5JJ

Tel: 020 7420 7200
Fax: 020 7420 7201
Website: www.bccca.org.uk

Enquiries to: Director

Founded: 1901

Organisation type and purpose: Trade association.

Subject coverage: Cocoa, chocolate, confectionery products, cakes and biscuits.

Trade and statistical information: Data on the sales of biscuits, cakes, chocolate and confectionery for the home market and for export

Publications: Printed, and electronic and video

Member of: CAOBISCO, the corresponding EC professional organisation; Food and Drink Federation

BISHOP AUCKLAND COLLEGE LEARNING CENTRE

Woodhouse Lane, Bishop Auckland, Co Durham, DL14 6JZ

Tel: 01388 443000
Fax: 01388 609294
E-mail: enquiries@bacoll.ac.uk
Website: www.bishopaucklandcollege.ac.uk

Enquiries to: Learning Resources Manager
Direct tel: extn 2219

History of institution: formerly called Bishop Auckland College Library (year of change 2011)

Organisation type and purpose: Suitable for ages: 16+.
College library.

Subject coverage: Engineering, construction, business studies, creative and community subjects, hairdressing, crafts, caring, art and design, information technology, leisure and tourism.

Non-library collection catalogue: All or part available in-house

Library catalogue: All or part available in-house

Access to staff: Contact by letter, by telephone, by fax and by e-mail
Hours: Term time: Mon, Wed and Thu, 0900 to 1830; Tue and Fri, 0900 to 1630
Vacations: on request

Access for disabled people: Parking provided, ramped entry, level entry, access to all public areas, toilet facilities
Special comments: Library is on first floor.

BISHOPSGATE INSTITUTE

230 Bishopsgate, London, EC2M 4QH

Tel: 020 7392 9270
Fax: 020 7392 9275
E-mail: library@bishopsgate.org.uk
Website: www.bishopsgate.org.uk/library

Enquiries to: Library Manager
Other contacts: Deputy Library Manager

Founded: 1894

Organisation type and purpose: Independent free public library.

Subject coverage: London history and topography, labour and trade union history, economic and political history, co-operation and the co-operative movement in London and the South East, secularism, humanism, republicanism, pacifism, anarchism.

Collection: London Collection (50,000 volumes); Howell Collection (7,000 volumes); Labour History (10,000 volumes); Holyoake Collection (1,000 items); Bradlaugh Papers (3,000 items); London Cooperative Society Collection (20,000 items); archives of: Raphael Samuel; Bernie Grant; Republic; British Humanist Association; Rationalist Association; Stop the War Coalition.

Non-library collection catalogue: All or part available online and in-house

Library catalogue: All or part available online and in-house

Publications: Printed

Access to staff: Contact by letter, by telephone, by e-mail and in person
Hours: Mon, Tue, Thu and Fri, 1000 to 1730; Wed, 1000 to 2000
Special comments: Library closes at 1400 on the 1st Fri of each month.

Access to building: No prior appointment required

BISHOPTHORPE LOCAL HISTORY GROUP

39 Acaster Lane, Bishopthorpe, York, YO23 2SA

Tel: 01904 704584
E-mail: historygroup@bishopthorpe.net
Website: www.bishopthorpe.net/mt/history

Enquiries to: Chairman

Founded: 1998

Organisation type and purpose: Membership association (membership is by subscription), present number of members: 11, voluntary organisation.

Subject coverage: Local and family history relating to the parish of Bishopthorpe.

Collection: Bishopthorpe photographs, ephemera and administration records of local groups.

Non-library collection catalogue: All or part available in-house

Publications: Printed

Access to staff: Contact by letter, by telephone and by e-mail
Hours: Mon to Fri, 0900 to 1700

BITTER OWNERS CLUB

Treasurer and Membership Secretary, 6 Swanston Field, Whitchurch on Thames, RG8 7HP UK

Tel: 01189 845214
E-mail: info@bitter-owners-club.com
Website: www.bitter-owners-club.com/

Enquiries to: Secretary

Founded: 1988

Organisation type and purpose: Membership association (membership is by subscription), present number of members: 55, service industry.
Classic car club.
To promote and encourage Bitter owners and prospective buyers of the cars.

Subject coverage: Bitter cars.

Collection: Collection of over 5,000 pictures of Bitter cars
Collection of archive press articles and road tests

Trade and statistical information: Values and numbers of Bitter cars

Non-library collection catalogue: All or part available in-house

Publications: Printed

Access to staff: Contact by letter, by telephone, by fax and by e-mail. Appointment necessary.
Hours: Mon to Sun, 0900 to 2100

Member of: Classic Car Association

BITUMEN WATERPROOFING ASSOCIATION (UK) LTD (BWA)

19 Regina Crescent, Ravenshead, Nottingham, NG15 9AE

Tel: 01623 430574
Fax: 01623 798098
E-mail: info@bwa-europe.com
Website: www.bwa-europe.com

Enquiries to: Chief Executive

Founded: 1968

Organisation type and purpose: International organisation, trade association (membership is by subscription, qualification, election or invitation), manufacturing industry, service industry.

Subject coverage: Technical investigations, market survey projects, PR role.

continued overleaf

Publications: Printed

Access to staff: Contact by letter, by telephone, by fax, by e-mail, in person and via website
Hours: Mon to Fri, 0900 to 1700

UK registered office: Bitumen Waterproofing Association (UK) Ltd; Newstead House, Pelham Road, Nottingham, NG5 1AP; tel: 0115 960 8412; fax: 0115 969 1878

BLABY DISTRICT COUNCIL

Council Offices, Desford Road, Narborough, Leicestershire, LE19 2EP

Tel: 0116 275 0555, 0116 284 9786 (Minicom)
Fax: 0116 275 0368
E-mail: customer.services@blaby.gov.uk
Website: www.blaby.gov.uk

Enquiries to: Public Relations Manager
Direct tel: 0116 272 7556
Direct e-mail: djm@blaby.gov.uk

Organisation type and purpose: Local government body.

Subject coverage: Local government services.

Publications: Printed

Publications list: Available online

Access to staff: Contact by letter, by telephone, by fax, by e-mail, in person and via website
Hours: Mon to Thu, 0845 to 1715; Fri, 0845 to 1645

Access for disabled people: Parking provided, level entry, access to all public areas, toilet facilities
Special comments: Access to all public areas.

BLACK COUNTRY CHAMBER OF COMMERCE (BCCOC)

Chamber of Commerce House, Ward Street, Walsall, WS1 2AG

Tel: 0845 002 1234
Fax: 01922 645721
E-mail: info@blackcountrychamber.co.uk
Website: www.blackcountrychamber.co.uk/

Enquiries to: PR Coordinator
Direct tel: 0845 8724 297
Direct e-mail: gemmahall@blackcountrychamber.co.uk

Founded: 2001

Organisation type and purpose:
Membership association (membership is by subscription). We are the voice of business across Dudley, Sandwell, Walsall & Wolverhampton. We represent 1,500 members who employ over 56,000 employees, which is 13% of the Black Country workforce from sectors including manufacturing, engineering, construction and the professional services.

We are passionate, focused and committed to our members' success. We offer business advice, help and support on a huge range of issues, from helping you to raise your company profile and develop a wider sales network, to helping you find new overseas markets through our International Trade team and lobby to Government on your behalf. We also offer great cost saving services! We strive to help businesses in the local area.

Subject coverage: Business information and services for business.

Non-library collection catalogue: All or part available online

Library catalogue: All or part available online and in-house

Access to staff: Contact by letter, by telephone, by fax, by e-mail, in person and via website. Non-members charged.
Hours: Mon to Fri: 0900 to 1700
Special comments: SME business within the Black Country and members of the Black Country Chamber of Commerce.

Access for disabled people: Access to all public areas, toilet facilities

BLACK COUNTRY INVESTMENT

The Deckhouse, Waterfront West, Dudley Road, Brierley Hill, DY5 1LW

Tel: 0845 815 1515
E-mail: enquiries@bci-uk.com
Website: www.bci-uk.com

Enquiries to: Enquiry Officer
Direct e-mail: jane_mcgreen@blackcountryconsortium.co.uk

Founded: 2001; formerly called Business Link Sandwell (year of change 2001)

Organisation type and purpose: Local government body.

Subject coverage: Property location information within the Black Country, general information concerning the Black Country.

Publications: Printed

Access to staff: Contact by letter, by telephone, by fax, by e-mail and via website
Hours: Mon to Fri, 0900 to 1700

BLACK COUNTRY SOCIETY (BCS)

PO Box 71, Kingswinford, West Midlands, DY6 9YN

E-mail: editor@blackcountrysociety.co.uk
Website: www.blackcountrysociety.co.uk

Enquiries to: Editor
Other contacts: Membership Secretary (for subscriptions)

Founded: 1967

Organisation type and purpose: Learned society (membership is by subscription), present number of members: 2,000, voluntary organisation.
To foster interest in the Black Country area of the West Midlands past, present and future.

Subject coverage: Local history, industrial archaeology, geography and culture; the past, present and future of the Black Country region; family and social history in the Black Country

Collection: Photographic collection (now deposited in the Black Country Living Museum)

Publications: Printed, and electronic and video
Order printed publications from: Publications, BCS
PO Box 71, Kingswinford, West Midlands, DY6 9YN, tel: 01384 295606

Publications list: Available online and in print

Access to staff: Contact by letter, by telephone, by e-mail and via website
Hours: Mon to Fri, 0900 to 1700

Access to building: No access other than to staff

Also at: Advertising/Distribution/Publications; 32 Lawnswood Avenue, Wordsley, Stourbridge, West Midlands, DY8 5LP; tel: 01384 295606

Constituent bodies: Four subsidiary groups, all with same contact details as BCS

BLACK WELSH MOUNTAIN SHEEP BREEDERS ASSOCIATION

Strathearn, Ruthwell, Dumfries, DG1 4NN

Tel: 0387 870653
E-mail: enquiries@blackwelshmountain.org.uk
Website: www.blackwelshmountain.org.uk

Enquiries to: Secretary

Founded: 1920

Organisation type and purpose:
Membership association (membership is by subscription), present number of members: 250, registered charity.
Sheep breeders association.

Access to staff: Contact by letter, by telephone and by fax
Hours: Mon to Fri, 0900 to 1700

BLACKBURN COLLEGE LIBRARY

Feilden Street, Blackburn, Lancashire, BB2 1LH

Tel: 01254 292120
Fax: 01254 682700
Website: catalogue.blackburn.ac.uk

Enquiries to: Learning Resources Manager

Organisation type and purpose: College of Further Education.

Subject coverage: Wide subject coverage for FE and HE in FE curriculum.

Library catalogue: All or part available online

Publications: Printed

Access to staff: Contact by letter, by telephone and in person. Appointment necessary. Non-members charged.
Hours: Term time: Mon to Thu, 0845 to 2000; Fri, 0845 to 1500; Sat, 0900 to 1230
Vacations: Mon to Fri, 0900 to 1630
Special comments: Associate membership is available (annual subscription) to members of the public; occasional users may prefer single admission fee for each visit.

Access for disabled people: Access to all public areas

Associate college of: Lancaster University

BLACKBURN WITH DARWEN BOROUGH COUNCIL

King William Street, Town Hall, Blackburn, Lancashire, BB1 7DY

Tel: 01254 585585
Fax: 01254 680870
E-mail: info@blackburn.gov.uk
Website: www.council.blackburnworld.com

Enquiries to: Public Relations Manager

Organisation type and purpose: Local government body.

BLACKFRIARS LIBRARY

64 St Giles, Oxford, OX1 3LY

Tel: 01865 278441
Fax: 01865 278403
Website: www.bfriars.ox.ac.uk

Enquiries to: Librarian
Direct e-mail: librarian@blackfriars.ox.ac.uk

Organisation type and purpose: Library.

Subject coverage: Philosophy, theology and scripture (particularly in relation to the Roman Catholic tradition and the medieval contribution of Dominican authors such as St Thomas Aquinas); life, work and history of the Dominican Order.

Collection: 1 papyrus, 5 MSS, some cuneiform tablets, 26 incunabula and some 350 books printed before 1700, including many Dominican authors
Autograph letters of George Tyrrell SJ
Private press items, including many from St Dominic's Press
Works from the Library of André Raffalovich

Library catalogue: All or part available online

Access to staff: Contact by letter, by telephone, by e-mail, in person and via website. Access for members only. Letter of introduction required.
Hours: Mon to Fri, 0900 to 1700

Access to building: Prior appointment required

A permanent private hall of: University of Oxford

In collaboration with other libraries of the: English Dominicans

Serves a priory and *studium generale* of the: English Province of the Friars of the Order of Preachers (Dominicans)

BLACKHEATH SCIENTIFIC SOCIETY

Mycenae House Community Centre, Mycenae Road, London, SE3 7SE

Tel: 020 8854 3389
E-mail: richardjbuchanan@aol.com
Website: www.bss.btik.com

Founded: 1857

Organisation type and purpose: Learned society (membership is by subscription, election or invitation), voluntary organisation.
Airing of information on developments in science and technology to qualified and non-qualified public; members.

Subject coverage: Current scientific and technological developments. Coverage is wide and does include occasionally an historical lecture.

Publications: Printed

Access to staff: Contact by letter, by telephone and by e-mail. Appointment necessary.
Hours: Mon to Fri, 0900 to 2200

BLACKPOOL AND THE FYLDE COLLEGE

Ashfield Road, Bispham, Blackpool, Lancashire, FY2 0HB

Tel: 01253 352352
Fax: 01253 356127
E-mail: lrc@blackpool.ac.uk
Website: www.blackpool.ac.uk

Enquiries to: Learning Resources
Direct tel: 01253 352352
Direct e-mail: lrc@blackpool.ac.uk

Founded: 1934

Organisation type and purpose: Education for ages 16+.

Library catalogue: All or part available online

Access to staff: Contact by letter, by telephone, by fax and by e-mail. Appointment necessary.
Hours: Mon to Fri, 0900 to 1700

BLACKPOOL CENTRAL LIBRARY

Queen Street, Blackpool, Lancashire, FY1 1PX

Tel: 01253 478080
Fax: 01253 478082
E-mail: central.library@blackpool.gov.uk
Website: www.blackpool.gov.uk

Organisation type and purpose: Local government body, public library.

Subject coverage: General, local history of Blackpool and Fylde area.

Library catalogue: All or part available online

Access to staff: Contact by letter, by telephone, by fax, by e-mail and in person
Hours: Closed – undergoing refurbishment and remodelling until Sept 2011
Special comments: Local history items are for use in the library only.

Access for disabled people: Access to all public areas

BLACKWELL PUBLISHING LIMITED

9600 Garsington Road, Oxford, OX4 2DQ

Tel: 01865 776868
Fax: 01865 714591
Website: www.blackwell-science.com
Website: www.blackwellpublishers.co.uk
Website: www.blackwellpublishing.com
Website: www.blackwell-synergy.com

Enquiries to: Marketing Co-ordinator

Founded: 1939; formerly called Blackwell Scientific Publications Limited (BSPL) (year of change 1995); formerly called Blackwell Publishers Limited (BPL), Blackwell Science Limited (BSL) (year of change 2001)

Organisation type and purpose: Publishing house.

Subject coverage: Books and journals in medicine, humanities, life and social sciences, as listed in catalogues.

Publications: Printed, and electronic and video

Publications list: Available online and in print

Access to staff: Contact by letter and by telephone
Hours: Mon to Fri, 0900 to 1700

Other addresses: Blackwell Publishing Asia; 54 University Street, Carlton South 3053, Victoria, Australia; tel: 00 61 3 9374 0300; fax: 00 61 3 9347 5001; Blackwell Publishing Limited; 108 Cowley Road, Oxford, OX4 1JF; Blackwell Publishing Limited; 10 rue Casimir Delavigne, 75006 Paris, France; tel: +33 1 53 10 33 10; fax: +33 1 53 10 33 15; e-mail: aboydsquires@compuserve.com; Blackwell Publishing, Inc; Commerce Place, 350 Main Street, Malden, MA 02148–5018, USA; tel: 00 1 781 388 8250; fax: 00 1 781 388 8255; Blackwell Wissenschaft-Verlag; Kurfürstendamm 57, Charlottenburg, Berlin, D-10707, Germany; tel: +49 30/32 79 06 -0; fax: +49 30/32 79 06 -10; e-mail: verlag@ blackwis.de

Sister company: B H Blackwell Limited

BLACKWELL UK LIMITED (Blackwell's)

Beaver House, Hythe Bridge Street, Oxford, OX1 2ET

Tel: 01865 792792
Fax: 01865 200285
E-mail: sales@blackwell.co.uk
Website: www.blackwell.com

Enquiries to: International Sales Manager
Direct fax: 01865 200285

Founded: 1879; also known as Blackwell's, Blackwell's Book Services

Organisation type and purpose: International organisation, service industry. Booksellers.
Academic Library Suppliers.

Subject coverage: Academic books, CD-ROM, music, microform, cataloguing and bibliographic services, eBook services.

Non-library collection catalogue: All or part available online

Publications: Printed, and electronic and video

Publications list: Available online

Access to staff: Contact by letter, by telephone, by fax, by e-mail and via website. Appointment necessary.
Hours: Mon to Fri, 0900 to 1700

BLAENAU GWENT COUNTY BOROUGH COUNCIL

Municipal Offices, Civic Centre, Ebbw Vale, Gwent, NP23 6XB

Tel: 01495 350555
Fax: 01495 301255
Website: www.blaenau-gwent.gov.uk

Enquiries to: Public Relations Officer
Direct tel: 01495 355112
Direct fax: 01495 355093

Organisation type and purpose: Local government body.
Unitary authority.

Subject coverage: Local government services.

Publications: Printed

Access to staff: Contact by letter, by telephone and by fax
Hours: Mon to Fri, 0900 to 1700

BLAENAU GWENT COUNTY BOROUGH LIBRARIES

Anvil Court, Church Street, Abertillery, Blaenau Gwent, NP13 1DB

Tel: 01495 355950
Fax: 01495 355900
E-mail: sue.white@blaenau-gwent.gov.uk

Enquiries to: Principal Librarian
Direct tel: 01495 355950
Direct fax: 01495 355900
Direct e-mail: sue.white@blaenau-gwent.gov.uk

Organisation type and purpose: Local government body, public library.

Subject coverage: General subjects, local studies and self-help, adult basic information.

Collection: Main information collections housed at Ebbw Vale Library
Main local history collections housed at Tredegar Library

Non-library collection catalogue: All or part available online and in-house

Library catalogue: All or part available online and in-house

Publications: Printed

Publications list: Available in print

Access to staff: Contact by letter, by telephone, by fax, by e-mail and in person. Appointment necessary.
Hours: Mon to Fri, 0900 to 1700; Sat 0900 to 1300

Library HQ: Blaenau Gwent County Borough Council; Leisure Services, Anvil Court, Church Street, Abertillery, NP13 1DB; tel: 01495 355950; fax: 01495 355900; e-mail: sue.white@blaenau-gwent.gov.uk

BLATCHINGTON COURT TRUST (BCT)

Ridgeland House, 165 Dyke Road, Hove, East Sussex, BN3 1TL

Tel: 01273 727222
Fax: 01273 722244
E-mail: info@blatchingtoncourt.org.uk
Website: www.blatchingtoncourt.org.uk/

Enquiries to: Client Services Manager

Founded: 1993

Organisation type and purpose: Voluntary organisation, registered charity (charity number 306350), suitable for ages: 0 to 30. Primarily grant giving charity to promote education and employment and provide grants for young visually impaired people for computers and sensory equipment. Also help with Family Support and Advocacy.

Subject coverage: Services and facilities for visually impaired young people, mainly in Sussex; help includes: family support service, advocacy service, IT training, education and employment.

Publications: Printed

Access to staff: Contact by letter, by telephone, by fax, by e-mail, in person and via website
Hours: Mon to Fri, 0900 to 1700

Access to building: No prior appointment required

Access for disabled people: Parking provided, ramped entry

BLC LEATHER TECHNOLOGY CENTRE (BLC)

Kings Park Road, Moulton Park, Northampton, NN3 6JD

Tel: 01604 679999
Fax: 01604 679998
E-mail: info@blcleathertech.com
Website: www.blcleathertech.com

Enquiries to: Sales Manager
Direct tel: 01604 679999
Direct fax: 01604 679998
Direct e-mail: info@blcleathertech.com

Founded: 1920; formerly called British Leather Confederation

Organisation type and purpose: International Organisation providing a range of services to the leather industry.

Subject coverage: Product, leather, material and chemical testing, support on chemical and product safety legislation and compliance, problem solving, leather training courses, consultancy, LWG audits and research projects.

Publications: Printed

Access to staff: Contact by letter, by telephone, by fax, by e-mail, in person and via website. Appointment necessary.
Hours: Mon to Fri, 0900 to 1700

BLENHEIM PROJECT

321 Portobello Road, London, W10 5SY

Tel: 020 8960 5599
Fax: 020 8960 0508
E-mail: blenpro@dircon.co.uk

Enquiries to: Administrator

Founded: 1966

Organisation type and purpose: Voluntary organisation, registered charity (charity number 1015237).
Drugs counselling.

Subject coverage: Counselling for drug users, their friends and family, use and effects, alternative therapies, detox teas.

Publications: Printed

Publications list: Available in print

Access to staff: Contact by letter, by telephone, by fax, by e-mail, in person and via website
Hours: Mon to Fri, 1000 to 1700; Drop in: Mon to Fri, 1300 to 1600; Tue, 1800 to 2100

BLIND VETERANS UK

Formal name: Blind Veterans UK – Life beyond sight loss.

12–14 Harcourt Street, London, W1H 4HD

Tel: 020 7616 7980
Fax: 020 7262 6199
E-mail: laura.luxton@blindveterans.org.uk
Website: www.blindveterans.org.uk

Enquiries to: PR and Communications
Direct tel: 020 76167900
Direct e-mail: enquiries@blindveterans.org.uk

Founded: 1915; formerly called St Dunstan's (year of change 2012)

Organisation type and purpose: Registered charity (charity number 216227).
To provide an independent future through rehabilitation and training for blind ex-Service men and women.

Publications: Printed

Access to staff: Contact by letter, by telephone and by e-mail
Hours: Mon to Fri, 0900 to 1700

BLOOD PRESSURE ASSOCIATION

60 Cranmer Terrace, London, SW17 0QS

Tel: 020 8772 4994 (head office); 0845 241 0989 (information line)
Website: www.bpassoc.org.uk

Founded: 2000

Organisation type and purpose: Registered charity in England and Wales (charity number 1058944), membership organisation (membership is by subscription).
Dedicated to lowering the nation's blood pressure to prevent disability and death from stroke and heart disease.
To help people take control of, or prevent, high blood pressure.

Subject coverage: The vision is that everyone will know their blood pressure numbers, in the same way that they know their height or weight, and take steps to keep them healthy both now and in the future.

Information services: Booklets, magazine, e-newsletters, website, information line and other activities.

Special visitor services: UK's biggest blood pressure testing event, Know your Numbers! Week.

Publications: Printed, and electronic and video
Order electronic and video publications from: via website

Publications list: Available online

Access to staff: Contact by letter and by telephone
Hours: Information line: Mon to Fri, 1100 to 1500

BLOOMSBURY HEALTHCARE LIBRARY

Ground Floor, Bonham Carter House, 52 Gower Street, London, WC1E 6EB

Tel: 020 3447 9097
Fax: 020 7436 5111
E-mail: bloomsbury.library@uclh.nhs.uk
Website: www.chllib.demon.co.uk

Enquiries to: Librarian

Founded: 1997

Organisation type and purpose: NHS Library.
Library services for all healthcare staff in associated organisations.

Subject coverage: Nursing, midwifery, health visiting, sociology, psychology, education, management, physiotherapy, occupational therapy, dietetics, clinical governance, NHS policy, radiography, librarianship.

Non-library collection catalogue: All or part available online

Library catalogue: All or part available online

Publications: Printed

Access to staff: Contact by letter, by telephone and by fax. Appointment necessary. Non-members charged.
Hours: Mon, Wed and Thu 0900 to 1900, Tue 1000 to 2000, Fri 0900 to 1700

Access to building: No prior appointment required

BLUEFACED LEICESTER SHEEP BREEDERS ASSOCIATION (BFLSBA)

The Secretary, Riverside View, Warwick Road, Carlisle CA1 2BS

Tel: 01228 598022
Fax: 01228 598021
E-mail: info@blueleicester.co.uk
Website: www.blueleicester.co.uk

Founded: 1962

Organisation type and purpose: National government body, membership association (membership is by subscription).
Sheep breeders' association.
Sheep registration.

Subject coverage: Bluefaced Leicester sheep.

Access to staff: Contact by letter, by telephone, by fax, by e-mail and via website
Hours: Mon to Fri, 0900 to 1500

Access to building: Prior appointment required

BMS WORLD MISSION

PO Box 49, Baptist House, 129 Broadway, Didcot, Oxfordshire, OX11 8XA

Tel: 01235 517700
Fax: 01235 517601
E-mail: mail@bmsworldmission.org
Website: www.bmsworldmission.org

Enquiries to: General Director

Founded: 1792; formerly called Baptist Missionary Society (BMS)

Organisation type and purpose: Voluntary organisation, registered as a charity in England and Wales (number 233782) and in Scotland (number SC037767).
BMS World Mission is a Christian mission organisation aiming to share life in all its fullness with the world's peoples by: enabling them to know Christ; alleviating suffering and injustice; improving the quality of life with people as the primary agent of change – motivating, training, sending and resourcing them. Has missions in 4 continents.

Subject coverage: Christian missions worldwide involving church planting and evangelism; development initiatives; disaster relief; educational programmes; health programmes; and other specialised activities.

Collection: Archives of the 19th century relating to the establishment of missions and some rare books at Regents Park College, Oxford

Publications: Printed
Order printed publications from: Resources, tel: 01235 517617; e-mail: resources@bmsworldmission.org

Publications list: Available online

Access to staff: Contact by letter, by telephone, by fax, by e-mail and via website. Appointment necessary.
Hours: Mon to Fri, 0900 to 1700

BMT GROUP LTD

Goodrich House, 1 Waldegrave Road, Teddington, Middlesex, TW11 8LZ

Tel: 020 8943 5544
Fax: 020 8943 5347
E-mail: dgriffiths@bmtmail.com
Website: www.bmt.org
Website: www.marinescienceandtechnology.com
Website: www.marinetechnologyabstracts.com

Enquiries to: Librarian
Direct tel: 020 8614 4277

Founded: 1985

Organisation type and purpose: Consultancy, research organisation.

Subject coverage: Fluid mechanics, naval architecture, ocean engineering, industrial aerodynamics as related to the commercial shipping, maritime defence, ports and harbours, and offshore oil and gas industries.

Collection: Report material of former National Maritime Institute
Report material of former ship, aero and maritime science divisions of the National Physical Laboratory
Transactions of Royal Institution of Naval Architects, Society of Naval Architects and Marine Engineers, North-east Coast Institution of Engineers and Shipbuilders, Institution of Engineers and Shipbuilders in Scotland

Library catalogue: All or part available in-house

Publications: Printed, and electronic and video

Publications list: Available in print

Access to staff: Contact by letter, by telephone, by fax, by e-mail and via website. All charged.
Hours: Mon to Thu, 0830 to 1700; Fri, 0830 to 1630

Access to building: No prior appointment required

Also at: BMT Group Ltd; Northumbria House, Davy Bank, Wallsend, Tyne and Wear, NE28 6UY; tel: 0191 263 6899; fax: 0191 263 8754; e-mail: gsmith@bmtmail.com

BMT GROUP LTD – WALLSEND (BMT)

Northumbria House, Oceana Business Park, Wallsend, Tyne and Wear, NE28 6UZ

Tel: 0191 262 5242
Fax: 0191 263 8754
E-mail: gilliansmith@bmtmail.com
Website: www.bmt.org
Website: www.marinescienceandtechnology.com
Website: www.marinetechnologyabstracts.com

Enquiries to: Librarian

Founded: 1985

Organisation type and purpose: Consultancy, research organisation.

Subject coverage: Maritime and civil engineering research, naval architecture, fluid mechanics, ocean engineering, marine engineering, wind engineering, offshore technology, industrial aerodynamics, marine traffic operations, port and harbour design operations and related subjects.

Collection: Stock/Holdings: 1,000 books and 10,000 reports on related subjects
Reports and Technical Memoranda of British Ship Research Association (BSRA)
Special Collections:
Transactions of Royal Institution of Naval Architects
Transactions of Society of Naval Architects & Marine Engineers
Transactions of North East Coast Institution of Engineers and Shipbuilders
Transactions of Engineers and Shipbuilders in Scotland
Reports and Technical Memoranda of British Ship Research Association (BSRA)
Transactions of Engineers and Shipbuilders in Scotland
Transactions of North East Coast Institution of Engineers and Shipbuilders
Transactions of Royal Institution of Naval Architects
Transactions of Society of Naval Architects & Marine Engineers

Library catalogue: All or part available in-house

Publications: Printed, and electronic and video
Order electronic and video publications from: website: http://www.marinetechnologyabstracts.com

Publications list: Available in print

Access to staff: Contact by letter, by telephone, by fax and by e-mail. All charged.
Hours: Mon to Thu, 0830 to 1700; Fri, 0830 to 1630

continued overleaf

Access to building: Prior appointment required

Constituent part of: BMT Group Ltd; Goodrich House, 1 Waldegrave Road, Teddington, Middlesex, TW11 8LZ; tel: 020 8943 5544; fax: 020 8943 5347; e-mail: dgriffiths@bmtmail.com

BMT MARINE & OFFSHORE SURVEYS LTD. (SA)

4th Floor, Holland House, 1–4 Bury Street, London, EC3A 5AW

Tel: 0207 648 9650
Fax: 0207 929 5564
E-mail: enquiries@bmtmarinerisk.com
Website: www.wreckage.org

Enquiries to: Director, Business Development
Direct tel: 020 7648 9652
Other contacts: Chief Executive; Managing Director

Founded: 1856

Organisation type and purpose:
International organisation, professional body, membership association (membership is by election or invitation), service industry, consultancy.
Marine survey and risk management.
From offices around the world, the SA's surveyors, marine engineers and master mariners are on call; being involved in loss prevention and pre-risk assessment, they travel constantly to ships that are in trouble.

Subject coverage: Marine surveying and consultancy, insurance loss prevention, marine damage assessment, marine casualty investigation.

Publications: Printed

Access to staff: Contact by letter, by telephone, by fax, by e-mail and via website
Hours: Mon to Fri, 0900 to 1730

Has: offices worldwide

Parent body: British Maritime Technology Limited (BMT); Goodrich House, 1 Waldegrave Road, Teddington, TW11 8LZ; tel: 020 8943 5544; fax: 020 8943 5347; e-mail: enquiries@bmtmail.com

BOARD OF DEPUTIES OF BRITISH JEWS (BoD)

6 Bloomsbury Square, London, WC1A 2LP

Tel: 020 7543 5400
Fax: 020 7543 0010
E-mail: info@bod.org.uk
Website: www.bod.org.uk

Enquiries to: Researcher
Direct e-mail: jci@bod.org.uk

Founded: 1760

Organisation type and purpose:
Membership association (membership is by election or invitation), voluntary organisation, registered charity.
Lay representative body for Jewish community in the UK.

Subject coverage: Information about Judaism and about the British Jewish community.

Collection: Jewish Way of Life Exhibition

Order printed publications from: As above

Publications list: Available online

Access to staff: Contact by letter, by telephone, by fax, by e-mail and via website
Hours: Mon to Fri, 0930 to 1730
Closed for public and Jewish holidays, early closing on Fridays and evenings of Jewish holidays

Access to building: Prior appointment required

BOARD OF GRADUATE STUDIES (BGS)

Formal name: University of Cambridge Board of Graduate Studies

University of Cambridge, 4 Mill Lane, Cambridge, CB2 1RZ

Tel: 01223 760606
Fax: 01223 338723
E-mail: graduate.admissions@admin.cam.ac.uk
Website: www.admin.cam.ac.uk/univ/gsprospectus
Website: www.admin.cam.ac.uk/offices/gradstud

Enquiries to: Admissions Office

Founded: 1284

Organisation type and purpose: University department or institute.
University graduate admissions.

Subject coverage: All academic subjects studied at the university: arts, humanities, social sciences, physical sciences, biological sciences, engineering, management, technology.

Publications: Printed

Access to staff: Contact by letter, by telephone, by fax and by e-mail
Hours: Mon to Fri, 1000 to 1600

Access to building: Mon to Fri, 1000 to 1600

Access for disabled people: Mon to Fri, 1000 to 1600

Parent body: University of Cambridge; Cambridge; website: http://www.cam.ac.uk

BOARDING SCHOOLS' ASSOCIATION (BSA)

Grosvenor Gardens House, 35–37 Grosvenor Gardens, London, SW1W 0BS

Tel: 020 7798 1580
Fax: 020 7798 1581
E-mail: bsa@boarding.org.uk
Website: www.boarding.org.uk

Enquiries to: National Director
Direct e-mail: office@boarding.org.uk

Founded: 1965

Organisation type and purpose: National professional society of schools with boarding facilities.

Subject coverage: Boarding school education in both independent and maintained sectors, with specialist areas in: training, publication, information, National Boarding Standards.

Publications: Printed

Publications list: Available online and in print

Access to staff: Contact by letter, by telephone, by fax, by e-mail, in person and via website. Appointment necessary. Access for members only. Non-members charged.
Hours: Mon to Fri, 0900 to 1700

Links with: GSA; HMC; IAPS; ISA; ISC; SHMIS; State Boarding Schools' Association (SBSA)

BOBATH CENTRE FOR CHILDREN WITH CEREBRAL PALSY

Bradbury House, 250 East End Road, London, N2 8AU

Tel: 020 8444 3355
Fax: 020 8444 3399
E-mail: info@bobathlondon.co.uk
Website: www.bobathlondon.co.uk

Enquiries to: Director for Referrals
Other contacts: (1) Course Organiser (2) Appointments Organiser for (1) training (2) treatment information.

Founded: 1957; formerly called Western Cerebral Palsy Centre

Organisation type and purpose: Registered charity (charity number 229663), treatment organisation, training organisation, research organisation.
Treatment of children with cerebral palsy and related conditions; training of therapists; research. Treatment of adults with neurological disability.

Subject coverage: Cerebral palsy, brain damage, treatment of these conditions.

Publications: Printed, and electronic and video

Publications list: Available online and in print

Access to staff: Contact by letter, by telephone, by fax, by e-mail and via website. Appointment necessary.
Hours: Mon to Fri, 0900 to 1700

Access for disabled people: Parking provided, level entry, access to all public areas, toilet facilities

Connections with: Bobath Children's Therapy Centre Wales; 19 Park Road, Whitchurch, Cardiff, CF4 7BP; tel: 029 2052 2600; fax: 029 2052 1477; Bobath Scotland; Golden Jubilee National Hospital, Beardmore Street, Clydebank, G81 4HX; tel: 0141 435 3270; fax: 0141 435 3279; British Association of Bobath Trained Therapists

BODLEIAN HEALTH CARE LIBRARIES

Cairns Library, John Radcliffe Hospital, Headington, Oxford, OX3 9DU

Tel: 01865 221936
Fax: 01865 221941
E-mail: hcl-library@bodleian.ox.ac.uk
Website: www.bodleian.ox.ac.uk/medicine

Enquiries to: Head of Health Care Libraries

History of institution: formerly called Oxford Postgraduate Medical Library (year of change 1973); formerly called Cairns

Library (year of change 2002); formerly called Institute of Health Sciences Library (year of change 2002)

Organisation type and purpose: University library, library of the Faculty of Clinical Medicine, University of Oxford.
Also serves as an information source for NHS staff in the Oxford University Hospitals NHS Trust and the Oxford Deanery.

Subject coverage: Health care including clinical medicine, nursing, physiotherapy, radiography and other paramedical subjects. Satellite libraries have specialities in cancer, diabetes, neurosciences, gerontology, public health medicine and statistics.

Library catalogue: All or part available online

Access to staff: Contact by letter, by telephone, by fax and by e-mail. Appointment necessary.

Access to building: No access other than to staff
Hours: 24 hours
Special comments: Members only.

Access for disabled people: Access to all public areas
Special comments: Ramped or level entry – varies on different sites.

Also at: Knowledge Centre; University of Oxford Old Road Campus Research Building, Headington, Oxford, OX3 7DQ; tel: 01865 221936; fax: 01865 289406; e-mail: hcl-library@bodleian.ox.ac.uk; website: http://www.bodleian.ox.ac.uk/medicine

Links with: University of Oxford; Wellington Square, Oxford, OX1 2JD; tel: 01865 270001

BODLEIAN JAPANESE LIBRARY (BJL)

27 Winchester Road, Oxford, OX2 6NA

Tel: 01865 284506
Fax: 01865 284500
E-mail: japanese@bodleian.ox.ac.uk
Website: www.bodleian.ox.ac.uk/bjl
Website: solo.bodleian.ox.ac.uk/

Enquiries to: Bodleian Japanese Librarian
Direct e-mail: japanese@bodleian.ox.ac.uk

Founded: 1993; created by the merger of The Japanese collections of the Bodleian Library and the former Nissan Institute Library (year of change 1993)

Organisation type and purpose: University library.

Subject coverage: Japanese studies.

Library catalogue: All or part available online

Access to staff: Contact by letter, by telephone, by fax, by e-mail, in person and via website. Non-members charged.

Access to building: *Hours:* Term time: Mon to Fri, 0915 to 1900; Sat, 1000 to 1300
Vacations: Mon to Fri, 0915 to 1700
Special comments: Must be accredited readers of the Bodleian Library.

Access for disabled people: Ramped entry, toilet facilities

Parent body: Bodleian Library; Broad Street, Oxford, OX1 3BG; tel: 01865 277000; fax: 01865 277182; website: http://www.bodleian.ox.ac.uk

BODLEIAN LAW LIBRARY

St Cross Building, Manor Road, Oxford, OX1 3UR

Tel: 01865 271462
Fax: 01865 271475
E-mail: law.library@bodleian.ox.ac.uk
Website: www.bodleian.ox.ac.uk/law

Enquiries to: Bodleian Law Librarian
Other contacts: Academic Services Librarian for services offered by the library, ILL, copies of materials.

Founded: c.1602

Organisation type and purpose: University library.

Subject coverage: Law; criminology; legal bibliography.

Collection: Law from the jurisdictions of the British Isles, most Commonwealth countries, USA, most European countries; public international law; European Documentation Centre

Library catalogue: All or part available online

Access to staff: Contact by letter, by telephone, by fax, by e-mail and via website. Appointment necessary.
Hours: Mon to Fri, 0900 to 1700

Access for disabled people: Ramped entry, toilet facilities, lift

Constituent part of: Bodleian Libraries; Broad Street, Oxford, OX1 3BG; tel: 01865 277162; fax: 01865 277182; e-mail: reader.services@bodleian.ox.ac.uk; website: http://www.bodleian.ox.ac.uk

BODLEIAN LIBRARY

Broad Street, Oxford, OX1 3BG

Tel: 01865 277000
Fax: 01865 277182
E-mail: enquiries@bodley.ox.ac.uk
Website: www.lib.ox.ac.uk/olis/
Website: www.ouls.ox.ac.uk/bodley

Enquiries to: Librarian
Other contacts: Director of University Library Services and Bodley's Librarian

Founded: 1598

Organisation type and purpose: University library.
University and copyright library, of the University of Oxford.

Subject coverage: Comprehensive range of a university and copyright library dating from 1602; strong coverage in Orientalia, Hebraica, medieval MSS, incunabula, English 16th- and 17th-century literature and history, modern political papers, music (manuscripts and printed); maps.

Collection: Clarendon State Papers
Douce, Francis (1757–1834) Collection (MSS and early printed works)
Gough, Richard (1735–1809) Collection (British topography)
Harding Collection (music, scores and libretti)
John Johnson Collection of Printed Ephemera
Locke, John (1632–1704) Papers and library
Malone Collection of Shakespearean and British drama
Opie, Peter Mason (1918–1982) Collection (children's literature)
Rawlinson, Richard (1690–1755) Collection
Rawlinson, Thomas (1681–1725) Collection
Selden, John (1584–1654) Collection
UN and EC documents

Non-library collection catalogue: All or part available online and in print

Library catalogue: All or part available online and in print

Publications: Printed, and electronic and video, and microform publications
Order printed publications from: Marketing and Publishing Division, Bodleian Library Broad Street, Oxford, OX1 3BG, tel: 01865 277091, fax: 01865 277218, e-mail: sales@bodley.ox.ac.uk

Publications list: Available online and in print

Access to staff: Contact by letter, by telephone, by fax and by e-mail. Non-members charged.
Hours: Mon to Fri, 0900 to 1900 or 2200
Special comments: Admission Form (available on web) required. No access below undergraduate level; access to undergraduates of other universities only during vacations.

Central Bodleian site: Admissions Office (for enquiries about becoming a reader at the library); tel: 01865 277180; fax: 01865 277105; e-mail: admissions@bodley.ox.ac.uk; Bodleian Japanese Library at the Nissan Institute (for Japanese collections); 27 Winchester Road, Oxford, OX2 6NA; tel: 01865 284506; fax: 01865 284500; e-mail: japanese@bodley.ox.ac.uk; Bodleian Law Library (for law, excluding ecclesiastical law); Manor Road, Oxford, OX1 3UR; tel: 01865 271463; fax: 01865 271475; e-mail: law.library@bodley.ox.ac.uk; Department of Oriental Books and Manuscripts (books and manuscripts in Oriental languages, except Japanese and the languages of the Indian subcontinent); tel: 01865 277034; fax: 01865 277029; e-mail: oriental@bodley.ox.ac.uk; Department of Special Collections & Western Manuscripts (manuscripts, rare and early printed books, modern political papers in Western languages); tel: 01865 277158; fax: 01865 277182; e-mail: western.manuscrpts@bodley.ox.ac.uk; Eastern Art Library; Pusey Lane, Oxford, OX1 2LE; tel: 01865 278202; fax: 01865 278190; e-mail: eastern.art.library@bodley.ox.ac.uk; European Documentation Centre (receives all European Union publications); Bodleian Law Library, Manor Road, Oxford, OX1 3UR; tel: 01865 271463; fax: 01865 271475; e-mail: edc@bodley.ox.ac.uk; Hooke Library (for science); South Parks Road, Oxford, OX1 3UB; tel: 01865 272812; fax: 01865 272821; e-mail: hooke@bodley.ox.ac.uk; Imaging Services (all photocopy and photographic enquiries); tel: 01865 277061; fax: 01865 287127; e-mail: repro@bodley.ox.ac.uk; Indian Institute Library (for books and manuscripts from the Indian subcontinent); Bodleian Library, Broad Street, Oxford, OX1

continued overleaf

3BG; tel: 01865 277081; fax: 01865 277182; e-mail: indian.institute@bodley.ox.ac.uk; Institute for Chinese Studies Library; Walton Street, Oxford, OX1 2HG; tel: 01865 280430; fax: 01865 280431; e-mail: chinese.studies .library@bodley.ox.ac.uk; John Johnson Collection (printed ephemera); tel: 01865 277047; fax: 01865 277182; e-mail: jjcoll@ bodley.ox.ac.uk; Map Room (for maps and geography-related resources); tel: 01865 277013; fax: 01865 277139; e-mail: maps@ bodley.ox.ac.uk; Marketing & Publishing Division (library publications and merchandise, publication of material from the library); tel: 01865 277091; fax: 01865 277218; e-mail: sales@bodley.ox.ac.uk; Modern Papers (modern political papers); tel: 01865 277046; fax: 01865 277182; e-mail: modern.papers@bodley.ox.ac.uk; Music Room (for music resources); tel: 01865 277063; fax: 01865 277182; e-mail: music@ bodley.ox.ac.uk; Oriental Institute Library; Pusey Lane, Oxford, OX1 2LE; tel: 01865 278202; fax: 01865 278190; e-mail: library@ orinst.ox.ac.uk; Philosophy Library (admission restricted to University members); 10 Merton Street, Oxford, OX1 4JJ; tel: 01865 276927; fax: 01865 276932; e-mail: philosophy.library@bodley.ox.ac.uk; Preservation & Conservation Department (preservation and conservation of the collections); tel: 01865 277086; fax: 01865 277182; e-mail: prescons@bodley.ox.ac.uk; Radcliffe Science Library (for science, covering the physical and life sciences); Parks Road, Oxford, OX1 3QP; tel: 01865 272800; fax: 01865 272821; e-mail: rsl .enquiries@bodley.ox.ac.uk; Reader Services Department (reader services relating to printed books and journals in Western languages); tel: 01865 277162; fax: 01865 287112; e-mail: reader.services@bodley.ox.ac .uk; Rhodes House Library (for African and Commonwealth history and politics); South Parks Road, Oxford, OX1 3RG; tel: 01865 270908; fax: 01865 270912; e-mail: rhodes .house.library@bodley.ox.ac.uk; Systems Section (Bodleian's database network and www pages); tel: 01865 277074; fax: 01865 277182; e-mail: systems@bodley.ox.ac.uk; Technical Services Department (status of items on order, receipt of legal deposit material, reporting errors in the Oxford union catalogue, OLIS); tel: 01865 277017; fax: 01865 277036; e-mail: technical.services@ bodley.ox.ac.uk; Vere Harmsworth Library (for American history and politics); South Parks Road, Oxford, OX1 3TG; tel: 01865 282700; fax: 01865 282709; e-mail: vhl@ bodley.ox.ac.uk

Parent body: University of Oxford; tel: 01865 270000; fax: 01865 270708

BODLEIAN LIBRARY OF COMMONWEALTH AND AFRICAN STUDIES AT RHODES HOUSE

South Parks Road, Oxford, OX1 3RG

Tel: 01865 270908
E-mail: rhodes.house.library@bodleian.ox.ac .uk
Website: www.bodleian.ox.ac.uk/rhodes

Enquiries to: Subject Consultant or Archivist

Founded: 1929; formerly called Rhodes House Library

Organisation type and purpose: University library.

Subject coverage: History of the Commonwealth (excluding the Indian sub-continent) and Africa south of the Sahara.

Collection: C J Rhodes Papers
Colonial Records (collection of papers of colonial servants)
Papers of the Anti-Apartheid Movement
Papers of the Anti-Slavery Society
Papers of the United Society for the Propagation of the Gospel
Scicluna Collection (Malta)
Sir Roy Welensky Papers

Library catalogue: All or part available online

Publications: Printed, and microform publications

Publications list: Available in print

Access to staff: Contact by letter, by telephone, by e-mail and in person. Letter of introduction required. Non-members charged.
Hours: Term time: Mon to Fri, 0900 to 1900; Sat, 0900 to 1300
Vacations: Mon to Fri, 0900 to 1700

Access for disabled people: Access difficult due to steps at building entrance and within building. Please contact staff in advance for material to be moved to an accessible reading room.

Constituent part of: Bodleian Library; University of Oxford

BOLSOVER DISTRICT COUNCIL (BDC)

Sherwood Lodge, Bolsover, Derbyshire, S44 6NF

Tel: 01246 242424, 01246 242450 (minicom)
Fax: 01246 242423
E-mail: enquiries@bolsover.gov.uk
Website: www.bolsover.gov.uk

Enquiries to: Communications Officer
Direct tel: 01246 242323
Direct e-mail: scott.chambers@bolsover.gov .uk

Founded: 1974

Organisation type and purpose: Local government body.

Publications: Printed, and electronic and video
Order printed publications from: Contact Centres, Bolsover District Council, Sherwood Lodge, Bolsover, Derbyshire S44 6NF

Publications list: Available online and in print

Access to staff: Contact by letter, by telephone, by fax, by e-mail, in person and via website
Hours: Mon to Fri, 0900 to 1700

Access for disabled people: Parking provided, ramped entry, toilet facilities

BOLTON LIBRARIES

Central Library, Civic Centre, Le Mans Crescent, Bolton, Lancashire, BL1 1SE

Tel: 01204 333173
Fax: 01204 332225
E-mail: josie.butterworth@bolton.gov.uk
Website: www.bolton.gov.uk/libraries

Enquiries to: Team Librarian
Direct tel: 01204 333173
Direct e-mail: central.library@bolton.gov.uk

Founded: 1853

Organisation type and purpose: Local government body, public library.

Subject coverage: General, science and technology, textiles, local studies, business information, childcare information, career information, health and social care information.

Information services: In-depth information service, tourist information service, Bolton NHS library, social care library

Collection: Textiles collection, special periodicals collection, rare books collection, Lancashire collection, British Standards, childcare information, careers

Trade and statistical information: Mainly official British statistics, EU statistics, UN statistics

Library catalogue: All or part available online

Access to staff: Contact by letter, by telephone, by fax, by e-mail and in person
Hours: Mon, Tue and Thu, 0900 to 1930; Wed, 0930 to 1730; Fri, 0900 to 1730; Sat, 0900 to 1700; Sun, 1000 to 1600. Bank Holidays, 1000 to 1600.

Access to building: *Hours:* Mon, Tue and Thu, 0815 to 1930; Wed, 0930 to 1730; Fri, 0815 to 1730; Sat, 0900 to 1700; Sun, 1000 to 1600. Bank Holidays, 1000 to 1600.

Access for disabled people: Ramped entry, toilet facilities
Hours: Mon, Tue and Thu, 0815 to 1930; Wed, 0930 to 1730; Fri, 0815 to 1730; Sat, 0900 to 1700; Sun, 1000 to 1600. Bank Holidays, 1000 to 1600.

BOLTON METROPOLITAN BOROUGH COUNCIL (Bolton Council)

Town Hall, Bolton, Greater Manchester, BL1 1RU

Tel: 01204 333333
Fax: 01204 392808
E-mail: bolton@bolton.gov.uk
Website: www.bolton.gov.uk

Organisation type and purpose: Local government body.

Subject coverage: Local government services.

BOND OWNERS' CLUB (BOC)

42 Beaufort Avenue, Hodge Hill, Birmingham, B34 6AE

Tel: 0121 784 4626
Fax: 0121 784 4626
E-mail: bondownersclub@sky.com
Website: www.bondownersclub.co.uk

Enquiries to: General Secretary

Founded: 1951

Organisation type and purpose: International organisation, membership association.

Subject coverage: Information on Bond cars and the Bond Owners' Club, spares availability and technical advice.

Collection: Production records and original archive material

Publications: Printed

Access to staff: Contact by letter, by telephone and by fax. Appointment necessary.
Hours: Evenings and weekends

BOOK AID INTERNATIONAL

39–41 Coldharbour Lane, London, SE5 9NR

Tel: 020 7733 3577
Fax: 020 7978 8006
E-mail: info@bookaid.org
Website: www.bookaid.org

Enquiries to: Administrator

Founded: 1954

Organisation type and purpose: Registered charity (charity number 313869).
Working in partnership with organisations in developing countries to support their work in literacy, education, training and publishing.

Subject coverage: Education, book provision and publishing in developing countries, especially Africa.

Publications: Printed

Access to staff: Contact by letter, by telephone, by fax, by e-mail and via website. Appointment necessary.
Hours: Mon to Fri, 0900 to 1700

BOOK PRODUCTION CONSULTANTS LTD (BPC)

25–27 High Street, Chesterton, Cambridge, CB4 1ND

Tel: 01223 352790
Fax: 01223 460718
E-mail: bpc@bpccam.co.uk
Website: www.bpccam.co.uk

Enquiries to: Marketing Manager
Direct e-mail: jl@bpccam.co.uk

Founded: 1973

Organisation type and purpose: The complete design, editorial, production and printing service for publishers, companies, organisations and institutions.

Subject coverage: Service publishing including: guides, catalogues and magazines, corporate manuals, brochures and histories, books and journals, all subjects covered.

Publications list: Available in print

Access to staff: Contact by letter, by telephone, by fax and by e-mail
Hours: Mon to Fri, 0900 to 1730

Constituent bodies: Granta Editions; website: http://grantabooks.com/

BOOK TRUST

Formal name: Book Trust

Book House, 45 East Hill, London, SW18 2QZ

Tel: 020 8516 2977
Fax: 020 8516 2978
E-mail: query@booktrust.org.uk
Website: www.booktrust.org.uk

Organisation type and purpose: To provide reviews, information and advice giving readers the widest possible access to books.

Subject coverage: Books, publishing, reading, literary prizes

Access to staff: Contact by letter, by telephone, by fax, by e-mail and via website

BOOKPLATE SOCIETY

Yarkhill, Upper Bucklebury, Reading, Berkshire, RG7 6QH

E-mail: publications@bookplatesociety.org
Website: www.bookplatesociety.org/

Enquiries to: Honorary Secretary

Founded: 1972

Organisation type and purpose: International organisation, membership association (membership is by subscription), present number of members: 250, registered charity (charity number 295678), publishing house.
Voluntary association of bookplate collectors, artists and bibliophiles.
To promote the collection and study of bookplates.

Subject coverage: History of bookplates, bookplate artists, bookplate literature.

Collection: Society Archive

Publications: Printed
Order printed publications from: The Bookplate Society
Address as above

Publications list: Available online

Access to staff: Contact by letter and by e-mail
Hours: Weekends and evenings

Affiliated to: Fédération Internationale des Sociétés d'Amateurs d'Ex-Libris (FISAE)

BOOKS EXPRESS

Unit 4, Dencora Park, Shirehill Industrial Estate, Saffron Walden, Essex, CB11 3GB

Tel: 01799 513726
Fax: 01799 513248
E-mail: info@books-express.co.uk
Website: www.books-express.co.uk

Enquiries to: Senior Partner
Direct e-mail: duncan@books-express.co.uk
Other contacts: Bibliographic Services Manager (for website enquiries, bibliographic enquiries)

Founded: 1983

Organisation type and purpose: Service industry.
Specialist bookseller and information service. North American and European academic publishers.

Subject coverage: Official publications, government documents and electronic information from Commonwealth of Australia (AGPS), Federal Government of Canada (CCG-P), Federal Government of USA (USGPO), Queensland Department of Primary Industry, and Library Cataloguing Materials from United States Library of Congress.

Collection: Comprehensive database of official publications for sale from Australia, Canada, USA and Queensland
US and European academic publications

Publications: Printed

Access to staff: Contact by letter, by telephone, by fax, by e-mail and via website. Appointment necessary.
Hours: Mon to Fri, 1000 to 1800

BOOKSELLERS ASSOCIATION OF THE UK & IRELAND LIMITED (BA)

6 Bell Yard, London WC2A 2JR

Tel: 020 7421 4640
Fax: 020 7421 4641
E-mail: mail@booksellers.org.uk
Website: www.booksellers.org.uk

Enquiries to: Chief Executive

Founded: 1895

Organisation type and purpose: Trade association, present number of members: 4,400 mostly retail outlets.
Representing and promoting retail booksellers nationwide.

Subject coverage: Book trade regulations, market conditions, legislation, shopfitting, distribution, national book tokens, careers, etc.

Publications: Printed

Publications list: Available in print

Wholly owned companies: Batch Ltd; e-mail: mail@batch.co.uk

Wholly-owned companies: Book Tokens Limited; e-mail: mail@booktokens.co.uk

BORDER HERITAGE

Loophill, Canonbie, Dumfries & Galloway, DG14 0XF

Tel: 01387 371780
Fax: 01387 381243
Website: www.borderheritage.com

Enquiries to: Managing Director

Founded: 1997

Organisation type and purpose: Local history society.

Subject coverage: Scottish/English border history, films, books.

Collection: Extensive video tape collection on Border family history
Books

Non-library collection catalogue: All or part available online

Publications: Printed

Publications list: Available online

Access to staff: Contact by letter, by telephone, by fax and by e-mail

continued overleaf

Hours: Mon to Fri, 0900 to 1700

Access to building: Prior appointment required

BORDER UNION AGRICULTURAL SOCIETY

Showground Office, Springwood Park, Kelso, Borders, TD5 8LS

Tel: 01573 224188
Fax: 01573 226778
E-mail: bordunion@aol.com

Enquiries to: Secretary

Founded: 1813

Organisation type and purpose: Voluntary organisation, publishing house.
Agricultural Society.
Organisation and promotion of agricultural, rural and canine activities.

Subject coverage: Shows and exhibitions, agricultural, canine and general, rural life. Access to rural historical records for the locality. Information on present day rural activities.

Collection: Society records dating from 1813

Publications: Printed

Access to staff: Contact by letter, by telephone and by fax
Hours: Mon to Fri, 0900 to 1700

Member of: Association of Show and Agricultural Organisations

BORGWARD DRIVERS' CLUB

158 Willow Avenue, Edgbaston, Birmingham, B17 8HG

Tel: 0121 429 7169
E-mail: borgwardclub@btinternet.com
Website: www.borgward.co.uk

Enquiries to: Secretary

Founded: 1980

Organisation type and purpose: Membership association (membership is by subscription), present number of members: 70, voluntary organisation.
To further the promotion of Borgward, Lloyd, Goliath, and Hansa cars in the United Kingdom.

Subject coverage: Borgward cars, Lloyd cars, Goliath cars, Hansa cars and spares for same.

Publications: Printed

Access to staff: Contact by letter, by telephone, by e-mail and via website
Hours: Sun to Sat, 0900 to 2000

BORTHWICK INSTITUTE FOR ARCHIVES

University of York, Heslington, York, YO10 5DD

Tel: 01904 321166
E-mail: bihr500@york.ac.uk
Website: www.york.ac.uk/inst/bihr

Enquiries to: Archive assistants
Direct tel: 01904 321166
Direct e-mail: bihr500@york.ac.uk

Founded: 1953

Organisation type and purpose: University department or institute.
Historical research institute and archives.

Subject coverage: Ecclesiastical, social, economic, local and political history, medical history, architectural history and the history of Southern Africa.

Collection: Archive of the Archbishopric of York c. 1200 to present day, including c. 500,000 wills and inventories 1320–1858, for Yorkshire and the north of England, and ecclesiastical cause papers from the 14th century
Archives of Church of England houses, the Community of the Resurrection and the Society of the Sacred Mission
Anglican parish records for the archdeaconry of York, Methodist and Congregational records for the York area
Archive of the Catholic Apostolic Church
Archive of the Earls of Halifax, including Viceroy's papers and war diaries of the first Earl
Archives of architectural practices based in York (Atkinson-Brierley and Pace and Simms)
York Health Trust Archive, including psychiatric and general hospitals from the 18th century and NHS managing bodies from 1948
The Archive of Rowntree plc
The Archive of Terry of York
Archives of the Rowntree Trusts, and the research papers of Seebohm Rowntree
Storey Collection of the archives of modern dramatists, including Sir Alan Ayckbourn, Marks and Gran, David Storey and others.
Many private family, charity and business archives
Archive of the University of York
Archives collected by the Centre for Southern African Studies

Non-library collection catalogue: All or part available online, in-house and in print

Publications: Printed
Order printed publications from: Borthwick Institute, University of York, Heslington, York, YO10 5DD

Publications list: Available online and in print

Access to staff: Contact by letter, by telephone, by e-mail, in person and via website
Hours: Mon to Fri, 0915 to 1645

Access to building: Open to the public
Hours: Sun to Sat, 0800 to 2200

Access for disabled people: Lift available to building and within building, height-adjustable desks available

Constituent part of: University of York; tel: 01904 32 0000; fax: 01904 32 3433; e-mail: web-office@york.ac.uk; website: http://www.york.ac.uk/

BOSS FEDERATION

Formal name: British Office Supplies and Services Federation

c/o BPIF, 2 Villiers Court, Meriden Business Park, Copse Drive, Coventry CV5 9RN

Tel: 0845 450 1565
E-mail: info@bossfederation.co.uk
Website: www.bossfederation.co.uk

Founded: 1905; formerly called Stationers Proprietary Articles Trade Association

Organisation type and purpose: A non-profit making organisation, the trade association that serves the UK office supplies and services industry.
Provides a range of initiatives, cost-saving benefits and services to enhance the business performance of its members, and plays a strategic role in the support, promotion and protection of the office products industry.

Subject coverage: Represents all businesses, from the smallest retailer to the largest manufacturer, along the distribution chain in the office products industry, covering stationery, office machines and supplies, office furniture, office systems and related product areas.

Access to staff: Contact by letter, by telephone, by fax and by e-mail

Branches: Has 8 regional committees throughout the UK

Federation includes: Rubber Stamp Manufacturers Guild (RSMG); Writing Instruments Associaton (WIA)

BOTANICAL SOCIETY OF SCOTLAND (BSS)

c/o Royal Botanic Garden Edinburgh, 20a Inverleith Row, Edinburgh, EH3 5LR

Tel: 0131 552 7171
Fax: 0131 248 2901
Website: www.botsocscot.org.uk

Enquiries to: General Secretary

Founded: 1836

Organisation type and purpose: Learned society (membership is by subscription, election or invitation), voluntary organisation, recognised Scottish charity (charity number 016283).
Incorporates the Cryptogamic Society of Scotland.

Subject coverage: Plant science; Scottish flora: plant identification, ecological studies and botanical conservation.

Collection: Library is incorporated within that of the Royal Botanic Garden Edinburgh

Publications: Printed

Access to staff: Contact by letter

BOTANICAL SOCIETY OF THE BRITISH ISLES (BSBI)

Department of Botany, Natural History Museum, Cromwell Road, London, SW7 5BD

Tel: 020 7492 5002 (answerphone only)
E-mail: dpearman4@aol.com
Website: www.bsbi.org.uk

Enquiries to: Honorary General Secretary (for specific plant enquiries)
Other contacts: Honorary Assistant Secretary (for all general enquiries)

Founded: 1836

Organisation type and purpose: Learned society (membership is by subscription), present number of members: 2,800 approx, voluntary organisation, research organisation, publishing house.

The study and conservation of the British and Irish vascular plant and charophyte flora, its form and distribution. Research into the taxonomy, ecology, biogeography of the flora, maintenance of a botanical recording network and collaboration with other statutory and voluntary bodies.

Subject coverage: British flowering plants and ferns, identification of wild plants, local floras.

Collection: Database at University of Leicester, c/o Dr R J Gornall, University Road, Leicester, LE1 7RH

Publications: Printed
Order printed publications from: Botanical Society of the British Isles Publications, c/o Summerfield Books, 3 Phoenix Park, Skelton, Penrith, Cumbria, CA11 95DE; tel: 01768 484909; fax: 01768 484910; e-mail: info@summerfieldbooks.com

Publications list: Available in print

Access to staff: Contact by letter, by telephone and by e-mail
Hours: Mon to Fri, 0900 to 1700
Special comments: Answerphone provides a letter reply only.

BOTANIX LIMITED

Hop Pocket Lane, Paddock Wood, Tonbridge, Kent, TN12 6DQ

Tel: 01892 833415
Fax: 01892 836905
E-mail: sales@botanix.co.uk
Website: www.botanix.co.uk

Enquiries to: Sales Director

Founded: 1987

Organisation type and purpose: International organisation, manufacturing industry.

Subject coverage: Production and sales of hop-based products for the brewing industry; marketing of English hops and hop products.

Access to staff: Contact by letter, by telephone, by e-mail and via website. Appointment necessary.
Hours: Mon to Fri, 0900 to 1730

Member organisation of: Institute of Brewing and Distilling

BOUNDARY COMMISSION FOR SCOTLAND

Thistle House, 91 Haymarket Terrace, Edinburgh, EH12 5HD

Tel: 0131 538 7510
Fax: 0131 538 7511
E-mail: secretariat@scottishboundaries.gov.uk
Website: www.bcomm-scotland.gov.uk

Enquiries to: Secretary

Founded: 1945

Organisation type and purpose: Statutory body, advisory non-departmental public body, constituted under the Parliamentary Constituencies Act 1986, reporting to the Scotland Office.

Subject coverage: Parliamentary boundaries.

Publications: Printed, and electronic and video
Order printed publications from: The Stationery Office

Publications list: Available online

Access to staff: Contact by letter, by telephone, by fax, by e-mail and via website
Hours: Mon to Fri, 0900 to 1700

BOURNEMOUTH AND POOLE COLLEGE

North Road, Parkstone, Poole, Dorset, BH14 0LS

Tel: 01202 747600
Fax: 01202 205477
E-mail: enquiries@thecollege.co.uk
Website: www.thecollege.co.uk

Enquiries to: Librarian
Direct tel: 01202 205631

Subject coverage: FE courses (GCSE, A-level, AS-level, AVCE, GMVQ, NVQ) in the following subjects: construction, engineering, social care, child care, theatre and performing arts, hairdressing, floristry, beauty therapy, catering, tourism, hotel operations, business studies, computing, media studies, management, teacher training, art and design, science, languages, social sciences, law.
HE courses (BSC and BEng Foundation, HND, HNC) in the following subjects: conservation sciences, computing, electronics, design engineering, business, business information technology, computer-aided design, geography and coastal conservation, popular music, tourism and leisure management, mechanical and production engineering, building studies.

Collection: 249 journals
6,000 audio visual items (videos, tapes)
70,776 books to support courses listed

Library catalogue: All or part available in-house

Access to staff: Contact by letter and by e-mail
Hours: Mon to Thu, 0900 to 1900; Fri, 0900 to 1700

Access for disabled people: Parking provided, ramped entry, access to all public areas, toilet facilities

BOURNEMOUTH UNIVERSITY

The Sir Michael Cobham Library, Talbot Campus, Fern Barrow, Poole, Dorset, BH12 5BB

Tel: 01202 965959
Fax: 01202 965475
Website: www.bournemouth.ac.uk/library

Enquiries to: Library & Learning Support Librarian
Direct tel: 01202 965044
Direct fax: 01202 965475
Direct e-mail: jascott@bmth.ac.uk
Other contacts: Service Development Manager

Founded: 1979

Organisation type and purpose: University library.

Subject coverage: Computing, IT, electronics and information systems, psychology, communications and sociology, economics and industry, finance, taxation and accountancy, law, management, marketing, retailing, advertising and public relations, health and community studies, social policy, nursing and midwifery, biological and environmental sciences, design, production and manufacture, food hospitality, tourism, recreation and leisure, media studies, archaeology and heritage conservation.

Collection: Wedlake and Greening: Archaeology
Ernst and Young: Taxation and Revenue Law
BBC Radio 4 Analysis Programme
Broadcasting Audience Research
Independent Local Radio Programme
Sharing Digitization Project Archive
Segrue Journalism Collection
TV Times Project
Printed and electronic sources covering history of broadcasting, public relations and advertising; product design, interior design and engineering

Trade and statistical information: Collection of government and EC official statistics.
A range of unofficial statistics.
Business information.
Company data.
Market Research

Library catalogue: All or part available online

Access to staff: Contact by letter, by e-mail and via website. Appointment necessary.
Hours: Term time: Mon to Thu, 0900 to 2100; Fri, 0915 to 1715; Sat, 1200 to 1800; Sun 1200 to 1800

Members: Southern Universities Purchasing Consortium (SUPC)

BOVIS LEND LEASE LIMITED (EUROPE) (BLLE)

20 Triton Street, Regent's Place, London, NW1 3BF

Tel: 020 3430 9000
Fax: 020 3430 9001
Website: www.bovislendlease.com

Enquiries to: Librarian
Direct tel: 020 8271 8124 (Information Centre)
Direct e-mail: caroline.massey@eu.bovislendlease.com

Founded: 1885

Organisation type and purpose: Service industry.
Construction company.
Project and construction management, consultancy, creative solutions.

Subject coverage: Building construction.

Library catalogue: All or part available in-house

Access to staff: Contact by letter, by e-mail and via website. Appointment necessary.
Hours: Mon to Fri, 0900 to 1700

Access to building: No access other than to staff

Parent body: Lend Lease Limited

Regional offices in: Birmingham, Bristol, Edinburgh, Glasgow, Manchester, Dublin, Belfast

BOWLS ENGLAND (BE)

Lyndhurst Road, Worthing, West Sussex, BN11 2AZ

Tel: 01903 820222
Fax: 01903 820444
E-mail: enquiries@bowlsengland.com
Website: www.bowlsengland.com

Enquiries to: Chief Executive

Founded: 1903

Organisation type and purpose: National organisation, professional body, present number of members: 132,000.
National governing body of the game.

Subject coverage: The game of bowls.

Access to staff: Contact by letter, by telephone and by fax. Appointment necessary.
Hours: Mon to Fri, 0900 to 1700

Access for disabled people: Parking provided, level entry

Also at: Bowls England; Victoria Park, Archery Road, Royal Leamington Spa, Warwickshire, CV31 3PT; tel: 01926 430686; fax: 01926 332024

BOX CULVERT ASSOCIATION (BoxCA)

60 Charles Street, Leicester, LE1 1FB

Tel: 0116 253 6161
Fax: 0116 251 4568
E-mail: boxca@britishprecast.org
Website: www.boxculvert.org.uk/

Enquiries to: Secretary

Organisation type and purpose: Trade association.

Subject coverage: Precast concrete box culverts.

Publications: Printed

Access to staff: Contact by letter, by telephone, by fax and by e-mail
Hours: Mon to Fri, 0900 to 1700

Product association of the: British Precast Concrete Federation

BOYS' BRIGADE (BB)

Felden Lodge, Felden Lane, Hemel Hempstead, Hertfordshire, HP3 0BL

Tel: 01442 231681
Fax: 01442 235391
E-mail: felden@boys-brigade.org.uk
Website: www.boys-brigade.org.uk

Enquiries to: Chief Executive

Founded: 1883

Organisation type and purpose: Voluntary organisation.
Youth organisation.

Subject coverage: Church-based youth work with boys and young men in nearly 3,000 churches of most denominations.

Collection: Archives relating to the founding (in 1883) and subsequent history of the Brigade

Publications: Printed
Order printed publications from: The Supplies Manager, The Boys' Brigade
Alington Road, Eynesbury, St Neots, Cambridgeshire, PE19 2RD, tel: 01480 470515, fax: 01480 470516, e-mail: bus-cent@boys-brigade.org.uk

Access to staff: Contact by letter, by fax and by e-mail
Hours: Mon to Fri, 0900 to 1700

BP VIDEO LIBRARY

52–54 Southwark Street, London, SE1 1UN

Tel: 020 7357 7521
Fax: 020 7357 9953
E-mail: bpvl@bp.com
Website: www.bpvideolibrary.com

Enquiries to: Librarian

Organisation type and purpose: Suitable for ages: all.
Distribution library.

Subject coverage: Oil industry, refining, exploration, energy, environment, motoring, power and engineering.

Collection: Video programmes covering wide area of the oil industry

Library catalogue: All or part available in print

Publications: Electronic and video

Publications list: Available in print

Access to staff: Contact by letter, by telephone, by fax and by e-mail
Hours: Mon to Fri, 0900 to 1700

BPA CONSULTING LIMITED

Dorset House, Regent Park, 297 Kingston Road, Leatherhead, Surrey, KT22 7PL

Tel: 01306 875500
Fax: 01306 888179
E-mail: bpa@bpaconsulting.com
Website: www.bpaconsulting.com/

Enquiries to: Director

Founded: 1971

Organisation type and purpose: Consultancy.

Subject coverage: Strategic consultants to the electronics industry, specialising in interconnection and packaging.

Publications list: Available online and in print

Access to staff: Contact by letter, by telephone, by fax and by e-mail
Hours: Mon to Fri, 0900 to 1730

BRACE

Formal name: Bristol Research into Alzheimer's and Care of the Elderly

Frenchay Hospital, Frenchay, Bristol, BS16 1LE

Tel: 0117 340 4831
Fax: 0117 340 4831
E-mail: admin@alzheimers-brace.org
Website: www.alzheimers-brace.org

Founded: 1987

Organisation type and purpose: Registered charity (charity number 297965).
One of only a few charities that exists specifically to finance dementia research. Aims to help support a continuing programme of research into conditions of the elderly, particularly Alzheimer's Disease, and also to raise awareness of the disease and its effects, not only on the sufferer but also on family life. Supports research projects undertaken in universities and hospitals in the South West of the UK, particularly in Bristol, which is a centre of excellence for neuroscience research.

Subject coverage: High quality, peer-reviewed research projects in different aspects of dementia research. The projects range from the development of more accurate methods of diagnosis and evaluating treatments to examining a person's genetic make-up to see why some people suffer from dementia when others live into old age without developing the condition.

Information services: Provides speakers for external events and group meetings.

Publications: Electronic and video
Order electronic and video publications from: Website

Access to staff: Contact by letter, by telephone, by fax, by e-mail and via website

BRACKENHURST LIBRARY

The Nottingham Trent University, Brackenhurst, Nottingham Road, Southwell, Nottinghamshire, NG25 0QF

Tel: 01636 817000 (switchboard); 01636 817049 (library)
Fax: 01636 815404

Enquiries to: Information Specialist
Direct e-mail: heather.parsonage@ntu.ac.uk

Organisation type and purpose: University library, suitable for ages: 16+.

Subject coverage: Agriculture, food science, horticulture and floristry, equine studies and horse management, land management, small animal care.

Access to staff: Contact by telephone
Hours: Term time: Mon to Thu, 0830 to 2100; Fri, 0830 to 1730

Department of: Nottingham Trent University

BRACKNELL AND WOKINGHAM COLLEGE

Church Road, Bracknell, Berkshire, RG12 1DJ

Tel: 01344 766200
E-mail: study@bracknell.ac.uk
Website: www.bracknell.ac.uk

Enquiries to: Learning Resources Centre Manager
Direct tel: 01344766470
Direct e-mail: lrc@bracknell.ac.uk

Founded: 1962

Organisation type and purpose: Suitable for ages: 16+.

Subject coverage: GCSE, A Level, BTEC Diploma and Extended Diploma
Art, Design and Media
Photography

Performing Arts
Business and Leisure
Marketing, Personnel and Accountancy
IT and Computer Aided Design
Engineering and Motor Vehicle
Electrical Installation and Construction
Hairdressing and Beauty Therapy
Health and Social Care
Childcare and Early Years
Sport and Public Services
Travel and Tourism
EFL and ESOL
Modern Languages
Access to HE
Teacher Training, PTLLS, CTLLS and DTLLS
Wide range of leisure courses

Library catalogue: All or part available online

Access to staff: Contact by letter, by telephone, by e-mail, in person and via website
Hours: Mon, 0830 to 1700; Tue to Thu, 0830 to 2000; Fri 0830 to 1600
Special comments: Limited opening in College vacation.

Access for disabled people: Parking provided, access to all public areas, toilet facilities

Other addresses: Bracknell & Wokingham College; Wick Hill Centre, Wick Hill, Sandy Lane, Bracknell, RG12 2JG; tel: 01344 766 600; Bracknell & Wokingham College; Woodley Hill House, Eastcourt Avenue, Earley, Reading, RG6 1HH; tel: 0118 984 7600

BRACKNELL FOREST BOROUGH COUNCIL

Easthamstead House, Town Square, Bracknell, Berkshire, RG12 1AQ

Tel: 01344 352000 \ Minicom no. 01344 352045
Fax: 01344 352810
E-mail: customer.services@bracknell-forest.gov.uk
Website: www.bracknell-forest.gov.uk

Enquiries to: Public Relations Manager
Other contacts: Borough Administrator

Organisation type and purpose: Local government body.

Subject coverage: Leisure, environmental health, housing services, planning, development and control, council tax, refuse collection, street lighting, landscape maintenance, drains, sewer clearance and cesspools, services for residents of the borough of Bracknell Forest.

Trade and statistical information: Data on the local population of Bracknell, amenities, services and employment

Publications: Printed, and electronic and video

Access to staff: Contact by letter, by telephone and by fax
Hours: Mon to Fri, 0900 to 1700

BRACKNELL FOREST COUNCIL LIBRARY AND INFORMATION SERVICE

Bracknell Central Library, Town Square, Bracknell, Berkshire, RG12 1BH

Tel: 01344 423149
Fax: 01344 411392
E-mail: bracknell.library@bracknell-forest.gov.uk
Website: www.bracknell-forest.gov.uk/libraries

Organisation type and purpose: Local government body, public library.

Collection: Photographic collection of the development of Bracknell town, and local studies collection.

Library catalogue: All or part available online

Access to staff: Contact by letter, by telephone, by fax, by e-mail and in person
Hours: Mon, 0930 to 1700; Tue, Thu, Fri, 0930 to 1900; Sat, 0930 to 1600
Closed Wed and Sun

Access to building: *Special comments:* No lift access at Bracknell Library.

Access for disabled people: Ramp and automatic doors

BRACKNELL FOREST HERITAGE

Environment & Leisure, Time Square, Market Street, Bracknell, RG12 1JD

Tel: 01344 351754
E-mail: heritage@bracknell-forest.gov.uk
Website: www.bracknell-forest.gov.uk/leis-heritage

Enquiries to: Heritage Officer

Organisation type and purpose: Heritage strategy arm of Bracknell Forest Borough Council.

Subject coverage: The heritage strategy covers a broad range of heritage concerns and interests across the borough.

Access to staff: Contact by letter, by telephone and by e-mail

BRADFORD CATHEDRAL

Formal name: Cathedral Church of St Peter, Bradford

Cathedral Office, Stott Hill, Bradford, West Yorkshire, BD1 4EH

Tel: 01274 777720
Fax: 01274 777730
E-mail: info@bradfordcathedral.org
Website: www.bradfordcathedral.org

Enquiries to: Cathedral Secretary

Founded: 7th century

Organisation type and purpose: Place of worship, historic listed building, concert and exhibition venue, education resource – visits programme, Bradford heritage.

Subject coverage: Christian worship and faith; local history; William Morris Glass.

Education services: For school and group visits contact the Education Officer

Access to staff: Contact by letter, by telephone, by fax, by e-mail, in person and via website
Hours: Mon to Fri, 0900 to 1700; Sun, services only
Special comments: Groups by prior appointment.

Access to building: *Hours:* Mon to Fri, 0900 to 1630; Sat, 0900 to 1600 (phone ahead for confirmation)

Access for disabled people: Access for most areas, parking provided, level entry, toilet facilities

Constituent part of: Diocese of Bradford; Kadugli House, Elmsley Street, Steeton, Keighley, BD20 6SE; tel: 01535 650555; fax: 01535 650550; e-mail: office@kadugli.org.uk; website: http://www.bradford.anglican.org

BRADFORD CHAMBER OF COMMERCE & INDUSTRY (CMS)

Devere House, Vicar Lane, Little Germany, Bradford, West Yorkshire, BD1 5AH

Tel: 01274 772777
Fax: 01274 771081
E-mail: information@bradfordchamber.co.uk
Website: www.bradfordchamber.co.uk

Enquiries to: Chief Executive
Other contacts: Enterprise and Marketing Manager

Organisation type and purpose: Trade association (membership is by subscription), present number of members: 1,100.
Chamber of Commerce.
Provision of business services to members.

Subject coverage: All business information, international trade documentation, business representation, training services.

Publications: Printed

Access to staff: Access for members only. Non-members charged.
Hours: Mon to Fri, 0900 to 1700

BRADFORD LIBRARIES, ARCHIVES AND INFORMATION

Central Library, Princes Way, Bradford, West Yorkshire, BD1 1NN

Tel: 01274 433600
Fax: 01274 395108
E-mail: public.libraries@bradford.gov.uk
Website: www.bradford.gov.uk

Enquiries to: Head of Service: Libraries Archives & Information

Founded: 1872

Organisation type and purpose: Local government body, public library.

Subject coverage: Business information; local studies including oral history; photography; Indic languages especially Urdu; multicultural material, particularly children's material.

Collection: Arthur Blackburn Monumental Inscriptions Collection
Bradford Heritage Recording Unit (local oral history)
Dickons Collection (mainly Bradford history)
Federer Collection (Yorkshire books and pamphlets)
Lees Botanical Collection (19th century flora)
Snowdon Collection (political and social history of the late 19th and early 20th centuries)

Library catalogue: All or part available online

continued overleaf

Publications: Printed, and electronic and video

Publications list: Available in print

Access to staff: Contact by letter, by telephone, by fax, by e-mail and in person

Access for disabled people: Access to all public areas, toilet facilities

Houses the library of: Bradford Antiquarian Society

BRADFORD MECHANICS' INSTITUTE LIBRARY

76 Kirkgate, Bradford, West Yorkshire, BD1 1SZ

Tel: 01274 722857
E-mail: bmi-library@tiscali.co.uk

Enquiries to: Administrator

Founded: 1832

Organisation type and purpose: Registered charity (charity number 509231).
Independent subscription library.

Subject coverage: Lending library; local history collection, history of Bradford and environs, history of the Institute.

Publications: Printed

Access to staff: Contact by letter and by telephone. Access for members only.

Access to building: *Hours:* Mon to Fri, 0900 to 1630; Sat, 0900 to 1200
Special comments: Library open to members only by subscription.

Member organisation of: Association of Independent Libraries

BRADFORD SCHOOL OF MANAGEMENT

Emm Lane, Bradford, West Yorkshire, BD9 4JL

Tel: 01274 234393
Fax: 01274 234405
E-mail: management@bradford.ac.uk
Website: www.brad.ac.uk/management/
Website: www.brad.ac.uk/acad/management

Enquiries to: Director
Direct tel: 01274 234466
Other contacts: Programme Administrators

Founded: 1962

Organisation type and purpose: University department or institute.
Creation and delivery of executive education and development programmes.

Subject coverage: Management development; marketing; finance and accounting; human resource management; strategic management; negotiation skills; effective manager programmes; company programmes.

Collection: Business Library

Publications: Printed

Publications list: Available online and in print

Access to staff: Contact by letter, by telephone, by fax, by e-mail and in person
Hours: Mon to Fri, 0900 to 1700

Access to building: No prior appointment required
Hours: Mon, Tue, Thu, Fri, 0900 to 1700; Wed, 0900 to 2100; Sat, 0900 to 1200

Access for disabled people: Parking provided, level entry, toilet facilities

Parent body: University of Bradford; tel: 01274 232323

BRADFORD UNIVERSITY SCHOOL OF MANAGEMENT LIBRARY

Emm Lane, Bradford, West Yorkshire, BD9 4JL

Tel: 01274 234402
Fax: 01274 234398
E-mail: j.finder@bradford.ac.uk
Website: www.brad.ac.uk/lss/library

Enquiries to: Librarian

Founded: 1962

Organisation type and purpose: University library, consultancy.

Subject coverage: All aspects of management.

Collection: Research publications, projects and theses on a wide variety of management topics
Library with business information services

Library catalogue: All or part available online

Access to staff: Contact by letter, by telephone, by fax, by e-mail and in person. Non-members charged.
Hours: Mon to Fri, 0900 to 1700

Access to building: No prior appointment required
Hours: Term Time: Mon, Tue, Thu, Fri, 0845 to 1730; Wed, 0845 to 2000; Sat, 1000 to 1400
Vacation: Mon to Fri, 0845 to 1730

Parent body: University of Bradford Library; Richmond Road, Bradford, West Yorkshire, BD7 1DP; tel: 01274 233400; fax: 01274 233398; e-mail: j.j.horton@bradford.ac.uk (university librarian)

BRAIN AND SPINE FOUNDATION

3.36 Canterbury Court, Kennington Park, 1–3 Brixton Road, London, SW9 6DE

Tel: 020 7793 5900
Fax: 020 7793 5939
E-mail: info@brainandspine.org.uk
Website: www.brainandspine.org.uk

Enquiries to: Administrator

Founded: 1992

Organisation type and purpose: Registered charity (charity number 1098528).
To provide information and support to anyone affected by a brain and spine condition in the UK.

Subject coverage: Disorders of the brain and spine.

Information services: tel: 0808 808 1000

Publications: Printed, and electronic and video

Publications list: Available online and in print

Access to staff: Contact by letter, by telephone, by fax, by e-mail and via website. Appointment necessary.
Hours: Mon to Fri, 0900 to 1700

Member organisation of: Brain Tumour Research; website: http://www.braintumourresearch.org/
Neurological Alliance; website: http://www.neural.org.uk/
Spinal Injuries Forum; website: http://spinal-injury.net/forums/

BRAIN RESEARCH TRUST (BRT)

15 Southampton Place, London, WC1A 2AJ

Tel: 020 7404 9982
Fax: 020 7404 9983
E-mail: info@brt.org.uk
Website: www.brt.org.uk

Enquiries to: Chief Executive

Founded: 1971

Organisation type and purpose: Registered charity (charity number 263064).
Promotes and supports neurological research at UCL, Institute of Neurology, Queen Square, London.

Subject coverage: World class neurological research.

Publications: Printed

Publications list: Available online

Access to staff: Contact by letter, by telephone, by fax and by e-mail. Appointment necessary.
Hours: Mon to Fri, 0900 to 1700

BRAINTREE DISTRICT COUNCIL

Causeway House, Braintree, Essex, CM7 9HB

Tel: 01376 552525, 01376 557766 (minicom)
Fax: 01376 552626
Website: www.braintree.gov.uk

Enquiries to: Public Relations Manager
Direct tel: 01376 557752

Founded: 1974

Organisation type and purpose: Local government body.

Publications list: Available online

Access to staff: Contact by letter and by telephone. Appointment necessary.
Hours: Mon to Fri, 0900 to 1700

Access for disabled people: Parking provided, ramped entry, access to all public areas, toilet facilities

BRAINWAVES NI

Tel: 028 9335 3995
E-mail: brainwavesni@hotmail.com
Website: www.brainwaves-ni.org

Enquiries to: Secretary

Founded: 1994

Organisation type and purpose: Registered charity (charity number XO 1519/94) dedicated to providing support and information to those people affected by brain tumour. Free membership is open to all.

Subject coverage: Provides information and signposts to appropriate and accurate quality materials, raises awareness of the needs of those just recently diagnosed or living with a brain tumour, and the needs of their families and carers, organises and runs social activities for members, provides financial support, where appropriate, makes donations towards research.

Information services: Hosts a number of information and networking meetings – see website.

Publications: Electronic and video
Order electronic and video publications from: Download from website

Publications list: Available online

Access to staff: Contact by telephone and by e-mail
Hours: Answerphone available if phone is not answered

BRAM STOKER SOCIETY (B S Society)

c/o 43 Castle Court, Killiney Hill Road, Killiney, Co. Dublin, Ireland

E-mail: gothicalbert@eircom.net
Website: www.bibliomania.com
Website: www.vampyreempire.com

Enquiries to: Registrar & Journal Editor

Founded: 1980

Organisation type and purpose: Learned society (membership is by subscription), present number of members: 120.
The promotion of the serious study and appreciation of Bram Stoker, his works, and influence in the areas of fiction, cinema, theatre and music, as well as his importance in the Gothic Horror literary genre.

Subject coverage: The Vampire in fiction, Count Dracula, Bram Stoker, the Gothic Horror genre in film and literature and the Irish Supernatural tradition in folklore and literature.

Collection: An archive of 5,000 books, MSS and documents relating to Bram Stoker held at The Chairperson's address

Publications: Printed
Order printed publications from: Editor (Dr Albert Power), The B S Society Journal
43 Castle Court, Killiney Hill Road, Killiney, County Dublin, Ireland

Publications list: Available in print

Access to staff: Contact by letter, by e-mail and in person. Appointment necessary. Access for members only. Non-members charged.
Hours: Mon to Fri, 0900 to 1700

Access to building: Prior appointment required
Special comments: Prior appointment by application to Chairperson in advance, to consult archives held at his private house. The Annual Summer School held in Dublin, 1st weekend of July.

Affiliated to: The Bram Stoker Club; Trinity College, Dublin; The Bram Stoker Memorial Association of New York

Chairperson's address: The B S Society; 1 Lakelands Close, Stillergan, County Dublin, Ireland; tel: 00 35 31 288 1970; fax: 00 35 31 288 1970

Close links with: Dracula Society of London

BRANCH LINE SOCIETY (BLS)

73 Norfolk Park Avenue, Sheffield, S2 2RB

Tel: 0114 275 2303
Fax: 0114 275 2303
Website: www.branchline.org.uk

Enquiries to: General Secretary
Other contacts: Sales Officer (for sales and membership recruitment enquiries only)

Founded: 1955

Organisation type and purpose: Membership association (membership is by subscription), present number of members: 900, voluntary organisation.

Subject coverage: Minor and branch railway lines, primarily in the British Isles but also in the rest of Europe and other parts of the world.

Publications: Printed
Order printed publications from: Sales Officer, Branch Line Society, 37 Osberton Place, Sheffield, S11 8XL; tel: 0114 263 1094; fax: 0114 263 1094; e-mail: bls.sales@tesco.net

Access to staff: Contact by letter, by telephone and by fax. Appointment necessary.
Hours: Mon to Sun, 0900 to 2200

BRASS BAND HERITAGE TRUST (BBHT)

1 Clumber Close, Poynton, Cheshire, SK12 1PG

E-mail: pehindmarsh@btinternet.com

Enquiries to: Director
Direct tel: 01625 873820

Founded: 1996

Organisation type and purpose: Registered charity (charity number 1037552).
To promote, present activities and foster the future of the Brass Band movement in the UK. The Trust is an active commissioner of new repertoire for brass bands.

Subject coverage: Commissioning new works for brass band for national and regional events; supporting the activities of young composers and youth brass bands nationwide.

Access to staff: Contact by letter, by telephone and by e-mail
Hours: Mon to Fri, 0900 to 1700

BREAKTHROUGH DEAF/HEARING INTEGRATION (Breakthrough)

Alan Geale House, The Close, Westhill Campus, Bristol Road, Birmingham, B29 6LN

Tel: 0121 415 2289 (voice and text)
Fax: 0121 415 2323
E-mail: info@breakthrough-dhi.org.uk
Website: www.breakthrough-dhi.org.uk

Enquiries to: Information Officer

Founded: 1971

Organisation type and purpose: National organisation, voluntary organisation, registered charity (charity number 261951), training organisation.
Self help group.
Development of innovative work with deaf and hearing people through contact, information and training.

Subject coverage: Integration between deaf and hearing adults through contact, information and training.

Collection: Information service on all aspects of deafness

Publications: Printed

Access to staff: Contact by letter and via website
Hours: Mon to Fri, 0900 to 1700

Access for disabled people: Parking provided, toilet facilities

Regional centres at: Breakthrough (London) Ealing & Hammersmith & Fulham; 2 Erconwald Street, East Acton, London, W12 0BS; tel: 020 8749 4111 (voice/fax); 020 8749 8186 (text); 020 8749 7854 (video); e-mail: london.ealing@breakthrough-dhi.org.uk and london.hammersmith; Breakthrough (London) Ealing & Hammersmith & Fulham; The Hall, Peyton Place, Greenwich, London, SE10 8RS; tel: 020 8853 5661; 020 8858 7689 (text); 020 8858 2954 (video); fax: 020 8853 5661; e-mail: london.greenwich@breakthrough-dhi.org.uk; Breakthrough (London) Harrow; 2nd Floor, Premier House, 1 Canning Road, Wealdstone, HA7 7TS; tel: 020 8424 0983 (voice/fax); 020 8424 4626 (text); 020 8861 4625 (video); e-mail: london.harrow@breakthrough-dhi.org.uk; Breakthrough (London) Tower Hamlets; Trinity Centre, Key Close, London, E1 4HG; tel: 010 7790 8478 (voice/fax); 020 7791 0105 (text); 020 7790 7453 (video); e-mail: london.tower.hamlets@breakthrough-dhi.org.uk; Breakthrough (North); John Haswell House, 8/9 Gladstone Terrace, Gateshead, Tyne and Wear, NE8 4DY; tel: 0191 478 7920 (voice/fax) 0191 478 6363 (text) 0191 478 4369 (video phone); e-mail: north@breakthrough-dhi.org.uk; Breakthrough (Southern Counties); Farnborough Centre, 67 Albert Road, Farnborough, Hampshire, GU14 6SL, Text 01252 372978 (video); tel: 01252 510051; 522765; fax: 01252 524642; e-mail: southern.counties@breakthrough-dhi.org.uk; Breakthrough (Southern Counties); Aldershot Centre, Princess Gardens, 2A High Street, Aldershot, Hants, GU11 1BJ; tel: 01252 313882 (voice/text) 01242 310041 (video); fax: 01252 337546; e-mail: southern.counties@breakthrough-dhi.org.uk; Breakthrough (West Midlands); 1 College Walk, Bristol Road, Selly Oak, Birmingham, B29 6LE; tel: voice/fax 415 5900, Minicom 0121 472 5488; Breakthrough London Services Team; The Hall, Peyton Place, London, SE10 8RS; tel: 020 8269 0307 (voice/fax); 020 8269 0287 (text); 020 8269 0242 (video); e-mail: london.services@breakthrough-dhi.org.uk

BREAST CANCER CARE – GLASGOW (BCC)

2nd Floor, 40 St Enoch Square, Glasgow, G1 4DH

Tel: 0141 221 2244

continued overleaf

Fax: 0141 221 9499
E-mail: sco@breastcancercare.org.uk
Website: www.breastcancercare.org.uk

Enquiries to: Head of National Development
Direct e-mail: press@breastcancercare.org.uk
Other contacts: National Manager responsible for all services provided in Scotland.

Founded: 1973

Organisation type and purpose: National organisation, voluntary organisation, registered charity (charity number 1017658).

Subject coverage: Breast cancer in women and men, information, help and support.

Library catalogue: All or part available online and in print

Publications: Printed, and electronic and video
Order printed publications from: Publications Department, Breast Cancer Care
Kiln House, 210 New Kings Road, London, SW6 4NZ, tel: 0808 800 6000 or 0141 221 2244, fax: 020 7384 3387, e-mail: bcc@breastcancercare.org.uk

Publications list: Available online and in print

Access to staff: Contact by letter, by telephone, by fax, by e-mail and via website. Appointment necessary.
Hours: Mon to Fri, 0900 to 1700

Access for disabled people: Level entry, toilet facilities

BREAST CANCER CARE – LONDON (BCC)

5–13 Great Suffolk Street, London SE1 0NS

Tel: 0845 077 1895
Fax: 020 7384 3387
E-mail: src@breastcancercare.org.uk
Website: www.breastcancercare.org.uk

Enquiries to: Administrator

Founded: 1973

Organisation type and purpose: National organisation, membership association, present number of members: 400, voluntary organisation, registered charity (charity number 1017658).
To provide information and support to those affected by breast cancer.

Subject coverage: Breast cancer; treatments, general information, prostheses, after-care, support groups.

Publications: Printed, and electronic and video

Publications list: Available online and in print

Access to staff: Contact by letter, by telephone, by fax, by e-mail and via website
Hours: Helpline: Mon to Fri, 1000 to 1700; Sat, 1000 to 1400

Access to building: Prior appointment required

Access for disabled people: Parking provided, ramped entry, toilet facilities
Special comments: Parking must be requested prior to visit.

Also at Northern Office: Breast Cancer Care; Volsenc House, 14–18 West Bar Green, Sheffield, S1 2DA; tel: 0114 276 0296; fax: 0114 276 0293

Also at Scotland Office: Breast Cancer Care; 46 Gordon Street, Glasgow, G1 3PU; tel: 0141 221 2244; fax: 0141 221 9499

Subsidiary body: Lavender Trust Charity

BRECON BEACONS NATIONAL PARK AUTHORITY (BBNPA)

Plas y Ffynnon, Cambrian Way, Brecon, Powys, LD3 7HP

Tel: 01874 624437
Fax: 01874 622574
E-mail: enquiries@breconbeacons.org
Website: www.breconbeacons.org

Enquiries to: Public Relations Officer
Other contacts: Chief Executive for statutory and legal matters.

Founded: 1957

Organisation type and purpose: Local government body, advisory body, statutory body, present number of members: 24, public library, research organisation, publishing house.
National park authority, two thirds of the authority members are appointed by the constituent unitary authorities; one third are appointed by the Welsh Assembly.
To protect and conserve wildlife, landscape and cultural heritage; to promote opportunities for quiet enjoyment of the countryside; a local planning authority.

Subject coverage: Landscape conservation and countryside recreation within the Brecon Beacons National Park. Ecology/archaeology/planning, local area knowledge.

Publications: Printed

Publications list: Available in print

Access to staff: Contact by letter, by telephone, by fax, by e-mail and in person. Appointment necessary.
Hours: Mon to Fri, 0900 to 1700

BRECON BEACONS NATIONAL PARK VISITOR CENTRE

Libanus, Brecon, Powys, LD3 8ER

Tel: 01874 623366
Fax: 01874 624515
E-mail: visitor.centre@breconbeacons.org
Website: www.breconbeacons.org

Enquiries to: Information Officer

Founded: 1957

Organisation type and purpose: Local government body, service industry, suitable for ages: all.
To provide an information and education service relating to the Brecon Beacons National Park.

Subject coverage: Activities within the Brecon Beacons National Park, specialised publications on offer, education resources.

Library catalogue: All or part available in-house

Publications: Printed

Publications list: Available in print

Access to staff: Contact by letter, by telephone, by fax, by e-mail, in person and via website
Hours: Sun to Sat, 0930 to 1700

Access to building: No prior appointment required
Hours: Sun to Sat, 0930 to 1700

Access for disabled people: Parking provided, ramped entry, access to all public areas, toilet facilities
Special comments: Hearing loop/induction installed.

Other addresses: Brecon Beacons National Park Authority; Plas y Ffynnon, Cambrian Way, Brecon, Powys, LD3 7HP; tel: 01874 624437

BRENT ARCHIVES

Willesden Green Library Centre, 95 High Road, Willesden, London NW10 2SF

Tel: 020 8937 3541
Fax: 020 8937 3601
E-mail: archives@brent.gov.uk
Website: www.brent.gov.uk/archives

Enquiries to: Borough Archivist
Direct tel: 020 8937 3677

Founded: 1976/7

Organisation type and purpose: Local government body.
Archive.

Subject coverage: Government and local history of London Borough of Brent and predecessors (Willesden, Wembley, etc).

Education services: Schools sessions and lectures, talks and sessions for adult learners.

Non-library collection catalogue: All or part available online and in-house

Library catalogue: All or part available online

Publications: Printed
Order printed publications from: Brent Archives, Willesden Green Library Centre, 95 High Road, Willesden, London NW10 2SF.

Publications list: Available online and in print

Access to staff: Contact by letter, by telephone, by fax, by e-mail, in person and via website
Hours: Tue and Wed, 0900 to 1700; Thu, 1300 to 2000; Sat, 0900 to 1700

Access for disabled people: Fully accessible

Links with: Brent Museum; Willesden Green Library Centre, 95 High Road, Willesden, London, NW10 2SF; tel: 020 937 3600

BREWER'S COMPANY

Brewer's Hall, Aldermanbury Square, London, EC2V 7HR

Tel: 020 7600 1801
Fax: 020 7776 8939
E-mail: clerksecretary@brewershall.co.uk
Website: www.brewershall.co.uk

Enquiries to: The Clerk

Founded: 1438

Organisation type and purpose: Membership association (membership is by election or invitation).
City of London Livery Company.

Access to staff: Contact by letter, by telephone, by fax and by e-mail

BREWERY HISTORY SOCIETY

Brewery History Society, Manor Side East, Mill Lane, Byfleet, Surrey, KT14 7RS

Tel: 020 8642 7189
E-mail: membership@breweryhistory.com

Enquiries to: Archivist

Founded: 1971

Organisation type and purpose: Membership association (membership is by subscription), present number of members: 700, voluntary organisation, research organisation, publishing house.

Subject coverage: History of the British brewery industry.

Collection: Histories of brewing industry, yearbooks, directories, periodicals

Non-library collection catalogue: All or part available in-house

Library catalogue: All or part available in-house

Publications: Printed
Order printed publications from: Paul Travis Long High Top, Heptonstall, Hebden Bridge, West Yorkshire, HX7 7PF

Publications list: Available in print

Access to staff: Contact by letter, by telephone and in person. Appointment necessary.
Hours: Mon to Fri, 0900 to 1700

BREWING, FOOD & BEVERAGE INDUSTRY SUPPLIERS ASSOCIATION (BfBi)

3 Brewery Road, Wolverhampton, West Midlands, WV1 4JT

Tel: 01902 422303
Fax: 01902 795744
E-mail: info@bfbi.org.uk
Website: www.bfbi.org.uk

Enquiries to: Chief Executive

Founded: 1907

Organisation type and purpose: Trade association (membership is by subscription), present number of members: 430.

Publications: Printed

Publications list: Available in print

Access to staff: Contact by letter, by telephone, by fax and by e-mail
Hours: Mon to Fri, 0900 to 1700

BRIDGEMAN ART LIBRARY LIMITED

17–19 Garway Road, London, W2 4PH

Tel: 020 7727 4065
Fax: 020 7792 8509
E-mail: info@bridgeman.co.uk
Website: www.bridgeman.co.uk

Enquiries to: Marketing Manager

Founded: 1972

Organisation type and purpose: Service industry.
Commercial company; formerly Cooper-Bridgeman Library; fine art photographic library/agency; agency agreements with photographic libraries outside the UK.
Fine art photo archive (commercial).

Subject coverage: Large format colour transparencies of paintings, sculpture, prints, manuscripts, the decorative arts, antiques and antiquities.

Collection: Over 150,000 large format colour transparencies growing by more than 500 new pictures each week, of the works from more than 1,000 museums, galleries and private collections, including contemporary artists

Library catalogue: All or part available online and in print

Publications: Printed, and electronic and video

Publications list: Available online and in print

Access to staff: Contact by telephone, by fax, by e-mail and via website.
Appointment necessary.
Hours: Mon to Fri, 0930 to 1730

Access to building: Prior appointment required

Members of: British Association of Picture Libraries & Agencies (BAPLA); Vine Hill, London, EC1

Other address: Bridgeman Art Library International; 65 East 93rd Street, New York, NY 10128, USA; tel: 00 1 212 828 1238; fax: 00 1 212 828 1255; e-mail: info@bridgemanart.com; Bridgeman Giraudon; 36 rue des Bourdonnais, 75001 Paris, France; tel: +33 1 55 80 79 10; fax: +33 1 55 80 79 11; e-mail: paris@bridgeman.fr

BRIDGEND COUNTY BOROUGH COUNCIL

Civic Offices, Angel Street, Bridgend, CF31 4WB

Tel: 01656 643643
Fax: 01656 668126
E-mail: talktous@bridgend.gov.uk
Website: www.bridgend.gov.uk

Enquiries to: Public Relations Manager
Direct tel: 01656 643210/17
Direct fax: 01656 643215

Founded: April 1996

Organisation type and purpose: Local government body.

Subject coverage: Economic and business database, traffic surveys, transport infrastructure, trading standards, public protection, planning, local plan, mineral extraction, design and print, information technology, demographic information.

Access to staff: Contact by letter, by telephone, by fax and by e-mail
Hours: Mon to Fri, 0800 to 1730

Access for disabled people: Ramped entry, toilet facilities

BRIDGEND LIBRARY AND INFORMATION SERVICE

Coed Parc, Park Street, Bridgend, Mid Glamorgan, CF31 4BA

Tel: 01656 754800
Fax: 01656 645719
E-mail: blis@bridgend.gov.uk
Website: www.bridgend.gov.uk/libraries

Enquiries to: Librarian

Founded: 1996

Organisation type and purpose: Public library.

Subject coverage: Local history (Mid Glamorgan), family history (Glamorgan area).

Collection: Local studies (Mid Glamorgan and areas surrounding Bridgend County Borough)

Non-library collection catalogue: All or part available online

Library catalogue: All or part available online

Access to staff: Contact by letter, by telephone, by fax, by e-mail and in person
Hours: Mon to Fri, 0830 to 1900; Sat, 0830 to 1700

Access for disabled people: Parking provided, ramped entry

BRIDGNORTH & DISTRICT HISTORICAL SOCIETY

Barn Cottage, Bridge Street, Bridgnorth, Shropshire, WV15 6AF

Tel: 01746 765159

Enquiries to: Treasurer and Publicity

Organisation type and purpose: Membership association (membership is by subscription), present number of members: 120, voluntary organisation, registered charity.

Subject coverage: History of Bridgnorth and district.

BRIDGNORTH DISTRICT COUNCIL

Westgate, Bridgnorth, Shropshire, WV16 5AA

Tel: 01746 765131
Fax: 01746 764414
E-mail: townclerk@bridgnorthtowncouncil.gov.uk
Website: www.bridgnorth.gov.uk

Enquiries to: Public Relations Manager
Direct tel: 01746 713111
Direct e-mail: lscreen@bridgnorth-dc.gov.uk

Founded: 1974

Organisation type and purpose: Local government body.

Access to staff: Contact by letter, by telephone, by fax, by e-mail and in person
Hours: Mon to Fri, 0900 to 1700

Access for disabled people: Ramped entry

BRIDLEDOWN CHILDREN'S FARM AND WILDLIFE CENTRE

Bridledown, West Hougham, Dover, Kent, CT13 7AG

Tel: 01304 201382
Fax: 01304 204757
E-mail: bridledown.dover@virgin.net

Enquiries to: Information Officer

Founded: 1968

Organisation type and purpose: Suitable for ages: Key Stages 1 and 2.
Stray dogs' kennels and children's activity farm.
Finding homes for stray dogs.

Subject coverage: Teaching the importance of wildlife, farming in the community and hands-on fun for the family.

Access to staff: Contact by letter, by telephone, by fax, by e-mail, in person and via website
Hours: Daily, 1000 to 1700

Access for disabled people: Access to all public areas

BRIGHTON AND HOVE CITY LIBRARIES

Jubilee Library, Jubilee Street, Brighton, BN1 1GE

Tel: 01273 296969; 01273 290800
Fax: 01273 296976
E-mail: libraries@brighton-hove.gov.uk
Website: www.citylibraries.info

Enquiries to: Library Manager

Founded: 1869

Organisation type and purpose: Local government body, public library.

Subject coverage: Local studies, fine arts, early printed books, business and European studies.

Collection: Bloomfield Collection (rare books)
Cobden Collection (2,500 items from Richard Cobden's library)
Elliot Collection (3,000 Greek and Hebrew texts)
Lewes Collection (3,000 European language books in fine arts)
Long Collection (3,000 classical texts)
Matthews Collection (3,500 oriental (Middle East) books)
Wolseley Collection (late 19th-century British military history and horticulture and topography of Sussex, including Field Marshal Wolseley's letters)

Library catalogue: All or part available online

Access to staff: Contact by letter, by telephone, by fax, by e-mail and in person

Access to building: *Hours:* Mon and Tue, 1000 to 1900; Wed, Fri and Sat, 1000 to 1700; Thu, 1000 to 2000; Sun, 1100 to 1600
Special comments: Some special collections materials and rare books require membership of rare books scheme. Baby changing area available.

Access for disabled people: Jubilee Library is fully accessible and has adult change facilities; guide dogs are welcome

BRINSBURY CAMPUS

Formal name: Chichester College

North Heath, Pulborough, West Sussex, RH20 1DL

Tel: 01243 786321
Fax: 01243 539481
E-mail: info@chichester.ac.uk
Website: www.chichester.ac.uk

Enquiries to: Information Officer

History of institution: formerly called Brinsbury College (year of change 2002)

Organisation type and purpose: Suitable for ages: 16+, training organisation.

Subject coverage: Land-based training.

Library catalogue: All or part available online

Publications: Printed

Access to staff: Contact by letter, by telephone, by fax, by e-mail and in person
Hours: Mon to Fri, 0900 to 1700

Access for disabled people: Parking provided, ramped entry, toilet facilities, lifts

Headquarters address: Chichester College; Westgate Fields, Chichester, West Sussex PO19 1SB; tel: 01243 786321; fax: 01243 539481; e-mail: info@chichester.ac.uk; website: http://www.chichester.ac.uk

BRISTOL AND GLOUCESTERSHIRE ARCHAEOLOGICAL SOCIETY (BGAS)

Stonehatch, Oakridge Lynch, Stroud, Gloucestershire, GL6 7NR

Tel: 01285 760460
E-mail: john@looseleyj.freeserve.co.uk
Website: www.bgas.org.uk

Enquiries to: General Secretary
Other contacts: Chairman (for special correspondence); Editor

Founded: 1876

Organisation type and purpose: Learned society (membership is by subscription), present number of members: 900, voluntary organisation, registered charity (charity number 202014), suitable for ages: 18+, publishing house.
Promotes the study of the history and antiquities of Bristol and Gloucestershire, including South Gloucestershire; encourages their conservation and publishes records, reports and papers.

Subject coverage: History, archaeology and antiquities of Gloucestershire including South Gloucestershire and Bristol.

Collection: Archaeological Library: Bristol, Gloucestershire and neighbouring counties

Non-library collection catalogue: All or part available online

Library catalogue: All or part available online

Publications: Printed
Order printed publications from: Stockholder, Bristol and Gloucestershire Archaeological Society, 17 Estcourt Road, Gloucester, GL1 3LU; tel. 01452 528930

Publications list: Available online and in print

Access to staff: Contact by letter, by telephone, by e-mail and via website

Links with: Committee for Archaeology in Gloucestershire (CAG); at same address

BRISTOL AND WESTERN ENGINEERING MANUFACTURERS ASSOCIATION LIMITED (BEMA)

Engineers House, The Promenade, Clifton Down, Bristol, BS8 3NB

Tel: 0117 906 4830
Fax: 0117 906 4827
E-mail: enquiries@bema.co.uk

Enquiries to: Director

Founded: 1936

Organisation type and purpose: Trade association.
Engineering Companies in South West and South Wales.

Subject coverage: Personnel matters including employment law, wage rates, technical and business matters affecting small engineering companies, health and safety legislation and training courses.

Trade and statistical information: Sources of engineering products and services in the South West and South Wales

Publications: Printed

Access to staff: Contact by letter and by fax
Hours: Mon to Fri, 0900 to 1700

Affiliated to: Engineering Industries Association

Member of: CBI

BRISTOL CENTRAL LIBRARY

Central Library, College Green, Bristol, BS1 5TL

Tel: 0117 903 7200
Fax: 0117 922 1081
E-mail: bristol_library_service@bristol-city.gov.uk
Website: www.bristol-city.gov.uk/librarycatalogue

Enquiries to: Reference enquiries
Direct tel: 0117 903 7202
Direct e-mail: refandinfo@bristol-city.gov.uk

Founded: 1613

Organisation type and purpose: Local government body, public library.
Central lending, music, reference and business libraries.

Subject coverage: Bristol local history; slave trade; modern literature; caving and potholing; doctrinal theology; genealogy; British Standards and British Patents; non-performing arts, both fine and applied.

Collection: Private Press books; Early Printed books (Bristol)
Stuckey Lean Collection (folklore and proverbs)
(Bristol)
Thomas Chatterton Collection (Bristol)

Non-library collection catalogue: All or part available online

Library catalogue: All or part available online

Access to staff: Contact by letter, by telephone, by fax, by e-mail and in person. Appointment necessary.
Hours: Mon, Tue and Thu, 0930 to 1930; Wed 1000 to 1700, Fri and Sat, 0930 to 1700; Sun, 1300 to 1700

Access for disabled people: Ramped entry, toilet facilities

Parent body: Bristol City Council; Culture and Leisure Services

BRISTOL CITY COUNCIL

The Council House, College Green, Bristol, BS1 5TR

Tel: 0117 922 2000
Fax: 0117 922 2024
E-mail: simon_caplan@bristol-city.gov.uk
Website: www.bristol-city.gov.uk

Enquiries to: Head of Corporate Communications
Direct tel: 0117 922 2650
Direct fax: 0117 922 4330

Organisation type and purpose: Local government body.

Subject coverage: Full range of local authority information.

Access to staff: Contact by letter, by telephone, by fax, by e-mail, in person and via website. Appointment necessary.
Hours: Mon to Fri, 0900 to 1700

BRISTOL RECORD OFFICE

B Bond Warehouse, Smeaton Road, Bristol, BS1 6XN

Tel: 0117 922 4224
Fax: 0117 922 4236
E-mail: bro@bristol.gov.uk
Website: www.bristol.gov.uk/recordoffice

Enquiries to: Archivist

Organisation type and purpose: Local government body.

Subject coverage: Historical archives relating to the city of Bristol from the 12th century to the present day.

Non-library collection catalogue: All or part available online and in-house

Library catalogue: All or part available online and in-house

Publications: Printed, and electronic and video

Publications list: Available in print

Access to staff: Contact by letter, by telephone, by fax, by e-mail and in person
Hours: Tue to Fri, 0930 to 1630; first two Thu of month, 0930 to 1900; first two Sat of month, 1000 to 1600

Access for disabled people: Parking provided, ramped entry, access to all public areas, toilet facilities

BRISTOL SOCIETY, THE

Leigh Court, Abbots Leigh, Bristol, BS8 3RA

Tel: 0117 915 2335

Fax: 01275 374423

Enquiries to: Membership Secretary
Direct e-mail: sally.allen@bcci.westec.co.uk
Other contacts: Chairman

Founded: 1992

Organisation type and purpose: Learned society (membership is by subscription), present number of members: 300.
Lecture society.

Access to staff: Contact by letter and by telephone
Hours: Mon to Fri, 0900 to 1700

Other addresses: The Bristol Society; Somerset House, 18 Canynge Road, Clifton, Bristol, BS8 3JX; tel: 0117 923 9234; fax: 0117 923 9237

BRISTOL-MYERS SQUIBB PHARMACEUTICALS LIMITED

Uxbridge Business Park, Sanderson Road, Uxbridge, Middlesex UB8 1DH

Tel: 01895 523000
Fax: 01895 523010
Website: www.b-ms.co.uk/

Enquiries to: Librarian
Direct tel: 020 8754 3610
Direct fax: 020 8572 7370

Organisation type and purpose: Manufacturing industry.

Subject coverage: Pharmaceutical industry, cardiovascular disease, oncology.

Library catalogue: All or part available in-house

Access to staff: Contact by letter
Hours: Mon to Fri, 0900 to 1700

Access to building: No access other than to staff

BRITAIN-AUSTRALIA SOCIETY

c/o Swire House, 59 Buckingham Gate, London, SW1E 6AJ

Tel: 020 7630 1075
Fax: 020 7828 2260
Website: www.britain-australia.org.uk

Enquiries to: National Director
Direct e-mail: natdir@britain-australia.org.uk

Founded: 1971

Organisation type and purpose: Membership association (membership is by subscription).
Society for development of strong Anglo-Australian relations.

Subject coverage: All aspects of life in Australia.

Publications: Printed

Access to staff: Contact by letter, by telephone, by fax, by e-mail and via website. Appointment necessary.
Hours: Mon to Fri, 1000 to 1630

BRITAIN-RUSSIA CENTRE (BRC)

11 Belgrave Road, London, SW1V 1RB

Tel: 020 7931 6455
Fax: 020 7233 9736
E-mail: mail@bewc.org
Website: www.bewc.org

Enquiries to: Information Officer

Founded: 1959

Organisation type and purpose: Membership association.
To promote understanding and contacts between UK and countries of former USSR, excluding Baltic States.

Subject coverage: General information on Russia and other republics of former USSR; arts and humanities, literature, history, geography and travel, politics and society.

Library catalogue: All or part available in-house

Access to staff: Contact by letter and via website. Appointment necessary.
Special comments: The Centre is not a public body.

Also known as: British East-West Centre (BEWC); at the same address; tel: 020 7823 1990

BRITISH & INTERNATIONAL FEDERATION OF FESTIVALS FOR MUSIC, DANCE AND SPEECH

Festivals House, 198 Park Lane, Macclesfield, Cheshire, SK11 6UD

Tel: 0870 774 4290
Fax: 0870 774 4292
E-mail: liz@federationoffestivals.org.uk
Website: www.federationoffestivals.org.uk/

Enquiries to: Chief Executive
Direct tel: 01625 611578

Founded: 1921

Organisation type and purpose: Membership association (membership is by qualification), voluntary organisation, registered charity (charity number 213125), training organisation.
Consists of festival organisers, adjudicators, accompanists and private members.

Subject coverage: Amateur festivals, all aspects of the performing arts, particularly music, speech, drama and dance, adjudication in all these disciplines.

Publications: Printed

Access to staff: Contact by letter, by telephone, by fax and by e-mail
Hours: Mon to Fri, 0930 to 1730

Headquarters of the: Amateur Competitive Festival Movement

BRITISH ABRASIVES FEDERATION (BAF)

Toad Hall, Hinton Road, Horst, Berkshire, RG10 0BS

Tel: 08456 121380
Fax: 08456 121380
E-mail: info@thebaf.org.uk
Website: www.the-british-abrasives-federation.org.uk

Enquiries to: Secretary General

Organisation type and purpose: Trade association.

continued overleaf

Subject coverage: Use, care and protection of grinding wheels and other abrasive products; British and European safety standards.

Publications: Printed

Access to staff: Contact by letter, by telephone, by fax, by e-mail and via website
Hours: Mon to Fri, 0900 to 1700

Affiliated to: Fédération Européenne des Fabricants de Produits Abrasifs (FEPA); Secretariat, 20 avenue Reille, 75014 Paris, France; tel: 00 331 4581 2590; fax: 00 331 4581 6294; e-mail: fepa@compuserve.com

Product groups: Abrasive Grain; Bonded Abrasives; Coated Abrasives; Superabrasives

BRITISH ACADEMY

Formal name: British Academy: The National Academy for the Humanities and Social Sciences

10 Carlton House Terrace, London, SW1Y 5AH

Tel: 020 7969 5200
Fax: 020 7969 5300
E-mail: secretary@britac.ac.uk
Website: www.britac.ac.uk

Enquiries to: Secretary
Direct fax: 020 7969 5414

Founded: 1902

Organisation type and purpose: National organisation, learned society (membership is by election or invitation), present number of members: 851 ordinary, 307 corresponding, 18 hon fellows, registered charity (charity number 233176).
Directory of all UK Learned Bodies in the social sciences and humanities.
Promotes advanced research in humanities and social sciences.

Subject coverage: Humanities and social sciences.

Publications: Printed

Publications list: Available online and in print

Access to staff: Contact by letter, by fax and by e-mail
Hours: Mon to Fri, 0930 to 1730

Access to building: No access other than to staff

Access for disabled people: Access to all public areas

BRITISH ACADEMY OF COMPOSERS, SONGWRITERS AND AUTHORS (BASCA)

British Music House, 26 Berners Street, London, W1T 3LR

Tel: 020 7636 2929
Fax: 020 7636 2212
E-mail: info@basca.org.uk
Website: www.basca.org.uk

Enquiries to: Information Officer

Founded: 1999

Organisation type and purpose: Professional body, trade association.

Subject coverage: Advice on publishing contracts in classical music, recommended commissioning fees, copyright advice, music hire fees, competitions.
Music, songwriting; music industry; copyright; authors' royalties from broadcast and public performances; music publishing; creative workshops.

Publications: Printed

Access to staff: Contact by letter, by telephone, by fax and by e-mail.
Appointment necessary.
Hours: Mon to Fri, 1000 to 1700

BRITISH ACADEMY OF DRAMATIC COMBAT (BADC)

3 Castle View, Helmsley, North Yorkshire, YO62 5AU

Tel: 01439 770546
E-mail: info@badc.co.uk
Website: www.badc.co.uk

Enquiries to: Communications Officer
Direct e-mail: info@badc.co.uk

Founded: 1969; formerly called Society of British Fight Directors (year of change 1996)

Organisation type and purpose: Professional body.

Subject coverage: The BADC is dedicated to the advance of the art of stage combat in all forms of performance media. This includes the provision of training and qualifications in all weapon and combat systems employed throughout the performing arts and entertainment industries including theatre, television, film and new media technologies. The central principle of the Academy is to raise the standards of stage combat safety, performance and teaching within the industry. The BADC offers training and qualifications for all those interested in working in the performing arts and entertainment industries.

Library catalogue: All or part available in-house

Access to staff: Contact by letter, by telephone, by e-mail and via website
Hours: Any reasonable time

BRITISH ACADEMY OF FILM AND TELEVISION ARTS (BAFTA)

195 Piccadilly, London, W1J 9LN

Tel: 020 7734 0022
Fax: 020 7734 1792
E-mail: website@bafta.org
Website: www.bafta.org

Enquiries to: Public Relations Manager
Direct fax: 020 7734 1009
Other contacts: Membership Officer

Founded: 1947

Organisation type and purpose: Professional body (membership is by subscription, qualification, election or invitation), registered charity (charity number 216726).

Access to staff: Contact by letter and by fax.
Appointment necessary.
Hours: Mon to Fri, 0900 to 1700

Access to building: Prior appointment required

Access for disabled people: Level entry

Also at: BAFTA Cymru; Chapter Arts Centre, Market Road, Canton, Cardiff, CF5 1QE; tel: 029 2022 3898; fax: 029 2066 4189; BAFTA East Coast; 31 West 56th Street, New York, NY 10019, USA; tel: 00 1 212 254 2681; fax: 00 1 212 258 2653; BAFTA LA; 930 South Robertson Boulevard, Los Angeles, California, CA 90035–1626, USA; tel: 00 1 310 652 4121; fax: 00 1 310 854 6002; BAFTA North; International Media Centre, Adelphi House, The Crescent, Salford, Manchester, M3 3EN; tel: 0161 831 9733; fax: 0161 831 9733; BAFTA Scotland; 74 Victoria Crescent Road, Glasgow, G12 9JN; tel: 0141 357 4317; fax: 0141 337 1432

BRITISH ACADEMY OF MANAGEMENT (BAM)

Ground Floor, 137 Euston Road, London, NW1 2AA

Tel: 0207 383 7770
Fax: 0207 383 0377
E-mail: bam@bam.ac.uk
Website: www.bam.ac.uk

Founded: 1986

Organisation type and purpose: Professional association representing the community of management academics.

Subject coverage: Management studies.

Publications: Electronic and video

Access to staff: Contact by letter, by telephone, by fax and by e-mail

BRITISH ACCREDITATION COUNCIL (BAC)

Formal name: British Accreditation Council for Independent Further and Higher Education

76 Shoe Lane, London EC4A 3JB

Tel: 0300 330 1400
Fax: 0300 330 1401
E-mail: info@the-bac.org
Website: www.the-bac.org

Enquiries to: Chief Executive
Other contacts: Head of Administration

Founded: 1984

Organisation type and purpose: Registered charity (charity number 326652).
Inspection and accreditation of privately funded institutions of further and higher education.

Publications: Printed

Publications list: Available online

Access to staff: Contact by letter, by telephone, by fax, by e-mail and via website
Hours: Mon to Fri, 0830 to 1630

Access for disabled people: Lift
Hours: Mon to Fri, 0830 to 1630

BRITISH ACTIVITY HOLIDAY ASSOCIATION (BAHA)

The Hollies, Oak Bank Lane, Hoole Village, Chester, CH2 4ER

Tel: 01244 301342
E-mail: info@baha.org.uk

Website: www.baha.org.uk

Enquiries to: Secretary

Founded: 1986

Organisation type and purpose: Trade association (membership is by qualification), present number of members: 31, service industry, suitable for ages: all.

Subject coverage: Activities offered by members; recommended standards of safety in activity holidays; legislation covering activity holidays.

Publications: Printed

Access to staff: Contact by letter, by telephone, by fax and by e-mail
Hours: Mon to Thu, 0930 to 1230

Access to building: No access other than to staff

BRITISH ACUPUNCTURE COUNCIL (BAcC)

63 Jeddo Road, London, W12 9HQ

Tel: 020 8735 0400
Fax: 020 8735 0404
E-mail: info@acupuncture.org.uk
Website: www.acupuncture.org.uk

Enquiries to: Administrator

Founded: 1995

Organisation type and purpose: Advisory body, professional body, membership association (membership is by subscription, qualification), present number of members: 3,000. Research organisation.
Governing body of the acupuncture profession working to maintain common standards of education, ethics, discipline and codes of practice to ensure the health and safety of the public at all times. It is committed to promoting research and enhancing the role that traditional acupuncture can play in the health of the nation.

Subject coverage: Acupuncture, ethics, practice, research, training and educational developments.

Publications: Printed, and electronic and video

Access to staff: Contact by letter, by telephone, by fax, by e-mail and via website. Appointment necessary.
Hours: Mon to Fri, 0930 to 1730
Special comments: Office not open to the public.

BRITISH ADHESIVE AND SEALANTS ASSOCIATION (BASA)

5 Alderson Road, Worksop, Nottinghamshire, S80 1UZ

Tel: 01909 480888
Fax: 01909 473834
E-mail: secretary@basaonline.org
Website: www.basaonline.org

Enquiries to: Secretary

Organisation type and purpose: Trade association.

Subject coverage: Information on the manufacturers and suppliers of adhesives and sealants.

Publications: Printed

Access to staff: Contact by letter
Hours: Mon to Fri, 0900 to 1700

BRITISH AEROSOL MANUFACTURERS' ASSOCIATION (BAMA)

Kings Buildings, Smith Square, London, SW1P 3JJ

Tel: 020 7828 5111
Fax: 020 7834 8436
E-mail: enquiries@bama.co.uk
Website: www.bama.co.uk

Enquiries to: Director
Direct e-mail: enquiries@bama.co.uk
Other contacts: PR Manager (for press, statistics)

Founded: 1961

Organisation type and purpose: Trade association.

Subject coverage: Aerosols.

Trade and statistical information: Data on UK production of aerosols

Publications: Printed

Access to staff: Contact by letter, by telephone, by fax and by e-mail
Hours: Mon to Fri, 0900 to 1700

Access to building: Prior appointment required

Affiliated to: European Aerosol Federation; Brussels

BRITISH AGENTS REGISTER (BAR)

24 Mount Parade, Harrogate, North Yorkshire, HG1 1BP

Tel: 01423 560608
Fax: 01423 561204
E-mail: info@agentsregister.com
Website: www.agentsregister.com

Enquiries to: Director
Other contacts: Membership Secretary

Founded: 1963

Organisation type and purpose: Membership association (membership is by subscription), service industry.

Subject coverage: Commercial sales agents and their advantages in developing sales plus payable services to assist manufacturers in finding sales agents and a monthly publication detailing agencies, available by annual subscription.

Publications: Printed

Access to staff: Contact by letter, by telephone, by fax, by e-mail and via website
Hours: Mon to Fri, 0900 to 1700

Access to building: Prior appointment required

BRITISH AGRICULTURAL & GARDEN MACHINERY ASSOCIATION (BAGMA)

Middleton House, 2 Main Road, Middleton Cheney, Banbury, Oxon, OX17 2TN

Tel: 01295 713 344
Fax: 01295 711 665
E-mail: info@bagma.com
Website: www.bagma.com

Enquiries to: Information Officer
Direct e-mail: information@bhfgroup.co.uk
Other contacts: Director General

Founded: 1917

Organisation type and purpose: Trade association (membership is by subscription, qualification), service industry, training organisation.

Subject coverage: Agricultural and garden machinery dealer industry.

Publications: Printed
Order printed publications from: Indices Publications Ltd
14–16 Church Street, Rickmansworth, Hertfordshire, WD31 1RQ, tel: 01923 711434, fax: 01923 896063

Access to staff: Contact by letter, by telephone, by fax and by e-mail. Appointment necessary.
Hours: Mon to Fri, 0900 to 1700

BRITISH AGRICULTURAL HISTORY SOCIETY (BAHS)

University of Exeter, Department of History, Amory Building, Rennes Drive, Exeter, Devon, EX4 4RJ

Tel: 01392 263284
Fax: 01392 263305
E-mail: bahs@exeter.ac.uk
Website: www.bahs.org.uk

Enquiries to: Membership Secretary
Other contacts: Editorial, tel no: 0118 931 8662

Founded: 1952

Organisation type and purpose: Learned society (membership is by subscription), present number of members: 970.
To further the study of rural and agricultural history.

Subject coverage: British agricultural history and rural economics.

Publications: Printed

Access to staff: Contact by letter, by e-mail and via website
Hours: Mon to Fri, 0900 to 1700

BRITISH AIKIDO BOARD

6 Halkingcroft, Langley, Slough, Berkshire, SL3 7AT

Tel: 01753 577878
Fax: 01753 577331
E-mail: babsecretary@bab.org.uk

Enquiries to: General Secretary

Founded: 1975

Organisation type and purpose: National government body, membership association (membership is by subscription), voluntary organisation, training organisation.
Governing body for Aikido in UK.

Subject coverage: Aikido.

Access to staff: Contact by letter and by telephone
Hours: Mon to Fri, 0900 to 1700
Special comments: Enclose an sae for reply to letter.

BRITISH AMATEUR RUGBY LEAGUE ASSOCIATION (BARLA)

West Yorkshire House, 4 New North Parade, Huddersfield, West Yorkshire, HD1 5JP

Tel: 01484 599113
Fax: 01484 519985
E-mail: info@barla.org.uk
Website: www.barla.org.uk

Enquiries to: Membership Secretary
Direct e-mail: msd@barla.org.uk

Founded: 1973

Organisation type and purpose:
Membership association (membership is by subscription), present number of members: 42 leagues.
Controlling body of the sport.

Subject coverage: Rugby League.

Publications: Printed

Publications list: Available online and in print

Access to staff: Contact by letter, by telephone, by fax, by e-mail and in person
Hours: Mon to Fri, 0900 to 1700

Access to building: No prior appointment required

Access for disabled people: Parking provided

Links with: Rugby League Coach Education Programme (RLCEP)

BRITISH AMBULANCE SOCIETY

21 Victoria Road, Horley, Surrey, RH6 9BN

Tel: 01293 776636 (answerphone)
Fax: 01293 776636
E-mail: basochq@aol.com
Website: www.britambsoc.org.uk

Enquiries to: General Secretary

Founded: 1974

Organisation type and purpose:
International organisation, advisory body, membership association (membership is by subscription), present number of members: 300, voluntary organisation, museum, research organisation.
To encourage the research of the British Ambulance Service and its vehicles. To provide an educational medium for all ambulance-related subjects. To create a museum appertaining to the history of the British ambulance service.

Subject coverage: Ambulances, the ambulance service, history and operation (past, present and future).

Collection: Vehicles and uniforms
Reference library of model and badge collection
Journals, documents, pictures, photographs, publications, statistical information, videos

Publications: Printed

Access to staff: Contact by letter, by telephone, by fax and by e-mail.
Appointment necessary. Non-members charged.
Hours: After 2000 for phone contact or 24-hour answerphone
Special comments: Access by prior appointment.

Access to building: No prior appointment required

Links with: Council Vehicle Society / Fleet Data Register; Fire Service Preservation Group; Professional Car Society (USA); St John Ambulance Brigade

Membership Secretary: British Ambulance Society; Falklands, 251 Kings Drive, Eastbourne, East Sussex, BN21 2UR; tel: 01323 508233

Public Relations Officer: British Ambulance Society; 25 West Rise, Tonbridge, Kent, TN9 2PG; tel: 01732 508525; e-mail: chrisbatten@virgin.net

BRITISH AMERICAN BUSINESS INC (BABi)

75 Brook Street, London, W1K 4AD

Tel: 020 7467 7400
Fax: 020 7493 2394
E-mail: ukinfo@babinc.org
Website: www.babinc.org

Enquiries to: Director – Commercial
Direct e-mail: cwells@babinc.org
Other contacts: Director – Membership

Founded: 2000

Organisation type and purpose:
International organisation, membership association (membership is by subscription), present number of members: 630 corporate, 2,400 individuals, service industry, suitable for ages: 20 to 60.
Leading transatlantic business organisation dedicated to helping its member companies build and expand their international business.
As a not-for-profit organisation, BABi's mission is to provide practical business benefits for its member companies.

Subject coverage: Focuses closely on US and UK company information and trading relationships. Through BABi's collection of databases, it is possible to trace and highlight the ownership of company affiliates and subsidiaries worldwide, including information on US subsidiaries in the UK and UK subsidiaries in the US.

Trade and statistical information: US company data

Publications: Printed
Order printed publications from: Publications Manager, BABi

Publications list: Available online and in print

Access to staff: Contact by letter, by telephone, by fax, by e-mail and via website. Appointment necessary. Non-members charged.
Hours: Mon to Fri, 0900 to 1700

Affiliated to: British-American Business Inc; 20th Floor, 52 Vanderbilt Avenue, New York, NY, 1022, USA; tel: +1 212 661 4060; fax: +1 212 661 4074; e-mail: info@babinc.org

BRITISH AMERICAN TOBACCO (BAT)

Regent's Park Road, Southampton, SO15 8TL

Tel: 023 8077 7155
Fax: 023 8078 0332
Website: www.bat.com

Enquiries to: Information Manager

Founded: 1956

Organisation type and purpose:
Manufacturing industry.

Subject coverage: Tobacco growing, cigarette manufacture, tobacco history.

Library catalogue: All or part available in-house

Access to staff: Contact by letter, by fax and by e-mail
Hours: Mon to Fri, 0900 to 1700

Parent body: British American Tobacco (Investments) Limited; tel: 020 7845 1000; fax: 020 7845 0555

BRITISH AND FOREIGN SCHOOL SOCIETY ARCHIVES (BFSS Archives)

BFSS Archives, c/o Brunel University Archives, Brunel University, Kingston Lane, Uxbridge, Middlesex UB8 3PH

Tel: 01895 265911
E-mail: bfss.archive@brunel.ac.uk
Website: www.bfss.org.uk
Website: www.brunel.ac.uk/about/administration/archivesandrecords

Enquiries to: Archivist

Founded: 1808

Organisation type and purpose: Registered charity (charity number 314286).

Subject coverage: The Archive documents the history of 19th- and 20th-century elementary education and teacher training.

Collection: Surviving records of the BFSS from the beginning of the 19th century including minute books 1808–1834, correspondence of the Secretaries of the Society 1814–1897, overseas correspondence, annual reports
Letters of Joseph Lancaster 1810–1812
Records of the Society's teacher training colleges, mainly 1830–1976, including Borough Road College, Saffron Walden College, Stockwell College and some from Darlington College
Student registers and other official records of student progress
Lists of British Schools and some original records including pamphlets, annual reports and Newcastle Commission returns
The Educational Record 1848–1929
Student magazines
Student photos from 19th century
Prints and photographs, paintings and engravings, architects' plans
Books and pamphlets on education dating from the 19th century, including works by Lancaster, Bell, Pestalozzi and Froebel.

Non-library collection catalogue: All or part available online

Access to staff: Contact by letter, by telephone, by e-mail, in person and via website. Appointment necessary.
Hours: Reading room open by appointment only, Mon to Thu, 0930 to 1430

Access to building: The Archive is 5 mins walk from Brunel University in Uxbridge. Contact the archivist for address and directions

Hours: Reading room open by appointment only, Mon to Thurs, 0930 to 1430

Access for disabled people: Reading room is upstairs with no lift, but arrangements will be made for researchers to view documents elsewhere at the university if they are unable to use the stairs. Advance notice needed.
Hours: As above

Administered by: Brunel University Archives; Brunel University Archives, Brunel University, Kingston Lane, Uxbridge, Middlesex, UB8 3PH; tel: 01895 265911; e-mail: bfss.archive@brunel.ac.uk; website: http://www.brunel.ac.uk/about/administration/archivesandrecords

BRITISH AND IRISH ASSOCIATION OF LAW LIBRARIANS (BIALL)

Lincoln's Inn Library, London, WC2A 3TN

Tel: 020 7242 4371
Fax: 020 7404 1864
E-mail: susanfrost@compuserve.com
Website: www.biall.org.uk

Enquiries to: Administrator

Founded: 1969

Organisation type and purpose:
Professional body.
To provide better administration and exploitation of law libraries and legal information units; unite and co-ordinate the interests, opinions and activities of legal information professionals into a single influential voice.

Subject coverage: Law librarianship, exchange of information and improvement of service, history of law and the courts, legal bibliography. Salary information in legal information sector.

Trade and statistical information: Salary survey

Publications: Printed
Order printed publications from: BIALL Administrator, BIALL
26 Myton Crescent, Warwick, CV34 6QA, tel: 01926 491717, fax: 01926 491717, e-mail: susanfrost@compuserve.com

Access to staff: Contact by letter, by telephone, by fax, by e-mail and via website
Hours: Administrator available Mon to Fri, 0900 to 1200, or answerphone available

Administrator's Office: British and Irish Association of Law Librarians (BIALL); 26 Myton Crescent, Warwick, CV34 6QA; tel: 01926 491717; fax: 01926 491717; e-mail: susanfrost@compuserve.com

Cooperation with: other national law librarianship associations such as CALL and AALL

BRITISH AND IRISH ORTHOPTIC SOCIETY (BIOS)

British & Irish Orthoptic Society, 62 Wilson Street, London, EC2A 2BU

Tel: 01353 66 55 41
E-mail: bios@orthoptics.org.uk
Website: www.orthoptics.org.uk

Enquiries to: Executive Officer

Founded: 1937

Organisation type and purpose:
Professional body, trade union, present number of members: 1,400.

Subject coverage: Orthoptics, binocular vision, amblyopia.

Collection: National archive of orthoptics

Publications: Printed, and electronic and video
Order printed publications from: email: membership@orthoptics.org.uk

Publications list: Available online and in print

Access to staff: Contact by e-mail
Hours: Mon to Fri, 0900 to 1700

Access to building: Prior appointment required

Access for disabled people: *Special comments:* By appointment.

BRITISH ANTARCTIC SURVEY (BAS)

High Cross, Madingley Road, Cambridge, CB3 0ET

Tel: 01223 221400
Fax: 01223 362616
E-mail: information@bas.ac.uk
Website: www.antarctica.ac.uk

Enquiries to: Information Officer

Organisation type and purpose:
International organisation, national government body, research organisation.

Subject coverage: Antarctic research as follows: atmospheric sciences: upper air and surface meteorology (including ozone observations), geomagnetism, aurora and airglow, ionosphere and whistlers; earth sciences: glaciology and physical oceanography, marine and land geophysics (including seismology), geology (including economic geology), topographical survey, hydrography and hydrographic surveys, quaternary studies; life sciences: taxonomy, biogeography, bioclimatology, marine biology, freshwater biology, pedology, terrestrial ecology, physiology (including human physiology); also: polar equipment and travel techniques, including the operation of ships, aircraft and vehicles.

Collection: BAS Archive Collection – Expeditions from 1943
BAS Herbaria – Code: AAS (Antarctic and Sub-Antarctic plants)
Geology Rock Collection
Sea ice records, and field data and maps for all scientific work carried out

Library catalogue: All or part available in-house

Publications: Printed, and electronic and video

Access to staff: Contact by letter, by fax, by e-mail and via website
Hours: Mon to Fri, 0900 to 1700

Access to building: Prior appointment required
Special comments: Access to library by prior appointment only.

Access for disabled people: Parking provided, level entry, toilet facilities

Funded institute of the: Natural Environment Research Council (NERC); Polaris House, North Star Avenue, Swindon, SN2 1EU; tel: 01793 411500; fax: 01793 411501

BRITISH ANTIQUE DEALERS' ASSOCIATION (BADA)

20 Rutland Gate, London, SW7 1BD

Tel: 020 7589 4128
Fax: 020 7581 9083
E-mail: info@bada.org
Website: www.bada.org

Enquiries to: Secretary-General

Founded: 1918

Organisation type and purpose: Trade association (membership is by election or invitation), present number of members: 400.

Subject coverage: Buying, selling, valuation and care of antiques.

Publications: Printed

Publications list: Available in print

Access to staff: Contact by letter, by telephone, by fax, by e-mail, in person and via website
Hours: Mon to Fri, 0930 to 1700

Links with: Confédération des Négociants en Oeuvres d'Art

BRITISH ANTIQUE FURNITURE RESTORERS ASSOCIATION LTD (BAFRA)

Head Office, Rushbrook House, Benville Lane, Corscombe, Dorset, DT2 0NN

Tel: 01935 83213
Fax: 01935 83213
E-mail: headoffice@bafra.org.uk
Website: www.bafra.org.uk

Enquiries to: Chief Executive Officer
Direct tel: 01935 83213
Direct fax: 01935 83213
Direct e-mail: headoffive@bafra.org.uk
Other contacts: Chief Executive Officer

Founded: 1979

Organisation type and purpose:
International organisation, national organisation, advisory body, professional body, trade association (membership is by subscription, qualification), present number of members: 102 in all categories, suitable for ages: 18 to 80, publishing house.
Although a trade association, BAFRA is also a professional body in the conservation and restoration field.
To provide the public and private heritage sector and antique trade with a network of highly skilled and accredited conservators/restorers across Britain.

Subject coverage: Furniture conservation and restoration, furniture history, training in furniture conservation and restoration.

Information services: Unlimited, in the areas of furniture, clocks, barometers, mechanical music, textile conservation.

Education services: BAFRA-designed training in all aspects of furniture conservation and restoration.

continued overleaf

Publications: Printed
Order printed publications from: BAFRA Head Office

Publications list: Available in print

Access to staff: Contact by letter, by telephone, by fax, by e-mail and via website. Appointment necessary.
Hours: Mon to Fri, 0900 to 1700

BRITISH APPAREL & TEXTILE CONFEDERATION (BATC)

5 Portland Place, London, W1B 1PW

Tel: 020 7636 7788
Fax: 020 7636 7515
E-mail: batc@dial.pipex.com

Enquiries to: Director General

Organisation type and purpose: Trade association.

Subject coverage: Apparel and textile industry.

Access to staff: Contact by letter, by fax and by e-mail
Hours: Mon to Fri, 0900 to 1700

Access to building: Prior appointment required

Member of: European Clothing and Textile Association (EURATEX)

BRITISH APPROVALS FOR FIRE EQUIPMENT (BAFE)

Bridges 2, The Fire Service College, London Road, Moreton in Marsh, Gloucestershire GL56 0RH

Tel: 0844 335 0897
Fax: 01608 653359
E-mail: info@bafe.org.uk
Website: www.bafe.org.uk/

Enquiries to: General Secretary
Direct e-mail: info@bafe.org.uk
Other contacts: BAFE Scheme Administrator

Founded: 1984

Organisation type and purpose: The organisation writes and adopts schemes of third party accreditation for the fire protection industry.

Subject coverage: Active fire protection equipment, services.

Publications: Printed

Access to staff: Contact by letter, by telephone and by fax
Hours: Mon to Fri, 0900 to 1700

BRITISH ARACHNOLOGICAL SOCIETY (BAS)

31 Duxford Close, Redditch, Worcestershire, B97 5BY

E-mail: secretary@britishspiders.org.uk
Website: www.britishspiders.org.uk

Enquiries to: Honorary Secretary

Organisation type and purpose: Learned society (membership is by subscription), present number of members: 700, registered charity (charity number 260346).

Subject coverage: Arachnida (spiders, harvestmen, pseudoscorpions).

Collection: Library of books, papers and microfiche available to members

Publications: Printed
Order printed publications from: Francis Farr -Cox, 1 Winchester Road, Burnham on Sea, Somerset, TA8 1HY; e-mail: sales@britishspiders.org.uk

Access to staff: Contact by letter, by e-mail and via website
Hours: Mon to Fri, 0900 to 1700

Links with: American Arachnological Society; Centre de Documentation Arachnologique

BRITISH ARCHITECTURAL LIBRARY (BAL)

Royal Institute of British Architects, 66 Portland Place, London, W1B 1AD

Tel: 020 7580 5533
Fax: 020 7631 1802
E-mail: info@riba.org
Website: www.architecture.com

Enquiries to: Director
Other contacts: Archivist; Curator of Drawings

Founded: 1834

Organisation type and purpose: Professional body.
Library of a professional organisation; the title given above was designated in 1975; includes the Sir Banister Fletcher Library.

Subject coverage: Architecture; architectural history; building; construction; planning; landscape architecture; conservation; design; applied and decorative arts; interior design; topography.

Collection: Biography Files (over 15,000 vertical files on architects and others)
Books Collection (some 135,000 volumes)
Collection on the Modern Movement
Drawings and Archives Collection (some 500,000 drawings, predominantly British from the 15th century onwards, at the RIBA Study Rooms in the Victoria and Albert Museum)
Early Imprints Collection (some 4,000 books on architecture, printed before 1841)
Handley-Read Collection on Victorian decorative arts
Manuscripts Collection (important papers of architects, architectural historians, practices, firms and societies, 17th century to present, at the RIBA Study Rooms in the Victoria and Albert Museum)
Periodicals Collection (700 current titles and 1,400 that have ceased publication)
Photographs Collection (some 1.5m. images including postcards and slides)

Non-library collection catalogue: All or part available online and in print

Library catalogue: All or part available online and in-house

Publications: Printed, and electronic and video, and microform publications
Order printed publications from: Directory of British Architects 1834–1914 (2001)

Publications list: Available online

Access to staff: Contact by letter, by telephone, by fax, by e-mail, in person and via website
Hours: Tue, Wed, Fri, 1000 to 1700; Sat, 1000 to 1330; Mon, Thu, closed
Special comments: Appointment necessary for access to Photographs Collection.

Access for disabled people: Ramped entry, level entry

BRITISH ART MEDAL SOCIETY (BAMS)

c/o Department of Coins and Medals, British Museum, London, WC1B 3DG

Tel: 020 7323 8568
Fax: 020 7323 8171
E-mail: jlarkin@thebritishmuseum.ac.uk
Website: www.bams.org.uk

Enquiries to: Secretary

Founded: 1982

Organisation type and purpose: Learned society, voluntary organisation, registered charity (charity number 288869).
To encourage, develop and support the practice and study of medallic art.

Subject coverage: Medals and coins; commissioning of medals; sculpture; history of art; contemporary art.

Publications: Printed
Order printed publications from: Galata Print Ltd, The Old White Lion, Market Street, Llanfyllin, Powys, SY22 5BX; fax: 01691 648765

Publications list: Available in print

Access to staff: Contact by letter, by telephone, by fax and by e-mail. Appointment necessary.
Hours: Mon to Fri, 1000 to 1700

BRITISH ARTS FESTIVALS ASSOCIATION (BAFA)

1 Goodwins Court, London, WC2N 4LL

Tel: 020 7240 4532
E-mail: info@artsfestivals.co.uk
Website: www.artsfestivals.co.uk

Enquiries to: Co-ordinator

Founded: 1970

Organisation type and purpose: Membership association (membership is by subscription), voluntary organisation, registered charity (charity number 1010867).
BAFA is the meeting point of arts festivals in the UK, and is a point of information for member festivals.
Promotes and co-ordinates information in more than 100 arts festivals.

Subject coverage: Arts festivals, dates, and programmes etc.

Publications: Printed

Publications list: Available in print

Access to staff: Contact by letter, by telephone, by fax, by e-mail and via website
Hours: Mon to Fri, 0900 to 1700

Access to building: No access other than to staff

Affiliated to: European Festivals Association (EFA); Chateau di Coppet, Case Postale 26, Coppet, CH 1296, Switzerland;

tel: 00 41 22 776 8673; fax: 00 41 22 776 4275; e-mail: geneva@euro-festival.net; website: http://www.euro-festival.net

BRITISH ASSOCIATION FOR AMERICAN STUDIES (BAAS)

Department of English, University of Exeter, Queens Drive, Exeter, EX4 4QH

Tel: 01392 264256
E-mail: joe.gill@baas.ac.uk
Website: www.baas.ac.uk

Enquiries to: Secretary
Other contacts: Chair

Founded: 1955

Organisation type and purpose: Learned society, professional body.
To promote, support and encourage the study of the USA in the United Kingdom.

Subject coverage: History, literature, politics, sociology, geography, film, culture of the USA.

Publications: Printed, and microform publications

Publications list: Available in print

Access to staff: Contact by letter, by telephone and by e-mail
Hours: Variable hours

Links with: American Studies Association (US); Canadian Association for American Studies; European Association for American Studies; International American Studies Association; Irish Association for American Studies; United Kingdom Council for Area Studies

BRITISH ASSOCIATION FOR APPLIED LINGUISTICS (BAAL)

c/o Dovetail Management Consultancy, London, SE15 3WB

Tel: 020 7639 0090
Fax: 020 7635 6014
E-mail: admin@baal.org.uk
Website: www.baal.org.uk

Enquiries to: Administrator

Founded: 1967

Organisation type and purpose: Learned society, membership association (membership is by subscription), present number of members: 750 individual, 6 associate (publishers), 21 university departments and libraries.
To promote the study of language in use, to foster interdisciplinary collaboration and to provide a common forum for those engaged in the theoretical study of language and those interested in its practical use.

Subject coverage: Applied linguistics.

Publications: Printed

Access to staff: Contact by letter, by telephone, by fax and by e-mail
Hours: Thu, 0900 to 1700
Special comments: Call to confirm

Links with: Association Internationale de Linguistique Appliquée (AILA)

BRITISH ASSOCIATION FOR CANADIAN STUDIES (BACS)

31 Tavistock Square, London, WC1H 9HA

Tel: 020 7862 8687
Fax: 020 7117 1875
E-mail: jodie.robson@canadian-studies.net
Website: www.canadian-studies.net

Enquiries to: Administrator

Founded: 1975

Organisation type and purpose: Learned society.

Subject coverage: General information on Canadian studies in Britain, on Canadian academics visiting the UK, travel grants to scholars, specialist groups on Canada/UK architecture, business and economic studies, Canada in schools, history, social policy, library and resources, Aboriginal studies.

Publications: Printed
Order printed publications from: BACS

Access to staff: Contact by letter, by telephone, by e-mail and via website. Appointment necessary.
Hours: Mon to Fri, 0900 to 1700

Member organisation of: International Council for Canadian Studies; 250 City Centre Avenue, Suite 303, Ottawa, Ontario, K1R 6K7, Canada; website: http://www.iccs-ciec.ca

BRITISH ASSOCIATION FOR CANCER RESEARCH (BACR)

c/o Leeds Institute of Molecular Medicine, Clinical Sciences Building, St James's University Hospital, Beckett Street, Leeds, LS9 7TF

Tel: 0113 206 5611
Fax: 0113 206 5611
E-mail: bacr@leeds.ac.uk
Website: www.bacr.org.uk

Enquiries to: BACR Administrative Secretary

Founded: 1960

Organisation type and purpose: National organisation, learned society (membership is by election or invitation), present number of members: 1,100, representing all aspects of clinical and experimental research.
Registered charity (charity number 289297).
Organises scientific meetings/workshops on cancer research within the United Kingdom, and provides a platform for presentation of original clinical and experimental research. Funds exchanges between laboratories to encourage knowledge transfer and engender collaboration both nationally and internationally; provides opportunities for senior investigators to undergo further training to enable them to keep abreast of new investigative/research methods, and for junior investigators and research students to present their work at other meetings/ conferences.

Subject coverage: Cancer research.

Publications: Printed

Access to staff: Contact by letter, by telephone, by fax, by e-mail and via website
Hours: Mon to Fri, 0830 to 1630

Links with: European Association for Cancer Research; Institute of Biology

BRITISH ASSOCIATION FOR CEMETERIES IN SOUTH ASIA (BACSA)

135 Burntwood Lane, London, SW17 0AJ

E-mail: rosieljai@clara.co.uk
Website: www.bacsa.org.uk

Enquiries to: Honorary Secretary

Founded: 1976

Organisation type and purpose: Membership association (membership is by subscription), present number of members: over 1,400, registered charity (charity number 273422), research organisation, publishing house.

Subject coverage: Information on cemeteries in South Asia.

Collection: An archive maintained in the British Library – Oriental and India Office Collections.

Publications: Printed

Publications list: Available in print

Access to staff: Contact by letter, by e-mail and via website

BRITISH ASSOCIATION FOR CHEMICAL SPECIALITIES (BACS)

Simpson House, Windsor Court, Clarence Drive, Harrogate, HG1 2PE

Tel: 01423 700249
Fax: 01423 520297
E-mail: enquiries@bacsnet.org
Website: www.bacsnet.org

Enquiries to: Secretariat

Founded: 1977

Organisation type and purpose: Trade association (membership is by subscription), present number of members: 155.

Subject coverage: The British Association for Chemical Specialities (BACS) is the trade association representing manufacturers and formulators of speciality chemicals and intermediates. Major classes of performance and effect chemicals covered by BACS include maintenance products for consumer and industrial use, disinfectants and industrial biocides, including water treatment chemicals and services, speciality surfactants and personal care and cosmetic ingredients.

Publications: Printed

Publications list: Available online

Access to staff: Contact by letter, by telephone, by fax and by e-mail. Appointment necessary.
Hours: Mon to Fri, 0900 to 1700

BRITISH ASSOCIATION FOR COMMUNITY CHILD HEALTH (BACCH)

5–11 Theobalds Road, London, WC1X 8SH

Tel: 020 7092 6082/4
Fax: 020 7092 6001
E-mail: bacch@rcpch.ac.uk
Website: www.bacch.org.uk

Enquiries to: Executive Officer

continued overleaf

Subject coverage: Community child health, paediatrics, child development

Publications: Printed

Publications list: Available online

Access to staff: Contact by letter, by telephone, by fax, by e-mail, in person and via website
Hours: Mon to Fri, 0930 to 1700

Affiliate group: British Academy for Childhood Disability (BACD); at the same address; tel: 020 7092 6083; e-mail: bacd@rcpch.ac.uk; website: www.bacdis.org.uk
British Association of Paediatricians in Audiology; website: http://www.bapa.uk.com/
British Paediatric Mental Health Group; website: http://www.bpmhg.org.uk/
Child Protection Special Interest Group (CPSIG); at the same address; e-mail: cpsig@rcpch.ac.uk; website: www.cpsig.org.uk

Affliate group: Child Public Health Interest Group (CPHIG); at the same address; e-mail: cphig@rcpch.ac.uk; website: www.cphig.org.uk

BRITISH ASSOCIATION FOR COUNSELLING & PSYCHOTHERAPY (BACP)

15 St John's Business Park, Lutterworth, LE17 4HB

Tel: 01455 883300, 01455 550243 (minicom)
E-mail: bacp@bacp.co.uk
Website: www.counselling.co.uk
Website: www.bacp.co.uk/

Enquiries to: Information Officer
Other contacts: Membership Services Manager (for membership); Accreditation Manager (for accreditation)

Founded: 1977

Organisation type and purpose: National organisation, learned society, professional body (membership is by subscription), present number of members: 15,000 individuals, 800+ organisations, registered charity (charity number 298361).
Counselling help in local areas of England, Wales, Scotland and Northern Ireland; agencies and individuals, available on the website or on receipt of an SAE.

Subject coverage: Counselling, psychotherapy, training, personal development, stress management, employee assistance programmes, post-trauma.

Publications: Printed, and electronic and video

Publications list: Available online and in print

Access to staff: Contact by letter, by fax and by e-mail
Hours: Mon to Fri, 0845 to 1700

Divisions of BAC: Association for Pastoral Care and Counselling (APCC); Association for Student Counselling (ASC); Association of Independent Practitioners (AIP); BACP Healthcare; BACP Workplace; Counselling Children & Young People (CCYP)

Member of: Standing Conference for the Advancement of Counselling

BRITISH ASSOCIATION FOR CRYSTAL GROWTH (BACG)

BAE Systems Infra-red Limited, PO Box 217, Millbrook Industrial Estate, Southampton, SO15 0EG

Tel: 023 8070 2300
Fax: 023 8031 6777
E-mail: pete.capper@baesystems.com
Website: bacg.co.uk

Enquiries to: Honorary Secretary

Founded: 1969

Organisation type and purpose:
International organisation, national organisation, membership association (membership is by qualification), present number of members: 400, registered charity (charity number 261780), suitable for ages: 21+.
Interdisciplinary in nature and representing crystal growth in industry, research laboratories and higher education in the UK. To encourage scientific and technological communication on crystal growth including all types of inorganic and organic crystals.

Subject coverage: Crystal growth of inorganic and organic crystalline materials including metals, ceramics, polymers and electronic-device materials.

Publications: Printed

Access to staff: Contact by letter, by telephone, by fax and by e-mail
Hours: Mon to Fri, 0900 to 1700

Affiliated to: International Organisation for Crystal Growth (IOCG)

BRITISH ASSOCIATION FOR IMMEDIATE CARE (BASICS)

Turret House, Turret Lane, Ipswich, Suffolk, IP4 1DL

Tel: 01473 218407
Fax: 01473 280585
E-mail: admin@basics.org.uk
Website: www.basics.org.uk

Enquiries to: Chief Executive

Founded: 1977

Organisation type and purpose:
Membership association (membership is by subscription), present number of members: 1,400, registered charity (charity number 276054), training organisation.

Subject coverage: Emergency medical care.

Publications: Printed

Access to staff: Contact by letter, by telephone, by fax, by e-mail and via website
Hours: Mon to Thu, 0830 to 1700; Fri, 0830 to 1630

BRITISH ASSOCIATION FOR INFORMATION AND LIBRARY EDUCATION AND RESEARCH (BAILER)

c/o Dr Vesna Brujic-Okretic, Head of Department of Information Science, School of Informatics, City University London, Northampton Square, London, EC1V 0HB

Tel: 020 7040 8551
E-mail: v.brujic-okretic@city.ac.uk
Website: www.bailer.org.uk

Enquiries to: Chairman

Founded: 1992

Organisation type and purpose:
Professional body, university department or institute.
Comprising teaching and research staff of information and library schools and departments in the UK and Ireland. Acts as a national forum for matters relating to information and library education and research and aims to reflect and focus the evolution of the field of information and library studies through the development and encouragement of its members.

Subject coverage: Education and research in library and information studies, including theory and practice in digital information management and dissemination.

Publications: Printed

Access to staff: Contact by e-mail
Hours: Mon to Fri, 0900 to 1700

BRITISH ASSOCIATION FOR LOCAL HISTORY (BALH)

PO Box 6549, Somersal Herbert, Ashbourne, DE6 5WH

Tel: 01283 585947
E-mail: info@balh.co.uk
Website: www.balh.co.uk

Enquiries to: Secretary General
Direct e-mail: mail@balh.co.uk

Founded: 1982

Organisation type and purpose:
Membership association (membership is by subscription), present number of members: 2,500, voluntary organisation, registered charity (charity number 285467), publishing house.

Subject coverage: Local history, family history, genealogy, industrial archaeology, vernacular architecture, archive services, library services, museum services.

Publications: Printed

Publications list: Available online and in print

Access to staff: Contact by letter and by fax
Hours: Mon to Fri, 0900 to 1700

BRITISH ASSOCIATION FOR MUSIC THERAPY (BAMT)

2nd Floor, 24–27 White Lion Street, London, N1 9PD

Tel: 020 7837 6100
Fax: 020 7837 6142
E-mail: info@bamt.org
Website: www.bamt.org

Enquiries to: Administrator
Other contacts: Chairperson

Founded: 1958; created by the merger of British Society for Music Therapy and Association of Professional Music Therapists (year of change 2011)

Organisation type and purpose:
International organisation, professional and associate membership, present number of members: 938, registered charity (charity number 1137807).

To promote the use and development of music therapy.

Subject coverage: Use and development of music therapy.

Non-library collection catalogue: All or part available online, in-house and in print

Library catalogue: All or part available online, in-house and in print

Publications: Printed, and electronic and video

Publications list: Available online and in print

Access to staff: Contact by letter, by telephone, by fax and by e-mail. Appointment necessary.
Hours: Mon to Thu, 0930 to 1530

Access to building: No access other than to staff

BRITISH ASSOCIATION FOR PAEDIATRIC NEPHROLOGY (BAPN)

Renal Unit, Royal Hospital for Sick Children, Yorkhill, Glasgow, G3 8SJ

Tel: 0141 201 0200
Fax: 0141 201 0859
E-mail: lynda.lawson@ggc.scot.nhs.uk
Website: bapn.uwcm.ac.uk

Enquiries to: Speciality Coordinator

Organisation type and purpose: Professional body.

Subject coverage: All aspects of kidney disease in children, including the treatment of renal failure; research.

Publications: Printed

Access to staff: Contact by letter
Hours: Mon to Fri, 0900 to 1700

Close links with: Renal Association; Royal College of Paediatrics and Child Health

BRITISH ASSOCIATION FOR PERFORMING ARTS MEDICINE (BAPAM)

4th Floor, Totara Park House, 34–36 Gray's Inn Road, London, WC1X 8HR

Tel: 020 7404 5888
Fax: 020 7404 3222
E-mail: admin@bapam.org.uk
Website: www.bapam.org.uk

Enquiries to: Chief Executive
Other contacts: (1) Administrator; (2) Clinic Manager; for (1) Membership; (2) Volunteering, helpline, clinic.

Founded: 1984

Organisation type and purpose: National organisation, membership association, registered charity (charity number 10823295), training organisation, research organisation.
To provide medical assessment and diagnosis for performers with performance-related injury and/or illness.

Subject coverage: Medical and psychological problems of performing artists.

Collection: Small specialist library

Trade and statistical information: Data on specific medical problems of performers

Publications: Printed

Access to staff: Contact by letter, by telephone and by e-mail. Appointment necessary.
Hours: Tues to Fri, 0900 to 1830; Mon, 0900 to 1500

Access to building: Prior appointment required

Access for disabled people: Lift and level floors

Subsidiary body: Association of Medical Advisors to British Orchestras

BRITISH ASSOCIATION FOR PERINATAL MEDICINE (BAPM)

5–11 Theobalds Road, London, WC1X 8SH

Tel: 020 7092 6085
Fax: 020 7092 6001
E-mail: bapm@rcpch.ac.uk
Website: www.bapm-london.org

Enquiries to: Administrator
Direct e-mail: bryan.gill@leedsth.nhs.uk

Founded: 1976

Organisation type and purpose: Professional body.

Subject coverage: All aspects of perinatal medicine.

Publications: Printed

Publications list: Available online

Access to staff: Contact by letter, by telephone, by fax and by e-mail
Hours: Mon to Fri, 0900 to 1700

BRITISH ASSOCIATION FOR PSYCHOLOGICAL TYPE (BAPT)

17 Royal Crescent, Cheltenham, Gloucestershire, GL50 3DA

Tel: 01242 282990
Fax: 01242 282990
E-mail: office@bapt.org.uk
Website: www.bapt.org.uk

Enquiries to: General Secretary

Founded: 1989

Organisation type and purpose: Professional body (membership is by subscription), present number of members: 200, voluntary organisation, registered charity (charity number 1045772), consultancy.

Subject coverage: Advice on Psychological Type including workshops and register of practitioners.

Information services: Library of Psychological Type.

Library catalogue: All or part available in-house and in print

Publications list: Available online

Access to staff: Contact by letter, by telephone and by e-mail
Hours: Mon to Fri, 0900 to 1700

Access to building: No access other than to staff

BRITISH ASSOCIATION FOR PSYCHOPHARMACOLOGY (BAP)

36 Cambridge Place, Hills Road, Cambridge, CB2 1NS

Tel: 01223 358395
Fax: 01223 321268
E-mail: susan@bap.org.uk
Website: www.bap.org.uk

Enquiries to: Executive Officer
Direct tel: 01223 358428

Founded: 1974

Organisation type and purpose: International organisation, learned society (membership is by subscription), present number of members: 1,000, registered charity (charity number 277825).

Subject coverage: Psychopharmacology: behavioural pharmacology, neurochemical pharmacology, psychopharmacological treatment in psychiatry.

Publications: Printed

Access to staff: Contact by letter, by e-mail and via website
Hours: Mon to Fri, 0900 to 1700

BRITISH ASSOCIATION FOR SEXUAL AND RELATIONSHIP THERAPY (BASRT)

PO Box 13686, London, SW20 9ZH

Tel: 020 8543 2707
Fax: 020 8543 2707
E-mail: info@basrt.org.uk
Website: www.basrt.org.uk

Enquiries to: Administrator

Founded: 1976

Organisation type and purpose: National organisation, membership association (membership is by subscription, qualification), present number of members: 760, voluntary organisation, registered charity (charity number 1101961).
Professional body for clinicians and therapists who treat sexual and relationship problems.
To further education of professionals working in field of sexual and relationship therapy, to set and maintain ethical standards, to promote research and raise public awareness of sexual and relationship therapy.

Subject coverage: A professional body for clinicians and therapists who treat sexual and relationship problems.

Publications: Printed
Order printed publications from: Taylor & Francis plc, Rankine Road, Basingstoke, RG24 8PR; tel: 020 7017 6318; e-mail: info@tandf.co.uk

Publications list: Available in print

Access to staff: Contact by letter, by telephone, by fax, by e-mail and via website
Hours: Mon to Fri, 0900 to 1430

BRITISH ASSOCIATION FOR SHOOTING AND CONSERVATION

Marford Mill, Chester Road, Rossett, Wrexham, Clwyd, LL12 0HL

Tel: 01244 573000

continued overleaf

Fax: 01244 573001
E-mail: enq@basc.org.uk
Website: www.basc.org.uk

Enquiries to: Head of Media and Communications
Direct tel: 01244 573032
Direct fax: 01244 573040
Other contacts: Press Officer

Founded: 1908

Organisation type and purpose:
Membership association (membership is by subscription), present number of members: 120,000.
Cross-party lobbying organisation, representing United Kingdom shooting sports.

Subject coverage: Firearms, political lobbying, public relations, land management, education and training, ecology, quarry species management, research.

Trade and statistical information: Data on shooting sports, quarry species, firearms ownership, access issues, and shooting and conservation

Publications: Printed

Publications list: Available in print

Access to staff: Contact by letter, by telephone, by fax, by e-mail and via website
Hours: Mon to Fri, 0900 to 1700

Other addresses: BASC Northern Ireland; Courtyard Cottage, Galgorm Castle, Ballymena, Co Antrim, BT42 1HL; BASC Scotland; Trochry, Dunkeld, Tayside, PH8 0DY; tel: 01350 723226; fax: 01350 723227; e-mail: scotland@basc.org.uk

BRITISH ASSOCIATION FOR THE STUDY AND PREVENTION OF CHILD ABUSE AND NEGLECT (BASPCAN)

17 Priory Street, York, YO1 6ET

Tel: 01904 613605
Fax: 01904 642239
E-mail: baspcan@baspcan.org.uk
Website: www.baspcan.org.uk

Founded: 1979

Organisation type and purpose:
Professional body (membership is by subscription), present number of members: 1,800, registered charity (charity number 279119).
Networking.
Multi-disciplinary networking association for professionals working in the field of child protection. Membership applications invited.

Subject coverage: Child abuse.

Publications: Printed

Access to staff: Contact by letter, by telephone, by e-mail and via website
Hours: Mon to Fri, 0900 to 1700

BRITISH ASSOCIATION OF ADVISERS AND LECTURERS IN PHYSICAL EDUCATION (BAALPE)

Sports Development Centre, Loughborough University, Loughborough, Leicestershire, LE11 3TU

Tel: 01509 228378
Fax: 01509 228378
E-mail: baalpe@lboro.ac.uk
Website: www.baalpe.org

Enquiries to: General Secretary
Direct tel: 01746 769487
Direct fax: 01746 769487
Other contacts: 1) Finance and Membership Officer; 2) Continuing Professional Development (CPD) Manager for (1) Finance and membership issues (2) CPD/training.

Founded: 1921

Organisation type and purpose: National organisation, professional body, trade union (membership is by qualification, election or invitation), present number of members: 450.
The development and maintenance of high standards in all areas and all phases of physical education in schools.

Subject coverage: Teaching and coaching of physical activities; equipment and apparatus; training of teachers in primary and secondary schools; health of young people; safety in physical activities; consultancy on safe practice providing expert witnesses for court cases related to physical education/leisure; recreation, leisure, health, safety related to physical education and recreation; curriculum and management issues in physical education; initial teacher's training and CPD for PE.

Collection: Bulletin copies since 1920s (foundation time)

Non-library collection catalogue: All or part available online

Publications: Printed, and electronic and video
Order printed publications from: Dudley LEA (BAALPE Publications)
Saltwells EDC, Bowling Green Road, Dudley, West Midlands, tel: 01384 813706/7, fax: 01384 813801

Publications list: Available online and in print

Access to staff: Contact by letter, by telephone, by fax, by e-mail and via website
Hours: Permanent 24-hour answerphone on 01509 228378.

Affiliated to: Central Council of Physical Recreation; Fédération Internationale Éducation Physique

BRITISH ASSOCIATION OF ART THERAPISTS (BAAT)

24–27 White Lion Street, London N1 9PD

Tel: 020 7686 4216
Fax: 020 7837 7945
E-mail: info@baat.org
Website: www.baat.org

Enquiries to: Honorary Secretary

Founded: 1964

Organisation type and purpose:
Professional body, voluntary organisation.

Subject coverage: Art therapy and art education in special schools; training in art therapy; research in art therapy; professional standards; conditions of work; art therapy in all areas of child, adult and elderly care; mental health; learning disabilities; physical and neurological problems; dementia; autism etc.

Publications: Printed

Access to staff: Contact by letter, by telephone, by fax, by e-mail and via website
Hours: Mon to Fri, 0900 to 1700

Access to building: No access other than to staff

BRITISH ASSOCIATION OF AUDIOLOGICAL PHYSICIANS (BAAP)

Department of Audiovestibular Medicine, Queen Alexandra Hospital, Southwick Hill Road, Cosham, Portsmouth, Hampshire, PO6 3LY

Tel: 020 7837 3611 ext 3386
Fax: 029 7829 8775
E-mail: honsec.baap@virgin.net or adminsec@baap.org.uk
Website: www.baap.org.uk

Enquiries to: Honorary Secretary

Founded: 1976

Organisation type and purpose: National organisation, professional body (membership is by subscription, qualification, election or invitation), present number of members: 90.

Subject coverage: Audiological medicine; audiology; hearing aids; auditory rehabilitation; hearing loss; balance disorders; neuro-otology; auditory electrophysiology. Vestibular medicine; vestibular rehabilitation; noise-induced hearing loss; cochlear implants; universal newborn screening for hearing loss; auto-immune inner ear disease.

Publications: Printed

Publications list: Available online

Access to staff: Contact by letter, by telephone, by fax, by e-mail and via website
Hours: Mon to Fri, 0900 to 1700

Connections with: National Council for Professionals in Audiology (NCPA); c/o Ellen Godden BSA, Brighton Road, Reading

BRITISH ASSOCIATION OF AVIATION CONSULTANTS (BAAC)

c/o Jacobs Consultancy, 16 Connaught Place, London, W2 2ES

Tel: 0207 630 5358
Fax: 0207 828 0667
E-mail: committee@baac.org.uk
Website: www.baac.org.uk

Enquiries to: Chairman
Direct e-mail: peter.mw@jacobs-consultancy.com
Other contacts: Honorary Secretary for administration.

Founded: 1972

Organisation type and purpose:
Professional body (membership is by qualification), present number of members: 80.
Aviation consultancy.

Subject coverage: Aviation worldwide.

Publications: Printed

Publications list: Available online and in print

Access to staff: Contact by e-mail
Hours: Mon to Fri, 0900 to 1700

BRITISH ASSOCIATION OF COLLIERY MANAGEMENT, TECHNICAL, ENERGY AND ADMINISTRATIVE MANAGEMENT (BACM-TEAM)

17 South Parade, Doncaster, South Yorkshire, DN1 2DR

Tel: 01302 815551
Fax: 01302 815552
E-mail: enquiries@bacmteam.org.uk
Website: www.bacmteam.org.uk

Enquiries to: General Secretary
Other contacts: Office Manager

Founded: 1947

Organisation type and purpose: Trade union (membership is by subscription), present number of members: 4,300.

Subject coverage: Mining, European energy, employment law.

Publications: Printed

Access to staff: Contact by letter, by telephone and by e-mail
Hours: Mon to Fri, 0830 to 1700

Access to building: No prior appointment required

Affiliated to: TUC

Member of: ECSC; FICME; MIF

BRITISH ASSOCIATION OF CONFERENCE DESTINATIONS (BACD)

6th Floor, Charles House, 148–149 Great Charles Street, Birmingham, B3 3HT

Tel: 0121 212 1400
Fax: 0121 212 3131
E-mail: info@bacd.org.uk
Website: www.bacd.org.uk

Enquiries to: Executive Director
Other contacts: Marketing Executive for library and information services.

Founded: 1969

Organisation type and purpose: Trade association.
Association of local authorities, convention bureaux and tourist boards.
To promote the British Isles as a conference destination.

Subject coverage: Conference and exhibition facilities in British Isles, information/research on the conference industry, consultancy advice on conference infrastructure developments.

Collection: Library of reports and publications

Trade and statistical information: Data on the value, size, and trends etc, in the conference and business tourism sectors

Publications: Printed, and electronic and video

Access to staff: Contact by letter, by telephone, by fax and by e-mail. Appointment necessary.
Hours: Mon to Fri, 0900 to 1700

Member of: The Council for Travel and Tourism; LGM House, Mill Green Road, Haywards Heath, West Sussex, RH16 1XQ; tel: 01444 452277; fax: 01444 452244

BRITISH ASSOCIATION OF DENTAL NURSES (BADN)

Room 200, Hillhouse Intl Business Centre, Thornton-Cleveleys, FY5 4QD

Tel: 01253 338360
E-mail: admin@badn.org.uk
Website: www.badn.org.uk

Enquiries to: Chief Executive
Direct tel: 01253 338365
Direct e-mail: pam@badn.org.uk

Founded: 1940

Organisation type and purpose: Professional body, trade union (membership is by subscription).

Subject coverage: Education, training, employment, salaries and conditions of employment, advice seminars, annual conference, local group network, national groups for DNs in specific areas of dentistry.

Publications: Printed

Publications list: Available in print

Access to staff: Contact by letter, by telephone, by e-mail and via website
Hours: Mon to Fri, 0900 to 1700

BRITISH ASSOCIATION OF DERMATOLOGISTS (BAD)

4 Fitzroy Square, London, W1T 5HQ

Tel: 020 7383 0266
Fax: 020 7388 5263
E-mail: admin@bad.org.uk
Website: www.skinhealth.co.uk
Website: www.bad.org.uk

Enquiries to: Executive Officer

Founded: 1920

Organisation type and purpose: Learned society, professional body (membership is by qualification, election or invitation), present number of members: 800.
A body of international specialists of dermatology formed to promote and represent the best interests of dermatologists and patients affected by diseases of the skin. Its objects are: to promote for public benefit greater knowledge and understanding of diseases of the skin, and improve the teaching of dermatology at all levels by organising and sponsoring scientific meetings, conferences and seminars; to stimulate and promote appropriate medical and scientific research; to collect, evaluate and disseminate data and information on all matters relating to the well-being of patients.

Subject coverage: Dermatology.

Collection: A small specialised library of historically significant books in relation to dermatology, which can only be viewed privately since it is a private collection controlled from the Association's offices Willan Library

Publications: Printed

Access to staff: Contact by letter
Hours: Mon to Fri, 0900 to 1700

BRITISH ASSOCIATION OF DRAMATHERAPISTS (BADth)

Waverley, Battledown Approach, Cheltenham, Gloucestershire, GL52 6RE

Tel: 01242 235515
E-mail: enquiries@badth.org.uk
Website: www.badth.org.uk

Enquiries to: Administrator

Founded: 1977

Organisation type and purpose: Professional body (membership is by qualification, election or invitation), present number of members: 680, voluntary organisation, training organisation, research organisation, publishing house.

Information services: Information about dramatherapy and dramatherapy training.

Publications: Printed, and electronic and video
Order printed publications from: e-mail: enquiries@badth.org.uk
Order electronic and video publications from: e -mail: enquiries@badth.org.uk

Access to staff: Contact by letter, by telephone, by e-mail and via website
Hours: Mon to Fri, variable hours

BRITISH ASSOCIATION OF FASTENER DISTRIBUTORS (BAFD)

Formal name: British Association of Fastener Distributors Limited

35 Calthorpe Road, Edgbaston, Birmingham, B15 1TS

Tel: 0121 454 4141
E-mail: info@bafd.org
Website: www.bafd.org

Enquiries to: General Secretary

Founded: 1945

Organisation type and purpose: National organisation, trade association (membership by subscription), present number of members: 60.

Subject coverage: Distribution of fasteners and construction fixings.

Access to staff: Contact by e-mail
Hours: Mon to Fri, 0900 to 1700

Affiliated to: European Fastener Distributors Association (EFDA); Germany

BRITISH ASSOCIATION OF FRIENDS OF MUSEUMS (BAFM)

141a School Road, Brislington, Bristol. BS4 4LZ

Tel: 01179 77435
E-mail: admin@bafm.org.uk
Website: www.bafm.org.uk

Enquiries to: Honorary Secretary
Other contacts: Administrator

Organisation type and purpose: National organisation, membership association, voluntary organisation, registered charity

continued overleaf

(charity number 270253), museum, art gallery, historic building, house or site, consultancy.
To inform, encourage and support all those, whether in groups or as individuals, who wish to work in and for museums in a voluntary capacity.

Subject coverage: Museums, the organisation and management of friends, groups, supporters and volunteers in museums of all kinds. Setting up a group, good practice, model constitution, contacts worldwide.

Publications: Printed

Publications list: Available online and in print

Access to staff: Contact by letter, by telephone, by fax, by e-mail and via website. Appointment necessary.
Hours: Mon to Fri, 0900 to 1700

Links with: Association of Independent Museums; Museum Association; World Federation of Friends of Museums; Paris, France

BRITISH ASSOCIATION OF GREEN CROP DRIERS LIMITED (BAGCD)

March Hares, Montagu Road, Canwick, Lincoln, LN4 2RW

Tel: 01522 523322
Fax: 01522 568539
E-mail: info@bagcd.org
Website: www.bagcd.org

Enquiries to: Secretary

Founded: 1963

Organisation type and purpose: National organisation, trade association (membership is by election or invitation), present number of members: 30, manufacturing industry.

Subject coverage: All production, political and nutritional aspects of drying grass and lucerne for animal feed.

Access to staff: Contact by letter, by telephone, by fax and by e-mail
Hours: Mon to Fri, 0900 to 1700

Access to building: No access other than to staff

Links with: European Dehydrators Association – Commission Intersyndicale des Deshydrateurs Européens (CIDE); tel: +33 2 33 85 12 38; fax: +33 2 33 85 12 38; e-mail: ericguillemot@aol.com

BRITISH ASSOCIATION OF LANDSCAPE INDUSTRIES (BALI)

Landscape House, NAC, Stoneleigh Park, Warwickshire, CV8 2LG

Tel: 024 7669 0333
Fax: 024 7669 0077
E-mail: contact@bali.org.uk
Website: www.bali.co.uk

Enquiries to: Chief Executive

Founded: 1972

Organisation type and purpose: Trade association (membership is by subscription, qualification), present number of members: 645, training organisation.
Industry training organisation for landscaping.
BALI is the national body representing Landscape Contractors in the UK.

Subject coverage: Environmental landscaping, all landscape work and supplies, all facets of landscaping.

Publications: Printed

Access to staff: Contact by letter and by telephone
Hours: Mon to Fri, 0900 to 1700

Founder member of: Confederation of British Industry (CBI); Industry Lead Body for Amenity Horticulture (ILBAH); Joint Council for Landscape Industries (JCLI); National Specialist Contractors Council (NSCC)

BRITISH ASSOCIATION OF LIBERTARIAN FEMINISTS

25 Chapter Chambers, Esterbrook Street, London, SW1P 4NN

Tel: 020 7821 5502
Fax: 020 7834 2031
E-mail: sean@libertarian.co.uk
Website: www.libertarian.co.uk

Enquiries to: Director
Direct e-mail: chris@rand.demon.co.uk

Publications list: Available online

BRITISH ASSOCIATION OF MOUNTAIN GUIDES (BMG)

Siabod Cottage, Capel Curig, Conwy, LL24 0ES

Tel: 01690 720386
Fax: 01690 720248
E-mail: guiding@bmg.org.uk
Website: www.bmg.org.uk

Enquiries to: Honorary Secretary
Direct tel: 07878 303229
Other contacts: President (for discipline, conduct)

Founded: 1975

Organisation type and purpose: Professional body (membership is by qualification), present number of members: 183, service industry.

Subject coverage: Guides for climbing and mountaineering, climbing instruction, advice and consultancy on mountaineering affairs.

Publications: Electronic and video

Access to staff: Contact by letter, by telephone, by fax and by e-mail
Hours: Mon to Fri, 0900 to 1700

Links with: Union Internationale des Associations de Guides de Montagne (The International Federation of Mountain Guide Associations); Armin Oehrli, Sekretar IVBV/ UIAGM, Badweidli, 3780 Gstaad, Switzerland; tel: +41 (0) 33 744 54 77; fax: +41 (0) 33 744 54 77; website: htp://www .ivbv.info

BRITISH ASSOCIATION OF NUMISMATIC SOCIETIES (BANS)

The Manchester Museum, The University of Manchester, Oxford Road, Manchester, M13 9PL

Tel: 0161 275 2643
E-mail: phyllis.stoddart@manchester.ac.uk
Website: www.coinclubs.freeserve.co.uk

Enquiries to: Honorary Secretary

Founded: 1953

Organisation type and purpose: National organisation, membership association (membership is by subscription), present number of members: 60.
A coordinating body for liaison and research among local numismatics societies.

Subject coverage: Numismatics.

Collection: Collections of slides of coins for lecturing purposes (for loan to affiliated societies)

Publications: Printed, and electronic and video

Publications list: Available in print

Access to staff: Contact by letter, by telephone and by e-mail
Hours: Mon to Fri, 0900 to 1700

BRITISH ASSOCIATION OF PAPER HISTORIANS (BAPH)

BAPH, 24 Heol Beca, Carmarthen, SA31 3LS

Tel: 01665 577988
E-mail: terry@baph.org.uk
Website: www.baph.org.uk

Enquiries to: Membership Secretary

Founded: 1989

Organisation type and purpose: Membership association (membership is by subscription).

Subject coverage: Paper making history, paper mill sites, raw materials, communities; paper watermarks, users and conservation.

Publications: Printed

Publications list: Available online

Access to staff: Contact by letter, by e-mail and via website
Hours: Mon to Fri, 0900 to 1700

BRITISH ASSOCIATION OF PHARMACEUTICAL WHOLESALERS (BAPW)

90 Long Acre, London, WC2E 9RA

Tel: 020 7031 0590
Fax: 020 7031 0591
E-mail: secretariat@bapw.net
Website: www.bapw.net/

Enquiries to: Executive Director

Founded: 1967

Organisation type and purpose: Trade association (membership is by subscription).

Subject coverage: Pharmaceuticals.

Publications: Printed

Access to staff: Contact by letter, by telephone, by fax and by e-mail. Appointment necessary.
Hours: Mon to Thu, 0900 to 1700; Fri, 0900 to 1600

Affiliated to: Groupement International de la Répartition Pharmaceutique Européenne (GIRP); International Federation of Pharmaceutical Wholesalers (IFPW)

BRITISH ASSOCIATION OF PICTURE LIBRARIES AND AGENCIES (BAPLA)

59 Tranquil Vale, Blackheath, London, SE3 0BS

Tel: 020 8297 1198
Fax: 020 8852 7211
E-mail: enquiries@bapla.org.uk
Website: www.bapla.org.uk

Enquiries to: Administrator

Founded: 1975

Organisation type and purpose: National organisation, trade association (membership is by subscription), present number of members: 200+
Free referral service to picture researchers to assist them in locating the best source of photographic imagery.
To develop and maintain a professional framework for the industry.

Subject coverage: Picture libraries, Picture Agencies

Collection: Members' specialist collections

Non-library collection catalogue: All or part available online

Publications list: Available online

Access to staff: Contact by telephone, by e-mail and via website. Appointment necessary.
Hours: Mon to Fri, 1000 to 1800

Access to building: By appointment only

Member organisation of: British Copyright Council; CEPIC; Picture Agency Council of America

BRITISH ASSOCIATION OF PSYCHOTHERAPISTS (BAP)

British Association of Psychotherapists, 37 Mapesbury Road, London NW2 4HJ

Tel: 020 8452 9823
Fax: 020 8452 0310
E-mail: library@bap-psychotherapy.org
Website: www.bap-psychotherapy.org

Enquiries to: Librarian

Founded: 1951

Organisation type and purpose: National organisation, professional body, membership association (membership is by qualification, election or invitation), present number of members: 500, registered charity (charity number 281720), training organisation.

Subject coverage: Analytic psychotherapy (child, adolescent and adult), registration of psychotherapists, training in adult and child psychotherapy (Jungian and Freudian), clinical assessment and referral service.

Collection: Books and journals on psychotherapy

Library catalogue: All or part available online

Publications: Printed
Order printed publications from: Administrator

Publications list: Available in print

Access to staff: Contact by letter, by telephone, by fax, by e-mail and via website. Appointment necessary.
Hours: Mon to Fri, 0930 to 1700

Access for disabled people: Parking provided, toilet facilities
Special comments: No lift to the 1st floor.

Member organisation of: British Psychoanalytic Council; Suite 7, 19–23 Wedmore Street, London, N19 4RU; tel: 020 7561 9240; fax: 020 7561 9005; e-mail: mail@psychoanalytic-council.org; website: http://www.psychoanalytic-council.org

BRITISH ASSOCIATION OF REMOVERS (BAR)

Tangent House, 62 Exchange Road, Watford, Herts, WD18 0TG

Tel: 01923 699480
Fax: 01923 699481
E-mail: info@bar.co.uk
Website: www.bar.co.uk/

Enquiries to: General Secretary
Direct e-mail: james.falkner@bar.co.uk
Other contacts: Executive Assistant

Founded: 1900

Organisation type and purpose: Trade association.

Subject coverage: Removal, storage, shipping etc, of household goods and effects and commercial, office furniture and effects.

Publications: Printed

Access to staff: Contact by letter, by telephone, by fax, by e-mail and via website
Hours: Mon to Fri, 0900 to 1700

Affiliated to: Fédération des Entreprises de Déménagement du Marché Commun (FEDEMAC); Fédération Internationale des Déménageurs Internationaux (FIDI)

Associated with: Freight Transport Association; Road Haulage Association

BRITISH ASSOCIATION OF SETTLEMENTS AND SOCIAL ACTION CENTRES (bassac)

33 Corsham Street, London, N1 6DR

Tel: 0845 241 0375
Fax: 0845 241 0376
E-mail: info@bassac.org.uk

Enquiries to: Administrator

Founded: c. 1919–20

Organisation type and purpose: National organisation, membership association (membership is by subscription), present number of members: 100, voluntary organisation, registered charity (charity number 1028784).
Network of 70 independent organisations.

Subject coverage: Social welfare, community development, member settlements and social action centres, inner-city projects, urban regeneration, community work, funding (members only).

Library catalogue: All or part available in-house

Publications: Printed

Publications list: Available online

Access to staff: Contact by letter, by telephone, by fax, by e-mail and via website. Appointment necessary.
Hours: Mon to Fri, 0930 to 1730
Special comments: Primarily information provided to members.

Access for disabled people: Level entry, access to all public areas, toilet facilities; lift

Member organisation of: International Federation of Settlements (IFS); Canada; tel: +1 416 469 5711; e-mail: ifs.agnes@woodgreen.org

BRITISH ASSOCIATION OF SKI PATROLLERS (BASP UK LTD) (BASP)

20 Lorn Drive, Glencoe, Ballachulish, Argyll, PH49 4HR

Tel: 01855 811443
E-mail: firstaid@basp.org.uk
Website: www.basp.org.uk

Enquiries to: Administrator

Founded: 1987

Organisation type and purpose: Professional body (membership is by subscription), present number of members: 120, education, suitable for ages: 18+, training organisation.
Training and grading of ski patrollers, first aid training.

Subject coverage: Ski patrolling, first aid training, specialist advanced mountain medicine.

Publications: Printed

Publications list: Available in print

Access to staff: Contact by letter, by telephone, by e-mail and via website
Hours: Mon to Fri, 0900 to 1700

BRITISH ASSOCIATION OF SNOWSPORTS INSTRUCTORS (BASI)

Morlich House, 17 The Square, Grantown-on-Spey, Morayshire, PH26 3HG

Tel: 01479 861717
Fax: 01479 873657
E-mail: basi@basi.org.uk
Website: www.basi.org.uk

Enquiries to: Chief Executive
Direct e-mail: fergus@basi.org.uk

Founded: 1963; formerly called British Association of Ski Instructors BASI (year of change 2005)

Organisation type and purpose: Membership association (membership is by subscription, qualification), present number of members: 5,700, training organisation.

Subject coverage: Training and grading of snowsport instructors; skiing and ski teaching; snowboard teaching.

Publications: Printed, and electronic and video
Order electronic and video publications from: roz@basi.org.uk

Publications list: Available online and in print

Access to staff: Contact by letter, by telephone, by fax, by e-mail, in person and via website. Appointment necessary. Letter of introduction required.

continued overleaf

Hours: Mon to Fri, 0900 to 1700

Access to building: Through reception
Hours: Mon to Fri, 0900 to 1700

Access for disabled people: Parking provided, ramped entry
Hours: as above
Special comments: Ground floor access only.

Affiliated to: Snowsports GB

BRITISH ASSOCIATION OF SOCIAL WORKERS (BASW)

16 Kent Street, Birmingham, B5 6RD

Tel: 0121 622 3911
Fax: 0121 622 4860
E-mail: reception@basw.co.uk
Website: www.basw.co.uk

Founded: 1970

Organisation type and purpose: Professional body.

Subject coverage: Social work and social welfare in all field and residential settings (public, charitable and private agencies and independent practice), including child care, child abuse, mental health, learning disabilities, old age, physical handicap, personal and family problems, adult and juvenile offenders, community work, poverty, social services management, education and training in social services, social services employment.

Collection: Archives of the founding associations

Publications: Printed

Publications list: Available in print

Access to staff: Contact by letter, by telephone, by fax and by e-mail

Affiliated to: International Federation of Social Workers

BRITISH ASSOCIATION OF SPORTS AND EXERCISE SCIENCES (BASES)

Rooms G07 and G08 Leeds Metropolitan University Carnegie Faculty of Sport and Education Fairfax Hall Headingley Campus, Beckett Park, Leeds, LS6 3QS

Tel: 0113 8126162 OR 0113 8126163
Fax: +44 (0)113 8126162
E-mail: enquiries@bases.org.uk
Website: www.bases.org.uk

Enquiries to: Executive Officer
Direct e-mail: cpalmer@bases.org.uk
Other contacts: Office Manager for general information and membership.

Founded: 1983

Organisation type and purpose: Learned society, professional body, membership association (membership is by subscription, qualification), present number of members: 2,855.

Subject coverage: Sport and exercise sciences; psychology, physiology, biomechanics, nutrition, elite sport, health promotion, exercise and associated careers.

Publications: Printed

Access to staff: Contact by letter, by telephone, by fax, by e-mail and via website
Hours: Mon to Fri, 0830 to 1645

Access to building: No prior appointment required
Hours: Mon to Fri, 0900 to 1700

Access for disabled people: Parking provided, ramped entry, toilet facilities

Affiliated to: European Federation of Sports Psychology; International Society of Biomechanics

BRITISH ASSOCIATION OF SURGICAL ONCOLOGY (BASO~ACS)

at the Royal College of Surgeons, 35–43 Lincoln's Inn Fields, London, WC2A 3PE

Tel: 020 7869 6817
Fax: 020 7869 6851
E-mail: admin@baso.org.uk
Website: www.baso.org.uk

Enquiries to: Honorary Secretary

Founded: 1972

Organisation type and purpose: Learned society (membership is by subscription), present number of members: 650, registered charity (charity number 269736).

Subject coverage: Cancer surgery; oncology.

Library catalogue: All or part available online

Publications: Printed

Access to staff: Contact by letter
Hours: Mon to Fri, 0900 to 1700

BRITISH ASSOCIATION OF TEACHERS OF DANCING (BATD)

The British Association of Teachers of Dancing, Pavilion 8, Upper Level, Watermark Business Park, 315 Govan Road, Glasgow, Scotland, G51 2SE

Tel: 0141 427 3699
Fax: 0141 419 9783
E-mail: enquiries@batd.co.uk
Website: www.batd.co.uk

Enquiries to: General Secretary

Founded: 1892

Organisation type and purpose: International organisation, professional body (membership is by qualification, election or invitation), present number of members: 3,000, suitable for ages: 16+. Registered Friendly Society, no. 11SA(S). To promote the art of dancing and aid members in times of distress.

Subject coverage: All dancing activities.

Publications: Printed

Access to staff: Contact by letter, by telephone, by fax, by e-mail, in person and via website
Hours: Mon to Fri, 0900 to 1700

Affiliated to: Central Council of Physical Recreation

Representation on: British Council of Ballroom Dancing; Scottish Official Board of Highland Dancing; Stage Dance Council International

BRITISH ASSOCIATION OF TEACHERS OF THE DEAF (BATOD)

21, Keating Close, Rochester, Kent, ME1 1EQ

Tel: 0845 643 5181
Fax: 0845 643 5181
E-mail: exec@batod.org.uk
Website: www.batod.org.uk

Enquiries to: National Executive Officer
Other contacts: Magazine Editor for matters related to magazine and publications.

Founded: 1977

Organisation type and purpose: National organisation, professional body (membership is by subscription), present number of members: 1,520, voluntary organisation, suitable for ages: all, training organisation, consultancy, research organisation, publishing house.

Subject coverage: National curriculum (hearing-impaired), communication, Teacher of the Deaf training, examination special arrangements, special education (hearing-impaired), educational audiology, educational legislation.

Collection: Archived history at University of Birmingham

Publications: Printed

Publications list: Available online and in print

Access to staff: Contact by letter, by telephone, by fax, by e-mail and via website. Appointment necessary.
Hours: Answerphone 24-hours

Affiliated to: European Federation of Associations of Teachers of the Deaf (FEAPDA); c/o 21, Keating Close, Rochester, Kent, ME1 1EQ; tel: 0845 643 5181; fax: 0845 643 5181; e-mail: president@feapda.org; website: http://www.feapda.org

BRITISH ASSOCIATION OF UROLOGICAL SURGEONS (BAUS)

Royal College of Surgeons of England, 35–43 Lincoln's Inn Fields, London, WC2A 3PE

Tel: 020 7869 6950
Fax: 020 7404 5048
E-mail: admin@baus.org.uk
Website: www.baus.org.uk/

Enquiries to: Chief Executive

Founded: 1945

Organisation type and purpose: Professional body.

Subject coverage: Urology; urological surgery.

Access to staff: Contact by letter, by fax and by e-mail
Hours: Mon to Fri, 0900 to 1700

BRITISH AUTOMOBILE RACING CLUB LIMITED (BARC)

Thruxton Circuit, Andover, Hampshire, SP11 8PN

Tel: 01264 882200
Fax: 01264 882233
E-mail: info@barc.net
Website: www.barc.net

Enquiries to: Chief Executive

Founded: 1912

Organisation type and purpose: Membership association. Motor Sport organisation.

Subject coverage: Motor racing, motor racing and motor racing safety.

Collection: Early photographs, motoring books, minutes, Brooklands programmes, etc.

Publications: Printed

Access to staff: Contact by letter, by telephone, by fax, by e-mail, in person and via website
Hours: Mon to Fri, 0900 to 1700
Special comments: By appointment for research.

Access for disabled people: Parking provided, toilet facilities

Affiliated to: Royal Automobile Club Motor Sports Association; tel: 01753 681736; fax: 01753 682938

BRITISH AVIATION PRESERVATION COUNCIL (BAPC)

19 Acton Place, High Heaton, Newcastle upon Tyne, NE7 7RL

Tel: 0191 266 2049
Fax: 0191 266 2049
E-mail: secretarybapc@btconnect.com
Website: www.bapc.org.uk

Enquiries to: Secretary

Founded: 1967

Organisation type and purpose: International organisation, advisory body, membership association (membership is by subscription), present number of members: 100+.
Co-ordinating body.
To link national, local authority, independent and service museums with private collections, voluntary groups and other organisations in the advancement of the preservation of Britain's aviation heritage.

Subject coverage: Preservation, restoration and exhibition of historic aviation, archives and associated records.

Publications: Printed
Order printed publications from: British Aviation Preservation Council
19 Acton Place, High Heaton, Newcastle upon Tyne, NE7 7RL

Access to staff: Contact by letter, by telephone, by fax and by e-mail
Hours: Mon to Sun, 0700 to 2200

Affiliated to: Association of British Transport Museums; European Aviation Preservation Council; Transport Trust

There are some: 3 honorary members, 100 member organisations and 12 affiliated member organisations

BRITISH BALLET ORGANIZATION (BBO)

39 Lonsdale Road, Barnes, London, SW13 9JP

Tel: 020 8748 1241
Fax: 020 8748 1301
E-mail: info@bbo.org.uk
Website: www.bbo.org.uk

Enquiries to: Director

Founded: 1930

Organisation type and purpose: Membership association, registered charity (charity number 277177), suitable for ages: all.
Examining body for ballet, tap, jazz and modern dancing at all ages. Teaching qualifications in ballet and tap dancing. Teacher training programme.

Subject coverage: Examinations in ballet, tap, jazz and modern dancing, in the UK, Australia, New Zealand, Spain, Cyprus, Jordan and Kuwait. Dance and teacher training and examinations.

Collection: Archives of the British Ballet Organization
Archives of the Espinosa Family (founders)

Publications: Printed, and electronic and video
Order printed publications from: BBO Dance Supplies Limited
39 Lonsdale Road, Barnes, London, SW13 9JP; tel: 020 8748 1241; fax: 020 8748 1301; e-mail: info@bbo.org.uk

Access to staff: Contact by letter, by fax and by e-mail
Hours: Mon to Fri, 0900 to 1700
Special comments: Open to anyone wishing to join and study the British Ballet Organization method.

Access for disabled people: Parking provided

Registered with: The Council for Dance Education and Training (CDET(UK))

BRITISH BANDSMAN

66–78 Denington Road, Wellingborough, Northamptonshire, NN8 2QH

Tel: 01933 445442
Fax: 01933 445435
E-mail: info@britishbandsman.com
Website: www.britishbandsman.com

Enquiries to: Information Officer
Other contacts: Managing Editor

Founded: 1887

Organisation type and purpose: Publishing house.

Subject coverage: Brass bands.

Publications: Printed

Access to staff: Contact by letter
Hours: Mon to Fri, 0900 to 1630

Parent body: Kapitol Media and Events Limited; 64 London End, Beaconsfield, Buckinghamshire, HP18 9QH; tel: 01494 674411; fax: 01494 670932; e-mail: info@britishbandsman.com

BRITISH BANKERS' ASSOCIATION (BBA)

Pinners Hall, 105–108 Old Broad Street, London, EC2N 1EX

Tel: 020 7216 8800
Fax: +44 (0) 20 7216 8811
E-mail: info@bba.org.uk
Website: www.bba.org.uk

Founded: 1919

Organisation type and purpose: Trade association.

Subject coverage: Banks and banking; specific information for member banks; some limited information for general public.

Trade and statistical information: Monthly statistical information of bank lending (available on website)

Publications: Printed

Publications list: Available online and in print

Access to staff: Contact by letter
Hours: Mon to Fri, 0900 to 1700

Access to building: By appointment only

Member of: European Banking Federation

BRITISH BANKING HISTORY SOCIETY (BBHS)

British Banking History Society, P Michael Lord Esq, Treasurer, 38 Ingleton Road, Newsome, Huddersfield, HD4 6QX

Tel: 024 7650 3245
E-mail: enquiries@banking-history.co.uk
Website: www.banking-history.co.uk

Enquiries to: Honorary Secretary

Founded: 1980

Organisation type and purpose: Membership association (membership is by subscription).

Subject coverage: The collection of cheques and research into banking history.

Publications: Printed

Access to staff: Contact by letter, by telephone and by e-mail
Hours: Mon to Fri, 0900 to 1700

BRITISH BASKETBALL ASSOCIATION (BBA)

Linen Hall, Suite 446, 162–168 Regent Street, London, W1B 5TE

Tel: 020 7993 6864
E-mail: info@bbauk.com
Website: www.bbauk.com

Founded: 2007

Organisation type and purpose: Formed by a consortium of business, sports, marketing and basketball professionals primarily to create a commercially viable professional basketball league in the United Kingdom.

BRITISH BATTERY MANUFACTURERS ASSOCIATION (BBMA)

BBMA, The Registry, Royal Mint Court, London, EC3N 4QN

Tel: 020 7457 2018
Fax: 020 7866 7900
E-mail: info@bbma.co.uk
Website: www.bbma.co.uk

Enquiries to: Secretary
Other contacts: Executive

Founded: 1986

continued overleaf

Organisation type and purpose: Trade association.

Subject coverage: Standards, safety, statistics, UK and European legislation, environmental interest, disposal and recycling of portable batteries, both primary (non-rechargeable) and secondary (rechargeable).

Publications: Printed

Publications list: Available online and in print

Access to staff: Contact by letter, by telephone, by fax and by e-mail
Hours: Mon to Fri, 0900 to 1700

Member of: European Portable Battery Association

BRITISH BAVARIAN WARMBLOOD ASSOCIATION (BBWA)

Sittyton, Straloch, Newmachar, Aberdeen, AB21 0RP

Tel: 01651 882226
Fax: 01651 882313
E-mail: bbwa@bbwa.co.uk
Website: www.bbwa.co.uk

Enquiries to: Secretary

Founded: 1987

Organisation type and purpose: Membership association (membership is by subscription), present number of members: 80.

Subject coverage: Bavarian Warmblood horses, breeding, registration, grading and performance testing.

Access to staff: Contact by telephone
Hours: Mon to Fri, 0900 to 1700

Parent body: Landesverband Bayerischer Pferdezuechter eV; Landshamer Str. 11, 81929 Munich, Germany; tel: +49 89 926967; fax: +49 89 907405

BRITISH BEEKEEPERS' ASSOCIATION (BBKA)

National Beekeeping Centre, National Agricultural Centre, Stoneleigh Park, Warwickshire, CV8 2LG

Tel: 024 7669 6679
Fax: 024 7669 0682
E-mail: bbka@britishbeekeepers.com
Website: www.bbka.org.uk
Website: www.pollinationdating.com

Enquiries to: General Secretary
Direct e-mail: general.secretary@bbka.org.uk

Founded: 1874

Organisation type and purpose: Membership association (membership is by subscription), present number of members: 23,000, registered charity (charity number 212025).
To further the craft of beekeeping.

Subject coverage: Bees and beekeeping; examinations in beekeeping.

Education services: Educational resources for beekeepers and educational information on the honey bee for the general public

Collection: AVA library of slides, tapes etc
Library of numerous collections

Non-library collection catalogue: All or part available online

Library catalogue: All or part available online

Publications: Printed, and microform publications
Order printed publications from: www.bbka.org.uk

Publications list: Available in print

Access to staff: Contact by letter, by telephone, by fax, by e-mail and via website. Appointment necessary.
Hours: Mon to Fri, 0900 to 1230 and 1300 to 1700

Access to building: By Appointment

Access for disabled people: By Appointment

BRITISH BEER & PUB ASSOCIATION

British Beer & Pub Association, Brewers' Hall, Aldermanbury Square, London, EC2V 7HR

Tel: 020 7627 9191
Fax: 020 7627 9123
E-mail: contact@beerandpub.com
Website: www.beerandpub.com

Enquiries to: Secretary

Founded: 1904

Organisation type and purpose: Trade association.

Subject coverage: Beer, brewing, the brewing industry, public houses, licensing system.

Collection: Trade periodicals and annuals back to 1880

Publications: Printed

Publications list: Available in print

Access to staff: Contact by letter
Hours: Mon to Fri, 0900 to 1700

Access for disabled people: Level entry

Member of: Confederation of British Industry

BRITISH BERRICHON DU CHER SHEEP SOCIETY LIMITED (BdC)

Tregwynt, Three Ashes, Hereford, HR2 8LY

Tel: 01989 770 071
E-mail: berrichon@btconnect.com

Enquiries to: Secretary

Founded: 1986

Organisation type and purpose: Membership association (membership is by subscription).
Breed Society.

Subject coverage: British Berrichon Du Cher sheep breed.

Publications: Printed

Access to staff: Contact by letter, by telephone and by fax
Hours: Mon to Fri, 0900 to 1700

BRITISH BIOMAGNETIC ASSOCIATION (BBA)

The Gables Gunthorpe North Lincs DN9 1BQ

Tel: 01427 728386
Fax: 01427 728386
E-mail: secretary@britishbiomagneticassoc.fsnet.co.uk

Enquiries to: Secretary
Other contacts: Course Administrator

Founded: 1976

Organisation type and purpose: Professional body (membership is by qualification), present number of members: 250, training organisation, research organisation.
Postgraduate Training.

Subject coverage: Magnetic effects on acupuncture points, acupuncture at postgraduate level, radionic practice.

Access to staff: Contact by letter, by telephone, by fax and by e-mail

BRITISH BIRD COUNCIL (BBC)

1st Floor Offices, 1159 Bristol Road South, Northfield, Birmingham, B31 2SL

Tel: 0121 476 5999
E-mail: info@britishbirdcouncil.com
Website: www.britishbirdcouncil.com

Enquiries to: Administrator
Direct tel: 01902 700319
Direct fax: 01902 701140
Direct e-mail: rogercaton@birdexpert.fsnet.co.uk

Founded: 1970

Organisation type and purpose: Non-governmental organisation.
Department for the Environment, Food & Rural Affairs approved supplier of rings for birds.

Subject coverage: Rings to identify British birds.

Access to staff: Contact by letter
Hours: Mon to Fri, 0900 to 1700

Access to building: No access other than to staff

Affiliated society: Cleveland British Bird Club; Eastern Federation of British Bird Fanciers; Lancashire British Bird & Hybrid Club; London & Home Counties British Bird & Mule Club; National British Bird & Mule Club; North Derbyshire British Bird & Mule Club; Sandwell British Bird & Hybrid Club; Scottish British Bird & Mule Club; Severn Counties Foreign & British Bird Society; South Coast British Bird & Hybrid Club; Staffordshire British Bird & Mule Club; Welsh British Bird & Mule Club; Yorkshire British Bird & Hybrid Club

Affiliated to: National Council for Aviculture

BRITISH BIRDWATCHING FAIR (Birdfair)

Fishponds Cottage, Hambleton Road, Oakham, Rutland, LE15 8AB

Tel: 01572 771079
Fax: 01572 756611

E-mail: etate@birdfair.org.uk
Website: www.birdfair.org.uk

Enquiries to: Administrator

Founded: 1989

Organisation type and purpose: Voluntary organisation.
Conservancy organisation.
Three-day event at Egleton Nature Reserve, Rutland Water, the purpose of which is a celebration of birdwatching and a way of raising funds for international bird conservation.

Subject coverage: Birdwatching and conservation.

Trade and statistical information:
Approximately 300 exhibitions and 23,000 visitors

Access to staff: Contact by letter, by telephone, by fax and by e-mail
Hours: Mon to Fri, 0900 to 1700
Special comments: Preferred access order: e-mail, letter, fax, telephone.

Access for disabled people: Parking provided, toilet facilities

Links with: Leicestershire & Rutland Wildlife Trust; tel: 0116 2720444; fax: 0116 2720404; e-mail: info@lrwt.org.uk; website: http://www.lrwt.org.uk
Royal Society for the Protection of Birds; tel: 01767 680551; website: http://www.rspb.org.uk

BRITISH BLIND AND SHUTTER ASSOCIATION (BBSA)

British Blind and Shutter Association, PO Box 232, Stowmarket, Suffolk, IP14 9AR

Tel: 01449 780 444
Fax: 01827 310827
E-mail: info@bbsa.org.uk
Website: www.bbsa.org.uk

Enquiries to: Secretary

Founded: 1919

Organisation type and purpose: National organisation, advisory body, trade association (membership is by subscription), present number of members: 390.
Represents manufacturers and suppliers.

Subject coverage: Internal and external blinds, awnings and security grilles and shutters.

Publications: Printed

Access to staff: Contact by letter, by telephone, by fax and by e-mail
Hours: Mon to Thu, 0900 to 1700; Fri, 0900 to 1630

BRITISH BLIND SPORT (BBS)

British Blind Sport, Pure Offices, Plato Close, Tachbrook Park, Leamington Spa, Warwickshire, CV34 6WE

Tel: 01926 424247
Fax: 01926 427775
E-mail: info@britishblindsport.org.uk
Website: www.britishblindsport.org.uk

Enquiries to: Admin. Manager

Founded: 1975

Organisation type and purpose:
Membership association, voluntary organisation, registered charity (charity number 271500).
Providing sport and recreation for blind and partially sighted people.

Subject coverage: General information about sports for the blind and partially sighted, specialist sports, classification of sight categories.

Access to staff: Contact by letter and by e-mail
Hours: Mon to Thu, 0900 to 1700; Fri, 0900 to 1630

Affiliated to: International Blind Sport Association

BRITISH BOARD OF AGRÉMENT (BBA)

Bucknalls Lane, Garston, Watford, Hertfordshire, WD25 9BA

Tel: 01923 665300
Fax: 01923 665301
E-mail: mail@bba.star.co.uk
Website: www.bbacerts.co.uk

Enquiries to: Information Officer
Direct e-mail: athomas@bba.star.co.uk
Other contacts: Sales and Communications Director

Founded: 1966

Organisation type and purpose: Approvals body for the construction industry.

Subject coverage: Testing and approval of building and civil engineering products (successful assessments are published as Agrément Certificates, which contain essential technical data for designers and users).

Collection: 3,500 agrément certificates dating from 1966

Non-library collection catalogue: All or part available online

Library catalogue: All or part available online

Publications: Printed, and electronic and video, and microform publications

Publications list: Available in print

Access to staff: Contact by letter, by fax, by e-mail and via website
Hours: Mon to Fri, 0900 to 1730

Access to building: Mon to Fri
Hours: Mon to Fri, 0900 to 1730

Member organisation of: European Organisation for Technical Approvals (EOTA); tel: +32 2 502 6900; fax: +32 2 502 3814; e-mail: info@eota.be; European Union of Agrément (UEATC); tel: 01923 665412; fax: 01923 665301; e-mail: jblaisdale@bba.star.co.uk

BRITISH BOTTLERS' INSTITUTE (BBI)

53 Basepoint, Caxton Close, Andover, Hampshire, SP10 3FG

Tel: 01264 326478
Fax: 01264 326477
E-mail: info@bbi.org.uk
Website: www.bbi.org.uk

Enquiries to: President
Direct e-mail: info@bbi.org.uk

Founded: 1953

Organisation type and purpose: Trade association

Subject coverage: Bottling, canning and packaging of beverages, including beers, mineral waters, soft drinks, fruit juices, ciders, wines, spirits

Access to staff: Contact by letter, by telephone, by fax, by e-mail and via website
Hours: Mon to Thu, 0930 to 1700

BRITISH BRICK SOCIETY (BBS)

19 Woodcroft Avenue, Stanmore, Middx, HA7 3PT

Tel: 020 8954 4976
E-mail: micksheila67@hotmail.com
Website: www.britishbricksoc.free-online.co.uk

Enquiries to: Honorary Secretary

Founded: 1972

Organisation type and purpose: Learned society (membership is by subscription), present number of members: c. 300.
To promote the study and recording of all aspects of the archaeology and history of bricks, brickmaking and brickwork.

Subject coverage: Historical aspects of brickmaking in the United Kingdom and of brickwork structures.

Publications: Printed

Access to staff: Contact by letter, by telephone, by fax and by e-mail
Hours: Mon to Fri, 0900 to 1700

Also at: Honorary Secretary; 9 Bailey Close, High Wycombe, Buckinghamshire, HP13 6QA; tel: 01494 520299; e-mail: michael@mhammett.freeserve.co.uk

Links with: British Archaeological Association, Brick Section

BRITISH BRYOLOGICAL SOCIETY (BBS)

6 Church View, Wootton, Northampton, NN4 7LJ

Website: www.britishbryologicalsociety.org.uk

Enquiries to: General Secretary

Founded: 1896

Organisation type and purpose: Learned society (membership is by subscription), present number of members: 600, registered charity (charity number 228851).
To promote a wide interest in bryology.

Subject coverage: Study and conservation of mosses and liverworts (bryophytes) worldwide.

Collection: Bryological library
Herbarium of approximately 30,000 dried specimens of bryophytes

Publications: Printed

Access to staff: Contact by letter
Hours: Mon to Fri, 0900 to 1700

BRITISH BUDDHIST ASSOCIATION (BBA)

The Buddhist Society, 58 Eccleston Square, London, SW1V 1PH

Tel: 020 7834 5858
Fax: 020 7976 5238
E-mail: info@thebuddhistsociety.org
Website: thebuddhistsociety.org/

Enquiries to: Director

Founded: 1974

Organisation type and purpose: Voluntary organisation.
Specialists in teaching and practice of early Buddhism. The BBA is non-sectarian and seeks to express devotion in ways suitable to Western practitioners.

Subject coverage: Educational, religious and meditation aspects of the Buddha's teaching. The Association promotes educational, religious and meditation aspects of the Buddha's teaching at evening and weekend sessions both in London and at country retreats, to augment private study and practice.

Access to staff: Contact by letter and by fax
Hours: Mon to Fri, 0900 to 1700

Access to building: Prior appointment required

BRITISH BULGARIAN CHAMBER OF COMMERCE (BBCC)

PO Box 123, Bromley, Kent, BR1 4ZX

Tel: 020 8464 5007
E-mail: info@bbcc.bg
Website: www.bbcc.bg

Enquiries to: Executive Director

Founded: 1993

Organisation type and purpose:
International organisation, membership association (membership is by subscription).

Subject coverage: Promotion of business between the United Kingdom and Bulgaria.

Publications: Electronic and video

Access to staff: Contact by e-mail
Hours: Mon to Fri, 0900 to 1700

Access to building: No access other than to staff

BRITISH BURN ASSOCIATION (BBA)

35–43 Lincoln's Inn Fields, London, WC2A 3PE

Tel: 020 7869 6923
Fax: 020 7869 6929
E-mail: info@britishburnassociation.org
Website: www.britishburnassociation.co.uk

Enquiries to: Honorary Secretary

Founded: 1967

Organisation type and purpose:
Professional body (membership is by subscription, qualification), registered charity (charity number 260167).
Disseminate knowledge and research into the care of, recovery from and prevention of burns.

Subject coverage: Burn prevention; burn treatment, care and rehabilitation.

Publications: Printed

Access to staff: Contact by letter, by telephone, by fax and by e-mail
Hours: Mon to Fri, 0900 to 1700

Affiliated to: International Society for Burn Injuries

BRITISH BUSINESS AWARDS ASSOCIATION

The Stables, Highfield Park, Creaton, Northampton, NN6 8NT

Tel: 01604 505480
Fax: 01604 505861
E-mail: info@bbaa.co.uk
Website: www.bbaa.co.uk/

Enquiries to: Information Officer

BRITISH BUTTON SOCIETY (BBS)

Angela Clark, 36 Avebury Avenue, Tonbridge, Kent TN9 1TQ

Tel: 01732 364309
E-mail: angelaclarkbuttons@btinternet.com
Website: www.britishbuttonsociety.org

Enquiries to: Secretary
Other contacts: Membership Secretary for information regarding membership.

Founded: 1976

Organisation type and purpose:
Membership association (membership is by subscription), present number of members: 350 (approx).
Members, collect and research the background to old, interesting buttons; uniform and dress.

Subject coverage: History of button manufacturers, collection and research into all types of buttons i.e. modern/antique dress, military/service uniform, all types of civilian uniform, livery. Not present day manufacturers or sources of supply.

Publications: Printed

Access to staff: Contact by letter
Hours: Mon to Fri, 0900 to 1700

Membership Secretary: British Button Society; Jersey Cottage, Parklands Road, Patchway, Bower Ashton, Bristol, BS3 2JR

BRITISH CABLES ASSOCIATION (BCA)

37a Walton Road, East Molesey, Surrey, KT8 0DH

Tel: 020 8941 4079
Fax: 020 8783 0104
Website: www.bcauk.org/

Enquiries to: Secretary General
Direct e-mail: peter.smeeth@btconnect.com

Organisation type and purpose: Trade association.

Subject coverage: Insulated cables.

Access to staff: Contact by e-mail
Hours: Mon to Fri, 0900 to 1700

Access to building: No access other than to staff

BRITISH CACTUS AND SUCCULENT SOCIETY (BCSS)

49 Chestnut Glen, Hornchurch, Essex, RM12 4HL

Tel: 01708 447778
Fax: 01444 454061
E-mail: bcss@bcss.org.uk
Website: www.bcss.org.uk

Enquiries to: Membership Secretary
Direct tel: 01455 614410
Direct e-mail: membership@bcss.org.uk
Other contacts: Secretary (for general enquiries); Publicity Officer

Founded: 1983

Organisation type and purpose: Learned society (membership is by subscription), present number of members: 3,500, registered charity (charity number 290786).
To educate the general public on all aspects of the subject.

Subject coverage: All aspects concerned with the growing, propagation and conservation of succulent plants.

Publications: Printed
Order printed publications from: Publications Manager, BCSS, Brenfield, Bolney Road, Ansty, West Sussex, RH17 5AW; tel: 01444 459151; fax: 01444 454061; e-mail: bcss@bcss.org.uk

Publications list: Available online

Access to staff: Contact by letter, by telephone, by fax, by e-mail and via website
Hours: Mon to Fri, 0900 to 1700

Access to building: No prior appointment required
Special comments: Members only for reference library, no borrowing.

Also at: Membership Secretary, British Cactus and Succulent Society; 6 Castlemaine Drive, Hinckley, Leicester, LE10 1RY; tel: 01455 614410; e-mail: membership@bcss.org.uk; website: http://www.bcss.org.uk

BRITISH CALCIUM CARBONATES FEDERATION (BCCF)

c/o Omya UK Ltd, Omya House, Stephensons Way, Wyvern Business Park, Chaddesden, Derby, DE21 6LY

Tel: 01332 887435
Fax: 01332 887049
E-mail: mike.nocivelli@omya.com
Website: www.calcium-carbonate.org.uk

Enquiries to: Secretary

Founded: 1943

Organisation type and purpose: Trade association.

Subject coverage: Calcium carbonates (chalk whiting), production and uses.

Publications: Printed

Access to staff: Contact by letter, by telephone, by fax and by e-mail
Hours: Mon to Fri, 0900 to 1700

BRITISH CANOE UNION (BCU)

18 Market Place, Bingham, Nottingham, NG13 8AP

Tel: 0845 370 9500

Fax: 0845 370 9501
E-mail: info@bcu.org.uk
Website: www.bcu.org.uk

Enquiries to: Chief Executive
Other contacts: PA to Chief Executive

Organisation type and purpose: Membership association (membership is by subscription), present number of members: 23,000.
Governing body for the sport and recreation of canoeing and kayaking.

Subject coverage: All aspects of canoeing.

Collection: Archival films

Publications: Printed

Access to staff: Contact by letter and by e-mail
Hours: Mon to Fri, 0900 to 1700

Access to building: No prior appointment required

Affiliated to: British Olympic Association; tel: 020 8871 2677; fax: 020 8871 9104; Central Council of Physical Recreation; tel: 020 7828 3163; fax: 020 7630 8820; Commonwealth Games Federation for England; tel: 020 7388 6643; fax: 020 7388 6744; European Canoe Association; International Canoe Federation

BRITISH CARTOGRAPHIC SOCIETY (BCS)

BCS Administration, 15, The Crescent, Stanley Common, Ilkeston, Derby, DE7 6 GL

Tel: 0115 9328684
Fax: 0115 9328684
E-mail: admin@cartography.org.uk
Website: www.cartography.org.uk

Enquiries to: Administrator

Founded: 1963

Organisation type and purpose: Learned society (membership is by subscription), present number of members: 700, registered charity (charity number 240034).
To promote the art and science of map-making.

Subject coverage: Cartography, history of cartography, map libraries curatorship, GIS, technical developments and automation in cartography, design, technology, education and careers in cartography.

Collection: Library housed at the National Library of Scotland
Exchange and subscription journals
Map design awards entries
Reference works

Publications: Printed
Order printed publications from: The Cartographic Journal from Maney Publishing, tel: 0113 243 2800; website: http://www.maney.co.uk
All other publications from the Administration address

Publications list: Available in print

Access to staff: Contact by letter, by telephone, by fax, by e-mail and via website
Hours: Mon to Fri, 0900 to 1700; answerphone when absent

Also at: British Cartographic Society (Administration); 15 The Crescent, Stanley Common, Ilkeston, Derby, DE7 6GL; tel: 0115 9328684; fax: 0115 9328684

BRITISH CARTON ASSOCIATION

Farringdon Point, 29–35 Farringdon Road, London, EC1M 3JF

Tel: 020 7915 8300
Fax: 020 7405 7785
Website: bpif.org.uk

Enquiries to: Manager
Direct e-mail: chris.selby@bpif.org.uk

Founded: 1933

Organisation type and purpose: Trade association.
To represent manufacturers of printed folding cartons.

Subject coverage: Cartons, folding cartons, carton board, employment affairs, technical, legal, training advice, statistics, health and safety, environment.

Trade and statistical information: Printing industry statistics, consumption and production of cartons

Publications: Printed

Publications list: Available in print

Access to staff: Contact by letter and by e-mail
Hours: Mon to Fri, 0900 to 1700

Affiliated to: British Printing Industries Federation; tel: 020 7915 8300; fax: 020 7405 7784

BRITISH CARTOON ARCHIVE (BCA)

Templeman Library, University of Kent, Canterbury, Kent, CT2 7NU

Tel: 01227 823127
Fax: 01227 823127
E-mail: j.m.newton@kent.ac.uk
Website: www.cartoons.ac.uk

Founded: 1973; formerly called Centre for the Study of Cartoons and Caricature

Organisation type and purpose: Created as a research centre and picture library with the objectives of conserving and cataloguing cartoons; encouraging research into all aspects and periods of cartooning; planning and promoting exhibitions of cartoon originals; and servicing teaching in a variety of disciplines.

Subject coverage: Cartoons.

Collection: Archive of 150,000 pieces of original cartoon artwork, plus 90,000 cuttings, with 140,000 cartoons available for viewing online in the database.
Library of more than 5,000 books, periodicals, cuttings, slides, videos and cassettes about cartoons, caricature and humour.

Non-library collection catalogue: All or part available online

Library catalogue: All or part available online

Publications list: Available online

Access to staff: Contact by letter, by telephone, by fax, by e-mail, in person and via website. Appointment necessary.
Hours: Mon to Fri, 0900 to 1700

Access to building: Varies during University terms and holidays

BRITISH CATTLE VETERINARY ASSOCIATION (BCVA)

BCVA, Unit B4, Pure Offices, Kestrel Court, Waterwells Drive, Quedgeley, Glos., GL2 2AT

Tel: 01452 260125
Fax: 01452 886484
E-mail: office@cattlevet.co.uk
Website: www.bcva.org.uk

Enquiries to: Secretariat

Organisation type and purpose: Learned society.

Subject coverage: Veterinary science related to cattle and cattle production.

Publications: Printed

Access to staff: Contact by letter, by telephone, by fax, by e-mail and via website
Hours: Mon to Fri, 0900 to 1700

Affiliated to: British Veterinary Association

BRITISH CAVE RESEARCH ASSOCIATION (BCRA)

The Old Methodist Chapel, Great Hucklow, Buxton, Derbyshire, SK17 8RG

Tel: 01298 873810
Fax: 01298 873801
E-mail: bcra-enquiries@bcra.org.uk
Website: www.bcra.org.uk

Enquiries to: Secretary

Founded: 1973

Organisation type and purpose: National organisation, membership association (membership is by subscription), present number of members: 1,000, registered charity (charity number 267828), research organisation, publishing house.
The national organisation for the study of sciences associated with caving, caves and karst.

Subject coverage: Speleology (British and foreign), biospeleology, hydrology, cave chemistry, physics and geophysics, cave archaeology and palaeontology, cave survey and photography, regional studies (NW Yorkshire, Derbyshire, Mendip, South Wales and Devon limestone regions), geology, geomorphology, erosion of limestones, cave rescue and medicine, ropes, ladders, lights.

Collection: National Caving Library, including old and rare works, British and foreign publications virtually a complete collection of published material on speleology

Non-library collection catalogue: All or part available in-house

Publications: Printed, and electronic and video
Order printed publications from: Publications Sales Officer, BCRA
Village Farm, Great Thirkleby, Thirsk, YO7 2AT, tel: 01845 501424

continued overleaf

Access to staff: Contact by letter, by telephone and by e-mail
Hours: Usually 0900 to 2100 but not guaranteed

Access to building: Prior appointment required for access to library
Hours: Mon to Fri, 0900 to 1700
Special comments: Contact: BCRA, Holt House, Holt Lane, Lea, Matlock, Derbyshire, DE4 5GQ, tel: 01629 534775, email: librarian@bcra.org.uk

Associated with the: British Caving Association

BRITISH CAVING ASSOCIATION (BCA)

The Old Methodist Chapel, Great Hucklow, Buxton, Derbyshire, SK17 8RG

E-mail: secretary@british-caving.org.uk
Website: www.british-caving.org.uk

Enquiries to: Publications and Information Officer
Direct e-mail: publications@british-caving.org.uk
Other contacts: Training coordinator for leadership qualification queries.

Founded: 1969

Organisation type and purpose: Advisory body, statutory body, membership association (membership is by subscription), present number of members: 5,000, voluntary organisation, training organisation.
Governing body of the sport of caving in the UK.

Subject coverage: Caving training and equipment, cave conservation and access, research and science, rescue, registry data, diving; mine history, overseas caving expeditions, caving in general, caving clubs.

Trade and statistical information: Statistics on caving accidents

Publications: Printed, and electronic and video

Publications list: Available online and in print

Access to staff: Contact by letter, by telephone, by e-mail, in person and via website
Hours: 24 hours every day
Special comments: Voluntary organisation, officers have other occupations.

Affiliated to: European Speleological Federation; International Speleological Union

Umbrella organisation of the: 5 Regional Caving Councils; British Cave Rescue Organisation; British Cave Research Association; National Association on Mining History Organisations; William Pengelly Cave Studies Trust

BRITISH CERAMIC CONFEDERATION (BCC)

Federation House, Station Road, Stoke-on-Trent, Staffordshire, ST4 2SA

Tel: 01782 744631
Fax: 01782 744102
E-mail: bcc@ceramfed.co.uk
Website: www.ceramfed.co.uk

Enquiries to: Chief Executive

Organisation type and purpose: Trade association.
Representative body for UK ceramics manufacturing industry.

Subject coverage: Ceramics manufacturing industry.

Publications: Printed

Access to staff: Contact by letter, by fax and by e-mail
Hours: Mon to Fri, 0900 to 1700
Special comments: No personal callers.
Information available to members only.

Links with: Cerame Unie

BRITISH CERAMIC PLANT AND MACHINERY MANUFACTURERS ASSOCIATION (BCPMMA)

P O Box 28, Biddulph, Stoke-on-Trent, United Kingdom, ST8 7AZ

Tel: 01782 513010
E-mail: sales@bcpmma.com

Founded: 1962

Organisation type and purpose: Trade association (membership is by subscription), present number of members: 75, manufacturing industry, publishing house. Exhibition Organisers.

Subject coverage: Plant, machinery and raw materials and/or turn-key projects for the manufacture of the complete range of ceramic products, including building bricks, sewer pipes, roofing/wall/floor tiles, tableware, sanitary ware, art pottery, porcelain insulators, refractories etc.

Publications: Printed

Access to staff: Contact by letter, by telephone, by fax, by e-mail, in person and via website. Appointment necessary. Access for members only. Non-members charged.
Hours: Mon to Fri, 0900 to 1700

Affiliated to: British Ceramic Confederation

BRITISH CHAMBERS OF COMMERCE (BCC)

65 Petty France, London, SW1H 9EU

Tel: 020 7654 5800
Fax: 020 7654 5819
E-mail: info@britishchambers.org.uk
Website: www.britishchambers.org.uk

Enquiries to: Managing Director
Direct e-mail: s.turvey@britishchambers.org.uk

Organisation type and purpose: Membership association.
Chamber of commerce.

Subject coverage: Export advice and guidance, international trade advice, links to local and overseas chambers of commerce.

Trade and statistical information: European economics.
UK economics and business statistics

Publications: Printed
Order printed publications from: 65 Petty France, St James's Park, London, SW1H 9EU

Publications list: Available online and in print

Access to staff: Contact by letter, by telephone, by fax, by e-mail and via website. Appointment necessary.
Hours: Mon to Fri, 0845 to 1645 (Coventry Office), 0900 to 1700 (London Office)

Parent body: The British Chambers of Commerce; 65 Petty France, St James Park, London, SW1H 9EU; tel: 020 7654 5800; fax: 020 7654 5819; e-mail: info@britishchambers.org.uk

BRITISH CHEMICAL ENGINEERING CONTRACTORS ASSOCIATION (BCECA)

1–4 Regent Street, London, SW1Y 4NR

Tel: 020 7839 6514
Fax: 020 7930 3466
E-mail: rod.dean@bceca.org.uk
Website: www.bceca.org.uk

Enquiries to: Director

Founded: 1966

Organisation type and purpose: Trade association (membership is by subscription, qualification, election or invitation), present number of members: 20.

Subject coverage: Process plant contracting and the activities of member companies, their qualifications and experience.

Trade and statistical information: Industry statistics, member companies order, intake and exports

Publications: Printed

Access to staff: Contact by letter, by telephone and by e-mail
Hours: Mon to Thu, 1000 to 1600

BRITISH CHINESE ARTISTS' ASSOCIATION (BCAA)

Tel: 020 7813 0086
Fax: 020 7482 5292

Enquiries to: Information Officer
Other contacts: Arts & Education for education work.

Founded: 1991

Organisation type and purpose: Voluntary organisation, registered charity (charity number 1059823), suitable for ages: 5+, training organisation, consultancy, research organisation.
To raise the profile of Chinese arts and artists through education for the public benefit through the promotion of the full spectrum of arts practised by artists of Chinese origins in Britain.

Subject coverage: Database of Chinese artists in London and UK, in performing arts, visual arts, design, music and film. Education projects, research, general advice to public, media sector.

Access to staff: Contact by letter, by telephone, by fax and by e-mail. Appointment necessary.
Hours: Mon to Fri, 0900 to 1700

BRITISH CHIROPODY AND PODIATRY ASSOCIATION (BChA)

The New Hall, Bath Road, Maidenhead, Berkshire, SL6 4LA

Tel: 01628 632449
Fax: 01628 674483
E-mail: smae_institute@compuserve.com

Enquiries to: Membership Secretary

Founded: 1959

Organisation type and purpose: Professional body (membership is by qualification, election or invitation), present number of members: over 10,000, service industry, training organisation, consultancy, research organisation, publishing house.

Subject coverage: Chiropody, chiropodists, podiatry, all matters pertaining to feet and footware care.

Publications: Printed

Publications list: Available in print

Access to staff: Contact by letter, by telephone, by fax, by e-mail and via website
Hours: Mon to Fri, 0900 to 1700

Access to building: No prior appointment required

Affiliated to: School of Surgical Chiropody

BRITISH CHIROPRACTIC ASSOCIATION (BCA)

59 Castle Street, Reading, Berkshire, RG1 7SN

Tel: 0118 950 5950
Fax: 0118 958 8946
E-mail: enquiries@chiropractic-uk.co.uk
Website: www.chiropractic-uk.co.uk

Enquiries to: Press Officer
Direct e-mail: jdoyle@publicasity.co.uk

Founded: 1925

Organisation type and purpose: Advisory body, statutory body, professional body (membership is by subscription), present number of members: 816, voluntary organisation.

Subject coverage: Chiropractic within the UK.

Collection: Library of resource material
Photographs and slides of chiropractors, their work and related topics

Publications: Printed

Access to staff: Contact by letter, by telephone, by fax, by e-mail and via website. Appointment necessary. Access for members only.
Hours: Mon to Fri, 0900 to 1700

Access to building: No access other than to staff

BRITISH CHRISTMAS TREE GROWERS ASSOCIATION (BCTGA)

Fynn Valley Farm, Main Road, Tuddenham St Martin, Ipswich, IP6 9BZ

Tel: 01473210519
E-mail: secretary@bctga.co.uk
Website: www.bctga.co.uk

Enquiries to: General Secretary

Founded: 1979

Organisation type and purpose: National organisation, trade association (membership is by subscription), present number of members: 380.
Promotion of real Christmas trees.

Subject coverage: Growing, cultivating and marketing real Christmas trees.

Publications: Printed

Access to staff: Contact by letter, by telephone, by fax and by e-mail. Appointment necessary.
Hours: Mon to Fri, 0900 to 1700

BRITISH CLEANING COUNCIL LIMITED (BCC Ltd)

PO Box 1328, Kidderminster, Worcestershire, DY11 5ZJ

Tel: 01562 851129
Fax: 01562 851129

Enquiries to: General Secretary/Treasurer
Direct e-mail: info@britishcleaningcouncil.org
Other contacts: Press Office, tel no: 01942 612616 for public relations

Founded: 1982

Organisation type and purpose: Trade association (membership is by election or invitation), research organisation.
Co-ordinating body for UK cleaning industry.

Subject coverage: All matters relating to cleaning and hygiene, including cleaning of buildings, internally and externally, and cleaning of outside areas.

Publications list: Available in print

Access to staff: Contact by letter, by telephone, by fax and by e-mail. Appointment necessary. Non-members charged.
Hours: Mon to Fri, 0900 to 1700

Member organisations: 18 member organisations

BRITISH CLOTHING INDUSTRY ASSOCIATION LIMITED (BCIA)

5 Portland Place, London, W1B 1PW

Tel: 020 7636 7788
Fax: 020 7636 7515
E-mail: bcia@dial.pipex.com

Enquiries to: Director

Organisation type and purpose: Trade association.

Subject coverage: Clothing industry.

Publications: Printed

BRITISH COFFEE ASSOCIATION (BCA)

British Coffee Association, PO Box 5, Chipping Norton, Oxfordshire, OX7 5UD

Tel: 01608 644 995
Fax: 01608 644 996
E-mail: info@britishcoffeeassociation.org
Website: www.britishcoffeeassociation.org/

Enquiries to: Executive Secretary

Founded: 2001; amalgamated with Coffee Trade Federation (year of change 2008); created by the merger of British Soluble Coffee Manufacturers' Association (BSCMA) and the Roast and Ground Coffee Association (RGCA)

Organisation type and purpose: Trade association.

Subject coverage: Representative organisation for the UK coffee trade and industry; promotes and safeguards members' interests in all matters relating to the growth, preparation, shipment, warehousing, transport, insurance, manufacturing, distribution and consumption of coffee.

Access to staff: Access for members only.
Hours: Mon to Fri, 0900 to 1700

Member of: Food and Drink Federation

BRITISH COLOSTOMY ASSOCIATION (BCA)

15 Station Road, Reading, Berkshire, RG1 1LG

Tel: 0118 939 1537
Fax: 0118 956 9095
E-mail: sue@bcass.org.uk
Website: www.bcass.org.uk

Enquiries to: Secretary

Founded: 1967

Organisation type and purpose: Membership association, voluntary organisation, registered charity (charity number 298299).
25 area organisers, to help people who have, or are about to have, a colostomy.

Subject coverage: Help and advice to anyone who has, or is about to have, a colostomy.

Publications: Printed

Publications list: Available in print

Access to staff: Contact by letter, by telephone, by fax, by e-mail and via website. Appointment necessary.
Hours: Mon to Thu, 0900 to 1700; Fri, 0900 to 1500

Access to building: Prior appointment required

Connections with: Macmillan Cancer Relief (MCR); tel: 020 7840 7840; fax: 020 7840 7841; website: http://www.macmillan.org.uk

BRITISH COMPLEMENTARY MEDICINE ASSOCIATION (BCMA)

PO Box 5122, Bournemouth, BH8 0WG

Tel: 0845 345 5977
E-mail: office@bcma.co.uk
Website: www.bcma.co.uk

Enquiries to: Administrator

Founded: 1992

Organisation type and purpose: National organisation, professional body, membership association (membership is by subscription, qualification), present number of members: 86 organisations, voluntary organisation.

continued overleaf

Subject coverage: Complementary therapies and therapists.

Publications: Printed

Access to staff: Contact by letter, by telephone, by e-mail and via website
Hours: Mon, Tue, Thu and Fri, 1000 to 1700

Access to building: No access other than to staff

BRITISH COMPRESSED AIR SOCIETY (BCAS)

33 Devonshire Street, London, W1G 6PY

Tel: 020 7935 2464
Fax: 020 7935 3077
E-mail: enquiries@bcas.org.uk
Website: www.bcas.org.uk

Enquiries to: Executive Director

Organisation type and purpose: Trade association.
Technical body for the compressed air industry.

Subject coverage: Compressed air, gas and vacuum equipment and use; European and British legislation affecting the industry.

Publications: Printed

Publications list: Available in print

Access to staff: Contact by letter, by telephone, by fax and by e-mail. Appointment necessary.
Hours: Mon to Fri, 0900 to 1700

BRITISH COMPRESSED GASES ASSOCIATION (BCGA)

British Compressed Gases Association, 4A Mallard Way, Pride Park, Derby, DE24 8GX

Tel: 01332 225120
Fax: 01332 225101
E-mail: enquiries@bcga.co.uk
Website: www.bcga.co.uk

Enquiries to: Secretary

Founded: 1971

Organisation type and purpose: National organisation, trade association.
Representation of about 35 companies who manufacture or distribute gases, or manufacture cylinders to contain them or equipment to use them. It does not represent the interests of the compressed air or natural gas industries.

Subject coverage: Compressed and liquefied industrial, medical and food gases e.g. oxygen, nitrogen, carbon dioxide, acetylene, chlorine etc; cylinders, regulators, valves etc; safety in handling, transport and use.

Publications: Printed

Publications list: Available online

Access to staff: Contact by e-mail
Hours: Mon to Fri, 0900 to 1700

Affiliated to: European Industrial Gases Association (EIGA)

BRITISH COMPUTER ASSOCIATION OF THE BLIND (BCAB)

c/o RNIB, 58–72 John Bright Street, Birmingham, B1 1BN

Tel: 0845 643 9811
E-mail: secretary@bcab.org.uk
Website: www.bcab.org.uk

Enquiries to: Administrator

Founded: 1969

Organisation type and purpose: National government body, professional body, membership association (membership is by subscription, qualification), present number of members: 400, voluntary organisation, registered charity (charity number SCO232324), suitable for ages: all, training organisation.
A society pursuing all matters of interest to blind people in the computer field.

Subject coverage: Training, advice on computer access devices for the visually impaired, support groups.

Information services: General advice on website and access to user group for members, plus monthly helpline.

Education services: We organise seminars on subjects, usually attached to our AGM and we have a series of Get to Grips with... CDs.

Publications: Printed, and electronic and video

Access to staff: Contact by letter, by telephone, by fax and by e-mail
Hours: Mon to Fri, 0900 to 1700

Access to building: No access other than to staff.

BRITISH COMPUTER SOCIETY (BCS)

1st Floor, Block D, North Star House, North Star Avenue, Swindon, SN2 1FA

Tel: 01793 417417
Fax: 01793 417444
E-mail: bcsacademy@hq.bcs.org.uk
Website: www.bcs.org.uk

Enquiries to: Public Relations Manager
Direct tel: 01793 417433
Direct e-mail: aduckworth@hq-bcs.org.uk

Founded: 1957

Organisation type and purpose: Professional body.

Subject coverage: Computers and their applications, commercial data processing, programming and programming languages, information technology, safety-critical and business-critical systems, computers for the disabled and computer misuse (including hacking and viruses).

Collection: The Society's Library is online

Library catalogue: All or part available online

Publications: Printed

Publications list: Available in print

Access to staff: Contact by letter, by telephone, by fax and by e-mail
Hours: Mon to Fri, 0915 to 1715

Associated with: numerous similar Information Technology Societies

Member of: Council of European Professional Information Societies

UK member of: IFIP

BRITISH CONSTRUCTIONAL STEELWORK ASSOCIATION LIMITED (BCSA)

Head Office, 4 Whitehall Court, Westminster, London, SW1A 2ES

Tel: 020 7839 8566
Fax: 020 7976 1634
E-mail: postroom@steelconstruction.org
Website: www.steelconstruction.org

Enquiries to: Director General
Direct fax: 020 7839 4729
Direct e-mail: derek.tordoff@steelconstruction.org

Founded: 1906

Organisation type and purpose: Trade association.

Subject coverage: Constructional steelwork.

Publications list: Available online and in print

Access to staff: Contact by letter, by telephone, by fax and by e-mail
Hours: Mon to Fri, 0900 to 1700

BRITISH CONTRACT FURNISHING ASSOCIATION (BCFA)

Project House, 25 West Wycombe Road, High Wycombe, Buckinghamshire, HP11 2LQ

Tel: 01494 896790
Fax: 01494 896779
E-mail: enquiries@bcfa.org.uk
Website: www.thebcfa.com

Enquiries to: Chief Executive

Founded: 1970

Organisation type and purpose: Trade association.

Subject coverage: British manufacture or supply of goods and services for the contract furnishing sector.

Publications: Printed
Order printed publications from: BCFA

Access to staff: Contact by telephone, by fax, by e-mail and via website
Hours: Mon to Fri, 0900 to 1700

Access for disabled people: Ramped entry

BRITISH COPYRIGHT COUNCIL (BCC)

29–33 Berners Street, London, W1T 3AB

Tel: 01986 788122
E-mail: info@britishcopyright.org
Website: www.britishcopyright.org

Enquiries to: Secretary

Organisation type and purpose: Membership association (membership is by subscription), present number of members: 31.
Liaison committee.
Discussion forum for the Council's member associations on matters of common concern relating to copyright in literary, musical, dramatic and artistic works.

Subject coverage: Copyright and rights in performances in the UK.

Access to staff: Contact by letter and by e-mail

BRITISH CORRESPONDENCE CHESS ASSOCIATION (BCCA)

6 Milner Avenue, Penistone, Sheffield, S36 9DB

Tel: 01226 763536
E-mail: neil.limbert@tiscali.co.uk
Website: www.bcca.info

Enquiries to: General Secretary

Founded: 1906

Organisation type and purpose:
Membership association (membership is by subscription), present number of members: 220, voluntary organisation.

Subject coverage: Internet chess, postal chess, e-mail chess and chess in general.

Collection: Archive of Minutes 1906 to date; Archive of Yearbooks & Magazines 1910 to date.

Publications: Printed

Access to staff: Contact by letter, by telephone, by e-mail and via website
Hours: Mon to Fri, 0900 to 1700

Links with: British Federation for Correspondence Chess; tel: 01206 542753

BRITISH COUNCIL – INFORMATION CENTRE (BC)

Bridgewater House, 58 Whitworth Street, Manchester, M1 6BB

Tel: 0161 957 7755, 0161 957 7188 (minicom)
Fax: 0161 957 7762
E-mail: general.enquiries@britishcouncil.org
Website: www.britishcouncil.org

Founded: 1934

Organisation type and purpose:
International organisation, service industry, registered charity (charity number 209131).
Non-government organisation.
Promoting art, cultural, and educational co-operation between Britain and other countries.

Subject coverage: British education system, English language teaching and learning, higher education courses, English literature, visual arts, science and technology education, overseas development, work of the British Council overseas, environment, government, law and social development.

Collection: The unit holds small collections of leaflets, prospectuses, reports, etc. in its fields of interest, but it has no major holdings of books or runs of periodicals

Publications: Printed

Access to staff: Contact by letter, by telephone, by fax, by e-mail and via website
Hours: Mon to Fri, 1000 to 1645

Access to building: No access other than to staff
Hours: Mon to Fri, 1000 to 1700

Funded by: Foreign and Commonwealth Office

BRITISH COUNCIL – VISUAL ARTS DEPARTMENT

10 Spring Gardens, London, SW1A 2BN

Tel: 020 7389 3050
Fax: 020 7389 3101
E-mail: visual.arts@britishcouncil.org
Website: www.britishcouncil.org/arts

Enquiries to: Resources Officer
Other contacts: Research Officer for bibliographic enquiries.

Founded: 1934

Organisation type and purpose:
International organisation, national organisation, registered charity (charity number 209131).
To develop and enlarge overseas knowledge and appreciation of British achievements in the fields of contemporary visual art.

Subject coverage: Painting, sculpture, printmaking, design, photography, crafts, architecture, video, installation, performance.

Collection: Art collection specialising in British Art, especially post-1945

Non-library collection catalogue: All or part available online, in-house and in print

Library catalogue: All or part available online and in-house

Publications: Printed
Order printed publications from: Cornerhouse Publications
70 Oxford Street, Manchester, M1 5NH, tel: 0161 200 1503, fax: 0161 200 1504, e-mail: publications@cornerhouse.org

Publications list: Available online

Access to staff: Appointment necessary.
Hours: Mon to Fri, 1000 to 1700
Special comments: Library: by appointment only.
Art Collection: online only.

Access to building: By appointment only
Hours: Mon to Fri, 1000 to 1700

BRITISH COUNCIL EDUCATION AND TRAINING GROUP

10 Spring Gardens, London, SW1A 2BN

Tel: 0161 957 7755
Fax: 0161 957 7762
E-mail: general.enquiries@britishcouncil.org
Website: www.educationuk.org
Website: www.globalgateway.org
Website: www.britishcouncil.org/learning

Enquiries to: Information Officer
Other contacts: Director

Organisation type and purpose:
International organisation, registered charity (charity number 209131).
The British Council Education and Training Group promotes and enhances quality education and training in the UK and world-wide by strengthening education, training and youth co-operation between the UK and other countries; increasing international recognition of the range and quality of learning opportunities, including English language teaching, provided by the UK; supporting education and training reform; sharing creativity, innovation and best practice between the UK and other countries; delivering a range of quality programmes in international education, training, youth and sport.

Subject coverage: For international students: information and advice on studying in the UK and on British courses, qualifications and examinations.
For the UK education and training field: information and advice on working internationally, setting up educational partnerships, international professional development and exchange opportunities, the promotion of UK education and training overseas.

Access to staff: Contact by letter, by telephone, by fax, by e-mail and via website
Hours: Mon to Fri, 1000 to 1645

Also at: Belfast Office; Norwich Union Building, 7 Fountain Street, Belfast, BT1 5EG; tel: 028 9024 8220; fax: 028 9023 7592; Cardiff Office; 1 Kingsway, Cardiff, CF10 3AQ; tel: 029 2092 4300; fax: 029 2092 4301; Edinburgh Office; 3rd Floor, The Tun, 4 Jackson's Entry, Holyrood Road, Edinburgh, EH8 8PJ; tel: 0131 524 5700; fax: 0131 524 5701; Manchester Office; Bridgewater House, 58 Whitworth Street, Manchester, M1 6BB; tel: 0161 957 7755; fax: 0161 957 7762

Parent body: British Council; 10 Spring Gardens, London, SW1A 2BN

BRITISH COUNCIL FOR OFFICES (BCO)

78–79 Leadenhall Street, London, EC3A 3DH

Tel: 020 7283 0125
Fax: 020 7626 1553
E-mail: mail@bco.org.uk
Website: www.bco.org.uk

Enquiries to: Chief Executive
Other contacts: Assistant Secretary

Founded: 1990

Organisation type and purpose:
Membership association (membership is by subscription), present number of members: 1,553.
The British Council for Offices' mission is to research, develop and communicate best practice in all aspects of the office sector. It delivers this by providing a forum for the discussion and debate of relevant issues.

Publications: Printed
Order printed publications from: website: http://www.bco.org.uk/research

Publications list: Available online

Access to staff: Contact by letter, by telephone, by fax, by e-mail and via website. Appointment necessary.
Hours: Mon to Fri, 0930 to 1730

BRITISH COUNCIL FOR PREVENTION OF BLINDNESS (BCPB)

4 Bloomsbury Square, London, WC1A 2RP

Tel: 020 7404 7114
E-mail: info@BCPB.org
Website: www.bcpb.org

Founded: 1976

continued overleaf

Organisation type and purpose: Registered charity (number 270941).
Funds both UK-based and overseas research into the causes of blindness throughout the world, together with specific community-based disease prevention projects in developing countries. Also funds the training of eyecare professionals from developing countries through Fellowship programmes.

Subject coverage: Prevention of blindness.

Access to staff: Contact by letter, by telephone and by e-mail

BRITISH COUNCIL OF CHINESE MARTIAL ARTS

c/o 110 Frensham Drive, Nuneaton, Warwickshire, CV10 9QL

Tel: 024 7639 4642
E-mail: enquiries@bccma.com
Website: www.bccma.com

Enquiries to: Secretary General

Organisation type and purpose: Membership association (membership is by subscription, qualification).
Governing body of the sport.

Subject coverage: Traditional Chinese martial arts, freestyle martial arts, Tai Chi and Chi Gung and Chinese boxing (Sanshou).

Access to staff: Contact by letter, by telephone, by e-mail and via website
Hours: Mon to Fri, 1000 to 1600

Affiliated to: European Wu Shu Federation; International Wu Shu Federation

Member of: Sports Council

BRITISH COUNCIL OF DISABLED PEOPLE (BCODP)

Suites 1–2, Litchurch Plaza, Litchurch Lane, Derby, DE24 8AA

Tel: 01332 295551, 01332 295581 (minicom)
Fax: 01332 295580
E-mail: bcodp@bcodp.org.uk
Website: www.bcodp.org.uk

Enquiries to: Chief Executive

Founded: 1981

Organisation type and purpose: Registered charity.

Subject coverage: Campaigning and lobbying, representing the interests of disabled people at national level and above; supporting new and existing organisations run by and for disabled people to represent their interests.

Publications: Printed

Publications list: Available in print

Access to staff: Contact by letter, by telephone, by fax and by e-mail
Hours: Mon to Fri, 0900 to 1700

Access for disabled people: Parking provided, ramped entry, access to all public areas, toilet facilities

BRITISH COUNCIL OF SHOPPING CENTRES (BCSC)

1 Queen Anne's Gate, Westminster, London, SW1H 9BT

Tel: 0845 270 0775
Fax: 020 7227 3452
E-mail: info@bcsc.org.uk
Website: www.bcsc.org.uk

Enquiries to: Head of Secretariat
Other contacts: Events Manager for BCSC Events.

Founded: 1984

Organisation type and purpose: Membership association.
To provide a forum for all those involved in the development and management of shopping centres.

Subject coverage: Matters relating to shopping centres.

Publications list: Available in print

Access to staff: Contact by letter, by telephone and by e-mail
Hours: Mon to Fri, 0900 to 1730

Access to building: No access other than to staff

BRITISH CROWN GREEN BOWLING ASSOCIATION (BCGBA)

94 Fishers Lane, Pensby, Wirral, Merseyside, CH61 8SB

Tel: 0151 648 5740
Fax: 0151 648 0733
E-mail: jac21up@aol.com
Website: www.bowls.org

Enquiries to: Chief Executive
Other contacts: Financial Officer

Founded: 1907

Organisation type and purpose: Membership association.
Governing body of crown green bowls.

Subject coverage: Crown green bowls; coaching; manufacture and maintenance of crown greens.

Publications: Printed

Access to staff: Contact by letter, by telephone and by fax
Hours: Mon to Fri, 0900 to 1700

BRITISH CUTLERY AND SILVERWARE ASSOCIATION (BCSA)

Unit 10 Edmund Road Business Centre, Sheffield, S2 4ED

Tel: 0114 252 7550
Fax: 0114 252 7555
E-mail: enquiries@secas.co.uk
Website: www.secas.co.uk

Enquiries to: Chief Executive

Organisation type and purpose: Trade association.

Subject coverage: Trade marks, patterns, care of cutlery and silverware, sources of supply.

Publications: Printed

BRITISH CYCLING FEDERATION (BCF)

National Cycling Centre, Stuart Street, Manchester, M11 4DQ

Tel: 0161 274 2000
Fax: 0161 274 2001
E-mail: info@britishcycling.org.uk
Website: new.britishcycling.org.uk

Enquiries to: Company Secretary
Direct tel: 0161 274 2038

Founded: 1959

Organisation type and purpose: Membership association (membership is by subscription), present number of members: 32,000.
Promotional and governing body for the sport and pastime of cycling.

Subject coverage: All forms of cycling, including cycle racing, coaching, touring, leisure cycling.

Publications: Printed

Access to staff: Contact by letter, by telephone, by fax, by e-mail, in person and via website. Non-members charged.
Hours: Mon to Thu, 0845 to 1700; Fri, 0845 to 1545

Access for disabled people: Access to all public areas

BRITISH DANCE COUNCIL (BDC)

Terpsichore House, 240 Merton Road, South Wimbledon, London, SW19 1EQ

Tel: 020 8545 0085
Fax: 020 8545 0225
E-mail: secretary@british-dance-council.org
Website: www.british-dance-council.org

Enquiries to: Company Secretary
Direct e-mail: secretary@british-dance-council.org

Founded: 1929

Organisation type and purpose: Membership association.
Official Board of Ballroom Dancing.
Promotion and regulation of ballroom and Latin American dancing, dance sport and social dancing in Great Britain.

Subject coverage: Ballroom and Latin American dancing.

Publications: Printed
Order printed publications from: BDC, 240 Merton Road, London, SW19 1EQ

Publications list: Available in print

Access to staff: Contact by letter, by telephone, by fax, by e-mail and via website
Hours: Mon to Fri, 1000 to 1600

Corporate member: ADFP; tel: 01543 577440; e-mail: mail@adfp.co.uk; Allied Dancing Association; tel: 0151 7241829; Associated Board of Dance; tel: 0121 694 0012; e-mail: abd.hq@hotmail.com; Blackpool Council, CECL; tel: 01253 625252; British Association of Teachers of Dancing; tel: 0141 427 3699; Dancesport Scotland; tel: 0141 563 2001; e-mail: fraser.hillfoot@ntlworld.com; Dancesport Wales; tel: 01443 691978; e-mail: m.webley@homecall.co.uk; Imperial Society of Teachers of Dancing; tel: 020 7377 1577; International Dance Teachers Association; tel: 01273 685652/3; fax: 01273

674388; e-mail: inf@idta.co.uk; National Association of Teachers of Dancing; tel: 01635 868888; fax: 01635 872301; Northern Counties Dance Teachers' Association; tel: 0191 268 1830; Scottish Dance Teachers' Alliance; tel: 0141 339 8944; United Kingdom Alliance; tel: 01253 408828; fax: 01253 408066

BRITISH DARTS ORGANISATION (BDO)

2 Pages Lane, Muswell Hill, London, N10 1PS

Tel: 020 8883 5544
Fax: 020 8883 0109
E-mail: britishdarts.org@btconnect.com
Website: www.bdodarts.com

Enquiries to: Director

Founded: 1973

Organisation type and purpose:
Membership association (membership is by subscription), voluntary organisation.
Incorporates 66 member county darts organisations in England, Scotland and Wales; plus associations with over 60 countries worldwide.
Promoters of darts.

Subject coverage: Promotion and organisation of the sport of darts at all levels, i.e. local darts league, Inter County Championships and International and World Championships; rules and regulations governing the sport of darts (updated annually). Promoters of the BBC televised Lakeside World Professional Darts Championships and Winmau World Masters annually.

Publications: Printed

Access to staff: Contact by letter
Hours: Mon to Fri, 0900 to 1700

Member of: Central Council of Physical Recreation; World Darts Federation (WDF)

BRITISH DEAF ASSOCIATION (BDA)

18 Leather Lane, London, EC1N 7SU

Tel: 020 7405 0090
E-mail: admin@bda.org.uk
Website: www.bda.org.uk

Founded: 1890

Organisation type and purpose:
Membership association, voluntary organisation, registered charity.
Membership-led charity campaigning on behalf of nearly 70,000 deaf people in Britain.
To advance and protect the interests of the Deaf Community, to increase deaf people's access to the facilities and lifestyles of hearing people, and to ensure a greater awareness of their rights and responsibilities as members of society.

Subject coverage: Profound deafness; British sign language; deaf community, culture and heritage.

Publications: Printed

Publications list: Available online

Access to staff: Contact by letter, by telephone, by fax, by e-mail, in person and via website
Hours: Mon to Fri, 0900 to 1700
Textphone also available during evening hours.
Special comments: Voice and textphone also available for access.

Access for disabled people: Level entry, toilet facilities

Has regional offices in: Belfast, Cardiff, Glasgow and Preston

Representative organisation of UK on the: European Union of the Deaf; World Federation of the Deaf (affiliated to the United Nations)

BRITISH DEAF HISTORY SOCIETY (BDHS)

11–13 Wilson Patten Road, Warrington, Cheshire, WA1 1PG

Tel: 01925 632463
E-mail: info.bdhs@btconnect.com
Website: www.bdhs.org.uk

Organisation type and purpose:
Membership organisation focusing on history related to deafness.

Subject coverage: History related to deafness.

BRITISH DEAF SPORTS COUNCIL (BDSC)

Bridge Street, Otley, West Yorkshire, LS21 1B

Tel: 01943 850214 / Minicom: 01943 850081
Fax: 01943 850828
E-mail: enquiries@britishdeafsportscouncil.org.uk
Website: www.britishdeafsportscouncil.org.uk/

Enquiries to: Administrator

Founded: 1930

Organisation type and purpose:
Membership association (membership is by subscription), registered charity (charity number 1014541).

Subject coverage: Sports for hearing impaired people.

Access to staff: Contact by letter, by telephone and by fax
Hours: Mon to Thu, 0930 to 1330 and 1430 to 1730; Fri, 0930 to 1330 and 1430 to 1700
Special comments: Stamped addressed envelope preferred.

BRITISH DEER FARMERS ASSOCIATION (BDFA)

Old Stoddah, Penruddock, Penrith, Cumbria, CA11 0RY

Tel: 01768 483810
Fax: 01768 483809
E-mail: info@bdfpa.org
Website: www.deer.org.uk

Enquiries to: Secretary

Organisation type and purpose: National organisation, trade association (membership is by subscription).
National association representing deer farmers and venison processors.

Subject coverage: Deer farming; farmed venison.

Publications: Printed

Access to staff: Contact by e-mail and via website
Hours: Mon to Fri, 0900 to 1700

BRITISH DENTAL ASSOCIATION (BDA)

64 Wimpole Street, London, W1G 8YS

Tel: 020 7563 4545
Fax: 020 7935 6492
E-mail: r.farbey@bda.org
Website: www.bda.org

Enquiries to: Librarian
Other contacts: Head of Library Services

Founded: 1880

Organisation type and purpose: National organisation, professional body (membership is by subscription).

Subject coverage: Dentistry and the dental profession.

Collection: Rare historical dental texts, DVD and video collection.

Publications: Printed

Access to staff: Contact by letter. Appointment necessary. Letter of introduction required.
Hours: Mon to Fri, 0900 to 1800

Access to building: Prior appointment required for non-members, except to museum
Hours: Mon to Fri, 0900 to 1800

BRITISH DENTAL HEALTH FOUNDATION (BDHF)

Smile House, 2 East Union Street, Rugby, Warwickshire, CV22 6AJ

Tel: 01788 546 365
Fax: 01788 541 982
E-mail: mail@dentalhealth.org
Website: www.dentalhealth.org.uk
Website: www.dentalhelpline.org

Enquiries to: Public Relations Department
Direct tel: 0870 770 4014
Direct e-mail: pr@dentalhealth.org.uk

Founded: 1971

Organisation type and purpose:
International organisation (membership is by subscription, election or invitation), present number of members: 1,400, voluntary organisation, registered charity (charity number 263198).
To promote dental health to the public.

Subject coverage: Free, impartial and independent advice on dental health for the public and the media.

Library catalogue: All or part available online and in print

Publications: Printed, and electronic and video

Publications list: Available online and in print

Access to staff: Contact by letter, by telephone, by fax and by e-mail
Hours: Mon to Fri, 0900 to 1700

BRITISH DISABLED WATER SKI ASSOCIATION (BDWSA)

The Tony Edge National Centre, Heron Lake, Hythe End, Wraysbury, Middlesex, TW19 6HW

Tel: 01784 483664
Fax: 01784 482747
E-mail: southern@bdwsa.org
Website: www.bdwsa.org

Enquiries to: Honorary Secretary
Other contacts: Chairman

Founded: 1979

Organisation type and purpose:
Membership association (membership is by subscription), present number of members: 200, registered charity (charity number 1063678).
Teaching disabled people to water ski.

Subject coverage: Tuition and equipment for disabled water skiers.

Publications: Printed

Publications list: Available in print

Access to staff: Contact by letter, by telephone, by fax, by e-mail, in person and via website
Hours: Mon to Fri, 0900 to 1700

Access for disabled people: Parking provided, level entry, access to all public areas, toilet facilities

Parent body: British Water Ski Federation; 390 City Road, London, EC1V 2QA; tel: 020 7833 2856

BRITISH DRAGON BOAT RACING ASSOCIATION (BDA)

13 The Prebend, Northend, Southam, Warwickshire, CV47 2TR

Tel: 01295 770734
Fax: 01295 770734
E-mail: dacogswell@aol.com
Website: www.dragonboat.com

Enquiries to: Company Secretary and Treasurer

Founded: 1987

Organisation type and purpose: National government body, membership association (membership is by subscription), present number of members: 867, voluntary organisation.
Governing body of the sport.

Subject coverage: The BDA in general, dragon boat racing, boats, sponsoring of dragon boat racing, dragon boat purchase and specification, dragon boat events.

Publications: Printed

Access to staff: Contact by letter, by telephone, by fax, by e-mail and via website
Hours: Mon to Fri, 0900 to 2100

Access to building: Prior appointment required

Parent body: International Dragon Boat Federation; HKTA , 35th Floor, Jardine House, Central, Hong Kong

Subsidiary body: Dragon Boats UK

BRITISH DRILLING ASSOCIATION LIMITED (BDA)

Wayside, 55 London End, Upper Boddington, Daventry, Northamptonshire, NN11 6DP

Tel: 01327 264622
Fax: 01327 264623
E-mail: office@britishdrillingassociation.co.uk
Website: www.britishdrillingassociation.co.uk

Enquiries to: Executive Secretary

Founded: 1975

Organisation type and purpose:
Professional body, trade association.

Subject coverage: Ground drilling, including ground investigation, ground improvement, water well drilling, mining and quarrying, mineral exploration and some aspects of tunnelling.

Publications: Printed

Access to staff: Contact by letter, by telephone, by fax, by e-mail and via website
Hours: Mon to Fri, 0900 to 1700

BRITISH DRIVING SOCIETY (BDS)

83 New Road, Helmingham, Stowmarket, Suffolk, IP14 6EA

Tel: 01473 892001
Fax: 01473 892005
E-mail: email@britishdrivingsociety.co.uk
Website: www.britishdrivingsociety.co.uk

Enquiries to: Executive Secretary

Founded: 1957

Organisation type and purpose:
Membership association (membership is by subscription), present number of members: 6,000, voluntary organisation.
To encourage and assist those interested in the driving of horses and ponies.

Subject coverage: Driving of horses and ponies.

Publications: Printed

Publications list: Available online and in print

Access to staff: Contact by letter, by telephone, by fax, by e-mail and via website
Hours: Mon to Fri, 0900 to 1700

Affiliated to: Joint National Horse Education and Training Council

BRITISH DYSLEXIA ASSOCIATION (BDA)

Unit 8, Bracknell Beeches, Old Bracknell Lane, Bracknell, RG12 7BW

Tel: 0845 251 9002 (helpline); 0845 251 9003 (office)
Fax: 0845 215 9005
E-mail: helpline@bdadyslexia.org.uk
Website: www.bdadyslexia.org.uk

Founded: 1960

Organisation type and purpose:
Membership association, voluntary organisation, registered charity (charity number 289243), training organisation.
Co-ordinates 120 independent local associations.

Subject coverage: Dyslexia; education and training for the young, adults and professionals in education, health and employment, medical and psychological information. The charity offers advice, information and help to dyslexic people, their families and the professionals who support them, and works to raise awareness and understanding and to effect change.

Publications: Printed

Publications list: Available online and in print

Access to staff: Contact by letter, by telephone, by fax, by e-mail and via website
Hours: Mon to Fri, 1000 to 1600; Wed, 1700 to 1900

Member organisations: local dyslexia associations and corporate members

BRITISH EARTH SHELTERING ASSOCIATION (BESA)

15 Maes-y-Fron Terrace, Abercrave, Swansea Valley, SA9 1XE

Tel: 01639 730006
E-mail: caerllan@compuserve.com, undergroundwoods@hotmail.co.uk
Website: besa-uk.org/

Enquiries to: Honorary Secretary

Founded: 1981

Organisation type and purpose:
Membership association.

Subject coverage: Design and construction of earth sheltering structures, energy efficiency and architecture.

Publications: Printed

Access to staff: Contact by letter, by telephone, by fax, by e-mail and via website. Appointment necessary.
Hours: Mon to Fri, 0900 to 1700

BRITISH ECOLOGICAL SOCIETY (BES)

Charles Darwin House, 12 Roger Street, London, WC1N 2JU

Tel: 020 7685 2500
Fax: 020 7685 2501
E-mail: info@britishecologicalsociety.org
Website: www.BritishEcologicalSociety.org

Enquiries to: Executive Director

Founded: 1913

Organisation type and purpose: Learned society.
To promote the science of ecology through research, and to use the findings of such research to educate the public and influence policy decisions that involve ecological matters.

Subject coverage: Ecology, as a branch of natural science.

Publications: Printed, and electronic and video

Publications list: Available in print

Access to staff: Contact by letter, by telephone, by fax and by e-mail

BRITISH EDITORIAL SOCIETY OF BONE AND JOINT SURGERY (BESBJS)

22 Buckingham Street, London, WC2N 6ET

Tel: 020 7782 0010
Fax: 020 7782 0995
E-mail: info@jbjs.org.uk
Website: www.jbjs.org.uk

Enquiries to: Managing Director
Other contacts: Circulations Manager (for ordering subscriptions)

Founded: 1948

Organisation type and purpose: Registered charity (charity number 209299), publishing house.
The advancement and improvement of education in orthopaedic surgery and allied branches of surgery.

Subject coverage: Bone and joint surgery.

Collection: Watson-Jones Library Bequest

Non-library collection catalogue: All or part available online

Library catalogue: All or part available in-house

Publications: Printed, and electronic and video, and microform publications

Publications list: Available online and in print

Access to staff: Contact by letter, by telephone, by fax, by e-mail and via website. Appointment necessary.
Hours: Mon to Fri, 0900 to 1700

Access to building: Prior appointment required

BRITISH EDUCATIONAL SUPPLIERS ASSOCIATION LIMITED (BESA)

20 Beaufort Court, Admirals Way, London, E14 9XL

Tel: 020 7537 4997
Fax: 020 7537 4846
E-mail: besa@besa.org.uk
Website: www.besa.org.uk

Enquiries to: Information Manager / Research Assistant

Founded: 1933

Organisation type and purpose: Trade association.

Subject coverage: Educational equipment and materials, home and export.

Publications: Printed, and electronic and video

Access to staff: Contact by letter, by telephone, by fax, by e-mail and via website
Hours: Mon to Fri, 0900 to 1700

Special interest group the: British Educational Distributors and Contractors Group; British Educational Furniture Manufacturers Group; Educational Software Publishers Association

BRITISH ELASTIC ROPE SPORTS ASSOCIATION (BERSA)

33a Canal Street, Oxford, OX2 6BQ

Tel: 01865 311179
Fax: 01865 426007
E-mail: info@bersa.org
Website: www.bersa.org

Enquiries to: Chairman

Founded: 1989

Organisation type and purpose:
Professional body.
National governing body for the safety and regulation of bungee jumping and other sports involving elastic ropes.

Subject coverage: General and specialist information on current clubs and their locations, history of the sport and of the Association, recognised equipment and its safe use. Training of operatives within clubs, insurance and accident investigation, inspection of sites, risk assessment and product development to BERSA Certification Mark standard.

Publications: Printed

Access to staff: Contact by letter, by telephone, by fax and by e-mail. Appointment necessary.
Hours: Mon to Fri, 0900 to 1700
Special comments: Charges made for some services.

BRITISH ELECTROTECHNICAL COMMITTEE (BEC)

389 Chiswick High Road, London, W4 4AL

Tel: 020 8996 9001
Fax: 020 8996 7001
E-mail: cservices@bsigroup.com
Website: www.bsi-global.com

Enquiries to: Secretary

Founded: 1908

Organisation type and purpose: Advisory body.
Represents the UK in European and international electrotechnical bodies.

Subject coverage: International and European electrotechnical standardisation and its relationship with British Standards.

Collection: Full Collection of British, European and international standards

Library catalogue: All or part available in-house

Order printed publications from: Customer Services, BSI
at the same address
Order microform publications from: Technical Indexes Ltd, Willoughby Road, Bracknell, Berkshire, RG12 4DW

Publications list: Available online and in print

Access to staff: Contact by letter, by telephone, by fax and by e-mail
Hours: Mon to Fri, 0900 to 1700

Access to building: Prior appointment required

Access for disabled people: Parking provided, ramped entry, level entry, access to all public areas, toilet facilities

Links with: BSI; at the same address

BRITISH ENERGY

GSO Business Park, East Kilbride, G74 5PG

Tel: 01355 846000
Fax: 01355 846001
Website: www.british-energy.co.uk

Enquiries to: Corporate Librarian

Organisation type and purpose: Electricity generator.

Subject coverage: Nuclear engineering, electrical engineering, heat transfer, physics and mechanical engineering, health and safety, management.

Access to staff: Appointment necessary.
Hours: Mon to Thu, 0900 to 1700; Fri, 0900 to 1600

BRITISH ENGINEERS' CUTTING TOOLS ASSOCIATION (BECTA)

c/o Institute of Spring Technology, Henry Street, Sheffield, S3 7EQ

Tel: 0114 278 9143
E-mail: nstamp@mta.org.uk

Enquiries to: Secretary

Organisation type and purpose: Trade association.

Subject coverage: Cutting tools manufactured from high-speed steel.

Access to staff: Contact by letter, by telephone, by fax and by e-mail
Hours: Mon to Fri, 0900 to 1700

Affiliated to: Federation of British Engineers' Tool Manufacturers

BRITISH EQUESTRIAN FEDERATION (BEF)

National Agricultural Centre, Stoneleigh, Kenilworth, Warwickshire, CV8 2RH

Tel: 024 7669 8871
Fax: 024 7669 6484
E-mail: info@bef.co.uk
Website: www.bef.co.uk

Enquiries to: Chief Executive

Organisation type and purpose:
International organisation, national government body, advisory body, membership association (membership is by election or invitation).
Represents the sport on the National Olympic Committee of the British Olympic Association.

Subject coverage: BEF provides knowledge regarding international equestrian matters concerning competition, rules and regulations. Member disciplines provide specialist discipline knowledge.

Access to staff: Contact by letter, by telephone, by fax, by e-mail and via website. Appointment necessary.
Hours: Mon to Fri, 0900 to 1700

Access to building: Prior appointment required

Access for disabled people: Level entry

Member disciplines: Association of British Riding Schools (ABRS); tel: 01736 369440; fax: 01736 351390; e-mail: office@abrs.org; British Dressage Limited; tel: 024 7669 8843; e-mail: name.surname@britishdressage.co.uk; British Equestrian Trade Association (BETA); tel: 01937 587062; fax: 01937 582728;

continued overleaf

e-mail: clairewilliams@beta-uk.org; British Equestrian Vaulting Limited; tel: 0976 421789; fax: 01203 463027; e-mail: julievaulting@hotmail.com; British Eventing; tel: 024 7669 8856; e-mail: name.surname@britisheventing.com; British Horse Driving Trials Association; tel: 01347 878789; e-mail: bhdta@dial.pipex.com; British Horse Society; tel: 01926 707700; fax: 01926 707800; British Reining Horse Association (BRHA); tel: 01342 892203; fax: 01342 893441; British Show Jumping Association; tel: 024 7669 8800; e-mail: nameinitial@bsja.co.uk; Endurance GB; tel: 024 7669 8863; Pony Club; tel: 024 7669 8300; fax: 024 7669 6386; e-mail: name@pcuk.org; Scottish Equestrian Association (SEA); tel: 01475 540687; fax: 01475 540348; e-mail: patsypup@aol.com

BRITISH EQUESTRIAN TRADE ASSOCIATION (BETA)

East Wing, Stockeld Park, Wetherby, West Yorkshire, LS22 4AW

Tel: 01937 587062
Fax: 01937 582728
E-mail: info@beta-uk.org
Website: www.beta-uk.org/

Enquiries to: Secretary
Direct e-mail: tinar@beta-int.com

Founded: 1977

Organisation type and purpose: Trade association.

Subject coverage: Equestrian business and trade, including saddlery, pharmaceutical products, breeding, feedstuffs, transport, stalling, exporting, importing and other related matters.

Information services: BETA International Trade Fair

Publications: Printed

Access to staff: Contact by letter, by telephone, by fax and by e-mail
Hours: Mon to Fri, 0900 to 1700

Links with: EMC Limited, publishers

Subsidiary body: BETA Trade Fairs

BRITISH ESSENCE MANUFACTURERS ASSOCIATION (BEMA)

PO Box 172, Cranleigh, GU6 8WU

Tel: 01483 275411
E-mail: secretariat@bemaorg.org
Website: www.bemaorg.org

Enquiries to: Secretary

Founded: 1917

Organisation type and purpose: Trade association.

Subject coverage: Food and drink flavourings, UK, EEC and global legislation.

Access to staff: Contact by letter and by e-mail
Hours: Mon to Fri, 0900 to 1700

Links with: British Fragrance Association; Food and Drink Federation

BRITISH EXPERTISE

10 Grosvenor Gardens, London, SW1W 0DH

Tel: 020 7824 1920
Fax: 020 7824 1929
E-mail: mail@britishexpertise.org
Website: www.britishexpertise.org

Enquiries to: Chief Executive

Founded: 1965; formerly called BCCB (British Consultants & Construction Bureau) (year of change 2006)

Organisation type and purpose: Trade association.
Bureau of multi-disciplined consultants.
Primary information source on business prospects worldwide.
Promotion of British Consultancy of all disciplines worldwide.

Subject coverage: Overseas projects and British consultancy expertise in all disciplines and specialisations; engineers, architects, planners, management and economics, surveyors, agriculture, mining, healthcare, education and training, environment, tourism, security, legal, banking, catering, energy, transportation, leisure, IT, maritime, water engineering, fire, telecommunications, corrosion, acoustics, chemical, contractors and construction.

Trade and statistical information: Knowledge of all countries and multilateral funding agencies

Access to staff: Contact by letter, by telephone, by fax, by e-mail and via website. Appointment necessary.
Hours: Mon to Thu, 0900 to 1715; Fri, 0900 to 1700

BRITISH EXPORTERS ASSOCIATION (BExA)

Broadway House, Tothill Street, Westminster, London, SW1H 9NQ

Tel: 020 7222 5419
Fax: 020 7799 2468
E-mail: hughbailey@bexa.co.uk
Website: www.bexa.co.uk

Enquiries to: Director

Founded: 1940

Organisation type and purpose: Trade association.
Lobby organisation.

Subject coverage: Exporting with a slant towards trade finance and credit insurance.

Publications: Printed
Order printed publications from: Available to members. Can also be downloaded from www.bexa.co.uk

BRITISH FALCONERS' CLUB (BFC)

Westfield, Meeting Hill, Worstead, North Walsham, Norfolk, NR28 9LS

Tel: 01692 404057
Fax: 01692 404057
E-mail: admin@britishfalconersclub.co.uk
Website: www.britishfalconersclub.co.uk

Enquiries to: Director
Other contacts: Public Relations Officer (for publicity and press releases)

Founded: 1927

Organisation type and purpose: Membership association (membership is by subscription), present number of members: 1,266.

Subject coverage: Promotion of falconry in the British Isles and promotion of captive breeding for birds of prey.

Collection: The Alexander Library, Oxford University Zoological Department Library The A. K. Bell Library, Perth

Publications: Printed

Access to staff: Contact by letter, by telephone, by fax, by e-mail and via website
Hours: Mon and Tue, 0900 to 1500; Wed and Thu, 0900 to 1300

Access to building: No access other than to staff

Branches: 12 regional clubs in the United Kingdom, and overseas members

Member organisation of: Countryside Alliance; Federation of Field Sports Associations of the EEC (FACE); International Association of Falconry and Conservation of Birds of Prey (IAF); Standing Conference on Countryside Sports (SCCS)

BRITISH FASHION COUNCIL (BFC)

Somerset House, South Wing, Strand, London, WC2R 1LA

Tel: 020 7759 1999
Fax: 020 7636 7515
E-mail: info@britishfashioncouncil.com
Website: www.britishfashioncouncil.com
Website: www.londonfashionweek.co.uk

Enquiries to: Administrator

Organisation type and purpose: Trade association.

Subject coverage: Fashion; fashion exhibitions and London Fashion Week.

Publications: Printed

BRITISH FEDERATION OF BRASS BANDS (BFBB)

Unit 12, Maple Estate, Stocks Lane, Barnsley, South Yorkshire, S75 2BL

Tel: 01226 771015
Fax: 01226 732630
E-mail: natoffice@bfbb.co.uk
Website: www.bfbb.co.uk

Enquiries to: Secretary

Founded: 1968

Organisation type and purpose: Membership association (membership is by subscription), present number of members: 310, registered charity (charity number BFBB 1065181; BBHT 1037552).
National umbrella body.
Working for all brass bands in the UK.

Subject coverage: Amateur brass band movement in the UK.

Collection: Brass Band Music Library

Non-library collection catalogue: All or part available in-house

Library catalogue: All or part available in-house

Access to staff: Contact by letter, by telephone, by fax, by e-mail, in person and via website
Hours: Mon to Fri, 0900 to 1700

Also at: British Federation of Brass Bands (BFBB); 122 Main Street, Bingley, BD16 2HL; tel: 01274 511280; fax: 01274 511281

BRITISH FEDERATION OF WOMEN GRADUATES (BFWG)

4 Mandeville Courtyard, 142 Battersea Park Road, London, SW11 4NB

Tel: 020 7498 8037
E-mail: office@bfwg.org.uk
Website: www.bfwg.org.uk

Other contacts: President/Vice-Presidents

Founded: 1907

Organisation type and purpose:
International organisation, membership association (membership is by subscription), present number of members: over 500 in England and Wales; 180,000 Worldwide, voluntary organisation, registered charity (charity number 273043).
BFWG is a non-profit, international non-governmental organisation working locally, nationally and globally to improve the status of women and girls, to promote lifelong education, and to enable graduate women to use their expertise to effect change.

Subject coverage: National pre-doctoral research scholarships for women entering their final year towards a PhD degree, lobbying of government, EU, UN; educational exchange plus international fellowships for members of IFUW.

Collection: Archives held in The Women's Library, Old Castle Street, London, E1 7NT and Sybil Campbell Collection Trust held on permanent loan at the University of Winchester.

Library catalogue: All or part available online

Publications: Printed

Access to staff: Contact by letter, by telephone, by e-mail and via website. Appointment necessary.
Hours: Varied – by arrangement

Access to building: Prior appointment required

Access for disabled people: The rear entrance to the courtyard is flat; however, entrance to the office is by steps. There is no disabled access.

Other branches: Approximately 15 Associations in England and Wales divided into 4 regions.

Other offices in: 79 Countries

Parent body: International Federation of University Women; 10 Rue de Lac, Geneva, CH-1207; tel: 00 41 22 731 2380; fax: 00 41 22 738 0440; e-mail: ifuw@ifuw.org; website: http://www.ifuw.org

Subsidiary: British Federation of Women Graduates Charitable Foundation (BFWG (CF)); Contact details as per BFWG above

BRITISH FENCING

1 Baron's Gate, 33–35 Rothschild Rd, London, W4 5HT

Tel: 020 8742 3032
Fax: 020 8742 3033
E-mail: headoffice@britishfencing.com
Website: www.britishfencing.com

Organisation type and purpose: National governing body for the Olympic sport of fencing in the British Isles (excluding the Republic of Ireland).
To promote and develop the sport of fencing in the British Isles (excluding the Republic of Ireland).

Subject coverage: The sport of fencing.

Publications: Electronic and video

Publications list: Available online

Access to staff: Contact by letter, by telephone, by fax and by e-mail
Hours: Mon to Thu, 0930 to 1700; Fri, 0930 to 1600
Special comments: Telephone contact.

Links with: England Fencing; at the same address; Guernsey Union d'Escrime; Jersey Fencing; Northern Ireland Fencing; Scottish Fencing
Welsh Fencing

BRITISH FILM INSTITUTE – LIBRARY (BFI)

BFI Southbank , Belvedere Road, South Bank, Waterloo, SE1 8XT

Tel: 020 7928 3535
E-mail: library@bfi.org.uk
Website: www.bfi.org.uk/library

Enquiries to: Librarian – Research & Enquiries
Direct e-mail: library@bfi.org.uk
Other contacts: Curator of Special Collections (for access to special collections)

Founded: 1933

Organisation type and purpose: National organisation, registered charity.
Grant-aided education/cultural body.
To enable everyone to experience, enjoy and discover more about the world of film and television.

Subject coverage: All aspects of world cinema; UK broadcast television, with some restrictions.

Collection: Rare and old books on cinema and pre-cinema
The following are accessed via the library:
Collections, over 200, donated by organisations associated with film and TV
Newspaper cuttings (over 1.5m. dating back to 1930s)
Includes the former ITC (Independent Television Commission) Library collection
Periodicals collection (believed to be largest of its kind in the world)
Published and unpublished scripts (over 20,000)

Trade and statistical information: Film production statistics, television viewing figures

Non-library collection catalogue: All or part available online and in-house

Library catalogue: All or part available online and in-house

Publications: Printed, and electronic and video, and microform publications
Order printed publications from: Some items from BFI only
Order microform publications from: Cinema Pressbooks 1920–40 and Picturegoer via Proquest Chadwyck-Healey
Order electronic and video publications from: Via Proquest Chadwyck-Healey

Publications list: Available online and in print

Access to staff: Contact by letter, by e-mail, in person and via website

Access to building: No prior appointment required
Hours: Library opening times Tue to Sat 1030 to 1900
Special comments: Special collections access by appointment

Access for disabled people: Lifts, toilet facilities

Constituent bodies: Collections and Information: National Film and Television Archive

BRITISH FIRE ADVISORY SERVICES LIMITED

3 Otterbourne Place, Willington, Maidstone, Kent, ME15 8JL

Tel: 01622 755365
Fax: 01622 755365
E-mail: bfas@zoom.co.uk

Enquiries to: Director
Other contacts: Senior Consultant

Founded: 2000

Organisation type and purpose:
Consultancy.
A non-political organisation not funded by public money.

Subject coverage: Fire risk assessment; advice on all fire safety-related legislation; fire fighting procedures; means of escape from fire for disabled persons.

Access to staff: Contact by letter, by telephone, by fax and by e-mail. Appointment necessary. All charged.
Hours: Mon to Fri, 0900 to 1700

BRITISH FLUE AND CHIMNEY MANUFACTURERS' ASSOCIATION (BFCMA)

2 Waltham Court, Milley Lane, Hare Hatch, Reading, Berkshire, RG10 9TH

Tel: 0118 940 3416
Fax: 0118 940 6258
E-mail: info@feta.co.uk
Website: www.feta.co.uk

Enquiries to: Commercial Manager

Founded: 1977

Organisation type and purpose: Trade association.

Subject coverage: Natural draught flues and chimneys for all fuels.

Publications: Printed

Publications list: Available online

continued overleaf

Access to staff: Contact by letter, by telephone, by fax and by e-mail
Hours: Mon to Thu, 0830 to 1630; Fri, 0830 to 1600

Links with: Federation of Environmental Trade Associations; at the same address

BRITISH FLUID POWER ASSOCIATION (BFPA)

Cheriton House, Cromwell Park, Chipping Norton, Oxfordshire, OX7 5SR

Tel: 01608 647900
Fax: 01608 647919
E-mail: enquiries@bfpa.co.uk
Website: www.bfpa.co.uk

Enquiries to: Director

Founded: 1959

Organisation type and purpose: Trade association.
Trade association for manufacturers and distributors of hydraulic and pneumatic equipment.

Subject coverage: Hydraulic and pneumatic equipment.

Trade and statistical information: General production and trade statistics UK and Europe (specific data available to members only), technical information, product sourcing, exhibitions

Publications: Printed

Publications list: Available online and in print

Access to staff: Contact by letter, by telephone, by fax, by e-mail and via website
Hours: Mon to Thu, 0900 to 1700; Fri, 0900 to 1520

Access for disabled people: Parking provided

Sister association: British Fluid Power Distributors Association; at the same address

BRITISH FLUORIDATION SOCIETY (BFS)

PO Box 18, Uppermill, OL3 6WU

Tel: 01457238507
E-mail: bfs@bfsweb.org
Website: www.bfsweb.org/

Enquiries to: Admin Officer
Direct e-mail: bfs@bfsweb.org
Other contacts: Administrator, tel: 01457 23 8507

Founded: 1969

Organisation type and purpose: Learned society (membership is by subscription), research organisation.

Subject coverage: Fluoridation of public water supplies; safety, benefits, effectiveness; fluoride supplements.

Publications: Printed

Publications list: Available online

Access to staff: Contact by letter, by telephone, by e-mail and via website
Hours: Mon to Fri, 0900 to 1700

BRITISH FLUTE SOCIETY (BFS)

The Nook, How Mill, Brampton, Cumbria, CA8 9JY

Tel: 01228 670306
E-mail: membership@bfs.org.uk

Enquiries to: Membership Secretary

Organisation type and purpose: Membership association.
To promote the flute and flute playing, provide an opportunity for enthusiasts to contact each other.

Subject coverage: Flutes and flute making, music, instruments, history, players, events worldwide.

Publications: Printed

Access to staff: Contact by letter, by telephone and by e-mail
Hours: Mon to Fri, 0900 to 1700

BRITISH FOOTWEAR ASSOCIATION (BFA)

3 Burystead Place, Wellingborough, Northamptonshire, NN8 1AH

Tel: 01933 229005
Fax: 01933 225009
E-mail: info@britishfootwearassociation.co.uk
Website: www.britishfootwearassociation.co.uk

Founded: 1890

Organisation type and purpose: National organisation, trade association (membership is by subscription), present number of members: 100+, manufacturing industry, service industry.

Subject coverage: Footwear manufacture: labour relations, working conditions, environmental and safety legislation, export information, trade shows.

Access to staff: Contact by letter, by telephone, by fax, by e-mail and via website. Non-members charged.
Hours: Mon to Fri, 0900 to 1700

Access to building: Staff only.

BRITISH FRANCHISE ASSOCIATION (bfa)

Centurion Court, 85f Milton Park, Abingdon, OX14 4RY

Tel: 01235 820470
Fax: 01235 832158
E-mail: mailroom@thebfa.org
Website: www.thebfa.org

Enquiries to: Director General
Direct e-mail: mailroom@thebfa.org

Founded: 1977

Organisation type and purpose: The bfa is the only voluntary self-regulatory body for the UK franchise industry, with a standards-based approach to membership. Its aim is to promote ethical franchising practice in the UK and help the industry develop credibility, influence and favourable circumstance for growth.

Subject coverage: One of the bfa's main jobs is to help potential franchisees recognise the pros and cons of their organisation. Another is to help businesses involved in franchising to secure their own position amongst the 'good' operators.

Trade and statistical information: Annual survey and statistics on the extent and performance of franchising in the UK

Publications: Printed

Publications list: Available online

Access to staff: Contact by letter, by telephone, by fax and by e-mail
Hours: Mon to Fri, 0900 to 1700

BRITISH FRIENDS OF RAMBAM MEDICAL CENTRE (BFRMC)

Formal name: The British Friends of Rambam Medical Center

The Director, 10 North Crescent, London, N3 3LL

Tel: 020 8371 1500
Fax: 020 8271 1501
E-mail: alexanderpasse@dsl.pipex.com

Enquiries to: Director

Founded: 1993

Organisation type and purpose: Registered charity (charity number 1028061).
The purchase of medical equipment for all departments of the Rambam Medical Centre.

Access to staff: Contact by letter
Hours: Mon to Fri, 0900 to 1700

BRITISH FRIESLAND SHEEP SOCIETY

Weir Park Farm, Christow, Exeter, Devon, EX6 7PB

Tel: 01647 252549
E-mail: peter@baber.co.uk
Website: www.baber.co.uk

Founded: 1980

Subject coverage: British Friesland sheep.

BRITISH FUCHSIA SOCIETY (BFS)

Formal name: The British Fuchsia Society

PO Box 8177, Reading, Berkshire, RG6 9PH

Tel: 0118 375 7462
E-mail: secretary@thebfs.org.uk
Website: www.thebfs.org.uk

Enquiries to: Honorary Secretary

Founded: 1938

Organisation type and purpose: Membership association (membership is by subscription), present number of members: 3,500, registered charity (charity number 1038334).
To encourage, improve and research the cultivation of fuchsias and their various cultivars.

Subject coverage: All matters related to the culture of fuchsias, availability of specific cultivars (limited to those grown in the UK).

Publications: Printed

Access to staff: Contact by letter, by telephone and via website
Hours: Mon to Fri, 0900 to 1700

Affiliated to the: Royal Horticultural Society

Has: 300 affiliated local societies

BRITISH FURNITURE MANUFACTURERS FEDERATION (BMF)

Wycombe House, 9 Amersham Hill, High Wycombe, Bucks, HP13 6NR

Tel: 01494 523021
Fax: 01494 474270
E-mail: info@bfm.org.uk
Website: www.bfm.org.uk/

Organisation type and purpose: Trade Association

Subject coverage: British Furniture Manufacturers (BFM) is a trade association that has represented the interests of the British furniture industry in all sectors for more than 60 years. Membership is open to manufacturing companies, suppliers and ancillary companies to the trade.

Members: High Wycombe Furniture Manufacturers Society; London and South Eastern Furniture Manufacturers Association; Midlands and North West Furniture Manufacturers Association; Northern Furniture Manufacturers Association; Scottish Furniture Manufacturers Association; West of England & South Wales Furniture Manufacturers Association

BRITISH GEAR ASSOCIATION (BGA)

Suite 43, Imex Business Park, Shobnall Road, Burton-on-Trent, Staffordshire, DE14 2AU

Tel: 01283 515521
Fax: 01283 515841
E-mail: admin@bga.org.uk
Website: www.bga.org.uk

Enquiries to: Office Manager
Other contacts: Technical Executive for technical enquiries.

Organisation type and purpose: Trade association, membership association (membership is by subscription).
Association for the Mechanical Power Transmission Industry.

Subject coverage: Technical, research, education, training and economic aspects related to the mechanical power transmissions industry.

Collection: Congress papers on mechanical power transmission subjects

Trade and statistical information: Statistical Profile of the Power Transmission Industry, members: 1 CD copy free of charge, UK non-members: £250 for hard copy, £120 + VAT for CD, outside UK: please ask for quote

Publications: Printed

Publications list: Available online and in print

Access to staff: Contact by letter, by telephone, by fax, by e-mail and via website
Hours: Mon to Fri, 0900 to 1700

Member of: European Committee of Associations of Manufacturers of Gears and Transmission Parts; tel: +49 69 66 03 1526; fax: +49 69 66 03 1459

BRITISH GEOLOGICAL SURVEY (BGS)

Natural History Museum, Cromwell Road, London, SW7 5BD

Tel: 020 7589 4090
Fax: 020 7589 4090
E-mail: bgslondon@bgs.ac.uk
Website: www.bgs.ac.uk
Website: www.geologyshop.com

Enquiries to: Manager

Founded: 1845

Organisation type and purpose: Research organisation.
Scientific research (earth sciences).

Subject coverage: Geological sciences, earth sciences, geology and associated subjects, economic resources, environmental geology, hydrogeology, geochemistry, regional geology (UK and overseas), geophysics, palaeontology, engineering geology, minerals, remote sensing, seismology, volcanology, petrology, biostratigraphy, petroleum geology, fluid processes, marine geology, coastal geology, geological maps, natural hazards.

Collection: 1:10,000 / 1:10,560 National Grid and County Series Geological maps of the British Isles and other scale geological maps
Indexes to field notebooks and BGS archives
Manuscript graphic indexes to BGS maps
All BGS publications including:
BGS Memoirs, open file, technical and research reports

Trade and statistical information: World mineral statistics.
UK Minerals Year-book

Library catalogue: All or part available online

Publications: Printed

Publications list: Available online and in print

Access to staff: Contact by letter, by telephone, by fax, by e-mail, in person and via website
Hours: Mon to Fri; tel., 0900 to 1700; visitors, 1000 to 1700

Access for disabled people: Toilet facilities
Special comments: Lift available to office level.

BRITISH GEOLOGICAL SURVEY – MARINE OPERATIONS AND ENGINEERING

Formal name: British Geological Survey

2A Nivensknowe Road, Loanhead, Midlothian, EH20 9AU

Tel: 0131 448 2700
Fax: 0131 448 2545
E-mail: enquiries@bgs.ac.uk
Website: www.bgs.ac.uk/science/marine_operations/home.html

Enquiries to: Information Officer
Direct tel: 0131 667 1000 (Murchison House); 01159 363 100 (Keyworth)
Direct fax: 0131 668 4140 (Murchison House); 01159 363 200 (Keyworth)
Other contacts: Head of Marine Operations and Engineering

Founded: 1835

Organisation type and purpose: National government body, professional body, research organisation.
National onshore and offshore data archive for geology and geoscience.
Geological survey, geophysical survey and monitoring (geomagnetism and earthquakes).

Subject coverage: Geological, geophysical, geotechnical field data maps, reports, computer databased archive files and maps, seismic hazards. Geomagnetic observations and predictions. Offshore geophysical and geological surveys. Specialised offshore sampling and coring equipment. Coastal and environmental monitoring and data collection.

Trade and statistical information: Documentation relating to mineral statistics, earthquake statistics and similar data

Non-library collection catalogue: All or part available in-house

Library catalogue: All or part available in-house

Publications: Printed, and electronic and video, and microform publications
Order printed publications from: Information Officer, British Geological Survey, Murchison House, West Main Road, Edinburgh, EH9 3LA; tel: 0131 667 1000; fax: 0131 668 2683
Information Officer, British Geological Survey, Keyworth, Nottingham, NG12 5GG; tel: 0115 936 3100; fax: 0115 936 3200

Publications list: Available online and in print

Access to staff: Contact by letter, by fax, by e-mail and via website. Appointment necessary. All charged.
Hours: Mon to Thu, 0900 to 1700; Fri, 0900 to 1630
Special comments: There may be data exchange arrangements.
Access times may vary. Please check with staff concerned.

Access for disabled people: Parking provided
Special comments: Access varies dependent on building.

Constituent part of: The Natural Environment Research Council (NERC); Polaris House, North Star Avenue, Swindon, Wiltshire, SN2 1EU; tel: 01793 411500; fax: 01793 411501

Main Office: British Geological Survey; Platt Lane, Nicker Hill, Keyworth, Nottingham, NG12 5GG; tel: 01159 363 100; fax: 01159 363 200; e-mail: enquiries@bgs.ac.uk; website: http://www.bgs.ac.uk

North UK Office: British Geological Survey; Murchison House, West Main Road, Edinburgh, EH19 3LA; tel: 0131 667 1000; fax: 0131 668 4140; e-mail: enquiries@bgs.ac.uk; website: http://www.bgs.ac.uk

BRITISH GEOLOGICAL SURVEY LIBRARY SERVICE – DE LA BECHE LIBRARY

Environmental Science Centre, Keyworth, Nottingham, NG12 5GG

Tel: 0115 936 3205
E-mail: libuser@bgs.ac.uk

continued overleaf

Website: www.bgs.ac.uk
Website: nora.nerc.ac.uk

Enquiries to: Library Service Manager

Founded: 1835

Organisation type and purpose: National government body, consultancy, research organisation, publishing house.
The mission of the BGS is to: advance geoscientific knowledge of the United Kingdom landmass and its adjacent continental shelf; provide comprehensive, objective and up-to-date geoscientific information, advice and services; enhance the United Kingdom science base.

Subject coverage: Earth sciences and related subjects.

Collection: 500,000 volumes
14,000 serials incl world-wide
BGS archives
National collection of field survey records (NGRC)
BGS and British Association for the Advancement of Science geological photographs (80,000)
World-wide collections of geological maps and related texts (200,000)

Trade and statistical information: Minerals statistics

Non-library collection catalogue: All or part available online and in-house

Library catalogue: All or part available online

Publications: Printed, and electronic and video
Order printed publications from: Sales Desk, British Geological Survey
Order electronic and video publications from: Sales at http://www.bgs.ac.uk/contacts/sales.html

Publications list: Available online and in print

Access to staff: Contact by letter, by telephone, by e-mail, in person and via website. Appointment necessary.
Hours: Mon to Thu, 0900 to 1700; Fri, 0900 to 1630

Access to building: Prior appointment required
Hours: Mon to Thu, 0900 to 1700; Fri, 0900 to 1630
Special comments: Library available for reference only.

Access for disabled people: Parking provided, ramped entry, level entry, toilet facilities

Also at: British Geological Survey; Maclean Building, Crowmarsh Gifford, Wallingford, Oxfordshire, OX10 8BB; tel: 01491 838800; fax: 01491 692345; website: http://www.bgs.ac.uk/contacts/sites/wallingford/wahome.html
British Geological Survey; Columbus House, Greenmeadow Springs, Tongwynlais, Cardiff, CF15 7NE; tel: 029 2052 1962; fax: 029 2052 1963; website: http://www.bgs.ac.uk/contacts/sites/cardiff/home.html
British Geological Survey; Hydrogeological Enquiries and National Wells Records Archive; tel: 01491 692299; fax: 01491 692345; e-mail: hydro@bgs.ac.uk; British Geological Survey; Murchison House, West Mains Road, Edinburgh, EH9 3LA; tel: 0131 667 1000; fax: 0131 668 2683; e-mail: enquiry@bgs.ac.uk; website: http://www.bgs.ac.uk/contacts/sites/edinburgh/mhhome.html
British Geological Survey; London Information Office, Natural History Museum Earth Galleries, Exhibition Road, South Kensington, London, SW7 2DE; tel: 020 7589 4090; fax: 020 7584 8270; e-mail: bgslondon@bgs.ac.uk; website: http://www.bgs.ac.uk/contacts/sites/london/liohome.html
Geological Survey of Northern Ireland; Colby House, Stranmills Court, Belfast, BT9 5BF; tel: 028 9038 8462; fax: 028 9038 8461; National Geological Records Centre (North); tel: 0131 650 0307; fax: 0131 667 2785; e-mail: ngrcn@bgs.ac.uk; National Geological Records Centre (South); tel: 0115 936 3109; fax: 0115 936 3276; e-mail: ngis@bgs.ac.uk

Parent body: Natural Environment Research Council; Polaris House, North Star Avenue, Swindon, SN2 1EU; tel: 01793 411500; fax: 01793 411501; website: http://www.nerc.ac.uk

BRITISH GEOTECHNICAL ASSOCIATION (BGA)

Institution of Civil Engineers, 1 Great George Street, London, SW1P 3AA

Tel: 020 7665 2233
Fax: 020 7799 1325
E-mail: bga@icc.org.uk
Website: www.ice.org.uk

Enquiries to: Administrator

Organisation type and purpose: Learned society.

Subject coverage: Soil mechanics; foundation engineering; rock and ice mechanics; geotechnical engineering; details of conferences and proceedings in the field.

Publications: Printed

Access to staff: Contact by letter
Hours: Mon to Fri, 0900 to 1700

Affiliated to: Institution of Civil Engineers

Member of: International Society for Rock Mechanics; International Society for Soil Mechanics and Ground Engineering

BRITISH GERIATRICS SOCIETY (BGS)

Marjory Warren House, 31 St John's Square, London, EC1M 4DN

Tel: 020 7608 1369
Fax: 020 7608 1041
E-mail: general.information@bgs.org.uk
Website: www.bgs.org.uk

Enquiries to: Administrator

Founded: 1947

Organisation type and purpose: Advisory body, professional body (membership is by qualification), voluntary organisation, registered charity (charity number 268762).
Voluntary association of physicians and scientists concerned with improving standards of treatment, and encouraging research in the illnesses of elderly people.

Subject coverage: Promotion of high standards of health and treatment for the elderly, the teaching of geriatric medicine, the training of medical and paramedical staff, and research into age-related disease.

Publications: Printed

Publications list: Available online and in print

Access to staff: Contact by letter, by telephone, by fax, by e-mail and via website
Hours: Mon to Fri, 0900 to 1700
Special comments: The society does not deal specifically with the public, but aims its activities at doctors with an interest in elderly care.

BRITISH GLASS MANUFACTURERS CONFEDERATION (BGMC)

9 Churchill Way, Sheffield, S35 2PY

Tel: 0114 290 1850
Fax: 0114 290 1851
E-mail: info@britglass.co.uk
Website: www.britglass.co.uk

Enquiries to: Information Officer
Direct e-mail: t.green@britglass.co.uk
Other contacts: Recycling Officer

Founded: 1959

Organisation type and purpose: Advisory body, trade association (membership is by subscription, qualification), present number of members: 144, training organisation, consultancy, research organisation.

Subject coverage: Glass, recycling, statistics, education, economics, legislation, safety, specifications, HSE, training and consultancy, environmental services.

Trade and statistical information: Production and recycling statistics

Library catalogue: All or part available in-house

Publications: Printed, and electronic and video

Publications list: Available in print

Access to staff: Contact by letter, by telephone and by e-mail. Appointment necessary. Non-members charged.
Hours: Mon to Fri, 0900 to 1700

Access to building: Prior appointment required
Hours: Mon to Fri, 0900 to 1700

Access for disabled people: Parking provided, toilet facilities

Member of: (ETSU); British Standards Institution; European Domestic Glassware Organisation; European Glass Manufacturers; Scientific Glassware Association

BRITISH GLIDING ASSOCIATION (BGA)

British Gliding Association Limited, 8 Merus Court, Meridian Business Park, Leicester, LE19 1RJ

Tel: 0116 289 2956
Fax: 0116 289 5025
E-mail: office@gliding.co.uk
Website: www.gliding.co.uk

Enquiries to: Secretary
Direct e-mail: keith@gliding.co.uk

Founded: 1929

Organisation type and purpose:
Membership association (membership is by election or invitation), present number of members: 9,500, voluntary organisation.
Governing body for the sport.

Subject coverage: Gliding.

Publications: Printed

Access to staff: Contact by letter, by telephone, by fax, by e-mail and in person
Hours: Mon to Fri, 0900 to 1700

Affiliated to: Fédération Aéronautique Internationale; Royal Aero Club of the United Kingdom

BRITISH GLOVE ASSOCIATION (BGA)

Sussex House, 8–10 Homesdale Road, Bromley, Kent, BR2 9LZ

Tel: 020 8464 0131
Fax: 020 8464 6018
E-mail: tradeassn@craneandpartners.com
Website: www.gloveassociation.org

Enquiries to: Secretary

Organisation type and purpose: Trade association.

Subject coverage: Glove production, glove types (dress, sports, industrial and protective).

Collection: The Worshipful Company of Glovers is responsible for two glove collections, both at the Museum of Costume, Bath
The Duplicate Royal Coronation Gloves Collection
The Spence Collection

Sponsors the: Worshipful Company of Glovers

BRITISH GOAT SOCIETY (BGS)

Jane Wilson, Secretary, British Goat Society, Gibshiel, Tarset, Hexham, Northumberland, NE48 1RR

Tel: 01434 240 866
E-mail: secretary@allgoats.com
Website: www.allgoats.com

Enquiries to: Secretary

Founded: 1879

Organisation type and purpose: Voluntary organisation.
Registration body, over 90 local and regional societies are affiliated.

Subject coverage: Goat husbandry and management; registration of stock.

Publications: Printed

Publications list: Available in print

Access to staff: Contact by letter, by telephone and by e-mail
Hours: Mon to Fri, 0900 to 1700

BRITISH GRASSLAND SOCIETY (BGS)

Unit 32C Stoneleigh Deer Park, Stareton, Kenilworth, Warwickshire, CV8 2LY

Tel: 02476 696 600
E-mail: bgsoffice@britishgrassland.com
Website: www.britishgrassland.com

Enquiries to: Administrator

Founded: 1945

Organisation type and purpose: Learned society, present number of members: 650, registered charity (charity number 261800).
BGS is a forum for those with an active interest in the science and practice of temperate grassland production and utilisation.

Subject coverage: The advancement of methods of production and utilisation of grass and forage crops for the promotion of agriculture and the public benefit; the advancement of education and research in grass and forage crop production and utilisation, and the publication of the results of such research.

Publications list: Available in print

Access to staff: Contact by letter, by telephone, by e-mail and via website
Hours: Mon to Thu, 0830 to 1630 and Fri 0830 to 1600

BRITISH GREYHOUND RACING BOARD LIMITED (BGRB)

32 Old Burlington Street, London, W1S 3AT

Tel: 020 7292 9900
Fax: 020 7292 9909

Enquiries to: Chief Executive

Founded: 1976

Organisation type and purpose: Advisory body, statutory body, trade association.

Subject coverage: Greyhound racing.

Trade and statistical information:
Information and statistics on greyhound racing

Access to staff: Contact by letter and by telephone
Hours: Mon to Fri, 0930 to 1700

BRITISH GUILD OF TRAVEL WRITERS (BGTW)

335 Lordship Road, London, United Kingdom, N16 5HG

Tel: 020 8144 8713
Fax: 020 8181 6663
E-mail: secretariat@bgtw.org
Website: www.bgtw.org

Enquiries to: Administrator

Founded: 1960

Organisation type and purpose:
Membership association (membership is by election or invitation), present number of members: 250.
Professional travel writers, authors, broadcasters and photographers.

Subject coverage: Travel, tourism, journalism, photography, radio, television, video.

Publications: Printed

Publications list: Available in print

Access to staff: Contact by letter, by telephone, by fax and by e-mail
Hours: Mon to Fri, 0900 to 1700

BRITISH GYMNASTICS (BG)

Ford Hall, Lilleshall National Sports Centre, Newport, Shropshire, TF10 9NB

Tel: 0845 129 7 129
E-mail: information@british-gymnastics.org
Website: www.british-gymnastics.org

Enquiries to: Head of Media
Direct fax: 0845 129 7 129 (2533)
Direct e-mail: tim.peake@british-gymnastics.org
Other contacts: Chief Executive for policy of the association.

Founded: 1888

Organisation type and purpose:
Membership association (membership is by subscription), present number of members: 150,000, training organisation.
National governing body of the sport.

Subject coverage: Gymnastics, women's and men's; rhythmic gymnastics, trampolining, acrobatic gymnastics, general gymnastics, gymnastics for people with disabilities, aerobic gymnastics, competitions, courses, membership, technical information, awards and publications, events, promotion and publicity, judging.

Non-library collection catalogue: All or part available in-house

Publications: Printed, and electronic and video
Order printed publications from: GEL- Liz Liebman: 0845 129 7 129 (2384); liz.liebman@british-gymnastics.org
Order electronic and video publications from: Mark Young: mark.young@british-gymnastics.org ; 0845 129 7 129 (2503)

Publications list: Available online

Access to staff: Contact by letter, by telephone, by fax, by e-mail, in person and via website. Appointment necessary.
Hours: Mon to Thu, 0900 to 1700; Fri, 0900 to 1630

Access to building: Prior appointment required
Hours: Mon to Thu, 0900 to 1700; Fri, 0900 to 1630

Access for disabled people: Parking provided

Constituent part:

European governing body is: UEG; Switzerland; tel: +41 21 613 7332; fax: +41 21 613 7331; e-mail: info@ueg.org

World governing body is: FIG; Switzerland; tel: +41 21 321 55 10; fax: +41 21 321 55 19; e-mail: info@fig-gymnastics.org; website: www.fig-gymnastics.com

BRITISH HALLMARKING COUNCIL

No 1 Colmore Square, Birmingham, B4 6AA

Tel: 0870 763 1455
Fax: 0870 763 1855

continued overleaf

E-mail: geraldine.swanton@martineau-uk.com
Website: www.britishhallmarkingcouncil.gov.uk/

Enquiries to: Secretary

Founded: 1973

Organisation type and purpose: Statutory body.
Created by the Hallmarking Act of 1973; supervisory body for the activities of the Independent Assay Offices.

Subject coverage: Hallmarking in the United Kingdom.

Publications: Printed

Access to staff: Contact by letter
Hours: Mon to Fri, 0900 to 1700

BRITISH HANG GLIDING AND PARAGLIDING ASSOCIATION (BHPA)

8 Merus Court, Meridian Business Park, Leicester, LE19 1RJ

Tel: 0116 289 4316
Fax: 0116 281 4949
E-mail: office@bhpa.co.uk
Website: www.bhpa.co.uk

Enquiries to: Office Manager

Founded: 1992

Organisation type and purpose: Membership association.
Governing body of the sport.

Subject coverage: Hang gliding and paragliding; availability, training, licensing of instructors, safety regulations, national competitions, development of new techniques and equipment, courses, conventions.

Publications: Printed

Access to staff: Contact by letter, by telephone, by fax, by e-mail and via website
Hours: Mon to Fri, 0900 to 1700

Affiliated to: Féderation Aéronautique Internationale

Constituent bodies: British Association of Parascending Clubs; British Hang Gliding Association

Representation on: Royal Aero Club of the United Kingdom

BRITISH HARDMETAL ASSOCIATION (BHA)

c/o Institute of Spring Technology, Henry Street, Sheffield, S3 7EQ

Tel: 0114 278 9143

Enquiries to: Secretary

Organisation type and purpose: Trade association.

Subject coverage: Hardmetal and associated products.

Access to staff: Contact by letter, by telephone, by fax and by e-mail
Hours: Mon to Fri, 0900 to 1700

Affiliated to: Federation of British Engineers' Tool Manufacturers

BRITISH HEALTH CARE ASSOCIATION (BHCA)

PO Box 6752, Elgin, IV30 9BN

Tel: 01343 830148
E-mail: info@bhca.org.uk
Website: www.bhca.org.uk

Enquiries to: National Secretary
Other contacts: President

Founded: 1947

Organisation type and purpose: Trade association (membership is by subscription).
To promote and advance the interest of member organisations; to lobby, consult and negotiate on their behalf and undertake and arrange for the arbitration of disputes. To determine and administer an ethical code of conduct for the resolution of disputes.

Subject coverage: Health care cash plan insurance.

Collection: History of the Association

Non-library collection catalogue: All or part available in-house and in print

Library catalogue: All or part available in-house and in print

Access to staff: Contact by letter, by e-mail and via website
Special comments: Office operates irregular part-time hours only.

Member organisations: BHSF; Gamgee House, 2 Darnley Road, Birmingham, B16 8TE; tel: 0800 622 552; e-mail: enquiries@bhsf.co.uk; website: http://www.bhsf.co.uk
Engage Mutual Assurance; Hornbeam Park Avenue, Harrogate, HG2 8XE; tel: 0800 169 4321; e-mail: mail@engagemutual.com; website: http://www.engagemutual.com
Gwent Hospitals Contributory Fund; 13 Cardiff Road, Newport, NP20 2EH; tel: 0800 479 8003; e-mail: admin@ghcf.co.uk; website: http://www.ghcf.co.uk
HSF health plan; 24 Upper Ground, London, SE1 9PD; tel: 020 7928 6662; e-mail: marketing@hsf.eu.com; website: http://www.hsf.eu.com
Medicash; One Derby Square, Liverpool, L2 1AB; tel: 0800 011 2222; e-mail: info@medicash.org; website: http://www.medicash.org
Paycare; George Street, Wolverhampton, WV2 4DX; tel: 01902 371000; e-mail: enquiries@paycare.org; website: http://www.paycare.org
Simplyhealth; Hambleden House, Waterloo Court, Andover, SP10 1LQ; tel: 0800 980 7890; e-mail: customerservices@simplyhealth.co.uk; website: http://www.simplyhealth.co.uk
Sovereign Health Care; Royal Standard House, 26 Manningham Lane, Bradford, West Yorkshire, BD1 3DN; tel: 01274 841130; e-mail: cs@sovereignhealthcare.co.uk; website: http://www.sovereignhealthcare.co.uk
UK Healthcare; Regent House, Folds Point, Folds Road, Bolton, BL1 2RZ; tel: 0845 2088 632; e-mail: info@ukhealthcare.org.uk; website: http://www.ukhealthcare.org.uk
Westfield Health; Westfield House, 87 Division Street, Sheffield S1 1HT; tel: 0114 250 2000; e-mail: enquiries@westfieldhealth.com; website: http://www.westfieldhealth.com
WHA Healthcare; 60 Newport Road, Cardiff, CF2 1YG; tel: 029 2048 5461; e-mail: mail@whahealthcare.co.uk; website: http://www.whalhealthcare.co.uk
WHCA; Worcester House, 9 St Mary's Street, Worcester, WR1 1HA; tel: 01905 729090; e-mail: orchard@whcaorchard.com; website: http://www.whcaorchard.com

BRITISH HEALTHCARE TRADES ASSOCIATION (BHTA)

New Loom House, Suite 4.06, 101 Back Church Lane, London, E1 1LU

Tel: 020 7702 2141
Fax: 020 7680 4048
E-mail: bhta@bhta.com
Website: www.bhta.com

Enquiries to: Director

Founded: 1917

Organisation type and purpose: Trade association (membership is by subscription), present number of members: 320.

Subject coverage: BHTA's aim is to be seen as the body that effectively represents the sector of the British health care industry that serves those with special physical needs.

Trade and statistical information: Membership lists available for general circulation. All other information available to members only

Publications: Printed

Publications list: Available in print

Access to staff: Contact by letter, by telephone, by fax, by e-mail and via website
Hours: Mon to Fri, 0900 to 1700

Access to building: No access other than to staff

BRITISH HEART FOUNDATION (BHF)

British Heart Foundation, Greater London House, 180 Hampstead Road, London, NW1 7AW

Tel: 020 7554 0000
Fax: 020 7554 0100
Website: www.bhf.org.uk

Enquiries to: Director of Communications
Direct tel: 020 7487 7183
Direct fax: 020 7224 5082
Other contacts: Editor

Founded: 1961

Organisation type and purpose: Registered charity (charity number 225971), research organisation.
Medical research charity working in the field of cardiovascular disease. Producers of a statistical database.
Funds vital research, rehabilitation programmes, life-saving cardiac equipment and educational initiatives, BHF nurses and co-ordinates heart support groups.
Encourages people to learn emergency life support skills.

Subject coverage: Research into the causes, diagnosis, treatment and prevention of heart disease, public education and information, information to the medical profession, rehabilitation, heart support groups, emergency life support skills training.

Trade and statistical information: Coronary heart disease statistics

Publications: Printed, and electronic and video

Publications list: Available online and in print

Access to staff: Contact by letter and by telephone. Appointment necessary.
Hours: Mon to Fri, 0900 to 1700

Has: 9 regional offices

Member of: International Society and Federation of Cardiologists

Regional Offices: Region 1; 4–6 Bridge Street, Tadcaster, North Yorkshire, LS24 9AL; tel: 01937 835421; Region 10; 6 Terrace Walk, Bath, BA1 1LN; tel: 01225 463616; Region 2; 2 Kiln House Yard, Baldock Street, Royston, Hertfordshire, SG8 5AY; tel: 01763 242414; Region 3; 4 Shore Place, Edinburgh, EH6 6UU; tel: 0131 555 5891; Region 5; Oak House B, Ransom Wood Business Park, Southwell Road West, Mansfield, Nottinghamshire, NG21 0HJ; tel: 01623 624558; Region 6; 21 Cathedral Road, Cardiff, CF11 9HA; tel: 029 2038 2368; Region 7; 7 Queen Avenue, Dale Street, Liverpool, L2 4TZ; tel: 0151 236 6988; Region 8; 239A High Street, Erdington, Birmingham, B23 6SS; tel: 0121 382 3168; Region 9; 33 High Street, Ticehurst, Wadhurst, East Sussex, TN5 7AS; tel: 01580 200443

BRITISH HEDGEHOG PRESERVATION SOCIETY (BHPS)

Hedgehog House, Dhustone, Ludlow, Shropshire, SY8 3PL

Tel: 01584 890801
Fax: 01584 891313
E-mail: info@britishhedgehogs.org.uk
Website: www.britishhedgehogs.org.uk

Enquiries to: Chief Executive

Founded: 1982

Organisation type and purpose: National organisation, membership association (membership is by subscription), present number of members: 11,000, registered charity (charity number 326885).
National organisation with some foreign members.
To heighten awareness of needs of hedgehogs.

Subject coverage: Hedgehog care.

Publications: Printed

Access to staff: Contact by letter, by telephone, by e-mail and via website
Hours: Mon to Fri, 0900 to 1700

BRITISH HELICOPTER ADVISORY BOARD LIMITED (BHAB)

Graham Suite, West Entrance, Fairoaks Airport, Chobham, Woking, Surrey, GU24 8HX

Tel: 01276 856100
Fax: 01276 856126
Website: www.bhab.demon.co.uk

Enquiries to: Chief Executive

Other contacts: Executive Assistant for information regarding membership or helicopter charter, services.

Founded: 1969

Organisation type and purpose: Trade association (membership is by subscription). To promote and advise on civil helicopter operations.

Subject coverage: All aspects of helicopter operations.

Publications: Printed

BRITISH HERBAL MEDICINE ASSOCIATION (BHMA)

PO Box 583, Exeter, EX1 9GX

Tel: 0845 680 1134
Fax: 0845 680 1136
E-mail: secretary@bhma.info
Website: www.bhma.info

Enquiries to: Secretary

Founded: 1964

Organisation type and purpose: Trade association.
BHMA provides an advisory service to government and is involved in scientific research and legislation.

Subject coverage: Herbs and herbal medicine; herbal products; Medicines Act (1968); advertising regulations on herbs, suppliers etc.; training facilities for herbal practitioners; research.

Publications: Printed

Access to staff: Contact by letter, by telephone, by fax and by e-mail
Hours: Mon to Fri, 1000 to 1600

BRITISH HERNIA CENTRE

87 Watford Way, Hendon Central, London, NW4 4RS

Tel: 020 8201 7000
E-mail: experts@hernia.org
Website: www.hernia.org

Enquiries to: Chief Executive

Founded: 1990

Organisation type and purpose: Specialist hospital.
The largest tension-free specialist hernia centre in the world.

Subject coverage: All aspects of hernias, treatment and cure.

Library catalogue: All or part available online

Publications: Printed

Publications list: Available online

Access to staff: Contact by letter, by telephone, by fax, by e-mail and via website. Appointment necessary.
Hours: Mon to Fri, 0900 to 1700
Special comments: Telephone lines open 24 hours.

Links with: BHC – Grosvenor Hospitals Group Limited

BRITISH HERPETOLOGICAL SOCIETY (BHS)

Zoological Society of London, Regent's Park, London, NW1 4RY

Tel: 01674 671676
E-mail: secretary@thebhs.org
Website: www.thebhs.org

Enquiries to: Secretary

Founded: 1947

Organisation type and purpose: Learned society (membership is by subscription), present number of members: 600, voluntary organisation, registered charity.
Study of herpetology.

Subject coverage: Herpetology, study and protection of amphibians and reptiles, particularly British and European; captive breeding of species in vivaria as a conservation tool.

Collection: Scientific journals from various countries
Corkhill Collection of books and bound papers

Publications: Printed
Order printed publications from: Secretary

Access to staff: Contact by letter, by telephone and by e-mail
Hours: Mon to Fri, 1730 to 1930

Constituent bodies: Conservation committee, research committee, captive breeding committee, education committee, including a young members' group (Young Herpetologists Club)

BRITISH HOLIDAY AND HOME PARKS ASSOCIATION (BH & HPA Ltd)

6 Pullman Court, Great Western Road, Gloucester, GL1 3ND

Tel: 01452 526911
Fax: 01452 508508
E-mail: enquiries@bhhpa.org.uk
Website: www.bhhpa.org.uk/

Enquiries to: Director General

Founded: 1950

Organisation type and purpose: Trade association.

Subject coverage: The interests of owners and managers of holiday and residential parks nationwide.

Publications: Printed

Access to staff: Contact by letter
Hours: Mon to Fri, 0900 to 1700

BRITISH HOLISTIC MEDICAL ASSOCIATION (BHMA)

5 Sea Lane Close, East Preston, West Sussex, BN16 1NQ

Tel: 01278 722000
E-mail: admin@bhma.org
Website: www.bhma.org

Enquiries to: Chairman

Founded: 1983

Organisation type and purpose:
Membership association (membership is by subscription), present number of members:

continued overleaf

650, voluntary organisation, registered charity (charity number 289459), training organisation, research organisation, publishing house.
BHMA is an organisation of professionals and members of the public who care about the future of healthcare and want to adopt a more holistic approach in their own life and work.
The BHMA is furthering the development of holistic healthcare through bringing together the many people who can contribute to a system for the 21st century by holding conferences, workshops, seminars and by facilitating a network of regional groups.

Subject coverage: Holistic medical practice; complementary therapies, their application in and outside orthodox medical practice; training.

Publications: Printed, and electronic and video

Access to staff: Contact by letter, by telephone, by e-mail and via website
Hours: Mon to Fri, 1000 to 1600
Answerphone checked regularly
Special comments: If contacting by letter please enclose an sae.

Access to building: Prior Appointment Required

BRITISH HOMEOPATHIC ASSOCIATION (BHA)

Hahnemann House, 29 Park Street West, Luton, LU1 3BE

Tel: 01582 408675
Fax: 01582 723032
E-mail: info@trusthomeopathy.org
Website: www.britishhomeopathic.org

Enquiries to: Chief Executive

Founded: 1902

Organisation type and purpose:
Membership association, registered charity (charity number 235900).
To promote homeopathy and raise funds for research and education.

Subject coverage: Homeopathy practised by statutorily registered healthcare professionals – doctors, dentists, nurses, vets, pharmacists, podiatrists, midwives, osteopaths

Information services: Information on medical homeopathy.

Publications: Printed
Order printed publications from: British Homeopathic Association

Access to staff: Contact by letter, by telephone, by e-mail and via website. Appointment necessary.
Hours: Mon to Fri, 0900 to 1700

Access to building: Prior appointment required

Access for disabled people: *Hours:* Mon to Fri, 0900 to 1700

BRITISH HOROLOGICAL FEDERATION (BHF)

Upton Hall, Upton, Newark, Nottinghamshire, NG23 5TE

Tel: 01636 813795
Fax: 01636 812258
E-mail: clocks@bhi.co.uk
Website: www.bhi.co.uk/bhfhome.htm

Enquiries to: Secretary General

Founded: 1932

Organisation type and purpose: Trade association.

Subject coverage: Clocks and watches, manufacturers and suppliers, horological technology (including standards), horological trade fairs, European directives for the horological industry.

Publications: Printed

Access to staff: Contact by fax
Hours: Mon to Fri, 0900 to 1700

Member of: European Committee for the Industry

Other address: British Horological Federation; tel: 01636 706965; fax: 01636 706965; e-mail: gevansbhf@aol.com

Sister organisation at the same address the: British Horological Institute

BRITISH HOROLOGICAL INSTITUTE (BHI)

Upton Hall, Upton, Newark, Nottinghamshire, NG23 5TE

Tel: 01636 813795
Fax: 01636 812258
E-mail: clocks@bhi.co.uk
Website: www.bhi.co.uk

Enquiries to: General Manager
Other contacts: Education Team for education related services and facilities.

Founded: 1858

Organisation type and purpose:
Professional body, membership association (membership is by subscription), present number of members: 3,500, museum, historic building, house or site, training organisation.
To protect and further the science and art of horology.

Subject coverage: Horology.

Collection: Library and museum

Publications: Printed

Access to staff: Contact by letter, by telephone, by fax, by e-mail and via website. Appointment necessary. Letter of introduction required. Non-members charged.
Hours: Mon to Fri, 0900 to 1700

Access to building: Prior arrangement necessary
Hours: By appointment for members only. Group visits for non-mems by prior arrangement

Access for disabled people: Parking provided, level entry, toilet facilities
Special comments: Access to ground floor only.

BRITISH HORSE SOCIETY (BHS)

Abbey Park, Stareton, Kenilworth, Warwickshire CV8 2XZ

Tel: 02476 840500 or 0844 848 1666
Fax: 02476 840501
E-mail: enquiry@bhs.org.uk
Website: www.bhs.org.uk
Website: www.britishhorse.com

Enquiries to: Director of Membership, Marketing and Communications
Direct tel: 02476 840506
Other contacts: Chief Executive

Founded: 1947; created by the merger of Institute of the Horse and Pony Club and the National Horse Association of Great Britain

Organisation type and purpose:
Membership association (membership is by subscription), registered charity (charity number 210504 and SC038516).
Represents all equine interests and has the following objectives: to promote and advance the education, training and safety of the public in all matters relating to the horse; to promote the use, breeding, well-being, safety, environment, health and management of the horse for the public benefit; to promote community participation in healthy recreation involving the horse; to promote and facilitate the prevention of cruelty, neglect or harm to horses and to promote the relief, safety, sanctuary, rescue and welfare of horses in need of care, attention and assistance; to promote and secure the provision, protection and preservation of rights of way and of access for ridden and driven horses over public roads, highways, footpaths, bridleways, carriageways, public paths and other land.

Subject coverage: Equine welfare, equestrian safety, access and riding rights of way, qualifications, training and careers, riding schools, horse and pony breeds, riding clubs, competitions.

Collection: Library deposited with Warwickshire College, Moreton Morrell

Trade and statistical information: Data on statistics relating to equestrian activities

Publications: Printed, and electronic and video
Order printed publications from: website: http://www.britishhorse.com

Access to staff: Contact by letter, by telephone, by fax, by e-mail and in person
Hours: Mon to Thu, 0835 to 1700; Fri, 0835 to 1500

Access for disabled people: Ramped entry, level entry, toilet facilities

Affiliated to: The British Equestrian Federation (BEF); National Agriculture Centre, Stoneleigh Park, Kenilworth, Warwickshire, CV8 2RH; tel: 01203 698871; fax: 01203 696484

Affiliates: British Riding Clubs; The British Horse Society, Abbey Park, Stareton, Kenilworth, Warwickshire, CV8 2XZ; tel: 01926 707700; fax: 01926 707764

Represented by the BEF in matters concerned with the: Fédération Equestre Internationale (FEI)

BRITISH HORSEBALL ASSOCIATION (BHA)

67 Clifford Road, New Barnet, Barnet, Hertfordshire, EN5 5NZ

Tel: 020 8441 1799
Fax: 020 8441 1060

Website: www.british-horseball-association.btck.co.uk/

Enquiries to: Chairman
Direct e-mail: jim@horseball.org.uk

Founded: 1991

Organisation type and purpose:
Membership association.
National governing body.
To control and develop the game of horseball.

Subject coverage: The game of horseball.

Publications: Printed

Publications list: Available online and in print

Access to staff: Contact by letter, by telephone, by fax, by e-mail and via website. Appointment necessary.
Hours: Mon to Fri, 0900 to 1700

BRITISH HOSPITALITY ASSOCIATION (BHA)

Queen's House, 55–56 Lincoln's Inn Fields, London, WC2A 3BH

Tel: 020 7404 7744
Fax: 020 7404 7799
E-mail: bha@bha.org.uk
Website: www.bha.org.uk/

Enquiries to: Information Officer
Direct e-mail: bill@bha.org.uk

Founded: 1910

Organisation type and purpose: Trade association (membership is by subscription).

Subject coverage: Hotels, restaurants, industrial catering, motorway catering, employment in the hotel and catering industry (legislation and conditions), computer software for hotels etc, licensing law, food hygiene.

Trade and statistical information: Contract catering survey.
Starting a small hotel or restaurant business

Publications: Printed
Order printed publications from: Office Manager

Publications list: Available in print

Access to staff: Contact by letter, by telephone, by fax, by e-mail and via website. Access for members only.
Hours: Mon to Fri, 0900 to 1700

Access to building: No prior appointment required

Member of: European Federation of Contract Catering Organisations (FERCO); Brussels; European Hotel, Restaurant and Catering Association (HOTREL); Brussels; International Hotel and Restaurants Association (IHRA); Paris

Other addresses: British Hospitality Association; c/o Dundas & Wilson, Saltire Court, Edinburgh, EH1 2EN; tel: 0131 200 7484; fax: 0131 228 8888; e-mail: john.a.loudon@dundas.wilson.com

BRITISH HUMANIST ASSOCIATION (BHA)

1 Gower Street, London, WC1E 6HD

Tel: 020 7079 3580
Fax: 020 7079 3588
E-mail: info@humanism.org.uk
Website: www.humanism.org.uk

Enquiries to: Reception
Other contacts: Assistant to the Chief Executive

Founded: 1896

Organisation type and purpose: Learned society, membership association (membership is by subscription), present number of members: 4,000, service industry, registered charity (charity number 285987), suitable for ages: all.

Subject coverage: Humanism, moral education, ethics, law as it relates to religious privilege, reform of religious education and collective worship, non-religious funerals, weddings and baby namings.

Collection: Archive, books, international journals

Publications: Printed, and electronic and video

Publications list: Available online and in print

Access to staff: Contact by letter, by telephone, by fax, by e-mail and via website. Appointment necessary.
Hours: Mon to Fri, 0900 to 1700

Affiliated to: Religious Education Council

Has: 50 regional and local groups, parliamentary group; branch details are available from Head Office

Member organisation of: European Humanist Federation; International Humanist and Ethical Union

BRITISH HUMANITARIAN AID

11 Devon Road, Canterbury, Kent, CT1 1RP

Tel: 01227 453434
Fax: 01227 787728
E-mail: office@britishhumanitarianaid.co.uk
Website: www.britishhumanitarianaid.co.uk/

Enquiries to: Director
Direct tel: 07774 100 273 (mobile)

Founded: 1992

Organisation type and purpose: Voluntary organisation, registered charity (charity number 1031547).
Aid to the needy abroad, mainly children, presently Ukraine.

Subject coverage: Convoying of humanitarian aid to those in need, Ukraine, supplying aid. Ukraine – centre for adults and children in need, helping 4 orphanages in Ukraine for physically and mentally handicapped children.

Publications: Printed

Access to staff: Contact by letter, by telephone, by fax, by e-mail and via website
Hours: Mon to Fri, 0900 to 1700

BRITISH HYPNOTHERAPY ASSOCIATION (BHA)

30 Cotsford Avenue, New Malden, Surrey KT3 5EU

Tel: 020 8942 3988 or 020 8579 5533
E-mail: bha@bethere.co.uk
Website: www.british-hypnotherapy-association.org

Enquiries to: Secretary

Founded: 1958

Organisation type and purpose:
International organisation, national organisation, advisory body, learned society, professional body (membership is by qualification), present number of members: 348, training organisation, consultancy, research organisation.
The organisation of practitioners who have had at least four years of relevant training and who comply with professional standards of competence and ethics in psychotherapy involving hypnotherapy.
To maintain a register of competent qualified practitioners and raise standards in the treatment of nervous problems.

Subject coverage: Hypnotherapy; hypnoanalysis; psychotherapy; psychodynamics; nervous problems; emotional problems; birth; parenthood; human relationships; phobias; compulsions, lack of confidence; fears; learning difficulties; parent problems; migraine; psoriasis; psychosexual problems; anxiety etc.

Publications: Printed

Publications list: Available in print

Access to staff: Contact by letter and by telephone. Appointment necessary.
Hours: Mon to Fri, 0900 to 1700

BRITISH IMAGING AND PHOTOGRAPHIC ASSOCIATION (BIPA)

Ambassador House, Brigstock Road, Thornton Heath, Surrey, CR7 7JG

Tel: 020 8665 5395
Fax: 020 8665 6447
E-mail: bipa@admin.co.uk
Website: www.bipa.org

Enquiries to: Chief Executive

Founded: 1918

Organisation type and purpose: Trade association.

Subject coverage: Photographic and imaging products.

Access to staff: Contact by letter, by fax and by e-mail
Hours: Mon to Fri, 0900 to 1700

BRITISH IN VITRO DIAGNOSTIC ASSOCIATION (BIVDA)

1 Queen Anne's Gate, London, SW1H 9BT

Tel: 020 7957 4633
Fax: 020 7957 4644
E-mail: enquiries@bivda.co.uk
Website: www.bivda.co.uk

Founded: 1992

Organisation type and purpose: Trade association (membership is by subscription), present number of members: 120 companies.

Subject coverage: in vitro diagnostics; laboratory medicine.

continued overleaf

Access to staff: Contact by letter, by telephone, by fax, by e-mail, in person and via website. Appointment necessary.
Hours: Mon to Fri, 0900 to 1700

BRITISH INDEPENDENT RETAILERS ASSOCIATION (bira)

225 Bristol Road, Edgbaston, Birmingham, B5 7UB

Tel: 0121 4466688
Fax: 0121 4465215
E-mail: info@bira.co.uk
Website: www.bira.co.uk

Organisation type and purpose: trade association; lobbying organization; membership (by subscription).

Subject coverage: independent retailing across a range of sectors.

Publications: Printed

Member organisations: British Agricultural and Garden Machinery Association; British Hardware Federation; Fashion Association of Britain; Home Decoration Retailers Association; Pet Product Retail Association; The Cookshop and Housewares Association

BRITISH INDUSTRIAL FURNACE CONSTRUCTORS ASSOCIATION (BIFCA)

National Metalforming Centre, 47 Birmingham Road West Bromwich B70 6PY

Tel: 0121 601 6350
Fax: 0121 601 6387
E-mail: enquiry@bifca.org.uk
Website: www.bifca.org.uk

Enquiries to: Secretary

Organisation type and purpose: Trade association.

Subject coverage: Design and manufacture of furnaces, refurbishment, ancillary equipment and control systems.

Access to staff: Contact by letter, by telephone, by fax, by e-mail and via website. Appointment necessary.
Hours: Mon to Fri, 0900 to 1700

Access to building: Prior appointment required

Federated member of the: Metcom Organisation (Mechanical and Metal Trades Confederation) (METCOM); tel: 0141 332 0826; fax: 0141 332 5788; website: http://www.metcon.org.uk

Founder member of: European Committee of Furnace and Heating Equipment Associations (CECOF); Frankfurt, Germany; tel: +49 69 66031413; fax: +49 69 66031692; e-mail: cecof@vdma.org

BRITISH INDUSTRIAL TRUCK ASSOCIATION (BITA)

5–7 High Street, Sunninghill, Berkshire, SL5 9NQ

Tel: 01344 623800
Fax: 01344 291197
E-mail: info@bita.org.uk
Website: www.bita.org.uk/

Enquiries to: Secretary General
Other contacts: Technical Officer for technical matters.

Founded: 1942

Organisation type and purpose: Trade association, present number of members: 130.
Represents UK manufacturers of industrial trucks, UK suppliers to the industry and importers of trucks, components and accessories.

Subject coverage: Industrial trucks (lift trucks), operator safety, code books and guidance notes for the industry.

Publications: Printed

Publications list: Available online and in print

Access to staff: Contact by letter, by telephone, by fax and by e-mail
Hours: Mon to Thu, 0900 to 1700; Fri, 0900 to 1630

Member of: British Materials Handling Federation; tel: 0121 200 2100; fax: 0121 200 1306

BRITISH INFECTION SOCIETY (BIS)

Department of Infection and Tropical Medicine, Leicester Royal Infirmary, Infirmary Square, Leicester, LE1 5WW

Tel: 0116 258 6952
Fax: 0116 258 5067
E-mail: martin.wiselka@uhl-tr.nhs.uk
Website: www.britishinfectionsociety.org

Enquiries to: Honorary Secretary

Founded: 1997

Organisation type and purpose: Learned society.

Subject coverage: Infection and communicable diseases and within that general context, public health, microbiology, zoonoses.

Publications: Printed

Access to staff: Contact by letter, by fax and by e-mail
Hours: Mon to Fri, 0900 to 1700

BRITISH INSTITUTE AT ANKARA (BIAA)

10–11 Carlton House Terrace, London, SW1Y 5AH

Tel: 020 7969 5204
Fax: 020 7969 5401
E-mail: biaa@britac.ac.uk
Website: www.biaa.ac.uk

Enquiries to: London Manager

Founded: 1948

Organisation type and purpose: Learned society, registered charity (charity number 313940), research organisation, publishing house.
The British Institute at Ankara (BIAA) supports, promotes and publishes British research focused on Turkey and the Black Sea littoral in all academic disciplines within the arts, humanities and social sciences, whilst maintaining a centre of excellence in Ankara focused on the archaeology and related subjects of Turkey.

Subject coverage: British research focused on Turkey and the Black Sea littoral in all academic disciplines within the arts, humanities and social sciences.

Collection: Library (53,000 vols), maps, inscription squeezes, pottery, botanical and bone collections, field work archives, photographs and slides

Non-library collection catalogue: All or part available online and in-house

Library catalogue: All or part available online and in-house

Publications: Printed
Order printed publications from: Oxbow Books, Park End Place, Oxford, OX1 1HN; tel: 01865 241249; website: http://www.oxbowbooks.com

Publications list: Available online and in print

Access to staff: Contact by letter, by telephone, by fax, by e-mail, in person and via website. Appointment necessary.
Hours: Mon to Fri, 0900 to 1700

Also at: British Institute at Ankara; Tahran Caddesi 24, 06700 Kavaklidere, Ankara, Turkey; tel: +90 312 427 5487; fax: +90 312 428 0159

Parent body: British Academy; 10–11 Carlton House Terrace, London, SW1Y 5AH

BRITISH INSTITUTE FOR ALLERGY AND ENVIRONMENTAL THERAPY (BIAET)

Ffynnonwen, Llangwyryfon, Aberystwyth, Ceredigion, SY23 4EY

Tel: 01974 241376
Fax: 01974 241795
E-mail: allergy@onetel.com
Website: www.allergy.org.uk

Enquiries to: Principal

Founded: 1987

Organisation type and purpose: Professional body.

Subject coverage: Allergies; clinical ecology.

Education services: Diploma:The Identification and Treatment of Allergic Disorders (DipAET).

Access to staff: Contact by letter, by telephone and by fax
Hours: Mon to Fri, 0900 to 1500

BRITISH INSTITUTE FOR LEARNING & DEVELOPMENT (BILD)

The British Institute for Learning & Development, WestPoint, 78 Queens Road, Clifton, Bristol, BS8 1QU

Tel: 0117 985 6949
Fax: 0117 959 6518
E-mail: info@thebild.org
Website: www.thebild.org/

Enquiries to: Marketing and Development Manager
Other contacts: General Manager

Founded: 1990; formerly called the British Learning Association (formed by merger in 2003 of the British Association for Open Learning and The Forum for Technology in Training) (year of change 2007)

Organisation type and purpose: International organisation, national organisation, trade association, membership association (membership is by subscription), present number of members: 300, registered charity (charity number 328229).
To build a dynamic community, with global reach, committed to inculcating excellence and best practice in learning.

Subject coverage: Open, flexible and distance learning and e-learning. All aspects associated with this area.

Publications: Printed

Access to staff: Contact by letter, by telephone, by fax, by e-mail and via website. Appointment necessary.
Hours: Mon to Fri, 0900 to 1700

BRITISH INSTITUTE IN EASTERN AFRICA (BIEA)

10 Carlton House Terrace, London, SW1Y 5AH

Tel: 020 7969 5201
Fax: 020 7969 5401
E-mail: biea@britac.ac.uk
Website: www.biea.ac.uk

Enquiries to: London Secretary

Founded: 1960

Organisation type and purpose: Learned society (membership is by subscription), registered charity (charity number 1061622).

Subject coverage: Research into the history, archaeology and related subjects of eastern Africa.

Non-library collection catalogue: All or part available online and in-house

Library catalogue: All or part available online and in-house

Publications: Printed
Order printed publications from: Membership enquires via website: http://www.biea.ac.uk
Sponsored publications can be ordered through Oxbow Books, 10 Hythe Bridge St, Oxford, OX1 1EW, tel: 01865 241249, fax: 01865 794449

Access to staff: Contact by letter, by telephone, by fax, by e-mail and via website
Hours: Tue and Thu, 0930 to 1730

Also at: British Institute in Eastern Africa; PO Box 30710, Nairobi, Kenya; tel: 00 254 2 43721; fax: 00 254 2 43365; e-mail: office@biea.ac.uk

BRITISH INSTITUTE OF AGRICULTURAL CONSULTANTS (BIAC)

The Estate Office, Torry Hill, Milstead, Sittingbourne, Kent, ME9 0SP

Tel: 01795 830100
Fax: 01795 830243
E-mail: info@biac.co.uk
Website: www.biac.co.uk

Enquiries to: Chief Executive
Direct e-mail: anthony.hyde@farmline.com

Founded: 1957

Organisation type and purpose: Professional body.

Subject coverage: Agriculture, horticulture, forestry, silviculture, arboriculture, crop production, livestock production, mechanisation, land drainage and reclamation, landscape planning, chemicals and fertilisers, plant pathology, farm and estate management, farm buildings, pollution, soils, management, finance, planning appeals, agricultural education and law, fish farming, photography, snail farming, deer farming, historic houses and gardens, leisure and amenity, environment and conservation, arbitration.

Publications: Printed, and electronic and video

Access to staff: Contact by letter, by telephone, by fax, by e-mail and via website
Hours: Mon to Fri, 0900 to 1700

BRITISH INSTITUTE OF CLEANING SCIENCE (BICSc)

9 Premier Court, Boarden Close, Moulton Park, Northampton, NN3 6LF

Tel: 01604 678710
Fax: 01604 645988
E-mail: info@bics.org.uk
Website: www.bics.org.uk

Enquiries to: Executive Director
Direct tel: 01604 678715
Direct e-mail: stan@bics.org.uk
Other contacts: Business Development Manager

Founded: 1961

Organisation type and purpose: Membership association (membership is by qualification), present number of members: 5,000, service industry, suitable for ages: 18+. Education and training body for the cleaning industry.

Subject coverage: Education, training and general information regarding the cleaning industry, cleaning of buildings, internally and externally; cleaning of outside areas; education and training.

Publications: Printed, and electronic and video

Publications list: Available online and in print

Access to staff: Contact by letter, by telephone, by fax, by e-mail and via website. Appointment necessary.
Hours: Mon to Fri, 0830 to 1700

Links with: British Cleaning Council

BRITISH INSTITUTE OF FACILITIES MANAGEMENT (BIFM)

Number One Building, The Causeway, Bishop's Stortford, Hertfordshire, CM23 2ER

Tel: 0845 058 1356
Fax: 01279 712 669
E-mail: info@bifm.org.uk
Website: www.bifm.org.uk

Enquiries to: Membership Team
Direct tel: 0845 058 1356
Direct fax: 01279 712 669
Direct e-mail: membership@bifm.org.uk

Founded: 1993

Organisation type and purpose: Professional body (membership is by subscription, election or invitation), present number of members: 12,500.
To promote awareness of facilities management and provide support, education, training and information to members.

Subject coverage: All aspects of facilities management, including space planning, lighting, business continuity planning, measurement protocol.

Trade and statistical information: Survey of members' responsibilities.
Research Directory

Publications: Printed, and electronic and video

Publications list: Available online and in print

Access to staff: Contact by letter, by telephone, by fax, by e-mail and via website. Appointment necessary.
Hours: Mon to Fri, 0900 to 1715

BRITISH INSTITUTE OF GRAPHOLOGISTS (BIG)

PO Box 3060, Gerrards Cross, Buckinghamshire, SL9 9XP

Tel: 01753 891 241
Website: www.britishgraphology.org

Enquiries to: General Secretary

Founded: 1983

Organisation type and purpose: Learned society.
To promote understanding and recognition of graphology.

Subject coverage: Graphology consultancy in: vocational guidance; information and professional training; personnel selection, etc.

Publications: Printed

Access to staff: Contact by letter, by telephone and by e-mail
Hours: Mon to Fri, 0900 to 1700

Also at: Association of Disabled Professionals; Netley Lodge, 134 Old Woking Road, Woking, Surrey, GU22 8NY

Subsidiary body: Graphology Research & Education Trust (GRET); 55 Whitton Avenue East, Greenford, Middlesex, UB6 0BQ; tel: 020 8902 4183

BRITISH INSTITUTE OF HOMEOPATHY (BIH)

Endeavour House, 80 High Street, Egham, Surrey, TW20 9HE

Tel: 01784 473800
Fax: 01784 473801
E-mail: britinsthom@compuserve.com
Website: www.britinsthom.com

Enquiries to: Managing Director

Founded: 1986

Organisation type and purpose: International organisation, training organisation.

continued overleaf

Subject coverage: Homoeopathic medicine, homoeopathic pharmacy, herbal medicine, anatomy, physiology, pathology, nature of disease. Bach flower therapy, nutrition, differential diagnosis, aromatherapy.

Publications: Printed, and electronic and video

Access to staff: Contact by letter, by telephone, by fax, by e-mail and in person. Appointment necessary.
Hours: Mon to Fri, 0900 to 1700

Access to building: No prior appointment required

Parent body: The British Institute of Homeopathy Limited; tel: 01784 440467; fax: 01784 449887; e-mail: britinsthom@compuserve.com

BRITISH INSTITUTE OF HUMAN RIGHTS (BIHR)

School of Law, Queen Mary University of London, Mile End Road, London, E1 4NS

Tel: 020 7882 5850
E-mail: info@bihr.org.uk
Website: www.bihr.org.uk

Enquiries to: Administrator

Founded: 1970

Organisation type and purpose: Registered charity (charity number 1101575).
Conducting research, organising lectures, conferences, etc. in the human rights field.

Subject coverage: Human rights with particular application to education; European Convention on Human Rights.

Publications: Printed

Access to staff: Contact by letter and by e-mail
Hours: Mon to Fri, 0930 to 1730

Close links with: King's College, London

Connections with: Council of Europe; Other human rights organisations through the Human Rights Network

BRITISH INSTITUTE OF INDUSTRIAL THERAPY (BIIT)

243 Shelley Road, Wellingborough, Northamptonshire, NN8 3EN

Tel: 01933 675327
Fax: 01933 675327

Enquiries to: Administrator

Founded: 1981

Organisation type and purpose:
Professional body (membership is by subscription), present number of members: 110, voluntary organisation, registered charity (charity number 283951), consultancy.
National charitable organisation with members from both statutory and voluntary sector units.

Subject coverage: Rehabilitation through work therapy and associated social education and training for the relief and rehabilitation of the mentally disabled. Advancement of science and practice of industrial therapy. Educational courses for those working in the field of industrial therapy. Consultancy service on work rehabilitation for members.

Publications: Printed

Access to staff: Appointment necessary.
Hours: Mon to Fri, 0900 to 1700
Special comments: Answerphone if not available.

Chairman: British Institute of Industrial Therapy; Lewin Cottage, Jeremy's Lane, Bolney, Haywards Heath, West Sussex, RH17 5QE; tel: 01444 881054

BRITISH INSTITUTE OF INNKEEPING (BII)

Wessex House, 80 Park Street, Camberley, Surrey, GU15 3PT

Tel: 01276 684449
Fax: 01276 23045
E-mail: info@bii.org
Website: www.bii.org
Website: www.barzone.co.uk

Enquiries to: Reception
Direct fax: 01276 682214
Direct e-mail: reception@bii.org

Founded: 1981

Organisation type and purpose:
Professional body (membership is by qualification, election or invitation), present number of members: 16,000, registered charity (charity number 283945), training organisation.
BII is the professional body for the licensed retail sector. BII's aim is to provide skills, information and qualifications to help members run more successful businesses. BIIAB is a wholly owned subsidiary awarding qualifications for licensed hospitality.

Subject coverage: Qualifications for those entering or already in the licensed retail sector (pubs) and off licences. Information on careers in licensed retailing.

Trade and statistical information: Data relating to careers in the licensed retail sector (pubs)

Publications: Printed

Publications list: Available online

Access to staff: Contact by letter, by telephone, by fax, by e-mail, in person and via website
Hours: Mon to Fri, 0900 to 1700

Links with: BIIAB – qualifications for licensed hospitality; tel: 01276 684449; fax: 01276 23045; e-mail: info@bii.org

BRITISH INSTITUTE OF INTERIOR DESIGN (BIID)

109 Design Centre East, Chelsea Harbour, London, SW10 0XF

Tel: 0207 349 0800
Fax: 0207 349 0500
E-mail: info@biid.org.uk
Website: www.biid.org.uk

Founded: 2002; created by the merger of Interior Decorators & Designers Association (originally set up in 1966) and International Interior Design Association (UK Chapter) (year of change 2002); formerly called The British Interior Design Association (BIDA) (year of change 2009)

Organisation type and purpose:
Professional organisation for interior designers in the UK, its growing national and international membership represents both the commercial and residential sectors, from heritage to cutting edge.
Committed to encouraging and supporting creativity and competence in the field of interior design through facilitating best practice, practical professional support, development opportunities and education.

Subject coverage: Interior design.

Order printed publications from: http://www.ribabookshops.com

Publications list: Available online

Access to staff: Contact by letter, by telephone, by fax and by e-mail

Member organisation of: Construction Industry Council

Represented on the board of: International Federation of Interior Architects and Designers

BRITISH INSTITUTE OF INTERNATIONAL AND COMPARATIVE LAW (BIICL)

Charles Clore House, 17 Russell Square, London, WC1B 5JP

Tel: 020 7862 5151
Fax: 020 7862 5152
E-mail: info@biicl.org
Website: www.biicl.org

Enquiries to: Director

Founded: 1952

Organisation type and purpose:
International organisation, consultancy, research organisation.
Commonwealth Legal Advisory Service.

Subject coverage: Public international law; EC law; human rights law; private international law; comparative law; Commonwealth law.

Publications: Printed

Publications list: Available online and in print

Access to staff: Contact by letter, by telephone, by fax and by e-mail
Hours: Mon to Fri, 0930 to 1730

BRITISH INSTITUTE OF LEARNING DISABILITIES (BILD)

Campion House, Green Street, Kidderminster, Worcestershire, DY10 1JL

Tel: 01562 723010
Fax: 01562 723029
E-mail: enquiries@bild.org.uk
Website: www.bild.org.uk

Enquiries to: Information Administrator
Direct tel: 01562 723014
Direct e-mail: k.brackley@bild.org.uk

Founded: 1972

Organisation type and purpose:
Professional body (membership is by subscription), registered charity (charity

number 1019663), training organisation, consultancy, research organisation, publishing house.
Receives financial support from the Department of Health.
Aims to improve the quality of life of people with learning disabilities, through advancing education, research and practice and by promoting better ways of working with and for children and adults with learning difficulties.

Subject coverage: Learning disability and multi-handicap, medical, nursing, social, educational and environmental needs.

Library catalogue: All or part available in-house

Publications: Printed
Order printed publications from: BookSource, 32 Finlas Street, Cowlair's Estate, Glasgow, G22 5DU; tel: 08702 402182; fax: 0141 557 0189

Publications list: Available online and in print

Access to staff: Contact by letter, by telephone, by fax, by e-mail and via website. Appointment necessary.
Hours: Mon to Thu, 0900 to 1300 and 1400 to 1700; Fri, 0900 to 1300 and 1400 to 1630

Access to building: Prior appointment required

Access for disabled people: Parking provided, level entry, access to all public areas, toilet facilities

BRITISH INSTITUTE OF MUSCULOSKELETAL MEDICINE (BIMM)

The British Institute of Musculoskeletal Medicine, PO Box 1116, Bushey, Herts, WD23 9BY

Tel: 0208 421 9910
Fax: 0208 386 4183
E-mail: deena@bimm.org.uk
Website: www.bimm.org.uk

Enquiries to: Honorary Secretary
Direct e-mail: deena@bimm.org.uk
Other contacts: Secretary for non-medical enquiries.

Founded: 1992

Organisation type and purpose:
Professional body (membership is by subscription), present number of members: 340, registered charity, training organisation, research organisation.
Dissemination of knowledge to medical profession of musculoskeletal medicine.

Subject coverage: Musculoskeletal medicine, including manual/manipulative medicine, all aspects of mechanical disorders of the spine and peripheral joints, and sports injuries. This specifically includes soft tissue disorders/injuries of muscles, ligaments, tendons and fascia.

Publications: Printed

Access to staff: Contact by letter, by telephone, by fax and by e-mail
Hours: Mon to Fri, 0900 to 1700

Access to building: No access other than to staff

Affiliated to: British League Against Rheumatism (BLAR); Fédération Internationale de Médecine Manuelle (FIMM)

BRITISH INSTITUTE OF NON-DESTRUCTIVE TESTING (BINDT)

Newton Building, St George's Avenue, Northampton, NN2 6JB

Tel: 01604 893811
Fax: 01604 893861
E-mail: info@bindt.org
Website: www.bindt.org

Enquiries to: Secretary

Founded: 1954

Organisation type and purpose: Learned society.
To promote the science and practice of non-destructive testing and all other associated materials testing disciplines.

Subject coverage: Non-destructive testing, condition and health monitoring and all other materials and quality testing disciplines. Various specialist groups for NDT application, e.g. aerospace, service inspection, condition monitoring and diagnostic technology group.

Library catalogue: All or part available in-house

Publications: Printed, and electronic and video
Order printed publications from: website: http://www.bindt.org
Order electronic and video publications from: tel: 01604 893811

Publications list: Available online

Access to staff: Contact by letter, by telephone, by fax, by e-mail and via website

A nominated body of the: Engineering Council

Member organisation of: European Federation for Non-Destructive Testing; International Committee for Non-Destructive Testing

BRITISH INSTITUTE OF OCCUPATIONAL HYGIENISTS (BIOH)

5–6 Melbourne Business Court, Millennium Way, Pride Park, Derby, DE24 8LZ

Tel: 01332 298101
Fax: 01332 298099
E-mail: admin@bohs.org
Website: www.bioh.org

Enquiries to: Media Enquiries
Direct tel: 01332 250701
Direct e-mail: anthea@bohs.org

Founded: 1997

Organisation type and purpose:
Professional body (membership is by subscription, qualification), registered charity (charity number 1066537).

Subject coverage: Occupational hygiene.

Access to staff: Contact by letter, by telephone, by fax and by e-mail
Hours: Mon to Fri, 0830 to 1630

Access to building: No access other than to staff

BRITISH INSTITUTE OF ORGAN STUDIES (BIOS)

Ashcroft, 10 Ridgegate Close, Reigate, Surrey, RH2 0HT

Tel: 01737 241355
E-mail: secretary@bios.org.uk
Website: www.bios.org.uk

Enquiries to: Secretary
Direct e-mail: c.kearl@blueyonder.co.uk
Other contacts: Hon. Archivist; Membership Secretary

Founded: 1976

Organisation type and purpose: Learned society (membership is by subscription), present number of members: c. 650, voluntary organisation, registered charity (charity number 283936), suitable for ages: 11–80.

Subject coverage: Conservation, history and restoration of historic British pipe organs; information on repertoire and performance practice.

Collection: British Organ Archive (largest single collection of original records, order books, designs, working drawings, etc. of organ builders from 1820); housed in Birmingham Central Library

Non-library collection catalogue: All or part available online

Publications: Printed
Order printed publications from: Positif Press, British Institute of Organ Studies, 130 Southfield Road, Oxford, OX4 1PA, tel: 01865 243220; fax: 01865 243272; e-mail: john .f.brennan@btinternet.com

Publications list: Available online

Access to staff: Contact by letter, by fax, by e-mail and via website. Appointment necessary. Letter of introduction required.
Hours: Mon to Fri, 0900 to 1700
Special comments: Visitors to British Organ Archive require a letter of introduction and should arrange a prior appointment with Birmingham Central Library (City Archives), where the Archive is held.

Access to building: Prior appointment required
Hours: Mon, Tue, Fri, Sat, 0900 to 1700; Thu, 0900 to 2000

Constituent bodies: British Organ Archive (BOA); National Pipe Organ Register (NPOR)

BRITISH INSTITUTE OF PROFESSIONAL PHOTOGRAPHY (BIPP)

The Coach House, The Firs, High Street, Whitchurch, Buckinghamshire, HP22 4SJ

Tel: 01296 642020
Fax: 01296 641553
E-mail: info@bipp.com
Website: www.bipp.com

Enquiries to: Project Manager
Direct e-mail: marketing@bipp.com

Founded: 1901

Organisation type and purpose:
Professional body.

Subject coverage: Imaging/Photography

continued overleaf

Information services: Find professional photographers alongside hints and tips on booking a photographer.

Education services: Qualifications, education & training are at the core of the BIPP

Publications: Printed
Order printed publications from: www.bipp.com

Publications list: Available online

Access to staff: Contact by letter, by telephone, by fax and by e-mail
Hours: Mon to Fri, 0900 to 1700

BRITISH INSTITUTE OF RADIOLOGY (BIR)

131–151 Great Titchfield Street, London, W1W 5BB

Tel: 020 3586 8325
Fax: 020 3008 7759
E-mail: admin@bir.org.uk
Website: www.bir.org.uk

Enquiries to: General Secretary
Direct tel: 020 7307 1406
Other contacts: Information Centre Manager

Founded: 1897

Organisation type and purpose:
Professional body, registered charity (charity number GB 233 7553 63).

Subject coverage: Radiology, radiography, diagnostic imaging, ultrasound, radiation protection, radiation physics, radiotherapy and oncology, computed tomography, radiobiology, nuclear medicine, NMR, MRI (magnetic resonance imaging), history of radiology.

Collection: Hugh Davies Bequest
KC Clark Slide Collection of 3,500 glass slides

Library catalogue: All or part available online

Publications: Printed

Publications list: Available online and in print

Access to staff: Contact by letter, by telephone, by fax and by e-mail. Appointment necessary. All charged.
Hours: Mon, Wed and Fri, 0900 to 1700; Tue and Thu, 1000 to 1800

BRITISH INSURANCE BROKERS' ASSOCIATION (BIBA)

8th Floor, John Stow House, 18 Bevis Marks, London, EC3A 7JB

Tel: 0870 950 1790
Fax: 020 7626 9676
E-mail: enquiries@biba.org.uk
Website: www.biba.org.uk

Enquiries to: Chief Executive

Founded: 1978

Organisation type and purpose: Trade association.
Representing insurance brokers and independent intermediaries for the sale of general insurance.

Subject coverage: The sale of general insurance products through an insurance broker or independent intermediary.

Publications: Printed

Access to staff: Contact by letter, by telephone, by fax, by e-mail and via website
Hours: Mon to Fri, 0900 to 1700

BRITISH INSURANCE LAW ASSOCIATION (BILA)

British Insurance Law Association, 47 Bury Street, Stowmarket, Suffolk, IP14 1HD

Tel: 07776 115795
Fax: 01449 770941
E-mail: bila@insuranceevents.com
Website: www.bila.org.uk

Enquiries to: Administrator

Founded: 1964

Organisation type and purpose: Learned society.
Education and exchange of ideas.

Subject coverage: Law affecting any branch of insurance.

Publications: Printed

Access to staff: Contact by letter, by fax, by e-mail and via website
Hours: Mon to Fri, 0900 to 1700

Affiliated to: International Insurance Law Association (AIDA)

BRITISH INTERIOR TEXTILES ASSOCIATION (BITA)

3 Queen Square, Bloomsbury, London, WC1N 3AR

Tel: 020 7843 9460
Fax: 020 7843 9478
E-mail: enquiries@interiortextiles.com
Website: www.interiortextiles.co.uk

Enquiries to: Secretary

Founded: 1917

Organisation type and purpose: Trade association.

Subject coverage: Furnishing textiles industry, manufacture and distribution. UK and EC legislation affecting the industry.

Publications: Printed, and electronic and video

Publications list: Available in print

Access to staff: Contact by letter, by fax, by e-mail and via website. Appointment necessary.
Hours: Mon to Fri, 0900 to 1730

Access to building: Prior appointment required

BRITISH INTERNATIONAL FREIGHT ASSOCIATION (BIFA)

Redfern House, Browells Lane, Feltham, Middlesex, TW13 7EP

Tel: 020 8844 2266
Fax: 020 8890 5546
E-mail: bifa@bifa.org
Website: www.bifa.org

Direct e-mail: information@bifa.org

Founded: 1944

Organisation type and purpose: Trade association.
To represent the international freight services industry.

Subject coverage: Practical help and advice on any aspect of running a freight forwarding business or any industry-related issues that may affect member companies.

Publications list: Available online and in print

Access to staff: Contact by letter, by telephone, by fax and by e-mail. Access for members only. Non-members charged.
Hours: Mon to Fri, 0900 to 1700

Incorporates: Institute of Freight Professionals

BRITISH INTERNATIONAL STUDIES ASSOCIATION (BISA)

BISA office, International Politics Building, Aberystwyth University, Aberystwyth, Ceredigion, SY23 3DA

Tel: 01970 628672
Fax: 01970 622709
E-mail: pkellybisa@compuserve.com
Website: www.bisa.ac.uk

Enquiries to: Administrator

Founded: 1975

Organisation type and purpose:
Membership association (membership is by subscription), present number of members: c. 1,000, registered charity.
To promote the study of International Relations and related subjects through teaching, research and the facilitation of contact between scholars.

Subject coverage: International studies, IR theory, strategy, IPE, environment, UN and International organisations.

Publications: Printed

Publications list: Available in print

Access to staff: Contact by letter, by e-mail and via website
Hours: Mon to Fri, 0900 to 1700

BRITISH INTERPLANETARY SOCIETY (BIS)

27–29 South Lambeth Road, London, SW8 1SZ

Tel: 020 7735 3160
Fax: 020 7587 5118
E-mail: mail@bis-space.com
Website: www.bis-space.com

Enquiries to: Executive Secretary

Founded: 1933

Organisation type and purpose: Learned society, registered charity (charity number 250556).
Promotion of studies in space research, technology and applications.

Subject coverage: Space research and technology, space applications and astronomy.

Collection: Specialised library contains about 8,000 books and reports (members only)

Publications: Printed, and electronic and video
Order printed publications from: www.bis-space.com
Order electronic and video publications from: www.bis-space.com

Publications list: Available online

Access to staff: Contact by letter, by telephone, by fax, by e-mail and via website
Hours: Mon to Fri, 0930 to 1700

Founder member of: International Astronautical Federation

BRITISH INVESTMENT CASTING TRADE ASSOCIATION (BICTA)

National Metalforming Centre, 47 Birmingham Road, West Bromwich, West Midlands, B70 6PX

Tel: 0121 601 6390
Fax: 0121 601 6391
E-mail: admin@cmfed.co.uk

Enquiries to: Manager
Founded: 1958

Organisation type and purpose: Trade association.

Subject coverage: All aspects of the foundry process known as investment (or lost wax) casting – technology of process, markets for investment castings, equipment and consumables used in process, related (foundry) subjects.

Collection: Books on investment casting
Copies of proceedings of: BICTA Conferences, EICF (European Investment Casters' Federation) Conferences, World Investment Casting Conference, US Investment Casting Institute Conferences
Miscellaneous technical papers

Trade and statistical information: Data on output of investment castings

Publications: Printed

Publications list: Available online and in print

Access to staff: Contact by letter, by telephone, by fax and by e-mail. Appointment necessary. Non-members charged.
Hours: Mon to Thu, 0900 to 1700; Fri, 0900 to 1530

BRITISH IRIS SOCIETY (BIS)

Aulden Farm, Aulden, Leominster, Herefordshire, HR6 0JT

Tel: 01568 720129
E-mail: jill@auldenfarm.co.uk
Website: www.britishirissociety.org.uk

Enquiries to: Enrolment Secretary
Direct tel: 01243 781887
Direct e-mail: jillchar@btinternet.com
Other contacts: Membership Secretary

Founded: 1922

Organisation type and purpose: Voluntary organisation, registered charity (charity number 261896), research organisation.

Subject coverage: Irises and iridaceae: origins, breeding, cultivation, taxonomy, history.

Collection: The Genus Iris: original paintings by W R Dykes
Miscellaneous printed material not available in public libraries
Slide library
Paintings by Paul Furse
Paintings by Caparne

Publications: Printed
Order printed publications from: Postal address; or e-mail: jill@auldenfarm.co.uk

Access to staff: Contact by letter, by telephone and by e-mail
Hours: Mon to Fri, 0900 to 1700

Affiliated to: Iris societies around the world; Royal Horticultural Society

Member organisation of: National Plant Societies Federation

BRITISH JEWELLERS' ASSOCIATION (BJA)

10 Vyse Street, Birmingham, B18 6LT

Tel: 0121 237 1110
Fax: 0121 237 1113
E-mail: info@bja.org.uk
Website: www.bja.org.uk

Enquiries to: Senior Co-ordinator

Organisation type and purpose: Membership association (membership is by subscription).

Subject coverage: Jewellery manufacturing and silversmithing, designers, jewellery tools, members who supply these services.

Publications: Printed
Order printed publications from: British Jewellers' Association
338 Goswell Road, London, EC1V 7QP

Access to staff: Contact by letter, by telephone, by fax, by e-mail and via website
Hours: Mon to Fri, 0900 to 1700

BRITISH JEWELLERY GIFTWARE AND FINISHING FEDERATION (BJGF)

Federation House, 10 Vyse Street, Birmingham, B18 6LT

Tel: 0121 236 2657
Fax: 0121 236 3921
Website: www.bjgf.org.uk

Founded: 1887; formerly called Birmingham Jewellers & Silversmiths Association (BJSA) (year of change 1946); formerly called British Joint Association of Goldsmiths, Silversmiths, Horological and Kindred Trades (BJA) (year of change 1970); formerly called British Jewellery & Giftware Federation (year of change 2004); incorporates the former Fancy Goods Association (changed name to Giftware Association in 1966) (year of change 1948)

Organisation type and purpose: Represents the interests of 2,500 member companies operating in the jewellery, gift and home, leathergoods and surface engineering industries, employing between them 46,000 people.
To provide professional central services to the six trade associations operating within it.

Access to staff: Contact by letter, by telephone and by fax

Federated associations: British Jewellers' Association (BJA); British Travelgoods and Accessories Association (BTAA); Giftware Association (GA); Jewellery Distributors' Association (JDA); Surface Engineering Association (SEA)

BRITISH JIGSAW PUZZLE LIBRARY (BJPL)

Clarendon, Parsonage Road, Herne Bay, Kent, CT6 5TA

Tel: 01227 742222
E-mail: jigsawinfo@aol.com
Website: www.britishjigsawpuzzlelibrary.co.uk

Enquiries to: Secretary

Founded: 1933

Organisation type and purpose: Membership association (membership is by subscription).
Library of wooden jigsaw puzzles.
Leisure and therapy.

Subject coverage: Jigsaw puzzles (subscription loan service).
Lending library of wooden jigsaw puzzles.
Puzzles exchanged by post.
Stock contains jigsaws with large pieces suitable for stroke victims and people with disabilities.

Trade and statistical information: Collection of over 3,500 high quality craftsman-cut wooden puzzles

Publications: Printed

Access to staff: Contact by letter, by telephone, by e-mail and via website. Appointment necessary.
Hours: Mon to Fri, 0900 to 1700

Access to building: No access other than to staff

BRITISH JUDO COUNCIL (BJC)

1A Horn Lane, Acton, London, W3 9NJ

Tel: 01692 580900
Fax: 01692 580909
E-mail: admin@britishjudocouncil.org
Website: www.britishjudocouncil.org/

Enquiries to: General Secretary

Organisation type and purpose: Voluntary organisation.

Subject coverage: Judo.

Access to staff: Contact by letter and by telephone. Appointment necessary.
Hours: Mon to Fri, 0900 to 1500

BRITISH KENPO KARATE UNION (BKKU)

16 York Road, Exeter, Devon, EX4 6BA

Tel: 0560 3319 558
E-mail: info@bkku.com
Website: www.bkku.com

Enquiries to: Secretary
Founded: 1981

Organisation type and purpose: Membership association (membership is by subscription), present number of members: 100, service industry, training organisation.

continued overleaf

Subject coverage: Kenpo karate.

Access to staff: Contact by e-mail
Hours: Mon to Fri, 0900 to 1700

BRITISH KIDNEY PATIENT ASSOCIATION (BKPA)

The British Kidney Patient Association (BKPA), 3 The Windmills, St Mary's Close, Turk Street, Alton, GU34 1EF

Tel: 01420 541424
Fax: 01420 89438
E-mail: info@britishkidney-pa.co.uk
Website: www.britishkidney-pa.co.uk/

Enquiries to: Chief Executive

Organisation type and purpose: National Charity.
To help kidney patients and their families.

Subject coverage: Renal dialysis and transplantation, material and physical needs of patients and their relatives, lobbying for more facilities.

Publications: Printed, and electronic and video

Publications list: Available in print

Access to staff: Contact by letter, by telephone and by fax. Appointment necessary.
Hours: Mon to Fri, 0900 to 1700

BRITISH KORFBALL ASSOCIATION (BKA)

Registrations Officer, 50 Mayfair Avenue, Worcester Park, Surrey, KT4 7SL

Tel: 020 8337 6729
E-mail: secretary@korfball.co.uk
Website: www.korfball.co.uk

Enquiries to: General Secretary
Direct e-mail: secretary@korfball.co.uk
Other contacts: Development Officer

Founded: 1946

Organisation type and purpose: Voluntary organisation.
Governing body for the sport.

Subject coverage: Rules of Korfball, lists of clubs, coaches and referees, coaching and refereeing courses.

Publications: Printed

Access to staff: Contact by letter and by e-mail
Hours: Answerphone, if unavailable during office hours; personal contact by phone, normally in the evenings

Affiliated to: International Korfball Federation; PO Box 85394, 3508 AJ Utrecht, The Netherlands; tel: +31 30 6566354; fax: +31 30 6570468; e-mail: office@ihf.org; website: http://www.ihf.org

General Secretary: British Korfball Association; PO Box 179, Maidstone, Kent, ME14 1LU; e-mail: secretary@korfball.co.uk

BRITISH LIBRARY – ASIA, PACIFIC AND AFRICA COLLECTIONS (APAC)

96 Euston Road, London, NW1 2DB

Tel: 020 7412 7873
Fax: 020 7412 7641
E-mail: apac-enquiries@bl.uk
Website: www.bl.uk/collections/asiapacificafrica.html

Enquiries to: Reference Services

Founded: 1753

Organisation type and purpose: Non-departmental public body.

Subject coverage: Languages, literature, religion, art, social and political life of the various regions of Asia and North Africa, both historical and contemporary; principal linguistic and geographical sections are: Hebrew (with Coptic, Syriac, Ethiopian, etc.), Islamic (Arabic, Turkish, Iranian, etc.), South Asian, South-East Asian, Far Eastern.
Official British records relating to the Indian sub-continent from 1600 to 1947, humanities and social sciences relating to the sub-continent, activities of the British in the sub-continent and in other areas of Asia where the East India Company was active, material in Indian vernacular languages, Indian studies in the broadest sense.

Education services: Free monthly training sessions for first-time users of the family history sources.

Collection: Drawings and prints, including miniatures (over 29,000 items)
Each language section contains rare and specialised collections of manuscripts and printed books
East India Company material, including collections on factories or early trading stations, and the Company's maritime activities
Government of India Publications (70,200 vols)
Manuscripts in European languages (over 100 major collections)
Manuscripts in Oriental languages (over 27,000 items)
Maps: topographical, subject (railways, canals, irrigation, etc.)
Oriental language newspapers and official publications
Photographs, including some 187,000 photographs of scenes in India, pre-1947 and 2,300 negative plates of Indian inscriptions and antiquities
Records of the Crown Representative and of the Residents in the Indian Princely States

Non-library collection catalogue: All or part available online, in-house and in print

Library catalogue: All or part available online, in-house and in print

Publications: Printed

Publications list: Available in print

Access to staff: Contact by letter, by telephone, by fax, by e-mail and in person
Hours: Mon, 1000 to 1700; Tue to Sat, 0930 to 1700

Access for disabled people: Ramped entry, access to all public areas, toilet facilities
Special comments: Parking spaces for disabled people are in Midland Road.

Constituent part of: British Library

BRITISH LIBRARY – BUSINESS AND INTELLECTUAL PROPERTY CENTRE

96 Euston Road, London, NW1 2DB

Tel: 020 7412 7454 (enquiries and holdings information)
Fax: 020 7412 7453
E-mail: bipc@bl.uk
Website: www.bl.uk/bipc

Organisation type and purpose: Information service.

Subject coverage: Business and intellectual property information on patents, designs, trademarks, copyright, markets, companies, and products covering all sectors in the United Kingdom and overseas.

Collection: Various electronic databases, patent specifications, market research reports, trade directories, trade journals and trade literature collection

Trade and statistical information: Range of national and international trade statistics

Non-library collection catalogue: All or part available online and in-house

Library catalogue: All or part available online

Access to staff: Contact by letter, by telephone, by fax, by e-mail, in person and via website

Access to building: *Hours:* Mon, 1000 to 2000; Tue to Thu, 0930 to 2000; Fri to Sat, 0930 to 1700
Special comments: No access to first-time users after 1700.

Access for disabled people: Ramped entry, toilet facilities
Special comments: Parking spaces for disabled people are in Midland Road.

BRITISH LIBRARY – CARTOGRAPHIC AND TOPOGRAPHIC MATERIALS (BL)

96 Euston Road, London, NW1 2DB

Tel: 020 7412 7702
Fax: 020 7412 7780
E-mail: maps@bl.uk
Website: www.bl.uk

Enquiries to: Head of Cartographic and Topographic Materials
Direct tel: 020 7412 7701
Direct e-mail: peter.barber@bl.uk

Organisation type and purpose: Non-departmental public body.

Subject coverage: Cartographic materials (atlases, maps, globes), cartobibliography, celestial atlases and maps, history of cartography, remotely sensed imagery, topographical views and panoramas, gazeteers, geographical information systems, digital mapping.

Collection: Crace Collection (maps of London)
King George III Topographical and Maritime Collections
Ministry of Defence mapping archive
Ordnance Survey manuscript drawings
Ordnance Survey publications, including large-scale plans (the United Kingdom's definitive collection)

Royal United Services Institution map collection

Non-library collection catalogue: All or part available online, in-house and in print

Library catalogue: All or part available online, in-house and in print

Publications: Printed
Order printed publications from: Turpin Distribution Ltd, Blackhorse Road, Letchworth, Hertfordshire, SG6 1HN; tel. 01462 672555; fax 01462 480497; e-mail turpin@turpinltd.com

Publications list: Available online and in print

Access to staff: Contact by letter, by telephone, by fax, by e-mail, in person and via website. Appointment necessary.
Hours: Mon, 1000 to 1700; Tue to Sat, 0930 to 1700

Access for disabled people: Ramped entry, toilet facilities
Special comments: Parking spaces for disabled people are in Midland Road.

BRITISH LIBRARY – DEPARTMENT OF MANUSCRIPTS (BL MSS)

Formal name: British Library Department of Western Manuscripts

96 Euston Road, London, NW1 2DB

Tel: 020 7412 7513
Fax: 020 7412 7745
E-mail: mss@bl.uk
Website: www.bl.uk/collections/manuscripts.html

Enquiries to: Reading Room Manager
Other contacts: Manuscripts Librarian (for subject enquiries)

Founded: 1753

Organisation type and purpose: Non-departmental public body.

Subject coverage: Primarily material written by hand in Western languages, covering virtually all aspects of history, literature and culture, including maps dating from the classical period to the present day and early (pre-1500) music.

Collection: Additional MSS
Arundel MSS
Ashley MSS
Burney MSS
Collections of Charters, Rolls, Seals, Papyri and Ostraca
Cotton MSS
Egerton MSS
Hargrave MSS
Harley MSS
King's MSS
Lansdowne MSS
Lord Chamberlain's Plays
Modern Playscripts
Photocopies of exported manuscripts
Royal MSS
Sloane MSS
Stowe MSS
Yates Thompson MSS
Zweig MSS
Facsimile collection

Non-library collection catalogue: All or part available online and in print

Publications: Printed

Access to staff: Contact by letter, by telephone, by fax, by e-mail and via website
Hours: Mon, 1000 to 1700; Tue to Sat, 0930 to 1700

Access for disabled people: Ramped entry, access to all public areas, toilet facilities
Special comments: Parking spaces for disabled people are in Midland Road.

BRITISH LIBRARY – DIALTECH

96 Euston Road, London, NW1 2DB

Tel: 020 7412 7951 or 7946
Fax: 020 7412 7947
E-mail: dialtech@bl.uk
Website: www.gemcatcher.com
Website: www.bl.uk/

Enquiries to: Manager
Direct e-mail: roy.kitley@bl.uk

Organisation type and purpose: To provide the UK national centre for EINS (European Information Network Services) which gives access to the GEM online information service in science, technology and business information. Support is also given to customers in Australia, New Zealand, Ireland, Canada and the USA.

Subject coverage: Bibliographic and factual databases in science, technology and business information.

Publications: Printed

Access to staff: Contact by letter, by telephone, by fax, by e-mail and via website. Appointment necessary. All charged.
Hours: Mon to Fri, 0930 to 1700

Access for disabled people: Ramped entry, toilet facilities
Special comments: Parking spaces for disabled people are in Midland Road.

Represents the: European Information Network Services (EINS)

BRITISH LIBRARY – DOCUMENT SUPPLY (BLDS)

Boston Spa, Wetherby, West Yorkshire, LS23 7BQ

Tel: 01937 546060
Fax: 01937 546333
E-mail: dsc-customer-services@bl.uk
Website: www.bl.uk/catalogue
Website: www.bl.uk/docsupply
Website: www.bl.uk/inside
Website: www.bl.uk

Enquiries to: Customer Services
Direct tel: 01937 546060
Direct fax: 01937 546333
Direct e-mail: dsc-customer-services@bl.uk

Founded: 1962

Organisation type and purpose: National Library Service.
To provide a document supply and loan service to researchers in every field of enquiry anywhere in the world. A small Reading Room also operates on-site (open Mon to Fri, 0930 to 1600: tel: 01937 546070).

Subject coverage: Science, technology, law, finance, industry, medicine, humanities, social sciences and all allied subjects.

Collection: Over 250,000 journal series in total (50,000 current subscriptions)
Over 3 million books
All British official publications since 1962
All EC official publications since 1973
Conference Proceedings (over 370,000)
Local authority material (28,000)
Music (over 129,000 scores)
Reports (over 4,300,000, mainly US and in microform)
Russian science and technology monographs (over 220,000)
Theses and Dissertations (over 580,000 UK, US, and some European)
Translations (over 570,000)
Microform research collections – includes one of the largest medieval manuscript collections in Europe
Access to all United Kingdom and international patents

Non-library collection catalogue: All or part available online and in print

Publications: Printed, and electronic and video
Order printed publications from: Turpin Distribution Services Ltd
Blackhorse Road, Letchworth, Hertfordshire, SG6 1HN, tel: 01462 488900, fax: 01462 480947, e-mail: turpin@rsc.org

Publications list: Available in print

Access to staff: Contact by letter, by telephone, by fax, by e-mail, in person and via website
Hours: Customer Services open: Mon to Fri, 0830 to 1700 (except for English public holidays)
Document supply staff work 'around the clock' from Mon at 0800 to Sat at 0200 (except for English public holidays)
Special comments: Charges made for document supply and interlibrary loan. Orders must be sent online or by email.

Access for disabled people: For visitors to the Boston Spa site, parking provided, ramped entry, toilet facilities

Affiliated to: National Bibliographic Service; Boston Spa; tel: 01937 546585; fax: 01937 546586; e-mail: nbs-info@bl.uk

Parent body: British Library; tel: 020 7412 7111; fax: 020 7412 7168; e-mail: press-and-pr@bl.uk

BRITISH LIBRARY – ECCLES CENTRE FOR AMERICAN STUDIES

96 Euston Road, London, NW1 2DB

Tel: 020 7412 7551
E-mail: eccles-centre@bl.uk
Website: www.bl.uk/ecclescentre

Enquiries to: Director

Founded: 1991

Organisation type and purpose:
Information agency.
To support the study and understanding of North America in the United Kingdom through the resources of the British Library.

Subject coverage: North American collections in the British Library, North American educational activities in the United Kingdom, general information on the USA and Canada.

Publications list: Available online

continued overleaf

Access to staff: Contact by letter, by telephone, by e-mail and via website. Appointment necessary.
Hours: Mon to Fri, 0900 to 1700

Access to building: No prior appointment required

Parent body: The British Library; 96 Euston Road, London, NW1 2DB

BRITISH LIBRARY – ENVIRONMENTAL INFORMATION SERVICE (EIS)

96 Euston Road, London, NW1 2DB

Tel: 020 7412 7477
Fax: 020 7412 7954
E-mail: eis@bl.uk
Website: www.bl.uk/environment

Enquiries to: Information Officer
Other contacts: Head of Science and Technology Information Services

Founded: 1989

Organisation type and purpose: Consultancy, research organisation. Information service.

Subject coverage: Scientific and technological aspects of environmental information.

Collection: Access to all British Library collections including environmental newsletters and corporate environmental reports

Publications: Printed

Publications list: Available in print

Access to staff: Contact by letter, by telephone, by fax and by e-mail
Hours: Mon to Fri, 0930 to 1700
Special comments: Reader Pass needed. Charges made for on-line searches and detailed enquiries.

Access for disabled people: Ramped entry, toilet facilities
Special comments: Parking spaces for disabled people are in Midland Road.

Part of: British Library (same address)

BRITISH LIBRARY – HEALTH CARE INFORMATION SERVICE (HCIS)

96 Euston Road, London, NW1 2DB

Tel: 020 7412 7489
Fax: 020 7412 7954
E-mail: hcis@bl.uk
Website: www.bl.uk/health
Website: www.bl.uk/services/publications/onlineshop.html

Enquiries to: Information Officer
Direct fax: 020 7412 7947
Direct e-mail: fiona.mclean@bl.uk
Other contacts: Head of HCIS

Founded: 1995

Organisation type and purpose: Non-departmental public body.

Subject coverage: Biomedicine and healthcare, medical information, consumer health information, complementary medicine, allied healthcare, occupational therapy, physiotherapy, palliative care, rehabilitation, nursing, health informatics.

Collection: UK Publications (and selected overseas) including patents and historical material, as well as a wide range of relevant books, journals, grey literature and databases

Trade and statistical information: Health Care Statistics for the United Kingdom

Non-library collection catalogue: All or part available in-house

Library catalogue: All or part available online

Publications: Printed, and electronic and video
Order printed publications from: Health Care Information Service (North)
Boston Spa, Wetherby, West Yorkshire, LS23 7BQ, tel: 01937 546361, fax: 01937 546458, e-mail: anita.jackson@bl.uk

Publications list: Available online and in print

Access to staff: Contact by letter, by telephone, by fax, by e-mail and via website. Appointment necessary.
Hours: Mon to Fri, 1000 to 1700
Special comments: Voicemail out of hours.

Access for disabled people: Ramped entry, toilet facilities
Special comments: Parking spaces for disabled people are in Midland Road.

Other address: Health Care Information Service (North) and Reading Room (North); The British Library; Boston Spa, Wetherby, West Yorkshire, LS23 7BQ; tel: 01937 546364; fax: 01937 546458

Parent body: British Library

BRITISH LIBRARY – LIBRARIANSHIP AND INFORMATION SCIENCES SERVICE (LIS)

96 Euston Road, London, NW1 2DB

Tel: 020 7412 7676
Fax: 020 7412 7691
E-mail: lis@bl.uk
Website: www.bl.uk
Website: www.catalogue.bl.uk

Enquiries to: Reference Specialist

Organisation type and purpose: National library.

Subject coverage: All aspects of librarianship and information science.

Collection: Collections include British material acquired by legal deposit and selected non-British material on librarianship, information science and related subjects

Non-library collection catalogue: All or part available online

Library catalogue: All or part available online

Publications: Printed

Access to staff: Contact by letter, by telephone, by fax, by e-mail and in person
Hours: Mon, 1000 to 2000; Tue, Wed, Thu, 0930 to 2000; Fri, Sat, 0930 to 1700
Special comments: A Reader's Pass is required for entry to the Reading Rooms, see details on website.

Access for disabled people: Accessible to the disabled

BRITISH LIBRARY – METADATA SERVICES

Boston Spa, Wetherby, West Yorkshire, LS23 7BQ

Tel: 01937 546548
Fax: 01937 546586
E-mail: bd-info@bl.uk
Website: www.bl.uk

Founded: 2002; formerly called National Bibliographic Service; Bibliographic Development (year of change 2010)

Organisation type and purpose: National government body, public library.
To develop metadata standards with reference to their application in British Library bibliographic products and services, and in a variety of EC and other projects.

Subject coverage: The development of bibliographic standards at national and international levels; the British National Bibliography; support for metadata products and services; projects in support of the UK library and information community.

Collection: Metadata Services does not have its own collections but makes available the MARC records of the British National Bibliography and the British Library collections

Library catalogue: All or part available online

Access to staff: Contact by letter, by telephone, by fax and by e-mail. Appointment necessary.
Hours: Mon to Fri, 0900 to 1700

BRITISH LIBRARY – MUSIC COLLECTIONS

96 Euston Road, London, NW1 2DB

Tel: 020 7412 7772
Fax: 020 7412 7751
E-mail: music-collections@bl.uk
Website: www.bl.uk/collections/music/music.html
Website: www.bl.uk/reshelp/findhelprestype/music

Enquiries to: Head of Music Collections
Direct tel: 020 7412 7529

Founded: 1973

Organisation type and purpose: Non-departmental public body.

Subject coverage: All aspects of printed and manuscript music, including music history, music printing, bibliography of music, availability of music, music copyright, popular music, etc. NB for recorded music, see British Library Sound Archive.

Information services: Music Reference Service.

Collection: Hirsch Collection
Royal Music Library
Royal Philharmonic Society Archive

Non-library collection catalogue: All or part available in-house

Library catalogue: All or part available online and in print

Publications: Printed, and electronic and video

Publications list: Available in print

Access to staff: Contact by letter, by telephone, by fax, by e-mail and via website. Appointment necessary.
Hours: Mon, 1000 to 2000; Tue, Wed, Thu, 0930 to 2000; Fri, Sat, 0930 to 1700
Special comments: Reader's Pass required to use reading rooms.

Access for disabled people: Ramped entry, access to all public areas, toilet facilities
Special comments: 3 parking bays in Ossulton Street.

BRITISH LIBRARY – NATIONAL PRESERVATION OFFICE (NPO)

96 Euston Road, London, NW1 2DB

Tel: 020 7412 7612
Fax: 020 7412 7796
E-mail: blpac@bl.uk
Website: www.bl.uk/npo/
Website: www.bl.uk/services/npo/npo.html

Enquiries to: Information Officer
Other contacts: Director

Founded: 1984

Organisation type and purpose: Research organisation.
Independent national advisory body.
Independent national focus for debate and information on preservation, conservation and security in libraries and archives.

Subject coverage: Preservation, conservation, disaster control, security, surrogacy.

Publications: Printed

Access to staff: Contact by letter, by telephone, by fax, by e-mail and via website
Hours: Mon to Fri, 0900 to 1700
Special comments: Visitors by prior appointment only (no casual callers).

Funded by: British Library; Cambridge University Library; The Bodleian Library, Oxford University; The National Archives; The National Library of Scotland; The National Library of Wales; Trinity College Library, Dublin

Policies guided by the: National Preservation Office Board

BRITISH LIBRARY – NEWSPAPERS

Colindale Avenue, London, NW9 5HE

Tel: 020 7412 7353
Fax: 020 7412 7379
E-mail: newspaper@bl.uk
Website: www.bl.uk/collections/newspapers.html

Organisation type and purpose: The national archive collections in the United Kingdom of British and overseas newspapers; the only large, integrated national newspaper service in the world, combining facilities for the collection, preservation, and use of newspapers all on one site.
Our collections, which also include popular magazines and periodicals, are made available in hard copy, in microform, and on CD-ROM in the Newspaper Reading Rooms in Colindale, north west London. Subject to restrictions, facilities are available for the photocopying, microfilming, and photographic and film reproduction of items from the collections in our care.

Collection: British Library Newspapers Web Catalogue
The British Library Online Newspaper Archive (Pilot version only)
British and Irish Newspapers
Overseas Newspapers
Periodicals and Comics
Visual Arts collections
Microform Series
Chatham House Press Cuttings
Special collections:
British and Irish Cinema and Film Periodicals
British Comics Collection
British Football Programmes
British Military History Collections 1801–1945
The Burney Collection of Newspapers
Current Foreign (Non-British Isles) Newspapers
The Dutch Underground Press 1940–1945
Early American Newspapers
Early English Newspapers
Early Indian Newspapers
The Francis Place Collection (British Politics and Economics)
General Strike Newspapers 1926
German-language Newspapers and Journals Published in London since 1810
Modern Music Periodicals: Pop and Jazz
Northern Ireland Politicial Literature: Periodicals 1966–1989
The Thomason Tracts (English Newsbooks, 1640–61)
Tuskegee Institute News Clippings File (African-Americans 1899–1966)
Victorian Illustrated Newspapers and Journals

Publications: Printed, and electronic and video

Access to staff: *Hours:* Mon to Fri, 0900 to 1700

BRITISH LIBRARY – PHILATELIC COLLECTIONS

96 Euston Road, London, NW1 2DB

Tel: 020 7412 7635
Fax: 020 7412 7780
E-mail: philatelic@bl.uk
Website: www.bl.uk/collections/philatelic

Founded: 1973

Organisation type and purpose: Non-departmental public body.

Subject coverage: Philately, postal history, philatelic literature, history of philately.

Collection: Over 50 main collections, including:
Board of Inland Revenue Stamping Department Archive
Crown Agents Philatelic and Security Printing Archive
Fletcher Collection
Foreign and Commonwealth Office Collection
Harrison Collection
Tapling Collection (perhaps the most important and unique)

Non-library collection catalogue: All or part available in-house

Publications: Printed

Access to staff: Contact by letter, by telephone, by fax and by e-mail. Appointment necessary.
Hours: Mon to Fri, 0900 to 1700

Access to building: Prior appointment required
Hours: Mon to Fri, 1000 to 1600
Special comments: Reader's pass required

Access for disabled people: Ramped entry, toilet facilities

BRITISH LIBRARY – READER REGISTRATION OFFICE

96 Euston Road, London, NW1 2DB

Tel: 020 7412 7676
Fax: 020 7412 7794
E-mail: reader-registration@bl.uk
Website: www.bl.uk

Founded: 1973

Organisation type and purpose: Non-departmental public body.

Subject coverage: Applications for a Reader's Pass and information about access to the Library.

Publications: Printed

Access to staff: Contact by letter, by telephone, by fax, by e-mail and in person
Hours: Mon, 1000 to 1800; Tue, Wed, Thu, 0930 to 1800; Fri, Sat, 0930 to 1630

Access for disabled people: Ramped entry, toilet facilities
Special comments: Parking spaces for disabled people are in Midland Road and Ossulton Street

BRITISH LIBRARY – READING ROOMS AT ST PANCRAS

96 Euston Road, London, NW1 2DB

Tel: 020 7412 7676
Fax: 020 7412 7609
E-mail: reader-services-enquiries@bl.uk
Website: www.bl.uk

Organisation type and purpose: Non-departmental public body.

Access to staff: Contact by letter, by telephone, by fax, by e-mail, in person and via website
Hours: Mon to Fri, 0900 to 1700
Special comments: Reader's Pass required, apply to the Reader Admissions Office.

Direct lines: General enquiries; reader services and advance reservations; tel: 020 7412 7676; fax: 020 7412 7789; e-mail: reader-services-enquiries@bl.uk; Humanities 1 and 2; includes the Library and Information Sciences Service and the Recorded Sound Information Service; tel: 020 7412 7440 (Humanities and LISS), 020 7412 7676 (RSIS); Manuscripts; tel: 020 7412 7513; Maps; tel:

continued overleaf

020 7412 7702; Oriental and India Office; tel: 020 7412 7873; Rare Books and Music; includes the Music Service and the Listening and Viewing Service; tel: 020 7412 7772 (Early Printed Collections), 020 7412 7673 (Music Service); Reader Admissions Office; information about access to the Library; tel: 020 7412 7677; fax: 020 7412 7794; Readers' Advisor; information about assistance for users with disabilities; tel: 020 7412 7666; fax: 020 7412 7557; e-mail: lydia.butler@bl .uk; Science, Technology & Innovation Information Services; British and EPO patents; tel: 020 7412 7919; Science, Technology & Innovation Information Services; Business; tel: 020 7412 7454/7977; Science, Technology & Innovation Information Services; Foreign patents; tel: 020 7412 7902; Science, Technology & Innovation Information Services; Science and Technology; tel: 020 7412 7288/7494/ 7496; Science, Technology & Innovation Information Services; Social Sciences; tel: 020 7412 7536

BRITISH LIBRARY – RESEARCH SERVICE

96 Euston Road, London, NW1 2DB

Tel: 020 7412 7903
Fax: 020 7412 7930
E-mail: research@bl.uk
Website: www.bl.uk/reshelp/experthelp/researchservice

Enquiries to: Information Expert

Founded: 1973

Organisation type and purpose: Information service.

Subject coverage: Intellectual property (patents, trademarks and registered desgins) and company information.

Collection: The Business & IP Centre has a very extensive collection of business and patent material

Library catalogue: All or part available online

Publications: Printed
Order printed publications from: Turpin Distribution Services, Blackhorse Road, Letchworth, Hertfordshire, SG6 1HN; tel. 01462 672555; fax 01462 480947; e-mail turpin@turpinltd.com

Publications list: Available online and in print

Access to staff: Contact by letter, by telephone, by fax, by e-mail, in person and via website

Access to building: *Hours:* Mon to Fri, 1000 to 1300 and 1400 to 1700
Special comments: Reader Pass required by visitors. Ring for details of admission procedure.

Access for disabled people: Ramped entry, toilet facilities

BRITISH LIBRARY – SOCIAL SCIENCES AND OFFICIAL PUBLICATIONS REFERENCE SERVICE

96 Euston Road, London, NW1 2DB

Tel: 020 7412 7676
Fax: 020 7412 7761
E-mail: social-sciences@bl.uk
Website: catalogue.bl.uk
Website: www.bl.uk/socialsciences

Enquiries to: Social Sciences Reference Service

Founded: 1753

Organisation type and purpose: Non-departmental public body.

Subject coverage: Government, national and local; politics and administration; sociology; economics; education and training policy and administration; transport and the environment; social care, health and welfare services; social security; theory of management; housing and homelessness; law.

Collection: Legal deposit collection of British official publications
Electoral registers for whole of United Kingdom from 1947 and extensive earlier collection
Depository for United Nations publications, some UN agencies, World Bank, International Labour Organization, European Union, OECD and World Health Organization
Worldwide collections of publications of governments and inter-governmental organisations, including microfiche of US Federal GPO publications (both depository and non-depository) from 1982 (extensive earlier collection in hard copy) and full-text electronic resources including Congressional Serial Set Online, Congressional Hearings Digital Collection 1823–1979, Congressional Record, Declassified Documents Reference System and Digital National Security Archive
Reading room open access collections include:
National Statistics Collection
Social Sciences collection of recent English-language books and serials
UK Parliamentary materials and legislation
Note: The British Library has one of the largest collections of social science publications worldwide, accessible through the Social Sciences Reading Room, but this is not organised as a discrete collection

Trade and statistical information: The National Statistics Collection based in SS&OP (focus on social and demographic statistics for the UK)

Library catalogue: All or part available online

Publications: Electronic and video

Access to staff: Contact by letter, by telephone, by fax, by e-mail and in person
Hours: Telephone enquiries: Mon to Fri, 0930 to 1700

Access to building: No access other than to reading rooms
Hours: Reading Room: Mon, 1000 to 2000; Tue, Wed, Thu, 0930 to 2000; Fri, Sat, 0930 to 1700
Special comments: Reader's Pass required.

Access for disabled people: Ramped entry, access to all public areas, toilet facilities

Constituent part of: British Library, Operations and Services

BRITISH LIBRARY SOUND ARCHIVE

96 Euston Road, London, NW1 2DB

Tel: 020 7412 7676
Fax: 020 7412 7441
E-mail: sound-archive@bl.uk
Website: www.bl.uk/soundarchive
Website: cadensa.bl.uk
Website: sounds.bl.uk

Enquiries to: Head of the Sound Archive
Direct tel: 020 7412 7424
Direct fax: 020 7412 7422
Direct e-mail: richard.ranft@bl.uk

Founded: 1955; formerly called British Institute of Recorded Sound (year of change 1983)

Organisation type and purpose: Registered charity (charity number 292096).
Non-departmental public body.

Subject coverage: All aspects of recorded sound, in particular music, including classical music, world and traditional music, popular music and jazz; spoken word, including poetry and drama, oral history, language and dialect; wildlife sounds including birds, mammals, insects, reptiles, amphibians and fish; sound effects; also the United Kingdom music business, broadcasting and the technology of recording.

Information services: Sound Archive Information Service, e-mail: sound-archive@bl.uk

Special visitor services: Listening & Viewing Service, website: http://www.bl.uk/reshelp/inrrooms/stp/sound/listening.html

Collection: Classical Music Collection
Drama and Literature Collection
Library of printed reference sources
Music video
National Deposit Collection of published phonograms
Oral History Collection
Popular Music Collection
Radio recordings
Record catalogues, national and international
Wildlife Sounds
World and Traditional Music Collection
Broadcast TV and radio news

Trade and statistical information: Data on the United Kingdom record industry

Non-library collection catalogue: All or part available online

Library catalogue: All or part available online

Publications: Printed

Publications list: Available online

Access to staff: Contact by letter, by telephone, by fax, by e-mail and in person
Hours: Mon, 1000 to 2000; Tue, Wed and Thu, 0930 to 2000; Fri and Sat, 0930 to 1700
Special comments: Listening and viewing service by appointment.

Access to building: *Special comments:* Reader's Pass required.

Access for disabled people: Ramped entry, access to all public areas, toilet facilities
Special comments: Parking spaces for disabled people are in Midland Road.

Parent body: British Library; 96 Euston Road; website: htpp://www.bl.uk

BRITISH LIMBLESS EX-SERVICE MEN'S ASSOCIATION (BLESMA)

Frankland Moore House, 185–187 High Road, Chadwell Heath, Romford, Essex, RM6 6NA

Tel: 020 8590 1124
Fax: 020 8599 2932
E-mail: headquarters@blesma.org
Website: www.blesma.org

Enquiries to: General Secretary
Other contacts: National Welfare Officer (for all welfare matters)

Founded: 1932

Organisation type and purpose: National organisation, membership association (membership is by subscription), present number of members: 5,000 including widows, voluntary organisation, registered charity (charity number: England – 1084189; Scotland – SCO10315).
National charity dealing specifically with amputation and rehabilitation. Operates residential and nursing homes. Grant-making organisation providing advice on pensions and allowances.

Subject coverage: Amputation and rehabilitation, general welfare, prosthetics and orthotics, pension advice and casework, financial grants, research and development, residential homes, counselling.

Publications: Printed, and electronic and video

Publications list: Available in print

Access to staff: Contact by letter, by telephone, by fax, by e-mail and via website
Hours: Mon to Fri, 0900 to 1700

Access for disabled people: Parking provided, ramped entry, toilet facilities

Also at: The Ancaster BLESMA Home, Crieff; Alligan Road, Crieff, Perthshire, PH7 3JU; tel: 01764 652480; fax: 01764 652550; e-mail: crieff@blesma.org; The Elizabeth Frankland Moore Home; 539 Lytham Road, Blackpool, Lancashire, FY4 1RA; tel: 01253 343313; fax: 01253 408994; e-mail: blackpool@blesma.org

Headquarters address: International Society of Prosthetics and Orthotics (ISPO)

Links with: Royal Association for Disability and Rehabilitation (RADAR); World Veterans Federation (WVF)

BRITISH LIME ASSOCIATION (BLA)

156 Buckingham Palace Road, London, SW1W 9TR

Tel: 020 7730 8194
Fax: 020 7730 4355
Website: www.bla.org
Website: www.britishlime.org
Website: www.qpa.org

Enquiries to: Public Relations Manager
Direct e-mail: clements@qpa.org
Other contacts: Lime Product Officer

Organisation type and purpose: Trade association.

Subject coverage: Lime, limestone, chalk dolomite, health and safety, environmental matters.

Trade and statistical information: Data on industry statistics

Publications: Printed

Publications list: Available in print

Access to staff: Contact by letter, by telephone, by fax, by e-mail and via website
Hours: Mon to Fri, 0900 to 1700

Parent body: Quarry Products Association (QPA); tel: 020 7730 8194; fax: 020 7730 4355; e-mail: info@qpa.org

BRITISH LIVER TRUST

2 Southampton Road, Ringwood, Hampshire, BH24 1HY

Tel: 01425 481320
Fax: 01425 481335
E-mail: info@britishlivertrust.org.uk
Website: www.britishlivertrust.org.uk

Founded: 1988

Organisation type and purpose: National organisation, registered charity (charity number 298858), suitable for: adults, research organisation.
Education on liver disease. The charity produces information on all aspects of liver disease and funds research.

Subject coverage: Information on liver disease.

Information services: Liver disease information helpline: 0800 652 7330

Publications: Printed
Order printed publications from: e-mail: publications@britishlivertrust.org.uk

Publications list: Available online and in print

Access to staff: Contact by letter, by telephone, by fax, by e-mail and via website
Hours: Mon to Fri, 0900 to 1700 and Wed to 2000

Access to building: No access other than to staff

BRITISH LLAMA AND ALPACA ASSOCIATION (BLAA)

Seebeck House, One Seebeck Place, Knowlhill, Milton Keynes, MK5 8FR

Tel: 01608 661893
Fax: 01608 661893
Website: www.llama.co.uk
Website: www.alpaca.co.uk

Enquiries to: Honorary Secretary

Founded: 1987

Organisation type and purpose:
Membership association (membership is by subscription), present number of members: 432, registered charity (charity number 802688).
Owners and breeders association.
To promote good husbandry and the establishment of sound breeding programmes to improve and increase British stock; to guide and foster the growing interest in camelids.

Subject coverage: Welfare guidelines, trekking, sheep guarding, pets, information from conference proceedings, social days, showing and judging camelids, contacts to visit, camelid fibre.

Publications: Printed

Publications list: Available in print

Access to staff: Contact by letter, by telephone and by fax
Hours: Mon to Fri, 0900 to 1700

Access to building: No access other than to staff

BRITISH LUGGAGE AND LEATHERGOODS ASSOCIATION (BLLA)

Federation House, 10 Vyse Street, Birmingham, B18 6LT

Tel: 0121 237 1107
Fax: 0121 236 3921
E-mail: enquries@blla.org.uk
Website: www.blla.org.uk

Enquiries to: Chief Executive
Direct e-mail: diana.fiveash@blla.org.uk

Founded: 1918

Organisation type and purpose: Trade association (membership is by subscription, election or invitation), present number of members: 102.
National trade body for those manufacturing and supplying luggage, travel goods, briefcases, handbags, small leathergoods and accessories.

Subject coverage: Luggage, travel goods, briefcases, handbags, small leathergoods and accessories.

Publications: Printed

Publications list: Available online

Access to staff: Contact by letter, by telephone, by fax, by e-mail and via website. Appointment necessary.
Hours: Mon to Thu, 0930 to 1630; Fri, 0900 to 1600

Access to building: Prior appointment required

Access for disabled people: Parking provided, access to all public areas, toilet facilities

Parent body: British Jewellery and Giftware Federation Limited; Federation House, 10 Vyse Street, Birmingham, B18 6LT; tel: 0121 236 2657; fax: 0121 236 3921

BRITISH LUNG FOUNDATION

73–75 Goswell Road, London EC1V 7ER

Tel: 020 7831 5831
Fax: 020 7831 5832
E-mail: enquiries@blf.org.uk
Website: www.lunguk.org/

Enquiries to: Press Officer
Direct tel: 020 7688 5564
Direct e-mail: casey.purkiss@blf-uk.org

Founded: 1984

Organisation type and purpose: Registered charity (charity number 326730).
Raising funds for, and promoting research into, diseases of the lung.

continued overleaf

Subject coverage: Diseases of the chest and lungs, their prevalence, treatment, social and economic effects and research into these diseases; maintaining healthy lungs; effects of atmospheric pollution and occupational respiratory disease.

Publications: Printed

Publications list: Available online and in print

Access to staff: Contact by letter, by telephone, by fax and by e-mail
Hours: Mon to Fri, 0900 to 1700

Member of: Association of Medical Research Charities; Long-Term Medical Conditions Alliance

Regional Offices: British Lung Foundation; The Nuffield House, Queen Elizabeth Hospital, Birmingham, B15 2TH; tel: 0121 627 2260; fax: 0121 697 8323; British Lung Foundation; Orchard Street Business Centre, 3 Charles Place, Bristol, BS8 4QW; tel: 0117 925 5810; fax: 0117 925 5809; e-mail: susan@blfsw.fsnet.co.uk; British Lung Foundation; Sir G B Hunter Memorial Hospital, The Green, Wallsend, Tyne & Wear, NE28 7PB; tel: 0191 263 0276; fax: 0191 262 2660; British Lung Foundation (North West); Moroney House, Cardiothoracic Centre, Thomas Drive, Liverpool, L14 3LB; tel: 0151 228 4723; fax: 0151 228 4723; British Lung Foundation Scotland; The Beacon, 176 St Vincent Street, Glasgow, G2 5SG; tel: 0141 249 6810; e-mail: redballoon@blfscotland.org.uk

BRITISH LYMPHOLOGY SOCIETY (BLS)

PO Box 196, Shoreham, Sevenoaks, TN13 9BF

Tel: 01959 525524
Fax: 01959 525524
E-mail: info@thebls.com
Website: www.lymphoedema.org/bls

Enquiries to: Administrator

Founded: 1985

Organisation type and purpose:
Professional body (membership is by subscription), present number of members: 600, registered charity (charity number 1042561).

Subject coverage: Lymphoedema.

Publications: Printed

Publications list: Available online and in print

Access to staff: Contact by letter, by telephone, by fax, by e-mail and via website
Hours: Tue to Thu, 0900 to 1700

Access to building: Prior appointment required

BRITISH MARINE FEDERATION

Marine House, Thorpe Lea Road, Egham, Surrey, TW20 8BF

Tel: 01784 473377
Fax: 01784 439678
E-mail: info@britishmarine.co.uk
Website: www.britishmarine.co.uk
Direct tel: 01784 223663
Direct e-mail: membership@britishmarine.co.uk

Founded: 1913; formerly called Boat, Yacht and Allied Trades Association (year of change 1947); formerly called Ship and Boat Builders National Federation (year of change 1986); formerly called British Marine Industries Federation (year of change since 1986)

Organisation type and purpose: Trade association for the leisure and small commercial marine industry, including leisure boats – seagoing and inland, small commercial workboats, superyachts, hire fleets, and all the equipment and services needed for those craft. Members come from over 4,300 businesses in the UK leisure, superyacht and small commercial marine markets.

Subject coverage: Promotes the marine industry, provides showcases for its products in the UK and overseas, liaises with governments, authorities and agencies, conducts research on UK and international marine markets, provides technical, regulatory and manufacturing information and advice, provides strategy, advice and practical assistance on environmental issues, assists with training and recruitment, advises and represents on legal and financial matters.

Trade and statistical information:
Numerous statistics and market research projects to provide members with valuable information on the marine industry and to enable BMF to highlight the size and importance of the industry to government and the media

Publications: Printed, and electronic and video
Order electronic and video publications from: Many available to download from website.

Publications list: Available online

Access to staff: Contact by letter, by telephone, by fax and by e-mail

Constituent bodies: 12 Region and 18 Group Associations

BRITISH MARINE INDUSTRIES FEDERATION SCOTLAND (BMIF Scotland)

Westgate, Toward, Dunoon, Argyll, PA23 7UA

Tel: 01369 870251
Fax: 01369 870251
E-mail: bmif-s@clydemarinepress.co.uk

Enquiries to: Administrator

Founded: 1921

Organisation type and purpose: Trade association (membership is by election or invitation), present number of members: 55, training organisation.
Representing members of the Scottish Marine industry.

Subject coverage: Yacht and boat building in Scotland, chandlery manufacture, wholesale and retail, marina operations, marine electronics, yacht chartering and other related marine operations in Scotland.

Access to staff: Contact by letter, by telephone, by fax and by e-mail
Hours: Mon to Fri, 0900 to 1700

Member of: British Marine Industries Federation; Meadlake Place, Thorpe Lea Road, Egham, Surrey, TW20 8HE

BRITISH MARITIME LAW ASSOCIATION (BMLA)

Andrew Taylor, Reed Smith LLP, The Broadgate Tower, 20 Primrose Street, London, EC2A 2RS

Tel: 020 3116 3000
Fax: 020 3116 3999
E-mail: adtaylor@reedsmith.com
Website: www.bmla.org.uk

Enquiries to: Secretary and Treasurer

Founded: 1908

Organisation type and purpose:
Professional association, acts as an adviser to UK government bodies responsible for maritime legislation or regulation and co-operates with its international parent body, the CMI, in research and drafting of international instruments for the harmonisation of maritime and mercantile law. Membership consists of representatives from the following groups: shipowners, shippers, merchants, manufactures, insurers, insurance brokers, tug owners, shipbuilders, port and harbour authorities, bankers, classifications societies or other societies or bodies interested in the objects of the Association. The Association also has a number of individual members who may be employees of corporate or institute members or barristers or others without a corporate identity.
To promote the study and the advancement of British maritime and mercantile law; to promote and consider with foreign and other maritime law associations proposals for the unification of maritime and mercantile law in the practice of different nations; to afford opportunities for members to discuss matters of national and international maritime law; to collect and circulate amongst its members information regarding maritime and mercantile law and to establish a collection of publications and documents of interest to members.

Subject coverage: Maritime and mercantile law.

Access to staff: Contact by letter, by telephone, by fax and by e-mail

Member organisation of: Comité Maritime International

BRITISH MATCHBOX LABEL AND BOOKMATCH SOCIETY (BML&BS)

122 High Street, Melbourn, Cambridgeshire, SG8 6AL

Tel: 01763 260399
E-mail: secretary@phillumeny.com
Website: www.phillumeny.com

Enquiries to: Secretary

Founded: 1945

Organisation type and purpose:
Membership association (membership is by subscription), present number of members: 450.

Subject coverage: Matchbox labels and bookmatch collecting, hardware, advertising and other material pertaining to the hobby of collecting these items.

Publications: Printed
Order printed publications from: Bookshop Manager, BML&BS, e-mail: webmaster@phillumeny.com

Access to staff: Contact by letter, by telephone, by e-mail and via website
Hours: Mon to Fri, 0900 to 1700

BRITISH MATERIALS HANDLING FEDERATION (BMHF)

British Materials Handling Federation, Airport House, Purley Way, Croydon, Surrey, CR0 0XZ

Tel: 0208 253 4504
Fax: 0208 253 4510
E-mail: bmhf@admin.co.uk
Website: www.bmhf.org.uk

Enquiries to: General Secretary

Organisation type and purpose: Trade association.
The UK's voice in Europe on materials handling matters.

Subject coverage: Heavy lifting and handling equipment, continuous handling equipment, industrial trucks, mobile cranes, lifts, escalators, passenger conveyors, series lifting equipment, storage equipment and methods, powered access vehicles.

Publications: Printed

Access to staff: Contact by letter, by telephone, by fax and by e-mail
Hours: Mon to Fri, 0900 to 1700

BRITISH MEASUREMENT AND TESTING ASSOCIATION (BMTA)

East Malling Enterprise Centre, New Road, East Malling, Kent, ME19 6BJ

Tel: 01732 897452
Fax: 01732 897453
E-mail: enquiries@bmta.co.uk
Website: www.bmta.co.uk

Enquiries to: Executive Secretary
Other contacts: Assistant Secretary

Founded: 1990

Organisation type and purpose: Membership association (membership is by subscription), present number of members: 90.
An Association for organisations concerned with measurement or testing.

Subject coverage: Testing and calibration; European issues relating to testing and product conformity.

Publications: Printed

Access to staff: Contact by telephone, by fax, by e-mail and via website
Hours: Mon to Fri, 0900 to 1700

UK member of: EUROLAB

BRITISH MEDICAL ACUPUNCTURE SOCIETY (BMAS)

BMAS House, 3 Winnington Court, Northwich, Cheshire, CW8 1AQ

Tel: 01606 786782
Fax: 01606 786783
E-mail: admin@medical-acupuncture.org.uk
Website: www.medical-acupuncture.co.uk

Enquiries to: Support Manager to Medical Director
Direct e-mail: bmaslondon@aol.com

Founded: 1980

Organisation type and purpose: National organisation, professional body (membership is by subscription, election or invitation), registered charity (charity number 1057942).

Subject coverage: Medical acupuncture; medically qualified practitioners who practise acupuncture; education, promotion, professional support.

Publications: Printed, and electronic and video

Publications list: Available online

Access to staff: Contact by letter, by telephone, by fax, by e-mail and via website
Hours: Mon to Fri, 0900 to 1700 (Head Office); Mon to Fri, 1000 to 1800 (London office)

Access to building: No access other than to staff

Also at: Medical Director; BMAS, The Royal London Hospital for Integrated Medicine, 60 Great Ormond Street, London, WC1N 3HR; tel: 020 7713 9437; fax: 020 7713 6286; e-mail: bmaslondon@aol.com; website: http://www.medical-acupuncture.co.uk

Links with: International Council for Medical Acupuncture and Related Techniques (ICMART); Rue de l'Amazone 62, 1050 Brussels, Belgium

BRITISH MEDICAL ASSOCIATION (BMA)

BMA House, Tavistock Square, London, WC1H 9JP

Tel: 020 7383 6625
Fax: 020 7388 2544
E-mail: bma.library@bma.org.uk
Website: www.bma.org

Enquiries to: Librarian

Organisation type and purpose: Professional body, trade union.

Subject coverage: Current clinical information, medical ethics, computers and medicine.

Collection: Hastings, Sir Charles (1794–1866) Collection (c. 400 volumes pre-1866 which belonged to the founder of the Association)

Access to staff: Contact by letter. Appointment necessary. Access for members only. Letter of introduction required. Non-members charged.
Hours: Mon to Fri, 0900 to 1700

BRITISH MEDICAL ASSOCIATION SCOTLAND (BMA)

14 Queen Street, Edinburgh, EH2 1LL

Tel: 0131 247 3000
Fax: 0131 247 3001
E-mail: bmascotland@bma.org.uk
Website: www.bma.org.uk
Website: www.bma.org.uk/scotland

Enquiries to: Scottish Secretary

Founded: 1832

Organisation type and purpose: National organisation, professional body, trade union (membership is by subscription).
Represents the interests of and provides services for 140,044 members in UK, including 19,000 medical students and 3,000 overseas members.

Access to staff: Contact by letter, by telephone, by fax and by e-mail. Access for members only.
Hours: Mon to Fri, 0900 to 1700

Access to building: Prior appointment required

Access for disabled people: Parking provided, disabled lift, toilet facilities

Headquarters address: BMA; BMA House, Tavistock Square, London, WC1H 9JP; tel: 020 7387 4499

BRITISH MEDICAL ULTRASOUND SOCIETY (BMUS)

36 Portland Place, London, W1B 1LS

Tel: 020 7636 3714
Fax: 020 7323 2175
E-mail: secretariat@bmus.org
Website: www.bmus.org

Enquiries to: Chief Executive Officer

Founded: 1984

Organisation type and purpose: Learned society, present number of members: 2,200.
The advancement of science and technology in medical ultrasound; maintenance of the highest standards in these fields; to advance and encourage education and research in these areas.

Subject coverage: Diagnostic medical ultrasound.

Publications: Printed

Access to staff: Contact by letter, by telephone, by fax, by e-mail and via website
Hours: Mon to Fri, 0900 to 1700

Links with: European Federation of Ultrasound in Medicine & Biology (EFSUMB); 36 Portland Place, London, W1B 1LS; fax: 020 7099 7140; e-mail: 020 7436 7934; website: http://www.efsumb.org

BRITISH MENSA LIMITED (MENSA)

St John's House, St John's Square, Wolverhampton, West Midlands, WV2 4AH

Tel: 01902 772771
Fax: 01902 392500
E-mail: enquiries@mensa.org.uk
Website: www.mensa.org.uk

Enquiries to: Financial Controller
Direct e-mail: info@mensa.org.uk
Other contacts: PA to GM

Founded: 1946

Organisation type and purpose: Learned society, membership association (membership is by qualification), present number of members: 27,000.

continued overleaf

Society for people with high IQ.
Association for people of high intelligence (IQ scope above 98th percentile).

Subject coverage: Measurement of intelligence, gifted children, puzzles.

Publications: Printed

Access to staff: Contact by letter, by telephone, by fax and by e-mail
Hours: Mon to Fri, 0830 to 1630

BRITISH MENSWEAR GUILD (BMG)

5 Portland Place, London, W1B 1PW

Tel: 020 7580 8783
Fax: 020 7436 8833
E-mail: director@british-menswear-guild.co.uk
Website: www.british-menswear-guild.co.uk

Enquiries to: Director

Founded: 1959

Organisation type and purpose: Trade association.

Subject coverage: Manufacturing of top quality men's clothing and accessories, clothing trade exhibitions in the United Kingdom and Europe.

Trade and statistical information: Available from the Department of Trade and Industry

Publications: Printed

Access to staff: Contact by letter, by telephone, by fax and by e-mail
Hours: Mon to Fri, 0900 to 1700

BRITISH METALS RECYCLING ASSOCIATION (BMRA)

16 High Street, Brampton, Huntingdon, Cambridgeshire, PE28 4TU

Tel: 01480 455249
Fax: 01480 453680
E-mail: admin@recyclemetals.org

Enquiries to: Director General

Founded: 1919

Organisation type and purpose: Trade association.

Subject coverage: Ferrous and non-ferrous scrap metal recycling.

Access to staff: Contact by letter, by telephone, by fax, by e-mail and via website
Hours: Mon to Fri, 0900 to 1700

Access to building: No access other than to staff

BRITISH MICROCIRCULATION SOCIETY (BMS)

c/o Prof Giovanni E. Mann, Cardiovascular Division, King's College London, 150 Stamford Street, London, SE1 9NH

Tel: 020 7848 4306
Fax: 020 7848 4500
E-mail: giovanni.mann@kcl.ac.uk
Website: www.microcirculation.org.uk

Enquiries to: President

Founded: 1963

Organisation type and purpose: Learned society, present number of members: 225.
Promotion of all aspects of research into microvascular function.

Subject coverage: Microcirculation, blood flow in small vessels, capillary function, endothelial function, tissue fluid balance, vessel growth, vasculature in disease, nitric oxide, inflammation, oedema.

Collection: Annual proceedings

Publications: Printed

Access to staff: Contact by fax and by e-mail
Hours: Mon to Fri, 0900 to 1700

Affiliated to: European Society for Microcirculation

BRITISH MICROLIGHT AIRCRAFT ASSOCIATION (BMAA)

Bullring, Deddington, Banbury, Oxfordshire, OX15 0TT

Tel: 01869 338888
Fax: 01869 337116
E-mail: general@bmaa.org
Website: www.bmaa.org

Enquiries to: Chief Executive

Founded: 1978

Organisation type and purpose: National organisation, membership association (membership is by subscription), present number of members: 4,000, service industry.
Promotion of affordable aviation in microlight aircraft.

Subject coverage: Information on every aspect of microlight flying.

Access to staff: Contact by letter, by telephone, by fax, by e-mail and via website
Hours: Mon to Fri, 0900 to 1700

Authorised company of: Civil Aviation Authority (CAA)

Links with: Fédération Aéronautique Internationale (FAI); Royal Aero Club of Great Britain

BRITISH MILKSHEEP SOCIETY (BMS)

St. Kenelms, Broad Lane, Tanworth-in-Arden, Solihull. B94 5HX

Tel: 01564 742398
E-mail: whopkins@britishmilksheep.com
Website: www.britishmilksheep.apt-sites.com/

Enquiries to: Secretary

Founded: 1982

Organisation type and purpose:
Membership association (membership is by subscription, qualification), present number of members: 131, voluntary organisation.
To promote the British Milksheep, advertise the breed, assist members with exports, collate pedigree breeding data, organise meetings for members.

Subject coverage: Information on the British Milksheep, on milking sheep and pedigree data of British Milksheep.

Affiliation to: National Sheep Association (NSA); Sheep Centre, Malvern, Worcestershire

BRITISH MINIGOLF ASSOCIATION (BMGA)

E-mail: via website for (general enquiries); membership@minigolf.org.uk (fo
Website: www.minigolf.org.uk

Enquiries to: Chairman
Direct e-mail: chairman@minigolf.org.uk

Organisation type and purpose: A non-profit making organisation, a membership association (membership is by subscription).
The UK's governing body for minigolf sport, including crazy golf and adventure golf.
To promote and increase the profile of minigolf in the UK, to represent the interests of its members at both national and international level, with regards to the authorities, other sport associations, the media and the public, to bring together those who enjoy playing minigolf, including adventure golf and crazy golf, to encourage the playing of minigolf as a competitive sport, to organise national tournaments, including a British Open and British Championship, to encourage the development of new, skill-based, minigolf courses in the UK.

Subject coverage: Minigolf of all types.

Publications: Electronic and video
Order electronic and video publications from: Download from website

Publications list: Available online

Access to staff: Contact by e-mail and via website

Member organisation of: European Minigolf Federation; World Minigolf Federation

BRITISH MODEL FLYING ASSOCIATION (BMFA)

Chacksfield House, 31 St Andrews Road, Leicester, LE2 8RE

Tel: 0116 244 0028
Fax: 0116 244 0645
E-mail: admin@bmfa.org
Website: www.bmfa.org

Enquiries to: Chief Executive

Founded: 1922

Organisation type and purpose:
Membership association (membership is by subscription, election or invitation), present number of members: 28,000, voluntary organisation.
National governing body for model flying.

Subject coverage: Model flying legislation, model aircraft building and flying, flying site retention, national and international model flying competitions.

Publications: Printed

Access to staff: Contact by letter, by telephone, by fax, by e-mail, in person and via website
Hours: Mon to Fri, 0900 to 1700

Links with: Fédération Aéronautique Internationale (FAI); General Aviation Awareness Council (GAAC); Royal Aero Club of the United Kingdom (RAeC)

BRITISH MODEL SOLDIER SOCIETY (BMSS)

12 Savay Lane, Denham, Buckinghamshire, UB9 5NH

Tel: 01895 832757
E-mail: model.soldiers@btinternet.com
Website: www.model.soldiers.btinternet.co.uk

Enquiries to: Honorary Secretary

Founded: 1935

Organisation type and purpose:
International organisation, voluntary organisation.
To promote research and scholarship of military history, weaponry, uniforms, etc. through the media of military models.

Subject coverage: Collecting, making and painting model soldiers, military vehicles and weapons, military uniforms and operations of all periods, campaigns of all military bodies of all nationalities and periods.

Collection: The Society's National Collection of all types of figures of a military nature

Publications: Printed

Access to staff: Contact by letter, by telephone and by e-mail. Access for members only.
Hours: Mon to Fri, 0900 to 1700

BRITISH MUSEUM (BM)

Great Russell Street, London, WC1B 3DG

Tel: 020 7323 8000
Fax: 020 7323 8616
E-mail: information@thebritishmuseum.ac.uk
Website: www.thebritishmuseum.ac.uk
Website: www.britishmuseum.co.uk

Enquiries to: Information Officer
Direct tel: 020 7323 8299
Other contacts: Visitor Information Manager

Founded: 1753

Organisation type and purpose: Museum. National museum.

Subject coverage: The history, culture and ethnography of much of the world from prehistoric times to the present day.
The collections are displayed in the following departments:
Greek and Roman Department
Ancient Near East Department
Oriental Department
Japanese Department
Prehistory and Early Europe Department
Medieval and Modern Europe Department
Coins and Medals Department
Egyptian Department
Ethnography Department
Prints and Drawings Department.

Information services: Helpline available, tel: 020 7323 8299.

Special visitor services: Guided tours, tape recorded guides, materials and/or activities for children.

Education services: Group education facilities, resources for Key Stages 1 and 2, 3 and 4.

Services for disabled people: For the visually impaired; for the hearing impaired.

Collection: Records of the buildings, staff and administration, 1753 to the present day, are in the Central Archives
The departments hold manuscript records relating to the history of the collections
These include the papers of Charles Townley relating to his collection of classical antiquities, 1760–1805

Non-library collection catalogue: All or part available online and in-house

Publications: Printed
Order printed publications from: British Museum Company Ltd, 46 Bloomsbury Street, London, WC1B 3QQ; tel: 020 7323 1234; fax: 020 7436 7315; e-mail: sales.products@bmcompany.co.uk

Publications list: Available in print

Access to staff: Contact by letter, by telephone, by fax, by e-mail, in person and via website
Hours: Mon to Sun, 0900 to 1730

Access for disabled people: Parking provided, ramped entry, level entry, access to all public areas, toilet facilities
Special comments: Pre-booking required for parking.

BRITISH MUSIC HALL SOCIETY (BMHS)

82 Fernlea Road, London, SW12 9RW

Tel: 020 8673 2175

Enquiries to: Honorary Secretary

Founded: 1963

Organisation type and purpose: Learned society (membership is by subscription), present number of members: 950, consultancy, research organisation.
Study group.
To preserve the history of British Music Hall and Variety, and recall the artists who created it.

Subject coverage: The British music halls and variety theatre from 1800 to present day.

Collection: Removed from Passmore Edwards Museum, now in storage awaiting a new venue, information from the Historian/Archivist

Publications: Printed

Access to staff: Contact by letter and by telephone. Non-members charged.
Hours: Mon to Fri, 1830 to 2230

Access to building: No prior appointment required
Special comments: Contact Historian/Archivist, 76 Royal Close, Chichester, West Sussex, PO19 2FL, enclose sae, tel 01243 783322.

BRITISH MUSIC SOCIETY (BMS)

7 Tudor Gardens, Upminster, Essex, RM14 3DE

Tel: 01708 224795
E-mail: sct.bms1943@amserve.com
Website: www.britishmusicsociety.co.uk

Enquiries to: Honorary Treasurer

Founded: 1978

Organisation type and purpose:
Membership association (membership is by subscription), present number of members: 600, voluntary organisation, registered charity (charity number 1043838).
To promote an interest in the music of lesser-known British composers of serious music, especially between 1850 and 1975 and where they do not have their own society or trust.

Subject coverage: Promotion of British composers from about 1800 to the present day, especially between 1850 and 1975.

Publications: Printed, and electronic and video

Publications list: Available online and in print

Access to staff: Contact by letter, by telephone and by e-mail. Appointment necessary.
Hours: Mon to Fri, 0900 to 1700

BRITISH MYCOLOGICAL SOCIETY (BMS)

City View House, 5 Union Street, Ardwick, Manchester, M12 4JD

Tel: 0161 277 7638 / 7639
Fax: 0161 277 7634
E-mail: admin@britmycolsoc.info
Website: www.britmycolsoc.org.uk

Enquiries to: General Secretary
Direct tel: 0151 231 2203
Direct fax: 0151 207 4726
Direct e-mail: g.p.sharples@livjm.ac.uk
Other contacts: Membership Secretary for membership application.

Founded: 1896

Organisation type and purpose: Learned society, registered charity (charity number 276503).
To promote mycology in all its aspects by publications, meetings and such other means as the society deems appropriate.

Subject coverage: Mycology, biodiversity, biotechnology, conservation, ecology, genetics, fungal pathogens of plants and animals, systematics.

Collection: Books

Publications: Printed
Order printed publications from: Books, The Librarian and Archivist
British Mycological Society, c/o Herbarium, Royal Botanic Gardens, Kew, Richmond, Surrey, TA9 3AE, tel: 020 8332 5720, e-mail: v.barkham@rbgkew.org.uk

Publications list: Available in print

Access to staff: Contact by letter, by fax and by e-mail
Hours: Mon to Fri, 0900 to 1700

Book collection housed with: Librarian and Archivist; British Mycological Society, c/o Herbarium, Royal Botanic Gardens, Kew, Richmond-upon-Thames, Surrey, TW9 3AE; tel: 020 8332 5720; e-mail: v.barkham@rbgkew.org.uk

BRITISH NATIONAL CARNATION SOCIETY (BNCS)

Linfield, Duncote, Towcester, Northamptonshire, NN12 8AH

continued overleaf

Tel: 01327 351594
E-mail: betty@induncote.freeserve.co.uk

Enquiries to: Membership Secretary

Founded: 1948

Organisation type and purpose: National organisation, membership association (membership is by subscription), present number of members: c. 400, voluntary organisation.

Subject coverage: Carnations and pinks (Dianthus family); culture and hybridisation; exhibitions and competitions.

Publications: Printed

Access to staff: Contact by e-mail
Hours: Evenings

Affiliated to: Royal Horticultural Society

BRITISH NATIONAL LYMPHOMA INVESTIGATION (BNLI)

UCL & CRC Cancer Trials Centre, 222 Euston Road, London, NW1 2DA

Tel: 020 7679 8060
Fax: 020 7679 6061
E-mail: bnli@ctc.ucl.ac.uk
Website: www.bnli.ucl.ac.uk/

Enquiries to: Senior Data Manager

Founded: 1970

Organisation type and purpose:
Professional body, registered charity (charity number 263424).

Subject coverage: Lymphoma investigation.

Publications list: Available in print

Access to staff: Contact by letter and by e-mail
Hours: Mon to Fri, 0900 to 1700

BRITISH NATIONAL TEMPERANCE LEAGUE (BNTL)

30 Keswick Road, Worksop, Nottinghamshire, S81 7PT

Tel: 01909 531858
E-mail: bntl@btconnect.com
Website: www.bntl.org

Enquiries to: Chief Executive Officer

Founded: 1834

Organisation type and purpose: Voluntary organisation, registered charity (charity number 224555), suitable for ages: 5–18. Promoting drug-free lifestyles; providing education and resources on the subject.

Subject coverage: Alcohol and drug education, history of temperance organisations (general), training.

Collection: Livesey Library held at the University of Central Lancashire in Preston: temperance history and 19th-century social reform, includes items bequeathed by William E. Moss

Publications: Printed, and electronic and video

Access to staff: Contact by letter, by telephone, by e-mail and in person
Hours: Mon to Thu, 0900 to 1700

BRITISH NATURALISTS' ASSOCIATION (BNA)

General Secretary, BM 8129, London, WC1N 3XX

Tel: 0844 892 1817
E-mail: marketing@bna-naturalists.org
Website: www.bna-naturalists.org

Enquiries to: Marketing Officer

Founded: 1905

Organisation type and purpose:
Membership association (membership is by subscription), registered charity (charity number 296551).
One of the oldest natural history societies in the UK.
Educational charity.

Subject coverage: Natural history in general.

Collection: Books, magazines, Papers and documents

Trade and statistical information:
Phenology Records

Publications: Printed

Access to staff: Contact by letter, by telephone and by e-mail
Hours: Mon to Fri, 1000 to 1700

Has: 12 branches; 24 affiliated societies

BRITISH NON-FERROUS METALS FEDERATION (BNFMF)

5 Grovelands Business Centre, Boundary Way, Hemel Hempstead, HP2 7TE

Tel: 01442 275705
Fax: 01442 275716
E-mail: bnfmf@copperuk.org.uk

Founded: 1945

Organisation type and purpose: Trade association.

Subject coverage: Trade association for producers in the UK of copper and copper alloy semi-fabricated products: strip, tube, wire, rod, bar and profiles, for electrical and other engineering purposes.

Access to staff: Contact by letter, by fax and by e-mail
Hours: Mon to Fri, 0900 to 1700

Administered by: Copper Development Association; 5 Grovelands Business Centre, Boundary Way, Hemel Hempstead, HP2 7TE; tel: 01442 275705; fax: 01442 275716; website: http://www.copperinfo.co.uk

BRITISH NUCLEAR ENERGY SOCIETY (BNES)

Institution of Civil Engineers, 1–7 Great George Street, London, SW1P 3AA

Tel: 020 7665 2241
Fax: 020 7799 1325
E-mail: ianandrews@ice.org.uk
Website: www.bnes.org.uk

Enquiries to: Secretary

Founded: 1962

Organisation type and purpose: Learned society, professional body (membership is by subscription), present number of members: 1,100, registered charity (charity number 261687).

Subject coverage: Nuclear energy for power generation; fuel; safety.

Publications: Printed
Order printed publications from: Stk Publishing Ltd; 6 Yarde Hill Orchard, Sidmouth, Devon, EX10 9J2

Access to staff: Contact by letter, by telephone, by fax and by e-mail
Hours: Mon to Fri, 0900 to 1700

Affiliated to: European Nuclear Society; tel: +41 31 382 6111; fax: +41 31 382 6845; Institution of Civil Engineers; tel: 020 7222 7722; fax: 020 7222 7500

Constituent bodies: Institute of Energy; tel: 020 7580 7124; fax: 020 7580 4420; Institute of Marine Engineers; tel: 020 7382 2600; fax: 020 7382 2670; e-mail: imare@imare.org.uk; Institute of Materials; tel: 020 7839 4071; fax: 020 7839 1702; Institute of Measurement and Control; tel: 020 7387 4989; fax: 020 7388 8431; Institute of Physics; tel: 020 7470 4800; fax: 020 7470 4848; Institution of Chemical Engineers; tel: 01788 578214; fax: 01788 560833; Institution of Civil Engineers; tel: 020 7222 7722; fax: 020 7222 7500; Institution of Electrical Engineers; tel: 020 7240 1871; Institution of Incorporated Engineers; Institution of Mechanical Engineers; tel: 020 7222 7899; fax: 020 7222 4557; Institution of Nuclear Engineers; tel: 020 8698 1500; fax: 020 8695 6409; Royal Society of Chemistry; tel: 020 7437 8658; fax: 020 7437 8883

BRITISH NUCLEAR FUELS PLC

Magnox Generation, Berkeley Centre, Berkeley, Gloucestershire, GL13 9PB

Tel: 01453 810451
Fax: 01453 812529

Enquiries to: Information Officer
Direct tel: 01453 812562
Direct fax: 01453 813914

Founded: 1996

Organisation type and purpose: Electricity generator.

Subject coverage: Nuclear engineering, electrical engineering, physics, mechanical engineering, health and safety, robotics.

Access to staff: Contact by telephone and by fax
Hours: Mon to Fri, 0900 to 1700

BRITISH NUCLEAR MEDICINE SOCIETY (BNMS)

Regent House, 291 Kirkdale, London, SE26 4QD

Tel: 020 8676 7864
Fax: 020 8676 8417
E-mail: office@bnms.org.uk
Website: www.bnms.org.uk

Enquiries to: Administrator

Founded: 1969

Organisation type and purpose: Learned society.
Affiliated to the European Nuclear Medicine Society and to the World Federation of Nuclear Medicine; the British Association for Radiopharmacy is an affiliate society.

Subject coverage: Nuclear medicine; clinical uses of unsealed radioactive isotopes and radiopharmaceuticals.

Publications: Printed, and electronic and video

BRITISH NUMBER PLATE MANUFACTURERS ASSOCIATION (BNMA)

PO Box 23, South Shore, Blackpool, Lancs FY4 3DA

Tel: 01253 345287
Fax: 01253 344595
Website: www.bnma.org/

Enquiries to: Press Officer

Organisation type and purpose: Trade association.

Subject coverage: Road vehicle number plates.

Access to staff: Contact by letter, by fax and by e-mail
Hours: Mon to Fri, 0900 to 1700

BRITISH NUMISMATIC SOCIETY (BNS)

c/o Warburg Institute, Woburn Square, London, WC1H 0AB

Tel: 01223 332915
E-mail: secretary@britnumsoc.org
Website: www.britnumsoc.org

Enquiries to: Honorary Secretary

Founded: 1903

Organisation type and purpose: Learned society.

Subject coverage: British numismatics: coins, currency, medals and tokens of Great Britain and Ireland, Empire and Commonwealth; numismatics more generally, especially the literature; history of minting techniques.

Collection: Library

Publications: Printed

Affiliated to: British Association of Numismatic Societies

BRITISH NUMISMATIC TRADE ASSOCIATION (BNTA)

PO Box 2, Rye, East Sussex, TN31 7WE

Tel: 01797 229988
E-mail: secretary@bnta.net
Website: www.bnta.net

Enquiries to: General Secretary

Founded: 1973

Organisation type and purpose: Trade association.

Subject coverage: The purchase and sale of numismatic items including coins, medals and decorations.

Publications: Printed

Publications list: Available in print

Access to staff: Contact by letter, by telephone and by e-mail
Hours: Mon to Fri, 0900 to 1700

BRITISH NURSING ASSOCIATION (BNA)

Group House, 92–96 Lind Road, Sutton, SM1 4PL

Tel: 0871 873 3324
Fax: 0871 873 3325
E-mail: info@bna.co.uk
Website: www.bna.co.uk

Founded: 1949

Organisation type and purpose: Professional body, service industry.
Provision of nurses and carers to support people in their own homes, hospitals, NHS Trusts, social services departments, prisons and industry.

Subject coverage: Nursing, staffing, occupational health, first aid courses, social services, nursing homes, family health services authorities, insurance companies, GP practices, prisons, individual clients in their own homes.

Publications: Printed

Access to staff: Contact by letter, by telephone, by e-mail, in person and via website
Hours: Mon to Fri, 0900 to 1700
Special comments: 24 hour emergency on-call at local BNA branches.

Has: over 160 branches nationwide

Holding Group: Nestor Healthcare Group; The Colonnades, Beaconsfield Close, Hatfield, Hertfordshire; tel: 01707 255635; fax: 01707 255633

Member of: REC; UKHCA

Other companies in the group include: Abigail Care; At Home Care; Forensic Medical Services; Grosvenor Nursing Agency; Home Nursing Agency; Kensington and Knightsbridge Nurses Bureau; Mayfair Specialist Nurses; Medic International; Medico Nursing; Nestor Medical Duty Services; Nestor Primecare; Nightingales; United Kingdom Underwriting Services; Worldwide Healthcare Exchange

BRITISH NUTRITION FOUNDATION (BNF)

High Holborn House, 52–54 High Holborn, London, WC1V 6RQ

Tel: 020 7404 6504
Fax: 020 7404 6747
E-mail: postbox@nutrition.org.uk
Website: www.nutrition.org.uk

Founded: 1967

Organisation type and purpose: National organisation, registered charity (charity number 251681), suitable for ages: 5 to 18, consultancy, publishing house.
Independent scientific charity.
Provides scientifically based information on nutrition and related health matters, also provides health education resources for primary and secondary schools.

Subject coverage: Nutrition and related health matters, science of nutrition and its application, food and diet, diet-related health problems, nutrition education, food labelling, food safety.

Publications: Printed, and electronic and video

Publications list: Available online and in print

Access to staff: Contact by letter, by fax, by e-mail and via website
Hours: Mon to Fri, 0900 to 1700
Special comments: Stamped addressed envelope is useful for information.

BRITISH OAT AND BARLEY MILLERS ASSOCIATION (BOBMA)

4A Torphichen Street, Edinburgh, EH3 8JQ

Tel: 0131 229 9415
Fax: 0131 229 9407

Enquiries to: Executive Secretary
Direct e-mail: tom.hollis@fdf.org.uk

Organisation type and purpose: Trade association.
Acts as a lobbying organisation for trade sector.

Subject coverage: Supply of oats and barley.

Access to staff: Contact by telephone and by e-mail. Appointment necessary. Access for members only.
Hours: Mon to Fri, 0900 to 1700

Affiliated to the European organisation: CEEREAL; Rond-Point Schuman 9, bte 11, Brussels, B-1040, Belgium; tel: 00 3 22 230 4354; fax: 00 3 22 230 9493

Umbrella organisation: Food and Drink Federation (FDF); 6 Catherine Street, London, WC2B 5JJ; tel: 020 7836 2460; fax: 020 7836 0580; e-mail: fdf@fdf.org.uk

BRITISH OCCUPATIONAL HYGIENE SOCIETY (BOHS)

5–6 Melbourne Business Court, Millennium Way, Pride Park, Derby, DE24 8LZ

Tel: 01332 298101
Fax: 01332 298099
E-mail: admin@bohs.org
Website: www.bohs.org

Enquiries to: Press Officer
Direct e-mail: anthea@bohs.org

Founded: 1953

Organisation type and purpose: Learned society, registered charity (charity number 801417).

Subject coverage: Occupational hygiene; recognition, evaluation and control of the workplace; physical and chemical factors affecting the health or well-being of workers or the community, emphasis on health hazards at work and indoor air quality.

Publications: Printed

Access to staff: Access for members only.
Hours: Mon to Thu, 0830 to 1630; Fri, 0830 to 1600

Access to building: No access other than to staff

BRITISH OLYMPIC ASSOCIATION (BOA)

60 Charlotte Street, London, W1T 2NU

Tel: 020 7842 5700

continued overleaf

E-mail: boa@boa.org.uk
Website: www.olympics.org.uk

Founded: 1905

Organisation type and purpose: BOA is the national Olympic committee for the United Kingdom, with sole responsibility for raising funds for Team GB. Working with the Olympic governing bodies, it selects Team GB from the best sportsmen and women who will go on to compete in the 26 summer and 7 winter Olympic sports. BOA is the strong, independent voice for British Olympic Sport.
BOA's role is to prepare and lead the nation's finest athletes at the Olympic Games and it has the responsibility for developing the Olympic Movement throughout the UK. In addition, it delivers extensive support services to Britain's Olympic athletes and their national governing bodies throughout each Olympic cycle to assist them in their preparations for, and performances at the Games.

Subject coverage: Preparation of Team GB for the Olympic Games.

Access to staff: Contact by letter, by telephone and by e-mail

Member organisations: The 33 national governing bodies of each Olympic sport, both summer and winter

BRITISH ORCHID COUNCIL (BOC)

Hall Farm House, Shelton, Newark on Trent, NG23 5JG

Tel: 01949 850713
E-mail: bocsecretary@tiscali.co.uk
Website: www.british-orchid-council.info

Enquiries to: Secretary

Founded: 1971

Organisation type and purpose:
Membership association (membership is by subscription), registered charity (charity number 1002945).

Subject coverage: Orchids: their study, cultivation, breeding and conservation.

Collection: Slide (35mm) Library

Library catalogue: All or part available in-house

Publications: Printed

Access to staff: Contact by letter, by telephone and by e-mail
Hours: Sun to Sat, 0800 to 2100

BRITISH ORGAN DONOR SOCIETY (BODY)

Balsham, Cambridge, CB21 4DL

Tel: 01223 893636
Fax: 01223 893636 (telephone first)
E-mail: body@argonet.co.uk
Website: www.argonet.co.uk/body

Enquiries to: Administrator

Founded: 1984

Organisation type and purpose: Voluntary organisation, registered charity (charity number 294925).

Subject coverage: Aspects of transplantation and organ donation other than specific medical details; help available to donor recipient and waiting recipient families, especially where there are emotional problems; information to nurses and researchers about the emotional side of organ donation.

Publications: Printed, and electronic and video

Access to staff: Contact by letter, by telephone, by fax, by e-mail and via website
Hours: Mon to Fri, 0900 to 1700
Special comments: 24 hour answerphone, no office access or personal answers.

Member organisation of: Council of TIME (transplants in mind)

BRITISH ORIENTEERING FEDERATION (BOF)

8a Stancliffe House, Whitworth Road, Darley Dale, Matlock, Derbyshire, DE4 2HJ

Tel: 01629 734042
Fax: 01629 733769
E-mail: info@britishorienteering.org.uk
Website: www.britishorienteering.org.uk/

Enquiries to: Secretary General
Other contacts: (1) Director of Coaching (2) Marketing and Membership Manager

Founded: 1967

Organisation type and purpose: Governing body of the sport.

Subject coverage: Orienteering, maps, forests and adventure; competitive events, specialised coaching awards, teachers' and leaders' certificates, NVQ qualifications.

Publications list: Available in print

Access to staff: Contact by letter, by telephone, by fax and in person
Hours: Mon to Fri, 0900 to 1700

Affiliated to: International Orienteering Federation (IOF); Radio Katu 20, FI-00093 SLU, Finland

BRITISH ORNITHOLOGISTS' UNION (BOU)

PO Box 417, Peterborough, PE7 3FX

Tel: 01733 844820
Fax: 01733 844820
E-mail: bou@bou.org.uk
Website: www.bou.org.uk

Enquiries to: Senior Administrator
Direct tel: 01733 844820
Direct fax: 01733 844820
Direct e-mail: stevedudley@bou.org.uk

Founded: 1858

Organisation type and purpose:
International organisation, learned society, registered charity (charity number 249877).

Subject coverage: Ornithology.

Publications: Printed, and electronic and video

Publications list: Available online and in print

Access to staff: Contact by e-mail
Hours: Mon to Fri, 0900 to 1700

BRITISH OVERSEAS TRADE BOARD (BOTB)

China and Hong Kong Branch: China; tel: 020 7215 5252 or 4827; Hong Kong; tel: 020 7215 4829

Exports to North America Branch: consumer goods; tel: 020 7215 4595 or 4593; industrial goods; tel: 020 7215 4608 or 4606

Latin America, Caribbean and Australasia Branch: Australia, Papua New Guinea; tel: 020 7215 5319/21; Caribbean; tel: 020 7215 5297; Latin America; tel: 020 7215 5059; New Zealand, the Pacific Islands; tel: 020 7215 4760

Market branches: East Europe Branch; tel: 020 7215 5258; Exports to Europe Branch; tel: 020 7215 5336

Middle East Branch: Arabian Gulf; tel: 020 7215 5096; Egypt; tel: 020 7215 4947; North Africa; tel: 020 7215 5358; other Middle East countries; tel: 020 7215 5501

South Asia and Far East Branch: Burma, Indonesia; tel: 020 7215 4738; India, Sri Lanka; tel: 020 7215 4825; Indo-China, North Korea; tel: 020 7215 4736; Japan; tel: 020 7215 4804; Pakistan, Bangladesh, Nepal; tel: 020 7215 4821/4; Singapore, Malaysia, Brunei; tel: 020 7215 5143; South Korea; tel: 020 7215 4808; Thailand, the Philippines; tel: 020 7215 5253

Sub-Saharan Africa Branch: Sub-Saharan Africa; tel: 020 7215 4969/70

BRITISH PARACHUTE ASSOCIATION (BPA)

5 Wharf Way, Glen Parva, Leicester, LE2 9TF

Tel: 0116 278 5271
Fax: 0116 247 7662
E-mail: skydive@bpa.org.uk
Website: www.bpa.org.uk
Website: www.skydivemag.com

Enquiries to: Membership Services

Founded: 1962

Organisation type and purpose:
Membership association.
Governing body for Sport Parachuting in the United Kingdom.
Parachuting in the UK.

Subject coverage: Sport parachuting, technical information, safety information, diary of events, skydiving and people in the sport.

Publications: Printed, and electronic and video

Publications list: Available online

Access to staff: Contact by letter, by telephone, by fax, by e-mail, in person and via website
Hours: Mon to Fri, 0900 to 1700

Links with: Fédération Aéronautique Internationale, through the Royal Aero Club of the United Kingdom

BRITISH PEST CONTROL ASSOCIATION (BPCA)

4A Mallard Way, Pride Park, Derby, DE24 8GX

Tel: 01332 294288

E-mail: sofi@bpca.org.uk
Website: www.BPCA.org.uk

Enquiries to: Administrator
Direct tel: 01332 225114
Direct e-mail: sofi@bpca.org.uk

Founded: 1942

Organisation type and purpose: National organisation, trade association (membership is by qualification), present number of members: 420, training organisation.

Subject coverage: Public hygiene, pest control.

Publications: Printed

Publications list: Available online

Access to staff: Contact by letter, by telephone, by fax, by e-mail and via website
Hours: Mon to Thu, 0830 to 1700; Fri, 0830 to 1600

Access to building: No access other than to staff

Access for disabled people: Parking provided, ramped entry, level entry, access to all public areas, toilet facilities

BRITISH PHARMACOLOGICAL SOCIETY (BPS)

16 Angel Gate, City Road, London, EC1V 2PT

Tel: 020 7417 0171
Fax: 020 7417 0114
E-mail: info@bps.ac.uk
Website: www.bps.ac.uk

Founded: 1931

Organisation type and purpose: Learned society (membership is by qualification, election or invitation), present number of members: 3,000, registered charity (charity number 1030623).
To promote and advance pharmacology (including without limitation clinical pharmacology).

Subject coverage: Pharmacology, drug use.

Publications: Printed

Access to staff: Contact by letter, by telephone, by fax and by e-mail
Hours: Mon to Fri, 0900 to 1700
Special comments: Press enquiries only – no general information service.

Access to building: No access other than to staff

BRITISH PIG ASSOCIATION (BPA)

Trumpington Mews, 40B High Street, Trumpington, Cambridge, CB2 2LS

Tel: 01223 845100
Fax: 01223 846235
E-mail: bpa@britishpigs.org
Website: www.britishpigs.org.uk

Enquiries to: Chief Executive

Founded: 1884

Organisation type and purpose: Trade association.
Representative body for the UK pig industry and pedigree recording society.

Subject coverage: Pig industry matters; non-technical aspects of pig breeding and production in the UK; UK pedigree pig breeds.

Collection: Herd Books for Pedigree Pig Breeds from 1884

Publications: Printed

Access to staff: Appointment necessary.
Hours: Mon to Fri, 0900 to 1700

BRITISH PLASTICS FEDERATION (BPF)

6 Bath Place, Rivington Street, London, EC2A 3JE

Tel: 020 7457 5000
Fax: 020 7457 5020
E-mail: reception@bpf.co.uk
Website: www.bpf.co.uk/

Direct e-mail: mcairns@bpf.co.uk

Founded: 1933

Organisation type and purpose: National organisation, trade association (membership is by subscription), present number of members: 400 companies.
To promote and safeguard the UK plastics industry.

Subject coverage: Plastics industry, commercial and technical; economic trends and statistics, biological safety, environmental information, fire hazards and prevention, industrial health and safety, plastics in building, processing and moulding, reinforced plastics, thermoplastics, thermosets.

Collection: Many and varied publications, photographs, illustrations related to the plastics industry

Non-library collection catalogue: All or part available online

Library catalogue: All or part available online

Publications: Printed

Publications list: Available online and in print

Access to staff: Contact by letter, by telephone, by fax, by e-mail and via website
Hours: Mon to Fri, 0900 to 1700

Access for disabled people: Parking provided, ramped entry, access to all public areas, toilet facilities

Affiliated associations: Association of Flexible Calendared uPVC Sheet Manufacturers; British Laminated Fabricators Association Limited; British Rigid Urethane Foam Manufacturers Association; Flexible Packaging Association; Gauge and Toolmakers Association; Northern Ireland Polymers Association; Packaging and Industrial Films Association; Plastics Consultancy Network; Polymer Machinery Manufacturers and Distributors Association; Scottish Plastics and Rubber Association

Member of: European Plastics Converters Association

BRITISH POLAROGRAPHIC RESEARCH INSTITUTE (BPRI)

6 Beechvale, Hillview Road, Woking, Surrey, GU22 7NS

Enquiries to: Director of Research

Founded: 1955

Organisation type and purpose: Advisory body, research organisation.

Subject coverage: Polarographic operational research (theory and methodology); polarographic mathematical, physical and chemophysical depolarisational processes and phenomena; polarophilosophy, polarology, polaronomy, polarometry, polaroscopy, polarography, polarological sciences; polaroengineering sciences, radiopolarography, communication-radiopolarography, medical communication-radiopolarography, deaf-mute communication radiopolarography, stroke-communication radiopolarography. Cardiopolarographic therapy, cardiac-immobility polarography, cancer diagnostic polarography, psychoanalytical polarography, psychomotivation polarography. Space-communication radiopolarography, fog-prevention gas-phase polarography, fog and (CO) jet-stream-dispersal polarography, cot death (CO) poisoning (prevention) polarography, learning disabilities, (communication), photon-polarography, and very many other applications and uses of polarography.

Publications: Printed

Access to staff: Contact by letter
Hours: Mon to Fri, 0900 to 1700

Links with: Institute of Pure Polarology Research; National Institute of Applied Polarology Research; Polarographic Society; UK Polaromatics R E – National Centres for Polarological and Polarographic Operational Research

Parent body: British Polarological Research Society (BPRS); 6 Beechvale, Hillview Road, Woking, Surrey, GU22 7NS

BRITISH POLIO FELLOWSHIP (BPF)

Ground Floor Unit A, Eagle Office Centre, The Runway, South Ruislip, Middlesex, HA4 6SE

Tel: 0800 018 0586
Fax: 020 8842 0555
E-mail: info@britishpolio.org.uk
Website: www.britishpolio.org.uk

Enquiries to: Chief Executive
Other contacts: Information and Benefits Manager (for support and information)

Founded: 1939

Organisation type and purpose: Registered charity (charity number 1108335, England; SC038863, Scotland).

Subject coverage: Support for people who have had polio and their carers, information available on the late effects of polio, often referred to as post-polio syndrome.

Information services: Information in relation to post-polio syndrome, benefits.

Publications: Printed, and electronic and video

continued overleaf

Publications list: Available online and in print

Access to staff: Contact by letter, by telephone, by fax, by e-mail and in person. Appointment necessary.
Hours: Mon to Thu, 0900 to 1700; Fri, 0900 to 1600

Access for disabled people: Parking provided, level entry, access to all public areas, toilet facilities

BRITISH PORTS ASSOCIATION (BPA)

4th Floor, Carthusian Court, 12 Carthusian Street, London, EC1M 6EZ

Tel: 020 7260 1780
E-mail: info@britishports.org.uk
Website: www.britishports.org.uk

Enquiries to: Director
Direct e-mail: monica.williams@britishports.org.uk
Other contacts: Association Secretary

Founded: 1993

Organisation type and purpose: Trade association.

Subject coverage: Port industry and policy.

Access to staff: Contact by letter, by telephone, by fax, by e-mail and via website. Appointment necessary.
Hours: Mon to Fri, 0900 to 1700

Affiliated to: European Seaports Organisation (ESPO); International Association of Ports and Harbours (IAPH)

BRITISH POSTAL MUSEUM AND ARCHIVE (BPMA)

Freeling House, Phoenix Place, London, WC1X 0DL

Tel: 020 7239 2570
Fax: 020 7239 2576
E-mail: info@postalheritage.org.uk
Website: www.postalheritage.org.uk

Enquiries to: Archive Assistant
Other contacts: Head of Archive/Collections Manager (for offers of donation of records/ objects); Philatelic Curator (for appointments for access to philatelic collections)

Founded: 1896; formerly called Post Office Heritage (year of change 2001); incorporates the former National Postal Museum; incorporates the former Post Office Archives (year of change 1998); incorporates the former Consignia Heritage Services (year of change 2004)

Organisation type and purpose: Archive and museum service.

Subject coverage: All aspects of British postal history.

Collection: An archive of historical records of Royal Mail Group plc, from 1636 to the present day, including working files, staff records, reports and visual records such as maps, posters, artwork and photographs.
Stamps of Great Britain from the Penny Black onwards, and their artwork, and British postal markings from 1661.
Museum collection: letter boxes, vehicles, uniforms, postal equipment, paintings, signs, etc.

Non-library collection catalogue: All or part available online and in-house

Publications: Printed

Publications list: Available online

Access to staff: Contact by letter, by telephone, by fax, by e-mail and in person
Hours: Mon, Tue, Wed, Fri, 1000 to 1700; Thu, 1000 to 1900; Sat, see website
Special comments: Philatelic collections available by appointment only. Cannot undertake research on behalf of members of the public, although will provide access to the records.

Access for disabled people: Level entry, access to all public areas, toilet facilities

BRITISH POSTMARK SOCIETY (BPS)

12 Dunavon Park, Strathaven, Lanarkshire, ML10 6LP

Tel: 01357 522430
E-mail: johlen@stracml10.freeserve.co.uk
Website: www.britishpostmarksociety.org.uk

Enquiries to: General Secretary

Founded: 1958

Organisation type and purpose:
Membership association (membership is by subscription), present number of members: 237, voluntary organisation; registered charity (charity number 1102748).

Subject coverage: British postmarks, postal history, postal mechanisation markings.

Collection: Cuttings and reprints (10 titles by W G Stitt-Dibden and 29 titles by J A Mackay)
Cuttings collected under subject headings, available for loan to members; information provided to non-members by the Librarian Postmark Library

Library catalogue: All or part available online and in-house

Publications: Printed
Order printed publications from: Publications, British Postmark Society, 19 Moorland Road, Hemel Hempstead, Hertfordshire, HP1 1NH

Publications list: Available online and in print

Access to staff: Contact by letter, by telephone, by e-mail and via website
Hours: Mon to Fri, 0900 to 1700

BRITISH POTATO TRADE ASSOCIATION (BPTA)

12 Buckstone Hill, Edinburgh, EH10 6TH

Tel: 0131 623 0183
Fax: 0131 623 5295
E-mail: charlie.greenslade@bpta.org.uk
Website: www.bpta.org.uk

Enquiries to: Secretary

Founded: 1940; created by the merger of National Association of Seed Potato Merchants (NASPM) and Scottish Potato Trade Association (SPTA) (year of change 2006)

Organisation type and purpose: Trade association (membership is by subscription, election or invitation), present number of members: 110.

Subject coverage: All matters pertaining to seed potato merchanting.

Access to staff: Contact by letter, by telephone, by fax, by e-mail, in person and via website
Hours: Mon to Thu, 0830 to 1330

BRITISH POULTRY COUNCIL (BPC)

Europoint House, 5 Lavington Street, London, SE1 0NZ

Tel: 020 7202 4760
Fax: 020 7928 6366
E-mail: info@britishpoultry.org.uk
Website: www.poultry.uk.com

Enquiries to: Chief Executive

Founded: 2001; incorporates the former BCA (Co-operative & Export) Limited; incorporates the former British Chicken Association; incorporates the former British Goose Producers Association; incorporates the former British Poultry Breeders and Hatcheries Association; incorporates the former British Turkey Federation; incorporates the former Duck Producers Association; incorporates the former Hen Packers Association; incorporates the former Poultry Industry Conference

Organisation type and purpose: Trade association (membership is by election or invitation).

Subject coverage: Poultry meat industry.

Access to staff: Contact by letter, by telephone and by e-mail. Appointment necessary.
Hours: Mon to Fri, 0900 to 1700

BRITISH PRECAST CONCRETE FEDERATION (BPCF)

60 Charles Street, Leicester, LE1 1FB

Tel: 0116 253 6161
Fax: 0116 251 4568
E-mail: info@britishprecast.org
Website: www.britishprecast.org

Enquiries to: Secretary

Organisation type and purpose: Trade association.

Subject coverage: Precast concrete.

Publications list: Available online

Access to staff: Contact by letter, by telephone, by fax, by e-mail and via website
Hours: Mon to Fri, 0900 to 1700

Access to building: No access other than to staff

Members: Concrete Lighting Column Association; Concrete Lintel Association

BRITISH PREGNANCY ADVISORY SERVICE (bpas)

20 Timothy's Bridge Road, Stratford Enterprise Park, Stratford upon Avon, CV37 9BF

Tel: 0845 730 4030
Fax: 0845 365 5051
E-mail: info@bpas.org
Website: www.bpas.org

Founded: 1968

Organisation type and purpose: National organisation, advisory body and registered charity (charity number 289145). bpas is the UK's leading provider of abortion care.

Subject coverage: Pregnancy testing; pre- and post-abortion counselling; abortion assessment, treatment and aftercare; vasectomy; female sterilisation; vasectomy reversal; contraception; unplanned pregnancy and online STI testing and treatment.

Publications: Printed
Order printed publications from: e-mail: marketing@bpas.org

Publications list: Available online and in print

Access to staff: Contact by letter, by telephone, by fax, by e-mail and via website
Hours: Mon to Fri, 0800 to 2100; Sat, 0830 to 1800; Sun, 0930 to 1430

Branches: Branches nation-wide; tel: 0845 730 4030

BRITISH PRINTING INDUSTRIES FEDERATION (BPIF)

2 Villiers Court, Meriden Business Park, Copse Drive, Coventry, West Midlands, CV5 9RN

Tel: 0845 250 7050
Fax: 01676 526 033
E-mail: info@bpif.org.uk
Website: www.britishprint.com

Enquiries to: Director of Corporate Affairs
Direct tel: 020 7915 8378
Direct fax: 020 7915 8395
Direct e-mail: andrew.brown@bpif.org.uk

Founded: 1901

Organisation type and purpose: National organisation, advisory body, trade association, present number of members: 2,500, training organisation, consultancy. The British Printing Industries Federation is the leading trade association and business support organisation for the UK printing industry. The BPIF runs a strong regional network of advisors and business centres to support printing companies in the UK, offering a 'one-stop shop' for skills solutions, and delivering expert assistance across the full range of business activities from sales and marketing to environmental and risk management, from training to insurance and pensions.
As a leading trade association the BPIF also works closely with government and international institutions. Regularly consulted by government and other national and international trade associations, the BPIF is in a strong position to lobby and influence public policy on behalf of the industry both in the UK, in Europe and other parts of the globe.

Subject coverage: British printing industry and paper; employment affairs, education and training, industrial relations, technical, consultancy, environment, health and safety, waste management.

Trade and statistical information: Surveys for the UK printing industry

Publications: Printed
Order printed publications from: Information Officer

Publications list: Available in print

Access to staff: Contact by letter, by telephone, by fax, by e-mail and via website. Appointment necessary. Non-members charged.
Hours: Mon to Fri, 0900 to 1700

Access to building: No access other than to staff
Hours: Mon to Fri, 0930 to 1630

Access for disabled people: Parking provided, ramped entry, access to all public areas, toilet facilities

Affiliated to: Intergraf

Regional business centres: BPIF Eastern (Bedfordshire, Buckinghamshire, Cambridgeshire, Essex (East and North), Hertfordshire, Norfolk and Suffolk); 7 Kings Court, Willie Snaith Road, Newmarket, Suffolk, CB8 7SG; tel: 01638 565180; fax: 01638 665235; e-mail: east@bpif.org.uk; BPIF Midland (Derbyshire (except High Peak and Chesterfield areas), Leicestershire, Lincolnshire, Northamptonshire, Nottinghamshire, Shropshire, Staffordshire, Warwickshire, West Midlands and Worcestershire); Unit 2 Villiers Court, Meridien Business Park, Birmingham Road, Coventry, West Mids, CV5 9RN; tel: 01676 526030; fax: 01676 526033; e-mail: mid@bpif.org.uk; BPIF North Eastern (Cleveland, Derbyshire (Chesterfield area), Durham, Humberside, Northumberland, Tyne and Wear, North Yorkshire, South Yorkshire and West Yorkshire); 142 Thornes Lane, Wakefield, West Yorkshire, WF2 7XG; tel: 01924 203330; fax: 01924 290092; e-mail: ne@bpif.org.uk; BPIF North Western (Cheshire, Cumbria, Derbyshire (High Peak district), Lancashire, Greater Manchester, Merseyside, Isle of Man, Clwyd, Gwynedd and Northern Ireland); 8th Floor, Trafford House, Chester Road, Stretford, Manchester, M32 0RS; tel: 0161 886 8400; fax: 0161 877 4455; e-mail: nw@bpif.org.uk; BPIF South Eastern (Berkshire, Hampshire, Kent, Greater London, Surrey, Sussex and the Isle of Wight); Farringdon Point, 29–35 Farringdon Road, London, EC1M 3JF; tel: 020 7915 8400; fax: 020 7404 7304; e-mail: se@bpif.org.uk; BPIF South Western (Avon, Cornwall, Devon, Dorset, Gloucestershire, Herefordshire, Oxfordshire, Somerset, Wiltshire, Dyfed, Mid Glamorgan, South Glamorgan, West Glamorgan, Gwent and Powys); Lindsey House, Oaklands Business Park, Bristol, BS37 5NA; tel: 01454 333 331; fax: 01454 333 331; e-mail: sw@bpif.org.uk

Subsidiary of BPIF, access through BPIF Head Office: Book Production Section; British Binders and Finishers Association (BBFA); British Carton Association (BCA); British Engraved Stationery Association (BESA); British Roll Label Association (BRLA); Business Documents Section; Digital Interest Group; Direct Marketing Special Products Section; Heidelberg Users Group; Inplant Printers; Magazine & Media Section; Promotional Finishers Association (PFA); Young Managing Printers (YMP)

BRITISH PROMOTIONAL MERCHANDISE ASSOCIATION (BPMA)

Formal name: British Promotional Merchandise Association Limited
52–53 Russell Square, London, WC1B 4HP

Tel: 020 7631 6960
Fax: 020 7631 6944
E-mail: enquiries@bpma.co.uk
Website: www.bpma.co.uk

Enquiries to: Secretary

Founded: 1965

Organisation type and purpose: Trade association, present number of members: 800. Members are manufacturers and suppliers of products and services to the sales promotion industry.

Publications: Printed

Access to staff: Contact by letter, by telephone, by fax, by e-mail and via website
Hours: Mon to Fri, 0900 to 1700

BRITISH PROPERTY FEDERATION (BPF)

5th Floor, St Albans House, 57–59 Haymarket, London, SW1Y 4QX

Tel: 020 7828 0111
Fax: 020 7834 3442
E-mail: info@bpf.org.uk
Website: www.bpf.org.uk

Enquiries to: Operations Manager
Direct tel: 020 7802 0100
Direct e-mail: mhoyte@bpf.org.uk

Founded: 1974

Organisation type and purpose: Trade association, present number of members: 450.

Subject coverage: Property taxation (direct and indirect) accounting standards, private rented sector, planning and environment, property legislation, landlord/tenant relationship, impact of development on archaeology.

Publications: Printed

Publications list: Available in print

Access to staff: Contact by letter, by telephone, by fax and by e-mail. Appointment necessary.
Hours: Mon to Fri, 0930 to 1700

Access to building: 24-hour access

Access for disabled people: Access to all public areas

Subsidiary company: BPF Commercial Ltd; at the same address

BRITISH PSYCHIC AND OCCULT SOCIETY (BPOS)

PO Box 1112, London, N10 3XE

Tel: 020 8442 1233
Fax: 020 8442 1233
Website: www.dfarrant.co.uk

Enquiries to: General Secretary

Founded: 1967

continued overleaf

Organisation type and purpose: Learned society, present number of members: 374, research organisation.
Psychic research and investigation, including ghosts, poltergeists, unexplained apparitions and other phenomena, unsolved mysteries etc.

Subject coverage: Psychic research in general, i.e. unexplained phenomena, psychic disturbances, mysterious or unexplained events relating to 'ghosts', 'vampires' etc.

Publications: Printed, and electronic and video
Order printed publications from: BPOS Publications

Access to staff: Contact by letter and by fax
Hours: Mon to Fri, 0900 to 1700

Access to building: No access other than to staff

BRITISH PSYCHOANALYTIC COUNCIL (BPC)

Formal name: The British Psychoanalytic Council

British Psychoanalytic Council, Suite 7, 19–23 Wedmore Street, London, N19 4RU

Tel: 020 7561 9240
Fax: 020 7561 9005
E-mail: mail@psychoanalytic-council.org
Website: www.psychoanalytic-council.org

Enquiries to: Honorary Secretary
Other contacts: Chief Executive Officer; Head of Services

Founded: 1993; formerly called British Confederation of Psychotherapists (year of change 2005)

Organisation type and purpose:
Professional body, voluntary organisation.
To publish a register of appropriately qualified psychotherapists.

Subject coverage: Register lists psychoanalysts, Jungian analysts, psychoanalytic psychotherapists and child psychotherapists.

Publications: Printed

Access to staff: Contact by letter, by telephone, by fax, by e-mail and via website
Hours: Mon to Fri, 0930 to 1730

Members: British Association of Psychotherapists; 37 Mapesbury Road, London, NW2 4HJ; tel: 020 8452 9823; fax: 020 8452 5182; e-mail: admin@bap-psychotherapy.org; website: http://www.bap-psychotherapy.org
British Psychoanalytical Society and the Institute of Psychoanalysis; 112A Shirland Road, London, W9; tel: 020 7563 5000; fax: 020 7563 5001; website: http://www.psychoanalysis.org.uk
Lincoln Clinic and Centre for Psychotherapy; 23 Abbeville Mews, 88 Clapham Park Road, London, SW4 7BX; tel: 020 7978 1545; fax: 020 7720 4721; e-mail: info@lincoln-psychotherapy.org.uk; London Centre of Psychotherapy; 32 Leighton Road, London, NW5 2QE; tel: 020 7482 2002; fax: 020 7482 4222; e-mail: info@lcp-psychotherapy.org.uk; website: http://www.lcp-psychotherapy.org.uk
North of England Association of Psychoanalytic Psychotherapists; Claremont House, off Framlington Place, Newcastle upon Tyne, NE2 4AA; tel: 0191 282 4547; fax: 0191 282 4542; Northern Ireland Association for the Study of Psycho-Analysis; 32 Upper Malone Park, Upper Malone Road, Belfast, BT9 6PP; tel: 028 9047 3254; Scottish Association of Psychoanalytical Psychotherapists; 172 Leith Walk, Edinburgh, EH6 5EA; tel: 0131 454 3240; fax: 0131 454 3241; Scottish Institute of Human Relations; 172 Leith Walk, Edinburgh, EH6 5EA; tel: 0131 226 9610; fax: 0131 454 3241; e-mail: info@sihr.org.uk; website: http://www.sihr.org.uk
Severnside Institute for Psychotherapy; 11 Orchard Street, Bristol, BS1 5EH; tel: 0117 923 2354; fax: 0117 923 2354; e-mail: sipsychotherapy@blueyonder.co.uk; Society of Analytical Psychology; 1 Daleham Gardens, London, NW3 5BY; tel: 020 7435 7696; fax: 020 7731 1495; e-mail: office.sap@btconnect.com; website: http://www.jungian-analysis.org
Tavistock Clinic and Tavistock Society of Psychotherapists; 120 Belsize Lane, London, NW3 5BA; tel: 020 7435 7111; fax: 020 7447 3709; e-mail: info@tavi-port.org; website: http://www.tavi-port.org

Partner organisation: Association of Psychoanalytic Psychotherapists in the National Health Service; 5 Windsor Road, London, N3 3SN; tel: 020 8349 9873; fax: 020 8343 3197; e-mail: joycepiper@compuserve.com

BRITISH PSYCHOLOGICAL SOCIETY (BPS)

St Andrews House, 48 Princess Road East, Leicester, LE1 7DR

Tel: 0116 254 9568
Fax: 0116 227 1314
E-mail: enquiries@bps.org.uk
Website: www.bps.org.uk

Enquiries to: Help Desk

Founded: 1901

Organisation type and purpose: Learned society, professional body.
Empowered to maintain Register of Chartered Psychologists; 20 specialist divisions or sections.

Subject coverage: Psychology, specialist groups in educational, medical, clinical, criminological and legal, mathematical, statistical and computing, social, developmental, cognitive, consciousness and experimental psychology, counselling psychology, occupational psychotherapy, history and philosophy of psychology, neuropsychology, teaching of psychology, psychology of women, transpersonal psychology.

Collection: Archives

Publications: Printed

Access to staff: Contact by telephone, by e-mail and via website
Hours: Mon to Fri, 0900 to 1700

Affiliated to: European Federation of Professional Psychological Associations; International Union of Psychological Science

BRITISH PTERIDOLOGICAL SOCIETY (BPS)

Department of Botany, Natural History Museum, Cromwell Road, South Kensington, London, SW7 5BD

Tel: 020 8850 3218
Fax: 020 8850 3218
E-mail: secretary@ebps.org.uk
Website: www.ebps.org.uk

Enquiries to: Honorary Secretary
Direct e-mail: horticulturalinformation@ebps.org.uk
Other contacts: Horticultural Information Officer for horticultural information.

Founded: 1891

Organisation type and purpose:
International organisation, learned society (membership is by subscription), present number of members: 760, voluntary organisation.
Membership comprises amateur and professional pteridologists.
To promote the growing, study and conservation of ferns and fern allies, both of wild species and cultivated varieties and to encourage interest in their taxonomy, distribution and ecology.

Subject coverage: Ferns and fern allies: their morphology, ecology, distribution, taxonomy, conservation. All aspects of fern growing.

Publications: Printed

Access to staff: Contact by letter, by telephone, by fax and by e-mail
Hours: Mon to Fri, 0900 to 1700

Affiliated to: National Council for the Conservation of Plants and Gardens; National Plant Societies Federation; Plantlife; Royal Horticultural Society

BRITISH PUMP MANUFACTURERS ASSOCIATION (BPMA)

National Metalforming Centre, 47 Birmingham Road, West Bromwich, B70 6PY

Tel: 0121 601 6350
Fax: 0121 601 6387
E-mail: enquiry@bpma.org.uk
Website: www.bpma.org.uk

Enquiries to: Administration
Direct e-mail: admin@bpma.org.uk
Other contacts: Technical Director

Founded: 1941

Organisation type and purpose: Trade association, present number of members: 80.

Subject coverage: Manufacture and marketing of pumps.

Education services: Training in pump technology.

Publications: Printed
Order printed publications from: http://www.bpma.org.uk or admin@bpma.org.uk

Publications list: Available online and in print

Access to staff: Contact by telephone, by fax, by e-mail and via website
Hours: Mon to Fri, 0900 to 1700

Affiliated to: European Committee of Pump Manufacturers (EUROPUMP)

Parent body: Mechanical and Metal Trades Confederation (METCOM)

BRITISH PUPPET AND MODEL THEATRE GUILD (BPMTG)

65 Kingsley Avenue, West Ealing, London, W13 0EH

Tel: 020 8997 8236
E-mail: peter@peterpuppet.co.uk
Website: www.puppetguild.org.uk

Enquiries to: Honorary Chairman
Direct tel: 07931 550365

Founded: 1924

Organisation type and purpose: Membership association (membership is by subscription), voluntary organisation.
To promote and encourage the art of puppetry in all its forms.

Subject coverage: Puppetry, model theatre, workshops, technical assistance, festivals, exhibitions.

Collection: Archive, books on puppetry and collection of puppets including the Lanchester Marionettes, stored in Bridgnorth, Shropshire; viewing by appointment

Non-library collection catalogue: All or part available online

Publications: Printed

Access to staff: Contact by letter and by telephone. Non-members charged.
Hours: Any reasonable time

Access to building: Prior appointment required

BRITISH RACING SPORTS CAR CLUB (BRSCC)

Homesdale Business Centre, Platt Industrial Estate, Maidstone Road, Borough Green, Kent, TN15 8JL

Tel: 01732 780 100
E-mail: Judith@brscc.co.uk
Website: www.brsccse.co.uk/

Enquiries to: Vice President
Direct e-mail: jo@brscc.co.uk

Founded: 1946

Organisation type and purpose: Membership association (membership is by subscription), present number of members: 4,500.

Access to staff: Contact by letter, by telephone, by fax, by e-mail and via website
Hours: Mon to Fri, 0900 to 1700

BRITISH RECORDS ASSOCIATION (BRA)

c/o Finsbury Library, 245 St John Street, London, EC1V 4NB

Tel: 020 7833 0428
Fax: 020 7833 0416
E-mail: info@britishrecordsassociation.org.uk
Website: www.britishrecordsassociation.org.uk

Enquiries to: Honorary Secretary
Direct tel: 020 7834 6242
Direct fax: 020 7828 8317
Direct e-mail: secretary@britishrecordsassociation.org.uk
Other contacts: Chairman, Vice-Chair, Chair – Records Preservation Section; Administrative Officer

Founded: 1932

Organisation type and purpose: National organisation, membership association (membership is by subscription), present number of members: 800, registered charity (charity number 227464). Council includes representatives of the British Academy, the Library Association, the National Archives, the Society of Archivists, etc.
Preservation and promotion of archival material as an historical source.

Subject coverage: Archive management, archive services, use of documentary sources (in general), information management, preservation, conservation, care; deposit and use of historical records, manuscripts and archives, advice to record owners and keepers, friends of record offices, publication of records and archive user guides.

Publications: Printed
Order printed publications from: BRA

Publications list: Available online and in print

Access to staff: Contact by letter, by telephone, by fax and by e-mail. Appointment necessary.
Hours: Mon, Tue, Thu, 0900 to 1700
Special comments: Please telephone for an appointment.

Constituent bodies: Records Preservation Section

Links with: Scottish Records Association

BRITISH RED CROSS SOCIETY (British Red Cross)

UK Office, 44 Moorfields, London, EC2Y 9AL

Tel: 0844 871 1111
Fax: 020 7562 2000
E-mail: information@redcross.org.uk
Website: www.redcross.org.uk

Enquiries to: Information Officer
Direct tel: 0844 412 2804

Founded: 1870

Organisation type and purpose: Voluntary organisation, registered charity (England and Wales charity number 220949; Scotland charity number SC037738).

Subject coverage: Improvement of health, prevention of disease, first aid, nursing, welfare, training, community services, family reunions, transport, medical equipment loans, fundraising, voluntary work.

Collection: Collection of international humanitarian law documents and Red Cross policies, practices and procedures

Publications: Printed

Publications list: Available online and in print

Access to staff: Contact by letter, by telephone, by fax, by e-mail and via website. Appointment necessary.
Hours: Mon to Fri, 0930 to 1730

Access to building: Prior appointment required
Hours: Mon to Fri, 0900 to 1700

Access for disabled people: Ramped entry, access to all public areas, toilet facilities

Also at: British Red Cross Museum and Archives; same address; tel: 020 7201 5153; e-mail: enquiry@redcross.org.uk; website: http://www.redcross.org.uk/museumandarchives

Links with: International Committee of the Red Cross; International Federation of Red Cross and Red Crescent Societies

BRITISH REED GROWER'S ASSOCIATION (BRGA)

c/o Brown & Co, The Atrium, St George's Street,, Norwich, Norfolk, NR3 1AB

Tel: 01603 629871
Fax: 01603 616199
E-mail: ian.lonsdale@brown-co.com
Website: www.brga.org.uk

Enquiries to: Secretary

Founded: 1965

Organisation type and purpose: Trade association (membership is by subscription), present number of members: 38, suitable for ages: all.
Promotion of reed and sedge growing; co-ordination of supply to thatchers, monitoring supply and demand; promotion of research into improved production, maintaining close links with the thatching trade, environmental groups, government agencies and local authorities; lobbying over important relevant issues.

Subject coverage: Reed bed management and creation, marketing reed and sedge.

Trade and statistical information: Guideline information on cost of reed and sedge

Publications: Printed

Publications list: Available in print

Access to staff: Contact by letter, by telephone, by fax, by e-mail and via website. Non-members charged.
Hours: Mon to Fri, 0900 to 1700

BRITISH REFLEXOLOGY ASSOCIATION (BRA)

Monks Orchard, Whitbourne, Worcester, WR6 5RB

Tel: 01886 821207
E-mail: bra@britreflex.co.uk
Website: www.britreflex.co.uk

Enquiries to: Chairman

Founded: 1985

Organisation type and purpose: Membership association, training organisation.

Subject coverage: Reflexology and reflexology training.

Publications: Printed, and electronic and video

Publications list: Available online and in print

continued overleaf

Access to staff: Contact by letter, by telephone, by e-mail and via website. Appointment necessary.
Hours: Mon to Thu, 0900 to 1600

Official teaching body: The Bayly School of Reflexology; Monks Orchard, Whitbourne, Worcestershire, WR6 5RB; tel: 01886 821207; e-mail: bayly@britreflex.co.uk; website: http://www.britreflex.co.uk

BRITISH REFRACTORIES & INDUSTRIAL CERAMICS ASSOCIATION (BRICA)

Federation House, Station Road, Stoke-on-Trent, Staffordshire, ST4 2SA

Tel: 01782 744631
Fax: 01782 744102
E-mail: bcc@ceramfed.co.uk
Website: www.ceramfed.co.uk

Enquiries to: Secretary
Direct e-mail: andrewm@ceramfed.co.uk

Organisation type and purpose: Trade association.

Subject coverage: Refractory and ceramics materials industry, commercial and industrial relations within it.

Publications: Printed

Access to staff: Contact by letter, by telephone, by fax and by e-mail
Hours: Mon to Fri, 0900 to 1700

Member of: British Ceramic Confederation; at the same address

BRITISH RETAIL CONSORTIUM (BRC)

MWB Business Exchange, 10 Greycoat Place, London, SW1P 1SB

Tel: 020 7854 8900
Fax: 020 7854 8901
E-mail: info@brc.org.uk
Website: www.brc.org.uk

Enquiries to: Marketing and Business Information Director
Direct e-mail: krishan.rama@brc.org.uk

Founded: 1992

Organisation type and purpose: Trade association.

Subject coverage: Retailing, consumer affairs.

Trade and statistical information: Retailing

Publications list: Available online

Access to staff: Contact by letter, by fax, by e-mail and via website
Hours: Mon to Fri, 0900 to 1700

Branch office: Scottish Retail Consortium; PO Box 13737, Gullane, EH31 2WX; tel: 07830 152423; e-mail: src@brc.org.uk

BRITISH RETINITIS PIGMENTOSA SOCIETY (BRPS)

Formal name: RP Fighting Blindness

PO Box 350, Buckingham, MK18 1GZ

Tel: 01280 821334
E-mail: info@brps.org.uk
Website: www.brps.org.uk
Website: www.fightingblindness.org.uk

Enquiries to: Chief Executive Officer

Founded: 1975

Organisation type and purpose: Membership association (membership is by subscription), present number of members: 3,000, charity, research organisation.
Run by volunteers, it aims to raise funds for scientific research to provide treatments leading to a cure for RP.
Provides welfare support and guidance service to members and their families.

Subject coverage: Retinitis pigmentosa (RP), medical advice, progress of research, aids to sufferers.

Publications: Printed, and electronic and video

Publications list: Available in print

Access to staff: Contact by letter, by telephone, by fax and by e-mail

BRITISH RIGID URETHANE FOAM MANUFACTURERS' ASSOCIATION LIMITED (BRUFMA)

12a High Street East, Glossop, Derbyshire, SK13 8DA

Tel: 01457 855884
Fax: 01457 855884
E-mail: brufma@brufma.co.uk
Website: www.brufma.co.uk

Enquiries to: Chief Executive
Direct e-mail: mel.price@brufma.co.uk

Founded: 1967

Organisation type and purpose: Trade association.

Subject coverage: BRUFMA is a trade association that was incorporated in 1978 to represent the manufacturers of the wide range of PIR/PUR insulation products produced in the UK. Its membership comprises the major companies in the industry, both manufacturers of finished insulation products and suppliers of the various raw materials.

Publications list: Available online

Access to staff: Contact by e-mail and via website. Appointment necessary.
Hours: Mon to Fri, 0915 to 1700

Affiliated to: Construction Products Association

BRITISH ROSE GROWERS ASSOCIATION (BRGA)

c/o Horticultural Trades Association, 19 High Street, Theale, Reading, Berkshire, RG7 5AH

Tel: 0118 930 3132
Fax: 0118 930 4989
E-mail: info@the-hta.org.uk

Enquiries to: Administrator
Direct e-mail: info@the-hta.org.uk

Founded: 1976

Organisation type and purpose: Trade association (membership is by election or invitation), present number of members: 70.

Publications: Printed
Order printed publications from: The Editor, British Rose Growers Association
303 Mile End Road, Colchester, CO4 5EA

Access to staff: Contact by letter, by telephone and by fax
Hours: Mon to Fri, 0900 to 1700

BRITISH ROWING

GB Rowing Team Office, British Rowing, 6 Lower Mall, Hammersmith, London, W6 9DJ

Tel: 020 8237 6767
Fax: 020 8563 2265
E-mail: info@britishrowing.org
Website: http:www.britishrowing.org

Founded: 1882; formerly called Amateur Rowing Association (year of change 2009)

Organisation type and purpose: Membership association, voluntary organisation, publishing house, training organisation.
Governing body of the sport in England.

Subject coverage: All aspects of rowing: learning, training, coaching, rules, organisation, clubs, competitions, international and Olympic representation.

Collection: British Rowing Almanack & Year Book (from 1869)
Reference library of historic and contemporary books associated with rowing

Library catalogue: All or part available in-house

Publications: Printed

Access to staff: Contact by letter, by telephone, by fax and in person
Hours: Mon to Fri, 0900 to 1700
Special comments: Library by prior appointment.

Also at: International Office, British Rowing; tel: 020 8237 6767; fax: 020 8563 2265; e-mail: info@gbrowingteam.org.uk; Satellite Office, British Rowing; Bedford Satellite Office, Unit 3, Greensbury Farm, Thurleigh Road, Bolnhurst, Beds, MK44 2ET; fax: 01234 378899; e-mail: 01234 37886

Members: British Olympic Association; tel: 020 8871 2677; fax: 020 8871 9104; Central Council of Physical Recreation; tel: 020 7854 8500; fax: 020 7854 8501; Commonwealth Games Federation; tel: 020 7388 6643; Fédération Internationale des Sociétés d'Aviron; tel: +41 21 617 8373; fax: +41 21 617 8375; e-mail: info@fisa.org

BRITISH SAFETY COUNCIL (BSC)

70 Chancellors Road, London, W6 9RS

Tel: 020 8741 1231
Fax: 020 8741 4555
E-mail: info@britsafe.org
Website: www.britsafe.org

Founded: 1957

Organisation type and purpose: Advisory body, professional body (membership is by subscription), present number of members: 10,000, registered charity, training organisation.
To promote health, safety and environmental best practice for the increase of productivity and the benefit of society.

Subject coverage: Occupational health, safety and environmental issues, training, risk management, audits, award schemes, advisory and assessment schemes, and related publications.

Publications: Printed

Access to staff: Contact by letter, by telephone, by fax, by e-mail and via website. Appointment necessary.
Hours: Mon to Fri, 0900 to 1700

Access for disabled people: Level entry, access to all public areas, toilet facilities

BRITISH SAFETY INDUSTRY FEDERATION (BSIF)

BSIF House, 3 Austins Mews, Hemel Hempstead, Hertfordshire, HP1 3AF

Tel: 01442 248744
E-mail: enquiries@bsif.co.uk

Enquiries to: Secretary General

Founded: 1994

Organisation type and purpose: Trade association (membership is by qualification), present number of members: 180, service industry.
Single voice for UK safety industry.

Subject coverage: Lead association for the PPE directive, access to supply chain for safety products, access to information on safety industry.

Access to staff: Contact by letter, by telephone and by fax. Non-members charged.
Hours: Mon to Fri, 0900 to 1600

Access to building: No access other than to staff

Access for disabled people: Parking provided, ramped entry, toilet facilities

BRITISH SCHOOL OF OSTEOPATHY (BSO)

275 Borough High Street, London, SE1 1JE

Tel: 020 7407 0222
Fax: 020 7089 5300
E-mail: admin@bso.ac.uk
Website: www.bso.ac.uk

Enquiries to: Librarian
Direct tel: 020 7089 5324
Direct e-mail: willp@bso.ac.uk

Founded: 1917

Organisation type and purpose: Registered charity (charity number 312873).
Private institution of higher education.

Subject coverage: Medicine, complementary medicine, osteopathy.

Collection: J. M. Littlejohn collection of osteopathic books
Special collection of osteopathic books and periodicals

Library catalogue: All or part available online

Publications: Printed

Access to staff: Contact by letter, by telephone, by fax, by e-mail and in person. Non-members charged.
Hours: Mon to Fri, 0900 to 1700

Access for disabled people: Parking provided, ramped entry, access to all public areas, toilet facilities

Links with: University of Bedfordshire; Park Square, Luton, Bedfordshire, LU1 3JU; tel: 01234 793006; website: http://www.beds.ac.uk

BRITISH SCHOOL OF SHIATSU-DO (BSS-Do)

Unit 3, Thane Works, Thane Villas, London, N7 7NU

Tel: 020 7700 3355
Fax: 020 7700 3355
E-mail: london@shiatsu-do.co.uk
Website: www.shiatsu-do.co.uk

Enquiries to: Registrar
Direct tel: 020 7700 3355

Founded: 1983

Organisation type and purpose: Training organisation.

Subject coverage: Shiatsu-Do, Shiatsu.

Publications: Printed, and electronic and video

Access to staff: Contact by letter, by telephone, by fax, by e-mail and in person
Hours: Mon to Fri, 1100 to 1300 and 1400 to 1800

Access to building: No prior appointment required
Hours: Mon to Fri, 0900 to 1900

Access for disabled people: Parking provided
Special comments: No wheelchair access

BRITISH SCHOOL OF YOGA (BSY GROUP)

Stanhope Square, Holsworthy, Devon, EX22 6DF

Tel: 0800 731 9271
E-mail: info@bsygroup.co.uk
Website: www.bsygroup.co.uk

Enquiries to: Information Officer

Founded: 1946

Organisation type and purpose: Learned society (membership is by qualification), training organisation.

Subject coverage: Complementary therapies, stress management, counselling, alternative therapies, self improvement, beauty therapies, yoga, new age, fitness training.

Publications list: Available online and in print

Access to staff: Contact by letter, by telephone, by fax, by e-mail and via website. Appointment necessary.
Hours: Mon to Fri, 0900 to 1800

BRITISH SCHOOLBOY MOTORCYCLE ASSOCIATION

20 Glenpark Crescent, Kingscourt, Stroud, Gloucestershire, GL5 5DT

Tel: 01453 766516
Fax: 01453 764877

Enquiries to: Information Officer

Founded: 1969

Organisation type and purpose: Membership association.

Subject coverage: Motorcycling for those of school age.

Access to staff: Contact by letter
Hours: Mon to Fri, 0900 to 1700

BRITISH SCHOOLS CYCLING ASSOCIATION (BSCA)

21 Bedhampton Road, North End, Portsmouth, Hampshire, PO2 7JX

Tel: 023 9264 2226
Fax: 023 9266 0187
E-mail: susanknight@bsca.fsnet.co.uk
Website: www.bsca.org.uk

Enquiries to: General Secretary

Founded: 1967

Organisation type and purpose: Membership association (membership is by subscription).
School sports governing body.

Access to staff: Contact by letter, by telephone and by fax
Hours: Answerphone in operation

Connections with: National Council for Schools' Sport

BRITISH SCHOOLS EXPLORING SOCIETY (BSES Expeditions)

Royal Geographical Society, 1 Kensington Gore, London, SW7 2AR

Tel: 020 7591 3141
Fax: 020 7591 3140
E-mail: info@bses.org.uk
Website: www.bses.org.uk

Enquiries to: Executive Director

Founded: 1932

Organisation type and purpose: Learned society (membership is by qualification), registered charity (charity number 802196), suitable for ages: 16 to 24, training organisation.
The British Schools Exploring Society is a pioneering youth development charity undertaking scientific research expeditions. For over 75 years its aim has been to recruit, train and develop the leaders and scientists of the future who are able to inspire others.

Subject coverage: Expeditions to areas such as Svalbard, Greenland, northern Norway, Peruvian Amazon, Ladakh and South Georgia. Other destinations include Canada, Kenya, Botswana, Zimbabwe, Australia, Papua New Guinea, Iceland and Namibia. Field work in associated sciences, e.g. glaciology, geology, botany, survey, art and photography. All associated expedition planning and logistics, including budgets.

Collection: Library (private) of exploration books
Slides of past expeditions
Video collection made from 8mm/16mm film etc, of BSES expeditions, mainly Arctic areas, since 1932

Publications: Printed, and electronic and video

continued overleaf

Access to staff: Contact by letter, by telephone, by fax, by e-mail and in person. Appointment necessary.
Hours: Mon to Fri, 0930 to 1730

Links with: Royal Geographical Society; at the same address

BRITISH SCHOOLS GYMNASTIC ASSOCIATION (BSGA)

Orchard House, 15 North Common Road, Uxbridge, Middlesex, UB8 1PD

Tel: 01895 233377
Fax: 01895 814031
E-mail: crhamilton@lineone.net

Enquiries to: General Secretary

Organisation type and purpose: National organisation, voluntary organisation.
National schools sports organisation – voluntarily staffed.

Subject coverage: Coaching of gymnastics for boys and girls; organisation of national gymnastic competitions.

Publications: Printed

Affiliated to: British Amateur Gymnastics Association

BRITISH SCIENCE ASSOCIATION

Wellcome Wolfson Building, 165 Queen's Gate, London, SW7 5HD

Tel: 0870 770 7101
Fax: 0870 770 7102
E-mail: via website
Website: www.britishscienceassociation.org/web

Enquiries to: Chief Executive

Founded: 1831; formerly called British Association for the Advancement of Science (BA) (year of change 2009)

Organisation type and purpose: A registered charity (charity number 212479 in England and Wales and SCO39236 in Scotland) that exists to advance the public understanding, accessibility and accountability of the sciences and engineering in the UK.

Subject coverage: Organises major initiatives across the UK, including the annual British Science Festival, National Science and Engineering Week, programmes of regional and local events, and an extensive programme for young people in schools and colleges.

Education services: Extensive programme for young people in schools and colleges.

Publications: Electronic and video
Order electronic and video publications from: Download from website

Publications list: Available online

Access to staff: Contact by letter, by telephone, by fax and by e-mail

BRITISH SCIENCE FICTION ASSOCIATION LIMITED (BSFA)

8 West Avenue Road, London, E17 9SE

E-mail: bsfachair@gmail.com
Website: www.bsfa.co.uk
Website: www.mjckeh.demon.co.uk/

Enquiries to: Administrator

Founded: 1958

Organisation type and purpose: Voluntary organisation.
Amateur association and company limited by guarantee dedicated to the enjoyment and promotion of science fiction.

Subject coverage: Science fiction in general; publication sources; writers' forum; book reviews.

Collection: BSFA Library (based at Science Fiction Foundation, Liverpool University)

Publications: Printed

Publications list: Available online

Access to staff: Contact by letter, by e-mail and via website
Hours: Mon to Fri, 0900 to 1700

BRITISH SECURITY INDUSTRY ASSOCIATION LIMITED (BSIA)

Kirkham House, John Comyn Drive, Worcester, WR3 7NS

Tel: 0845 389 3889
Fax: 0845 389 0761
E-mail: info@bsia.co.uk
Website: www.bsia.co.uk

Enquiries to: Press contacts
Direct e-mail: a.beesley@bsia.co.uk

Founded: 1967

Organisation type and purpose: Trade association (membership is by subscription).
To promote and encourage high standards of ethics, equipment and service throughout the industry.

Subject coverage: All aspects of security, including guard and patrol services, security equipment manufacture and installation, physical and electronic security, access control, closed circuit television, locks and safes.

Trade and statistical information: UK security industry market size by sector

Publications: Printed

Publications list: Available online and in print

Access to staff: Contact by letter, by telephone, by e-mail and via website
Hours: Mon to Fri, 0900 to 1715

BRITISH SHOOTING SPORTS COUNCIL (BSSC)

PO Box 53608, London, SE24 9YN

Tel: 020 7095 8181
Fax: 020 7095 8181
E-mail: djpbssc@btconnect.com
Website: www.bssc.org.uk

Enquiries to: Secretary

Founded: 1956

Organisation type and purpose: Advisory body.
To promote and safeguard the lawful use of firearms and air weapons for sporting and recreational purposes in the United Kingdom amongst all sections of the community, to co-ordinate and present the views of member associations and other bodies.

Subject coverage: The lawful manufacture and use of firearms, air weapons and ammunition in the United Kingdom, for sporting and recreational purposes. National policy for the use of firearms and air weapons.

Collection: Archive of Council

Publications: Printed, and electronic and video
Order printed publications from: BSSC, PO Box 53608, London, SE24 9YN

Access to staff: Contact by letter, by telephone and by e-mail
Hours: Mon to Fri, 0900 to 1700

Access to building: No access other than to staff

Links with: Home Office Consultee on Shooting Issues; tel: 020 7273 2623; fax: 020 7273 4284; World Forum of Shooting Sports Associations (WFSA); tel: +39 06 592 5971; fax: +39 06 322 0016

Member organisations: Association of Professional Clay Target Shooting Grounds; tel: 01234 707003; Association of Professional Shooting Instructors; tel: 01782 397961; fax: 01782 394896; British Association for Shooting and Conservation; tel: 0124 4457 3000; fax: 0124 4457 3013; Clay Pigeon Shooting Association; tel: 01483 485400; fax: 01483 485410; Countryside Alliance; tel: 020 7582 5432; fax: 020 7793 8484; Gun Trade Association; tel: 01684 291868; fax: 01684 291864; Institute of Clay Shooting Instructors; tel: 01347 888312; Muzzle Loaders Association; tel: 01734 590080; fax: 01734 590080; National Rifle Association; tel: 01483 797777; fax: 01483 797285; National Small Bore Rifle Association; tel: 01483 485500; fax: 01483 476392; Sportsman Association; tel: 0208789 1211; fax: 0208789 1211; United Kingdom Practical Shooting Association; tel: 07010703845; fax: 08707657721

BRITISH SHOW JUMPING ASSOCIATION (BSJA)

British Equestrian Centre, National Agricultural Centre, Stoneleigh Park, Kenilworth, Warwickshire, CV8 2LR

Tel: 024 7669 8800
Fax: 024 7669 6685
E-mail: bsja@bsja.co.uk
Website: www.bsja.co.uk

Enquiries to: Chief Executive

Founded: 1925

Organisation type and purpose: Membership association.
National governing body.

Subject coverage: National and international show jumping.

Publications: Printed

Access to staff: Contact by letter, by telephone, by fax and by e-mail
Hours: Mon to Fri, 0900 to 1700

BRITISH SIGN & GRAPHICS ASSOCIATION (BSGA)

5 Orton Enterprise Centre, Bakewell Road, Orton Southgate, Peterborough, Cambridgeshire, PE2 6XU

Tel: 01733 230033
E-mail: info@bsga.co.uk
Website: www.bsga.co.uk

Enquiries to: Director

Founded: 1978

Organisation type and purpose: Trade association.

Subject coverage: Illuminated and non-illuminated signs, graphics, printing.

Trade and statistical information: Data on UK and European sign manufacturing markets

Publications: Printed

Publications list: Available in print

Access to staff: Contact by letter, by telephone, by e-mail and via website. Appointment necessary.
Hours: Mon to Thu, 0900 to 1700; Fri 0900 to 1600

Affiliated to: European Sign Federation (ESF)

BRITISH SIKH FEDERATION (BSF)

PO Box 242, Wolverhampton, West Midlands, WV4 5DH

Tel: 01242 226517
Fax: 01242 226517
E-mail: british_sikh_fed@btopenworld.com
Website: www.british-sikh-federation.org

Enquiries to: General Secretary
Direct tel: 07221 507055

Founded: 1984

Organisation type and purpose: Voluntary organisation.
Tackles UK political and religious issues of a serious nature for the British Sikh community.

Subject coverage: Politics, religion, legal and business issues as they relate to the Sikh community, contacts for other Sikh organisations, interests of 600,000 British Sikhs.

Access to staff: Contact by letter and by e-mail. Access for members only.
Hours: Mon to Fri, 0900 to 1700

BRITISH SIMMENTAL CATTLE SOCIETY

National Agricultural Centre, Stoneleigh Park, Kenilworth, Warwickshire, CV8 2LG

Tel: 024 7669 6513
Fax: 024 7669 6724
E-mail: info@britishsimmental.co.uk
Website: www.britishsimmental.co.uk

Enquiries to: General Secretary

Founded: 1970

Organisation type and purpose: Membership association (membership is by subscription), registered charity (charity number 985570).
Registration and promotion of Simmentals.

Subject coverage: Breeds of beef cattle.

Publications: Printed

Access to staff: Contact by letter, by telephone and by fax. Appointment necessary.
Hours: Mon to Fri, 0900 to 1700

BRITISH SMALL ANIMAL VETERINARY ASSOCIATION (BSAVA)

Woodrow House, 1 Telford Way, Waterwells Business Park, Quedgeley, Gloucestershire, GL2 2AB

Tel: 01452 726700
Fax: 01452 726701
E-mail: administration@bsava.com
Website: www.bsava.com

Enquiries to: Administration Officer

Founded: 1957

Organisation type and purpose: Membership association (membership is by subscription, qualification), present number of members: 5,700, registered charity (charity number 1024811).
To foster and promote high scientific and educational standards of small animal medicine and surgery in practice, teaching and research.

Subject coverage: Health, welfare and diseases of small animals, birds and fish; veterinary science and medicine.

Publications: Printed, and electronic and video

Parent body: British Veterinary Association

BRITISH SNORING AND SLEEP APNOEA ASSOCIATION LIMITED (BSSAA)

Chapter House, 33 London Road, Reigate, Surrey, RH2 9HZ

Tel: 01737 245638
Fax: 0870 052 9212
E-mail: info@britishsnoring.co.uk
Website: www.britishsnoring.co.uk

Enquiries to: Helpline staff
Other contacts: Information Officer, Help Line Manager

Founded: 1991

Organisation type and purpose: International organisation, national organisation, membership association, voluntary organisation.

Subject coverage: Snoring and sleep apnoea and related topics, including surgery, treatment and prevention.

Publications: Printed

Access to staff: Contact by letter, by telephone, by fax, by e-mail and via website
Hours: Mon to Fri, 0900 to 1700

BRITISH SOCIETY FOR ALLERGY AND CLINICAL IMMUNOLOGY (BSACI)

Studio 16, Cloisters House, 8 Battersea Park Road, London, SW8 4BG

Tel: 020 7501 3910
Fax: 020 7627 2599
E-mail: info@bsaci.org
Website: www.bsaci.soton.ac.uk/bsaci/

Enquiries to: Administrator
Other contacts: President, Secretary, Newsletter Editor

Founded: 1948

Organisation type and purpose: Learned society (membership is by qualification), present number of members: 580, registered charity.
The recognition of allergy and clinical immunology as a specialised branch of medicine; to advance and encourage study of the subject.

Subject coverage: Allergy, clinical immunology.

Publications: Printed

Access to staff: Contact by letter, by telephone, by fax and by e-mail
Hours: Mon to Fri, 0900 to 1700

Affiliated to: EAACI; IAACI

BRITISH SOCIETY FOR CELL BIOLOGY (BSCB)

School of Biosciences, Faculty of Medical Sciences, University of Newcastle, Newcastle upon Tyne, NE2 4HH

Tel: 0191 222 5264
Fax: 0191 222 6706
E-mail: michael.whitaker@ncl.ac.uk
Website: www.bscb.org

Enquiries to: Secretary

Founded: 1965

Organisation type and purpose: Learned society.

Subject coverage: Research in the general field of cell and molecular biology and cytology, applications of cell biology in the commercial and biomedical fields.

Publications: Printed

Access to staff: Contact by letter, by telephone, by fax and by e-mail. Appointment necessary.
Hours: Mon to Fri, 0900 to 1700

Constituent society of the: European Cell Biology Organization

BRITISH SOCIETY FOR CLINICAL CYTOLOGY (BSCC)

12 Coldbath Square, London, EC1R 5HL

Tel: 029 20715596
Fax: 029 20716469
E-mail: mail@bscc.uk.net
Website: www.clinicalcytology.co.uk

Enquiries to: Secretariat
Direct e-mail: mail@bscc.uk.net

Organisation type and purpose: Learned society.

Subject coverage: Clinical cytology; diagnostic cytopathology; education and training for medical and non-medical personnel.

Publications: Printed

Access to staff: Contact by letter, by telephone, by fax and by e-mail
Hours: Mon, Wed, Thu, 0900 to 1700

continued overleaf

Access to building: No access other than to staff

Affiliated to: International Academy of Cytology

Has: 9 affiliated regional cytology societies

Member of: European Federation of Cytology Societies

BRITISH SOCIETY FOR DENTAL RESEARCH (BSDR)

Restorative Dentistry, The Dental School, Framlington Place, Newcastle upon Tyne, NE2 4BW

Tel: 0191 222 7823
Fax: 0191 222 8191
E-mail: a.w.g.walls@ncl.ac.uk
Website: www.bsdr.org.uk

Enquiries to: Honorary Secretary

Founded: 1952

Organisation type and purpose: International organisation, learned society, registered charity, research organisation.

Subject coverage: Dental public health, forensic dentistry, oral and dental sciences, dental materials, implant research, restorative dentistry, oral medicine, oral microbiology and immunology, oral pathology, oral surgery, mineralised tissues, oral anatomy and histology, oral biochemistry and physiology.

Publications: Printed

Access to staff: Contact by letter, by telephone, by fax, by e-mail and via website
Hours: Mon to Fri, 0900 to 1700

Affiliated to: International Association for Dental Research; 1619 Duke Street, Alexandria, VA, USA

BRITISH SOCIETY FOR DEVELOPMENTAL BIOLOGY (BSDB)

Department of Developmental Neurobiology, UMDS, Guy's Hospital, London, SE1 9RT

Tel: 020 7955 4798
Fax: 020 7955 4886
E-mail: bsdb@kcl.ac.uk

Enquiries to: Secretary
Direct tel: 020 7848 6547
Direct fax: 020 7848 6550
Direct e-mail: ivor.mason@kcl.ac.uk

Founded: 1964

Organisation type and purpose: Learned society.

Subject coverage: Developmental biology.

Publications: Printed

Access to staff: Contact by letter
Hours: Mon to Fri, 0900 to 1700

Affiliated to: United Kingdom Life Sciences Council

BRITISH SOCIETY FOR GEOMORPHOLOGY (BSG)

Royal Geographical Society (with IBG), 1 Kensington Gore, London, SW7 2AR

E-mail: bsg@rgs.org
Website: www.geomorphology.org.uk

Enquiries to: Honorary Secretary
Other contacts: Administrator

Founded: 1960

Organisation type and purpose: Learned society.

Subject coverage: Geomorphology: landforms, earth surface processes, sedimentology, earth materials, hydrology, Quaternary stratigraphy, Quaternary studies; fluvial, coastal, glacial, periglacial, tropical and arid environment processes and landforms; land deposits.

Publications: Printed
Order printed publications from: John Wiley & Sons, 43 Leinster Gardens, London, W2 3AN

Access to staff: Contact by letter and by e-mail
Hours: Mon to Fri, 0900 to 1700

Links with: Royal Geographical Society (with IBG)

BRITISH SOCIETY FOR HAEMATOLOGY (BSH)

100 White Lion Street, London, N1 9PF

Tel: 020 7713 0990
Fax: 020 7837 1931
E-mail: info@b-s-h.org.uk
Website: www.b-s-h.org.uk

Enquiries to: Administrator

Founded: 1962

Organisation type and purpose: Learned society, registered charity (charity number 1005735).

Subject coverage: General haematology, including diagnosis and treatment of blood diseases, leukaemia, haemophilia and other bleeding diseases, lymphomas. Equipment used in haematological laboratories, quality control and standards in haematological laboratories, blood transfusion and blood products (preparation and clinical use).

Publications: Printed

Access to staff: Contact by letter, by telephone, by fax, by e-mail and via website
Hours: Flexible

BRITISH SOCIETY FOR IMMUNOLOGY (BSI)

Vintage House, 37 Albert Embankment, London, SE1 7TL

Tel: 020 3031 9800
Fax: 020 7582 2882
E-mail: onlinecommunity@immunology.org
Website: www.immunology.org

Founded: 1956

Organisation type and purpose: Learned society (membership is by subscription, qualification, election or invitation), present number of members: 4,000, registered charity (charity number 1043255).

Subject coverage: Immunology; biochemical immunology, materno-foetal immunology, comparative and veterinary immunology, mucosal immunology, neuroimmunology, histocompatibility and immunogenetics, clinical immunology.

Publications: Printed, and electronic and video

Publications list: Available in print

Access to staff: Contact by letter, by telephone, by fax, by e-mail and via website. Appointment necessary.
Hours: Mon to Fri, 0900 to 1700

Member organisation of: European Federation of Immunological Societies; International Union of Immunological Societies; Society of Biology

BRITISH SOCIETY FOR MEDICAL AND DENTAL HYPNOSIS (BSMDH (MET&S))

(Metropolitan and South), Flat 23, Broadfield Heights, Broadfield Avenue, Edgware, Middlesex, HA8 8PF

Tel: 020 8905 4342
Fax: 020 8958 8069

Enquiries to: Referral Secretary

Founded: 1960

Organisation type and purpose: Learned society.

Subject coverage: Use of hypnosis in dentistry and medicine. Training of doctors, dentists and clinical psychologists. Referral service for members of public, medical and dental practitioners.

Access to staff: Contact by letter and by telephone
Hours: Mon to Fri, 0900 to 1700
Special comments: Telephone for referral requests.

Links with: European Society for Hypnosis; International Society of Hypnosis

BRITISH SOCIETY FOR MERCURY FREE DENTISTRY (BSMFD)

The British Society for Mercury Free Dentistry, The Weathervane, 22A Moorend Park Road, Cheltenham, GL53 0JY

Tel: 020 7373 3655
Fax: 020 7736 2480
E-mail: info@mercuryfreedentistry.org.uk
Website: mercuryfreedentistry.org.uk/

Enquiries to: President

Organisation type and purpose: Advisory body, professional body, registered charity.

Subject coverage: Mercury poisoning from dental amalgam filling.

Access to staff: Contact by letter and by telephone. All charged.
Hours: Mon to Fri, 0900 to 1700

BRITISH SOCIETY FOR PARASITOLOGY (BSP)

87 Gladstone Street, Bedford, Bedfordshire, MK41 7RS

Tel: 01234 211015
Fax: 01234 481015
E-mail: info@bsp.uk.net
Website: www.bsp.uk.net

Enquiries to: Honorary General Secretary
Direct e-mail: info@bsp.uk.net; at info@bsp.uk .net (Secretariat)
Other contacts: Secretariat

Founded: 1962

Organisation type and purpose: International organisation, national organisation, learned society (membership is by subscription), present number of members: 1,000, registered charity (charity number 206847), suitable for ages: 18 plus.

Subject coverage: All aspects of parasitology including human, animal, fish and plant diseases caused by parasites; study of parasites including physiology, biochemistry, immunology, ecology, pathology.

Publications: Printed

Access to staff: Contact by letter, by telephone, by fax, by e-mail and via website
Hours: Mon to Fri, 0900 to 1700

BRITISH SOCIETY FOR RESTORATIVE DENTISTRY (BSRD)

Department of Restorative Dentistry, The Royal London Hospital, Whitechapel, London, E1 1BB

Website: www.bsrd.org.uk/

Enquiries to: Honorary Secretary

Organisation type and purpose: Learned society.

Subject coverage: General or specialised information on restorative dentistry, the conservation of teeth and the improvement of their appearance (the Society does not recommend by name individual dentists able to carry out this work).

Publications: Printed

Access to staff: Contact by letter
Hours: Mon to Fri, 0900 to 1700

BRITISH SOCIETY FOR RHEUMATOLOGY (BSR)

Bride House, 18–20 Bride Lane, London, EC4Y 8EE

Tel: 020 7842 0900
Fax: 020 7842 0901
E-mail: bsr@rheumatology.org.uk
Website: www.rheumatology.org.uk

Enquiries to: Chief Executive

Founded: 1984

Organisation type and purpose: Learned society, registered charity.

Subject coverage: Rheumatology, education for medical staff, research conferences, information for providers/purchasers of rheumatology services, also runs British Health Professionals in Rheumatology (BHPR) and Arthritis and Musculoskeletal Alliance (ARMA).

Collection: The Heberden Library – based at the Royal College of Physicians

Trade and statistical information: Can provide access to epidemiological information eg number of people with osteoarthritis in UK

Publications: Printed

Access to staff: Contact by letter
Hours: Mon to Fri, 0830 to 1730

Access to building: Prior appointment required

Access for disabled people: Parking provided

Member of: Arthritis & Musculoskeletal Alliance (ARMA); at the same address; European League Against Rheumatism (EULAR)

BRITISH SOCIETY FOR STRAIN MEASUREMENT (BSSM)

71 Hillview Drive, Clarkston, Glasgow, G76 7JJ

Tel: 0141 577 6297
Fax: 0141 577 6281
E-mail: jerry.lord@npl.co.uk
Website: www.bssm.org/

Enquiries to: Honorary Secretary

Founded: 1964

Organisation type and purpose: Learned society.

Subject coverage: Strain measurement by strain gauges, brittle lacquers, photoelasticity extensometers, strain transducers and other optical methods; experimental stress analysis and other experimental engineering evaluation, theoretical analysis, engineering measurements by transducers; data logging and data handling.

Publications: Printed

Access to staff: Contact by letter, by telephone, by fax and by e-mail
Hours: Mon to Fri, 0900 to 1700

BRITISH SOCIETY FOR THE HISTORY OF PHARMACY (BSHP)

Q House, Troon Way Business Centre, Humberstone Lane, Thurmaston, Leicester, LE4 9HA

Tel: 0116 274 7350
Fax: 0116 274 7365
E-mail: bshp@associationhq.org.uk
Website: www.bshp.org

Enquiries to: Secretary

Founded: 1967

Organisation type and purpose: Learned society.

Subject coverage: History of pharmacy in Britain, pharmaceutical antiques.

Publications: Printed

Access to staff: Contact by letter and by e-mail
Hours: Mon to Fri, 0900 to 1700

Affiliated to: Royal Pharmaceutical Society of Great Britain

BRITISH SOCIETY FOR THE HISTORY OF SCIENCE (BSHS)

PO Box 3401, Norwich, Norfolk, NR7 7JF

Tel: 01603 516236
Fax: 01603 208563
E-mail: office@bshs.org.uk
Website: www.bshs.org.uk

Enquiries to: Executive Secretary

Founded: 1947

Organisation type and purpose: International organisation, learned society (membership is by subscription), present number of members: 700, registered charity (charity number 258854).
To promote and further the study of the history and philosophy of science.

Subject coverage: History and philosophy of science.

Non-library collection catalogue: All or part available online

Publications: Printed, and electronic and video
Order printed publications from: British Journal for the History of Science, Cambridge University Press, FREEPOST, The Edinburgh Building, Shaftesbury Road, Cambridge, CB2 1BR

Publications list: Available online and in print

Access to staff: Contact by letter, by telephone, by fax, by e-mail and via website. Appointment necessary.
Hours: Mon to Fri, 0900 to 1700

Links with: Association for Science Education; History of Science Society (USA); e-mail: info@hssonline.org; website: http://www.hssonline.org

BRITISH SOCIETY FOR THE STUDY OF PROSTHETIC DENTISTRY (BSSPD)

Division of Restorative Dentistry, University Dental School and Hospital, Wilton, Cork, Republic of Ireland

Tel: 00 353 21 490 1186
Fax: 00 353 21 490 1193
E-mail: finbarralen@hotmail.com

Enquiries to: Honorary Secretary

Organisation type and purpose: Learned society.

Subject coverage: Prosthetic dentistry.

Access to staff: Contact by letter, by fax and by e-mail
Hours: Mon to Fri, 0900 to 1700

Affiliated to: European Prosthodontic Association

Conference organiser: British Society for the Study of Prosthetic Dentistry; Birmingham Dental School, St Chad's Queensway, Birmingham; e-mail: c.w.barclay@bham.ac.uk

BRITISH SOCIETY OF AESTHETICS (BSA)

c/o Kathleen Stock, Dept of Philosophy, University of Sussex, Falmer, Brighton, BN1 9QN

E-mail: kathleen@british-aesthetics.org
Website: www.british-aesthetics.org

Enquiries to: Honorary Secretary

Founded: 1965

Organisation type and purpose: International organisation, learned society (membership is by subscription).

Subject coverage: Aesthetics, philosophy of the arts and criticism, theory of beauty.

continued overleaf

Publications: Printed

Access to staff: Contact by letter, by e-mail and via website
Hours: Mon to Fri, 0900 to 1700

Member of: British Philosophical Association; International Association of Aesthetics

Organisers of the: Collaborative European Conferences

BRITISH SOCIETY OF ANIMAL SCIENCE (BSAS)

PO Box 3, Penicuik, Midlothian, EH26 0RZ

Tel: 0131 650 8784
Fax: 0131 650 8821
E-mail: bsas@sac.ac.uk
Website: www.bsas.org.uk

Enquiries to: Secretary
Direct tel: 01848 331437
Direct fax: 01848 331437
Other contacts: Finance Officer for membership and financial matters.

Founded: 1943

Organisation type and purpose: National organisation, learned society (membership is by subscription), present number of members: 1,100, service industry, registered charity, suitable for ages: 18+.
Educational society.

Subject coverage: Animal science in most areas and species, research, welfare, nutrition, breeding/genetics.

Publications: Printed, and electronic and video

Publications list: Available in print

Access to staff: Contact by letter, by telephone, by fax and by e-mail
Hours: Mon to Fri, 0900 to 1700

Member of: Biological Society; European Association for Animal Production (EAAP); Via A Torlonia 15/A, Rome, I-00161, Italy

BRITISH SOCIETY OF AUDIOLOGY (BSA)

80 Brighton Road, Reading, Berkshire, RG6 1PS

Tel: 0118 966 0622
Fax: 0118 935 1915
E-mail: bsa@thebsa.org.uk
Website: www.thebsa.org.uk

Enquiries to: Administrator

Founded: 1966

Organisation type and purpose: National organisation, professional body (membership is by subscription), present number of members: 1,400, registered charity (charity number 1143782).
Umbrella organisation in audiology services.

Subject coverage: Audiology; otology; hearing; hearing loss; balance; clinical audiological practice.

Collection: Hearing aid museum (now at Thackray Museum, Leeds)

Library catalogue: All or part available in-house

Publications: Printed

Access to staff: Contact by letter, by telephone, by fax and by e-mail
Hours: Mon to Fri, 0900 to 1700

Access to building: No access other than to staff

BRITISH SOCIETY OF CLINICAL AND ACADEMIC HYPNOSIS (BSCAH)

134 Garfield Road, London, SW19 8SB

Tel: 0844 884 3116
Fax: 020 8543 5900
E-mail: bscah@btinternet.com
Website: www.bscah.com

Enquiries to: Secretary
Direct tel: 020 8543 5900

Founded: 1952; created by the merger of British Society of Medical and Dental Hypnosis (BSMDH) and British Society of Experimental and Clinical Hypnosis (BSECH – founded 1977) (year of change 2007); formerly called British Society of Dental Hypnosis (year of change 1955); formerly called Dental and Medical Society for the Study of Hypnosis (year of change 1968); formerly called British Society of Medical and Dental Hypnosis (BSMDH) (year of change 2007)

Organisation type and purpose: A non-profit making registered charity (charity number 1012806), a national organisation of healthcare professionals and academics.
To promote the safe and responsible use of hypnosis in medicine, dentistry, and psychology, and to educate both professional colleagues and the public about hypnosis and its uses; to promote and maintain the highest professional standards in the practice of hypnosis for clinical or experimental purposes and in the dissemination of information concerning hypnosis; to advance the science of hypnosis and promote the evidence-base for clinical hypnosis as a therapeutic tool, by using research to guide interventions and clinical practice to guide research.

Subject coverage: Clinical hypnosis.
Believes that the safe use of clinical hypnosis as a therapeutic tool is best in the hands of practitioners who are qualified to treat patients without hypnosis. Encourages the conduct of research and audit of practices of the subject of clinical hypnosis and the publication of the useful results of that research.

Publications: Printed
Order printed publications from: Crown House Publishing Ltd., Bancyfelin, Camarthenshire SA33 5ND

Publications list: Available online

Access to staff: Contact by letter, by telephone, by fax, by e-mail and via website

Constituent part of: European Society of Hypnosis; International Society of Hypnosis

BRITISH SOCIETY OF DOWSERS (BSD)

4–5 Cygnet Centre, Worcester Road, Hanley Swan, Worcs, WR8 0EA

Tel: 01684 576969
Fax: 01684 311388
E-mail: info@britishdowsers.org
Website: www.britishdowsers.org

Enquiries to: Director

Founded: 1933

Organisation type and purpose: International organisation, learned society (membership is by subscription), present number of members: 1,600, registered charity (charity number 295911), training organisation.

Subject coverage: Dowsing (water divining) for geophysical, medical, agricultural and other purposes; radiesthesia; professional operators.

Collection: Library of books on dowsing, radiesthesia and allied subjects

Non-library collection catalogue: All or part available online

Publications: Printed, and electronic and video

Access to staff: Contact by letter, by telephone, by fax, by e-mail, in person and via website. Appointment necessary.
Hours: Mon to Fri, 0900 to 1300 and 1400 to 1700

Access to building: Mon to Fri, 1030 to 1500

BRITISH SOCIETY OF GASTROENTEROLOGY (BSG)

3 St Andrews Place, Regent's Park, London, NW1 4LB

Tel: 020 7935 3150
Fax: 020 7487 3734
E-mail: enquiries@bsg.org.uk
Website: www.bsg.org.uk

Enquiries to: Chief Executive

Founded: 1937

Organisation type and purpose: Learned society, professional body (membership is by qualification), registered charity (charity number 258713), research organisation.

Subject coverage: Clinical and scientific aspects of the structure and function of the gastrointestinal system and its appendages; liver disease; gastrointestinal endoscopy.

Publications: Printed, and electronic and video

Publications list: Available online

Access to staff: Contact by letter, by telephone, by fax, by e-mail and via website
Hours: Mon to Fri, 0900 to 1700

BRITISH SOCIETY OF GERONTOLOGY (BSG)

PO Box 607, 8 Queenswood Grove, York, YO24 4PP

Tel: 07532 248 835
E-mail: britishgerontology@yahoo.co.uk
Website: www.britishgerontology.org

Enquiries to: Administrator

Founded: 1971

Organisation type and purpose: Learned society (membership is by subscription), present number of members: 650, registered charity (charity number 264385).

Subject coverage: Quality of life in old age. Implications of ageing societies and populations. Social care of older people.

Publications: Printed

Publications list: Available in print

Access to staff: Contact by letter and by e-mail
Hours: Mon to Fri, 0900 to 1700

Member organisation of: Academy of Learned Societies for the Social Sciences (ALSISS); tel: 020 7468 2296; fax: 020 7468 2296; e-mail: andy.cawdell@the-academy.org.uk; International Association of Gerontology – European Region; tel: +34 91 807 0874; fax: +34 91 807 5637; International Association of Gerontology (IAG); tel: +61 8 8201 7552; fax: +61 8 8201 7551; e-mail: cas@flinders.edu.au

BRITISH SOCIETY OF HEARING AID AUDIOLOGISTS (BSHAA)

Formal name: British Society of Hearing Aid Audiologists Limited

9 Lukins Drive, Great Dunmow, Essex, CM6 1XQ

Tel: 01371 876623
Fax: 01371 876623
E-mail: secretary@bshaa.com
Website: www.bshaa.com

Enquiries to: Executive Secretary

Founded: 1954

Organisation type and purpose: Professional body, trade association, membership association (membership is by subscription), present number of members: 1,200

Subject coverage: Hearing aid audiology; education and research in acoustics relating to hearing aids, operation of a customer care scheme to help resolve complaints if they cannot be resolved with the HAD

Publications: Printed

Access to staff: Contact by letter, by telephone, by e-mail and via website
Hours: Mon to Friday, 0900 to 1700

Hearing Aid Dispenser regulator: Health Professions Council; Park House, 184 Kennington Park Road, London, SE11 4BU; tel: 020 7582 0866; website: www.hpc-uk.org

BRITISH SOCIETY OF HYPNOTHERAPISTS (BSH)

37 Orbain Road, Fulham, London, SW6 7JZ

Tel: 020 7385 1166
Fax: 020 7385 1166
E-mail: enquiries@britishhypnotherapists.org.uk
Website: www.britishhypnotherapists.org.uk/

Enquiries to: Secretary

Founded: 1950

Organisation type and purpose: Professional body.

Subject coverage: Clinical and educational applications of hypnotherapy; information on training courses, training standards and qualifications; hypnotherapy for patients suffering from functional nervous problems and unwanted habits such as smoking; phobias, depression and insomnia; stammering, asthma, etc. (psychosomatic conditions); hypnotherapy as complementary to orthodox medicine.

Access to staff: Contact by letter, by telephone, by fax, by e-mail and via website
Hours: Mon to Fri, 0900 to 1700

Access to building: No access other than to staff

BRITISH SOCIETY OF MAGAZINE EDITORS (BSME)

Administrator, c/o Gill Branston & Associates, 137 Hale Lane, Edgware, Middlesex, HA8 9QP

Tel: 020 8906 4664
E-mail: via website
Website: www.bsme.com

Direct fax: 020 8959 2137
Direct e-mail: info@gillbranston.com

Organisation type and purpose: A membership association (membership is by subscription), the only society exclusively for magazine editors in the UK. Full membership is open to serving editors, website editors, editors-in-chief and editorial directors of recognised consumer, business or customer magazines published in the UK; members include the editors of magazines and websites as diverse as Prima, Glamour, YOU Magazine, Supply Management, Elle, Take a Break, Handbag.com and Waitrose Food Illustrated.
To represent the needs and views of all magazine editors, and enhance their status, acting as a voice for the industry.

Subject coverage: Editing magazines.

Access to staff: Contact by letter, by telephone, by fax, by e-mail and via website

BRITISH SOCIETY OF MASTER GLASS PAINTERS (BSMGP)

6 Queen Square, London, WC1N 3AR

Tel: 01643 862807
E-mail: bsmgp@cix.co.uk
Website: www.bsmgp.org.uk

Enquiries to: Honorary Secretary

Founded: 1921

Organisation type and purpose: Learned society, voluntary organisation.
To promote and elevate the art and craft of glass painting and staining and the conservation and appreciation of historic stained glass.

Subject coverage: Glass painting, use of decorative glass in churches and secular buildings, conservation and restoration services by accredited craftsmen.

Publications: Printed

Access to staff: Contact by letter, by e-mail and via website
Hours: Mon to Fri, 0900 to 1700
Special comments: Please enclose sae for reply.

BRITISH SOCIETY OF NEURORADIOLOGISTS (BSNR)

Department of Radiology, Hull Royal Infirmary, Anlaby Road, Hull, East Yorkshire

Tel: 01482 674083
Fax: 01482 320137
E-mail: rjvbartlett50@hotmail.com

Enquiries to: Honorary Secretary

Founded: 1970

Organisation type and purpose: Learned society.

Subject coverage: Neuroradiology: training, post availability and career prospects.

Publications: Printed

Access to staff: Contact by letter, by telephone, by fax and by e-mail
Hours: Mon to Fri, 0900 to 1700

Recognised by the: Royal College of Radiologists

BRITISH SOCIETY OF PERIODONTOLOGY (BSP)

PO BOX 228, Bubwith, Selby, YO8 1EY

Tel: 0844 335 1915
Fax: 0844 335 1915
Website: www.bsperio.org.uk

Enquiries to: Administrator

Founded: 1949

Organisation type and purpose: Learned society, registered charity (charity number 265815).

Subject coverage: Dentistry, periodontology, periodontics, periodontal diseases, dental hygiene.

Publications: Printed

Access to staff: Contact by letter, by telephone, by fax, by e-mail and via website
Hours: Mon to Fri, 0900 to 1700

BRITISH SOCIETY OF PLANT BREEDERS LIMITED (BSPB)

Woolpack Chambers, Market Street, Ely, Cambridgeshire, CB7 4ND

Tel: 01353 653200
Fax: 01353 661156
E-mail: enquiries@bspb.co.uk
Website: www.bspb.co.uk

Enquiries to: Chief Executive
Other contacts: Technical Liaison Manager

Organisation type and purpose: Membership association (membership is by subscription, qualification).
To liaise with official bodies and other organisations on technical and legislative matters concerning plant breeding, issue licences and to collect and redistribute royalties.

Subject coverage: Plant breeding, technical and legislative matters.

Publications: Printed

Access to staff: Contact by letter, by telephone, by fax and by e-mail
Hours: Mon to Fri, 0900 to 1700

Access to building: Prior appointment required

BRITISH SOCIETY OF SOIL SCIENCE (BSSS)

c/o Macaulay Land Use Research Institute, Craigiebuckler, Aberdeen, AB9 2QJ

Tel: 01224 318611
Fax: 01224 208065
E-mail: j.gauld@mluri.sari.ac.uk

Enquiries to: Administrator

Organisation type and purpose: Learned society (membership is by subscription), voluntary organisation.

Subject coverage: Soil science, soil management, environmental management, education, agriculture, agricultural management.

Publications: Printed

Access to staff: Contact by telephone, by fax and by e-mail
Hours: Mon to Fri, 0900 to 1700

BRITISH SOCIOLOGICAL ASSOCIATION (BSA)

Bailey Suite, Palatine House, Belmont Business Park, Belmont, Durham, DH1 1TW

Tel: 0191 383 0839
Fax: 0191 383 0782
E-mail: enquiries@britsoc.org.uk
Website: www.britsoc.co.uk

Enquiries to: Enquiries
Other contacts: Communications Officer (for member enquiries); Events Officer (for events); Publications Officer (for publications)

Founded: 1951

Organisation type and purpose: The BSA is the professional association for sociology in Britain, representing the intellectual interests of members. Membership is open to anyone who is engaged in, has influenced, or is interested in contributing to the promotion of sociology. Members include individuals in research, teaching and learning, as well as practitioners in many fields. Present number of members: 2,500. Registered charity (charity number 1080235).

Subject coverage: Sociology.

Information services: Website/IT Officer

Publications: Printed
Order printed publications from: website: http://www.britsoc.co.uk/publications/pubsjournals.htm

Access to staff: Contact by letter, by telephone, by fax, by e-mail and via website
Hours: Mon to Fri, 0900 to 1700

Access to building: Prior appointment required
Hours: Mon to Fri, 0900 to 1700

Access for disabled people: Parking provided

BRITISH SOFT DRINKS ASSOCIATION LIMITED (BSDA)

20–22 Bedford Row, London, WC1R 4EB

Tel: 020 7405 0300
Fax: 020 7831 6014
E-mail: bsda@britishsoftdrinks.com
Website: www.britishsoftdrinks.com

Enquiries to: Media Director
Other contacts: Administration (for publications)

Founded: 1987

Organisation type and purpose: Trade association.

Subject coverage: UK soft drinks, fruit juices, bottled water industries.

Publications list: Available online and in print

Access to staff: Contact by letter, by telephone, by fax, by e-mail and via website. Appointment necessary. Non-members charged.
Hours: Mon to Fri, 0900 to 1700

Member organisation of: AIJN; EFBW; UNESDA

Subsections are: Bottled Waters Group; Fruit Juice Committee

BRITISH SOFTBALL FEDERATION (BSF)

c/o Baseball Softball UK, Ariel House, 74A Charlotte Street, London W1T 4QJ

Tel: 020 7453 7055
Fax: 020 7453 7007
E-mail: carmel.keswick@britishsoftball.org
Website: www.baseballsoftballuk.com

Enquiries to: Executive Secretary

Founded: 1984

Organisation type and purpose:
Membership association.
Governing body of the sport.

Subject coverage: Playing and coaching of softball, umpiring, team locations, national teams.

Publications: Printed

Publications list: Available online and in print

Access to staff: Contact by letter, by e-mail and via website
Hours: Mon to Fri, 0900 to 1700

Affiliated to: European Softball Federation; International Softball Federation

BRITISH SPORTING ART TRUST (BSAT)

99 High Street, Newmarket, Suffolk, CB8 8JL

Tel: 01638 664429
E-mail: bsatrust@btconnect.com
Website: www.bsat.co.uk

Founded: 1977

Organisation type and purpose: An independent registered charity (charity number 274156) with membership by subscription.

Subject coverage: Sporting art.

Collection: Representative collection of British sporting paintings
Library of books, transparencies, catalogues, magazines and archive material

Publications: Printed

BRITISH STAMMERING ASSOCIATION (BSA)

15 Old Ford Road, London, E2 9PJ

Tel: 020 8983 1003
Fax: 020 8983 3591
E-mail: mail@stammering.org
Website: www.stammering.org

Enquiries to: Helpline
Direct tel: 0845 603 2001

Organisation type and purpose: National organisation, membership association (membership is by subscription), present number of members: 1,200, voluntary organisation, registered charity (charity number 278170).
To help stammerers help themselves and promote wider understanding of condition.

Subject coverage: Stammering, speech therapy, medical/health, self-help.

Collection: Postal library
Regional directories of speech therapy provision
Research information database.

Library catalogue: All or part available online

Publications: Printed, and electronic and video

Publications list: Available online and in print

Access to staff: Contact by letter, by telephone, by fax, by e-mail and via website. Appointment necessary.
Hours: Mon to Fri, 0900 to 1700

Member organisation of: European League of Stuttering Associations (ELSA); tel: 0191 281 8003; e-mail: via website; website: http://www.stuttering.ws/

BRITISH STANDARDS SOCIETY (BSS)

389 Chiswick High Road, London, W4 4AL

Tel: 020 8996 9001
Fax: 020 8996 7001
E-mail: cservices@bsigroup.com
Website: www.bsigroup.com/

Enquiries to: Secretary
Direct tel: 01923 252361
Direct fax: 01923 252361
Direct e-mail: pam.hall@bsi-global.com

Founded: 1960

Organisation type and purpose:
Professional body (membership is by subscription), present number of members: 500.
Voluntary association of individuals concerned with the application of standards; established and administered by BSI.

Subject coverage: Application of standards in design, manufacturing, services, quality assurance, information technology and in-service support; special interest groups on building, electronics and management systems, health and environment, consumer products and services, information technology.

Collection: Library of papers on various aspects of standardisation available to members only

Publications: Printed
Order printed publications from: Customer Services, BSI
389 Chiswick High Road, London, W4 4AL, tel: 020 8996 9001, fax: 020 8996 7001, website: http://www.bsi-global.com

Access to staff: Contact by letter, by telephone, by fax and by e-mail
Hours: Mon to Fri, 0900 to 1700

Parent body: British Standards Institution; tel: 020 8996 9000; fax: 020 8996 7001; website: http://www.bsi-global.com

UK member of: International Federation of Standards Users (IFAN); tel: +41 22 749 0331; fax: +41 22 749 0155; e-mail: ifan@iso.ch

BRITISH STARCH INDUSTRY ASSOCIATION (BSIA)

Federation House, 6 Catherine Street, London, WC2B 5JJ

Tel: 020 7836 2460
Fax: 020 7836 0580

Enquiries to: Executive Secretary
Direct e-mail: tom.hollis@fdf.org.uk

Organisation type and purpose: Trade association.

Subject coverage: Maize refining and wheat refining, production of starch, glucose and other derived products.

Access to staff: Contact by letter, by fax and by e-mail
Hours: Mon to Fri, 0930 to 1730

BRITISH SUB-AQUA CLUB (BSAC)

Telford's Quay, South Pier Road, Ellesmere Port, Cheshire, CH65 4FL

Tel: 0151 350 6200
E-mail: info@bsac.com
Website: www.bsac.com

Founded: 1953

Organisation type and purpose: The UK national governing body for underwater activities.
Works in conjunction with the Health & Safety Executive, the Marine Coastguard Association, the RNLI, HM Treasury's Receiver of Wrecks, DEFRA and other diving agencies to ensure the continued development, safety and enjoyment of scuba diving for all; also works in partnership with a wide range of conservation and environmental organisations to help safeguard the UK's precious waters and marine life for divers – both now and for future generations – to enjoy.

Subject coverage: Run by divers, for divers, BSAC provides all the training and support needed to get the best out of this exciting sport.

Publications: Electronic and video
Order electronic and video publications from: Download from website

Publications list: Available online

Access to staff: Contact by letter, by telephone and by e-mail

BRITISH SUNDIAL SOCIETY (BSS)

c/o The Royal Astronomical Society, Burlington House, Piccailly, London,W1J 0BQ

Tel: 01663 762415
E-mail: graham@sheardhall.co.uk
Website: www.sundialsoc.org.uk

Enquiries to: Secretary

Founded: 1989

Organisation type and purpose: Learned society (membership is by subscription), present number of members: 500, voluntary organisation, registered charity (charity number 1032530).
A society for those interested in gnomonics and sundials generally.

Subject coverage: Constructing sundials, makers of sundials, sundial bibliography, history of sundials, location of sundials (British), restoration of sundials, gnomonics, speakers' panel.

Collection: Photographs of most existing British sundials
Detailed records of over 6,000 existing sundials in the British Isles
Books on sundials
Quarterly all-colour Bulletin with learned articles and descriptions and mathematics of sundials

Trade and statistical information: List of dial makers in the UK who are members of the society

Non-library collection catalogue: All or part available in print

Publications: Printed, and electronic and video, and microform publications
Order printed publications from: British Sundial Society

Publications list: Available online

Access to staff: Contact by letter, by telephone, by e-mail and via website. Appointment necessary.
Hours: Mon to Fri, 0900 to 1700

Links with: European sundial societies; North American Sundial Society; Public Monuments and Sculpture Association

BRITISH SURFING ASSOCIATION (BSA)

c/o The International Surfing Centre, Fistral Beach, Newquay, Cornwall, TR7 1HY

Tel: 01637 876474
Fax: 01637 878608
E-mail: info@britsurf.co.uk
Website: www.nationalsurfingcentre.com
Website: www.gbsurf.org
Website: www.britsurf.co.uk

Enquiries to: National Director
Other contacts: Assistant to National Director

Founded: 1966

Organisation type and purpose: Membership association.
Governing body of the sport.

Subject coverage: Surfing; courses for beginners, teachers and coaches.

Trade and statistical information: Information on surfing related business available

Publications: Printed

Access to staff: Contact by letter, by telephone, by fax and by e-mail
Hours: Mon to Fri, 0900 to 1700

Access to building: No prior appointment required

Affiliated to: Central Council of Physical Recreation; International Surfing Association

BRITISH SUZUKI INSTITUTE (BSI)

British Suzuki Institute, Unit 1.01, The Lightbox, 111 Power Road, Chiswick, London, W4 5PY

Tel: 020 7471 6780
Fax: 020 7471 6778
E-mail: info@britishsuzuki.com
Website: www.britishsuzuki.org.uk/

Enquiries to: General Secretary

Founded: 1978

Organisation type and purpose: Membership association (membership is by subscription), present number of members: c. 1,600, registered charity (charity number 278005), training organisation.
To further education by Suzuki method.

Subject coverage: Information about the Suzuki approach to instrumental teaching, provision of training courses in music and general education. The emphasis is on teaching very young children with parental involvement.

Collection: A small library on Suzuki method includes musical tapes and CDs

Publications: Printed, and electronic and video

Publications list: Available in print

Access to staff: Contact by letter, by telephone, by fax and by e-mail. Appointment necessary.
Hours: Mon to Fri, 0930 to 1630
Special comments: 24 hour answerphone.

Affiliated to: European Suzuki Association; at the same address; International Suzuki Association; 3–10–3 Fukhshi, Matsumoto, Nagawo, 390, Japan

BRITISH TARANTULA SOCIETY (BTS)

81 Phillimore Place, Radlett, Hertfordshire, WD7 8NJ

Tel: 01923 856071
Website: thebts.co.uk/

Enquiries to: Honorary Secretary
Direct e-mail: angehale@thebts.co.uk

Founded: 1984

Organisation type and purpose: Membership association (membership is by subscription), present number of members: over 700, voluntary organisation, suitable for ages: all, research organisation.
Membership is predominantly UK but is also worldwide.

Subject coverage: Keeping, conservation, captive breeding and management of tropical arachnids (tarantulas and scorpions).

continued overleaf

Collection: Reference library

Library catalogue: All or part available online

Publications: Printed

Access to staff: Contact by letter and by telephone. Non-members charged.
Hours: 24-hour answerphone

BRITISH TAXPAYERS ASSOCIATION LIMITED (British Taxpayers)

Barclays House, 51 Bishopric, Horsham, West Sussex, RH12 1BS

Tel: 01403 271919
Fax: 01403 271912
E-mail: enquiries@britishtaxpayers.com
Website: www.britishtaxpayers.com

Enquiries to: Managing Director
Direct fax: 01403 271912

Founded: 1919

Organisation type and purpose: Consultancy.

Subject coverage: Income, capital gains and inheritance tax, overseas income and trusts, expatriate taxation, national insurance contributions, tax return preparation, personal financial planning, remuneration planning, employee benefits, revenue investigations, incentive schemes.

Collection: Research library on all UK taxation matters

Trade and statistical information: Full data on UK personal taxation

Publications: Printed

Publications list: Available online

Access to staff: Contact by letter, by telephone, by fax, by e-mail and in person
Hours: Mon to Fri, 0900 to 1700

Affiliated to: British Taxpayers Financial Planning; tel: 020 7456 0450; fax: 020 7247 0411; e-mail: mail@british-taxpayers.com; The Taxpayers' Society; tel: 01403 271919; fax: 01403 271912; e-mail: tps@british-taxpayers.com

Also at: British Taxpayers; 78 Park Street, Horsham, West Sussex, RH12 1BS; tel: 01403 271919; fax: 01403 271912; e-mail: mail@british-taxpayers.co.uk

BRITISH TECHNION SOCIETY

62 Grosvenor Street, London, W1K 3JF

Tel: 020 7495 6824
Fax: 020 7355 1525
E-mail: bts62@britishtechnionsociety.org
Website: www.britishtechnionsociety.org

Enquiries to: Executive Director

Founded: 1951

Organisation type and purpose: Registered charity (charity number 206922).
To raise funds for Technion, Haifa, Israel.

Subject coverage: Promotion of Technion, fund-raising for Technion.

Publications: Printed

Access to staff: Contact by letter, by telephone, by fax and in person
Hours: Mon to Fri, 0900 to 1700

Parent body: Technion; Israel Institute of Technology, Haifa, 32000, Israel

BRITISH TENPIN BOWLING ASSOCIATION (BTBA)

114 Balfour Road, Ilford, Essex, IG1 4JD

Tel: 0208 478 1745
Fax: 0208 514 3665
E-mail: admin@btba.org.uk
Website: www.btba.org.uk

Founded: 1961

Organisation type and purpose: Governing body of the tenpin bowling sport in Britain. Provides official rules; recognises bowling achievements in sanctioned play; provides tournament competition; and provides services to sanctioned leagues.

Subject coverage: Tenpin bowling in Britain at all levels.

Access to staff: Contact by letter, by telephone, by fax and by e-mail

BRITISH TEXTILE MACHINERY ASSOCIATION (BTMA)

Mount Pleasant, Glazebrook Lane, Glazebrook, Warrington, WA3 5BN

Tel: 0161 775 5740
Fax: 0161 775 5485
E-mail: btma@btma.org.uk
Website: www.btma.org.uk

Enquiries to: Director

Founded: 1940

Organisation type and purpose: Trade association (membership is by subscription), present number of members: 50, manufacturing industry.
To promote the British textile machinery industry world-wide.

Subject coverage: Textile machinery for natural and synthetic products.

Publications: Printed

Access to staff: Contact by letter, by telephone, by fax, by e-mail and via website. Appointment necessary.
Hours: Mon to Fri, 0700 to 1600

BRITISH THYROID FOUNDATION (BTF)

2nd Floor, 3 Devonshire Place, Harrogate, HG1 4AA

Tel: 01423 709707
E-mail: info@btf-thyroid.org
Website: www.btf-thyroid.org

Enquiries to: Membership Secretary

Founded: 1991

Organisation type and purpose: Voluntary organisation, registered charity.
To support sufferers of thyroid disorders.

Subject coverage: Thyroid disorders.

Publications: Printed

Access to staff: Contact by letter and by telephone
Hours: Mon to Fri, 1000 to 1400

BRITISH TINNITUS ASSOCIATION (BTA)

Acorn Business Park, Woodseats Close, Sheffield, S8 0TB

Tel: 0114 250 9933, 0114 258 5694 (minicom)
Fax: 0114 258 2279
E-mail: info@tinnitus.org.uk
Website: www.tinnitus.org.uk/

Enquiries to: Communications Manager
Direct tel: 0114 250 9933
Direct fax: 0114 258 2279
Direct e-mail: info@tinnitus.org.uk
Other contacts: Chief Executive

Founded: 1992

Organisation type and purpose: The British Tinnitus Association (BTA) is a world leader in providing support and advice about tinnitus. We provide accurate, reliable and authoritative information.
The BTA also works with medical professionals to support medical and clinical research and provide training.
The BTA is a registered charity, registered charity (charity number 1011145).

Subject coverage: Tinnitus advice, support, information, training, education and research.

Information services: We work to help individuals with tinnitus and the wider public understand more about tinnitus via:
A confidential freephone helpline – 0800 018 0527
Over 30 information leaflets, written by leading medical professionals
Quiet, the BTA's quarterly magazine
Our website, which contains information and advice for all audiences

Education services: The BTA provide information and training for health professionals, as well as information for the general public

Services for disabled people: A textphone is available

Publications: Printed, and electronic and video
Order printed publications from: Call 0800 018 0527 to request or visit our website to download
Order electronic and video publications from: Call 0800 018 0527 to request a product catalogue or visit website www.tinnitus.org.uk to download

Publications list: Available online and in print

Access to staff: Contact by letter, by telephone, by fax, by e-mail and via website
Hours: Mon to Fri, 0915 to 1645 (plus 24hr answerphone)

BRITISH TOY & HOBBY ASSOCIATION LIMITED (BTHA)

80 Camberwell Road, London, SE5 0EG

Tel: 020 7701 7271
Fax: 020 7708 2437
E-mail: admin@btha.co.uk
Website: www.btha.co.uk

Enquiries to: Director General

Founded: 1944

Organisation type and purpose: Trade association.

Subject coverage: Toys and hobbies, toy industry, UK toy exports and imports, toy safety, advertising of toys and responsible manufacturing.

Publications: Printed

Access to staff: Contact by letter, by telephone, by fax and by e-mail
Hours: Jun to Sep, Mon to Thu, 0830 to 1700; Fri, 0830 to 1630

Houses the: British Toy Council; British Toy Fairs (International) Limited; website: http://www.toyfair.co.uk

Member of: International Council of Toy Industries; website: http://www.toy-icti.org
Toy Industries of Europe; website: http://www.tietoy.org

BRITISH TOY COUNCIL LIMITED

80 Camberwell Road, London, SE5 0EG

Tel: 020 7701 7271
Fax: 020 7708 2437
E-mail: admin@btha.co.uk

Enquiries to: Secretary

Founded: 1967

Organisation type and purpose: Trade association.

Subject coverage: Standards of design, development, quality and safety of toys; preparation and implementation of these standards UK and international.

Collection: Some international toy safety standards

Access to staff: Contact by letter
Hours: Mon to Fri, 0900 to 1700

Subsidiary of: British Toy and Hobby Association; website: http://www.btha.co.uk

BRITISH TOYMAKERS GUILD (BTG)

PO Box 4498, Bradford-on-Avon, BA15 5BB

Tel: 0845 474 7905
E-mail: info@toymakersguild.co.uk
Website: www.toymakersguild.co.uk

Enquiries to: Manager

Founded: 1956

Organisation type and purpose:
International organisation, trade association (membership is by subscription, qualification), present number of members: 200.

Subject coverage: Toys.

Trade and statistical information: Data on the traditional toy sector

Publications: Printed

Access to staff: Contact by letter, by telephone, by e-mail and via website. Appointment necessary.
Hours: Mon to Fri, 0900 to 1700

BRITISH TROLLEYBUS SOCIETY (BTS)

2 Josephine Court, Southcote Road, Reading, Berkshire, RG30 2DG

Tel: 0118 958 3974
E-mail: librarian@britishtrolley.org.uk

Enquiries to: Honorary Secretary

Founded: 1961

Organisation type and purpose:
Membership association (membership is by subscription), present number of members: 320, voluntary organisation, registered charity (charity number 1033666).

Subject coverage: History and development of British trolleybus systems in particular, and foreign systems in general; history and development of bus operation in the Thames Valley area, development of public transport in West Yorkshire area.

Publications: Printed

Access to staff: Contact by letter and by telephone
Hours: Mon to Fri, 0900 to 1700

Associated with: Sandtoft Transport Centre

There are groups in: Bradford and Reading

BRITISH TROUT ASSOCIATION (BTA)

British Trout Association, The Rural Centre, West Mains, Ingliston, EH28 8NZ

Tel: 0131 472 4080
Fax: 0131 472 4083
E-mail: mail@britishtrout.co.uk
Website: www.britishtrout.co.uk

Enquiries to: Honorary Secretary

Organisation type and purpose: National organisation, trade association (membership is by subscription).
Information for members only.

Access to staff: Contact by e-mail
Hours: Mon to Fri, 0900 to 1700

BRITISH TRUST FOR ORNITHOLOGY (BTO)

The Nunnery, Thetford, Norfolk, IP24 2PU

Tel: 01842 750050
Fax: 01842 750030
E-mail: emily.coleman@bto.org
Website: www.bto.org

Enquiries to: Senior Development Officer
Direct e-mail: sandra.sparkes@bto.org

Founded: 1933

Organisation type and purpose:
Membership association (membership is by subscription), present number of members: 12,500, registered charity (charity number 216652 England & Wales, SC039193 Scotland), research organisation.

Subject coverage: British and migratory birds, their habitats and population levels, breeding season, mortality, migration, using information gathered by members.
Understanding, appreciation and conservation of birds.

Collection: Largest data collection on British birds in the UK
Second largest ornithological library of books and journals in the UK
Breeding Bird Survey (data from 1994 onwards)
Common Birds Census (data from 1962 to 2000)
Ornithological Sites Register (data from 1960s onwards)
Waterway Bird Survey (data 1974 onwards)
Wetland Bird Survey (data from 1993 onwards)
Nest Record Scheme (data from 1930s onwards)
National Ringing Scheme (data from 1909 onwards)

Non-library collection catalogue: All or part available online, in-house and in print

Library catalogue: All or part available in-house

Publications: Printed

Publications list: Available online and in print

Access to staff: Contact by letter, by telephone, by fax and by e-mail
Hours: Mon to Fri, 0900 to 1700

Access to building: Prior appointment required
Special comments: Members only, preferably by prior appointment.

Access for disabled people: Parking provided, level entry, toilet facilities

Also at: British Trust for Ornithology (Scottish Office) (BTO Scotland); School of Biological & Environmental Sciences, Cottrell Building, University of Stirling, Stirling, FK9 4LA; tel: 01786 466560; fax: 01786 466561

BRITISH TUNNELLING SOCIETY (BTS)

Institution of Civil Engineers, 1 Great George Street, London, SW1P 3AA

Tel: 020 7665 2229
Fax: 020 7799 1325
E-mail: bts@ice.org.uk
Website: www.ice.org.uk
Website: www.britishtunnelling.org.uk

Founded: 1971

Organisation type and purpose: Learned society.

Subject coverage: All aspects of tunnel design, construction and maintenance.

Collection: Library tunnelling section of the ICE library

Publications: Printed

Access to staff: Contact by letter, by telephone and via website
Hours: Mon to Fri, 0900 to 1700
Special comments: Access to library/archives of Institution of Civil Engineers on payment of a fee.

Affiliated to: Institution of Civil Engineers

National section of the: International Tunnelling Association

BRITISH TURNED PARTS MANUFACTURERS ASSOCIATION (BTMA)

77 Greyhound Lane, Norton, Stourbridge, West Midlands, DY8 3AD

Tel: 01789 730877
Fax: 01789 730899
E-mail: chrisgladwin@btma.org
Website: www.btma.org

Enquiries to: Director

continued overleaf

Organisation type and purpose: Trade association.

Subject coverage: Precision-turned parts and machined components.

Education services: CNC setter training courses for members.

Non-library collection catalogue: All or part available online and in print

Publications: Printed
Order printed publications from: Postal address

Access to staff: Contact by letter, by telephone, by fax, by e-mail and via website

Access to building: *Special comments:* No access

BRITISH UNIDENTIFIED FLYING OBJECT RESEARCH ASSOCIATION (BUFORA)

PO Box 241, Business House, Herts, SG6 9AJ

Tel: 08445 674 694
E-mail: enquiries@bufora.org.uk
Website: www.bufora.org.uk

Founded: 1962

Organisation type and purpose: Non-membership Association conducting objective/scientific based investigative research into the UFO phenomenon.

Subject coverage: Field investigations, research, investigator training, support in all areas pertaining to UFOs and related paranormal phenomena

Publications: Printed

Access to staff: Contact by letter, by telephone, by e-mail and via website
Hours: Access via e-mail 24 hours
Special comments: Telephone evenings after 3pm

BRITISH UNION CONFERENCE OF SEVENTH-DAY ADVENTISTS (BUC)

Stanborough Park, Garston, Watford, Hertfordshire, WD25 9JZ

Tel: 01923 672251
Fax: 01923 893212
E-mail: info@adventist.org.uk
Website: www.adventist.org.uk

Enquiries to: Communications Director
Direct e-mail: vhulbert@adventist.org.uk

Organisation type and purpose: Registered charity (charity number 209780).
British Isles Headquarters of the Seventh-day Adventist Church.

Subject coverage: Seventh-day Adventist beliefs and history, health and temperance.

Collection: Rare collections relating to Church history are housed at the denominational college, Newbold College, Binfield, nr Bracknell, Berkshire, RG42 4AN

Publications: Printed, and electronic and video

Access to staff: Contact by letter, by telephone, by fax, by e-mail and via website
Hours: Mon to Thu, 0900 to 1700; Fri, 0900 to 1200

Access to building: *Hours:* Mon to Thu, 0900 to 1700; Fri, 0900 to 1200

Access for disabled people: Disabled access available

Also at the same address: Seventh-day Adventist Association Limited; website: http://www.adventist.org.uk

Parent body: General Conference of Seventh-day Adventists; 12501 Old Columbia Pike, Silver Spring, MD 20904-6600, USA

Subsidiary body: Adventist Development and Relief Agency (ADRA-uk); at the same address; tel: 01923 681723; website: http://adra.org.uk

BRITISH UNION FOR THE ABOLITION OF VIVISECTION (BUAV)

16a Crane Grove, Islington, London, N7 8NN

Tel: 020 7700 4888
Fax: 020 7700 0252
E-mail: info@buav.org
Website: www.buav.org

Other contacts: Media Manager for media enquiries

Founded: 1898

Organisation type and purpose: The BUAV works to create a world where nobody wants to or believes in the need to experiment on animals. It campaigns peacefully to end animal testing. Through undercover investigations, political lobbying, the promotion of cruelty-free products, legal and scientific expertise and media activities, it works to make the world a better place for animals.

Subject coverage: Animal protection, campaigning, Cruelty Free, laboratory animals and the campaign against vivisection.

Collection: BUAV archive material (1898 to present day) held at Brynmor Jones Library, University of Hull, available to bona fide researchers by appointment

Library catalogue: All or part available in-house

Publications: Printed

Access to staff: Contact by letter, by telephone, by fax, by e-mail and via website. Appointment necessary. Letter of introduction required.
Hours: Mon to Fri, 0900 to 1700

Access to building: *Hours:* Mon to Fri, 0900 to 1700

Access for disabled people: via lift
Hours: Mon to Fri, 0900 to 1700

Affiliated to: European Coalition to End Animal Experiments; at the same address

BRITISH UNION OF SOCIAL WORK EMPLOYEES (BUSWE)

BUSWE House, 208 Middleton Road, Manchester, M8 4NA

Tel: 0161 720 7727
Fax: 0161 795 4524
E-mail: buswe@buswe.fsnet.co.uk

Enquiries to: General Secretary

Founded: 1976

Organisation type and purpose: Trade union, present number of members: 3,500.

Subject coverage: UK social work structure and services, industrial relations.
Development of a broad knowledge base; education of the public and others as to the purpose and impact of social care practices and procedures; creation of the optimal circumstances for the employment of social care practitioners; participation in the setting and evolution of professional standards of social care; support of initiatives that promote the expansion of opportunities within which individuals can expand their development potential; re-establishment of education and training of social care employees in order that the demands of evolving standards and practices can be met.

Access to staff: Contact by letter, by telephone and by e-mail. Appointment necessary.
Hours: Mon to Fri, 0900 to 1700

Access to building: Prior appointment required
Hours: Mon to Fri, 0900 to 1700

Access for disabled people: Parking provided

BRITISH UNIVERSITIES FILM & VIDEO COUNCIL (BUFVC)

77 Wells Street, London, W1T 3QJ

Tel: 020 7393 1500
Fax: 020 7393 1555
E-mail: ask@bufvc.ac.uk
Website: www.bufvc.ac.uk

Enquiries to: Head of Information
Direct tel: 020 7393 1508
Direct e-mail: luke@bufvc.ac.uk
Other contacts: Library and Database Manager for general Information. Also newsreels@bufvc.ac.uk and rgo@bufvc.ac.uk

Founded: 1948; merged with Learning on Screen (year of change 2004)

Organisation type and purpose: Registered charity (charity number 313582), research organisation, publishing house.
Reference Library founded 1972; instrumental in founding the Consortium for Drama and Media in Higher Education, providing the secretariat since 1974; assumed responsibility for administration of Slade Film History Register, 1975; took over production of HELPIS catalogue from Council for Educational Technology, 1976; Audio-Visual Reference Centre opened, 1978; took over distribution of the films of the Interuniversity History Film Consortium, 1981, launched British Universities Newsreel Project 1995; launched British Universities Newsreel (Scripts) Project 1999; launched Researcher's Guide Online and Moving Image Gateway (2001); launched Television & Radio Index for Learning and Teaching (2002).

Subject coverage: Audio-visual media, including computer-based multi-media, materials and techniques for degree-level teaching and research, resource lists on the history of science and invention, Shakespeare, post-war British history, physics and astronomy, teaching, guides to film, and newsreel collections.

Collection: BKSTS book library
Issue sheets for all British newsreels and cinemagazines, as well as details of unissued material, held in the Slade Film History Register
Newsreel commentary scripts, dope sheets and other original documents from Reuters Television
Records of the Scientific Film Association
Subject index to television documentary programmes broadcast by BBC and ITV from 1987 to 2001

Publications: Printed, and electronic and video, and microform publications

Publications list: Available in print

Access to staff: Contact by letter, by telephone, by fax and by e-mail. Appointment necessary. Non-members charged.
Hours: Mon to Fri, 0930 to 1730
Special comments: Information service open for enquiries 1200 to 1730.

Supported by: the Joint Information Systems Committee (JISC)

BRITISH UNIVERSITIES SPORTS ASSOCIATION (BUSA)

8 Union Street, London, SE1 1SZ

Tel: 020 7357 8555
Fax: 020 7403 1218
E-mail: office@busa.org.uk

Enquiries to: Public Relations Manager

Organisation type and purpose: National government body, membership association (membership is by qualification), present number of members: 147, registered charity (charity number 223324).

Subject coverage: Governing body for University Sport in the UK. Organises tournaments in 42 sports for 147 member institutions.

BRITISH URBAN REGENERATION ASSOCIATION (BURA)

63–66 Hatton Garden, London, EC1N 8LE

Tel: 020 7539 4030
Fax: 020 7404 9614
E-mail: info@ukregeneration.org.uk

Enquiries to: Business Development Director

Founded: 1990

Organisation type and purpose: Trade association (membership is by subscription, election or invitation), present number of members: 550, voluntary organisation.
Promoting an integrated approach to improving the quality of life in urban areas, taking fully into account the interdependence of the social, economic and environmental issues involved.

Subject coverage: Urban regeneration; contaminated land; sustainable development; annual awards: BURA Award for Best Practice in Urban Regeneration; The Secretary of State for the Environment, Transport and the Regions' Award for Partnership in Regeneration; Best Practice in Community Regeneration Awards; Best Practice in Promoting Sport in the Community Awards.

Publications: Printed

Access to staff: Contact by letter, by telephone, by fax and by e-mail. Appointment necessary.
Hours: Mon to Fri, 0930 to 1730

Standing committees and working groups include: Contaminated Land Working Group; Urban Policy Group

Works in partnership with: Association of Town Centre Management; Civic Trust; Local Government Association; Royal Town Planning Institute; Town and Country Planning Association; Urban Villages Forum

BRITISH URUGUAYAN SOCIETY

BUS Secretary Mrs. Linda Curiel, 28a Reynards Rd, Welwyn, Herts, AL6 9TP

Tel: 01438715803
Fax: 01438715803
E-mail: info@britishuruguayansociety.org
Website: www.britishuruguayansociety.org/

Enquiries to: Secretary

Founded: 1945

Organisation type and purpose:
Membership association (membership is by subscription), present number of members: 270, registered charity (charity number 275362).
Educational charity promoting knowledge of Uruguay in Britain and of Britain in Uruguay.

Subject coverage: History, geography and culture of Uruguay; educational contacts for students; some limited information on business, trade and travel, not specialists but have contacts and are willing to help wherever possible.

Collection: The Society's library is on permanent loan to the Library of the Hispanic and Luso-Brazilian Council at 2 Belgrave Square, London, SW1, where it is open to the public weekdays, 0930 to 1730

Publications: Printed

Access to staff: Contact by letter and by telephone
Hours: Mon to Fri, 0900 to 1700

Affiliated to: Hispanic and Luso-Brazilian Council; tel: 020 7235 2303; fax: 020 7235 3587

BRITISH VALVE & ACTUATOR ASSOCIATION (BVAMA)

9 Manor Park, Banbury, OX16 3TB

Tel: 01295 221270
Fax: 01295 268965
E-mail: enquiry@bvaa.org.uk
Website: www.bvaa.org.uk

Enquiries to: Director

Founded: 1939

Organisation type and purpose: Trade association.

Subject coverage: Industrial valves for the control of fluids.

Publications: Printed

Publications list: Available online and in print

Access to staff: Contact by letter, by telephone, by fax and by e-mail
Hours: Mon to Fri, 0900 to 1700

Access to building: Prior appointment required

BRITISH VENDEEN SHEEP SOCIETY (BVSS)

Formal name: British Vendeen Sheep Society Ltd

Darkes House, Conderton, Tewkesbury, Gloucestershire, GL20 7PP

Tel: 01386 725229
Fax: 01386 725229
E-mail: info@vendeen.co.uk
Website: www.vendeen.co.uk

Enquiries to: Secretary

Founded: 1985

Organisation type and purpose: National organisation, membership association (membership is by subscription), present number of members: 40, registered charity.
To promote and improve the breed of British Vendeen sheep.

Subject coverage: Breeding of and breeding from British Vendeen sheep.

Publications: Printed

Access to staff: Contact by letter, by telephone, by fax, by e-mail and in person. Appointment necessary.
Hours: Any reasonable time

BRITISH VETERINARY ASSOCIATION (BVA)

7 Mansfield Street, London, W1G 9NQ

Tel: 020 7636 6541
Fax: 020 7908 6349
E-mail: bvahq@bva.co.uk
Website: www.bva.co.uk

Enquiries to: Head of Media
Direct e-mail: press@bva.co.uk

Founded: 1882

Organisation type and purpose:
Professional body (membership is by subscription, election or invitation), present number of members: 10,000.
Houses the BVA Animal Welfare Foundation. There are 2 branches (Scottish and Welsh), 30 territorial divisions and 20 specialist divisions within the Association.
The national representative body for the British veterinary profession.

Subject coverage: Veterinary science, including animal health and welfare and public health.

Publications: Printed
Order printed publications from: Ten Alps Subscriber Services, Coach House, Turners Drive, Thatcham, Berkshire, RG19 4QB
6 Bourne Enterprise Centre, Wrotham Road, Borough Green, Wrotham, Kent, TN15 8DG, tel: 01732 884023, fax: 01732 884034

Publications list: Available online and in print

Access to staff: Contact by letter, by telephone, by e-mail and via website. Access for members only.
Hours: Mon to Fri, 0930 to 1700

continued overleaf

Member organisation of: Commonwealth Veterinary Association; Federation of Veterinarians in Europe; Inter-Professional Group; Parliamentary and Scientific Committee; Pet Advisory Committee; Pet Health Council; World Veterinary Association

Specialist divisions at the same address: Association for Veterinary Teaching and Research Work; Association of Government Vets; Association of Veterinarians in Industry; Association of Veterinary Students; British Cattle Veterinary Association; British Equine Veterinary Association; British Laboratory Animals Veterinary Association; British Small Animal Veterinary Association; British Veterinary Hospitals Association; British Veterinary Poultry Association; British Veterinary Zoological Society; Fish Veterinary Society; Goat Veterinary Society; Pig Veterinary Society; Royal Army Veterinary Corps Division; Sheep Veterinary Society; Society for the Study of Animal Breeding; Society of Greyhound Veterinarians; Society of Practising Veterinary Surgeons; Veterinary Deer Society; Veterinary Public Health Association

BRITISH VETERINARY NURSING ASSOCIATION (BVNA)

82 Greenway Business Centre, Harlow Business Park, Harlow, Essex, CM19 5QE

Tel: 01279 408644
Fax: 01279 408645
E-mail: bvna@bvna.co.uk
Website: www.bvna.org.uk

Founded: 1965

Organisation type and purpose: The only national representative body for veterinary nurses.
To promote animal health and welfare through the ongoing development of professional excellence in veterinary nursing.

Subject coverage: Veterinary nursing.

Information services: BVNA Members Helpline

Publications: Printed, and electronic and video
Order electronic and video publications from: Download from website

Access to staff: Contact by letter, by telephone, by fax and by e-mail
Hours: Mon to Thu, 0900 to 1700; Fri, 0900 to 1600

BRITISH VIDEO ASSOCIATION (BVA)

167 Great Portland Street, London, W1W 5PE

Tel: 020 7436 0041
Fax: 020 7436 0043
E-mail: general@bva.org.uk
Website: www.bva.org.uk

Enquiries to: Director General

Founded: 1980

Organisation type and purpose: Trade association.
Represent the interests of UK video rights owners.

Subject coverage: Trends in market of video rental and retail sales.

Trade and statistical information: Quarterly statistical press release

Publications: Printed

Access to staff: Contact by letter, by telephone, by fax, by e-mail and via website. Appointment necessary.
Hours: Mon to Fri, 0930 to 1730

Affiliated to: British Screen Advisory Council; tel: 020 7287 1111; International Video Federation; tel: 00 322 503 4063

BRITISH VOICE ASSOCIATION (BVA)

330 Grays Inn Road, London, WC1X 8EE

Tel: 0300 123 2773
Fax: 020 7915 1388
E-mail: administrator@britishvoiceassociation.org.uk
Website: www.britishvoiceassociation.org.uk

Enquiries to: Administrator

Founded: 1991

Organisation type and purpose: Professional body, registered charity.
An umbrella group for all professionals involved with the care of the human voice – from laryngologists and speech and language therapists to voice and singing teachers.

Subject coverage: Multidisciplinary voice; otolaryngology; speech and language therapy; teachers of singing; singers; voice trainers, students of all of the above.

Publications: Printed, and electronic and video

Publications list: Available online and in print

Access to staff: Contact by letter, by telephone, by fax, by e-mail and via website
Hours: Mon to Fri, 0900 to 1700

Access for disabled people: Parking provided, ramped entry, toilet facilities
Special comments: Please check for parking availability.

BRITISH WATCH AND CLOCKMAKERS GUILD (BWCMG)

PO Box 2368, Romford, Essex, RM1 2YZ

Tel: 01708 750616
E-mail: sec@bwcmg.org
Website: www.bwcmg.org

Enquiries to: Honorary Secretary

Founded: 1907

Organisation type and purpose: Trade association (membership is by election or invitation).
Trade organisation to protect the interests of those engaged in the watch, clock and general horological industry.

Subject coverage: Horological and allied crafts.

Publications: Printed

Access to staff: Contact by letter, by telephone and by e-mail
Hours: Mon to Fri, 1300 to 1800

BRITISH WATER

1 Queen Anne's Gate, London, SW1H 9BT

Tel: 020 7957 4554
Fax: 020 7957 4565
E-mail: info@britishwater.co.uk
Website: www.britishwater.co.uk

Enquiries to: Chief Executive
Other contacts: (1) International Director (2) Technical Director (3) UK Director for (1) inward/outward trade missions (2) standards/regulations/technology (3) industrial/municipal/domestic (POU) equipment.

Founded: 1993

Organisation type and purpose: Trade association (membership is by subscription).
The British water and waste water industry worldwide.

Subject coverage: Plant for the treatment of water for potable or industrial use; disinfection of swimming pools; plant for the treatment of domestic and municipal sewage and liquid industrial waste, and for industrial and waterworks sludges; domestic water softeners etc; statistics. With some 200 members, it promotes the involvement of all sectors in water-related projects, working closely with government and government departments at home and overseas; it organises outward and inward missions, seminars, exhibitions and other platforms to promote the technical, financial and administrative expertise of the British water sector. The organisation operates technical committees concerned with all aspects of the industry's activities and collaborates with British and European agencies in the development of standards.

Non-library collection catalogue: All or part available online and in-house

Library catalogue: All or part available online

Publications: Printed

Publications list: Available online

Access to staff: Contact by letter, by telephone, by fax, by e-mail and via website. Appointment necessary.
Hours: Mon to Fri, 0900 to 1700

Access to building: Prior appointment required

Links with: Aqua Europa; Geelseweg 56, B-2250, Olen, Belgium; METCOM; Savoy Tower, Glasgow, G2 3BZ; tel: 0141 332 5788; fax: 0141 332 0826

BRITISH WATER SKI & WAKEBOARD

Unit 3 The Forum, Hanworth Lane, Chertsey, Surrey, KT16 9JX

Tel: 01932 560007
Fax: 01932 570028
E-mail: via website
Website: www.britishwaterski.org.uk

Founded: 1951; formerly called British Water Ski; formerly called British Water Ski Federation (BWSF) (year of change 1999)

Organisation type and purpose: The national governing body for water skiing in Great Britain, a non-profit making organisation.

Subject coverage: Responsible for the development of the sport; co-ordination of national and international competition; selection of national teams; training and registration of coaches and officials; increasing the opportunities for participation in water skiing for all residents, including the disabled; actively encourages newcomers to the sport, promotes good practice and safety and works to enhance and improve standards of coaching and driving; has highly active competition programmes in all divisions of the sport.

Access to staff: Contact by letter, by telephone, by fax and via website

Affiliated to: International Water Ski & Wakeboard Federation (IWWF)

Member organisation of: Boating Alliance; Central Council for Physical Recreation (CCPR); European Boating Association; Parliamentary Waterways Group; ROSPA

BRITISH WEIGHT LIFTING (BWL)

110 Cavendish, Leeds Metropolitan University, Headingley Campus, Leeds, LS6 3QS

Tel: 0113 812 7098
E-mail: enquiries@britishweightlifting.org
Website: www.bwla.netcalm.co.uk

Enquiries to: Chief Executive Officer

Organisation type and purpose: Membership association (membership is by subscription), present number of members: 4,000, voluntary organisation.
Sports governing body.

Subject coverage: Weightlifting, powerlifting, weight training and fitness training with weights.

Publications: Printed

Publications list: Available in print

Access to staff: Contact by letter, by telephone and by fax
Hours: Mon to Fri, 0900 to 1700

Affiliated to: European Powerlifting Federation; European Weightlifting Federation; International Powerlifting Federation; International Weightlifting Federation

Links with: British Olympic Committee; Central Council of Physical Recreation; Commonwealth Games Council

Welsh Divisional Association: British Amateur Weight Lifters Association; Pennant Blaenau, Ammanford, Dyfed, SA18 3BZ

BRITISH WEIGHTS AND MEASURES ASSOCIATION (BWMA)

98 Eastney Road, Croydon, Surrey CR0 3TE.

Tel: 01738 783936
E-mail: bwma@email.com
Website: www.bwmaonline.com
Website: www.footrule.org

Enquiries to: President

Founded: c. 1868

Organisation type and purpose: Membership association.
To oppose compulsory metrication and to explain the good reasons for using traditional weights and measures.

Subject coverage: The advantages of British weights and measures and the disadvantages of metrication.

Publications: Printed

Access to staff: Contact by letter, by telephone and by fax
Hours: Mon to Fri, 0900 to 1700

Access to building: Prior appointment required

Access for disabled people: Level entry, toilet facilities

BRITISH WHEEL OF YOGA, THE

25 Jermyn Street, Sleaford, Lincolnshire, NG34 7RU

Tel: 01529 306851
Fax: 01529 303233
E-mail: mchapmanbwy@googlemail.com
Website: www.bwy.org.uk

Enquiries to: Central Office Manager
Direct tel: 01529 303881
Direct e-mail: office@bwy.org.uk

Founded: 1965

Organisation type and purpose: National organisation, membership association (membership is by subscription), present number of members: 8,400, registered charity (charity number 264993), training organisation.
The governing body for yoga in Great Britain, non-political, non-sectarian.
To encourage and help all persons to a greater knowledge and understanding of all aspects of Yoga and its practice by the provision of study, education and training, to maintain and improve the standard of teaching.

Subject coverage: Yoga: philosophy involving meditation and physical discipline; training of yoga teachers; yoga for therapy and for the elderly and less able.

Publications: Printed, and electronic and video
Order printed publications from: BWY Services e-mail: office@bwy.org.uk

Access to staff: Contact by letter, by telephone, by fax, by e-mail and via website
Hours: Mon to Fri, 0900 to 1700

Affiliated to: European Union of National Federations of Yoga

Member of: Central Council of Physical Recreation

BRITISH WHEELCHAIR SPORTS FOUNDATION (BWSF)

Guttmann Road, Stoke Mandeville, Aylesbury, Buckinghamshire, HP21 9PP

Tel: 01296 395995
Fax: 01296 424171
Website: www.bwsf.org.uk

Enquiries to: Chief Executive
Other contacts: Head of Public Relations

Founded: 1952

Organisation type and purpose: National organisation, membership association (membership is by subscription, election or invitation), present number of members: 1,500, voluntary organisation, registered charity (charity number 265498).
National body for wheelchair sport – sport for disabled people.

Subject coverage: Wheelchair sports; archery, athletics, basketball, bowls, fencing, rugby, shooting, snooker, swimming, table tennis, tennis, weightlifting, wintersports – sledge hockey and handcycling.

Publications: Printed

Access to staff: Contact by letter, by telephone, by e-mail and via website. Appointment necessary.
Hours: Mon to Fri, 0900 to 1700

Access to building: Prior appointment required

Access for disabled people: Access to all public areas

Affiliated to: British Paralympic Association; tel: 020 8681 9655

Member of: International Paralympic Committee; International Stoke Mandeville Wheelchair Sports Federation; tel: 01296 436179; Royal Association for Disability and Rehabilitation; tel: 020 7250 3222

BRITISH WILDLIFE PUBLISHING LTD

The Old Dairy, Milton on Stour, Gillingham, Dorset, SP8 5PX

Tel: 01747 835511
Fax: 01747 835522
E-mail: enquiries@britishwildlife.com
Website: www.britishwildlife.com

Enquiries to: Information Officer

Founded: 1989

Organisation type and purpose: Publishing house.

Subject coverage: Natural history, environment, conservation.

Publications: Printed
Order printed publications from: British Wildlife Publishing, The Old Dairy, Milton on Stour, Gillingham, Dorset, SP8 5PX; tel: 01747 835511

Access to staff: Contact by letter and by fax
Hours: Mon to Fri, 0900 to 1700

BRITISH WILDLIFE RESCUE CENTRE (BWRC)

Amerton Working Farm, Amerton, Stafford, ST18 0LA

Tel: 01889 271308
E-mail: admin@thebwrc.com
Website: www.britishwildliferescue.co.uk

Founded: 1991

Organisation type and purpose: Voluntary organisation, suitable for ages: all.

continued overleaf

Subject coverage: Rescue and rehabilitation of British wildlife, animal hospital, centre open to the public, school parties welcome, visits to schools, national curriculum subjects covered.

Publications: Printed

Access to staff: Contact by letter, by telephone and in person
Hours: Summer: Sun to Sat, 1000 to 1800
Winter: Sun to Sat, 1000 to dark
Special comments: Closed Christmas Day, New Year's Day

Access for disabled people: *Hours:* Summer: Sun to Sat, 1000 to 1800
Winter: Sun to Sat, 1000 to dark

Member and working links with: Royal Society for the Prevention of Cruelty to Animals (RSPCA)

Member of: British Wildlife Rehabilitation Council; website: http://www.bwrc.co.uk

BRITISH WIRELESS FOR THE BLIND FUND (BWBF)

10 Albion Place, Maidstone, Kent, ME14 5DZ

Tel: 01622 754757
Fax: 01622 751725
E-mail: info@blind.org.uk
Website: www.blind.org.uk

Founded: 1929

Organisation type and purpose: Registered charity (charity number 211849).
To provide the comfort of radio listening to the registered blind in need.

Subject coverage: Free permanent loan of radio, radio/cassette players, CD/radio/ cassette and internet radio for registered blind people and partially sighted people.

Services for disabled people: Provision of radios and associated equipment to registered blind and registered partially sighted people resident in the United Kingdom, over the age of 8 and in need. Sets can be sold to those who do not qualify through the trading arm of the charity.

Publications: Printed

Access to staff: Contact by letter, by telephone, by fax, by e-mail and via website. Appointment necessary.
Hours: Mon to Fri, 0900 to 1700

Access for disabled people: Full disabled access

BRITISH WOMEN PILOTS' ASSOCIATION (BWPA)

White Waltham Airfield, Waltham Road, Maidenhead, Berkshire, SL6 3NJ

E-mail: info@bwpa.co.uk
Website: www.bwpa.co.uk

Enquiries to: Chairman
Direct e-mail: info@bwpa.co.uk

Founded: 1955

Organisation type and purpose: Membership association (membership is by subscription).

Subject coverage: Women in aviation, careers in aviation.

Information services: Careers, recreational pilot training.

Education services: Talks to schools.

Publications: Printed

Access to staff: Contact by letter, by e-mail and via website
Hours: Mon to Fri, 0900 to 1700

BRITISH WOODWORKING FEDERATION (BWF)

Royal London House, 22–25 Finsbury Square, London, EC2A 1DX

Tel: 0844 209 2610
E-mail: bwf@bwf.org.uk
Website: www.bwf.org.uk

Enquiries to: Chief Executive
Other contacts: Membership Director; Technical Manager

Organisation type and purpose: Membership organisation (membership is by subscription), trade association.
Represents leading manufacturers, distributors and installers of a variety of joinery and woodworking products and ensures that they comply with the highest technical and regulatory standards.

Subject coverage: Joinery and woodworking.

Publications: Electronic and video
Order electronic and video publications from: Most publications can be downloaded free by members; further copies can be ordered direct

Publications list: Available online

Access to staff: Contact by letter, by telephone and via website

Access to building: Entrance via north-east corner of Finsbury Sq.

Member organisation of: Construction Confederation; Construction Products Association; TRADA; Trade Association Forum

BRITISH YOUTH COUNCIL (BYC)

British Youth Council, CAN Mezzanine, 49–51 East Road, London, N1 6AH

Tel: 0845 458 1489
Fax: 0845 458 1847
E-mail: mail@byc.org.uk
Website: www.byc.org.uk

Enquiries to: Policy and Press Officer
Direct tel: 0845 458 1489
Direct e-mail: helen.deakin@byc.org.uk

Founded: 1948

Organisation type and purpose: Membership association (membership is by subscription), present number of members: 130 member organisations, voluntary organisation, registered charity (charity number 305973).
The British Youth Council is the independent voice of young people in the UK.
Representing the views of young people to government and decision-makers at national and international levels.

Subject coverage: Interests and views of young people, advocacy for the increased participation of young people in society.

Publications: Printed
Order printed publications from: Policy and Research Officer, British Youth Council at the same address, tel: 020 7422 8644, e-mail: louise.king@byc.org.uk

Publications list: Available in print

Access to staff: Contact by letter, by telephone, by e-mail and via website. Appointment necessary.
Hours: Mon to Fri, 0930 to 1800

Access to building: Prior appointment required

Access for disabled people: Ramped entry

BRITISH-GERMAN ASSOCIATION (BGA)

34 Belgrave Square, London, SW1X 8QB

Tel: 020 7235 1922
Fax: 020 7235 1902
E-mail: info@britishgermanassociation.org
Website: www.britishgermanassociation.org/

Enquiries to: Honorary Treasurer
Direct tel: 020 7244 7663
Direct fax: 020 7373 3415

Founded: 1951

Organisation type and purpose: Membership association (membership is by subscription), present number of members: 1,000, registered charity (charity number 206062).
Promotion of Anglo-German relations on an educational and cultural basis.

Subject coverage: All aspects of German affairs and British-German cultural and educational relations.

Publications: Printed
Order printed publications from: Editor-in-Chief, British-German Review
April House, Balcombe, Sussex, RH17 6LF, tel: 01444 811237, fax: 01444 811237

Access to staff: Contact by letter, by telephone and by fax
Hours: Mon to Fri, 1100 to 1600

Connected with: Deutsch Englische Gesellschaft (DEG); Jaegerstrasse 54/5, 10112 Berlin, Germany; tel: 030 203 983

BRITISH-ISRAEL-WORLD FEDERATION (BIWF)

121 Low Etherley, Bishop Auckland, DL14 0HA

Tel: 01388 834395
Fax: 01388 835957
E-mail: admin@britishisrael.co.uk
Website: www.britishisrael.co.uk

Enquiries to: Administrator

Founded: 1919

Organisation type and purpose: International organisation, national organisation (membership is by subscription), present number of members: 300, registered charity (charity number 208079), research organisation, publishing house.
Christian heritage research into Anglo-Saxon-Celtic peoples as the modern-day descendants of the ancient Hebrew race and

nation of Israel which spread to the west from the Assyrian and Babylonian Captivities.

Subject coverage: Migrations of Israel in Europe; scriptural evidence, bible prophecy, early Christian Church, 1st century in Britain, charts of royal descent, heraldry showing British links with Israel, current events.

Collection: Books in library, not open to public

Publications: Printed
Order printed publications from: The Covenant Publishing Company Limited
at the same address

Publications list: Available online and in print

Access to staff: Contact by letter, by telephone, by fax, by e-mail and via website. Appointment necessary.
Hours: Mon to Fri, 0900 to 1700

Access to building: Prior appointment required
Hours: Access for publications by prior appointment

Access for disabled people: Parking provided, toilet facilities
Special comments: Level entry at rear from parking area.

Associated with similar: Christian Israel Organisations in: Australia, Canada, Holland, New Zealand, South Africa and USA

BRITISH-ITALIAN SOCIETY

The Membership Secretary, The British-Italian Society, 9 Durham Lodge, 74 Durham Road, London, SW20 0TN

Tel: 020 8150 9167
E-mail: jj@british-italian.org
Website: www.british-italian.org

Enquiries to: General Secretary

Founded: 1941

Organisation type and purpose: Learned society, membership association (membership is by subscription), present number of members: 500, registered charity (charity number 253386).
To increase understanding of Italy in this country and to promote friendship between Great Britain and Italy.

Subject coverage: General information on Italy.
No employment contacts.

Publications: Printed

Access to staff: Contact by letter, by telephone, by fax and by e-mail
Hours: 3 days per week variable

Access to building: Prior appointment required

BRITISH-KAZAKH SOCIETY

Formal name: British-Kazakh Society

105 Salisbury Road, London, NW6 6RG

Tel: 020 7596 5176
Fax: 020 7596 5115
E-mail: info@bksoc.org.uk
Website: www.bksoc.org.uk

Founded: 2002

Organisation type and purpose: Individual and corporate membership organisation (membership by subscription)
To promote relations between the UK and Kazakhstan.

Access to staff: Contact by letter, by telephone, by fax, by e-mail and via website

BRITISH–SERBIAN BENEVOLENT TRUST (B-SBT)

Glebelands, Star Lane, Rockland St Mary, Norwich, NR14 7BX

Tel: 01508 480262
Fax: 01508 480262
E-mail: orns@lineone.net

Enquiries to: Chairman

Founded: 1917

Organisation type and purpose: National organisation, registered charity (charity number 254179).
Charitable trust.

Subject coverage: The relief of children resident in Serbia who are in conditions of need, hardship or distress.

Access to staff: Contact by letter, by telephone, by fax and by e-mail.
Appointment necessary.
Hours: Mon to Fri, 0900 to 1700

BRITTEN-PEARS LIBRARY

Formal name: Britten-Pears Foundation

The Red House, Golf Lane, Aldeburgh, Suffolk, IP15 5PZ

Tel: 01728 451700
E-mail: N.Clark@brittenpears.org
Website: www.britten-pears.org

Enquiries to: Director of Collections and Heritage
Other contacts: Archivist; Curator; Librarian; Promotions Manager

Founded: 1980

Organisation type and purpose: A company limited by guarantee, registered in England and Wales (number 2071223). Registered as a charity (number 295595).

Subject coverage: Benjamin Britten's life, career and music, Peter Pears's life and career, English song (books and music), Gustav Holst's music, English Opera Group/ English Music Theatre, Aldeburgh Festival, music in general.

Collection: Benjamin Britten's manuscripts (some on permanent loan from the British Library)
Britten's collection of printed music
Britten's personal papers (including correspondence and diaries)
Printers' copies, proofs and early editions of Britten's works
Peter Pears's collection of printed music
Pears's personal papers (including correspondence)
Extensive collection of sound recordings and video cassettes (chiefly relating to Britten and Pears)
English Opera Group/English Music Theatre Archive
Aldeburgh Festival Archive
Archive of press cuttings and programmes (chiefly relating to Britten and Pears)
Photographic archives (chiefly relating to Britten and Pears)
Manuscripts of works by other composers, including Bax, Bedford, L Berkeley, M Berkeley, Bridge, Crosse, Maxwell Davies, C A Gibbs, Greene, Harvey, Henze, G Holst, I Holst, Knussen, Lehmann, Lutoslawski, Maconchy, C Matthews, D Matthews, Maw, Moeran, Nash, Oldham, Quilter, Rainier, Saxton, Seiber, Shostakovich, Stanford, Tippett, Turnage, Weir, Wellesz, Williamson
Literary manuscripts, including those of W H Auden, Ronald Duncan, E M Forster, Thomas Hardy, Wilfred Owen, Myfanwy Piper, William Plomer, Edith Sitwell
English Song (from 16th century to present day)
Julian Herbage material relating to Thomas Arne
Holst Library, a lending library for use of students attending the Britten-Pears School for Advanced Musical Studies

Non-library collection catalogue: All or part available online

Library catalogue: All or part available online

Publications: Printed

Publications list: Available online and in print

Access to staff: Contact by letter, by telephone, by fax, by e-mail and via website. Appointment necessary.
Hours: Mon to Fri, 1000 to 1300 and 1415 to 1715; closed on bank holidays

Access to building: Prior appointment required

Access for disabled people: Level entry, toilet facilities

Administers the: Holst Library

BRITTEN-PEARS YOUNG ARTIST PROGRAMME (BPP)

Snape Maltings Concert Hall, Snape, Saxmundham, Suffolk, IP17 1SP

Tel: 01728 687100
Fax: 01728 687120
E-mail: enquiries@aldeburgh.co.uk
Website: www.aldeburgh.co.uk

Enquiries to: Assistant
Other contacts: Administrator for orchestral enquiries.

Founded: 1972

Organisation type and purpose: Music school.
The Britten-Pears Programme offers a unique opportunity for young professionals and advanced students to study intensively with some of the world's most respected musicians.

Access to staff: Contact by letter, by telephone, by fax, by e-mail and via website
Hours: Mon to Fri, 0930 to 1730

Parent body: Aldeburgh Productions; Snape Maltings Concert Hall, Snape, Saxmundham, Suffolk, IP17 1SP; tel: 01708 687100; fax: 01728 687120; e-mail: info@ aldeburgh.co.uk

BRITTLE BONE SOCIETY (BBS)

Grant-Paterson House, 30 Guthrie Street, Dundee, DD1 5BS

Tel: 01382 204446
Fax: 01382 206771

Enquiries to: Chief Executive
Direct e-mail: annette@brittlebone.org

Founded: 1968

Organisation type and purpose: Registered charity (Scottish registered charity SCO10951).
Promoting research and providing information and support for people and their relatives.

Subject coverage: The society seeks to promote research into the causes, inheritance and treatment of osteogenesis imperfecta, characterised by excessive fragility of the bones. It also provides advice, encouragement and practical help for patients and their relatives facing the difficulties of living with brittle bones, practical aspects of living with brittle bones, education, wheelchairs and other equipment.

Publications list: Available in print

Access to staff: Contact by letter, by telephone and by e-mail. Appointment necessary.
Hours: Mon to Fri, 0900 to 1700

Access to building: *Hours:* Mon to Fri, 0900 to 1700

Charity Shop: BBS Shop; 112 City Road, Dundee; tel: 01382 667603

BROADCASTING GROUP OF THE SOCIETY OF AUTHORS

84 Drayton Gardens, London, SW10 9SB

Tel: 020 7373 6642
Fax: 020 7373 5768
E-mail: info@societyofauthors.org

Organisation type and purpose: Trade union.

Subject coverage: Writing for radio and television.

Access to staff: Contact by letter and by e-mail
Hours: 0930 to 1730

BROADCASTING, ENTERTAINMENT, CINEMATOGRAPH AND THEATRE UNION (BECTU)

373–377 Clapham Road, London, SW9 9BT

Tel: 020 7346 0900
Fax: 020 7346 0901
E-mail: info@bectu.org.uk
Website: www.bectu.org.uk

Enquiries to: Administrator

Founded: 1991; incorporates the former ABS, ACTT, BETA, FAA, NATTKE (year of change 1991)

Organisation type and purpose: Trade union, present number of members: 26,000.

Subject coverage: The interests of workers in broadcasting, film, theatre and related areas of the arts and media.

Collection: Documents of the Unions dating back to 1890 (uncatalogued)

Publications: Printed

Access to staff: Contact by letter, by telephone, by e-mail and via website. Access for members only.
Hours: Mon to Fri, 0900 to 1700

Access for disabled people: Wheelchair lift, toilet facilities, induction loop

Affiliated to: Trades Union Congress

Affiliated via Federation of Entertainment Unions to: Irish Congress of Trade Unions; Labour Party; Uni-Media Entertainment International; Wales Trades Union Congress

Member organisations: Scottish Trades Union Congress

BROADLAND DISTRICT COUNCIL

Thorpe Lodge, 1 Yarmouth Road, Thorpe St Andrew, Norwich, Norfolk, NR7 0DU

Tel: 01603 431133
Fax: 01603 300087
E-mail: reception@broadland.gov.uk
Website: www.broadland.gov.uk

Enquiries to: Communications Manager
Direct tel: 01603 430523
Direct fax: 01603 430614
Direct e-mail: angi.doy@broadland.gov.uk

Founded: 1974

Organisation type and purpose: Local government body.

Subject coverage: Broadland District Council area, services and amenities.

Education services: Broadland Council Training Services

Publications: Printed
Order printed publications from: e-mail: news@broadland.gov.uk
Order electronic and video publications from: website: http://www.broadland.gov.uk

Access to staff: Contact by letter, by telephone, by fax, by e-mail and via website. Appointment necessary.
Hours: Mon to Fri, 0900 to 1700

Access to building: *Hours:* Mon to Fri, 0900 to 1700

Access for disabled people: Parking provided, ramped entry

BROADS AUTHORITY, THE

Dragonfly House, 2 Gilders Way, Norwich, Norfolk, NR3 1UB

Tel: 01603 610734
Fax: 01603 765710
E-mail: broads@broads-authority.gov.uk
Website: www.broads-authority.gov.uk

Enquiries to: Information Officer

Founded: 1989

Organisation type and purpose: Local government body.
Equivalent to national park.

Subject coverage: The Broads: conservation (including planning), recreation, navigation.

Publications: Printed

Publications list: Available online and in print

Access to staff: Contact by letter, by telephone, by fax and by e-mail. Appointment necessary.
Hours: Mon to Fri, 0900 to 1700

BROADS SOCIETY

Solar Via, Happisburgh, Norwich, Norfolk, NR12 0QU

Tel: 01692 651321
E-mail: broads_society.admin@bigfoot.com
Website: www.broads-society.org.uk

Enquiries to: Administrator
Other contacts: Chairman

Founded: 1956

Organisation type and purpose: Membership association (membership is by subscription), present number of members: 1,700, voluntary organisation, registered charity (charity number 1078434).
Voluntary body dedicated to securing a sustainable future for The Broads as a unique and protected landscape in which leisure, tourism and the local economy can thrive in harmony with the natural environment.

Subject coverage: Wetland conservation, navigation on inland waters.

Collection: Collection of all back issues of quarterly magazine

Publications: Printed

Access to staff: Contact by letter, by telephone, by e-mail and via website
Hours: Any reasonable time; 24-hour answering service

Also at: Broads Society Editor; Grebe Cottage, New Road, Catfield, Great Yarmouth, NR29 5BQ; tel: 01692 584179; e-mail: harnser2006@yahoo.co.uk

BROMLEY COLLEGE OF FURTHER AND HIGHER EDUCATION (BCFHE)

Rookery Lane, Bromley, Kent, BR2 8HE

Tel: 020 8295 7000
Fax: 020 8295 7099
E-mail: info@bromley.ac.uk
Website: www.bromley.ac.uk

Enquiries to: Librarian
Direct tel: 020 8295 7024
Direct e-mail: judym@bromley.ac.uk

Founded: 1959

Organisation type and purpose: Suitable for ages: all.
Library of a college of further and higher education.

Subject coverage: Life science, engineering (electrical, mechanical and motor vehicle), social work, business, finance, law, IT, software engineering, hairdressing and beauty therapy, leisure, travel and tourism, counselling, teaching and training, media, built environment, sport.

Library catalogue: All or part available online and in-house

Access to staff: Contact by telephone, by e-mail and via website. Appointment necessary.
Hours: Mon to Fri, 0900 to 1700

Access for disabled people: Parking provided, ramped entry, toilet facilities

Also at: Old Town Hall Site; Tweedy Road, Bromley, BR2 8HE; tel: 020 8295 7091

BROMLEY HOUSE LIBRARY (BHL)

Bromley House, Angel Row, Nottingham, NG1 6HL

Tel: 0115 947 3134
E-mail: enquiries@bromleyhouse.org
Website: www.bromleyhouse.org

Enquiries to: Librarian

Founded: 1816

Organisation type and purpose: Membership association (membership is by subscription), present number of members: 1,000, registered charity (charity number 1074752).
Private library for research purposes.

Subject coverage: Victorian fiction, history, local history, biography, travel, theology.

Publications: Printed

Access to staff: Contact by letter, by telephone and by e-mail. Appointment necessary. Access for members only. Letter of introduction required.
Hours: Mon to Fri, 0930 to 1700

Access for disabled people: No disabled access
Special comments: Situated on first floor and above.

BROMLEY PUBLIC LIBRARIES

Central Library, High Street, Bromley, Kent, BR1 1EX

Tel: 020 8460 9955
Fax: 020 8466 7860
E-mail: informationservices@bromley.gov.uk
Website: www.bromley.gov.uk/libraries

Enquiries to: Principal Library Service Manager

Organisation type and purpose: Local government body, public library.

Subject coverage: General; geography, travel and history of all countries, excluding Europe, history and studies of the London Borough of Bromley.

Collection: Crystal Palace collection
H. G. Wells collection
Harlow bequest (Orpington and Kent)
Walter de la Mare collection

Library catalogue: All or part available online

Publications: Printed
Order printed publications from: Local Studies Librarian, Central Library, High Street, Bromley, BR1 1EX; tel. 020 8461 7170; fax 020 8466 7860; e-mail localstudies.library@bromley.gov.uk

Access to staff: Contact by letter, by telephone, by e-mail and in person
Hours: Central Library: Mon, Wed, Fri, 0930 to 1800; Tue, Thu, 0930 to 2000; Sat, 0930 to 1700
Branch Libraries: open at 0930, but are all closed one day a week (Burnt Ash three days, Hayes three days), so telephone first

Branch libraries: Anerley Library; Anerley Town Hall, Anerley Road, Anerley, SE20 8BD; tel: 020 8778 7457; Beckenham Library; Beckenham Road, Beckenham, BR3 4PE; tel: 020 8650 7292; Biggin Hill Library; Church Road, Biggin Hill, TN16 3LB; tel: 01959 574468; Burnt Ash Library; Burnt Ash Lane, Bromley, BR1 5AF; tel: 020 8460 3405; Chislehurst Library; Red Hill, Chislehurst, BR7 6DA; tel: 020 8467 1318; Hayes Library; Hayes Street, Hayes, BR2 7LH; tel: 020 8462 2445; Mottingham Library; 31 Mottingham Road, Mottingham, SE9 4QZ; tel: 020 8857 5406; Orpington Library; The Priory, Church Hill, Orpington, BR6 0HH; tel: 01689 831551; Penge Library; 186 Maple Road, Penge, SE20 8HT; tel: 020 8778 8772; Petts Wood Library; Frankswood Road, Petts Wood, BR5 1BP; tel: 01689 821607; Shortlands Library; 110 Shortlands Road, Bromley, BR2 0JP; tel: 020 8460 9692; Southborough Library; Southborough Lane, Bromley, BR2 8HP; tel: 020 8467 0355; St Paul's Cray Library; Mickleham Road, St Paul's Cray, Kent, BR5 2RW; tel: 020 8300 5454; West Wickham Library; Glebe Way, West Wickham, BR4 0SH; tel: 020 8777 4139

Parent body: The London Borough of Bromley

BROMYARD AND DISTRICT LOCAL HISTORY SOCIETY

5 Sherford Street, Bromyard, Herefordshire, HR7 4DL

Tel: 01885 488755
E-mail: bromyard.history@virgin.net
Website: www.bromyardhistorysociety.org.uk

Founded: 1966

Organisation type and purpose: A registered charity (charity number 1051572), with a local history centre run by volunteers.

Subject coverage: History of Bromyard and the surrounding area.

Collection: Archive of documents, books, maps, newspapers and photographs

Publications: Printed

Publications list: Available online

Access to building: *Hours:* Thu and Fri, 1000 to 1300 and 1400 to 1630; Sat, 1000 to 1230

BRONTË SOCIETY

The Brontë Parsonage Museum, Church Street, Haworth, Keighley, West Yorkshire, BD22 8DR

Tel: 01535 642323
Fax: 01535 647131
E-mail: bronte@bronte.org.uk
Website: www.bronte.info

Enquiries to: Library and Information Officer
Direct tel: 01535 640199
Direct e-mail: sarah.laycock@bronte.org.uk
Other contacts: Director, Brontë Parsonage Museum for all matters concerning the museum.

Founded: 1893

Organisation type and purpose: Learned society (membership is by subscription), present number of members: 1,750, voluntary organisation, registered charity (charity number 529952), suitable for ages: all.
Entrusted with the ownership and care of the Brontë Parsonage Museum.
To stimulate interest in the writing and the history of the Brontë Family and to promote understanding of their contemporary significance as an integral part of the intellectual, cultural and historical heritage of world literature.

Subject coverage: The writings of the Brontës and those associated with them; interpretations of their lives and works, subsequent biographies, monographs and scholarly criticism.

Collection: Books, manuscripts, drawings, furnishings and artefacts owned by the Brontës
Bonnell Collection: archive of manuscripts, drawings, first editions, Brontës' own books
Brontë Society General Collection: archive of manuscripts, letters, drawings, first editions, Brontës' own books, furniture, personal memorabilia
Grolier Collection of manuscripts
Seton Gordon Collection of manuscripts

Non-library collection catalogue: All or part available in-house

Publications: Printed

Access to staff: Contact by letter, by telephone, by fax, by e-mail and via website. Appointment necessary.
Hours: Mon to Fri, 1000 to 1630
Special comments: Visitors to the research library by prior appointment. Academic reference required in advance for access to primary sources.

Links with: Irish Brontë Society

Member organisation of: Alliance of Literary Societies (ALS); Association of Independent Museums (AIM); Yorkshire and Humberside Museums Council (YMHC)

BROOKLANDS SOCIETY LIMITED

The Brooklands Society Ltd, Registered Office: Copse House, Coxheath Road, Fleet, Hants, GU52 6QG

Tel: 01252 408877
Fax: 01252 408878
E-mail: graham.skillen@brooklands.org.uk
Website: www.brooklands.org.uk

Enquiries to: Chairman

Founded: 1967

Organisation type and purpose: International organisation, learned society, membership association (membership is by subscription), present number of members: 1,350, voluntary organisation.

Subject coverage: Brookland motor course and airfield, history and preservation of relics.

continued overleaf

Collection: Large archive of films, photographs and artefacts related to the Brooklands motor course and the personalities involved for the period 1907–1987

Publications: Printed

Publications list: Available online and in print

Access to staff: Contact by letter, by telephone, by fax, by e-mail and via website. Appointment necessary.
Hours: Mon to Fri, 0900 to 1700

Access to building: Prior appointment required

Affiliated to: Brooklands Museum Trust; Brooklands Museum, Brooklands Road, Weybridge, Surrey, KT13 0QN

Website management: Brooklands Society Limited; Hartland, Copse Corner, 38 Coxheath Road, Church Crookham, Hampshire, GU13 0QC; tel: 01252 408877; fax: 01252 408878; e-mail: brooklands@hartland.co.uk

BROOM'S BARN RESEARCH STATION

Higham, Bury St Edmunds, Suffolk, IP28 6NP

Tel: 01284 812200
Fax: 01284 811191
Website: www.broomsbarn.ac.uk

Enquiries to: Information Officer
Direct tel: 01284 812230
Direct e-mail: mike.may@bbsrc.ac.uk

Organisation type and purpose: Research organisation.
Agricultural research station for English sugar beet crop.

Subject coverage: Sugar beet crop rotation: seed quality, fertiliser practice, irrigation, crop agronomy; sugar beet crop protection: seedling pests and diseases, beet cyst nematode, virus yellows and vector aphids, leaf diseases, rhizomania, weed control.

Library catalogue: All or part available in-house

Publications: Printed

Access to staff: Contact by letter, by telephone, by fax and by e-mail
Hours: Mon to Thu, 0830 to 1700; Fri, 0830 to 1630

Funded by: Biotechnology and Biological Sciences Research Council

BROUGH SUPERIOR CLUB

Flint Cottage, St Pauls Walden, Hitchin, Hertfordshire, SG4 8DN

Tel: 01438 871714
E-mail: webmaster@broughsuperiorclub.com
Website: www.broughsuperiorclub.com/home.htm

Enquiries to: Secretary

Organisation type and purpose: Voluntary organisation.

Subject coverage: Preservation and use of W.E. Brough and Brough Superior Motorcycles, and any knowledge relating to these.

BROUGHAM HALL CHARITABLE TRUST (BHCT)

Brougham Hall, Brougham, Penrith, Cumbria, CA10 2DE

Tel: 01768 868184
Fax: 01768 862306
E-mail: juliachurchill@sky.com
Website: www.broughamhall.co.uk

Enquiries to: Administrator

Founded: 1986

Organisation type and purpose: Registered charity (charity number 517943), museum, historic building, house or site, suitable for ages: school leavers and undergraduates; training organisation, consultancy, research organisation, publishing house.

Subject coverage: Vernacular crafts, architecture, stone masonry, political history.

Collection: A collection of books, documents, manuscripts, pictures, photographs and other materials.

Library catalogue: All or part available in-house

Publications: Printed
Order printed publications from: Brougham Hall, Brougham, Penrith, Cumbria, CA10 2DE

Publications list: Available in print

Access to staff: Contact by letter
Hours: Mon to Fri, 0900 to 1700
Special comments: Prior appointment preferred.

Access to building: No prior appointment required
Hours: Mon to Fri, 0900 to 1700

Access for disabled people: Parking provided, ramped entry, level entry, toilet facilities
Special comments: Access to most areas, including cafe.

BROXBOURNE BOROUGH COUNCIL

Borough Offices, Bishops' College, Churchgate, Cheshunt, Hertfordshire, EN8 9XQ

Tel: 01992 785555
Fax: 01992 785578
E-mail: enquiry@broxbourne.gov.uk
Website: www.broxbourne.gov.uk

Enquiries to: Senior Communications Officer

Founded: 1974

Organisation type and purpose: Local government body.

Subject coverage: Local information, tourism, recycling, refuse, environment, leisure facilities, social housing, building control, planning and development, council tax.

Access to staff: Contact by letter, by telephone, by fax, by e-mail and via website
Hours: Mon, Wed, Thu, 0800 to 1800; Tue, 0800 to 1930; Fri, 0800 to 1730; Sat, 0900 to 1300

Access for disabled people: Parking provided, level entry, access to all public areas, toilet facilities

Also at: Broxbourne Borough Council; Unit 5, Broxbourne Business Centre, New River Estate, Cheshunt, Waltham Cross, Hertfordshire, EN8 0NP; tel: 01992 642240; fax: 01992 642216; e-mail: broxserv@broxbourne.gov.uk

BRUNEL INSTITUTE FOR BIOENGINEERING (BIB)

Information Unit, Brunel University, Uxbridge, Middlesex, UB8 3PH

Tel: 01895 266927
Fax: 01895 274608
E-mail: dawn.brandl@brunel.ac.uk
Website: www.brunel.ac.uk

Enquiries to: Information Officer

Founded: 1983

Organisation type and purpose: University department or institute.
Commercial institute attached to Brunel University.

Subject coverage: Mainly countercurrent chromatography and centrifugal partition chromatography, but will compile bibliographies on any relevant subject

Publications: Printed

Access to staff: Contact by letter, by telephone, by fax, by e-mail and in person. Appointment necessary. Non-members charged.
Hours: Fri, 0730 to 1500

Access for disabled people: Toilet facilities

BRUNEL UNIVERSITY

Library, Uxbridge, Middlesex, UB8 3PH

Tel: 01895 266154
Fax: 01895 203263
E-mail: library@brunel.ac.uk
Website: www.brunel.ac.uk/life/study/library
Direct tel: 01896 266154

Founded: 1965

Organisation type and purpose: University library.

Subject coverage: Biology, computer science, economics, electrical engineering, government, human sciences, law, mathematics, health sciences, arts and media, education, design, management, government, social work, sports science, occupational therapy, physiotherapy, sports medicine, sports science, education, social work, arts and humanities.

Collection: Bill Griffiths Collection
British and Foreign School Society Archives (University Archives)
Burnett Archive of Working Class Autobiographies
Cult Film Archive
D C Watt Collection
I K Brunel photographs
Maria Grey Archives (University Archives)

National Jazz Reserve Collection
Neglected Voices
OR Society Library
Poetry of the Now
SALIDAA (South Asian Diaspora Literature and Arts Archive)
Shakespearean Collections
Shoreditch College Collection (University Archives)
Transport History Collection
Library catalogue: All or part available online
Access to staff: Contact by letter, by telephone and by e-mail. Appointment necessary.
Hours: Hours may vary during weekends, vacations and semesters
Access for disabled people: Access to all public areas, toilet facilities

BSA FRONT-WHEEL DRIVE CLUB (BSAFWDC)

93 Barkby Road, Syston, Leicestershire, LE7 2AH

Tel: 0116 260 9663
Website: www.bsafwdc.co.uk

Enquiries to: Information Officer

Founded: 1959

Organisation type and purpose: To preserve the BSA front-wheel drive car and to maintain its position in the history of motor-engineering.

Subject coverage: BSA front-wheel drive 3- and 4-wheel cars produced from 1929 to 1939. Also caters for RWD cars.

Publications: Printed

BSA OWNERS' CLUB

Formal name: Birmingham Small Arms Owners' Club

PO Box 27, Crewe, Cheshire, CW1 6GE

E-mail: librarian@bsaownersclub.co.uk
Website: www.bsaownersclub.co.uk/

Enquiries to: National Secretary

Founded: 1958

Organisation type and purpose: Membership association (membership is by subscription), present number of members: 4,000.
Support for owners of BSA Motorcycles worldwide in terms of technical help and opportunity to get together with other motorcyclists.

Subject coverage: Information and technical advice on motorcycles produced by the Birmingham Small Arms Co. This includes original factory machine dispatch books, an archive of technical and publicity material. The club also offers social events for BSA owners through regional branch meetings and national and international rallies. International branches also exist.

Library catalogue: All or part available in-house

Publications: Printed

Access to staff: Contact by letter, by e-mail and via website. Non-members charged.
Hours: Mon to Fri, 0900 to 1700

BSEM

Formal name: British Society for Ecological Medicine

Administrator, BSEM, c/o New Medicine Group, 144 Harley St, London, W1G 7LE

E-mail: thebsem@gmail.com
Website: www.ecomed.org.uk

Enquiries to: Administrator

Founded: 1993

Organisation type and purpose: Membership association (membership is by subscription), present number of members: 160, registered charity (charity number 326372).

Subject coverage: Nutritional and environmental medicine.

Publications list: Available in print

Access to staff: Contact by letter, by telephone and by e-mail
Hours: Mon, Tue and Thu, 0900 to 1700

BSI

Formal name: British Standards Institution

389 Chiswick High Road, London, W4 4AL

Tel: 020 8996 9001
Fax: 020 8996 7001
E-mail: cservices@bsigroup.com
Website: www.bsi-global.com

Enquiries to: Librarian
Direct tel: 020 8996 7041
Direct e-mail: mary.yates@bsi-global.com

Founded: 1901

Organisation type and purpose: Professional body (membership is by subscription), present number of members: 20,000.
National Standards body.

Subject coverage: British, international and overseas standards and technical requirements covering most subject areas, certification schemes, European Community legislation, environmental issues.

Collection: BSI current and obsolete standards
Books on quality and environmental management
International and overseas national standards and related specifications (Library)

Publications: Printed, and electronic and video, and microform publications

Publications list: Available online and in print

Access to staff: Contact by letter, by telephone, by fax, by e-mail, in person and via website. Non-members charged.
Hours: Mon to Fri, 0900 to 1700
Special comments: Free to members and students.

Access for disabled people: Parking provided, access to all public areas, toilet facilities

Controls: BSI Product Services, Hemel Hempstead

Member of: European Committee for Electrotechnical Standardization (CENELEC); European Committee for Standardization (CEN); International Electrotechnical Commission (IEC); International Organization for Standardization (ISO)

BSI PRODUCT SERVICES (BSI)

Formal name: British Standards Institution Product Services

Kitemark House, Maylands Avenue, Hemel Hempstead Industrial Estate, Hemel Hempstead, Hertfordshire, HP2 4SQ

Tel: 08450 765600
Fax: 01442 278630
E-mail: product.services@bsigroup.com
Website: www.bsigroup.com
Website: www.kitemark.com

Enquiries to: Customer Service

Founded: 1901

Organisation type and purpose: Service industry.
Product testing and certification services.

Subject coverage: Product testing information in the following areas: construction, engineering, fire, personal protective equipment, electrical and electronic, lighting, environmental, healthcare, services, automotive services, combustion equipment, building and construction products, engineering and scientific products, transport and recreation, electronics, communications systems, electrical machines, lighting, cables, Canadian Standards Association, electromagnetic compatibility, electrical and mechanical calibration. Support for product development, product certification, voluntary (Kitemark schemes) and mandatory (CE marking).

Collection: National and International Standards
National Standards Body Library based at HQ Chiswick

Library catalogue: All or part available online and in print

Publications: Printed
Order printed publications from: BSI Customer Services
389 Chiswick High Road, London, W4 4AL, tel: 020 8996 9001

Access to staff: Contact by letter, by telephone, by fax, by e-mail and via website. Appointment necessary.
Hours: Mon to Fri, 0900 to 1700

Access for disabled people: Parking provided, ramped entry

Parent body: British Standards Institution; 389 Chiswick High Road, London, W4 4AL; tel: 020 8996 9000; website: http://www .bsigroup.com

BSI-DISC

389 Chiswick High Road, London, W4 4AL

Tel: 020 8996 9000
Fax: 020 8996 7448
E-mail: disc.enquiries@bsi-global.com

Enquiries to: Membership Secretary

continued overleaf

Direct tel: 020 8996 7180

Founded: 1990

Organisation type and purpose: International organisation, membership association (membership is by subscription), present number of members: 5,000, training organisation, publishing house.
The standards development and publishing service for the information and communications technology sector.

Subject coverage: Information management systems, data protection, document scanning and storage, IT service management, risk assessment, disaster recovery, training and workshops, records management, telecommunications.

Publications: Printed, and electronic and video

Publications list: Available online and in print

Access to staff: Contact by letter, by telephone, by fax, by e-mail and via website
Hours: Mon to Fri, 0900 to 1700

Access to building: Prior appointment required

Access for disabled people: Parking provided, level entry, access to all public areas, toilet facilities

Parent body: British Standards Institution

BSRIA

Old Bracknell Lane West, Bracknell, Berkshire, RG12 7AH

Tel: 01344 465600
Fax: 01344 465626
E-mail: bsria@bsria.co.uk
Website: www.bsria.co.uk

Enquiries to: Information and Knowledge Manager
Direct tel: 01344 465522
Direct e-mail: information@bsria.co.uk

Founded: 1955; formerly called Heating and Ventilating Research Association (year of change 1959); formerly called Building Services Research and Information Association (year of change 1975)

Organisation type and purpose: Membership association (membership is by subscription), present number of members: 650, consultancy, research organisation.
An independent research testing and information organisation offering laboratory facilities, site investigations and consultancy for building services.

Subject coverage: Heating; ventilation and air conditioning; building and energy management; technical information; equipment consultancy and testing; water quality and legionella; research; marketing research; management consultancy.

Information services: Building services and construction online, physical and phone enquiry services for BSRIA members.

Trade and statistical information: Market research facilities for building service industry

Library catalogue: All or part available online, in-house and in print

Publications: Printed
Order printed publications from: BSRIA Bookshop
Address as before

Publications list: Available online and in print

Access to staff: Contact by letter, by telephone, by fax, by e-mail and via website. Appointment necessary. Non-members charged.
Hours: Mon to Fri, 0830 to 1700

Access to building: Prior appointment required
Hours: Mon to Fri, 0830 to 1700
Special comments: Members only.

Access for disabled people: Parking provided, level entry, access to all public areas

BSS

Formal name: Broadcasting Support Services

bss Head Office, 163 Eversholt Street, London, NW1 1BU

Tel: 0207 419 3800
Fax: 0207 419 3899
Website: www.bss.org

Enquiries to: Business Development Executive
Direct tel: 0845 600 1317
Direct fax: 020 8799 9099
Direct e-mail: marketing@bss.org

Founded: 1975

Organisation type and purpose: National organisation, registered charity (charity number 282264), consultancy.
BSS provides tailored communications solutions to broadcasters, charities and organisations, through the provision of helplines, and distribution services. BSS also processes credit card and online donations.

Subject coverage: Charity providing communications solutions through: helplines provision, donation processing for appeals, design, print and distribution services.

Publications: Printed, and electronic and video

Access to staff: Contact by telephone, by fax, by e-mail and via website
Hours: Mon to Fri, 0930 to 1730

Access to building: Prior appointment required

Access for disabled people: Parking provided

Offices in: Leicester, Manchester and London

BT ARCHIVES

Formal name: British Telecommunications plc

Third Floor, Holborn Telephone Exchange, 268–270 High Holborn, London, WC1V 7EE

Tel: 020 7440 4220
Fax: 020 7242 1967
E-mail: archives@bt.com
Website: www.bt.com/archives
Website: www.connected-earth.com
Website: www.bt.com/archivesonline
Website: www.bt.com/archives-telefocus

Enquiries to: BT Curator

Founded: 1846

Organisation type and purpose: BT Archives is the corporate memory of the world's oldest communications company; prior to 1984 records are public records, which BT Archives looks after on behalf of the nation.

Subject coverage: The unique and nationally significant archive charts the development of communications in the UK and across the world, from the birth of the electric telegraph in the 1830s to the explosion of the internet and the rise of competition.
The collection illustrates the leading role that the UK, BT and its predecessors played in the progress of communications technology and its influence on society.

Collection: Archives of British Telecommunication plc and its predecessors, including private telegraph and telephone companies, Post Office Telecommunications and BT (public corporation)
Major collections include:
Private telegraph and telephone companies, 1830s–1910s
Post Office Telecommunications, 1870 (nationalisation) to 1981
Records of BT plc, 1984 to date
Historical phone books, 1880 to date
Photographic records, 19th century to date
Film and audio, 1930 to date
Reference library of printed sources including journals, periodicals, technical and historical works, 1769 to date.

Non-library collection catalogue: All or part available online and in-house

Library catalogue: All or part available online and in-house

Publications: Printed
Order printed publications from: http://www.bt.com/history

Access to staff: Contact by letter, by telephone, by fax, by e-mail, in person and via website. Appointment necessary.
Hours: Mon to Fri, 0900 to 1700; research appointments Tue and Thu, 1000 to 1600

Access to building: By appointment
Hours: Tue and Thu, 1000 to 1600

BT GROUP

Antares Building, Room 1/3, Martlesham Heath, Ipswich, Suffolk, IP5 3RE

E-mail: library@bt.com
Website: www.bt.com

Enquiries to: Library and information services manager

Organisation type and purpose: Research organisation.

Subject coverage: Telecommunications, electronics, computing, internet, information technology, business, management, learning and development.

Library catalogue: All or part available in-house

Access to staff: Contact by e-mail
Hours: Mon to Fri, 0900 to 1700

Access to building: No access other than to staff

BTCV – BARN COUNTRYSIDE CENTRE

Formal name: British Trust for Conservation Volunteers

Philips Park, Whitefield, Manchester, M45 7QJ

Tel: 0161 796 6404
Fax: 0161 796 8846
Website: www.btcv.org

Enquiries to: Manager

Founded: 1959

Organisation type and purpose: Membership association (membership is by subscription), voluntary organisation, registered charity.

Access to staff: Contact by letter, by telephone and by fax
Hours: Mon to Fri, 0900 to 1700

Access for disabled people: Parking provided, ramped entry, access to all public areas, toilet facilities

BTCV – WALLINGFORD (BTCV)

Formal name: British Trust for Conservation Volunteers

36 St Mary's Street, Wallingford, Oxfordshire, OX10 0EU

Tel: 01491 821600
Fax: 01491 839646
E-mail: information@btcv.org.uk
Website: www.btcv.org

Enquiries to: Information Officer
Direct e-mail: e.hudson@btcv.org.uk
Other contacts: PR Manager for media contacts.

Founded: 1959

Organisation type and purpose: Membership association (membership is by subscription), present number of members: 5000, voluntary organisation, registered charity (charity number 261009), training organisation.
BTCV is the UK's leading practical conservation charity supporting people from all sectors of the community in positive action to improve our environment.
BTCV's purpose is to ensure that the potential of voluntary action for the environment is fully realised.

Subject coverage: Volunteering, particularly in relation to conservation and the environment. Practical conservation operations in woodlands, waterways, wetlands, footpaths and sand dunes, hedging, dry stone walling and fencing. Environmental skills training, e.g. hedge-laying, dry stone walling. Community groups – support network for groups involved in conservation. BTCV is the UK's leading conservation charity supporting over 84,000 volunteers each year in action to improve their local environment.
Information on conservation working holidays both in Britain and abroad.

Collection: Slide-photo library

Publications: Printed
Order printed publications from: BTCV Enterprises, The Conservation Centre, Balby Road, Doncaster, South Yorkshire, DN4 0RH, tel: 01302 572200, fax: 01308 310167

Publications list: Available in print

Access to staff: Contact by letter, by telephone, by fax, by e-mail and via website
Hours: Mon to Fri, 0900 to 1700

Has: 130 offices throughout the UK

BTTG

Formal name: British Textile Technology Group

Wira House, West Park Ring Road, Leeds, West Yorkshire, LS16 6QL

Tel: 0113 259 1999
Fax: 0113 278 0306
E-mail: info@bttg.co.uk
Website: www.bttg.co.uk

Enquiries to: Customer Services
Direct tel: 0161 445 8141
Direct fax: 0161 434 9957
Other contacts: Pat Widdowson

Founded: 1988

Organisation type and purpose: International organisation, membership association (membership is by subscription), present number of members: 120, training organisation, consultancy, research organisation.

Specialised centre of excellence in textile-related testing, investigation and evaluation.

UKAS accredited textile testing laboratory.

Research and technical services for the textile and related industries.

Subject coverage: Textiles of all types (sourcing, processing, use, performance), carpets, cleaning science, biotechnology, polymers, testing of textiles and many other products including toys, flammability research, forensic science, water, effluent, energy, noise, safety etc.
Technical textiles, personal protective equipment, fire testers, chemical and biochemical sciences, laundry products, textile ecology (Oeko-Tex), microscopy, toys, spinning and non-wovens, certification, training etc.

Collection: Research results

Publications: Printed

Access to staff: Contact by letter, by telephone, by fax, by e-mail and via website
Hours: Mon to Fri, 0900 to 1700

Other addresses: BTTG (British Textile Technology Group); Shirley House, Wilmslow Road, Didsbury, Manchester, M20 2RB; tel: 0161 445 8141; fax: 0161 434 4957; e-mail: info@bttg.co.uk; BTTG Fire Technology Services; Unit 4B, Stag Industrial Estate, Atlantic Street, Broadheath, Altrincham, Cheshire, WA14 5DW; tel: 0161 929 8056; fax: 0161 929 8070; e-mail: pmeaton@bttg.co.uk; BTTG Spinning and Non-Wovens; Unit B6, Newton Business Park, Talbot Road, Hyde, SK14 4UQ; tel: 0161 368 2630; fax: 0161 368 1305; e-mail: info@bttg.co.uk

BUCKINGHAMSHIRE ARCHAEOLOGICAL SOCIETY (BAS)

Formal name: Buckinghamshire Archaeological and Architectural Society

County Museum, Church Street, Aylesbury, Buckinghamshire, HP20 2QP

Tel: 01296 387341
E-mail: bucksas@buckscc.gov.uk
Website: www.bucksas.org.uk

Enquiries to: Honorary Librarian/Archivist

Founded: 1847

Organisation type and purpose: Learned society (membership is by subscription), present number of members: 569 plus 16 affiliated societies.

Subject coverage: History and archaeology of Buckinghamshire in all aspects.

Non-library collection catalogue: All or part available in-house and in print

Library catalogue: All or part available in-house and in print

Publications: Printed

Publications list: Available in print

Access to staff: Contact by letter, by telephone, by e-mail and in person. Appointment necessary. Non-members charged.
Hours: Members only: Mon to Sat, 1000 to 1700;
Non-members: Wed, 1000 to 1600

Access for disabled people: Parking provided, ramped entry to building, level entry to library

BUCKINGHAMSHIRE CHILTERNS UNIVERSITY COLLEGE

Queen Alexandra Road, High Wycombe, Buckinghamshire, HP11 2JZ

Tel: 01494 522141
Fax: 01494 524392
E-mail: advice@bcuc.ac.uk
Website: www.bcuc.ac.uk

Enquiries to: Marketing Officer
Direct fax: 01494 471585

Organisation type and purpose: College of higher education; formerly High Wycombe College of Technology and Art and Newland Park College of Education; connection with Missenden Abbey Management Centre.

Subject coverage: Art and design, arts and social sciences, built environment, business and management, computing, engineering and technology, furniture, health studies, leisure and tourism.

Publications: Printed

Publications list: Available in print

Access to staff: Contact by letter
Hours: Mon to Fri, 0900 to 1700

Access to building: Prior appointment required

Access for disabled people: Parking provided, ramped entry

BUCKINGHAMSHIRE FAMILY HISTORY SOCIETY

PO Box 403, Aylesbury, Buckinghamshire, HP21 7GU

Website: www.bucksfhs.org.uk/

Subject coverage: Buckinghamshire family history.

Access to staff: Contact by letter
Hours: Mon to Fri, 0900 to 1700

BUCKINGHAMSHIRE LIBRARY SERVICE

Reference and Information Service, County Hall, Walton Street, Aylesbury, Buckinghamshire, HP20 1UU

Tel: 0845 230 3132
E-mail: lib-ref@buckscc.gov.uk
Website: www.buckscc.gov.uk/lis

Enquiries to: Head of Culture and Learning

Organisation type and purpose: Local government body, public library.

Subject coverage: General, Buckinghamshire, business information, careers and courses information.

Information services: Information services: Reference and Information Service (see below)

Collection: Buckinghamshire Collection (at the Centre for Buckinghamshire Studies, Aylesbury)
Early Children's Book Collection (at Chesham), County Museum (Aylesbury)

Library catalogue: All or part available online

Access to staff: Contact by letter, by telephone, by fax, by e-mail, in person and via website
Hours: Mon to Fri, 0900 to 1700
Special comments: Access hours to libraries vary.

Branch libraries: Aylesbury Study Centre; County Hall, Walton Street, Aylesbury, Buckinghamshire, HP20 1UU; tel: 0845 2303132; Centre for Buckinghamshire Studies; County Hall, Walton Street, Aylesbury, Buckinghamshire, HP20 1UU; tel: 01296 382250; fax: 01296 382771; Chesham Study Centre; Chesham Library, Elgiva Lane, Chesham, Buckinghamshire, HP5 2JD; tel: 0845 2303132; High Wycombe Study Centre; High Wycombe Library, 5 Eden Place, High Wycombe, Buckinghamshire, HP11 2DH; tel: 0845 2303132

Member organisation of: Buckinghamshire Culture and Learning Department; Libraries Information Service; County Hall, Walton Street, Aylesbury, Buckinghamshire, HP20 1UU; tel: 0845 230 3132; fax: 01296 382405; e-mail: lib-info@buckscc.gov.uk; website: http://www.bucks.gov.uk

BUCKINGHAMSHIRE RECORD SOCIETY

c/o Centre for Buckinghamshire Studies, County Hall, Aylesbury, Buckinghamshire, HP20 1UU

Tel: 01296 383013
Fax: 01296 382771
E-mail: archives@buckscc.gov.uk
Website: www.bucksinfo.net/brs

Enquiries to: Honorary Secretary

Founded: 1947; formerly called Buckinghamshire Archaeological Society (Records Branch)

Organisation type and purpose: Learned society (membership is by subscription), voluntary organisation, registered charity (charity number 262004).
To publish volumes based on original records illustrative of the history of Buckinghamshire; to concern itself with the collection, preservation and listing of public and private records relating to the county, including, if necessary, the raising of separate funds for this purpose.

Subject coverage: Local history of Buckinghamshire.

Publications: Printed, and electronic and video, and microform publications
Order printed publications from: The Society
Order microform publications from: The Society

Publications list: Available online and in print

Access to staff: Contact by letter, by telephone, by fax and by e-mail. Appointment necessary.
Hours: Tue to Fri, 0900 to 1715

Access for disabled people: Ramped entry, access to all public areas, toilet facilities.

BUDDHIST SOCIETY

58 Eccleston Square, London, SW1V 1PH

Tel: 020 7834 5858
Fax: 020 7976 5238
E-mail: info@thebuddhistsociety.org
Website: www.the buddhistsociety.org

Enquiries to: Librarian (for enquiries related to the literature of Buddhism)
Direct e-mail: library@thebuddhistsociety.org

Founded: 1924

Organisation type and purpose: Membership association (membership is by subscription), present number of members: 2,000.
Religious society.

Subject coverage: All aspects of Buddhism.

Library catalogue: All or part available online and in-house

Publications: Printed, and electronic and video

Publications list: Available online and in print

Access to staff: Contact by letter, by telephone, by fax, by e-mail and in person
Hours: Mon to Fri, 1400 to 1800; Sat, 1400 to 1700

Links with: European Buddhist Union; e-mail: president@e-b-u.org; website: http://www.e-b-u.org/
World Fellowship of Buddhists; e-mail: info@thebuddhistsociety.org.uk; website: http://www.thebuddhistsociety.org/

BUGATTI OWNERS' CLUB LIMITED

Prescott Hill, Gotherington, Cheltenham, Gloucestershire, GL52 9RD

Tel: 01242 673136
Fax: 01242 677001
E-mail: club@bugatti.co.uk
Website: www.prescott-hillclimb.com
Website: www.prescott-hillclimb-school.uk

Enquiries to: Secretary

Founded: 1929

Organisation type and purpose: Membership association (membership is by subscription).

Subject coverage: Speed Hill Climb meetings, Speed Hill Climb driver school, Bugatti information.

Access to staff: Contact by letter, by telephone, by fax and by e-mail
Hours: Mon to Fri, 0900 to 1700

Access for disabled people: Parking provided, toilet facilities

BUILDERS CONFERENCE

Crest House, 19 Lewis Road, Sutton, Surrey, SM1 4BR

Tel: 020 8770 0111
Fax: 020 8770 7736
E-mail: info@buildersconf.co.uk
Website: www.buildersconference.co.uk

Enquiries to: General Manager

Founded: 1935

Organisation type and purpose: Trade association, registered charity (charity number 281742), research organisation.

Subject coverage: Building.

Trade and statistical information: A comprehensive tender reporting and market information service in the UK market

Access to staff: Contact by letter, by telephone, by fax and by e-mail. Appointment necessary.
Hours: Mon to Thu, 0830 to 1700; Fri 0830 to 1630

BUILDING COST INFORMATION SERVICE (BCIS)

Royal Institution of Chartered Surveyors, Parliament Square, London, SW1P 3AD

Tel: 020 7695 1500
Fax: 020 7695 1501
E-mail: contact@bcis.co.uk
Website: www.bcis.co.uk

Enquiries to: Executive Director
Direct tel: 020 7695 1502

Founded: 1961

Organisation type and purpose: Membership association, consultancy, research organisation.
Voluntary association for the exchange of information; open to all those willing to exchange information.
To provide information on the construction and property markets.

Subject coverage: Construction industry information; statistical and econometric studies, facilities management information, building cost information, building economic forecasting, analysis of prices; property occupancy and costs; building maintenance management and costs; facilities management; life cycle costs.

Trade and statistical information: Statistics on price and cost trends in UK construction.
Statistics on the level of prices for UK building construction.
Data on occupancy costs.
Data on expenditure on maintenance of buildings in the UK

Publications: Printed, and electronic and video

Access to staff: Contact by letter, by telephone, by fax, by e-mail and via website. Access for members only. All charged.
Hours: Mon to Fri, 0900 to 1700

Constituent part of: Royal Institution of Chartered Surveyors

BUILDING RESEARCH ESTABLISHMENT LIMITED (BRE)

Bucknalls Lane, Garston, Watford, Hertfordshire, WD25 9XX

Tel: 01923 664000
Fax: 01923 664010
E-mail: enquiries@bre.co.uk
Website: www.bre.co.uk
Website: www.brebookshop.com
Website: www.greenbooklive.com/
Website: www.redbooklive.com/index.jsp
Website: www.breeam.org/

Enquiries to: Librarian

Founded: 1921; incorporates the former Princes Risborough Laboratory, Fire Research Station, Loss Prevention Certification Board (year of change 1972.)

Organisation type and purpose: Consultancy, research organisation.

Subject coverage: Building materials, building services, construction industry, structural design, fire science, timber construction, indoor environment (sick building syndrome), energy conservation, contaminated land.
Fire statistics; self-heating, ignition and growth of fire; structural aspects of fire in buildings; detection, extinction and suppression of fire; heat and smoke detectors; explosion hazards; combustion products, smoke, toxicity; smoke control and ventilation; human behaviour, escape and risk; combustion theory and modelling; sprinklers and extinguishing agents; special fire hazards in industries and materials.

Library catalogue: All or part available in-house

Publications: Printed
Order printed publications from: BRE Press, distributed by IHS, Willoughby Road, Bracknell, Berkshire, RG12 8FB, tel: 01344 328038, e-mail: brepress@ihsatp.com, website http://www.brebookshop.com

Publications list: Available online and in print

Access to staff: Contact by letter, by telephone, by fax, by e-mail and via website. Appointment necessary. All charged.
Hours: Mon to Fri, 0900 to 1700
Special comments: Not normally open to visitors.

Access to building: BRE Innovation Park open by appointment for tours
Special comments: Collections not open to the public

Access for disabled people: Access to all public areas, toilet facilities

Member of: Construction Industry Information Group (CIIG); 26 Store Street, London, WC1E 7BT; European Network of Building Research Institutions (ENBRI); International Council for Research and Innovation in Building and Construction (CIB); International Network for Fire Information and Reference Exchange (INFIRE)

Other addresses: BRE Scotland; Orion House, Scottish Enterprise Technology Park, East Kilbride, G75 0RD; tel: 01355 576200

BUILDING SOCIETIES ASSOCIATION (BSA)

6th Floor, York House, 23 Kingsway, London, WC2B 6UJ

Tel: 020 7520 5900
Fax: 020 7240 5290
E-mail: simon.rex@bsa.org.uk
Website: www.bsa.org.uk

Enquiries to: Information Services Manager

Organisation type and purpose: Trade association.

Subject coverage: Building society industry, housing finance, the mortgage market, savings markets, related financial services.

Library catalogue: All or part available in-house

Publications list: Available online

Access to staff: Contact by letter, by telephone, by fax, by e-mail and via website. Appointment necessary.
Hours: Mon to Fri, 0900 to 1700

Access to building: Appointment required
Hours: Mon to Fri, 0900 to 1700

BURDEN NEUROLOGICAL INSTITUTE (BNI)

Frenchay Park Road, Bristol, BS16 1JB

Tel: 0117 918 6720
E-mail: burdeninstitute@hotmail.com

Enquiries to: Director
Direct e-mail: n.j.scolding@bris.ac.uk

Founded: 1939

Organisation type and purpose: University department or institute, research organisation.

Subject coverage: Research in neurological diseases and stem-cell therapies.

Collection: Research journals in the fields of neurology, neurophysiology, neuropsychology, psychiatry, psychophysiology

Access to staff: Contact by letter, by telephone and by e-mail
Hours: Mon to Fri, 0900 to 1700

Access to building: Prior appointment required

Access for disabled people: Level entry, access to all public areas, toilet facilities

Associated institute of the: University of Bristol

BUREAU OF ANALYSED SAMPLES LIMITED (BAS)

Newham Hall, Newby, Middlesbrough, Cleveland, TS8 9EA

Tel: 01642 300500
Fax: 01642 315209
E-mail: enquiries@basrid.co.uk
Website: www.basrid.co.uk

Enquiries to: Managing Director

Founded: 1935

Organisation type and purpose: Manufacturing industry.

Subject coverage: Certified reference materials (CRM), sources of supply.

Non-library collection catalogue: All or part available online, in-house and in print

Library catalogue: All or part available online, in-house and in print

Publications: Printed

Publications list: Available online and in print

Access to staff: Contact by letter, by telephone, by fax, by e-mail and via website
Hours: Mon to Thu, 0900 to 1700; Fri, 0900 to 1630

BUREAU VAN DIJK ELECTRONIC PUBLISHING LIMITED

Northburgh House, 10 Northburgh Street, London, EC1V 0PP

Tel: 020 7549 5000
Fax: 020 7549 5010
E-mail: uk@bvdep.com
Website: www.bankscope.bvdep.com
Website: www.cameo.bvdep.com
Website: www.mintforbusiness.com
Website: www.fame.bvdep.com
Website: www.bvdep.com
Website: www.amadeus.bvdep.com

Enquiries to: Marketing Manager

Founded: 1970

Organisation type and purpose: Publishing house.
Provider of business information solutions on disk and via the Internet.

Subject coverage: Company information for the UK, Europe and worldwide.
Detailed information on banks worldwide.
Detailed information on insurance companies worldwide.
UK electoral roll on the internet.

Access to staff: Contact by letter, by telephone, by fax, by e-mail and via website
Hours: Mon to Fri, 0830 to 1830

BURNLEY BOROUGH COUNCIL

Town Hall, Manchester Road, Burnley, Lancashire, BB11 9SA

Tel: 01282 425011
Fax: 01282 438772
E-mail: enquiries@burnley.gov.uk
Website: www.burnley.gov.uk/

Enquiries to: Public Relations Manager
Direct tel: 01282 477180
Direct fax: 01282 424764
Direct e-mail: srichardson@burnley.gov.uk

Organisation type and purpose: Local government body.

Subject coverage: Local government services.

BURTON AND SOUTH DERBYSHIRE COLLEGE LIBRARY (BSDC)

Lichfield Street, Burton-on-Trent, Staffordshire, DE14 3RL

Tel: 01283 494431
Fax: 01283 494800
E-mail: library@bsdc.ac.uk
Website: www.bsdc.ac.uk

Enquiries to: Librarian

History of institution: formerly called Burton College Library (year of change 2011)

Organisation type and purpose: Further Education College with Higher Education provision.

Library catalogue: All or part available online

Links with: Staffordshire University Regional Federation (SURF)

BURTON HOSPITALS NHS FOUNDATION TRUST LIBRARY & INFORMATION SERVICE

Queen's Hospital, Belvedere Road, Burton-on-Trent, Staffordshire, DE13 0RB

Tel: 01283 511511 extn 2104
Fax: 01283 593174
E-mail: library.bur@burtonft.nhs.uk

Enquiries to: Library Services Manager

Founded: 1973

Organisation type and purpose: NHS Medical Library.

Subject coverage: Medicine, general aspects and specialities, including nursing.

Library catalogue: All or part available online

Access to staff: Contact by letter, by telephone, by fax, by e-mail and in person. Non-members charged.
Hours: Mon to Fri, 0900 to 1630

BURTON UPON TRENT FAMILY AND LOCAL HISTORY CENTRE (F&LHC)

Burton upon Trent Public Library, Riverside, High Street, Burton upon Trent, Staffordshire, DE14 1AH

Tel: 01283 239556
Fax: 01283 239571
E-mail: burton.library@staffordshire.gov.uk
Website: www.staffordshire.gov.uk/libraries
Website: www.staffordshire.gov.uk/leisure/archives/burtoncentre

Enquiries to: Library Development Officer
Direct tel: 01283 239564

Founded: 1977

Organisation type and purpose: Public library.

Subject coverage: Civic, educational, Burton Workhouse, and church (including some nonconformist) records, etc.; copies of census from 1841–1901 inclusive; pre- and post-WWII local newspapers; and a range of material relating to Burton and the surrounding areas in East Staffordshire and South Derbyshire.

Information services: Free computer and internet access for all. Free access to online subscriptions such as Ancestry.com and a range of Oxford Reference titles such as the Dictionary of National Biography and Oxford English Dictionary.

Special visitor services: Cafe facilities are available during library opening hours, serving hot and cold drinks and snacks.

Education services: Guided tours can be arranged for groups or classes.

Services for disabled people: The F&LHC is located on the ground floor. A large-print keyboard and trackerball mouse are available on request. A reader-magnifier is located on the first floor (accessible by a passenger lift).

Non-library collection catalogue: All or part available online and in-house

Library catalogue: All or part available online

Access to staff: Contact by letter, by telephone, by fax, by e-mail and in person
Hours: Mon, Tue, Wed and Fri, 0900 to 1800; Thu, 0900 to 2000; Sat, 0900 to 1630

Access to building: *Hours:* Same as access to staff hours.

Access for disabled people: Limited parking available at the front of the building, ramped entry, access to all public areas, toilet facilities

BURY ARCHIVES + LOCAL STUDIES

Moss Street, Bury, BL9 0DR

Tel: 0161 253 6782
Fax: 0161 253 5878
E-mail: archives@bury.gov.uk
Website: www.bury.gov.uk
Website: archives.bury.gov.uk

Enquiries to: The Archivist
Other contacts: The Archives Assistant

Founded: 1986

Organisation type and purpose: Public Archive Service.

Subject coverage: Local history, family history, geography, government of Bury and district, other local information, photographic collection.

Collection: The archives of local authorities in the Bury area, 1675 to present
Deposited archives of various local organisations (business, trade union, church, voluntary, sports, etc.) and individuals, mostly c. 1780 to present.

Non-library collection catalogue: All or part available online, in-house and in print

Publications: Printed

Access to staff: Contact by letter, by telephone, by fax, by e-mail and in person. Appointment necessary.
Hours: Tue to Fri, 1000 to 1300, 1400 to 1630; Sat, 2nd of the month, 1000 to 1300, 1400 to 1600
Special comments: Appointment recommended but not always essential.

Access to building: *Hours:* Tue to Fri, 1000 to 1700; Sat, 1000 to 1630

Access for disabled people: Ramp and lift access, bathrooms

Location: Bury Council, Environment and Development Services; Knowsley Place, Bury

BURY COLLEGE

Learning Resources Centre, Bury College, Market Street, Bury, Lancashire, BL9 0DB

Tel: 0161 280 8280
Website: www.burycollege.ac.uk

Enquiries to: Resource Librarian
Direct tel: 0161 280 8214/59
Direct e-mail: louise.minta@burycollege.ac.uk
Other contacts: Learning Resources Manager

Organisation type and purpose: Further education college, suitable for ages: 16+.

Subject coverage: Art and Design, Business studies, Catering, Childcare, Computing, Construction, Electrical Installation, Engineering, Hair and Beauty, Health and Social Care, Humanities, Maths, Media, Music, Performing Arts, Science, Sport, Teacher Ed., Travel and Tourism, Uniformed Services.

Library catalogue: All or part available online and in-house

Access to staff: Contact by letter, by telephone, by fax and by e-mail. Appointment necessary.
Hours: Mon to Fri, 0900 to 1700

Access to building: No prior appointment required

Access for disabled people: Access to all public areas

BURY COUNCIL LIBRARIES

Reference and Information Services, Bury Library, Manchester Road, Bury, BL9 0DG

Tel: 0161 253 5871
Fax: 0161 253 5857
E-mail: information@bury.gov.uk
Website: www.bury.gov.uk/libraries

Enquiries to: Reference and Information Services Librarian

Founded: 1901

Organisation type and purpose: Local government body, public library.

Subject coverage: General, business, local history and genealogical information, careers, social science.

Information services: Online library services.

Services for disabled people: Visual impairment unit, hearing impairment unit, housebound library service.

Non-library collection catalogue: All or part available online

Library catalogue: All or part available online

Publications: Printed, and electronic and video
Order printed publications from: Reference Information Services, Bury Library
Order electronic and video publications from: Website

Publications list: Available online and in print

Access to staff: Contact by letter, by telephone, by fax, by e-mail, in person and via website

Access to building: *Hours:* Mon, Tue, Thu, Fri, 0930 to 1730; Wed, 0930 to 1930; Sat, 0930 to 1630

Access for disabled people: Disabled access available
Hours: As above

Branch libraries: 16 branch libraries throughout Bury Metroplitan Borough Council

BUS USERS UK

PO Box 119, Shepperton, TW17 8UX

Tel: 01932 232574
E-mail: enquiries@bususers.org
Website: www.bususers.org

Enquiries to: General Manager

Founded: 1985; formerly called National Federation of Bus Users (year of change c. 2004)

Organisation type and purpose: National organisation, membership association, voluntary organisation.

Subject coverage: An independent group, formed to give bus passengers a voice. Has the ear of all the major bus companies and a lot of the smaller ones too, of their trade organisation and of the Government and local authorities. Resolves complaint appeals for bus users.

Publications: Printed

Access to staff: Contact by letter, by telephone and by e-mail
Hours: Mon to Fri, 0900 to 1700

Access to building: No access other than to staff

BUSINESS AND PROFESSIONAL WOMEN UK LIMITED (BPW UK Ltd)

74 Fairfield Rise, Billericay, Essex, CM12 9NU

Tel: 01277 623867
E-mail: hq@bpwuk.co.uk
Website: www.bpwuk.co.uk

Founded: 1938

Organisation type and purpose: Membership association (membership is by subscription), present number of members: 500, voluntary organisation.
Lobbying and networking organisation.

Subject coverage: The interests of all working women, equality, women in the workplace and public life, support for them personally or in their work, networking system.

Publications: Printed

Access to staff: Contact by letter, by telephone, by e-mail and via website

Links with: International Federation of Business and Professional Women; tel: +1631 422 7849; fax: +1631 792 1192; e-mail: presidents.office@bpw-international.org

Member organisations: There are 26 clubs in the United Kingdom

BUSINESS AND TRADE STATISTICS LIMITED (BTS)

Lancaster House, More Lane, Esher, Surrey, KT10 8AP

Tel: 01372 463121
Fax: 01372 469847
E-mail: info@worldtradestats.com
Website: www.worldtradestats.com

Enquiries to: Managing Director

Founded: 1986

Organisation type and purpose: Service industry.

Subject coverage: External trade statistics for the UK, all the European Community countries and Switzerland, Norway, USA, Canada, Mexico, Japan, Hong Kong, South Korea, Taiwan, Singapore, Australia, New Zealand.

Collection: Historical data back to 1979

Trade and statistical information: Statistical databases.
Production Statistics (PRODCOM) for UK.
UK consumption statistics for beer, wine, spirits, tobacco, hydrocarbons and expenditure in betting and gambling

Publications: Printed, and electronic and video

Publications list: Available in print

Access to staff: Contact by letter, by telephone, by fax and by e-mail.
Appointment necessary.
Hours: Mon to Fri, 0900 to 1700

BUSINESS ARCHIVES COUNCIL OF SCOTLAND (BACS)

c/o University of Glasgow Archive Services, 77 Dumbarton Road, Glasgow, G11 6PW

Tel: 0141 330 4159
Fax: 0141 330 4158
E-mail: bacs@archives.gla.ac.uk
Website: www.gla.ac.uk/archives/bacs

Enquiries to: Surveying Officer
Direct e-mail: k.king@archives.gla.ac.uk

Founded: 1960

Organisation type and purpose: National organisation, membership association (membership is by subscription), registered charity (charity number SCO 02565).

Subject coverage: Scottish business history, locating records of Scottish business history, preserving, appraising and listing.

Publications: Printed, and electronic and video
Order printed publications from: Editor, Scottish Business and Industrial History, c/o Business Archives Council of Scotland; e-mail: bacs@archives.gla.ac.uk

Publications list: Available online

Access to staff: Contact by letter, by telephone, by fax, by e-mail, in person and via website. Appointment necessary.
Hours: Mon to Fri, 0900 to 1700

Access to building: No access other than to staff

BUSINESS CONTINUITY INSTITUTE (BCI)

10 Southview Park, Marsack Street, Caversham, RG4 5AF

Tel: 0118 947 8215
E-mail: bci@thebci.org
Website: www.thebci.org

Founded: 1994

Organisation type and purpose: Membership association, professional organisation for business continuity management, number of members: 5,000 in 90 countries.
To enable individual members to obtain guidance and support from fellow business continuity practitioners; to promote the highest standards of professional competence and commercial ethics in the provision and maintenance of business continuity planning and services.

Subject coverage: The art and science of business continuity management world-wide.

Publications: Printed, and electronic and video
Order printed publications from: Online bookstore.

Publications list: Available online

Access to staff: Contact by letter, by telephone and by e-mail

Links with: Risk Management Institution of Australasia (RMIA)

Member organisation of: Risk Federation

BUSINESS IN THE COMMUNITY (BITC)

137 Shepherdess Walk, London, N1 7RQ

Tel: 020 7566 8650
Fax: 020 7253 1877
E-mail: information@bitc.org.uk
Website: www.bitc.org.uk

Enquiries to: Executive Secretary
Other contacts: Information Officer for publications

Founded: 1982

continued overleaf

Organisation type and purpose: Membership association (membership is by subscription, election or invitation), present number of members: 650 companies, voluntary organisation, registered charity (charity number 297716).
BITC's mission is to inspire businesses to increase the quality and extent of their contribution to social and economic regeneration by making corporate social responsibility an essential part of business excellence.

Subject coverage: Development of companies' positive impact on society through specialised campaigns.

Publications: Printed

Publications list: Available in print

Access to staff: Contact by telephone
Hours: Mon to Fri, 0900 to 1700

Offices at: Business in the Community, East Midlands; 3rd Floor, 30–34 Hounds Gate, Nottingham, NG1 7AB; tel: 0115 911 6666; fax: 0115 911 6667; Business in the Community, East of England; PO Box 93, 58 High Street, Newmarket, CB8 8ZN; tel: 01638 663272; fax: 01638 666841; Business in the Community, North East; Design Works, William Street, Felling, Tyne & Wear, NE10 0JP; tel: 0191 469 5333; fax: 0191 469 5353; Business in the Community, North West; Suite 17, St James Court, Wilderspool Causeway, Warrington, WA4 6RS; tel: 01925 230317; fax: 01925 652644; Business in the Community, Northern Ireland; c/o TK-ECC Limited, 770 Upper Newtownards Road, Dundonald, Belfast, BT16 1UL; tel: 028 9041 0410; fax: 028 9041 9030; Business in the Community, South East; 137 Shepherdess Walk, London, N1 7RQ; tel: 0870 600 2482; fax: 020 7253 1877; Business in the Community, South West; 165 Whiteladies Road, Bristol, BS8 2RN; tel: 0117 923 8750; fax: 0117 923 8270; Business in the Community, Wales; Fourth Floor, Empire House, Mount Stuart Square, Cardiff, CF10 5FN; tel: 029 2048 3348; fax: 029 2046 1513; Business in the Community, West Midlands; c/o Cadbury Limited, 83 Bournville Lane, Birmingham, B30 2HP; tel: 0121 451 2227; fax: 0121 451 2782; Business in the Community, Yorkshire & Humberside; Progress House, 99 Bradford Road, Pudsey, Leeds, LS28 6AT; tel: 0113 236 1888; fax: 0113 236 0555

Sister organisation: Scottish Business in the Community; PO Box 408, Bankhead Avenue, Edinburgh, E11 4EX; tel: 0131 442 2020; fax: 0131 442 3555

BUSINESS SERVICES ASSOCIATION (BSA)

BSA, 2nd Floor, 130 Fleet Street, London, EC4A 2BH

Tel: 020 7822 7421
Fax: 020 7786 6309
E-mail: sarah.fd@bsa-org.com
Website: www.bsa-org.com

Enquiries to: Director General
Direct tel: 020 7786 6301
Direct e-mail: norman.rose@bsa-org.com

Founded: 1993

Organisation type and purpose: Trade association (membership is by subscription), present number of members: 19, service industry.
Leading representative of major companies in the business services industry. BSA is secretary of the Parliamentary All Party Group for Business Services and represents the views of the industry to government. Has close links with UK and EU government monitoring policies and legislation. It develops policy papers on issues of employment and social policy including Best Value in local government contracting, public sector pensions and National Minimum Wage.

Subject coverage: Support services, public sector market testing, employment legislation, government tendering, EU markets, PFI, local government contracting, pensions, training.

Trade and statistical information: Data on private companies competing for public sector markets

Publications: Printed

Access to staff: Contact by letter, by telephone, by fax and by e-mail
Hours: Mon to Fri, 0900 to 1700

Access to building: No access other than to staff

BUSINESS SOFTWARE ALLIANCE (BSA)

79 Knightsbridge, London, SW1X 7RB

Tel: 020 7245 0304
Fax: 020 7245 0310
Website: www.bsa.org

Enquiries to: Communications Manager

Founded: 1988

Organisation type and purpose: International organisation, trade association. Alliance of Microsoft, Novell/WordPerfect, Adobe, Autodesk, Bentley Systems, Apple, Borland, CNC/Mastercam, Macromedia, Symantec and Unigraphics Solutions.

Subject coverage: Software piracy, its occurrence and prevention, software management.

Trade and statistical information: Statistics on software piracy and what this has cost in jobs and taxes in Europe

Publications: Electronic and video

Access to staff: Contact by letter, by telephone and by fax
Hours: Mon to Fri, 0900 to 1700

Access to building: No access other than to staff

Headquarters of the: BSA; 1180 18th Street NW, Suite 700, Washington, DC, 20036, USA; tel: +1 202 872 5500; fax: +1 202 872 5501

BUSINESS WEST

Formal name: Bristol Chamber of Commerce and Initiative (trading as Business West)

Leigh Court Business Centre, Abbots Leigh, Bristol, BS8 3RA

Tel: 01275 373373
Fax: 01275 370706
E-mail: info@businesswest.co.uk
Website: www.businesswest.co.uk

Enquiries to: Information Services Manager

Founded: 1826

Organisation type and purpose: Membership association (membership is by subscription), present number of members: 2,400, service industry.
Business Link.

Subject coverage: Industrial, commercial and financial affairs in Bristol and region: overseas trade, travel and marketing; overseas trade documentation; transport and shipping procedures; general business information; export credit insurance; EU legislation and public sector tenders information; credit referencing.

Collection: Company Information and Market Information, UK and worldwide
EC legislation: Official journal (L, C and S series)
Electronic Database Information
Standard reference material for business information

Trade and statistical information: UK and European statistics.
CSO data.
Tradstats

Publications: Printed

Access to staff: Contact by telephone, by fax and by e-mail. Non-members charged.
Hours: Mon to Fri, 0900 to 1700

Affiliated to: Bristol Euro Info Centre (EIC); at the same address

BUSINESS-COMMUNITY CONNECTIONS, CRAIGMILLAR AND SOUTH EDINBURGH

Castlebrae Community High School, 2a Greendykes Road, Edinburgh, EH16 4DP

Tel: 0131 652 0367
Fax: 0131 661 9811
E-mail: janet@ednet.co.uk

Enquiries to: Manager

Founded: 1991; formerly called Friends of Craigmillar (year of change 2000)

Organisation type and purpose: Registered charity.
To act as a link between the business and community sector to generate jobs for local people and to create innovative working links.

Subject coverage: Links between community groups and the private sector.

Publications: Printed, and microform publications

Access to staff: Contact by letter, by telephone and by fax
Hours: Mon to Fri, 0900 to 1700

Access to building: Prior appointment required

Access for disabled people: Parking provided, level entry

BUTTERFLY CONSERVATION (BC)

Manor Yard, East Lulworth, Wareham, Dorset, BH20 5QP

Tel: 01929 400209
Fax: 01929 400210
E-mail: info@butterfly-conservation.org
Website: www.butterfly-conservation.org

Enquiries to: Publicity Officer
Direct e-mail: cmallinson@butterfly-conservation.org

Founded: 1968; formerly called British Butterfly Conservation Society Limited (BBCS)

Organisation type and purpose: Membership association (membership is by subscription), present number of members: 11,500, registered charity (charity number 254937), the UK charity taking action to save butterflies, moths and their habitats. Conservation society.

Subject coverage: Butterfly and moth conservation, species information, habitat information, research, monitoring, nature reserves.

Publications: Printed

Publications list: Available in print

Access to staff: Contact by letter, by telephone, by fax and by e-mail
Hours: Mon to Fri, 0900 to 1700

Associated with: Butterfly Recording Scheme; English Nature; JCCBI; Wildlife Link

Has: 32 branches

BUTTERFLY HOUSE

Formal name: Seaforde Gardens and Tropical Butterfly House

Seaforde Demense, Seaforde, Downpatrick, Co Down, BT30 8PG

Tel: 028 4481 1225
Fax: 028 4481 1370
E-mail: plants@seafordegardens.com

Enquiries to: Owner

Founded: 1988

Subject coverage: Gardens, maze and tropical butterfly house

Access to staff: Contact by letter, by fax and by e-mail

Access to building: *Hours:* Easter to end September: Mon to Sat, 1000 to 1700; Sun, 1300 to 1800

Access for disabled people: Parking provided, access to all public areas, toilet facilities

BUTTERWORTH-HEINEMANN

Linacre House, Jordan Hill, Oxford, OX2 8DP

Tel: 01865 310366
Fax: 01865 314519
E-mail: bhmarketing@repp.co.uk

Enquiries to: Administrator
Direct tel: 01865 314492
Direct e-mail: maggie.harte@repp.co.uk

Founded: 1990; formerly called Butterworth Scientific Limited, Heinemann Professional Publishing

Organisation type and purpose: Publishing house.
Books and electronic products. An Imprint of Elsevier Science.

Subject coverage: Software development; information systems; strategy formulation and implementation, architecture, networking, data communications, programming, IS/IT management, personal computing, internet, business, open learning fields for tertiary and professional qualification.

Publications: Printed
Order printed publications from: Customer Services Department, Reed Publishers, Oxford
PO Box 382, Halley Court, Jordan Hill, Oxford, OX2 8RU, tel: 01865 888110, fax: 01865 314029, e-mail: bhuk.orders@repp.co.uk

Publications list: Available online and in print

Access to staff: Contact by letter, by fax, by e-mail and via website
Hours: Mon to Fri, 0900 to 1700

Parent body: Elsevier Science

BUTTONHOOK SOCIETY

PO Box 1089, Maidstone, Kent, ME14 9BA

Tel: 01622 752949
Fax: 01622 752949
E-mail: buttonhooksociety@tiscali.co.uk
Website: www.thebuttonhooksociety.com

Enquiries to: Chairman

Founded: 1979

Organisation type and purpose: International organisation, learned society (membership is by subscription), research organisation.
Archives of over 150,000 buttonhooks.
Research into origins and social history associated with buttonhooks.

Subject coverage: Buttonhooks, their origins, history, social context, materials and construction, costume, sources of information and areas of further research.

Information services: Speakers list available

Collection: Computerised Compendium of archival material on known buttonhooks in collections, sorted by type and material

Non-library collection catalogue: All or part available in-house

Publications: Printed

Publications list: Available in print

Access to staff: Contact by letter, by telephone, by e-mail and via website
Hours: Mon to Fri, 0900 to 1700

Associated with: Button Society; e-mail: angelaclarkbuttons@btinternet.com; website: http://www.britishbuttonsociety.org
Costume Society; website: http://costumesociety.org.uk

Other addresses: Overseas coordinator for American members; Box 287, White Marsh, Maryland, 21162–0287, USA

BYRON SOCIETY

Byron House, 6 Gertrude Street, London, SW10 0JN

Tel: 020 7352 5112
E-mail: thebyronsociety@btconnect.com
Website: www.thebyronsociety.com/

Enquiries to: Honorary Director

Founded: 1972

Organisation type and purpose: Learned society.

Subject coverage: Lord Byron's life and works, and those of his contemporaries (1788–1824).

Publications: Printed

Access to staff: Contact by letter
Hours: Mon to Fri, 0900 to 1700

Includes the: International Byron Society; maintains contact with many literary societies

CAB INTERNATIONAL (CABI)

Formal name: Centre for Agriculture and Biosciences International

Nosworthy Way, Wallingford, Oxfordshire, OX10 8DE

Tel: 01491 832111
Fax: 01491 833508
E-mail: enquiries@cabi.org
Website: www.cabi.org/

Enquiries to: Director General

Founded: 1929; formerly called Imperial Agricultural Bureaux (year of change 1948); formerly called Commonwealth Agricultural Bureaux (year of change 1985); incorporates Bureau of Hygiene and Tropical Diseases (year of change 1993)

Organisation type and purpose: International organisation, membership association (membership is by election or invitation), present number of members: 41 countries, training organisation, consultancy, research organisation.
Intergovernmental organisation, granted international status under the International Organisations Act of 1985.
Provides information, scientific and development services in the applied life sciences.

Subject coverage: Agriculture, forestry and forest products, field crops, grasslands, horticulture, crop protection, plant and animal breeding, veterinary science, water pollution and quality, leisure, recreation and tourism. Rural sociology and development. Public health, communicable diseases, tropical diseases, community health and medicine, environmental science, soils, land and water management, biotechnology, biodiversity, biosystematics, integrated pest management, biological control, human and animal nutrition, human and animal parasitology, AIDS.

Publications: Printed, and electronic and video, and microform publications
Order printed publications from: Publishing Division, CAB International
Wallingford, Oxfordshire, OX10 8DE

Publications list: Available in print

Access to staff: Contact by letter, by fax, by e-mail and via website
Hours: Mon to Fri, 0900 to 1700

continued overleaf

Access for disabled people: Parking provided, level entry

Member countries: Australia, Bahamas, Bangladesh, Belize, Botswana, Brunei Darussalam, Canada, People's Republic of China, Chile, Colombia, Cyprus, Fiji, Gambia, Ghana, Guyana, Hungary, India, Indonesia, Jamaica, Kenya, Malawi, Malaysia, Mauritius, Myanmar, New Zealand, Nigeria, Pakistan, Papua New Guinea, Philippines, Sierra Leone, Solomon Islands, South Africa, Sri Lanka, Tanzania, Trinidad & Tobago, Uganda, United Kingdom, UK Dependent Territories, Vietnam, Zambia, Zimbabwe

Other addresses: CAB International; Headquarters, CABI Publishing, Wallingford, Oxfordshire, OX10 8DE; tel: 01491 832111; fax: 01491 829292; e-mail: publishing@cabi.org; CAB International Africa Regional Centre; ICRAF Complex, PO Box 633, Village Market, Nairobi, Kenya; tel: +254 2 524462; fax: +254 2 522150; e-mail: arc@cabi.org; CAB International Caribbean Regional Centre; Gordon Street, Curepe, Trinidad & Tobago, West Indies; tel: +1 868 645 7628; fax: +1 868 663 2859; e-mail: crc@ cabi.org; CAB International North America; CABI Publishing, 10 East 40th Street, Suite 3203, New York, NY 10016, USA; tel: +1 212 481 7018 and +1 800 528 4841; fax: +1 212 686 7993; e-mail: cabi-nao@cabi.org; CAB International South-East Asia Regional Centre; MARDI, PO Box 210, 43409 UPM Serdang, Malaysia; tel: +60 3 894 32921; fax: +60 3 894 36400; e-mail: searc@cabi.org; CABI Bioscience Switzerland Centre; 1 Rue des Grillons, CH-2800 Delémont, Switzerland; tel: +41 32 421 4870; fax: +41 32 421 4871; e-mail: swiss.centre@cabi -bioscience.ch; CABI Bioscience UK Centre; Bakeham Lane, Egham, Surrey, TW20 9TY; tel: 0178 470111; fax: 01491 829100; e-mail: bioscience.egham@cabi.org; CABI Bioscience UK Centre; Silwood Park, Buckhurst Road, Ascot, Berkshire, SL5 7TA; tel: 01491 829129; fax: 01212 686 7993

Registered with the: United Nations

CABRINI CHILDREN'S SOCIETY

49 Russell Hill Road, Purley, Surrey, CR8 2XB

Tel: 020 8668 2181
Fax: 020 8763 2274
E-mail: info@cabrini.org.uk
Website: www.cabrini.org.uk

Enquiries to: Executive Director

Founded: 1887; formerly called Catholic Children's Society (Arundel & Brighton, Portsmouth and Southwark (year of change 2009)

Organisation type and purpose: The Cabrini Children's Society is a regional social care agency. It works primarily in disadvantaged communities helping to improve the emotional wellbeing and outcomes for children, young people and families. It supports people from a diverse range of backgrounds, cultures and faiths. It places children's needs at the centre of everything it does.

Subject coverage: Adoption, post-adoption care, fostering, schools counselling, community projects and catechetical programmes and residential care for people with learning difficulties.

Access to staff: Contact by letter, by telephone, by fax and by e-mail
Hours: Mon to Fri, 0930 to 1730

Access to building: *Hours:* Mon to Fri, 0930 to 1730

Also at: Cabrini Children's Society Fostering; 7a Bridge Street, Winchester, SO23 0HN; tel: 01962 842024; e-mail: fostering.@cabrini.org; Hove Adoption, Cabrini Children's Society Adoption; Linkline House, 65 Church Road, Hove, BN3 2BD; tel: 01273 821234; e-mail: hoveadoption@cabrini.org; Reading Adoption, Cabrini Children's Society Adoption; 50 Mount Pleasant, Reading, RG1 2TD; tel: 0118 987 5121; e-mail: reading@ cabrini.org; Winchester Adoption, Cabrini Children's Society Adoption; 7 Bridge Street, Winchester, SO23 0HN; tel: 01962 842024; e-mail: adoption,winchester@cabrini.org

Cabrini Residential Care: Cabrini; 3a Healy Drive, Orpington, Kent, BR6 9LB; tel: 01689 891401; e-mail: residential@cabrini.org

Dartford Community Project: Hubert House, Dartford; Mallard Close, Knights Manor Estate, Dartford, DA1 5HU; tel: 01322 224500; e-mail: huberthouse@cabrini .org

Parish Work: Fountains Centre; 24 Knebworth Road, Bexhill on Sea, TN39 4JJ; tel: 01424 730536; e-mail: fountainscentre@ cabrini.org

Peckham Community Project: Bird in Bush, Peckham; 616 Old Kent Road, Peckham, London, SE15 1JB; tel: 020 7639 3030; e-mail: birdinbush@cabrini.org

Schools Counselling: Schools Counselling; 49 Russell Hill Road, Purley, CR8 2XB; tel: 020 8668 2181; e-mail: info@cabrini.org

Vauxhall Community Project: St Anne's, Vauxhall; 42–46 Harleyford Road, Vauxhall, London, SE11 5AY; tel: 020 7735 7049; e-mail: vauxhall@cabrini.org

CAERNARFON AREA RECORD OFFICE

County Offices, Shirehall Street, Caernarfon, Gwynedd, LL55 1SH

Tel: 01286 679088
Fax: 01286 679637
E-mail: annrhydderch@gwynedd.gov.uk
Website: www.llgc.org.uk/cac/cac0053.htm
Website: www.gwynedd.gov.uk/archives

Enquiries to: Archivist

Founded: 1947

Organisation type and purpose: Local government body.

Subject coverage: Local government archives, parish material, estates, industrial (predominantly slate), maritime records.

Non-library collection catalogue: All or part available online

Publications: Printed

Publications list: Available online

Access to staff: Contact by letter, by telephone, by fax, by e-mail and in person
Hours: Mon, closed; Tue, Thu, Fri, 0930 to 1230 and 1330 to 1700; Wed, 0930 to 1230 and 1330 to 1900
Special comments: CARN Reader's ticket required.

Access for disabled people: Level entry, access to all public areas, toilet facilities

CAERNARVONSHIRE HISTORICAL SOCIETY

County Offices, Caernarfon, Gwynedd, LL55 1SH

Tel: 01286 679088
Fax: 01286 679637

Enquiries to: Honorary Secretary

Founded: 1939

Organisation type and purpose: Learned society, voluntary organisation, registered charity.
Historical Society.

Subject coverage: Local history in the former county of Caernarvon (now Gwynedd).

Publications: Printed

Access to staff: Contact by letter, by telephone and by fax
Hours: Mon to Fri, 0900 to 1700

Member of: Federation of Local History Societies in Caernarvonshire

CAERPHILLY COUNTY BOROUGH COUNCIL

Nelson Road, Tredomen, Ystrad Mynach, Mid Glamorgan, CF82 7WF

Tel: 01443 815588 or 01495 226622
Fax: 01443 863029
E-mail: info@caerphilly.gov.uk
Website: www.caerphilly.gov.uk

Enquiries to: Communications Manager
Direct tel: 01443 864262
Direct fax: 01443 864246
Direct e-mail: rosemarymathews@caerphilly .gov.uk

Founded: 1996; formerly called Gwent County Council, Islwyn Borough Council, Mid Glamorgan County Council, Rhymney Valley District Council

Organisation type and purpose: Local government body.

Subject coverage: Socio-economic data about the county borough.

Publications: Printed

Access to staff: Contact by letter
Hours: Mon to Thu, 0830 to 1700; Fri, 0830 to 1630

CAIRNGORM REINDEER CENTRE, THE

Glenmore Forest Park, Visitors Centre, Aviemore, Inverness-shire, PH22 1QU

Tel: 01479 861228
Fax: 01479 861228
E-mail: info@cairngormreindeer.co.uk

Enquiries to: Director

Founded: 1952

Organisation type and purpose: Promotion and research of reindeer.

Subject coverage: Reindeer breeding and general husbandry, training to harness, import/export of reindeer to and from the UK.

Publications: Printed

Publications list: Available in print

Access to staff: Contact by letter, by fax and by e-mail
Hours: Mon to Fri, 0900 to 1700

CAITHNESS ARCHIVE CENTRE (CAC)

Wick Library, Sinclair Terrace, Wick, Caithness, KW1 5AB

Tel: 01955 606432
Fax: 01955 603000
E-mail: north.highlandarchive@highlifehighland.com
Website: www.highlandarchives.org.uk/caithness.asp

Enquiries to: Caithness Archivist

Founded: 1995; formerly called North Highland Archive (year of change 2009)

Organisation type and purpose: Local archive and record office.

Subject coverage: Maritime history, poor relief, council administration, police activity, education, planning (building development). Less significant: WWII, archaeology, trade, estates and agriculture, nursing, church activity.

Collection: Local and family history sources including census/OPR microfilms, maps, valuations rolls, school records, council and parochial board records, and private collections of major local significance such as Wick Harbour Trust
A number of smaller private collections come from local businesses or major landowning professional families

Non-library collection catalogue: All or part available online and in-house

Library catalogue: All or part available in-house

Publications: Printed

Access to staff: Contact by letter, by telephone, by fax, by e-mail and in person
Hours: Mon, Tue, Thu, Fri, 1000 to 1300 and 1400 to 1730
Special comments: May be advisable to book in the summer months to ensure access to microfilm readers.

Access to building: No access other than to staff

Access for disabled people: On request

Parent body: Highland Archive Service, Inverness

CALDERDALE COLLEGE

Learning Resources Centre, Francis Street, Halifax, West Yorkshire, HX1 3UZ

Tel: 01422 357 357
Fax: 01422 399 320
E-mail: info@calderdale.ac.uk
Website: www.calderdale.ac.uk

Enquiries to: Head of Learning Resources

History of institution: formerly called Percival Whitley College of Further Education Library and Resources

Organisation type and purpose: Further educational college

Subject coverage: All subjects covered by the further education curriculum; building construction; information technology; health and safety; further and adult education; chemistry; physics; biology; mathematics; computing; commercial art; business; strongest subjects are business and social care, graphic and fine arts, photography, service industries, health and caring.

Library catalogue: All or part available online

Access to staff: Contact by letter, by telephone, by fax and by e-mail. Appointment necessary. Letter of introduction required.
Hours: Mon to Thu, 0845 to 2000; Fri, 0915 to 1600; Sat, 1000 to 1300 (term only).
Special comments: Restricted hours during college vacations.

Access for disabled people: Level entry, access to all public areas, toilet facilities

Member organisation of: Leeds Metropolitan University Regional University Network; website: http://www.leedsmet.ac.uk/regional/new
Welcome!; website: http://welcome.hud.ac.uk

CALDERDALE FAMILY HISTORY SOCIETY (CFHS)

4 Rawson Avenue, Halifax HX3 0JP

Tel: 01422 345164
E-mail: mail@cfhsweb.co.uk
Website: www.cfhsweb.com

Enquiries to: Chairman

Founded: 1985

Organisation type and purpose: Membership association (membership is by subscription).
The Society exists to encourage interest in, and assist in, matters relating to genealogy and family history, and to record and preserve genealogical material for future generations.

Subject coverage: Genealogy, family history, particularly with relation to Halifax (West Yorkshire) and surrounding areas.

Collection: Calderdale War Dead, other local summary information

Non-library collection catalogue: All or part available in print

Library catalogue: All or part available in-house

Publications: Electronic and video
Order electronic and video publications from: Publications Officer, Calderdale Family History Society, 22 Well Grove, Hove Edge, Brighouse, HD6 2LT; tel: 01484 714311; e-mail: publications@cfhsweb.co.uk

Publications list: Available online and in print

Access to staff: Contact by letter, by telephone, by e-mail and via website
Hours: Sun to Sat, 1000 to 2100; Research Room, Brighouse Library, Tue, 1330 to 1630 and Thu, 1000 to 1300

CALDERDALE LIBRARIES

Central Library, Northgate, Halifax, West Yorkshire, HX1 1UN

Tel: 01422 392630
Fax: 01422 392615
E-mail: libraries@calderdale.gov.uk
Website: www.calderdale.gov.uk

Enquiries to: Information Services Team Leader
Direct tel: 01422 392631
Direct fax: 01422 349458
Direct e-mail: reference.library@calderdale.gov.uk

Founded: 1882; formerly called Halifax Central Library, Halifax Public Libraries

Organisation type and purpose: Local government body, public library, suitable for all ages.

Subject coverage: General; Calderdale local history.

Services for disabled people: Access to all units, including assistive technology for full access to IT services

Collection: Edwards Bindings (Halifax late 18th and early 19th centuries)
Horsfall Turner Local History Collection (Calderdale)
Milner Collection (publications of William Milner dating 1834–1913)
Phyllis Bentley Collection (MS books and work books)
Some incunabula

Library catalogue: All or part available online and in-house

Access to staff: Contact by letter, by telephone, by fax, by e-mail and in person
Hours: Mon, Tue, Thu and Fri, 0930 to 1900; Sat, 0930 to 1700

Access for disabled people: Access to all public areas

Branch libraries: 21 local branches, 2 mobile libraries

Parent body: Calderdale Metropolitan Borough Council; Town Hall, Crossley Street, Halifax, HX1 1UJ; tel: 01422 357257; fax: 01422 393102

CALEDONIAN RAILWAY ASSOCIATION (CRA)

63 Andrew Drive, Clydebank, Dunbartonshire, G81 1BU

E-mail: dwhind@ukonline.co.uk
Website: www.crassoc.org.uk

Enquiries to: Secretary

Founded: 1983

Organisation type and purpose: Voluntary organisation, research organisation.

Subject coverage: Research and study of former Caledonian Railway Company, including locomotive drawings, coach and wagon drawings, signal box track diagrams,

continued overleaf

industrial relations, architecture, publicity material, shipping services, tickets and history.

Collection: At University of Glasgow Business Archive, 13 Thurso Street, Glasgow, G11 6PE; website: http://www.gla.ac.uk/archives; e-mail: enquiries@gla.ac.uk; tel: 0141 330 5515

Publications: Printed
Order printed publications from: Sales Officer, Caledonian Railway Association, 73 Victoria Park Drive North, Glasgow, G14 9PS

Publications list: Available online

Access to staff: Contact by letter, by telephone and by e-mail

CALOUSTE GULBENKIAN FOUNDATION

50 Hoxton Square, London, N1 6PB

Tel: 020 7012 1400
Fax: 020 7739 1961
E-mail: info@gulbenkian.org.uk
Website: www.gulbenkian.org.uk

Enquiries to: Information Officer

Founded: 1956

Organisation type and purpose: Charitable foundation.

Subject coverage: Arts, education, social welfare, Anglo-Portuguese cultural relations.

Publications: Printed
Order printed publications from: Central Books Ltd, 99 Wallis Road, London, E9 5LN, tel: 0845 458 9911, fax: 0845 458 9912; e-mail: orders@centralbooks.com website: www.centralbooks.co.uk

Publications list: Available online and in print

Access to staff: Contact by letter, by telephone, by fax and by e-mail
Hours: Mon to Fri, 0930 to 1730
Special comments: Telephone messages taken all day.

Parent body: Calouste Gulbenkian Foundation; Avenida de Berna 45A, Lisbon, 1067–001, Portugal; tel: 00 35121 782 3000; fax: 00 35121 782 3021; e-mail: info@gulbenkian.pt; website: www.gulbenkian.pt

CAMANACHD ASSOCIATION

Alton House, 4 Ballifeary Road, Inverness, IV3 5PJ

Tel: 01463 715931
Fax: 01463 226551
E-mail: admin@shinty.com
Website: www.shinty.com

Enquiries to: Executive Officer
Direct e-mail: executive@camanachd.co.uk

Founded: 1893

Organisation type and purpose:
Membership association (membership is by subscription).
National governing body of the game.
To foster and develop the game of Shinty.

Subject coverage: The game of Shinty.

Access to staff: Contact by fax
Hours: Mon to Fri, 0900 to 1700

CAMBERWELL COLLEGE OF ARTS

Peckham Road, London, SE5 8UF

Tel: 020 7514 6302
Fax: 020 7514 6310
E-mail: info@camberwell.arts.ac.uk
Website: www.camberwell.arts.ac.uk

Enquiries to: Information Assistant
Direct tel: 020 7514 6302
Direct e-mail: info@camberwell.arts.ac.uk

Founded: 1898; formerly called Camberwell College of Arts and Crafts

Organisation type and purpose: College of higher and further education.

Subject coverage: Fine art (drawing, painting, photography and sculpture); ceramics; textiles; graphic design; illustration; 3D Design, printing; print making; typographic design; bookbinding; silversmithing and metalwork; conservation of prints, drawings, textiles and artefacts; book illustration; photography and film.

Collection: Books and ephemera by and about Walter Crane
Books on poster art
Thorold Dickinson Cinema Collection

Non-library collection catalogue: All or part available online

Library catalogue: All or part available online

Access to staff: Contact by letter, by telephone and by e-mail. Appointment necessary. Access for members only.
Hours: Mon, Fri, 1000 to 1700; Tue, Thu, 1000 to 2000; Wed, 1000 to 1930

Parent body: University of the Arts London; 272 High Holborn, London; tel: 0207 514 6130; e-mail: info@arts.ac.uk; website: htp://www.arts.ac.uk

CAMBRIDGE ASSESSMENT

Syndicate Buildings, 1 Hills Road, Cambridge, CB1 2EU

Tel: 01223 553311
Fax: 01223 460278
E-mail: info@cambridgeassessment.org.uk

Enquiries to: Chief Executive

Founded: 1858; formerly called University of Cambridge Local Examinations Syndicate

Organisation type and purpose: Examining body.
UK Examinations offered through OCR (which is part of Cambridge Assessment) include GCSE, GCE at A/AS, and vocational qualifications

Subject coverage: Specifications and question papers in all subjects for which papers are set, numerous examinations and assessment services.

Publications: Printed

Subsidiary body: Oxford Cambridge and RSA Examinations (OCR); 1 Hills Road, Cambridge; tel: 01223 552552; fax: 01223 552553

CAMBRIDGE BIBLIOGRAPHICAL SOCIETY

University Library, West Road, Cambridge, CB3 9DR

Tel: 01223 333123
Fax: 01223 333160
E-mail: cbs@lib.cam.ac.uk
Website: www.lib.cam.ac.uk/cambibsoc

Enquiries to: Secretary
Direct e-mail: cbs@lib.cam.ac.uk
Other contacts: Treasurer (for subscription enquiries)

Founded: 1949

Organisation type and purpose: Learned society.

Subject coverage: Bibliography (historical), rare books, manuscripts, book collecting.

Publications: Printed
Order printed publications from: The Secretary (address as above)

Publications list: Available in print

Access to staff: Contact by letter, by telephone and by e-mail
Hours: Mon to Fri, 0930 to 1245 and 1400 to 1730

CAMBRIDGE CRYSTALLOGRAPHIC DATA CENTRE (CCDC)

12 Union Road, Cambridge, CB2 1EZ

Tel: 01223 336408
Fax: 01223 336033
E-mail: admin@ccdc.cam.ac.uk
Website: www.ccdc.cam.ac.uk

Enquiries to: Executive Director

Founded: 1987

Organisation type and purpose: Registered charity (charity number 800579). Research organisation.
Independent non-profit institution.

Subject coverage: Chemical structure and substructure searching, crystal structures of organic, organometallic compounds.

Collection: Reprint collection
Structural data on CD-ROM

Access to staff: Contact by e-mail and via website
Hours: Mon to Fri, 0900 to 1700
Special comments: Academic and industrial scientists.

Access to building: No access other than to staff

Access for disabled people: Level entry

Links with: International Union of Crystallography; University of Cambridge

CAMBRIDGE PHILOSOPHICAL SOCIETY

Bene't Street, Cambridge, CB2 3PY

Tel: 01223 334743
E-mail: philosoc@hermes.cam.ac.uk
Website: www.cambridgephilosophicalsociety.org

Enquiries to: Executive Secretary

Founded: 1819

Organisation type and purpose: Learned society.
To promote scientific enquiry.

Subject coverage: Science, biology and mathematics.

Publications: Printed, and microform publications
Access to staff: Contact by letter and by e-mail. Appointment necessary.
Hours: Mon to Fri, 0900 to 1630

CAMBRIDGE REFRIGERATION TECHNOLOGY (CRT)

140 Newmarket Road, Cambridge, CB5 8HE

Tel: 01223 365101
Fax: 01223 461522
E-mail: crt@crtech.co.uk
Website: www.crtech.co.uk

Enquiries to: Information Officer
Direct tel: 01223 461352

Founded: 1965

Organisation type and purpose: Research organisation.
Research association; connection with IIR (Paris), RIB, Institute of Refrigeration.

Subject coverage: Transportation of perishable cargoes; specialist knowledge on all storage and stowage techniques of fruits and vegetables; transport, both road vehicles and sea freight – reefers and containers; refrigeration equipment; refrigerants; CFCs; food legislation.

Collection: Early books and ship drawings from 1850s of refrigeration equipment and refrigerated ships

Trade and statistical information: Data on UNEP and all environmental organisations, especially connected with use of solvents, refrigerants, and foams

Non-library collection catalogue: All or part available online

Publications: Printed

Publications list: Available in print

Access to staff: Contact by letter, by telephone, by fax, by e-mail and via website. Appointment necessary. Non-members charged.
Hours: Mon to Fri, 0900 to 1700

Access to building: Prior appointment required

Access for disabled people: Parking provided

CAMBRIDGE UNIVERSITY LIBRARY

West Road, Cambridge, CB3 9DR

Tel: 01223 333000
Fax: 01223 333160
E-mail: library@lib.cam.ac.uk
Website: www.lib.cam.ac.uk

Founded: 1400

Organisation type and purpose: University library.
Legal Deposit Library.

Subject coverage: Extensive and general.

Collection: Acton Library
Adversaria
Almanacks
Armorial bindings
Bible Society Library and Archives
Book sales (English sales catalogues)
Bookplates and book stamps
Bradshaw Collection (Irish books)
Cambridge Collection
Chapbooks
Darwin Library and papers
Early English printed books
Ely Diocesan and Chapter Records
Gerhardie Collection
Hunter-McAlpine Collection (history of psychiatry)
Incunabula
Jardine-Matheson Archives
Keynes Collection (Sir Geoffrey Keynes' personal library)
Madden Collection of Ballads
Madden Collection of Maps
Music
Norton Collection (early European printing 1501–1520)
Official Publications
Peterborough Cathedral Library
Portraits
Royal Commonwealth Society's Library
Royal Greenwich Observatory Archives
Taylor-Schechter Genizah Collection
University Archives
Vickers Archives
Wade Collection (Chinese books)
War Collection 1914–1919

Non-library collection catalogue: All or part available online, in-house and in print

Publications: Printed
Order printed publications from: Library Offices, Cambridge University Library; tel: 01223 333048; e-mail: admin@lib.cam.ac.uk

Publications list: Available online and in print

Access to building: Prior appointment required
Hours: Mon to Fri, 0900 to 1915; Sat, 0900 to 1700
Easter Full Term: Mon to Fri, 0900 to 2200
Special comments: Closed between Christmas and New Year, Bank Holidays, Sept 16 to 23. A prior appointment is advised to obtain reader's ticket.

Access for disabled people: Parking provided, ramped entry, toilet facilities
Special comments: Recommended to contact Library before first visit.

Also at the same address: Cambridge Bibliographical Society; University Archives; tel: 01223 333147/8

Organisationally, it includes the: Betty & Gordon Moore Library; Centre for Mathematical Sciences, Wilberforce Road, Cambridge, CB3 0WD; tel: 01223 765670; fax: 01223 765678; e-mail: moore-library@lib.cam.ac.uk; Cambridge University Medical Library; Clinical School Building, Box 111, Addenbrooke's Hospital, Hills Road, Cambridge, CB2 2SP; tel: 01223 336750; fax: 01223 331918; e-mail: library@medschl.cam.ac.uk; Central Science Library; Bene't Street, Cambridge, CB2 3PY; tel: 01223 334742; fax: 01223 334748; e-mail: lib-csl-inquiries@lists.cam.ac.uk; Squire Law Library; 10 West Road, Cambridge, CB3 9DZ; tel: 01223 330077; fax: 01223 330048; e-mail: dfw1003@cam.ac.uk

CAMBRIDGE UNIVERSITY PRESS (CUP)

The Edinburgh Building, Shaftesbury Road, Cambridge, CB2 8RU

Tel: 01223 312393
Fax: 01223 325959
E-mail: information@cambridge.org
Website: www.cambridge.org

Enquiries to: Sales Manager

Founded: 1534

Organisation type and purpose: University department or institute, publishing house.

Subject coverage: The Press publishes in all main academic and educational subject areas, including English Language Teaching, Schoolbooks, Humanities, Social Sciences, STM and Reference books, Bibles and prayer books, educational software and CD-ROMs.

Publications: Printed

Publications list: Available online and in print

Access to staff: Contact by letter, by telephone, by fax, by e-mail and via website
Hours: Mon to Fri, 0900 to 1700

CAMBRIDGESHIRE ARCHIVES

Box RES 1009, Shire Hall, Castle Hill, Cambridge, CB3 0AP

Tel: 01223 699399
Fax: 01223 718823
E-mail: cambs.archives.cambridge@cambridgeshire.gov.uk
Website: www.cambridgeshire.gov.uk/leisure/archives

Enquiries to: Senior Archivist Public Services
Other contacts: Archives and Local Studies Manager (for matters of general policy, broad issues); Principal Archivist (for collections-related matters)

Founded: 1930; formerly called Cambridgeshire Record Office (alias County Record Office Cambridge) (year of change 2008)

Organisation type and purpose: Local government body.
Record office.

Subject coverage: Historical matters of all kinds relating to the area of the former county of Cambridgeshire and the Isle of Ely; matters relating to the County Council of Cambridgeshire since 1974.

Collection: Cambridge Borough, 13th to 20th centuries
Land drainage authorities including the former Bedford Level Corporation 1663–1920

Non-library collection catalogue: All or part available online and in-house

Library catalogue: All or part available in-house

Publications: Printed, and microform publications
Order printed publications from: See website
Order microform publications from: Cambridgeshire Family History Society; website: http://www.cfhs.org.uk

Publications list: Available in print

Access to staff: Contact by letter, by telephone, by e-mail and in person
Hours: Tue, Wed, Thu, 0900 to 1245 and 1345 to 1715; Fri, 0900 to 1245 and 1345 to 1615; Tue, 1715 to 2100 by appointment only

continued overleaf

Branches: Huntingdonshire Archives; Huntingdon; tel: 01480 375842

Constituent part of: Cambridgeshire Archives and Local Studies (CALS)

Parent body: Cambridgeshire County Council; tel: 01223 717111

CAMBRIDGESHIRE CHAMBERS OF COMMERCE

Vision Park, Histon, Cambridge, CB24 9ZR

Tel: 01223 237414
Fax: 01223 237405
E-mail: enquiries@cambscci.co.uk

Enquiries to: Chief Executive

Founded: 1917; formerly called Cambridge and District Chamber of Commerce and Industry

Organisation type and purpose: Membership association (membership is by subscription), present number of members: 1,100.
Chamber of Commerce.

Subject coverage: International trade services, relevant information and back-up services.

Collection: UK, Local and International Trade Library

Trade and statistical information: On-line access to trade statistics

Publications: Printed

Access to staff: Contact by letter, by telephone, by fax, by e-mail and in person
Hours: Mon to Fri, 0900 to 1700

Access to building: No access other than to staff
Hours: Mon to Fri, 0900 to 1700

Member of: Association of British Chambers of Commerce

CAMBRIDGESHIRE RECORDS SOCIETY

Cambridgeshire Archives, Box RES1009, Shire Hall, Castle Hill, Cambridge, CB3 0AP

Tel: 01223 716858; 01223 699399
Fax: 01223 718823
E-mail: cambs.archives@cambridgeshire.gov.uk
Website: www.cambsrecordsociety.co.uk/index.php

Enquiries to: Secretary

Founded: 1972; formerly called Cambridge Antiquarian Records Society (year of change 1987)

Organisation type and purpose: A not-for-profit record publishing society of around 120 individual and institutional members publishing texts of documentary sources and reproductions of maps, etc., relating to Cambridgeshire and adjoining areas.

Subject coverage: History of Cambridgeshire, documentary sources.

Publications: Printed
Order printed publications from: from the Society

Publications list: Available online and in print

Access to staff: Contact by letter, by telephone, by fax and by e-mail

Links with: Cambridge Antiquarian Society (CAS); Haddon Library, Faculty of Archaeology and Anthropology, Pembroke Street, Cambridge, CB2 3RA

CAMDEN LOCAL STUDIES AND ARCHIVES CENTRE

Holborn Library, 32–38 Theobalds Road, London, WC1X 8PA

Tel: 020 7974 6342
Fax: 020 7974 6284
E-mail: localstudies@camden.gov.uk
Website: www.camden.gov.uk/localstudies

Enquiries to: Senior Officer: Local Studies and Archives

Organisation type and purpose: Local government body, public library.
Archives service.

Subject coverage: Local studies, local history of Camden including Hampstead, Holborn and St Pancras, archives, conservation.

Collection: Local books and printed materials
Local newspapers
Ephemera
Local directories
Electoral registers
Illustrations
Maps
Census returns for Camden Area 1841–1901 (microfilm)
Archives of the London Borough of Camden and its predecessor bodies
Deposited archives including Highgate Cemetery registers (microfilm)
Special collections including:
Bellmoor Collection (compiled by Hampstead historian Thomas J. Barratt)
Eleanor Farjeon Collection
Heal Collection (compiled by local historian Sir Ambrose Heal on St Pancras to 1913)
Kate Greenaway Collection (available by special application only)

Non-library collection catalogue: All or part available in-house

Publications: Printed

Publications list: Available online and in print

Access to staff: Contact by letter, by telephone, by fax, by e-mail, in person and via website
Hours: Mon, Tue, 1000 to 1800, Thu, 1000 to 1900, Fri by appointment; alternate Sats, 1100 to 1700; Wed and Sun closed.
Special comments: Appointments needed for some archives held in outstore.

Parent body: London Borough of Camden; website: http://www.camden.gov.uk/

CAMPAIGN AGAINST ARMS TRADE (CAAT)

11 Goodwin Street, London, N4 3HQ

Tel: 020 7281 0297
Fax: 020 7281 4369
E-mail: enquiries@caat.org.uk
Website: www.caat.org.uk

Enquiries to: Research Co-ordinator

Founded: 1974

Organisation type and purpose: Voluntary organisation.

Subject coverage: The international arms trade.

Publications list: Available online and in print

Access to staff: Appointment necessary.
Hours: Mon to Fri, 1030 to 1730

CAMPAIGN FOR AN INDEPENDENT BRITAIN (CIB)

81 Ashmole Street, London, SW8 1NF

Tel: 020 8340 0314
Fax: 020 7582 7021

Enquiries to: Honorary Secretary
Direct tel: 020 8348 3784
Direct fax: 020 8347 8246
Other contacts: Chairman

Founded: 1976; formerly called Safeguard Britain Campaign (year of change 1983); formerly called British Anti-Common Market Campaign (year of change 1989)

Organisation type and purpose: Membership association (membership is by subscription), present number of members: 3,000.
To recoup self-government from the European Union.

Subject coverage: European Community and its impact on the United Kingdom.

Publications: Printed

Publications list: Available in print

Access to staff: Contact by letter, by telephone and by fax
Hours: Mon to Fri, 0900 to 1700

CAMPAIGN FOR FREEDOM OF INFORMATION (CFoI)

Suite 102, 16 Baldwins Gardens, London, EC1N 7RJ

Tel: 020 7831 7477
Fax: 020 7831 7461
E-mail: admin@cfoi.demon.co.uk
Website: www.cfoi.org.uk

Founded: 1984

Organisation type and purpose: Not-for-profit organisation working to improve public access to official information and ensure that the Freedom of Information Act is implemented effectively.

Subject coverage: Freedom of information. Data protection/access to personal files.

Publications: Printed

Publications list: Available online and in print

Access to staff: Contact by letter, by telephone, by fax and by e-mail
Hours: Mon to Fri, 1000 to 1600

Access to building: Prior appointment required

CAMPAIGN FOR HOMOSEXUAL EQUALITY (CHE)

CHE, c/o London Friend, 86 Caledonian Road, London, N1 9DN

Tel: 07941 914340
E-mail: secretary@c-h-e.org.uk
Website: www.c-h-e.org.uk/

Enquiries to: Secretary

Founded: 1969

Organisation type and purpose: Membership association (membership is by subscription), present number of members: 200, voluntary organisation.
Pressure group.
To promote acceptance of homosexuality.

Subject coverage: Discrimination against homosexuals and bisexuals.

Publications: Printed, and electronic and video

Publications list: Available in print

Access to staff: Contact by letter and by telephone
Hours: Mon to Fri, 0900 to 1700

CAMPAIGN FOR NATIONAL PARKS (CNP)

6–7 Barnard Mews, London, SW11 1QU

Tel: 020 7924 4077
Fax: 020 7924 5761
E-mail: info@cnp.org.uk
Website: www.cnp.org.uk

Enquiries to: Chief Executive

Founded: 1936

Organisation type and purpose: Voluntary organisation, registered charity (charity number 295336).

Subject coverage: National Parks of England and Wales; conservation and protection.

Publications: Printed

Publications list: Available online and in print

Access to staff: Contact by letter, by telephone, by e-mail and via website. Appointment necessary. Non-members charged.
Hours: Mon to Fri, 0900 to 1700

Access to building: Prior appointment required

Member organisations: over 40 organisations

CAMPAIGN FOR PRESS AND BROADCASTING FREEDOM (CPBF)

2nd Floor, Vi & Garner Smith House, 23, Orford Road, Walthamstow, London, E17 9NL

Tel: 07729 846146
E-mail: freepress@cpbf.org.uk
Website: www.cpbf.org.uk

Enquiries to: National Organiser

Founded: 1979

Organisation type and purpose: Membership association, voluntary organisation, research organisation.
Campaign for diversity and democracy in the media.

Subject coverage: Media ownership, right of reply, new media technologies, democracy and diversity in the media.

Collection: Books and videos on media issues

Publications: Printed
Order printed publications from: CPBF

Access to staff: Contact by letter, by telephone, by e-mail, in person and via website. Appointment necessary.
Hours: Mon to Fri, 1000 to 1800

Access to building: Prior appointment required

Access for disabled people: Level entry

CAMPAIGN FOR REAL ALE LIMITED (CAMRA)

230 Hatfield Road, St Albans, Hertfordshire, AL1 4LW

Tel: 01727 867201
Fax: 01727 867670
E-mail: camra@camra.org.uk
Website: www.camra.org.uk

Enquiries to: Research and Information Manager
Direct tel: 01727 798449
Direct e-mail: iain.loe@camra.org.uk

Founded: 1971

Organisation type and purpose: National organisation, membership association (membership is by subscription), present number of members: 118,000, voluntary organisation, publishing house.
Consumer organisation.
To act as the champion of the consumer in relation to the UK drinks industry.

Subject coverage: Brewing industry, traditional beer and public houses, consumer protection, foreign breweries and beer.

Services for disabled people: Tapes of members' newspaper available.

Collection: Issues of What's Brewing – the newspaper of the campaign – back to the early 70s
Good Beer Guides back to 1st edition 1974

Trade and statistical information: Some statistics on the UK Brewing Industry

Publications: Printed

Access to staff: Contact by letter, by telephone, by fax, by e-mail and via website. Appointment necessary.
Hours: Mon to Fri, 0900 to 1700

Access to building: Prior appointment required
Hours: Mon to Fri, 0900 to 1700

Access for disabled people: Parking provided

Links with: European Beer Consumer Union (EBCU); 230 Hatfield Road, St Albans, Hertfordshire, AL1 4LW; tel: 01727 867201; fax: 01727 867670; e-mail: ebcu@camra.org.uk

CAMPAIGN FOR STATE EDUCATION (CASE)

98 Erlanger Road, London, SE14 5TH

Tel: 07932 149942
E-mail: case@casenet.org.uk
Website: www.casenet.org.uk

Enquiries to: Contact

Founded: 1963; formerly called Campaign for the Advancement of State Education

Organisation type and purpose: Membership association (membership is by subscription), voluntary organisation.
Education campaign group.

Subject coverage: State education, funding, class size, contacts, government policy, comprehensive education.

Publications: Printed

Publications list: Available online and in print

Access to staff: Contact by letter, by telephone, by fax and by e-mail

Access to building: No access other than to staff

CAMPAIGN FOR THE PROTECTION OF RURAL WALES (CPRW)

Ty Gwyn, 31 High Street, Welshpool, Powys, SY21 7YD

Tel: 01938 552525 or 556212
Fax: 01938 552741
E-mail: info@cprwmail.org.uk
Website: www.cprw.org.uk

Enquiries to: Liaison Officer

Founded: 1928; formerly called Council for the Protection of Rural Wales

Organisation type and purpose: Voluntary organisation, registered charity (charity number 239899).
Protection of Wales countryside and coasts from inappropriate development.

Subject coverage: Active protection of the Welsh countryside and its villages; planning; amenities; legislation.

Collection: Library of environmental publications

Publications: Printed

Access to staff: Contact by e-mail and via website. Appointment necessary.
Hours: Mon to Fri, 0900 to 1700

CAMPAIGN TO PROTECT RURAL ENGLAND – DORSET BRANCH (Dorset CPRE)

The Little Keep, Bridport Road, Dorchester, Dorset, DT1 1SQ

Tel: 01305 265808
E-mail: info@dorset-cpre.org.uk
Website: www.dorset-cpre.org.uk

Enquiries to: Director

Founded: 1926

Organisation type and purpose: Membership association (membership is by subscription), voluntary organisation, registered charity (charity number 211974).

continued overleaf

To improve, protect and preserve for the benefit of the public, the countryside and the country towns and villages of the county of Dorset.

Subject coverage: Planning procedures appropriate to county structure plan, minerals and waste local plans, district and borough local plans and planning applications within the county; issues relevant to the protection of the countryside; litter and transport issues.

Publications: Printed

Access to staff: Contact by letter, by telephone, by e-mail and via website. Appointment necessary.
Hours: Tue, 0900 to 1600; and most Thu, 0900 to 1500
Special comments: 24-hour answerphone

National office: Campaign to Protect Rural England (CPRE); 5–11 Lavington Street, London, SE1 0NZ; tel: 020 7981 2800; fax: 020 7981 2899; e-mail: info@cpre.org.uk; website: www.cpre.org.uk

CAMPAIGN TO PROTECT RURAL ENGLAND – OXFORDSHIRE BRANCH (CPRE Oxfordshire)

Punches Barn, Waterperry Road, Holton, Oxfordshire, OX33 1PP

Tel: 01865 874780
E-mail: campaign@cpreoxon.org.uk
Website: www.cpreoxon.org.uk

Enquiries to: Campaign Manager
Direct e-mail: campaign@cpreoxon.org.uk

Founded: 1931

Organisation type and purpose:
Membership association (membership is by subscription).
A company limited by guarantee, registered in England, number 04443278.
Registered charity (charity number 1093081).
Branch of the national charity.

Subject coverage: Protection of the local countryside, planning applications, transport, development, conservation issues relating to rural environment, hedgerows, dry stone walls.

Publications: Printed
Order printed publications from: Order directly from the office. Please send cheques payable to CPRE Oxfordshire.

Access to staff: Contact by letter, by telephone, by e-mail and via website. Appointment necessary.
Hours: Mon, Tue, Thu and Fri, 1000 to 1300
Special comments: Officer is only part-time.

CAMPAIGN TO PROTECT RURAL ENGLAND – SHROPSHIRE BRANCH (CPRE Shropshire)

c/o Stags Head, New Invention, Bucknell, Shropshire, SY7 0BS

Tel: 01547 528546
E-mail: admin@cpreshropshire.org.uk
Website: www.cpreshropshire.org.uk

Enquiries to: Administrator

Founded: 1926

Organisation type and purpose:
Membership association (membership is by subscription), present number of members: 550, voluntary organisation, registered charity (charity number 218782), suitable for ages: all. Promotes the beauty, tranquillity and communities of Shropshire.

Subject coverage: Environmental conservation.

Access to staff: Contact by letter, by telephone and by e-mail
Hours: Mon to Fri, 1000 to 1600
Special comments: The regional office is not open to visitors. National office is open Monday to Friday inclusive.

National Office at: Campaign to Protect Rural England; 5–11 Lavington Street, London, SE1 0NZ; tel: 020 7981 2800; fax: 020 7981 2899

CAMPBELL HOOPER

35 Old Queen Street, London, SW1H 9JD

Tel: 020 7222 9070
Fax: 020 7222 5591
E-mail: sa@campbellhooperco.co.uk

Enquiries to: Partner
Direct tel: 020 7654 5115
Direct fax: 020 7654 5226

Founded: 1760

Organisation type and purpose: Solicitors. Legal advice, transactional work and litigation.

Subject coverage: Computer software copyright issues, intellectual property advice and litigation, employment, commercial property, company law and commercial law, private client and trust issues.
Order printed publications from: Marketing Administrator, Campbell Hooper
35 Old Queen Street, London, SW1H 9JD, tel: 020 7222 9070, fax: 020 7222 5591, e-mail: marketing@campbellhooper.com

Publications list: Available online

Access to staff: Contact by letter, by telephone, by fax, by e-mail and via website. Appointment necessary.
Hours: Mon to Fri, 0900 to 1800

CAMPDEN BRI

Chipping Campden, Gloucestershire, GL55 6LD

Tel: 01386 842000
Fax: 01386 842100
E-mail: info@campden.co.uk
Website: www.campden.co.uk

Enquiries to: Information Officer
Direct tel: 01386 842045
Direct e-mail: info@campden.co.uk

Founded: 1919; created by the merger of Campden & Chorleywood Food Research Association and Brewing Research International (year of change 2008); formerly called Campden Food and Drink Research Association (year of change 1995); formerly called Campden & Chorleywood Food Research Association (year of change 2008)

Organisation type and purpose:
Consultancy, research organisation.

Subject coverage: Food science and technology associated with the preservation (canning, aseptic, chill, modified atmosphere packaging, freezing, dehydration) of foods, microbiology, chemistry, biochemistry and sensory quality evaluation of processed foods, suitability of raw materials for processing.

Collection: Old books on milling and baking equipment and products

Publications list: Available online

Access to staff: Contact by letter, by telephone, by fax, by e-mail and via website. Non-members charged.
Hours: Mon to Fri, 0900 to 1700

CAMPING AND CARAVANNING CLUB

Greenfield House, Westwood Way, Coventry, Warwickshire, CV4 8JH

Tel: 0845 130 7632
Website: www.campingandcaravanningclub.co.uk

Enquiries to: Public Relations Manager
Direct e-mail: jon.dale@thefriendlyclub.co.uk
Other contacts: Public Relations Executive

Founded: 1901; formerly called Camping Club of Great Britain and Ireland

Organisation type and purpose:
Membership association.
Owning and running over 100 campsites on behalf of members, although most sites are also open to non-members.

Subject coverage: Technical assistance to members with tents, caravans, trailer tents, motor caravans. General assistance on camping law and information to official bodies, media, trade, etc.

Collection: Historical archives relative to the club and camping in general

Access to staff: Contact by letter, by telephone and by e-mail
Hours: Mon to Fri, 0845 to 1645

Access for disabled people: Parking provided, lift
Special comments: Access to all floors

CANADA WOOD UK

PO Box 1, Farnborough, Hampshire, GU14 6WE

Tel: 01252 522545
Fax: 01252 522546
E-mail: office@canadawooduk.org
Website: www.canadawooduk.org

Enquiries to: UK Consultant

History of institution: incorporates the former CertiWood, Coastal Forest Products Association (CFPA), Council of Forest Industries (COFI), Ontario Wood Products Export Association (OWPEA), Quebec Wood Export Bureau (QWEB), Western Red Cedar Export Association (WRCEA).

Organisation type and purpose: Industry association and advisory body representing, in the United Kingdom, Canadian timber and wood products manufacturers through various agencies and associations.

Providing technical information and advice on member-company products to architects, engineers, specifiers, consumers and the construction and wood-utilising industries generally.

Subject coverage: Technical advisory service for application and use of wood and plywood in construction.

Information services: RIBA-accredited CPD presentations, technical literature and free advice over the phone.

Education services: RIBA-accredited CPD presentations on Canadian wood products, western red cedar, temperate hardwoods, timber buildings and green design.

Trade and statistical information: Worldwide exports of Canadian timber and plywood

Publications: Printed

Access to staff: Contact by letter, by telephone, by fax and by e-mail. Appointment necessary.
Hours: Mon to Fri, 0900 to 1700

Also at: Maritime Lumber Bureau; PO Box 459, Amherst, Nova Scotia, B4H 4A1, Canada; tel: +1 902 667 3889; fax: +1 902 667 0401

CANADA-UNITED KINGDOM CHAMBER OF COMMERCE

38 Grosvenor Street, London, W1K 4DP

Tel: 020 7258 6578
Fax: 020 7258 6594
E-mail: info@canada-uk.org
Website: www.canada-uk.org

Enquiries to: Membership & Events Co-ordinator
Direct tel: 020 7258 6578

Founded: 1921

Organisation type and purpose: Membership association (membership is by subscription), present number of corporate members: 300 approx.

Subject coverage: Enquiries about trade and investment between Canada and the UK in both directions.

Publications: Printed

Access to staff: Contact by letter, by telephone, by fax, by e-mail, in person and via website. Appointment necessary. Non-members charged.
Hours: Mon to Fri, 0900 to 1730

CANAL & RIVER TRUST

First Floor North, Station House, 500 Elder Gate, Milton Keynes, MK9 1BB

Tel: 0303 040 4040
E-mail: customer.services@canalrivertrust.org.uk
Website: canalrivertrust.org.uk

Direct tel: 24-hour emergency contact: tel. 0800 4799947

Founded: 2012

Organisation type and purpose: Registered charity (charity number 1146792) been set up to care for 2,000 miles of historic waterways in England and Wales.

Subject coverage: 200-year-old network of canals and rivers, as well as docks and reservoirs, along with museums, archives and the country's third largest collection of protected historic buildings.

Access to staff: *Hours:* Mon to Fri, 0800 to 1800

CANCER PREVENTION RESEARCH TRUST

231 Roehampton Lane, London, SW15 4LB

Tel: 020 8785 7786
Fax: 020 8785 6466
E-mail: cprt@talk21.com
Website: www.cancerpreventionresearch.org.uk

Enquiries to: Director

Founded: 1973

Organisation type and purpose: International organisation, national organisation, voluntary organisation, registered charity (charity number 265985), research organisation.

Subject coverage: Cancer prevention, cancer research.

Publications: Printed

Access to staff: Contact by letter, by telephone, by fax, by e-mail, in person and via website
Hours: Mon to Fri, 0900 to 1700

Access to building: No prior appointment required.

Access for disabled people: Toilet facilities.

CANNING HOUSE LIBRARY (HLBC)

Formal name: Hispanic and Luso-Brazilian Council

Hispanic and Luso-Brazilian Council, Canning House, 2 Belgrave Square, London, SW1X 8PJ

Tel: 020 7235 2303
Fax: 020 7838 9258
E-mail: library@canninghouse.org
Website: www.canninghouse.org

Enquiries to: Library and Information Services Manager
Direct tel: ext. 208
Direct e-mail: library@canninghouse.org

Founded: 1943

Organisation type and purpose: Registered charity, cultural lending and reference library (65,000 vols).
Promotes relations between the UK and Latin America, Spain and Portugal.

Subject coverage: Most subjects relating to Latin America, the Caribbean, Portugal and its former colonies, and Spain, including history, archaeology, politics, economics, sociology, anthropology, religion, geography, natural history, travel, literature, language, art, music, cinema, food and drink.

Collection: R. B. Cunninghame Graham Collection
W. H. Hudson Collection
George Canning Collection
Rare books (travel accounts, history, literature and language, religion, anthropology, natural history, etc.)
Feature films from Latin America, Spain and Portugal, on DVD and video

Non-library collection catalogue: All or part available online and in-house

Library catalogue: All or part available online

Publications: Printed
Order printed publications from: Worldwide Subscription Services, e-mail: enquiries@worldwidesubscriptions.com

Publications list: Available online

Access to staff: Contact by letter, by telephone, by fax, by e-mail, in person and via website
Hours: Mon to Fri, 1400 to 1800

Links with: ACLAIIR, REDIAL, SALALM

CANTERBURY CATHEDRAL ARCHIVES (CCA)

The Precincts, Canterbury, Kent, CT1 2EH

Tel: 01227 865330, 01622 605249 (minicom)
Fax: 01227 865222
E-mail: archives@canterbury-cathedral.org
Website: www.canterbury-cathedral.org/archives.html

Enquiries to: Archivist / Manager
Other contacts: Canon Librarian

Founded: 597

Organisation type and purpose: Local government body.
Cathedral archives.

Subject coverage: Archives relating to Canterbury, especially the Cathedral, City, Diocese and Archdeaconry parishes.

Collection: Archives of Christ Church, dating from the 8th century, including charters, financial records and manorial records
Archives of the post-Reformation Dean and Chapter, to the present day, including photographs and architectural drawings
Records of the City of Canterbury, dating from the 12th century
Records of the Diocese of Canterbury
Parish records for Church of England parishes in the Archdeaconry of Canterbury
Records of individuals, families, businesses and organisations in the district of Canterbury
Collections of artefacts

Non-library collection catalogue: All or part available online and in-house

Publications: Microform publications

Publications list: Available online and in print

Access to staff: Contact by letter, by telephone, by fax, by e-mail, in person and via website. Appointment necessary.
Hours: Mon to Thu, 0900 to 1700; 1st and 3rd Sat, 0900 to 1300

Access for disabled people: Parking provided, subject to availability
Special comments: Lift to search room; hearing loop.

continued overleaf

Parent body: Dean and Chapter of Canterbury; Cathedral House, The Precincts, Canterbury, CT1 2EH; tel: 01227 762862; fax: 01227 865222; Kent County Council; Sessions House, County Hall, Maidstone, Kent, ME14 1XQ; tel: 08458 247247; fax: 01622 697186

CANTERBURY CATHEDRAL LIBRARY (CCL)

The Precincts, Canterbury, Kent, CT1 2EH

Tel: 01227 865287
Fax: 01227 865222
E-mail: library@canterbury-cathedral.org
Website: www.canterbury-cathedral.org
Website: opac.ukc.ac.uk

Enquiries to: Librarian
Direct tel: 01227 865288
Direct e-mail: librarian@canterbury-cathedral.org
Other contacts: Canon Librarian

Founded: 597

Organisation type and purpose: Registered charity.
Cathedral library.

Subject coverage: Church history, Kentish history, bibliography, anti-slavery literature, early natural science books, printed historical sources, Oxford Movement, Roman Catholic controversy.

Collection: 50,000 books in total: 30,000 pre-19th-century books and pamphlets held on computer database
Anti-slave trade tracts (19th century)
Herbals and other natural history books
Howley-Harrison Library (12,800 books bequeathed by Benjamin Harrison, Archdeacon of Maidstone, 1887)
Local history and cathedral history collection
Mendham Collection on Roman Catholic Controversy
Parish collections for Elham and Preston-next-Wingham

Library catalogue: All or part available online and in print

Publications: Printed
Order printed publications from: e-mail: canterburysources@canterbury-cathedral.org
Adam Matthews Publications, Marlborough, Wiltshire (for the Cathedral pre-1801 catalogue)

Access to staff: Contact by letter, by telephone, by e-mail and via website. Appointment necessary.
Hours: Mon to Thu, 0900 to 1700; 1st and 3rd Sat, 0900 to 1300

Access for disabled people: Parking provided
Special comments: Lift to first floor where library is situated.

Affiliated to the: University of Kent at Canterbury; tel: 01227 764000

Parent body: Dean and Chapter of Canterbury Cathedral; The Precincts, Canterbury, CT1 2EH; tel: 01227 762862

CANTERBURY CHRIST CHURCH UNIVERSITY – LIBRARY

North Holmes Road, Canterbury, Kent, CT1 1QU

Tel: 01227 767700
Fax: 01227 470442
Website: www.canterbury.ac.uk/library

Enquiries to: Director of Library Services
Direct tel: 01227 782352

Founded: 1962

Organisation type and purpose: University library.

Subject coverage: Applied social sciences, art, business and management studies, education, English and language studies, geography, history, IT, law and criminal justice studies, media, music, nursing and allied health professions, religious studies, social work, and sports science.

Collection: Elizabeth Gaskell Collection

Library catalogue: All or part available online

Access to staff: Contact by letter, by telephone, by e-mail, in person and via website. Non-members charged.
Hours: Mon to Fri, 0900 to 1700

Access to building: *Hours:* Main library: Mon to Fri, 0730 to 2100; Sat, Sun, 0900 to 1700

Access for disabled people: Building is fully accessible

Also at: Broadstairs Learning Centre; Northwood Road, Broadstairs, CT10 2WA; tel: 01843 609103; website: http://www.canterbury.ac.uk/library
Salomons Campus; David Salomons Estate, Broomhill Road, Southborough, Tunbridge Wells, TN3 0TG; tel: 01895 507516; website: http://www.canterbury.ac.uk/library

CANTERBURY CITY COUNCIL

Military Road, Canterbury, Kent, CT1 1YW

Tel: 01227 862000
Fax: 01227 862020
E-mail: firstname.familyname@canterbury.gov.uk
Website: www.canterbury.co.uk

Enquiries to: Chief Executive

Founded: 1974

Organisation type and purpose: Local government body.

Subject coverage: Local government.

Access to staff: Contact by letter, by telephone, by fax, by e-mail, in person and via website. Appointment necessary.
Hours: Mon to Fri, 0900 to 1700

CAPEL

Formal name: Capel: The Chapels Heritage Society

5 Cuffnell Close, Liddell Park, Llandudno, Conwy, LL30 1UX

Tel: 01492 860449
E-mail: obadiah1@btinternet.com
Website: www.capeli.org.uk

Enquiries to: Honoury Secretary
Other contacts: Treasurer for subscription/membership

Organisation type and purpose: Membership association (membership is by subscription), present number of members: 300, voluntary organisation, registered charity (charity number 518411).
Presentation of the nonconformist heritage of Wales.

Subject coverage: Nonconformist history, chapels in Wales.

Publications: Printed

Publications list: Available online and in print

Access to staff: Contact by letter and by e-mail
Hours: Mon to Fri, 0900 to 1700

CAPEL MANOR COLLEGE

Bullsmore Lane, Enfield, Middlesex, EN1 4RQ

Tel: 08456 122122
Fax: 01992 717544
E-mail: enquiries@capel.ac.uk
Website: www.capel.ac.uk/

Enquiries to: Student Registrar

History of institution: formerly called Capel Manor Horticultural and Environmental Centre

Organisation type and purpose: Further education college.
Specialist horticultural college and gardens open to the public.

Subject coverage: Horticulture, garden design, arboriculture, countryside management, floristry, balloon artistry.

Library catalogue: All or part available in-house

Access to staff: Contact by letter, by telephone and by e-mail. Appointment necessary.
Hours: Mon to Fri, 0900 to 1700

Access for disabled people: Parking provided, level entry, access to all public areas, toilet facilities

Also at: Capel Manor College at Castle Green; Gale Street, Dagenham, RM9 4UN; tel: 020 8724 1528; Capel Manor College at Crystal Palace; Crystal Palace Park, Ledrington Road, SE19 2BS; tel: 020 8778 5572; Capel Manor College at Gunnersbury Park; Popes Lane, Gunnersbury Park, Acton, W3 8LQ; tel: 020 8993 6266; fax: 020 8993 6266; Capel Manor College at Regent's Park; The Store Yard, Inner Circle, Regent's Park, NW1 4NR; tel: 020 7486 7930

CAPRI CLUB (INTERNATIONAL) (CCI)

Capri Club HQ, Badgers Hill, Sheriffs Lench, Evesham, Worcestershire, WR11 4SN

Tel: 01386 860860
Fax: 01386 861455
E-mail: capriclub@btclick.com
Website: www.capriclub.co.uk/

Enquiries to: Membership Secretary
Founded: 1983; formerly called Capri 70 Owners Club, Capri Owners Club.

Organisation type and purpose: Membership association (membership is by subscription), present number of members: 8,000.

Subject coverage: Ford Capris 1969 to 1987.

Publications: Printed, and electronic and video

Access to staff: Contact by letter, by telephone, by fax, by e-mail and in person
Hours: Mon to Fri, 0900 to 1700

CARADON DISTRICT COUNCIL

Luxstowe House, Liskeard, Cornwall, PL14 3DZ

Tel: 01579 341000, 01579 341010 (minicom)
Fax: 01579 341001
E-mail: postroom@caradon.gov.uk
Website: www.caradon.gov.uk

Enquiries to: Chief Executive
Direct tel: 01579 341022
Direct fax: 01579 341002
Other contacts: Corporate Communications Officer for public relations and media enquiries.

Founded: 1974

Organisation type and purpose: Local government body.

Access to staff: Contact by letter, by telephone, by fax, by e-mail and in person. Appointment necessary.
Hours: Mon to Fri, 0830 to 1700

Access for disabled people: Parking provided, ramped entry, toilet facilities

CARDIFF LIBRARIES

Cardiff Central Library, The Hayes, Cardiff, CF10 1FL

Tel: 029 2038 2116
Fax: 029 2078 0989
E-mail: centrallibrary@cardiff.gov.uk
Website: www.cardiff.gov.uk/libraries

Enquiries to: Central Library Manager
Direct e-mail: nrichards@cardiff.gov.uk
Other contacts: Adult Non-Fiction; Children's Librarian; Community Languages Librarian; Information Librarian; Leisure Librarian; Local Studies Librarian; Music Librarian; Stock Manager; Welsh Librarian

Founded: 1882; formerly called South Glamorgan County Libraries (year of change 1996)

Organisation type and purpose: Local government body, public library.

Subject coverage: Adult Non-Fiction department: business, law, education, history, art, language and literature, military studies, social sciences, religion and philosophy, transport, life sciences, geography, science and technology, travel, gardening, food and drink.
Music department: books, scores, CDs, DVDs, performance area and baby grand piano.
Information department: business and commercial directories for UK and worldwide, telephone directories for UK, Eire, Jersey and Guernsey, British Standards online, statistical information, European Union information, census statistics, maps and atlases, community information, National Assembly for Wales linked libraries collection, trade journals.
Cardiff Capital Collection: local studies and geneaology, census returns.
The Wales Collection: material in Welsh and English relating to Wales.
Leisure Library includes: fiction, talking books, DVDs, biographies, newsroom.
Children's Library Service.
Community Languages Department: 14 community languages.

Collection: Manuscripts, fine bindings, private press books, early printed books, limited editions
Cardiff Local Collection including photographs, maps and newspapers

Non-library collection catalogue: All or part available in-house

Library catalogue: All or part available online

Access to staff: Contact by letter, by telephone, by fax, by e-mail, in person and via website
Hours: Mon, Tue, Wed, Fri, 0900 to 1800; Thu, 0900 to 1900; Sat, 0900 to 1730; Sun, 1100 to 1500 ground floor only

Access for disabled people: Level entry, access to all public areas, toilet facilities, lifts to all floors.

Parent body: Cardiff County Council; Housing and Neighbourhood Renewal

CARDIFF METROPOLITAN UNIVERSITY (Cardiff Met)

Western Avenue, Llandaff, Cardiff, CF5 2YB

Tel: 029 2041 6240
Fax: 029 2041 6908
Website: www.cardiffmet.ac.uk/lis

Enquiries to: Head of Library Division
Direct tel: 029 2041 6240
Direct e-mail: eadamson@cardiffmet.ac.uk

Founded: 1976

Organisation type and purpose: University department or institute.

Subject coverage: Business; computing; food science and technology; education; art education; physical education; human movement and sport studies; art and design; applied sciences; health and social sciences; product design.

Services for disabled people: Hearing loops, lift access, toilet facilities, seating, assistance with accessing items from shelves.

Collection: Cardiff School of Art & Design Ceramic Archive; Artist's books collection.

Trade and statistical information: N/A

Library catalogue: All or part available online

Access to staff: Contact by letter, by telephone, by fax, by e-mail and via website. Letter of introduction required.
Hours: Mon to Fri, 0900 to 1700, Sat, 1000 to 1530; (All). Sun, 1200 to 1630 (Cyncoed and Llandaff only).

Access to building: Prior appointment required

Access for disabled people: Parking provided (pay and display payment), level entry, access to all public areas, toilet facilities

Other addresses: Cyncoed Learning Centre, Cardiff Metropolitan University; Cyncoed Road, Cardiff, CF23 6XD; tel: 029 2041 6242; e-mail: Cyncoedlibrary@cardiffmet.ac.uk; Howard Gardens Learning Centre, Cardiff Metropolitan University; Howard Gardens, Cardiff, CF24 0SP; tel: 029 2041 6243; e-mail: Howardgardenslibrary@cardiffmet.ac.uk; Llandaff Learning Centre, Cardiff Metropolitan University; Western Avenue, Llandaff, Cardiff, CF5 2YB; tel: 029 2041 6244; e-mail: Llandafflibrary@cardiffmet.ac.uk

CARDIFF NATURALISTS SOCIETY

The Library, National Museum Wales, Cathays Park, Cardiff, CF10 3NP

Tel: 029 2057 3202
E-mail: library@museumwales.ac.uk

Enquiries to: Librarian

Founded: 1867

Organisation type and purpose: Learned society.

Subject coverage: Natural history of the Glamorgan area; zoology; ornithology; botany; entomology.

Collection: Library, mainly periodicals via exchange agreements
Morrey Salmon Ornithology Archive

Library catalogue: All or part available in-house

Publications: Printed

Access to staff: Contact by letter, by telephone and by fax. Appointment necessary.
Hours: Tue to Fri, 1000 to 1700

Access for disabled people: Parking provided, ramped entry, toilet facilities
Special comments: Lift.

CARDIFF UNIVERSITY – HEALTH LIBRARY

Heath Park, Cardiff, CF14 4YU

Tel: 029 2068 8131
E-mail: healthlibrary@cf.ac.uk
Website: cardiff.ac.uk/insrv/libraries

Enquiries to: Director of Library Services
Direct e-mail: library@cf.ac.uk

Founded: 1931; formerly called Welsh National School of Medicine Library; formerly called University of Wales College of Medicine (year of change 2004); incorporates the former Combined Training Institute, Institute of Healthcare Studies, South East Wales Institute of Nursing and Midwifery

Organisation type and purpose: University library.
NHS library.

Subject coverage: Medicine; dentistry; nursing (including relevant sociology and social sciences); basic medical sciences;

continued overleaf

professions allied to medicine; library and information sciences (especially academic medical and life sciences).

Collection: Health and Safety
Historical collection (medicine and some dentistry)

Non-library collection catalogue: All or part available online and in-house

Library catalogue: All or part available online

Publications: Printed

Access to staff: Contact by letter, by telephone, by fax and by e-mail. Appointment necessary.
Hours: Duthie Library: Sep to Jun: Mon to Fri, 0900 to 2100; Sat, 0900 to 1700; Jul and Aug: Mon to Fri, 0900 to 1900; Sat, 0900 to 1230
Special comments: Full library service provided to NHS employees in South Glamorgan; extension services to NHS employees throughout Wales; fee for some services for external users. Certain services to staff and students of Welsh HE institutions.

Access for disabled people: Parking provided, level entry, access to all public areas
Special comments: Located within hospital building.

Branch libraries: Cardiff University; Library, School of Nursing Studies, Grounds of St Cadoc's Hospital, Caerleon, Newport, NP6 1XR; tel: 01633 430919; fax: 01633 430717; e-mail: caerleonliby@cf.ac.uk; Cardiff University; Library, School of Nursing & Healthcare Studies, Ty Dewi Sant Building, Heath Park, Cardiff, CF4 4XN; tel: 029 2068 7713; fax: 029 2068 7715; e-mail: healthcliby@cardiff.ac.uk; Cardiff University; Sir Herbert Duthie Medical Library, Heath Park, Cardiff, CF14 4XN; tel: 029 2074 2875; fax: 029 2074 3651; e-mail: duthieliby@cf.ac.uk; Cardiff University; Brian Cooke Dental Library, Heath Park, Cardiff, CF4 4XY; tel: 029 2074 2523; fax: 029 2074 3651; e-mail: dentliby@cf.ac.uk; University of Wales College of Medicine; Cancer Research Wales Library, Velindre Hospital, Whitchurch, Cardiff, CF4 7XL; tel: 029 2031 6291; fax: 029 2031 6927; e-mail: crwlibrary@wales.nhs.uk; University of Wales College of Medicine; Archie Cochrane Library, University Hospital Llandough, Penarth, CF64 2XX; tel: 029 2071 1711, extn 5497; e-mail: cochraneliby@cf.ac.uk

Member organisation of: All-Wales Health Information and Libraries Extension Service (AWHILES); NHS Regional Librarians Group; Standing Conference of National University Libraries; University Medical School Librarians Group; Welsh Higher Education Libraries' Forum (WHELF)

CARDIFF UNIVERSITY – INFORMATION SERVICES

PO Box 430, Cardiff, CF24 0DE

Tel: 029 2087 4818
Fax: 029 2037 1921
E-mail: library@cardiff.ac.uk
Website: www.cardiff.ac.uk/insrv

Enquiries to: Director of Libraries and University Librarian.
Direct e-mail: petersjm@cardiff.ac.uk

Founded: 1883; formerly called University of Wales, Cardiff, Library

Organisation type and purpose: University library.
Information service.

Subject coverage: Humanities, religious studies, education, music, social sciences, law, Welsh language, literature, history and culture, archaeology, language, literature and history of other Celtic countries, engineering, biosciences, optometry, pharmacy, physics, chemistry, earth sciences, architecture, business studies, town planning, computer studies, journalism, mathematics, medicine, nursing and health care.

Collection: Library:
- British, EU, and UN official publications collections (19th–20th C.)
- Newspapers (Welsh and British, 19th–20th C.)
- Salisbury Library (Welsh and Celtic, 16th–20th C.)
- Ballads and Almanacks collections (18th–19th C.)
- Ann Griffiths collection (18th–20th C.)
- Carmarthen Presbyterian College collection (17th–19th C)
- Architecture Rare Books collection (18th–20th C.)
- Tennyson collection (19th C.)
- Prints and Illustrations collections (17th–19th C.)
- Marburger Index (Art and Architecture)
- History Research Collection (Ancient and Medieval reprints)
- Trade Union, Labour and Cabinet collections (print and microfilm)
- History of Human/Medical Genetics (20th C.)
- Historical Music Collections (18th–20th C.)
- Historical Travel and Atlases collection (17th–20th C.)
- History of Medicine collections (16th–20th C.)
- Bibles collection (15th–20th C.)
- Incunabula collection (15th C.)
- Continental rare books (16th–18th C.)
- Private Presses collection (19th–20thC.)
- Restoration Drama collection (17th C.)
- British rare books collection (16th–18th C.)
- Children's Literature collections (19th C.)
- Corvey Collection (microfiche 18th C.)
- Medieval Welsh literary manuscripts (microfilm, 12th–15th C.)
- Osman photojournalism collection (20th C.)
- Historical British Journals (19th–20th C.)
- Spanish Civil War collections (pamphlets, microfilm, newspapers)

Archives:
- Archive and Manuscript collections including those of Edward Thomas (d. 1917), Enoch Salisbury, Hugh Cudlipp, Morfydd Owen, Grace Williams, Herbert Mackworth, Sir Julian Hodge, Archie Cochrane and associates in the CHEHC archives, Daily Mirror journalists papers, UCAC archive, Ben Morse papers, Pharmacy Prescription volumes, etc.

Non-library collection catalogue: All or part available online

Library catalogue: All or part available online

Publications list: Available online

Access to staff: Contact by letter, by telephone, by e-mail and in person
Hours: 0900 to 1700

Access to building: No prior appointment required

Access for disabled people: Parking provided, ramped entry, level entry, toilet facilities
Special comments: Cardiff University Information Services are distributed across the campus. All areas are accessible but by different means – some areas ramped or level entry.

CARDIFF UNIVERSITY – RESEARCH AND COMMERCIAL DIVISION

7th Floor, 30–36 Newport Road, Cardiff, CF24 0DE

Tel: 029 2087 5834
Fax: 029 2087 4189
E-mail: whittinghamj@cf.ac.uk
Website: www.cardiff.ac.uk/racdv

Enquiries to: Research Information Officer

History of institution: formerly called Cardiff University, Research and Consultancy Division, Cardiff University

Organisation type and purpose: University Division, consultancy, research policy, research support, research funding, University expertise, technology transfer, IP, business development, commercial support.

Subject coverage: Architecture, semiconductors, engineering, pharmacy, computing, geology, marine research, magnetics technology, aerospace, chemistry, motors, astronomy, insect biology, systems dynamics, EDI, Cardiff University Innovation Network, planning, optometry, medicine, dentistry, nursing, health care, social sciences, history, archaeology, religion, politics, music, Welsh, journalism, English, philosophy, business, physics, biosciences, languages, psychology, law.

Library catalogue: All or part available online

Publications: Printed

Access to staff: Contact by e-mail and via website
Hours: Mon to Fri, 0800 to 1600

CARE FOR THE WILD INTERNATIONAL (CWI)

The Granary, Tickfold Farm, Marches Road, Kingsfold, Horsham, West Sussex, RH12 3SE

Tel: 01306 627900
Fax: 01306 627901
E-mail: info@careforthewild.com
Website: www.careforthewild.com

Enquiries to: Reception & Administration
Other contacts: Cashier & Administration

Founded: 1984

Organisation type and purpose: Registered charity (charity number 288802).
To alleviate suffering and the exploitation of wildlife around the world.

Subject coverage: A charity dedicated to the conservation and welfare of wildlife around the world. Working with partners, to protect wildlife and its habitat, rescue and rehabilitate displaced wild animals, and act as a global voice for wildlife protection through campaigns, research and education.

Information services: Information on wildlife issues and the charity's work.

Publications: Printed
Order printed publications from: tel: 01306 627900; or e-mail: info@careforthewild.com

Publications list: Available in print

Access to staff: Contact by letter, by telephone, by fax, by e-mail, in person and via website. Appointment necessary.
Hours: Mon to Fri, 0900 to 1700

Also at: Care for the Wild Kenya; PO Box 34334, Nairobi, Kenya; tel: +254 2 21977/8; fax: +254 2 219717

CARE PROGRAMME APPROACH ASSOCIATION (CPA Association)

Walton Hospital, Whitecoats Lane, Chesterfield, Derbyshire, S40 3HW

Tel: 01246 515975
Fax: 01246 515976
E-mail: cpa.association@derbyshcft.nhs.uk

Enquiries to: CPAA Lead Officer
Direct tel: 01246 515 975
Direct fax: 01246 515974
Direct e-mail: cpa.association@derbyshcft.nhs.uk
Other contacts: Secretary

Founded: 1996

Organisation type and purpose: The CPAA has been established to support the implementation, operation and development of the Care Programme Approach and care standards. The Association is endorsed by the Department of Health in their document 'Modernising the CPA' and membership is recommended in the CPA Audit pack. The main objections and functions of the CPA Association are to:
Act as a learned society promoting and supporting professional practice by developing, collecting, analysing, and disseminating information on the CPA to its members
Promote and support the delivery of quality mental health and learning disability care
To lend support to all those involved in the operation of the CPA
Develop and share good professional standards and practice in mental health and learning disability
Seek to influence national policy, strategy and activity, as well as regional and local processes and protocols
Develop and influence the provision of high quality relevant professional training to all.

Subject coverage: Application of CPA in mental health/learning disabilites, CPAA standards and criteria.

Information services: Application / implementation of CPA in mental health and learning disabilities, CPAA standards and criteria. Annual CPAA Good Practice Awards for members.

Special visitor services: No access other than to staff, prior appointment required.

Education services: Education establishments who deliver mental health/ CPA training can become members.

Services for disabled people: Parking provided, toilet facilities.

Publications: Printed
Order printed publications from: www.cpaa.org.uk; cpa.association@derbyshcft.nhs.uk; telephone 01246 515975 or at postal address.

Access to staff: Contact by letter, by telephone, by e-mail and via website
Hours: Mon to Thu, 0830 to 1430

Access to building: No access other than to staff, prior appointment required.

Access for disabled people: Parking provided, toilet facilities.

CPAA Regional Leads and Committee members details: Obtainable from CPAA.

CAREERS GROUP, UNIVERSITY OF LONDON

Stewart House, 32 Russell Square, London, WC1B 5DN

Tel: 020 7863 6014
Fax: 020 7863 6003
E-mail: careers@careers.lon.ac.uk
Website: www.careers.lon.ac.uk

Enquiries to: Information & Research Specialist

Organisation type and purpose: University department or institute.
Careers service.

Subject coverage: Careers advice, recruitment information, occupational information.

Publications: Printed

Access to staff: Contact by letter, by telephone, by fax, by e-mail and via website. Non-members charged.
Hours: Mon to Thu, 0930 to 1700; Fri, 1100 to 1700

CARERS UK

20 Great Dover Street, London, SE1 4LX

Tel: 020 7378 4999; 0808 808 7777 (carers' line)
Fax: 020 7378 9787
E-mail: info@carersuk.org
Website: www.carersuk.org

Enquiries to: Chief Executive
Other contacts: Information Officer (for professional enquiries); Advice Officer / Carers' line (for carers)

Founded: 1988; formerly called Carers National Association (year of change 2001)

Organisation type and purpose: National organisation, voluntary organisation, registered charity (charity number 246329). Campaigning organisation.
To give information and advice to carers and professionals, develop support groups, campaign at all levels of national and local government, and with service providers, on behalf of carers.

Subject coverage: Information on any subject of concern or interest to carers, e.g. benefits, community care, residential care, practical caring, money worries, emotional support, housing, holdings, council tax, etc.

Trade and statistical information: Data on the numbers of carers in the United Kingdom

Publications: Printed

Publications list: Available online and in print

Access to staff: Contact by letter, by telephone, by fax, by e-mail and via website
Hours: Mon to Fri, 0900 to 1700
Carers' line: Wed, Thu, 1000 to 1200 and 1400 to 1600

Branches: Carers Northern Ireland; 58 Howard Street, Belfast, BT1 6PJ; tel: 028 9043 9843; fax: 028 9032 9299; e-mail: info@carersni.co.uk; website: http://www.carersni.org
Carers Scotland; The Cottage, 21 Pearce Street, Glasgow, G51 3UT; tel: 0141 445 3070; fax: 0141 445 3096; e-mail: info@carerscotland.org; website: http://www.carerscotland.org
Carers Wales; River House, Ynys Bridge Court, Gwaelod-y-Garth, Cardiff, CF15 9SS; tel: 029 2081 1370; fax: 029 2081 1575; e-mail: info@carerswales.org; website: http://www.carerswales.org

CARITAS SOCIAL ACTION NETWORK (CSAN)

39 Eccleston Square, London, SW1V 1BX

Tel: 020 7901 4875
E-mail: admin@csan.org.uk
Website: www.csan.org.uk

Founded: 2002; formerly called Catholic Child Welfare Council

Organisation type and purpose: CSAN (Caritas Social Action Network) is the social action arm of the Catholic Church in England & Wales. (charity number 1101431).

Subject coverage: We are a family of social action charities collectively known as the Caritas network which is supported by the CSAN team.

The Caritas network works for the most vulnerable people of society across England and Wales, providing support for families and children, the elderly, the homeless, refugees, the disabled, and prisoners.

The national team of CSAN, based in London, works to strengthen and facilitate the network, conduct policy and advocacy work and use its 'voice' at a national level.

CSAN is a member of Caritas Internationalis, within the Caritas Europa group.

Access to staff: Contact by letter, by telephone and by e-mail. Appointment necessary.
Hours: Mon to Fri, 0930 to 1730

CARLISLE CITY COUNCIL

Civic Centre, Carlisle, Cumbria, CA3 8QG

Tel: 01228 817000

continued overleaf

Fax: 01228 817013
E-mail: customerservices@carlisle.gov.uk
Website: www.carlisle.gov.uk

Organisation type and purpose: Local government body.

Subject coverage: Policy and performance, property, community services, building and mechanised services, leisure and amenity services and housing, environmental services.

Access to staff: Contact by letter, by telephone, by fax and by e-mail
Hours: Mon to Thu, 0900 to 1700; Fri, 0900 to 1600

CARLISLE COLLEGE LEARNING RESOURCE CENTRE (Carlisle College LRC)

Victoria Place, Carlisle, Cumbria, CA1 1HS

Tel: 01228 822760
Fax: 01228 822710
E-mail: lrc@carlisle.ac.uk
Website: www.carlisle.ac.uk

Enquiries to: LRC Officer

History of institution: formerly called Carlisle Technical College

Organisation type and purpose: College of further and higher education.

Library catalogue: All or part available online

Access to staff: Contact by letter, by telephone and by e-mail. Appointment necessary.
Hours: Term time: Mon, Wed, 0830 to 1700; Tue, Thu, 0830 to 1900; Fri, 0830 to 1600
Special comments: For reference only.

CARLISLE PUBLIC LIBRARY

11 Globe Lane, Carlisle, Cumbria, CA3 8NX

Tel: 01228 227310
Fax: 01228 607333
E-mail: carlisle.library@cumbriacc.gov.uk
Website: www.cumbria.gov.uk/libraries

Enquiries to: Area Library Manager

Organisation type and purpose: Local government body, public library.

Subject coverage: General.

Library catalogue: All or part available online

Access to staff: Contact by letter, by telephone, by fax, by e-mail and in person
Hours: Mon, Wed and Fri, 0930 to 1730; Tue and Thu, 0930 to 1900; Sat 0930 to 1600; Sun 1200 to 1600

Parent body: Cumbria Library Services

CARMARTHENSHIRE ARCHIVE SERVICE

Parc Myrddin, Richmond Terrace, Carmarthen, SA31 1HQ

Tel: 01267 228232
Fax: 01267 228237
E-mail: archives@carmarthenshire.gov.uk

Enquiries to: Archivist

Founded: 1959; formerly a part of Dyfed Archive Service (year of change 1996)

Organisation type and purpose: Local government body.

Subject coverage: Aspects of the history of Carmarthenshire, church and chapel records 16th–20th century, estate records 13th–20th century, business records 18th–20th century, local government records 16th–20th century, maps of the county 18th–20th century.

Collection: Cawdor Collection containing the Golden Grove Book, an 18th-century collection of pedigrees relating to the whole of Wales.
Records of local historical interest, including parish registers.

Publications: Printed

Publications list: Available in print

Access to staff: Contact by letter, by telephone, by fax, by e-mail and in person. Appointment necessary.
Hours: Mon, closed; Tue, 0930 to 1900 (1700 to 1900 by appointment only); Wed to Thu, 0930 to 1700; Fri 0930 to 1630.
Special comments: For reservations at other times, phone for appointment.

Links with: Carmarthen Reference Library; St Peter's Street, Carmarthen; tel: 01267 224822; Carmarthenshire Museums Service; Abergwili, Carmarthen; tel: 01267 231691

CARMARTHENSHIRE COLLEGE (COLEG SIR GAR)

Graig Campus, Sandy Road, Llanelli, Carmarthenshire, SA15 4DN

Tel: 01554 748000
Fax: 01554 756088
E-mail: admissions@colegsirgar.ac.uk
Website: www.colsirgar.ac.uk

Enquiries to: Marketing Officer
Direct tel: 01554 748112
Direct e-mail: debbie.williams@colegsirgar.ac.uk

Founded: 1984; formerly called Llanelli Technical College

Organisation type and purpose: Suitable for ages: 16+.
Higher and further education establishment.

Subject coverage: Access and general education; business, management, and office technology, catering, hairdressing and beauty therapy, computing and applied science, creative and performing arts, engineering and construction, foundation and community education, health, social and child care, sport, leisure, tourism and land-based studies.

Publications: Printed

Access to staff: Contact by letter, by telephone, by fax, by e-mail, in person and via website. All charged.
Hours: Mon to Thu, 0845 to 2100; Fri, 0845 to 1630

Access for disabled people: Parking provided, toilet facilities

Has: 5 sites (11,000 students, 500 staff)

Parent body: Funding Council for Wales; Lambourne House, Cardiff Business Park, Llanishen, Cardiff, CF4 5GL

Subsidiary body: CCTA Enterprises Ltd

CARMARTHENSHIRE COUNTY LIBRARIES

Carmarthen Library, St. Peter's Street, Carmarthen, SA31 1LN

Tel: 01267 224824
Fax: 01267 223189
E-mail: library@carmarthenshire.gov.uk

Enquiries to: Regional Library Manager

Founded: 1996; formerly called Dyfed County Library, Llanelli Borough Library (year of change 1996)

Organisation type and purpose: Local government body, public library.

Subject coverage: General, local history and other matters relating to the county of Carmarthenshire, history of Wales, Welsh languages and literature.

Collection: Carmarthenshire Antiquarian Society Collection
Video collection on physical and mental disabilities

Library catalogue: All or part available online and in-house

Publications: Printed
Order printed publications from: Carmarthen Library

Publications list: Available online and in print

Access to staff: Contact by letter, by telephone, by fax, by e-mail and in person
Hours: Mon to Wed and Fri, 0900 to 1900; Thu and Sat, 0900 to 1700

Access to building: No prior appointment required

Access for disabled people: Ramped entry

CARNEGIE LEADERS IN LEARNING PARTNERSHIP

Churchwood, Headingley Campus, Leeds Metropolitan University, Leeds, LS6 3QS

Tel: 0113 812 6138
Fax: 0113 275 5927
E-mail: info@carnegieleaders.org.uk
Website: www.carnegieleaders.org.uk

History of institution: please select
Carnegie Leaders in Learning Partnership is a partnership between CCDU Ltd and Leeds Metropolitan University.

Organisation type and purpose: Carnegie Leaders in Learning Partnership exists to enable individuals, teams and organisations to achieve their potential.

Subject coverage: Consultancy – working collaboratively with clients to understand requirements and design and deliver solutions. Examples of solutions delivered include: competency development, coaching, impact evaluation, quality improvement, leadership development and assessment and moderation.

Publications: Printed

Publications list: Available online and in print

Access to staff: Contact by letter, by telephone, by fax, by e-mail and via website
Hours: Mon to Fri, 0900 to 1700

CARNEGIE UNITED KINGDOM TRUST

Comely Park House, New Row, Dunfermline, Fife, KY12 7EJ

Tel: 01383 721445
Fax: 01383 620682
E-mail: raji@carnegieuk.org
Website: www.carnegieuktrust.org.uk

Enquiries to: Chief Executive
Other contacts: Communications Director

Founded: 1913

Organisation type and purpose: Registered charity (charity number SCO 12799).

Collection: Archives (held in National Archives of Scotland)

Publications: Printed

Publications list: Available online and in print

Access to staff: Contact by letter, by telephone and by e-mail
Hours: Mon to Fri, 0900 to 1700

CARNIVOROUS PLANT SOCIETY (CPS)

1 Orchard Close, Ringwood, Hampshire, BH24 1LP

Enquiries to: Chairman
Other contacts: Membership Secretary for membership enquiries.

Founded: 1978

Organisation type and purpose: Membership association (membership is by subscription), present number of members: 600, voluntary organisation, registered charity (charity number 281423).
To bring together all those interested in carnivorous plants whether beginners or experts. To increase people's knowledge both in horticulture and in the wild, including conservation.

Subject coverage: Botany and horticulture of carnivorous plants; seed bank; conservation of carnivorous plants in their habitats.

Publications: Printed

Access to staff: Contact by letter
Hours: Mon to Fri, 0900 to 1700

Affiliated to: Royal Horticultural Society

Membership Secretary: Carnivorous Plant Society; 100 Lambley Lane, Burton Joyce, Nottingham, NG14 5BL

CARPENTERS' COMPANY

Carpenters' Hall, Throgmorton Avenue, London, EC2N 2JJ

Tel: 020 7588 7001
Fax: 020 7638 6286
E-mail: info@carpentersco.com
Website: www.thecarpenterscompany.co.uk

Enquiries to: The Clerk

Founded: 1271

Organisation type and purpose: Professional body (membership is by election or invitation), present number of members: 150.
City of London Livery Company that supports the construction industry, craft of carpentry and charitable giving.

Access to staff: Contact by letter
Hours: Mon to Fri, 0900 to 1700

CARPET FOUNDATION, THE

MCF Complex, 60 New Road, Kidderminster, Worcestershire, DY10 1AQ

Tel: 01562 755568
Fax: 01562 565405
E-mail: info@carpetfoundation.com
Website: www.carpetfoundation.com

Enquiries to: Commercial Director

Founded: 1999

Organisation type and purpose: Membership association (membership is by subscription), present number of members: 12.
To promote the image of carpets and to improve knowledge about them to this end.

Subject coverage: Pile carpets (especially wool carpets), carpet tiles and most other wall-to-wall textile floor coverings – but NOT oriental or machine washable rugs.

Publications: Printed

Access to staff: Contact by letter, by telephone, by fax, by e-mail and via website
Hours: Mon to Fri, 0900 to 1700

CARSHALTON COLLEGE

Nightingale Road, Carshalton, Surrey, SM5 2EJ

Tel: 020 8544 4444
Fax: 020 8544 4440
E-mail: cs@carshalton.ac.uk
Website: www.carshalton.ac.uk

Enquiries to: Systems Librarian
Direct tel: 020 8544 4344
Other contacts: e-Learning Librarian

Subject coverage: Art and design, media, multimedia, music technology, business studies, secretarial and administration, accounting, early years, health and social care, residential care, dental care, construction, electrical installation, motor vehicle engineering, hairdressing, beauty therapy, hospitality and catering, information technology, software engineering, sports science, uniformed services, ESOL, pre-entry and entry level vocational studies, and teacher training. Level 4 courses in management, accounting, care, early years, teaching and learning support, and teacher training.

Library catalogue: All or part available in-house

Publications: Printed

Access to staff: Contact by letter, by telephone, by fax, by e-mail and in person. Appointment necessary.
Hours: Mon to Fri, 0900 to 1700

Access to building: Prior appointment required

Access for disabled people: Parking provided, level entry, lifts to all floors, toilet facilities

CAST METALS FEDERATION (CMF)

National Metalforming Centre, 47 Birmingham Road, West Bromwich, West Midlands, B70 6PY

Tel: 0121 601 6390
Fax: 0121 601 6391
Website: www.castmetalsfederation.com

Enquiries to: Chief Executive

Founded: 2001; formed from British Foundry Association (BFA), British Investment Casting Trade Association (BICTA), British Metal Castings Association (BMCA) (year of change 2001)

Organisation type and purpose: National organisation, trade association (membership is by subscription).
The single trade body for the UK cast metals sector.

Subject coverage: Promotion of Best Of British castings, influencing and forming legislation, guidance and information on environmental, health, safety, statistics, markets, costs, prices, contracts, best practice, benchmarking.

Publications: Printed

Access to staff: Appointment necessary.
Hours: Mon to Fri, 0900 to 1700

CASTINGS TECHNOLOGY INTERNATIONAL

Advanced Manufacturing Park, Brunel Way, Rotherham, S60 5WG

Tel: 0114 254 1144
Fax: 0114 254 1155
E-mail: info@castingstechnology.com
Website: www.castingstechnology.com

Enquiries to: Information Officer

Founded: 1996; formerly called British Cast Iron Research Association and the Castings Development Centre (year of change 2001)

Organisation type and purpose: International organisation, membership association (membership is by subscription), present number of members: 300, research organisation.

Subject coverage: Cast metals technology includes environmental and working conditions, melting and molten metal treatment, moulding and coremaking, process and quality control, NDE guaranteed quality, automation and advanced manufacturing technology (AMT), new cast materials, new applications for castings, casting design and choice of materials ferrous and non-ferrous, operating economics, design and production control, and costing.

Collection: National and International Standards
The Cti Library is devoted solely to the technology of metal castings production

Non-library collection catalogue: All or part available in-house

Library catalogue: All or part available in-house

Publications list: Available online and in print

continued overleaf

Access to staff: Contact by letter, by telephone, by fax and by e-mail. Access for members only.
Hours: Mon to Fri, 0800 to 1600

CASTLE BROMWICH HALL GARDENS TRUST (CBHGT)

Chester Road, Castle Bromwich, Birmingham, B36 9BT

Tel: 0121 749 4100
Fax: 0121 749 4100
E-mail: Admin@cbhgt.org.uk
Website: www.cbhgt.swinternet.co.uk

Enquiries to: Secretary

Founded: 1985

Organisation type and purpose: Registered charity (charity number 516855), historic building, house or site.
Historic gardens and maze.
Restoration of walled gardens to their 18th-century glory.

Subject coverage: Historical and horticultural. The Hall and Gardens were built in 1599 by Sir Edward Devereux who was MP for Tamworth. In 1657 the estate was purchased by Sir John Bridgeman I and later extended by his son Sir John Bridgeman II to its present boundaries. The gardens are of some 10 acres and include a 19th-century holly maze.

Information services: Lectures by special arrangement.

Special visitor services: Guided tours.

Library catalogue: All or part available in-house

Publications: Printed

Access to staff: Contact by letter and by telephone
Hours: Mon to Fri, 0900 to 1700

Access for disabled people: Level entry, access to all public areas, toilet facilities

CASTLE COMBE CIRCUIT LIMITED

Castle Combe, Chippenham, Wiltshire, SN14 7EY

Tel: 01249 782417
Fax: 01249 782392
E-mail: sales@castlecombecircuit.co.uk
Website: www.castlecombecircuit.co.uk

Enquiries to: Managing Director

Founded: 1950

Organisation type and purpose: Service industry.
Racing circuit.

Subject coverage: All usages of the circuit, racing and other, motorsports, learning to race.

Publications: Printed

Access to staff: Contact by letter, by telephone, by fax, by e-mail, in person and via website
Hours: Mon to Fri, 0900 to 1700; Sat, 0900 to 1600

Subsidiary body: Castle Combe Exhibitions Limited; tel: 01249 782417; fax: 01249 782392; e-mail: sales@castlecombecircuit.co.uk; Castle Combe Racing School; tel: 01249 782929; fax: 01249 782392; e-mail: sales@castlecombecircuit.co.uk

CASTOR MANUFACTURERS ASSOCIATION (CMA)

1 Perch Close, Marlow, Buckinghamshire, SL7 2BQ

Tel: 01628 475648
Fax: 01628 475648

Enquiries to: General Secretary

Founded: 1963

Organisation type and purpose: Trade association.

Subject coverage: Furniture, hospital and industrial castors.

Publications: Printed

Access to staff: Contact by letter, by telephone and by fax
Hours: Mon to Fri, 0900 to 1700

Member of: British Materials Handling Federation; BSI; FIRA

CASUALTIES UNION (CU)

Casualties Union Headquarters, PO Box 1942, London, E17 6YU

Tel: 08700 780590
E-mail: hq.cu@casualtiesunion.org.uk
Website: www.casualtiesunion.org.uk

Enquiries to: Headquarters Administrator
Other contacts: Honorary Treasurer (for financial matters)

Founded: 1942

Organisation type and purpose: Membership association (membership is by subscription or invitation), present number of members: 430, voluntary organisation, registered charity (charity number 234672), suitable for ages: 8+.
To advance for the public benefit education and training in first aid, the treatment of illness, nursing, rescue, accident prevention, care in the community and similar activities, particularly through casualty simulation.

Subject coverage: Casualty simulation, training and provision of skilled acting casualties, demonstrations and emergency exercises for training first aid, rescue, ambulance and hospital personnel.

Collection: Some archives are stored at the Wellcome Trust, London.

Publications: Printed
Order printed publications from: e-mail: hq.cu@casualtiesunion.org.uk

Access to staff: Contact by letter, by telephone and by e-mail
Hours: Mon to Fri, 1100 to 2000

CATERHAM AND DISTRICT LOCAL HISTORY CENTRE

Caterham Valley Library, Stafford Road, Caterham, Surrey, CR3 6JG

Tel: 08456 009009
Fax: 01883 330872
E-mail: libraries@surreycc.gov.uk
Website: www.surreycc.gov.uk/caterhamlocalhistory

Organisation type and purpose: A partnership between Surrey Libraries, Surrey History Centre, the Bourne Society, East Surrey Museum and East Surrey Family History Society.

Subject coverage: Local and family history of the parishes of Caterham, Chaldon, Chelsham, Farleigh, Godstone, Tatsfield, Titsey, Warlingham, Whyteleafe and Woldingham.

Access to building: *Hours:* 1st Tue of the month, 1400 to 1600; 2nd and 4th Sat of the month, 1000 to 1200

CATERING EQUIPMENT DISTRIBUTORS ASSOCIATION OF GREAT BRITAIN (CEDA)

PO Box 683, Inkberrow, Worcestershire, WR7 4WQ

Tel: 01386 793911
E-mail: peterkay@ceda.co.uk
Website: www.ceda.co.uk

Enquiries to: Managing Director

Founded: 1972

Organisation type and purpose: Trade association, membership association (membership is by subscription).
The official organisation of the catering equipment dealer and supply industry.

Subject coverage: Provision, installation, service and design of commercial kitchens, catering equipment and kitchen utensils.

Publications: Printed

Publications list: Available online

Access to staff: Contact by letter, by telephone, by e-mail and via website. Appointment necessary.
Hours: Mon to Fri, 0900 to 1700

CATES

Formal name: Campaign Against the Trade of Endangered Species

23 Clifton Road, Henlow, Bedfordshire, SG16 6BL

Enquiries to: Secretary
Other contacts: Director

Founded: 1985; formerly called North Herts FOE Endangered Species Campaign (year of change 1985)

Organisation type and purpose: Advisory body (membership is by subscription), present number of members: 200, voluntary organisation, research organisation.

Subject coverage: Environmental subjects including: tropical rainforests, endangered species campaign, tree planting/woodland management, introduction/reintroduction (i.e. plant or animal species), behavioural and genetic extinction, pesticides and architecture.

Collection: Earth Matters Magazines (Friends of the Earth)
TRAFFIC Bulletins

Non-library collection catalogue: All or part available in-house

Publications: Printed

Publications list: Available in print

Access to staff: Contact by letter
Hours: Mon to Fri, 0900 to 1700

CATHEDRAL ORGANISTS' ASSOCIATION (COA)

Royal School of Church Music, 19 The Close, Salisbury, SP1 2EB

Tel: 01722 424841
Fax: 01722 424849
E-mail: coa@rscm.com

Enquiries to: Secretary

Founded: 1946

Organisation type and purpose:
Professional body.
To provide opportunities for all cathedral organists to meet at 2 conferences per year and for the exchange of useful information.

Subject coverage: Cathedral music today, education of choristers and the choir school situation today.

Access to staff: Contact by letter, by telephone, by fax and by e-mail. Access for members only.
Hours: Mon to Fri, 0900 to 1700

CATHEDRALS AND CHURCH BUILDINGS LIBRARY

Formal name: Cathedrals and Church Buildings Division of the Archbishops' Council of the Church of England

Church House, Great Smith Street, London, SW1P 3AZ

Tel: 020 7898 1884
Fax: 020 7898 1881
E-mail: vaughan.whibley@c-of-e.org.uk
Website: www.churchcare.co.uk
Website: www.cofe.anglican.org/about/librariesandarchives

Enquiries to: Honorary Librarian

Founded: 1921

Organisation type and purpose: The Library supports the work of the Church Buildings Council (CBC) and the Cathedrals Fabric Commission for England (CFCE). The CBC advises churches and dioceses on matters relating to architecture and ecclesiastical planning regulations; it also dispenses grants, for conservation of furnishings of historical or artistic significance in Church of England churches, on behalf of charitable organisations. The CFCE oversees the Church's own system of planning controls for cathedrals and provides guidance and advice on such issues.

Subject coverage: Ecclesiastical art and architecture, with special reference to the cathedral and church buildings and furnishings of the Church of England; conservation of works of art in Church of England churches, general and specific information on a wide range of topics relating to churches and their contents including ecclesiology; liturgy; heraldry; ecclesiastical history; symbolism; hagiography.

Collection: Library of c.13,000 books and over 100 periodical titles on ecclesiastical art and architecture; liturgy; ecclesiology; National Association of Decorative and Fine Arts Society (NADFAS) church recorders reports; National Survey of English Churches, with documentary and photographic material, postcards and guide books relating to about 18,000 churches

Library catalogue: All or part available in print

Access to staff: Contact by letter, by telephone, by fax, by e-mail and in person. Appointment necessary.
Hours: Tue, Wed, 1030 to 1600

Constituent part of: Cathedrals Fabric Commission for England; Church House, Great Smith Street, London, SW1P 3AZ; tel: 020 7898 1884; fax: 020 7898 1881; e-mail: vaughan.whibley@c-of-e.org.uk; Church Buildings Council

Parent body: Archbishops' Council of the Church of England

CATHEDRALS FABRIC COMMISSION FOR ENGLAND (CFCE)

Church House, Great Smith Street, London, SW1P 3NZ

Tel: 020 7898 1888
Fax: 020 7898 1881
E-mail: maggie.goodall@churchofengland.org

Enquiries to: Secretary

Founded: 1991; formerly called Cathedrals Advisory Committee (CAC) (year of change 1991)

Organisation type and purpose: Advisory and research body.
Statutory church body.

Subject coverage: Care of cathedrals in England.

Library catalogue: All or part available in-house

Access to staff: Contact by letter
Hours: Mon to Fri, 0930 to 1630
Special comments: By appointment only.

Access to building: Prior appointment required

Access for disabled people: Ramped entry, access to all public areas

Parent body: Cathedral and Church Buildings Division, ChurchCare

CATHOLIC AGENCY FOR OVERSEAS DEVELOPMENT (CAFOD)

Romero Close, Stockwell Road, London, SW9 9TY

Tel: 020 7733 7900
Fax: 020 7274 9630
E-mail: hqcafod@cafod.org.uk
Website: www.cafod.org.uk

Enquiries to: Information Services Manager
Direct tel: 020 7326 5600

Founded: 1962

Organisation type and purpose: Voluntary organisation, registered charity (charity number 285776).
Specialised library.
Development and relief NGO working in the third world.

Subject coverage: Computing, development economics, debt, trade, environment, land, information technology, theology, women, children in Africa, Asia, the Pacific, Latin America, the Caribbean and Eastern Europe.

Trade and statistical information: A number of UN and World Bank statistical reports

Library catalogue: All or part available in-house

Publications: Printed, and electronic and video
Order printed publications from: e-mail: afarragh@cafod.org.uk

Publications list: Available in print

Access to staff: Contact by letter, by telephone, by fax, by e-mail and via website. Appointment necessary.
Hours: Mon to Fri, 1030 to 1630

Access to building: No access other than to staff

Regional Offices: CAFOD East; Chigwell Convent, 803 Chigwell Road, Woodford Green, Essex, IG8 8AX; tel: 020 8502 9722; CAFOD East Midlands; 61 Staton Road, Rearsby, Leicestershire, LE7 4YY; tel: 01664 424346; CAFOD Leeds and Hallam; St William of York, Eccleshall Road, Sheffield, S11 8TL; tel: 0114 268 7817; CAFOD Liverpool; St Joseph's, Upholland, Lancashire, WN8 0PZ; tel: 01695 633284; CAFOD North East; Ushaw College, Durham, DH7 9BJ; tel: 0191 373 5001; CAFOD North West; St Walburge, Weston Street, Preston, Lancashire, PR2 2QE; tel: 01772 733310; CAFOD South; St John's Seminary, Wonersh, Surrey, GU5 0QX; tel: 01483 898866; CAFOD South West; The Mount, Taunton, Somerset, TA1 3NR; tel: 01823 338903; CAFOD Southwark; Hubert House, Mallard Close, Temple Hill, Dartford, Kent, DA1 5HU; tel: 01322 294924; fax: 01322 279223; e-mail: southwark@cafod.org.uk; CAFOD Wales; St Mary's Parish Centre, Union Street, Carmarthen, Dyfed, SA31 3DE; tel: 01267 221549; CAFOD West Midlands; 23 Glebe Street, Walsall, West Midlands, WS1 3NX; tel: 01922 722944; CAFOD Westminster; The Benedictine Centre for Spirituality, 29 Bramley Road, Cockfosters, London, N14 4HE; tel: 020 8449 6970

CATHOLIC BISHOPS' CONFERENCE OF ENGLAND AND WALES

Department for International Affairs, 39 Eccleston Square, London, SW1V 1BX

Tel: 020 7901 4861
Fax: 020 7901 4821

Enquiries to: Secretary

Founded: 1968; formerly called Commission for International Justice and Peace

Organisation type and purpose: Advisory body, professional body, registered charity.
Promotion of international justice and peace including development. The Department is an advisory body for the Catholic Bishops of England and Wales, and has four analytical groups dealing with: international justice and peace, European affairs, refugees and migrants, environmental issues.

continued overleaf

Subject coverage: Catholic teaching on international affairs, development, and justice and peace issues.

Access to staff: Contact by letter
Hours: Mon to Fri, 0900 to 1700

Subsidiary body: National Liaison Committee of Diocesan Justice and Peace Groups

CATHOLIC CENTRAL LIBRARY

Lancing Street, London, NW1 1ND

Tel: 020 7383 4333
Fax: 020 7388 6675
E-mail: librarian@catholic-library.org.uk
Website: www.catholic-library.org.uk

Enquiries to: Librarian
Other contacts: Director

Organisation type and purpose: Registered charity (charity number 1064460/0).
A theological library.

Subject coverage: Catholic Church in England and in countries of the world, Roman Catholic current affairs, theology, ecumenism, scripture, ecclesiastical history, comparative religion and Christian sociology.

Collection: 19th-century Roman Catholic pamphlets, tracts and directories
Ecumenism
Papal documents and magisterial statements
Post-Reformation English Catholic history
Vatican Council II

Publications: Printed

Access to staff: Contact by letter, by telephone, by fax, by e-mail, in person and via website
Hours: Mon, Tue, Thu, Fri, 1030 to 1700; Wed, 1030 to 1900

Access for disabled people: Level entry, access to all public areas, toilet facilities

CATHOLIC EDUCATION SERVICE (CESEW)

Formal name: Catholic Education Service for England and Wales

39 Eccleston Square, London, SW1V 1BX

Tel: 020 7901 1900
Fax: 020 7901 1939
E-mail: general@cesew.org.uk
Website: www.cesew.org.uk

Enquiries to: Office Manager

Founded: 1847; formerly called Catholic Poor Schools Committee

Organisation type and purpose: Promoting and supporting Catholic education in England and Wales.

Subject coverage: Catholic education.

Publications: Printed
Order printed publications from: general@cesew.orguk

Publications list: Available online and in print

Access to staff: Contact by letter, by telephone, by fax, by e-mail and via website. Appointment necessary.
Hours: Mon to Fri, 0900 to 1700

The education agency of the: Bishops' Conference of England and Wales

CATHOLIC INSTITUTE FOR INTERNATIONAL RELATIONS (CIIR)

Unit 3 Canonbury Yard, 190a New North Road, London, N1 7BJ

Tel: 020 7288 8600
Fax: 020 7359 0017
E-mail: info@ciir.org
Website: www.ciir.org

Enquiries to: Information Officer
Other contacts: Advocacy Officer for issue/region based information request.

Organisation type and purpose: Membership association (membership is by subscription), registered charity (charity number 294329).
CIIR works for justice, development and the eradication of poverty through a combination of technical assistance and advocacy for political change.

Subject coverage: Social, economic, cultural and political analysis and expertise in geographic regions: Dominican Republic, El Salvador, Nicaragua, Honduras, Ecuador, Peru, Namibia, Zimbabwe, Somalia, Yemen, East Timor.

Publications: Printed

Publications list: Available in print

Access to staff: Contact by e-mail and via website. Appointment necessary.
Hours: Mon to Fri, 0930 to 1730

Access to building: Prior appointment required

Other addresses: International Cooperation for Development (ICD); At the same address

CATHOLIC RECORD SOCIETY (CRS)

12 Melbourne Place, Wolsingham, Co. Durham, DL13 3EH

Tel: 01388 527747
E-mail: secretary@catholicrecordsociety.co.uk
Website: www.catholicrecordsociety.co.uk

Enquiries to: Honorary Secretary

Founded: 1904

Organisation type and purpose: Learned society, present number of members: 600.

Subject coverage: Catholic history of England and Wales from the Reformation (not genealogical).

Non-library collection catalogue: All or part available online

Publications: Printed

Access to staff: Contact by letter and by telephone
Hours: Mon to Fri, 0900 to 1700

CATHOLIC YOUTH SERVICES (CYS)

39 Eccleston Square, London, SW1V 1BX

Tel: 020 7901 4870
Fax: 020 7901 4873
E-mail: cys@btinternet.com

Enquiries to: Director

Organisation type and purpose: Statutory body, voluntary organisation, registered charity.
Training agency.

Subject coverage: Youth, youth service, youth work.

Publications: Printed

Access to staff: Contact by letter, by telephone and by fax. Appointment necessary.
Hours: Mon to Fri, 0900 to 1700

Also at: Assistant Director; Newman College, Genners Lane, Bartley Green, Birmingham, B32 3NT; tel: 0121 411 1033; fax: 0121 475 0012

Member of: British Youth Council; Council of Churches for Britain and Ireland (Youth Unit); National Council for Voluntary Youth Services

Sponsored by: Roman Catholic Bishops' Conference

CBD RESEARCH LIMITED

Chancery House, 15 Wickham Road, Beckenham, Kent, BR3 5JS

Tel: 020 8650 7745
Fax: 020 8650 0768
E-mail: cbd@cbdresearch.com
Website: www.cbdresearch.com

Enquiries to: Company Secretary

Founded: 1961

Organisation type and purpose: Publishing house.

Subject coverage: Sources of business information; directories and guides to associations, societies and institutions of all kinds in Great Britain and Europe.

Library catalogue: All or part available in-house and in print

Publications: Printed, and electronic and video

Publications list: Available online and in print

Access to staff: Contact by letter, by telephone, by e-mail and via website
Hours: Mon to Fri, 0900 to 1700

CCUSA

Formal name: Camp Counsellors USA

1st Floor North, Devon House, 171–177 Great Portland Street, London, W1W5PQ

Tel: 020 7637 0779
Fax: 0207 580 6209
E-mail: info@ccusa.co.uk
Website: www.ccusa.com

Enquiries to: Marketing Manager
Direct e-mail: jamiem@ccusa.co.uk

Founded: 1986; formerly called Camp Counsellors USA (CCUSA) (year of change 2001)

Organisation type and purpose: International organisation.
Student work & travel specialists.

Recruitment for summer work placements in the USA and gap years to Australia or New Zealand, work experience in Brazil or Russian summer camps.

Subject coverage: Work experience placements and travel.

Publications: Printed

Access to staff: Contact by letter, by telephone, by fax, by e-mail, in person and via website
Hours: Mon to Fri, 0900 to 1700

Also at the same address: Work Experience USA (WEUSA)

CEEBIS

Formal name: Central and East European Business Information Service

Glasgow University Library, Hillhead Street, Glasgow, G12 8QE

Tel: 0141 330 6735
Fax: 0141 330 4952
E-mail: t.konn@lib.gla.ac.uk

Enquiries to: Information Officer

Founded: 1990; formerly called Soviet and East European Business Information Service

Organisation type and purpose: University library, consultancy.

Subject coverage: Economic, social and political background for all countries of Eastern Europe and the former Soviet Union, general and specialised business information services.

Collection: 50 current newspaper titles
75,000 monographs
600 journals
Back runs of newspapers held on microfilm

Trade and statistical information: Statistics, company data, legislation

Access to staff: Appointment necessary. All charged.
Hours: Mon to Fri, 0900 to 1700

CELTIC MEDIA FESTIVAL

249 West George Street, Glasgow, G2 4QE

Tel: 0141 302 1737
Fax: 0141 302 1738
E-mail: info@celticmediafestival.co.uk
Website: www.celticmediafestival.co.uk

Enquiries to: Festival Producer

Founded: 1980; formerly called Celtic Film and Television Festival; formerly called Celtic Film and Television Association

Organisation type and purpose:
International organisation, trade association (membership is by subscription, election or invitation), registered charity (charity number SC 028708).
Celebrates and showcases the best of film and broadcasting from the Celtic countries and regions of Scotland, Ireland, Wales, Cornwall and Brittany. The festival is a unique platform for debate and international co-production development.

Access to staff: Contact by letter, by telephone and by e-mail
Hours: Mon to Fri, 0930 to 1730

CEMENT ADMIXTURES ASSOCIATION (CAA)

38a Tilehouse Green Lane, Knowle, West Midlands, B93 9EY

Tel: 01564 776362
Fax: 01564 776362
E-mail: info@admixtures.org.uk
Website: www.admixtures.org.uk

Enquiries to: Secretary

Organisation type and purpose: Trade Association.

Subject coverage: Admixtures for concrete, mortar, grout and sprayed concrete; curing compounds for concrete.

Publications: Printed

Member organisation of: European Federation of Concrete Admixtures Associations (EFCA); Cobblers Cottage, Chester Road, Daresbury, Warrington, Cheshire, WA4 4AJ; tel: 01925 740581; fax: 01925 740581; e-mail: roland.harbron@talktalk.net; website: http://www.efca.info

CENTER FOR AUTISM & RELATED DISORDERS (CARD)

Acorn House, 13 Moorfield Road, Orpington, Kent, BR6 0HG

Tel: 01689 837373
Fax: 01689 896656
E-mail: carduk@kentseuk.freeserve.co.uk
Website: www.cardhq.com

Enquiries to: Clinic Supervisor

Founded: 1998

Organisation type and purpose: National organisation, suitable for ages: 2–8. Special Needs Education.

Subject coverage: Design and implementation of home-based teaching programmes for children with autism and related disorders based on the Lovaas technique.

Publications: Printed

Access to staff: Contact by letter, by telephone and by e-mail
Hours: Mon to Fri, 0900 to 1700

Access to building: Prior appointment required

Headquarters: Center for Autism & Related Disorders; 2330 Ventura Boulevard, Woodland Hills, California, CA 91364, USA; tel: +1 818 223 0123

CENTRAL ARBITRATION COMMITTEE (CAC)

Euston Tower, 22nd Floor, 286 Euston Road, London, NW1 3JJ

Tel: 020 7904 2300
Fax: 020 7904 2301
E-mail: enquiries@cac.gov.uk
Website: www.cac.gov.uk

Founded: 1976

Organisation type and purpose: National government body, permanent independent arbitration body.
To promote fair and efficient arrangements in the work place, by resolving collective disputes (in England, Scotland and Wales), either by voluntary agreement or, if necessary, through adjudication.

Subject coverage: Disclosure of information (Trade Union and Labour Relations (Consolidation) Act 1992: Section 183); voluntary arbitration (1992 Act: Section 212); industrial relations; statutory recognition (Employment Relations Act 1999). Considers applications and complaints under the Information and Consultation of Employees Regulations 2004 and performs a similar role in relation to European Works Councils, European Companies, European Co-operative Societies and Cross-Border Mergers.

Collection: Copies of past awards as issued by the Industrial Court, Industrial Arbitration Board and Central Arbitration Committee, from 1919,
Applications and decisions on all cases, Guidelines to Statutory Recognition Procedures.

Publications: Printed

Publications list: Available online

Access to staff: Contact by letter, by telephone, by fax, by e-mail and via website
Hours: Mon to Fri, 0900 to 1700.

Access to building: Prior appointment required

Access for disabled people: Access to all public areas, toilet facilities

CENTRAL BEDFORDSHIRE LIBRARIES

Operations Unit, Dunstable Library, Vernon Place, Dunstable, LU5 4HA

Tel: 0300 300 8060
Fax: 01582 471290
E-mail: dunstable.library@centralbedfordshire.gov.uk
Website: www.galaxy.bedfordshire.gov.uk/cgi-bin/vlib.sh

Enquiries to: Libraries Manager
Other contacts: Service Development Manager, Adult, Community & Information

Organisation type and purpose: Local government body. Public library service offering access to information, books, spoken word, DVDs and CDs for all ages and interests.

Subject coverage: Local information on Bedfordshire and its history, agriculture; local government information; life and works of John Bunyan; medieval English history; aeronautics; automobile engineering.

Education services: Homework centres and a virtual homework centre.

Non-library collection catalogue: All or part available online and in-house

Library catalogue: All or part available online

Publications: Printed, and microform publications
Order printed publications from: Download free from the Virtual Library

continued overleaf

Access to staff: Contact by letter, by telephone, by fax, by e-mail, in person and via website
Hours: Mon to Sat

CENTRAL COUNCIL FOR BRITISH NATURISM (CCBN)

30–32 Wycliffe Road, Northampton, NN1 5JF

Tel: 01604 620361
Fax: 01604 230176
E-mail: headoffice@british-naturism.org.uk
Website: www.british-naturism.org.uk

Enquiries to: Secretary General
Other contacts: Public Relations Office, 07799 677732, Archivist 01223 840947

Founded: 1964

Organisation type and purpose: National organisation, membership association (membership is by subscription), present number of members: 20,000, voluntary organisation.
National organisation of clubs and individuals.

Subject coverage: History of, and present facilities for, naturism and naturist sunbathing throughout the world.

Collection: Archives of CCBN and its predecessors
Magazines and books concerning naturism throughout the world

Publications: Printed

Publications list: Available online and in print

Access to staff: Contact by letter, by telephone, by fax, by e-mail and via website
Hours: Mon to Fri, 0900 to 1630

Affiliated to: International Naturist Federation

CENTRAL COUNCIL OF CHURCH BELL RINGERS (CCCBR)

E-mail: secretary@cccbr.org.uk
Website: www.cccbr.org.uk

Enquiries to: Library Steward
Direct e-mail: librarysteward@cccbr.org.uk

Founded: 1891

Organisation type and purpose: Advisory body, membership association (membership is by election or invitation), present number of members: 200, voluntary organisation, registered charity (charity number 270036).
To promote and foster the ringing of church bells for Christian worship and on other occasions, to represent ringers to national bodies, etc., to advise on all matters concerned with bells and bellringing.

Subject coverage: Bells and their fittings (both historical and engineering aspects); technical aspects of change ringing; history of change ringing; assistance with disposal of bells from redundant churches; advice on fund-raising for bells and their maintenance.

Collection: Unique collection of books and manuscripts on bells, bellfounders, bell-ringers and bell-ringing in the English tradition, covering the British Isles and overseas

Non-library collection catalogue: All or part available online, in-house and in print

Library catalogue: All or part available in-house and in print

Publications: Printed, and electronic and video
Order printed publications from: Central Council Publications: The Ringing World, 35A High Street, Andover, Hampshire, SP10 1LJ; tel: 01264 366620; e-mail: pubs@cccbr.org.uk; website: http://www.ringingworld.co.uk; http://www.cccbr.org.uk/pubs

Publications list: Available online

CENTRAL GURDWARA LONDON

Formal name: The Central Gurdwara (Khalsa Jatha) London

62 Queensdale Road, London, W11 4SQ

Tel: 020 7603 2789
Fax: 0207 480 7636
E-mail: ksg@khalsa.com
Website: www.centralgurdwara.org.uk

Enquiries to: General Secretary
Direct tel: 020 7481 8176

Founded: 1908; formerly called Central Gurdwara (British Isles Khalsa Jatha) London

Organisation type and purpose: Membership association (membership is by subscription), present number of members: 1,000, registered charity (charity number 258324), public library, suitable for all ages. Sunday school.
Religious congregations; education; births, marriages, death rites; library; music.

Subject coverage: Sikhism

Non-library collection catalogue: All or part available in-house

Library catalogue: All or part available in-house

Publications: Printed

Access to staff: Contact by letter, by telephone, by fax, by e-mail and in person
Hours: Access to the Executive Committee by phone, or Sunday evening on the premises. Wed and Fri, 1900 to 2030

Access to building: No access other than to staff
Hours: Daily, 0500 to 2030

CENTRAL LIBRARY, DERBY

The Wardwick, Derby, DE1 1HS

Tel: 01332 641702
Fax: 01332 369570
E-mail: central.library@derby.gov.uk

Direct e-mail: askusaquestion@derby.gov.uk

Founded: 1879

Organisation type and purpose: Local government body, public library.

Collection: An extensive manuscript collection, files of newspapers, Derbyshire census (both on microfilm), photographs, engravings, maps and family records
Local studies collection incorporates the Devonshire and Bemrose family libraries
The collection of printed books and pamphlets includes works published in 17th, 18th, 19th and 20th centuries. This is housed at the Local Studies Library, 25B Irongate, Derby, DE1 3GL

Library catalogue: All or part available online and in-house

Access to staff: Contact by letter, by telephone, by fax, by e-mail, in person and via website

Access for disabled people: Ramped entry, access to all public areas, toilet facilities

Part of: Derby City Libraries; website: http://www.derby.gov.uk/libraries

CENTRAL SCHOOL OF BALLET (CSB)

10 Herbal Hill, Clerkenwell Road, London, EC1R 5EG

Tel: 020 7837 6332
Fax: 020 7833 5571
E-mail: info@csbschool.co.uk
Website: www.centralschoolofballet.co.uk

Enquiries to: Assistant Administrator
Other contacts: Senior School Administrator (for admission process)

Founded: 1982

Organisation type and purpose: Registered charity (charity number 285398), dance training organisation.
Affiliate Member of the Conservatoire for Dance & Drama.

Access to staff: Contact by letter, by telephone, by fax, by e-mail, in person and via website
Hours: Mon, Wed, Fri, Sat, 0900 to 1830; Tue, Thu, 0900 to 2100

Access to building: Prior appointment required

Graduate touring company: Ballet Central; at the same address; e-mail: info@csbschool.co.uk; website: http://www.balletcentral.co.uk

CENTRAL SCHOOL OF SPEECH AND DRAMA (CSSD, Central)

Embassy Theatre, 64 Eton Avenue, London, NW3 3HY

Tel: 020 7559 3942
Fax: 020 7722 4132
E-mail: library@cssd.ac.uk
Website: www.cssd.ac.uk/pages/library.htmll

Enquiries to: Head of Library Services
Other contacts: Library, Media, Computer Services Managers (for library, media, computer enquiries)

Founded: 1906

Organisation type and purpose: University library, HE College library.
Higher education.

Subject coverage: Theatre, drama, art and design, drama education.

Collection: Library of c. 32,000 vols

Library catalogue: All or part available online

Publications: Electronic and video

Access to staff: Contact by telephone. Appointment necessary. Non-members charged.
Hours: Telephone for hours as times vary for term time and holidays

Access to building: Prior appointment required
Hours: Hours vary, see website for details
Special comments: Charges for borrowing and copying.

Access for disabled people: Toilet facilities
Special comments: Access via side-entrance, phone beforehand.

CENTRAL SCOTLAND FAMILY HISTORY SOCIETY (CSFHS)

11 Springbank Gardens, Dunblane, Perthshire, FK15 9JX

Website: www.csfhs.org.uk

Enquiries to: Honorary Secretary

Founded: 1990

Organisation type and purpose: Membership association (membership is by subscription).

Subject coverage: Family history of the area.

Publications: Printed

Publications list: Available online

CENTRAL ST MARTINS COLLEGE OF ARTS AND DESIGN (CSM)

Granary Building, 1 Granary Square, London, N1C 4AA

Tel: 020 7514 7000
Website: www.csm.arts.ac.uk
Website: www.arts.ac.uk/library

Enquiries to: Learning Resources Manager
Direct tel: 020 7514 7029
Direct e-mail: s.gilmour@csm.arts.ac.uk
Other contacts: Assistant Learning Resources Manager (for requests for access by potential external users)

Founded: 1896; incorporates the former ILEA Art Schools; incorporates the former Central School of Art and Design, St Martins School of Art (year of change 1989); incorporates the former Drama Centre London (year of change 2000); incorporates the former Byam Shaw School of Art (year of change 2003)

Organisation type and purpose: University department or institute, suitable for ages: 18+
College of Higher Education.

Subject coverage: Fine arts, graphic design, product and industrial design, fashion design, textile design, jewellery design, ceramic design, photography, animation, film and video, theatre design and scenography, performing arts.

Collection: Materials and Products Collection
Fashion files

Non-library collection catalogue: All or part available online

Library catalogue: All or part available online

Publications: Printed

Publications list: Available online

Access to staff: Contact by letter, by telephone, by fax, by e-mail and via website. Appointment necessary.
Hours: Mon to Fri, 0900 to 1700

Parent body: University of the Arts London; 272 High Holborn, London, WC1; tel: 020 7514 6000; e-mail: p.christie@arts.ac.uk

CENTRAL SUSSEX COLLEGE

Learning Resource Centre (LRC), Crawley Campus, College Road, Crawley, West Sussex, RH10 1NR

Tel: 01293 442281
Fax: 01293 442399
E-mail: lrc@centralsussex.ac.uk

Enquiries to: LRC Manager
Other contacts: Deputy LRC Manager

Founded: 2005; created by the merger of Crawley College and Haywards Heath Sixth Form College (year of change 2005)

Organisation type and purpose: Further education, higher education.

Subject coverage: Business and finance, beauty therapy, catering, computing and IT, engineering, construction, hairdressing, health and social care, languages, management, education, the arts, social sciences, travel and tourism.

Library catalogue: All or part available in-house

Access to staff: Contact by letter, by telephone and by e-mail. Appointment necessary.
Hours: Mon to Fri, 1000 to 1600

Access for disabled people: Access to most areas

CENTRE FOR ACCESSIBLE ENVIRONMENTS (CAE)

70 South Lambeth Road, Vauxhall, London, SW8 1RL

Tel: 020 7840 0125
Fax: 020 7840 5811
E-mail: info@cae.org.uk
Website: www.cae.org.uk

Enquiries to: Team
Direct tel: 020 7840 0125
Direct fax: 020 7840 5811
Direct e-mail: info@cae.org.uk
Other contacts: Consultancy Team (provide guidance on inclusive design and fulfil access audit / consultancy requests)

Founded: 1970; formerly called Centre on Environment for the Handicapped

Organisation type and purpose: Registered charity (charity number: 1050820).

Subject coverage: Information and advice on the design of the built environment for disabled and older people.

Information services: CAE provides guidance to enquirers by phone and email. For advice and consultancy work, the Consultancy Team can quote and assist further. Publications, a quarterly journal and a monthly newsletter available.

Collection: Specialist library on the disability and environments.

Non-library collection catalogue: All or part available in-house

Library catalogue: All or part available in-house

Publications: Printed, and electronic and video, and microform publications
Order printed publications from: membership@cae.org.uk
Order microform publications from: CAE: info@cae.org.uk

Publications list: Available in print

Access to staff: Contact by letter, by telephone, by fax, by e-mail and via website. Appointment necessary.
Hours: Mon to Fri, 0900 to 1700
Special comments: CAE operates with a very small team so it may take us a little longer to respond to queries but we are happy to help.

Access to building: By appointment only.
Hours: Mon to Fri, 0900 to 1700.
Special comments: Buzzer entry for shared building.

Access for disabled people: Level access to building entrance and CAE office.
Hours: Mon to Fri, 0900 to 1700
Special comments: Entry to building by digital key pad. CAE can be buzzed (relief button indicates CAE's office) and a member of staff will come to the door.

CENTRE FOR AGRICULTURAL STRATEGY (CAS)

The University of Reading, PO Box 237, Earley Gate, Reading, Berkshire, RG6 6AR

Tel: 0118 931 8150
Fax: 0118 935 3423
E-mail: casagri@reading.ac.uk
Website: www.rdg.ac.uk/AgriStrat

Enquiries to: Director

Founded: 1980

Organisation type and purpose: University department or institute, research organisation.

Subject coverage: Agriculture, including food, horticulture, forestry, agroforestry, fish production; environment; long-term planning and forecasting for the agricultural industries, worldwide.

Publications: Printed
Order printed publications from: Publications Department, Centre for Agricultural Strategy at the same address, tel: 0118 931 8152, fax: 0118 935 3423, e-mail: t.m.hicks@rdg.ac.uk

Publications list: Available in print

Access to staff: Contact by letter, by telephone, by fax, by e-mail, in person and via website
Hours: Mon to Fri, 0900 to 1700

Established by the: Nuffield Foundation as an independent, non-profit distributory organisation

Part of: University of Reading within the Faculty of Agriculture and Food

CENTRE FOR ALTERNATIVE TECHNOLOGY (CAT)

Machynlleth, Powys, SY20 9AZ

continued overleaf

Tel: 01654 705989
E-mail: info@cat.org.uk
Website: www.cat.org.uk

Enquiries to: Free Information Service

Founded: 1975

Organisation type and purpose:
International organisation, national organisation, membership association (membership is by subscription), registered charity (charity number 265239), suitable for ages: all, training organisation, consultancy, research organisation, publishing house.
Visitor Centre.
Display and research in sustainable, environmental, alternative technology and energy conservation issues.

Subject coverage: Small-scale renewable energy, wind, water and solar energy, energy efficiency, environmentally sound buildings, organic gardening, alternative sewage systems, reed beds, compost toilets, green tourism, environmental visitor centres, green building technology, education.

Publications: Printed
Order printed publications from: CAT Mail Order, at the same address; tel: 01654 705959 or 0845 330 4592; fax: 01654 705999; e-mail: mail.order@cat.org.uk

Publications list: Available online and in print

Access to staff: Contact by letter, by telephone, by e-mail, in person and via website
Hours: Mon to Fri, 0930 to 1730
Also Sat, Sun for visitors to the centre
Special comments: In person access may be restricted – please phone for details.

Access to building: No prior appointment required
Hours: Mon to Sun, 1000 to 1730
Special comments: Entrance fee.

Access for disabled people: Parking provided, level entry, access to most public areas, toilet facilities

CENTRE FOR APPLIED RESEARCH IN EDUCATION (CARE)

School of Education and Professional Development, University of East Anglia, Norwich, Norfolk, NR4 7TJ

Tel: 01603 456161
Fax: 01603 451412
E-mail: c.stephens@uea.ac.uk
Website: www.uea.ac.uk/care/

Enquiries to: Director's Secretary
Direct tel: 01603 592638

Founded: 1970

Organisation type and purpose: University department or institute, consultancy, research organisation.
University policy and curriculum research centre with degree teaching function; a constituent of the School of Education while maintaining its own identity.

Subject coverage: Curriculum research, evaluation, development, dissemination, particularly in relation to centralised innovation projects; policy research and evaluation; information technology in education; computer-based education; bilingual education; in-service teacher education, particularly school-focused with an action research element; naturalistic methods of inquiry; problems and effects of teaching about race relations; library access and independent study for sixth-form students; performing arts evaluation; police training; AIDS/HIV education; research on youth; funding and contracting of social research, higher education research, disaffected pupils and curriculums; research/evaluation of nurse, midwife and GP education.

Collection: Archive of major research and curriculum development projects

Publications: Printed

Publications list: Available in print

Access to staff: Contact by e-mail
Hours: Mon to Fri, 0900 to 1700

CENTRE FOR ARMENIAN INFORMATION AND ADVICE

Hayashen, 105A Mill Hill Road, London, W3 8J

Tel: 020 8992 4621
Fax: 020 8993 8953
E-mail: info@caia.org.uk
Website: www.caia.org.uk

Founded: 1986

Organisation type and purpose: To enhance the quality of life for disadvantaged members of the Armenian community in London, specifically those in poverty and isolation, through the provision of welfare, educational and cultural services.
To promote understanding of the Armenian heritage, history and culture among the Armenian community and the wider public.
Registered charity (charity number 1088534)

Publications: Printed

Access to staff: Contact by letter, by telephone, by fax, by e-mail and via website.
Appointment necessary.
Hours: Mon to Fri, 0900 to 1600 (phone for appointment)

CENTRE FOR BUCKINGHAMSHIRE STUDIES

County Hall, Aylesbury, Buckinghamshire, HP20 1UU

Tel: 01296 382587 (Archives); 01296 382250 (Local Studies)
Fax: 01296 382771
E-mail: archives@buckscc.gov.uk; localstudies@buckscc.gov.uk
Website: www.buckscc.gov.uk/archives
Website: www.buckscc.gov.uk (click on P in A-Z index, then Photographs of Buckinghamshire)
Website: www.nationalarchives.gov.uk/a2a
Website: www.buckscc.gov.uk/libraries

Enquiries to: Archivist

Founded: 1938; formerly called Buckinghamshire Record Office (year of change 1997); formerly called Buckinghamshire Records and Local Studies Service (year of change 2002)

Organisation type and purpose: Local government body.

Subject coverage: Local authority records, including Buckinghamshire Quarter Sessions (from1678) and County Council (from 1889), Church of England parish records, also records of non-conformist churches, records of Archdeaconry of Buckinghamshire (including wills 1483–1858) etc., family and estate records, business records.

Collection: Microfiche copies of National Probate Index, 1858–1943
Microfiche copies of General Register Office index to births, deaths and marriages, 1837–2004
Microfilm copies of most of the Buckinghamshire Parish Registers held in the archives are available in the Local Studies Library

Non-library collection catalogue: All or part available online

Library catalogue: All or part available online and in-house

Publications: Printed

Publications list: Available online and in print

Access to staff: Contact by letter, by telephone, by fax, by e-mail, in person and via website
Hours: Tue, Wed and Fri, 0900 to 1730; Thu 0900 to 2000; Sat, 0900 to 1600.
(Archive Searchroom closes Tue to Fri, 1715; Sat, 1545)
Special comments: CARN Readers Ticket required for archive searchroom; can be issued on presentation of proof of identity, name, address, signature.
A reservation is strongly advised for a microfilm/microfiche reader in the Local Studies Library and for a seat in the archive searchroom.

Access for disabled people: Ramped entry, toilet facilities
Special comments: Access to all public areas.

Parent body: Culture and Learning Service of Buckinghamshire County Council

CENTRE FOR BUSINESS AND PUBLIC SECTOR ETHICS (CBPSE)

Suite 131, 23 King Street, Cambridge, CB1 1AH

Tel: 01954 710086
Fax: 01954 710103
E-mail: info@ethicscentre.org
Website: www.ethicscentre.org
Website: www.ethicspress.com

Enquiries to: Director

Founded: 1988

Organisation type and purpose:
International organisation, registered charity (charity number 1045986), training organisation, consultancy, research institute, publishing house.

Subject coverage: Business ethics, corporate governance, government and political ethics, corporate and social responsibility, ethical systems, ethical audit, public administration and policy, environmental ethics, sustainable development, anti-corruption.

Non-library collection catalogue: All or part available online and in print

Library catalogue: All or part available online and in print

Publications: Printed, and electronic and video
Order printed publications from: Ethics International Press Ltd, St. Andrew's Castle, St. Andrew's Street South, Bury St. Edmunds
Order electronic and video publications from: www.bookmasters.com/ebooks/30079.htm

Publications list: Available online and in print

Access to staff: Contact by letter, by telephone, by fax, by e-mail and via website. Appointment necessary.
Hours: Mon to Fri, 0900 to 1700

Access to building: No access other than to staff.

Also at: Centre for Business and Public Sector Ethics; St Andrew's Castle, St Andrew's Street South, Bury St Edmunds, IP33 3PH; tel: 01954 710086; fax: 01954 710103; e-mail: info@ethicscentre.org

CENTRE FOR CELL & TISSUE RESEARCH (CCTR)

Department of Biology, University of York, PO Box 373, York, YO10 5YW

Tel: 01904 432936
Fax: 01904 432936
E-mail: cmj4@york.ac.uk

Enquiries to: Marketing Coordinator
Other contacts: Director

Founded: 1981

Organisation type and purpose: University department or institute.
Commercial Unit.
The development and use of equipment.

Subject coverage: Low temperature preparation techniques for electron microscopy, rapid freezing, cryo-sem, cryo ultra-microtomy freeze fracture for transmission electron microscopy, freeze-etching, low temperature embedding.

Access to staff: Contact by letter, by telephone, by fax and by e-mail
Hours: Mon to Fri, 0900 to 1700

CENTRE FOR CLASSICAL HOMOEOPATHY

Homoeopathy Clinic, 2a Meal Market, Hexham, Northumberland, NE46

Tel: 01434 322084
E-mail: francishannon@hotmail.com
Website: www.hompath.club24.co.uk
Website: www.yell.co.uk/sites/homeopathy

Enquiries to: Director

Founded: 1979; formerly called Hannon Clinic of Natural Medicine

Organisation type and purpose: Service industry, consultancy. To treat sick people by means of homoeopathic medicine.
Specialising in chronic diseases such as arthritis, asthma, eczema and psoriasis.

Subject coverage: Treatment of chronic diseases by means of homoeopathic medicine.

Publications: Printed

Access to staff: Contact by letter, by telephone, by e-mail and via website. Appointment necessary.
Hours: Mon to Fri, 0900 to 1700

Also at: Homoeopathy Clinic; Lindisfarne, 71 Westgate Road, Newcastle Upon Tyne; Homoeopathy Clinic; 1 Red Gables, Chatsworth Road, Carlisle, CA1

CENTRE FOR COACHING (CfC)

156 Westcombe Hill, London, SE3 7DH

Tel: 0845 680 2065
E-mail: cope@ciafpd.com
Website: www.centreforcoaching.com

Enquiries to: Director

Founded: 2001

Organisation type and purpose: Training organisation, consultancy, research organisation.

Subject coverage: Coaching, life coaching, performance coaching, business coaching, executive coaching, stress management coaching, health coaching, psychological coaching, cognitive coaching, training.

Non-library collection catalogue: All or part available online

Publications: Printed, and electronic and video

Publications list: Available online

Access to staff: Contact by letter, by telephone and by e-mail. Appointment necessary.
Hours: Mon to Fri, 1000 to 1700

Links with: Centre for Stress Management; 156 Westcombe Hill, London, SE3 7DH; International Academy for Professional Development Ltd; website: http://iafpd.com

Member organisation of: Association for Coaching; British Institue for Learning and Development

CENTRE FOR COMBUSTION AND ENERGY STUDIES

University of Leeds, Leeds, West Yorkshire, LS2 9JT

Tel: 0113 343 2498
Fax: 0113 244 0572
Website: www.mech-eng.leeds.ac.uk/cces/ce.html

Enquiries to: Deputy Director
Direct tel: 0113 343 2108
Direct fax: 0113 242 4611
Direct e-mail: comb-energy@mech-eng.leeds.ac.uk

Organisation type and purpose: University department or institute, consultancy, research organisation.
Consortium of University Departments of Chemistry, Fuel and Energy Engineering and Mechanical Engineering.

Subject coverage: Combustion; fundamentals and applications in engines, furnaces, power generation; flames; control and diagnostics; heat transfer; pollution emission control; energy; analysis, conservation, cogeneration; alternative sources; fuels; analysis, reserves, conversion technologies; fire and explosion hazards.

Publications: Printed

Access to staff: Contact by letter, by telephone and by e-mail
Hours: Mon to Fri, 0900 to 1700

Access for disabled people: Access to all public areas

CENTRE FOR COMPLEMENTARY AND INTEGRATED MEDICINE

56 Bedford Place, Southampton, SO15 2DT

Tel: 023 8033 4752
Fax: 023 8023 1835
E-mail: info@complemed.co.uk
Website: www.complemed.co.uk

Enquiries to: Manager

Founded: 1982

Organisation type and purpose: Service industry, training organisation, research organisation.
Medical Practice.
To provide services, planning and research within complementary medicine.

Subject coverage: A multi-disciplinary, medically based clinical practice within the field of complementary medicine encompassing training and research in homoeopathy, osteopathy, acupuncture, environmental medicine, clinical ecology (food and chemical sensitivity).

Publications: Printed

Publications list: Available in print

Access to staff: Contact by letter, by telephone, by fax and via website
Hours: Mon to Thu, 0900 to 1300

Also at: 21 Harcourt House, 19 Cavendish Square, London, W1G 0PL; tel: 020 7935 7848

CENTRE FOR COMPOSITE MATERIALS

Imperial College of Science, Technology and Medicine, Prince Consort Road, London, SW7 2BY

Tel: 020 7594 5084
Fax: 020 7594 5083
E-mail: composites@ic.ac.uk
Website: www.cm.ic.ac.uk

Enquiries to: Director

Founded: 1983

Organisation type and purpose: University department or institute.
MSc in composite materials, research degrees, contract research and testing for industry.

Subject coverage: Testing, characterisation, design, mathematical modelling of fibre-reinforced plastics, metals and ceramics.

Publications: Printed

Access to staff: Contact by letter, by telephone, by fax and by e-mail. Appointment necessary.
Hours: Mon to Fri, 0900 to 1700

CENTRE FOR CONSERVATION STUDIES

Department of Archaeology, University of York, The Kings Manor, York, YO1 7EP

Tel: 01904 433997
Fax: 01904 433902
E-mail: pab11@york.ac.uk
Website: www.york.ac.uk/depts/arch

Enquiries to: Postgraduate Administrator

History of institution: created by the merger of Institute of Advanced Architectural Studies (IAAS), Institute of Advanced Architectural Studies Centre for the Conservation of Parks and Gardens (year of change 1997)

Organisation type and purpose: University department or institute, suitable for ages: 18+.
Award of MA and DPhil degrees. Short courses open to the public.

Subject coverage: Architectural conservation, cultural heritage management, landscape studies.

Collection: Library housed at the Kings Manor Library, University of York

Library catalogue: All or part available online

Publications list: Available in print

Access to staff: Contact by letter, by telephone, by fax, by e-mail, in person and via website. Appointment necessary.
Hours: Mon to Fri, 0900 to 1700

Access to building: No access other than to staff
Hours: Mon to Fri, 0900 to 1700
Special comments: Borrowing restricted to university members and subscribers, but access is free.

CENTRE FOR CONTEMPORARY ART AND THE NATURAL WORLD (CCANW)

Haldon Forest Park, Exeter, Devon, EX6 7XR

Tel: 01392 832277
E-mail: info@ccanw.co.uk
Website: www.ccanw.co.uk
Founded: 2001

Organisation type and purpose: A registered limited company (charity number 4141506) and registered charity (charity number 1092019), seeking to increase access to the arts by breaking down physical, psychological and intellectual barriers, while working with different communities, embracing cultural diversity and social inclusion.

Subject coverage: Man's artistic relationship with the natural world.

CENTRE FOR CONTEMPORARY ARTS (CCA)

350 Sauchiehall Street, Glasgow, G2 3JD

Tel: 0141 332 7521
Fax: 0141 332 3226
E-mail: gen@cca-glasgow.com
Website: www.cca-glasgow.com

Enquiries to: Head of Administration & Resources

Founded: 1993

Organisation type and purpose: Voluntary organisation, registered charity, art gallery. Arts centre.
To support artists in making possible the creation of original works, increasing the accessibility and strengthening the understanding of contemporary arts through a range of activities including talks, tours, writers' events, classes and workshops.

Subject coverage: Contemporary visual and performing arts especially in Scotland.

Publications: Printed

Publications list: Available in print

Access to staff: Contact by telephone and by e-mail
Hours: Mon to Fri, 0900 to 1700

Access for disabled people: Access to all public areas

CENTRE FOR CONTEMPORARY BRITISH HISTORY (CCBH)

K.6.52, King's College London, Strand, London, WC2R 2LS

Tel: 020 7836 5454 ext. 7045
E-mail: virginia.preston@kcl.ac.uk
Website: www.ccbh.ac.uk

Founded: 1986; formerly called Institute of Contemporary British History

Organisation type and purpose: University department or institute, age range: higher, research organisation, publishing house.

Subject coverage: British history since 1945, oral history, information about research and scholars in these fields both in the UK and overseas, Conservative Party in the 20th century, Labour Party in the 20th century, current affairs (political), political economy.

Publications: Printed

Publications list: Available in print

Access to staff: Contact by letter, by telephone, by fax, by e-mail and via website. Appointment necessary.

CENTRE FOR COUPLE RELATIONSHIPS (TCCR)

Tavistock Centre, 120 Belsize Lane, London, NW3 5BA

Tel: 020 8938 2353
Fax: 020 7435 1080
E-mail: tccr@tccr.org.uk
Website: www.tccr.org.uk

Enquiries to: Information Officer
Other contacts: Director

Founded: 1948

Organisation type and purpose: Voluntary organisation, registered charity (charity number 211058), training organisation, consultancy, research organisation.
Psychotherapy Organisation working nationally and internationally; learned institute concerned with the couple relationship.

Subject coverage: Training, consultancy and research organisation offering psychotherapy to couples, teaching, training and consultancy to other practitioners working with couples, research. Areas of particular interest: couple psychotherapy, divorce, infertility, unemployment, family transitions, divorce court welfare, mediation, inter-agency collaboration.

Publications: Printed, and electronic and video
Order printed publications from: Karnac (Books) Ltd
58 Gloucester Road, London, SW7 4DQ, tel: 020 7584 3303, fax: 020 7823 7743

Publications list: Available online and in print

Access to staff: Contact by letter, by telephone, by fax, by e-mail and via website. Appointment necessary.
Hours: Mon to Fri, 0900 to 1700

Member of: International Union of Family Organisations; United Kingdom Council for Psychotherapy

Parent body: Tavistock Institute of Medical Psychology

CENTRE FOR CRIME AND JUSTICE STUDIES (CCJS)

King's College London, Strand, WC2R 2LS

Tel: 020 7848 1688
Fax: 020 7848 1689
E-mail: info@crimeandjustice.org.uk
Website: www.kcl.ac.uk/ccjs
Website: www.crimeinfo.org
Website: www.kcl.ac.uk/istd

Enquiries to: Director
Other contacts: Research and Development Officer

Founded: 1931; formerly called Institute for the Study and Treatment of Delinquency (ISTD)

Organisation type and purpose: Membership association (membership is by subscription), present number of members: 926, voluntary organisation, registered charity (charity number 251588), research organisation.
To promote the exchange of knowledge, experience and understanding of criminal justice matters among interested individuals and to provide an independent, objective and non-campaigning forum for debate.

Subject coverage: Criminology, criminal justice, delinquency.

Collection: The E T Jensen Library (over 2000 volumes on Criminology) now in the King's College Library

Publications: Printed

Publications list: Available online and in print

Access to staff: Contact by letter, by telephone, by fax, by e-mail and via website
Hours: Mon to Fri, 0900 to 1700

CENTRE FOR CRIMINOLOGY (CCR)

Formal name: The Centre for Criminology

Manor Road Building, Manor Road, Oxford, OX1 3UQ

Tel: 01865 274444/8
Fax: 01865 281924

E-mail: ccr@crim.ox.ac.uk
Website: www.crim.ox.ac.uk
Website: www.lib.ox.ac.uk/olis

Enquiries to: Administrator

Founded: 1996; formerly called Penal Research Unit (year of change 1973); formerly called The Centre for Criminological Research and Probation Studies Unit (year of change 2004)

Organisation type and purpose: University department or institute, research organisation.
Research centre. Provider of graduate programmes at Master's and DPhil level.

Subject coverage: Policing and security; sentencing and punishment; public opinion, politics and crime control; victims; extra-legal governance and organized crime, and crime, rehabilitation and desistance.

Publications: Printed

Access to staff: Contact by letter, by telephone, by fax, by e-mail and via website. Appointment necessary.
Hours: Mon to Fri, 0915 to 1700

Access to building: Please arrange appointment in advance
Hours: Mon to Fri, 0900 to 1700
Special comments: University card required.

Access for disabled people: Please arrange appointment in advance
Hours: Mon to Fri, 0900 to 1700
Special comments: University card required.

CENTRE FOR DEAF EDUCATION (CfDE)

City Lit, Keeley Street, Covent Garden, London, WC2B 4BA

Tel: 020 7492 2725
Fax: 020 7492 2745
E-mail: deafedu@citylit.ac.uk
Website: www.citylit.ac.uk

Enquiries to: Centre administrators
Other contacts: Centre Co-ordinators, Head of Centre

History of institution: formerly called Central London AEI Centre for the Deaf; formerly called Deaf Education and Learning Support (year of change 2010)

Organisation type and purpose: Professional body, suitable for ages: 18+, training organisation.
Academic institution, formerly under the Inner London Education Authority.

Subject coverage: Training, courses and support for deaf people and for those wishing to work with deaf people. Provides support for deaf students in over 30 further education and higher education colleges.

Library catalogue: All or part available in-house

Publications: Printed

Publications list: Available online

Access to staff: Contact by letter, by telephone, by fax and by e-mail. Appointment necessary.
Hours: Mon to Fri, 0900 to 1700

Access to building: No prior appointment required

Access for disabled people: Street-level entry, toilet facilities

CENTRE FOR DEFENCE AND INTERNATIONAL SECURITY STUDIES (CDISS)

Cartmel College, University of Lancaster, Bailrigg, Lancaster, LA1 4YL

Tel: 01524 594254
Fax: 01524 594258
E-mail: cdiss@lancaster.ac.uk
Website: www.cdiss.org

Enquiries to: Executive Secretary
Direct e-mail: p.elliott@lancaster.ac.uk
Other contacts: Director

Founded: 1990; formed by the merger of Centre for Defence and Security Analysis (CDSA), Centre for the Study of Arms Control and International Security (CSACIS) (year of change 1990)

Organisation type and purpose: Membership association (membership is by election or invitation), present number of members: 54, university department or institute, research organisation.

Subject coverage: Ballistic missile defence; defence management; civil-military relations; military technology; maritime and naval policy.

Collection: 150+ Defence Journal Titles 1983–1999 as Abstracts and indexed in The Lancaster Index

Non-library collection catalogue: All or part available online and in print

Library catalogue: All or part available in-house

Publications: Printed, and electronic and video

Publications list: Available in print

Access to staff: Contact by letter, by telephone, by fax, by e-mail and via website
Hours: Mon to Fri, 0900 to 1700

Access to building: No access other than to staff
Hours: University Library: 0900 to 2100 term time
Special comments: Permission required.

Connections with: ANEPE; Santiago, Chile; CERSA Toulouse University; CISSM Maryland University; Defence Research Centre; Tokyo, Japan; SIIA; Johannesburg, South Africa

CENTRE FOR DEVELOPMENT STUDIES (CDS)

University of Wales, Swansea, Singleton Park, Swansea, West Glamorgan, SA2 8PP

Tel: 01792 295332
Fax: 01792 295682
E-mail: h.lewis@swansea.ac.uk
Website: www.swan.ac.uk/cds/index.htm
Website: www.swan.ac.uk/cds/devres/index.htm

Enquiries to: Admissions Secretary

Founded: 1976

Organisation type and purpose: International organisation, university department or institute, training organisation, consultancy, research organisation, publishing house.

Subject coverage: Development planning, in particular social development; monitoring, evaluation and impact assessment; development policy; regional development; rights-based approaches; development management; environmental planning; population and development; participatory development; health planning; sexual and reproductive health; crime and justice systems; children's rights; governance; poverty reduction; sustainable livelihoods; corporate social responsibility.

Publications: Printed

Publications list: Available online and in print

Access to staff: Contact by letter, by telephone, by fax, by e-mail, in person and via website. Appointment necessary.
Hours: Mon to Fri, 0900 to 1700

Links with: Resource Centre for Department for International Development, in the fields of social development, health and population

CENTRE FOR ECOLOGY & HYDROLOGY (CEH)

Maclean Building, Crowmarsh Gifford, Wallingford, Oxfordshire, OX10 8BB

Tel: 01491 838800
Fax: 01524 61536
E-mail: enquiries@ceh.ac.uk
Website: nerc.worldcat.org/

Enquiries to: Library Manager
Direct tel: 01524 595906
Direct e-mail: cehlib@ceh.ac.uk
Other contacts: Assistant Librarian

Founded: 2000; formed from Institute of Freshwater Ecology (IFE), Institute of Hydrology (IH), Institute of Terrestrial Ecology (ITE), Institute of Virology and Environmental Microbiology (IVEM) (year of change 2000)

Organisation type and purpose: Research organisation.
One of the Centres and Surveys of the Natural Environment Research Council. UK body for research, survey and monitoring in terrestrial and freshwater environments.

Subject coverage: Environmental science, aquatic ecology, terrestrial ecology, hydrology, microbiology, environmental chemistry, hydrobiology.

Collection: Various collections of original (unpublished) data; NERC Open Research Archive (NORA)

Library catalogue: All or part available online

Publications: Printed

Publications list: Available online

Access to staff: Contact by letter, by telephone and by e-mail. Appointment necessary.
Hours: Mon to Fri, 0900 to 1630
Special comments: CEH Bangor and CEH Edinburgh Libraries unmanned

continued overleaf

Access to building: Prior appointment required
Special comments: Any bona fide researcher with a scientific not-for-profit research need which cannot easily be met through their own organisation's resources may use the libraries at the discretion of the Head of Site

Access for disabled people: Parking provided
CEH Wallingford; Maclean Building, Crowmarsh Gifford, Wallingford, Oxfordshire, OX10 8BB; tel: 01491 838800; fax: 01491 692424; **Other addresses:** CEH Bangor; Environment Centre Wales, Deiniol Road, Bangor, Gwynedd, LL57 2 UW; tel: 01248 374500; fax: 01248 3553656; CEH Edinburgh; Bush Estate, Penicuik, Midlothian, EH26 0QB; tel: 0131 445 4343; fax: 0131 445 3943; CEH Lancaster; Lancaster Environment Centre, Library Avenue, Bailrigg, Lancaster LA1 4AP; tel: 01524 595800; fax: 01524 61536

Parent body: Natural Environment Research Council (NERC); Polaris House, North Star Avenue, Swindon, SN2 1EY; tel: 01793 411500; fax: 01793 411501

CENTRE FOR ECOLOGY AND HYDROLOGY – EDINBURGH RESEARCH STATION

Bush Estate, Penicuik, Midlothian, EH26 0QB

Tel: 0131 445 4343
Fax: 0131 445 3943
E-mail: bulib@ceh.ac.uk
Website: www.ceh.ac.uk

Enquiries to: Librarian
Direct tel: 0131 445 8509

Founded: 2000; created by the merger of Institute of Freshwater Ecology (IFE), Institute of Hydrology (IH), Institute of Terrestrial Ecology (ITE), Institute of Virology and Environmental Microbiology (IVEM) (year of change 2000); formerly a part of Nature Conservancy Council (year of change 1973)

Organisation type and purpose: Research organisation.

Subject coverage: Factors determining the structure, composition and processes of terrestrial ecological systems and the abundance and performance of individual species and organisms, scientific bases for predicting and modelling future environmental trends, human impact, land use, conservation and the protection and management of the environment.

Library catalogue: All or part available online

Publications: Printed
Order printed publications from: Publications Section, CEH Wallingford, OX10 8BB

Access to staff: Contact by letter, by telephone, by fax, by e-mail and via website. Appointment necessary.
Hours: Mon to Fri, 0900 to 1700
Special comments: Researchers only.

Also at: Bangor Research Unit; Environment Centre for Wales, Deiniol Road, Bangor, Gwynedd, LL57 2UW; tel: 01248 374500; CEH Lancaster; Lancaster Envionment Centre, Library Avenue, Bailrigg, LA1 4AP; tel: 01524 595906; fax: 01539 534705; Centre for Ecology and Hydrology; Maclean Building, Crowmarsh Gifford, Wallingford, Oxfordshire, OX10 8BB; tel: 01491 838800

Parent body: Natural Environment Research Council

CENTRE FOR ECONOMIC PERFORMANCE (CEP)

London School of Economics, Houghton Street, London, WC2A 2AE

Tel: 020 7955 7673
Fax: 020 7955 7595
E-mail: cep.info@lse.ac.uk
Website: cep.lse.ac.uk
Website: cep.lse.ac.uk/papers/

Enquiries to: Administrator

Founded: 1990

Organisation type and purpose: University department or institute, research organisation.
Researching the factors affecting the economic performance of nations and firms.

Subject coverage: Economic aspects of the labour market, including employment, unemployment, inflation and income distribution; economics of education and human capital, economic growth, corporate performance, industrial relations, skills and job satisfaction, globalisation, internet economy, productivity and innovation, and wellbeing.

Library catalogue: All or part available online

Publications list: Available online and in print

Access to staff: Contact by e-mail and via website
Hours: Mon to Fri, 0900 to 1700

Access to building: No access other than to staff.
Location: 4th floor, Lionel Robbins Building, 10 Portugal Street, London, WC2A 2HD

Access for disabled people: Access to all public areas

Parent body: London School of Economics (LSE); Houghton Street, London, WC2A 2AE

CENTRE FOR ECONOMIC POLICY RESEARCH (CEPR)

90–98 Goswell Road, London, EC1V 7RR

Tel: 020 7878 2900
Fax: 020 7878 2999
E-mail: cepr@cepr.org
Website: www.cepr.org

Enquiries to: External Relations Manager

Founded: 1983

Organisation type and purpose: Registered charity, research organisation.

Subject coverage: Economic policy.

Publications: Printed
Order printed publications from: tel: 020 7878 2903, e-mail: orders@cepr.org

Publications list: Available online and in print

Access to staff: Contact by e-mail
Hours: Mon to Fri, 0900 to 1700

Links with: Centre for Economic Policy Research International Foundation (US)

CENTRE FOR EFFECTIVE DISPUTE RESOLUTION (CEDR)

70 Fleet Street, London, EC4Y 1EU

Tel: 020 7536 6000
Fax: 020 7536 6001
E-mail: info@cedr.co.uk
Website: www.cedr.co.uk

Enquiries to: Administration Manager, Corporate Resources

Founded: 1990

Organisation type and purpose:
International organisation, advisory body, membership association (membership is by subscription), present number of members: 450, registered charity (charity number 106369), training organisation, consultancy, research organisation.
Experts in mediation and other forms of effective dispute resolution for commercial disputes.
CEDR is an independent organisation supported by industry and professional advisers and founded to promote and encourage more effective commercial resolution of disputes.

Subject coverage: Alternative dispute resolution (ADR) information services and training, negotiating training, mediation and alternative dispute resolution techniques, mediation training for lawyers, UK and worldwide, commercial alternative dispute resolution services, extensive mediation and conflict resolution training.

Publications: Printed, and electronic and video

Publications list: Available online and in print

Access to staff: Contact by letter, by telephone, by fax, by e-mail, in person and via website. Appointment necessary.
Hours: Mon to Fri, 0900 to 1800

CENTRE FOR ENERGY, PETROLEUM AND MINERAL LAW AND POLICY (CEPMLP)

CEPMLP Information Service, Carnegie Building, Geddes Quadrangle, University of Dundee, Dundee, DD1 4HN

Tel: 01382 384302
Fax: 01382 385854
E-mail: r.m.carstairs@dundee.ac.uk
Website: www.cepmlp.org

Enquiries to: Information Services Manager
Direct e-mail: r.m.carstairs@dundee.ac.uk

History of institution: formerly called Centre for Petroleum and Mineral Law and Policy (CPMLP) (year of change 1997)

Organisation type and purpose: University library, training organisation, consultancy, research organisation, publishing house.

Subject coverage: Oil and gas law, policy and economics; mineral law, policy and economics; natural resources law, policy and economics; environmental law and policy.

Education services: Access given to external research scholars, but by prior arrangement only.

Collection: Petroleum, mining and environmental laws, worldwide
Contracts and agreements collection

Library catalogue: All or part available online and in-house

Publications: Printed, and electronic and video
Order electronic and video publications from: Online store

Publications list: Available online and in print

Access to staff: Contact by letter, by telephone, by fax, by e-mail, in person and via website. Appointment necessary. Non-members charged.
Hours: Mon to Fri, 0930 to 1230 and 1400 to 1700

CENTRE FOR ENGLISH LANGUAGE TEACHING (CELT)

Airthrey Castle, University of Stirling, Stirling, FK9 4LA

Tel: 01786 467934
Fax: 01786 466131
E-mail: celt@stir.ac.uk
Website: www.celt.stir.ac.uk/

Enquiries to: Associate Director
Other contacts: Director

Founded: 1981

Organisation type and purpose: University department or institute.
Provides English language courses for non-native speakers of English.

Subject coverage: Courses in English as a foreign language lasting from 4 weeks to 3 years for anyone over the age of 17; courses in the teaching of English as a foreign language.

Publications: Printed

Access to staff: Contact by letter, by telephone, by fax, by e-mail and via website
Hours: Mon to Fri, 0900 to 1700

CENTRE FOR ENVIRONMENT, FISHERIES AND AQUACULTURE SCIENCE, THE (Cefas)

Lowestoft Laboratory, Lowestoft, Suffolk, NR33 0HT

Tel: 01502 562244
Fax: 01502 513865
E-mail: lowlibrary@cefas.co.uk
Website: www.cefas.defra.gov.uk

Enquiries to: Library and Information Officer

Organisation type and purpose: National government body.
Main Cefas laboratory.

Subject coverage: Fisheries, fishing and aquatic environmental research; marine biology; oceanography; aquaculture; marine pollution; fish diseases; marine radiobiology.

Library catalogue: All or part available in-house

Publications: Printed
Order printed publications from: tel: 01502 527735, e-mail: lowlibrary@cefas.co.uk

Publications list: Available online and in print

Access to staff: Contact by letter, by telephone, by fax, by e-mail and via website. Appointment necessary.
Hours: Mon to Fri 0900 to 1600

Access to building: No access other than to staff

Access for disabled people: Parking provided, ramped entry, toilet facilities

Also at: Cefas Weymouth Laboratory; Barrack Road, The Nothe, Weymouth, Dorset, DT4 8UB; tel: 01305 206600; e-mail: weylibrary@cefas.co.uk

Constituent part of: Department for Environment, Food and Rural Affairs (DEFRA)

CENTRE FOR ENVIRONMENTAL DATA AND RECORDING (CEDaR)

National Museums Northern Ireland, 153 Bangor Road, Cultra, Holywood, County Down, Northern Ireland

Tel: 028 9039 5256
E-mail: damian.mcferran@nmni.com
Website: www.nmni.com/cedar

Enquiries to: Records Centre Manager

Organisation type and purpose: National government body, museum, university department or institute, research organisation.
Funded by Northern Ireland Environment Agency (NIEA) and funding in-kind from NMNI.

Subject coverage: Natural history, flora and fauna, and geology of Northern Ireland and its coastal waters.

Collection: Databases of the location, date, vice-county, recorder, species and grid reference
Over 200,000 local natural history records
Over 1m. species and site records

Non-library collection catalogue: All or part available in-house

Library catalogue: All or part available in-house

Access to staff: Contact by letter, by telephone, by fax, by e-mail and via website. Appointment necessary.
Hours: Mon to Fri, 0900 to 1700

Access to building: Prior appointment required

CENTRE FOR ENVIRONMENTAL INITIATIVES (The CEI)

Old School House, Mill Lane, Carshalton, Surrey, SM5 2JY

Tel: 020 8770 6611
Fax: 020 8647 0719
E-mail: info@ecolocal.org.uk
Website: www.thecei.org.uk

Enquiries to: Director

Founded: 1987; formerly called Centre for Environmental Information (year of change 1993)

Organisation type and purpose: Voluntary organisation, registered charity (charity number 800377), suitable for ages: all, training organisation, consultancy, research organisation.
Local agenda 21, sustainable development, community involvement in sustainability.
The CEI's aim's to achieve and sustain strong, vibrant communities within a healthy environment.

Subject coverage: Local agenda 21, sustainable development, community involvement and participation in sustainable development, community consultation techniques.

Publications: Printed

Publications list: Available in print

Access to staff: Contact by letter. Appointment necessary.
Hours: Mon to Fri, 1000 to 1630
Special comments: Building accessible to the disabled, but there are no disabled toilets.

Access to building: Prior appointment required
Hours: Mon to Fri, 1000 to 1630

CENTRE FOR ENVIRONMENTALLY RESPONSIBLE TOURISM

PO Box 14, Benfleet, Essex, SS7 3LW

Tel: 01268 752827
Fax: 0870 139 2802
E-mail: cert.desk@virgin.net

Enquiries to: Chief Executive

Founded: 1994

Organisation type and purpose: International organisation (membership is by subscription), voluntary organisation.

Access to staff: Contact by e-mail
Hours: Mon to Fri, 0900 to 1700

Access to building: No access other than to staff

CENTRE FOR EUROPEAN REFORM (CER)

14 Great College Street, Westminster, London, SW1P 3RX

Tel: 020 7233 1199
Fax: 020 7233 1117
E-mail: info@cer.org.uk
Website: www.cer.org.uk

Organisation type and purpose: Think tank. Discussion forum. Conducts research and seminars.

Subject coverage: Political, economic and social challenges facing Europe. Pro-European but not uncritical.

Publications: Printed, and electronic and video

Publications list: Available online

CENTRE FOR FACILITIES CONSULTANCY LIMITED

PO Box 7490, Chelmsford, CM2 8YW

Tel: 0870 607 0201
Fax: 01245 403 262

continued overleaf

E-mail: centre@globalnet.co.uk
Website: www.facilities-centre.com

Enquiries to: Chairman
Other contacts: Office Manager for absence of the Chairman.

Founded: 1992

Organisation type and purpose: Service industry, training organisation, consultancy. Facilities management consulting and training.

Subject coverage: All aspects of facilities management consultancy including strategic reviews, accommodation strategy, outsourcing, cost savings, business continuity, performance measurement, health and safety, skills training, specifications, impartial advice and information on facilities management in UK and overseas. Training in non-clinical aspects of NHS Trusts, e.g.: violence, aggression, quality aspects.

Publications: Printed

Access to staff: Contact by letter, by telephone, by fax, by e-mail and via website. Appointment necessary.
Hours: Mon to Fri, 0900 to 1700

Access for disabled people: Access to all public areas

CENTRE FOR GLOBAL ENERGY STUDIES (CGES)

17 Knightsbridge, London, SW1X 7LY

Tel: 020 7235 4334
Fax: 020 7235 4338
E-mail: marketing@cges.co.uk
Website: www.cges.co.uk

Enquiries to: Marketing Manager
Direct tel: 020 7309 3610
Direct e-mail: jenni.wilson@cges.co.uk

Founded: 1990

Organisation type and purpose: International organisation, research institute (oil and gas).

Subject coverage: Oil market subscription reports, studies, special reports, events and oil market consulting.

Trade and statistical information: Oil and gas/energy

Publications: Printed
Order printed publications from: website: http://www.cges.co.uk, e-mail: marketing @ cges.co.uk

Publications list: Available online and in print

Access to staff: Contact by letter, by telephone, by fax, by e-mail and via website
Hours: Mon to Fri, 0930 to 1730

CENTRE FOR HEALTH ECONOMICS (CHE)

University of York, Heslington, York, YO10 5DD

Tel: 01904 433707
Fax: 01904 433644
E-mail: jmg1@york.ac.uk
Website: www.york.ac.uk/inst/che/welcome .html

Enquiries to: Information Service Manager
Direct e-mail: cheweb@york.ac.uk
Other contacts: Director for research opportunities.

Founded: 1983

Organisation type and purpose: University department or institute, training organisation, research organisation.
Centre for research and training in the factors affecting the demand for and supply of health, and the consequences for the provision of care.

Subject coverage: Health economics, health technology assessment, community care, economics of addiction, health services manpower, quality of life.

Collection: Health economics working papers

Library catalogue: All or part available in-house

Publications: Printed
Order printed publications from: Publications Office, Centre for Health Economics at same address, tel: 01904 433648, fax: 01904 433644, e-mail: chepub@york.ac.uk

Publications list: Available online and in print

Access to staff: Contact by letter, by telephone, by fax, by e-mail and via website. Appointment necessary.
Hours: Mon to Fri, 0900 to 1700
Special comments: Closed 23 Dec to 2 Jan.

Connections with: NHS Centre for Reviews and Dissemination (CRD); tel: 01904 433707; fax: 01904 433661; e-mail: revdis@york.ac.uk

Parent body: University of York; tel: 01904 430000; fax: 01904 433433

Part of: Institute for Research into the Social Sciences (IRISS); tel: 01904 433523; fax: 01904 433524

CENTRE FOR HEALTH INFORMATICS (CHI)

City University London, Northampton Square, London, EC1V 0HB

Tel: 020 7040 8367
Fax: 020 7040 8364
E-mail: a.v.roudsari@city.ac.uk
Website: www.city.ac.uk/chi

Enquiries to: Director

Founded: 1983; formerly called Centre for Measurement and Information in Medicine (year of change 2005)

Organisation type and purpose: University department or institute, research organisation.

Subject coverage: e-health and telecare, high-dependency medicine and public health; decision support systems (including computer-aided learning); integrated policy modelling for ICT-enhanced public healthcare; healthcare technologies, with emphasis upon methodologies for assessment and evaluation.

Collection: Annual Reports

Publications: Printed

Access to staff: Contact by letter, by telephone, by fax, by e-mail and via website. Appointment necessary.
Hours: Mon to Fri, 0900 to 1700; other times by arrangement

Constituent part of: Cass Business School of City University London

Links with: School of Engineering and Mathematical Sciences of City University London; School of Informatics of City University London

CENTRE FOR HUMAN GENETICS

Children's Hospital, Western Bank, Sheffield, South Yorkshire, S10 2TH

Tel: 0114 271 7000
Fax: 0114 273 7467
E-mail: o.quarrell@sheffield.ac.uk

Enquiries to: Director
Other contacts: Head of Department

Organisation type and purpose: Professional body.

Subject coverage: Genetics, medical genetics, cytogenetics.

Access to staff: Contact by letter
Hours: Mon to Fri, 0900 to 1700

Links with: Sheffield Children's Hospital

CENTRE FOR INDEPENDENT TRANSPORT RESEARCH IN LONDON (CILT)

Room 208, The Colourworks, 2 Abbot Street, London, E8 3DP

Tel: 020 7275 9900, 020 7275 9123 (minicom)
Fax: 020 7254 6777
Website: www.cilt.dial.pipex.com/

Enquiries to: Researchers

Founded: 1983; formerly called The Campaign to Improve London's Transport (CILT) (year of change 1988)

Organisation type and purpose: Membership association (membership is by subscription), present number of members: 30, voluntary organisation, registered charity (charity number 1001580), consultancy, research organisation, publishing house. Research and resource unit.
To explore ways of making public transport more accessible, efficient and safe for all those who want to use it.

Subject coverage: Transport, environment, transport planning, operational issues, women's transport needs, disability access, related issues.

Collection: Books, documents, reports, own publications, transport journals

Publications: Printed, and electronic and video

Publications list: Available online and in print

Access to staff: Contact by letter, by telephone, by fax, by e-mail and via website. Appointment necessary.
Hours: Mon to Fri, by arrangement

Access to building: Prior appointment required

Access for disabled people: Ramped entry, access to all public areas, toilet facilities

Special comments: Lift to second floor. Heavy gates and doors, but staff will come down to assist if requested. Very poor pavements in the surroundings.

CENTRE FOR INFORMATION QUALITY MANAGEMENT (CIQM)

Penbryn, Bronant, Aberystwyth, Ceredigion, SY23 4TJ

Tel: 01974 251302
E-mail: lisqual@cix.co.uk
Website: www.i-a-l.co.uk/index.htm

Enquiries to: Managing Director
Direct tel: 01974 251302

Founded: 1993

Organisation type and purpose:
Professional body, training organisation, consultancy, research organisation.
CIQM represents the professional interests of the information community with respect to the quality, evaluation and selection of informational resources and databases.

Subject coverage: CIQM acts as a clearing house for database and internet resource quality issues, and as a research and consulting organisation for all matters concerning the provision of good quality electronic information.

Publications list: Available online

Access to staff: Contact by letter, by telephone, by e-mail and via website. Appointment necessary.
Hours: Mon to Fri, 0900 to 1700

Access to building: Prior appointment required

Access for disabled people: Parking provided

Affiliated to: CILIP; 7 Ridgmount Street, London; UKeiG: UK electronic information Group; Piglet Cottage, Redmire, Leyburn, North Yorkshire, DL8 4EH; tel: 01969 625751

Parent body: Information Automation Limited (IAL); at the same address; tel: 01974 251302

CENTRE FOR INSTITUTIONAL STUDIES (CIS)

Duncan House, Stratford High Street, London, E15 2JB

Tel: 020 8223 3333 \ Minicom 020 8223 2853
Website: www.uel.ac.uk

Enquiries to: Press Officer
Direct tel: 020 8223 8194
Direct e-mail: h.esselink@uel.ac.uk

Founded: 1970

Organisation type and purpose: University department or institute, research organisation.

Subject coverage: Public policy and institutions, education policy, administration, local government, the voluntary sector, volunteering, urban regeneration, management of voluntary organisations, youth justice, community safety, social enterprise, community action, philosophy of Karl Popper.

Collection: Reference library

Publications: Printed

Publications list: Available in print

Access to staff: Contact by letter, by telephone, by fax and by e-mail
Hours: Mon to Fri, 0900 to 1700

Access for disabled people: Ramped entry, toilet facilities

CENTRE FOR INTER-CULTURAL DEVELOPMENT (CI-CD)

Formal name: Diversity Works Ltd

Diversity Works Ltd, 27 Langland Gardens, London, NW3 6QE

Tel: 020 7431 1712
E-mail: johntwitchin@diversityworks.co.uk
Website: www.diversityworks.co.uk OR www.cicd.uk.com

Enquiries to: Director
Direct tel: 020 431 1712
Direct e-mail: johntwitchin@diversityworks .co.uk
Other contacts: Co-Director

Founded: 1993

Organisation type and purpose:
Consultancy, research, coaching and training provision for (a) international business (b) domestic public services (c) university courses and international students.

Subject coverage: Managing diversity: policy implementation and understanding of Equality Act. Awareness and skills of cross-cultural communication; Training DVD production; Recruiting, Performance measuring and appraisal, and delivery of Customer care across cultures.

Information services: DVD resources for training in diversity and in cross-cultural communication available on request.

Special visitor services: Visitors welcome to examine DVD training resources and library of 5,000 books and articles.

Education services: Visiting lectures in cross-cultural communication for global graduates on MBA/MSC courses, for linguistics courses; for meeting needs of international students.

Collection: Library of training resources: research papers, books and DVD/video packages.

Non-library collection catalogue: All or part available online

Library catalogue: All or part available in-house

Publications: Printed, and electronic and video
Order printed publications from: Diversity Works Ltd. via www.cicd.uk.com
Order electronic and video publications from: Diversity Works Ltd

Publications list: Available online and in print

Access to staff: Contact by letter, by telephone, by fax, by e-mail, in person and via website. Appointment necessary.
Hours: Mon to Fri, 1030 to 1700

Access to building: *Hours:* 1030 to 1700

Associates in: Australia, Malaysia, Hong Kong, USA, Finland, South Africa

CENTRE FOR INTERFIRM COMPARISON (CIFC)

32 St Thomas Street, Winchester, Hampshire, SO23 9HJ

Tel: 01962 844144
Fax: 01962 843180
E-mail: enquiries@cifc.co.uk
Website: www.cifc.co.uk

Enquiries to: Managing Director

Founded: 1959

Organisation type and purpose:
Consultancy, research organisation.
To organise benchmarking projects and properly conducted interfirm comparisons between firms or organisations in the same industry or trade, as a service to them.

Subject coverage: Benchmarking studies, interfirm comparison, management ratios, financial information systems, industry surveys, industry statistics.

Access to staff: Contact by letter, by telephone, by fax, by e-mail and via website. Appointment necessary.
Hours: Mon to Fri, 0900 to 1700

CENTRE FOR JAPANESE AND EAST ASIAN STUDIES (CJEAS)

PO Box 427, Pinner, Middlesex, HA5 3FX

Tel: 020 8429 2839
Fax: 020 8429 9236
E-mail: ruth.taplin@btinternet.com
Website: www.jie.org.uk

Enquiries to: Director
Direct tel: 020 8429 2839
Direct fax: 020 8429 9236
Direct e-mail: ruth.taplin@btinternet.com

Founded: 1989

Organisation type and purpose: Briefings, research, translation of Japanese, Chinese, Korean from English and into English, interpreters

Subject coverage: East and South-East Asia. Specialised translations and interpretations of the languages of the region, bespoke marketing strategies, research, cultural training such as company briefings. Content analysis of medical and pharmaceutical clinical trials, and legal reports. Japanese, Chinese and Korean Intellectual Property Law consultancy.

Publications: Printed
Order printed publications from: Routledge, 2 Park Square, Milton Park, Abingdon, Oxford, OX14 4RN (for other publications by Dr Taplin in Asian Studies, Economics and Law)

Publications list: Available online and in print

Access to staff: Contact by letter, by telephone, by fax, by e-mail and in person. Appointment necessary.
Hours: Mon to Fri, 0900 to 1700

CENTRE FOR LAW AND SOCIETY (CLS)

Formal name: Criminology & Law

Faculty of Law, University of Edinburgh, Old College, South Bridge, Edinburgh, EH8 9YL

Tel: 0131 650 2025
Fax: 0131 650 2005
E-mail: elizabeth.goodwin-andersson@ed.ac.uk

Enquiries to: Director

History of institution: formerly called Centre for Criminology and the Social and Philosophical Study of Law

Organisation type and purpose: University department or institute.

Subject coverage: Official data on crime, crime surveys, policy analysis on crime and punishment, policy advice on crime and punishment, comparative knowledge on criminal justice policy, legal theory.

Access to staff: Contact by letter, by telephone, by fax and by e-mail
Hours: Mon to Fri, 0900 to 1700

Access for disabled people: Ramped entry, toilet facilities
Special comments: Lifts.

CENTRE FOR LEBANESE STUDIES (CLS)

c/o 14a Airlie Gardens, London, W8 7AL

Tel: 020 7221 3809
E-mail: info@lebanesestudies.com
Website: lebanesestudies.com

Enquiries to: Director
Direct e-mail: shehadi@herald.ox.ac.uk

Founded: 1984

Organisation type and purpose: Learned society (membership is by subscription), registered charity (charity number 298375), research organisation, publishing house.

Subject coverage: The Centre initiates and publishes research papers and books on relevant historical, economic, political, sociological and cultural issues affecting Lebanon.

Publications: Printed

Publications list: Available in print

Access to staff: Contact by letter, by telephone, by fax, by e-mail and via website. Appointment necessary.
Hours: Mon to Fri, 1030 to 1730

Access to building: Prior appointment required

Access for disabled people: Ramped entry, access to all public areas, toilet facilities

CENTRE FOR LOCAL ECONOMIC STRATEGIES (CLES)

Express Networks, 1 George Leigh Street, Manchester, M4 5DL

Tel: 0161 236 7036
Fax: 0161 236 1891
E-mail: info@cles.org.uk
Website: www.cles.org.uk

Enquiries to: Information Officer

Founded: 1986

Organisation type and purpose: Membership association, registered charity (charity number 1089503).

Subject coverage: Regeneration, economic development, local government, employment and labour markets, sector studies, urban and regional economics, community initiatives, European issues, European legislation and links.

Publications list: Available online

Access to staff: Contact by letter, by telephone, by fax and by e-mail. Appointment necessary. Non-members charged.
Hours: Mon to Fri, 0900 to 1700

Subsidiary body: CLES European Research Network (CERN)

CENTRE FOR MANAGEMENT CREATIVITY (CMC)

High Trenhouse, Malham Moor, Settle, North Yorkshire, BD24 9PR

Tel: 01729 830322
Fax: 01729 830519
E-mail: helen@centreformanagementcreativity.com
Website: www.centreformanagementcreativity.com

Enquiries to: Business Development Manager

Founded: 1985

Organisation type and purpose: Service industry, training organisation, consultancy. Managing change.

Subject coverage: Strategic thinking, team development, culture change, management techniques, personal development.

Publications: Printed, and electronic and video

Access to staff: Contact by letter, by telephone, by fax, by e-mail and via website. Appointment necessary.
Hours: Mon to Fri, 0900 to 1700

Access for disabled people: Parking provided, ramped entry, toilet facilities

CENTRE FOR MANX STUDIES (CMS)

Formal name: Department of Archaeology, Classics and Egyptology, University of Liverpool.

The Stables, University Centre, Old Castletown Road, Douglas, Isle of Man, IM2 1QB

Tel: 01624 695777
Fax: 01624 695783
E-mail: cms@liv.ac.uk
Website: www.liv.ac.uk/manxstudies

Enquiries to: Administrator
Direct e-mail: gillw@liverpool.ac.uk
Other contacts: Secretary

Founded: 1992

Organisation type and purpose: Centre for the academic study of anything Manx; undergraduate and postgraduate research organisation.

Subject coverage: Research related to the Isle of Man, particularly earth sciences, archaeology, architecture, history, music, language and social studies.

Education services: BA in History and Heritage Management (with IOM Dept Education); MA in Manx Studies; MPhil; PhD.

Collection: Collection of reference-only books on Manx topics.

Non-library collection catalogue: All or part available online

Library catalogue: All or part available online

Publications: Printed
Order printed publications from: Secretary

Publications list: Available online and in print

Access to staff: Contact by letter, by telephone, by fax, by e-mail, in person and via website
Hours: Mon to Fri, 0900 to 1700

Access to building: No prior appointment required
Hours: Mon to Fri, 0900 to 1700

Links with: Isle of Man Department of Education; St George's Court, Upper Church Street, Douglas, Isle of Man, IM1 2SG

Parent body: Department of Archaeology, Classics and Egyptology, University of Liverpool; PO Box 147, Liverpool, L69 3BX; tel: 0151 794 2000; fax: 0151 708 6502; website: http://www.liv.ac.uk

CENTRE FOR MARINE TECHNOLOGY

University of Salford, 43 The Crescent, Salford, Manchester, M5 4WT

Tel: 0161 295 5081
Fax: 0161 295 5380
E-mail: r.hughes@salford.ac.uk

Enquiries to: Director

Organisation type and purpose: University department or institute.

Subject coverage: Offshore processing of oil and gas; enhanced oil recovery; simulation of oil and gas production; underwater life support systems.

Access to staff: Contact by letter, by telephone, by fax and by e-mail
Hours: Mon to Fri, 0900 to 1700

Associated with: Marinetech North West

CENTRE FOR MASS COMMUNICATION RESEARCH (CMCR)

University of Leicester, 104 Regent Road, Leicester, LE1 7LT

Tel: 0116 252 5293
Fax: 0116 252 5276
E-mail: cmcr@le.ac.uk
Website: www.le.ac.uk/cmcr/
Website: www.le.ac.uk/cmcr/dl

Enquiries to: General Office Manager/PA to Head of Department
Direct e-mail: hlh7@leicester.ac.uk

Founded: 1966

Organisation type and purpose: University department or institute, suitable for ages: 18+, research organisation.

Subject coverage: Mass media, sociological research on mass media and communications, media and health, science communications, media and environment, media and politics, popular music industry, film, globalisation, culture, national identity, television and food.

Collection: Current and pre-current year British national newspapers, limited access available

Trade and statistical information: Data on use of media in health education, structure of the media industries, viewing, listening, reading behaviour

Access to staff: Contact by telephone and by e-mail. Appointment necessary.
Hours: Mon to Fri, 0900 to 1700

Access to building: Prior appointment required

CENTRE FOR MEDICAL EDUCATION (CME)

Tay Park House, 484 Perth Road, Dundee, DD2 1LR

Tel: 01382 631968
Fax: 01382 645748
E-mail: p.a.wilkie@dundee.ac.uk
Website: www.dundee.ac.uk/meded/

Enquiries to: Director
Direct tel: 01382 631973
Direct e-mail: r.m.harden@dundee.ac.uk
Other contacts: AMEE Administrator for membership of Association for Medical Education in Europe.

Organisation type and purpose: University department or institute.

Subject coverage: Medical education: curriculum design, development and assessment; teaching and learning methods, evaluation management and administration, technology-based learning in medicine and health sciences, distance learning, vocational training and continuing medical and nursing education; diploma and masters of medical education; diploma in advanced nursing studies, degree in nursing studies, masters in palliative care.

Collection: Extensive collection of books and journals on medical and general education

Library catalogue: All or part available in-house

Publications: Printed

Publications list: Available in print

Access to staff: Contact by letter, by telephone, by fax, by e-mail and via website. Appointment necessary.
Hours: Mon to Fri, 0900 to 1700

Access for disabled people: Parking provided, ramped entry

CENTRE FOR MEDIEVAL STUDIES (CMS)

King's Manor, York, YO1 7EP

Tel: 01904 433910
Fax: 01904 433918
E-mail: cms-office@york.ac.uk
Website: www.york.ac.uk/medieval-studies/

Enquiries to: Administrator

Founded: 1968

Organisation type and purpose: University department or institute.

Subject coverage: Medieval studies.

Education services: Taught postgraduate and research degrees

Library catalogue: All or part available in print

Access to staff: Contact via website

CENTRE FOR MULTIMODAL THERAPY

156 Westcombe Hill, Blackheath, London, SE3 7DH

Tel: 0845 680 2065
E-mail: admin@managingstress.com
Website: www.centreforcoaching.com
Website: www.managingstress.com

Enquiries to: Director
Other contacts: Co-ordinator

Founded: 1990

Organisation type and purpose: Training organisation, consultancy, research organisation, publishing house.

Subject coverage: Multimodal therapy, stress management, stress counselling, training for counsellors, psychologists and therapists.

Publications: Electronic and video

Publications list: Available online

Access to staff: Contact by letter, by telephone, by e-mail and via website. Appointment necessary.
Hours: Mon to Fri, 1000 to 1700

Parent body: Centre for Stress Management

CENTRE FOR ORGANISATIONAL MANAGEMENT

Zenith House, Craigholm, Shooters Hill, London, SE18 3RR

Tel: 020 8319 1449
E-mail: almeric.powerone@btinternet.com
Website: Under review

Enquiries to: Director & Founder
Direct tel: 07523 528 895; 020 8319 1449

Founded: 1985; formerly called Centre for Performance Improvement (year of change 1990)

Organisation type and purpose: Organisational leadership coaching and transference consultancy practice.
To transfer understanding and skills that will directly transmit into an organisation's overall performance. To support the development of understanding and skills enabling the development of the collective use of both human resources and technical assets to reinforce an organisation's overall performance.

Subject coverage: The development and application of skills in the following areas: Organisational Leadership, Organisational Design and Development, Organisational and Personal Decision-making, Motivational Skills Transference, Creating and Developing Focused Effective Teams and Work-Groups, Influencing and Negotiating, Conflict Resolution, Organisational Communication, Systems Design, Development, and Management, Contract Management, Simultaneous Problem-solving; many other problems that naturally present themselves in any continuous performance improvement programme.

Access to staff: Contact by letter, by telephone, by e-mail and in person. Appointment necessary.
Hours: Mon to Fri, 0900 to 1700

Access for disabled people: Parking provided, ramped entry

CENTRE FOR PERSONAL AND PROFESSIONAL DEVELOPMENT

The Brewery, High Street, Twyford, Winchester, Hampshire, SO21 2RG

Tel: 01962 715838
Fax: 01962 711419
E-mail: ann@cppd.co.uk

Enquiries to: Managing Director
Other contacts: Administrator

Founded: 1994

Organisation type and purpose: Training organisation, consultancy.
Counselling services.
To provide counselling, training and consultancy services to both individuals and organisations, personal and professional development.

Subject coverage: Counselling, psychotherapy, family and marital therapy, hypnotherapy, personal and professional development, training.

Access to staff: Contact by letter, by telephone and by e-mail. Appointment necessary.
Hours: Mon to Fri, 0900 to 1700

Access to building: Prior appointment required

Access for disabled people: Parking provided

CENTRE FOR POLICY ON AGEING (CPA)

25–31 Ironmonger Row, London, EC1V 3QP

Tel: 020 7553 6500
Fax: 020 7553 6501
E-mail: ageinfo@cpa.org.uk
Website: www.cpa.org.uk

Enquiries to: Director
Other contacts: Librarian

Founded: 1947

Organisation type and purpose: Registered charity (charity number 207163).
Independent policy and information unit promoting and formulating effective policies to improve services etc. for older people.

Subject coverage: Social aspects of gerontology in Britain and, to a lesser extent, Europe, USA, etc.; includes health care, housing, adult education/leisure, employment, retirement, social policy, etc. for older people.

continued overleaf

Collection: Reference library (by appointment only)
International collection on gerontology, over 500 core journals and 49,000 monographs, reports, statistical sources, legislation, etc.

Library catalogue: All or part available online and in-house

Publications: Printed, and electronic and video
Order printed publications from: Central Books, 99 Wallis Road, London, E9 5LN, tel: 020 8986 5488, fax: 020 8533 5821, e-mail: peter@centralbooks.com

Publications list: Available online and in print

Access to staff: Contact by letter, by telephone, by fax and by e-mail. Appointment necessary.
Hours: Mon, 1400 to 1700; Tue to Fri, 1000 to 1700

Access to building: Prior appointment required

Established by: Nuffield Foundation

CENTRE FOR RADIOGRAPHIC AND MEDICAL STUDIES

Cranfield University, Shrivenham, Swindon, Wiltshire, SN6 8LA

Tel: 01793 785756
Fax: 01793 785744
E-mail: j.laxon@rmcs.cranfield.ac.uk

Enquiries to: Director
Direct tel: 01793 785227
Direct e-mail: berridge@rcms.cranfield.ac.uk
Other contacts: Undergraduate Admissions Officer (for undergraduate admissions through UCAS)

Founded: 1992; formerly called Oxford Centre for Radiographic Studies (year of change 1997); incorporates the former Joint Services School of Radiography, Northampton School of Radiography, Oxford Regional School of Radiography

Organisation type and purpose: University department or institute.

Subject coverage: Radiography, radiobiology, radiation physics, radiation dosimetry, medical ultrasound, veterinary radiography and ultrasound, dental radiography, radiation protection, imaging, oncology, forensic radiography, radiation effects on materials.

Publications: Printed

Publications list: Available in print

Access to staff: Contact by letter, by telephone, by fax and by e-mail
Hours: Mon to Fri, 0900 to 1700

Access for disabled people: Parking provided, ramped entry, access to all public areas, toilet facilities

CENTRE FOR RATIONAL EMOTIVE BEHAVIOUR THERAPY

Broadway House, 3 High Street, Bromley, Kent, BR1 1LF

Tel: 020 8228 1185
Website: www.managingstress.com

Enquiries to: Director
Direct e-mail: jason.jones@bsmhft.nhs.uk
Other contacts: Co-ordinator

Founded: 1990; formerly called Centre for Rational Emotive Therapy

Organisation type and purpose: Training organisation, consultancy, research organisation, publishing house. Counselling and training centre.

Subject coverage: Rational emotive behaviour therapy, counselling, coaching and training.

Publications: Printed, and electronic and video

Publications list: Available online

Access to staff: Contact by letter, by telephone, by e-mail and via website. Appointment necessary.
Hours: Mon to Fri, 1000 to 1700

Affiliated to: Centre for Coaching; Centre for Multimodel Therapy; Centre for Problem Focused Training and Therapy; Centre for Stress Management

CENTRE FOR RESEARCH IN ETHNIC RELATIONS (CRER)

University of Warwick, Coventry, Warwickshire, CV4 7AL

Tel: 024 7652 3605
Fax: 024 7652 4324
E-mail: crer@warwick.ac.uk
Website: www.warwick.ac.uk/CRER

Enquiries to: Librarian
Direct tel: 024 7652 2972
Other contacts: Publications Manager for publications.

Organisation type and purpose: University department or institute, research organisation.

Subject coverage: All aspects of British, and increasingly of European, race and ethnic relations: employment, health, housing, education, politics, social services, etc.; migrant workers in Europe; refugees; community studies.

Collection: Large indexed press clippings collection; videos and ephemera collection
Over 200 periodicals and newspapers
Over 8,000 pamphlets and reports
Resources Centre maintained and staffed part-time, reinforcing the university library's collection of material on race and ethnic relations

Trade and statistical information: National Ethnic Minority Data Archive (statistical, survey and census data, primarily for Britain)

Library catalogue: All or part available online

Publications: Printed
Order printed publications from: Publications Manager, Centre for Research in Ethnic Relations
tel: 024 7652 3607, fax: 024 7652 4324, e-mail: bains@warwick.ac.uk

Publications list: Available online and in print

Access to staff: Contact by letter, by telephone, by fax and by e-mail
Hours: Mon to Fri, 0900 to 1600

Access for disabled people: Ramped entry, toilet facilities

Parent body: University of Warwick; tel: 024 7652 3523

CENTRE FOR REVIEWS AND DISSEMINATION (CRD)

University of York, Heslington, York, YO10 5DD

Tel: 01904 321040
Fax: 01904 321041
E-mail: crd-info@york.ac.uk
Website: www.york.ac.uk/inst/crd

Enquiries to: Information Service Manager

Founded: 1994

Organisation type and purpose: Part of the National Institue of Health Research and an academic department of the University of York.
To provide information to the NHS on the effects of treatments and the delivery and organisation of care.

Subject coverage: Systematic reviews of the effects of health care interventions. Cost-effectiveness information.

Library catalogue: All or part available in-house

Publications: Printed, and electronic and video
Order printed publications from: Publications Officer, Centre for Reviews and Dissemination, at same address, tel: 01904 321441; fax: 01904 321035

Publications list: Available online

Access to staff: Contact by e-mail

Parent body: University of York; York, YO10 5DD; tel: 01904 430000; fax: 01904 433433

CENTRE FOR SOCIAL ANTHROPOLOGY AND COMPUTING (CSAC)

University of Kent, Canterbury, Kent, CT2 7NS

Tel: 01227 764000
Fax: 01227 827289
E-mail: csa-c@lucy.ukc.ac.uk
Website: www.lucy.ukc.ac.uk/
Website: www.csac.anthropology.ac.uk/
Website: www.era.anthropology.ac.uk/
Website: www.lucy.ukc.ac.uk/online_pubs.html
Website: www.lucy.ukc.ac.uk/AIO.html
Website: www.aio.anthropology.org.uk/

Enquiries to: Director
Direct e-mail: m.d.fischer@ukc.ac.uk
Other contacts: Deputy Director

Organisation type and purpose: University department or institute.

Subject coverage: Anthropology, anthropological computing, teaching and learning materials.

Publications: Printed, and electronic and video
Order printed publications from: CSAC Office Eliot College, University of Kent, Canterbury, CT2 7NS

Publications list: Available online and in print

Access to staff: Contact by letter, by e-mail and via website
Hours: Mon to Fri, 0900 to 1700

Affiliated to: Department of Anthropology; University of Kent, Canterbury, CT2 7NS; tel: 01227 764000

CENTRE FOR SOCIO-LEGAL STUDIES (CSLS)

University of Oxford, Manor Road Building, Manor Road, Oxford, OX1 3UQ

Tel: 01865 284220
Fax: 01865 284221
E-mail: admin@csls.ox.ac.uk
Website: www.cslc.ox.ac.uk

Enquiries to: Administrator

Founded: 1972

Organisation type and purpose: University department or institute, research organisation.

Subject coverage: Role and function of law in societies, law and the media, human rights, social history, procedures for adjudication and dispute settlement, law and psychology, law and economics, families and the law especially divorce, compensation for illness and injury, medicine and law, regulation of health and safety at work, regulation of public and private sector, regulation of business practice.

Collection: Small specialised socio-legal library, open for outside use by appointment

Publications: Printed

Publications list: Available in print

Access to staff: Contact by letter, by fax, by e-mail and via website. Appointment necessary.
Hours: Mon to Fri, 0900 to 1700

CENTRE FOR SPEECH TECHNOLOGY RESEARCH (CSTR)

University of Edinburgh, 2 Buccleuch Place, Edinburgh, EH8 9LW

Tel: 0131 650 2804
Fax: 0131 650 4587
E-mail: evelcen@cogsci.ed.ac.uk
Website: www.cstr.ed.ac.uk/

Enquiries to: Secretary

Founded: 1984

Organisation type and purpose: University department or institute, research organisation.

Subject coverage: Phonetics, dialogue engineering, speech synthesis, speech signal processing and coding, hidden markov modelling, neural networks, transputer DSP and PC prototyping, speaker verification, expert software.

Publications: Printed

Access to staff: Contact by letter, by telephone, by fax and by e-mail
Hours: Mon to Fri, 0900 to 1700

Links with: research organisations throughout Europe

Member of: European Network in Language and Speech (ELSNET)

CENTRE FOR STRESS MANAGEMENT (CFSM)

156 Westcombe Hill, Blackheath, London, SE3 7DH

Tel: 0845 680 2065
E-mail: admin@managingstress.com
Website: www.managingstress.com

Enquiries to: Director
Other contacts: Co-ordinator

Founded: 1987

Organisation type and purpose: Training organisation, consultancy, research organisation, publishing house.

Subject coverage: Stress management, stress counselling, stress audits, positive approaches to managing pressure and stress, assertion and communication skills, self-esteem and self-acceptance, challenging irrational beliefs and public beliefs.

Publications: Printed, and electronic and video

Publications list: Available in print

Access to staff: Contact by letter, by telephone, by e-mail and via website. Appointment necessary.
Hours: Mon to Fri, 1000 to 1700

Affiliated to: Centre for Multimodal Therapy; tel: 020 8318 4448; Centre for Problem Focused Training and Therapy; Centre for Rational Emotive Behaviour Therapy; Institute for Complementary Medicine; UK Centre for Cognitive Behaviour Therapy, Centre for Coaching, International Academy for Professional Development, Centres of Expertise

Also at: Centre for Stress Management; Porthleven, Cornwall

CENTRE FOR STUDIES ON INCLUSIVE EDUCATION LIMITED (CSIE)

The Park, Daventry road, Knowle, Bristol, BS4 1DQ

Tel: 0117 353 3150
Fax: 0117 353 3150
E-mail: admin@csie.org.uk
Website: www.csie.org.uk

Enquiries to: Director
Direct e-mail: admin@csie.org.uk

Founded: 1982; formerly called Centre for Studies on Integration in Education (CSIE) (year of change 1994)

Organisation type and purpose: The Centre for Studies on Inclusive Education (CSIE) is a registered charity (charity number 327805) working to promote equality and eliminate discrimination in education. The Centre works towards raising public awareness and transforming education so that everyone can benefit from, and contribute to, day to day life in ordinary local schools. CSIE activities include talks, training, consultancy, research and the production of a wide range of resources to support the development of inclusive education. CSIE was set up in 1982 and is also a registered company (2253521).

Publications: Printed

Publications list: Available online and in print

Access to staff: Contact by letter, by telephone, by fax and via website. Appointment necessary.
Hours: Mon to Fri, 0900 to 1700

Access to building: Prior appointment required

Access for disabled people: Parking provided, ramped entry, access to all public areas, toilet facilities

Links with: Alliance for Inclusive Education (ALLFIE); Council for Exceptional Children (ERIC); 1920 Association Drive, Reston, Virginia, 20191–1589, USA; Parents for Inclusion

CENTRE FOR SUSTAINABLE ENERGY (CSE)

3 St Peter's Court, Bedminster Parade, Bristol, BS3 4AQ

Tel: 0117 934 1400
Fax: 0117 934 1410
E-mail: info@cse.org.uk
Website: www.cse.org.uk

Enquiries to: Office Administrator
Direct tel: 0117 9341408

Founded: 1979; formerly called Urban Centre for Appropriate Energy (UCAT)

Organisation type and purpose: National government body.
Established to stimulate the development of new and renewable energy sources wherever they have the prospect of being economically attractive and environmentally acceptable, in order to contribute to diverse, secure and sustainable energy supplies, reduction in the emission of pollutants, and encouragement of internationally competitive industries.

Subject coverage: Biosciences, commercialisation, energy from waste, solar energy, wave and tidal energy, wind energy.

Publications: Printed
Order printed publications from: e-mail: kirsty .mitchell@cse.org.uk

Publications list: Available online

Access to staff: Contact by letter, by telephone, by fax, by e-mail and via website. Appointment necessary.
Hours: Mon to Fri, 0900 to 1730

Links with: Centre for Alternative Energy; Machynlleth, Powys, Wales, SY20 9AZ; tel: 01654 702782; website: http://www.cat.org .uk

CENTRE FOR THE ECONOMICS AND MANAGEMENT OF AQUATIC RESOURCES (CEMARE)

University of Portsmouth, Boathouse No. 6, College Road, HM Naval Base, Portsmouth, PO1 3LJ

Tel: 023 9284 4082
Fax: 023 9284 4614
E-mail: christopher.martin@port.ac.uk
Website: www.port.ac.uk/cemare

Enquiries to: Librarian

continued overleaf

Founded: 1970; formerly called Centre for Marine Resource Economics, Marine Resources Research Unit

Organisation type and purpose: University department or institute, consultancy, research organisation.

Subject coverage: Fisheries economics, agricultural economics, environmental economics, coastal zone management, aquaculture, recreational fisheries.

Collection: 2,000 books, 10,000 reports, 5,000 reprints, 165 serial titles (60 current)
Large collection of FAO Fisheries publications on hard copy and microfiche

Non-library collection catalogue: All or part available online and in-house

Publications: Printed

Publications list: Available online and in print

Access to staff: Contact by e-mail and via website. Appointment necessary.
Hours: Mon to Fri, 1000 to 1700

Member of: BIASLIC; EURASLIC; IAALD; IAMSLIC

CENTRE FOR THE HISTORY OF TECHNOLOGY, SCIENCE AND SOCIETY (HOTRU)

Formal name: renamed 2011 as 'History of Technology Research Unit'

University of Bath, Claverton Down, Bath, BA2 7AY

Tel: 01225 311508
E-mail: hssraab@bath.ac.uk

Enquiries to: Honorary Director

Founded: 1964

Organisation type and purpose: University department or institute, research organisation.
The National Cataloguing Unit for the Archives of Contemporary Scientists has now left the University

Subject coverage: History of technology in all periods and all forms, technology and society, history of engineering, especially in Britain, engineering biography, Victorian engineering, history of stationary steam power, industrial archaeology, national heritage and conservation.

Collection: Watkins collection (photographs and documentation of stationary steam engines), now with the National Buildings Record, English Heritage, Swindon

Publications: Printed

Access to staff: Contact by letter and by e-mail. Appointment necessary.
Hours: by appointment

CENTRE FOR THE STUDY OF FINANCIAL INNOVATION (CSFI)

5 Derby Street, London, W1J 7AB

Tel: 020 7493 0173
Fax: 020 7493 0190
E-mail: info@csfi.org.uk
Website: www.csfi.org.uk

Enquiries to: Director
Direct e-mail: andrew@csfi.org.uk

Other contacts: Director of Studies (for research, themes); Sponsorship Manager (for membership)

Founded: 1993

Organisation type and purpose: Membership association (membership is by subscription), present number of members: c. 70, registered charity (charity number 1017352), research organisation.

Subject coverage: Banking, regulation, risk, e-finance, SMEs, development finance, Europe, insurance, technology.

Publications: Printed, and electronic and video

Publications list: Available online and in print

Access to staff: Contact by letter, by fax and by e-mail
Hours: Mon to Fri, 0900 to 1700

Access to building: Prior appointment required

CENTRE FOR THE STUDY OF GLOBALISATION AND REGIONALISATION (CSGR)

Department of Economics, University of Warwick, Coventry, Warwickshire, CV4 7AL

Tel: 024 7657 2533
Fax: 024 7657 2548
E-mail: csgr@warwick.ac.uk
Website: www.warwick.ac.uk/fac/soc/CSGR
Website: www.csgr.org

Enquiries to: Research Fellow

Organisation type and purpose: University department or institute, research organisation.

Subject coverage: Globalisation, regionalisation, trade, finance

CENTRE FOR THE STUDY OF INTERRELIGIOUS RELATIONS (CSIR)

University of Birmingham, Elmfield House, Bristol Road, Birmingham, B29 6LQ

Tel: 0121 415 8373
Fax: 0121 415 8376
E-mail: d.r.thomas.1@bham.ac.uk
Website: www.bham.ac.uk/theology

Enquiries to: Administrative Secretary
Direct e-mail: h.ingram@bham.ac.uk

Founded: 2007; formerly called Centre for the Study of Islam and Christian-Muslim Relations (year of change 2007)

Organisation type and purpose: University department, research organisation

Subject coverage: Interreligious relations; Christian-Muslim relations; philosophy of religion; religion in South Asia.

Collection: Mingana Collection of Islamic Arabic, Christian Arabic and Syriac Manuscripts

Library catalogue: All or part available online

Publications: Printed, and electronic and video
Order printed publications from: h.ingram@bham.ac.uk
Order electronic and video publications from: Taylor & Francis

Publications list: Available online and in print

Access to staff: Contact by letter, by telephone, by fax, by e-mail, in person and via website. Appointment necessary.
Hours: Mon to Fri, 0900 to 1700

Access to building: Doors security locked; wall phone to secretaries available
Hours: 0900 to 1700

Access for disabled people: Parking provided, toilet facilities

CENTRE FOR THE STUDY OF PUBLIC POLICY (CSPP)

Edward Wright Building, University of Aberdeen, Aberdeen, AB24 3QY

E-mail: cspp@abdn.ac.uk
Website: www.abdn.ac.uk/cspp
Website: www.russiavotes.org

Enquiries to: Director
Direct e-mail: cspp@abdn.ac.uk

Founded: 1976

Organisation type and purpose: University department or institute, research organisation.
Concerned with the problems of public policy, especially post-Communist societies and new democracies in the European Union. Specialised databases of public opinion, surveys of 20 countries.

Subject coverage: Public policy generally; the growth of government; public finance and political economy; elections, transformation of post-Communist societies; social capital.

Collection: A variety of machine-readable survey data sets

Non-library collection catalogue: All or part available online and in print

Publications: Printed, and electronic and video

Publications list: Available online and in print

Access to staff: Contact by letter, by e-mail and via website. Appointment necessary.
Hours: Mon to Fri, 0900 to 1700

Headquarters address: research institutes in Eastern and Western Europe and the United States

CENTRE FOR TRADITIONAL CHINESE MEDICINE

78 Haverstock Hill, London, NW3 2BE

Tel: 020 7284 2898
Fax: 020 7485 8875
E-mail: centcm@netcomuk.co.uk

Enquiries to: Director

Founded: 1992

Organisation type and purpose: Professional body, consultancy.

Subject coverage: Chinese herbal medicine, acupuncture and Chinese massage.

Collection: Chinese herbal samples
Chinese medical books

Access to staff: Contact by letter, by telephone, by fax and by e-mail
Hours: Mon to Fri, 0930 to 1730

CENTRE OF AFRICAN STUDIES LIBRARY

Centre of African Studies Library, Alison Richard Building, 7 West Road, Cambridge, CB3 9DT

Tel: 01223 334398
Fax: 01223 769325
E-mail: afrlib@hermes.cam.ac.uk
Website: www.african.cam.ac.uk/library.htm
Website: www.african.cam.ac.uk

Enquiries to: Librarian
Direct e-mail: meg23@cam.ac.uk
Other contacts: Assistant Librarian

Founded: 1965

Organisation type and purpose: University department or institute (library).

Subject coverage: Africa (mainly sub-Saharan): its history, geography, literature, economics and politics and its social, developmental, cultural and artistic affairs.

Library catalogue: All or part available online

Publications list: Available in print

Access to staff: Contact by letter, by telephone, by fax, by e-mail, in person and via website. Appointment necessary.
Hours: Mon to Fri, 0900 to 1730
Special comments: The library hours may be shortened during the summer vacation, so please check before visiting.

Access to building: *Hours:* Mon to Fri, 0900 to 1730
Special comments: After hours and at weekend, authorised card entry only (no access to library).

Access for disabled people: By side door; intercom to request door opening
Hours: Mon to Fri, 0900 to 1730

Links with: UK Libraries and Archives Group on Africa (SCOLMA)

Parent body: University of Cambridge

CENTRE OF CANADIAN STUDIES

University of Edinburgh, 15A George Square, Edinburgh, EH8 9LD

Tel: 0131 650 4129
Fax: 0131 650 6535
E-mail: centreofcanadianstudies@ed.ac.uk
Website: www.cst.ed.ac.uk

Enquiries to: Administrator
Other contacts: Director

Organisation type and purpose: University department or institute.

Subject coverage: Canada.

Publications list: Available online

Access to staff: Contact by letter, by telephone, by fax, by e-mail, in person and via website. Appointment necessary.
Hours: Mon to Thu, 0900 to 1700; Fri, 0900 to 1230

Access to building: No access other than to staff

CENTRE OF MEDICAL LAW AND ETHICS (CMLE)

King's College London, Strand, London, WC2R 2LS

Tel: 020 7848 2382
Fax: 020 7848 2575
E-mail: cmle.enq@kcl.ac.uk
Website: www.kcl.ac.uk/cmle

Enquiries to: Administrator
Other contacts: Director

Founded: 1978

Organisation type and purpose: University department or institute.

Subject coverage: Medical ethics, medical and healthcare law.

Collection: Specialist collection of medical, law and ethics books and periodicals held by King's College Library, Chancery Lane, London, WC2

Publications: Printed

Publications list: Available in print

Access to staff: Contact by letter, by telephone, by fax and by e-mail. Appointment necessary.
Hours: Mon to Fri, 0930 to 1300, 1400 to 1730

Part of: School of Law; King's College London, London

CENTRE OF SOUTH ASIAN STUDIES

Laundress Lane, Cambridge, CB2 1SD

Tel: 01223 338094
Fax: 01223 767094
E-mail: webmaster@s-asian.cam.ac.uk
Website: www.s-asian.cam.ac.uk

Enquiries to: Librarian

Founded: 1964

Organisation type and purpose: University library, university department or institute, research organisation.

Subject coverage: South Asia (India, Sri Lanka, Pakistan, Bangladesh, Nepal) and Southeast Asia (Burma, Thailand, Laos, Cambodia, Vietnam, Malaysia, Singapore, Indonesia, Philippines); social sciences, history (17th century onwards), geography, agriculture, economics, development, etc.

Collection: 7,500 microforms on South and Southeast Asia
30,000 monographs on South and Southeast Asia
Cambridge South Asian Archive of the personal papers relating to the British period in India
Indian Newspapers on microfilm from the 19th century onwards
50 hours of cinefilm now on DVD

Non-library collection catalogue: All or part available online and in print

Library catalogue: All or part available online

Publications: Printed

Access to staff: Contact by letter and via website. Appointment necessary. Letter of introduction required.
Hours: Mon to Fri, 0930 to 1730
Special comments: Closed Christmas and Easter.

Constituent part of: University of Cambridge

CENTRE OF WEST AFRICAN STUDIES (CWAS)

University of Birmingham, Edgbaston, Birmingham, B15 2TT

Tel: 0121 414 5128
Fax: 0121 414 3228
E-mail: cwas@bham.ac.uk
Website: www.bham.ac.uk/WestAfricanStudies

Enquiries to: Director
Direct tel: 0121 414 5125
Direct e-mail: tmccaskie@aol.com
Other contacts: Secretary, CWAS for routine requests for information, publications.

Founded: 1963

Organisation type and purpose: Museum, university department or institute, suitable for ages: 18+, research organisation.

Subject coverage: History (social, Islamic, South African), geography, political science, Yoruba language, literature (African and Caribbean), popular culture, sociology – all related to West Africa and, in some cases, Eastern or Southern Africa. Specialisms in Benin, Ghana, Mali, Nigeria, Senegambia and Sierra Leone, African development studies, African cultural anthropology.

Collection: Cadbury Papers
CMS archives
Danford Collection of African Art and Artefacts
Early West African newspapers
Extensive holdings of books on Africa
John Figueroa Papers
Joseph Chamberlain Papers
R E Bradbury Papers (Benin)
William Bascom Collection (Yoruba)

Publications: Printed

Publications list: Available online

Access to staff: Contact by letter, by e-mail and via website. Appointment necessary.
Hours: Mon to Fri, 0930 to 1700

Access to building: Prior appointment required

CENTREPOINT

Central House, 25 Camperdown Street, London, E1 8DZ

Tel: 0845 4663400
Website: www.centrepoint.org.uk

Enquiries to: Information Officer
Direct e-mail: john.raynham@centrepoint.org

Organisation type and purpose: Voluntary organisation, registered charity (charity number 292411).

Subject coverage: Housing and support to homeless 16–25-year-olds, research with young people at risk.

Publications list: Available online and in print

Access to staff: Contact by letter and by telephone
Hours: Mon to Fri, 0900 to 1700

Access to building: No prior appointment required

CEP ASSOCIATES

1st Floor NYMCA, North View, Ashington, Northumberland, NE63 9XQ

Tel: 01670 521805
Fax: 01670 521805
E-mail: patdreyer@cepassociates.fsnet.co.uk
Website: www.cepassociates@fsnet.co.uk

Enquiries to: Information Officer

Founded: 1991; formerly called Community Education Project

Organisation type and purpose: Suitable for ages: 18+, training organisation, consultancy.

Subject coverage: Community education.

Access to staff: Contact by letter, by telephone, by fax, by e-mail, in person and via website. Appointment necessary.
Hours: Mon to Fri, 0900 to 1700

Access for disabled people: Ramped entry

CERAM RESEARCH LTD

Queens Road, Penkhull, Stoke-on-Trent, Staffordshire, ST4 7LQ

Tel: 01782 764444
Fax: 01782 412331
E-mail: enquiries@ceram.com
Website: www.ceram.com

Enquiries to: Information Manager
Direct tel: 01782 764241
Direct e-mail: ann.pace@ceram.com

Founded: 1948

Organisation type and purpose:
Membership association (membership is by subscription), present number of members: 300, research organisation.
Research and technology organisation for ceramics and materials industries.

Subject coverage: Production and service behaviour of ceramic materials and pottery (tableware, tiles, sanitary ware, electrical porcelain); refractories; technical ceramics for engineering and electrical applications; clay and calcium silicate-based building products (bricks, sewer pipes) and their behaviour in structures; evaluation of properties, and physical and chemical testing methods.

Collection: Graves Library (on bricks and building)
Mellor Memorial Library

Trade and statistical information: Statistical information on ceramics industry (worldwide).
Material information on ceramics industry (worldwide)

Non-library collection catalogue: All or part available in-house

Library catalogue: All or part available in-house

Publications: Printed, and electronic and video

Publications list: Available online and in print

Access to staff: Contact by letter, by telephone, by fax, by e-mail, in person and via website. Appointment necessary. Access for members only. Letter of introduction required. Non-members charged.
Hours: Mon to Thu, 0845 to 1715; Fri, 0845 to 1645

CEREDIGION ARCHIVES

County Office, Marine Terrace, Aberystwyth, Ceredigion, SY23 2DE

Tel: 01970 633697
Fax: 01970 633663
E-mail: archives@ceredigion.gov.uk
Website: www.archifdy-ceredigion.org.uk

Enquiries to: Archivist

Founded: 1974; formerly called Dyfed Archives, Cardiganshire Area Office (year of change 1996)

Organisation type and purpose: Local government body.
Local government county record office.

Non-library collection catalogue: All or part available online and in-house

Access to staff: Contact by letter, by telephone, by fax, by e-mail, in person and via website
Hours: Mon, 1400 to 1900; Tue to Fri, 1400 to 1630

Access to building: No prior appointment required

Access for disabled people: Toilet facilities
Special comments: Disability lift

Parnet body: Ceredigion County Council

CEREDIGION COUNTY COUNCIL

Neuadd Cyngor Ceredigion, Penmorfa, Aberaeron, Ceredigion, SA46 0PA

Tel: 01545 570881
Fax: 01545 572009
E-mail: info@ceredigion.gov.uk
Website: www.ceredigion.cix.co.uk/cyngor/

Enquiries to: Public Relations Manager
Direct tel: 01545 572002

Founded: 1996; formerly called Cardiganshire County Council, Dyfed County Council; formerly called Cyngor Dosbarth Ceredigion (year of change 1996)

Organisation type and purpose: Local government body.

Access to staff: Contact by letter, by telephone, by fax, by e-mail, in person and via website
Hours: Mon to Fri, 0900 to 1700

CERTIFICATION OFFICE FOR TRADE UNIONS AND EMPLOYERS' ASSOCIATIONS

22nd Floor, Euston Tower, 286 Euston Road, London, NW1 3JJ

Tel: 020 7210 3734
Fax: 020 7210 3612
E-mail: info@certoffice.org
Website: www.certoffice.org

Enquiries to: Operations Manager
Direct tel: 020 7210 3719

Founded: 1976

Organisation type and purpose: National government body.
Independent statutory body.
To ensure trade unions and employers' associations comply with the relevant legislation.

Subject coverage: Financial returns of trade unions and employers' associations, source documents and guidance in respect of mergers between trade unions and employers' associations, trade union independence, guidance on trade union political fund rules.

Collection: Certification Officer's annual reports from 1976
Trade union and employers' association annual returns, rules and constitutions from 1976
Trade union and employers' association merger documents from 1976

Publications: Printed

Publications list: Available in print

Access to staff: Contact by letter, by telephone and by e-mail
Hours: Mon to Fri, 0900 to 1700

Access to building: No prior appointment required
Hours: Mon to Fri, 0930 to 1630

Access for disabled people: Toilet facilities

CHAMBER BUSINESS

The Business Competitiveness Centre, Kimpton Road, Luton, Bedfordshire, LU2 0LB

Tel: 01582 522448
Fax: 01582 522450

Enquiries to: Information Officer
Direct e-mail: info@chamber-business.com

Founded: 2001; formerly called Bedfordshire & Luton Chamber of Commerce, Business Link Bedfordshire (year of change 2001)

Organisation type and purpose:
Membership association (membership is by subscription), present number of members: 1,400, service industry, training organisation, consultancy, research organisation.

Subject coverage: Business, companies, grants, funding, employment, exporting, HR, credit.

Access to staff: Contact by e-mail
Hours: Mon to Fri, 0900 to 1700

Access for disabled people: Parking provided, ramped entry, access to all public areas, toilet facilities

CHAMBER OF COMMERCE HEREFORDSHIRE AND WORCESTERSHIRE

Head Office, Severn House, Prescott Drive, Warndon Business Park, Worcester, WR4 9NE

Tel: 0845 641 1641
Fax: 0845 641 4641
E-mail: enquiries@hwchamber.co.uk
Website: www.hwchamber.co.uk

Enquiries to: Information Services & Quality Executive

Founded: 1993; formerly called HAWTEC Hereford & Worcester (year of change 1996/97); formerly called Business Link Herefordshire and Worcestershire (year of change 1998/99)

Organisation type and purpose: National organisation, advisory body, professional body, membership association (membership is by subscription), present number of members: 1,400.
Business support services, business advice and information, membership services.

Subject coverage: Information on Herefordshire and Worcestershire.

Information services: Business Reference Library for Chamber Members; On-line Resource Centre.

Collection: Business Reference library

Library catalogue: All or part available online

Publications: Printed

Access to staff: Contact by letter, by telephone, by fax, by e-mail, in person and via website. Appointment necessary. Access for members only. Non-members charged.
Hours: Mon to Fri, 0830 to 1730

Access for disabled people: Parking provided, ramped entry, level entry, access to all public areas, toilet facilities

Affiliated to: British Chamber of Commerce Accredited Chamber (BCC)

Also at: Chamber of Commerce Herefordshire and Worcestershire; Crossway House, Holmer Road, Hereford, HR4 9SS; tel: 0845 641 1641; e-mail: enquiries@hwchamber.co.uk

CHAMBER OF COMMERCE TRAINING COMPANY LIMITED

Enterprise House, Castle Street, Worcester, WR1 3EN

Tel: 01905 744450
Fax: 01905 744451

Enquiries to: Chief Executive
Direct e-mail: jennyj@hwchamber.co.uk
Other contacts: Administrator

Founded: 1982

Organisation type and purpose: Training organisation.

Subject coverage: Offers broad range of training services from IT internet training through to MIG and TIG welding training.

Publications: Printed

Access to staff: Contact by letter, by telephone, by fax and by e-mail
Hours: Mon to Fri, 0830 to 1730

Access for disabled people: Parking provided, ramped entry, level entry, access to all public areas, toilet facilities

CHANGING FACES

The Squire Centre, 33/37 University Street, London, WC1E 6JN

Tel: 0845 4500 275
Fax: 0845 4500 276
E-mail: info@changingfaces.org.uk
Website: changingfaces.org.uk

Enquiries to: National Infomation and Advice Worker

Founded: 1992

Organisation type and purpose: Registered charity (charity number 1011222).
To provide information, advice and counselling to children, adults (and families) affected by disfigurement. Also provides training and resources to health and social care professionals, schools and employers.

Subject coverage: Facial disfigurement.

Information services: Online counselling via young people's website: http://www.iface.org.uk.

Library catalogue: All or part available in-house

Publications: Printed, and electronic and video
Order printed publications from: Full details on website; available from same address

Publications list: Available online and in print

Access to staff: Contact by letter, by telephone, by fax, by e-mail, in person and via website. Appointment necessary.
Hours: Mon to Fri, 0900 to 1700

Access for disabled people: Full access

CHANNEL CROSSING ASSOCIATION, THE (CCA)

Bolden's Wood, Fiddling Lane, Stowting, Ashford, Kent, TN25 6AP

Tel: 01303 812011
Fax: 01303 812011
E-mail: channelcrossings@aol.com
Website: www.channelcrossingassociation.com

Enquiries to: Information Officer

Founded: 2001

Organisation type and purpose:
International organisation, membership association (membership is by subscription).
To act as a body competent to organise and/or control selected sporting activities which take place in the Channel (e.g. Channel swims and crossings undertaken by unorthodox craft) and to liaise with the British and French Coastguards and Maritime Authorities, to maintain a register of professional pilots with experience of providing escort and pilotage for these activities.

Subject coverage: Professional escort and pilotage across Strait of Dover and effective liaison with coastguard agencies of UK and France.

Publications: Printed

Access to staff: Contact by telephone, by e-mail and via website
Hours: Mon to Fri, 0900 to 1700

Access to building: No access other than to staff

Wholly owned subsidiary of: Channel Crossings Association Limited; at the same address

CHANNEL SWIMMING ASSOCIATION LIMITED (CSA)

Bolden's Wood, Fiddling Lane, Stowting, Ashford, Kent, TN25 6AP

Tel: 01303 814788
Fax: 01303 813835
E-mail: swimsecretary@aol.com
Website: www.channelswimmingassociation.com

Enquiries to: General Secretary

Founded: 1927

Organisation type and purpose: Voluntary organisation.

Subject coverage: All information on Channel swimming since 1875, assistance for channel swimmers, observation and ratification of swims.

Collection: Photographs and press cuttings from 1875

Publications: Printed

Access to staff: Contact by telephone and by e-mail
Hours: Mon to Fri, 0900 to 1700

CHANNEL VIEW PUBLICATIONS LTD (CVP)

St Nicholas House, 31–34 High Street, Bristol, BS1 2AW

Tel: 0117 315 8562
Fax: 0117 315 8563
E-mail: info@multilingual-matters.com
Website: www.multilingual-matters.com

Enquiries to: Managing Director

Founded: 1980; formerly called Multilingual Matters Limited (year of change 2008)

Organisation type and purpose: Publishing house.

Subject coverage: Languages, linguistics, translations, education, bilingualism, travel and tourism.

Order printed publications from: http://www.channelviewpublications.com

Publications list: Available online and in print

Access to staff: Contact by letter, by telephone, by fax, by e-mail and via website
Hours: Mon to Fri, 0900 to 1700

CHANTRAINE SCHOOL OF DANCE

25A Menelik Road, London, NW2 3RJ

Tel: 020 7435 4247 and 07956 308031
E-mail: patricia.woodall@yahoo.com
Website: htttp://www.chantrainedance.co.uk

Enquiries to: Director
Direct e-mail: info@chantrainedance.co.uk

Founded: 1978

Organisation type and purpose:
International organisation.
Dance school.
The School teaches the Chantraine Dance of Expression, created in France since 1958 by Alain and Françoise Chantraine, for the harmony and development of the person. Open to all ages – children from 4, to adults

continued overleaf

without age limit – and all levels – beginners to professional dancers; it aims to broaden and deepen the scope of dance as an expressive art linked with life, and to promote well-being and joy. It offers regular classes, short courses, choreographic ensemble and professional training.

Subject coverage: The Chantraine Dance of Expression has three dimensions – artistic, pedagogic and human. They cover an extensive choreographic repertoire and a teaching method with five main aspects – rhythm, interiority, technique, creativity and choreography. The approach takes in the main styles – contemporary, classical, jazz and dances of other cultures – while going beyond style alone, as well as relationships with the other arts and the natural world.

Publications: Printed

Access to staff: Contact by letter, by telephone, by fax, by e-mail, in person and via website. Appointment necessary.
Hours: Daily, 0830 to 2100

Also at: High Wycombe Chantraine Centre; 13 Queens Road, High Wycombe, Buckinghamshire, HP13 6AQ; tel: 01494 447741; e-mail: jgreenstreet@live.co.uk; website: http://www.chantrainedance.co.uk; Wanstead Chantraine Centre; 27 Blake Hall Crescent, London, E11 3RH; tel: 020 8989 8604; e-mail: kategreen@yahoo.co.uk; website: http://www.chantrainedance.co.uk

Parent body: Ecole de Danse Chantraine; 12 avenue Ste-Foy, 92200 Neuilly sur Seine, France; tel: +33 1 46 24 01 89; fax: +33 1 46 24 64 11; e-mail: centredeneuilly@dansechantraine.com; website: http://www.dansechantraine.com

CHAPELS SOCIETY

c/o 47 Salisbury Drive, Midway, Swadlincote, DE11 7LD

Tel: 01283 558169
E-mail: chapelssociety@gmail.com
Website: www.britarch.ac.uk/chapelsoc/index.html

Enquiries to: Honorary Secretary

Founded: 1988

Organisation type and purpose: Seeks to promote knowledge of the architectural and historical importance of places of worship outside the established Church, primarily the buildings of Christian bodies (Protestant, Roman Catholic, and Orthodox) but also those of other faiths.
The Chapels Society is a learned society administered by volunteers and is a registered charity in England (number 1014207). Membership of the Chapels Society is by annual subscription.

Subject coverage: Nonconformist places of worship in England and comparable buildings throughout UK.

Publications: Printed
Order printed publications from: Honorary Editor, Chapels Society, c/o 31 Melrose Avenue, Reading, RG6 7BN

Publications list: Available online

Access to staff: Contact by letter, by e-mail and via website
Special comments: Contact by e-mail.

Links with: Capel (Welsh Chapels Heritage Society); website: http://www.capeli.org.uk/index.php
Historic Chapels Trust; website: http://www.hct.org.uk/
The Association of Denominational Historical Societies & Cognate Libraries; website: http://www.adhscl.org.uk/

CHAPTER 1

Formal name: Christian Alliance Housing Services Limited

2 Exton Street, London, SE1 8UE

Tel: 020 7593 0470
Fax: 020 7593 0478
E-mail: mail@ch1.org.uk
Website: www.ch1.org.uk

Enquiries to: Director

Organisation type and purpose: Membership association (membership is by election or invitation), registered charity.

Subject coverage: Residential accommodation and information.

Access to staff: Contact by letter, by telephone, by e-mail and via website
Hours: Mon to Fri, 0900 to 1700

CHARITIES AID FOUNDATION (CAF)

Kings Hill, West Malling, Kent, ME19 4TA

Tel: 01732 520000
Fax: 01732 520001
E-mail: enquiries@cafonline.org
Website: www.cafonline.org/research
Website: www.cafonline.org/info
Website: www.cafonline.org

Enquiries to: Information Officer
Direct tel: 01732 520081/2/3
Other contacts: Press Officer for PR enquiries.

Founded: 1924

Organisation type and purpose: International organisation, registered charity (charity number 268369), consultancy, research organisation.
CAF provides a range of services to charities and their supporters worldwide.
Exists to increase the flow of funds to the voluntary sector. Advises on how to give tax-effectively and provide charities with banking, investment and administration services.

Subject coverage: Tax-effective giving, resources in the voluntary sector, loans for charities, international giving, administration and investment services for charities. Information on the charitable sector, lists of specific areas of charities, advice and support for charities seeking to use the Internet.

Trade and statistical information: Income and expenditure of top 500 charities.
Size and scope of UK voluntary sector.
Levels of individual giving.
Corporate giving in the UK.
Local Authority and central government support for the voluntary sector.
Grant-making Trusts in the UK

Publications: Printed

Publications list: Available in print

Access to staff: Contact by letter, by telephone, by fax, by e-mail and via website. Appointment necessary.
Hours: Mon to Fri, 0900 to 1700

Access for disabled people: Parking provided, level entry, access to all public areas, toilet facilities

Offices also at: Charities Aid Foundation; 114–118 Southampton Row, London, WC1B 5AA; tel: 020 7400 2300; fax: 020 7831 0134; e-mail: enquiries@cafonline.org

Overseas offices: CAF America; King Street Station, 1800 Diagonal Road, Suite 150, Alexandria, Virginia 22314–2840, USA; tel: 00 1 703 549 8931; fax: 00 1 703 549 8934; e-mail: info@cafamerica.org; CAF Brussels; Rue Dejonckerstraat 46, Brussels, B-1060, Belgium; tel: 00 32 2 544 0050; fax: 00 32 2 544 0880; e-mail: cafbrussels@cafonline.org; CAF Bulgaria; 65 Vitosha Blvd, 2nd Floor, Sofia, 100, Bulgaria; tel: 00 359 2 981 1901; fax: 00 359 2 981 1901; e-mail: bcaf@cafonline.org; CAF India; 25 Navjeevan Vihar, Ground Floor, New Delhi, 110017, India; tel: 00 91 11 652 2206; fax: 00 91 11 618 6646; e-mail: cafindia@cafonline.org; CAF Russia (based in Moscow); 14/6 Ulitsa Sadovnicheskaya 57, Moscow, 113035, Russia; tel: 00 7 095 792 5929; fax: 00 7 095 792 5929; e-mail: cafrussia@cafonline.org; CAF Southern Africa; 41 de Korte Street, Braamfontein 2017, Gauteng, South Africa; tel: 00 27 11 339 1136; fax: 00 27 11 339 1152; e-mail: cafsouthafrica@cafonline.org; CAF West Africa; F-146/5 Second Soula Street, North Labone Estates, PO Box 05–2956, OSU, Accra, Ghana; tel: 00 233 21 771 953; fax: 00 233 21 7011 260; e-mail: cafwestafrica@cafonline.org

CHARITIES EVALUATION SERVICES (CES)

4 Coldbath Square, London, EC1R 5HL

Tel: 020 7713 5722
Fax: 020 7713 5692
E-mail: enquiries@ces-vol.org.uk
Website: www.ces-vol.org.uk

Enquiries to: Information Officer

Organisation type and purpose: Registered charity (charity number 803602), training organisation.

Access to staff: Contact by letter, by telephone, by fax, by e-mail and via website. Appointment necessary.
Hours: Mon to Fri, 0900 to 1730

Access for disabled people: Parking provided, level entry, toilet facilities

CHARITY COMMISSION FOR ENGLAND AND WALES

Charity Commission Direct, PO Box 1227, Liverpool, L69 3UG

Tel: 0845 300 0218
Fax: 0151 703 1555
E-mail: enquiries@charitycommission.gsi.gov.uk
Website: www.charitycommission.gov.uk

Direct e-mail: pressenquiries@charitycommission.gsi.gov.uk

Organisation type and purpose: Central government body; includes the Central Register of Charities.

Subject coverage: General advice to charity trustees, information on the Commission to members of the public, effective use of charitable monies, charity law, history, administration and management.

Collection: 19th-century reports of the former Commissioners for Inquiring concerning Charities
Unreported vols concerning charities (mid-19th century to 1947)

Library catalogue: All or part available in-house

Publications: Printed
Order printed publications from: The Stationery Office

Publications list: Available online

Access to staff: Contact by letter, by telephone, by fax, by e-mail, in person and via website. Appointment necessary.
Hours: Mon to Fri, 0900 to 1700
Special comments: Central Register of Charities open 1000 to 1600 by appointment only.

Access to building: Prior appointment required

Access for disabled people: Level entry, access to all public areas, toilet facilities

CHARLES WILLIAMS SOCIETY

Flat 8, 65 Cadogan Gardens, London, SW3 2RA

Tel: 020 7581 9917
E-mail: brian.horne2@btinternet.com
Website: www.charleswilliamssociety.org.uk

Enquiries to: Librarian

Founded: 1976

Organisation type and purpose: Learned society.
To promote interest in and provide opportunities for study of Charles Williams' writings.

Subject coverage: Life and works of Charles Walter Stansby Williams, author, theologian and poet, 1886–1945.

Collection: Members' lending and reference libraries are located at CMRS, St Michael's Hall, Shoe Lane, Oxford, OX1 2DP

Publications: Printed

Access to staff: Contact by letter, by telephone, by e-mail and via website
Hours: Mon to Fri, 0900 to 1700

CHARLOTTE M. YONGE FELLOWSHIP (CMYF)

8 Anchorage Terrace, Durham, DH1 3DL

E-mail: clemence.schultze@gmail.com
Website: www.cmyf.org.uk

Enquiries to: Chairman

Founded: 1995

Organisation type and purpose: Membership association (membership is by subscription), present number of members: 160.
Literary society for all those interested in the work of Victorian novelist, Charlotte M. Yonge.

Subject coverage: The works, life and milieu of Victorian novelist, Charlotte M. Yonge (1823–1901).

Collection: Collection of books by and relating to Charlotte M. Yonge, accessible to members, located in Oxford, United Kingdom

Publications: Printed
Order printed publications from: Details on website

Publications list: Available online

Access to staff: Contact by letter, by e-mail and via website
Hours: Mon to Fri, 0900 to 1700

Access to building: No access other than to staff

CHARTERED INSTITUTE FOR SECURITIES & INVESTMENT (CISI)

8 Eastcheap, London, EC3M 1AE

Tel: 020 7645 0600
Fax: 020 7645 0601
Website: www.secinst.co.uk

Enquiries to: Client Services
Direct tel: 020 7645 0680
Direct e-mail: clientservices@cisi.org

Founded: 1992; royal charter granted (year of change 2009)

Organisation type and purpose: A registered charity, a professional body for those who work in the securities and investment industry in the UK and in a growing number of major financial centres round the world. Has more than 40,000 members in 89 countries.
To promote, for the public benefit, the advancement and dissemination of knowledge in the field of securities and investments; to develop high ethical standards for practitioners in securities and investments and to promote such standards in the UK and overseas; to act as an authoritative body for the purpose of consultation and research in matters of education or public interest concerning investment in securities.

Subject coverage: Securities and investments industry.

Publications: Electronic and video
Order electronic and video publications from: Download from website; for multiple hard copies, contact Client Services, tel: 0207 645 0600; e-mail: clientservices@cisi.org

Publications list: Available online

Access to staff: Contact by letter, by telephone, by fax and by e-mail

Also at: CISI Northern Ireland; CISI Scotland

Branches: 10 network branches in England and Wales, 3 offshore branches

CHARTERED INSTITUTE OF ARBITRATORS (CIArb)

International Centre for Arbitration and Mediation, 12 Bloomsbury Square, London, WC1A 2LP

Tel: 020 7421 7444
Fax: 020 7404 4023
E-mail: info@ciarb.org
Website: www.ciarb.org

Enquiries to: Member Services Assistant
Direct tel: 020 7421 7439
Direct e-mail: kmurray@ciarb.org
Other contacts: The Legal Counsel (for legal enquiries)

Founded: 1915

Organisation type and purpose: The Institute is globally recognised as the professional home for all dispute resolvers and is a resource centre for those who benefit from cost-effective, private dispute resolution; number of members: 11,000 worldwide; the CIArb is a global authority on dispute resolution. CIArb membership offers individuals from a variety of sectors internationally recognised standards of excellence. The Institute also provides dispute resolution services for public sector, consumer and commercial markets, providing bespoke solutions for the efficient settlement of disputes.

Subject coverage: Commercial arbitration, mediation, adjudication, dispute resolution, aspects of law, arbitration clauses, appointment of arbitrators, arbitration acts, international arbitration, international conventions on arbitration, enforcement of arbitration awards, training of arbitrators, duties of expert witnesses and advocacy, alternative dispute resolution procedures.

Collection: Volumes on arbitration procedure and practice throughout the world
Legal texts covering dispute resolution

Library catalogue: All or part available online and in-house

Publications: Printed

Access to staff: Contact by letter, by telephone, by fax, by e-mail and via website. Appointment necessary.
Hours: Mon to Fri, 0830 to 1730

Access to building: Library available to members
Hours: Mon to Fri, 0830 to 1730

Access for disabled people: Toilet facilities, lifts

Branches: 30 branches world-wide

CHARTERED INSTITUTE OF ARCHITECTURAL TECHNOLOGISTS (CIAT)

397 City Road, Islington, London, EC1V 1NH

Tel: 020 7278 2206
Fax: 020 7837 3194
E-mail: info@ciat.org.uk
Website: www.ciat.org.uk

Enquiries to: Communications Director
Other contacts: Assistant Communications Director

continued overleaf

Founded: 1965; formerly called Society of Architectural & Associated Technicians (year of change 1986); formerly called British Institute of Architectural Technicians (year of change 1994); formerly called British Institute of Architectural Technologists (year of change 2005)

Organisation type and purpose: Professional body (membership is by subscription), present number of members: 9,500.
International qualifying body for Chartered Architectural Technologists and Professional Architectural Technicians.

Subject coverage: Careers advice, practice and technical advice, education guidance, recognition of the CIAT qualifications, continuing professional development, consultative panel for construction documents, architecture and construction awards.

Publications: Printed

Publications list: Available in print

Access to staff: Contact by letter, by telephone, by fax, by e-mail, in person and via website
Hours: Mon to Fri, 0900 to 1700

Access to building: Prior appointment required

Member organisation of: Construction Industry Council

CHARTERED INSTITUTE OF BANKERS IN SCOTLAND (CIOBS)

38B Drumsheugh Gardens, Edinburgh, EH3 7SW

Tel: 0131 473 7777
Fax: 0131 473 7788
E-mail: info@ciobs.org.uk
Website: www.ciobs.org.uk

Enquiries to: Chief Executive
Other contacts: Director of Education (for information on qualifications and courses; Business Development Manager (for marketing and development issues)

Founded: 1875; formerly called Institute of Bankers in Scotland (year of change 1991)

Organisation type and purpose: Professional body (membership is by subscription, qualification, election or invitation), present number of members: 11,500, registered charity (charity number SCO 13927).

Subject coverage: Banking and finance, administration and management.

Collection: Scottish Bank Notes from 1727 to the present

Publications: Printed

Publications list: Available in print

Access to staff: Contact by letter, by telephone, by fax, by e-mail and via website. Appointment necessary.
Hours: Mon to Fri, 0900 to 1700

CHARTERED INSTITUTE OF BUILDING (CIOB)

Englemere, Kings Ride, Ascot, Berkshire, SL5 7TB

Tel: 01344 630700
Fax: 01344 630777
E-mail: reception@ciob.org.uk
Website: library.ciob.org.uk/liberty3
Website: www.ciob.org.uk

Enquiries to: LIS Officer
Direct tel: 01344 630 737
Direct fax: 01344 630 764
Direct e-mail: lis@ciob.org.uk

Founded: 1834

Organisation type and purpose: International organisation, professional body (membership is by qualification), present number of members: 48,000 individuals, 320 firms, registered charity (charity number 280795), suitable for ages: 18+, research organisation, publishing house.

Subject coverage: Processes of management in construction: e.g., law; contracts; human resources; costs; planning and programming; education and training.

Information services: Full access permitted to members of the Institute; limited access for non-members, who may use the collection for reference. Free postal loan service and technical enquiry handling. Preferential rates on document delivery service for members. Non-members welcome to request copies of documents for a charge.

Collection: Building Law Reports
Conference Proceedings, 1970 to date
Construction Law Reports

Library catalogue: All or part available online

Publications: Printed
Order printed publications from: Construction Books Direct, Englemere Limited
The White House, Englemere, Kings Ride, Ascot, SC5 7JR, tel: 01344 630810

Publications list: Available online

Access to staff: Contact by letter, by telephone, by fax, by e-mail and via website. Appointment necessary. Access for members only. Non-members charged.
Hours: Mon to Fri, 0900 to 1700 (phone)

Access to building: Appointment preferred
Hours: Mon to Fri, 0930 to 1630

Access for disabled people: Parking provided, ramped entry, access to all public areas, toilet facilities.

CHARTERED INSTITUTE OF ENVIRONMENTAL HEALTH (CIEH)

Chadwick Court, 15 Hatfields, London, SE1 8DJ

Tel: 020 7928 6006
Fax: 020 7827 5862
E-mail: info@cieh.org
Website: www.cieh.org

Enquiries to: Information Officer
Direct tel: 020 7827 5821
Direct fax: 020 7827 6322

Founded: 1883; formerly called Association of Public Sanitary Inspectors (year of change 1891); formerly called Sanitary Inspectors Association (year of change 1957); formerly called Association of Public Health Inspectors (year of change 1975); formerly called Environmental Health Officers Association (year of change 1981); formerly called Institution of Environmental Health Officers (year of change 1994)

Organisation type and purpose: Professional body (membership is by qualification), registered charity (charity number 290350).
Registration board and examining body for Environmental Health Officers.

Subject coverage: Environmental health, housing, pollution control, food safety, health and safety at work, and noise.

Collection: Complete set of the CIEH journal: Environmental Health Practitioner 1895 to 2009

Library catalogue: All or part available in-house

Publications: Printed

Publications list: Available online

Access to staff: Contact by letter, by telephone, by fax, by e-mail and via website. Appointment necessary.
Hours: Mon to Fri, 0900 to 1700

Access to building: Library access for CIEH members and researchers, by appointment
Hours: Library: Mon to Fri, 0900 to 1700

CHARTERED INSTITUTE OF HOUSING (CIH)

Octavia House, Westwood Way, Coventry, Warwickshire, CV4 8JP

Tel: 024 7685 1700
Fax: 024 7669 5110
Website: www.cih.org

Enquiries to: Information Officer
Other contacts: Good Practice Manager

History of institution: formerly called Institute of Housing; merged with Institute of Rent Officers and Rental Valuers, date of change, February 1999

Organisation type and purpose: Professional body (membership is by subscription), present number of members: over 17,000, registered charity (charity number 244067/R), training organisation, research organisation.

Subject coverage: Housing (social and private rented sector), housing finance, CCT, homelessness, housing management and good practice.

Collection: 15,000 books and reports and about 35 journal titles held in library

Trade and statistical information: Housing statistics, stock sizes, tenure type

Publications: Printed, and electronic and video
Order printed publications from: Publications Officer
tel: 02476 851700

Publications list: Available online and in print

Access to staff: Contact by letter, by telephone and by e-mail. Access for members only.
Hours: Mon to Fri, 0900 to 1700
Special comments: Members only.

Access to building: No prior appointment required

Other addresses: CIH London; 9 White Lion Street, Islington, London, N1 9XJ; tel: 020 7837 4280; fax: 020 7278 2705; CIH Scotland; 6 Palmerston Place, Edinburgh, EH12 5AA; tel: 0131 225 4544; fax: 0131 225 4566; CIH Wales; 4 Purbeck House, Lambourne Crescent, Cardiff Business Park, Llanishen, Cardiff, CF4 5GJ; tel: 029 2076 5760; fax: 029 2076 5761

CHARTERED INSTITUTE OF JOURNALISTS (CIOJ)

2 Dock Offices, Surrey Quays Road, London, SE16 2XU

Tel: 020 7252 1187
Fax: 020 7232 2302
E-mail: memberservices@cioj.co.uk
Website: www.ioj.co.uk

Enquiries to: General Secretary
Other contacts: Treasurer (for all financial matters)

Founded: 1884; formerly called Institute of Journalists (IOJ) (year of change 1978)

Organisation type and purpose:
International organisation, professional body, trade union (membership is by subscription, election or invitation), present number of members: 1,150.

Subject coverage: Journalism, broadcasting.

Collection: Newspaper and journalistic library

Publications: Printed

Access to staff: Contact by letter, by telephone, by fax, by e-mail and via website. Appointment necessary.
Hours: Mon to Fri, 0900 to 1700

Access to building: No prior appointment required

Links with: British Copyright Council; Campaign for Freedom of Information; Independent Unions Training Council; Journalists' Copyright Fund; Media Society; National Council for the Training of Journalists

CHARTERED INSTITUTE OF LIBRARY AND INFORMATION PROFESSIONALS (CILIP)

7 Ridgmount Street, London, WC1E 7AE

Tel: 020 7255 0500; 020 7255 0505 (minicom, textphone)
Fax: 020 7255 0501
E-mail: info@cilip.org.uk
Website: www.cilip.org.uk

Enquiries to: Customer Services
Direct tel: 020 7255 0574
Direct e-mail: info@cilip.org.uk
Other contacts: Chief Executive

Founded: 1877; formerly called The Institute of Information Scientists (IIS), The Library Association (LA) (year of change 2002)

Organisation type and purpose: CILIP maintains, monitors and promotes standards of excellence in the creation, management, exploitation and sharing of information and knowledge resources. We enable our Members to achieve and maintain the highest professional standards in delivering an information service.

Subject coverage: Librarianship, information and knowledge management, libraries, education for the profession, qualifications and continuing professional development, advocacy and campaigns, policy, sector related events and conferences, Facet publications, Update magazine.

Library catalogue: All or part available in-house

Publications: Printed

Publications list: Available in print

Access to staff: Contact by letter, by telephone, by fax and by e-mail. Appointment necessary.
Hours: Mon to Fri, 0900 to 1700
Special comments: Tel. enquiries taken 0900 to 1700

Access to building: *Hours:* 0830 to 1700

CHARTERED INSTITUTE OF LIBRARY AND INFORMATION PROFESSIONALS IN SCOTLAND (CILIPS)

Office 511, 151 West George Street, Glasgow, G2 2JJ

Tel: 0141 228 4790
E-mail: cilips@slainte.org.uk
Website: www.cilips.org.uk

Enquiries to: Director
Direct e-mail: e.fulton@slainte.org.uk

Founded: 1908; created by the merger of The Scottish Library Association and the Institute of Information Scientists (IIS) (year of change 2002)

Organisation type and purpose:
Professional body, registered charity (charity number 313014).

Subject coverage: Librarianship and library resources in Scotland.

Publications: Printed, and electronic and video

Access to staff: Contact by letter, by telephone and by e-mail

Access to building: Appointment only
Hours: 0900 to 1700

Affiliated to: CILIP; website: http://www.cilip.org.uk

CHARTERED INSTITUTE OF LINGUISTS (IoL)

Saxon House, 48 Southwark Street, London, SE1 1UN

Tel: 020 7940 3100
Fax: 020 7940 3101
E-mail: info@iol.org.uk
Website: www.iol.org.uk

Enquiries to: Director of Communications
Direct tel: 020 7940 3135
Direct fax: 020 7940 3121
Direct e-mail: cetty.zambrano@iol.org.uk
Other contacts: (1) Central Registration Department (2) Registrar for (1) examination queries (2) membership eligibility.

Founded: 1910

Organisation type and purpose:
International organisation, professional body (membership is by qualification), present number of members: 6,500.
To promote the interests of professional linguists and maintain standards within the language world.

Subject coverage: Language learning; courses; methods; availability and training of translators and interpreters; qualifications; language grammar books and dictionaries; employment of translators; examinations in languages; careers with languages; language in general; public service interpreters; language assessments.

Collection: Journals and magazines relating to languages or linguistics received from appropriate organisations overseas
Monolingual minor language works
Technical and/or specialised multilingual dictionaries

Trade and statistical information: Survey of freelance notes for translators and interpreters

Library catalogue: All or part available in-house

Publications: Printed
Order printed publications from: Membership Department

Publications list: Available online and in print

Access to staff: Contact by letter, by telephone, by fax, by e-mail and via website
Hours: Mon to Fri, 0900 to 1700

Access to building: By appointment with a contact
Hours: Mon to Fri, 0900 to 1700

Access for disabled people: Wheelchair access not available due to the heritage condition and age of the building, disabled persons can be assisted by staff at the main entrance

CHARTERED INSTITUTE OF LOGISTICS AND TRANSPORT (UK) (CILT (UK))

Logistics and Transport Centre, Earlstrees Court, Earlstrees Road, Corby, Northamptonshire, NN17 4AX

Tel: 01536 740100
Fax: 01536 740101
E-mail: enquiry@ciltuk.org.uk
Website: www.ciltuk.org.uk

Enquiries to: Chief Executive
Other contacts: Director Corporate Communications

Founded: 1999

Organisation type and purpose:
Professional body (membership is by qualification), present number of members: 23,000, registered charity (charity number 1004963).

Subject coverage: Information technology, logistics, warehousing, transport, materials management, materials handling, inventory systems, stock control, storage, distribution, road, rail, air and sea transport, transport planning, transport operations, transport infrastructure provision.

continued overleaf

Library catalogue: All or part available online and in-house

Publications: Printed

Publications list: Available in print

Access to staff: Contact by letter, by telephone, by fax, by e-mail and via website. Appointment necessary.
Hours: Mon to Fri, 0900 to 1700

Access to building: No access other than to staff and members
Hours: Mon to Fri, 0900 to 1700
Special comments: Charge to non-members.

CHARTERED INSTITUTE OF LOSS ADJUSTERS (CILA)

Warwick House, 65/66 Queen Street, London, EC4R 1EB

Tel: 020 7337 9960
Fax: 020 7929 3082
E-mail: info@cila.co.uk
Website: www.cila.co.uk

Enquiries to: Executive Director

Founded: 1941

Organisation type and purpose: Professional body (membership is by qualification), present number of members: Approx 2,600.

Subject coverage: Insurance, loss adjusting, property, liability.

Publications: Printed

Publications list: Available in print

Access to staff: Contact by letter
Hours: Mon to Fri, 0900 to 1700

CHARTERED INSTITUTE OF MARKETING (CIM)

Moor Hall, Cookham, Maidenhead, Berkshire, SL6 9QH

Tel: 01628 427500
Fax: 01628 427499
E-mail: info@cim.co.uk
Website: www.cim.co.uk

Enquiries to: Head of Information Services
Direct tel: 01628 427333
Direct fax: 01628 427349
Direct e-mail: library@cim.co.uk
Other contacts: Corporate Affairs Manager

Founded: 1911

Organisation type and purpose: Professional body.

Subject coverage: Consumer and industrial products and services, retail, wholesale and distribution sectors, marketing planning, implementation and control techniques, marketing communications, marketing support services, human resources.

Collection: 4,000 books held on marketing and management specifically, relevant marketing journals, market research reports, miscellaneous other reports
Members also have access to online journals/reports/books from their desktops

Trade and statistical information: Market research reports and government statistics

Non-library collection catalogue: All or part available in-house

Library catalogue: All or part available online and in-house

Publications: Printed, and electronic and video
Order printed publications from: CIM Direct, at the same address: tel: 01628 427427; fax: 01628 427439; e-mail: cimdirect@cim.co.uk
Go to www.cim.co.uk for more information on training and events.

Publications list: Available online and in print

Access to staff: Contact by letter, by telephone, by fax, by e-mail, in person and via website. Appointment necessary. Non-members charged.
Hours: Mon to Fri, 0900 to 1700 for telephone and e-mail enquiries
Wed to Fri, 0900 to 1700 for personal visits
Special comments: Charges may be made to non-members for usage, prior appointment required.
Some services free to members.

Member organisation of: European Marketing Council (EMC); tel: +32 2 7421780; fax: +32 2 7421785; e-mail: infodesk@emc.be

CHARTERED INSTITUTE OF PATENT ATTORNEYS (CIPA)

95 Chancery Lane, London, WC2A 1DT

Tel: 020 7405 9450
Fax: 020 7430 0471
E-mail: mail@cipa.org.uk
Website: www.cipa.org.uk

Enquiries to: Chief Executive

Founded: 1882; formerly called The Chartered Institute of Patent Agents (year of change 2006)

Organisation type and purpose: Professional body.

Subject coverage: Intellectual property: patents, designs, trade marks, copyright.

Publications: Printed
Order printed publications from: publications@cipa.org.uk

Access to staff: Contact by letter, by telephone, by fax, by e-mail and via website
Hours: Mon to Fri, 0900 to 1730

CHARTERED INSTITUTE OF PERSONNEL AND DEVELOPMENT (CIPD)

151 The Broadway, London, SW19 1JQ

Tel: 020 8612 6200
Fax: 020 8612 6232
E-mail: cipd@cipd.co.uk
Website: www.cipd.co.uk

Enquiries to: Head of Library and Information Services
Direct tel: 020 8612 6210
Direct fax: 020 8612 6232
Direct e-mail: lis@cipd.co.uk

Founded: 2000

Organisation type and purpose: Professional body, registered charity (charity number 1079797), training organisation, research organisation.

Subject coverage: Personnel management, industrial relations, employment law, training.

Publications: Printed, and electronic and video

Publications list: Available online

Access to staff: Contact by letter, by telephone, by fax, by e-mail, in person and via website. Non-members charged.
Hours: Mon to Fri, 0900 to 1730
Special comments: Primarily for members only.

UK contact for: European Association for People Management (EAPM); International Federation of Training and Development Organisations (IFTDO)

CHARTERED INSTITUTE OF PUBLIC FINANCE AND ACCOUNTANCY (CIPFA Scotland)

22 Logie Mill, Edinburgh, EH7 4HG

Tel: 0131 551 2100
Fax: 0131 551 2223
E-mail: scotland@cipfa.org.uk
Website: www.cipfascotland.org.uk

Founded: 1885

Organisation type and purpose: Professional body (membership is by qualification), present number of members: 13,000, registered charity (charity number 231060).

Subject coverage: Financial management in the public services, especially as regards Scotland.
Accountancy and finance training and qualifications.

Trade and statistical information: Information published on the expenditure and income of all Scottish local authorities; two annual publications of statistics (Rating Review)

Publications: Printed

Publications list: Available in print

Access to staff: Contact by letter, by telephone, by fax, by e-mail and via website
Hours: Mon to Fri, 0900 to 1700
Special comments: Not a public office.

Headquarters address: CIPFA; 3 Robert Street, London, WC2N 6BH; tel: 020 7543 5600; fax: 020 7543 5700; e-mail: info@cipfa.org.uk

CHARTERED INSTITUTE OF PUBLIC RELATIONS (CIPR)

32 St James's Square, London, SW1Y 4JR

Tel: 020 7766 3333
Fax: 020 7766 3344
E-mail: info@cipr.co.uk
Website: www.cipr.co.uk

Founded: 1948

Organisation type and purpose: Professional body, present number of members: 9,000.

Subject coverage: Public relations practice in central and local government, industry and commerce, consultancies and voluntary organisations.

Publications: Printed
Order printed publications from: website: http://www.cipr.co.uk/publications

Publications list: Available in print

Access to staff: Contact by letter, by telephone, by fax, by e-mail and via website. Appointment necessary.
Hours: Mon to Fri, 0900 to 1800

Member organisation of: European Confederation of Public Relations (CERP); Global Alliance

CHARTERED INSTITUTE OF TAXATION (CIOT)

12 Upper Belgrave Street, London, SW1X 8BB

Tel: 020 7235 9381
Fax: 020 7235 2562
Website: www.tax.org.uk

Enquiries to: Head of Education Department
Direct e-mail: rbaxter@ciot.org.uk

Founded: 1930; formerly called Institute of Taxation (year of change 1994)

Organisation type and purpose: Professional body, registered charity (charity number 1037771), training organisation.

Subject coverage: UK taxation, information on examinations in taxation and careers in the profession.

Collection: Tax Library at King's College London (members only)

Publications: Printed

Access to staff: Contact by letter, by telephone, by fax, by e-mail and via website
Hours: Mon to Fri, 0900 to 1700

Access to building: No access other than to staff

Sister body to: Association of Taxation Technicians; at the same address; tel: 020 7235 2544; fax: 020 7235 4571; e-mail: info@att.org.uk

UK Representative Body on the: Confédération Fiscale Européenne

CHARTERED INSTITUTION OF BUILDING SERVICES ENGINEERS (CIBSE)

222 Balham High Road, London, SW12 9BS

Tel: 020 8675 5211
Fax: 020 8675 5449
Website: www.cibse.org

Enquiries to: Information Officer

Founded: 1977; formerly called Illuminating Engineering Society (IES), Institution of Heating and Ventilating Engineers (IHVE) (year of change 1977); formerly called Chartered Institution of Building Services (CIBS) (year of change 1982)

Organisation type and purpose: Professional body, registered charity (charity number 278104).
Provides the Secretariat of the National Illumination Committee of Great Britain.

Subject coverage: All engineering services within buildings: design, installation, commissioning, maintenance, acoustics, air conditioning, communications, controls, electrical services, energy management, fire protection, heating, internal transportation, lighting, maintenance, public health, refrigeration, safety, security, ventilating, facilities management.

Publications: Printed, and electronic and video

Publications list: Available online and in print

Access to staff: Contact by letter, by telephone, by fax and by e-mail
Hours: Mon to Fri, 0900 to 1700

CHARTERED INSTITUTION OF WASTES MANAGEMENT (CIWM)

9 Saxon Court, St Peter's Gardens, Northampton, NN1 1SX

Tel: 01604 620426
Fax: 01604 621339
E-mail: technical@ciwm.co.uk
Website: www.ciwm.co.uk

Enquiries to: Technical Officer

Founded: 1898; formerly called Institute of Public Cleansing (IPC), Institute of Solid Wastes Management (ISWM), Institute of Wastes Management (IWM)

Organisation type and purpose: National organisation, professional body, registered charity, training organisation, research organisation.

Subject coverage: Refuse collection; refuse disposal; street cleaning; litter abatement and control; resource recovery; incineration of waste and heat utilisation; analysis of wastes, best practice and technical articles and publications on waste and resource management, biological treatment, strategy, healthcare waste.

Collection: Comprehensive technical library on all aspects of wastes management

Library catalogue: All or part available online

Publications: Printed, and electronic and video

Publications list: Available online and in print

Access to staff: Contact by letter, by telephone, by fax, by e-mail and via website. Appointment necessary.
Hours: Mon to Fri, 0900 to 1630

Access to building: Prior appointment required
Hours: Mon to Fri, 0900 to 1700

Access for disabled people: Toilet facilities

Member organisation of: International Solid Waste Association (ISWA); Overgarden Oven Vandet 48E, 1415 Copenhagen, Denmark; tel: +45 32 96 15 88; fax: +45 32 96 15 84; e-mail: iswa@inet.vni2.dk

CHARTERED INSTITUTION OF WATER AND ENVIRONMENTAL MANAGEMENT (CIWEM)

15 John Street, London, WC1N 2EB

Tel: 020 7831 3110
Fax: 020 7405 4967
E-mail: admin@ciwem.org
Website: www.ciwem.org

Enquiries to: Executive Director

Founded: 1895; created by the merger of Institute of Water Pollution Control, Institution of Public Health Engineers, Institution of Water Engineers and Scientists (year of change 1987); formerly called Institution of Water and Environmental Management (year of change 1995)

Organisation type and purpose: Professional body (membership is by qualification), present number of members: 11,500, registered charity (charity number 1043409).

Subject coverage: Water treatment, water pollution control, treatment and disposal of sewage and trade waste, sewers and sewerage waste disposal, environmental issues.

Publications: Printed

Access to staff: Contact by letter, by telephone, by fax, by e-mail and via website. Appointment necessary.
Hours: Wed, 1000 to 1600

Access to building: Prior appointment required

Access for disabled people: *Hours:* Mon to Fri, 0900 to 1700

Founder member of: Society of Environment

Nominated body of: Engineering Council; Science Council

CHARTERED INSURANCE INSTITUTE (CII)

20 Aldermanbury, London, EC2V 7HY

Tel: 020 7417 4416/5
Fax: 020 7417 0110
E-mail: knowledge@cii.co.uk
Website: www.cii.co.uk
Website: www.cii.co.uk/knowledge

Founded: 1934

Organisation type and purpose: Professional body for those working in the insurance and financial services industry, with 92,000 members.

Subject coverage: Insurance, United Kingdom and overseas, risk, financial services and related subjects.

Trade and statistical information: Overseas insurance markets, UK insurance market

Non-library collection catalogue: All or part available online

Library catalogue: All or part available online

Publications: Printed, and electronic and video
Order printed publications from: 31 Hillcrest Road, London, E18 2JB, tel: 020 8989 8464, fax: 020 8530 3052, e-mail: customer.serv@cii.co.uk

Access to staff: Contact by letter, by telephone, by fax, by e-mail, in person and via website. Non-members charged.
Hours: Mon to Fri, 0900 to 1700

Access for disabled people: Ramped entry, access to all public areas, toilet facilities

continued overleaf

Branches: Insurance Institute of London and 60 others

Constituent bodies: Personal Finance Society; same address; tel: 020 8989 8464; Society of Mortgage Professionals; same address; tel: 020 8989 8464

CHARTERED MANAGEMENT INSTITUTE (CMI)

Management House, Cottingham Road, Corby, Northamptonshire, NN17 1TT

Tel: 01536 204222
Fax: 01536 201651
E-mail: mic.enquiries@managers.org.uk
Website: www.managers.org.uk
Website: www.managers.org.uk/bookshop

Enquiries to: Head of Information Services
Direct tel: 01536 207423
Direct fax: 01536 401013
Direct e-mail: bob.norton@managers.org.uk

Founded: 1992

Organisation type and purpose:
Professional body, membership association (membership is by subscription, qualification, election or invitation), present number of members: 74,000, registered charity (charity number 1091035), research organisation.

Subject coverage: Techniques, skills, theories and practices of management.

Non-library collection catalogue: All or part available online

Publications: Printed, and electronic and video

Publications list: Available online

Access to staff: Contact by letter, by telephone, by fax, by e-mail, in person and via website
Hours: Mon to Fri, 0900 to 1700
Special comments: Non-members may use the library for reference free of charge. Use of other services will incur a charge.

Access for disabled people: Parking, level entry, access to all areas, toilet facilities
Special comments: Ramped fire exits

Administrative Office: Chartered Management Institute; 3rd Floor, 2 Savoy Court, London, WC2R 0EZ; tel: 020 7497 0580; fax: 020 7497 0463; e-mail: secretariat@managers.org.uk

CHARTERED PHYSIOTHERAPISTS IN MENTAL HEALTHCARE (CPMH)

14 Bedford Row, London, WC1R 4ED

Tel: 01926 406 782
E-mail: heather.grimwade@covwarkpt.nhs.uk
Website: www.csp.org.uk

Enquiries to: General Secretary

History of institution: formerly called Association of Chartered Physiotherapists in Psychiatry (ACPP) (year of change 1994)

Organisation type and purpose:
International organisation, advisory body, professional body (membership is by subscription, qualification, election or invitation), present number of members: 150, training organisation.

Subject coverage: Physiotherapy, psychiatry, mental healthcare.

Publications: Printed

Access to staff: Contact by letter, by telephone and by fax
Hours: Mon to Fri, 0900 to 1700

Group within the: Chartered Society of Physiotherapy

CHARTERED QUALITY INSTITUTE (CQI)

2nd Floor North, Chancery Exchange, 10 Furnival Street, London, EC4A 1AB

Tel: 020 7245 6722
Fax: 020 7245 6788
E-mail: info@thecqi.org
Website: www.thecqi.org

History of institution: formerly called Institute of Quality Assurance (year of change 2007)

Organisation type and purpose:
Professional body.

Subject coverage: All aspects of quality assurance and quality management.

Publications: Printed
Order printed publications from: via website

Publications list: Available in print

Access to staff: Contact by letter, by telephone, by fax, by e-mail and via website. Appointment necessary.
Hours: Mon to Thu, 0900 to 1700; Fri, 0900 to 1600

Access to building: Prior appointment required

Constituent part of: International Register of Certificated Auditors; tel: 020 7245 6833; fax: 020 7245 6755; e-mail: irca@irca.org; website: http://www.irca.org

CHARTERED SOCIETY OF DESIGNERS (CSD)

1 Cedar Court, Royal Oak Yard, Bermondsey Street, London, SE1 3GA

Tel: 020 7357 8088
Fax: 020 7407 9878
E-mail: info@csd.org.uk
Website: www.csd.org.uk

Enquiries to: Director

Founded: 1930; formerly called Society of Industrial Artists & Designers (year of change 1977)

Organisation type and purpose:
Professional body (membership is by subscription, qualification, election or invitation). Registered charity (charity number 279393).

Subject coverage: Industrial, product and engineering design, fashion and textile design, interior and exhibition design, graphic design and illustration, professional practice in all the foregoing, design copyright and registration, intellectual property law.

Publications: Printed, and electronic and video

Access to staff: Contact by letter, by fax and by e-mail
Hours: Mon to Fri, 0930 to 1730

Member of: Bureau of European Designers Association (BEDA)

CHARTERED SOCIETY OF PHYSIOTHERAPY (CSP)

14 Bedford Row, London, WC1R 4ED

Tel: 020 7306 6666
Fax: 020 7306 6611
E-mail: enquiries@csp.org.uk
Website: www.csp.org.uk

Enquiries to: Chief Executive

Founded: 1894

Organisation type and purpose:
Professional body, educational body, trade union (membership is by subscription, qualification), present number of members: 51,000.

Subject coverage: Physical rehabilitation and therapy, treatment techniques, conditions such as back pain, physiotherapy.

Services for disabled people: Facilities in the Learning Resource Centre for literature searching, reading documents and accessing the Internet are available for blind, visually impaired, dyslexic and disabled members. These include a scanner and speech synthesis system, a magnifier/screen reader, a screen reader and a braille keyboard. CCTV is also available.

Collection: CSP Learning Resource Centre holding 180 English language journals (paper and full text); CSP journal 'Physiotherapy' from 1916; foreign language physiotherapy journals; relevant books, dissertations, theses, grey literature.

Non-library collection catalogue: All or part available in-house

Library catalogue: All or part available in-house

Publications: Printed, and electronic and video

Publications list: Available online and in print

Access to staff: Contact by letter, by telephone, by fax, by e-mail, in person and via website. Appointment necessary.
Hours: Mon to Fri, 0900 to 1700

Connections with: Universities for validation of courses

CHARTERED SURVEYORS TRAINING TRUST (CSTT)

6–8 Gunnery Terrace, The Royal Arsenal, London, SE18 6SW

Tel: 020 7871 0454
E-mail: info@cstt.org.uk
Website: www.cstt.org.uk

Enquiries to: Chief Executive

Organisation type and purpose: Registered charity (charity number 327456), training organisation.
Training for the professions of the built environment.

Access to staff: Contact by letter, by telephone and by e-mail
Hours: Mon to Fri, 0900 to 1730

CHARTERED SURVEYORS' COMPANY

75 Meadway Drive, Horsell, Woking, Surrey, GU21 4TF

Tel: 01483 727113
E-mail: wccsurveyors@btinternet.com
Website: www.surveyorslivery.org.uk

Enquiries to: The Clerk
Direct tel: 01483 727113
Direct e-mail: wccsurveyors@btinternet.com

Founded: 1977

Organisation type and purpose:
Membership association (membership is by election or invitation).
City of London Livery Company.

Access to staff: Contact by letter, by telephone, by e-mail and via website

CHATHAM DOCKYARD HISTORICAL SOCIETY (CDHS)

The Museum of The Royal Dockyard, The Historic Dockyard, Chatham, Kent, ME4 4TZ

Tel: 01634 832028
Website: www.cdhs.org.uk

Enquiries to: Honorary Secretary
Direct tel: 01634 718546
Direct e-mail: john_lambert@talk21.com

Founded: 1980

Organisation type and purpose: Learned society, registered charity (charity number 287263), museum, historic building, house or site, suitable for ages: 8+, research organisation.
To spread the knowledge of the dockyard and promote the museum.

Subject coverage: History of the Navy and its men, ships, etc. Workers and trades in the dockyard.

Information services: Catalogue in preparation.

Special visitor services: Guided tours, materials and/or activities for children.

Services for disabled people: Displays and/or information at wheelchair height.

Collection: Extensive reference library
Reserve Collection of artefacts in addition to those on show

Publications: Printed

Access to staff: Contact by letter, by telephone, by e-mail, in person and via website
Hours: Mon to Fri, 1030 to 1700
Special comments: via historic dockyard.

Access to building: No prior appointment required
Hours: Apr to end Oct: Daily, 1030 to 1700
Nov, Feb, Mar: Wed, Sat, Sun, 1030 to 1700
Special comments: Closed to the public Dec and Jan.

Access for disabled people: Parking provided, level entry, toilet facilities

CHELMSFORD BOROUGH COUNCIL

Civic Centre, Duke Street, Chelmsford, Essex, CM1 1JE

Tel: 01245 606606
Fax: 01245 606747
E-mail: mailbox@chelmsford.gov.uk
Website: www.chelmsford bc.gov.uk

Enquiries to: Chief Executive
Other contacts: Head of Publicity and Marketing

Organisation type and purpose: Local government body.

Subject coverage: All local authority services.

Collection: Chelmsford Museum
Essex Regiment Museum

Publications: Printed

Access to staff: Contact by letter and by telephone. Appointment necessary.
Hours: Mon to Thu, 0845 to 1645; Fri, 0845 to 1615
Special comments: Closed until 1000 last Wed of month for staff training.

CHELMSFORD CATHEDRAL LIBRARY

The Cathedral Centre, New Street, Chelmsford, Essex, CM1 1TY

Tel: 01245 294489
Fax: 01245 294499
E-mail: office@chelmsfordcathedral.org.uk
Website: www.chelmsfordcathedral.org.uk

Enquiries to: Librarian
Other contacts: Canon Theologian

Organisation type and purpose: Voluntary organisation, suitable for ages: adults.
Theological lending library.
Early collections reference only, together with those Cathedral Archives that are not in the County Record Office.

Subject coverage: 19th- and early 20th-century theology; contemporary works in biblical, liturgical, missionary, ecumenical and behavioural, inter-faith studies; Essex church history.

Collection: Appointment required to view the collections marked *:
Ante-Nicene Fathers, 10 vols
*Historic Collection
*Essex Church History
*Knightbridge Library (mainly Puritan theology and patristics: 571 vols of 16th and 17th centuries)
Nicene; Past Nicene Fathers, 2 series, 28 vols

Non-library collection catalogue: All or part available in-house

Library catalogue: All or part available in-house

Access to staff: Contact by letter, by telephone, by fax, by e-mail, in person and via website
Hours: Mon to Fri, 0900 to 1600
Special comments: Appointment required for certain collections.

Access to building: No prior appointment required
Hours: Mon to Fri, 0900 to 1600
Special comments: Prior appointment is required for Historic and Essex Collections.

Access for disabled people: Level entry, toilet facilities

Constituent part of: Chelmsford Cathedral; Cathedral Centre, New Street, Chelmsford, CM1 1TY; tel: 01245 294489; fax: 01245 294499; e-mail: office@chelmsfordcathedral.org.uk; website: http://www.chelmsfordcathedral.org.uk

Member organisation of: Cathedral Libraries and Archives Associations

CHELSEA PHYSIC GARDEN

66 Royal Hospital Road, London, SW3 4HS

Tel: 020 7352 5646
Fax: 020 7376 3910
E-mail: enquiries@chelseaphysicgarden.co.uk
Website: www.cpgarden.demon.co.uk

Enquiries to: Curator
Direct tel: 020 7352 5646 ext .3

Founded: 1673

Organisation type and purpose: Registered charity (charity number 286513), research organisation.
Botanic garden.
Research and education in botany, horticulture especially medicinal plants.

Subject coverage: Medicinal plants and herbalism, history of plant introductions, history of the Chelsea Physic Garden and its curators.

Services for disabled people: One wheelchair available to reserve.

Collection: Library ex Society of Apothecaries
Thomas Moore Clematis Herbarium
Photographic archive of the Chelsea Physic Garden

Non-library collection catalogue: All or part available in-house

Library catalogue: All or part available in-house

Publications: Printed

Publications list: Available in print

Access to staff: Appointment necessary.
Hours: Mon to Fri, 0900 to 1700

Access to building: *Hours:* Public openings: April to October, Wed, Thu, Fri, 1200 to 1700, Sun and Bank Holidays, 1200 to 1800.
Members: all year Mon to Fri, 0930 to 1700 (or dusk if earlier); April to October, Sun, 1200 to 1800.

Access for disabled people: Through 66 Royal Hospital Road

CHELTENHAM LIBRARY

Clarence Street, Cheltenham, Gloucestershire, GL50 3JT

Tel: 01242 532686/7
Fax: 01242 532684
E-mail: cheltenham.library@gloucestershire.gov.uk
Website: www.gloucestershire.gov.uk

Enquiries to: Librarian
Direct tel: 0845 230 5421

continued overleaf

Direct e-mail: ask@gloucestershire.gov.uk

Founded: 1897

Organisation type and purpose: Local government body, public library.

Subject coverage: General reference, local studies – Cheltenham and environs, art.

Collection: Art collection – 6,000 items covering fine and applied arts

Library catalogue: All or part available online

Access to staff: Contact by letter, by telephone, by fax, by e-mail and in person
Hours: Mon, Wed, Fri, 0900 to 1900; Tue, Thu, 0900 to 1730; Sat, 0900 to 1600

Access for disabled people: Ramped entry.

Member organisation of: ARLIS

Parent body: Gloucestershire County Council, Libraries & Information

CHEMICAL INDUSTRIES ASSOCIATION (CIA)

Kings Buildings, Smith Square, London, SW1P 3JJ

Tel: 020 7834 3399
Fax: 020 7834 4469
E-mail: enquiries@cia.org.uk
Website: www.chemistry-industry.org.uk
Website: www.sourcerer.co.uk
Website: www.cia.org.uk

Enquiries to: General Secretary
Other contacts: Head of Media Relations for press enquiries.

Founded: 1965

Organisation type and purpose: National organisation, advisory body, trade association, membership association (membership is by subscription), present number of members: 200, manufacturing industry, training organisation, publishing house.
Employers' Federation.

Subject coverage: Chemical and allied industries economic aspects, e.g. production, investment, employees and employment, safety, law, trade, tariffs, statistics; not information on individual companies, technical information limited to the extent of staff expertise. Comprehensive product information on Sourcerer (See Internet home pages), health, safety, and environment.

Publications: Printed, and electronic and video
Order printed publications from: Publications Orders
at the same address, fax: 020 7834 4469, e-mail: publications@cia.org.uk

Publications list: Available in print

Access to staff: Contact by letter, by telephone, by fax, by e-mail and via website. Appointment necessary. Access for members only.
Hours: Mon to Fri, 0900 to 1700
Special comments: No library facilities available. CIA and Sourcerer online 24 hours a day.

Access to building: Prior appointment required

Affiliated associations: Association of the British Pharmaceutical Industry (ABPI); tel: 020 7930 3477; fax: 020 7747 1411; British Aerosol Manufacturers Association (BAMA); tel: 020 7828 5111; fax: 020 7834 8436; e-mail: bama@compuserve.com; British Agrochemicals Association (BAA); tel: 01733 349225; fax: 01733 562523; e-mail: reception@brit-agro.prestel.co.uk; British Association for Chemical Specialities (BACS); tel: 01524 849606; fax: 01524 849194; British Chemical Distributors & Traders Association (BCDTA); tel: 020 8686 4545; fax: 020 8686 7768; Fertiliser Manufacturers Association (FMA); tel: 01733 331303; fax: 01733 332909; National Sulphuric Acid Association (NSAA); tel: 01244 322200; fax: 01224 345155; Picon Ltd; tel: 01372 824513; fax: 01372 824628; Soap and Detergent Industry Association (SDIA); tel: 01444 450884; fax: 01444 450951; Solvents Industry Association (SIA); tel: 01206 252268; fax: 01206 252268

Member of: Confederation of British Industry (CBI); tel: 020 7395 8247; fax: 020 7240 1578; European Chemical Industry Council (CEFIC); Brussels, Belgium; tel: 00 32 2 676 7211; fax: 00 32 2 676 7300; e-mail: mde@cefic.be

CHERWELL DISTRICT COUNCIL

Bodicote House, Bodicote, Banbury, Oxfordshire, OX15 4AA

Tel: 01295 252535, 01295 221572 (minicom)
Fax: 01295 270028
E-mail: liz.matthews@cherwell-dc.gov.uk
Website: www.cherwell.gov.uk

Enquiries to: Communications Manager
Direct tel: 01295 221577

Organisation type and purpose: Local government body.

Subject coverage: Local government services.

Access to staff: Contact by letter, by telephone, by fax, by e-mail and via website. Appointment necessary.
Hours: Mon to Thu, 0840 to 1715; Fri, 0840 to 1620

CHESHIRE ARCHIVES AND LOCAL STUDIES SERVICE

Cheshire Record Office, Duke Street, Chester, Cheshire, CH1 1RL

Tel: 01244 972574
Fax: 01244 973812
E-mail: recordoffice@cheshire.gov.uk
Website: www.cheshire.gov.uk/recordoffice

Enquiries to: County Archivist

Founded: 1949; created by the merger of Cheshire County Record Office and Chester City Record Office (year of change 2000); formerly called Cheshire County Record Office (year of change 2000); formerly called Cheshire and Chester Archives and Local Studies (year of change 2009)

Organisation type and purpose: Local government body.

Subject coverage: History of ancient county of Cheshire, development of Cheshire and its communities.

Collection: Antiquarian Collections
Archives of local authorities, courts, the diocese, parishes, nonconformist churches, private estates and businesses
Central Local Studies Collection includes books, journals, maps, pamphlets, etc.

Non-library collection catalogue: All or part available online, in-house and in print

Library catalogue: All or part available online

Publications: Printed, and microform publications

Publications list: Available online and in print

Access to staff: Contact by letter, by telephone, by fax, by e-mail, in person and via website
Hours: Mon, 1300 to 1700; Tue to Fri, 0900 to 1700; 3rd Sat in month, 0900 to 1600

Access to building: *Special comments:* CARN Readers' Ticket required, booking recommended.

Access for disabled people: Ramped entry, level entry, access to all public areas, toilet facilities, parking available

Parent body: Cheshire West and Chester Council

CHESHIRE COMMUNITY ACTION (CCA)

96 Lower Bridge Street, Chester, Cheshire, CH1 1RU

Tel: 01244 323602
Fax: 01244 401036
E-mail: enquiries@cheshireaction.org.uk
Website: www.cheshireaction.org.uk

Enquiries to: Chief Executive
Direct e-mail: alison.roylance@cheshireaction.org.uk
Other contacts: Assistant Chief Executive

Founded: 1930; formerly called Cheshire Community Council (year of change 2008)

Organisation type and purpose: Advisory body, membership association (membership is by subscription), voluntary organisation, registered charity (charity number 1074676). To promote the quality of life in Cheshire communities, especially rural communities.

Subject coverage: Management and funding of charities and voluntary bodies, community development and voluntary action, rural community services.

Information services: Community development, grants, funding.

Collection: Data on rural communities and services in Cheshire
Directories of funding sources
Grantfinder national computer database on funding sources

Publications: Printed
Order printed publications from: Website, or see contact details
Order electronic and video publications from: Website

Publications list: Available online

Access to staff: Contact by letter, by telephone, by fax, by e-mail, in person and via website. Appointment necessary.

Hours: Mon to Thu, 0900 to 1630; Fri, 0900 to 1600

Access to building: *Hours:* Mon to Fri, 0900 to 1700
Special comments: Parking can be a problem.

Access for disabled people: No disabled access
Special comments: Stairs; no lifts or ramps.

Also at: Satellite office; Unit 20, Blakemere Craft Centre, Chester Road, Sandiway, Cheshire, CW8 2EB

Parent body: ACRE (Action with Communities in Rural England); Somerford Court, Somerford Road, Cirencester, Gloucestershire, GL7 1TW

CHESHIRE EAST LIBRARIES

Macclesfield Library, Jordangate, Macclesfield, Cheshire, SK10 1EE

Tel: 01625 374000
Fax: 01625 612818
E-mail: macclesfield.infopoint@cheshireeast.gov.uk
Website: www.cheshireeast.gov.uk/libraries

History of institution: formerly called Cheshire Libraries and Archives

Organisation type and purpose: Local government body, public library.

Subject coverage: Full range of general reference and information from local to international, e.g. community, business, travel, law, leisure.

Collection: Collection of books written by, and with paintings or drawings by, Charles F. Tunnicliffe, bird artist.
Extensive local history collection including works on the silk industry of Macclesfield.

Library catalogue: All or part available online

Access to staff: Contact by letter, by telephone, by fax, by e-mail, in person and via website
Hours: Mon, Tue, Thu, 0900 to 1900; Wed, Fri, 0900 to 1700; Sat, 0900 to 1300

Access for disabled people: Level entry, access to all public areas, toilet facilities.

Headquarters address: Cheshire East Council; Westfields, Middlewich Road, Sandbach, Cheshire

CHESHIRE MUSEUMS SERVICE

162 London Road, Northwich, Cheshire, CW9 8AB

Tel: 01606 271640
Fax: 01606 350420
E-mail: cheshiremuseums@cheshire.gov.uk
Website: www.saltmuseum.org.uk

Enquiries to: Heritage and Museums Officer

Founded: 1974

Organisation type and purpose: Local government body, museum.

Subject coverage: Archaeology and field monuments, excavations at Northwich and Middlewich, museology, curatorship, history of the salt industry.

Collection: Main collections relate to the industrial and social history of Mid-Cheshire with particular emphasis on salt. Material held ranges from industrial equipment, packaging, domestic items and art, to photographs, also archaeological excavation archives for Cheshire, excluding Chester district

Non-library collection catalogue: All or part available in-house

Publications list: Available online and in print

Access to staff: Contact by letter, by telephone and by e-mail
Hours: Mon to Fri, 0900 to 1700

Access for disabled people: Parking provided, ramped entry, toilet facilities lift access to first floor

Administers: Salt Museum; Stretton Watermill

CHEST HEART & STROKE SCOTLAND (CHSS)

Rosebery House, 9 Haymarket Terrace, Edinburgh, EH12 5EZ

Tel: 0131 225 6963
Fax: 0131 220 6313
E-mail: admin@chss.org.uk
Website: www.chss.org.uk

Enquiries to: Finance Director

Founded: 1959; formerly called Chest Heart and Stroke Association (year of change 1991)

Organisation type and purpose: Registered charity (charity number SC 018761).

Subject coverage: Medical welfare.

Information services: Advice Line, tel: 0845 077 6000

Order printed publications from: Website, e-mail or telephone.

Publications list: Available online and in print

Access to staff: *Hours:* Mon to Fri, 0900 to 1630

Access to building: No access other than to staff

Regional Offices: Glasgow; tel: 0141 633 1666; Inverness; tel: 01463 713433

CHESTER COMMUNITY HISTORY & HERITAGE (CHH)

Formal name: Chester Community History & Heritage

St Michael's Church, Bridge Street Row East, Chester, Cheshire, CH1 1NW

Tel: 01244 402110
Fax: 01244 312243
E-mail: chh@cheshirewestandchester.gov.uk
Website: www.chester.gov.uk/heritage/history/home.html
Website: www.chester.gov.uk/heritage/history/family-history.html
Website: www.chesterimagebank.com

Enquiries to: Community Heritage Officer

Founded: 2000; formerly called Chester Archives, Chester City Record Office (year of change 2000)

Organisation type and purpose: Local government body, suitable for ages: all.

Subject coverage: Family history, local history, community history, conservation archaeology.

Information services: Library available for reference (for conditions see Access); Guided tours for parties – walks and talks.

Special visitor services: Materials and/or activities for children.

Education services: Group education facilities, resources for Key Stages 1 and 2.

Collection: General Register Office Index 1837–1969
Census for Chester District 1841–1901
1881 census for UK
Electoral registers for Chester, IGI for Cheshire, Lancashire, Shropshire, Staffordshire, Derbyshire and Wales
Parish registers for Chester
Local newspapers, maps
Chester photographic survey team, street by street ongoing record since 1950s with some early photographs
Local history library
Archaeological library

Publications: Printed, and electronic and video

Access to staff: Contact by letter, by telephone, by fax, by e-mail and in person
Hours: Mon to Thu, 1000 to 1600

Access to building: *Hours:* Mon to Thu, 1000 to 1600

CHESTER-LE-STREET AND CITY OF DURHAM ENTERPRISE AGENCY (CDC Enterprise Agency)

7 Millennium Place, Durham City, DH1 1WA

Tel: 0191 384 5407
Fax: 0191 386 3934
E-mail: enquiries@cdcbp.org.uk
Website: www.cdcbp.org.uk

Enquiries to: Chief Executive

Founded: 1986

Organisation type and purpose: Voluntary organisation, consultancy, training organisation.
Business advice, information and training.

Subject coverage: Business information.

Publications: Printed

Access to staff: Contact by letter, by telephone, by fax, by e-mail, in person and via website. Appointment necessary.
Hours: Mon to Fri, 0900 to 1700

Access for disabled people: Ramped entry, full disabled access

Also at: Chester-le-Street and City of Durham Enterprise Agency; Mile House, Newcastle Road, Chester-le-Street, Co Durham, DH3 3RA; tel: 0191 389 2648; fax: 0191 387 1684; e-mail: enquiries@cdcbp.org.uk

Links with: Chester-le-Street District Council; tel: 0191 387 1919; Durham City Council; tel: 0191 386 6111

CHESTERFIELD BOROUGH COUNCIL (CBC)

Town Hall, Chesterfield, Derbyshire, S40 1LP

Tel: 01246 345345
Fax: 01246 345252
E-mail: info@chesterfieldbc.gov.uk
Website: www.chesterfieldbc.gov.uk

Enquiries to: Public Relations Manager

Organisation type and purpose: Local government body.

Subject coverage: Local government services and amenities.

Publications: Printed

Access to staff: Contact by letter, by e-mail and via website
Hours: Mon to Fri, 0900 to 1700

CHESTERFIELD LIBRARY

New Beetwell Street, Chesterfield, Derbyshire, S40 1QN

Tel: 01629 533400
Fax: 01246 209304
E-mail: contact.centre@derbyshire.gov.uk
Website: www.derbyshire.gov.uk/leisure/libraries

Enquiries to: Senior Librarian
Direct tel: 01629 533444

Organisation type and purpose: Local government body, public library.

Subject coverage: Marketing information, disabled services, music and drama.

Information services: Library Information Service, tel: 01629 533444

Collection: Asa Lees collection (dogs, especially s.c. fox terriers): a collection of printed items (including Kennel Gazette 1880–1973 and Stud Book 1859–1973) and manuscript correspondence, pedigrees and show reports
Stephenson Collection (railway history)

Non-library collection catalogue: All or part available online

Library catalogue: All or part available online

Access for disabled people: Level entry, access to all public areas, toilet facilities

CHESTERTON LTD

10 Gillingham Street, London, SW1V 1HJ

Tel: 020 3040 8240
Website: www.chesterton.co.uk

Enquiries to: Senior Information Officer

Organisation type and purpose: Service industry, consultancy.
Commercial Company.
Property agents and consultants.

Subject coverage: Property, including offices, retail, industrial, residential, leisure, investment, UK, Europe, USA, Japan, South East Asia, companies.

Library catalogue: All or part available in-house

Publications: Printed

Publications list: Available online

Access to staff: Contact by letter, by telephone, by fax and by e-mail
Hours: Mon to Fri, 0900 to 1730

Access to building: No prior appointment required

Other addresses: Chesterton Ltd; Head Office, 54 Brook Street, London, W1A 2BU; tel: 020 7499 0404; fax: 020 7629 7804

CHESTERTON SOCIETY, THE

11 Lawrence Leys, Bloxham, Near Banbury, Oxfordshire, OX15 4NU

Tel: 01295 720869/ 07766 711984 (Mobile)
Fax: 01295 720869
E-mail: contactus@gkchesterton.org.uk

Enquiries to: Honorary Secretary

Founded: 1964

Organisation type and purpose: International organisation, national organisation, learned society (membership is by subscription), present number of members: 1,500, voluntary organisation.
To inform and educate members on the writing of G K Chesterton.

Subject coverage: Words and writings of G K Chesterton.

Non-library collection catalogue: All or part available in-house and in print

Library catalogue: All or part available in-house and in print

Publications: Printed
Order printed publications from: Secretary, Chesterton Society
As main address

Publications list: Available in print

Access to staff: Contact by letter, by telephone, by fax, by e-mail and in person
Hours: Any reasonable time

CHETHAM'S LIBRARY

Long Millgate, Manchester, M3 1SB

Tel: 0161 834 7961
Fax: 0161 839 5797
E-mail: librarian@chethams.org.uk
Website: www.chethams.org.uk

Enquiries to: Librarian
Other contacts: Archivist (for archival enquiries); Senior Librarian (for systems)

Founded: 1653

Organisation type and purpose: Registered charity (charity number DG/526702C-1/E), museum, historic building, house or site.
Free public library, founded in 1653, for research and consultation.

Subject coverage: History and topography of the North-West of England, rare books.

Collection: Archival Collections re Manchester
Halliwell-Phillipps Collection of broadsides
History of Lancashire and Cheshire
Incunabula
John Byrom's Collection

Non-library collection catalogue: All or part available online

Library catalogue: All or part available online

Publications: Printed

Access to staff: Contact by letter, by telephone, by fax and by e-mail.
Appointment necessary.
Hours: Mon to Fri, 0930 to 1630

Access for disabled people: Parking provided, ramped entry

CHEVIOT SHEEP SOCIETY

Holm Cottage, Langholm, Dumfries & Galloway, DG13 0JP

Tel: 013873 80222
Website: www.cheviotsheep.org

Enquiries to: General Secretary

Organisation type and purpose: Membership association (membership is by subscription), present number of members: 114, registered charity.
To promote and encourage the breeding of Cheviot sheep.

Subject coverage: South country Cheviot sheep; record of ram pedigrees.

Publications: Printed

Member of: National Sheep Association; The Sheep Centre, Malvern, Worcestershire

CHICHESTER CHAMBER OF COMMERCE & INDUSTRY (CCCI)

3 Chapel Street, Chichester, West Sussex, PO19 1BU

Tel: 01243 531765
Fax: 01243 531765
E-mail: office@chichestercci.org.uk
Website: www.chichesteri.org.uk

Enquiries to: Membership Secretary

Founded: 1970

Organisation type and purpose: Advisory body, membership association (membership is by subscription), voluntary organisation.

Subject coverage: Local business information.

Publications: Printed

Access to staff: Contact by letter, by telephone, by fax and by e-mail.
Appointment necessary.
Hours: Mon to Fri, 0900 to 1700

CHICHESTER DISTRICT COUNCIL

East Pallant House, 1 East Pallant, Chichester, West Sussex, PO19 1TY

Tel: 01243 785166
Fax: 01243 776766
E-mail: helpline@chichester.gov.uk
Website: www.chichester.gov.uk

Enquiries to: Information Services Officer
Direct tel: 01243 534679

Founded: 1974

Organisation type and purpose: Local government body.

Subject coverage: Archaeology in Chichester district, tourist information, local government information, business information, housing needs, environmental health, waste management, recycling, development control and building control, council tax, business and economic development.

Trade and statistical information: Local business information (including statistics), local tourism information (including statistics), crime audit information (including statistics)

Publications: Printed, and electronic and video
Order printed publications from: Information Services Officer, Chichester District Council tel: 01234 534679

Access to staff: Contact by letter, by telephone, by fax and by e-mail
Hours: Mon to Thu, 0845 to 1710; Fri, 0845 to 1700

Access for disabled people: Parking provided, ramped entry, level entry, toilet facilities

Other area offices: Midhurst Area Office; North Street, Midhurst, West Sussex, GU29 9DW; tel: 01730 812251; Petworth Area Office; The Old Bakery, Golden Square, Petworth, West Sussex, GU28 0AP; tel: 01798 342241

CHILD ACCIDENT PREVENTION TRUST (CAPT)

Canterbury Court 1.09, 1–3 Brixton Road, London, SW9 6DE

Tel: 020 7608 3828
Fax: 020 7608 3674
E-mail: safe@capt.org.uk
Website: www.capt.org.uk

Founded: 1981

Organisation type and purpose: Advisory body, voluntary organisation, registered charity (charity number 1053549), consultancy, research organisation.
Researches childhood accidents, examines modes of prevention, promotes the importance of a child's safe environment, spreads information about nature and prevention of accidents to children and young people.

Subject coverage: Prevention of children's accidents, child development, child's environment, road accidents, home accidents, leisure accidents, injury types (burns, scalds, poisonings, falls, suffocations, etc.), accident prevention (United Kingdom, international), product safety, accident prevention and health services, safety education, accident compensation and post-accident disability.

Publications list: Available in print

Access to staff: Contact by letter, by telephone, by fax, by e-mail and via website. Appointment necessary.
Hours: Mon to Fri, 0930 to 1700

CHILD BEREAVEMENT CHARITY (CBC)

The Saunderton Estate, Wycombe Road, Saunderton, Bucks HP14 4BF

Tel: 01494 568900 (information and support)
Fax: 01494 568920
E-mail: enquiries@childbereavement.org.uk
Website: www.childbereavement.org.uk

Enquiries to: Chief Executive

Founded: 1994; formerly called Child Bereavement Trust (year of change 2007)

Organisation type and purpose: CBC is the UK's leading national organisation that supports families and provides training to professionals across the entire spectrum of child bereavement.

Subject coverage: We provide ongoing professional support to bereaved children and families and also support the individuals and organisations that become involved with these families. We do this through training, over the phone, via our website and face to face.

Information services: Support and information for bereaved families and the professionals who care for them.

Education services: Educating professionals and offering bereavement training in schools.

Collection: Resources include DVDs, CD-ROMs, books, leaflets, research.

Publications: Printed
Order printed publications from: website: http://www.childbereavement.org.uk

Publications list: Available online and in print

Access to staff: Contact by letter, by telephone, by fax, by e-mail and via website. Appointment necessary.
Hours: Mon to Fri, 0900 to 1700

Access to building: No access other than to staff

Access for disabled people: Disabled Access and parking provided

CHILD DEATH HELPLINE (CDH)

York House, 37 Queen Square, London, WC1N 3BH

Tel: 0800 282986; 0808 800 6019 (Helpline)
Fax: 020 7813 8516
E-mail: contact@childdeathhelpline.org
Website: www.childdeathhelpline.org.uk

Enquiries to: Head of Department
Direct tel: 020 7813 8551
Other contacts: Administrator

Founded: 1995

Organisation type and purpose: Voluntary organisation.
A national freephone service for all those affected by the death of a child of any age, from pre-birth to adult, under any circumstances, however recently or long ago.

Subject coverage: Support for those bereaved by the death of a child whether recent or many years ago.

Publications: Printed

Publications list: Available online and in print

Access to staff: Contact by letter, by telephone, by fax and by e-mail
Hours: Mon to Fri, 0900 to 1700
Special comments: Helpline open: Mon, Thu and Fri, 1000 to 1300 and 1900 to 2200; Tue and Wed, 1000 to 1600 and 1900 to 2200

Also at: Child Death Helpline Department; Great Ormond Street Hospital NHS Trust, London, WC1N 3JH; tel: 020 7813 8551; fax: 020 7813 8516; The Alder Centre; Alder Hey Children's Hospital, Eaton Road, Liverpool, L12 2AP; tel: 0151 252 5391; fax: 0151 252 5513

CHILD GROWTH FOUNDATION (CGF)

2 Mayfield Avenue, Chiswick, London, W4 1PW

Tel: 020 8994 7625 or 8995 0257
Fax: 020 8995 9075
E-mail: cgflondon@aol.com
Website: www.heightmatters.org.uk
Website: www.tss.org.uk

Enquiries to: Administrator

Founded: 1977

Organisation type and purpose: Membership association (membership is by subscription), present number of members: 1,100, registered charity (charity number 274325).
Parent support and to promote public and professional awareness of growth and growth related problems.

Subject coverage: All aspects of growth disorders and related problems, including Silver Russell Syndrome; Soto's Syndrome; Turner's Syndrome; growth hormone deficiency and insufficiency, multiple pituitary hormone deficiency, achondroplasia and bone dysplasias, premature sexual maturation, intrauterine growth retardation.

Publications: Printed

Publications list: Available in print

Access to staff: Contact by letter, by telephone and by fax
Hours: Mon to Fri, 0900 to 1600

CHILD POVERTY ACTION GROUP (CPAG)

94 White Lion Street, London, N1 9PF

Tel: 020 7837 7979
Fax: 020 7837 6414
E-mail: info@cpag.org.uk
Website: www.cpag.org.uk

Founded: 1965

Organisation type and purpose: Membership association (membership is by subscription), voluntary organisation, registered charity (charity number 294841), training organisation, research organisation, publishing house.
Promotes action for relief of poverty among families with children.

Subject coverage: Poverty in the United Kingdom; social policy and administration; welfare rights and benefits; social security; children; social security law, appeals and reviews.

Collection: CPAG Library

Library catalogue: All or part available in-house

Publications: Printed, and electronic and video
Order printed publications from: CPAG

continued overleaf

Publications list: Available online and in print

Access to staff: Contact by letter, by telephone, by fax, by e-mail and via website. Appointment necessary.
Hours: Mon to Fri, 0900 to 1700

Access to building: Prior appointment required
Hours: Mon to Fri, 0900 to 1700

Access for disabled people: Parking provided for disabled visitors only, ramped entry, access to all public areas, toilet facilities, hearing loop
Hours: Mon to Fri, 0900 to 1700

Administers: National Association of Welfare Rights Advisers (NAWRA); 94 White Lion St, London, N1 9PF; tel: 020 7837 7979; fax: 020 7837 6414; e-mail: nawra@cpag.org.uk; website: www.nawra.org.uk

Also at: Child Poverty Action Group in Scotland; Unit 9, Ladywell, 94 Duke St, Glasgow, G4 0UW; tel: 0141 552 3303; fax: 0141 552 4404; e-mail: staff@cpagscotland.org.uk; website: http://www.cpag.org.uk/scotland

CHILD PSYCHOTHERAPY TRUST (CPT)

Star House, 104–108 Grafton Road, Kentish Town, London, NW5 4BD

Tel: 020 7284 1355
Fax: 020 7284 2755
E-mail: cpt@globalnet.co.uk
Website: www.childpsychotherapytrust.org.uk

Enquiries to: Administrator

Founded: 1987

Organisation type and purpose: Voluntary organisation, registered charity (charity number 327361).
Provide information on children's behaviour and emotional development, promote understanding of psychoanalytic work, promote the training of child psychotherapists, and increase the access of children in need of help to child psychotherapy provision.

Subject coverage: Concerned with providing information about child psychotherapy within the National Health Service. Child and adolescent mental health, emotional and behavioural problems, and supporting psychotherapists through providing training awards.

Library catalogue: All or part available in-house

Publications: Printed, and electronic and video

Publications list: Available in print

Access to staff: Contact by letter, by telephone, by fax and by e-mail
Hours: Mon to Fri, 0900 to 1700

CHILDLINE

2nd Floor, Royal Mail Building, Studd Street, London, N1 0QW

Tel: 020 7239 1000 (Admin only)
Fax: 020 7239 1001 (Admin only)
E-mail: info@childline.org.uk
Website: www.childline.org.uk

Enquiries to: Executive Director
Other contacts: Information Officer

Founded: 1986

Organisation type and purpose: Voluntary organisation, registered charity (charity number 1003758).
To provide help and support to children and young people in trouble or danger. It also brings to public attention issues affecting children's welfare and rights.

Subject coverage: ChildLine is the free, national helpline for children and young people in danger and distress. It provides a confidential phone counselling service for any child with any problem 24 hours a day, every day. It listens, comforts and protects. Trained counsellors provide support and advice, and refer children in danger to appropriate helping agencies. ChildLine also raises public awareness of issues affecting children's welfare and rights.

Publications: Printed

Publications list: Available online and in print

CHILDLINK ADOPTION SOCIETY

10 Lion Yard, Tremadoc Road, Clapham, London, SW4 7NQ

Tel: 020 7501 1700
Fax: 020 7498 1791
E-mail: enquiries@adoptchildlink.org.uk
Website: www.adoptchildlink.org.uk

Enquiries to: Administrator

Founded: 1913; formerly called Church Adoption Society (year of change 1990)

Organisation type and purpose: Voluntary organisation, registered charity (charity number 211419).
Adoption.

Subject coverage: Adoption; counselling for children, parents and adopters; relevant childcare.

Publications: Printed

Access to staff: Contact by letter, by telephone, by fax, by e-mail and via website
Hours: Mon to Fri, 0930 to 1700

Access to building: No access other than to staff

CHILDREN 1ST (RSSPCC)

Formal name: Royal Scottish Society for Prevention of Cruelty to Children

83 Whitehouse Loan, Edinburgh, EH9 1AT

Tel: 0131 446 2300
Fax: 0131 446 2339
E-mail: info@children1st.org.uk
Website: www.children1st.org.uk

Enquiries to: Chief Executive

Founded: 1884

Organisation type and purpose: Voluntary organisation (charity number SCO 16092).

Subject coverage: Child protection, child abuse and neglect, parent support.

Publications: Printed
Order printed publications from: website: http://www.children1st.org.uk/shop

Publications list: Available online

Access to staff: Contact by letter, by telephone, by fax, by e-mail, in person and via website. Appointment necessary.
Hours: Mon to Fri, 0900 to 1700

Links with: NSPCC; tel: 020 7825 2500

CHILDREN IN SCOTLAND

Princes House, 5 Shandwick Place, Edinburgh, EH2 4RG

Tel: 0131 228 8484
Fax: 0131 228 8585
E-mail: info@childreninscotland.org.uk
Website: www.childreninscotland.org.uk/children

Enquiries to: Communications Manager

History of institution: formerly called Scottish Child and Family Alliance

Organisation type and purpose: Membership association (membership is by subscription), present number of members: 406, voluntary organisation, registered charity (charity number SCO 03527).
National co-ordinating agency of over 300 members who work with children and families throughout Scotland.

Subject coverage: Information relevant to children and families in Scotland, e.g. education, welfare, health, services, special needs, early years and rural development.

Publications: Printed

Publications list: Available online and in print

Access to staff: Contact by letter, by telephone, by fax, by e-mail and via website. Appointment necessary.
Hours: Mon to Fri, 0900 to 1700

Affiliated to: Children in Wales; National Children's Bureau

CHILDREN LAW UK

44 Queen Anne Street, London, W1G 8HG

Tel: 020 7224 3566
Fax: 020 7224 3577
E-mail: philip@childlawpartnership.co.uk

Enquiries to: Secretary

Founded: 1974; formerly called British Juvenile and Family Courts Society (BJFCS) (year of change 2001)

Organisation type and purpose: Registered charity (charity number 265966).
Working for children and families in legal proceedings throughout the UK.
Aims to inform and educate professionals, to commission research and disseminate findings and to enrich national policy development in order to foster a judicial process that works in the interests of children, young people, families and the wider community.

Subject coverage: Forum for information and debate on national and international policy and practice; best European practice and research; authoritative and independent contribution to youth and family court policy across the UK.

Access to staff: Contact by letter, by telephone, by fax and by e-mail
Hours: Mon to Fri, 0900 to 1700

Affiliated to: The International Association of Juvenile and Family Court Magistrates

CHILDREN WITH AIDS CHARITY (CWAC)

Acorn House, 314–320 Gray's Inn Road, London, WC1X 8DP

Tel: 020 7033 8620
Fax: 020 7739 3902
E-mail: info@cwac.org
Website: www.cwac.org

Enquiries to: CEO
Other contacts: Hardship Fund Manager, Campaigns Officer, Fund raiser

Founded: 1992

Organisation type and purpose:
Membership association (membership registration), present number of members: 160 voluntary and statutory organisations, registered charity (charity number 1027816), suitable for ages: under 18.
Leaflets, DVDs and resources available re paediatric HIV in the UK.

Subject coverage: Medicine, HIV/Aids.

Non-library collection catalogue: All or part available in-house

Library catalogue: All or part available in-house

Publications: Printed, and electronic and video
Order printed publications from: e-mail: info@cwac.org

Access to staff: Contact by letter, by telephone, by e-mail and via website. Appointment necessary.
Hours: Mon to Fri, 1000 to 1800

Access to building: No access other than to staff

CHILDREN WITH LEUKAEMIA

Formal name: Children with Cancer UK

51 Great Ormond Street, London, WC1N 3JQ

Tel: 020 7404 0808
Fax: 020 7404 3666
E-mail: info@leukaemia.org
Website: www.leukaemia.org

Enquiries to: Media Enquiries
Direct e-mail: tina@tinapriceconsultants.com

Founded: 1989; formerly called Foundation for Children with Leukaemia; formerly called Children with Leukaemia UK; formerly called Paul O'Gorman Foundation for Children with Leukaemia

Organisation type and purpose: Voluntary organisation, registered charity (charity number 1035538).

Subject coverage: Childhood leukaemia; other childhood cancers.

Access to staff: Contact by letter, by telephone and by fax
Hours: Mon to Fri, 0900 to 1700

CHILDREN'S CLINIC AT DOLPHIN HOUSE

Formal name: Dolphin House Children's Clinic

14 New Road, Brighton, East Sussex, BN1 1UF

Tel: 01273 324790
Fax: 01273 729491
E-mail: info@dolphin-house.org.uk

Enquiries to: Practice Manager

Founded: 1983; formerly called Foundation for Traditional Medicine

Organisation type and purpose: Registered charity (charity number 288174), suitable for ages: 0 to 18.
Registered charity that focuses on providing a comprehensive range of complementary therapies to babies, children and young people, regardless of family means, mainly focusing on familes and children who are socially and economically excluded.

Subject coverage: Complementary therapies for children: treating children with acupuncture, homoeopathy, paediatric/cranial osteopathy, creative art therapy, nutritional advice, herbal medicine, reflexology, healing.

Access to staff: Contact by letter, by telephone, by fax and in person
Hours: Mon to Sat, 0900 to 1730

CHILDREN'S LEGAL CENTRE (CLC)

The University of Essex, Wivenhoe Park, Colchester, Essex, CO4 3SQ

Tel: 01206 877910 (administration)
Fax: 01206 877963
E-mail: clc@essex.ac.uk
Website: www.childrenslegalcentre.com; www.lawstuff.org.uk

Enquiries to: Child Law Advice Line Freephone
Direct tel: 0808 802 0008

Founded: 1981

Organisation type and purpose: Advisory body, registered charity (charity number 281222).
Independent national charity concerned with law and policy affecting children and young people.
To give free and confidential advice for children, young people and their advisers, on any aspect of children's legal rights; to lobby for changes in the law.

Subject coverage: Law and policy affecting children and young people in England and Wales, welfare and rights of children and young people.

Publications: Printed

Access to staff: Contact by letter, by telephone, by fax, by e-mail and via website
Hours: Mon to Fri, 0900 to 1700

CHILDREN'S LIVER DISEASE FOUNDATION (CLDF)

36 Great Charles Street, Birmingham, B3 3JY

Tel: 0121 212 3839
Fax: 0121 212 4300
E-mail: info@childliverdisease.org
Website: www/childliverdisease.org

Enquiries to: Chief Executive

Founded: 1980

Organisation type and purpose: Registered charity (charity number 1067331).
To raise awareness of paediatric liver disease, to give support both to children with liver disease and to their families, to promote research and to provide new facilities and trained staff.

Subject coverage: Children's liver diseases.

Publications: Printed

Access to staff: Contact by letter, by telephone, by fax, by e-mail, in person and via website. Appointment necessary.
Hours: Mon to Fri, 0900 to 1700

CHILDREN'S SOCIETY, THE (TCS)

Formal name: Church of England Children's Society

Edward Rudolf House, Margery Street, London, WC1X 0JL

Tel: 020 7841 4400
E-mail: supportercare@childrenssociety.org.uk
Website: www.the-childrens-society.org.uk

Founded: 1881

Organisation type and purpose: Voluntary organisation, registered charity (charity number 221124).

Subject coverage: Child care; neighbourhood and community work with the Church; advocacy; independent living; runaways; conciliation; fundraising; voluntary organisations.

Collection: Archive material documenting the development of the Society since it was founded in 1881
Collection of 10,000 photographic images depicting child welfare mainly at the turn of the century

Publications: Printed
Order printed publications from: Publishing Department, The Children's Society
tel: 020 7837 4415, e-mail: publishing@the-childrens-society.org.uk

Publications list: Available in print

Access to staff: Contact by letter, by telephone, by e-mail and via website
Hours: Mon to Fri, 0930 to 1700
Special comments: Enquiries from the general public by telephone, letter or email only. No visitors.

Access to building: No access other than to staff

CHILLED FOOD ASSOCIATION (CFA)

PO Box 6434, Kettering, NN15 5XT

Tel: 01536 514365
E-mail: cfa@chilledfood.org

continued overleaf

Website: www.chilledfood.org

Enquiries to: Secretary-General

Founded: 1989

Organisation type and purpose: Trade association (membership is by qualification), present number of members: 21, manufacturing industry.

Subject coverage: Food safety, food hygiene, HACCP, technology, chilled food manufacture.

Library catalogue: All or part available online, in-house and in print

Publications: Printed
Order printed publications from: http://www.chilledfood.org/shop

Publications list: Available online and in print

Access to staff: Contact by letter, by telephone, by e-mail and via website. Appointment necessary. Access for members only.
Hours: Mon to Fri, 0900 to 1700
Special comments: Detailed information available to members only.

Access to building: No access other than to staff

Links with: European Chilled Food Federation; website: http://www.ecff.net

CHILTERN SOCIETY

The White Hill Centre, White Hill, Chesham, Buckinghamshire, HP5 1AG

Tel: 01494 771250
Fax: 01494 793745
E-mail: office@chilternsociety.org.uk
Website: www.chilternsociety.org.uk

Enquiries to: Office Manager

Founded: 1965

Organisation type and purpose: Membership association (membership is by subscription), present number of members: 7,250, voluntary organisation, registered charity (charity number 1085163).
Local amenity society.

Subject coverage: Conservation in the Chilterns, trees and woodlands, rivers and wetlands, rights of way, waymarking, historic works and buildings, planning, mineral resources and water supplies, etc.

Library catalogue: All or part available online, in-house and in print

Publications: Printed, and electronic and video
Order printed publications from: Chiltern Society office

Publications list: Available online and in print

Access to staff: Contact by letter, by telephone, by fax, by e-mail and via website. Appointment necessary.
Hours: Mon to Fri, 0900 to 1700

Affiliated to: Civic Trust; CPRE

Founders of: Chiltern Open Air Museum; The Chiltern Woodland Project Limited

CHINA SOCIETY

16 Bridge Street, Christchurch, Dorset, BH23 1EB

Tel: 01202 482717

Enquiries to: Chairman

Founded: 1906

Organisation type and purpose: Learned society.

Subject coverage: Generalised information only on Chinese art, history and current affairs.

Publications: Printed

Access to staff: Contact by letter and by telephone
Hours: Mon to Fri, 0900 to 2000

CHINA-BRITAIN BUSINESS COUNCIL (CBBC)

1 Warwick Row, London, SW1E 5ER

Tel: 020 7802 2000
Fax: 020 7802 2029
Website: www.cbbc.org

Enquiries to: Information Centre Manager
Direct tel: 020 7802 2014
Direct fax: 020 7802 2029
Direct e-mail: leo.liu@cbbc.org

Founded: 1998

Organisation type and purpose: National government body, advisory body.

Subject coverage: People's Republic of China: business and trade, economy.

Collection: Business guides, reference books, China statistical year books

Trade and statistical information: UK-China trade statistics

Library catalogue: All or part available in-house

Publications: Printed

Access to staff: Contact by letter, by telephone, by fax, by e-mail and via website. Appointment necessary.
Hours: Mon to Fri, 0900 to 1700

Access to building: Prior appointment required
Hours: Mon to Fri, 0900 to 1700

CHINESE INFORMATION AND ADVICE CENTRE (CIAC)

1st Floor, 53 New Oxford Street, London, WC1A 1BL

Tel: 020 7692 3471
Fax: 020 7692 3476
E-mail: ciac@ciac.co.uk

Enquiries to: Information Officer
Direct tel: 020 7692 3473
Direct e-mail: cheng@ciac.co.uk
Other contacts: Tel: 020 7692 3474

Founded: 1983

Organisation type and purpose: National government body, advisory body, voluntary organisation, registered charity, training organisation.
Advice agency for Chinese community, specialising in immigration, asylum, matrimonial, employment law to Chinese Community ONLY.
Also undertakes specific project work and undertakes cases re: domestic violence issues; matrimonial law; only sees women users.

Subject coverage: Immigration, matrimonial, employment law advice only; only sees women users re matrimonial advice.

Non-library collection catalogue: All or part available in-house

Library catalogue: All or part available in-house

Publications: Printed

Access to staff: Contact by letter, by telephone, by fax and by e-mail. Appointment necessary.
Hours: Mon to Fri, 0930 to 1800
Special comments: Not accessible to wheelchairs.

CHIPPENDALE SOCIETY

Temple Newsam House, Leeds, West Yorkshire, LS15 0AE

Tel: 0113 264 7321
Fax: 0113 260 2285

Enquiries to: Honorary Curator

Founded: 1965

Organisation type and purpose: Learned society (membership is by subscription), registered charity.

Subject coverage: Life and work of Thomas Chippendale Senior and Junior, furniture, wood carving.

Collection: Furniture, manuscripts, designs

Publications: Printed

Access to staff: Contact by letter
Hours: Mon to Fri, 0900 to 1700

CHIROPRACTIC PATIENTS' ASSOCIATION (CPA)

Twingley Centre, The Portway, Winterbourne Gunner, Salisbury, Wiltshire, SP4 6JL

Tel: 01980 610218
Fax: 01980 611947
E-mail: c.p.a@dial.pipex.com
Website: www.chiropatients.org.uk

Enquiries to: Chairman
Other contacts: Membership Secretary

Founded: 1966; formerly called British Pro Chiropractic Association; formerly called Chiropractic Advancement Association (CAA) (year of change 1996)

Organisation type and purpose: National organisation, membership association (membership is by subscription), voluntary organisation, registered charity (charity number 328135), suitable for all ages.
Voluntary association of chiropractic patients that aims to ensure patient welfare, provide a patient helpline, make chiropractic treatment more easily accessible via the NHS, and fund chiropractic research and education.

Subject coverage: All aspects that relate patients to the provision of chiropractic treatment in the United Kingdom.

Publications: Printed

Access to staff: Contact by letter, by telephone, by fax, by e-mail and via website
Hours: Mon to Fri, 0900 to 1700

Access to building: No access other than to staff

CHOIR SCHOOLS ASSOCIATION (CSA)

The Minster School, Deangate, York, YO1 7JA

Tel: 01904 624900
Fax: 01904 557232

Enquiries to: Administrator

Organisation type and purpose:
Professional body, registered charity (charity number 326868).
To supply information about choir schools. The Bursary Trust provides financial help to families in need of assistance.

Subject coverage: Choir schools, information about entry, location, bursaries.

Publications: Printed

Access to staff: Contact by letter and by telephone
Hours: Mon to Fri, 0900 to 1700
Special comments: Office is open on Monday and Wednesday only during term-time.

At the same address is the: CSA Bursary Trust

CHRIS MCALLISTER ASSOCIATES

2 Riverside Walk, Annan, Dumfries and Galloway, DG12 6BE

Tel: 01461 205831
E-mail: chris@chrismca.com
Website: www.chrismca.com

Enquiries to: Principal Consultant
Direct tel: 01461 205831
Direct e-mail: chris@chrismca.com

Founded: 1985; formerly called Chris McAllister Limited (year of change 2010)

Organisation type and purpose: Training organisation, consultancy.

Subject coverage: Trainer training, management and leadership training, assessor and verifier training, open learning, customer service training, advice and guidance training, team leadership training.

Special visitor services: Delivers NVQs and SVQs and QCFs anywhere in the United Kingdom (and abroad, usually by telephone and e-mail).

Education services: NVQs/SVQs in Management, Learning and Development, etc., PTLLS

Services for disabled people: Telephone tutoring (as required). Home or work visits (as required)

Non-library collection catalogue: All or part available online, in-house and in print

Library catalogue: All or part available online, in-house and in print

Publications: Electronic and video
Order electronic and video publications from: http://www.chrismca.com

Publications list: Available online

Access to staff: Contact by letter, by telephone, by fax, by e-mail, in person and via website. Appointment necessary.
Hours: Mon to Fri, 0900 to 1700

Access to building: Only by appointment
Hours: Mon to Fri, 0900 to 1700

Access for disabled people: No disabled access, but wheelchairs can be admitted and accommodated

Links with: Chartered Institute of Personnel and Development (CIPD); tel: 020 8971 9000; Independent Association of Verifiers and Assessors (IVA); tel: 01782 644418; Institute for Leadership and Management (ILM); tel: 01593 251346

CHRIST CHURCH LIBRARY

Christ Church, Oxford, OX1 1DP

Tel: 01865 276169
E-mail: library@chch.ox.ac.uk
Website: www.chch.ox.ac.uk/library

Enquiries to: Librarian

Founded: 1546

Organisation type and purpose: College library.

Subject coverage: Manuscript and printed music of the 16th and 17th centuries; theology, particularly the Vulgate; theatre.

Collection: Brady Collection of theatrical prints and plays
Manuscript and printed music of 16th and 17th centuries
Medieval and Renaissance manuscripts, especially Greek
Printed books and pamphlets of 17th and 18th centuries

Non-library collection catalogue: All or part available online, in-house and in print

Publications: Microform publications
Order microform publications from: See website http://www.chch.ox.ac.uk/library

Access to staff: Contact by letter and by e-mail. Appointment necessary. Letter of introduction required.
Hours: Mon to Fri, 0900 to 1700

Constituent part of: University of Oxford

CHRIST'S COLLEGE LIBRARY

St Andrew Street, Cambridge, CB2 3BU

Tel: 01223 334905
E-mail: library@christs.cam.ac.uk
Website: www.christs.cam.ac.uk/college-life/library/

Enquiries to: College Librarian

Founded: 1505

Organisation type and purpose: University library.

Subject coverage: General academic subjects.

Collection: C. Lesingham Smith Collection of early scientific books
Collection of editions of the works of John Milton
Robertson Smith Oriental Collection
Stephen Gazelee Coptic Collection
W. H. D. Rouse Indian Collection
Wratislaw Slavonic Collection
David Stanbury Darwin Collection
Donald Dickson C. P. Snow Collection

Non-library collection catalogue: All or part available in-house

Library catalogue: All or part available online, in-house and in print

Access to staff: Contact by letter, by telephone and by e-mail. Appointment necessary. Letter of introduction required.
Hours: Mon to Fri, 0900 to 1700

Access for disabled people: Parking provided, ramped entry, access to all public areas

CHRISTCHURCH BOROUGH COUNCIL

Civic Offices, Bridge Street, Christchurch, Dorset, BH23 1AZ

Tel: 01202 495000
Fax: 01202 482200
E-mail: post@christchurch.gov.uk
Website: www.dorsetforyou.com
Website: www.christchurchtourism.info

Enquiries to: Chief Executive
Direct tel: 01202 495126
Direct fax: 01202 482060
Direct e-mail: m.turvey@christchurch.gov.uk

Organisation type and purpose: Local government body.

Access to staff: Contact by letter, by telephone, by fax, by e-mail, in person and via website. Appointment necessary.
Hours: Mon to Thu, 0845 to 1715; Fri, 0845 to 1645

Access for disabled people: Parking provided, ramped entry, toilet facilities, hearing loop, interpreting (by appointment)

CHRISTIAN AID

PO Box 100, London SE1 7RT

Tel: 020 7620 4444
E-mail: info@christian-aid.org
Website: www.christian-aid.org.uk

Founded: 1945

Organisation type and purpose:
International organisation, registered charity (charity number 1105851).
International development aid agency committed to working with all people to combat poverty.

Subject coverage: Combatting poverty. Information on 700 partners in 60 countries that it works with. Campaign work on cancellation of 3rd World debt and Trade for Life. Emergency work around the world.

Publications: Printed, and electronic and video

Publications list: Available online and in print

Access to staff: Contact by letter, by telephone, by fax, by e-mail, in person and via website

continued overleaf

Hours: Mon to Fri, 0930 to 1615

Access for disabled people: Level entry, access to all public areas, toilet facilities
Special comments: Lift available.

Also at: Christian Aid; 35 Lower Marsh, London, SE1 7RL; tel: 020 7620 4444

Parent body: The British Council of Churches

CHRISTIAN AID SCOTLAND

Sycamore House, 290 Bath Street, Glasgow, G2 4JR

Tel: 0141 221 7475
E-mail: glasgow@christian-aid.org
Website: www.christianaid.org.uk/scotland/

Founded: 1955

Organisation type and purpose:
International organisation, registered charity (Scottish Charity number SC039150).

Access to staff: Contact by letter, by telephone, by e-mail and in person. Appointment necessary.
Hours: Mon to Fri, 0900 to 1700

Also at: Christian Aid; 41 George IV Bridge, Edinburgh, EH1 1EL; tel: 0131 240 1254; Christian Aid; 28 Glasgow Road, Perth, PH2 0NX; tel: 01738 643982

CHRISTIAN AID, INFORMATION RESOURCES CENTRE

PO Box 100, London, SE1 7RT

Tel: 020 7523 2414
Fax: 020 7620 0719
E-mail: irc@christian-aid.org
Website: www.christian-aid.org

Enquiries to: Senior Information Officer

Organisation type and purpose: Voluntary organisation, registered charity.
An official agency of the British and Irish Churches working with local organisations in 60 countries, strengthening their efforts to eradicate poverty and increase self-reliance; also provides grants to refugees and disaster victims.

Subject coverage: Needs of the world's poor; poverty issues; development education; emergencies, refugees and interchurch aid.

Library catalogue: All or part available in-house

Order printed publications from: Supporter Relations Department

Access to staff: Contact by letter, by telephone, by e-mail, in person and via website. Appointment necessary.
Hours: Mon to Fri, 1000 to 1700

CHRISTIAN ASSOCIATION OF BUSINESS EXECUTIVES (CABE)

24 Greencoat Place, London, SW1P 1BE

Tel: 020 7798 6040
Fax: 020 7798 6044

Enquiries to: Director

Founded: 1943

Organisation type and purpose:
Membership association, registered charity.

Access to staff: Contact by letter
Hours: Mon to Fri, 1000 to 1700

CHRISTIAN BUSINESSMEN'S COMMITTEE (BROMLEY) (CBMC)

Fair Winds, Goatsfield Road, Tatsfield, Westerham, Kent, TN16 2 BU

Tel: 01959 577745
E-mail: roy@lifesroadmap.co.uk
Website: www.cbmcbromley.org.uk

Enquiries to: Secretary

Founded: 1967

Organisation type and purpose:
International organisation, membership association (membership is by election or invitation).
Religious – Christian Gospel.
A Christian organisation witnessing to businessmen sharing Christ with businessmen and professional men in the market place.

Access to staff: Contact by letter, by telephone, by fax and by e-mail
Hours: Mon to Fri, 0900 to 1700

CHRISTIAN COMMUNITY

22 Baylie Street, Stourbridge, DY8 1AZ

Tel: 01384 377190
E-mail: info@thechristiancommunity.co.uk
Website: www.thechristiancommunity.co.uk

Founded: 1922

Organisation type and purpose: Movement for religious renewal.

Subject coverage: Ordained priests, both men and women, work together with the members of the congregations to create free sacramental communities for celebrating The Act of Consecration of Man and the other sacraments.

Publications: Electronic and video
Order printed publications from: Floris Books, see website: http://www.florisbooks.co.uk

Access to staff: Contact by letter, by telephone and by e-mail

Christian Community sites in: North America, Australia and New Zealand, Germany and France

Christian Community training centres in: Chicago, USA, and Hamburg and Stuttgart, Germany

CHRISTIAN COPYRIGHT LICENSING (EUROPE) LTD (CCL)

PO Box 1339, Eastbourne, East Sussex, BN21 1AD

Tel: 01323 417711
Fax: 01323 417722
E-mail: info@ccli.co.uk
Website: www.ccli.com

Enquiries to: Church/School Representative

Founded: 1991

Organisation type and purpose:
International organisation.
Copyright licensing.

Subject coverage: Hymn and worship song copyright, non-commercial licences for reproducing and photocopying text or audio/visual recordings of hymns and worship songs by churches, schools and Christian organisations.

Publications: Printed

Access to staff: Contact by letter, by telephone, by fax, by e-mail and via website
Hours: Mon to Fri, 0830 to 1630

Parent body: Christian Copyright Licensing International; 17201, NE Sacramento Street, Portland, OR 97230, USA

CHRISTIAN EDUCATION

1020 Bristol Road, Selly Oak, Birmingham, B29 6LB

Tel: 0121 472 4242
Fax: 0121 472 7575
E-mail: enquiries@christianeducation.org.uk
Website: www.christianeducation.org.uk

Enquiries to: Director

Founded: 2001; formerly called National Sunday School Union (NSSU), SCM in Schools (SCM) (year of change 1965); formerly called Christian Education Movement (CEM), National Christian Education Council (NCEC) (year of change 2001)

Organisation type and purpose: National organisation, membership association (membership is by subscription), registered charity (charity number 1086990), suitable for ages: life-long, training organisation, consultancy, research organisation, publishing house.

Subject coverage: Religious education for all ages; ecumenism.

Publications: Printed, and electronic and video

Publications list: Available in print

Access to staff: Contact by letter, by telephone, by fax and via website
Hours: Mon to Fri, 0900 to 1700

Other addresses: RE Today Services; 1020 Bristol Road, Selly Oak, Birmingham, B29 6LB; tel: 0121 472 4242; fax: 0121 472 7575

Subsidiary body: Professional Council for Religious Education (PCfRE); tel: 0191 213 5227; fax: 0191 213 5227; e-mail: rachel@retoday.org.uk

CHRISTIAN ENQUIRY AGENCY (CEA)

Selsdon House, 212–220 Addington Road, South Croydon, CR2 8LD

Tel: 020 3490 3315
E-mail: enquiry@christianity.org.uk
Website: www.christianity.org.uk

Enquiries to: Administrator

Founded: 1988

Organisation type and purpose: Registered charity (charity number 297393).
To provide information about the Christian faith.

Subject coverage: Christian faith.

Publications: Printed

Access to staff: Contact by letter, by telephone, by e-mail and via website
Hours: Mon to Fri, 0800 to 1600
Special comments: Hours are variable, but voicemail and answerphone operate.

Works in association with: all major churches in Britain and Ireland, and many Christian organisations.

CHRISTIAN POLICE ASSOCIATION (CPA)

Bedford Heights, Manton Lane, Bedford, MK41 7PH

Tel: 01234 272 865
E-mail: info@cpauk.net
Website: www.cpauk.net

Enquiries to: Executive Director

Organisation type and purpose: Membership association (membership is by election or invitation), present number of members: 2,000, registered charity (charity number 220482).

Access to staff: Contact by letter, by telephone, by fax and by e-mail
Hours: Mon to Fri, 0900 to 1700

CHRISTIAN SCIENCE COMMITTEES ON PUBLICATION

Formal name: District Manager for the United Kingdom and Republic of Ireland, Christian Science Committees on Publication

90 Long Acre, London, WC2E 9RZ

Tel: 020 8150 0245
Fax: 020 7849 3200
E-mail: londoncs@csps.com
Website: www.christianscience.co.uk

Enquiries to: District Manager

Founded: 1909

Organisation type and purpose: Registered charity (charity number 230940).
To engage withe the media on issues of spirituality and health, and especially Christian Science and its healing practice.

Subject coverage: Connecting the dots between consciousness and wellbeing, spirituality and health and prayer and healing. Christian Science, the writings of Mary Baker Eddy, the Bible and general information on The Church of Christ Scientist.

Information services: Blogger on spirituality and health from a Christian Science perspective and media contact for information about Christian Science, Mary Baker Eddy, and Church of Christ, Scientist.

Access to staff: Contact by letter, by telephone, by e-mail, in person and via website. Appointment necessary.

CHRISTIANS ABROAD (Cab)

The Bon Marche Centre, 241–251 Ferndale Road, London, SW9 8BJ

Tel: 08707 707990
Fax: 08707 707991
E-mail: director@cabroad.org.uk
Website: www.cabroad.org.uk
Website: www.wse.org.uk

Enquiries to: Information Officer

Founded: 1972

Organisation type and purpose: Voluntary organisation, registered charity (charity number 265867).
To offer opportunities for individuals with Christian commitment to work for development overseas through Christians Abroad, and debriefing sessions for review and reflection for those returning from overseas service.
To provide a consultancy for overseas recruitment and personnel management to agencies placing persons overseas in mission, and development on all matters deriving from the organisation's experience in the international movement of personnel.
As World Service Enquiry, providing information and advice about volunteering or working in the developing world.

Subject coverage: Work in aid, development and mission overseas; recruitment and personnel management in mission work overseas.

Publications: Printed

Publications list: Available online and in print

Access to staff: Contact by telephone, by e-mail and via website
Hours: Mon to Fri, 0900 to 1700

Access to building: No access other than to staff

CHRISTIE CHARITY

Formal name: The Christie NHS Foundation Trust

Appeals Office, Wilmslow Road, Withington, Manchester, M20 4BX

Tel: 0161 446 3988
Fax: 0161 446 3991
E-mail: via website
Website: www.christies.org

Founded: 1901

Organisation type and purpose: Registered charity (charity number 1049751).
Raises money to fund projects at The Christie hospital that are outside the scope of the NHS, such as a new radiopharmacy, communications skills training for nursing staff, a new state-of-the-art surgical robot, groundbreaking cancer research and the wig service.

Publications: Printed, and electronic and video
Order printed publications from: Website
Order electronic and video publications from: Website

Access to staff: Contact by letter, by telephone, by fax and via website

CHRISTIE HOSPITAL & PATERSON INSTITUTE FOR CANCER RESEARCH

Medical Library, Wilmslow Road, Withington, Manchester, M20 4BX

Tel: 0161 446 3000
Fax: 0161 446 3454
E-mail: sglover@picr.man.ac.uk
Website: www.christie.nhs.uk

Enquiries to: Librarian
Direct tel: 0161 446 3456

Founded: 1932

Organisation type and purpose: Research organisation.
Medical library.
Cancer.

Subject coverage: Oncology; radiotherapy; treatment and research.

Library catalogue: All or part available in-house

Access to staff: Contact by telephone and by e-mail
Hours: Mon to Wed, 0900 to 1900; Thu, 0800 to 1730; Fri, 0800 to 1700; Sat, 0900 to 1300
Special comments: NHS or academic staff only.

CHURCH MISSION SOCIETY (CMS)

Watlington Road, Oxford, OX4 6BZ

Tel: 01865 787552
Fax: 01865 776375
E-mail: margaret.acton@cms-uk.org
Website: www.cms-uk.org

Enquiries to: Records Manager

Founded: 1799; formerly called Church Missionary Society

Organisation type and purpose: Registered charity (charity number 220297).
Anglican Missionary Society.

Subject coverage: Mission work and local church growth, particularly in Asia and Africa.

Collection: Extensive archive collection located at Birmingham University Library. Contact Special Collections, Main Library, University of Birmingham, Edgbaston, Birmingham, B15 2TT

Library catalogue: All or part available online

Publications: Printed

Access to staff: Appointment necessary.
Hours: Mon to Fri, 0900 to 1700

CHURCH MONUMENTS SOCIETY (CMS)

The Membership Secretary, 55 Bowden Park Road, Crownhill, Plymouth, PL6 5NG

E-mail: churchmonuments@aol.com
Website: www.churchmonumentssociety.org

Enquiries to: Honorary Secretary
Other contacts: Honorary Publicity Officer

Founded: 1979

Organisation type and purpose: Learned society, registered charity (charity number 279597).
To promote, for the public benefit, the study, care and conservation of funerary monuments of all countries and all periods.

Subject coverage: Art, architecture, history, costume, heraldry, lettering, geology, genealogy, iconography, epigraphy.

continued overleaf

Publications: Printed
Order printed publications from: Honorary Membership Secretary, Church Monuments Society, 55 Bowden Park Road, Crownhill, Plymouth, PL6 5NG; tel. 01752 773634

Access to staff: Contact by letter, by telephone, by fax, by e-mail and via website

CHURCH OF ENGLAND BOARD OF EDUCATION (BOE)

Church House, Great Smith Street, London, SW1P 3AZ

Tel: 020 7898 1500
Fax: 020 7898 1520
E-mail: janina.ainsworth@c-of-e.org.uk
Website: www.cofe.anglican.org/about/education
Website: www.churchschools.co.uk
Website: www.natsoc.org.uk

History of institution: formerly called General Synod Board of Education

Organisation type and purpose: Advisory body, voluntary organisation, suitable for ages: all.
To promote the Church's interest in education.

Subject coverage: Church of England schools, church colleges, chaplains in colleges and universities, adult work in the Church, children's work (including Sunday schools), religious education, history of church colleges of education, training/adult education, youth work/youth council.

Publications list: Available in print

Access to staff: Contact by letter, by telephone, by fax, by e-mail and via website
Hours: Mon to Fri, 0900 to 1700

Constituent bodies: Lifelong Learning Team; tel: 020 7898 1505; fax: 020 7898 1520; e-mail: gabriella.disalvo@c-of-e.org.uk; Schools Strategy Team; tel: 020 7898 1491; fax: 020 7898 1520; e-mail: veronica.elks@c-of-e.org.uk; Training & Development Team; tel: 020 7898 1512; fax: 020 7898 0520; e-mail: julia.eden@c-of-e.org.uk

Links with: National Society (CofE) for Promoting Religious Education; tel: 020 7898 1518; fax: 020 7898 1493; e-mail: peter.churchill@c-of-e.org.uk

Parent body: Archbishops' Council of the Church of England; tel: 020 7898 1000

CHURCH OF ENGLAND RECORD CENTRE (CERC)

15 Galleywall Road, South Bermondsey, London, SE16 3PB

Tel: 020 7898 1030
Fax: 020 7898 1043
E-mail: archives@churchofengland.org
Website: www.lambethpalacelibrary.org/content/cerc

Enquiries to: Operations Manager

Founded: 1990; formerly called Church Commissioners' Archives, General Synod Archives, National Society Archives (year of change 1990)

Organisation type and purpose: Church Administration.

Subject coverage: Church of England; administration, buildings, education, finance, history, legislation, liturgy, ministry, mission, social responsibility.

Collection: Church Commissioners' Archives
General Synod Archives
National Society Archives

Non-library collection catalogue: All or part available in print

Library catalogue: All or part available online

Publications: Printed, and electronic and video

Access to staff: Contact by letter, by telephone, by fax and by e-mail. Appointment necessary.
Hours: Tue to Thu, 1000 to 1700
Special comments: Readers' ticket required

Access to building: Prior appointment required for reading room

Access for disabled people: Parking provided, toilet facilities

CHURCH OF JESUS CHRIST OF LATTER-DAY SAINTS

Church Offices, 751 Warwick Road, Solihull, West Midlands, B91 3DQ

Tel: 0121 712 1200
Website: www.familysearch.org
Website: www.lds.org/newsroom
Website: www.mormon.org
Website: www.lds.org

Founded: 1830; also known as Mormons (nickname)

Organisation type and purpose: International organisation, membership association (membership is by qualification), present number of members: 180,000 UK and Ireland, 11,000,000 worldwide, registered charity (charity number 242451). Church, religious organisation.

Subject coverage: Theology, especially early Christian church, revelation; certain fields of health, especially cancer; self-sufficiency; family relationships; genealogy, especially the use of computer held genealogical records, such as the IGI (International Genealogical Index).

Publications: Printed, and electronic and video
Order printed publications from: Latter-Day Saints Distribution
399 Garrett Green Lane, Birmingham, B33 0UH, tel: 0121 785 2200
Order electronic and video publications from: Latter-Day Saints Distribution
399 Garrett Green Lane, Birmingham, B33 0UH, tel: 0121 785 2200

Access to staff: Contact by letter, by telephone, by fax, by e-mail and via website. Appointment necessary.
Hours: Mon to Fri, 0900 to 1700

Access for disabled people: Access to all public areas, toilet facilities

CHURCH OF SCOTLAND

121 George Street, Edinburgh, EH2 4YN

Tel: 0131 225 5722
Fax: 0131 220 3133
E-mail: fmacdonald@cofscotland.org.uk
Website: www.churchofscotland.org.uk

Enquiries to: Principal Clerk

Founded: 500 AD

Organisation type and purpose: National church.

Subject coverage: Church of Scotland.

Publications: Printed

Access to staff: Contact by letter
Hours: Mon to Fri, 0900 to 1700

CHURCH UNION (CU)

Formal name: The Church Union

2A The Cloisters, Gordon Square, London, WC1H 0AG

Tel: 020 7388 3588
E-mail: secretary@churchunion.co.uk
Website: www.churchunion.co.uk

Enquiries to: The Secretary
Direct tel: 020 7388 3588
Other contacts: Chairman, tel: 01371 830132; Treasurer, tel: 020 8467 3809; Membership, tel: 01884 34563

Founded: 1859; formerly called Tufton Books; formerly called Church Literature Association (publication arm of CU) (year of change 1997)

Organisation type and purpose: Membership association (membership is by subscription), present number of members: 2,000, registered charity (charity number 243535), publishing house.

Subject coverage: The Catholic Movement within the Church of England, founded at the time of the Oxford Movement, to promote catholic faith and order, it continues this work today by providing support and encouragement to those lay people and priests who wish to see catholic faith, order, morals and spirituality maintained and upheld, and who wish to promote catholic unity. The Union is a publisher of books and tracts and has part-time staff who can advise on matters liturgical, legal and musical.

Collection: Lord Halifax's personal Library: history of the English Church Union and Anglo-Catholic congresses

Publications: Printed, and electronic and video
Order printed publications from: Canterbury Press, St Mary's Works, St Mary Plain, Norwich, NR3 3BH, tel: 01603 612914
Order electronic and video publications from: Canterbury Press

Publications list: Available in print

Access to staff: Contact by letter, by telephone and by e-mail. Appointment necessary.
Hours: Mon to Fri, 0900 to 1700
Special comments: Via telephone only

Access to building: Prior appointment required

Also trades as: Tufton Books

CHURCHES RACIAL JUSTICE NETWORK (CRJN)

39 Eccleston Square, London, SW1V 1BX

Tel: 020 7901 4890
Fax: 020 7901 4894
E-mail: info@ctbi.org.uk
Website: www.ctbi.org.uk

Enquiries to: RJN Desk

Founded: 1992

Organisation type and purpose: National organisation, voluntary organisation, registered charity (charity number 259688). Church organisation.

Subject coverage: Racial justice and community relations in Britain.

Library catalogue: All or part available online

Publications: Printed

Publications list: Available online and in print

Access to staff: Contact by letter, by telephone, by fax, by e-mail and via website. Appointment necessary.
Hours: Mon to Fri, 0930 to 1700

Access for disabled people: Level entry

Affiliated to: All community race relations bodies.

CHURCHES TOGETHER IN BRITAIN AND IRELAND (CTBI)

39 Eccleston Square, London, SW1V 1BX

Tel: 020 7901 4890
Fax: 020 79014894
E-mail: info@ctbi.org.uk
Website: www.ctbi.org.uk

Enquiries to: General Secretary

Founded: 1947; formerly called British Council of Churches (year of change 1990)

Organisation type and purpose: National organisation, membership association (membership is by subscription, qualification), present number of members: 37 member churches, registered charity (charity number 1113299).
Fellowship of Churches in the United Kingdom and the Republic of Ireland; member churches – Protestant, Anglican, Orthodox, Roman Catholic, Pentecostal, Salvation Army, Quaker, Ecumenical.

Subject coverage: Ecumenical co-operation: Christianity; relations with other churches and other faiths; Christian perspectives on public affairs, international affairs, race relations, mission and evangelisation, women's issues, inter-faith relations.

Publications: Printed
Order printed publications from: CTBI Publications, Church House Bookshop, Great Smith Street, London, SW1P 3BN

Publications list: Available online and in print

Access to staff: Contact by letter, by telephone, by fax, by e-mail and via website. Appointment necessary.
Hours: Mon to Fri, 0900 to 1700

Access to building: Prior appointment required

Access for disabled people: Level entry, access to all public areas, toilet facilities

Affiliated to: Conference of European Churches; World Council of Churches

Links with: Churches Together in England, Scotland, Wales; Irish Council of Churches

CHURCHES' CONSERVATION TRUST, THE

1 West Smithfield, London, EC1A 9EE

Tel: 020 7213 0660
Fax: 020 7213 0678
E-mail: central@tcct.org.uk
Website: www.visitchurches.org.uk

Founded: 1969; formerly called Redundant Churches Fund (year of change 1994)

Organisation type and purpose: The Churches Conservation Trust is the national charity protecting historic churches at risk. We've saved over 340 beautiful buildings which attract more than a million visitors a year. We are a registered charity (number 258612).

Subject coverage: Conservation, community use for historic churches

Publications: Printed

Publications list: Available online and in print

Access to staff: Contact by letter, by telephone, by fax, by e-mail, in person and via website
Hours: Mon to Fri, 0900 to 1700

Access to building: No prior appointment required
Special comments: Please check our website for detailed information about opening arrangements to our churches

Access for disabled people: Please check the website for detailed information

CHURCHILL ARCHIVES CENTRE

Churchill College, Cambridge, CB3 0DS

Tel: 01223 336087
Fax: 01223 336135
E-mail: archives@chu.cam.ac.uk
Website: www.chu.cam.ac.uk/archives

Enquiries to: Director of the Archives

Founded: 1973

Organisation type and purpose: University department or institute.
College library and archive.

Subject coverage: Churchill Family; diplomacy, foreign policy and international relations, 1900 to date; political life and government policy, 1900 to date; military and naval history, 1900 to date; history of science and technology, 1900 to date.

Collection: Papers of Sir Winston Churchill, together with papers of about 570 other individuals and institutions

Non-library collection catalogue: All or part available online and in-house

Library catalogue: All or part available in-house

Access to staff: Contact by letter, by telephone, by fax, by e-mail and via website. Appointment necessary.
Hours: Mon to Fri, 0900 to 1700

Access to building: Prior appointment required, ID required

Access for disabled people: Parking provided, ramped entry, toilet facilities, lift to reading rooms

CIBA SPECIALTY CHEMICALS PLC

Hawkhead Road, Paisley, Renfrewshire, PA2 7BG

Tel: 0141 887 1144
Fax: 0141 840 2283

Enquiries to: Information Manager
Direct tel: 0141 887 1144 ext 5287
Direct e-mail: ailsa.morrison@cibasc.com
Other contacts: Library Assistant for general.

History of institution: formerly called Ciba-Geigy Pigments (year of change 1997)

Organisation type and purpose: Manufacturing industry.

Subject coverage: Organic pigments, colour chemistry.

Library catalogue: All or part available in-house

Access to staff: Contact by letter, by telephone and by e-mail. Appointment necessary.
Hours: Mon to Fri, 0900 to 1700

Access to building: Prior appointment required

CILT, THE NATIONAL CENTRE FOR LANGUAGES (CiLT)

20 Bedfordbury, London, WC2N 4LB

Tel: 020 7379 5110
Fax: 020 7379 5082
E-mail: library@cilt.org.uk
Website: www.nacell.org.uk
Website: www.blis.org.uk
Website: www.cilt.org.uk

Enquiries to: Librarian

Founded: 1966

Organisation type and purpose: Registered charity (charity number 313938).
Supported by Central Government grants.

Subject coverage: Promotion of a greater national capability in languages, including languages for employment, and to support the work of all those concerned with language teaching and learning from primary to graduate level. Research into teaching methods and learning resources in French, German, Italian, Russian, Spanish, and many other languages; English as a second language in Britain; community languages; examinations.

Collection: Books and periodicals
Teaching materials, textbooks, visual aids, software, video and audio recordings

Trade and statistical information: Education statistics and labour market data at http://www.cilt.org.uk/statistics

Non-library collection catalogue: All or part available online

Library catalogue: All or part available online

continued overleaf

Publications: Printed, and electronic and video
Order printed publications from: Central Books Ltd, 99 Wallis Road, London, E9 5LN, tel: 0845 458 9910 (mail order/enquiries) 0845 458 9911 (trade orders), fax: 0845 458 9912, e-mail: mo@centralbooks.com

Publications list: Available online and in print

Access to staff: Contact by letter, by telephone, by fax, by e-mail and in person
Hours: Mon to Fri, 1030 to 1700
Extended opening hours during school terms: Wed, 1030 to 2000; Sat, 1000 to 1300

Affiliated to: A network of Comenius Centres in England; CILT Cymru; tel: 029 2048 0137; fax: 029 2048 0145; e-mail: bethan.enticott@ciltcymru.org.uk; website: http://www.ciltcymru.org.uk
Northern Ireland CILT; tel: 028 9097 5955; fax: 028 9032 6571; e-mail: nicilt@qub.ac.uk; website: http://www.qub.ac.uk/edu/nicilt
Scottish CILT; tel: 01786 466290; fax: 01786 466291; e-mail: scilt@stir.ac.uk; website: http://www.scilt.stir.ac.uk/

CIMA

Formal name: Chartered Institute of Management Accountants

26 Chapter Street, London, SW1P 4NP

Tel: 020 7663 5441
Fax: 020 7663 5442
Website: www.cimaglobal.com
Website: www.cimaglobal.com/main/resources/knowledge

Enquiries to: Information Manager (TAS)
Direct tel: 020 8849 2259
Direct fax: 020 8849 2464
Direct e-mail: tas@cimaglobal.com

Founded: 1919; formerly called Institute of Cost and Management Accountants

Organisation type and purpose: Professional body (membership is by qualification).

Subject coverage: Cost, financial and management accountancy; finance and financial management.

Collection: Archive of own publications from 1934
Historical collection of books relating to cost and management accounting

Library catalogue: All or part available in-house

Publications: Printed, and electronic and video
Order printed publications from: Publishing Sales Department
tel: 020 8849 2270, fax: 020 8849 2465, e-mail: publishing-sales@cimaglobal.com

Publications list: Available online

Access to staff: Contact by letter, by telephone, by fax, by e-mail, in person and via website. Access for members only.
Hours: Mon to Fri, 1000 to 1600
Special comments: Members and bona fide researchers only.

Access to building: Prior appointment required

CIMTECH LIMITED

University of Hertfordshire, Innovation Centre, College Lane, Hatfield, Herts, AL10 9AB

Tel: 01707 281060
Fax: 01707 281061
E-mail: c.cimtech@herts.ac.uk
Website: www.cimtech.co.uk

Enquiries to: Office Manager

Founded: 1967; formerly called HERTIS Information and Research, National Centre for Information Management and Technology (CIMTECH)

Organisation type and purpose: Membership association (membership is by subscription), service industry, training organisation, consultancy, publishing house.

Subject coverage: Image processing, electronic content, document and records management, microfilm, optical disks, CD-ROM, electronic publishing, document imaging, recognition technology, workflow management, business process re-engineering, data and document capture.

Publications: Printed, and electronic and video

Publications list: Available online

Access to staff: Contact by letter, by telephone, by fax, by e-mail and via website. Appointment necessary. All charged.
Hours: Mon to Thu, 0900 to 1700; Fri, 0900 to 1600

Parent body: University of Hertfordshire; website: http://www.herts.ac.uk/home-page.cfm

CINE GUILDS OF GREAT BRITAIN (CGGB)

72 Pembroke Road, London, W8 6NX

Tel: 0560 294 2610
Fax: 0560 294 2610
E-mail: cineguildsgb@btinternet.com
Website: www.cineguilds.org

Enquiries to: Secretary

Founded: 1990

Organisation type and purpose: To promote the British film industry.

Subject coverage: The British film industry.

Access to staff: Contact by letter, by e-mail and via website
Hours: Mon to Fri, 0900 to 1700

Access to building: No access other than to staff

CINEMA ADVERTISING ASSOCIATION LIMITED (CAA)

12 Golden Square, London, W1F 9JE

Tel: 020 7534 6363
Fax: 020 7534 6227

Enquiries to: Secretary
Direct e-mail: sam.newsom@carltonscreen.com

Organisation type and purpose: Trade association.

Subject coverage: Cinema advertising medium (UK), standards of advertising practice, research.

Collection: Advertising Film Archives

Publications: Printed

Access to staff: Contact by telephone and by e-mail
Hours: Mon to Fri, 0900 to 1700

Access to building: No access other than to staff

Access for disabled people: Access to all public areas, toilet facilities

Member of: Advertising Association

CINEMA THEATRE ASSOCIATION (CTA)

59 Harrowdene Gardens, Teddington, Middlesex, TW11 0DJ

Tel: 020 8977 2608
E-mail: atunger@blueyonder.co.uk
Website: www.cta-uk.org.

Enquiries to: Honorary Secretary
Other contacts: Chairman (for cinemas threatened by planning proposals); Public Relations Officer (for press releases and enquiries); Archivist (for archive)

Founded: 1967

Organisation type and purpose: Advisory body, membership association (membership is by subscription), present number of members: 1,400, voluntary organisation, research organisation.
To promote interest in Britain's cinema-building legacy, to visit and research cinema buildings, to monitor threatened cinemas of architectural importance and campaign for their protection, to maintain an archive.
The Association arranges visits to cinemas and theatres in the UK and abroad. The CTA is often consulted by local planning authorities on planning applications.

Subject coverage: Cinema buildings, history, architecture, ownership, lighting, projection, stage facilities, programmes, publicity, etc. (primarily in the United Kingdom).

Collection: Archive of photographs and related material
George Coles (cinema architect) photograph collection, plans and drawings
John Squires colour slide collection of cinemas
Kine Year Books (incomplete run)
Opening programmes of cinemas, photo collection, plans and drawings, and related material

Publications: Printed

Publications list: Available online and in print

Access to staff: Contact by letter, by telephone and by e-mail. Non-members charged.
Special comments: Collections available for reference by appointment.

Access to building: Prior appointment required

CINTO

Formal name: Cleaning Industry National Training Organisation

3 Moulton Court, Anglia Way, Moulton Park, Northampton, NN3 6JA

Tel: 01604 645731
Fax: 01604 645988
Website: www.cleaningnto.org

Enquiries to: Executive Director

Founded: 1997; formerly called Cleaning and Support Services Industry Training Organisation (CSSITO); formerly called Cleaning Industry Lead Body (year of change 1997); formerly called Cleaning and Support Services National Training Organisation (CSSNTO) (year of change 2000)

Organisation type and purpose: Training organisation.

Subject coverage: Education and training for the cleaning and support services industry, both private and public sectors, National Standards, National Vocational Qualifications (NVQs), Scottish Vocational Qualifications (SVQs), modern apprenticeships, labour market information, skills needs, qualification structures, how to start a cleaning business.

Trade and statistical information: Labour market information

Publications: Printed

Publications list: Available online and in print

Access to staff: Contact by letter, by telephone, by fax, by e-mail and via website. Appointment necessary.
Hours: Mon to Fri, 0830 to 1600

Links with: DfES; QCA; SQA

CIRIA

Formal name: Construction Industry Research and Information Association

Classic House, 174–180 Old Street, London, EC1V 9BP

Tel: 020 7549 3300
Fax: 020 7253 0523
E-mail: enquiries@ciria.org
Website: www.ciria.org.uk

Enquiries to: Customer Services

Founded: 1960

Organisation type and purpose: Advisory body, professional body, membership association (membership is by subscription), research organisation, publishing house.
Providing best practice guidance for construction and the environment.

Subject coverage: Building; structural design; construction management; materials; ground engineering; site operations; contaminated land; water engineering and environmental management; structural engineering; health and safety; quality management; information technology.

Library catalogue: All or part available online and in print

Publications: Printed

Publications list: Available online and in print

Access to staff: Contact by letter, by telephone, by fax, by e-mail, in person and via website
Hours: Mon to Fri, 0900 to 1700

CISION UK

Cision House, 16–22 Baltic Street West, London, EC1Y 0UL

Tel: 020 7251 7220
Fax: 020 7689 1164
E-mail: info.uk@cision.com
Website: uk.cision.com/

Enquiries to: Information Officer

Founded: 1852; formerly called Romeike Limited

Organisation type and purpose: Media monitoring and press clipping agency.
Media monitoring and analysis.

Subject coverage: Press clippings; media analysis; online summaries.

Access to staff: Contact by letter, by telephone, by fax, by e-mail and in person
Hours: Mon to Fri, 0900 to 1700

Member of: Association of Media Evaluation Companies (AMEC); Fédération Internationale des Bureaux d'Extraits de Presse (FIBEP); International Association of Broadcast Monitors (IABM); Public Relations Consultants Association (PRCA)

CITB-CONSTRUCTIONSKILLS (CITB)

Head Office, Bircham Newton, King's Lynn, Norfolk, PE31 6RH

Tel: 01485 577577
Fax: 01485 577684
E-mail: robert.dale@cskills.org
Website: www.cskills.org

Enquiries to: Cskills Awards
Direct tel: 0344 994 4020
Direct e-mail: cskillsawards@cskills.org

Founded: 1964

Organisation type and purpose: Statutory body, registered charity (charity number 264289), training organisation.
Statutory body.
An integral part of the construction industry concerned with craft, technicians, safety, supervisory, management training and manpower.

Subject coverage: Building; civil engineering and related management; training; health and safety in the industry.

Publications: Printed, and electronic and video
Order printed publications from: CITB Publications Department
tel: 01485 577800, fax: 01485 577758

Access to staff: Appointment necessary.
Hours: Mon to Fri, 0900 to 1700

CITIZENS ADVICE CYMRU (CAC)

Quebec House, 5–19 Cowbridge Road East, Cardiff, CF11 9AB

Tel: 029 2037 6750
Fax: 029 2034 1541
Website: www.adviceguide.org.uk

Enquiries to: Office Manager

Organisation type and purpose: Registered charity.
Advice and information service.
CAC provides central administrative support for Citizens Advice Bureaux.

Subject coverage: Information on services provided by, and levels of use of, the Citizens Advice Bureaux in the South Wales area.

Trade and statistical information: Number and type of enquiries received and financial grant aid achieved

Access to staff: Contact by letter, by telephone and by fax
Hours: Mon to Fri, 0900 to 1700

Parent body: National Association of Citizens Advice Bureaux; Myddelton House, 115–123 Pentonville Road, London, N1 9LZ

CITIZENS ADVICE SCOTLAND (CAS)

Formal name: Scottish Association of Citizens Advice Bureaux – Citizens Advice Scotland

Spectrum House, 2 Powderhall Road, Edinburgh, EH7 4GB

Tel: 0131 550 1000
Fax: 0131 550 1001
E-mail: info@cas.org.uk
Website: www.cas.org.uk

Enquiries to: Press Officer
Other contacts: Chief Executive

Founded: 1975

Organisation type and purpose: Membership association, voluntary organisation, registered charity (Scottish charity number SC016637).
Policy-making body and provider of services to Citizens Advice Bureaux in Scotland.

Subject coverage: Citizens Advice Bureau services in Scotland and advice centres generally; all aspects of welfare law, Commissioners' decisions, social security, employment, housing, consumer affairs, money advice, Scots Law; expertise in training, volunteer development and advice service development.

Collection: Library of information related to Welfare Law

Non-library collection catalogue: All or part available online

Library catalogue: All or part available in-house

Publications: Printed, and electronic and video, and microform publications

Publications list: Available online and in print

Access to staff: Contact by letter and by telephone
Hours: Mon to Fri, 0900 to 1700

CITIZENS' BAND RADIO GOOD PUBLICITY GROUP (CB Radio Good Publicity Group)

Hillview, Mid-Holmwood Lane, Dorking, RH5 4HD

Tel: 01306 881137

continued overleaf

E-mail: cbrgpg@muddymail.com
Website: www.4x4cb.com/cbrgpg/

Enquiries to: Manager

Founded: 1997; incorporates the former Communication Eleven, County Hunters DX Group

Organisation type and purpose: Advisory body, voluntary organisation.
Increase public awareness of the positive sides to citizens band radio (CB Radio). Practical help and advice on installation and use of CB radio equipment in vehicles, homes and business premises.

Subject coverage: Citizens' band radio, advice on which radios are legal and which are not, help with keeping a CB station within legal limits; specific installation advice regarding CB in a wide variety of vehicles, especially Land Rovers & other off-road vehicles, tractors & farm machines, motorhomes & motorcaravans, canal & narrow boats, Classic Minis, Fiat X1/9's and other cars; information on specialist products available; microphone wiring database to stop mic compatibility problems; CB radio advice for potential new users, who may be curious as to what CB radio could do for them or their business.

Publications: Printed

Access to staff: Contact by letter, by telephone and by e-mail. Appointment necessary.
Hours: Mon to Fri, 10.00 – 18.00

Also at: Citizens' Band Radio Good Publicity Group; PO Box 198, Reigate, Surrey, RH2 0FX

CITROËN CAR CLUB (CCC)

PO Box 348, Bromley, Kent, BR2 8QT

Tel: 07000 248 258
Fax: 07000 248 258
E-mail: member@citroencarclub.net
Website: www.citroencarclub.org.uk

Enquiries to: Membership Administration

Founded: 1949

Organisation type and purpose: Membership association (membership is by subscription), present number of members: 3,000, voluntary organisation.

Subject coverage: Citroën cars, past and present.

Collection: Comprehensive library of all back issues of Citroënian and most English language publications and books on Citroën

Publications: Printed

Access to staff: Contact by letter, by telephone, by fax, by e-mail and via website
Hours: 1000 to 1900 only
Special comments: Club membership list enquiries are not normally available, but all enquiries will be considered on merit.

CITY & GUILDS LAND BASED SERVICES

Building 500, Abbey Park, Stareton, Warwickshire, CV8 2LG

Tel: 024 7685 7300
Fax: 024 7669 6128
E-mail: information@cityandguilds.com
Website: www.nptc.org.uk

Enquiries to: Customer Support

Founded: 1970

Organisation type and purpose: City & Guilds Land Based Services is an awarding body for the land-based industries. It seeks to promote competence and professionalism in the workforce of land-based and related industries by the encouragement of continous learning and the recognition of skill. To this end, it oversees a range of qualifications, including Certificates of Competence, NVQs, SVQs, work-based qualifications, Certificates, Extended Certificates, Diplomas, Subsidiary and Extended Diplomas.

Subject coverage: Agriculture, horticulture, forestry and timber, floristry, animal care, equine, countryside and environment, land-based machinery.

Publications: Printed

Access to staff: Contact by letter, by telephone, by fax, by e-mail and via website. Appointment necessary.
Hours: Mon to Fri, 0830 to 1700

CITY AND COUNTY OF SWANSEA LIBRARY & INFORMATION SERVICE

Library HQ, Civic Centre, Oystermouth Road, Swansea, SA1 3SN

Tel: 01792 636430
Fax: 01792 636235
E-mail: swansea.libraries@swansea.gov.uk
Website: www.swansea.gov.uk/libraries
Website: www.libraries.swansea.gov.uk

Enquiries to: Librarian
Direct tel: 01792 636464
Direct fax: 01792 636235
Direct e-mail: libraryline@swansea.gov.uk

Founded: 1996

Organisation type and purpose: Local government body, public library.

Subject coverage: Welsh language material, culture and history of Wales, history of Swansea, Dylan Thomas.

Information services: Library Line, a dedicated enquiry service to help with any issues about Swansea Libraries, and local studies and general information enquiries, is available: Mon to Fri, 0830 to 1800; Sat, 1000 to 1600.

Collection: Local studies collections focussing on the history, culture and people of Swansea, but also in relation to Wales in general; antiquarian collection of books and periodicals covering Wales and the Celtic nations.

Non-library collection catalogue: All or part available online and in-house

Library catalogue: All or part available online and in-house

Publications: Electronic and video

Access to staff: Contact by letter, by telephone, by fax, by e-mail, in person and via website. Appointment necessary.
Hours: Central Library open Tue to Fri, 0830 to 2000; Sat and Sun, 1000 to 1600
Local Studies Librarian available by appointment

Parent body: City and County of Swansea; Civic Centre, Oystermouth Road, Swansea, SA1 3SN; tel: 01792 636000

CITY AND ISLINGTON COLLEGE

The Marlborough Building, 383 Holloway Road, London, N7 0RN

Tel: 020 7700 9333
Fax: 020 7700 4268
Website: www.candi.ac.uk

Enquiries to: Director of Students
Direct tel: 020 7700 9214
Other contacts: Head of Learning Resources

History of institution: formed by the amalgamation of City and East London College, Islington 6th Form Centre and Adult Education Service, North London College

Organisation type and purpose: Suitable for ages: 16+.
Further education college.

Subject coverage: Applied optics, engineering technology, access courses, GNVQ and A levels, business studies, health and leisure, ESOL, wide range of adult education courses, health and community care, wide range of IT resources, media, visual and performing arts.

Library catalogue: All or part available online

Publications list: Available online and in print

Access to staff: Contact by letter, by telephone, by fax and by e-mail
Hours: Mon to Thu, 0900 to 2000; Fri, 0900 to 1700; Sat, 1100 to 1600 at Camden, Springhouse and Willen

Access to building: No access other than to staff

CITY BUSINESS LIBRARY (CBL)

Aldermanbury, London, EC2V 7HH

Tel: 020 7332 1812 (enquiries)
E-mail: cbl@cityoflondon.gov.uk
Website: www.cityoflondon.gov.uk/cbl

Enquiries to: Head of City Business Library
Direct e-mail: goretti.considine@cityoflondon.gov.uk

Founded: 1970

Organisation type and purpose: Free public reference library, open to all; current worldwide business information; free business training events.

Subject coverage: Company data (including facility to create free B2B mailing lists), market research, country economies, import/export, management, finance, marketing.

Services for disabled people: Induction loop; Jaws and ZoomText software for those with visual impairment.

Collection: Worldwide trade directories
Worldwide company data – financials and profiles
Worldwide market research

Trade and statistical information: Worldwide financial statistics

Library catalogue: All or part available online

Publications: Printed

Publications list: Available online and in print

Access to staff: Contact by letter, by telephone, by e-mail, in person and via website
Hours: Mon to Fri, 0930 to 1700

Access for disabled people: Internal lift for Library entry, access to all public areas, toilet facilities

Constituent part of: City of London library service

CITY COLLEGE BRIGHTON AND HOVE (CCBH)

Pelham Tower, Pelham Street, Brighton, East Sussex, BN1 4FA

Tel: 01273 667733
Fax: 01273 667748
E-mail: lrc@ccb.ac.uk
Website: www.ccb.ac.uk

Enquiries to: LRC Manager

History of institution: formerly called Brighton College of Technology (BCT) (year of change 2001)

Organisation type and purpose: College of further education library.

Subject coverage: Art and design, business, child care and education, construction, digital media and photography, ESOL, electrical, electronic, mechanical and motor vehicle engineering, general humanities, hairdressing and beauty therapy, hospitality and catering, media and journalism, music and performing arts, science, travel and tourism.

Library catalogue: All or part available online

Access to staff: Contact by letter, by telephone and by e-mail. Appointment necessary.
Hours: Term time: Mon to Thu, 0900 to 2000; Fri, 0900 to 1700; vacation: 0900 to 1700 (variable)

Access to building: *Special comments:* Visitors who wish to use the LRC should come during less busy times (after 1600) and report to the Enquiry Desk on arrival.

CITY LITERARY INSTITUTE (City Lit)

Keeley Street, London, WC2B 4BA

Tel: 020 7492 2600
E-mail: infoline@citylit.ac.uk
Website: www.citylit.ac.uk

Enquiries to: Head of Learning Centre
Direct tel: 020 7492 2666
Direct fax: lc-enquiries@citylit.ac.uk

Organisation type and purpose: Adult education institute.

Subject coverage: Education of deaf and partially hearing adults, speech therapy for stammerers and hearing impaired people.

Collection: Sign language videos, CD-ROMs and books, deaf culture and deaf awareness, aural rehabilitation, speech therapy

Non-library collection catalogue: All or part available online

Library catalogue: All or part available online

Access to staff: Contact by telephone
Hours: Term Time: Mon, 1200 to 2000; Tue to Fri, 1030 to 2000; Sat, 1200 to 1600

Access to building: No prior appointment required
Hours: Mon, 1200 to 2000; Tue to Fri, 1030 to 2000; Sat, 1200 to 1600

CITY OF BRADFORD METROPOLITAN DISTRICT COUNCIL

City Hall, Bradford, West Yorkshire, BD1 1HY

Tel: 01274 432111
Fax: 01274 432065
Website: www.bradford.gov.uk

Organisation type and purpose: Local government body.

Subject coverage: Local government services.

CITY OF GLASGOW COLLEGE, RIVERSIDE CAMPUS

Library, 21 Thistle Street, Glasgow, G5 9XB

Tel: 0141 565 2582
Fax: 0141 565 2599
E-mail: resources@cityofglasgowcollege.ac.uk
Website: www.cityofglasgowcollege.ac.uk

Enquiries to: Librarian
Direct e-mail: margaret.scalpello@cityofglasgowcollege.ac.uk

Founded: 2011; formerly called Glasgow College of Nautical Studies (year of change 2011)

Organisation type and purpose: Suitable for ages: 16+.
Further education college.

Subject coverage: Maritime studies, marine engineering, telecommunications, instrumentation and control, nautical science, social science, social care, sport and leisure, beauty therapy, child care, drama.

Non-library collection catalogue: All or part available in-house

Library catalogue: All or part available online

Publications: Printed

Access to staff: Contact by letter, by telephone, by fax, by e-mail, in person and via website
Hours: Term time: Mon, Tue, Thu, 0830 to 1900; Wed, Fri, 0830 to 1630
Vacations: Mon to Fri, 0830 to 1630

Links with: Glasgow Colleges Librarians Group (GCLG)

CITY OF LONDON SOLICITORS' COMPANY (CLSC)

4 College Hill, London, EC4R 2RB

Tel: 020 7329 2173
Fax: 020 7329 2190
E-mail: mail@citysolicitors.org.uk
Website: www.citysolicitors.org.uk

Enquiries to: The Clerk

Founded: 1908

Organisation type and purpose: Membership association (membership is by election or invitation).
City of London Livery Company.

Access to staff: Contact by letter, by telephone, by fax, by e-mail and via website

CITY OF SALFORD

Civic Centre, Chorley Road, Swinton, Salford, Greater Manchester, M27 5FJ

Tel: 0161 794 4711
Fax: 0161 794 6595
E-mail: public.relations@salford.gov.uk
Website: www.salford.gov.uk

Enquiries to: Public Relations Manager
Direct tel: 0161 793 3157
Direct fax: 0161 793 3234
Direct e-mail: margaret.hynes@salford.gov.uk
Other contacts: Chief Executive for formal complaints.

Organisation type and purpose: Local government body.

Subject coverage: Business of a local authority – metropolitan authority – Greater Manchester. Arts and leisure, libraries, museums, education, social services, housing, planning issues, environmental issues.

Publications: Printed

Access to staff: Contact by letter, by telephone, by fax, by e-mail, in person and via website
Hours: Mon to Fri, 0830 to 1630

Access for disabled people: Parking provided, ramped entry, access to all public areas, toilet facilities

Includes: Rushmoor Local History Gallery; at the same address

CITY OF SUNDERLAND

Civic Centre, Sunderland, Tyne and Wear, SR2 7DN

Tel: 0191 553 1000
Website: www.sunderland.gov.uk

Enquiries to: Chief Executive

Organisation type and purpose: Local government body.

Subject coverage: Local government services.

Access to staff: Contact by letter, by telephone, by fax and by e-mail. Appointment necessary.
Hours: Mon to Fri, 0900 to 1700

CITY OF WESTMINSTER ARCHIVES CENTRE (COWAC)

10 St Ann's Street, London, SW1P 2DE

Tel: 020 7641 5180, 020 7641 4879 (minicom)
Fax: 020 7641 5179
E-mail: archives@westminster.gov.uk

continued overleaf

Website: www.westminster.gov.uk/archives

Enquiries to: Librarian
Other contacts: City Archivist, Manager for the Business Unit Manager.

Organisation type and purpose: Local government body, public library.
Archive.

Subject coverage: Local studies, conservation, local history, archives, Westminster history, Marylebone history, Paddington history.

Collection: A M Broadley Collections (Annals of the Haymarket, and Some Social, Political and Literary Landmarks of Bath and Piccadilly)
Artisans', Labourers' & General Dwellings Company Limited (annual reports and accounts 1880–1956)
Francis Edwards Limited (booksellers catalogues 1938–1982)
Manuscript notes on local subjects including an 82-volume scrapbook, Inns, Taverns, Alehouses, Coffee Houses, etc. in and around London, compiled by D Foster c. 1900
Marylebone Gardens (over 50 songs of the 18th century sung in the gardens, some by William Defesch and James Hook)
The Ashbridge Collection (books, maps, prints, watercolours and drawings relating to St Marylebone)
The parliamentary representation of Westminster from the 13th century to the present day
The Preston Blake Collection: books by and about William Blake, papers, letters, periodicals, catalogues, transparencies.
Theatre Collection (some 28,000 theatre programmes, and playbills, news cuttings, portraits, financial records, correspondence)
St Marylebone Housing Association
Whiteley's (catalogues for general goods, wines, cigars, provisions, etc., staff magazine 1885–1958)
Books and pamphlets; rare books; newspapers and periodicals; official local government records; prints and photographs; census; parish registers; wills, from 1460 onwards; maps and plans; directories and electoral registers; business records

Non-library collection catalogue: All or part available online and in-house

Library catalogue: All or part available online

Publications: Printed, and microform publications
Order printed publications from: Publications Officer, City of Westminster Archives Centre
Address as main
Order microform publications from: St Marylebone Census Name Index for 1821 and 1831, published by The Family History Shop, Norwich

Publications list: Available online and in print

Access to staff: Contact by letter, by telephone, by fax, by e-mail, in person and via website
Hours: Mon, Closed, Fri, Sat, 1000 to 1700; Tue to Thu, 1000 to 1900

Access to building: No prior appointment required

Access for disabled people: Ramped entry, access to all public areas, toilet facilities
Special comments: Parking provided by prior arrangement.

CITY OF YORK & DISTRICT FAMILY HISTORY SOCIETY

The Raylor Centre, James Street, Lawrence Street, York, YO10 3DW

Tel: 01904 412204
E-mail: secretary@yorkfamilyhistory.org.uk
Website: www.yorkfamilyhistory.org.uk/

Enquiries to: Secretary

Founded: 1975

Organisation type and purpose: Membership association (membership is by subscription), registered charity.

Subject coverage: Family history.

Publications: Printed, and electronic and video, and microform publications

Publications list: Available online and in print

Access to staff: Contact by letter, by e-mail and via website

CITY OF YORK LIBRARIES

Museum Street, York, YO1 7DS

Tel: 01904 655631
Fax: 01904 611025
E-mail: reference.library@york.gov.uk
Website: www.york.gov.uk
Website: www.york.gov.uk/libraries

Enquiries to: Head of Library Service
Direct tel: 01904 553316
Other contacts: Information Services Librarian tel: 01904 552824 reference.library@york.gov.uk.

Founded: 1891

Organisation type and purpose: Local government body, public library.

Subject coverage: General, York and Yorkshire.

Collection: Rowland Collection of oboe music
Sir John Marriott Memorial Library on modern European history from the French Revolution

Non-library collection catalogue: All or part available in-house

Library catalogue: All or part available online

Access to staff: Contact by letter, by telephone, by fax, by e-mail and in person
Hours: Lending library: Mon, Tue, Fri, 0930 to 2000; Wed, Thu, 0930 to 1730; Sat, 0930 to 1600
Reference library: Mon, Tue, Wed, Fri, 0900 to 2000; Thu, 0900 to 1730; Sat, 0900 to 1600

Access to building: No prior appointment required

Access for disabled people: Lift, ramped entry, access to all public areas, toilet facilities
Hours: as above

Has: 15 libraries and 1 mobile library covering the City of York Council area

Parent body: City of York Council; tel: 01904 613161

CITY UNIVERSITY LONDON – DEPARTMENT OF COMPUTING

Northampton Square, London, EC1V 0HB

Tel: 020 7040 8432
Fax: 020 7040 8587
Website: www.soi.city.ac.uk/doc/

Enquiries to: Administrator

History of institution: formerly called Department of Business Computing, Department of Computer Science

Organisation type and purpose: University department or institute.

Subject coverage: Undergraduate courses in computer science, computer science with distributed systems or AI, software engineering, business computing and information systems. Postgraduate courses in business systems analysis and design and object oriented software systems.

Publications list: Available online

Access to staff: Contact by letter and by e-mail. Appointment necessary.
Hours: Mon to Fri, 0900 to 1700

Access to building: Prior appointment required

Access for disabled people: Ramped entry, access to all public areas, toilet facilities

CITY UNIVERSITY LONDON – DEPARTMENT OF LANGUAGE AND COMMUNICATION SCIENCE

Northampton Square, London, EC1V 0HB

Tel: 020 7040 8281
Fax: 020 7040 8577
E-mail: lcsadmin@city.ac.uk
Website: www.city.ac.uk/lcs

Enquiries to: Programme Officer

Organisation type and purpose: University department or institute.

Subject coverage: Disorders of speech, training of speech therapists, research into disorders of speech, alternative and augmentative aids to human communication.

Collection: MSc and MPhil/PhD theses in field of disorders of human communication

Access to staff: Contact by telephone and by e-mail
Hours: Mon to Fri, 0900 to 1700

CITY UNIVERSITY LONDON – LIBRARY

Northampton Square, London, EC1V 0HB

Tel: 020 7040 8191
Fax: 020 7040 8194
E-mail: library@city.ac.uk
Website: www.city.ac.uk/library

Enquiries to: Director of Information Services and Libraries
Direct tel: 020 7040 8162

Founded: 1894

Organisation type and purpose: University library.

Subject coverage: Cultural policy and management; banking; business; finance; language and communication science; computer science; engineering; information science; journalism; law; management; mathematics; music; optometry; property valuation; social science; nursing; midwifery.

Collection: Erna Auerbach Collection (art history)
Kipling Society Collection
Rosencweig Collection (Jewish music), now transferred to the School of Oriental and African Studies
Walter Fincham Collection (optics)

Library catalogue: All or part available online

Publications: Printed

Access to staff: Contact by e-mail
Hours: Mon to Fri, 0900 to 1700

Access for disabled people: Ramped entry, toilet facilities

CIVIC TRUST

17 Carlton House Terrace, London, SW1Y 5AW

Tel: 020 7930 0914
Fax: 020 7321 0180
E-mail: pride@civictrust.org.uk
Website: www.civictrust.org.uk

Enquiries to: Librarian

Founded: 1957

Organisation type and purpose: National organisation, membership association (membership is by subscription), present number of members: 3,000 members, 60 corporate members, voluntary organisation, registered charity (charity number 1068759).
Working in partnership to improve the built environment for the benefit of the community.

Subject coverage: Urban environment, architecture, planning, transport, conservation, regeneration, community involvement, civic societies.

Publications: Printed

Publications list: Available online and in print

2nd Office: Civic Trust Northern Office; 6th Floor, The View, Gostins Building, 32–36 Hannover Street, Liverpool, L1 4LN; tel: 0151 709 1969; fax: 0151 709 2022; e-mail: northernoffice@civictrust.org.uk

Partner organisations: Civic Trust for Wales; 3rd Floor, Empire House, Mount Stuart Square, Cardiff, CF10 5FN; tel: 01222 484606; website: http://www.civictrustwales.org; North East Civic Trust; Blackfriars, Monk Street, Newcastle upon Tyne, NE1 4XN; Scottish Civic Trust; 42 Miller Street, Glasgow, G2 1DT; tel: 0141 221 1466

CIVIL AID (NVCAS)

Formal name: National Voluntary Civil Aid Services

c/o Crinoids, 106 Church Road, Teddington, Middlesex, TW11 8EY

Tel: 020 8977 2806
Fax: 020 8943 5556

Enquiries to: President
Other contacts: General Secretary, tel no: 020 8942 9126

Founded: 1968; emerged for reasons of political expediency Civil Defence Corps (year of change 1968)

Organisation type and purpose: National organisation, membership association (membership is by subscription), present number of members: 300, voluntary organisation, registered charity (charity number 266349), suitable for ages: 16+, training organisation.
An autonomous, self-funded organisation which emerged in 1968 when the Civil Defence Corps was stood down for reasons of political expediency. Duke of Edinburgh's Award training organisation.
To train its members and the public in disaster mitigation and relief, and to provide aid for any peace-time disaster.

Subject coverage: First aid, fire prevention and control, emergency feeding, rescue techniques, communications, rest centres, information centres.

Publications: Printed

Access to staff: Contact by letter, by telephone and by fax
Hours: Mon to Fri, 0900 to 1700

Links with: The Institute of Civil Defence and Disaster Studies; The National Council for Civil Protection

Registered Office: Civil Aid; Phoenix House, Greenlands Avenue, Kingsway, Derby

CIVIL AVIATION AUTHORITY (CAA)

Library and Information Centre, Civil Aviation Authority Safety Regulation Group, Aviation House, South Area, Gatwick Airport, West Sussex, RH6 0YR

Tel: 01293 573725
Fax: 01293 573181
E-mail: infoservices@caa.co.uk
Website: www.caa.co.uk

Enquiries to: Manager
Direct tel: 01293 573966
Direct e-mail: vagn.pedersen@caa.co.uk
Other contacts: Librarian for information enquiries

Founded: 1972; carries out the functions of the former Air Registration Board, Air Transport Licensing Board; incorporates the former Safety Regulation Group Library

Organisation type and purpose: Statutory body, public authority, aviation regulatory body.

Subject coverage: Civil aviation, electronics including air traffic control, aircraft, flightcrew, airports, telecommunications, radar, etc.

Collection: Historical aviation collection

Trade and statistical information: UK airlines and airports statistics

Library catalogue: All or part available in-house

Publications list: Available in print

Access to staff: Contact by letter, by telephone, by fax, by e-mail and in person
Hours: Mon to Fri, 0930 to 1630; 1st Wed of each month, 1000 to 1630
Special comments: Reference use only to visitors.

Access to building: No prior appointment required

Access for disabled people: Parking provided, level entry, access to all public areas

CIVIL ENGINEERING CONTRACTORS ASSOCIATION (CECA)

1 Birdcage Walk, London, SW1H 9JJ

Tel: 020 7340 0450
Fax: 020 7222 7514
E-mail: enquiries@ceca.co.uk
Website: www.ceca.co.uk

Direct e-mail: lauraellis@ceca.co.uk

Founded: 1996

Organisation type and purpose: Trade association.

Subject coverage: Construction, including training and careers, legal affairs, industrial relations, safety, economics, statistics.

Publications: Printed

Access to staff: Contact by letter, by telephone, by fax, by e-mail and via website
Hours: Mon to Fri, 0900 to 1730

Member of: Construction Confederation

CIVIL SERVICE APPEAL BOARD (CSAB)

22 Whitehall, London, SW1A 2WH

Tel: 020 7276 3832
Fax: 020 7276 3836
E-mail: COparliamentarybranch@cabinet-office.gsi.gov.uk
Website: www.cabinet-office.gov.uk/civilservice/1999/appealboard/csab.htm
Website: www.civilserviceappealboard.gov.uk

Enquiries to: Secretary
Direct e-mail: keith.wright@cabinet-office.x.gsi.gov.uk

Founded: 1971

Organisation type and purpose: Advisory body.
An advisory non-departmental public body that hears appeals from civil servants against: dismissal and early retirement; part- or non-payment of the amount of compensation paid to civil servants dismissed on inefficiency grounds; refusal to allow participation in political activities or forfeiture of superannuation benefits.

Publications: Printed

Access to staff: Contact by letter, by telephone, by fax and by e-mail
Hours: 0900 to 1700

CIVITAS: THE INSTITUTE FOR THE STUDY OF CIVIL SOCIETY

The Mezzanine, Elizabeth House, 39 York Road, London, SE1 7NQ

Tel: 020 7401 5470
Fax: 020 7401 5471
E-mail: robert.whelan@civitas.org.uk
Website: www.civitas.org.uk

Enquiries to: Deputy Director

History of institution: formerly called Health & Welfare Unit of the Institute of Economic Affairs (year of change 2000)

Organisation type and purpose: Registered charity (charity number 1085494), research organisation, publishing house.

Subject coverage: Health, education, welfare, criminal justice, the family.

Publications list: Available online and in print

Access to staff: Contact by letter, by telephone, by fax, by e-mail and via website
Hours: Mon to Fri, 0900 to 1700

CLACKMANNANSHIRE COUNCIL

Greenfield, Alloa, Clackmannanshire, FK10 2AD

Tel: 01259 450000
Fax: 01259 452010
E-mail: info@clacksweb.org.uk
Website: www.clacksweb.org.uk

Enquiries to: Communications and Marketing Manager
Direct tel: 01259 452023
Direct fax: 01259 452117
Direct e-mail: rfry@clacks.gov.uk
Other contacts: Chief Executive

Founded: 1996; formerly called Central Regional Council, Clackmannan District Council

Organisation type and purpose: Local government body.

Subject coverage: Scottish local government; Clackmannanshire as an inward investment area.
Schools, nurseries, adult and community education, trading standards, environmental health, roads maintenance, property maintenance and design, social work, housing, licensing, council tax.

Publications: Printed
Order printed publications from: http://www.clacksweb.org.uk

Publications list: Available in print

Access to staff: Contact by letter, by telephone, by fax, by e-mail and via website
Hours: Mon to Fri, 0900 to 1700

Access for disabled people: Parking provided, level entry, toilet facilities

CLACKMANNANSHIRE LIBRARIES (CL)

Alloa Library, 26–28 Drysdale Street, Alloa, Clackmannanshire, FK10 1JL

Tel: 01259 722262
Fax: 01259 219469
E-mail: libraries@clacks.gov.uk
Website: www.clacksweb.org.uk/culture/libraryservice

Enquiries to: Information Librarian and Archivist
Other contacts: Special Services Co-ordinator; Team Leader of Public Services

Founded: 1996; formerly called Clackmannan District Libraries (year of change 1996); formerly called Central Region Archives Department; Central Region Schools Library Service (year of change 1997)

Organisation type and purpose: Local government body, museum, public library. Archive service.

Subject coverage: General, local studies, archives, schools material.

Collection: Walter Murray Local Studies Collection; Clackmannanshire Archives

Non-library collection catalogue: All or part available in-house

Library catalogue: All or part available online

Publications: Printed
Order printed publications from: Special Services Co-ordinator, at the same address

Publications list: Available online and in print

Access to staff: Contact by letter, by telephone, by fax, by e-mail and in person

Access to building: No prior appointment required
Hours: Alloa Library: Mon, Wed, Thu, Fri, 0930 to 1900; Tue, 0930 to 1630; Sat, 0900 to 1600
Other libraries vary, all close for lunch, telephone first
Special comments: Orders for items from Archive Store (Mon to Fri only) to be lodged no later than 1700 for delivery same day.

Access for disabled people: Level entry

Branch libraries: Alva Community Access Point; 153 West Stirling Street, Alva; tel: 01259 760652; fax: 01259 760364; Clackmannan Community Access Point; Main Street, Clackmannan; tel: 01259 721579; fax: 01259 212493; Dollar Community Access Point; Dollar Civic Centre, Park Place, Dollar; tel: 01259 743253; fax: 01259 743328; Menstrie Community Access Point; Dumyat Leisure Centre, Main Street East, Menstrie; tel: 01259 769439; fax: 01259 762941; Sauchie Community Access Point; 42–48 Main Street, Sauchie; tel: 01259 721679; fax: 01259 218750; Tillicoultry Branch Library; 99 High Street, Tillicoultry; tel: 01259 751685; Tullibody Branch Library; Leisure Centre, Abercromby Place, Tullibody; tel: 01259 218725

Parent body: Clackmannanshire Council; tel: 01259 450000; fax: 01259 452230

CLAN RANALD TRUST FOR SCOTLAND

Unit 35 New Street, Warsely Car Park, Edinburgh, EH8 8DW

Tel: 0131 558 9191
Website: www.clanranald.org

Enquiries to: Chief Executive
Direct e-mail: info@clanranald.org
Other contacts: Administrator

Founded: 1996

Organisation type and purpose: Membership association (membership is by election or invitation), present number of members: 50 (charity number SCO 24881), suitable for ages: 14+.
Promotes Scottish Medieval History through education and entertainment. Constructing large motte and baille fortress in the Carronn Valley near Stirling for tourism and education.

Subject coverage: Film, TV, combat team, period room dressing, entertainment, gala days and open events, pipers and drummers, actors, special events, walk-ons, experienced extras for film.

Library catalogue: All or part available online

Publications: Printed, and electronic and video

Publications list: Available online

Access to staff: Contact by letter, by telephone, by e-mail and via website. Appointment necessary.
Hours: Mon to Fri, 1200 to 1800

Access for disabled people: Parking provided, level entry

Links with: Kirkpatrick McAndrew Clan Trust; McFarlane Clan Trust; Wallace Clan Trust

CLAN TARTAN CENTRE (EWM)

Formal name: Edinburgh Woollen Mills

James Pringle Weavers at Leith Mills, Leith Mills, 70–74 Bangor Road, Leith, Edinburgh, EH6 5JU

Tel: 0131 553 5161
Fax: 0131 553 4415
Website: www.foreverscotland.com

Enquiries to: Public Relations Manager
Other contacts: Manager

Subject coverage: Clan history, research and retail tartan and accessories, gifts, crystal, cashmere, woollens, ladies and gents fashion, designer labels, shoes, whisky shop, golf company and Scottish foods.

Publications: Printed

Access to staff: Contact by letter, by telephone, by fax and by e-mail. Appointment necessary.
Hours: Mon to Sat, 0900 to 1700; Sun, 1000 to 1700

Access for disabled people: Parking provided, level entry

Head Office: Edinburgh Woollen Mill; Waverley Mill, Langholm, Dumfriesshire, DG13 2BR; tel: 01387 380611

CLARINET HERITAGE SOCIETY (CHS)

47 Hambalt Road, London, SW4 9EQ

Tel: 020 8675 3877

Enquiries to: Honorary Secretary

Founded: 1980

Organisation type and purpose: International organisation, advisory body, learned society, professional body (membership is by subscription), training organisation, consultancy, research organisation, publishing house.
To promote new and rare music and general awareness for the clarinet, research, recording, study and performance.

Subject coverage: Discovery, publication and sound recordings of rare, unknown music for the clarinet; history; performance and teaching; inventions and innovations.

Education services: Clarinet lessons from beginner to professional coaching by internationally acclaimed teacher and performer.

Collection: Book manuscript
Musical instruments and tools of a noted master clarinettist
Various limited music for clarinet

Publications: Printed, and electronic and video

Access to staff: Contact by letter, by telephone, by e-mail and via website. Appointment necessary. Non-members charged.
Hours: Mon to Fri, 0900 to 1700

Access to building: Prior appointment required

CLASSIC SALOON CAR CLUB (GB) (CSCC)

15 Biddenham Turn, Garston, Hertfordshire, WD2 6PU

Tel: 01923 893518
E-mail: peter.edwards@classictouringcars.com
Website: www.csccgb.co.uk

Enquiries to: Registrar
Direct e-mail: robslater@csccgb.co.uk

Founded: 1975

Organisation type and purpose: Membership association (membership is by subscription).

Subject coverage: Recreating the great touring car racing of the past in the spirit of the period but to the standards of modern motorsport, showing, racing and enjoying historic racing touring cars.

Access to staff: Contact by letter, by e-mail and via website
Hours: Mon to Fri, 0900 to 1700

Affiliated club: British Automobile Racing Club; Thruxton Circuit, Andover, Hants, SP11 8PN; tel: 01264 772696

Registered with Sport Governing Body: The Motorsports Association; Motorsports House, Riverside Park, Colnbrook, Berks, SL3 0HG; tel: 01753 765000; fax: 01753 682938

CLASSICAL ASSOCIATION (CA)

Senate House, Malet Street, London, WC1E 7HU

Tel: 020 7862 8706
Fax: 020 7862 8729
E-mail: office@classicalassociation.org
Website: www.classicalassociation.org

Enquiries to: Secretary

Founded: 1904

Organisation type and purpose: Membership association (membership is by subscription), present number of members: 4,000, registered charity.

Subject coverage: Classical studies generally.

Publications: Printed
Order printed publications from: The Secretary, Classical Association, at the same address

Access to staff: Contact by letter, by telephone, by fax and by e-mail
Hours: Mon to Thu, 0900 to 1700

Affiliated to: International Federation for Classical Studies (FIEC)

CLEANING AND HYGIENE SUPPLIERS ASSOCIATION (CHSA)

PO Box 770, Marlow, Buckinghamshire, SL7 2SH

Tel: 01628 478273
Fax: 01628 478286
E-mail: secretary@chsa.co.uk
Website: www.chsa.co.uk

Enquiries to: General Secretary

Founded: 1969

Organisation type and purpose: Trade association (membership is by subscription), present number of members: 200.

Subject coverage: Supply chain issues.

Access to staff: Contact by letter, by telephone, by fax, by e-mail and via website
Hours: Mon to Fri, 0900 to 1700

Access to building: No access other than to staff

CLEANING AND SUPPORT SERVICES ASSOCIATION (CSSA)

478–480 Salisbury House, London Wall, London, EC2M 5QQ

Tel: 020 7920 9632
Fax: 020 7256 9360
E-mail: alarge@cleaningassoc.org
Website: www.cleaningindustry.org

Enquiries to: Director General

Founded: 1967

Organisation type and purpose: Trade association.

Subject coverage: Site support services, industry; especially, cleaning, hygiene, building maintenance.

Trade and statistical information: Trade information

Publications: Printed

Publications list: Available online and in print

Access to staff: Contact by letter, by telephone, by fax, by e-mail and via website
Hours: Mon to Fri, 0800 to 1630

Links with: AssetSkills; European Federation of Cleaning Industries (EFCI); Trade Association Forum (TAF); World Federation of Building Service Contractors (WFBSC)

CLEAPSS

The Gardiner Building, Brunel Science Park, Kingston Lane, Uxbridge, Middlesex, UB8 3PQ

Tel: 01895 251496
Fax: 01895 814372
E-mail: science@cleapss.org.uk
Website: www.cleapss.org.uk

Enquiries to: Director

Founded: 1963; formerly called CLEAPSE (year of change 1988)

Organisation type and purpose: Local government body, advisory body, membership association (membership is by subscription), present number of members: all state-funded, local authority schools in all 182 local authorities in England, Wales and Northern Ireland and off-shore islands (not Scotland), 2,000 associate members, training organisation, consultancy.
Information service.
To offer guidance on practical science and technology in schools and colleges, including health and safety, facilities, resources, laboratories, technicians, etc.

Subject coverage: Primary and secondary school and college practical science and design & technology, facilities, resources and health and safety.

Library catalogue: All or part available online

Publications: Printed
Order printed publications from: Members can access via security password on website

Publications list: Available online

Access to staff: Contact by letter, by telephone, by fax, by e-mail and via website. Access for members only. Non-members charged.
Hours: Mon to Fri, 0900 to 1700

CLECKHEATON LIBRARY & INFORMATION CENTRE

Cleckheaton Library & Information Centre, Whitcliffe Road, Cleckheaton, West Yorkshire, BD19 3DX

Tel: 01274 335170
Fax: 01274 335171
E-mail: cleckheaton.lic@kirklees.gov.uk
Website: www.kirklees.gov.uk/libraries
https://www.facebook.com/cleckheatonlibrary

Enquiries to: Customer Service Manager

Founded: 1930

Organisation type and purpose: Public library.

Subject coverage: Your library is a one stop shop for access to all council services. We love books but offer so much more for everyone including free use of computers and internet.

Information services: Reference, Information and Study facilities. Public photocopying and fax machines (charge applies) Kirklees Passports issued. Please bring proof of benefit, photo and fee. Gateway to Care enquiries including Blue Badge applications. Access to all Council services

continued overleaf

Special visitor services: Audio books, DVD hire

Education services: Quick reads, Teen Space, All Aboard collection for children with special needs, Graphic novels, Local History and reference collection and free access to the libraries on-line databases including Ancestry Library.com. Free Public access computers with internet access

Services for disabled people: Disabled lift, toilets and ramp

Collection: Spen Valley Historical Society Collection

Non-library collection catalogue: All or part available in-house

Library catalogue: All or part available online and in-house

Access to staff: Contact by letter, by telephone, by fax, by e-mail, in person and via website
Hours: Mon, 0900 to 2000; Tue and Thu, 0900 to 1930; Wed, 0900 to 1300; Fri, 0900 to 1700; Sat, 0900 to 1600

Access to building: Baby changing facilities

Access for disabled people: Parking provided, ramped entry, toilet facilities, wheelchair lift,

CLEFT LIP AND PALATE ASSOCIATION (CLAPA)

First Floor, Green Man Tower, 332b Goswell Road, London, EC1V 7LQ

Tel: 020 7833 4883
Fax: 020 7833 5999
E-mail: info@clapa.com
Website: www.clapa.com

Enquiries to: Chief Executive
Other contacts: Community Fundraiser (for volunteers wanting to get involved in CLAPA)

Founded: 1979

Organisation type and purpose: Registered charity (England and Wales charity number 1108160, Scotland SC041034).
To offer support to families affected by cleft lip and/or palate.

Subject coverage: Cleft lip and/or palate.

Information services: Information via website, email, letter and phone enquiries.

Publications: Printed

Publications list: Available online and in print

Access to staff: Contact by letter, by telephone, by fax, by e-mail and via website
Hours: Mon to Fri, 0900 to 1700

CLEVELAND COLLEGE OF ART AND DESIGN LIBRARY (CCAD)

Green Lane, Linthorpe, Middlesbrough, Cleveland, TS5 7RJ

Tel: 01642 288000 or 01429 422000
Fax: 01642 288828
Website: www.ccad.ac.uk

Enquiries to: Library Manager
Direct tel: 01642 856170/01429 858327
Direct e-mail: ann.kenyon@ccad.ac.uk

Organisation type and purpose: College of further and higher education.

Subject coverage: Fine art, applied arts and crafts, 3D, entertainment crafts, jewellery, ceramics, textiles, graphics, painting, photography, fashion, interactive media and film.

Library catalogue: All or part available online

Publications: Printed

Access to staff: Contact by letter, by telephone and by e-mail. Appointment necessary.
Hours: Mon, Tue, 0900 to 1900; Thu, 0900 to 1700; Fri, 0900 to 1630
Special comments: Limited access during vacation periods.

Access for disabled people: Ramped entry

CLEVELAND COLLEGE OF ART AND DESIGN LIBRARY – HARTLEPOOL ANNEXE

Church Square, Hartlepool, Cleveland, TS24 7EX

Tel: 01429 422000
Fax: 01429 422122

Enquiries to: Librarian
Other contacts: Learning Resource Manager

Organisation type and purpose: HE students, full and part time

Subject coverage: Fine and applied arts and crafts, art history, design history, history of architecture, interior design and layout, jewellery, ceramics, textiles, printmaking and photography.

Library catalogue: All or part available online

Publications: Printed

Access to staff: Contact by letter and by telephone. Appointment necessary.
Hours: Mon to Fri, 0900 to 1700

Access to building: *Hours:* 0900 to 1700

Access for disabled people: Fully accessible

Parent body: Cleveland College of Art and Design; Green Lane, Linthorpe, Middlesbrough, TS5 7RJ; tel: 01642 288000; fax: 01642 288828; website: http://www.ccad.ac.uk

CLEVELAND, NORTH YORKS & SOUTH DURHAM FHS

1 Oxgang Close, Redcar, Cleveland, TS10 4ND

Tel: 01642 486615
Fax: 01642 486615
E-mail: pjoiner@lineone.net
Website: www.wesite.lineone.net/~pjoiner/cfhs/cfhs.html

Enquiries to: General Secretary

Founded: 1980

Organisation type and purpose: International organisation, membership association (membership is by subscription), number of members: 2,000, voluntary organisation, research organisation.

Subject coverage: Family history.

Publications: Printed, and microform publications
Order microform publications from: as for printed publications

Publications Manager, Cleveland, North Yorkshire & South Durham FHS
106 The Avenue, Nunthorpe, Middlesbrough, Cleveland, TS7 0AH

Publications list: Available in print

Access to staff: Contact by letter, by fax and by e-mail
Hours: Mon to Fri, 0900 to 1700

CLIFFORD CHANCE

200 Aldersgate Street, London, EC1A 4JJ

Tel: 020 7600 1000
Fax: 020 7600 5555
Website: www.cliffordchance.com

Enquiries to: Head of Information Sourcing

Founded: 1987; formerly called Clifford Turner Coward Chance (year of change 1987)

Organisation type and purpose: Service industry.
Law Firm.

Subject coverage: Commercial aspects of UK, European and international law, publications for clients and professional contacts.

Non-library collection catalogue: All or part available in-house

Library catalogue: All or part available in-house

Publications: Printed
Order printed publications from: Clifford Chance Publications
c/o Jevons Brown, 19 Bedford Row, London, WC1R 4EB, tel: 020 7404 2917, fax: 020 7600 5555

Publications list: Available online and in print

Access to staff: Access for members only.
Hours: Mon to Fri, 0900 to 1730
Special comments: Publications for clients and professional contacts.

Has: offices worldwide

CLIMB

Formal name: Children Living with Inherited Metabolic Diseases

Climb Building, 176 Nantwich Road, Crewe, CW2 6BG

Tel: 0800 652 3181 (freephone); 0845 241 2173
Fax: 0845 241 2174
E-mail: info.svcs@climb.org.uk
Website: www.climb.org.uk

Enquiries to: Information Research Officer
Other contacts: Membership Services

Organisation type and purpose: A registered charity (number 1089588).
The National Information Centre for Metabolic Diseases. A national organisation working on behalf of children, young people and families affected by metabolic disease and providing a resource for children, adults, families and professionals.

To maintain and advance its position as the primary provider of Metabolic Disease-specific information and support to children, young people, adults, families and professionals in the United Kingdom and to provide information and support to families world-wide; to fund educational and primary research programmes; and to investigate treatments and medical services.

Subject coverage: Funding research and facilitating medical treatment, providing information, advice and support for families and professionals, supporting families through grants to help meet equipment and other costs, educating professionals and others about this group of diseases.

Information services: Up-to-date, sourced information covering over 730 metabolic conditions, each supported disorder having an information pack containing information for professionals and families. For disease-specific information and support, e-mail: info.svcs@climb.org.uk. Additional information and support available in relation to the health system, benefits, welfare rights, medicine, empowerment, personal issues, education and jobs, links with other specialists and families, care, social services, accessing education or special needs support, attaining services available locally, diagnosis, sharing information with family members, and advice on genetic counselling and issues around genetic testing.

Publications: Printed, and electronic and video
Order electronic and video publications from: Download from website

Publications list: Available online

Access to staff: Contact by letter, by telephone and by e-mail
Hours: Mon to Fri, 1000 to 1600

CLOTHWORKERS' COMPANY, THE

Formal name: Worshipful Company of Clothworkers of the City of London

Clothworkers' Hall, Dunster Court, Mincing Lane, London, EC3R 7AH

Tel: 020 7623 7041
Fax: 020 7397 0107
E-mail: enquiries@clothworkers.co.uk
Website: www.clothworkers.co.uk

Founded: 1528

Organisation type and purpose:
Membership association (membership is by election or invitation).
City of London Livery Company.

Collection: Archive
Plate Collection

Non-library collection catalogue: All or part available in-house

Library catalogue: All or part available in-house

Publications list: Available online

Access to staff: Contact by letter, by telephone, by fax, by e-mail, in person and via website. Appointment necessary. Letter of introduction required.

Access to building: No public access

Access for disabled people: Wheelchair access, lift access

CLUB FOR ACTS AND ACTORS (CAA)

20 Bedford Street, London, WC2E 9HP

Tel: 020 7836 3172
Fax: 020 7836 3172
E-mail: office@thecaa.org

Enquiries to: Secretary
Other contacts: Chairman (for initiations); Treasurer (for financial matters)

Founded: 1897; formerly called Concert Artistes' Association (CAA) (year of change early 1990s)

Organisation type and purpose:
Membership association (membership is by subscription, election or invitation), present number of members: 1,010 plus a few Honorary Members, registered charity (charity number 211012).

Collection: Archive Material: old members list, photographs, concert programmes, posters, etc.

Publications: Printed

Access to staff: Contact by letter, by telephone, by fax and by e-mail.
Appointment necessary.
Hours: Mon to Fri, 0930 to 1700

Access to building: *Special comments:* Entry door, stairs to first floor office.

CLUB GTI

PO Box 6506, Sutton in Ashfield, Nottinghamshire, NG17 1NG

Tel: 07891 963823
E-mail: info@clubgti.com
Website: www.clubgti.com

Enquiries to: Chairman
Direct e-mail: secretary@clubgti.com

Organisation type and purpose:
International organisation, national organisation, membership association (membership is by subscription), present number of members: 3,600.

Subject coverage: Club GTI is a non-profit making organisation for enthusiasts of the Volkswagen GTI and associated models within the Volkswagen group of companies. The club is independent of the manufacturer, importer or dealer network.

Publications: Printed

Access to staff: Contact by letter, by telephone, by e-mail and via website
Hours: Mon to Fri, 0900 to 1700

CLUB LOTUS

58 Malthouse Court, Dereham, Norfolk, NR20 4UA

Tel: 01362 694459 or 691144
Fax: 01362 695522
E-mail: jane@clublotus.co.uk
Website: www.club-lotus.co.uk/

Enquiries to: Membership Secretary
Direct e-mail: annemarie@clublotus.co.uk

Founded: 1956

Organisation type and purpose:
International organisation, membership association (membership is by subscription), present number of members: 10,000.
Lotus enthusiasts.

Subject coverage: Lotus cars, technical information and all aspects.

Collection: Complete book list of current titles

Access to staff: Contact by letter, by telephone, by fax and by e-mail.
Appointment necessary.
Hours: Fri, 0900 to 1500

CLUB MARCOS INTERNATIONAL (CMI)

26 Blackberry Close, Chippenham, Wiltshire, SN14 6RG

Tel: 01249 464795
E-mail: info@clubmarcos.net
Website: www.clubmarcos.org.uk

Enquiries to: Membership Secretary

Founded: 1986

Organisation type and purpose:
Membership association (membership is by subscription).

Subject coverage: The Marcos marque.

Access to staff: Contact by letter, by telephone, by e-mail and via website
Hours: Evenings and weekends; 24-hour answerphone

CLUB TRIUMPH

42 Greenlands Road, Staines, Middlesex, TW18 4LR

Tel: 01784 465351
Fax: 01784 465351
E-mail: enquiries@club.triumph.org.uk
Website: www.club.triumph.org.uk

Enquiries to: Secretary

Founded: 1954

Organisation type and purpose:
Membership association (membership is by subscription), present number of members: 1,500, voluntary organisation.
Classic car club.

Subject coverage: Technical and other advice on Triumph cars.

Library catalogue: All or part available in-house

Publications: Printed

Access to staff: Contact by letter, by telephone, by fax, by e-mail and via website
Hours: Mon to Fri, 0900 to 1700

Public Relations Officer: Club Triumph; 1 Bure Homage Gardens, Mudeford, Christchurch, Dorset, BH23 4DR; tel: 01425 278320; e-mail: charles.collin@ntlworld.com

CLUB TRIUMPH (EASTERN)

39 Maltings Road, Great Baddow, Chelmsford, Essex, CM2 8HQ

E-mail: enquiries@clubtriumph.org
Website: clubtriumph.org

continued overleaf

Enquiries to: Publicity Officer
Direct e-mail: enquiries@clubtriumph.org

Founded: 1960; formerly called Triumph Sports Owners Association; incorporates the former Club Triumph Limited

Organisation type and purpose: Membership association (membership is by subscription), voluntary organisation.
To bring together like-minded enthusiasts of the Triumph Marque and to provide technical back-up. To promote enjoyment of the Triumph marque of motor car in a social environment.

Subject coverage: The Triumph motor car: the technology, enjoyment and use of all models.

Collection: Triumph motor car history
Triumph-related technical information (hard copy only)

Publications: Printed

Access to staff: Contact by letter, by e-mail and via website. Appointment necessary.

Affiliated to: RACMSA

CLUBS FOR YOUNG PEOPLE (CYP)

371 Kennington Lane, London, SE11 5QY

Tel: 020 7793 0787
Fax: 020 7820 9815
E-mail: office@clubsforyoungpeople.org.uk
Website: www.clubsforyoungpeople.org.uk/
Website: www.nacyp.org.uk

Enquiries to: National Director
Other contacts: Director of Fundraising Officer for communications.

Founded: 1925; formerly called National Association of Boys' Clubs (NABC) (year of change 2005)

Organisation type and purpose: Membership association, present number of members: 400,000, voluntary organisation, registered charity (charity number 306065), suitable for ages: 11 to 25, training organisation.
To offer young people the knowledge, understanding and help they need which will utilise their full potential as they prepare for life in society and their responsibilities as adults.

Subject coverage: Youth leadership training; sports; creative activities; adventure opportunities, development training, youth clubs.

Publications: Printed

Access to staff: Contact by letter, by fax, by e-mail and via website
Hours: Mon to Fri, 0900 to 1700

Affiliated to: British Youth Council; National Council for Voluntary Youth Services; National Youth Agency

Has: 3,000 youth clubs affiliated

CLYDEBANK LOCAL HISTORY SOCIETY

Mrs C Ward (Secretary) 14 Birch Road, Parkhall, Clydebank, Strathclyde, G81 3NZ

Tel: 0141 562 3212
E-mail: cath.ward@ntlworld.com

Enquiries to: Chairman, S D Carson
Direct tel: 01389 383043
Direct e-mail: s_david.carson@ntlworld.com

Founded: 1977

Organisation type and purpose: Voluntary organisation.

Subject coverage: Local history of Clydebank and district.

Publications: Printed

Access to staff: Contact by letter, by telephone and by e-mail

Access for disabled people: Access via ramp at side entrance in Hall Street.

Links with: Scottish Civic Trust

CMR INTERNATIONAL LIMITED

Formal name: Centre for Medicines Research International

Novellus Court, 61 South Street, Epsom, Surrey, KT18 7PX

Tel: 01372 846100
Fax: 01372 846101
E-mail: information@cmr.org
Website: www.cmr.org

Enquiries to: Information Assistant

Founded: 1981; formerly called Centre for Medicines Research (CMR)

Organisation type and purpose: Membership association (membership is by subscription), present number of members: 55, consultancy, research organisation.
To collect data and conduct research into the development of medicines.

Subject coverage: Innovation of new chemical entities, safety evaluation of medicines, international medicines regulations, research and development in the pharmaceutical industry and benchmarking.

Collection: Small collection of c. 400 books on the drug development process

Trade and statistical information: International pharmaceutical research and development expenditure. New chemical entities reaching the world market.
Development times for new medicines.
Regulatory review times in major markets

Publications: Printed

Publications list: Available in print

Access to staff: Contact by letter, by e-mail and via website
Hours: Mon to Fri, 0900 to 1700

CO-OPERATIVE AND SOCIAL ENTERPRISE DEVELOPMENT AGENCY LTD (CASE-DA)

1st Floor, 1 The Crescent, King Street, Leicester, LE1 6RX

Tel: 0116 222 5010
E-mail: enquiries@case-da.co.uk
Website: www.case-da.co.uk

Enquiries to: Information Officer

Organisation type and purpose: Voluntary organisation.
Advice, training and support to people who want to set up Social Enterprise.

Subject coverage: Industrial and service co-operatives; how to set up and run co-operatives and social enterprises; their projects, markets, available skills and finance, legal and taxation problems, education, training, publicity.

Publications: Printed

Access to staff: Contact by letter, by telephone, by fax, in person and via website
Hours: Mon to Fri, 0900 to 1700

CO-OPERATIVE COLLEGE

Formal name: National Co-operative Archive

Holyoake House, Hanover Street, Manchester, M60 0AS

Tel: 0161 246 2937
Fax: 0161 246 2946
E-mail: archive@co-op.ac.uk
Website: www.archive.coop

Enquiries to: Archivist
Direct tel: 0161 246 2937
Direct e-mail: archive@co-op.ac.uk

Founded: 1911; formerly called Co-operative College, J J Worley Memorial Library; formerly called Co-operative Union Library (year of change 2000)

Organisation type and purpose: Registered charity, suitable for ages: adults, consultancy, research organisation.

Subject coverage: Co-operation, co-operative history and co-operative society history and histories, nationally and internationally; co-operative film archive, co-operative archive, international economic development centre for alternative industrial and technological systems archive, co-operative oral history archive.

Collection: CAITS Archive
Co-operation and Owenism history collection (c. 2,000 items)
Co-operative Society History
J J Worley Memorial Library
Midlands Co-operative Society Archive
Robert Owen Collection (3,000 items)
George Jacob Holyoake Collection (4,000 items)
National Co-operative Film Archive
Co-operative Oral History Archive
Edward Owen Greening Collection
Co-operative Women's Guild
Rochdale Equitable Pioneers Society Collection
Co-operative Party Collection
Co-operative Press Collection
Co-operative Group South East, South Midlands and Northern Region Collection
Co-operative Youth Movements

Non-library collection catalogue: All or part available online

Library catalogue: All or part available online

Publications: Printed

Publications list: Available in print

Access to staff: Contact by letter, by telephone, by fax, by e-mail and via website. Appointment necessary.
Hours: Mon to Fri, 1000 to 1700

Access to building: By appointment
Hours: Mon to Fri, 1000 to 1700

Access for disabled people: By appointment
Hours: Mon to Fri, 1000 to 1700

COBALT DEVELOPMENT INSTITUTE (CDI)

167 High Street, Guildford, Surrey, GU1 3AJ

Tel: 01483 578877
Fax: 01483 573873
E-mail: info@thecdi.com
Website: www.thecdi.com

Enquiries to: General Manager
Other contacts: Administration Manager

Founded: 1982; formerly called Centre d'Information du Cobalt (CIC) (year of change 1970)

Organisation type and purpose: Trade association (membership is by subscription). Representing the world's main cobalt producers and users; purpose is to promote cobalt and provide information on it to any interested party.

Subject coverage: All aspects of cobalt – sources, statistics, uses, properties, extraction, environmental aspects.

Non-library collection catalogue: All or part available in-house

Library catalogue: All or part available in-house

Publications: Printed

Publications list: Available online and in print

Access to staff: Contact by letter, by telephone, by fax, by e-mail and via website. Appointment necessary.
Hours: Mon to Fri, 0900 to 1700

COCKBURN ASSOCIATION

Formal name: Cockburn Association (The Edinburgh Civic Trust)

Trunk's Close, 55 High Street, Edinburgh, EH1 1SR

Tel: 0131 557 8686
Fax: 0131 337 9387
E-mail: admin@cockburnassociation.org.uk
Website: www.cockburnassociation.org.uk

Founded: 1875

Organisation type and purpose: A registered Scottish charity.

Subject coverage: Conservation and enhancement of Edinburgh's landscape and historic and architectural heritage.

CODRINGTON LIBRARY

All Souls College, High Street, Oxford, OX1 4AL

Tel: 01865 279379
Fax: 01865 279299
E-mail: codrington.library@all-souls.ox.ac.uk
Website: www.all-souls.ox.ac.uk/library

Enquiries to: Librarian in Charge
Direct tel: 01865 279318

Organisation type and purpose: College Library.

Subject coverage: Law, history, strategic studies.

Collection: 400 manuscripts including the Luttrell-Wynne Papers
British and continental early-printed books
18th-century English newspapers
Material relating to the letters of Junius
Neo-Latin and inscriptional literature

Library catalogue: All or part available online

Access to staff: Contact by letter and by e-mail. Appointment necessary. Letter of introduction required.
Hours: Term time: Mon to Fri, 0930 to 1830
Vacations: Mon to Fri, 0930 to 1630

COELIAC UK

3rd floor, Apollo Centre, Desborough Road, PO Box 220, High Wycombe, Buckinghamshire, HP11 2HY

Tel: 01494 437278
Fax: 01494 474349
E-mail: info@coeliac.co.uk

Enquiries to: Chief Executive
Direct tel: Helpline: 0845 305 2060

Founded: 1968; formerly called Coeliac Society of the United Kingdom, The Coeliac Society (year of change 2001)

Organisation type and purpose: Registered charity (charity number 1048167 in England and Wales and SC039804 in Scotland).
To support the health, welfare and rights of coeliacs, those with Dermatitis Herpetiformis (DH). Supports other medically diagnosed patients whose health and quality of life can be improved by following the dietary regime beneficial to coeliacs. To provide easily accessible written, verbal and electronic advice, information and resources to these individuals and groups. To educate the public and those in appropriate sectors of health, government, commerce and industry on the conditions and the issues. To promote and commission research into the causes, alleviation, treatment, care and cure of the coeliac and DH conditions.

Subject coverage: General management of a gluten-free diet for those medically diagnosed as having the coeliac condition or dermatitis herpetiformis.

Publications: Printed, and electronic and video

Access to staff: Contact by letter, by telephone, by fax and by e-mail
Hours: Mon to Fri, 0900 to 1700
Helpline: Mon, Tue, Thu, Fri, 1000 to 1600; Wed, 1100 to 1600

COIL WINDING INTERNATIONAL MAGAZINE

Formal name: Coil Winding International & Electrical Insulation Magazine

PO Box 936, Alder Hills, Poole, Dorset, BH12 3HB

Tel: 01202 743906
Fax: 01202 736018
E-mail: coilwind@bournemouth-net.co.uk
Website: www.coilwinding.co.uk

Enquiries to: Editor

Founded: 1976

Organisation type and purpose: Publishing house.

Subject coverage: Electric motors; transformers; electromagnetic materials and components.

Publications: Printed

Access to staff: Contact by fax and by e-mail
Hours: Mon to Fri, 0900 to 1700

Access to building: Prior appointment required

COKE OVEN MANAGERS' ASSOCIATION (COMA)

Otto Simon Ltd, Churchfield House, 5, The Crescent, Cheadle, Cheshire, SK8 1PS

Tel: 0161 491 7440
Fax: 0161 491 3369
Website: coke-oven-managers.org

Enquiries to: Honorary Secretary
Direct e-mail: familymills@msn.com

Founded: 1915

Organisation type and purpose: Professional body.

Subject coverage: Coke ovens, coking, carbonisation.

Collection: Complete set of COMA Yearbooks

Library catalogue: All or part available online

Publications: Printed
Order printed publications from: Honorary Secretary

COLCHESTER BOROUGH COUNCIL

PO Box 884, Town Hall, Colchester, Essex, CO1 1FR

Tel: 01206 282222
Fax: 01206 282288
Website: www.colchester.gov.uk

Enquiries to: Chief Executive

Organisation type and purpose: Local government body.

Access to staff: Contact by letter, by telephone, by fax and in person
Hours: Mon to Fri, 0900 to 1700

COLCHESTER INSTITUTE LIBRARY

Sheepen Road, Colchester, Essex, CO3 3LL

Tel: 01206 712642
Fax: 01206 711712
E-mail: library.helpdesk@colchester.ac.uk
Website: library.colchester.ac.uk

Enquiries to: Head of Learning Resources and Student Services
Direct tel: 01206 712280
Direct e-mail: cilla.summers@colchester.ac.uk

Organisation type and purpose: Suitable for ages: 16+.
College of further and higher education.

Subject coverage: Music, art and design, catering and hospitality studies, health studies, business studies, leisure and

continued overleaf

recreation, construction, automobile and general engineering, humanities, social sciences, science, education.

Collection: Music scores, including wind band scores

Library catalogue: All or part available online

Access to staff: Contact by letter, by telephone, by fax, by e-mail, in person and via website. Non-members charged.
Hours: Mon to Fri, 0900 to 1700

Links with: Essex University

COLD ROLLED SECTIONS ASSOCIATION (CRSA)

National Metalforming Centre, 47 Birmingham Road, Birmingham, B70 6PY

Tel: 0121 601 6350
Fax: 0121 601 6373
E-mail: crsa@crsauk.com
Website: www.crsauk.com

Enquiries to: Secretary

Organisation type and purpose: Trade association.

Subject coverage: Cold roll-formed steel sections.

Publications: Printed

Access to staff: Contact by telephone and by e-mail
Hours: Mon to Fri, 0900 to 1700

Connections with: Confederation of British Metalforming (CBM); National Metalforming Centre, 47 Birmingham Road, Birmingham, B70 6PY; tel: 0121 601 6350; fax: 0121 601 6373; e-mail: info@britishmetalforming.com; website: http://www.britishmetalforming.com

COLEG LLANDRILLO LIBRARY RESOURCE CENTRE

Formal name: Library Learning Technology Service

Llandudno Road, Rhos-on-Sea, Colwyn Bay, Conwy, LL28 4HZ

Tel: 01492 546666
Fax: 01492 543052
E-mail: info@llandrillo.ac.uk
Website: www.llandrillo.ac.uk

Enquiries to: Library Resource Manager
Direct tel: 01492 542342
Direct fax: 01492 548267
Direct e-mail: library1@llandrillo.ac.uk

Organisation type and purpose: Library resource centre for a college of further education, higher education and work-based learning.

Subject coverage: A Level, GCSE and International Baccalaureate; business and management, further education, computer studies, special needs, hospitality management, leisure and tourism, health care and counselling, engineering, construction, motor vehicle technology, languages, art, office technology and secretarial studies.

Non-library collection catalogue: All or part available online

Library catalogue: All or part available online

Publications: Printed

Access to staff: Contact by letter, by telephone, by fax, by e-mail and via website. Appointment necessary. Non-members charged.
Hours: Term time: Mon, 0830 to 1600; Tue to Thu, 0830 to 2000; Fri, 0930 to 1630; Sat, 1000 to 1500
Vacations: Mon to Thu, 0830 to 1700; Fri 0830 to 1630

Branches: Abergele Community College; Denbigh Community College; Rhyl Community College

COLLECTIONS TRUST

Downstream Building, CAN Mezzanine, 1 London Bridge, London, SE1 9BG

Tel: 020 7022 1889
E-mail: office@collectionstrust.org.uk
Website: www.collectionstrust.org.uk

Enquiries to: Marketing Officer

History of institution: incorporates the former MDA (year of change 2008)

Organisation type and purpose: Professional body, registered charity (charity number 273984).

Subject coverage: Professional collections management and related information technology and legal issues.

Publications: Printed
Order printed publications from: website: http://www.collectionstrust.org.uk/books

Publications list: Available online and in print

Access to staff: Contact by letter, by telephone, by fax, by e-mail and via website. Appointment necessary.
Hours: Mon to Fri, 0900 to 1700

Access to building: No prior appointment required

COLLEGE OF ARMS

Formal name: Corporation of the Kings, Heralds and Pursuivants of Arms; also known as Heralds' College.

Queen Victoria Street, London, EC4V 4BT

Tel: 020 7248 2762
Fax: 020 7248 6448
E-mail: enquiries@college-of-arms.gov.uk
Website: www.college-of-arms.gov.uk

Enquiries to: Officer in Waiting
Other contacts: Archivist for study of books or manuscripts.

Founded: 1484

Organisation type and purpose: Advisory body, professional body (membership is by election or invitation), present number of members: 11, historic building, house or site, consultancy, research organisation.
Repository of the official registers of armorial bearings and genealogies of England, Wales, Northern Ireland and Commonwealth families.
Heraldry and genealogy.

Subject coverage: Heraldry, grants of arms, genealogy, ceremonial, precedence, changes of name.

Collection: Some of the Arundel MSS
Unique manuscript collections of heraldic and genealogical material

Non-library collection catalogue: All or part available in-house and in print

Library catalogue: All or part available in-house

Publications: Printed

Access to staff: Contact by letter, by telephone, by fax, by e-mail, in person and via website
Hours: Mon to Fri, 1000 to 1600
Special comments: Groups of visitors by appointment with Officer in Waiting.

Access to building: Prior appointment required
Hours: Mon to Fri, 1000 to 1600
Special comments: Contact Archivist, telephone 020 7236 1627

COLLEGE OF CRANIO-SACRAL THERAPY (CCST)

9 St Georges Mews, Primrose Hill, London, NW1 8XE

Tel: 020 7586 0148 or 7483 0120
Fax: 020 7586 9550
E-mail: info@ccst.co.uk
Website: www.ccst.co.uk

Enquiries to: Administrator

Founded: 1986

Organisation type and purpose: Training organisation, research organisation.
Clinic.

Subject coverage: Cranio-sacral therapy, general health and wellbeing, physical and psychological; birth trauma, baby and child health, learning difficulties, meningitis, resolution of obscure and intractable conditions.

Publications: Printed

Access to staff: Contact by letter, by telephone, by fax and by e-mail
Hours: Mon to Fri, 0900 to 1800

Access to building: No prior appointment required

Also at: Primrose Hill Natural Health Centre; 9 St George's Mews, London, NW1 8XE; tel: 020 7586 0148; fax: 020 7586 9550

COLLEGE OF EMERGENCY MEDICINE (CEM)

Churchill House, 35 Red Lion Square, London, WC1R 4SG

Tel: 020 7404 1999
Fax: 020 7067 1267
E-mail: cem@collemergencymed.ac.uk
Website: www.collemergencymed.ac.uk

Organisation type and purpose: Became a College by Royal Charter 2008. Seeks to advance education and research in emergency medicine. Sets standards for training. Administers examinations in emergency medicine for the award of fellowship and membership of the College. Recommends trainees for CCT in Emergency

Medicine. Present number of fellows and members: 2,900. Registered charity (charity number 1122689).

Subject coverage: Emergency medicine.

Access to staff: Contact by letter, by telephone, by e-mail and via website
Hours: 0900 to 1700

COLLEGE OF ESTATE MANAGEMENT (CEM)

Whiteknights, Reading, Berkshire, RG6 6AW

Tel: 0800 019 9697
Fax: 0118 921 4620
E-mail: courses@cem.ac.uk
Website: www.cem.ac.uk

Enquiries to: Admission Officer
Direct e-mail: prospectuses@cem.ac.uk

Founded: 1919

Organisation type and purpose: Registered charity (charity number 313223), suitable for ages: 18+, research organisation.

Subject coverage: Undergraduate, professional and postgraduate courses for the property professions, construction industry and those associated. Course subjects include estate management, arbitration, shopping centre management, property investment, building conservation, construction and real estate, project management, construction, surveying, facilities management, valuation.

Publications: Printed, and electronic and video

Publications list: Available online and in print

Access to staff: Contact by letter, by telephone, by fax, by e-mail and via website. Appointment necessary.
Hours: Mon to Fri, 0830 to 1730

Access to building: No prior appointment required

COLLEGE OF HARINGEY ENFIELD AND NORTH EAST LONDON (COHENEL)

High Road, Tottenham, London, N15 4RU

Tel: 020 8802 3014
Fax: 020 8442 3091
E-mail: jdunster.conel.ac.uk
Website: www.conel.ac.uk

Enquiries to: Head of Learner Support
Direct tel: 020 8442 3877

Founded: 1990; formerly called College of North East London

Organisation type and purpose: College of further education.

Subject coverage: Subjects Basic Skills to Foundation Degrees, accountancy; business studies; building and engineering; health care; art; design; media; hairdressing; beauty therapy; information technology; environmental health; housing; public administration; electronics; general education; sports and recreation, teacher training

Library catalogue: All or part available in-house

Access to staff: Contact by letter, by telephone, by e-mail and via website
Hours: Mon to Thu, 0900 to 2000; Fri 0900 to 1630;

Access to building: Prior appointment required

Access for disabled people: Ramped entry, toilet facilities

COLLEGE OF HEALTH CARE CHAPLAINS (CHCC)

Unite Health Sector, 128 Theobald's Road, London, WC1X 8TN

Tel: 020 3371 2004
Fax: 0870 731 5043
E-mail: william.sharpe@unitetheunion.org
Website: www.healthcarechaplains.org

Enquiries to: Registrar

Founded: 1993

Organisation type and purpose: Trade union (membership is by subscription), present number of members: 1,000, training organisation, research organisation, Allied Health Care Chaplains.

Subject coverage: Pastoral care, ethics in health care, inter-faith relationships in health care.

Library catalogue: All or part available online and in-house

Publications: Printed

Publications list: Available online and in print

Access to staff: Contact by letter, by telephone, by fax, by e-mail and via website
Hours: Mon to Fri, 0900 to 1700

Autonomous section of: Unite the Union; website: http://www.unitetheunion.org

COLLEGE OF INTEGRATED CHINESE MEDICINE (CICM)

19 Castle Street, Reading, Berkshire, RG1 7SB

Tel: 0118 950 8880
Fax: 0118 950 8890
E-mail: info@cicm.org.uk
Website: www.cicm.org.uk

Enquiries to: Reception

Founded: 1992

Organisation type and purpose: Training organisation.

Subject coverage: Training in acupuncture, tuina and Chinese herbal medicine.

Library catalogue: All or part available online, in-house and in print

Access to staff: Contact by letter, by fax, by e-mail and in person. Appointment necessary. Letter of introduction required.
Hours: Mon to Fri, 0900 to 1800

Access to building: *Hours:* Every day except over Christmas and Easter, 0900 to 1800

Access for disabled people: None to library, but provision would be made for access to requested books or journals

Member organisations: British Acupuncture Acreditation Board; 63 Jeddo Road, London, W12 9HQ; tel: 020 8735 0466; website: http://www.baab.co.uk

COLLEGE OF MASONS

42 Magdalen Road, Wandsworth, London, SW18 3NP

Tel: 020 8874 8363
Fax: 020 8871 1342

Enquiries to: Honorary Secretary

Founded: 1893

Organisation type and purpose: Membership association.

Subject coverage: Masonry and all worked materials: building, decoration, carving, lettering, sculpture, restoration, cleaning, fixings, memorials and monuments, granite, marble, slate and stone.

Access to staff: Contact by letter, by telephone and by fax
Hours: Mon to Fri, 0900 to 1700

COLLEGE OF NORTH WEST LONDON (CNWL)

Dudden Hill Lane, Willesden, London, NW10 2XD

Tel: 020 8208 5000
Fax: 020 8451 2718
E-mail: cic@cnwl.ac.uk
Website: www.cnwl.ac.uk

Enquiries to: Head of Learning Resources
Direct tel: 020 8208 5145

Organisation type and purpose: Further education.

Subject coverage: Fashion; catering; creative and media studies; building services, plumbing, electrical and electronics engineering; construction; refrigeration; business studies; auto engineering; access provision; ESOL, EFL, modern foreign languages, interpreting, IELTS.

Collection: Technical index – for construction

Trade and statistical information: Available from website

Library catalogue: All or part available online

Access to staff: Contact by letter, by telephone and by e-mail
Hours: Mon to Fri, 0900 to 1700

Also at: College of North West London; Wembley Park, North End Road, Middlesex, HA9 0AD; College of North West London; Willesden Centre, Denzil Road, London, NW2 7BZ; tel: 020 8208 5050; fax: 020 8451 2718

COLLEGE OF OCCUPATIONAL THERAPISTS

106–114 Borough High Street, London, SE1 1LB

Tel: 020 7450 2316
Fax: 020 7450 2364

Enquiries to: Librarian
Direct e-mail: library@cot.co.uk

continued overleaf

Organisation type and purpose: Professional body (membership is by subscription), present number of members: c. 29,000, registered charity.

Subject coverage: All aspects of occupational therapy in a variety of formats.

Collection: Archives
Code of Practice documents (for reference only)
Conferences file
Government and legal publications
National collection of occupational therapy literature
Organisations file
Practice records and references

Publications: Printed
Order printed publications from: Sales department

Publications list: Available online and in print

Access to staff: Contact by letter, by telephone, by fax, by e-mail, in person and via website. Access for members only. Non-members charged.
Hours: Mon to Fri, 0900 to 1700

Access for disabled people: Level entry, toilet facilities

Parent body: British Association of Occupational Therapists

COLLEGE OF OPTOMETRISTS

Library, The College of Optometrists, 42 Craven Street, London, WC2 5NG

Tel: 020 7839 6000
Fax: 020 7839 6800
E-mail: library@college-optometrists.org
Website: www.college-optometrists.org

Enquiries to: Librarian

Founded: 1901

Organisation type and purpose: Learned society, professional body (membership is by qualification).

Subject coverage: Anatomy and physiology of the eye, physiology and psychology of vision, vision defects and their correction, spectacles and contact lenses, geometric and visual optics, optometry and its history.

Collection: Early books on vision

Library catalogue: All or part available online

Access to staff: Contact by letter, by telephone, by fax, by e-mail, in person and via website. Appointment necessary. Non-members charged.
Hours: Mon to Fri, 0900 to 1300 and 1400 to 1700

Administered by: College of Optometrists

COLLEGE OF PIPING

16–24 Otago Street, Glasgow, G12 8JH

Tel: 0141 334 3587
Fax: 0141 587 6068
E-mail: college@college-of-piping.co.uk
Website: www.college-of-piping.co.uk/index.html

Enquiries to: Chairman
Other contacts: Principal for day to day responsibility.

Founded: 1944

Organisation type and purpose: Voluntary organisation, museum.

Subject coverage: Highland bagpipe and its music.

Publications: Printed

Access to staff: Contact by letter, by telephone, by fax, by e-mail and in person
Hours: Mon to Fri, 0900 to 1700

Access for disabled people: Parking provided

COLLEGE OF PSYCHIC STUDIES (CPS)

16 Queensberry Place, London, SW7 2EB

Tel: 020 7589 3292
Fax: 020 7589 2824
E-mail: admin@collegeofpsychicstudies.co.uk
Website: www.psychic-studies.org.uk

Enquiries to: Administrator
Direct tel: 020 7838 4401
Other contacts: Librarian for books and research.

Founded: 1884; formerly called London Spiritualist Alliance (year of change 1955); formerly called College of Psychic Science (year of change 1970)

Organisation type and purpose: Membership association (membership is by subscription), present number of members: 2,190, registered charity (charity number 212728), suitable for ages: 18+, training organisation, research organisation.
Educational charity, advice and resource centre.

Subject coverage: Psychic research, parapsychology, occult, healing, meditation, New Age, psychic development, spiritual philosophy.

Collection: Small specialist collection of books, manuscripts, photographs and artefacts relating to psychic research and the college's history. No public access. Research by prior arrangement with the Librarian

Publications: Printed, and electronic and video

Publications list: Available in print

Access to staff: Contact by letter, by telephone, by fax, by e-mail and via website. Appointment necessary.
Hours: Mon to Fri, 1030 to 1900; Sat, 0915 to 1415
Special comments: Library for members only, no direct access to archives unless by special appointment with the Librarian.

COLLEGE OF TEACHERS

3rd Floor, 33 John Street, London, WC1N 2AT

Tel: 020 7404 2008
Fax: 020 7404 2008
E-mail: gen@cot4.freeserve.co.uk

Enquiries to: Chief Executive

Founded: 1849; formerly called College of Preceptors

Organisation type and purpose: Professional body.
To make public the concerns of the teaching profession and to support the profession through its publications and qualifications.

Subject coverage: Professional development of teachers, education, especially teacher education.

Publications: Printed

Publications list: Available in print

Access to staff: Appointment necessary.
Hours: Mon to Fri, 0930 to 1700

COLLEGE OF TRADITIONAL ACUPUNCTURE (CTA)

Haseley Manor, Hatton, Warwickshire, CV35 7LU

Tel: 01926 484158
Fax: 01926 485444
E-mail: jeanette.harper@cta-uk.net
Website: www.acupuncture-coll.ac.uk

Enquiries to: Administrator

Founded: 1960s; formerly called Oriental Medical College Ltd t/a The College of Traditional Acupuncture UK (year of change 1994)

Organisation type and purpose: Registered charity (charity number 1039702), suitable for ages: 20+.
Private college offering 3-year part-time licentiate in acupuncture for qualification as professional practitioners. Programme is fully accredited by the British Acupuncture Accreditation Board and validated as BA(Hons) by Oxford Brookes University.

Subject coverage: Acupuncture, complementary medicine.

Access to staff: Contact by letter, by telephone, by fax and by e-mail
Hours: Mon to Fri, 0900 to 1700

Access for disabled people: Parking provided, ramped entry, access to all public areas, toilet facilities

COLOMBIAN EMBASSY

3 Hans Crescent, Knightsbridge, London, SW1X 0LN

Tel: 020 7589 9177
Fax: 020 7581 1829
E-mail: mail@colombianembassy.co.uk
Website: www.colombiaemb.co.uk

Enquiries to: Ambassador

Organisation type and purpose: National government body.
Embassy.

Subject coverage: Colombia, general information and economic statistics.

Publications: Printed

Also at: Colombian Consulate General; 3rd Floor, 15–19 Great Titchfield Street, London, W1P 7FB; tel: 020 7637 9893; fax: 020 7637 5604; e-mail: consulco@consulco.demon.co.uk

Links with: Proexport (Trade Office); 9 Berkeley Street, London, W1X 5AD; tel: 020 7491 3535; fax: 020 7491 4295; e-mail: cici@proexport-london.co.uk

COMBAT STRESS

Formal name: Ex-Services Mental Welfare Society

Tyrwhitt House, Oaklawn Road, Leatherhead, Surrey, KT22 0BX

Tel: 01372 841600
Fax: 01372 841601
E-mail: contactus@combatstress.org.uk
Website: www.combatstress.org.uk/

Enquiries to: Director Fundraising & Communications
Direct tel: 01372 841615
Direct e-mail: robert.marsh@combatstress.org.uk; faye.waters@combatstress.org,uk

Founded: 1919

Organisation type and purpose: Registered charity (charity number 206002). Supports three treatment centres and 15 welfare officers in the UK and Republic of Ireland. The Ex-Services Mental Welfare Society, also known as Combat Stress, is the only charity to specialise in helping those of all ranks of the Armed Forces and Merchant Navy who suffer from psychological disorders caused through or exacerbated by service.

Publications: Printed, and microform publications

Access to staff: Contact by letter, by telephone, by fax, by e-mail and via website. Appointment necessary.
Hours: Mon to Fri, 0730 to 1600

Branches: Combat Stress Regional Offices; Hollybush House, Hollybush by Ayr, Ayrshire, KA6 7EA; tel: 01292 561315; fax: 01292 561351; e-mail: bill.middleton@combatstress.org.uk; website: http://www.combatstress.org.uk
Combat Stress Welfare Support Team North; Audley Court, Audley Avenue, Newport, Shropshire, TF10 7BP; tel: 01952 822712; fax: 01952 811751; e-mail: mike.burrows@combatstress.org.uk; website: http://www.combatstress.org.uk

COMHAIRLE NAN EILEAN SIAR (CNES)

Council Offices, Sandwick Road, Stornoway, Isle of Lewis, HS1 2BW

Tel: 01851 703773
Fax: 01851 705349
Website: www.w-isles.gov.uk

Enquiries to: Chief Executive
Direct tel: 01851 709500
Direct fax: 01851 706022
Direct e-mail: m.burr@cne-siar.gov.uk
Other contacts: Communications Officer

Founded: 1975; formerly called Western Isles Council (WIC) (year of change 1998)

Organisation type and purpose: Local government body.

Subject coverage: All areas of community service.

Collection: Library (open to the public)

Access to staff: Contact by letter, by telephone, by fax, by e-mail and in person
Hours: Mon to Fri, 0900 to 1700

Access for disabled people: Parking provided, ramped entry, level entry, access to all public areas, toilet facilities

Affiliated to: Conference of Peripheral Maritime Regions

Council Offices: Comhairle Nan Eilean Siar; Castlebay, Isle of Barra; tel: 01871 810431; fax: 01871 810254; Comhairle Nan Eilean Siar; Tarbert, Isle of Harris; tel: 01859 502367; fax: 01859 502283; Comhairle Nan Eilean Siar; Balivanich, Benbecula; tel: 01870 602425; fax: 01870 602332

COMIC BOOK POSTAL AUCTIONS LIMITED (COMPAL)

PO Box 58386, London, NW1W 9RE

Tel: 020 7424 0007
Fax: 020 7424 0008
E-mail: comicbook@compalcomics.com
Website: www.compalcomics.com

Enquiries to: Managing Director

Founded: 1992

Organisation type and purpose: Publishing house.
Comic book auctions by post.

Subject coverage: Comics.

Non-library collection catalogue: All or part available online

Library catalogue: All or part available online

Access to staff: Contact by letter, by telephone, by fax and via website
Hours: Mon to Fri, 0900 to 1700

COMIC RELIEF EDUCATION DISTRIBUTION

Education House, Drywall Estate, Castle Road, Sittingbourne, Kent, ME10 3RL

Tel: 01795 437988
Fax: 01795 474871
E-mail: info@edist.co.uk

Enquiries to: Information Officer

Organisation type and purpose: Registered charity (charity number 326568).

Access to staff: Contact by letter, by telephone, by fax and by e-mail
Hours: Mon to Fri, 0900 to 1700

Access to building: No access other than to staff

Head Office: Comic Relief; 5th Floor, 89 Albert Embankment, London, SE1 7TP

COMMEMORATIVE COLLECTORS SOCIETY

Lumless House, Gainsborough Road, Winthorpe, Newark, Nottinghamshire, NG24 2NR

Tel: 01636 671377
E-mail: commemorativecollectorssociety@hotmail.com
Website: www.commemorativecollecting.co.uk

Enquiries to: Honorary Secretary

Founded: 1972

Organisation type and purpose: International organisation, membership association (membership is by subscription), present number of members: 3,649, voluntary organisation, research organisation.
International society of private collectors of all types of popular commemorabilia.
To represent the interests of members, research and record/maintain archive of commemorative items and commemorative collections.

Subject coverage: Popular/mass-produced commemorative items of any kind, in any material or medium, identification of items/events/manufacturer (if known) and historical background.

Collection: Archive of information on 12,731 different items, worldwide events, 1660–2006
Commemorative Museum Trust Collection of over 5762 pieces from 1761–2006
Library of related material
Photographic Library of over 10,822 black and white photographs of popular commemorative items in any medium from 1660 to the present day. These include foreign commemoratives covering 71 countries to date

Trade and statistical information: Market size and value for commemorative items

Publications: Printed

Access to staff: Contact by letter, by telephone, by e-mail and in person. Appointment necessary.
Hours: Mon to Sun, 0900 to 1700

Access to building: Prior appointment required
Hours: 0930 to 1700

Access for disabled people: Level entry
Hours: 0930 to 1700

COMMITTEE OF SCOTTISH CLEARING BANKERS (CSCB)

Drumsheugh House, 38b Drumsheugh Gardens, Edinburgh, EH3 7SW

Tel: 0131 473 7770
Fax: 0131 473 7799
E-mail: info@scotbanks.co.uk

Enquiries to: Operations Co-ordinator

Organisation type and purpose: Trade association, present number of members: 4.

Subject coverage: Most aspects of Scottish banking.

Trade and statistical information: Aggregate statistics of Scottish clearing banks

Access to staff: Contact by letter, by telephone, by fax and by e-mail
Hours: Mon to Fri, 0900 to 1700

COMMITTEE ON THE ADMINISTRATION OF JUSTICE (CAJ)

2nd Floor, Sturgen Building, 9–15 Queen Street, Belfast, BT1 6EA

Tel: 028 9031 6000
Fax: 028 9031 4583

continued overleaf

E-mail: info@caj.org.uk
Website: www.caj.org.uk

Enquiries to: Office Manager

Founded: 1981

Organisation type and purpose:
Membership association, voluntary organisation, research organisation.
Civil liberties group.

Subject coverage: Civil liberties and human rights in Northern Ireland.

Collection: Information from newspaper cuttings, legislation, conference reports, government publications, etc. on a variety of subjects including administration of the courts, bill of rights, right to silence, miscarriages of justice, police and policing, equality and criminal justice

Publications: Printed

Publications list: Available online and in print

Access to staff: Contact by letter, by telephone, by fax and by e-mail.
Appointment necessary.
Hours: Mon to Fri, 0900 to 1700

Links with: International Federation of Human Rights; 17 passage de la Main d'Or, 75011 Paris, France

COMMONWEAL COLLECTION

J B Priestley Library, University of Bradford, Richmond Road, Bradford, West Yorkshire, BD7 1DP

Tel: 01274 233404
Fax: 01274 233398
E-mail: commonweal@bradford.ac.uk
Website: www.bradford.ac.uk/library/services/commonweal/index.php

Enquiries to: Secretary to the Trustees
Other contacts: Special Collections Librarian (archives)

Founded: 1958

Organisation type and purpose: Voluntary organisation, registered charity (charity number 1053157), public library.
To provide a resource for all issues relating to non-violence and non-violent social change.
Mission Statement: The Commonweal Collection is an independent specialist library devoted to issues around non-violent social change, working to promote justice and peace. Commonweal aims to provide literature.

Subject coverage: Theory and practice of non-violence; non-violence and peace research; Gandhi and other pacifists and political radicals; peace education; critique of war; disarmament; nuclear power and weaponry; alternative society; spirituality; ecological issues; human rights; gender issues.

Collection: Over 11,000 books and pamphlets available for loan, over 230 current alternative journals available for reference
Archival material documenting non-violent campaigns and the peace movement in Britain, including:
Collection of printed materials on Gandhi
Peace News Archives
Papers from the International Seminar on Training in Nonviolent Action
Papers from the London Office of the United Farm Workers, USA
Papers of Hugh Brock (Editor of Peace News, 1955–1964)

Library catalogue: All or part available online

Publications: Printed, and electronic and video

Access to staff: Contact by letter, by telephone and in person
Hours: Term time: Mon to Thu, 0800 to 2400; Fri, 0800 to 2100; Sat, Sun, 0845 to 2100
Vacations: Mon to Fri, 0845 to 2100; Sat, Sun, 0845 to 1800

Access for disabled people: Level entry, access to all public areas, toilet facilities, lifts

Parent body: Commonweal Trust

COMMONWEALTH ASSOCIATION OF SURVEYING AND LAND ECONOMY (CASLE)

University of the West of England, Faculty of Environment & Technology, Frenchay Campus, Coldharbour Lane, Bristol, BS16 1QY

Tel: 0117 328 3036
Fax: 0117 328 3036
E-mail: susan.spedding@uwe.ac.uk
Website: www.casle.org
Website: www.casle.conferences.co.uk

Enquiries to: Assistant Secretary General

Founded: 1969

Organisation type and purpose:
Membership association.

Subject coverage: Education and training in surveying and land management subjects throughout the Commonwealth.

Publications: Printed
Order printed publications from: CASLE Room 2Q20A, Faculty of the Built Environment, University of the West of England, Bristol, BS16 1QY, tel: As main numbers

Access to staff: Contact by letter, by telephone, by fax and by e-mail.
Appointment necessary.
Hours: Mon to Fri, 0900 to 1200

COMMONWEALTH BROADCASTING ASSOCIATION (CBA)

17 Fleet Street, London, EC4Y 1AA

Tel: 020 7853 5550
Fax: 020 7583 5549
E-mail: cba@cba.org.uk
Website: www.cba.org.uk

Enquiries to: Secretary General

Founded: 1945

Organisation type and purpose:
International organisation, professional body, membership association (membership is by election or invitation), present number of members: 100, training organisation, consultancy, research organisation.

To support quality broadcasting throughout the Commonwealth.

Subject coverage: Broadcasting in Commonwealth countries.

Publications: Printed, and electronic and video
Order printed publications from: Postal address or email: cba@cba.org.uk

Publications list: Available online

Access to staff: Contact by letter, by telephone, by fax, by e-mail and via website
Hours: Mon to Fri, 0930 to 1730

Access to building: No access other than to staff and visitors

COMMONWEALTH FORCES HISTORY TRUST

37 Davis Road, Acton, London, W3 7SE

Tel: 020 8749 1045

Enquiries to: Secretary

Founded: 1988

Organisation type and purpose: Registered charity.

Subject coverage: All the different units of the Defence Forces of the British Commonwealth and Empire outside the United Kingdom, from 1066 to 1946, including the American Loyalists and the Indians who fought as Allies of the King in the American Revolution and/or the War of 1812.

Collection: Books and Journals
Indices
Letters
Photographs
Tape recordings

Access to staff: Contact by letter and by telephone. Appointment necessary.
Hours: Mon to Fri, 0900 to 1600

COMMONWEALTH FORESTRY ASSOCIATION (CFA)

The Crib, Dinchope, Craven Arms, Shropshire, SY7 9JJ

Tel: 01588 672868
Fax: 0870 0116645
E-mail: cfa@cfa-international.org
Website: www.cfa-international.org

Enquiries to: Membership Manager
Direct e-mail: jenny@cfa-international.org

Founded: 1921

Organisation type and purpose:
Professional body.

Subject coverage: Forestry, forest products, related environmental subjects.

Collection: Commonwealth Forestry Conference Proceedings
Commonwealth Forestry Review

Publications: Printed

Access to staff: Contact by letter, by telephone, by fax, by e-mail and via website
Hours: Mon to Fri, 0900 to 1700

Member organisation of: Commonwealth Professional Associations; Commonwealth Trust

COMMONWEALTH HUMAN ECOLOGY COUNCIL (CHEC)

Church House, Newton Road, London, W2 5LS

Tel: 020 7792 5934
Fax: 020 7792 5948
E-mail: chec@btopenworld.com
Website: www.checinternational.org

Enquiries to: Chief Executive
Other contacts: Chairman, Governing Board

Founded: 1969; formerly called Committee on Nutrition in the Commonwealth

Organisation type and purpose: Promotion of a human ecological approach to sustainable development, international organisation, professional body, present number of members: 92 individuals and 3 corporate, voluntary organisation, registered charity (charity number 272018), research organisation.
Joint government and non-government composition.

Subject coverage: Human ecology, Commonwealth, human settlements, poverty programmes, health education, sustainable fisheries.

Non-library collection catalogue: All or part available in-house

Library catalogue: All or part available in-house

Publications: Printed
Order printed publications from: from CHEC

Publications list: Available in print

Access to staff: Contact by letter, by telephone, by fax and by e-mail. Appointment necessary.
Hours: Mon to Thu, 1030 to 1700

Access to building: By Appointment

Access for disabled people: No access

Links with: Commission on Sustainable Development; Economic and Social Council for Asia and the Pacific (ESCAP); IUCN Education Commission; UN Centre for Human Settlements; UN ECOSOC; UN Environment Programme (UNEP); UNESCO Education; World Health Organisation (WHO)

COMMONWEALTH JEWISH COUNCIL (CJC)

BCM Box 6871, London, WC1N 3XX

Tel: 020 7222 2120
Fax: 020 7222 1781
E-mail: info@cjc.org.uk
Website: www.cjc.org.uk

Enquiries to: Administrator

Founded: 1982

Organisation type and purpose: Registered charity (charity number 287564).
Commonwealth Jewish Trust.
CJC is the political arm of the organisation that provides the Commonwealth link between countries, high commissioners and ambassadors.

Subject coverage: Commonwealth, Jewish communities, Judaism.

Publications: Printed

Access to staff: Contact by letter, by telephone, by fax and by e-mail
Hours: Mon to Fri, 0915 to 1745

Access to building: No access other than to staff

COMMONWEALTH LOCAL GOVERNMENT FORUM (CLGF)

16A Northumberland Avenue, London, WC2N 5AP

Tel: 020 7389 1490
Fax: 020 7389 1499
E-mail: linfo@clgf.org.uk
Website: www.clgf.org.uk

Founded: 1995

Organisation type and purpose:
International organisation, local government body, membership association, present number of members: 160.

Subject coverage: Local government in Commonwealth countries.

Special visitor services: Only for CLGF members.

Collection: Documentation on local government in Commonwealth countries

Non-library collection catalogue: All or part available in-house and in print

Library catalogue: All or part available online

Publications: Printed, and electronic and video

Publications list: Available online and in print

Access to staff: Contact by letter, by fax and by e-mail
Hours: Mon to Fri, 0900 to 1700

Access to building: Prior appointment required

COMMONWEALTH PARLIAMENTARY ASSOCIATION (CPA)

Suite 700, Westminster House, 7 Millbank, London, SW1P 3JA

Tel: 020 7799 1460
Fax: 020 7222 6073
E-mail: hq.sec@cpahq.org
Website: www.cpahq.org

Enquiries to: Secretary General

Founded: 1911

Organisation type and purpose:
International organisation, professional body (membership is by qualification), present number of members: 14,000, registered charity, training organisation, research organisation, publishing house.
To promote knowledge and education about the constitutional, legislative, economic, social and cultural systems within a parliamentary democratic framework, with particular reference to countries of the Commonwealth.

Subject coverage: Parliaments of the Commonwealth (membership, practice and procedures etc), constitutions, standing orders, names of Commonwealth MPs, elections.

Collection: Books on parliamentary practice and procedure, the Commonwealth, Commonwealth constitutions and standing orders
PA publications, including specialist monographs

Publications: Printed, and electronic and video

Publications list: Available online

Access to staff: Contact by letter, by telephone, by fax, by e-mail and via website. Appointment necessary. Non-members charged.
Hours: Fri, 0900 to 1600

Access to building: Prior appointment required

Access for disabled people: Ramped entry

Has: branches in more than 165 national, state, provincial and territorial parliaments in the Commonwealth

COMMONWEALTH PHARMACEUTICAL ASSOCIATION (CPA)

1 Lambeth High Street, London, SE1 7JN

Tel: 020 7572 2364
Fax: 020 7572 2508
Website: www.rpsgb.org.uk/international.html

Enquiries to: Administrator

Founded: 1970

Organisation type and purpose:
Membership association (membership is by subscription), present number of members: 600.
An association of professional pharmaceutical bodies and personal members from 39 Commonwealth countries.
To establish, develop and maintain the highest possible professional standards of pharmacy throughout the Commonwealth in order to achieve better health outcomes within communities.

Subject coverage: Pharmacy.

Access to staff: Contact by telephone, by fax and by e-mail. Appointment necessary.
Hours: Mon to Fri, 0900 to 1700

Access for disabled people: Ramped entry, toilet facilities

COMMONWEALTH SCIENCE COUNCIL (CSC)

Formal name: Commonwealth Science Council

Marlborough House, Pall Mall, London, SW1Y 5HX

Tel: 020 7747 6220/6219
Fax: 020 7839 6174
E-mail: science@commonwealth.int
Website: www.commonwealthknowledge.net

Enquiries to: Information Officer
Direct tel: 020 7747 6219
Direct e-mail: t.ruredzo@commonwealth.int

Organisation type and purpose:
International organisation.

continued overleaf

The CSC is an innovative, creative and proactive organisation that seeks to leverage the science and technology capability in the public and industry domain within the Commonwealth through networking of both knowledge and finance, using modern information technologies to facilitate the application of S&T by member countries for sustainable economic, environmental, social and cultural development.

Subject coverage: Science and technology.

Publications: Printed
Order printed publications from: The Publications Unit
tel: 020 7747 6342, fax: 020 7839 9081

Access to staff: Contact by e-mail
Hours: Mon to Fri, 0900 to 1700

Access to building: Prior appointment required
Hours: Mon to Fri, 0930 to 1730

Access for disabled people: Level entry, toilet facilities

COMMONWEALTH SECRETARIAT

Marlborough House, Pall Mall, London, SW1Y 5HX

Tel: 020 7747 6164
Fax: 020 7747 6168
E-mail: library@commonwealth.int
Website: www.thecommonwealth.org

Enquiries to: Head of Library and Archives

Founded: 1965

Organisation type and purpose: International organisation.

Subject coverage: Commonwealth, development, trade, agriculture, statistics, economics, technology, industry, politics, education, women and development, youth, health and science.

Collection: Collection of Commonwealth Secretariat Publications
Commonwealth Secretariat Archive, released after 30 years

Library catalogue: All or part available in-house

Publications: Printed
Order printed publications from: Publications Manager, Communications and Public Affairs Division, Commonwealth Secretariat; tel. 020 7747 6342; fax 020 7839 9081

Publications list: Available online and in print

Access to staff: Contact by letter, by telephone, by e-mail and in person. Appointment necessary.
Hours: Mon to Fri, 0915 to 1700

Access for disabled people: Access to all public areas, toilet facilities
Special comments: Lift from ground floor.

COMMONWEALTH WAR GRAVES COMMISSION (CWGC)

2 Marlow Road, Maidenhead, Berkshire, SL6 7DX

Tel: 01628 634221
Fax: 01628 771208
E-mail: general.enq@cwgc.org
Website: www.cwgc.org

Enquiries to: Enquiries Section
Direct tel: 01628 507200
Direct e-mail: casualty.enq@cwgc.org

Founded: 1917; formerly called Imperial War Graves Commission (year of change 1964)

Organisation type and purpose: An international organisation, the Commonwealth War Graves Commission was established by Royal Charter of 21 May 1919, the provisions of which were amended and extended by a Supplemental Charter of 8 June 1964.
Its duties are to mark and maintain the graves of the members of the forces of the Commonwealth who died in the two world wars, to build and maintain memorials to the dead whose graves are unknown, and to keep records and registers.

Subject coverage: The Commission's work is guided by four fundamental principals:
1) that each of the dead should be commemorated individually by name either on the headstone on the grave or by an inscription on a memorial;
2) that the headstones and memorials should be permanent;
3) that the headstones should be uniform;
4) that there should be no distinction made on account of military or civil rank, race or creed.

Information services: media@cwgc.org

Education services: education@cwgc.org

Non-library collection catalogue: All or part available in-house

Library catalogue: All or part available in-house

Publications: Printed, and electronic and video
Order printed publications from: website: http://www.cwgc.org
Order electronic and video publications from: website: http://www.cwgc.org

Publications list: Available online and in print

Access to staff: Contact by letter, by telephone, by fax, by e-mail and via website. Appointment necessary.
Hours: Mon to Thu, 0830 to 1700; Fri, 0830 to 1630

Access to building: Prior appointment required

Access for disabled people: Level entry, toilet facilities

Branches: Outer Area Office (not Europe or the Mediterranean); 2 Marlow Road, Maidenhead, Berkshire, SL6 7DX; tel: 01628 634221; fax: 01628 771643; e-mail: outer .area@cwgc.org; United Kingdom Area Office; Jenton Road, Sydenham, Leamington Spa, Warwickshire, CV31 1XS; tel: 01926 330137; fax: 01926 456595; e-mail: ukaoffice@cwgc.org

COMMONWEALTH YOUTH EXCHANGE COUNCIL (CYEC)

7 Lion Yard, Tremadoc Road, London, SW4 7NQ

Tel: 020 7498 6151
Fax: 020 7720 5403
E-mail: mail@cyec.org.uk
Website: www.cyec.org.uk

Enquiries to: Chief Executive
Other contacts: Grants and Administration Officer for Youth Exchange Information Enquiries

Founded: 1970

Organisation type and purpose: Voluntary organisation, registered charity (charity number 1086375).
National voluntary youth organisation.
Education – informal (young people's social and personal education via youth work) via international youth exchange projects.
Not able to help individuals interested in an international experience or overseas applicants.

Subject coverage: Group youth exchanges between Britain and other Commonwealth countries for young people aged 16–25 years.

Publications: Printed

Publications list: Available in print

Access to staff: Contact by letter, by telephone, by fax and by e-mail. Appointment necessary.
Hours: Mon to Fri, 1100 to 1800
Special comments: Send stamped addressed envelope.

Access to building: *Hours:* Mon to Fri, 1000 to 1700

Branch Office: CYEC Scotland; Development Officer, 30 Wyvis Crescent, Conon Bridge, Dingwall, Highland, IV7 8BZ; tel: 01349 861110; fax: 01349 861110; e-mail: cyecscotland@btinternet.com

COMMUNICATIONS POLICY PROGRAMME (CPJRU)

City University, Northampton Square, London, EC1V 0HB

Tel: 020 7040 8908
Fax: 020 7040 8558
E-mail: socscipg@city.ac.uk
Website: www.city.ac.uk/human/sociology
Website: www.staff.city.ac.uk/p.iosifidis

Enquiries to: Director
Direct e-mail: p.iosifidis@city.ac.uk

Founded: 1984; formerly called Communications Policy and Journalism Research Unit, Communications Policy Centre

Organisation type and purpose: University department or institute.

Subject coverage: Communications Policy; New Media Technologies; Information Society.

Access to staff: Contact by letter, by telephone, by fax and by e-mail
Hours: Mon to Fri, 0900 to 1700

COMMUNIST PARTY OF BRITAIN (CPB)

BCM Box 928, London WC1N 3XX

Tel: 020 7254 8444
E-mail: office@cpgb.org.uk
Website: www.cpgb.org.uk

Enquiries to: Organiser

Founded: 1998; formerly called Communist Party of Great Britain (CPGB) (year of change 1991)

Organisation type and purpose: National organisation (membership is by subscription), present number of members: 1,350.
Political party.

Publications: Printed

Publications list: Available in print

Access to staff: Contact by letter, by telephone, by fax and by e-mail
Hours: Mon to Fri, 0900 to 1700

Access for disabled people: Parking provided, access to all public areas

COMMUNITIES AND LOCAL GOVERNMENT AND DEPARTMENT FOR TRANSPORT (CLG/DfT)

Information Centre, Eland House, Bressenden Place, London, SW1E 5DU

Tel: 0303 444 1111
Website: www.dft.gov.uk
Website: www.communities.gov.uk

Founded: 2002

Organisation type and purpose: National government body.

Subject coverage: Provides an internal service to policy divisions of Communities and Local Government and Department for Transport. Subject areas cover devolution and the regions, housing, homelessness, urban policy, planning, local and regional government, neighbourhood renewal, social exclusion, rent assessment panels and fire services. For DfT: railways and aviation, transport strategy, roads, local transport, maritime transport.

Non-library collection catalogue: All or part available in-house

Library catalogue: All or part available in-house

Order printed publications from: CLG and DfT Publications, Cambertown Ltd, Cambertown House, Goldthorpe Industrial Estate, Goldthorpe, Rotherham, S63 9BL; tel: 0300 123 1124

Publications list: Available online

Access to staff: Contact by letter, by telephone, by e-mail and via website. Appointment necessary.
Hours: Mon to Fri, 0900 to 1700

COMMUNITIES SCOTLAND

Thistle House, 91 Haymarket Terrace, Edinburgh, EH12 5HE

Tel: 0131 313 0044
Fax: 0131 313 2680
E-mail: ceu@scotland.gsi.gov.uk
Website: www.communitiesscotland.gov.uk

Enquiries to: Librarian
Direct tel: 0131 479 5016
Direct e-mail: johnstoner@communitiesscotland.gov.uk

Founded: 2001; formerly called Housing Corporation in Scotland, Scottish Special Housing Association; formerly called Scottish Homes (year of change 1989–2001)

Organisation type and purpose: National government body.
The national housing agency for Scotland.

Subject coverage: Wide-ranging information on all aspects of housing in Scotland, including joint funding arrangements, establishment and funding of housing associations and housing co-operatives; approval of landlords; urban renewal; housing management; modernisation and rehabilitation techniques; private developers; rural housing.

Library catalogue: All or part available in-house

Publications: Printed

Access to staff: Contact by letter, by telephone and by e-mail. Appointment necessary.
Hours: Mon to Thu, 0830 to 1700; Fri, 0830 to 1630

Access to building: Prior appointment required

Access for disabled people: Ramped entry, toilet facilities

COMMUNITY ACTION NORTHUMBERLAND (CAN)

Tower Buildings, 9 Oldgate, Morpeth, Northumberland, NE61 1PY

Tel: 01670 517178
Fax: 01670 511400
E-mail: info@ca-north.org.uk
Website: www.ca-north.org.uk

Enquiries to: Director
Direct e-mail: davidfrancis@ca-north.org.uk

Founded: 1951; formerly called Northumberland Rural Community Council; (year of change 1974); formerly called Community Council of Northumberland (year of change 2007)

Organisation type and purpose: Voluntary organisation, registered charity (charity number 224798). Community development and voluntary sector support.

Subject coverage: Voluntary organisations, community initiatives and parish councils in Northumberland. Information needed by these groups, e.g. grant aid, law, project development, working together, further sources of help.

Publications: Printed

Access to staff: Contact by letter, by telephone, by fax, by e-mail and in person. Appointment necessary.
Hours: Mon to Thu, 0900 to 1700; Fri, 0900 to 1630

Affiliated to: ACRE; NAVCA; Voluntary Organisations Network North East

COMMUNITY AND DISTRICT NURSING ASSOCIATION (CDNA)

32–38 Uxbridge Road, Ealing, London, W5 2BS

Tel: 020 8280 5342
Fax: 020 8280 5341
E-mail: info@cdnaonline.org
Website: www.cdna.tvu.ac.uk

Enquiries to: Chairman
Other contacts: Professional Officer for information on professional and clinical issues.

Founded: 1971

Organisation type and purpose: Professional body, trade union (membership is by subscription), present number of members: 5,500.

Access to staff: Contact by letter, by telephone, by fax, by e-mail and via website
Hours: Mon to Fri, 0900 to 1700

COMMUNITY AND YOUTH WORKERS' UNION, THE (CYWU)

302 The Argent Centre, 60 Frederick Street, Birmingham, B31 3HS

Tel: 0121 233 3344
Fax: 0121 344 3345
E-mail: kerry@cywu.org.uk
Website: www.cywu.org.uk

Enquiries to: Administrator
Direct e-mail: kerry.jenkins@unitetheunion.org

Founded: 1938

Organisation type and purpose: Trade union (membership is by subscription), present number of members: 4,500.

Subject coverage: Community and youth work.

Publications: Printed
Order printed publications from: CYWU

Pepar Publications
The Gatehouse, 112 Park Hill Road, Harborne, Birmingham, B17 0HD
Russell House Publishing Limited
4 St George's House, Uplyme Road Business Park, Lyme Regis, DT7 3LS

Publications list: Available in print

Access to staff: Contact by e-mail
Hours: Mon to Fri, 0900 to 1700

Affiliated to: GFTU; TUC

COMMUNITY COMPOSTING NETWORK (CCN)

67 Alexandra Road, Sheffield, South Yorkshire, S2 3EE

Tel: 0114 258 0483
Fax: 0114 258 0483
E-mail: info@communitycompost.org
Website: www.communitycompost.org

Enquiries to: Co-ordinator

Founded: 1995

Organisation type and purpose: National organisation, membership association (membership is by subscription), present number of members: 200, voluntary organisation.
Provides advice and support to existing and 'would be' community composting projects across the UK.

Publications: Printed

continued overleaf

Access to staff: Contact by letter, by telephone, by fax, by e-mail and via website. Appointment necessary.
Hours: Mon to Fri, 0900 to 1700

COMMUNITY COUNCIL FOR BERKSHIRE (CCB)

Abbey House, 1650 Arlington Business Park, Theale, RG7 4SA

Tel: 0118 961 2000
Fax: 0118 961 2600
E-mail: admin@ccberks.org.uk
Website: www.ccberks.org.uk

Founded: 1973

Organisation type and purpose: Voluntary organisation, registered charity (charity number 1056367).
To enable all people, communities and organisations to work better by working together.

Subject coverage: Information on rural communities in Berkshire, funding advice, community buildings information and advice service, village shops, rural disadvantage, community developments, community training, training on how to connect with hard-to-reach groups, etc.

Access to staff: Contact by letter, by telephone, by fax and by e-mail. Appointment necessary.
Hours: Mon to Fri, 0900 to 1700

Access to building: Prior appointment required

COMMUNITY COUNCIL OF DEVON

First Floor, 3 & 4 Cranmere Court, Lustleigh Close, Matford Business Park, Exeter, EX2 8PW

Tel: 01392 248919
E-mail: info@devonrcc.org.uk
Website: www.devonrcc.org.uk

Enquiries to: Chief Executive
Other contacts: (1) Parish Councils Officer (2) Playing Fields Officer for (1) information on Parish Councils (2) information and advice on playing fields.

Founded: 1961

Organisation type and purpose: Voluntary organisation, registered charity (charity number 1074047).
Rural community council.

Subject coverage: Village halls in Devon, Parish Council contacts in Devon, Charities Information Bureau, Devon Playing Fields Association, information on sources of funding, community development, parish appraisals, children's play in Devon.

Publications: Printed

Access to staff: Contact by letter, by telephone, by e-mail and in person
Hours: Mon to Fri, 0900 to 1700

COMMUNITY COUNCIL OF SHROPSHIRE (CCS)

1 College Hill, Shrewsbury, Shropshire, SY1 1LT

Tel: 01743 360641
Fax: 01743 233335
E-mail: Julia.baron@shropshire-rcc.org.uk
Website: www.collegehill.org.uk

Enquiries to: Director

Founded: 1961

Organisation type and purpose: Registered charity (charity number 218783), training organisation.

Subject coverage: Advice for voluntary organisations, especially in rural areas, rural transport, rural housing, promotion of volunteering, funding, training, charities, parish councils.

Publications: Printed

Publications list: Available in print

Access to staff: Contact by letter, by telephone, by fax, by e-mail and in person
Hours: Mon to Fri, 0900 to 1700

Member of: Federation of Rural Community Councils; William House, Skipton Road, Skelton, York, YO3 6XW

COMMUNITY DEVELOPMENT FOUNDATION (CDF)

Unit 5, Angel Gate, 320–326 City Road, London, EC1V 2PT

Tel: 020 7833 1772
Fax: 020 7837 6584
E-mail: admin@cdf.org.uk
Website: www.cdf.org.uk

Founded: 1968; formerly called Community Projects Foundation

Organisation type and purpose: Social enterprise, registered charity (charity number 1139975), consultancy, research organisation.
Promotion of community development.

Subject coverage: Community development, community work, social policy, environment and planning, housing, health, education, social welfare, local government, economic development, employment and unemployment, voluntary sector; youth work, ethnic and racial issues, poverty, regeneration, social inclusion and capacity building.

Non-library collection catalogue: All or part available in-house

Library catalogue: All or part available in-house

Publications: Printed, and electronic and video

Publications list: Available online and in print

Access to staff: Contact by letter, by telephone, by fax, by e-mail and via website. Appointment necessary.
Hours: Mon to Fri, 0900 to 1700

Access to building: Prior appointment required

Access for disabled people: *Special comments:* No wheelchair access.

COMMUNITY FIRST

Wyndhams, St Joseph's Place, Devizes, Wiltshire, SN10 1DD

Tel: 01380 722475
Fax: 01380 728476
E-mail: reception@communityfirst.org.uk

Enquiries to: Director

Founded: 1965

Organisation type and purpose: Membership association (membership is by subscription), voluntary organisation, registered charity (charity number 288117).
Working in partnership with communities and funders to encourage and support social, economic and environmental initiatives in Wiltshire and Swindon.

Subject coverage: Rural community development, village halls, sports clubs, children's play, parish and town councils, funding and support for voluntary groups, rural projects and services, rural housing, community transport, rural policy, rural economic development.

Publications: Printed

Publications list: Available in print

Access to staff: Contact by letter, by telephone and by e-mail. Appointment necessary.
Hours: Mon to Thu, 0900 to 1700; Fri, 0900 to 1600

Access for disabled people: Parking provided, ramped entry, toilet facilities

Member of: ACRE Network of Rural Community Councils

COMMUNITY FIRST IN HEREFORDSHIRE AND WORCESTERSHIRE

141 Church Street, Malvern, Worcestershire, WR14 2AN

Tel: 01684 573334
Fax: 01684 573367
E-mail: info@comfirst.org.uk
Website: www.comfirst.org.uk

Enquiries to: Chief Executive Officer

Founded: 1975; formerly called Rural Community Council; formerly called Community Council of Hereford and Worcester (year of change 2001)

Organisation type and purpose: Voluntary organisation, registered charity (charity number 703072).
Sub-regional development agency working with communities and voluntary organisations in Herefordshire and Worcestershire.
Mission – To build better communities.

Subject coverage: Rural transport initiatives, learning and skills in the voluntary sector, information and training for voluntary sector, community resource centres, village halls in Herefordshire and Worcestershire; ICT support for voluntary sector, business advice, social enterprise support.

Publications: Printed

Publications list: Available in print

Access to staff: Contact by letter, by telephone, by fax, by e-mail and via website. Appointment necessary.
Hours: Mon to Fri, 0900 to 1700

Access to building: Prior appointment required

Access for disabled people: Parking provided, ramped entry, toilet facilities

Other offices: Community First – Hereford Office; 41a Bridge Street, Hereford; tel: 01432 267820

COMMUNITY FOUNDATION FOR NORTHERN IRELAND (NIVT)

City Link, Albert House, Belfast, BT12 4HQ

Tel: 028 9024 5927
Fax: 028 9032 9839
E-mail: info@communityfoundation.org

Enquiries to: Director

Founded: 1979

Organisation type and purpose: Registered charity (charity number XN45242).

Access to staff: Contact by letter
Hours: Mon to Fri, 0900 to 1700

COMMUNITY FOUNDATION NETWORK

Arena House, 66–68 Pentonville Road, London, N1 9HS

Tel: 020 7713 9326
Fax: 020 7713 9327
E-mail: network@communityfoundations.org.uk
Website: www.communityfoundations.org.uk

Enquiries to: Director

Founded: 1991; formerly called Association of Community Trusts and Foundations (ACTAF) (year of change 1999)

Organisation type and purpose:
Membership association (membership is by subscription), present number of members: 68, voluntary organisation, registered charity (charity number 1004630).
Membership is restricted to active community foundations, although any interested body may subscribe as an associate.
Promotion, support and development of community foundations throughout the UK.

Subject coverage: Community foundation development and management.

Trade and statistical information: Fund development and grant-making in community foundations in UK. Advice on the development of community foundations

Library catalogue: All or part available in-house

Publications: Printed

Publications list: Available online and in print

Access to staff: Contact by letter, by telephone, by fax, by e-mail and via website. Appointment necessary.
Hours: Mon to Fri, 0900 to 1700

COMMUNITY LINCS

The Old Mart, Church Lane, Sleaford, Lincolnshire, NG34 7DF

Tel: 01529 302466
Fax: 01529 414267
E-mail: office@communitylincs.com
Website: www.communitylincs.com

Enquiries to: Chief Executive's PA
Direct e-mail: teresa.palmer@communitylincs.com

Founded: 1927

Organisation type and purpose: Voluntary organisation, registered charity (charity number 1046569). Rural Community Development.

Subject coverage: Rural development in Lincolnshire.

Publications: Printed

Publications list: Available in print

Access to staff: Contact by letter, by telephone, by fax and by e-mail. Appointment necessary.
Hours: Mon to Fri, 0900 to 1700

Access for disabled people: Ramped entry, access to all public areas, toilet facilities

Affiliated to: Federation of Rural Community Councils

Connections with: Lincolnshire Association of Local Councils; Lincolnshire Playing Fields Association

COMMUNITY MATTERS

12–20 Baron Street, Islington, London, N1 9LL

Tel: 020 7837 7887
Fax: 020 7278 9253

Enquiries to: Chief Executive
Other contacts: Performance Improvement & Information Manager

Founded: 1945; formerly called National Federation of Community Organisations (NFCO)

Organisation type and purpose:
Membership association (membership is by subscription), present number of members: 1,500 member organisations, voluntary organisation, registered charity (charity number 1002383), training organisation, consultancy, research organisation, publishing house.
To support and help develop local community groups and associations and make sure their interests are represented locally and nationally.

Subject coverage: Good management of charities and community organisations; managing community activities; managing social contractual relations; managing community premises, legislation affecting charities and voluntary organisations managing buildings.

Publications: Printed, and electronic and video

Publications list: Available in print

Access to staff: Contact by letter, by telephone, by fax and by e-mail. Appointment necessary. Non-members charged.
Hours: Mon to Fri, 0900 to 1700

Affiliated to: Community Sector Coalition; International Federation of Settlements; National Council for Voluntary Organisations

COMMUNITY MEDIA ASSOCIATION (CMA)

15 Paternoster Row, Sheffield, South Yorkshire, S1 2BX

Tel: 0114 279 5219
Fax: 0114 279 8976
E-mail: admin@commedia.org.uk
Website: www.commedia.org.uk

Enquiries to: Financial/Office Manager

Founded: 1983; formerly called Community Radio Association (CRA) (year of change 1997)

Organisation type and purpose: National organisation, membership association (membership is by subscription), present number of members: 600, voluntary organisation, training organisation, consultancy.
The CMA's primary purpose is to support the development of local media projects for community-based, creative and cultural expression, community development, information and entertainment. Media forms include community radio, community TV, cable broadcasting and multimedia on the internet.

Subject coverage: Community Radio – general information on start up, training, fundraising, consultancy, licence application. Community media including TV, cable and internet broadcasting.

Collection: Airflash – Complete Set
Broadcast – Hard Copies Only
The Radio Magazine – Hard Copies Only

Non-library collection catalogue: All or part available in-house and in print

Publications: Printed

Publications list: Available online and in print

Access to staff: Contact by letter, by telephone, by fax, by e-mail and via website. Appointment necessary.
Hours: Mon to Fri, 0930 to 1730

Access to building: Prior appointment required
Hours: Mon to Fri, 0930 to 1730

Access for disabled people: Access to all public areas, toilet facilities

Member organisation of: World Association of Community Radio Broadcasters (AMARC); 705 Bourget, bureau 100, Montreal, Quebec, H2C 2M6, Canada; tel: +1 514 982 0351; fax: +1 514 849 7129; website: http://www.amarc.org

COMMUNITY MUSIC WALES (CMW)

2 Leckwith Place, Canton, Cardiff, CF11 6QA

Tel: 029 2038 7620
Fax: 029 2023 3022
E-mail: admin@communitymusicwales.org.uk
Website: www.communitymusicwales.org.uk

Enquiries to: Administrator
Direct e-mail: gethin.evans@communitymusicwales.org.uk

Founded: 1990

continued overleaf

Organisation type and purpose: Voluntary organisation, registered charity (charity number 1009867), training organisation. Concerned with developing music projects, targeting groups of people who, through reasons of disability or disadvantage, have little chance of taking part in mainstream music activities.

Subject coverage: Use of music technology in working with people with disabilities, training for community practitioners, role of music in working with young people at risk.

Collection: Small library of reference books

Access to staff: Contact by letter, by telephone and by fax. Appointment necessary.
Hours: Mon to Fri, 0900 to 1700

Access for disabled people: Level entry, toilet facilities

COMMUNITY PRACTITIONERS AND HEALTH VISITING ASSOCIATION (Unite/CPHVA)

128 Theobald's Road, London, WC1X 8TN

Tel: 020 7611 2500
E-mail: infocphva@unitetheunion.org
Website: www.unitetheunion.org/cphva
Website: www.cphvabookshop.com

Founded: 1896

Organisation type and purpose: National organisation, trade union, membership association (membership is by subscription). The CPHVA is an autonomous body of Unite. It gives information on professional issues and labour relations to members.

Subject coverage: Health visiting, child care and development, community care of elderly and handicapped, health promotion, accident prevention, community nursing, clinical effectiveness, practice nursing, school nursing, mental health.

Information services: Archives of the Association, available from The Wellcome Institute, 183 Euston Road, London, NW1 2BE.

Non-library collection catalogue: All or part available online and in-house

Library catalogue: All or part available online and in-house

Publications: Printed
Order printed publications from: McMillan Scott, Garrard House, 2–6 Homesdale Road, Bromley, Kent, BR2 2WL; tel. 020 8249 4454; fax 020 8289 7955

Publications list: Available online and in print

Access to staff: Contact by letter, by telephone, by fax, by e-mail, in person and via website. Access for members only.

Access to building: *Special comments:* Library and information service for members only.

Constituent part of: Unite – The Union; 128 Theobald's Road, London, WC1X 8TN; tel: 020 7611 2500; fax: 020 7611 2555; website: http://www.unitetheunion.org

COMMUNITY SELF BUILD AGENCY (CSBA)

Swale Foyer, Bridge Road, Sheerness, Kent, ME12 1RH

Tel: 01795 663 073
Fax: 01795 581 804
E-mail: info@communityselfbuildagency.org.uk
Website: www.communityselfbuildagency.org.uk

Enquiries to: Director
Direct e-mail: j.gillespie@communityselfbuildagency.org.uk

Founded: 1989

Organisation type and purpose: National organisation.
To promote and advise on the development of community self build housing projects for those in housing need.

Subject coverage: Community Self Build, where a group of local people in housing need come together to build homes for themselves.

Publications: Printed

Publications list: Available in print

Access to staff: Contact by letter, by telephone and by e-mail. Appointment necessary.
Hours: Mon to Fri, 0930 to 1730

COMMUNITY SERVICE VOLUNTEERS (CSV)

237 Pentonville Road, London, N1 9NJ

Tel: 020 7278 6601
Fax: 020 7833 0149
E-mail: information@csv.org.uk
Website: www.csv.org.uk

Founded: 1962

Organisation type and purpose: National organisation, voluntary organisation, registered charity (charity number 291222).

Subject coverage: Volunteering and employment and media training.
Volunteering for young people, older people, employees and students. Mentoring and befriending, work with young offenders, social action broadcasting, citizenship in schools, the environment, Millennium Awards, Millennium Volunteers, advice and expertise in volunteer management. Make a Difference Day – the largest single day of volunteering – is co-ordinated by CSV.

Publications: Printed

Publications list: Available online and in print

Access to staff: Contact by letter, by telephone, by fax, by e-mail and via website
Hours: Mon to Fri, 0900 to 1730

Access for disabled people: Level entry, toilet facilities

COMMUNITY TRANSPORT ASSOCIATION (CTA)

Highbank, Halton Street, Hyde, Cheshire, SK14 2NY

Tel: 0161 351 1475
Fax: 0161 351 7221
E-mail: info@ctauk.org
Website: www.ctauk.org

Enquiries to: Advice Service
Direct tel: 0845 130 6195
Direct e-mail: advice@ctauk.org

Founded: 1978

Organisation type and purpose: National organisation, advisory body, trade association (membership is by subscription), present number of members: 1,500, voluntary organisation, registered charity (charity number 1002222), training organisation, consultancy.
Representation and support services for non-profit transport sector.

Subject coverage: All aspects of non-profit transport operations; service planning and development; accessibility and technical equipment; community development; employment and volunteering issues.

Information services: Advice and information for operators of not-for-profit transport.

Collection: Historical records of CTA
Photograph library

Publications: Printed

Publications list: Available online

Access to staff: Contact by letter, by telephone, by fax and by e-mail
Hours: Mon to Fri, 0900 to 1700

COMPANIES HOUSE

Crown Way, Cardiff, CF14 3UZ

Tel: 030 3123 4500
Fax: 029 2038 0900
E-mail: enquiries@companieshouse.gov.uk
Website: www.companieshouse.gov.uk

Enquiries to: Cardiff Contact Centre
Direct e-mail: press@companieshouse.gov.uk

Founded: 1844

Organisation type and purpose: National government body. To incorporate limited companies and to maintain a register of information on them for public information.

Subject coverage: Information on limited companies entered in the register.

Publications: Printed, and electronic and video

Access to staff: Contact by letter, by telephone, by fax, by e-mail, in person and via website. All charged.
Hours: Mon to Fri, 0900 to 1700

Also at: Companies House; London Search Room, 21 Bloomsbury Street, London, WC1B 3XD; tel: 0870 333 3636; fax: 029 2038 0900

Executive Agency of: Department for Business, Enterprise and Regulatory Reform

COMPANIES HOUSE SCOTLAND

37 Castle Terrace, Edinburgh, EH1 2EB

Tel: 0870 333 3636
Fax: 0131 535 5820
Website: www.companieshouse.gov.uk

Enquiries to: Registrar
Direct tel: 0131 535 5855
Direct fax: 0131 535 5879

Direct e-mail: jhenderson@companieshouse.gov.uk

Founded: 1856; formerly called Companies Registration Office (year of change 1988)

Organisation type and purpose: National government body, statutory body.
Executive agency within the Department of Trade and Industry.
To incorporate and dissolve limited companies, to examine and file documents relating to the Companies Act, to make this information available to the public.

Subject coverage: Information on Scottish limited companies from statutory documents filed by the company directors, including financial information, details of directors, capital changes and members.

Publications: Printed, and electronic and video, and microform publications

Publications list: Available in print

Access to staff: Contact by letter, by telephone, by fax, by e-mail and via website. Appointment necessary.
Hours: Mon to Fri, 0900 to 1700
Special comments: Closed on Public and Bank Holidays.

Head Office: Companies House; Crown Way, Cardiff, CF4 3UZ; tel: 0870 3333636; fax: 029 2038 0900

Other branches at: Companies House; 25 Queen Street, Leeds, LS 2TW; tel: 0113 233 8338; fax: 0113 233 8335; Companies House; 75 Mosley Street, Manchester, M2 2HR; tel: 0161 236 7500; fax: 0161 237 5258; Companies House; Central Library, Chamberlain Square, Birmingham, B3 3HQ; tel: 0121 233 9047; fax: 0121 233 9052; Companies House; 7 West George Street, Glasgow, G2 1BQ; tel: 0141 221 5513; fax: 0141 221 3244

COMPANY OF DESIGNERS

232 Kempshott Lane, Basingstoke, Hampshire, RG22 5LR

Tel: 01256 472757
E-mail: mike-preedy@company-of-designers.co.uk

Enquiries to: Managing Director

Founded: 1995

Organisation type and purpose: Service industry, consultancy, publishing house.
Design consultancy.
Design for print: books, annual reports and accounts, brochures, leaflets, promotional literature

Access to staff: Contact by letter, by telephone and by e-mail
Hours: Mon to Fri, 0900 to 1700

Access to building: Prior appointment required

COMPANY OF SECURITY PROFESSIONALS

Formal name: Worshipful Company of Security Professionals

Willowcroft, Old Forest Road, Winnersh, Wokingham, Berkshire, RG41 1HY

Tel: 01189 794675
Fax: 01189 794675
E-mail: clerk@wcosp.org
Website: www.professionalsecurity.co.uk/company

Enquiries to: Clerk
Direct e-mail: john@troon.wanadoo.co.uk

Organisation type and purpose: To promote, support and encourage standards of excellence, integrity and honourable practice in conducting the profession of security practitioners and to aid societies and other organisations connected to the security profession.

Access to staff: Contact by letter, by telephone and by e-mail

COMPANY OF WATERMEN AND LIGHTERMEN OF THE RIVER THAMES (Company of Watermen)

Watermen's Hall, 16 St Mary Hill, London, EC3R 8EF

Tel: 020 7283 2373
Fax: 020 7283 0477
E-mail: admin@watermenshall.org
Website: www.watermenshall.org

Enquiries to: Clerk

Founded: 1555

Organisation type and purpose: Statutory body, membership association (membership is by election or invitation), present number of members: 400, voluntary organisation, training organisation.
A working guild promoting the work of watermen and lightermen on the River Thames, training apprentices and having charitable interests.

Subject coverage: Watermen and Lightermen of the River Thames.

Library catalogue: All or part available in-house

Publications: Printed
Order printed publications from: Watermen's Hall

Publications list: Available online and in print

Access to staff: Contact by letter, by telephone, by fax, by e-mail, in person and via website. Appointment necessary. Non-members charged.
Hours: Mon to Fri, 0900 to 1700

Access to building: By appointment
Hours: Mon to Fri, 0900 to 1700

Access for disabled people: Accessible, lift to all floors
Special comments: Disabled access entrance at 16 St Mary-at-Hill

COMPASSIONATE FRIENDS, THE (TCF)

53 North Street, Bedminster, Bristol, BS3 1EN * from Aug. 1st will be 14 New King Street, Deptford, London, SE8 3HS

Tel: 0845 120 3785
Fax: 0845 120 3786
E-mail: helpline@tcf.org.uk
Website: www.tcf.org.uk

Enquiries to: Helpline Co-ordinator
Direct tel: 0845 123 2304

Founded: 1969

Organisation type and purpose: National organisation, registered charity (charity number 1082335).
Offers support and friendship to bereaved parents and their families after the death of a child or children of any age and from any cause

Subject coverage: Support and friendship for bereaved parents and their families by those with a similar experience.

Publications: Printed

Publications list: Available online and in print

Access to staff: Contact by letter, by telephone, by fax, by e-mail and via website
Hours: Mon to Fri, 0930 to 1700.

Subsidiary body: Support in Bereavement for Brothers and Sisters (SIBBS); At same address

COMPETITION COMMISSION (CC)

Victoria House, Southampton Row, London, WC1B 4AD

Tel: 020 7271 0100
Fax: 020 7271 0367
E-mail: info@cc.gsi.gov.uk
Website: www.competition-commission.org.uk

Enquiries to: Information Centre Manager

History of institution: formerly called Monopolies and Mergers Commission (MMC) (year of change 1999)

Organisation type and purpose: Statutory body.

Subject coverage: Monopolies; mergers; industrial economics; competition policy.

Publications list: Available online and in print

Constituent part of: Department for Business, Enterprise and Regulatory Reform (BERR)

COMPLEMENTARY THERAPISTS ASSOCIATION

PO Box 6955, Towcester, NN12 6WZ

Tel: 0845 202 2941
Fax: 0844 779 8898
E-mail: info@complementary.assoc.org.uk
Website: www.complementary.assoc.org.uk

Enquiries to: Administrator

Founded: 2003; created by the merger of The International Therapists Examination Council (ITEC) and the Guild of Complementary Practitioners (GCP, which had previously merged with the Holistic Association of Reflexologists)

Organisation type and purpose: National organisation, professional body (membership is by subscription, qualification).
Member of the Parliamentary Group for Alternative & Complementary Medicine.
To maintain a national and international register of professional members, available to the general public and to other professionals.

continued overleaf

To establish standards of professional training and qualification appropriate to the various disciplines.

Subject coverage: Complementary medicine including aromatherapy, massage, reflexology, sports therapy, nutrition, Shiatsu, homoeopathy and Reiki.

Publications: Printed, and electronic and video, and microform publications

Access to staff: Contact by letter, by telephone, by fax, by e-mail and via website
Hours: Mon to Fri, 0900 to 1700

Affiliated to: British School of Reflexology

Member of: British Complementary Medicine Association

COMPLIANCE INSTITUTE

107 Barkby Road, Leicester, LE4 9LG

Tel: 0116 246 1316
Fax: 0116 274 2239
E-mail: hlacey.compinst@nsconnect.co.uk
Website: www.complianceinstitute.co.uk/

Enquiries to: Secretary

Founded: 1990; formerly called UK Association of Compliance Officers (year of change 1997)

Organisation type and purpose: Professional body (membership is by subscription).

Subject coverage: Regulation – guide and assistance to Compliance staff.

Publications: Printed

Access to staff: Contact by letter
Hours: Mon to Fri, 0900 to 1700

COMPOSITES PROCESSING ASSOCIATION LIMITED (CPA)

Sarum Lodge, St Anne's Court, Talygarn, Pontyclun, Mid Glamorgan, CF72 9HH

Tel: 01443 228867
Fax: 01443 239083
E-mail: info@composites-proc-assoc.co.uk
Website: www.composites-proc-assoc.co.uk

Enquiries to: Association Secretary

Founded: 1989

Organisation type and purpose: Trade association, consultancy.

Subject coverage: Raw materials, manufacturing processes, applications, research and development activity, technical exchange, international activity as related to reinforced plastic composites.

Trade and statistical information: National and international composites industry, market statistics, market sectors, data on composite shipments worldwide

Access to staff: Contact by letter, by telephone, by fax, by e-mail and via website. Appointment necessary.
Hours: Mon to Fri, 0900 to 1700

Member of: American Composites Manufacturers Association; Composites Fabricators Association, 1655 North Fort Myer Drive, Suite 510, Arlington, VA22209, USA; tel: +1 703 525 0511; fax: +1 703 525 0743; e-mail: info@acmanet.org; website: http://www.acmanet.org

COMPUTER USERS FORUM (CUF)

95 Galpins Road, Thornton Heath, Surrey CR7 6EN

Tel: 0791 7117 279
E-mail: tyneham@yahoo.com

Enquiries to: Parveez

Founded: 1980

Organisation type and purpose: Advisory body, professional body, membership association (membership is by subscription, election or invitation), present number of members: over 5,000, training organisation, consultancy, research organisation.

Subject coverage: Expertise and knowledge in the use of computers.

Education services: Training

Access to staff: Contact by e-mail. All charged.
Hours: Mon to Fri, 0900 to 1700

Access to building: No access other than to staff

COMPUTING SUPPLIERS FEDERATION (CSF)

26–27 Brookside Business Park, Colde Meece, Stone, Staffordshire, ST15 0TZ

Tel: 01785 769090
Fax: 01785 769082
Website: www.csf.org.uk

Enquiries to: Managing Director

Founded: 1985; formerly called Computer Graphics Suppliers Association (CGSA) (year of change 1995); formerly called Association of Visual Communicators (AVC) (year of change 1997)

Organisation type and purpose: Trade association (membership is by subscription, qualification, election or invitation), present number of members: 200.
The CSF is a not-for-profit trade association representing specialist sectors of the IT industry.

Subject coverage: Information management, imaging and workflow. CAD, CAM, PDM, EDM and other engineering applications, platforms and IT peripherals (including monitors, printers, workstations and storage equipment). Electronic presentations equipment (including projectors, video communications and conferencing systems).

Non-library collection catalogue: All or part available online and in print

Publications: Printed

Publications list: Available online

Access to staff: Contact via website
Hours: Mon to Fri, 0900 to 1700

Access for disabled people: Parking provided, level entry, access to all public areas

CONCHOLOGICAL SOCIETY OF GREAT BRITAIN AND IRELAND (CSGBI)

1 Court Farm, Hillfarrance, Taunton, Somerset, TA4 1AN

Tel: 01823 461482
E-mail: c_m_gillard@compuserve.com
Website: www.conchsoc.org

Enquiries to: General Secretary

Founded: 1876

Organisation type and purpose: Learned society (membership is by subscription), present number of members: 420, registered charity (charity number 208205), suitable for ages: all.
To promote the study of the Mollusca in all its aspects.

Subject coverage: Distribution of molluscs, marine and non-marine in the United Kingdom, conservation of molluscan species and their habitats, environmental impact assessment, in general all aspects of conchology world-wide, marine, non-marine and fossil.

Collection: Distribution records
Non-marine held at NHM
Marine computerised database

Trade and statistical information: Holds national records of non-marine and marine biogeographical distribution

Non-library collection catalogue: All or part available in-house and in print

Publications: Printed
Order printed publications from: CSGBI, Hilliers
Freith, Henley on Thames, Oxon, RG9 6PJ

Publications list: Available in print

Access to staff: Contact by letter, by telephone, by e-mail and via website
Hours: After 1700 weekdays and weekends
Special comments: Please note that all officers of the Society are volunteers.

Affiliated to: Council for Nature

CONCORD MEDIA

The Rosehill Centre, 22 Hines Road, Ipswich, Suffolk, IP3 9BG

Tel: 01473 726012
E-mail: sales@concordmedia.org.uk
Website: www.concordmedia.org.uk

Enquiries to: Office Manager

Founded: 1965; formerly called Concord Film Council (year of change 1984); formerly called Concord Video & Film Council (year of change 2006)

Organisation type and purpose: Registered charity, public library.
Video and film library.

Subject coverage: Social sciences, arts, development education, peace, counselling, medical and mental health.

Library catalogue: All or part available online

Publications: Printed, and electronic and video

Publications list: Available online and in print

Access to staff: Contact by letter, by telephone and by e-mail
Hours: Mon, Tue, Thu, Fri, 0900 to 1700; closed Wed

Access for disabled people: Parking provided, level entry, toilet facilities

CONCRETE ADVISORY SERVICE (CAS)

Riverside House, 4 Meadows Business Park, Station Approach, Blackwater, Camberley, Surrey, GU17 9AB

Tel: 01276 607140
Fax: 01276 607141
Website: www.concrete.org.uk

Organisation type and purpose: National organisation, advisory body, membership association (membership is by subscription), consultancy.
Specialist consultancy in concrete and cementitious materials and applications.

Subject coverage: Concrete and cementitious materials, design, construction, application, trouble-shooting.

Non-library collection catalogue: All or part available online

Publications: Printed

Publications list: Available online and in print

Access to staff: Contact by letter and by telephone. Access for members only. All charged.
Hours: Mon to Fri, 0900 to 1730

Parent body: Concrete Society; At the same address

CONCRETE PIPE ASSOCIATION (CPA)

Tournai Hall, Evelyn Woods Road, Aldershot, Hampshire, GU11 2LL

Tel: 01252 357834
Fax: 01252 357831
E-mail: lauren.fairley@corrosionprevention.org.uk
Website: www.corrosionprevention.org.uk

Enquiries to: Director

Founded: 1932

Organisation type and purpose: Trade association.

Subject coverage: Manufacture and use of precast concrete pipe products for drainage systems; foul and surface water drainage systems.

Publications: Printed, and electronic and video

Publications list: Available in print

Access to staff: Contact by letter, by telephone and by fax
Hours: Mon to Fri, 0900 to 1700
Special comments: Library for members only. Information freely available to enquirers.

Affiliated to: British Precast Concrete Federation; International Bureau of Concrete Manufacturers; International Concrete Pipe Commission

CONCRETE REPAIR ASSOCIATION (CRA)

Tournai Hall, Evelyn Woods Road, Aldershot, Hampshire, GU11 2LL

Tel: 01252 357835
Fax: 01252 357831
E-mail: admin@cra.org.uk
Website: www.concreterepair.org.uk

Enquiries to: Secretary
Direct e-mail: publications@cra.org.uk

Founded: 1989

Organisation type and purpose: Trade association, present number of members: 32.
Represents contractors, manufacturers and consultants involved in the concrete repair industry.

Publications: Printed

Publications list: Available in print

Access to staff: Contact by letter, by telephone, by fax, by e-mail and via website
Hours: Mon to Fri, 0900 to 1700

CONCRETE SOCIETY

Riverside House, 4 Meadows Business Park, Station Approach, Blackwater, Camberley, Surrey, GU17 9AB

Tel: 01276 607140
Fax: 01276 607141
Website: www.concrete.org.uk
Website: www.concretebookshop.com

Founded: 1966

Organisation type and purpose: Learned society.

Subject coverage: Concrete in the construction industry.

Information services: contact: Manager, Information Services

Education services: contact: Head, Training & Education

Collection: Library, archives and photographic collection established by the former Cement & Concrete Association in 1937

Library catalogue: All or part available online, in-house and in print

Publications: Printed
Order printed publications from: e-mail: enquiries@concretebookshop.com

Publications list: Available online and in print

Access to staff: Contact by letter, by telephone, by fax, by e-mail, in person and via website. Appointment necessary. Non-members charged.
Hours: Mon to Fri, 0900 to 1700

Access to building: *Hours:* Mon to Fri, 0900 to 1700

Administers: Glassfibre Reinforced Concrete Society; tel: 01276 607140; fax: 01276 607141; e-mail: grc_advisor@concrete.org.uk

Links with: Institute of Concrete Technology; tel: 01276 607140; e-mail: k.calverley@concrete.org.uk

CONCRETE TILE MANUFACTURERS' ASSOCIATION (CTMA)

60 Charles Street, Leicester, LE1 1FB

Tel: 0116 253 6161
Fax: 0116 251 4568
E-mail: info@britishprecast.org
Website: www.britishprecast.org

Enquiries to: Secretary

Organisation type and purpose: Trade association.

Subject coverage: Precast concrete roof tiles.

Publications list: Available online

Access to staff: Contact by letter, by telephone, by fax and by e-mail
Hours: Mon to Fri, 0900 to 1700

Links with: British Precast Concrete Federation

CONFED

Formal name: Confederation of Education Service Managers

The Humanities Building, University of Manchester, Oxford Road, Manchester, M13 9PL

Tel: 0161 275 8810
Fax: 0161 275 8811
E-mail: confedoffice@confed.org.uk
Website: www.confed.org.uk

Enquiries to: General Secretary
Other contacts: Administrator, President

Founded: 1972; formed by the merger of Association of Chief Education Officers (ACEO), Society of Chief Inspectors and Advisers (SCIA), Society of Education Officers (SEO) (year of change 2002)

Organisation type and purpose: Professional body (membership is by subscription, qualification), present number of members: 900.

Subject coverage: Administration and management of the education service in local authorities in England and Wales.

Publications list: Available in print

Access to staff: Contact by letter, by telephone, by fax and by e-mail
Hours: Mon to Thu, 0900 to 1700; Fri, 0900 to 1300

CONFEDERATION OF AERIAL INDUSTRIES LIMITED (CAI)

Fulton House Business Centre, Fulton Road, Wembley Park, Middlesex, HA9 0TF

Tel: 020 8902 8998
Fax: 020 8903 8719
E-mail: office@cai.org.uk
Website: www.cai.org.uk

Enquiries to: Secretary
Direct e-mail: suzanne@cai.org.uk

Founded: 1978

Organisation type and purpose: Trade association.

Subject coverage: Aerials, satellite dishes, cables and allied equipment, manufacture, supply, installation.

Trade and statistical information: Training for the industry

Publications: Printed

Access to staff: Contact by letter, by telephone, by fax and by e-mail
Hours: Mon to Fri, 0900 to 1700

CONFEDERATION OF AFRICAN PROFESSIONALS (CAP) UK (CAP UK)

BBI Business Centre, 53 Peckham Park Road, Peckham, London, SE15 6TU

E-mail: capuk@bbinitiative.com

Enquiries to: Chairman/President
Direct e-mail: sunny@sunnylambe.com

Founded: 1998

Organisation type and purpose: International organisation, national organisation, professional body, membership association (membership is by subscription, qualification, election or invitation), present number of members: 200, voluntary organisation, suitable for ages: all, consultancy, research organisation.
To provide a voice and networking opportunity for professionals of African origin.

Access to staff: Contact by letter, by telephone, by fax and by e-mail. Appointment necessary. Letter of introduction required.
Hours: Mon to Fri, 0900 to 1700

Access to building: Prior appointment required

Access for disabled people: Parking provided, level entry, access to all public areas, toilet facilities

CONFEDERATION OF BRITISH INDUSTRY (CBI)

Centre Point, 103 New Oxford Street, London, WC1A 1DU

Tel: 020 7379 7400
Fax: 020 7240 0988 or 1578
Website: www.cbi.org.uk

Enquiries to: Information Officer
Direct tel: 020 7395 8247
Direct e-mail: press.office@cbi.org.uk

Founded: 1965

Organisation type and purpose: Membership association (membership is by subscription), manufacturing industry, service industry.
Representative organisation for member companies, employers organisations and trade associations.

Subject coverage: Public policy (international, national and regional), economic situation and trends, taxation, human resources, industrial relations, conditions of employment, education and training, manufacturing, research and development, overseas affairs, commercial and company law, industrial property law, industrial effluent, energy and water resources, innovation, information society.

Trade and statistical information: See publications

Library catalogue: All or part available in-house

Publications: Printed
Order printed publications from: CBI Publications, tel: 020 7395 8071

Access to staff: Contact by letter, by telephone, by fax and by e-mail. Appointment necessary.
Hours: Mon to Fri, 0930 to 1730

CONFEDERATION OF BRITISH WOOL TEXTILES LIMITED (CBWT)

Textile House, Red Doles Lane, Huddersfield, HD2 1YF

Tel: 01484 346500
Fax: 01484 346501
E-mail: info@cbwt.co.uk
Website: www.cbwt.co.uk

Enquiries to: Administation
Direct e-mail: slawka@cbwt.co.uk

Founded: 1979

Organisation type and purpose: Trade association (membership is by subscription), present number of members: 180.
Promotion and protection of interests of the British wool textiles industry, provision of services to member companies.

Subject coverage: UK wool textile industry; international trade practice and technical specifications relating to the raw materials and end products.

Trade and statistical information: Data on the British wool textile industry

Access to staff: Contact by fax, by e-mail and via website
Hours: Mon to Fri, 0900 to 1700

Member of: British Apparel and Textile Confederation (BATC); tel: 020 7636 7788; fax: 020 7636 7515; e-mail: batc@dial.pipex.com; INTERLAINE (EEC); tel: +32 2 513 06 20; fax: +32 2 514 06 65; International Wool Textile Organization (IWTO); tel: +32 2 513 06 20; fax: +32 2 514 06 65; e-mail: info@iwto.org

CONFEDERATION OF FOREST INDUSTRIES (UK) LTD (ConFor)

59 George Street, Edinburgh, EH2 2JG

Tel: 0131 240 1410
Fax: 0131 240 1411
E-mail: mail@confor.org.uk
Website: www.confor.org.uk

Enquiries to: Chief Executive

Founded: 1983; formed from merged with Forestry and Timber Association (FTA), 2006; formed from Association of Professional Foresters (APF), Timber Growers Association (TGA) (year of change 2002); formerly called Timber Growers United Kingdom Limited (year of change 1994)

Organisation type and purpose: Trade association (membership is by subscription).

Subject coverage: Forestry and woodland ownership. Timber production.

Publications: Printed

Access to staff: Contact by letter, by telephone, by fax, by e-mail and via website

CONFEDERATION OF INDIAN ORGANISATIONS (UK) (CIO)

5 Westminster Bridge Road, London, SE1 7XW

Tel: 020 7928 9889
Fax: 020 7620 4025
E-mail: headoffice@cio.org.uk
Website: www.cio.org.uk

Enquiries to: Chief Executive
Other contacts: Information Officer

Founded: 1975

Organisation type and purpose: National organisation, membership association (membership is by subscription), present number of members: 150, voluntary organisation, registered charity (charity number 1075501), training organisation, research organisation.
A national South Asian umbrella organisation.
Representation of the needs of South Asian community and voluntary organisations.

Subject coverage: Information about South Asians in the UK including statistics, organisations, health issues, information resources in ethnic languages, issue-based participatory research, social policy, service provision, development of innovative models of good practice, promotion of anti-racist practices.

Library catalogue: All or part available in-house

Publications: Printed

Publications list: Available in print

Access to staff: Contact by letter, by telephone and by fax. Appointment necessary.
Hours: Mon to Fri, 0900 to 1700

Other addresses: CIO Leicester Office; 5th Floor, Epic House, Lower Hill Street, Leicester, LE1 3SH; tel: 0116 225 9299; fax: 0116 225 9298

CONFEDERATION OF PAPER INDUSTRIES (CPI)

1 Rivenhall Road, Swindon, Wiltshire, SN5 7BD

Tel: 01793 889600
Fax: 01793 878700
E-mail: cpi@paper.org.uk
Website: www.corrugated.org.uk

Founded: 1974

Organisation type and purpose: Represents the paper chain from the recovery of used paper through papermaking and conversion to distribution.
To be recognised by the UK government, and the community at large, as the authoritative and effective voice of the UK paper-related industry, defending its interests and promoting its achievements and potential.

Subject coverage: Supporting members by identifying, analysing, and resolving issues; informing government, the media and the public; presenting the industry's views in a coherent, consistent and targeted manner.

Information services: Information section on website, including glossary of terms, recycling, papermaking process.

Education services: School information packs for either primary/junior or secondary pupils.

Trade and statistical information: Reference guide of industry statistics, 1989–2009

Publications: Electronic and video
Order electronic and video publications from: Download from website

Publications list: Available online

Access to staff: Contact by letter, by telephone, by fax and by e-mail. Appointment necessary.
Hours: Mon to Fri, 0900 to 1700

Access to building: No access other than to staff

Access for disabled people: Parking provided, toilet facilities

Constituent bodies: Association of Makers of Packaging Papers; Association of Makers of Printing and Writing Papers; Association of Makers of Soft Tissue Papers; Corrugated Case Materials Association

Member organisation of: Confederation of European Paper Industries; Brussels, Belgium

CONFEDERATION OF PASSENGER TRANSPORT UK (CPT)

Drury House, 34–43 Russell Street, London, WC2B 5HA

Tel: 020 7240 3131
Fax: 020 7240 6565
E-mail: chairman@cpt-uk.org
Website: www.cpt-uk.org/

Enquiries to: Public Affairs Officer
Direct e-mail: chrisnice@cpt-uk.org
Other contacts: Assistant Director Public Affairs for media and press enquiries.

History of institution: formerly called Bus and Coach Council

Organisation type and purpose: Trade association.

Subject coverage: Public road passenger transport, bus and coach industry, fixed track operators, technical and operations, legal matters, statistics, informed comment.

Publications: Printed

Publications list: Available in print

Access to staff: Contact by letter, by telephone, by fax, by e-mail and via website. Appointment necessary.
Hours: Mon to Fri, 0900 to 1700

Subsidiary of: Confederation of British Road Passenger Transport; Transfed

CONFEDERATION OF ROOFING CONTRACTORS 2000 LIMITED (CoRC)

Association House: 22d Victoria Place, Brightlingsea, Colchester, Essex, CO7 0BX

Tel: 01206 306600
Fax: 01206 306200
E-mail: enquiries@corc.co.uk
Website: www.corc.co.uk

Enquiries to: Membership Co-ordinator
Direct e-mail: mike@corc.co.uk

Founded: 1985

Organisation type and purpose: Trade association (membership is by subscription), present number of members: 586.
To protect the general public from unscrupulous roofing contractors.

Subject coverage: All aspects of the roofing industry.

Library catalogue: All or part available in-house

Publications: Printed, and electronic and video
Order printed publications from: mike@corc.co.uk
Order electronic and video publications from: lisa@corc.co.uk

Publications list: Available online

Access to staff: Contact by letter, by telephone, by fax, by e-mail and via website
Hours: Mon to Fri, 0900 to 1700

Access to building: *Hours:* 0900 to 1700
Special comments: Disabled access via rear door.

Access for disabled people: Parking provided, level entry, access to all public areas, toilet facilities

CONFEDERATION OF SHIPBUILDING AND ENGINEERING UNIONS (CSEU)

140–142 Walworth Road, Walworth, London, SE17 1JW

Tel: 020 7703 2215
Fax: 020 7252 7397

Enquiries to: General Secretary
Direct e-mail: smehta@hwfisher.co.uk

Founded: 1936; formed from Federation of Engineering & Shipbuilding Trades (FESTUK) (year of change 1936)

Organisation type and purpose: Trade union (membership is by subscription), present number of members: 1,093,001.

Subject coverage: Co-ordination and policy of shipbuilding and engineering unions throughout the UK.

Access to staff: Contact by letter, by telephone and by fax
Hours: Mon to Fri, 0900 to 1700

CONFERENCE INTERPRETERS GROUP (CIG)

50 Ellington Street, London, N7 8PL

Tel: 07733 887765
E-mail: info@cig-interpreters.com
Website: www.cig-interpreters.com

Enquiries to: Executive Secretary

Founded: 1979

Organisation type and purpose: Service industry.
Cooperative grouping; membership restricted to members of AIIC (Association Internationale des Interprètes de Conférence).

Subject coverage: Interpretation, simultaneous and consecutive.

Access to staff: Contact by letter, by telephone and by fax
Hours: Mon to Fri, 0900 to 1700

CONGREGATIONAL LIBRARY

c/o 14 Gordon Square, London, WC1H 0AR

Tel: 020 7387 3727

Enquiries to: Librarian

Founded: 1831

Organisation type and purpose: Registered charity (charity number 260601), public library.
Managed by Dr Williams's Library.

Subject coverage: English religious dissent. Congregationalism.

Library catalogue: All or part available in-house

Publications: Printed

Publications list: Available in print

Access to staff: Contact by letter, by telephone and in person. Appointment necessary.
Hours: Mon, Wed, Fri, 1000 to 1700; Tue, Thu, 1000 to 1830

Parent body: Congregational Memorial Hall Trust (1978) Limited; c/o Dr Williams's Library, 14 Gordon Square, London, WC1H 0AR

CONNECT

30 St George's Road, Wimbledon, London, SW19 4BD

Tel: 020 8971 6000
Fax: 020 8971 6002
E-mail: info@connectinternetsolutions.com
Website: www.connect.org.uk
Website: www.connectuk.org

Enquiries to: Researcher
Direct tel: 020 8971 6025
Direct fax: 020 8971 6026
Direct e-mail: research@connect.uk.org
Other contacts: Assistant Secretary for overseas publications.

History of institution: formerly called Society of Telecom Executives (year of change 2000)

Organisation type and purpose: Trade union (membership is by subscription), present number of members: 18,500, service industry.
Members are managers and professionals in the Communications and IT industry.

Publications: Printed

Access to staff: Contact by letter, by telephone and by e-mail. Access for members only. Non-members charged.
Hours: Mon to Fri, 0900 to 1715

Access to building: No access other than to staff

Access for disabled people: Parking provided, ramped entry, access to all public areas, toilet facilities

Field offices at: CONNECT; 22a Caroline Street, St Paul's Square, Birmingham, B3 1VE; tel: 0121 236 0596 or 2637; fax: 0121 233 2616

CONSERVATION FOUNDATION

1 Kensington Gore, London, SW7 2AR

Tel: 020 7591 3111
Fax: 020 7591 3110
E-mail: info@conservationfoundation.co.uk
Website: www.conservationfoundation.co.uk

continued overleaf

Enquiries to: Executive Director

Founded: 1982

Organisation type and purpose: International organisation, registered charity (charity number 284656).

Subject coverage: Initiation and management of environmental projects.

Publications: Printed

Access to staff: Contact by letter, by telephone, by fax and by e-mail
Hours: Mon to Fri, 0930 to 1730

CONSORTIUM OF PROFESSIONAL AWARDING BODIES

40 Archdale Road, East Dulwich, London, SE22 9HJ

E-mail: info@snnp.org.uk
Founded: 2012

CONSTRUCTION EMPLOYERS FEDERATION (CEF)

143 Malone Road, Belfast, BT9 6SU

Tel: 028 9087 7143
Fax: 028 9087 7155
E-mail: mail@cefni.co.uk
Website: www.cefni.co.uk
Website: www.constructionfocus.co.uk

Enquiries to: Deputy Secretary
Direct e-mail: nlucas@cefni.co.uk
Other contacts: Information Officer

Founded: 1945; formerly called Federation of Building and Civil Engineering (FBCE)

Organisation type and purpose: Advisory body, trade association (membership is by subscription), service industry, voluntary organisation.

Subject coverage: Construction output data, expenditure, contract problems.

Trade and statistical information: State of Trade Survey

Non-library collection catalogue: All or part available online

Publications: Printed

Publications list: Available in print

Access to staff: Contact by letter. Access for members only. Letter of introduction required.
Hours: Mon to Fri, 0900 to 1700

CONSTRUCTION EQUIPMENT ASSOCIATION (CEA)

Ambassador House, Brigstock Road, Thornton Heath, Surrey, CR7 7JG

Tel: 020 8665 5727
Fax: 020 8665 6447
E-mail: cea@admin.co.uk
Website: www.coneq.org.uk

Enquiries to: Information Officer

Founded: 1942; formerly called Federation of Manufacturers of Construction Equipment and Cranes (FMCEC) (year of change 2000)

Organisation type and purpose: Trade association (membership is by subscription), present number of members: 100.
The UK trade association serving construction equipment manufacturers, their component and accessory suppliers and service providers.

Subject coverage: Subjects relating to UK-based manufacturers of construction equipment, relevant components and accessories in the UK.

Publications: Electronic and video

Access to staff: Contact by letter, by telephone, by fax, by e-mail and via website
Hours: Mon to Fri, 0900 to 1700

Member of: Committee for European Construction Equipment (CECE); Fédération Européenne de la Manutention (FEM)

CONSTRUCTION FIXINGS ASSOCIATION (CFA)

Light Trades House, 3 Melbourne Avenue, Sheffield, South Yorkshire, S10 2QJ

Tel: 0114 266 3084
Fax: 0114 267 0910
E-mail: light.trades@virgin.net

Enquiries to: Secretary

Organisation type and purpose: Trade association.

Subject coverage: Construction fixings.

Access to staff: Contact by letter, by telephone, by fax and by e-mail
Hours: Mon to Fri, 0900 to 1700

Affiliated to: Federation of British Hand Tool Manufacturers

CONSTRUCTION HEALTH AND SAFETY GROUP (CHSG)

John Ryder Training Centre, St Ann's Road, Chertsey, Surrey, KT16 9EH

Tel: 01932 561871 or 563121
Fax: 01932 560193
E-mail: info@chsg.co.uk
Website: www.chsg.co.uk

Enquiries to: Manager
Direct e-mail: gm@chsg.co.uk

Founded: 1953

Organisation type and purpose: Membership association (membership is by subscription), present number of members: 430, registered charity, training organisation.

Subject coverage: Construction safety training courses.

Access to staff: Contact by letter, by telephone, by fax, by e-mail and via website
Hours: Mon to Fri, 0900 to 1700

CONSTRUCTION HISTORY SOCIETY (CHS)

c/o Library and Information Services Manager, The Chartered Institute of Building, Englemere, Kings Ride, Ascot, Berkshire, SL5 7TB

Tel: 01344 630741
Fax: 01344 630764
E-mail: secretary@constructionhistory.co.uk
Website: www.constructionhistory.co.uk

Enquiries to: Secretary

Founded: 1982; formerly called Construction History Group (year of change 1985)

Organisation type and purpose: Learned society (membership is by subscription), present number of members: 300, registered charity.

Subject coverage: Construction history, construction techniques and materials, company histories, etc.

Publications: Printed
Order printed publications from: Society, as above, or via website

Publications list: Available online

Access to staff: Contact by letter, by e-mail and via website
Hours: Mon to Fri, 0900 to 1700

Links with: Building and Construction Industry Interest Group; Society for the History of Technology; Panel for Historical Engineering Works; Institution of Civil Engineers

CONSTRUCTION INDUSTRY COMPUTING ASSOCIATION (CICA)

National Computing Centre, Oxford House, Oxford Road, Manchester, M1 7ED

Tel: 0161 242 2121
E-mail: michael.dean@ncc.co.uk
Website: www.cica.org.uk

Enquiries to: Managing Director

Founded: 1973

Organisation type and purpose: Membership association (membership is by subscription), consultancy, research organisation.
To provide impartial information and advice on the use of computers in the construction industry.

Subject coverage: All areas of construction, including CAD, communications, management, engineering software, building services, quantity surveying; computing services, expert systems, IT strategy and standards.

Collection: Directory of software for the construction industry

Trade and statistical information: Data on use of computers in the UK and European Construction Industry.
Data on sales of CAD systems to construction

Publications: Printed

Publications list: Available online and in print

Access to staff: Contact by letter, by telephone, by e-mail and via website
Hours: Mon to Fri, 0900 to 1700

Commercial branch for consultancy and training: CICA Services Ltd

CONSTRUCTION INDUSTRY COUNCIL (CIC)

26 Store Street, London, WC1E 7BT

Tel: 020 7399 7400
Fax: 020 7399 7425

E-mail: cic@cic.org.uk
Website: www.cic.org.uk

Founded: 1988

Organisation type and purpose: The Construction Industry Council (CIC) is the representative forum for the professional bodies, research organisations and specialist business associations in the construction industry.

Non-library collection catalogue: All or part available in print

Publications: Printed
Order printed publications from: CIC
26 Store Street, London, WC1E 7BT, tel: 020 7399 7400, fax: 020 7399 7425, e-mail: cic@cic.org.uk

Publications list: Available online and in print

Access to staff: Contact by letter, by telephone, by fax, by e-mail and via website. Appointment necessary.
Hours: Mon to Fri, 0900 to 1700

Access for disabled people: lift, toilet facilities

Other address: Construction Industry Council; 26 Store Street, London, WC1E 7BT; tel: 020 7399 7400; fax: 020 7399 7425; e-mail: mail@cic.org.uk

CONSTRUCTION PLANT-HIRE ASSOCIATION (CPA)

52 Rochester Row, London, SW1P 1JU

Tel: 020 7630 6868
Fax: 020 7630 6765
E-mail: enquiries@cpa.uk.net
Website: www.c-p-a.co.uk

Enquiries to: Director

Founded: 1941

Organisation type and purpose: Trade association.

Subject coverage: Construction plant-hire, health and safety, training, statistics and legal aspects.

Publications: Printed, and electronic and video

Publications list: Available in print

Access to staff: Contact by letter, by telephone and by fax
Hours: Mon to Fri, 0930 to 1700

CONSTRUCTION PRODUCTS ASSOCIATION (CPA)

The Building Centre, 26 Store Street, London, WC1E 7BT

Tel: 020 7323 3770
Fax: 020 7323 0307
E-mail: enquiries@constructionproducts.org.uk
Website: www.constructionproducts.org.uk

Enquiries to: Director
Other contacts: Communications and External Affairs Director

Founded: 2000; formed from the merger of Association of Construction Product Supplies (ACPS), Building Materials Export Group (BMEG), National Council of Building Material Producers (NCBMP)

Organisation type and purpose: National organisation, trade association (membership is by subscription), present number of members: 60.
To demonstrate the importance of a growing and profitable construction products sector to the UK economy.

Subject coverage: Building materials, components and fittings, industry in general; non-specialist information on availability and sources of materials; forecasts of construction industry output; statistics.

Collection: Economic, technical, wide-ranging other information on construction industry structure and organisation

Publications: Printed

Publications list: Available online and in print

Access to staff: Contact by letter, by telephone, by fax, by e-mail and via website. Appointment necessary. Non-members charged.
Hours: Mon to Fri, 0900 to 1700

Member organisation of: Confederation of British Industry (CBI); tel: 020 7379 8001; Council of European Producers of Materials for Construction

CONSUMER CREDIT ASSOCIATION (CCA)

Queens House, Queens Road, Chester, Cheshire, CH1 3BQ

Tel: 01244 312044
Fax: 01244 318035
E-mail: cca@ccauk.org
Website: www.ccauk.org

Enquiries to: Director
Direct tel: 01244 505907
Direct fax: 01244 322528
Direct e-mail: cca@ccauk.org

Founded: 1978; created by the merger of National Personal Finance Association (NPFA) and Retail Credit Federation (RCF) (year of change 1978)

Organisation type and purpose: Trade association.
Represents over 500 companies operating in the home credit market.

Subject coverage: Consumer credit, home credit.

Publications: Printed

Access to staff: Contact by letter, by telephone, by fax and by e-mail
Hours: Mon to Fri, 0900 to 1700

CONSUMER FOCUS

Fleetbank House, Salisbury Square, London EC4Y

Tel: 020 7799 7900
Fax: 020 7799 7901
E-mail: contact@consumerfocus.org.uk
Website: www.consumerfocus.org.uk

Enquiries to: Communications Assistant

Founded: 2008; created by the merger of energywatch, Postwatch and National Consumer Council (NCC) (year of change 2008)

Organisation type and purpose: NDPB (Non-departmental public body).

Subject coverage: Consumer Focus is the independent champion for consumers in the UK, giving a strong voice to consumers on the issues that matter to them and working to secure a fair deal on their behalf. It works with consumers and a range of organisations to tackle the problems customers face and to achieve creative solutions that make a difference to peoples' lives.
It has legislative powers, including the right to investigate any complaint if it is of wider interest; the right to open up information from providers; and the ability to make an official super-complaint about failing services.
It is not a complaints-handling body or a statutory regulator. Consumer complaints or advice requests should be directed to the Citizens Advice consumer service.

Publications list: Available online

Access to staff: Contact by letter, by telephone, by fax and by e-mail
Hours: Mon to Fri, 0900 to 1700

Also at: Consumer Focus Post (Northern Ireland); Elizabeth House, 116 Holywood Road, Belfast, BT4 1NY; tel: 028 9067 4833; website: http://www.consumerfocus.org.uk/northern-ireland
Consumer Focus Scotland; Royal Exchange House, 100 Queen Street, Glasgow, G1 3DN; tel: 0141 226 5261; fax: 0141 221 0731; website: http://www.consumerfocus.org.uk/scotland
Consumer Focus Wales; Portcullis House, 21 Cowbridge Road East, Cardiff; tel: 02920 787100; fax: 02920 787101; website: http://www.consumerfocus.org.uk/wales

CONSUMER FOCUS SCOTLAND

Royal Exchange House, 100 Queen Street, Glasgow, G1 3DN

Tel: 0141 226 5261, 0141 226 8459 (minicom)
Fax: 0141 221 9695
E-mail: mail@consumerfocus-scotland.org.uk
Website: www.consumerfocus.org.uk/scotland

Founded: 2008; created by the merger of Scottish Consumer Council (founded 1975), energywatch, Postwatch (year of change 2008)

Organisation type and purpose: National government body.
Set up by the government to promote the interests of Scottish consumers, particularly those experiencing disadvantage in society.

Subject coverage: Consumer issues, including access to information, advice, debt, education, food, health, housing, legal matters, local authorities, rural problems, social security, transport, social services, environmental affairs, food and diet, disability issues.

Publications: Printed

Publications list: Available online and in print

Access to staff: Contact by letter, by telephone, by fax, by e-mail and via website. Appointment necessary.
Hours: Mon to Fri, 0900 to 1700

continued overleaf

Part of: National Consumer Council; 20 Grosvenor Gardens, London, SW1W 0DH; tel: 020 7730 3469; fax: 020 7730 0191

CONSUMERS' ASSOCIATION (CA)

Head Office, 2 Marylebone Road, London, NW1 4DF

Tel: 020 7770 7400
Fax: 01992 827485
E-mail: support@which.net
Website: www.which.net

Enquiries to: Customer Services Officer
Direct tel: 01992 589031 ext 4504

Founded: 1957

Organisation type and purpose: Membership association (membership is by subscription), registered charity, research organisation, publishing house.
The company is Which Limited.

Subject coverage: Consumer affairs, product testing, consumer law, standards.

Collection: Local Consumer Group magazines and Overseas Consumer magazines on microfiche

Non-library collection catalogue: All or part available online and in print

Publications: Printed, and electronic and video

Publications list: Available in print

Access to staff: Contact by letter, by telephone, by fax, by e-mail and via website
Hours: Which queries Mon to Fri, 0830 to 2000; Sat, 0900 to 1300
Which online Mon to Fri, 0830 to 2100; Sat 0900 to 1500

Connections with: BEUC; IOCU

Links with: Research Institute for Consumer Affairs

Other addresses: Membership Queries; Consumers' Association, Castlemead, Gascoyne Way, Hertford, SG1 1LH

CONTACT A FAMILY

209–211 City Road, London, EC1V 1JN

Tel: 020 7608 8700, 020 7608 8702 (minicom)
Fax: 020 7608 8701
E-mail: info@cafamily.org.uk
Website: www.cafamily.org.uk

Enquiries to: Information Officer

Founded: 1979

Organisation type and purpose: Voluntary organisation, registered charity.
Support for families who care for children with disabilities and special needs.

Subject coverage: Children with special needs, parent carers, parents' support groups, rare conditions affecting children.

Information services: Helpline, tel: 0808 808 3555 (Mon to Fri); textphone, tel: 0808 808 3556.

Non-library collection catalogue: All or part available in-house

Library catalogue: All or part available in-house

Publications: Printed, and electronic and video

Publications list: Available online and in print

Access to staff: Contact by letter, by telephone, by fax, by e-mail and via website
Hours: Mon to Fri, 0900 to 1700

Access to building: Prior appointment required
Hours: Mon to Fri, 0900 to 1700

Access for disabled people: Ramped entry, toilet facilities

CONTACT THE ELDERLY

15 Henrietta Street, Covent Garden, London, WC2E 8QG

Tel: 020 7240 0630
Fax: 020 7379 5781
E-mail: info@contact-the-elderly.org.uk
Website: www.contact-the-elderly.org.uk

Enquiries to: Friendship Line Officer

Founded: 1965; formerly called CONTACT

Organisation type and purpose: Voluntary organisation, registered charity (charity number 244681 in England and Wales and SC039377 in Scotland).

Subject coverage: Contact the Elderly provides monthly Sunday afternoon tea parties for people over 75, who live alone with little or no contact with family and friends. Members are picked up by volunteer drivers and spend afternoons full of fun and laughter at a volunteer host's home: a real lifeline.

Publications: Printed, and electronic and video

Access to staff: Contact by letter, by telephone, by fax, by e-mail and via website
Hours: Mon to Fri, 0900 to 1700

CONTEMPORARY APPLIED ARTS

2 Percy Street, London, W1P 9FA

Tel: 020 7436 2344
Fax: 020 7436 2446
Website: www.caa.org.uk

Enquiries to: Press and Promotions Officer

Founded: 1948; formerly called British Crafts Centre (year of change 1989)

Organisation type and purpose: Membership association (membership is by qualification), present number of members: 250 approx, registered charity.
Gallery.

Subject coverage: Ceramics, glass, jewellery, furniture, textiles, wood, metalwork.

Publications: Printed

Access to staff: Contact by letter and by telephone
Hours: Mon to Sat, 1030 to 1730
Special comments: Closed Bank Holidays and from Christmas to early Jan.

Member of: Federation of British Crafts Societies (FBCS)

CONTEMPORARY ART SOCIETY (CAS)

11–15 Emerald Street, London, WC1N 3QL

Tel: 020 7831 1243
Fax: 020 7831 1214
E-mail: info@contemporaryartsociety.org
Website: www.contemporaryartsociety.org

Founded: 1910

Organisation type and purpose: The Contemporary Art Society exists to support and develop public collections of contemporary art in the UK.

Subject coverage: Promotion of the understanding, enjoyment and collecting of contemporary art; acquisition of works of contemporary art for gifts to public museums and galleries; an extensive knowledge of British contemporary art.

Collection: Extensive data on contemporary artists
Information is held on all CAS purchases since 1910
Office used as a gallery space, rotating exhibitions

Access to staff: Contact by letter, by telephone, by fax and by e-mail.
Appointment necessary.
Hours: Mon to Fri, 0930 to 1730

CONTEMPORARY GLASS SOCIETY (CGS)

c/o Broadfield House Glass Museum, Compton Drive, Kingswinford, West Midlands, DY6 9NS

Tel: 01379 741120
E-mail: admin@cgs.org.uk
Website: www.cgs.org.uk

Enquiries to: Administrator
Direct e-mail: admin@cgs.org.uk

Founded: 1997; please select

Organisation type and purpose: The CGS is the UK's foremost organisation for supporting established artists, for supporting up-and-coming makers and for promoting contemporary glass in the wider art world.

The CGS is the first port of call for information about contemporary glass. Our extensive knowledge and international networks mean we can help you source scarce materials, find exhibitions and events, or find workshops to improve technical or business skills.

Subject coverage: Glass art in all its forms. For artists, designers, makers, exhibitions, educators, students, collectors and supporters.

Information services: Advice, support, information and contacts for all things glass-related

Education services: Workshops, exhibitions, conferences and events

Collection: Online exhibitions and portfolios of members' work

Non-library collection catalogue: All or part available online

Library catalogue: All or part available online and in print

Publications: Printed
Order printed publications from: admin@cgs.org.uk

Publications list: Available online

Access to staff: Contact by letter, by telephone, by e-mail and via website
Hours: Mon to Fri, 0900 to 1700

CONTENT MARKETING AGENCY (CMA)

Queens House, 55–56 Lincoln's Inn Fields, London, WC2A 3LJ

Tel: 020 7404 4166
Fax: 020 7404 4167
E-mail: info@the-cma.com
Website: www.the-cma.com

Enquiries to: Director
Other contacts: Marketing Executive for other principal contact.

Founded: 1993; formerly called Association of Publishing Agencies

Organisation type and purpose: Trade association (membership is by subscription, qualification).

Subject coverage: Content marketing agencies.

Trade and statistical information: Statistics on the size of the UK content marketing industry. Data on content marketing published by UK agencies

Publications: Printed

Access to staff: Contact by letter, by telephone, by fax, by e-mail and via website
Hours: Mon to Fri, 0900 to 1730

CONTINYOU

Unit C1, Grovelands Court, Grovelands Est., Longford Road, Exhall, Coventry, Warwickshire, CV7 9NE

Tel: 024 7658 8440
Fax: 024 7658 8441
E-mail: generalenquiries@continyou.org.uk
Website: www.continyou.org.uk

Enquiries to: Publications Co-ordinator
Direct tel: 024 7658 8465

Founded: 2003

Organisation type and purpose: Voluntary organisation, registered charity (charity number 1097596).

Subject coverage: Education, supplementary education, extra-curricular activities, health improvement, community focused schools

Publications: Printed
Order printed publications from: www.continyou.org.uk/shop

Publications list: Available online

Access to staff: Contact by letter, by telephone, by e-mail and via website. Appointment necessary.
Hours: Mon to Thu, 0900 to 1700; Fri 0900 to 1630

CONTRACT FLOORING ASSOCIATION (CFA)

4C Saint Mary's Place, The Lace Market, Nottingham, NG1 1PH

Tel: 0115 941 1126
Fax: 0115 941 2238
E-mail: info@cfa.org.uk
Website: www.cfa.org.uk

Founded: 1974

Organisation type and purpose: Trade association.

Subject coverage: All types of floorcoverings, incl. carpet, timber, resilient.

Publications: Printed

Publications list: Available in print

Access to staff: Contact by letter, by telephone, by fax, by e-mail and via website
Hours: Mon to Fri, 0900 to 1700

Member organisation of: National Specialist Contractors Council (NSCC)

CONTROL SYSTEMS CENTRE (CSC)

UMIST, Department of Electrical Engineering & Electronics, PO Box 88, Manchester, M60 1QD

Tel: 0161 200 4665
Fax: 0161 200 4647
E-mail: neil@csc.umist.ac.uk
Website: www.csc.umist.ac.uk

Enquiries to: Head of Centre

Founded: 1966

Organisation type and purpose: University department or institute, consultancy. University unit within the Department of Electrical and Electronic Engineering. Interdisciplinary research in control and systems engineering.

Subject coverage: Control and information technology, multivariable control system design, computer-aided design, self-tuning regulators, 2-D system theory, robust control, fault detection, symbolic programming, nonlinear systems, optimisation.

Publications: Printed
Order printed publications from: IEE, RSP and J Wiley

Publications list: Available in print

Access to staff: Contact by letter, by telephone, by fax and by e-mail
Hours: Mon to Fri, 0900 to 1700

CONVENTION OF SCOTTISH LOCAL AUTHORITIES (COSLA)

Rosebery House, 9 Haymarket Terrace, Edinburgh, EH12 5XZ

Tel: 0131 474 9200
Fax: 0131 474 9292
E-mail: carol@cosla.gov.uk
Website: www.cosla.gov.uk

Enquiries to: Head of Media and Communications
Direct tel: 0131 474 9205
Direct e-mail: davidk@cosla.gov.uk

Founded: 1975

Organisation type and purpose: Local government body.

Subject coverage: Scottish local government, people, boards, and public bodies.

Publications: Printed
Order printed publications from: COSLA Connections

Publications list: Available online and in print

Access to staff: Contact by letter, by telephone, by fax, by e-mail and via website
Hours: Mon to Fri, 0900 to 1700

Access to building: Main Reception
Hours: Mon to Fri, 0900 to 1700

Also at: COSLA; Brussels Office, The House of Cities, Municipalities & Regions, Square de Meeus 1 , B-1000 Brussels, Belgium; tel: +32 (0)2 213 8120; fax: +32 (0)2 213 8129; e-mail: cosla@pophost.eunet.be; COSLA; Glasgow Office, Suite 203, 69 Buchanan Street, Glasgow, G1 3HL; tel: 0141 314 3700; fax: 0141 314 3836

CONWY COUNTY BOROUGH COUNCIL (CCBC)

Bodlondeb, Conwy, LL32 8DU

Tel: 01492 574000
Fax: 01492 592114
E-mail: information@conwy.gov.uk
Website: www.conwy.gov.uk

Enquiries to: Chief Executive
Direct fax: 01492 576003
Other contacts: Corporate Information and Complaints Manager

Founded: 1996; created by the merger of Colwyn Borough Council and Aberconwy Borough Council (year of change 1996)

Organisation type and purpose: Local government body.

Subject coverage: Information on services provided by the Authority for those who live in, work in or visit Conwy County Borough.

Information services: Corporate Information and Complaints Service, Library and Information Services, Corporate Research and Information Unit, Marketing and Communications Unit, Tourist Information Services

Education services: Education Services

Services for disabled people: Physical Disability and Sensory Impairment Service

Trade and statistical information: Local census information available, business directory, community information directory

Library catalogue: All or part available online

Publications: Printed
Order printed publications from: Corporate Information and Complaints Service, Publications Circulation, Reception and Information Desk, Civic Offices, Colwyn Bay, LL29 8AR

Access to staff: Contact by letter, by telephone, by fax, by e-mail, in person and via website
Hours: Mon to Thu, 0845 to 1715; Fri, 0845 to 1645

Access to building: Access is different for each council building, contact for further details

Access for disabled people: Access is different for each council building, contact for further details

CONWY LIBRARY SERVICE (CLIS)

Formal name: Conwy County Borough Council – Community Development Service – Culture and Information

The Old Board School, Lloyd Street, Llandudno, LL30 2YG

Tel: 01492 576139
Fax: 01492 577550
E-mail: library@conwy.gov.uk
Website: www.conwy.gov.uk/library
Website: www.conwy.gov.uk/llyfrgell
Website: www.conwy.gov.uk
Website: prism.talis.com/conwy

Enquiries to: Section Head: Culture and Information
Direct e-mail: rhian.williams@conwy.gov.uk

Founded: 1996; formerly a part of Gwynedd and Clwyd Library Services (year of change 1996)

Organisation type and purpose: Local government body, statutory body, public library.
Information and archives service.

Subject coverage: Local government information; Welsh history; Welsh language and literature; Welsh reference material, local information.

Collection: Alice in Wonderland Books Collection at Llandudno library
Archive access points (held at Llandudno and Colwyn Bay libraries)

Trade and statistical information: Statistical information, e.g. population, social data, etc

Non-library collection catalogue: All or part available online

Library catalogue: All or part available online

Access to staff: Contact by letter, by telephone, by fax, by e-mail and via website
Hours: Mon to Fri, 0900 to 1700
Special comments: Headquarters visitors by prior appointment only.

Access to building: *Hours:* Opening times vary; contact for further details

Access for disabled people: *Special comments:* Headquarters on first floor, with no lift.

Branch libraries: Abergele Library; Market Street, Abergele, LL22 7BP; tel: 01492 577505; fax: 01745 823376; e-mail: llyfr.lib.abergele@conwy.gov.uk; website: http://www.conwy.gov.uk/library/abergele
Cerrigydrudion Library; King Street, Cerrigydrudion, Corwen, LL21 9UB; tel: 01490 420501; e-mail: llyfr.lib.cerrig@conwy.gov.uk; website: http://www.conwy.gov.uk/library/cerrigydrudion
Colwyn Bay Library; Woodland Road West, Colwyn Bay, LL29 7DH; tel: 01492 577510; fax: 01492 534474; e-mail: llyfr.lib.baecolwynbay@conwy.gov.uk; website: http://www.conwy.gov.uk/library/colwynbay
Conwy Library; Civic Hall, Castle Street, Conwy, LL32 6AY; tel: 01492 596242; fax: 01492 582359; e-mail: llyfr.lib.conwy@conwy.gov.uk; website: http://www.conwy.gov.uk/library/conwy
Deganwy Library; Station Road, Deganwy, Conwy, LL31 9EX; tel: 01492 584705; e-mail: llyfr.lib.deganwy@conwy.gov.uk; website: http://www.conwy.gov.uk/library/deganwy
Kinmel Bay Library; Community Centre, Kendal Road, Kinmel Bay, LL18 5BT; tel: 01745 353499; e-mail: llyfr.lib.kinmel@conwy.gov.uk; website: http://www.conwy.gov.uk/library/kinmelbay
Llandudno Junction Library; Maes Derw, Llandudno Junction, LL31 9AL; tel: 01492 582266; e-mail: llyfr.lib.cyffordd@conwy.gov.uk; website: http://www.conwy.gov.uk/library/llandudnojunction
Llandudno Library; Victoria Centre, Mostyn Street, Llandudno, LL30 2RS; tel: 01492 574010; 01492 574020; fax: 01492 876826; e-mail: llyfr.lib.llandudno@conwy.gov.uk; website: http://www.conwy.gov.uk/library/llandudno
Llanfairfechan Library; Village Road, Llanfairfechan, LL33 0AA; tel: 01248 681014; e-mail: llyfr.lib.llanfairfechan@conwy.gov.uk; website: http://www.conwy.gov.uk/library/llanfairfechan
Llangernyw Library; Ysgol Bro Cernyw, Llangernyw, Abergele, LL22 8PF; tel: 01745 860413; e-mail: llyfr.lib.llangernyw@conwy.gov.uk; website: http://www.conwy.gov.uk/library/llangernyw
Llanrwst Library; Plas yn Dre, Station Road, Llanrwst, LL26 0DF; tel: 01492 577545; e-mail: llyfr.lib.llanrwst@conwy.gov.uk; website: http://www.conwy.gov.uk/library/llanrwst
Penmaenmawr Library; Bangor Road, Penmaenmawr, LL34 6DA; tel: 01492 623619; e-mail: llyfr.lib.penmaenmawr@conwy.gov.uk; website: http://www.conwy.gov.uk/library/penmaenmawr
Penrhyn Bay Library; Llandudno Road, Penrhyn Bay, Llandudno, LL30 3HN; tel: 01492 548873; e-mail: llyfr.lib.penrhyn@conwy.gov.uk; website: http://www.conwy.gov.uk/library/penrhynbay

Constituent part of: Conwy County Borough Council; Bodlondeb, Conwy, North Wales, LL32 8DU; tel: 01492 574000; e-mail: information@conwy.gov.uk; website: http://www.conwy.gov.uk

COPELAND BOROUGH COUNCIL

The Copeland Centre, Catherine Street, Whitehaven, Cumbria, CA28 7SJ

Tel: 0845 095 2100
Fax: 0845 095 2140
Website: www.copelandbc.gov.uk

Enquiries to: General Manager
Direct tel: 01946 598320
Direct fax: 01946 598303
Direct e-mail: jstanforth@copelandbc.gov.uk

Organisation type and purpose: Local government body.

Subject coverage: Corporate services, education, environmental services, finance, housing, legal services, personnel services, planning development and tourism, property and technical services, roads and transportation, social services, council tax and other payments, registration of births, deaths and marriages.

Access to staff: Contact by letter, by telephone, by fax, by e-mail and via website
Hours: Mon to Fri, 0900 to 1700

COPPER DEVELOPMENT ASSOCIATION (CDA)

5 Grovelands Business Centre, Boundary Way, Hemel Hempstead, HP2 7TE

Tel: 01442 275705
Fax: 01442 275716
E-mail: cda@copperalliance.org.uk
Website: www.copperinfo.co.uk

Founded: 1933

Organisation type and purpose: Advisory body, service industry, non-trading organisation, sponsored by copper producers and fabricators.

Subject coverage: Copper, its alloys and compounds, non-ferrous metals, market development and technical data.

Publications list: Available online

Access to staff: Contact by letter, by fax, by e-mail and via website
Hours: Mon to Fri, 0900 to 1700, lunch 1230 to 1330

COPYRIGHT LICENSING AGENCY (CLA)

Saffron House, 6–10 Kirby Street, London, EC1N 8TS

Fax: 020 7400 3100
E-mail: cla@cla.co.uk
Website: www.cla.co.uk

Enquiries to: PR Manager
Other contacts: Marketing Manager

Founded: 1982

Organisation type and purpose: Service industry.
To license photocopying and scanning of extracts and clippings from copyright books, journals and magazines.

Subject coverage: Copyright licensing, copyright, electronic copying, internet issues.

Trade and statistical information: Photocopy fees for specific publications

Publications: Printed

Access to staff: Contact by letter, by telephone and by e-mail
Hours: Mon to Fri, 0900 to 1700
Special comments: Internet online 24 hrs.

Affiliated to: Association of Learned and Professional Society Publishers; International Federation of Reproduction Rights Organisations; Publishers Association; Publishers Licensing Society (PLS); 37–41 Gower Street, London, WC1E 6HH; tel: 020 7299 7730; fax: 020 7299 7780; e-mail: pls@pls.org.uk; Society of Authors; Writers' Guild of Great Britain

Parent body: Authors' Licensing and Collecting Society (ALCS); Marlborough Court, 14–18 Holborn, London, EC1N 2LE; tel: 020 7395 0600; fax: 020 7395 0660; e-mail: alcs@alcs.co.uk

CORBY BOROUGH COUNCIL

Deene House, New Post Office Square, Corby, Northamptonshire, NN17 1GD

Tel: 01536 402551
Fax: 01536 464640

Website: www.corby.gov.uk

Enquiries to: Public Relations Manager

Founded: 1993; formerly called Corby District Council

Organisation type and purpose: Local government body.

Subject coverage: Corby Borough, services and amenities.

Access to staff: Contact by letter, by telephone, by fax and by e-mail. Appointment necessary.
Hours: Mon to Fri, 0900 to 1700

CORD

Formal name: Christian Outreach – Relief and Development

1 New Street, Leamington Spa, Warwickshire, CV1 1HP

Tel: 01926 315301
Fax: 01926 885786
E-mail: info@cord.org.uk

Enquiries to: Director

Founded: 1967; formerly called Christian Outreach Project Vietnam Orphans (year of change 1999)

Organisation type and purpose:
International organisation, registered charity (charity number 1070684).
An international Christian-based relief and development organisation.

Publications: Printed

Access to staff: Contact by letter and by e-mail
Hours: Mon to Fri, 0900 to 1700

CORE

3 St Andrew's Place, Regent's Park, London, NW1 4LB

Tel: 020 7486 0341
Fax: 020 7224 2012
E-mail: info@corecharity.org.uk
Website: www.corecharity.org.uk

Enquiries to: Public Affairs Coordinator
Direct tel: 020 7034 4972

Founded: 1971; formerly called Digestive Disorders Foundation (year of change 2004)

Organisation type and purpose: Registered charity (charity number 1137029), research organisation.
Core supports research into all aspects of digestive disease.

Subject coverage: Gastroenterology, including the physiology and pathology of the digestive system; research into causes, prevention and treatment of digestive disorders.

Publications: Printed
Order printed publications from: Leaflets available from: Core, 3 St Andrews Place, London, NW1 4LB

Publications list: Available in print

Access to staff: Contact by letter, by telephone, by fax, by e-mail and via website
Hours: Mon to Fri, 0900 to 1700
Special comments: Please send sae if requiring information.

Close association with: British Liver Trust; Children's Liver Disease Foundation; Coeliac Society; Crohn's in Childhood Research Appeal; IA – The Ileostomy and Internal Pouch Support Group; IBS Network; National Association for Colitis and Crohn's Disease

CORK INDUSTRY FEDERATION (CIF)

13 Felton Lea, Sidcup, Kent, DA14 6BA

Tel: 020 8302 4801
Fax: 020 8302 4801
Website: www.cork-products.co.uk

Enquiries to: Honorary Secretary
Other contacts: Chairman

Founded: 1969

Organisation type and purpose: Trade association (membership is by subscription).

Subject coverage: All aspects of cork, for domestic, decorative, industrial and architectural uses, and for use in the wine and spirit trades; advice can be given on roof drainage and insulation, material selection and design.

Collection: Details of cork products

Access to staff: Contact by letter, by telephone and by fax
Hours: Mon to Fri, 0900 to 1700

Member organisation of: European Cork Industry Federation

CORNWALL CENTRE (KRESENN KERNOW)

Alma Place, Redruth, Cornwall, TR15 2AT

Tel: 01209 216760
Fax: 01209 210283
E-mail: cornishstudies.library@cornwall.gov.uk
Website: www.cornwall.gov.uk/cornwallcentre

Enquiries to: Librarian

Founded: 1974

Organisation type and purpose: Local government body, public library.
Local studies library and visitor centre.

Subject coverage: Cornwall

Collection: Ashley Rowe Collection (general Cornish)
Hambly and Rowe Collection (general Cornish)
A. K. Hamilton Jenkin Collection (Cornish mining)
Cornish Newspapers (around 50 titles, microfilm)
Photographs (over 150,000)
Cornish Census returns
Maps
Parish Register transcriptions
Books and pamphlets about Cornwall

Library catalogue: All or part available online

Publications: Printed, and electronic and video

Access to staff: Contact by letter, by telephone, by fax, by e-mail and in person
Hours: Mon to Fri, 1000 to 1700; Sat, 1000 to 1600
Special comments: Prior appointment is advisable to view microforms.

Access for disabled people: Level entry, access to all public areas, toilet facilities

Parent body: Cornwall Council; Cornwall Library Service, Unit 17, Threemilestone Industrial Estate, Truro, Cornwall, TR4 9LD; tel: 0300 123 4111; fax: 01872 223509; e-mail: libraries@cornwall.gov.uk; website: http://www.cornwall.gov.uk

CORNWALL COLLEGE GROUP (CCLS)

Learning Services, Cornwall College St Austell, Tregonissey Road, St Austell, Cornwall, PL25 4DJ

Tel: 01726 226401
E-mail: peter.sampson@cornwall.ac.uk
Website: www.cornwall.ac.uk

Organisation type and purpose: Further and higher education.

Subject coverage: General.

Library catalogue: All or part available online and in-house

Publications: Printed

Access to staff: Access for members only. Non-members charged.
Hours: Mon to Fri, 0900 to 1630 (minimum)

Also at: Cornwall College Camborne; Trevenson Road, Redruth, TR15 3RD; tel: 01209 616242; Cornwall College Newquay; Centre for Applied Zoology, Wildflower Lane, Trenance Gardens, Newquay, TR7 2LZ; tel: 01637 857930; Cornwall College Saltash; Church Road, Saltash, PL12 4AE; tel: 01752 850215; Duchy College Rosewarne; Rosewarne, Cambourne, TR14 0AB; tel: 01209 722134; Duchy College Stoke Climsland; Stoke Climsland, Callington, PL17 8PB; tel: 01579 372213; Falmouth Marine School; Killigrew Street, Falmouth, TR11 3QS; tel: 01326 310319; fax: 01326 310331

CORNWALL FAMILY HISTORY SOCIETY (CFHS)

18 Lemon Street, Truro, Cornwall, TR1 2LS

Tel: 01872 264044
E-mail: secretary@cornwallfhs.com
Website: www.cornwallfhs.com

Enquiries to: Administrator

Founded: 1976

Organisation type and purpose:
International organisation, membership association (membership is by subscription), present number of members: 4000, voluntary organisation, registered charity (charity number 288686), research organisation.
To promote interest in family history research into Cornish families.

Subject coverage: All records concerning the tracing of Cornish family histories.

Collection: Books, documents, indexes, photographs of Cornish families
Much held on computer database
1837–1992 GRO index (microfiche)
1841–1901 Censuses (microfiche)

Publications: Printed

continued overleaf

Publications list: Available online

Access to staff: Contact by letter, by telephone, by e-mail, in person and via website. Non-members charged.
Hours: Mon, 1100 to 1500; Wed to Fri, 1100 to 1500; Tue, closed

CORNWALL LIBRARY SERVICE

Unit 17, Threemilestone Industrial Estate, Truro, Cornwall, TR4 9LD

Tel: 01872 324316
Fax: 01872 223509
E-mail: library@cornwall.gov.uk
Website: www.cornwall.gov.uk

Organisation type and purpose: Local government body, public library.

Subject coverage: General; metalliferous mining in Cornwall; county local studies (at Redruth); performing arts (at St Austell); art (at Penzance); maritime studies (at Falmouth); law and business (at Truro).

Collection: Ashley Rowe Collection (local studies)
Cornish Methodist Historical Association (on deposit)
Hambley Rowe Collection (local studies)
Hamilton Jenkin Collection (local studies)
Rosewarne Collection (local studies)

Non-library collection catalogue: All or part available online

Library catalogue: All or part available online

Publications: Printed

Parent body: Cornwall County Council

CORNWALL REFERENCE AND INFORMATION LIBRARY

Union Place, Truro, Cornwall, TR1 1EP

Tel: 01872 272702; Freephone 0800 032 2345
Fax: 01872 223772
E-mail: reference.library@cornwall.gov.uk
Website: www.cornwall.gov.uk/library

Enquiries to: Librarian

Founded: 1896; formerly called Cornwall County Reference and Information Library

Organisation type and purpose: Public reference library, Cornwall Centre for Europe Direct

Subject coverage: Law and business, European information, general reference.

Trade and statistical information: General statistics

Non-library collection catalogue: All or part available online

Library catalogue: All or part available online

Publications: Electronic and video

Access to staff: Contact by letter, by telephone, by fax, by e-mail, in person and via website
Hours: Mon, Tue, Thu and Fri, 0900 to 1800; Wed, 0930 to 1800; Sat, 0900 to 1600

Access for disabled people: Parking provided, level entry, access to all public areas

Parent body: Chief Executive's Department; New County Hall, Truro, Cornwall, TR1 3EW; tel: 01872 322000; fax: 01872 323818

CORONA WORLDWIDE (CWW)

Southbank House, Black Prince Road, London, SE1 7SJ

Tel: 020 7793 4020
Fax: 020 7793 4020
E-mail: corona@coronaworldwide.org
Website: www.corona_worldwide.org
Website: www.coronaworldwide.org

Enquiries to: Administrative Secretary

Founded: 1950; formerly called Women's Corona Society (year of change 2006)

Organisation type and purpose: International organisation, voluntary organisation, registered charity (charity number 204802), suitable for ages: adults. Notes for newcomers to over 100 countries worldwide.
To support people going to work and live in other countries by giving them information about living conditions there, to welcome people coming to live in Britain; aim is to promote friendship and understanding around the world.

Subject coverage: Living and working in foreign countries.

Publications: Printed

Access to staff: Contact by letter, by telephone, by fax and by e-mail
Hours: Tue, Thu, 0900 to 1700

Access to building: *Hours:* 0900 to 1700
Special comments: Security pass at reception.

CORONERS' SOCIETY OF ENGLAND AND WALES

HM Coroner's Court, The Cotton Exchange, Old Hall Street, Liverpool, L3 9UF

Tel: 0151 233 4708
Fax: 0151 233 4710
E-mail: andre.rebello@liverpool.gov.uk
Website: www.coroner.org.uk

Enquiries to: Honorary Secretary

Founded: 1846

Organisation type and purpose: Professional body (membership is by election or invitation), present number of members: 400.
Membership restricted to coroners, deputies and assistant deputies, and retired coroners.

Subject coverage: Law and practice concerning coroners.

Collection: Minutes and reports 1846–

Access to staff: Contact by letter and by e-mail
Hours: Mon to Fri, 0900 to 1700

CORPORATION OF INSURANCE, FINANCIAL AND MORTGAGE ADVISERS (CIFMA)

174 High Street, Guildford, Surrey, GU1 3HW

Tel: 01483 539121
Fax: 01483 301847

Enquiries to: General Secretary

Founded: 1968; formerly called Corporation of Mortgage Brokers (year of change 1972)

Organisation type and purpose: Professional body, membership association (membership is by subscription, qualification), present number of members: c. 700.
To raise the professional standards in mortgage broking and the associated life assurance industry and general insurance industry.

Subject coverage: Mortgage broking, life insurance and general insurance.

Publications: Printed

Access to staff: Contact by letter, by telephone and by fax
Hours: Mon to Fri, 0900 to 1700

CORPORATION OF LONDON RECORDS OFFICE (CLRO)

c/o London Metropolitan Archives, 40 Northampton Road, London, EC1R 0HB

Tel: 020 7332 3820
Fax: 020 7833 9136
E-mail: ask.lma@cityoflondon.gov.uk
Website: www.cityoflondon.gov.uk/archives/lma

Enquiries to: Enquiries Team

Founded: 1876; formerly called City of London Record(s) Office, Guildhall Record(s) Office

Organisation type and purpose: Local government body.
Record office.
Custody of the official archives of the Corporation of the City of London.

Subject coverage: Archives of national as well as civic interest, reflecting the interests and activities of the Corporation, from the 11th to the 20th centuries.

Collection: Administrative records, such as: Proceedings of the Courts of Aldermen and Common Council, 15th century onwards
Financial records
Judicial records, from the civic courts and the Sessions of Gaol Delivery and Peace, 13th century onwards
Medieval compilations of City law and custom
Records of admission to the Freedom of the City
Records of the City of London Police
Rentals and deeds relating to property, some of which lay outside the City
Royal Charters 1067 onwards

Non-library collection catalogue: All or part available online, in-house and in print

Publications: Printed, and microform publications

Publications list: Available online and in print

Access to staff: Contact by letter, by telephone, by fax, by e-mail, in person and via website

Access to building: *Hours:* Mon, Wed and Fri, 0930 to 1645; Tue and Thu, 0930 to 1930; Sat, contact for details
Special comments: Appointments required to view rare books.

Access for disabled people: Toilet facilities

CORPORATION OF TRINITY HOUSE

Trinity House, Tower Hill, London, EC3N 4DH

Tel: 020 7481 6900
Fax: 020 7480 7662
E-mail: enquiries@thls.org
Website: www.trinityhouse.co.uk

Direct e-mail: paul.howe@thls.org
Other contacts: Media and Communication Officer

Founded: 1514

Organisation type and purpose: Statutory body, registered charity.
General lighthouse authority for England, Wales and Channel Islands, a deep sea pilotage authority and marine charitable organisation.

Subject coverage: History and current operations of Trinity House. Aids to navigation – lighthouses, light vessels, buoyage and radio navigation.

Collection: Corporations archives dating from 1660 held by Guildhall Library
Library – mainly nautical books

Publications: Printed
Order printed publications from: Publications Office
at the same address, tel: 020 7481 6900

Access to staff: Contact by letter, by telephone, by fax, by e-mail and via website. Appointment necessary.
Hours: Mon to Fri, 0900 to 1700

CORPS OF COMMISSIONAIRES MANAGEMENT LIMITED (The Corps)

85 Cowcross Street, London, EC1M 6PF

Tel: 020 7566 0500
Fax: 020 7566 0522
E-mail: info@the-corps.co.uk
Website: www.the-corps.co.uk

Enquiries to: Executive Director
Other contacts: Sales and Marketing Director

Founded: 1859

Organisation type and purpose: National organisation, present number of members: 3,000, service industry.
Providers of security and facilities support services.
To help (former) members of HM's Uniformed Services find employment (worldwide).

Subject coverage: Availability of employment using former military/police skills.
Security – manned guarding, receptionists, patrols and key-holding, training.
Recruitment agency, international projects and consultancy.
Facilities support: mailrooms, file management, building administration and management, receptionists.

Collection: Uncatalogued collection, archive stored photographs of corps members (informal), may or may not be identifiable

Library catalogue: All or part available in-house

Publications: Printed, and electronic and video

Access to staff: Contact by letter, by telephone and by fax. Appointment necessary.
Hours: Mon to Fri, 0900 to 1700

Affiliations with: Similar associations with the same name exist in Commonwealth countries – Canada and Australia

Branches at: Corps of Commissionaires Management Limited; In 16 major UK towns, See local Yellow Pages; website: http://www.the-corps.co.uk

CORROSION PREVENTION ASSOCIATION (CPA)

Kingsley House, Ganders Business Park, Kingsley, Bordon, Hampshire, GU35 9LU

Tel: 01420 471614
Fax: 01420 471611
E-mail: admin@corrosionprevention.org.uk
Website: www.corrosionprevention.org.uk

Enquiries to: Secretary

Founded: 1991; formerly called Society for the Cathodic Protection of Re-Inforced Concrete (SCPRC) (year of change 1998)

Organisation type and purpose:
Construction industry association representing consultants, contractors and manufacturers working in the field of corrosion prevention for concrete and masonry-encased steel.

Subject coverage: The CPA acts as the leading authority and source of information on the subject of cathodic protection and other corrosion techniques and encourages research to ensure better understanding of the preservation of reinforced concrete structures and masonry-clad steel-framed buildings

Library catalogue: All or part available online

Publications: Printed

Publications list: Available online and in print

Access to staff: Contact by letter, by telephone, by fax, by e-mail and via website
Hours: Mon to Fri, 0900 to 1700

CORUS RESEARCH, DEVELOPMENT & TECHNOLOGY

Swinden Technology Centre, Library & Information Services, Moorgate, Rotherham, South Yorkshire, S60 3AR

Tel: 01709 820166
Fax: 01709 825464
E-mail: stc.library@corusgroup.com

Enquiries to: Information Officer
Direct tel: 01709 825335
Direct e-mail: mike.nott@corusgroup.com

History of institution: formerly called British Steel plc (year of change 1999)

Organisation type and purpose: Research organisation.

Subject coverage: Iron and steel product applications, carbon, alloy and stainless steels, physical metallurgy, environmental sciences, welding, machinability, advanced machining, steel specifications, iron and steel roll technology, iron and steel plant.

Collection: Steel specifications and standards

Access to building: Prior appointment required

Access for disabled people: Ramped entry

Other services: Corus Construction Centre; Piling Advisory Service; PO Box 1, Frodingham House, Scunthorpe, South Humberside, DN16 1BP; tel: 01724 404040; Plates Technical Advisory Centre; PO Box 30, Motherwell, ML1 1AA; tel: 01698 266233; Stainless Steel Advisory Centre, not now part of British Steel, now Avesta; Strip Products Advisory Service; PO Box 10, Newport, Gwent; tel: 01633 290011; Technical Hotline; PO Box 1, Brigg Road, Scunthorpe, DN16 1BP; tel: 01724 405060; Tubes and Open Sections Structural Advisory Service; PO Box 101, Weldon Road, Corby, Northamptonshire, NN17 1UA; tel: 01536 402121

COSMETIC, TOILETRY AND PERFUMERY ASSOCIATION LIMITED (CTPA)

Josaron House, 5–7 John Princes Street, London, W1G 0JN

Tel: 020 7491 8891
Fax: 020 7493 8061
Website: www.ctpa.org.uk

Enquiries to: Company Secretary
Direct e-mail: info@ctpa.org.uk

Founded: 1945

Organisation type and purpose: Trade association.

Subject coverage: Cosmetic, toiletry and perfumery industry, legislation, technical information (no market information).

Information services: Consumer website: http://www.thefactsabout.co.uk

Education services: Online resource for schools: http://www.catie.org.uk

Publications: Electronic and video

Publications list: Available online

Access to staff: Access for members only.
Hours: Mon to Fri, 0900 to 1700

Member organisation of: European Association of Cosmetic Industries (COLIPA); Brussels

COSTUME AND TEXTILE STUDY CENTRE, CARROW HOUSE

301 King Street, Norwich, Norfolk, NR1 2TS

Tel: 01603 223870; text phone 0844 800 8011
E-mail: museums@norfolk.gov.uk
Website: www.museums.norfolk.gov.uk

Organisation type and purpose: Study centre, with specialist facilities for students and enthusiasts.

Subject coverage: Period costume, textiles and related material.

COSTUME SOCIETY OF SCOTLAND (CSS)

16 Muirpark, Eskbank, Dalkeith

Tel: 0131 663 0967
E-mail: tandd@muirpark.plus.com
Website: www.costumesocietyofscotland .org

Enquiries to: Secretary
Other contacts: Chairman

Founded: 1965

Organisation type and purpose: Membership association (membership is by subscription), present number of members: 90, suitable for ages: all, meet on a monthly basis for relevant talks.
To promote interest in all matters relating to costume, design and textiles.

Subject coverage: Mourning jewellery, Scottish costume, including fisherfolks' dress, textiles and embellishment, historical and contemporary.

Collection: A small collection of donated clothes from different eras is used for study, illustrating talks and exhibition purposes and may be borrowed for a fee.
Small library of books available to members.

Library catalogue: All or part available in-house

Publications: Printed
Order printed publications from: Treasurer, Costume Society of Scotland, 28 Cameron Park, Newington, Edinburgh, EH16 5LA.

Access to staff: Contact by letter, by e-mail and via website
Hours: Mon to Fri, 0900 to 1700

COTSWOLD DISTRICT COUNCIL (CDC)

Council Offices, Trinity Road, Cirencester, Gloucestershire, GL7 1PX

Tel: 01285 623000
Fax: 01285 623900
Website: www.cotswold.gov.uk

Enquiries to: Information Officer
Direct tel: 01285 623132
Direct e-mail: claire.mcgine@cotswold.gov.uk

Founded: 1974

Organisation type and purpose: Local government body.

Subject coverage: Local government, economic development, tourism, planning, housing, enabling, environmental health; conservation, landscape; arts, leisure, museums; benefits, elections, waste collection, recycling, landcharges.

Publications: Printed

Access to staff: Contact by letter, by telephone, by fax, by e-mail, in person and via website. Appointment necessary.
Hours: Mon to Fri, 0900 to 1700

Access to building: Prior appointment required

Access for disabled people: Parking provided, ramped entry, level entry

Branch Office: Cotswold District Council; Moreton in Marsh, Gloucestershire; tel: 01608 650881; fax: 01608 651542

COTTAGE AND RURAL ENTERPRISES LIMITED (CARE)

CARE Central Office, 9 Weir Road, Kibworth, Leicestershire, LE8 0LQ

Tel: 0116 279 3225
Fax: 0116 279 6384
E-mail: jp@care-ltd.co.uk
Website: www.care-ltd.co.uk

Enquiries to: Chief Executive

Founded: 1966

Organisation type and purpose: Voluntary organisation, registered charity (charity number 250058).
CARE is a national charity that responds creatively and innovatively to the changing needs of people with learning disabilities.

Subject coverage: Care of adults with a learning disability in communities where they live and work.

Publications: Printed

Access to staff: Contact by letter, by telephone, by fax, by e-mail and via website
Hours: Mon to Fri, 0900 to 1700

COUGAR CLUB OF AMERICA (CCOA)

International Office, 19A Lorne Road, Oxton, Birkenhead, CH43 2JW

Tel: 0151 652 3984
E-mail: international@cougarclub.org
Website: www.cougarclub.org

Enquiries to: International Manager

Founded: 1980

Organisation type and purpose: International organisation, membership association (membership is by subscription), present number of members: 1,000.

Subject coverage: Information regarding 1967 to present, Mercury Cougars, i.e. options, identifications, parts availability, parts suppliers. All this information is free to members.

Publications: Printed

Access to staff: Contact by letter and by e-mail
Hours: Mon to Sat, 1000 to 1900

Parent body: Cougar Club of America; e-mail: membership@cougarclub.org

COUNCIL FOR ADVANCEMENT AND SUPPORT OF EDUCATION (EUROPE) (CASE)

Entrance A, Tavistock House North, Tavistock Square, London, WC1H 9HX

Tel: 020 7387 4404
Fax: 020 7387 4408
E-mail: membership@case.org
Website: www.case.org

Enquiries to: Executive Director
Direct e-mail: jmotion@eurocase.org.uk

Founded: 1994

Organisation type and purpose: International organisation, registered charity (charity number 1042724), training organisation, consultancy, research organisation, publishing house.
Dissemination of Best Practice in the advancement of education.

Subject coverage: Educational external relations, in particular alumni relations, communications, fund raising, marketing, philanthropy, public relations, student recruitment.

Publications: Printed, and electronic and video

Publications list: Available in print

Access to staff: Contact by letter, by telephone, by fax and by e-mail. Access for members only. Non-members charged.
Hours: Mon to Fri, 0900 to 1700

Connections with: CASE; Suite 400, 11 Dupont Circle, Washington, DC, 20036–1261, USA

COUNCIL FOR ALUMINIUM IN BUILDING (CAB)

Bank House, Bond's Mill, Stonehouse, Gloucestershire, GL10 3RF

Tel: 01453 828851
Fax: 01453 828861
E-mail: enquiries@c-a-b.org.uk
Website: www.c-a-b.org.uk

Enquiries to: Chief Executive
Direct tel: 01453 828856

Founded: 1995; incorporates the former Aluminium Window Association (AWA), Architectural Aluminium Association (AAA), Patent Glazing Contractors' Association (PGCA) (year of change 1995)

Organisation type and purpose: Trade association.

Subject coverage: Aluminium in building, patent glazing, curtain wall, aluminium windows, doors, cladding and roofing in aluminium, aluminium powder coatings, anodising, hardware, systems suppliers.

Publications: Printed

Publications list: Available online

Access to staff: Contact by letter, by telephone, by fax and by e-mail
Hours: Mon to Fri, 0900 to 1700

Member organisation of: Centre for Window and Cladding Technology (CWCT); Construction Products Association

COUNCIL FOR AWARDS IN CHILDREN'S CARE AND EDUCATION (CACHE)

8 Chequer Street, St Albans, Hertfordshire, AL1 3XZ

Tel: 01727 847636
Fax: 01727 867609
E-mail: info@cache.org.uk
Website: www.cache.org.uk

Enquiries to: Chief Executive
Other contacts: Information and Publications Officer, Marketing Officer

Founded: 1994; formed by the merger of Council for Early Years Awards (CEYA), National Nursery Examination Board (NNEB), date of change, April 1994; formed by the merger of National Association for Maternal and Child Welfare (NAMCW) (year of change 2000)

Organisation type and purpose: Registered charity (charity number 1036232).
Awarding body.
Offers courses and NVQ assessment in childcare, education and playwork.

Subject coverage: Vocational training in childcare, education and playwork; NVQs; early years workers, A&V units for assessors and verifiers.

Collection: Archive material regarding the history of the NNEB and CEYA, and the development of their awards and courses in child care and education.
Pass lists of candidates who have successfully completed course and awards.

Trade and statistical information: Numbers of candidates registered as training with the Council.
Post-qualifying employment and progression.
Equal opportunities monitoring.
Number of study centres approved to run Council awards and which particular courses they offer.
Number of candidates registered for NVQ assessment.
Number of NVQ Assessment Centres approved by CACHE to offer NVQ assessment and the awards they offer

Publications: Printed, and electronic and video

Publications list: Available online and in print

Access to staff: Contact by letter, by telephone, by fax, by e-mail and via website. Appointment necessary.
Hours: Mon to Fri, 0900 to 1700

COUNCIL FOR BRITISH ARCHAEOLOGY (CBA)

St Mary's House, 66 Bootham, York YO30 7BZ

Tel: 01904 671417
Fax: 01904 671384
E-mail: info@britarch.ac.uk
Website: www.britarch.ac.uk

Enquiries to: Office Administrator

Founded: 1944

Organisation type and purpose:
Membership association (membership is by subscription), present number of members: 10,000 individuals and institutions, registered charity (charity number 1760254), research organisation, publishing house.
To promote the study of Britain's historic environment, provide a forum for archaeological opinion and improve public knowledge and enjoyment of the past through participation, discovery and advocacy.

Subject coverage: Information on all aspects of Britain's historic environment (organisation, research in progress, conservation, legislation, management); specialises in countryside and urban archaeology, archaeology of buildings, archaeological science, nautical archaeology, archaeology in education, calendar of events and excavations, annual Festival of British Archaeology and presenting archaeology to young people.

Publications: Printed, and electronic and video

Publications list: Available online and in print

Access to staff: Contact by letter, by telephone, by fax, by e-mail, in person and via website. Appointment necessary.
Hours: Mon to Fri, 0900 to 1700

Subsidiary body for 8- to 16-year-olds: Young Archaeologists' Club (YAC)

COUNCIL FOR DANCE EDUCATION AND TRAINING (UK) (CDET)

Old Brewer's Yard, 17–19 Neal Street, Covent Garden, London, WC2H 9UY

Tel: 020 7240 5703
Fax: 020 7240 2547
E-mail: info@cdet.org.uk
Website: www.cdet.org.uk

Enquiries to: Administrator

Founded: 1979

Organisation type and purpose:
Professional body, registered charity (charity number 277729).
Professional and representative body for dance education and training matters.

Subject coverage: Vocational dance training, including accredited courses, sources of funding and grants, careers advice.

Collection: The first comprehensive source of information in dance training

Publications: Printed

Access to staff: Contact by letter, by fax and by e-mail
Hours: Mon to Fri, 0930 to 1700
Special comments: Appointment necessary.

Member organisation of: CDET; Conference of Professional Dance Schools

COUNCIL FOR MOSQUES

Formal name: Bradford Council for Mosques

Khidmat Centre, 36 Spencer Road, Bradford BD8 2EU

Tel: 01274 521 792
E-mail: info@khidmat.org.uk
Website: councilformosques.org.uk/

Enquiries to: Press Officer

Founded: 1985

Organisation type and purpose: Voluntary organisation.

Access to staff: Contact by letter, by telephone, by fax, by e-mail and in person. Appointment necessary.
Hours: Mon to Fri, 0930 to 1900

Access for disabled people: Ramped entry, toilet facilities

COUNCIL FOR REGISTERED GAS INSTALLERS, THE (CORGI)

1st Floor, Unit 7, Prisma Park, Berrington Way, Basingstoke, RG24 8WG

Tel: 0870 401 2200
Fax: 0870 401 2600
E-mail: answers@trustcorgi.com
Website: www.trustcorgi.com

Enquiries to: Press Officer
Direct tel: 01256 372254
Direct e-mail: publications@corgi-gas.co.uk
Other contacts: Public Relations Manager

Founded: 1991; formerly called Confederation of Registered Gas Installers (CORGI) (year of change 1991)

Organisation type and purpose:
Membership organisation for gas engineering profession. National watchdog for gas safety until 2009 (when this role passed to Gas Safe Register). Gas safety advice, technical information, events and exhibition, safety equipment.

Publications: Printed
Order printed publications from: CORGI Direct, 4 Elmwood, Chineham Park, Crockford Lane, Basingstoke, Hampshire, RG24 8WG

Publications list: Available online and in print

Access to staff: Contact by letter, by telephone, by fax and by e-mail
Hours: Mon to Thu, 0900 to 1730; Fri, 0900 to 1700

Access for disabled people: Parking provided, ramped entry, access to all public areas, toilet facilities

See also: Gas Safe Register; website: www.gassaferegister.co.uk
Gas Safety Trust; website: www.gas-safety-trust.org.uk

COUNCIL FOR THE ADVANCEMENT OF ARAB-BRITISH UNDERSTANDING (CAABU)

21 Collingham Road, London, SW5 0NU

Tel: 020 7373 8414
Fax: 020 7835 2088
E-mail: caabu@caabu.org

Enquiries to: Information Officer

Founded: 1967

Organisation type and purpose:
International organisation, membership association (membership is by subscription), present number of members: 900, research organisation.
Lobby, education, non-governmental. To promote understanding between peoples of Arab countries and Britain.

Subject coverage: The Arab world, Palestine, Iraq.

Collection: Comprehensive information about all Arab countries

Trade and statistical information:
Newspaper clippings on the Middle East, information service, speakers for schools

Publications: Printed

Publications list: Available online and in print

Access to staff: Contact by letter, by telephone, by fax and by e-mail. Appointment necessary.
Hours: Mon to Thu, 0930 to 1730; Fri, 0930 to 1630

continued overleaf

Access to building: Prior appointment required
Hours: Mon to Fri, 0930 to 1730

Chairs the: European Co-ordinating Committee of Non-governmental Organisations (ECCP) on the question of Palestine

COUNCIL FOR THE HOMELESS (NI) (CHNI)

4th floor, Andras House, 60 Great Victoria Street, Belfast BT2 2BB

Tel: 028 9024 6440
Fax: 028 9024 1266
E-mail: info@chni.org.uk
Website: www.chni.org.uk

Enquiries to: Information Officer

Founded: 1983

Organisation type and purpose: Voluntary organisation, registered charity (charity number XO544/83), training organisation.

Subject coverage: Homelessness, housing benefits, children, finance, health, poverty, legislation, Northern Ireland Housing Executive, organisations and organisational development, individuals' rights, special needs, temporary accommodation, types of housing, women, young people.

Access to staff: Contact by letter, by telephone, by fax, by e-mail, in person and via website
Hours: Mon to Fri, 1000 to 1600

Member organisation of: European Federation of National Organisations Working with the Homeless (FEANTSA); Rue Defacqz 1, 1050 Brussels, Belgium; tel: +32 2 538 6669; fax: +32 2 539 4174

COUNCIL FOR VOLUNTARY SERVICE – SOUTH LAKELAND (SLCVS)

Stricklandgate House, 92 Stricklandgate, Kendal, Cumbria, LA9 4PU

Tel: 01539 742627
Fax: 01539 742628

Enquiries to: Information Officer

Organisation type and purpose: Advisory body, membership association (membership is by election or invitation), voluntary organisation, registered charity (charity number 503635), training organisation.
Concerning voluntary organisations in South Lakeland.

Subject coverage: Advice on voluntary organisations in South Lakeland. Advice on fundraising, recruitment, training and management of voluntary organisations. Advice on charity law. Liaison with health and social care providers.

Collection: Includes the Roger Wilson Library – all on computerised database

Publications: Printed

Access to staff: Contact by letter, by telephone, by fax, by e-mail and in person. Appointment necessary.
Hours: Mon to Fri, 0930 to 1630
Special comments: Wheelchair access to all areas.

COUNCIL FOR WORLD MISSION (CWM)

32–34 Great Peter Street, London, SW1P 2DB

Tel: 020 7222 4214
Fax: 020 7233 1747
E-mail: council@cwmission.org
Website: www.cwmission.org

Enquiries to: Communications Officer
Direct tel: 020 7227 2505
Direct fax: 020 7222 3510
Direct e-mail: kenwyn.pierce@cwmission.org

Founded: 1795; formerly called London Missionary Society (year of change 1977)

Organisation type and purpose: International organisation, registered charity.
Ecumenical organisation.
World mission (Reformed Churches and United Churches).

Subject coverage: Christian world mission.

Collection: Archives of the former London Missionary Society

Publications: Printed

Publications list: Available in print

Access to staff: Contact by letter, by fax, by e-mail and via website. Appointment necessary.
Hours: Mon to Fri, 0900 to 1700

COUNCIL OF DISABLED PEOPLE (CDP)

Formal name: Council of Disabled People – Warwickshire and Coventry

Independent Options, Hillmorton Road, Rugby, Warwickshire, CV22 5AB

Tel: 01926 413334
Fax: 01926 413334

Enquiries to: Director

Organisation type and purpose: Membership association (membership is by subscription), present number of members: 150, registered charity (charity number 1028144).
Meeting the needs of disabled people.

Subject coverage: Benefit information, resource teams.

Publications list: Available in print

Access to staff: Contact by letter
Hours: Mon to Fri, 0900 to 1700

Access to building: Prior appointment required

Access for disabled people: Parking provided, level entry, access to all public areas, toilet facilities

Other addresses: The Council of Disabled People – Warwickshire and Coventry; Fordsfield Centre, Bury Road, Leamington Spa, CV31 3HW

COUNCIL OF MORTGAGE LENDERS (CML)

North West Wing, Bush House, Aldwych, London, WC2B 4PJ

Tel: 0845 373 6771
Fax: 0845 373 6778
Website: www.cml.org.uk

Enquiries to: Information Officer
Direct e-mail: tamsin.askew@cml.org.uk

Founded: 1989

Organisation type and purpose: Trade association.

Subject coverage: Mortgage lending; housing market; financial services.

Publications: Printed, and electronic and video

Publications list: Available online and in print

Access to staff: Contact by letter, by fax, by e-mail and via website
Hours: Mon to Fri, 0900 to 1630

Access to building: No access other than to staff

COUNCIL OF NATIONAL GOLF UNIONS (CONGU)

1 Peerswood Court, Little Neston, Neston, CH64 0US

Tel: 0151 336 3936
E-mail: secretary@congu.com
Website: www.congu.com

Enquiries to: Secretary

Founded: 1924; formerly called British Golf Unions Joint Advisory Committee (year of change 1960)

Organisation type and purpose: Membership association.

Subject coverage: Golf handicaps.

Access to staff: Contact by letter, by telephone and by e-mail
Hours: Mon to Fri, 0900 to 1700

Links with: English Golf Union; Golfing Union of Ireland; Royal and Ancient Golf Club of St. Andrews; Scottish Golf Union; Welsh Golfing Union

COUNCIL OF SIKH GURDWARAS IN BIRMINGHAM (CSGB)

627 Stratford Road, Sparkhill, Birmingham, B11 4LS

Tel: 0121 773 0399
Fax: 0121 773 0699
E-mail: info@sikhcouncil.org.uk

Enquiries to: General Secretary
Direct e-mail: csgb@sikh-council.demon.co.uk

Founded: 1989

Organisation type and purpose: Membership association (membership is by election or invitation), present number of members: 13 organisations, voluntary organisation.
Consultancy on Sikh issues.
To serve and provide a collective voice for Birmingham's Sikh community.

Access to staff: Contact by letter, by telephone, by fax and by e-mail. Appointment necessary.
Hours: Mon to Fri, 1000 to 1800
Special comments: No alcohol, drugs, tobacco.

COUNCIL ON INTERNATIONAL EDUCATIONAL EXCHANGE (CIEE)

52 Poland Street, London, W1F 7AB

Tel: 020 7478 2020
Fax: 020 7734 7322
E-mail: info@ciee.org
Website: www.councilexchanges.org.uk

Enquiries to: Regional Director
Direct e-mail: jccooper@fie.org.uk
Other contacts: Programme Co-ordinator for specific programme enquiries.

Founded: 1947; formerly called Council Exchanges (year of change 1999)

Organisation type and purpose: International organisation, registered charity (charity number 293969).
To arrange international educational exchanges.

Subject coverage: Work abroad and study abroad opportunities for students and recent graduates: work abroad in USA, Canada, Australia, China and Japan; studies abroad in the USA, France, Spain, Italy and Germany.

Publications: Printed

Access to staff: Contact by letter, by telephone, by fax, by e-mail and via website. Appointment necessary.
Hours: Mon to Fri, 0930 to 1730

Founder member of the: Year Out Group

Offices in many cities world-wide including: New York, Paris, Tokyo, Rome, Berlin and Madrid

COUNSEL AND CARE

Formal name: Counsel and Care for the Elderly
Twyman House, 16 Bonny Street, London, NW1 9PG

Tel: 020 7241 8555
Fax: 020 7267 6877
E-mail: advice@counselandcare.org.uk
Website: www.counselandcare.org.uk

Enquiries to: Advicework Department
Direct tel: 0845 300 7585

Founded: 1954; formerly called Elderly Invalids Fund

Organisation type and purpose: National organisation, membership association (membership is by subscription), voluntary organisation, registered charity (charity number 203429).
To provide practical help and advice to people over 60, their families and carers.

Subject coverage: Advice for older people on welfare benefits, community care, hospital discharge, going into care and help at home. One-off grants for older people.

Publications: Printed

Publications list: Available online and in print

Access to staff: Contact by letter, by telephone, by fax, by e-mail and via website. Appointment necessary.
Hours: Mon, Tue, Thu, Fri, 1000 to 1600; Wed, 1000 to 1300

Access for disabled people: Level entry, toilet facilities

COUNTERFEITING INTELLIGENCE BUREAU (CIB)

Formal name: The International Chamber of Commerce – Commercial Crime Services (CCS)
Cinnabar Wharf, 26 Wapping High Street, London, E1W 1NG

Tel: 020 7423 6960
Fax: 020 7423 6961
E-mail: ccs@icc-ccs.org
Website: www.icc-ccs.org/cib/overview.php

Enquiries to: Director

Founded: 1985

Organisation type and purpose: International organisation, membership association (membership is by subscription), consultancy, research organisation.

Subject coverage: Intellectual property rights, trademarks, counterfeiting, infringements, proactive monitoring, reactive intelligence and investigations, anti-counterfeiting technology assistance.

Collection: Special reports on counterfeiting

Publications: Printed

Access to staff: Contact by letter, by telephone, by fax, by e-mail and via website. Appointment necessary.
Hours: Mon to Fri, 0900 to 1700

Access for disabled people: Ramped entry

Specialised division of: International Chamber of Commerce

COUNTRY LAND & BUSINESS ASSOCIATION (CLA)

16 Belgrave Square, London, SW1X 8PQ

Tel: 020 7235 0511
Fax: 020 7235 0528
Website: www.cla.org.uk

Enquiries to: Public Relations Manager
Direct e-mail: richardb@cla.org.uk
Other contacts: Finance and Administration Secretary

Founded: 1907; formerly called Country Landowners Association (CLA) (year of change 2000)

Organisation type and purpose: Membership association (membership is by subscription).
Owners of rural land in England and Wales. 43 branches in England and Wales.

Subject coverage: Legal, tax and economic aspects of rural landowning; land use, conservation, water and minerals interests.

Publications: Printed

Publications list: Available in print

Access to staff: Contact by letter. Access for members only.
Hours: Mon to Fri, 0900 to 1700

Connections with: CBI; Confederation of European Agriculture; European Landowners Organisation; FACE; FWAG; Rural; Rural Voice; Standing Conference on Countryside Sports

Regional Office: CLA, North West Region; Dalton Hall, Stable Yard, Burton, Carnforth, Lancashire, LA6 1NJ; tel: 01524 782209; fax: 01524 782248

COUNTRYSIDE AGENCY

John Dower House, Crescent Place, Cheltenham, Gloucestershire, GL50 3RA

Tel: 01242 521381
Fax: 01242 584270
Website: www.countryside.gov.uk

Enquiries to: Librarian

Founded: 1999; formed by the merger of Countryside Commission; formed by the merger of Rural Development Commission (RDC); formed by the merger of Rural Industries Bureau (RIB); formed by the merger of National Parks Commission (NPC); formed by the merger of Council for Small Industries in Rural Areas (CoSIRA); formed by the merger of Development Commission of CoSIRA; formerly called Development Commission (DC)

Organisation type and purpose: Statutory body.
The 1968 Countryside Act widened its remit to become the Countryside Commission as part of the Department of the Environment; the 1981 Wildlife and Countryside Act gave the Countryside Commission independent status as an independent grant-in-aid corporate body. The Environmental Protection Act 1990 removed the Commission's responsibilities for Wales. From 1 April 1991 these were incorporated in the newly formed Countryside Council for Wales and the Countryside Commission became responsible for England only. In April 1999 the Countryside Commission merged with the Rural Development Commission to become the Countryside Agency responsible for advising government and taking action on issues relating to the social, economic and environmental well-being of the English countryside.
To conserve and enhance England's countryside; to spread social and economic opportunity for people who live there; to help everyone, wherever they live and whatever their background, to enjoy the countryside and share in this priceless asset. The Countryside Agency works to achieve the aims by: influencing those whose decisions affect the countryside through their expertise and research and by spreading good practice; implementing specific work programmes reflecting priorities set by Parliament, the Government and the Agency Board.

Subject coverage: Bulk of stock is from the Countryside Commission Library and covers: conservation and enhancement of landscape beauty; provision and improvement of facilities for countryside recreation, access and rights of way, particularly national trails; planning and management of the countryside, specifically national parks, areas of outstanding natural beauty, heritage coasts. Subject coverage is being broadened to include the rural economy and rural communities.

Library catalogue: All or part available in-house

Publications: Printed, and electronic and video
Order printed publications from: Countryside Agency Postal Sales (Ref: CA2)
PO Box 124, Walgrave, Northampton, NN6 0TL, tel: 01604 781848, fax: 01604 781714

continued overleaf

Publications list: Available online and in print

Access to staff: Contact by letter and by telephone
Hours: Mon to Fri, 0900 to 1700
Special comments: The library closes at 1630 on Fridays.

Access to building: No access other than to staff
Special comments: Currently in temporary accommodation with no access for visitors.

Affiliated to: Council of Europe; Federation of Nature and National Parks of Europe; International Union for the Conservation of Nature and Natural Resources (IUCNNR)

Funded by: Department for Environment, Food and Rural Affairs

Other addresses: Also some national functions; Dacre House, 19 Dacre Street, London, SW1H 0DH; tel: 020 7340 2900; fax: 020 7340 2911; East Midlands; 18 Market Place, Bingham, Nottingham, NG13 8AP; tel: 01949 876200; fax: 01949 876222; East of England; Ortona House, 110 Hills Road, Cambridge, CB2 1LQ; tel: 01223 354462; fax: 01223 313850; North East; Cross House, Westgate Road, Newcastle upon Tyne, NE1 4XX; tel: 0191 269 1600; fax: 0191 269 1601; North West; Haweswater Road, Penrith, CA11 7EH; tel: 01768 865752; fax: 01768 890414; North West; 7th Floor, Bridgewater House, Whitworth Street, Manchester, M1 6LT; tel: 0161 237 1061; fax: 0161 237 1062; South East & London; Sterling House, 7 Ashford Road, Maidstone, ME14 5BJ; tel: 01622 765222; fax: 01622 662102; South West; 2nd Floor, 11–15 Dix's Field, Exeter, EX1 1QA; tel: 01392 477150; fax: 01392 477151; South West; Bridge House, Sion Place, Clifton Down, Bristol, BS8 4AS; tel: 0117 973 9966; fax: 0117 923 8086; West Midlands; Strickland House, The Lawns, Park Street, Wellington, Telford, TF1 3BX; tel: 01952 247161; fax: 01952 248700; West Midlands and Doorstep Greens National Project Team; 1st Floor, Vincent House, Tindal Bridge, 92–93 Edward Street, Birmingham, B1 2RA; tel: 0121 233 9399; fax: 0121 233 9286; Yorkshire & The Humber; 4th Floor, Victoria Wharf, No 4 The Embankment, Sovereign Street, Leeds, LS1 4BA; tel: 0113 246 9222; fax: 0113 246 0353

COUNTRYSIDE ALLIANCE

367 Kennington Road, London, SE11 4PT

Tel: 020 7840 9200
Fax: 020 7793 8484
E-mail: info@countryside-alliance.org
Website: www.countryside-alliance.org

Enquiries to: Information Officer
Other contacts: Membership for membership queries.

Founded: 1930; formed from British Field Sports Society (BFSS), Countryside Movement; formed from Countryside Business Group (year of change 1997)

Organisation type and purpose: Advisory body, membership association (membership is by subscription), present number of members: 85,000, suitable for ages: 10 to 18. To champion the countryside, country sports and the rural way of life.

Subject coverage: Rural issues – rural livelihood, businesses, lifestyles and country sports. Land management, access to the countryside and conservation.

Trade and statistical information: Economic facts relating to country sports and countryside in general

Publications: Printed

Access to staff: Contact by letter, by telephone, by fax, by e-mail and via website
Hours: Mon to Fri, 0900 to 1700

Regional Offices: Countryside Alliance

COUNTRYSIDE COUNCIL FOR WALES (CCW)

Maes y Ffynnon, Penrhosgarnedd, Bangor, Gwynedd, LL57 2DW

Tel: 01248 385500
Fax: 01248 355782
E-mail: enquiries@ccw.gov.uk
Website: www.ccw.gov.uk

Enquiries to: Librarian
Other contacts: Public Relations Officer for press.

History of institution: formerly called Countryside Commission Wales, Nature Conservancy Council (year of change 1991)

Organisation type and purpose: National government body.
Statutory body funded by a grant from the Welsh Assembly Government.
The Countryside Council for Wales is the government's statutory adviser on wildlife, countryside and maritime conservation matters in Wales.

Subject coverage: Wildlife, countryside and maritime conservation matters, conservation of plants, mammals, reptiles and amphibians, promotes protection of landscape, opportunities for recreation, planning and management of the countryside.

Publications: Printed

Publications list: Available online and in print

Access to staff: Contact by letter, by telephone, by fax, by e-mail and via website. Appointment necessary.
Hours: Mon to Fri, 0900 to 1700

Access for disabled people: Parking provided, ramped entry, toilet facilities

Branches: North Area Office, Countryside Council for Wales; Llys y Bont, Ffordd y Parc, Parc Menai, Bangor, Gwynedd, LL57 4BN; tel: 01248 672500; fax: 01248 679259; e-mail: s.williams@ccw.gov.uk; South and East Area Office, Countryside Council for Wales; Unit 7, Castleton Court, Fortran Road, St Mellons, Cardiff, CF3 0LT; tel: 02920 772400; fax: 02920 772412; e-mail: annmorgan@ccw.gov.uk; West Area Office, Countryside Council for Wales; Plas Gogerddan, Aberystwyth, Ceredigion, SY23 3EE; tel: 01970 821100; fax: 01970 828314; e-mail: i.frost@ccw.gov.uk

COUNTRYWIDE HOLIDAYS (COUNTRYWIDE)

Miry Lane, Wigan, Lancashire, WN3 4AG

Tel: 01942 823456
Fax: 01942 242518
E-mail: info@ramblersholidays.co.uk
Website: www.countrywidewalking.com

Enquiries to: Manager
Direct tel: 01942 823529
Direct fax: 01942 825034
Other contacts: (1) Marketing Manager (2) Product Manager for (1) advertising and promotion (2) new products and contracting.

Founded: 1893; formerly called CHA (year of change 1992)

Organisation type and purpose:
Membership association (membership is by subscription).
Holiday company and guest house accommodation provider.

Subject coverage: Countrywide Holidays specialises in walking and special interest holidays, including bridge, dancing, painting, photography and countryside appreciation. Holidays are offered throughout the UK to individuals, special arrangements are available for groups.

Collection: Guest House collection brochure
Historical information
Holiday brochures
Newsletters
Transparencies available for loan to journalists for promotion purposes

Publications: Printed

Access to staff: Contact by letter, by telephone, by fax, by e-mail and via website
Hours: Mon to Sat, 0900 to 1700

COUNTY OF HEREFORDSHIRE DISTRICT COUNCIL (Herefordshire Council)

Brockington, 35 Hafod Road, Hereford, HR1 1SH

Tel: 01432 260000
Fax: 01432 260384
Website: www.herefordshire.gov.uk

Enquiries to: Chief Executive
Direct tel: 01432 260044
Direct fax: 01432 340189

Founded: 1998

Organisation type and purpose: Local government body.

Subject coverage: Local government services.

Access to staff: Contact by letter, by telephone and by fax
Hours: Mon to Fri, 0900 to 1700

Access to building: No access other than to staff

COURT BARN MUSEUM (Court Barn)

Formal name: The Guild of Handicraft Trust

Church Street, Chipping Campden, Gloucestershire, GL55 6JE

Tel: 01386 841951
E-mail: admin@courtbarn.org.uk
Website: www.courtbarn.org.uk

Enquiries to: Administrator
Other contacts: Curator

Founded: 1990

Organisation type and purpose: Registered charity (charity number 1007696), museum, suitable for ages: 5+.
Collections of material relating to art, craft and design in Chipping Campden and the North Cotswolds.
To preserve, promote and encourage an understanding of the work of artists, craftsmen and women, and designers of Chipping Campden and the North Cotswolds.

Subject coverage: Information and material relating to C R Ashbee's Guild of Handicraft in Chipping Campden 1902–1919, a permanent exhibition of the work of: CR Ashbee in silverwork, jewellery and printed books; Katharine Adams, bookbinder; FL Griggs, illustrator and etcher; Paul Woodroffe, illustrator and stained-glass artist; Alex Miller, carver and sculptor; Gordon Russell, furniture designer; the Winchcombe Pottery; the Hart workshop, silversmiths; and Robert Welch, silversmith and industrial designer.

Special visitor services: The exhibition at Court Barn accommodates about 20 people; groups of 15 or more should book with the Administrator.

Education services: Children are welcome; family packs and drawing materials provided. There is a space for classes, workshops, temporary exhibitions and work with schools.

Collection: The gallery houses the Trust's collections, including the working archive of Robert Welch.

Non-library collection catalogue: All or part available in-house

Publications: Printed

Publications list: Available in print

Access to staff: Contact by letter, by telephone and by e-mail. Appointment necessary.
Hours: Any reasonable time during museum opening hours

Access to building: *Hours:* April to September: Tue to Sun, 1000 to 1700
October to March: Tue to Sun 1000 to 1600
Special comments: Closed on Mondays (except bank holidays) and from 24 December, reopening second Tuesday in January.

Access for disabled people: *Special comments:* Wheelchair access except in the archive. Staff will bring archive material to disabled visitors.

COURT OF THE LORD LYON KING OF ARMS

HM New Register House, Edinburgh, EH1 3YT

Tel: 0131 556 7255
Fax: 0131 557 2148
Website: www.lyon-court.com

Enquiries to: Lyon Clerk

Organisation type and purpose: Court of Law.
Court of heraldic jurisdiction.

Subject coverage: The granting and control of heraldry in Scotland.

Collection: Heraldic, genealogical and associated library (non-lending library, not public)

Non-library collection catalogue: All or part available in-house

Library catalogue: All or part available in-house

Access to staff: Contact by letter, by fax and via website. Appointment necessary.
Hours: Mon to Fri, 1000 to 1230 and 1400 to 1600

COURTAULD INSTITUTE OF ART, BOOK LIBRARY

Somerset House, Strand, London, WC2R 0RN

Tel: 020 7848 2701
Fax: 020 7848 2887
E-mail: booklib@courtauld.ac.uk
Website: www.courtauld.ac.uk

Founded: 1933

Organisation type and purpose: University department or institute.
Library.

Subject coverage: Fine arts (painting, sculpture, architecture) in the Western tradition from classical antiquity to the present.

Collection: Extensive photographic collections administered separately from the Book Library

Non-library collection catalogue: All or part available online

Library catalogue: All or part available online and in-house

Access to staff: Contact by letter, by telephone, by fax, by e-mail and via website. Appointment necessary.
Hours: Term time: 0930 to 2100 (last admission before 1900)
Vacations: 1030 to 1730
Special comments: A last-resort reference library.

Constituent part of: University of London

COVENT GARDEN MARKET AUTHORITY (CGMA)

Covent House, New Covent Garden Market, London, SW8 5NX

Tel: 020 7720 2211
Fax: 020 7622 5307
E-mail: info@cgma.gov.uk
Website: www.cgma.gov.uk

Enquiries to: Information Officer

Founded: 1961

Organisation type and purpose: Statutory body.
Wholesale market operator.

Subject coverage: Wholesaling of horticultural produce; operation of the market with over 300 market tenants including wholesalers, catering distributors, importers, hauliers and trade and official bodies.

Trade and statistical information: Annual turnover figures for traders on New Covent Garden Market

Publications: Printed

Access to staff: Contact by telephone
Hours: Mon to Fri, 0900 to 1700

Links with: Department for Environment, Food and Rural Affairs

COVENTRY & WARWICKSHIRE CHAMBER OF COMMERCE

Chamber House, Unit 8–9 Innovation Village, Cheetah Road, Coventry, Warwickshire, CV1 2TL

Tel: 024 7665 4321
Fax: 024 7645 0242
E-mail: info@cw-chamber.co.uk
Website: www.cw-chamber.co.uk

Enquiries to: Information Officer

Founded: 2001; formerly called Business Link Coventry & Warwickshire; formerly called Coventry & Warwickshire Chamber of Commerce Training & Enterprise (year of change 2001)

Organisation type and purpose: National government body, membership association (membership is by subscription), present number of members: 1800.
Chamber of Commerce.

Subject coverage: Market research, export, design and innovation, information technology, manufacturing, personal business advisors, finance, start-up advice, training advice.

Collection: Reference Directories

Trade and statistical information: Local economic assessments

Publications list: Available online

Access to staff: Contact by letter, by telephone, by fax, by e-mail, in person and via website
Hours: Mon to Fri, 0900 to 1700

Access for disabled people: Parking provided, ramped entry, access to all public areas, toilet facilities.

Other addresses: Coventry & Warwickshire Chamber of Commerce; Progress House, Avenue Farm, Birmingham Road, Stratford Upon Avon, CV37 0HR

COVENTRY CITY ARCHIVES

Formal name: Coventry History Centre

Herbert Art Gallery & Museum, Jordan Well, Coventry, CV1 5QP

Tel: 024 7683 4060
Fax: 024 7683 4060

Enquiries to: Archivist/Librarian

Founded: 1937; formerly called Coventry Record Office (CRO) (year of change 1995); formerly called Coventry Archives (year of change 2008)

Organisation type and purpose: Local government body, local government archives service.

Subject coverage: Family history, local history of Coventry including destruction in World War II and post-war reconstruction. Local authority records, Coventry Borough Archives 1182–1881, records of non-conformist churches.

continued overleaf

Information services: Combined Archive and Local History Centre. Resources for local and family history.

Collection: Archive collections of organisations and individuals who are or have been active in Coventry from the 12th to the 20th centuries.
Freemans and Apprentice Records from Coventry 1714 onwards.
Cancelled vehicle registration cards to the early 1960s.
Local public records, including quarter sessions, magistrates court, coroner's court and hospital records.
Large collection of architect plans, building plans and byelaws for all areas of Coventry, from1900 onwards.
Collection of oral history tapes (with transcripts) covering most aspects of Coventry's recent history, especially the motor cars and allied trades.
Microfilms of Church of England and Roman Catholic registers for Coventry and environs and local cemetery records.
Detailed 1851 map of Coventry prepared for the local Board of Health.
Plans for reconstruction of Coventry after World War II.
Medieval records of the city from 12th century onwards, including minutes of the Court Leet 1421 and records of Coventry's trading companies, Guilds.
Records of the Blitz and post-war reconstruction of the city.
Deposited and donated collections also include local and district trade union records, business records, notably Rootes (and constituent companies, e.g. Singer Motors), Armstrong-Siddley, Armstrong Whitworth, Daimler and Clarke Cluley, records of non-conformist churches, clubs, societies, schools and other local organisations.
A large majority of the Coventry City Archives catalogues are computerised on the CALM database, direct customer access on site is available and also at other heritage facilities in the city.
Card indexes for Coventry Freemen (women included from the 1930s), microfiche indexes of apprenticeship enrolments 1781–1841, microfiche index of building plans and byelaws, card indexes for architects plans (all of these are gradually being transferred to computer catalogue).

Non-library collection catalogue: All or part available online and in-house

Library catalogue: All or part available in-house

Publications: Printed

Publications list: Available in print

Access to staff: Contact by letter, by telephone, by fax, by e-mail and in person
Hours: Mon to Fri, 0930 to 1645
Special comments: Identification required to obtain County Archive Research Network (CARN) reader ticket.

Access to building: No prior appointment required
Special comments: Preparing to move to new premises.

Access for disabled people: Lift, access to all public areas, toilet facilities
Special comments: Minimal parking provided.

Links with: Coventry Arts and Heritage; Herbert Art Gallery and Museum, Jordan Well, Coventry; tel: 02476 832386; fax: 02476 220171; e-mail: info@theherbert.org; website: http://www.theherbert.org

COVENTRY FAMILY HISTORY SOCIETY (COVFHS)

12 Knoll Drive, Styvechale, Coventry, CV3 5BT

Tel: 024 7669 3904
E-mail: enquiries@covfhs.org
Website: www.covfhs.org

Enquiries to: General Secretary

Founded: 1994

Organisation type and purpose: Membership association (membership is by subscription), present number of members: 450, voluntary organisation, registered charity (charity number 1070160).
To promote genealogy, family history and local history studies of Coventry and surrounding parishes and villages.

Subject coverage: Tracing ancestry, genealogy of local areas.

Publications: Printed, and microform publications
Order printed publications from: Bookshop Manager, Coventry Family History Society, 88 Howes Lane, Coventry, West Midlands, CV3 6PJ

Publications list: Available online and in print

Access to staff: Contact by letter, by telephone, by e-mail and via website. Appointment necessary. Non-members charged.
Hours: Mon to Fri, 0900 to 1700

Links with: Federation of Family History Societies

COVENTRY LIBRARIES AND INFORMATION SERVICES

Central Library, Smithford Way, Coventry, Warwickshire, CV1 1FY

Tel: 024 7683 2314; 024 7683 2395 (minicom)
Fax: 024 7683 2440
E-mail: central.library@coventry.gov.uk
Website: www.coventry.gov.uk/libraries

Enquiries to: Libraries & Information Services Manager
Direct fax: 024 7683 2470

Organisation type and purpose: Public library.

Subject coverage: General, industrial relations and trade union affairs, current and historical; Coventry local studies collection; automobile engineering; history of automobiles (local studies, auto engineering, auto history now at Herbert Art Gallery and Museum)

Collection: Angela Brazil Collection (at Herbert Art Gallery and Museum)
Bartleet Collection on development of the bicycle (at Herbert Art Gallery and Museum)
Workshop Manuals Collection (at Herbert Art Gallery and Museum)
George Eliot Collection (at Herbert Art Gallery and Museum)
Tom Mann Centre for Trade Union and Labour Studies
Waring Brown Collection of newscuttings on engineering (at Herbert Art Gallery and Museum)

Library catalogue: All or part available online and in-house

Publications: Printed, and electronic and video

Publications list: Available online and in print

Access to staff: Contact by letter, by telephone, by fax, by e-mail and in person. Appointment necessary.
Hours: Mon to Fri, 0900 to 2000; Sat, 0900 to 1630; Sun, 1200 to 1600

Access to building: No access to non-public areas other than with staff permission

Access for disabled people: Access to all public areas, lifts, toilet facilities

COVENTRY UNIVERSITY – LANCHESTER LIBRARY

Gosford Street, Coventry, Warwickshire, CV1 5DD

Tel: 024 7688 7541
Fax: 024 7688 7525
Website: wwwm.coventry.ac.uk/cu/library

Enquiries to: University Librarian

History of institution: formerly called Lanchester Library of Lanchester Polytechnic; incorporates the former Art & Design Library (year of change 2000)

Organisation type and purpose: University library.

Subject coverage: Biology, building construction, business studies, chemistry, civil engineering, communication studies, computer science, control engineering and systems, economics, electrical engineering, geography and topography, health sciences, industrial design, life sciences, linguistics, materials science, mathematics, mechanical engineering, microbiology, motor vehicle engineering, operational research, physics, physiotherapy, politics, production engineering, social science, social work, statistics, town and country planning, performing arts, nursing and midwifery.
Art in general, art history, design, films and cinema, graphic art and design, photography, television, communication studies, computer graphics and industrial design.

Collection: Lanchester Collection (manuscripts and archives of Dr F W Lanchester, pioneer motor car designer and engineer, and early theory of flight)

Non-library collection catalogue: All or part available online

Library catalogue: All or part available online

Access to staff: Contact by letter, by telephone, by fax, in person and via website
Hours: Term-time: Mon to Thu, 0845 to 1900; Fri, 0900 to 1715; Sat, Sun, 1300 to 1700
Vacations: Mon to Fri, 0900 to 1700

Access for disabled people: Level entry, access to all public areas, toilet facilities, parking

CPRE

Formal name: Council for the Protection of Rural England

128 Southwark Street, London, SE1 0SW

Tel: 020 7981 2800
Fax: 020 7981 2899
E-mail: info@cpre.org.uk
Website: www.cpre.org.uk

Enquiries to: Librarian
Direct e-mail: publications@cpre.org.uk
Other contacts: Library & Information Unit for CPRE history and archive information requests.

Founded: 1926; formerly called Council for the Preservation of Rural England (year of change 1969)

Organisation type and purpose: Membership association (membership is by subscription), present number of members: 49,000, registered charity (charity number 242809), research organisation.
Independent environment group.
Lobbying locally, Parliament, Whitehall and the EC for countryside protection.

Subject coverage: Improvement, protection and management of the rural scenery and amenities of the countryside and its towns and villages, in particular, planning, green belts, development control, access to the countryside, transport policies, motorways, heavy lorries, mineral extraction, farmed landscape, land drainage, water resources, tourism/recreation and impact on the countryside, forestry and woodlands, hedgerows, environmental assessment, energy policies, rural development, housing and urban regeneration.

Collection: CPRE documents and archives

Non-library collection catalogue: All or part available in-house

Library catalogue: All or part available in-house

Publications: Printed

Publications list: Available in print

Access to staff: Contact by letter, by telephone, by fax and by e-mail.
Appointment necessary.
Hours: Mon to Fri, 0930 to 1730
Special comments: Access only to bona fide researchers on the work of CPRE.

Access to building: Prior appointment required

Has: 43 branches and district committees; in every English county. Contact numbers available, from national office

CPRE HERTFORDSHIRE (CPRE Herts.)

31A Church Street, Welwyn Garden City, Hertfordshire, AL6 9LW

Tel: 01438 717587
Fax: 01438 714984
E-mail: office@cpreherts.org.uk
Website: www.cpreherts.org.uk

Enquiries to: Executive Secretary

Founded: 1936; formerly called The Hertfordshire Conservation Society (HCS) (year of change 1997)

Organisation type and purpose: Membership association, present number of members: 1,350 in Hertfordshire, 60,000 nationally, voluntary organisation, registered charity (charity number 211299). Protection of the countryside.

Subject coverage: Promotes beauty, tranquillity and diversity of rural Hertfordshire by encouraging the sustainable use of land and other natural resources in town and country. Operates through the planning system, screening planning applications countywide and raising the alarm where the countryside is threatened. Influences planning policy through the local plan process. Offers advice and support to individuals and local groups embarking on planning campaigns. Lobbies for sustainable transport polices and safer country lanes. Organises the Hertfordshire Village of the Year competition.

Publications: Printed

Access to staff: Contact by letter, by telephone, by fax, by e-mail and via website
Hours: Mon to Thu, 0930 to 1700

Parent body: Campaign to Protect Rural England (CPRE); 128 Southwark Street, London, SE1 0SW; tel: 020 7981 2800; fax: 020 7981 2899; e-mail: info@cpre.org.uk; website: http://www.cpre.org.uk

CPRE LANCASHIRE

Formal name: Campaign to Protect Rural England Lancashire Branch

Hazelwell's House, Station Road, Bamber Bridge, Preston, PR5 6TT

Tel: 01772 627510
E-mail: ruralengland@btconnect.com

Enquiries to: Administration Officer

Founded: 1933

Organisation type and purpose: Membership association (membership is by subscription), voluntary organisation, registered charity (charity number 1107376). To protect the countryside and the country towns and villages of Lancashire and parts of Greater Manchester and Merseyside.

Subject coverage: Rural land use, planning policy and development control, material from a wide range of sources.

Collection: Library set of CPRE publications (campaigners' guides, authoritative reports and free leaflets); stock can be obtained

Publications: Printed

Publications list: Available online

Access to staff: Contact by letter, by telephone, by e-mail and in person.
Appointment necessary.
Hours: Mon, Tue and Thu, 0930 to 1230
Special comments: No information service, only access to the collection and files.

Constituent part of: CPRE; Warwick House, 128 Southwark St, London, SE1 0SW; tel: 020 7981 2800; e-mail: info@cpre.org.uk; website: http://www.cpre.org.uk

CRAFTS COUNCIL

44A Pentonville Road, Islington, London, N1 9BY

Tel: 020 7278 7700
Fax: 020 7837 6891
Website: www.craftscouncil.org.uk

Enquiries to: Research and Information Assistants
Direct tel: 020 7806 2501
Direct e-mail: reference@craftscouncil.org.uk
Other contacts: Research and Information Officer

Founded: 1971; formerly called Crafts Advisory Committee (year of change 1979)

Organisation type and purpose: National organisation, registered charity (charity number 280956). National development agency for contemporary craft.

Subject coverage: Contemporary British craft: retail outlets, suppliers of materials, exhibitions, funding sources, business practice, guilds and societies, techniques.

Information services: Enquiry service by telephone, email and post.

Collection: Crafts Council Collection, the national collection of works by leading contemporary crafts people, available for loan to public institutions
Online image library of more than 30,000 images of contemporary work

Non-library collection catalogue: All or part available in-house

Library catalogue: All or part available in-house

Publications: Printed

Access to staff: Contact by letter, by telephone, by e-mail, in person and via website. Appointment necessary.
Hours: Research Library: Wed, Thu, 1000 to 1700
Special comments: By appointment only.

Access to building: Reception open to the public, Research Library available by appointment
Hours: Reception: Mon to Fri, 1000 to 1700; Research Library: Wed, Thu, 1000 to 1700

Access for disabled people: There is disabled access
Hours: Mon to Fri, 1000 to 1700

Funded by: Arts Council England; 14 Great Peter Street, London, SW1P 3NQ; website: http://www.artscouncil.org.uk

CRAFTS STUDY CENTRE

University of the Creative Arts, Falkner Road, Farnham, Surrey, GU9 7DS

Tel: 01252 891450
Fax: 01252 891451
E-mail: craftscentre@ucreative.ac.uk
Website: www.csc.ucreative.ac.uk

Enquiries to: Information & Administration Officer

Founded: 1977

Organisation type and purpose: A registered charity (261109) functioning as a specialist museum and a research centre of the University for the Creative Arts.

Subject coverage: Modern calligraphy, furniture and crafts in ceramics, textiles and wood.

continued overleaf

Education services: Research visits welcome by appointment; please telephone 01252 891450

Collection: Supporting material includes makers' diaries, working notes and photographs dating from the 1920s

Access to staff: Contact by letter, by telephone, by fax, by e-mail, in person and via website
Hours: Tue to Fri, 1000 to 1700; Sat, 1000 to 1600

Access to building: *Hours:* Tue to Fri, 1000 to 1700; Sat, 1000 to 1600

Access for disabled people: The Centre is accessible to wheelchair users, induction loop at reception

CRANFIELD PRECISION (CP)

Formal name: Cranfield Precision, Divison of Unova UK Limited

Woburn House, 3 Adams Close, Kempston, Bedfordshire, MK42 7JE

Tel: 01234 312820
Fax: 01535 367121
E-mail: cpsales@landis-lund.co.uk
Website: www.cranfieldprecision.com

Enquiries to: Marketing Department

Founded: 1968; formerly called Cranfield Unit for Precision Engineering (CUPE) (year of change 1987)

Organisation type and purpose:
Manufacturing industry, university department or institute, consultancy, research organisation.
OEM design, manufacture and application in machine tools.

Subject coverage: Precision engineering, including metrology, machine design, servo system design and development, measuring systems (linear and angular), control systems. Applications in semiconductor processing and computer peripheral manufacturing, as well as in automotive, advanced optics, optoelectronics and other ultra-precision manufacturing industries.

Access to staff: Contact by telephone and by e-mail
Hours: Mon to Fri, 0830 to 1700

Parent body: Landis Lund, Division of Unova UK Limited; tel: 01535 633211

CRANFIELD UNIVERSITY (CU)

Cranfield, Bedfordshire, MK43 0AL

Tel: 01234 750111
Fax: 01234 752391
E-mail: e.hartill@cranfield.ac.uk
Website: www.cranfieldlibrary.cranfield.ac.uk
Website: diglib.shrivenham.cranfield.ac.uk
Website: www.cranfield.ac.uk

Enquiries to: University Librarian
Direct tel: 01234 754446

Organisation type and purpose: University library.

Subject coverage: Aerospace engineering; electronics; mechanical engineering; advanced materials; advanced manufacturing techniques, defence science and technology, agricultural engineering; food production; land use; management, water and waste technology, biotechnology, health science, logistics, natural resources.

Collection: Aeronautical history
Aerospace Technology Reports (NASA, AGARD, AIAA, ARC)
History of ballooning (Kings Norton Library)
British Balloon Library; Kings Norton Collection.

Library catalogue: All or part available online

Includes the: Defence College of Management and Technology,; Shrivenham

CREATIVESHEFFIELD (SF4I)

1st Floor, The Fountain Precinct, Balm Green, Sheffield, S1 2JA

Tel: 0114 223 2345
Fax: 0114 223 2346
E-mail: info@creativesheffield.co.uk
Website: www.creativesheffield.co.uk

Enquiries to: Director – Operations

Founded: 2007; formerly called Sheffield First for Investment; formerly called Sheffield One

Organisation type and purpose: Local government body.
Provides a single point of contact for inward investment, relocation and business development enquiries, marketing Sheffield and visitor attractions.

Subject coverage: Industrial and commercial property, sources of financial assistance, the development climate, local partner organisations, statistical information on Sheffield, local labour market and economy.

Information services: All information on Sheffield as a place to live, work and visit.

Trade and statistical information: Database of available industrial and commercial property
General information and statistics on Sheffield

Publications: Printed

Access to staff: Contact by letter, by telephone, by fax, by e-mail and via website. Appointment necessary.
Hours: Mon to Fri, 0830 to 1715

Links with: Yorkshire Forward

Parent body: Sheffield City Council

CREDIT PROTECTION ASSOCIATION

CPA House, 350 King Street, London, W6 0RX

Tel: 020 8846 0000; freephone: 0800 634 0187
Fax: 020 8741 7459
E-mail: via website
Website: www.cpa.co.uk

Founded: 1914

Organisation type and purpose:
Membership association providing credit management services to members.

Subject coverage: Innovative IT connects client-members to essential financial data, enabling instant decision making relating to the granting of credit. Client-members can also instantaneously refer their overdue accounts, which usually results in full settlement days later.

Access to staff: Contact by letter, by telephone, by fax and via website

Branches: in or near Falkirk, Bolton, Harrogate, Birmingham, Newmarket and Bristol

CREMATION SOCIETY OF GREAT BRITAIN (CSGB)

Brecon House, 1st Floor, 16–16A Albion Place, Maidstone, Kent, ME14 5DZ

Tel: 01622 688292/3
Fax: 01622 686698
E-mail: info@cremation.org.uk
Website: www.cremation.org.uk

Enquiries to: Secretary

Founded: 1874

Organisation type and purpose: Advisory body, membership association, registered charity.

Subject coverage: Cremation and its religious, legal, technical, architectural and statistical aspects; crematorium administration.

Collection: Society's records since 1874. From 1999 these have been transferred to University of Durham Library (Special Collections)

Publications: Printed

Access to staff: Contact by letter, by telephone, by fax and by e-mail
Hours: Mon to Fri, 0900 to 1700

Founder member of the: International Cremation Federation; tel: +31 70 3518836; fax: +31 70 3518827; e-mail: keizer@facultatieve.com; website: http://www.int-crem-fed.org

CRIME CONCERN TRUST

Beaver House, 147–150 Victoria Road, Swindon, Wiltshire, SN1 3UY

Tel: 01793 863500
Fax: 01793 514654
Website: www.crimeconcern.org.uk
Website: www.safer-community.net

Direct e-mail: john.skillicorn-aston@catch-22.org.uk

Founded: 1988

Organisation type and purpose: Registered charity (charity number 800735).
Working with local and national partners to reduce crime and create safer communities.

Subject coverage: Crime prevention, burglary reduction, domestic violence, racial harassment, youth crime, car crime, neighbourhood safety, drug misuse prevention, and personal safety.

Library catalogue: All or part available online

Publications: Printed

Publications list: Available online and in print

Access to staff: Contact by letter, by

telephone, by fax, by e-mail and via website
Hours: Mon to Fri, 0900 to 1715

CRIMESTOPPERS TRUST (Crimestoppers)

Apollo House, 66A London Road, Morden, Surrey, SM4 5BE

Tel: 020 8254 3200
Fax: 020 8254 3201
E-mail: cst@crimestoppers-uk.org
Website: www.crimestoppers-uk.org

Enquiries to: Director
Other contacts: Head of Marketing & Fundraising for any marketing or fundraising enquiries.

Founded: 1986; formed from Community Action Trust (year of change 1995)

Organisation type and purpose: Registered charity (charity number 1108687).
To create an alliance to fight crime.

Subject coverage: Crimestoppers Trust publicises the Crimestoppers Scheme and supports specific crime-fighting initiatives. To date Crimestoppers have received 320,000 anonymous phone calls leading to 30,000 arrests and the recovery of property valued at £44 million. With other offences taken into consideration, it is estimated that information given to Crimestoppers has helped to clear up almost 100,000 crimes.

Trade and statistical information: The only UK charity dedicated to solving crimes

Publications: Printed

Publications list: Available online and in print

Access to staff: Contact by letter, by telephone, by fax, by e-mail and via website. Appointment necessary. Letter of introduction required.
Hours: Mon to Fri, 0900 to 1700

Access to building: No access other than to staff, prior appointment required

CRIMINAL BAR ASSOCIATION (CBA)

2–3 Cursitor Street, London, EC4A 1NE

Tel: 020 7242 1289
Fax: 020 7242 1107
E-mail: videoconference@dial.pipex.com
Website: www.criminalbar.com

Enquiries to: Administrator

Founded: 1969

Organisation type and purpose: Professional body (membership is by qualification), present number of members: 2,700.

Subject coverage: Criminal procedure and practice, policy of the specialist organisation for members of the Criminal Bar, criminal justice system.

Publications: Printed

Access to staff: Contact by letter, by fax and by e-mail
Hours: Mon to Fri, 0900 to 1700

Links with: General Council of The Bar; 3 Bedford Row, London, WC1R 4DB; tel: 020 7240 0082; fax: 020 7831 9217

CRIMINAL INJURIES COMPENSATION AUTHORITY (CICA)

Tay House, 300 Bath Street, Glasgow, G2 4LN 0800 358 3601 0141 331 2287

Tel: 0300 003 3601
Fax: 0141 331 2287
E-mail: general.enquiries@cica.gsi.gov.uk
Website: www.cica.gov.uk

Enquiries to: Media Enquiries
Direct e-mail: media.contact@cica.gsi.gov.uk

Founded: 1964; formerly called Criminal Injuries Compensation Board (year of change 1995)

Organisation type and purpose: National government body.
Government board.

Subject coverage: Compensates blameless victims of violent crime for physical and mental injuries, based on the rules Parliament sets in the criminal injuries compensation scheme(s).

Publications: Printed

CRISIS

Formal name: Crisis UK trading as Crisis

66 Commercial Street, London, E1 6LT

Tel: 0870 011 3335
Fax: 0870 011 3336
E-mail: enquiries@crisis.org.uk
Website: www.crisis.org.uk

Enquiries to: Marketing Executive

Founded: 1967; formerly called Crisis at Christmas

Organisation type and purpose: National organisation, voluntary organisation, registered charity (charity number 1082947).
Crisis is a national charity for homeless people.

Subject coverage: Homelessness, housing, volunteering, fundraising.

Collection: Photograph library
Reports on homelessness issues

Trade and statistical information: Statistics on homelessness and housing

Publications: Printed

Publications list: Available online and in print

Access to staff: Contact by letter, by telephone, by fax, by e-mail and via website
Hours: Mon to Fri, 0930 to 1730; Sat, Sun, closed

Access to building: No access other than to staff

CROFTING COMMISSION

Great Glen House, Leachkin Road, Inverness

Tel: 01463 663450
Fax: 01463 711820
E-mail: info@crofting.scotland.gov.uk
Website: www.crofting.scotland.gov.uk

Enquiries to: Head of Communications
Direct tel: 01463 663479
Direct e-mail: jane.thomas@crofting.scotland.gov.uk

Founded: 2012; formerly called Crofters Commission (year of change 2012)

Organisation type and purpose: National government body, advisory body, statutory body.
Non-departmental government body.

Subject coverage: Crofting regulation
Croft house grants

Non-library collection catalogue: All or part available online and in print

Publications: Printed

Publications list: Available online and in print

Access to staff: Contact by letter, by telephone, by fax, by e-mail, in person and via website. Appointment necessary.
Hours: Mon to Thu, 0830 to 1700; Fri, 0830 to 1630

Access to building: *Hours:* Mon to Fri, 0900 to 1630

Access for disabled people: Fully accessible, toilet facilities

CROHN'S IN CHILDHOOD RESEARCH ASSOCIATION (CICRA)

Parkgate House, 356 West Barnes Lane, Motspur Park, Surrey, KT3 6NB

Tel: 020 8949 6209
Fax: 020 8942 2044
E-mail: support@cicra.org
Website: www.cicra.org

Enquiries to: Charity Co-ordinator

Founded: 1978

Organisation type and purpose: Membership association, present number of members: 1,500, registered charity (charity number England and Wales 278212, Scotland SC040700).
Free membership offered to all interested parties, including medical professionals.

Subject coverage: Telephone advice and support for individuals and families of children sufferering from Crohn's Disease and Ulcerative Colitis (inflammatory bowel disease). Literature on all aspects of inflammatory bowel disease, especially as it affects children and young people. Membership (free of charge) to all relevant individuals and families, and the medical profession. Annual meeting/open day attended by senior medical professionals.

Publications: Printed

Publications list: Available in print

Access to staff: Contact by letter, by telephone, by fax, by e-mail and via website. Appointment necessary.
Hours: Mon to Fri, 0930 to 1730

Access to building: Prior appointment required

Access for disabled people: Parking provided

CRONER CCH GROUP LIMITED

145 London Road, Kingston Upon Thames, Surrey, KT2 6SR

Tel: 020 8547 3333

continued overleaf

Fax: 020 8547 2638
E-mail: info@croner.cch.co.uk
Website: www.croner.cch.co.uk

Enquiries to: Customer Services Manager

Organisation type and purpose: Publishing house.
Publishers of business information solutions.

Subject coverage: Human resources; consumer, business and specialist industry law; exporting, importing, health and safety, transport; freight and haulage, VAT and finance, IT, education, charities, care homes, catering, health service management, environmental management and the control of hazardous substances.

Publications: Printed

Publications list: Available in print

Access to staff: Contact by letter, by telephone, by fax, by e-mail and via website
Hours: Mon to Fri, 0830 to 1730

Part of: Wolters Kluwer Group

CROP PROTECTION ASSOCIATION (UK) LIMITED (CPA)

4 Lincoln Court, Lincoln Road, Peterborough, Cambridgeshire, PE1 2RP

Tel: 01733 349225
Fax: 01733 562523
E-mail: info@cropprotection.org.uk

Enquiries to: Director General

History of institution: formerly called British Agrochemicals Association Limited (BAA)

Organisation type and purpose:
International organisation, trade association.
Represents companies who manufacture and formulate pesticides, and distributors.

Subject coverage: Agrochemicals, pesticides.

Publications: Printed

Publications list: Available in print

Access to staff: Appointment necessary.
Hours: Mon to Fri, 0900 to 1700

Member of: Crop Life; European Crop Protection Association (ECPA)

CROQUET ASSOCIATION (CA)

c/o The Cheltenham Croquet Club, Old Bath Road, Cheltenham, GL53 7DF

Tel: 01242 242318
E-mail: caoffice@croquet.org.uk
Website: www.croquet.org.uk

Enquiries to: Manager

Founded: 1897

Organisation type and purpose:
Membership association (membership is by subscription), present number of individual members: 1,700, member clubs; 185, voluntary organisation.
Governing body of the game.
Organises tournaments and coaching for players of all abilities.

Subject coverage: Croquet, handicap ratings, laws of croquet, history.

Publications: Printed
Order printed publications from: Croquet Association Shop

Publications list: Available in print

Access to staff: Contact by letter, by telephone, by e-mail and via website.
Appointment necessary.
Hours: Mon to Fri, 0900 to 1700

CROSS & COCKADE INTERNATIONAL (CCI)

Hamilton House, Church Street, Wadenhoe, Peterborough, PE8 5ST

Tel: 01832 720522
Fax: 07092 172286
E-mail: chairman@crossandcockade.com
Website: www.crossandcockade.com

Enquiries to: Membership Secretary
Direct tel: 01237 474703
Direct e-mail: membership.secretary@crossandcockade.com
Other contacts: Managing Editor for journal material

Founded: 1969; also known as First World War Aviation Historical Society; formerly called Cross and Cockade Great Britain 1969; incorporates the former Essex Chapter Cross and Cockade

Organisation type and purpose:
International organisation, learned society (membership is by subscription), present number of members: 1,400, voluntary organisation, consultancy, research organisation, publishing house.
To enable those with a common interest in any aspect of World War I aviation to share those interests, and to meet fellow enthusiasts.

Subject coverage: Factual information about all aspects of the 1914–1918 war in the air.

Collection: Photographs and some original documents
Reference books

Publications: Printed, and electronic and video
Order printed publications from: Sales Manager, Cross and Cockade, 6 Cowper Road, Southgate, London, N14 5RP

Publications list: Available in print

Access to staff: Contact by letter, by telephone, by e-mail and via website.
Appointment necessary. Non-members charged.
Hours: Mon to Fri, 0900 to 1700

Also at: Advertising Manager, Cross & Cockade International; 6 Cowper Road, Southgate, London, N14 5RP; tel: 020 8361 8482; e-mail: advertising.manager@crossandcockade.com; Membership Secretary, Cross & Cockade International; 11 Francis Drive, Westward Ho!, EX39 1XE; tel: 01237 474703; e-mail: membership.secretary@crossandcockade.com

CROSSLEY REGISTER

Willow Cottage, Lexham Road, Great Dunham, King's Lynn, Norfolk, PE32 2LS

Tel: 01328 701240
E-mail: malcolmhatfield@globalnet.co.uk
Website: www.crossley-motors.org.uk

Enquiries to: General Secretary
Direct e-mail: anthonycourtney@tiscali.co.uk
Other contacts: Editor

Founded: 1985

Organisation type and purpose:
Membership association (membership is by subscription), voluntary organisation.

Subject coverage: The Crossley motor car.

Collection: Archive material on Crossley Motors Limited
Records from the company of Crossley Motors Limited

Publications: Printed

Access to staff: Contact by letter, by telephone, by fax and by e-mail
Hours: Mon to Fri, 0900 to 1700

Access to building: Prior appointment required

Access for disabled people: Parking provided

CROSSWORD CLUB

Coombe Farm, Awbridge, Romsey, Hampshire, SO51 0HN

Tel: 01794 524346
Fax: 01794 514988
E-mail: bh@thecrosswordclub.co.uk
Website: www.thecrosswordclub.co.uk

Enquiries to: Editor

Founded: 1978

Organisation type and purpose:
Membership association.

Subject coverage: All aspects of crosswords, especially difficult examples involving gimmicks; composition; history, etc.

Collection: Collections of crossword and general dictionaries
Library of books of and about crosswords

Publications: Printed

Access to staff: Contact by letter, by telephone, by fax and by e-mail.
Appointment necessary.
Hours: Generally 1600 to 2000; other times on spec; 24-hour answerphone

CROWN PROSECUTION SERVICE (CPS)

50 Ludgate Hill, London, EC4M 7EX

Tel: 020 7273 8000
Fax: 020 7796 8651
Website: www.cps.gov.uk

Enquiries to: Information Officer
Direct tel: 020 7796 8023
Direct fax: 020 7796 8030
Direct e-mail: cps.pressoffice@cps.gsi.gov.uk

Founded: 1986

Organisation type and purpose: National government body.

Subject coverage: Criminal law.

Library catalogue: All or part available in-house

Publications: Printed
Order printed publications from: Communications Branch, CPS

Publications list: Available online

Access to staff: Contact by letter, by fax and by e-mail
Hours: Mon to Fri, 0900 to 1700

Access to building: No access other than to staff

Access for disabled people: Ramped entry, level entry, access to all public areas, toilet facilities
Special comments: Parking provided in The Courtyard, 1st left turn in Old Bailey.

CROWTHER CENTRE FOR MISSION EDUCATION

Watlington Road, Oxford, OX4 6BZ

Tel: 01865 787400
Fax: 01865 776375
E-mail: info@cms-uk.org
Website: www.cms-uk.org

Enquiries to: Librarian
Direct tel: 01865 787552
Direct e-mail: ken.osborne@cms-uk.org

Founded: 1987; please select Partnership House Mission Studies Library

Organisation type and purpose: Registered charity (charity number 1131655).
Provides library service to the Anglican missionary societies. The Partnership House Mission Studies Library was formed in 1987 from the post-1945 library collections of CMS and the USPG, to which has been added the library of the South American Missionary Society. All interested in Christian Mission are welcome to use the library.

Subject coverage: Missiology; world-wide Christian church, especially history; growth and work of Anglicanism; the ecumenical movement; other faiths; spirituality; social concerns of the church (e.g. race, poverty, human rights); area studies.

Collection: CMS Max Warren collection (comprises the books from the former Church Missionary Society Library that were published prior to 1946, plus copies of all CMS publications)

Non-library collection catalogue: All or part available online

Library catalogue: All or part available online and in-house

Publications: Printed

Access to staff: Contact by letter, by telephone, by fax, by e-mail, in person and via website
Hours: Mon to Fri, 0930 to 1700
Special comments: Reference services free of charge. Loan of books (other than to missions staff) by annual subscription.

CROYDON COLLEGE LIBRARY

College Road, Fairfield, Croydon, Surrey, CR9 1DX

Tel: 020 8760 5843
E-mail: library@croydon.ac.uk
Website: www.croydon.ac.uk/library

Enquiries to: Librarian

Founded: 1952

Organisation type and purpose: Croydon College (FE) – 14–16 and 16+ General FE. University Centre Croydon – Higher Education College

Subject coverage: Further Education College – BTEC/A-Levels and HE Access courses in Art and design, Business, IT, nursing, health studies, child care, social work, law, construction, education, travel and tourism, sport. University Centre Croydon – Foundation Degree and Degrees in Art and Design, Buisness, Early Childhood Studies, Education, Health and Social Care, Law, Management

Library catalogue: All or part available online

Access to staff: Access for members only.
Hours: Term time, Mon to Thu, 0830 to 2130; Fri, 0830 to 1700; Weekends, closed. Vacations, Mon to Fri, 1300 to 1700; occasionally closed.
College closes for two weeks over Christmas and library is closed during College enrolment in late August and early September.
Special comments: Library for the use of Croydon College staff and students only.

Access for disabled people: Ramped entry, access to all public areas, toilet facilities, lifts

CROYDON LIBRARIES

Central Library, Katharine Street, Croydon, Surrey, CR9 1ET

Tel: 020 8726 6900
Fax: 020 8253 1004
E-mail: aileen.cahill@croydon.gov.uk
Website: www.croydon.gov.uk/libraries

Enquiries to: Assistant Director, Libraries
Direct tel: 020 8253 1001

Founded: 1888; formerly called Croydon Public Library

Organisation type and purpose: Local government body, public library.

Subject coverage: General collection, strong in the following areas: computers, business information, European information, law, visual arts, Croydon local history.

Information services: Online access to encyclopedias, dictionaries, newspaper archives and business sources.

Services for disabled people: Zoomtext on public PCs, Kurzweil reader, CCTV enlarger.

Collection: Archives
Croydon Local Studies Library
IGI complete
1881 Census Index, Surrey only
Riesco Collection of Chinese Ceramics

Library catalogue: All or part available online

Publications: Printed

Access to staff: Contact by letter, by telephone, by fax, by e-mail, in person and via website
Hours: Main Library: Mon, 0900 to 1900; Tue, Wed and Fri, 0900 to 1800; Thu, 0930 to 1800; Sat, 0900 to 1700; Sun, 1400 to 1700

Access to building: No access other than to staff
Hours: Main Library: Mon, 0900 to 1900; Tue, Wed and Fri, 0900 to 1800; Thu, 0930 to 1800; Sat, 0900 to 1700; Sun, 1400 to 1700

Access for disabled people: Ramped entry, access to all public areas, toilet facilities, lifts to all floors

CROYDON LOCAL STUDIES LIBRARY AND ARCHIVES SERVICE

Central Library, Katharine Street, Croydon, Surrey, CR9 1ET

Tel: 020 8726 6900 etn 61112
Fax: 020 8253 1012
E-mail: localstudies@croydon.gov.uk
Website: www.croydon.gov.uk/researchcroydon

Enquiries to: Senior Borough Archivist
Other contacts: Local Studies Librarian

Organisation type and purpose: Public library.

Subject coverage: Local history of the Borough of Croydon and the surrounding area. By virtue of the range of the collections, local and family history of many parts of England.

Information services: Free internet access for family and local history, including Ancestry library edition.

Collection: IGI (microfiche)
1841–1901 Census
Books
Maps
Photographs
Newspapers and local periodicals
Large collection of volumes of English local history societies, records and transcriptions
Harleian Society volumes
Street directories
Electoral rolls
Telephone directories
Parish registers
GRO indexes of births, marriages and deaths, 1837–1897
Rate books (advance notice may be required)
Records of Croydon Council and predecessor bodies, Croydon schools, Croydon Board of Guardians and Workhouse, other local organisations and individuals (advance notice may be required for some or all of these)

Library catalogue: All or part available online and in-house

Access to staff: Contact by letter, by telephone, by fax, by e-mail, in person and via website
Hours: Mon, 1030 to 1900; Tue, Wed, Fri, 1030 to 1700; 1st and 3rd Sat in month, 1030 to 1700

Access to building: No prior appointment required; situated off Level 3
Hours: Mon, 1030 to 1900; Tue, Wed, Fri, 1030 to 1700; 1st and 3rd Sat in month, 1030 to 1700

Access for disabled people: Ramped entry, access to all public areas, toilet facilities
Hours: As above

CROYDON NATURAL HISTORY AND SCIENTIFIC SOCIETY LIMITED (CNHSS)

96A Brighton Road, South Croydon, Surrey, CR2 6AD

Tel: 020 8688 3593
Website: www.croydononline.org/hs/cnhss/index.asp

Enquiries to: Librarian
Other contacts: Membership Secretary for membership

Founded: 1870; formed from Croydon Microscopical & Natural History Club (1877–1901), Croydon Microscopical Club (1870–1877)

Organisation type and purpose: Learned society (membership is by subscription), present number of members: 360, voluntary organisation, registered charity (charity number 260739).
Research and education concerned with the geology, natural history, archaeology, local history, etc. of Croydon and adjoining parts of east Surrey and west Kent.

Subject coverage: Archaeology, botany, entomology, geography, geology, industrial archaeology and history, local history, ornithology, zoology, all pertaining to the Croydon area and some parts of NE Surrey, NW Kent and adjoining London Boroughs; particularly strong in natural history, geology and industrial history, and archaeology of the extractive and transport industries.

Collection: C C Fagg Collection (early land-use surveying, regional survey, etc.)
Strong holdings relating to economic, geological, civil engineering, water supply, etc.
W H Bennett Collection (geological and palaeontological books and journals)

Non-library collection catalogue: All or part available in-house

Library catalogue: All or part available in-house

Publications: Printed

Publications list: Available in print

Access to staff: Contact by letter and by telephone. Appointment necessary.
Hours: Any reasonable time

Access to building: Prior appointment required
Hours: Any mutually convenient time
Special comments: By arrangement with the librarian.

CRUISING ASSOCIATION (CA)

1 Northey Street, Limehouse Basin, London, E14 8BT

Tel: 020 7537 2828
Fax: 020 7537 2266
E-mail: office@cruising.org.uk
Website: www.cruising.org.uk

Enquiries to: Information Officer

Founded: 1908

Organisation type and purpose: Voluntary organisation.

Subject coverage: Cruising under sail or power, pilotage, accounts of cruises historical and modern, navigation, seamanship and boat maintenance.
Extensive maritime chart collection.

Information services: Extensive library and information centre of yachting information, available to members of the association.

Collection: Nautical books (said to be the largest collection in private ownership in Europe)

Non-library collection catalogue: All or part available online

Library catalogue: All or part available online

Publications: Printed

Access to staff: Contact by letter, by telephone, by e-mail, in person and via website. Appointment necessary. Access for members only.
Hours: Mon to Fri, 0930 to 1730

Access for disabled people: Ramped entry, access to all public areas, toilet facilities

Affiliated to: Royal Yachting Association

CRUSE BEREAVEMENT CARE

PO Box 800, Richmond, TW9 1RG

Tel: 020 8939 9530
Fax: 020 8940 1671
E-mail: info@cruse.org.uk
Website: www.cruse.org.uk

Founded: 1959; formerly called National Organisation for the Widowed and their Children

Organisation type and purpose: National organisation, registered charity (charity number 208278).
To provide bereavement support, counselling and advice to anyone who is bereaved by death. This help also includes support groups, a monthly newsletter and a wide variety of leaflets and publications. Includes specialist support and website for children and young people.

Subject coverage: Welfare of bereaved people; counselling, social support and courses for counsellors.

Publications: Printed

Publications list: Available online and in print

Access to staff: Contact by letter, by telephone, by fax, by e-mail and via website
Hours: Mon to Fri, 0930 to 1700

Access to building: No access other than to staff

Branches: Local Cruse branches throughout England, Wales and Northern Ireland and a National Helpline

CRY-SIS HELP LINE (CRY-SIS)

BM CRY-SIS, London, WC1N 3XX

Tel: 08451 228669
E-mail: info@cry-sis.org.uk
Website: www.cry-sis.org.uk

Enquiries to: Administrator

Founded: 1981; formerly called The Cry-sis Support Group (year of change 1986); formerly called Serene (year of change 1997)

Organisation type and purpose: National organisation, voluntary organisation, registered charity (charity number 295470).
Self-help and support group for families with excessively crying, sleepless and demanding babies.

Subject coverage: Self-help and support for parents of excessively crying, sleepless and demanding babies.

Publications: Printed, and electronic and video
Order printed publications from: BM CRY-SIS, London, WC1N 3XX

Publications list: Available online and in print

Access to staff: Contact by letter, by telephone, by e-mail and via website
Hours: Mon to Sun, 0900 to 2200
Special comments: Telephone access and postal enquiries only (sae please).

CUED SPEECH ASSOCIATION UK

9 Jawbone Hill, Dartmouth, Devon, TQ6 9RW

Tel: 01803 832784
Fax: 01803 835311
E-mail: info@cuedspeech.co.uk
Website: www.cuedspeech.co.uk

Enquiries to: Executive Director

Founded: 1975; formerly called National Centre for Cued Speech (NCCS) (year of change 2000)

Organisation type and purpose: National organisation, membership association (membership is by subscription, election or invitation), present number of members: 75, registered charity (charity number 279523), training organisation.
To provide information and training in cued speech throughout the UK.

Subject coverage: Cued speech is a simple sound-based system comprising 8 handshapes used in 4 positions near the mouth, in conjunction with the lip patterns of normal speech, to make all the sounds of spoken language fully comprehensible to deaf and hearing-impaired people.

Publications: Printed

Access to staff: Contact by letter, by telephone, by fax and by e-mail. Appointment necessary.
Hours: Mon to Fri, 0900 to 1700

Access to building: No access other than to staff

CULHAM CENTRE FOR FUSION ENERGY (INCORPORATING EFDA-JET) (CCFE)

Formal name: United Kingdom Atomic Energy Authority

Culham Centre for Fusion Energy, Culham Science Centre, Abingdon, Oxfordshire, OX14 3DB

Tel: 01235 466647
Fax: 01235 466706
E-mail: chris.warrick@ccfe.ac.uk

Website: www.jet.efda.org
Website: www.fusion.org.uk

Enquiries to: Communications Manager.

Founded: 1965

Organisation type and purpose: Research organisation, which is part of a Europe- and world-wide effort to realise nuclear fusion as a viable source of carbon-free, abundant electricity in the future. JET is funded by the EU fusion research organisations under the European Fusion Development Agreement (EFDA) and operated on behalf of the research organisations by CCFE.

Subject coverage: Research into realising nuclear fusion electricity production in the future.

Information services: Information on the science and engineering challenges of nuclear fusion research.

Special visitor services: Open evenings throughout the year – see website: http://www.ccfe.ac.uk.

Education services: School visits accommodated – see website: http://www.ccfe.ac.uk.

Collection: Annual reports, annual progress reports and detailed scientific reports in the various fields of relevance to fusion research in the site library

Library catalogue: All or part available online, in-house and in print

Publications: Printed, and electronic and video, and microform publications
Order printed publications from: 1. Communications Dept, CCFE, Culham Science Centre, Abingdon, Oxon, OX14 3DB or via website: http://www.ccfe.ac.uk
2. Public Information Officer, EFDA-JET Close Support Unit, Culham Science Centre, Abingdon, Oxon, OX14 3DB or via website: http://www.jet.efda.org

Publications list: Available online and in print

Access to staff: Contact by letter, by telephone, by fax and by e-mail. Appointment necessary.

Access to building: Prior appointment required for all visitors. For open evenings or group visits of any kind, registration is required
Hours: As required for the visit

Access for disabled people: Parking provided, ramped entry to buildings; most parts of tour routes are disabled-accessible
Hours: As required for the visit

CULT INFORMATION CENTRE (CIC)

BCM CULTS, London, WC1N 3XX

Tel: 0845 4500 868
Website: www.cultinformation.org.uk

Enquiries to: General Secretary

Founded: 1987

Organisation type and purpose: National organisation, voluntary organisation, registered charity (charity number 1012914), suitable for ages: all, training organisation, consultancy, research organisation.
Information and advice to families, ex-members, the media and researchers on cults. Gives lectures on the dangers of cults to a wide variety of audiences.

Subject coverage: Cults.

Education services: The cult information centre gives lectures/talks on the topic of cults to schools, professional groups, clubs, religious institutions, UK companies and community groups.

Collection: Archive of books and publicity material published relating to cults
Newscuttings
Relevant articles

Publications: Printed, and electronic and video

Publications list: Available online and in print

Access to staff: Contact by letter and by telephone
Hours: Mon to Fri, 0900 to 1700

Access to building: No access other than to staff

CUMBERLAND AND WESTMORLAND ANTIQUARIAN AND ARCHAEOLOGICAL SOCIETY (CWAAS)

E-mail: info@cumbriapast.com
Website: www.cumbriapast.com

Enquiries to: Honorary Secretary
Direct e-mail: general.secretary@cumbriapast.com
Other contacts: Publications, tel: 01228 544120; e-mail: librarian@cumbriapast.com

Founded: 1866

Organisation type and purpose: Learned society (membership is by subscription), present number of members: 850, registered charity (charity number 227786).

Subject coverage: Archaeology and all aspects of history and customs of Cumberland and Westmorland, including genealogy, heraldry, parish registers, industrial archaeology, historic buildings, etc.

Collection: Artefacts are held at Carlisle Museum, Tullie House, Castle Street, Carlisle, access by application Curator of Archaeology.
Library is now c/o University of Cumbria Library, Fusehill Street, Carlisle CA1 2HH http://www.cumbria.ac.uk
Society's archives are held at Cumbria Record Offices in Carlisle and Kendal, The Castle, Carlisle Carlisle, Carlisle: Petteril Bank Carlisle CA1 3AJ; Kendal, Kendal County Offices, Kendal LA9 4RQ
Society's archives are held at Cumbria Record Office, The Castle, Carlisle

Library catalogue: All or part available in-house

Publications: Printed
Order printed publications from: Publications Officer, Cumberland and Westmorland Antiquarian and Archaeological Society
10 Peter Street, Carlisle, Cumbria, CA3 8QP; tel: 01228 544120; e-mail: elizabethallnutt@btinternet.com

Publications list: Available in print

Access to staff: Contact by e-mail and via website

Access to building: No prior appointment required
Special comments: New arrangements are under discussion.

Affiliated to: Council of British Archaeology (CBA)

Library is now at: Cumbrian Institute of the Arts; Brampton Road, Carlisle, Cumbria, CA3 9AY; tel: 01228 400300; fax: 01228 514491; website: http://www.cumbria.ac.uk

CUMBRIA ARCHIVE SERVICE – BARROW-IN-FURNESS

Cumbria Record Office & Local Studies Library, 140 Duke Street, Barrow in Furness, Cumbria, LA14 1XW

Tel: 01229 407377; minicom no. 01228 606336
Fax: 01229 894364
E-mail: barrow.record.office@cumbriacc.gov.uk
Website: www.cumbria.gov.uk/archives
Website: www.cumbria.gov.uk/archives/pubs.asp
Website: www.a2a.pro.gov.uk/default.asp

Enquiries to: Area Archivist

Founded: 1975; formerly called Central Library (Local Studies), Ramsden Square, Barrow, Cumbria Record Office (Barrow) (year of change 1998)

Organisation type and purpose: Local government body.
Record office.

Subject coverage: General local history of Barrow-in-Furness and South West Cumbria, genealogy, iron-mining and production, the Furness Railway, naval armaments production and design by Vickers Ltd, Barrow, urban growth and architecture.
Printed sources on Cumbria, chiefly the Furness area, including books, newspapers, journals; also transactions of local academic societies.

Special visitor services: Has operated a combined searchroom since Oct 1998, jointly controlled by Cumbria Archive Service and Cumbria Library Service.

Collection: Manorial records for various Furness Manors, 16th to 20th centuries.
Microfilm of minute books of Furness Railway 1844–1923 and station staff registers, late 19th century.
Records of the Furness Estate of the Duke of Buccleuch, c. 1820–1960.
Ships armament drawings (mainly gun mountings) from Vickers Ltd, Barrow, 20th century.
Early 19th century handbills, etc. from J Soulby, Ulverston and other local printers.

Non-library collection catalogue: All or part available online and in-house

Library catalogue: All or part available online

Publications: Printed, and microform publications
Order microform publications from: Microform Academic Publishers, East Ardsley, Wakefield, WF3 2AT

Publications list: Available in print

continued overleaf

Access to staff: Contact by letter, by telephone, by fax, by e-mail and in person
Hours: Usual opening hours: Mon to Fri, 0930 to 1300 and 1400 to 1700
Offers a full archive and local studies service on the 1st Sat of every month, 1000 to 1300 and 1400 to 1600
Closed the first Mon of every month following the 1st Sat
Local studies and searchroom sources only: Wed, 1700 to 1900

Access for disabled people: Ramped entry, access to all public areas, toilet facilities

Constituent part of: Cumbria (County Council) Archive Service

Links with: Record Offices in Carlisle, Whitehaven and Kendal

CUMBRIA ARCHIVE SERVICE – CARLISLE (CACC)

Formal name: Cumbria Archive Centre, Carlisle

Cumbria Archive Centre, Lady Gillford's House, Petteril Bank Road, Carlisle, CA1 3AJ

Tel: 01228 227285 or 227284; minicom no. 01228 226336
Fax: 01228 607270 (office hours only)
E-mail: carlisle.record.office@cumbriacc.gov.uk
Website: www.cumbria.gov.uk/archives

Enquiries to: Assistant County Archivist
Direct tel: 01228 227283
Other contacts: Senior Archivist, Carlisle

Founded: 1962; incorporates the former Joint Archives Committee for the Counties of Cumberland and Westmorland, and The City of Carlisle (year of change 1974)

Organisation type and purpose: Local government body.
Record office.

Subject coverage: History of Cumberland, Carlisle and Cumbria, history of property, mining and transport, etc., genealogy.

Collection: Archive of Catherine Marshall, suffragist and pacifist
Archive of Sir Esme Howard, diplomat

Non-library collection catalogue: All or part available online and in-house

Publications: Printed, and microform publications

Publications list: Available online and in print

Access to staff: Contact by letter, by telephone, by fax, by e-mail, in person and via website
Hours: Mon to Fri, 0900 to 1700
Special comments: CARN readers' ticket system.

Access to building: There is visitor car parking

Access for disabled people: Parking provided, ramped entry, toilet facilities; lifts; platform lift

CUMBRIA ARCHIVE SERVICE – KENDAL

Cumbria Record Office, County Offices, Kendal, Cumbria, LA9 4RQ

Tel: 01539 773540; minicom no. 01228 606336
Fax: 01539 773538
E-mail: kendal.record.office@cumbriacc.gov.uk
Website: www.cumbria.gov.uk/archives

Enquiries to: Archivist

Founded: 1962; formerly called Westmorland Record Office (year of change 1974)

Organisation type and purpose: Local government body.
Record office.

Subject coverage: Records of: the historic county of Westmorland, the Cartmel area formerly in Lancashire north of the sands, Sedbergh, Garsdale and Dent area, formerly in West Riding of Yorkshire.

Collection: Records of Lady Anne Clifford of Appleby Castle (1590–1676)
Records of Sir Daniel Fleming MP of Rydal Hall (1633–1701)
Records of Thomas H Mawson (1861–1933), landscape architect of Lancaster

Non-library collection catalogue: All or part available online and in-house

Publications: Printed

Publications list: Available in print

Access to staff: Contact by letter, by fax, by e-mail and in person
Hours: Mon to Fri, 0900 to 1700
Special comments: Readers' ticket required.

Access for disabled people: Parking provided, level entry, access to all public areas, toilet facilities

Parent body: Cumbria (County Council) Archive Service; The Castle, Carlisle

CUMBRIA CHAMBER OF COMMERCE AND INDUSTRY

The Enterprise Centre, James Street, Carlisle, Cumbria, CA2 5DA

Tel: 01228 534120
Fax: 01228 515602
E-mail: info@cumbriachamber.co.uk

Enquiries to: Chief Executive
Direct e-mail: info@cumbriachamber.co.uk

Founded: May 2001

Organisation type and purpose: Membership association (membership is by subscription).

Publications: Printed

Access to staff: Contact by letter
Hours: Mon to Fri, 0900 to 1700

Has: 41 county groups

CUMBRIA COLLEGE OF ART AND DESIGN LIBRARY (CCAD)

Brampton Road, Carlisle, Cumbria, CA3 9AY

Tel: 01228 400312
Fax: 01228 514491
E-mail: enquirycentre@cumbria.ac.uk
Website: www.libraryopac.cumbriacad.ac.uk

Enquiries to: Librarian
Direct e-mail: cdaniel@cumbriacad.ac.uk

Subject coverage: Ceramics, textiles, painting, sculpture, printmaking, photography, graphic design, media studies, fashion, product design, heritage management, performing arts, archaeology, history, local history, writing.

Non-library collection catalogue: All or part available online

Library catalogue: All or part available online

Access to staff: Contact by letter, by telephone and by fax. Appointment necessary.
Hours: Mon to Thu, 0845 to 2000; Fri, 0845 to 1600; Sat, 0900 to 1300

Access for disabled people: Parking provided

Member of: HCLRG; Northern Regional Library System and ARLIS

CUMBRIA ENVIRONMENTAL AND GEOLOGICAL SERVICES (CEGS)

Watch Hill, Aspatria, Wigton, Cumbria, CA7 3SB

Tel: 016973 22565
Fax: 016973 21375
E-mail: sales@cumbriaenvironmental.co.uk

Enquiries to: Proprietor

Founded: 1992

Organisation type and purpose: Consultancy.

Subject coverage: Contaminated ground investigations (including mine gas monitoring and mine shaft investigations) and reports; knowledge of geology in relation to mine design, geomorphology, mapping and evaluation of mineral reserves; geotechnical site investigations and reports; geological appraisals, investigations, mapping and report writing; environmental surveys (including wildlife – amphibian handling licences held); environmental forestry and habitat management; extensive knowledge of the farming year and farming practices in UK; footpath surveys and countryside management practical skills.

Access to staff: Contact by letter, by telephone and by e-mail
Hours: Mon to Fri, 0830 to 1900

Access to building: *Hours:* Mon to Fri, 0830 to 1900; other times by appointment

CUMBRIA RECORD OFFICE AND LOCAL STUDIES LIBRARY

Scotch Street, Whitehaven, Cumbria, CA28 7NL

Tel: 01946 506420
Fax: 01946 852919
E-mail: whitehaven.record.office@cumbriacc.gov.uk
Website: www.cumbria.gov.uk/archives/whrec.asp
Website: www.a2a.org.uk
Website: www.cumbria.gov.uk/archives/Online_catalogues/default.asp

Founded: 1996

Organisation type and purpose: Local government body.

Subject coverage: History of West Cumbria and Whitehaven.

Collection: Whitehaven Local Studies Library (formerly in the Daniel Hay Library, Whitehaven)

Non-library collection catalogue: All or part available online and in-house

Library catalogue: All or part available online and in-house

Publications: Printed
Order printed publications from: http://www.cumbria.gov.uk/archives/onlineshop

Publications list: Available online

Access to staff: Contact by letter, by telephone, by fax, by e-mail and in person

Access to building: Mon, Tue, Thu and Fri, 0930 to 1230 and 1330 to 1700; Wed, 0930 to 1230 and 1330 to 1900; alternate Sat, 0900 to 1300
Special comments: CARN readers' ticket required.

Access for disabled people: Ramped entry, access to all public areas, toilet facilities

Constituent part of: Cumbria Archive Service

CUMBRIA TOURISM

Windermere Road, Staveley, Cumbria, LA8 9PL

Tel: 01539 822222
Fax: 01539 825079
E-mail: info@cumbriatourism.org
Website: www.golakes.co.uk

Enquiries to: Chief Executive

Founded: 1974

Organisation type and purpose:
Membership association (membership is by subscription).

Subject coverage: Tourism in Cumbria and the Lake District.

Publications list: Available in print

Access to staff: Contact by letter, by telephone, by fax and by e-mail
Hours: Mon to Fri, 0900 to 1700

Links with: local authorities and commercial members; Visit Britain

CURATIVE HYPNOTHERAPY REGISTER (CHR)

584 Derby Road, Nottingham, NG7 2GZ

Tel: 0115 970 1233
E-mail: info@curativehypnotherapyregister.co.uk
Website: www.curativehypnotherapyregister.co.uk

Enquiries to: The Directors

Founded: 1985

Organisation type and purpose:
International organisation, advisory body, professional body (membership is by subscription, qualification, election or invitation).
To enhance the understanding of hypnotherapy, to provide advice/information on the subject of hypnosis/hypnotherapy; maintains a register of qualified practitioners nationwide.

Subject coverage: Improving standards of hypnotherapy, list of qualified practitioners nationwide, information about hypnotherapy.

Publications: Printed

Publications list: Available online

Access to staff: Contact by e-mail and via website
Hours: Mon to Fri, 0900 to 1700

CUTLERY AND ALLIED TRADES RESEARCH ASSOCIATION (CATRA)

Henry Street, Sheffield, South Yorkshire, S3 7EQ

Tel: 0114 276 9736
Fax: 0114 272 2151
E-mail: info@catra.org
Website: www.catra.org

Enquiries to: Director of Research

Founded: 1952

Organisation type and purpose:
Consultancy, research organisation.

Subject coverage: Corrosion, grinding, heat treatment, metal finishing, electroplating, metallography, polishes and polishing, stainless steel, silver plate, automation, robotics, quality control, quality testing, cutlery, machine knives, knives, scissors, tools, sharpening, cookware, kitchen gadgets, surgical instruments, hand tools and garden tools.

Publications: Printed

Access to staff: Contact by letter, by telephone, by fax, by e-mail and via website. Appointment necessary. All charged.
Hours: Mon to Fri, 0900 to 1700

Access to building: Prior appointment required

Member of: BSI

CYCLING TIME TRIALS (CTT)

Moor End, Etherley Moor, Bishop Aukland, Co. Durham, DL14 0JU

Tel: 01388 609824
E-mail: andy.cosgrove@cyclingtimetrials.org.uk
Website: cyclingtimetrials.org.uk

Enquiries to: National Secretary (Corporate & Administration)

Founded: 1937; formerly called Road Time Trials Council (year of change 2002)

Organisation type and purpose: National organisation, membership association (membership is by subscription), present number of members: 1,064 clubs, voluntary organisation.
National governing body for cycling road time trials.

Subject coverage: Cycle road time trials.

Publications: Printed, and electronic and video

Publications list: Available online and in print

Access to staff: Contact by letter, by telephone, by e-mail and via website. Appointment necessary.
Hours: Mon to Fri, 0900 to 1700

Access to building: No access other than to staff

Links with: Sport and Recreation Alliance; 14–16 Caxton Street, London, SW1H 0QT; tel: 020 7976 3900

CYCLISTS' TOURING CLUB (CTC)

Parklands, Railton, Road, Guildford, Surrey, GU2 9JX

Tel: 0870 873 0060
Fax: 0870 873 0064
E-mail: cycling@ctc.org.uk
Website: www.ctc.org.uk

Enquiries to: Public Relations Manager
Other contacts: Director

Founded: 1878

Organisation type and purpose:
Membership association.
Promotes cycling for leisure, travel and transport.

Subject coverage: All aspects of cycling; recreational and utility cycling; technical; legal aid; cycle insurance; mail order; campaigning; information for local/central government; rights and safety of all cyclists; touring; third party insurance; publications; all ages and abilities of cyclists helped.

Collection: Cycle Archive (CTC est. 1878)

Publications: Printed

Affiliated to: Alliance Internationale de Tourisme (AIT); BCF; European Cycling Federation (ECF); RTTC

CYFA

Formal name: Church Youth Fellowships Association

CPAS, Athena Drive, Tachbrook Park, Warwick, CV34 6NG

Tel: 01926 458458
Fax: 01926 458459
E-mail: thehub@cpas.org.uk
Website: www.cpas.org.uk

Enquiries to: Head
Direct tel: 01926 458438

Founded: 1930

Organisation type and purpose: To equip, encourage and enable churches in youth ministry and discipleship.

Subject coverage: Christian teaching and training for older teenagers, training of adults for youth leadership.

Publications: Printed, and electronic and video
Order printed publications from: 24-hour sales orderline
tel: 01926 458400

Publications list: Available online and in print

Access to staff: Contact by letter, by telephone, by fax, by e-mail and via website. Appointment necessary.

continued overleaf

Hours: Mon to Fri, 0900 to 1700

Affiliated to: Church Pastoral Aid Society (CPAS); at the same address

CYNGOR GWYNEDD COUNCIL

Stryd y Jêl, Shirehall Street, Caernarfon, Gwynedd, LL55 1SH

Tel: 01286 672255
Fax: 01286 673993
E-mail: enquiries@gwynedd.gov.uk
Website: www.gwynedd.gov.uk

Enquiries to: Communications Manager
Direct tel: 01286 679310
Direct fax: 01286 679488
Direct e-mail: siongwilliams@gwynedd.gov.uk

Founded: 1996; Gwynedd County Council (year of change 1996)

Organisation type and purpose: Local government body.

Subject coverage: Local government services.

Library catalogue: All or part available online

Access to staff: Contact by letter, by telephone, by fax, by e-mail, in person and via website. Appointment necessary.
Hours: Mon to Fri, 0900 to 1700

Other addresses: Arfon Area Office; Penrallt, Caernarfon, Gwynedd, LL55 1BN; tel: 01286 673113; fax: 01286 672635; Dwyfor Area Office; Ffordd y Cob, Pwllheli, Gwynedd, LL53 5AA; tel: 01758 613131; fax: 01758 613265; Meirionnydd Area Office; Cae Penarlag, Dolgellau, Gwynedd, LL40 1HL; tel: 01341 422341; fax: 01341 423984

CYNGOR LLYFRAU CYMRU – WELSH BOOKS COUNCIL

Castell Brychan, Aberystwyth, Ceredigion, SY23 2JB

Tel: 01970 624151
Fax: 01970 625385
E-mail: castellbrychan@cllc.org.uk
Website: www.gwales.com
Website: www.wbc.org.uk

Enquiries to: Director of Administration and Services
Direct e-mail: moelwen.gwyndaf@cllc.org.uk
Other contacts: Distribution Centre Manager (for visiting the Distribution Centre); Head of Children's Books Department (for visiting the Children's Books Collection)

Founded: 1961

Organisation type and purpose: National organisation, trade association.

Subject coverage: Welsh language and English language Welsh-interest books and magazines, books for learning Welsh, books for children (Welsh and Welsh interest).

Education services: The service of School Officers in Wales to supply information on the latest children's books.

Collection: Complete collection of Welsh language and Welsh interest Children's books published during previous 10 years and that are still in print

Library catalogue: All or part available online

Publications: Printed
Order printed publications from: Head of Sales and Marketing, Welsh Books Council, Uned 16 Parc Menter Glanyrafon, Llanbadarn, Aberystwyth, Ceredigion, SY23 3AQ; tel: 01970 624455

Publications list: Available online

Access to staff: Contact by letter, by telephone, by fax, by e-mail and via website. Appointment necessary.
Hours: Mon to Fri: 0900 to 1700
Special comments: Only account holders at Distribution Centre may purchase titles during visit.

Access to building: Prior appointment required

Access for disabled people: Parking provided, level entry

Also at: Cyngor Llyfrau Cymru/Welsh Books Council (CLLC); Uned 16 Parc Menter Glanyrafon, Llanbadarn, Aberystwyth, Ceredigion, SY23 3AQ; tel: 01970 624455; fax: 01970 625506; e-mail: canolfan.ddosbarthu@cllc.org.uk

CYSTIC FIBROSIS TRUST

11 London Road, Bromley, Kent, BR1 1BY

Tel: 020 8464 7211
Fax: 020 8313 0472
E-mail: enquiries@cftrust.org.uk
Website: www.cftrust.org.uk

Enquiries to: Chief Executive

Founded: 1964; formerly called Cystic Fibrosis Research Trust

Organisation type and purpose: Registered charity (charity number 1079049), research organisation.
Affiliated to the International Cystic Fibrosis (Mucoviscidosis) Association and the European Working Group for Cystic Fibrosis.

Subject coverage: Research into the condition, and advice in coping with cystic fibrosis.

Collection: Library of books and documents relating to cystic fibrosis

Publications: Printed, and electronic and video

Publications list: Available in print

Access to staff: Contact by letter, by telephone, by fax, by e-mail and via website. Appointment necessary.
Hours: Mon to Fri, 0900 to 1700

Affiliated to: European Working Group for Cystic Fibrosis; International Cystic Fibrosis (Mucoviscidosis) Association

Has: local self-help groups

CYSTITIS AND OVERACTIVE BLADDER FOUNDATION (COB Foundation)

Kings Court, 17 School Road, Hall Green, Birmingham, B28 8JG

Tel: 0121 702 0820
E-mail: info@cobfoundation.org
Website: www.cobfoundation.org

Enquiries to: Membership Secretary

Founded: 1994

Organisation type and purpose: Membership association (membership is by subscription), registered charity (charity number 1047714).
Support for those with a specific medical condition.

Subject coverage: Interstitial cystitis, treatments, therapies, medical research data.

Publications: Printed, and electronic and video

Publications list: Available in print

Access to staff: Contact by letter, by telephone, by e-mail and via website
Hours: Mon to Fri, 0900 to 1400

CZECH AND SLOVAK TOURIST CENTRE (CTC)

16 Frognal Parade, Finchley Road, London, NW3 5HG

Tel: 020 7794 3264
Fax: 020 7794 3265
E-mail: reservations@cztc.co.uk
Website: www.czech-wedding.co.uk
Website: www.czechtravel.co.uk
Website: www.czech-slovak-tourist.co.uk

Enquiries to: Director

Founded: 1994; formerly called Czech Tourist Centre

Organisation type and purpose: National Slovak Tourist Board/Tour Operator.

Publications: Printed, and electronic and video

Access to staff: Contact by letter, by telephone, by fax, by e-mail and in person
Hours: Mon to Fri, 1000 to 1800

CZECH CENTRE

13 Harley Street, London, W1G 9QG

Tel: 020 7307 5180
Fax: 020 7323 3709
E-mail: info@czechcentre.org.uk
Website: www.czechcentres.cz/london

Enquiries to: Administration and Marketing
Direct e-mail: storchova@czechcentre.org.uk

Founded: 1993

Organisation type and purpose: International organisation.
Information centre of the Czech Republic.

Subject coverage: Cultural information, activities, tourism, local and foreign investment, exhibitions, trade.

Access to staff: Contact by letter, by telephone, by fax, by e-mail and via website
Hours: Tue, 1000 to 1900; Wed to Fri, 1000 to 1800

D H LAWRENCE SOCIETY

1 Church Street, Swepstone, Leics, LE67 2SA

Tel: 01530 270367

Enquiries to: Joint Secretary
Direct tel: 0115 950 3008

Founded: 1974

Organisation type and purpose: Learned society (membership is by subscription), present number of members: 200.
Study of life and works of D H Lawrence.

Subject coverage: Life and works of D H Lawrence.

Publications: Printed

Access to staff: Contact by letter and by telephone
Hours: Mon to Fri, 0900 to 1700

DAFFODIL SOCIETY

105 Bramcote Road, Nottingham, NG9 3GZ

Tel: 0115 925 5498
E-mail: rogerbb@lineone.net
Website: www.thedaffodilsociety.com

Enquiries to: Secretary
Other contacts: Membership Secretary (tel. 01264 790745)

Founded: 1898

Organisation type and purpose: Membership association (membership is by subscription), societies and individual members, voluntary organisation, registered charity (charity number 1055817).
To encourage the cultivation of the genus Narcissus.

Subject coverage: Daffodils (genus Narcissus): breeding of new cultivars; control of pest and disease; general cultivation and exhibition.

Publications: Printed
Order printed publications from: Merchandising Manager, The Daffodil Society, 8 Foxdalls, Birch Green, Hertford, SG14 2LS; e-mail: baxterdaffs@hotmail.com

Access to staff: Contact by letter, by telephone, by e-mail and via website

DAIRY COUNCIL

Henrietta House, 17–18 Henrietta Street, Covent Garden, London, WC2E 8QH

Tel: 020 7395 4030
Fax: 020 7240 9679
E-mail: info@dairycouncil.org.uk
Website: www.milk.co.uk

Enquiries to: Communications Manager
Direct e-mail: amanda.ball@dairyco.org.uk

Founded: 1920; formerly called The National Dairy Council (year of change 2001)

Organisation type and purpose: Trade association.
Promotional organisation for the whole dairy industry in Britain.

Subject coverage: Dairy industry, milk, dairy products, nutrition, careers in the dairy industry, market data.

Collection: Foreign Dairy Industry journals
Historical exhibits
Photographic library
United Kingdom and European Community Dairy Facts and Figures

Trade and statistical information: Consumption data and market research on the liquid milk market, top line data for other dairy products

Library catalogue: All or part available in-house

Publications: Printed, and electronic and video

Access to staff: Contact by letter and by fax. Appointment necessary.
Hours: Mon to Fri, 0900 to 1700

Links to: The Dairy Industry Federation (for processors); The Milk Development Council (for farmers)

Other addresses: Dairy Council for Northern Ireland; 456 Antrim Road, Belfast, BT15 5GB; tel: 028 9077 0113

DAIRY UK

93 Baker Street, London, W1U 6QQ

Tel: 020 7486 7244
Fax: 020 7487 4734
E-mail: info@dairyuk.org
Website: www.dairyuk.org/

Enquiries to: Secretary
Direct tel: 020 7486 7244
Direct e-mail: khunter@dairyuk.org

History of institution: created by the merger of Dairy Industry Federation (DIF) and the National Dairymen's Association (NDA); formerly called Dairy Trade Federation (DTF) (year of change 1993)

Organisation type and purpose: Trade association.
Represents the interests of UK dairy companies.

Subject coverage: Milk and milk products.

Publications: Printed

Access to staff: Contact by letter, by telephone, by fax and by e-mail
Hours: Mon to Fri, 0900 to 1700

Access for disabled people: Step entry

Member of: European Dairy Association; United Kingdom Dairy Association

Member organisation of: International Dairy Federation

Parent body: The Dairy Council

DAIRY UK (NORTHERN IRELAND)

Shaftesbury House, Edgewater Road, Belfast BT3 9JQ

Tel: 02890770116
Fax: 02890781224
E-mail: mike.johnston@dairycouncil.co.uk

Enquiries to: Northern Ireland Director

Founded: 1995

Organisation type and purpose: Trade association (membership is by subscription), present number of members: 9.

Subject coverage: Dairy processing industry in Northern Ireland.

Access to staff: Contact by letter, by telephone, by fax and by e-mail
Hours: Mon to Fri, 0900 to 1700

Access to building: Prior appointment required

Access for disabled people: Parking provided, level entry, access to all public areas, toilet facilities

DAIWA ANGLO-JAPANESE FOUNDATION (DAJF)

Daiwa Foundation Japan House, 13–14 Cornwall Terrace, London, NW1 4QP

Tel: 020 7486 4348
Fax: 020 7486 2914
E-mail: office@dajf.org.uk
Website: www.dajf.org.uk

Enquiries to: Receptionist
Direct fax: 020 7486 3049

Founded: 1988

Organisation type and purpose: Registered charity (charity number 299955).
To support links between the UK and Japan by awarding Daiwa Scholarhips, grant-making, and a year-round programme of events.

Subject coverage: Japan, Japanese culture and the Japanese people.

Collection: Library (open to the public)

Access to staff: Contact by letter, by telephone, by fax, by e-mail and in person. Appointment necessary.
Hours: Mon to Fri, 0930 to 1700
Special comments: Non-commercial enquiries only.

Links with: Daiwa Anglo-Japanese Foundation; Bancho Building 103 Gobancho 12–1 Chiyoda-ku Tokyo 102–0076; tel: +81 (0)3 3222 1205; fax: +81 (0)3 3222 1208; e-mail: tokyo.office@dajf.org

DARTINGTON COLLEGE OF ARTS

Dartington Hall Estate, Totnes, Devon, TQ9 6EJ

Tel: 01803 862224
Fax: 01803 861666
E-mail: admissions@falmouth.ac.uk
Website: www.dartington.ac.uk

Enquiries to: Librarian
Direct tel: 01803 861651

Founded: 1961

Organisation type and purpose: Higher education in the performing arts.

Subject coverage: Music, theatre, visual arts, arts management, writing for performance.

Library catalogue: All or part available online

Access to staff: Contact by letter, by telephone, by fax, by e-mail, in person and via website. Non-members charged.
Hours: Mon to Fri, 0900 to 2100; Sat, Sun, 1330 to 1730

Access to building: No prior appointment required
Hours: Mon to Fri, 0900 to 2100; Sat, Sun, 1330 to 1730

Access for disabled people: Level entry, toilet facilities

DARTMOOR NATIONAL PARK AUTHORITY (DNP/DNPA)

Parke, Bovey Tracey, Devon, TQ13 9JQ

Tel: 01626 832093
Fax: 01626 834684
E-mail: hq@dartmoor-npa.gov.uk
Website: www.dartmoor-npa.gov.uk

Enquiries to: Chief Executive
Other contacts: Directors

Founded: 1951

Organisation type and purpose: Local government body.
National Park Authority.

Subject coverage: Moorland and woodland management, upland archaeology, recreation management, development control, urban and rural enhancement, listed building protection, farm conservation, species conservation, community support, information and interpretation, design techniques.

Collection: Books, photographs and slides pertaining to Dartmoor only
Taylor Collection, photographs
Parminter Collection, photographs
Minter Collection (copy archaeological excavations)
French Collection (assorted papers, photographs and artefacts)

Trade and statistical information: Corporate Plan

Library catalogue: All or part available in-house

Publications: Printed, and electronic and video, and microform publications

Publications list: Available online and in print

Access to staff: Contact by letter, by telephone, by fax, by e-mail, in person and via website. Appointment necessary.
Hours: Mon to Thu, 0900 to 1700; Fri, 0900 to 1630

Access to building: Prior appointment required

Access for disabled people: Parking provided, ramped entry, toilet facilities
Special comments: Disabled access to ground floor only.

Also at: High Moorland Visitor Centre (HMVC); Princetown, Devon; tel: 01822 890414; e-mail: hmvc@dartmoor-npa.fsbusiness.co.uk

Parent body: Association of National Park Authorities (ANPA)

DARTMOOR PRESERVATION ASSOCIATION (DPA)

Duchy Hotel, Tavistock Road, Princetown, Yelverton, Devon, PL20 6QF

Tel: 01822 890646
E-mail: info@dartmoorpreservation.com
Website: www.dartmoorpreservation.com

Enquiries to: Chief Executive

Founded: 1883

Organisation type and purpose: Membership association (membership is by subscription), present number of members: 2,400, voluntary organisation, registered charity (charity number 215665).
Conservation and amenity interests; campaigning to conserve the special qualities of Dartmoor.

Subject coverage: All information relevant to Dartmoor.

Publications: Printed

Access to staff: Contact by letter, by telephone, by e-mail and via website. Appointment necessary.
Hours: Tue and Thu, 0930 to 1430

DARTMOOR SHEEP BREEDERS ASSOCIATION (DSBA)

Lower Stocksdon Farm, St Mellion, Saltash, Cornwall PL12 6QF

Tel: 01579 350920
E-mail: secretary@greyface-dartmoor.org.uk
Website: www.greyface-dartmoor.org.uk

Enquiries to: Hon. Secretary

Founded: 1909

Organisation type and purpose: Membership association (membership is by subscription), present number of members: 220, registered charity (charity number 266083).
Sheep Breeding Association (Greyface Dartmoor).

Subject coverage: Sheep breeding.

Access to staff: Contact by letter, by telephone, by e-mail and via website
Hours: Evenings preferred

DARTMOUTH TOURIST INFORMATION CENTRE

The Engine House, Mayors Avenue, Dartmouth, Devon, TQ6 9YY

Tel: 01803 834224
Fax: 01803 835631
E-mail: holidays@discoverdartmouth.com
Website: www.discoverdartmouth.com

Enquiries to: Manager

Founded: 1993

Organisation type and purpose: Advisory body, museum, suitable for ages: 8+.

Subject coverage: Features the Newcomen Atmospheric Engine, a preserved working steam atmospheric engine which was re-erected here in Thomas Newcomen's home town in 1963 to mark the 300th anniversary of his birth. In 1993 it was combined with a new tourist information centre.

Publications: Printed

Access to staff: Contact by letter, by telephone, by e-mail, in person and via website
Hours: Mon to Fri, 0930 to 1600

Access to building: No prior appointment required
Hours: Apr to Oct: Mon to Sat, 0930 to 1700; Sun, 1000 to 1400
Nov to Mar: Mon to Sat, 0930 to 1600

Access for disabled people: Level entry, access to all public areas

DATA AND ARCHIVAL DAMAGE CONTROL CENTRE (DADCC)

4 Bridge Wharf, 156 Caledonian Road, London, N1 9UU

Tel: 020 7837 8215
E-mail: info@dadcc.com
Website: www.dadcc.com

Enquiries to: Managing Director
Direct tel: 07973 295155

Founded: 1986

Organisation type and purpose: Training organisation, consultancy; forensic disaster management.

Subject coverage: Salvage and restoration of books and documents damaged by fires, floods and terrorist activities; disaster planning, health and safety equipment that should be worn when entering disaster sites, training on pre-disaster planning and post-disaster recovery operations; educational literature.

Education services: Training, talks and papers.

Collection: Slide reference library in UK disaster case studies

Publications: Printed

Access to staff: Contact by letter, by telephone, by e-mail, in person and via website. Appointment necessary.
Hours: Mon to Fri, 0900 to 1700

Access to building: No access other than to staff

Access for disabled people: Toilet facilities

DATSUN OWNERS CLUB

40 Humber Way, Donnington, Telford, Shropshire, TF2 8LJ

Tel: 01342 321000
Website: www.datsunworld.com

Enquiries to: Archivist
Direct e-mail: datsunownersclub@hotmail.com

Founded: 1993

Organisation type and purpose:
International organisation, membership association (membership is by subscription), present number of members: 300, voluntary organisation.
Preservation of Datsun cars, help with obtaining parts, bringing together owners of this marque.

Subject coverage: History of Datsuns, technical information, whereabouts of parts or cars.

Collection: Newspaper and magazine articles
Owners' manuals
Photographs
Spare parts available for Datsun cars
Workshop manuals

Trade and statistical information:
Production numbers of Datsun cars, numbers of examples surviving

Publications: Printed

Access to staff: Contact by letter, by telephone, by e-mail and via website. Appointment necessary.

Hours: Mon to Fri, 1000 to 1900

Archivist: Datsun Owners Club; 7 School Road, Fritton, Norwich, Norfolk, NR15 2QN; tel: 01508 499620; e-mail: nigelg@tinyonline.co.uk

DAVID LEWIS CENTRE FOR EPILEPSY (DLC)

Mill Lane, Warford, Alderley Edge, Cheshire, SK9 7UD

Tel: 01565 640000
Fax: 01565 640100
E-mail: enquiries@davidlewis.org.uk
Website: www.davidlewis.org.uk

Enquiries to: Chief Executive

Founded: 1904

Organisation type and purpose: Registered charity (charity number 1000392).
The David Lewis Centre provides a unique range of services for adults and children with complicated epilepsy. Services include The David Lewis School, The David Lewis College, Children's Epilepsy Outreach Assessments, Adult Social Care Provision, Residential Behaviour Service, Adult Assessment Unit and Residential High Dependency Unit.

Subject coverage: Epilepsy and associated disabilities, in adults and children, including behaviour problems, understanding, treatment care, stabilisation, rehabilitation, research of adults and children.
Adults and children – severe epilepsy and associated problems, assessment, treatment, residential care, education, training and rehabilitation service for children and young people with acquired brain injuries.

Access to staff: Contact by letter, by telephone, by fax and by e-mail. Appointment necessary.
Hours: Mon to Fri, 0900 to 1700

Access to building: Prior appointment required

Access for disabled people: Ramped entry, toilet facilities

DAVID WILLIAMS PICTURE LIBRARY

Allt-na-Craobh, Old Shore Road, Connel, Argyll, PA37 1PT

Tel: 01631 710586
Fax: 01631 710586

Enquiries to: Proprietor
Direct e-mail: enquiries@bapla.org.uk

Founded: 1989

Organisation type and purpose: Commercial picture library.

Subject coverage: Colour photographic transparencies of Scotland, Iceland, Spain and a number of other countries, photographs of landscapes, landforms, buildings, towns and sites of historical interest.

Collection: Colour photographic transparencies of Scotland, Iceland, Spain and a number of other countries

Access to staff: Contact by letter, by telephone, by fax and by e-mail. Appointment necessary.
Hours: ordinary business hours, also evenings and weekends

Member of: British Association of Picture Libraries and Agencies

DAWSON BOOKS LIMITED

Foxhills House, Rushden, Northamptonshire, NN10 6DB

Tel: 01933 417500
Fax: 01933 417501
Website: www.dawsonbooks.co.uk

Enquiries to: Marketing Manager
Direct e-mail: marketing@dawsonbooks.co.uk

Founded: 1809

Organisation type and purpose: International organisation, service industry, supplier of books.

Subject coverage: A market leader in the use of information technology to expedite the book-buying process, providing a total acquisitions package for professional librarians worldwide. Provides the industry with web interfaces, shelf-ready book supply and delivery of eContent through dawsonera.

Publications: Printed, and electronic and video

Access to staff: Contact by letter, by telephone, by fax and by e-mail
Hours: Mon to Thu, 0845 to 1645, Fri 0845 to 1600

Access to building: Prior appointment required

Access for disabled people: Parking provided, level entry, access to all public areas, toilet facilities

Constituent part of: Dawson Holdings plc

DAYCARE TRUST

2nd Floor, Novas Contemporary Urban Centre, 73–81 Southwark Bridge Road, London, SE1 0NQ

Tel: 020 7940 7510
Fax: 020 7940 7515
E-mail: info@daycaretrust.org.uk
Website: www.daycaretrust.org.uk
Website: www.payingforchildcare.org.uk

Enquiries to: Information Officer

Founded: 1986; formerly called National Childcare Campaign

Organisation type and purpose: Voluntary organisation, registered charity (charity number 327279).

Subject coverage: Childcare, policy and practice; family-friendly employment practices; sources of information on childcare and children's services, consultancy and training.

Trade and statistical information: Data on childcare in the UK

Publications: Printed
Order printed publications from: e-mail: publications@daycaretrust.org.uk

Publications list: Available online and in print

Access to staff: Contact by letter, by telephone, by fax, by e-mail and via website. Appointment necessary.
Hours: Mon to Fri, 0900 to 1700

Access for disabled people: Toilet facilities, lift

DE MONTFORT UNIVERSITY

The Gateway, Leicester, LE1 9BH

Tel: 0116 255 1551
Fax: 0116 255 0307
Website: www.library.dmu.ac.uk

Enquiries to: Librarian
Direct tel: 0116 257 7165
Direct fax: 0116 257 7046

Organisation type and purpose: University library.

Subject coverage: Chemistry, physics, electronics, mechanical engineering, architecture, building, fashion, textiles, graphic art and design, information technology, law, public administration, economics, education, performing arts, speech and speech therapy, sport and physical education, business, health, nursing, midwifery, humanities.

Collection: HATRA Collection (former Hosiery and Allied Trades Research Association)
Hockliffe Collection of early children's books (Polhill Site)

Library catalogue: All or part available online

Access to staff: Contact by letter and by telephone
Hours: Varies between campuses – please consult website for full details.

Access for disabled people: Parking provided, ramped entry, access to all public areas, toilet facilities
Special comments: Facilities may vary slightly from campus to campus.

Includes the: Kimberlin Library; City Campus; tel: 0116 255 1551 ext 2677; Polhill Campus Library (Bedford); tel: 01234 793077

Site libraries: De Montfort University; Polhill Campus, Polhill Avenue, Bedford, MK41 9EA; tel: 01234 793077; fax: 01234 217738; De Montfort University; Charles Frears Campus, 266 London Road, Leicester, LE2 1RQ; tel: 0116 270 0661; fax: 0116 270 9722; De Montfort University; Kimberlin Library, The Gateway, Leicester, LE1 9BH; tel: 0116 257 7042; fax: 0116 257 7170

DE TOMASO DRIVERS CLUB

Flint Barn, Malthouse Lane, Ashington, West Sussex, RH20 3BU

Tel: 01903 893870
Fax: 01903 893870

Enquiries to: Secretary

Founded: 1982

Organisation type and purpose: Membership association.

Subject coverage: De Tomaso cars.

continued overleaf

Collection: De Tomaso Books
Club Magazines

DEAFAX

The Saunderton Estate, Wycombe Road, Saunderton, Buckinghamshire, HP14 4BF

Tel: 01494 568885
E-mail: info@deafax.org
Website: www.deafax.org

Enquiries to: Administrator (for all initial enquiries)

Founded: 1985

Organisation type and purpose:
International organisation, voluntary organisation, registered charity (new charity number 1095398), suitable for ages: all, training organisation, research organisation.
To deliver ICT and English literacy training and provide other support services for deaf children and adults in the UK and internationally.

Subject coverage: Deaf issues: communications technology, training, literacy, education, support services.

Publications: Printed, and electronic and video
Order printed publications from: Deafax website

Publications list: Available online

Access to staff: Contact by letter, by telephone and by e-mail. Appointment necessary.
Hours: Mon to Thursday, 0900 to 1700

Access for disabled people: Parking provided, ramped entry, access to cafe, toilet facilities.
Special comments: Wheelchair accessible.

DEAFBLIND SCOTLAND

21 Alexandra Avenue, Lenzie, Glasgow, G66 5BG

Tel: 0141 777 6111
Fax: 0141 775 3311
E-mail: info@deafblindscotland.org.uk
Website: www.deafblindscotland.org.uk

Enquiries to: Information Officer
Direct e-mail: Information@deafblindscotland.org.uk
Other contacts: Chief Executive

Founded: 1928

Organisation type and purpose: Registered charity (charity number 802976).
To serve deafblind people and reduce their isolation through clubs, outings, holidays and provision of information; provide trained guide/communicator service where funding available, training in communication and guiding skills, awareness-raising.

Subject coverage: Deafblind awareness, communication and guiding skills with deafblind people.

Collection: Small resource centre of books, articles, reports and publications

Publications: Printed, and electronic and video

Access to staff: Contact by letter, by telephone, by fax, by e-mail and via website
Hours: Mon to Fri, 0900 to 1700
Special comments: Helpline.

DEAFBLIND UK (DBUK)

The National Centre for Deafblindness, John and Lucille van Geest Place, Cygnet Road, Hampton, Peterborough, PE7 8FD

Tel: 01733 358100; Free helpline 0800 132320; Minicom 01733 358100
Fax: 01733 358356
E-mail: info@deafblind.org.uk
Website: www.deafblind.org.uk

Enquiries to: Information Officer
Direct e-mail: enquiries@deafblind.org.uk
Other contacts: Chief Executive

Founded: 1928; formerly called National Deaf-Blind Helpers League; formerly called National Deafblind League (year of change 1996)

Organisation type and purpose: Voluntary organisation, registered charity.
To enable those people with a dual sensory impairment to live full and active lives despite their disability. To raise awareness of deafblindness in the caring professions and amongst the wider public, to ensure sufferers' needs are met in care planning.

Subject coverage: Activities include visiting/assessing deafblind individuals.
Participation in national development/lobbying groups. Contributing to individual community care plans. Information and advice on dual sensory loss. Counselling. Training. Social activities for deafblind people, rehabilitation services, holiday flat, independent living accommodation. Linking deafblind people through magazines and newspapers in touch-based media. Free helpline accessible to deafblind people, their carers and professionals working with deafblind people.

Information services: Information for people who have a combined sight and hearing loss, and for their families and friends.

Services for disabled people: Volunteer befriending; interpreters; communicator guides; free helpline; case worker; formatted publications and letters; deafblind clubs; campaigning and raising awareness.

Collection: Heritage exhibition at the National Centre for Deafblindness explaining the history of combined sight and hearing loss.

Publications: Printed
Order printed publications from: 01733 358100

Access to staff: Contact by letter, by telephone, by fax, by e-mail and via website. Appointment necessary.
Hours: Mon to Thu, 0830 to 1700; Fri, 0830 to 1600
Free Helpline available daily, 0900 to 2130

Access for disabled people: Level entry, toilet facilities, handrails, wheelchair and assistance dog friendly, Braille, Moon, Large Print and Audio room markings, tactile map of building.

Also at: Deafblind UK Training and Rehabilitation Centre; 18 Rainbow Court, Paston Ridings, Peterborough, Cambridgeshire, PE4 7UP; tel: 01733 325353; fax: 01733 323101

DEAFNESS RESEARCH UK

330–332 Gray's Inn Road, London, WC1X 8EE

Tel: 020 7833 1733, 020 7915 1412 (minicom) (text phone)
Fax: 020 7278 0404
E-mail: contact@deafnessresearch.org.uk
Website: www.deafnessresearch.org.uk

Enquiries to: Office Manager
Other contacts: Information Officer

Founded: 1985; formerly called Defeating Deafness (year of change 2005)

Organisation type and purpose: Voluntary organisation, registered charity.
Aims to encourage and finance research into the prevention, diagnosis, treatment and cure of hearing difficulties. It also aims to educate people about hearing problems and their treatments, offering information and advice based upon the most up-to-date evidence available.

Subject coverage: Cochlear implants, glue ear, hearing aids, tinnitus, hyperacusis, hair cell research, genetics of hearing loss, auditory processing disorder, otosclerosis, Meniere's Disease, cholesteatoma

Publications: Printed

Publications list: Available in print

Access to staff: Contact by letter, by telephone, by fax, by e-mail and via website
Hours: Office hours: Mon to Fri, 0930 to 1730
Helpline: Mon to Fri, 0900 to 1700

Parent body: The Hearing Research Trust

DEBRA

Debra House, 13 Wellington Business Park, Dukes Ride, Crowthorne, Berkshire, RG45 6LS

Tel: 01344 771961
Fax: 01344 762661
E-mail: debra@debra.org.uk
Website: www.debra.org.uk
Website: www.debra-international.org

Enquiries to: Director of Nursing and Social Care
Direct e-mail: claire.mather@debra.org.uk
Other contacts: PR and Press Officer; CEO; Director of Fundraising; Director of Research

Founded: 1978; formerly called Dystrophic Epidermolysis Bullosa Research Association

Organisation type and purpose: Registered charity (charity number 1084958).
Funds nursing and welfare teams.
Commissions research into EB (Epidermolysis Bullosa).

Subject coverage: Epidermolysis bullosa, all types; education, self-help, care and management, counselling and research.

Library catalogue: All or part available online

Publications: Printed, and electronic and video

Publications list: Available online and in print

Access to staff: Contact by letter, by telephone, by fax, by e-mail, in person and via website
Hours: Mon to Fri, 0900 to 1700

Access for disabled people: Access to all public areas, toilet facilities

DEBRETT'S PEERAGE LIMITED

Formal name: Debrett's Limited

18–20 Hill Rise, Richmond, Surrey, TW10 6UA

Tel: 020 8939 2250
Fax: 020 8939 2251
E-mail: people@debretts.co.uk
Website: www.debretts.co.uk

Enquiries to: Finance and Operations Manager

Founded: 1769

Organisation type and purpose: Publishing house.

Subject coverage: Biographical information – general, peerage, baronetage. Etiquette and manners.

Publications: Printed, and electronic and video

Access to staff: Contact by letter, by e-mail and via website
Hours: Mon to Fri, 0900 to 1700
Special comments: By appointment only.

DECORATIVE ARTS SOCIETY (DAS)

Formal name: The Decorative Arts Society 1850 to the Present

PO Box 136, Woodbridge, Suffolk, IP12 1TG

Website: www.decorativeartssociety.org.uk/

Enquiries to: Honorary Secretary
Direct e-mail: links@thedecorativeartssociety.org.uk
Other contacts: Membership Secretary for membership applications, subscription rates, etc.

Founded: 1975

Organisation type and purpose: Learned society (membership is by subscription), present number of members: 650, registered charity (charity number 271838).
To encourage the study and appreciation of the Decorative Arts in Britain, Europe and America from 1850 to the present.

Subject coverage: Decorative arts, 1850 to the present.

Publications: Printed
Order printed publications from: Richard Dennis Publications, The Old Chapel Middle Street, Shepton Beauchamp, Ilminster, Somerset, TA19 0LE

Publications list: Available in print

Access to staff: Contact by letter
Hours: Mon to Fri, 0900 to 1700

Membership applications: The Decorative Arts Society; PO Box 136, Woodbridge, Suffolk, IP12 1TG

DEESIDE COLLEGE

Kelsterton Road, Connah's Quay, Deeside, Flintshire, CH5 4BR

Tel: 01244 831531
Fax: 01244 814305
E-mail: enquiries@deeside.ac.uk
Website: www.deeside.ac.uk

Enquiries to: Manager
Direct tel: 01244 834516
Direct fax: 01244 834526
Direct e-mail: forresl@deeside.ac.uk

Founded: 1993

Organisation type and purpose: College of Further Education.

Subject coverage: All subjects including computer studies, management and business studies.

Access to staff: Contact by letter, by telephone, by fax, by e-mail and via website
Hours: Term time: Mon to Thu, 0830 to 1925; Fri, 0830 to 1625
Vacations: Mon to Thu, 0830 to 1625; Fri, 0830 to 1555

Access for disabled people: Level entry, access to all public areas

DEFENCE ACADEMY, COLLEGE OF MANAGEMENT AND TECHNOLOGY (DA-CMT)

Cranfield University, Shrivenham, Swindon, Wiltshire, SN6 8LA

Tel: 01793 785743
Fax: 01793 785555
E-mail: library.barrington@cranfield.ac.uk
Website: www.cranfield.ac.uk
Website: diglib.shrivenham.cranfield.ac.uk

Enquiries to: Head of Library Services
Direct tel: 01793 785481

Organisation type and purpose: University library.

Subject coverage: Military science, military technology, computing science, mathematics, ballistics, operational research, statistics, defence procurement, management, political science, social science, international affairs, chemistry, materials science, metallurgy, engineering design, mechanical engineering, aeronautical engineering, military vehicles, thermal power, control and guidance, information technology, electromagnets, electronic engineering, physics, electro-optics, electrical engineering, telecommunications, electronic warfare, command and control, guided weapons, explosives and ammunition, weapons systems, surveillance and target acquisition, military management, defence administration, military affairs, disaster management, security and resilience, forensic science, forensic archaeology, anthropology.

Collection: Reports collection of about 50,000 items, reflects the specialised nature of some of the campus courses

Library catalogue: All or part available online

Publications: Electronic and video

Access to staff: Contact by telephone and via website. Appointment necessary.
Hours: Mon to Fri, 0800 to 1900; Sat, 1000 to 1500

Access for disabled people: Parking provided, level entry

Constituent bodies: Defence Academy

DEFENCE MEDICAL LIBRARY SERVICE (DMLS)

Formal name: DMLS Central Library

DMS Whittington, Lichfield, Staffordshire WS14 9PY

Tel: 01543 4317
Fax: N/A
E-mail: SGSCCorpSvcs-KIMDMLSMailbox@mod.uk

Enquiries to: Militatry Medical Librarian
Direct tel: 01543 4175
Other contacts: Head of Defence Medical Library Service, HQ SGD

Founded: 1827

Organisation type and purpose: Central medical library for the Ministry of Defence; linked with the Ministry of Defence medical libraries.

Subject coverage: Military medicine, primary and secondary care, mental health.

Collection: Defence Medical Services dissertations; Historical military medicine collection.

Library catalogue: All or part available online and in-house

Publications: Printed

Publications list: Available online

Access to staff: Contact by letter, by telephone and by e-mail. Access for members only.
Hours: Mon to Thu, 0800 to 1630; Fri, 0800 to 1600
Special comments: Services to Defence medical staff and Ministry of Defence staff; to others by written appointment only.

Access to building: Prior appointment required

Library for: Defence Medical Services

DELIUS SOCIETY

c/o Crosland Communications Ltd., The Railway Station, Newmarket CB8 9WT

Tel: 07941 188617
E-mail: secretary@thedeliussociety.org.uk

Enquiries to: Honorary Secretary

Founded: 1962

Organisation type and purpose: Membership association.
Society for all who appreciate the music of Delius.

Subject coverage: Life and works of the composer Frederick Delius.

Publications: Printed

Access to staff: Contact by letter
Hours: Mon to Fri, 0900 to 1700

Independent from, but works closely with, the: Delius Trust

DELPHINIUM SOCIETY (DS)

2 The Grove, Ickenham, Uxbridge, Middlesex, UB10 8QH

Tel: 01895 464694
Fax: 01895 235365
E-mail: roger.beauchamp@btinternet.com
Website: www.delphinium-society.co.uk

Enquiries to: Promotions and Publicity Secretary

Founded: 1928

Organisation type and purpose:
International organisation, membership association (membership is by subscription), present number of members: 1,000.
For the study, dissemination and collection of all information concerning the genus Delphinium and the closely related genus Consolida. Also to study the relationship of the genus to other members of the family Ranunculaceae.

Subject coverage: All aspects of the genus Delphinium and related-genus Consolida. Scientific interest in Aconitum.

Information services: from Promotions and Publicity Secretary

Publications: Printed

Publications list: Available in print

Access to staff: Contact by letter, by telephone, by fax, by e-mail and via website

DELTA

Formal name: Deaf Education through Listening and Talking

The Con Powell Centre, Alfa House, Molesey Road, Walton-on-Thames, Surrey, KT12 3PD

Tel: 0845 108 1437
E-mail: enquiries@deafeducation.org.uk
Website: www.deafeducation.org.uk

Founded: 1980

Organisation type and purpose: Voluntary organisation, registered charity (charity number 1115603).
To guide parents and teachers in helping deaf children to develop normal spoken language and to live independently within the hearing society, the practice and philosophy of the natural aural approach to the education of deaf children.

Subject coverage: Deaf young people, the development of independence and communication, the attainment levels achieved by severely and profoundly deaf young people.

Publications: Printed, and electronic and video
Order electronic and video publications from: e-mail: enquiries@deafeducation.org.uk

Publications list: Available online and in print

Access to staff: Contact by letter, by telephone, by e-mail and via website. Appointment necessary.
Hours: Mon to Fri, 0900 to 1700

DELTA BIOTECHNOLOGY LIMITED

Castle Court, Castle Boulevard, Nottingham, NG7 1FD

Tel: 0115 955 3355
Fax: 0115 955 1299
E-mail: office@datagate.co.uk

Enquiries to: Information Manager
Direct e-mail: alison.mitson@aventis.com

Organisation type and purpose: Research organisation.

Subject coverage: Recombinant technology.

Access to staff: Contact by letter, by fax and by e-mail
Hours: Mon to Fri, 0900 to 1700

Parent body: Aventis Behring

DENBIGHSHIRE COUNTY COUNCIL

Council Offices, Wynnstay Road, Ruthin, Denbighshire, LL15 1YN

Tel: 01824 706000
Fax: 01824 705026
Website: www.denbighshire.gov.uk

Enquiries to: Public Relations Manager
Direct tel: 01824 706222
Direct fax: 01824 707446
Direct e-mail: sue.appleton@denbighshire.gov.uk

Founded: 1996; formed from Clwyd County Council, Glyndwr District Council, Rhuddlan Borough Council (year of change 1996)

Organisation type and purpose: Local government body.

Subject coverage: Education, social services, housing and environment, planning, economic development, highways, transport.

Access to staff: Contact by telephone
Hours: Mon to Fri, 0900 to 1700

DENBIGHSHIRE HERITAGE SERVICE

46 Clwyd Street, Ruthin, Denbighshire, LL15 1HP

Tel: 01824 708281
Fax: 01824 708258
E-mail: heritage@denbighshire.gov.uk
Website: www.denbighshire.gov.uk

Enquiries to: Curator
Direct tel: 01824 708223
Direct e-mail: curatorialmanager@denbighshire.gov.uk

Organisation type and purpose: Local government body.
Administrative body for the libraries, museums, art galleries and historical sites that are under the care of Denbighshire County Council.

Subject coverage: The conservation of Denbighshire heritage. Ruthin Gaol, Plas Newydd, Rhyl Museum and Nantclwyd y Dre.

Information services: Information on DCC museum collections.

Special visitor services: Site audio guides; multimedia presentations.

Education services: For all ages, but focusing on KS2 history.

Access to staff: Contact by letter, by telephone, by fax, by e-mail and via website. Appointment necessary.

Parent body: Denbighshire County Council; tel: 01824 706000

DENBIGHSHIRE HISTORICAL SOCIETY

Formal name: Cymdeithas Hanes Sir Ddinbych / Denbighshire Historical Society

1 Green Park, Erddig, Wrexham, LL13 7YE.

Tel: 01978 353 363
Website: www.glyndwr.ac.uk/dhs

Enquiries to: Chairman

Founded: 1950

Organisation type and purpose: Learned society (membership is by subscription), present number of members: 350, registered charity (charity number 519210).

Subject coverage: General, social, personal and industrial history of the former county of Denbighshire, defined by the boundaries prior to 1974 reorganisation.

Publications: Printed
Order printed publications from: The Treasurer, Ysgubor Isa, Llanfair D.C., Ruthin, LL15 2UN

Access to staff: Contact by letter and by telephone
Hours: Mon to Fri, 0900 to 1700

DENBIGHSHIRE RECORD OFFICE

46 Clwyd Street, Ruthin, Denbighshire, LL15 1HP

Tel: 01824 708250
Fax: 01824 708222
E-mail: archives@denbighshire.gov.uk
Website: www.denbighshire.gov.uk/archives

Enquiries to: Archivist

Founded: 1972; formerly called Clwyd Record Office (year of change 1996)

Organisation type and purpose: Local government body.
Archive.
County record office holding material relating to the pre-1974 county of Denbigh and the present area.

Subject coverage: Local history: former county of Clwyd, and the historic and present county of Denbighshire.

Collection: Collections relating to historic county of Denbighshire, including quarter sessions; county council; district councils; parish (microfilm); schools; family and estates; census (microfilm); newspapers (microfilm and original)

Non-library collection catalogue: All or part available online and in-house

Publications list: Available online and in print

Access to staff: Contact by letter, by telephone, by fax, by e-mail, in person and via website
Hours: Tue to Fri, 0930 to 1630
Special comments: Reader's ticket, prior appointment for microfilm users.

Access for disabled people: Parking provided, ramped entry, access to most public areas, toilet facilities

DENTAL LABORATORIES ASSOCIATION LIMITED (DLA)

44–46 Wollaton Road, Beeston, Nottingham, NG9 2NR

Tel: 0115 925 4888
Fax: 0115 925 4800
E-mail: info@dla.org.uk
Website: www.DLA.ORG.UK

Enquiries to: Chief Executive

Founded: 1961

Organisation type and purpose: Trade association.

Subject coverage: Dental technology; commercial dental laboratories; Department of Health current guidelines and regulations within mechanical dentistry.

Publications: Printed

Access to staff: Contact by letter and by e-mail. Appointment necessary. Non-members charged.
Hours: Mon to Fri, 0900 to 1700

Links with: Federation of European Dental Laboratory Owners (FEPPD)

DENTAL PRACTITIONERS' ASSOCIATION (DPA)

61 Harley Street, London, W1G 8QU

Tel: 020 7636 1072
Fax: 020 7636 1086
E-mail: info@uk-dentistry.org
Website: www.uk-dentistry.org/

Enquiries to: Chief Executive

Founded: 1954

Organisation type and purpose: Professional body (membership is by subscription), number of members: 1,200 practices, 3,000 members.
Founded in 1954 by General Dental Practitioners for GDPs. Exclusively promotes the interests of dentists in general practice, providing support, advice and representation at all levels.

Subject coverage: Dentistry, statistics, dental politics, dento-legal matters, business briefing, management consultancy.

Non-library collection catalogue: All or part available online and in-house

Publications: Printed

Publications list: Available online

Access to staff: Contact by letter, by telephone, by fax, by e-mail and via website. Appointment necessary. Access for members only.
Hours: Mon to Fri, 1000 to 1600

Access for disabled people: No

DENTISTS' MEDIA GROUP (DMG)

PO Box 15, Sindalthorpe House, Ely, Cambridgeshire, CB7 4SG

Tel: 01353 688456
Fax: 01353 688451

Enquiries to: Administrator
Direct e-mail: peter@dentalconfidence.com

Founded: 1996

Organisation type and purpose: National organisation, membership association (membership is by election or invitation), present number of members: 170, voluntary organisation, training organisation, consultancy.
To encourage, and to enhance the quality of, broadcasting and writing by dentists on radio and television, local radio in particular and in the press and magazines.

Subject coverage: The Dentists' Media Group is a source of spokespeople on all aspects of oral health.

Access to staff: Contact by letter, by telephone, by fax and by e-mail
Hours: Mon to Fri, 0900 to 1700

Access to building: Prior appointment required

Access for disabled people: Ramped entry

Affiliated to and at the same address as: Association of Broadcasting Doctors (ABD)

DEPARTMENT FOR BUSINESS INNOVATION AND SKILLS (BIS)

1 Victoria Street, London, SW1H 0ET

Tel: 020 7215 5000; minicom no. 020 7215 6740
E-mail: enquiries@bis.gsi.gov.uk
Website: www.bis.gov.uk

Enquiries to: Librarian
Direct tel: 0207 215 5006
Direct e-mail: infosource@bis.gsi.gov.uk

Founded: 2009; created by the merger of Department for Business Enterprise and Regulatory Reform, and Department for Innovation, Universities and Skills (year of change 2009); formerly called Department of Trade and Industry (year of change 2007)

Organisation type and purpose: National government body.
Government library.

Subject coverage: Trade policy, export promotion, corporate and consumer affairs, employment relations, innovation and technology, small firms, regional development and inward investment.

Collection: Archive of publications from the DTI, Department of Energy, Board of Trade, etc.

Library catalogue: All or part available in-house

Order printed publications from: BIS Publications Orderline, ADMAIL 528, London, SW1W 8YT; tel. 0845 015 0010; or via website: http://www.bis.gov.uk/publications

Publications list: Available online

Access to staff: Contact by letter and by telephone. Appointment necessary.
Hours: Mon to Fri, 0900 to 1700

DEPARTMENT FOR CULTURE, MEDIA AND SPORT (DCMS)

Library, Room L21, 2–4 Cockspur Street, London, SW1Y 5DH

Tel: 020 7211 6041
Fax: 020 7211 6032
Website: www.lottery.culture.gov.uk
Website: www.culture.gov.uk

Enquiries to: Libraries services to DCMS staff

Founded: 1992; formerly called Department of National Heritage (year of change 1997)

Organisation type and purpose: National government body.

Subject coverage: The arts, sport, the National Lottery, libraries, museums and galleries, broadcasting, gambling, film, press freedom and regulation, the built heritage, tourism, the creative industries, cultural property and the Government Art Collection.

Collection: On the subjects listed

Library catalogue: All or part available online and in-house

Publications: Printed

Publications list: Available online

Access to staff: Contact by letter, by telephone, by fax, by e-mail and via website. Appointment necessary.
Hours: Mon to Fri, 0900 to 1730

Access for disabled people: Access to all public areas

DEPARTMENT FOR EDUCATION LIBRARY (DfE)

Sanctuary Buildings, Great Smith Street, London, SW1P 3BT

Tel: 0870 000 2288
Website: www.education.gov.uk
Website: publications.dcsf.gov.uk

Organisation type and purpose: National government body.

Subject coverage: Education policy, children and families policy.

Library catalogue: All or part available in-house

Access to building: *Special comments:* Library is not open to the public, please use the public enquiries contact for the Department.

DEPARTMENT FOR ENVIRONMENT, FOOD AND RURAL AFFAIRS – LIBRARY (Defra)

Lower Ground Floor, Ergon House, c/o 17 Smith Square, London, SW1P 3JR

Tel: 020 7238 6575
Fax: 020 7238 6609
E-mail: defra.library@defra.gsi.gov.uk
Website: www.defra.gov.uk

Enquiries to: Librarian
Direct tel: 020 7238 3327
Direct e-mail: kevin.jackson@defra.gsi.gov.uk

continued overleaf

Founded: 2001; formerly called Ministry of Agriculture, Fisheries & Food (MAFF) (year of change 2001)

Organisation type and purpose: National government body.
Government departmental library.

Subject coverage: Agriculture, fisheries, food, particularly temperate agriculture, environment, nature conservation, sustainable environment, biodiversity, climate change adaptation.

Information services: Helpdesk, tel: 08459 335577

Library catalogue: All or part available in-house

Order printed publications from: Defra Library at above address

Publications list: Available online

Access to staff: Contact by e-mail and via website. Appointment necessary.
Hours: Mon to Fri, 0900 to 1700

Access to building: Prior appointment required

Access for disabled people: Toilet facilities

Also at: Department for Environment, Food and Rural Affairs (DEFRA); Nobel House, 17 Smith Square, London, SW1P 3JR

DEPARTMENT FOR INTERNATIONAL DEVELOPMENT (DFID)

Abercrombie House, Eaglesham Road, East Kilbride, Glasgow, G75 8EA

Tel: 01355 843880
Fax: 01355 843632
E-mail: library@dfid.gov.uk
Website: www.dfid.gov.uk

Enquiries to: Librarian
Direct tel: 020 7023 0574
Direct fax: 020 7023 0523
Direct e-mail: s-skelton@dfid.gov.uk

History of institution: formerly called Overseas Development Administration (ODA) (year of change 1997)

Organisation type and purpose: National government body.
Central government library.

Subject coverage: Social and economic development of developing countries; development aid and policy (especially for the Third World, but now also for Eastern Europe).

Access to staff: Contact by letter, by telephone, by fax, by e-mail and via website. Appointment necessary.
Hours: Mon to Fri, 0900 to 1700

Access to building: Prior appointment required

London Office: Department for International Development; 1 Palace Street, London, SW1E 5HE; tel: 020 7023 0000; fax: 020 7023 0019

DEPARTMENT FOR WORK AND PENSIONS (DWP)

Information and Library Services, Room 114, Adelphi, 111 John Adam Street, London, WC2N 6NT

Tel: 020 7712 2500
Fax: 020 7962 8491
E-mail: library.services@dwp.gsi.gov.uk
Website: www.dwp.gov.uk

Founded: 2001

Organisation type and purpose: National government body.
Government departmental library.

Subject coverage: Social security, social welfare (including National Insurance, industrial injuries, supplementary benefits, state and occupational pensions, family benefits); social policy, poverty, taxation, distribution of income, public administration, management; unemployment, employment.

Trade and statistical information: UK government statistics and worldwide statistics on social security and social welfare

Library catalogue: All or part available in-house

Publications: Printed

Access to staff: Contact by letter, by telephone, by fax and by e-mail. Appointment necessary.
Hours: Mon to Fri, 0900 to 1700
Special comments: Library of last resort – if there is no other service for the information.

Access for disabled people: Access to all public areas, toilet facilities

DEPARTMENT OF AGRICULTURE AND RURAL DEVELOPMENT LIBRARY (DARD Library)

Room 615, Dundonald House, Upper Newtownards Road, Belfast, BT4 3SB

Tel: 028 9052 4401
Fax: 028 9052 5546
E-mail: library@dardni.gov.uk
Website: www.dardni.gov.uk

Enquiries to: Librarian

Founded: 1999; formerly called Ministry of Agriculture (year of change 1973); formerly called Department of Agriculture (year of change 1983)

Organisation type and purpose: Government department.

Subject coverage: Agriculture, animal health, fisheries, forestry, horticulture, rural development, public administration, rivers, veterinary.

Information services: Online catalogue: http://library.nics.gov.uk

Library catalogue: All or part available online

Publications: Printed

Access to staff: Contact by letter, by telephone and by e-mail. Appointment necessary.
Hours: Mon to Fri, 0900 to 1700

Access to building: Access for general public, by arrangement only. Part of Inspire network.
Hours: 0900 to 1700

Access for disabled people: Disabled access available

DEPARTMENT OF COMPLEMENTARY THERAPIES

School of Integrated Health, University of Westminster, 115 New Cavendish Street, London, W1W 6UW

Tel: 020 7911 5000
Fax: 020 7911 5028
E-mail: course-enquiries@westminster.ac.uk
Website: www.westminster.ac.uk/sih

Founded: 1983; created by the merger of Centre for Community Care and Primary Health, and London School of Acupuncture and Traditional Chinese Medicine (year of change 1997)

Organisation type and purpose: Advisory body, university department or institute, training organisation, consultancy, research organisation.

Subject coverage: Homoeopathy, nutritional therapy, medical herbalism, remedial massage, professional entry education in traditional Chinese medicine, acupuncture and other complementary therapies, development of research base of traditional Chinese acupuncture in the United Kingdom and other complementary therapies.

Library catalogue: All or part available online and in-house

Publications: Printed
Order printed publications from: Course Enquiries: course-enquiries@westminster.ac.uk, tel. 020 7911 5000

Access to staff: Contact by letter, by telephone, by fax, by e-mail and via website
Hours: Mon to Fri, 0900 to 1700

Access to building: Prior appointment required
Hours: Mon to Fri, 0900 to 1700

Access for disabled people: Ramped entry, toilet facilities

DEPARTMENT OF GEOGRAPHY, UNIVERSITY OF CAMBRIDGE

University of Cambridge, Downing Site, Cambridge, CB2 3EN

Tel: 01223 333399
Fax: 01223 333392
E-mail: enquiries@geog.cam.ac.uk
Website: www.geog.cam.ac.uk

Founded: 1945

Organisation type and purpose: University library.

Subject coverage: Indexed collection of 500,000 vertical and oblique aerial photographs of United Kingdom and Ireland from 1945 onwards. Smaller collection of air photographs of France, the Netherlands and Denmark taken from 1966 to 1974. Emphasis on areas of ecological, historical and archaeological interest.

Non-library collection catalogue: All or part available online and in-house

Library catalogue: All or part available in-house

Access to staff: Contact by letter, by telephone, by fax, by e-mail and in person

Access to building: Appointment required.

DEPARTMENT OF HEALTH

5E01, Quarry House, Quarry Hill, Leeds, LS2 7UE

Tel: 0113 2545080
Fax: 0113 2545084
E-mail: knowledgecentre-qh@dh.gsi.gov.uk
Website: www.dh.gov.uk

Enquiries to: Customer Services Librarian (Leeds)

Founded: 1834

Organisation type and purpose: National government body.
Government Department Library Service provided to all staff within the Department of Health.

Subject coverage: Public health, health services, health services policy and management, social care policy and management, hospital buildings.

Collection: 250,000 monographs
565 printed periodicals
Various databases and e-journals

Library catalogue: All or part available online and in-house

Publications: Electronic and video
Order printed publications from: DH Publications Order Line, PO Box 777, London, SE1 6XH,; fax: 0870 1555 455; e-mail: dh@prolog.uk.com

Access to staff: Contact by letter, by telephone, by fax and by e-mail.
Appointment necessary.
Hours: Mon to Fri, 0900 to 1700

Access to building: No access other than to staff
Special comments: Not open to the public. Email requests for access should be addessed to the Customer Services Librarian

Also at: Senior Librarian, Department of Health Library; 5E25, Quarry House, Quarry Hill, Leeds LS2 7UE; tel: 0113 2545071; fax: 0113 2545084; e-mail: knowledgecentre-qh@dh.gsi.gov.uk; website: http://www.dh.gov.uk

DEPARTMENT OF HEALTH – LIBRARY INFORMATION SERVICES

Skipton House, 80 London Road, London, SE1 6LH

Tel: 020 7972 2000
Fax: 020 7972 1609
Website: www.doh.gov.uk

Enquiries to: Librarian
Direct tel: 020 7972 6541
Direct fax: 020 7972 5976

Organisation type and purpose: National government body.
Government department library.

Subject coverage: Health and social care services, management of the National Health Service, hospitals, public health, environmental health, services for older people and those with disabilities and learning difficulties.

Collection: Collection of early Poor Law pamphlets
Government Medical Inspectors Local Reports on Public Health, 1869–1907
Local Reports to the General Board of Health, 1848–1857

Library catalogue: All or part available in-house

Publications: Printed, and electronic and video, and microform publications
Order printed publications from: DH publications Orderline, PO Box 777, London, SE1 6XH; tel: 08701 555455; fax: 01623 724524; e-mail: dh@prolog.uk.com

Access to staff: Appointment necessary.
Hours: Mon to Fri, 0900 to 1700

Access to building: Prior appointment required

DEPARTMENT OF MATERIALS: LOUGHBOROUGH UNIVERSITY

Loughborough University, Loughborough, Leicestershire, LE11 3TU

Tel: 01509 223331
Fax: 01509 223949
E-mail: materials@lboro.ac.uk
Website: www.lboro.ac.uk/materials

Enquiries to: Development Officer
Direct tel: 01509 228592
Direct e-mail: m.e.white@lboro.ac.uk

Founded: 1967; formerly called Institute of Polymer Technology and Materials Engineering — IPTME (year of change 2008)

Organisation type and purpose: University department or institute.
Postgraduate education, research and consultancy.

Subject coverage: Polymers; metals; ceramics; materials characterisation centre with advanced thermal method units; Institute of Surface Science and Technology; electron microscope unit; X-ray unit.

Publications: Printed

Publications list: Available in print

Access to staff: Contact by letter, by telephone, by fax, by e-mail and via website
Hours: Mon to Fri, 0900 to 1700

Links with: Loughborough Materials Characterisation Centre (LMCC); address as Department of Materials; tel: 01509 223387; fax: 01509 234225; e-mail: lmcc@lboro.ac.uk

DEPARTMENT OF REGIONAL DEVELOPMENT (DRD)

Library, Room G-40, Clarence Court, 10–18 Adelaide Street, Belfast, BT2 8GB

Tel: 028 9054 1046
Fax: 028 9054 1081
E-mail: library@drdni.gov.uk

Enquiries to: Librarian

History of institution: formerly called Department of the Environment for Northern Ireland (DOE) (year of change 2000)

Organisation type and purpose: National government body.
There is a Core Department and two Next Steps agencies.

Subject coverage: Planning, roads, road safety, environmental protection and conservation, local government, urban regeneration and disposal and management of the department's land and property holdings, transport, fire services, pollution, historic monuments, archaeology, water and sewerage services, building construction, public records.

Non-library collection catalogue: All or part available online and in-house

Library catalogue: All or part available online and in-house

Access to staff: Access for members only.
Hours: Mon to Fri, 0900 to 1700
Special comments: Loans and personal access to civil servants only. Brief subject enquiries by letter or telephone from non-civil servants will be dealt with where possible.

Access to building: No prior appointment required

Next Steps agencies: Roads Service; website: http://www.roadsni.gov.uk
Water Service; website: http://www.waterni.gov.uk

DEPAUL UK

1st Floor, 291–299 Borough High Street, London, SE1 1JG

Tel: 020 7939 1220
Fax: 020 7939 1221
E-mail: depaul@depauluk.org
Website: www.depauluk.org

Enquiries to: Administrator

Founded: 1989

Organisation type and purpose: Voluntary organisation, registered charity (charity number 802384).

Subject coverage: Depaul Trust helps young people across the UK who are homeless, vulnerable and disadvantaged, working in the very heart of local communities. It protects young people who become homeless by finding them a place to call their home. Each year it provides over 100,000 bed nights and it is open every day and night.
It prevents young people from becoming homeless by rebuilding family relationships and offering through-the-gate support to young offenders.
It provides young people with the chance to fulfil their potential in the community through education, volunteering, training and jobs.
Since Depaul Trust started in 1989, it has made a difference to over 40,000 young people.

Publications list: Available online

Access to staff: Contact by letter, by telephone, by fax, by e-mail and via website
Hours: Mon to Fri, 0900 to 1730

DEPRESSION ALLIANCE

35 Westminster Bridge Road, London, SE1 7JB

Tel: 020 7633 0557
Fax: 020 7633 0559
E-mail: information@depressionalliance.org
Website: www.depressionalliance.org

Enquiries to: Office and Communications Co-ordinator

continued overleaf

Founded: 1974; formerly called Depressives Associated (year of change 1995); formerly called National Depression Campaign (year of change 2000)

Organisation type and purpose: Membership association (membership is by subscription), present number of members: 3000, voluntary organisation, registered charity (charity number 278532).
To provide support and understanding, information, education, self-help.

Subject coverage: Depression.

Publications: Printed, and electronic and video
Order printed publications from: Office Manager, Depression Alliance
As above

Publications list: Available online and in print

Access to staff: Contact by letter, by telephone, by fax, by e-mail and via website
Hours: Mon to Fri, 1000 to 1700

Access to building: Prior appointment required

Other addresses: Depression Alliance Cymru; 11 Plas Melin, Westbourne Road, Whitchurch, Cardiff, CF4 2BT; tel: 029 2069 2891; fax: 029 2052 7774; Depression Alliance Scotland; 3 Grosvenor Gardens, Edinburgh, EH12 5JU; tel: 0131 467 3050; fax: 0131 467 7701

DEPRESSION–UK (D–UK)

Self Help Nottingham, Ormiston House, 32–36 Pelham Street, Nottingham, NG1 2EG

E-mail: info@depressionuk.org
Website: www.depressionuk.org.uk

Enquiries to: Honorary Secretary
Direct tel: 0870 774 4320
Direct e-mail: info@depressionuk.org

Founded: 1973; formerly called Depressives Anonymous (year of change 1973); formerly called Fellowship of Depressives Anonymous (year of change 2007)

Organisation type and purpose: Membership association (membership is by subscription), present number of members: 300, voluntary organisation, registered charity (charity number 294482).
Encouragement and support for those with depression and those concerned for them.

Subject coverage: Depression Self-Help Group.

Information services: Have a few leaflets about depression. Our phone number 0870 774 4320 is for information only.

Publications: Printed, and electronic and video
Order printed publications from: Postal address

Publications list: Available in print

Access to staff: Contact by letter, by telephone and by e-mail
Hours: Mon to Fri, 0900 to 1700
Special comments: The charity is run by a team of volunteers who work from their own homes.

Access for disabled people: Our AGM and other meetings are usually held in venues that offer access for the disabled.

DERBY CITY COUNCIL

Council House, Corporation Street, Derby, DE1 2FS

Tel: 01332 293111\ Minicom no. 01332 256666
Fax: 01322 255500
E-mail: customerservices@derby.gov.uk
Website: www.derby.gov.uk

Enquiries to: Chief Executive

Organisation type and purpose: Local government body.

Subject coverage: All local authority services.

Access to staff: Contact by letter, by telephone, by fax, by e-mail and in person
Hours: Mon to Thu, 0830 to 1700; Fri, 0830 to 1630

DERBY CITY LIBRARIES

Derby Local Studies Library, 25B Irongate, Derby, DE1 3GL

Tel: 01332 255393
E-mail: localstudies.library@derby.gov.uk
Website: www.derby.gov.uk/libraries/about/local_studies.htm

Enquiries to: Librarian

Founded: 1879

Organisation type and purpose: Public library.
Local studies library providing research facilities.

Subject coverage: Local studies materials of all types relating to Derby and Derbyshire.

Education services: Informal family history and local history courses.

Collection: Printed materials, over 40,000 items including histories of Derby and Derbyshire, street and trade directories, poll books and registers of electors for Derby Periodicals and newspapers dating from 1732
Maps from 1577
Illustrations and engravings including over 8,500 photographs dating from 1860s to present day
Broadsheets mostly 19th-century items depicting events
Family History including Census returns on microfilm for the whole of Derbyshire 1841 to 1901
IGI (microfiche) for UK
Special collections including family papers, deeds, manuscripts, business records, etc.

Non-library collection catalogue: All or part available in-house

Library catalogue: All or part available online and in-house

Publications: Printed, and electronic and video

Access to staff: Contact by letter, by telephone, by e-mail, in person and via website
Hours: Mon, 0900 to 1900; Thu, Fri, 0930 to 1230; Sat, 0930 to 1600
Special comments: Opening hours subject to change; please check website or phone for current opening.

Access to building: *Hours:* As above

Access for disabled people: Ramped entry
Special comments: Please ring to book a parking space.

Parent body: Derby City Council; Derby City Libraries, Regeneration & Community, Heritage Gate, Friary Street, Derby, DE1 1QX; tel: 01332 715549; fax: 01332 716607

DERBYSHIRE AND NOTTINGHAMSHIRE CHAMBER OF COMMERCE (DNCC)

Canal Wharf, Chesterfield, Derbyshire, S41 7NA

Tel: 0845 601 1038
Fax: 01246 233228
E-mail: information@dncc.co.uk
Website: www.dncc.co.uk

Enquiries to: Information & Research Officer

Founded: 1899; formerly called Derbyshire Chamber and Business Link; Nottinghamshire Chamber of Commerce and Industry (year of change 2006 and 2007)

Organisation type and purpose: Membership association.
Chamber of Commerce.

Subject coverage: Training, business information, business support, with emphasis on Derbyshire and Nottinghamshire. Export advice.

Information services: Telephone and e-mail enquiry service for business

Publications: Printed, and electronic and video

Access to staff: Contact by letter, by telephone, by fax, by e-mail and via website
Hours: Mon to Fri, 0900 to 1700
Special comments: Charges made for incurred costs and research time.

Member of: Association of British Chambers of Commerce

DERBYSHIRE COUNTY COUNCIL

Cultural and Community Services Department, County Hall, Matlock, Derbyshire, DE4 3AG

Tel: 01629 580000
Fax: 01629 585363
E-mail: derbyshire.libraries@derbyshire.gov.uk
Website: www.derbyshire.gov.uk
Website: www.peaklandheritage.org.uk
Website: picturethepast.org.uk

Enquiries to: Strategic Director of Cultural and Community Services
Other contacts: Assistant Director (for information on resources and publications)

Organisation type and purpose: Local government body, museum, art gallery, public library.
County and Diocesan Record Office.

Subject coverage: Derbyshire local studies; local government information; family history; lead mining.

Collection: British Cave Research Association Library (at HQ)
George Stephenson Collection of early railway history (at Chesterfield)

Non-library collection catalogue: All or part available online and in-house

Library catalogue: All or part available online

Publications: Printed, and electronic and video

Publications list: Available online and in print

Access to staff: Contact by letter, by telephone, by fax, by e-mail, in person and via website
Hours: Mon to Fri, 0900 to 1700

Links with: County local studies library at Matlock; Derbyshire County Council; Main public library at Chesterfield

DERBYSHIRE FAMILY HISTORY SOCIETY (DFHS)

Bridge Chapel House, St Mary's Bridge, Sowter Road, Derby, DE1 3AT

Tel: 01332 363876
Website: www.dfhs.org.uk

Enquiries to: Honorary Secretary

Founded: 1976

Organisation type and purpose:
Membership association (membership is by subscription), present number of members: 2000, registered charity (charity number 517162).
Family history research.

Subject coverage: Family history in Derbyshire.

Services for disabled people: Quarterly journal on tape for the partially sighted.

Library catalogue: All or part available in-house and in print

Publications: Printed, and electronic and video, and microform publications
Order printed publications from: Booksales Officer, Derbyshire Family History Society 17 Penrhyn Avenue, Littleover, Derby, DE23 6LB
Order microform publications from: Booksales Officer

Publications list: Available online and in print

Access to staff: Contact by letter and via website
Hours: Tue, Thu, Sat, 1000 to 1600
Special comments: Telephone 01332 363876 during these hours only.

Access to building: *Hours:* Tue, Thu, Sat, 1000 to 1600

Access for disabled people: *Special comments:* Grade 2 listed building; please telephone to make arrangements before visiting.

Affiliated to: Federation of Family History Societies

DERBYSHIRE GRITSTONE SHEEP BREEDERS SOCIETY

The Secretary, 5 Bridge Close, Waterfoot, Rossendale, Lancashire, BB4 9SN

Tel: 07766 448854
E-mail: susan@pmcoppack.com
Website: www.derbyshiregritstone.org.uk

Enquiries to: Honorary Secretary

Founded: 1906

Organisation type and purpose:
Membership association (membership is by subscription), registered charity (charity number 265539).
Support for members and to maintain/develop standard of Derbyshire Gritstone sheep.

Publications: Printed

Access to staff: Contact by letter, by telephone, by e-mail and via website
Hours: Mon to Fri, 0900 to 1700

DERBYSHIRE RECORD OFFICE

County Hall, Matlock, Derbyshire, DE4 3AG

Tel: 01629 539202
Fax: 01629 57611
E-mail: record.office@derbyshire.gov.uk
Website: www.derbyshire.gov.uk/recordoffice

Enquiries to: County and Diocesan Archivist
Direct tel: 01629 539201
Direct e-mail: margaretosullivan@derbyshire.gov.uk

Organisation type and purpose: Local government body.
County Record Office.

Subject coverage: Archives of the County of Derbyshire, the City of Derby and the Diocese of Derby; public records of Derbyshire origin; business, industrial, diocesan, parish, family and estate, manorial, hospital, school, voluntary society and other records from Derby and Derbyshire.

Non-library collection catalogue: All or part available online, in-house and in print

Publications: Printed, and electronic and video
Order printed publications from: Derbyshire Record Office
Order electronic and video publications from: Derbyshire Record Office

Publications list: Available online and in print

Access to staff: Contact by letter, by telephone, by fax, by e-mail and in person. Appointment necessary.

Access to building: *Hours:* Mon to Fri, 0930 to 1645, one Sat per month, 1000 to 1600
Special comments: Reader registration required, with proof of identity and address

Parent body: Derbyshire County Council; Cultural and Community Services Department, Libraries and Heritage Division

DERBYSHIRE WILDLIFE TRUST (DWT)

East Mill, Bridgefoot, Belper, Derbyshire, DE56 1XH

Tel: 01773 881188
Fax: 01773 821826
E-mail: enquiries@derbyshirewt.co.uk
Website: www.derbyshirewildlifetrust.org.uk

Enquiries to: Administration Assistant

Founded: 1962

Organisation type and purpose: Voluntary organisation, registered charity (charity number 222212).

Publications: Printed

Publications list: Available in print

Access to staff: Contact by letter, by telephone, by fax, by e-mail and via website
Hours: Mon to Thu, 0900 to 1700; Fri, 0900 to 1630

Access to building: No prior appointment required

Also at: Carsington Water Wildlife Discovery Room; Countryside Centre, Derbyshire Wildlife Trust; The Whistlestop Countryside Centre, Matlock Bath Railway Station, Matlock Bath, Derbyshire, DE4 3PT; tel: 01629 580958

DERMATITIS AND ALLIED DISEASES RESEARCH TRUST (DERMATRUST)

40 Queen Anne Street, London, W1G 9EL

Tel: 01604 781903
Fax: 01604 781514

Enquiries to: Chairman

Founded: 1996

Organisation type and purpose: Registered charity (charity number 1016315).
To support the care of patients with skin diseases and to fund research into their causes and develop new treatments.

Subject coverage: Dermatological diseases, dermatology research.

Access to staff: Contact by letter and by fax
Hours: Mon to Fri, 0900 to 1700

DESIGN AND ARTISTS COPYRIGHT SOCIETY (DACS)

33 Great Sutton Street, London, EC1V 0DX

Tel: 020 7336 8811
Fax: 020 7336 8822
E-mail: info@dacs.org.uk

Enquiries to: Membership Secretary

Founded: 1983

Organisation type and purpose:
International organisation, membership association (membership is by subscription).
DACS is the copyright and collecting society for visual arts in the UK; acting as exclusive licensee on behalf of its national members and as agent for foreign artists and estates. It also actively campaigns to create a fairer working environment for visual creators through collective administration and lobbying on behalf of all artists at both national and international levels on rights-related issues.

Publications: Printed

Publications list: Available online and in print

Access to staff: Contact by letter, by fax and by e-mail. Appointment necessary.
Hours: Mon to Fri, 0900 to 1800

continued overleaf

Special comments: DACS can only act on behalf of its members, but offers general copyright information to all.

Access to building: No prior appointment required

DESIGN HISTORY SOCIETY (DHS)

28 New High Street, Oxford, OX3 7AQ

Tel: 01264 353058
E-mail: webadmin@designhistorysociety.org
Website: www.designhistorysociety.org

Enquiries to: Secretary

Founded: 1977

Organisation type and purpose: Learned society (membership is by subscription), registered charity (charity number 327326), research organisation.

Subject coverage: History of architecture and design, including design of fashion and textiles; graphic design; product design; cultural studies.

Publications: Printed

Access to staff: Contact by letter, by telephone, by e-mail and via website
Hours: Mon to Fri, 0900 to 1700

DESIGNER BOOKBINDERS

6 Queen Square, London, WC1N 3AR

Tel: 01225 342793
E-mail: secretary@designerbookbinders.org.uk
Website: www.designerbookbinders.org.uk

Enquiries to: Secretary

Founded: 1951; formerly called Guild of Contemporary Bookbinders; formerly called Hampstead Guild of Scribes and Bookbinders (year of change 1955)

Organisation type and purpose: Membership association, present number of members: 600, voluntary organisation, registered charity (charity number 282018). Maintenance and improvement of standards of design and craft in hand bookbinding by means of exhibitions, teaching and publications.

Subject coverage: Art of the hand-bound book, design, craftsmanship, repair and restoration.

Publications: Printed
Order printed publications from: Designer Bookbinders Publications Limited
Email: publications@designerbookbinders.org.uk

Publications list: Available in print

Access to staff: Contact by letter, by telephone, by e-mail and via website

Member of: Federation of British Crafts Societies (FBCS)

DEUX CHEVAUX CLUB OF GREAT BRITAIN (2CVGB)

PO Box 602, Crick, Northampton, NN6 7UW

E-mail: secretary@2cvgb.com
Website: www.2cvgb.co.uk

Enquiries to: Secretary

Founded: 1978

Organisation type and purpose: International organisation, membership association (membership is by subscription), number of members: 3,000.

Subject coverage: Information and parts for all Citroën A-series vehicles.

Collection: Archive on A-series vehicles

Publications: Printed

Access to staff: Contact by letter, by e-mail and via website
Hours: Mon to Fri, 0800 to 2200

DEVELOPMENT EDUCATION ASSOCIATION (DEA)

1st Floor, River House, 143–145 Farringdon Road, London EC1R 3AB

Tel: 020 7812 1282
Fax: 020 7812 1272
E-mail: dea@dea.org.uk
Website: www.dea.org.uk
Website: www.globaldimension.org.uk

Enquiries to: Communications Team

Founded: 1993

Organisation type and purpose: Membership association (membership is by subscription), present number of members: 300, voluntary organisation, registered charity (charity number 291696), suitable for ages: all.
To promote and strengthen the development education movement in UK; to raise public awareness of global and development issues.

Subject coverage: Provides information on availability of development education resources for researchers, youth and community workers; information and support base to development education practitioners, global perspectives in formal education (schools, higher and further education), youth work, adult and community education.

Collection: Small resource centre for internal use

Trade and statistical information: Contact and resource information on development education sector in UK

Publications: Printed
Order printed publications from: Contact the DEA

Publications list: Available online and in print

Access to staff: Contact by letter, by telephone, by fax, by e-mail and via website. Appointment necessary.
Hours: Mon to Fri, 1000 to 1700

DEVON AND EXETER INSTITUTION LIBRARY

7 Cathedral Close, Exeter, Devon, EX1 1EZ

Tel: 01392 251017
Website: www.lib.ex.ac.uk/search
Website: www.ex.ac.uk/library/devonex.html

Enquiries to: Librarian in Charge
Direct e-mail: c.j.faunch@exeter.ac.uk

Founded: 1813

Organisation type and purpose: Membership association, registered charity. Independent subscription library.

Subject coverage: History of Exeter, Devon, Cornwall, Somerset, Dorset, 19th-century periodicals, biography, history and topography.

Collection: 18th- and 19th-century local newspapers
Early 19th-century pamphlets, including medical history and locally published
South West Collection
Topographical prints and early maps

Library catalogue: All or part available online

Publications: Printed

Access to staff: Contact by letter, by telephone and by e-mail. Appointment necessary. Access for members only.
Hours: Mon to Fri, 0900 to 1700

Affiliated to: University of Exeter

Houses the: Devon & Cornwall Record Society; Devon Archaeological Society (as Library); Devon Gardens Trust; Devon History Society

DEVON ARCHAEOLOGICAL SOCIETY (DAS)

c/o Royal Albert Memorial Museum, Queen Street, Exeter, Devon, EX4 3RX

E-mail: dasmail@devonarchaeologicalsociety.org.uk
Website: devonarchaeologicalsociety.org.uk

Enquiries to: Honorary Secretary
Direct e-mail: dasonline.wanadoo.co.uk

Organisation type and purpose: Learned society, registered charity.

Subject coverage: Archaeology of Devon, historic buildings.

Library catalogue: All or part available online and in-house

Publications: Printed

Publications list: Available online and in print

Access to staff: Contact by letter and by e-mail

DEVON ART SOCIETY

27 Barchington Avenue, Torquay, TQ2 8LB

Tel: 01803 310600
E-mail: lynn@drake55.fsnet.co.uk

Enquiries to: Honorary Secretary
Other contacts: Chairman

Founded: 1912

Organisation type and purpose: Membership association (membership is by qualification), present number of members: 144.

Subject coverage: Society for professional and non-professional artists in the Torbay area. Exhibitions held twice yearly. Members meet regularly for workshops and demonstrations. Membership by selection.

Access to staff: Contact by letter and by telephone
Hours: Mon to Fri, 0900 to 1700

DEVON CATTLE BREEDERS' SOCIETY (DCBS)

Wisteria Cottage, Iddesleigh, Winkeigh, Devon, EX19 8BG

Tel: 01837 810845
E-mail: lane@dcbs.fsbusiness.co.uk

Enquiries to: Secretary

Founded: 1884; formerly called Devon Cattle Society (year of change 2000)

Organisation type and purpose: Membership association (membership is by subscription, qualification, election or invitation), present number of members: c. 330, registered charity (charity number 248836).
Cattle breed society.
To maintain and further the breeding of the Devon breed of cattle.

Subject coverage: The Herd books of the society, which are published on an annual basis and are available for reference in the reference sections of the Devon County Library Service at Barnstaple and Exeter.

Publications: Printed

Access to staff: Contact by letter, by telephone, by fax, by e-mail and via website. Appointment necessary.
Hours: Mon to Fri, 0900 to 1700

DEVON COUNTY FOOTBALL ASSOCIATION LIMITED

County Headquarters, Coach Road, Newton Abbot, Devon, TQ12 1EJ

Tel: 01626 332077
Fax: 01626 336814
E-mail: anne.kemp@devonfa.com

Enquiries to: General Secretary

Subject coverage: Association football in Devon.

DEVON HERITAGE SERVICE (DHS)

Great Moor House, Bittern Road, Sowton Industrial Estate, Exeter, EX2 7NL

Tel: 01392 384253 (Tue to Fri, 1000 to 1700)
Fax: 01392 384256
E-mail: devrec@devon.gov.uk
Website: www.devon.gov.uk/index/community/the_county/record_office.htm

Enquiries to: Heritage Services Manager

Founded: 1952

Organisation type and purpose: Local government body.
Archive office.

Subject coverage: Mainly local political, administrative, ecclesiastical, maritime, social and economic history, including the history of towns, parishes, local institutions, farms and estates, families, houses, crime and punishment, and transport.

Collection: City of Exeter records, and the County and City of Exeter quarter sessions
Devon quarter sessions records
Ecclesiastical records of the Diocese of Exeter
Exeter Cathedral Archives in the Cloister Library
Records of the ancient Borough of Barnstaple, in the North Devon Record Office

Non-library collection catalogue: All or part available online

Library catalogue: All or part available online

Publications: Printed
Order printed publications from: http://www.devon.gov.uk/index/councildemocracy/record_office/publications-shop.htm
Order microform publications from: devrec@devon.gov.uk

Publications list: Available online

Access to staff: Contact by letter, by telephone, by e-mail and in person
Hours: Tues to Fri, 1000 to 1700; some Sats, 0930 to 1230
Special comments: Charges for some postal enquiries.

Constituent bodies: North Devon Record Office; North Devon Library and Record Office, Tuly Street, Barnstaple, Devon, EX31 1EL; tel: 01271 388607; fax: 01271 388608; e-mail: ndevrec@devon.gov.uk

Links with: Plymouth and West Devon Record Office

Parent body: Devon County Council; County Hall, Topsham Road, Exeter; tel: 01392 382000

DEVON LIBRARIES

Great Moor House, Bittern Road, Sowton, Exeter, EX2 7NL

Tel: 01392 384315
Fax: 01392 384316
E-mail: devlibs@devon.gov.uk
Website: www.devon.gov.uk/libraries

Enquiries to: Head of Libraries

Organisation type and purpose: Local government body, public library.

Subject coverage: General.

Collection: Early children's books collection; Railway Studies collection; Westcountry Studies Library; Pocknell collection of shorthand books; Napoleonic material.

Non-library collection catalogue: All or part available online

Library catalogue: All or part available online

Publications: Printed

Access to staff: Contact by letter, by telephone, by fax, by e-mail and via website
Hours: Mon to Fri, 0900 to 1700

DEVON LIBRARY SERVICES – NORTH DEVON LIBRARY AND RECORD OFFICE

Tuly Street, Barnstaple, Devon, EX31 1EL

Tel: 01271 388596
Fax: 01271 388599
E-mail: geoff.king@devon.gov.uk
Website: www.devon.gov.uk/library

Enquiries to: Manager

History of institution: formerly called Barnstaple Central Library (year of change 1988)

Organisation type and purpose: Local government body, public library.

Subject coverage: General, local and family history of North Devon, business, commercial and technical information.

Collection: Community information database

Non-library collection catalogue: All or part available online

Library catalogue: All or part available online

Publications: Printed

Access to staff: Contact by letter, by telephone, by fax, by e-mail and in person. Appointment necessary.
Hours: Mon, 0930 to 1900; Tue, Fri, 0900 to 1900; Wed, 0930 to 1300; Thu, 0930 to 1700; Sat, 0930 to 1600

Access for disabled people: Level entry, access to all public areas, toilet facilities

Accommodates the: Devon Schools Library Service; tel: 01271 388623; North Devon Athenaeum; tel: 01271 388607; North Devon Branch of the Devon Record Office; tel: 01271 388608

Parent body: Devon County Council, Library Services

DEVON LIBRARY SERVICES – RAILWAY STUDIES LIBRARY (RSC)

Formal name: Railway Studies Collection

Newton Abbot Library, Market Street, Newton Abbot, Devon, TQ12 2RJ

Tel: 01626 206422
E-mail: railway.library@devon.gov.uk
Website: www.devon.gov.uk/library/catalogue

Enquiries to: Librarian
Direct e-mail: moira.andrews@devon.gov.uk

Organisation type and purpose: Local government body, public library.

Subject coverage: All aspects of railways in United Kingdom.

Collection: Back and current issues of a very large range of railway journals and magazines, including many now discontinued, also those relating to railway modelling

Library catalogue: All or part available online

Publications: Printed, and electronic and video

Publications list: Available online and in print

Access to staff: Contact by letter, by telephone, by e-mail and in person
Hours: Wed, 1000 to 1300 and 1400 to 1700; Thu, 1000 to 1300; Sat, 1000 to 1300 and 1400 to 1600
Special comments: Staffed by the Friends of the Railway Studies Collection on Saturdays.

Access for disabled people: Toilet facilities, lift

Administered by: Devon Library Services

DEVON WILDLIFE TRUST (DWT)

Cricklepit Mill, Commercial Road, Exeter, Devon, EX2 4AB

Tel: 01392 279244
Fax: 01392 433221
E-mail: contactus@devonwildlifetrust.org
Website: www.devonwildlifetrust.org

Enquiries to: Chief Executive

Founded: 1962; formerly called Devon Trust for Nature Conservation

Organisation type and purpose: Registered charity (charity number 213224).
Conservation organisation.

Subject coverage: Wildlife conservation in Devon.

Collection: Biological Data

Publications: Printed, and electronic and video
Order electronic and video publications from: e-mail: contactus@devonwildlifetrust.org

Publications list: Available online

Access to staff: Contact by letter, by telephone, by fax and by e-mail
Hours: Mon to Fri, 0900 to 1700

Access to building: *Hours:* Mon to Fri, 0900 to 1700

Access for disabled people: *Hours:* Mon to Fri, 0900 to 1700

Links with: Royal Society for Nature Conservation; The Kiln, Waterside, Mather Lane, Newark, NG24 1WT; tel: 01636 677711; fax: 01636 670001

DEWSBURY COLLEGE

Halifax Road, Dewsbury, West Yorkshire, WF13 2AS

Tel: 01924 465916 ext 286
Fax: 01924 457047
E-mail: info@kirkleescollege.ac.uk
Website: www.dewsbury.ac.uk

Enquiries to: Learning Resources Manager
Direct tel: 01924 465916 ext 240
Direct e-mail: abismillah@dewsbury.ac.uk
Other contacts: Art and Design Specialist

History of institution: formed from Wheelwright 6th Form Centre; formerly called DABTAC (year of change 1993)

Subject coverage: Fashion, graphics, design, media studies, surface pattern design, photography, general subjects in humanities and social studies up to A level, business studies up to HND level.

Library catalogue: All or part available in-house

Access to staff: Contact by letter and by e-mail
Hours: Mon to Thurs, 0850 to 2000; Fri 1000 to 1600

Access for disabled people: Level entry, toilet facilities

Associate college of: Huddersfield University

DIABETES UK

10 Parkway, London, NW1 7AA

Tel: 020 7424 1000
Fax: 020 7424 1001
E-mail: info@diabetes.org.uk
Website: www.diabetes.org.uk

Enquiries to: Assistant Media Relations Officer

Founded: 1934; formerly called British Diabetic Association (BDA) (year of change 2000)

Organisation type and purpose: Advisory body, membership association (membership is by subscription), voluntary organisation, registered charity (charity number 215199), research organisation.
Helping people with diabetes and supporting diabetes research.

Subject coverage: Diabetes and all aspects of living with diabetes.

Publications: Printed, and electronic and video
Order printed publications from: Distribution Department, British Diabetic Association PO Box 1, Portishead, Bristol, BS20 8DJ, tel: 0800 585088

Publications list: Available in print

Access to staff: Contact by letter, by telephone, by fax, by e-mail, in person and via website
Hours: Mon to Fri, 0900 to 1700

Has: 450 branches in the UK

Regional offices: North West; 65 Bewsey Street, Warrington, WA2 7JG; tel: 01925 653281; fax: 01925 653288; Northern & Yorkshire; Birch House, 80 East Mount, Darlington, DL1 1LE; tel: 01325 488606; fax: 01325 488816; Northern Ireland; John Gibson House, 257 Lisbon Road, Belfast, BT9 7EN; tel: 028 9066 6646; fax: 028 9066 6333; Scotland; Unit 3, 4th Floor, 34 West George Street, Glasgow, G2 1AD; tel: 0141 332 2700; fax: 0141 332 4880; Wales; The Board Room, Plas Gwynt, Sophia Close, 30 Cathedral Road, Cardiff, CF1 9TD; tel: 029 2066 8276; fax: 029 2066 8329; West Midlands; 1 Eldon Court, Eldon Street, Walsall, West Midlands, WS1 2JP; tel: 01922 614500; fax: 01922 646789

DIAL UK

Formal name: Disablement Information and Advice Line

Birch View, St Catherine's, Tickhill Road, Doncaster, West Yorkshire, DN4 8QN

Tel: 01302 310123; minicom no. 01302 310123
Fax: 01302 310404
E-mail: dialuk@scope.org.uk
Website: www.dialuk.org.uk

Enquiries to: Head of DIAL UK
Other contacts: Information Officer

Founded: 1981; now part of scope's information and advice services (year of change 2008)

Organisation type and purpose: National organisation, advisory body, registered charity (charity number 208231).
The national organisation for the DIAL network of approx 90 disability advice centres run by and for people with disabilities.
Promotes the interests and usage of disability advice centres controlled by disabled people and provides information and support servies to DIAL groups and other disability information providers.
DIAL groups give free, independent advice on all aspects of disability over the telephone, at drop-in centres and in some cases through a home visit.

Subject coverage: Help for people with disabilities. Information and advice on social, medical or economic problems of all mental, physical and sensory disablements.

Access to staff: Contact by letter, by telephone and by e-mail
Hours: Mon to Fri, 1000 to 1600

Access for disabled people: Fully accessible, toilet facilities

DIALOG CORPORATION, THE

Oxford Office, 2 Des Roches Square, Witney, Oxford, OX28 4BE

Tel: 01993 899300
Fax: 01993 899333
E-mail: ondisc@dialog.com
Website: www.dialog.com

Enquiries to: Manager
Direct e-mail: mike_sullivan@dialog.com
Other contacts: Marketing Executive

Founded: 1972; formerly called DIALOG, DIALOG Europe; formerly called KR OnDisc (year of change 1997)

Organisation type and purpose: International organisation, publishing house.
Providing access to online databases and publishing CD-ROMs and DVD-ROMS.

Subject coverage: Databases on CD-ROM in science, technology, chemistry, medicine, health, biomedicine, engineering, materials, social sciences, business, law, government, economics, education, humanities, current events, newspapers and journals, indexes to book reviews, companies, and people and associations. Also web browser access to above databases (Intranet/extranet solutions).

Publications: Electronic and video

Access to staff: Contact by letter, by telephone, by fax, by e-mail and via website
Hours: Mon to Fri, 0900 to 1730

Parent body: The Dialog Corporation

DIECASTING SOCIETY (DCS)

The National Metalforming Centre, 47 Birmingham Road, West Bromwich B70 6PY

Tel: 0121 601 6365
Fax: 0870 138 9714
E-mail: dcs@alfed.org.uk
Website: www.dcsoc.org.uk

Enquiries to: Secretary

Founded: 1967

Organisation type and purpose: Professional body.

Subject coverage: Diecasting.

Access to staff: Contact by letter, by telephone, by fax and by e-mail. Appointment necessary.

Hours: Mon to Fri, 0900 to 1700

Administered by: The Aluminium Federation

DIGNITY IN DYING

181 Oxford Street, London, W1D 2JT

Tel: 020 7479 7730
E-mail: info@dignityindying.org.uk
Website: www.dignityindying.org.uk

Direct e-mail: jo.cartwright@dignityindying.org.uk

Founded: 1935; formerly called EXIT (year of change 1982)

Organisation type and purpose: Voluntary organisation.
Promoting living wills, campaigning to change the law so that a competent incurably ill adult who is suffering unbearably can choose medical assistance to die.

Subject coverage: Voluntary euthanasia, advance directives, living wills, patients' rights, physician-assisted suicide, refusal of medical treatment.

Collection: Newsletters of World Federation Members
Press cuttings and articles
Extensive collection of books and journal articles

Publications: Printed

Access to staff: Contact by letter, by telephone, by fax, by e-mail and via website
Hours: Mon to Fri, 1000 to 1600
Special comments: Visitors strictly by prior appointment.

Access to building: No prior appointment required
Hours: Mon to Fri, 1000 to 1600

Affiliated to: World Federation of Right to Die Societies

DIRECT MAIL INFORMATION SERVICE (DMIS)

5 Carlisle Street, London, W1D 3JX

Tel: 020 7494 0483
Fax: 020 7494 0455
Website: www.dmis.co.uk

Founded: 1991

Organisation type and purpose: Consultancy, research organisation.
Run by HBH on behalf of the Royal Mail to provide information to assist the direct mail and marketing industry.

Subject coverage: Direct mail statistics and research reports.

Collection: Direct mail research by DMIS and DMSB from 1982 onwards

Publications: Printed

Publications list: Available in print

Access to staff: Contact by letter, by telephone, by fax, by e-mail and via website
Hours: Mon to Fri, 0900 to 1700

Parent body: HBH Partnership Limited; at the same address; tel: 020 7494 0482

DIRECT SELLING ASSOCIATION LIMITED (DSA)

29 Floral Street, London, WC2E 9DP

Tel: 020 7497 1234
Fax: 020 7497 3144
E-mail: info@globalnet.co.uk
Website: www.dsa.org.uk

Enquiries to: Director

Founded: 1965

Organisation type and purpose: Trade association (membership is by subscription, election or invitation).
To promote high trading standards in the direct selling of consumer goods.

Subject coverage: General industry data on direct selling of consumer goods, industry codes of practice, direct selling legislation, details of member companies.

Trade and statistical information: Annual statistical survey of direct selling of consumer goods in UK, includes DSA members and non-members

Publications: Printed

Access to staff: Contact by letter, by fax, by e-mail and via website. Appointment necessary.
Hours: Mon to Fri, 0930 to 1700

Affiliated to: Federation of European Direct Selling Associations (FEDSA); Avenue de Tervueren 14, 1040 Brussels, Belgium; tel: + 32 2 7361014; fax: + 32 2 7363497; World Federation of Direct Selling Associations (WFDSA); Washington, DC, USA; tel: + 1 202 293 5760; fax: + 1 202 463 4569

DIRECTORS GUILD OF GREAT BRITAIN (DGGB)

4 Windmill Street, London, W1T 2HZ

Tel: 020 7580 9131
Fax: 020 7580 9132
E-mail: info@dggb.org
Website: www.dggb.co.uk
Website: www.directorstraining.org.uk

Enquiries to: Chief Executive
Direct e-mail: malcolm@dggb.co.uk

Founded: 1985

Organisation type and purpose: Trade union (membership is by subscription), number of members: 1,250.

Subject coverage: Directors' rates, contract advice, guidance to the profession, information on contacting directors and/or other relevant organisations, organising events, masterclasses and conferences. Training website and information.

Non-library collection catalogue: All or part available online

Publications: Printed, and electronic and video

Access to staff: Contact by letter, by telephone, by fax, by e-mail and via website. Appointment necessary.
Hours: 1000 to 1800

Access for disabled people: Level entry

Member of: Federation of European Film Directors (FERA); Avenue Everard 59, 1190 Brussels, Belgium; Informal European Theatre Meeting (IETM); International Association of Audiovisual Writers and Directors (AIDAA)

DISABILITY ALLIANCE

Universal House, 88–94 Wentworth Street, London, E1 7SA

Tel: 020 7247 8776
Fax: 020 7247 8765
E-mail: office@disabilityalliance.org
Website: www.disabilityalliance.org

Enquiries to: Membership and Office Administrator

Founded: 1974

Organisation type and purpose: National organisation, present number of members: 230 paid member organisations, registered charity (charity number 1063115).
Disability Alliance is committed to breaking the link between poverty and disability by providing information about social security benefits to disabled people, their carers and advisers through publications.

Subject coverage: Social Security benefits and related services for disabled people.

Publications: Printed, and electronic and video
Order printed publications from: website; e-mail: zuzana@disabilityalliance.org

Publications list: Available online and in print

Access to staff: Contact by letter, by telephone, by fax, by e-mail and via website
Hours: Mon to Fri, 1000 to 1600
Special comments: Access for the purchase of publications only.

Access to building: Prior appointment required
Special comments: Library is only available to Disability Alliance member organisations.

Access for disabled people: Level entry, toilet facilities

Connections with Disability Benefits Consortium; Coalition on Charging: 230 Alliance Member Organisations

DISABILITY ARTS CYMRU

Sbectrwm, Bwlch Road, Fairwater, Cardiff, CF5 3EF

Tel: 029 2055 1040
Fax: 029 2055 1036
E-mail: post@dacymru.com
Website: www.dacymru.com

Enquiries to: Director

Organisation type and purpose: Registered charity (charity number 514083), membership association (membership is free to the disabled and the unwaged).
Committed to working with individuals and organisations to celebrate the diversity of disabled and deaf people's arts and culture, and develop equality across all art forms.

Subject coverage: Creates opportunities for disabled and deaf people to develop their skills in the arts, raises the profile of arts by disabled and deaf people, works in

continued overleaf

partnership with other organisations on arts-related projects, advises on issues related to disability and the arts, provides a consultancy service around policy development and offers arts-specific disability equality training.

Information services: Information and advice service, free of charge, to arts organisations on a wide range of issues relating to disability and the arts and to individuals on a wide range of issues, including marketing work, making funding applications and skills development.

Publications: Printed, and electronic and video
Order electronic and video publications from: Download from website

Publications list: Available online

Access to staff: Contact by letter, by telephone, by fax and by e-mail
Special comments: In some circumstances it may be possible to arrange for someone from Disability Arts Cymru to visit an organisation, or for a visit to be made to the office in Cardiff. Please contact the Disability Arts Cymru office to make an appointment.

Funded by: Arts Council of Wales

DISABILITY INFORMATION SERVICES (DISS)

Oaklawn Road, Leatherhead, Surrey KT22 0BT

Tel: 01372 841396

Enquiries to: Manager
Direct e-mail: hue.schoenemann@diss.org.uk

Founded: 1989; formerly called Disability Information Service Surrey (DISS) (year of change 2001)

Organisation type and purpose: Voluntary organisation, registered charity (charity number 251051).
Information service.

Subject coverage: Anything connected with disabilities, e.g. equipment, care, employment, holidays, education, social security benefits, self-help groups, recreation, transport and access.

Collection: Journal articles, leaflets, statistical materials, directories, equipment guides

Publications: Printed, and electronic and video

Access to staff: Contact by letter, by telephone, by fax, by e-mail, in person and via website. Appointment necessary.
Hours: Mon to Fri, 1000 to 1300 and 1400 to 1600
Special comments: Also textphone and typetalk.

Access for disabled people: Parking provided, level entry, access to all public areas, toilet facilities

Parent body: Queen Elizabeth's Foundation for Disabled People; Leatherhead Court, Leatherhead, Surrey, KT22 0BN; tel: 01372 841100; fax: 01372 844072; website: http://www.qefd.org

Subsidiary body: DISS network

DISABILITY PREGNANCY AND PARENTHOOD INTERNATIONAL (DPPI)

336 Brixton Road, London SW7 9AA

Tel: 020 7263 3088
E-mail: office@dppi.org.uk
Website: www.dppi.org.uk

Enquiries to: Information Officer
Direct tel: 0800 018 4730; minicom number: 0800 018 9949
Direct e-mail: info@dppi.org.uk

Founded: 1993

Organisation type and purpose:
International organisation, voluntary organisation, registered charity (charity number 1070303).
To provide an information service to disabled parents, professionals and others.

Subject coverage: Information related to all aspects of pregnancy and parenting for disabled people, including: condition-specific information, equipment, adaptations, specialist deaf parenting project, parents' rights, advocacy, local support groups.

Library catalogue: All or part available in-house

Publications: Printed, and electronic and video
Order printed publications from: tel. 0800 018 4730, info@dppi.org.uk, or via the website
Order electronic and video publications from: Same as printed publications.

Publications list: Available online and in print

Access to staff: Contact by letter, by telephone, by e-mail and via website. Appointment necessary.
Hours: Mon to Thu, 1000 to 1600

Access for disabled people: Access to all public areas, toilet facilities

DISABILITY SPORT ENGLAND (DSE)

Disability Sport Events, Belle Vue Centre, Pink Bank Lane, Manchester, M12 5GL

Tel: 0161 953 2499
Fax: 0161 953 2420
E-mail: info@dse.org.uk
Website: www.disabilitysport.org.uk

Enquiries to: Marketing and Communications Manager
Direct e-mail: sarah@dse.org.uk
Other contacts: tel no: 01325 369554 for information re the BT/DSE swimming programme.

Founded: 1961; formerly called British Sports Association for the Disabled (BSAD)

Organisation type and purpose:
Membership association (membership is by subscription), present number of members: 80,000, voluntary organisation, registered charity (charity number 297035).
Provision, development and coordination of sport for the inclusion of people with disabilities.

Subject coverage: Sport and recreation for people with disabilities.

Publications: Printed

Access to staff: Contact by letter, by telephone, by fax and by e-mail
Hours: Mon to Fri, 1000 to 1600

Access for disabled people: Access to all public areas

Links with: regional branches and associations

Other address: Disability Sport England (Water Sports); Darlington, DL1 5QU; tel: 01325 369554

DISABILITY SPORT ENGLAND – DARLINGTON

The Dolphin Centre, The Horse Centre, Darlington, Co Durham, DL1 5QU

Tel: 01325 369554

Enquiries to: Coordinator for swimming events
Direct e-mail: patbennett@darlingtondse.freeserve.co.uk

Founded: 1961

Organisation type and purpose:
Membership association (membership is by subscription), present number of members: 80,000, voluntary organisation, registered charity (charity number 297035).

Subject coverage: Water sports, information re the BT/DSE swimming programme.

Access to staff: Contact by letter, by telephone and by e-mail
Hours: Mon to Fri, 0900 to 1700

Access for disabled people: Access to all public areas, toilet facilities

Other address: Disability Sport England; London, N17 0DA; tel: 020 8801 4466; fax: 020 8801 6644; e-mail: info@dse.org.uk

DISABILITY SPORT ENGLAND – WEST MIDLANDS REGION

Wyndley Lane, Sutton Coldfield, West Midlands, B73 6ES

Tel: 0121 354 5369
Fax: 0121 355 5702

Enquiries to: Administrator

History of institution: formerly called BSAD

Organisation type and purpose: Voluntary organisation, registered charity (charity number 297035).

Subject coverage: Advice on sports opportunities for disabled people.

Publications: Printed

Access to staff: Contact by letter and by telephone
Hours: 24-hour answerphone

Other addresses: Disability Sport England; Darlington, DL1 5QU; tel: 01325 369554

Parent body: Disability Sport England; Unit 4G, 784–788 High Road, Tottenham, London, N17 0DA; tel: 020 8801 4466; fax: 020 8801 6644

DISABLED DRIVERS INSURANCE BUREAU

Formal name: Chartwell Insurance

292 Hale Lane, Edgware, Middlesex, HA8 8NP

Tel: 020 8958 0901/0900
Fax: 020 8958 3220
E-mail: info@chartwellinsurance.co.uk
Website: www.chartwellinsurance.co.uk

Enquiries to: Partner
Direct tel: 020 8958 0919
Other contacts: Manager

Founded: 1965; formed from Chartwell Insurance

Organisation type and purpose: Service industry.
Insurance intermediary.

Subject coverage: Motor car insurance for the disabled driver, adapted vehicles i.e. vans, powerchairs, travel and household, breakdown cover.

Publications: Printed

Access to staff: Contact by letter, by telephone, by fax and in person
Hours: Mon to Fri, 0900 to 1730

Access to building: Mon to Fri, 0900 to 1730

Access for disabled people: Parking provided, ramped entry, access to all public areas, toilet facilities

Affiliated to: Chartwell Insurance; at the same address; tel: 020 8958 0900 or 0845 260 7051; fax: 020 8958 3220; e-mail: info@chartwellinsurance.co.uk; website: http://www.chartwellinsurance.co.uk

DISABLED LIVING FOUNDATION (DLF)

380–384 Harrow Road, London, W9 2HU

Tel: 020 7289 6111, 0870 603 9176 (minicom)
Fax: 020 7266 2922
E-mail: info@dlf.org.uk
Website: www.dlf.org.uk

Enquiries to: Information Officer
Other contacts: Director

Founded: 1970

Organisation type and purpose: Advisory body, voluntary organisation, registered charity (charity number 290069), training organisation, publishing house.

Subject coverage: The DLF works for freedom, empowerment and choice for disabled people and others who use equipment or technology to enhance their independence. It runs a helpline and letter enquiry service offering information and advice about disability equipment, and the London Disability Living Centre with over 600 items for people to try. It produces a wide range of publications on choosing and using equipment and offers a specialist subscriber service and training for healthcare professionals and organisations.

Publications: Printed, and electronic and video
Order printed publications from: Marketing and Publication Department, Disabled Living Foundation; at same address

Publications list: Available online and in print

Access to staff: Contact by letter, by telephone, by fax, by e-mail and in person. Appointment necessary.
Hours: Office: Mon to Fri, 0900 to 1700; helpline, Mon to Fri, 1000 to 1600

Access to building: Prior appointment required
Hours: Equipment Centre: Mon to Fri, 1000 to 1600

Access for disabled people: Level entry, toilet facilities

Has: 40 centres in the UK

DISABLED MOTORING UK (DMUK)

National Office Ashwellthorpe, Norwich, Norfolk, NR16 1EX

Tel: 01508 489449
E-mail: info@disabledmotoring.org
Website: www.disabledmotoring.org

Enquiries to: Information Officer

Founded: 2005; created by the merger of Disabled Drivers' Association and Disabled Drivers' Motor Club (year of change 2011)

Organisation type and purpose: Membership, campaigning charity (membership is by subscription, qualification), present number of members: 15,000, voluntary organisation, registered charity (charity number 1111826).

Subject coverage: Mobility benefits and queries, assessment centres, licensing problems, car/vehicle insurance for disabled people, car acquisition and adaptation, holidays, ferry concessions, legislation on transport and parking.

Information services: Brief information services for non-members; members are entitled to unlimited access to Information Officers who will take up case work, help with appealing against parking tickets, etc.

Services for disabled people: Provides case work for members, help with appealing against parking tickets, acts on behalf of members by contacting local authorities, etc.

Collection: Archive of Magic Carpet and Disabled Motorinst magazines (bound vols) dating back to foundation in 1948 and 1922, respectively, which form a valuable historical resource.

Publications: Printed

Publications list: Available in print

Access to staff: Contact by letter, by telephone, by fax, by e-mail, in person and via website
Hours: Mon to Fri, 0900 to 1645
Special comments: Answerphone outside office hours.

Access to building: Fully accessible

Access for disabled people: Parking provided, level entry, access to all public areas, toilet facilities

DISABLED MOTORISTS FEDERATION (DMF)

c/o Chester-le-Street and District CVS Volunteer Centre, Clarence Terrace, Chester-le-Street, Co Durham, DH3 3DQ

Tel: 0191 416 3172
Fax: 0191 416 3172
E-mail: jkillick2214@yahoo.co.uk
Website: www.dmfed.org.uk

Enquiries to: Honorary Secretary
Other contacts: Vice-President

Founded: 1973

Organisation type and purpose: National organisation, membership association (membership is by subscription, qualification), voluntary organisation, registered charity (charity number 1012874). Qualification for membership is registered disabled or carer.
To provide information to disabled people and their carers on matters of travel whether by road, rail or air, including advice on suitable hotel accommodation; to act for and on behalf of disabled motorist clubs.

Subject coverage: Motoring and mobility for the disabled; setting up a local base or club for disabled drivers; vehicle choice; overseas and UK travel; wheelchairs; home adaptations; lifts and hoists; camping and caravanning; route-planning service and route maps.

Information services: Free information on travel by road, rail, air or sea to all disabled people and their carers.

Publications: Printed
Order printed publications from: from the Honorary Secretary, by letter or e-mail, or see website.

Access to staff: Contact by telephone, by fax and by e-mail. Appointment necessary.
Hours: Mon to Fri, 0900 to 1700

Also at: Honorary Secretary; 145 Knoulberry Road, Black Fell, Washington, Tyne & Wear, NE37 1JN; tel: 0191 416 3172; fax: 0191 416 3172; e-mail: jkillick2214@yahoo.co.uk

Constituent bodies: 10 member clubs for disabled drivers throughout Britain; website: http://www.dmfed.org.uk

DISABLED PHOTOGRAPHERS' SOCIETY (DPS)

PO Box 85, Longfield, Kent, DA3 9BA

E-mail: enquiries@disabledphotographers.co.uk
Website: www.disabledphotographers.co.uk

Founded: 1968

Organisation type and purpose: Membership association (membership is by subscription), present number of members: 500 individuals, 55 groups, voluntary organisation, registered charity (charity number 262866).
Encourages disabled people to take an active interest in photography as a therapeutic and creative pursuit primarily by collecting surplus photographic equipment and redistributing it to disabled users who are members of the society.

Subject coverage: Adaptation of photographic equipment for specific handicaps; advice on equipment and techniques; assistance in adopting

continued overleaf

photography as a therapeutic/leisure pursuit for disabled and handicapped persons of all ages.

Publications: Printed

Access to staff: Contact by letter and by e-mail

DISCRIMINATION LAW ASSOCIATION

PO Box 7722, Newbury, RG20 5WD

Tel: 0845 478 6375
E-mail: info@discriminationlaw.org.uk
Website: www.discriminationlaw.org.uk

Enquiries to: Administrator

Founded: 1995

Organisation type and purpose: A non-profit network that brings together a broad range of discrimination law practitioners, policy experts, academics and concerned individuals, all united around a commitment to improving equality law, practice, education and advice for those who face discrimination; has 350 members.

Subject coverage: Activities include submitting responses to government consultations, sharing experiences and expertise through practitioner group meetings, disseminating information and knowledge via the Briefings journal, e-mail updates, conferences and seminars.

Publications: Electronic and video
Order electronic and video publications from: website

Publications list: Available online

Access to staff: Contact by letter, by telephone, by fax and by e-mail
Hours: Office functions part-time and therefore may not be able to respond to communications immediately
Special comments: Not an advice service; cannot provide advice to the public.

DISFIGUREMENT GUIDANCE CENTRE/LASERFAIR (DGC)

PO Box 7, Cupar, Fife, KY15 4PF

Tel: 01337 870 281
Fax: 01337 870310
Website: www.dgc.org.uk

Enquiries to: Director
Other contacts: Publications Officer, tel no: 0133 787 0281, fax: 0133 787 0310

Founded: 1969

Organisation type and purpose: Voluntary organisation, registered charity, research organisation, publishing house.
UK corporate voice and centre for the disfigured, specialist resource Skin Laser Services and information.

Subject coverage: All aspects of disfigurement, including treatment developments, especially medical lasers, insurance, compensation advice, research, family problems; skin problems.

Non-library collection catalogue: All or part available online and in print

Publications: Printed

Publications list: Available in print

Access to staff: Contact by letter, by telephone and by fax. Appointment necessary.
Hours: Mon to Fri, 0900 to 1700
Special comments: Please send sae for information.

DIVINE INFORMATION SERVICES

PO Box 2530, Windsor, Berkshire, SL4 1WS

Website: www.divineinformationservices.co.uk

Enquiries to: UK Marketing Manager

History of institution: formerly called RoweCom (year of change 2001)

Organisation type and purpose:
International organisation, service industry.
To provide librarians and information specialists with a complete information solution in acting not only as a subscription agent for both print and electronic information resources but also in providing librarians and information specialists with content and information management, content classification, search and taxonomy.

Collection: Northern Light – Single Point Print and Electronic Subscription Services

Publications: Electronic and video

Access to staff: Contact by telephone, by fax and by e-mail
Hours: Mon to Fri, 0900 to 1730

Other offices: Has 19 other offices throughout the world

DOCUMENT OPTIONS LTD

Priestley Way, Crawley, West Sussex, RH10 9NT

Tel: 01293 426677
Fax: 01293 403453
E-mail: sales@document-options.co.uk
Website: www.document-options.co.uk
Website: www.document-options.net

Enquiries to: Director

Founded: 1970

Organisation type and purpose: Service industry.
Microfilming and scanning bureau.

Subject coverage: Reprographic procedures, raster to vector conversion, conversion of microfilm/microfiche to digital data.

Access to staff: Contact by telephone
Hours: Mon to Fri, 0900 to 1700

DOLMETSCH FOUNDATION INCORPORATED

27 Gilmour Gardens, Alton, Hampshire, GU34 2NR

Tel: 01420 541892
Website: www.dolmetsch.com

Enquiries to: Secretary

Organisation type and purpose: Learned society.

Subject coverage: Early music and instruments, c. 1000 to c. 1750.

Collection: File from 1929 of the annual journal, The Consort

Access to staff: Contact by letter
Hours: Mon to Fri, 0900 to 1700

Other addresses: Dolmetsch Foundation Incorporated; Jesses, Grayswood Road, Haslemere, Surrey, GU27 2BS

DOLMETSCH HISTORICAL DANCE SOCIETY (DHDS)

17 Well Lane, Stock, Ingatestone, Essex, CM4 9LT

Tel: 01277 840473
Fax: 01277 840473
E-mail: secretary@dhds.org.uk
Website: www.dhds.org.uk

Enquiries to: Honorary Secretary

Founded: 1970

Organisation type and purpose: National organisation, membership association, present number of members: 120, registered charity (charity number 270896), research organisation.
To promote the practice of and research into social dance in Europe from the 15th to the 19th century.

Subject coverage: Information on dances, dancers and dancing masters of the past; information on source material and secondary sources, including society publications; information on teachers and dance classes available; information on performing groups.

Publications: Printed, and electronic and video
Order printed publications from: Secretary, Dolmetsch Historical Dance Society, 17 Well Lane, Stock, ingatestone, Essex, CM4 9LT

Publications list: Available online and in print

Access to staff: Contact by letter, by telephone, by fax and by e-mail
Hours: No fixed hours.

DOMESTIC APPLIANCE SERVICE ASSOCIATION (DASA)

2nd Floor, 145–157 St John Street, London, EC1V 4PY

Tel: 0870 224 0343
Fax: 0870 224 0358
E-mail: dasa@dasa.org.uk
Website: www.dasa.org.uk

Enquiries to: Administrator
Direct e-mail: admin@dasa.org.uk

Founded: 1978

Organisation type and purpose: Trade association (membership is by qualification), present number of members: 180, service industry. To promote quality service, efficiency and courtesy in the servicing of domestic appliances.

Subject coverage: Promotion of good service, efficiency and courtesy to all members of the public, investigation of complaints against member firms, quality management, insurance, training.

Publications: Printed

Access to staff: Contact by letter, by telephone, by fax and by e-mail. Appointment necessary.

Hours: Mon to Fri, 0900 to 1700

Access to building: Appointment required

Member organisation of: British Quality Foundation; tel: 020 7654 5000; fax: 020 7654 5001; e-mail: mail@quality-foundation.co.uk; Electrical and Electronics Servicing Training Council (EESTC); tel: 020 7836 3357; fax: 020 7497 9006; e-mail: ccrouch@eeb.iie.org.uk

DOMESTIC FOWL TRUST

Station Road, Honeybourne, Evesham, Worcestershire, WR11 5QG

Tel: 01386 833083
Fax: 01386 833364
E-mail: clive@domesticfowltrust.co.uk
Website: www.domesticfowltrust.co.uk

Enquiries to: Director

Founded: 1975

Organisation type and purpose: Professional body, consultancy, research organisation.

Subject coverage: Poultry breeding, old breeds of hens, ducks, geese, turkeys; housing and management of outdoor poultry, poultry health.

Publications: Printed

Access to staff: Contact by letter, by telephone, by fax, by e-mail and in person
Hours: Mon to Sun, 1030 to 1700

Access to building: No access other than to staff
Hours: Mon to Fri, 1030 to 1700

Access for disabled people: Parking provided, ramped entry, toilet facilities

DOMINICA HIGH COMMISSION

Formal name: High Commission for the Commonwealth of Dominica

1 Collingham Gardens, London, SW5 0HW

Tel: 020 7370 5194
Fax: 020 7373 8743
E-mail: info@dominicahighcommission.co.uk
Website: www.dominicahighcommission.co.uk

Enquiries to: Secretary

Organisation type and purpose: National government body.

Subject coverage: Dominica, tourism, trade, consular, general information.

Access to staff: Contact by letter, by fax and by e-mail. Appointment necessary.
Hours: Mon to Fri, 0930 to 1730

DOMINICAN REPUBLIC TOURIST BOARD

18–21 Hand Court, London, WC1V 6JF

Tel: 020 7242 7778
Fax: 020 7405 4202
E-mail: uk@godominicanrepublic.com
Website: www.godominicanrepublic.com

Enquiries to: Executive Director

Founded: 1996

Organisation type and purpose: International organisation, national government body.
Promotion of tourism.

Information services: Dominican Republic visitor information.

Publications: Printed
Order printed publications from: e-mail: uk@godominicanrepublic.com
Order electronic and video publications from: e-mail: uk@godominicanrepublic.com

Publications list: Available online and in print

Access to staff: Contact by letter, by telephone, by fax, by e-mail, in person and via website
Hours: Mon to Fri, 1000 to 1700

Access to building: *Hours:* Mon to Fri, 1000 to 1700

Access for disabled people: Level entry, access to public areas, no toilet facilities

DONCASTER AND DISTRICT FAMILY HISTORY SOCIETY (DDFHS)

8 Tenter Lane, Warmsworth, Doncaster, South Yorkshire, DN4 9PT

Tel: 01302 854809
E-mail: honsecretary@doncasterfhs.co.uk
Website: www.doncasterfhs.co.uk

Enquiries to: Honorary Secretary

Founded: 1980; formerly called Doncaster Family History Society (year of change 1990)

Organisation type and purpose: Membership association (membership is by subscription), voluntary organisation, registered charity (charity number 516226).

Subject coverage: Genealogy, family history.

Collection: Archives held at: Palgrave Research Centre, King Edward Road, Balby.

Library catalogue: All or part available in-house and in print

Publications: Printed, and electronic and video, and microform publications
Order printed publications from: Doncaster and District Family History Society
Mr D Valentine, Badger's Bench, Top Street, North Wheatley, Retford, Nottinghamshire, DN22 9DE
Order microform publications from: Doncaster and District Family History Society
Mr D Valentine, Badger's Bench, Top Street, North Wheatley, Retford, Nottinghamshire, DN22 9DE
Order electronic and video publications from: Doncaster and District Family History Society
Mr D Valentine, Badger's Bench, Top Street, North Wheatley, Retford, Nottinghamshire, DN22 9DE

Publications list: Available online and in print

Access to staff: Contact by letter, by e-mail and via website
Hours: Mon to Fri, 0900 to 1700
Special comments: Not after 2100

Access to building: Prior appointment required
Special comments: Contact the Palgrave Research Centre – tel: 01302 311930.

Access for disabled people: Access to the Palgrave Research Centre is by way of four steps. It may be possible to arrange wheelchair access by prior arrangement – tel: 01302 311930.
Special comments: Contact the Palgrave Research Centre – tel: 01302 311930.

DONCASTER ARCHIVES

Formal name: Doncaster Metropolitan Borough Council: Library and Information Services, Doncaster Archives

King Edward Road, Balby, Doncaster, South Yorkshire, DN4 0NA

Tel: 01302 859811
E-mail: doncaster.archives@doncaster.gov.uk
Website: www.doncaster.gov.uk/doncasterarchives

Enquiries to: Principal Archivist

Founded: 1973; formerly called Doncaster Archives Department

Organisation type and purpose: Local government body.
Doncaster Archives collects, preserves and gives public access to the documentary heritage of Doncaster Metropolitan Borough from 1194 to the present.

Subject coverage: The full range of records usually to be found in a local record office, including local government archives, local public records, Church of England parish records, nonconformist church records, family and landed estate records, business archives, political party archives, trade union archives, voluntary society archives, local maps and plans.

Collection: Includes:
Parish Registers of 36 ancient parishes, transcribed with surname index up to 1837 and many to later dates

Non-library collection catalogue: All or part available online and in-house

Library catalogue: All or part available in-house

Publications: Printed
Order printed publications from: Doncaster Archives, King Edward Road, Balby, Doncaster, South Yorkshire, DN4 0NA

Access to staff: Contact by letter, by telephone, by e-mail and in person. Appointment necessary.
Hours: Mon to Fri, 0900 to 1245 and 1400 to 1645

Access to building: *Special comments:* Reader's ticket required

DONCASTER COLLEGE

The Hub Learning Resource Centre, Doncaster, South Yorkshire, DN1 2RF

Tel: 01302 553553
Fax: 01302 553559
Website: www.don.ac.uk

Enquiries to: Site Librarian at The Hub
Direct tel: 01302 553745
Direct e-mail: infocentre@don.ac.uk

continued overleaf

Other contacts: Head of Learning Resources (responsible for all site Learning Resource Centres)

History of institution: created by the merger of 4 Doncaster Colleges of Technology, Art and Design and Education

Organisation type and purpose: College of further education.

Subject coverage: Business studies, environmental sciences, engineering (construction, mechanical, production, electrical, mining and mineral), catering, hairdressing and beauty, nursing, modern languages, computing, education and related fields, art and design, sociology, geography and history, travel and tourism, animal care, floristry.

Library catalogue: All or part available online

Access to staff: Contact by letter. Appointment necessary. Non-members charged.
Hours: Term time: Mon to Thu, 0845 to 2000; Fri, 0845 to 1700
Vacations: Mon to Fri, 0900 to 1230 and 1330 to 1645

Also at: Doncaster College; The University Centre LRC, High Melton, Doncaster, South Yorkshire, DN5 7SZ

DONCASTER LIBRARY AND INFORMATION SERVICES

Doncaster Central Library, Waterdale, Doncaster, South Yorkshire, DN1 3JE

Tel: 01302 734305
Fax: 01302 369749
E-mail: reference.library@doncaster.gov.uk
Website: www.doncaster.gov.uk

Enquiries to: Reference Manager
Direct tel: 01302 734320

Founded: 1869

Organisation type and purpose: Local government body, public library.

Subject coverage: General, local studies, railways, horse racing.

Information services: Reference and information service.

Education services: Classes held in Library premises.

Services for disabled people: Reading Aids Unit – serving the visually impaired.

Collection: Archives: official, ecclesiastical, family and private records held at King Edward Road, Balby, Doncaster, DN4 0NA; tel: 01302 859811
Local Studies Library – 1984–85 Miners' Strike Collection
Local Studies Library – Family Album Project
Local Studies Library – Doncaster Community Archive (CD ROM)
British Standards (online)
Britannica Online
Oxford Online

Trade and statistical information: Mint UK online

Library catalogue: All or part available online

Publications: Printed
Order printed publications from: Reference Department

Access to staff: Contact by letter, by telephone, by fax, by e-mail, in person and via website
Hours: Mon to Thu, 0900 to 1800; Fri, 1000 to 1800; Sat, 0900 to 1700

Access for disabled people: Access to all public areas, toilet facilities

Member organisation of: Doncaster Chamber of Commerce; European Public Information Centre; SINTO; South Yorkshire Joint Archives Service; Yorkshire and Humberside Association of Library Services

DONKEY BREED SOCIETY (DBS)

The Hermitage, Pootings, Edenbridge, Kent, TN8 6SD

Tel: 01732 864414
Fax: 01732 864414
E-mail: showsecretary@donkeybreedsociety.co.uk
Website: www.donkeybreedingsociety.co.uk

Enquiries to: Secretary

Founded: 1967

Organisation type and purpose: Membership association, registered charity (charity number 292268).
To work for the welfare of all donkeys.

Subject coverage: The care, management and breeding of donkeys, also their welfare, education and general activities such as trekking, showing, driving and light draught work.

Collection: Library of limited donkey related books (for hire by members)
Stud Book

Publications: Printed

Access to staff: Contact by letter, by telephone and by fax
Hours: Mon to Fri, 0900 to 1700

DONKEY SANCTUARY

Sidmouth, Devon, EX10 0NU

Tel: 01395 578222
Fax: 01395 579266
E-mail: enquiries@thedonkeysanctuary.com
Website: www.thedonkeysanctuary.org.uk

Founded: 1969; incorporates the International Donkey Protection Trust

Organisation type and purpose: International organisation, registered charity (charity number 264818).

Subject coverage: Provision of high quality, professional advice, training and support on donkey welfare world-wide.

Publications: Printed, and electronic and video

Publications list: Available in print

Access to staff: Contact by letter, by telephone, by fax, by e-mail, in person and via website. Appointment necessary.
Hours: Mon to Fri, 0830 to 1630

Access for disabled people: Parking provided, level entry, toilet facilities

Connections at the same address with: The Elisabeth Svendsen Trust for Children and Donkeys; tel: 01395 578222; fax: 01395 579266; e-mail: info@elisabethsvendsentrust.org

DOROTHY L SAYERS SOCIETY

Rose Cottage, Malthouse Lane, Hurstpierpoint, West Sussex, BN6 9JY

Tel: 01273 833444
Fax: 01273 835988
E-mail: jasmine@sayers.org.uk
Website: www.sayers.org.uk

Enquiries to: Chairman
Other contacts: info@sayers.org.uk

Founded: 1976; formerly called Dorothy L Sayers Historical and Literary Society

Organisation type and purpose: Membership association (membership is by subscription), present number of members: 500, registered charity (charity number 272120), suitable for ages: all.

Subject coverage: Life, biographical details and works of Dorothy L Sayers and the subjects in which she was involved such as: Christian theology and apologetics, campanology, genealogy, Dante, drama (secular and religious), literary and theological criticism, broadcasting, the Wimsey family, Sherlock Holmes, detective fiction, the Detection Club, Wimsey chronology, poetry, painting and stage sets, locations and social references in DLS fiction.

Collection: Archives include writings by DLS (articles, poetry, speeches, letters (personal and press), reviews and introductions and pamphlets); other writings on DLS and her subjects, commentaries and essays, press cuttings, certificates, memorabilia, reviews of her plays and biographies. Most of these items can be copied for members only; copies of much of the work are available at Witham County Library

Publications: Printed
Order printed publications from: Dorothy L Sayers Society

Access to staff: Contact by letter, by telephone, by fax, by e-mail and via website. Appointment necessary.
Hours: Mon to Fri, 0900 to 1700

DORSET DOWN SHEEP BREEDERS' ASSOCIATION (DDSBA)

Havett Farm, Dobwalls, Liskeard, Cornwall, PL14 6HB

Tel: 01579 320273
E-mail: secretary@dorsetdownsheep.org.uk
Website: www.dorsetdownsheep.org.uk

Enquiries to: Breed Secretary

Founded: 1906

Organisation type and purpose: National organisation, membership association (membership is by subscription), present number of members: 80, registered charity (charity number 84799).

Promotion of the breed of Dorset Down sheep.

Subject coverage: Breeding and whereabouts of Dorset Down sheep, and administration of the association since 1906.

Collection: Flock Books, 1906 to present day

Publications: Printed

Publications list: Available in print

Access to staff: Contact by letter, by telephone and by e-mail

DORSET LIBRARY SERVICE

Headquarters, Colliton Park, Dorchester, Dorset, DT1 1XJ

Tel: 01305 225000
Fax: 01305 224344
E-mail: dorsetlibraries@dorsetcc.gov.uk
Website: www.dorsetforyou.com/libraries

Enquiries to: Head of Cultural Services

Organisation type and purpose: Local government body, public library.

Subject coverage: General lending and reference and information services; also specialist information on all aspects of the County of Dorset.

Collection: Collections on T E Lawrence and Percy Westerman (Wareham Library)
Collections on Thomas Hardy, the Powys family and William Barnes, John Fowles, Sir Frederick Treves, Sylvia Townsend Warner (Dorchester Library)
Drama and Playsets Collection
Local Studies Collections (Dorset History Centre; Dorchester Library; Weymouth Library; Christchurch Library; Bridport Library)

Non-library collection catalogue: All or part available online

Library catalogue: All or part available online

Publications list: Available in print

Access to staff: Contact by letter, by telephone, by fax, by e-mail, in person and via website
Hours: Hours vary dependent on service point

Access to building: No access other than to staff

Parent body: Dorset County Council

DORSET NATURAL HISTORY AND ARCHAEOLOGICAL SOCIETY

Dorset County Museum, High West Street, Dorchester, Dorset, DT1 1XA

Tel: 01305 262735
Fax: 01305 257180
Website: www.dorsetcountymuseum.org

Enquiries to: Director

Founded: 1846

Organisation type and purpose: Learned society, museum.
Private library.

Subject coverage: Dorset: local history, natural history, archaeology, social history, fine arts, geology, literature.

Collection: Dorset Archaeological Archive
Lock and Mann Hardy Collection
Mansel-Pleydell Herbarium
Photographic Collection
Sanders Hardy Collection
Sylvia Townsend Warner (author 1893–1985), manuscripts, notebooks, diaries, letters and publications
Thomas Hardy Memorial Collection
William Barnes (Dorset poet, 1801–1886), manuscripts, notebooks, letters, diaries, scrapbooks and publications

Non-library collection catalogue: All or part available in-house

Publications: Printed

Publications list: Available in print

Access to staff: Appointment necessary.
Hours: Mon to Fri, 1000 to 1700

DORSET RECORD OFFICE

Bridport Road, Dorchester, Dorset, DT1 1RP

Tel: 01305 250550, 01305 267933 (minicom) (at County Hall)
Fax: 01305 257184
E-mail: archives@dorset-cc.gov.uk
Website: www.dorset-cc.gov.uk/archives

Enquiries to: County Archivist

Founded: 1955

Organisation type and purpose: Local government body.
Archives and record office.
The preservation of archives of Dorset and making them accessible, providing an archives service on behalf of Dorset County Council, Bournemouth Borough Council and the Borough of Poole.

Subject coverage: Standard range of public and private archives, including local government, parishes, estates, businesses, families, suitable for history, local history, family history and much else.

Collection: Standard local record office archives, documents, manuscripts, photographs, sound film
Parish registers, probate records, census records, General Register Office index (microfilm and microfiche)

Non-library collection catalogue: All or part available in-house

Publications: Printed, and microform publications

Publications list: Available in print

Access to staff: Contact by letter, by telephone, by fax, by e-mail and via website. Appointment necessary.
Hours: Mon, Tue, Thu, Fri, 0900 to 1700; Wed, 1000 to 1700; Sat, 0930 to 1230
Special comments: Proof of identity required.

Access for disabled people: Level entry, toilet facilities

Other addresses: Dorset Record Office; Archives Management Unit, County Hall, Dorchester, Dorset, DT1 1XJ; tel: 01305 225191; fax: 01305 225175

Parent bodies: Borough of Poole; Bournemouth Borough Council; Dorset County Council

DOUGLAS PUBLIC LIBRARY

Formal name: Henry Bloom Noble Library

10/12 Victoria Street, Douglas, Isle of Man, IM1 2LH

Tel: 01624 696461
Fax: 01624 696400
E-mail: jmacartney@douglas.gov.im
Website: www.douglas.gov.im

Enquiries to: Librarian

Founded: 1886

Organisation type and purpose: Local government body, public library.

Subject coverage: Isle of Man: historical, social, political, economic and other aspects.

Collection: Manx Collection

Non-library collection catalogue: All or part available in-house

Library catalogue: All or part available online and in-house

Access to staff: Contact by letter, by telephone, by fax, by e-mail, in person and via website
Hours: Mon to Sat, 0915 to 1730

Access to building: *Hours:* Mon, Tue, Thu, Fri and Sat, 0915 to 1730; Wed, 1000 to 1730

Access for disabled people: Fully compliant with DOA requirements

DOVE MARINE LABORATORY

Cullercoats, North Shields, Tyne and Wear, NE30 4PZ

Tel: 0191 222 3053
Fax: 0191 252 1054
E-mail: marineweb@ncl.ac.uk
Website: www.ncl.ac.uk/marine

Enquiries to: Secretary
Direct e-mail: c.a.weiss@ncl.ac.uk
Other contacts: Deputy Director

Founded: 1908

Organisation type and purpose: Research organisation.

Subject coverage: Marine biology; oceanography; fisheries.

Special visitor services: Laboratory and meeting room hire.

Education services: School pupil science classes; UG- and CPO-level training.

Library catalogue: All or part available in-house

Publications: Printed

Access to staff: Contact by letter, by telephone, by fax and by e-mail
Hours: Mon to Fri, 0900 to 1700

Access to building: By appointment
Hours: Mon to Fri, 0900 to 1700

Access for disabled people: Access to ground floor only

Part of: School of Marine Science and Technology; tel: 0191 222 6661; fax: 0191 222 7891

DOVER HARBOUR BOARD

Harbour House, Dover, Kent, CT17 9BU

Tel: 01304 240400

continued overleaf

Fax: 01304 240465
Website: www.doverport.co.uk

Enquiries to: Public Relations Officer
Direct tel: 01304 240400 ext 4801
Direct fax: 01304 241274
Direct e-mail: val.crimmin@doverport.co.uk

Founded: 1606; also known as Port of Dover

Organisation type and purpose: Statutory body.

Subject coverage: Port administration, particularly cross-channel passenger trade and roll-on roll-off traffic, cruise terminal, marina operation and fresh produce cargo facilities.

Publications: Printed

Access to staff: Contact by letter, by telephone, by fax and via website
Hours: Mon to Fri, 0800 to 1800

DOWN'S HEART GROUP (DHG)

PO Box 4260, Dunstable, Bedfordshire, LU6 2ZT

Tel: 0844 288 4800
Fax: 0844 288 4808
E-mail: info@dhg.org.uk
Website: www.dhg.org.uk

Enquiries to: Information Officer
Direct e-mail: sarah@dhg.org.uk
Other contacts: Director

Founded: 1989

Organisation type and purpose: UK national charity.

Subject coverage: Heart defects with Down's Syndrome; pre-natal screening for heart defects with Down's Syndrome; bereavement; support for families.

Information services: Information and support offered via phone, e-mail, website, newsletters and conferences.

Special visitor services: One-to-one visits at hospitals, if possible.

Services for disabled people: Provides information, research, support for people with Down's Syndrome and heart problems.

Collection: Archive information at National Office and Information Office.

Non-library collection catalogue: All or part available in-house

Library catalogue: All or part available online and in print

Publications: Printed, and electronic and video
Order printed publications from: National Office
Order electronic and video publications from: National Office.

Publications list: Available online

Access to staff: Contact by letter, by telephone, by fax, by e-mail and via website
Hours: 24-hour in emergency; contact or answerphone always available.

Access to building: Prior appointment required.

Member organisation of: Children's Heart Federation; tel: 020 7422 0630; fax: 020 7247 2087; website: http://www.chfed.org.uk

DOWN'S SYNDROME ASSOCIATION (DSA)

Langdon Down Centre, 2a Langdon Park, Teddington, TW11 9PS

Tel: 0845 230 0372
Fax: 0845 230 0373
E-mail: info@downs-syndrome.org.uk
Website: www.downs-syndrome.org.uk

Enquiries to: Information Officer

Founded: 1971

Organisation type and purpose: National organisation, membership association (membership is by subscription), present number of members: 12,000, voluntary organisation, registered charity (charity number 1061474).

Subject coverage: Down's Syndrome: medical, educational and psychological issues, counselling new parents, and general aspects.

Publications: Printed, and electronic and video

Publications list: Available in print

Access to staff: Contact by letter, by telephone, by fax, by e-mail and via website. Appointment necessary.
Hours: Mon to Fri, 0900 to 1700

DOWN'S SYNDROME SCOTLAND

158–160 Balgreen Road, Edinburgh, EH11 3AU

Tel: 0131 313 4225
Fax: 0131 313 4285
E-mail: info@dsscotland.org.uk
Website: www.dsscotland.org.uk

Founded: 1982; formerly called Scottish Down's Syndrome Association (SDSA) (year of change 2001)

Organisation type and purpose: Membership association (membership is by subscription), present number of members: 1500+, voluntary organisation, registered charity (charity number SC011012).

Subject coverage: Down's Syndrome.

Information services: Telephone, e-mail helplines, website resources, ebulletins and archive.

Education services: Provides training to parents and professionals on all aspects connected with Down's syndrome.

Services for disabled people: Making Your Way Through Life Project provides training for adults with Down's syndrome.

Collection: Resource centre of books and DVDs available for loan

Non-library collection catalogue: All or part available online, in-house and in print

Library catalogue: All or part available online

Publications: Printed

Publications list: Available online and in print

Access to staff: Contact by letter, by telephone, by fax, by e-mail, in person and via website. Appointment necessary.
Hours: Mon to Fri, 0900 to 1700

Access for disabled people: Level entry, access to all public areas, toilet facilities

Branches: in Ayrshire, Central, Grampian, Lothian, Tayside, West of Scotland

Sister organisation for England, Wales and Northern Ireland: Down's Syndrome Association; Langdon Down Centre, 2A Langdon Park, Teddington, Middlesex, TW11 9PS; tel: 0845 230 0372; fax: 0845 230 0373; e-mail: info@downs-syndrome.org.uk; website: http://www.downs-syndrome.org.uk

DOZENAL SOCIETY OF GREAT BRITAIN (DSGB)

32 Lansdowne Crescent, Carlisle, Cumbria, CA3 9EW

Tel: 01228 596834
E-mail: dsgb@dozenalsociety.org.uk
Website: www.dozenalsociety.org.uk

Enquiries to: Secretary

Founded: 1958; formerly called Duodecimal Society of Great Britain (year of change 1978)

Organisation type and purpose:
International organisation, learned society (membership is by subscription), present number of members: 60, research organisation.
Metrological and numbering systems past, present and future. Informed consideration of attempts to impose decimal-metric methods on areas for which they are not appropriate.
To replace base ten with base twelve.
Technical and social metrologies have differing requirements and purposes. The first postulates abstract concepts which need not relate to anything but one another, to be operated on by multi-figured calculations. Social use requires human-sized units that are designated by small numbers and are in the simple proportions commonly required and instinctively employed when making comparisons of size, weight, value, etc., such as have been evolved down the ages for our convenience and understanding.

Subject coverage: Measurement systems and methods of numeration and arithmetic, past, present and future; principles, practical imperatives and efficiency in applied metrology and computation; historical, scientific and social metrology; derivation, relationships and purposes of basic units; application of twelve-based arithmetic; informed criticism of decimal-metric methods.

Collection: Books, papers and references on numeration, calculation and metrology
Duodecimal Bulletins of the Dozenal Society of America since 1945
Journals of the DSGB from 1960 to date
Media cuttings over present decimalisation era
Wide bibliography of references

Non-library collection catalogue: All or part available in-house

Library catalogue: All or part available in-house

Publications: Printed

Publications list: Available in print

Access to staff: Contact by letter, by telephone, by e-mail and via website. Appointment necessary.
Hours: Mon to Sun, 0900 to 2100

Links with: British Weights and Measures Association; 11 Greensleeves Avenue, Broadstone, Dorset, BH18 8BJ; tel: 020 8922 0089; fax: bwma@email.com; website: http://www.footrule.org
Dozenal Society of America (DSA); 472 Village Oaks Lane, Babylon Village, NY 11702–3123, USA; tel: +1 631 669 0273; fax: contact@dozenal.org; website: http://www.dozenal.org

DR WILLIAMS'S LIBRARY

14 Gordon Square, London, WC1H 0AR

Tel: 020 7387 3727
E-mail: enquiries@dwlib.co.uk
Website: www.dwlib.co.uk

Founded: 1729

Organisation type and purpose: Registered charity (charity number 214926), public library.

Subject coverage: Theology, ecclesiastical history (particularly early nonconformist history), philosophy, humanities in general.

Collection: Henry Crabb Robinson, diaries and correspondence
New College, London, Collection
Norman Baynes Byzantine Library
George Henry Lewes Library
Philip Doddridge Correspondence
Richard Baxter Correspondence
Roger Morrice Collection

Non-library collection catalogue: All or part available online, in-house and in print

Library catalogue: All or part available online, in-house and in print

Publications: Printed

Publications list: Available online

Access to staff: Contact by letter, by telephone and by e-mail. Appointment necessary.
Hours: Mon, Wed, Fri, 1000 to 1700; Tue, Thu, 1000 to 1830

Parent body: Dr Williams's Trust; 14 Gordon Square, London, WC1H 0AR

DRAKE MUSIC

Rich Mix, 35–47 Bethnal Green Road, London, E1 6LA

Tel: 020 7739 5444
Fax: 020 7729 8942
E-mail: LONinfo@drakemusic.org
Website: www.drakemusicproject.org

Organisation type and purpose: Registered charity (charity number 1034374).
Removes disabling barriers to music through innovative approaches to teaching, learning and making music. Focuses on nurturing musical and creative ability through exploring music and technology in imaginative ways. Enables access to music making and connects disabled and non-disabled musicians locally, nationally and internationally.

Subject coverage: The team works in areas surrounding London, Bristol and Manchester, offering training in disability equality for music, an introduction to music technology and disability, accessible singing and Soundbeam. It provides consultancy services to universities, colleges, PGCE course providers, venues, music studios and others who wish to ensure their music facilities and resources are fully accessible to disabled people. It works in partnership with schools, universities, arts organisations, local authorities, music services, software developers as well as individual artists, composers, musicians and music technologists to deliver creative learning for schools, playschemes, young people and adults.

Publications: Electronic and video
Order electronic and video publications from: Download from website

Access to staff: Contact by letter, by telephone, by fax, by e-mail and via website

Also at: Drake Music North West; Zion Arts Centre, 335 Stretford Road, Hulme, Manchester, M15 5ZA; tel: 0161 232 6079; e-mail: gemmanash@drakemusicproject.org;
Drake Music South West; C/o Claremont School, Henleaze Park, Westbury-On-Trym, Bristol, BS9 4LR; tel: 0117 353 3614; fax: 0117 942 6942 (please add: FAO Drake Music); e-mail: annamacgregor@drakemusicproject.org

DRAMA ASSOCIATION OF WALES (DAW)

Unit 2, The Maltings, East Tyndall Street, Cardiff, CF24 5EA

Tel: 029 2045 2200
E-mail: teresa@dramawales.org.uk
Website: www.dramawales.org.uk

Enquiries to: PR & Member Services Officer
Direct e-mail: teresa@dramawales.org.uk
Other contacts: Library & Publications Officer; Training & Festivals Officer; Marketing Officer; General Assistant.

Founded: 1934

Organisation type and purpose: National organisation, advisory body, membership association (membership is by subscription), present number of members: 420, voluntary organisation, registered charity (charity number 502186), public library, training organisation, publishing house.

Subject coverage: Information on all aspects of amateur theatre, including funding, training, supplies of costumes, etc., festivals, lottery funding, international activities and contacts.

Collection: Largest playscript lending library in the world
Part reference collection of former British Theatre Association (BTA)
Playsets of the former British Theatre Association (BTA) and Inner London Education Authority
Part collection BBC Research Library
Playsets collection of Kensington and Chelsea Libraries
Entire collection of the Greater Manchester Drama Federation (GMDF)
Various collections donated by private individuals

Non-library collection catalogue: All or part available online and in print

Library catalogue: All or part available online and in print

Publications: Printed
Order printed publications from: Drama Association of Wales, Unit 2, The Maltings, East Tyndall Street, Cardiff, CF24 5EA

Publications list: Available online and in print

Access to staff: Contact by letter, by telephone, by e-mail, in person and via website
Hours: Mon to Fri, 0900 to 1630

Links with: All England Theatre Festival; website: http://www.aetf.org.uk
Association of Ulster Drama Festivals (AUDF); website: http://www.audf.org.uk
Scottish Community Drama Association (SCDA); website: http://www.scda.org.uk
Theatre Information Group (TIG); website: http://www.theatreinfo.specialistnetwork.org.uk
Wales Association of the Performing Arts (WAPA); website: http://www.waparts.org.uk

DRAPERS' COMPANY

Formal name: Worshipful Company of Drapers

Drapers' Hall, Throgmorton Avenue, London, EC2N 2DQ

Tel: 020 7588 5001
Fax: 020 7628 1988
E-mail: mail@thedrapers.co.uk
Website: www.thedrapers.co.uk

Organisation type and purpose:
Membership association (membership is by election or invitation).
City of London Livery Company.
To administer charitable trusts relating to relief of need, education and almshouses, to provide banqueting and catering services, and to foster the Company's heritage and traditions of good fellowship.

Access to staff: Contact by letter, by telephone, by fax, by e-mail and via website

DRAUGHT PROOFING ADVISORY ASSOCIATION LIMITED (DPAA)

PO Box 12, Haslemere, Surrey, GU27 3AH

Tel: 01428 654011
Fax: 01428 651401
E-mail: info@dpaa-association.org.uk
Website: www.dpaa-association.org.uk

Enquiries to: Director

Founded: 1985

Organisation type and purpose: Trade association (membership is by qualification).

Subject coverage: Draught proofing.

Publications: Printed

Access to staff: Contact by letter, by telephone, by fax, by e-mail and via website
Hours: Mon to Fri, 0900 to 1700

DRIVER AND VEHICLE AGENCY (DVA)

County Hall, Castlerock Road, Coleraine, BT51 3HS

Tel: 0845 601 4094; textphone 028 7034 1351
Fax: 028 7034 1422
Website: www.dvani.gov.uk

Organisation type and purpose: Executive Agency within the Department of the Environment (Northern Ireland Government).

Constituent bodies: Driver and Vehicle and Licensing Northern Ireland (DVLNI);
County Hall, Castlerock Road, Coleraine, BT51 3TA; tel: 0845 402 4000; e-mail: dvlni@doeni.gov.uk; website: http://www.dvlni.gov.uk
Driver and Vehicle Testing Agency (DVTA); County Hall, Castlerock Road, Coleraine, BT51 3HS; tel: 0845 601 4094; fax: 028 7034 1422; e-mail: dvta@doeni.gov.uk; website: http://www.dvtani.gov.uk

DRIVING INSTRUCTORS ASSOCIATION (DIA)

Safety House, Beddington Farm Road, Croydon, Surrey, CR0 4XZ

Tel: 020 8665 5151
Fax: 020 8665 5565
E-mail: dia@driving.org
Website: www.driving.org

Enquiries to: General Manager

Founded: 1978

Organisation type and purpose: Trade association (membership is by subscription), present number of members: 10,000.

Subject coverage: Nation-wide, looking after the interests of driving instructors and road safety educationalists. Providing information, producing magazines and manuals, resource material towards raising standards of driver education, professional qualifications including Diploma in Driving Instruction and degree courses – BSc and BA (Driver Education) Masters and Doctorates. Mail order supplies and requisites – everything for driving schools and driving instructors.

Publications: Printed

Access to staff: Contact by letter, by telephone, by fax, by e-mail and in person
Hours: Mon to Fri, 0900 to 1700

Links with: International Association of Driver Education (IVV); tel: 020 8665 5151; fax: 020 8665 5565; e-mail: ivv@driving.org

DRIVING STANDARDS AGENCY (DSA)

Stanley House, 56 Talbot Street, Nottingham, NG1 5GU

Tel: 0115 901 2500
Fax: 0115 901 2940
E-mail: pressoffice@dsa.gsi.gov.uk
Website: www.dsa.gov.uk

Enquiries to: Customer Service Manager
Direct tel: 0115 901 2515/6
Direct fax: 0115 901 2510
Direct e-mail: customerservices@dsa.gov.uk

Founded: 1990

Organisation type and purpose: National government body.
Government Executive Agency.
To promote road safety in Great Britain through the advancement of driving standards and by testing drivers, riders and driving instructors fairly and efficiently.

Subject coverage: Driving standards, testing drivers, riders and driving instructors.

Trade and statistical information: Data on pass and fail characteristics of the theory and practical driving tests

Publications: Printed, and electronic and video
Order printed publications from: Publications Unit, Driving Standards Agency
Paul Waller Avenue, Harrowden Lane, Cardington, Bedfordshire, MK14 3ST, tel: 01234 742297, fax: 01234 742581, e-mail: publications@dsa.gsi.gov.uk

Publications list: Available in print

Access to staff: Contact by letter, by telephone, by fax, by e-mail and via website
Hours: Mon to Fri, 0800 to 1800

Access to building: Yes
Hours: Mon to Fri, 0800 to 1800

Access for disabled people: Yes

Executive Agency of: Department for Transport (DfT)

DRUGSCOPE

Prince Consort House, Suite 204, Second Floor, 109–111 Farringdon Road, London, EC1R 3BW

Tel: 020 7520 7550
Fax: 020 7520 7555
E-mail: info@drugscope.org.uk
Website: www.drugscope.org.uk

Founded: 2000; created by the merger of Institute for the Study of Drug Dependence (ISDD), Standing Conference on Drug Abuse (SCODA) (year of change 2000)

Organisation type and purpose:
Membership association (membership is by subscription), voluntary organisation, registered charity (charity number 255030), policy organisation. Centre of expertise on drugs.
Aims to inform policy development and reduce drug-related risk by providing quality drug information, promoting effective responses to drug taking, advising on policy-making and encouraging debate.

Subject coverage: Drug misuse.

Publications: Printed

Publications list: Available online

Access to staff: Contact by letter, by telephone, by fax, by e-mail and via website. Appointment necessary.
Hours: Mon to Fri, 0930 to 1630

DRY STONE WALLING ASSOCIATION OF GREAT BRITAIN (DSWA)

Lane Farm, Crooklands, Milnthorpe, Cumbria, LA7 7NH

Tel: 01539 567953
E-mail: information@dswa.org.uk
Website: www.dswa.org.uk

Enquiries to: Secretary

Founded: 1968

Organisation type and purpose:
Membership association (membership is by subscription), voluntary organisation, registered charity (charity number 289678), training organisation.
To further all aspects of the craft of dry stone walling.

Subject coverage: All aspects of the craft of dry stone walling, craft training – formal and informal, skills assessment and certification scheme.

Collection: Small collection of printed material on the craft

Publications: Printed, and electronic and video

Publications list: Available online and in print

Access to staff: Contact by letter, by e-mail and via website
Hours: Mon to Fri, 0900 to 1700

Branches: 19 branches throughout the United Kingdom (all honorary/volunteers)

Works closely with: Conservation Bodies; Government Agencies

DSTL KNOWLEDGE AND INFORMATION SERVICES (Dstl)

Formal name: Defence Science and Technology Laboratory

Dstl Porton Down, Salisbury, Wiltshire, SP4 0JQ

Tel: 01980 613971
Fax: 01980 614273
E-mail: kisenquiries@dstl.gov.uk
Website: www.dstl.gov.uk/athena

Founded: 2001

Organisation type and purpose: National government body, research organisation.

Subject coverage: Operational analysis, military policy, naval systems, general business and management, special operations, radar, electronic warfare, explosives, weapon technologies including pyrotechnics and obscurants research, countermeasures, detection, ordnance, forensics, electronic warfare, electronic detection technologies, operational research, military history, general military- and defence-related topics, biological sciences, chemistry, materials science, historical analysis incl. history of battles, WW1 and WW2, aeronautics and space, military aviation, psychology, physiology, mathematics, statistics, biological sciences, computing and other technology areas at undergraduate/postgraduate level including signal processing, radar, lasers, acoustics and management.

Collection: KIS has over 700,000 scientific and technical reports, which are not publicly available, comprising:
The output from UK government-funded defence R&D and intelligence programmes since World War ll
Scientific, technical and intelligence reports from non-UK government defence R&D programmes over the same period

15,000 books and access to over 1,000 electronic journals

Non-library collection catalogue: All or part available in-house

Library catalogue: All or part available in-house

Publications: Printed

Access to staff: Contact by letter, by telephone, by fax, by e-mail and via website. Appointment necessary.
Hours: Mon to Fri, 0900 to 1600

Access to building: Prior appointment required

Agency of: Ministry of Defence (MOD)

DUDLEY ARCHIVES AND LOCAL HISTORY SERVICE (DALHS)

Mount Pleasant Street, Coseley, West Midlands, WV14 9JR

Tel: 01384 812770
E-mail: archives.centre@dudley.gov.uk
Website: www.dudley.gov.uk/archives

Enquiries to: Archivist

Founded: 1947; relocated from Dudley Library (year of change 1992)

Organisation type and purpose: Local government body.

Subject coverage: History of Dudley and the Black Country, in particular the area of the present Metropolitan Borough of Dudley.

Collection: Printed material re: Dudley and the Black Country and Archives – for details see entry in British Archives (Foster and Sheppard, 3rd edn)
The Dudley Estate Archive (the Earls of Dudley) 12th to 20th century

Non-library collection catalogue: All or part available online and in-house

Library catalogue: All or part available online and in-house

Publications: Printed, and electronic and video, and microform publications

Access to staff: Contact by letter, by telephone, by e-mail, in person and via website
Hours: Mon: closed; Tue, Wed, Fri: 0900 to 1700; Thu: 0930 to 1900; 1st and 3rd Sat in month: 0930 to 1230
Closed for last full week of every month; see website for details
Special comments: CARN readers' tickets issued with two proofs of identity with name, address and signature; appointments advisable, particularly for microform material; appointments for Saturdays.

Access for disabled people: Ramped entry, access to all public areas, toilet facilities
Special comments: On-site parking on level.

Parent body: Dudley Metropolitan Borough Council

DUDLEY COLLEGE

The Broadway, Dudley, West Midlands, DY1 4AS

Tel: 01384 363000
Fax: 01384 363311
Website: www.dudleycol.ac.uk

Enquiries to: Library Co-ordinator
Direct tel: 01384 363353
Direct e-mail: library@dudleycol.ac.uk

Organisation type and purpose: College of further and higher education.

Subject coverage: Management; secretarial and office practice; work study; production control; construction; structural engineering; welding; brickwork; carpentry; joinery; electrical engineering; electronic engineering; microcomputer technology; hairdressing; beauty therapy; mechanical engineering; production engineering; motor vehicle work, local history, science, humanities.

Non-library collection catalogue: All or part available in-house

Library catalogue: All or part available in-house

Access to staff: Contact by letter, by telephone and by e-mail. Appointment necessary.
Hours: Term time: Mon to Thu, 0900 to 2000; Fri, 0900 to 1630
Vacations: Mon to Thu, 0900 to 1700; Fri, 0900 to 1630
Special comments: Reference facilities for non-students £5 per annum; borrowing facilities for non-students £25 per annum.

Access for disabled people: Parking provided, level entry, toilet facilities, lift access from disabled parking to ground floor library

Subsidiary body: International Glass Centre; tel: 01384 363067

DUDLEY PUBLIC LIBRARIES

Dudley Library, St James's Road, Dudley, West Midlands, DY1 1HR

Tel: 01384 815568 (library office)
Fax: 01384 815543
E-mail: dudley.library@dudley.gov.uk
Website: www.dudley.gov.uk/libraries

Founded: 1909

Organisation type and purpose: Local government body, public library.

Subject coverage: Dudley and Black Country local studies.

Library catalogue: All or part available online and in-house

Access to staff: Contact by letter, by telephone, by fax, by e-mail, in person and via website
Hours: Mon, Wed, Thu, Fri, 0900 to 1900; Tue, 0930 to 1900; Sun, 1000 to 1400

Access for disabled people: Disabled entrance, public lift.

Branch libraries: Brierley Hill; Coseley; Cradley; Gornal; Halesowen; Kingswinford; Long Lane; Lye; Netherton; Sedgley; Stourbridge; Wordsley

DUGDALE SOCIETY

Shakespeare Centre, Stratford-upon-Avon, Warwickshire, CV37 6QW

E-mail: dugdale-society@hotmail.co.uk
Website: www.dugdale-society.org.uk

Enquiries to: Secretary

Founded: 1920

Organisation type and purpose: Learned society, membership association (membership is by subscription), present number of members: 350, registered charity (charity number 1051033).

Subject coverage: Warwickshire: historical records, local history and topography.

Publications: Printed

Publications list: Available online and in print

Access to staff: Contact by letter and by e-mail

DUKE OF EDINBURGH'S AWARD, THE (the DofE)

Formal name: The Duke of Edinburgh's Award Charity

Gulliver House, Madeira Walk, Windsor, Berkshire, SL4 1EU

Tel: 01753 727400
Fax: 01753 810666
E-mail: info@DofE.org
Website: www.DofE.org

Enquiries to: Director
Other contacts: Head of Marketing

Founded: 1956

Organisation type and purpose: Registered charity (charity number 1072490).
The Duke of Edinburgh's Award is the world's leading achievement award for young people. It provides a balanced programme of activities that develops the whole person – mind, body and soul – in an environment of social interaction and teamworking. Young people aged between 14 and 24 progress through three levels of DofE programmes to achieve a Bronze, Silver or Gold Award.
The DofE Head Office is advised by national co-ordinating bodies concerned with individual activities.

Subject coverage: Over 300 different activities from bee-keeping to ballet, first aid to farming, etc; the specialist advice and expertise of the assisting organisations is relied upon by the DofE Head Office, especially in the field of expeditioning.

Publications: Printed

Access to staff: Contact by letter, by telephone, by fax and by e-mail
Hours: Mon to Fri, 0900 to 1700

DUMFRIES AND GALLOWAY ARCHIVE CENTRE

33 Burns Street, Dumfries, DG1 2PS

Tel: 01387 269254
Fax: 01387 264126
E-mail: libs&i@dumgal.gov.uk
Website: www.dumgal.gov.uk/lia

Enquiries to: Resources Development
Other contacts: Research Officer; tel no: 01387 253820 for genealogical research.

Founded: 1987

Organisation type and purpose: Local government body. Record office.
Preservation of, and research using, local archives.

continued overleaf

Subject coverage: Local and family history, civic, religious, economic and social history, architecture and genealogical studies.

Collection: Dumfries Burgh archives
Local Authority archives
Papers of local businesses, societies and families
Sanquhar Burgh archives
Stewart of Shambellie family papers
Walter Newall architectural drawings

Non-library collection catalogue: All or part available online, in-house and in print

Publications: Printed

Publications list: Available in print

Access to staff: Contact by letter, by telephone, by fax, by e-mail and in person. Appointment necessary.
Hours: Tue, Wed, Fri, 1100 to 1300 and 1400 to 1700; Thu, 1800 to 2100

Links with: Ewart Library; Catherine Street, Dumfries, DG1 1JB; tel: 01387 253820; fax: 01387 260294; e-mail: alastairj@dumgal.gov.uk

Parent body: Libraries, Information and Archives Service, Dumfries and Galloway Council; tel: 01387 253820; fax: 01387 260294; e-mail: alastairj@dumgal.gov.uk

DUMFRIES AND GALLOWAY COLLEGE (DAGCOL)

Bankend Road, Dumfries, DG1 4FD

Tel: 01387 734000
Fax: 01387 734040
E-mail: info@dumgal.ac.uk
Website: www.dumgal.ac.uk

Enquiries to: Admissions Team
Direct tel: 01387 734059 / 60
Direct e-mail: admissions@dumgal.ac.uk

History of institution: formerly called Dumfries and Galloway College of Technology

Organisation type and purpose: Suitable for ages: 16+.
College of further and higher education.

Subject coverage: Mechanical, electrical, electronic and motor vehicle engineering, construction and allied industries, health & safety, business studies, computing, accounting, office management, art and design, media/communications, photography, hairdressing, health & social studies, hospitality, education, sport.

Library catalogue: All or part available online, in-house and in print

Access to staff: Contact by letter, by telephone, by e-mail and via website. Non-members charged.
Hours: Mon to Thu, 0845 to 1630; Fri, 0845 to 1630

Access for disabled people: Parking provided, ramped entry, toilet facilities

Also at: Stranraer Campus; Lewis Street, Stranraer; tel: 01776 706633; website: http://www.dumgal.ac.uk

DUMFRIES AND GALLOWAY COUNCIL

Council Offices, English Street, Dumfries, DG1 2DD

Tel: 01387 260000
Fax: 01387 260034
Website: www.dumgal.gov.uk

Enquiries to: Communications Manager
Direct tel: 01387 260330
Direct fax: 01387 260334
Direct e-mail: susanbl@dumgal.gov.uk

Founded: 1996; formerly called Annandale and Eskdale District Council, Dumfries and Galloway Regional Council, Nithsdale District Council, Stewartry District Council, Wigtown District Council (year of change 1996)

Organisation type and purpose: Local government body.

Subject coverage: All information covering Dumfries and Galloway.

Publications: Printed

Access to staff: Contact by letter, by telephone, by fax, by e-mail, in person and via website
Hours: Mon to Fri, 0900 to 1700

Access for disabled people: Ramped entry, access to all public areas

DUMFRIES AND GALLOWAY FAMILY HISTORY SOCIETY (D&GFHS)

Family History Centre, 9 Glasgow Street, Dumfries, DG2 9AF

Tel: 01387 248093
E-mail: publications@dgfhs.org.uk
Website: www.safhs.org.uk
Website: www.dgfhs.org.uk
Website: homepages.rootsweb.com/~scottish

Enquiries to: Honorary Secretary

Founded: 1987

Organisation type and purpose: Learned society (membership is by subscription), present number of members: 1,700, voluntary organisation, registered charity (charity number SC 020596), research organisation, publishing house.
Family history research.

Subject coverage: Genealogy, family history, local history, especially pertaining to Dumfriesshire, Kircudbrightshire and Wigtownshire.

Collection: Wigtown Free Press newspaper indexes 1850–1920 and all these newspapers on fiche
Bank of family trees
Books, documents, manuscripts
Dumfries newspapers' indexes 1777–1930
OPRs, IGI and 1841–1901 Census records (film)

Publications: Printed, and electronic and video

Publications list: Available online and in print

Access to staff: Contact by letter, by telephone, by e-mail, in person and via website. Non-members charged.
Hours: Tue to Fri; Apr to Oct, 1000 to 1600; Nov to Mar 1100 to 1500; Sat, 1000 to 1300

Access to building: No prior appointment required

Access for disabled people: Level entry

DUMFRIES AND GALLOWAY LIBRARIES, INFORMATION AND ARCHIVES

Ewart Library, Catherine Street, Dumfries, DG1 1JB

Tel: 01387 253820
Fax: 01387 260294
E-mail: libs&i@dumgal.gov.uk
Website: www.dumgal.gov.uk/lia

Enquiries to: Cultural Services, Libraries Information & Archives Manager
Other contacts: Reference Librarian

Founded: 1903; formerly called Dumfries and Galloway Libraries (year of change 1995)

Organisation type and purpose: Local government body, public library.

Subject coverage: General, local studies of Dumfries and Galloway region; civic, religious, genealogy, architecture, economic and social history; Lockerbie Air Disaster at Ewart.

Collection: Burns Club Collection (at Archive Centre)
Local Authority Archives
Local Studies Collection
Lockerbie Air Disaster Archive
Lord Glendyne Collection
R C Reid Manuscripts (at Ewart)

Non-library collection catalogue: All or part available online and in-house

Library catalogue: All or part available online and in-house

Publications: Printed
Order printed publications from: http://www.dumgal.gov.uk/lia

Publications list: Available online and in print

Access to staff: Contact by letter, by telephone, by fax, by e-mail, in person and via website
Hours: Ewart: Mon, to Wed, Fri, 0900 to 1930; Thu, Sat, 0900 to 1700

Access for disabled people: Parking provided, ramped entry, access to all public areas, toilet facilities

Branches at: Annan Library; Charles Street, Annan, DG12 5AG; tel: 01461 202809; fax: 01461 20280901461 202809; Castle Douglas Library; King Street, Castle Douglas, DG7 1AE; tel: 01556 502643; fax: 01556 502643; Dalbeattie Library; High Street, Dalbeattie Library, DG5 4AD; tel: 01556 610898; fax: 01556 610898; Dalry Library; Dalry, Castle Douglas, DG7 3UP; tel: 01644 430234; fax: 01644 430234; Dumfries and Galloway Archives; Archive Centre, 33 Burns Street, Dumfries, DG1 2PS; tel: 01387 269254; fax: 01387 264126; Eastriggs Library; Eastriggs Community School, Eastriggs, Annan, DG12 6PZ; tel: 01461 40844; fax: 01461 40844; Gatehouse Library; 63 High Street, Gatehouse of Fleet, DG7 2HS; tel: 01557 814646; fax: 01557 814646; Georgetown Library; Gillbrae Road, Dumfries, DG1 4EJ; tel: 01387 256059; fax: 01387 256059; Gretna Library; Richard Greenhow Centre, Central Avenue, Gretna, DG16 5AQ; tel: 01461 338000; fax: 01461 338000; Kirkconnel Library; Greystone Avenue, Kelloholm, DG4 6RA; tel: 01659 67191; fax: 01659 67191; Kirkcudbright Library; Sheriff Court House,

Kirkcudbright, DG6 4JW; tel: 01557 331240; fax: 01557 331240; Langholm Library; Charles Street Old, Langholm, DG13 0AA; tel: 01387 380040; fax: 01387 380040; Lochmaben Library; High Street, Lochmaben, Lockerbie, DG11 1NQ; tel: 01387 811865; fax: 01387 811865; Lochside Library; Lochside Road, Dumfries, DG2 0LW; tel: 01387 268751; fax: 01387 268751; Lochthorn Library; Lochthorn, Dumfries, DG1 1UF; tel: 01387 265780; fax: 01387 266424; Lockerbie Library; 31–33 High Street, Lockerbie, DG11 2JL; tel: 01576 203380; fax: 01576 203380; Moffat Library; Town Hall, High Street, Moffat, DG10 9HF; tel: 01683 220952; fax: 01683 220952; Newton Stewart Library; Church Street, Newton Stewart, DG8 6ER; tel: 01671 403450; fax: 01671 403450; Port William Library; Church Street, Port William, Newton Stewart, DG8 9QL; tel: 01988 700406; fax: 01988 700406; Sanquhar Library; 106 High Street, Sanquhar, DG4 6DZ; tel: 01659 50626; fax: 01659 50626; Stranraer Library; North Strand Street, Stranraer, DG9 7LD; tel: 01776 707400; fax: 01776 703565; Thornhill Library; Townhead Street, Thornhill, DG3 5NW; tel: 01848 330654; fax: 01848 330654; Whithorn Library; St John Street, Whithorn, DG8 8PF; tel: 01988 500406; fax: 01988 500406; Wigtown Library; Wigtown County Buildings, Wigtown, DG8 9JH; tel: 01988 403329; fax: 01988 403329

DUNDEE AND TAYSIDE CHAMBER OF COMMERCE AND INDUSTRY

Chamber of Commerce Buildings, Panmure Street, Dundee, DD1 1ED

Tel: 01382 228545
Fax: 01382 228441
E-mail: admin@dundeechamber.co.uk
Website: www.dundeechamber.co.uk

Enquiries to: Communications Manager
Direct e-mail: juliechristie@dundeechamber .co.uk

Organisation type and purpose: Advisory body, trade association (membership is by subscription).
To represent the business interests of companies in Tayside.

Subject coverage: Business services.

Publications: Printed

Publications list: Available online and in print

Access to staff: Contact by letter, by telephone, by fax, by e-mail, in person and via website
Hours: Mon to Fri, 0900 to 1700

Access to building: No prior appointment required

Access for disabled people: Access to all public areas

DUNDEE CITY ARCHIVES

21 City Square, Dundee, DD1 3BY

Tel: 01382 434494
Fax: 01382 434666
E-mail: archives@dundeecity.gov.uk
Website: www.dundeecity.gov.uk/archive
Website: www.fdca.org.uk

Enquiries to: City Archivist

Founded: 1969; formerly called City of Dundee District Council Archive & Record Centre Acting On An Agency Basis for Tayside Regional Council (year of change 1996)

Organisation type and purpose: Local government body.

Subject coverage: Local history from the formation of the Burgh of Dundee in 1191, shipbuilding, Port of Dundee, Customs and Excise, Presbytery records.

Non-library collection catalogue: All or part available in-house

Publications: Printed
Order printed publications from: Honorary Sales Secretary, Friends of Dundee City Archive (at same address)

Access to staff: Contact by letter, by telephone, by fax and by e-mail. Appointment necessary.
Hours: Mon to Fri, 0915 to 1300 and 1400 to 1645

Access to building: Report to City Square Reception, 18 City Square
Hours: Mon to Fri, 0915 to 1300 and 1400 to 1645; for local holidays check council website A–Z
Special comments: Visitors will be escorted to City Archives from 18 City Square.

Access for disabled people: No lift available to Archives; special arrangements can be made to consult records elsewhere for those with difficulty walking

Links with: Friends of Dundee City Archives; c/o Dundee City Archives; website: http://www.fdca.org.uk

DUNDEE CITY COUNCIL – ARTS & HERITAGE

The McManus: Dundee's Art Gallery & Museum, Albert Square, Meadowside, Dundee, DD1 1DA

Tel: 01382 307200
Fax: 01382 307207
E-mail: themcmanus@dundeecity.gov.uk
Website: www.themcmanus-dundee.gov.uk
Website: www.dundeecity.gov.uk

Enquiries to: Arts & Heritage Manager
Direct tel: 01382 307210
Direct e-mail: john.stewart-young@ dundeecity.gov.uk

Founded: 1867; formerly called Dundee Art Galleries & Museums (year of change 1994); formerly called Arts & Heritage Dept (year of change 2002); formerly called Leisure & Arts Dept (year of change 2006); formerly called Leisure & Communities Dept (year of change 2008)

Organisation type and purpose: Local government body, museum, art gallery. Heritage facilities.

Subject coverage: Tayside and North Fife region: archaeology, including sites research, history, natural sciences and environmental studies; museum education services; fine and applied art; Egyptology; astronomy; numismatics; field archaeology.

Collection: Recognised collections of fine and decorative art and whaling

Non-library collection catalogue: All or part available online

Publications: Printed

Access to staff: Contact by letter, by telephone, by fax, by e-mail, in person and via website
Hours: Mon to Fri, 0900 to 1700

Access to building: *Hours:* Mon to Sat 1000 to 1700; Sun 1230 to 1600

Access for disabled people: Level access to both entrances to the building; full wheelchair access to all public areas and a lift to all floors; room thresholds have lighting to assist visitors with partial sight; larger text sizes and colour coding on displays; guide dogs, hearing dogs and other recognised assistance dogs are admitted; accessible toilets incorporating adult changing are available in the main toilet suite

Branch museums: Broughty Castle Museum; Castle Approach, Broughty Ferry, Dundee, DD5 2TF; tel: 01382 436916; fax: 01382 436951; e-mail: broughty@dundeecity .gov.uk; website: http://www.dundeecity .gov.uk/broughtycastle
Mills Observatory; Glamis Road, Balgay Park, Dundee, DD2 2UB; tel: 01382 435967; fax: 01382 435962; e-mail: mills .observatory@dundeecity.gov.uk; website: http://www.dundeecity.gov.uk/mills

DUNDEE CITY COUNCIL LIBRARIES

Leisure and Communites Department, Central Library, The Wellgate, Dundee, DD1 1DB

Tel: 01382 431500
Fax: 01382 431558
E-mail: central.library@dundeecity.gov.uk
Website: www.dundeecity.gov.uk/library
Website: opac.dundeecity.gov.uk/cgi-bin/ spydus.exe/MSGTRN/OPAC/HOME
Website: www.wighton.com
Website: www.dundeecity.gov.uk/photodb

Enquiries to: Head of Libraries, Information & Cultural Services
Direct tel: 01382 307462
Direct fax: 01382 307487
Direct e-mail: moira.methven@dundeecity .gov.uk
Other contacts: Manager, Central Library

Founded: 1869

Organisation type and purpose: Local government body, public library.

Subject coverage: General, business information, ethnic minority languages, local history, genealogy, art, music, architecture, patents, Scottish literature, open learning materials, Scottish Parliament, European information and early Scottish music.

Collection: Antiquarian Collection
British Standards
Cynicus Collection (early 20th century cartoons)
Dundee Photographic Survey 1916
Dundee Photographic Survey 1991
Lamb Collection (local history ephemera including posters, news cuttings, pamphlets, etc.)
Ower Collection (architecture)

continued overleaf

Sir James Ivory Collection (early mathematical and scientific works)
Sturrock Collection (fine printing and binding; private press books)
Whaling Logbooks
Wighton Collection (1,200 volumes of early music of UK, particularly Scottish; some unique items)
William McGonagall Collection
Wilson Collection (late 19th-/early 20th-century photographs, mainly of Dundee)

Trade and statistical information: The Central Library has a collection of government and inter-governmental publications

Non-library collection catalogue: All or part available online

Library catalogue: All or part available online

Publications: Electronic and video

Access to staff: Contact by letter, by telephone, by fax, by e-mail, in person and via website
Hours: Central Library: Mon, Tue, Thu, Fri, 0900 to 2000; Wed, 1000 to 2000; Sat, 0930 to 1700
Opening times of neighbourhood libraries vary

Access for disabled people: Parking provided, ramped entry, level entry, access to all public areas, toilet facilities

Branch libraries: Ardler Complex; Turnberry Avenue, Dundee, DD3 3TP; tel: 01382 432863; fax: 01382 432862; e-mail: ardler.library@dundeecity.gov.uk; Arthurstone Community Library; Arthurstone Terrace, Dundee, DD4 6RT; tel: 01382 438881; fax: 01382 438886; e-mail: arthurstone.library@dundeecity.gov.uk; Blackness Community Library; 225 Perth Road, Dundee, DD2 1EJ; tel: 01382 435936; fax: 01382 435942; e-mail: blackness.library@dundeecity.gov.uk; Broughty Ferry Community Library; Queen Street, Broughty Ferry, Dundee, DD5 2HN; tel: 01382 436919; fax: 01382 436913; e-mail: broughty.library@dundeecity.gov.uk; Charleston Community Centre and Library; 60 Craigowan Road, Dundee, DD2 4NL; tel: 01382 436639; fax: 01382 436640; e-mail: charleston.library@dundeecity.gov.uk; Coldside Community Library; 150 Strathmartine Road, Dundee, DD3 7SE; tel: 01382 432849; fax: 01382 432850; e-mail: coldside.library@dundeecity.gov.uk; Douglas Community and Library Centre; Balmoral Avenue, Dundee, DD4 8SD; tel: 01382 436944; fax: 01382 436922; e-mail: douglas.library@dundeecity.gov.uk; Fintry Community Library; Findcastle Street, Dundee, DD4 9EW; tel: 01382 432560; fax: 01382 432559; e-mail: fintry.library@dundeecity.gov.uk; Hub Community Centre and Library; Pitkerro Road, Dundee, DD4 8ES; tel: 01382 438648; fax: 01382 438627; e-mail: hub.library@dundeecity.gov.uk; Kirkton Community Centre and Library; Derwent Avenue, Dundee, DD3 0BW; tel: 01382 432851; fax: 01382 436321; e-mail: kirkton.library@dundeecity.gov.uk; Lochee Community Library; High Street, Lochee, Dundee, DD2 3AU; tel: 01382 431835; fax: 01382 431837; e-mail: lochee.library@dundeecity.gov.uk; Menzieshill Community Centre and Library; Orleans Place, Dundee, DD2 4BH; tel: 01382 432945; fax: 01382 432968; e-mail: menzieshill.library@dundeecity.gov.uk; Whitfield Library and Learning Centre; Whitfield Drive, Dundee, DD4 0DX; tel: 01382 432561; fax: 01382 432562; e-mail: whitfield.library@dundeecity.gov.uk

Parent body: Dundee City Council; City Chambers, Dundee, DD1 3BY; tel: 01382 434000; fax: 01382 434666; e-mail: helpline@dundeecity.gov.uk

DUNDEE HERITAGE TRUST

Verdant Works, West Henderson's Wynd, Dundee, DD1 5BT

Tel: 01382 226659
Fax: 01382 225891
E-mail: info@dundeeheritage.co.uk
Website: www.rrrdiscovery.com

Enquiries to: Museums Officer

Founded: 1985

Organisation type and purpose: Registered charity (charity number SC 002268). Museum.

Subject coverage: Dundee's industrial history, specifically textiles (linen and jute). Textile engineering and mill architecture. RRS Discovery, polar exploration, Captain Scott and ship restoration and conservation.

Collection: Archives (not business archives), photographs and objects relating to Dundee textile industries, especially linen and jute
Archival photographs and objects relating to RRS Discovery and 1901–04 British National Antarctic Expedition under Captain Scott

Publications: Printed
Order printed publications from: Shop Manager, Dundee Industrial Heritage Ltd Discovery Point, Discovery Quay, Dundee, DD1 4XA, tel: 01382 309060, fax: 01382 225891, e-mail: info@dundeeheritage.co.uk

Access to staff: Contact by letter, by telephone, by fax and by e-mail. Appointment necessary.
Hours: Mon to Fri, 0900 to 1700

Access to building: No access other than to staff
Hours: Verdant Works: April to October, Mon and Sat 1000 to 1800, Sun 1100 to 1800; November to March, Wed and Sat 1030 to 1630, Sun 1100 to 1630. Closed Mon and Tue from November to March. Closed 25 and 26 December and 1 and 2 January. Last admission is 1 hour prior to closing

Also at: Discovery Point; Discovery Quay, Dundee, DD1 5BT; tel: 01382 309060; fax: 01382 225891; e-mail: info@dundeeheritage.co.uk

DUNFERMLINE CARNEGIE LIBRARY

Formal name: Fife Council Libraries & Museums

Dunfermline Carnegie Library, Abbot Street, Dunfermline, Fife, KY12 7NL

Tel: 01383 312600
Fax: 01383 312608
E-mail: dunfermline.library@fife.gov.uk

Enquiries to: Librarian
Direct tel: 01383 312602
Direct e-mail: libraries.museums@fife.gov.uk

Founded: 1883; formerly called Dunfermline District Libraries; formerly called Fife Council Libraries (year of change 2008)

Organisation type and purpose: Local government body, public library.

Subject coverage: General, local history.

Collection: Andrew Carnegie Collection
George Reid Collection (medieval manuscripts and early printed books)
Local History Collection of books, maps, photographs, slides
Murison Burns Collection (works of Robert Burns, contains no manuscripts)

Non-library collection catalogue: All or part available online and in-house

Library catalogue: All or part available online and in-house

Publications: Printed, and electronic and video

Publications list: Available in print

Access to staff: Contact by letter and by e-mail

Access for disabled people: Parking provided, level entry, access to all public areas, toilet facilities

Parent body: Fife Council, Housing & Communitites; Fife House, North Street, Glenrothes; website: http://www.fife.gov.uk

DURHAM CATHEDRAL LIBRARY

The College, Durham, DH1 3EH

Tel: 0191 386 2489
Fax: 0191 386 4267 (Chapter Office)
E-mail: library@durhamcathedral.co.uk
Website: www.durhamcathedral.co.uk/library

Enquiries to: Head of Collections

Founded: 995

Organisation type and purpose: Cathedral library.

Subject coverage: Durham Cathedral; manuscripts and early printed books; Durham local history; pre-1800 sacred and secular music; monasticism; Saxon and medieval monastic manuscripts.

Collection: Antiquarian mss collections: Allan, Hunter, Longstaffe, Randall, Raine, Sharp
Churchmen's papers: Henson, I.T. Ramsey, J.B. Lightfoot
Music MS part books for organ and choir
Collection of over 12,000 17th- and 18th-century printed theses, mainly from German universities
Falle Collection of 17th- and 18th-century printed music
Pre-conquest and medieval books of the monastic house of Durham (manuscripts, c. 300 vols)

Non-library collection catalogue: All or part available online, in-house and in print

Library catalogue: All or part available online, in-house and in print

Publications: Printed, and microform publications

Access to staff: Contact by letter, by telephone, by e-mail, in person and via website. Appointment necessary. Letter of introduction required.
Hours: Mon to Fri, 0930 to 1645
Special comments: Closed Bank Holidays and Christmas to Easter, any exceptional closures noted on Cathedral website.
For Search Room use an appointment is required.

Parent body: Durham Cathedral; The College, Durham, DH1 3EH; tel: 0191 386 4266; fax: 0191 386 4267; e-mail: enquiries@durhamcathedral.co.uk; website: http://www.durhamcathedral.co.uk

DURHAM COUNTY LOCAL HISTORY SOCIETY (DCLHS)

St Mary's Grove, Tudhoe, Spennymoor, DL16 6LR

Tel: 01388 816209
E-mail: johnbanham@tiscali.co.uk
Website: www.durhamweb.org.uk/dclhs

Enquiries to: Secretary

Founded: 1964

Organisation type and purpose: Learned society, publishing house.

Subject coverage: Durham, local history, mainly 15th century to present day.

Publications: Printed

Publications list: Available online

Access to staff: Contact by letter and by e-mail
Hours: Voluntary service – best to e-mail or write

DURHAM COUNTY RECORD OFFICE (DCRO)

County Hall, Durham, DH1 5UL

Tel: 0191 383 3253
Fax: 0191 383 3474
E-mail: record.office@durham.gov.uk
Website: www.durhamrecordoffice.org.uk

Enquiries to: County Archivist
Direct tel: 0191 383 4211

Founded: 1961

Organisation type and purpose: Local government body.
Record office.

Collection: Archives and records of County Durham and Darlington
All catalogues of these records are in online database

Non-library collection catalogue: All or part available online

Publications: Printed

Publications list: Available online and in print

Access to staff: Contact by letter, by telephone, by fax, by e-mail, in person and via website. Appointment necessary.
Hours: Mon, Tue, 0845 to 1645; Wed, 0845 to 2000
Special comments: Thursday, Fri, Sat, Sun and bank holidays closed.

Access to building: Prior appointment required

Access for disabled people: Parking provided, ramped entry, access to all public areas, toilet facilities, visual aids for viewing records, priority microfilm readers

DURHAM HISTORICAL ENTERPRISES

3 Briardene, Margery Lane, Durham, DH1 4QU

Tel: 0191 386 1500
E-mail: dhent@dhent.fsnet.co.uk
Website: www.dhent.fsnet.co.uk

Enquiries to: Proprietor

Founded: 1991

Organisation type and purpose: Consultancy, research organisation, publishing house.

Subject coverage: Durham local history, Durham family histories.

Publications: Printed

Access to staff: Contact by letter, by telephone and by e-mail
Hours: Mon to Fri, 0900 to 1700

DURHAM LEARNING RESOURCES (DLR)

Sevenhills, Unit 1, Greenhills Industrial Estate, Spennymoor, Co Durham, DL16 6JB

Tel: 03000 263 781
Fax: 01388 817099
E-mail: dlr@durham.gov.uk
Website: www.durham.gov.uk/dlr

Enquiries to: Learning Support Asst. Coordinator (Durham Learning Resources)
Direct tel: 03000 263 780
Direct e-mail: patricia.brown@durham.gov.uk

Founded: 1991

Organisation type and purpose: Local government body, public library.
To support reading and learning in schools by providing: a multimedia loans service to schools in support of the National Curriculum; advice and courses on schools resource centres and learning using books and other resources; books for sale to schools.

Subject coverage: Information and advice in school resource centre management; information and training on study and library skills; knowledge of loans of museum objects, books, art and other media in support of the National Curriculum; sales of books to schools.

Non-library collection catalogue: All or part available online

Access to staff: Contact by letter, by telephone, by fax, by e-mail, in person and via website. Appointment necessary.
Hours: Mon to Thu, 0830 to 1700; Fri, 0830 to 1630

Access for disabled people: Parking provided

DURHAM UNIVERSITY

Formal name: University of Durham

Mountjoy Research Centre, Stockton Road, Durham, DH1 3UR

Tel: 0191 334 4649
Fax: 0191 334 4634

Enquiries to: Busienss Relations Manager
Direct e-mail: jonathon.lee@durham.ac.uk

Founded: 1832

Organisation type and purpose: University department or institute, consultancy, research organisation.

Subject coverage: All academic departments, particularly, mathematics/statistics; chemistry; physics; geological sciences; computing; business development; economics and finance; engineering; manufacturing, environment. Particular expertise includes photonics, nanotechnology, materials, nuclear magnetic resonance, electronics.

Library catalogue: All or part available online

DURHAM WILDLIFE TRUST

Bowlees Visitor Centre, Bowlees, Middleton in Teesdale, Co Durham, DL12 0XE

Tel: 01833 622292
Fax: 01833 622292
E-mail: durhamwt@cix.co.uk
Website: www.wildlifetrust.org.uk/durham

Enquiries to: Manager
Other contacts: Education Officer (tel: 0191 548 0152)

Founded: 1975; formerly called Durham County Conservation Trust

Organisation type and purpose: National organisation, membership association (membership is by subscription), service industry, voluntary organisation, registered charity (charity number 501038), suitable for ages: all.
Visitor Centre.
To highlight the natural history of Teesdale.

Subject coverage: Wildlife and conservation in Teesdale and tourist information leaflets.

Collection: The Fitzhugh Library, previously held here, is now housed at Witham Hall in Barnard Castle

Publications: Printed

Publications list: Available online and in print

Access to staff: Contact by letter, by telephone, by fax, by e-mail, in person and via website
Hours: 1 Apr to 31 Oct: daily, 1030 to 1730
Special comments: Other times by prior appointment.

Access to building: By prior appointment
Hours: Daily, 1030 to 1700

Access for disabled people: Parking provided, ramped entry, level entry, access to all public areas
Hours: As above
Special comments: Toilet facilities in main car park.

continued overleaf

For membership details: Rainton Meadows Site; tel: 0191 584 3112; fax: 0191 584 3934; e-mail: durhamwt@cix.compulink.co.uk

Head Office and Visitor Centre: Durham Wildlife Trust; Rainton Meadows, Chilton Moor, Houghton-le-Spring, Tyne & Wear, DH4 6PU; tel: 0191 584 3112; fax: 0191 584 3934; e-mail: durhamwt@cix.compulink.co.uk

Visitor Centre at: Low Barns; Witton-le-Wear, Bishop Auckland, Co Durham, DL14 0AG; tel: 01388 488728; fax: 01388 488529

DVORAK SOCIETY

Formal name: The Dvorak Society for Czech and Slovak Music

The Secretary, 13 Church Lane, Knutton, Newcastle-under-Lyme, Staffordshire, ST5 6DU

Tel: 01782 631274
E-mail: secretary@dvorak-society.org
Website: www.dvorak-society.org

Enquiries to: Membership Secretary
Direct tel: 01962 864184
Direct e-mail: membership@dvorak-society.org

Founded: 1974; formerly called Dvorák Society of Great Britain (year of change 1986)

Organisation type and purpose: Learned society (membership is by subscription, election or invitation), present number of members: 582, registered charity (charity number 267336), suitable for all ages. The promotion of Czech and Slovak music.

Subject coverage: History of Czech and Slovak music composers and musicians; contemporary Czech and Slovak music. Concert promotion, record reviews and regular listings of available recordings of Czech and Slovak music.

Collection: All collections are held c/o The Dvorak Society Library, Cardiff School of Music, Corbett Road, Cardiff, CF10 3ED
John Clapham Collection
Recorded Music Library
Tausky Collection
Melville-Mason Collection
Belohlavek Collection
Dvorak Society Archive

Non-library collection catalogue: All or part available in-house

Library catalogue: All or part available in-house

Publications: Printed

Access to staff: Contact by letter, by telephone, by e-mail and via website
Hours: Mon to Fri, 0900 to 1700

Access to building: No access other than to staff
Special comments: Members only.

Links with: British Czech and Slovak Association

DYLAN THOMAS SOCIETY OF GREAT BRITAIN, THE

Fernhill, 124 Chapel Street, Mumbles, Swansea, West Glamorgan, SA3 4NH

Tel: 01792 363875

Enquiries to: Chair

Founded: 1977

Organisation type and purpose: Learned society (membership is by subscription).

Subject coverage: Life and works of Dylan Thomas.

Non-library collection catalogue: All or part available in-house

Publications: Printed, and electronic and video

DYNIX USERS GROUP (DUG)

Thompson Library, Staffordshire University, College Rd, Stoke on Trent, ST4 2XS

Tel: 01782 294755
Fax: 01782 295799
E-mail: i.haydock@staffs.ac.uk
Website: www.dynixusers.org.uk

Enquiries to: Honorary Secretary

Founded: 1995; incorporates the former Horizon Users Group (year of change 2004)

Organisation type and purpose: Membership association.

Subject coverage: SirsiDynix Horizon and Dynix Classic library management system.

Access to staff: Contact by letter, by telephone, by fax and by e-mail
Hours: Mon to Fri, 0900 to 1700

DYSLEXIA ACTION

Park House, Wick Road, Egham, Surrey, TW20 0HH

Tel: 01784 222300
Fax: 01784 222333
E-mail: info@dyslexiaaction.org.uk
Website: www.dyslexiaaction.org.uk

Enquiries to: Information Officer

Founded: 1972

Organisation type and purpose: Professional body, registered charity (charity number 268502).

Subject coverage: Dyslexia: assessment of difficulties, teaching children and adults, teacher training, advisory service.

Non-library collection catalogue: All or part available online

Publications: Printed
Order printed publications from: DI Trading Limited; at the same address

Publications list: Available online and in print

Access to staff: Contact by letter, by telephone, by e-mail and via website. Appointment necessary.
Hours: Mon to Fri, 0900 to 1700

Parent body: Dyslexia Trust

DYSLEXIA INFORMATION CENTRE (DIC)

Hampton Grange, 21 Hampton Lane, Solihull, West Midlands, B91 2QJ

Tel: 0121 705 4547
Website: www.dyslexiabooks.biz

Enquiries to: Director
Direct e-mail: petercongdon@blueyonder.co.uk

Founded: 1978

Organisation type and purpose: Suitable for ages: all, consultancy, publishing house. The primary purpose of the Centre is to disseminate advice and information on the subject of specific learning difficulties/dyslexia.

Subject coverage: Gifted children, dyslexic children and adults, left-handed children and adults.

Education services: Assessment of children and adults suffering from dyslexia, dyspraxia, ADHD, Asperger Syndrome.

Publications: Printed
Order printed publications from: GCIC, 21 Hampton Lane, Solihull, B91 2QJ

Publications list: Available online and in print

Access to staff: Contact by letter, by telephone, by e-mail, in person and via website. Appointment necessary.
Hours: Mon to Fri, 0900 to 1700

Connections with: Gifted Children's Information Centre; at the main address

DYSLEXIA SCOTLAND (DS)

Stirling Business Centre, Wellgreen, Stirling, FK8 2DZ

Tel: 01786 446650
Fax: 01786 471235
E-mail: info@dyslexiascotland.org.uk
Website: www.dyslexiascotland.org.uk

Enquiries to: Administrator
Direct e-mail: sharon@dyslexiascotland.org.uk

Founded: 1981

Organisation type and purpose: National organisation, voluntary organisation, registered charity (charity number SCO 00951).

Subject coverage: All aspects of dyslexia and its related difficulties.

Publications: Printed

Publications list: Available in print

Access to staff: Contact by letter, by telephone, by fax and by e-mail. Appointment necessary.
Hours: Helpline: Mon to Fri, 1000 to 1600

Branches: a wide number of locations throughout Scotland

DYSTONIA SOCIETY

2nd Floor, 89 Albert Embankment, London, SE1 7TP

Tel: 0845 458 6211
Fax: 0845 458 6311
E-mail: info@dystonia.org.uk
Website: www.dystonia.org.uk

Enquiries to: Helpline
Direct tel: 0845 458 6322

Founded: 1983

Organisation type and purpose: Membership association (membership is by subscription), present number of members: 3,627, registered charity (charity number 1062595).
The Dystonia Society exists to support people who are affected by any form of the neurological movement disorder known as dystonia, and their families and carers, through the promotion of awareness, research and support and information.

Subject coverage: Neurological disorders known as the dystonias; methods of treatment and care; research to find a cure.

Services for disabled people: Helpline, support and information for those affected by dystonia.

Publications: Printed, and electronic and video

Publications list: Available online and in print

Access to staff: Contact by letter, by telephone, by fax, by e-mail, in person and via website. Appointment necessary.
Hours: Mon to Fri, 0900 to 1700;
Answerphone operates at other times
Access to Helpline: Mon to Fri, 1000 to 1600

Access to building: Via main reception, 24 hours

Links with: Dystonia Medical Research Foundation, USA; tel: +1 312 755 0198; website: http://www.dystonia-foundation.org
Parkinson's Disease Society; tel: 020 7931 8080; fax: 020 7233 5373

E F BENSON SOCIETY

Allan Downend, The Old Coach House, High Street, Rye, East Sussex, TN31 7JF

Tel: 01797 223114
E-mail: info@efbensonsociety.org
Website: www.efbensonsociety.org

Enquiries to: Secretary

Founded: 1985

Organisation type and purpose: Literary society.

Subject coverage: E. F. Benson and the Benson Family.

Education services: Talks and exhibitions can be arranged.

Publications: Printed
Order printed publications from: The Secretary

Publications list: Available online and in print

Access to staff: Contact by letter, by telephone, by e-mail and via website. Appointment necessary. Access for members only.
Hours: Sun to Sat, 0900 to 1700

E2V TECHNOLOGIES (UK) LTD

Waterhouse Lane, Chelmsford, Essex, CM1 2QU

Tel: 01245 493493 ext. 3320
Fax: 01245 45341
E-mail: doug.spencer@e2v.com
Website: www.e2v.com

Enquiries to: Information Specialist

Founded: 1946; formerly called English Electric Valve Co Ltd (year of change 1999); formerly called Marconi Applied Technologies (year of change 2002)

Organisation type and purpose: Manufacturing industry.

Subject coverage: Microwave technology, CCD & CMOS sensors, magnetrons, thyratrons, spark gaps, modulators and power supplies.

Collection: Company library

Non-library collection catalogue: All or part available in-house

Library catalogue: All or part available in-house

Access to staff: Contact by telephone and by e-mail. Appointment necessary.
Hours: Mon to Fri, 0800 to 1600

Access to building: Prior appointment required

Access for disabled people: Parking provided, ramped entry

EALING LIBRARY AND INFORMATION SERVICE

Ealing Central Library, 103 Ealing Broadway Centre, London, W5 5JY

Tel: 020 8825 9278
E-mail: libuser@ealing.gov.uk
Website: www.ealing.gov.uk/libraries

Enquiries to: Manager

Founded: 1965

Organisation type and purpose: Local government body, public library.

Services for disabled people: The home library service will deliver books to your home every month if you are unable to visit your local library due to an illness, disability or if you are elderly.

Collection: Selborne Society Library (Gilbert White's work)

Non-library collection catalogue: All or part available in-house

Library catalogue: All or part available online and in-house

Publications: Printed

Access to staff: Contact by letter, by telephone, by e-mail and in person

Access for disabled people: Level entry, access to all public areas

Branch libraries: Acton, Southall, Greenford and West Ealing and seven Community Libraries

EALING, HAMMERSMITH AND WEST LONDON COLLEGE (EHWLC)

Hammersmith Campus, Learning Centre, Gliddon Road, London, W14 9BL

Tel: 0207 565 1339
E-mail: library@wlc.ac.uk
Website: www.wlc.ac.uk

Enquiries to: Learning Centre Manager

Organisation type and purpose: College of further education.

Subject coverage: Art & design, beauty & holistic therapies, business, construction, engineering, ESOL, hairdressing, health, care & early years, hospitality & catering, information technology, media, performing arts, public services, science, sport, travel, leisure & tourism.

Library catalogue: All or part available online

Access to staff: Contact by letter, by telephone and by e-mail
Hours: Mon to Thu, 0800 to 2030; Fri, 0800 to 1800; Sat, 1000 to 1600

Also at: Acton Campus; Gunnersbury Lane, Acton, London, W3 8UX; tel: 020 8231 6344; Ealing Campus; The Green, Ealing, W5 5EW; tel: 020 8231 6037; Southall Campus; Beaconsfield Road, Southall, Middlesex, UB1 1DP; tel: 020 8231 6142

EAR INSTITUTE & RNID LIBRARIES (ILO)

Royal National Throat Nose and Ear Hospital, 330 Gray's Inn Road, London, WC1X 8EE

Tel: 020 7915 1445
E-mail: rnidlib@ucl.ac.uk
Website: www.ucl.ac.uk/library/rnidlib.shtml

Enquiries to: Librarian

Founded: 1946

Organisation type and purpose: University library. The UCL Ear Institute and RNID Libraries are a collaborative venture between UCL, RNID and the NHS. The libraries are based at the Royal National Throat Nose & Ear Hospital (RNTNEH) and together constitute the largest specialist collection for audiology, deaf studies, and ear, nose and throat (ENT) or otorhinolaryngolgic (ORL) medicine in Europe.
As well as providing services to staff and students at UCL, RNID, and the Royal Free Hampstead NHS Trust, the libraries are open to the public and provide reference and enquiry services to anybody conducting research connected with ENT medicine, hearing or deafness.

Subject coverage: Otorhinolaryngology, audiology, medical research, facial plastic surgery; deafness & deaf history.

Collection: Historical works on otorhinolaryngology, deaf history & related topics

Library catalogue: All or part available online

Publications: Printed

Access to staff: Contact by letter, by telephone, by fax, by e-mail, in person and via website. Appointment necessary.
Hours: Mon, Tue, 0900 to 1900; Wed to Fri, 0900 to 1730

Access for disabled people: Arrange in advance
Special comments: No wheelchair access.

Constituent part of: Royal Free and University College Medical School; University College London Library Services

EARLY EDUCATION

Formal name: British Association for Early Childhood Education

136 Cavell Street, London, E1 2JA

Tel: 020 7539 5400
Fax: 020 7539 5409
E-mail: office@early-education.org.uk
Website: www.early-education.org.uk

Enquiries to: Chief Executive

Founded: 1923; formerly called Nursery Schools Association (year of change 1974)

Organisation type and purpose:
Membership association (membership is by subscription), present number of members: 7,000, voluntary organisation, registered charity (charity number 313082), suitable for ages: 0 to 8.
Promotes the right of all children to an education of the highest quality. Provides a multi-disciplinary network of support for all concerned with the education and care of young children.

Subject coverage: Information regarding the care and early childhood education of children of up to 8 years.

Collection: Books concerning early childhood education

Library catalogue: All or part available in-house

Order printed publications from: Website

Publications list: Available online and in print

Access to staff: Contact by letter, by telephone, by fax and by e-mail. Appointment necessary.
Hours: Mon to Fri, 0900 to 1700

Access to building: Prior appointment required
Hours: Mon to Fri, 0900 to 1700

Access for disabled people: Access to all public areas, toilet facilities
Special comments: Four steps to entrance and no ramp to front door.

Member organisation of: National Children's Bureau; National Council for Voluntary Organisations; Women's National Commission; World Organization for Early Childhood Education

EARLY ENGLISH TEXT SOCIETY (EETS)

Lady Margaret Hall, Oxford, OX2 6QA

Website: www.eets.org.uk
Website: www.boydell.co.uk/eets.htm

Enquiries to: Executive Secretary
Direct e-mail: vincent.gillespie@ell.ox.ac.uk

Founded: 1864

Organisation type and purpose: Learned society (membership is by subscription), present number of members: 1,034.

Subject coverage: Publications of English texts earlier than 1558; medieval studies, especially the history of English language and literature, medieval theology and sociology, medieval history.

Publications: Printed
Order printed publications from: Oxford University Press, Saxon Way West, Corby, Northamptonshire, NN18 9ES (for publications from 2006)
Boydell & Brewer, PO Box 9, Woodbridge, Suffolk, IP12 3DF (for publications up to 2006)

Publications list: Available online and in print

Access to staff: Contact by letter and by e-mail
Hours: Mon to Fri, 0900 to 1700

EARLY MUSIC NETWORK (EMN)

31 Abdale Road, London, W12 7ER

Founded: 1972; formerly called Early Music Centre (EMC) (year of change 1996)

EARLY YEARS – THE ORGANISATION FOR YOUNG CHILDREN

6C Wildflower Way, Belfast, BT12 6TA

Tel: 028 9066 2825
Fax: 028 9038 1270
E-mail: info@early-years.org
Website: www.early-years.org

Enquiries to: Information Officer
Direct tel: 028 9038 7935

Founded: 1965

Organisation type and purpose:
Membership association (membership is by subscription), present number of members: c. 900, voluntary organisation, registered charity, suitable for ages: up to 12, training organisation.

Subject coverage: Information about early childhood, care and education.

Library catalogue: All or part available online

Publications: Printed

Publications list: Available online and in print

Access to staff: Contact by telephone, by e-mail, in person and via website
Hours: Mon to Fri, 0900 to 1700

Access for disabled people: Parking provided, level entry, access to all public areas, toilet facilities

EARTH SCIENCE TEACHERS' ASSOCIATION (ESTA)

E-mail: contact@esta-uk.net
Website: www.esta-uk.net

Enquiries to: Chairman

Founded: 1967

Organisation type and purpose:
Membership association (membership is by subscription), present number of members: 700, voluntary organisation, registered charity (charity number 1005331).
To encourage and support the teaching of earth sciences at all levels, whether as a single subject or as part of science or geography courses.

Subject coverage: Geology, education, earth science.

Publications: Printed

Access to staff: Contact by e-mail and via website

Constituent bodies: 8 Committees

EAST ASIAN HISTORY OF SCIENCE LIBRARY

8 Sylvester Road, Cambridge, CB3 9AF

Tel: 01223 311545
Fax: 01223 362703
E-mail: jm10019@cam.ac.uk
Website: www.nri.org.uk/library.html

Enquiries to: Librarian

Founded: 1976

Organisation type and purpose: Registered charity.
Private research institute and library.

Subject coverage: History of traditional Chinese science, technology and medicine.

Collection: Based on personal collection of Dr Joseph Needham

Non-library collection catalogue: All or part available online and in-house

Library catalogue: All or part available online

Publications: Printed

Access to staff: Contact by letter, by telephone, by fax, by e-mail and via website. Appointment necessary.
Hours: Mon to Fri, 0900 to 1700

Access for disabled people: Parking provided, level entry, access to all public areas, toilet facilities

EAST AYRSHIRE COUNCIL

Council Headquarters, London Road, Kilmarnock, Ayrshire, KA3 7BU

Tel: 01563 576000
Fax: 01563 576500
E-mail: the.council@east-ayrshire.gov.uk
Website: www.east-ayrshire.gov.uk

Enquiries to: Head of Public Relations and Marketing
Direct tel: 01563 576135
Direct fax: 01563 576068

Founded: 1996; formerly called Cumnock and Doon Valley District Council, Kilmarnock and Loudoun District Council; formerly part of Strathclyde Regional Council

Organisation type and purpose: Local government body.
Public relations and marketing.

Subject coverage: Services and amenities; corporate services, education, environmental services, finance, housing, legal services, personnel services, planning development and tourism, property and technical services, roads and transportation, social services, council tax and other payments, registration of births, deaths and marriages.

Access to staff: Contact by letter, by telephone, by fax, by e-mail and via website
Hours: Mon to Thu, 0900 to 1700; Fri, 0900 to 1600

EAST AYRSHIRE LIBRARY, REGISTRATION AND INFORMATION SERVICES (EALRIS)

Headquarters (North), Dick Institute, 14 Elmbank Avenue, Kilmarnock, Ayrshire, KA1 3BU

Tel: 01563 554300
Fax: 01563 554311
E-mail: libraries@east-ayrshire.gov.uk
Website: www.east-ayrshire.gov.uk/thelibrary

Enquiries to: Library, Registration and Information Services Manager
Direct e-mail: gerald.cairns@east-ayrshire.gov.uk

Founded: 1901; created by the merger of Cumnock and Doon Valley District Libraries, Kilmarnock and Loudoun District Libraries (year of change 1996); formerly called East Ayrshire Library and Information Services (EALIS)

Organisation type and purpose: Local government body, public library.

Subject coverage: General, Robert Burns, Ayrshire history and place names, genealogy, archaeological and historical sites, remains and monuments in South-West Scotland.

Services for disabled people: ICT training in JAWS software.

Collection: Braidwood Collection of incunabula and early printed books
Hutton Collection of early printed Bibles
Papers of the Boyd Family, the Earls of Kilmarnock
Robert Burns Collection

Library catalogue: All or part available online and in-house

Publications: Printed

Publications list: Available online and in print

Access to staff: Contact by letter, by telephone, by fax, by e-mail, in person and via website

Access to building: *Hours:* Mon, Tue, Thu and Fri, 0900 to 2000; Wed, 1000 to 1700; Sat, 0900 to 1700;
other libraries vary, telephone for times

Access for disabled people: Parking provided, ramped entry, access to all public areas, toilet facilities

Also at: Council Offices; Library Headquarters (South), Lugar, Cumnock, KA18 3JQ; tel: 01563 555459; e-mail: libraries@east-ayrshire.gov.uk

Branch libraries: Auchinleck; Community Centre, Well Road, Auchinleck, KA18 2LA; tel: 01209 422829; e-mail: libraries@east-ayrshire.gov.uk; Bellfield; 79 Whatriggs Road, Kilmarnock, KA1 3RB; tel: 01563 534266; e-mail: libraries@east-ayrshire.gov.uk; Catrine; A. M. Brown Institute, Catrine, KA5 6RT; tel: 01290 551717; e-mail: libraries@east-ayrshire.gov.uk; Crosshouse; Crosshouse Area Centre, Annandale Gardens, Crosshouse, KA2 0LE; tel: 01563 503290; e-mail: libraries@east-ayrshire.gov.uk; Cumnock; 25–27 Ayr Road, Cumnock, KA18 1EB; tel: 01290 422804; e-mail: libraries@east-ayrshire.gov.uk; Dalmellington; Townhead, Dalmellington, KA6 7QZ; tel: 01292 550159; e-mail: libraries@east-ayrshire.gov.uk; Dalrymple; Barbieston Road, Dalrymple, KA6 6DZ; tel: 01292 560511; e-mail: libraries@east-ayrshire.gov.uk; Darvel; Town Hall, West Main Street, Darvel, KA17 0AQ; tel: 01560 322754; e-mail: libraries@east-ayrshire.gov.uk; Drongan; Mill O'Shield Road, Drongan, KA6 7AY; tel: 01292 591718; e-mail: libraries@east-ayrshire.gov.uk; Galston; Henrietta Street, Galston, KA4 8HQ; tel: 01563 821994; e-mail: libraries@east-ayrshire.gov.uk; Hurlford; Blair Road, Hurlford, KA1 5BN; tel: 01563 539899; e-mail: libraries@east-ayrshire.gov.uk; Kilmaurs; Irvine Road, Kilmaurs, KA3 2RJ; tel: 01563 539895; e-mail: libraries@east-ayrshire.gov.uk; Mauchline; 2 The Cross, Mauchline, KA5 5DA; tel: 01290 550824; e-mail: libraries@east-ayrshire.gov.uk; Muirkirk; Burns Avenue, Muirkirk, KA18 3RQ; tel: 01290 661505; e-mail: libraries@east-ayrshire.gov.uk; New Cumnock; Community Centre, The Castle, New Cumnock, KA18 4AH; tel: 01290 338710; e-mail: libraries@east-ayrshire.gov.uk; Newmilns; Craigview Road, Newmilns, KA16 9DQ; tel: 01560 322890; e-mail: libraries@east-ayrshire.gov.uk; Ochiltree; Main Street, Ochiltree, KA18 2PE; tel: 01290 700425; e-mail: libraries@east-ayrshire.gov.uk; Patna; Doonside Avenue, Patna, KA6 7LX; tel: 01292 531538; e-mail: libraries@east-ayrshire.gov.uk; Stewarton; Stewarton Area Centre, Avenue Street, Stewarton, KA3 5AP; tel: 01563 553670; e-mail: libraries@east-ayrshire.gov.uk

Constituent bodies: Burns Monument Centre; Kay Park; tel: 01563 553655; e-mail: libraries@east-ayrshire.gov.uk; website: http://www.burnsmonumentcentre.co.uk

Parent body: East Ayrshire Council (EAC); Council HQ, London Road, Kilmarnock, KA1 5BU; tel: 01563 576000; fax: 01563 576500; website: http://www.east-ayrshire.gov.uk

EAST CAMBRIDGESHIRE DISTRICT COUNCIL (ECDC)

The Grange, Nutholt Lane, Ely, Cambridgeshire, CB7 4PL

Tel: 01353 665555
Fax: 01353 665240
E-mail: info@eastcambs.gov.uk
Website: www.eastcambs.gov.uk

Enquiries to: Chief Executive
Other contacts: Press and PR Officer for corporate communication.

Founded: 1974

Organisation type and purpose: Local government body.

Subject coverage: Many subjects relating to East Cambridgeshire district, including Ely, Soham and Littleport. Information about projects both economic and community based, new initiatives and all aspects of tourism.

Non-library collection catalogue: All or part available online

Publications: Printed

Access to staff: Contact by letter, by telephone, by fax and by e-mail. Appointment necessary.
Hours: Mon to Thu, 0845 to 1700; Fri, 0845 to 1630

Access for disabled people: Level entry, toilet facilities

EAST DORSET DISTRICT COUNCIL (EDDC)

Council Offices, Furzehill, Wimborne, Dorset, BH21 4HN

Tel: 01202 886201
Fax: 01202 841390
Website: www.eastdorset.gov.uk/tourism
Website: www.eastdorset.gov.uk

Enquiries to: Public Relations Manager
Direct tel: ext 2289
Direct e-mail: chief.exec@eastdorset.gov.uk

Organisation type and purpose: Local government body.

Subject coverage: Local government, elections and elected members, electoral roll, environmental health, planning, council tax and housing benefit, recycling and refuse collection, tourism, local plan and grants.

Access for disabled people: Parking provided, ramped entry, toilet facilities

EAST DUNBARTONSHIRE LEISURE & CULTURAL SERVICES

Library Headquarters, William Patrick Library, 2–4 West High Street, Kirkintilloch, Glasgow, G66 1AD

Tel: 0141 777 3143
Fax: 0141 777 3140
E-mail: libraries@eastdunbarton.gov.uk
Website: www.eastdunbarton.gov.uk

Enquiries to: Leisure & Cultural Services Manager
Direct e-mail: mark.grant@eastdunbarton.gov.uk

Founded: 1996; created by the merger of Bearsden and Milngavie District Libraries, Strathkelvin District Libraries (year of change 1996)

Organisation type and purpose: Local government body; public library service.

Subject coverage: Local history of Dunbartonshire, Stirlingshire, Lanarkshire and Glasgow; community and government information; leisure, educational and cultural; learning and outreach.

Collection: Archives of East Dunbartonshire Council and its predecessor authorities, including the former Burghs of Kirkintilloch, Milngavie, Bearsden and Bishopbriggs, the parishes of Baldernock, Cadder, Campsie, Kirkintilloch and New Kilpatrick, and Strathkelvin District Council and Bearsden and Milngavie District Council; also, deposited collections of businesses, organisations and individuals within East Dunbartonshire, including J. F. McEwan Transport History Collection, Lion Foundry Co. Ltd., J. & J. Hay Boatbuilders and Glasgow Garden Suburb Tenants Ltd.

Non-library collection catalogue: All or part available online

Library catalogue: All or part available online

continued overleaf

Publications: Printed, and microform publications

Publications list: Available online and in print

Access to staff: Contact by letter, by telephone, by fax, by e-mail, in person and via website
Hours: Mon to Fri, 0900 to 1700

Access to building: No prior appointment required
Hours: Bishopbriggs, Brookwood, Milngavie, William Patrick Libraries: Mon to Thu, 1000 to 2000; Fri and Sat, 1000 to 1700
Lennoxtown, Lenzie, Milton of Campsie, Westerton Libraries: Mon and Thu, 1300 to 2000; Tue, Wed and Fri, 1000 to 1700

Access for disabled people: Parking provided, ramped entry, level entry, access to all public areas, toilet facilities

Branch libraries: Bishopbriggs Library; 170 Kirkintilloch Road, Bishopbriggs, G64 2LX; tel: 0141 772 4513; fax: 0141 762 5363; Brookwood Library, Bearsden; 166 Drymen Road, Bearsden, G61 3RJ; tel: 0141 777 3021; fax: 0141 777 3022; Lennoxtown Library; 31 Main Street, Lennoxtown, G65 7HA; tel: 01360 311436; fax: 01360 311436; Lenzie Library; 13 Alexandra Avenue, Lenzie, G66 5BG; tel: 0141 776 3021; Milngavie Library; Milngavie Community Education Centre, Allander Road, Milngavie, G62 8PN; tel: 0141 956 2776; fax: 0141 956 2776; Milton of Campsie Library; School Lane, Milton of Campsie, G66 8DL; tel: 01360 311925; Westerton Library; 82 Maxwell Avenue, Westerton, Bearsden, G61 1NZ; tel: 0141 943 0780; fax: 0141 943 0780; William Patrick Library; 2–4 West High Street, Kirkintilloch, G66 1AD; tel: 0141 777 3141; fax: 0141 777 3140

EAST DURHAM COLLEGE (EDC)

Houghall Centre, Durham, DH1 3SG

Tel: 0191 375 4710; 0191 375 4756
Fax: 0191 3860419
E-mail: enquiry@edhcc.ac.uk
Website: www.eastdurham.ac.uk

Enquiries to: Learning Resources Manager
Direct e-mail: jill.forbes@eastdurham.ac.uk

Founded: 1999; created by the merger of Durham College of Agriculture and Horticulture, East Durham Community College (year of change 1999); formerly called Houghall College

Organisation type and purpose: Vocational, further and higher education.

Subject coverage: Agriculture, horticulture, equestrianism, arboriculture, environmental management, small animal care.

Library catalogue: All or part available in-house

Access to staff: Contact by letter, by telephone, by fax and by e-mail
Hours: Mon to Thu, 0900 to 2000; Fri, 0900 to 1600

Access to building: No access other than to staff

Access for disabled people: Parking provided, ramped entry, toilet facilities

EAST ENGLAND ARTS

Eden House, 48–49 Bateman Street, Cambridge, CB2 1LR

Tel: 01223 454400, 01223 306893 (minicom)
Fax: 0870 242 1271
Website: www.eastenglandarts.co.uk
Website: www.axisartists.org.uk

Enquiries to: Helpdesk

History of institution: formed with Arts Council of England and the other Regional Arts Boards (year of change 2002); formerly called Eastern Arts Board

Organisation type and purpose: Service industry, registered charity (charity number 1036733).
On 1 April 2002, East England Arts joined with the Arts Council of England and the other regional arts boards to form a single development organisation for the arts.
East England Arts is the government arts and culture development agency for the East of England.

Subject coverage: Arts funding, including National Lottery, design, dance, mime and new circus, theatre and puppetry, literature, music, new media, visual arts, regeneration, audience development.

Publications: Printed

Publications list: Available in print

Access to staff: Contact by letter, by telephone, by fax, by e-mail and via website
Hours: Mon to Fri, 0900 to 1700

Access to building: Prior appointment required
Hours: Mon to Fri, 0900 to 1700

Access for disabled people: Parking provided, ramped entry, access to all public areas, toilet facilities. Lift/elevator access.

EAST HAMPSHIRE DISTRICT COUNCIL (EHDC)

Penns Place, Petersfield, Hampshire, GU31 4EX

Tel: 01730 266551; 01730 234103 (minicom)
Fax: 01730 267760
E-mail: info@easthants.gov.uk
Website: www.easthants.gov.uk

Enquiries to: Chief Executive

Founded: 1974

Organisation type and purpose: Local government body.

Subject coverage: East Hampshire demographic and environmental information, council service information: planning, council tax, housing, refuse collection and recycling, benefits, tourism and leisure, grants for community groups, animal welfare, countryside, environmental health, business information and advice, and local democracy.

Publications: Printed

Publications list: Available online and in print

Access to staff: Contact by letter, by telephone, by fax, by e-mail, in person and via website
Hours: Mon to Fri, 0900 to 1700

Access to building: No prior appointment required

Access for disabled people: Parking provided, ramped entry

EAST HERTFORDSHIRE DISTRICT COUNCIL (EHDC)

Wallfields, Pegs Lane, Hertford, SG13 8EQ

Tel: 01279 655261, 01279 658512 (minicom)
Fax: 01992 552280
E-mail: enquiries@eastherts.gov.uk
Website: www.eastherts.gov.uk

Enquiries to: Public Relations Manager
Direct tel: 01279 655261 ext 449
Direct fax: 01992 505710
Other contacts: Chief Executive for complaints.

Founded: 1974

Organisation type and purpose: Local government body.

Subject coverage: Local government services.

Access to staff: Contact by letter, by telephone, by fax and by e-mail. Appointment necessary.
Hours: Mon to Fri, 0830 to 1700

Other addresses: Council Offices; The Causeway, Bishop's Stortford, Hertfordshire, CM23 2EN; tel: 01279 655261; e-mail: ce@ehdc.gov.uk

EAST HERTS ARCHAEOLOGICAL SOCIETY (EHAS)

41 St Leonard's Road, Bengeo, Hertford, Hertfordshire, SG14 3JW

Tel: 01992 423725
E-mail: ehasoc@googlemail.com
Website: www.ehas.org.uk

Enquiries to: Honorary Secretary

Founded: 1898

Organisation type and purpose: Learned society (membership is by subscription), present number of members: 86, registered charity (charity number 257254).

Subject coverage: Archaeological, architectural information, local history in Eastern Hertfordshire.

Library catalogue: All or part available in-house

Publications: Printed

Access to staff: Contact by letter, by telephone, by e-mail and via website
Hours: Mon to Fri, 0900 to 1700
Special comments: Membership: adult £10, family £12 a year.

Member of: Council for British Archaeology; Hertfordshire Archaeological Council; Hertfordshire Archaeological Trust

EAST KENT ARCHIVES CENTRE (EKAC)

Enterprise Zone, Honeywood Road, Whitfield, Dover, Kent, CT16 3EH

Tel: 01304 829306
Fax: 01304 820783
E-mail: eastkentarchives@kent.gov.uk

Website: www.kent.gov.uk/archives

Enquiries to: Manager

Founded: 2000; formerly called South East Area Office, Folkestone Library (year of change 1999); formerly called Thanet Branch Archives, Ramsgate Library (year of change 1999)

Organisation type and purpose: Local government body.
Archive service.

Subject coverage: Archives relating to Thanet, Dover and Shepway District Council areas, except Church of England and civil registration records.

Collection: Local government, hospital, family and estate and nonconformist records
Business, schools, shipping registers

Non-library collection catalogue: All or part available online and in-house

Access to staff: Contact by letter, by telephone, by e-mail and in person. Appointment necessary.
Hours: Tue, Wed, Thu, 0900 to 1700

Access for disabled people: Free parking provided, ramped entry, access to all public areas including toilet facilities

Also at: Centre for Kentish Studies (CKS); Sessions House, County Hall, Maidstone, ME14 1XQ; tel: 01622 694363; e-mail: archives@kent.gov.uk

Links with: Kent County Council

EAST LANCASHIRE CHAMBER OF INDUSTRY AND COMMERCE

Red Rose Court, Clayton Business Park, Clayton-le-Moors, Accrington, Lancashire, BB5 5JR

Tel: 01254 356400
Fax: 01254 388900
E-mail: info@chamberelancs.co.uk
Website: www.chamberelancs.co.uk
Website: www.chamberinternet.co.uk

Enquiries to: Chief Executive

History of institution: formerly called Blackburn Chamber of Commerce and Industry

Organisation type and purpose: Membership association.
Chamber of Commerce.

Subject coverage: Export and import information; general business advice; business expansion; sources of finance and grants.

Publications: Printed

EAST LOTHIAN ANTIQUARIAN AND FIELD NATURALISTS SOCIETY (ELFNSoc)

Inchgarth, East Links, Dunbar, East Lothian, EH42 1LT

Tel: 01368 863335
E-mail: s.bunyan@yahoo.co.uk
Website: eastlothianantiquarians.org.uk/site

Enquiries to: President
Other contacts: The Editor, for publications and transactions.

Founded: 1924

Organisation type and purpose: Learned society (membership is by subscription), present number of members: c. 200, voluntary organisation. Stimulates and develops knowledge and awareness of the history and natural history of East Lothian.

Subject coverage: East Lothian antiquities, local architecture, history and natural history, flora and fauna.

Collection: Local history books
Pictures of local interest (in the care of East Lothian Council Library and Museums Service)
Society's Transactions

Publications: Printed
Order printed publications from: S. A. Bunyan

Publications list: Available in print

Access to staff: Contact by letter, by telephone and by e-mail
Hours: Mon to Fri, 0900 to 1700
Special comments: Telephone calls may only get through to an answerphone.

EAST LOTHIAN COUNCIL

John Muir House, Haddington, East Lothian, EH41 3HA

Tel: 01620 827827
Fax: 01620 827888
Website: www.eastlothian.gov.uk

Enquiries to: Corporate Communications Manager
Direct tel: 01620 827655
Direct fax: 01620 827442

Founded: 1996; formerly called East Lothian District Council, Lothian Regional Council

Organisation type and purpose: Local government body.

Subject coverage: All matters relating to local government; law and administration, policy and performance, property, personnel, finance, information technology, community services, building design direct, mechanised services, leisure and amenity services, libraries, education, social services and housing, environmental services.

Publications: Printed

Access to staff: Contact by letter, by telephone, by fax and by e-mail
Hours: Mon to Thu, 0900 to 1700; Fri, 0900 to 1600

Access for disabled people: Parking provided, level entry, toilet facilities

EAST LOTHIAN COUNCIL LIBRARY SERVICE

Library and Museum Headquarters, Dunbar Road, Haddington, East Lothian, EH41 3PJ

Tel: 01620 828200
Fax: 01620 828201
E-mail: jstevenson@eastlothian.gov.uk
Website: www.eastlothian.gov.uk

Enquiries to: Librarian
Direct tel: 01620 823307
Direct e-mail: localhistory@eastlothian.gov.uk
Other contacts: Senior Librarian: Local History & Promotions

Founded: 1996

Organisation type and purpose: Local government body, public library.

Subject coverage: General; local history and genealogy for the County of East Lothian, previously Haddingtonshire and Inveresk (Musselburgh).

Services for disabled people: Wi-Fi provided whether building is open or closed. Staff will assist downstairs with information or books that are portable. Assistance will be given with genealogy enquiries, which can also be handled by e-mail or post. Please contact 01620 823307 for details.

Collection: Library of the East Lothian Antiquarian and Field Naturalists Society, Latto Collection on Musselburgh, Gordon photograph collection
Local history collection (at the Local History Centre, Haddington Library, Newtonport, Haddington)

Non-library collection catalogue: All or part available online

Library catalogue: All or part available online

Publications: Printed
Order printed publications from: East Lothian, Library & Museum HQ, Dunbar Road, Haddington, EH41 3PJ; e-mail: jstevenson@eastlothian.gov.uk

Publications list: Available online

Access to staff: Contact by letter, by telephone, by e-mail, in person and via website
Hours: Mon to Fri, 0930 to 1700

Access for disabled people: Public parking nearby, level entry, access to public areas, toilet facilities, except Local History Centre

EAST MALLING RESEARCH (EMR)

New Road, East Malling, Kent, ME19 6BJ

Tel: 01732 843833
Fax: 01732 849067
E-mail: enquiries@emr.ac.uk
Website: www.eastmallingresearch.com

Enquiries to: Information Officer

Founded: 1913

Organisation type and purpose: Independent company, professional body, registered charity (charity number 211581), research organisation.
Research on fruit and other perennial crops including hardy nursery stock, farm woodland and hops.

Subject coverage: Horticulture, particularly temperate fruit culture, forestry, woody ornamentals, hops, related plant science, particularly plant physiology, plant pathology, entomology, biochemistry, IPDM, postharvest storage and quality of horticultural crops.

Collection: Cherry gene database
European apple inventory
Historical books on fruit breeding and horticulture
Index of graft transmittable diseases

Non-library collection catalogue: All or part available in-house

Library catalogue: All or part available in-house

continued overleaf

Access to staff: Contact by telephone and by e-mail. Appointment necessary.
Hours: Mon to Fri, 0900 to 1700

Access to building: Prior appointment required
Special comments: Open to members of the East Malling Research Association.

EAST MIDLANDS MUSEUMS SERVICE (EMMS)

Centre for Museum and Heritage Management, Nottingham Trent University, Clifton Lane, Nottingham, NG11 8NS

Tel: 0115 848 3562
E-mail: emms@emms.org.uk
Website: www.emms.org.uk

Enquiries to: Executive Director
Direct tel: 0115 848 3572
Other contacts: Administrator

Founded: 1981

Organisation type and purpose: Regional museum network (membership is by subscription), present number of members: 112 (local authorities, independent museums, universities, national bodies and individuals), registered charity (charity number 1009683).
Offers support, communication, networking, training, consultancy. Aims to enhance and improve standards in care and public use of museum collections in the East Midlands.

Subject coverage: Museum management, organisation and practice, museum collections in the East Midlands, collections care, training and advice, Regional Emergencies and Disaster Support Service (prevention, preparedness, reaction and recovery).

Information services: Advice and information relating to museums in the East Midlands
Regional Emergency and Disaster Support (REDS) Service.

Publications: Printed, and electronic and video

Publications list: Available online

Access to staff: Contact by letter, by telephone, by fax, by e-mail, in person and via website. Appointment necessary. Non-members charged.
Hours: Variable

Access to building: By appointment
Hours: University opening hours

Access for disabled people: No restrictions

EAST MIDLANDS ORAL HISTORY ARCHIVE (EMOHA)

Centre for Urban History, University of Leicester, LE1 7RH

Tel: 0116 252 5065
Fax: 0116 252 5769
E-mail: emoha@le.ac.uk
Website: www.le.ac.uk/emoha

Organisation type and purpose: A partnership between the University of Leicester's Centre for Urban History, Leicestershire County Council and Leicester City Museums and Library Services.

Subject coverage: Oral history of the East Midlands (Leicestershire and Rutland).

Collection: Among the Archive's resources are the collections of the former Leicester Oral History Archive, the Mantle Archive from north-west Leicestershire, the Community History archive of Leicester City Libraries and the sound archive of BBC Radio Leicester

Access to building: The Archive is housed on the University of Leicester's satellite campus, at 1 Salisbury Road, Leicester, LE1 7QR

EAST NORTHAMPTONSHIRE COUNCIL

East Northamptonshire House, Cedar Drive, Thrapston, Kettering, Northamptonshire, NN14 4LZ

Tel: 01832 742000
Fax: 01832 734839
Website: www.east-northamptonshire.gov.uk

Founded: 1974

Organisation type and purpose: Local government body.

Subject coverage: Local government services, economic development, tourism.

Access to staff: Contact by letter and by telephone
Hours: Mon to Fri, 0900 to 1700

Other office at: Rushden Centre (One Stop Shop); Newton Road, Rushden, Northamptonshire, NN10 0PT; tel: 01933 412000; fax: 01933 410564

EAST OF ENGLAND TOURISM (EET)

Formal name: East of England Tourist Board

Dettingen House, Dettingen Way, Bury St Edmunds, Suffolk, IP33 3TU

Tel: 01284 727470
Fax: 01284 706657
E-mail: info@eet.org.uk
Website: www.visiteadtofengland.com
Website: www.eet.org.uk

Founded: 1972; formerly called East Anglia Tourist Board (year of change 1996); formerly called East of England Tourist Board (year of change 2007)

Organisation type and purpose: Promotion of sustainable tourism throughout the East of England.

Subject coverage: Tourism in Bedfordshire, Cambridgeshire, Essex, Hertfordshire, Norfolk and Suffolk. Information on research.

Access to staff: Contact by letter, by telephone, by fax, by e-mail and via website
Hours: Mon to Fri, 0900 to 1700
Special comments: Closed Bank Holidays.

Access to building: No public access

EAST OF LONDON FAMILY HISTORY SOCIETY (EoLFHS)

23 Louvaine Avenue, Wickford, Essex, SS12 0DP

E-mail: society.secretary@eolfhs.org.uk
Website: www.eolfhs.org.uk

Enquiries to: General Secretary
Direct e-mail: society.secretary@eolfhs.org.uk

Founded: 1978

Organisation type and purpose: Membership association (membership is by subscription), present number of members: over 3,000, suitable for ages: all.
Family history society.

Subject coverage: Family history and genealogy.

Library catalogue: All or part available online

Publications: Printed
Order printed publications from: East of London Family History Society, Bookstall Manager, 68 Stanfield Road, Dagenham, RM10 8JT

Publications list: Available online

Access to staff: Contact by letter, by e-mail and via website
Hours: Mon to Fri, 0900 to 1700
Special comments: Advice only provided, no research undertaken.

Member organisation of: The Federation of Family History Societies

EAST RENFREWSHIRE COUNCIL

Council Headquarters, Eastwood Park, Giffnock, East Renfrewshire, G42 6UG

Tel: 0141 577 3000
Fax: 0141 620 0884

Enquiries to: Public Relations Manager
Direct tel: 0141 577 3851
Direct fax: 0141 577 3852
Direct e-mail: RelationsP@eastrenfrewshire.gov.uk

Founded: 1996

Organisation type and purpose: Local government body.

Subject coverage: Local government; services and amenities; corporate services, education, environmental services, finance, housing, legal services, personnel services, planning development and tourism, property and technical services, roads and transportation, social services, council tax and other payments, registration of births, death and marriages.

Publications: Printed

Access to staff: Contact by letter, by telephone, by fax and by e-mail. Appointment necessary.
Hours: Mon to Fri, 0900 to 1700

EAST RIDING ARCHIVES AND LOCAL STUDIES SERVICE (Treasure House)

County Hall, Beverley, East Yorkshire, HU17 9BA

Tel: 01482 392790
Fax: 01482 392791
E-mail: archives.service@eastriding.gov.uk
Website: www.eastriding.gov.uk

History of institution: created by the merger of East Riding Archives Service and Beverley Local Studies Library (year of change 2007)

Organisation type and purpose: Archive and local studies library.

Subject coverage: East Riding of Yorkshire local history, topography and culture.

Special visitor services: Meeting rooms available for hire.

Collection: Archive with collections of public, local government, church, family and estate and other local records
Local studies library with local studies books, pamphlets and journals, newspapers and directories

Non-library collection catalogue: All or part available online and in-house

Library catalogue: All or part available online and in-house

Publications: Printed

Access to staff: Contact by letter, by telephone, by fax, by e-mail and in person

Access to building: *Hours:* Mon, Wed, Fri, 0930 to 1700; Tue, Thu, 0930 to 2000; Sat, 0900 to 1600

Access for disabled people: Disabled access and lift access to all public parts of building

Also at: East Riding Archives and Local Studies Service; Treasure House, Champney Road, Beverley, HU17 8HE

Parent body: East Riding of Yorkshire Council

EAST RIDING OF YORKSHIRE COUNCIL (ERYC)

County Hall, Cross Street, Beverley, East Yorkshire, HU17 9BA

Tel: 01482 887700
Website: www.eastriding.gov.uk

Enquiries to: Chief Executive
Direct tel: 01482 884832

Founded: 1996

Organisation type and purpose: Local government body.

Subject coverage: All local government services.

Collection: Archives of documents collected by Humberside County Council and former East Riding County Council and former East Riding Registry of Deeds held by the East Riding of Yorkshire Council Archives and Records Service

Access to staff: Contact by letter, by telephone and by fax. Appointment necessary.
Hours: Mon to Fri, 0900 to 1700

EAST STAFFORDSHIRE BOROUGH COUNCIL

The Maltsters, Wetmore Road, Burton-on-Trent, Staffordshire, DE14 1LS

Tel: 01283 508000
Fax: 01283 35412
E-mail: reception@eaststaffsbc.gov.uk
Website: www.eaststaffsbc.gov.uk

Organisation type and purpose: Local government body.

Access to staff: Contact by letter, by telephone, by fax, by e-mail and via website
Hours: Mon to Fri, 0800 to 1700

Access for disabled people: Parking provided, level entry, toilet facilities

EAST SURREY BADGER PROTECTION SOCIETY (ESBPS)

30 Church Road, Warlingham, Surrey CR6 9NU

Tel: 01883 380321
Fax: 01883 349699
E-mail: esbps.badgers@gmail.com
Website: badger-groups.org.uk/east-surrey

Enquiries to: Honorary Secretary

Founded: 1979; formerly called Surrey Badger Protection Society (year of change 1997)

Organisation type and purpose: Registered charity (charity number 800270).

Subject coverage: Badgers.

Publications: Printed

Access to staff: Contact by letter, by telephone and by e-mail
Hours: Mon to Fri, 0900 to 1700
Special comments: Also available in evenings and at weekends in emergencies

Affiliated to the: Badger Trust

EAST SURREY FAMILY HISTORY SOCIETY

119 Keevil Drive, London, SW19 6TF

Tel: 01737 554071
E-mail: secretary@eastsurreyfhs.co.uk
Website: scorpio.gold.ac.uk/genuki/sry/esfhs

Enquiries to: Honorary Secretary

Founded: 1977

Organisation type and purpose: International organisation, membership association (membership is by subscription), present number of members: 2,000, registered charity (charity number 286659), suitable for ages: all, research organisation.

Subject coverage: Family history (genealogy) data relating to East Surrey, which includes parts of South London previously in Surrey.

Publications: Printed, and microform publications
Order printed publications from: Census Indexes and Other Publications, East Surrey Family History Society
4 Constance Road, Croydon, Surrey, CR0 2RS

Publications list: Available online and in print

Access to staff: Contact by letter and by e-mail
Hours: Mon to Fri, 0900 to 1700

EAST SUSSEX LIBRARY AND INFORMATION SERVICE

County Hall, Lewes, East Sussex, BN7 1UE

Tel: 01273 481870
Fax: 01273 481716
E-mail: anita.cundall@eastsussex.gov.uk
Website: www.eastsussex.gov.uk/libraries

Founded: 1974

Organisation type and purpose: Local government body, public library.

Library catalogue: All or part available online and in-house

Access to staff: Contact by letter, by telephone, by fax, by e-mail, in person and via website
Hours: Mon to Fri, 0900 to 1700

Group Headquarters at: Hastings, Eastbourne, Lewes, Bexhill and Uckfield

EAST SUSSEX RECORD OFFICE (ESRO)

The Maltings, Castle Precincts, Lewes, East Sussex, BN7 1YT

Tel: 01273 482349
Fax: 01273 482341
E-mail: archives@eastsussex.gov.uk
Website: www.eastsussex.gov.uk/useourarchives
Website: www.nationalarchives.gov.uk/archon
Website: www.nationalarchives.gov.uk/a2a

Founded: 1949

Organisation type and purpose: Local government body.
To preserve the documentary heritage of East Sussex, and of the Brighton and Hove Council area, and to make its resources available to the public for research. To act as a Diocesan Record Office for Chichester (East Sussex Parish records).

Subject coverage: Most aspects of the history and historical geography of East Sussex (including Brighton and Hove), its communities, people, public authorities and organisations, c. 1100 to date.

Collection: Archives of the usual local authority holdings
Deposited collections, including:
Battle Abbey Archives
Danny Archives
Frewen Archives
Hickstead Place Archives
Sheffield Park Archives concerning John Baker Holroyd, 1st Earl of Sheffield, politician and authority on commercial and agricultural topics, late 18th century
Sussex Archaeological Society records, including papers of the Gage family (American material) and the Fuller family of Rosehill (West Indian material)

Non-library collection catalogue: All or part available online and in-house

Publications: Printed, and microform publications

Publications list: Available in print

Access to staff: Contact by letter, by telephone, by fax, by e-mail, in person and via website
Hours: Mon, Tue and Thu, 0845 to 1645; Wed, 0930 to 1645; Fri, 0845 to 1615; Sat 2nd and 4th in the month (booking required), 0900 to 1300 and 1400 to 1645

continued overleaf

Special comments: Although it is not compulsory to book in advance, it is strongly recommended.

Access for disabled people: Parking provided, ramped entry
Special comments: The public search room is on the first floor and is only accessible via two flights of stairs; there are no disabled toilet facilities on site. Only one parking space, but it is bookable.

EAST YORKSHIRE FAMILY HISTORY SOCIETY (EYFHS)

Carnegie Heritage Centre, 342 Anlaby Road, Kingston upon Hull, HU3 6JA

Tel: 01482 561216
E-mail: secretary@eyfhs.org.uk
Website: www.eyfhs.org.uk
Website: www.eyreg.co.uk
Website: www.heroesofhull.co.uk

Enquiries to: Secretary

Founded: 1977

Organisation type and purpose: Membership association (membership is by subscription), present number of members: 1,700, registered charity (charity number 519743). Extensive local and family history library. Publisher of over 500 family/local history titles.

Subject coverage: Family history in East Yorkshire.

Information services: Extensive library and publications catalogue. Local archives 'look-up' service.

Special visitor services: Free family history help desks across the whole East Riding and every Monday afternoon at the Carnegie.

Education services: Various family and local history courses at the Carnegie all year round.

Services for disabled people: Full access to the Carnegie Heritage Centre (ambulant toilets only).

Non-library collection catalogue: All or part available online, in-house and in print

Library catalogue: All or part available online, in-house and in print

Publications: Printed, and electronic and video, and microform publications
Order printed publications from: The Publications Officers, East Yorkshire Family History Society, 5 Curlew Close, Molescroft, Beverley, East Yorkshire, HU17 7QN
Order microform publications from: The Publications Officers, East Yorkshire Family History Society, 5 Curlew Close, Molescroft, Beverley, East Yorkshire, HU17 7QN
Order electronic and video publications from: The Publications Officers, East Yorkshire Family History Society, 5 Curlew Close, Molescroft, Beverley, East Yorkshire, HU17 7QN

Publications list: Available online and in print

Access to staff: Contact by letter, by telephone, by e-mail, in person and via website
Hours: Mon to Fri, 0900 to 1700

Access to building: Open to the general public
Hours: Mon, 1330 to 1530; Tue and Thu, 1000 to 1600
Special comments: For details of other times and events please contact the Carnegie.

Access for disabled people: Full disabled access
Hours: No restrictions – as per public timetable
Special comments: No disabled toilet.

Branches: EYFHS Beverley; e-mail: beverley@eyfhs.org.uk; website: http://www.eyfhs.org.uk
EYFHS Bridlington; e-mail: bridlington@eyfhs.org.uk; website: http://www.eyfhs.org.uk
Scarborough; e-mail: scarborough@eyfhs.org.uk; website: http://www.eyfhs.org.uk

EASTERN AFRICA ASSOCIATION (EAA)

2 Vincent Street, London, SW1P 4LD

Tel: 020 7828 5511
Fax: 020 7828 5251
E-mail: jcsmall@eaa-lon.co.uk
Website: www.eaa-lon.co.uk

Enquiries to: Asst Company Secretary

Founded: 1964; formerly called East Africa Association (year of change 1995)

Organisation type and purpose: Trade association (membership is by subscription), present number of members: 340
To support and promote investment in Eastern Africa.

Subject coverage: Trade and investment matters in Kenya, Uganda, Tanzania, Ethiopia, Eritrea, Seychelles and Rwanda.

Publications: Printed

Access to staff: Contact by letter, by telephone, by fax, by e-mail and via website. Appointment necessary. Access for members only.
Hours: Mon to Fri, 0930 to 1730

Administered by: The Eastern Africa Association; PO Box 41272, 5th Floor, Room 512, Jubilee Place, Mama Ngina Street/ General Kago Street, Nairobi, Kenya 00100; tel: +254 20 340341; fax: +254 20 214898; e-mail: info@eaa.co.ke; website: http://www.eea-lon.co.uk
The Eastern Africa Association; Dar-es-Salaam, Tanzania; tel: +255 22 2617124; fax: +255 22 2617145; e-mail: dcrobertsontz@gmail.com; The Eastern Africa Association; Kampala, Uganda; tel: +256 752 757025; e-mail: aaslund@infocom.co.ug; The Eastern Africa Association; Kigali, Rwanda; tel: +250 575075; +250 0830 8276; e-mail: steve.caley@finabank.co.rw; The Eastern Africa Association; Addis Ababa, Ethiopia; tel: + 251 11 662 3372; +251 91 125 0745; e-mail: demissie.demissie@gmail.com

EASTLEIGH BOROUGH COUNCIL

Civic Offices, Leigh Road, Eastleigh, Hampshire, SO50 9YN

Tel: 023 8068 8000
Fax: 023 8064 3952
Website: www.eastleigh.gov.uk

Enquiries to: Chief Executive
Other contacts: Public Relations Officer

Organisation type and purpose: Local government body.

Subject coverage: Local government services.

Access to staff: Contact by letter, by telephone, by fax, by e-mail and in person. Appointment necessary.
Hours: Mon to Thu, 0830 to 1700; Fri, 0830 to 1630

Access to building: No prior appointment required

Access for disabled people: Parking provided, ramped entry, access to all public areas, toilet facilities

ECCTIS LIMITED (ECCTIS)

Oriel House, Oriel Road, Cheltenham, Gloucestershire, GL50 1XP

Tel: 0871 330 7303
Fax: 01242 258600
E-mail: info@ecctis.co.uk
Website: www.ecctis.co.uk

Enquiries to: Head of Policy and Communications
Direct tel: 01242 258616
Direct e-mail: communications@ecctis.co.uk

Founded: 1990; carries out the functions of the former ECCTIS Ltd (trading as UK NARIC) operates the NARIC service for the UK under contract from the Department of Business Innovation and Skills.
As the national agency responsible for providing information, advice and data on qualifications from overseas, it offers services to those bringing individuals into the UK to work or study. (year of change 1997); carries out the functions of the former ECCTIS Ltd is also the UK National Europass Centre (UK NEC) for the UK.
UK NEC is the national agency responsible for promoting Europass within the UK to individuals, awarding bodies, employers, education institutions and other stakeholders. The agency is jointly funded by the European Commission and the UK Department of Business, Innovation and Skills (BIS) and sits within a network of 31 other Europass Centres within the EU / EEA. Europass helps individuals highlight their abilities in an effective way. It can help to remove barriers to working, studying or training in Europe. It is free and enables people to present their competencies, skills and qualifications in a clear way. This European-wide initiative consists of five documents that help potential employers, educational establishments and training providers understand which subjects have been studied, what training has been completed or how much experience has been gained working. (year of change 2005)

Organisation type and purpose: International organisation (membership is by subscription), training organisation, consultancy, research organisation, publishing house.

Subject coverage: All award-bearing courses, from non-advanced to postgraduate level, in further and higher education throughout the UK, in colleges and universities, including standard entry requirements, course content and institutional data; non-standard entry opportunities (i.e. credit transfer).

Publications: Printed

Publications list: Available in print

Access to staff: Contact by e-mail
Hours: Mon to Fri, 0830 to 1730

Parent body: Hobsons Ltd

ECHO LANGUAGE SCHOOL (ECHO)

23 Rutland Gardens, Hove, East Sussex, BN3 5PD

Tel: 01273 202802
Fax: 01273 746464
E-mail: info@echolanguageschool.co.uk
Website: www.echolanguageschool.co.uk

Enquiries to: Information Officer
Other contacts: Director of Studies

Founded: 1989

Organisation type and purpose: Service industry, suitable for ages: 12+.
Residential language school, home tuition.

Subject coverage: English residential language courses.

Publications: Printed

Access to staff: Contact by letter, by telephone, by fax, by e-mail, in person and via website
Hours: Daily, 0800 to 2000

Access to building: No prior appointment required

ECONOMIC AND SOCIAL RESEARCH COUNCIL (ESRC)

Polaris House, North Star Avenue, Swindon, SN2 1UJ

Tel: 01793 413000
Fax: 01793 413001
Website: www.esrcsocietytoday.ac.uk

Founded: 1965; formerly called Social Science Research Council (year of change 1983)

Organisation type and purpose: An independent organisation, established by Royal Charter.
Funds research and training in social and economic issues.

Subject coverage: Provides high-quality research on issues of importance to business, the public sector and government, and is committed to training world-class social scientists; nearly two-thirds of the budget is allocated to research and just under one-third to postgraduate training.

Publications: Printed, and electronic and video
Order printed publications from: ESRC Publications, Tangent Communications, PO Box 757, Cheltenham, GL52 2YZ; tel: 01242 283100 Mon to Fri, 0900 to 1730; fax: 01242 283131; e-mail: esrc@tangentuk.com
Order electronic and video publications from: website

Publications list: Available online

Access to staff: Contact by letter, by telephone and by fax

Funded by: Department for Business, Innovation and Skills

ECONOMIC HISTORY SOCIETY

University of Glasgow, Department of Economic and Social History, Lilybank House, Bute Gardens, Glasgow, G12 8RT

Tel: 0141 330 4662
Fax: 0141 330 4889
E-mail: ehsocsec@arts.gla.ac.uk
Website: www.ehs.org.uk

Enquiries to: Honorary Secretary

Founded: 1926

Organisation type and purpose: Learned society, registered charity (charity number 228494; SCO38304).
To promote the study of economic history and to establish closer relations between students and teachers of economic and social history.

Subject coverage: Economic and social history.

Non-library collection catalogue: All or part available online and in print

Publications: Printed
Order printed publications from: e-mail: ehsocsec@arts.gla.ac.uk

Publications list: Available online and in print

Access to staff: Contact by letter, by telephone, by fax, by e-mail and via website
Hours: Mon to Fri, 0900 to 1700

ECONOMIC RESEARCH COUNCIL (ERC)

7 St James's Square, London, SW17 4JU

Tel: 020 7439 0271
Website: www.ercouncil.org

Enquiries to: Honorary Secretary

Founded: 1943

Organisation type and purpose: Membership association, registered charity.
To promote education in economics, particularly monetary practice.

Subject coverage: Education in the science of economics, particularly monetary policy; inflation, taxation, use of resources etc.

Non-library collection catalogue: All or part available online

Publications: Printed

Access to staff: Contact by letter
Hours: Mon to Fri, 0900 to 1700

ECONOMIC RESEARCH INSTITUTE OF NORTHERN IRELAND LTD (ERINI)

Pearl Assurance House, 1–3 Donegall Square East, Belfast, BT1 5HB

Tel: 028 9023 2125 or 028 261 8000
Fax: 028 9033 1250/3054
E-mail: lwalker@niec.org.uk
Website: www.niec.org.uk

Enquiries to: Director
Direct e-mail: e.moore@erini.ac.uk
Other contacts: Administrator

Founded: 2004

Organisation type and purpose: Economic research and policy development body.

Subject coverage: Economics.

Publications: Printed
Order printed publications from: The Administration Group, Economic Research Institute of Northern Ireland Ltd
tel: 028 90 232125, fax: 028 90 331250, e-mail: info@niec.org.uk

Publications list: Available online and in print

Access to staff: Contact by letter, by telephone, by fax, by e-mail, in person and via website. Appointment necessary.
Hours: Mon to Fri, 0900 to 1700

Also at: Economic Research Institute of Northern Ireland Ltd; 22–24 Mount Charles, Belfast, BT7 6NN

ECONOMIST INTELLIGENCE UNIT LIMITED (EIU)

26 Red Lion Square, London, WC1R 4HQ

Tel: 020 7576 8000
E-mail: london@eiu.com
Website: www.eiu.com
Website: store.eiu.com

Enquiries to: Client Relations Department
Direct tel: 020 7576 8181
Direct fax: 020 7572 8476
Direct e-mail: london@eiu.com

Organisation type and purpose: To provide country, industry and management analysis.
To assess and forecast the political, economic and business climates of 201 countries.
To produce intelligence on key industries.

Subject coverage: Country specific reports – economic and political studies; forecasts; country credit risk; commodities; industry studies – consumer markets, energy, rubber, travel and tourism, automotive, financial services, food, beverages and tobacco, healthcare and pharmaceuticals.

Trade and statistical information: International business and economic information

Publications list: Available online and in print

Incorporates: Business International Limited

Other offices: Hong Kong; 60F Central Plaza, 18 Harbour Road, Wanchai, Hong Kong; tel: +852 2802 7288; New York; The Economist Building, 111 West 57th Street, New York, NY 10019, USA; tel: +1 212 698 9745

Parent body: Economist Group

EDEXCEL

One90 High Holborn, London, WC1V 7BH

Tel: 0870 240 9800
E-mail: enquiries@edexcel.org.uk
Website: www.edexcel.org.uk

Enquiries to: Corporate Information Resource Centre Manager
Direct e-mail: sarah.whybrow@pearson.com

continued overleaf

Other contacts: Customer Response Centre (CRC) for information and guidance on the full range of Edexcel programmes of study and qualifications.

Founded: 1983

Organisation type and purpose: Body concerned with academic and vocational qualifications in secondary and tertiary education.

Subject coverage: The CIRC provides a 'first step' information service for all users of Edexcel qualifications. Guidance, contents, procedures and availability can be given on a wide range of qualifications, both academic and vocational, from Entry Level right through to Professional Development Awards.

Non-library collection catalogue: All or part available in-house and in print

Library catalogue: All or part available in-house

Publications: Printed
Order printed publications from: Edexcel Publications
Adamsway, Mansfield, Nottinghamshire, NG18 4FN, tel: 01623 467467, fax: 01623 450481, e-mail: publications@linneydirect.com

Publications list: Available in print

Access to staff: Contact by letter, by telephone, by fax, by e-mail and via website
Hours: Mon to Fri, 0900 to 1700

EDF ENERGY

Corporate Library, EDF Energy, Nuclear Generation Ltd.,Barnett Way, Barnwood, Gloucester, GL4 3RS

Tel: 01452 652769
Fax: 01452 654163
Website: www.edf-energy.com

Enquiries to: Library and Information Officer
Direct tel: 01452 652769
Direct e-mail: bwd.library@edf-energy.com

Founded: 1996; formerly called British Energy (year of change 2011)

Organisation type and purpose: Service industry.
Electricity generator.

Subject coverage: Power generation; nuclear technology; electricity supply industry.

Library catalogue: All or part available in-house

Access to staff: Contact by telephone and by e-mail
Hours: Mon to Thurs, 0900 to 1600

Access to building: Prior appointment required

EDGE HILL COLLEGE OF HIGHER EDUCATION

St Helens Road, Ormskirk, Lancashire, L39 4QP

Tel: 01695 584284
Fax: 01695 579997
E-mail: nicky.speed@edgehill.ac.uk
Website: www.ehche.ac.uk/ims

Enquiries to: Manager
Direct e-mail: mary.bernia@edgehill.ac.uk

History of institution: formerly called Edge Hill College of Further Education, Edge Hill University College

Organisation type and purpose: University library, university department or institute.
College awards are validated by Lancaster University.

Subject coverage: Afro-Asian studies, social science, community and race relations, drama, religious studies, English language and literature, biology, science, French, geography (human and physical), British and world history, mathematics, information technology, politics, European literature and culture, organisation and management, teacher education and educational studies, urban development, women's studies, sport studies and health.

Collection: Education Resource collection
Local history collection

Non-library collection catalogue: All or part available online

Access to staff: Contact by letter, by telephone, by e-mail and via website
Hours: Term time: Mon to Fri, 0845 to 2100; Sat, Sun, 1300 to 1700

Affiliated to: University of Lancaster

EDINBURGH ASSAY OFFICE (EAO)

Goldsmiths' Hall, 24 Broughton Street, Edinburgh, EH1 3RH

Tel: 0131 556 1144
Fax: 0131 556 1177
E-mail: admin@assay-office.co.uk
Website: www.assayofficescotland.co.uk

Enquiries to: Assay Master

Organisation type and purpose: Statutory body.
Established in accordance with the requirements of the Hallmarking Act 1973.

Subject coverage: Assaying and hallmarking over the past 500 years of gold, silver and platinum.

Collection: Records of wares hallmarked at Edinburgh since 1799 to present day

Publications: Printed

Access to staff: Contact by letter, by fax, by e-mail and in person
Hours: Mon to Fri, 0800 to 1600

Controlled by the: Incorporation of Goldsmiths of the City of Edinburgh

EDINBURGH BIBLIOGRAPHICAL SOCIETY

c/o National Library of Scotland, George IV Bridge, Edinburgh, EH1 1EW

Tel: 0131 623 3894
E-mail: H.Vincent@nls.uk
Website: www.edinburghbibliographicalsociety.org.uk

Enquiries to: Secretary

Founded: 1890

Organisation type and purpose: Learned society.

Subject coverage: Bibliography (especially Scottish).

Publications: Printed
Order printed publications from: website: http://www.edinburghbibliographicalsociety.org.uk/

Publications list: Available online and in print

Access to staff: Contact by letter, by telephone and by e-mail

EDINBURGH CENTRE FOR TROPICAL FORESTS (ECTF)

Pentlands Science Park, Bush Loan, Penicuik, Midlothian, EH26 0PH

Tel: 0131 440 0400
Fax: 0131 440 4141
E-mail: R.Clarkson@ed.ac.uk
Website: www.nmw.ac.uk/ectf

Enquiries to: Administrator

Founded: 1991

Organisation type and purpose: Training organisation, consultancy, research organisation.
Coordinates the expertise of the members of ECTF for potential clients.

Subject coverage: Tropical forestry, land management and sustainable development of natural resources.

Publications: Printed, and electronic and video

Access to staff: Contact by letter, by e-mail and via website
Hours: Mon to Fri, 0900 to 1700

Member organisations: Centre for Ecology and Hydrology; Bush Estate, Penicuik, Midlothian, EH26 0QB; Forestry Commission; 231 Corstorphine Road, Edinburgh, EH12 7AT; LTS International Limited; Pentlands Science Park, Bush Loan, Penicuik, Midlothian, EH26 0PH; Royal Botanic Garden; 20A Inverleith Row, Edinburgh, EH3 5LR; University of Edinburgh; Darwin Building, Mayfield Road, Edinburgh, EH9 3JU

EDINBURGH CITY LIBRARIES AND INFORMATION SERVICE

George IV Bridge, Edinburgh, EH1 1EG

Tel: 0131 242 8000
Fax: 0131 242 8009
E-mail: eclis@edinburgh.gov.uk
Website: www.edinburgh.gov.uk/libraries

Enquiries to: Head of Library and Information Services

Organisation type and purpose: Local government body, public library.

Subject coverage: Architecture, art, design and photography, business, community information, Edinburgh past and present, English literature, genealogy, government information, courses and careers, consumer information, music, dance (particularly Scottish), geography, science and technology, travel, painting, Scotland, Sir Walter Scott and R L Stevenson, Scottish Parliament.

Collection: Architectural Copy Books
British Standards (CD-ROM)
Children's Illustrated Books
Cowan Bequest (music)
Dance of Death Collection

Donald Scottish Dance Collection
Early Photography of Edinburgh and Scotland
Early Scottish Printed Music
Edinburgh Printing before 1700
Genealogy Records – Microform
General Register Office Index to Births Deaths and Marriages 1837–1997 (microfiche)
Henry Dyer Collection of Japanese Prints
Highland Life Collection of Photographs
Individual Family Histories
James Skene Watercolours
Krishnamurti Collection
Robert Louis Stevenson Collection
Marr Collection (music/handbills)
Scottish Artists' Sketchbooks
Scottish Parliament Offficial Publications
Sir Walter Scott Collection

Trade and statistical information: Business directories UK, government information, yearbooks and statistics

Non-library collection catalogue: All or part available online

Library catalogue: All or part available online

Publications: Printed, and electronic and video

Branch libraries: Access Services; 343 Oxgangs Road North, Edinburgh, EHB 9NE; tel: 0131 529 5683; Balerno; 1 Main Street, Edinburgh, EH14 7EQ; tel: 0131 529 5500; fax: 0131 529 5502; e-mail: balerno.library@edinburgh.gov.uk; Balgreen; 173 Balgreen Road, Edinburgh, EH11 3AT; tel: 0131 529 5585; fax: 0131 529 5583; e-mail: balgreen.library@edinburgh.gov.uk; Blackhall; 56 Hillhouse Road, Edinburgh, EH4 5EG; tel: 0131 529 5595; fax: 0131 336 5419; e-mail: blackhall.library@edinburgh.gov.uk; Colinton; 14 Thorburn Road, Edinburgh, EH13 0BQ; tel: 0131 529 5603; fax: 0131 529 5607; e-mail: colinton.library@edinburgh.gov.uk; Corstorphine; 12 Kirk Loan, Edinburgh, EH12 7HD; tel: 0131 529 5506; fax: 0131 529 5508; e-mail: costorphine.library@edinburg.gov.uk; Craigmillar; 7 Niddrie Marischal Gardens, Edinburgh, EH16 4LX; tel: 0131 529 5597; fax: 0131 529 5601; e-mail: craigmillar.library@edinburgh.gov.uk; Currie; 210 Lanark Road West, Edinburgh, EH14 5NN; tel: 0131 529 5609; fax: 0131 529 5613; e-mail: currie.library@edinburgh.gov.uk; Fountainbridge; 137 Dundee Street, Edinburgh, EH11 1BG; tel: 0131 529 5616; fax: 0131 529 5621; website: fountainbridge.library'edinburgh.gov.uk Gilmerton; 64 Gilmerton Dykes Street, Edinburgh, EH17 8PL; tel: 0131 529 5628; fax: 0131 529 5627; e-mail: gilmerton.library@edinburgh.gov.uk; Granton; Wardieburn Terrace, Edinburgh, EH5 2DA; tel: 0131 529 5630; fax: 0131 529 5634; e-mail: granton.library@edinburgh.gov.uk; Kirkliston; Station Road, Kirkliston, Edinburgh, EH29 9BE; tel: 0131 529 5510; fax: 0131 529 5514; e-mail: kirkliston.library@edinburgh.gov.uk; Leith; 28–30 Ferry Road, Edinburgh, EH6 4AE; tel: 0131 529 5517; fax: 0131 554 2720; e-mail: leith.library@edinburgh.gov.uk; McDonald Road; 2 McDonald Road, Edinburgh, EH7 4LU; tel: 0131 529 5636 (also Ethnic Services tel: 0131 529 5644); fax: 0131 529 5646; e-mail: mcdonaldrd.library@edinburgh.gov.uk; Moredun; 92 Moredun Park Road, Edinburgh, EH17 7HL; tel: 0131 529 5652; fax: 0131 447 5651; e-mail: moredun.library@edinburgh.gov.uk; Morningside; 184 Morningside Road, Edinburgh, EH10 4PU; tel: 0131 529 5654; fax: 0131 447 4685; e-mail: morningside.library@edinburgh.gov.uk; Muirhouse; 15 Pennywell Court, Edinburgh, EH4 4TZ; tel: 0131 529 5528; fax: 0131 529 5532; e-mail: muirhouse.library@edinburgh.gov.uk; Newington; 17–21 Fountainhall Road, Edinburgh, EH9 2LN; tel: 0131 529 5536; fax: 0131 667 5491; e-mail: newington.library@edinburgh.gov.uk; Oxgangs; 343 Oxgangs Road North, Edinburgh, EH13 9NE; tel: 0131 529 5549; fax: 0131 529 5554; e-mail: oxgangs.library@edinburgh.gov.uk; Piershill; 30 Piersfield Terrace, Edinburgh, EH8 7BQ; tel: 0131 529 5685; fax: 0131 529 5685; e-mail: piershill.library@edinburgh.gov.uk; Portobello; 14 Rosefield Terrace, Edinburgh, EH15 1AU; tel: 0131 529 5558; fax: 0131 669 2344; e-mail: portobello.library@edinburgh.gov.uk; Ratho; 6 School Wynd, Ratho, Newbridge, Edinburgh, EH28 8TT; tel: 0131 333 5297; fax: 0131 333 5297; e-mail: ratho.library@edinburgh.gov.uk; Sighthill; 6 Sighthill Wynd, Edinburgh, EH11 4BL; tel: 0131 529 5569; fax: 0131 539 5572; e-mail: sighthill.library@edinburgh.gov.uk; South Queensferry; 9 Shore Road, Edinburgh, EH30 9RD; tel: 0131 529 5576; fax: 0131 529 5578; e-mail: southqueensferry.library@edinburgh.gov.uk; Stockbridge; Hamilton Place, Edinburgh, EH3 5BA; tel: 0131 529 5665; fax: 0131 529 5681; e-mail: stockbridge.library@edinburgh.gov.uk; Wester Hailes; 1 West Side Plaza, Edinburgh, EH14 2ET; tel: 0131 529 5667; fax: 0131 529 5671; e-mail: westerhailes.library@edinburgh.gov.uk

Mobile Libraries: c/o Access Services

Resource Centre (for people with disabilities): Central Library; George IV Bridge, Edinburgh, EH1 1EG; tel: 0131 242 8136

EDINBURGH COLLEGE OF ART LIBRARY SERVICE (ECA)

Lauriston Place, Edinburgh, EH3 9DF

Tel: 0131 221 6180
Fax: 0131 221 6293
E-mail: library@eca.ac.uk
Website: www.lib.eca.ac.uk

Enquiries to: Reader Services Librarian
Other contacts: Technical Services Librarian

Founded: 1907

Organisation type and purpose: University library, suitable for ages: adult, research organisation; SFC Small Specialist Institution status.

Subject coverage: Architecture; landscape architecture; painting and drawing; sculpture; applied arts (jewellery and silversmithing, glass and architectural glass); applied design (furniture and interior and product design, fashion, textiles); visual communications (graphics, photography, animation, film and TV, illustration); urban design; architectural conservation; Islamic architecture, and urbanism.

Library catalogue: All or part available online

Access to staff: Contact by letter, by telephone, by e-mail and in person
Hours: Term time: Mon to Thu, 0915 to 2000; Fri, 1000 to 1700; vacations: Mon to Thu, 0915 to 1600; Fri, 1000 to 1600

Access to building: *Hours:* Term time: Mon to Thu, 0915 to 2000; Fri, 0900 to 1700; vacations: Mon to Thu, 0915 to 1600; Fri, 0900 to 1600

EDINBURGH COLLEGE OF PARAPSYCHOLOGY (ECP)

2 Melville Street, Edinburgh, EH3 7NS

Tel: 0131 220 1433
Fax: 0131 220 1433
Website: www.parapsychology.org.uk

Enquiries to: Secretary

Founded: 1932; formerly called Edinburgh Psychic College and Library (year of change 1973)

Organisation type and purpose: Membership association (membership is by subscription), present number of members: 300, voluntary organisation, registered charity (charity number SC 000571), suitable for ages: 18+.
To help the bereaved understand that life continues after physical death, to assist enquirers in this area plus provision of education, in a non-religious context. To promote all aspects of non-religious spiritualism.

Subject coverage: Parapsychology, mediumship, psychism, survival after death, physical phenomena, spiritualism, spiritual healing, clairvoyance, counselling.

Collection: Library of 2,000 books (catalogue on computer)

Library catalogue: All or part available in-house

Publications: Printed

Access to staff: Contact by letter, by telephone, by fax, by e-mail and in person
Hours: Mon to Fri, 1000 to 1600

EDINBURGH DISTRICT ENGINEERING TRAINING ASSOCIATION LIMITED (EDETA Ltd)

Fleming House, Kinnaird Park, Edinburgh, EH15 3RD

Tel: 0131 454 4840
Fax: 0131 454 4841
E-mail: administration@edeta.org.uk
Website: www.edeta.org.uk

Enquiries to: Manager

Founded: 1970

Organisation type and purpose: National organisation, advisory body, learned society (membership is by election or invitation), service industry, registered charity, suitable for ages: 18+, training organisation.

Subject coverage: VQ training in engineering, administration, IT, customer care, health and safety training.

Publications list: Available online and in print

continued overleaf

Access to staff: Contact by letter, by telephone, by fax, by e-mail, in person and via website. Appointment necessary.
Hours: Mon to Fri, 0900 to 1700

Access for disabled people: Parking provided, level entry, access to all public areas, toilet facilities

EDINBURGH FESTIVAL FRINGE

180 High Street, Edinburgh, EH1 1QS

Tel: 0131 226 0026, 0131 220 5594 (minicom)
Fax: 0131 226 0016
E-mail: admin@edfringe.com
Website: www.edfringe.com

Enquiries to: Administrator

Founded: 1947

Organisation type and purpose: Registered charity.
Arts festival.
Promotion of the performing and visual arts in Edinburgh.

Subject coverage: Edinburgh Festival Fringe; performance, production, marketing and technical information. Advice and support year-round.

Publications: Printed

Access to staff: Contact by letter, by telephone, by fax and by e-mail. Appointment necessary.
Hours: Mon to Fri, 1000 to 1800

EDINBURGH FILM FOCUS (EFF)

20 Forth Street, Edinburgh, EH1 3LH

Tel: 0131 622 7337
Fax: 0131 622 7338
E-mail: info@edinfilm.com
Website: www.edinfilm.com

Enquiries to: Film Commissioner
Other contacts: Location Liaison

Founded: 1989; formerly called Edinburgh and Lothian Screen Industries Office (ELSIO) (year of change 1997)

Organisation type and purpose: Advisory body, service industry. Local government-funded, independent film commission. A first point of contact for information and help on filming in Edinburgh, the Lothians and Scottish Borders.

Publications: Printed

Access to staff: Contact by letter, by telephone, by fax, by e-mail and via website. Appointment necessary.
Hours: Mon to Fri, 0900 to 1700

Access to building: By appointment
Hours: Mon to Fri, 0930 to 1700

EDINBURGH INTERNATIONAL FESTIVAL

The Hub, Castlehill, Edinburgh, EH1 2NE

Tel: 0131 473 2000, 0131 473 2098 (minicom/textphone)
Fax: 0131 473 2003
E-mail: info@eif.co.uk
Website: www.eif.co.uk

Enquiries to: Marketing Manager
Direct tel: 0131 473 2020
Direct fax: 0131 473 2002
Direct e-mail: marketing@eif.co.uk

Founded: 1947

Organisation type and purpose: Registered charity (charity number SC 004694).
For promotion of annual arts festival.
Three-week festival presenting over 200 performances of the world's best music, opera, theatre and dance.

Subject coverage: Performances in music, opera, dance, theatre.

Publications: Printed

Access to staff: Contact by letter, by telephone, by fax, by e-mail and via website. Appointment necessary.
Hours: Mon to Fri, 0930 to 1730

Access to building: No prior appointment required
Hours: Mon to Sun, 0930 to 1700
Special comments: Restricted access when functions are on.

Access for disabled people: Level entry, access to all public areas, toilet facilities

EDINBURGH INTERNATIONAL JAZZ & BLUES FESTIVAL

89 Giles Street, Edinburgh, EH6 6BZ

Tel: 0131 467 5200
Fax: 0131 554 0454
E-mail: fiona@adjazz.co.uk
Website: www.edinburghjazzfestival.com

Enquiries to: Producer

Founded: 1979

Organisation type and purpose: Registered charity (charity number SC012211).
Running an annual jazz and blues festival.

Publications: Printed

Access to staff: Contact by letter, by telephone, by fax and by e-mail
Hours: Mon to Fri, 0900 to 1700

EDINBURGH INTERNATIONAL SCIENCE FESTIVAL (EISF)

4 Gayfield Place Lane, Edinburgh, EH1 3NZ

Tel: 0131 558 7666
Fax: 0131 557 9177
E-mail: Pat@scifest.co.uk
Website: www.sciencefestival.co.uk

Enquiries to: Marketing Manager
Other contacts: Festival Manager

Founded: 1988

Organisation type and purpose: Registered charity, events suitable for all ages, plus an extensive schools touring programme.
To reveal science and the excitement of discovery to the widest possible audience.

Subject coverage: Public understanding of science. Science communication. Science shows, workshops and hands-on events.

Non-library collection catalogue: All or part available online

Publications: Printed

Access to staff: Contact by letter, by telephone, by fax and by e-mail. Appointment necessary.
Hours: Mon to Fri, 0930 to 1730

Also known as: The Science Festival

EDINBURGH MATHEMATICAL SOCIETY (EMS)

School of Mathematics, Edinburgh University, The King's Buildings, Mayfield Road, Edinburgh, EH9 3JZ

Tel: 0131 650 5040
Fax: 0131 650 6553
E-mail: edmathsoc@ed.ac.uk
Website: www.maths.ed.ac.uk/~ems

Enquiries to: Honorary Secretary

Founded: 1883

Organisation type and purpose: Learned society.
Promotion and extension of the mathematical sciences, pure and applied, particularly in Scotland.

Subject coverage: Pure and applied mathematics.

Publications: Printed

EDINBURGH NAPIER UNIVERSITY INFORMATION SERVICES

Craiglockhart Campus, Edinburgh, EH14 1DJ

Tel: 0131 455 4269
Fax: 0131 455 4276
Website: www.napier.ac.uk/about/campuses/Pages/home.aspx
Website: www.napier.ac.uk

Enquiries to: Director of Information Services
Direct tel: 0131 455 4270
Direct fax: 0131 455 4242
Direct e-mail: c.pinder@napier.ac.uk

Organisation type and purpose: University IT and library services.

Subject coverage: Accounting, economics and statistics; arts and creative industries; computing; engineering and the built environment; health and social sciences; life sciences; management and law; marketing, tourism and languages; nursing, midwifery and social care.

Collection: Edward Clark Collection on printing and book production
War Poets' collection, material relating to Wilfred Owen, Siegfried Sassoon and war poetry generally.

Non-library collection catalogue: All or part available online

Library catalogue: All or part available online

Publications: Printed

Access to staff: Contact by letter, by telephone and by e-mail. Non-members charged.
Hours: Term time: Mon to Thu, 0845 to 2100; Sat and Sun, 1000 to 1600

EDINBURGH ROYAL CHORAL UNION (ERCU)

Criagroyston, Broadgate, Gullane, EH31 2DH

Tel: 01620 843299
E-mail: jane.kirk@ed.ac.uk
Website: www.ercu.org.uk

Enquiries to: President

Other contacts: Librarian for hire of choral music.

Founded: 1858

Organisation type and purpose: Membership association (membership is by qualification), present number of members: 120, voluntary organisation, registered charity (charity number SC012050). Self-governing amateur society whose objects are the study, practice and performance of music, one of Scotland's largest independent amateur choirs, promoting at least three concerts in a season, with professional orchestras and conductors.

Subject coverage: Choral music.

Collection: Large library of choral music available for hire

Library catalogue: All or part available online

Publications: Printed

Publications list: Available online

Access to staff: Contact by letter, by telephone, by fax, by e-mail and via website
Hours: Mon to Fri, 0900 to 1700

Member of: National Federation of Music Societies (NFMS); 7–15 Rosebery Avenue, London, EC1R 4SP; tel: 020 7841 0110; fax: 020 7841 0115; e-mail: nfms@nfms.org.uk

EDINBURGH SIR WALTER SCOTT CLUB (ESWSC)

9, Burnbank Grove, Straiton, Loanhead, Midlothian, EH20 9NX

Tel: 0131 448 1976
E-mail: hontreas@walterscottclub.org.uk
Website: www.walterscottclub.org.uk

Enquiries to: Hon. Secretary
Direct tel: 0131 228 2430
Direct e-mail: honsec@walterscottclub.org.uk

Founded: 1894

Organisation type and purpose: Learned society (membership is by subscription), present number of members: 250.

Subject coverage: Life and works of Sir Walter Scott.

Collection: A few books of Scott minutes of club and council meetings
Tapes of annual dinner speeches

Publications: Printed

Access to staff: Contact by e-mail and via website. Appointment necessary.

Links with: University of Edinburgh, Department of Literature

EDUCATION CENTRE LIBRARY

Formal name: South Warwickshire NHS Foundation Trust

Education Centre, Warwick Hospital, Lakin Road, Warwick, CV34 5BW

Tel: 01926 495321 ext 4287
Fax: 01926 608087
E-mail: Nicholas.Harden@swft.nhs.uk
Website: covw.ent.sirsidynix.net.uk/client/WARECL

Enquiries to: Librarian

Founded: 1986

Organisation type and purpose: Hospital.

Subject coverage: Medicine and related disciplines.

Library catalogue: All or part available online

Access to staff: Contact by letter, by telephone, by fax, by e-mail, in person and via website. Appointment necessary.
Hours: Mon, Tue, Wed, 0900 to 1700; Thu, 0900 to 1945; Fri, 0900 to 1645

Access to building: Prior appointment required. Please ring library ext (4287) on arrival

Access for disabled people: Parking within c.200m, lift to first floor, access to toilet facilities

EDUCATION LAW ASSOCIATION (ELAS)

37 Grimston Avenue, Folkestone, Kent, CT20 2QD

Tel: 01303 211570
Fax: 01303 211570
E-mail: secretary@educationlawassociation.org.uk

Enquiries to: Executive Secretary

Founded: 1992

Organisation type and purpose: Professional body (membership is by subscription), present number of members: 325, registered charity (charity number 1053614), suitable for ages: all, training organisation.

Subject coverage: Education law.

Access to staff: Contact by letter, by telephone, by fax and by e-mail
Hours: Mon to Fri, 0900 to 1700
Special comments: No visitors, part-time staff.

EDUCATIONAL AND TELEVISION FILMS LIMITED (ETV)

247a Upper Street, Highbury Corner, London, N1 1RU

Tel: 020 7226 2298
Fax: 020 7226 8016
E-mail: zoe@etvltd.demon.co.uk
Website: www.etvltd.demon.co.uk

Enquiries to: Librarian

Founded: 1950

Organisation type and purpose: Film library.

Subject coverage: Footage of and from the history of the British Labour Movement and a wide variety of documentary and technical subjects from the former socialist countries and from the former Soviet Union, former Eastern Bloc countries, Afghanistan, China, Chile, Cuba, Korea and Viet Nam, as well as a complete collection from the Spanish Civil War from the Republican side.

Collection: British Labour History films
Spanish Civil War films
A wide spectrum of international films that have a political relevance to today's news stories

Non-library collection catalogue: All or part available in-house

Library catalogue: All or part available in-house

Publications: Printed

Publications list: Available in print

Access to staff: Contact by letter, by telephone, by fax, by e-mail and via website
Hours: Mon to Fri, 0930 to 1730

Access to building: Prior appointment required
Hours: Mon to Fri, 0930 to 1730

EDUCATIONAL DISTRIBUTION SERVICE

Education House, Drywall Estate, Castle Road, Murston, Sittingbourne, Kent, ME10 3RL

Tel: 01795 427614
Fax: 01795 437988
E-mail: info@edist.co.uk

Enquiries to: Managing Director

Founded: 1971

Organisation type and purpose: International organisation, suitable for ages: all.
Library and distribution service for film and video, and all resources and other goods as contracted.

Collection: GPO classic films

Publications: Printed

Publications list: Available in print

Access to staff: Contact by letter, by telephone, by fax and by e-mail. Appointment necessary.
Hours: Mon to Fri, 0900 to 1700

Access to building: Prior appointment required

EDUCATIONAL GRANTS ADVISORY SERVICE (EGAS)

501–505 Kingsland Road, London, E8 4AU

Tel: 020 7254 6251 (Tue, Wed and Thu 1400 to 1600 only)
Fax: 020 7249 5443
E-mail: egas.enquiry@family-action.org.uk
Website: www.family-action.org.uk

Enquiries to: Educational and Grants Manager

Founded: 1962; parent body formerly called Family Welfare Association (year of change 2008)

Organisation type and purpose: Information and grant giving service. A service provided by Family Action, registered charity number 264713.

Subject coverage: Post-16 education in England, specialising in charitable funding.

Information services: Guide to Student Funding, Educational Grants Search

Access to staff: Contact by letter and by telephone
Hours: Mon to Fri, 0900 to 1700
Special comments: Telephone service only available on Tue, Wed and Thu, from 1400 to 1600

continued overleaf

Parent body: Family Action; 501–505 Kingsland Road, London E8 4AU; tel: 020 7254 6251; fax: 020 7249 5443; e-mail: info@family-action.org.uk; website: http://www.family-action.org.uk

EDUCATIONAL INSTITUTE OF SCOTLAND (EIS)

46 Moray Place, Edinburgh, EH3 6BH

Tel: 0131 225 6244
Fax: 0131 220 3151
E-mail: enquiries@eis.org.uk
Website: www.eis.org.uk

Enquiries to: General Secretary

Organisation type and purpose: Trade union (membership is by subscription), present number of members: 58,000.
All sectors of Scottish education.

Subject coverage: Education and teachers in all sectors (Scotland).

Publications: Printed

Access to staff: Contact by letter, by fax and by e-mail
Hours: Mon to Fri, 0900 to 1700

Affiliated to: Trades Union Congress

EDUSERV

Royal Mead, Railway Place, Bath, BA1 1SR

Tel: 01225 474300
Fax: 01225 474301
E-mail: contact@eduserv.org.uk
Website: www.eduserv.org.uk

Founded: 1988

Organisation type and purpose: Non-profit IT services group, dedicated to developing and delivering technology services for education and the public sector through services, including access and identity management; institution connections to online resources such as Athens and OpenAthens; licence negotiation and management; offers on software and data licences to the education community; web development and hosting and consultancy. Eduserv also undertakes forward-thinking research and innovation that leads to a greater understanding of technology and shared services, which it provides to the academic community.

Subject coverage: Access to protected online resources, web development and hosting and licence negotiation for software and data licences.

Access to staff: Contact by letter, by telephone, by fax, by e-mail and via website. Appointment necessary.
Hours: Mon to Fri, 0800 to 1800

EEF – THE MANUFACTURERS' ORGANISATION (EEF)

Broadway House, Tothill Street, Westminster, London, SW1H 9NQ

Tel: 020 7222 7777
Fax: 020 7222 2782
E-mail: enquiries@eef.org.uk
Website: www.eef.org.uk

Enquiries to: Information Services Manager
Direct tel: 020 7654 1574
Direct e-mail: crochester@eef-fed.org.uk

Founded: 1896

Organisation type and purpose: Trade association.
Employers' organisation.

Subject coverage: Representation of the engineering industry's employer interests, employee relations, personnel management, education and skills, environmental issues, health and safety, economics. (Information derived from surveys of members is not generally available.)

Non-library collection catalogue: All or part available in-house

Library catalogue: All or part available in-house

Publications: Printed

Publications list: Available in print

Access to staff: Contact by letter, by telephone, by fax, by e-mail and via website. Access for members only.
Hours: Mon to Fri, 0900 to 1530

Affiliated to: 15 autonomous organisations, 14 regional associations; Engineering Construction Industry Association; Federation of Engineering Design Companies

Links with: Engineering Council; SEMTA

Member of: Council of European Employers of the Metal, Engineering and Technology-based Industries

EEF YORKSHIRE AND HUMBERSIDE

Fieldhead, Thorner, Leeds, West Yorkshire, LS14 3DN

Tel: 0113 289 2671
Fax: 0113 289 3170
Website: www.eef.org.uk

Enquiries to: Director
Direct tel: 0113 289 2863

Founded: 1890; formerly called Engineering and Ship Building Employers Association (Yorkshire and Humberside)

Organisation type and purpose:
Membership association.
Employers trade association.
Supports engineering and manufacturing companies.

Subject coverage: All matters relating to the employment of people.

Publications: Printed

Publications list: Available in print

Access to staff: Contact by letter and by fax. Appointment necessary. Non-members charged.
Hours: Mon to Fri, 0900 to 1700

Affiliated to: EEF; Tothill Street, London, SW1H 9NQ

EEMA

Formal name: European Electronic Messaging Association

Alexander House, High Street, Inkberrow, Worcester, WR7 4DT

Tel: 01386 793028
Fax: 01386 793268
E-mail: info@eema.org
Website: www.eema.org

Enquiries to: Membership Director
Direct e-mail: jim.dickson@eema.org

Founded: 1987

Organisation type and purpose:
International organisation, trade association.

Subject coverage: All aspects of electronic business including security, directory, e-commerce, XML, unified messaging, legal issues surrounding secure digital identity and trusted third-party products and services, change management, e-Government and public sector, CA's and regulation authorities.

Non-library collection catalogue: All or part available online

Publications: Printed

Publications list: Available online and in print

Access to staff: Contact by letter, by telephone, by fax and by e-mail
Hours: Mon to Fri, 0900 to 1700

Access to building: Prior appointment required

EFFECTIVE TECHNOLOGY MARKETING LIMITED (ETM)

PO Box 171, Grimsby, Lincolnshire, DN35 0TP

Tel: 01472 816660
Fax: 01472 816660
Website: www.dataresources.co.uk

Enquiries to: Managing Director

Founded: 1987

Organisation type and purpose: Publishing house.
Publishers' distributor.

Subject coverage: Business information, Central and Eastern Europe and the CIS, Russia.

Publications: Printed

Publications list: Available in print

Access to staff: Contact by letter, by telephone, by fax and by e-mail
Hours: Mon to Fri, 0900 to 1700

EFNARC (EFNARC)

Formal name: Experts for Specialised Construction and Concrete Systems

EFNARC Secretary, Cobblers Cottage, Chester Road, Daresbury, Warrington, WA4 4AJ

Tel: 01925 740581
Fax: 01925 740581
E-mail: secretary@efnarc.org
Website: www.efnarc.org

Founded: 1998; formerly called European Federation of Producers and Applicators of Specialist Products for Structures

Organisation type and purpose: Trade association, present number of members: 11.

Represents major international manufacturers, raw material suppliers, contractors and consultants involved in specialised construction and concrete systems industry.

Subject coverage: Specialised construction and concrete systems.

Non-library collection catalogue: All or part available online

Publications: Printed

Publications list: Available online and in print

Access to staff: Contact by letter, by telephone, by fax, by e-mail and via website
Hours: Mon to Fri, 0900 to 1700

EGG CRAFTERS GUILD OF GREAT BRITAIN

The Studio, 7 Hylton Terrace, North Shields, Tyne and Wear, NE29 0EE

Tel: 0191 258 3648
E-mail: joanccutts@aol.com
Website: www.geocities.com/eggcraftersguild
Website: www.freewebs.com/eggcraftersguild

Enquiries to: Life President/Founder

Founded: 1979

Organisation type and purpose:
International organisation, membership association (membership is by subscription, election or invitation), present number of members: 800 world-wide, voluntary organisation.
Craft organisation.
Members meet at various venues to exhibit and enter competitions; many members sell their eggs, some give Guild talks to organisations.

Subject coverage: Egg craft (painting and other art work on eggshell); exhibitions; teaching; cutting designs with electric drill. Many eggs are created in the style of Fabergé, and all are made from real eggs.

Publications: Printed

Access to staff: Contact by letter, by fax and by e-mail. Appointment necessary.
Hours: Mon to Fri, 0900 to 1600

EGYPT EXPLORATION SOCIETY (EES)

3 Doughty Mews, London, WC1N 2PG

Tel: 020 7242 1880
Fax: 020 7404 6118
E-mail: contact@ees.ac.uk
Website: www.ees.ac.uk

Enquiries to: Administrator
Direct tel: 020 7242 1880
Direct e-mail: contact@ees.ac.uk

Founded: 1882; formerly called The Egypt Exploration Fund (EEF) (year of change 1915)

Organisation type and purpose:
International organisation, learned society (membership is by subscription), present number of members: 3,200, registered charity (charity number 212384), research organisation.

Subject coverage: Ancient Egypt; archaeology and history of Egypt to AD1900.

Information services: Library, archives, online resources.

Education services: Publications, events.

Collection: Library of Egyptology, archive of photographs, correspondence and other documents relating to the Society and its work.
Archive

Non-library collection catalogue: All or part available online

Library catalogue: All or part available online

Publications: Printed
Order printed publications from: The EES, 3 Doughty Mews, London, WC1N 2PG; e-mail: @ees.ac.uk; tel: 020 7242 2266; fax: 020 7404 6118; website: http://www.ees.ac.uk

Publications list: Available online and in print

Access to staff: Contact by letter, by telephone, by fax, by e-mail, in person and via website. Appointment necessary. Non-members charged.
Hours: Tue to Fri, 1030 to 1630

Access to building: No prior appointment required

Links with: Foundation for Science and Technology

EGYPTIAN STATE TOURIST OFFICE

Egyptian House, 170 Piccadilly, London, W1V 9DD

Tel: 020 7493 5283
Fax: 020 7408 0295
E-mail: egypt@freenetname.co.uk
Website: www.interoz.com/Egypt

Enquiries to: Director
Direct tel: 020 7495 6489
Other contacts: Deputy Manager

History of institution: formerly called Egyptian Tourist Authority (UK)

Organisation type and purpose: National government body.
Promotion of tourism to Egypt.

Subject coverage: Tourism, travel and transport, schedules and prices in Egypt; visa forms and information; Nile cruises; places of interest; tourist villages, destinations in Egypt. Conference and meeting facilities.

Collection: A collection of slides of Egypt
Promotional videos on the country
Posters

Publications: Printed, and electronic and video

Access to staff: Contact by letter, by telephone, by fax and by e-mail
Hours: Mon to Fri, 0930 to 1630

Links with: Egyptian Embassy and the Egyptian Consulate; tel: 020 7235 9777; fax: 020 7235 5684

Parent body: Ministry of Tourism in Egypt; tel: + 202 685 3576/9658; fax: + 202 685 4363/4788

EIL CULTURAL AND EDUCATIONAL TRAVEL (EIL UK)

287 Worcester Road, Malvern, Worcestershire, WR14 1AB

Tel: 01684 562577
Fax: 01684 562212
E-mail: info@eiluk.org
Website: www.eiluk.org

Founded: 1936; formerly called BAEIL

Organisation type and purpose:
International organisation, membership association, registered charity (charity number 1070440), suitable for ages: 16+. Non-profit making organisation. Recognised by the Economic and Social Council of the UN (ECOSOC) as category II non-governmental organisation.
Cultural and educational exchange.

Subject coverage: Understanding between countries of the world, cross-cultural education.

Access to staff: Contact by letter, by telephone, by fax, by e-mail and via website
Hours: Mon to Fri, 0900 to 1700

Affiliated to: UNESCO, category B

ELDERLY ACCOMMODATION COUNSEL (EAC)

3rd Floor, 89 Albert Embankment, London, SE1 7TP

Tel: 020 7820 1343
Fax: 020 7820 3970
E-mail: enquiries@eac.org.uk
Website: www.housingcare.org

Founded: 1985

Organisation type and purpose: Registered charity (charity number 292552).
A national charity offering advice and information about all forms of accommodation and care for older people.

Subject coverage: Accommodation options for older people. Elderly Accommodation Counsel (EAC) is a national charity, maintaining nation-wide databases of accommodation specifically for older people – sheltered, retirement housing to buy and to rent, extra care schemes and close care housing (sheltered accommodation where there is a care home on site), and care homes, both for personal care and for nursing. The free, independent advice line offers guidance, advice and detailed information to help older people choose and fund the support or accommodation options most suited to their needs and wishes.

Publications: Printed

Access to staff: Contact by letter, by telephone, by fax, by e-mail and via website
Hours: Mon to Fri, 0900 to 1700

Access to building: No access other than to staff

ELECTORAL REFORM INTERNATIONAL SERVICES

6 Chancel Street, Blackfriars, London, SE1 0UU

Tel: 020 7620 3794
Fax: 020 7928 4366
E-mail: erisuk@eris.org.uk

continued overleaf

Website: www.eris.org.uk

Organisation type and purpose: To provide support to emerging democracies for the further consolidation of democracy and good governance around the world, with a particular emphasis of the conduct of credible and transparent elections

Access to staff: Contact by letter, by telephone, by fax, by e-mail and via website

ELECTORAL REFORM SOCIETY LIMITED (ERS)

6 Chancel Street, Blackfriars, London, SE1 0UU

Tel: 020 7928 1622
Fax: 020 7401 7789
Website: www.electoral-reform.org.uk

Enquiries to: Chief Executive
Direct e-mail: ers@electoral-reform.org.uk

Founded: 1884; formerly called Proportional Representation Society (year of change 1969)

Organisation type and purpose: Learned society, membership association (membership is by subscription), present number of members: 2,000, voluntary organisation.
Campaigning organisation.
To campaign for the introduction of proportional representation by the single transferable vote method for all elections.

Subject coverage: All aspects of elections, including electoral law and practice; voting systems, especially proportional representation; election monitoring; election campaigns; balloting in professional, trade union and other common interest organisations, etc.

Collection: The Lakeman Library (formerly the Arthur McDougall Library) houses a collection of works and papers on political science, elections, election observations, voting systems, electoral reform, especially proportional representation in the United Kingdom and elsewhere. The Library is maintained by the McDougall Trust

Trade and statistical information: Statistical information relating to elections in the UK and elsewhere

Library catalogue: All or part available in-house

Publications: Printed

Publications list: Available online and in print

Access to staff: Contact by letter, by telephone, by fax and by e-mail. Appointment necessary.
Hours: Mon to Fri, 0930 to 1730
Special comments: Letter of introduction preferred. Charges may be made to users.

Access to building: No prior appointment required
Hours: Mon to Fri, 0930 to 1730

Access for disabled people: Toilet facilities

Associated charity: The McDougall Trust; tel: 020 7620 1080; fax: 020 7928 1528; e-mail: admin@mcdougall.org.uk

Consultative status with: Economic and Social Council of the United Nations

Enquiries concerning the conduct of ballots and surveys only: Electoral Reform (Services) Ltd; The Elections Centre, 33 Clarendon Road, Hornsey, London, N8 0NW; tel: 020 8365 8909; fax: 020 8365 8587

ELECTRIC RAILWAY SOCIETY (ERS)

17 Catherine Drive, Sutton Coldfield, West Midlands, B73 6AX

Tel: 0121 354 8332
E-mail: iwfrew@tiscali.co.uk
Website: www.electric-rly-society.org.uk

Enquiries to: Honorary Secretary

Founded: 1946

Organisation type and purpose: Learned society (membership is by subscription).

Subject coverage: History and development of electric railway and light railway services and equipment in the British Isles.
Development of rail services around major cities worldwide. Development of high-speed intercity passenger services worldwide.

Collection: Some material available for educational purposes
Collection of colour slides depicting tramways, electric railways, in the United Kingdom
Collection of colour slides depicting coastal ferries and pleasure steamers in British waters

Publications: Printed
Order printed publications from: Hon. Secretary

Access to staff: Contact by letter and by e-mail
Hours: Mon to Fri, 0900 to 2200

Access to building: No access other than to staff

Affiliated to: Asociación Uruguaya Amigos del Riel; Cas Correos 857, Montevideo, Uruguay; Railway Society of Southern Africa; PO Box 12375, Jacobs, SA 4026

ELECTRICAL CONTRACTORS' ASSOCIATION (ECA)

ESCA House, 34 Palace Court, London, W2 4HY

Tel: 020 7313 4800
Fax: 020 7221 7344
E-mail: electricalcontractors@eca.co.uk
Website: www.eca.co.uk

Enquiries to: Head of Marketing
Other contacts: Departmental Heads

Founded: 1901

Organisation type and purpose: Trade association.

Subject coverage: Electrical installation work; engineering and contracting.

Publications: Printed

Access to staff: Contact by letter, by fax and by e-mail
Hours: Mon to Fri, 0900 to 1700

ELECTRICAL INSTALLATION EQUIPMENT MANUFACTURERS' ASSOCIATION LIMITED (EIEMA)

Westminster Tower, 3 Albert Embankment, London, SE1 7SL

Tel: 020 7793 3013
Fax: 020 7735 4158
E-mail: info@beama.org.uk
Website: www.eiema.org.uk

Enquiries to: Director
Direct tel: 020 7793 3009
Direct e-mail: dd@eiema.demon.co.uk

Organisation type and purpose: Trade association.

Subject coverage: Electrical accessories; fuses; switch and fuse gear; miniature, earth leakage and moulded case circuit-breakers; distribution switchboards (cubicle and non-cubicle types); cablejoints and terminators.

Trade and statistical information: Statistical information is strictly for members only

Publications: Printed

Access to staff: Contact by letter, by telephone, by fax and by e-mail
Hours: Mon to Thu, 0900 to 1700; Fri, 0900 to 1545

Affiliated to: British Electrotechnical and Allied Manufacturers Association (BEAMA)

ELECTROPHYSIOLOGICAL TECHNOLOGISTS ASSOCIATION (EPTA)

Department of Clinical Neurophysiology, Great Ormond St Hospital, Great Ormond Street, London, WC1N 3JH

E-mail: eptasec@hotmail.com
Website: www.epta.50megs.com

Enquiries to: Honorary Secretary

Founded: 1949

Organisation type and purpose: National organisation, professional body (membership is by subscription), present number of members: over 600.

Subject coverage: Electrophysiology especially neurophysiology.

Publications: Printed

Access to staff: Contact by letter and by e-mail
Hours: Mon to Fri, 0900 to 1700

Links with: International Organisation of Societies for Electophysiology (OSET); tel: 01785 258672

ELGAR SOCIETY

The Hon Secretary, 12 Monkhams Drive, Woodford Green, IG8 0LQ

Tel: 020 8504 0292
E-mail: hon.sec@elgar.org
Website: www.elgar.org
Website: www.cornucopia.org.uk

Enquiries to: Honorary Secretary

Founded: 1951; created by the merger of Friends of Elgar's Birthplace

Organisation type and purpose: International organisation, learned society (membership is by subscription), present number of members: 1,500 UK & world, registered charity (charity number 298062). Trading Company formed in 2000.
To supply books, CDs, scores and other merchandise.

Subject coverage: Sir Edward Elgar, his life and music; study, appreciation and performance of his works. Publicity for concerts, talks and lectures via website.

Collection: Scores of all Compositions
Memorabilia
Research biographies, etc.

Publications: Printed, and electronic and video
Order printed publications from: Elgar Editions, c/o 20 High Street, Rickmansworth, Hertfordshire, WD3 1ER; or via the website

Publications list: Available online and in print

Access to staff: Contact by letter, by telephone, by e-mail and via website
Hours: Any reasonable time

Branches: Bristol (Great Western Branch); tel: 01434 776503; Edinburgh (Scottish Branch); tel: 01383 727491; London Branch; tel: 01707 876079; Manchester (North West Branch); tel: 0161 998 4404; Southampton (Southern Branch); tel: 023 9281 6488; Worcester (West Midlands Branch); tel: 01453 882091

ELIZABETH FINN CARE (EFC)

Hythe House, 200 Shepherds Bus Road, London, W6 7NL

Tel: 020 8834 9200
E-mail: info@elizabethfinn.org.uk
Website: www.elizabethfinncare.org.uk
Website: www.turn2us.org.uk

Enquiries to: Grants Department
Direct tel: 0800 413 220
Direct e-mail: enquiries@elizabethfinn.org.uk

Founded: 1897; formerly called Distressed Gentlefolks Aid Association (DGAA); formerly called Homelife DGAA (year of change 1994); formerly called Elizabeth Finn Trust (year of change 2005)

Organisation type and purpose: Voluntary organisation, registered charity (charity number 207812).
Elizabeth Finn Care is one of the UK's largest independent direct grant-giver, dedicated specifically to helping those in poverty. As such, EFC provides support and care for people, including their immediate families, who are permanent residents in the UK, regardless of gender, religious denomination or political opinion.

Subject coverage: High quality care in 9 residential and nursing homes and 10 almshouses cottages; financial support and assistance to people of all ages who live in their own homes or those requiring financial assistance toward care in other homes. The financial support we can provide includes ongoing support and one-off grants to cover specific items, such as wheelchairs, or for household repair and maintenance.

Access to staff: Contact by letter, by telephone, by fax, by e-mail and via website
Hours: Mon to Fri, 0900 to 1700
Special comments: No personal callers.

ELMBRIDGE BOROUGH COUNCIL (EBC)

Civic Centre, High Street, Esher, Surrey, KT10 9SD

Tel: 01372 474474, 01372 474219 (minicom)
Fax: 01372 474972
E-mail: civiccentre@elmbridge.gov.uk
Website: www.elmbridge.gov.uk

Enquiries to: Communications and Consultation Officer
Direct tel: 01372 474391
Direct fax: 01372 474931
Direct e-mail: lballinger@elmbridge.gov.uk

Founded: 1974

Organisation type and purpose: Local government body.

Subject coverage: All aspects of Elmbridge Borough and Elmbridge Borough Council; services, amenities, housing and planning.

Publications: Printed

Access to staff: Contact by letter, by telephone, by fax, by e-mail and via website. Appointment necessary.
Hours: Mon to Fri, 0845 to 1700

Access for disabled people: Level entry, toilet facilities

Parent body: Surrey County Council; tel: 020 8541 8800

ELSEVIER SCIENCE BIBLIOGRAPHIC DATABASES

Customer Service Department, Linacre House, Jordan Hill, Oxford, OX2 8DP

Tel: 01865 474010
Fax: 01865 474011
E-mail: directenquiries@elsevier.com
Website: www.elsevier.com

Enquiries to: Press Officer
Direct e-mail: pressoffice@elsevier.com
Other contacts: Product Manager for telephone queries, email: a.munns@elsevier.co.uk.

Founded: 1960

Organisation type and purpose: Publishing house.

Subject coverage: Geology, development studies, human geography, physical geography, textiles, fluids, civil engineering, process engineering, ecology, physical geography, oceanography, geomechanics.

Collection: Back issues and indexes for 1966 until present

Publications: Printed, and electonic and video
Order printed publications from: Elsevier Science, Regional Sales Office
Customer Support Department, PO Box 211, Amsterdam, NL-1000 AE, The Netherlands, tel: 00 31 20 485 3757, fax: 00 31 20 485 3432, e-mail: nlinfo-f@elsevier.nl

Publications list: Available in print

Access to staff: Contact by letter, by telephone, by fax, by e-mail and via website
Hours: Mon to Fri, 0900 to 1700

Other addresses: Elsevier Science Bibliographic Databases; Molenwerf 1, 1014 AE Amsterdam, The Netherlands; tel: 00 31 20 485 3507; fax: 00 31 20 485 3222

Parent body: Elsevier Science Limited; The Boulevard, Langford Lane, Kidlington, Oxford, OX5 1GB; tel: 01865 843000; fax: 01865 843010

ELVA OWNERS CLUB (EOC)

c/o Elva Racing Components Ltd, Unit 3, Gaugemaster Way, Ford Road, Ford, Arundel, BN18 0RX

Tel: 01903 882911
Fax: 01903 882911
E-mail: roger.dunbar@elva.com; elvacars@gmail.com
Website: www.elva.com
Website: www.elvacourier.com
Website: www.elva-ale.com

Enquiries to: Honorary Secretary
Direct tel: 07976 234470
Direct e-mail: roger@elva.com

Founded: 1979

Organisation type and purpose: Membership association (membership is by election or invitation), present number of members: 400.
Support for owners and enthusiasts of Elva cars.

Subject coverage: Information about Elva racing and sports racing cars.

Information services: A focal point for information relating to ELVA Cars.

Access to staff: Contact by letter, by telephone, by e-mail and via website. Appointment necessary.
Hours: Mon to Fri, 0900 to 1700

EMBASSY OF DENMARK

55 Sloane Street, London, SW1X 9SR

Tel: 020 7333 0200
Fax: 020 7333 0270
E-mail: lonamb@um.dk
Website: storbritannien.um.dk

Enquiries to: Information Officer

Organisation type and purpose: National government body.

Subject coverage: Denmark and Danish governmental matters; Danish commerce and culture.

Publications: Printed

Access to staff: Contact by letter, by telephone, by fax and by e-mail

EMBASSY OF FINLAND

38 Chesham Place, London, SW1X 8HW

Tel: 020 7838 6200
Fax: 020 7235 3680
E-mail: sanomat.lon@formin.fi
Website: www.finemb.org.uk

Enquiries to: Information Officer

Organisation type and purpose: Embassy.

Access to staff: Contact by letter, by

continued overleaf

telephone and via website
Hours: Mon to Fri, 0830 to 1230 and 1330 to 1630
Special comments: Passport and Visa Department Open: Mon to Fri, 0900 to 1200 only; telephone enquiries: Mon to Fri, 1400 to 1600.

EMBASSY OF HONDURAS

115 Gloucester Place, London, W1U 6JT

Tel: 020 7486 4880
Fax: 020 7486 4550
E-mail: hondurasuk@lineone.net

Enquiries to: Information Officer

Organisation type and purpose: National embassy.

Subject coverage: Honduras Republic; Central America.

Access to staff: Contact by letter, by telephone and by e-mail
Hours: 1000 to 1700

EMBASSY OF ICELAND

2A Hans Street, London, SW1X 0JE

Tel: 020 7259 3999
Fax: 020 7245 9649
E-mail: icemb.london@utn.stjr.is
Website: www.statice.is
Website: www.icetourist.is
Website: www.iceland.org/uk
Website: www.iceland.is

Enquiries to: Information Officer

Organisation type and purpose: International organisation.

Subject coverage: Icelandic government matters, Icelandic trade.

Access to staff: Contact by letter, by fax and by e-mail
Hours: Mon to Fri, 0930 to 1600

EMBASSY OF MONGOLIA

7 Kensington Court, London, W8 5DL

Tel: 020 7937 5238
Fax: 020 7937 1117
E-mail: office@embassyofmongolia.co.uk
Website: www.embassyofmongolia.co.uk

Enquiries to: Information Officer

Founded: 1969

Organisation type and purpose: National government body.

Subject coverage: General information about Mongolia.

Trade and statistical information: Statistics and information about Mongolian economy

Publications: Printed

Access to staff: Contact by letter, by telephone, by fax, by e-mail and in person. Appointment necessary.
Hours: Mon to Fri, 0900 to 1700

EMBASSY OF PERU

52 Sloane Street, London, SW1X 9SP

Tel: 020 7235 1917
Fax: 020 7235 4463
E-mail: postmaster@peruembassy-uk.com
Website: www.peruembassy-uk.com

Enquiries to: Economic Advisor (for trade and investment opportunities, for economic information)

Organisation type and purpose: National government body.
Diplomatic representation of Peru in the UK and Ireland.

Subject coverage: Peruvian information.

Information services: Trade and investment opportunities, tourism and cultural information and advice.

Education services: Information and advice.

Trade and statistical information: UK trade with Peru; Peruvian exports and imports; British investment in Peru; foreign investment in Peru; economic indicators for Peru; general statistical information

Non-library collection catalogue: All or part available in-house

Library catalogue: All or part available in-house

Publications: Printed
Order printed publications from: e-mail: postmaster@peruembassy-uk.com

Publications list: Available in print

Access to staff: Contact by letter, by telephone, by fax, by e-mail, in person and via website. Appointment necessary.
Hours: Mon to Fri, 0900 to 1700

Access to building: *Hours:* Mon to Fri, 0900 to 1700

Links with: Consulate General of Peru; 52 Sloane Street, London, SW1X 9SP; Naval Attaché Office; 5 Falstaff House, 24 Barldolph Road, Richmond, London, TW9 2LH

EMBASSY OF RWANDA (AMBARWA)

Uganda House, 58–59 Trafalgar Square, London, WC2N 5DS

Tel: 020 7930 2570
Fax: 020 7930 2572
E-mail: ambarwanda@compuserve.com
Website: www.ambarwanda.org.uk

Enquiries to: Administrator
Other contacts: First Secretary for detailed enquiries.

Founded: 1995

Organisation type and purpose: National government body.
Embassy or Diplomatic Mission.
Consular and diplomatic relations.

Subject coverage: Any information regarding Rwanda.

Trade and statistical information: Trade or statistical information regarding Rwanda

Access to staff: Contact by letter, by telephone, by fax and by e-mail.
Appointment necessary.
Hours: Mon to Fri, 0930 to 1300 and 1400 to 1730

Access for disabled people: Level entry

EMBASSY OF SWEDEN

Press and Information, 11 Montagu Place, London, W1H 2AL

Tel: 020 7917 6400
Fax: 020 7724 4174
E-mail: ambassaden.london@foreign.ministry.se
Website: www.swedenabroad.com/london

Enquiries to: Information Officer

Organisation type and purpose: Embassy.

Subject coverage: General information on Sweden.

Access to staff: *Hours:* Mon to Fri, 0900 to 1230 and 1400 to 1600

EMBASSY OF THE FEDERAL REPUBLIC OF GERMANY

23 Belgrave Square, London, SW1X 8PZ

Tel: 020 7824 1300
Fax: 020 7824 1470
E-mail: info@london.diplo.de
Website: www.london.diplo.de
Website: www.auswaertiges-amt.de

Enquiries to: Information Centre

Organisation type and purpose: Government diplomatic representation.

Subject coverage: Life, science, economy and culture in Germany.

EMBASSY OF THE REPUBLIC OF BULGARIA

186–188 Queens Gate, London, SW7 5HL

Tel: 020 7584 9433
Fax: 020 7584 4948
E-mail: bgembasy@globalnet.co.uk
Website: www.bulgarianembassy.org.uk

Enquiries to: Secretary
Other contacts: Trade Counsellor for trade information.

Founded: 1920

Organisation type and purpose: National government body.
Embassy.
Diplomatic.

Access to staff: Contact by letter and by fax. Appointment necessary.
Hours: Mon to Fri, 0900 to 1700

EMBASSY OF THE REPUBLIC OF CROATIA

21 Conway Street, London, W1T 6BN

Tel: 020 7387 2022/1640
Fax: 020 7387 0310

Enquiries to: Information Officer

Organisation type and purpose: National government body.
Diplomatic mission.

Subject coverage: Information regarding the Republic of Croatia, the Croatian language, economic data, culture, etc.

Access to staff: Contact by letter, by telephone, by fax and by e-mail.
Appointment necessary.
Hours: Mon to Fri, 0900 to 1700

Consular Department: Mon to Thu, 1100 to 1400

EMBASSY OF THE REPUBLIC OF LITHUANIA

84 Gloucester Place, London, W1U 6AU

Tel: 020 7486 6401/6402; Consular section 020 7486 6404
Fax: 020 7486 6403
E-mail: lralon@globalnet.co.uk
Website: www.users.globalnet.co.uk/~lralon

Enquiries to: Head of Chancery
Other contacts: Private Secretary to the Ambassador

Organisation type and purpose: National government body.

Subject coverage: Lithuania.

Access to staff: Contact by letter, by telephone, by fax and by e-mail. Appointment necessary.
Hours: Consular Section: Mon to Fri, 1000 to 1300

EMBASSY OF THE REPUBLIC OF SLOVENIA

10 Little College Street, London, SW1P 3SH

Tel: 020 7222 5400
Fax: 020 7222 5722
E-mail: vlo@mzz-dkp.gov.si
Website: www.embassy-slovenia.org.uk

Enquiries to: Information Officer

Founded: 1991

Organisation type and purpose: National government body.

Subject coverage: Slovenia and Slovene governmental matters, Slovene commerce, visa information.

Access to staff: Contact by letter, by telephone, by fax, by e-mail and via website. Appointment necessary.
Hours: Mon to Fri, 0900 to 1700
Visas: Mon to Fri, 1000 to 1200

Access to building: Prior appointment required

Other address: Embassy of the Republic of Slovenia; Consular Section, 10 Cowley Street, London, SW1P

EMBASSY OF THE SLOVAK REPUBLIC (Slovak Embassy)

25 Kensington Palace Gardens, London, W8 4QY

Tel: 020 7313 6470
Fax: 020 7313 6481
E-mail: mail@slovakembassy.co.uk
Website: www.slovakembassy.co.uk

Enquiries to: Information Officer

Founded: 1993

Organisation type and purpose: National government body.
Embassy.

Subject coverage: General information on the Slovak Republic and tourist information.

Trade and statistical information: General economy and trade information and statistics obtainable from the commercial attaché, telephone: 020 7727 3099; fax: 020 7727 3667 or via website

Non-library collection catalogue: All or part available in-house

Library catalogue: All or part available in-house

Publications list: Available online

Access to staff: Contact by letter, by telephone, by fax and by e-mail. Appointment necessary.
Hours: General: Mon to Thu, 0900 to 1645; Fri, 0900 to 1530
Visa Department: Mon, Wed, 0900 to 1600; Tue,Thu, Fri, 0900 to 1200

Access to building: Prior appointment required
Hours: Open to public: Mon to Thu, 0900 to 1645; Fri, 0900 to 1530
Special comments: Visa Information: tel. 020 7313 6470.

EMBASSY OF THE SYRIAN ARAB REPUBLIC

8 Belgrave Square, London, SW1X 8PH

Tel: 020 7245 9012
Fax: 020 7235 4621

Enquiries to: Information Officer

Organisation type and purpose: Diplomatic Mission.

EMBASSY OF THE UNION OF MYANMAR

19a Charles Street, London, W1J 5DX

Tel: 020 7499 4340 Option 1 Consular Section; 09001 600 306 Visa Information
Fax: 020 7493 7399
E-mail: memblondon@aol.com
Website: www.myanmar.com

Enquiries to: Information Officer – Consular Office
Direct tel: 020 7499 4340

History of institution: formerly called Embassy of the Union of Burma

Organisation type and purpose: Diplomatic relations and consular services.

Subject coverage: Consular, travel, investing opportunities, trade.

Publications: Printed, and electronic and video

Access to staff: Contact by letter, by telephone and by fax. Appointment necessary.
Hours: Mon to Fri, 0930 to 1630
Visa Section: Mon to Fri, 1000 to 1300

Access to building: *Hours:* Mon to Fri, 0930 to 1630
Special comments: Via Charles Street

EMBASSY OF THE UNITED ARAB EMIRATES

30 Princes Gate, London, SW7 1PT

Tel: 020 7581 1281
Fax: 020 7581 9616
E-mail: information@uaeebassyuk.net
Website: www.uaeebassyuk.net

Enquiries to: Information and Resources
Direct e-mail: commerce@uaeembassyuk.net

Organisation type and purpose: National government body.
Embassy.

Subject coverage: United Arab Emirates.

EMBROIDERERS' GUILD

Apartment 41, Hampton Court Palace, Kingston Upon Thames, Surrey, KT8 9AU

Tel: 020 8943 1229
Fax: 020 8977 9882
E-mail: administrator@embroiderersguild.com
Website: www.embroiderersguild.com

Enquiries to: CEO
Direct e-mail: ceo@embroidersguild.com
Other contacts: Head of Heritage

Founded: 1906

Organisation type and purpose: Membership association (membership is by subscription), present number of members: 14,000, registered charity (charity number 234239), museum, suitable for ages: 5+, publishing house.
To promote the craft of embroidery for all.

Subject coverage: Historical and contemporary embroidery – workshops, library, bookshop and educational resources. Branches nationwide and Young Embroiderers available for children.

Collection: Collection of 11,000 pieces of historical and contemporary embroidery from the 17th century onwards, under the care of a professional curator; exhibitions from the collection travel to museums throughout the UK
Specialised library (by appointment)

Publications: Printed
Order printed publications from: Magazine Secretary, Embroiderers' Guild, PO Box 42B, East Molesey, Surrey, KT8 9BB; tel: 020 8943 1229 extn 28; fax: 020 8977 9882; e-mail: jjardine@embroiderersguild.com

Publications list: Available online and in print

Access to staff: Contact by letter, by telephone, by fax, by e-mail and via website. Appointment necessary.
Hours: Mon to Fri, 1000 to 1630
Special comments: Day pass required on arrival at Hampton Court Palace.

Access to building: No prior appointment required
Hours: Mon to Fri, 1030 to 1630

EMERSON COLLEGE

Formal name: Emerson College Trust Ltd

Forest Row, East Sussex, RH18 5JX

Tel: 01342 822238
Fax: 01342 826055
E-mail: mail@emerson.org.uk
Website: www.emerson.org.uk

Enquiries to: Information Officer

Founded: 1962

continued overleaf

Organisation type and purpose: International organisation, registered charity (charity number 312101), suitable for ages: 18+ no upper limit, training organisation.
Emerson College is an international centre for adult education, training and research based on the work of Rudolph Steiner.

Subject coverage: Steiner and Waldorf teacher training, anthroposophy and Rudolf Steiner.
Bio-dynamic, organic agriculture training.

Publications: Printed

Access to staff: Contact by letter, by telephone, by fax, by e-mail and via website. Appointment necessary.
Hours: Mon to Fri, 0830 to 1645; Reception is closed 1245 to 1400

Access to building: Prior appointment required
Special comments: Library is only open to current full-time students.

Access for disabled people: Parking provided, ramped entry

Accredited by the: British Accreditation Council (BAC); Westminster Central Hall, Storey's Gate, London, SW1H 9NH; tel: 020 7233 3468; fax: 020 7233 3470; e-mail: info@the-bac.org

EMI MUSIC SOUND FOUNDATION

27 Wrights Lane, London, W8 5SW

Tel: 020 7795 7000
Fax: 020 7795 7296
E-mail: enquiries@emimusicsoundfoundation.com
Website: www.emimusicsoundfoundation.com

Enquiries to: Chief Executive

Founded: 1997

Organisation type and purpose: Registered charity (charity number 1104027).

Subject coverage: Improvement of people's access to music education.

Publications: Printed

Publications list: Available in print

Access to staff: Contact by letter, by telephone, by fax, by e-mail and via website
Hours: Mon to Fri, 0900 to 1730

EMIE AT NFER

NFER, The Mere, Upton Park, Slough, Berkshire, SL1 2DQ

Tel: 01753 574123
Fax: 01753 691632
E-mail: enquiries@nfer.ac.uk
Website: www.nfer.ac.uk/emie

Enquiries to: Head of Service
Other contacts: EMIE Information Officers

Founded: 1981

Organisation type and purpose: Local government body, research organisation.

Subject coverage: Information services on educational management policy and practice provided principally to local authority staff and members in England, Wales, Scotland and Northern Ireland. Not curriculum but other matters pertaining to the operation of education and children's services in the UK.

Collection: Certain categories of documentation only accessible by local authority personnel. Extensive collection of policy level documentation contributed by education and children's services authorities in England, Wales, Scotland and Northern Ireland

Trade and statistical information: Surveys conducted on various aspects of education and children's service provision

Publications: Printed

Publications list: Available online and in print

Access to staff: Contact by letter, by telephone, by fax, by e-mail and via website. Appointment necessary.
Hours: Mon to Fri, 0915 to 1715
Special comments: Queries dealt with if resources permit, but full range of services limited to local authorities and subscribers to the service.

Funded by: Education and Library Boards in Northern Ireland; Local Authorities in England, Wales, Scotland and Northern Ireland; National Foundation for Educational Research (NFER)

Housed with the: National Foundation for Educational Research,; with whose researchers, and library and information services, EMIE co-operates closely

EMMS INTERNATIONAL (EMMS)

7 Washington Lane, Edinburgh, EH11 2HA

Tel: 0131 313 3828
Fax: 0131 313 4662
E-mail: via website
Website: www.emms.org

Enquiries to: Chief Executive

Founded: 1841; formerly called Edinburgh Medical Missionary Society; incorporates the former Emmanuel Healthcare

Organisation type and purpose: Registered charity (charity number SC032327, company number 224402).
Medical missionary society.

Subject coverage: History of medical missions; the Nazareth Hospital; placement of medical students for elective periods; medical missions.

Collection: Records of the Society since its foundation in 1841

Publications: Printed

Access to staff: Contact by letter, by telephone, by fax and by e-mail
Hours: Mon to Fri, 0900 to 1700

Links with: Church of Central Africa Presbyterian; Malawi; Dr Stephen Alfred; India; Emmanuel Hospital Association; India; International Nepal Fellowship

EMPICS

Formal name: EMPICS, A PA Group Photos Company

Pavilion House, 16 Castle Boulevard, Nottingham, NG7 1FC

Tel: 0115 844 7447
Fax: 0115 844 7448
E-mail: info@empics.com
Website: www.empics.com

Enquiries to: Sales and Marketing Director

Founded: 1867

Organisation type and purpose: National organisation, service industry.
Picture library.

Subject coverage: News, sport, and entertainment pictures, past and present.

Collection: PA
Empire Sport
AP
Emoics Entertainment

Non-library collection catalogue: All or part available online

Library catalogue: All or part available online

Publications: Electronic and video

Access to staff: Contact by telephone, by e-mail and via website
Hours: Mon to Fri, 0900 to 1700

Access to building: Prior appointment required
Hours: Mon to Fri, 0930 to 1800

Access for disabled people: Access to all public areas, toilet facilities

EMPLOYMENT OPPORTUNITIES FOR PEOPLE WITH DISABILITIES (Employment Opportunities)

Crystal Gate, 3rd Floor, 28–30 Worship Street, London, EC2A 2AH

Tel: 020 7448 5420
Website: www.opportunities.org.uk

Enquiries to: Administrator
Direct e-mail: samantha.jobber@shaw-trust.org.uk

Founded: 1980; formerly called Opportunities for the Disabled

Organisation type and purpose: National organisation, registered charity (charity number 280112).
Helps people with disabilities find employment via a network of regional centres around the country.

Subject coverage: Disability in relation to employment.

Publications: Printed

Publications list: Available online and in print

Access to staff: Contact by letter, by telephone, by fax, by e-mail and via website. Appointment necessary.
Hours: Mon to Fri, 0900 to 1700

Regional Centres: Bath; tel: 01225 461005 and minicom; fax: 01225 461158; e-mail: eopps.diropsbath@connectfree.co.uk; Bristol and West; Bristol; tel: 0117 925 5751 and minicom; fax: 0117 925 5751; e-mail: eopps.bristol@connectfee.co.uk; East Midlands; Leicester; tel: 0116 280 7450; minicom 7451; fax: 0116 280 7449; e-mail: eopps.leicester@connectfree.co.uk; Greater London; London; tel: 020 7580 7545 and minicom; fax: 020 7255 3115; e-mail: eopps.grtlondon@connectfree.co.uk; Greater Manchester;

Manchester; tel: 0161 431 8889 and minicom; fax: 0161 431 8889; e-mail: eopps .manchester@connectfree.co.uk; Merseyside and Deeside; Wirral; tel: 0151 645 2346 and minicom; fax: 0151 645 2346; e-mail: eopps .mersey@connectfree.co.uk; Newcastle and North East; Newcastle upon Tyne; tel: 0191 232 1994 and minicom; fax: 0191 233 0945; e-mail: eopps.newcastle@connectfree.co.uk; Scotland; Glasgow; tel: 0141 429 8429 and minicom; fax: 0141 429 4023; e-mail: eopps .glasgow@connectfree.co.uk; South East Wales; Cardiff; tel: 029 2039 4363 and minicom; fax: 029 2039 8886; e-mail: eopps .cardiff@connectfree.co.uk; South Essex; Essex; tel: 01227 201984 and minicom; fax: 01227 202355; e-mail: eopps.brentwood@ connectfree.co.uk; South Hampshire; Southampton; tel: 02380 228010 and minicom; fax: 01329 233911; e-mail: eopps .fareham@connectfree.co.uk; South Yorkshire & North Midlands; Sheffield; tel: 0114 279 5362; fax: 0114 279 7303 and minicom; e-mail: eopps.sheffield@ connectfree.co.uk; Surrey and East Sussex; West Sussex; tel: 01403 262021; minicom 262031; fax: 01403 262021; e-mail: eopps .horsham@connectfree.co.uk; West Midlands; Birmingham; tel: 0121 331 4121 and minicom; fax: 0121 344 4470; e-mail: eopps.birmingham@connectfree.co.uk

EMPLOYMENT RIGHTS ADVICE SERVICE (ERAS)

Low Pay Unit, 10 Dukes Road, London, WC1H 9AD

Tel: 020 7387 2911
Fax: 020 7387 2250
E-mail: enquiries@lowpayunit.org.uk
Website: www.lowpayunit.org.uk

Enquiries to: Director
Direct e-mail: bharti.patel@lowpayunit.org.uk
Other contacts: On-line Officer for web site.

Founded: 1974

Organisation type and purpose: Voluntary organisation, research organisation.
Advice and campaigning body on issues related to low pay and in-work poverty, campaigning for better protection for the low paid.

Subject coverage: Employment legislation and advice, information on better employment practice.

Trade and statistical information: Labour market data and earnings.
Poverty statistics

Publications: Printed

Publications list: Available online and in print

Access to staff: Contact by letter, by telephone, by fax, by e-mail and via website
Hours: Mon to Fri, 0930 to 1730
Special comments: No disabled access.

EMPLOYMENT TRIBUNALS SERVICE (ETS)

The Secretary to the Tribunals, ETS/FSU, First Floor, 100 Southgate Street, Bury St Edmunds, IP33 2AQ

Tel: 0845 795 9775, 0845 757 3722 (minicom)
E-mail: buryet@ets.gsi.gov.uk
Website: www.employmenttribunals.gov.uk

Enquiries to: Senior Secretariat Officer

History of institution: formerly called Central Office of the Industrial Tribunals (COIT)

Organisation type and purpose: National government body.

Subject coverage: Procedures for Employment Tribunals, statistics etc.

Collection: Public registers of applications and tribunal decisions held in Bury St Edmunds and Glasgow for England and Wales and for Scotland, respectively

Non-library collection catalogue: All or part available in-house

Publications: Printed, and electronic and video
Order printed publications from: DTI Orderline tel: 0870 1502 500, fax: 0870 1502 333

Publications list: Available online

Access to staff: Contact by letter, by telephone and by fax
Hours: Mon to Fri, 0900 to 1700

Access to building: No prior appointment required
Hours: Mon to Fri, 0900 to 1700

Access for disabled people: Ramped entry

ENABLE SCOTLAND

2nd Floor, 146 Argyle Street, Glasgow, G2 8BL

Tel: 0141 226 4541
Fax: 0141 204 4398
E-mail: enable@enable.org.uk
Website: www.enable.org.uk

Enquiries to: Information Service
Direct e-mail: info@enable.org.uk
Other contacts: Chief Executive

Founded: 1954; formerly called Scottish Society for the Mentally Handicapped (year of change 1993)

Organisation type and purpose: Voluntary organisation, registered charity (charity number SC 09024).

Subject coverage: Rights, services, employment, advocacy, education, community care relating to people with learning disabilities and their families.

Information services: A telephone and e-mail enquiry service, a lending library.

Services for disabled people: ENABLE Scotland supports people with learning disabilities and their families in Scotland; provides accessible, easy-to-read information on many topics.

Collection: Small library

Non-library collection catalogue: All or part available online

Library catalogue: All or part available online and in-house

Publications: Printed, and electronic and video
Order printed publications from: Information Service

Publications list: Available online and in print

Access to staff: Contact by letter, by telephone, by fax, by e-mail and via website. Appointment necessary.
Hours: Enquiry line: Mon to Fri, 1300 to 1600

Access to building: Prior appointment required
Hours: Appointments to use the library may be made Mon to Fri, 0900 to 1600

Access for disabled people: Steps into building, lift, level access thereafter, toilet facilities
Special comments: Steps into building, lift, level access thereafter.

Member organisation of: Inclusion Europe

ENDANGERED DOGS DEFENCE AND RESCUE LIMITED (EDDR Ltd)

PO Box 1544, London, W7 2ZB

Tel: 0844 856 3303
E-mail: info@endangereddogs.com
Website: www.endangereddogs.com

Enquiries to: Secretary
Direct e-mail: office@endangereddogs.com

Founded: 1999; formerly called Endangered Dogs Defence and Rescue (year of change 1999)

Organisation type and purpose: Advisory body, voluntary organisation.
Advice and guidance concerning canine legislation and welfare.

Subject coverage: Canine legislation and legal actions, canine rescue/re-homing, dogs with special needs, promoting responsible dog ownership, telephone helplines.

Publications: Printed

Access to staff: Contact by letter, by telephone, by e-mail and via website
Hours: All hours

ENERGY INFORMATION CENTRE (EIC)

Rosemary House, Lanwades Business Park, Newmarket, Suffolk, CB8 7PW

Tel: 01638 751400
Fax: 01638 751801
E-mail: info@eic.co.uk

Enquiries to: Membership Manager

Founded: 1975

Organisation type and purpose: Membership association (membership is by subscription), present number of members: 650 corporate members, training organisation, consultancy, research organisation, publishing house.

Subject coverage: Utilities market information, advice and support, covering electricity, gas, oil and water.

Trade and statistical information: Data on the production and use of utility services; electricity, gas, oil and water

Publications: Printed

Access to staff: Access for members only.
Hours: Mon to Fri, 0900 to 1730

Access to building: Prior appointment required

Access for disabled people: Toilet facilities

continued overleaf

Parent Company: Metal Bulletin plc; Park House, Park Terrace, Worcester Park, Surrey, KT4 7HY

ENERGY INSTITUTE (EI)

61 New Cavendish Street, London, W1G 7AR

Tel: 020 7467 7100
Fax: 020 7255 1472
E-mail: info@energyinst.org
Website: www.energyinst.org

Enquiries to: Library and Information Service Manager
Direct tel: 020 7467 7111
Direct e-mail: ccosgrove@energyinst.org
Other contacts: Information Officer

Founded: 2003; created by the merger of Institute of Petroleum (founded 1913), Institute of Energy (founded 1927) (year of change 2003)

Organisation type and purpose: Membership association (membership is by subscription), present number of members: 12,000 individuals and 400 corporate, registered charity (charity number 1097899).

Subject coverage: All forms of energy including renewables, wind, wave, electricity, nuclear, oil and gas. Especially strong on petroleum technology, petroleum geology, exploration, production, refining, transportation, physical and chemical properties of hydrocarbons, methods of analysis, petroleum products and petrochemicals, statistics, business.

Information services: Quick queries; extended desk research; online searching; statistics service.

Special visitor services: Access to on-line databases.

Education services: Training courses.

Collection: Books dating from the mid-19th century to present day
Periodicals relating to petroleum and other energy industries dating from 1890s

Trade and statistical information: UK petrol retailing market statistics.
UK refining statistics.
Worldwide petroleum industry statistics

Non-library collection catalogue: All or part available online and in-house

Library catalogue: All or part available online and in-house

Publications: Printed, and electronic and video
Order printed publications from: Portland Customer Services, tel: 01206 796351; e-mail: sales@portland-services.com
Order electronic and video publications from: EI Publications available for purchase electronically, see website: http://www.energyinst.org

Publications list: Available online and in print

Access to staff: Contact by letter, by telephone, by fax, by e-mail, in person and via website. Non-members charged.
Hours: Mon to Fri, 0915 to 1700
Special comments: Letter of introduction is required from students.

Access for disabled people: *Special comments:* Steps from pavement to front door.

Administers: Information for Energy Group – IFEG; at the same address; tel: 020 7467 7115; fax: 020 7255 1472; e-mail: ifeg@energyinst.org; website: http://www.energyinst.org
UKWEC – UK Member Committee of the World Energy Council; at the same address; tel: 020 7467 7111; fax: 020 7255 1472; e-mail: ukwec@energyinst.org; website: http://www.energyinst.org/ukwec

ENFIELD & DISTRICT VETERAN VEHICLE TRUST (EDVVT)

Whitewebbs Museum, Whitewebbs Road, Enfield, Middlesex, EN2 9HW

Tel: 020 8367 1898
Fax: 020 8363 1904
E-mail: museum@whitewebbs.fsnet.co.uk

Enquiries to: Information Officer

Founded: 1979; formerly called Enfield and District Veteran Vehicle Society

Organisation type and purpose: Museum.

Subject coverage: Vintage and classic cars, motorcycles and commercial vehicles.

Access to staff: Contact by letter, by telephone, by fax and by e-mail. Appointment necessary.
Hours: Tue, 1200 to 1600
Special comments: Otherwise access by arrangement.

Access for disabled people: Parking provided, ramped entry, toilet facilities

ENFIELD LIBRARIES

First Stop Information, Central Library, Cecil Road, Enfield Town, EN2 6TW

Tel: 020 8379 8341
Fax: 020 8379 8401
Website: www.enfield.gov.uk

Organisation type and purpose: Local government body, public library.

Subject coverage: General; local history including material in the museum at Forty Hall; European fiction; linguistics.

Collection: European Fiction Collection
Linguistics (under the London and SE Region Scheme)
Local History Collection
Sound recordings of J S Bach, jazz artists BAJ to BH and Folk Music (Argentina, Bolivia, Chile, Paraguay, Uruguay) (under the Greater London Audio Specialising Scheme)

Access to staff: Contact by letter, by telephone, by fax and by e-mail
Hours: Mon to Fri, 0900 to 1700
Special comments: No appointment necessary for general libraries. Appointments are required for local history collections and other special collections.

ENFIELD LOCAL HISTORY UNIT

Formal name: Enfield Local Studies Library & Archives

Thomas Hardy House, 39 London Road, Enfield, EN2 6DS

Tel: 020 8379 2724
E-mail: local.history@enfield.gov.uk
Website: www.enfield.gov.uk/info/1062/libraries-local_collections/1011/enfield_local_studies_library_and_archive

Enquiries to: Local Studies Officer

Founded: 1975

Organisation type and purpose: Archive.

Subject coverage: Local history material for Local Borough of Enfield area.

Non-library collection catalogue: All or part available in-house

Library catalogue: All or part available in-house

Access to staff: Contact by letter, by telephone, by e-mail and in person. Appointment necessary.
Hours: Mon, Tue, Thu, Fri, 0930 to 1630

Access to building: *Hours:* As above.

Access for disabled people: Lift.

ENGINEERING AND PHYSICAL SCIENCES RESEARCH COUNCIL (EPSRC)

Polaris House, North Star Avenue, Swindon, Wiltshire, SN2 1ET

Tel: 01793 444000
E-mail: infoline@epsrc.ac.uk
Website: www.epsrc.ac.uk

Enquiries to: Head of Communications & Stakeholder Engagement
Direct tel: 01793 444502
Direct e-mail: david.reid@epsrc.ac.uk

Founded: 1965; formerly called Science Research Council (SRC) (year of change 1981); formerly called Science and Engineering Research Council (SERC) (year of change 1994)

Organisation type and purpose: EPSRC is a non-departmental public body funded by the UK government through the Department for Business Innovation and Skills. It employs around 300 staff in Swindon.

Subject coverage: The main UK government agency for funding research and training in engineering and the physical sciences, investing more than £850m. a year. Supports research into engineering, mathematics, physics, chemistry, materials science, information and communications technologies.

Publications: Printed

Publications list: Available online

Access to staff: Contact by letter, by telephone, by e-mail and via website
Hours: Mon to Fri, 0900 to 1700

ENGINEERING COUNCIL

246 High Holborn, London, WC1V 7EX

Tel: 020 3206 0500
Fax: 020 3206 0501
E-mail: staff@engc.org.uk
Website: www.engc.org.uk

Enquiries to: Marketing and Communications Director
Direct e-mail: sbrough@engc.org.uk

Founded: 1983; formerly called Engineering Council UK (year of change 2009)

Organisation type and purpose: Regulatory authority for professional engineers and engineering technicians in the UK. Operates through 35 engineering institutions, which it licenses to assess individuals for inclusion on the ECUK register of Chartered Engineers, Incorporated Engineers and Engineering Technicians (titles that are protected by Royal Charter).

Subject coverage: The engineering profession, education and training of Chartered Engineers, Incorporated Engineers and Engineering Technicians, continuing professional development.

Publications: Printed

Publications list: Available online and in print

Access to staff: Contact by letter, by telephone, by fax, by e-mail and via website
Hours: Mon to Fri, 0900 to 1700

Access to building: Prior appointment required

Nominated institutions: Association of Cost Engineers; British Computer Society; British Institute of Non-Destructive Testing; Chartered Institution of Building Services Engineers; Chartered Institution of Water and Environmental Management; Energy Institute; IEE; Institute of Acoustics; Institute of Cast Metals Engineers; Institute of Healthcare Engineering & Estate Management; Institute of Highway Incorporated Engineers; Institute of Marine Engineering, Science and Technology; Institute of Materials, Minerals and Mining; Institute of Measurement and Control; Institute of Physics; Institute of Physics & Engineering in Medicine; Institute of Plumbing & Heating Engineers; Institution of Agricultural Engineers; Institution of Chemical Engineers; Institution of Civil Engineers; Institution of Electrical Engineers; Institution of Engineering Designers; Institution of Fire Engineers; Institution of Gas Engineers and Managers; Institution of Highways & Transportation; Institution of Incorporated Engineers; Institution of Lighting Engineers; Institution of Mechanical Engineers; Institution of Nuclear Engineers; Institution of Plant Engineers; Institution of Railway Signal Engineers; Institution of Structural Engineers; Institution of Water Officers; Royal Aeronautical Society; Royal Institution of Naval Architects; Society of Environmental Engineers; Society of Operations Engineers; Welding Institute

ENGINEERING EDUCATION SCHEME IN ENGLAND (EES)

Weltech Centre, Ridgeway, Welwyn Garden City, Hertfordshire, AL7 2AA

Tel: 01707 393323
Fax: 01707 393133
E-mail: info@etrust.org.uk
Website: www.engineering-education.org .uk

Enquiries to: Director
Direct e-mail: a.ritchie@eeswgc.demon.co.uk

Founded: 1984

Organisation type and purpose: Registered charity (charity number 1002459), suitable for ages: year 12 students.
To encourage year 12 students into engineering.

Subject coverage: Engineering education scheme for schools.

Publications: Printed

Access to staff: Contact by letter, by telephone and by e-mail
Hours: Mon to Fri, 0900 to 1700

Administered by: Engineering Development Trust

Part of: Royal Academy of Engineering's Best Programme

ENGINEERING EQUIPMENT AND MATERIALS USERS' ASSOCIATION (EEMUA)

10–12 Lovat Lane, London, EC3R 8DN

Tel: 020 7621 0011
Fax: 020 7621 0022
E-mail: info@eemua.org
Website: www.eemua.org
Website: www.eemua.co.uk/pub-folder/index.htm

Enquiries to: Executive Director

Founded: 1950

Organisation type and purpose: Industry Association.
Members are purchasers, specificiers and users of engineering products and services in the chemical process industries, power generation and utilities sectors.
Aims to reduce costs and improve safety and operational effectiveness by sharing experiences and expertise, and by promotion of engineering users' interests.

Subject coverage: Storage tanks, mechanical, electrical, instrumentation and control engineering, inspection and maintenance, quality assurance and control, health and safety at work.

Library catalogue: All or part available online

Publications: Printed

Publications list: Available online

Access to staff: Contact by letter, by telephone, by fax, by e-mail and via website. Appointment necessary. Access for members only.
Hours: Mon to Fri, 0900 to 1700

Administers: Secretariat for the European Committee of User Inspectorates (ECUI)

ENGINEERING INDUSTRIES ASSOCIATION (EIA)

62 Bayswater Road, London, W2 3PS

Tel: 020 7298 6455
Fax: 020 7298 6456
E-mail: head.office@eia.co.uk
Website: www.eia.uk

Enquiries to: Director
Other contacts: Administrator (for general enquiries)

Founded: 1940

Organisation type and purpose: Trade association.

Subject coverage: Engineering industry; legislation, particularly health and safety and employment law; export practice; overseas missions and exhibitions.

Publications: Printed

Access to staff: Contact by letter, by telephone, by fax, by e-mail and via website. Appointment necessary.
Hours: Mon to Fri, 0900 to 1700

Constituent bodies: five regional groups

Member organisation of: Bristol and Western Engineering Manufacturers Association (BEMA); tel: 0117 906 4830; fax: 0117 906 4827; e-mail: enquiries@bema.co.uk

ENGINEERING INTEGRITY SOCIETY (EIS)

5 Wentworth Avenue, Sheffield, South Yorkshire, S11 9QX

Tel: 0114 262 1155
Fax: 0114 262 1120
E-mail: cpinder@e-i-s.org.uk
Website: www.e-i-s.org.uk

Enquiries to: Secretariat Administrator

Founded: 1985

Organisation type and purpose:
Membership association (membership is by subscription), registered charity (charity number 327121).
Arrangement of courses and conferences to advance the education of persons working in the field of engineering by providing a forum for the interchange of ideas and information on engineering integrity.

Subject coverage: Durability and fatigue; simulation; test and measurement, noise, vibration and harshness; these are the three Groups that make up the society.

Publications: Printed

Access to staff: Contact by letter, by telephone, by fax, by e-mail and via website
Hours: Mon to Fri, 0900 to 1700

ENGINEERING TRAINING COUNCIL FOR NORTHERN IRELAND (ETC (NI))

Interpoint, 20–24 York Street, Belfast, BT15 1AQ

Tel: 028 9032 9878
Fax: 028 9031 0301
E-mail: info@etcni.org.uk
Website: www.etcni.org.uk

Enquiries to: Chief Executive

Founded: 1990

Organisation type and purpose: Training organisation.

Subject coverage: Industrial training, employment, qualifications, education and technical issues associated with careers and development of engineers in manufacturing industries.

Access to staff: Contact by letter, by telephone, by e-mail and via website
Hours: Mon to Fri, 0900 to 1700

ENGINEERINGUK

Weston House, 2nd Floor, 246 High Holborn, London, WC1V 7EX

Tel: 020 3206 0400
Fax: 020 3206 0401
E-mail: info@engineeringuk.com
Website: www.engineeringuk.com

Enquiries to: Communications Director
Direct e-mail: belgood@engineeringuk.com

Founded: 2002; formerly called Engineering and Technology Board (ETB) (year of change 2002)

Organisation type and purpose: An independent, not-for-profit organisation.
To promote the vital contribution that engineers, and engineering and technology, make to society; to inspire people at all levels to pursue careers in engineering and technology; to improve the perception of engineers, engineering and technology and to improve the supply of engineers.
Works with partners across business and industry, education and skills, the professional engineering institutions, the Engineering Council and the wider science and engineering communities.

Subject coverage: The engineering profession, education and training, qualifications of engineers and technicians, careers advice, salary surveys, continuing education and training, career breaks for women, Young Engineers for Britain and the Environment Award for Engineers, Women Into Science and Engineers (WISE) campaign, schools and industry liaison, engineering and technology.

Publications: Printed

Access to staff: Contact by letter, by telephone, by fax, by e-mail and via website
Hours: Mon to Fri, 0900 to 1700

ENGLAND AND WALES CRICKET BOARD (ECB)

Lord's Cricket Ground, St John's Wood Road, London, NW8 8QZ

Tel: 020 7432 1200
Fax: 020 7289 5619
E-mail: feedback@ecb.co.uk
Website: lords.org
Website: www.ecb.co.uk

Enquiries to: Administration Manager

Founded: 1997; formed from Cricket Council, National Cricket Association (NCA), Test and County Cricket Board (TCCB) (year of change 1997)

Organisation type and purpose: Governing body for cricket at all levels in England and Wales.

Subject coverage: Cricket: coaching, pitches (turf and non-turf), grant aid, competitions, laws of the game, insurance.

Collection: MCC Cricket Memorial Gallery (information from the Curator, MCC, Lords Cricket Ground)

Publications: Printed, and electronic and video

Access to staff: Contact by letter, by telephone, by fax and by e-mail.
Appointment necessary.
Hours: Mon to Fri, 0900 to 1700

Composed of: Marylebone Cricket Club; National Cricket Association; Test and County Cricket Board

Member of: Sports Council

ENGLAND AND WALES CRICKET BOARD ASSOCIATION OF CRICKET OFFICIALS (ECB ACO)

The England and Wales Cricket Board, Lord's Cricket Ground, London, NW8 8QZ

Tel: 020 7432 1200
Fax: 020 7286 5583
E-mail: ecbaco@ecb.co.uk
Website: www.ecb.co.uk/ecbaco

Enquiries to: Membership Services Team
Direct tel: 020 7432 1240

Founded: 1953; created by the merger of the Association of Cricket Umpires and Scorers and the ECB Officials Association (year of change 2008); formerly called Association of Cricket Umpires & Scorers (ACUS) (year of change 1993)

Organisation type and purpose: International organisation, membership association (membership is by subscription, qualification), present number of members: 9,500, voluntary organisation, training organisation.
Examination organisation.
To improve the standard of umpiring and scoring by training, examination and example, and by any other means.

Subject coverage: The interpretation and application of the laws of cricket.

Publications: Printed, and electronic and video

Access to staff: Contact by letter, by telephone, by e-mail and via website
Hours: Mon to Fri, 0900 to 1700

ENGLAND SQUASH

Ground Floor, Bell Vue Athletics Centre, Pink Bank Lane, Manchester, M12 5GL

Tel: 0161 231 4499
Fax: 0161 231 4231
E-mail: enquiries@englandsquashandracketball.com
Website: www.englandsquash.com

Enquiries to: Chair
Other contacts: Administration Manager

Founded: 1930; formerly called Squash Rackets Association (SRA) (year of change 2001)

Organisation type and purpose: Membership association.
Governing body of squash in England.

Subject coverage: Coach training and qualification, referee training and qualification, technical and court specification, tournament organisation, grass roots development both player and participation, membership, club and individual.

Trade and statistical information: Some statistics held for playing numbers in UK

Publications: Printed

Publications list: Available online and in print

Access to staff: Contact by letter and by e-mail
Hours: Mon to Fri, 0900 to 1700

Access to building: No prior appointment required

Access for disabled people: Parking provided, level entry, toilet facilities

ENGLAND SQUASH & RACKETBALL

National Squash Centre, Sportcity, Manchester, M11 3FF

Tel: 01612314499
E-mail: enquiries@englandsquashandracketball.com
Website: www.englandsquashandracketball.com

Founded: 1984; formerly called British Racketball Association (BRA) and Squash Rackets Association (SRA) (year of change 1998)

Organisation type and purpose: Voluntary organisation.
Governing body of the sport.

Subject coverage: England Squash & Racketball is the national governing body for squash and racketball.

At our Head Office at the National Squash Centre in Manchester, we have staff covering areas such as competitions and events, coaching and coach education, performance, marketing, membership, and finance.

Access to staff: Contact by letter, by telephone and by fax
Hours: Mon to Fri, 0900 to 1700

ENGLISH ASSOCIATION (EA)

University of Leicester, University Road, Leicester, LE1 7RH

Tel: 0116 229 7622
Fax: 0116 229 7623
E-mail: engassoc@le.ac.uk
Website: www.le.ac.uk/engassoc

Enquiries to: Chief Executive

Founded: 1906

Organisation type and purpose: International organisation, learned society, professional body (membership is by subscription), present number of members: 1,500, registered charity (charity number 1124890), publishing house.

Subject coverage: English language and literature; standards of English writing and speech; educational matters relating to the teaching of English.

Collection: Own publications back to 1906

Publications: Printed
Order printed publications from: www.le.ac.uk/engassoc

Publications list: Available online and in print

Access to staff: Contact by letter, by telephone, by fax, by e-mail and via website
Hours: Mon to Fri, 0900 to 1700

ENGLISH BASKETBALL ASSOCIATION (EBBA)

c/o English Institute of Sport, Coleridge Road, Sheffield, S9 5DA

Tel: 0870 77 44 225
Fax: 0870 77 44 226
E-mail: info@englandbasketball.co.uk
Website: www.englandbasketball.co.uk

Enquiries to: Chief Executive
Other contacts: General Manager

Organisation type and purpose: Membership association (membership is by subscription), present number of members: 900 clubs; 20,000 individuals.
Governing body of sport.

Subject coverage: Sport of basketball, coaching, officiating, playing indoor and outdoor basketball.

Publications: Printed, and electronic and video

Publications list: Available in print

Access to staff: Contact by letter, by telephone, by fax and by e-mail. Appointment necessary.
Hours: Mon to Fri, 0900 to 1700

Affiliated to: British Olympic Association; Central Council of Physical Recreation; International Basketball Association

ENGLISH BOWLING FEDERATION (EBF)

The Secretary, 14 Field Close, Worksop, Nottinghamshire, S81 0PF

Tel: 01909 474346
Fax: 01909 474346
E-mail: j.heppel@btinternet.com
Website: www.fedbowls.co.uk

Enquiries to: Publicity Officer
Direct e-mail: d.nash1@tiscli.co.uk

Founded: 1926

Organisation type and purpose: National governing body, membership association, present number of members: 13 county bowling associations.
National governing body of the sport.

Subject coverage: Flat green bowls.

Publications: Printed

Access to staff: Contact by letter, by telephone and by fax
Hours: Mon to Fri, 0900 to 1700

ENGLISH BRIDGE UNION LIMITED (EBU)

Broadfields, Bicester Road, Aylesbury, Buckinghamshire, HP19 8AZ

Tel: 01296 317200
Fax: 01296 317220
E-mail: postmaster@ebu.co.uk
Website: www.ebu.co.uk

Enquiries to: General Manager
Other contacts: Bridge for All helpline for students/teachers wishing to join Bridge for All education programme.

Founded: 1940

Organisation type and purpose: Membership association (membership is by subscription), present number of members: 30,000.
National governing body for the card game of Duplicate Bridge.

Subject coverage: Duplicate bridge in England, membership, Master Points, bridge supplies, competition entry, laws and ethics, educating and teaching, Bridge for All, overseas information.

Collection: Some archive material – books, trophies

Publications: Printed, and electronic and video

Access to staff: Contact by letter, by telephone, by fax, by e-mail, in person and via website
Hours: Mon to Fri, 0830 to 1715

Access for disabled people: Parking provided, ramped entry, toilet facilities

Member of: European Bridge League; World Bridge Federation

ENGLISH CHESS FEDERATION (ECF)

The Watch Oak, Chain Lane, Battle, East Sussex, TN33 0YD

Tel: 01424 775222
Fax: 01424 775904
E-mail: office@englishchess.org.uk
Website: www.bcf.org.uk

Enquiries to: Manager
Direct e-mail: cynthia@englishchess.org.uk

Founded: 1904; formerly called British Chess Federation (year of change 2005)

Organisation type and purpose: To control, direct and promote the playing of chess in England, to institute and maintain British Chess Championships, to promote national and international chess tournaments in England.

Collection: National Chess Library of 8,000 vols (housed at University Centre Hastings)

Library catalogue: All or part available online

Publications: Printed

Publications list: Available online

Access to staff: Contact by letter, by telephone, by fax and by e-mail
Hours: Mon to Fri, 1000 to 1530 (by telephone only)

Access to building: *Hours:* Daily, 0900 to 1730

Access for disabled people: *Hours:* Daily, 0900 to 1730

Affiliated to: World Chess Federation (FIDE)

ENGLISH CIVIL WAR SOCIETY LIMITED (ECWS)

E-mail: press@english-civil-war-society.org.uk
Website: www.english-civil-war-society.org.uk

Enquiries to: Public Relations Manager

Founded: 1981; formed from King's Army, Roundhead Association

Organisation type and purpose: Membership association (membership is by subscription), present number of members: 2,000, voluntary organisation.
Re-enactment society specialising in period 1638–1651.

Subject coverage: Historical re-enactment, English Civil War 1638–1651, film, television and media contacts and expertise, educational interpretation of history, living history, museum activity.

Access to staff: Contact by e-mail and via website

ENGLISH COLLECTIVE OF PROSTITUTES

Crossroads Women's Centre, PO Box 287, London, NW6 5QU

Tel: 020 7482 2496, 020 7482 2496 (minicom)
Fax: 020 7209 4761
E-mail: crossroadswomenscentre@compuserve.com
Website: www.prostitutescollective.net

Enquiries to: Information Officer

Organisation type and purpose: Voluntary organisation.
Pressure group.
To establish workers' rights in the sex industry, to be recognised as workers with legal, economic and civil rights. To campaign for the abolition of the prostitution laws, for the right to protection from violence, to health care, to form or join unions and for financial alternatives to prostitution.
To oppose illegal and racist enforcement of the law, and state run prostitution including toleration zones.

Subject coverage: Prostitution laws, police legality and racism, child custody, taxes, health including HIV and AIDS, benefits.

Publications: Printed

Access to staff: Contact by letter, by telephone, by fax, by e-mail, in person and via website. Appointment necessary.
Hours: Tue and Wed, 1200 to 1600; Thu, 1700 to 1900
Telephone lines: Mon to Wed, Fri, 1000 to 1600; Thu, 1000 to 1600, 1700 to 1900

Access for disabled people: Access to all public areas, toilet facilities

Initiated: Legal Action for Women (LAW); e-mail: law@crossroadswomen.net; website: http://www.allwomencount.net

Member of: International Prostitutes Collective; website: http://www.prostitutescollectives.net; International Wages for Housework Campaign; Wages for Housework Campaign

ENGLISH CROSS-COUNTRY ASSOCIATION (ECCA)

22 Denham Drive, Berg Estate, Basingstoke, Hampshire, RG22 6LR

Tel: 01256 328401

Enquiries to: Honorary Secretary

Founded: 1992

continued overleaf

Organisation type and purpose: Membership association, voluntary organisation.
National governing body, controlling body of the sport in England.
Organises and develops cross-country running.

Subject coverage: Cross-country running.

Publications: Printed

Access to staff: Contact by letter, by telephone and by fax
Hours: Mon to Fri, 0900 to 1700

Affiliated to: United Kingdom Athletics

Member of: Amateur Athletics Association of England

ENGLISH CURLING ASSOCIATION (ECA)

14 Donnelly Drive, Bedford, MK14 9TV

Tel: 01234 315174 (home); 01223 372752 (business)
E-mail: jmbroons@ntlworld.com
Website: www.englishcurling.org.uk

Enquiries to: Secretary

Founded: 1971

Organisation type and purpose: Membership association, present number of members: 150, suitable for ages: 13+, training organisation.
National governing body of the sport.

Subject coverage: Sport of curling in general from beginners to world championships.

Access to staff: Contact by letter, by telephone, by fax, by e-mail and in person. Appointment necessary.
Hours: Mon to Fri, 0900 to 1700

ENGLISH FOLK DANCE AND SONG SOCIETY (EFDSS)

Formal name: Vaughan Williams Memorial Library

Vaughan Williams Memorial Library, Cecil Sharp House, 2 Regent's Park Road, London, NW1 7AY

Tel: 020 7485 2206
Fax: 020 7284 0534
E-mail: library@efdss.org
Website: www.efdss.org

Enquiries to: Library Director
Direct e-mail: library@efdss.org

Founded: 1932

Organisation type and purpose: Learned society (membership is by subscription), present number of members: 5,000, registered charity.
To document and promote folk arts in England.

Subject coverage: Folk music including song, dance and drama, customs involving dance and song, singing games, social history, folk tales, oral history, dialects, mainly British material but much information on other English-speaking countries, notably the USA.

Collection: BBC archive of folk music recordings
Broadwood Collection (manuscripts, and folk song books on loan)
Butterworth Collection (manuscripts, dance and song)
Carpenter Collection (manuscripts and tapes from wax cylinders, folk song and drama)
Cecil Sharp Collection (books and manuscripts on folk song and dance)
Collection of 18th-century dancing masters
Gardiner Collection (folk song)
Gilchrist Collection (folk music)
Melusine Wood (historical dance)
Percy Grainger Collection of phonograph recordings from wax cylinders (on tape)
Vaughan Williams manuscripts in the British Library (microfilm)

Library catalogue: All or part available online and in-house

Publications: Printed, and electronic and video
Order electronic and video publications from: website: http://folkshop.efdss.org

Publications list: Available online

Access to staff: Contact by letter, by telephone, by fax, by e-mail, in person and via website. Access for members only. Non-members charged.
Hours: Tue to Fri, 0930 to 1730; 1st and 3rd Sat each month, 1000 to 1600

Access to building: *Hours:* Tue to Fri, 0930 to 1730; 1st and 3rd Sat each month, 1000 to 1600
Special comments: Sound/audio-visual collections closed daily, 1200 to 1400.

Access for disabled people: To library reading room level only
Hours: Tue to Fri, 0930 to 1730; 1st and 3rd Sat each month, 1000 to 1600
Special comments: To library level, to which materials will be retrieved by staff for disabled users.

ENGLISH GARDENING SCHOOL

c/o The Chelsea Physic Gardens, 66 Royal Hospital Road, London, SW3 4HS

Tel: 020 7352 4347
Fax: 020 7376 3936
E-mail: egs@dircon.co.uk
Website: www.englishgardeningschool.co.uk

Enquiries to: Principal

Founded: 1984

Organisation type and purpose: Suitable for ages: 18+, training organisation, consultancy.

Subject coverage: Teaching a wide range of amateur and professional gardening courses; horticultural/garden design consultancy; resource for garden designers.

Publications list: Available in print

Access to staff: Contact by letter, by telephone, by fax, by e-mail and via website. Appointment necessary.
Hours: Mon to Fri, 0900 to 1700

ENGLISH GOLF UNION (EGU)

The National Golf Centre, Broadway, Woodhall Spa, Lincolnshire, LN10 9PU

Tel: 01526 354500
Fax: 01526 354020
E-mail: info@englishgolfunion.org
Website: www.englishgolfunion.org

Enquiries to: Chief Executive

Founded: 1924

Organisation type and purpose: National government body.
Governing body for the amateur game of men's golf in England.

Subject coverage: Amateur golf in England, handicapping, standard scratch scores of golf courses.

Non-library collection catalogue: All or part available online and in-house

Library catalogue: All or part available in-house

Publications: Printed
Order printed publications from: e-mail: nhayward@englishgolfunion.org

Publications list: Available in print

Access to staff: Contact by letter, by fax and by e-mail
Hours: Mon to Fri, 0900 to 1700

Access to building: Prior appointment required

Access for disabled people: Parking provided, ramped entry, toilet facilities

ENGLISH HERITAGE (HBMC or EH)

Fortress House, 23 Savile Row, London, W1S 2ET

Tel: 0870 333 1181 Customer Services
Fax: 01793 414926
Website: www.open.gov.uk/heritage/ehehome.htm
Website: www.english-heritage.org.uk

Enquiries to: Customer Services Department
Other contacts: Nine Regional Education Officers at the appropriate English Heritage Regional offices

Founded: 1984; formerly called Historic Buildings and Monuments Commission for England, Ministry of Works (MOW); formerly called Department of the Environment (DOE) (year of change 1983)

Organisation type and purpose: National government body, advisory body, statutory body, membership association (membership is by subscription).
Heritage conservation.

Subject coverage: The governments' official adviser on all matters concerning the conversation of the historic environment and the major source of public funding for rescue archaeology, conservation areas, and repairs to historic buildings and ancient monuments.

Collection: Historical Research Library (mainly architectural)
Listed historic buildings
Historic Plans Collection of over 200,000 plans of buildings
Mayson Beeton Collection (London social history)
Lists of scheduled monuments
Photographic library
Register of historic parks and gardens

Non-library collection catalogue: All or part available in print

Library catalogue: All or part available in print

Publications: Printed, and electronic and video
Order printed publications from: Customer Services, English Heritage
PO Box 569, Swindon, SN2 2YP, tel: 0870 333 1181

Publications list: Available online and in print

Access to staff: Contact by letter, by telephone, by fax and in person. Appointment necessary.
Hours: Mon to Fri, 0900 to 1730

Other address: English Heritage; Customer Services Department, PO Box 569, Swindon, Wiltshire, SN2 5YP

Other office: National Monuments Record Centre; Kemble Drive, Swindon, Wiltshire, SN2 2GZ; tel: 01793 414600; e-mail: nmrinfo@english-heritage.org.uk

Parent body: Department for Culture, Media and Sport; 2–4 Cockspur Street, London, SW1Y 5DH

Regional Offices: English Heritage (East Midlands Region); 44 Derngate, Northampton, NN1 1UH; tel: 01604 735400; fax: 01604 735401; English Heritage (East of England Region); Brooklands, 24 Brooklands Avenue, Cambridge, CB2 2BU; tel: 01223 582700; fax: 01223 582701; English Heritage (London Region); 23 Savile Row, London, W1S 2ET; tel: 020 7973 3000; fax: 020 7973 3000; English Heritage (North East Region); Bessie Surtees House, 41–44 Sandhill, Newcastle upon Tyne, NE1 3JF; tel: 0191 261 1585; English Heritage (North West Region); Canada House, 3 Chepstow Street, Manchester, M1 5FW; tel: 0161 242 1400; English Heritage (South East Region); Eastgate Court, 195–205 High Street, Guildford, Surrey, GU1 3EH; tel: 01483 252000; fax: 01483 252001; English Heritage (South West Region); 29 Queen Square, Bristol, BS1 4ND; tel: 0117 975 0700; English Heritage (West Midlands Region); 112 Colemore Row, Birmingham, B3 3AG; tel: 0121 625 6820; English Heritage (Yorkshire Region); 37 Tanner Row, York, YO1 6WP; tel: 01904 601901

ENGLISH HERITAGE – EDUCATION

1 Waterhouse Square, 138–142 Holborn, London, EC1N 2ST

Tel: 020 79733000
E-mail: education@english-heritage.org.uk
Website: www.english-heritage.org.uk/education

Enquiries to: Director of Education
Direct e-mail: sandra.stancliffe@english-heritage.org.uk

Founded: 1984; formerly called Historic Buildings and Monuments Commission for England (year of change 1984)

Organisation type and purpose: National government body, advisory body, statutory body, membership association (membership is by subscription), suitable for ages: 5 to 18 (formal and informal).
To provide an advisory and support service for primary and secondary schools in the teaching of history and the use of the historic environment.

Subject coverage: The historic environment of England, its preservation and use.
Archaeology, architecture, ancient monuments, conservation and listed buildings.

Publications: Printed
Order printed publications from: English Heritage, c/o Gillards, Trident Works, Temple Cloud, Bristol, BS39 5AZ; tel: 01761 452966; fax: 01761 453408

Publications list: Available online and in print

Access to staff: Contact by letter, by telephone, by fax and by e-mail
Hours: Mon to Fri, 0900 to 1700
Special comments: Access for visitors with disabilities should be checked with the regional office before booking a visit.

Also at: English Heritage; Customer Services Department, National Monuments Record Centre, Kemble Drive, Swindon, Wiltshire, SN2 2GZ; tel: 01793 414926

Branches: English Heritage; Education Officer, East of England Region; tel: 01223 582715; English Heritage; Education Officer, North of England, 37 Tanner Row, York, YO1 6WP; tel: 01904 601917; English Heritage; Education Officer, West Midlands Region; tel: 0121 625 6864; English Heritage; Education Officer, East Midlands Region, 44 Derngate, Northampton, NN1 1UH; tel: 01604 735440; English Heritage; Education Officer, London Region; tel: 020 7499 5676; English Heritage; Education Officer, South West Region, 29–30 Queen Square, Bristol, BS1 4ND; tel: 0117 975 0720; English Heritage; Education Officer, South East Region, Eastgate Court, 195–205 High Street, Guildford, GU1 3EH; tel: 01483 252013

ENGLISH HERITAGE – NATIONAL MONUMENTS RECORD (NMR)

Kemble Drive, Swindon, Wiltshire, SN2 2GZ

Tel: 01793 414600
Fax: 01793 414606
E-mail: nmrinfo@english-heritage.org.uk
Website: www.english-heritage.org.uk/nmr
Website: www.imagesof england.org.uk
Website: www.pastscape.org.uk
Website: www.english-heritager.org.uk/viewfinder
Website: www.englishheritagearchives.org.uk

Enquiries to: Enquiry and Research Services
Other contacts: Customer Services Section

Founded: 1908; formerly called Historic Buildings and Monuments Commission for England (HBMCE) (year of change 1984); incorporates the former National Archaeological Record, National Buildings Record, National Library of Air Photography; incorporates the former Royal Commission on the Historical Monuments of England (RCHME) (year of change 1999)

Organisation type and purpose: National government body.
Public archive of English Heritage.

Subject coverage: Architecture, archaeology, aerial photographs and maritime sites. The archive is of use to anyone interested in the historic built environment, local historians, researchers, archaeologists, architectural historians and environmental consultants.

Collection: Archive comprises over 10m. photographs, drawings and reports and an extensive book library specialising in architecture, archaeology and the historic environment
Aerial photograph collection includes complete RAF post-war coverage of England, early photographs of sites such as Stonehenge and more recent Ordnance Survey and English Heritage photography
Architectural archive includes interior and exterior photographs of buildings from the early days of photography to the present day. The National Buildings Record collection and photographs taken by Bedford Lemere, Eric De Mare, John Gay and many others are held in the NMR
Archaeological collections include earthwork surveys, aerial photograph interpretations and photographs of historic excavations

Trade and statistical information: Data on archaeological sites, Scheduled Ancient Monuments and Listed Buildings

Non-library collection catalogue: All or part available in-house

Library catalogue: All or part available in-house

Publications: Printed
Order printed publications from: http://www.english-heritageshop.org.uk

Publications list: Available online

Access to staff: Contact by letter, by telephone, by fax, by e-mail, in person and via website
Hours: Tue to Fri, 0930 to 1700
Special comments: Closed over Christmas and New Year (please contact for details)

Access to building: *Hours:* Tue to Fri, 0930 to 1700
Special comments: Limited visitor parking.

Funded by: Department of Culture, Media and Sport

Links with: county councils and local planning departments

Parent body: English Heritage; 1 Waterhouse Square, 138–142 Holborn, London, EC1N 2ST

ENGLISH HERITAGE (EAST MIDLANDS REGION)

44 Derngate, Northampton, NN1 1UH

Tel: 01604 735400
Fax: 01604 735401
Website: www.english-heritage.org.uk

Enquiries to: Marketing Executive

Organisation type and purpose: National organisation, advisory body, membership association (membership is by subscription), suitable for ages: all.
Independent but government-sponsored body.
English Heritage site administration and information service, including dates, times of opening and special events.

Subject coverage: English Heritage East Midlands Region, administers and cares for properties and sites in Derbyshire, Northamptonshire, Rutland, Lincolnshire and Leicestershire; the conservation and preservation of the historic environment.

continued overleaf

Access to staff: Contact by letter, by telephone and by fax
Hours: Mon to Fri, 0900 to 1700

Heritage sites: Ashby-de-la-Zouch Castle; South Street, Ashby-de-la-Zouch, Leicestershire, LE6 5PR; tel: 01530 413343; Bolsover Castle; Castle Street, Bolsover, Chesterfield, Derbyshire, S44 6PR; tel: 01246 822844; fax: 01246 241569; Gainsborough Old Hall; Parnell Street, Gainsborough, Lincolnshire, DN21 2NB; tel: 01427 612669; fax: 01427 612779; Hardwick Old Hall; Doe Lea, Chesterfield, Derbyshire, S44 5QJ; tel: 01246 850431; Kirby Hall; Deene, Corby, Northamptonshire, NN17 3EN; tel: 01536 203230; Kirby Muxloe Castle; Oakcroft Avenue, Kirby Muxloe, Leicestershire, LE9 9MD; tel: 01162 386886; Lyddington Bede House; Blue Coat Lane, Uppingham, Rutland, LE15 9LZ; tel: 01572 822438; Medieval Bishops' Palace; Minster Yard, Lincoln, LN2 1PU; tel: 01522 527468; Peveril Castle; Market Place, Castleton, Derbyshire, S33 8WQ; tel: 01422 620613; Rushton Triangular Lodge; Rushton, Kettering, Northamptonshire, NN14 1RP; tel: 01536 710761; Sibsey Trader Windmill; Sibsey, Boston, Lincolnshire, PE22 0SY; tel: 01205 460647; Wingfield Manor; Garner Lane, South Wingfield, Alfreton, Derbyshire, DE5 7NH; tel: 01773 832060

ENGLISH HERITAGE (EAST OF ENGLAND REGION)

Brooklands, 24 Brooklands Avenue, Cambridge, CB2 2BU

Tel: 01223 582700
Fax: 01223 582701
Website: www.english-heritage.org.uk

Enquiries to: Regional Marketing Executive – East of England

Organisation type and purpose: National organisation, suitable for ages: all.
Independent but government-sponsored body.
English Heritage site information service, including dates, times of opening and special events.

Subject coverage: The conservation and preservation of the historic environment of Eastern England.

Access to staff: Contact by letter, by telephone, by fax and by e-mail
Hours: Mon to Fri, 0900 to 1700

Heritage sites: Audley End House & Gardens; Saffron Walden, Essex, CB11 4JF; tel: 01799 522399; Berney Arms Windmill; 8 Manor Road, Southtown, Norfolk, NR31 0QA; tel: 01493 85700; Castle Acre Priory and Castle; Stocks Green, Castle Acre, Kings Lynn, Norfolk, PE32 2XD; tel: 01760 755394; Castle Rising Castle; King's Lynn, Norfolk; tel: 01553 631330; Denny Abbey & The Farmland Museum; Near Waterbeach, Cambridge; tel: 01223 860489; Framlingham Castle; Framlingham, Suffolk, IP8 9BT; tel: 01728 724189; Great Yarmouth Row Houses; South Quay, Great Yarmouth, Norfolk, IP13 2RQ; tel: 01493 857900; Grime's Graves; Lynford, Thetford, Norfolk, IP26 5DE; tel: 01842 810656; Hill Hall; Epping, Essex; tel: 01223 582700; Landguard Fort; Felixstowe, Suffolk; tel: 01473 218245; Longthorpe Tower; Thorpe Road, Longthorpe, Cambridgeshire, PE1 1HA; tel: 01760 755394; Orford Castle; Orford, Woodbridge, Suffolk; tel: 01394 450472; Saxtead Green Post Mill; The Mill House, Saxtead Green, Suffolk, IP13 9QQ; tel: 01728 685789; Tilbury Fort; No 2 Office Block, The Fort, Tilbury, Essex, RM18 7NR; tel: 01375 858489; West Park Gardens; Silsoe, Luton, Bedfordshire, MK45 4HS; tel: 01525 860152 (weekends only)

ENGLISH HERITAGE (LONDON REGION)

23 Savile Row, London, W1X 1AB

Tel: 020 7973 3000
Fax: 020 7937 3001
Website: www.english-heritage.org.uk

Enquiries to: Marketing Officer

Organisation type and purpose: National organisation, membership association, suitable for ages: all.
Independent but government-sponsored body.
English Heritage sites administration and information service, including dates, times of opening and special events.

Subject coverage: Conservation and preservation of the historic environment. English Heritage London Region, administers and cares for its properties and sites in the London area.

Education services: Group education facilities.

Access to staff: Contact by letter and by telephone. Appointment necessary.
Hours: Mon to Fri, 0900 to 1700

Heritage sites: Chapter House; East Cloisters, Westminster Abbey, London, SW1P 3PE; tel: 020 7222 5897; fax: 020 7222 0960; Chiswick House; Burlington Lane, London, W4 2RP; tel: 020 8995 0508; fax: 020 8742 3104; Downe House; Luxted Road, Downe, Biggin Hill, Kent, BR6 7JT; tel: 01689 859119; fax: 01689 862755; Eltham Palace; Court Yard, Eltham, London, SE9 5QE; tel: 020 8294 2548; fax: 0208 8294 2621; Jewel Tower; Abingdon Street, Westminster, London, SW1P 3JY; tel: 020 7222 2219; fax: 020 7222 2219; Kenwood House; The Iveagh Bequest, Kenwood, Hampstead Lane, London, NW3 7JR; tel: 020 8348 1286; fax: 020 8793 3891; Marble Hill House; Richmond Road, Twickenham, Middlesex, TW1 2NL; tel: 0208 892 5115; fax: 020 8607 9976; The Wernher Collection at Ranger's House; Chesterfield Walk, Blackheath, London, SE10 8QX; tel: 020 8853 0035; fax: 020 8853 0090; Wellington Arch; Hyde Park Corner, London, W1J 7JZ; tel: 020 7930 2726; fax: 020 7925 1019

ENGLISH HERITAGE (NORTH EAST REGION)

Bessie Surtees House, 41–44 Sandhill, Newcastle upon Tyne, NE1 3JF

Tel: 0191 269 1200
Website: www.english-heritage.org.uk

Enquiries to: Marketing Manager

Organisation type and purpose: National organisation, advisory body, membership association (membership is by subscription), suitable for ages: all.
Independent but government-sponsored body.
English Heritage site administration and information service, including dates, times of opening and special events.

Subject coverage: English Heritage North East Region administers and cares for properties and sites in Northumberland, Tyne and Wear, County Durham and Teesside; the conservation and preservation of the historic environment.

Access to staff: Contact by letter and by telephone. Appointment necessary.
Hours: Mon to Fri, 0900 to 1700

Heritage sites: Aydon Castle; Corbridge, Northumberland, NE45 5PJ; Barnard Castle; Castle House, Barnard Castle, County Durham, DL12 9AT; Belsay Hall, Castle and Gardens; Belsay, Ponteland, Northumberland, NE20 0DX; Berwick Barracks; The Parade, Berwick upon Tweed, Northumberland, TD15 1DF; Brinkburn Priory; Long Framlington, Morpeth, Northumberland, NE65 8AR; Chesters Roman Fort and Museum; Chollerford, Humshaugh, Hexham, Northumberland, NE46 4EP; Dunstanburgh Castle; 14 Queen Street, Alnwick, Northumberland, NE66 1RD; Etal Castle; Etal Village, Berwick upon Tweed, Northumberland, TD12 4TN; Finchale Priory; Brasside, Newton Hall, County Durham, DH1 5SH; Hadrian's Wall Museums; Hadrian's Wall Tourism Partnership; Housesteads Roman Fort; Haydon Bridge, Hexham, Northumberland, NE46 6NN; Lindisfarne Priory; Holy Island, Berwick upon Tweed, Northumberland, TD15 2RX; Norham Castle; Berwick upon Tweed, Northumberland, TD15 2JY; Prudhoe Castle; Prudhoe, Northumberland, NE42 6NA; Tynemouth Castle and Priory; North Shields, Tyne and Wear, NE30 4BZ; Warkworth Castle and Hermitage; Morpeth, Northumberland, NE66 0UJ

ENGLISH HERITAGE (NORTH WEST REGION)

Canada House, 3 Chepstow Street, Manchester, M1 5FW

Tel: 0161 242 1400
Fax: 0161 242 1401
E-mail: northwest@english-heritage.org.uk
Website: www.english-heritage.org.uk

Organisation type and purpose: National organisation, advisory body, membership association (membership is by subscription), suitable for ages: all.
Independent but government-sponsored body.
English Heritage site administration and information service, including dates, times of opening and special events.

Subject coverage: English Heritage North West Region advises local planning authorities on proposals for highly graded listed buildings, and major new development in historic areas, and allocates financial support to the historic environment of the North West.

Publications list: Available online

Access to staff: Contact by letter and by telephone. Appointment necessary.
Hours: Mon to Fri, 0900 to 1700

Heritage sites: Ambleside Roman Fort; Ambleside, Cumbria; Beeston Castle; Beeston, Tarporley, Cheshire, CW6 9TX; Brough Castle; Brough, Kirby Stephen, Cumbria; Brougham Castle; Brougham, Penrith, Cumbria, CA10 2AA; Carlisle Castle; Carlisle, Cumbria, CA3 8UR; Furness Abbey; Barrow-in-Furness, Cumbria, LA13 0TJ; Hadrian's Wall Museums; The Roman Site, Corbridge, Northumberland, NE45 5NT; Lanercost Priory; Lanercost, Brampton, Cumbria, CA8 2HQ; Stott Park Bobbin Mill; Low Stott Park, Ulverston, Cumbria, LA12 8AX

ENGLISH HERITAGE (SOUTH EAST REGION)

Eastgate Court, 195–205 High Street, Guildford, Surrey, GU1 3EH

Tel: 01483 252000
Fax: 01483 252001
E-mail: southeast@english-heritage.org.uk
Website: www.english-heritage.org.uk/southeast

Enquiries to: Marketing Assistant

Organisation type and purpose: National organisation, advisory body, suitable for ages: all.
Independent but government-sponsored body.
English Heritage site administration and information service, including dates, times of opening and special events.

Subject coverage: English Heritage South East Region administers and cares for properties and sites in Kent, Surrey, Sussex, Hampshire and the Isle of Wight; conservation and preservation of the historic environment.

Access to staff: Contact by letter, by telephone and by fax
Hours: Mon to Fri, 0900 to 1700

Heritage sites: Abingdon County Hall; Oxfordshire, 0X14 3HG; tel: 01235 523703; Appuldurcombe House; Wroxall, Ventnor, Isle of Wight, PO38 3EW; tel: 01983 852484; fax: 01983 840188; Battle Abbey and Battlefield; High Street, Battle, East Sussex, TN33 0AD; tel: 01424 773792; Bayham Old Abbey; Bayham, Lamberhurst, Kent, TN8 8DE; tel: 01892 890381; Bishop's Waltham Palace; Bishop's Waltham, Hampshire, SO32 1DH; Calshot Castle; Hampshire, SO4 1BR; tel: 02380 892023; Camber Castle; tel: 01797 223862; Carisbrooke Castle and Museum; Carisbrooke, Newport, Isle of Wight, PO30 6JY; tel: 01983 522107; e-mail: carismus@lineone.net; Deal Castle; Victoria Road, Deal, Kent, CT14 7BA; tel: 01304 372762; Dover Castle; The Keep, Dover, Kent, CT16 1HU; tel: 01304 211067; Down House; Luxted Road, Downe, Biggin Hill, Kent, BR6 7JT; tel: 01689 859119; Dymchurch Martello Tower; High Street, Dymchurch, Kent, CT16 1HU; Farnham Castle Keep; Castle Hill, Farnham, Surrey, GU6 0AG; Fort Brockhurst; Gunners Way, Elson, Hampshire, PO12 4DS; tel: 02392 378291; Hurst Castle; Hampshire, SO14 0TP; tel: 01590 642344; Lullingstone Roman Villa; Lullingstone Lane, Eynsford, Kent, DA4 0JA; tel: 01322 863467; Medieval Merchant's House; 58 French Street, Southhampton, SO23 8NB; tel: 02380 221503; Osborne House; York Avenue, East Cowes, Isle of Wight, PO32 6JY; tel: 01983 200022; fax: 01983 281380; Pevensey Castle; Pevensey, East Sussex, BN24 5LE; tel: 01323 762604; Portchester Castle; Portchester, Hampshire, PO16 9QW; tel: 023 923 78291; Richborough Roman Fort; Sandwich, Kent, CT13 9JW; Rochester Castle; Boley Hill, Rochester, Kent, ME1 1SW; tel: 01634 402276; St Augustine's Abbey and Museum; Longport, Canterbury, Kent, CT1 1TF; tel: 01227 767345; fax: 01227 767345; Temple Manor; Strood, Rochester, Kent; tel: 01634 827980; Upnor Castle; Wainscott, Rochester, Kent; tel: 01634 718742; Walmer Castle & Gardens; Kingsdown Road, Deal, Kent, CT14 7LJ; tel: 01304 364288; fax: 01304 364826; Wolvesey Castle (Old Bishop's Palace); College Street, Winchester, SO23 8NB; Yarmouth Castle; Quay Street, Yarmouth, Isle of Wight, PO41 0PB; tel: 01983 760678

ENGLISH HERITAGE (SOUTH WEST REGION) (HMBCE)

Formal name: Historic Monuments & Building Commission for England

29 Queen Square, Bristol, BS1 4ND

Tel: 0117 975 0700
Fax: 0117 975 0701
E-mail: southwest@english-heritage.org.uk
Website: www.english-heritage.org.uk/southwest

Founded: 1984

Organisation type and purpose: National organisation, advisory body, membership association (membership is by subscription), suitable for ages: all, publishing house.
English Heritage South West Region administers and cares for properties and sites in Bristol, Cornwall, Devon, Dorset, Gloucestershire, Isles of Scilly, Somerset and Wiltshire.

Subject coverage: The conservation and preservation of the historic environment.

Access to staff: Contact by letter, by telephone, by fax, by e-mail and in person. Appointment necessary.
Hours: Mon to Fri, 0900 to 1700

Heritage sites: Berry Pomeroy Castle; Totnes, Devon, TQ9 6NJ; tel: 01803 866618; e-mail: customers@english-heritage.org.uk; website: http://www.english-heritage.org.uk/berrypomeroy
Chysauster Ancient Village; Newmill, Penzance, Cornwall, TR20 8XA; tel: 07831 757934; e-mail: customers@english-heritage.org.uk; website: http://www.english-heritage.org.uk/chysauster
Cleeve Abbey; Washford, Watchet, Somerset, TA23 0PS; tel: 01984 640377; e-mail: customers@english-heritage.org.uk; website: http://www.english-heritage.org.uk/cleeve
Dartmouth Castle; Castle Road, Dartmouth, Devon, TQ6 0JN; tel: 01803 833588; e-mail: customers@english-heritage.org.uk; website: http://www.english-heritage.org.uk/dartmouth
Farleigh Hungerford Castle; Farleigh Hungerford, Bath, Somerset, BA3 6RS; tel: 01225 754026; e-mail: customers@english-heritage.org.uk; website: http://www.english-heritage.org.uk/farleighhungerford
Hailes Abbey; Winchcombe, Cheltenham, Gloucester, GL54 5PB; tel: 01242 602398; e-mail: customers@english-heritage.org.uk; website: http://www.english-heritage.org.uk/hailes
Launceston Castle; Castle Lodge, Launceston, Cornwall, PL15 7DR; tel: 01566 772365; e-mail: customers@english-heritage.org.uk; website: http://www.english-heritage.org.uk/launceston
Muchelney Abbey; Muchelney, Langport, Somerset, TA10 0DQ; tel: 01458 250664; e-mail: customers@english-heritage.org.uk; website: http://www.english-heritage.org.uk/muchelney
Okehampton Castle; Castle Lodge, Okehampton, Devon, EX20 1JB; tel: 01837 52844; e-mail: customers@english-heritage.org.uk; website: http://www.english-heritage.org.uk/okehampton
Old Sarum; Castle Road, Salisbury, Wiltshire, SP1 3SD; tel: 01722 335398; e-mail: customers@english-heritage.org.uk; website: http://www.english-heritage.org.uk/oldsarum
Old Wardour Castle; Tisbury, Salisbury, Wiltshire, SP3 6RR; tel: 01747 870487; e-mail: customers@english-heritage.org.uk; website: http://www.english-heritage.org.uk/oldwardour
Pendennis Castle; Falmouth, Cornwall, TR11 4LP; tel: 01326 316594; e-mail: customers@english-heritage.org.uk; website: http://www.english-heritage.org.uk/pendennis
Portland Castle; Castleton, Portland, Dorset, DT5 1AZ; tel: 01305 820539; e-mail: customers@english-heritage.org.uk; website: http://www.english-heritage.org.uk/portland
Restormel Castle; Lostwithiel, Cornwall, PL22 0BD; tel: 01208 872687; e-mail: customers@english-heritage.org.uk; website: http://www.english-heritage.org.uk/restormel
Sherborne Old Castle; Castleton, Sherborne, Dorset, DT9 3SA; tel: 01935 812730; e-mail: customers@english-heritage.org.uk; website: http://www.english-heritage.org.uk/sherborne
St Mawes Castle; St Mawes, Cornwall, TR2 3AA; tel: 01326 270526; e-mail: customers@english-heritage.org.uk; website: http://www.english-heritage.org.uk/stmawes
Stonehenge; Stone Circle, Wiltshire, SP4 7DE; tel: 01980 624715 (Information line); e-mail: customers@english-heritage.org.uk; website: http://www.english-heritage.org.uk/stonehenge
Tintagel Castle; Tintagel, Cornwall, DL34 0AA; tel: 01840 770328; e-mail: customers@english-heritage.org.uk; website: http://www.english-heritage.org.uk/tintagel
Totnes Castle; Castle Street, Totnes, Devon, TQ9 5NU; tel: 01803 864406; e-mail: customers@english-heritage.org.uk; website: http://www.english-heritage.org.uk/totnes

ENGLISH HERITAGE (WEST MIDLANDS REGION)

The Axis, 10 Holliday Street, Birmingham, B1 1TG

Tel: 0121 625 6820

continued overleaf

Website: www.english-heritage.org.uk

Organisation type and purpose: National organisation, advisory body.
Independent but government-sponsored body.
English Heritage West Midlands Region administers and cares for properties and sites in Herefordshire, Shropshire, Staffordshire, Warwickshire, West Midlands and Worcestershire.

Subject coverage: The conservation and preservation of the historic environment.
English Heritage site administration and information service, including dates, times of opening and special events.

Access to staff: Contact by letter, by telephone and in person
Hours: Mon to Fri, 0900 to 1700

Heritage Sites: Boscobel House and the Royal Oak; Brewood, Bishops Wood, Staffordshire, ST19 9AR; Buildwas Abbey; Ironbridge, Telford, TF8 7BW; Goodrich Castle; Goodrich, Ross on Wye, Worcestershire, HR9 6HY; Halesowen Abbey; Haughmond Abbey; Upton Magna, Uffington, Shropshire, SY4 4RW; Kenilworth Castle; Kenilworth, Warwickshire, CV8 1NE; Stokesay Castle; Craven Arms, Shropshire, SY7 9AH; Wall Roman Site (Letocetum); Watling Street, Lichfield, Staffordshire, WS14 0AW; Wenlock Priory; Much Wenlock, Shropshire, TF13 6HS; Witley Court; Great Witley, Worcestershire, WR6 6JT; Wroxeter Roman City; Wroxeter, Shropshire, SY5 6PH

ENGLISH HERITAGE (YORKSHIRE REGION)

37 Tanner Row, York, YO1 6WP

Tel: 01904 601901
Website: www.english-heritage.org.uk

Organisation type and purpose: National organisation, advisory body.
Independent but government-sponsored body.
English Heritage Yorkshire Region administers and cares for properties and sites in East Riding of Yorkshire, North East Lincolnshire, North Lincolnshire, North Yorkshire, South Yorkshire and West Yorkshire.

Subject coverage: The conservation and preservation of the historic environment.
English Heritage site administration and information service, including dates, times of opening and special events.

Access to staff: Contact by letter, by telephone and in person
Hours: Mon to Fri, 0900 to 1700

Heritage Site: Scarborough Castle; Castle Road, Scarborough, North Yorkshire, YO11 1HY

Heritage sites: Aldborough Roman Site; Main Street, Boroughbridge, Yorkshire, YO5 9EF; Brodsworth Hall and Gardens; Brodsworth, Doncaster, South Yorkshire; Byland Abbey; Coxwold, North Yorkshire, YO6 4BD; Clifford's Tower; Clifford Street, York, YO11 1HY; Conisbrough Castle; Helmsley Castle; Helmsley, North Yorkshire, YO6 5AB; Kirkham Priory; Whitwell-on-the-Hill, North Yorkshire, YO6 7JS; Middleham Castle; Middleham, Leyburn, North Yorkshire, DL8 4QG; Mount Grace Priory; Saddle Bridge, Northallerton, North Yorkshire, DL6 3JG; Pickering Castle; Pickering, North Yorkshire, YO18 7AX; Richmond Castle; Richmond, North Yorkshire, DL10 4QW; Rievaulx Abbey; Rievaulx, Helmsley, North Yorkshire, DL10 5LB; Roche Abbey; Maltby, Rotherham, South Yorkshire, S66 8NW; Whitby Abbey; Whitby, North Yorkshire, YO22 4JT

ENGLISH HOCKEY (EHA)

The Stadium, Silbury Boulevard, Milton Keynes, Buckinghamshire, MK9 1HA

Tel: 01908 544644
Fax: 01908 241106
E-mail: info@englandhockey.org
Website: www.hockeyonline.co.uk

Enquiries to: Marketing Director

Founded: 1886; formerly called Hockey Association (HA) from 1886 to 1997; formerly called All England Womens Hockey Association (AEWHA) from 1895 to 1997; formerly called Mixed Hockey Association (MHA), National Hockey Foundation (NHF) (year of change 1997)

Organisation type and purpose: Membership association (membership is by subscription), present number of members: 70,000, suitable for ages: 5 to 65.
Governing body of hockey in England.

Subject coverage: Hockey in England, its history, past, present and future development, English hockey in European and world arenas; league and competition management, coaching, umpiring and teaching, technical information, sponsorship and partnership, international teams, advice on all aspects of hockey including clubs.

Collection: Minute books and cash account books from the formation of the Association in 1896
Pictorial history
Trophies, gifts and artefacts presented by guest and host nations

Trade and statistical information: Data on the market profile and on the number of participants in hockey, at club level split into regions and counties

Publications: Printed, and microform publications

Access to staff: Contact by letter, by telephone, by fax, by e-mail and via website. Appointment necessary.
Hours: Mon to Fri, 0900 to 1700

Affiliated to: European Hockey Federation (EHF); International Hockey Federation (FIH)

Constituent member of: Great Britain Olympic Hockey Board

ENGLISH INDEPENDENCE PARTY (EIP)

27 Old Gloucester Street, London, WC1N 3XX

Tel: 020 7278 5221
E-mail: eip_enquiries@yahoo.com
Website: www.englishindependenceparty.com

Enquiries to: Chairman

Founded: 1991; formerly called English National Party (ENP)

Organisation type and purpose: National organisation, membership association (membership is by subscription), voluntary organisation.
Political party.

Subject coverage: English nationalism, knowledge about the English people, UK devolution, UK politics, English politics, nationalism, English history, culture and language.

Collection: Books related to English nationalism, etc.

Publications: Printed

Access to staff: Contact by letter and by telephone. Appointment necessary.
Hours: Mon to Fri, 1100 to 2200

Access to building: No access other than to staff

ENGLISH INDOOR BOWLING ASSOCIATION LTD (EIBA)

David Cornwell House, Bowling Green, Leicester Road, Melton Mowbray, Leicestershire, LE13 0FA

Tel: 01664 481900
Fax: 01664 482888
E-mail: enquiries@eiba.co.uk
Website: www.eiba.co.uk

Enquiries to: Chief Operating Executive

Founded: 1971

Organisation type and purpose: National organisation, membership association (membership is by subscription), present number of members: 327 clubs.
National governing body, level-green, indoor bowling.

Subject coverage: Development of facilities for indoor bowling for men and women, details of events and programme, player profiles.

Publications: Printed, and electronic and video

Access to staff: Contact by letter, by telephone, by fax, by e-mail, in person and via website. Appointment necessary.
Hours: Mon to Fri, 0900 to 1700

Access to building: By appointment

Affiliated to: British Isles Indoor Bowls Council; World Indoor Bowls Council

ENGLISH LACROSSE ASSOCIATION (ELA)

Belle Vue Athletics Centre, Pink Bank Lane, Manchester, M12 5GL

Tel: 0161 227 3626
Fax: 0161 227 3625
E-mail: info@englishlacrosse.co.uk
Website: www.englishlacrosse.co.uk

Founded: 1996; created by the merger of All England Women's Lacrosse Association and English Lacrosse Union

Organisation type and purpose: National governing body for lacrosse in England, membership association (membership is by subscription).

To control, promote and develop lacrosse throughout the country, and in the long term to make lacrosse one of the major team sports in England by substantially increasing participation for all.

Subject coverage: Lacrosse at all levels.

Education services: Education programme develops, administers, organises and implements courses and resources for lacrosse coaches, officials, teachers and volunteers.

Publications: Printed

Access to staff: Contact by letter, by telephone, by fax, by e-mail and via website

ENGLISH NATIONAL BALLET

Markova House, 39 Jay Mews, London, SW7 2ES

Tel: 020 7581 1245
Fax: 020 7225 0827
E-mail: info@ballet.org.uk
Website: www.ballet.org.uk

Enquiries to: Assistant to Managing Director
Other contacts: Marketing Manager for general source of information about performances and other activities.

Founded: 1950; formed from Festival Ballet, London Festival Ballet

Organisation type and purpose:
Membership association (membership is by subscription), registered charity (charity number 214005).
English National Ballet is a performing arts organisation. Individuals and companies can provide support and receive services/ benefits by joining the Association of English National Ballet or the Council of English National Ballet or by becoming a corporate member/sponsor of the Company.

Subject coverage: Ballet.

Collection: English National Ballet Archive includes photographs, designs, set models, music scores, press clippings and books

Publications: Printed

Access to staff: Contact by letter, by telephone, by fax and by e-mail
Hours: Mon to Fri, 1000 to 1800

Access to building: Prior appointment required
Special comments: English National Ballet Archive is available to those undertaking serious study.

ENGLISH NATIONAL OPERA (ENO)

Lilian Baylis House, 165 Broadhurst Gardens, London, NW6 3AX

Tel: 020 7624 7711
E-mail: ccolvin@eno.org
Website: www.eno.org

Enquiries to: Archivist

Founded: 1931; formerly called Sadler's Wells Opera (year of change 1974)

Organisation type and purpose: Registered charity (charity number 257210), historic building, house or site.
Opera production in English.
Encouragement of understanding and appreciation of the dramatic art by providing, presenting, producing, organising, managing and conducting performances of classical and educational plays, opera, ballet, films and concerts.

Subject coverage: History and performance of opera at Sadler's Wells Theatre until 1968 and The Coliseum from 1968.

Collection: Original documents relating to the history and performance of Sadler's Wells Opera and English National Opera

Non-library collection catalogue: All or part available online and in-house

Access to staff: Contact by letter, by telephone and by e-mail. Appointment necessary.
Hours: Archives: by appointment

Access for disabled people: Toilet facilities

ENGLISH PÉTANQUE ASSOCIATION (EPA)

41 Warwick Road, Southam, Warwickshire, CV47 0HW

Tel: 01926 815982
E-mail: mike.pegg@fipjp.com
Website: www.englishpetanque.org.uk

Enquiries to: National President

Founded: 1974

Organisation type and purpose:
Membership association.
Governing body of the sport.

Subject coverage: Pétanque: starting a club, facilities, equipment, coaching, umpiring, competition organisation, leagues.

Publications: Printed

Publications list: Available in print

Access to staff: Contact by e-mail. Appointment necessary.
Hours: Mon to Fri, 0900 to 1700

Member organisation of: CCPR; Fédération Internationale de Pétanque et Jeu Provençal; Sports Council

ENGLISH PEWTER COMPANY

1 Blackmore Street, Sheffield, South Yorkshire, S4 7TZ

Tel: 0114 272 3920
Fax: 0114 276 1416
E-mail: asharp@englishpewter.co.uk
Website: www.englishpewter.co.uk

Enquiries to: Managing Director
Direct e-mail: sales@englishpewter.co.uk

Founded: 1977

Organisation type and purpose:
Manufacturing industry.

Subject coverage: Pewterware.

Non-library collection catalogue: All or part available online

Library catalogue: All or part available online

Publications list: Available online

Access to staff: Contact by letter, by telephone, by fax and by e-mail. Appointment necessary.
Hours: Mon to Fri, 0900 to 1700

Access to building: Prior appointment required

Also at: English Pewter Company; 1 Blackmoor Street, Sheffield, S4 7TZ; e-mail: sales@englishpewter.co.uk

ENGLISH PLACE-NAME SOCIETY (EPNS)

Department of English Studies, University of Nottingham, Nottingham, NG7 2RD

Tel: 0115 951 5919
Fax: 0115 951 5924
Website: www.nottingham.ac.uk/english/research/EPNS/index.html

Enquiries to: Administrator

Founded: 1923

Organisation type and purpose: Learned society (membership is by subscription), registered charity (charity number 257891), research organisation, publishing house.

Subject coverage: Etymologies of English place-names, surveyed on a county basis.

Collection: English and Scandinavian onomastics
Library including the Olof von Feilitzen bequest

Library catalogue: All or part available in-house

Publications: Printed

Publications list: Available online and in print

Access to staff: Contact by letter, by telephone and by fax. Appointment necessary. Non-members charged.
Hours: Mon to Fri, 0900 to 1700

Affiliated to: AHRB; Institute for Navneforskning; University of Copenhagen; Ortnamnssällskapets; University of Uppsala; Sydsvenska Ortnamnssällskapets; University of Lund

Supported by: British Academy

ENGLISH PLAYING CARD SOCIETY (EPCS)

Little Paddock, Charlton Mackrell, Somerton, Somerset, TA11 7BG

Tel: 01458 223812
E-mail: secretary@epcs.org
Website: www.wopc.co.uk/epcs

Enquiries to: Secretary

Founded: 1984

Organisation type and purpose:
Membership association (membership is by subscription), present number of members: 120.

Subject coverage: All aspects of the manufacture and designs of English playing cards/card games and related subjects, including ephemera.

Publications: Printed

Access to staff: Contact by telephone and by e-mail. Appointment necessary.
Hours: Mon to Fri, 0900 to 1700

ENGLISH SCHOOLS' ATHLETIC ASSOCIATION (ESAA)

26 Newborough Green, New Malden, Surrey, KT3 5HS

Tel: 020 8949 1506
Fax: 020 8942 0943

Enquiries to: Honorary Secretary

Founded: 1925

Organisation type and purpose: Voluntary organisation.

Subject coverage: Schools' athletics.

Publications: Printed

Access to staff: Contact by letter, by telephone and by fax
Hours: Mon to Fri, 0900 to 1700

Affiliated to: Amateur Athletic Association of England; Central Council of Physical Recreation; National Council for School Sports; UK Athletics

ENGLISH SCHOOLS' FOOTBALL ASSOCIATION (ESFA)

4 Parker Court, Staffordshire Technology Park, Stafford, ST18 0WP

Tel: 01785 785970
Fax: 01785 256246
E-mail: office@esfa.co.uk
Website: www.esfa.co.uk/esfa

Enquiries to: Chief Executive

Founded: 1904

Organisation type and purpose: Membership association, registered charity (charity number 306003).

Subject coverage: Organisation of extra-curricular football for schools in England, regulations for schoolboy or schoolgirl footballers, competition rules.

Publications: Printed

Publications list: Available in print

Access to staff: Contact by letter, by telephone, by fax and by e-mail. Appointment necessary.
Hours: Mon to Fri, 0900 to 1700

Affiliated to: Football Association; tel: 020 7745 4545

Has: 500 member associations

ENGLISH SHORT MAT BOWLING ASSOCIATION (ESMBA)

Wytheford Hall, Shawbury, Shrewsbury, Shopshire, SY4 4JJ

Tel: 01952 770218
Fax: 01952 770567
Website: www.shortmatbowlsesmba.com

Enquiries to: General Secretary
Other contacts: Umpires Director; Competition Secretary; Membership Secretary

Founded: 1984

Organisation type and purpose: Membership association (membership is by subscription), present number of members: c. 27,000, voluntary organisation.
National governing body of the game in England, sports association.

Subject coverage: The game of short mat bowls.

Publications: Printed, and electronic and video

Access to staff: Contact by letter
Hours: Daily, 0900 to 1700

ENGLISH SPEAKING BOARD (INTERNATIONAL) LIMITED (ESB)

26a Princes Street, Southport, Merseyside, PR8 1EQ

Tel: 01704 501730
Fax: 01704 539637
E-mail: admin@esbuk.org
Website: www.esbuk.org

Enquiries to: Chief Administration Officer

Founded: 1953

Organisation type and purpose: International organisation, advisory body, professional body, voluntary organisation, registered charity (charity number 272565), suitable for ages: 5+, training organisation. Examining body.

Subject coverage: Oral education, communication, speech, English language, English teaching.

Publications: Printed

Publications list: Available in print

Access to staff: Contact by letter, by telephone, by fax, by e-mail and via website
Hours: Mon to Fri, 0900 to 1700

Access for disabled people: Parking provided

Affiliated to: Australia Speech Communication Association; ESB New South Wales; New Zealand Speech Board

ENGLISH SPEAKING UNION OF THE COMMONWEALTH (ESU)

Page Memorial Library, Dartmouth House, 37 Charles Street, London, W1J 5ED

Tel: 020 7529 1550
Fax: 020 7495 6108
E-mail: esu@esu.org
Website: www.esu.org

Enquiries to: Librarian
Direct e-mail: library@esu.org

Founded: 1948

Organisation type and purpose: International organisation, membership association (membership is by subscription), present number of members: 6,104, registered charity (charity number 273136). Promotion of international understanding; scholarships, exchange programmes, cultural events.

Subject coverage: History, literature and culture of the USA.

Collection: ESU Archive (photographs, letters, documents)
Adlai Stevenson Memorial Collection
Main collection c. 12,000 books of US interest (history, literature, arts, social sciences)
Winifred Nerney Collection: publishers and literary figures

Access to staff: Contact by letter, by telephone, by fax and by e-mail. Appointment necessary.
Hours: Mon to Fri, 1000 to 1700

Affiliated to: The English Speaking Union of the United States; 144 East 39th Street, New York, NY 10016, USA; tel: +1 212 818 1200; fax: +1 212 867 4177; e-mail: info@esuus.org; website: http://www.esuus.org

ENGLISH STRING ORCHESTRA LIMITED/ENGLISH SYMPHONY ORCHESTRA (ESO)

Formal name: English Symphony Orchestra

The Old Hop Store, Three Counties Showground, Malvern, Worcestershire, WR13 6SP

Tel: 01684 560696
Fax: 01684 560656
E-mail: info@eso.co.uk

Enquiries to: Head of Finance and Administration
Direct e-mail: alison@eso.co.uk
Other contacts: Administrator

Founded: 1980

Organisation type and purpose: Registered charity (charity number 293345). Orchestra.

Subject coverage: Orchestral performance and touring, music, orchestration, programme notes.
3 Youth Orchestras for grades 1–8, regular courses, bespoke concerts/programmes, indoor and outdoor. Box office services for customer events.

Publications: Electronic and video

Publications list: Available in print

Access to staff: Contact by letter, by telephone, by fax, by e-mail and via website
Hours: Mon to Fri, 1000 to 1700

ENGLISH TABLE TENNIS ASSOCIATION (ETTA)

Queensbury House, Havelock Road, Hastings, East Sussex, TN34 1HF

Tel: 01424 722525
Fax: 01424 422103
E-mail: admin@etta.co.uk
Website: www.etta.co.uk

Enquiries to: National Communications Officer
Direct e-mail: richard.pettit@etta.co.uk

Founded: 1901; formerly called Ping Pong Association (PPA) (year of change 1901); formerly called Table Tennis Association (year of change 1903); formerly called United Table Tennis and Ping Pong Association (UTTPPA) (year of change 1904); formerly called Table Tennis Association (TTA) (year of change 1922); formerly called English Table Tennis Association (ETTA) (year of change 1927); formerly called English Table Tennis Association Limited (year of change 2001)

Organisation type and purpose: Governing body of the sport.

Subject coverage: Table tennis: competition and administration; historical, technical and developmental aspects of table tennis.

Publications: Printed

Access to staff: Contact by letter, by telephone, by fax and by e-mail. Appointment necessary.
Hours: Mon to Fri, 0900 to 1700

Links with: European Table Tennis Union (ETTU); 25 rue des Capucins, 1313, Luxembourg; tel: +352 223030; +352 223031; fax: +352 223060; e-mail: ettu@pt.lu; International Table Tennis Federation (ITTF); Avenue Mon-Repos 30, Lausanne, 1005, Switzerland; tel: + 41 21 340 7090; fax: + 41 21 340 7099; e-mail: ittf@ittf.com

ENGLISH TOURING OPERA (ETO)

52–54 Rosebery Avenue, London, EC1R 4RP

Tel: 0207 833 2555
Fax: 0207 713 8686
E-mail: admin@englishtouringopera.org.uk
Website: www.englishtouringopera.org.uk

Enquiries to: Chief Executive
Other contacts: Marketing Manager, Education Manager, Head of Development & Marketing – Fundraising

Founded: 1979; formerly called Opera 80 Limited (year of change 1979–1992)

Organisation type and purpose: Service industry, registered charity.
To take opera throughout England to venues that otherwise would receive little or no professional opera and in so doing to provide opportunities for singers in the early stages of their careers.

Subject coverage: Opera, touring opera, opera in education and for special needs.

Access to staff: Contact by letter, by telephone, by fax and by e-mail
Hours: Mon to Fri, 1000 to 1800

ENGLISH VOLLEYBALL ASSOCIATION (EVA)

27 South Road, West Bridgford, Nottinghamshire, NG2 7AG

Tel: 01509 631699
Fax: 01509 631699

Enquiries to: Chief Executive
Other contacts: Director

Founded: 1972

Organisation type and purpose: Membership association (membership is by subscription), present number of members: 23,000, voluntary organisation.

Subject coverage: Volleyball; coaching; refereeing; competitions (domestic and international); equipment recommendations, rules, qualifications, awards, beach volleyball, mini volleyball.

Publications: Printed, and electronic and video

Publications list: Available online and in print

Access to staff: Contact by letter, by telephone, by fax, by e-mail and via website. Appointment necessary.
Hours: Mon to Fri, 0930 to 1630

Affiliated to: European Volleyball Confederation; International Volleyball Federation

ENGLISH WOMEN'S GOLF ASSOCIATION (EWGA)

11 Highfield Road, Edgbaston, Birmingham, B15 3EB

Tel: 0121 456 2088
Fax: 0121 452 5978
E-mail: office@englishwomensgolf.org
Website: www.englishwomensgolf.org

Enquiries to: Chief Executive

Founded: 1952

Organisation type and purpose: Membership association (membership is by subscription), present number of members: 135,000, voluntary organisation.
National governing body of the game, training organisation for juniors.
Administers ladies golf in England.

Subject coverage: Ladies golf, entry to golf clubs, queries on handicaps and rules of golf, championship organisation.

Collection: Yearbook
Histories and Centenary Books from County Associations and Golf Clubs

Publications: Printed

Access to staff: Contact by letter, by telephone, by e-mail and via website. Appointment necessary.
Hours: Mon to Fri, 0830 to 1730

Affiliated to: Ladies Golf Union; The Scores, St Andrews, Fife, KY16 9AT

ENGLISH-SPEAKING UNION SCOTLAND (ESU Scotland)

23 Atholl Crescent, Edinburgh, EH3 8HQ

Tel: 0131 229 1528
Fax: 0131 229 1533
E-mail: secretary@esuscotland.org.uk
Website: www.esuscotland.org.uk

Enquiries to: Secretary

Founded: 1918

Organisation type and purpose: International organisation, membership association (Scottish charity number 000653).
World-wide educational charity, represented in over 50 countries. Members contribute to a wide range of international and cultural events; the promotion of the awareness of current affairs; the use of the English language to create a more harmonious world. Runs international scholarships and exchanges, organises conferences and cultural events, and teaches English as a foreign language. The main providers of training and competitions in speech and debate for Scottish schools, also providing training in public speaking and presentation skills for adults.

Subject coverage: Public speaking and debating, English language, culture, current affairs.

Education services: Training for schools in speech and debate. Training for adults in public speaking and presentation skills. Teaching English as a foreign language. Resources for school debate online. Cultural events and public debates. Scholarships.

Collection: American Studies Library, over 1,200 vols of North American interest, covering literature, criticism, history, politics and society

Non-library collection catalogue: All or part available online

Library catalogue: All or part available online

Publications: Printed

Access to staff: Contact by letter, by telephone, by fax, by e-mail and via website. Appointment necessary.
Hours: Mon to Fri, 0900 to 1700

Links with: English-Speaking Union of the Commonwealth; Dartmouth House, 37 Charles Street, London, W1J 5ED; tel: 020 7529 1550; fax: 020 7495 6108; e-mail: esu@esu.org; website: http://www.esu.org

ENT UK

Formal name: Trading as: British Academic Conference in Otolaryngology (BACO) and British Association of Otorhinolaryngology-Head and Neck Surgery (BAO-HNS)

The Royal College of Surgeons, 35–43 Lincoln's Inn Fields, London, WC2A 3PE

Tel: 020 7404 8373
Fax: 020 7404 4200
E-mail: entuk@entuk.org
Website: www.entuk.org

Enquiries to: Administration Manager
Direct tel: 020 7611 1731
Direct fax: 020 7404 4200
Other contacts: Honorary Secretary

Founded: 2008; created by the merger of British Association of Otorhinolaryngologists-Head and Neck Surgeons and the British Academic Conference in Otolaryngology (year of change 2008)

Organisation type and purpose: Professional body (membership is by subscription, election or invitation), present number of members: 1,353, registered charity (charity number 1125524).
The Association aims to promote the highest quality and standards of medical and surgical practice of the specialty for the benefit of patients and to encourage its future advancement through education, research and audit.

Subject coverage: Laryngology, otology, rhinology, head and neck surgery.

Publications list: Available in print

Access to staff: Contact by letter, by telephone, by fax, by e-mail and via website. Appointment necessary.
Hours: Mon to Fri, 0930 to 1730
Special comments: For doctors only.

ENTERPRISE EUROPE NETWORK

E-mail: info@eiscltd.eu
Website: www.enterprise-europe-network.ec.europa.eu/network_en.htm

Founded: 2008

Organisation type and purpose: An initiative of the European Commission to establish a network of contact points, in the Member States of the European Union (EU)

continued overleaf

and in a number of non-EU countries, offering information and advice to companies (particularly small and medium-sized enterprises) on EU matters.

ENTERPRISE EUROPE NETWORK YORKSHIRE

7th Floor, Jacob's Well, Bradford, West Yorkshire, BD1 5RW

Tel: 01274 434262
Fax: 01274 432136
E-mail: info@ee-yorkshire.com
Website: www.ee-yorkshire.com

Enquiries to: Manager

Founded: 1990; incorporates the former West Yorkshire European Information Centre (WYEIC) (year of change 2008)

Organisation type and purpose: Member of Enterprise Europe Network.
Provision of information and advice to business on EU legislation, innovation and technology transfer, and trading in Europe.

Subject coverage: EU legislation and policies, European business information, innovation, technical standards, research and development, and the environment.

Information services: Enquiry service, tenders information service, alerting service, European partner search service.

Publications: Electronic and video
Order electronic and video publications from: via website

Access to staff: Contact by letter, by telephone, by fax, by e-mail, in person and via website. Appointment necessary.
Hours: Mon to Fri, 0900 to 1700

Parent body: Bradford City Council; Department of Regeneration & Culture

ENTRUST CARE

Clifton House, 3 St Paul's Road, Foleshill, Coventry, Warwickshire, CV6 5DE

Tel: 024 7666 5450
Fax: 024 7666 5450
E-mail: admin@entrustcare.co.uk
Website: www.entrustcare.co.uk

Enquiries to: General Manager

Founded: 1969; Association for Brain-Damaged Children and Young Adults (year of change 2005)

Organisation type and purpose:
Membership association (membership is by subscription), present number of members: 70, voluntary organisation, registered charity (charity number 500452).
Localised.
Respite and residential care in the Coventry area only.

Subject coverage: Self-help group providing respite care to children and residential care to adults with learning and physical disabilities.

Publications: Printed

Access to staff: Contact by letter, by telephone, by fax and by e-mail.
Appointment necessary. Access for members only. All charged.
Hours: Mon to Fri, 0900 to 1500

Access for disabled people: Parking provided, ramped entry

Links with: CVS Coventry

ENVIRONMENT AGENCY – BRISTOL

Rio House, Waterside Drive, Aztec West, Almondsbury, Bristol, BS32 4UD

Tel: 01454 624400
Fax: 01454 624409
E-mail: enquiries@environment-agency.gov.uk
Website: www.environment-agency.gov.uk
Website: www.environment-agency.gov.uk/fish

Enquiries to: Information & Marketing Manager
Direct tel: 0117 914 2856
Direct fax: 0117 914 2760

Founded: 1 April 1996; formed from County Council Waste Regulatory Functions; formed from London Waste Regulation Authority (year of change 1996); formerly called Her Majesty's Inspectorate of Pollution (HMIP), National Rivers Authority (NRA)

Organisation type and purpose: National government body.
Non departmental public body.
Environmental regulation.

Subject coverage: Water quality, water resources, conservation, water recreation, navigation, waste management, pollution control, sustainable development, environmental policy, environmental legislation, fisheries.

Collection: Principal Public Registers are:
Integrated Pollution Control (IPC) Register (industrial processes; applications, authorisations, variations, appeals, restrictions, monitoring records, enforcement and prohibition notices, revocations, convictions and appeals)
Register of Industrial Works (the 'Air Register'; industrial processes with the potential to cause air pollution)
Radioactive Substances (RAS) Register (use, accumulation and disposal of radioactive materials; applications, registrations, authorisations, variations, cancellations, enforcement and prohibition notices, convictions and appeals)
Water Quality & Pollution Control Register (discharge consent applications, decisions and appeals, changes of holder, revocations, water quality objectives, monitoring records including bathing waters, maps of freshwater limits, maps of 'controlled' coastal waters)
Water Abstraction and Impounding Register (licence applications, decisions and appeals, successions, revocations)
Maps of Waterworks (location of resource mains, water mains, discharge pipes and underground works)
Maps of Main Rivers (for each area covered by the Agency's Regional Flood Defence Committees)
Waste Management Licence Register (relating to the recovery or disposal of waste; applications, working plans, inspection reports, monitoring information, modifications, revocations, suspensions, appeals, surrenders, convictions, exemptions to licences)
Carriers and Brokers of Controlled Waste Register (applications to carry waste)
Other Registers:
Works Discharge Register (information on owners or occupiers of premises that abut watercourses who have requested to be registered in order to receive notification of discharges caused by the Agency)
Genetically Modified Organisms Register, held on behalf of the Department of the Environment, Food and Rural Affairs (releases of genetically modified organisms)
Chemical Release Inventory (releases from processes regulated under Integrated Pollution Control)
Special Waste Notifications (consignment notes: disposal and location records – non-commercially confidential, summaries of Special Waste – when prepared by the disposal authority)

Trade and statistical information: Public Registers in a combination of paper and computer files, details of water quality, consents to discharge to water, water and effluent sample data

Non-library collection catalogue: All or part available in-house

Library catalogue: All or part available in-house

Publications: Printed
Order printed publications from: Free publications, Environment Agency
Rio House, Waterside Drive, Aztec West, Almondsbury, Bristol, BS12 4UD
Priced publications, The Stationery Office
PO Box 276, London, SW8 5DT
R&D Reports, Foundation for Water Research
Allen House, The Listons, Liston Road, Marlow, Buckinghamshire, SL7 1FD
Regional publications, Environment Agency Regional Offices

Publications list: Available in print

Access to staff: Contact by letter, by telephone, by fax, by e-mail and via website. Appointment necessary.
Hours: Mon to Fri, 0900 to 1700

Access to building: Prior appointment required
Hours: Mon to Fri, 0900 to 1700

Access for disabled people: Parking provided, ramped entry, toilet facilities

Libraries and Information Service: Agency Libraries are open to the public for reference purposes, by appointment during working hours. They hold publications of the former National Rivers Authority and Her Majesty's Inspector of Pollution; Environment Agency Anglian; Kingfisher House, Goldhay Way, Orton Goldhay, Peterborough, Cambridgeshire, PE2 5ZR; tel: 01733 371811; fax: 01733 464397; Environment Agency Head Office; Rio House, Waterside Drive, Aztec West, Almondsbury, Bristol, BS32 4UD; tel: 01454 624400; fax: 01454 624004; Environment Agency North East Region; Tyneside House, Skinnerburn Road, Newcastle Business Park, Newcastle upon Tyne, NE4 7AR; tel: 0191 203 4000; fax: 0191 203 4004; Environment Agency North West; Richard Fairclough House, Knutsford Road, Warrington, WA4 1HG; tel: 01925 653999;

fax: 01925 639670; Environment Agency South West Region; Manley House, Kestrel Way, Exeter, EX2 7LQ; tel: 01392 444000; fax: 01392 444238; Environment Agency Southern Region; Guildbourne House, Chatsworth Road, Worthing, West Sussex, BN11 1LD; tel: 01903 832000; fax: 01903 821832; Environment Agency Thames; Kings Meadow House, Kings Meadow Road, Reading, RG1 8DQ; tel: 0118 953 5000; fax: 0118 950 0388; Environment Agency Welsh; Rivers House/Plas-yr-Afon, St Mellons Business Park, Fortran Road, Cardiff, CF3 0LT; tel: 029 2077 0088; fax: 029 2036 1437

Sponsoring department: Department of the Environment, Transport and the Regions

ENVIRONMENT AGENCY – TEWKESBURY

Area Office, Riversmeet House, Newtown Industrial Estate, Northway Lane, Tewkesbury, Gloucestershire, GL20 8JG

Tel: 01684 850951
Fax: 01684 293599
Website: www.environment-agency.gov.uk

Enquiries to: Customer Contact Team

Founded: 1996; formerly called Her Majesty's Inspectorate of Pollution, National Rivers Authority, Waste Regulation Authorities

Organisation type and purpose: National government body, professional body.
To protect and improve the environment and contribute towards sustainable development through the integrated management of air, land and water. We have specific responsibilities for water resources, pollution prevention and control, flood defence, fisheries, conservation, recreation and navigation throughout England and Wales.

Collection: Public Register Information

Publications: Printed, and electronic and video

Access to staff: Contact by letter, by telephone and by fax
Hours: Mon to Fri, 0900 to 1700

Links with: DEFRA; The Welsh Office

Main sponsor in the Government is: The Department for Environment, Food & Rural Affairs (DEFRA)

Sub-Area Office: Environment Agency; Brooke House, Spartan Close, Tachbrook Park Industrial Estate, Leamington Spa, Warwickshire, CV34 6RR; tel: 01926 889474; fax: 01926 887657

ENVIRONMENTAL AWARENESS TRUST (EAT)

23 High Street, Wheathampstead, Hertfordshire, AL4 8BB

Tel: 01582 834580
Fax: 01582 834547

Enquiries to: Executive Director

Founded: 1990

Organisation type and purpose: Registered charity (charity number 100042).
Prime purpose is the development of a National Exploratorium of the Global Environment open to members of the public of all ages.

Subject coverage: Global environment.

Access to staff: Contact by letter, by telephone and by fax
Hours: Mon to Fri, 0900 to 1700

ENVIRONMENTAL COMMUNICATORS' ORGANIZATION (ECO Journalists)

8 Hooks Cross, Watton-at-Stone, Hertford, SG14 3RY

Tel: 01920 830527
Fax: 01920 830538
E-mail: alanmassam@btinternet.com

Enquiries to: Chairman
Direct tel: 01920 830527
Other contacts: Press spokesman for press releases.

Founded: 1972

Organisation type and purpose:
Membership association (membership is by election or invitation).
Pressure group.
To bring a green interpretation of significant events to the attention of professional journalists and broadcasters.

Subject coverage: Information on environmental topics provided for journalists.

Publications: Printed

Access to staff: Contact by letter, by fax and by e-mail
Hours: Mon to Fri, 0900 to 1700

Affiliated to: Foundation for Ethnobiology; tel: 01992 893632; e-mail: conradgorinsky@hotmail.com

ENVIRONMENTAL HEALTH REGISTRATION BOARD (EHRB)

Chartered Institute of Environmental Health, Chadwick Court, 15 Hatfields, London, SE1 8DJ

Tel: 020 7928 6006
E-mail: g.telfer@cieh.org
Website: www.ehrb.co.uk

Enquiries to: Principal Education Officer
Direct tel: 020 7827 5929

History of institution: formerly called Public Health Inspectors Registration Board (PHIEB)
Environmental Health Officers Registration Board (year of change 2003)

Organisation type and purpose: Publicly listed company.

Subject coverage: Registration of student and qualified environmental health officers. Development and accreditation of courses for other environmental professional staff.

Information services: Provides information on how to become an environmental health officer, lists accredited environmental health degree courses in the UK and accredited courses for technician qualifications such as Higher Certificate in Food Premises Inspection.

Access to staff: Contact by letter, by telephone, by e-mail and via website
Hours: Mon to Fri, 0900 to 1700

Administered by: Chartered Institute of Environmental Health; Chadwick Court, 15 Hatfields, London, SE1 8DJ; tel: 020 7928 6006

ENVIRONMENTAL INDUSTRIES COMMISSION LIMITED, THE (EIC)

45 Weymouth Street, London, W1G 8ND

Tel: 020 7935 1675
Fax: 020 7486 3455
E-mail: info@eic-uk.co.uk
Website: www.eic-uk.co.uk

Enquiries to: Director

Founded: 1995; formed from Association of Environmental Consultancies (AEC)

Organisation type and purpose: National organisation, trade association (membership is by subscription), present number of members: 210.

Subject coverage: Contact with members. Information about EIC members and in which fields they specialise. Information about membership for potential members.

Publications: Printed

Publications list: Available in print

Access to staff: Contact by telephone
Hours: Mon to Fri, 0930 to 1800

ENVIRONMENTAL INVESTIGATION AGENCY (EIA)

62–63 Upper Street, London, N1 0NY

Tel: 020 7354 7960
Fax: 020 7354 7961
E-mail: ukinfo@eia-international.org
Website: www.eia-international.org

Enquiries to: Administrator

Founded: 1984

Organisation type and purpose: Voluntary organisation, registered charity.
Independent wildlife and environmental campaigning organisation.

Subject coverage: Research, investigations and monitoring of illegal trade in endangered animal species and environmentally damaging commodities. Provision of documented information on such activities to governmental authorities and the media to generate improved enforcement measures.

Publications: Printed, and microform publications

Access to staff: Contact by letter, by telephone, by fax and by e-mail
Hours: Mon to Fri, 0930 to 1800

ENVIRONMENTAL LAW FOUNDATION (ELF)

Suite 309, 16 Baldwins Gardens, London, EC1N 7RJ

Tel: 020 7404 1030
Fax: 020 7404 1032
E-mail: info@elflaw.org
Website: www.elflaw.org

continued overleaf

Enquiries to: Administrator
Direct e-mail: membership@elflaw.org
Other contacts: Director

Founded: 1992

Organisation type and purpose: Advisory body, present number of members: 450, voluntary organisation, registered charity, research organisation.
Provides advice and assistance, refers communities to lawyers and experts to resolve environmental problems.

Subject coverage: Environmental law; how the law can be used to resolve environmental problems, access to justice.

Collection: Case information (not available to the public)

Trade and statistical information: Data on communities taking legal action to protect and improve the environment of the UK

Publications: Printed

Publications list: Available in print

Access to staff: Contact by letter, by telephone, by fax and by e-mail
Hours: Mon to Fri, 1030 to 1630
Special comments: Information provided in response to specific requests only.

ENVIRONMENTAL NETWORK LIMITED (ENL)

The Hillocks, Tarland, Aboyne, Aberdeenshire, AB34 4TJ

Tel: 01339 881446
Fax: 01339 881618
E-mail: mail@env-net.com
Website: www.env-net.com

Enquiries to: Managing Director

Founded: 1993

Organisation type and purpose: Multi-disciplinary European network organisation for R&D in environmental management and sustainable development.

Subject coverage: Environmental assessment, planning and management, sustainable development, rural resource management and development; software development.

Access to staff: Contact by letter, by telephone, by fax, by e-mail and via website. Appointment necessary.
Hours: Britain: Mon to Fri, 0900 to 1700 GMT
Germany: Mon to Fri, 0900 to 1700 GMT+1

Also at: Umweltnetzwerk Deutschland; Oberilfingerstrasse 3, 72160 Horb, Germany; tel: +49 1577 6826343

ENVIRONMENTAL PROTECTION UK

44 Grand Parade, Brighton, East Sussex, BN2 9QA

Tel: 01273 878770
Fax: 01273 606626
E-mail: info@environmental-protection.org.uk
Website: www.environmental-protection.org.uk

Enquiries to: Administration Officer
Direct tel: 01273 878775

Founded: 1899; formerly called National Society for Clean Air and Environmental Protection

Organisation type and purpose: National organisation, membership association (membership is by subscription), present number of members: 1,775, registered charity (charity number 221026).
The society is a non-governmental, non-political organisation, bringing together pollution expertise from industry, local and central government and technical, academic and institutional bodies.
Seeks to inform debate and influence changes in policy and practice in the areas of air quality, climate change, noise and land quality.

Subject coverage: Air quality, noise, contaminated land; policy and legislation.

Collection: Archive Collection on Air Pollution and Environment

Non-library collection catalogue: All or part available in-house

Library catalogue: All or part available in-house

Publications: Printed
Order printed publications from: shop@environmental-protection.org.uk

Publications list: Available online and in print

Access to staff: Contact by letter, by telephone, by fax, by e-mail and via website. Appointment necessary.
Hours: Mon to Fri, 0900 to 1700

Access to building: Prior appointment required

ENVIRONMENTAL SERVICES ASSOCIATION (ESA)

154 Buckingham Palace Road, London, SW1W 9TR

Tel: 020 7824 8882
Fax: 020 7824 8753
E-mail: info@esauk.org
Website: www.esauk.org
Website: www.epolitix.com/forum/esa

Enquiries to: Chief Executive
Other contacts: Deputy Chief Executive/ Members' Services

Founded: 1969; formerly called National Association of Waste Disposal Contractors (NAWDC) (year of change 1996); incorporates the former Energy from Waste Association (EWA) (year of change 2001)

Organisation type and purpose: Trade association.
ESA is the UK's sectoral trade association for waste and secondary resource management, an industry accounting for 0.5% of GDP.

Subject coverage: Information on integrated solutions to waste across the full spectrum of biological, mechanical and thermal treatment processing options, to achieve sustainable waste management.

Collection: Library containing printed products

Non-library collection catalogue: All or part available in-house

Library catalogue: All or part available in-house

Publications: Printed, and electronic and video

Publications list: Available online and in print

Access to staff: Contact by letter, by telephone, by fax, by e-mail, in person and via website. Appointment necessary. Access for members only. All charged.
Hours: Mon to Fri, 0900 to 1700

Access to building: Prior appointment required

Access for disabled people: Ramped entry

Member of: European Waste Management Association (FEAD); Avenue des Gaulois 19, Brussels, B-1040, Belgium; tel: 00 32 2 732 3213; fax: 00 32 2 734 9592; e-mail: wg@fead.be; WAMITAB; 3 The Lakes, Peterbridge House, Northampton, NN4 7HE; tel: 01604 231950; fax: 01604 232457; e-mail: info.admin@wamitab.org.uk

Other addresses: Northern Ireland Environmental Services Association (NIESA); PO Box 21, Belfast, BT1 4WD; tel: 0870 241 3298; e-mail: niesa@esauk.org; Scottish Environmental Services Association (SESA); 48 Edinburgh Road, Coatbridge, Lanarkshire, ML5 4UG; tel: 01236 437480; e-mail: sesa@esauk.org; Welsh Environmental Services Association (WESA); PO Box 4061, Cardiff, CF14 3YY; tel: 020 7591 3205; e-mail: wesa@esauk.org

ENVIRONMENTAL TRANSPORT ASSOCIATION (ETA)

ETA Services Limited, 10 Church Street, Weybridge, Surrey, KT13 8RS

Tel: 01932 828882
Fax: 01932 829015
E-mail: eta@eta.co.uk
Website: www.eta.co.uk

Enquiries to: Public Relations Co-ordinator

Founded: 1990

Organisation type and purpose: National organisation, membership association (membership is by subscription), present number of members: 20,000, service industry.
Breakdown recovery and other insurance issues.
Motoring breakdown organisation campaigning for greener transport.

Subject coverage: Specialist information on transport and environment issues.

Publications: Printed

Publications list: Available online and in print

Access to staff: Contact by letter, by telephone, by fax, by e-mail and via website
Hours: Mon to Fri, 0800 to 1800

Access to building: Prior appointment required

Access for disabled people: Parking provided

Affiliated to: European Federation for Transport and Environment (T&E); Boulevard de Waterloo 34, 1000 Brussels, Belgium; tel: 00 322 502 9909; fax: 00 322 502

9908; Transport 2000 (T2000); The Impact Centre, 12 Hoxton Street, London, N1 6NG; tel: 020 7613 0743; fax: 020 7615 5280

ENVIROWISE

Harwell International Business Centre, Harwell, Didcot, Oxfordshire, OX11 0QJ

Tel: 0800 585794
Fax: 0870 190 6713
E-mail: press.office@wrap.org.uk
Website: www.envirowise.gov.uk

Enquiries to: Helpline Advisor

Founded: 1994

Organisation type and purpose: Government-funded advice and information service for business.

Subject coverage: Waste minimisation, cleaner technology, environment: all subjects including legislation, for all industry and service sectors.

Publications: Printed, and electronic and video

Publications list: Available online and in print

Access to staff: Contact by letter, by telephone, by fax, by e-mail and via website
Hours: Mon to Fri, 0900 to 1700
Special comments: UK only except for Web access.

Access for disabled people: Access to all public areas, toilet facilities

EPHEMERA SOCIETY

PO Box 112, Northwood, Middlesex, HA6 2WT

Tel: 01923 829079
Fax: 01923 825207
Website: www.ephemera-society.org.uk

Enquiries to: Secretary

Founded: 1975

Organisation type and purpose: Membership association.

Subject coverage: Preservation, study and presentation of printed and handwritten ephemera, identification, dating and conservation, valuation and disposal of collections of ephemera.

Collection: Centre for Ephemera Studies Collection based on Rickards Collection at University of Reading

Publications: Printed

Access to staff: Contact by letter, by telephone and by fax
Hours: Mon to Fri, 0900 to 1700

Associated with: Foundation for Ephemera Studies

Associated with offshoot ephemera societies in: The USA, Australia, Canada and Austria

Contact Centre for Ephemera Studies: University of Reading

EPILEPSY ACTION

New Anstey House, Gateway Drive, Yeadon, Leeds, West Yorkshire, LS19 7XY

Tel: 0113 210 8800
Fax: 0113 391 0300
E-mail: epilepsy@epilepsy.org.uk
Website: www.epilepsy.org.uk

Direct tel: 0808 800 5050
Direct fax: 0808 800 5555
Direct e-mail: helpline@epilepsy.org.uk

Founded: 1950

Organisation type and purpose: Voluntary organisation.
Provides information and support to people with epilepsy, their families and any professionals involved.

Subject coverage: Epilepsy Action represents the interests of people with epilepsy. Services include a national information service, an epilepsy helpline, consultation to professionals, staging of conferences, etc. The Association assists in the formation of local groups, funds social research and promotes a greater awareness of epilepsy among lay and professional people.

Information services: Advice and information in a variety of languages for people with epilepsy, their families and carers.

Education services: Advice and information for education professionals on working with children and young people with epilepsy.

Publications: Printed, and electronic and video

Publications list: Available online and in print

Access to staff: Contact by letter, by telephone, by fax, by e-mail and via website
Hours: Mon to Thu, 0900 to 1630; Fri, 0900 to 1600

Affiliated to: International Bureau for Epilepsy; International League Against Epilepsy

Also at: International Bureau for Epilepsy; PO Box 21, 2100, AA Heemstede, Netherlands

EPILEPSY CONNECTIONS

100 Wellington Street, Glasgow, G2 6DH

Tel: 0141 248 4125
Fax: 0141 248 5887
E-mail: info@epilepsyconnections.org.uk
Website: www.epilepsyconnections.org.uk

Founded: 2000

Organisation type and purpose: A registered Scottish charity (number SC030677) that provides information and support to people with epilepsy, their families, friends and those with whom they live and work.
Runs a variety of projects within the Greater Glasgow & Clyde and Forth Valley Health Board areas.

Subject coverage: Epilepsy.

Special visitor services: Counselling appointments are available from time to time in the Glasgow office to adults affected by epilepsy, and to their family and carers.

Education services: Training and Education Programmes for anyone with a personal or professional interest in epilepsy.

Publications: Electronic and video
Order electronic and video publications from: Download from website

Publications list: Available online

Access to staff: Contact by letter, by telephone, by fax and by e-mail
Hours: Mon to Fri, 0900 to 1700

Access to building: *Hours:* Mon to Fri, 0900 to 1700

Access for disabled people: Wheelchair accessible
Hours: Mon to Fri, 0900 to 1700

EPILEPSY RESEARCH UK (ERUK)

PO Box 3004, London, W4 1XT

Tel: 020 8995 4781
Fax: 020 8995 4781
E-mail: info@eruk.org.uk
Website: www.epilepsyresearch.org.uk

Enquiries to: Research and Information Executive
Other contacts: Information Executive (for research enquiries)

Founded: 2007; created by the merger of The Epilepsy Research Foundation and the Fund for Epilepsy (year of change 2007); formerly called British Epilepsy Research Foundation (year of change 2003)

Organisation type and purpose: Voluntary organisation, registered charity (charity number 1100394), research organisation.
Promotes and supports basic and clinical scientific research into epilepsy throughout the United Kingdom. Independent research is supported, carried out by the best available research team.

Subject coverage: Epilepsy.

Collection: Information available relating to epilepsy research

Publications: Printed

Access to staff: Contact by letter, by telephone, by fax, by e-mail and via website. Appointment necessary.
Hours: Mon to Fri, 0900 to 1700

Access to building: Prior appointment required

Member organisation of: Association of Medical Research Charities (AMRC); Joint Epilepsy Council (JEC)

EPILEPSY SCOTLAND

48 Govan Road, Glasgow, G51 1JL

Tel: 0808 800 2200
Fax: 0141 419 1709
E-mail: enquiries@epilepsyscotland.org.uk
Website: www.epilepsyscotland.org.uk

Enquiries to: Helpline

Founded: 1954

Organisation type and purpose: National organisation, membership association (membership is by subscription), present number of members: 500, voluntary organisation, registered charity (charity number SCO 00067), training organisation, consultancy.
Campaigning, lobbying and policy organisation.

continued overleaf

Helpline and information service.
Training.
Support services in Edinburgh and Glasgow

Subject coverage: Social aspects of epilepsy and associated disabilities, epilepsy in relation to employment, driving, the law, the family, etc., understanding of epilepsy, support systems, professional training, community care, research and policy comment.

Publications: Printed, and electronic and video
Order printed publications from: e-mail: enquiries@epilepsyscotland.org.uk; tel: 0808 800 2200

Publications list: Available online and in print

Access to staff: Contact by letter, by telephone, by fax, by e-mail, in person and via website. Appointment necessary.
Hours: Mon to Fri, 0900 to 1700

Access to building: Prior appointment required

Access for disabled people: Parking provided, ramped entry, toilet facilities

Affiliated to: International Bureau for Epilepsy; Joint Epilepsy Council of UK and Ireland

EPPING FOREST DISTRICT COUNCIL (EFDC)

Civic Offices, High Street, Epping, Essex, CM16 4BZ

Tel: 01992 564000
Fax: 01992 578018
Website: www.eppingforestdc.gov.uk

Enquiries to: Information Officer
Direct e-mail: contactus@eppingforestdc.gov.uk
Other contacts: Public Relations Manager

Founded: 1974

Organisation type and purpose: Local government body.

Subject coverage: All areas relating to local council matters. Most areas relating to the district.

Collection: EFDC Museum, Sun Street, Waltham Abbey, Essex, EN9 1OZ

Access to staff: Contact by letter, by telephone, by fax and by e-mail
Hours: Mon to Fri, 0900 to 1700

Access to building: *Hours:* Mon to Fri, 0900 to 1700

Access for disabled people: Accessible for disabled

EPPING FOREST FIELD CENTRE (FSC)

Pauls Nursery Road, High Beech, Loughton, Essex, IG10 4AF

Tel: 020 8502 8500
Fax: 020 8502 8502
E-mail: enquiries.ef@field-studies-council.org

Founded: 1970; formerly called Epping Forest Conservation Centre (year of change 1992)

Organisation type and purpose: Membership association (membership is by qualification), registered charity.
Environmental education.

Subject coverage: Environmental field work for schools at all levels, environmental and natural history courses for adults, out-of-school activities and environmental birthday parties.

Education services: Environmental field work for schools at all levels. Environmental and natural history courses for adults.

Publications: Printed
Order printed publications from: FSC Publications, Preston Montford, Montford Bridge, Shrewsbury, Shropshire, SY4 1HW; tel. 01743 852140; fax 01743 852101; e-mail publications@field-studies-council.org

Publications list: Available in print

Access to staff: Contact by letter, by telephone, by fax and by e-mail. Appointment necessary.
Hours: Mon to Fri, 0900 to 1700
Special comments: Centre must be booked for teaching, lectures, use of library, etc.

Access to building: Prior appointment required

Access for disabled people: Parking provided

Constituent part of: Field Studies Council; tel: 01743 852100; fax: 01743 852101

EQUALITY & HUMAN RIGHTS COMMISSION (EHRC)

2nd Floor, Arndale House, Arndale Centre, Manchester, M4 3AQ

Tel: 0161 829 8100
Fax: 0161 829 8110
E-mail: info@equalityhumanrights.com; library@equalityhumanrights.com
Website: www.equalityhumanrights.com

Enquiries to: Library & Information Services Manager
Direct tel: 0161 829 8308
Direct e-mail: david.sparrow@equalityhumanrights.com

Founded: 1 October 2007

Information services: Workplace library & information services

Library catalogue: All or part available in-house

Publications: Printed

Publications list: Available online and in print

Access to staff: Contact by letter, by telephone, by fax, by e-mail and via website. Appointment necessary.
Hours: Mon to Fri, 0900 to 1700
Special comments: Access by arrangement only.

Access for disabled people: Fully accessible.

EQUALITY COMMISSION FOR NORTHERN IRELAND (ECNI)

Equality House, 7–9 Shaftesbury Square, Belfast, BT2 7DP

Tel: 028 9050 0600
Fax: 028 9024 8687; textphone 028 9050 0589
E-mail: information@equalityni.org
Website: www.equalityni.org

Enquiries to: Information Officer

Founded: 1999; created by the merger of Commission for Racial Equality for Northern Ireland, Equal Opportunities Commission for Northern Ireland, Fair Employment Commission for Northern Ireland, Northern Ireland Disability Council (year of change 1999)

Organisation type and purpose: Statutory body for promotion of equality in Northern Ireland.

Subject coverage: Equality of opportunity in employment, education, goods, facilities and services; issues related to women in society.

Collection: Women in employment and in society generally, women's education, discrimination law, race issues

Library catalogue: All or part available in-house

Publications: Printed

Publications list: Available online and in print

Access to staff: Contact by letter, by telephone, by fax, by e-mail, in person and via website. Appointment necessary.
Hours: Mon to Fri, 0900 to 1700

Access to building: *Special comments:* Library is reference only.

Access for disabled people: Parking provided, level entry, access to all public areas, toilet facilities

EQUITY

Guild House, Upper St Martin's Lane, London, WC2H 9EG

Tel: 020 7379 6000
Fax: 020 7379 7001
E-mail: info@equity.org.uk
Website: www.equity.org.uk

Enquiries to: General Secretary
Direct fax: 020 7379 6074

Founded: 1930

Organisation type and purpose: Trade union (membership by subscription).
To represent artists from across the entire spectrum of arts and entertainment, to negotiate minimum terms and conditions of employment throughout the entire world of entertainment and to endeavour to ensure these take account of social and economic changes, to lobby government and other bodies on issues of paramount importance to the membership.

Publications: Printed

Access to staff: Contact by letter, by telephone, by fax, by e-mail and via website. Access for members only.
Hours: Mon to Fri, 0930 to 1730

Access to building: *Hours:* Mon to Fri, 0930 to 1730

Access for disabled people: *Hours:* Mon to Fri, 0930 to 1730

Affiliated to: Trades Union Congress (TUC)

ERC GROUP LTD (ERC)

3 Kings Court, Newmarket, Suffolk, CB8 7SG

Tel: 01638 667733
Fax: 01638 667744
E-mail: marketing@erc-world.com
Website: www.erc-world.com

Enquiries to: Director

Founded: 1961

Organisation type and purpose:
International organisation, service industry, consultancy, research organisation.

Subject coverage: Food, drinks, tobacco, ophthalmics, OTC pharmaceuticals, cosmetics and toiletries, personal care, home goods. Geographical research specialisation extends to Eastern and Western Europe, Pacific Rim, Latin America, China, the USA, Middle East, India, South Africa, plus other global markets.

Publications: Printed, and electronic and video

Publications list: Available online

Access to staff: Contact by letter, by telephone, by fax, by e-mail and via website. Appointment necessary.
Hours: Mon to Fri, 0930 to 1730

Access for disabled people: Level entry

EREWASH BOROUGH COUNCIL

Town Hall, Ilkeston, Derbyshire, DE7 5RP

Tel: 0115 907 2244, 0115 949 9478 (minicom)
Fax: 0115 907 1121
E-mail: enquiries@erewash.gov.uk
Website: www.erewash.gov.uk

Enquiries to: Public Relations Manager
Direct tel: 0115 9071159

Organisation type and purpose: Local government body.

Subject coverage: Local government services.

Access to staff: Contact by letter
Hours: Mon to Thu, 0830 to 1700; Fri, 0830 to 1630

Access for disabled people: Ramped entry, access to all public areas, toilet facilities

ERGONOMICS INFORMATION ANALYSIS CENTRE (EIAC)

Electronic, Electrical and Computer Engineering, University of Birmingham, Edgbaston, Birmingham, B15 2TT

Tel: 0121 414 4239
Fax: 0121 414 3476
E-mail: ergo-abs@bham.ac.uk
Website: www.eee.bham.ac.uk/eiac

Enquiries to: Manager

Founded: 1968

Organisation type and purpose: University department or institute.

Subject coverage: Ergonomics, human factors, human-computer interaction.

Publications: Electronic and video
Order electronic and video publications from: Taylor and Francis Ltd, 4 Park Square, Milton Park, Abingdon, Oxfordshire; tel. 020 7017 6000; fax 020 7017 6336; e-mail richard .steele@tandf.co.uk

Access to staff: Contact by letter, by telephone, by fax and by e-mail. Appointment necessary. All charged.
Hours: Mon to Fri, 0800 to 1600

Access for disabled people: Parking provided, ramped entry, access to all public areas, toilet facilities

ERGONOMICS SOCIETY (ES)

Devonshire House, Devonshire Square, Loughborough, Leicestershire, LE11 3DW

Tel: 01509 234904
Fax: 01509 235666
E-mail: ergsoc@ergonomics.org.uk
Website: www.ergonomics.org.uk
Website: www.ergonomics4schools.com

Enquiries to: Honorary Secretary
Other contacts: Business Manager

Founded: 1949

Organisation type and purpose:
Professional body.

Subject coverage: Ergonomics and human factors, work design, environmental sciences, equipment design, human and computer interaction.

Publications: Printed, and electronic and video

Access to staff: Contact by letter, by telephone, by fax and by e-mail
Hours: Mon to Fri, 0900 to 1630

Affiliated to: International Ergonomics Association

ERIC (EDUCATION AND RESOURCES FOR IMPROVING CHILDHOOD CONTINENCE)

36 Old School House, Britannia Road, Kingswood, Bristol, BS15 8DB

Tel: Helpline: 0845 370 8008
Fax: 0117 3012106
E-mail: info@eric.org.uk
Website: www.eric.org.uk
Website: www.eric.org.uk

Enquiries to: Training and media enquiries
Direct tel: 0117 301 2102

Founded: 1988

Organisation type and purpose: Registered Charity (number 1002424), national child health charity.
Support and information on potty training, childhood bedwetting, daytime wetting, constipation and soiling.

Subject coverage: Potty training, bedwetting (nocturnal enuresis), daytime wetting, soiling and constipation in children and young people.

Information services: ERIC Helpline.

Education services: ERIC Training.

Publications: Printed, and electronic and video

Publications list: Available online and in print

Access to staff: Contact by letter, by telephone, by fax, by e-mail and via website
Hours: Mon to Fri, 1000 to 1600

Member organisation of: THA

ESCP-EAP EUROPEAN SCHOOL OF MANAGEMENT (ESCP-EAP)

Formal name: Ecole Supérieure de Commerce de Paris-Ecole des Affaires de Paris

Parsifal College, 527 Finchley Road, Hampstead, London, NW3 7BG

Tel: 020 7443 8800
Fax: 020 7443 8845
E-mail: kstokes@escp-eap.net
Website: www.escp-eap.net

Enquiries to: Business Librarian
Direct tel: 020 7443 8875

Founded: 1973; formed by the merger of Ecole des Affaires de Paris (EAP) and Ecole Supérieure de Commerce de Paris (ESCP) (year of change 1999)

Organisation type and purpose: Registered charity (charity number 293027), suitable for ages: c. 18–30.

Subject coverage: Management.

Library catalogue: All or part available in-house

Access to staff: Contact by letter, by telephone, by fax, by e-mail and via website
Hours: Mon to Fri, 0900 to 1700
ESCP-EAP European School of Management; Heubnerweg 6, 14059 Berlin, Germany; ESCP-EAP European School of Management; Corso Stati Uniti 38, 10128 Turin, Italy; **Other addresses:** ESCP-EAP European School of Management; Arroyofresno 1, 28035 Madrid, Spain

Parent body: ESCP-EAP; 79 avenue de la République, 75543 Paris Cedex 11, France

ESDU

133 Houndsditch, London, EC3A 7BX

Tel: 020 3159 3300
Fax: 020 3159 3299
E-mail: esdu@ihs.com
Website: www.esdu.com

Enquiries to: Sales Office Supervisor
Other contacts: Technical Director; Director of Finance

Founded: 1940; formerly called Engineering Sciences Data Unit; formerly called Royal Aeronautical Society (RAeS) (year of change 1970)

Organisation type and purpose:
International organisation, service industry, research organisation, publishing house.
Profit-making company, but utilising large number of committees where (250+) members give time voluntarily.
Suppliers of validated engineering data and software.

Subject coverage: Acoustic fatigue; aerodynamics; composites; dynamics; fatigue (endurance data and fracture mechanics); fluid mechanics, internal flow; heat transfer; metallic materials data; mechanisms; noise; aircraft performance; physical data (in chemical and mechanical engineering); stress and strength; structures; transonic aerodynamics; tribology; wind engineering; computer software.

continued overleaf

Publications: Printed, and electronic and video

Publications list: Available online

Access to staff: Contact by letter, by telephone, by fax, by e-mail and via website. Appointment necessary.
Hours: Mon to Fri, 0900 to 1700

Access to building: No access other than to staff

Access for disabled people: Level entry

Work is endorsed by the: Institution of Chemical Engineers; Institution of Mechanical Engineers; Royal Aeronautical Society

ESI LTD (ESI)

Formal name: Endat Standard Indexes Ltd

Ochil House, Springkerse Business Park, Stirling, FK7 7XE

Tel: 01786 407000
Fax: 01786 407003
E-mail: info@esi.info
Website: www.esi.info

Enquiries to: Managing Director

Founded: 1989; formerly called Environmental Data Research Limited (EDR), Landscape Promotions (year of change 1999)

Organisation type and purpose: Research organisation, publishing house.

Subject coverage: Landscape, civil engineering, horticulture, architectural landscape, products, users, local authorities, consulting engineers, facilities managers, engineers, process engineering, regulatory authorities, environmental management, water utilities, manufacturing industry, interior design.

Trade and statistical information: Product information for designers and specifiers involved with process engineering and environmental management. Produce information for specifiers, buyers and estimators in the design and construction industry in both private and public sectors

Publications: Printed

Publications list: Available online

Access to staff: Contact by letter, by fax, by e-mail and via website
Hours: Mon to Fri, 0900 to 1700

ESPERANTO – ASOCIO DE BRITIO (EAB)

Formal name: Esperanto Association of Britain

Esperanto House, Station Road, Barlaston, Stoke-on-Trent, Staffordshire, ST12 9DE

Tel: 01782 372141
E-mail: eab@esperanto-gb.org
Website: www.esperanto-gb.org

Enquiries to: Office Manager
Direct tel: 0845 230 1887
Other contacts: Honorary Librarian

Founded: 1976; formerly called British Esperanto Association (BEA) (year of change 1976)

Organisation type and purpose: National organisation, membership association (membership is by subscription), present number of members: 700, voluntary organisation, registered charity (charity number 272676), suitable for all ages.
Esperanto library, book sales, courses, etc.
For the promotion of the international language Esperanto.

Subject coverage: Esperanto, international language movements in general, and related subjects.

Collection: Rare publications dating from 1887

Non-library collection catalogue: All or part available in-house

Library catalogue: All or part available in-house

Publications: Printed, and electronic and video

Publications list: Available in print

Access to staff: Contact by letter, by telephone, by fax, by e-mail and via website. Appointment necessary.
Hours: Mon to Fri, 0900 to 1700, telephone transfer in operation when the office is not manned

Access to building: Prior appointment required

Access for disabled people: Parking provided, level entry, access to all public areas

Links with: Esperanto Teachers Association; 1 Regent Avenue, Skipton, Yorkshire, BD23 1AZ; tel: 01756 799912; Regional federations in the United Kingdom; World Esperanto Organisation; Rotterdam, The Netherlands; tel: + 31 10 436 1044; fax: + 31 10 436 1751; e-mail: uea@inter.nl.net

ESSENTIA GROUP, THE

Lower Ground, Skypark, 72 Finnieston Square, Glasgow, G3 8ET

Tel: 0141 568 4000
Fax: 0141 568 4001
E-mail: info@essentiagroup.com

Enquiries to: Managing Director
Other contacts: Accounts Manager, Information Officer

Founded: 1979; formerly called Network Scotland (year of change 2000)

Organisation type and purpose: Advisory body, registered charity (charity number SCO 02866).

Subject coverage: Telephone counselling and information services on predominantly health-related topics.

Access to staff: Contact by letter, by telephone and by e-mail
Hours: Mon to Fri, 0900 to 1700 (office)

Access to building: No access other than to staff

Access for disabled people: Access to all public areas

Connections with: NHS Helpline; tel: 0800 22 44 88; Sexwise; tel: 0800 28 29 30; Smokeline; tel: 0800 84 84 84

ESSEX ARCHAEOLOGICAL AND HISTORICAL CONGRESS (Essex Congress)

c/o Cllr Norman Jacobs, Honorary Secretary, 101 Farmleigh Ave, Clacton-on-Sea, Essex, CO15 4UL

Fax: 01621 890868
E-mail: essexahc@aol.com

Founded: 1964

Organisation type and purpose: Membership association (membership is by subscription), registered charity (charity number 27604).

Subject coverage: Archaeology, local history and conservation of geographical county of Essex.

Publications: Printed

Connections with: British Association for Local History; Council for British Archaeology; Rural Community

ESSEX COUNTY COUNCIL LIBRARIES

County Hall, Market Road, Chelmsford, Essex CM1 1LQ

Tel: 0845 603 7628
E-mail: answers.people@essex.gov.uk
Website: www.essex.gov.uk/libraries

Founded: 1926

Organisation type and purpose: Local government body, public library.

Subject coverage: General library service with 73 service points and 11 mobile libraries.

Collection: Performing Arts Service
Business Information Service
Castle Collection example 18th century subscription library (Colchester)
Jazz archive (Loughton)
Victorian Studies Centre (Saffron Walden)

Non-library collection catalogue: All or part available online

Library catalogue: All or part available online

Access to staff: Contact by letter, by telephone, by e-mail, in person and via website
Hours: Mon to Fri, 0900 to 1900; Sat 0900 to 1730; Sun 1300 to 1600

Access for disabled people: Access to all public areas

Parent body: Essex County Council

ESSEX COUNTY COUNCIL LIBRARIES – BASILDON LIBRARY

St Martin's Square, Basildon, Essex, SS14 1EE

Tel: 01268 288533
Fax: 01268 286326
E-mail: basildon.library@essex.gov.uk
Website: askchris.essexcc.gov.uk
Website: www.essexcc.gov.uk/libraries

Enquiries to: Customer Service Supervisor – Basildon
Direct tel: 0845 438438

Organisation type and purpose: Local government body, public library.

Subject coverage: General.

Information services: 0845 438438

Access to staff: Contact by letter, by telephone, by fax, by e-mail, in person and via website
Hours: Mon, Fri, 0900 to 1800; Tue, 0900 to 1900; Wed, 0900 to 1800; Thu, 1000 to 1800; Sat, 0900 to 1700; Sun, 1300 to 1600

Access for disabled people: Level entry, access to all public areas.

ESSEX COUNTY COUNCIL LIBRARIES – BRAINTREE LIBRARY

Fairfield Road, Braintree, Essex, CM7 3YL

Tel: 01376 320752
Fax: 01376 553316
E-mail: braintree.library@essex.gov.uk

Enquiries to: Group Manager

Organisation type and purpose: Local government body, public library.

Subject coverage: General.

Access to staff: Contact by letter, by telephone, by fax, by e-mail and in person
Hours: Mon to Fri, 0900 to 1900; Sat, 0900 to 1700; Sun, 1300 to 1600

ESSEX COUNTY COUNCIL LIBRARIES – CHELMSFORD CENTRAL LIBRARY

PO Box 882, Market Road, Chelmsford, Essex, CM1 1LH

Tel: 01245 492758
Fax: 01245 436503
E-mail: chelmsford.library@essex.gov.uk
Website: www.essex.gov.uk/libraries
Website: askchris.essex.gov.uk

Enquiries to: Group Manager – Chelmsford

Organisation type and purpose: Local government body, public library.
District library for Chelmsford.

Subject coverage: General, local history and studies, particularly of Chelmsford from c.1903, business, Learndirect Centre, statistics, Europe.

Library catalogue: All or part available online

Access to staff: Contact by letter, by telephone, by fax, by e-mail, in person and via website
Hours: Mon to Fri, 0830 to 1900; Sat, 0830 to 1730; Sun, 1230 to 1630

Access for disabled people: Ramped entry, access to all public areas, toilet facilities
Special comments: Induction loop to counter and enquiry desks, minicom (textphone), automatic doors.

ESSEX COUNTY COUNCIL LIBRARIES – COLCHESTER CENTRAL LIBRARY

Trinity Square, Colchester, Essex, CO1 1JB

Tel: 01206 245900
Fax: 01206 254901
E-mail: contact@essex.gov.uk
Website: www.essex.gov.uk/libraries

Organisation type and purpose: Local government body, public library.

Subject coverage: General, local & family history.

Services for disabled people: Home library service, hearing loop, additional services for visually impaired & learning-disabled customers.

Collection: Castle Library (18th-century subscription library)
Essex Local Studies Collection

Library catalogue: All or part available online and in-house

Access to staff: Contact by letter, by telephone, by fax, by e-mail, in person and via website
Hours: Mon to Fri, 0830 to 1930; Sat, 0830 to 1700; Sun, 1230 to 1630

Access for disabled people: Level entry, access to all public areas, toilet facilities
Special comments: Escalator to 1st floor; lift available.

Branch libraries: Greenstead Library; Hawthorne Avenue, Colchester, Essex, CO4 3QE; tel: 01206 862758; fax: 01206 798754; e-mail: greenstead.library@essex.gov.uk; Prettygate Library; Prettygate Road, Colchester, Essex, CO3 4EQ; tel: 01206 563700; fax: 01206 571283; e-mail: prettygatelibrary@essexcc.gov.uk; Stanway Library; 10 Villa Road, Stanway, Colchester, Essex, CO3 0RH; tel: 01206 545022; e-mail: stanway.library@essexcc.gov.uk

Headquarters address: Essex County Council Libraries; Goldlay Gardens, Chelmsford, Essex, CM2 0EW; tel: 01245 284981

Mobile libraries: Three mobile libraries serving surrounding area.

ESSEX COUNTY COUNCIL LIBRARIES – HARLOW LIBRARY

The High, Harlow, Essex, CM20 1HA

Tel: 01279 413772
Fax: 01279 424612
E-mail: harlow.library@essexcc.gov.uk
Website: www.essexcc.gov.uk/libraries

Enquiries to: District Manager – Harlow/ Saffron Walden

Organisation type and purpose: Local government body, public library.
District Library – Harlow/Epping Forest District.

Subject coverage: Essex County Council Libraries Language and Literature Librarian is based at Harlow Library, responsible for County collection of language books, audio and video courses, non-English fiction and literature stock.

Library catalogue: All or part available online

Access to staff: Contact by letter, by telephone, by fax and in person
Hours: Mon, 0900 to 1900; Tue, 0900 to 1900; Wed, CLOSED; Thu, 0900 to 1900, Fri, 0900 to 1900; Sat, 0900 to 1700; Sun, CLOSED

Access for disabled people: Level entry, access to all public areas
Special comments: Induction loop at counter and enquiry desk.

Parent body: Essex County Council Libraries; website: http://www.essex.gov.uk/libraries-archives/libraries/Pages/Essex-Libraries.aspx

ESSEX COUNTY COUNCIL LIBRARIES – SAFFRON WALDEN LIBRARY

2 King Street, Saffron Walden, Essex, CB10 1ES

Tel: 01799 523178
Fax: 01799 513642
E-mail: saffronwalden.library@essex.gov.uk
Website: www.essex.gov.uk

Enquiries to: Librarian

Organisation type and purpose: Local government body, public library.
Houses a Victorian studies centre based on the old Town Library Collection.

Subject coverage: Victorian studies with special emphasis on art, literature and natural history, local studies relating to Saffron Walden and its environs.

Collection: Herts and Essex Observer (1939–2004, microfilm)
Saffron Walden Observer (1994–2004)
Saffron Walden Weekly News (1881–2004, microfilm)
Local census returns 1841, 1851, 1861, 1871, 1881, 1891 and 1901 (microfilm)
The Library of Saffron Walden Literary and Scientific Institute
Victorian Studies collection

Non-library collection catalogue: All or part available online and in-house

Library catalogue: All or part available online

Access to staff: Contact by letter, by telephone, by fax, by e-mail and in person
Hours: Mon to Fri, 0900 to 1900; Sat, 0900 to 1700; Sun, 1300 to 1600

Access for disabled people: Level entry, access to all public areas, toilet facilities

ESSEX RECORD OFFICE – CHELMSFORD (ERO)

Wharf Road, Chelmsford, Essex, CM2 6YT

Tel: 01245 244644
Fax: 01245 244655
E-mail: ero.enquiry@essex.gov.uk
Website: www.essex.gov.uk/ero

Enquiries to: Archive Service Manager

Founded: 1938; incorporates the former Essex Record Office – Colchester (year of change 2007)

Organisation type and purpose: Local government body.
Record office.

Subject coverage: Topography and history of Essex, genealogy.

Special visitor services: Conference facilities.

Education services: Heritage Education Officer.

Collection: Extensive collections of local government, parish, estate and family, business and other archives relating to the county of Essex; library of Essex local history

continued overleaf

books, journals and newspapers; Essex Sound and Video Archive; Essex Ancestors subscription service

Non-library collection catalogue: All or part available online, in-house and in print

Library catalogue: All or part available in-house

Publications: Printed, and electronic and video, and microform publications
Order printed publications from: Address above
Order microform publications from: Address above
Order electronic and video publications from: Address above

Publications list: Available online and in print

Access to staff: Contact by letter, by telephone, by fax, by e-mail, in person and via website
Hours: Mon, 0900 to 2030; Tue to Thu, 0900 to 1700; Fri and Sat, 0900 to 1600

Access to building: Public entrance is situated on river side of building, not on Wharf Road side
Hours: From 0830

Access for disabled people: Parking provided, level entry, access to all public areas, toilet facilities
Hours: From 0830

Links with: Saffron Walden Archive Access Point; Saffron Walden Library, 2 King Street, Saffron Walden, CB10 1ES; tel: 01799 523178; e-mail: ero.saffronwalden@essex.gov.uk

ESSEX SOCIETY FOR ARCHAEOLOGY AND HISTORY

Hollytrees Museum, High Street, Colchester, Essex, CO1 1UG

Enquiries to: Secretary
Direct tel: 01277 363106

Founded: 1852; formerly called Essex Archaeological Society

Organisation type and purpose: Learned society.

Subject coverage: Essex archaeology and history.

Collection: Library is now housed at the University of Essex
17th- and 18th-century books (history and religion)
Archaeological journals
Brass rubbing collection (A H Brown)
Definitive collection of rubbings of Essex brasses (Christy, Porteous and Smith)
Essex Parish histories and county biography
Essex prints and photographs
Transcripts of Essex Parish Registers

Non-library collection catalogue: All or part available in print

Library catalogue: All or part available in print

Publications: Printed
Order printed publications from: Secretary

Access to staff: Contact by letter.
Appointment necessary.
Hours: Mon to Fri, 0900 to 1700

Affiliated to: Council for British Archaeology; Essex Historical and Archaeological Congress

ESTONIAN EMBASSY

Formal name: Embassy of the Republic of Estonia

16 Hyde Park Gate, London, SW7 5DG

Tel: 020 7589 3428
Fax: 020 7589 3430
E-mail: embassy.london@estonia.gov.uk
Website: www.estonia.gov.uk

Enquiries to: Secretary
History of institution: formerly called Estonian Information Bureau (year of change 1992)

Organisation type and purpose: National government body.
Diplomatic mission/Embassy.

Subject coverage: All information on Estonia: travel, economical, political, cultural, etc.

Access to staff: Contact by letter, by telephone, by fax, by e-mail and via website
Hours: The Consular Section (for visas): Mon, Fri, 1000 to 1300; Tue, Thu, 1300 to 1600

Access to building: Prior appointment required

ETHICAL INVESTMENT RESEARCH SERVICE (EIRIS)

80–84 Bondway, London, SW8 1SF

Tel: 020 7840 5700
Fax: 020 7735 5323
E-mail: ethics@eiris.org
Website: www.eiris.org

Enquiries to: Partnerships and Development Manager

Founded: 1983

Organisation type and purpose: Registered charity (charity number 1020068), consultancy, research organisation.
Provides research on the ethical aspects of corporate activities for ethical investors.
Provides (non-financial) information on ethical or socially responsible investment.

Subject coverage: Helping investors match their investments with their ethical (incl. environmental) principles. Providing (non-financial) information on ethical or socially responsible investment.

Trade and statistical information: Collated information on retail ethical funds

Publications: Printed, and electronic and video
Order printed publications from: EIRIS Orderline
tel: 0845 606 0324

Publications list: Available online and in print

Access to staff: Contact by letter, by telephone, by fax, by e-mail and via website
Hours: Mon to Fri, 0900 to 1700
Special comments: Charges for some services made to all users. Some information available free via website.

Member of: Global Partners for Corporate Responsibility Research; UK Social Investment Forum

ETON COLLEGE LIBRARY

Eton College, Windsor, Berkshire, SL4 6DB

Tel: 01753 671221
Fax: 01753 801507
E-mail: collections@etoncollege.org.uk

Founded: 1440

Organisation type and purpose: Registered charity.
A rare book and manuscript library, maintained by collegiate body (Provost and Fellows). A research library.

Collection: 16th-century continental books
17th- and 18th-century English pamphlets (to c.1730)
Armenian printed books (16th–19th centuries)
Bibliography
Classical school books (15th–19th centuries)
Drawings and engravings after the antique (Topham Collection)
Drawings of Rome and its environs
English literature 19th and 20th centuries (Hardy, Browning, Swinburne, Anne Thackeray Ritchie, Edward Gordon Craig, Susan Hill, Moelwyn Merchant, Anthony Powell, Etonian authors)
Fine bindings
Incunabula
Local history collections (Eton and Windsor)
Photographic collection
Pre-Restoration English drama
Private presses
Topographical prints and drawings (mostly local)
Western and oriental manuscripts

Non-library collection catalogue: All or part available in-house

Library catalogue: All or part available in-house and in print

Access to staff: Contact by letter, by telephone, by fax, by e-mail and via website.
Appointment necessary.
Hours: Mon to Fri, 0930 to 1300 and 1400 to 1700

ETON FIVES ASSOCIATION (EFA)

3 Bourchier Close, Sevenoaks, Kent, TN13 1PD

Tel: 01732 458775
E-mail: efa@etonfives.co.uk
Website: www.etonfives.co.uk

Enquiries to: Secretary

Founded: c. 1928

Organisation type and purpose: National organisation, membership association (membership is by subscription, election or invitation), present number of members: 700 plus 50 friends.
Controlling body of the game.
To promote the playing of Eton Fives; to review and publish the rules and laws of the game.

Subject coverage: Eton Fives court specifications; lighting; equipment (gloves and balls); laws of the game; court location; court availability; archives.

Collection: Archives: include books, documents, manuscripts, pictures, photographs and other material

Library catalogue: All or part available online

Publications: Printed

Access to staff: Contact by letter, by telephone, by e-mail and via website
Hours: Sun to Sat, 0800 to 2200

EUROMONITOR INTERNATIONAL

60–61 Britton Street, London, EC1M 5UX

Tel: 020 7251 8024
Fax: 020 7608 3149
E-mail: info@euromonitor.com
Website: www.euromonitor.com

Enquiries to: Marketing Manager

Founded: 1972

Organisation type and purpose: Professional body, consultancy, research organisation, publishing house.

Subject coverage: International marketing information and analysis, food, drinks, tobacco, tourism, household cleaning, healthcare, cosmetics and toiletries, household goods, domestic electrical appliances, consumer electronics, leisure, automotives, catering, financial, consumer lifestyles, retailing, Europe, Eastern Europe, North and South America, Australasia, Japan and China, South East Asia.

Collection: Large in-house international library which includes directories, national statistics (Europe), trade and marketing press (Europe), company reports (international) and key data and surveys on consumer goods markets around the world

Trade and statistical information: Data on overall and specific consumer markets to include key trends and developments, market size, sources of supply, market sectors, usership and purchasing patterns, prices and margins, brands and manufacturers, advertising, promotions and new products, retail distribution, future outlook

Library catalogue: All or part available in print

Publications: Printed, and electronic and video

Publications list: Available online and in print

Access to staff: Contact by letter, by telephone, by fax, by e-mail and via website
Hours: Mon to Fri, 0930 to 1730

EUROPEAN ASSOCIATION FOR BRAZING AND SOLDERING (EABS)

Secure Hold Business Centre, Studley Road, Redditch, B98 7LG

Tel: 0845 521 4094
Fax: 01527 518 718
E-mail: admin@eabs.org.uk
Website: www.eabs.org.uk

Enquiries to: Secretariat

Founded: 1970; formerly called British Association for Brazing and Soldering (BABS) (year of change 2008)

Organisation type and purpose: Training organisation.
To provide a consultancy service and technical information in the promotion of brazing and soldering technology.

Subject coverage: Brazing (low and high temperature), diffusion bonding, ceramics, metals, process equipment, consumables, standards.

Publications: Printed

Access to staff: Contact by letter, by telephone, by fax, by e-mail and via website. Non-members charged.
Hours: Mon to Fri, 0830 to 1630

EUROPEAN ASSOCIATION FOR PASSIVE FIRE PROTECTION (EAPFP)

Tournai Hall, Evelyn Woods Road, Aldershot, Hampshire, GU11 2LL

Tel: 01252 357836
Fax: 01252 357831
E-mail: admin@eapfp.com
Website: www.eapfp.com

Enquiries to: Secretary

Founded: 1988; formerly called European Association for Specialist Fire Protection (EASFP)

Organisation type and purpose: Trade association, present number of members: 7.
Corporate voice for European manufacturers and contractors involved in passive fire protection to steelwork, timber and other specialist applications.

Subject coverage: Fire protection to steelwork, timber and other specialist fire protection applications including penetration seals and ductwork.

Publications: Printed

Publications list: Available online and in print

Access to staff: Contact by letter, by telephone, by fax, by e-mail and via website
Hours: Mon to Fri, 0900 to 1700

EUROPEAN ASSOCIATION OF SCIENCE EDITORS (EASE)

West Trethellan, Trethellan Water, Lanner, Redruth, Cornwall, TR16 6BP

Tel: 01209 860450
Fax: 01209 860450
E-mail: secretary@ease.org.uk
Website: www.ease.org.uk

Enquiries to: Secretary
Direct tel: 01209 860450
Direct fax: 01209 860450
Direct e-mail: secretary@ease.org.uk;

Founded: 1982; created by the merger of European Association of Earth Science Editors (Editerra), European Life Sciences Editors' Association (ELSE) (year of change 1982)

Organisation type and purpose: International organisation, professional body.

Subject coverage: Editing and copy-editing in the sciences.

Publications: Printed
Order printed publications from: e-mail: secretary@ease.org.uk; website: http://www.ease.org.uk

Access to staff: Contact by letter, by telephone, by fax, by e-mail and via website
Hours: Tues to Fri, 0900 to 1300
Special comments: No visitors.

Links with: International Union of Biological Sciences (IUBS); International Union of Geological Sciences (IUGS)

EUROPEAN BANK FOR RECONSTRUCTION AND DEVELOPMENT – BUSINESS INFORMATION CENTRE (EBRD)

One Exchange Square, London, EC2A 2JN

Tel: 020 7338 7269
Fax: 020 7338 6155
E-mail: stanojes@ebrd.com
Website: www.ebrd.com

Enquiries to: Senior Information Officer

Founded: 1991

Organisation type and purpose: International organisation.
Financing the economic transition in Central and Eastern Europe and the former Soviet Union.

Subject coverage: Business information for Central and Eastern Europe and the CIS.

Collection: Collection of books, periodicals, CD-ROMs and other documents relating to the area of Central and Eastern Europe and the CIS

Trade and statistical information: Economic and business-related data covering the countries of Central and Eastern Europe and the CIS

Publications: Printed, and electronic and video
Order printed publications from: ETM Ltd, PO Box 171, Grimsby, DN35 0TP; tel. 01472 816660; fax 01472 816660; e-mail sales@dataresources.co.uk

Publications list: Available online and in print

Access to staff: Contact by letter, by fax and by e-mail. Appointment necessary. Letter of introduction required.
Hours: Mon to Fri, 0900 to 1700

Access for disabled people: Toilet facilities
Special comments: Access by lift in Exchange Square and access by lift to Exchange Square from Appold Street

EUROPEAN BEER CONSUMER UNION (EBCU)

230 Hatfield Road, St Albans, Hertfordshire, AL1 4LW

Tel: 01727 798449
Fax: 01727 867670
E-mail: ebcu@camra.org.uk
Website: www.camra.org.uk

Enquiries to: Communications Manager
Direct e-mail: iain.loe@camra.org.uk

Founded: 1990

continued overleaf

Organisation type and purpose: International organisation (membership is by subscription), present number of members: 100,000.

Subject coverage: Beer and brewing. Legislation relating to beer, brewing, sale of alcohol. Historical information on beer and brewing.

Trade and statistical information: Some statistical information on UK brewing, less on the rest of Europe

Publications: Printed

Access to staff: Contact by letter, by telephone and by e-mail. Appointment necessary.
Hours: Mon to Fri, 0900 to 1700

Access for disabled people: Parking provided, level entry

EUROPEAN CENTRE FOR MEDIUM-RANGE WEATHER FORECASTS (ECMWF)

Shinfield Park, Reading, Berkshire, RG2 9AX

Tel: 0118 949 9000
Fax: 0118 986 9450
E-mail: dra@ecmwf.int
Website: www.ecmwf.int

Enquiries to: Director
Direct tel: 0118 949 9101

Founded: 1975

Organisation type and purpose: International organisation, research organisation.

Subject coverage: Numerical weather prediction in the medium range.

Library catalogue: All or part available in-house

Publications: Printed, and electronic and video

Access to staff: Contact by letter and by e-mail. Appointment necessary.
Hours: Mon to Fri, 0900 to 1700

Access to building: No access other than to staff

EUROPEAN CHRISTIAN MISSION

50 Billing Road, Northampton, NN1 5DH

Tel: 01604 621092
E-mail: ecm.gb@ecmi.org
Website: www.ecmbritain.org

Enquiries to: Information Officer

Founded: 1904

Organisation type and purpose: International organisation, voluntary organisation, registered charity.

Access to staff: Contact by letter, by telephone, by e-mail and via website
Hours: Mon to Fri, 0900 to 1700

Access for disabled people: Parking provided, ramped entry

EUROPEAN COMMISSION – EDINBURGH (EC or EU)

9 Alva Street, Edinburgh, EH2 4PH

Tel: 0131 225 2058
Fax: 0131 226 4105
E-mail: diana.hart@cec.eu.int
Website: europa.eu.int
Website: www.cec.org.uk
Website: www.europe.org.uk

Enquiries to: Information Officer

Founded: 1975; formerly called European Economic Community (EEC)

Organisation type and purpose: International organisation.
Representation of the EC/EU in Scotland.

Subject coverage: Information on the European Union.

Collection: Official publications of the European Community

Trade and statistical information: Eurostat

Publications: Printed
Order printed publications from: The Stationery Office

Publications list: Available in print

Access to staff: Contact by letter, by telephone, by fax, by e-mail and via website. Appointment necessary.
Hours: Mon to Fri, 0900 to 1700

Access to building: Prior appointment required

EUROPEAN COMMISSION – LONDON

Formal name: European Commission Representation in the United Kingdom

Europe House, 32 Smith Square, London, SW1P 3EU

Tel: 020 7973 1992
Fax: 020 7973 1900/10
Website: europa.eu
Website: www.europarl.org.uk/view/en/index.html
Website: ec.europa.eu/unitedkingdom

History of institution: formerly called Commission of the European Communities

Organisation type and purpose: International organisation.
Representation of the European Commission.

Subject coverage: European Community polices, legislation and documentation.

Information services: http://ec.europa.eu/unitedkingdom/information/index_en.htm

Publications: Printed
Order printed publications from: See list of agents in the UK at http://publications .europa.eu/others/agents/index_en.htm

Publications list: Available online and in print

Access to staff: Contact by letter, by telephone, by fax and by e-mail. Appointment necessary.
Hours: Mon to Fri, 0900 to 1700
Special comments: The Representation in the UK is now supporting a national network of information centres — see http://ec.europa.eu/unitedkingdom/information/index_en.htm — to whom all enquiries should be addressed. Visits strictly by appointment.

Also at: European Commission; Publications Office of the European Union, 2 rue Mercier, 2985, Luxembourg; tel: 00 352 29291; e-mail: info@publications.europa.eu; website: http://publications.europa.eu/index_en.htm
European Commission; Rue de la Loi 200, 1049, Brussels, Belgium; tel: 00 32 2 235 1111; website: http://europa.eu/about-eu/institutions-bodies/european-commission/index_en.htm
European Commission Office in Northern Ireland; Windsor House, 9–15 Bedford Street, Belfast, BT2 7EG; tel: 028 9024 0708; fax: 028 9024 8241; European Commission Office in Scotland; 9 Alva Street, Edinburgh, EH2 4PH; tel: 0131 225 2058; fax: 0131 226 4105; European Commission Office in Wales/Swyddfa'r Comisiwn Ewropeaidd yng Nghymru; 2 Caspian Point/2 Pentir Caspian, Caspian Way/Ffordd Caspian, Cardiff/Caerdydd, CF10 4QQ; tel: 029 2089 5020; fax: 029 2089 5035; European Commission Statistical Office (Eurostat); Bâtiment Bech, 11 rue Alphonse Weicker, 2721, Luxembourg; tel: 00 352 43011; website: http://epp.eurostat.ec.europa.eu/portal/page/portal/eurostat/home

Links with: Members of the European Parliament (MEPs) London Office of the EP; Europe House, 32 Smith Square, London, SW1P 3EU; tel: 020 7227 4300; e-mail: eplondon@europarl.europa.eu; website: http://www.europarl.org.uk/office/TheOfficeMain.htm

EUROPEAN COMPUTER LEASING AND TRADING ASSOCIATION (ECLAT)

1285 Stratford Road, Hall Green, Birmingham, B28 9AJ

Tel: 0121 778 5327
Fax: 0121 778 5924
E-mail: jgsewel@attglobal.net
Website: www.eclat.net
Website: www.ascdi.com

Enquiries to: Director General

Founded: 1979

Organisation type and purpose: Trade association (membership is by qualification, election or invitation), present number of members: 230.

Represents the interests of the computer leasing and trading industry.

Subject coverage: Specialised knowledge on computer leasing and on purchase and sale of used computers.

Access to staff: Contact by letter, by telephone, by fax and by e-mail. Appointment necessary. Non-members charged.
Hours: Mon to Fri, 0900 to 1730

Connections with: Association of Service and Computer Dealers International (ASCDI); 131 NW 1st Avenue, Derray Beach, FL 33444, USA; tel: +561 266 9016; fax: +561 266 9017; e-mail: jmarion@ix.netcom.com

EUROPEAN CONSTRUCTION INSTITUTE (ECI)

Loughborough University, Sir Frank Gibb Annex, Loughborough, Leicestershire, LE11 3TU

Tel: 01509 223526
Fax: 01509 260118
E-mail: eci@lboro.ac.uk
Website: www.eci-online.org

Enquiries to: Administrator
Direct tel: 01509 223643

Founded: 1990

Organisation type and purpose:
International organisation, membership association (membership is by subscription), research organisation.
To improve the performance of the European construction industry.

Subject coverage: Construction in Europe.

Collection: Business Roundtable (USA) publications
Construction Industry Institute (USA) publications

Publications: Printed

Publications list: Available in print

Access to staff: Contact by letter, by telephone, by fax, by e-mail and via website. Appointment necessary.
Hours: Mon to Fri, 0900 to 1730

Has: over 70 member companies

EUROPEAN COUNCIL OF INFORMATION ASSOCIATIONS (ECIA)

Aslib, Holywell Centre, 1 Phipp Street, London, EC2A 4PS

Tel: 020 7613 3031
Fax: 020 7613 5080
E-mail: eric@eia.org.uk
Website: www.aslib.com/ecia/index.html

Enquiries to: Honorary Secretary
Direct e-mail: roger.bowes@aslib.com
Other contacts: President

Founded: 1979; formerly called WERTID (year of change 1992)

Organisation type and purpose:
International organisation.

Subject coverage: Management of information.

Publications: Printed

Access to staff: Contact by e-mail
Hours: Mon to Fri, 0900 to 1700

Members: Associação Portuguesa para a Gestao da Informação Edificio (INCITE); Portugal; e-mail: incite@net.sapo.pt; website: www.incite.pt
Association Belge de Documentation, Belgische Vereniging voor Documentatie (ABD-BVD); Belgium; e-mail: abdbrd@abd-bvd.be; website: www.abd-bvd.be
Associazione Italiana per la Documentazione Avanzata (AIDA); Italy; e-mail: aida-cd@inroma.roma; website: www.aidaweb.it
Deutsche Gesellschaft für Informationswissenschaft und Informationspraxis (DGI); Germany; e-mail: zentrale@dgi-info.de; website: www.dgi-info.de
L'Association des professionnels de l'information et de la documentation (ADBS); France; e-mail: ADBS@adbs.fr; website: www.adbs.fr
Sociedad Española de Documentación e Información Científica (SEDIC); Spain; e-mail: sedic@sedic.es; website: www.sedic.es
Swedish Association for Information Specialists (TLS); Sweden; e-mail: kansliet@tls.se; website: www.tls.se
The Association for Information Management (ASLIB); UK; e-mail: ecia@aslib.com; website: www.aslib.com
Tietopalveluseura ry – Finnish Society for Information Services; Finland; e-mail: info@tietopalveluseura.fi; website: www.tietopalveluseura.fi

EUROPEAN COUNCIL OF INTERNATIONAL SCHOOLS (ECIS)

Formal name: European Council of International Schools

21 Lavant Street, Petersfield, Hampshire, GU32 3EL

Tel: 01730 268244
Fax: 01730 267914
E-mail: ecis@ecis.org
Website: www.ecis.org

Enquiries to: Executive, Information & Resources

Founded: 1965

Organisation type and purpose:
International organisation, membership association, present number of members: 515 schools, 400 colleges and universities, suitable for ages: 3 to 18.
Provides services to international schools worldwide including: conferences, teacher/senior administrator recruitment, school accreditation and publications.

Subject coverage: Arranges and conducts professional meetings, publishes directories, newsletters and journals, assists member schools with finding staff, evaluates and accredits schools, conducts research and acts as a consultant, encourages the professional development of teachers and provides a link to higher education.

Publications: Printed

Access to staff: Contact by letter, by telephone, by fax, by e-mail and via website
Hours: Mon to Fri, 0830 to 1700

Other offices: European Council of International Schools; PO Box 6066, 28080 Madrid, Spain; tel: +34 91 562 6722; fax: +34 91 745 1310; e-mail: ecismadrid@ecis.org;
European Council of International Schools; 105 Tuxford Terrace, Basking Ridge, NJ 07920, USA; tel: +1 908 903 0552; fax: +1 908 480 9381; e-mail: malyecisna@aol.com;
European Council of International Schools; Cumburri IEC, PO Box 367, Kilmore 3764, Victoria, Australia; tel: +61 35 781 1351; fax: +61 35 781 1151

EUROPEAN COUNCIL OF OPTOMETRY AND OPTICS (ECOO)

61 Southwark Street, London, SE1 0HL

Tel: 020 7928 9269
Fax: 020 7261 0228
E-mail: richardecoo@aop.org.uk
Website: www.ecoo.info

Enquiries to: Secretary General

Founded: 1992; formerly called GOOMAC, PEG

Organisation type and purpose:
Professional body.

Subject coverage: Optometry, optics, eyecare, optical appliances, eye conditions and examinations, co-operation with ophthalmology.

Access to staff: Contact by letter
Hours: Mon to Fri, 0900 to 1700

EUROPEAN DESIGN CENTRE, WALSALL COLLEGE OF ARTS AND TECHNOLOGY

St Pauls Street, Walsall, West Midlands, WS1 1XN

Tel: 01922 657000
Fax: 01922 657083
E-mail: j.pearson@walcat.ac.uk
Website: www.walcat.ac.uk

Enquiries to: Library Manager
Direct tel: ext 7078

Organisation type and purpose: training organisation.

Subject coverage: Engineering: mechanical, production, electronic; building; business studies; catering; community care; hair and beauty; robotics, CADCAM; leisure and tourism; computing; creative arts; design; performing arts; GCSEs; A levels; management; accounts and law; photography; languages; humanities; teacher training; counselling; adult education and return to learn; access to HE; motor vehicles; science; painting and decorating; interior design and soft furnishing.

Non-library collection catalogue: All or part available online

Library catalogue: All or part available online

Access to staff: Contact by e-mail
Hours: Term time: Mon to Thu, 0900 to 2200; Fri, 0945 to 1630; Sat, 0930 to 1230, 1300 to 1530.
Vacations: Mon to Fri, 0900 to 1630
Special comments: There is a small charge for computer usage for non-members.

Access for disabled people: Parking provided, ramped entry, toilet facilities

EUROPEAN DOCUMENTATION CENTRE – COVENTRY UNIVERSITY (EDC)

Lanchester Library, Gosford Street, Coventry, Warwickshire, CV1 5DD

Tel: 024 7688 7541
Fax: 024 7688 7525
E-mail: lbx203@coventry.ac.uk
Website: www.coventry.ac.uk

Enquiries to: EDC Librarian

Organisation type and purpose: University library.

Subject coverage: European Union.

continued overleaf

Trade and statistical information: Eurostats

Library catalogue: All or part available online

Access to staff: Contact by letter, by telephone, by fax, by e-mail, in person and via website
Hours: Term-time: Mon to Fri, 0900 to 1930; Sat, Sun, 1300 to 1700
Vacations: Mon to Fri, 0900 to 1700

Access for disabled people: Level entry, access to all public areas, toilet facilities, parking

EUROPEAN DOCUMENTATION CENTRE – DURHAM UNIVERSITY

Official Publications Collection, Durham University Library, Stockton Road, Durham, DH1 3LY

Tel: 0191 334 2944
Fax: 0191 334 2971
E-mail: n.p.davies@durham.ac.uk
Website: www.dur.ac.uk/library/resources/european/edc

Enquiries to: European Documentation Officer

Founded: 1969

Organisation type and purpose: University library.

Subject coverage: European Communities legislation; preparing legislation; statistical material, background information; reports and periodicals; information on EC grants and loans; UK government publications in all fields.

Non-library collection catalogue: All or part available online and in-house

Publications: Printed

Publications list: Available in print

Access to staff: Contact by letter, by telephone and by e-mail. Appointment necessary.
Hours: Mon to Fri, 0900 to 1700 (staffed)
Special comments: For unstaffed access, see Durham University opening hours online

Access for disabled people: Level entry, access to all public areas, toilet facilities

EUROPEAN DOCUMENTATION CENTRE – UNIVERSITY OF CAMBRIDGE

Cambridge University Library, West Road, Cambridge, CB3 9DR

Tel: 01223 333138
Fax: 01223 333160
E-mail: wani000@cam.ac.uk

Enquiries to: Under-Librarian

Founded: 1963

Organisation type and purpose: University library.

Subject coverage: All subjects.

Collection: Council of Europe publications
EU Publications
ECE publications
EFTA publications
NATO publications
Nordic Council publications
OECD publications
OSCE publications
Very many in the rest of the library

Trade and statistical information: Worldwide collection of statistical abstracts, EC statistics, UN statistics

Library catalogue: All or part available online

Access to staff: Contact by letter, by telephone, by fax and by e-mail. Appointment necessary. Letter of introduction required.
Hours: Mon to Fri, 0930 to 1845; Sat, 0930 to 1245

Access for disabled people: Parking provided, ramped entry, access to all public areas, toilet facilities

EUROPEAN DOCUMENTATION CENTRE – UNIVERSITY OF DUNDEE

Law Library, Scrymgeour Building, Park Place, Dundee, DD1 4HN

Tel: 01382 384101
Fax: 01382 381019
E-mail: edc-library@dundee.ac.uk
Website: www.dundee.ac.uk/edc

Enquiries to: Senior Assistant Librarian

Founded: 1972

Organisation type and purpose: University library.
To promote and consolidate studies and research in European Union matters, particularly European legislation; to make the policies of the EU known to citizens.

Subject coverage: Legislation of the European Union, via the Official Journal and websites. General information on all institutions and agencies of the EU.

Collection: Official documentation of the institutions of the European Communities, reports and studies

Non-library collection catalogue: All or part available online

Library catalogue: All or part available online

Access to staff: Contact by letter, by telephone, by fax, by e-mail, in person and via website
Hours: Term time: Mon to Fri, 0900 to 1700; Vacations: Mon to Fri, 0900 to 1700

Access to building: No prior appointment required

Member organisation of: European Information Association (EIA); Central Library, St Peter's Square, Manchester, M2 5PD; tel: 0161 228 3691; fax: 0161 236 6547; e-mail: eia@manchester.gov.uk

Parent body: University of Dundee; Perth Road, Dundee, DD1 4HN; tel: 01382 383000; fax: 01382 201604; e-mail: university@dundee.ac.uk; website: http://www.dundee.ac.uk

EUROPEAN DOCUMENTATION CENTRE – UNIVERSITY OF ESSEX

Albert Sloman Library, University of Essex, PO Box 24, Colchester, Essex, CO4 3UA

Tel: 01206 873333
Fax: 01206 873598
Website: libwww.essex.ac.uk/

Enquiries to: EDC Librarian
Direct tel: 01206 873181
Direct fax: 01206 872289

Founded: 1976

Organisation type and purpose: University library.

Subject coverage: Specialised EDC, concentrating on social and economic affairs.

Trade and statistical information: UK and EC trade statistics

Library catalogue: All or part available online

Access to staff: Contact by letter, by telephone, by fax and by e-mail. Appointment necessary.
Hours: Term time: Mon to Fri, 0900 to 2000; Sat, 0900 to 1800; Sun, 1400 to 1900

Access for disabled people: Access to all public areas, toilet facilities

EUROPEAN DOCUMENTATION CENTRES

Organisation type and purpose: European Documentation Centres (EDCs) are set up to stimulate European awareness and the study of Europe in academic institutions. They hold copies of all documentation on the Community legislative process that has been published by the European Commission. In addition, they hold preparatory documents and reports from the Commission, European Parliament and Economic and Social Committee. They do not hold stocks of documents for sale. Some produce guides and bulletins.

Contacts: Aberdeen; Aberdeen University, Taylor Library, Dunbar Street, Aberdeen, AB9 2UE; tel: 01224 273819; fax: 01224 273819; e-mail: e.a.mackie@abdn.ac.uk; Aberystwyth; University of Wales, The Library, Hugh Owen Building, Penglais Campus, Aberystwyth, SY23 3DZ; tel: 01970 622401; fax: 01970 622404; e-mail: llis@aber.ac.uk; Ashford; Wye College, The Library, Wye, Ashford, Kent, TN25 5AH; tel: 01223 812401 ext 512; fax: 01223 813320; e-mail: w.sage@wye.ac.uk; Bath; Bath University, University Library, Claverton Down, Bath, BA2 7AY; tel: 01225 826826 ext 5594; fax: 01225 826229; e-mail: a.holbrook@bath.ac.uk; Belfast; Queen's University of Belfast, Main Library, Belfast, BT7 1LS; tel: 028 9024 5133 ext 3605; fax: 028 9032 3340; e-mail: a.mcmillan@qub.ac.uk; Birmingham; Birmingham University, Main Library, Edgbaston, Birmingham, B15 2TT; tel: 0121 414 7574 or 6570; fax: 0121 471 4691; e-mail: p.a.robinson@bham.ac.uk; Birmingham; University of Central England in Birmingham, William Kendrick Library, Perry Bar, Birmingham, B42 2SU; tel: 0121 331 5298; fax: 0121 356 2875; e-mail: linda.garratt@uce.ac.uk; Bradford; Bradford University, J B Priestley Library, Richmond Road, Bradford, West Yorkshire, BD7 1DP; tel: 01274 383402; fax: 01274 383398; e-mail: g.l.hudson@bradford.ac.uk; Brighton; University of Sussex, Library Information Services, Falmer, Brighton, East Sussex, BN1 9QL; tel: 01273 678159; fax: 01273 678441; e-mail: library@sussex.ac.uk; Bristol; Bristol

University, Wills Memorial Library, Queen's Road, Bristol, BS8 1RJ; tel: 0117 928 7944; fax: 0117 925 1870; e-mail: sue.pettit@bristol .ac.uk; Cambridge; Cambridge University, University Library, West Road, Cambridge, CB3 9DR; tel: 01223 333138; fax: 01223 333160; e-mail: wan@ula.cam.ac.uk; Canterbury; University of Kent, Templeman Library, Canterbury, CT2 7NU; tel: 01227 764000 ext 3111; fax: 01227 823984; e-mail: s .h.carter@ukc.ac.uk; Cardiff; UWCC, The Guest Library, PO Box 430, Cardiff, CF1 3XT; tel: 029 2087 4262; fax: 029 2022 9340; e-mail: edc@cardiff.ac.uk and thomson@cardiff.ac .uk; Colchester; University of Essex, Albert Sloman Library, PO Box 24, Colchester, CO4 3UA; tel: 01206 873181; fax: 01206 872289; e-mail: helenb@essex.ac.uk; Coleraine; University of Ulster, The Library, Cromore Road, Coleraine, Co Londonderry, BT52 1SA; tel: 028 9132 4029; fax: 028 9132 4928; e-mail: p.j.compton@ulst.ac.uk; Coventry; University of Warwick, The Library, Gibbet Hill Road, Coventry, CV4 7AL; tel: 024 7652 3523 ext 2041; fax: 024 7652 4211; e-mail: j .bennett@warwick.ac.uk; Coventry; Coventry University, The Lanchester Library, Much Park Street, Coventry, CV1 2HF; tel: 024 7683 8295; fax: 024 7683 8686; e-mail: lbx029@coventry.ac.uk; Dundee; Dundee University, The Law Library, Perth Road, Dundee, DD1 4HN; tel: 01382 344102; fax: 01382 228669; e-mail: a.duncan@dundee.ac .uk; Durham; Durham University, The University Library, Stockton Road, Durham, DH1 3LY; tel: 0191 374 3041/3044; fax: 0191 374 7481; e-mail: r.I.caddel@durham.ac.uk; Edinburgh; Edinburgh University, Europa Library, Old College, South Bridge, Edinburgh, EH8 9YL; tel: 0131 650 2041; fax: 0131 650 6343; e-mail: kdt@festival.ed.ac.uk; Exeter; Exeter University, Law Library, Amory Building, Rennes Drive, Exeter, EX4 4RL; tel: 01392 263356; fax: 01392 263196; e-mail: p.c.overy@exeter.ac.uk; Glasgow; Glasgow University, University Library, Hillhead Street, Glasgow, G12 8QE; tel: 0141 330 6722; fax: 0141 330 4952; e-mail: gxlr30@ lib.gla.ac.uk; Guildford; Surrey University, George Edwards Library, Guildford, Surrey, GU2 5XH; tel: 01483 259233; fax: 01483 259500; e-mail: s.telfer@surrey.ac.uk; Hull; Hull University, Brynmor Jones Library, Cottingham Road, Hull, HU6 7RX; tel: 01482 465941; fax: 01482 466205; e-mail: w.m .carroll@lib.hull.ac.uk or e.b.davies@lib.hull .ac.uk; Keele; Keele University, Library, Keele, Staffordshire, ST5 5BG; tel: 01782 583283; fax: 01782 711553; e-mail: b.g .finnemore@cc.keele.ac.uk; Lancaster; Lancaster University, The Library, Bailrigg, Lancaster, LA1 4YH; tel: 01524 65201; fax: 01524 63806; e-mail: m.dunne@lancaster.ac .uk; Leeds; Leeds University, Faculty of Law Library, 20 Lydon Terrace, Leeds, LS2 9JT; tel: 0113 233 5040; fax: 0113 233 5561; e-mail: j.m.porter@leeds.ac.uk; Leeds; Leeds Metropolitan University, Calverley Street, Leeds, LS1 3HE; tel: 0113 283 3126; fax: 0113 283 3123; e-mail: m.message@lmu.ac.uk; Leicester; Leicester University, Library, University Road, Leicester, LE1 9RH; tel: 0116 252 2044; fax: 0116 252 2066; e-mail: arsi@leic.ac.uk; London; London School of Economics and Political Science, British Library of Political and Economic Science, 10 Portugal Street, London, WC2A 2HD; tel: 020 7955 7273/7229; fax: 020 7955 7454; e-mail: f.m.shipsey@lse.ac.uk; London; University of London, Queen Mary and Westfield College Library, Mile End Road, London, E1 4NS; tel: 020 7775 3321; fax: 020 7981 0028; e-mail: r.d.burns@qmw.ac.uk; Loughborough; Loughborough University, Pilkington Library, Loughborough, Leicestershire, LE11 3TU; tel: 01509 222352 or 222343; fax: 01509 234806; e-mail: l.a .mcgarry@lut.ac.uk; Manchester; Manchester University, John Rylands University Library, Oxford Road, Manchester, M13 9PP; tel: 0161 275 3770; fax: 0161 273 7488; e-mail: h.j.blackhurst@ man.ac.uk; Newcastle; University of Northumbria at Newcastle, The City Campus Library, Ellison Place, Newcastle upon Tyne, NE1 8ST; tel: 0191 227 4136; fax: 0191 227 4563; e-mail: maimie.balfour@unn .ac.uk; Norwich; University of East Anglia, University Library, University Plain, Norwich, Norfolk, NR4 7TJ; tel: 01603 592412; fax: 01603 259490 (Library); Nottingham; Nottingham University, Hallward Library, Nottingham, NG7 2RD; tel: 0115 951 4579; fax: 0115 951 4558; e-mail: susan.heaster@nottingham.ac.uk; Oxford; Oxford University, Bodleian Law Library, St Cross Building, Oxford, OX1 3UR; tel: 01865 271463; fax: 01865 271475; e-mail: elizabeth .martin@bodley.ox.ac.uk; Portsmouth; Portsmouth University, The Frewen Library, Cambridge Road, Portsmouth, PO1 2ST; tel: 023 9284 3239; fax: 023 9284 3233; e-mail: mayfield@libr.port.ac.uk; Reading; Reading University, The Library, Whiteknights, PO Box 223, Reading, RG6 6AE; tel: 0118 931 8782; fax: 0118 931 2335; e-mail: vlsedc@ reading.ac.uk; Salford; Salford University, The Library, Academic Information Services, Salford, M5 4WT; tel: 0161 745 5846; fax: 0161 745 5888; e-mail: j.m.wilson@als.salford .ac.uk; Sheffield; Sheffield Hallam University, The Library, Pond Street, Sheffield, S1 1WB; tel: 0114 253 2126; fax: 0114 253 2125; e-mail: g.h.wills@shu.ac.uk; Southampton; Southampton University, Hartley Library, Southampton, SO9 5NH; tel: 023 8059 3451; fax: 023 8059 3939; e-mail: rfy@soton.ac.uk; Wolverhampton; Wolverhampton University, Robert Scott Library, St Peter's Square, Wolverhampton, West Midlands, WV1 1RH; tel: 01902 322300; fax: 01902 322668; e-mail: a .edwards@wlv.ac.uk

EUROPEAN FEDERATION OF FOUNDATION CONTRACTORS (EFFC)

Forum Court, 83 Copers Cope Road, Beckenham, Kent, BR3 1NR

Tel: 020 8663 0948
Fax: 020 8663 0949
E-mail: effc@effc.org
Website: www.effc.org

Enquiries to: Secretary

Founded: 1988

Organisation type and purpose: International organisation, trade association (membership is by qualification), present number of members: 17 countries, 350 companies.

Access to staff: Contact by letter, by telephone, by fax and by e-mail
Hours: Mon to Fri, 0900 to 1700

EUROPEAN FITTINGS MANUFACTURERS ASSOCIATION (EFMA)

55 Bryanston Street, London, W1H 7AA

Tel: 020 7868 8930
Fax: 020 7868 8819
E-mail: efma@coppercouncil.org

Enquiries to: Secretary

History of institution: formerly called European Capillary Fittings Manufacturers Association (ECFMA)

Organisation type and purpose: International organisation, trade association, present number of members: 4.

Access to staff: Contact by letter, by telephone, by fax and by e-mail. Appointment necessary. Access for members only.
Hours: Mon to Fri, 0900 to 1700

EUROPEAN FLEXIBLE INTERMEDIATE BULK CONTAINER ASSOCIATION (EFIBCA)

18 Wellesley Road, Colchester, Essex, CO3 3HF

Tel: 01206 575584
Fax: 01206 575584
E-mail: efibca@aspects.net
Website: www.efibca.com

Enquiries to: Director General

Founded: 1983

Organisation type and purpose: Trade association (membership is by qualification), present number of members: 36.

Subject coverage: Flexible intermediate bulk containers.

Publications: Printed

Access to staff: Contact by letter, by telephone, by fax and by e-mail
Hours: Mon to Fri, 0900 to 1700

EUROPEAN GENERAL GALVANIZERS ASSOCIATION (EGGA)

Maybrook House, 97 Godstone Road, Caterham, Surrey, CR3 6RE

Tel: 01883 331277
Fax: 01883 331287
E-mail: mail@egga.com
Website: www.egga.com

Enquiries to: Director

Organisation type and purpose: Trade association.

Subject coverage: Galvanizing.

Publications: Printed

Access to staff: Contact by letter, by fax and by e-mail
Hours: Mon to Fri, 0830 to 1630

EUROPEAN GUILD (Euroguild)

Media House, 11b High Street, Sandbach, Cheshire, CW11 1HH

Tel: 01270 753133
Fax: 01270 753444

continued overleaf

E-mail: europeanguild@tesco.net
Enquiries to: Administrator
Direct tel: 01270 753444

Founded: 1988; formerly called European Guild of Media and Marketing, European Guild of Sales and Marketing

Organisation type and purpose: International organisation, membership association (membership is by subscription), service industry, training organisation, consultancy, research organisation.
Support to develop new projects in Europe with PR, VT production and in rare cases sponsorship, TV, radio, newspapers, tourism attractions, music, art.

Subject coverage: Radio development, applications for licence etc, design and production of tourist attractions, voice/over production (in-house), VT production, public relations, tourism development.

Publications: Printed, and electronic and video

Access to staff: Contact by letter, by telephone, by fax and by e-mail. Letter of introduction required.
Hours: Mon to Fri, 0930 to 1700
Special comments: A charge of £10 per hour or 17 euros may apply for certain assistance.

Access to building: Prior appointment required

EUROPEAN INFORMATION ASSOCIATION (EIA)

Central Library, St Peter's Square, Manchester, M2 5PD

Tel: 0161 228 3691
Fax: 0161 236 6547
E-mail: eia@libraries.manchester.gov.uk
Website: www.eia.org.uk

Founded: 1980; formerly called Association of European Documentation Centre Librarians (year of change 1991)

Organisation type and purpose: Membership association (membership is by subscription), present number of members: 500, registered charity (charity number 294502).
To assist information workers dealing with European information to network, share experience and train. To improve EU information provision.

Subject coverage: The European Union, its policies and legislative process.

Publications list: Available online and in print

Access to staff: Contact by letter, by telephone, by fax, by e-mail and via website. Access for members only.
Hours: Mon to Fri, 0900 to 1700
Special comments: Please phone before personal visits.

EUROPEAN INSTITUTE OF GOLF COURSE ARCHITECTS (EIGCA)

Meadow View House, Tannery Lane, Bramley, Surrey, GU5 0AJ

Tel: 01483 891831
Fax: 01483 891846
E-mail: info@eigca.org
Website: www.eigca.org
Enquiries to: Executive Officer

Founded: 2000; created by the merger of British Institute of Golf Course Architects (BIGCA), Association Française des Architectes de Golf (AFAG), European Society of Golf Architects (ESGA) (year of change 2000); formerly called British Association of Golf Course Architects (BAGCA)

Organisation type and purpose: International organisation, advisory body, professional body (membership is by subscription, qualification, election or invitation), present number of members: 133, training organisation, consultancy.

Subject coverage: Design of golf courses.

Information services: The Librarian is happy to help with any enquiries relating to golf course architecture.

Collection: The EIGCA Library contains some 800 books and a dozen or so journals on golf course architecture and related subjects. Of particular interest is the collection of golf club histories generally produced to mark a club's centenary, which now numbers over 300 titles.

Non-library collection catalogue: All or part available online

Library catalogue: All or part available online

Publications: Printed, and electronic and video
Order electronic and video publications from: the website

Access to staff: Contact by letter, by telephone, by fax, by e-mail and via website. Appointment necessary.
Hours: Mon to Fri, 0930 to 1430

Access to building: Prior appointment required

EUROPEAN LEAD SHEET INDUSTRY ASSOCIATION (ELSIA)

c/o 17A Welbeck Way, London, W1G 9YJ

Tel: 020 7499 8422
Fax: 020 7493 1555
E-mail: info@elsia.eu
Website: www.elsia-web.org

Enquiries to: Administrator

Founded: 1985

Organisation type and purpose: Trade association.

Subject coverage: Applications and specifications of rolled lead sheet in the construction industry.

Access to staff: Contact by letter, by telephone, by fax, by e-mail and via website. Appointment necessary.
Hours: Mon to Fri, 0900 to 1700

EUROPEAN LEISURE SOFTWARE PUBLISHERS ASSOCIATION (ELSPA)

Station Road, Offenham, Evesham, Worcestershire, WR11 8JJ

Tel: 01386 830642
Fax: 01386 833871
E-mail: info@elspa.com
Website: www.elspa.com

Enquiries to: Deputy Director General
Direct tel: 01386 835811
Direct e-mail: press@ukie.info

Organisation type and purpose: Trade association.

Subject coverage: Publishing and development of computer and video games.

Trade and statistical information: Sales data for computer and video games

Publications: Printed

Access to staff: Contact by letter, by telephone, by fax and by e-mail
Hours: Mon to Fri, 0900 to 1700

EUROPEAN LIQUID WATERPROOFING ASSOCIATION (ELWA)

Fields House, Gower Road, Haywards Heath, West Sussex, RH16 4PL

Tel: 01444 417458
Fax: 01444 415616
E-mail: info@elwassociation.org.uk
Website: www.elwassociation.org.uk

Enquiries to: Secretary

Founded: 1979; formerly called Bituminous Roof Coatings Manufacturers Association; formerly called European Liquid Roofing Association

Organisation type and purpose: Trade association.
Seeks to raise the level of awareness of the technical and financial benefits of specifying liquid waterproofing systems and to establish product and installation standards.

Subject coverage: Bituminous and polymer-based waterproofing membranes, codes of practice, installation, specification and application.

Publications: Printed

Access to staff: Contact by letter, by telephone, by fax, by e-mail and via website
Hours: Mon to Fri, 0900 to 1700

Affiliated to: Flat Roofing Alliance (FRA); Fields House, Gower Road, Haywards Heath, West Sussex, RH16 4PL; tel: 01444 440027; fax: 01444 415616

EUROPEAN MARKETING SYSTEMS (EMS)

100 New Kings Road, London, SW6 4LX

Tel: 020 7736 0350
E-mail: ems@emsbase.co.uk
Website: www.emsbase.co.uk

Enquiries to: Managing Director

Founded: 1991

Organisation type and purpose: Service industry, consultancy.
Database agency for corporate marketing.

Subject coverage: Corporate data for marketing to the UK and Europe, Central and Eastern Europe, energy and environmental industries and financial sectors, telecoms and IT sectors, government and EU across Europe.

Collection: News extracts on Central and Eastern Europe (1989 to date)

Publications: Electronic and video

Publications list: Available in print

Access to staff: Contact by letter, by telephone, by e-mail and via website. Appointment necessary.
Hours: Mon to Fri, 0900 to 1800 (24-hr answerphone)

Subsidiary body: EPIC books

EUROPEAN MOVEMENT (SCOTTISH COUNCIL)

12B Cumberland Street, South East Lane, Edinburgh, EH3 6RU

Tel: 0131 557 9790
Fax: 0131 557 9790
E-mail: scotland@euromove.org.uk

Enquiries to: National Organiser

Founded: 1990

Organisation type and purpose:
International organisation, membership association (membership is by subscription), present number of members: 430, voluntary organisation.
Independent, cross-party, membership organisation which believes in European unity and seeks to ensure that Scotland's interests are safeguarded and developed as Europe evolves.

Subject coverage: The European Union, Europe, information and activities for schools and universities. Visiting speakers including senior European figures. Study visits to Europe. Annual conference and dinner. Links with other national and international councils. Regular newsletters and information packs.

Access to staff: Contact by letter, by telephone, by fax and by e-mail
Hours: Tue to Thu, 0900 to 1600

EUROPEAN ORTHODONTIC SOCIETY (EOS)

Flat 20, 49 Hallam Street, London, W1W 6JN

Tel: 020 7637 0367
Fax: 020 7637 0367
E-mail: eoslondon@aol.com

Enquiries to: Honorary Secretary

Founded: 1907

Organisation type and purpose:
International organisation, professional body (membership is by subscription), registered charity (charity number 238836), training organisation, research organisation.

Subject coverage: Orthodontics, orthodontic services in Europe.

Publications: Printed, and electronic and video

Publications list: Available in print

Access to staff: Contact by letter, by telephone, by fax and by e-mail
Hours: Mon to Fri, 0900 to 1700

EUROPEAN PARLIAMENT UK OFFICE

Europe House, 32 Smith Square, London, SW1P 3EU

Tel: 020 7227 4300
Fax: 020 7227 4302
E-mail: eplondon@europarl.europa.eu
Website: www.europarl.org.uk
Website: www.europarl.europa.eu

Enquiries to: Information Officer
Direct tel: 0207 227 4300
Direct fax: 020 7227 4301
Direct e-mail: eplondon@europarl.europa.eu

Organisation type and purpose: European institution, European Parliament (EP) press and information office.

Subject coverage: Reports, debates and minutes of the EP, EP activities in Committee and elsewhere, election results and systems for the EP elections.

Collection: EP debates and minutes from 1973

Publications: Printed

Publications list: Available online and in print

Access to staff: Contact by letter, by telephone, by fax, by e-mail and in person
Hours: Mon to Fri, 1000 to 1300, 1400 to 1730

EUROPEAN PHENOLIC FOAM ASSOCIATION (EPFA)

Tournai Hall, Evelyn Woods Road, Aldershot, Hampshire, GU11 2LL

Tel: 01252 357837
Fax: 01252 357831
E-mail: admin@epfa.org.uk
Website: www.epfa.org.uk

Enquiries to: Honorary Secretary

Founded: before 1989; formerly called Phenolic Foam Manufacturers Association (PFMA)

Organisation type and purpose: Trade association, present number of members: 8. Members all share an interest in phenolic foam products, either as producers or as providers of raw materials.

Subject coverage: Phenolic foam in insulation applications, its use based on the technical data available especially that relating to performance in fire.

Publications: Printed

Publications list: Available online and in print

Access to staff: Contact by letter, by telephone, by fax, by e-mail and via website
Hours: Mon to Fri, 0900 to 1700

EUROPEAN PIANO TEACHERS' ASSOCIATION, UK LIMITED (EPTA UK)

6, Ripley Close, Hazel Grove, Stockport, Cheshire, SK7 6EX

Tel: 08456 581054
Fax: 08456 581054
E-mail: admin@epta-uk.org
Website: www.epta-uk.org

Enquiries to: Administrator

Other contacts: Chairman for policy matters.

Founded: 1978

Organisation type and purpose:
International organisation, membership association (membership is by election or invitation), registered charity (charity number 293698), suitable for ages: 6+.

Subject coverage: Piano teaching and performance.

Collection: Extensive collection of audio and video tapes, books and other printed matter available for reference by members only

Publications: Printed, and electronic and video

Publications list: Available in print

Access to staff: Contact by letter, by telephone, by fax and by e-mail
Hours: Mon to Fri, 0900 to 1700

Access to building: Prior appointment required

Has: 31 Regional Organisers

Members reference collection: Piano Teachers Information Centre; c/o The Office, 6 Ripley Close, Hazel Grove, Stockport, Cheshire, SK7 6EX; tel: please contact the administrator for more details

Parent body: European Piano Teachers' Association; Secretary, 34 Carver Road, London, SE24 9LT; tel: 020 7274 6821; fax: 020 7737 5015

EUROPEAN POLICY FORUM LIMITED

125 Pall Mall, London, SW1Y 5EA

Tel: 020 7839 7565
Fax: 020 7839 7339
E-mail: epfltd@compuserve.com
Website: www.epfltd.org

Enquiries to: President

Founded: 1992

Organisation type and purpose: Research organisation.
International research institute.

Publications: Printed

Publications list: Available in print

Access to staff: Contact by letter, by telephone, by fax, by e-mail and via website. Appointment necessary.
Hours: Mon to Fri, 0900 to 1700

Access to building: No prior appointment required

EUROPEAN PUBLIC INFORMATION RELAYS

Organisation type and purpose: Based in public libraries to provide the general public with access to information about EU policies and programmes.

England East Midlands: Chesterfield; tel: 01246 209292; Derby; tel: 01332 255398; Grimsby; tel: 01472 323600; Leicester; tel: 0116 255 6699; Lincoln; tel: 01522 549160; Matlock; Derbyshire; tel: 01629 580000 ext 6578; Northampton; tel: 01604 30404; Nottingham; tel: 0115 941 2121; Oakham; Rutland; tel: 01572 723654; Scarborough; tel: 01724 860161

continued overleaf

England Eastern: Bedford; tel: 01234 350931; Cambridge; tel: 01223 712017; Chelmsford; tel: 01245 492758; Dunstable; tel: 01582 477073; Hatfield; tel: 01707 281558; Ipswich; tel: 01473 583705; King's Lynn; tel: 01553 772568 or 761393; Luton; tel: 01582 454580; Norwich; Norfolk; tel: 01603 215255; Peterborough; tel: 01733 348343

England Greater London: Barking; tel: 020 8517 8666; Battersea; tel: 020 8871 7467; Bexley Heath; tel: 020 8301 5151; Brixton; tel: 020 7926 1067; Bromley; Kent; tel: 020 8460 9955 ext 250; City; tel: 020 7638 8215; Croydon; tel: 020 8760 5400; Ealing; tel: 020 8567 3656; Elephant & Castle; tel: 020 7708 0516; Enfield; tel: 020 8443 1701; Hackney; tel: 020 8525 2576; Hammersmith; tel: 020 8576 5053; Harringay; tel: 020 8365 1155; Harrow; tel: 020 8424 1055/6; Hendon; tel: 020 8359 2883; Highbury; tel: 020 7619 6931; Ilford; tel: 020 8478 7145 ext 222; Kensington; tel: 020 7937 2542; Kingston; tel: 020 8547 6425; Lewisham; tel: 020 8297 9430; Marylebone; tel: 020 7641 1039; Morden; tel: 020 8545 4089; Richmond; tel: 020 8940 5529; Romford; Essex; tel: 01708 772393/4; Stratford; tel: 020 8519 6346; Sutton; Surrey; tel: 020 8770 4785; Swiss Cottage; London; tel: 020 7413 6527; Uxbridge; tel: 01895 250603; Walthamstow; tel: 020 8520 3017; Wembley; Middlesex; tel: 020 8937 3500; Westminster; tel: 020 7641 2034; Woolwich; tel: 020 8312 5750

England North East: Altrincham; Cheshire; tel: 0161 912 5923; Ashton-under-Lyne; tel: 0161 342 2031; Darlington; tel: 01325 462034; Durham; tel: 0191 383 4231; Gateshead; Tyne & Wear; tel: 0191 477 3478; Hartlepool; tel: 01429 272905; Middlesbrough; tel: 01642 263364; Morpeth; tel: 01670 512385; Newcastle upon Tyne; tel: 0191 261 0691; North Shields; tel: 0191 200 5424; South Shields; tel: 0191 427 1818 ext 2133; Sunderland; tel: 0191 514 8435

England North West: Birkenhead; tel: 0151 652 6106; Bolton; Lancashire; tel: 01204 522173; Crosby; tel: 0151 928 6487/8; Ellesmere Port; tel: 0151 356 7606; Knowsley; tel: 0151 443 3738; Liverpool; tel: 0151 225 5435; Manchester; tel: 0161 234 1996; Oldham; tel: 0161 911 4643; Preston; Lancashire; tel: 01772 404010; Salford; tel: 0161 793 3016; Southport; tel: 0151 934 2119; St Helens; Merseyside; tel: 01744 456989/51; Stockport; tel: 0161 474 4524; Warrington; tel: 01925 442889; Wigan; tel: 01942 827619/27; Workington; Cumbria; tel: 01900 325170/77

England South East: Aylesbury; tel: 01296 383252; Bracknell; tel: 01344 423149; Brighton; East Sussex; tel: 01273 296969; Camberley; tel: 01276 683626; Hastings; tel: 01424 716481; Maidenhead; tel: 01628 625657; Maidstone; Kent; tel: 01622 696503/511; Milton Keynes; tel: 01908 835008; Newbury; tel: 01635 40972; Newport; Isle of Wight; tel: 01983 823800; Oxford; tel: 01865 810182; Reading; Berkshire; tel: 0118 923 3234; Slough; Berkshire; tel: 01753 535166; Southampton; tel: 023 8083 2958; Worthing; Sussex; tel: 01903 212414

England South West: Bristol; tel: 0117 929 9148; Dorchester; Dorset; tel: 01305 224448; Exeter; tel: 01392 384206; Gloucester; tel: 01452 425027; Plymouth; Devon; tel: 01752 305906; Poole; Dorset; tel: 01202 671496; Swindon; Wiltshire; tel: 01793 463240; Taunton; Somerset; tel: 01823 336354; Trowbridge; Wiltshire; tel: 01225 713727; Truro; Cornwall; tel: 01872 272702; Yate; Bristol; tel: 01454 865818

England West Midlands: Birmingham; tel: 0121 235 4545/6; Coventry; tel: 024 7683 2325; Dudley; tel: 01384 815554/560; Kidderminster; tel: 01562 512900; Nuneaton; tel: 024 7638 4027; Shrewsbury; Shropshire; tel: 01743 255380; Solihull; tel: 0121 704 6974; Stafford; tel: 01785 278351; Stoke-on-Trent; tel: 01782 238431; Walsall; tel: 01922 653110; West Bromwich; tel: 01902 322300; Wolverhampton; tel: 01902 312026

England Yorkshire: Barnsley; South Yorkshire; tel: 01226 773935; Beverley; tel: 01482 885081; Bradford; West Yorkshire; tel: 01274 383402; Doncaster; tel: 01302 734320; Halifax; tel: 01422 392631/2; Huddersfield; tel: 01484 221967; Hull; tel: 01482 883025; Leeds; tel: 0113 247 8282; Northallerton; North Yorkshire; tel: 01609 776202; Rotherham; tel: 01709 823614; Scarborough; North Yorkshire; tel: 01723 364285; Sheffield; tel: 0114 273 4736

Northern Ireland: Ballymena; tel: 028 2532 3456; Ballynahinch; tel: 028 9756 6400; Belfast; tel: 028 9024 3233; Omagh; tel: 028 8224 4821; Portadown; tel: 028 3833 5247

Scotland: Aberdeen; tel: 01224 652534; Alloa; tel: 01259 722262; Ardrossan; tel: 01294 469137; Ayr; tel: 01292 282109; Bathgate; tel: 01506 776335; Bearsden; tel: 0141 943 0121; Carrick; tel: 01292 288820; Clydebank; tel: 0141 952 1416 or 8765; Clydesdale; tel: 01555 661144; Cumbernauld; tel: 01236 725664; Cummock & Doon; tel: 01290 422111; Cupar; tel: 01334 653722 ext 111; Dumbarton; tel: 01389 763129; Dumfries; tel: 01387 253820; Dundee; tel: 01382 434336; Dunfermline; tel: 01383 723661; Dunoon; tel: 01436 679567; East Kilbride; tel: 01355 220046; Eastwood; tel: 0141 638 6511; Edinburgh; tel: 0131 225 5584; Elgin; tel: 01343 542746; Falkirk; tel: 01324 503605/08; Forfar; tel: 01307 461460; Galashiels; tel: 01896 752512; Giffnock; tel: 0141 544 4976; Glasgow; G3; tel: 0141 287 2850; Glasgow; G2; tel: 0141 621 3424; Glenrothes; tel: 01592 755866; Greenock; tel: 01475 726211; Haddington; tel: 01620 828202; Hamilton; tel: 01698 452403; Inverness; tel: 01463 235713; Kilmarnock; tel: 01563 526401; Kirkcaldy; tel: 01592 412879; Kirkintilloch; tel: 0141 776 8090; Kirkwall; Orkney; tel: 01856 873166; Lanark; tel: 01555 661144; Lerwick; Shetlands; tel: 01595 693868; Loanhead; tel: 0131 225 5584; Methil; tel: 01333 592470; Monklands; tel: 01236 424150 or 434847; Moray; tel: 01343 544475; Motherwell; tel: 01698 251311; Oldmeldrum; tel: 01651 872707; Paisley; tel: 0141 889 2360; Perth; tel: 01738 477060; Selkirk; tel: 01750 20842; Stepps; tel: 0141 304 1800; Stirling; tel: 01786 432106; Stornoway; Lewis; tel: 01851 703064

Wales: Barry; tel: 01446 735722; Blackwood; tel: 01495 223345; Bodlondeb; tel: 01492 860101; Bridgend; tel: 01656 767451; Caernarfon; tel: 01286 679465; Cardiff; tel: 029 2038 2116; Cwnbran; tel: 01633 867584; Ebbw Vale; tel: 01495 303069; Llanelli; tel: 01554 773538; Llangefni; tel: 01248 752092; Merthyr Tydfil; tel: 01685 723057; Mold; tel: 01352 704400; Neath; tel: 01639 764230; Newport; tel: 01633 211376; Rhyl; tel: 01745 353814; Swansea; tel: 01792 655521; Wrexham; tel: 01978 261932

EUROPEAN REFERENCE CENTRES

Organisation type and purpose: The European Reference Centres (ERCs) hold collections of EC documents.

Other addresses: Aberystwyth; European Liaison Office, University College of Wales Aberystwyth, Laura Place, Aberystwyth, SY23 3AX; tel: 01970 622401; fax: 01970 623364; Brighton; Brighton Central Library, Reference Library and Information Service, Church Street, Brighton, East Sussex, BN1 2UE; tel: 01273 601197; fax: 01273 695882; Chalfont St Giles; Buckinghamshire College of Higher Education, Library, Newlands Park, Chalfont St Giles, Buckinghamshire, HP8 4AD; fax: 01494 874441; Chelmsford; Anglia Polytechnic University, Victoria Road South, Chelmsford, Essex, CM1 1LL; tel: 01245 493131 ext 3757; fax: 01245 490935; Edinburgh; National Library of Scotland, George IV Bridge, Edinburgh, EH1 1EW; tel: 0131 650 2041; fax: 0131 667 9780; Exmouth; The European Reference Centre, University of Plymouth Library, Exmouth Campus, Douglas Avenue, Exmouth, Devon, EX8 2AT; tel: 01395 255352; Halifax; Calderdale College, Francis Street, Halifax, West Yorkshire, HX1 3UZ; tel: 01422 358221 ext 2117; Hatfield; Hertfordshire University, College Lane, Hatfield, Hertfordshire, AL10 9AD; tel: 01707 84678; fax: 01707 284670; Ipswich; Suffolk County Reference Library, Northgate Street, Ipswich, Suffolk, IP1 3DE; tel: 01473 583705; fax: 01473 583700; London; Thames Valley University, Ealing Campus, St Mary's Road, Ealing, London, W5 5RF; tel: 020 8231 2246; fax: 020 8231 2631; Middlesbrough; Teesside University, Borough Road, Middlesbrough, Cleveland, TS1 3BA; tel: 01642 218123; fax: 01642 342067; Northampton; Nene College, Boughton Green Road, Moulton Park, Northampton, NN2 7AL; tel: 01604 715000; fax: 01604 720636; Preston; University of Central Lancashire, Library and Resources Service, St Peter's Square, Preston, Lancashire, PR1 2TQ; tel: 01772 53191/22141; Reading; Reading University, Bulmershe Library, Woodlands Avenue, Reading, RG6 1HY; tel: 0118 931 8651; Sheffield; Sheffield University, Crookesmoor Library, Crookesmoor Building, PO Box 598, Sheffield, S10 1FL; tel: 0114 276 8555 ext 6779; fax: 0114 275 4670; Stirling; Stirling University, Library, Stirling, FK9 4LA; tel: 01786 467227; fax: 01786 466866; Swansea; University College of Swansea, Natural Sciences Library, Singleton Park, Swansea, SA2 8PP; tel: 01792 205678 ext 4037; Wrexham; European Reference Centre, North East Wales Institute of Higher Education, Information Services, Plas Coch, Mold Lane, Wrexham, Clwyd, LL11 2AW; tel: 01978 293261 or 293237; fax: 01978 293254

EUROPEAN REGIONS AIRLINE ASSOCIATION (ERAA)

The Baker Suite, Fairoaks Airport, Chobham, Woking, Surrey, GU24 8HX

Tel: 01276 856495

Fax: 01276 857038
E-mail: info@eraa.org
Website: www.eraa.org

Enquiries to: Corporate Communications Manager
Direct e-mail: lesley.shepherd@eraa.org
Other contacts: Director General

Founded: 1980; formerly called European Regional Airline Association

Organisation type and purpose: Trade association.
To protect and promote the interests of regional airlines throughout Europe.
To be the principal body representing the interests of organisations involved in air transport in Europe's regions.

Subject coverage: Airlines, air safety issues, operations, maintenance, infrastructure, environmental issues, air transport policy.

Trade and statistical information: Traffic statistics of European regional airlines and airports (ERA members only)

Publications: Printed

Publications list: Available online

Access to staff: Contact by letter, by telephone, by fax, by e-mail and via website
Hours: Mon to Fri, 0800 to 1730

EUROPEAN RELAY CENTRES

Made up of: European Documentation Centres; European Information Centres; European Public Information Relays; European Reference Centres

EUROPEAN RESOURCE CENTRES FOR SCHOOLS & COLLEGES

Central Bureau for Educational Visits and Exchanges, 10 Spring Gardens, London, SW1A 2BN

Tel: 020 7389 4004

Organisation type and purpose: To provide teachers and pupils with information on Europe, and to support the development of the European dimension in the curriculum.

Collection: Extensive stocks of directories, journals, books and brochures on Europe, the EU and European issues

Publications: Printed

Contacts: East Anglia (ACER); The Association of Colleges in the Eastern Region, Merlin Place, Milton Road, Cambridge, CB4 4DP; tel: 01223 424022; fax: 01223 423389; East Midlands; Leicestershire Comenius Centre, Quorn Hall, Meynell Road, Quorn, Leicestershire, LE12 8BG; tel: 01509 416950; fax: 01509 416993; London and the Home Counties; Kent County Council Education Department, Springfield, Maidstone, Kent, ME14 2LJ; tel: 01622 605704; fax: 01622 605704; London and the Home Counties; Wheathampstead Education Centre (drop-in centre only), Butterfield Road, Wheathampstead, St Albans, Hertfordshire, AL4 8PY; London and the Home Counties; Colchester Curriculum Development Centre (drop-in centre only, telephone to arrange a visit), Acacia Avenue, Greenstead, Colchester, CO4 3TQ; tel: 01206 863839; London and the Home Counties; Central Bureau (written and telephone enquiries only), 10 Spring Gardens, London, SW1A 2BN; tel: 020 7389 4697 or 4723; fax: 020 7389 4426; London and the Home Counties (CiLT); Centre for Information on Language Teaching and Research, (drop-in centre only), 20 Bedfordbury, London, WC2N 4LB; tel: 020 7379 5110; North East; European Information and Education Centre, John Smith House, 1 South View, Jarrow, NE32 5JP; tel: 0191 420 1711/428 2436; fax: 0191 489 0643; North West; European Information Unit (drop-in centre only), Central Library, St Peter's Square, Manchester, M2 5PD; North West; Liverpool Quality Assurance Service, Dulcie Cottages, Riverside Road, Liverpool, L19 3QN; tel: 0151 225 8110; fax: 0151 494 2846; Southern; West Sussex County Council, Education Department, County Hall, Chichester, PO19 1RF; tel: 01243 777578; fax: 01243 777229; Southern; International Education Office, The Hucclecote Centre, Churchdown Lane, Hucclecote, Gloucester, GL3 3QN; tel: 01452 427204 or 427270; fax: 01452 427204; Wales; Ysgol Leithoedd Modern, School of Modern Languages, Prifysgol Cymru, Bangor, Gwynedd, LL57 2DG; tel: 01248 383874; fax: 01248 382551; Wales; National Comenius Centre of Wales, WJEC, 245 Western Avenue, Cardiff, CF5 2YX; tel: 029 2026 5043; fax: 029 2057 6201; West Midlands; Matthew Boulton College, 3rd Floor, Magnolia House, 73 Conybere Street, Birmingham, B12 0YL; tel: 0121 446 3400; fax: 0121 446 3401; Yorkshire & Humberside; Elmete Professional Development Centre, Elmete Lane, Leeds, LS8 2LJ; tel: 0113 214 4072; fax: 0113 214 4069; Yorkshire & Humberside; Hull University, Curriculum Development, Brynmor Jones Library, Cottingham Road, Hull, HU6 7RX; tel: 01482 466843; fax: 01482 466839

Incorporates the: UK Centre for European Education Partners Overseas

Parent body: British Council

EUROPEAN SCHOOL OF OSTEOPATHY (ESO)

Formal name: Osteopathic Education and Research Limited

Boxley House, Boxley, Kent, ME14 3DZ

Tel: 01622 671558
Fax: 01622 662165
E-mail: esolibrary@eso.ac.uk
Website: www.eso.ac.uk

Enquiries to: Library Supervisor

Founded: 1971; formerly called Ecole Européenne d'Ostéopathie (EEO) (year of change 1974)

Organisation type and purpose: Registered charity. College of higher education.

Subject coverage: Osteopathy and other manual and alternative medical therapies.

Library catalogue: All or part available in-house

Access to staff: Contact by letter, by telephone, by fax and by e-mail. Appointment necessary.
Hours: Mon to Fri, 0900 to 1700
Special comments: No loans to non-members.

Also at: European School of Osteopathy Clinic; 104 Tonbridge Road, Maidstone, Kent, ME16 8SL; tel: 01622 685913; fax: 01622 661812

EUROPEAN STUDIES PROGRAMME

The Southern Education and Library Board, 3 Charlemont Place, The Mall, Armagh, BT61 9AX

Tel: 028 3751 2247
Fax: 028 3751 2285
E-mail: office@esp.dnet.co.uk
Website: www.european-studies.org

Enquiries to: Information Officer

Founded: 1986; formerly called European Studies (Ireland and Great Britain) Project

Organisation type and purpose: Membership association (membership is by election or invitation), present number of members: 500 schools, suitable for ages: 11 to 18.
European Studies is a joint partnership between the Dept of Education NI and Dept of Education ROI promoting joint study and communication among students and teachers in 20 different jurisdications, aiming to promote mutal understanding, awareness and tolerance in the youth of contemporary Europe.

Subject coverage: Various units of study/ topics in both the junior and senior programmes have been designed to assist students in examining not only areas of shared interest today, but also areas of conflict in the past. They are intended to broaden the student's knowledge and understanding of their own place and their relationship to others in the Europe of today.

Publications list: Available in print

Access to staff: Contact by letter, by telephone, by fax, by e-mail and via website
Hours: Mon to Fri, 0900 to 1700

Access to building: Prior appointment required

Access for disabled people: Ramped entry

EUROPEAN-ATLANTIC GROUP (E-AG)

4 St Paul's Way, Finchley, London, N3 2PP

Tel: 020 8632 9253
Fax: 020 8343 3532
E-mail: info@eag.org.uk
Website: www.eag.org.uk

Enquiries to: Director

Founded: 1954

Organisation type and purpose: Registered charity (charity number 274898).
Provides a regular forum in the United Kingdom for informed discussion between European and Atlantic countries.
Discusses problems and possibilities for better economic, strategic and political co-operation with each other and with the rest of the world.
Disseminates authoritative information concerning the work of international organisations, such as the Council of Europe, the North Atlantic Treaty Organization, the Organisation for Economic Co-operation

continued overleaf

and Development, the European Union, the World Trade Organization and the Organization for European Security and Co-operation.

Subject coverage: Economic, strategic and political co-operation between European and Atlantic countries, and with the rest of the world.

Publications: Printed
Order printed publications from: E-AG office

Publications list: Available online

Access to staff: Contact by letter, by telephone, by fax and by e-mail. Appointment necessary.

EURYDICE UNIT FOR ENGLAND, WALES AND NORTHERN IRELAND (Eurydice at NFER)

NFER, The Mere, Upton Park, Slough, Berkshire, SL1 2DQ

Tel: 01753 637036
Fax: 01753 531458
E-mail: eurydice@nfer.ac.uk
Website: www.nfer.ac.uk/eurydice

History of institution: formerly called Education Policy Information Centre (EPIC Europe) (year of change 1998)

Organisation type and purpose: International organisation, research organisation.
Part of the Eurydice Network, part of the EU's Lifelong Learning Programme.

Subject coverage: Education policy in EU Member States, EFTA countries, Croatia and Turkey.

Publications: Printed
Order printed publications from: Eurydice at NFER, Wales and Northern Ireland, The Mere, Upton Park, Slough, Berkshire, SL1 2DQ or online from the Eurydice Network website.

Access to staff: Contact by letter, by telephone and by e-mail
Hours: Mon to Fri, 0915 to 1715
Special comments: Service restricted to national and local education policymakers.

Links with: International Review of Curriculum and Assessment Frameworks Internet Archive (INCA), which describes curriculum and assessment frameworks for the 3–19 age range using information from national authorities; website: http://www.inca.org.uk;
the EU's Education, Audiovisual and Culture Executive Agency in Brussels, which co-ordinates the Network; the 37 Eurydice National Units in 33 European countries; website: http://eacea.ec.europa.eu/education/eurydice

Parent body: National Foundation for Educational Research; tel: 01753 574123; fax: 01753 691632; website: http://www.nfer.ac.uk

EVANGELICAL ALLIANCE (EA)

Whitefield House, 186 Kennington Park Road, London, SE11 4BT

Tel: 020 7207 2100
Fax: 020 7207 2150
E-mail: info@eauk.org
Website: www.eauk.org

Enquiries to: Information Officer
Direct tel: 020 7207 2110

Founded: 1846

Organisation type and purpose: Membership association (membership is by subscription), present number of members: 38,000 individuals, 3,000 churches, 700 organisations, registered charity (charity number 212325).
National para-church body representing the concerns of more than 1m. Christians from over a dozen denominations to the state, society and the wider Church.

Subject coverage: Evangelical Christian activity in Britain.
Information on the views and beliefs of Evangelicals across the United Kingdom.

Collection: 19th-century documents of the Evangelical Alliance; uncatalogued collection

Publications: Printed

Publications list: Available online and in print

Access to staff: Contact by letter, by telephone, by fax, by e-mail and via website. Appointment necessary.
Hours: Mon, Wed, Thu, 0900 to 1600

Access to building: Please book to arrange appointmant

Access for disabled people: Level entry, toilet facilities

Also at: Evangelical Alliance Northern Ireland; Downview House, 440 Shore Road, Newtownabbey, BT37 9RU; tel: 028 9029 2266; fax: 028 9029 2277; e-mail: nireland@eauk.org; Evangelical Alliance Scotland; Challenge House, 29 Canal Street, Glasgow, G4 0AD; tel: 0141 332 8700; fax: 0141 332 8704; e-mail: scotland@eauk.org; Evangelical Alliance Wales; 20 High Street, Cardiff, CF10 1PT; tel: 029 2022 9822; fax: 029 2022 9741; e-mail: wales@eauk.org; cymru@eauk.org

Links with: European Evangelical Alliance; World Evangelical Alliance

EVANGELICAL LIBRARY (EL)

5/6 Gateway Mews, Ringway, Bounds Green, London, N11 2UT

Tel: 020 8362 0868
E-mail: stlibrary@zen.co.uk
Website: www.evangelical-library.org.uk

Enquiries to: Librarian
Other contacts: Treasurer (for advice on donations)

Founded: 1945

Organisation type and purpose: Membership association (membership is by subscription), present number of members: 1,100, research organisation.
Lending, reference and research library.

Subject coverage: Evangelical faith, hymnology, revivals, reformers, Puritans, denominational and biographical history.

Collection: Journals from 1766
Manuscripts of unpublished letters, etc.
Robinson Collection of Puritan works
Slides – Bible scene slide tours

Non-library collection catalogue: All or part available in print

Library catalogue: All or part available online

Publications: Printed

Publications list: Available in print

Access to staff: Contact by letter, by telephone, by e-mail, in person and via website. All charged.
Hours: Mon to Sat, 1000 to 1700

Access to building: No prior appointment required
Hours: Mon to Sat, 1000 to 1700

EVELYN OLDFIELD UNIT

London Voluntary Sector Resource Centre, 356 Holloway Road, London, N7 6PA

Tel: 020 7700 8213
Fax: 020 7700 8136
E-mail: administrator@evelynoldfield.co.uk
Website: www.evelynoldfield.co.uk

Founded: 1994

Organisation type and purpose: Established by a consortium of funding bodies (including the City Parochial Foundation, Thames Telethon, London Borough Grants, the Refugee Working Party and the Refugee Council) to develop specialist support for refugee organisations to enable them to tackle the pressing needs of the communities that they served.

EVENT SUPPLIER AND SERVICES ASSOCIATION (ESSA)

119 High Street, Berkhamsted, Herts, HP4 2DJ

Tel: 0845 122 1880
Fax: 01442 875551
E-mail: info@essa.uk.com
Website: www.essa.uk.com

Direct e-mail: paula.ripoll@essa.uk.com

History of institution: created by the merger of British Exhibition Contractors Association (BECA) and Association of Exhibition Contractors (AEC) (year of change 2008)

Organisation type and purpose: Trade association.

Subject coverage: Employment, legislation, health and safety, quality assurance.

Constituent member of: CBI

EVESHAM LIBRARY

Oat Street, Evesham, Worcestershire, WR11 4PJ

Tel: 01905 822722
Fax: 01386 765855
E-mail: eveshamlib@worcestershire.gov.uk
Website: www.worcestershire.gov.uk/libraries

Enquiries to: Library Manager

Organisation type and purpose: Public library.

Subject coverage: General; local history.

Collection: Barnard Bequest (local history)

Non-library collection catalogue: All or part available online

Library catalogue: All or part available online

Publications: Microform publications

Access to staff: Contact by letter, by telephone, by fax, by e-mail and in person. Appointment necessary.
Hours: Mon, Wed, Fri, 0930 to 1730; Tue, Thu, 0930 to 1900; Sat, 0930 to 1700

Access to building: *Hours:* As above

Access for disabled people: *Hours:* As above

Parent body: Worcestershire County Council Cultural Services

EVESHAM TOURIST INFORMATION AND ALMONRY HERITAGE CENTRE

Almonry Heritage Centre, Abbey Gate, Evesham, Worcestershire, WR11 4BG

Tel: 01386 446944
Fax: 01386 442348
E-mail: tic@almonry.ndo.co.uk
Website: www.almonryevesham.org

Enquiries to: Tourist Information and Heritage Centre Manager

Founded: 1957

Organisation type and purpose: Local government body, museum, suitable for ages: all.
Heritage and Tourist Information Centre.

Subject coverage: Tourist information housed in the local heritage centre with its collection of archaeology and local history of the Evesham area, displays relating to the Battle of Evesham (1265), Evesham Abbey (701–1540) and the crafts and history of the Vale, civic regalia of the former Evesham Borough and artefacts belonging to the former Evesham Abbey, display of Anglo-Saxon jewellery and weapons found on a burial site just outside the town.

Publications: Printed

Publications list: Available in print

Access to staff: Contact by letter, by telephone, by fax, by e-mail, in person and via website
Hours: Mon to Sat, 1000 to 1700; Sun, 1400 to 1700
Special comments: Closed Sun, in Nov, Dec, Jan and Feb, and for 2 weeks at Christmas and New Year.

Access for disabled people: Level entry

Parent body: Evesham Town Council; Community Contact Centre, Abbey Road, Evesham, Worcs, WR11 4SB; tel: 01386 47070; fax: 01386 423811; e-mail: townclerk@eveshamtowncouncil.gov.uk

EXEMPLAS BUSINESS INTELLIGENCE (EXEMPLAS)

45 Grosvenor Road, St Albans, Hertfordshire, AL1 3AW

Tel: 01727 813813
Fax: 01727 813404
E-mail: info@exemplas.com
Website: www.exemplas.com

Enquiries to: Information Manager
Direct e-mail: ClareN@exemplas.com

Founded: 1994

Organisation type and purpose: Advisory body, research organisation.
Information and advice service.
Designed to improve business competitiveness through an outstanding range and quality of business information, advice and services to Hertfordshire, UK and international firms.

Subject coverage: Business, science and technology, intellectual property, pharmaceuticals, current affairs, management and products.

Library catalogue: All or part available in-house

Access to staff: Contact by letter, by telephone, by fax, by e-mail and in person
Hours: Mon, Wed to Fri, 0900 to 1700; Tue, 0900 to 1600

Links with: Hertfordshire Chamber of Commerce and Industry; Hertfordshire County Council; Hertfordshire Learning and Skills Council; University of Hertfordshire

EXERCISE, MOVEMENT AND DANCE PARTNERSHIP (EMDP)

1 Grove House, Foundry Lane, Horsham, West Sussex, RH13 5PL

Tel: 01403 266000
Fax: 01403 266111
E-mail: office@emdp.org
Website: www.emdp.org.uk

Enquiries to: Support Administrator
Direct e-mail: sara@emdp.org

Founded: 2006; created by the merger of the Keep Fit Association, the Fitness League and the Medau Society (1952)

Organisation type and purpose: Professional body.

Subject coverage: Medau rhythmic movement.

Publications: Printed

Access to staff: Contact by letter, by telephone, by fax and by e-mail. Access for members only.
Hours: Term time: 0930 to 1500

Links with: Medau College; Coburg

EXETER CATHEDRAL LIBRARY

Diocesan House, Palace Gate, Exeter, Devon, EX1 1HX

Tel: 01392 272894, Library; 01392 495954, Archives
Fax: 01392 285986
E-mail: reception@exeter-cathedral.org.uk
Website: www.exeter-cathedral.org.uk

Enquiries to: Librarian
Other contacts: Assistant Librarian

Founded: 11th century

Organisation type and purpose: Cathedral library.

Subject coverage: Theological subjects, in early printed books, tracts etc. Early printed works on travel, law, literature, linguistics, history, local history, history of medicine, bibliography.

Collection: Cathedral archives and manuscripts
Collection of tracts (Civil War period)
Cook Collection (early foreign language material, 19th-century linguistics)
Exeter Book of Anglo-Saxon poetry c. 965–75
Exon Domesday 1086
Glass Collection and Exeter Medical Library (early medicine and science)
Harington Collection (theology, history, 16th to 19th century)
Manuscript books, 10th century onwards
Printed books, 15th century onwards, including a large proportion of early imprints

Non-library collection catalogue: All or part available in-house

Library catalogue: All or part available in-house

Publications: Printed, and microform publications

Access to staff: Contact by letter, by telephone, by e-mail and in person
Hours: Library: Mon to Fri, 1400 to 1700
Archives: Mon to Wed, 1400 to 1700, by appointment
Special comments: Casual visitors restricted to exhibition area; browsing not permitted.

Archives jointly administered and financed by the: Dean and Chapter of Exeter and the Devon Record Office; Devon Record Office, Great Moor House, Bitton Road, Sowton, Exeter, EX2 7NL; tel: 01392 384253 (DRO); fax: 01392 384256 (DRO); e-mail: devrec@devon.gov.uk

Parent body: Dean and Chapter of Exeter Cathedral; Cathedral Office, 1 The Cloisters, Exeter, EX1 1HS; tel: 01392 255573; fax: 01392 285986; e-mail: admin@exeter-cathedral.org.uk

EXETER CENTRAL LIBRARY

Castle Street, Exeter, Devon, EX4 3PQ

Tel: 01392 384206
Fax: 01392 384208
E-mail: exeter.central.library@devon.gov.uk
Website: www.devon.gov.uk/library

Enquiries to: Group Librarian (South and East)
Direct tel: 01392 384222

Organisation type and purpose: Local government body, public library.
The Central Library for South and East Devon of the Devon Library & Information Services, houses the Westcountry Studies Library.

Subject coverage: General; music and drama, West Country local history, business information, careers, official publications.

Collection: British Standards
Drama Collection (play sets)
HMSO collection (selective subscription from 1975)
Pocknell Collection (early books on shorthand)
Pre-1800 Book Collection (2,000 volumes)

continued overleaf

Trade and statistical information: Keynote market research reports, UK business monitors, government trade statistics

Library catalogue: All or part available online

Publications: Printed

Access to staff: Contact by letter, by telephone, by fax, by e-mail, in person and via website
Hours: Mon, Tue, Thu, Fri, 0930 to 1900; Wed 1000 to 1700; Sat 0930 to 1600; Sun 1100 to 1430

Access for disabled people: Ramped entry, access to all public areas, toilet facilities

EXETER CHAMBER OF COMMERCE & INDUSTRY

10 Southernhay West, Exeter, Devon, EX1 1JG

Tel: 01392 431133
Fax: 01392 278804
E-mail: enquiries@exeterchamber.co.uk
Website: www.exeterchamber.co.uk

Enquiries to: Administrator

Founded: 1992

Organisation type and purpose: Trade association (membership is by subscription), present number of members: over 450.

Subject coverage: Business information, trade and business contacts.

Publications: Printed

Access to staff: Contact by letter, by telephone, by fax, by e-mail and via website. Appointment necessary.
Hours: Mon to Fri, 0900 to 1730

EXETER CITY CENTRE CONSORTIUM

PO Box 209, Exeter, Devon, EX1 1YJ

Tel: 01392 494980

Enquiries to: Administrator

Founded: 1991

Organisation type and purpose: Trade association (membership is by subscription), present number of members: 80.
To represent the interest of members; to promote Exeter City Centre by whatever means with intention of improving the prosperity of business dependent upon Exeter City Centre; to work with others for the enhancement of the city centre environment; to provide the Christmas illuminations each year; to provide and run the Storewatch Radio System.

Subject coverage: City centre improvement.

Access to staff: Contact by letter, by telephone and by e-mail
Hours: Mon to Fri, 0900 to 1700

EXETER CITY COUNCIL

Civic Centre, Paris Street, Exeter, Devon, EX1 1JN

Tel: 01392 277888
Fax: 01392 265265
E-mail: customer.services@exeter.gov.uk
Website: www.exeter.gov.uk

Enquiries to: Communications Manager
Direct tel: 01392 265319
Direct fax: 01392 265247
Direct e-mail: mandy.pearse@exeter.gov.uk

Organisation type and purpose: Local government body.

Subject coverage: Local government.

Publications: Printed

Access to staff: Contact by letter, by telephone, by fax and by e-mail
Hours: Mon to Fri, 0900 to 1700

Access for disabled people: Parking provided, ramped entry, access to all public areas, toilet facilities

EXETER HEALTH LIBRARY (EHL)

Peninsula Medical School Building, Royal Devon and Exeter NHS Foundation Trust, Barrack Road, Exeter, Devon, EX2 5DW

Tel: 01392 406800
Fax: 01392 406728
E-mail: medlib@exeter.ac.uk
Website: www.exeter.ac.uk/library/eml

Enquiries to: Library Manager

Organisation type and purpose: NHS/ Medical School library.

Subject coverage: Medicine, healthcare.

Collection: Collection of pre-19th century medical books (housed in Exeter Cathedral Library)

Non-library collection catalogue: All or part available online

Library catalogue: All or part available online

Access to staff: Contact by letter, by telephone, by fax, by e-mail, in person and via website
Hours: Mon to Fri, 0830 to 1730

Parent body: Royal Devon and Exeter NHS Foundation Trust; Barrack Road, Exeter EX2 5DW

EXMOOR NATIONAL PARK AUTHORITY

Exmoor House, Dulverton, Somerset, TA22 9HL

Tel: 01398 323665
Fax: 01398 323150
E-mail: info@exmoor-nationalpark.gov.uk
Website: www.exmoor-nationalpark.gov.uk

Enquiries to: Head of Education and Interpretation
Other contacts: External Relations Manager for media and general enquiries

Founded: 1954

Organisation type and purpose: Local government body, planning authority, statutory body.
Statutory purposes of the National Park are to conserve and enhance the natural beauty, wildlife and cultural heritage of the area. To promote opportunities for the understanding and enjoyment of the park's special qualities. To seek to foster the economic and social well-being of the communities within the National Park without incurring significant expenditure in so doing. The Authority is also the planning authority for Exmoor.

Subject coverage: Exmoor, its natural history, history, culture, access, recreation and tourist facilities.

Information services: 3 National Park Centres.

Education services: Residential outdoor education centre, sleeps 40.

Services for disabled people: Easy access trails.

Collection: Books, maps and photographs of Exmoor, including aerial photography

Publications: Printed
Order printed publications from: Centre Head, National Park Centre, Dulverton TA22 9EX, tel: 01398 323841

Publications list: Available online and in print

Access to staff: Contact by letter, by telephone, by fax, by e-mail and via website. Appointment necessary.
Hours: Mon to Thu, 0900 to 1700; Fri, 0900 to 1600

Access for disabled people: Parking provided, ramped entry, toilet facilities, lift to committee room

Member of: UK Association of National Park Authorities (ANPA); 126 Bute Street, Cardiff, CF10 5LE; tel: 02920 499966; e-mail: enquiries@anpa.gov.uk

National Park Centre: ENPA; Fore Street, Dulverton, TA22 3EX; tel: 01398 323841; e-mail: npcdulverton@exmoor-nationalpark.gov.uk

EXMOOR SOCIETY

Parish Rooms, Rosemary Lane, Dulverton, Somerset, TA22 9DP

Tel: 01398 323335
Fax: 01398 323335
E-mail: exmoorsociety@yahoo.co.uk
Website: www.exmoorsociety.org.uk

Enquiries to: Secretary

Founded: 1959

Organisation type and purpose:
Membership association (membership is by subscription), present number of members: 2,200, voluntary organisation, registered charity (charity number 245761).
Conservation.

Subject coverage: Conservation of Exmoor.

Collection: Archives from Roger Miles including:
Forestry Commission Reports
NPC Reports
Alfred Vowles Photographic Archive

Non-library collection catalogue: All or part available in-house

Library catalogue: All or part available in-house

Publications: Printed

Access to staff: Contact by letter, by telephone, by fax, by e-mail and in person
Hours: Tue to Thu, 0900 to 1600

EXMOUTH LIBRARY

40 Exeter Road, Exmouth, Devon, EX8 1PS

Tel: 01395 272677
Fax: 01395 271426
E-mail: exmouth.library@devon.gov.uk
Website: www.devon.gov.uk/libraries

Enquiries to: Senior Library Supervisor

Founded: 1946

Organisation type and purpose: Local government body, public library.
Part of the Devon Library & Information Services.

Subject coverage: General, Exmouth local history.

Collection: Exmouth local history

Trade and statistical information: A selection of standard printed sources

Library catalogue: All or part available online

Publications: Microform publications

Access to staff: Contact by letter, by telephone, by e-mail, in person and via website
Hours: Mon, Tue, Thu, Fri, 0900 to 1800; Sat, 0900 to 1600.

Access for disabled people: Ramped entry

Parent body: Devon County Council, Devon Library & Information Services; Great Moor House, Sowton, Exeter, EX2 7NL; tel: 01392 384315; fax: 01392 384316; e-mail: devlibs@devon.gov.uk

EXPORT CREDITS GUARANTEE DEPARTMENT (ECGD)

PO Box 2200, 2 Exchange Tower, Harbour Exchange Square, London, E14 9GS

Tel: 020 7512 7000
Fax: 020 7512 7649
E-mail: help@ecgd.gsi.gov.uk
Website: www.ecgd.gov.uk

Enquiries to: ECGD Help Desk
Direct tel: 020 7512 7887

Founded: 1919

Organisation type and purpose: National government body.
Government department.
UK's official export credit agency.

Subject coverage: Export credit insurance for UK exporters, overseas investment insurance, export finance guarantees for banks.

Publications: Printed

Access to staff: Contact by letter, by telephone, by fax, by e-mail and via website
Hours: Mon to Fri, 0800 to 1800

Responsible to the: Secretary of State for Trade and Industry

EXTEND EXERCISE TRAINING LTD (EXTEND)

Formal name: Movement to Music for the over Sixties and the Less Able of Any Age

2 Place Farm, Wheathampstead, Hertfordshire, AL4 8SB

Tel: 01582 832760
Fax: 01582 832760
E-mail: admin@extend.org.uk
Website: www.extend.org.uk

Enquiries to: Head Office Senior Administrator
Other contacts: Director of Training, Assistant Administrator

Founded: 1976

Organisation type and purpose: Registered charity (charity number 802498), training organisation.
Provides recreational movement to music for the over sixties and for the less able of any age.
To promote good health and enhance the quality of life through stimulating physical and mental health, increasing mobility and independence, improving strength, stamina, posture and coordination and to overcoming loneliness and isolation.

Subject coverage: Recreational movement to music, recreational rehabilitation, use of music and rhythm, diet and nutrition.

Information services: Details of how to train as an Extend Teacher and contact a teacher for a nearby class.

Services for disabled people: Provision of exercise classes.

Publications: Printed

Access to staff: Contact by letter, by telephone, by fax, by e-mail and via website. Appointment necessary. Access for members only.
Hours: Mon to Fri, 0900 to 1500

EXXONMOBIL

ExxonMobil House, Ermyn Way, Leatherhead, Surrey, KT22 8UX

Tel: +44 1372 222000
Fax: 020 7026 4728

Enquiries to: IMS Administrator
Direct tel: 023 8089 6113
Direct fax: 023 8089 6334
Direct e-mail: rob.gostt@exxonmobil.com

Organisation type and purpose: Manufacturing industry.

Subject coverage: Chemical engineering; combustion; corrosion; petroleum and petroleum products; oil refining; oil transport and storage; plant maintenance; pollution.

Collection: British and American industrial standards

Access to staff: Contact by telephone, by fax and by e-mail
Hours: Mon to Fri, 0830 to 1630

EYECARE TRUST, THE (EIS)

PO Box 804, Aylesbury, Buckinghamshire, HP20 9DF

Tel: 0845 129 5001
Fax: 0845 129 5001
E-mail: info@eyecaretrust.org.uk
Website: www.eye-care.org.uk

Enquiries to: Membership Secretary
Direct e-mail: pr@eyecaretrust.org.uk
Other contacts: Administrator

Founded: 2001; formerly called Eyecare Information Bureau (ECIB), Optical Information Council (OIC); formerly called Eyecare Information Service (EIS) (year of change 2001)

Organisation type and purpose: National organisation, advisory body, membership association (membership is by subscription), present number of members: 500, voluntary organisation, registered charity (charity number 1086146).
Public relations and promotions for the whole of optics.

Subject coverage: All aspects of eyes and optics.

Trade and statistical information: Statistics relating to the optical sector

Publications: Printed, and electronic and video

Publications list: Available online and in print

Access to staff: Contact by letter, by telephone, by fax, by e-mail and via website
Hours: Mon to Fri, 1000 to 1600

Members: Association of British Dispensing Opticians (ABDO); Association of Contact Lens Manufacturers (ACLM); Association of Optometrists (AOP); British College of Optometrists (BCO); Federation of Manufacturing Opticians (FMO); Federation of Ophthalmic and Dispensing Opticians (FODO)

FABIAN SOCIETY

11 Dartmouth Street, London, SW1H 9BN

Tel: 020 7227 4900
Fax: 020 7976 7153
E-mail: info@fabian-society.org.uk
Website: www.fabians.org.uk

Enquiries to: Membership Secretary
Direct e-mail: members@fabian-society.org.uk
Other contacts: Editor

Founded: 1884

Organisation type and purpose: Membership association (membership is by subscription), present number of members: 6,700, research organisation, publishing house.
Senior Think Tank for the Labour Party and the oldest socialist society affiliated to the Labour Party.

Subject coverage: Politics, current affairs, social policy and economics.

Publications list: Available online and in print

Access to staff: Contact by letter, by telephone, by fax, by e-mail and via website. Appointment necessary.
Hours: Mon to Fri, 0930 to 1300 and 1400 to 1730

FACULTY OF CREATIVE ARTS LIBRARY, UNIVERSITY OF THE WEST OF ENGLAND, BRISTOL (UWE, Bristol)

Bower Ashton Campus, Kennel Lodge Road, Bristol, BS3 2JT

Tel: 0117 328 4750

continued overleaf

Fax: 0117 328 4745
E-mail: library.sca@uwe.ac.uk
Website: www.uwe.ac.uk/library

Enquiries to: Campus/Faculty Librarian
Direct tel: 0117 328 4731

Founded: 1992; formerly called Bristol Polytechnic (year of change 1992)

Organisation type and purpose: University library.

Subject coverage: Art and design, media studies, cinema films.

Collection: Cinema films (video and DVD format)
Collection of slides
Collection of artists' books
Exhibition catalogues

Library catalogue: All or part available online

Access to staff: Contact by letter, by telephone, by fax and by e-mail.
Appointment necessary.
Hours: Mon to Fri, 0900 to 1700

Member organisation of: ARLIS (UK and Eire)

FACULTY OF DENTAL SURGERY (FDS RCSEng)

Royal College of Surgeons of England, 35–43 Lincoln's Inn Fields, London, WC2A 3PN

Tel: 020 7869 6810
Fax: 020 7869 6816
E-mail: fds@rcseng.ac.uk
Website: www.rcseng.ac.uk/public/fds/fds.htm

Enquiries to: Administrative Assistant

Founded: 1947

Organisation type and purpose: International organisation, advisory body, professional body (membership is by subscription, qualification, election or invitation), present number of members: 4,222, registered charity, training organisation.

Subject coverage: Postgraduate dental education and training, and oral and maxillofacial surgery.

Collection: Odontological collection

Non-library collection catalogue: All or part available in-house

Publications list: Available online

Access to staff: Contact by e-mail
Hours: Mon to Fri, 0900 to 1700

Access to building: Prior appointment required

Access for disabled people: Parking provided

FACULTY OF PROFESSIONAL BUSINESS AND TECHNICAL MANAGEMENT (FPBTM)

Warwick Corner, 42 Warwick Road, Kenilworth, Warwickshire, CV8 1HE

Tel: 01926 259342
E-mail: info@pbtm.org.uk
Website: www.pbtm.org.uk

Enquiries to: Executive Administrator

Founded: 1983

Organisation type and purpose: International organisation, professional body (membership is by subscription, qualification), management, manufacturing, industry, training organisation, professional diploma courses available.

Subject coverage: Industrial, computing, technological and associated management, education and training.

Publications: Electronic and video

Access to staff: Contact by letter, by telephone, by e-mail and via website

Links with: Academy of Multi-Skills (AMS); website: www.academyofmultiskills.org.uk
Institute of Management Specialists (IMS); website: www.instituteofmanagementspecialists.org.uk
Institute of Manufacturing (IManf); website: www.instituteofmanufacturing.org.uk
The Academy of Executives and Administrators (AEA); website: www.academyofexecutivesandadministrators.org.uk

FACULTY OF SEXUAL AND REPRODUCTIVE HEALTHCARE (FSRH)

27 Sussex Place, Regent's Park, London NW1 4RG, UK

Tel: 020 7724 5681
Fax: 020 7723 5333
E-mail: journal@fsrh.org
Website: jfprhc.bmj.com/

Enquiries to: Secretary

Founded: 1993

Organisation type and purpose: Professional body (membership is by qualification), registered charity (charity number 1019969), training organisation. Training for medical professionals (doctors).

Subject coverage: All fields of family planning and reproductive health.

Publications: Printed, and electronic and video
Order printed publications from: For ALL subscription enquiries/orders contact:
BMJ Journals, BMA House, Tavistock Square, London WC1H 9JR, UK
Email: support@bmjgroup.com
Tel: +44 (0)20 7383 6270
Fax: +44 (0)20 7383 6402
Order electronic and video publications from: For ALL subscription enquiries/orders contact:
BMJ Journals, BMA House, Tavistock Square, London WC1H 9JR, UK
Email: support@bmjgroup.com
Tel: +44 (0)20 7383 6270
Fax: +44 (0)20 7383 6402

Access to staff: Access for members only.
Hours: Mon to Fri, 0900 to 1700

Parent body: Royal College of Obstetricians and Gynaecologists; at the same address

FAIR ISLE BIRD OBSERVATORY TRUST (FIBOT)

Fair Isle Bird Observatory, Fair Isle, Shetland, ZE2 9JU

Tel: 01595 760258
Fax: 01595 760258 (telephone first)
E-mail: fairisle.birdobs@zetnet.co.uk
Website: www.fairislebirdobs.oc.uk

Enquiries to: Warden
Other contacts: Administrator for office business.

Founded: 1948

Organisation type and purpose: Registered charity, research organisation.
Ornithological research and holiday accommodation.

Subject coverage: Seabird monitoring and migration studies at Fair Isle Bird Observatory. Accommodation for paying guests/visitors to Observatory/Isle.

Collection: Richard Richardson Library

Publications: Printed
Order printed publications from: Fair Isle Bird Observatory Reports

Access to staff: Contact by letter, by telephone, by e-mail, in person and via website
Hours: Any time, any day.

Access to building: Prior appointment required
Special comments: Open to visitors end April to end October.

FAIR ORGAN PRESERVATION SOCIETY (FOPS)

43 Woolmans, Fullers Slade, Milton Keynes, Buckinghamshire, MK11 2BA

Tel: 01908 263707
Fax: 01908 263707
Website: www.fops.org

Enquiries to: Membership Secretary
Direct e-mail: membership@fops.org

Founded: 1958

Organisation type and purpose: Membership association (membership is by subscription), present number of members: 900 in 13 countries.
Promotion and encouragement of interest in, and the preservation of, fairground organs and mechanical musical instruments.

Subject coverage: Fairground organs, Dutch and German street organs, Belgian dance organs.

Collection: Documentary archive held within the National Fairground Archive at Sheffield University

Publications: Printed

Access to staff: Contact by letter, by telephone, by fax, by e-mail and via website
Hours: Answerphone out of office hours

FALKIRK ARCHIVES

Formal name: Falkirk Community Trust Archives

Callendar House, Callendar Park, Falkirk, FK1 1YR

Tel: 01324 503778
Fax: 01324 503771
E-mail: callendar.house@falkirk.gov.uk
Website: www.falkirkcommunitytrust.org/heritage/archives

Enquiries to: Archivist
Direct tel: 01324 503779
Direct e-mail: archives@falkirkcommunitytrust.org
Other contacts: Archives Assistants

Founded: 1992; formerly called Falkirk Council Archives (year of change 2011)

Organisation type and purpose: Registered charity and company limited by guarantee; manages culture, leisure & sport for Falkirk Council.

Collection: Local authority records, including Falkirk Burgh 1803–1975, Grangemouth Burgh 1872–1975, Bo'ness Burgh, Denny & Dunipace Burgh 1833–1975, Stirling County District Councils 1930–1975, West Lothian County District Councils 1930–1975, parish councils and parochial boards; Falkirk District Council, 1975–1995 and Falkirk Council, 1995 to present
Photograph collection, over 43,000 images of local places, events and people
Records of local businesses, organisations, trade unions, professional associations, churches, families and estates.
Small reference library

Non-library collection catalogue: All or part available online and in-house

Library catalogue: All or part available in-house

Access to staff: Contact by letter, by telephone, by fax, by e-mail and in person
Hours: Mon to Fri, 1000 to 1230 and 1330 to 1700
Special comments: Closed on local public holidays.

Access to building: No prior appointment required
Hours: Mon to Sat, 1000 to 1700

Access for disabled people: Parking available, level entry, access to all public areas, toilet facilities

Parent body: Falkirk Community Trust; Suite 1A, The Falkirk Stadium, 4 Stadium Way, Falkirk FK2 9EE; tel: 01324 590900

FALKIRK COLLEGE OF FURTHER AND HIGHER EDUCATION

Grangemouth Road, Falkirk, Strathclyde, FK2 9AD

Tel: 01324 403045
Fax: 01324 403046
E-mail: library@falkirkcollege.ac.uk

Enquiries to: Librarian

Founded: 1963

Organisation type and purpose: College of further education.

Subject coverage: Automobile, electrical, electronic, mechanical, and plant engineering, construction and building, food technology, catering, health, social care, business studies, office services, leisure management, sport and recreation, computer studies, art and design, environmental management.

Library catalogue: All or part available in-house

FALKIRK COMMUNITY TRUST LIBRARIES

Victoria Buildings, Queen Street, Falkirk, FK2 7AF

Tel: 01324 506800
Fax: 01324 506801
E-mail: library.support@falkirkcommunitytrust.org
Website: www.falkirkcommunitytrust.org/libraries

Enquiries to: Team Leader Library Support
Direct tel: 01324 506804
Direct e-mail: shona.hill@falkirkcommunitytrust.org

History of institution: formerly called Falkirk Council Library Services (year of change 2011)

Organisation type and purpose: Local government body, public library.

Subject coverage: General, local history.

Non-library collection catalogue: All or part available online and in-house

Library catalogue: All or part available online and in-house

Publications: Printed
Order printed publications from: Library Support, Victoria Buildings, Queen Street, Falkirk, FK2 7AF, tel: 01324 506800

Publications list: Available online and in print

Access to staff: Contact by letter, by telephone, by fax, by e-mail, in person and via website
Hours: Mon to Fri, 0900 to 1700

FALKLAND ISLANDS GOVERNMENT OFFICE (FIGO)

Falkland House, 14 Broadway, London, SW1H 0BH

Tel: 020 7222 2542
Fax: 020 7222 2375
E-mail: rep@falklands.gov.fk
Website: www.falklands.gov.fk
Website: www.visitorfalklands.com

Enquiries to: Representative

Founded: 1983

Organisation type and purpose: National government body.
To provide an information source and trade links in the United Kingdom. Point of contact for UK Parliament.

Subject coverage: All aspects relating to the government, development of trade, tourism and travel to the Falklands. Dissemination of all information of a general nature in connection with the Falklands.

Trade and statistical information: General and specific information on trade to and from the Islands

Publications: Printed, and electronic and video
Order printed publications from: Falkland Islands Government Office, Falkland House, 14 Broadway, Westminster, London, SW1H 0BH
Order electronic and video publications from: Falkland Islands Government Office, Falkland House, 14 Broadway, Westminster, London, SW1H 0BH

Publications list: Available in print

Access to staff: Contact by letter, by telephone, by fax, by e-mail, in person and via website
Hours: Mon to Fri, 0900 to 1300 and 1400 to 1730

Access to building: Prior appointment required
Hours: Mon to Fri, 0900 to 1300 and 1400 to 1730

Links with: Falkland Islands Development Corporation; Shackleton House, Davis Street East, Stanley, Falkland Islands, FIQQ 1ZZ; tel: +500 27211; fax: +500 27210; e-mail: develop@fidc.co.fk; website: http://www.fidc.co.fk
Falkland Islands Tourist Board; Jetty Visitor Centre, Stanley, Falkland Islands, FIQQ 1ZZ; tel: +500 22215; fax: +500 22619; e-mail: jettycentre@horizon.co.fk; website: http://www.visitorfalklands.com

Parent body: Falkland Islands Government; The Secretariat, Stanley, Falkland Islands, FIQQ 1ZZ; tel: +500 27242; fax: +500 27109; e-mail: lbrownlee@sec.gov.fk

FAMILIES NEED FATHERS

134–146 Curtain Road, London, EC2A 3AR

Tel: 020 7613 5060
Fax: 020 7739 3410
E-mail: fnf@fnf.org.uk
Website: www.fnf.org.uk

Enquiries to: Secretary

Founded: 1974

Organisation type and purpose:
Membership association (membership is by subscription), present number of members: 3,000, voluntary organisation, registered charity (charity number 276899).
Support group, self-help society and pressure group to change and improve the present legal process and to eliminate unnecessary and protracted legal conflict. Keeping children in contact with both parents after separation or divorce. Promoting shared-parenting.

Publications: Printed

Publications list: Available online and in print

Access to staff: Contact by telephone, by e-mail and via website
Hours: Mon to Fri, 0900 to 1700

FAMILY AND COMMUNITY HISTORICAL RESEARCH SOCIETY (FACHRS)

Formal name: Family and Community Historical Research Society Limited

Fir Trees, 12 Fryer Close, Chesham, Bucks, HP5 1RD

E-mail: honsec@fachrs.org.uk
Website: www.fachrs.com

Enquiries to: Hon. Sec.

Organisation type and purpose:
Membership organisation (membership by subscription), registered charity (charity number 3965865).

continued overleaf

To promote and communicate research in family and community history within a scholarly framework.

Publications: Printed
Order printed publications from: website: http://www.fachrs.com

Access to staff: Contact by letter, by e-mail and via website

FAMILY FUND

Unit 4, Alpha Court, Monks Cross Drive, Huntington, York, YO32 9WN

Tel: 01904 621115, 01904 658085 (minicom)
Fax: 01904 652625
E-mail: info@familyfund.org.uk
Website: www.familyfund.org.uk

Enquiries to: Information Officer
Direct tel: 0845 130 4542

Founded: 1973; formerly called Family Fund (year of change 1994)

Organisation type and purpose: Registered charity (charity number 1053866).
To ease the stress on families who care for severely disabled children under 16, by providing grants related to the care of the child.

Subject coverage: Families with disabled children.

Publications: Printed

Publications list: Available online and in print

Access to staff: Contact by letter, by telephone, by fax, by e-mail and via website
Hours: Mon to Fri, 0900 to 1700

FAMILY HISTORY SOCIETY OF CHESHIRE (FHSC)

Little Trees, Gawsworth Road, Gawsworth, Macclesfield, SK11 9RA

Tel: 01625 426173
E-mail: info@fhsc.org.uk
Website: www.fhsc.org.uk

Enquiries to: Secretary

Founded: 1969

Organisation type and purpose: Membership association (membership is by subscription), present number of members: 3,000, voluntary organisation, registered charity (charity number 515168), suitable for ages: all.
To promote interest in family history research in Cheshire by organising monthly meetings of the 18 local groups, hosting conferences, open days, and publishing transcriptions and indexes of local records.

Subject coverage: Family history in Cheshire.

Collection: Over 2,000 books and magazines, and exchange journals from other family history societies
Many films of Cheshire Parish Registers and Bishop's Transcripts
Microfiche of the IGI, GRO BMD 1837 to 1900
1881 Census on CD-ROM

Library catalogue: All or part available in-house

Publications: Printed, and electronic and video, and microform publications
Order printed publications from: Family History Society of Cheshire, 91 Stretford House, Chapel Lane, Stretford, Manchester, M32 9AY
Order microform publications from: Family History Society of Cheshire
10 Daleswood Avenue, Whitefield, Manchester, M45 7WP tel: 0161 766 5997
Order electronic and video publications from: 10 Daleswood Avenue, Whitefield, Manchester, M45 7WP tel: 0161 766 5997

Publications list: Available online and in print

Access to staff: Contact by letter, by telephone, by e-mail and via website
Hours: Mon to Fri, 0900 to 1700

Access to building: No prior appointment required; non-members please tel: 01625 599722,
Hours: Library: Mon to Fri, 1000 to 1600
Special comments: Library and Research Centre, Festival Hall, Alderley Edge, Cheshire; Mon to Fri, 1000 to 1600. Members only and joining facility.

Access for disabled people: Please tel: 01625 599722, Mon to Fri, 1000 to 1600

Has local groups in: Alsager, Altrincham, Bebington, Birkenhead, Bramhall, Chester, Congleton, Crewe, Dukinfield, Macclesfield, Middlesex, Nantwich, Northwich, Runcorn, Stockton Heath, Tarporley, Wallasey, West Kirby

FAMILY LIVES (FORMERLY PARENTLINE PLUS) (FL)

CAN Mezzanine, 49–51 East Road, London, N1 6AH

Tel: 0808 800 2222, 0800 783 6783 (minicom)
Fax: 020 7284 5501
E-mail: parentsupport@familylives.org.uk
Website: www.familylives.org.uk

Enquiries to: Chief Executive
Direct tel: 0207 553 3080

Founded: 1983

Organisation type and purpose: Voluntary organisation, registered charity (charity number 1077722).
Provision of advice, support and information, research and training, represents issues to government, encourages informed media coverage.

Subject coverage: Any family issue including stepfamilies, stepparents, stepmothering, stepchildren, shared parenting, post-divorce, remarriage, re-partnering, teenagers and bullying.

Publications: Printed, and electronic and video

Publications list: Available in print

Access to staff: Contact by letter, by telephone, by fax, by e-mail and via website
Hours: Mon to Fri, 0900 to 1700

Branches: Family Lives; Gloucestershire; tel: 01453 768160; Family Lives; Nottinghamshire; tel: 01623 494320; Family Lives; Essex; tel: 01702 554782; Family Lives; Hampshire; tel: 02380 557130; Family Lives; London, South East, Herts, Bucks and Beds.; tel: 01707 630100; Family Lives; South London; tel: 0208 655 2402; Family Lives; Tyne and Wear; tel: 0191 215 3282/3

FAMILY WELFARE ASSOCIATION (FWA)

501–505 Kingsland Road, Dalston, London, E8 4AU

Tel: 020 7254 6251
Fax: 020 7249 5443
E-mail: fwa.headoffice@fwa.org.uk

Enquiries to: Chief Executive

Founded: 1869; formerly called Charity Organisation Society (year of change 1946)

Organisation type and purpose: Registered charity, voluntary organisation (charity number 264713).
Support for families, children and others in need.

Subject coverage: Educational grants advice for students/potential students who are ineligible for statutory grants. Information and advice to people requiring help through various services in certain areas.

Collection: Archives of Charity Organisation Society and the Family Welfare Association held by London Metropolitan Archives

Publications list: Available in print

Access to staff: Contact by letter
Hours: Mon to Fri, 0900 to 1700

FANY (PRVC)

Formal name: FANY (Princess Royal's Volunteer Corps)

TA Headquarters, 95 Horseferry Rd, London, SW1P 2DY

Tel: 020 7976 5459
Fax: 020 7630 8019
E-mail: hq@fany.org.uk
Website: www.fany.org.uk

Enquiries to: Adjutant

Founded: 1907

Organisation type and purpose: Voluntary organisation, suitable for women aged: 18 to 45.
To serve the country in peace and war; volunteer Emergency Response units providing support to the City of London and Metropolitan Police in major incidents and to the British Army as required, particularly in the protection of the capital against terrorism.

Subject coverage: Provides emergency response teams of women able to cope in a variety of circumstances.

Collection: Archive documents and photographs, WWI, WWII and to the present day

Non-library collection catalogue: All or part available online

Access to staff: Contact by letter, by telephone, by fax, by e-mail and via website. Appointment necessary. Letter of introduction required.

Hours: Mon to Thu, 0900 to 1800

Access to building: Prior appointment required

FAREHAM COLLEGE

Bishopsfield Road, Fareham, Hampshire, PO14 1NH

Tel: 01329 815200
Fax: 01329 822483
Website: www.fareham.ac.uk

Enquiries to: Learning Resources Coordinator
Direct tel: 01329 815322
Direct e-mail: cathie.stevenson@fareham.ac.uk

Founded: 1969

Organisation type and purpose: College of education, suitable for ages: 16+.

Subject coverage: Full time A-level, BTEC Introductory, First, BTEC National Diplomas, NVQs Levels1, 2 and 3, Entry Level Certificates, VRQ and City and Guilds.

Non-library collection catalogue: All or part available online and in-house

Library catalogue: All or part available online and in-house

Access to staff: Contact by letter, by telephone, by e-mail and in person
Hours: Mon, 0830 to 1700; Tue to Thu, 0830 to 1900; Fri, 0830 to 1630

Access for disabled people: Parking provided, ramped entry, access to all public areas, toilet facilities

FARM ANIMAL WELFARE COMMITTEE (FAWC)

Area 8B, 9 Millbank, c/o Nobel House, 17 Smith Square, London, SW1P 3JR

Tel: 020 7238 6340
E-mail: fawcsecretariat@defra.gsi.gov.uk
Website: www.defra.gov.uk/fawc

Founded: 2011

Organisation type and purpose: Advisory body to Government; membership is by Ministerial appointment. FAWC's membership includes farmers, researchers, consumers, animal welfarists and veterinarians.
To keep under review welfare of farm animals and to advise the Government of legislative or other changes.

Subject coverage: Farm animal welfare: studies on farm assurance schemes, cloning, broiler breeders, outdoor pigs, farmed fish, laying hens and dairy cattle have been completed. Other areas addressed include sheep, turkeys, wild boar, ostriches, broilers and transport.

Collection: Reports on all subject coverage

Publications: Printed
Order printed publications from: MAFF Publications, London, SE99 7TP; tel: 0645 556000

Publications list: Available online

Access to staff: Contact by letter, by telephone, by fax and by e-mail
Hours: Mon to Fri, 0900 to 1700

Access to building: No access other than to staff

Parent body: Department for Environment, Food and Rural Affairs

FARM STAY (UK) LIMITED (FSUK)

National Agricultural Centre, Stoneleigh Park, Kenilworth, Warwickshire, CV8 2LZ

Tel: 024 7669 6909
Fax: 024 7669 6930
E-mail: admin@farmstayuk.co.uk
Website: www.farmstayuk.co.uk

Enquiries to: Chief Executive
Other contacts: Office Manager for administrative queries, requests for information, promotional material.

Founded: 1983; formerly called Farm Holiday Bureau (UK) Limited (FHB) (year of change 2000)

Organisation type and purpose: National organisation, membership association (membership is by qualification), present number of members: 1,000.
Self-funding Agricultural Cooperative.
Producing a full colour brochure promoting members' businesses.

Subject coverage: Farm-based holiday accommodation; information for farmers and customers; farm and rural tourism; tourism markets.

Publications: Printed

Access to staff: Contact by letter, by telephone, by fax, by e-mail and via website. Appointment necessary.
Hours: Mon to Fri, 0900 to 1700

Access to building: No prior appointment required

FARMDATA LIMITED

Westertown, Rothienorman, Inverurie, Aberdeenshire, AB51 8US

Tel: 01467 671457
Fax: 01467 671448
E-mail: sales@farmdata.co.uk
Website: www.farmdata.co.uk

Enquiries to: Information Officer

Founded: 1978

Organisation type and purpose: Service industry.

Access to staff: Contact by letter, by telephone, by fax, by e-mail and via website
Hours: Mon to Fri, 0900 to 1700

FARNHAM CASTLE INTERNATIONAL BRIEFING & CONFERENCE CENTRE

Farnham Castle, Farnham, Surrey, GU9 0AG

Tel: 01252 721194
Fax: 01252 719277
E-mail: info@farnhamcastle.com
Website: www.farnhamcastle.com

Enquiries to: Sales Manager
Direct tel: 01252 720418
Direct e-mail: lroberts@farnhamcastle.com
Other contacts: Client Services Administrator

Founded: 1953; formerly called Centre for International Briefing (CIB) (year of change 2001)

Organisation type and purpose: International organisation, registered charity (charity number 313648), training organisation.
Not-for-profit organisation offering intercultural awareness training, international assignment briefings, business briefings for people proposing to live and work overseas.

Subject coverage: Briefings on any country, including current economics, politics, the people and their social and business culture, the business environment, social and domestic conditions, constructive and efficient conducting of verbal and non-verbal communications, agreements, discussions, negotiations; practical aspects of moving overseas; information on leisure and recreation, health, education and security. Business briefings for home-based international personnel. Intercultural workshops and repatriation programmes.

Publications: Printed

Access to staff: Contact by letter, by telephone, by fax, by e-mail, in person and via website. Appointment necessary.
Hours: Mon to Fri, 0900 to 1700

FASHION MUSEUM, BATH – STUDY FACILITIES

The Assembly Rooms, Bennett Street, Bath, BA1 2QH

Tel: 01225 477754
E-mail: fashion_bookings@bathnes.gov.uk
Website: www.fashionmuseum.co.uk

Founded: 1974; formerly called Fashion Research Centre (year of change 2007)

Organisation type and purpose: Museum's study facilities.

Subject coverage: History of fashionable dress.

Information services: 24-hour information line tel: 01225 477867

Special visitor services: To book a reading space or a study table, tel: 01225 477754 or e-mail: fashion_enquiries@bathnes.gov.uk

Collection: Designated collection of historical and contemporary fashionable dress, mostly 18th- to 20th-century, archives

Non-library collection catalogue: All or part available in-house

Library catalogue: All or part available in-house

Publications: Printed
Order printed publications from: Fashion Museum Shop, email: museumshop_enquiries@bathnes.gov.uk

Access to staff: Contact by telephone and by e-mail
Hours: Mon to Fri, 0930 to 1700
Special comments: Closed on public holidays.

Access to building: *Hours:* Mon to Sun, 1030 to 1700
Special comments: Closed 25 and 26 Dec.

continued overleaf

Access for disabled people: Study facilities are on the first floor of the Assembly Rooms, so access may be difficult for those with limited mobility; telephone the Study Facilities to discuss individual requirements.
Parent body: Bath and North East Somerset Council; Heritage Services Division

FATHER HUDSON'S SOCIETY

Coventry Road, Coleshill, Birmingham, B46 3ED

Tel: 01675 434 000
E-mail: enquiries@fatherhudsons.org.uk
Website: www.fatherhudsons.org.uk

Founded: 1902; formerly called Birmingham Diocesan Rescue Society for the Protection of Homeless and Friendless Catholic Children (year of change 1984)

Organisation type and purpose: A registered charity (number 512992).
The Social Care Agency of the Roman Catholic Archdiocese of Birmingham, covering the counties of Staffordshire, Worcestershire, West Midlands, Warwickshire and Oxfordshire.
Offers services to children, young people, adults and families in need, without favour or discrimination, in order to improve their quality of life.

Subject coverage: Provides adult residential and day care, adoption and fostering services, and community projects.

Information services: Origin Services providing information from over a hundred years of archive records regarding personal origins to all those who, as children, were involved wth Father Hudson's because of being adopted, in care, or part of child migration schemes.

Access to staff: Contact by letter, by telephone and by e-mail

FAVERSHAM SOCIETY

Fleur de Lis, 10–13 Preston Street, Faversham, Kent, ME13 8NS

Tel: 01795 534542
Fax: 01795 533261
E-mail: ticfaversham@btconnect.com
Website: www.faversham.org/society

Enquiries to: Honorary Director

Founded: 1977

Organisation type and purpose:
Membership association, present number of members: 1,000, voluntary organisation, registered charity (charity number 250945).
The Society is run by 100% voluntary effort for the good of the area. It is completely independent and open to all sharing its interests.

Subject coverage: History of Faversham area, including the port of Faversham, and industries; family history in Faversham area, history of explosives industry.

Special visitor services: Networker (officer), Tourist Information Centre

Collection: Museum, gallery, two libraries

Non-library collection catalogue: All or part available in-house

Library catalogue: All or part available in-house

Publications: Printed, and electronic and video
Order electronic and video publications from: above address

Publications list: Available online and in print

Access to staff: Contact by letter, by telephone, by fax, by e-mail, in person and via website
Hours: Mon to Sat, 1000 to 1600; Sun, 1000 to 1300

Access to building: *Hours:* Mon to Sat, 1000 to 1600; Sun, 1000 to 1300

Access for disabled people: Available over most of complex
Hours: Mon to Sat, 1000 to 1600; Sun, 1000 to 1300

Manages the: Chart Gunpowder Mills; Westbrook Walk, Faversham

Manages the: Fleur de Lis Heritage Centre; at the same address

Manages the: Maison Dieu Museum; Ospringe Street, Faversham

FEDERATION AGAINST COPYRIGHT THEFT LIMITED (FACT)

7 Victory Business Centre, Worton Road, Isleworth, Middlesex, TW7 6DB

Tel: 020 8568 6646
Fax: 020 8560 6364
E-mail: contact@fact-uk.org.uk

Enquiries to: Director General
Direct e-mail: eddy.leviten@fact-uk.org.uk
Other contacts: Company Secretary

Founded: 1983

Organisation type and purpose: National organisation, membership association (membership is by subscription, election or invitation), present number of members: 20. Private company.

Subject coverage: Copyright protection of motion pictures.

Access to staff: Contact by letter and by e-mail
Hours: Mon to Fri, 0900 to 1700

Affiliated to: Motion Picture Association

FEDERATION AGAINST SOFTWARE THEFT (FAST)

York House, 18 York Road, Maidenhead, Berkshire, SL6 1SF

Tel: 01628 622121
Fax: 01628 760355
E-mail: fast@fast.org
Website: www.fast.org.uk

Enquiries to: Public Relations Manager
Other contacts: Account Manager for membership.

Founded: 1984

Organisation type and purpose: National organisation, advisory body, trade association, membership association (membership is by subscription), present number of members: 150.

Subject coverage: Software control and management, auditing, the law governing software copyright, forensic examination of counterfeits, software piracy.

Publications: Printed

Access to staff: Contact by letter, by telephone, by fax, by e-mail and via website
Hours: Mon to Fri, 0900 to 1700

Access to building: Prior appointment required

Access for disabled people: Parking provided, ramped entry, level entry, toilet facilities

FEDERATION OF BAKERS (FoB)

6 Catherine Street, London, WC2B 5JW

Tel: 020 7420 7190
Fax: 020 7379 0542
Website: www.bakersfederation.org.uk

Founded: 1942

Organisation type and purpose:
Membership association, represents the interests of the UK's largest baking companies that manufacture sliced and wrapped bread, bakery snacks and other bread products. The Federation has 7 member companies running 44 bakeries in the United Kingdom.
To deliver professional services to members and other users of its services to an excellent standard and in genuine partnership with all stakeholders; this may be in the provision of advice, training or leadership in health and safety, or in a representational role lobbying on technical issues or promoting the consumption of bread through PR work.

Subject coverage: Bread baking industry.

Information services: Annual conference presentations available on website.

Publications: Printed, and electronic and video
Order printed publications from: website
Order electronic and video publications from: website

Publications list: Available online

Access to staff: Contact by letter, by telephone and by fax

FEDERATION OF BRITISH AQUATIC SOCIETIES (FBAS)

2 Cedar Avenue, Wickford, Essex, SS12 9DT

Tel: 01268 472095
E-mail: chris@cheswright.freeserve.co.uk

Enquiries to: General Secretary

Founded: 1938

Organisation type and purpose:
Membership association (membership is by subscription), voluntary organisation.
Central governing body for all UK aquarist clubs.

Subject coverage: All fields of aquatics associated with fishkeeping: coldwater, tropical, marine; the environment, keeping, breeding and showing of fish; fish diseases and cures.

Publications: Printed
Order printed publications from:
Merchandising Officer, FBAS
28 The Mall, Binstead, Isle of Wight, PO33 3SF, tel: 01983 566810

Publications list: Available in print

Access to staff: Contact by fax
Hours: Telephone after 1800

FEDERATION OF BRITISH ARTISTS (FBA)

17 Carlton House Terrace, London, SW1Y 5BD

Tel: 020 7930 6844
Fax: 020 7839 7830
E-mail: info@mallgalleries.com
Website: www.mallgalleries.org.uk

Enquiries to: Secretary
Other contacts: Marketing and Communications Officer

Founded: 1961

Organisation type and purpose:
Membership association (membership is by election or invitation), present number of members: 600, voluntary organisation, registered charity (charity number 200048).
Federation of voluntary art societies (see list).
The FBA promotes the visual arts in Britain and is the umbrella organisation for nine autonomous national art societies.

Subject coverage: Arranging art exhibitions in the Mall Galleries, London SW1, advice on commissioning portraits or other art work, visual arts by contemporary artists, past and present society members.

Collection: Catalogues of previous exhibitions

Non-library collection catalogue: All or part available in print

Publications: Printed

Access to staff: Contact by letter, by telephone, by fax, by e-mail and via website
Hours: Mon to Fri, 0930 to 1700

Access to building: Prior appointment required
Hours: Mon to Fri, 0930 to 1700

Access for disabled people: Toilet facilities, stair lift

Links with: FBA Friends Society; contact through the FBA; Hesketh Hubbard Art Society; contact through the FBA; Mall Galleries; contact through the FBA; New English Art Club; contact through the FBA; Pastel Society; contact through the FBA; Royal Institute of Oil Painters; contact through the FBA; Royal Institute of Painters in Watercolours; contact through the FBA; Royal Society of British Artists; contact through the FBA; Royal Society of Marine Artists; contact through the FBA; Royal Society of Portrait Painters; contact through the FBA; Society of Wildlife Artists; contact through the FBA

FEDERATION OF BRITISH BONSAI SOCIETIES (FOBBS)

17 Woodland Park, Ynystawe, Swansea, West Glamorgan, SA6 5AR

Tel: 01792 845659
E-mail: ukbonsai@ntlworld.com
Website: www.fobbs.co.uk
Website: uk.geocities.com/fobbs_uk

Enquiries to: General Secretary

Founded: 1982

Organisation type and purpose:
Membership association (membership is by subscription), voluntary organisation, registered charity.

Subject coverage: Bonsai and bonsai clubs, national bonsai collection, bonsai traders, bonsai events.

Collection: National Bonsai Collection at Birmingham Botanical Gardens

Publications: Printed

Access to staff: Contact by letter, by telephone, by e-mail and via website
Hours: Any reasonable time

Affiliated to: Friends of the National Bonsai Collection; (charitable trust); tel: 0121 378 4837; fax: 0121 311 1912

FEDERATION OF BRITISH HAND TOOL MANUFACTURERS (FBHTM)

c/o Manufacturing Technologies Association, 62 Bayswater Road, London, W2 3PS

Tel: 020 7298 6400
Fax: 020 7298 6430
E-mail: info@britishtools.co.uk
Website: www.britishtools.co.uk

Enquiries to: Secretary

Organisation type and purpose: Trade association.

Subject coverage: British hand tool manufacturing industry, exhibition and export activity, publicity for the industry.

Member organisation of: Comité Européen d'Outillage (CEO – European Hand Tool Committee)

Member organisations: Construction Fixings Association; website: http://www.fixingscfa.co.uk

FEDERATION OF BUILDING SPECIALIST CONTRACTORS (FBSC)

Unit 9 Lakeside Industrial Estate, Stanton Harcourt, Oxfordshire OX29 5SL

Tel: 01865 883557
Fax: 01865 884467
E-mail: enquiries@fbsc.org.uk
Website: www.fbsc.org.uk/

Enquiries to: Membership Secretary

Organisation type and purpose: Trade association (membership is by subscription).

Subject coverage: Details of member companies covering a wide range of specialist trades in the building industry.

Access to staff: Contact by letter, by telephone, by fax and by e-mail
Hours: Mon to Fri, 0900 to 1700

Access to building: No prior appointment required

Member of: Construction Confederation

FEDERATION OF BURIAL AND CREMATION AUTHORITIES (FBCA)

41 Salisbury Road, Carshalton, Surrey, SM5 3HA

Tel: 020 8669 4521
Website: www.fbca.org.uk

Enquiries to: Secretary
Direct e-mail: fbcasec@btconnect.com

Founded: 1924; formerly called Federation of British Cremation Authorities (year of change 2006)

Organisation type and purpose: Trade association and technical advisory service.

Subject coverage: All matters connected with the management and operation of cemeteries and crematoria.

Publications: Printed

Access to staff: Contact by letter, by telephone, by fax, by e-mail and via website
Hours: Mon to Fri, 0900 to 1700

FEDERATION OF CHILDREN'S BOOK GROUPS (FCBG)

Hampton Farm, Bowerhill, Melksham, Wiltshire SN12 6QZ

Tel: 01225 353710
E-mail: info@fcbg.org.uk
Website: www.fcbg.org.uk

Enquiries to: National Secretary

Founded: 1968

Organisation type and purpose:
Membership association (membership is by subscription), present number of members: 30 book groups, plus individual and professional members, voluntary organisation, registered charity (charity number 268289).
To promote enjoyment and interest in children's books and reading.

Subject coverage: Children's booklists, book group details and locations, children's book award information, annual conference details.

Publications: Printed

Access to staff: Contact by letter, by telephone, by e-mail and via website
Hours: Mon to Fri, 0900 to 1700

FEDERATION OF CITY FARMS AND COMMUNITY GARDENS (FCFCG)

The Green House, Hereford Street, Bedminster, Bristol, BS3 4NA

Tel: 0117 923 1800
Fax: 0117 923 1900
E-mail: admin@farmgarden.org.uk
Website: www.farmgarden.org.uk

Enquiries to: Director
Other contacts: Information Officer

Founded: 1980; formerly called National Federation of City Farms (NFCF) (year of change 1999)

continued overleaf

Organisation type and purpose: Membership association (membership is by subscription), present number of members: 398 projects and affiliates, registered charity (charity number 294494).
To promote community development and advance education in animal husbandry and gardening.

Subject coverage: Farming and gardening in urban areas, legal requirements for setting up a charity or company limited by guarantee, community management of a voluntary project.

Collection: Teacher Resource Centre

Library catalogue: All or part available in-house

Publications: Printed

Publications list: Available in print

Access to staff: Contact by letter, by fax and by e-mail. Appointment necessary.
Hours: Mon to Fri, 0900 to 1700

Access to building: No prior appointment required

Access for disabled people: Ramped entry, access to all public areas, toilet facilities
Hours: Mon to Fri, 0900 to 1700

Member farms and gardens: More than 350 in the UK

Member of: Black Environment Network; Council for Environmental Education; European Federation of City Farms; National Council for Voluntary Organisations; NCVCCO

FEDERATION OF CLOTHING DESIGNERS AND EXECUTIVES (FCDE)

56 Eden Park Avenue, Beckenham, Kent, BR3 3HW

Tel: 020 8650 5429
Fax: 020 8663 0073
E-mail: maggiewatts@compuserve.com
Website: www.ntu.ac.uk/fas/fcde/index.htm

Enquiries to: General Secretary

Founded: 1935; formerly called Federation of Clothing Designers and Production Managers

Organisation type and purpose: Trade association (membership is by election or invitation).
Improving knowledge and skills of members by technical meetings and conventions.

Subject coverage: Technical information on clothing manufacturing in the areas of pattern technology, design, clothing and manufacturing techniques on all types of outerwear.

Access to staff: Contact by letter, by telephone, by fax, by e-mail and via website. Non-members charged.
Hours: Mon to Fri, 0900 to 1700

Branches in: London, Manchester, the Midlands, and Nottingham

FEDERATION OF COCOA COMMERCE LTD (FCC)

Cannon Bridge House, 1 Cousin Lane, London, EC4R 3XX

Tel: 020 7379 2884
Fax: 020 7379 2389
E-mail: fcc@nyx.com
Website: www.cocoafederation.com

Enquiries to: Chief Executive
Direct tel: 020 7379 2882

Founded: 1929

Organisation type and purpose: International organisation, trade association.

Subject coverage: Cocoa trading.

Access to staff: Contact by letter, by telephone, by fax, by e-mail and via website
Hours: Mon to Fri, 0900 to 1700

FEDERATION OF COMMUNICATION SERVICES LIMITED (FCS)

Burnhill Business Centre, Provident House, Burrell Row, High Street, Beckenham, Kent, BR3 1AT

Tel: 020 8249 6363
Fax: 0844 870 5927
E-mail: fcs@fcs.org.uk
Website: www.fcs.org.uk

Enquiries to: Chief Executive

Founded: 1981

Organisation type and purpose: National organisation, trade association (membership is by subscription), present number of members and associates: 360, manufacturing industry, service industry.
Mobile and telecoms services communication trade association.

Subject coverage: Mobile communications, telecommunications, radio communications.

Publications: Printed

Access to staff: Contact by e-mail and via website. Appointment necessary.
Hours: Mon to Fri, 0900 to 1730

Access to building: No access other than to staff

FEDERATION OF ECONOMIC DEVELOPMENT AUTHORITIES (FEDA)

7 Franklin's Yard, Fossgate, York, YO1 9TN

Tel: 01904 670534
Fax: 01904 670536
E-mail: feda@btconnect.com

Enquiries to: Director

Founded: 1943

Organisation type and purpose: Membership association (membership is by subscription), present number of members: local authorities in the UK.

Subject coverage: Economic development issues in relation to impact on local authorities.

Publications: Printed

Access to staff: Contact by letter, by telephone, by fax and by e-mail
Hours: Mon to Fri, 0930 to 1730

FEDERATION OF ENGINE RE-MANUFACTURERS (FER)

59 Mewstone Avenue, Wembury, Plymouth, PL9 OJT

Tel: 01752 863681
Fax: 01752 863682
E-mail: ferm@btinternet.com
Website: www.fer.co.uk

Enquiries to: Director

Founded: 1938

Organisation type and purpose: Trade association.

Subject coverage: Re-manufacture of internal combustion engines.

Publications: Printed

Access to staff: Contact by letter
Hours: Mon to Fri, 0900 to 1700

FEDERATION OF ENVIRONMENTAL TRADE ASSOCIATIONS (FETA)

2 Waltham Court, Milley Lane, Hare Hatch, Reading, Berkshire, RG10 9TH

Tel: 0118 940 3416
Fax: 0118 940 6258
E-mail: info@feta.co.uk
Website: www.feta.co.uk

Enquiries to: Director-General

Organisation type and purpose: Trade association.

Subject coverage: Building services, heating, ventilating, air conditioning and refrigeration.

Publications: Printed

Publications list: Available online and in print

Access to staff: Contact by letter, by telephone, by fax and by e-mail
Hours: Mon to Thu, 0830 to 1630; Fri, 0830 to 1600

Member organisations: British Flue and Chimney Manufacturers' Association (BFCMA); at same address; British Refrigeration Association (BRA); at same address; Chilled Beam and Ceiling Association (CBCA); at same address; Fan Manufacturers Association (FMA); at same address; Heat Pump Association (HPA); at same address; Heating, Ventilating and Air-Conditioning Manufacturers' Association (HEVAC); at same address; Hose Manufacturers' and Suppliers' Association (HMSA); at same address; Residential Ventilation Association (RVA); at same address; Smoke Control Association (SCA); at same address

FEDERATION OF FAMILY HISTORY SOCIETIES (FFHS)

PO Box 8857, Lutterworth, Leicestershire, LE17 9BJ

Tel: 01455 203133
E-mail: info@ffhs.org.uk
Website: www.ffhs.org.uk

Enquiries to: Administrator

Founded: 1974

Organisation type and purpose: International organisation, trade association, membership association (membership is by subscription), present number of members: 200, registered charity (charity number 1038721), suitable for all ages.

Subject coverage: Family history, local history, genealogy, heraldry, demography, historical research.

Publications: Printed, and electronic and video

Access to staff: Contact by letter, by telephone, by e-mail and via website

Access to building: No access.

FEDERATION OF HOLISTIC THERAPISTS (FHT)

18 Shakespeare Business Centre, Hathaway Close, Eastleigh, Hampshire, SO50 4SR

Tel: 0844 875 2022
Fax: 023 8062 4399
E-mail: info@fht.org.uk
Website: www.fht.org.uk

Enquiries to: Chief Executive
Other contacts: Marketing Manager for information about International Therapist Magazine – advertising, editorial etc.

Founded: 1962; formerly called International Federation of Health and Beauty Therapists

Organisation type and purpose: International organisation, professional body (membership is by qualification), present number of members: 18,000.
Oldest and largest professional association for the health and beauty industry.
Publishers of the International Therapist Journal.
Services to members, teachers and employers, advisory and information service to health and beauty employers and to the media regarding the nature of the work, to arrange insurance and provide a code of practice for hygiene in salons and clinics.

Subject coverage: Health and beauty including physical treatment through massage, colour, sports and beauty therapy, aromatherapy, reflexology. All aspects of health and beauty therapy including employment.

Publications: Printed

Access to staff: Contact by letter, by telephone, by fax, by e-mail and via website
Hours: Mon to Fri, 0900 to 1700
Special comments: No visitors in person.

Founder member of the industry lead body: Health and Beauty Therapy Training Board

Links with: Association of Therapy Lecturers; Federation of Professional Sugaring; fraternal organisations in many overseas countries; Health and Beauty Employers Federation; International Council of Health, Fitness and Sports Therapists; International Council of Holistic Therapists; International Federation of Health and Beauty Therapists

FEDERATION OF INDEPENDENT DETECTORISTS (FID)

Detector Lodge, 44 Heol Dulais, Birchgrove, Swansea, West Glamorgan, SA7 9LT

Tel: 07866 914253
Fax: 07866 914253
E-mail: hon.sec.fid@detectorists.net
Website: www.fid.newbury.net

Enquiries to: Honorary Secretary
Direct tel: 01635 522578

Founded: 1982

Organisation type and purpose: International organisation, membership association, voluntary organisation.
A lobby on behalf of the members' interests; information service to the press, media, parliament and local authorities.

Subject coverage: The recreational use of metal detectors.

Publications: Printed, and electronic and video

Access to staff: Contact by letter, by telephone, by e-mail and via website
Hours: Mon to Fri, 0900 to 1700

Affiliated to: Detector Information Group; Heritage 2100; Heritage for All

Also at: Press and Public Relations Officer, Federation of Independent Detectorists; 61 Newtown Road, Newbury, Berkshire, RG14 7BU; tel: 01635 522578

Member organisation of: Standing Conference of European Metal Detecting

FEDERATION OF IRISH SOCIETIES (FIS)

52 Camden Square, London, NW1 9XB

Tel: 020 7916 2725
Fax: 020 7916 2753

Enquiries to: Administrator

Founded: 1973

Organisation type and purpose: National organisation, membership association (membership is by qualification), present number of members: 100, voluntary organisation, research organisation.
Representation of the Irish community in Britain.

Subject coverage: Information relative to the Irish community in Britain.

Publications: Printed
Order printed publications from: Community Administrative Assistant, Federation of Irish Societies;
tel: 020 7916 2729, fax: 020 7916 2753

Publications list: Available in print

Access to staff: Contact by letter, by telephone and by fax
Hours: Mon to Fri, 0900 to 1700

FEDERATION OF LICENSED VICTUALLERS ASSOCIATIONS (FLVA)

128 Bradford Road, Brighouse, West Yorkshire, HD6 4AU

Tel: 01484 710534
Fax: 01484 718647
E-mail: admin@flva.co.uk
Website: www.flva.co.uk

Founded: 1992

Organisation type and purpose: Professional body, trade association.
To provide help and advice to licensed victuallers.

Subject coverage: All aspects of the licensing trade, up-to-date legislation of employment law, health and safety, food and hygiene.

Publications: Printed

Access to staff: Contact by letter, by telephone, by fax and by e-mail
Hours: Mon to Fri, 0900 to 1700

FEDERATION OF LONDON YOUTH CLUBS (The Fed; London Youth)

Bridge House, Bridge House Quay, Prestons Road, London, E14 9QA

Tel: 020 7537 2777
Fax: 020 7537 7072
E-mail: hello@londonyouth.org.uk

Enquiries to: Chief Executive

Founded: 1887; formed by the merger of London Federation of Clubs for Young People (LFCYP), London Union of Youth Clubs (LUYC) (year of change 1999); formerly called London Federation of Boys Clubs (LFBC) (year of change 1994–1999)

Organisation type and purpose: Voluntary organisation, registered charity (charity number 303324).
Youth work.

Subject coverage: Youth work in London since 1887.

Access to staff: Contact by letter, by fax and by e-mail
Hours: Mon to Fri, 0900 to 1700

Access for disabled people: Parking provided

Other locations at: Hindleap Warren; Wych Cross, Forest Row, East Sussex, RH18 5JS; tel: 01342 822625; fax: 01342 822913; e-mail: hindleap@londonyouth.org.uk; Woodrow High House; Cherry Tree Lane, Amersham, Buckinghamshire, HP7 0QG; tel: 01494 433531; fax: 01494 431391; e-mail: woodrow@londonyouth.org.uk

FEDERATION OF MASTER BUILDERS (FMB)

Gordon Fisher House, 14–15 Great James Street, London, WC1N 3DP

Tel: 020 7242 7583
Fax: 020 7404 0296
Website: www.fmb.org.uk

Enquiries to: Information Officer

Founded: 1941

Organisation type and purpose: Trade association.

Subject coverage: Building industry; all aspects affecting the building employer; health and safety, employment law, product and manufacturer traces, contract law, EC law, technical.

continued overleaf

Trade and statistical information: Quarterly state of trade survey (based on response from members)

Library catalogue: All or part available in-house

Publications: Printed

Publications list: Available in print

Access to staff: Contact by letter
Hours: Mon to Fri, 0900 to 1700
Special comments: Not open to the public, no loan facilities.

Member of: European Builders Confederation

With the: Transport and General Workers Union formed the Building & Allied Trades Joint Industrial Council

FEDERATION OF OILS, SEEDS AND FATS ASSOCIATIONS LIMITED (FOSFA)

20 St Dunstans Hill, London, EC3R 8NQ

Tel: 020 7283 5511
Fax: 020 7623 1310
E-mail: membership@fosfa.org
Website: www.fosfa.org

Enquiries to: Chief Executive

Organisation type and purpose:
International organisation, trade association.

Subject coverage: Oil seed and animal, vegetable and margarine oils and fats; HPS groundnuts; trading conditions; analysis, sampling and specification.

Access to staff: Access for members only.
Hours: Mon to Fri, 0900 to 1700

Associated with: National Farmers' Union; UK Agricultural Supply Trade Association

Incorporating the: Incorporated Oil Seed Association; London Copra Association; London Oil and Tallow Trades Association; Seed, Oil, Cake and General Produce Association

Liaison with: over 50 kindred organisations throughout the world

FEDERATION OF OPHTHALMIC AND DISPENSING OPTICIANS (FODO)

199 Gloucester Terrace, London, W2 6LD

Tel: 020 7298 5151
Fax: 020 7298 5111
E-mail: Pamela@fodo.com
Website: www.fodo.com

Founded: 1985; formerly called Guild of British Dispensing Opticians (year of change 1985)

Organisation type and purpose:
Membership association (membership is by subscription), registered charity (charity number 368950).

Subject coverage: Optical practice and dispensing, sources of optics, training, memberships.

Publications: Printed

Access to staff: Contact by letter and by telephone
Hours: Mon to Fri, 0900 to 1700
Special comments: By letter in the first instance.

FEDERATION OF PATIDAR ASSOCIATIONS

Patidar House, 22 London Road, Wembley, Middlesex, HA9 7EX

Tel: 020 8795 1648
Fax: 020 8795 1648
E-mail: info@patidars.org
Website: www.patidars.org

Enquiries to: Honorary Secretary
Other contacts: President

Founded: November 1976

Organisation type and purpose:
Membership association (membership is by subscription), present number of members: 13 organisations, voluntary organisation, registered charity (charity number 1076284), suitable for ages: 2 to 25.
Drop-in centre for elderly; performing arts classes; yoga; youth club.

Subject coverage: Nursery; day centre for elderly; performing arts classes (Bhart Natyam, Kathak, folk dances, music); yoga; Bollywood dance; sitar

Access to staff: Contact by letter, by telephone and by e-mail
Hours: Mon to Fri, 1000 to 1800

Access to building: *Hours:* Mon to Sun, 0800 to 2200

Access for disabled people: *Hours:* Mon to Fri, 1000 to 1400

FEDERATION OF PILING SPECIALISTS (FPS)

Forum Court, 83 Copers Cope Road, Beckenham, Kent, BR3 1NR

Tel: 020 8663 0947
Fax: 020 8663 0949
E-mail: fps@fps.org.uk
Website: www.fps.org.uk

Enquiries to: Executive Secretary

Organisation type and purpose: Trade association.

Subject coverage: Ground engineering, foundation and pile construction techniques, geotechnical engineering, ground improvement.

Access to staff: Contact by letter, by telephone, by fax and by e-mail
Hours: Mon to Fri, 0900 to 1700

Member organisation of: European Federation of Foundation Contractors (EFFC); Ground Forum; National Specialist Contractors Council (NSCC)

FEDERATION OF PLASTERING AND DRYWALL CONTRACTORS (FPDC)

1st Floor, 8–9 Ludgate Square, London, EC4M 7AS

Tel: 020 7634 9480
Fax: 020 7248 9263
E-mail: membership@fpdc.org
Website: www.fpdc.org

Enquiries to: Director
Other contacts: Administrator

Founded: 1942; formerly called Dry Lining and Partition Association, National Federation of Plastering Contractors (year of change 1990); incorporates the London Master Plasterers Association (year of change 1997)

Organisation type and purpose: Trade association.

Subject coverage: Plastering and drywall construction.

Publications: Printed

Publications list: Available online

Access to staff: Contact by letter, by telephone and by fax
Hours: Mon to Fri, 0930 to 1715

Member of: National Specialist Contractors Council (NSCC); tel: 020 7608 5090; fax: 020 7608 5081

FEDERATION OF RECORDED MUSIC SOCIETIES LIMITED (FRMS)

FRMS Secretary, 6 Oakroyd Close, Brighouse, HD6 4BP

Tel: 01484 717865
E-mail: secretary@thefrms.co.uk
Website: www.thefrms.co.uk

Enquiries to: Secretary

Founded: 1936; formerly called National Federation of Gramophone Societies

Organisation type and purpose: Voluntary organisation, present number of members: 205 affiliated societies with members numbering 11,000.

Subject coverage: Organisation, establishment and conduct of recorded music societies, reproducing equipment, copyright and related subjects applying to gramophone records and all forms of tape, audio matters in general.

Publications: Printed

Access to staff: Contact by letter, by telephone and by e-mail
Hours: Any time

FEDERATION OF SMALL BUSINESSES (FSB)

2 Catherine Place, London, SW1E 6HF

Tel: 020 7592 8100
Fax: 020 7828 5919
E-mail: press@fsb.org.uk
Website: www.fsb.org.uk

Enquiries to: Head of Public Affairs
Direct tel: 020 7592 8112
Direct e-mail: stephen.alambritis@fsb.org.uk
Other contacts: Press Office

Founded: 1974; formerly called National Federation of Self-Employed and Small Businesses (year of change 1990)

Organisation type and purpose: Trade association, membership association (membership is by subscription), present number of members: 215,000.
To represent the small business sector in the UK.

Subject coverage: Small business issues.

Trade and statistical information: Statistics on small businesses

Publications: Printed

Access to staff: Contact by letter, by telephone and by e-mail. Appointment necessary. Access for members only.
Hours: Mon to Fri, 0900 to 1700

Access to building: Prior appointment required

Links with: ESBA – European Small Business Alliance

FEDERATION OF THE RETAIL LICENSED TRADE NORTHERN IRELAND (FRLT)

91 University Street, Belfast, BT7 1HP

Tel: 028 9032 7578
Fax: 028 9032 7578
E-mail: enquiries@ulsterpubs.com
Website: www.ulsterpubs.com

Enquiries to: Chief Executive

Founded: 1872

Organisation type and purpose: Trade association (membership is by subscription, qualification), present number of members: 1200, training organisation.

Subject coverage: Licensing legislation and statistics relating to Northern Ireland. Licensed trade training.

FEDERATION OF ZOOLOGICAL GARDENS OF GREAT BRITAIN AND IRELAND (FZGB)

Regent's Park, London, NW1 4RY

Tel: 020 7586 0230
Fax: 020 7722 4427
E-mail: fedzoo@zsl.org
Website: www.zoofederation.org.uk

Enquiries to: Administrator
Other contacts: Director, Conservation Co-ordinator

Founded: 1966; formerly called National Federation of Zoological Gardens of Great Britain and Ireland

Organisation type and purpose:
Professional body, membership association (membership is by subscription, qualification, election or invitation), present number of members: 61, registered charity (charity number 248553).
The Federation of Zoos, the principal professional body representing the zoo community in Britain and Ireland, is a conservation, education and scientific wildlife charity dedicated to the maintenance of the world's biodiversity, the welfare of animals in zoos and the advancement of scientific knowledge.
The Federation achieves its objectives through: conservation breeding programmes and support for projects in the wild; inspiring an understanding of the natural world through environmental education; and non-invasive scientific studies of animals.

Subject coverage: Data concerning zoos in the UK and including details of species stocked, breeding schemes, education service, conservation projects; zoo legislation; zoo standards and management; careers in zoos.

Publications: Printed, and electronic and video

Publications list: Available in print

Access to staff: Contact by letter, by fax, by e-mail, in person and via website. Appointment necessary. Access for members only. Non-members charged.
Hours: Mon to Fri, 0900 to 1700

Access for disabled people: Parking provided, ramped entry, access to all public areas, toilet facilities

A member of: Association of Zoos and Aquariums (WAZA); tel: +22 999 07 90; fax: +22 999 07 91; European Association of Zoos and Aquaria (EAZA); tel: + 31 20 5200 753; fax: + 31 20 5200 754; e-mail: corinne.bos@ndvzoos; World Conservation Union (IUCN); tel: +22 999 00 01; fax: +22 999 00 02

Has: 66 Member Collections (list available, £15) and 63 Associates; tel: 020 7586 0230; fax: 020 7722 4427; e-mail: fedzoo@zsl.org

Members: Amazon World; Watery Lane, Newchurch, Isle of Wight, PO36 0LX; tel: 01983 867122; fax: 01983 868560; e-mail: amaozonworld@dialstart.net; Aquarium & Vivarium, National Museums & Galleries on Merseyside; Liverpool Museum, William Brown Street, Liverpool, L3 8EN; tel: 0151 207 0001; fax: 0151 478 4390; Banham Zoo Ltd; The Grove, Banham, Norfolk, NR16 2HE; tel: 01953 887771; fax: 01953 888445; website: http://www.banhamzoo.co.uk
Battersea Park Children's Zoo; Battersea Park, London, SW11 4NJ; tel: 020 8871 7540; fax: 020 7350 0477; Birdland; Rissington Road, Bourton-on-the-Water, Cheltenham, Gloucestershire, GL54 2BN; tel: 01451 820480; fax: 01451 822398; e-mail: sb.birdland@virgin.net; Birdworld; Holt Pound, Farnham, Surrey, GU10 4LD; tel: 01420 22140; fax: 01420 23715; website: http://www.birdworld.co.uk
Blackpool Zoo Park; East Park Drive, Stanley Park, Blackpool, Lancashire, FY3 8PP; tel: 01253 830830; fax: 01253 830800; e-mail: zookeeper@blackpool-zoo.freeserve.co.uk; Brent Lodge Park Animal Centre; Brent Lodge Park, Church Road, Hanwell, London, W7 3BP; tel: 020 8758 5019; fax: 020 8840 4244; Bristol, Clifton & West of England Zoological Society; Bristol Zoo Gardens, Clifton, Bristol, BS8 3HA; tel: 0117 974 7300; fax: 0117 973 6814; e-mail: information@bristolzoo.org.uk; website: http://www.bristolzoo.org.uk
Butterfly & Wildlife Park; Long Sutton, Spalding, Linclonshire, PE12 9LE; tel: 01406 363833; fax: 01406 363182; e-mail: butterflypark@hotmail.com; Camperdown Wildlife Centre; Camperdown Country Park, Coupar Angus Road, Dundee, DO2 4TF, and education department; tel: 01382 432661; fax: 01382 432660; Chester Zoo; North of England Zoological Society, Caughall Road, Upton-by-Chester, Cheshire, CH2 1LH; tel: 01244 380280; fax: 01244 371273; e-mail: f.jaques@chesterzoo.co.uk; website: http://www.chesterzoo.co.uk
Chestnut Centre Conservation Park; Castleton Road, Chapel-en-le-Frith, Derbyshire, SK23 0QS; tel: 01298 814099; fax: 01298 816213; City of Belfast Zoo; Antrim Road, Newtownabbey, Co Antrim, BT36 7PN; tel: 028 9077 6277; fax: 028 9037 0578; website: http://www.belfastzoo.co.uk
Colchester Zoo; Maldon Road, Stanway, Colchester, Essex, CO3 5SL; tel: 01206 331292; fax: 01206 331392; e-mail: colchester.zoo@btinternet.com; website: http://www.colchester-zoo.uk
Cotswold Wild Life Park; Burford, Oxfordshire, OX18 4JW; tel: 01993 823006; fax: 01993 823807; Curraghs Wildlife Park; Ballaugh, Isle of Man, IN7 5EA; tel: 01624 897323; fax: 01624 897327; Drusillas Zoo Park; Alfriston, East Sussex, BN26 5QS; tel: 01323 870656; fax: 01323 870846; e-mail: drusilla@drusilla.demon.co.uk; Dublin Zoo; Zoological Society of Ireland, Phoenix Park, Dublin, 8, Republic of Ireland; tel: 00 353 1 677 1425; fax: 00 353 1 677 1660; website: http://www.dublinzoo.ie
Dudley and West Midlands Zoological Society Ltd; Dudley Zoo, 2 The Broadway, Dudley, DY1 4QB; tel: 01384 215300; fax: 01384 456048; e-mail: marketing@dudleyzoo.org.uk; Durrell Wildlife Conservation Trust; Jersey Zoo, Les Augres Manor, Trinity, Jersey, JE3 5BF; tel: 01534 860000; fax: 01534 860001; e-mail: jerseyzoo@durrell.org; East Midlands Zoological Society Ltd; Twycross Zoo Park, Norton-juxta-Twycross, Atherstone, Warwickshire, CV9 3PX; tel: 01827 880250; fax: 01827 880700; e-mail: twycross.zoo@btinternet.com; Edinburgh Zoo; Royal Zoological Society of Scotland, 134 Corstorphine Road, Edinburgh, EH12 6TS; tel: 0131 334 9171 (press 0 for operator); fax: 0131 316 4050; e-mail: amanda@edinburghzoo.org.uk; website: http://www.edinburghzoo.org.uk
Exmoor Zoological Park; Bratton Fleming, Barnstaple, North Devon, EX31 4SG; tel: 01598 763352; fax: 01598 763352; Fota Wildlife Park; Zoological Society of Ireland, Carrigtwohill, Co Cork, Republic of Ireland; tel: 00 353 21 812 678; fax: 00 353 21 812 744; e-mail: fota@indigo.ie; Gatwick Zoo; Russ Hill, Charlwood, Surrey, RH6 0EG; tel: 01293 862312; fax: 01293 862550; Harewood Bird Garden; Harewood House, Harewood, Leeds, LS17 9LQ; tel: 0113 288 6238; fax: 0113 288 6784; e-mail: birdgdn@harewood.org; website: http://www.harewood.org
Hawk Conservancy; Weyhill, Andover, Hampshire, SP11 8DY; tel: 01264 773850; fax: 01264 773772; website: http://www.hawk-conservancy.org
Highland Wildlife Park; Royal Zoological Society of Scotland, Kincraig, Kingussie, Inverness-shire, PH21 1NL; tel: 01540 651270; fax: 01540 651236; e-mail: wildlife@rzss.org.uk; website: http://www.kincraig.com/wildlife
Kirkleatham Owl Centre; Kirkleatham Village, Redcar, TS10 5NW; tel: 01642 480512; fax: 01642 492790; e-mail: stan@kirk58.freeserve.co.uk; website: http://www.jillsowls.co.uk
Knowsley Safari Park; Prescot, Merseyside, L34 4AN; tel: 0151 430 9009; fax: 0151 426 3677; website: http://www.knowsley.com
Lakeland Wildlife Oasis; Hale, Milnthorpe, Cumbria, LA7 7BW; tel: 01539 563027; e-mail: wildlifeoasis@hotmail.com; Linton Zoological Gardens; Hadstock Road, Linton, Cambridgeshire, CB1 6NT; tel: 01223 891308; fax: 01223 891308; London Zoo; Zoological Gardens, Regent's Park, London, NW1 4RY,

continued overleaf

tel: 020 7449 6551 education department; tel: 020 7722 3333; fax: 020 7586 5743; website: http://www.zsl.org
Lotherton Hall Bird Garden; Towton Road, Near Aberford, Leeds, LS25 3EB; tel: 0113 281 3723; Manor House Wildlife and Leisure Park; St Florence, Tenby, Dyfed, SA70 8RJ; tel: 01646 651201; fax: 01646 651201;
Marwell Zoological Park; Colden Common, Winchester, Hampshire, SO21 1JH; tel: 01962 777407; fax: 01962 777511; e-mail: marwel@marwell.org.uk; Mole Hall Wildlife Park; Widdington, Saffron Walden, Essex, CB11 3SS; tel: 01799 540400; fax: 01799 540400; e-mail: molehall@aol.com; National Birds of Prey Centre; Newent, Gloucestershire, GL18 1JJ; tel: 01531 821581; fax: 01531 821389; e-mail: jpj@nbpc.demon.co.uk; Newquay Zoo; Trenance Park, Newquay, Cornwall, TR7 2LZ; tel: 01637 873342; fax: 01637 851318; e-mail: mark@newquayzoo.demon.co.uk; Owl Centre; Muncaster Castle, Ravenglass, Cumbria, CA18 1RQ; tel: 01229 717393; fax: 01229 717107; Paignton Zoo Environmental Park; Totnes Road, Paignton, Devon, TQ4 7EU; tel: 01803 697500; fax: 01803 523457; e-mail: amy@paigntonzoo.demon.co.uk; Palacerigg Country Park; Cumbernauld, G67 3HU; tel: 01236 720047; fax: 01236 458271; e-mail: pccreception@northlan.gw.uk; Paradise Wildlife Park; White Stubbs Lane, Broxbourne, Hertfordshire, EN10 7QA; tel: 01992 470490; fax: 01992 440525; website: http://www.pwpark.com
Shaldon Wildlife Trust Ltd; Ness Drive, Shaldon, Devon, TQ14 0HP; tel: 01626 872234; fax: 01626 872234; website: http://www.the-zoo.demon.co.uk
Southport Zoo and Conservation Trust; Princes Park, Southport, Merseyside, PR8 1RX; tel: 01704 538102; fax: 01704 548102; e-mail: 100534.35@compuserve.com; Suffolk Wildlife Park; Whites Lane, Kessingland, Lowestoft, Suffolk, NR33 7TF; tel: 01502 740291; fax: 01953 888427; website: http://www.suffolkwildlifepark.co.uk
Thrigby Hall Wildlife Gardens; Thrigby Hall, Filby, Great Yarmouth, Norfolk, NR29 3DR; tel: 01493 369477; fax: 01493 368256; Tilgate Nature Centre; Tilgate Park, Crawley, West Sussex, RH10 5PQ; tel: 01293 521168; fax: 01293 533981; Tropical World; Canal Gardens, Roundhay Park, Leeds, LS8 1DF; tel: 0113 266 1850; fax: 0113 237 0077; Welsh Mountain Zoo; Zoological Society of Wales, Colwyn Bay, Clwyd, LL28 5UY; tel: 01492 532938; fax: 01492 530498; e-mail: welshmountainzoo@enterprise.net;
Whipsnade Wild Animal Park; Zoological Society of London, Dunstable, Bedfordshire, LU6 2LF; tel: 01582 872171; fax: 01582 872649; e-mail: nick.lindsay@zsl.org; website: http://www.zsl.org
Wildfowl & Wetland Trust; Mill Road, Arundel, West Sussex, BN18 9PB; tel: 01903 883355; fax: 01903 884834; e-mail: wwt.arundel@virgin.net; website: http://www.wwt.org.uk
Wildfowl & Wetland Trust; District 15, Washington, Tyne & Wear, NE38 8LE; tel: 0191 416 5454; fax: 0191 416 5801; website: http://www.wwt.org.uk
Wildfowl & Wetland Trust; Martin Mere, Fish Lane, Burscough, Ormskirk, Lancashire, L40 0TA; tel: 01704 895181; fax: 01704 892343; website: http://www.wwt.org.uk
Wildfowl & Wetland Trust; Slimbridge, Gloucestershire, GL2 7BT; tel: 01453 890333; fax: 01453 890827; website: http://www.wwt.org.uk
Wildfowl & Wetland Trust; Canolfan Llanelli Centre, Penclacwydd, Llwynhendy, Llanelli, Dyfed, SA14 9SH; tel: 01554 741087; website: http://www.wwt.org.uk
Wildfowl & Wetland Trust; Castle Espie, Ballydrain Road, Comber, Co Down, BT23 6EA; tel: 028 9187 4146; fax: 028 9187 3857; website: http://www.wwt.org.uk
Woburn Safari Park; Woburn, Bedfordshire, MK17 9QN; tel: 01525 290407; fax: 01525 290489; e-mail: WobSafari@aol.com;
Yorkshire Dales Falconry and Conservation Centre; Crows Nest, Near Giggleswick, Settle, North Yorkshire, LA2 8AS; tel: 01729 822832 Direct 01729 825164 Information; fax: 01729 825160

FEED THE MINDS

Park Place, 12 Lawn Lane, London, SW8 1UD

Tel: 020 7582 3535
Fax: 020 7735 7617
E-mail: info@feedtheminds.org
Website: www.feedtheminds.org

Enquiries to: Administrator

Founded: 1964

Organisation type and purpose: Registered charity (charity number 291333).
An ecumenical Christian organisation that supports education in the world's poorest regions.

Publications: Printed

Access to staff: Contact by letter, by telephone, by fax and by e-mail. Appointment necessary.
Hours: Mon to Fri, 0900 to 1700

Constituent bodies: 22 agencies and mission societies from Anglican, Baptist, Catholic, Methodist and Reformed backgrounds

Links with: Council of Churches for Britain and Ireland; United Society for Christian Literature; at the same address

Member organisation of: Churches' Commission on Mission; World Association for Christian Communication (WACC)

FELINE ADVISORY BUREAU (FAB)

Taeselbury, High Street, Tisbury, Wiltshire, SP3 6LD

Tel: 01747 871872
Fax: 01747 871873
E-mail: information@fabcats.org
Website: www.fabcats.org
Website: www.web.ukonline.co.uk/fab

Enquiries to: Chief Executive

Founded: 1958

Organisation type and purpose: Advisory body, membership association (membership is by subscription), present number of members: 3,000, registered charity (charity number 1117342), suitable for ages: adults, publishing house.
To provide information on the health and welfare of cats.

Subject coverage: Disease, treatment, management and welfare of the feline species, particularly the domestic cat. Information on design, construction and management of boarding catteries and rescue facilities. Approved Boarding Cattery listing. Boarding Cattery Information Service: constructing and management of boarding catteries. Advice to owners on all feline problems, behavioural or sickness, and general cat care.

Access to staff: Contact by letter, by telephone, by fax, by e-mail and via website
Hours: Mon to Fri, 0900 to 1700

Constituent bodies: Central Fund for Feline Studies

Subsidiary body: Boarding Cattery Information Service

Supports the: International Society of Feline Medicine (ESFM)

FELL & ROCK CLIMBING CLUB OF THE ENGLISH LAKE DISTRICT (FRCC)

Library, Lancaster University Library, Bailrigg, Lancaster, LA1 4YH

Tel: 01524 65201

Enquiries to: Honorary Librarian

Founded: 1907

Organisation type and purpose: Climbing club library housed in the University Library.

Subject coverage: Fell walking and rock climbing, particularly in the English Lake District; protection of the amenities of the District; mountaineering in other parts of Great Britain, the Alps, the Himalayas and other great ranges.

Collection: Himalayan Journal
Journals of Alpine Club, American and Canadian Alpine Clubs
Journals of FRCC, Climbers' Club, Scottish Mountaineering Club, etc

Publications: Printed

Access to staff: Contact by letter
Hours: Mon to Fri, 0900 to 1700

FELL RUNNERS ASSOCIATION (FRA)

8 Leygate View, New Mills, High Peak, SK22 3EF

Tel: 01663 746476
Website: www.fellrunner.org.uk

Enquiries to: General Secretary
Direct e-mail: alan.brentnall@btinternet.com

Founded: 1970

Organisation type and purpose: National organisation, membership association (membership is by subscription), present number of members: 7,000.
Governing body of the sport in England.

Subject coverage: Fell running in the British Isles.

Publications: Printed

Publications list: Available in print

Access to staff: Contact by letter, by telephone and by e-mail
Hours: Mon to Fri, 0900 to 1700

FELLOWSHIP OF CHRISTIAN MOTORCYCLISTS (FCM)

17 Brackenbury, Andover, Hampshire SP10 3XJ

Tel: 01264 350135
E-mail: secretary@fcm-mail.org.uk
Website: www.fcm-bikers.org.uk

Enquiries to: Chairman
Direct e-mail: chairman@fcm-mail.org.uk
Other contacts: Publicity Officer

Founded: 1976

Organisation type and purpose: Membership association (membership is by subscription), present number of members: 100.

Subject coverage: We provide opportunities for Christian and non-Christian motorcyclists to meet and enjoy motorcycling.

Publications: Printed, and electronic and video

Publications list: Available online and in print

Access to staff: Contact by letter, by e-mail and via website
Hours: Mon to Fri, 0900 to 1700
Special comments: As everyone is a volunteer, you might not get an immediate response to an email.

FELLOWSHIP OF INDEPENDENT EVANGELICAL CHURCHES (FIEC)

39 The Point, Market Harborough, LE16 7QU

Tel: 01858 434540
E-mail: admin@fiec.org.uk
Website: www.fiec.org.uk

Enquiries to: Administrator
Direct e-mail: rod@fiec.org.uk
Other contacts: Office Manager

Founded: 1922

Organisation type and purpose: Advisory body, registered charity (charity number 263354).
Association of churches, ministers and Christian workers.

Subject coverage: Church-related practical issues, evangelism, pastoral care guidance.

Publications: Printed

Access to staff: Contact by letter, by telephone, by e-mail and via website
Hours: Mon to Fri, 0900 to 1700

Access for disabled people: *Special comments:* Ground floor only

Affiliated to: Affinity; PO Box 246, Bridgend, CF31 9FD; tel: 01656 646152; fax: info@affinity.org.uk; website: www.affinity .org.uk

FELLOWSHIP OF MAKERS AND RESEARCHERS OF HISTORICAL INSTRUMENTS (FoMRHI)

c/o Lewis Jones, London Metropolitan University, 41 Commercial Road, London, E1 1LA

E-mail: secretary@fomrhi.org
Website: www.hrinstruments.demon.co.uk/ fomrhi.html

Enquiries to: Honorary Secretary

Founded: 1975

Organisation type and purpose: Learned society (membership is by subscription).

Subject coverage: Reconstruction of early musical instruments (from the Stone Age to about 1900, but mostly from the Middle Ages to c. 1800), conservation and restoration of instruments of the same periods.

Publications: Printed

Access to staff: Contact by letter and by e-mail
Hours: Mon to Fri, 0900 to 1700

FELLOWSHIP OF POSTGRADUATE MEDICINE (FPM)

12 Chandos Street, London, W1G 9DR

Tel: 020 7636 6334
Fax: 020 7436 2535
E-mail: admin@fpm-uk.org
Website: www.fpm-uk.org

Enquiries to: Administrator

Organisation type and purpose: Learned society (membership is by election or invitation), present number of members: c. 50, registered charity (charity number 313355).
Medical education and publishing.

Subject coverage: Postgraduate medical education.

Access to staff: Contact by letter and by e-mail
Hours: Tue, Wed and Thu, 1000 to 1730

FELLOWSHIP OF ST ALBAN AND ST SERGIUS (FSASS)

1 Canterbury Road, Oxford, OX2 6LU

Tel: 01865 552991
Fax: 01865 316700
E-mail: gensec@sobornost.org
Website: www.sobornost.org

Enquiries to: General Secretary
Other contacts: Treasurer for subscription enquiries.

Founded: 1928

Organisation type and purpose: Membership association (membership is by subscription), present number of members: 1,218, registered charity (charity number 245112).
To promote understanding between Western and Eastern Christian churches.

Subject coverage: Information on the Orthodox Churches in the British Isles, information on the unity between Christians of East and West.

Collection: Small orthodoxy and theological library with emphasis on Russian Church Studies

Publications: Printed, and microform publications

Publications list: Available online and in print

Access to staff: Contact by letter, by telephone, by e-mail and via website
Hours: Mon to Fri, 0900 to 1300

Access to building: Prior appointment required
Special comments: Library open to members of the Fellowship.

FEMINIST LIBRARY RESOURCE AND INFORMATION CENTRE (FLRIC)

5 Westminster Bridge Road, London, SE1 7XW

Tel: 020 7928 7789
E-mail: feministlibrary@beeb.net
Website: www.genesis.ac.uk

Enquiries to: Information Officer

Founded: 1975; formerly called Women's Research and Resource Centre (year of change 1982)

Organisation type and purpose: Membership association (membership is by subscription), voluntary organisation, registered charity (charity number 272410).

Subject coverage: Women, feminism, black women, lesbians, disabled women and women's studies.

Collection: Archive material relating to second wave women's movement (WLM) 1970s
Women's Liberation Movement – Archives
Extensive journals collection from UK and around the world
10,000 books, 1,500 journals, 1,200 articles, 9,000 pamphlets and ephemera

Library catalogue: All or part available in-house

Publications: Printed

Access to staff: Contact by letter and by telephone. Appointment necessary.
Hours: Tue, 1100 to 2000; Wed, 1500 to 2000; Sat, 1400 to 1700

FENCING CONTRACTORS ASSOCIATION (FCA)

Hillside Grange, Warren Road, Trellech, Monmouth, Gwent, NP25 4PQ

Tel: 07000 560722
Fax: 01600 860888
E-mail: info@fencingcontractors.org
Website: www.fencingcontractors.org

Enquiries to: Chief Executive

Founded: 1942

Organisation type and purpose: Trade association.

Subject coverage: All types of fencing and gates including vehicle restraint systems and electric security fencing.

Collection: British Standards Parts – 1,722 fences

continued overleaf

FCA Code of Practice (PAS 48)
Publicly available specification (PAS 47) for electric fences

Publications: Printed

Access to staff: Contact by letter, by telephone, by fax and by e-mail
Hours: Mon to Fri, 0900 to 1700

Access to building: Prior appointment required

Access for disabled people: Parking provided, ramped entry, access to all public areas, toilet facilities

Connections with: Association of Safety Fencing Contractors (ASFC); as main address; Electric Security Fencing Federation (ESFF); as main address

FERFA: THE RESIN FLOORING ASSOCIATION

16 Edward Road, Farnham, Surrey, GU9 8NP

Tel: 01252 714250
Website: www.ferfa.org.uk

Enquiries to: Secretary

Founded: 1969

Organisation type and purpose: Trade association (membership is by subscription and election), present number of members: 85.
Represents UK manufacturers, contractors and associated companies involved in industrial resin flooring systems and surface preparation.

Subject coverage: UK manufacturers, contractors and associated companies involved in industrial resin flooring systems and surface preparation.

Publications: Printed
Order printed publications from: PPE booklet available from FeRFA, 16 Edward Road, Farnham, Surrey GU9 8NP; tel: 01252 714250

Publications list: Available online and in print

Access to staff: Contact by letter, by telephone, by fax, by e-mail and via website
Hours: Mon to Fri, 0900 to 1700

Access to building: By appointment only

FERRARI OWNERS' CLUB OF GREAT BRITAIN (FOCGB)

14 Lynn Road, Snettisham, King's Lynn, Norfolk, PE31 7PT

Tel: 01485 544500
Fax: 01485 544515
E-mail: foc.info@btconnect.com
Website: www.ferrariownersclub.co.uk

Enquiries to: General Secretary

Founded: 1967

Organisation type and purpose:
Membership association (membership is by subscription, qualification).
To provide events, activities, information and news for Ferrari owners and enthusiasts.

Subject coverage: Club activities including Ferrari competition, racing, sprints and hillclimb, concours events, international Ferrari events and activity, Ferrari cars old and new, technical guidance through established outlets, market trends, advertising outlets and publications.

Collection: Club library and OC register of cars

Publications: Printed

Access to staff: Contact by letter, by telephone, by fax and by e-mail
Hours: Mon to Fri, 0900 to 1700

FIBRE CEMENT MANUFACTURERS' ASSOCIATION LIMITED (FCMA)

ATSS House, Station Road East, Stowmarket, Suffolk, IP14 1RQ

Tel: 01449 676053
Fax: 01449 770028
E-mail: fcma@ghyllhouse.co.uk

Enquiries to: Secretary General
Other contacts: Chairman

Founded: 1985; formerly called Asbestos Cement Manufacturers Association

Organisation type and purpose: Trade association.

Subject coverage: Manufacture of fibre cement building products; technical development; health and safety, occupational training.

Access to staff: Contact by letter, by telephone, by fax and by e-mail
Hours: Mon to Fri, 0900 to 1700

Access to building: No access other than to staff

Member of: CBI; NFRC

FIBREOPTIC INDUSTRY ASSOCIATION (FIA)

The Manor House, Buntingford, Hertfordshire, SG9 9AB

Tel: 01763 273039
Fax: 01763 273255
E-mail: jane@fiasec.demon.co.uk
Website: www.fia-online.co.uk

Enquiries to: Secretary

Founded: 1990

Organisation type and purpose: Trade association (membership is by subscription), present number of members: 200.
Technology-based trade association for the fibre optics industry.

Subject coverage: Fibre optics, data communications, telecommunications.

Publications: Printed

Publications list: Available online

Access to staff: Contact by letter, by telephone, by fax, by e-mail and via website
Hours: Mon to Fri, 0930 to 1630

FIELD

Formal name: Foundation for International Environmental Law and Development

3 Endsleigh Street, London, WC1H 0DD

Tel: 020 7872 7200
Fax: 020 7388 2826
E-mail: field@field.org.uk
Website: www.field.org.uk

Enquiries to: Administrator
Direct e-mail: clare.duckney@field.org.uk
Other contacts: Director for Project Co-ordinator and fundraising.

Founded: 1989; formerly called Centre for International Environment Law (CIEL) (year of change 1989)

Organisation type and purpose: Advisory body, registered charity (charity number 802934), training organisation, research organisation.
To promote the progressive development of EU and international law through research, teaching, training and publishing.

Subject coverage: Environmental law related to climate and energy; trade, environment and sustainable development; international courts and tribunals; biological diversity and marine resources, international law and sustainable development and EC environmental law.

Collection: Field Brochure/Folder
FIELD in Brief
RECIEL Journal

Publications: Printed

Publications list: Available online and in print

Access to staff: Contact by letter, by telephone, by fax, by e-mail and via website
Hours: Mon to Fri, 0900 to 1700

Access to building: No access other than to staff

Connections with: IUCN; World Conservation for Nature

FIELD STUDIES COUNCIL (FSC)

Preston Montford, Montford Bridge, Shrewsbury, Shropshire, SY4 1HW

Tel: 01743 852100
Fax: 01743 852101
E-mail: enquiries@field-studies-council.org
Website: www.field-studies-council.org

Founded: 1943; formerly called Council for the Promotion of Field Studies

Organisation type and purpose:
Membership association (membership is by subscription), registered charity (charity number 313364), suitable for ages: 4 to adult.
Educational charity.
Environmental understanding for all.

Subject coverage: Biology, botany, geography, ecology, environment, environmental auditing, natural history, photography, birds, butterfly safaris, archaeology, walking, painting, crafts.

Publications: Printed
Order printed publications from: FSC Publications; tel: 01952 208910; e-mail: publications@field-studies-council.org

Publications list: Available online

Access to staff: Contact by telephone, by fax, by e-mail and via website.
Appointment necessary.
Hours: Mon to Fri, 0900 to 1700

FIELDEN-CEGOS LIMITED

The Towers, Towers Business Park, Wilmslow Road, Didsbury, Manchester, M20 2FZ

Tel: 0161 445 2426
Fax: 0161 446 2051
E-mail: customerservices@fielden-cegos.co.uk
Website: www.fielden-cegos.co.uk

Enquiries to: Course Registrar
Direct e-mail: jeremy.blain@cegos.co.uk

Founded: 1949; formerly called Fielden House Limited (year of change 1989)

Organisation type and purpose: Training organisation, consultancy.
Management training centre.

Subject coverage: Management development, supervisory training, trainer training, health and safety, administrative/secretarial, personnel/HR, supply chain management, quality management, consultancy, sales, marketing.

Publications: Printed, and electronic and video

Access to staff: Contact by letter, by telephone, by fax, by e-mail and via website
Hours: Mon to Fri, 0900 to 1700

Subsidiary of: CEGOS; France

FIELDS IN TRUST (FIT)

15 Crinan Street, London, N1 9SQ

Tel: 020 8 7427 2110
Fax: 020 74272128
E-mail: info@fieldsintrust.org
Website: www.fieldsintrust.org
Website: www.qe2fields.com

Enquiries to: Director

Founded: 1925; formerly called National Playing Fields Association (NPFA) (year of change 2007)

Organisation type and purpose: Advisory body, membership association (membership is by subscription), registered charity (charity number 306070), consultancy, publishing house.

Subject coverage: Playing fields, their establishment, conservation and development. Includes King George's Fields and the Queen Elizabeth II Fields.

Publications: Printed
Order printed publications from: Publications Department, FIT;
tel: 02074272110, e-mail: publications@npfa.co.uk

Publications list: Available online and in print

Access to staff: Contact by letter, by telephone, by e-mail, in person and via website. Appointment necessary.
Hours: 9.00 am to 5.00 pm

Affiliated to: National Council for Voluntary Organisations

Also at: FIT Cymru; Sport Wales National Centre, Sophia Gardens, Cardiff, CF11 9SW; tel: 029 2033 4935; e-mail: rhodri.edwards@fieldsintrust.org; FIT Scotland; Dewar House, Staffa Place, Dundee, DD2 3SX; tel: 01382 817427

FIFE COUNCIL

Fife House, North Street, Glenrothes, Fife, KY7 5LT

Tel: 01592 414141, 01592 414201 (minicom)
Fax: 01592 414142

Enquiries to: Co-ordination Assistant
Direct tel: 01592 413991
Direct fax: 01592 413939

Founded: 1 April 1996

Organisation type and purpose: Local government body.

FIFE COUNCIL LIBRARIES – EAST AREA

Library Headquarters, County Buildings, St Catherine Street, Cupar, Fife, KY15 4TA

Tel: 01334 412737
Fax: 01334 412941

Enquiries to: Libraries Information Services Co-ordinator

History of institution: formerly called North East Fife District Libraries (year of change 1996)

Organisation type and purpose: Local government body, public library.

Subject coverage: Local history of East Fife area and St. Andrews, local agriculture and fisheries, genealogical records relating to North East Fife, community information.

Non-library collection catalogue: All or part available in-house

Publications: Printed

Publications list: Available in print

Access to staff: Contact by letter, by telephone and by fax
Hours: Mon to Fri, 0900 to 1700

Parent body: Fife Council

FIFE COUNCIL LIBRARIES, ARTS, MUSEUMS & ARCHIVES

LAMA Headquarters, East Fergus Place, Kirkcaldy, Fife, KY1 1XT

Tel: 01592 583204
E-mail: libraries.museums@fife.gov.uk
Website: www.fifedirect.org.uk/libraries

Enquiries to: Service Manager, Libraries, Arts, Museums & Archives
Other contacts: Administration Officer

Founded: 1883; created by the merger of Libraries & Museums Service with Cultural Partnerships and Events Team in 2010 and Archives in 2011 (year of change 2011)

Organisation type and purpose: Public Libraries & Museums.
Has a network of 51 libraries, 9 museums, 2 heritage sites and hundreds of access points in schools, sheltered housing complexes and homes, bringing enjoyment, learning and enlightenment to all of Fife's citizens.

Subject coverage: Libraries provide a gateway to the world of information and cultural resources, offer leisure reading and learning support on the local doorstep, open the door further with free membership, free internet access and free requests, and stock, conserve and exploit family and local history resources.
Museums collect, document, conserve and interpret objects and materials relating to Fife, encourage others to take an interest in and preserve Fife's heritage, make the objects and their history accessible, and maximise the learning potential of the collections for adults and children.

Collection: Genealogical material
Local newspapers (microfilm and hard copy)
Local studies collection Fife
Natural, social and industrial artefacts and photographs relating to Fife
Art Gallery – focusing on Scottish artists

Trade and statistical information: General trades directories

Non-library collection catalogue: All or part available online and in-house

Library catalogue: All or part available online

Publications list: Available in print

Access to staff: Contact by letter, by telephone, by e-mail and in person
Hours: Mon to Fri, 0900 to 1700

Access to building: No prior appointment required
Hours: Hours vary between locations

Access for disabled people: Access varies between locations

Parent body: Fife Council; Fife House, North Street, Glenrothes; tel: 0845 155 0000; e-mail: fife.council.fife.gov.uk; website: http://fifedirect.org.uk

FIFE COUNCIL MUSEUMS WEST (FCMW)

Museum HQ, Dunfermline Museum, Viewfield Terrace, Dunfermline, Fife, KY12 7HY

Tel: 01383 313838
Fax: 01383 313837
E-mail: lesley.botten@fife.gov.uk

Founded: 1996; formerly called Dunfermline District Museum and Small Gallery (year of change 1997)

Organisation type and purpose: Local government body, museum, suitable for ages: all.
Headquarters of Fife Council Museums West.

Subject coverage: Local history and archaeology; 19th- and 20th-century luxury linen damask weaving industry history; costume; coal mining; of the west Fife area.

Collection: Comprehensive collection of machinery, designs and products from the luxury damask linen and silk industry of 19th- and 20th-century Dunfermline

Access to staff: Contact by letter, by telephone, by fax and by e-mail. Appointment necessary.
Hours: Mon to Fri, 0900 to 1700

Access to building: Prior appointment required

Access for disabled people: Ramped entry, level entry

Branch museums: Dunfermline Museum; Viewfield Terrace, Dunfermline, Fife, KY12 7HY; Inverkeithing Museum; The Friary, Queen Street, Inverkeithing; Pittencrieff

continued overleaf

House Museum; Pittencrieff Park, Dunfermline; St. Margaret's Cave (Dunfermline)

Parent body: Fife Council

FIFE FAMILY HISTORY SOCIETY (FFHS)

Glenmoriston, Durie Street, Leven, Fife, KY8 4HF

E-mail: via website
Website: www.fifefhs.org

Enquiries to: Secretary

Founded: 1989

Organisation type and purpose:
Membership association (membership is by subscription), voluntary organisation, registered charity.

Access to staff: *Hours:* Mon to Fri, 0900 to 1700

Access to building: *Hours:* Mon to Fri, 0900 to 1700

Chairman: Fife Family History Society; Hallfield, Blebo Craigs, Cupar, KY15 5UQ

FILM DISTRIBUTORS' ASSOCIATION LIMITED

22 Golden Square, London, W1F 9JW

Tel: 020 7437 4383
Fax: 020 7734 0912
E-mail: info@fda.uk.net
Website: www.launchingfilms.com

Enquiries to: Chief Executive

Founded: 1915; formerly called Society of Film Distributors Limited (SFD) (year of change 2001)

Organisation type and purpose: Trade association.

Subject coverage: UK film distribution.

Publications: Electronic and video

Publications list: Available online

Access to staff: Contact by letter, by telephone, by fax, by e-mail and via website
Hours: Mon to Fri, 0930 to 1730

FILMLINK (FL)

South Way, Leavesden, Hertfordshire, WD25 7LZ

Tel: 01923 495051
Fax: 01923 333007
E-mail: locations@film-link.co.uk

Enquiries to: Centre Administrator

Founded: 1996; formed from South West Herts Business Partnership (SWHBP); formed from Herts Film Link (HFL) (year of change 1996); formerly called Business Link Hertfordshire, South West Herts Centre

Organisation type and purpose: Advisory body.
A film and television commission office.

Subject coverage: Filmlink is the point of contact for all film enquiries in the county. Services include location searching, location library, private and public authority liaison, production guide to the county.

Trade and statistical information: 200 location enquiries processed a month. 40 shooting days a month

Publications: Printed

Access to staff: Contact by e-mail
Hours: Mon to Fri, 0800 to 1800

Access to building: No prior appointment required
Special comments: No prior appointment required for locations library.

FILTON COLLEGE LEARNING RESOURCE CENTRE

Filton Avenue, Filton, Bristol, BS34 7AT

Tel: 0117 931 2121
Fax: 0117 931 2233
Website: www.filton.ac.uk

Enquiries to: Learning Resources Manager

Founded: 1960

Organisation type and purpose: Suitable for ages: 16+.
Library.

Subject coverage: A Level subjects; foundation degrees; national and first diplomas.

Library catalogue: All or part available online

Access to staff: Contact by letter, by telephone, by fax and by e-mail
Hours: Mon to Thu, 0830 to 1930; Fri, 0830 to 1630

Access to building: Prior appointment required
Hours: Mon to Thu, 0830 to 1930; Fri, 0830 to 1630

Access for disabled people: Parking provided, ramped entry, toilet facilities

FINANCE AND LEASING ASSOCIATION (FLA)

2nd Floor, Imperial House, 15–19 Kingsway, London, WC2B 6UN

Tel: 020 7836 6511
Fax: 020 7420 9655
E-mail: info@fla.org.uk
Website: www.fla.org.uk

Enquiries to: Head of Government Affairs
Direct tel: 020 7420 9654
Direct e-mail: edward.simpson@fla.org.uk

Founded: 1992; formerly called Finance Houses Association (FHA) (year of change 1992); incorporates the former Equipment Leasing Association (ELA) (year of change 1992)

Organisation type and purpose: Trade association.

Subject coverage: The FLA is the trade association for companies offering business finance and leasing, consumer credit and motor finance in the UK, and holds information on all of these subjects.

Trade and statistical information: Asset finance and leasing, business finance, consumer credit, motor finance

Publications: Printed

Publications list: Available online

Access to staff: Contact by letter, by telephone, by fax and by e-mail
Hours: Mon to Fri, 0900 to 1700

Access to building: No access other than to staff

Access for disabled people: Ramped entry

FINANCIAL OMBUDSMAN SERVICE

South Quay Plaza, 183 Marsh Wall, London, E14 9SR

Tel: 020 7964 1000
Fax: 020 7964 1001
E-mail: enquiries@financial-ombudsman.org.uk
Website: www.financial-ombudsman.org.uk

History of institution: formed by the merger of Banking Ombudsman (BO), Building Societies Ombudsman (BSO), Insurance Ombudsman Bureau (IOB), Investment Ombudsman Bureau (IOB), Office of the Investment Ombudsman (OIO)

Organisation type and purpose: Statutory body.
Set up by law to help settle individual disputes between consumers and financial firms.

Subject coverage: Banking, insurance, pensions, savings and investments, credit cards and store cards, loans and credit, hire purchase and pawnbroking, financial advice, stocks, shares, unit trusts and bonds.

Publications: Printed, and electronic and video

Publications list: Available online and in print

Access to staff: Contact by letter, by telephone, by fax, by e-mail and via website
Hours: Mon to Fri, 0900 to 1700

FINANCIAL SERVICES AUTHORITY, THE (FSA)

25 The North Colonnade, London, E14 5HS

Tel: 020 7066 1000
Fax: 020 7066 1097
Website: www.fsa.gov.uk

Enquiries to: Public Enquiry Officer

Founded: 1986; formerly called Securities and Investments Board (SIB), date of change, October 1997; incorporating the former Building Societies Commission (BSC), Friendly Societies Commission (FSC), date of change, December 2001

Organisation type and purpose: Statutory body.
Financial services regulation and investor protection.

Subject coverage: Financial services regulation.

Publications list: Available in print

Access to staff: Contact by letter and by telephone
Hours: Mon to Fri, 0900 to 1700

FINANCIAL SERVICES COMPENSATION SCHEME (FSCS)

7th Floor, Lloyds Chambers, 1 Portsoken Street, London, E1 8BN

Tel: 020 7892 7300
Fax: 020 7892 7301
E-mail: enquiries@fscs.org.uk
Website: www.fscs.org.uk

Enquiries to: Customer Services Team
Other contacts: Head of Communications for press enquiries.

Founded: Dec 2001; formerly called Deposit Protection Board (DPB), Investors Compensation Scheme (ICS), Policyholders Protection Board (PPB) (year of change 2001)

Organisation type and purpose: Statutory body.
FSCS is a final safety net for customers of authorised financial services firms. It compensates consumers if an authorised firm is unable to pay claims against it. The Scheme covers deposits, insurance and investments.

Subject coverage: Set up under the Financial Services and Markets Act (FSMA) 2000.

Publications: Printed

Publications list: Available online and in print

Access to staff: Contact by letter, by telephone, by fax and by e-mail. Appointment necessary.
Hours: Mon to Fri, 0900 to 1700

Access to building: No access other than by appointment

Access for disabled people: Access to all public areas

Independent but accountable to: FSA

FINANCIAL SERVICES SKILLS COUNCIL

51 Gresham Street, London, EC2V 7HQ

Tel: 020 7216 7366
Fax: 020 7216 7370
E-mail: fsp@flamepr.com
Website: www.fssc.org.uk

Enquiries to: Sector Support Executive
Direct e-mail: info@fsnto.org

History of institution: formerly called Banking Industry Training and Development Council (BITDC), BBS NTO, IRFS NTO, FS NTO

Organisation type and purpose: Sector Skills Council.

Subject coverage: Labour market information for the financial services sector.

Publications: Printed, and electronic and video
Order printed publications from: e-mail: www.fssc.org.uk

Publications list: Available online

Access to staff: Contact by e-mail and via website
Hours: Mon to Fri, 0900 to 1700

Access to building: No access other than to staff

Access for disabled people: Access to all public areas

FINE ART SOCIETY PLC (FAS)

148 New Bond Street, London, W1S 2JT

Tel: 020 7629 5116
Fax: 020 7491 9454
E-mail: art@faslondon.com
Website: www.faslondon.com

Enquiries to: Information Officer

Founded: 1876

Organisation type and purpose: Service industry, art gallery.
Art dealers.

Subject coverage: Dealers in 19th- and 20th-century fine and contemporary arts.

Collection: Past and present exhibition catalogues held by Victoria and Albert Museum National Art Library

Publications: Printed

Access to staff: Contact in person
Hours: Mon to Fri, 1000 to 1800; Sat, 1000 to 1300
Special comments: Closed Saturdays in August.

FINE ART TRADE GUILD

16–18 Empress Place, London, SW6 1TT

Tel: 020 7381 6616
Fax: 020 7381 2596
E-mail: info@fineart.co.uk
Website: www.fineart.co.uk

Enquiries to: Managing Director
Other contacts: Editor, Art Business Today (for wide industry knowledge and insight)

Founded: 1910; formerly called The Printsellers Association; broadened scope to become the Fine Art Trade Guild (year of change 1910)

Organisation type and purpose: International organisation, trade association (membership is by subscription), present number of members: 1,000, service industry, manufacturing industry, publishing house.

Subject coverage: Pictures, print publishing, limited-edition prints, picture framing industry.

Collection: Archives of limited edition prints

Publications: Printed

Access to staff: Contact by letter, by telephone, by fax, by e-mail and via website. Appointment necessary.
Hours: Mon to Fri, 0930 to 1730

FINISHING PUBLICATIONS LIMITED

105 Whitney Drive, Stevenage, Hertfordshire, SG1 4BL

Tel: 01438 745115
Fax: 01438 364536
E-mail: finpubs@compuserve.com
Website: www.finishingpublications.com
Website: www.surfacequery.com

Enquiries to: Manager

Founded: 1964

Organisation type and purpose: Publishing house.

Subject coverage: Surface engineering and treatment, metal finishing, electroplating, anodizing, etching, pickling, plating, printed circuit board fabrication, effluent treatment for these industries. Books relating to St Ives and its literary/artistic community

Collection: In-house Metal-Finishing Library (UK, USA, German serials, books)

Trade and statistical information: Statistical information available from in-house database (costs, market size, etc)

Non-library collection catalogue: All or part available online

Publications: Printed, and electronic and video

Publications list: Available online

Access to staff: Contact by letter, by telephone, by fax, by e-mail and via website. Appointment necessary.
Hours: Mon to Fri, 0900 to 1700

Access for disabled people: Parking provided, level entry

FIRA INTERNATIONAL LTD (FIRA)

Formal name: Furniture Industry Research Association

Maxwell Road, Stevenage, Hertfordshire, SG1 2EW

Tel: 01438 777700
Fax: 01438 777800
E-mail: info@fira.co.uk
Website: www.fira.co.uk

Enquiries to: Technical Advisors

Organisation type and purpose: FIRA International is acknowledged as the UK centre of excellence for furniture research, testing, consultancy and information which provides a suite of products and services to a number of global businesses.

Subject coverage: Furniture design and manufacturing methods, tests for furniture materials and complete items of furniture, upholstery, standards, environmental issues, ergonomics, flammability, fault investigations, market research and marketing, consultancy in product costing, factory layout etc, machinery and material selection, statistics for the industry.

Publications: Printed

Publications list: Available online

Access to staff: Contact by letter, by telephone and by fax. Access for members only.
Hours: Mon to Fri, 0900 to 1700

Access to building: No access other than to staff

FIRE BRIGADE SOCIETY (FBS)

17 Kinsbourne Way, Southampton, SO19 6HB

Website: www.firebrigadesociety.freeserve.co.uk/fbs/welcome.htm

Enquiries to: General Secretary

Founded: 1963

continued overleaf

Organisation type and purpose: International organisation, membership association (membership is by subscription). Voluntary association.

Subject coverage: Fire service, past, present and future.

Access to staff: Contact by letter
Hours: Mon to Fri, 0900 to 1700

FIRE BRIGADES UNION (FBU)

Bradley House, 68 Coombe Road, Kingston upon Thames, Surrey, KT2 7AE

Tel: 020 8541 1765
Fax: 020 8546 5187
E-mail: office@fbu.org.uk
Website: www.fbu.org.uk

Enquiries to: General Secretary

Founded: 1918

Organisation type and purpose: Trade union, present number of members: 51,600.

Subject coverage: Fire services.

Publications: Printed

Access to staff: Contact by letter, by telephone, by e-mail and via website
Hours: Mon to Fri, 0900 to 1700

Access to building: Prior appointment required

Affiliated to: TUC

FIRE FIGHTING VEHICLE MANUFACTURERS ASSOCIATION (FFVMA)

Forbes House, Halkin Street, London, SW1X 7DS

Tel: 020 7344 9232
Fax: 020 7235 7112
E-mail: cford@smmt.co.uk
Website: www.smmt.co.uk

Enquiries to: Director

Founded: 1972

Organisation type and purpose: Trade association.
Subject coverage: Legislation and standards regarding fire appliances and associated vehicles and equipment.

Trade and statistical information: UK Vehicle Registration Statistics

Access to staff: Contact by letter, by telephone, by fax and via website. Appointment necessary.
Hours: Mon to Fri, 0900 to 1700

Affiliated to the: Society of Motor Manufacturers & Traders (SMMT); tel: 020 7235 7000; fax: 020 7235 7112

FIRE INDUSTRY ASSOCIATION (FIA)

Thames House, 29 Thames Street, Kingston Upon Thames, Surrey, KT1 1PH

Tel: 020 8549 5855
Fax: 020 8547 1564
E-mail: info@fia.uk.com
Website: www.fia.uk.com

Enquiries to: General Manager
Other contacts: Committee Secretary

History of institution: created by the merger of the Fire Extinguishing Trades Association (FETA) and the British Fire Protection Systems Association (BFPSA)

Organisation type and purpose: Trade association.

Subject coverage: Development, manufacture and specialist distribution of fire extinguishers of all types, portable fire fighting equipment fillings.

Publications: Printed

Access to staff: Contact by letter, by telephone and by fax
Hours: Mon to Fri, 0900 to 1700

Affiliated to, and premises and secretarial services shared with, the: Association of British Fire Trades (ABFT); British Approvals for Fire Equipment (BAFE); Fire Industry Confederation (FIC)

FIRE MARK CIRCLE

44 Kings Road, East Sheen, London, SW14 8PF

Tel: 020 8878 7123
Fax: 020 8878 7123
E-mail: saunders_mj@hotmail.com
Website: www.firemarkcircle.fsnet.co.uk

Enquiries to: Honorary Secretary

Founded: 1934

Organisation type and purpose: Learned society.
For persons interested in the origin and history of fire insurance companies, their fire marks, fire brigades and all that pertains to the past of fire insurance.

Subject coverage: History of fire insurance and fire-fighting.

Publications: Printed

Publications list: Available in print

Access to staff: Contact by letter, by telephone, by fax, by e-mail and via website
Hours: Mon to Fri, 0900 to 1700

FIRE SERVICE COLLEGE (FSC)

Moreton-in-Marsh, Gloucestershire, GL56 0RH

Tel: 01608 812050
Fax: 01608 812048
E-mail: library@fireservicecollege.ac.uk
Website: www.fireservicecollege.ac.uk

Enquiries to: Library Manager
Direct e-mail: jmason@fireservicecollege.ac.uk
Other contacts: Customer Services for enquiries

Organisation type and purpose: National government body, training organisation, Government agency.
Training personnel from UK fire service and industry in fire, fire safety and related subjects.

Subject coverage: Fire and emergency, technology, engineering, safety, operational aspects and disaster management, related subjects and history of the Fire Service.

Collection: Archives of Fire Service History
Fire Journal from first issue
Library of over 80,000 books

Non-library collection catalogue: All or part available online

Library catalogue: All or part available online, in-house and in print

Access to staff: Contact by letter, by telephone, by fax, by e-mail and via website. Appointment necessary.
Hours: Mon to Thu, 0900 to 1700; Fri, 0900 to 1400

Access to building: No public access

FIRE SERVICE PRESERVATION GROUP (FSPG)

50 Old Slade Lane, Iver, Buckinghamshire, SL0 9DR

Website: www.f-s-p-g.org

Enquiries to: Membership Secretary

Founded: 1968

Organisation type and purpose: Membership association (membership is by subscription), present number of members: 1200.
Preservation of all types of fire appliances and equipment.

Subject coverage: Fire appliances and equipment, equipment of the NFS and AFS, equipment dating back to the formation of the Fire Brigades, clothing spare parts, hand pumps, horse-drawn appliances and extinguishers, legislation and registration of appliances.

Collection: Library of books and reference manuals

Publications: Printed

Access to staff: Contact by letter and via website
Hours: Mon to Fri, 0900 to 1700

Member of: Federation of British Historic Vehicle Clubs (FBHVC)

FIRST DIVISION ASSOCIATION (FDA)

2 Caxton Street, London, SW1H 0QH

Tel: 020 7343 1111
Fax: 020 7343 1105
E-mail: head-office@fda.org.uk
Website: www.fda.org.uk
Website: www.fda.org.uk/members

Enquiries to: General Secretary

Founded: 1919; formerly called Association of First Division Civil Servants (FSA) (year of change 2001)

Organisation type and purpose: Professional body, trade union (membership is by subscription), present number of members: 11,000.

Subject coverage: Civil Service; modernising government; freedom of information.

Publications: Printed

Publications list: Available online

Access to staff: Contact by letter, by telephone, by fax, by e-mail and via website
Hours: Mon to Fri, 0900 to 1700

Access to building: Prior appointment required

Affiliated to the: Trades Union Congress (TUC)

FIRST KEY

Oxford Chambers, Oxford Place, Leeds, West Yorkshire, LS1 3AX

Tel: 0113 244 3898
Fax: 0113 243 2541
E-mail: information@firstkeyleeds.com or admin@firstkeyleeds.com
Website: www.first-key.co.uk

Enquiries to: Administrator

Founded: 1984

Organisation type and purpose: Voluntary organisation, registered charity (charity number 289552).
To improve the life chances of young people leaving public care, through training, advice, consultancy.

Subject coverage: Young people leaving public care.

Publications: Printed

Publications list: Available in print

Access to staff: Contact by letter, by telephone, by fax and by e-mail. Appointment necessary.
Hours: Mon to Fri, 1000 to 1600

Other addresses: First Key; London Voluntary Sector Resource Centre, 356 Holloway Road, London, N7 6PA; tel: 020 7700 8130; fax: 020 7700 8174; e-mail: admin@firstkeylondon.com; First Key; Room 14 Koco Building, Unit 15, The Arches, Spon End, Coventry, CV1 3JQ; tel: 02476 716259; fax: 02476 677554; e-mail: information@firstkeycoventry.com

FIRST STEPS TO FREEDOM (FSTF)

PO Box 476, Newquay, TR7 1WQ

Tel: 0845 120 2916
E-mail: first.steps@btconnect.com
Website: www.first-steps.org

Enquiries to: Secretary

Founded: 1991

Organisation type and purpose: Membership association (membership is by subscription), present number of members: 1,400, voluntary organisation, registered charity (charity number 1006837).
To offer help, advice and support to those suffering from stress-related disorders such as phobias, panic attacks and Obsessive Compulsive Disorder

Subject coverage: Generalised anxiety disorder (GAD), phobias, compulsive disorders
FSTF offers a confidential helpline, practical advice, telephone self-help groups, one-to-one telephone counselling and befriending, leaflets, self-help booklets and videos.

Publications: Printed, and electronic and video

Publications list: Available online and in print

Access to staff: Contact by letter, by telephone, by fax, by e-mail and via website
Hours: Helpline, daily, 1000 to 2200

Links with: Queen Elizabeth's Hospital; Department of Psychiatry, Welwyn Garden City, Hertfordshire

Member organisation of: Telephone Helplines Association

FIRST STOP CENTRE

29 Bocking End, Braintree, Essex, CM7 9AE

Tel: 01376 346535
E-mail: via website
Website: www.firststopcentre.org.uk

Founded: 1990

Organisation type and purpose: Registered charity (charity number 803170).
To relieve the condition of disadvantaged persons in mid-Essex experiencing difficulties with homelessness, joblessness, substance misuse, physical and mental health and related problems, or learning disabilities by the provision of support services; to assist such persons in maintaining normal relationships with and within the community in which they reside.

Subject coverage: Services include a drop-in centre open to all ages and backgrounds, where staff can help with many issues such as form-filling, housing, employment and debts; a free needle exchange; basic skills education, free, for numeracy and literacy; a formal counselling service for individuals and couples; a postal holding address for those who are homeless or do not have a secure mailing address. Help is offered for any adult in need of help in a crisis.

Education services: Free-of-charge basic skills training for numeracy and literacy.

Publications: Electronic and video
Order electronic and video publications from: Download from website

Publications list: Available online

Access to staff: Contact by letter, by telephone, in person and via website
Hours: Mon, Tue, Thu, Fri, 1030 to 1330
Special comments: Answer machine service out of hours.

Access to building: *Hours:* Drop-in centre (incl. needle exchange): Mon, Tue, Thu, Fri, 1030 to 1330
Special comments: Other activities take place outside these core hours, including basic skills education, counselling, anger and anxiety groups.

FISHERIES RESEARCH SERVICES MARINE LABORATORY LIBRARY (FRS)

PO Box 101, 375 Victoria Road, Aberdeen, AB11 9DB

Tel: 01224 876544
Fax: 01224 295309
Website: www.marlab.ac.uk

Enquiries to: Librarian
Direct tel: 01224 295391
Direct e-mail: k.mutch@marlab.ac.uk

Organisation type and purpose: Research organisation.
Executive Agency of the Scottish Office.

Subject coverage: Marine biology, oceanography, fisheries, fishing methods and gear, pollution and aquaculture, marine ecology, fish diseases, sonar.

Collection: Ogilvie Collection on diatomaceae

Non-library collection catalogue: All or part available in-house

Library catalogue: All or part available in-house

Publications: Printed

Publications list: Available online

Access to staff: Contact by letter, by telephone, by fax and by e-mail. Appointment necessary. Non-members charged.
Hours: Mon to Thu, 0900 to 1700; Fri, 0900 to 1630
Special comments: Charges made for photocopying.

Access for disabled people: Toilet facilities

Branch library at the: Freshwater Fisheries Laboratory; Pitlochry

Parent body: Scottish Executive Environment and Rural Affairs Department (SEERAD)

FISHERIES SOCIETY OF THE BRITISH ISLES (FSBI)

Martineau Johnson , No. 1 Colmore Square, Birmingham, B4 6AA

Tel: 0870 763 1487
E-mail: membership@fsbi.org.uk
Website: www.fsbi.org.uk

Enquiries to: Secretary
Direct e-mail: secretary@fsbi.org.uk

Founded: 1967

Organisation type and purpose: Learned society.

Subject coverage: Scientific aspects of freshwater and marine fisheries, fish biology.

Publications: Printed

Access to staff: Contact by letter, by telephone, by fax, by e-mail and via website
Hours: Mon to Fri, 0900 to 1700

FITNESS INDUSTRY ASSOCIATION (FIA)

Castlewood House, 77–91 New Oxford Street, London, WC1A 1PX

Tel: 020 7420 8560
Fax: 020 7420 8561
Website: www.fia.org.uk

Enquiries to: Executive Director
Direct e-mail: davidstalker@fia.org.uk

Founded: 1990

Organisation type and purpose: A not-for-profit organisation and trade body that represents the interests of members in the health and fitness industry across the UK, currently represents over 2,800 operators in the public and private sectors, as well as 250 supplier organisations, including multi-site operators, individual local gyms, and many leading suppliers.

continued overleaf

Regularly responds to government consultations, publishes research and engages with the political community.

Subject coverage: Collective purchasing; professional development seminars and events to develop staff and share best practice; community engagement programmes; government campaigns; sponsoring opportunities.

Publications: Electronic and video
Order electronic and video publications from: Website

Access to staff: Contact by letter, by telephone, by fax and via website

Runs the following government-funded programmes: MoreActive4Life, Fit for the Future, Active Schools, Go, Active at Work

FITNESS WALES

1B Clarke Street, Cardiff, CF5 5AL

Tel: 029 2057 5155
Fax: 029 2056 8886
E-mail: enquiries@fitnesswales.co.uk

Enquiries to: Director
Other contacts: Manager for general enquiries.

Founded: 1966

Organisation type and purpose: Training organisation.
Governing body of exercise and fitness.
To promote exercise and physical fitness and to monitor standards in the fitness sector in Wales.

Subject coverage: Training opportunities to teach exercise and fitness. Qualifications needed in fitness industry (national standards). Registration of fitness instructors. Fitness events in Wales.

Publications: Printed

Access to staff: Contact by letter, by telephone, by fax, by e-mail, in person and via website
Hours: Mon to Fri, 0900 to 1700

FITZWILLIAM COLLEGE LIBRARY

Formal name: Fitzwilliam Information Services Trust

Storey's Way, Cambridge, CB3 0DG

Tel: 01223 332042
Fax: 01223 477976
E-mail: library@fitz.cam.ac.uk
Website: www.fitz.cam.ac.uk/library

Enquiries to: Librarian

Founded: 1963

Organisation type and purpose: University department or institute. College library.

Subject coverage: Some specialisation in international law.

Library catalogue: All or part available online

Access to staff: Contact by letter, by telephone, by fax, by e-mail and via website. Appointment necessary.
Hours: Mon to Fri, 0900 to 1700

FITZWILLIAM MUSEUM

Library, Trumpington Street, Cambridge, CB2 1RB

Tel: 01223 332900
Fax: 01223 332923
E-mail: fitzmuseum-enquiries@lists.cam.ac.uk
Website: www.fitzmuseum.cam.ac.uk

Enquiries to: Librarian
Other contacts: Keeper of Manuscripts and Printed Books

Organisation type and purpose: Museum, university department or institute.

Subject coverage: The collection is valuable for its form rather than subject coverage: illuminated manuscripts, music manuscripts and printed music, autograph letters, rare books of all periods, art reference works, literary manuscripts, fine arts and antiquities.

Collection: Collections include:
Most of music and some of the other manuscript material on microfilm
Music by Patrick Hadley, MacFarren, Handel
William Hayley papers
W. S. Blunt papers

Non-library collection catalogue: All or part available online and in print

Library catalogue: All or part available online

Publications: Printed, and microform publications

Access to staff: Contact by letter, by telephone, by e-mail and in person. Appointment necessary. Letter of introduction required.
Hours: Tue to Fri, 1000 to 1200 and 1330 to 1630
Special comments: Access restrictions apply only to the users of curatorial materials (i.e. manuscripts and rare books). Introductory letter required for use of special collections.

Access to building: No access other than to staff
Hours: Tue to Fri, 1000 to 1200 and 1330 to 1630

Parent body: University of Cambridge

FLAG INSTITUTE

38 Hill Street, Mayfair, London, W1J 5NS

Website: www.flaginstitute.org

Enquiries to: Editor

Founded: 1971

Organisation type and purpose: Voluntary organisation.

Subject coverage: Flags and related emblems both historical and modern, with particular reference to national flags, flag protocol and usage, flag design, the publication of flag information in various formats, charts and information packs.

Collection: Country-by-country flag dossiers
Frederick Warne collection
John Sharpe Collection of flag books
Library of flag books, charts and pictures
Louis Loynes Collection of flag paintings and drawings

Trade and statistical information: Information on the flag trade (manufacture and distribution) in Britain and abroad

Publications: Printed

Publications list: Available in print

Access to staff: Contact by letter and via website. All charged.
Hours: Mon to Fri, 1000 to 1800

Member of: Fédération Internationale des Associations Vexillologiques

FLINTSHIRE COUNTY COUNCIL

County Hall, Mold, Flintshire, CH7 6NB

Tel: 01352 752121
E-mail: info@flintshire.gov.uk
Website: www.flintshire.gov.uk

Enquiries to: Corporate Communications Manager

Founded: 1996

Organisation type and purpose: Local government body.

Access to staff: Contact by letter, by telephone, by fax, by e-mail, in person and via website
Hours: Mon to Fri, 0830 to 1700

FLINTSHIRE HISTORICAL SOCIETY

Flintshire Record Office, The Old Rectory, Hawarden, Flintshire, CH5 3NR

Tel: 01244 532414
Fax: 01244 538344

Enquiries to: Honorary Secretary
Direct tel: 01745 332220

Founded: 1911

Organisation type and purpose: Learned society (membership is by subscription), present number of members: 280 individual, 38 corporate, registered charity (charity number 218288).

Subject coverage: History and archaeology of the historical county of Flintshire.

Publications: Printed
Order printed publications from: Flintshire Records Office

Publications list: Available in print

Access to staff: Contact by letter and by telephone. Non-members charged.
Hours: Mon to Fri, 0900 to 1700

FLINTSHIRE LIBRARY AND INFORMATION SERVICE

Library Headquarters, County Hall, Mold, Flintshire, CH7 6NW

Tel: 01352 704400
Fax: 01352 753662
E-mail: libraries@flintshire.gov.uk
Website: www.flintshire.gov.uk/libraries

Enquiries to: Head of Libraries, Culture & Heritage

Founded: 1996

Organisation type and purpose: Local government body, public library.

Subject coverage: Arthurian legend, Wales and Welsh literature, general public reference service.

Collection: Arthurian Legend Collection
Local history collection
Daniel Owen Museum
Mold Gold Cape replica
Buckley pottery museum collection

Library catalogue: All or part available online

Publications: Printed
Order printed publications from: As above

Access to staff: Contact by letter, by telephone, by fax, by e-mail, in person and via website
Hours: Mon to Fri, 0900 to 1700

Access for disabled people: At Library HQ: parking provided, ramped entry, toilet facilities, lift.

FLINTSHIRE MUSEUM SERVICE

County Hall, Mold, Flintshire, CH7 6NW

Tel: 01352 704409
Fax: 01352 753662
E-mail: museums@flintshire.gov.uk
Website: www.flintshire.gov.uk

Enquiries to: Principal Museums Officer
Direct e-mail: deborah.seymour@flintshire.gov.uk

Founded: 1996; formerly called Clwyd County Museum Service (year of change 1996)

Organisation type and purpose: Local government body.
Local authority museum service.

Subject coverage: The support of local culture and history.

Collection: Flintshire historical artefacts

Non-library collection catalogue: All or part available in-house

Access to staff: Contact by letter, by telephone, by fax, by e-mail and via website. Appointment necessary.
Hours: Mon to Fri, 0900 to 1700

Access to building: No prior appointment required

Branch museums: Buckley Library and Heritage Centre; The Precinct, Buckley, Flintshire, CH7 2EF; tel: 01244 549210; e-mail: museums@flintshire.gov.uk; website: http://www.flintshire.gov.uk
Mold Library and Museum; Earl Road, Mold, Flintshire, CH7 1AP; tel: 01352 754791; e-mail: museums@flintshire.gov.uk; website: http://www.flintshire.gov.uk

Links with: Greenfield Valley Heritage Park; Greenfield, Holywell, CH8 7GH; tel: 01352 714172; e-mail: info@greenfieldvalley.com; website: http://www.greenfieldvalley.com

FLINTSHIRE RECORD OFFICE (FRO)

The Old Rectory, Hawarden, Flintshire, CH5 3NR

Tel: 01244 532364
Fax: 01244 538344
E-mail: archives@flintshire.gov.uk
Website: www.flintshire.gov.uk/archives

Enquiries to: Searchroom
Direct tel: 01244 532364
Direct fax: 01244 538344
Direct e-mail: archives@flintshire.gov.uk
Other contacts: Conservator for conservation enquiries

Founded: 1951; formerly called Flintshire Record Office (year of change 1974); formerly called Clwyd Record Office (year of change 1996)

Organisation type and purpose: Local government body.
Archives, conservation, records management.

Subject coverage: All aspects of the history of Flintshire from 12th to 20th century, official, public and deposited records for Flintshire and North East Wales.

Information services: Research Service available at £25 per hour

Special visitor services: One-to-one sessions available

Collection: Family papers of W. E. Gladstone

Non-library collection catalogue: All or part available online and in-house

Library catalogue: All or part available in-house

Publications: Printed, and electronic and video

Access to staff: Contact by letter, by telephone, by fax, by e-mail, in person and via website. Appointment necessary.

Access to building: *Hours:* Mon/Tue/Thu/Fri, 1000 to 1630; documents not produced between 1200 and 1330
Special comments: CARN Reader's Ticket required; can be issued on production of proof of ID with address and signature.

Access for disabled people: Parking provided, level entry

Constituent part of: Flintshire County Council; tel: 01352 752121; website: http://www.flintshire.gov.uk

FLOUR ADVISORY BUREAU LIMITED (FAB)

21 Arlington Street, London, SW1A 1RN

Tel: 020 7493 2521
Fax: 020 7493 6785
Website: www.grainchain.com
Website: www.fabflour.co.uk

Enquiries to: Head of Communications/Communications Assistant
Direct e-mail: fab@nabim.org.uk

Founded: 1956

Organisation type and purpose: Trade association.
A central source of information on matters relating to bread and flour in the UK.

Subject coverage: Generic information on wheat, flour and bread; usage, recipes, educational material, nutritional information and market trends.

Education services: See website.

Publications: Printed

Access to staff: Contact by letter, by telephone, by fax, by e-mail and via website
Hours: Mon to Fri, 0900 to 1700

Public relations arm of the: National Association of British and Irish Millers (NABIM); at the same address

FLOWERS & PLANTS ASSOCIATION (F&PA)

266 Flower Market, New Covent Garden Market, London, SW8 5NB

Tel: 020 7738 8044
Fax: 020 7738 8083
E-mail: press-office@flowers.org.uk
Website: www.flowers.org.uk
Website: www.tryflowers.org.uk

Enquiries to: Chief Executive

Founded: 1984

Organisation type and purpose: Trade association (membership is by subscription), present number of members: 200 companies.
Promotion of fresh cut flowers and indoor pot plants.

Subject coverage: Commercially grown cut flowers, commercially grown pot plants (indoor), statistical data on market; care advice; product information; general related topics of interest.

Trade and statistical information: Statistics for members only.
Data on cut flower market.
Data on pot plants market

Publications: Printed

Access to staff: Contact by letter, by telephone, by fax, by e-mail and via website. Appointment necessary. Non-members charged.
Hours: Mon to Fri, 0900 to 1700
Special comments: Certain information is available to members only.

FOCUS

10 Great Pulteney Street, London, W1F 9NB

Tel: 020 3214 0100
Fax: 020 3214 0126
Website: www.focusnet.co.uk

Enquiries to: Director

Founded: 1984; still trading and formed from Property Intelligence Limited (year of change 2004)

Organisation type and purpose: Service industry, research organisation.
Provides information on commercial properties UK-wide.

Subject coverage: Commercial properties in the UK; socioeconomic and geo-demographic data on major UK towns, 17 million property records, 1 million deals, 900 retailers' requirements, 2.1 million occupiers, 7 town reports, planning details, auction information, property history, rating information, office availability, office requirements.

Collection: Company prospectuses
Property journals
Property company and fund reports
Press releases

Publications: Printed, and electronic and video

continued overleaf

Access to staff: Contact by letter, by telephone, by fax, by e-mail and via website. Appointment necessary. All charged.
Hours: Mon to Fri, 0830 to 1800

Access for disabled people: Ramped entry, toilet facilities

Connections with: Scottish Property Network Limited; 26 New Street, Paisley, PA1 1YB; tel: 0141 561 7300; fax: 0141 561 7319; e-mail: info@scottishproperty.co.uk

FOLKESTONE LIBRARY, MUSEUM AND SASSOON GALLERY

2 Grace Hill, Folkestone, Kent, CT20 1HD

Tel: 01303 850123, 01303 240258 (minicom)
Fax: 01303 242907

Enquiries to: Librarian
Direct tel: 01303 256710
Direct fax: 01303 256710
Direct e-mail: janet.adamson@kent.gov.uk
Other contacts: (1) Information Officer (2) Heritage Officer for (1) reference (2) local studies.

Founded: 1888

Organisation type and purpose: Local government body, museum, art gallery, public library, suitable for ages: all.

Subject coverage: General and local information, including Channel Tunnel, local and family history.

Collection: Heritage Room, historical records, maps, photographs and newspapers for Folkestone and the Shepway area
Bishop's Transcripts and Archdeacon's Transcripts and Parish Registers for many parishes (microfilm)
Census enumerator's returns for 1841–1891 for Shepway and Capel-le-Ferne
Photographic collection
Map collection
Newspapers

Publications: Printed

Access to staff: Contact by letter, by telephone, by fax, by e-mail and in person
Hours: Mon, Tue, Thu, 0930 to 1800; Fri, 0930 to 1900; Sat, Wed, 0930 to 1700

Access for disabled people: Level entry, access to all public areas, toilet facilities

Part of: Kent County Council, Education and Libraries Department

FOLLY FELLOWSHIP (F/F)

7 Inch's Yard, Market Street, Newbury, Berkshire, RG14 5DP

Tel: 01635 42864
E-mail: andrew@follies.fsnet.co.uk
Website: www.follies.org.uk

Enquiries to: Secretary
Other contacts: Membership Secretary

Founded: 1988

Organisation type and purpose: International organisation, learned society (membership is by subscription), registered charity (charity number 1002646).
To protect, preserve and promote follies, grottoes and garden buildings.

Subject coverage: Architectural follies, grottoes and landscape buildings in the United Kingdom and worldwide.

Collection: Picture and photographic library

Publications: Printed, and electronic and video
Order printed publications from: e-mail: membership@follies.org.uk

Access to staff: Contact by letter, by telephone, by e-mail and via website. Appointment necessary.
Hours: Mon to Fri, 0900 to 1700

FOOD AND DRINK FEDERATION (FDF)

6 Catherine Street, London, WC2B 5JJ

Tel: 020 7836 2460
Fax: 020 7836 0580
E-mail: generalenquiries@fdf.org.uk
Website: www.fdf.org.uk

Enquiries to: Information Manager

History of institution: formerly called Food Manufacturers Federation

Organisation type and purpose: Trade association.

Subject coverage: UK food manufacturing industry.

Publications: Electronic and video

Publications list: Available online

Access to staff: Contact by letter, by telephone, by fax, by e-mail and via website. Access for members only.
Hours: Mon to Fri, 0930 to 1730
Special comments: Visitors not normally permitted.

European link is the: CIAA

Members: Association of Cereal Food Manufacturers; British Pasta Products Association; British Starch Industry Association; Cereal Ingredient Manufacturers' Association; Frozen and Chilled Potato Processors' Association; tel: 0131 229 9415; Infant & Dietetic Foods Association; Margarine and Spreads Association; National Association of Cider Makers; Potato Processors' Association; tel: 0131 229 9415; Seasoning and Spice Association; UK Association of Manufacturers of Bakers' Yeast; UK Preserves Manufacturers' Association; UK Tea Association

FOOD AND ENVIRONMENT RESEARCH AGENCY (FERA)

Sand Hutton, York, North Yorkshire, YO41 1LZ

Tel: 01904 462000
Fax: 01904 462111
E-mail: science@fera.gsi.gov.uk
Website: www.fera.defra.gov.uk/contactUs

Enquiries to: Information Centre Manager
Direct tel: 01904 462272

Founded: 1992; formerly called Central Science Laboratory (year of change 2009)

Organisation type and purpose: National government body, research organisation.

Subject coverage: Plant pathology (bacteriology, plant health and disease assessment, disease control, mycology, virology), agricultural entomology (general entomology, vertebrate pest assessment, biology and control, fumigation, insect systematics), crop protection, biochemistry, chemistry (biological efficiency, analytical methods for pest formulations and residues in crops, safety to users), toxicology and industrial hygiene related to pesticides. Biology and control of invertebrate pests of stored products, moulds on stored products, mycotoxins. Food safety, food quality, food authenticity, pesticide residues in food and water. Microbiology. Alternative crops, GMOs. Conservation, environmental protection and environmental effects of pesticides, ecotoxicology. Mammal and bird ecology, invasive species, avian risks to aviation ('birdstrike'), animal health and welfare, zoonoses. Risk assessment, epidemiology, modelling and bioinformatics relevant to the above areas.

Collection: Cowan collection on Bees and Beekeeping – a collection containing works from the 17th century to date.
Original drawings of invertebrate pest species
Photographic images of pest species and plant diseases

Trade and statistical information: Annual Pesticide Usage Survey Reports

Library catalogue: All or part available in-house

Publications: Printed

Publications list: Available online

Access to staff: Contact by letter, by telephone and by e-mail. Appointment necessary.
Hours: Mon to Thu, 0900 to 1700, Fri 0900 to 1630
Special comments: Some charges may be made.

Access to building: Appointment necessary

Constituent part of: Department for Environment, Food and Rural Affairs (DEFRA)

FOOD COMMISSION

94 White Lion Street, London, N1 9PF

Tel: 020 7837 2250
Fax: 020 7837 1141
E-mail: enquiries@foodcomm.org.uk
Website: www.foodcomm.org.uk

Enquiries to: Information Officer

Founded: 1990; formerly called London Food Commission (year of change 1990)

Organisation type and purpose: Registered charity, voluntary organisation (charity number 1000358), consultancy, research organisation.
Consumer watchdog, campaigning for better food.

Subject coverage: Food policy, food labelling, irradiation, claims, nutrition and health, food composition analysis, agriculture and the environment, pesticides, contaminants, food adulteration, baby foods, genetic engineering, advertising.

Collection: Books, magazines and press cuttings

Publications: Printed

Publications list: Available online and in print

Access to staff: Contact by letter, by telephone and by fax. Appointment necessary.
Hours: Mon to Fri, 1030 to 1800

Subsidiary body: Food Additives Campaign Team; Food Commission Research Charity; Food Irradiation Campaign

FOOD STORAGE AND DISTRIBUTION FEDERATION (FSDF)

7 Diddenham Court, Lamb Wood Hill, Grazeley, Reading, Berkshire, RG7 1JQ

Tel: 0118 988 4468
Fax: 0118 988 7035
E-mail: info@fsdf.org.uk
Website: www.fsdf.org.uk

Enquiries to: Chief Executive

Founded: 1911; formerly called Cold Storage and Distribution Federation (CSDF); formerly called National Cold Storage Federation

Organisation type and purpose: Trade association (membership is by subscription).

Subject coverage: All aspects of controlled storage and distribution including operations temperature, health and safety, legislative aspects, fire, construction and related food processing acts.

Publications: Printed

Publications list: Available in print

Access to staff: Contact by letter, by telephone, by fax and by e-mail. Appointment necessary.
Hours: Mon to Fri, 0900 to 1700

Affiliated to: Refrigerated Food Industry Confederation (RFIC)

Associated European and international links: European Cold Storage and Logistics Association (ECSLA)

Associated European and International links: European Consortium for the Responsible Application of Refrigerants; International Association of Cold Store Contractors

FOODSERVICE CONSULTANTS SOCIETY INTERNATIONAL (FCSI)

Bourne House, Horsell Park, Woking, Surrey, GU21 4LY

Tel: 01483 761122
Fax: 01483 751991
E-mail: admin@fcsi.org.uk
Website: www.fcsi.org.uk

Enquiries to: Administrator

Founded: 1970; formerly called Society of Catering and Hotel Management Consultants (year of change 1996)

Organisation type and purpose: International organisation, professional body.

Subject coverage: Market research, design and planning facilities, catering and hotel systems and procedures, recruitment, equipment, human resources, all related to hotel and catering industry.

Access to staff: Contact by letter, by telephone, by fax and by e-mail. Appointment necessary.
Hours: Mon to Fri, 0900 to 1700

Parent body: Foodservices Consultants Society International; Suite 201, 304 West Liberty Street, Louisville, KY 40202 – 3068, USA; tel: +1 502 589 3783; fax: +1 502 589 3602; e-mail: fcsi@fcsi.org

FOOTBALL ASSOCIATION (FA)

25 Soho Square, London, W1D 4FA

Tel: 020 7745 4545
Fax: 020 7745 4546
E-mail: david.fowkes@londonfa.com
Website: www.fa.premier.com

Enquiries to: Chief Executive

Founded: 1863

Organisation type and purpose: Membership association.
To promote the sport of association football.

Subject coverage: Football: coaching, competitions, refereeing and registrations.

Publications: Printed
Order printed publications from: FACA Resources
tel: 0113 279 1395, fax: 0113 231 9606

Publications list: Available in print

Access to staff: Contact by letter, by telephone, by fax and by e-mail. Appointment necessary.
Hours: Mon to Fri, 0900 to 1700

Affiliated to: FIFA; UEFA; world and European governing bodies

Has: 42,000 affiliated clubs

Other address: Football Association; 62 Lancaster Mews, London, W2 3QG

FOOTBALL ASSOCIATION OF WALES (FAW)

11–12 Neptune Court, Vanguard Way, Cardiff, CF24 5PJ

Tel: 029 2043 5830
Fax: 029 2049 6953
E-mail: info@faw.co.uk
Website: www.faw.org.uk

Enquiries to: Secretary General

Founded: 1876

Organisation type and purpose: Governing body for association football in Wales.

Subject coverage: In addition to its administration responsibilities for football in Wales also has responsibility for running the 8 international teams: A, U21, U19, U17, Semi-Professional, Women's, Women's U19 and Women's U17.

Publications: Electronic and video
Order electronic and video publications from: Download from website

Access to staff: Contact by letter, by telephone, by fax and by e-mail

Constituent part of: International Football Association Board (with FIFA, the FA, SFA and IFA)

Member organisation of: FIFA; UEFA

FOOTBALL LICENSING AUTHORITY (FLA)

27 Harcourt House, 19 Cavendish Square, London, W1G 0PL

Tel: 020 7491 7191
Fax: 020 7491 1882
E-mail: info@sgsamail.org.uk
Website: www.flaweb.org.uk

Enquiries to: Office Manager

Founded: 1990

Organisation type and purpose: Statutory body.
Application of Safety of Sports Ground Act 1975 amended and Football Spectators Act 1989.

Subject coverage: Safety of sports grounds and spectators, accommodation including seating, terracing and accommodation for spectators with disabilities.

Publications: Printed, and electronic and video

Access to staff: Contact by letter, by telephone, by fax and by e-mail. Appointment necessary.
Hours: Mon to Fri, 0900 to 1700

Parent body: Department for Culture, Media and Sport (DCMS); Sport and Recreation Division, 2–4 Cockspur Street, London, SW1Y 5DY; tel: 020 7211 6200; e-mail: enquiries@culture.gov.uk; website: www.culture.gov.uk

FORCE

Formal name: FORCE (Friends of the Oncology and Radiotherapy Centre) Cancer Charity

FORCE Cancer Support Centre, Corner House, Barrack Road, Exeter, EX2 5DW

Tel: 01392 406151 (patient suppport)
E-mail: support@forcecancercharity.co.uk
Website: www.forcecancercharity.co.uk

Enquiries to: Information Manager
Direct tel: 01392 406151
Other contacts: Support Information Assistant

Founded: 1987

Organisation type and purpose: Registered charity (charity number 296884).
Cancer charity.
Provides a relaxed and comfortable environment where people can seek information and discuss their needs with experienced staff and also meet other Centre users and talk with trained volunteers.

Subject coverage: Finances improvements in patient care through research, the purchase of advanced equipment and a Cancer Support and Information Centre located in the grounds of the RD&E Hospital.

Information services: Benefits advice service, run in partnership with the Citizens Advice Bureau.

continued overleaf

Collection: Library of leaflets, helpful articles, books to borrow and audio-visual materials, as well as guided internet access

Publications: Electronic and video
Order electronic and video publications from: Download from website

Access to staff: Contact by letter, by telephone, by e-mail, in person and via website
Hours: Benefits advice service appointments: Thu

FORD 400E OWNERS CLUB

1 Maltings Farm Cottages, Witham Road, White Notley, Witham, Essex, CM81 1SE

E-mail: sandy@thames400e.freeserve.co.uk

Enquiries to: Membership Secretary

Founded: 1991

Organisation type and purpose: Membership association (membership is by subscription), present number of members: 120.

Subject coverage: Ford medium commercial vehicle range 1957–1965, 400E models.

Collection: Sales and technical literature

Publications: Printed

Access to staff: Contact by letter and by e-mail. Appointment necessary.
Hours: Telephone: Mon and Fri only, 1900 to 2100.

FORD CORSAIR OWNERS' CLUB (FCOC)

4 Bexley Close, Hailsham, East Sussex, BN27 1NH

Tel: 01323 840655
E-mail: checkleylizandray@yahoo.co.uk
Website: www.fordcorsairownersclub.co.uk

Enquiries to: Membership Secretary
Direct tel: 01245 287519
Direct e-mail: michelestafford155@btinternet.com

Founded: 1985

Organisation type and purpose: Membership association (membership is by subscription), present number of members: 130.

Subject coverage: Technical advice for Ford Corsair cars.

Access to staff: Contact by letter, by telephone, by e-mail and via website
Hours: Mon to Fri, 0900 to 1700; Sat and Sun, 1000 to 2000

FORD EXECUTIVE OWNERS REGISTER

3 Shanklin Road, Stonehouse Estate, Coventry, Warwickshire, CV3 4EE

Tel: 024 7651 1822

Enquiries to: Information Officer

Founded: 1985

Organisation type and purpose: Membership association (membership is by subscription).
Classic car club.

Subject coverage: Ford Cortina 1600E, Ford Cortina 2000E, Ford Corsair 2000E, Ford Capri 3000E, Ford Escort 1300E, Ford Zodiac Executive.

Publications: Printed

Publications list: Available in print

Access to staff: Contact by letter and by telephone
Hours: Mon to Fri, 0900 to 1700

FORD MADOX FORD SOCIETY

Department of English, The Open University, Walton Hall, Milton Keynes, Buckinghamshire, MK7 6AA

Tel: 01908 653453
Fax: 01908 653750
E-mail: s.j.haslam@open.ac.uk
Website: www.open.ac.uk/Arts/fordmadoxford-society

Enquiries to: Chair
Direct e-mail: p.skinner370@btinternet.com (Treasurer)

Founded: 1996

Organisation type and purpose: International organisation, learned society, present number of members: c. 140, voluntary organisation, registered charity.
Provides information on and generates research into Ford Madox Ford. Co-ordinates conferences and publications.

Subject coverage: Ford Madox Ford, modernism, research/conferences.

Publications: Printed

Publications list: Available online

Access to staff: Contact by letter, by telephone, by fax, by e-mail and via website
Hours: Any reasonable time

Access to building: No access other than to staff

Links with: Joseph Conrad Society

FORD MK II INDEPENDENT OC INTERNATIONAL

173 Sparrow Farm Drive, Feltham, Middlesex, TW14 0DG

Tel: 020 8384 3559
Fax: 020 8890 3741
E-mail: brian.enticknap@mypostoffice.co.uk

Enquiries to: President

Founded: 1988

Organisation type and purpose: Membership association, present number of members: 500.
Motor vehicle authenticator for RAC and MSA.

Subject coverage: All aspects, and information on the Ford MKII Consul, Zephyr, Zodiac; technical advice, modification; classic car meetings and rallies, national and international.

Collection: Original parts books
Workshop manuals

Publications: Printed

Access to staff: Contact by letter, by telephone and by fax
Hours: Mon to Fri, 0900 to 2100

Officially recognised by: DVLA; Swansea; Ford Motor Company

FORD MODEL 'T' REGISTER OF GB

195 Bradford Road, Riddlesden, Keighley, West Yorkshire, BD20 5JR

Tel: 01535 607978
E-mail: jma195@aol.com
Website: www.t-ford.co.uk

Enquiries to: Secretary

Founded: 1960

Organisation type and purpose: Advisory body, membership association, voluntary organisation.

Subject coverage: Register of Model T Ford vehicles, help with such and supply of parts; magazine; events held throughout the year.

Publications: Printed
Order printed publications from: The Secretary

Publications list: Available in print

Access to staff: Contact by letter, by telephone, by e-mail and via website
Hours: Mon to Fri, 1730 to 2100

FORD MOTOR COMPANY LIMITED

Eagle Way, Brentwood, Essex, CM13 3BW

Tel: 01277 253000

Enquiries to: Secretary

Founded: 1928

Organisation type and purpose: Manufacturing industry.
The principal activity in which the Company is engaged is the manufacture and sale of motor vehicles and components.

Subject coverage: Motor vehicle manufacture; industrial engines; parts and accessories.

Access to staff: Contact by letter
Hours: Mon to Fri, 0900 to 1700

FORECAST INTERNATIONAL/DMS INC

Templehurst House, 48 New Street, Chipping Norton, Oxfordshire, OX7 5LJ

Tel: 01608 643281
Fax: 01608 641159
E-mail: hawk@hawk.co.uk
Website: www.hawk.co.uk

Enquiries to: Managing Director

Founded: 1975

Organisation type and purpose: Research organisation, publishing house.

Subject coverage: Aircraft maintenance, budget, funding, commercial aircraft, commercial inventories, contractors, electronics, avionics, emerging technologies, gas turbines, military aircraft, military inventories, military vehicles, missiles, ordnance, munitions, power systems, space systems and satellites, component and niche market analysis.

Collection: Library containing hardcopy and CD-ROM formats for market intelligence for aerospace, defence, electronics, power systems and transportation industries

Trade and statistical information: Production forecasts and analysis for aerospace, weapons systems, power systems, naval systems, electronic systems, US defence budget including inventories and product life cycle analysis

Publications: Electronic and video

Publications list: Available in print

Access to staff: Contact by telephone, by fax, by e-mail and via website
Hours: Mon to Fri, 0900 to 1700

Head office: Forecast International/DMS; 22 Commerce Road, Newtown, Connecticut, 06470, USA

FOREIGN AND COMMONWEALTH OFFICE (FCO)

Downing Street, London, SW1A 2AL

Tel: 020 7270 3925
Fax: 020 7270 3270
E-mail: library.historical@fco.gov.uk

Enquiries to: Librarian
Other contacts: Head of Library Enquiry Services; e-mail library.current@fco.gov.uk for current affairs

History of institution: formerly called Colonial Office (CO), Commonwealth Relations Office (CRO); formerly called Foreign Office (FO) (year of change 1968)

Organisation type and purpose: National government body.

Subject coverage: International relations, international law, diplomacy and politics, history, administration, economics and laws of overseas countries.

Collection: Historic collections of books of the former colonial and foreign offices
Photographic collection mainly of Commonwealth countries and former UK colonies
Portraits of diplomats and colonial governors, places and events c. 1850 to current

Non-library collection catalogue: All or part available in-house

Access to staff: Contact by letter, by telephone and by e-mail. Appointment necessary.
Hours: Mon to Fri, 0900 to 1700

Access to building: Prior appointment required

Access for disabled people: Ramped entry, toilet facilities

FOREIGN AND COMMONWEALTH OFFICE – TRAVEL ADVICE UNIT (TAU)

Consular Directorate, Old Admiralty Building, Whitehall, London, SW1A 2PA

Tel: 0845 850 2829
Fax: 020 7008 0155
Website: www.fco.gov.uk

Enquiries to: Travel Advice Clerk

Organisation type and purpose: National government body, advisory body.

Subject coverage: Up-to-date travel advice on threats to personal safety, arising from political unrest, lawlessness, violence, natural disasters, epidemics, anti-British demonstrations and aircraft safety, is given to help British travellers avoid trouble when overseas.

Publications: Printed

Access to staff: Contact by letter, by telephone, by fax and by e-mail. Appointment necessary.
Hours: Mon to Fri, 0930 to 1600

FOREIGN AND COMMONWEALTH OFFICE (FCO) – KNOWLEDGE AND LEARNING CENTRE

Room G6, Building 17, Hanslope Park, Hanslope, Milton Keynes, Buckinghamshire, MK19 7BH

Tel: 01908 515960
Fax: 01908 515943
Website: www.fco.gov.uk

Enquiries to: Librarian
Other contacts: Librarian (London address) for non-central-government enquiries to FCO's main library in first instance.

Organisation type and purpose: National government body.
Support and IT services for the FCO at home and abroad.

Subject coverage: Hanslope Park Knowledge and Learning Centre is an information unit and open learning centre primarily serving FCO staff based on site. Stock is available for loan to other central government departments and agencies. Other enquirers are requested to contact the main FCO library in London, in the first instance, or consult the FCO's website, www.fco.gov.uk, for advice on foreign travel.

Non-library collection catalogue: All or part available in-house

Order printed publications from: Stationery Office Ltd (formerly HMSO)

Access to staff: Contact by letter, by telephone and by fax. Appointment necessary.
Hours: Mon to Fri, 0830 to 1630

Access to building: Prior appointment required

Other address: Foreign and Commonwealth Office (FCO); Library, Room E213, King Charles Street, London, SW1A 2AH; tel: 020 7270 3925; fax: 020 7270 3270/3682

FOREIGN PRESS ASSOCIATION IN LONDON (FPA)

25 Northumberland Avenue, London, WC2N 5AP

Tel: 020 7930 0445
E-mail: briefings@foreign-press.org.uk
Website: www.foreign-press.org.uk

Enquiries to: Director
Direct e-mail: christopherwyld@foreign-press.org.uk

Founded: 1888

Organisation type and purpose: International organisation, professional body (membership is by annual subscription), present number of members: 450.
Professional body/club for foreign journalists based in the UK.

Subject coverage: Foreign media in the UK.

Publications: Printed

Access to staff: Contact by telephone and by e-mail
Hours: Mon to Fri, 0900 to 1800

Links with: Commonwealth Club; 25 Northumberland Avenue; tel: 02077669200; e-mail: events@thercs.org; website: http://www.thercs.org

FORENSIC SCIENCE SOCIETY (FSSoc)

Clarke House, 18A Mount Parade, Harrogate, North Yorkshire, HG1 1BX

Tel: 01423 506068
Fax: 01423 566391
E-mail: president@forensic-science-society.org.uk
Website: www.forensic-science-society.org.uk

Enquiries to: Secretary

Founded: 1959

Organisation type and purpose: Learned society (membership is by subscription), present number of members: 2,300, registered charity (charity number 205992), publishing house.
To advance the study, application and standing of forensic science and to facilitate co-operation among persons interested in forensic science throughout the world.

Subject coverage: Forensic sciences, pathology and medicine, forensic chemistry and biology, forensic serology, forensic science in connection with textiles, tyres, metallurgy, photographs and marks; forensic identification, handwriting and documents examination, explosion investigation, firearms and ballistics, aspects of alcohol.

Publications: Printed

Access to staff: Contact via website
Hours: Mon to Fri, 0900 to 1700

FORESIGHT

28 The Paddock, Godalming, Surrey, GU7 1XD

Tel: 01483 427839
Fax: 01483 427668
Website: www.foresight-preconception.org.uk

Enquiries to: Chairman

Founded: 1978; formerly called Foresight, The Association for the Promotion of Preconceptual Care

Organisation type and purpose: Registered charity (charity number 279160).

Subject coverage: Preparing couples for pregnancy.

Library catalogue: All or part available in print

continued overleaf

Publications: Printed
Order printed publications from: Resource Centre, Foresight
Mead House, Littlemead Estate, Alfold Road, Cranleigh, Surrey, GU6 8ND, tel: 01483 548071

Publications list: Available in print

Access to staff: Contact by letter, by telephone, by fax and in person. Appointment necessary.
Hours: Mon to Fri, 0900 to 1700
Special comments: Organisation works almost always by letter/telephone etc.

Access to building: Prior appointment required

Access for disabled people: Parking provided, ramped entry

FOREST

Formal name: Freedom Organisation for the Right to Enjoy Smoking Tobacco

Sheraton House, Castle Park, Cambridge, CB3 0AX

Tel: 01223 370156
E-mail: contact@forestonline.org
Website: www.forestonline.org

Enquiries to: Media Enquiries
Direct tel: 07774 781840

Founded: 1979

Organisation type and purpose: National organisation, membership association (membership is by subscription), voluntary organisation.
To promote equal rights for smokers of tobacco, and those who wish to accommodate them.

Subject coverage: Smoking, a sensible smoking policy and different aspects of the smoking debate.

Publications: Printed

Publications list: Available online and in print

Access to staff: Contact by letter, by telephone, by fax, by e-mail and via website. Appointment necessary.
Hours: Mon to Fri, 0930 to 1730

Access to building: No prior appointment required

FOREST HEATH DISTRICT COUNCIL

College Heath Road, Mildenhall, Suffolk, IP28 7EY

Tel: 01638 719000
Fax: 01638 716493
E-mail: info@forest-heath.gov.uk
Website: www.forest-heath.gov.uk

Enquiries to: Public Relations Manager

Organisation type and purpose: Local government body.

Access to staff: Contact by letter, by telephone, by fax, by e-mail, in person and via website
Hours: Mon to Fri, 0900 to 1700

Access for disabled people: Parking provided, level entry, toilet facilities

FOREST OF DEAN RAILWAY LIMITED (DFR)

Formal name: T/A Dean Forest Railway Company Limited

Forest Road, Lydney, GL15 4ET

Tel: 01594 843423 (information line, recorded times & dates of services)
E-mail: infodfr@btconnect.com
Website: www.dfr.co.uk

Enquiries to: Commercial Director
Direct tel: 01594 845840
Direct e-mail: membership@dfr.co.uk
Other contacts: DFR Society – Membership Applications

Founded: 1970; formerly called Dean Forest Railway Preservation Society

Organisation type and purpose: Operators of the Dean Forest Railway Co. Ltd and Dean Forest Railfreight Ltd.

Subject coverage: Dean Forest Railway is a predominantly steam-powered standard gauge tourist heritage railway operating between Parkend and Lydney Junction. It is adjacent, and connected, to Railtrack. The railway is the sole surviving remnant of the Severn and Wye Railway. The headquarters at Norchard are on the site of the former West Gloucestershire Power Station and Norchard Colliery. Railway artefacts plus a working telephone system.

Publications: Printed, and electronic and video
Order printed publications from: Dean Forest Railway Co. Ltd at the above address
Order electronic and video publications from: Dean Forest Railway Co. Ltd at the above address

Access to staff: Contact by letter. Appointment necessary.
Hours: 1100 to 1600; longer opening hours when trains are running

Access to building: No prior appointment required
Hours: Museum and gift shop: daily, except Christmas Day and Boxing Day, 1100 to 1600
Special comments: Longer opening hours when trains are running.

Access for disabled people: Parking provided, ramped entry, toilet facilities
Hours: As above
Special comments: Access to shop, station, etc. only at Norchard.

FORESTRY AND TIMBER ASSOCIATION (FTA)

Formal name: Association of Timber Growers and Forestry Professionals Ltd

5 Dublin Street Lane South, Edinburgh, EH1 3PX

Tel: 0131 538 7111
Fax: 0131 538 7222
E-mail: stuart.goodall@confor.org.uk

Enquiries to: Chief Executive

Founded: 1957; formed from Ulster Timber Growers Organisation (UTGA) (year of change 2001); formed from Association of Professional Foresters (APF), Timber Growers Association (TGA) (year of change 2002)

Organisation type and purpose: Membership association (membership is by subscription), present number of members: 2,500.

Access to staff: Contact by letter, by telephone and by e-mail

FORESTRY COMMISSION

Silvan House, 231 Corstorphine Road, Edinburgh, EH12 7AT

Tel: 0131 334 0303
Fax: 0131 334 3047
E-mail: enquiries@forestry.gsi.gov.uk
Website: www.forestry.gov.uk

Enquiries to: Information Officer

Founded: 1919

Organisation type and purpose: National government body.

Subject coverage: Forestry.

Publications list: Available online and in print

Access to staff: Contact by letter, by telephone, by fax, by e-mail and in person. Appointment necessary.
Hours: Mon to Fri, 0900 to 1700

Access for disabled people: Parking provided, ramped entry, access to all public areas, toilet facilities

Also at: Forestry Commission England; England National Office, 620 Bristol Business Park, Coldharbour Lane, Bristol, BS16 1EJ; tel: 0117 906 6000; fax: 0117 931 2859; Forestry Commission Scotland; Silvan House, 231 Corstorphine Road, Edinburgh, EH12 7AT; tel: 0131 334 0303; fax: 0131 334 3047; Forestry Commission Wales; Welsh Assembly Government, Rhodfa Padarn, Llanbadarn Fawr, Aberystwyth, Ceredigion, SY23 3UR; tel: 0300 068 0300; fax: 0300 068 0301

FORESTRY COMMISSION LIBRARY, RESEARCH INFORMATION SERVICE

Forest Research, Alice Holt Lodge, Wrecclesham, Farnham, Surrey, GU10 4LH

Tel: 01420 22255
Fax: 01420 23653
E-mail: library@forestry.gsi.gov.uk
Website: www.forestry.gov.uk

Enquiries to: Librarian
Direct tel: 01420 526260
Direct e-mail: research.info@forestry.gsi.gov.uk

Founded: 1919

Organisation type and purpose: National government body, research organisation.

Subject coverage: Forestry in temperate regions; arboriculture (information provided by the independent Arboricultural Advisory and Information Service).

Trade and statistical information: http://www.forestry.gov.uk/statistics

Non-library collection catalogue: All or part available in-house

Library catalogue: All or part available in-house

Publications: Printed
Order printed publications from: Forestry Commission Publications, PO Box 785, Stockport SK3 3AT; tel: 0161 495 4845; Fax: 0161 495 4840; e-mail: forestry@apsgroup.co.uk

Publications list: Available online

Access to staff: Contact by letter, by telephone, by fax, by e-mail and via website. Appointment necessary. All charged.
Hours: Mon to Thu, 0900 to 1700; Fri, 0900 to 1630

Access to building: As Library
Hours: Mon to Thu, 0900 to 1700; Fri, 0900 to 1630

Access for disabled people: Level entry, toilet facilities

Also at: Forestry Commission; 231 Corstorphine Road, Edinburgh, EH12 7AT; tel: 0131 334 0303; fax: 0131 334 3047; e-mail: enquiries@forestry.gsi.gov.uk; website: http://www.forestry.gov.uk
Forestry Commission; tel: 0845 FORESTS (0845 367 3787); Tree Helpline (Arboriculture Advisory and Information Service); tel: 09065 161147 (£1.50 per minute)

FORESTRY CONTRACTING ASSOCIATION (FCA)

Dalfling, Blairdaff, Inverurie, Aberdeenshire, AB51 5LA

Tel: 01467 651368
Fax: 01467 651595
E-mail: members@fcauk.com
Website: www.fcauk.com

Enquiries to: Executive Director
Direct e-mail: gordon@fcauk.com
Other contacts: Membership Services

Founded: 1992

Organisation type and purpose: Trade association.

Subject coverage: All forestry matters; training, running a business, insurance, finance, health and safety and other legislation, wood fuel and biomass.

Publications: Printed, and electronic and video

Access to staff: Contact by letter, by telephone, by fax, by e-mail and via website. Appointment necessary.
Hours: Mon to Fri, 0900 to 1700

FORGOTTEN RACING CLUB (FRC)

Hillside, Holt Road, Hackney, Matlock, Derbyshire, DE4 2QD

Tel: 01629 733898

Enquiries to: Membership Secretary

Founded: 1986; formerly called Forgotten Era Racing Club

Organisation type and purpose: Membership association.

Subject coverage: Racing motorcycles predominantly from the period 1963 to 1986, their restoration and use.

Publications: Printed

Access to staff: Contact by letter and by telephone
Hours: Evenings and weekends

FORK LIFT TRUCK ASSOCIATION

Manor Farm Buildings, Lasham, Alton, Hampshire, GU34 5SL

Tel: 01256 381441
Fax: 01256 381735
E-mail: mail@fork-truck.org.uk

Enquiries to: Chief Executive

Founded: 1992; formerly called Fork Truck Hire Association; formerly called Fork Truck Association

Organisation type and purpose: Trade association.

Subject coverage: Fork lift trucks.

Non-library collection catalogue: All or part available online

Publications list: Available online and in print

Access to staff: Contact by letter, by telephone, by fax and via website. Appointment necessary.
Hours: Mon to Fri, 0900 to 1700

FORTRESS STUDY GROUP (FSG)

6 Lanark Place, London, W9 1BS

Tel: 0020 7286 5512
Website: www.fsgfort.com

Enquiries to: Honorary Secretary

Founded: 1975

Organisation type and purpose: Learned society (membership is by subscription), registered charity (charity number 288790).
To advance the education of the public in the study of all aspects of fortifications and their armaments, especially works constructed to mount or resist artillery.

Subject coverage: Fortification since the introduction of artillery.

Publications: Printed

Access to staff: Contact by letter, by telephone and by e-mail
Hours: Evenings

Affiliated to: International Fortress Council

FORUM FOR THE BUILT ENVIRONMENT (FBE)

35 Hayworth Road, Sandiacre, Nottingham, NG10 5LL

Tel: 0115 949 0641
Fax: 0115 949 1664
Website: www.fbe-org.co.uk

Enquiries to: Chief Executive
Direct e-mail: phil.laycock@fbe-org.co.uk

Founded: 1946

Organisation type and purpose: Learned society.
Multi-professional society for all engaged in construction.
Construction networking.

Subject coverage: There are 154 technical advice panels covering a very wide range of building and civil engineering, and related subjects, including acoustics, asphalt technology, bridge construction, building construction and maintenance, ceramics, contract law and procedure, demolition, district and group heating, drainage, gas engineering and technology, geodetic engineering, lift installation, materials handling, testing and purchasing, piling, quarrying, sewerage technology, timber technology.

Publications: Printed

Access to staff: Contact by letter, by telephone, by fax and by e-mail. Appointment necessary.
Hours: Mon to Fri, 0900 to 1730

Has: 19 regional UK branches and overseas representation

FORUM OF PRIVATE BUSINESS (The Forum)

Ruskin Chambers, Drury Lane, Knutsford, Cheshire, WA16 6HA

Tel: 01565 634467
Fax: 0870 241 9570
E-mail: info@fpb.org
Website: www.fpb.org

Enquiries to: Research Projects Manager
Other contacts: Media and PR Manager

Founded: 1977

Organisation type and purpose: Business support organisation (SMEs), research organisation.
Parliamentary representative body for SMEs.

Subject coverage: Structure and needs of UK small businesses, concerns and priorities of SME problems, financial, administrative and legal; research on specific issues, bank/SME relationships, late payment, legal identities, crime, ISO and others.

Collection: Reports, consultation responses and research on SME-related topics

Trade and statistical information: Quarterly report on current SME issues and longitudinal survey research on specific concerns, detailed academic reports on specialised areas (banking, etc.)

Publications: Printed, and electronic and video

Access to staff: Contact by letter, by telephone, by fax and by e-mail. Appointment necessary.
Hours: Mon to Fri, 0900 to 1730

Access to building: Appointment required

FOSTERING NETWORK (tFN)

87 Blackfriars Road, London, SE1 8HA

Tel: 020 7620 6400; Infoline: 020 7261 1884
Fax: 020 7620 6401
E-mail: info@fostering.net
Website: www.fostering.net

Enquiries to: Information Officer

Founded: 1974; formerly called National Foster Care Association (NFCA) (year of change 2001)

Organisation type and purpose: Membership association (membership is by subscription), voluntary organisation,

continued overleaf

registered charity (charity number 280852), training organisation, consultancy, research organisation, publishing house.
To improve the quality of life for all children in foster care.

Subject coverage: Foster care, including allowances for foster carers, dealing with difficult behaviour, dealing with allegations of abuse, after-care needs of young people, needs of foster children with disabilities, needs of teenagers in foster care.

Information services: E-mail and telephone information service – deals with general fostering enquiries.

Collection: Foster Care Resource Centre

Trade and statistical information: One of the largest collections of resources relating to foster care in the UK.

Library catalogue: All or part available online

Publications: Printed, and electronic and video
Order printed publications from: website: http://www.fosteringresources.co.uk

Publications list: Available online and in print

Access to staff: Contact by letter, by telephone, by fax, by e-mail, in person and via website. Appointment necessary.
Hours: Infoline: Mon to Fri, 1000 to 1600
Special comments: Appointments to use the Foster Care Resource Centre are necessary to ensure library and information staff are available.

Access to building: By appointment with the Information Officer
Hours: Office: Mon to Thu, 0900 to 1700; Fri, 0900 to 1630

Constituent bodies: The Fostering Network Northern Ireland; Unit 10, 40 Montgomery Road, Belfast, BT6 9HL; tel: 028 9070 5056; fax: 028 9079 9215; e-mail: ni@fostering.net; The Fostering Network Scotland; Ingram House, 2nd Floor, 227 Ingram Street, Glasgow, G1 1DA; tel: 0141 204 1400; fax: 0141 204 6588; e-mail: scotland@fostering .net; The Fostering Network Wales; 1 Caspian Point, Pierhead Street, Cardiff Bay, CF10 4DQ; tel: 029 2044 0940; fax: 029 2044 0941; e-mail: wales@fostering.net

Member organisations: Almost all local authorities in the UK

FOUNDATION FOR ASSISTIVE TECHNOLOGY (FAST)

12 City Forum, 250 City Road, London, EC1V 8AF

Tel: 020 7253 3303
Fax: 020 7253 5990
E-mail: info@fastuk.org
Website: www.fastuk.org

Enquiries to: Administrator
Direct e-mail: pat@fastuk.org

History of institution: some services taken over from Disability Information Trust (DIT) (year of change 2001)

Organisation type and purpose: National organisation, registered charity (charity number 1061636).
The Foundation for Assistive Technology (FAST) is an independent networking organisation funded by the Department of Health. We will:
- enable you to contact other people active in the Assistive Technology research and development community via our database which contains information on over 1,500 organisations and individuals.
- keep you up to date and act as a signpost to useful and related information about research and development activity in assistive technology.

Subject coverage: Assistive technology.

Publications: Printed

Access to staff: Contact by e-mail and via website
Hours: Mon to Fri, 0900 to 1700
Special comments: Online service.

FOUNDATION FOR CREDIT COUNSELLING (CCCS)

Formal name: Consumer Credit Counselling Service

2 Ridgmount Street, London, WC1E 7AA

Tel: 020 7636 5214
Fax: 020 7580 0016
E-mail: mhurlston@hurlstons.com

Enquiries to: Chairman
Other contacts: (1) Public Relations Officer; (2) Chief Executive Operations for (1) political, media; (2) technical.

Founded: 1993; also CCCS Scotland

Organisation type and purpose: Registered charity.

Subject coverage: Consumer debt.

Trade and statistical information: Data on levels of enquiries and debts

Publications: Printed

Access to staff: Contact by e-mail
Hours: Mon to Fri, 0900 to 1700

Access to building: No access other than to staff

Other addresses: Customer Access; Merrion Centre, Leeds; tel: 0800 138 1111; 0800 138 DEBT; Foundation for Credit Counselling; Merrion Centre, Leeds; tel: 0800 138 1111; 0800 138 DEBT

FOUNDATION FOR EDUCATION AND RESEARCH IN CHILD BEARING

27 Walpole Street, London, SW3 4QS

Tel: 020 7730 2800
Fax: 020 7730 0710

Enquiries to: Information Officer

Founded: 1972

Organisation type and purpose: Registered charity (charity number 262318).

Subject coverage: Prevention of handicaps of perinatal origin.

Publications: Printed

Access to staff: Contact by letter, by telephone and by fax. Appointment necessary.
Hours: Mon to Fri, 0900 to 1700

FOUNDATION FOR PROFESSIONALS IN SERVICES FOR ADOLESCENTS (FPSA)

Holtwood, Red Lion Street, Cropredy, Banbury, Oxon, OX171PD

Tel: 01295750182
E-mail: secretariat@foundationpsa.org.uk
Website: www.foundationpsa.org.uk

Enquiries to: Administrator

Founded: 1970

Organisation type and purpose: Grant giving foundation

Subject coverage: Subjects related to disturbed adolescents.

Publications: Printed

Access to staff: Contact by letter, by telephone, by e-mail and via website
Hours: Mon to Fri, 0900 to 1700

FOUNDATION FOR THE STUDY OF INFANT DEATHS (FSID)

11 Belgrave Road, London, SW1V 1RB

Tel: 020 7802 3200
E-mail: office@fsid.org.uk
Website: www.fsid.org.uk

Enquiries to: Communications Officer

Founded: 1971

Organisation type and purpose: Voluntary organisation, registered charity (charity number 262191), research organisation. Library holding SIDS articles and related topics.
To raise funds for research, to support families whose baby has died suddenly and unexpectedly, to disseminate information about cot death and infant health to health professionals and the general public.

Subject coverage: Research into cot death and sudden infant death, information for bereaved families and for professionals who may have to deal with this, general information on infant health and care. The scope of FSID is all infant deaths, not just cot death.

Information services: Helpline, tel 020 7233 2090, e-mail helpline@fsid.org.uk.

Publications: Printed, and electronic and video

Publications list: Available in print

Access to staff: Contact by letter, by telephone, by fax, by e-mail and via website. Appointment necessary.
Hours: Mon to Fri, 0900 to 1700

FOUNDATION FOR WOMEN'S HEALTH RESEARCH AND DEVELOPMENT (FORWARD)

Suite 2.1, Chandelier Building, 2nd Floor, 8 Scrubs Lane, London, NW10 6RB

Tel: 020 8960 4000
Fax: 020 8960 4014
E-mail: forward@forwarduk.org.uk
Website: www.forwarduk.org.uk

Enquiries to: Administrator

Founded: 1985

Organisation type and purpose: International organisation, voluntary organisation, registered charity (charity number 292403), suitable for ages: all, consultancy, research organisation.
Leading voluntary organisation in the UK campaigning against female genital mutilation (FGM). Provision of training and education to women affected by FGM, and for health, social work, education and child protection professionals.

Subject coverage: Minority health issues with focus on African women and children's reproductive and sexual health. FGM in the UK and Africa.

Publications: Printed

Publications list: Available in print

Access to staff: Contact by letter, by telephone, by fax and by e-mail
Hours: Mon to Fri, 0900 to 1700

FOUNDRY EQUIPMENT AND SUPPLIERS ASSOCIATION (FESA)

Queensway House, 2 Queensway, Redhill, Surrey, RH1 1QS

Tel: 01737 768611
Fax: 01737 855469
Website: www.fesa.org.uk

Enquiries to: Secretary
Direct tel: 01737 855280
Direct e-mail: marywhite@uk.dmgworldmedia.com

Founded: 1925

Organisation type and purpose: Trade association (membership is by subscription), present number of members: 34.

Access to staff: Contact by letter
Hours: Mon to Fri, 0800 to 1300

Access to building: No access other than to staff

FOUNTAIN SOCIETY, THE

26 Binney Street, London, W1K 5BL

Tel: 020 7355 2002 answerphone
Fax: 020 7355 2002
Website: www.fountainsoc.org.uk

Enquiries to: Chairman
Direct tel: 01306 883874
Direct fax: 01306 883874
Direct e-mail: knowlsonpm@cix.co.uk
Other contacts: Projects Officer

Founded: 1986

Organisation type and purpose: International organisation, membership association (membership is by subscription), present number of members: 320, voluntary organisation, registered charity (charity number 292778).

Subject coverage: Conservation and restoration of fountains of aesthetic merit for public enjoyment, promotion of the provision of fountains in new developments and the restoration of cascades and waterfalls.

Collection: Bibliography available to members

Publications: Printed

Access to staff: Contact by letter, by telephone, by fax, by e-mail and via website
Hours: Mon to Fri, 0900 to 1700

FPA

Formal name: Family Planning Association

50 Featherstone Street, London, EC1Y 8QU

Tel: 020 7608 5240
Fax: 0845 123 2349
E-mail: library.information@fpa.org.uk
Website: www.fpa.org.uk

Direct tel: 020 7923 5228

Founded: 1930

Organisation type and purpose: Membership association (membership is by subscription), voluntary organisation, registered charity (charity number 250187).
To advance the sexual health and reproductive rights and choices of all people throughout the United Kingdom.

Subject coverage: Family planning, contraception, sexual health, fertility control, unplanned pregnancy, sexually transmitted infections, sex education.

Collection: Archives of the Family Planning Association, 1920–1977 (held at the Wellcome Institute for the History of Medicine, Contemporary Medical Archives Centre, London)

Library catalogue: All or part available in-house

Publications: Printed, and electronic and video
Order printed publications from: fpa Direct
50 Featherstone Street, London, EC1Y 8QU

Publications list: Available in print

Access to staff: Contact by letter, by telephone, by fax and by e-mail. Appointment necessary.
Hours: Mon to Fri, 0900 to 1700

Access to building: Prior appointment required

Access for disabled people: Level entry, toilet facilities

Other offices: fpa Cymru; Greenhouse, Trevelyan Terrace, Bangor, Gwynedd, LL57 1AX; tel: 01248 353534; fax: 01248 371138; fpa Cymru; Suite D1, Canton House, 435–451 Cowbridge Road East, Cardiff, CF5 1JH; tel: 029 2064 4034; fax: 029 2064 4306; fpa Northern Ireland; 2nd Floor, Northern Counties Building, Custom House Street, Derry, BT48 6AE; tel: 028 7126 0016; fax: 028 7136 1254; fpa Northern Ireland; 113 University Street, Belfast, BT7 1HP; tel: 028 9032 5488; fax: 028 9031 2212; fpa Scotland; Unit 10, Firhill Business Centre, 76 Firhill Road, Glasgow, G20 7BA; tel: 0141 576 5088; fax: 0141 576 5006

FRAGILE X SOCIETY

Rood End House, 6 Stortford Road, Great Dunmow, Essex, CM6 1DA

Tel: 01371 875100
E-mail: info@fragilex.org.uk
Website: www.fragilex.org.uk

Enquiries to: National Contact
Direct tel: 01371 875100

Founded: 1990

Organisation type and purpose: Registered charity (charity number 1127861).
To provide support, information and advice to families whose children and adult relatives have fragile X syndrome; offers national support and information, telephone helplines on education statementing, benefits and epilepsy, family support workers, family conferences and reports, access to latest research, free UK family membership of the society, free attendance at society conferences. Fragile X shows itself in a wide range of difficulties with learning and development delay, as well as social, language, attentional, emotional and behavioural problems.

Subject coverage: Fragile X is the second most common cause of inherited learning disabilities.

Publications: Printed, and electronic and video

Publications list: Available online and in print

Access to staff: Contact by letter, by telephone, by e-mail and via website
Hours: Mon to Fri, 0900 to 1700

FRAME

Formal name: Fund for the Replacement of Animals in Medical Experiments

Russell & Burch House, 96–98 North Sherwood Street, Nottingham, NG1 4EE

Tel: 0115 958 4740
Fax: 0115 950 3570
E-mail: frame@frame.org.uk
Website: www.frame.org.uk

Enquiries to: Communications Officer
Direct e-mail: info@frame.org.uk; science@frame.org.uk

Founded: 1969

Organisation type and purpose: Registered as a national charity (charity number 259464).
FRAME's ultimate aim is the elimination of the need to use laboratory animals in any kind of medical or scientific procedure. FRAME believes that the current scale of animal experimentation is unacceptable, but recognises that an immediate abolition of all laboratory animal use is not possible. It works towards the development, validation and acceptance of replacement alternative methods. Until this goal is reached, FRAME promotes ways to reduce the numbers of animals used, through better experimental design and data analysis, and refining procedures, so that the suffering of any animals necessarily used is minimised. Supports a research laboratory at the University of Nottingham.

Subject coverage: The Three Rs approach to this problem: Replacement, Reduction and Refinement.

Information services: Online information of relevance to laboratory technicians, statisticians and scientists who are actively engaged in animal experimentation or developing alternatives to using animals in medical experiments.

continued overleaf

Education services: FRAME scientists give talks to school students or to other groups interested in the use of animals in science (limited to the Nottinghamshire area). Some publications are available.

Publications: Electronic and video
Order electronic and video publications from: Download from website

Publications list: Available online

Access to staff: Contact by letter, by telephone, by fax and by e-mail

FRANCIS BACON RESEARCH TRUST (FBRT)

Old Rick Barn, Mill Lane, Shenington, Oxfordshire, OX15 6NB

Tel: 01295 678623
E-mail: secretary@fbrt.org.uk
Website: www.fbrt.org.uk

Enquiries to: Secretary
Direct e-mail: sarah@fbrt.org.uk

Founded: 1980

Organisation type and purpose: International organisation, membership association (membership is by subscription), training organisation, consultancy, research organisation.
Educational charity.

Subject coverage: Study of the life and works of Sir Francis Bacon and of all those associated with him, and to make known and further the Great Instauration... a worldwide scheme intended to create understanding between peoples through which illumined peace may be acquired; ancient wisdom and traditions, the wisdom of Shakespeare.

Publications: Printed

Publications list: Available in print

Access to staff: Contact by letter, by telephone, by e-mail and via website. Appointment necessary. Non-members charged.
Hours: Mon to Fri, 1000 to 1700

FRANCIS BRETT YOUNG SOCIETY (FBY Society)

92 Gower Road, Halesowen, West Midlands, B62 9BT

Tel: 0121 422 8969
Website: www.fbysociety.co.uk

Enquiries to: Chairman
Direct e-mail: michael.hall10@gmail.com

Founded: 1978

Organisation type and purpose: Learned society (membership is by subscription), present number of members: 210, registered charity (charity number 1075904).
Literary society.
To provide opportunities for members to meet, correspond, and to share the enjoyment of the author's works.

Subject coverage: Life and literary works of Francis Brett Young.

Publications: Printed

FRANCIS-BARNETT OWNERS CLUB (FBOC)

307 Lower Hillmorton Road, Rugby, Warwickshire, CV21 4AD

Tel: 01788 544909
E-mail: mrs.eileen.lloyd@virgin.net
Website: www.francis-barnett.freeserve.co.uk

Enquiries to: Secretary

Founded: 1986

Organisation type and purpose: Company limited by guarantee, registered in England and Wales, no. 4750767 (membership is by subscription), present number of members: 550.
To encourage ownership, use and preservation of Francis-Barnett motorcycles.

Subject coverage: All models of Francis Barnett motorcycles produced by that company in Coventry from 1919 until the demise of AMC (AJS, Matchless, Norton) in the late 1960s.

Collection: A library of model information manuals and spares lists for most models.

Non-library collection catalogue: All or part available in print

Library catalogue: All or part available in print

Publications: Printed

Access to staff: Contact by letter
Hours: Mon to Fri, 0900 to 1700
Special comments: There are no full-time staff.

Registered office: at the same address

FRANCO-BRITISH COUNCIL

16–18 Strutton Ground, London, SW1P 2HP

Tel: 020 7976 8380
Fax: 020 7976 8181
E-mail: fbc@cix.co.uk
Website: www.francobritishcouncil.org.uk

Enquiries to: Secretary General

Founded: 1972

Organisation type and purpose: International organisation, membership association (membership is by election or invitation), registered charity.
Promoting Franco-British relations.

Publications: Printed

Publications list: Available online and in print

Access to staff: Contact by letter, by telephone, by fax and by e-mail
Hours: Tue to Thu, 0930 to 1730

FREE CHURCHES' GROUP (FCG)

Churches Together in England, 27 Tavistock Square, London, WC1H 9HH

Tel: 020 7539 8131
Fax: 020 7529 8134
E-mail: freechurch@cte.org.uk
Website: www.cte.org.uk

Enquiries to: Secretary
Direct tel: 020 7387 8413
Other contacts: Health Care Chaplaincy

Founded: 1940

Organisation type and purpose: Voluntary organisation.
Representative body for Free Church opinion.

Subject coverage: Free Church tradition and opinion, Free Church and ecumenical relations.

Access to staff: Contact by letter, by telephone, by fax and by e-mail. Appointment necessary.
Hours: Mon to Fri, 0900 to 1700

Access to building: No access other than to staff

Also at: Free Church Education Unit; 27 Tavistock Square, London WC1H 9HH; tel: 020 7529 8131; fax: 020 7529 8134; e-mail: sarah.lane@cte.org.uk

Members: Afro Westindian United Council of Churches (AWUCOC); tel: 020 8888 9427; fax: 020 8888 2877; Baptist Union of Great Britain (BUGB); tel: 01235 517700; fax: 01235 517715; e-mail: baptistuniongb@baptist.org.uk; Baptist Union of Wales; tel: 01792 655468; fax: 01792 469489; Congregational Federation; tel: 0115 911 1460; fax: 0115 911 1462; e-mail: michael.heaney@congregational.org.uk; Council of African and Afro-Caribbean Churches (UK) (CAAC-UK); tel: 020 7582 4209, Work: 020 7620 4444; Countess of Huntingdon's Connexion; tel: 0118 933 2569; e-mail: brianbrendabaldwin@talk21.com; Fellowship of Churches of Christ; tel: 0121 373 7942; fax: 0121 373 7942; e-mail: hazelwilson@bigfoot.com; Free Church of England; tel: 01273 845092; fax: 01273 845092; e-mail: rtal799@aol.com; Independent Methodist Churches; tel: 01942 223526; fax: 01942 227768; e-mail: resourcecentre@imcgb.org.uk; Methodist Church; tel: 020 7486 5502; fax: 020 7467 5226; e-mail: conferenceoffice@methodistchurch.org.uk; Moravian Church; tel: 020 8883 3409/1912; fax: 020 8365 3371; New Testament Church of God; tel: 01604 643311/645944; fax: 01604 790254; Old Baptist Union; tel: 01625 422404; fax: 01625 422404; Presbyterian Church of Wales; tel: 029 2049 4913; fax: 029 2046 4293; Salvation Army; tel: 020 7367 4614; fax: 020 7367 4718; e-mail: webmajor@salvationarmy.org.uk; Undeb yr Annibynwyr Cymraeg (Union of Welsh Independents); tel: 01792 652542/467040; fax: 01792 650647; e-mail: tyjp@tyjp.co.uk; United Reformed Church in the United Kingdom; tel: 020 7916 2020; fax: 020 7916 2021; e-mail: david.cornick@urc.org.uk; Wesleyan Reform Union; tel: 0114 272 1938; fax: 0114 272 1965; e-mail: john@wesleyan-reform.freeserve.co.uk

FREIGHT TRANSPORT ASSOCIATION LIMITED (FTA)

Hermes House, 157 St John's Road, Tunbridge Wells, Kent, TN4 9UZ

Tel: 01892 526171
Fax: 01892 534989
E-mail: enquiries@fta.co.uk
Website: www.fta.co.uk
Website: supplychain.fta.co.uk

Enquiries to: Director of Communications
Direct tel: 01892 552255
Direct fax: 01892 552323
Direct e-mail: jtanner@fta.co.uk

Other contacts: Media Relations Manager

Founded: 1889; formerly called Traders Road Transport Association (year of change 1969)

Organisation type and purpose: Trade association.

Subject coverage: Freight transport, including transport law, costs and rates, statistics, education and training, vehicle maintenance, international transport, shipping, hazardous cargoes.

Publications: Printed

Access to staff: Contact by letter, by telephone, by fax, by e-mail and via website
Hours: Mon to Fri, 0900 to 1700

Includes the: British Shippers Council

FRENCH CHAMBER OF COMMERCE IN GREAT BRITAIN (FCCGB)

21 Dartmouth Street, Westminster, London, SW1H 0BP

Tel: 020 7304 4040
Fax: 020 7304 7034
E-mail: jpintore@ccfgb.co.uk
Website: www.ccfgb.co.uk

Enquiries to: Public Relations Manager
Direct tel: 020 7304 7017
Direct e-mail: atassi@ccfgb.co.uk

Founded: 1883

Organisation type and purpose:
Membership association (membership is by subscription), present number of members: c. 550, consultancy.
Chamber of Commerce.
Increase Franco-British trade.

Subject coverage: Publications for settling in France or Great Britain as an individual or a professional.

Collection: Databases of French companies in the UK and British companies in France, exporters/importers in the UK and France
Directories of members of the French Chamber

Publications: Printed, and electronic and video

Publications list: Available online and in print

Access to staff: Contact by letter and by e-mail. Appointment necessary.
Hours: Mon to Fri, 0900 to 1700

Access to building: Prior appointment required

Access for disabled people: Level entry

FRENCH EMBASSY – CULTURAL DEPARTMENT

23 Cromwell Road, London, SW7 2EL

Tel: 020 7073 1300
Fax: 020 7073 1320
E-mail: cultural@ambafrance.org.uk
Website: www.institut_francais.org.uk/lb_about.htm

Enquiries to: Cultural Counsellor

Organisation type and purpose: Diplomatic mission.

Subject coverage: Education in France; studies in France; teaching in France; sport exchanges; theatre; cinema; literature and publishing; music; dance; concerts and recitals; art exhibitions in France and Great Britain.

Library catalogue: All or part available online

Publications: Printed, and electronic and video

Access to staff: Contact by letter, by fax and by e-mail
Hours: Mon to Fri, 0900 to 1700

Other addresses: Institut Français; 17 Queensberry Place, London, SW7 2DT; tel: 020 7073 1350; fax: 020 7073 1355; e-mail: box.office@ambafrance.org.uk

FRENCH EMBASSY – SCIENCE AND TECHNOLOGY DEPARTMENT

6 Cromwell Place, London, SW7 2JN

Tel: 020 7073 1380
Fax: 020 7073 1390
E-mail: visas.londres-fslt@diplomatie.gouv.fr
Website: www.ambascience.co.uk

Enquiries to: Information Officer
Other contacts: Counsellor for Science and Technology

Organisation type and purpose: National government body.
Embassy.

Subject coverage: French and English research in: humanities and social sciences, chemical sciences, life sciences, sciences of the universe, physical sciences and mathematics, engineering sciences, information sciences and technology, medicine and health.

Non-library collection catalogue: All or part available in-house

Library catalogue: All or part available in-house

Publications: Printed, and electronic and video

Publications list: Available online and in print

Access to staff: Contact by letter, by telephone, by fax and by e-mail
Hours: Mon to Fri, 0900 to 1730

Parent body: Ministère des affaires étrangères et européennes (French Ministry for Foreign and European Affairs); Paris, France

FRENCH INSTITUTE (IFE)

Formal name: Institute Français d'Ecosse

13 Randolph Crescent, Edinburgh, EH3 7TT

Tel: 0131 225 5366
Fax: 0131 220 0648
E-mail: library@ifecosse.org.uk
Website: www.ifecosse.org.uk

Enquiries to: Librarian

Founded: 1946

Organisation type and purpose:
International organisation, membership association (membership is by subscription).
To promote French language and culture.

Subject coverage: French language and culture, for adults and children, contemporary France, French cinema, documentary exhibitions.

Collection: Books: 20,000 volumes, mostly in French, relating to various aspects of French life and culture
Videos and DVDs: 1,100 films and documentary films with or without subtitles; 962 films of French cinema from classics to recent productions; 747 documentary films on a diversity of topics related to contemporary France
CDs: talking books, classical, contemporary, popular music and jazz; 1,000 CDs of popular music from traditional chansons to current trends
CD-ROMs: 200 CD-ROMs for adults and children including many games
Newspapers and magazines: 50 titles on a wide range of topics to suit everyone including daily papers
Reference: many dictionaries and encyclopaedic books.

Non-library collection catalogue: All or part available online and in-house

Library catalogue: All or part available in-house

Access to staff: Contact by letter, by telephone, by fax, by e-mail, in person and via website. Appointment necessary.
Hours: Mon, 1400 to 1830; Tue to Fri, 0930 to 1830; Sat, 0930 to 1300

Access to building: No access other than to staff
Hours: Mon to Fri, 0930 to 1830; Sat, 0930 to 1300

FRESHWATER BIOLOGICAL ASSOCIATION (FBA)

The Ferry House, Far Sawrey, Ambleside, Cumbria, LA22 0LP

Tel: 015394 42468
Fax: 015394 46914
E-mail: info@fba.org.uk
Website: www.fba.org.uk

Enquiries to: Collections Manager
Direct e-mail: dis@fba.org.uk

Founded: 1929

Organisation type and purpose:
International organisation, learned society (membership is by subscription), registered charity (charity number 214440), research organisation.
The Freshwater Biological Association is an independent body that conducts research into all aspects of freshwater science, usually by awarding grants and studentships.

Subject coverage: Limnology, freshwater biology (hydrobiology), freshwater algae, microbiology, fish, invertebrates, physics and chemistry of lakes and rivers.

Information services: Document supply; literature searches; subject reviews; digitisation services; data management

continued overleaf

Collection: Fritsch Collection of illustrations of the freshwater algae; FBA freshwater data collection

Non-library collection catalogue: All or part available online, in-house and in print

Library catalogue: All or part available online, in-house and in print

Publications: Printed
Order microform publications from: Fritsch Collection
Order electronic and video publications from: see website: http://www.freshwaterlife.org

Publications list: Available online and in print

Access to staff: Contact by letter, by telephone, by fax, by e-mail and via website. Appointment necessary. Non-members charged.
Hours: Mon to Fri, 0900 to 1700

FRIENDS OF ANIMALS LEAGUE (Foal Farm)

Foal Farm, Jail Lane, Biggin Hill, Kent, TN16 3AX

Tel: 01959 572386
Fax: 01959 572386
E-mail: info@foalfarm.org.uk
Website: www.foalfarm.org.uk

Enquiries to: Customer Services Manager
Direct tel: 01959 572386

Founded: 1960

Organisation type and purpose: Voluntary organisation, registered charity (charity number 201654).
Animal rescue and re-homing centre.

Subject coverage: Care of sick, distressed or unwanted animals; restoring them to health; organisation and functioning of an animal sanctuary.

Publications: Printed

Access to staff: Contact by letter
Hours: Mon, Wed, Thu, Fri, Sat, Sun, 1400 to 1700

Access for disabled people: Toilet facilities

Member organisation of: The Association of British Dogs' and Cats' Homes

FRIENDS OF BIRZEIT UNIVERSITY (FoBZU)

1 Gough Square, London, EC4A 3DE

Tel: 020 7832 1340
Fax: 020 7832 1349
E-mail: director@fobzu.org
Website: www.fobzu.org

Enquiries to: Development Director

Founded: 1978

Organisation type and purpose: Registered charity (charity number 1114343).
To support education at Birzeit University and its right to academic freedom. Birzeit University is the leading Palestinian university on the West Bank.

Subject coverage: Palestinian higher education; human rights violations affecting university community; projects (development/education); workcamps; Arabic and social science courses for internationals at Birzeit University.

Publications: Printed

Access to staff: Contact by letter, by telephone, by fax and by e-mail. Appointment necessary.
Hours: Mon to Thurs, 0930 to 1730

FRIENDS OF CATHEDRAL MUSIC (FCM)

27 Old Gloucester Street, London, WC1N 3XX

Tel: 0845 644 3721
E-mail: roger.bishton1@btinternet.com
Website: www.fcm.org.uk

Enquiries to: General Secretary

Founded: 1956

Organisation type and purpose: Membership association (membership is by subscription), present number of members: 2,500, voluntary organisation, registered charity (charity number 285121).

Subject coverage: Details and times of choral services at cathedrals and collegiate establishments in the UK.

Publications: Printed

Access to staff: Contact by letter and by e-mail
Hours: Mon to Fri, 0900 to 1700

FRIENDS OF CONSERVATION (FOC)

Southcombe Business Centre, 11–12 Southcombe Street, London, W14 0RA

Tel: 020 7348 3408
E-mail: focinfo@aol.com
Website: www.foc-uk.com

Enquiries to: Director

Founded: 1982

Organisation type and purpose: Registered charity (charity number 328176).
FOC is a registered charity, with offices in the UK, USA and Kenya, that aims to protect endangered species and habitats.

Subject coverage: Conservation education, habitat conservation, wildlife monitoring, forestry projects, community projects for local people and tourist education worldwide.

Publications: Printed

Access to staff: Contact by letter and by e-mail
Hours: Mon to Fri, 0900 to 1700

FRIENDS OF ENGLISH NATIONAL OPERA

London Coliseum, St Martin's Lane, London, WC2N 4ES

Tel: 020 7845 9420
Fax: 020 7845 9272
E-mail: friends@eno.org

Enquiries to: Membership Administrator
Direct tel: 020 7845 9441
Direct e-mail: rreiss@eno.org

Organisation type and purpose: Membership association, registered charity (charity number 257210).
Supporting English National Opera.

Subject coverage: Current activities of English National Opera.

Access to staff: Contact by letter, by telephone, by fax and by e-mail
Hours: Mon to Fri, 1000 to 1800

FRIENDS OF REAL LANCASHIRE

1 Belvidere Park, Great Crosby, Lancashire, L23 0SP

Tel: 0151 928 2770
E-mail: csd@forl.co.uk
Website: www.forl.co.uk

Enquiries to: Chairman
Direct tel: 01539 535507 (membership)
Direct e-mail: janet.m.ainsworth@btinternet.com (membership)
Other contacts: Membership Secretary

Founded: 1992

Organisation type and purpose: Membership association (membership is by subscription), voluntary organisation.
To promote the true identity of the traditional county of Lancashire.

Subject coverage: The true identity of the traditional county of Lancashire.

Publications: Printed

Access to staff: Contact by letter, by telephone and by e-mail
Hours: Sun to Sat, 0900 to 1700, and evenings

Member organisation of: Association of British Counties

FRIENDS OF THE EARTH

26–28 Underwood Street, London, N1 7JQ

Tel: 020 7490 1555
Fax: 020 7490 0881
E-mail: info@foe.co.uk
Website: www.foe.co.uk

Enquiries to: Supporter Information Team

Founded: 1971

Organisation type and purpose: Membership association (membership is by subscription), voluntary organisation, registered charity (charity number 281681), research organisation.
Environmental group, largely funded by subscriptions, donations and grants.

Subject coverage: Environmental issues in general, climate change, natural resources, environmental justice and green economics.

Publications: Printed
Order printed publications from: Information Service, Friends of the Earth, 26–28 Underwood St, London, N1 7JQ

Publications list: Available online and in print

Access to staff: Contact by letter, by telephone, by fax, by e-mail and via website
Hours: Mon to Fri, 0900 to 1700

Also at: Friends of the Earth Membership Services; 56–58 Alma Street, Luton, Bedfordshire, LU1 2PH; tel: 020 7490 1555; e-mail: info@foe.co.uk; website: http://www.foe.co.uk

FRIENDS OF THE ELDERLY

40–42 Ebury Street, London, SW1W 0LZ

Tel: 020 7730 8263
Fax: 020 7259 0154
E-mail: enquiries@fote.org.uk
Website: www.fote.org.uk

Founded: 1905

Organisation type and purpose: Registered charity (number 226064).
Supports older people, particularly those in need due to frailty, isolation or lack of adequate resources, by providing high quality caring services, personalised to the needs of the individual, integrated with local communities and dedicated to promoting the independence, well-being, dignity and peace of mind of each person with whom it works.

Subject coverage: Provides direct services including residential care homes, nursing homes and dementia care homes. Its day clubs, home support, home visiting, telephone befriending and grant-giving services help older people live independently at home.

Access to staff: Contact by letter, by telephone, by fax and by e-mail

FRIENDS OF THE LAKE DISTRICT (FLD)

Murley Moss, Oxenholme Road, Kendal, Cumbria, LA9 7SS

Tel: 01539 720788
Fax: 01539 730355
E-mail: info@fld.org.uk
Website: www.fld.org.uk

Enquiries to: Executive Director
Direct e-mail: andrew-forsyth@fld.org.uk
Other contacts: Communications officer

Founded: 1934

Organisation type and purpose:
Membership association, present number of members: 7,100, voluntary organisation, registered charity (charity number 11000759), conservation and landscape society.
To promote and organise concerted action for the protection and conservation of the landscape and natural beauty of the Lake District and the county of Cumbria.

Subject coverage: Subjects relating to conservation and protection of landscape and natural beauty in the Lake District National Park and Cumbria, representations to planning authorities, and policies on access, tourism, development pressures, roads, transport, agriculture, forestry.

Collection: Library of books, documents and photographs (including slides)

Publications: Printed

Access to staff: Appointment necessary.
Hours: Mon to Fri, 0900 to 1700

Affiliated to: CPRE; 128 Southwark Street, London, SE1 0SW; tel: 020 7981 2800; fax: 020 7981 2899; e-mail: info@cpre.org.uk; website: www.cpre.org.uk

Represents: Council for the Protection of Rural England (CPRE) in Cumbria

FRIENDS OF THE NATIONAL LIBRARIES (FNL)

c/o Department of MSS, British Library, 96 Euston Road, London, NW1 2DB

Tel: 020 7412 7559
E-mail: secretary@fnlmail.org.uk
Website: www.friendsofnationallibraries.org.uk

Enquiries to: Honorary Secretary

Founded: 1931

Organisation type and purpose:
Membership association (membership is by subscription), present number of members: 723, registered charity (charity number 313020).
To give grants for the purchase of printed books, manuscripts and archives by libraries and other institutions that provide public access within the United Kingdom.

Subject coverage: Raising of funds to save rare books and manuscripts for national and local institutions.

Publications: Printed

Access to staff: Contact by letter, by telephone and via website
Hours: 24-hour answerphone
Special comments: Voicemail only.

FRIENDS OF THE PEAK DISTRICT

The Stables, 22A Endcliffe Crescent, Sheffield, South Yorkshire, S10 3EF

Tel: 0114 2665822
Fax: 0114 2685514
E-mail: mail@friendsofthepeak.org.uk
Website: www.friendsofthepeak.org.uk

Enquiries to: Communications Officer
Direct e-mail: liz@friendsofthepeak.org.uk
Other contacts: Office Manager

Founded: 1924

Organisation type and purpose: Local charity.
Campaigning work to safeguard Peak District landscapes.

Subject coverage: Peak District.

Publications: Printed
Order printed publications from:
Downloadable at: http://www.friendsofthepeak.org.uk

Access to staff: Contact by letter, by telephone, by fax, by e-mail and via website. Appointment necessary.
Hours: Mon to Fri, 1000 to 1600

Access to building: Please make appointment

Access for disabled people: Ramped entry

Links with: Campaign to Protect Rural England (CPRE); 128 Southwark Street London SE1 0SW; tel: 020 7981 2800

Member organisation of: Campaign for National Parks; 6–7 Barnard Mews, London, SW11 1QU; tel: 020 7924 4077; website: http://www.cnp.org.uk

FRIENDS OF UCLH

Ground Floor, University College London Hospital, 250 Euston Road, London, NW1 2PG

Tel: 0845 155 5000 extn 73038
E-mail: friendsuclh@uclh.nhs.uk
Website: www.uclh.nhs.uk/Charities+at+UCLH/Friends+at+UCLH

Founded: 2005; created by the merger of Leagues of Friends of four major London hospitals

Organisation type and purpose: A registered charity (charity number 266669).
To help the hospital, its patients and staff by providing facilities and amenities that are not available from the National Health Service. This covers many items that cannot otherwise be afforded.

Subject coverage: Grant requests from various wards and departments in the hospital.

Access to staff: Contact by letter, by telephone and by e-mail

Links with: University College London Hospitals NHS Foundation Trust (UCLH); 250 Euston Road, London, NW1 2PG; tel: 0845 1555 000

FRISKY REGISTER

Graces Cottage, Tregagle, Monmouth, Gwent, NP25 4RZ

Tel: 01600 860420
Fax: 01600 860420

Enquiries to: Registrar

Founded: 1974

Organisation type and purpose:
Membership association.
Car register.

Subject coverage: The restoration of the Frisky car, engines, body, chassis, electrics, history, components.

Collection: Maintenance manuals
Press releases
Technical information, handbooks, engine books, article reprints

Publications: Printed

Access to staff: Contact by letter, by telephone and by fax. Appointment necessary.
Hours: Mon to Fri, 0900 to 1700

FRONTIER: THE SOCIETY FOR ENVIRONMENTAL EXPLORATION (Frontier)

50–52 Rivington Street, London, EC2A 3QP

Tel: 020 7613 2422
Fax: 020 7613 2992
E-mail: info@frontier.ac.uk
Website: www.frontier.ac.uk

Enquiries to: Marketing Manager
Direct e-mail: marketing@frontier.ac.uk

Founded: 1989

continued overleaf

Organisation type and purpose: International organisation, voluntary organisation, training organisation, research organisation.
To conduct development projects and conservation research in Fiji, Nepal, Peru, Tibet, Guatemala, India, Tanzania, Madagascar, Cambodia and Nicaragua. To provide opportunities for volunteers to carry out conservation work and obtain tropical field experience.

Subject coverage: Conservation and environmental research, development of natural resources, volunteer work abroad, teaching, community development, language courses.

Publications: Printed

Publications list: Available online and in print

Access to staff: Contact by letter, by telephone, by fax, by e-mail and via website
Hours: Mon to Fri, 0930 to 1730
Special comments: No visits without appointment.

Branches: Frontier–Cambodia; PO Box 1275, General Post Office, Phlauv 13, Phnom Penh, Cambodia; tel: +855 23 221 163; Frontier–Costa Rica; c/o Amigos de Osa, Apartido 54, 8203 Puerto Jiménez Golfito, Costa Rica; tel: +506 87562183; Frontier–Madagascar; BP 413, Tulear 1 Zone Portuaire, Madagascar; tel: +261 20 94 430 38; Frontier–Tanzania; PO Box 9473, Dar es Salaam, Tanzania; tel: +255 22 2780063; fax: +255 22 2780063; e-mail: frontier@raha.com

FRS FRESHWATER LABORATORY (FRS FL)

Formal name: Fisheries Research Service Freshwater Laboratory

Faskally, Pitlochry, Perthshire, PH16 5LB

Tel: 01224 294408 or 01796 472060
Fax: 01796 473523
E-mail: FL_Library@marlab.ac.uk
Website: www.frs-scotland.gov.uk

Enquiries to: Librarian

Founded: 1948

Organisation type and purpose: National government body, research organisation.

Subject coverage: Salmonid ecology, salmon fisheries, coarse fish, freshwater biology, fish biology, environmental chemistry (inorganic), fisheries science, environmental pollution, fish culture, aquaculture.

Collection: The Library is the only government research library in Great Britain devoted to the subject of freshwater fisheries

Trade and statistical information: Statistical Bulletin: Scottish Salmon and Sea Trout Catches

Library catalogue: All or part available in-house

Publications: Printed
Order printed publications from: ML_Library@marlab.ac.uk

Publications list: Available online

Access to staff: Contact by letter, by telephone, by fax, by e-mail and via website. Appointment necessary.
Hours: Mon to Fri, 0900 to 1700

Access to building: *Hours:* Mon to Fri, 0900 to 1700

Constituent part of: FRS Marine Laboratory Library; 375 Victoria Road, Aberdeen, AB11 9DB; tel: 01224 876544; fax: 01224 295309; e-mail: ML_Library@marlab.ac.uk; website: www.frs-scotland.gov.uk

FULL TIME MOTHERS

PO Box 43690, London, SE22 9WN

Tel: 020 8653 8786
Fax: 020 8761 6574
E-mail: fulltimemothers@hotmail.com
Website: www.fulltimemothers.org

Enquiries to: Chairman

Founded: 1990

Organisation type and purpose: Membership association (membership is by subscription, election or invitation).
To promote understanding of the child's need for a full-time mother, enhance the status and self esteem of mothers at home, campaign for changes in the tax and benefits system and in employment policies to give women a chance to be full-time mothers.

Subject coverage: The voice of the mother at home; information or quotes on: caring for children; mothers at home; childcare; tax and benefits relative to the family; psychology of the child; isolation and self-esteem of mothers; general motherhood; family-friendly employment policies.

Publications: Printed

Access to staff: Contact by letter, by telephone and by e-mail
Hours: Mon to Fri, 0900 to 1700

Affiliated to: Fédération des Femmes au Foyer (FEFAF)

FURNITURE HISTORY SOCIETY (FHS)

1 Mercedes Cottages, St John's Road, Haywards Heath, West Sussex, RH16 4EH

Tel: 01444 413845
Fax: 01444 413845
E-mail: furniturehistorysociety@hotmail.com
Website: www.furniturehistorysociety.org

Enquiries to: Membership Secretary and Publications Officer
Direct e-mail: brian.austen@zen.co.uk

Founded: 1966

Organisation type and purpose: International organisation, learned society (membership is by subscription), present number of members: 1,700.
International learned society dedicated to the study and publication of research on the history of furniture and furnishings.

Subject coverage: All aspects of the history of furniture and furnishings of all periods, especially that of Europe and North America.

Publications: Printed
Order printed publications from: Furniture History Society, via website, post, telephone, fax, or email

Publications list: Available online and in print

Access to staff: Contact by letter, by telephone, by fax, by e-mail, in person and via website. Appointment necessary.
Hours: Telephone calls accepted 0800 to 2200, Sun to Sat

FUTURES AND OPTIONS ASSOCIATION (FOA)

2nd Floor, 36–38 Botolph Lane, London, EC3R 8DE

Tel: 020 7929 0081
Fax: 020 7621 0223
Website: www.foa.co.uk

Organisation type and purpose: The principal European association for the futures and options industry, representing its interests in the public and regulatory domain.
Membership includes banks, financial institutions, brokers, commodity trade houses, energy market participants, fund managers, exchanges, clearing houses, systems providers, lawyers, accountants, consultants.

Subject coverage: Principally concerned with financial and commodity exchange-traded derivatives markets, but also addresses related issues arising in other markets (e.g. OTC markets) or issues that have a cross-sectoral impact. In such cases, it liaises, as appropriate, with other affected trade associations.

Education services: Provides a variety of training courses to supplement core activities and provide a benchmark in industry best practice.

Publications: Electronic and video
Order electronic and video publications from: Download from website

Access to staff: Contact by letter, by telephone, by fax and via website

Member organisation of: European Parliamentary Financial Services Forum (EPFSF); Brussels; Industry Advisory Group of the Associate Parliamentary Group (APG) on Wholesale Financial Markets and Services

GALLOWAY CATTLE SOCIETY OF GREAT BRITAIN & IRELAND

15 New Market Street, Castle Douglas, Kirkcudbrightshire, DG7 1HY

Tel: 01556 502753
Fax: 01556 502753
E-mail: info@gallowaycattlesociety.co.uk

Enquiries to: Secretary

Founded: 1877

Organisation type and purpose: Trade association (membership is by subscription), present number of members: 450, registered charity (charity number CR 36927).
Registration and promotion of beef cattle known as Galloway. Galloway cattle are found throughout the world and, whilst they have their own societies, this society is considered the parent body by many.

Subject coverage: History of Galloway Cattle. Pedigrees held of all registered Galloway Cattle in Britain and Ireland.

Publications: Printed

Access to staff: Contact by letter, by telephone and by fax
Hours: Wed, Fri, 0930 to 1630

GALPIN SOCIETY

37 Townsend Drive, St. Albans, Hertfordshire, AL3 5RF

E-mail: administrator@galpinsociety.org
Website: www.galpinsociety.org

Enquiries to: Administrator
Other contacts: Editor for publications & contributions to them.

Founded: 1946

Organisation type and purpose:
International organisation, learned society (membership is by subscription), present number of members: 800, registered charity (charity number 306012).
The study of development, history, construction and use of musical instruments.

Subject coverage: History, construction, development and use of musical instruments.

Collection: The Society's archives (for members only)
Documents relating to the history of the Society (for members only)

Publications: Printed

Publications list: Available online

Access to staff: Contact by letter and by e-mail

GAMBICA ASSOCIATION LIMITED

Formal name: Association for Instrumentation, Control, Automation & Laboratory Technology

Broadwall House, 21 Broadwall, London, SE1 9PL

Tel: 020 7642 8080
Fax: 020 7642 8096
E-mail: assoc@gambica.org.uk
Website: www.gambica.org.uk

Enquiries to: Executive Secretary
Direct e-mail: schenery@gambica.org.uk

Founded: 1915; formerly called Association for the Laboratory Supply Industry (ALSI), British Instrument Control and Automation Manufacturers (BIMCAM), Control and Automation Manufacturers Association (CAMA), Scientific Instrument Manufacturers Association (SIMA); formerly called British Laboratory Ware Association (BLWA) (year of change 1991); formerly called BWLA Limited (year of change 2001)

Organisation type and purpose: Trade association.

Subject coverage: Instrumentation, control, automation and laboratory technology, sources of supply, etc.

Publications: Printed

Publications list: Available online

Access to staff: Contact by letter, by fax, by e-mail and via website
Hours: Mon to Thu, 0900 to 1700; Fri, 0900 to 1545

Member organisation of: European Association of Optical and Scientific Instrument Manufacturers (EUROM); ORGALIME

Secretaries of: EROM II Optics, Lasers and Laboratory Instrumentation

GAMBLERS ANONYMOUS (UK) (GA)

PO Box 5382 London W1A 6SA

Tel: 020 7384 3040
E-mail: via website
Website: www.gamblersanonymous.org.uk

Enquiries to: Secretary
Direct e-mail: info@gamblersanonymous.org.uk

Organisation type and purpose: Voluntary organisation.
A self-help fellowship of compulsive gamblers.

Subject coverage: Group therapy and advice on the best ways to stop gambling.

Non-library collection catalogue: All or part available in-house

Library catalogue: All or part available in-house

Publications: Printed

Access to staff: Contact by telephone
Hours: 24-hour helpline

Links with: GAM-ANON, for wives and/or relatives of the compulsive gambler

GAMCARE

Formal name: National Association for Gambling Care, Educational Resources and Training

2nd Floor, 7–11 St John's Hill, Clapham Junction, London, SW11 1TR

Tel: 020 7801 7000
Fax: 020 7801 7033
E-mail: director@gamcare.org.uk
Website: www.gamcare.org.uk

Enquiries to: Business Administrator
Other contacts: Chairman

Founded: 1990; formerly called UK Forum on Young People and Gambling (UKF) from 1990 to 1997

Organisation type and purpose:
Membership association (membership is by subscription), present number of members: 100, registered charity (charity number 1060005), suitable for ages: all.
Friends Association, National Centre for information.

Subject coverage: Gambling, information, advice and practical help in relation to the social impact of gambling, damage done by such activities, strategies to reduce potential and actual harm to young people.

Trade and statistical information: Statistical information on gambling, particularly in relation to the number of calls to the Helpline
Information on social impact of gambling in the UK

Publications: Printed, and electronic and video

Publications list: Available in print

Access to staff: Contact by letter, by telephone, by fax, by e-mail and via website. Appointment necessary.
Hours: Helpline: Mon to Fri, 1000 to 2200; Sat, 1000 to 1800; Sun, 1800 to 2200

Affiliated to: European Association for the Study of Gambling; Society for Study of Gambling; Youth Access

GAME AND WILDLIFE CONSERVATION TRUST (GWCT)

Burgate Manor, Fordingbridge, Hampshire, SP6 1EF

Tel: 01425 652381
Fax: 01425 655848
E-mail: info@gwct.org.uk
Website: www.gwct.org.uk

Enquiries to: Librarian
Direct tel: 01425 651019
Direct e-mail: library@gwct.org.uk

Founded: 1931; formerly called Game Conservancy Trust (year of change 2007)

Organisation type and purpose: Registered charity (charity number 1112023), research organisation.

Subject coverage: Game management and conservation; habitat requirements; problems imposed by intensive farming methods on wildlife populations; predators, upland wildlife; advises government and other decision makers on wildlife policy.

Publications: Printed
Order printed publications from: Membership Department, Game and Wildlife Conservation Trust, Burgate Manor, Fordingbridge, SP6 1EF

Access to staff: Contact by letter, by telephone, by fax, by e-mail and via website. Appointment necessary.
Hours: Mon to Fri, 0900 to 1700

Access to building: Library facilities only
Hours: Mon to Fri, 0900 to 1700
Special comments: By appointment only.

Constituent bodies: Game and Wildlife Conservation Trust Trading Ltd

GANDHI FOUNDATION (GF)

c/o G. Paxton, 87 Barrington Drive, Glasgow, G4 9ES

Tel: 0845 313 8419
E-mail: contact@gandhifoundation.org
Website: www.gandhifoundation.org

Enquiries to: Administrator
Other contacts: The Editor, The Gandhi Way (e-mail gpaxton@phonecoop.coop)

Founded: 1983

Organisation type and purpose:
International organisation, membership association (membership is by subscription), voluntary organisation, registered charity (charity number 292629).

Subject coverage: Spreading Gandhian principles through multifaith celebration, annual summer gathering, annual lectures, Peace Award, seminars and conferences, AGM and workshops, newsletter.

Publications: Printed

continued overleaf

Access to staff: Contact by letter, by telephone, by e-mail, in person and via website. Appointment necessary.

GARAGE EQUIPMENT ASSOCIATION LIMITED (GEA)

2–3 Church Walk, Daventry, Northamptonshire, NN11 4BL

Tel: 01327 312616
Fax: 01327 312606
E-mail: john@gea-ltd.demon.co.uk
Website: www.gea.co.uk

Enquiries to: Administrator

Founded: 1945

Organisation type and purpose: Trade association.

Subject coverage: Garage equipment selection, design, layout, distribution, installation and importation.

Collection: Trade catalogues dating back to 1950s and 1960s

Publications: Printed

Publications list: Available in print

Access to staff: Contact by letter, by telephone, by fax, by e-mail and in person
Hours: Mon to Fri, 0830 to 1300 and 1400 to 1700

Affiliated to: Aftermarket Association Liaison Group (AALG)

GARDEN HISTORY SOCIETY, THE (GHS)

70 Cowcross Street, London, EC1M 6EJ

Tel: 020 7608 2409
E-mail: enquiries@gardenhistorysociety.org
Website: www.gardenhistorysociety.org

Enquiries to: Chairman

Founded: 1965

Organisation type and purpose:
International organisation, learned society. Also statutory consultee on planning applications affecting listed historic designed landscapes. The Society's aims are to promote the study of the history of gardening, landscape gardening and horticulture in all its aspects; to promote the protection and conservation of historic parks, gardens and designed landscapes, and to promote and advise on their conservation; and to encourage the creation of new parks, gardens and designed landscapes.

Subject coverage: Garden history, landscape design, architectural features, horticultural use of plants, conservation.

Collection: The Society's library is housed at King's Manor Library, University of York and Department of Art History, University of Bristol. Further collections at University of Bath.

Non-library collection catalogue: All or part available online

Library catalogue: All or part available online

Publications: Printed
Order printed publications from: Back issues department

Publications list: Available online

Access to staff: Contact by letter, by telephone and by e-mail. Appointment necessary.
Special comments: Staff work part time

Access to building: *Special comments:* Appointment necessary

GARDEN INDUSTRY MANUFACTURERS ASSOCIATION (1999) LIMITED (GIMA)

225 Bristol Road, Edgbaston, Birmingham, B5 7UB

Tel: 0121 446 5213
Fax: 0121 446 5215
E-mail: info@gima.org.uk
Website: www.gima.org.uk

Enquiries to: Director
Direct tel: 01428 712513
Direct fax: 01428 712513
Direct e-mail: marshpr1@aol.com

Founded: 1999; formerly known as Garden Products Association (GPA)

Organisation type and purpose: Trade association.

Subject coverage: Trade specific information made available to members.

Access to staff: Access for members only.
Hours: Mon to Fri, 0900 to 1700

Access to building: No access other than to staff

Secretariat: British Hardware Federation (BHF); tel: 0121 446 6688; fax: 0121 446 5215

GATESHEAD COLLEGE

Formal name: Gateshead College Library

Quarryfield Road, Baltic Business Quarter, Gateshead, Tyne and Wear, NE8 3BN

Tel: 0191 490 2249; 0191 490 2289
Fax: 0191 490 2313
E-mail: library.manager@gateshead.ac.uk
Website: www.gateshead.ac.uk

Enquiries to: Library and Learning Officers
Direct tel: 0191 490 2249
Direct e-mail: library@gateshead.ac.uk

Founded: 1956; formerly called Gateshead College Learning Centre, Gateshead College Library and Resources Unit, Centre 4... Knowledge.

Organisation type and purpose: College of further education. Suitable for ages: 16 upwards.

Subject coverage: General subjects spread over wide range of qualifications including some higher education.

Library catalogue: All or part available online

Access to staff: Contact by letter, by telephone, by fax, by e-mail and in person. All charged.
Hours: Mon to Thu, 0830 to 2000; Fri, 1000 to 1630

Access for disabled people: Pay and display parking provided, ramped entry, toilet facilities, internal lifts for access to floors

GATESHEAD LIBRARIES AND ARTS

Central Library, Prince Consort Road, Gateshead, Tyne and Wear, NE8 4LN

Tel: 0191 433 8400
Fax: 0191 433 8424
E-mail: libraries@gateshead.gov.uk
Website: www.gatesheadlibraries.com
Website: www.gateshead.gov.uk
Website: isee.gateshead.gov.uk

Enquiries to: Head of Libraries and Arts
Direct e-mail: annborthwick@gateshead.gov.uk
Other contacts: Principal Library Manager

Founded: 1885

Organisation type and purpose: Local government body, public library.

Subject coverage: Reading, readers' groups, local history, heritage, tourism, learning, children's library, community rooms, music, film, internet access, wi-fi.

Collection: Gateshead Local Studies collection including:
Brockett Collection of items relating to Gateshead in the 1830s
Oxberry Collection of Local History relating to Gateshead and Felling
Local newspapers from 1711
Collection relating to the General Strike, including several national newspapers for 1926
Suffragette publications
Collection of reports and magazines on women workers
Felling collection of Joan Hewitt
Maughan collection on Ryton and Blaydon.

Non-library collection catalogue: All or part available online

Library catalogue: All or part available online

Publications: Printed

Access to staff: Contact by letter, by telephone, by fax, by e-mail, in person and via website
Hours: Mon, Tue, Thu and Fri, 0900 to 1900; Wed, 0900 to 1700; Sat, 0900 to 1300

Access to building: *Hours:* Mon, Tue, Thu and Fri, 0900 to 1900; Wed, 0900 to 1700; Sat, 0900 to 1300

Access for disabled people: Wheelchair accessible parking provided, ramped entry, level entry, access to all public areas, toilet facilities, staff with signing skills
Hours: Mon, Tue, Thu and Fri, 0900 to 1900; Wed, 0900 to 1700; Sat, 0900 to 1300

Links with: BALTIC: The Centre for Contemporary Art; The Sage Gateshead

Parent body: Gateshead Council

GAUGE AND TOOL MAKERS' ASSOCIATION (GTMA)

3 Forge House, Summerleys Road, Princes Risborough, Buckinghamshire, HP27 9DT

Tel: 01844 274222
Fax: 01844 274227
E-mail: gtma@gtma.co.uk
Website: www.gtma.co.uk

Enquiries to: Executive Manager
Other contacts: Business Manager for technical enquiries.

Founded: 1942

Organisation type and purpose: Trade association.

Subject coverage: Gauge and toolmaking, precision machining, rapid prototyping, metrology.

Publications: Printed

Access to staff: Contact by telephone, by fax and by e-mail
Hours: Mon to Fri, 0900 to 1700

GB-RUSSIA SOCIETY, THE

Formal name: GB-Russia Society, The

24 Maida Avenue, London, W2 1ST

Website: www.gbrussia.org

Enquiries to: Secretary
Other contacts: Via online form at website www.gbrussia.org

Organisation type and purpose: Registered charity (charity number 1105296)

Publications: Printed

Access to staff: Contact by letter, by e-mail and via website

GEDLING BOROUGH COUNCIL

Civic Centre, Arnot Hill Park, Arnold, Nottingham, NG5 6LU

Tel: 0115 901 3901, 0115 901 3935 (minicom)
Fax: 0115 901 3921

Enquiries to: Public Relations Manager
Direct tel: 0115 901 3801
Direct fax: 0115 901 3807
Direct e-mail: carolyn.iwanowski@gedling.gov.uk

Founded: 1974

Organisation type and purpose: Local government body.

Publications: Printed

Access to staff: Contact by letter
Hours: Mon to Thu, 0845 to 1715; Fri, 0845 to 1645

Access for disabled people: Parking provided, level entry, access to all public areas, toilet facilities

GEM MOTORING ASSIST (GEM)

Station Road, Forest Row, East Sussex, RH18 5EN

Tel: 01342 825676
Fax: 01342 824847
E-mail: info@motoringassist.com
Website: www.motoringassist.com

Enquiries to: Chief Executive
Direct e-mail: david.williams@motoringassist.com

Founded: 1932; formerly called Company of Veteran Motorists (year of change 1983)

Organisation type and purpose: Membership association.
Promotion of road safety, provision of motoring services to members.

Subject coverage: Promotion of road safety, motoring law, motoring technology, motor insurance and claims.

Information services: Advice given on road safety and motoring matters

Publications: Printed

Publications list: Available online

Access to staff: Contact by letter, by telephone, by e-mail and via website. Appointment necessary.
Hours: Mon to Fri, 0900 to 1700

Access to building: By invitation only

GEMMOLOGICAL ASSOCIATION AND GEM TESTING LABORATORY OF GREAT BRITAIN (GAGTL)

27 Greville Street (Saffron Hill Entrance), London, EC1N 8TN

Tel: 020 7404 3334 or 020 7405 3351
Fax: 020 7404 8843
E-mail: gagtl@btinternet.com
Website: www.gagtl.ac.uk/gagtl

Enquiries to: Director
Other contacts: Director of Education for member of Council of Management.

Founded: 1908; formed by the merger of Gem Testing Laboratory of Great Britain (1925), Gemmological Association of Great Britain (1908) (year of change 1990)

Organisation type and purpose: Professional body, service industry, suitable for ages: 16+, training organisation, publishing house.
Gemmological education, with gem testing and grading services.

Subject coverage: Gemmology, gemstones, diamonds, pearls, gem minerals, gem materials, gem identification, gem testing methods and equipment, gemmological education.

Non-library collection catalogue: All or part available in-house

Library catalogue: All or part available in-house

Publications: Printed

Access to staff: Contact by telephone, by e-mail and via website
Hours: Mon to Fri, 0900 to 1700

Access to building: Prior appointment required

Wholly owned subsidiary: Gemmological Instruments Limited, which sells gemmological books and instruments; tel: 020 7404 3334; fax: 020 7404 8843; e-mail: gagtl@btinternet.com

GENDER TRUST (GT)

Formal name: Gender Trust Association

Community Base, 113 Queens Road, Brighton, BN1 3XG

Tel: 0845 231 0505 (helpline, Mon to Fri, 1000 to 2200, Sat and Sun, 1300 to 2200)
E-mail: info@gendertrust.org.uk
Website: www.gendertrust.org.uk

Enquiries to: Project Manager
Direct tel: 01273 234024
Other contacts: Administrator

Founded: 1990

Organisation type and purpose: National organisation, registered charity (charity number 1088150).
To support any adult affected by gender identity issues, throughout the United Kingdom.

Subject coverage: Gender identity, gender dysphoria, transsexuality.

Publications: Printed

Publications list: Available online and in print

Access to staff: Contact by letter, by telephone, by e-mail and via website. Appointment necessary.
Hours: Tue to Thu, 0900 to 1700

GENERAL CONFERENCE OF THE NEW CHURCH

Swedenborg House, 20 Bloomsbury Way, London, WC1A 2TH

Tel: 020 7229 9340
Fax: 01206 302932

Enquiries to: Chief Executive
Direct tel: 01206 303800
Other contacts: Treasurer (for financial matters)

Founded: 1789

Organisation type and purpose: Registered charity (charity number 253206).
Free Church organisation.
Propagation of the Christian teachings of Emanuel Swedenborg (1688–1772).

Subject coverage: Faith and doctrines of the New Church (Swedenborgian) and the history of the organisation; life and teaching of Emanuel Swedenborg.

Collection: Archives and records of the General Conference of the New Church and individual congregations of the organisation
Works of Emanuel Swedenborg

Non-library collection catalogue: All or part available in-house

Library catalogue: All or part available in-house

Publications: Printed, and electronic and video
Order printed publications from: North of England New Church House, 34 John Dalton Street, Manchester, M2 6LE; tel: 0161 834 4192

Publications list: Available in print

Access to staff: Contact by letter, by telephone and by e-mail. Appointment necessary.
Hours: Mon to Fri, 0900 to 1700

Chief Executive: General Conference of the New Church; 59 Campernell Close, Brightlingsea, Colchester, Essex, CO7 0PP; tel: 01206 303800; fax: 01206 303800; e-mail: michael.hindley@generalconference.org.uk

Close links with: Swedenborg Society; 20 Bloomsbury Way, London, WC1A 2TH; tel: 020 7405 7986

Organisation is made up of: 23 churches in the UK and 8 groups

Treasurer: General Conference of the New Church; 42 Hillside, Findern, Derby, DE65 6AZ; tel: 01283 702764; e-mail: nigel.sutton@generalconference.org.uk

GENERAL CONSUMER COUNCIL FOR NORTHERN IRELAND

Elizabeth House, 116 Holywood Road, Belfast, BT4 1NY

Tel: 028 9067 2488, 028 9067 2488 (minicom)
Fax: 028 9065 7701
E-mail: info@consumercouncil.org.uk
Website: www.consumercouncil.org.uk
Website: www.consumerline.org

Enquiries to: Chief Executive

Founded: 1985; formed from Northern Ireland Consumer Council, Transport Users Committee (year of change 1985)

Organisation type and purpose: Advisory body, statutory body, professional body, membership association, present number of members: 14, research organisation.
The General Consumer Council is Northern Ireland's official consumer organisation, set up by the Government in 1985.
Membership is by open competition.
To promote and safeguard the interests of consumers in Northern Ireland.

Subject coverage: Consumer affairs; generally, food, energy, electricity, coal, natural gas, transport, consumer education.

Publications: Printed, and electronic and video

Publications list: Available online and in print

Access to staff: Contact by letter, by telephone, by fax, by e-mail and in person
Hours: Mon to Fri, 0900 to 1700

Access for disabled people: Access to all public areas, toilet facilities

Affiliated to: BEUC – the European Consumer organization

GENERAL COUNCIL AND REGISTER OF NATUROPATHS (GCRN)

1 Green Lane Avenue, Street, Somerset, BA16 0QS

Tel: 01458 840072
E-mail: admin@naturopathy.org.uk
Website: www.naturopathy.org.uk

Enquiries to: Secretary

Founded: 1964

Organisation type and purpose: Professional body (membership is by qualification).
To register suitably qualified practitioners, to enforce a code of professional conduct and maintain educational standards.

Subject coverage: Naturopathy, natural medicine, alternative medicine, complementary medicine.

Publications: Printed

Access to staff: Contact by letter, by telephone, by e-mail and via website
Hours: Mon to Fri, 0900 to 1300

Links with: British Naturopathic Association; 1 Green Lane Avenue, Street, Somerset, BA16 0QS, UK; tel: 01458 840072; e-mail: admin@naturopaths.org.uk; website: http://www.naturopaths.org.uk

GENERAL COUNCIL OF THE BAR OF ENGLAND AND WALES (Bar Council)

289–293 High Holborn London WC1V 7HZ

Tel: 020 7242 0082
Fax: 020 7831 9217
Website: www.barprobono.org.uk
Website: www.barcouncil.org.uk

Enquiries to: Library/Registry Officer
Direct e-mail: library@barcouncil.org.uk

Founded: 1894; formerly called Senate of the Inns of Court and the Bar

Organisation type and purpose: National organisation, professional body (membership is by qualification), present number of members: 20,000.
Central governing body of the profession of the Bar of England and Wales.
Regulation of the profession and promotion of the interests of barristers.

Subject coverage: Barristers' profession in England and Wales; official records of names and addresses of practising barristers.
Provision of legal services by barristers; information on entry to the profession; recruiting information; complaints against barristers.

Publications: Printed

Access to staff: Contact by letter, by telephone, by fax and by e-mail
Hours: Mon to Fri, 0900 to 1700

Access to building: Prior appointment required

Access for disabled people: Ramped entry, toilet facilities

Other departments: Complaints Department; Northumberland House, 303/306 High Holborn, London, WC1V 7JZ; Education and Training Departments; 2–3 Cursitor Street, London, EC4A 1NE; tel: 020 7440 4002 (Complaints) 020 7440 4000 (Education & Training); fax: 020 7440 4001

GENERAL DENTAL COUNCIL (GDC)

37 Wimpole Street, London, W1G 8DQ

Tel: 0845 222 4141 (Typetalk calls accepted)
Fax: 020 7224 3294
E-mail: information@gdc-uk.org
Website: www.gdc-uk.org

Founded: 1956

Organisation type and purpose: Statutory body.
The General Dental Council's purpose is to protect the public by regulating dental professionals in the UK.
Registers qualified professionals; sets standards of dental practice and conduct; assures the quality of dental education; ensures professionals keep up to date with developments in their profession; helps patients with complaints about dental professionals; and works to strengthen patient protection.

Subject coverage: All aspects of the dental profession: regulation, registration, qualifications, education, undergraduate training and continuing professional development, specialist training in oral surgery, surgical dentistry, endodontics, periodontics, prosthodontics, restorative dentistry, dental public health, orthodontics, paediatric dentistry, oral medicine, oral microbiology, oral pathology and dental and maxillofacial radiology.

Publications: Printed, and electronic and video

Publications list: Available online

Access to staff: Contact by letter, by telephone, by fax, by e-mail, in person and via website
Hours: Mon to Fri, 0900 to 1700

GENERAL FEDERATION OF TRADE UNIONS (GFTU)

Headland House, 308–312 Gray's Inn Road, London, WC1X 8DP

Tel: 0207 520 8340
Fax: 0207 520 8350
E-mail: gftuhq@gftu.org.uk
Website: www.gftu.org.uk

Enquiries to: General Secretary

Founded: 1899

Organisation type and purpose: Trade union.

Subject coverage: Services, education and research for trade unions.

Publications: Printed

Access to staff: Contact by letter
Hours: Mon to Fri, 0900 to 1700

GENERAL OPTICAL COUNCIL (GOC)

41 Harley Street, London, W1G 8DJ

Tel: 020 7307 3939
Fax: 020 7436 3525
E-mail: goc@optical.org
Website: www.optical.org

Enquiries to: Registrar and Chief Executive

Founded: 1958

Organisation type and purpose: The GOC is the regulator for the optical professions in the UK. Its purpose is to protect the public by promoting high standards of education and conduct amongst opticians. The Council currently registers around 23,500 optometrists, dispensing opticians, student opticians and optical businesses.

Subject coverage: It holds: statutory registers of all those registered and fit to practise, train, or carry out optical business; information relating to education and training prior to registration; advice on the application of the Opticians Act 1989; information on professional conduct.

Information services: Opticians registers – an online statutory register of all optometrists and dispensing opticians who are registered and fit to practise in the UK.

Education services: Careers information available.

Trade and statistical information: Data on the number and distribution of registered opticians

Publications: Printed, and electronic and video

Publications list: Available online

Access to staff: Contact by letter, by telephone, by fax, by e-mail and via website. Appointment necessary.
Hours: Mon to Thur, 0900 to 1700; Fri, 0900 to 1645

Access to building: *Hours:* Mon to Thur, 0900 to 1700; Fri, 0900 to 1645

Access for disabled people: Ramp available; please call or email in advance

GENERAL OSTEOPATHIC COUNCIL (GOsC)

Osteopathy House, 176 Tower Bridge Road, London, SE1 3LU

Tel: 020 7357 6655
E-mail: info@osteopathy.org.uk
Website: www.osteopathy.org.uk

Enquiries to: Osteopathic Information Service
Direct tel: Extn 242

Founded: 1993

Organisation type and purpose: Statutory body.
To regulate, promote and develop the profession of osteopathy.

Subject coverage: Osteopathy.

Trade and statistical information: Osteopathic profession

Publications: Printed

Access to staff: Contact by letter, by telephone, by fax, by e-mail and via website
Hours: Mon to Fri, 0900 to 1700

GENERAL REGISTER OFFICE (NORTHERN IRELAND) (NISRA)

Formal name: Northern Ireland Statistics and Research Agency

Oxford House, 49–55 Chichester Street, Belfast, BT1 4HL

Tel: 03002007890 or 028 9151 3101 from outside Northern Ireland.
Fax: 028 9025 2044
E-mail: gro.nisra@dfpni.gov.uk
Website: www.nidirect.gov.uk

Founded: 1922

Organisation type and purpose: National government body.
Central government department.

Subject coverage: Births, deaths, marriages.

Collection: Birth, death and marriage statistics from 1922.

Publications: Printed

Access to staff: Contact by letter, by telephone, by fax, by e-mail, in person and via website. All charged.
Hours: Mon to Fri, 0930 to 1700

Access to building: *Hours:* Mon to Fri, 0930 to 1600

GENERAL TEACHING COUNCIL FOR SCOTLAND (GTC Scotland)

Clerwood House, 96 Clermiston Road, Edinburgh, EH12 6UT

Tel: 0131 314 6000
Fax: 0131 314 6001
E-mail: gtcs@gtcs.org.uk
Website: www.gtcs.org.uk

Enquiries to: Chief Executive
Other contacts: (1) Exceptional Admissions Secretary; (2) Communications Officer for all enquiries about registration from outwith Scotland and for press enquiries and enquiries of a general nature.

Founded: 1965

Organisation type and purpose: National organisation, advisory body, statutory body, professional body (membership is by qualification), present number of members: 83,000.
Regulatory body for the teaching profession in Scotland. Registration with the Council is required for teaching in local authority and independent schools in Scotland.

Subject coverage: Teaching in Scotland, accreditation of teacher education courses in Scotland, probationary teaching service.

Trade and statistical information: Certain limited statistics on numbers of teachers registered with the Council, including applications under EC directive 89/48 (mutual recognition of professional qualifications)

Publications: Printed, and electronic and video

Access to staff: Contact by letter, by telephone, by fax, by e-mail and via website. Appointment necessary.
Hours: Mon to Thu, 0900 to 1645; Fri, 0900 to 1530

Access for disabled people: Ramped entry, access to all public areas, toilet facilities

GENERAL TEACHING COUNCIL FOR WALES (GTCW)

4th Floor, Southgate House, Wood Street, Cardiff, CF10 1EW

Tel: 029 2055 0350
Fax: 029 2055 0360
E-mail: information@gtcw.org.uk
Website: www.gtcw.org.uk

Enquiries to: Deputy Chief Executive
Direct e-mail: hayden.llewellyn@gtcw.org.uk

Founded: 2000

Organisation type and purpose: Professional body.

Subject coverage: Information concerning registered teachers.

Publications: Printed
Order printed publications from: publications@gtcw.org.uk

Access to staff: Contact by letter, by telephone, by fax, by e-mail, in person and via website
Hours: Mon to Fri, 0900 to 1700

Access to building: Prior appointment required

Access for disabled people: Access to all public areas

GENETICS SOCIETY (GENSOC)

Wallace Building, Roslin BioCentre, Roslin, Midlothian, EH25 9PS

Tel: 0131 200 6391
Fax: 0131 200 6394
E-mail: theteam@genetics.org.uk
Website: www.genetics.org.uk

Enquiries to: Executive Officer

Founded: 1919

Organisation type and purpose: Learned society (membership is by subscription), present number of members: 2,000, registered charity (charity number 261062).

Subject coverage: Genetics.

Publications: Printed

Access to staff: Contact by letter, by telephone, by fax and by e-mail

GENOME DAMAGE & STABILITY CENTRE (GDSC)

Science Park Road, University of Sussex, Falmer, Brighton, East Sussex, BN1 9RQ

Tel: 01273 678123
Fax: 01273 678121
E-mail: qhfa1@sussex.ac.uk
Website: www.biols.susx.ac.uk/gdsc

Enquiries to: Director
Direct e-mail: gdsc@sussex.ac.uk
Other contacts: Centre Administrator

Founded: 2001

Organisation type and purpose: National government body, university department or institute, research organisation.

Subject coverage: The GDSC is a research centre investigating the responses of cells to genome damage and their relationship to cancer and other aspects of human disease. The purpose-built laboratories, funded by the Joint Infrastructure Fund (JIF), the Wolfson Foundation and the University, are located adjacent to the School of Life Sciences and provide a dynamic and collaborative environment for carrying out state-of-the-art research. Much of this research is supported by the Medical Research Council via a Centre Development Grant and Programme Grants. The Centre currently houses ten research groups.

Publications: Printed

Access to staff: Contact by telephone, by fax, by e-mail and via website. Appointment necessary.
Hours: Mon to Fri, 0900 to 1700

Access to building: Prior appointment required
Hours: Mon to Fri, 0900 to 1700

Access for disabled people: Ramped entry, toilet facilities

Parent body: Sussex University; Falmer, Brighton, BN1 9RH; tel: 01273 606755; website: http://www.sussex.ac.uk

GEOGRAPHICAL ASSOCIATION (GA)

160 Solly Street, Sheffield, South Yorkshire, S1 4BF

Tel: 0114 296 0088
Fax: 0114 296 7176
E-mail: info@geography.org.uk
Website: www.geographyshop.org.uk
Website: www.geography.org.uk

continued overleaf

Founded: 1893

Organisation type and purpose: Membership association (membership is by subscription), present number of members: 6,000, voluntary organisation, registered charity (charity number 1135148), publishing house.
Resource centre for the teaching of geography.

Subject coverage: The teaching of geography, its promotion nationally and in schools.

Publications: Printed
Order printed publications from: sales@geography.org.uk

Publications list: Available online and in print

Access to staff: Contact by letter, by telephone, by fax, by e-mail, in person and via website. Appointment necessary.
Hours: Mon to Fri, 0900 to 1700

GEOGRAPHY OUTDOORS

Formal name: Geography Outdoors: the centre supporting field research, exploration and outdoor learning

Royal Geographical Society (with IBG), 1 Kensington Gore, London, SW7 2AR

Tel: 020 7591 3030
Fax: 020 7591 3031
E-mail: go@rgs.org
Website: www.rgs.org/go

Enquiries to: Head of Expeditions and Fieldwork
Direct e-mail: s.winser@rgs.org

Founded: 1980; formerly called Royal Geographical Society and Young Explorer's Trust; formerly called Expedition Advisory Centre (year of change 2006)

Organisation type and purpose: Advisory body, registered charity, suitable for ages: university undergraduates and adult leaders and teachers, training organisation, publishing house.
Information, training and advice for those planning expeditions and field research overseas.

Subject coverage: Scientific expeditions and adventure travel overseas: planning, fieldwork, equipment, safety, medicine; logistics of operating in tropical, desert and arctic environments; environmental information, training.

Collection: Expedition reports dating back to 1965

Non-library collection catalogue: All or part available online

Library catalogue: All or part available in-house

Publications: Printed, and electronic and video
Order electronic and video publications from: http://www.rgs.org/JE

Publications list: Available online and in print

Access to staff: Contact by letter, by telephone, by fax, by e-mail and via website. Appointment necessary.
Hours: Mon to Fri, 0900 to 1700

Access to building: Prior appointment required
Hours: Mon to Fri, 1100 to 1700

Access for disabled people: Ramped entry, toilet facilities

Office of the: Royal Geographical Society (with IBG); tel: 020 7591 3000; fax: 020 7591 3001; e-mail: info@rgs.org

GEOLOGICAL CURATORS GROUP (GCG)

Natural History Division, National Museum of Ireland, Merrion St, Dublin 2, Republic of Ireland

Tel: +353 87 122 1967
E-mail: mparkes@museum.ie
Website: www.geocurator.org

Enquiries to: Secretary

Founded: 1974

Organisation type and purpose: Professional body.
To improve the status of geology in museums and the standard of geological curation in general.

Subject coverage: All aspects of geology in museums; protection/care of collections; collecting; display; conservation; history; research, etc.

Publications: Printed

Access to staff: Contact by letter, by e-mail and via website
Hours: Mon to Fri, 0900 to 1700

Affiliated to: Geological Society of London

GEOLOGICAL SOCIETY

Burlington House, Piccadilly, London, W1J 0BG

Tel: 020 7434 9944
Fax: 020 7439 8975
E-mail: enquiries@geolsoc.org.uk
Website: www.geolsoc.org.uk

Enquiries to: Science & Communications Officer
Direct e-mail: sarah.day@geolsoc.org.uk
Other contacts: Librarian (for bibliographical enquiries, tel: 020 7432 0999)

Founded: 1807; incorporates the former Institution of Geologists

Organisation type and purpose: Learned society, professional body (membership is by qualification, election or invitation), present number of members: 8,800, registered charity (charity number 210161), publishing house.
To serve the science and profession of geology in the UK.

Subject coverage: Geology and allied sciences.

Collection: Murchison Letters and Diaries Rare Book Collection

Library catalogue: All or part available online and in-house

Publications: Printed
Order printed publications from: Geological Society Publishing House, Unit 7, Brassmill Lane, Bath, Somerset, BA1 3JN; tel: 01225 445046; fax: 01225 442836; e-mail: http://bookshop.geolsoc.org.uk

Publications list: Available online and in print

Access to staff: Contact by letter, by fax, by e-mail and via website. Appointment necessary. Non-members charged.
Hours: Mon to Fri, 0930 to 1730
Special comments: Charges made to non-members for use of the Library and information.

Has: 23 specialist groups and joint associations

GEOLOGISTS' ASSOCIATION (GA)

Burlington House, Piccadilly, London, W1V 9AG

Tel: 020 7434 9298
Fax: 020 7287 0280
E-mail: geol.assoc@btinternet.com
Website: www.geologist.demon.co.uk

Enquiries to: Executive Secretary

Founded: 1858

Organisation type and purpose: Learned society (membership is by election or invitation), present number of members: 2,000, registered charity (charity number 233199), suitable for ages: 18+.

Subject coverage: Geological sciences.

Publications: Printed

Access to staff: Contact by letter, by telephone, by fax, by e-mail and via website
Hours: Mon to Fri, 0930 to 1600

GEORGE ELIOT FELLOWSHIP

71 Stepping Stones Road, Coventry, Warwickshire, CV5 8JT

Tel: 024 7659 2231

Enquiries to: Honorary Secretary

Founded: 1930

Organisation type and purpose: Membership association (membership is by subscription, election or invitation), present number of members: 600, voluntary organisation, registered charity (charity number 1054060).
Literary society to promote interest in George Eliot.

Subject coverage: George Eliot's life, works, family and friends.

Publications: Printed, and electronic and video

Publications list: Available in print

Access to staff: Contact by letter and by telephone
Hours: Mon to Fri, 0900 to 2200

Affiliated to the: Alliance of Literary Societies; 22 Belmont Grove, Havant, Hampshire, PO9 3PU; tel: 01705 475855; fax: 01705 788842; e-mail: rosemary@sndc.demon.co.uk

Branches at: George Eliot Fellowship; 2006–13–212 Yamakuni, Yashiro-Cho, Kato-Gun, Hyogo 673–1421, Japan; George Eliot Fellowship; PO Box 10167, Springfield, MO 65808–0167, USA

GEORGE MACDONALD SOCIETY, THE

9 Medway Drive, Forest Row, East Sussex, RH18 5NU

Tel: 01342 823859
Fax: 01342 823859
E-mail: macdonald-society@britishlibrary.net
Website: www.george-macdonald.com
Website: www.gmsociety.org.uk

Enquiries to: Honorary Secretary
Other contacts: Membership Secretary for membership enquiries.

Founded: 1981

Organisation type and purpose:
Membership association (membership is by subscription), present number of members: 190, registered charity.
Literary society.

Subject coverage: All matters connected with the Victorian writer, lecturer and preacher George MacDonald.

Library catalogue: All or part available in-house

Publications: Printed
Order printed publications from: The George MacDonald Society, 18 Tapanhall Road Fernhill Heath, Worcester, WR3 7TR, tel: 01905 453214, fax: 01905 453214, e-mail: terryandrachel@puzzlejug.co.uk

Access to staff: Contact by letter, by telephone, by fax and by e-mail
Hours: Any reasonable time

Other addresses: The George MacDonald Society; The Library, King's College, Strand, London, WC2R 2LS

GEORGE PADMORE INSTITUTE (GPI)

76 Stroud Green Road, Finsbury Park, London, N4 3EN

Tel: 020 7272 8915
Fax: 020 7281 4662
Website: www.georgepadmoreinstitute.org

Organisation type and purpose: A registered charity (no. 1003001) offering an archive, an educational resource and a research centre.

Subject coverage: The black community of Caribbean, African and Asian descent in Britain and continental Europe.

GEORGIAN GROUP

6 Fitzroy Square, London, W1T 5DX

Tel: 0871 750 2936
Fax: 0871 750 2937
E-mail: office@georgiangroup.org.uk
Website: www.georgiangroup.org.uk

Enquiries to: Secretary

Founded: 1937

Organisation type and purpose: Voluntary organisation, registered charity (charity number 209934).
National amenity society.

Subject coverage: Conservation of Georgian architecture, 1700–1840; advice to owners and public authorities; uses to which such buildings can be adapted.

Non-library collection catalogue: All or part available in-house and in print

Library catalogue: All or part available in-house

Publications: Printed

Publications list: Available online and in print

Access to staff: Contact by letter, by telephone, by fax and by e-mail
Hours: Mon to Fri, 0930 to 1730

Liaison with: 20th Century Society; English Heritage; Society for the Protection of Ancient Buildings; Victorian Society

GERMAN HISTORICAL INSTITUTE LONDON (GHIL)

17 Bloomsbury Square, London, WC1A 2NJ

Tel: 020 7309 2050
Fax: 020 7309 2055
E-mail: ghil@ghil.ac.uk
Website: www.ghil.ac.uk

Enquiries to: Librarian
Direct tel: 020 7309 2022; 020 7309 2019
Direct e-mail: library@ghil.ac.uk
Other contacts: Head Librarian

Founded: 1975

Organisation type and purpose: Research organisation.
Academic institute.

Subject coverage: German history and politics (apart from the library, the Institute's staff of German historians are experts in various periods of German and English history from the late Middle Ages onwards).

Collection: 75,000 vols, including microforms
c. 220 current periodicals on German, English, European and global history
German and English newspapers

Library catalogue: All or part available online

Publications: Printed
Order printed publications from: For English publications: Oxford University Press, Great Clarendon Street, Oxford, OX2 6DP; tel. 01865 556767; fax 01865 556646
For German publications: Oldenbourg, Rosenheimerstrasse 145, 81671 Munich, Germany; tel. +49 8945 0510

Publications list: Available online and in print

Access to staff: Contact by letter, by telephone, by fax, by e-mail, in person and via website

Access to building: No prior appointment required (but check on website for short notice closures)
Hours: Mon, Tue, Wed and Fri, 1000 to 1700; Thu, 1000 to 2000
Special comments: Readers' tickets required (photograph and proof of address needed), free access, reference only.

Links with: Partner institutes in Rome, Paris, Washington, Warsaw, Moscow, Tokyo, Beirut, Istanbul

Parent body: The Foundation of German Humanities Institutes Abroad (DGIA); Rheinallee 6, 53173 Bonn, Germany; tel: +49 228 377860; fax: +49 228 377861; e-mail: dgia@stiftung-dgia.de; website: http://www.stiftung-dgia.de

GERMAN NATIONAL TOURIST OFFICE (GNTO)

PO Box 2695, London, W1A 3TN

Tel: 020 7317 0908
Fax: 020 7317 0917
E-mail: gntolon@d-z-t.com
Website: www.germany-tourism.de
Website: www.germany-christmas-market.org.uk

Enquiries to: Information Officer

Founded: 1951

Organisation type and purpose: National government body.
National tourist office.
Promotion of Germany as a travel destination.

Subject coverage: Information on travel to and within Germany, including list of tour operators, accommodation lists, tourist information, events, conferences and fairs in Germany.

Collection: Picture library (online at http://www.images-dzt.de)

Trade and statistical information: Data on travel and tourism from the UK and Ireland to Germany.
Data on the German travel industry (incoming only)

Publications: Printed

Publications list: Available online and in print

Access to staff: Contact by letter, by telephone, by fax, by e-mail and via website
Hours: Mon to Fri, 0900 to 1700
Special comments: Telephone hours are 1000 to 1600. No counter service.

Access to building: No access other than to staff

Branches: 30 branch offices world-wide and representative agencies world-wide

Parent body: Head Office (GNTB); German National Tourist Board, Beethoven str 69, 60325 Frankfurt am Main, Germany; tel: +49 69 974640; fax: +49 69 751903; e-mail: info@d-z-t.com

GERMAN-BRITISH CHAMBER OF INDUSTRY & COMMERCE

16 Buckingham Gate, London, SW1E 6LB

Tel: 020 7976 4100
Fax: 020 7976 4101
E-mail: mail@ahk-london.co.uk
Website: www.germanbritishchamber.co.uk

Enquiries to: PA to Director General

Founded: 1971; formerly called German Chamber of Industry & Commerce in the UK (year of change 1993)

Organisation type and purpose: Chamber of Commerce.

continued overleaf

Subject coverage: Promotion of trade and investment between Germany and the United Kingdom.
Specialist groups: membership, events, business information, legal, business partner search, marketing services, business promotion, trade fairs, VAT refund, green dot.

Publications list: Available online and in print

Access to staff: Contact by letter, by telephone, by fax, by e-mail, in person and via website. Appointment necessary. Non-members charged.
Hours: Mon to Fri, 0900 to 1700

GERMANISCHER LLOYD INDUSTRIAL SERVICES (UK) LIMITED (GLIS (UK))

Enterprise Court, Gapton Hall, Great Yarmouth, Norfolk, NR31 0ND

Tel: 01493 442112
Fax: 01493 444365
E-mail: glocb-great.yarmouth@gl-group.com
Website: www.ocbgl.com

Enquiries to: Company Secretary

Founded: 1976

Organisation type and purpose: Professional body.

Subject coverage: Verification services – i.e. oilrigs, offshore and onshore structures etc.

Publications: Printed

Publications list: Available in print

Access to staff: Contact by letter
Hours: Mon to Fri, 0900 to 1700

Main shareholding company: Germanischer Lloyd AG

GFK NOP

Ludgate House, 245 Blackfriars Road, London, SE1 9UL

Tel: 020 7890 9000
Fax: 020 7890 9001
E-mail: ukinfo@gfk.com
Website: www.gfknop.co.uk

Enquiries to: Chief Executive

Founded: 1957

Organisation type and purpose: Market research organisation.

Subject coverage: automotive, business, consumer (including CPR, travel, new media), financial services, healthcare, media, mystery shopping, technology, social research, omnibus surveys.

Access to staff: Contact by letter, by telephone, by fax, by e-mail and via website. Appointment necessary.
Hours: Mon to Fri, 0930 to 1730

Access for disabled people: Access to all public areas

Affiliated to: MRS, GfK Group

GIFTED CHILDREN'S INFORMATION CENTRE (GCIC)

Hampton Grange, 21 Hampton Lane, Solihull, West Midlands, B91 2QJ

Tel: 0121 705 4547
Fax: 0121 705 4547
E-mail: petercongdon@blueyonder.co.uk
Website: www.ukselfhelp.info/giftedchildren

Enquiries to: Director

Founded: 1978

Organisation type and purpose: Advisory body, suitable for ages: all, consultancy, publishing house.

Subject coverage: Gifted children; dyslexic children and adults; left-handed individuals; attention deficit and hyperactivity disorder; Asperger's Syndrome.

Collection: Books and guides on the above subjects

Publications: Printed

Publications list: Available in print

Access to staff: Contact by letter, by telephone and by fax. Appointment necessary.
Hours: 24-hour service

Connections with: British Dyslexia Association; Dyslexia Information Centre; Dyslexia Institute; Irlen Institute; at the same address; National Association for Gifted Children (NAGC)

GIFTWARE ASSOCIATION (GA)

Federation House, 10 Vyse Street, Birmingham, B18 6LT

Tel: 0121 236 2657
Fax: 0121 236 3921
E-mail: enquiries@ga-uk.org
Website: www.ga-uk.org

Organisation type and purpose: Membership organisation, the trade association for the UK gift and home industry.
Represents companies from across the gift and home industry – manufacturers, designers, wholesalers, importers, exporters, retailers (independents, multiples and online), from sole traders to major plcs.

Subject coverage: UK gift and home industry.

Access to staff: Contact by letter, by telephone, by fax and by e-mail

Constituent part of: British Jewellery Giftware and Finishing Federation; at the same address

GILBERT AND SULLIVAN SOCIETY

7–20 Hampden Gurney Street, London, W1H 5AX

Enquiries to: Honorary Secretary

Founded: 1924

Organisation type and purpose: Membership association (membership is by subscription), registered charity (charity number 1062970).

Subject coverage: The operas of Gilbert and Sullivan, their lives and their other works.

Collection: Society library held at the Barbican music library, London

Publications: Printed

Access to staff: Contact by letter
Hours: Mon to Fri, 0900 to 1700

Links with: Affiliated societies throughout the English-speaking world

GILERA APPRECIATION SOCIETY (GAS)

Fox House, Moor Road, Langham, Colchester, Essex, CO4 5NR

Tel: 01206 272737
Fax: 01206 273064
E-mail: ged@fox-house.freeserve.co.uk
Website: www.gilera.com

Enquiries to: Information Officer

Founded: 1982; formerly called Gilera Owners Club (GOC) (year of change 1987)

Organisation type and purpose: Voluntary organisation.

Subject coverage: History, and technical assistance on all models of the Gilera motorcycle from the earliest in 1909 until the final models in 1993; contemporary articles, road tests, manuals, sources of spare parts and relevant information appropriate to Gilera.

Collection: Sales brochures, handbooks, workshop manuals
Spare parts lists, exploded diagrams, contemporary magazine road tests, period photographs

Non-library collection catalogue: All or part available online and in-house

Library catalogue: All or part available in-house

Publications: Printed, and electronic and video

Access to staff: Contact by letter, by telephone, by e-mail and via website
Hours: Mon to Fri, 0900 to 2230 via telephone

Affiliated to: Italian Motorcycle Owners Club; 34 Pictor Road, Fairfield, Buxton, SK17 7TB; tel: 01298 79899

GILGAL SOCIETY

PO Box 53515, London, SE19 2TX

E-mail: info@gilgalsoc.org
Website: www.gilgalsoc.org
Website: www.circinfo.com

Enquiries to: Information Officer

Founded: 1988

Organisation type and purpose: Voluntary organisation, publishing house, not-for-profit publisher.
Provision of accurate, medically approved, information regarding male sexual health, with special reference to circumcision.

Subject coverage: Male genital health with special reference to circumcision.

Information services: Medically approved information about male circumcision for all ages.

Publications: Printed, and electronic and video
Order printed publications from: website: http://www.gilgalsoc.org/sterlingorder.html
Order electronic and video publications from: website: http://www.gilgalsoc.org/sterlingorder.html

Publications list: Available online and in print

Access to staff: Contact by letter, by e-mail and via website. Appointment necessary.
Hours: Daily, 0900 to 2000
Special comments: No direct access, no opening hours.

Access to building: No access other than to staff

GILLETTE ADVANCED TECHNOLOGY CENTRE UK

460 Basingstoke Road, Reading, Berkshire, RG2 0QE

Tel: 0118 987 5222
Fax: 0118 975 2822

Enquiries to: Library and Information Services Manager

History of institution: formerly called Gillette Research & Development Laboratory (year of change 2002)

Organisation type and purpose: Research organisation.

Subject coverage: Shaving devices, toiletries, writing instruments.

Access to staff: Contact by letter, by fax and by e-mail
Hours: Mon to Fri, 0800 to 1600

Access to building: No access other than to staff

Subsidiary of: Gillette Company, USA

GIN AND VODKA ASSOCIATION (GVA)

Formal name: Gin and Vodka Association of Great Britain

Cross Keys House, Queen Street, Salisbury, Wiltshire, SP1 1EY

Tel: 01722 415892
Fax: 01722 415840
Website: www.ginvodka.org.

Enquiries to: Director-General

Founded: 1991; created by the merger of Gin Rectifiers and Distillers Association, and Vodka Trade Association

Organisation type and purpose: Trade association.

Subject coverage: Gin and vodka industries; neutral alcohol industry, specific regulations in sector, nationally and internationally.

Trade and statistical information: Data on UK gin and vodka industries, data on EC spirits industry

Publications: Printed

Access to staff: Contact by fax and by e-mail
Hours: Mon to Fri, 0900 to 1700

GINGERBREAD

255 Kentish Town Road, London, NW5 2LX

Tel: 0808 802 0925 (helpline); 020 7428 5400 (office)
Fax: 020 7482 4851
E-mail: info@gingerbread.org.uk
Website: www.gingerbread.org.uk

Enquiries to: Helpline.

Founded: 1918; created by the merger of One Parent Families and Gingerbread (year of change 2007)

Organisation type and purpose: Voluntary organisation, registered charity (charity number 230750).
Campaigning and lobbying organisation.

Subject coverage: Single-parent families with reference to poverty, social security, welfare rights, housing and homelessness, equality of women, family law, divorce, pregnancy and parenthood, child care.

Publications: Printed

Publications list: Available online and in print

Access to staff: Contact by telephone
Hours: Mon to Fri, 0900 to 1700, Wed 0900 to 2000

Access to building: No access other than to staff

GIRLGUIDING SCOTLAND

16 Coates Crescent, Edinburgh, EH3 7AH

Tel: 0131 226 4511
Fax: 0131 220 4828
E-mail: administrator@girlguiding-scot.org.uk

Founded: 1910; formerly called Guide Association Scotland; formerly called The Girl Guide Association (Scotland) (year of change 1995)

Organisation type and purpose: Helps girls to reach their potential through programme of activities.

Subject coverage: Guiding in Scotland.

Access to staff: Contact by letter, by telephone and by fax. Appointment necessary.
Hours: Mon to Fri, 0900 to 1700

Also at: The Guide Association Scotland; Netherurd House, Blyth Bridge, West Linton, EH46 7AQ; tel: 01968 682208; fax: 01968 682371

GIRLGUIDING UK

17–19 Buckingham Palace Road, London, SW1W 0PT

Tel: 020 7834 6242
Fax: 020 7828 8317
E-mail: chq@girlguding.org.uk
Website: www.girlguiding.org.uk

Enquiries to: Receptionist

Founded: 1910; formerly called Guide Association; formerly called Girl Guides Association (year of change 1994)

Organisation type and purpose: Membership organisation, present number of members: 575,000, voluntary organisation, registered charity (charity number 306016).
Voluntary interdenominational international uniformed movement for girls.

Subject coverage: Guide training, outdoor pursuits, skills training, service to community.

Collection: Archives from 1910 to date
Books, documents, badges, uniforms, photographs, exhibits

Non-library collection catalogue: All or part available in-house

Library catalogue: All or part available in-house

Publications: Printed
Order printed publications from: The Guide Association, Trading Service, Atlantic Street, Broadheath, Altrincham, Cheshire, WA14 5EQ, tel: 0161 941 2237, fax: 0161 941 6326, e-mail: tradings@girlguiding.org.uk

Publications list: Available in print

Access to staff: Contact by letter, by telephone, by fax, by e-mail and via website. Appointment necessary.
Hours: Mon to Fri, 0900 to 1700

Access to building: Prior appointment required
Hours: Archives: Mon to Fri, 1000 to 1600

Access for disabled people: Ramped entry, access to all public areas, toilet facilities

Links with: Scout Association

GIRLS' BRIGADE ENGLAND AND WALES, THE (GB (England and Wales))

PO Box, 129 Broadway, Didcot, Oxfordshire, OX11 8XN

Tel: 01235 510425
Fax: 01235 510429
E-mail: admin@girlsbrigadeew.org.uk
Website: www.girlsbrigadeew.org.uk

Enquiries to: National Director

Founded: 1965; formerly called Girls' Brigade of Ireland, Girls' Guildry, Girls' Life Brigade (year of change 1965)

Organisation type and purpose:
International organisation, membership association, registered charity (charity number 206655).
Christian youth organisation.

Subject coverage: Children and youth issues; Duke of Edinburgh Award scheme; Christian teaching.

Collection: History of organisation – bound copies of GB Chronicle since 1900

Publications: Printed

Access to staff: Contact by letter, by telephone, by fax, by e-mail, in person and via website. Appointment necessary.
Hours: Mon to Fri, 0900 to 1700

Affiliated to: The Girls' Brigade Ireland; The Girls' Brigade N Ireland; The Girls' Brigade Scotland

GIRLS' FRIENDLY SOCIETY (GFS Platform)

GFS Platform, Unit 2, Angel Gate, 326 City Road, London EC1V 2PT

Tel: 020 7837 9669

continued overleaf

E-mail: annualreport@gfsplatform.org.uk
Website: www.gfsplatform.org.uk

Enquiries to: Director

Founded: 1875; formerly called Girls' Friendly Society and Townsend Fellowship

Organisation type and purpose: Membership association (membership is by subscription), present number of members: 1,000, voluntary organisation, registered charity (charity number 1054310).

Subject coverage: Parish-based work with girls and women. Youth and community work with women.

Collection: Girls' Friendly Society Archives from 1875

Publications: Printed

Access to staff: Contact by letter, by telephone, by fax and by e-mail. Appointment necessary.
Hours: Mon to Fri, 0900 to 1700

Member of: Anglican Voluntary Societies Forum; National Council for Voluntary Organisations; National Council for Voluntary Youth Services

GLADSTONE'S LIBRARY

Church Lane, Hawarden, Flintshire, CH5 3DF

Tel: 01244 532350
Fax: 01244 520643
E-mail: patsy.williams@gladlib.org
Website: www.gladstoneslibrary.org

Enquiries to: Librarian

Founded: 1896; formerly called St Deiniol's Library (year of change 2010)

Organisation type and purpose: Residential research library founded by the Rt Hon. W. E. Gladstone.

Subject coverage: Theology/religion; history/politics; literature/culture; Victorian studies

Collection: W. E. Gladstone Foundation Collection
Glynne-Gladstone Manuscripts (over 250,000 family letters, estate, household and business papers)
Bishop JRH Moorman Franciscan Collection
Radical Theology Archive (inc. papers of Don Cupitt, John AT Robinson, Anthony Freeman)
Richard L. Hills History of Technology Collection

Library catalogue: All or part available online

Access to staff: Contact by letter, by telephone, by fax, by e-mail, in person and via website. Access for members only.
Hours: Mon to Sat, 0900 to 1700

Access to building: *Hours:* Day readers: Mon to Sat, 0900 to 1700: Resident readers: daily, 0900 to 2200

Access for disabled people: Wheelchair accessible, ramp to residential wing and coffee shop

GLAMORGAN ARCHIVES

Glamorgan Archives, Clos Parc Morgannwg, Leckwith, Cardiff, CF11 8AW

Tel: 029 2087 2200
E-mail: glamro@cardiff.gov.uk
Website: www.glamarchives.gov.uk

Founded: 1939; formerly called Glamorgan Record Office (year of change 2010)

Organisation type and purpose: Local government body.
Serving the authorities of Bridgend, Caerphilly, Cardiff, Merthyr Tydfil, Rhondda Cynon Taff and the Vale of Glamorgan.

Subject coverage: History of Glamorgan.

Collection: Records of:
Glamorgan Quarter Sessions, Petty Sessions
Glamorgan County Council, Mid
Glamorgan County Council, South
Glamorgan County Council, urban and district councils, boroughs
Local boards of health, burial boards, highway boards
Coroners, Poor Law unions, hospitals, police, vehicle licensing
Port of Cardiff Shipping Registers, crew agreements (Cardiff-registered ships)
Land tax assessments, registers of electors, schools and education
Business and industry (including iron companies – Dowlais Iron Company, Rhymney Iron Company, etc. and records of the South Wales Coalfield)
Estates, families and individuals
Maps and plans
Parish records for Glamorgan parishes in the Diocese of Llandaff
Civil parishes
Non-conformist chapels and churches
Jewish synagogues and individuals
Quaker records for Wales
Societies and associations
Political records
Manorial records
Pictorial records

Non-library collection catalogue: All or part available in-house

Publications: Printed

Publications list: Available online and in print

Access to staff: Contact by letter, by telephone, by e-mail and in person. Appointment necessary.
Hours: Mon, 1300 to 1700; Tue to Fri 0900 to 1700
Every 2nd Sat of the month, 0900 to 1200
Every 3rd Mon of the month, 1700 to 2000
For dates of our of Saturday and Monday openings please see http://www.glamarchives.gov.uk/content.asp?nav=2,13&parent_directory_id=1
Special comments: Closed Bank Holidays.

GLASGOW & WEST OF SCOTLAND FAMILY HISTORY SOCIETY (G&WSFHS)

Unit 13, 32 Mansfield Street, Glasgow, G11 5QP

Tel: 0141 339 8303
Website: www.gwsfhs.org.uk

Enquiries to: Librarian
Other contacts: Publications Secretary (for details of publications)

Founded: 1977

Organisation type and purpose: Membership association (membership is by subscription), present number of members: 1,750–2,000, voluntary organisation, registered charity (charity number SC 010866), research organisation.
To promote the study of family history, particularly in Glasgow and the west of Scotland.

Subject coverage: Genealogical research in Glasgow and the west of Scotland i.e. Argyll, Ayrshire, Bute, Dunbartonshire, Lanarkshire, Renfrewshire and Stirlingshire (part).

Non-library collection catalogue: All or part available online and in-house

Library catalogue: All or part available online and in-house

Publications: Printed, and electronic and video, and microform publications

Publications list: Available online and in print

Access to staff: Contact by letter, by telephone and in person. Access for members only.
Hours: Tue, Sat, 1400 to 1630; Thu, 1000 to 2030
Special comments: Only members have access to the research facilities.

Access to building: No prior appointment required
Hours: Tue, Sat, 1400 to 1630; Thu, 1000 to 2030
Special comments: Members only.

Member of: Scottish Association of Family History Societies; e-mail: longerlive@tiscali.co.uk

GLASGOW ARCHAEOLOGICAL SOCIETY (GAS)

Flat 1–2, 27 Kirkland Street, Glasgow, G22 6SY

Tel: 0141 287 3625
Website: www.glasarchsoc.org.uk

Enquiries to: Secretary
Direct tel: 0141 945 0447 (evenings)
Direct e-mail: james_mearns@yahoo.co.uk

Founded: 1856

Organisation type and purpose: Learned society (membership is by subscription), present number of members: 350.
Encouragement of interest and research in archaeology, especially in the West of Scotland.

Subject coverage: Archaeology, architecture, archives.

Publications: Printed

Publications list: Available in print

Access to staff: Contact by letter, by telephone, by e-mail and via website
Hours: Mon to Fri, 0900 to 1700

Member of: Council for Scottish Archaeology

GLASGOW ASSOCIATION FOR MENTAL HEALTH (GAMH)

St. Andrews by the Green, 33 Turnbull Street, Glasgow, G1 5PR

Tel: 0141 552 5592
E-mail: info@gamh.org.uk
Website: www.gamh.org.uk

Enquiries to: Advice and Resource Centre

Founded: 1979

Organisation type and purpose: Membership association (membership is by subscription), voluntary organisation, registered charity (charity number SC 011684).
Advice and resource centre.

Subject coverage: Mental health in Glasgow, community-based services, befriending home support, advocacy, equalities project.

Publications: Printed

Access to staff: Contact by letter, by telephone, by fax, by e-mail and via website. Appointment necessary.
Hours: Office 0900 to 1700, Fri, 0900 to 1630; Advice and Resource Centre Tue, Fri, 1000 to 1600

Access for disabled people: Parking provided, level entry, toilet facilites

Citywide services: Advice and Resource Centre; tel: 0141 552 5592; e-mail: info@gamh.org.uk; Advocacy Matters; tel: 0141 559 5491; e-mail: advocacy@gamh.org.uk; Carers Support Project; tel: 0141 429 7593; e-mail: carers@gamh.org.uk; Homeless Support Project; tel: 0141 554 6200; e-mail: homelesssupport@gamh.org.uk; Supported Living Project; tel: 0141 429 6307; e-mail: supportedliving@gamh.org.uk

Services in North and East Glasgow: Active Outreach Team; tel: 0141 554 6200; e-mail: activeoutreach@gamh.org.uk; Housing Support Project – East; tel: 0141 564 1206; e-mail: hspeast@gamh.org.uk; Housing Support Project – North; tel: 0141 587 1018; e-mail: hspnorth@gamh.org.uk; North and East Community Project; tel: 0141 558 0943; e-mail: northeast@gamh.org.uk; Scotia Clubhouse; tel: 0141 556 7766; e-mail: scotiaclubhouse@gamh.org.uk

Services in South Glasgow: Housing Support Project – South; tel: 0141 433 9393; e-mail: hspsouth@gamh.org.uk; South Community Project; tel: 0141 423 0408; e-mail: south@gamh.org.uk; Young Carers Southside; tel: 0141 424 1708; e-mail: youngcarers@gamh.org.uk

Services in West Glasgow: Housing Support Project – West; tel: 0141 579 0013; e-mail: hspwest@gamh.org.uk; West Community Project; tel: 0141 357 2570; e-mail: west@gamh.org.uk; Young Carers Riverside; tel: 0141 424 1708; e-mail: youngcarers@gamh.org.uk

GLASGOW CALEDONIAN UNIVERSITY LIBRARY IN THE SALTIRE CENTRE (GCU)

70 Cowcaddens Road, Glasgow, G4 0BA

Tel: 0141 273 1000
Fax: 0141 273 1000
Website: www.gcal.ac.uk/library

Enquiries to: Director of Library Services
Direct tel: 0141 273 1180

Founded: 1992; formed by the merger of Glasgow Polytechnic and Queen's College, Glasgow

Organisation type and purpose: University library.

Subject coverage: Biology, building and surveying, business administration, computer studies, economics, engineering, finance and accounting, health and nursing studies, law and public administration, management, mathematics, ophthalmic optics, optometry and vision science, psychology, risk and financial services, social sciences, social work, hospitality and leisure, consumer studies, physiotherapy, radiography, podiatry, nutrition, orthoptics and occupational therapy.

Collection: Norman and Janey Buchan collection (left-wing politics)
David Donald collection (left-wing politics)
Gallacher Memorial Library (left-wing politics)
Sandy Hobbs Collection
George H Johannes Collection (South Africa, ANC, struggle against apartheid)
William Kemp Collection (left-wing politics)
John Lenihan Collection
Norrie McIntosh Collection (left-wing politics)
Jim Milligan Collection (left-wing politics)
Queen's College Collection (home economics, domestic science)
Samuel Stewart Collection (left-wing politics)
Michael Scott Collection (left-wing politics)
Scottish and Northern Book Distribution Centre Limited Collection (alternative politics, pressure groups)

Library catalogue: All or part available online

Publications: Printed

Publications list: Available in print

Access to staff: Letter of introduction required. Non-members charged.
Hours: Mon to Thu, 0830 to 2100; Fri, 0830 to 1700; Sat, Sun, 1000 to 1800

Access for disabled people: Parking provided, access to all public areas, toilet facilities

GLASGOW CITY COUNCIL

City Chambers, George Square, Glasgow, G2 1DU

Tel: 0141 287 2000
Fax: 0141 287 5666
E-mail: pr@glasgow.gov.uk
Website: www.glasgow.gov.uk

Enquiries to: Public Relations Manager
Direct tel: 0141 287 0901
Direct fax: 0141 287 0904

Founded: April 1996

Organisation type and purpose: Local government body, statutory body.
Local government.

Subject coverage: Local government services.

Publications: Printed

Publications list: Available online and in print

Access to staff: Contact by letter, by telephone, by e-mail and via website
Hours: Mon to Fri, 0900 to 1700

GLASGOW COUNCIL ON ALCOHOL (GCA)

Seventh Floor, Newton House, 457 Sauchiehall Street, Glasgow G2 3LG

Tel: 0141 353 1800
Fax: 0141 353 1030
E-mail: email@thegca.org.uk
Website: www.thegca.org.uk

Enquiries to: Director

Founded: 1965

Organisation type and purpose: Voluntary organisation, registered charity (charity number SC 014501).
The aim of GCA is to reduce alcohol abuse in the community of Greater Glasgow.

Subject coverage: Counselling, education and advice on alcohol and alcohol abuse.

Access to staff: Contact by letter, by telephone, by fax and in person
Hours: Mon to Thu, 0900 to 2030; Fri, 0900 to 1645

Access for disabled people: Toilet facilities

Affiliated to: Alcohol Focus Scotland; 2nd Floor, 166 Buchanan Street, Glasgow, G1 2NH; tel: 0141 333 9677; fax: 0141 333 1606; e-mail: enquiries@alcohol-focus-scotland.org.uk

GLASGOW INTERNATIONAL JAZZ FESTIVAL (GIJF)

Formal name: Royal Bank Glasgow Jazz Festival

81 High Street, Glasgow, G1 1NB

Tel: 0141 552 3552
Fax: 0141 552 3592
E-mail: glasgow@jazzfest.co.uk
Website: www.jazzfest.co.uk

Enquiries to: Director
Direct e-mail: olive@jazzfest.co.uk

Founded: 1987

Organisation type and purpose: Annual jazz festival organiser.
To present the best of international jazz and jazz related music.

Subject coverage: Jazz and blues.

Collection: Photographic library
Previous festival programmes

Publications: Printed

Publications list: Available online and in print

Access to staff: Contact by letter, by telephone, by fax, by e-mail and via website
Hours: Mon to Fri, 1000 to 1700

GLASGOW LIBRARIES, INFORMATION & LEARNING

Mitchell Library, North Street, Glasgow, G3 7DN

Tel: 0141 287 2999
Fax: 0141 287 2815
E-mail: lil@csglasgow.org
Website: www.glasgowlibraries.org

Enquiries to: Head of Libraries and Archives
Direct tel: 0141 287 5114
Direct fax: 0141 287 5151

continued overleaf

Other contacts: Information Services Manager for specific remit for Mitchell Library.

Founded: 1877; formerly called Glasgow City Libraries and Archives

Organisation type and purpose: Local government body.
Public reference library.

Subject coverage: General and business information, newspapers, philosophy, religion, social sciences, language, literature, science, technology, arts, recreation, music, history and topography, particularly Scottish, Glasgow collection.

Collection: Andrew Bain Memorial Collection (4,000 vols local history)
Archives (records of the City of Glasgow)
Armour Donation (3,600 vols German literature)
Bell Collection (450 pamphlets, Scottish Union)
British Standards (complete set)
Clem Edwards Donation (2,000 vols Labour Movement)
Cumming Pamphlets (185 pamphlets, Scottish religion and education – 19th-century)
Dante Collection (216 vols)
Donald Purchase (400 vols shorthand)
E A Reynolds Collection (711 vols Rationalist literature)
E J Thomson Collection (500 vols Scottish topography)
Forrester Pamphlets (500 pamphlets, religion – 19th century)
Gardyne Collection (1,800 vols Scottish poetry)
Glasgow Collection (20,000 vols)
Gourlay Donation (1,042 vols India)
Graham Collection (local history)
Henderson Purchase (2800 vols Celtic languages)
Hillhouse Purchase (300 vols draughts)
Inverclyde Donation (Inverclyde Family albums, etc.)
J H Thomson Collection (1,230 vols Covenanting history)
Jenkins Donation (500 vols Spain)
Jervise Collection (1,300 vols provincial poets of Scotland)
Kidson Collection (9,000 vols 18th-century popular music)
Lipton Collection (Sir Thomas Lipton albums, etc.)
McClelland Donation (350 vols phrenology)
Moncrieff Mitchell Collection (3,000 vols and 100 prints, local history)
Moody Manners Collection (2,900 vols vocal and orchestral opera scores)
Morgan Collection (6,000 vols pure and applied science)
Morrison Collection (7,000 vols theology)
New Church Collection (2,000 vols)
North British Locomotive Company Collection (10,000 items)
Patent Specifications (5,000,000 UK, US, European)
Private Press Collection (1,600 vols)
R L Stevenson Collection (200 vols)
Reid Collection (850 vols angling)
Reid Donation (134 vols Social Credit)
Russell-Fergus Collection (20 vols history of the harp)
Scottish Poetry Collection (15,000 vols including 4,000 vols on Robert Burns)
Scouler Collection (2,000 vols science and philosophy, 16th to 19th centuries)
Slains Castle Collection (3,100 vols theology, literature, travel, 16th to 18th centuries)
Smeal Collection (117 vols anti-slavery)
Trade Unions Collection (2,500 vols)
UK and Scottish Newspapers
UK patents and specifications
United Nations Collection (10,000 vols)
Wallace and Bruce Collection (310 vols)
Whitton Bequest (347 vols botany, horticulture, etc.)
William ('Crimea') Simpson Collection (103 items)
Wotherspoon Collection (41 vols Clyde steamships)

Trade and statistical information: A wide selection of trade and statistical information, including market research reports, is available in the business information and social sciences sections

Non-library collection catalogue: All or part available in-house

Library catalogue: All or part available in-house

Publications: Printed
Order printed publications from: Stock control at the same address, tel: 0141 287 2812, fax: 0141 287 2815

Publications list: Available in print

Access to staff: Contact by letter, by telephone, by fax, by e-mail and in person
Hours: Mon to Thu, 0900 to 2000; Fri, Sat, 0900 to 1700
Archives: Mon to Thu, 0930 to 1645; Fri, 0930 to 1600; or by appointment

Access for disabled people: Parking provided, toilet facilities
Special comments: Parking by prior arrangement via duty librarian.
Level entry via Kent Road.

GLASGOW METROPOLITAN COLLEGE

230 Cathedral Street, Glasgow, G1 2TG

Tel: 0141 566 1664
Fax: 0141 566 1666
E-mail: tony.donnelly@glasgowmet.ac.uk
Website: www.glasgowmet.ac.uk/library

Enquiries to: Chief Librarian
Direct tel: 0141 566 1550

Founded: 2005; created by the merger of Glasgow College of Food Technology (f. 1972) and Glasgow College of Building and Printing (year of change 2005)

Organisation type and purpose: Further education.

Subject coverage: Construction, design, ESOL, commmunication and media, printing, sports science, tourism, health and safety, food technology, food science, food processing, hospitality and catering, professional cookery, travel and tourism.

Library catalogue: All or part available online

Access to staff: Contact by letter, by telephone, by fax, by e-mail, in person and via website. Appointment necessary. Non-members charged.
Hours: Term time: Mon to Wed, 0800 to 1930; Thu, 1000 to 1700; Fri, 0800 to 1700.
Vacation: Mon to Fri, 0900 to 1600

Access for disabled people: Parking provided, ramped entry, access to all public areas, toilet facilities

Links with: Glasgow Caledonian University (GCU); Cowcaddens Road, Glasgow, G4 0BA

GLASGOW MUSEUMS

Glasgow Life, 220 High Street, Glasgow, G4 0QW

Tel: 0141 287 4350
E-mail: museums@glasgowlife.org.uk
Website: www.glasgowmuseums.com

Enquiries to: Director
Direct tel: 0141 287 2600
Other contacts: Marketing Officer

Founded: 1901; formerly called Glasgow Museums and Art Galleries

Organisation type and purpose: Local government body, museum, art gallery, suitable for all ages.
Glasgow Museums is the corporate title for Glasgow City Council, Culture & Leisure Services, Museums Service, and administers Glasgow's 12 municipal museums and art galleries.

Subject coverage: The subjects covered by the twelve museums of Glasgow include art, history, British history, worldwide ethnography, sociology, natural history, history of science, history of transport, religious history, and content and conservation science.

Information services: Selective dissemination services; the Open Museum Department lends objects and displays to community groups in Glasgow and Strathclyde. Glasgow Museums offers touring exhibitions to venues in UK and elsewhere. For Museum Education Department tel: 0141 276 9368.

Special visitor services: Materials and/or activities for children, guided tours.

Education services: Group education facilities.

Trade and statistical information: Glasgow's municipal art and design collections of over 1 million objects, a substantial proportion of which relate to the city's artistic, cultural, political and social history

Non-library collection catalogue: All or part available online and in print

Publications: Printed

Publications list: Available online and in print

Access to staff: Contact by letter, by telephone, by fax and by e-mail. Appointment necessary.
Hours: Mon to Thu, Sat, 1000 to 1700; Fri, Sun, 1100 to 1700

Access to building: Prior appointment required

Access for disabled people: Parking provided, level entry, access to all public areas, toilet facilities

Museum and Galleries: Riverside Museum (formally Museum of Transport); 100 Pointhouse Place, Glasgow, G3 8RS

Museums and Galleries: Burrell Collection; 2060 Pollokshaws Road, Glasgow, G43 1AT; tel: 0141 287 2550; fax: 0141 287 2597; Gallery of Modern Art (GoMA); Royal Exchange Square, Glasgow, G1 3AH; tel: 0141 229 1996; fax: 0141 204 5316; Glasgow Museums Resource Centre (GMRC); 200 Woodhead Road, Nitshill, Glasgow, G53 7NN; tel: 0141 276 9300; fax: 0141 276 9305; Kelvingrove Art Gallery & Museum; Argyle Street, Glasgow, G3 8AG; tel: 0141 287 2699; fax: 0141 287 2690; Open Museum; Glasgow Museums Resource Centre, 200 Woodhead Road, Nitshill, Glasgow, G53 7NN; tel: 0141 276 9368; fax: 0141 276 9305; People's Palace and Winter Gardens; Glasgow Green, Glasgow, G40 1AT; tel: 0141 271 2951; fax: 0141 271 2960; Pollok Country Park, Pollok House (managed by The National Trust for Scotland); Pollok Country Park, 2060 Pollokshaws Road, Glasgow, G43 1AT; tel: 0141 616 6410; fax: 0141 616 6521; website: www.nts.org.uk
Provand's Lordship; 3 Castle Street, Glasgow, G4 0RB; tel: 0141 552 8819; fax: 0141 552 4744; Scotland Street School Museum; 225 Scotland Street, Glasgow, G5 8QB; tel: 0141 287 0500; fax: 0141 287 0515; St Mungo Museum of Religious Life and Art; 2 Castle Street, Glasgow, G4 0RH; tel: 0141 553 2557; fax: 0141 552 4744

Parent body: Glasgow Life; 220 High Street, Glasgow, G4 0QW; tel: 0141 287 4350; fax: 0141 287 5558

GLASGOW PHILHARMONIC MALE VOICE CHOIR

c/o John McFarlane, 5 Chapelton Avenue, Bearsden, Glasgow, G61 2RE

Tel: 0141 586 5195
E-mail: john.mcfarlane4@ntlworld.com
Website: www.glasphilmvc.org.uk

Enquiries to: General Secretary

Founded: 1925

Organisation type and purpose: Membership association (membership is by subscription), present number of members: 60.

Subject coverage: Male voice choral singing.

Collection: Large library of male voice music, now accommodated in the Mitchell Library, Glasgow.

Non-library collection catalogue: All or part available in-house

Access to staff: Contact by letter, by e-mail and via website
Hours: daily, before 2200

GLASGOW WOMEN'S LIBRARY (GWL)

15 Berkeley Street, Glasgow, G3 7BW

Tel: 0141 248 9969
E-mail: info@womenslibrary.org.uk
Website: www.womenslibrary.org.uk

Founded: 1991

Organisation type and purpose: A registered charity (charity number SC 029881) and a registered company (number 178507), maintaining a lending library, archive collections and historical artifacts.

Subject coverage: Women's lives, histories and achievements.

Education services: Lifelong Learning Programme, Adult Literacy and Numeracy Project and a Black and Minority Ethnic Women's Project.

Non-library collection catalogue: All or part available online

Library catalogue: All or part available online

Access to staff: Contact by letter, by telephone, by e-mail, in person and via website
Hours: Mon to Fri, 0930 to 1700

Access to building: Pending major refurbishment of new premises, the majority of the collection is in storage and access is limited.
Hours: Mon to Fri, 0930 to 1700

Access for disabled people: Please contact the Library about accessibility

GLASSFIBRE REINFORCED CONCRETE ASSOCIATION (GRCA)

c/o The Concrete Society, Riverside House, 4 Meadows Business Park, Station Approach, Blackwater, Camberley, Surrey, GU17 9AB

Tel: 01276 607140
Fax: 01276 607141
E-mail: enquiries@grca.org.uk
Website: www.grca.co.uk

Enquiries to: Adviser

Founded: 1975

Organisation type and purpose: International organisation, advisory body, trade association (membership is by subscription).
Technical database for GRC industry.
Creation of CEN standards and representation on non-UK trade associations, relevant to the CRC (GFRC) industry.

Subject coverage: Technical advice and sourcing of suppliers of glassfibre reinforced concrete.

Publications: Printed, and electronic and video
Order printed publications from: The Concrete Bookshop, Riverside House, 4 Meadows Business Park, Station Approach, Blackwater, Camberley, Surrey, GU17 9AB; tel: 01276 607140; fax: 01276 607141; e-mail: enquiries@concretebookshop.com; website: http://www.concretebookshop.com
Order electronic and video publications from: The Concrete Bookshop

Publications list: Available online and in print

Access to staff: Contact by letter, by telephone, by fax, by e-mail and via website. Appointment necessary.
Hours: Mon to Fri, 0900 to 1700

Access to building: No prior appointment required

Administered by: The Concrete Society; Riverside House, 4 Meadows Business Park, Station Approach, Blackwater, Camberley, Surrey, GU17 9AB; tel: 01276 607140; fax: 01276 607141; website: http://www.concrete.org.uk

GLAXOSMITHKLINE

North Lonsdale Road, Ulverston, Cumbria, LA12 9DR

Tel: 01229 582261
Fax: 01229 482282

Enquiries to: Technical Information Officer
Direct tel: 01229 482232
Direct fax: 01229 482257

History of institution: formerly called Glaxo Wellcome Operations

Organisation type and purpose: Manufacturing industry, research organisation.

Subject coverage: Pharmaceutical development and production.

GLAXOSMITHKLINE, RESEARCH AND DEVELOPMENT

New Frontiers Science Park (North), Third Avenue, Harlow, Essex, CM19 5AW

Tel: 01279 622000
Fax: 01279 622100
Website: www.gsk.com

Enquiries to: Librarian

History of institution: formerly called Beecham Pharmaceuticals Research Division, SmithKline Beecham Pharmaceuticals, Research and Development

Organisation type and purpose: Research organisation.

Subject coverage: Organic chemistry, pharmacology, neurosciences.

Non-library collection catalogue: All or part available in-house

Library catalogue: All or part available in-house

Access to staff: Contact by letter and by e-mail
Hours: Mon to Fri, 0900 to 1700

Access to building: No access other than to staff
Special comments: No access to library.

Subsidiary of: GlaxoSmithKline

GLOBAL EDUCATION MILTON KEYNES (GEMK)

Global Education Milton Keynes, Queensway Centre, Bletchley MK2 2HB

Tel: 07952038268
E-mail: info@gemk.org.uk
Website: www.gemk.org.uk
Website: www.gemkresources.co.uk

Enquiries to: Information Officer
Other contacts: Centre Co-ordinator

Founded: 1980; formerly called Milton Keynes World Development Education Centre (year of change 2001)

Organisation type and purpose: Charitable company (charity number 1086858; company number 4102062), training organisation, resource centre.
Public education in the field of sustainability, global issues and world development.

continued overleaf

Subject coverage: Materials for teachers and community workers on world development issues, e.g. food, water, population, India, Ghana, Tanzania, schools-linking, recycling and disability, sustainable development and citizenship.

Special visitor services: Resource Centre with loan facility for members.

Education services: Provides support for Sustainable Schools, Global Schools, Sustainable Communities and for teachers and others seeking to bring a global dimension to their work.

Collection: Everyday items from India, Ghana, Tanzania
Recycled items commonly made in Ghana and Zambia

Publications: Printed, and electronic and video

Access to staff: Contact by letter, by telephone and by e-mail. Appointment necessary.
Hours: By appointment; restricted availability in the school holidays

Links with: Development Education Association; CAN Mezzanine 32–36 Loman Street London SE1 0EH; tel: 020 7922 7930; fax: 020 7922 7929; e-mail: dea@dea.org.uk

GLOBAL SCHOOL PARTNERSHIPS (GSP)

British Council, 10 Spring Gardens, London, SW1A 2BN

Tel: 020 7389 4031
Fax: 020 7389 4426
E-mail: globalschools@britishcouncil.org
Website: www.dfid.gov.uk/globalschools.htm

Enquiries to: Marketing, Sales and Communications Manager
Direct e-mail: andrea.mason@britishcouncil.org

Founded: 2003

Organisation type and purpose: Registered charity.

Publications: Printed, and electronic and video
Order electronic and video publications from: Website: http://www.difid.gov.uk/globalschools

Publications list: Available in print

Access to staff: Contact by letter, by telephone, by fax and by e-mail
Hours: Mon to Fri, 0900 to 1730

Constituent part of: British Council

GLOSCAT

Formal name: Gloucestershire College of Arts and Technology

Princess Elizabeth Way, Cheltenham, Gloucestershire, GL51 7SJ

Tel: 01242 532000
Fax: 01242 532196
E-mail: info@gloscat.ac.uk
Website: www.gloscat.ac.uk

Enquiries to: Librarian
Direct tel: 01242 532185

Organisation type and purpose: College of further education.

Subject coverage: Cheltenham site: bakery, beauty therapy, business studies, caring, catering, clerical, computing, GCSEs, hairdressing, home economics, hotels, languages, leisure studies, science, secretarial, textiles, tourism.
Brunswick site: building studies, construction, design, electronic communication engineering, electronic engineering, manufacturing engineering, motor vehicles, surveying.

Library catalogue: All or part available in-house

Access to staff: Contact by letter, by telephone, by fax, by e-mail and via website
Hours: Mon to Fri, 0900 to 1700

Access to building: No prior appointment required
Hours: Cheltenham: term time: Mon, Wed, Thu, 0830 to 2000; Tue 0930 to 2000; Fri, 0830 to 1700
Brunswick: term time: Mon, Wed, Thu, 0830 to 2000; Tue 0930 to 2000; Fri, 0830 to 1700; Sat, 1015 to 1345
Both sites, vacations: Mon to Fri, 0900 to 1700
Special comments: Reference only.

Access for disabled people: Level entry, access to all public areas, toilet facilities

Other site at: GLOSCAT; Brunswick Campus, Brunswick Road, Gloucester, GL1 1HU; tel: 01452 426530; fax: 01452 426531

GLOUCESTER CITY COUNCIL

North Warehouse, The Docks, Gloucester, GL1 2EP

Tel: 01452 522232
Fax: 01452 396140
E-mail: thecouncil@gloucester.gov.uk
Website: www.gloucester.gov.uk

Enquiries to: Head of Communications and Marketing
Direct tel: 01452 396133
Direct fax: 01452 396334

Organisation type and purpose: Local government body.

Subject coverage: Local government services.

Access to staff: Contact by letter, by telephone, by fax, by e-mail, in person and via website. Appointment necessary.
Hours: Mon to Fri, 0830 to 1700

GLOUCESTER LIBRARY

Brunswick Road, Gloucester, GL1 1HT

Tel: 01452 426979, 01452 426975 (minicom)
Fax: 01452 521468
Website: www.gloscc.gov.uk/pubserv/gcc/clams

Enquiries to: Librarian

Founded: 1900

Organisation type and purpose: Public library.

Non-library collection catalogue: All or part available online and in-house

Library catalogue: All or part available in-house

Access to staff: Contact by letter, by telephone, by fax, by e-mail, in person and via website
Hours: Mon, Tue, Thu, 1000 to 1930; Wed, Fri, 1000 to 1700; Sat, 0900 to 1300

Access for disabled people: Access to all public areas, toilet facilities

Parent body: Gloucestershire County Library, Arts and Museum Service; Quayside House, Shire Hall, Gloucester, GL1 2HY

GLOUCESTERSHIRE ARCHIVES (GA)

Clarence Row, Alvin Street, Gloucester, GL1 3DW

Tel: 01452 425295
Fax: 01452 426378
E-mail: archives@gloucestershire.gov.uk
Website: www.gloucestershire.gov.uk/archives

Enquiries to: Head of Information Management and Archives
Other contacts: Customer Services Manager (for specific historical enquiries)

Founded: 1936; formerly called Gloucestershire Record Office (year of change 2006); incorporates the former Gloucestershire Collection (local studies collection) (year of change 2005)

Organisation type and purpose: Local government body.
An amalgamation of the County Record Office, the Gloucester Diocesan Archives and the Gloucester City Archives; also houses the Victoria History of Gloucestershire and the Gloucester Local Studies Collection.
Aims to preserve locally generated historical records of the county and all its communities dating from earliest times to the present day. The documents are kept in strongrooms at the Record Office but ownership is retained by depositors.

Subject coverage: Local history and topography of Gloucestershire and all its towns and parishes; biography, demography, genealogy, history of churches, landed estates, organisations, businesses, charities within the county; contribution of Gloucestershire to regional and national history.

Collection: Archives of: the diocese of Gloucester, Gloucestershire County Council and its predecessors, all district councils and predecessor town and borough councils, City of Gloucester, boroughs of Tewkesbury and Cheltenham, also nonconformist churches, charities, schools, businesses and antiquarian collections
Many family collections including St Aldwyn, Lloyd-Baker, Bathurst, Hicks-Beach, Beaufort, Blathwayt, Codrington, Sherborne
Gloucestershire Local Studies Collection

Non-library collection catalogue: All or part available online and in-house

Publications: Microform publications

Publications list: Available online and in print

Access to staff: Contact by letter, by telephone, by fax, by e-mail, in person and via website
Hours: Tue, Wed, Fri, 0900 to 1700; Thu, 0900 to 1830; Sat, 0900 to 1300

Access for disabled people: Access to all public areas

Also at: Gloucestershire Archives; Shire Hall Record Centre, Westgate Street, Gloucester, GL1 2TG; tel: 01452 425289

Parent body: Gloucestershire County Council

GLOUCESTERSHIRE LIBRARIES & INFORMATION

Quayside House, Shire Hall, Gloucester, GL1 2HY

Tel: 0845 230 5420
Fax: 01452 452042
E-mail: libraryhelp@gloucestershire.gov.uk
Website: www.gloucestershire.gov.uk/libraries
Website: www.searchourshelves.gloucestershire.gov.uk/TalisPrism

Enquiries to: Ask Us Enquiry Service.
Direct tel: 0845 230 5421
Direct e-mail: ask@gloucestershire.gov.uk

Organisation type and purpose: Local government body, public library.
Library headquarters, there are 39 libraries in the County.

Subject coverage: General reference, business information, Gloucestershire local studies & family history, Gloucestershire arts and crafts.

Information services: Ask Us Enquiry Service offers information support by telephone, e-mail, letter and website form. The Ask Us service supports reference services in all Gloucestershire Libraries. Gloucester library holds the Europe Direct service and official publications collection. Cheltenham also has a reference collection, including Art collection.

Education services: Library Services for Education, tel: 01452 427240

Services for disabled people: For the visually impaired; for the hearing impaired.

Collection: Art Collection – Cheltenham
Europe Direct – Gloucester
Cheltenham Local & Family History Library
Tewkesbury, Stroud, Cirencester, Stow on the Wold & Cinderford Libraries all have local & family history collections.

Trade and statistical information: From Ask Us Enquiry Service

Non-library collection catalogue: All or part available online

Access to staff: Contact by letter, by telephone, by fax, by e-mail and via website
Hours: Mon to Fri, 0900 to 1700

Parent body: Gloucestershire County Council

Strategic libraries at: Cheltenham, Cinderford, Cirencester, Gloucester, Stroud and Tewkesbury

GLOUCESTERSHIRE LOCAL HISTORY COMMITTEE

Community House, 15 College Green, Gloucester, GL1 2LZ

Tel: 01452 528491
Fax: 01452 528493
E-mail: glosrcc@grcc.org.uk
Website: www.gloshistory.org.uk

Enquiries to: Secretary

Founded: 1948

Organisation type and purpose: Voluntary organisation.

Subject coverage: Local history and archaeology of Gloucestershire, local history and activities within Gloucestershire.

Publications: Printed

Access to staff: Contact by letter, by telephone, by fax and by e-mail
Hours: 0900 to 1700

Constituent part of: Gloucestershire Rural Community Council (GRCC)

GLUED LAMINATED TIMBER ASSOCIATION (GLTA)

Formal name: Glued Laminated Timber Association – GLULAM

Chiltern House, Stocking Lane, Hughenden Valley, High Wycombe, Buckinghamshire, HP14 4ND

Tel: 01494 565180
Fax: 01494 565487
E-mail: info@glulam.co.uk
Website: www.glulam.co.uk

Enquiries to: Secretary

Founded: 1987

Organisation type and purpose: Trade association (membership is by subscription), present number of members: 8 (in two categories).
To promote the awareness and use of glued laminated timber in the UK.

Non-library collection catalogue: All or part available online

Publications: Printed, and electronic and video

Access to staff: Contact by letter, by telephone, by fax, by e-mail and via website
Hours: Mon to Fri, 0900 to 1700
Special comments: Visitors not normally received by secretariat.

GLYNDWR UNIVERSITY

Library, Postal Point 22L, Glyndwr Univeristy, Mold Road, Wrexham, LL11 2AW

Tel: 01978 293237
E-mail: enquirydesk@glyndwr.ac.uk
Website: www.glyndwr.ac.uk

Enquiries to: Library Services Manager
Other contacts: University Librarian

Founded: 2008; formerly called North East Wales Institute of Higher Education (year of change 2008)

Organisation type and purpose: University library, suitable for ages: 18+.

Subject coverage: Creative industries, computing, engineering, education, art and design, health, sciences, social work, business and management, humanities.

Library catalogue: All or part available online

Access to staff: Contact by letter, by telephone, by fax, by e-mail and in person
Hours: Term time: Mon to Thu, 0845 to 2200; Fri, 0845 to 2100; Sat, 1000 to 1700; some Sunday openings
Vacation: Mon to Fri, 0845 to 1200

Access for disabled people: Parking provided, level entry, toilet facilities

GMB

22–24 Worple Road, Wimbledon, London, SW19 4DD

Tel: 020 8947 3131
Fax: 020 8944 6552
E-mail: info@gmb.org.uk
Website: www.gmb.org.uk

Enquiries to: General Secretary

Founded: 1889; formerly called FTAT, National Union of Tailor and Garment Workers (NUTGW); formerly called General & Municipal Workers (GMW) (year of change 1987)

Organisation type and purpose: Trade union (membership is by subscription), present number of members: 600,000, voluntary organisation.

Subject coverage: Industrial relations, collective bargaining, employment law, occupational pensions, health and safety at work, job education, work study.

Collection: Agreements on wages and conditions of work with companies where GMB is recognised (accessible to public only by special arrangement)

Publications: Printed

Publications list: Available in print

Access to staff: Contact by letter and by fax
Hours: Mon to Fri, 0900 to 1700

Access for disabled people: Parking provided, ramped entry, access to all public areas, toilet facilities

Affiliated to: The Labour Party; Trades Union Congress

GO! SIGN

Formal name: Go! Sign – Christ in the Deaf Community

E-mail: via website
Website: www.gosign.org.uk

Founded: 1998

Organisation type and purpose: Registered charity dedicated to serving the spiritual and social needs of deaf people, their families and friends.
To advance the Christian faith, particularly amongst deaf people, to support deaf people, to promote full participation for deaf people in their communities.

Subject coverage: GRACE programme:

continued overleaf

- Growth in the network of deaf Christian groups, leaders, churches, fellowship and individuals.
- Renewal and spiritual growth through training, support, events and conferences.
- Access to information promoting deaf Christian issues, support and service provisions.
- Churches: strengthening members through deaf spiritual awareness, network support and equipping.
- Evangelism via drama shows, video resources and training.

Education services: Summer school.

Publications: Electronic and video
Order electronic and video publications from: Website

Access to staff: Contact via website

GOETHE-INSTITUT

Library, 50 Princes Gate, Exhibition Road, London, SW7 2PH

Tel: 020 7596 4040
Fax: 020 7594 0230
E-mail: library@london.goethe.org
Website: www.goethe.de/london
Website: www.goethe.de/ins/gb/lon/inz/bib/enindex.htm

Enquiries to: Information Officer

Organisation type and purpose:
International organisation.
Cultural organisation.

Subject coverage: Germany: general information on all aspects, German books with some English translations covering all fields in the arts, history, humanities and social sciences; emphasis on German literature, contemporary history, art and language.

Library catalogue: All or part available online and in-house

Publications: Printed

Access to staff: Contact by letter, by telephone, by fax, by e-mail, in person and via website
Hours: Mon to Thu, 1300 to 1830; Sat, 1300 to 1700

Links with: Goethe-Institut München; Dachauer Strasse 122, München, D-80637, Germany

GOETHE-INSTITUT GLASGOW, GERMAN CULTURAL INSTITUTE

3 Park Circus, Glasgow, G3 6AX

Tel: 0141 332 2555
Fax: 0141 343 1656
E-mail: library@glasgow.goethe.org
Website: www.goethe.de/glasgow

Enquiries to: Librarian
Other contacts: Language Office (for language courses in Glasgow and Germany, scholarships for Scottish teachers of German and seminars)

Founded: 1973; formerly called Goethe-Institut Inter Nationes; formerly called Goethe-Institut (year of change 2001)

Organisation type and purpose:
International organisation.
Promotion of the German language at all levels of education and of international cultural co-operation, library and information service.

Subject coverage: German language, literature, culture and teaching.

Collection: Library, books, videos, cassettes, CD-ROMs, DVDs, CDs

Non-library collection catalogue: All or part available online and in-house

Library catalogue: All or part available online and in-house

Publications: Printed

Access to staff: Contact by letter, by telephone, by fax, by e-mail, in person and via website
Hours: Language Department: Mon to Thu, 1000 to 1700; Fri, 1000 to 1500
Library & Information Service: Mon, 1600 to 18.30; Tue,Thu, 1200 to 1830; Wed, 1200 to 2000; Sat, 1000 to 1330
Special comments: A membership fee is applicable for borrowing rights. Reference use of the library is free.
Full: £20 annually, £14 monthly.
Concession (students, unemployed, senior citizens: £14 annually, £10 monthly).
Membership for Goethe-Institut students is free.
Concessionary membership for members of the Alliance Française de Glasgow.

Access for disabled people: There are steps into the building

Headquarters address: Goethe-Institut; Zerntrale München, München, D-80637, Germany

GOFAL CYMRU

26 Dunraven Place, Bridgend, CF31 1JD

Tel: 01656 647722
E-mail: centraloffice@gofalcymru.org.uk
Website: www.gofalcymru.org.uk

Founded: 1990

Organisation type and purpose: A mental health registered charity (charity number 1000889) with more than 20 years' experience of service provision. Currently working across 11 counties in Wales, Gofal Cymru provides innovative support and advice to people experiencing mental ill health.

Subject coverage: The services Gofal Cymru provides assist service users with various aspects of daily life including applying for benefits, tenancy issues, health appointments, advocacy, daily living skills, accessing work and training, debt management and budgeting, crisis prevention, advice in accessing suitable housing, and liaison with other health professionals such as CPNs, CMHTs, GPs and psychiatrists. Its services range from supported housing for people unable to live independently to tenancy support for people who already have a home but require assistance and support to maintain and retain their tenancy.

Publications: Electronic and video

Publications list: Available online

Access to staff: Contact by letter, by telephone and by e-mail

Branches: Offices in Swansea, Neath Port Talbot, Bridgend, Rhondda Cynon Taff, Vale of Glamorgan, Blaenau Gwent, Caerphilly and Merthyr, Cardiff, Torfaen and Newport

GOLD COCKEREL BOOKS

Kennerleigh, Crediton, Devon, EX17 4RS

Tel: 01363 866750
Fax: 01363 866750
Website: www.goldcockerelbooks.co.uk

Enquiries to: Director

Founded: 1987

Organisation type and purpose: Research organisation, publishing house.

Subject coverage: Poultry history, poultry breeding, old breeds of hens, ducks, geese, turkeys, poultry health, and small holding and countryside.

Publications: Printed

Publications list: Available in print

Access to staff: Contact by letter, by telephone, by fax, by e-mail and via website
Hours: Mon to Fri, 0900 to 1700

GOLDSMITHS

Formal name: Goldsmiths' College

Library, University of London, Lewisham Way, New Cross, London, SE14 6NW

Tel: 020 7919 7171
Fax: 020 7919 7165
E-mail: library@gold.ac.uk
Website: www.goldsmiths.ac.uk

Enquiries to: Librarian
Direct tel: 020 7919 7150

Founded: 1891

Organisation type and purpose: University library.

Subject coverage: Anthropology, education, music, social sciences, creative arts, humanities.

Collection: A L Lloyd Collection of European and North American Folk Music
Ewan MacColl and Peggy Seeger Collection
Centre for Russian Music Collection
Serge Prokofiev Archive
Women's Art Library
LIFT Living Archive
Bush Collection
Stevens Collection
Deac Rossell Collection
Angus Fairhurst Collection
John Thomas Collection
Glen Baxter Collection
Artist's books and ephemera collections
Constance Howard Centre for Textiles collections

Non-library collection catalogue: All or part available online and in-house

Library catalogue: All or part available online

Publications list: Available online

Access to staff: Contact by letter, by telephone, by fax and by e-mail. Appointment necessary.

Hours: Term time and Christmas and Easter holidays: Mon to Fri, 0915 to 2045; Sat and Sun, 1130 to 1700
Summer holidays: Mon to Fri, 0915 to 1645; Sat, 1130 to 1700; Sun closed
Special comments: No access for visitors to computers (except the library catalogue), audiovisual collections or to electronic databases.

Access to building: No prior appointment required

Access for disabled people: Level entry, access to all public areas, toilet facilities

College of the: University of London

GOLF FOUNDATION

Foundation House, The Spinney, Hoddesdon Road, Stanstead Abbotts, Hertfordshire, SG12 8GF

Tel: 01920 876200
Fax: 01920 876211
Website: www.golf-foundation.org

Enquiries to: Executive Director
Direct e-mail: hayley@golf-foundation.org

Founded: 1952

Organisation type and purpose: Registered charity (charity number 285917).
To promote and develop junior golf for young people in full-time education.

Subject coverage: Coaching and tournaments for junior golfers. Development initiatives for grass-roots junior golf.

Publications: Printed

Publications list: Available in print

Access to staff: Contact by letter, by telephone, by fax and by e-mail
Hours: Mon to Fri, 0900 to 1700

GONVILLE AND CAIUS COLLEGE

Library, Cambridge, CB2 1TA

Tel: 01223 332419
E-mail: library@cai.cam.ac.uk
Website: www.cai.cam.ac.uk/college/library/index.php

Enquiries to: College Librarian

Founded: 1349

Organisation type and purpose: University library.
College library.

Subject coverage: Broad-based; covers most subjects taught within the University Tripos; some postgraduate and research level material.

Collection: 15,000 early-printed books
900 medieval and later manuscripts
Music manuscripts, e.g. Charles Wood, Patrick Hadley
Venn manuscripts

Library catalogue: All or part available online

Publications: Electronic and video, and microform publications
Order microform publications from: College Librarian
Order electronic and video publications from: College Librarian

Access to staff: Contact by letter, by telephone, by e-mail and via website. Appointment necessary. Letter of introduction required.
Hours: Mon to Fri, 0930 to 1245 and 1415 to 1645

GOOD GARDENERS ASSOCIATION (GGA)

4 Lisle Place, Wotton-under-Edge, Gloucestershire, GL2 7AZ

Tel: 01453 520322
E-mail: info@goodgardeners.org.uk

Enquiries to: Secretary General
Other contacts: Soil Scientist

Founded: 1961

Organisation type and purpose: International organisation, membership association (membership is by subscription), voluntary organisation, registered charity (charity number 255300), suitable for ages: adults.
To teach the 'No Dig' method of growing fruit and vegetables on natural soil for the nutritional benefits that this provides in the maintenance of health worldwide.

Subject coverage: Organics, soil fertility – nature's way, soil science, organic marketing, community supported agriculture, composting, nutrition, health from plant-orientated foods.

Publications: Printed

Publications list: Available in print

Access to staff: Contact by letter, by telephone and by e-mail. Access for members only. Non-members charged.
Hours: Mon to Fri, 0900 to 1700

GOOD SCHOOLS GUIDE (GSG)

3 Craven Mews, London, SW11 5PW

Tel: 020 7801 0191
Fax: 0870 052 4067
E-mail: editor@goodschoolsguide.co.uk
Website: www.goodschoolsguide.co.uk

Enquiries to: Editor

Founded: 1985

Organisation type and purpose: Consultancy, research organisation, publishing house.
Describes United Kingdom schools and international schools worldwide as they really are, advising parents on them through the web and one-to-one; provides information on schools and schooling over the internet and in printed form.

Subject coverage: Primary and secondary schools in the United Kingdom, both private and state; international schools worldwide.

Information services: The Good Schools Guide Advice Service offers parents one-to-one consultations on school choice.

Trade and statistical information: School examination and other statistics

Publications: Printed, and electronic and video
Order printed publications from: e-mail: orders@goodschoolsguide.co.uk
Order electronic and video publications from: website: http://www.goodschoolsguide.co.uk

Access to staff: Contact by letter, by telephone, by fax, by e-mail, in person and via website. Appointment necessary.
Hours: Mon to Fri, 0900 to 1700

Administers: The Good Schools Guide International; website: http://www.gsgi.co.uk

Parent body: Lucas Publications Ltd

GOOLE LOCAL STUDIES LIBRARY

Carlisle Street, Goole, East Riding of Yorkshire, DN14 5DS

Tel: 01405 762187
Fax: 01405 768329
E-mail: gooleref.library@eastriding.gov.uk

Enquiries to: Librarian

Organisation type and purpose: Public library.

Subject coverage: Collections on Goole and the surrounding area, local family history resources.

Collection: 2,500 books covering Goole and the historic East, North and West Ridings of Yorkshire
Collections of books and 3,000 photographs

Non-library collection catalogue: All or part available online and in-house

Library catalogue: All or part available online

Access to staff: Contact by letter, by telephone, by fax, by e-mail and in person
Hours: Mon, Wed, 1000 to 1900; Tue, Thu, Fri, 1000 to 1700; Sat, 0900 to 1300

Access to building: No prior appointment required
Special comments: For detailed enquiries preferable to advise staff beforehand.
Prior appointment required for booking microform readers.

Access for disabled people: Level entry
Special comments: Lift to Local Studies Library on first floor.

Parent body: East Riding of Yorkshire Council

GORDON KEEBLE OWNERS CLUB

26 Burford Park Road, Kings Norton, Birmingham, B38 8PB

Tel: 0121 459 8700
Fax: 0121 459 9587

Enquiries to: Secretary

Founded: 1970

Organisation type and purpose: Membership association (membership is by subscription).

Subject coverage: The Gordon Keeble car marque parts availability, location of cars.

Access to staff: Contact by letter, by telephone and by fax. Appointment necessary.
Hours: Mon to Fri, 0900 to 1700

GOSPORT BOROUGH COUNCIL

Town Hall, Gosport, Hampshire, PO12 1EB

Tel: 023 9258 4242
Fax: 023 9251 1279
E-mail: enquiries@gosport.gov.uk
Website: www.gosport.gov.uk

Enquiries to: Marketing Manager
Direct tel: 023 9254 5258
Direct fax: 023 9254 5238

Organisation type and purpose: Local government body.

Subject coverage: Local government.

Access to staff: Contact by letter, by fax and by e-mail. Appointment necessary.
Hours: Mon to Fri, 0900 to 1700

GOSS COLLECTORS CLUB

22 Littlebrook Gardens, Cheshunt, Hertfordshire, EN8 8QQ

Tel: 01992 627033
E-mail: registrar@gosscollectorsclub.org
Website: www.gosschina.com
Website: www.gosscollectorsclub.org

Enquiries to: Registrar
Direct e-mail: auctionsecretary@gosscollectorsclub.org
Other contacts: Auction Secretary for enquiries re the postal auction.

Founded: 1970

Organisation type and purpose: International organisation, membership association (membership is by subscription).

Subject coverage: The works of William Henry Goss, Goss china collecting and identification, associated heraldry.

Collection: Various collection of books, documents, etc., including comprehensive slide bank, held by archivist (available to members only)

Publications: Printed

Access to staff: Contact by letter, by telephone, by e-mail and via website
Hours: Up to 2100

GOVERNING COUNCIL OF THE CAT FANCY, THE (GCCF)

4–6 Penel Orlieu, Bridgwater, Somerset, TA6 3PG

Tel: 01278 427575
E-mail: GCCF_CATS@compuserve.com
Website: www.gccfcats.org

Enquiries to: Secretary

Founded: 1910

Organisation type and purpose: Voluntary organisation.
Council made up of affiliated cat clubs. Registration body for pedigree cats.

Subject coverage: Pedigree cats breeds, shows and cat clubs.

Collection: Cat registration records from 1910
Own records 1910 onwards

Trade and statistical information: Analysis of cats registered

Publications: Printed

Publications list: Available in print

Access to staff: Contact by letter, by telephone, by e-mail and via website. Appointment necessary.
Hours: Mon to Fri, 0900 to 1700

GOVERNMENT ACTUARY'S DEPARTMENT (GAD)

Finlaison House, 15–17 Furnival Street, London, EC4A 1AB

Tel: 020 7211 2600
Fax: 020 7211 2650
E-mail: enquiries@gad.gov.uk
Website: www.gad.gov.uk

Enquiries to: Director
Direct tel: 020 7211 2620
Other contacts: Directing Actuary (for advice on pensions)

Founded: 1919

Organisation type and purpose: National government body, consultancy. Central government department. Actuarial and financial consultancy.

Subject coverage: Demography (including national population projections), survey of occupational pension schemes, social security projection, public sector pensions.

Publications: Printed
Order printed publications from: Publications Officer, Government Actuary Department; tel: 020 7211 2620; fax: 020 7211 2650; e-mail: marilyn.estrick@gad.gov.uk

Access to staff: Contact by letter, by fax and by e-mail
Hours: Mon to Fri, 0900 to 1700

GOWER PUBLISHING LIMITED

Gower House, Croft Road, Aldershot, Hampshire, GU11 3HR

Tel: 01252 331551
Fax: 01252 344405
E-mail: info@gowerpub.com
Website: www.gowerpub.com

Enquiries to: Customer Service Manager

Founded: 1967

Organisation type and purpose: Publishing house. Academic, business and professional publishing.

Subject coverage: Business, management, personal skills, specialist areas of business activity, information management, training.

Publications: Printed, and electronic and video
Order printed publications from: Bookpoint Limited, Gower Publishing Direct Sales 130 Milton Park, Abingdon, Oxon, OX14 4SB, tel: 01235 827730, fax: 01235 400454, e-mail: orders@bookpoint.co.uk

Publications list: Available online and in print

Access to staff: Contact by letter, by telephone, by fax, by e-mail and via website
Hours: Mon to Fri, 0900 to 1700

Access to building: Prior appointment required

Parent body: Ashgate Group Publishing Limited; at the same address

Subsidiary body: Dartmouth Press; Scolar Press; Variorum Press

GRADUATE PROSPECTS LTD (HECSU)

Formal name: Higher Education Careers Services Unit

Prospects House, Booth Street East, Manchester, M13 9EP

Tel: 0161 277 5200
Fax: 0161 277 5210
E-mail: enquiries@prospects.ac.uk
Website: www.prospects.ac.uk

Enquiries to: Marketing Communications Manager

History of institution: formerly called Central Services Unit for Graduate Careers and Appointments Services

Subject coverage: Graduate trends and predictions, graduate training, graduate salaries, university output, college output, graduate supply and demand, postgraduate training, higher education careers services.

Trade and statistical information: Statistics on the graduate recruitment market

Publications list: Available online

Access to staff: Contact by letter, by telephone, by fax and by e-mail
Hours: Mon to Fri, 0900 to 1700

Access to building: No access other than to staff

Access for disabled people: Parking provided, ramped entry, level entry, access to all public areas, toilet facilities

Commercial subsidiary of the: Higher Education Careers Services Unit (HECSU)

Jointly owned by: Universities UK and the Guild HE

Publishing house for the: Association of Graduate Careers Advisory Services (AGCAS)

GRADUATE SCHOOL OF EUROPEAN AND INTERNATIONAL STUDIES (GSEIS)

University of Reading, Whiteknights, PO Box 218, Reading, Berkshire, RG6 2AA

Tel: 0118 931 8378
Fax: 0118 975 5442
E-mail: gseis@reading.ac.uk
Website: www.rdg.ac.uk/AcaDepts/ce/GSEIS/home.html

Enquiries to: Secretary

Founded: 1960

Organisation type and purpose: University department or institute, research organisation.

Subject coverage: Postgraduate teaching and training in the fields of European and international studies, international security studies, political theory and public ethics, governance and international law and world order, diplomacy.

Library catalogue: All or part available in-house

Publications: Printed

Publications list: Available in print

Access to staff: Contact by telephone and by e-mail
Hours: Mon to Fri, 1000 to 1600

Access for disabled people: Ramped entry, access to all public areas

GRAHAM GREENE BIRTHPLACE TRUST

9 Briar Way, Berkhamsted, Hertfordshire, HP4 2JJ

Tel: 01442 873604
E-mail: secretary@grahamgreenebt.org
Website: www.grahamgreenebt.org

Enquiries to: Secretary

Founded: 1997

Organisation type and purpose: International organisation, membership association (membership is by subscription), present number of members: 200, voluntary organisation, registered charity (charity number 1064839).

Subject coverage: Life and works of Graham Greene.

Collection: Archive and specialist library

Library catalogue: All or part available in print

Publications: Printed, and electronic and video

Publications list: Available online and in print

Access to staff: Contact by letter, by telephone, by e-mail and via website. Appointment necessary.
Hours: Sun to Sat, 0900 to 2100
Special comments: Answerphone out of hours.

GRAIN AND FEED TRADE ASSOCIATION (GAFTA)

GAFTA House, 6 Chapel Place, Rivington Street, London, EC2A 3SH

Tel: 020 7814 9666
Fax: 020 7814 8383
E-mail: post@gafta.com
Website: www.gafta.com

Enquiries to: Director-General

Organisation type and purpose: International organisation, trade association (membership is by subscription), present number of members: more than 1,000.

Subject coverage: Grain, animal feedstuffs, pulses and rice, contracts, arbitration, trade policy.

Publications list: Available online

Access to staff: Contact by letter, by e-mail and via website
Hours: Mon to Fri, 0900 to 1700

Access to building: Prior appointment required

Access for disabled people: Level entry, toilet facilities

GRAPHIC ENTERPRISE SCOTLAND (GES)

112 George Street, Edinburgh, EH2 4LH

Tel: 0131 220 4353
Fax: 0131 220 4344
E-mail: info@graphicenterprisescotland.org
Website: www.graphicenterprisescotland.org

Enquiries to: Director

Founded: 1910; formerly called Society of Master Printers of Scotland (SMPS) (year of change 1991); formerly called Scottish Print Employers Federation (SPEF) (year of change 2009)

Organisation type and purpose: Trade association (membership is by subscription).

Subject coverage: Employee relations; training; health and safety; commercial information.

Access to staff: Contact by letter, by telephone and by fax. Appointment necessary.
Hours: Mon to Fri, 0900 to 1700

Links with: Intergraf (International Confederation for Printing and Allied Industries)

GRAPHICAL, PAPER AND MEDIA UNION (GPMU)

Birmingham and West Midlands Branch, Union House, 9 William Street North, Birmingham, B19 3QH

Tel: 0121 236 2963 or 8860
Fax: 0121 233 1731
E-mail: gpmuwestmidlands@btclick.com
Website: www.gmpu.org.uk

Enquiries to: Branch Secretary

History of institution: formerly called Birmingham Typographical Society (year of change 1995)

Organisation type and purpose: Trade union (membership is by subscription), present number of members: 8,000.

Subject coverage: Information on general print, finishings, graphics, lithography, flexography, silk screen. Electronic and digital generations, employment legislation, health and safety, pension information, state benefits, welfare advice.

Access to staff: Contact by letter, by telephone, by fax and in person
Hours: Mon to Fri, 0900 to 1700

Affiliated to: Graphical, Paper and Media Union; Keys House, Bromham Road, Bedford; tel: 01234 351521; fax: 01234 270580; website: www.gpmu.org.uk

GRAY CANCER INSTITUTE (GLCRT)

PO Box 100, Mount Vernon Hospital, Northwood, Middlesex, HA6 2JR

Tel: 01923 828611
Fax: 01923 835210
Website: www.gci.ac.uk

Enquiries to: Deputy Director

Founded: 1955

Organisation type and purpose: Registered charity, research organisation.
Research into cancer.

Subject coverage: Experimental cancer therapy, especially with radiation; tumour biology; tumour kinetics; tumour vasculature; radiation physics; radiation chemistry; radiation biology; neutrons; X-rays; radiation sources.

Collection: Fowler-Scott Library of books and journals related to cancer research and biological effects of radiation

Publications: Printed

Publications list: Available in print

Access to staff: Contact by letter, by telephone and by e-mail. Letter of introduction required.
Hours: Mon to Fri, 0900 to 1700

Access to building: Prior appointment required

GRAY'S INN LIBRARY

Formal name: The Honourable Society of Gray's Inn

The Honourable Society of Gray's Inn, 5 South Square, Gray's Inn, London, WC1R 5ET

Tel: 020 7458 7822
Fax: 020 7458 7850
E-mail: library.information@graysinn.org.uk
Website: www.graysinnlibrary.org.uk

Enquiries to: Librarian
Other contacts: Archivist (for historical material)

Founded: c. 15th century

Organisation type and purpose: Legal library.

Collection: Core collection of 60,000 vols on all aspects of the the law, but specifically entertainment and sport, IT and communications law, and the law of education
Manuscripts (medieval to 19th century)

Library catalogue: All or part available online

Access to staff: Contact by letter, by telephone, by fax and by e-mail. Access for members only. Letter of introduction required.

Access to building: *Hours:* Student and legal terms: Mon to Fri, 0900 to 2000; holidays: see website for details
Special comments: Open to all barrister and student mems of Gray's Inn and barrister mems of all Inns of Court; other researchers by appointment with the Librarian

Access for disabled people: Wheelchair lift
Hours: Telephone for assistance and advice

GRAYS CENTRAL LIBRARY

Orsett Road, Grays, Essex, RM17 5DX

Tel: 01375 413973
Fax: 01375 385504
E-mail: grays.library@thurrock.gov.uk
Website: www.thurrock.gov.uk/libraries

Enquiries to: Librarian
Direct tel: 01375 413977

Organisation type and purpose: Local government body, public library.

Subject coverage: General, local studies.

continued overleaf

Collection: Museum

Non-library collection catalogue: All or part available online

Library catalogue: All or part available online

Access to staff: Contact by letter, by telephone, by fax, by e-mail, in person and via website
Hours: Mon, Tue, Thu, 1000 to 1900; Wed, Fri, Sat, 1000 to 1700

Access to building: No access other than to staff

Access for disabled people: Parking provided, access to all public areas, toilet facilities

Constituent part of: Thurrock Libraries

GREAT BRITAIN POSTCARD CLUB

34 Harper House, St James Crescent, London, SW9 7LW

Tel: 020 7771 9404

Enquiries to: Executive Director

Founded: 1961

Organisation type and purpose: Membership association.

Subject coverage: Postcard collecting throughout the world, ephemera under 100 subjects.

Publications: Printed

Access to staff: Contact by letter
Hours: Mon to Fri, 0900 to 1700

GREAT BRITAIN RACQUETBALL FEDERATION (GBRF)

78 Suffolk Drive, Rendlesham, Woodbridge, Suffolk, IP12 2TP

Tel: 01394 461069
E-mail: aburrow.newman@btinternet.com

Enquiries to: General Secretary

Founded: 1984

Organisation type and purpose: National government body, membership association (membership is by subscription), voluntary organisation, suitable for ages: 8+.
Promote the game of racquetball and racquetball education.

Subject coverage: Racquetball rules, regulations, court specifications.

Access to staff: Contact by letter and by telephone
Hours: Mon to Fri, 0900 to 1700

Affiliated to: European Racquetball Federation; International Racquetball Federation

GREAT BRITAIN WHEELCHAIR BASKETBALL ASSOCIATION (GBWBA)

GBWBA Office, Sport Park, 3 Oakwood Drive, Loughborough, Leicestershire, LE11 3QF

Tel: 01509 279900
Fax: 01509 6279909
E-mail: office@gbwba.org.uk
Website: www.gbwba.org.uk

Enquiries to: Chief Executive
Direct e-mail: c.bethel@gbwba.org.uk ; info@gbwba.org.uk
Other contacts: League Secretary, Chairman, General Secretary

Founded: 1973

Organisation type and purpose: Membership association (membership is by subscription), present number of members: over 700, registered charity (charity number 298045).
National governing body for the sport.

Subject coverage: All matters relating to the sport of wheelchair basketball in Great Britain.

Collection: Records of Association, member clubs, registered players and officials etc.

Publications: Printed, and electronic and video

Publications list: Available in print

Access to staff: Contact by letter, by telephone, by fax, by e-mail and via website. Appointment necessary.
Hours: Mon to Fri, 0900 to 1700
Special comments: Not after 2200.

Affiliated to: International Wheelchair Basketball Federation (IWBF); IWBF Secretariat, 108–109 Watson Street, Winnipeg, Manitoba, Canada, R2P 2E1; tel: (204) 632 6475; e-mail: iwbfpresident@aol.com

GREAT BRITAIN-SASAKAWA FOUNDATION (GBSF)

Dilke House, 1 Malet Street, London, WC1E 7JN

Tel: 020 7436 9042
E-mail: gbsf@gbsf.org.uk
Website: www.gbsf.org.uk

Enquiries to: Chief Executive

Founded: 1984

Organisation type and purpose: Registered charity (charity number 290766).
To improve relations between the United Kingdom and Japan by promoting a deeper understanding between the peoples of both nations. Awards grants to organisations for cultural events, youth exchanges, Japanese language/studies and academic research collaboration.

Subject coverage: Promotion of Anglo-Japanese understanding.

Publications list: Available in print

Access to staff: Contact by letter and by e-mail
Hours: Mon to Fri, 0900 to 1700

Also at: Great Britain-Sasakawa Foundation; The Nippon Foundation Building 4F, 1–2-2 Akasaka, Tokyo, 107–0052, Japan; tel: +81 3 6229 5465; fax: +81 3 6229 5467; e-mail: gbsf@spf.or.jp

GREAT WESTERN AIR AMBULANCE

Appeals Office, Eastwood Park Training and Conference Centre, Falfield, Wotton under Edge, Gloucestershire, GL12 8DA

Tel: 0303 444 4999; 0845 838 8492
E-mail: info@greatwesternairambulance.org.uk
Website: www.greatwesternairambulance.com

Founded: 2008

Organisation type and purpose: Registered charity (charity number 1121300).
The provision of a sustainable Helicopter Emergency Medical Service (HEMS) within the area covered by the Great Western Ambulance Service NHS Trust.

Subject coverage: Covering the counties of Avon, Gloucestershire, North Somerset and Wiltshire, an area of 3,000 sq. km and serving a resident population of 2.2m. people, together with a transient and visiting population, heavy industrial sector, and sporting and leisure activity, the service helps to provide a fully effective and integrated road and air response emergency medical system that meets best practice response standards and outcomes for patients.

Access to staff: Contact by letter, by telephone and by e-mail
Hours: Appeals Office: Mon to Fri, 0830 to 11.40

GREAT WESTERN SOCIETY LIMITED (GWS)

Didcot Railway Centre, Didcot, Oxfordshire, OX11 7NJ

Tel: 01235 817200
Fax: 01235 510621
E-mail: didrlyc@globalnet.co.uk
Website: www.didcotrailwaycentre.org.uk

Enquiries to: Secretary

Founded: 1961

Organisation type and purpose: Membership association (membership is by subscription), voluntary organisation, registered charity (charity number 272616), museum.

Subject coverage: Great Western Railway.

Non-library collection catalogue: All or part available online and in print

Publications: Printed

Access to staff: Contact by letter, by telephone, by e-mail and via website
Hours: Mon to Fri, 0900 to 1700

Affiliated to: Heritage Railway Association; Transport Trust

GREAT YARMOUTH CENTRAL LIBRARY

Tolhouse Street, Great Yarmouth, Norfolk, NR30 2SH

Tel: 01493 844551/842279
Fax: 01493 857628
E-mail: yarmouth.lib@norfolk.gov.uk
Website: www.library.norfolk.gov.uk

Enquiries to: Librarian

Organisation type and purpose: Local government body, public library.

Subject coverage: General, history and current information on Great Yarmouth and East Norfolk including newspaper cuttings; backfiles of local newspapers on microfilm, illustrations, maps etc; herring fishing, town walls and rows (narrow passageways), Dickens, Nelson, local genealogical information.

Collection: Francis Frith Collection of photographs of Great Yarmouth and East Norfolk early/mid-twentieth century
Herbert Tinkler MSS (early 20th-century entertainments in Great Yarmouth)
W A S Wynne Collection (history of SE Norfolk and NE Suffolk)
William de Castre MSS (early 20th-century writings and indexes on Great Yarmouth and Caister)
Yallop Collection of glass plate negatives of Great Yarmouth Victorian/Edwardian era

Publications: Printed

Parent body: Norfolk Library and Information Service

Part of: Anglian Libraries Information Exchange Scheme

GREATER GLASGOW & CLYDE VALLEY TOURIST BOARD

11 George Square, Glasgow, G2 1DY

Tel: 0141 204 4480
Fax: 0141 204 4772
E-mail: enquiries@seeglasgow.com
Website: www.seeglasgow.com

Enquiries to: Director
Other contacts: (i) Marketing Manager; (ii) Manager for (1) Leisure Tourism (2) Convention Bureau.

Organisation type and purpose: Statutory body, membership association (membership is by subscription), present number of members: 700+.
Destination marketing organisation.

Subject coverage: Information on the Greater Glasgow Clyde Valley area for visitors, i.e. accommodation information, things to see and do, and assistance to tour operators and travel trade, e.g. itinerary planning.
Trade and statistical information: Statistics relating to visitors to the Greater Glasgow & Clyde Valley Area

Publications: Printed, and electronic and video

Publications list: Available online

Access to staff: Contact by letter, by telephone, by fax, by e-mail, in person and via website. Appointment necessary.
Hours: Mon to Fri, 0900 to 1700
Special comments: Seasonal weekend opening for tourist information offices.

Access for disabled people: Toilet facilities

GREATER LONDON ACTION ON DISABILITY (GLAD)

336 Brixton Road, London, SW9 7AA

Tel: 020 7346 5800, 020 7326 4554 (minicom)
Fax: 020 7346 8844

Enquiries to: Information Officer
Direct tel: 020 7346 5819
Other contacts: Head of Policy for information on disability equality, training and DDA training.

History of institution: formerly called Greater London Association of Disabled People (GLAD) (year of change 1999)

Organisation type and purpose: Membership association (membership is by subscription, qualification), voluntary organisation, registered charity (charity number 293158), training organisation. Centre of network of affiliated disability organisations throughout Greater London.

Subject coverage: All non-medical disability issues such as access, aids, benefits, education, employment, holidays, housing, leisure and sport.

Publications: Printed, and electronic and video

Publications list: Available online and in print

Access to staff: Contact by letter, by telephone, by fax and by e-mail. Appointment necessary.
Hours: Information line: Mon, Wed, Fri, 1330 to 1630

Access for disabled people: Parking provided, ramped entry, access to all public areas, toilet facilities

Links with: Alliance of Disability Advice and Information Providers; British Council of Disabled People; London Voluntary Service Council (LVSC); National Council for Voluntary Organisations; National Information Forum; Rights Now!; Royal Association for Disability and Rehabilitation (RADAR)

GREATER LONDON AUTHORITY (GLA) INFORMATION SERVICES

City Hall, The Queen's Walk, London, SE1 2AA

Tel: 020 7983 4455
Fax: 020 7983 4674
E-mail: isinfo@london.gov.uk
Website: www.london.gov.uk

Founded: 2000

Organisation type and purpose: Local government body, research organisation. GLA Information Services is a specialist library and provides information services for urban and social policy planners.

Subject coverage: Planning and transport, business, the economy, labour market, education and training, health, housing and social exclusion, equalities policy, environment, culture, governance, police and community safety.

Collection: Library collection includes more than 250,000 books, reports and journal articles (including grey literature), and 500 regular periodicals and statistical series.

Non-library collection catalogue: All or part available in-house

Library catalogue: All or part available in-house

Publications: Printed, and electronic and video

Publications list: Available online and in print

Access to staff: Appointment necessary. Non-members charged.
Hours: Mon to Fri, 0930 to 1700

Access for disabled people: Lift and ramp entry, toilet facilities

GREATER LONDON FUND FOR THE BLIND

12 Whitehorse Mews, 37 Westminster Bridge Road, London, SE1 7QD

Tel: 020 7620 2066
Fax: 020 7620 2016
E-mail: info@glfb.org.uk
Website: www.glfb.org.uk

Enquiries to: Information Officer

Founded: 1921

Organisation type and purpose: Registered charity (charity number 1074958).

Subject coverage: Blind and partially sighted people

Access to staff: Contact by letter, by telephone, by fax, by e-mail and in person. Appointment necessary.
Hours: Mon to Fri, 0915 to 1715

Member organisations: BlindAid; Lantern House, 102 Bermondsey Street, London SE1 3UB; e-mail: enquiries@blindaid.org.uk; website: www.blindaid
Clarity: Employment for Blind People; 276 York Way, London N7 9PH; tel: 0207 619 1650; website: www.clarityefbp.org
Croydon Voluntary Association for the Blind; 72–74 Wellesley Road, Croydon CR0 2AR; tel: 0208 688 2486; e-mail: cvab@croydonvisual.plus.com;
Kingston-upon-Thames Association for the Blind; Adams House, Dickerage Lane, New Malden KT3 3SF; tel: 0208 546 4899; e-mail: jcooper52@yahoo.com; website: www.kingstonassociationfortheblind.org
MertonVision; Guardian Centre, 67 Clarendon Road, London SW19 0JX; tel: 0208 540 5446; website: www.mertonvision.org.uk
SeeAbility; SeeAbility House, Hook Road, Epsom KT19 8SQ; tel: 01372 755000; e-mail: enquiries@seeability.org; Surrey Association for Visual Impairment; Rentwood, School Lane, Fetcham, Leatherhead KT22 9JX; tel: 01372 377701; website: www.surreywebsight.org.uk
Sutton Association for the Blind; 3 Robin Hood Lane, Sutton Surrey SM1 2SW; tel: 0208 409 7166; website: sab.gb.org
The Middlesex Association for the Blind

GREATER MANCHESTER CENTRE FOR VOLUNTARY ORGANISATION (GMCVO)

St Thomas Centre, Ardwick Green North, Manchester, M12 6FZ

Tel: 0161 277 1000
Fax: 0161 273 8296
E-mail: gmcvo@gmcvo.org.uk
Website: www.gmcvo.org.uk

Enquiries to: Policy and Information Officer

Founded: 1975

Organisation type and purpose: Voluntary organisation.
To strengthen the voluntary and community sector, build bridges with other sectors and influence local and national policy.

continued overleaf

Publications: Printed, and electronic and video

Access to staff: Contact by letter, by telephone, by fax, by e-mail and via website. Appointment necessary.
Hours: Phone lines open Mon to Fri, 0900 to 1700

Access for disabled people: Ramped entry, toilet facilities

Member of: National Association for Voluntary and Community Action; National Council for Voluntary Organisations; Voluntary Sector North West

GREATER MANCHESTER COUNTY RECORD OFFICE (WITH MANCHESTER ARCHIVES) (GMCRO)

56 Marshall Street, New Cross, Manchester, M4 5FU

Tel: 0161 832 5284
Fax: 0161 839 3808
E-mail: archiveslocalstudies@manchester.gov.uk
Website: www.gmcro.co.uk

Enquiries to: County Archivist

Founded: 1976

Organisation type and purpose: Local government body.
Archive service, storage, reprographics, conservation.

Subject coverage: Industrial and business records of Greater Manchester county, family and estate records, probate and registration indexes. Family history, public records, maps, newspapers, documentary photography archive, records of Greater Manchester County Council, societies, organisations and trade unions in Greater Manchester.

Collection: Archives relating to Greater Manchester region from 1197 to modern day
Photographs – documentary photography archive
Photographs – Manchester Ship Canal Collection

Non-library collection catalogue: All or part available online and in-house

Access to staff: Contact by letter, by telephone, by fax, by e-mail, in person and via website

Access to building: *Hours:* Mon, Tue, Thu and Fri, 0900 to 1700; Wed, closed; 2nd and 4th Sat, 0900 to 1700
Special comments: CARN ticket required; essential to book a place in the searchroom in advance; essential to reserve archives in advance (2 working days' notice for on-site collections; 2 weeks' notice for off-site collections).

Access for disabled people: Access to all public areas
Special comments: Private study room available for those with special access requirements.

Administers: From Jun 2010, provides access to Manchester Archives' collections (during closure of Manchester Central Library for refurbishment) alongside GMCRO's own collections

Parent body: Managed by Manchester City Council on behalf of Association of Greater Manchester Authorities (AGMA)

GREEK NATIONAL TOURISM ORGANISATION (EOT/GNTO)

4 Conduit Street, London, W1S 2DJ

Tel: 020 7495 9300
Fax: 020 7495 4057
E-mail: info@gnto.co.uk
Website: www.visitgreece.gr
Website: www.tourist-offices.org.uk
Website: www.antor.com/greece

Enquiries to: Information Officer

Organisation type and purpose: International organisation, national government body.

Subject coverage: All forms of tourism to Greece including mainland and islands, special interest and conferences, information regarding transport, accommodation, tour operators, local festivals and cultural events.

Publications: Printed, and electronic and video, and microform publications

Access to staff: Contact by letter, by telephone, by fax, by e-mail and in person
Hours: Mon to Fri 10:00 to 1500

Access for disabled people: Level entry

Headquarters address: EOT; Tsocha 7, Athens, Greece; tel: +30 210 8707000; e-mail: info@gnto.gr; website: http://www.visitgreece.gr

GREEN PARTY

1a Waterlow, London, N19 5NJ

Tel: 020 7272 4474
Fax: 020 7272 6653
E-mail: office@greenparty.org.uk
Website: www.greenparty.org.uk

Enquiries to: Chair of the Executive
Other contacts: Head of Office

Founded: 1973; formerly called People (year of change 1975); formerly called Ecology Party (year of change 1985)

Organisation type and purpose: Political party.

Subject coverage: Green politics, party policies.

Publications: Printed

Access to staff: Contact by letter, by telephone, by e-mail and via website. Appointment necessary.
Hours: Mon to Fri, 0900 to 1700

GREEN TEMPLETON COLLEGE

Green Templeton College, Woodstock Road, Oxford, OX2 6HG

Tel: 01865 274770
Fax: 01865 274796
E-mail: hilary.binks@gtc.ox.ac.uk
Website: www.gtc.ox.ac.uk

Enquiries to: Information Centre Manager

Founded: 1965

Organisation type and purpose: Management studies college.

Subject coverage: Management studies in general; retailing (Oxford Centre of Retail Management); employee relations; information management; food and drink industry; human resource management; industrial relations.

Publications: Printed

Publications list: Available online

Access to staff: Contact by letter, by telephone and by e-mail
Hours: Mon to Fri, 0830 to 1700

Access to building: Prior appointment required
Special comments: Restricted, please telephone for information.

Access for disabled people: Parking provided, ramped entry

Member of: British Business Schools Librarians Group; European Business Schools Librarians Group

GREENPEACE UK

Canonbury Villas, London, N1 2PN

Tel: 020 7865 8100
Fax: 020 7865 8200
E-mail: info@uk.greenpeace.org
Website: www.greenpeace.org.uk

Enquiries to: Information Officer

Founded: 1977

Organisation type and purpose: International organisation.
Environmental campaigning.

Subject coverage: Global warming, toxic waste, civil nuclear, nuclear disarmament, renewable energy, ancient forests, oceans.

Publications: Printed, and electronic and video

Publications list: Available in print

Access to staff: Contact by letter, by telephone, by fax, by e-mail and via website
Hours: Mon to Fri, 0900 to 1700

Parent body: Greenpeace Environmental Trust; at the same address

GREENWICH COMMUNITY COLLEGE LEARNING RESOURCES CENTRE

95 Plumstead Road, Plumstead, London, SE18 7DQ

Tel: 020 8488 4813
Fax: 020 8488 4899
E-mail: lib-help@gcc.ac.uk
Website: www.gcc.ac.uk

Enquiries to: Learning Resources Service Manager

History of institution: formerly called Woolwich & Greenwich Community College Learning Resource Service; formerly called Woolwich College (year of change 1998)

Organisation type and purpose: College of education learning resources centre.

Subject coverage: General.

Non-library collection catalogue: All or part available online

Library catalogue: All or part available online and in-house

Access to staff: Contact by letter, by telephone, by fax and by e-mail
Hours: Mon to Fri, 0900 to 1700

Access for disabled people: Level entry, toilet facilities, lift access

GREENWICH HERITAGE CENTRE

Artillery Square, Royal Arsenal, Woolwich, SE18 4DX

Tel: 020 8854 2452
E-mail: heritage.centre@greenwich.gov.uk
Website: www.greenwich.gov.uk/greenwich/leisureculture/historyandheritage/heritagecentre

Enquiries to: Search Room

Founded: 2003; created by the merger of London Borough of Greenwich's Borough Museum and Local History Library

Organisation type and purpose: Museum, library and archive for exhibitions, research and education.

Subject coverage: The history of the area now designated the London Borough of Greenwich.

Collection: Museum objects relating to the archaeology, social and natural history of the area
Paintings and drawings collection
Books, pamphlets, periodicals manuscripts, maps and illustrations relating to the people, topography and history of the area
Official repository of the records of the London Borough of Greenwich and its predecessors

Non-library collection catalogue: All or part available in-house

Library catalogue: All or part available in-house

Publications: Printed

Access to staff: Contact by letter, by telephone, by fax, by e-mail and in person
Hours: Tue to Sat, 0900 to 1700

Access to building: Open to the public
Hours: Tue to Sat, 0900 to 1700

Access for disabled people: Full access
Hours: Tue to Sat, 0900 to 1700

Parent body: Greenwich Council; tel: 020 8854 8888

GREENWICH LIBRARY AND INFORMATION SERVICE

Woolwich Reference Library, Calderwood Street, Woolwich, London, SE18 6QZ

Tel: 020 8921 5748
Fax: 020 8316 1545
E-mail: reference.library@greenwich.gov.uk
Website: www.greenwich.gov.uk

Enquiries to: Librarian
Direct tel: 020 8921 5749

Founded: 1965

Organisation type and purpose: Local government body, public library.

Subject coverage: Metropolitan Special Collection in the following fields: recreation; indoor and outdoor games and sports; dancing (excluding ballet); official books of most sports associations.

Collection: Greenwich Local History and Archives Collection (history, topography and archaeology, at the Greenwich Heritage Centre)
Metropolitan Special Collection (recreation, sports) at Library Headquarters, Plumstead Library

Non-library collection catalogue: All or part available online

Library catalogue: All or part available online

Publications: Printed
Order printed publications from: Greenwich Heritage Centre, Artillery Square, Royal Arsenal, Woolwich, SE18 4DX. tel: 020 8854 2452, fax: 020 8854 2490

Access to staff: Contact by letter, by telephone, by fax, by e-mail, in person and via website

Access to building: No prior appointment required

Constituent bodies: Library and Information Service

Headquarters address: Greenwich Library and Information Service; c/o Plumstead Library, High Street, Plumstead, London, SE18 1JL; tel: 020 8317 4466; fax: 020 8317 4868

Links with: Greenwich Heritage Centre; Building 41, Royal Arsenal, Woolwich, SE18 6SP; tel: 020 8854 2452; e-mail: heritage .centre@greenwich.gov.uk; website: http://www.greenwich.gov.uk

Parent body: Greenwich Council, Culture and Community Services; tel: 020 8854 8888

GREEVES RIDERS ASSOCIATION (GRA)

4 Longshaw Close, North Wingfield, Chesterfield, Derbyshire, S42 5QR

Tel: 01246 853846

Enquiries to: Membership Secretary

Founded: 1984

Organisation type and purpose: Membership association.

Subject coverage: Information on all Greeves motorcycles, technical, for restoration, parts supply, clarification of models and month of manufacture.

Access to staff: Contact by letter and by telephone
Hours: Mon to Fri, 1800 to 2100

GROUDLE GLEN RAILWAY

29 Hawarden Avenue, Douglas, Isle of Man, IM1 4BP

Tel: 01624 622138 (evenings only); 01624 670453 (weekends only)
E-mail: lbeard@manx.net

Enquiries to: Honorary Secretary

Founded: 1982

Organisation type and purpose: Membership association (membership is by subscription), present number of members: 700, voluntary organisation, registered charity (charity number Isle of Man No. 406). Restoration and operation of a narrow gauge railway.

Subject coverage: Railway restoration and operation of a 2ft gauge line with steam and diesel locomotives over 3/4 mile track.

Publications: Printed

Access to staff: Contact by letter. Appointment necessary.
Special comments: No access to staff.

Access for disabled people: *Special comments:* Please telephone for advice before your visit.

Affiliated to: Isle of Man Steam Railway Supporters Association; at the same address

GROWTH THROUGH TRAINING (GTT) LIMITED (GTT Ltd)

55 Curlew Drive, Chippenham, Wiltshire, SN14 6YG

Tel: 01249 661231
Fax: 01249 447442
E-mail: csimons@dircon.co.uk

Enquiries to: Managing Director

Founded: 1985

Organisation type and purpose: Organisational and human resource development, consultancy.
Management Development, Investors in People practitioners.

Subject coverage: Organisational development, management development training. Investors in People consultancy, counselling at work.

Publications: Printed

Access to staff: Contact by letter, by telephone, by fax and by e-mail. Appointment necessary.
Hours: Any reasonable time

GRUBB INSTITUTE

Formal name: Grubb Institute of Behavioural Studies Limited

Cloudesley Street, London, N1 0HU

Tel: 020 7278 8061
Fax: 020 7278 0728
E-mail: info@grubb.org.uk
Website: www.grubb.org.uk

Enquiries to: Executive Director

Founded: 1969

Organisation type and purpose: Registered charity (charity number 313460), training organisation, consultancy, research organisation.

Subject coverage: Analysis of organisation: theory, including organisational behaviour, group dynamics, systems psychology, religious behaviour; applications in the following fields: leadership and organisation of institutions, the educational process in secondary and higher education, industrial organisation and structure, management in central and local government agencies, religious institutions in society, community service and voluntary organisations, probation and after-care, prisons and penal establishments, transition from childhood to adult life, management training, group and inter-group relations, unemployment.

continued overleaf

Publications: Printed
Order printed publications from: Publications Secretary, e-mail: purchases@grubb.org.uk

Publications list: Available online and in print

Access to staff: Contact by letter, by telephone, by fax, by e-mail and via website. Appointment necessary.
Hours: Mon to Fri, 0900 to 1730

GS1 UK

10 Maltravers Street, London, WC2R 3BX

Tel: 020 7655 9000
Fax: 020 7681 2290
E-mail: info@gs1uk.org
Website: www.gs1uk.org

Enquiries to: Chief Executive
Direct e-mail: suraya.adnan@gs1uk.org
Other contacts: Director, Business Development, for marketing issues.

Founded: 1976

Organisation type and purpose: Advisory body, trade association (membership is by subscription), present number of members: 16,000 members, training organisation.
Trusted source of the best standards for business data and the best practices for electronic commerce.
The system provides the foundation for improved supply chain management and electronic trading.

Subject coverage: Best practice code for doing business electronically across the extended enterprise. One-stop organisation for help and advice on electronic commerce to UK organisations. Supports and promulgates EAN UCC standards, and electronic commerce standards. Strong lobbying position on behalf of 'UK plc'.

Library catalogue: All or part available in-house

Publications: Printed, and electronic and video

Publications list: Available in print

Access to staff: Contact by letter, by fax, by e-mail and via website
Hours: Mon to Fri, 0900 to 1700

Access to building: Prior appointment required

Access for disabled people: Parking provided, ramped entry

Affiliated to: International Article Numbering Association (EAN Int); tel: + 32 2 2271020; fax: + 32 2 2271021

Founder member of: EAN

GUARDIAN NEWS & MEDIA LTD (GNM)

Research & Information, The Guardian, Kings Place, 90 York Way, London N1 9GU

E-mail: richard.nelsson@guardian.co.uk
Website: www.guardian.co.uk

Enquiries to: Information Manager

Organisation type and purpose: Publishing house.
Media.

GUILD OF AID FOR GENTLEPEOPLE (The Guild)

Formal name: Professionalsaid

10 St Christopher's Place, London, W1U 1 HZ

Tel: 020 7935 0641
E-mail: thead@professionalsaid.org.uk
Website: www.professionalsaid.org.uk
Website: www.guild-of-aid.org.uk
Website: www.charitygiving.co.uk/donate/professionalaid

Enquiries to: Welfare & Support Officer

Founded: 1904

Organisation type and purpose: National organisation, voluntary organisation, registered charity (charity number 31/BEN).
Providing assistance to those of gentle birth and good education.

Subject coverage: Financial assistance to people of gentle birth and good education who have fallen into poverty.

Information services: General.

Education services: Education and further education.

Publications: Printed

Access to staff: Contact by letter, by telephone, by fax and by e-mail
Hours: Mon to Fri, 0930 to 1700

Access to building: No access other than to staff

Affiliated to: Professional Classes Aid Council; administered from the same address

GUILD OF AIR PILOTS AND AIR NAVIGATORS (GAPAN)

Cobham House, 9 Warwick Court, Gray's Inn, London, WC1R 5DJ

Tel: 020 7404 4032
Fax: 020 7404 4035
E-mail: gapan@gapan.org
Website: www.gapan.org

Enquiries to: Clerk

Founded: 1929

Organisation type and purpose: Professional body (membership is by subscription, qualification, election or invitation), present number of members: 1,650, voluntary organisation, suitable for ages: 17+.
Livery company of the City of London.
To promote air safety and aviation knowledge.

Subject coverage: Air safety, aircrew licensing and training, technical developments in aviation and the allocation of flying scholarships and awards.

Access to staff: Contact by letter, by fax, by e-mail and in person. Appointment necessary.
Hours: Mon to Fri, 0900 to 1700

GUILD OF ALL SOULS (GAS)

Royal London House, 22–25 Finsbury Square, London, EC2A 1DX

Tel: 020 7920 6468
E-mail: contact@guildofallsouls.org.uk
Website: www.guildofallsouls.org.uk

Enquiries to: General Secretary

Founded: 1873

Organisation type and purpose: Membership association (membership is by subscription), present number of members: 1,800, registered charity (charity number 240234).
Religious guild and patron of 40 livings.

Collection: 40 Advowson documents (some dating back to the 18th century)

Publications list: Available online

Access to staff: Contact by letter, by telephone, by e-mail, in person and via website. Appointment necessary. Access for members only.

GUILD OF ANTIQUE DEALERS AND RESTORERS (GADAR)

111 Belle Vue Road, Shrewsbury, Shropshire, SY3 7NJ

Tel: 01743 271852

Enquiries to: Membership Secretary
Other contacts: Chairman

Founded: 1989

Organisation type and purpose: Advisory body, learned society, professional body, trade association (membership is by subscription), present number of members: 300, consultancy, research organisation.
Advice to trade and public regarding restoration of furniture, ceramics, glass, silver, paintings, etc.

Subject coverage: All restoration to antiques. Information regarding courses on restoration. Valuations for probate and insurance.

Collection: Reference books on all aspects of restoration and antiques

Publications: Printed

Access to staff: Contact by letter, by telephone and in person
Hours: Mon and Fri, 0930 to 1700; 24-hour answering service

Access to building: Prior appointment required

GUILD OF ARCHITECTURAL IRONMONGERS (GAI)

8 Stepney Green, London, E1 3JU

Tel: 020 7790 3431
Fax: 020 7790 8517
E-mail: info@gai.org.uk
Website: www.gai.org.uk

Enquiries to: Chief Executive

Founded: 1961

Organisation type and purpose: International organisation, trade association (membership is by subscription), present number of members: 400, service industry.

Subject coverage: Architectural ironmongery and industry training.

Publications: Printed

Publications list: Available in print

Access to staff: Contact by letter, by fax, by e-mail and via website
Hours: Mon to Fri, 0900 to 1700

GUILD OF BRITISH BUTLERS, ADMINISTRATORS AND PERSONAL ASSISTANTS

12 Little Bornes, Alleyn Park, Dulwich, London, SE21 8SE

Tel: 020 8670 5585
Fax: 020 8670 0055
Website: www.ivorspencer.com

Enquiries to: Chief Executive
Direct tel: 020 8670 5585

Founded: 1981

Organisation type and purpose:
Professional body, voluntary organisation, training organisation.

Subject coverage: Controlling large households; banqueting; purchasing for large parties; training staff for service in hotels and private households; organisation of Royal and State banquets world-wide.

Access to staff: Contact by letter, by telephone and by fax
Hours: Mon to Fri, 0900 to 1700

Links with: Ivor Spencer School for Butler Administrators; at the same address

GUILD OF BUILDERS AND CONTRACTORS

Crest House, 102–104 Church Road, Teddington, Middlesex, TW11 8PY

Tel: 020 8977 1105
Fax: 020 8943 3151
E-mail: info@buildersguild.co.uk
Website: www.BuildersGuild.co.uk

Enquiries to: Director General

Founded: 1992

Organisation type and purpose: National organisation, trade association (membership is by subscription, election or invitation), present number of members: 1,700.

Subject coverage: Building.

Access to staff: Contact by letter, by telephone, by fax and by e-mail
Hours: Mon to Fri, 0930 to 1600

Access to building: No access other than to staff

Access for disabled people: Parking provided

GUILD OF CHURCH MUSICIANS (GCM)

Hillbrow, Godstone Road, Bletchingley, Surrey, RH1 4PJ

Tel: 01883 743168
E-mail: JohnMusicsure@orbix.co.uk

Enquiries to: General Secretary

Founded: 1888; formerly called Incorporated Guild of Church Musicians (IGCM) (year of change 1988)

Organisation type and purpose:
International organisation, professional body (membership is by election or invitation), present number of members: 700, registered charity, suitable for ages: all, training organisation.
Examining body for Archbishop's Certificate in Church Music and Fellowship of the Guild of Church Musicians, and the Archbishop's Certificate in Public Worship.

Subject coverage: Church music; administration of Archbishops' Certificates in Church Music and Public Worship, associate and fellowship examinations.

Non-library collection catalogue: All or part available in print

Library catalogue: All or part available in-house

Publications: Printed

Access to staff: Contact by letter, by telephone, by e-mail and via website. Appointment necessary.
Hours: Mon to Fri, 0930 to 1800

Liaison with the: Royal School of Church Music

Other addresses: St Katharine Cree Church; 86 Leadenhall Street, London, EC3; tel: 020 7283 5733

GUILD OF DISABLED HOMEWORKERS

23 Fountain Street, Nailsworth, Gloucestershire, GL6 0BL

Tel: 01453 835623
Fax: 01453 835623
E-mail: godcl@tiscali.co.uk

Enquiries to: Membership Secretary

Founded: 1972

Subject coverage: Homeworking for the disabled.

Access to staff: Contact by letter, by telephone, by fax and by e-mail
Hours: Mon to Fri, 0930 to 1630

Access for disabled people: Ramped entry

GUILD OF FOOD WRITERS

255 Kent House Road, Beckenham, Kent, BR3 1JQ

Tel: 020 8659 0422
E-mail: guild@gfw.co.uk
Website: www.gfw.co.uk

Enquiries to: Administrator

Founded: 1984

Organisation type and purpose:
Professional body, membership association (membership is by subscription, election or invitation), present number of members: 390.

Publications list: Available online

Access to staff: Contact by letter, by telephone, by e-mail and via website
Hours: Mon to Fri, 0900 to 1700

GUILD OF FREEMEN OF THE CITY OF LONDON

PO Box 1202, Kingston upon Thames, Surrey, KT2 7XB

Tel: 020 8541 1435
Fax: 020 8541 1455
E-mail: clerk@guild-freemen-london.co.uk
Website: www.guild-freemen-london.co.uk

Enquiries to: The Clerk

Founded: 1908

Organisation type and purpose:
Membership association (membership is by subscription, qualification, election or invitation), present number of members: 2,500.
Guild, whose Patron is The Lord Mayor of the City of London. Membership restricted to individuals having the freedom of the City of London.
To bring together Freemen of the City of London, for the purposes of charity, benevolence, education and social activities.

Subject coverage: History of Guild of the Freemen of the City of London and current information.

Publications: Printed
Order printed publications from: The Clerk

Access to staff: Contact by letter, by telephone, by fax, by e-mail and via website
Hours: Mon to Fri, 0900 to 1700

GUILD OF GLASS ENGRAVERS (GGE)

87 Nether Street, London, N12 7NP

Tel: 020 8446 4050
Fax: 020 8446 4050
E-mail: enquiries@gge.org.uk
Website: www.gge.org.uk

Enquiries to: Secretary

Founded: 1975

Organisation type and purpose:
International organisation, membership association (membership is by subscription), present number of members: 300, voluntary organisation, registered charity (charity number 1016162).

Subject coverage: Glass engraving; methods, the copper wheel lathe, the hand-held stylus, acid etch, electrically driven hand-held drill.

Collection: Images of Fellows' and Associate Fellows' engraved glass, books, slides, DVDs on different techniques of glass engraving

Publications: Printed, and electronic and video
Order printed publications from: e-mail: enquiries@gge.org.uk; tel: 0208 0446 4050
Order electronic and video publications from: website: http://www.gge.org.uk

Publications list: Available online and in print

Access to staff: Contact by letter, by telephone, by e-mail and via website
Hours: Mon, 0930 to 1530; Tue, 0930 to 1530; Wed, 0930 to 1430

GUILD OF INTERNATIONAL PROFESSIONAL TOASTMASTERS

12 Little Bornes, Alleyn Park, Dulwich, London, SE21 8SE

Tel: 020 8670 5585
Fax: 020 8670 0055
Website: www.ivorspencer.com

Enquiries to: Life President

continued overleaf

Direct tel: 020 8670 8424

Founded: 1992; formerly called Guild of Professional Toastmasters (year of change 1992)

Organisation type and purpose: Advisory body, professional body.

Subject coverage: Organisation of functions of all types, including Royal events, in the UK and abroad; award of Best Speaker of the Year.

Access to staff: Contact by letter and by telephone
Hours: Mon to Fri, 0900 to 1700

Links with: Guild of Professional After Dinner Speakers

GUILD OF MACE-BEARERS

C/o The Mayor's Parlour, Town Hall, Katharine Street, Croydon, CR9 1XW

Tel: 020 8760 5764
E-mail: info@macebearer.com
Website: www.macebearer.com

Enquiries to: Guild Clerk

Founded: 1933

Organisation type and purpose: National organisation, membership association (membership is by subscription), present number of members: 250.

Subject coverage: Ceremonial activities, protocol matters and advice, toastmastering duties, chauffeuring duties.

Access to staff: Contact by letter, by telephone, by e-mail, in person and via website
Hours: Monday to Friday, 0900 to 1700

GUILD OF NATUROPATHIC IRIDOLOGISTS INTERNATIONAL (GNI Int)

94 Grosvenor Road, London, SW1V 3LF

Tel: 020 7821 0255
Fax: 020 7821 0255
E-mail: info@gni-international.org
Website: www.gni-international.org

Enquiries to: Vice President and Registrar
Other contacts: Managing Director, General Secretary

Founded: 1993; formerly called Holistic Health Consultancy and College (year of change 1993); formerly called British Register of Iridologists (MBRI) (year of change 1997); formerly called UK College of Clinical Iridologists (year of change 1999)

Organisation type and purpose: International organisation, advisory body, professional body (membership is by qualification), present number of members: 120 + 84 Licentiates + 62 Student members, training organisation, research organisation. Now the UK's only umbrella body for iridologists.
Affiliates 11 training colleges.

Subject coverage: Iridology, naturopathic medicine, herbal medicine, nutrition.

Collection: Iridiagnosis (Kritzer, J Maskel MD, original manuscript)
Prospectuses re Accredited Training Courses
Teaching Models
EU & US Iridology Books

Trade and statistical information: Data on recognised professional training courses, events and postgraduate training dates and venues

Non-library collection catalogue: All or part available in print

Library catalogue: All or part available in-house

Publications: Printed, and electronic and video

Publications list: Available online and in print

Access to staff: Contact by letter, by telephone, by fax, by e-mail and in person. Appointment necessary. Access for members only.
Hours: Mon to Wed, 0900 to 1700; Thu and Fri, 0800 to 1100
Special comments: Telephone Monday to Wednesday only.

Access to building: Prior appointment required

Access for disabled people: Access to all public areas, toilet facilities

GUILD OF ONE-NAME STUDIES (GOONS)

Box G, 14 Charterhouse Buildings, Goswell Road, London, EC1M 7BA

Tel: 0800 011 2182
E-mail: guild@one-name.org
Website: www.one-name.org

Enquiries to: Secretary
Direct e-mail: Apply for membership online at the Guild website

Founded: 1979

Organisation type and purpose: International organisation, membership association (membership is by subscription), present number of members: 2,500, registered charity (charity number 802048). Furtherance of family history.

Subject coverage: Study of surnames.

Information services: Members supply information about the registered surname that they are studying. Register of names available on website.

Education services: Techniques for one-name (surname) study available in the Forum, Journal, Seminars, Help Desk (see website for more details).

Publications: Printed

Publications list: Available in print

Access to staff: Contact by letter, by telephone, by e-mail and via website
Hours: 24 hours

GUILD OF PHOTOGRAPHERS (UNITED KINGDOM) (GWP)

59 Fore Street, Trowbridge, Wiltshire, BA14 8ET

Tel: 01225 760088
Fax: 01225 759159
E-mail: via website
Website: www.gwp-uk.co.uk

Enquiries to: Administrator

Founded: 1988; formerly called Guild of Wedding Photographers UK (year of change 1999)

Organisation type and purpose: Membership association (membership is by subscription), present number of members: 1,200, service industry, suitable for ages: 18+, training organisation.
Training, qualifying and marketing services for photographers engaged in wedding and portrait photography.

Subject coverage: Photography at weddings and other similar social functions in the UK and overseas.

Publications: Printed, and electronic and video

Publications list: Available in print

Access to staff: Contact by letter, by telephone, by fax, by e-mail and via website
Hours: Mon to Fri, 0900 to 1730

GUILD OF PROFESSIONAL VIDEOGRAPHERS (GPV)

11 Telfer Road, Coventry, Warwickshire, CV6 3DG

Tel: 024 7627 2548
Fax: 024 7627 2548
E-mail: info@gpv4u.co.uk
Website: www.professional-videographers.co.uk

Enquiries to: General Secretary

Founded: 1991

Organisation type and purpose: Advisory body, trade association (membership is by subscription, qualification), present number of members: 215, training organisation.

Subject coverage: Information concerning copyright law. Investigations into new equipment available. Widespread international freelance videographers available for work.

Access to staff: Contact by letter, by telephone, by fax, by e-mail, in person and via website
Hours: Mon to Fri, 0900 to 1700

GUILD OF PSYCHOTHERAPISTS, THE

47 Nelson Square, London, SE1 0QA

Tel: 020 8540 4454
E-mail: guild@psycho.org.uk
Website: www.psycho.org.uk

Enquiries to: Administrator

Founded: 1974

Organisation type and purpose: Professional body, registered charity, training organisation.

Subject coverage: All aspects of training in psychoanalytic psychotherapy leading to UKCP registration. Referrals to psychoanalytic psychotherapists.

Publications: Printed

Access to staff: Contact by letter
Hours: Mon to Fri, 0900 to 1700

Member of: UK Council for Psychotherapy; Psychoanalytic and Psychodynamic Psychotherapy Section, 167–169 Great

Portland Street, London, WIN 5FB; tel: 020 7436 3002; fax: 020 7436 3013; e-mail: ukcp@psychotherapy.org.uk

GUILD OF REGISTERED TOURIST GUIDES

Guild House, 52D Borough High Street, London, SE1 1XN

Tel: 020 7403 1115
Fax: 020 7378 1705
E-mail: guild@blue-badge.org.uk
Website: www.visitbritain.com
Website: www.blue-badge.org.uk

Enquiries to: Office Manager

Founded: 1950; formerly called Guild of Guide Lecturers (GGL) (year of change 1995)

Organisation type and purpose: National organisation, advisory body, membership association (membership is by subscription, qualification), present number of members: 1,800, voluntary organisation.
The Guild is the national professional association for tourist board registered guides in the United Kingdom.
It represents 1,800 guides in England, Northern Ireland, Scotland, Wales, Jersey and the Isle of Man, who between them speak 38 different languages.

Subject coverage: Tourism, guide training, organisation of tours, sources of information for tourist guides and tour operators, tourist guides, the languages spoken, special interests offered.

Publications: Printed

Publications list: Available online and in print

Access to staff: Contact by letter, by telephone, by fax, by e-mail and via website. Appointment necessary.
Hours: Mon to Fri, 0900 to 1700

Member of: Federation of European Guides; London and Regional Tourist Boards; World Federation of Tourist Guides

GUILD OF TAXIDERMISTS (GOT)

Glasgow Museums Resource Centre, 200 Woodhead Road, South Nitshill, Glasgow, G53 7NN

Tel: 0141 276 9445/9311
Fax: 0141 276 9305

Enquiries to: Honorary Secretary
Direct e-mail: james.dickinson@lancashire.gov.uk

Founded: 1976

Organisation type and purpose: International organisation, membership association (membership is by subscription), present number of members: 210, voluntary organisation, museum, suitable for ages: all, training organisation, consultancy.

Subject coverage: Taxidermy and natural history display work.

Collection: Photograph library plus slide collection covering many techniques

Publications: Printed

Access to staff: Contact by letter, by telephone, by fax, by e-mail and in person. Appointment necessary.
Hours: Mon to Fri, 0900 to 1700

Member organisation of: European Taxidermy Federation; at the same address

GUILD OF TRAVEL AND TOURISM

Suite 193 Temple Chambers, 3–7 Temple Avenue, London, EC4Y 0DB

Tel: 020 7583 6333
E-mail: nigel.bishop@traveltourismguild.com
Website: www.traveltourismguild.com

Enquiries to: Chief Executive
Direct tel: 00 44 (0) 20 7583 6333
Direct e-mail: enquiries@traveltourismguild.com
Other contacts: Director Guild Asia

Founded: 1994

Organisation type and purpose: Travel industry trade association.

Publications: Printed

Access to staff: Contact by telephone and by e-mail

Branches: Guild of Travel and Tourism Asia Chapter in Hong Kong

GUILDFORD BOROUGH COUNCIL

Millmead House, Millmead, Guildford, Surrey, GU2 4BB

Tel: 01483 505050
Fax: 01483 444444
Website: www.guildford.gov.uk

Enquiries to: Chief Executive

Organisation type and purpose: Local government body.

Publications: Printed

Access to staff: Contact by letter, by telephone, by fax, by e-mail and in person
Hours: Mon to Fri, 0900 to 1700

Access to building: Mon to Wed, 0830 to 1700; Thu, 0830 to 2000; Fri, 0830 to 1630

Access for disabled people: Parking spaces, lift, stair-lift

Parent body: Surrey County Council

GUILDFORD COLLEGE OF FURTHER AND HIGHER EDUCATION

Stoke Park, Guildford, Surrey, GU1 1EZ

Tel: 01483 448611
Fax: 01483 448606
Website: www.guildford.ac.uk

Enquiries to: Librarian
Direct e-mail: dmarshall@guildford.ac.uk

Organisation type and purpose: Further Education College.

Subject coverage: Health, social studies, education, mathematics, engineering, catering, management, business studies, computing, travel and tourism, geography, sport, leisure, media studies, art, graphic, printing, science, construction, humanities.

Library catalogue: All or part available in-house

Publications: Printed

Access to staff: Contact by letter, by telephone, by e-mail, in person and via website
Hours: Term time: Mon to Thu, 0830 to 2000; Fri, 0830 to 1700; Sat, 1000 to 1300

Access for disabled people: Toilet facilities
Special comments: Lift available

GUILDFORD INSTITUTE

Ward Street, Guildford, Surrey, GU1 4LH

Tel: 01483 562142
Fax: 01483 451034
E-mail: info@guildford-institute.org.uk
Website: www.guildford-institute.org.uk

Enquiries to: Manager

Founded: 1834

Organisation type and purpose: The Guildford Institute is registered in England and Wales as a company limited by guarantee (company number 6571640; registered charity number 1125031).
Educational institute and library.
Membership organisation (membership by subscription).

Subject coverage: A selection of the latest fiction and non-fiction and a unique local history collection.

Collection: Library of 13,000 vols, newspapers, periodicals, local history books, ephemera, photographs, prints and drawings relating to the history, people, antiquities and topography of Guildford and the county of Surrey.
The institutional archive is held by the Surrey History Service: 130 Goldsworth Road, Woking, Surrey, GU21 1ND

Publications: Printed

Access to staff: Contact by letter, by telephone, by e-mail and in person. Non-members charged.
Hours: Tue to Fri, 1000 to 1500; Sat, 1000 to 1300
Special comments: Library closed Mon.

GUILDHALL LIBRARY

Aldermanbury, London, EC2V 7HH

Tel: 020 7332 1868/1870
E-mail: guildhall.library@cityoflondon.gov.uk
Website: www.cityoflondon.gov.uk/guildhalllibrary

Enquiries to: Head of Guildhall Library

Founded: 1828

Organisation type and purpose: Local government body, public library.

Subject coverage: London history, English topography, local societies, historical horology, historical technology, clockmaking, maritime history, cookery, wine trade, genealogy, parliamentary and statutory materials, business history, English law reports, history of shorthand.

Collection: Acts (public, private and local)
Antiquarian Horological Society Library
Clockmakers' Company Library
Alfred Cock Collection (Thomas More)

continued overleaf

English Law Reports from the 17th century onwards
Fletchers' Company Library (archery)
Gardeners' Company Library
Gresham College Collection (early music)
Elizabeth David Collection (food and wine)
Institute of Masters of Wine Library
International Genealogical Index (microfiche) compiled by the Church of Jesus Christ of the Latter-Day Saints: British Isles and Ireland
International Wine and Food Society Library
Charles Lamb Society Collection
Lloyds Marine Collection
Sir Thomas More Collection
Parliamentary Papers from 1801
Public Record Office Publications
André Simon Collection (food and wine)
Stock Exchange Reports and Prospectuses c.1824–1964
Pepys Collection
Wilkes Collection (John Wilkes and 18th-century radical history)

Library catalogue: All or part available online and in-house

Publications: Printed
Order printed publications from: http://www.cityoflondon.gov.uk/librarycatalogue

Access to staff: Contact by letter, by telephone, by e-mail and in person

Access to building: No prior appointment required
Hours: Mon to Sat, 0930 to 1700
Special comments: Closed on Sat before Bank Holidays.

Access for disabled people: Lift entry, access to all public areas, toilet facilities

Parent body: City of London Corporation

GUILDHALL SCHOOL OF MUSIC AND DRAMA (GSMD)

Silk Street, Barbican, London, EC2Y 8DT

Tel: 020 7382 7178
Fax: 020 7786 9378
E-mail: library@gsmd.ac.uk
Website: www.gsmd.ac.uk

Enquiries to: Senior Librarian
Direct tel: 020 7382 7174
Direct e-mail: keaton@gsmd.ac.uk
Other contacts: Deputy Librarian

Founded: 1880

Organisation type and purpose: Suitable for ages: 18+ (HE).
Conservatoire of music and drama.

Subject coverage: Music, drama.

Collection: Alkan Society Collection (material on or by Charles Alkan)
Appleby Collection of guitar music
Goossens Collection of oboe music
Harris Opera Collection
Lute Society Collection of art reproductions depicting early instruments
Merrett Collection of double bass music
Westrup Library of music and books on music

Non-library collection catalogue: All or part available in-house

Library catalogue: All or part available in-house

Publications: Printed

Access to staff: Contact by letter, by telephone, by e-mail and in person. Appointment necessary.
Hours: Mon to Fri, 0900 to 1900

Access to building: Prior appointment required

Parent body: Corporation of London

GUILDHE

20 Tavistock Square, Woburn House, London, WC1H 9HB

Tel: 020 7387 7711
Fax: 020 7387 7712
E-mail: business@guildhe.ac.uk
Website: www.guildhe.ac.uk

Enquiries to: PA to Chief Executive
Direct tel: 020 7529 8795

Founded: 1978; formerly called Standing Conference of Principals (year of change 2006)

Organisation type and purpose: National organisation, membership association (membership is by subscription), registered charity (charity number 1012218), research organisation.

Subject coverage: Higher education issues relating especially to colleges of higher education in England and Northern Ireland.

Publications list: Available online

Access to staff: Contact by letter, by telephone, by fax, by e-mail and via website
Hours: Mon to Fri, 0900 to 1700

GUN TRADE ASSOCIATION LIMITED (GTA)

PO Box 43, Tewkesbury, Gloucestershire, GL20 5ZE

Tel: 01684 291868
Fax: 01684 291864
E-mail: enquiries@guntradeassociation.com
Website: www.gtaltd.co.uk

Enquiries to: Director
Direct e-mail: john@guntradeassociation.com

Founded: 1912

Organisation type and purpose: Trade association.
Represents all sectors of the British sporting gun and allied trades.

Subject coverage: The manufacture, supply and legitimate use of firearms and ammunition, the law relating to the above.

Publications: Printed

Access to staff: Contact by letter, by telephone, by fax and by e-mail
Hours: Mon to Fri, 0900 to 1700

Access to building: No access to building.

Member organisation of: British Shooting Sports Council; European Association for the Civil Commerce of Weapons; Standing Conference on Countryside Sports; World Forum on the Future of Sport Shooting Activities

GURKHA WELFARE TRUST

2nd Floor, Cross Keys House, PO Box 2170, 22 Queen Street, Salisbury, SP2 2EX

Tel: 01722 323955
Fax: 01722 343119
E-mail: staffassistant@gwt.org.uk
Website: www.gwt.org.uk

Founded: 1969

Organisation type and purpose: Registered charity (charity number 1103669).
Founded to support Gurkha soldiers and/or dependents and widows of soldiers who had served in World War II, but did not qualify for an army pension.
To relieve poverty and distress among Gurkha veterans of the Crown and their dependents. Supports Gurkhas through welfare pensions, a first-class medical scheme, hardship grants, emergency aid, community projects, and education grants to the dependants of retired Gurkhas.

Subject coverage: The Trust distributes funds in Nepal and responds to welfare needs as they arise in the UK.
It supports around 10,000 welfare pensioners in Nepal. Most are in their 80s and are totally reliant on the Trust for a dignified comfortable old age. Increasing numbers of Gurkhas will settle in the UK and the Trust is ready to respond. As the lead charity for Gurkha welfare, it has a co-ordinating role for helping those in need in the UK and other service charities. However, its firm focus remains Nepal and the some 10,000 veterans who will spend their final days in the mountain villages.

Publications: Electronic and video
Order electronic and video publications from: Download from website

Publications list: Available online

Access to staff: Contact by letter, by telephone, by fax, by e-mail and in person. Appointment necessary.
Hours: By appointment

Grant in aid funding from: Ministry of Defence

Links with: The Gurkha Museum; Peninsula Barracks, Romsey Road, Winchester, SO23 8TS; tel: 01962 843659; fax: 01962 877597; e-mail: curator@thegurkhamuseum.co.uk; website: http://www.thegurkhamuseum.co.uk

GUT TRUST

Unit 5, 53 Mowbray Street, Sheffield, S3 8EN

Tel: 0114 272 3253
E-mail: info@theguttrust.org
Website: www.theguttrust.org

Enquiries to: Membership Officer

Founded: 1991; formerly called IBS Network (year of change 2007)

Organisation type and purpose:
Membership association (membership is by subscription), voluntary organisation, registered charity (charity number 1057563).
A self-help organisation.
To inform, support and educate those with irritable bowel syndrome (IBS).

Subject coverage: Irritable bowel syndrome.

Collection: Art Works: entries to Living with IBS competition (2000, 2001)
Assorted books on IBS
Gut Reaction Journal (issue 1 to date)

Non-library collection catalogue: All or part available in-house

Publications: Printed, and electronic and video
Order printed publications from: A Complete Guide To Relief, order from IBS, Robinson Publishing, 7 Kensington Church Court, London, W8 4SP

Publications list: Available online and in print

Access to staff: Contact by letter, by telephone, by e-mail and via website
Hours: Office: Mon to Fri, 1000 to 1500
Helpline: Tue and Thu, 1930 to 2130

Access to building: Prior appointment required

GUYANA HIGH COMMISSION

3 Palace Court, Bayswater Road, London, W2 4LP

Tel: 020 7229 7684
Fax: 020 7727 9809
E-mail: ghc.1@ic24.net

Enquiries to: First Secretary

Organisation type and purpose: National body of the Republic of Guyana.
Guyana's diplomatic representation.

Subject coverage: Political, social, economic and cultural aspects of Guyana.

Access to staff: Contact by letter, by telephone, by fax and by e-mail
Hours: Office Hours: Mon to Fri, 0930 to 1730
Consular Matters: Mon to Fri, 0930 to 1430

GUYS' AND ST THOMAS' POISONS UNIT, GUY'S AND ST THOMAS' NHS FOUNDATION TRUST (GTPU)

Mary Sheridan House,15 St Thomas Street , London, SE1 9RY

Tel: 020 7188 0600
Fax: 020 7188 0800
E-mail: esms@gstt.nhs.uk
Website: www.medtox.co.uk

Organisation type and purpose: Poisons centre; part of Guy's and St Thomas' NHS Foundation Trust.

Subject coverage: Medical toxicology.

Information services: Poisons information service.

Library catalogue: All or part available in-house

Access to staff: Contact by letter, by telephone, by fax, by e-mail and via website. Appointment necessary.
Hours: Mon to Fri, 0930 to 1730

Access to building: *Special comments:* Researchers and NHS staff only, 24 hours notice required.

Links with: Guy's and St Thomas' NHS Foundation Trust; St Thomas' Hospital, Lambeth Palace Road, London, SE1 7EH; tel: 020 7188 7188; website: http://www.guysandstthomas.nhs.uk

GWE BUSINESS WEST LTD

Leigh Court, Abbots Leigh, Bristol, BS8 3RA

Tel: 01275 373373
Fax: 01275 370 706
E-mail: info@businesswest.co.uk
Website: www.businesswest.co.uk

Enquiries to: Receptionist

Founded: 2008; created by the merger of Great Western Enterprise (GWE) Ltd and Business West (year of change 2008)

Organisation type and purpose: Business support and chamber membership

Subject coverage: Bath and Bristol Chambers of Commerce; office space to let; virtual office services; meeting room hire; conferencing facilities and venue hire; business training (courses and bespoke); mentoring; international trade advice and support; event management; networking; business advice; business workshops; business information.

Publications: Printed

Access to staff: Contact via website

Branches: Bristol Chamber of Commerce; Leigh Court, Abbey Meads, Bristol, BS8 3RA; tel: 01275 373373; website: http://www,gwebusinesswest.co.uk
Business Link (Berkshire); The Crossbow Centre, Crossbow House, 40 Liverpool Road, Slough, Berkshire, SL1 4QZ; tel: 0845 600 9006; website: http://www,gwebusinesswest.co.uk

Links with: Bath Chamber of Commerce; 16 Abbey Churchyard, Bath, BA1 1PB; website: http://www,gwebusinesswest.co.uk
Business Link (South West); Leigh Court, Abbey Meads, Bristol, BS8 3RA; tel: 0845 600 9006; website: http://www,gwebusinesswest.co.uk

GWENT ARCHIVES

Gwent Archives , Steelwork Road, Ebbw Vale NP23 6DN

Tel: 01495 353363
E-mail: enquiries@gwentarchives.gov.uk

Founded: 1939; formerly called Gwent Record Office (year of change 2011)

Organisation type and purpose: Local government body.
County record office.

Subject coverage: Public records; manorial and tithe records; turnpike trusts; highways boards; health and services records; estate and family records; church parochial records etc.

Collection: Archive

Non-library collection catalogue: All or part available in-house

Publications: Printed

Access to staff: Contact by letter, by telephone, by e-mail, in person and via website
Hours: Mon to Fri, 0930 to 1700; one Sat per month, 1000 to 1600

Host authority: Torfaen County Borough Council; Civic Centre, Pontypool, Torfaen, NP4 6YB; tel: 01495 762200; fax: 01495 755513; website: www.torfaen.gov.uk

Parent body: Gwent Joint Records Committee

GWENT LOCAL HISTORY SOCIETY

Ty Derwen, Church Road, Newport, NP19 7EJ

Tel: 01633 241564
E-mail: karen.vowles@gavowales.org.uk
Website: www.gavowales.org.uk/gwent_local_history/index.htm

Enquiries to: Secretary

Founded: 1954

Organisation type and purpose: Voluntary organisation.
Provides forum for local history societies within Gwent.

Subject coverage: Gwent local history.

Publications: Printed

Access to staff: Contact by letter, by telephone, by fax and by e-mail
Hours: Mon to Fri, 0900 to 1700

Member of: British Association of Local History

GWENT WILDLIFE TRUST

16 White Swan Court, Monmouth, Gwent, NP25 3NY

Tel: 01600 715501
Fax: 01600 715832
E-mail: gwentwildlife@cix.co.uk
Website: www.wildlifetrust.org.uk

Enquiries to: Chairman

Organisation type and purpose: Membership association (membership is by subscription), present number of members: 2,500, voluntary organisation.
Aims to protect and enhance wildlife sites in Gwent.

Subject coverage: Conservation management, species protection, site protection and enhancement, ecological surveying, advice and education, trust nature reserves, Gwent wildlife.

Trade and statistical information: Species recording, site recording

Publications: Printed

Affiliated to: RSNC and Wildlife Trusts Partnership

Education Centre: Gwent Wildlife Trust; Festival Park, Ebbw Vale, NP23 6UF; tel: 01495 305289

GWYNEDD ARCHIVES & MUSEUMS SERVICE

Victoria Dock, Caernarfon, Gwynedd

Tel: 01286 679095
Fax: 01286 679637
E-mail: archives.caernarfon@gwynedd.gov.uk
Website: www.gwynedd.gov.uk/archives

Enquiries to: Archivist

Organisation type and purpose: County Record Office.

Subject coverage: Usual county archive collection with particular strengths in the industrial (quarrying), maritime and estate records.

continued overleaf

Education services: Group education facilities, resources for Key Stages 1, 2 and 3.

Non-library collection catalogue: All or part available online and in-house

Publications list: Available online

Access to staff: Contact by telephone, by fax, by e-mail and in person
Hours: Closed Mon; Tue, Thu, Fri, 0930 to 1230 and 1330 to 1700; Wed, 0930 to 1230 and 1330 to 1900

Access to building: No prior appointment required
Hours: Closed Mon; open Tue, Thu, Fri, 0930 to 1230 and 1330 to 1700; Wed, 0930 to 1230 and 1330 to 1900
Special comments: CARN readers ticket required.
Appointment advised for microfiche and microfilm readers

Access for disabled people: Level entry, access to all public areas, toilet facilities

Other address: Gwynedd Archives; Dolgellau Area Record Office

GWYNEDD COUNTY COUNCIL

Development Directorate, Culture and Leisure, County Offices, Caernarfon, Gwynedd, LL55 1SH

Tel: 01286 672255
Fax: 01286 677347
E-mail: celf@gwynedd.gov.uk
Website: www.gwynedd.gov.uk

Enquiries to: Assistant Director: Culture

Founded: 1996; formerly called Arfon Borough Council, Dwyfor District Council, Gwynedd County Council, Meirionydd District Council (year of change 1996)

Organisation type and purpose: Local government body, museum, art gallery, public library, suitable for ages: 4 to 18. Archives, arts organisation.

Subject coverage: General reference materials, local history, county archives, artefacts.

Collection: County archives collections
European Community publications
Local history collections
Maritime records, including Lloyd's Registers, Lloyd's Lists, registers, crew lists and log books
Reports, Hansard etc., of Welsh Assembly
Welsh periodicals and local newspapers

Non-library collection catalogue: All or part available online and in-house

Library catalogue: All or part available online

Publications: Printed

Access to staff: Contact by letter, by telephone, by fax, by e-mail and in person
Hours: Mon to Fri, 0900 to 1700; late nights to 1900
Library also Sat, 1000 to 1300

Access to building: No access other than to staff

Other addresses: Archives and Museum Service; County Offices, Caernarfon, Gwynedd; tel: 01286 679093; fax: 01286 679637; e-mail: archifau@gwynedd.gov.uk; County Library Headquarters; Allt Pafiliwn, Caernarfon, Gwynedd; tel: 01286 679465; fax: 01286 671137; e-mail: llyfrgell@gwynedd.gov.uk

GYPSUM PRODUCTS DEVELOPMENT LIMITED (GPDA)

PO Box 35084, London, NW1 4XE

Tel: 020 7935 8532
E-mail: admin@gpda.com
Website: www.gpda.com

Enquiries to: General Secretary

Founded: 1889

Organisation type and purpose: Trade association (membership is by subscription).

Subject coverage: Gypsum product usage (gypsum plaster, plasterboard); mainly in the fields of building and refurbishment.

Publications: Printed

Publications list: Available online

Access to staff: Contact by letter, by telephone, by fax, by e-mail and via website
Hours: Mon to Fri, 0900 to 1700

Links with: Construction Products Association; tel: 020 7323 3770; fax: 020 7323 0307; e-mail: enquiries@constprod.org.uk; website: http://www.constrprod.org.uk
Eurogypsum (European Gypsum Industry Association); tel: +32 2 521 3890; e-mail: info@eurogypsum.org; website: http://www.eurogypsum.org

GYPSY COUNCIL, THE (NGC)

Greenacres Caravan Park, Common Lane, Hapsford, Frodsham, Cheshire, WA6 0JS

Tel: 01928 723138
Fax: 01928 723138

Enquiries to: President

Founded: 1966; formerly called National Gypsy Council (NGC)

Organisation type and purpose: Voluntary organisation.
Membership restricted to Gypsies as defined in legislation.

Subject coverage: Site provision for travellers, including information of site facilities, design and management; statistical information on numbers of Gypsy families in England, Wales and Scotland; existing sites and sites needed; movement of travellers; development and diversity of the travelling community in Britain; Gypsies and government policy; Gypsies and local government; Gypsy education; new age travellers, hippies.

Publications: Printed

Publications list: Available in print

Access to staff: Contact by letter, by telephone and by fax
Hours: Mon to Fri, 0900 to 1700

Links with: Romani Kris (West European Gypsy Council)

H C STARCK LIMITED (HCST)

UK Sales Office, Aizlewood's Mill, Nursery Street, Sheffield, S3 8GG

Tel: 0114 282 3158
E-mail: malcolm.greaves@hcstarck.com
Website: www.hcstarck.com

Founded: 1969

Organisation type and purpose: International organisation, manufacturing industry.

Subject coverage: Refractory metals; corrosion-resistant metals e.g. tantalum, titanium, tungsten, hastelloy, zirconium, molybdenum, nickel and nickel alloys.

Publications list: Available online

Access to staff: Contact by letter, by telephone, by fax, by e-mail and via website. Appointment necessary.
Hours: Mon to Fri, 0900 to 1700

Access to building: Prior appointment required

Subsidiary of: H C Starck Inc (HCSI); 45 Industrial Place, Newton, MA 0241–1951, USA; tel: 00 1 617 630 5800; fax: 00 1 617 630 5919; website: www.hcstarck.com

UK production site: H C Starck Limited; 1 Harris Road, Calne, Wiltshire, SN11 9PT; tel: 01249 822122; fax: 01249 823800

H G WELLS SOCIETY, THE (HGWS)

20 Upper Field Close, Hereford, HR2 7SW

E-mail: secretaryhgwellssociety@hotmail.com
Website: hgwellsusa.50megs.com

Enquiries to: General Secretary

Founded: 1960

Organisation type and purpose: International organisation, learned society.
To promote and encourage an interest in, and appreciation of, the life, work and thought of H G Wells.

Subject coverage: The life and work of Herbert George Wells (1866–1946).

Publications: Printed

HABERDASHERS' COMPANY, THE

Formal name: Worshipful Company of Haberdashers

Haberdashers' Hall, 18 West Smithfield, London, EC1A 9HQ

Tel: 020 7246 9988
Fax: 020 7246 9989
E-mail: enquiries@haberdashers.co.uk
Website: www.haberdashers.co.uk

Enquiries to: The Clerk

Founded: 1448

Organisation type and purpose: Membership association (membership is by election or invitation).
City of London Livery Company.

Access to staff: Contact by letter, by telephone, by fax and by e-mail

HACKNEY ARCHIVES

Dalston CLR James Library and Hackney Archives, Dalston Square, London, E8 3SQ

Tel: 020 5386 8925
E-mail: archives@hackney.gov.uk

Website: www.hackney.gov.uk/archives

Founded: 1965

Organisation type and purpose: Local government body.
Record office.

Non-library collection catalogue: All or part available online, in-house and in print

Library catalogue: All or part available online and in-house

Publications list: Available online and in print

Access to staff: Contact by letter, by telephone, by e-mail and via website
Hours: Tue to Thu, 0930 to 1730; Fri, 0930 to 1300; Sat, 1000 to 1700.

Access to building: *Special comments:* Car park is restricted to permit holders (residential and staff).

Access for disabled people: Lift.

HACKNEY HORSE SOCIETY

Fallowfields, Little London, Heytesbury, Warminster, Wiltshire, BA12 0ES

Tel: 01985 840717
Fax: 01985 840616
E-mail: dawn@hackney-horse.org.uk
Website: www.hackney-horse.org.uk

Enquiries to: Secretary General

Organisation type and purpose: Membership association.

Breed society.

Subject coverage: Breeding of hackney horses and ponies.

Collection: Stud Books from 1884
Year Books from 1967

Publications: Printed

Access to staff: Contact by letter, by telephone, by fax, by e-mail and via website

Links with: British Horse Society

HAEMOPHILIA SOCIETY

3rd Floor, Chesterfield House, 385 Euston Road, London, NW1 3AU

Tel: 020 7380 0600
Fax: 020 7387 8220
E-mail: info@haemophilia.org.uk
Website: www.haemophilia.org.uk

Enquiries to: Information Officer
Direct e-mail: dan@haemophilia.org.uk

Founded: 1950

Organisation type and purpose: Membership association (membership is by subscription), registered charity (charity number 288260).

Subject coverage: Haemophilia and related bleeding disorders, treatment and care, education, employment, welfare benefits, HIV, hepatitis C.

Publications: Printed

Publications list: Available online and in print

Access to staff: Contact by letter, by telephone, by fax, by e-mail and via website
Hours: Mon to Fri, 0900 to 1700

Affiliated to: European Haemophilia Consortium; World Federation of Haemophilia

HAIG HOMES

Formal name: Douglas Haig Memorial Homes

Alban Dobson House, Green Lane, Morden, Surrey, SM4 5NS

Tel: 020 8685 5777
Fax: 020 8685 5778
E-mail: haig@haighomes.org.uk
Website: www.haighomes.org.uk

Founded: 1929; incorporates the former Housing Association for Officers' Families (HAOF)

Organisation type and purpose: Established as a charitable trust.
To provide housing assistance to ex-Service people and/or their dependants. Currently this object is achieved by letting homes at affordable rents. To be considered for housing, applicants must have a British Armed Forces connection and be in housing need.

Subject coverage: The Association has over 1,300 houses, flats, maisonettes and bungalows throughout the UK, built mostly in the 1930s, 1950s and 1990s.

Publications: Electronic and video
Order electronic and video publications from: Download from website

Access to staff: Contact by letter, by telephone, by e-mail and via website
Hours: Mon to Fri, 0900 to 1700
Out of office hours: answerphone

HAIR AND BEAUTY INDUSTRY AUTHORITY (HABIA)

Fraser House, Nether Hall Road, Doncaster, South Yorkshire, DN7 2PH

Tel: 0845 230 6080
Fax: 01302 623171
E-mail: info@habia.org
Website: www.habia.org
Website: www.qualifications.org
Website: www.salon.org.uk

Enquiries to: Reception
Other contacts: Entry to the Workforce Manager for specific training, careers and education information.

Founded: January 1997; formed from Beauty Industry Authority (BIA), Hairdressing Training Board (HTB), Hairdressing Training Board Scotland; formerly called Health and Beauty Therapy Training Board (HBTTB)

Organisation type and purpose: Advisory body.
Lead body.

Subject coverage: Hairdressing and beauty therapy.

Trade and statistical information: Data on UK hairdressing and beauty industry

Non-library collection catalogue: All or part available online

Publications: Printed

Publications list: Available online and in print

Access to staff: Contact by letter, by telephone, by fax, by e-mail and via website. Appointment necessary.
Hours: Mon to Thu, 0830 to 1700; Fri, 0830 to 1530

Access to building: No access other than to staff

Links to: City & Guilds; 2 Giltspur Street, London, EC1A 9DD; tel: 020 7294 2468; Thomson Learning

HAIRDRESSING COUNCIL (HC)

30 Sydenham Road, Croydon, Surrey, CRO 2EF

Tel: 020 8760 7010
Fax: 020 8688 5372
E-mail: registrar@haircouncil.org.uk
Website: www.haircouncil.org.uk

Enquiries to: Registrar

Founded: 1964

Organisation type and purpose: Statutory body.
Maintains state register of qualified hairdressers.

Subject coverage: Hairdressing profession and industry; details of State Registered Hairdressers who are properly trained and qualified (to NVQ Hairdressing Certificate level). Details of personnel on state register; what to do in the event of a bad or unsatisfactory hairdressing experience.

Publications: Printed

Publications list: Available online

Access to staff: Contact by telephone, by fax, by e-mail and via website
Hours: Mon to Fri, 0900 to 1600

Access to building: No access other than to staff

Links with: The Guild of Hairdressers; The National Hairdressers Federation; Union of Shop Distributive and Allied Workers

Member organisations: Association of Hairdressing Teachers in Colleges of Further Education; British Medical Association; Hairdressing Employers' Association; individuals include Members of Parliament, teachers, trichologists and other experts; Institute of Trichologists; Royal College of Physicians

HAKLUYT SOCIETY

Map Library, British Library, 96 Euston Road, London, NW1 2DB

Tel: 01428 641850
Fax: 01428 641933
E-mail: office@hakluyt.com
Website: www.hakluyt.com

Enquiries to: Administrator

Founded: 1846

Organisation type and purpose: Learned society (membership is by subscription), present number of members: 1,800, registered charity (charity number 313168).

continued overleaf

Subject coverage: Original narratives of important and historical voyages, travels, expeditions and other geographical records.

Non-library collection catalogue: All or part available online

Publications: Printed, and microform publications
Order printed publications from: Publishers, Ashgate Ltd (non-members)
Order microform publications from: University Publications of America, UPA

Publications list: Available online and in print

Access to staff: Contact by letter, by telephone, by fax, by e-mail and via website

HALIFAX ANTIQUARIAN SOCIETY

356 Oldham Road, Sowerby Bridge, Halifax, HX6 4QU

Tel: 01422 823966
E-mail: anne@boothwoodnook.fsnet.co.uk
Website: www.halifaxhistory.org.uk

Enquiries to: Secretary

Founded: c. 1900

Organisation type and purpose: Learned society (membership is by subscription), present number of members: c. 300, voluntary organisation.

Subject coverage: History of Parish of Halifax.

Collection: Books and documents re Parish of Halifax

Library catalogue: All or part available in-house

Publications: Printed
Order printed publications from: Publications Officer, Halifax Antiquarian Society, 6 Baker Fold, Raglan Street, Halifax, HX1 5TX

Publications list: Available online

Access to staff: Contact by letter, by telephone and via website

HALL-CARPENTER ARCHIVES (HCA)

Archives Division, Library of the London School of Economics and Political Science, 10 Portugal Street, London, WC2A 2HD

Tel: 020 7955 7223
E-mail: document@lse.ac.uk
Website: www2.lse.ac.uk/library/archive/holdings/lesbian_and_gay_archives.aspx

Organisation type and purpose: An archive of gay activism in Britain including the archives of LGBT organisations and activists, newspapers and magazines from the gay press, and series of ephemera from campaigns and individuals.

Subject coverage: Gay activism in Britain.

Collection: Archive collection

Non-library collection catalogue: All or part available online

Access to staff: Contact by letter, by telephone, by e-mail, in person and via website. Appointment necessary.
Hours: Term-time and Easter vacation: Mon to Thu, 1000 to 2000; Fri, 1000 to 1700; Sat, 1100 to 1800
Special comments: Opening hours differ on public holidays and around Easter and Christmas; please contact for further details.

HALLMARK IP LIMITED

1 Pemberton Row, London. EC4A 3BG

Tel: 020 3102 9000
Fax: 020 3102 9001
E-mail: info@hallmark-ip.com
Website: www.hallmark-ip.com

Enquiries to: Company Secretary
Other contacts: Senior Attorney

Founded: 1886; formerly called Trade Mark Owners Association Limited (year of change 2004)

Organisation type and purpose: Service industry, trade mark attorneys.

Subject coverage: Advisers into the availability for use and registration of trade marks, designs and copyright; attorneys obtaining rights in trade marks, continued protection of those marks, including through renewal of trade mark registrations, and subsequent enforcement of trade mark rights; design protection, including searching, registration, renewal and enforcement of design rights; copyright protection and enforcement; all throughout the UK, EU and worldwide.

Access to staff: Contact by letter, by telephone, by fax, by e-mail, in person and via website
Hours: Mon to Fri, 0800 to 1800

Links with: Nucleus Limited; John Loftus House, Summer Road, Thames Ditton, Surrey, KT7 0RD; tel: 020 8398 9133; fax: 020 8398 8785; e-mail: enquiries@nucleus.co.uk; website: http://www.nucleus.co.uk

HAMBLETON DISTRICT COUNCIL

Civic Centre, Stone Cross, Northallerton, North Yorkshire, DL6 2UU

Tel: 0845 1211 555
Fax: 01609 767228
E-mail: info@hambleton.gov.uk
Website: www.hambleton.gov.uk

Enquiries to: Chief Executive
Other contacts: Press Officer for press enquiries.

Organisation type and purpose: Local government body.

Subject coverage: Local government services.

Access to staff: Contact by letter, by telephone, by fax, by e-mail and in person
Hours: Mon to Fri, 0900 to 1700

Access to building: No access other than to staff
Hours: The World of James Herriott:
Mar to Oct, 1000 to 1800 (last admission 1700)
Nov to Feb, 1000 to 1700 (last admission 1600)

Access for disabled people: Parking provided, level entry, toilet facilities

Administers: The World of James Herriot; 23 Kirkgate, Thirsk, North Yorkshire, YO7 1PL; tel: 01845 524234; fax: 01845 525333

HAMMERSMITH AND FULHAM ARCHIVES AND LOCAL HISTORY CENTRE

The Lilla Huset, 191 Talgarth Road, London, W6 8BJ

Tel: 020 8741 5159
E-mail: archives@lbhf.gov.uk
Website: www.lbhf.gov.uk

Enquiries to: Archivist

Founded: 1992

Organisation type and purpose: Local government body.
Combined record office and local history library.

Subject coverage: Local history of Hammersmith and Fulham, family history sources for Hammersmith and Fulham, records of Hammersmith and Fulham Council and its predecessors, deposited archives of local organisations and individuals.

Collection: Special Collections:
William Morris
Kelmscott Press
A. P. Herbert
White City Exhibitions
Sir William Bull
Cecil French Bequest of pictures (British art of the late 19th and early 20th centuries, especially Sir Edward Burne-Jones)
Old Ordnance Survey Maps and other maps
Old postcards and photographs
Old local newspapers
Topographical collection of paintings and prints of the Borough
Books and pamphlets
Archives relating to the history of the Borough

Non-library collection catalogue: All or part available in-house

Library catalogue: All or part available in-house

Publications: Printed

Publications list: Available in print

Access to staff: Contact by letter, by telephone, by e-mail and in person

Access to building: *Hours:* Mon, 0930 to 1630; Tue, 0930 to 1945; Thu, 0930 to 1630; closed Wed and Fri; 2nd and 4th Sat in month (excluding bank holiday weekends), 0930 to 1630

Access for disabled people: Parking provided, level entry, access to all public areas, toilet facilities

Parent body: London Borough of Hammersmith and Fulham; Hammersmith Town Hall, King Street, London, W6 9JU; tel: 020 8748 3020

HAMMERSMITH AND FULHAM LIBRARIES

Hammersmith Library, Shepherds Bush Road, London, W6 7AT

Tel: 020 8753 3813
Fax: 020 8753 3815

E-mail: myaccountsupport@lbhf.gov.uk
Website: www.lbhf.gov.uk

Enquiries to: Head of Library Services

Organisation type and purpose: Local government body, public library.

Subject coverage: English law, United Kingdom government publications, EC Public Information Relay at Hammersmith library, theology, fine art at Fulham Library.

Collection: Audio Collections: Mendelssohn, Vaughan Williams, jazz composers HP-JEF, British poetry, folk music of Iran, Iraq, Lebanon, Syria and Jordan
Doves Press (Archive Centre)
Early children's books
Special Fiction Collection: Authors CRI-DEL

Library catalogue: All or part available online and in-house

Publications: Printed

Access to staff: Contact by letter, by telephone, by fax and in person
Hours: Fulham and Hammersmith Libraries: Mon, Tue, Thu, 0930 to 2000; Wed, Fri, Sat, 0930 to 1700; Sun, 1315 to 1700

Branch libraries: Askew Road Library; 87–91 Askew Road, London, W12 9AS; tel: 020 8753 3863; Barons Court Library; North End Crescent, London, W14 8TG; tel: 020 8753 3888; Fulham Library; 598 Fulham Road, London, SW6 5NX; tel: 020 8753 3879; fax: 020 7736 3741; Hammersmith Library; Shepherds Bush Road, London, W6 7AT; tel: 020 8753 3827; fax: 020 8753 3815; Sands End Library; The Community Centre, 59–61 Broughton Road, London, SW6 2LA; tel: 020 8753 3885; Shepherds Bush Library; 7 Uxbridge Road, London, W12 8LJ; tel: 020 8753 3842; fax: 020 8740 1712

Member of: Art Reference Libraries Information Service (ARLIS); Association of British Theological and Philosophical Libraries; British and Irish Association of Law Librarians; Greater London Audio Specialisation Scheme; International Association of Music Libraries

Participates in: Joint Fiction Reserve Scheme; LASER Special Collections Scheme

HAMPSHIRE AND WIGHT TRUST FOR MARITIME ARCHAEOLOGY (HWTMA)

Room W1/95, National Oceanography Centre, Empress Dock, Southampton, SO14 3ZH

Tel: 023 8059 3290
Fax: 023 8059 3052
E-mail: info@hwtma.org.uk
Website: www.hwtma.org.uk

Organisation type and purpose: A charitable organisation that relies on grants, donations and assistance in kind.

Subject coverage: British maritime archaeology, with emphasis on Hampshire, the Isle of Wight and adjacent areas.

Education services: Education and outreach programme. Educational display at the Underwater Archaeology Centre at Fort Victoria. Public lectures and talks.

HAMPSHIRE ARCHIVES AND LOCAL STUDIES (HALS)

Hampshire Record Office, Sussex Street, Winchester, Hampshire, SO23 8TH

Tel: 01962 846154; textline 0808 100 2484
Fax: 01962 878681
E-mail: enquiries.archives@hants.gov.uk
Website: www.hants.gov.uk/record-office

Enquiries to: Archivist

Founded: 1947; created by the merger of Hampshire Record Office and Hampshire Local Studies Service (year of change 2008)

Organisation type and purpose: Local government body.

Subject coverage: Records relating to Hampshire and Hampshire families, includes records of local government (Quarter Sessions, County Council, civil, parish, etc.), Church of England, individuals, families, businesses, societies, chapels, schools, etc.

Collection: Archives relating to Hampshire and Hampshire families
Wessex Film and Sound Archive – film, video and audio tapes from the wider Wessex region
Local Studies collection of books, pamphlets, periodicals and other printed materials

Non-library collection catalogue: All or part available in-house

Library catalogue: All or part available online and in-house

Publications: Printed, and electronic and video, and microform publications

Publications list: Available online and in print

Access to staff: Contact by letter, by telephone, by fax, by e-mail, in person and via website
Hours: Mon to Fri, 0900 to 1900; Sat, 0900 to 1600

Access for disabled people: Parking provided, level entry, access to all public areas, toilet facilities

HAMPSHIRE COUNTY COUNCIL LIBRARY AND INFORMATION SERVICE, BASINGSTOKE DISCOVERY CENTRE

1920 Westminster House, Festival Place, Basingstoke, Hampshire, RG21 7LS

Tel: 0845 603 5631
E-mail: basingstoke.library@hants.gov.uk
Website: libcat.hants.gov.uk
Website: www3.hants.gov.uk/library/reference-online.htm

Enquiries to: Library Manager

Organisation type and purpose: Local government public library.

Subject coverage: General and local history.

Services for disabled people: Learning at the Centre Project, Changing Places Suite.

Collection: Local History Collection

Trade and statistical information: General trade directories and statistical volumes

Library catalogue: All or part available online

Publications: Microform publications

Access to staff: Contact by letter, by e-mail and in person
Hours: During normal opening hours
Special comments: If specific member of staff required, please make arrangments in advance.

Access to building: *Hours:* Mon, Tue, Wed, Thurs and Fri 0830 to 1830; ; Sat 0830 to 1600; Sun 1100 to 1500

Access for disabled people: Level entry
Special comments: Lift to Discovery Centre on first floor.

Links with: Basingstoke Citizens Advice Bureau; at same address, first floor

Parent body: Hampshire County Council

HAMPSHIRE COUNTY COUNCIL MUSEUMS SERVICE HEADQUARTERS

Chilcomb House, Chilcomb Lane, Winchester, Hampshire, SO23 8RD

Tel: 01962 826700
Fax: 01962 869836
E-mail: musmga@hants.gov.uk
Website: www.hants.gov.uk/museums

Enquiries to: Senior Keeper of Printed and Topographical Collections
Direct e-mail: gill.arnott@hants.gov.uk

Founded: 1944

Organisation type and purpose: Local government body.
The museums headquarters houses administration, documentation, and the conservation workshops that assist the work of the specialist and community museums operated by Hampshire County Council but also has a role in supporting museums across the South East Region.

Subject coverage: Collections are subdivided into six subject disciplines under a Senior Keeper: Archaeology; Decorative Arts, including ceramics and historic textiles and dress and the childhood collections; Natural Science, including geology; Printed and Topographical Collections, including historic photographs; Social History; and Transport and Technology. Each discipline holds relevant reference material which is available for examination by appointment.

Special visitor services: Researchers welcome by appointment with relevant Keepers.

Collection: Archaeological site archives
Blair Collection (entomologist's notes)
Thornycroft archive relating to vehicle manufacture in Basingstoke
Small collection of material relating to William Curtis, botanist of Alton
Tasker Collection (steam machinery, engineering drawings, archives and plans)
Paintings by WH Allen (searchable online)
Tichborne Archive (image database searchable online, documents shared with Hampshire Records Office)

Non-library collection catalogue: All or part available in-house

Library catalogue: All or part available in-house

continued overleaf

Access to staff: Contact by letter, by telephone, by fax, by e-mail and in person. Appointment necessary.
Hours: Mon to Fri, 0900 to 1630

Access to building: *Hours:* Mon to Fri, 0900 to 1630

Access for disabled people: *Special comments:* Access only to part of the site.

Branch museums: Aldershot Military Museum; Queens Avenue, Aldershot, Hampshire, GU11 2LG; tel: 0845 603 5635; Allen Gallery; Church Street, Alton, Hampshire, GU34 2BW; tel: 0845 603 5635; Andover Museum & Museum of the Iron Age; 6 Church Close, Andover, Hampshire, SP10 1DP; tel: 0845 603 5635; Basing House; Redbridge Lane, Basing, Basingstoke, Hampshire, RG24 7HB; tel: 0845 603 5635; Bursledon Windmill; Windmill Lane, Bursledon, Southampton, SO31 8BG; tel: 0845 603 5635; Curtis Museum; High Street, Alton, Hampshire, GU34 1BA; tel: 0845 603 5635; Eastleigh Museum; 25 High Street, Eastleigh, Hampshire, SO50 5LF; tel: 0845 603 5635; Gosport Discovery Centre; Walpole Road, Gosport, Hampshire, PO12 1NS; tel: 023 9258 8035; fax: 023 9250 1951; Milestones: Hampshire's Living History Museum; Leisure Park, Churchill Way West, Basingstoke, Hampshire, RG21 6YR; tel: 0845 603 5635; Red House Museum; Quay Road, Christchurch, Hampshire, BH23 1BU; tel: 0845 603 5635; Rockbourne Roman Villa; Rockbourne, Fordingbridge, Hampshire, SP6 3PG; tel: 0845 603 5635; SEARCH; 50 Clarence Road, Gosport, Hampshire, PO12 1BU; tel: 0845 603 5635; St Barbe Museum; New Street, Lymington, Hampshire, SO41 9BH; tel: 01590 676969; fax: 01590 679997; Westbury Manor Museum; 84 West Street, Fareham, Hampshire, PO16 0JJ; tel: 0845 603 5635; Willis Museum & Sainsbury Gallery; Old Town Hall, Market Place, Basingstoke, Hampshire, RG21 7QD; tel: 0845 603 5635

Parent body: Hampshire County Council

HAMPSHIRE COUNTY LIBRARY, WINCHESTER DISCOVERY CENTRE

Jewry Street, Winchester, Hampshire, SO23 8SB

Tel: 01962 873600
E-mail: winchester.discoverycentre@hants.gov.uk

Enquiries to: Library Manager

Organisation type and purpose: Local government body, public library.
To provide information to all who live, work and study in the county of Hampshire.

Subject coverage: General.

Collection: Comprehensive collection of broadsheet newspapers from 1979 onward on microfilm and CD-ROM
Official publications from 1972

Trade and statistical information: Statistics collection including all relevant official publications (UK) and selected EC and UN publications; trade directories collection covering the United Kingdom

Non-library collection catalogue: All or part available online

Library catalogue: All or part available online

Access to staff: Contact by letter, by telephone, by fax, by e-mail and in person
Hours: Mon to Fri, 0900 to 1900; Sat, 0900 to 1700; Sun 1000 to 1600

HAMPSHIRE FIELD CLUB AND ARCHAEOLOGICAL SOCIETY (Hants Field Club)

14 Smeeton Road, Lee-on-the-Solent, Gosport, Hampshire, PO13 8LH

Tel: 01202 408376
E-mail: martin.goodchild@baesystems.com
Website: www.fieldclub.hants.org.uk

Enquiries to: General Secretary

Founded: 1885

Organisation type and purpose: Learned society (membership is by subscription), present number of members: 611, registered charity (charity number 243773).

Subject coverage: Archaeology, local history, natural history, industrial archaeology, geology, landscape and historical buildings of Hampshire.

Collection: Library in the Southampton University Library Archives
Photographic Collection in the Hampshire Record Office

Publications: Printed

Access to staff: Contact by letter and by e-mail
Hours: Mon to Fri, 0900 to 1700

Member of: Council for British Archaeology

HAMPSHIRE LIBRARY AND INFORMATION SERVICE

Library and Information Service Headquarters, 56 Moorside Place, Moorside Road, Winchester, SO23 7FZ

Tel: 01962 826688
Fax: 01962 856615
E-mail: library@hants.gov.uk
Website: www.hants.gov.uk/library

Enquiries to: Head of Operations

Organisation type and purpose: Local government body, public library.

Subject coverage: General; business information, local government information service, naval studies, railways, military history, aeronautics.

Collection: British Standards
Local Studies Collections
Aeronautics Collection (Farnborough)
Military Collection (Aldershot)
Naval Collection (Gosport)
Railway Collection (Winchester)

Trade and statistical information: Published United Kingdom, European Union and world trade directories, statistical series and marketing information

Non-library collection catalogue: All or part available online

Library catalogue: All or part available online

Publications: Printed

Access to staff: Contact by letter, by telephone, by fax, by e-mail, in person and via website
Hours: Mon to Fri, 0900 to 1700

Access for disabled people: Parking provided, level entry

Branch libraries: include Basingstoke, Fareham, Farnborough and Winchester

Member organisation of: European RELAY Network

Parent body: Hampshire County Council; tel: 01962 841841

HAMPSHIRE LIBRARY AND INFORMATION SERVICE – FARNBOROUGH (HLIS)

Farnborough Library, Pinehurst, Farnborough, Hampshire, GU14 7JZ

Tel: 01252 513838
Fax: 01252 511149
E-mail: CLNOREF@Hants.gov.uk
Website: www.hants.gov.uk/library

Enquiries to: Information and Lifelong Learning Librarian

Organisation type and purpose: Local government body, public library.

Subject coverage: General; business and aviation; local studies for Farnborough area.

Collection: Aviation and aerospace
British standards (online)
Local studies: books, maps, photographs, news cuttings, periodicals etc for Farnborough and surrounding area

Trade and statistical information: UK and other official, unofficial statistics.
Trade and business directories.
Company reports

Library catalogue: All or part available online and in-house

Access to staff: Contact by letter, by telephone, by fax, by e-mail, in person and via website
Hours: Mon, Tue, Thu, Fri, 0930 to 1900; Wed, 0930 to 1700; Sat, 0930 to 1600

Access for disabled people: Parking provided, level entry, access to all public areas

HANNAH RESEARCH INSTITUTE (HRI)

Kirkhill, St Quivox, Ayr, KA6 5HL

Tel: 01292 674000
Fax: 01292 674005
E-mail: enquiry@hannahresearch.org.uk
Website: www.hri.sari.ac.uk

Enquiries to: Librarian
Direct tel: 01292 674116

Founded: 1928

Organisation type and purpose: Consultancy, research organisation.

Subject coverage: Biological research, biochemistry, molecular biology, integrative biology, biological science and technology, food research, food science and technology, physical chemistry.

Publications: Printed

Access to staff: Contact by telephone. Appointment necessary.
Hours: Mon to Fri, 0900 to 1700

Connections with: University of Glasgow

Funded by: Scottish Office Agriculture, Environment and Fisheries Department

Research programme agreed in consultation with the: Agricultural and Food Research Council; Biotechnology and Biological Sciences Research Council

HANSEL FOUNDATION

Broadmeadows, Symington, Ayrshire, KA1 5PU

Tel: 01563 830340
E-mail: info@hansel.org.uk
Website: www.hansel.org.uk

Founded: 1963

Organisation type and purpose: Registered Scottish charity (charity number SC001514). To help people with disabilities have a future that is interesting, meaningful and fulfilling. Supports people in finding and keeping work, building their own social lives, living in their own homes, planning their own futures, getting the kind of support they want, to do the things they want to do.

Subject coverage: Services include: small group living, specialist residential services, housing support services, care at home, short breaks and employment services

Publications: Printed
Order printed publications from: Hansel Foundation, tel: 10563 830340

Access to staff: Contact by letter, by telephone, by e-mail and via website

HARINGEY ARCHIVE SERVICE

Bruce Castle Museum, Lordship Lane, London, N17 8NU

Tel: 020 8808 8772
Fax: 020 8808 4118
E-mail: museum.services@haringey.gov.uk

Enquiries to: Local History Officer

Organisation type and purpose: Local government body, museum.

Subject coverage: Archives and local history of the present local authority (Borough of Haringey) and its predecessors (Tottenham, Wood Green and Hornsey).
Collections of maps, photographs, postcards, 1841 to 1891 census returns on 35mm microfilm for Tottenham, Wood Green and Hornsey, newspapers, directories.

Non-library collection catalogue: All or part available in-house

Access to staff: Contact by letter and by telephone. Appointment necessary.
Hours: Wed to Fri, 1300 to 1645; alternate Sat, 1300 to 1645
Special comments: Appointment required.

HARINGEY LIBRARIES, ARCHIVES AND MUSEUM SERVICE

Wood Green Central Library, High Road, Wood Green, London, N22 6XD

Tel: 020 8489 2700
Fax: 020 8489 2722
Website: www.haringey.gov.uk

Enquiries to: Head of Library Services
Other contacts: Principal Librarian Systems and Support Services for Head of Bibliographic Computer Services.

History of institution: formerly called Haringey Library Services

Organisation type and purpose: Local government body, public library.

Subject coverage: General; instrumental recitals and the works of Telemann (under the Greater London Audio Subject Specialisation scheme GLASS).

Information services: Enquiries desk; Online information services, printed information

Collection: Public health engineering under the LASCRA specialisation
Heath Robinson Collection (at Wood Green Library)

Non-library collection catalogue: All or part available online

Library catalogue: All or part available online

Publications: Printed

Access to staff: Contact by letter, by telephone, by fax, by e-mail and in person. Appointment necessary.
Hours: Central Library: Mon to Fri, 0900 to 1900; Sat, 0900 to 1700; Sun, 1200 to 1600 (Wood Green only)
Special comments: Contact other branch libraries for information regarding opening times and disabled access facilities.

Access to building: No access other than to staff
Hours: Central Library: Mon to Fri, 0700 to 1930; Sat, 0700 to 1730; Sun, 1100 to 1630
Special comments: Staff only or by appointment before usual opening hours

Access for disabled people: Level entry, access to all public areas, toilet facilities, lift
Hours: Central Library: Mon to Fri, 0900 to 1900; Sat, 0900 to 1700; Sun, 1200 to 1600 (Wood Green only)

Branch libraries: Alexandra Park; Alexandra Park Road, London, N22 7UJ; tel: 020 8883 8553; Coombes Croft; Tottenham High Road, London; tel: 020 8348 3443; Highgate; Shepherd's Hill, London, N6 5QT; tel: 020 8348 3443; Hornsey; Haringey Park, London, N8 9JA; tel: 020 8489 1427; Marcus Garvey; Tottenham Green Leisure Centre, 1 Philip Lane, London, N15 4JA; tel: 020 8489 5350; Muswell Hill; Queens Avenue, London, N10 3PE; tel: 020 8883 6734; St Ann's; Cissbury Road, London, N15 5PU; tel: 020 8800 4390; Stroud Green; Quernomore Road, London, N4 4QR; tel: 020 8348 4363

Parent body: London Borough of Haringey Education Service; Civic Centre, High Road, Wood Green, London, N22 7UJ; tel: 020 8849 0000 (ask for Education Services)

HARLEIAN SOCIETY

Formal name: Harleian Society Incorporated 1902, The

College of Arms, Queen Victoria Street, London, EC4V 4BT

Tel: 020 7236 7728
Fax: 020 7248 6448
E-mail: info@harleian.org.uk
Website: harleian.org.uk

Enquiries to: Honorary Secretary

Founded: 1869

Organisation type and purpose: Learned society (membership is by subscription), present number of members: 280, registered charity (charity number 253659), publishing house.

Subject coverage: Transcribing, printing and publishing of the Heraldic Visitations of the counties of England and Wales and other unpublished manuscripts relating to genealogy, family history and heraldry.

Publications: Printed

Publications list: Available online and in print

Access to staff: Contact by letter, by telephone, by fax and by e-mail
Hours: Mon to Fri, 0900 to 1700

HARLOW COLLEGE

Velizy Avenue, Town Centre, Harlow, Essex, CM20 3LH

Tel: 01279 868000
Fax: 01279 868260

Enquiries to: Learning Resources Centre Manager

Organisation type and purpose: College of further education.

Subject coverage: Education, catering, art, hairdressing, floristry, engineering, construction, journalism, social care, social sciences, business, secretarial, computing, performing arts, mathematics, sciences, leisure and community.

Library catalogue: All or part available in-house

Publications: Printed

Access to staff: Contact by letter and by telephone. Appointment necessary. Access for members only.
Hours: Mon to Fri, 0900 to 1700

HARLOW DISTRICT COUNCIL

Town Hall, Harlow, Essex, CM20 1HJ

Tel: 01279 446611, 01279 446026 (minicom)
Fax: 01279 446767
E-mail: postroom@harlow.gov.uk
Website: www.harlow.gov.uk/community/info
Website: www.harlow.gov.uk/harlow_council/index.htm
Website: www.harlow.gov.uk

Enquiries to: Chief Executive

Founded: 1974; formerly called Harlow Development Corporation Commission for New Towns, Harlow District Council (year of change 1974)

Organisation type and purpose: Local government body.
Provision of services to local people.

Subject coverage: Social, economic, historic or local government related information specific to Harlow.

continued overleaf

Collection: Archive held at Harlow Study Centre and the Museum of Harlow

Publications: Printed

Access to staff: Contact by letter, by telephone, by fax, by e-mail and via website. Appointment necessary.
Hours: Mon to Fri, 0830 to 1700

Access for disabled people: Ramped entry

Other sites: Details available on request

HARPER ADAMS UNIVERSITY COLLEGE LIBRARY

Newport, Shropshire, TF10 8NB

Tel: 01952 820280
Fax: 01952 814783
Website: www.harper-adams.ac.uk

Enquiries to: Library Service Manager
Direct tel: 01952 815220
Direct fax: 01952 815391
Direct e-mail: kgreaves@harper-adams.ac.uk

Founded: 1901

Organisation type and purpose: research organisation.

Subject coverage: Animal production (sheep, cattle, pigs, poultry), crop production (cereals, potatoes, sugar beet, grass, oilseeds), farm management; agricultural economics and policy, agricultural marketing, agricultural engineering, rural land and estate management, the environment.

Collection: 18th-, 19th- and early 20th-century agricultural books and journals
Library of the National Institute of Poultry Husbandry
Sir Edward Brown Library (18th-, 19th- and early 20th- century poultry books)

Non-library collection catalogue: All or part available in-house

Library catalogue: All or part available online

Publications: Printed

Access to staff: Contact by letter, by telephone and in person
Hours: Term time: Mon to Fri, 0900 to 2200, Sat and Sun, 1000 to 1700
Outside Term time: Mon to Fri, 0900 to 1700
Special comments: Charges for external borrowers.

HARRIS MANCHESTER COLLEGE LIBRARY

Mansfield Road, Oxford, OX1 3TD

Tel: 01865 271016
Fax: 01865 271012
E-mail: librarian@hmc.ox.ac.uk
Website: www.hmc.ox.ac.uk

Enquiries to: Fellow Librarian
Direct tel: 01865 281472
Other contacts: Library Assistant

Founded: 1786; formerly called Manchester Academy (year of change 1786); formerly called Manchester College (year of change 1803); formerly called Manchester New College (year of change 1840); formerly called Manchester College (year of change 1889); incorporates the former Harris Manchester College (year of change 1996)

Organisation type and purpose: A college library of the University of Oxford.

Subject coverage: Provision of undergraduate and graduate reading for University of Oxford degrees.

Services for disabled people: Collection is accessible to all visitors through service delivery.

Collection: Carpenter Library of World Religions
Manuscripts and printed notes of lectures in Dissenting Academies
Manuscripts collections, especially letters of 19th- and 20th-century Unitarians
Old Library (pre-1800, especially Enlightenment and nonconformist authors)
Sociniana
Tract Collection (pamphlets, etc. on politics and dissent, 1500–1914)
Unitariana

Non-library collection catalogue: All or part available online and in print

Library catalogue: All or part available online

Publications: Printed

Access to staff: Contact by letter, by telephone, by fax, by e-mail, in person and via website. Appointment necessary. Letter of introduction required.
Hours: Mon to Fri, 0900 to 1630
Special comments: Library is also closed during College closure.
Vacations: Library may be closed due to staff holidays.

Access to building: *Hours:* Mon to Fri, 0900 to 1630

Access for disabled people: Ramped entry
Special comments: A reading room is available on the ground floor and staff will fetch items for individuals, e.g. parts of the old catalogue, books, periodicals, anything within reason; toilet facilities: doorway is very narrow.

Member organisation of: Association of British Theological and Philosophical Libraries; University of Oxford; website: http://www.ox.ac.uk

HARRIS TWEED AUTHORITY (HTA)

6 Garden Road, Stornoway, Isle of Lewis, HS1 2QJ

Tel: 01851 702269
Fax: 01851 702600
E-mail: enquiries@harristweed.org
Website: www.harristweed.org

Enquiries to: Chief Executive

Founded: 1909

Organisation type and purpose: Statutory body, trade association (membership is invitation), present number of members: 10. Harris Tweed certification body.

Subject coverage: Harris Tweed industry.

Education services: information packs

Trade and statistical information: Marketing and certification of Harris Tweed

Publications: Printed, and electronic and video

Access to staff: Contact by letter, by telephone, by fax, by e-mail, in person and via website. Appointment necessary.
Hours: Mon to Thu, 0900 to 1700; Fri, 0900 to 1200

HARROW LIBRARY SERVICE

PO Box 4, Civic Centre, Harrow, Middlesex, HA1 2UU

Tel: 020 8424 1059
Fax: 020 8424 1971
E-mail: library@harrow.gov.uk

Enquiries to: Interim Head of Service – Library Services
Direct tel: 020 8424 1055/1056 (for general information and local history enquiries)
Other contacts: Principal Librarian (Reference and Information Services)

Organisation type and purpose: Local government body, public library.

Subject coverage: General, architecture and building, civil engineering, town and country planning and the local history of Harrow and Middlesex. Also a section on family history and genealogy in general (e.g. IGI, 1881 Census for England and Wales on file).

Library catalogue: All or part available online

Branch libraries: Bob Lawrence Library; 6–8 North Parade, Mollison Way, Edgware, HA8 5QH; tel: 020 8952 4140; e-mail: boblawrence.library@harrow.gov.uk; Civic Centre Library; Central Reference Library, Station Road, Harrow, HA1 2UU; tel: 020 8424 1055/6 (enquiries); 020 8424 1051 (renewals); e-mail: civiccentre.library@harrow.gov.uk; Gayton Library (Central Lending Library and main music library); Garden House, 5 St John's Road, Harrow, Middlesex, HA1 2EE; tel: 020 8427 6012 or 8986; e-mail: gayton.library@harrow.gov.uk; Hatch End Library; Uxbridge Road, Hatch End, HA5 4EA; tel: 020 8428 2636; e-mail: hatchend.library@harrow.gov.uk; Kenton Library; Kenton Lane, Kenton, HA3 8UJ; tel: 020 8907 2463; e-mail: kenton.library@harrow.gov.uk; Local History Library; e-mail: localhistory.library@harrow.gov.uk; North Harrow Library; 429–433 Pinner Road, North Harrow, HA1 4HN; tel: 020 8427 0611; e-mail: northharrow.library@harrow.gov.uk; Pinner Library; Marsh Road, Pinner, HA5 5NQ; tel: 020 8866 7827; e-mail: pinner.library@harrow.gov.uk; Rayners Lane Library; Imperial Drive, Rayners Lane, HA2 7HJ; tel: 020 8866 9185; e-mail: raynerslane.library@harrow.gov.uk; Roxeth Library; Northolt Road, South Harrow, HA2 8EQ; tel: 020 8422 0809; e-mail: roxeth.library@harrow.gov.uk; Stanmore Library; 8 Stanmore Hill, Stanmore, HA7 3BQ; tel: 020 8954 9955; e-mail: stanmore.library@harrow.gov.uk; Wealdstone Library; Wealdstone Centre, 38–40 High Street, Wealdstone, HA3 7AE; tel: 020 8420 9333; e-mail: wealdstone.library@harrow.gov.uk

HARTLEPOOL CENTRAL LIBRARY

Reference and Information Service, 124 York Road, Hartlepool, TS26 9DE

Tel: 01429 263778
Fax: 01429 283400
E-mail: infodesk@hartlepool.gov.uk
Website: www.hartlepool.gov.uk

Enquiries to: Reference manager

Founded: 1895

Organisation type and purpose: Public library.

Subject coverage: All subjects, specialist coverage: local studies, family history, local organisations database.

Collection: William Gray and Co – Ships Particulars Books 1872 to 1941
Luke Blumer and Son – Shipbuilders and Ship Repairs Accounts 1853 to 1868
Music scores
Family History Collection
Local Studies Collection
Map Collection – local area and port
Photograph Collection – local area

Library catalogue: All or part available online and in-house

Access to staff: Contact by letter, by telephone, by fax, by e-mail, in person and via website
Hours: Mon to Thu, 0930 to 1900; Fri to Sat, 0930 to 1700; Sun, 1130 to 1530

Access to building: No prior appointment required
Hours: Mon to Thu, 0930 to 1900; Fri to Sat, 0930 to 1700; Sun, 1130 to 1530

Access for disabled people: Level entry, access to all public areas, toilet facilities

HARVEIAN SOCIETY OF LONDON

11 Chandos Street, Cavendish Square, London, W1M 0EB

Tel: 020 7580 1043
Fax: 020 7580 5793

Enquiries to: Executive Secretary

Founded: 1831

Organisation type and purpose: Learned society (membership is by election or invitation), present number of members: 330, registered charity.

Subject coverage: Medicine in general, history of medicine.

Collection: Archives of Society

Access to staff: Contact by letter and by fax
Hours: Mon to Fri, 0900 to 1700

HASTINGS REFERENCE LIBRARY

Brassey Institute, 13 Claremont, Hastings, East Sussex, TN34 1HE

Tel: 0345 608 0195
Fax: 01424 724698
E-mail: library.hastings.ref@eastsussex.gov.uk
Website: www.eastsussex.gov.uk/libraries

Enquiries to: Information and Local Studies Librarian

Organisation type and purpose: Local government body, public library.

Subject coverage: General reference material; large local studies collection including photographs, newspapers, maps (especially Hastings, with some Sussex).

Collection: Brassey Collection (material by, about, and relating to Thomas, 1st Earl Brassey, and his family)

Library catalogue: All or part available online and in-house

Access to staff: Contact by letter, by telephone, by fax, by e-mail and in person
Hours: Mon, 0930 to 1800; Tue, Thu, 0930 to 1830; Wed, 0930 to 1300; Fri, 1030 to 1830; Sat, 0930 to 1700; Sun, closed

Access for disabled people: Access to all public areas

Parent body: East Sussex Libraries

HAUGHTON INTERNATIONAL FAIRS

15 Duke Street, St James's, London, SW1Y 6DB

Tel: 020 7389 6555
Fax: 020 7389 6556
E-mail: info@haughton.com
Website: www.haughton.com

Enquiries to: Public Relations Manager

Founded: 1989

Organisation type and purpose: Organiser of international fine art and antiques fairs, including the International Fine Art & Antique Dealers Show, and Art Antiques London.

Subject coverage: Art and antiques from all periods and countries, including pictures, sculpture, furniture, ceramics, jewellery, silver, manuscripts, textiles, ethnographica.

Collection: Catalogues of past fairs

Publications: Printed

Access to staff: Contact by letter, by telephone, by fax and by e-mail
Hours: Mon to Fri, 1000 to 1800

Access for disabled people: Yes

HAVANT BOROUGH COUNCIL (HBC)

Civic Offices, Civic Centre Road, Havant, Hampshire, PO9 2AX

Tel: 023 9247 4174, 023 9244 6602 (minicom)
Fax: 023 9248 0263
E-mail: customer.services@havant.gov.uk
Website: www.havant.gov.uk

Enquiries to: Public Relations Manager
Direct tel: 023 9244 6420
Direct fax: 023 9244 6490

Founded: 1974

Organisation type and purpose: Local government body.

Subject coverage: All matters relating to local government issues within the Borough of Havant.

Publications: Printed

Access to staff: Contact by letter, by telephone, by fax, by e-mail and in person
Hours: Mon to Fri, 0900 to 1700

Access for disabled people: Parking provided, level entry, access to all public areas, toilet facilities

HAVERFORDWEST PUBLIC LIBRARY

Dew Street, Haverfordwest, Pembrokeshire, SA61 1SU

Tel: 01437 765244
Fax: 01437 767092
E-mail: haverfordwestlibrary@pembrokeshire.gov.uk

Enquiries to: Librarian
Direct tel: 01437 775248
Other contacts: Principal Librarian (for main contacts for all County libraries)

Organisation type and purpose: Public library.

Subject coverage: General reference. Local studies of Pembrokeshire including: a multi-format collection relating to the people/places/events/subjects connected to the County of Pembrokeshire, past and present.

Collection: Francis Green Genealogical Collection covering the prominent families of Cardiganshire, Carmarthenshire and Pembrokeshire at the turn of the 19th century

Library catalogue: All or part available online

Publications: Printed
Order printed publications from: Local Studies Librarian, County Library, Dew St. Haverfordwest, SA61 1SU

Publications list: Available in print

Access to staff: Contact by letter, by telephone, by fax, by e-mail and in person
Hours: Mon, Wed, Thu, 0930 to 1700; Tue, Fri, 0930 to 1900; Sat 0930 to 1300

Access for disabled people: Parking provided, toilet facilities, customer lift

Branch libraries: Crymych Library; Preseli School, Crymych, SA41 3QF; tel: 01239 832092; e-mail: crymychlibrary@pembrokeshire.gov.uk; Fishguard Library; Town Hall, The Square, Fishguard, SA65 9HA; tel: 01437 776638; e-mail: fishguardlibrary@pembrokeshire.gov.uk; Milford Haven Library; Cedar Court, Milford Haven, SA73 3LS; tel: 01437 771888; e-mail: milfordhavenlibrary@pembrokeshire.gov.uk; Narberth Library; St James Street, Narberth, SA67 7BU; tel: 01437 775650; e-mail: narberthlibrary@pembrokeshire.gov.uk; Newport Library; Bank House, Bridge Street, Newport, SA42 0TB; tel: 01239 821169; e-mail: newportlibrary@pembrokeshire.gov.uk; Neyland Library; St Clements Road, Neyland, SA73 1SH; tel: 01437 775131; e-mail: neylandlibrary@pembrokeshire.gov.uk; Pembroke Dock Library; Water Street, Pembroke Dock, SA72 6DW; tel: 01437 775825; e-mail: pembrokedocklibrary@pembrokeshire.gov.uk; Pembroke Library; Commons Road, Pembroke, SA71 4EA; tel: 01437 776454; e-mail: pembrokelibrary@pembrokeshire.gov.uk; Saundersfoot Library; Regency Hall, Saundersfoot, SA69 9NG; tel: 01834 813958; e-mail: saundersfootlibrary@

continued overleaf

pembrokeshire.gov.uk; St Davids Library; City Hall, High Street, St Davids, SA62 6SD; tel: 01437 721170; e-mail: stdavidslibrary@pembrokeshire.gov.uk; Tenby Library; Greenhill House, Tenby, SA70 7LB; tel: 01834 843934; fax: 01834 843934; e-mail: tenbylibrary@pembrokeshire.gov.uk

Headquarters address: County Library; Dew Street, Haverfordwest, SA61 1SU; tel: 01437 775244; fax: 01437 769218; e-mail: haverfordwestlibrary@pembrokeshire.gov.uk

HAVERGAL BRIAN SOCIETY (HBS)

39 Giles Coppice, Gipsy Hill, Upper Norwood, London, SE19 1XF

Tel: 020 8761 8134
E-mail: damian_rees@yahoo.com
Website: www.havergalbrian.org

Enquiries to: Secretary

Founded: 1974

Organisation type and purpose:
Membership association (membership is by subscription, election or invitation), present number of members: 200, registered charity (charity number 275793).
To promote public knowledge of the work of William Havergal Brian (1876–1972) and, to this end, to support and sponsor its publication, performance and recording.

Subject coverage: Havergal Brian (1876–1972): the composer and his work.

Collection: Havergal Brian Society Archive in the University of Keele

Publications: Printed

Access to staff: Contact by letter, by telephone, by e-mail and via website

HAVERING COLLEGE OF FURTHER AND HIGHER EDUCATION (HCFHE)

Ardleigh Green Road, Hornchurch, Essex, RM11 2LL

Tel: 01708 462758; minicom no. 01708 462735
Fax: 01708 462788
E-mail: lrcag@havering-college.ac.uk
Website: www.havering-college.ac.uk
Website: svrautolib.havering-college.ac.uk/opac/opacreq.dll/new

Enquiries to: Head of Learning Centres
Direct tel: 01708 462831; 01708 462758 (Library)
Direct e-mail: astrande@havering-college.ac.uk

Founded: 1948

Organisation type and purpose: Library of a college of further and higher education.

Subject coverage: Art; design; hairdressing; beauty therapy; graphics; media production; business studies; management; accountancy; health services administration; motor vehicle engineering; mechanical engineering; electrical engineering; electronic engineering; computer studies; robotics; humanities; mathematics; science; secretarial and office studies; social services; social work; nursery nursing; teacher education; catering, fashion, sport & leisure, construction & building services.

Non-library collection catalogue: All or part available online

Library catalogue: All or part available online

Access to staff: Contact by letter, by telephone, by fax and by e-mail
Hours: Ardleigh Green Site: Mon to Thu, 0830 to 1900; Fri, 1000 to 1700
Quarles Site: Mon to Thu, 0830 to 1900; Fri, 0900 to 1700
Rainham Site: Mon, Tue, Thur 1000 to 1430; Wed, Fri 1030 to 1430

Access for disabled people: Parking provided, ramped entry, access to all public areas, toilet facilities
Special comments: No lift access to library at Rainham.

Branch libraries: Quarles Campus; Harold Hill, Romford, Essex; tel: 01708 462759; e-mail: jforsyth@havering-college.ac.uk; Rainham Construction Centre; Burnside House, New Road, Rainham, Essex; tel: 01708 462760; e-mail: ajrobinson@havering-college.ac.uk

HAWK AND OWL TRUST (HOT)

c/o Zoological Society of London, Regent's Park, London, NW1 4RY

Tel: 01626 334864
Fax: 01626 334864
E-mail: hawkandowl@aol.com
Website: www.hawkandowl.org

Enquiries to: Chairman
Direct tel: 01761 462017
Direct fax: 01761 462017
Other contacts: The Hawk and Owl Trust Membership Secretary: for administration of the Trust's Adopt a Box scheme, and issues periodic reports to subscribers.

Founded: 1969; formerly called The Hawk Trust

Organisation type and purpose:
Membership association (membership is by subscription), present number of members: c. 2,500, voluntary organisation, registered charity (charity number 1058565), suitable for all ages, research organisation.
The conservation of birds of prey in the wild and their habitat.

Subject coverage: Conservation of the barn owl and all birds of prey in the wild, nestboxes and habitat creation. The Law and Planning Regulations concerning birds of prey, particularly building regulations affecting barn owls.

Collection: Slide and picture library

Trade and statistical information: Barn owl road casualties survey.
Urban peregrine falcon survey

Publications: Printed
Order printed publications from: Publications Officer, The Hawk and Owl Trust Publications
PO Box 530, Windlesham, GU20 6XZ, e-mail: hawkowlpub@tiscali.co.uk

Publications list: Available in print

Access to staff: Contact by letter, by telephone, by fax, by e-mail and via website
Hours: Mon to Fri, 0900 to 1700

Adopt a Box: Adopt a Box; 2 Mill Walk, Wheathampstead, AL4 8DT; tel: 01582 832182; fax: 01582 832182; e-mail: hawkandowltrust@aol.com

Education Officer: The Hawk and Owl Trust; Exhibition and education parties at the Education Centre, Chalfont St Giles, Buckinghamshire, HP8 4AB; tel: 01494 876262; fax: 01494 876262; e-mail: hoteducation@tesco.net

Member of: Birdlife International

Membership Secretary: The Hawk and Owl Trust; 11 St Mary's Close, Abbotskerswell, Newton Abbot, Devon, TQ12 5QF; tel: 01626 334864; fax: 01626 334864; e-mail: hawkandowl@aol.com

Other addresses: Education Officer; c/o Chiltern Open Air Museum, Newland Park, Gorelands Lane, Chalfont St Giles, HP8 4AB; tel: 01494 876262; fax: 01494 876262; e-mail: hoteducation@tesco.net; The Hawk and Owl Trust National Conservation and Education Centre; The HOT Barn Owl Conservation Network; National Coordinator, c/o Sheepdrove Trust, Sheepdrove Organic Farm Centre, Lambourn, Berkshire, RG17 7UU; tel: 01488 674727; fax: 01488 72677

HAWTHORNS URBAN WILDLIFE CENTRE (The Hawthorns)

The Hawthorns, Southampton Common, Southampton, SO15 7NN

Tel: 023 8067 1921; minicom no. 023 8067 8079
Fax: 023 8067 6859
E-mail: lin.hand@southampton.gov.uk
Website: www.southampton.gov.uk/s-leisure/parksgreenspaces/thehawthorns

Enquiries to: Southampton City Council Natural Environment Manager
Direct e-mail: hawthorns.wildlife.centre@southampton.gov.uk

Founded: 1980

Organisation type and purpose: Local government body.
Urban wildlife centre.
Urban nature conservation displays, events, education and information.

Subject coverage: Biological records, wildlife information, urban habitat management.

Information services: Displays, expert staff, walks and talks.

Special visitor services: Room hire, cafe.

Education services: Education officer.

Services for disabled people: Centre fully accessible.

Access to staff: Contact by letter, by telephone, by fax, by e-mail, in person and via website. Appointment necessary.
Hours: Mon to Fri, 1000 to 1700; Sat, Sun, 1200 to 1600

Access for disabled people: Access to all public areas

Also at: Natural Environment Unit, Southampton City Council; as main address; tel: as main numbers

Parent body: Neighbourhoods, Southampton City Council; Civic Centre, Southampton, SO14 7LP; tel: 023 8022 3855; website: http://www.southampton.gov.uk

HAYDN SOCIETY OF GREAT BRITAIN

2 Hindley Hall, Stocksfield, Northumberland, NE43 7RY

Tel: 01661 842167
E-mail: d.mccaldin@lancaster.ac.uk
Website: www.haydnsocietyofgb.com

Enquiries to: Director

Founded: 1979

Organisation type and purpose: Learned society (membership is by subscription).

Subject coverage: Music of Joseph Haydn and his contemporaries, all matters concerning Haydn performances and research.

Publications: Printed, and electronic and video

Access to staff: Contact by letter, by telephone, by e-mail and via website. Appointment necessary.
Hours: Mon to Fri, 0900 to 1700

Links with: Similar societies world-wide

HCPT – THE PILGRIMAGE TRUST

Oakfield Park, 32 Bilton Rd, Rugby, Warwickshire, CV22 7HQ

Tel: 01788 564646, 01788 564642 (minicom)
Fax: 01788 564640
E-mail: hq@hcpt.org.uk
Website: www.hcpt.org.uk

Founded: 1956

Organisation type and purpose: Registered charity (number 281074).
Organises trips to Lourdes for over 7,000 people each year.

Subject coverage: Annually takes almost 2,000 children to Lourdes from the UK, Ireland and increasingly from other countries. The children have a wide range of physical and mental disabilities, or are physically and emotionally deprived or neglected. Cared for by voluntary helpers, including doctors, nurses and chaplains, most of whom pay for themselves, the total size of the Easter Pilgrimage is now about 5,000; the largest pilgrimage from the UK and Ireland and probably the largest children's pilgrimage from any country. The holiday pilgrimage is centred around the international shrine of Our Lady of Lourdes and gives children, aged 7–18, with many types of disability or special needs, the opportunity to experience a really stimulating and highly enjoyable group holiday. From HCPT grew the Hosanna House Trust, which was the response to a request from young adults for an opportunity to experience a similar holiday to that of the children. Today, Hosanna House, the Trust's residential centre just outside Lourdes in Bartres, takes nearly 2,000 pilgrims in groups of 40 to 50, many of whom have disabilities or special needs. These guests stay for a week between Easter and November.

Collection: Online photo gallery, film library and music

Publications: Printed, and electronic and video
Order printed publications from: e-mail: trust .news@hcpt.org.uk
Order electronic and video publications from: Download from website

Publications list: Available online

Access to staff: Contact by letter, by telephone, by fax and by e-mail

HDRA

Formal name: Henry Doubleday Research Association

Ryton Organic Gardens, Ryton-on-Dunsmore, Coventry, Warwickshire, CV8 3LG

Tel: 024 7630 3517
Fax: 024 7663 9229
E-mail: enquiry@hdra.org.uk
Website: www.hdra.org.uk

Enquiries to: Chief Executive

Founded: 1958

Organisation type and purpose: International organisation, membership association (membership is by subscription), present number of members: 30,000, registered charity (charity number 298104), suitable for ages: all, consultancy, research organisation.
Research, education, promotion of environmentally friendly organic gardening, farming and food.

Subject coverage: Organic gardening, organic horticulture, organic farming, organic food, recycling, composting, reafforestation, organic catering and retailing.

Collection: Organic gardening and farming book collection library and scientific papers

Trade and statistical information: Data on organic techniques in the UK and overseas. Data on reafforestation tree species in developing countries

Publications: Printed, and electronic and video
Order printed publications from: The Organic Gardening Catalogue – Retail, Chase Organics Ltd
River Dene Estate, Molesey Road, Hersham, Surrey, KT12 4RG, tel: 01932 253666, fax: 01932 252707

Access to staff: Contact by letter, by telephone, by fax, by e-mail, in person and via website
Hours: Mon to Fri, 0900 to 1700

Access for disabled people: Parking provided, access to all public areas, toilet facilities

Other addresses: Yalding Organic Gardens; Benover Lane, Yalding, Maidstone, Kent, ME18 6EX; tel: 01622 814650; fax: 01622 814650

HEADMASTERS' AND HEADMISTRESSES' CONFERENCE (HMC)

12 The Point, Rockingham Road, Market Harborough, Leicestershire, LE16 7QU

Tel: 01858 469059
Fax: 01858 469532
E-mail: hmc@hmc.org.uk

Enquiries to: Secretary
Other contacts: Chairman

Founded: 1869; formerly called Headmasters' Conference

Organisation type and purpose: Professional body, trade union.

Subject coverage: Independent education; boarding; curriculum matters; professional development of members and members' schools; school sport; community service.

Publications: Printed

Access to staff: Contact by letter, by telephone and by e-mail
Hours: Mon to Fri, 0900 to 1700

HEADWAY – THE BRAIN INJURY ASSOCIATION

Bradbury House, 190 Bagnall Road, Old Basford, Nottingham, NG6 8SF

Tel: 0115 924 0800
Fax: 0115 958 4446
E-mail: enquiries@headway.org.uk
Website: www.headway.org.uk

Enquiries to: Helpline
Direct tel: Helpline tel: 0115 924 0800/0808 800 2244 (freephone)
Direct e-mail: helpline@headway.org.uk

Founded: 1979

Organisation type and purpose: National organisation, voluntary organisation, registered charity (charity number 1025852).
Community services for people with head injuries.
We have over 100 local groups around the UK. Over one-half run Headway House day care centres. Contact details of local groups are available from us and we can also provide straightforward information on many aspects of head injury.

Subject coverage: Head injury; traumatic brain damage and its physical and psychological outcome; help and support of survivors and their families.

Publications: Printed, and microform publications

Publications list: Available online and in print

Access to staff: Contact by letter, by telephone, by fax, by e-mail and via website
Hours: Mon to Fri, 0900 to 1700 (helpline)

HEALTH AND SAFETY EXECUTIVE (HSE)

Rose Court, 2 Southwark Bridge, London, SE1 9HS

Tel: 020 7717 6000
Fax: 020 7717 6134
E-mail: public.enquiries@hse.gov.uk
Website: www.hse.gov.uk

Enquiries to: Manager Site Services

continued overleaf

Founded: 1975

Organisation type and purpose: National government body.

Subject coverage: Occupational health and safety policy.

Order printed publications from: HSE Books, PO Box 1999, Sudbury, Suffolk, CO10 2WA, tel: 01787 881165, fax: 01787 313995, e-mail: via http://www.hsebooks.co.uk

Publications list: Available in print

Access to staff: Contact by letter, by telephone, by fax, by e-mail and via website. Appointment necessary.
Hours: Mon to Fri, 0900 to 1700

Access for disabled people: Level entry
Department of Transport, Local Government and the Regions

HEALTH AND SAFETY EXECUTIVE – ELECTRICAL EQUIPMENT CERTIFICATION SERVICE (EECS)

Harpur Hill, Buxton, Derbyshire, SK17 9JN

Tel: 01298 28000
Fax: 01298 28244
E-mail: baseefa.info.eecs@hsl.gov.uk
Website: www.baseefa.com

Enquiries to: Director
Other contacts: Product Certification Support Team

Founded: 1926; formerly called British Approvals Service for Electrical Equipment in Flammable Atmosphere (BASEEFA) (year of change 1987)

Organisation type and purpose: National government body.
Government certification body, Electrical Equipment Certification Service (EECS) of the Health and Safety Executive.
Testing and certification of explosion protected electrical equipment. Safety in hazardous areas.

Subject coverage: Explosion protection (eg flameproof, intrinsic safety), equipment and systems for use in hazardous areas, flammable and explosive atmospheres, European conformity and directives, certification, testing, quality assurance, repairs.

Publications: Printed

Publications list: Available online and in print

Access to staff: Contact by letter, by telephone, by fax, by e-mail and via website. Appointment necessary.
Hours: Mon to Thu, 0900 to 1700; Fri, 0900 to 1630

Parent body: Department of the Environment

HEALTH AND SAFETY EXECUTIVE – INFORMATION SERVICES (HSE)

Caerphilly Business Park, Caerphilly, CF83 3GG

Tel: 0845 345 00 55
Fax: 0845 4089566
E-mail: hse.infoline@natbrit.com
Website: www.hse.gov.uk

Enquiries to: Public Enquiry Point

Organisation type and purpose: National government body.

Subject coverage: Occupational health and safety, particularly medical, chemical and technical information..

Order printed publications from: HSE Books PO Box 1999, Sudbury, Suffolk, CO10 2WA, tel: 01787 881165, fax: 01787 313995, e-mail: http://www.hsebooks.co.uk

Publications list: Available online and in print

Access to staff: Contact by letter, by telephone, by fax, by e-mail and via website
Hours: Mon to Fri, 0830 to 1700

Other address: Health and Safety Executive

Parent body: Department for Work and Pensions

HEALTH AND SAFETY LABORATORY (HSL)

Information Centre, Health & Safety Laboratory, Harpur Hill, Buxton, Derbyshire, SK17 9JN

Tel: 01298 218000
E-mail: hslinfo@hsl.gov.uk
Website: www.hsl.gov.uk

Enquiries to: Information Centre Manager
Direct tel: 01298 218218

Organisation type and purpose: Research laboratory in the field of occupational health and safety.

Subject coverage: Occupational health, hygiene and safety, engineering, human factors, analytical and biological sciences, fire and explosion safety, risk sciences.

Library catalogue: All or part available in-house

Publications: Printed, and electronic and video
Order printed publications from: Health and Safety Laboratory, Information Centre, Harpur Hill, Buxton, Derbyshire, SK17 9JN
Order electronic and video publications from: website: http://www.hse.gov.uk

Publications list: Available online

Access to staff: Contact by letter, by telephone, by fax, by e-mail and via website
Hours: Mon to Fri, 0930 to 1530

Parent body: Health and Safety Executive; Redgrave Court, Merton Road, Bootle, Merseyside, L20 7HS; tel: 0151 951 9000; website: http://www.hse.gov.uk

HEALTH FOOD MANUFACTURERS' ASSOCIATION (HFMA)

63 Hampton Court Way, Thames Ditton, Surrey, KT7 0LT

Tel: 020 8398 4066
Fax: 020 8398 5402
E-mail: pviner@hfma.co.uk
Website: www.hfma.co.uk

Enquiries to: Director
Direct e-mail: denise@hfma.co.uk

Founded: 1965; part of the now disbanded British Health Food Trade Association (year of change 1991)

Organisation type and purpose: Trade association (membership is by subscription), present number of members: 150, manufacturing industry, consultancy.

Subject coverage: Health foods, homoeopathic, herbal, dietetic products etc, food supplements, alternative medicines, natural beauty products, other health-related matters, import, export, labelling regulations etc.

Publications: Printed

Access to staff: Contact by letter, by telephone, by fax and by e-mail. Access for members only.
Hours: Mon to Fri, 0900 to 1700

HEALTH FOR ALL NETWORK (UK) LTD (HFAN (UK))

New Century House, 52 Tithebarn Street, Liverpool, L2 2SR

Tel: 0151 231 4283
Fax: 0151 231 4209
E-mail: ukhfan@livjm.ac.uk
Website: independent.livjm.ac.uk/healthforall

Enquiries to: Office Manager
Direct e-mail: a.boyd@livjm.ac.uk

Founded: 1989; formerly called United Kingdom Healthy Cities Network (year of change 1991); formerly called United Kingdom Health for All Network (year of change 1995)

Organisation type and purpose: Membership association (membership is by subscription), present number of members: 450, registered charity (charity number 1062376), suitable for ages: all, training organisation.

Subject coverage: Information on health for all, healthy cities, work and health, public policy.

Publications: Printed

Publications list: Available in print

Access to staff: Contact by letter, by telephone, by fax and by e-mail
Hours: Mon to Fri, 0900 to 1700

HEALTH MANAGEMENT LIBRARY AND INFORMATION SERVICE

Health Management Library, Scottish Health Service Centre, Crewe Road South, Edinburgh, EH4 2LF

Tel: 0131 275 7760
Fax: 0131 315 2369
E-mail: nss.hmlibrary@nhs.net
Website: www.healthmanagementonline.co.uk

Enquiries to: Librarian
Direct e-mail: hmlibrary@nhs.net

Founded: 1965; formerly called Common Services Agency – Management Education and Training Division (MET), Scottish Health Service Management Development Group (MDG); formerly called NHS in Scotland Development Group (DG) (year of change 1998)

Organisation type and purpose: National government body. Library and information service for NHS in Scotland staff.

Subject coverage: National Health Service, health services planning, administration, management, social welfare.

Library catalogue: All or part available online and in-house

Publications: Printed

Publications list: Available online and in print

Access to staff: Contact by letter, by telephone, by fax, by e-mail, in person and via website
Hours: Mon to Thu, 0830 to 1700; Fri, 0830 to 1630

Access to building: No prior appointment required

Access for disabled people: Ramped entry

Constituent part of: NHS National Services Scotland; Gyle Square, 1 South Gyle Crescent, Edinburgh, EH12 9EB; tel: 0131 275 6000

HEALTH PROFESSIONS COUNCIL (HPC)

Park House, 184 Kennington Park Road, London, SE11 4BU

Tel: 020 7582 0866
Fax: 020 7820 9684
Website: www.hpc-uk.org

Enquiries to: Registrar & Chief Executive

Founded: 2002; formerly called Council for Professions Supplementary to Medicine (CPSM) (year of change 2002)

Organisation type and purpose: Statutory body.
Independently regulating various health professions (arts therapists, biomedical scientists, chiropodists/podiatrists, clinical scientists, dietitians, hearing aid dispensers, occupational therapists, operating department practitioners, orthoptists, paramedics, physiotherapists, practitioner psychologists, prosthetists/orthotists, radiographers, social workers in England and speech and language therapists), whose practitioners must be registered with the HPC.
Protection of the public.

Subject coverage: Approval of training courses and programmes for the regulated professions.

Collection: Registers of the professions of chiropody, dietetics, medical laboratory sciences, occupational therapy, orthoptics, physiotherapy and radiography

Trade and statistical information: Data on numbers of professionals registered including those registered under European directives on mutual recognition of academic qualifications

Publications: Printed

Access to staff: Contact by letter, by telephone, by fax and in person
Hours: Mon to Fri, 0900 to 1700

Access to building: *Hours:* Mon to Fri, 0900 to 1700

Access for disabled people: Access to all public areas, toilet facilities
Hours: Mon to Fri, 0900 to 1700

HEALTH PROMOTION AGENCY FOR NORTHERN IRELAND (HPANI)

18 Ormeau Avenue, Belfast, BT2 8HS

Tel: 028 9031 1611
Fax: 028 9031 1711
E-mail: info@hpani.org.uk
Website: www.healthpromotionagency.org.uk
Website: www.drugsalcohol.info
Website: mindingyourhead.info
Website: www.up-2-you.net
Website: www.breastfedbabies.org

Enquiries to: Finance & Administration Manager
Other contacts: Resources Manager for availability of published resources and information

Founded: 1990

Organisation type and purpose: Advisory body, statutory body.
Special Agency of the Department of Health, Social Services and Public Safety.
To make health a top priority for everyone in Northern Ireland. Summarised under the following broad headings: policy development and advice; research, information and analysis; public and professional information; training and professional development; corporate business services.

Subject coverage: Information on health promotion related issues, including campaigns, research and training, topic information on alcohol and drugs, smoking, physical activity, nutrition and oral health, children and young people, mental health, social health, breastfeeding, Healthy Schools, Health Promoting Hospitals, Health Promoting Workplaces. The Confidential Enquiry into Maternal and Child Health (CEMACH) aims to improve the health of mothers, babies and children by carrying out confidential enquiries on a nationwide basis and widely disseminating the findings and recommendations.

Publications: Printed

Publications list: Available online

Access to staff: Contact by letter, by telephone, by fax, by e-mail and via website
Hours: Mon to Thurs, 0900 to 1700; Fri, 0900 to 1630
Special comments: Enquiries welcome from health professionals, members of the public should contact the central health promotion resource service of their local Health and Social Services Board area.

Access for disabled people: Ramped entry, access to all public areas, toilet facilities

HEALTH PROTECTION AGENCY (HPA)

Porton Down, Salisbury, Wiltshire, SP4 0JG

Tel: 01980 612711
Fax: 01980 612818
E-mail: porton.library@hpa.org.uk
Website: www.hpa.org.uk

Enquiries to: Librarian

Founded: 1979; formerly called Centre for Applied Microbiology and Research (year of change 2004)

Organisation type and purpose: National government body, research organisation.
Non-departmental public body.
Public health research and production of biopharmaceuticals.

Subject coverage: Infectious diseases; immunology; vaccine research and production; emergency response; molecular biology; therapeutic products; pathogens; virology

Library catalogue: All or part available in-house

Access to staff: Contact by letter, by telephone, by fax and by e-mail
Hours: Mon to Fri, 0900 to 1700

Access to building: No access other than to staff

Constituent part of: Department of Health

HEALTH PROTECTION AGENCY – CENTRE FOR INFECTIONS (HPA)

151 Buckingham Palace Road, London, SW1W 9SZ

Tel: 020 7811 7000
Fax: 020 7811 7750
Website: www.hpa.org.uk

Enquiries to: Library enquiries
Direct e-mail: colindale.library@hpa.org.uk

Founded: 2003

Organisation type and purpose: National government body

Subject coverage: Infectious diseases, medical microbiology and virology, vaccination, microbiological aspects of public health, microbiology of food and water.

Information services: Reference only, by prior appointment only

Library catalogue: All or part available online and in-house

Access to staff: Contact by letter, by telephone, by fax and by e-mail. Appointment necessary.
Hours: Mon to Fri, 0930 to 1700
Special comments: Prior appointment required

Access to building: Prior appointment required

HEALTH PROTECTION AGENCY – CENTRE FOR RADIATION, CHEMICAL AND ENVIRONMENTAL HAZARDS (HPA CRCE)

Chilton, Didcot, Oxfordshire, OX11 0RQ

Tel: 01235 831600
Fax: 01235 833891
E-mail: david.perry@hpa.org.uk
Website: www.hpa.org.uk

Enquiries to: Librarian
Direct tel: 01235 822649

Founded: 2005; formerly called National Radiological Protection Board

Organisation type and purpose: National government body, research organisation.
Government body established by statute to give advice on health effects of radiation, chemicals.

continued overleaf

Subject coverage: Radiological protection, biological and medical effects of ionising radiations, cytogenetics, health hazards posed by chemical exposures, health effects of non-ionising radiations; radioactivity in consumer protection; radioactivity in the natural environment and environmental modelling; radioactivity in man, dosimetry; training in radiological protection; epidemiology; medical physics.

Collection: ICRP, NCRP, ICRU, IAEA safety series, IARC Monographs and Scientific Publications

Library catalogue: All or part available in-house

Publications: Printed, and electronic and video

Publications list: Available online

Access to staff: Contact by letter, by fax and by e-mail. Appointment necessary.
Hours: Mon to Thu, 0815 to 1700; Fri, 0815 to 1600

Access to building: Prior appointment required

Access for disabled people: Ramped entry, toilet facilities

Also at: HPA Occupational Services; Leeds; HPA Radiation and Environmental Monitoring Scotland; Glasgow

HEALTH PROTECTION AGENCY – MYCOLOGY REFERENCE LABORATORY (HPA MRL)

Myrtle Road, Kingsdown, Bristol, BS2 8EL

Tel: 0117 929 1326
Fax: 0117 922 6611

Enquiries to: Director

Founded: 1946

Organisation type and purpose: National government body, service industry.

Subject coverage: Maintenance of the National Collection of Pathogenic Fungi, identification of fungi isolated from clinical sources.

Collection: National Collection of Pathogenic Fungi

Non-library collection catalogue: All or part available online and in print

Access to staff: Contact by letter, by telephone and by fax
Hours: Mon to Fri, 0900 to 1700

Access to building: Prior appointment required

HEALTH SERVICES MANAGEMENT CENTRE (HSMC)

School of Social Policy, University of Birmingham, Park House, 40 Edgbaston Park Road, Birmingham, B15 2RT

Tel: 0121 414 7060
Fax: 0121 414 7051
Website: www.bham.ac.uk/hsmc/library

Enquiries to: Librarian

Founded: 1972

Organisation type and purpose: University department or institute, consultancy. Education and research in the field of health service management.

Subject coverage: Health services management, quality in health services management, primary health care overseas.

Library catalogue: All or part available online

Publications: Printed
Order printed publications from: B. Earp, Health Services Management Centre, The University of Birmingham, Park House, 40 Edgbaston Park Road, Birmingham, B15 2RT, tel: 0121 414 2976, e-mail: b.earp@bham.ac.uk

Publications list: Available online and in print

Access to staff: Appointment necessary.
Hours: Mon to Fri, 0900 to 1700

HEALTHLINK WORLDWIDE

The Grayston Centre, 28 Charles Square, London, N1 6HT

Tel: 020 7250 6950
Fax: 020 7324 4740
E-mail: info@healthlink.org.uk
Website: www.healthlink.org.uk
Website: www.asksource.info

Enquiries to: Programme Manager Knowledge Sharing
Direct e-mail: source@ich.ucl.ac.uk

Founded: 1977

Organisation type and purpose: Voluntary organisation, registered charity (charity number 274260).
Non-governmental organisation.

Subject coverage: Primary healthcare in developing countries, information management, information production, disability-related issues in developing countries.

Collection: Reference collection of materials on primary healthcare and disability in developing countries

Library catalogue: All or part available online

Publications: Printed, and electronic and video
Order printed publications from: Programme Manager Knowledge Sharing

Publications list: Available online and in print

Access to staff: Contact by letter, by telephone, by fax and by e-mail. Appointment necessary. All charged.
Hours: Mon to Fri, 0900 to 1700

Access for disabled people: Lift at entrance, toilet facilities

HEARING CONCERN

95 Gray's Inn Road, London, WC1X 8TX

Tel: 020 7440 9871
Fax: 020 7440 9872
E-mail: info@hearingconcern.org.uk
Website: www.hearingconcern.org.uk

Enquiries to: Director

Founded: 1947; formerly called British Association of the Hard of Hearing

Organisation type and purpose: National organisation, membership association (membership is by subscription, election or invitation), present number of members: 4,416, voluntary organisation, registered charity (charity number 223322).

Subject coverage: Hearing loss, lip reading, noise, vocational and welfare matters, aids to hearing, assistive aids for the deaf, loop systems, education.

Trade and statistical information: Numbers of hearing impaired people in the UK stands at 8.4 million

Publications: Printed

Publications list: Available online and in print

Access to staff: Contact by letter, by telephone, by fax, by e-mail, in person and via website. Appointment necessary.
Hours: Mon to Fri, 0900 to 1700

Access to building: Prior appointment required

Access for disabled people: Parking provided, ramped entry, toilet facilities

Affiliated to: Disability Alliance

HEARING DOGS FOR DEAF PEOPLE

The Grange, Wycombe Road, Saunderton, Princes Risborough, Buckinghamshire, HP27 9NS

Tel: 01844 348 100 (voice and minicom)
Fax: 01844 348 101 info@hearingdogs.org.uk
E-mail: info@hearingdogs.org.uk
Website: www.hearingdogs.co.uk

Enquiries to: Managing Director
Other contacts: Client Secretary for applying for a hearing dog.

Founded: 1982; formerly called Hearing Dogs for the Deaf (year of change 1997)

Organisation type and purpose: National organisation, registered charity (charity number 293358).

Subject coverage: Hearing Dogs for Deaf People aims to offer greater independence, confidence and security to deaf people by providing dogs trained to alert them to chosen everyday sounds. Hearing dogs are free to deaf applicants.

Publications: Printed

Access to staff: Contact by letter, by telephone, by fax, by e-mail and via website. Appointment necessary.
Hours: Mon to Fri, 0900 to 1700

Access to building: Prior appointment required

Access for disabled people: Parking provided, ramped entry, level entry, toilet facilities

Other addresses: Hearing Dogs for Deaf People; 29 Craigiehall Crescent, West Freelands, Erskine, Renfrewshire, PA8 7DD; tel: 0141 812 6542; Hearing Dogs for Deaf People; 12 Main Street, Crawfordsburn, Bangor, Co Down, BT19 1JE; tel: 028 9185 3669; Hearing Dogs for Deaf People; The Beatrice Wright Training Centre, Hull Road,

Cliffe, North Yorkshire, YO8 7NG; Hearing Dogs for Deaf People; The Grange, Wycombe Road, Saunderton, Buckinghamshire, HPP27 9NS

HEART RESEARCH UK (HRUK)

Suite 12D, Joseph's Well, Leeds, West Yorkshire, LS3 1AB

Tel: 0113 234 7474
Fax: 0113 297 6208
E-mail: mail@heartresearch.org.uk
Website: www.heartresearch.org.uk

Enquiries to: National Director
Direct e-mail: info@heartresearch.org.uk
Other contacts: Grant Administrator

Founded: 1967; formerly called National Heart Research Fund (year of change 2005)

Organisation type and purpose: Registered charity (charity number 1044821), research organisation.

Subject coverage: Prevention, treatment and cure of heart disease

Information services: e-mail: info@heartresearch.org.uk.

Education services: e-mail: lifestyle@heartresearch.org.uk.

Publications: Printed
Order printed publications from: Lifestyle Department or Richard Gledhill

Access to staff: Contact by letter, by telephone, by fax, by e-mail and via website. Appointment necessary.
Hours: Mon to Thu, 0900 to 1700; Fri 0900 to 1600

Access for disabled people: Parking provided

Branches: Heart Research UK in the Midlands; Lee House, 6a Highfield Road, Edgbaston, Birmingham, B15 3ED; tel: 0121 454 1799; fax: 0121 454 1799; e-mail: midlands@heartresearch.org.uk; website: www.heartresearch.org.uk

HEAT PUMP ASSOCIATION (HPA)

2 Waltham Court, Milley Lane, Hare Hatch, Reading, Berkshire, RG10 9TH

Tel: 0118 940 3416
Fax: 0118 940 6258
E-mail: info@feta.co.uk
Website: www.feta.co.uk

Enquiries to: Commercial Manager

Founded: 1994

Organisation type and purpose: Trade association.

Subject coverage: The benefits and proper use of heat pumps and heat pump technology.

Access to staff: Contact by letter, by telephone, by fax and by e-mail
Hours: Mon to Thu, 0830 to 1630; Fri, 0830 to 1600

Member organisation of: Federation of Environmental Trade Associations

HEAT TRANSFER & FLUID FLOW SERVICE (HTFS)

Hyprotech UK Ltd, Harwell International Business Centre, Gemini Building, Fermi Avenue, Didcot, Oxfordshire, OX11 0QR

Tel: 01235 448330
Fax: 01235 448350
E-mail: htfs@hyprotech.com
Website: www.htfs.com

Enquiries to: Administrator

Founded: 1968

Organisation type and purpose: International organisation, research organisation.

Subject coverage: Heat transfer; condensation; boiling; evaporation; general fluid flow; cryogenic fluids; combustion; heat transfer in nuclear reactors, design of heat exchangers and furnaces.

Publications: Electronic and video

Access to staff: Contact by fax, by e-mail and via website
Hours: Mon to Fri, 0900 to 1700

Links with: Hyprotech Ltd; Canada; National Engineering Laboratory

HEATHER SOCIETY

c/o Tippitiwitchet Cottage, Hall Road, Outwell, Wisbech, Cambridgeshire, PE14 8PE

Tel: 01945 774077
Fax: 01202 829564 (mark all faxes 'Please forward')
E-mail: theheathersociety@phonecoop.coop
Website: www.heathersociety.org

Enquiries to: Administrator
Other contacts: Chairman; Treasurer; Secretary; Registrar

Founded: 1963

Organisation type and purpose: International organisation, membership association (membership is by subscription), present number of members: 250, registered charity in England & Wales (charity number 261407).
International Registration Authority for cultivars of heathers.

Subject coverage: Growing and propagation of heathers; nomenclature and identification; availability of individual cultivars in commerce.

Collection: Heather Society slide library (free access to members)

Publications: Printed

Publications list: Available online

Access to staff: Contact by letter, by telephone and by e-mail

Affiliated to: Royal Horticultural Society

Links with: North American and German Heather Societies

HEATHERSLAW LIGHT RAILWAY COMPANY LTD

Ford Forge, Heatherslaw, Etal, Cornhill on Tweed, Northumberland, TD12 4TJ

Tel: 01890 820244; 01890 820317
E-mail: info@heatherslawlightrailway.co.uk
Website: www.heatherslawlightrailway.co.uk

Enquiries to: Managing Director

Founded: 1988

Organisation type and purpose: Service industry.

Subject coverage: Operation of a light railway.

Publications: Printed

Access to staff: Contact by letter, by telephone, by e-mail and via website
Hours: Sun to Sat, 0900 to 1700

Subsidiary company: Errol Hut Smithy; Letham Hill, Etal, Cornhill-on-Tweed, Northumberland; tel: 01890 820317

HEBRIDEAN SHEEP SOCIETY

Knox Mill, Knox Mill Lane, Harrogate, North Yorkshire, HG3 2AE

Tel: 01423 507741
E-mail: info@hebrideansheep.org.uk

Enquiries to: General Secretary

Founded: 1986; formerly called Hebridean Sheep Breeders' Group (year of change 1994)

Organisation type and purpose: Membership association (membership is by subscription), present number of members: 230.
Sheep Breed Society.
Registration authority for Hebridean Sheep in UK.

Access to staff: Contact by letter, by telephone, by fax and by e-mail
Hours: Mon to Fri, 0900 to 1700

Affiliated to: National Sheep Association (NSA); Sheep Centre, Malvern, Worcestershire

HEBRON TRUST

12 Stanley Avenue, Norwich, Norfolk, NR7 0BE

Tel: 01603 439905
Fax: 01603 700799
E-mail: info@hebrontrust.org.uk
Website: www.hebrontrust.co.uk

Founded: 1993

Organisation type and purpose: Registered charity (number 1020095), voluntary organisation.
Provides a safe, nurturing and intensively supportive community environment in which to rehabilitate from drug and alcohol dependency and the life-dominating problems that serious substance misuse can cause.

Subject coverage: Residential rehabilitation for up to 10 women aged 18–65 who share the common goal of recovery.

Access to staff: Contact by letter, by telephone, by fax and by e-mail

HELP ADVISORY CENTRE (HAC)

57 Portobello Road, London, W11 3DB

Tel: 020 7221 9974
Website: www.helpcounselling.com

continued overleaf

Enquiries to: Administrator
Direct tel: 020 7221 7914

Founded: 1968

Organisation type and purpose: Voluntary organisation.
Counselling centre.

Subject coverage: Counselling, psychotherapy, communication skills, career direction, assertiveness, sexuality, life choices, life changes.

Access to staff: Contact by letter and by telephone
Hours: Mon to Fri, 1100 to 1830

Connections with: Virgin Co Limited; 120 Campden Hill Road, London, W8 7AR

HELP FOR HEROES (H4H)

Steynings House, Summerlock Approach, Salisbury, Wilts, SP2 7RJ

Website: www.helpforheroes.org.uk

Founded: 2007

Organisation type and purpose: Registered charity (number 1120920) helping wounded Servicemen and women.
To promote and protect the health of those who have been wounded whilst serving in the Armed Forces by making grants to purchase equipment for their rehabilitation; to make grants to other charities that assist members of the Armed Forces and their dependents.

Subject coverage: Current grants policy is to look for strategic partners that are developing the rehabilitation infrastructure required by those Servicemen and women injured in the line of duty, both in action and in more general service. Mindful of the work of other service charities, H4H currently restricts its grant making to supporting those affected by the current conflicts, i.e since 11 Sept 2001.

Access to staff: Contact by letter, by telephone and via website

Also at: Help for Heroes Donations Office; Unit 6, Aspire Business Centre, Ordnance Road, Tidworth, Hants, SP9 7QD; tel: 0845 673 1760; 01980 846 459; Help for Heroes Trading Company Ltd (H4HT) – a wholly owned trading subsidiary; 14 Parker's Close, Downton Business Centre, Salisbury, Wiltshire, SP5 3RB; tel: 01725 513212

HELP THE AGED

207–221 Pentonville Road, London, N1 9UZ

Tel: 020 7278 1114
Fax: 020 7278 1116
E-mail: info@helptheaged.org.uk
Website: www.helptheaged.org.uk

Other contacts: Policy Officer for awareness of local government policies.

Founded: 1961

Organisation type and purpose: Voluntary organisation, registered charity (charity number 272786).
To free disadvantaged older people from poverty, isolation, and neglect.
To campaign for change in government policy, to undertake research into the needs of older people, and to provide local services in communities across the UK and overseas.

Subject coverage: Age-related issues: demographics, welfare and disability benefits, community care, housing, residential care, health issues, home safety and security and more. Help the Aged cannot provide information on international or development issues – refer to Help Age International.

Publications: Printed, and electronic and video

Publications list: Available in print

Access to staff: Contact by letter, by telephone, by fax and by e-mail
Hours: Mon to Fri, 0900 to 1700

Access to building: No access other than to staff

Other addresses: Help the Aged Northern Ireland; Ascot House, Shaftesbury Square, Belfast, BT2 7DB; tel: 028 9023 0666; fax: 028 9024 8183; Help the Aged Scotland; 11 Granton Square, Edinburgh, EH5 1HX; tel: 0131 551 6331; fax: 0131 551 5415; Help the Aged Wales; 12 Cathedral Road, Cardiff, CF11 9LJ; tel: 029 2034 6550; fax: 029 2039 0898; e-mail: infocymru@helptheaged.org.uk

Part of: Help Age International Network, which currently has 16 members

HELP THE HOSPICES

Help the Hospices, Hospice House, 34–44 Britannia Street, London, WC1X 9JG

Tel: 0870 903 3903
Fax: 020 7278 1021
E-mail: info@hospiceinformation.info
Website: www.hospiceinformation.info

Enquiries to: Information Officer
Direct e-mail: m.hodson@helpthehospices.org.uk

Founded: 1977

Organisation type and purpose: International organisation, membership association (membership is by subscription), present number of members: 1,000, voluntary organisation, registered charity (charity number 1014851).
Hospice Information is a joint venture between St Christopher's Hospice and Help the Hospices. It is a world-wide resource for professionals and the public that encourages sharing of information and experience amongst those involved in palliative care.

Subject coverage: Hospice and palliative care services in the UK and overseas; care of people with advanced cancer, motor neurone disease, AIDS; research and education; nursing, medical, social work and other health professional material related to terminal and palliative care; pastoral care, bereavement issues and ethical aspects.

Publications: Printed, and electronic and video

Publications list: Available online and in print

Access to staff: Contact by letter, by telephone, by fax, by e-mail, in person and via website. Appointment necessary.
Hours: Mon to Fri, 0900 to 1700

Also at: St Christopher's Hospice; 51–59 Lawrie Park Road, London, SE26 6DZ; fax: 020 8776 9345; e-mail: info@stchristophers.org.uk

Parent body: Help the Hospices

HEMEL HEMPSTEAD CENTRAL LIBRARY

Combe Street, Hemel Hempstead, Hertfordshire, HP1 1HJ

Tel: 01438 737333
Fax: 01442 404660
E-mail: hemelhempstead.library@hertscc.gov.uk
Website: www.hertslib.hertscc.gov.uk

Enquiries to: Librarian

Organisation type and purpose: Public library.

Library catalogue: All or part available online

Access to staff: Contact by letter, by telephone, by fax, by e-mail and in person
Hours: Mon, Thu, Fri, 0930 to 2000; Tue, 1030 to 2000; Wed, 0930 to 1300; Sat, 0930 to 1600
Special comments: Reference library and local statistics collection on first floor, but no lift.

Access to building: No access other than to staff
Hours: Mon, Thu, Fri, 0930 to 2000; Tue, 1030 to 2000; Wed, 0930 to 1300; Sat, 0930 to 1600

Links with: Community Information Department; Hertfordshire County Council, County Hall, Hertford, SG13 8DE; tel: 01438 737333; fax: 01442 555614; e-mail: cidb@hertscc.gov.uk

HENLEY BUSINESS SCHOOL

Formal name: Henley Business School at the University of Reading

Greenlands, Henley-on-Thames, Oxfordshire, RG9 3AU

Tel: 01491 571454
Fax: 01491 571635
E-mail: arc@henley.com
Website: www.henley.reading.ac.uk

Enquiries to: ARC Manager
Direct tel: 01491 418823
Direct e-mail: arc@henley.com

Founded: 1945; formerly called Henley Management College; formerly called Administrative Staff College

Organisation type and purpose: Business School

Subject coverage: Accounting, banking, business studies, currency, economics, industrial relations, management, marketing, office management and practice, operational research, personnel recruitment and management, production management and control, sales management, information management, statistics.

Collection: Papers of Colonel L. F. Urwick

Access to staff: Appointment necessary. Access for members only. Letter of introduction required.
Hours: Mon to Fri, 0830 to 2130; Sat, 0900 to 1900; Sun, 1000 to 1800

HENRY GEORGE FOUNDATION OF GT BRITAIN LIMITED (Henry George Foundation)

212 Piccadilly, London, W1J 9HG

Tel: 020 7917 1899
Fax: 020 7917 1899
Website: www.henrygeorge.org.uk

Enquiries to: Secretary

History of institution: formerly called Economic and Social Science Research Association (ESSRA)

Organisation type and purpose:
Membership association, present number of members: 500, registered charity (charity number 259194), suitable for ages: 18+, research organisation, publishing house.
To promote a greater understanding of ways of improving the tax system to the benefit of the whole community.

Subject coverage: Economic theory; tax developments worldwide; history of the Georgist movement with archives; history of land tax and its implementation around the world.

Library catalogue: All or part available in-house

Publications: Printed

Publications list: Available in print

Access to staff: Contact by letter, by telephone, by fax, by e-mail and via website. Appointment necessary.
Hours: Mon to Fri, 0930 to 1700

Access to building: Prior appointment required

HENRY MOORE FOUNDATION

Dane Tree House, Perry Green, Much Hadham, Hertfordshire, SG10 6EE

Tel: 01279 843333
Fax: 01279 843647
Website: www.henry-moore-fdn.co.uk

Founded: 1977

Organisation type and purpose: A registered charity with the aim of advancing the education of the public by the promotion of their appreciation of the fine arts, and in particular of the works of Henry Moore.

Collection: Elmwood Library, specialising in Henry Moore studies
Henry Moore Archive
Henry Moore Image Archive of photographs recording the artist's life and works
Henry Moore Bibliography online

HENRY WATSON MUSIC LIBRARY

Central Library, St Peter's Square, Manchester, M2 5PD

Tel: 0161 234 1976
Fax: 0161 234 1961
E-mail: henrywatsonmusiclibrary@manchester.gov.uk
Website: www.manchester.gov.uk/libraries/central/hwml/index.htm

Enquiries to: Music Co-ordinator

Founded: 1899

Organisation type and purpose: Local government body, public library.

Subject coverage: Printed and manuscript music and the literature of music (principally classical music).

Collection: Early printed music (2,000 items)
Newman Flower Collection (Handel)
Collection of orchestral and choral music (for hire)
18th-century Italian manuscripts

Library catalogue: All or part available in-house

Publications: Printed, and microform publications

Access to staff: Contact by letter, by telephone, by fax, by e-mail, in person and via website
Hours: Mon to Thu, 0900 to 2000; Fri to Sat, 0900 to 1700

Access to building: No prior appointment required

Access for disabled people: Ramped entry, toilet facilities

Parent body: Manchester City Council

HENRY WILLIAMSON SOCIETY

7 Monmouth Road, Dorchester, Dorset, DT1 2DE

Tel: 01305 264092
E-mail: zseagull@aol.com
Website: www.henrywilliamson.co.uk

Enquiries to: General Secretary

Founded: 1980

Organisation type and purpose: Learned society (membership is by subscription), present number of members: 500, registered charity (charity number 288168).
To encourage interest in and a deeper understanding of the life and work of the writer, Henry Williamson.

Collection: Archive at Exeter University

Publications: Printed
Order printed publications from: Publications Manager, Henry Williamson Society
14 Nethergrove, Longstanton, Cambridge, CB4 5EL, tel: 01954 200598, e-mail: john@camnews.net

Publications list: Available in print

Access to staff: Contact by letter, by telephone and by e-mail
Hours: Mon to Fri, 0900 to 2000

Other addresses: Membership Secretary; 16 Doran Drive, Redhill, Surrey, RH1 6AX; e-mail: mm@misterman.freeserve.co.uk

HENSHAWS SOCIETY FOR BLIND PEOPLE (hsbp)

John Derby House, 88–92 Talbot Road, Old Trafford, Manchester, M16 0GS

Tel: 0161 872 1234
Fax: 0161 848 9889
E-mail: info@hsbp.co.uk
Website: www.hsbp.co.uk

Enquiries to: Chief Executive

Founded: 1837

Organisation type and purpose: Voluntary organisation, registered charity (charity number 221888).
Registered social landlord.

Subject coverage: Visual impairment and related issues.

Collection: Minute books and Annual Reports of the Society since 1837
Early minute books are housed at the John Rylands' Library, Manchester

Publications: Printed, and electronic and video

Publications list: Available in print

Access to staff: Contact by letter, by telephone, by fax and by e-mail. Appointment necessary.
Hours: Mon to Fri, 0900 to 1630

Access to building: No appointment necessary but staff members may not always be available if apppointment not made in advance.

Access for disabled people: Ramped entry, access to all public areas, toilet facilities, talking lift, loop system.

Now incorporating the: Manchester and Salford Blind Aid Society

Other addresses: Community Services North & West Yorkshire; 50 Bond End, Knaresborough, North Yorkshire, HG5 9AL; tel: 01423 541888; fax: 01423 541889; Harrogate Community Housing; 50 Bond End, Knaresborough, North Yorkshire, HG5 9AL; tel: 01423 541888; fax: 01423 541889; Henshaws Arts and Craft Centre; Bond End, Knaresborough, North Yorkshire, HG5 9AL; tel: 01423 541888; fax: 01423 541889; Henshaws College; Bogs Lane, Harrogate, North Yorkshire, HG1 4ED; tel: 01423 886451; fax: 01423 885095; Henshaws Training & Professional Development Centre; John Derby House, 88/92 Talbot Road, Old Trafford, Manchester, M16 0GS; tel: 0161 872 1234; fax: 0161 848 9889; Merseyside Resource Centre; Wellington Buildings, The Strand, Liverpool, L2 0PP; tel: 0151 227 1226; fax: 0151 236 3641; Old Trafford Resource Centre; John Derby House, 88–92 Talbot Road, Old Trafford, Manchester, M16 0GS; tel: 0161 872 1234; fax: 0161 848 9889; Patient Support Service; Manchester Royal Eye Hospital, Manchester; tel: 0161 276 5515

Works with: Liverpool Workshops and Birkenhead Society for the Blind

HENTY SOCIETY

205 Icknield Way, Letchworth, Hertfordshire, SG6 4TT

Tel: 01462 671357
E-mail: davidwalmsley@hentysociety.org

Enquiries to: Honorary Secretary

Founded: 1977

Organisation type and purpose:
International organisation, learned society (membership is by subscription), present number of members: 120.
To further knowledge of the life and work of George Alfred Henty (1832–1902), special correspondent, The Standard newspaper, writer of books for boys and young people.

Subject coverage: 19th-century children's literature.

Publications: Printed

continued overleaf

Access to staff: Contact by letter and by telephone
Hours: Mon to Fri, 0900 to 1800
Special comments: This society is run by volunteers from their own homes.

HER MAJESTY'S INSPECTORATE FOR EDUCATION AND TRAINING IN WALES (Estyn)

Anchor Court, Keen Road, Cardiff, CF24 5JW

Tel: 029 2044 6446
Fax: 029 2044 6448
E-mail: enquiries@estyn.gov.uk
Website: www.estyn.gov.uk

Enquiries to: Her Majesty's Chief Inspector of Education and Training in Wales
Direct tel: 029 2044 6475
Direct fax: 029 2044 6531
Direct e-mail: chief-inspector@estyn.gsi.gov.uk
Other contacts: Communications Team

Founded: 1992

Organisation type and purpose: National government body.
Non-ministerial government department in Wales.

Subject coverage: Inspects quality and standards in education and training in Wales, including: nursery schools and settings that are maintained by, or receive funding from, local education authorities (LEAs); primary schools; secondary schools; special schools; pupil-referral units; independent schools; further education; adult community-based learning; youth support services; LEAs; teacher education and training; work-based learning; careers companies; and the education, guidance and training elements of Department for Work and Pensions-funded training programmes. Estyn also provides advice on quality and standards in education and training in Wales to the National Assembly for Wales and others, and makes public good practice based on inspection evidence.

Access to staff: Contact by letter, by telephone, by fax, by e-mail and via website. Appointment necessary.
Hours: Mon to Fri, 0900 to 1700

Access to building: *Hours:* Mon to Fri, 0900 to 1700

Also at: Estyn; Broncoed House, Broncoed Business Park, Mold, Flintshire; tel: 029 2044 6319

HERALDRY SOCIETY

53 Hitchin Street, Baldock, Hertfordshire, SG7 6AQ

Tel: 01462 892062
E-mail: honsecheraldrysociety@googlemail.com

Enquiries to: Honorary Secretary

Founded: 1947

Organisation type and purpose:
International organisation, learned society (membership is by subscription), present number of members: 800+, registered charity (charity number 241456), suitable for ages: all.
Specialist library, special facilities available to members at Society of Antiquaries, London and Chetham Library, Manchester. Study of Heraldry.

Subject coverage: Heraldry, armoury, chivalry, genealogy.

Education services: Scheme of Examinations available – Basic, Intermediate and Advanced leading to the Award of the Diploma of The Heraldry Society.

Collection: Library on heraldry, for use of members only
Special facilities available to members at Society of Antiquaries, London and Chetham Library, Manchester.

Library catalogue: All or part available in-house

Publications: Printed

Publications list: Available in print

Access to staff: Contact by letter, by telephone and by e-mail
Hours: Mon to Fri, 0900 to 1700
Special comments: No premises for visits.

HERALDRY SOCIETY OF SCOTLAND

25 Craigentinny Crescent, Edinburgh, EH7 6QA

Website: www.heraldry-scotland.co.uk

Enquiries to: Treasurer

Founded: 1977

Organisation type and purpose: Learned society (membership is by subscription), present number of members: 400.

Subject coverage: Scottish heraldry; the Heraldic Executive in Scotland; use of heraldry in Scottish art and architecture; Scottish heraldic families; ceremonial in Scotland; the Order of the Thistle; the Order of Baronets of Nova Scotia.

Publications: Printed

Publications list: Available in print

Access to staff: Contact by letter

HERB SOCIETY

Sulgrave Manor, Sulgrave, Banbury, Oxfordshire, OX17 2SD

Tel: 01295 768899
Fax: 01295 768069
E-mail: info@herbsociety.org.uk
Website: www.herbsociety.co.uk

Enquiries to: Administrator

Founded: 1927

Organisation type and purpose:
Membership association (membership is by subscription).

Subject coverage: Herbs and herbal matters with emphasis on medicinal aspects, cultivation, uses and history.

Publications: Printed

Publications list: Available in print

Access to staff: Contact by letter, by telephone, by fax, by e-mail, in person and via website
Hours: Mon to Fri, 0900 to 1700

Access to building: No prior appointment required

Access for disabled people: Parking provided, level entry, access to all public areas, toilet facilities

HERBERT HOWELLS SOCIETY

32 Barleycroft Road, Welwyn Garden City, Hertfordshire, AL8 6JU

Tel: 01707 335315
E-mail: andrew.millinger@virgin.net

Enquiries to: Honorary Secretary

Founded: 1987

Organisation type and purpose:
Membership association (membership is by subscription), present number of members: 300.

Subject coverage: The Society exists to promote the performance, publication and recording of the works of Herbert Howells.

Access to staff: Contact by letter, by telephone and by e-mail. Appointment necessary.
Hours: Any reasonable time, answerphone available

Branches: Herbert Howells Society, North American Branch; Dr Jane Gamble; e-mail: drjanegamble@aol.com

HEREFORD CATHEDRAL LIBRARY AND ARCHIVES

The Cathedral, Hereford, HR1 2NG

Tel: 01432 374225/6
Fax: 01432 374220
E-mail: library@herefordcathedral.org
Website: www.herefordcathedral.org

Enquiries to: Librarian
Other contacts: Archivist

Founded: c. 12th century

Organisation type and purpose: Registered charity, research organisation.
Ecclesiastical library.

Subject coverage: Religion and theology, ecclesiastical history, history of Hereford Cathedral, local history, rare books and manuscripts, medieval maps ecclesiastical art and architecture, sacred (and some secular) music, including manuscripts of the 18th and 19th centuries.

Collection: 1,500 books (manuscripts and printed) chained to early 17th-century presses
229 medieval manuscripts, from the 8th to the early 16th centuries (microfilmed)
30,000 archives of the Dean and Chapter, dating from the 9th to 20th centuries (some microfilmed)
All Saints Chained Library (over 300 vols, 15th to 18th centuries, chained to early 18th-century presses)
Manuscript and printed music, 18th to 20th centuries (c. 350 vols)
Over 3,000 pre-1801 printed books, including 56 incunabula, 10,000 books published post-1800 on subjects listed above, many borrowable

Non-library collection catalogue: All or part available online, in-house and in print

Library catalogue: All or part available online and in-house

Publications: Printed, and microform publications

Access to staff: Contact by letter, by telephone, by fax, by e-mail, in person and via website

Access to building: *Hours:* Reading Room: Tue and Thu, 1000 to 1600; open other times by prior appointment

Access for disabled people: Level entry, access to all public areas, toilet facilities

Parent body: Dean and Chapter of Hereford; tel: 01432 374200; e-mail: office@herefordcathedral.org; website: http://www.herefordcathedral.org
Hereford Mappa Mundi Trustees

HEREFORD CATTLE SOCIETY

Hereford House, 3 Offa Street, Hereford, HR1 2LL

Tel: 01432 272057
Fax: 01432 377529
E-mail: postroom@herefordcattle.org
Website: www.herefordcattle.org

Enquiries to: The Secretary

Founded: 1878

Organisation type and purpose: National organisation, membership association (membership is by election or invitation), registered charity.

Subject coverage: Hereford cattle.

HEREFORDSHIRE COLLEGE OF TECHNOLOGY – HEREFORD CAMPUS (HCT)

Folly Lane, Hereford, HR1 1LS

Tel: 01432 352235
Fax: 01432 365395
E-mail: enquiries@hct.ac.uk
Website: www.hct.ac.uk

Enquiries to: Learning Resources Manager
Direct tel: 01432 365470
Direct e-mail: lrc@hct.ac.uk
Other contacts: LRC Co-ordinator

Founded: 1974; formerly called Herefordshire Technical College (year of change 1992)

Organisation type and purpose: College of further and higher education.

Subject coverage: Construction, business studies, caring, hospitality, tourism and leisure, engineering, farriery, blacksmithing, art and design, education, humanities, computing, agriculture, forestry, animal care, horticulture, sports, outdoor education.

Library catalogue: All or part available in-house

Access to staff: Contact by letter, by telephone, by fax, by e-mail and in person
Hours: Mon to Thu, 0830 to 2030; Fri, 0830 to 1630

Access to building: By prior arrangement with LRC staff

Access for disabled people: Parking provided, disabled access, toilet facilities

HEREFORDSHIRE COLLEGE OF TECHNOLOGY – HOLME LACY CAMPUS

Holme Lacy, Hereford, HR2 6LL

Tel: 01432 870316
Fax: 01432 870566
E-mail: enquiries@hct.ac.uk
Website: www.hct.ac.uk/

Enquiries to: Learning Resources Manager

Founded: 1963; formerly called Herefordshire College of Agriculture; incorporates the former Holme Lacy College (part of the Pershore Group of Colleges) (year of change 2007)

Organisation type and purpose: Suitable for ages: 16+.
Land based further education.

Subject coverage: Agriculture, horticulture, forestry, small animal care, equine studies, gamekeeping, floristry, environmental studies, sustainability, organic agriculture, leisure, recreation, business studies.

Collection: Workman collection of forestry-related material

Non-library collection catalogue: All or part available in-house

Library catalogue: All or part available in-house

Access to staff: Contact by letter, by telephone and by fax. Appointment necessary.
Hours: Open in term time only
Special comments: Reduced hours during college holidays as posted.

Access for disabled people: Parking provided, ramped entry, toilet facilities
Special comments: Access to all areas of the library.

HEREFORDSHIRE FAMILY HISTORY SOCIETY (HFHS)

6 Birch Meadow, Gosmore Road, Clehonger, Hereford, HR2 9RH

Tel: 01981 250974
E-mail: prosser_brian@hotmail.com
Website: www.rootsweb.com/~ukhfhs

Enquiries to: Secretary-General

Founded: 1980

Organisation type and purpose: Membership association (membership is by subscription), present number of members: 900, voluntary organisation, registered charity (charity number 517785).
Family history society with particular reference to Herefordshire.

Subject coverage: General family history enquiries.

Library catalogue: All or part available in-house

Order printed publications from: Publication Officer, Herefordshire FHS
79 College Road, Hereford, HR1 1ED

Publications list: Available online and in print

Access to staff: Contact by letter, by telephone, by e-mail and via website
Hours: Mon to Fri, 0900 to 1700

Access for disabled people: Parking provided

HEREFORDSHIRE LIBRARIES

Stock Unit, Herefordshire Libraries, Shirehall, Hereford, HR1 2HY

Tel: 01432 261570
Fax: 01432 260744
E-mail: libraries@herefordshire.gov.uk
Website: www.herefordshire.gov.uk/libraries

Enquiries to: Libraries manager
Direct tel: 01432 260557
Direct fax: 01432 383031
Direct e-mail: jchedgzoy@herefordshire.gov.uk

Founded: 1998; formerly called Hereford and Worcester County Libraries (year of change 1998)

Organisation type and purpose: Local government body, public library.

Subject coverage: Local studies, particularly history of the old county of Hereford; apple and pear cultivation; cidermaking; beekeeping.

Collection: Hopton Collection (local history, crosses)
Pilley Collection (local history, general and religious history, especially of the 19th century)
Alfred Watkins and F. C. Morgan Collections of photographic glass slides and negatives

Non-library collection catalogue: All or part available in-house

Library catalogue: All or part available online and in-house

Access to staff: Contact by letter, by telephone, by fax, by e-mail, in person and via website. Appointment necessary.
Hours: Mon to Fri, 0900 to 1700

Constituent bodies: Woolhope Naturalists' Field Club

Parent body: Herefordshire Council; Brockington, 35 Haford Road, Hereford, HR1 1SH; tel: 01432 260044; fax: 01432 340189; website: http://www.herefordshire.gov.uk

HEREFORDSHIRE RECORD OFFICE (HRO)

Harold Street, Hereford, HR1 2QX

Tel: 01432 260750
Fax: 01432 260066
E-mail: archives@herefordshire.gov.uk
Website: www.herefordshire.gov.uk/archives
Founded: 1958

Organisation type and purpose: Local government body.
Record office.

Subject coverage: All aspects of local and family history.

Collection: Hereford photographic survey

Publications: Printed

continued overleaf

Access to staff: Contact by letter, by telephone, by fax, by e-mail, in person and via website

Access to building: *Hours:* Mon Closed; Tue to Fri, 0915 to 1645; second Sat in each month, 0915 to 1645
Special comments: CARN Readers ticket needed for all records, ticket issued on production of identification of name and address. Searchers wishing to use microfilm readers should book in advance. Access to parish registers as well as some other heavily used material is normally only by microform.

Access for disabled people: *Special comments:* Lift, automatic doors, adapted furniture, large-print and Braille leaflets

HERIOT-WATT UNIVERSITY – HERITAGE AND INFORMATION GOVERNANCE (HIG)

Riccarton, Edinburgh, EH14 4AS

Tel: 0131 541 3219
E-mail: heritage@hw.ac.uk
Website: www.hw.ac.uk/heritage-information-governance

Enquiries to: Archivist

Founded: 1821; incorporates the former Heriot-Watt college, which became a university by royal charter in 1966, but its origins go back to the Edinburgh School of Arts, the first mechanics institute, founded in 1821.

Organisation type and purpose: University museum and archive.

Subject coverage: Collecting is governed by the University Acquisition and Disposal Policy. The university collects objects, works of art and archives in all formats including electronic and digital media. Collecting policy is focused on: the origins and development of Heriot-Watt University, its teaching and research activities, the achievements of its staff, students and other people associated with it, its links with business and industry, its campuses at Edinburgh, Galashiels, Orkney, Dubai and Malaysia; the history of Riccarton, home of the Edinburgh campus, and its communities; Scottish textile heritage and its development over four centuries from the paisley shawl to the Vivienne Westwood kilt; works of art, especially artists of the Edinburgh School, from Raeburn to Blackadder.

Special visitor services: Museum and Archive – Edinburgh campus; Textile Collection – Scottish Borders Campus

Collection: The Museum and Archive at the Edinburgh campus contains archives, plans, photographs, objects and works of art relating to the history of Heriot-Watt University and its predecessors – Heriot-Watt College (1885–1966) and The School of Arts and Watt Institution & School of Arts (1821–1885). Related collections include archives of Leith Nautical College and records relating to the engineering firm of Boulton and Watt.
Other collections relate to the history of the Edinburgh campus at Riccarton, including estate records dating back to the 15th century. There was a strong connection between the estate and the local communities of Currie, Balerno and Juniper Green and images and archives are also held relating to the history of these communities, including images of paper and snuff mills on the Water of Leith.
Works of art include portraits of the Gibson-Craig family by Sir Henry Raeburn, paintings by artists of the Edinburgh School such as Elizabeth Blackadder and John Bellany and sculptures including, James Watt by Peter Slater and A Stone for the Whales by Stan Wilson.
The Textile Collection held at the Scottish Borders Campus in Galashiels is a unique resource for the history of Scottish textiles from the mid-18th century to the present. Highlights include business records and pattern books from Borders mills; fabrics and apparel from designer and artist Bernat Klein; furnishing fabrics from Donald Brothers of Dundee; Paisley shawls, highland dress, tartan and costume. The Collection also includes records of textile professional education from the first classes provided by the Galashiels Manufacturers Corporation in 1883 to the Galashiels Combined Technical College (1889–1909), South of Scotland Combined Technical College (1909–1922), Scottish Woollen Technical College (1922–1968), Scottish College of Textiles (1968–1998) and Heriot-Watt University School of Textiles and Design (1998 to date).

Non-library collection catalogue: All or part available online and in-house

Publications: Printed
Order printed publications from: Corporate Communications, George Heriot Wing, Heriot-Watt University, Edinburgh EH14 4AS; website: http://www.hw.ac.uk/ppr/index.htm; e-mail: pr@hw.ac.uk

Publications list: Available online

Access to staff: Contact by letter, by telephone, by e-mail, in person and via website. Appointment necessary.
Hours: Mon to Fri, 0900 to 1700
Special comments: By appointment.

Access to building: No prior appointment required

HERIOT-WATT UNIVERSITY – SCOTTISH BORDERS CAMPUS

Netherdale, Galashiels, Selkirkshire, TD1 3HF

Tel: 01896 892185
Fax: 01896 758965 (Campus Reception)
E-mail: servicedesk@sbc.hw.ac.uk
Website: www.hw.ac.uk/sbc/library

Enquiries to: Campus Librarian
Direct tel: 01896 892155
Direct e-mail: sbclibhelp@hw.ac.uk
Other contacts: Further Education Liaison Librarian

Founded: 1922; formerly called Scottish Woollen Technical College (year of change 1968); formerly called Scottish College of Textiles (year of change 1998)

Organisation type and purpose: University department or institute.

Subject coverage: Art, business, clothing, chemistry, computing, design, fashion, management, marketing, textiles.

Information services: Enquiry Service for staff and students of Borders College and Heriot-Watt University.

Collection: The Co-operative College Collection at Heriot-Watt University, includes periodicals, books and pamphlets about the Co-operative Movement

Library catalogue: All or part available online

Access to staff: Contact by letter, by telephone, by e-mail, in person and via website. Appointment necessary.
Hours: Mon to Fri, 0900 to 1645

Access for disabled people: Parking provided, ramped entry, access to all public areas, toilet facilities

Constituent part of: Heriot-Watt University

HERIOT-WATT UNIVERSITY LIBRARY

Riccarton, Edinburgh, EH14 4AS

Tel: 0131 451 3577
Fax: 0131 451 3164
E-mail: libhelp@hw.ac.uk
Website: www.hw.ac.uk/library
Website: hwlibrary.wordpress.com

Enquiries to: Librarian
Direct tel: 0131 451 3570
Other contacts: University Archivist

Founded: 1821

Organisation type and purpose: University library.

Subject coverage: Librarianship and information science, history of the university, biological sciences, psychology, economics, modern European languages, building, chemical, civil, electrical, mechanical, offshore and petroleum engineering, physics, chemistry, mathematics, statistics, electronics, computer science.

Collection: History of the University
James Watt
Sir Robert Blair MSS

Non-library collection catalogue: All or part available online

Library catalogue: All or part available online

Access to staff: Contact by letter, by telephone, by fax, by e-mail, in person and via website
Hours: Mon to Fri, 0900 to 2145; Sat and Sun 1000 to 2000 (term time)

Access to building: No prior appointment required

Branch campuses: Dubai Campus; Dubai Academic City, PO Box 294345, Dubai, United Arab Emirates; tel: +971 4 3616999; fax: +971 4 3604800; e-mail: dubaienquiries@hw.ac.uk; Scottish Borders Campus; Galashiels, TD1 3HF; tel: 01896 892185; e-mail: sbclibhelp@hw.ac.uk

HERITAGE ENGINEERING

22 Carmyle Avenue, Glasgow, G32 8HJ

Tel: 0141 763 0007
Fax: 0141 763 0583

Enquiries to: Marketing Manager
Direct e-mail: sales@heritageengineering.com

Founded: 1991

Organisation type and purpose: Consultancy, research organisation. Restoration of historical artifacts.

Subject coverage: Cast- and wrought-iron founders; ships; trains; trams; machinery; bandstands and park furniture; architectural metal work.

Access to staff: Contact by letter, by telephone, by fax and by e-mail. Appointment necessary.

Connected with: The Industrial Heritage Company Limited; tel: 0141 763 0007; fax: 0141 763 0583; e-mail: indherco@aol.com

HERITAGE HUB

Formal name: Scottish Borders Archive and Local History Centre

Kirkstile, Hawick, TD9 0AE

Tel: 01450 360699
E-mail: archives@scotborders.gov.uk
Website: www.heartofhawick.co.uk/heritagehub

Organisation type and purpose: Local government body, archive and local history.

Subject coverage: Local history of the Scottish Borders.

Collection: Andrew Lang Collection
Census returns 1841–1901
IGI
Index to christenings and marriages in the pre-1855 old parish records for each county in Scotland (microfiche)
Information about and original records from pre-1975 counties of Roxburghshire, Berwickshire, Peeblesshire, Selkirkshire
James Hogg Collection
Local business records
Local newspapers (microfilm)
Maps and plans
Postcards
Pre-1855 parish records covering the counties of Roxburghshire, Berwickshire, Peebleshire, Selkirkshire
Sir Walter Scott Collection

Non-library collection catalogue: All or part available online and in-house

Access to staff: Contact by letter, by telephone, by e-mail, in person and via website
Hours: Mon, Fri, 0930 to 1300 1400 to 1645; Tue, Thu, 0930 to 1300 to 1400 to 1900; Wed, closed (pre-booked groups and school groups only); Sat 1000 to 1400
Special comments: Access to some collections may be covered by data protection legislation.

Access for disabled people: Disabled parking spaces, accessible building

Parent body: Scottish Borders Council

HERITAGE LOTTERY FUND (HLF)

7 Holbein Place, London, SW1W 8NR

Tel: 020 7591 6000; minicom no. 020 7591 6255
Fax: 020 7591 6001
E-mail: enquire@hlf.org.uk
Website: www.hlf.org.uk

Enquiries to: Information Team
Direct tel: 020 7591 6042
Direct fax: 020 7591 6271

Founded: 1993

Organisation type and purpose: Non-departmental public body. Distributes funds raised through the National Lottery. Grants are given to projects that help people to learn about, look after and celebrate heritage.

Subject coverage: Invests in every part of heritage, including museums, parks, historic places, archaeology, natural environment and cultural traditions.

Trade and statistical information: Statistics on grants awarded

Publications: Electronic and video
Order electronic and video publications from: Online

Publications list: Available online

Access to staff: Contact by letter, by telephone, by fax, by e-mail and via website. Appointment necessary.
Hours: Mon to Fri, 0930 to 1730

Access to building: Prior appointment required (if parking required)
Hours: Mon to Fri, 0930 to 1730

Access for disabled people: Parking provided, ramped entry, access to all public areas, toilet facilities

Administered by: The Trustees; National Heritage Memorial Fund; tel: 020 7591 6000; fax: 020 7591 6001; e-mail: enquire@hlf.org.uk

Also at: Heritage Lottery Fund (HLF); Hodge House, Guildhall Place, Cardiff, CF10 1DY; tel: 029 2034 3413; fax: 029 2034 3427; e-mail: wales@hlf.org.uk; Heritage Lottery Fund (HLF); 51–53 Adelaide Street, Belfast, BT2 8FE; tel: 028 9031 0120; fax: 028 9031 0121; e-mail: northernireland@hlf.org.uk; Heritage Lottery Fund (HLF); 28 Thistle Street, Edinburgh, EH2 1EN; tel: 0131 225 9450; fax: 0131 225 9454; e-mail: scotland@hlf.org.uk; Heritage Lottery Fund (HLF); Terrington House, 13–15 Hills Road, Cambridge, CB2 1NL; tel: 01223 224870; Heritage Lottery Fund (HLF); Chiltern House, St Nicholas Court, 25–27 Castle Gate, Nottingham, NG1 7AR; tel: 0115 934 9050; Heritage Lottery Fund (HLF); St Nicholas Building, St Nicholas Street, Newcastle upon Tyne, NE1 1RF; tel: 0191 255 7570; fax: 0191 255 7571; e-mail: northeastcontact@hlf.org.uk; Heritage Lottery Fund (HLF); 9th Floor, 82 King Street, Manchester, M2 4WQ; tel: 0161 831 0850; Heritage Lottery Fund (HLF); 7 Holbein Place, London, SW1W 8NR; tel: 020 7591 6171; e-mail: southeastengland@hlf.org.uk; Heritage Lottery Fund (HLF); Trinity Court, Southernhay East, Exeter, EX1 1PG; tel: 01392 223950; e-mail: southwest@hlf.org.uk; Heritage Lottery Fund (HLF); Bank House, 8 Cherry Street, Birmingham, B2 5AL; tel: 0121 616 6870; e-mail: westmidlands@hlf.org.uk; Heritage Lottery Fund (HLF); Carlton Tower, 34 St Paul's Street, Leeds, LS1 2QB; tel: 0113 388 8030; fax: 0113 388 8031; e-mail: y&hdevelopment@hlf.org.uk

HERITAGE RAILWAY ASSOCIATION (HRA)

10, Hurdeswell, Long Hanborough, Witney, Oxfordshire, OX29 8DH

Tel: 01993 883384/0800 756 5111 ext 702
Fax: 01993 883384
E-mail: john.crane@hra.gb.com
Website: www.heritagerailways.com

Enquiries to: Press Officer
Other contacts: Director

Founded: 1996; created by the merger of Association of Independent Railways (AIR); created by the merger of Association of Railway Preservation Societies Limited (ARPS) (year of change 1996)

Organisation type and purpose: Advisory body, trade association (membership is by subscription), present number of members: 800, service industry, voluntary organisation, training organisation, consultancy, research organisation.
National representation of preserved railways, railway museums and tramways.

Subject coverage: Preserved railways, details of locomotives, rolling stock, operating and maintenance equipment, setting up and operating railway preservation organisations.

Publications: Printed

Publications list: Available in print

Access to staff: Contact by letter, by telephone, by fax and by e-mail
Hours: Mon to Fri, 0900 to 1700
Special comments: Not by overnight fax.

Also at: Managing Director, Heritage Railway Association (HRA); Andrew Goyns, 28 George Street, Altofts, Normanton, West Yorkshire. WF6 2LT; tel: 0800 756 5111 ext 320; e-mail: andrew.goyns@hra.gb.com

Member organisation of: Association of Independent Museums; European Federation of Museum and Tourist Railways (FEDECRAIL); Institution of Railway Operators (IRO); Tourism Alliance; UKinbound; World Association of Tourist Trams and Trains (Wattrain)
Association of British Transport Engineering Museums (ABTEM)

HERPES VIRUSES ASSOCIATION (HVA, SPHERE)

41 North Road, London, N7 9DP

Tel: helpline: 0845 123 2305; office: 020 7607 9661
Fax: on request
E-mail: marian@herpes.org.uk
Website: www.herpes.org.uk

Enquiries to: Director
Other contacts: Administrator

Founded: 1985

Organisation type and purpose: Registered charity.

Subject coverage: Facial and genital herpes simplex, herpes zoster, shingles and other types of herpes viruses: research on drug trials, alternative treatments, psychological aspects of simplex.

Collection: Articles from media and medical press re herpes viruses

continued overleaf

Non-library collection catalogue: All or part available online

Library catalogue: All or part available online, in-house and in print

Publications: Printed, and electronic and video

Publications list: Available online and in print

Access to staff: Contact by letter, by e-mail and via website. Appointment necessary.
Hours: Mon to Fri, 1000 to 2000
Special comments: Please phone helpline number not office number. Fax number available on request.

HERTFORD COLLEGE LIBRARY

Catte Street, Oxford, OX1 3BW

Tel: 01865 279400
E-mail: library@hertford.ox.ac.uk

Enquiries to: Librarian
Direct tel: 01865 279409

Organisation type and purpose: University department or institute, College library of the University of Oxford.

Subject coverage: General, mainly for first degree course but with some provision for graduates; old library (16th to 18th centuries largely) in general subjects, but topography, science, theology, history and classics predominate.

Collection: Gilbert Library (geography)
Seiffert Bequest (German language and linguistics)

Non-library collection catalogue: All or part available online and in-house

Library catalogue: All or part available online and in-house

Access to staff: Contact by letter, by telephone, by e-mail and in person. Appointment necessary. Letter of introduction required.
Hours: Mon to Fri, 0900 to 1700

HERTFORD REGIONAL COLLEGE

Ware Centre, Scotts Road, Ware, Hertfordshire, SG12 9JF

Tel: 01992 411400
Fax: 01992 411885
E-mail: library@hertreg.ac.uk
Website: www.hrc.ac.uk
Website: colleges.herts.ac.uk

Enquiries to: Head of Library and Learning Services
Direct tel: 01992 411977
Direct fax: 01992 411978
Direct e-mail: smaskell@hrc.ac.uk

Founded: 1991; formerly called East Herts College, Ware College (year of change 1991)

Organisation type and purpose: College of further education.

Subject coverage: Child care, art and design, catering, hairdressing, beauty therapy, business studies, adult literacy, social care, computer studies, engineering, drama, media studies, leisure and tourism, information technology, special needs, management studies.

Library catalogue: All or part available online

Access to staff: Contact by letter, by telephone, by fax and by e-mail. Appointment necessary.
Hours: Term time: Mon to Thu, 0845 to 1930; Fri, 0845 to 1640
Vacations: Mon to Fri, 1000 to 1300 and 1400 to 1600

Access to building: No access other than to staff
Hours: Term time: Mon to Thu, 0900 to 1930; Fri, 0900 to 1640
Vacations: Mon to Fri, 1000 to 1300 and 1400 to 1600
Special comments: Reference use only for non staff or students.

Access for disabled people: Parking provided, level entry

Other addresses: Hertford Regional College; Broxbourne Centre, Broxbourne, Turnford, Hertford, EN10 6AF; tel: 01992 411400; fax: 01992 411650

HERTFORDSHIRE ARCHIVES AND LOCAL STUDIES (HALS)

County Hall, Hertford, SG13 8EJ

Tel: 01438 737333 (customer service centre – ask for archives/local studies)
Fax: 01992 555113
E-mail: hertsdirect@hertscc.gov.uk
Website: www.hertsdirect.org/hals

Founded: 1895; formerly called Hertfordshire Local Studies; formerly called Hertfordshire Record Office (HRO) (year of change 1997)

Organisation type and purpose: Local government body.
Archive, record office, local studies library.

Subject coverage: Hertfordshire: history; family history; local history; geography; topography and environment.

Collection: Manuscripts: estate collections: Cowper of Panshanger; Lytton of Knebworth; Grimston of Gorhambury
Ebenezer Howard papers
Photographs: John Dickinson; Stingemore collection

Non-library collection catalogue: All or part available online and in-house

Library catalogue: All or part available online

Access to staff: Contact by letter, by telephone, by fax, by e-mail, in person and via website

Access to building: No prior appointment required
Hours: Mon and Wed, 0900 to 1730; Tue, 1000 to 1930; Thu, 0900 to 1930; Fri, 0900 to 1700; Sat, 0900 to 1300

Access for disabled people: Parking provided, ramped entry, access to all public areas, toilet facilities

HERTFORDSHIRE FAMILY AND POPULATION HISTORY SOCIETY

30 Blenheim Way, Stevenage, Hertfordshire, SG2 8TE

E-mail: secretary@hertsfhs.org.uk

Website: www.hertsfhs.org.uk

Enquiries to: Membership enquiries.
Direct e-mail: registrar@hertsfhs.org.uk

Founded: 1977

Organisation type and purpose: Membership association (membership is by subscription), present number of members: 1,000, voluntary organisation, registered charity (charity number 285008), suitable for all ages.
To further the education of family history within the ancient county of Hertfordshire.

Subject coverage: Genealogy, family history, militia history, monumental inscription recording, hobbies, Hertfordshire.

Publications: Printed, and microform publications
Order printed publications from: Booksales Officer, Hertfordshire Family and Population History Society, 56 Dalkeith Road, Harpenden, Hertfordshire, AL5 5PW

Publications list: Available online and in print

Access to staff: Contact by letter, by e-mail and via website
Hours: Mon to Fri, 0900 to 1700
Special comments: Please enclose an sae or two international reply coupons for a reply to a letter.

Access to building: *Special comments:* Library open for members.

Member organisation of: Federation of Family History Societies

HERTFORDSHIRE MULTIPLE SCLEROSIS THERAPY CENTRE (HMSTC)

Unit 30, Campus Five, Letchworth, Hertfordshire, SG6 2JF

Tel: 01462 684214
Fax: 01462 487172
E-mail: info@hertsmstherapy.org.uk
Website: www.hertsmstherapy.org.uk

Enquiries to: Manager

Founded: 1983; formerly called North Hertfordshire Friends of Arms (year of change 1994)

Organisation type and purpose: Membership association (membership is by subscription), present number of members: 250, registered charity (charity number 299524).
To provide useful therapies, advice and support to people with MS in Hertfordshire.

Subject coverage: Hyperbaric oxygen therapy, physiotherapy, yoga, aromatherapy, reflexology, counselling, dietary advice, chiropody/podiatry.

Publications: Printed

Access to staff: Contact by letter, by telephone, by fax, by e-mail and in person
Hours: Mon to Fri, 0900 to 1700

Access for disabled people: Parking provided, ramped entry, toilet facilities

HERTFORDSHIRE NATURAL HISTORY SOCIETY (HNHS)

32 Mandeville Road, Hertford, SG13 8JQ

Tel: 01992 586150
Website: www.hnhs.org

Enquiries to: President
Direct e-mail: apreynolds22@hotmail.com

Founded: 1875

Organisation type and purpose: Voluntary organisation, registered charity (charity number 218418).

Subject coverage: Strengths at present are in botany, mammals, birds, geology, mycology, entomology, amphibians and reptiles, arachnology.

Collection: Pryor Bequest (valuable collection of rare old botanical books, held at University College under special storage conditions)

Publications: Printed

Access to staff: Contact by letter, by telephone and by e-mail
Hours: Mon to Fri, 0900 to 1700

Affiliated to: Hertfordshire Geological Society

Includes the: Hertfordshire Bird Club; Hertfordshire Dragonfly Group; Hertfordshire Mammal Group

HERTFORDSHIRE VISUAL ARTS FORUM (HVAF)

PO Box 894, St Albans, Hertfordshire AL1 9EG

E-mail: enquiries@hvaf.org.uk
Website: www.hvaf.org.uk

Enquiries to: Public Relations Manager
Other contacts: Membership Secretary for membership.

Founded: 1990

Organisation type and purpose:
Membership association (membership is by subscription), present number of members: 250, voluntary organisation.
Develop appreciation of visual arts in Hertfordshire.

Subject coverage: Visual arts: painting, sculpture, crafts, ceramics.

Publications: Printed

Access to staff: Contact by letter
Hours: Mon to Fri, 0900 to 1700

HESKETH OWNERS CLUB

97 Oakdale Avenue, Stanground, Peterborough, Cambridgeshire, PE2 8TE

Enquiries to: Secretary

Founded: 1982

Organisation type and purpose:
International organisation, membership association (membership is by subscription), present number of members: 52.
Provide a contact point for people interested in Hesketh motorcycles.

Subject coverage: Hesketh motorcycle, buying, selling, spares, mechanical and club services.

Collection: Large archive of material and technical information available within the club

Publications: Printed

Access to staff: Contact by letter
Hours: Mon to Fri, 0900 to 2100

Affiliated to: British Motorcyclists Federation

HEWLETT-PACKARD CDS (HP CDS)

Formal name: Hewlett-Packard Customer Delivery Services

Imperium Level 1, West Wing, Imperial Way, Reading RG2 0TD

Tel: 01189 227600
Fax: 01189 227601
E-mail: enquiries@synstar.com
Website: www.synstar.com

Enquiries to: Manager

Founded: 2004; incorporates the former Synstar plc

Organisation type and purpose: Service industry.

Subject coverage: Business continuity services, computer disaster recovery, mid-range systems and PC networks, mobile recovery, business recovery, business continuity planning, services and consultancy.
Business availability services: business continuity, networking, lifecycle and data management and computer services.

Trade and statistical information: Business continuity services throughout UK and Europe

Publications: Electronic and video

Access to staff: Contact by letter, by telephone, by fax and by e-mail
Hours: Mon to Fri, 0900 to 1730

Subsidiary of: Hewlett-Packard

HEWLETT-PACKARD LABORATORIES (HPLB)

Filton Road, Stoke Gifford, Bristol, BS34 8QZ

Fax: 0117 3128964
E-mail: bl@hplb.hpl.hp.com
Website: www.hpl.hp.com/techreports/index.html
Website: www.uk.hpl.hp.com

Enquiries to: Information Services

Founded: 1984

Organisation type and purpose:
International organisation, research organisation.

Subject coverage: Computing and telecommunications, networks and network security. Also e-services and personal appliances.

Trade and statistical information: Hewlett Packard Laboratories Technical Report Series

Order printed publications from: Via website

Publications list: Available online and in print

Access to staff: Contact by letter and by e-mail
Hours: Mon to Fri, 0900 to 1700
Special comments: Services outside HPLB very limited, therefore quick reference questions only please.

HEXHAM LIBRARY

Queen's Hall, Beaumont Street, Hexham, Northumberland, NE46 3LS

Tel: 01434 652488
Fax: 01434 652474
E-mail: mmason@northumberland.gov.uk

Enquiries to: Senior Librarian
Other contacts: Assistant Librarian for local history enquiries.

History of institution: formerly called Tynedale Area Library; formerly called West Area Library (year of change 1992); formerly called Hexham Group Library (year of change 1996); formerly called West Group Library (year of change 1998)

Organisation type and purpose: Local government body, public library.

Subject coverage: General, Hexham and Northumberland local history.

Collection: Brough Local Studies Collection
Census Returns (microfilm)
Electoral rolls, 1832 to 1950 (microfilm)
Local newspapers, 1864 to date (microfilm)
Parish Register transcripts
Photographs
Trades Directories

Library catalogue: All or part available in-house

Publications: Printed

Access to staff: Contact by letter, by telephone, by fax and in person
Hours: Mon, Fri, 0930 to 1930; Tue, Wed, 0930 to 1700; Thu, closed; Sat, 0930 to 1230

Parent body: Northumberland County Amenities Division

HEYDAY

Astral House, 1268 London Road London SW16 4ER

Tel: 0845 888 4444
Website: www.heyday.org.uk

Enquiries to: Public Relations Manager

Founded: 1988; formerly called Association of Retired and Persons Over Fifty (ARP/O50) (year of change 2006)

Organisation type and purpose:
Membership association (membership is by subscription), present number of members: 107,000, suitable for ages: 50+.

Subject coverage: Legislation affecting the retired and over 50s. Attitudes to all aspects of retirement including, finance, health, leisure and legislation as available.

Trade and statistical information: The members of the Association provide access to a research- and consumer-based data collection facility

Publications: Printed

Access to staff: Contact by telephone, by fax, by e-mail and via website
Hours: Mon to Fri, 0930 to 1730

Also at: Heyday; PO Box 87, Oakengates, TF3 3WT

HFT

Formal name: The Home Farm Trust

Merchants House, Wapping Road, Bristol, BS1 4RW

Tel: 0117 930 2600
Fax: 0117 922 5938
E-mail: marketing@hft.org.uk
Website: www.hft.org.uk

Enquiries to: Marketing Manager

Founded: 1962; formerly called The Home Farm Trust

Organisation type and purpose: Registered charity (charity number 313069).
Services for adults with learning disabilities.

Subject coverage: Provision of residential and other services for people with learning disabilities which develop their potential and sustain their rights.

Publications: Printed, and electronic and video

Access to staff: Contact by letter, by telephone, by fax, by e-mail, in person and via website. Appointment necessary.
Hours: Mon to Fri, 0900 to 1700

Access to building: *Hours:* Mon to Fri, 0900 to 1700

Access for disabled people: *Hours:* Mon to Fri, 0900 to 1700

Parent body: HFT Trading Limited; at the same address

HI KENT

18 Brewer Street, Maidstone, Kent, ME14 1RU

Tel: 01622 691151, 01622 691151 (minicom)
Fax: 01622 672436
E-mail: enquiries@hikent.org.uk
Website: www.hikent.org.uk

Enquiries to: Information Officer
Direct e-mail: d.lewis@hikent.org.uk

Founded: 1986; formerly called Hi Kent Association (year of change 1995)

Organisation type and purpose:
Membership association (membership is by subscription), present number of members: 72, registered charity (charity number 1052036).
Information and resource centre for hearing impaired.

Subject coverage: Assistive equipment for deaf people, sign language, deaf awareness, tinnitus.

Collection: Factsheets on assistive equipment for deaf people
Information sheets on deafness
Books and videos provided by Kent County Council Arts and Libraries for loan in Kent only on deaf subjects

Non-library collection catalogue: All or part available in-house

Library catalogue: All or part available in-house

Publications: Printed

Access to staff: Contact by letter, by telephone, by fax, by e-mail and in person
Hours: Mon to Fri, 0900 to 1700

Access for disabled people: Ramped entry, toilet facilities

Other addresses: Hi Kent; East Kent Centre, 46 Northgate, Canterbury, Kent, CT1 1BE; tel: 01227 760046; fax: 01227 760068; e-mail: jon.lambert@kent.gov.uk; Hi Kent Medway Centre; Audiology Unit, Medway Maritime Hospital, Windmill Road, Gillingham, Kent, ME7 5NY; tel: 01634 825043; e-mail: l.dray@hikent.org.uk

Works in partnership with: Kent County and Medway Council Social Services

HIGH COMMISSION OF THE REPUBLIC OF NAMIBIA

6 Chandos Street, London, W1G 9LU

Tel: 020 7636 6244
Fax: 020 7637 5694

Enquiries to: Information Officer
Other contacts: (1) First Secretary (2) Commercial Counsellor (3) Tourism Attaché (4) Counsellor for (1) educational/cultural matters (2) trade and investment in Namibia (3) geography and history of Namibia (4) passports/visas.

Organisation type and purpose: National government body.

Subject coverage: Any enquiry relating directly to Namibia, whether political, cultural, historical, geographical or economic; trade and investment information; tourism and travel information; diplomatic and consular matters, including enquiries about visa/passports; more generalised information on Africa and the Commonwealth.

Trade and statistical information: Statistical documents and reports from the respective ministries of the Government of Namibia. For specific enquiries regarding trade and investment contact the Commerical Counsellor

Access to staff: Contact by letter, by telephone, by fax and in person
Hours: Mon to Fri, 0900 to 1700

Parent body: Ministry of Foreign Affairs, Information and Broadcasting; Government Offices (4th Floor), Robert Mugabe Avenue, Private Bag 13347, Windhoek, Namibia; tel: +26461 282 9111; fax: +26461 22 3937

HIGH COMMSSION FOR THE REPUBLIC OF CYPRUS

13 St James' Square, London, SW1Y 4LB

Tel: 020 73214100
Fax: 020 7321 4167
E-mail: cyphclondon@dial.pipex.com
Website: www.cyprus.gov.cy
Website: www.mfa.gov.cy

Enquiries to: Press Counsellor
Direct tel: 020 7321 4141/3
Direct fax: 020 7321 4165
Direct e-mail: presscounsellor@chclondon.org.uk
Other contacts: Consular General (tel: 020 7321 4101, for Consular matters)

Organisation type and purpose: National government body.
Embassy and Consulate. Diplomatic.

Subject coverage: General information about Cyprus (press and office information). Consular enquiries (Consulate).

Library catalogue: All or part available in-house

Publications: Printed, and electronic and video

Access to staff: Contact by letter, by telephone, by fax and by e-mail
Hours: Mon to Fri, 0900 to 1630
Consulate Public Hours: Mon to Fri, 0930 to 1300

Links with: Cyprus Tourism Organisation; 17 Hanover Street, London, W1S 1YP; tel: 020 7569 8800; fax: 020 7499 4935; e-mail: informationcto@btconnect.com; website: http://www.visitcyprus.org.cy
Cyprus Trade Centre; 13 St James' Square, London, SW1Y 4LB; tel: 020 7321 4146; e-mail: cytradecentreuk@btinternet.com

Parent body: Ministry of Foreign Affairs of Cyprus; Dem Severis Avenue, Nicosia 1447, Cyprus; tel: + 357 22 300713; fax: + 37 7 22 665313; website: http://www.mfa.gov.cy

HIGH SHERIFFS' ASSOCIATION OF ENGLAND & WALES

PO Box 21, Heritage House, Baldock, Herts SG7 5SH

Tel: 01462 896688
Fax: 01462 896677
E-mail: secretary@highsheriffs.com

Enquiries to: Honorary Secretary

Founded: 1971

Organisation type and purpose:
Membership association (membership is by election or invitation).
To promote and strengthen the Office of High Sheriff in England and Wales.

Subject coverage: History and current activities of High Sheriffs in the Counties of England and Wales, relating to ceremonial matters. The prevention of crime and particularly juvenile crime through National Crimebeat, and debt and money management through DebtCred, both of which are charities established by the Association.

Publications: Printed

Access to staff: Contact by letter, by fax and by e-mail. Appointment necessary.
Hours: Mon to Fri, 0900 to 1700

HIGHBURY COLLEGE LEARNING CENTRE

Cosham, Portsmouth, Hampshire, PO6 2SA

Tel: 023 9231 3213
Fax: 023 9237 1972
E-mail: library@highbury.ac.uk

Enquiries to: Librarian

History of institution: formerly called Highbury Technical College

Organisation type and purpose: Suitable for ages: 16+ further education.
College of technology.

Subject coverage: Building, hospitality and catering, business and management studies, social welfare, leisure and tourism, electrical and electronic engineering, mechanical engineering.

Library catalogue: All or part available in-house

Access to staff: Contact by letter, by telephone, by fax, by e-mail and in person
Hours: Term time; Mon to Thu, 0900 to 2100; Fri, 0930 to 1700
Vacations; Mon to Thu, 0900 to 1700; Fri, 0900 to 1630

Access for disabled people: Access to all public areas

HIGHER EDUCATION FUNDING COUNCIL FOR ENGLAND (HEFCE)

Northavon House, Coldharbour Lane, Bristol, BS16 1QD

Tel: 0117 931 7317
Fax: 0117 931 7203
E-mail: hefce@hefce.ac.uk
Website: www.hefce.ac.uk

Enquiries to: Knowledge Centre Manager
Direct tel: 0117 931 7438
Direct fax: 0117 931 7082
Direct e-mail: s.roberts@hefce.ac.uk

Founded: 1993; created by the merger of Polytechnics and Colleges Funding Council (PCFC), Universities Funding Council (UFC) (year of change 1993); formerly called University Grants Committee (UGC) (year of change 1988)

Organisation type and purpose: The HEFCE is a non-departmental public body set up under the Further and Higher Education Act 1992. Its primary role is to distribute public funding for teaching and research and related activities in universities and colleges in England.

Subject coverage: Funding for higher education in England.

Collection: Books and documents related to the subject of higher education

Library catalogue: All or part available in-house

Order printed publications from: Some publications are available by post; all publications available via http://www.hefce.ac.uk/pubs

Publications list: Available online

Access to staff: Contact by letter, by telephone, by fax, by e-mail and via website
Hours: Mon to Fri, 0900 to 1700

Access to building: There is no public access

HIGHER EDUCATION FUNDING COUNCIL FOR WALES (HEFCW)

Linden Court, The Orchards, Ilex Close, Llanishen, Cardiff, CF14 5DZ

Tel: 029 2076 1861
Fax: 029 2076 3163
E-mail: wag-en@mailuk.custhelp.com
Website: www.elwa.ac.uk

Enquiries to: Clerk to the Council
Direct e-mail: info@elwa.ac.uk

Founded: 1992

Organisation type and purpose: National government body.
Non-departmental government body.
The Council is responsible for the administration of funds made available by the Welsh Assembly Government in support of the provision of higher education and the undertaking of research in higher education institutions in Wales.

Subject coverage: Funding for higher education in Wales. Student enrolment in Wales. Council funding for research in Welsh higher education institutions.

Publications: Printed, and electronic and video

Publications list: Available online and in print

Access to staff: Contact by letter, by telephone and by e-mail
Hours: Mon to Fri, 0900 to 1700

Access to building: No access other than to staff, prior appointment required

Access for disabled people: Parking provided, ramped entry

Parent body: National Assembly for Wales; Higher Education Division, Cathays Park, Cardiff, CF10 3NQ; tel: 029 2082 5111

HIGHER EDUCATION STATISTICS AGENCY (HESA)

95 Promenade, Cheltenham, Gloucestershire, GL50 1HZ

Tel: 01242 255577
Fax: 01242 211122
E-mail: www@hesa.ac.uk
Website: www.hesa.ac.uk

Enquiries to: Data Provision Manager

Founded: 1993

Organisation type and purpose: Registered charity (charity number 1039709).
HESA is the official agency for the collection, analysis and dissemination of quantitative information about higher education.

Subject coverage: Statistics of students and staff at all UK universities in six main record areas: undergraduates, postgraduates, first destinations of graduates, staff and short courses, finance.

Collection: Microfiche library of all statistical analyses produced 1972–1993 (in addition to original computerised database for same period)

Publications: Printed

Publications list: Available in print

Access to staff: Contact by letter, by telephone, by fax, by e-mail and via website
Hours: Mon to Thu, 0830 to 1700; Fri, 0830 to 1600

HIGHGATE LITERARY AND SCIENTIFIC INSTITUTION (HLSI)

11 South Grove, Pond Square, Highgate, London, N6 6BS

Tel: 020 8340 3343
Fax: 020 8340 5632
E-mail: librarian@hlsi.net
Website: www.hlsi.net

Enquiries to: Librarian
Direct tel: 020 8340 3343 (option 3)
Direct e-mail: librarian@hlsi.net

Founded: 1839

Organisation type and purpose: Membership association (membership is by subscription), voluntary organisation, lending library.

Subject coverage: Literature; biography; the arts; fiction; local history.

Collection: Highgate local history and archives
John Betjeman
Samuel Taylor Coleridge
London local history

Non-library collection catalogue: All or part available in-house

Library catalogue: All or part available in-house

Access to staff: Contact by letter, by telephone, by fax, by e-mail and in person
Hours: Tue to Fri, 1000 to 1700; Sat, 1000 to 1600

Access to building: *Hours:* Tue to Fri, 1000 to 1700; Sat, 1000 to 1600
Special comments: Closed for one week at Christmas and Easter, three weeks in August.

Links with: Association of Independent Libraries; website: http://www.independentlibraries.co.uk

HIGHLAND FAMILY HISTORY SOCIETY (HFHS)

Suite 4, Third Floor, Albyn House, 37A Union Street, Inverness, IV1 1QA

E-mail: info@highlandfamilyhistorysociety.org
Website: www.highlandfhs.org.uk
Website: www.genfair.com

Enquiries to: Honorary Secretary
Direct e-mail: abethune@highlandfhs.org.uk

Founded: 1981

Organisation type and purpose: Membership association (membership is by subscription).

Subject coverage: Genealogy, parish records, census returns, monumental inscriptions.

Order printed publications from: Public Library at Farraline Park, Genfair via http://www.genfair.com

Publications list: Available online and in print

Access to staff: Contact via website. Access for members only.
Hours: Tue only, 1000 to 1630

Access for disabled people: Lift to third floor

HIGHLAND LIBRARIES

Formal name: The Highland Council. Education, Culture & Sport Service

31A Harbour Road, Inverness, IV1 1UA

Tel: 01463 235713
Fax: 01463 236986
E-mail: libraries@highlifehighland.com

continued overleaf

Website: www.highland.gov.uk/leisureandtourism/libraries

Enquiries to: Library and Information Services Co-ordinator
Other contacts: Senior Librarian, Information Co-ordinator

Founded: 1975

Organisation type and purpose: Local government body, public library.

Subject coverage: General; specialised sections include local history, genealogy.

Information services: The Highland Council's Library and Information Service forms part of the Education Culture and Sport Service and operates through a network of joint and separate School, Community and Mobile Libraries and online services.

Collection: Held at Inverness:
Fraser Mackintosh Collection (local history, law and literature)
Gaelic Society of Inverness Library (Gaelic language and culture)
Highland Family History Society Library (extensive local history and genealogy collections)
Kirk Session Library (antiquarian interest)
Held at Wick:
John Mowat Collection (local history of Caithness and northern Scotland)

Non-library collection catalogue: All or part available online and in-house

Library catalogue: All or part available online and in-house

Access to staff: Contact by letter, by telephone, by fax, by e-mail and in person. Appointment necessary.
Hours: Mon to Fri, 0800 to 1700

Access to building: No prior appointment required
Hours: Mon to Fri, 0800 to 1700

Access for disabled people: Level entry

Parent body: The Highland Council; Education, Culture and Sport Service, Council Buildings, Glenurquhart Road, Inverness IV3 5NX; tel: 01463 702000; fax: 01463 711177; website: http://highlifehighland.com

HIGHLANDS & ISLANDS ENTERPRISE (HIE)

Cowan House, Inverness Retail & Business Park, Inverness, IV2 7GF

Tel: 01463 234171
Fax: 01463 244469
E-mail: hie.general@hient.co.uk
Website: www.hie.co.uk

Enquiries to: Librarian
Direct tel: 01463 234171
Direct fax: 01463 244469
Direct e-mail: library@hient.co.uk

Founded: 1991

Organisation type and purpose: National government body.
HIE is a government-sponsored development agency.
Economic and social development in the Highlands and Islands of Scotland.

Subject coverage: Business information, Highlands and Islands of Scotland, regional and industrial development, primary industries, fisheries, fish farming, land use, tourism, transport, community co-operatives, agriculture, renewable energy.

Library catalogue: All or part available in-house

Publications: Printed

Access to staff: Contact by e-mail, in person and via website. Appointment necessary. Access for members only.
Hours: Mon to Fri, 0900 to 1700

Access to building: Prior appointment required

Access for disabled people: Parking provided, level entry, toilet facilities

HILL TAYLOR DICKINSON

20–30 Irongate House, Duke's Place, London, EC3A 7HX

Tel: 020 7283 9033
Fax: 020 7283 1144
E-mail: via website

Enquiries to: Library and Information Manager

Organisation type and purpose: Solicitors.

Subject coverage: Law: shipping, insurance, company and commercial, litigation, property, taxation, probate.

Member of: British and Irish Association of Law Librarians (BIALL)

HILLCLIMB & SPRINT ASSOCIATION LIMITED

Spring Cottage, Gaydon Road, Bishops Itchington, Warwickshire, CV47 2QX

Tel: 01926 612432
Fax: 01926 612432

Enquiries to: Membership Secretary
Direct tel: 01926 424609
Direct fax: 01926 424609

Founded: 1955

Organisation type and purpose: Membership association (membership is by subscription), present number of members: 1,000.
Motor sport association whose members compete in speed hillclimb and sprint meetings.

Subject coverage: Speed hillclimb and sprint car racing.

Publications: Printed

Access to staff: Contact by letter, by telephone and by fax
Hours: Mon to Fri, 1800 to 2100; not weekends

HILLINGDON BOROUGH LIBRARIES

Central Library, 14–15 High Street, Uxbridge, Middlesex, UB8 1HD

Tel: 01895 250600
Fax: 01895 239794
E-mail: clibrary@lbhill.gov.uk or clibrary@hillingdon.gov.uk
Website: www.hillingdon.gov.uk

Enquiries to: Librarian
Direct tel: 01895 250603
Direct fax: 01895 811164

Organisation type and purpose: Local government body, public library.

Subject coverage: General; history of Hillingdon, Middlesex and surrounding areas.

Collection: Government Publications (SSS except for SI's)

Trade and statistical information: All current HMSO statistical series

Publications: Printed

Access to staff: Contact by letter, by telephone, by fax, by e-mail, in person and via website
Hours: Mon to Fri, 0900 to 1700

Access to building: No access other than to staff
Hours: Mon, Tue, Thu, 0930 to 2000; Wed, 0930 to 1730; Fri, 1000 to 1730; Sat, 0930 to 1600

Access for disabled people: Level entry, access to all public areas, toilet facilities

HILLINGDON FAMILY HISTORY SOCIETY

20 Moreland Drive, Gerrards Cross, Buckinghamshire, SL9 8BB

Tel: 01753 885602
E-mail: gillmay@dial.pipex.com
Website: www.hfhs.co.uk
Website: www.rootsweb.com/~enghfhs

Enquiries to: Honorary Secretary

Founded: 1987

Organisation type and purpose: Membership association (membership is by subscription).

Subject coverage: Family history and genealogy with particular reference to the London Borough of Hillingdon.

Collection: Collection of genealogical books, journals, CD-ROMs and microforms available to members

Non-library collection catalogue: All or part available online

Library catalogue: All or part available online

Publications: Printed, and microform publications

Publications list: Available online and in print

Access to staff: Contact by letter, by telephone and by e-mail
Hours: Mon to Fri, 0900 to 1700; evenings and weekends

Member of: Federation of Family History Societies

HILLINGDON LOCAL STUDIES, ARCHIVES AND MUSEUMS

Central Library, 14–15 High Street, Uxbridge, Middlesex, UB8 1HD

Tel: 01895 250702
Fax: 01895 811164

E-mail: archives@hillingdon.gov.uk
Website: www.hillingdon.gov.uk/heritage

Enquiries to: Local Studies and Archives Manager
Direct e-mail: ccotton@hillingdon.gov.uk
Other contacts: Assistant Archivist

Founded: 1922; formerly called Hillingdon Local Heritage Service; formerly called London Borough of Hillingdon Libraries (year of change 1991)

Organisation type and purpose: Museum, public library, archives.

Subject coverage: Local and family history of the Hillingdon area.

Education services: School visits and talks.

Collection: Challoner Collection of Uxbridge photographs
Gazette newspaper photographs 1920 to 1950
Minet Archives, deeds, etc. of Minet Properties in Hayes

Non-library collection catalogue: All or part available online

Library catalogue: All or part available online

Publications: Printed

Publications list: Available online and in print

Access to staff: Contact by letter, by telephone, by fax, by e-mail and in person
Hours: Mon, 0930 to 2000; Tue, Wed, Thu, 1300 to 1730; Fri, 1000 to 1230 and 13.30 to 17.30; Sat, 0930 to 1200 and 1300 to 1600

Access to building: Local Studies is located within the Central Library, Uxbridge
Hours: Mon, Tue, Thu, 0930 to 2000; Wed, 0930 to 1730; Fri, 1000 to 1730; Sat 0930 to 1600; Sun, 1230 to 1630

Access for disabled people: Access to all public areas, toilet facilities

HILLMAN COMMER & KARRIER CLUB (HCKC)

Capri House, Walton-on-Thames, Surrey, KT12 2LY

Tel: 01932 269109
Fax: 01932 269109

Enquiries to: Chairman

Founded: 1989

Organisation type and purpose:
International organisation, membership association (membership is by subscription), present number of members: 1,600 approx, voluntary organisation.

Subject coverage: Hillman, Commer and Karrier and other Rootes built vehicles, mechanical and technical information, insurance, registration, restoration.

Collection: Books, manuals, technical information, magazines, etc. relevant to Hillman, Commer, Karrier and Rootes vehicles

Library catalogue: All or part available in-house

Publications: Printed

Publications list: Available in print

Access to staff: Contact by letter and by fax
Hours: Mon to Fri, 0900 to 1700

Access to building: No prior appointment required

Parent body: Association of Rootes Vehicle Owners

HINCKLEY & BOSWORTH BOROUGH COUNCIL

Council Offices, Argents Mead, Hinckley, Leicestershire, LE10 1BZ

Tel: 01455 238141
Fax: 01455 251172
Website: www.hinckley-bosworth.gov.uk

Enquiries to: Chief Executive

Organisation type and purpose: Local government body.

Subject coverage: Local government services.

Publications: Printed

Access to staff: Contact by letter and by fax
Hours: Mon to Fri, 0900 to 1700

Health authority: Leicestershire, Northamptonshire and Rutland Health Authorities

Local education authority: Leicestershire Local Education Authority

HIRE ASSOCIATION EUROPE (HAE)

2 Holland Road West, Waterlinks, Birmingham, B6 4DW

Tel: 0121 380 4600
Fax: 0121 333 4109
E-mail: mail@hae.org.uk
Website: www.hae.org.uk

Enquiries to: Managing Director

Founded: 1971

Organisation type and purpose:
International organisation, trade association, membership association (membership is by subscription), present number of members: 1,000.
Membership body for hire equipment shops.

Subject coverage: Small plant and tool hire equipment, hire of equipment for leisure, catering, fencing and portable sanitation, training and safety supplies to the hire industry, audiovisual and powered access hire.

Trade and statistical information: Turnover and employment statistics

Publications: Printed

Publications list: Available in print

Access to staff: Contact by letter, by telephone, by fax and via website. Appointment necessary.
Hours: Mon to Fri, 0900 to 1700

Access to building: No prior appointment required
Hours: Mon to Fri, 0900 to 1700

Subsidiary body: Executive Hire News

HISTORIC COMMERCIAL VEHICLE SOCIETY (HCVS)

Iden Grange, Cranbrook Road, Staplehurst, Kent, TN12 0ET

Tel: 01580 892929
Fax: 01580 893227
E-mail: hcvs@btinternet.com
Website: www.hcvs.co.uk

Enquiries to: Membership Secretary

Founded: 1958

Organisation type and purpose:
International organisation, national organisation, membership association (membership is by subscription), present number of members: 3,500, registered charity (charity number 271123).

Subject coverage: Historic commercial vehicles.

Library catalogue: All or part available in-house

Access to staff: Contact by letter, by telephone, by fax, by e-mail and via website
Hours: Mon to Fri, 0900 to 1700

Access to building: No access other than to staff
Special comments: Prior appointment required for library research (situated in Cardiff)

HISTORIC FARM BUILDINGS GROUP (HFBG)

c/o Museum of English Rural Life, University of Reading, PO Box 229, Whiteknights, Reading, Berkshire, RG6 6AG

Tel: 0118 931 8663
Fax: 0118 975 1264
E-mail: r.d.brigden@reading.ac.uk
Website: www.chelt.ac.uk/ccru/hfbg

Enquiries to: Secretary

Founded: 1985

Organisation type and purpose: Learned society.

Subject coverage: History of old farm buildings.

Publications: Printed

Access to staff: Contact by letter and by e-mail
Hours: Mon to Fri, 0900 to 1700

HISTORIC HOUSES ASSOCIATION (HHA)

2 Chester Street, London, SW1X 7BB

Tel: 020 7259 5688
Fax: 020 7259 5590
E-mail: info@hha.org.uk
Website: www.hha.org.uk

Enquiries to: Executive Secretary

Founded: 1973

Organisation type and purpose:
Membership association (membership is by subscription).

Subject coverage: Preservation for the future of historic houses, parks, gardens and places of interest in Britain; pressure for a long-term policy based on private ownership.

Publications: Printed

continued overleaf

Access to staff: Contact by letter, by telephone, by fax, by e-mail and via website
Hours: Mon to Fri, 0900 to 1700

Access to building: Prior appointment required

Affiliated to: European Union of Historic Houses Association

Close liaison with: British Tourist Authority; Cadw Welsh Historic Monuments; Department of National Heritage; English Heritage; Historic Scotland; National Trust; National Trust for Scotland

HISTORIC LOTUS REGISTER (HLR)

Badgers Farm, Short Green, Winfarthing, Diss, Norfolk, IP22 2EE

Tel: 01953 860508

Enquiries to: Honorary Secretary

Founded: 1974

Organisation type and purpose: International organisation (membership is by subscription), present number of members: 1,000, voluntary organisation. Motor club.

Subject coverage: Historic Lotus cars manufactured prior to 1961, preservation and research.

Collection: Lotus factory records

Publications: Printed

Access to staff: Contact by letter and by telephone
Hours: Mon to Sun 0900 to 2000

HISTORIC SCOTLAND (HS)

Historic Scotland, Longmore House, Salisbury Place, Edinburgh, EH9 1SH

Tel: 0131 668 8600
Fax: 0131 668 8699
E-mail: hs.website@scotland.gsi.gov.uk
Website: www.historic-scotland.gov.uk

Founded: 1991

Organisation type and purpose: National government body, statutory body.

Subject coverage: Information on historic buildings and monuments under the guardianship of Scottish Ministers, architecture, archaeology, conservation and the environment.

Access to staff: Contact by letter, by telephone, by fax, by e-mail and via website
Hours: Mon to Fri, 1000 to 1600

Access for disabled people: Parking provided, ramped entry, toilet facilities

Constituent part of: Scottish Executive Education Department; tel: 0131 668 8600

HISTORIC SCOTLAND CONSERVATION GROUP

Room G20, Longmore House, Salisbury Place, Edinburgh, EH9 1SH

Tel: 0131 668 8668
Fax: 0131 668 8669
E-mail: hs.conservationgroup@scotland.gsi.gov.uk

Founded: 1980

Organisation type and purpose: National government body.
To provide information, advice and support to those concerned with the conservation of historic buildings in Scotland.

Subject coverage: Conservation of historic and traditional buildings in Scotland, careers in conservation, technical information on conservation.

Collection: Library of conservation books, videos, photographic material, samples

Library catalogue: All or part available in-house

Publications: Printed

Publications list: Available in print

Access to staff: Contact by letter, by telephone, by e-mail and via website. Appointment necessary.
Hours: Mon to Fri, 0900 to 1700

Part of: Historic Scotland

HISTORIC SOCIETY OF LANCASHIRE AND CHESHIRE (HSLC)

Flat 4, 3 Bramhall Road, Waterloo, Liverpool, L22 3XA

Tel: 0151 920 8213
E-mail: rch2949@yahoo.co.uk
Website: www.hslc.org.uk

Enquiries to: Secretary

Founded: 1848

Organisation type and purpose: Learned society (membership is by subscription), registered charity (charity number 224825).

Subject coverage: Local history of Lancashire and Cheshire.

Collection: Society's collections held at Liverpool Record Office, but see website as Record Office closed for major rebuilding work: http://www.liverpool.gov.uk/libraries

Library catalogue: All or part available online

Publications: Printed
Order printed publications from: Publications Officer, Historic Society of Lancashire and Cheshire, c/o School of History, 9 Abercromby Square, Liverpool, L69 7WZ; tel: 0151 428 4121

Publications list: Available in print

Access to staff: Contact by letter and by e-mail
Hours: Mon to Fri, 0900 to 1700

HISTORIC SPORTS CAR CLUB (HSCC)

Silverstone Circuit, Silverstone, Towcester, Northamptonshire, NN12 8TN

Tel: 01327 858400
Fax: 01327 858500
E-mail: office@hscc.org.uk

Enquiries to: Executive Director

Founded: 1966

Organisation type and purpose: International organisation, membership association (membership is by subscription), present number of members: 850.
Organiser of historic car race meetings and championships.
Appointed to coordinate European Championship for pre-1985 F1 cars by the FIA, now a major club.

Subject coverage: History of, and information regarding, historic motor racing.

Collection: Large archive of historic motor racing books and magazines dating back to 1940s

Publications: Printed

Access to staff: Contact by letter, by telephone, by fax, by e-mail, in person and via website. Appointment necessary.
Hours: Mon to Fri, 0900 to 1700

Affiliated to: RACMSA

HISTORIC VOLKSWAGEN CLUB

5 Gresley Close, Sutton Coldfield, West Midlands, B75 5HT

Tel: 0121 308 3693
E-mail: nigel.wallace@virgin.net
Website: www.historicvws.org.uk

Enquiries to: Membership Secretary

Founded: 1974

Organisation type and purpose: Membership association (membership is by subscription), voluntary organisation.
Provides a focal point for owners and enthusiasts of pre-1967 (Aug) Volkswagen vehicles. Provides technical information, spares location and historical information for members and others.

Subject coverage: Technical, historical, diary dates for gatherings of enthusiasts relating to Volkswagen products manufactured prior to August 1967.

Publications: Printed

Access to staff: Contact by letter, by telephone, by e-mail and via website
Hours: Mon to Fri, evenings only

HISTORICAL ASSOCIATION (HA)

59A Kennington Park Road, London, SE11 4JH

Tel: 020 7735 3901
Fax: 020 7582 4989
E-mail: enquiry@history.org.uk
Website: www.history.org.uk

Enquiries to: Membership Secretary

Founded: 1906

Organisation type and purpose: Membership association (membership is by subscription), registered charity (charity number 1120261).
Subject teaching association.

Subject coverage: General information on all areas of history, history teaching, careers in history.

Collection: The following collections not open to the public:
Bound copies Annual Bulletin of Historical Literature, 1907 to date

Bound copies of History, 1912 to date

Publications: Printed

Publications list: Available online and in print

Access to staff: Contact via website
Hours: Mon to Fri, 1000 to 1700

HISTORICAL METALLURGICAL SOCIETY LIMITED (HMS)

c/o The Institute of Materials, Minerals and Mining, 1 Carlton House Terrace, London, SW1Y 5DB

Tel: 01792 233223
Website: hist-met.org./ad_index.html
Website: hist-met.org/hmspub.htm
Website: hist-met.org/resources.html
Website: hist-met.org/hm_index.html
Website: hist-met.org

Enquiries to: General Secretary
Direct fax: 01792 233223
Direct e-mail: hon-sec@hist-met.org

Founded: 1979

Organisation type and purpose: Learned society.

Subject coverage: Metallurgical history and archaeometallurgy.

Collection: A collection of miscellaneous documents relating to metallurgical history. Includes the Charles Blick Archive, mainly conservation of metallurgical sites
A miscellaneous collection of largely metallurgical books, some scarce, mostly out of date

Non-library collection catalogue: All or part available online

Library catalogue: All or part available online

Publications: Printed, and electronic and video
Order printed publications from: Publications Officer, 22 Windley Crescent, Darley Abbey, Derbyshire, DE3 1BZ, tel: 01332 553430, e -mail: brian.read2@ntlworld.com

Publications list: Available online

Access to staff: Contact by letter, by telephone, by fax and by e-mail
Hours: Mon to Fri, 0900 to 2200

Affiliated to: Institute of Materials, Minerals aand Mining

HISTORICAL MODEL RAILWAY SOCIETY (HMRS)

c/o The Midland Railway Centre, Butterley Station, Ripley, Derbyshire, DE5 3QZ

Tel: 01773 745959
Fax: 01773 745959
E-mail: secretary@hmrs.org.uk
Website: www.hmrs.org.uk

Enquiries to: Museum and Study Centre Manager

Founded: 1950

Organisation type and purpose:
Membership association (membership is by subscription),
present number of members: 2,500,
registered charity (charity number 273110),
research organisation.
Educational organisation.

Subject coverage: Railways of Britain and the Commonwealth: all aspects from their invention to the present day.

Collection: Library of railway books and periodicals including some non-published documents of railway companies
Photographic library of over 50,000 items

Non-library collection catalogue: All or part available online and in-house

Library catalogue: All or part available online and in-house

Publications list: Available online and in print

Access to staff: Contact by letter, by fax, by e-mail and via website
Hours: Mon to Fri, 0900 to 1700

HISTORY OF ADVERTISING TRUST ARCHIVE (HAT Archive)

HAT House, 12 Raveningham Centre, Raveningham, Norwich, Norfolk, NR14 6NU

Tel: 01508 548623
Fax: 01508 548478
E-mail: enquiries@hatads.org.uk
Website: www.hatads.org.uk

Enquiries to: General Manager
Other contacts: Chief Executive; Curator

Founded: 1976

Organisation type and purpose: Registered charity (no. 276194), educational trust and research organisation. National archive of UK advertising and brand communication. Aims to rescue, collect and preserve the industry's archives and best work and to make it available to all.

Subject coverage: The history of advertising and brand communications 1800–present day, including advertising agencies; advertising controls; clubs and organisations; corporate and retail marketing; designers and creatives; professional interest bodies; special collections; TV commercials (over 70,000) 1950s to present.

Information services: Research and information service.

Special visitor services: Study visits by appointment only

Education services: Contextual downloadable resources and ideas for creative classroom activities

Collection: Specialist library of over 6,000 books
Large collections of proofs, posters, original artwork, market research and company records (see website for details)

Trade and statistical information: Over 130 advertising and marketing industry journal titles; published industry statistics and surveys; market research and trends; selected titles of consumer magazines

Non-library collection catalogue: All or part available in-house

Library catalogue: All or part available in-house

Publications: Printed, and electronic and video
Order printed publications from: enquiries@hatads.org.uk
Order electronic and video publications from: enquiries@hatads.org.uk

Publications list: Available online and in print

Access to staff: Contact by letter, by telephone, by fax, by e-mail, in person and via website. Appointment necessary. All charged.
Hours: Mon to Fri, 0900 to 1700

Access to building: Study visits by appointment only
Hours: Mon to Fri, 0900 to 1700
Special comments: Closed public holidays and weekends. UK student research visits free of charge.

Access for disabled people: Parking provided, level entry, access to all public areas, toilet facilities

HISTORY OF EDUCATION SOCIETY

Faculty of Education, Health and Social Care, University of Winchester, Sparkford Road, Winchester, Hampshire, SO22 4NR

Tel: 01962 827125
Fax: 01962 827479
E-mail: stephanie.spencer@winchester.ac.uk
Website: www.historyofeducation.org.uk

Enquiries to: Secretary

Founded: 1967

Organisation type and purpose: Learned society (membership is by subscription), present number of members: 300, registered charity (charity number 1055764).

Subject coverage: History of education, its study and teaching.

Publications: Printed
Order printed publications from: HEJ: order through Taylor and Francis
History of Education Society Researcher: contact Secretary

Access to staff: Contact by letter, by e-mail and via website
Hours: Mon to Fri, 0900 to 1700

Member organisation of: International Standing Conference for the History of Education

HISTORY OF PARLIAMENT TRUST

15 Woburn Square, London, WC1H 0NS

Tel: 020 7862 8800
Fax: 020 7255 1442
E-mail: s.macquire@histparl.ac.uk
Website: www.ihrinfo.ac.uk

Enquiries to: Administrator
Other contacts: Director

Founded: 1951

Organisation type and purpose: Registered charity, research organisation.

Subject coverage: History of Parliament.

Publications: Printed, and electronic and video
Order printed publications from: Available from, Sutton Publishing

continued overleaf

Phoenix Mill, Far Thrupp, Stroud, Gloucestershire, GL5 2BU, tel: 01453 731114, fax: 01453 731117

Publications list: Available in print

Access to staff: Contact by letter and by e-mail
Hours: Mon to Fri, 0900 to 1700

Access to building: No prior appointment required

HM GOVERNMENT OF GIBRALTAR (GIB)

Gibraltar House, 150 Strand, London, WC2R 1JA

Tel: 020 7836 0777
Fax: 020 7240 6612
E-mail: info@gibraltar.gov.uk
Website: www.gibraltar.gov.uk

Enquiries to: Director
Direct tel: 020 7836 0777
Direct fax: 020 7240 6612

History of institution: formerly called Gibraltar Tourist Board

Organisation type and purpose: National government body.
Information office.

Subject coverage: Gibraltar: all subjects including political, tourism, finance, trade and industry, property, conferences, stamps, ship repair, ship registry, yacht facilities etc.

Collection: Picture library

Library catalogue: All or part available online

Publications: Printed, and electronic and video

Publications list: Available online and in print

Access to staff: Contact by letter, by telephone, by fax, by e-mail and via website
Hours: Mon to Fri, 0900 to 1730

Access to building: No prior appointment required

Access for disabled people: Level entry

Other address: HM Government of Gibraltar; 6 Convent Place, Gibraltar, GX11 1AA; tel: + 350 20070071; fax: + 350 20076396

HM LAND REGISTRY (HMLR)

32 Lincoln's Inn Fields, London, WC2A 3PH

Tel: 020 7917 8888
Fax: 020 7955 0110
E-mail: enquiries@icr.gsi.gov.uk
Website: www.landreg.gov.uk

Enquiries to: Librarian
Direct tel: 020 7917 8888 ext 4800
Other contacts: Agency Customer Service Manager

Founded: 1862

Organisation type and purpose: National government body.
HM Land Registry is a government executive agency and trading fund.
It aims to: maintain and develop a stable and effective land registration system throughout England and Wales; guarantee title to registered estates and interests in land; provide ready access to up-to-date and guaranteed land information.

Subject coverage: Mapping of all the property boundaries, change of ownership of property, and land registration system in England and Wales, granting of legal title on behalf of the Crown, provides ready access to up-to-date and guaranteed information.

Trade and statistical information: Quarterly Residential Property Price Report (published free) on property prices in England and Wales, detailing average prices and volume of sales broken down by property type, counties and London Boroughs

Publications: Printed, and electronic and video

Publications list: Available in print

Access to staff: Contact by letter, by telephone, by fax, by e-mail, in person and via website. All charged.
Hours: Mon to Fri, 0900 to 1700

Access to building: No prior appointment required

District Land Registries: Birkenhead (Old Market) District Land Registry\ *For registered land titles in Merseyside and Staffordshire and Stoke-on-Trent*; Old Market House, Hamilton Street, Birkenhead, Merseyside, CH41 5FL; tel: 0151 473 1110; fax: 0151 473 0251; Birkenhead (Rosebrae) District Land Registry\ *For registered land titles in Cheshire and the London Boroughs of Kensington and Chelsea, and Hammersmith and Fulham*; Rosebrae Court, Woodside Ferry Approach, Birkenhead, Merseyside, CH41 5FL; tel: 0151 472 0666; fax: 0151 472 6789; Coventry District Land Registry\ *For registered land titles in West Midlands and Worcestershire districts of Wychavon, Bromsgrove and Redditch*; Leigh Court, Torrington Avenue, Tile Hill, Coventry, CV4 9XZ; tel: 024 7686 0860; fax: 024 7686 0021; Croydon District Land Registry\ *For registered land titles in London Boroughs of Bexley, Bromley, Merton, Croydon and Sutton*; Sunley House, Bedford Park, Croydon, CR9 3LE; tel: 020 8781 9100; fax: 020 8781 9110; Durham (Bolden House) District Land Registry\ *For registered land titles in Cumbria and Surrey*; Bolden House, Wheatlands Way, Pity Me, Durham, DH1 5GJ; tel: 0191 301 2345; fax: 0191 301 2300; Durham District Land Registry\ *For registered land titles in Durham, Hartlepool, Middlesbrough, Northumberland, Redcar and Cleveland, Stockton-on-Tees and Tyne & Wear*; Southfield House, Southfield Way, Durham, DH1 5TR; tel: 0191 301 3500; fax: 0191 301 0020; Gloucester District Land Registry\ *For registered land titles in Berkshire, Bristol, Gloucestershire, Oxfordshire, South Gloucestershire and Warwickshire*; Twyver House, Bruton Way, Gloucester, GL1 1DQ; tel: 01452 511111; fax: 01452 510050; Harrow District Land Registry\ *For registered land titles in Barnet, Brent, Camden, City of London, City of Westminster, Harrow, Inner & Middle Temples and Islington*; Lyon House, Lyon Road, Harrow, Middlesex, HA1 2EU; tel: 020 8235 1181; fax: 020 8862 0176; Hull District Land Registry\ *For registered land titles in Kingston upon Hull, Lincolnshire, Norfolk, North East Lincolnshire and Suffolk*; Earle House, Portland Street, Hull, Humberside, HU2 8JN; tel: 01482 223244; fax: 01482 224278; Lancashire District Land Registry\ *For registered land titles in Blackburn with Darwen, Blackpool and Lancashire*; Wrea Brook Court, Lytham Road, Warton, Preston, Lancashire, PR4 1TE; tel: 01772 836700; fax: 01772 836970; Leicester District Land Registry\ Leicester District Land Registry\ *For registered land titles in Buckinghamshire, Northamptonshire, Daventry and Leicestershire*; Westbridge Place, Leicester, LE3 5DR; tel: 0116 265 4000; fax: 0116 265 4008; Lytham District Land Registry\ *For registered land titles in Greater Manchester*; Birkenhead House, East Beach, Lytham St Annes, Lancashire, FY8 5AB; tel: 01253 840001; fax: 01253 840013; Nottingham (East) District Land Registry\ *For registered land titles in Nottinghamshire, South Yorkshire*; Robins Wood Road, Nottingham, NG8 3RQ; tel: 0115 906 5353; fax: 0115 936 0036; Nottingham (West) District Land Registry\ *For registered land titles in Derbyshire and West Yorkshire*; Chalfont Drive, Nottingham, NG8 3RN; tel: 0115 935 1166; fax: 0115 935 0038; Peterborough District Land Registry\ *For registered land titles in Bedfordshire, Cambridgeshire, Essex*; Touthill Close, City Road, Peterborough, Cambridgeshire, PE1 1XN; tel: 01733 288288; fax: 01733 280022; Plymouth District Land Registry\ *For registered land titles in Bath and North East Somerset, Cornwall, Devon, Isles of Scilly, North Somerset and Somerset*; Plumer House, Tailyour Road, Crownhill, Plymouth, PL6 5HY; tel: 01752 636000; fax: 01752 636161; Portsmouth District Land Registry\ *For registered land titles in East Sussex, Isle of Wight, West Sussex and Hampshire*; St Andrew's Court, St Michael's Road, Portsmouth, PO1 2JH; tel: 023 9276 8888; fax: 023 9276 8768; Stevenage District Land Registry\ *For registered land titles in Hertfordshire and the London Boroughs of Barking & Dagenham, Enfield, Hackney, Havering, Newham, Redbridge, Tower Hamlets and Waltham Forest*; Brickdale House, Swingate, Stevenage, Hertfordshire, SG1 1XG; tel: 01438 788888; fax: 01438 780107; Swansea District Land Registry\ *For registered land titles in Hereford & Worcester and the London Boroughs of Ealing, Hillingdon, Hounslow and Harringey*; Ty Bryn Glas, High Street, Swansea, SA1 1PW; tel: 01792 458877; fax: 01792 473236; Telford District Land Registry\ *For registered land titles in Shropshire and the London Boroughs of Greenwich, Kingston Upon Thames, Lambeth, Lewisham, Richmond Upon Thames, Southwark and Wandsworth*; Parkside Court, Hall Park Way, Telford, Shropshire, TF3 4LR; tel: 01952 290355; fax: 01952 290356; The Land Registry for Wales\ *For registered land in the principality of Wales*; Ty Cwm Tawe, Phoenix Way, Llansamlet, Swansea, SA7 9FQ; tel: 01792 355000; fax: 01792 355055; Tunbridge Wells District Land Registry\ *For registered land titles in Kent*; Forest Court, Forest Road, Tunbridge Wells, Kent, TN2 5AQ; tel: 01892 510015; fax: 01892 510032; Weymouth District Land Registry\ *For registered land titles in Dorset, Wiltshire, South Somerset and Mendip*; 1 Cumberland Drive, Weymouth, Dorset, DT4 9TT; tel: 01305 363636; fax: 01305 363646; York District Land Registry\ *For registered land titles in North Yorkshire, York and East Riding of Yorkshire*; James House, James Street, York, YO1 3YZ; tel: 01904 450000; fax: 01904 450086

Parent body: Lord Chancellor's Department

Subsidiary body: 23 District Land Registries in England and Wales

HM NAUTICAL ALMANAC OFFICE (HMNAO)

UK Hydrographic Office, Admiralty Way, Taunton, Somerset, TA1 2DN

Tel: 01823 337900
Fax: 01823 335396
E-mail: hmnao@ukho.gov.uk
Website: www.hmnao.com

Enquiries to: UKHO Helpdesk
Direct tel: 01823 723366
Direct fax: 01823 251816
Direct e-mail: helpdesk@ukho.gov.uk

Founded: 1831

Organisation type and purpose: National government body, professional body.

Subject coverage: Astronomy, navigation, land surveying using astronomy, astronomical phenomena, astronomical data, calendarial information, prayer times, first sighting of new moon, forensic astronomy, historical astronomy, astronomical software, astronomical data in various forms, e.g. camera-ready, floppy disc, e-mail and electronic.

Publications: Printed, and electronic and video
Order printed publications from: UK Hydrographic Office Admiralty Brand Distributor Network: http://www.admiraltyshop.co.uk

Publications list: Available in print

Access to staff: Contact by letter, by telephone, by fax, by e-mail and via website
Hours: Mon to Fri, 0800 to 1600

Links with: Astronomical Applications Department; US Naval Observatory, 3450 Massachusetts Avenue NW, Washington, DC 20392–5420, USA; tel: +1 (202) 762 1617; fax: +1 (202) 762 1612; website: http://aa.usno.navy.mil

Parent body: UK Hydrographic Office; Admiralty Way, Taunton, Somerset, TA1 2DN; tel: 01823 337900; 01823 251816 (helpdesk); e-mail: helpdesk@ukho.gov.uk; website: http://www.ukho.gov.uk

HOLBORN LIBRARY

32–38 Theobalds Road, London, WC1X 8PA

Tel: 020 7974 6354
Fax: 020 7974 6356
Website: www.camden.gov.uk

Enquiries to: Group Manager

Organisation type and purpose: Local government body, public library.

Subject coverage: General fiction and non-fiction. online databases (including Ancestry, Lexis)

Non-library collection catalogue: All or part available online

Library catalogue: All or part available online

Access to staff: Contact by letter, by telephone, by fax, in person and via website
Hours: Mon, Thu, 1000 to 1900; Tue, Fri, 1000 to 1800; Wed, 1000 to 1800; Sat, 1000 to 1700

Access for disabled people: Ramped entry, access to all public areas, toilet facilities

Parent body: London Borough of Camden, Culture and Environment Directorate

HOLIDAY CENTRES ASSOCIATION (HCA)

The Coppice, Rowe Close, Bideford, Devon, EX39 5XX

Tel: 01237 421 347
Fax: 01273 421 347
E-mail: holidaycentres@aol.com
Website: www.holidaycentres.com

Enquiries to: Chief Executive

Founded: 1936; formerly called National Association of Holiday Centres

Organisation type and purpose: Trade association.
Represents the majority of United Kingdom holiday centres and villages.

Subject coverage: Tourism, holiday centres and villages.

Trade and statistical information: Data on the holiday centre sector of the tourist industry

Publications: Printed

Access to staff: Appointment necessary.
Hours: Mon to Fri, 0900 to 1700

HOLISTIC HEALTH COLLEGE (HHC)

94 Grosvenor Road, London, SW1V 3LF

Tel: 020 7834 3579
Fax: 020 7821 0255
Website: www.gni-international.org

Enquiries to: General Secretary
Other contacts: Registrar

Founded: 1992; formed from Holistic Health Consultancy (year of change 1983); formerly called Holistic Health Consultancy and College (year of change 1992)

Organisation type and purpose: International organisation, training organisation, research organisation.

Subject coverage: Iridology, herbal medicine, nutrition, naturopathy and homoeopathy.

Library catalogue: All or part available in-house

Publications: Printed, and electronic and video

Publications list: Available in print

Access to staff: Contact by letter and by telephone. Appointment necessary.
Hours: Mon to Wed, 0900 to 1700; Thu and Fri, 0800 to 1100

Access for disabled people: Access to all public areas, toilet facilities

Affiliated to: Association of Master Herbalists; Holden Natural Health Centre, The Bield, Lewes Road, Forest Row, East Sussex, RH18 5AF; tel: 01342 826899; fax: 01342 826896; e-mail: kelly@holclinic.com; General Naturopathic Council Limited; 255 Lavender Hill, London, SW11 1JD; tel: 020 7498 9966; e-mail: maraia.harewood@btconnect.com; Guild of Naturopathic Iridologists International; at the same address; tel: 020 7821 0255; fax: 020 7821 0255; e-mail: info@gni_international.org

Connections with: Holistic Health Consultancy; at the same address; tel: 020 7834 3579; fax: 020 7821 0255

Parent body: Institute of Complementary Medicine; PO Box 194, London, SE16 1QZ; tel: 020 7237 5165; fax: 020 7237 5175

HOLLYCOMBE STEAM AND WOODLAND GARDEN SOCIETY

Iron Hill, Midhurst Road, Liphook, Hampshire, GU30 7LP

Tel: 01428 724900
Fax: 01428 723682
E-mail: hollycombe@talk21.com
Website: www.hollycombe.co.uk

Enquiries to: Information Officer

Founded: 1971

Organisation type and purpose:
Membership association (membership is by subscription), present number of members: 150, voluntary organisation, registered charity, museum, suitable for ages: all.
Operates Hollycombe Steam Collection, a working steam power museum of national importance in the UK. Open to the public as advertised.

Subject coverage: History and application of steam power to transport, agriculture, fairground, marine, industry. Shown working when open.

Publications: Printed, and electronic and video

Access to staff: Contact by letter, by telephone, by fax, by e-mail, in person and via website
Hours: Office: Mon to Fri, 0900 to 1700

Access to building: No prior appointment required
Hours: Collection open to public: Sun and Public holidays; Easter to mid-Oct; daily late Jul to late Aug, 1200 to 1700
Special comments: Admission charge published.
Prior appointment is required when closed to the public.

Access for disabled people: Parking provided, level entry, toilet facilities
Special comments: Access to most areas.

HOLLYHOCK SOCIETY, ENGLAND, SCOTLAND AND WALES

5 Clarence Road, Cheltenham, Gloucestershire, GL52 2AY

Tel: 01242 2621459

Subject coverage: Propagation and cultivation of hollyhocks.

Non-library collection catalogue: All or part available online

HOLSTEIN UK (HUK)

Scotsbridge House, Scots Hill, Rickmansworth, Hertfordshire, WD3 3BB

Tel: 01923 695200
Fax: 01923 770003
E-mail: info@holstein-uk.org
Website: www.holstein-uk.org

Enquiries to: Chief Executive

Founded: 1909; formed by the merger of British Holstein Society (BHS), Holstein-Friesian Society (HFS) (year of change 1999); formerly called British Friesian Cattle Society (BFCS) (year of change 1986)

Organisation type and purpose:
Membership association (membership is by subscription).
Cattle breed society.
Registration and promotion of the Holstein and Friesian breeds in the United Kingdom.

Subject coverage: Holstein breed history and present day facts and figures related to the breeding of Holstein cows; bull proofs, cow indexes. Ancestry details, production and conformation records and genetic indexes for production and conformation for over 4 million animals.

Publications: Printed

Access to staff: Contact by letter, by telephone, by fax, by e-mail and via website. Appointment necessary.
Hours: Mon to Fri, 0900 to 1700

Member of: European Confederation of Black and White Breed Societies; World Holstein Friesian Federation

HOME ACCIDENT PREVENTION NORTHERN IRELAND

Nella House, Dargan Crescent, Belfast, BT3 9JP

Tel: 028 9050 1160
Fax: 028 9050 1164
Website: www.rospa.co.uk

Enquiries to: Executive Secretary

Founded: 1965; formerly called Northern Ireland Home Accident Prevention Council; formerly called Northern Ireland Home Safety Council (year of change 1997)

Organisation type and purpose: Advisory body, voluntary organisation.

Subject coverage: Accident prevention in and around the home.

Collection: Variety of information on accidents and accident prevention

Publications: Printed

Access to staff: Contact by letter, by telephone, by fax, by e-mail and in person. Appointment necessary.
Hours: Closed, 1300 to 1400

Access to building: No prior appointment required

Parent body: Royal Society for the Prevention of Accidents (ROSPA); tel: 028 9050 1160; fax: 028 9050 1164

HOME DECORATION RETAILERS ASSOCIATION (HDRA)

BHF Group, 225 Bristol Road, Edgbaston, Birmingham B5 7UB

Tel: 0121 446 6688
Fax: 0121 446 5215
E-mail: membership@bhfgroup.co.uk

Enquiries to: Company Secretary

Founded: 1955; formerly called Wallpaper, Paint and Wallcovering Retailers Association (WPWRA); formerly called Wallcovering, Fabric and Décor Retailers Association Limited (WFDRA) (year of change 1995)

Organisation type and purpose: Advisory body, trade association (membership is by subscription), present number of members: 750, publishing house.

To promote the well-being of the independent home decorating specialist retailer.

Subject coverage: Home decor trade market, decorating materials, DIY materials, paint, wall coverings, co-ordination of decorative materials, design, fabrics, home furnishings.

Trade and statistical information: Data on home decor trade products

Publications: Printed

Access to staff: Contact by letter, by telephone, by fax and by e-mail
Hours: Mon to Fri, 0900 to 1700

Affiliated to: Trade and Professional Alliance (TPA)

Division of: The British Hardware Federation (BHF)

HOME MISSION DESK (HMD)

39 Eccleston Square, London. SW1V 1BX

Tel: 020 7901 4818
E-mail: homemission@cbcew.org.uk
Website: www.catholicchurch.org.uk
Website: www.life4seekers.co.uk

Enquiries to: Home Mission Advisor

History of institution: formerly called Catholic Missionary Society (year of change 2003); formerly called Catholic Agency to Support Evangelisation (year of change 2009)

Organisation type and purpose: To support Catholic communities and individuals to engage in mission in England and Wales.

Publications: Printed

Publications list: Available online

Access to staff: Contact by letter, by telephone and by e-mail. Appointment necessary.
Hours: Mon to Fri, 0900 to 1700

Access to building: Prior appointment required

HOME OFFICE: INFORMATION AND LIBRARY TEAM, INFORMATION MANAGEMENT SERVICE, SHARED SERVICES DIRECTORATE (ISC)

Formal name: Information Services Centre

Information Services Centre, Lower Ground Floor, Seacole Building, 2 Marsham Street, London, SW1P 4DF

Tel: 020 7035 6699
E-mail: informationservicescentre@homeoffice.gsi.gov.uk
Website: www.homeoffice.gov.uk

Founded: 1782

Organisation type and purpose: National government body, central government departmental library.

Subject coverage: Social sciences, especially parliamentary publications; community relations; criminal law; criminology; immigration and nationality; police; security; drugs; citizenship.

Trade and statistical information: The Home Office publishes a range of statistical data such as probation statistics and statistical bulletins. Many other statistics are published on behalf of the Home Office by The Stationery Office (e.g. criminal statistics)

Publications: Printed
Order printed publications from: Direct Communications Unit, 2 Marsham Street, London, SW1P 4DF; tel: 020 7035 4848; fax: 020 7035 4745; e-mail: public.enquiries@homeoffice.gsi.gov.uk

Access to staff: Appointment necessary.
Hours: Mon to Fri 0900 to 1700
Special comments: Access only for Home Office staff and staff of other government agencies, by prior appointment; no access to members of the public.

HOMEOPATHY COLLEGE (THC)

454 Hagley Road West, Quinton, Birmingham, B68 0DL

Tel: 0121 423 1913
E-mail: admin@homoeopathytraining.co.uk
Website: www.homoeopathytraining.co.uk

Enquiries to: Principal
Direct e-mail: enquirer@homoeopathytraining.co.uk

Founded: 1988; formerly called College of Practical Homeopathy, Midlands (year of change 2006)

Organisation type and purpose: Training organisation.
Training professional homeopathic practitioners.

Subject coverage: Homeopathy.

Access to staff: Contact by letter, by telephone, by e-mail, in person and via website. Appointment necessary.
Hours: Mon, Tue, Wed, Thu, 0930 to 1630

Access to building: Prior appointment required
Hours: Mon, Tue, Wed, Thu, 0930 to 1630

HOMERTON COLLEGE LIBRARY

Homerton College, Hills Road, Cambridge, CB2 8PH

Tel: 01223 507259

Enquiries to: Librarian

Organisation type and purpose: College library

Subject coverage: All subjects taken for the Cambridge Tripos

Collection: Children's Literature Collection

Non-library collection catalogue: All or part available in-house

Library catalogue: All or part available in-house

Access to staff: Contact by letter, by telephone, by e-mail and in person. Appointment necessary. Non-members charged.

Access to building: *Hours:* Term time: Mon to Fri, 0900 to 1700
Vacations: 1000 to 1700 (please telephone first)
Special comments: Closed to general public

Constituent part of: University of Cambridge

HOMERTON HOSPITAL NEWCOMB LIBRARY

Formal name: Homerton University Hospital NHS Foundation Trust Newcomb Library

Homerton Row, London, E9 6SR

Tel: 020 8510 7751
Fax: 020 8510 7281
E-mail: newcomb.library@homerton.nhs.uk
Website: www.homerton.nhs.uk/education/11573611372688.html

Enquiries to: Library Manager
Direct e-mail: isabel.cantwell@homerton.nhs.uk

History of institution: formerly called Hackney Hospital Medical Library (year of change 1986)

Organisation type and purpose: Multidisciplinary hospital library.

Subject coverage: Medicine and allied subjects.

Library catalogue: All or part available online

Publications: Printed

Access to staff: Contact by letter, by telephone, by fax, by e-mail and via website. Appointment necessary. Letter of introduction required.
Hours: Mon, 1100 to 2000; Tue to Fri, 0900 to 2000
Special comments: Staff availability permitting.

Links with: London Strategic Health Authority; Nursing Union List of Journals

Member organisation of: London Health Libraries; London Regional Library Scheme; Psychiatric Libraries Co-operative Scheme

HOMES FOR SCOTLAND (SHBA)

Forsyth House, 93 George Street, Edinburgh, EH2 3EJ

Tel: 0131 243 2595
Fax: 0131 243 2596
E-mail: info@homesforscotland.com
Website: www.homesforscotland.co.uk

Enquiries to: Manager
Other contacts: Manager, Marketing and Development

Founded: Early 1980s; formerly called Scottish Building Employers Federation (SBEF) (year of change 1985); formerly called Scottish House-Builders Association (SHBA) (year of change 2001)

Organisation type and purpose: Trade association.

Subject coverage: House building.

Trade and statistical information: Research and produce surveys etc on house building industry and economic factors affecting it in Scotland

Access to staff: Contact by letter, by telephone, by fax and by e-mail
Hours: Mon to Fri, 0900 to 1700

HONDA OWNERS CLUB (GB)

35 Mortimer Way, North Baddesley, Hampshire, SO52 9NE

Website: www.hoc.org.uk

Enquiries to: Secretary Classic

Founded: 1961

Organisation type and purpose: Membership association (membership is by subscription), present number of members: 6,000, voluntary organisation.

Subject coverage: Honda motorcycles, insurance, discounts, help and advice.

Publications: Printed

Access to staff: Contact by letter
Hours: Mon to Fri, 0900 to 1700

Subsidiary body: Honda Owners Club (GB); Classic Section

HONG KONG TOURISM BOARD (HKTB)

6 Grafton Street, London, W1S 4EQ

Tel: 020 7533 7100
Fax: 020 7533 7111
E-mail: lonwwo@hktb.com
Website: www.discoverhongkong.com

Enquiries to: Regional Director

Founded: 1957

Organisation type and purpose: National government body, statutory body, trade association (membership is by qualification), present number of members: 350.
Tourism board.
National tourist office.

Subject coverage: Tourist information on Hong Kong.

Publications: Printed

Access to staff: Contact by letter, by telephone, by fax, by e-mail and in person
Hours: Mon to Fri, 0930 to 1730

Location: Hong Kong Tourism Board; Citicorp Centre, 18 Whitfield Road, North Point, Hong Kong; tel: 00 852 2807 6543; fax: 00 852 2806 0303

HONOURABLE COMPANY OF MASTER MARINERS (HCMM)

HQS Wellington, Temple Stairs, Victoria Embankment, London, WC2R 2PN

Tel: 020 7836 8179
Fax: 020 7240 3082
E-mail: info@hcmm.org.uk
Website: www.hcmm.org.uk

Enquiries to: Clerk to the Company
Direct e-mail: clerk@hcmm.org.uk

Founded: 1926

Organisation type and purpose: Professional body (membership is by qualification, election or invitation).
City of London Livery Company.

Education services: School visits programme for KS1 and KS2.

Library catalogue: All or part available in print

Publications: Printed

Access to staff: Contact by letter, by telephone and by e-mail
Hours: Mon to Fri, 0900 to 1700

Access to building: No prior appointment required

HONOURABLE SOCIETY OF GRAY'S INN

8 South Square, Gray's Inn, London, WC1R 5ET

Tel: 020 7458 7800
Fax: 020 7458 7801

Enquiries to: Administration Secretary

Organisation type and purpose: Professional body.

Subject coverage: Legal education, records, professional conduct etc (in conjunction with the Council of Legal Education and the General Council of the Bar).

Publications: Printed

Access to staff: Contact by telephone
Hours: Mon to Fri, 1000 to 1600

HONOURABLE SOCIETY OF LINCOLN'S INN

Library, Holborn, London, WC2A 3TN

Tel: 020 7242 4371
Fax: 020 7404 1864
E-mail: library@lincolnsinn.org.uk
Website: www.lincolnsinn.org.uk
Website: www.lincolnsinnlibrary.org.uk

Enquiries to: Librarian

Founded: pre 1470

Organisation type and purpose: Professional body.
Library of an Inn of Court.

Subject coverage: Law, including the laws of the Commonwealth countries, legal history. Genealogical information and biographical information on past members and other barristers.

Collection: Continental legal dissertations (6,000 items, 17th and 18th centuries)
Manuscripts (medieval and later, including the Hale Collection)
Parliamentary Papers 1800 to date

continued overleaf

Roman, Canon and Foreign law (15th to 19th century)
Tracts and pamphlets (15,000 items, 16th to 19th century)

Library catalogue: All or part available online

Access to staff: Contact by letter, by telephone, by fax and by e-mail.
Appointment necessary. Letter of introduction required.
Hours: Mon to Fri, 0900 to 2000; Aug to mid-Sep, 0930 to 1800
Special comments: Current legal collection not available to the public or litigants in person. Genealogical enquiries by email or letter only.

Access for disabled people: Level entry
Special comments: Parking by prior arrangement.

HONOURABLE SOCIETY OF THE INNER TEMPLE

The Library, Inner Temple, London, EC4Y 7DA

Tel: 020 7797 8217/8/9
Fax: 020 7583 6030
E-mail: library@innertemple.org.uk
Website: www.innertemplelibrary.org.uk

Enquiries to: Deputy Librarian

Founded: 1500

Organisation type and purpose: Professional body.

Subject coverage: Law of the United Kingdom and Commonwealth countries.

Collection: Barrington manuscripts (57 vols)
Inner Temple Records (39 vols)
Miscellaneous manuscripts (211 vols)
Mitford manuscripts (79 vols)
Petyt manuscripts (386 vols)

Non-library collection catalogue: All or part available in print

Library catalogue: All or part available online

Publications: Printed

Access to staff: Contact by letter, by telephone, by fax, by e-mail and via website.
Appointment necessary.
Hours: Term time: Mon to Thu, 0900 to 2000; Fri, 0900 to 1900
Vacations: Mon to Fri, 0900 to 1730
Special comments: Non-members by letter only.

Member of: Aslib; BIALL; CILIP; NAG; UKSG

HONOURABLE SOCIETY OF THE MIDDLE TEMPLE (Middle Temple)

Library, Ashley Building, Middle Temple Lane, London, EC4Y 9BT

Tel: 020 7427 4830
Fax: 020 7427 4831
E-mail: library@middletemple.org.uk
Website: www.middletemplelibrary.org.uk

Enquiries to: Keeper of the Library
Direct e-mail: library@middletemple.org.uk

Founded: 1641

Organisation type and purpose: Learned society.
Library of an Inn of Court.

Subject coverage: Law and legal material covering the United Kingdom, Ireland, European Union and its member states, and the USA.

Services for disabled people: Lift access to all floors

Collection: 16th- and 17th-century tracts
Archives of the Inn and its members
Phillimore Collection (legal)
Incunabula
John Donne's Library
Robert Ashley's Collection
Ecclesiastical law collection
USA law collection
Capital punishment collection

Non-library collection catalogue: All or part available in print

Library catalogue: All or part available online

Publications: Printed
Order printed publications from: Middle Temple Treasury department

Publications list: Available in print

Access to staff: Contact by letter, by telephone, by fax and by e-mail.
Appointment necessary. Non-members charged.

Access to building: *Hours:* Term time: Mon to Thu, 0900 to 2000; Fri, 0900 to 1900; one Sat in every four, 1000 to 1700
Vacations: Mon to Fri, 0900 to 1730
Special comments: Open to all members of the Bar and Middle Temple students. Bone fide researchers admitted by prior appointment, at the discretion of the Librarian.

HOPE UK

25F Copperfield Street, London, SE1 0EN

Tel: 020 7928 0848
Fax: 020 7401 3477
E-mail: m.watson@hopeuk.org
Website: www.hopeuk.org

Enquiries to: Business Manager

Founded: 1855; formerly called UK Band of Hope Union (year of change 1995)

Organisation type and purpose: Registered charity in England, Wales and Scotland (England and Wales: 1044475; Scotland: SC040550); national voluntary organisation with membership; company limited by guarantee (number 3022470)
To prevent drug and alcohol-related harm to children and young people.

Subject coverage: Hope UK is a drug education charity working from a Christian basis. Its mission is to provide accurate information that enables children and young people to consider their attitudes to alcohol and drugs. It supports parents, teachers and youth leaders with quality resources, speakers and training events. Children and young people are at the centre of its work and it encourages positive peer influence and the ability to choose healthy options in the prevention of the abuse of alcohol, tobacco and other drugs.

Education services: Hope UK provides drug and alcohol awareness sessions for children and young people as well as those with responsibility for them (e.g., parents and youth workers). Two two-day courses accredited with the Open College Network are also available for youth and family workers.

Collection: The Liversey Collection, University of Central Lancashire, Lambeth Palace Library, London SE1 7JU

Publications: Printed

Publications list: Available online and in print

Access to staff: Contact by letter, by telephone, by fax, by e-mail, in person and via website
Hours: Mon to Fri, 0900 to 1700
Special comments: 24-hour answerphone.

Access to building: Parking limited as in central London – congestion charge applies

Affiliated to: Drug Education Forum; Evangelical Alliance

Member organisation of: DrugScope; National Council for Voluntary Organisations (NCVO); National Council for Voluntary Youth Services (NCVYS)

HORDER CENTRE

St Johns Road, Crowborough, East Sussex, TN6 1XP

Tel: 01892 665577
Fax: 01892 662142
E-mail: info@hordercentre.co.uk
Website: www.hordercentre.co.uk

Enquiries to: Main Reception

Founded: 1954

Organisation type and purpose: Service industry, registered charity (charity number 1046624).
Charitable and specialist hospital.
To offer help, advice and hospital services for people with arthritis and musculo-skeletal conditions.

Subject coverage: Medical unit offering total comprehensive care and attention to patients with arthritis and musculo-skeletal conndition, requiring medical treatment, surgical intervention or rehabilitation, major joint reconstruction surgery.

Publications: Printed

Access to staff: Contact by letter, by telephone and by e-mail. Appointment necessary.
Hours: Mon to Fri, 0900 to 1700

Access for disabled people: Parking provided, ramped entry, toilet facilities

HORSES AND PONIES PROTECTION ASSOCIATION (HAPPA)

Taylor Building, Shores Hey Farm, Black House Lane, Briercliffe, nr Burnley, BB10 3QU

Tel: 01282 455992
Fax: 01282 451992
E-mail: enquiries@happa.org.uk
Website: www.happa.org.uk

Enquiries to: General Secretary
Other contacts: Association Secretary

Founded: 1937

Organisation type and purpose: National organisation, membership association (membership is by subscription), present number of members: 5,000, registered charity (charity number 1085211).
Equine welfare.

Subject coverage: Horse care and welfare; prosecuting horse cruelty cases; investigation of complaints re neglect and ill treatment of equines.

Publications: Printed

Access to staff: Contact by letter, by telephone, by fax, by e-mail, in person and via website
Hours: Mon to Thu, 0900 to 1700; Fri, 0900 to 1600

HORSHAM DISTRICT COUNCIL

Park House, North Street, Horsham, West Sussex, RH12 1RL

Tel: 01403 215100
Fax: 01403 262985
E-mail: contact@horsham.gov.uk
Website: www.horsham.gov.uk

Enquiries to: Communications Manager
Direct tel: 01403 215549
Direct e-mail: richard.morris@horsham.gov.uk

Founded: 1974

Organisation type and purpose: Local government body.

Subject coverage: District Council services.

Publications: Printed, and electronic and video

Access to staff: Contact by letter, by telephone, by fax and by e-mail
Hours: Mon to Thu, 0840 to 1720; Fri, 0840 to 1620

Access to building: No access other than to staff, no prior appointment required, prior appointment required

Access for disabled people: Parking provided, ramped entry, level entry, access to all public areas, toilet facilities

HORTICULTURAL DEVELOPMENT COMPANY (HDC)

Bradbourne House, East Malling, West Malling, Kent, ME19 6DZ

Tel: 01732 848383
Fax: 01732 848498
E-mail: hdc@hdc.org.uk
Website: www.hdc.org.uk

Enquiries to: Communication Manager

Founded: 1986

Organisation type and purpose: Non-Departmental Public Body.
Statutory levy body.

Subject coverage: Horticulture.

Publications: Printed

Publications list: Available online and in print

Access to staff: Contact by letter, by telephone and by e-mail. Appointment necessary.
Hours: Mon to Fri, 0900 to 1700

Sponsoring department: Department for Environment, Food and Rural Affairs; Nobel House, 17 Smith Square, London, SW1P 3JR; tel: 020 7238 6000

HORTICULTURE RESEARCH INTERNATIONAL (HRI)

Wellesbourne, Warwickshire, CV35 9EF

Tel: 01789 470382
Fax: 01789 470552
Website: www.hri.ac.uk

Enquiries to: Business Development
Direct tel: 01789 470440
Direct fax: 01789 472069

Founded: 1990

Organisation type and purpose: University department or institute, research organisation.
The administrative headquarters, centre for strategic science and annual crops research, research and development organisation.

Subject coverage: Horticulture, botany, soil science, plant physiology, plant biochemistry, pesticides, weed control, entomology, plant pathology, biometrics, vegetable crops. Edible fungi, field vegetables, fruit, industrial crops, ornamentals, protected crops, tropical crops, crop production/agronomy, pest and disease control, environment, plant breeding, post-harvest technology, propagation and seed technology.

Collection: Historical books on horticulture
Vegetable gene bank

Publications: Printed

Access to staff: Contact by letter, by telephone and by fax
Hours: Mon to Fri, 0900 to 1700

Affiliated to: DEFRA

Has: some 500 staff sited at five locations, two of which have extensive libraries

Other addresses: Development research on field vegetables and bulbs; Willington Road, Kirton, Boston, Lincolnshire, PE20 1EJ; tel: 01205 723477; fax: 01205 722922;
Development research on glasshouse crops, nursery stock, micropropagation and soft fruit; Lymington, Hampshire, SO41 0LZ; tel: 01590 673341; fax: 01590 671553; Hops research; Department of Hop Research, Wye College, Wye, Ashford, Kent, TN25 5AH; tel: 01233 812179; fax: 01233 813126;
Horticultural Research International Efford; Horticultural Research International Kirton; Horticultural Research International Wye

HOSPITAL CHAPLAINCIES COUNCIL (HCC)

Church House, Great Smith Street, London, SW1P 3NZ

Tel: 020 7898 1892
Fax: 020 7898 1891
Website: www.nhs-chaplaincy-spiritualcare.org.uk

Enquiries to: Administrator

Organisation type and purpose: Advisory body, training organisation.

Subject coverage: Responsible to the General Synod of the Church of England for Anglican Hospital Chaplaincy, HCC relates to the Department of Health and NHS administration, assisting trusts in the selection, appointment and training of Healthcare Chaplains and co-operating with other Christian denominations and other faiths and traditions in promoting the highest standards of spiritual care for patients, relatives and staff.

Publications: Printed

Publications list: Available in print

Access to staff: Contact by letter, by telephone, by e-mail and via website
Hours: Mon to Fri, 0930 to 1730

Close liaison with: Department of Health

Co-operates with: Health Care Chaplaincy Boards of the Roman Catholic Church; Hospital Chaplaincy Boards of the Free Church Federal Council

Member of: Churches Committee for Hospital Chaplaincy

HOSPITAL CONSULTANTS AND SPECIALISTS ASSOCIATION (HCSA)

1 Kingsclere Road, Overton, Basingstoke, Hampshire, RG25 3JA

Tel: 01256 771777
Fax: 01256 770999
E-mail: conspec@hcsa.com
Website: www.hcsa.com

Enquiries to: Advisory Service Manager
Other contacts: Administrative Director.

Founded: 1945

Organisation type and purpose: Trade union, present number of members: 3,100.

Access to staff: Contact by letter, by telephone, by fax and by e-mail. Appointment necessary.
Hours: Mon to Thu, 0900 to 1700; Fri, 0900 to 1630

Access to building: Prior appointment required

Access for disabled people: Parking provided, ramped entry

HOSTELLING INTERNATIONAL NORTHERN IRELAND (YHANI)

22–32 Donegal Road, Belfast, BT12 5JN

Tel: 028 9032 4733
Fax: 028 9031 5889
E-mail: office@hini.org.uk
Website: www.hini.org.uk

Enquiries to: General Secretary

Founded: 1931

Organisation type and purpose: International organisation, membership association (membership is by subscription), registered charity.
To provide budget priced accommodation for travellers.

Subject coverage: Hostelling in Northern Ireland; knowledge, love and use of the countryside; preservation of the countryside; maintenance of rights-of-way.

continued overleaf

Publications: Printed

Access to staff: Contact by letter, by telephone and by fax
Hours: Mon to Fri, 0900 to 1700

HOTEL AND CATERING INTERNATIONAL MANAGEMENT ASSOCIATION (HCIMA)

191 Trinity Road, London, SW17 7HN

Tel: 020 8772 7400
Fax: 020 8772 7500
E-mail: Library@instituteofhospitality.org
Website: www.hcima.org.uk

Enquiries to: Director of ITS Services

Founded: 1971

Organisation type and purpose: Professional body.
Management in all sectors of industry; examining body.

Subject coverage: Hotels; restaurants; caterers; hospitals; school meals; staff; welfare; civic and industrial catering etc; hotel and catering industry abroad; research; tourism.

Publications: Printed, and electronic and video

Publications list: Available in print

Access to staff: Contact by letter, by telephone, by fax and by e-mail
Hours: Mon to Fri, 0900 to 1700
Special comments: Non-members can use the service, by appointment only, for a charge.

HOUNSLOW LIBRARY NETWORK (HLN)

Centre Space, 24 Treaty Centre, High Street, Hounslow, Middlesex, TW3 1ES

Tel: 020 8583 4545
Fax: 020 8583 4595
Website: www.cip.org.uk

Enquiries to: Strategic Library Manager (IT and Electronic Resources)
Direct tel: 020 8583 4623
Direct fax: 020 8583 4719
Other contacts: Borough Librarian

Organisation type and purpose: Local government body, public library.

Subject coverage: International or foreign affairs (to 1985): relations, policy, diplomacy etc; parliaments; legislative assemblies; political parties and the party systems; party organisation and tactics. Local history. Geology (from 1985).

Collection: Chiswick Press Collection (19th century)
GLASS Collection (Debussy, Wagner, Jazz)
GLASS: Greater London Audio Specialisation Scheme Collection (spoken word; American literature)
Laser Collection (international or foreign affairs 1976–1984 and geology from 1985)
Layton Collection (English historical and topographical antiquarian material, 16th to 19th centuries)

Library catalogue: All or part available in-house

Publications: Printed

Access to staff: Contact by telephone, by fax and in person
Hours: Mon to Sat, 0930 to 1730

Access for disabled people: Parking provided

Has links with: Community Initiative Partnerships (CIP); Centrespace, Treaty Centre, High Street, Hounslow, Middlesex, TW3 1FS; Other libraries in London Borough of Hounslow, including Chiswick Library and Feltham Library

HOUSE OF BEAULY LIMITED

Station Road, Beauly, Invernessshire, IV4 7EH

Tel: 01463 782578
Fax: 01463 782409
E-mail: info@houseofbeauly.com
Website: www.houseofbeauly.com

Enquiries to: Operations Manager

Founded: 1991

Organisation type and purpose: Visitor centre, retail.

Subject coverage: Scottish crafts, giftware and traditional textiles, marketing and retailing of crafts.

Access to staff: Contact by letter, by telephone, by fax, by e-mail, in person and via website. Appointment necessary.
Hours: Mon to Fri, 0900 to 1700

HOUSE OF COMMONS INFORMATION OFFICE (HCIO)

House of Commons, Westminster, London, SW1A 2TT

Tel: 020 7219 4272
Fax: 020 7219 5839
E-mail: hcinfo@parliament.uk
Website: www.parliament.uk

Founded: 1978

Organisation type and purpose: Information office.

Subject coverage: All matters concerning the work, history and membership of the House of Commons and parliamentary publications.

Publications: Printed

Publications list: Available in print

Access to staff: Contact by letter, by telephone, by fax and by e-mail
Hours: Mon to Thu, 0900 to 1800; Fri, 0900 to 1630

HOUSE OF LORDS INFORMATION

House of Lords, London, SW1A 0PW

Tel: 020 7219 3107
Fax: 020 7219 0620
E-mail: hlinfo@parliament.uk
Website: www.parliament.uk

Enquiries to: Head of Enquiry Services

Organisation type and purpose: National government body.
One of the Houses of Parliament.

Information services: Information Office

Special visitor services: Tours Office

Education services: Education Service

Services for disabled people: Black Rod's Office

Collection: Parliamentary archives

Publications: Printed, and electronic and video

Access to staff: Contact by letter, by telephone, by fax, by e-mail and via website
Hours: When the House of Lords is sitting: Mon to Thu, 1000 to 1800; Fri, 1000 to 1600
Recess: 1000 to 1600

HOUSE OF LORDS LIBRARY

House of Lords, London, SW1A 0PW

Tel: 020 7219 5242 or 5433
Fax: 020 7219 6396
E-mail: hllibrary@parliament.uk

Enquiries to: Librarian

Founded: 1826

Organisation type and purpose: Private library for members of the House of Lords.

Subject coverage: All matters concerning the House of Lords, parliament, parliamentary publications, British government, administration and politics, as well as the law of England and Wales, and of Scotland.

Collection: Collections of pamphlets made by Lords Truro and Farnham in the 19th century
Lord Truro's collection of English lawbooks
Peel Tracts (c. 2,000 pamphlets chiefly concerning 18th-century Ireland)

Library catalogue: All or part available in-house

Access to staff: Contact by letter, by telephone, by fax and by e-mail
Hours: Mon to Fri, 0930 to 1730
Special comments: No facilities for personal enquiries.

HOUSEBUILDER PUBLICATIONS (HBP)

Housebuilder Media Ltd, Byron House, 7–9 St. James's Street, London, SW1A 1EE

Tel: 020 7960 1630
Fax: 020 7960 1631
Website: www.house-builder.co.uk
Website: www.hbmedia.co.uk

Enquiries to: Publishing Manager
Direct tel: 020 7608 5128
Direct e-mail: ben.roskrow@hbmedia.co.uk
Other contacts: Editor

Founded: 1955

Organisation type and purpose: National organisation, trade association (membership is by subscription), publishing house.

Subject coverage: New housing development, new homes marketing, housing economics, building products information.

Trade and statistical information: UK data on new homes

Non-library collection catalogue: All or part available in-house

Library catalogue: All or part available in-house

Publications: Printed

Publications list: Available online

Access to staff: Contact by letter, by telephone, by fax, by e-mail and via website
Hours: Mon to Fri, 0900 to 1700

Access to building: No access other than to staff

Access for disabled people: Parking provided

Connections with: House Builders Federation (HBF); tel: 020 7608 5199

HOUSING OMBUDSMAN SERVICE (HOS)

81 Aldwych, London, WC2B 4HN

Tel: 020 7421 3800
Fax: 020 7831 1942
E-mail: info@housing-ombudsman.org.uk
Website: www.ihos.org.uk

Other contacts: Deputy Ombudsman (for handling complaints); Casework Manager (for deposit disputes)

Founded: 1997

Organisation type and purpose: National organisation, membership association (membership is by subscription), present number of members: 2,300.
To investigate complaints made by tenants against member landlords who are either RSLs or private landlords.

Subject coverage: Housing, complaints handling, dispute resolution.

Publications: Printed

Publications list: Available online and in print

Access to staff: Contact by letter, by telephone, by fax, by e-mail and via website
Hours: Mon to Fri, 0900 to 1700

Access to building: Prior appointment required

Access for disabled people: Toilet facilities, lift.

HOUSMAN SOCIETY

80 New Road, Bromsgrove, Worcestershire, B60 2LA

Tel: 01527 874136
E-mail: info@housman-society.co.uk
Website: www.housman-society.co.uk

Enquiries to: Chairman
Direct tel: 01527 878586

Founded: 1974

Organisation type and purpose: Learned society, present number of members: 280 (charity number 1001107), literary society.
Exists to promote knowledge and appreciation of the work of A. E. Housman. Also promotes the causes of literature and poetry in general. Sponsors an annual Housman lecture at the Hay Festival.

Subject coverage: A. E. Housman and his family, his writings, poetry and life.

Collection: Books published by the society

Publications: Printed
Order printed publications from: 80 New Road, Bromsgrove, Worcs, B60 2LA; e-mail: info@housman-society.co.uk

Publications list: Available in print

Access to staff: Contact by letter, by telephone, by e-mail and via website
Hours: Mon to Fri, 0900 to 1700

HOVERCRAFT CLUB OF GREAT BRITAIN (HCGB)

Formal name: HoverClub of Great Britain Ltd.

PO Box 328, Bolton, Lancashire, BL6 4RR

Tel: 01204 841248
E-mail: secretary@hovercraft.org.uk
Website: www.hovercraft.co.uk
Website: www.hoverclub.org.uk

Enquiries to: Information Officer
Direct e-mail: gordon.taylor61@hotmail.com
Other contacts: Secretary; Archivist (for historical information)

Founded: 1966

Organisation type and purpose: Membership association, voluntary organisation, suitable for ages: all.

Subject coverage: Construction and use of lightweight sporting hovercraft, history of light hovercraft development, details of manufacturers past and present, personalities in hovercraft.

Information services: See website or telephone for details.

Education services: By request to Secretary.

Services for disabled people: By request.

Collection: Archives include historical information on light hovercraft, history, development, club, people, manufacturers, etc.

Non-library collection catalogue: All or part available in-house

Publications: Printed, and electronic and video
Order printed publications from: Publications Officer, Po Box 328, Bolton, BL6 4FP
Order electronic and video publications from: As above

Publications list: Available online and in print

Access to staff: Contact by letter, by telephone, by e-mail, in person and via website. Appointment necessary.
Hours: Mon to Sat, 0900 to 1700

Access to building: No prior appointment required
Hours: By arrangement

Also at: Archivist, Hovercraft Club of Great Britain Limited; 29 Mytton View, Clitheroe, Lancashire, BB7 5AZ; tel: 01200 426689; e-mail: gordon.taylor61@hotmail.com

HOVERCRAFT MUSEUM TRUST

Argus Gate, Daedalus site, Chark Lane, off Broom Way, Lee-on-Solent, Gosport, Hampshire, PO13 9NY

Tel: 023 9255 2090
E-mail: enquiries@hovercraft-museum.org
Website: www.hovercraft-museum.org

Enquiries to: Trustee
Direct tel: 023 9260 1310 (for TV and film enquiries)
Direct e-mail: wjacobs@supanet.com

Founded: 1988

Organisation type and purpose: Learned society (membership is by subscription), registered charity, museum, suitable for ages: all, consultancy.

Subject coverage: Application of the air cushion principle; hovercraft applications in materials handling, civil engineering and medicine; ferries, transport, leisure, military.

Education services: School visits at £100 per class.

Collection: Early papers and books on the hovercraft principle, papers and proceedings, videos, photographs, films and slides
SRNI log book
2 Cross-Channel SRN4 Hovercraft
Many early historic craft – last of types
Last SRNS and many pioneer vehicles
A collection of 60 hovercraft, and over 5,000 books, pictures, etc.

Non-library collection catalogue: All or part available in-house and in print

Library catalogue: All or part available in-house and in print

Publications: Printed, and electronic and video

Publications list: Available online and in print

Access to staff: Contact by letter, by telephone, by e-mail, in person and via website. Appointment necessary. Non-members charged.
Hours: Any time
Special comments: Library access, by appointment.

Access to building: Prior appointment required
Hours: By appointment only or on open/show days

Access for disabled people: Parking provided, level entry, toilet facilities

HOVERCRAFT SEARCH AND RESCUE UK (HSR-UK)

2 Park Court, Pyrford Road, West Byfleet, Surrey, KT14 6SD

Tel: 01932 340492
E-mail: info@hsr-uk.org
Website: www.hsr-uk.org

Founded: 1997

Organisation type and purpose: Registered charity (charity number 1061801).
Specialist search and rescue services.

Access to staff: Contact by letter, by telephone and by e-mail
Hours: Mon to Fri, 0900 to 1700

HOWARD LEAGUE FOR PENAL REFORM

1 Ardleigh Road, London, N1 4HS

Tel: 020 7249 7373
Fax: 020 7249 7788
E-mail: info@howardleague.org

continued overleaf

Website: www.howardleague.org

Enquiries to: Director

Organisation type and purpose: Voluntary organisation, registered charity (charity number 251926).
To promote penal reform by evidence to government committees, working parties, public education and campaigning.

Subject coverage: Criminal justice, prison reform, penal history and alternatives to prison.

Library catalogue: All or part available online

Publications: Printed, and electronic and video

Publications list: Available online

Access to staff: Contact by telephone. Appointment necessary.
Hours: Mon to Fri, 0900 to 1700

HOWELL HARRIS MUSEUM

Coleg Trefeca, Brecon, Powys, LD3 0PP

Tel: 01874 711423
Fax: 01874 712212
E-mail: colegtrefeca@ebcpcw.org.uk
Website: www.trefeca.org.uk
Website: www.ebcpcw.org.uk

Enquiries to: Manager

Founded: 1752

Organisation type and purpose: Registered charity (charity number 258456), museum, historic building, house or site, suitable for ages: 8+.
Christian training, retreat and conference centre and museum.

Subject coverage: The Welsh Methodist revival by means of an audiovisual presentation. Artefacts include the Trefeca 'Family' period. Also features contacts with English Methodists such as Wesley, Whitefield and the Countess of Huntingdon. Library on Welsh Methodist history and related subjects, in English and Welsh, historic Grade II listed building (1752 onwards), extensive training, retreat and conference programme.

Information services: Library available for reference (for conditions see Access above)

Special visitor services: Guided tours, materials and/or activities for children.

Education services: Resources for Key Stages 1, 2, 3 and 4 and Further or Higher Education.

Services for disabled people: For the hearing impaired; displays and/or information at wheelchair height.

Collection: Electrifying Machine. 1763
Howell Harris Preaching Chair/Pulpit. Field Pulpit. c. 1741
Joseph Harris' Telescope (recorded the transit of Venus over sun – experiment presented to Royal Society) 1761
Pulpit from the Countess of Huntingdon's College, Trefeca
Turrett clock and bell. Rose drums of Yew. 1754 added to house, restored by Barometer Shop, Leominster, 1999
Swords and guns. Brecknock Militia ('Seven Year's War', 1756)
Books published by Treveka Press 1756–1800

Non-library collection catalogue: All or part available in-house

Library catalogue: All or part available in-house

Publications: Printed

Access to staff: Contact by letter, by telephone, by fax and by e-mail.
Appointment necessary.
Hours: Daily, 0900 to 1600

Access to building: Prior appointment required
Hours: Daily, 0900 to 1600
Special comments: Other times strictly by appointment only.
Dec to Feb: closed Sat, Sun.
Closed Good Friday to Easter Tuesday and Christmas.

Access for disabled people: Parking provided, ramped entry, toilet facilities
Special comments: Access to museum area by chair lift.
Access to historic house involves one step.

Parent body: Presbyterian Church of Wales (PCW EBC); Tabernacle Chapel, 81 Merthyr Road, Whitchurch, Cardiff, CF14 1DD; tel: 029 2062 7465; fax: 029 2061 6188; e-mail: swyddfa.office@ebcpcw.org.uk; website: http://www.ebcpcw.org.uk

HPI LIMITED

Formal name: Hire Purchase Information Limited

Dolphin House, New Street, Salisbury, Wiltshire, SP1 2PH

Tel: 01722 422422, Consumer Service; 01722 412888, Trade Service
Fax: 01722 412746
Website: www.hpi.co.uk

Enquiries to: Director
Direct tel: 01722 413434

Founded: 1938

Organisation type and purpose: Service industry.
Information provider on high-value mobile assets. Business-to-business and consumer services. Vehicle identity checks, written-off vehicle register, outstanding finance register and other information on used vehicles.

Subject coverage: Information on used vehicles for motor trade, motor auctions, finance and insurance companies by subscription.
Available to consumers by credit card, Switch etc.

Publications: Printed
Order printed publications from: Harrison Sadler
1 Bridgeman Road, Teddington, TW11 9AJ, tel: 01481 9779132

Access to staff: Contact by telephone, by fax and by e-mail
Hours: Mon to Sat, 0800 to 2000; Sun, 1000 to 1700
Special comments: On-line information service available 24 hours.

Access for disabled people: Access to all public areas, toilet facilities

Associate member of: Finance and Leasing Association (FLA); Retail Motor Industry Federation (RMIF)

HUDDERSFIELD AND DISTRICT FAMILY HISTORY SOCIETY (H&D FHS)

'The Root Cellar', 15 Huddersfield Road, Meltham, Holmfirth, HD9 4NJ

Tel: 01484 859229
E-mail: secretary@hdfhs.org.uk
Website: www.hdfhs.org.uk

Enquiries to: Research Officer
Direct e-mail: research@hdfhs.org.uk

Founded: 1987

Organisation type and purpose:
Membership association (membership is by subscription), present number of members: 1,100, registered charity (charity number 702199).
Research into family history.

Subject coverage: Family history in the metropolitan District of Kirklees including Batley, Colne Valley, Denby Dale, Dewsbury, Huddersfield, Holme Valley, Kirkburton, Meltham, Mirfield and Spen Valley.

Collection: Reference Library (borrowing facilities for UK members)
Lancashire 1861–1901
Yorkshire 1861–1901
Lincolnshire 1841–1901
Cheshire 1841–1901
Durham 1851–1901
1851 Census – Kirklees only
1851 for Norfolk, Devon, Warwickshire (fiche)
1881 Census England and Wales (microfiche)
1881 Census (CD-ROM)
IGI UK (microfiche)
National Probate Calendars – England and Wales 1858 to 1943 (fiche)
Soldiers Died in WWI (CD-ROM)

Publications: Printed
Order printed publications from: Librarian, Huddersfield and District Family History Society, Root Cellar, 15 Huddersfield Road, Meltham, Holmfirth, West Yorkshire, HD9 4NJ

Publications list: Available online and in print

Access to staff: Contact by letter, by telephone and by e-mail
Hours: Mon to Fri, 0900 to 1700

Access to building: No prior appointment required
Special comments: Tues, 1400 to 1630; Wed, 1000 to 1230 and 1400 to 1630; Thu, 1400 to 1630 and 1930 to 2200

HUDDERSFIELD CENTRAL LIBRARY

Princess Alexandra Walk, Huddersfield, West Yorkshire, HD1 2SU

Tel: 01484 221967
Fax: 01484 221974
E-mail: huddersfield.reference@kirklees.gov.uk
Website: www.kirklees.gov.uk/libraries

Enquiries to: Reference and Information Services Librarian

Organisation type and purpose: Local government body, public library.

Subject coverage: Local history; general reference; modern literature in the languages of India, Pakistan and Bangladesh.

Collection: Newspaper archives, wide range of hard copy and online reference sources
Family, local authority and other archives

Non-library collection catalogue: All or part available online and in-house

Library catalogue: All or part available online and in-house

Access to staff: Contact by letter, by telephone, by fax, by e-mail and in person

Parent body: Kirklees Council

HUDSON LIBRARY

Cathedral & Abbey Church of St Alban, Sumpter Yard, St Albans, Hertfordshire, AL1 1BY

Tel: 01727 830576
Fax: 01727 850944

Enquiries to: Librarian

Organisation type and purpose: Registered charity (charity number 280566).

Subject coverage: Comparative religion, Bible, history of Christianity, theology, philosophy, psychology, sociology, some history and literature, plus local history of Hertfordshire and Bedfordshire, particularly of St Albans City and Abbey.

Collection: Beardsmore Collection (History of Hertfordshire in book, pamphlet and ephemera)

Library catalogue: All or part available in-house

Access to staff: Contact by letter, by telephone and in person
Hours: Mon to Fri, 0900 to 1700

Located in: St Alban's Abbey Chapter House

Supported by: Diocese of St Albans and the Cathedral Council

HUGH BAIRD COLLEGE LIBRARY

Balliol Road, Bootle, Merseyside, L20 7EW

Tel: 0151 353 4409
Fax: 0151 353 4409
Website: www.hughbaird.ac.uk/llc/default.asp

Enquiries to: Learning Resources Manager
Direct tel: 0151 353 4455

Organisation type and purpose: Suitable for ages: 16+.

Subject coverage: Art, design and display; hairdressing and beauty therapy; floristry; construction; electrical engineering; business and secretarial studies; education; health and social care; child care; pre-uniform; visual merchandising; GCSE subjects, NVQs, AS, A2, motor vehicle engineering, foundation degrees, travel and tourism, visual merchandising BA (top up).

Library catalogue: All or part available online and in-house

Access to staff: Contact by letter, by telephone and via website. Appointment necessary.
Hours: Mon to Thu, 0845 to 1900; Fri, 0845 to 1600
Vacation times, contact Library direct, tel: 0151 353 4409
Special comments: Reference library only. Lending facilities to college staff and students enrolled at the College.

Access to building: ID card or visitor's pass required

HUGUENOT LIBRARY

UCL, Gower Street, London, WC1E 6BT

Tel: 020 7679 2046
E-mail: library@huguenotsociety.org.uk
Website: www.huguenotsociety.org.uk/library-and-archive.html

Enquiries to: Librarian

Founded: 1885

Organisation type and purpose: Learned society (membership is by subscription), present number of members: 1,500, registered charity.

Subject coverage: Huguenot history, general, ecclesiastical, economic, social, art and genealogy.

Collection: Archives of the French Protestant Hospital and other manuscript material
Huguenot Pedigrees
Library of the French Hospital (La Providence)
Royal Bounty Archives

Library catalogue: All or part available online and in print

Publications: Printed, and electronic and video, and microform publications
Order electronic and video publications from: See website for details.

Publications list: Available online and in print

Access to staff: Contact by letter, by telephone and by e-mail. Appointment necessary.
Hours: Tue and Wed, 0900 to 1700

Access to building: *Hours:* Tue and Wed, 0900 to 1700

Access for disabled people: *Hours:* Access during opening hours

Administered by: Huguenot Society of Great Britain and Ireland

Also at: French Protestant Hospital; Rochester, Kent

HULL & HUMBER CHAMBER OF COMMERCE AND INDUSTRY

34–38 Beverley Rd, Hull, HU3 1YE

Tel: 01482 324976
Fax: 01482 213962
E-mail: info@hull-humber-chamber.co.uk
Website: www.hull-humber-chamber.co.uk

Enquiries to: Membership and Business Manager
Direct e-mail: b.massie@hull-humber-chamber.co.uk

Founded: 1837

Organisation type and purpose: Business support organisation, membership association (membership is by subscription), service industry, training organisation.

Subject coverage: Export requirements, business information, economic surveys, training seminars, networking events, marketing.

Publications: Printed

Access to staff: Contact by letter, by telephone, by fax, by e-mail, in person and via website
Hours: 0830 to 1700

Also at: Hull & Humber Chamber of Commerce; Dock Offices, Cleethorpes Road, Grimsby, DN31 3LL; tel: 01472 342981; fax: 01472 349524; e-mail: a.tate@hull-humber-chamber.co.uk; website: http://www.hull-humber-chamber.co.uk

HULL AND HUMBER CHAMBER OF COMMERCE, INDUSTRY AND SHIPPING

34–38 Beverley Road, Hull, East Yorkshire, HU3 1YE

Tel: 01482 324976
Fax: 01482 213962
E-mail: info@hull-humber-chamber.co.uk

Enquiries to: Information Officer

Founded: 1837

Organisation type and purpose: Trade association, service industry.

Subject coverage: Exports, including export documentation.

Publications: Printed, and electronic and video

Access to staff: Contact by letter, by telephone and by fax. Appointment necessary.
Hours: Mon to Fri, 0900 to 1700

HULL CITY ARCHIVES

Hull History Centre, Worship Street, Kingston upon Hull, East Yorkshire, HU2 8BG

Tel: 01482 317500
E-mail: hullhistorycentre@hullcc.gov.uk
Website: www.hullhistorycentre.org.uk
Website: www.a2a.org.uk

Enquiries to: Archivist

Founded: 1968

Organisation type and purpose: Local government body.
Hull City Archives collects, preserves and makes available records of Kingston upon Hull City Council and its predecessor bodies back to 1299, as well as collections of records relating to local businesses, societies, charities and families.

Subject coverage: All aspects of the City of Hull from medieval times to the present day. The holdings are especially strong for the 16th to 17th centuries local government; the built environment and infrastructure (architecture and engineering); the administration of justice in the 19th and 20th centuries; the fishing industry in Hull. Important collections are held relating to maritime history of the Humber Region.

continued overleaf

Collection: Hellyer Bros. Trawler Owners c.1890 to 1975
Hull and Goole Port Sanitary Authority
Thomas Hamling and Co, Trawler Owners c.1890 to 1980
Pease family of Hull and Hesslewood archives 17th-20th centuries
Borough of Kingston upon Hull 1299 to 1835
Records of the Newlands Homes 1821–2001
Archives:
Archives of the City Council and its predecessors, 1299 to date; local courts 17th to 20th centuries, charities 13th to 19th centuries, churches 19th and 20th centuries, business 19th and 20th centuries, families 18th to 20th centuries
City of Kingston upon Hull 1835 to present

Non-library collection catalogue: All or part available online and in-house

Library catalogue: All or part available in-house

Publications: Printed

Publications list: Available online and in print

Access to staff: Contact by letter, by telephone, by fax, by e-mail, in person and via website. Appointment necessary.
Hours: Tue to Thu, 0900 to 1645; Fri 0900 to 1600
Special comments: Appointments are essential, closure can happen without notice.

Access to building: Tue to Thu, 0930 to 1645

Access for disabled people: By appointment

Parent body: Kingston upon Hull City Council; The Guildhall, Alfred Gelder Street, Kingston upon Hull, HU1 2AA; tel: 01482 300300

HULL LIBRARIES

Formal name: Kingston upon Hull City Libraries

Reference and Information Library, Central Library, Albion Street, Hull, Yorkshire, HU1 3TF

Tel: 01482 223344
Fax: 01482 616858
E-mail: jessica.leathley@hullcc.gov.uk
Website: www.hullcc.gov.uk/libraries
Website: prismcollect.hullcc.gov.uk

Enquiries to: Librarian

Founded: 1901; please select Humberside Libraries (year of change 1974–1996)

Organisation type and purpose: Local government body, public library.

Subject coverage: In Reference Library: general coverage; family history (national resources).
In Hull History Centre: the study of Hull and the surrounding area – its history, geology, geography, archaeology and flora and fauna; family history (local resources).

Collection: In Reference Library: British Standards Online, BvD MINT Company and market research, Lloyd's Register of Ships 1764 to date (with gaps), Napoleon, books published 1741–1759
In Hull History Centre: Andrew Marvell (1621–1678); Deposited records of Forster and Andrews, organ builders of Hull, 1843–1956; Hull City Health Department photographs 1890s to 1930s; whales and whaling; William Wilberforce and slavery; Winifred Holtby (1898–1935) correspondence, cuttings, photographs, publications, etc.; GRO indexes on microfiche 1837 onwards.

Trade and statistical information: Official statistical series

Library catalogue: All or part available online and in-house

Access to staff: Contact by letter, by telephone, by fax, by e-mail, in person and via website
Hours: Mon to Thu, 0930 to 2000; Fri, 0930 to 1730; Sat, 0900 to 1630

Access for disabled people: Ramped entry, toilet facilities, lift

HULL LOCAL STUDIES LIBRARY

Formal name: Hull History Centre

Hull History Centre, Worship Street, Hull, HU2 8BG

Tel: 01482 317500
E-mail: david.smith@hullcc.gov.uk
Website: www.hullhistorycentre.org.uk

Enquiries to: Senior Local Studies Librarian

Founded: 1960

Organisation type and purpose: Local government body, joint local studies library and archive.

Subject coverage: Family history, the study of Kingston upon Hull and the surrounding area – its history, people, geology, geography, archaeology, flora and fauna.

Collection: Kingston upon Hull Local Studies Library special collections include:
Amy Johnson correspondence
Andrew Marvell (1621–78)
Deposited records of Forster and Andrews, organ builders of Hull, 1843–1956
Hull City Health Department photographs, 1890s to 1930s
Whales and whaling
William Wilberforce and slavery
Winifred Holtby (1898–1935) correspondence, cuttings, photographs, publications, etc.

Non-library collection catalogue: All or part available online and in-house

Library catalogue: All or part available online and in-house

Publications: Printed

Access to staff: Contact by letter, by telephone, by fax, by e-mail, in person and via website

Access to building: *Hours:* Mon and Wed, 0930 to 1945; Tue, Thu and Fri, 0930 to 1730; Sat, 0900 to 1630

Access for disabled people: Full disabled access, all facilities on ground floor; toilet facilities

Links with: Hull City Archives; Worship Street, Hull, HU2 8BG; tel: 01482 317500; website: http://www.hullhistorycentre.org.uk
University of Hull Archives; Worship Street, Hull, HU2 8BG; tel: 01482 317500; website: http://www.hullhistorycentre.org.uk

HULTON ARCHIVE

Unique House, 21–31 Woodfield Road, London, W9 2BA

Tel: 020 7266 2662
Fax: 020 7266 3154
E-mail: info@getty-images.com
Website: www.hultonarchive.com
Website: www.getty-images.com

Enquiries to: Sales Manager
Other contacts: Picture enquiries tel no: 0171 266 2662, fax: 0171 266 3154

Founded: 1947

Organisation type and purpose: International organisation.
Commercial picture lending library.
Sale of reproduction rights for publishing, TV, and advertising, editorial, web usage, sale of prints (photographs, framed or unframed).

Subject coverage: Over 18 million images covering all subjects from pre-history to 1980s; especially strong on social history, royalty, performing arts, sport, fashion, transport. Engravings, woodcuts, maps, etchings, cartoons, etc. Large colour section.

Collection: Baron Collection (ballet)
Sasha Collection (theatre)
Keystone Collection
Topical Press Collection (general)
Picture Post Collection (general)
Studo Lisa Collection (royalty)
Evening Standard Collection (general)
Ernst Haas Collection
Slim Aarons Collection (personalities)
Fox Photos (general)
Central Press (general)
Weegee Collection (US crime)
Archive Photographs (general and US)

Non-library collection catalogue: All or part available online

Publications: Printed

Access to staff: Contact by letter, by telephone, by fax, by e-mail and via website. Appointment necessary.
Hours: Mon to Fri, 0915 to 1800
Special comments: Fees chargeable according to usage.

Access to building: Prior appointment required
Hours: Mon to Fri, 0930 to 1730

Affiliated to: British Association of Picture Libraries

Part of: Getty Images; 101 Bayham Street, London, NW1 0FG; tel: 020 7544 3333; fax: 020 7544 3334; e-mail: info@getty-images.com

HUMAN RIGHTS (HR)

Mariners Hard, High Street, Cley-next-the-Sea, Holt, Norfolk, NR25 7RX

Tel: 01263 740990
Fax: 01263 740990
E-mail: human-rights-society@ukgateway.net

Enquiries to: Executive Secretary

Founded: 1971

Organisation type and purpose: Voluntary organisation, registered charity (charity number 262328).

Subject coverage: Alternatives to euthanasia – i.e. hospice and home care services, relief of pain in terminal illness and other help.

Publications: Printed, and electronic and video

Publications list: Available in print

Access to staff: Contact by letter, by telephone, by fax and by e-mail
Hours: Variable hours

Membership body: Human Rights Society (HRS); at the same address

HUMANE RESEARCH TRUST

29 Bramhall Lane South, Bramhall, Stockport, SK7 2DN

Tel: 0161 439 8041
Fax: 0161 439 3713
E-mail: info@humaneresearch.org.uk
Website: www.humaneresearch.org.uk

Founded: late 1950s; carries out the functions of the former Lawson Tait Trust

Organisation type and purpose: A registered charity (number 267779) encouraging and supporting new medical research that does not include the use of animals, with the objectives of advancing the diagnosis and treatment of disease in humans.

Subject coverage: The Trust focuses upon human models for human diseases, to the permanent benefit of both people and animals.

Access to staff: Contact by letter, by telephone, by fax and by e-mail

HUMANE SLAUGHTER ASSOCIATION (HSA)

Formal name: Humane Slaughter Association and Council of Justice to Animals

The Old School, Brewhouse Hill, Wheathampstead, Hertfordshire, AL4 8AN

Tel: 01582 831919
Fax: 01582 831414
E-mail: info@hsa.org.uk
Website: www.hsa.org.uk

Enquiries to: Chief Executive & Scientific Director
Other contacts: Technical Director (for technical matters)

Founded: 1911

Organisation type and purpose: Membership association (membership is by subscription), present number of members: 650, registered charity (charity number 209563), suitable for ages: adults, training organisation, research organisation. Promotion of humane methods of slaughter and the introduction of reforms in livestock markets (including transport facilities).

Subject coverage: Welfare of livestock (including birds) destined for slaughter. Training of vets, farmers and slaughtermen in slaughter techniques. Improvements in market facilities. Improvements in transport facilities for livestock. Training of hauliers, stockmen, market staff.

Publications: Printed, and electronic and video

Publications list: Available online and in print

Access to staff: Contact by letter, by telephone, by fax, by e-mail and via website. Appointment necessary.
Hours: Mon to Fri, 0900 to 1600

Access to building: Prior appointment required
Hours: Mon to Fri, 0900 to 1600

HUMBER AND WOLDS RURAL COMMUNITY COUNCIL (HWRCC)

14 Market Place, Howden, East Yorkshire, DN14 7BJ

Tel: 01430 430904
Fax: 01430 432037
E-mail: info@hwrcc.org.uk
Website: www.hwrcc.org.uk

Enquiries to: Chief Executive

Founded: 1976

Organisation type and purpose: Membership association (membership is by qualification), present number of members: approx. 1,000, registered charity (charity number 505489), and company limited by guarantee (number 4606085). Administers grants and fosters community development.

Subject coverage: Rural issues; parish and town council issues; community buildings (e.g. village halls).

Publications: Printed

Access to staff: Contact by letter, by telephone, by fax and by e-mail. Appointment necessary.
Hours: Mon to Thu, 0900 to 1700; Fri, 0900 to 1630
Special comments: No disabled access but can arrange to meet visitors elsewhere.

HUMBER REGISTER

175 York Road, Broadstone, Dorset, BH18 8ES

Tel: 01202 695937
E-mail: thearmans@googlemail.com
Website: www.humberregister.org.uk

Enquiries to: Registrar

Founded: 1951

Organisation type and purpose: Membership association (membership is by subscription), present number of members: 300.

Subject coverage: All Humber models from 1896 to 1930 plus the inlet over exhaust (i.o.e.) engined cars from 1931 and 1932.

Collection: Large library, including all known statistical information

Publications: Printed

Access to staff: Contact by letter, by telephone and by e-mail
Hours: Any reasonable time

HUNGARIAN CULTURAL CENTRE (HCC)

10 Maiden Lane, Covent Garden, London, WC2E 7NA

Tel: 020 7240 8448
Fax: 020 7240 4847
E-mail: andrea.kos@hungary.org.uk
Website: www.hungary.org.uk

Founded: 1999

Organisation type and purpose: Associated with Hungary's Ministry of Culture.

Subject coverage: Hungarian culture and civilisation.

Special visitor services: Library (open Tue and Thu 1100 to 1900).

HUNGARIAN EMBASSY

35 Eaton Place, London, SW1X 8BY

Tel: 020 7235 5218
Fax: 020 7823 1348
E-mail: office.lon@kum.hu
Website: www.huemblon.org.uk

Enquiries to: Information Officer

Organisation type and purpose: International organisation.

Publications: Printed

Access to staff: Contact by letter, by telephone, by fax and via website
Hours: Mon to Thu, 0900 to 1700; Fri, 0900 to 1400
Special comments: Consular Department is open to personal callers Mon to Fri, 0930 to 1200 only.

Other office: The Hungarian Tourist Office; 46 Eaton Place, London, SW1X 8AL; tel: 020 7823 1032; fax: 020 7823 1459; The Hungarian Trade Commission; 46 Eaton Place, London, SW1X 8AL; tel: 020 7235 8767; fax: 020 7235 4319

HUNTINGDON LIFE SCIENCES (HLS)

Woolley Road, Alconbury, Huntingdon, Cambridgeshire, PE28 4HS

Tel: 01480 892000
Fax: 01480 892978
Website: www.huntingdon.com

Enquiries to: Information Officer

Organisation type and purpose: International organisation, research organisation, consultancy.

Subject coverage: Toxicology; environmental science; pathology; pharmacology; microbiology; cell biology; metabolic studies; analytical chemistry; veterinary science.

Library catalogue: All or part available in-house

Access to staff: Contact by letter, by telephone and by fax
Hours: Mon to Fri, 0900 to 1700

Access to building: No access other than to staff

HUNTINGDONSHIRE ARCHIVES (HA)

Huntingdon Library and Archives, Princes Street, Huntingdon PE29 3PA

Tel: 01480 372738
E-mail: hunts.archives@cambridgeshire.gov.uk

continued overleaf

Website: www.cambridgeshire.gov.uk/archives

Enquiries to: Senior Archivist

Founded: 1948; formerly called Huntingdonshire County Record Office (year of change 1968); formerly called County Record Office, Huntingdon (year of change 2008)

Organisation type and purpose: Local government body.
Record office.

Subject coverage: Local history of Huntingdonshire and to a lesser degree of the Soke of Peterborough, including genealogy and topography.

Collection: Records of the former Huntingdonshire and Soke of Peterborough County Councils. Deposited official and unofficial records relating to Huntingdonshire, including archdeaconry, parish and borough records and family and estate collections, including those of the Dukes of Manchester of Kimbolton and of the Earls of Sandwich of Hinchingbrooke, c.1200 to 20th century

Non-library collection catalogue: All or part available online and in-house

Library catalogue: All or part available online and in-house

Publications: Printed

Publications list: Available in print

Access to staff: Contact by letter, by telephone, by fax, by e-mail and in person

Access to building: *Hours:* Mon, Tue, Fri 0930 to 1700, Weds 0900 to 1900, second Saturday of every month 1000 to 1600.
Special comments: CARN ticket required

Access for disabled people: There is a lift to the archives floor

Parent body: Cambridgeshire County Council, Cambridgeshire Archives and Local Studies; Shire Hall, Castle Hill, Cambridge; tel: 01223 718131

HUNTINGDONSHIRE LOCAL HISTORY SOCIETY

3 The Lanes, Houghton, Huntingdon, Cambridgeshire, PE28 2BW

Tel: 01480 463007
E-mail: dam.coz@virgin.net

Enquiries to: Honorary Secretary

Founded: 1957

Organisation type and purpose: Voluntary organisation, registered charity (charity number 290741).
Local history society.

Subject coverage: Local history of Huntingdonshire, vernacular architecture.

Publications: Printed
Order printed publications from: Hon. Editor, Dr Philip Saunders
Deputy Country Archivist, Cambs. County Record Office, Shire Hall, Castle Hill, Cambridge, CB31 0PA, e-mail: philip.saunders@cambridgeshire.gov.uk

Access to staff: Contact by letter, by telephone and in person
Hours: Mon to Fri, 0900 to 1700, and evenings

Affiliated to: Cambridge Local History Association

Member of: British Association for Local History

HUNTINGDONSHIRE REGIONAL COLLEGE

California Road, Huntingdon, Cambridgeshire, PE29 1BL

Tel: 01480 379100
Fax: 01480 379127
E-mail: college@huntingdon.ac.uk

Enquiries to: Librarian

Organisation type and purpose: Suitable for ages: 16+.
Further education college.

Subject coverage: Art, business studies, engineering, photography, general education, hairdressing, beauty therapy, care, IT.

Library catalogue: All or part available in-house

Access to staff: Contact by letter and by telephone
Hours: Mon to Fri, 0900 to 1700

Access to building: Prior appointment required

HUNTINGTON'S DISEASE ASSOCIATION (HDA)

Suite 24, Liverpool Science Park

Tel: 0151 331 5444
Fax: 0151 331 5441
E-mail: info@hda.org.uk
Website: www.hda.org.uk

Other contacts: 24 regional care advisers around the country

Founded: 1974

Organisation type and purpose: Membership association, present number of members: 6,000, voluntary organisation, registered charity (charity number 296453).
To provide care, advice, support and education to anyone who is affected by Huntington's Disease.

Subject coverage: Information for families, carers, and health and social service professionals, to advise and support people with Huntington's Disease.

Publications: Printed, and electronic and video

Publications list: Available online and in print

Access to staff: Contact by letter, by telephone, by fax and by e-mail
Hours: Mon to Fri, 0900 to 1700

HURLINGHAM POLO ASSOCIATION, THE (HPA)

Manor Farm, Little Coxwell, Faringdon, Oxfordshire, SN7 7LW

Tel: 01367 242828
Fax: 01367 242829
E-mail: enquiries@hpa-polo.co.uk
Website: www.hpa-polo.co.uk

Enquiries to: Chief Executive

Founded: 1874

Organisation type and purpose: National government body, membership association (membership is by subscription), present number of members: 2,300, voluntary organisation.
Governing body of the game in the UK and the Commonwealth.

Subject coverage: Polo.

Library catalogue: All or part available in-house

Publications: Printed, and electronic and video

Access to staff: Contact by letter, by telephone, by fax, by e-mail and via website
Hours: Mon to Fri, 0900 to 1700

Access for disabled people: Parking provided, ramped entry

HYMN SOCIETY OF GREAT BRITAIN AND IRELAND (HSGBI)

7 Paganel Road, Minehead, Somerset, TA24 5ET

Tel: 01643 703530
Fax: 01643 703530
E-mail: g.wrayford@breathemail.net
Website: www.hymnsocgbi.org

Enquiries to: Honorary Secretary

Founded: 1936

Organisation type and purpose: Learned society (membership is by subscription), present number of members: 450.

Subject coverage: Use of hymns in Christian worship; research in hymnology.

Publications: Printed

Access to staff: Contact by letter, by telephone, by fax and by e-mail
Hours: Mon to Fri, 0900 to 1700

Member of: Hymn Society in the United States and Canada; International Fellowship of Hymnology (IAH)

HYPERACTIVE CHILDREN'S SUPPORT GROUP (HACSG)

71 Whyke Lane, Chichester, West Sussex, PO19 7PD

Tel: 01243 539966
E-mail: hacsg@hacsg.org.uk
Website: www.hacsg.org.uk

Enquiries to: Director

Founded: 1977

Organisation type and purpose: Membership association, registered charity (charity number 277643).
Parent support, research & information group.

Subject coverage: Hyperactivity in children and young people, its relationship to diet, nutrition, allergy and environment; organic brain dysfunction.

Publications: Printed

Publications list: Available in print

Access to staff: Contact by letter, by telephone, by e-mail and via website
Hours: Mon, Thu, Fri, 1000 to 1200; Wed, 1430 to 1630

Connections with: Autism Unravelled; British Society for Nutritional Medicine; Foresight Association for Preconceptual Care; Green Network

HYPERION RECORDS LIMITED

PO Box 25, London, SE9 1AX

Tel: 020 8318 1234
Fax: 020 8263 1230
E-mail: info@hyperion-records.co.uk
Website: www.hyperion-records.co.uk

Enquiries to: Managing Director

Founded: 1980

Organisation type and purpose: Publishing house.
Record company (classical CDs).

Subject coverage: Recording and sale of classical music under the Hyperion and Helios labels.

Publications: Printed, and electronic and video

Publications list: Available in print

Access to staff: Contact by letter, by telephone, by fax, by e-mail and via website
Hours: Mon to Fri, 0930 to 1730

HYPERLIPIDAEMIA EDUCATION & ATHEROSCLEROSIS RESEARCH TRUST UK (HEART UK)

7 North Road, Maidenhead, Berkshire, SL6 1PE

Tel: 01628 777046
Fax: 01628 628698
E-mail: ask@heartuk.org.uk
Website: www.heartuk.org.uk

Enquiries to: Nurse Advisor
Direct tel: 0845 450 5988
Other contacts: Dieticians

Founded: 2002; formerly called Familial Hypercholestrolaemia, Familial Hyperlipidaemia Association

Organisation type and purpose: Membership association (membership is by subscription, qualification), present number of members: 1,300, voluntary organisation, registered charity (charity number 1003904).
To help people at high risk of coronary heart disease.

Subject coverage: Diet, food nutrition and dietetics, lifestyle management, heart health, dietary and body/blood fats (lipids), origins of health and disease, prevention of coronary heart disease, cholesterol, familial hypercholesterolaemia, familial hyperlipidaemias.

Publications: Printed, and electronic and video

Publications list: Available online and in print

Access to staff: Contact by letter, by telephone, by fax, by e-mail and via website
Hours: Mon to Fri, 0930 to 1600

Access to building: No access other than to staff

I CAN

8 Wakley Street, London, EC1V 7QE

Tel: 0845 225 4071
Fax: 0845 225 4072
E-mail: info@ican.org.uk
Website: www.ican.org.uk
Website: www.talkingpoint.org.uk

Enquiries to: Marketing Officer
Direct e-mail: info@ican.org.uk

Founded: 1888

Organisation type and purpose: Registered charity (charity number 210031).
I CAN is the children's communication charity
I CAN's mission is to ensure no child who struggles to communicate is left out or left behind.
Our vision is a world where all children and young people who struggle to communicate receive the help they need so that they can have a happy childhood, make progress at school and thrive as adults.
For over 40 years we have been providing effective, practical solutions to change the lives of children with communication difficulties.

Subject coverage: Over 1 million children in the UK have severe difficulties speaking and understanding. They might find it hard to express themselves, understand words, speak in sentences and understand simple instructions. Daily life for these children can be distressing and frustrating. They can struggle to read, learn, join in, make friends and achieve. I CAN are the experts in helping children with communication difficulties. If we find and help these children and their families, we can unlock their potential.

Information services: Information – www.ican.org.uk/help
I CAN provides expert information to parents and practitioners about speech, language and communication. Call 020 7843 2544 or email enquiries@ican.org.uk to book your free and confidential call-back from a speech and language therapist.
www.talkingpoint.org.uk is the website dedicated to children's speech, language and communication. It is designed for parents and people who work with children as well as children and young people themselves. This information portal contains everything you need to know about supporting children's speech and language development.

Education services: Schools – www.ican.org.uk/schools
We run two specialist schools, both of which are rated Outstanding by Ofsted, for children aged 4–19 with very severe and complex communication difficulties. These provide high quality care, education and therapy to help pupils learn and grow into confident and independent young people.
Working with schools, early years settings and local authorities www.ican.org.uk/solutions
Our Talk programmes have been developed by specialist speech and language therapists (SLTs) and teachers. They provide training and accreditation to schools and settings to help them support children's speech, language and communication.
We also have developed activities to raise awareness and funds, including Chatterbox Challenge www.chatterboxchallenge.co.uk, Communication Triathlon www.communicationtriathlon.org.uk and Sponsored Silence www.ican.org.uk/sponsoredsilence

Collection: Archives (of 100 years)

Publications: Printed, and electronic and video
Order printed publications from: www.ican.org.uk/resources
Order electronic and video publications from: www.ican.org.uk/resources

Publications list: Available in print

Access to staff: Contact by letter, by telephone, by fax, by e-mail and via website
Hours: Mon to Fri, 0900 to 1700

Access for disabled people: Toilet facilities

IA – THE ILEOSTOMY AND INTERNAL POUCH SUPPORT GROUP (IA)

Peverill House, 1–5 Mill Road, Ballyclare, BT39 9DR

Tel: 0800 018 4724
Fax: 028 9332 4606
E-mail: info@iasupport.org
Website: www.iasupport.org

Enquiries to: National Secretary

Founded: 1956

Organisation type and purpose: Membership association (membership is by subscription), present number of members: 10,000, registered charity (charity number 234472).

Subject coverage: Ileostomy: care, mutual aid, rehabilitation, equipment and skin care for those who have had their colon removed.

Publications: Printed

Publications list: Available in print

Access to staff: Contact by letter, by telephone, by fax, by e-mail and via website
Hours: Mon to Fri, 0900 to 1700

Affiliated to: International Ostomy Association, over 59 branches

IAPA

IAPA International Secretariat, Old Chambers, 93–94 West Street, Farnham, Surrey, GU9 7EB

Tel: 01252 720810
Fax: 01252 720830
E-mail: admin@iapa.net
Website: www.iapa.net

Founded: 1979

Organisation type and purpose: A global association of independent accountancy and business advisory firms providing accounting, audit, tax advisory and business consultancy services. Comprises around 230 member firms with offices in more than 50 countries.
To support its members in providing their clients with a diverse range of professional, comprehensive and cost-effective business solutions, regardless of sector or location.
IAPA does not itself provide client services.

continued overleaf

Subject coverage: Accounting, audit, tax advisory and business consultancy services.

Access to staff: Contact by letter, by telephone, by fax and by e-mail

IATEFL

Formal name: International Association of Teachers of English as a Foreign Language

Darwin College, University of Kent, Canterbury, Kent, CT2 7NY

Tel: 01227 824430
Fax: 01227 824431
E-mail: generalenquiries@iatefl.org
Website: www.iatefl.org

Enquiries to: Executive Officer

Founded: 1967

Organisation type and purpose: International organisation, membership association (membership is by subscription), present number of members: 4000, voluntary organisation, registered charity (charity number 1090853).

Subject coverage: The teaching of English to those for whom it is a second language.

Publications list: Available online and in print

Access to staff: Contact by letter, by telephone, by fax, by e-mail and in person
Hours: Mon to Fri, 0900 to 1700

IBM UNITED KINGDOM LIMITED

Library (MP 149), Hursley Park, Winchester, Hampshire, SO21 2JN

Tel: 01962 818148
E-mail: library@uk.ibm.com
Website: www.ibm.com

Enquiries to: Librarian
Direct e-mail: library@uk.ibm.com

Organisation type and purpose: Research organisation.

Subject coverage: Data processing; computers; programming languages; computer applications; computer software.

Collection: IBM Manuals
IBM Technical Reports
IBM History
Computing History

Library catalogue: All or part available in-house

Access to staff: Contact by letter, by telephone, by e-mail, in person and via website. Access for members only.
Hours: Mon to Fri, 0830 to 1600

ICAEW

Formal name: The Institute of Chartered Accountants in England and Wales

Chartered Accountants' Hall, Moorgate Place, London, EC2P 2BJ

Tel: 020 7920 8620
Fax: 020 7920 8621
E-mail: library@icaew.com
Website: www.icaew.com/library
Website: www.icaew.com

Enquiries to: Head of Library and Information Services
Direct e-mail: library@icaew.com

Founded: 1880

Organisation type and purpose: International professional body for chartered accountants

Subject coverage: Accountancy, auditing, company law, taxation, management consultancy, financial management, financial services, information technology in accounting.

Information services: Fully staffed Enquiry Service

Services for disabled people: Lift access from street level

Collection: Files of comments on exposure drafts of accounting and auditing standards
Rare books on book-keeping, 1494–1914

Trade and statistical information: Business Confidence monitor, accountancy research, technical releases, press releases, subject and sectoral publications – all available on website: http://www.icaew.com

Non-library collection catalogue: All or part available online

Library catalogue: All or part available online

Publications: Printed, and electronic and video

Publications list: Available online

Access to staff: Contact by letter, by telephone, by fax, by e-mail, in person and via website. Letter of introduction required. Non-members charged.
Hours: Mon to Fri, 0830 to 1800
Special comments: Members of the public may have visiting access by providing a letter of introduction from a member of the ICAEW or by paying a daily or weekly fee.

Access to building: Use the main entrance at Moorgate Place, EC2. Disabled lift located at the Copthall Avenue entrance
Hours: 0800 to 1830

Access for disabled people: Yes.
Hours: Same as above

Member organisation of: Consultative Committee of Accountancy Bodies (CCAB); Global Accounting Alliance

ICC – INTERNATIONAL MARITIME BUREAU (ICC IMB)

Formal name: International Chamber of Commerce – International Maritime Bureau

Cinnabar Wharf, 26 Wapping High Street, London E1W 1NG

Tel: 020 7423 6960
Fax: 020 7423 6961
E-mail: imb@icc-ccs.org
Website: www.icc-ccs.org

Enquiries to: Director
Other contacts: Deputy Director (for piracy)

Founded: 1981

Organisation type and purpose: International organisation
The ICC–International Maritime Bureau (IMB) is a specialised membership division of the International Chamber of Commerce, the world business organisation. It is recognised by a special resolution of the International Maritime Organisation (IMO). The IMB was set up in 1981 to act as a focal point for the international trading community in the fight against trade fraud and malpractice. Its membership comprises some of the world's leading banks, insurance, shipping and trading companies and all those that have a legitimate interest in international trade.

Subject coverage: All types of maritime fraud and malpractice, piracy, investigations, cargo loss, document verification, loss prevention and due diligence.

Non-library collection catalogue: All or part available in-house

Library catalogue: All or part available in-house

Publications: Printed

Publications list: Available online and in print

Access to staff: Contact by telephone, by fax, by e-mail and via website. Appointment necessary. Non-members charged.
Hours: Mon to Fri, 0900 to 1700

Access for disabled people: Ramped entry

ICE CREAM ALLIANCE LIMITED (ICA)

3 Melbourne Court, Pride Park, Derby, DE24 8LZ

Tel: 01332 203333
Fax: 01332 203420
E-mail: info@ice-cream.org
Website: www.ice-cream.org

Enquiries to: Chief Executive Officer
Other contacts: Membership Adviser/Administrator

Founded: 1944

Organisation type and purpose: Trade Association.

Subject coverage: Ice cream, equipment and associated materials for manufacture and sale of the product.

Publications: Printed
Order printed publications from: Ice Cream Alliance

Publications list: Available online and in print

Access to staff: Contact by letter, by telephone, by fax, by e-mail and via website. Appointment necessary. Non-members charged.
Hours: Mon to Thu, 0900 to 1700; Fri, 0900 to 1600

Access to building: Appointment required

ICE ERGONOMICS LIMITED

Holywell Building, Holywell Way, Loughborough, Leicestershire, LE11 3UZ

Tel: 01509 283300
Fax: 01509 283360
Website: www.ice.co.uk

Enquiries to: Operations Director
Other contacts: Business Manager for business/financial matters.

Founded: 1970

Organisation type and purpose: University department or institute, consultancy, research organisation.

Subject coverage: Ergonomics in the design, development and evaluation of products, procedures, systems and environments, with application to consumer, industrial, commercial, automotive and transport areas. Special skills in occupational safety and health, accident research, and job assessment and allocation for disabled people.

Non-library collection catalogue: All or part available in-house

Library catalogue: All or part available in-house

Publications list: Available in print

Access to staff: Appointment necessary.
Hours: Mon to Fri, 0900 to 1700

Access to building: No prior appointment required

Access for disabled people: Parking provided, level entry, access to all public areas, toilet facilities

Parent body: Loughborough University; Ashby Road, Loughborough, Leicestershire, LE11 3TU; tel: 01509 263171

ICE HOCKEY UK (IHUK)

19 Heather Avenue, Rise Park, Romford, Essex, RM1 4SL

Tel: 020 8732 4505
Fax: 020 8952 9515
E-mail: ihukoffice@yahoo.co.uk
Website: www.icehockeyuk.co.uk

Enquiries to: Administrator

Founded: 1936

Organisation type and purpose: National organisation, training organisation. Governing body for ice hockey in UK and Northern Ireland.

Subject coverage: Ice hockey.

Collection: Photographs

Access to staff: Contact by letter, by telephone, by fax, by e-mail, in person and via website
Hours: Mon to Thu, 0900 to 1700; Fri, 0900 to 1600

Access to building: No prior appointment required

Affiliated to: BOA; CCPR; International Ice Hockey Federation (IIHF); Sports Council

Houses the: English Ice Hockey Association; Northern Ireland Ice Hockey Association; Scottish Ice Hockey Association

ICON

Formal name: Institute of Conservation

3rd Floor, Downstream Building, 1 London Bridge, London, SE1 9BG

Tel: 020 7785 3805
Fax: 020 7785 3806
E-mail: chantrylibrary@icon.org.uk
Website: www.icon.org.uk

Enquiries to: Administrator

Founded: 2005; created by the merger of The Scottish Society for Conservation and Restoration (year of change 2005)

Organisation type and purpose: International organisation, professional body, present number of members: 3,000, registered charity (charity number 1049444).

Subject coverage: All aspects of restoration and conservation of artistic and historic works, glass, ceramics, furniture, stone, easel paintings, wall paintings, books and paper, textiles, metals, stained glass, gilding, historical interiors, natural materials and archaeological objects.

Publications: Printed

Access to staff: Contact by letter, by telephone, by fax and by e-mail
Hours: Mon to Fri, 0900 to 1300 (best time to call)

IDOX INFORMATION SERVICE

7th Floor, 95 Bothwell Street, Glasgow G2 7HX

Tel: 0141 574 1920
E-mail: iu@idoxgroup.com
Website: is.idoxgroup.com/products/info_service.cfm

Enquiries to: Information Service Manager

Founded: 1973; formerly called Planning Exchange (year of change 2002)

Organisation type and purpose: Subscription-based service, specialising in the development and delivery of products, services and people for information management and knowledge sharing, for both public and private sector clients. Information service in the fields of economic, environmental and social development through a database of bibliographic abstracts, a telephone helpline and document supply.

Subject coverage: Economic and business development, regeneration, local government, finance and management, education and training, community development, the environment, housing, nature conservation, rural and urban areas, social work, town and country planning, regional development, transport, leisure and tourism

Collection: All Scottish planning appeal decision letters and reports from January 1976
All Scottish local plans

Non-library collection catalogue: All or part available online and in-house

Library catalogue: All or part available online and in-house

Publications: Printed, and electronic and video

Access to staff: Access for members only. Non-members charged.
Hours: Mon to Fri, 0900 to 1700
Special comments: By appointment for members.

IDOX INFORMATION SOLUTIONS LTD

First Floor, Alderley House, Alderley Road, Wilmslow, Cheshire SK9 1AT

Tel: 0844 874 0739
Fax: 0844 874 0719
Website: www.grantfinder.co.uk
Website: is.idoxgroup.com/products/info_service.cfm

Enquiries to: Marketing and Communications Director

Founded: 1985; formerly called Grantfinder Ltd (year of change 2010)

Organisation type and purpose: Consultancy, research organisation, publishing house, providers of information on grants and policy.

Subject coverage: Information on policy and funding available from the UK Government and European Community to organisations in the public, private and voluntary sectors.

Non-library collection catalogue: All or part available online and in-house

Library catalogue: All or part available online and in-house

Publications: Printed, and electronic and video

Publications list: Available online

Access to staff: Contact by e-mail and via website. Non-members charged.
Hours: Mon to Fri, 0900 to 1730

IEA COAL RESEARCH

The Clean Coal Centre, Gemini House, 10–18 Putney Hill, London, SW15 6AA

Tel: 020 8780 2111
Fax: 020 8780 1746
E-mail: mail@iea-coal.org.uk
Website: www.iea-coal.org.uk

Enquiries to: Information Services Group Manager

Founded: 1975

Organisation type and purpose: International organisation providing information on coal

Subject coverage: All aspects of coal production and use including coal reserves and exploration, mining, preparation, properties, processing, combustion, transport and handling, waste management, and political, legal, economic, environmental, health and safety aspects.

Library catalogue: All or part available in-house

Publications: Printed, and electronic and video
Order printed publications from: tel: 020 8789 0111, fax: 020 8789 0111, e-mail: sales@iea-coal.org.uk

Publications list: Available online and in print

Access to staff: Contact by letter, by telephone, by fax, by e-mail and via website. Appointment necessary. All charged.
Hours: Mon to Fri, 0900 to 1700

Links with: International Energy Agency (IEA); 2 rue André-Pascal, Paris cedex 16, 75775, France

continued overleaf

Member countries: Austria, Canada, Germany, Italy, Japan, Poland, Republic of Korea, Spain, Sweden, United Kingdom, USA

IEEM

Formal name: Institute of Ecology and Environmental Management

45 Southgate Street, Winchester, Hampshire, SO23 9EH

Tel: 01962 868626
Fax: 01962 868625
E-mail: enquiries@ieem.net
Website: www.ieem.net

Enquiries to: Executive Director

Founded: 1991

Organisation type and purpose: Professional body

Subject coverage: Ecology and environmental management.

Library catalogue: All or part available in-house

Publications: Printed

Publications list: Available online and in print

Access to staff: Contact by letter, by telephone, by fax and by e-mail
Hours: Mon to Fri, 0900 to 1700
Special comments: Members only

IEPRC

Formal name: International Electronic Publishing Research Centre Limited

PO Box 83, Leatherhead, Surrey, KT22 7AZ

Tel: 01372 373646
Fax: 01372 379732
E-mail: admin@ieprc.org
Website: www.ieprc.org

Enquiries to: Administrator
Direct tel: 01372 278335
Other contacts: (1) Chief Executive (2) Research Manager (3) Company Secretary for (1) strategic issues (2) research and development (3) finance and administration.

Founded: 1981

Organisation type and purpose: International organisation, membership association (membership is by subscription, qualification, election or invitation), present number of members: 70 organisations, research organisation.
Voluntary association of international multimedia publishers and related companies.

Subject coverage: Electronic publishing.

Trade and statistical information: Information for members only

Publications: Electronic and video

Publications list: Available online

Access to staff: Contact by letter, by telephone, by fax, by e-mail and via website. Access for members only.
Hours: Telephone is answered from 0800 to 2200, on 01372 278335 outside usual business hours

Access to building: No access other than to staff

IFPI

Formal name: International Federation of the Phonographic Industry

IFPI Secretariat, 10 Piccadilly, London, W1J 0DD

Tel: 020 7878 7900
Fax: 020 7878 7950
E-mail: info@ifpi.org
Website: www.ifpi.org

Founded: 1933

Organisation type and purpose: International organisation, trade association. Represents producers of sound recordings.

Subject coverage: Copyright in sound and video recordings, worldwide industry turnover, estimates of piracy of recordings.

Trade and statistical information: Annual and half-yearly sales statistics of the record industry

Access to staff: Contact by fax and by e-mail
Hours: Mon to Fri, 0900 to 1730

Access to building: Prior appointment required

Consultative status with: WIPO

IFS SCHOOL OF FINANCE

8th Floor, Peninsular House, 36 Monument Street, London, EC3R 8LJ

Tel: 020 7444 7100
Fax: 020 7444 7109
E-mail: knowledgebank@ifslearning.ac.uk
Website: www.ifslearning.ac.uk

Enquiries to: KnowledgeBank

Founded: 1879

Organisation type and purpose: Education. A registered charity.
To provide qualifications and lifelong career support services to those working within the financial services industry and formal education to customers.

Subject coverage: Financial services, banking, financial education for 14–19-year-olds, regulatory qualifications, accountancy, investment, economics, bank history, financial management, risk, e-commerce, financial technology, marketing in financial services, monetary and financial systems, financial services law.

Access to staff: Contact by letter, by telephone, by fax, by e-mail and via website

IHS

Willoughby Road, Bracknell, Berkshire, RG12 8FB

Tel: 01344 328000
Fax: 01344 328008
E-mail: customer.support@ihs.com
Website: uk.ihs.com

Enquiries to: Information Officer

Founded: 1964; formerly called Technical Indexes Ltd

Organisation type and purpose: Manufacturing industry.
Producers and distributors of information products on CD-ROM and online formats; registered to ISO 9002 by BSI Quality Assurance.

Subject coverage: Electronic engineering; process and chemical engineering; engineering components and materials; manufacturing and materials handling; construction and civil engineering; standards for construction industry; standards in health and safety; NATO Stock Numbers; laboratory equipment; British standards; defence standards and specifications; US industrial and military standards and specifications; Canadian, Japanese and world standards.

Publications: Printed, and electronic and video

Publications list: Available in print

Access to staff: Contact by letter, by telephone, by e-mail and via website. Appointment necessary.
Hours: Mon to Fri, 0845 to 1645

Links with: IHS Group – Information Handling Services (IHS Group); Colorado, USA

Other address: RAPIDOC – Hard Copy Supply Division; Willoughby Road, Bracknell; tel: 01344 861666; fax: 01344 714440; e-mail: rapidoc@techindex.co.uk

IMAGINATE

45A George Street, Edinburgh, EH2 2HT

Tel: 0131 225 8050
Fax: 0131 225 6440
E-mail: info@imaginate.org.uk

Enquiries to: Chief Executive

Founded: 1989

Organisation type and purpose: Registered charity, suitable for ages: 3 to 14.
Largest performing arts festival for 3- to 14-year-olds in the UK.

Subject coverage: Children's Theatre.

Publications: Printed

Access to staff: Contact by letter, by telephone, by fax and by e-mail. Appointment necessary. Letter of introduction required.
Hours: Mon to Fri, 0900 to 1700

IMERYS MINERALS LTD

Par Moor Centre, Par Moor, Par, Cornwall, PL24 2SQ

Tel: 01726 818007
Fax: 01726 811200
E-mail: adrian.mutton@imerys.com

Enquiries to: Property Surveyor

Organisation type and purpose: Company producing china clay and ball clay.

Subject coverage: China clay and ball clay.

Trade and statistical information: Information service provided to external solicitors in planning searches associated with house purchase, land development etc

Access to staff: Contact by letter, by telephone and by fax
Hours: Mon to Fri, 0900 to 1700

IMMIGRATION MANAGEMENT & BUSINESS GROUP (IMB Group)

75 Cannon Street, London, EC4N 5BN

Tel: 020 7556 7112
Fax: 020 7556 7001
E-mail: admin@immigration.co.uk
Website: www.workpermits.com
Website: www.immigration.co.uk

Enquiries to: General Manager

Founded: 1985

Organisation type and purpose: Service industry, consultancy.

Subject coverage: All categories of UK work permit, employment approval and fast extensions and foreign passport endorsement.

Publications list: Available online

Access to staff: Contact by letter, by telephone, by fax, by e-mail and via website. Appointment necessary.
Hours: Mon to Fri, 0830 to 1800

Access for disabled people: Parking provided, ramped entry, toilet facilities

Connections with: japanese-immigration.com; same address

IMP CLUB LIMITED

76 Star Lane, Folkestone, CT19 4QQ

Tel: 01438 741917
E-mail: membership@theimpclub.co.uk
Website: www.theimpclub.co.uk

Enquiries to: Chairman

Founded: 1980

Organisation type and purpose: Membership association (membership is by subscription).
Classic car club.

Subject coverage: All Hillman Imp cars and their variants (Singer, Sunbeam, Commer), Imp-based cars, technical advice, history, technical services.

Collection: Broad selection of technical reports and historical information
Comprehensive collection of photographs, sales literature and associated memorabilia

Non-library collection catalogue: All or part available online and in-house

Library catalogue: All or part available in-house

Publications: Printed

Access to staff: Contact by letter, by telephone, by e-mail and via website
Hours: Evenings and weekends

Links with: Association of Rootes Car Clubs

IMPERIAL COLLEGE LONDON – CENTRAL LIBRARY

Formal name: Imperial College of Science, Technology and Medicine – Central Library

South Kensington, London, SW7 2AZ

Tel: 020 7594 8820
Fax: 020 7584 8876
E-mail: library@imperial.ac.uk
Website: www.imperial.ac.uk/library

Organisation type and purpose: University library.

Subject coverage: Aeronautics; biotechnology; business; chemical engineering and chemical technology; chemistry; civil engineering; computing; electrical and electronic engineering; environment; earth sciences; geology; history of science; life sciences; materials; mathematics; mechanical engineering; medicine; physics.

Collection: Annan Collection (history of metals, mining and metallurgy)

Non-library collection catalogue: All or part available online

Library catalogue: All or part available online

Publications: Printed

Access to staff: Contact by letter, by telephone, by e-mail, in person and via website. Appointment necessary.
Hours: Please check the website

Access for disabled people: Access to all public areas, toilet facilities

Branch libraries: Charing Cross Campus Library; Imperial College London, The Reynolds Building, St Dunstan's Road, London, W6 8RP; tel: 020 7594 0755; e-mail: library@imperial.ac.uk; Chelsea and Westminster Campus Library; Imperial College London, Chelsea and Westminster Hospital, Fulham Road, London, SW10 9NH; tel: 020 3315 8107; e-mail: library@imperial.ac.uk; Hammersmith Campus Library; Imperial College London, Hammersmith Hospital, Du Cane Road, London, W12 0NN; tel: 020 8383 3246; e-mail: library@imperial.ac.uk; Royal Brompton Campus Library; Faculty of Medicine, Royal Brompton Hospital, Dove House Street, London, SW3 6LY; tel: 020 7351 8150; e-mail: library@imperial.ac.uk; Silwood Park Campus Library; Silwood Park Campus, Ascot, Berkshire, SL5 7TA; tel: 020 7594 2461; e-mail: library@imperial.ac.uk; St Mary's Campus Library; Faculty of Medicine, Norfolk Place, Paddington, London, W2 1PG; tel: 020 7594 3692; e-mail: library@imperial.ac.uk

Links with: Science Museum Library; tel: 020 7942 4242; fax: 020 7942 4243; e-mail: smlinfo@sciencemuseum.org.uk

IMPERIAL COLLEGE SCHOOL OF MEDICINE – ST MARY'S CAMPUS LIBRARY

Formal name: Imperial College of Science, Technology and Medicine – St Mary's Campus Library

Norfolk Place, Paddington, London, W2 1PG

Tel: 020 7594 3692
Fax: 020 7402 3971
E-mail: n.palmer@ic.ac.uk
Website: www.lib.ic.ac.uk/depts/stindex.htm

Enquiries to: Librarian

Founded: 1854

Organisation type and purpose: University department or institute.
Medical school.

Subject coverage: Medicine.

Access to staff: Contact by letter. Letter of introduction required. Non-members charged.
Hours: Term time: Mon to Fri, 0900 to 2100; Sat, 0900 to 1300
Vacations: Mon to Fri, 0900 to 1900; Sat, closed

Campus of: Imperial College of Science, Technology and Medicine

IMPERIAL PRESS

Pantiles, Garth Lane, Knighton, Powys, LD7 1HH

Tel: 01547 520360
E-mail: militarymuseums@tiscali.co.uk

Enquiries to: Proprietor

Founded: 1984

Organisation type and purpose: Publishing house.
Bookseller.

Subject coverage: War gaming, military history.

Publications: Printed

Publications list: Available in print

Access to staff: Contact by letter and by telephone
Hours: Mon to Fri, 0900 to 1700

Access to building: No access other than to staff

IMPERIAL SOCIETY OF TEACHERS OF DANCING (ISTD)

Imperial House, 22–26 Paul Street, London, EC2A 4QE

Tel: 020 7377 1577
Fax: 020 7247 8979
E-mail: marketing@istd.org
Website: www.istd.org

Enquiries to: Chief Executive

Founded: 1904

Organisation type and purpose: Professional body, present number of members: 9,500, registered charity (charity number 250397), training organisation.
Dance Examination Board.
The ISTD exists to promote knowledge of dance and to maintain and improve teaching standards.

Subject coverage: Ballroom dance, Latin American dance, sequence dance, disco/freestyle/rock-n-roll dance, classical ballet, modern theatre dance, tap dance, jazz dance, national dance, folk dance, classical Greek dance, South Asian dance, alternative rhythms.

Collection: Library collection related to dance

Publications: Printed

Publications list: Available in print

Access to staff: Contact by letter, by telephone, by e-mail and via website
Hours: Mon to Fri, 0900 to 1700

IMPERIAL TOBACCO LIMITED (ITL)

PO Box 525, Upton Road, Southville, Bristol, BS99 1LQ

Tel: 0117 963 6636
Website: www.imperial-tobacco.com

Founded: 1996

Organisation type and purpose:
Manufacturing industry.
Tobacco manufacturing.

Subject coverage: Tobacco industry.

Trade and statistical information: Tobacco trade volumes

Library catalogue: All or part available in-house

Access to staff: Contact by letter
Hours: Mon to Fri, 0900 to 1700

Access to building: No access other than to staff

IMPERIAL WAR MUSEUM (IWM)

Department of Printed Books, Lambeth Road, London, SE1 6HZ

Tel: 020 7416 5342
Fax: 020 7416 5246
E-mail: collections@iwm.org.uk
Website: www.iwm.org.uk

Enquiries to: Keeper, Department of Printed Books

Founded: 1917

Organisation type and purpose: Museum, suitable for ages: 16+.

Subject coverage: Study of conflicts in which British and Commonwealth forces were engaged in the 20th century, particularly the two World Wars, and early 21st century; naval, military and air operations; unit records; social, political, economic and literary aspects of modern warfare.

Collection: Over 100,000 books, 25,000 pamphlets, 8,000 periodical titles, 45,000 maps, and other special or ephemera collections, etc.
British, Commonwealth, French, German and American unit histories
Pamphlet Collection (wartime propaganda, ration books and other ephemera)
United States Strategic Bombing Survey Reports
Women's activities in the First World War

Non-library collection catalogue: All or part available online and in-house

Library catalogue: All or part available online and in-house

Publications: Printed, and electronic and video
Order printed publications from: Mail Order, Imperial War Museum, Duxford Air Field, Cambridge, CB2 4QR; tel. 01223 499348; fax 01223 839688; e-mail mailorder@iwm.org.uk
Order electronic and video publications from: Naval and Military Press; tel. 01825 749494; e-mail order.dept@naval-military-press.co.uk

Publications list: Available online

Access to staff: Contact by letter, by telephone, by fax, by e-mail and via website. Appointment necessary.
Hours: Telephone access: Mon to Fri, 0900 to 1700

Access for disabled people: Parking provided, ramped entry, toilet facilities
Special comments: Wheelchair-accessible study area available during opening hours, by appointment.

Constituent bodies: Museum Collection Division, Department of Art; tel: 020 7416 5342; e-mail: collections@iwm.org.uk; website: http://collections.iwm.org.uk
Museum Collection Division, Department of Documents; tel: 020 7416 5221; e-mail: docs@iwm.org.uk; website: http://collections.iwm.org.uk
Museum Collection Division, Department of Exhibits and Firearms; tel: 020 7416 5342; e-mail: collections@iwm.org.uk; website: http://collections.iwm.org.uk
Museum Collection Division, Photograph Archive; tel: 020 7416 5333; e-mail: photos@iwm.org.uk; website: http://collections.iwm.org.uk
Museum Collection Division, Sound Archive; tel: 020 7416 5342; e-mail: collections@iwm.org.uk; website: http://collections.iwm.org.uk
Museum Collection Division, United Kingdom National Inventory of War Memorials; tel: 020 7416 5353; e-mail: memorials@iwm.org.uk; website: http://www.ukniwm.org.uk

IMS PRUSSIA COVE (IMS)

Formal name: International Musicians Seminar, Prussia Cove

32 Grafton Square, London, SW4 0DB

Tel: 020 7720 9020
Fax: 020 7720 9033
E-mail: rosie@i-m-s.org.uk

Enquiries to: Administrator

Founded: 1972

Organisation type and purpose:
International organisation, registered charity (charity number 270204), suitable for ages: 16 to 30.
Music master classes, strings and piano for advanced international young musicians.

Subject coverage: Master classes/seminars provide a totally professional atmosphere and aim to foster the highest level of advanced study, drawing inspiration from the mid-European tradition.

Access to staff: Contact by letter, by telephone, by fax and by e-mail
Hours: Mon to Fri, 0900 to 1700

INCORE, UNIVERSITY OF ULSTER

Formal name: Institute for Conflict Resolution

Aberfoyle House, Northland Road, Londonderry, BT48 7JA

Tel: 028 7137 5500
Fax: 028 7137 5510
E-mail: incore@incore.ulst.ac.uk
Website: www.incore.ulst.ac.uk

Enquiries to: Administrator

Founded: 1991

Organisation type and purpose:
International organisation, membership association (membership is by election or invitation), present number of members: 700, university department or institute, research organisation.
Promote communication between networks of international scholars.

Subject coverage: Ethnic and community conflict, especially in relation to education, churches, voluntary and community groups, material conditions; controlled or regulated conflict; conflict resolution; international conflict resolution.

Collection: Collection of novels relating to the Northern Ireland conflict
Collection of political ephemera relating to the Northern Ireland conflict

Library catalogue: All or part available in-house

Publications: Printed

Publications list: Available online and in print

Access to staff: Contact by letter, by telephone, by fax, by e-mail and via website. Appointment necessary.
Hours: Mon to Fri, 0900 to 1700

Access to building: No access other than to staff

Access for disabled people: Parking provided, level entry

Collaborates with: Initiative on Conflict Resolution and Ethnicity (INCORE)

Links with: Conflict Archive on the Internet (CAIN)

INCORPORATED ASSOCIATION OF ORGANISTS (IAO)

13, St Flora's Road, Littlehampton, West Sussex BN17 6BD

Tel: 01903 725 002
E-mail: ikb13@live.co.uk
Website: www.iao.org.uk

Enquiries to: General Secretary

Founded: 1913

Organisation type and purpose:
Membership association (membership is by subscription), present number of members: 6,000, registered charity (charity number 269986).

Subject coverage: Organists and all lovers of the pipe organ and its music.

Publications: Printed

Access to staff: Contact by letter, by e-mail and via website
Hours: Mon to Fri, 0900 to 1700

INCORPORATED COUNCIL OF LAW REPORTING FOR ENGLAND AND WALES (ICLR)

Megarry House, 119 Chancery Lane, London, WC2A 1PP

Tel: 020 7242 6471
Fax: 020 7831 5247
E-mail: postmaster@iclr.co.uk
Website: www.iclr.co.uk

Enquiries to: Chief Executive Officer

Direct e-mail: enquiries@iclr.co.uk

Founded: 1865

Organisation type and purpose:
Professional body, registered charity (charity number 250605), publishing house.
Preparation and publication of reports of judicial decisions of the superior and appellate courts in England.

Subject coverage: Reports (prepared by barristers) of judicial decisions of the superior and appellate courts in England.

Publications: Printed, and electronic and video
Order electronic and video publications from: Available online at http://www.iclr.co.uk

Publications list: Available online and in print

Access to staff: Contact by letter, by telephone, by fax, by e-mail and via website. Appointment necessary.
Hours: Mon to Fri, 0900 to 1700

Access to building: No prior appointment required

INCORPORATED FROEBEL EDUCATIONAL INSTITUTE (IFEI)

Templeton Priory Lane, London, SW15 5JW

Tel: 020 8878 7546
Fax: 020 8876 2753

Enquiries to: Secretary

Founded: 1892

Organisation type and purpose: University department or institute, suitable for ages: 3 to 16, research organisation.

Collection: Froebel Education Archive

Publications: Printed

Access to staff: Contact by letter, by telephone and by fax. Appointment necessary.
Hours: Mon to Fri, 0900 to 1700

INCORPORATED PHONOGRAPHIC SOCIETY (IPS)

Bishopsgate Institute, 230 Bishopsgate, London, EC2M 4QH

Tel: 020 8684 9984
Fax: 020 8684 9984
Website: www.the-ipa.org.uk

Enquiries to: Administrator
Direct e-mail: jhdorrington@hotmail.com

Founded: 1872

Organisation type and purpose:
Membership association (membership is by subscription, qualification).
Examining body for shorthand and typewriting.

Subject coverage: Pitman's shorthand (otherwise known as phonography); history of shorthand (not restricted to Pitman's); history of writing machines (mainly typewriters).

Collection: Books about and printed in Pitman shorthand; books about typewriting

Publications: Printed

Access to staff: Contact by letter, by telephone, by fax and by e-mail
Hours: Mon to Fri, 0900 to 1700

INCORPORATED SOCIETY OF MUSICIANS (ISM)

10 Stratford Place, London, W1C 1AA

Tel: 020 7079 1202
Fax: 020 7408 1538
E-mail: membership@ism.org
Website: www.ism.org

Enquiries to: Chief Executive
Other contacts: Head of Professional Development (for policy development); Head of Legal and General Services (for casework)

Founded: 1882

Organisation type and purpose:
Professional body, training organisation.

Subject coverage: Private music teachers, musicians at all stages of education, solo, ensemble and orchestral performers, composers and conductors.

Publications: Printed, and electronic and video

Publications list: Available online and in print

Access to staff: Contact by letter, by telephone, by fax and by e-mail
Hours: Mon to Fri, 0930 to 1730

INDEPENDENT ASSOCIATION OF PREP SCHOOLS (IAPS)

11 Waterloo Place, Leamington Spa, Warwickshire, CV32 5LA

Tel: 01926 887833
Fax: 01926 888014
E-mail: iaps@iaps.org.uk
Website: www.iaps.org.uk

Enquiries to: Association Administrator

Founded: 1892

Organisation type and purpose:
International organisation, professional body, membership association (membership is by election).

Subject coverage: Preparatory school education.

Publications: Printed
Order printed publications from: Distribution Manager, Attain Magazine, Chapel Studios, High Street, Moreton-in-Marsh, Gloucestershire, GL56 0AX

Access to staff: Contact by letter, by telephone, by fax, by e-mail, in person and via website. Appointment necessary.
Hours: Mon to Fri, 0830 to 1700

Access to building: Prior appointment required

Member organisation of: Independent Schools Council; St Vincent House, 30 Orange Street, London, WC2H 7HH; tel: 020 7766 7070; fax: 020 7766 7071; e-mail: office@isc.co.uk; website: http://www.isc.co.uk

INDEPENDENT PANEL OF ARBITRATORS

c/o Retail Motor Industry Federation, 9 North Street, Rugby, Warwickshire, CV21 2AB

Tel: 01788 538317
Fax: 01788 538326

Enquiries to: Administrator

Organisation type and purpose: To provide an alternative complaint redress mechanism for motor trade related matters.

Subject coverage: Independent arbitration on complaints about motor vehicles.

Access to staff: Contact by letter and by fax
Hours: Mon to Fri, 0900 to 1700

Access to building: No access other than to staff

INDEPENDENT POLICE COMPLAINTS COMMISSION (IPCC)

PO Box 473, Sale, M33 0BW

Tel: 0300 020 0096 ; mincom: 020 7404 0431
Fax: 020 7404 0430
E-mail: julia.davies@ipcc.gsi.gov.uk
Website: www.ipcc.gov.uk

Enquiries to: Chairman
Direct e-mail: enquiries@ipcc.gsi.gov.uk

Founded: 1985; carries out the functions of the former Police Complaints Authority (year of change 2004)

Organisation type and purpose: Statutory body.

Trade and statistical information: Data on police complaints in England and Wales

Publications: Printed
Order printed publications from: For charged publications: Stationery Office, PO Box 276, London, SW8 5DT, tel. 0845 7023474 (for orders), fax: 0870 600 5533, e-mail: book .orders@theso.co.uk

Publications list: Available in print

Access to staff: Contact by letter, by telephone, by e-mail and via website. Appointment necessary.
Hours: Complaints against police can be made at any police station or in writing to the PCA

Parent body: Home Office; Queen Anne's Gate, London, SW1H 9AT

INDEPENDENT PUBLISHERS GUILD (IPG)

PO Box 93, Royston, Hertfordshire, SG8 5GH

Tel: 01763 247014
Fax: 01763 246293
E-mail: info@ipg.uk.com
Website: www.ipg.uk.com

Enquiries to: Executive Director
Direct e-mail: bridget@ipg.uk.com

Founded: 1962

Organisation type and purpose: Trade association (membership is by subscription), present number of members: 310.

Subject coverage: Publishing.

continued overleaf

Publications: Electronic and video

Access to staff: Contact by e-mail and via website. Access for members only.
Hours: Variable hours, e-mail is fastest

INDEPENDENT SCHOOLS COUNCIL (ISC)

St Vincent House, 30 Orange Street, London, WC2H 7HH

Tel: 0845 724 6657
Fax: 020 7766 7071
Website: www.isc.co.uk

Enquiries to: Senior Information Officer
Direct tel: 020 7766 7067
Direct e-mail: liam.butler@isc.co.uk

Founded: 1973

Organisation type and purpose: The Independent Schools Council works with its members to promote and preserve the quality, diversity and excellence of UK independent education both at home and abroad.
ISC's core principles are:
- The importance of a strong and diverse independent sector, founded on a belief in adding value for the individual child
- The widening of opportunity for children from all backgrounds to achieve their potential
- Access to Higher Education on merit, with each child treated as an individual, and with transparent information on the admissions process
- The widening of opportunity for parents to choose the best education for their child
- Open access to professional development, on equal terms, for teachers in the maintained and independent sectors
- The widening of opportunities for teachers to gain experience in both the maintained and independent sectors, and the removal of barriers to transfer between the sectors
- Co-operation between the maintained and independent sectors to improve outcomes for all children
- The importance of an independent sector participating fully in the national debate on educational issues.

Subject coverage: Independent schools.

Access to staff: Contact by letter, by telephone, by fax, by e-mail and via website
Hours: Mon to Fri, 0900 to 1700

Constituent bodies: Girls' Schools Association; Governing Bodies Association; Governing Bodies of Girls Schools Association; Headmasters' and Headmistresses' Conference; Incorporated Association of Preparatory Schools; Independent Schools Association Incorporated; Independent Schools Bursars' Association; Society of Headmasters and Headmistresses of Independent Schools

INDEPENDENT SCHOOLS COUNCIL INFORMATION SERVICE (ISCis)

Grosvenor Gardens House, 35–37 Grosvenor Gardens, London, SW1W 0BS

Tel: 020 7798 1500
Fax: 020 7798 1501
E-mail: info@iscis.uk.net
Website: www.isc.co.uk

Enquiries to: Press Officer
Direct tel: 020 7766 7067
Direct e-mail: hayley.dunlop@isc.co.uk

Founded: 1972

Organisation type and purpose:
Membership association, present number of members: 1,300 schools, suitable for ages: 1 to 19, consultancy.
Information service for parents, media, researchers, academics, government departments and politicians.

Subject coverage: Independent schools in the UK, details of nearly 1,300 schools, plus statistical surveys and services for the media and politicians, placement services for parents overseas who want their children educated in the UK (below university level).

Trade and statistical information: Statistical surveys of independent schools in the UK

Publications: Printed, and electronic and video

Publications list: Available in print

Access to staff: Contact by letter, by telephone, by fax, by e-mail, in person and via website
Hours: Mon to Fri, 0900 to 1700

Parent body: Independent Schools Council (ISC); tel: 020 7798 1590; fax: 020 7798 1591

Sponsored by: Governing Bodies Association; Governing Bodies of Girls Schools Association; Incorporated Association of Preparatory Schools; Independent Schools Association

INDEPENDENT WASTE PAPER PROCESSORS ASSOCIATION (IWPPA)

Heritage House, Vicar Lane, Daventry, NN11 4GD

Tel: 01327 703223
Fax: 01327 300612
E-mail: admin@iwppa.co.uk

Enquiries to: Chief Executive

Founded: 1975

Organisation type and purpose: Trade association.

Subject coverage: Waste paper; disposal and recycling.

Access to staff: Contact by letter and by e-mail
Hours: Mon to Fri, 0900 to 1700

INDEPENDENTAGE (FORMERLY THE ROYAL UNITED KINGDOM BENEFICENT ASSOCIATION) (RUKBA)

6 Avonmore Road, London, W14 8RL

Tel: 020 7605 4200
Fax: 020 7605 4201
E-mail: charity@independentage.org.uk
Website: www.independentage.org.uk

Enquiries to: Director

Founded: 1863

Organisation type and purpose:
Membership association, registered charity (charity number 210729).
To help elderly people on very low incomes to stay in their own homes.

Subject coverage: Care for elderly or infirm people who have devoted their personal or professional lives to others; IndependentAge maintains independence through the provision of a regular, small additional income and the practical support of over 1,000 volunteers.
RUKBA also runs three residential and nursing homes. Help may be available with care home fees.

Publications: Printed

Access to staff: Contact by letter, by telephone and by fax
Hours: Mon to Fri, 0900 to 1700

Trustees for: Universal Beneficent Society; at the same address

INDIA DEVELOPMENT GROUP (UK) LIMITED (IDG(UK))

68 Downlands Road, Purley, Surrey, CR8 4JF

Tel: 020 8668 3161
Fax: 020 8660 8541
E-mail: idguk@clara.co.uk

Enquiries to: Chief Executive
Other contacts: Administrator

Founded: April 1970

Organisation type and purpose: Voluntary organisation, registered charity (charity number 291167), training organisation, consultancy, research organisation.
To promote economic, social and educational development of India's rural areas where the majority of people live, to reverse drift to urban areas unable to absorb them.

Subject coverage: Alleviation of poverty and the generation of income in the backward areas of India. Development of appropriate technology.

Access to staff: Contact by letter, by telephone, by fax and by e-mail
Hours: Mon to Fri, 1000 to 1500

Links with: Schumacher Institute of Appropriate Technology; Village Melhaur, Chinhat, Lucknow (UP), India

INDIA HOUSE LIBRARY

High Commission of India, India House, Aldwych, London, WC2B 4NA

Tel: 020 7632 3166
E-mail: administration@hcilondon.in
Website: www.meagor.nic.in
Website: www.ficci.com
Website: www.culturopedia.com
Website: www.indiagov.nic.in
Website: www.nic.in
Website: www.ciionline.org.com
Website: www.nic.in/ncti
Website: www.hci.london.net
Website: www.mapsofindia.com/maps
Website: www.commin.nic.in

Enquiries to: Librarian

Founded: c. 1925

Organisation type and purpose:
Governmental body of the Indian Ministry of External Affairs, New Delhi.

Subject coverage: India and Indian affairs, mainly from 1950.

Collection: Indian Central Government Official publications from 1950 to approximately 1980, mainly economic (now in the Brynmor Jones Library, University of Hull)

Trade and statistical information: Available from the Economic Department in the High Commission

Library catalogue: All or part available in-house

Publications: Electronic and video
Order printed publications from: Publications Manager, Central News Agency Private Limited
P-23 Connaught Circus, PO Box 374, New Delhi, 110 001, India, tel: 00 91 11 3364448, fax: 00 91 11 7526036, e-mail: info@can-india.com
Order electronic and video publications from: CD Division, India High Commission
240 Okala Industrial Estate, Phase III, New Delhi, 110 020, fax: 00 91 11 6919073
Multisynic Trends Inc
186 Laauwe Avenue, Wayne, New Jersey, 07470, USA, fax: 00 1 201 595 8281

Access to staff: Contact by letter, by telephone and by fax
Hours: Mon to Fri, 0900 to 1700

Access to building: By appointment

INDIAN INSTITUTE READING ROOM

Bodleian Library, Broad Street, Oxford, OX1 3BG

Tel: 01865 287300
Fax: 01865 277182
E-mail: indian.institute@bodley.ox.ac.uk
Website: www.ouls.ox.ac.uk/bodley/library/rooms/iirr
Website: www.bodley.ox.ac.uk/oxlip

Enquiries to: Librarian
Direct tel: 01865 277083
Direct e-mail: gillian.evison@bodley.ox.ac.uk

Organisation type and purpose: University library.

Subject coverage: All subjects and languages of South Asia and Tibet, excluding natural sciences; secondary material only for Afghanistan, Burma (Myanmar).

Collection: Malan Collection
Monier Williams Collection
Whinfield Collection

Non-library collection catalogue: All or part available online

Library catalogue: All or part available online

Access to staff: Contact by letter, by telephone, by fax and by e-mail. Appointment necessary.
Hours: Mon to Fri, 0900 to 1700
Special comments: See details: http://www.ouls.ox.ac.uk/bodley/services/admissions

Access for disabled people: See details: http://www.ouls.ox.ac.uk/bodley/services/disability

Constituent part of: Bodleian Library, University of Oxford; Broad Street, Oxford, OX1 3BG; e-mail: reader.services@ouls.ox.ac.uk; website: http://www.ouls.ox.ac.uk/bodley/home

INDIAN MILITARY HISTORICAL SOCIETY (IMHS)

33 High Street, Tilbrook, Huntingdon, Cambridgeshire, PE28 0JP

Tel: 01480 860437
E-mail: info@imhs.org.uk
Website: www.imhs.org.uk

Enquiries to: Honorary Secretary

Founded: 1983

Organisation type and purpose: International organisation, membership association (membership is by subscription), present number of members: 230, research organisation.

Subject coverage: History of service units in India both before and after independence, including details of uniforms, medals, badges, buttons and other militaria. These include: Royal Navy, British Army and Royal Air Force units that have served in India; Units of the Honourable East India Company's Army and Marine prior to 1861; the Indian Army subsequent to 1861, including the European Volunteer Corps; the Royal Indian Marine and the Royal Indian Navy; the Army of Nepal and those of the Princely States; the present day Armed Services of India, Pakistan and Bangladesh, including Frontier Corps, Paramilitary and Police Units.

Non-library collection catalogue: All or part available online

Publications: Printed

Access to staff: Contact by letter, by e-mail and via website
Hours: Mon to Fri, 0900 to 1700

INDIAN MOTOCYCLE CLUB OF GB

2 Keswick Drive, Cullercoats, North Shields, Tyne & Wear, NE30 3EW

Tel: 01912 522840
E-mail: jdwright@netcomuk.co.uk
Website: www.indianmotocycle.co.uk

Enquiries to: Membership Secretary

Founded: 1989

Organisation type and purpose: Membership association (membership is by subscription), present number of members: 150.

Subject coverage: Indian motocycles manufactured in the USA between 1901 and 1953.

Collection: Part books and workshop manuals available for use by club members only

Publications: Printed

Access to staff: Contact by letter. Access for members only.
Hours: Mon to Fri, 0900 to 1700

INDIVIDUAL TRAVELLERS CO LTD (ITC Ltd)

Spring Mill, Earby, Barnoldswick, Lancashire, BB94 0AA

Tel: 0845 604 3877
E-mail: itcpno@holidaycottagesgroup.com
Website: www.individualtravellers.com

Enquiries to: Director

Founded: 1976

Organisation type and purpose: Service industry.
Tour operator.

Subject coverage: Self-catering in France, Italy, Spain and Portugal, New England, Sicily, Corsica, Mallorca.

Publications: Printed

Publications list: Available online

Access to staff: Contact by letter, by telephone, by fax, by e-mail, in person and via website
Hours: Mon to Fri, 0900 to 1730

Access to building: No prior appointment required

Links with: Individual Travellers Spain and Portugal; tel: 01798 869461; fax: 01798 869343; e-mail: spain@indiv-travellers.com; New England Country Homes; tel: 01798 869461; fax: 01798 869343; e-mail: newengland@indiv-travellers.com; Vacances en Campagne; tel: 01798 869461; fax: 01798 869343; e-mail: france@indiv-travellers.com; Vacanze in Italia; tel: 01798 869461; fax: 01798 869343; e-mail: italy@indiv-travellers.com

INDUSTRIAL CLEANING MACHINE MANUFACTURERS' ASSOCIATION (ICMMA)

PO Box 12492, Solihull, West Midlands, B91 9AX

Tel: 0121 703 0636
E-mail: icmma@icmma.org.uk
Website: www.icmma.org.uk

Enquiries to: Director

Founded: 1961

Organisation type and purpose: Trade association.

Subject coverage: Manufacture and marketing of industrial cleaning machines.

Access to staff: Contact by letter and via website
Hours: Mon to Fri, 0900 to 1700

Member of: BEAMA Ltd

INDUSTRIAL DEVELOPMENT BANGOR (UWB) LIMITED (IDB Ltd)

University of Wales Bangor, Dean Street, Bangor, Gwynedd, LL57 1UT

Tel: 01248 382749
Fax: 01248 372105
E-mail: info@idbsystems.co.uk
Website: www.idb.wales.com

Enquiries to: Managing Director
Direct tel: 01248 382748
Direct e-mail: emlyn@idb.wales.com

continued overleaf

Founded: 1978

Organisation type and purpose: Manufacturing industry, consultancy, research organisation.
Engineering company.
Strengthen links between industry and academia.

Subject coverage: Design and manufacture of specialist electronic instrumentation: in particular, portable simultaneous translation systems, navigation and location by satellite, electrostatic monitors, instrumentation for nuclear and hydro-electric power generation industries.

Publications: Printed

Publications list: Available online and in print

Access to staff: Appointment necessary.
Hours: Mon to Fri, 0900 to 1700

Access to building: Prior appointment required

Access for disabled people: Parking provided, ramped entry, level entry, access to all public areas

Parent body: University of Wales Bangor (UWB)

INDUSTRIAL INJURIES ADVISORY COUNCIL (IIAC)

2nd Floor, Caxton House, Tothill Street, London, SW1H 9NA

Tel: 020 7449 5618
E-mail: iiac@dwp.gsi.gov.uk
Website: iiac.independent.gov.uk

Other contacts: Secretary (for formal questions or comment to the Council)

Organisation type and purpose: IIAC is an independent body that advises the Secretary of State for Work and Pensions on the Industrial Injuries Disablement Benefit scheme.

Subject coverage: Industrial diseases.

Library catalogue: All or part available online and in print

Publications list: Available online and in print

INDUSTRIAL MARKETING RESEARCH ASSOCIATION (IMRA)

18 St Peters Steps, Brixham, Devon, TQ5 9TE

Tel: 01803 859575

Enquiries to: Director General
Other contacts: Chairman

Founded: 1963

Organisation type and purpose: Professional body (membership is by election or invitation).

Subject coverage: Industrial market research, international marketing research.

Non-library collection catalogue: All or part available in-house

Library catalogue: All or part available in-house

Publications: Printed

Access to staff: Contact by letter. Non-members charged.
Hours: Mon to Fri, 0900 to 1700

Access to building: No access other than to staff

Member of: European Council for Industrial Marketing (CEMI); Industrial Marketing Council (in the UK); International Marketing Federation

INDUSTRIAL RELATIONS RESEARCH UNIT (IRRU)

Warwick Business School, University of Warwick, Coventry, CV4 7AL

Tel: 024 7652 4268
Fax: 024 7652 4184
E-mail: irruoffice@wbs.ac.uk
Website: www2.warwick.ac.uk/fac/soc/wbs/research/irru

Enquiries to: Director
Direct tel: 024 7652 4272

Founded: 1970

Organisation type and purpose: University department or institute, research organisation.

Subject coverage: Industrial relations.

Publications: Printed

Publications list: Available online

Access to staff: Contact by letter, by telephone, by fax, by e-mail and via website
Hours: Mon to Fri, 0830 to 1630

INDUSTRIAL ROPE ACCESS TRADE ASSOCIATION (IRATA)

Evelyn Woods Road, Aldershot, Hampshire, GU11 2LL

Tel: 01252 357839
Fax: 01252 357831
E-mail: info@irata.org
Website: www.irata.org

Enquiries to: Administrator
Direct e-mail: wendy@irata.org

Organisation type and purpose: Trade association, present number of members: 38.
Equipment suppliers, trainers and operators involved in rope access for industrial purposes.

Publications: Printed

Publications list: Available in print

Access to staff: Contact by letter, by e-mail and via website
Hours: Mon to Fri, 0900 to 1700

INFERTILITY NETWORK UK (INUK)

Formal name: Infertility Network UK

114 Lichfield Street, Walsall, West Midlands, WS1 1SZ

Tel: 08701 188088
Fax: 01424 731858
Website: www.issue.co.uk
Website: www.moretolife.co.uk

Enquiries to: Chief Executive
Other contacts: Chair

Founded: 1976

Organisation type and purpose: National organisation, membership association (membership is by subscription), present number of members: 3,000, voluntary organisation, registered charity (charity number 1099960).
Support group.
To help people through the infertility maze with information, counselling and support at regional and national levels.

Subject coverage: Infertility, treatment, adoption and fostering, alternatives to childlessness, coping and living with childlessness.

Publications: Printed, and electronic and video

Publications list: Available online and in print

Access to staff: Contact by letter, by telephone, by fax, by e-mail and via website
Hours: Mon to Fri, 0830 to 1700

Access for disabled people: Yes

Member of the: International Federation of Infertility Patient Associations

INFLUENCE DESIGN ASSOCIATES LTD

Influence House, 10 Moorfield Grove, Heaton Moor, Stockport, Cheshire SK4 4BQ

Tel: 0870 228 2272
Fax: 0870 228 2202
E-mail: samueln@influencedesign.com
Website: www.influencedesign.com

Enquiries to: Administrator
Direct e-mail: info@influencedesign.com
Other contacts: Personal Assistant

Founded: 1992

Organisation type and purpose: Membership association (membership is by qualification), service industry, consultancy.
Design to print and production.

Library catalogue: All or part available online

Access to staff: Contact by letter, by fax and by e-mail
Hours: Mon to Fri, 0900 to 1700

INFONORTICS LIMITED

15 Market Place, Tetbury, Gloucestershire, GL8 8DD

Tel: 01666 505772
Fax: 01666 505774
E-mail: contact-1@infonortics.com
Website: www.infonortics.eu

Enquiries to: Managing Director

Founded: 1988

Organisation type and purpose: Conference organiser.

Subject coverage: Information, documentation, chemical information, competitive intelligence, information technology, search engines.

Publications list: Available online

Access to staff: Contact by letter, by telephone, by fax, by e-mail and via website

Hours: Mon to Fri, 0900 to 1700

Access to building: No access other than to staff

INFORMATION CENTRE, COBHAM TECHNICAL SERVICES

Cleeve Road, Leatherhead, Surrey, KT22 7SA

Tel: 01372 367007
Fax: 01372 367009
E-mail: era.info@cobham.com
Website: www.cobham.com/technicalservices

Enquiries to: Information Officer
Direct fax: 01372 367009
Direct e-mail: era.info@cobham.com

Founded: 1920

Organisation type and purpose: International organisation, service industry.
ERA Technology works at the leading edge of many advanced technologies and provides specialist, technology-based services including design and development, testing, assessment and expert advice. ERA has capabilities in electrical, electronic, software and communications engineering, RF microwave and radar, complex EMC, risk analysis, safety engineering, reliability and failure analysis, plant integrity, microelectronics and materials technologies.

Subject coverage: Electrotechnology; computing technology; electrical and electronic engineering; energy conservation; alternative energy; product design and prototype construction; new materials; testing and certification; regulatory compliance; national and international standardisation; explosion hazards; electromagnetic compatibility; servocomponents; electric motors; insulation; cables; radio frequency technology; electromechanical engineering; engineering materials; materials science; failure analysis.

Library catalogue: All or part available in-house

Publications: Printed

Publications list: Available online and in print

Access to staff: Contact by letter, by telephone, by fax, by e-mail and via website. Appointment necessary. Non-members charged.
Hours: Mon to Fri, 0900 to 1700
Special comments: Certain services are charged for.

Access to building: Prior appointment required

INFORMATION COMMISSIONER'S OFFICE (ICO)

Wycliffe House, Water Lane, Wilmslow, Cheshire, SK9 5AF

Tel: 01625 545745
Fax: 01625 524510
E-mail: mail@ico.gsi.gov.uk
Website: www.ico.gov.uk

Enquiries to: Marketing & Communications Officer

Founded: 1984

Organisation type and purpose: Statutory body; non-departmental government organisation.
To enforce the Data Protection Act and the Freedom of Information Act.

Subject coverage: Data Protection Act 1984 and its implications and application. The Freedom of Information Act 2000.

Publications: Printed, and electronic and video

Publications list: Available online and in print

Access to staff: Contact by letter, by telephone, by fax, by e-mail, in person and via website
Hours: Mon to Fri, 0900 to 1700

INFORMATION DIRECT

Central Library, Chamberlain Square, Birmingham, B3 3HQ

Tel: 0121 303 4531
Fax: 0121 303 4532
E-mail: information.direct@birmingham.gov.uk

Enquiries to: Information Officer

Founded: 1989

Organisation type and purpose: Local government body.
Fee-based business research and enquiry service.

Subject coverage: Business information, company information, market intelligence, mailing lists, company formations.

Access to staff: Contact by letter, by telephone, by fax and by e-mail. Appointment necessary. All charged.
Hours: Mon to Fri, 0900 to 1700

Parent body: Birmingham Library Service

INFORMATION FOR SCHOOL AND COLLEGE GOVERNORS (ISCG)

Avondale Park School, Sirdar Road, London, W11 4EE

Tel: 020 7229 0200
Fax: 020 7229 0651
E-mail: iscg@governors.fsnet.co.uk

Enquiries to: Secretary

Founded: 1991

Organisation type and purpose: Advisory body, research organisation.
An independent research and information service for governors.

Subject coverage: Current concerns and needs of school and college governors.

Publications: Printed

Publications list: Available in print

Access to staff: Contact by letter, by telephone, by fax, by e-mail and via website. Appointment necessary.
Hours: Mon to Fri, 1100 to 1600
Special comments: Answerphone when office closed.

Access to building: No access other than to staff

INFORMATION ON TRANQUILLISERS AND ANTIDEPRESSANTS (CITA)

Cavendish House, Brighton Road, Waterloo, Merseyside, L22 5NG

Tel: 0151 474 9626
Fax: 0151 284 8324
Website: www.citawithdrawal.org.uk

Enquiries to: Administrator

Founded: 1987; formerly called Council for Involuntary Tranquilliser Addiction

Organisation type and purpose: National organisation, advisory body, voluntary organisation, registered charity (charity number 519334), training organisation.
To provide support, counselling and GP clinics for those withdrawing from involuntary tranquilliser addiction.

Subject coverage: Sufferers as a result of taking tranquillisers, sleeping pills or anti-depressants, benzodiazepine and tranquilliser withdrawal, anxiety management.

Publications: Printed, and electronic and video

Publications list: Available in print

Access to staff: Contact by letter, by telephone and by fax
Hours: Mon to Fri, 1000 to 1300

INFORMATION WORLD REVIEW (IWR)

Bizmedia Ltd, 80–82 Chiswick High Road, London W4 1SY

Tel: 020 8995 9345
E-mail: peterw@bizmedia.co.uk
Website: www.iwr.co.uk

Enquiries to: Editor

Founded: 1977

Organisation type and purpose: Business publisher.

Subject coverage: Online information retrieval; optical publishing and storage; artificial intelligence software and tools.

Publications list: Available in print

Access to staff: Contact by letter, by telephone and by e-mail
Hours: Mon to Fri, 0930 to 1730

Parent body: Bizmedia Ltd

INFOTERRA LTD

Atlas House, 41 Wembley Road, Leicester, LE3 1UT

Tel: 0116 273 2300
Fax: 0116 273 2400
E-mail: info@infoterra-global.com
Website: www.infoterra.co.uk
Website: www.geostore.com

Organisation type and purpose: Geo-information products and services

Subject coverage: Provider of geographic information products and services, including airborne and satellite data acquisition, geo-information creation, database management and outsourced hosting. Provides geospatial knowledge to companies world-wide.

continued overleaf

Collection: Landsat and Spot satellites UK archive, a complete UK collection of photographic proof available with an image browse facility
IRS and IKONOS data
Remote Sensing Society Library

Publications: Printed

Publications list: Available online and in print

Access to staff: Contact by telephone and by e-mail. Appointment necessary. All charged.
Hours: Mon to Fri, 0900 to 1700

Also at: Infoterra France SAS; 31 rue des Cosmonautes, 31402 Toulouse, cedex 4, France; tel: +33 562 19 55 70; fax: +33 562 19 97 81; e-mail: info@infoterra-global.com; website: http://www.infoterra-global.com
Infoterra GmbH; tel: +49 7545 8 9969; fax: +49 7545 8 5650; e-mail: info@infoterra-global.com; website: http://www.infoterra-global.com
Infoterra Hungary Kft; Soroksari ut 48, 7ep, 11.em, 1095 Budapest. Hungary; tel: +361 468 3638; fax: +361 468 3640; e-mail: info@infoterra-global.com; website: http://www.infoterra.co.uk
Infoterra Ltd; Europa House, The Crescent, Southwood, Farnborough. Hampshire. GU14 0NL; tel: 01252 362000; fax: 01252 375016; e-mail: info@infoterra-global.com; website: http://www.infoterra.co.uk

Parent body: Astrium Limited; Anchorage Road, Portsmouth, Hampshire, PO3 5PU; website: http://www.astrium.eads.net

INLAND REVENUE LIBRARY AND INFORMATION SERVICE

1 Parliament Street, London, SW1A 2BQ

Enquiries to: Librarian

Organisation type and purpose: National government body.
Government library.

Subject coverage: Taxation (UK), Hansard, Public General Acts.

Access to staff: Contact by letter.
Appointment necessary.

INLAND WATERWAYS ASSOCIATION (IWA)

Island House, Moor Road, Chesham, HP5 1WA

Tel: 01494 783453
E-mail: iwa@waterways.org.uk
Website: www.waterways.org.uk

Enquiries to: Chief Executive
Direct e-mail: iwa@waterways.org.uk

Founded: 1946

Organisation type and purpose:
Membership association (membership is by subscription), present number of members: 18,000, registered charity (charity number 212342).
Campaigning for the retention, restoration, conservation and development of the inland waterways for the fullest possible commercial and recreational use.

Subject coverage: Restoration, retention and development of inland waterways in the British Isles, commercial and recreational use.

Collection: IWA John Heap Archive, at Boat Museum, Ellesmere Port

Publications: Printed, and electronic and video

Publications list: Available in print

Access to staff: Contact by letter, by telephone, by e-mail and via website
Hours: Mon to Fri, 0830 to 1630

Affiliated to: Inland Waterways Enterprises Ltd; IWA (Sales) Ltd; Waterway Recovery Group Ltd

INMARSAT

99 City Road, London, EC1Y 1AX

Tel: 020 7728 1777
Fax: 020 7728 1142
E-mail: customer_care@inmarsat.com
Website: www.inmarsat.com

Enquiries to: Information Officer
Direct e-mail: john_warehand@inmarsat.com

Founded: 1979

Organisation type and purpose: Mobile satellite communications operator.

Subject coverage: Satellite communications and related areas, mobile communications (land, sea, air), engineering; electronics, international communications etc.

Non-library collection catalogue: All or part available in-house

Publications list: Available online

Access to staff: Contact by letter and via website. Appointment necessary. Letter of introduction required.
Hours: Mon to Fri, 0900 to 1700

Access to building: Prior appointment required

Access for disabled people: Level entry, toilet facilities

INNER TEMPLE LIBRARY

Inner Temple, London, EC4Y 7DA

Tel: 020 7797 8217
Fax: 020 7583 6030
E-mail: library@innertemple.org.uk
Website: www.innertemplelibrary.org.uk

Enquiries to: Librarian and Keeper of Manuscripts
Direct e-mail: mclay@innertemple.org.uk

Founded: c.1500

Organisation type and purpose: Legal library.

Information services: General guides, database guides.

Collection: 70,000 vols on law of the United Kingdom and Commonwealth
Petyt Manuscripts (386 volumes)
Barrington Manuscripts (57 vols)
Inner Temple Records (39 vols)
Mitford Collection of Legal Manuscripts (79 vols)
Miscellaneous Manuscripts (211 vols)
Inner Temple Archives (16th century to present)

Library catalogue: All or part available online and in-house

Publications: Electronic and video

Access to staff: Contact by letter, by telephone, by fax and by e-mail.
Appointment necessary. Access for members only. Non-members charged.
Hours: Legal terms: Mon to Thu, 0900 to 2000; Fri, 0900 to 1900; every 4th Sat, during legal term time, in rotation with the other Inns of Court libraries, 1000 to 1700

Access to building: Open to all members of the Inns of Court; not open to the general public (researchers by written application to the Librarian)

INNERPEFFRAY LIBRARY

Innerpeffray by Crieff, Perthshire, PH7 3RF

Tel: 01764 652819
E-mail: info@innerpeffraylibrary.co.uk
Website: www.innerpeffraylibrary.co.uk

Enquiries to: Librarian

Founded: 1680

Organisation type and purpose: Registered charity (charity number SC 013843), museum, research organisation.
Reference library, library museum, first lending library in Scotland.

Subject coverage: Wide range of pre-1800 printed books, strong theological and religious content, natural history, history, agriculture, gardening, travel etc.

Collection: Accounts of Library etc
Borrowing records from 1747 to 1968
3,000 books published 1502 to 1800
1,400 volumes post 1801 AD
David Drummond Collection, 3rd Lord Maderty d.1692
Robert Hay-Drummond Collection, Archbishop of York d.1781
Visitor books

Library catalogue: All or part available online and in-house

Access to staff: Contact by letter, by telephone, by e-mail, in person and via website. All charged.
Hours: Wed to Sat, 1000 to 1645; Sun, 1400 to 1600

INNOVATION NORWAY

Charles House, 5–11 Lower Regent Street, London, SW1Y 4LR

Tel: 020 7389 8800
Fax: 020 7839 6014
E-mail: infouk@innovationnorway.no
Website: www.visitnorway.co.uk

Enquiries to: Consultant
Direct e-mail: infouk@innovationnorway.no

Organisation type and purpose: National organisation.
Government foundation.

Subject coverage: Tourism in Norway; hotel accommodation, camp sites and youth hostels; timetables and local or regional area brochures; conference facilities; tour operators; ferry companies and airlines.

Information is sent out on request.

Collection: Library of photographs and videos (strictly for use in travel promotion)

Access to staff: Contact by letter, by telephone, by fax, by e-mail and via website
Hours: Mon to Fri, 0900 to 1630
Special comments: Open to trade only – not public.

Parent body: Innovation Norway; PO Box 448, Sentrum, NO-0104, Oslo, Norway; tel: + 47 22 00 25 00; fax: + 47 22 00 25 01; e-mail: oslo@innovationnorway.no

INSOLVENCY PRACTITIONERS ASSOCIATION (IPA)

52–54 Gracechurch Street, London, EC3V 0EH

Tel: 020 7623 5108
Fax: 020 7623 5127
E-mail: secretariat@insolvency-practitioners.org.uk
Website: www.ipa.uk.com

Enquiries to: Secretary

Founded: 1961

Organisation type and purpose:
Professional body.
Association of 'full-time' insolvency practitioners (Recognised Professional Body under the Insolvency Act 1986).

Subject coverage: Insolvency.

Publications: Printed

Access to staff: Contact by letter
Hours: Mon to Fri, 0900 to 1700

Affiliated to: Insol International; SPI

INSPEC

Michael Faraday House, Six Hills Way, Stevenage, Hertfordshire, SG1 2AY

Tel: 01438 313311
Fax: 01438 767339
E-mail: inspec@theiet.org
Website: www.theiet.org/publications

Enquiries to: Managing Director

Organisation type and purpose: Learned society, professional body (membership is by qualification), publishing house.
Publishing, information and abstracting service; department of The Institution of Engineering and Technology.

Subject coverage: Physics, electrical engineering, electronics, control engineering, computing, information technology and manufacturing, mechanical and production engineering.

Publications: Printed, and electronic and video

Access to staff: Contact by letter, by telephone, by fax, by e-mail and via website
Hours: Mon to Fri, 0900 to 1700

Parent body: Institution of Engineering and Technology

INSTITUT FRANÇAIS – LA MÉDIATHÈQUE (IFRU)

Formal name: Institut Français du Royaume Uni

17 Queensberry Place, London, SW7 2DT

Tel: 020 7073 1350
Fax: 020 7073 1363
E-mail: library@ambafrance.org.uk
Website: www.institut-francais.org.uk

Enquiries to: Librarian
Direct tel: 020 7073 1354

Founded: 1910

Organisation type and purpose: National government body (membership is by subscription), present number of members: 4,500, public library.
French cultural centre.

Subject coverage: France: humanities, mainly literature, history, geography, travel guides, but also civilisation, history, philosophy, religion, social sciences, art, bibliography and linguistics (books mostly in French; a few in English).

Education services: Guided visits to school groups on request and by appointment.

Collection: 60,000 items (books, audio books, videos, DVDs, tapes)
French magazines and newspapers
Free French periodicals and special collection about France Libre and the French Resistance
Denis Saurat's archives

Non-library collection catalogue: All or part available online, in-house and in print

Library catalogue: All or part available online, in-house and in print

Publications: Printed, and electronic and video
Order electronic and video publications from: Conferences on line

Publications list: Available in print

Access to staff: Contact by letter, by telephone, by fax, by e-mail, in person and via website. Appointment necessary.
Hours: Tue to Fri, 1200 to 1900; Sat, 1200 to 1800
Children's Section: Tue to Sat, 1400 to 1800
Special comments: Closed 1 week at Christmas and all of August.

Access to building: No prior appointment required
Hours: 1200 to 1900

Access for disabled people: Access available for disabled, lift
Hours: 1200 to 1900

Also at: Institut Français; Language Centre, 14 Cromwell Place, London, SW7 2JR; tel: 020 7581 2701; fax: 020 7581 0061; e-mail: language-center@ambafrance.org.uk; website: http://www.institut-francais.org.uk
Institut Français; Children's Library, 29 Harrington Road, London SW7; tel: 020 7073 1350; fax: 020 7073 1363; e-mail: library@ambafrance.org.uk; website: http://www.institut-francais.org.uk

INSTITUTE AND FACULTY OF ACTUARIES

Staple Inn Hall, High Holborn, London, WC1V 7QJ

Tel: 020 7632 2114
Fax: 020 7632 2111
E-mail: libraries@actuaries.org.uk
Website: www.actuaries.org.uk

Enquiries to: Librarian
Direct e-mail: david.raymont@actuaries.org.uk

Founded: 1848; please select Institute of Actuaries
Faculty of Actuaries (year of change 2010)

Organisation type and purpose:
Professional body (membership is by qualification), present number of members: 16,850.

Subject coverage: Actuarial science, life assurance, general insurance, pensions, employee benefits, friendly societies, social security, investment, demography, mortality, probability, risk theory, histories of insurance and life assurance companies.

Collection: Small photograph collection
Small rare book and manuscript collection

Trade and statistical information:
Demographic statistics, mortality statistics

Non-library collection catalogue: All or part available online and in-house

Library catalogue: All or part available online

Publications: Printed, and electronic and video, and microform publications
Order printed publications from: Publications Officer

Publications list: Available online and in print

Access to staff: Contact by letter, by telephone, by fax, by e-mail and via website. Appointment necessary.

Access to building: *Hours:* Mon to Fri, 0900 to 1700

Access for disabled people: Level entry, toilet facilities

Also at: Institute and Faculty of Actuaries; Maclaurin House, 18 Dublin Street, Edinburgh, EH1 3PP; tel: 0131 240 1311; fax: 0131 240 1313; e-mail: libraries@actuaries.org.uk; Institute and Faculty of Actuaries, Staple Inn; Staple Inn Hall, High Holborn, London, WC1V 7QJ; tel: 020 7632 2111; e-mail: libraries@actuaries.org.uk

Member organisation of: Groupe Consultatif des Associations d'Actuaires des Pays des Communautés Européennes

INSTITUTE FOR ADVANCED STUDIES IN THE HUMANITIES

University of Edinburgh, Hope Park Square, Edinburgh, EH8 9NW

Tel: 0131 650 4671
Fax: 0131 668 2252
E-mail: iash@ed.ac.uk
Website: www.iash.ed.ac.uk/

Enquiries to: Director

Founded: 1970

continued overleaf

Organisation type and purpose: University department or institute.
Department of the University of Edinburgh. To promote scholarship in the Humanities and to further inter-disciplinary enquiries, by means of research fellowships, seminars, lectures and cultural events.

Subject coverage: All fields of the humanities very widely defined i.e. all departments of arts faculties, social sciences, theology, music and law.

Collection: Small private library available only to elected fellows of the Institute or by arrangement

Non-library collection catalogue: All or part available online

Library catalogue: All or part available in-house

Publications: Printed

Publications list: Available in print

Access to staff: Contact by letter, by telephone, by fax, by e-mail and via website
Hours: Mon to Fri, 0900 to 1700

Parent body: University of Edinburgh

INSTITUTE FOR ANIMAL HEALTH – COMPTON LABORATORY (IAH)

Compton, Newbury, Berkshire, RG20 7NN

Tel: 01635 577256
E-mail: compton.library@bbsrc.ac.uk
Website: www.iah.bbsrc.ac.uk

Enquiries to: IAH Libraries Manager (IAH Compton & IAH Pirbright Laboratories)
Direct e-mail: chris.gibbons@bbsrc.ac.uk

Organisation type and purpose: Research organisation.

Subject coverage: Diseases of economic importance in farm animals (exotic and endemic), immunology, molecular biology, veterinary science.

Collection: Specialist libraries on veterinary science

Library catalogue: All or part available in-house

Access to staff: Contact by letter, by telephone, by fax and by e-mail
Hours: Mon to Thu, 0900 to 1700; Fri, 0900 to 1630

Constituent part of: Biotechnology and Biological Sciences Research Council

INSTITUTE FOR ANIMAL HEALTH – PIRBRIGHT LABORATORY

Ash Road, Pirbright, Woking, Surrey, GU24 0NF

Tel: 01483 232441
Fax: 01483 232448
E-mail: pirbright.ill@bbsrc.ac.uk
Website: www.iah.bbsrc.ac.uk

Enquiries to: Librarian
Direct tel: 01483 231030

Founded: 1925

Organisation type and purpose: Research organisation.
Houses the World Reference Laboratory for Foot and Mouth Disease.
Research into infectious diseases of farm animals.

Subject coverage: Animal virology, particularly foot and mouth disease and other viruses exotic to the United Kingdom

Collection: Collection of reprints on foot and mouth disease and other viruses
Database of 100,000 virological references

Library catalogue: All or part available in-house

Publications: Printed

Access to staff: Contact by letter and by e-mail. Appointment necessary.
Hours: Mon to Fri, 0800 to 1430

Parent body: Biotechnology and Biological Sciences Research Council (BBSRC)

INSTITUTE FOR ARCHAEOLOGISTS (IfA)

Formal name: Institute of Field Archaeologists

SHES, Whiteknights, PO Box 227, Reading, RG6 6AB

Tel: 0118 931 6446
Fax: 0118 931 6448
E-mail: admin@archaeologists.net
Website: www.archaeologists.net

Enquiries to: Administrative Assistant

Founded: 1982

Organisation type and purpose:
Professional body, present number of members over 3,000.
To promote professional standards and ethics for conserving, managing, and understanding enjoyment of heritage.

Information services: Jobs Information Service (JIS)

Publications: Printed

Publications list: Available online and in print

Access to staff: Contact by letter, by telephone, by fax, by e-mail and via website
Hours: Mon to Fri, 0900 to 1730

INSTITUTE FOR ARTS IN THERAPY AND EDUCATION (IATE)

2–18 Britannia Row, Islington, London, N1 8PA

Tel: 020 7704 2534
Fax: 020 7704 0171
E-mail: info@artspsychotherapy.org
Website: www.artspsychotherapy.org

Enquiries to: Manager
Other contacts: Administrator

Founded: 1992

Organisation type and purpose: Training organisation.

Subject coverage: Integrative arts psychotherapy training.

Publications: Printed

Access to staff: Contact by letter, by telephone, by e-mail and via website. Appointment necessary.
Hours: Mon to Fri, 0900 to 1730

Access for disabled people: Ramped entry, toilet facilities

Full member of the: United Kingdom Council for Psychotherapy

INSTITUTE FOR COMPLEMENTARY AND NATURAL MEDICINE (ICNM)

Can-Mezzanine, 32–36 Loman Street, London, SE1 0EH

Tel: 020 7922 7980
Fax: 020 7922 7981
E-mail: info@icnm.org.uk
Website: www.i-c-m.org.uk

Enquiries to: Information Officer
Other contacts: Research Director

Founded: 1982; created by the merger of Nature Cure Clinic (NCC) and Institute for Complementary Medicine (ICM) (year of change 2007)

Organisation type and purpose: Advisory body, learned society (membership is by qualification), voluntary organisation, registered charity (charity number 326258).
To provide information on complementary medicine. To support research into complementary medicine. To develop professional standards of practice.

Subject coverage: Complementary medicine, practitioner training and qualification, membership of the register, contacts within the field and comments on the state and range of the subject, low technology methods of health care, traditional remedies and health care methods.

Collection: A modest library

Non-library collection catalogue: All or part available in-house

Library catalogue: All or part available in-house

Publications: Printed

Access to staff: Contact by letter, by telephone and by e-mail
Hours: Mon to Fri, 0930 to 1600
Special comments: Free information to public and media, fees required from commercial interests.

Access to building: Prior appointment required

Parent body: Healing Research Trust; tel: as for ICNM

INSTITUTE FOR EMPLOYMENT STUDIES (IES)

Sovereign House, Church Street, Brighton, BN1 1UJ

Tel: 01273 763400
Fax: 01273 763401
E-mail: askies@employment-studies.co.uk
Website: www.employment-studies.co.uk/pubs

Enquiries to: Communications Manager
Direct e-mail: andy.davidson@employment-studies.co.uk

Founded: 1969; formerly called Institute of Manpower Studies (year of change 1995)

Organisation type and purpose: Research organisation.

Subject coverage: Human resources, labour markets, public employment policy, training and skills analysis, careers, equality and diversity in employment, health and well-being at work.

Publications: Printed
Order printed publications from: website: http://www.employment-studies.co.uk/pubs

Publications list: Available online

Access to staff: Contact by letter, by telephone, by fax, by e-mail and via website
Hours: Mon to Fri, 0900 to 1700

Access to building: No access other than to staff

INSTITUTE FOR EUROPEAN ENVIRONMENTAL POLICY (IEEP)

Dean Bradley House, 52 Horseferry Road, London, SW1P 2AG

Tel: 020 7799 2244
Fax: 020 7799 2600
E-mail: central@ieep.eu
Website: www.ieep.org.uk

Enquiries to: Information Officer
Direct e-mail: aglynn@ieep.eu

Organisation type and purpose: Voluntary organisation, registered charity (charity number 802956), consultancy, research organisation.
Independent body with offices in Bonn, Paris, London, Brussels and Madrid.

Subject coverage: EU environmental policy including, environment, agriculture, water, air pollution, waste, chemicals, natural resources, fisheries, transport, rural development and strategic/horizontal issues.

Publications: Printed

Publications list: Available in print

Access to staff: Contact by letter, by fax, by e-mail and via website
Hours: Mon to Fri, 0900 to 1700

Brussels Office: IEEP; 18 Avenue des Gaulois, Brussels, B-1040; tel: + 32 2 732 4234/4004

INSTITUTE FOR FISCAL STUDIES (IFS)

7 Ridgmount Street, London, WC1E 7AE

Tel: 020 7291 4800
Fax: 020 7323 4780
E-mail: mailbox@ifs.org.uk
Website: www.ifs.org.uk

Enquiries to: External Relations Manager
Direct tel: 020 7291 4850

Founded: 1969

Organisation type and purpose:
Membership association (membership is by subscription), present number of members: 1,150, registered charity (charity number 258815); independent, non-profit-making economic research organisation.
To encourage debate and disseminate independent information about all aspects of taxation and government microeconomic policy. Promotes effective economic and social policies by understanding better their impact on individuals, families, businesses and government finances.

Subject coverage: Research in the fiscal regime, taxation (but not individual tax matters), public economic policy, government expenditure, local and European activities and international development economics.

Publications: Printed, and electronic and video
Order printed publications from: e-mail: mailbox@ifs.org.uk

Publications list: Available online

Access to staff: Contact by letter, by telephone, by fax, by e-mail and via website. Appointment necessary.
Hours: Mon to Fri, 0930 to 1730

Access to building: Prior appointment required

Access for disabled people: Ramped entry, access to all public areas, toilet facilities

INSTITUTE FOR JEWISH POLICY RESEARCH (JPR)

79 Wimpole Street, London, W1G 9RY

Tel: 020 7935 8266
Fax: 020 7935 3252
E-mail: jpr@jpr.org.uk
Website: www.jpr.org.uk
Website: www.axt.org.uk

Enquiries to: Director

Founded: 1941

Organisation type and purpose:
Membership association (membership is by subscription), present number of members: 500, registered charity (charity number 252626), consultancy, research organisation, publishing house.

Subject coverage: International Jewish affairs, anti-Semitism, race relations, civic society, human rights, neo-Nazism, Israel (domestic issues), the Middle East, migration and refugees, Jewish culture, history of Jewish communities, Jewish communities in Diaspora.

Publications: Printed, and electronic and video

Publications list: Available online and in print

Access to staff: Contact by letter, by fax, by e-mail and via website
Hours: Mon to Thu, 0930 to 1730

Access to building: No access other than to staff

INSTITUTE FOR METROPOLITAN STUDIES (IMS)

The Bartlett School of The Built Environment, UCL, Gower Street, London, WC1E 8BT

Tel: 020 7243 4205
Fax: 020 7727 5268

Enquiries to: Chief Executive

Organisation type and purpose: University department or institute, consultancy, research organisation.

Subject coverage: Metropolitan studies with particular focus on London.

Publications: Printed

Access to staff: Contact by fax. Appointment necessary.
Hours: Mon to Fri, 0900 to 1700

Access for disabled people: Toilet facilities

Affiliated to: University College London

INSTITUTE FOR MIDDLE EASTERN AND ISLAMIC STUDIES (IMEIS)

Al Qasimi Building, Elvet Hill Road, Durham, DH1 3TU

Tel: 0191 334 5660
Fax: 0191 334 5661
E-mail: a.ehteshami@durham.ac.uk
Website: www.dur.ac.uk/~dme0www

Enquiries to: Director

Founded: early 1900s

Organisation type and purpose: University department or institute.
Teaching and research on the Middle East.

Subject coverage: Extensive information and documentation on all matters related to the Middle East and North Africa, Islam, including Arabic, Persian and Turkish languages, politics, economy and social science of the contemporary Middle East.

Collection: Middle East Documentation Unit (University Library)
Sudan Archive

Trade and statistical information: Most relevant Middle East economic statistics

Publications: Printed

Publications list: Available in print

Access to staff: Contact by letter, by telephone, by fax and by e-mail
Hours: Mon to Fri, 0900 to 1700

Access to building: Prior appointment required

Access for disabled people: Parking provided, level entry

INSTITUTE FOR NATIONALIST AFFAIRS (INA)

National House, PO Box 83, Tonbridge, Kent, TN9 1YN

Tel: 01732 851259
E-mail: mikeeaster@dialstart.net

Enquiries to: Secretary

Founded: 1987

Organisation type and purpose: Research organisation.

Subject coverage: Research into fundamental matters concerning the government of the United Kingdom from the Nationalist viewpoint.

Publications: Printed

Access to staff: Contact by letter, by telephone and by e-mail
Hours: Mon to Fri, 0900 to 1700

INSTITUTE FOR OPTIMUM NUTRITION (ION)

Avalon House, 72 Lower Mortlake Road, Richmond, Surrey, TW9 2JY

Tel: 020 8614 7800
Fax: 0870 979 1133
E-mail: reception@ion.ac.uk
Website: www.ion.ac.uk

Founded: 1984

Organisation type and purpose:
Membership association, registered charity (charity number 1013084), research organisation.
Independent educational charity.

Subject coverage: Achieving optimum nutrition and reaching the highest level of health through nutrition.
To educate both the general public and health professionals about nutrition and nutritional therapy.

Collection: Information list available on request with sae
Library of books, journals and specific research papers, nutrition and medical related (alternative and complementary medicine related)

Publications: Printed

Publications list: Available in print

Access to staff: Contact by letter, by telephone, by fax, by e-mail and in person. All charged.
Hours: Mon to Fri, 0900 to 1700

Access to building: Prior appointment required
Hours: Mon to Fri, 1000 to 1700
Special comments: Library access to ION members and ION students only.

INSTITUTE FOR OUTDOOR LEARNING (IOL)

Warwick Mill Business Centre, Warwick Bridge, Carlisle, Cumbria CA4 8RR

Tel: 01228 564 580
Fax: 01228 564 581
E-mail: institute@outdoor-learning.org
Website: www.outdoor-learning.org

Enquiries to: Office Manager
Direct e-mail: louise@outdoor-learning.org

Organisation type and purpose: National organisation, membership association (membership is by subscription), present number of members: 1,400, registered charity (charity number 1085697), publishing house.
Supports, develops and promotes the achievement of learning through purposeful and planned outdoor education.

Subject coverage: Careers and qualifications in outdoor education, safety, insurance for outdoor education, outdoor training and development; school curriculum and outdoors, access and environment, urban adventure, equal opportunities and outdoors, insurance for outdoor education.

Collection: Small library of articles and books on all aspects of outdoor learning

Publications: Printed

Publications list: Available online and in print

Access to staff: Contact by letter, by telephone, by fax, by e-mail, in person and via website
Hours: Mon to Fri, 0900 to 1700

Access for disabled people: Parking provided, access to all public areas, toilet facilities

INSTITUTE FOR PUBLIC POLICY RESEARCH (ippr)

30–32 Southampton Street, London, WC2E 7RA

Tel: 020 7470 6100
Fax: 020 7470 6111
E-mail: info@ippr.org.uk
Website: www.ippr.org.uk

Enquiries to: Information Officer

Founded: 1989

Organisation type and purpose: Registered charity (charity number 800065).

Subject coverage: Health and social policy, education, economy, business and public private partnerships, public and democratic involvement, citizenship and governence, the digital society.

Publications: Printed
Order printed publications from: IPPR Orders, Central Books
99 Wallis Road, London, E9 5LN, tel: 0845 458 9911, fax: 0845 458 9912, e-mail: ippr@centralbooks.com

Publications list: Available in print

INSTITUTE FOR SOCIAL AND ECONOMIC RESEARCH (ISER)

University of Essex, Wivenhoe Park, Colchester, Essex, CO4 3SQ

Tel: 01206 872957
Fax: 01206 873151
E-mail: iser@essex.ac.uk
Website: www.iser.essex.ac.uk/
Website: www.iser.essex.ac.uk/pubs/index.php

Enquiries to: Enquiries
Direct e-mail: katet@essex.ac.uk
Other contacts: (1) Research Resources Unit Manager (2) Communications Manager for (1) library (2) press.

Founded: 1989

Organisation type and purpose: Research organisation.

Subject coverage: Household organisation, labour market, income and wealth, housing, health, socio-economic values, British Household Panel User Study and longitudinal studies methodology.

Collection: The Research Resource Unit (RRU) houses a collection of survey-related documents to support the centre's research. The collection largely consists of 'grey literature'. Outsiders can use the collection by prior appointment only

Non-library collection catalogue: All or part available online

Library catalogue: All or part available online

Publications: Printed, and electronic and video

Publications list: Available online and in print

Access to staff: Contact by letter, by telephone, by fax and by e-mail
Hours: Mon to Fri, 0930 to 1600
Special comments: Visitors by prior appointment to Research Resources Unit.

Access to building: Prior appointment required

Access for disabled people: Level entry, toilet facilities

Partly funded by: Economic and Social Science Research Council (ESRC)

INSTITUTE FOR SPORT, PARKS AND LEISURE (ISPAL)

Abbey House, 1650 Arlington Business Park, Theale, Reading

Tel: 0844 418 0077
Fax: 0118 929 8001
E-mail: infocentre@ispal.org.uk
Website: www.ispal.org.uk

Enquiries to: Research and Resources Manager

Founded: 1983; created by the merger of Institute of Leisure and Amenity Management (ILAM) and NASD (year of change 2006)

Organisation type and purpose:
Professional body.
Professional institute for sport, parks and leisure managers and aspiring managers.
To improve management in sport, parks and leisure industry and to enhance the quality of experience of those undertaking activities within these sectors.

Subject coverage: Leisure management, sport, recreation, arts, tourism, play, countryside, parks and open spaces, local government.

Non-library collection catalogue: All or part available online, in-house and in print

Library catalogue: All or part available online, in-house and in print

Publications: Printed
Order printed publications from: Research and Resources Manager

Publications list: Available online and in print

Access to staff: Contact by letter, by telephone, by fax, by e-mail, in person and via website. Appointment necessary. Access for members only. Non-members charged.
Hours: Mon to Fri, 0900 to 1700

Access for disabled people: Parking provided, level entry, toilet facilities
Special comments: Please notify beforehand.

INSTITUTE FOR THE MANAGEMENT OF INFORMATION SYSTEMS (IMIS)

Suite A, (Part) 2nd Floor, 3 White Oak Square, Swanley, Kent BR8 7AG

Tel: 0845 8500006
Fax: 0845 8500007
E-mail: central@imis.org.uk
Website: www.imis.org.uk

Enquiries to: Chief Executive

Founded: 1978

Organisation type and purpose: Professional body (membership is by subscription, qualification), registered charity (charity number 291495). Examining body.

Subject coverage: Management of information systems and information technology for commerce, industry and general business.

Publications: Printed

Access to staff: Contact by letter, by telephone, by fax, by e-mail and via website. Appointment necessary.
Hours: Mon to Fri, 0800 to 1600

INSTITUTE FOR THE STUDY OF THE AMERICAS (ISA)

University of London, School of Advanced Study, Senate House, South Block, London WC1E 7HU

Tel: 020 7862 8870
Fax: 020 7862 8886
E-mail: americas@sas.ac.uk
Website: www.americas.sas.ac.uk

Enquiries to: Information Resources Manager
Direct tel: 020 7862 8501
Direct e-mail: christy.palmer@sas.ac.uk
Other contacts: Latin American Bibliographer (in librarian's absence)

Founded: 1965; created by the merger of Institute of Latin American Studies (ILAS) with the Institute of United States Studies (IUSS) (year of change 2004)

Organisation type and purpose: University department or institute.

Subject coverage: Latin America, predominantly humanities and social sciences.

Collection: Archive collection (news sources, political party material)
Bibliography and reference
British Union Catalogue of Latin American (BUCLA) (author card catalogue, to 1988 closed)
Current affairs and political party ephemera (1960–)
Nissa Torrents video collection

Non-library collection catalogue: All or part available online and in-house

Publications: Printed

Publications list: Available in print

Access to staff: Contact by letter, by telephone, by fax, by e-mail, in person and via website. Letter of introduction required.
Hours: Mon to Fri, 0930 to 1730
Special comments: Letter of introduction required for undergraduate students.

Houses the editorial office of the: Journal of Latin American Studies

Member Institute of: University of London's School of Advanced Study

Member of: Red Europea de Información y Documentación sobre América Latina (REDIAL)

Member organisation of: Advisory Council on Latin American and Iberian Information Resources (ACLAIIR); Seminar on the Acquisition of Latin American Library Materials (SALALM)

INSTITUTE FOR TRANSPORT STUDIES (ITS)

University of Leeds, 34–40 University Road, Leeds, West Yorkshire, LS2 9JT

Tel: 0113 233 5325
Fax: 0113 233 5334
E-mail: info@its.leeds.ac.uk
Website: www.its.leeds.ac.uk

Founded: 1971

Organisation type and purpose: University department or institute, consultancy, research organisation.

Subject coverage: Public transport; transport economics; road safety and accident analysis; environmental economics and evaluation; information technology; surveys and data capture; transport policy and appraisal; land use and transport issues; transport demand management; travel demand forecasting; traffic management and control; transport network modelling; transport operations; microsimulation of traffic behaviour; traffic pollution monitoring and modelling.

Publications: Printed
Order printed publications from: www.its.leeds.ac.uk/research/outputs

Publications list: Available online and in print

Access to staff: Contact by letter, by telephone, by e-mail and via website. Appointment necessary.
Hours: Mon to Fri, 0900 to 1700

Access for disabled people: Parking provided, ramped entry, toilet facilities

Links with: For full list see: www.its.leeds.ac.uk/links

Member organisation of: For full list see: www.its.leeds.ac.uk/links

Parent body: University of Leeds

INSTITUTE OF ACOUSTICS (IOA)

77A St Peter's Street, St Albans, Hertfordshire, AL1 3BN

Tel: 01727 848195
Fax: 01727 850553
E-mail: ioa@ioa.org.uk
Website: www.ioa.org.uk

Enquiries to: Chief Executive

Founded: 1974

Organisation type and purpose: International organisation, learned society, professional body (membership is by qualification, election or invitation), present number of members: 2,600, registered charity (charity number 267026), publishing house.

Subject coverage: Acoustics, noise, vibration, ultrasonics.

Library catalogue: All or part available in-house and in print

Publications: Printed

Publications list: Available online and in print

Access to staff: Contact by letter, by telephone, by fax, by e-mail, in person and via website. Appointment necessary.
Hours: Mon to Fri, 0900 to 1700

Links with: European Acoustics Association (EAA); International Institute of Noise Control Engineering (IINCE)

INSTITUTE OF ADMINISTRATIVE MANAGEMENT (IAM)

6 Graphite Square, Vauxhall Walk, London, SE11 5EE

Tel: 020 7091 2600
Fax: 020 7091 2619
E-mail: info@instam.org
Website: www.instam.org

Founded: 1915

Organisation type and purpose: Established in 1915, the Institute of Administrative Management is the only professional body for both practising and aspiring Administrative Managers. Students and Members are professionals who are responsible for the management of: systems, human resources, communication, information technology, facilities, training and development, finance. The IAM supports managers (and aspiring managers) at all levels, aiming to improve both personal and organisational performance through a systematic approach to professional development.

Subject coverage: Administrative management, office supervision, business management.

Information services: Publications relating to the management of business.

Education services: A wide range of professional qualifications in business management.

Publications: Printed
Order printed publications from: info@instam.org

Publications list: Available online

Access to staff: Contact by letter, by telephone, by fax, by e-mail and via website. Appointment necessary.
Hours: Mon to Fri, 0900 to 1700

INSTITUTE OF ADVANCED LEGAL STUDIES LIBRARY (IALS)

17 Russell Square, London, WC1B 5DR

Tel: 020 7862 5800
Fax: 020 7862 5770
E-mail: ials@sas.ac.uk
Website: ials.sas.ac.uk

Enquiries to: Library Administrative Officer
Direct tel: 020 7862 5801

Founded: 1947

Organisation type and purpose: University department or institute.
Postgraduate legal research, other than Oriental and Eastern European law.

Subject coverage: Commonwealth Law; US Law; Western European Law; Public International Law.

continued overleaf

Collection: Commonwealth Law; US Law; Western European Law; Public International Law

Non-library collection catalogue: All or part available online and in-house

Library catalogue: All or part available online

Publications: Printed

Access to staff: Contact by letter, by telephone, by fax, by e-mail and via website
Hours: Mon to Fri, 0900 to 2000; Sat, 1000 to 1730
Special comments: Please apply to the library for admissions leaflet and subscription rates. There are restrictions, and charges for some users.

Access for disabled people: Toilet facilities

Member organisation of: School of Advanced Study of the University of London; tel: 020 7862 8659; fax: 020 7862 8657; e-mail: school@sas.ac.uk

Parent body: University of London; tel: 020 7862 8000

INSTITUTE OF ADVANCED MOTORISTS LIMITED (IAM)

IAM House, 510 Chiswick High Road, London, W4 5RG

Tel: 020 8996 9600
Fax: 020 8996 9601
Website: www.iam.org.uk

Enquiries to: Chief Executive

Founded: 1956

Organisation type and purpose:
Membership association (membership is by qualification), present number of members: 110,000, registered charity (charity number 249002), training organisation.
To improve road safety by raising driving standards.

Subject coverage: Driving standards, driving techniques.

Publications: Printed, and electronic and video

Publications list: Available in print

Access to staff: Contact by letter, by telephone and by fax
Hours: Mon to Fri, 0900 to 1700

Subsidiary bodies: IAM Fleet Training Ltd; at the same address; tel: 0845 3108311; fax: 020 8996 9701; IAM Group Services Ltd; at the same address

INSTITUTE OF AGRICULTURAL MANAGEMENT (IAgrM)

Portbury House, Sheepway, Portbury, Bristol BS20 7TE

Tel: 01275 843825
Fax: 01275 374747
E-mail: cooksleyandco@btconnect.com
Website: www.iagrm.org.uk

Enquiries to: Director

Founded: 1966

Organisation type and purpose: Learned society, professional body (membership is by subscription), present number of members: 850, registered charity.

Subject coverage: Business management in agriculture and associated industries; management techniques; management applications in agriculture.

Education services: Courses are available in Management and Supervisory Studies (in agriculture and associated subjects).

Publications: Printed

Publications list: Available online and in print

Access to staff: Contact by letter, by telephone, by fax, by e-mail and via website. Appointment necessary.
Hours: Mon to Fri, 0900 to 1700
Special comments: The office is manned during office hours. Answerphone at other times.

Links with: International Farm Management Association

INSTITUTE OF AGRICULTURAL SECRETARIES AND ADMINISTRATORS (IAgSA)

National Agricultural Centre, Stoneleigh, Kenilworth, Warwickshire, CV8 2LG

Tel: 024 7669 6592
Fax: 024 7641 7937
E-mail: iagsa@iagsa.co.uk
Website: www.iagsa.co.uk

Enquiries to: General Secretary

Founded: 1967

Organisation type and purpose:
Professional body (membership is by subscription), present number of members: 950

Subject coverage: Agricultural secretaryship and rural business administration.

Publications: Printed

Access to staff: Contact by letter, by telephone, by fax, by e-mail and via website
Hours: Mon to Fri, 0900 to 1700

INSTITUTE OF ALCOHOL STUDIES (IAS)

Alliance House, 12 Caxton Street, London, SW1H 0QS

Tel: 020 7222 4001
Fax: 020 7799 2510
E-mail: librarian@ias.org.uk
Website: www.ias.org.uk
Website: www.ias.org.uk/press.htm

Enquiries to: Librarian

Founded: 1982

Organisation type and purpose: National organisation, registered charity, research organisation.
A specialised reference library, which collects information on alcohol-related issues from a wide variety of sources.
To increase the knowledge of alcohol and the social and health consequences of its misuse.

Subject coverage: Library on alcohol-related issues with bibliographic database. Alcohol consumption and associated problems; alcohol control policies; social science research and policy studies. Historical archive of temperance-related material.

Collection: Historical (temperance) material, books, periodicals, etc.
Modern materials, books, scientific journals, etc.

Trade and statistical information: Data and reference material on alcohol consumption and harm principally in the UK

Library catalogue: All or part available in-house

Publications: Printed
Order printed publications from: e-mail: sales@ias.org.uk

Publications list: Available online and in print

Access to staff: Contact by letter, by telephone, by fax, by e-mail and via website. Appointment necessary.
Hours: Mon to Fri, 0930 to 1600
Special comments: Charges made for photocopies.

Affiliated to: Alliance House Foundation; at the same address; tel: 020 7222 4001; Eurocare (alliance of alcohol problems mainly in European Union); tel: 01480 466766

INSTITUTE OF AMATEUR CINEMATOGRAPHERS (IAC)

Global House, 1 Ashley Avenue, Epsom, Surrey, KT18 5NY

Tel: 01372 822812
E-mail: admin@theiac.org.uk
Website: www.theiac.org.uk

Enquiries to: Administrator

Founded: 1932

Organisation type and purpose:
Membership association (membership is by subscription), present number of members: 2,000, voluntary organisation, registered charity (charity number 260467).

Subject coverage: Amateur cinematography.

Collection: Archive library of amateur films

Publications: Printed

Access to staff: Contact by letter, by telephone and by e-mail. Appointment necessary.
Hours: Staffed part-time only

INSTITUTE OF ANIMAL TECHNOLOGY (IAT)

5 South Parade, Summertown, Oxford, OX2 7JL

E-mail: iat101@btconnect.com
Website: www.iat.org.uk

Enquiries to: IAT Administrator

Founded: 1950

Organisation type and purpose:
Professional body (membership is by qualification), present number of members: more than 2,200, voluntary organisation.
Advancing and promoting excellence in the care and welfare of animals in science.

Subject coverage: Laboratory animal technology; animal welfare; animal husbandry; advances in new technology; transgenic technology; seminars and symposiums.

Information services: Animal technology careers advice and opportunities.

Education services: Education and qualifications advice.

Publications: Printed, and electronic and video

Access to staff: Contact by letter, by e-mail and via website
Hours: Normal working hours

INSTITUTE OF ARCHITECTURAL IRONMONGERS (IAI)

8 Stepney Green, London, E1 3JU

Tel: 020 7790 3431
Fax: 020 7790 8517
E-mail: info@gai.org.uk
Website: www.iai.uk.com

Enquiries to: General Secretary

Founded: 1970

Organisation type and purpose: Professional body (membership is by qualification).
Parent body, the Guild of Architectural Ironmongers.

Subject coverage: Architectural ironmongery.

Access to staff: Contact by letter, by telephone, by fax, by e-mail and via website
Hours: Mon to Fri, 0900 to 1700

INSTITUTE OF ART AND LAW (IAL)

Pentre Moel, Crickadarn, Builth Wells, LD2 3BX

Tel: 01982 560 666
E-mail: info@ial.uk.com
Website: www.ial.uk.com

Enquiries to: Administrator

Founded: 1995

Organisation type and purpose: International organisation (membership is by subscription).

Subject coverage: Art, law, archaeology, museums.

Publications: Printed
Order printed publications from: www.ial.uk.com/publications.php

Publications list: Available online and in print

Access to staff: Contact by letter and by e-mail
Hours: Mon to Fri, 0900 to 1700

Access to building: Prior appointment required

INSTITUTE OF ASPHALT TECHNOLOGY, THE (IAT)

IAT Head Office, Paper Mews Place, 290 High Street, Dorking, Surrey, RH4 1QT

Tel: 01306 742792
Fax: 01306 888902
E-mail: secretary@instofasphalt.org
Website: www.instofasphalt.org

Enquiries to: Secretary

Founded: 1966

Organisation type and purpose: Learned society, professional body (membership is by subscription, election or invitation), present number of members: 1,650.
Furtherance of excellence in asphalt technology.

Subject coverage: Asphalt technology, bitumen, bituminous materials.

Collection: Past journals and Year Books

Non-library collection catalogue: All or part available in print

Library catalogue: All or part available in-house and in print

Publications: Printed, and electronic and video

Access to staff: Contact by letter, by telephone, by fax, by e-mail and via website
Hours: Mon to Fri, 0900 to 1700

Has: 11 regional branches thoughout the UK and an overseas branch; contact Head Office for details

Professional affiliate member of: The Engineering Council

INSTITUTE OF ASSOCIATION MANAGEMENT (IofAM)

Institute of Association Management, 2 Old College Court, 29 Priory Street, Ware, Hertfordshire, SG12 0DE

Tel: 0844 822 1736
Fax: 0844 822 5215
E-mail: info@iofam.co.uk
Website: www.iofam.co.uk

Founded: 1933; formerly called Society of Association Executives (year of change 2000); formerly called Secretaries Club (year of change prior to 2000)

Organisation type and purpose: An independent professional body made up of managers and senior staff responsible for the management, development and governance of trade bodies, professional institutes, societies, chambers of commerce, voluntary organisations, charities and other representative groups.
To develop, promote and share best practice for the benefit of IofAM members and all those involved in the governance of associations. To achieve its objectives, the IofAM offers a forum for education, training and development, dissemination of information, networking and research.

Subject coverage: Promotes best practice and professional standards in association management and governance; promulgates the role and contribution of associations in national life and the status and reputation of association management as a profession; provides services of value to members, by delivering information and advice on association management matters through means such as events, networking and member forums.

Access to staff: Contact by letter, by telephone, by fax, by e-mail and via website

INSTITUTE OF AUCTIONEERS AND APPRAISERS IN SCOTLAND

The Rural Centre – Westmains, Ingliston, Newbridge, Midlothian, EH28 8NZ

Tel: 0131 472 4067
Fax: 0131 472 4067
E-mail: iaas@auctioneersscotland.co.uk

Enquiries to: Executive Secretary
Direct e-mail: iaas@auctioneersscotland.co.uk

Founded: 1926

Organisation type and purpose: Professional body.

Subject coverage: Auction of livestock and chattels; urban and rural valuation; urban and rural estate agency; animal welfare; marketing; agricultural arbitration.

Publications: Printed

Access to staff: Access for members only.
Hours: Mon to Thu, 0900 to 1300

Links with: European Association of Livestock Markets; Livestock Auctioneers Market Committee for England and Wales

INSTITUTE OF BARRISTERS' CLERKS (IBC)

289–293 High Holborn, London, WC1V 7HZ

Tel: 020 7831 7144
Fax: 020 7831 7144
E-mail: admin@barristersclerks.com
Website: www.barristersclerks.com

Enquiries to: Administrator

Founded: 1922

Organisation type and purpose: Membership association (membership is by subscription), present number of members: 810.

Subject coverage: Work conditions, employment, education.

Access to staff: Contact by letter, by telephone and by e-mail. Appointment necessary. Non-members charged.
Hours: Mon to Fri, 0900 to 1700

Access for disabled people: Toilet facilities
Special comments: Wheelchair access by prior arangement, lift from basement.

INSTITUTE OF BIOLOGICAL, ENVIRONMENTAL AND RURAL SCIENCES (IBERS)

Aberystwyth University, Gogerddan, Aberystwyth, Ceredigion, SY23 3EB

Tel: 01970 823000
Fax: 01970 828357
E-mail: tns@aber.ac.uk
Website: www.aber.ac.uk/en/ibers

Enquiries to: Librarian
Direct tel: 01970 823051
Other contacts: Business Manager (for external liaison and research contract enquiries)

Founded: 1919; formerly called IGER – Institute of Grassland and Environmental Research (year of change 2008)

Organisation type and purpose: University research and teaching institute

Subject coverage: Grassland, agriculture, environment, cellular and molecular biology, genetic manipulation, plant development, environmental biology, plant physiology and biochemistry, pathology, nitrogen, fixation, plant genetics, forage and cereal breeding,

continued overleaf

ecology and environmental plant science including agricultural pollution, organic farming, ruminant nutrition and forage conservation, land use including low-input legume-based technology, alternative animals and crop systems.

Collection: Antiquarian agricultural and botanical collections of books
Flora (British and overseas), Prof. Harper reprint collection
Gene bank collections of herbage and cereal seeds, and germplasm
Herbarium flora and fauna collection
Pre-1840 books on grassland and agriculture
Works of Sir George Stapledon 1882–1960

Non-library collection catalogue: All or part available online and in-house

Library catalogue: All or part available online and in-house

Publications: Printed
Order printed publications from: Stapledon Library, Institute of Biological, Environmental and Rural Sciences, Aberystwyth University, Gogerddan, Aberystwyth, Ceredigion, SY23 3EB, Wales; e-mail gogstaff@aber.ac.uk

Publications list: Available online and in print

Access to staff: Contact by letter, by telephone, by fax, by e-mail and via website
Hours: Mon to Fri, 0900 to 1700

INSTITUTE OF BIOMEDICAL SCIENCE (IBMS)

12 Coldbath Square, London, EC1R 5HL

Tel: 020 7713 0214
Fax: 020 7436 4946
E-mail: mail@ibms.org
Website: www.ibms.org

Enquiries to: Publications Officer
Direct e-mail: mc@ibms.org

Founded: 1912

Organisation type and purpose:
Professional body, present number of members: 17,500, registered charity (charity number 261926).
To promote and develop biomedical science and its practitioners and to establish and maintain professional standards.

Subject coverage: Haematology, transfusion science, medical microbiology, virology, clinical chemistry, cellular pathology, immunology, pathology, all other biomedical science disciplines, laboratory administration and management, and laboratory safety.

Publications: Printed

Publications list: Available online and in print

Access to staff: Contact by letter, by telephone, by fax, by e-mail and via website. Non-members charged.
Hours: Mon to Fri, 0900 to 1700

Access to building: No prior appointment required

INSTITUTE OF BIOSCIENCE AND TECHNOLOGY

Cranfield University, Silsoe, Bedfordshire, MK45 4DT

Tel: 01525 863000
Fax: 01525 863001
Website: www.cranfield.ac.uk/ibst

Enquiries to: Commercial and Marketing Director
Direct tel: 01525 863168
Direct fax: 01525 863080
Direct e-mail: l.tigwell@cranfield.ac.uk

Founded: 1981

Organisation type and purpose: University department or institute.
Specialises in contract research, consultancy and postgraduate training, including short courses.

Subject coverage: Biotechnology, biosensors, environmental biotechnology, food and agricultural biotechnology, analysis of pollutants, medical diagnostics, molecular biology, education in biotechnology, food spoilage, environmental monitoring, oncology, in vitro toxicity testing, advanced imaging, clinical research in in vitro diagnostic assay technology, measurement science and instrumentation, computational intelligence, bioinformatics, process monitoring and integration, systems manufacture, computational chemistry, molecularly-imprinted polymers.

Publications: Printed, and electronic and video

Publications list: Available in print

Access to staff: Contact by e-mail
Hours: Mon to Fri, 0900 to 1700

Access to building: Prior appointment required

INSTITUTE OF BREWING AND DISTILLING (IBD)

33 Clarges Street, London, W1J 7EE

Tel: 020 7499 8144
Fax: 020 7499 1156
E-mail: enquiries@ibd.org.uk
Website: www.ibd.org.uk

Enquiries to: Executive Director

Founded: 1886

Organisation type and purpose: Learned society, present number of members: 4,000, registered charity (charity number 269830).

Subject coverage: Brewing science.

Collection: Historical Brewing Science Library (brewing, distilling, malting) now held at Oxford Brookes University

Publications: Printed, and electronic and video

Publications list: Available online and in print

Access to staff: Contact by letter, by telephone, by fax and by e-mail. Appointment necessary.

Access to building: Prior appointment required
Hours: Mon to Fri, 0900 to 1700; closed bank holidays, Christmas and Easter

Links with: American Society of Brewing Chemists; Brewing, Food and Beverage Industry Suppliers Association (BFBI); Master Brewers of America Assocation (MBAA)

INSTITUTE OF BUDDHIST STUDIES

PO Box 443, Tring, Hertfordshire, HP23 6PX

Tel: 01442 890882

Enquiries to: Managing Director
Direct e-mail: ts1@soas.ac.uk

Founded: 1966

Organisation type and purpose: Learned society (membership is by election or invitation), registered charity (charity number 314166).
Promotion of Buddhist Studies.

Subject coverage: Buddhism in Asian countries.

Publications: Printed

Publications list: Available in print

Access to staff: Contact by letter, by telephone and by e-mail
Hours: Mon to Fri, 0900 to 1700
Special comments: No access to public.

Access to building: No access other than to staff

INSTITUTE OF BUILDERS' MERCHANTS (IoBM)

2 Crab Apple Way, Gamlingay, Sandy, Beds, SG19 3LS

Tel: 01767 650662
E-mail: admin@instbm.co.uk
Website: www.iobm.co.uk

Enquiries to: Administrator

Founded: 1968

Organisation type and purpose:
Professional body.

Subject coverage: Building supplies.

Access to staff: Contact by letter, by telephone and by e-mail
Hours: Mon to Thu, 0900 to 1300

INSTITUTE OF BUSINESS ADVISERS (IBA)

Response House, Queen Street North, Chesterfield, Derbyshire, S41 9AB

Tel: 01246 453322
Fax: 01246 453300
Website: www.iba.org.uk

Enquiries to: Chief Executive
Direct e-mail: john.milburn@managers.org.uk
Other contacts: Membership & Communications Manager for membership and small business enquiries.

Founded: 1989

Organisation type and purpose:
Professional body (membership is by qualification, election or invitation), present number of members: 2,500.

Subject coverage: Small and medium enterprises, how to start up and run a small business, business planning, marketing, accounting, exporting, trade credit, raising finance, and all other aspects of small business growth, including related support services, business advisers, business counsellors, business mentors, business trainers and supporting staff.

Publications: Printed

Publications list: Available in print

Access to staff: Contact by letter, by telephone, by e-mail and via website. Appointment necessary.
Hours: Mon to Fri, 0900 to 1700

Professional Development and Accounts Departments: IBA; Response House, Queen Street North, Chesterfield, S41 9AB; tel: 01246 453322; fax: 01246 453300; e-mail: info@iba.org.uk

INSTITUTE OF BUSINESS CONSULTING

4th Floor, 2 Savoy Court, Strand, London, WC2R 0EZ

Tel: 020 7497 0580
Fax: 020 7497 0463
E-mail: welcome@iconsulting.org.uk
Website: www.ibconsulting.org.uk

Founded: 1961; created by the merger of Institute of Management Consultancy (IMC) and Chartered Management Institute (year of change 2005); created by the merger of Institute of Business Advisers (IBA) and the Institute of Management Consultancy (IMC) (year of change 2007); formerly called Institute of Management Consultants (IMC) (year of change 1990s); formerly called Institute of Management Consultancy (IMC) (year of change 2007)

Organisation type and purpose: The only professional body for all business consultants and advisers. Encompasses the entire profession of consultants and advisers with a membership touching on all areas of the UK economy.
To raise standards of professional practice in support of enhancing business performance. Offers a development path for the profession, supported by high quality online resources and a recognised qualification route.

Subject coverage: Business and management consultancy.

Access to staff: Contact by letter, by telephone, by fax and by e-mail

INSTITUTE OF BUSINESS ETHICS (IBE)

24 Greencoat Place, London, SW1P 1BE

Tel: 020 7798 6040
Fax: 020 7798 6044
E-mail: info@ibe.org.uk
Website: www.ibe.org.uk

Enquiries to: Director

Founded: 1986

Organisation type and purpose: Registered charity (charity number 1084014) with mission to encourage high standards of business behaviour based on ethical values. Offers training, research, advice.
Membership association (membership is by subscription).

Subject coverage: Codes of business ethics, business and the environment, management and health of employees, education and business. Ethical aspects of information technology, the teaching of business ethics, reputation risk management, supply chain.

Publications: Printed, and electronic and video
Order printed publications from: website: http://www.ibe.org.uk
Order electronic and video publications from: website: http://www.ibe.org.uk

Publications list: Available online and in print

Access to staff: Contact by letter, by telephone, by fax and by e-mail. Appointment necessary.
Hours: Mon to Fri, 0900 to 1700

Access to building: Appointment required

Partners of: Caux Round Table

INSTITUTE OF CANCER RESEARCH (ICR)

15 Cotswold Road, Sutton, Surrey, SM2 5NG

Tel: 020 8643 8901
Fax: 020 7352 6283

Enquiries to: Librarian
Direct tel: 020 7352 5946
Direct e-mail: press@icr.ac.uk

Organisation type and purpose: Research organisation.

Subject coverage: Oncology, cancer.

Library catalogue: All or part available in-house

Publications: Printed

Access to staff: Contact by letter, by telephone, by fax and by e-mail. Appointment necessary. Access for members only.
Hours: Reference only for non-ICR staff

Access to building: Prior appointment required

Affiliated to: University of London

INSTITUTE OF CAREER GUIDANCE (ICG)

27A Lower High Street, Stourbridge, West Midlands, DY8 1TA

Tel: 01384 376464
Fax: 01384 440830
E-mail: hq@icg-uk.org
Website: www.icg-uk.org

Enquiries to: Business Development Manager
Direct tel: 01384 445631
Other contacts: Marketing Department

Founded: 1922

Organisation type and purpose: Advisory body, professional body (membership is by subscription), present number of members: 3,500.
Building principles and practice of high quality careers guidance.

Subject coverage: All aspects of career guidance ware, including connections, careers service, information, advice and guidance partnerships, HE and FE.

Collection: Archive material on the work of Careers Service

Publications: Printed

Access to staff: Contact by letter, by telephone, by fax, by e-mail and via website
Hours: Mon to Fri, 0900 to 1700

INSTITUTE OF CARPENTERS (IOC)

32 High Street, Wendover, Bucks, HP22 6EA

Tel: 0844 879 7696
Fax: 01296 620981
E-mail: info@instituteofcarpenters.com
Website: www.instituteofcarpenters.com

Enquiries to: Administrator

Founded: 1890

Organisation type and purpose: Professional body for skilled woodworkers. Promotes and enhances the role and status of skilled craftsmen and women everywhere; encourages the highest standards of craftsmanship for all working with wood; maintains the best traditions of historic crafts; works to enhance and promote the status of the ancient profession and to ensure that members and their clients benefit from the superior knowledge and craftsmanship associated with the Institute.

Subject coverage: Membership open to carpenters, furniture and cabinet makers, boat builders (woodworking skills), joiners, shopfitters, heavy structural post and beam carpenters, wheelwrights, wood carvers, wood turners. Offers technical and practical information and advice, respected qualifications from Foundation through to Fellowship level, specialist service for members. Master Certificate Scheme

Publications: Printed, and electronic and video
Order electronic and video publications from: Back copies available free to members on line

Access to staff: Contact by letter, by telephone, by fax and by e-mail

INSTITUTE OF CAST METALS ENGINEERS (ICME)

National Metalforming Centre, 47 Birmingham Road, West Bromwich, Birmingham, B70 6HA

Tel: 0121 601 6979
Fax: 0121 601 6981
E-mail: info@icme.org.uk
Website: www.icme.org.uk

Enquiries to: Operations Director

Founded: 1904

Organisation type and purpose: Professional body.

Subject coverage: Cast metals technology, education, training.

Collection: Library available, with limited information service

Trade and statistical information: Summary of statistics

Publications: Printed
Order printed publications from: info@icme.org.uk

continued overleaf

Publications list: Available online and in print

Access to staff: Contact by letter, by telephone, by fax, by e-mail and via website. Appointment necessary.
Hours: Mon to Thu, 0900 to 1700; Fri, 0900 to 1330

Access to building: *Hours:* Mon to Thu, 0900 to 1700; Fri, 0900 to 1330

Access for disabled people: Fully accessible

Links with: International Committee of Foundry Technical Associations

INSTITUTE OF CHARTERED ACCOUNTANTS IN ENGLAND AND WALES (ICAEW)

Chartered Accountants' Hall, Moorgate Place, London, EC2R 6EA

Tel: 020 7920 8100
Fax: 020 7920 0547
E-mail: contactus@icaew.com
Website: www.icaew.com

Direct tel: 020 7920 8620 (for library enquiries)
Direct e-mail: library@icaew.com (for library enquiries)

Founded: 1880

Organisation type and purpose: The largest professional accountancy body in Europe, membership association, offers a number of routes to membership for both trainee and qualified accountants, as well as access to specialist technical and business groups. Responsible for protecting the public by ensuring that members maintain the highest standards of professional conduct and competence.

Subject coverage: Accountancy.

Information services: Library & Information Service located in the Business Centre in Chartered Accountants' Hall; the eLibr@ry provides fast online access to full text online resources for members and registered students; LibCat is the online catalogue of the Institute's Library and Information Service, containing details of over 40,000 books, 50,000 journal articles and other items held in the Library collection.

Collection: The Library holds an archive of all publicly available books and journals published by the Institute

Library catalogue: All or part available online

Publications: Printed
Order printed publications from: website or from Subscriber Services team, tel: 01635 588493

Access to staff: Contact by letter, by telephone, by fax and via website
Hours: Library & Information Service Enquiry Line: Mon to Thu, 0900 to 1730; Fri, 1000 to 1730

Also at: 11 regional UK offices and 6 overseas offices; ICAEW; Level 1, Metropolitan House, 321 Avebury Boulevard, Milton Keynes, MK9 2FZ; tel: 01908 248100; fax: 01908 248088

INSTITUTE OF CHARTERED ACCOUNTANTS IN IRELAND (ICAI)

11 Donegal Square South, Belfast, BT1 5JE

Tel: 028 9032 1600
Fax: 028 9023 0071
Website: www.icai.ie

Enquiries to: Librarian

Organisation type and purpose: Professional body (membership is by subscription, qualification).

Subject coverage: Taxation, accountancy, auditing.

Library catalogue: All or part available online

Access to staff: Access for members only. Non-members charged.
Hours: Mon to Fri, 0900 to 1700

INSTITUTE OF CHARTERED ACCOUNTANTS OF SCOTLAND (ICAS)

CA House, 21 Haymarket Yards, Edinburgh, EH12 5BH

Tel: 0131 347 0100
Fax: 0131 347 0105
E-mail: infoservice@icas.org.uk
Website: www.icas.org.uk

Enquiries to: Information Service Manager
Direct tel: 0131 347 0135
Other contacts: Information Officer

Founded: 1854

Organisation type and purpose: National organisation, professional body (membership is by subscription, qualification), present number of members: 18,300, training organisation.

Subject coverage: Accountancy, finance, auditing, taxation, management, company law, company accounts, company information, statutes and law reports.

Collection: Antiquarian collection on accounting and related topics, 1494–1930, now on deposit in National Library of Scotland but maintained by ICAS
Stock exchange daily official list (SEDOL) 1986 to date (mainly microfiche)

Non-library collection catalogue: All or part available online

Library catalogue: All or part available online

Publications: Printed
Order printed publications from: Research books, monographs and research publications from the ICAS Research Department or ICAS website
CA Magazine from ICAS or from the CA Magazine website

Publications list: Available online and in print

Access to staff: Contact by letter, by telephone, by fax, by e-mail, in person and via website
Hours: Mon to Fri, 0900 to 1700

Access to building: *Hours:* Mon to Fri, 0900 to 1700

Special comments: Limited car parking – please book a space in advance.

Access for disabled people: Parking provided, access to all public areas

INSTITUTE OF CHARTERED FORESTERS (ICF)

59 George Street, Edinburgh, EH2 2JG

Tel: 0131 240 1425
Fax: 0131 240 1424
E-mail: icf@charteredforesters.org
Website: www.charteredforesters.org

Enquiries to: Administrative Officer
Other contacts: Executive Director (for code of ethics queries)

Founded: 1926

Organisation type and purpose: Professional body.

Subject coverage: Amenity planting, arboriculture, tree surveys, farm forestry, timber valuations, forest landscaping, forest management, forest pathology, forest roads planning and construction, forest investment, taxation and economics, harvesting and marketing, integrated stock and site inventory, land use appraisals, environmental assessments, nature conservation, wood-based energy, negotiations on sale and purchase of land and woodlands, poplar cultivation, sawmilling, small woods, training and education, upland forestry, urban forestry.

Publications: Printed
Order printed publications from: e-mail: icf@charteredforesters.org

Publications list: Available online and in print

Access to staff: Contact by letter, by telephone, by fax, by e-mail and via website
Hours: Mon to Fri, 0900 to 1700

INSTITUTE OF CHARTERED SHIPBROKERS (ICS)

85 Gracechurch Street, London, EC3V 0AA

Tel: 020 7623 1111
Fax: 020 7623 8008
E-mail: info@ics.org.uk
Website: ics.org.uk

Enquiries to: Director-General
Direct e-mail: membership@ics.org.uk

Organisation type and purpose: International organisation, professional body.

Subject coverage: Ship-broking.

Publications: Printed

Access to staff: Contact by letter, by telephone, by e-mail and in person
Hours: Mon to Fri, 0900 to 1700

Member of: Federation of National Associations of Shipbrokers and Agents (FONASBA); tel: 020 7628 5559; fax: 020 7588 7836; e-mail: fonasba@ics.org.uk

INSTITUTE OF CHIROPODISTS AND PODIATRISTS (IOCP)

27 Wright Street, Southport, Merseyside, PR9 0TL

Tel: 01704 546141
Fax: 01704 500477
E-mail: secretary@iocp.org.uk
Website: www.iocp.org.uk

Enquiries to: General Secretary

Founded: 1955

Organisation type and purpose: Professional body.

Subject coverage: Foot care; training in foot health.

Publications: Printed

Access to staff: Contact by e-mail and via website. Appointment necessary.
Hours: Mon to Thu, 0845 to 1700; Fri, 0900 to 1600

INSTITUTE OF CIVIL DEFENCE AND DISASTER STUDIES (ICDDS)

2 Grosvenor Gardens, Muswell Hill, London, N10 3TE

Tel: 020 8883 3555
Website: www.icds.org

Enquiries to: Librarian

Founded: 1938

Organisation type and purpose: Learned society (membership is by subscription), voluntary organisation, registered charity (charity number 266522).
Educational charity.

Subject coverage: Civil defence, civil protection, emergency planning, disaster management.

Collection: Collection on civil defence and emergency planning from 1914 to present day

Publications: Printed, and electronic and video

Publications list: Available in print

Access to staff: Contact by letter
Hours: Mon to Fri, 0900 to 1700

Access to building: Prior appointment required

Member of: International Civil Defence Organization; 10–12 chemin de Surville, 1213 Petit-Lancy, Geneva, Switzerland

INSTITUTE OF CLASSICAL STUDIES LIBRARY (ICS)

3rd Floor, Senate House, Malet Street, London, WC1E 7HU

Tel: 020 7862 8709
Fax: 020 7862 8735
E-mail: sue.willetts@sas.ac.uk
Website: icls.sas.ac.uk/library/Home.htm

Enquiries to: Librarian
Direct tel: 020 7862 8710
Direct fax: 020 7862 8724
Direct e-mail: colin.annis@sas.ac.uk

Founded: 1953

Organisation type and purpose: University department or institute, Institute of London University and member of the University of London Research Library Services (ULRS).

Subject coverage: All aspects of classical civilisation, including archaeology, art and architecture, language and literature, history, law, politics, religion, philosophy and science of the Minoan, Mycenaean and Hellenic world, and the Byzantine Empire; also of the early Italic and Etruscan civilisations, and of the Roman Empire to 5th century AD, including Roman Britain.

Collection: Contains 110,000 monographs and pamphlets and 20,000 bound vols of periodicals
675 current periodicals taken
Slides collection (joint library) of 6,800

Library catalogue: All or part available online

Publications: Printed
Order printed publications from: Publications Department, Institute of Classical Studies, at the same address; tel. 020 7862 8700; fax 020 7862 8722; e-mail icls.publications@sas.ac.uk

Publications list: Available online and in print

Access to staff: Contact by letter, by telephone, by fax, by e-mail and in person. Access for members only.
Hours: Mon to Fri, 0930 to 1800; Sat, 1000 to 1630; term-time, Tue, Wed and Thu, 0930 to 2000

Links with: Society for the Promotion of Hellenic Studies; tel: 020 7862 8730; fax: 020 7862 8731; e-mail: office@hellenicsociety.org.uk; website: http://www.hellenicsociety.org.uk
Society for the Promotion of Roman Studies; tel: 020 7862 8727; fax: 020 7862 8728; e-mail: office@romansociety.org; website: http://www.romansociety.org

INSTITUTE OF CLERKS OF WORKS AND CONSTRUCTION INSPECTORATE (ICWCI)

Formal name: Institute of Clerks of Works and Construction Inspectorate of GB Incorporated

Equinox, 28 Commerce Road, Lynchwood, Peterborough, PE2 6LR

Tel: 01733 405160
Fax: 01733 405161
E-mail: info@icwci.org
Website: www.icwci.org

Enquiries to: Company Secretary
Other contacts: Editor and Event Organiser; Membership Officer

Founded: 1882

Organisation type and purpose: Professional body.

Subject coverage: Comprehensive and technical knowledge of the construction process of the built environment, particularly independent inspection of work in process in the construction industry.

Collection: Journal of the Institute of Clerks of Works from 1883 to the present day, now known as the Institute of Clerks of Works and Construction Inspectorate

Publications: Printed

Access to staff: Contact by letter, by telephone, by fax, by e-mail, in person and via website
Hours: Mon to Fri, 0900 to 1700

Access to building: No access other than to staff

INSTITUTE OF CLINICAL RESEARCH (ICR)

Institute House, Boston Drive, Bourne End, Buckinghamshire, SL8 5YS

Tel: 0845 521 0056
Fax: 01628 530641
E-mail: resources@icr-global.org
Website: www.icr-global.org

Enquiries to: Head of Information Services
Direct tel: 01628 536969
Direct e-mail: hkorjonen@icr-global.org
Other contacts: General Manager

Founded: 1978

Organisation type and purpose: Professional body, training organisation, conference organiser, publisher

Subject coverage: Pharmaceutical industry and clinical research.

Collection: Clinical research resources only.

Non-library collection catalogue: All or part available online, in-house and in print

Library catalogue: All or part available online

Publications: Printed
Order printed publications from: http://www.icr-global.org

Publications list: Available online and in print

Access to staff: Contact by letter, by telephone, by fax, by e-mail, in person and via website. Appointment necessary. Access for members only. Letter of introduction required. Non-members charged.

Access to building: No prior appointment required for members
Hours: Mon to Fri, 0800 to 1700

INSTITUTE OF COMMERCIAL MANAGEMENT (ICM)

ICM House, Castleman Way, Ringwood Hants, BH24 3BA

Tel: 01202 490555
Fax: 01202 409666
E-mail: info@icm.ac.uk
Website: www.icm.ac.uk

Enquiries to: Chief Executive

Founded: 1979

Organisation type and purpose: A professional body (membership is by qualification), present number of full and student members: 210,000, registered charity (charity number 1045370), suitable for ages: 19+, training organisation, consultancy, research organisation, publishing house.
A QCA/Ofqual accredited UK Examining and Awarding body. Operating in 120 countries, providing advisory and capacity-building services to business schools and colleges;

Subject coverage: Business and management education, tourism, trade and professional development.

Information services: Industry news, by sector, from 120 countries.

Education services: The design, development of business and management programmes from HND to degree levels and

continued overleaf

the examination and assessment of candidates. The design of CPD programmes for the corporate sector.

Publications: Printed

Access to staff: Contact by letter, by telephone, by fax, by e-mail, in person and via website

Access to building: *Hours:* Mon to Fri, 0900 to 1730

Access for disabled people: Fully accessible

Links with: a range of UK and overseas universities for HE progression purposes for student members

INSTITUTE OF COMMONWEALTH STUDIES LIBRARY (ICS)

University of London, Senate House, Malet Street, London, WC1E 7HU

Tel: 020 7862 8840
E-mail: icommlib@sas.ac.uk
Website: catalogue.ulrls.lon.ac.uk
Website: commonwealth.sas.ac.uk/library
Website: archives.ulrls.lon.ac.uk

Founded: 1949

Organisation type and purpose: University library, university department or institute, research organisation.

Subject coverage: Class, Commonwealth, culture, economics, environment, gender, health, history, human rights, international relations, literature, migration, Pacific, politics, race.
Antigua and Barbuda, Australia, The Bahamas, Bangladesh, Barbados, Belize, Botswana, Brunei Darussalam, Cameroon, Canada, Cyprus, Dominica, Fiji Islands, The Gambia, Ghana, Grenada, Guyana, India, Jamaica, Kenya, Kiribati, Lesotho, Malawi, Malaysia, Maldives, Malta, Mauritius, Mozambique, Namibia, Nauru, New Zealand, Nigeria, Pakistan, Papua New Guinea, Samoa, Seychelles, Sierra Leone, Singapore, Solomon Islands, South Africa, Sri Lanka, St Kitts and Nevis, St Lucia, St Vincent and the Grenadines, Swaziland, Tanzania, Tonga, Trinidad and Tobago, Tuvalu, Uganda, Vanuatu, Zambia, Zimbabwe.

Collection: Material on the contemporary history, economics, politics and social aspects of all Commonwealth countries. The collections (200,000 items) include monographs, government publications, research papers, statistical data, census and more than 9,000 periodicals and annual publications. Over 70% of the stock is published in Commonwealth countries
Special Collections or strengths include:
Caribbean, West Indies, including the West India Committee Library and minute books
Australia, New Zealand, the Pacific area, Canada
India, Pakistan, Bangladesh, Sri Lanka
African member countries
National bibliographies
Collection of more than 10,000 documents issued by political parties, pressure groups and trade unions in Commonwealth member countries
A number of important archive collections, including the papers of Ellis Ashmead-Bartlett, Sir Ivor Jennings, Richard Jebb and the West India Committee. Guides to archival materials are available
International Defence and Aid Fund newscutting microfiche archive South Africa, 1975–90 and Namibia, 1975–90

Trade and statistical information: Trade statistics, census statistics

Non-library collection catalogue: All or part available online

Library catalogue: All or part available online

Publications: Printed

Access to staff: Contact by letter, by telephone, by e-mail, in person and via website. Letter of introduction required. Non-members charged.

Access to building: *Hours:* Term time: Mon to Thurs, 0900 to 2100; Fri 0900 to 1830; Sat 0945 to 1730
Vacations: Mon to Fri, 0930 to 1800; Sat 0945 to 1730
Special comments: ID required. Membership open to all academic and academically related university staff and postgraduates.

Member organisation of: School of Advanced Study and Senate House Libraries; University of London

INSTITUTE OF CONCRETE TECHNOLOGY (ICT)

4 Meadows Business Park, Blackwater, Camberley, GU17 9AB

Tel: 01276 607140
Fax: 01276 607141
E-mail: ict@concrete.org.uk
Website: ict.concrete.org.uk

Enquiries to: Executive Officer

Founded: 1972

Organisation type and purpose: Professional body.

Subject coverage: Concrete technology.

Collection: Institute's own Convention and meeting papers
ACT reports

Non-library collection catalogue: All or part available online

Publications: Printed

Publications list: Available online and in print

Access to staff: Contact by letter, by telephone, by fax and by e-mail
Hours: Mon to Thurs, 0800 to 1400
Special comments: We do not offer a technical advisory service.

INSTITUTE OF CONFLICT MANAGEMENT (ICM)

840 Melton Road, Thurmaston, Leicester, LE4 8BN

Tel: 0116 260 6961
Fax: 0116 264 0141
E-mail: info@conflictmanagement.org
Website: www.conflictmanagement.org

Enquiries to: Executive Secretary

Founded: 1999

Organisation type and purpose: National organisation, advisory body, membership association, present number of members: 200+, service industry, age range: higher, training organisation, research organisation. Regulatory body, membership is by qualification and/or by experience.

Subject coverage: Education and training in conflict management and other physical and non-physical intervention skills and techniques. Prints and publishes journals, newspapers, periodicals, books and leaflets to advance and inform on subjects connected with the work, theory and practices relating to conflict management, including statistics, scientific investigation and similar subjects. Has established a library and other information bureau for the use of Members and others on all related subjects.

Publications: Printed, and electronic and video

Access to staff: Contact by letter, by telephone, by fax, by e-mail and via website. Appointment necessary.
Hours: Mon to Fri, 0900 to 1700

Access for disabled people: Level entry, access to all public areas

INSTITUTE OF CONTEMPORARY ARTS (ICA)

12 Carlton House Terrace, London, SW1Y 5AH

Tel: 020 7930 0493
Fax: 020 7873 0051
E-mail: info@ica.org.uk
Website: www.ica.org.uk

Enquiries to: Administrative Assistant
Other contacts: Education Officer for tel no: 020 7766 1423.

Founded: 1947

Organisation type and purpose: Membership association, registered charity (charity number 236848), art gallery, suitable for ages: 16+.
Arts Centre.

Subject coverage: Contemporary cultural activities, including film, theatre, dance and music; events and exhibitions.

Collection: Pre-1990 collection at the Tate

Publications: Electronic and video

Publications list: Available in print

Access to staff: Contact by letter, by telephone, by fax, by e-mail and via website. Appointment necessary. Non-members charged.
Hours: Mon to Fri, 1200 to 1930

Access to building: No prior appointment required
Hours: Mon to Fri, 1200 to 1930

Subsidiary body: ICA Projects Ltd

INSTITUTE OF CONTEMPORARY MUSIC PERFORMANCE (ICMP)

Foundation House, 1A Dyne Road, London, NW6 7XG

Tel: 020 7328 0222
E-mail: enquiries@icmp.co.uk

Website: www.icmp.co.uk

Enquiries to: Admissions Advisor

Founded: 1985; formerly called Guitar Institute & Basstech

Organisation type and purpose:
Membership association (membership is by subscription), suitable for ages: all, training organisation.
Music school, accredited by Institute of Thames Valley University.

Subject coverage: Music tuition and career advice for musicians.

Publications: Printed

Access to staff: Contact by letter, by telephone, by fax, by e-mail, in person and via website. Appointment necessary.
Hours: Mon to Fri, 0900 to 1700

Access to building: No prior appointment required

Parent body: University of East London; Docklands Campus, University Way, London, E16 2RD

INSTITUTE OF COST AND EXECUTIVE ACCOUNTANTS (ICEA)

Akhtar House, 2 Shepherd's Bush Road, London, W6 7PJ

Tel: 020 8749 7126
Fax: 020 8749 7127
E-mail: icea@enta.net
Website: www.icea.enta.net

Enquiries to: Secretary General
Other contacts: Membership Secretary

Founded: 1958

Organisation type and purpose:
International organisation, professional body (membership is by qualification).
Producing tomorrow's accountant.

Subject coverage: Accountancy, executive accountancy, financial decision making, management auditing, strategic management.

Non-library collection catalogue: All or part available online and in-house

Library catalogue: All or part available in-house

Publications: Printed

Access to staff: Contact by letter, by telephone, by fax and by e-mail
Hours: Mon to Fri, 1000 to 1600

Member of: European Accounting Association and Council for Education in the Commonwealth

INSTITUTE OF COUNSELLING (IoC)

6 Dixon Street, Glasgow, G1 4AX

Tel: 0141 204 2230
Fax: 0141 221 2841
E-mail: iofcounsel@aol.com
Website: www.collegeofcounselling.com

Enquiries to: General Manager

Founded: 1985

Organisation type and purpose:
Membership association (membership is by subscription, qualification), present number of members: 600, suitable for ages: adults, training organisation.

Subject coverage: Counselling, counselling training and bereavement.

Publications: Printed, and electronic and video

Publications list: Available in print

Access to staff: Contact by letter, by telephone, by fax, by e-mail, in person and via website. Appointment necessary. Non-members charged.
Hours: Mon to Fri, 0900 to 1700

Also at: Institute of Counselling; 10 High Street, Bromsgrove, B61 8HQ; tel: 01527 577803; fax: 01527 577803; e-mail: instofcoun@aol.com

INSTITUTE OF CREDIT MANAGEMENT (ICM)

The Water Mill, South Luffenham, Oakham, Leicestershire LE15 8NB

Tel: 01780 722900
Fax: 01780 721333
E-mail: info@icm.org.uk
Website: www.icm.org.uk

Enquiries to: Chief Executive's Office
Direct tel: 01780 722912
Direct e-mail: ceo@icm.org.uk

Founded: 1939

Organisation type and purpose:
Professional body (membership is by subscription, qualification, election or invitation), present number of members: 8,500, registered charity, training organisation, consultancy, research organisation.

Subject coverage: All aspects of credit management.

Publications: Printed
Order printed publications from: e-mail: bookshop@icm.org.uk

Publications list: Available online

Access to staff: Contact by letter, by telephone, by fax and by e-mail. Access for members only.
Hours: Mon to Fri, 0900 to 1700

Member organisation of: Federation of European Credit Management Associations (FECMA)

INSTITUTE OF CUSTOMER CARE (IOCC)

St John's House, Chapel Lane, Westcott, Dorking, Surrey, RH4 3PJ

Tel: 01306 876210
Fax: 01306 876249

Enquiries to: Membership Secretary

Founded: 1987

Organisation type and purpose: Advisory body, membership association (membership is by subscription), training organisation, consultancy.

Subject coverage: Customer care, total quality management, market research, complaint management, customer charters, mystery shopping, accreditation, customer satisfaction indices, quality audits, staff surveys, networking, benchmarking, training, facilities management.

Access to staff: Contact by letter and by telephone. Non-members charged.
Hours: Mon to Fri, 0900 to 1700

INSTITUTE OF CUSTOMER SERVICE (ICS)

2 Castle Court, St Peter's Street, Colchester, CO1 1EW

Tel: 01206 571716
E-mail: via website
Website: www.instituteofcustomerservice.com

Founded: 1996

Organisation type and purpose: The independent, professional membership body for customer service. Members are more than 300 organisations – from across the private, public and third sectors – and individuals.
To lead customer service performance and professionalism; to be the first port of call for every aspect of customer service, delivering high quality, tangible benefits to organisations, individuals and other stakeholders, so that the Institute's customers can improve their own customers' experiences and their business performance; to improve customer service performance and raise the status of people working directly or indirectly in customer service roles.

Subject coverage: Customer service.

Publications: Printed, and electronic and video
Order printed publications from: Online shop
Order electronic and video publications from: Downloadable PDFs, available from website or online shop

Publications list: Available online

Access to staff: Contact by letter, by telephone and via website

INSTITUTE OF DEVELOPMENT STUDIES LIBRARY (BLDS)

Formal name: British Library for Development Studies

BLDS, Institute of Development Studies, University of Sussex, Falmer, Brighton, East Sussex, BN1 9RE

Tel: 01273 915659
Fax: 01273 621202; 01273 691647
E-mail: blds@ids.ac.uk
Website: www.blds.ids.ac.uk
Website: www.ids.ac.uk/go/knowledge-services
Website: www.ids.ac.uk

Founded: 1966; formerly called IDS Library

Organisation type and purpose: Research/teaching institute library, with a local role to cater for the information needs of the parent institution and a wider remit to increase

continued overleaf

access to information for development practitioners, especially those in the global South.
Services to researchers, postgraduate students, and developing country users.

Subject coverage: Social, economic, political, technological and cultural aspects of societal change, primarily in developing countries. Over 50% of the collection originates from the global South.

Information services: Ask a Librarian – helpdesk providing advice on development-related resources.
BLDS Updates – updates by email or RSS giving details of the latest acquisitions. These are available for 24 different subject areas, and 5 regions, and are produced approximately every 2 weeks.
Document Delivery – the remote supply of scans or copies of material in the collection. This is available free of charge to users in developing countries who are members of GDNet.

Special visitor services: Visitors can access the collection for reference purposes free of charge.
External membership, allowing borrowing from the collection, is offered for a charge.

Services for disabled people: BLDS will ensure that all who need to use the collection or services have access to what they need during their visit.

Non-library collection catalogue: All or part available online

Library catalogue: All or part available online

Publications: Printed
Order printed publications from: via website: http://www.ids.ac.uk/go/bookshop

Publications list: Available online and in print

Access to staff: Contact by letter, by telephone, by fax, by e-mail, in person and via website
Hours: Mon to Fri, 0900 to 1700

Access to building: For all.
Hours: Mon to Fri, 0900 to 1700

Access for disabled people: For all
Hours: Standard hours
Special comments: Some open book stacks inaccessible to wheelchair users.

Funded by: Institute of Development Studies; UK Department for International Development (DfID)

Parent body: Institute of Development Studies (IDS)

INSTITUTE OF DIRECT MARKETING (IDM)

1 Park Road, Teddington, Middlesex, TW11 0AB

Tel: 020 8614 0274
Fax: 020 8614 0246
E-mail: enquiries@theidm.com
Website: www.theidm.com

Enquiries to: Information Services Manager
Direct tel: 020 8614 0253
Direct e-mail: juliethilditch@theidm.com

Founded: 1987

Organisation type and purpose: Professional body (membership is by qualification), present number of members: 5,000, registered charity (charity number 1001865), training organisation.

Subject coverage: Direct marketing.

Collection: Books, journals, press cuttings, reports

Non-library collection catalogue: All or part available online and in-house

Library catalogue: All or part available online and in-house

Publications: Printed, and electronic and video

Publications list: Available online

Access to staff: Contact by telephone, by fax, by e-mail and via website. Appointment necessary. Non-members charged.
Hours: Mon, Tues, 0930 to 1330; Wed, Thur, 0900 to 1600; Fri, 0900 to 1500

INSTITUTE OF DIRECTORS (IoD)

116 Pall Mall, London, SW1Y 5ED

Tel: 020 7839 1233
Fax: 020 7930 1949
E-mail: enquiries@iod.com
Website: www.iod.com

Enquiries to: Head of Information and Advisory Services
Direct tel: 020 7451 3100
Direct e-mail: businessinfo@iod.com

Founded: 1903

Organisation type and purpose: Professional body.

Subject coverage: Company directors, company law, boardroom practice, business, corporate governance.

Collection: Corporate governance collection

Library catalogue: All or part available online

Publications: Printed
Order printed publications from: Book Sales, Institute of Directors
116 Pall Mall, London, SW1Y 5ED, tel: 020 7766 8866, fax: 020 7766 8833, e-mail: pubs@iod.com

Access to staff: Appointment necessary. Access for members only.
Hours: Mon to Fri, 0900 to 1700

Access for disabled people: Toilet facilities

INSTITUTE OF DOMESTIC HEATING AND ENVIRONMENTAL ENGINEERS (IDHEE)

Unit 35A, New Forest Enterprise Centre, Chapel Lane, Totton, Southampton, SO40 9LA

Tel: 023 8066 8900
Fax: 023 8066 0888
E-mail: admin@idhee.org.uk
Website: www.idhee.org.uk

Enquiries to: Chairman
Direct tel: 07973 214574
Direct fax: 023 8081 4756
Direct e-mail: bill.bucknell@idhee.org.uk

Founded: 1964

Organisation type and purpose: National organisation, professional body (membership is by subscription, qualification), present number of members: 1,026.

Subject coverage: Domestic heating and environmental engineering.

Publications list: Available online

Access to staff: Contact by telephone, by e-mail and via website. Non-members charged.
Hours: Mon to Fri, 0900 to 1700

INSTITUTE OF ECONOMIC AFFAIRS (IEA)

2 Lord North Street, London, SW1P 3LB

Tel: 020 7799 8900
Fax: 020 7799 2137
E-mail: iea@iea.org.uk
Website: www.iea.org.uk

Enquiries to: Director General

Founded: 1955

Organisation type and purpose: Registered charity (charity number CC 235 351), research organisation, publishing house.

Subject coverage: Political economy, public choice, microeconomics.

Publications: Printed, and electronic and video

Publications list: Available online and in print

Access to staff: Contact by letter, by telephone, by fax, by e-mail and via website
Hours: Mon to Fri, 0900 to 1700

INSTITUTE OF ECOTECHNICS (IE)

24 Old Gloucester Street, Holborn, London, WC1N 3AL

Tel: 020 7405 1824
Fax: 020 7405 1851
E-mail: nelson@biospheres.com
Website: www.ecotechnics.edu

Enquiries to: Secretary

Founded: 1972

Organisation type and purpose: International organisation, learned society, training organisation, consultancy, research organisation.
Consultant to several businesses managing demonstration projects in varied biomes internationally: Tropic Ventures, Puerto Rico; Savannah Systems Pty Limited, West Australia; RV Heraclitus; Les Marroniers conference centre and Provençal farm, Aix-en-Provence, France; Synergia Ranch, New Mexico, USA.

Subject coverage: Ecological management, biospheric and closed systems.

Publications: Printed

Access to staff: Contact by letter, by fax and by e-mail. Appointment necessary.
Hours: Mon to Fri, 0900 to 1700

Access for disabled people: Ramped entry

INSTITUTE OF EDUCATION

Information Services, 20 Bedford Way, London, WC1H 0AL

Tel: 020 7612 6080
Fax: 020 7612 6093
E-mail: lib.enquiries@ioe.ac.uk
Website: www.ioe.ac.uk/is

Enquiries to: Library Enquiries
Other contacts: Archivist (for access to archives and special collections)

Founded: 1902

Organisation type and purpose: University department or institute, research organisation.

Subject coverage: All aspects of education.

Collection: Largest collection on education in the United Kingdom
Assorted deposited collections and archives

Non-library collection catalogue: All or part available online, in-house and in print

Library catalogue: All or part available online and in-house

Publications: Printed

Access to staff: Contact by letter, by telephone, by fax, by e-mail, in person and via website. Non-members charged.

Access to building: *Hours:* Mon to Thu, 0930 to 2000; Fri, 0930 to 1900; Sat, 0930 to 1700

Access for disabled people: Level entry, access to all public areas, toilet facilities, lift from Bedford Way

INSTITUTE OF EDUCATIONAL TECHNOLOGY (IET)

Open University, Walton Hall, Milton Keynes, Buckinghamshire, MK7 6AA

Tel: 01908 655581
Fax: 01908 654173
E-mail: j.taylor@open.ac.uk
Website: iet.open.ac.uk

Enquiries to: Director

Founded: 1970

Organisation type and purpose: University department or institute, consultancy, research organisation.
The role of the Institute of Educational Technology is to be a centre of international excellence for the teaching, research and development of educational technology in the service of effective learning.

Subject coverage: All aspects of distance and open teaching and learning, specialist areas: course design, education and quality assessment, use of media, information technology, multimedia, disabled students.

Trade and statistical information: National student data on media use and ownership. National student data on vocational intentions

Publications: Printed

Publications list: Available in print

Access to staff: Contact by letter
Hours: Mon to Fri, 0900 to 1700

INSTITUTE OF ELECTROLYSIS, THE

27 Emerson Valley, Milton Keynes, Buckinghamshire, MK4 2AF

Tel: 01908 503161
Fax: 0870 051 3611
E-mail: institute@electrolysis.co.uk
Website: www.electrolysis.co.uk

Enquiries to: Administrator

Founded: 1946

Organisation type and purpose: International organisation, professional body (membership is by qualification), present number of members: 200.

Access to staff: Contact by letter, by telephone and by e-mail
Hours: Mon to Fri, 0900 to 1700

INSTITUTE OF ENVIRONMENTAL MANAGEMENT & ASSESSMENT (IEMA)

St Nicholas House, 70 Newport, Lincoln, LN1 3DP

Tel: 01522 540069
Fax: 01522 540090
E-mail: info@iema.net
Website: www.iema.net

Enquiries to: Chief Executive
Other contacts: Membership Secretary for general membership enquiries.

Founded: 1990

Organisation type and purpose: National organisation, advisory body, professional body, membership association (membership is by subscription), present number of members: 6,500, training organisation, consultancy, research organisation.
To support environmental practitioners in careers by best practice advice in environmental assessment and environmental management, professional development and networking.

Subject coverage: Sustainability and environmental management in UK industry, commerce and local government.
Professional accreditation for environmental professionals; registration for environmental auditors and assessors; registration as Specialist in Land Condition (SiLC); registration for Environmental Impact Assessment (EIA); certification of training; networking and best practice; expert advice and technical support for corporate members.

Publications: Printed, and electronic and video

Publications list: Available online and in print

Access to staff: Contact by letter, by telephone, by fax, by e-mail and via website. Appointment necessary.
Hours: Mon to Fri, 0900 to 1700

Access to building: Prior appointment required
Hours: Mon to Fri, 0900 to 1700
Special comments: Library available to corporate members only.

Access for disabled people: Parking provided, toilet facilities
Special comments: Steps up to building

INSTITUTE OF EXPLOSIVES ENGINEERS (IExpE)

Wellington Hall 289, Cranfield University, Defence Academy of the UK, Shrivenham, Swindon, Wiltshire, SN6 8LA

Tel: 01793 785322
Fax: 01793 785772
E-mail: iexpe@cranfield.ac.uk
Website: www.iexpe.org

Enquiries to: Secretary

Founded: 1974

Organisation type and purpose: Professional body, membership association (membership is both by subscription and by qualification).
To represent companies and individuals who use explosives as part of the everyday tools of their trade.
A forum for demolition contractors, explosives manufacturers, underwater specialists, miners, tunnellers, quarrymen, disposal contractors, vibration specialists, oil industry contractors, special effects technicians (pyrotechnicians), firework display operators, police explosives liaison officers, legislators and members of the armed services.

Subject coverage: Use of explosives in civil engineering (demolition, tunnelling, shaft sinking, land clearance and excavation, underwater rock breaking and excavation) and in quarries and offshore oil operations; recording and interpreting disturbances occasioned by blasting operations.

Publications: Printed

Access to staff: Contact by letter, by telephone, by fax and by e-mail

Member organisation of: European Federation of Explosives Engineers

Professional affiliate of: Engineering Council UK (ECUK)

INSTITUTE OF EXPORT (IoE)

Export House, Minerva Business Park, Lynch Wood, Peterborough, Cambridgeshire, PE2 6FT

Tel: 01733 404400
Fax: 01733 404444
E-mail: institute@export.org.uk
Website: www.export.org.uk

Enquiries to: Information Officer

Founded: 1935

Organisation type and purpose: Professional body (membership is by qualification), registered charity, university department or institute, suitable for ages: Post-school and mature, training organisation.
Sets and raises standards in international trade management and export practice through professional qualifications and training.

Subject coverage: Sources of information on all aspects of international trade and training for exporters, leading to professional qualifications.

Publications: Printed, and electronic and video

Publications list: Available in print

continued overleaf

Access to staff: Contact by letter, by telephone, by fax, by e-mail and via website
Hours: Mon to Fri, 0900 to 1700

Access for disabled people: Parking provided, level entry, toilet facilities

INSTITUTE OF FAMILY THERAPY (LONDON) LIMITED (IFT)

24–32 Stephenson Way, London, NW1 2HX

Tel: 020 7391 9150
Fax: 020 7391 9169
E-mail: ift@psyc.bbk.ac.uk
Website: www.instituteoffamilytherapy.org.uk

Enquiries to: Director
Other contacts: Senior Administrator

Founded: 1977

Organisation type and purpose:
Professional body (membership is by qualification), present number of members: 204, voluntary organisation, registered charity (charity number 284858), training organisation, consultancy.

Subject coverage: Availability of family therapy resources across the country; advice, through appropriate professionals, on specialist subjects relating to the family, such as bereavement, divorce, child abuse, AIDS, adolescent problems, disability and many other issues.

Publications: Electronic and video

Publications list: Available in print

Access to staff: Contact by letter, by telephone, by fax, by e-mail and via website
Hours: Mon to Thu, 1000 to 1800; Fri, 1000 to 1700 (some evenings)

Affiliated to: Birkbeck College; London University; National Family Mediation

Member of: Association of Family Therapy; European Family Therapy Association; UK Council for Psychotherapy; UK Standing Conference for Psychotherapy

INSTITUTE OF FINANCIAL ACCOUNTANTS (IFA)

Burford House, 44 London Road, Sevenoaks, Kent, TN13 1AS

Tel: 01732 458080
Fax: 01732 455848
E-mail: mail@ifa.org.uk
Website: www.ifa.org.uk

Enquiries to: Chief Executive

Founded: 1916

Organisation type and purpose:
Professional body.
Examining and qualifying body.

Subject coverage: All aspects of accountancy, management, company law, data processing, information technology, taxation, economics and general administration.

Publications: Printed

Access to staff: Contact by letter, by telephone, by fax, by e-mail and via website. Appointment necessary.
Hours: Mon to Thu, 0900 to 1700; Fri, 0900 to 1600

Access to building: Prior appointment required

Access for disabled people: Parking provided

Junior body is the: International Association of Book-Keepers

INSTITUTE OF FINANCIAL PLANNING (IFP)

Southgate, Whitefriars, Lewins Mead, Bristol, BS1 2NT

Tel: 0117 945 2470
Fax: 0117 929 2214
E-mail: enquiries@financialplanning.org.uk
Website: www.financialplanning.org.uk

Enquiries to: Chief Executive

Founded: 1986

Organisation type and purpose:
International organisation, professional body (membership is by subscription, qualification), present number of members: 1,300, training organisation.
The principle aim of the Institute is to promote the understanding and recognition of the financial planning profession.

Subject coverage: Personal financial planning and management, business planning.

Collection: Reference works

Publications: Printed, and electronic and video

Access to staff: Contact by letter, by telephone, by fax, by e-mail and via website
Hours: Mon to Fri, 0915 to 1745

Member of: International Certified Financial Planner Council

INSTITUTE OF FOOD SCIENCE AND TECHNOLOGY (IFST)

5 Cambridge Court, 210 Shepherd's Bush Road, London, W6 7NJ

Tel: 020 7603 6316
Fax: 020 7602 9936
E-mail: info@ifst.org
Website: www.ifst.org

Enquiries to: Team Executive

Founded: 1964

Organisation type and purpose:
Professional body (membership is by qualification), present number of members: 2,500, registered charity (charity number 264044).

Subject coverage: Food Science and Technology.

Collection: Mounfield Collection of historic books relating to food science and technology (no public access)

Trade and statistical information: No

Non-library collection catalogue: All or part available in-house

Publications: Printed

Publications list: Available online and in print

Access to staff: Contact by letter, by telephone, by fax, by e-mail and via website. Appointment necessary.
Hours: Mon to Fri, 0930 to 1300 and 1400 to 1730

Access to building: No access other than to staff

INSTITUTE OF FUNDRAISING

Park Place, 12 Lawn Lane, London, SW8 1UD

Tel: 020 7840 1000
Fax: 020 7840 1001
Website: www.institute-of-fundraising.org.uk/

Enquiries to: Press Team
Direct e-mail: press@institute-of-fundraising.org.uk

Founded: 1983; formerly called Institute of Charity Fundraising Managers (ICFM)

Organisation type and purpose:
Professional body.

Subject coverage: Codes of practice, training, advice and techniques for fundraisers.

Collection: Fundraising in the UK and abroad, targets including trusts and companies

Publications: Printed

Publications list: Available online and in print

Access to staff: Contact by letter, by telephone and by e-mail. Appointment necessary.
Hours: Mon to Fri, 0900 to 1700

Access to building: Prior appointment required
Hours: Mon to Fri, 0900 to 1700

Access for disabled people: Ramped entry

INSTITUTE OF GROCERY DISTRIBUTION (IGD)

Grange Lane, Letchmore Heath, Watford, Hertfordshire, WD2 8DQ

Tel: 01923 857141
Fax: 01923 852531
E-mail: igd@igd.com
Website: www.igd.com

Enquiries to: Database Manager

Founded: 1909

Organisation type and purpose:
Professional body (membership is by subscription), present number of members: 500, registered charity (charity number 105680), training organisation, consultancy, research organisation.

Subject coverage: Leading source of information and analysis on the UK and European food industry.

Publications: Printed, and electronic and video
Order printed publications from: Publications Department, IGD
at same address, tel: 01923 851925, fax: 01923 852531, e-mail: publications@igd.org.uk

Publications list: Available in print

Access to staff: Contact by letter, by telephone, by fax, by e-mail and via website. Appointment necessary. Non-members charged.
Hours: Mon to Fri, 0900 to 1700

Access to building: Prior appointment required

INSTITUTE OF GROUNDSMANSHIP (IOG)

28 Stratford Office Village, Walker Avenue, Wolverton Mill East, Milton Keynes, MK12 5TW

Tel: 01908 312511
Fax: 01908 311140
E-mail: iog@iog.org
Website: www.iog.org

Enquiries to: Chief Executive
Direct e-mail: marketing@iog.org

Founded: 1934

Organisation type and purpose: Membership association, suitable for ages: 18+, training organisation, consultancy.

Subject coverage: All matters relating to grass, or turf, in sports amenity or leisure; organiser of the largest trade exhibition for the sports amenity and landscaping industry, IOGSALTEX, held annually at the Royal Windsor Racecourse in September; consultancy service on all aspects of the turf industry.

Publications: Printed

Access to staff: Contact by letter, by telephone, by fax, by e-mail and via website. Appointment necessary.
Hours: Mon to Fri, 0900 to 1700

Incorporates the: Association of Landscape Managers

Links with: FA Technical Pitch Committee; RHS; ROSPA; Sports Council

INSTITUTE OF HEALTH PROMOTION AND EDUCATION (IHPE)

University Dental Hospital, Higher Cambridge Street, Manchester, M15 6FH

Tel: 0161 275 6610
Fax: 0161 275 6299
E-mail: honsec@ihpe.org.uk
Website: www.ihpe.org.uk

Enquiries to: Honorary Secretary

Organisation type and purpose: Professional organisation.

Subject coverage: Health promotion and education.

Publications: Printed

INSTITUTE OF HEALTH RECORDS AND INFORMATION MANAGEMENT (IHRIM (UK))

IHRIM (UK) Headquarters, Marshall House, Heanor Gate Road, Heanor, Derbyshire DE75 7RG

Tel: 01773 713927
Fax: 01773 713927
E-mail: ihrim@zen.co.uk
Website: www.ihrim.co.uk

Enquiries to: Chief Executive
Direct tel: 01767 220650
Direct e-mail: ceo.ihrim@zen.co.uk

Founded: 1948; formerly called AMRO

Organisation type and purpose: Professional body for NHS and overseas staff employed in the fields of health informatics.

Subject coverage: Management of health records – systems and services, health record information management, clinical coding, information governance.

Education services: Certificate, Foundation and Diploma examinations in health informatics, National Clinical Coding Qualification

Publications: Printed
Order printed publications from: IHRIM Office

Publications list: Available online

Access to staff: Contact by letter, by telephone, by fax and by e-mail. Appointment necessary. Non-members charged.
Hours: Mon to Fri, 0930 to 1400

INSTITUTE OF HEALTH SCIENCES LIBRARY (IHS)

Old Road, Headington, Oxford, OX3 7LF

Tel: 01865 226688
Fax: 01865 226619
E-mail: reader.services@bodleian.ox.ac.uk
Website: www.library.ox.ac.uk

Enquiries to: Librarian
Direct tel: 01865 226618

Founded: 1996

Organisation type and purpose: University library.

Subject coverage: Health Services administration, evidence-based medicine, epidemiology, primary care and public health.

Library catalogue: All or part available online

Access to staff: Contact by letter, by telephone, by fax and by e-mail. Non-members charged.
Hours: Mon to Fri, 0900 to 1700

Access for disabled people: Access to all public areas, toilet facilities
Special comments: Lift to first floor

Parent body: University of Oxford

INSTITUTE OF HEALTHCARE ENGINEERING & ESTATE MANAGEMENT (IHEEM)

2 Abingdon House, Cumberland Business Centre, Northumberland Road, Portsmouth, Hampshire, PO5 1DS

Tel: 023 9282 3186
Fax: 023 9281 5927
E-mail: office@iheem.org.uk
Website: www.iheem.org.uk

Enquiries to: Administration Officer

Founded: 1943; formerly called Hospital of Engineering; incorporates the former X Ray Society

Organisation type and purpose: Learned society, professional body (membership is by qualification, election or invitation).

Subject coverage: Hospital engineering, medical equipment, estate management relating to the healthcare sector.

Publications: Printed
Order printed publications from: Main address

Access to staff: Contact by letter, by telephone, by fax, by e-mail and via website
Hours: Mon to Fri, 0900 to 1700

Administers: International Federation of Healthcare Engineering; website: http://www.ifhe.info

Links with: Engineering Council

INSTITUTE OF HERALDIC AND GENEALOGICAL STUDIES (IHGS)

79–82 Northgate, Canterbury, Kent, CT1 1BA

Tel: 01227 768664
Fax: 01227 765617
E-mail: librarian@ihgs.ac.uk
Website: www.ihgs.ac.uk

Enquiries to: Librarian

Founded: 1961

Organisation type and purpose: Membership association, registered charity (charity number 286429), research organisation.
Educational trust; training, study and research body.

Subject coverage: Family history, genealogy, heraldry, foreign heraldry, Coats of Arms, genetic diseases.

Collection: Catholic Marriage Index (London and Essex)
Complete Collection of Siebmacher's Wappenbuchen
Armorial Indexes
Manorial and early heraldic manuscripts
Marriage Indexes not collected elsewhere
Numerous family histories and pedigrees
Pallot Marriage Index (1780–1837, mainly London)
Sources and finding aids of special significance including International Genealogical Index and other indexes on microfiche; printout services available
Special collections for Kent, Sussex, Hampshire, London and Middlesex

Non-library collection catalogue: All or part available in-house

Library catalogue: All or part available in-house

Publications: Printed, and microform publications

Publications list: Available in print

Access to staff: Contact by letter, by telephone and by e-mail. Appointment necessary. Non-members charged.
Hours: Mon to Fri, 1000 to 1630

INSTITUTE OF HIGHWAY ENGINEERS (IHE)

De Morgan House, 58 Russell Square, London, WC1B 4HS

Tel: 020 7436 7487

continued overleaf

Fax: 020 7436 7488
E-mail: information@theihe.org
Website: www.theihe.org

Enquiries to: Chief Executive
Direct e-mail: secretary@theihe.org

Founded: 1965; formerly called Institute of Highway Incorporated Engineers (year of change 2009)

Organisation type and purpose:
Professional body, present number of members: 3,000.

Subject coverage: Highway engineering; traffic and transportation; highway maintenance.

Publications: Electronic and video

Publications list: Available online

Access to staff: Contact by letter, by telephone, by e-mail and via website. Appointment necessary.
Hours: Tues, Weds, Thurs, 0900 to 1700

Member organisation of: Engineering Council UK

INSTITUTE OF HISTORICAL RESEARCH (IHR)

University of London, Senate House, Malet Street, London, WC1E 7HU

Tel: 020 7862 8760
Fax: 020 7862 8762
E-mail: ihr.library@sas.ac.uk
Website: www.history.ac.uk
Website: catalogue.ulrls.lon.ac.uk/search~S10

Enquiries to: Librarian

Founded: 1921

Organisation type and purpose: University department or institute, postgraduate institute.

Subject coverage: History of Western Europe and its expansion overseas, c. AD450 to the present; imperial and colonial history; military and naval history; diplomatic history; history of international relations.

Library catalogue: All or part available online

Publications: Printed, and electronic and video
Order printed publications from: Publications Manager

Publications list: Available online and in print

Access to staff: Contact by letter, by telephone, by e-mail and in person. Appointment necessary.
Hours: Mon to Fri, 0900 to 2045; Sat, 0930 to 1715

Member organisation of: School of Advanced Study; University of London, Senate House, Malet Street, London, WC1E 7HU; website: http://www.sas.ac.uk
University of London Research Library Services (ULRLS); Senate House, Malet Street, London, WC1E 7HU; website: http://www.ulrls.lon.ac.uk

INSTITUTE OF HORTICULTURE (IoH)

Capel Manor College, Bullsmoor Lane, Enfield, EN1 4RQ

Tel: 01992 707025
Fax: 01992 707025
E-mail: ioh@horticulture.org.uk
Website: www.horticulture.org.uk

Enquiries to: Administration Manager

Founded: 1984

Organisation type and purpose:
Professional body (membership is by qualification), present number of members: 1,200.

Subject coverage: All aspects of horticulture, education, training and career progression in the amenity, commercial, research and advisory sectors.

Publications: Printed, and electronic and video

Access to staff: Contact by letter, by telephone, by fax, by e-mail and via website. Appointment necessary.
Hours: Mon to Fri, 08.30 to 17.15

INSTITUTE OF HOSPITALITY

Trinity Court, 34 West Street, Sutton, Surrey, SM1 1SH

Tel: 020 8661 4900
Fax: 020 8661 4901
Website: www.instituteofhospitality.org
Website: moodle.instituteofhospitality.org

Founded: 1971; created by the merger of Hotel and Catering Institute (HCI, created 1949) and the Institutional Management Association (IMA, created 1938) (year of change 1971); formerly called Hotel & Catering International Management Association (HCIMA) (year of change 2007)

Organisation type and purpose: A registered educational charity, the professional body for managers – and aspiring managers – working in the hospitality, leisure and tourism industries, a recognised and authoritative international body in the field of accreditation for hospitality, leisure and tourism programmes of learning; has over 10,000 members in the UK, and in more than 100 countries world-wide.
To promote the highest professional standards of management and education in the international hospitality, leisure and tourism industries; to benefit members in their professional and career development, while continuing to improve industry sector standards; to offer support to members throughout their careers in the industry.

Subject coverage: Covers all sectors of the industry including hotels, contract catering companies, restaurants, pubs and clubs, as well as leisure outlets, theme parks and sports venues. Works closely with all hospitality, leisure and tourism agencies, education and awarding bodies, and government departments, providing an interface between education and industry.

Information services: Library Staff, tel: 020 8661 4902; e-mail: library@instituteofhospitality.org.

Education services: Free online learning modules tailored to meet the needs of hospitality and tourism students and professionals.

Collection: Library and Information Service is a unique collection of resources in the field of hospitality, leisure & tourism (HLT); members have free access

Library catalogue: All or part available online

Publications: Printed, and electronic and video

Publications list: Available online

Access to staff: Contact by letter, by telephone, by fax and via website

INSTITUTE OF INDIAN CULTURE (BHARATIYA VIDYA BHAVAN) (BHAVAN)

Formal name: Bharatiya Vidya Bhavan – Institute of Indian Art and Culture

4A Castletown Road, West Kensington, London, W14 9HQ

Tel: 020 7381 3086 or 4608
Fax: 020 7381 8758
Website: www.bhavan.net

Enquiries to: Executive Director
Other contacts: Academic Director

Founded: 1972

Organisation type and purpose:
International organisation, professional body (membership is by subscription), present number of members: 1,220, voluntary organisation, registered charity (charity number 312879), public library, suitable for ages: 7+, training organisation, research organisation.
To popularise in the UK Indian art, archaeology, languages and culture in general.

Subject coverage: Indian philosophy, religion, languages, pilgrimage centres, festivals, calendar dates, music, dance, drama and all things connected with Indian art and culture.

Collection: Complete writings of Gandhi, Nehru and other Indian writers

Publications: Printed, and electronic and video

Publications list: Available in print

Access to staff: Contact by letter, by telephone, by fax and in person. Appointment necessary. All charged.
Hours: 0900 to 1900, seven days a week
Special comments: Wheelchair access to ground floor only.

Access to building: No prior appointment required
Hours: Mon to Fri, 0900 to 1700
Special comments: Books cannot be borrowed from Bhavan's library.

Bhavan's outreach classes at: Alperton Community School; Stanley Avenue, off Ealing Road, Wembley, Middlesex, HA0 4JE; tel: 020 7381 3086; fax: 020 7381 8758

Parent body and Head Office: Bharatiya Vidya Bhavan (BHAVAN); Munshi Sadan, Kulapati K M Munshi Marg, Chaupatti, Mumbai, Bombay, 400 007, India; tel: 00 91 22 363 0786; fax: 00 91 22 363 0058

INSTITUTE OF INDIRECT TAXATION (IIT)

Suite G1, The Stables, Station Road West, Oxted, RH5 9EE

Tel: 01883 730658
Fax: 01883 717778
E-mail: enquiries@theiit.org.uk
Website: www.theiit.org.uk

Enquiries to: Administrator
Direct e-mail: postmaster@theiit.org.uk

Founded: 1991

Organisation type and purpose: Professional body.

Subject coverage: Indirect taxes.

Publications: Printed

Access to staff: Contact by letter, by telephone, by fax, by e-mail and via website. Appointment necessary.
Hours: Mon to Fri, 0900 to 1700

Access to building: Mon to Fri, 0900 to 1700

Access for disabled people: Fully accessible

INSTITUTE OF INTERNAL AUDITORS UK & IRELAND (IIA UK & Ireland)

13 Abbeville Mews, 88 Clapham Park Road, London, SW4 7BX

Tel: 020 7498 0101
Fax: 020 7978 2492
E-mail: info@iia.org.uk
Website: www.iia.org.uk

Founded: 1975

Organisation type and purpose: Professional body (membership is by subscription), present number of members: 6,000.

Subject coverage: Corporate governance and risk management, internal control and internal auditing (general and computer).

Non-library collection catalogue: All or part available online and in print

Library catalogue: All or part available in-house

Publications: Printed

Publications list: Available online and in print

Access to staff: Contact by letter, by telephone, by fax, by e-mail and via website
Hours: Mon to Fri, 0900 to 1700

Affiliated to: European Confederation of Institutes of Internal Auditing; Institute of Internal Auditors Incorporate, USA

INSTITUTE OF INTERNAL COMMUNICATION (IoIC)

Suite GA2, Oak House, Woodlands Business Park, Linford Wood, Milton Keynes, MK14 6EY

Tel: 01908 313755
Fax: 01908 313661
E-mail: enquiries@ioic.org.uk
Website: www.ioic.org.uk

Founded: 1949; formerly called British Association of Industrial Editors (year of change 1995); formerly called British Association of Communicators in Business Ltd (CiB) (year of change 2010)

Organisation type and purpose: Professional body (membership is by subscription), present number of members: 1,000.

Subject coverage: Internal communication management and practice.

Publications: Printed, and electronic and video
Order printed publications from: Available to IoIC members

Access to staff: Contact by letter, by telephone, by fax and by e-mail

Liaison with: International Association of Business Communicators; USA

Member of: Federation of European Internal Communication Associations (FEIEA)

INSTITUTE OF INTERNATIONAL EDUCATION IN LONDON (IIEL)

Charlton House, Charlton Road, Charlton, London, SE7 8RE

Tel: 020 8331 3100
Fax: 020 8331 3149
E-mail: enquiries@iiel.org.uk
Website: www.iiel.org.uk

Enquiries to: Course Coordinator
Other contacts: Publicity Coordinator

Founded: 1989

Organisation type and purpose: International organisation, university department or institute, suitable for ages: 5+, training organisation, consultancy.
Japanese teacher training centre, EFL courses, JFL courses and consultancy on university and college entrance.

Subject coverage: Japanese language for younger learners (mother tongue Japanese), Japanese teacher training, the study of Japanese as a foreign language, the study of English as a foreign language and entrance to British universities.

Publications: Printed

Access to staff: Contact by letter, by telephone, by fax, by e-mail, in person and via website. Appointment necessary.
Hours: Mon to Fri, 0900 to 1730

Also at: ICJ – Japan Office; 2F Maeda Building, 2–13–2 Suido, Bunkyo-ku, Tokyo, 112–0005, Japan; tel: 00 81 3 5940 0506; fax: 00 81 3 5940 0507; e-mail: info@edu-icj.com

INSTITUTE OF INTERNATIONAL LICENSING PRACTITIONERS (IILP)

28 Main Street, Mursley, Milton Keynes, MK17 0RT

Tel: 01296 728136
Fax: 01296 720070
E-mail: enquiries@iilp.net
Website: www.iilp.net

Founded: 1969

Organisation type and purpose: International organisation, professional body (membership is by qualification, election or invitation).
To provide professional licensing assistance to companies requiring technology transfer services; to set professional standards for those engaged in licensing consultancy.

Subject coverage: Licensing, commercialising invention, technology transfer, distribution agreements, strategic alliances, joint ventures.

Publications: Printed

Access to staff: Contact by letter, by telephone, by fax and by e-mail. Non-members charged.
Hours: Mon to Fri, 0800 to 1800

Affiliated to: Licensing Innovation and Technology Consultants Association (LICTA); Let 2 Anaweg 25–27, Triesen, FL-9495, Liechtenstein; tel: +41 75 399 1000; fax: +41 75 399 1091; e-mail: enquiries@iilp.net; website: http://www.iilp.net

INSTITUTE OF INVENTORS (IoI)

19–23 Fosse Way, Ealing, London, W13 0BZ

Tel: 020 8998 3540/6372
E-mail: mikinvent@aol.com
Website: www.instituteofinventors.com

Enquiries to: President
Direct tel: 020 8998 6372; 020 8998 4372; 020 8998 3540
Direct e-mail: mikinvent@aol.com

Founded: 1964

Organisation type and purpose: International professional engineer inventor organisation for patents & rapid prototypes. Membership by subscription. Current number of members: 1,580.
A non-profit, voluntary Institute, to personally help inventor members' inventions with searches, evaluation, patenting, rapid prototypes, licence agreements, manufacture & sales.

Non-library collection catalogue: All or part available online

Library catalogue: All or part available online

Publications: Printed

Access to staff: Contact by letter, by telephone, by e-mail and via website. Appointment necessary.
Hours: Mon to Sun, 1000 to 1900

INSTITUTE OF IRISH STUDIES

Queen's University Belfast, 8 Fitzwilliam Street, Belfast, BT9 6AW

Tel: 028 9027 3386
Fax: 028 9043 9238
E-mail: irish.studies@qub.ac.uk
Website: www.qub.ac.uk/iis

Enquiries to: Director
Other contacts: Secretary for enquiries about courses, the work of the Institute etc.

Founded: 1965

continued overleaf

Organisation type and purpose: University department or institute, research organisation, publishing house.

Subject coverage: Academic research on Ireland, primarily in the humanities.

Order printed publications from: Institute of Irish Studies;
at the same address, tel: 028 9027 3235, fax: 028 9043 9238, e-mail: m.mcnulty@qub.ac.uk

Publications list: Available online and in print

Access to staff: Contact by letter and by fax
Hours: Mon to Fri, 0900 to 1700

INSTITUTE OF ISMAILI STUDIES (IIS)

210 Euston Road, London, NW1 2DA

Tel: 020 7756 2700
Fax: 020 7756 2740
E-mail: info@iis.ac.uk
Website: www.iis.ac.uk

Founded: 1977

Organisation type and purpose: Research institute, graduate studies, library.
To promote scholarship and learning of Islamic cultures and societies, historical as well as contemporary, Shi'ism in general, Isma'ilism in particular.

Subject coverage: Islamic studies, especially Shi'ism and Isma'ilism.

Collection: Library of 25,000 items, including manuscripts (in Arabic, Persian, and Khojki script)

Non-library collection catalogue: All or part available in-house and in print

Library catalogue: All or part available online and in-house

Publications: Printed
Order printed publications from: See website for details: http://www.iis.ac.uk

Publications list: Available online and in print

Access to staff: Contact by letter, by telephone, by fax, by e-mail and via website

INSTITUTE OF JEWISH STUDIES (IJS)

University College London, Foster Court, Gower Street, London, WC1E 6BT

Tel: 020 7679 3520
Fax: 020 7209 1026
E-mail: ijs@ucl.ac.uk
Website: www.ucl.ac.uk/hebrew-jewish/ijs

Organisation type and purpose: Affiliated with University College London's Department of Hebrew and Jewish Studies, the Institute is dedicated to the promotion of all aspects of Jewish scholarship and civilisation, with the aim of reaching every section of the Jewish community and of the interested non-Jewish public.
Holds public lectures, symposia, seminars and international conferences.

Subject coverage: Jewish scholarship and civilisation.

INSTITUTE OF LEADERSHIP & MANAGEMENT (ILM)

Stowe House, Netherstone, Lichfield, Staffordshire, WS13 6TJ

Tel: 01543 251346
Fax: 01543 266811
E-mail: customer@i-l-m.com
Website: www.nebsmgt.co.uk
Website: www.i-l-m.com
Website: www.ismstowe.com

Enquiries to: Information Services Manager
Direct e-mail: info@ismstowe-info.demon.co.uk

Founded: 1947

Organisation type and purpose:
Professional body (membership is by subscription, qualification), present number of members: 20,000, registered charity (charity number 248226), suitable for ages: normally 19+.
Professional institute for front-line managers and supervisors.

Subject coverage: Accreditation of management courses and NVQ/SVQs; customer care awards, training support awards, and world class qualifications, management and training topics.

Library catalogue: All or part available in-house

Publications: Printed, and electronic and video

Access to staff: Contact by letter, by telephone, by fax, by e-mail and via website.
Appointment necessary.
Hours: Mon to Fri, 0830 to 1700

Access to building: No access other than to staff
Hours: Mon to Fri, 1000 to 1600

Access for disabled people: Parking provided, ramped entry, toilet facilities

Second address: Institute of Leadership & Management; 1 Giltspur Street, London, EC1A 9DD; tel: 020 7294 3057; fax: 020 7294 2402; e-mail: nebsmgt@city-and-guilds.co.uk

INSTITUTE OF LEGAL CASHIERS & ADMINISTRATORS (ILCA)

146–148 Eltham Hill, Eltham, London, SE9 5DX

Tel: 020 8294 2887
Fax: 020 8859 1682
E-mail: info@ilca.org.uk
Website: www.ilca.org.uk

Enquiries to: Executive Secretary
Other contacts: Editor for press information.

Founded: 1978

Organisation type and purpose:
Professional body (membership is by subscription), present number of members: 2600, training organisation, research organisation, publishing house.
To promote excellence in legal finance and administration.

Subject coverage: Legal accounting, financial control, administration, marketing, personnel management, solicitors' accounts rules, VAT, law office management, accounting for legal aid.

Publications: Printed

Publications list: Available in print

Access to staff: Contact by letter, by telephone, by fax, by e-mail and via website.
Appointment necessary.
Hours: Mon to Fri, 0900 to 1700

Access for disabled people: Access to all public areas

Chairman: Institute of Legal Accountants of Ireland; c/o Wellfield House, Blessington Road, Naas, County Kildare, Eire

INSTITUTE OF LEGAL EXECUTIVES (ILEX)

Kempston Manor, Kempston, Bedford, MK42 7AB

Tel: 01234 841000
Fax: 01234 840989
E-mail: info@ilex.org.uk
Website: www.ilex.org.uk
Website: www.legal-executive-recruitment.com
Website: www.ilexjournal.com
Website: www.ilexpt.co.uk
Website: www.ilex-tutorial.ac.uk

Enquiries to: Secretary General
Other contacts: Head of Communications and Public Relations for press and media enquiries, articles etc.

Founded: 1963

Organisation type and purpose:
Professional body (membership is by qualification), present number of members: 22,000.
Examining body.

Subject coverage: Legal training services, for both lawyers and non-lawyers, law reform, distance learning.

Collection: Law Library (members only)

Publications: Printed, and electronic and video

Access to staff: Contact by letter, by telephone, by fax and by e-mail.
Appointment necessary.
Hours: Mon to Fri, 0900 to 1700

Subsidiary bodies: ILEX Paralegal Training; tel: 01234 348848; fax: 01234 266557; e-mail: ilex.pt@btconnect.com; ILEX Publishing and Advertising; tel: 01234 845721; fax: 01234 841999; e-mail: ipa@legal-executive-journal.co.uk; ILEX Tutorial College; tel: 01234 841010; fax: 01234 841373

INSTITUTE OF LICENSED TRADE STOCK AUDITORS (ILTSA)

7 Comely Bank Place, Edinburgh, EH4 1DT

Tel: 0131 315 2600
Fax: 0131 315 4346
Website: www.iltsa.co.uk

Enquiries to: Secretary
Direct e-mail: secretary@iltsa.co.uk

Founded: 1953

Organisation type and purpose: National organisation, professional body (membership is by qualification), present number of members: c. 400.
The only qualifying body for stock auditors within the licensed trade. The institute is also able to mediate in disputes concerning

stocktaking and can act in an advisory capacity to any company or individual who seeks advice.

Subject coverage: Qualified stocktakers, stocktaking, licensed trade, training, examinations, legislation affecting trade, specialist valuations.

Publications: Printed

Access to staff: Contact by letter, by telephone, by fax and by e-mail
Hours: Mon to Fri, 0900 to 1700

INSTITUTE OF MANAGEMENT CONSULTANCY (IMC)

3rd Floor, 17–18 Haywards Place, London, EC1R 0EQ

Tel: 020 7566 5220
Fax: 020 7566 5230
Website: www.imc.co.uk

Enquiries to: Chief Executive

Founded: 1962

Organisation type and purpose:
Professional body.
The IMC leads the profession of management consultancy by qualifying, supporting and regulating individual management consultants and providing a forum for all management consultancy stakeholders.

Subject coverage: Management consulting practice and careers.

Publications: Printed

Publications list: Available in print

Access to staff: Contact by letter, by telephone and by fax. Appointment necessary.
Hours: Mon to Fri, 0900 to 1700

INSTITUTE OF MANAGEMENT SERVICES (IMS)

Brooke House, 24 Dam Street, Lichfield, Staffordshire, WS13 6AA

Tel: 01543 266909
Fax: 01543 257848
E-mail: admin@ims-stowe.fsnet.co.uk
Website: www.ims-productivity.com

Enquiries to: Information Officer

Founded: 1941

Organisation type and purpose:
Professional body, present number of members: 1700.

Subject coverage: Work study; organisation and methods, business systems, work environment, motivation, information technology; quality management and control; industrial engineering, business process re-engineering.

Publications: Printed, and electronic and video

Publications list: Available in print

Access to staff: Contact by letter, by telephone, by fax, by e-mail and via website. Appointment necessary. Non-members charged.
Hours: Mon to Fri, 0930 to 1445

Links with: Alliance of Manufacturing and Management Organisations (AMMO); European Federation of Productivity Services (EFPS); World Confederation of Productivity Science (WCPS)

INSTITUTE OF MANAGEMENT SPECIALISTS (IMS)

Warwick Corner, 42 Warwick Road, Kenilworth, Warwickshire, CV8 1HE

Tel: 01926 259342
E-mail: info@instituteofmanagementspecialists.org.uk
Website: www.instituteofmanagementspecialists.org.uk

Enquiries to: Executive Administrator

Founded: 1971

Organisation type and purpose:
International organisation, professional body (membership is by subscription, qualification), training organisation, range of professional diploma courses available.

Subject coverage: Management; administration; technical and computer sciences.

Publications: Electronic and video

Access to staff: Contact by letter, by telephone, by e-mail and via website

Links with: Faculty of Professional Business and Technical Management (FPBTM); website: www.pbtm.org.uk
Institute of Manufacturing (IManf); website: www.instituteofmanufacturing.org.uk
The Academy of Executives and Administrators (AEA); website: www.academyofexecutivesandadministrators.org.uk
The Academy of Multi-Skills (AMS); website: www.academyofmultiskills.org.uk

INSTITUTE OF MANUFACTURING (IManf)

Warwick Corner, 42 Warwick Road, Kenilworth, Warwickshire, CV8 1HE

Tel: 01926 259342
E-mail: info@instituteofmanufacturing.org.uk
Website: www.instituteofmanufacturing.org.uk

Enquiries to: Executive Administrator

Founded: 1978

Organisation type and purpose:
Professional body (membership is by subscription, qualification), training organisation, range of professional diploma courses available.

Subject coverage: Manufacturing; industry; management – general and specialised; technical and computer sciences; education and training.

Publications: Electronic and video

Access to staff: Contact by letter, by telephone, by e-mail and via website

Links with: Faculty of Professional Business and Technical Management (FPBTM); website: www.pbtm.org.uk
Institute of Management Specialists (IMS); website: www.instituteofmanagementspecialists.org.uk
The Academy of Executives and Administrators (AEA); website: www.academyofexecutivesandadministrators.org.uk
The Academy of Multi-Skills (AMS); website: www.academyofmultiskills.org.uk

INSTITUTE OF MARINE ENGINEERING, SCIENCE AND TECHNOLOGY (IMarEST)

80 Coleman Street, London, EC2R 5BJ

Tel: 020 7382 2600
Fax: 020 7382 2670
E-mail: mic@imare.org.uk
Website: www.imare.org.uk

Enquiries to: Manager of Information Centre
Direct tel: 020 7382 2645
Direct e-mail: membership@imarest.org
Other contacts: Manager of Engineering, Science & Technology for technical information regarding marine engineering.

Founded: 1889

Organisation type and purpose: Learned society, professional body (membership is by qualification), present number of members: 17,000, registered charity (charity number 212992).
Promoting the maritime industries.

Subject coverage: Marine engineering; marine electrical engineering; ocean technology, offshore engineering, naval architecture, shipping, subsea technology.

Non-library collection catalogue: All or part available online

Publications: Printed, and electronic and video

Publications list: Available online and in print

Access to staff: Contact by letter, by telephone, by fax, by e-mail, in person and via website. All charged.
Hours: Mon to Fri, 0900 to 1700

Access for disabled people: Ramped entry

INSTITUTE OF MATERIALS, MINERALS AND MINING (IOM3)

1 Carlton House Terrace, London, SW1Y 5DB

Tel: 020 7451 7300
Fax: 020 7839 1702/020 7451 7406
E-mail: libraryservices@iom3.org
Website: www.iom3.org/content/library-services

Enquiries to: Information and Library Co-ordinator or Information Officer
Direct tel: 020 7451 7360/7324
Direct fax: 020 7451 7406
Direct e-mail: hilda.kaune@iom3.org; frances.perry@iom3.org

Founded: 1869

Organisation type and purpose:
Professional body (membership is by qualification), present number of members: 20,000.
The Institute of Materials, Minerals and Mining (IOM3) is a major UK engineering institution, the activities of which encompass the whole materials cycle, from exploration

continued overleaf

and extraction, through characterisation, processing, forming, finishing and application, to product recycling and land reuse. It exists to promote and develop all aspects of materials science and engineering, geology, mining and associated technologies, mineral and petroleum engineering and extraction metallurgy, as a leading authority in the world-wide materials and mining community.

Subject coverage: Science and technology of metals, polymers, rubbers, ceramics, composites, wood and packaging; production and use; physics and chemistry of materials and production processes. Economic geology, mining and processing of minerals, non-ferrous extractive metallurgy.

Information services: Enquiries, referral service, loans, photocopies, literature searches.

Collection: Historical collection: antiquarian books, biographies, photographs, portraits, technical drawings, artefacts.
Special Collection: Sir Henry Bessemer Room and artefacts

Non-library collection catalogue: All or part available in-house

Library catalogue: All or part available in-house

Publications: Printed, and electronic and video
Order printed publications from: Order Processing Dept, Maney Publishing, Suite 1C, Joseph's Well, Hanover Walk, Leeds, LS3 1AB; tel: 0113 243 2800; fax: 0113 386 8178; e-mail: maney@maney.co.uk

Publications list: Available online

Access to staff: Contact by letter, by telephone, by fax, by e-mail, in person and via website. Appointment necessary. Non-members charged.
Hours: Mon to Fri, 0930 to 1700

Also at: David West Library, Institute of Materials, Minerals and Mining; tel: 020 7451 7360; fax: 020 7451 7406; e-mail: hilda.kaune@iom3.org; frances.perry@iom3.org; Grantham Centre; The Boiler House, Springfield Business Park, Caunt Road, Grantham, Lincs NG31 7FZ; tel: 01476 513880; fax: 01476 513899; Stoke Regional Office; Shelton House, 12 Stoke Road, Stoke-on-Trent, Staffordshire, ST4 2DR; tel: 01782 221700; fax: 01782 221722

INSTITUTE OF MATHEMATICS AND ITS APPLICATIONS (IMA)

Catherine Richards House, 16 Nelson Street, Southend-on-Sea, Essex, SS1 1EF

Tel: 01702 354020
Fax: 01702 354111
E-mail: post@ima.org.uk
Website: www.ima.org.uk

Enquiries to: Executive Director

Founded: 1964

Organisation type and purpose:
Professional body, registered charity (charity number 1017777).

Subject coverage: Mathematics, mathematical education, statistics, applications of mathematics, operational research.

Publications: Printed

Publications list: Available online and in print

Access to staff: Contact by letter, by telephone, by fax, by e-mail and via website
Hours: Mon to Fri, 0900 to 1700

INSTITUTE OF MEASUREMENT AND CONTROL (INSTMC)

87 Gower Street, London, WC1E 6AF

Tel: 020 7387 4949
Fax: 020 7388 8431
E-mail: publications@instmc.org.uk
Website: www.instmc.org.uk

Enquiries to: Assistant CEO/ Communications Manager

Founded: 1944

Organisation type and purpose: Learned society (membership is by qualification, election or invitation), present number of members: 4,000, registered charity, publishing house.
To promote for the public benefit all aspects of measurement and control technology and its applications.

Subject coverage: Instrumentation, measurement, control engineering, automation.

Library catalogue: All or part available in-house

Publications: Printed

Publications list: Available online and in print

Access to staff: Contact by letter, by telephone, by fax, by e-mail, in person and via website. Appointment necessary.
Hours: Mon to Fri, 0900 to 1700

Access to building: Prior appointment required
Special comments: Library is open to members only.

INSTITUTE OF MEDICAL ILLUSTRATORS (IMI)

12 Coldbath Square, London, EC1R 5HL

Tel: 0207 837 2846
Website: www.imi.org.uk

Enquiries to: Hon. Secretary
Direct e-mail: secretary@imi.org.uk

Founded: 1968

Organisation type and purpose: A rich network of fellow professionals, working together to improve and develop medical illustration by means of conferences, courses and regional meetings.
To promote the role of the medical illustrator as a professional member of a multi-skilled team who offer a range of core clinical illustrative and communication services as part of the healthcare team for the benefit of patients and clients; to strive for the highest professional standards; to support, guide and motivate members to achieve success and personal recognition for the quality of their contribution to the healthcare team; to promote its standards to government, to employers and to potential members; to improve recognition of the profession; to seek national registration of all medical illustrators.

Subject coverage: Brings together the disciplines of clinical photography, medical art, illustration, graphic design and video within healthcare.

Publications: Printed, and electronic and video
Order electronic and video publications from: Free download for members from website

Publications list: Available online

Access to staff: Contact by letter, by telephone and by e-mail

Member organisation of: Committee for the Accreditation of Medical Illustration Practitioners (CAMIP)

INSTITUTE OF METAL FINISHING (IMF)

Exeter House, 48 Holloway Head, Birmingham, B1 1NQ

Tel: 0121 622 7387
Fax: 0121 666 6316
E-mail: exeterhouse@instituteofmetalfinishing.org

Enquiries to: Secretary

Organisation type and purpose: Learned society.
Technical and scientific society; eight regional branches; three technical groups.

Subject coverage: Metal finishing and all aspects of the surface treatment industry, metal finishing, printed circuits, anodizing, coating, all types of metal protection.

Publications: Printed

INSTITUTE OF MONEY ADVISERS (IMA)

Stringer House, 34 Lupton Street, Leeds, LS10 2QW

Tel: 0845 094 2384; 0113 270 8444
Fax: 0845 094 2175; 0113 270 2111
E-mail: office@i-m-a.org.uk
Website: www.i-m-a.org.uk

Founded: 2006; carries out the functions of the former Money Advice Association (founded 1984) (year of change 2006)

Organisation type and purpose: A charitable company, the only professional body acting solely for money advisers in England, Wales and Northern Ireland, current number of members: over 1,400.
To develop professional standards; to provide support services to members; to promote free money advice; to influence policy and practice relating to personal finance.

Subject coverage: Money and debt advice.

Education services: Offers free seminars on topics such as Insolvency Options, Managing Legal Advice Cases & Caseloads, and Utilities & Fuel Debt.

Publications: Printed, and electronic and video
Order printed publications from: Website
Order electronic and video publications from: Download from website

Publications list: Available online

Access to staff: Contact by letter, by telephone, by fax and by e-mail
Special comments: IMA is not able to give advice directly to members of the public.

Branches: 15 branches across England and Wales

INSTITUTE OF NATURAL THERAPY (INT)

PO Box 1418, Dorchester, Dorset, DT1 1YF

Tel: 01305 267069
Website: www.institute-natural-therapy.org.uk

Enquiries to: General Secretary

Founded: 1991

Organisation type and purpose: International organisation, advisory body, professional body (membership is by qualification).

Subject coverage: Hypnotherapy, healing, complementary therapies.

Access to staff: Contact by letter and by telephone
Hours: Mon to Fri, 0900 to 1700

Patron of: General Hypnotherapy Standards Council (GHSC); PO Box 204, Lymington, SO41 6WP; tel: 01590 683770; fax: 01590 683770

INSTITUTE OF NAVAL MEDICINE (INM)

Alverstoke, Gosport, Hampshire, PO12 2DL

Tel: 023 9276 8101
Fax: 023 9250 4823
E-mail: lib@inm.mod.uk

Enquiries to: Librarian

Organisation type and purpose: National government body, training organisation, research organisation.

Subject coverage: Underwater medicine, survival medicine, habitability, submarine environmental chemistry, heat, cold, toxicology, nuclear medicine and radiological protection, dosimetry, audiology and hearing conservation, submarine medicine, experimental physiology, occupational medicine and hygiene, microbiology, analytical chemistry, medical statistics, health and safety at work, ergonomics, human factors, anthropometry, psychology.

Library catalogue: All or part available in-house

Publications: Printed

Access to staff: Contact by letter, by telephone, by fax and by e-mail. Appointment necessary.
Hours: Mon to Fri, 0900 to 1700

Access to building: Prior appointment required

Access for disabled people: Parking provided, level entry, toilet facilities

Part of: Ministry of Defence, Medical Directorate (Naval)

INSTITUTE OF NAVAL MEDICINE – HISTORIC COLLECTIONS LIBRARY (INM H)

Alverstoke, Gosport, Hampshire, PO12 2DL

Tel: 023 0276 8238
Fax: 023 9250 4823
E-mail: inm-cs-infohistlib@mod.uk

Enquiries to: Historic Collections Librarian

Founded: 1948; formerly called Royal Naval Medical School (previously RNMS Clevedon) (year of change 1960s); historic collections installed. Previously the collections of the libraries of Royal Naval Hospitals Haslar and Stonehouse (Plymouth) (year of change 2001)

Organisation type and purpose: National government body.

Subject coverage: Naval history; history of naval medicine and surgery; natural history and exploration (small proportion); early printed books (small proportion).

Collection: Works of James Lind
Dr Robert McKinnal bequest
Dr Leonard Gillespie bequest
Navy List
Health of the Navy
Archive material (incomplete) from former staff of RNHs Haslar and Plymouth; some photographs
Small collection of papers relating to William J. Maillard, VC (1863–1903), holder of the only Royal Naval Medical Service Victoria Cross

Non-library collection catalogue: All or part available in-house

Library catalogue: All or part available in-house

Access to staff: Contact by letter, by telephone, by fax and by e-mail. Appointment necessary.
Hours: Mon to Fri, 1030 to 1730

Access to building: Prior appointment required
Hours: Mon to Fri, 1030 to 1600
Special comments: Visitors must call at main gate on arrival, and bring picture ID (for example, passport or bus pass)
No more than 25 people per group visit.

Access for disabled people: Parking provided by arrangement
Hours: Mon to Fri, 1030 to 1600
Special comments: Level entry to main building, steps with ramp and stair-climber to collections. Arrangements can be made to view items elsewhere on site if preferred.

Historic Collections holdings are in the ownership of: The Admiralty Library; Naval Historical Branch, PP 20, Main Road, HM Naval Base, Portsmouth, PO1 3LU; tel: 02392 725297; e-mail: cns-nhbal@mod.uk

INSTITUTE OF OCCUPATIONAL MEDICINE (IOM)

Research Avenue North, Riccarton, Edinburgh, EH14 4AP

Tel: 0870 850 5131
Fax: 0870 850 5132
E-mail: info@iom-world.org
Website: www.iom-world.org

Enquiries to: Information Officer

Founded: 1969

Organisation type and purpose: International organisation, service industry, registered charity, consultancy, research organisation.

Subject coverage: Health, hygiene and safety at work; occupational and environmental health, hygiene and epidemiology; ergonomics; hearing loss; respiratory diseases; asbestos; asbestosis; silica; pneumoconiosis; personal protective equipment.

Publications: Printed

Publications list: Available in print

Access to staff: Contact by letter, by telephone, by fax and by e-mail. Appointment necessary.
Hours: Mon to Fri, 0900 to 1700

INSTITUTE OF OPERATIONS MANAGEMENT (IOM)

CILT(UK), Earlstrees Court, Earlstrees Road, Corby, Northamptonshire, NN17 4AX

Tel: 01536 740105
Fax: 01536 740101
E-mail: info@iomnet.org.uk
Website: www.iomnet.org.uk

Enquiries to: Membership Enquiries
Direct e-mail: members@iomnet.org.uk

Founded: 1969

Organisation type and purpose: Professional body.
Professional institute for operations and production managers.

Subject coverage: Production management and control; inventory management; stock control; logistics; supply chain management; materials management; business process re-engineering; advanced planning and scheduling; ERP; MRPII; learn manufacturing; Just-in-Time (JIT).

Collection: Library of specialised technical books and journals on all aspects of operations management particularly production and inventory control

Library catalogue: All or part available in-house

Publications: Printed, and electronic and video

Publications list: Available online and in print

Access to staff: Contact by letter, by telephone, by fax, by e-mail and via website. Appointment necessary. Non-members charged.
Hours: Mon to Thu, 0900 to 1700; Fri, 0900 to 1600
Special comments: Members only may borrow from library.

Access for disabled people: Parking provided, level entry, access to all public areas, toilet facilities
Hours: Mon to Thu, 0900 to 1700; Fri, 0900 to 1600

INSTITUTE OF OPTOMETRY, THE

56 Newington Causeway, London, SE1 6DS

Tel: 020 7407 4183

continued overleaf

Fax: 020 7403 8007
E-mail: admin@ioo.org.uk
Website: www.ioo.org.uk

Enquiries to: Chief Executive

Founded: 1922

Organisation type and purpose: Registered charity (charity number 207965).

Subject coverage: Optometric examination and prescription/treatment for patients, vision-related dyslexia treatment, continuing education and training for optometrists, optometric research.

Access to staff: Contact by letter, by telephone, by fax and by e-mail
Hours: Mon to Fri, 0900 to 1700

INSTITUTE OF PAPER CONSERVATION (IPC)

Leigh Lodge, Leigh, Worcester, WR6 5LB

Tel: 01886 832323
Fax: 01886 833688
E-mail: admin@icon.org.uk
Website: www.ipc.org.uk

Enquiries to: Executive Secretary
Other contacts: Membership Secretary for membership.

Founded: 1976

Organisation type and purpose: International organisation, professional body (membership is by subscription, qualification), present number of members: 1,400, registered charity (charity number 280888), training organisation, publishing house.
Care and repair of artefacts on paper.

Subject coverage: Training in paper conservation, all types of paper-related materials including books, textiles, globes, wallpaper, archives, maps, works of art, photographs, manuscripts, frames, parchment. Collection care, conservation surveys, disaster planning, storage and preservation.

Collection: Specialist library at 1 Grove Cottage, St Cross Road, Oxford OX1 3TX

Trade and statistical information: Data on conservation profession.
Register of accredited book and paper conservators

Non-library collection catalogue: All or part available in print

Library catalogue: All or part available in print

Publications: Printed

Publications list: Available online and in print

Access to staff: Contact by letter, by telephone, by fax and by e-mail
Hours: Mon to Fri, 0915 to 1715

INSTITUTE OF PARALEGAL TRAINING, THE

The Mill, Climping Street, Climping, Littlehampton, West Sussex, BN17 5RN

Tel: 01903 714276
Fax: 01903 713710
E-mail: amanda@ibberson.fsbusiness.co.uk

Enquiries to: Secretary General

Founded: 1976

Organisation type and purpose: International organisation, professional body (membership is by qualification, election or invitation), service industry, training organisation.

Access to staff: Contact by letter, by telephone, by fax and by e-mail
Hours: Mon to Fri, 0900 to 1700

INSTITUTE OF PATENTEES AND INVENTORS (IPI)

PO Box 39296, London, SE3 7WH

Tel: 0871 226 2091
Fax: 020 8293 5920
E-mail: ipi@invent.org.uk
Website: www.invent.org.uk/

Enquiries to: Secretary

Founded: 1919

Organisation type and purpose: National organisation, advisory body, professional body, membership association (membership is by subscription), present number of members: 700.
A non-profit organisation offering its members advice and guidance on all aspects of inventing from idea conception to innovation and development.

Subject coverage: National and international patents, registered designs, trade-marks, copyright, the furtherance, protection and exploitation of inventions through to industrial innovation.

Publications: Printed

Publications list: Available in print

Access to staff: Contact by letter, by telephone, by fax, by e-mail and via website
Hours: Mon to Fri, 1000 to 1700

INSTITUTE OF PHYSICS (IOP)

76–78 Portland Place, London, W1B 1NT

Tel: 020 7470 4800
Fax: 020 7470 4848
E-mail: physics@iop.org
Website: www.iop.org
Website: www.iop.org/publications/index.html

Enquiries to: Corporate Communications Officer
Direct e-mail: corporatecomms@iop.org

Founded: 1874

Organisation type and purpose: The Institute of Physics is a scientific charity devoted to increasing the practice, understanding and application of physics. It has a world-wide membership of more than 37,000 and is a leading communicator of physics-related science to all audiences, from specialists through to government and the general public. Its publishing company, IOP Publishing, is a world leader in scientific publishing and the electronic dissemination of physics.

Subject coverage: Aspects of physics – pure and applied – in education, industry, government and public sector, and the media.

Publications: Printed, and electronic and video
Order printed publications from: Institute of Physics Publishing

Publications list: Available online

Access to staff: Contact by letter, by telephone, by fax, by e-mail and via website
Hours: Mon to Fri, 0900 to 1730

Access for disabled people: Ramped entry, toilet facilities

Links with: IOP Publishing; Dirac House, Temple Back, Bristol, BS1 6BE; tel: 0117 929 7481; fax: 0117 929 4318; e-mail: custserv@iop.org; website: http://publishing.iop.org

Member organisation of: European Optical Society; European Physical Society; International Union of Pure and Applied Physics (IUPAP); e-mail: admin.iupap@iop.org

INSTITUTE OF PHYSICS AND ENGINEERING IN MEDICINE (IPEM)

Fairmount House, 230 Tadcaster Road, York, YO24 1ES

Tel: 01904 610821
Fax: 01904 612279
E-mail: office@ipem.ac.uk
Website: www.ipem.ac.uk

Enquiries to: General Secretary

Founded: 1995

Organisation type and purpose: Professional body (membership is by qualification, election or invitation), registered charity (charity number 1047999), training organisation, publishing house.

Subject coverage: Physical science as applied to medicine, including radiation protection, radiotherapy, diagnostic radiology, nuclear magnetic resonance, nuclear medicine, ultrasonics, lasers, rehabilitation engineering, physiological measurement, bioengineering, non-ionising radiation.

Publications: Printed

Publications list: Available online and in print

Access to staff: Contact by telephone and by fax. Non-members charged.
Hours: Mon to Thu, 0900 to 1700: Fri, 0900 to 1600

Access to building: No prior appointment required

INSTITUTE OF PHYSICS PUBLISHING (IOP Publishing)

Dirac House, Temple Back, Bristol, BS1 6BE

Tel: 0117 929 7481
Fax: 0117 929 4318
E-mail: custserv@iop.org
Website: www.journals.iop.org

Enquiries to: Managing Director
Direct tel: 0117 930 1144
Direct fax: 0117 920 0775
Direct e-mail: jerry.cowhig@iop.org

Founded: 1874

Organisation type and purpose: International organisation, learned society, professional body (membership is by subscription, qualification, election or invitation), present number of members: 37,000, registered charity, publishing house. The Institute, which has its origins in the Physical Society established in 1874, is one of the world's leading publishers in physics and related subjects. Journals go back to 1874 and include several world leaders in their respective fields.
Dissemination of knowledge and education in physics.

Subject coverage: Physics.

Non-library collection catalogue: All or part available online

Publications: Printed, and electronic and video, and microform publications

Publications list: Available online and in print

Access to staff: Contact by letter, by telephone, by fax, by e-mail and via website
Hours: Mon to Fri, 0900 to 1700

Access for disabled people: Ramped entry, access to all public areas, toilet facilities

INSTITUTE OF PLUMBING AND HEATING ENGINEERING (IPHE)

64 Station Lane, Hornchurch, Essex, RM12 6NB

Tel: 01708 472791
Fax: 01708 448987
E-mail: info@iphe.org.uk
Website: www.iphe.org.uk

Enquiries to: Editor of Plumbing & Heating Engineering Magazine
Direct tel: 01708 463114
Direct e-mail: carolc@iphe.org.uk

Founded: 1906

Organisation type and purpose: Professional body (membership is by qualification), present number of members: 12,000, registered charity (charity number 278169), suitable for ages: 18 to 60.
To improve the standards of plumbing in the public interest.

Subject coverage: Plumbing, heating and allied subjects, names of registered plumbers.

Publications: Printed, and electronic and video

Access to staff: Contact by letter, by telephone, by fax, by e-mail and via website. Appointment necessary.
Hours: Mon to Fri, 0900 to 1700

INSTITUTE OF PRACTITIONERS IN ADVERTISING (IPA)

44 Belgrave Square, London, SW1X 8QS

Tel: 020 7235 7020
Fax: 020 7245 9904
E-mail: info@ipa.co.uk
Website: www.ipa.co.uk

Enquiries to: Head of Information Systems

Founded: 1917

Organisation type and purpose: Professional body, trade association (membership is by subscription).

Subject coverage: Advertising including European and international advertising, marketing, media, public relations, all aspects of communication, and related fields.

Publications: Printed

Publications list: Available online and in print

Access to staff: Contact by letter, by telephone, by fax and by e-mail. Access for members only.
Hours: Mon to Fri, 0900 to 1700
Special comments: IPA members only.

Access for disabled people: Access to all public areas, toilet facilities

Member organisation of: Advertising Association; European Association of Communication Agencies (EACA)

INSTITUTE OF PROFESSIONAL ADMINISTRATORS (IPA)

6 Graphite Square, Vauxhall Walk, London, SE11 5EE

Tel: 020 7091 2606
Fax: 020 7091 7340
E-mail: info@inprad.org
Website: www.inprad.org

Founded: 1957; formerly called Private Secretaries Association (year of change 1966); formerly called Institute of Qualified Private Secretaries (year of change 2007); formerly called Institute of Qualified Professional Secretaries (IQPS) (year of change 2009)

Organisation type and purpose: Professional body for all administration and office professionals. Membership includes secretaries, PAs, receptionists, general administrators, executive assistants and virtual assistants.
To be the leader in the field of administration and the institute of choice for administrators; to become a strong, professional and well-respected institute in the UK and overseas; to raise the profile of administration skills in the UK and overseas; to champion quality, good practice and professionalism.

Subject coverage: Professional administration.

Publications: Printed, and electronic and video

Access to staff: Contact by letter, by telephone, by fax and by e-mail

INSTITUTE OF PROFESSIONAL INVESTIGATORS LIMITED (IPI)

Claremont House, 70–72 Alma Road, Windsor, Berkshire SL4 3EZ

Tel: 0870 330 8622
Fax: 0870 330 8612
E-mail: admin@ipi.org.uk
Website: www.ipi.org.uk

Enquiries to: Secretary General

Founded: 1976

Organisation type and purpose: Professional body.

Subject coverage: Investigation services and practice; further education within the profession.

Publications: Printed

Access to staff: Contact by letter, by telephone, by fax and by e-mail
Hours: Mon to Fri, 1000 to 1600

Access to building: No access other than to staff

INSTITUTE OF PROFESSIONAL WILLWRITERS (IPW)

Trinity Point, New Road, Halesowen, B63 3HY

Tel: 08456 442042
Fax: 08456 442043
E-mail: office@ipw.org.uk
Website: www.ipw.org.uk

Enquiries to: Office Manager
Other contacts: Chairman for public relations.

Founded: 1991

Organisation type and purpose: Professional body (membership is by qualification), present number of members: 500, suitable for ages: 18+, training organisation.

Subject coverage: All aspects of wills and their writing, current members local to enquirer, membership requirements.

Education services: Willwriting courses

Publications: Printed
Order printed publications from: IPW Accounts

Access to staff: Contact by letter, by telephone, by fax, by e-mail, in person and via website. Appointment necessary.
Hours: Mon to Fri, 0900 to 1700

INSTITUTE OF PROMOTIONAL MARKETING LTD (IPM)

70 Margaret Street, London, W1W 8SS

Tel: 020 7291 7730
Fax: 020 7291 7731
E-mail: enquiries@theipm.org.uk
Website: www.theipm.org.uk

Enquiries to: Chief Executive Officer
Direct e-mail: annies@theipm.org.uk

Founded: 1933

Organisation type and purpose: Trade association.

Subject coverage: Promotional marketing.

Access to staff: Contact by letter, by telephone, by fax, by e-mail and via website
Hours: Mon to Fri, 0900 to 1700

Access to building: Prior appointment required
Hours: Mon to Fri, 0900 to 1700

INSTITUTE OF PSYCHIATRY

De Crespigny Park, Denmark Hill, London, SE5 8AF

Tel: 020 7848 0204
Fax: 020 7848 0209
E-mail: iop.library@iop.kcl.ac.uk
Website: www.iop.kcl.ac.uk/iopweb/departments/home/default.aspx?locator=12

continued overleaf

Enquiries to: Librarian

Organisation type and purpose: University department or institute.

Subject coverage: Psychiatry, psychology, neurology and neuroscience, psychopharmacology, genetics and genomics.

Collection: Guttmann-Maclay Collection of psychotic art
Henry Maudsley Collection of historic books in psychiatry
Mayer-Gross Collection of historic texts in European psychiatry

Non-library collection catalogue: All or part available online

Library catalogue: All or part available in-house

Publications: Printed

Publications list: Available in print

Access to staff: Contact by letter, by telephone, by e-mail and via website. Appointment necessary. Non-members charged.
Hours: Mon to Fri, 0900 to 2000; Term time: Sat, 1000 to 1700; Summer vacation: Sat, 1000 to 1500.

Parent body: King's College London

INSTITUTE OF PSYCHOANALYSIS (BPAS)

Formal name: British Psychoanalytical Society

112A Shirland Road, London, W9 2EQ

Tel: 020 7563 5000
Fax: 020 7563 5001
E-mail: ginette@goulston-lincoln.com
Website: www.psychoanalysis.org.uk

Enquiries to: Institute Manager

Founded: 1919

Organisation type and purpose: Professional body (membership is by qualification), present number of members: 510, registered charity (charity number 212330), training organisation.
The training organisation for psychoanalysis in Britain, also treats patients in The London Clinic of Psychoanalysis at the same addess.

Subject coverage: Psycho-analysis.

Collection: Archives

Non-library collection catalogue: All or part available in-house

Library catalogue: All or part available in-house

Publications: Printed, and electronic and video

Access to staff: Contact by letter, by telephone, by fax, by e-mail and in person. Appointment necessary. Non-members charged.
Hours: Mon to Fri, 0930 to 1730

Access to building: Appointment required
Hours: Mon to Fri, 0930 to 1730; Sat and Sun, closed
Special comments: Archives, apply to the Honorary Archivist for access.

Access for disabled people: Ramped entry, toilet facilities

Member organisation of: International Psycho-Analytical Association

INSTITUTE OF PSYCHOSEXUAL MEDICINE (IPM)

12 Chandos Street, Cavendish Square, London, W1G 9DR

Tel: 020 7580 0631
Fax: 020 7580 0631
E-mail: admin@ipm.org.uk

Enquiries to: Administrator
Other contacts: Referrals Secretary

Founded: 1974

Organisation type and purpose: National organisation, professional body (membership is by subscription), present number of members: 450, registered charity (charity number 298172), university department or institute, training organisation.
Referral service.
Refers members of the public to psychosexual doctors.

Subject coverage: Training for doctors in the field of psychosexual medicine (sexual difficulties and related marital or psychosomatic problems); training over 2 years for Diploma from Institute of Psychosexual Medicine and at 4 years for membership of Institute of Psychosexual Medicine.

Trade and statistical information: List of doctors qualified in the field of psychosexual medicine and able to receive referrals through our referrals secretary

Publications: Printed

Publications list: Available online and in print

Access to staff: Contact by letter, by telephone, by fax, by e-mail and via website
Hours: Mon to Fri, 0900 to 1700
Special comments: Answerphone also. Prefer sae from those wanting list of doctors.

INSTITUTE OF PSYCHOSYNTHESIS

65A Watford Way, London, NW4 3AQ

Tel: 020 8202 4525
Fax: 020 8202 6166
E-mail: institute@psychosynthesis.org
Website: www.psychosynthesis.org

Enquiries to: Administration

Founded: 1973

Organisation type and purpose: Membership association, training organisation.
Psychology, coaching, counselling and psychotherapy training, low-cost clinic open to members of the public.

Subject coverage: Psychotherapy and counselling, coaching, psychology.

Publications: Printed

Publications list: Available online

Access to staff: Contact by letter, by telephone, by e-mail and via website. Appointment necessary.
Hours: Mon to Fri, 1000 to 1700
Special comments: Appointments for the clinic are made in advance.

Access to building: Prior appointment required
Hours: Mon to Fri, 0700 to 2100

Access for disabled people: There is a staircase

Member of: British Association for Counselling and Psychotherapy (BACP); European Association for Psychotherapy; European Mentoring and Coaching Council; United Kingdom Council for Psychotherapy (UKCP)

INSTITUTE OF PUBLIC LOSS ASSESSORS (IPLA)

Ian Balcombe at Harris Balcombe at Assessor House, Daws Lane, London, NW7 4ST

Tel: 0844 879 3244
Website: www.lossassessors.org/

Enquiries to: General Secretary
Direct tel: 020 8959 4646
Direct fax: 020 8959 6156
Direct e-mail: london@harrisbalcombe.com

Founded: 1963

Organisation type and purpose: Professional body.
To represent the interests of professional loss assessors in their dealings with their clients.

Subject coverage: Loss assessment, preparation, submission and negotiation of all types of statutory and insurance claims on behalf of the public and corporate bodies.

Publications: Printed

Access to staff: Contact by letter and by telephone
Hours: Mon to Fri, 0900 to 1700

INSTITUTE OF PUBLIC RIGHTS OF WAY AND ACCESS MANAGEMENT (IPROW)

PO Box 222, Penrith, CA11 1BI

Tel: 01768 840428
E-mail: iprow@iprow.co.uk
Website: www.iprow.co.uk

Enquiries to: Executive Officer

Founded: 1986; formerly called Institute of Public Rights of Way Officers (year of change 2006)

Organisation type and purpose: Professional body.

Subject coverage: Public rights of way, outdoor access management.

Trade and statistical information: Some

Publications: Printed
Order printed publications from: e-mail: iprow@iprow.co.uk

Publications list: Available in print

Access to staff: Contact by letter, by telephone, by e-mail and via website
Hours: Mon to Fri, 0900 to 1700

Access to building: No access

INSTITUTE OF PYRAMIDOLOGY (IOP)

108 Broad Street, Chesham, Buckinghamshire, HP5 3ED

Tel: 01494 771774
E-mail: 101234.1734@compuserve.com

Enquiries to: Director

Founded: 1940

Organisation type and purpose: International organisation, membership association (membership is by subscription), voluntary organisation, research organisation.

Subject coverage: Pyramidology: study of the Great Pyramid of Egypt; books on pyramidology.

Publications: Printed

Access to staff: Contact by letter, by telephone and by e-mail
Hours: Mon to Fri, 0900 to 1700

INSTITUTE OF QUARRYING

7 Regent Street, Nottingham, NG1 5BS

Tel: 0115 941 1315
Fax: 0115 948 4035
E-mail: mail@quarrying.org
Website: www.quarrying.org

Enquiries to: The Secretary
Direct tel: 0115 945 3880
Direct e-mail: lyn.bryden@quarrying.org
Other contacts: Membership Co-ordinator

Founded: 1917

Organisation type and purpose: Professional body (membership is by qualification), present number of members: 5,000 world-wide, 3,000 UK, registered charity.

Subject coverage: Quarrying.

Publications: Printed
Order printed publications from: 7 Regent Street, Nottingham, NG1 5BS; tel: 0115 945 3880

Publications list: Available online and in print

Access to staff: Contact by letter, by telephone, by fax and by e-mail
Hours: Mon to Fri, 0900 to 1700

INSTITUTE OF RACE RELATIONS (IRR)

2–6 Leeke Street, London, WC1X 9HS

Tel: 020 7837 0041
Fax: 020 7278 0623
E-mail: info@irr.org.uk
Website: www.irr.org.uk

Founded: 1958

Organisation type and purpose: Registered charity (charity number 223989), research organisation.
Educational charity.

Subject coverage: Race and minority group relations; racism; imperialism; Third World issues.

Library catalogue: All or part available in-house

Publications: Printed, and electronic and video
Order printed publications from: IRR

Publications list: Available in print

Access to staff: Contact by telephone and by e-mail. Appointment necessary.
Hours: Mon to Thu, 1000 to 1300 and 1400 to 1700 (hours may be restricted)
Special comments: Access at librarian's discretion.

INSTITUTE OF REFRACTORIES ENGINEERS (IRE)

General Secretary and Treasurer, Joan Royd Cottage, Penistone, Sheffield, S36 9DA

Tel: 01226 762578
Fax: 01226 762673
E-mail: secretary@ireng.org
Website: ireng.org

Enquiries to: General Secretary
Direct e-mail: alanhey@ireng.org
Other contacts: Treasurer

Founded: 1961

Organisation type and purpose: Learned society (membership is by qualification, election or invitation), present number of members: 1,500.

Subject coverage: Refractories – manufacture and use, research and development, education and training.

Publications: Printed

Publications list: Available in print

Access to staff: Contact by letter, by telephone, by fax, by e-mail and via website
Hours: Mon to Fri, 0900 to 1700

INSTITUTE OF REFRIGERATION (IOR)

Kelvin House, 76 Mill Lane, Carshalton, Surrey, SM5 2JR

Tel: 020 8647 7033
Fax: 020 8773 0165
E-mail: ior@ior.org.uk
Website: www.ior.org.uk

Enquiries to: Secretary

Founded: 1899

Organisation type and purpose: Learned society (membership is by subscription).

Subject coverage: Refrigeration and air conditioning.

Collection: Reference library at Cambridge Refrigeration Technology

Non-library collection catalogue: All or part available online

Publications list: Available online

Access to staff: Contact by letter, by telephone, by fax, by e-mail and via website. Appointment necessary.
Hours: Mon to Fri, 0900 to 1700

Links with: Cambridge Refrigeration Technology

INSTITUTE OF REVENUES, RATING AND VALUATION (IRRV)

Northumberland House, 5th Floor, 303–306 High Holborn, London, WC1V 7JZ

Tel: 020 7831 3505
Fax: 020 7831 2048
E-mail: enquiries@irrv.org.uk
Website: www.irrv.org.uk

Founded: 1882

Organisation type and purpose: Local government body, professional body.

Subject coverage: Local taxation and property valuation issues including: Council Tax (Council Tax benefits, banding, enforcement), housing benefits, non-domestic rates.

Publications: Printed, and electronic and video
Order printed publications from: Communications Manager

Publications list: Available online and in print

Access to staff: Contact by letter, by fax and by e-mail. Appointment necessary.
Hours: Mon to Fri, 0900 to 1700

Access to building: Prior appointment required

Represents: over 5000 local authority revenues and benefits officers; private valuers and officers from appellate bodies

INSTITUTE OF RISK MANAGEMENT (IRM)

Lloyds Avenue House, 6 Lloyds Avenue, London, EC3N 3AX

Tel: 020 7709 9808
Fax: 020 7709 0716
E-mail: enquiries@theirm.org
Website: www.theIRM.org

Enquiries to: Executive Director
Other contacts: Examinations Officer, Membership Officer

Founded: 1986

Organisation type and purpose: International organisation, advisory body, professional body (membership is by subscription, qualification), present number of members: 1700, research organisation.
To provide a diploma in risk management.

Subject coverage: Business organisation and finance, occupational health and safety, public sector, finance, physical risk, liability exposures, contingency and disaster, risk analysis, business organisation and finance, local authority risk management, health sector.

Publications: Printed, and electronic and video

Publications list: Available in print

Access to staff: Contact by letter, by telephone, by fax and by e-mail. Appointment necessary.
Hours: Mon to Fri, 0900 to 1700

INSTITUTE OF ROAD SAFETY OFFICERS (IRSO)

Pin Point, 1–2 Rosslyn Crescent, Harrow, Middlesex, HA1 2SB

continued overleaf

Tel: 0870 010 4442
Fax: 0870 333 7772
E-mail: irso@dbda.co.uk
Website: www.irso.org.uk

Enquiries to: Executive Secretary
Direct tel: 01202 262051
Direct fax: 01202 262091
Direct e-mail: k.saunders@poole.gov.uk
Other contacts: National Secretary

Founded: 1971

Organisation type and purpose:
Professional body (membership is by subscription), training organisation.
Mainly local government officers.

Subject coverage: Road safety; education, training and publicity, engineering and enforcement.

Trade and statistical information: Accident statistics

Publications: Printed

Access to staff: Contact by letter, by telephone and by fax. Appointment necessary.
Hours: Mon to Fri, 0900 to 1700

Access to building: No access other than to staff

INSTITUTE OF ROOFING (IoR)

24 Weymouth Street, London, W1N 3FA

Tel: 020 7436 0103
Fax: 020 7637 5215
Website: www.instituteofroofing.org.uk

Enquiries to: Director
Direct fax: 020 7636 1287
Direct e-mail: info@instituteofroofing.org.uk

Founded: 1980

Organisation type and purpose:
Professional body (membership is by qualification).

Subject coverage: Education within the roofing industry.

Access to staff: Contact by letter, by telephone, by fax, by e-mail and via website
Hours: Tue, Wed, Thu, 1000 to 1500

Access to building: Prior appointment required

INSTITUTE OF SOUND AND COMMUNICATIONS ENGINEERS (ISCE)

PO Box 7966, Reading, Berkshire, RG6 7WY

Tel: 0118 954 2175
Fax: 0118 954 2175
E-mail: ros@isce.org.uk
Website: www.isce.org.uk

Enquiries to: Secretariat Manager

Founded: 1948

Organisation type and purpose:
Membership association (membership is by subscription), an independent institute, the specialist learned society for sound and communications engineers.
To unite those professionally engaged in the sound, video, communications, entertainment lighting and staging industries; to maintain and to raise technical standards throughout the profession; to disseminate technical and professional information through the publication of papers and by means of conferences, seminars and training courses; to promote educational and training programmes for those seeking advancement in the profession and to assist career development and continuing professional development within the industry; to promote the advancement and application of science and technology within the profession in the interests of society at large; to present the institute as an authoritative and influential professional body, representing trained, qualified and experienced practitioners within the profession; to establish and maintain a code of conduct in professional activities, embodying high ethical standards and concern for the environmental and sociological impacts of professional activities; to protect and promote the interests of members, collectively and individually.

Subject coverage: Sound and communications engineering.

Publications: Electronic and video
Order electronic and video publications from: Download from website

Access to staff: Contact by letter, by telephone, by fax and by e-mail

INSTITUTE OF SOUND AND VIBRATION RESEARCH (ISVR)

The University, Southampton, SO17 1BJ

Tel: 023 8059 2294
Fax: 023 8059 3190
E-mail: mzs@isvr.soton.ac.uk
Website: www.isvr.soton.ac.uk

Enquiries to: Director

Founded: 1963

Organisation type and purpose: University department or institute, consultancy, research organisation.

Subject coverage: Acoustics; structural dynamics; audiology; fluid dynamics; signal processing; active control; subjective acoustics; human response to vibration; automotive engineering; instrumentation; random process analysis; human response to noise and vibration; hearing conservation; urban planning and noise; vibration engineering and control; machinery noise and vibration, signal processing, etc.

Collection: Literature on the human response to vibration

Non-library collection catalogue: All or part available online

Library catalogue: All or part available online

Publications: Printed

Publications list: Available online and in print

Access to staff: Contact by letter, by telephone, by fax and by e-mail
Hours: Mon to Fri, 0900 to 1700

Access to building: Prior appointment required

Access for disabled people: Parking provided, ramped entry, toilet facilities

Links with: ISVR Consultancy Service; tel: 023 8059 2162; e-mail: djf@isvr.soton.ac.uk

INSTITUTE OF SPORT AND RECREATION MANAGEMENT (ISRM)

Sir John Beckwith Centre for Sport, Loughborough University, Loughborough, Leicestershire, LE11 3TU

Tel: 01509 226474
Fax: 01509 226475
E-mail: ralphriley@isrm.co.uk
Website: www.isrm.co.uk

Enquiries to: Chief Executive

Founded: 1921

Organisation type and purpose:
Membership association (membership is by qualification), present number of members: 2300, registered charity (charity number 250902).
Educational Charity.
National professional body for sport and recreation facility management and operation.

Subject coverage: Management and operation of public baths and recreation facilities, education and training.

Publications: Printed, and electronic and video

Publications list: Available online and in print

Access to staff: Contact by letter, by telephone, by fax and by e-mail
Hours: Mon to Fri, 0830 to 1630

INSTITUTE OF SPORTS AND EXERCISE MEDICINE (ISEM)

30 Devonshire Street, London, W1G 6PU

Tel: 020 7288 5310
E-mail: d.patterson@ucl.ac.uk
Website: www.fsem.co.uk

Enquiries to: Secretary

Founded: 1965

Organisation type and purpose: Learned society, professional body, registered charity (charity number 313301).
To encourage postgraduate medical research, teaching and treatment in all aspects of sports medicine.

Subject coverage: Sports and Exercise Medicine.

Access to staff: Contact by letter, by fax and by e-mail
Hours: Mon to Fri, 0900 to 1700
Special comments: No access – co-ordinating centre only.

Access to building: No access other than to staff

INSTITUTE OF SPRING TECHNOLOGY LIMITED (IST)

Henry Street, Sheffield, South Yorkshire, S3 7EQ

Tel: 0114 276 0771
Fax: 0114 252 7997
E-mail: ist@ist.org.uk
Website: www.ist.org.uk

Enquiries to: Information Manager
Direct tel: 0114 252 7982
Direct e-mail: mom@ist.org.uk

Founded: 1945; formerly called Spring Research and Manufacturers' Association (SRAMA) (year of change 1997)

Organisation type and purpose: Trade association (membership is by subscription), present number of members: 300, research organisation.

Subject coverage: Spring technology; design study and investigation of failures in springs and materials; technical, contract, testing and inspection services including SEM facilities; training; relevant British and foreign standards.

Information services: Technical information on all aspects of spring technology – free to members, chargeable to non-members

Education services: Training courses on all aspects of spring technology – including tailored in-house

Publications: Printed, and electronic and video

Publications list: Available in print

Access to staff: Contact by letter, by telephone, by fax and by e-mail. Appointment necessary. Non-members charged.
Hours: Mon to Thu, 0800 to 1630; Fri, 0800 to 1500

INSTITUTE OF SWIMMING POOL ENGINEERS LIMITED (ISPE)

PO Box 3083, Norwich NR6 7YL

Tel: 01603 499959
Fax: 01603 499959

Enquiries to: General Secretary

Founded: 1978

Organisation type and purpose: Professional body (membership is by qualification, election or invitation), present number of members: 850, training organisation, publishing house. Membership also by direct application. Professional membership, education and training to those in the swimming pool industry.

Subject coverage: All aspects of engineering related to swimming pools.

Publications: Printed

Publications list: Available in print

Access to staff: Contact by letter, by telephone, by fax and by e-mail
Hours: Mon to Fri, 0900 to 1700

INSTITUTE OF THE MOTOR INDUSTRY (IMI)

Fanshaws, Brickendon, Hertford, SG13 8PQ

Tel: 01992 511521
Fax: 01992 511548
E-mail: imi@motor.org.uk
Website: www.motor.org.uk

Enquiries to: Director of Marketing
Direct e-mail: kellysh@motor.org.uk
Other contacts: Director of Communications

Founded: 1920

Organisation type and purpose: International organisation, professional body, present number of members: 26,000.

Subject coverage: Professional guidance for individuals in the retail motor industry, including information on training and education and qualifications in all sectors.

Publications: Printed, and electronic and video

Publications list: Available in print

Access to staff: Contact by letter, by telephone, by fax, by e-mail and via website
Hours: Mon to Fri, 0900 to 1700

Access to building: Prior appointment required
Hours: Mon to Fri, 0900 to 1700

INSTITUTE OF TRADE MARK ATTORNEYS (ITMA)

Outer Temple, 222–225 Strand, London, WC2R 1BA

Tel: 020 7101 6090
Fax: 020 7101 6099
E-mail: tm@itma.org.uk
Website: www.itma.org.uk

Enquiries to: Chief Executive
Other contacts: Public Relations Manager (for press enquiries, presentations)

Founded: 1934

Organisation type and purpose: Professional body (membership is by subscription, election or invitation), present number of members: 1,500.

Subject coverage: Trade marks and allied matters.

Publications: Printed, and electronic and video

Access to staff: Contact by letter, by telephone, by fax and by e-mail
Hours: Mon to Fri, 0900 to 1700

INSTITUTE OF TRAFFIC ACCIDENT INVESTIGATORS (ITAI)

Column House, London Road, Shrewsbury, SY2 6NN

Tel: 08456 212066
Fax: 08456 212077
E-mail: admin@itai.org
Website: www.itai.org

Founded: 1988

Organisation type and purpose: A registered charity (number 1014784), professional body for traffic accident investigators. Membership includes forensic scientists, academics, specialist police officers, consultant investigators, engineers, vehicle assessors, lawyers, doctors and others; overseas membership has representatives from across the world. To promote the free and open exchange of knowledge between those involved in the field of investigating road traffic accidents, and through this, enhance expertise; to represent the interests of the profession in a collective way by arranging field days, lectures, seminars and other educational forums.

Subject coverage: Provides a forum for communication, education, representation and regulation in the field of traffic accident investigation. The Institute is committed to encouraging and, where possible, assisting with research programmes in connection with vehicles and roads.

Publications: Printed

Access to staff: Contact by letter, by telephone, by fax and by e-mail

INSTITUTE OF TRANSACTIONAL ANALYSIS (ITA)

Broadway House, 149–151 St Neots Road, Hardwick, Cambridge, CB23 7QJ

Tel: 01954 212468
Fax: 01954 212468
E-mail: admin@ita.org.uk
Website: www.ita.org.uk

Organisation type and purpose: Institute for practitioners of Transactional Analysis. Committed to effective personal and professional relationships. Advice is available on training and TA practice from ITA committees and council; Contractual Trainees, CTAs, PT/STAs or T/STAs may be included in the ITA Register of Practitioners provided certain criteria are met.

Subject coverage: Transactional Analysis – a theory of personality that offers a range of models that can be used to understand communication and relationships.

Publications: Electronic and video
Order electronic and video publications from: Download from website

Access to staff: Contact by letter, by telephone, by fax and by e-mail

INSTITUTE OF TRANSLATION AND INTERPRETING (ITI)

Suite 165, Milton Keynes Business Centre, Foxhunter Drive, Milton Keynes, MK14 6GD

Tel: 01908 325250
Fax: 01908 325259
E-mail: info@iti.org.uk
Website: www.iti.org.uk

Enquiries to: Operations Assistant

Founded: 1986

Organisation type and purpose: Professional body (membership is by qualification), present number of members: c. 3,000, training organisation.

Subject coverage: Translation and interpreting.

Publications: Printed

Publications list: Available in print

Access to staff: Contact by letter, by telephone, by fax and by e-mail. Appointment necessary.
Hours: Mon to Fri, 0900 to 1700

Access to building: No access other than to staff

Member organisation of: Fédération Internationale des Traducteurs (FIT); 63 rue La Fontaine, 75016 Paris, France; website: http://www.fit-ift.org

INSTITUTE OF TRANSPORT ADMINISTRATION (IoTA)

The Old Studio, 25 Greenfield Road, Westoning, Bedfordshire, MK45 5JD

Tel: 01525 634940
Fax: 01525 750016
E-mail: director@iota.org.uk
Website: www.iota.org.uk

Enquiries to: Director

Founded: 1944

Organisation type and purpose:
Professional body, present number of members: 2,500.

Subject coverage: Transport management and operations.

Publications: Printed

Access to staff: Contact by letter, by telephone, by fax, by e-mail and via website. Appointment necessary.
Hours: Mon to Fri, 0900 to 1600

INSTITUTE OF TRAVEL AND TOURISM (ITT)

PO Box 217, Ware, Hertfordshire, SG12 8WY

Tel: 0870 770 7960
Fax: 0870 770 7961
Website: www.itt.co.uk

Enquiries to: Chairman
Direct e-mail: press@itt.co.uk

Founded: 1956

Organisation type and purpose:
Professional body (membership is by qualification), present number of members: 3200.

Subject coverage: Education and training in the travel and tourism industry.

Publications: Printed

Access to staff: Contact by letter, by telephone, by fax and by e-mail. Appointment necessary.
Hours: Mon to Fri, 0900 to 1730

Access for disabled people: Level entry, toilet facilities

INSTITUTE OF TRICHOLOGISTS

Ground Floor Office, 24 Langroyd Road, London, SW17 7PL

Tel: 0845 604 4657
Fax: 01722 741380
E-mail: admin@trichologists.org.uk
Website: www.trichologists.org.uk

Founded: 1902

Organisation type and purpose:
Professional association for trichologists, the largest provider of trichology training in Europe, and the longest established body of its type.

Subject coverage: Advice and treatment for hair loss, scalp problems, hair texture problems, hair restoration, wigs, extensions, weaving, chemotherapy hair loss and many more hair- and scalp-related issues.

Access to staff: Contact by letter, by telephone, by fax and by e-mail

INSTITUTE OF VEHICLE ENGINEERS (IVehE)

31 Redstone Farm Road, Birmingham, B28 9NU

Tel: 0121 778 4354
Fax: 0121 702 2615
E-mail: secretary@iaea-online.co.uk
Website: www.ivehe.org

Enquiries to: Executive Director
Direct e-mail: james@ivehe.org

Founded: 1881

Organisation type and purpose:
Professional body.

Subject coverage: Manufacturing section of the vehicle industry, original equipment.

Collection: Library of books on historic automobiles and carriages

Publications: Printed

Access to staff: Contact by letter, by telephone, by fax, by e-mail and via website
Hours: Mon to Fri, 0900 to 1700

Access to building: No access other than to staff, prior appointment required

INSTITUTE OF VIDEOGRAPHY (IOV)

PO Box 625, Loughton, IG10 3GZ

Tel: 0845 741 3626; 020 8502 3817
Fax: 020 8508 9211
E-mail: info@iov.co.uk
Website: www.iov.co.uk
Website: www.videoskills.net

Founded: 1985

Organisation type and purpose: A UK-registered, not-for-profit limited company (number 2623169), professional body for those involved in video production.
To establish and maintain videography as a recognised profession; to establish the IOV as the leading body in professional videography; to establish recognised qualifications and training in videography; to provide members with a commercial advantage over non-members; to promote videography as an effective business tool; to promote videography as an art form; to promote videography as an archive medium; to promote the IOV's Code of Practice; to promote qualified members of the IOV.

Subject coverage: Professional video production.

Access to staff: Contact by letter, by telephone, by fax and by e-mail

INSTITUTE OF VITREOUS ENAMELLERS (IVE)

39 Sweetbriar Way, Heath Hayes, Cannock, Staffs, WS12 2UST

Tel: 01543 450596
Fax: 08700 941237
E-mail: info@ive.org.uk
Website: www.ive.org.uk

Enquiries to: Secretary General

Founded: 1934; incorporates the Vitreous Enamel Association (VEA, founded in 1956 as the Vitreous Enamel Development Council; name changed in 1995)

Organisation type and purpose: Trade association.
Represent the vitreous enamel industry by presentations to the public, industry and education also control the cleaner scheme – approval of cleaners for vitreous enamel.

Subject coverage: Nature and uses of vitreous enamel finishes.

Publications: Printed, and electronic and video

Access to staff: Contact by letter, by telephone, by fax and by e-mail. Appointment necessary.
Hours: Mon to Fri, 0900 to 1700

Access to building: No prior appointment required

Affiliated to: British Cookware Manufacturers Association

Parent body: The Institute of Vitreous Enamel (IVE)

INSTITUTE OF WATER (IWater)

4 Carlton Court, Team Valley, Gateshead, Tyne and Wear, NE11 0AZ

Tel: 0191 422 0088
Fax: 0191 422 0087
E-mail: info@instituteofwater.org.uk
Website: www.instituteofwater.org.uk

Enquiries to: Chief Executive
Direct e-mail: lynn@instituteofwaternrg.uk

Founded: 1945

Organisation type and purpose:
Membership association (membership is by subscription), present number of members: 1,700.

Subject coverage: Water industry.

Publications: Printed

Access to staff: Contact by letter, by telephone, by fax, by e-mail and via website. Appointment necessary.
Hours: Mon to Fri, 0900 to 1700

INSTITUTE OF WOMEN'S HEALTH (IWH)

PO Box 9010, Leicester, LE1 8BX

Tel: 0116 255 2100
E-mail: instituteofwomenshealth@yahoo.co.uk / info@iwhealth.co.uk
Website: www.iwhealth.co.uk

Enquiries to: Trustee

Founded: 1999

Organisation type and purpose: Registered charity (charity number 1065037/0), suitable for ages: Adults, training organisation.
To provide information and education on subject of menopause and related issues so that women feel able to make informed health choices.

Subject coverage: Menopause; osteoporosis; other gynaecological issues.
Management therapies: hormone replacement therapy, lifestyle aspects, complementary therapy.

Collection: Textbooks, leaflets, videos, audio tapes, journals on subject areas covered

Non-library collection catalogue: All or part available in-house

Publications: Printed

Access to staff: Contact by letter, by telephone, by e-mail and in person. Appointment necessary.
Hours: Wed, Thu, 1000 to 1400

Access for disabled people: Parking provided, level entry, toilet facilities

INSTITUTION OF AGRICULTURAL ENGINEERS (IAgrE)

The Bullock Building, University Way, Cranfield, Bedford, MK43 0GH

Tel: 01234 750876
Fax: 01234 751319
E-mail: secretary@iagre.org
Website: www.iagre.org

Enquiries to: Chief Executive
Direct e-mail: crw@iagre.org

Founded: 1938

Organisation type and purpose: Professional and learned body.

Subject coverage: Agricultural engineering; agricultural machinery; agriculture, horticulture, forest engineering; engineering for amenity areas; engineering for food storage and handling; food process engineering; environmental engineering; renewable energy.

Collection: Journal of Agricultural Engineering research (now Biosystems Engineering)

Non-library collection catalogue: All or part available online

Library catalogue: All or part available in print

Publications: Printed, and electronic and video, and microform publications

Access to staff: Contact by letter, by telephone, by fax, by e-mail, in person and via website
Hours: Mon to Fri, 0830 to 1630

Administers: Landbased Technician Accreditation scheme (LTA); website: www.iagretech.org
Landbased Technician Accreditation scheme for Milking Equipment (LTAmea); website: www.ltamea.org

Member organisation of: Engineering Council (EngC); website: http://www.engc.org.uk/
European Society of Agricultural Engineers; website: http://www.eurageng.eu/
Society for the Environment; website: http://www.socenv.org.uk/

Owner of the sector's scientific journal: Biosystems Engineering; website: http://www.journals.elsevier.com/biosystems-engineering/

INSTITUTION OF ANALYSTS AND PROGRAMMERS (IAP)

Charles House, 36 Culmington Road, London, W13 9NH

Tel: 020 8567 2118
Fax: 020 8567 4379
E-mail: dg@iap.org.uk
Website: www.iap.org.uk/iapdg

Enquiries to: Secretary

Founded: 1981

Organisation type and purpose: Professional body.
The Institution is Britain's leading specialised professional organisation for computer programmers and systems analysts.

Subject coverage: Advice on matters relating to training and career development in the IT industry.

Publications: Printed, and electronic and video

Access to staff: Contact by telephone and by e-mail
Hours: Mon to Fri, 0900 to 1700

INSTITUTION OF CIVIL ENGINEERING SURVEYORS (ICES)

Dominion House, Sibson Road, Sale, Cheshire, M33 7PP

Tel: 0161 972 3100
Fax: 0161 942 3118
E-mail: ices@ices.org.uk
Website: www.ices.org.uk

Enquiries to: Administrator

Founded: 1972

Organisation type and purpose: Advisory body, professional body (membership is by qualification, election or invitation), present number of members: 4,000, registered charity, suitable for ages: 18+.
Qualifying body for engineering and quantity surveyors involved with civil engineering.

Subject coverage: Construction, commercial management including: quantity surveying, project management, estimating, construction law, construction economics, planning, procurement engineering.
Geospacial engineering surveying including: land surveying, engineering surveying, hydrographic surveying, remote sensing, cartography, geographical information systems, photogrammetry.

Publications: Printed

Publications list: Available in print

Access to staff: Contact by letter, by telephone, by fax, by e-mail and via website
Hours: Mon to Fri, 0830 to 1700

Access for disabled people: Parking provided, access to all public areas, toilet facilities

Associated institution of the: Institution of Civil Engineers

Member of: Construction Industry Council; International Federation of Surveyors; Survey and Mapping Alliance

Wholly owned marketing and publications company is: SURCO Limited

INSTITUTION OF CIVIL ENGINEERS (ICE)

1 Great George Street, Westminster, London, SW1P 3AA

Tel: 020 7222 7722
Fax: 020 7976 7610
E-mail: library@ice.org.uk
Website: www.ice.org.uk

Enquiries to: Head Knowledge Transfer
Direct tel: 020 7665 2252
Other contacts: Archivist (for access for archives)

Founded: 1818

Organisation type and purpose: Learned society.
Qualifying body.

Subject coverage: Civil engineering and related theoretical and applied sciences; civil engineering, building, construction; concrete, iron, steel and timber in structures; geotechnical engineering; public health engineering; hydrology and hydraulics; municipal engineering; history of technology; transport, environment.

Collection: 18th- and 19th-century pamphlets
Archives of Council of Engineering Institutions
Archives of Institution of Civil Engineers
Archives of Institution of Municipal Engineers
Archives of Smeatonian Society
B L Vulliamy Horological Library
Films, videos and photographic collections
Gibb Collection
J G James Collection
Mackenzie Collection
MSS of Telford, Smeaton, the Rennies, Brunel and other early civil engineers

Non-library collection catalogue: All or part available online, in-house and in print

Library catalogue: All or part available online

Publications: Printed, and electronic and video

Publications list: Available online and in print

Access to staff: Contact by letter, by telephone, by fax, by e-mail, in person and via website. Appointment necessary. Access for members only. Letter of introduction required. Non-members charged.
Hours: Mon to Fri, 0915 to 1730
Special comments: Charges made to all users for certain services.

Houses the: British Dam Society; British Geotechnical Association; British Hydrological Society; British Tunnelling Society; Central Dredging Association – British Section; European Council of Civil Engineers; International Association for Hydraulic Research – British Section; International Commission on Irrigation and Drainage – British Section (ICID); International Navigation Association – British Section (PIANC); Nuclear Institute; Offshore Engineering Society; Railway Civil Engineers Association; Society for Earthquake and Civil Engineering Dynamics (SECED); Transport Planning Society; Wind Engineering Society

INSTITUTION OF DIESEL AND GAS TURBINE ENGINEERS (IDGTE)

Bedford Heights, Manton Lane, Bedford, MK41 7PH

Tel: 01234 214340
Fax: 01234 355493
E-mail: enquiries@idgte.org

continued overleaf

Website: www.idgte.org/

Enquiries to: Director General

Founded: 1913

Organisation type and purpose:
International organisation, learned society (membership is by subscription, qualification), present number of members: 450.
The institution is devoted to the advancement of diesel and gas engines, gas turbines and related products and technology.

Subject coverage: Diesel engines and gas turbines.

Publications: Printed, and electronic and video

Publications list: Available in print

Access to staff: Contact by letter, by telephone, by fax, by e-mail and via website
Hours: Mon to Fri, 0900 to 1500

Access to building: Prior appointment required

INSTITUTION OF ENGINEERING AND TECHNOLOGY (IET)

Savoy Place, London, WC2R 0BL

Tel: 020 7240 5461
Fax: 020 7240 8467
E-mail: libdesk@theiet.org
Website: www.theiet.org

Enquiries to: Librarian
Direct tel: 020 7344 5461
Direct fax: 020 7344 8467
Direct e-mail: jcoupland@theiet.org
Other contacts: Archivist

Founded: 1871; created by the merger of Institution of Electrical Engineers (IEE) and Institution of Incorporated Engineers (IIE) (year of change 2006)

Organisation type and purpose:
International organisation, learned society (membership is by subscription, qualification), present number of members: 150,000, registered charity (charity number 211014), publishing house.
Qualifying body.

Subject coverage: Electrical, electronic and control engineering, computer science, information technology, manufacturing, engineering, telecommunications.

Information services: Technical and business research service.

Special visitor services: PC access and wi-fi.

Collection: Silvanus Thompson Memorial Collection (rare books and manuscripts)
Sir Francis Ronalds Collection (19th-century rare books and manuscripts on electricity)

Trade and statistical information: Small collection of market reports

Non-library collection catalogue: All or part available online

Library catalogue: All or part available online

Publications: Printed, and electronic and video
Order printed publications from: Publications Sales, IET, PO Box 96, Stevenage, Hertfordshire, SG1 2SD; tel. 01438 767328; fax 01438 742792; e-mail sales@theiet.org
Order electronic and video publications from: Publications Sales, IET, PO Box 96, Stevenage, Hertfordshire, SG1 2SD; tel. 01438 767328; fax 01438 742792; e-mail sales@theiet.org

Publications list: Available online and in print

Access to staff: Contact by letter, by telephone, by fax, by e-mail, in person and via website. Non-members charged.
Hours: Mon to Fri, 0900 to 1700

Access to building: No prior appointment required
Hours: Mon to Fri, 0900 to 1700

Access for disabled people: Ramped entry, toilet facilities

Also at: IET; Michael Faraday House, Six Hills Way, Stevenage, Hertfordshire, SG1 2AY; tel: 01438 313311; fax: 01438 313465; e-mail: postmaster@theiet.org; website: http://www.theiet.org

Subsidiary: Inspec; Michael Faraday House, Six Hills Way, Stevenage, SG1 2AY; tel: 01438 767540; fax: 01438 742840; e-mail: inspec@theiet.org; website: http://www.theiet.org/inspec

INSTITUTION OF ENGINEERING DESIGNERS (IED)

Courtleigh, Westbury Leigh, Westbury, Wiltshire, BA13 3TA

Tel: 01373 822801
Fax: 01373 858085
E-mail: ied@ied.org.uk

Enquiries to: Secretary

Founded: 1945

Organisation type and purpose:
Professional body (membership is by qualification, election or invitation), present number of members: 5300, registered charity (charity number 269879).

Subject coverage: Engineering design, engineering drawing, design, design education.

Publications: Printed

Access to staff: Contact by letter, by telephone, by fax, by e-mail and via website
Hours: Mon to Fri, 0900 to 1700

Nominated body of the: Engineering Council; tel: 020 7240 7891

INSTITUTION OF ENVIRONMENTAL SCIENCES (IES)

PO Box 16, Bourne, Lincolnshire, PE10 9FB

Tel: 01778 394846
Fax: 01778 394846
E-mail: ies-uk@breathemail.net
Website: www.greenchannel.com/ies

Enquiries to: Honorary Secretary

Founded: 1971

Organisation type and purpose:
Professional body.

Subject coverage: Environmental science including ecology, pollution, public health, urban problems, genetic effects, climatic effects, effects of technology and transport.

Publications: Printed

Access to staff: Contact by letter and by e-mail
Hours: Mon to Fri, 0900 to 1700

INSTITUTION OF FIRE ENGINEERS (IFE)

London Road, Moreton-in-Marsh, Gloucestershire, GL56 0RH

Tel: 01608 812580
Fax: 01608 812581
E-mail: info@ife.org.uk
Website: www.ife.org.uk

Enquiries to: Membership Officer
Direct e-mail: gill.haynes@ife.org.uk

Organisation type and purpose:
Professional body (membership is by subscription).

Subject coverage: Fire engineering.

Publications: Printed

Access to staff: Contact by letter, by telephone, by fax, by e-mail and via website. Appointment necessary.
Hours: Mon to Fri, 0900 to 1700

Part of: Federation of British Fire Organisations

INSTITUTION OF GAS ENGINEERS AND MANAGERS (IGEM)

IGEM House, High Street, Kegworth, Derbyshire, DE74 2DA

Tel: 0844 375 4436
Fax: 01509 678198
E-mail: general@igem.org.uk
Website: www.igem.org.uk

Enquiries to: Librarian

Founded: 1863

Organisation type and purpose:
Professional body, registered charity (charity number 214011).

Subject coverage: Gas engineering, manufacture, transmission and distribution, gas utilisation, natural gas, LNG, gas by-products, gas industry administration and personnel, gas industry history.

Library catalogue: All or part available in-house

Publications: Printed

Publications list: Available online and in print

Access to staff: Contact by letter, by telephone, by fax, by e-mail and via website. Appointment necessary. Non-members charged.
Hours: Mon to Fri, 0900 to 1700

Member organisation of: Engineering Council; International Gas Union

INSTITUTION OF HIGHWAYS AND TRANSPORTATION (IHT)

6 Endsleigh Street, London, WC1H 0DZ

Tel: 020 7387 2525
Fax: 020 7387 2808
E-mail: iht@iht.org
Website: www.iht.org

Enquiries to: Chief Executive
Other contacts: Director of Technical Affairs for technical enquiries.

Founded: 1930

Organisation type and purpose: Learned society, registered charity (charity number 267321).

Subject coverage: Highways and transportation infrastructure, planning and design for: roads, traffic, light rail, safety, disabled access, environment.

Publications: Printed, and electronic and video

Publications list: Available in print

Access to staff: Contact by letter, by telephone, by fax, by e-mail and via website. Appointment necessary.
Hours: Mon to Fri, 0930 to 1700
Special comments: Access difficult for those with mobility handicaps.

Access to building: No prior appointment required
Hours: Library: Mon to Fri, 0930 to 1700
Special comments: Not open if meeting in library.

Close professional cooperation with the: Institute of Highways Incorporated Engineers (IHIE)

INSTITUTION OF LIGHTING ENGINEERS (ILE)

Lennox House, 9 Lawford Road, Rugby, Warwickshire, CV21 2DZ

Tel: 01788 576492
Fax: 01788 540145
E-mail: info@ile.co.uk
Website: www.ile.co.uk

Enquiries to: Chief Executive
Other contacts: Technical Services Manager for technical advice.

Founded: 1924

Organisation type and purpose: National organisation, professional body (membership is by qualification), present number of members: 2075, registered charity (charity number 268547), suitable for ages: all, training organisation, research organisation, publishing house.
To promote excellence in lighting.

Subject coverage: All aspects of lighting, particularly exterior including street, sports, flood, emergency, tunnel lighting.

Collection: Small library

Library catalogue: All or part available in-house

Publications: Printed, and electronic and video

Publications list: Available online and in print

Access to staff: Contact by letter, by telephone, by fax, by e-mail and via website. Appointment necessary. Non-members charged.
Hours: Mon to Fri, 0900 to 1700

Access to building: Prior appointment required

Nominated body of the: Engineering Council

INSTITUTION OF MECHANICAL ENGINEERS (IMechE)

1 Birdcage Walk, Westminster, London, SW1H 9JJ

Tel: 020 7222 7899; 020 7973 1274 (information and library service)
Fax: 020 7222 4557
E-mail: enquiries@imeche.org
Website: www.imeche.org

Enquiries to: Manager
Direct fax: 020 7222 8762
Other contacts: Archivist (for access to archives)

Founded: 1847

Organisation type and purpose: Professional body (membership is by subscription, qualification), registered charity (charity number 206882).
To create a natural home for all involved in mechanical engineering science that commands high regard in the community, whose members' expert views are sought on all important, relevant issues, and to membership of which every mechanical engineer aspires.

Subject coverage: Mechanical engineering and related fields: tribology, solid mechanics and machine systems, energy, materials, manufacturing technology and design, combustion engines, environmental engineering, offshore engineering, pressurised systems, aerospace and automotive engineering, maritime engineering, power engineering, railway engineering.

Collection: Archives of: Institution of Mechanical Engineers, Institution of Locomotive Engineers, Institution of Automobile Engineers
Manuscripts of: George Stephenson and Robert Stephenson; James Nasmyth; David Joy; FW Lanchester; Christopher Hinton; Joseph Whitworth; Livesey, Henderson and Company; many others
Library contains technical papers dating back to 1847
ESDU Data Sheets
More than 200 professional and trade journals, over 122,000 vols of books, some of which date back to the foundation of the Institution
American Society of Automotive Engineers, SAE, pre-prints

Non-library collection catalogue: All or part available online and in-house

Library catalogue: All or part available online

Publications: Printed, and electronic and video
Order printed publications from: Professional Engineering Publishing, 1 Birdcage Walk, London, SW1H 9JJ

Publications list: Available online and in print

Access to staff: Contact by letter, by telephone, by fax, by e-mail, in person and via website. Appointment necessary.

Access to building: No prior appointment required
Hours: Mon to Fri, 0915 to 1730
Special comments: Loans available to members only. Some services charged.

Access for disabled people: Access to all public areas, toilet facilities
Special comments: Lift

INSTITUTION OF NUCLEAR ENGINEERS (INucE)

Allan House, 1 Penerley Road, London, SE6 2LQ

Tel: 020 8698 1500 or 4750
Fax: 020 8695 6409
E-mail: London.branch@nuclearinst.com
Website: www.inuce.co.uk

Enquiries to: General Secretary
Other contacts: President

Founded: 1959

Organisation type and purpose: Learned society, professional body.

Subject coverage: Peaceful aspects of nuclear technology; nuclear engineering in relation to other disciplines, electronic/nuclear, mechanical/nuclear, nuclear physics, nuclear mathematics.

Publications: Printed, and microform publications
Order microform publications from: UMI, Bell and Howell Co
300 N Zeeb Road, Ann Arbor, MI 48106–1346, USA

Publications list: Available in print

Access to staff: Contact by letter, by telephone, by fax, by e-mail and via website. Appointment necessary.
Hours: Mon to Fri, 0830 to 1700

Affiliated to: The Engineering Council

Member society of the: European Nuclear Society

INSTITUTION OF OCCUPATIONAL SAFETY AND HEALTH (IOSH)

The Grange, Highfield Drive, Wigston, Leicestershire, LE18 1NN

Tel: 0116 257 3100
Fax: 0116 257 3101
E-mail: enquiries@iosh.co.uk
Website: www.iosh.co.uk

Enquiries to: Publishing and Media Assistant

Founded: 1945

Organisation type and purpose: Learned society, professional body (membership is by qualification), present number of members: 33,000, registered charity (charity number 210981), training organisation, publishing house.

Subject coverage: Occupational safety, health and hygiene; training; legislation; environmental management.

Publications: Printed

Publications list: Available in print

continued overleaf

Access to staff: Contact by letter, by telephone, by fax, by e-mail, in person and via website
Hours: Mon to Fri, 0900 to 1700

IOSH has: regional branches in the UK and Ireland and a number of special interest groups

INSTITUTION OF STRUCTURAL ENGINEERS (IStructE)

11 Upper Belgrave Street, London, SW1X 8BH

Tel: 020 7235 4535
Fax: 020 7235 4294
E-mail: mail@istructe.org
Website: www.istructe.org

Enquiries to: Manager, Library and Information Services
Direct tel: 020 7201 9105
Direct fax: 020 7201 9118
Direct e-mail: library@istructe.org

Founded: 1908; formerly called Concrete Institute (year of change 1922)

Organisation type and purpose: Learned society.

Subject coverage: Structural engineering, defined as the science and art of designing and making with economy and elegance, buildings, bridges, frames and other similar structures so that they can safely resist the forces to which they may be subjected.

Information services: Library service for IStructE members; non members by appointment

Library catalogue: All or part available online

Publications: Printed
Order printed publications from: Publications Department, at the same address

Publications list: Available online and in print

Access to staff: Contact by letter, by telephone, by fax, by e-mail, in person and via website. Access for members only.
Hours: Tues to Fri, 0930 to 1730
Special comments: Prior appointment required for non-members

Access to building: Prior appointment required for non-members
Hours: Tues to Fri, 0930 to 1730

Access for disabled people: Ramp available

Constituent bodies: Structural-Safety (incorporating SCOSS and CROSS)

Member organisation of: Construction Industry Council; Engineering Council

INSTOCK FOOTWEAR SUPPLIERS ASSOCIATION (IFSA)

Marlow House, Churchill Way, Fleckney, Leicester, LE8 8UD

Tel: 0116 240 3232
Fax: 0116 240 2762

Enquiries to: Information Officer

Organisation type and purpose: National organisation, trade association, membership association (membership is by subscription), present number of members: 8.

Subject coverage: Footwear wholesaling in the UK.

Access to staff: Contact by letter, by telephone and by fax
Hours: Mon to Fri, 0900 to 1700

Access to building: No access other than to staff

Affiliated to: Federation of Wholesale and Industrial Distributors and the Footwear Distributors

INSULATED RENDER AND CLADDING ASSOCIATION (INCA)

Royal London House, 22–25 Finsbury Square, London, EC2A 1DX

Tel: 0844 249 0040
Fax: 0844 249 0042
E-mail: info@inca.org.uk
Website: www.inca-ltd.org.uk

Enquiries to: Information Officer

Founded: 1983

Organisation type and purpose: Advisory body, trade association (membership is by qualification), present number of members: 60.

Subject coverage: Insulated render and cladding for solid or defective walled housing/buildings.

Trade and statistical information: UK insulated render and cladding market sales figures

Publications: Printed

Publications list: Available online

Access to staff: Contact by letter, by telephone, by fax, by e-mail and via website
Hours: Mon to Fri, 0900 to 1700

INSULATION AND ENVIRONMENTAL TRAINING TRUST LIMITED (IETTL)

TICA House, Allington Way, Yarm Road Business Park, Darlington, Co Durham, DL1 4QB

Tel: 01325 466704
Fax: 01325 487691
E-mail: enquiries@tica-acad.co.uk

Enquiries to: Director

Organisation type and purpose: Registered charity, training organisation.

Subject coverage: Industry training in insulation and asbestos removal.

Access to staff: Contact by letter, by fax and by e-mail
Hours: Mon to Thu, 0830 to 1700; Fri, 0830 to 1530

Access to building: Prior appointment required

Access for disabled people: Parking provided

Affiliated to: Insulation & Environmental Training Agency (IETA); tel: 01325 466704; fax: 01325 487691; e-mail: enquiries@tica-acad.co.uk; Thermal Insulation Contractors Association (TICA); tel: 01325 466704; fax: 01325 487691; e-mail: enquiries@tica-acad.co.uk

INSURANCE INSTITUTE OF LONDON (IIL)

5th Floor, 20 Aldermanbury, London, EC2V 7HY

Tel: 020 7600 1343
Fax: 020 7600 6857
E-mail: iil.london@cii.co.uk
Website: www.iilondon.co.uk

Founded: 1907

Organisation type and purpose:
Professional body.
To raise the professional knowledge of those working in insurance in the London Market.

Subject coverage: Insurance industry.

Publications: Printed
Order printed publications from: website: http://www.iilondon.co.uk

Publications list: Available online and in print

Access to staff: Contact by letter, by telephone, by fax, by e-mail, in person and via website. Appointment necessary.
Hours: Mon to Thu, 0900 to 1700; Fri, 0900 to 1645

Parent body: Chartered Insurance Institute; at the same address

INTER FAITH NETWORK FOR THE UK

2 Grosvenor Gardens, London SW1W 0DH

Tel: 020 7730 0410
Fax: 020 7730 0414
E-mail: ifnet@interfaith.org.uk
Website: www.interfaith.org.uk

Enquiries to: Director

Founded: 1987

Organisation type and purpose: Voluntary organisation, registered charity (charity number 1068934).

Subject coverage: Advice and information on inter faith matters.

Publications: Printed

Publications list: Available online and in print

Access to staff: Contact by letter, by telephone, by fax, by e-mail and via website. Appointment necessary.
Hours: Mon to Fri, 0930 to 1730

Access to building: Prior appointment required

INTER-CREDIT INTERNATIONAL

Formal name: Inter-Credit International Ltd

4th Floor, South Point House, 321 Chase Road, Southgate, London, N14 6JT

Tel: 020 8482 4444
Fax: 020 8482 4455
E-mail: collection@intercred.com
Website: www.intercred.com/

Enquiries to: Managing Director

Founded: 1971

Organisation type and purpose: Service industry.
National and international debt recovery agency and credit reference agency.

Subject coverage: Credit scoring.

INTERACT READING SERVICE

Room 8, Victoria Charity Centre, 11 Belgrave Road, London SW1V 1RB

Tel: 020 7931 6458
E-mail: info@interactreading.org
Website: www.interactreading.org
Direct e-mail: info@interactreading.org

Founded: 2000

Organisation type and purpose: A registered charity (number 1080046).
InterAct Reading Service is the only UK charity dedicated to supporting stroke recovery by using professional actors to deliver a live and interactive reading service to people who have had a stroke in hospitals and at stroke clubs.

Subject coverage: Over 200 professional actors visiting 22 hospitals and over 50 stroke clubs around the UK. In the hospitals the actors mainly read on a one-to-one basis at the patient's bedside. The Stroke Club readings are performance based; the reader performs a programme and reads to the whole group.
InterAct actors are professionally trained. They work for InterAct when not working in theatre, radio, film and television.

Access to staff: Contact by letter, by telephone and by e-mail

INTERACTIVE

Unit 2B07, London South Bank University, Technopark, 90 London Road, London, SE1 6LN

Tel: 020 7717 1699
E-mail: info@interactive.uk.net
Website: www.interactive.uk.net

Enquiries to: Office Co-ordinator

Founded: 1981

Organisation type and purpose:
Membership association (membership is by subscription, election or invitation), voluntary organisation, registered charity (charity number 1055683), suitable for ages: all, training organisation.
To develop sporting and recreational opportunities for all disabled people including those with learning disabilities, physical impairments, visual impairments and deaf people.

Subject coverage: Sporting and recreational activities for disabled people, training programmes, equipment.

Publications list: Available online

Access to staff: Contact by letter, by telephone, by fax, by e-mail and via website. Appointment necessary.
Hours: Mon to Fri, 0900 to 1700

Access for disabled people: Parking provided, ramped entry, toilet facilities

INTERCONTINENTAL CHURCH SOCIETY (ICS)

1 Athena Drive, Tachbrook Park, Warwick, CV34 6NL

Tel: 01926 430347
Fax: 01926 888092
E-mail: enquiries@ics-uk.org
Website: www.ics-uk.org

Enquiries to: General Manager

Founded: 1823; formerly called Colonial and Continental Church Society (year of change 1861); formerly called Commonwealth and Continental Church Society (year of change 1958)

Organisation type and purpose:
Membership association (membership is by subscription), present number of members: 830, voluntary organisation, registered charity (charity number 1072584).
ICS, an evangelical Anglican mission society, supports the ministry of English-speaking, international congregations in several continents, ministers to holidaymakers in Europe and the Mediterranean.

Subject coverage: English-language church services abroad.

Publications: Printed

Access to staff: Contact by letter, by telephone, by fax, by e-mail and via website
Hours: Mon to Fri, 0930 to 1700

Access to building: No access other than to staff

Access for disabled people: Level entry

Links with: Partnership for World Mission (PWM); Church House, 27 Great Smith Street, London, SW1P 3AZ; tel: 020 7898 1328

INTERMEDIATE TECHNOLOGY DEVELOPMENT GROUP LIMITED (ITDG)

The Schumacher Centre for Technology and Development, Bourton Hall, Bourton on Dunsmore, Rugby, Warwickshire, CV23 9QZ

Tel: 01926 634400
Fax: 01926 634401
E-mail: enquiries@practicalaction.org.uk
Website: www.itdg.org

Enquiries to: Information Officer
Direct e-mail: carolr@itdg.org.uk

Founded: 1966

Organisation type and purpose:
International organisation, registered charity (charity number 247257).
An international development agency working at the cutting edge of sustainable community development through country offices in Africa, Asia and South America.
To build the technical skills of poor people in developing countries, enabling them to improve the quality of their lives and that of future generations.

Subject coverage: Appropriate technology, low-cost and small-scale manufacturing processes suitable for the developing countries, in agriculture, water supply and sanitation, building materials and construction, energy, transport, food production, food processing, mining and small industries.

Collection: Books on appropriate technologies and grey literature

Publications: Printed
Order printed publications from: IT Publications
103–105 Southampton Row, London, WC1B 4HH, tel: 020 7436 9761, fax: 020 7436 2013, e-mail: itpubs@itpubs.org.uk

Publications list: Available in print

Access to staff: Contact by letter, by telephone, by fax, by e-mail and via website. Appointment necessary.
Hours: Mon to Fri, 0900 to 1700

INTERNATIONAL ACCOUNTING STANDARDS BOARD (IASB)

1st Floor, 30 Cannon Street, London, EC4M 6XH

Tel: 020 7246 6410
Fax: 020 7246 6411
E-mail: iasb@iasb.org.uk
Website: www.iasb.org.uk

Enquiries to: Secretary General
Other contacts: Publications Director

Founded: 1973

Organisation type and purpose:
Accountancy regulatory body.
To formulate international accounting standards and to promote their use worldwide.

Subject coverage: International accounting standards.

Publications: Printed, and electronic and video
Order printed publications from: Publications Department, IASB
tel: 020 7427 5927, fax: 020 7353 0562

Publications list: Available online and in print

Access to staff: Contact by letter and by telephone
Hours: Mon to Fri, 0900 to 1700
Special comments: Access for members only.

Access to building: No access other than to staff

INTERNATIONAL ACUPUNCTURE ASSOCIATION OF PHYSICAL THERAPISTS (IAAPT)

Hilltop, Benjamin Road, High Wycombe, Buckinghamshire, HP13 6SR

Tel: 01494 451295
Fax: 01494 451295
E-mail: merianmum@hotmail.com

Enquiries to: UK Representative
Direct e-mail: merianmum@hotmail.com

Founded: 1991

Organisation type and purpose:
Professional body.

Subject coverage: Acupuncture and physiotherapy.

Publications: Printed

Access to staff: Contact by letter and by fax
Hours: Unrestricted

Affiliated to: World Confederation for Physical Therapy (WCPT)

Links with: Acupuncture Association of Chartered Physiotherapists (AACP)

INTERNATIONAL AESTHETICIENNES

International Beauty Therapy Examination Board, Bache Hall, Bache Hall Estate, Chester, Cheshire, CH2 1BR

Tel: 01244 376539
Fax: 01244 373571
E-mail: info@iabeauty.com
Website: www.iabeauty.com

Enquiries to: Secretary

Founded: 1979

Organisation type and purpose:
International organisation, professional body (membership is by subscription, qualification).

Subject coverage: Beauty, body and electrolysis, examinations, membership with or without insurance.

Publications: Electronic and video

Access to staff: Contact by letter, by telephone, by fax and by e-mail
Hours: Sat, 0900 to 1700

INTERNATIONAL AFRICAN INSTITUTE (IAI)

SOAS, Thornhaugh Street, Russell Square, London, WC1H 0XG

Tel: 020 7898 4429
Fax: 020 7898 4410
E-mail: iai@soas.ac.uk
Website: www.internationalafricaninstitute.org

Enquiries to: Secretary

Founded: 1926

Organisation type and purpose:
International organisation, learned society (membership is by election or invitation), present number of members: 27, registered charity (charity number 1084798), research organisation, publishing house.
The International African Institute has been the foremost international association engaged in encouraging the study of African society and disseminating the results of research. Its prime objective is to facilitate communication between scholars within the continent and Africans throughout the world on issues that are of direct relevance to the peoples of this region. It achieves this objective through its publication programme, seminars, African and non-African scholars; and projects which are concerned with the infrastructure for learning and research in Africa.

Subject coverage: Communications between scholars in Africa and elsewhere, African societies and cultures.

Publications: Printed
Order printed publications from: Edinburgh University Press
22 George Square, Edinburgh, EH8 9LF
James Currey Publisher
73 Botley Road, Oxford, OX2 0BS

Publications list: Available online and in print

Access to staff: Contact by e-mail
Hours: Mon to Fri, 0900 to 1700

INTERNATIONAL AIRLINE PASSENGERS ASSOCIATION (IAPA)

Advertiser House, 19 Bartlett Street, South Croydon, Surrey, CR2 6TB

Website: www.iapa.com

Founded: 1960; formerly called Airways Club (year of change 1982)

Organisation type and purpose:
Membership association.
To represent the interests of frequent air travellers by providing them with special discounts on items such as hotel accommodation, car rental and insurance, in addition to protecting and promoting their rights as airline passengers.
Works in partnership with major companies world-wide to bring the best deals possible to members.

Subject coverage: Offers a range of services, from guaranteeing the 'best available rate' on key hotel chains and savings on car rental reservations, to a market-leading range of specialist insurance products for members; also provides a range of travel-planning services, helps members save money on mobile telephone bills when travelling, and represents their interests as frequent flyers to industry and government bodies.

Access to staff: Contact by letter, by telephone, by fax and by e-mail
Hours: London Membership Services: Mon to Fri, 0800 to 2000; Sat and public hols, 0900 to 1700; Sun and Dec 25, closed

Also at: Membership Services, IAPA; PO Box 380, Croydon, Surrey, CR9 2ZQ; tel: 020 8681 6555; fax: 020 8681 0234; e-mail: info.london@iapa.com; Membership Services, IAPA; PO Box 700188, Dallas, TX 75370–0188, USA; tel: +1 972 404 9980; toll-free in USA/Canada/Mexico: 800 821 4272; fax: +1 972 233 5348; toll-free in USA/Canada/Mexico: 800 647 4272; e-mail: info.dallas@iapa.com; Membership Services, IAPA; GPO Box 9200, Hong Kong; tel: +852 2528 4263; fax: +852 2865 6891; e-mail: info.hongkong@iapa.com

Constituent part of: Priority Travel Group

INTERNATIONAL ALUMINIUM INSTITUTE (IAI)

New Zealand House, Haymarket, London, SW1Y 4TE

Tel: 020 7930 0528
Fax: 020 7321 0183
E-mail: iai@world-aluminium.org
Website: www.world-aluminium.org

Enquiries to: Secretary General

Founded: 1972

Organisation type and purpose:
International organisation, trade association, membership association (membership is by qualification), present number of members: 22.
International association of the primary aluminium industry.

Subject coverage: Aluminium industry; aluminium products; energy requirements; statistics, developments; environmental health and safety.

Trade and statistical information: Information and statistics are available on the website

Publications list: Available online

Access to staff: Contact by letter, by telephone, by fax and by e-mail
Hours: Mon to Fri, 0900 to 1700

INTERNATIONAL ARTIST MANAGERS' ASSOCIATION (IAMA)

23 Garrick Street, Covent Garden, London, WC2E 9BN

Tel: 020 7379 7336
Fax: 020 7379 7338
E-mail: info@iamaworld.com
Website: www.iamaworld.com

Enquiries to: Chief Executive

Founded: 1954

Organisation type and purpose:
International organisation, membership association (membership is by election or invitation), present number of members: 230.

Subject coverage: Artist management, concert promotion (classical music).

Publications: Printed

Publications list: Available online and in print

Access to staff: Contact by letter, by telephone, by fax, by e-mail and via website
Hours: Mon to Fri, 0930 to 1730

INTERNATIONAL ASSOCIATION OF BOOK-KEEPERS (IAB)

Suite 5, 20 Churchill Square, Kings Hill, West Malling, Kent, ME19 4YU

Tel: 01732 897750
Fax: 01732 897751
E-mail: mail@iab.org.uk
Website: www.iab.org.uk

Enquiries to: Chief Executive

Founded: 1973

Organisation type and purpose:
Professional body.
Examining body.

Subject coverage: All aspects of book-keeping and accountancy.

Publications: Printed, and electronic and video

Access to staff: Contact by letter, by telephone, by fax, by e-mail and via website. Appointment necessary.
Hours: Mon to Fri, 0900 to 1700

Links with: International Association of Accounting Professionals; Suite 5, 20 Churchill Square, Kings HIll, West Malling, Kent, ME19 4YU; tel: 01732 897750; fax: 01732 897751; e-mail: mail@iaap.org.uk; website: www.intaap.org

INTERNATIONAL ASSOCIATION OF CLASSIFICATION SOCIETIES (IACS)

6th Floor, 36 Broadway, London, SW1H 0BH

Tel: 020 7976 0660
Fax: 020 7808 1100

E-mail: permsec@iacs.org.uk
Website: www.iacs.org.uk

Enquiries to: Permanent Secretary
Other contacts: Principal Technical Officer for technical enquiries.

Founded: 1992

Organisation type and purpose:
International organisation, membership association (membership is by qualification), present number of members: 13, voluntary organisation, registered charity, research organisation.
Trade association representing the world's 13 largest classification societies.

Subject coverage: Ship classification; vessel surveys; vessel repairs; vessel hull and essential engineering systems; international maritime conventions and regulations; safety at sea; prevention of marine pollution.

Trade and statistical information: IACS member societies classify the hull and essential engineering systems of over 90% of the world's merchant fleet by tonnage on behalf of well over 100 sovereign states worldwide

Publications: Printed, and electronic and video

Publications list: Available online

Access to staff: Contact by letter, by telephone, by fax, by e-mail and via website. Appointment necessary.
Hours: Mon to Fri, 0900 to 1700

Access to building: Prior appointment required

Access for disabled people: Level entry

Also at: IACS QSCS OPS; Suite 2, Orchard House, 51–67 Commercial Road, Southampton, SO15 1GG; tel: 023 8021 1369; e-mail: qscs.ops@iacs.org.uk

Links with: European Association of Classification Societies (EURACS)

Member organisations: American Bureau of Shipping; ABS Plaza, 16855 Northchase Drive, Houston, TX 77060, USA; tel: +1 281 877 6000; fax: +1 281 877 6001; e-mail: abs-worldhq@eagle.org; Bureau Veritas; Paris, France; tel: +33 1 42 91 52 91; fax: +33 1 42 91 52 93; e-mail: veristarinfo@bureauveritas.com; China Classification Society; Beijing, China; tel: +86 10 5811 2288; fax: +86 10 5811 2811; e-mail: ccs@ccs.org.cn; Croatian Register Of Shipping; 21000 Split Marasovića 67 P.O.B. 187 Croatia; tel: + 385 (0)21 408 111 (switchboard no.); fax: + 385 (0)21 358 159; e-mail: iacs@crs.hr; Det Norske Veritas; Hovik, Norway; tel: +47 67 57 99 00; fax: +47 67 57 99 11; e-mail: iacs@dnv.com; Germanischer Lloyd; Hamburg, Germany; tel: +49 40 36 14 90; fax: +49 40 36 14 9200; e-mail: headoffice@gl-group.com; Indian Register of Shipping; Mumbai, India; tel: +91 22 2570 3627; fax: +91 22 2570 3611; e-mail: ho@irclass.org; website: http://www.crs.hr
Korean Register of Shipping; Taejon, Korea; tel: +82 42 869 9114; fax: +82 42 862 6011; e-mail: krsiacs@krs.co.kr; Lloyd's Register of Shipping; London; tel: 020 7709 9166; fax: 020 7488 4796; e-mail: lloydsreg@lr.org; Nippon Kaiji Kyokai; Tokyo, Japan; tel: +81 3 3230 1201; fax: +81 3 3230 3524; e-mail: xad@classnk.or.jp; Polish Register of Shipping; Head Office: Polski Rejestr Statków S.A. al. Generåja Józefa Hallera 126 80–416 Gdańsk, Poland; tel: 58 346 17 00; fax: 58 346 03 92; e-mail: iacs@prs.pl; website: http://www.prs.pl
Register of Shipping (Russia); St Petersburg, Russia; tel: +7 812 312 3569; fax: +7 812 312 3569; e-mail: 004@rs-head.spb.ru; RINA; Genova, Italy; tel: +39 010 53 851; fax: +39 010 59 1877; e-mail: info@rina.org

INTERNATIONAL ASSOCIATION OF HYDROGEOLOGISTS (IAH)

PO Box 9, Kenilworth, Warwickshire, CV8 1JG

Tel: 01926 450677
Fax: 01926 856561
E-mail: iah@iah.org
Website: www.iah.org

Enquiries to: Secretary General

Founded: 1956

Organisation type and purpose:
International organisation, professional body (membership is by subscription), present number of members: 3500.

Subject coverage: Hydrogeology, groundwater, role in developing countries.

Publications: Printed, and electronic and video

Publications list: Available online

Access to staff: Contact by letter, by fax, by e-mail and via website
Hours: Irregular

Affiliated to: International Union of Geological Sciences

INTERNATIONAL ASSOCIATION OF INSTITUTES OF NAVIGATION (IAIN)

Royal Institute of Navigation, 1 Kensington Gore, London, SW7 2AT

Tel: 020 7591 3130
Fax: 020 7591 3131
E-mail: prentpage@aol.com
Website: www.rin.org.uk/iain/frame1.htm

Enquiries to: Secretary General
Direct tel: 01444 232405
Direct fax: 01444 232405

Organisation type and purpose:
International organisation.
Coordinating and consulting body of 19 national institutes of navigation throughout the world.

Subject coverage: Navigation by land, sea, air and in space.

Publications: Printed, and electronic and video

Access to staff: Contact by letter, by fax, by e-mail and via website
Hours: Mon to Fri, 0900 to 1700

Members are the institutes of navigation of: Arab States, Argentine, Austria, Australia, Czech Republic, China, France, Germany, Italy, Japan, Korea, Netherlands, Nordic States, Poland, Russia, Spain, Switzerland, UK, USA; Tel and fax numbers and e-mail address on IAIN website (http://www.rin.org.uk/iain/frame1.htm)

INTERNATIONAL ASSOCIATION OF MUSIC LIBRARIES, ARCHIVE AND DOCUMENTATION CENTRES (UNITED KINGDOM BRANCH) (IAML (UK & Irl))

Website: www.iaml-uk-irl.org

Founded: 1953

Organisation type and purpose:
International organisation, professional body (membership is by subscription, election or invitation), present number of members: 295.
Voluntary association in liaison with the Chartered Institute of Library Information Professionals.
Promotes music libraries and supports anyone working in music libraries or related fields.

Subject coverage: Music bibliography and librarianship.

Collection: A collection of books and magazines about music librarianship is held at the Department of Music, University of Oxford

Library catalogue: All or part available online and in print

Publications: Printed
Order printed publications from: Publications Officer, IAML (UK & Irl), County Library Headquarters, Walton Street, Aylesbury, Buckinghamshire, HP20 1UU, tel: 01296 382266, fax: 01296 382274, e-mail: mroll@buckscc.gov.uk

Publications list: Available online

Access to staff: Contact by letter, by telephone, by fax, by e-mail and in person. Appointment necessary.
Hours: Mon to Fri, 0900 to 1700

Links with: Chartered Institute of Library and Information Professionals

INTERNATIONAL ASSOCIATION OF TOUR MANAGERS (IATM)

397 Walworth Road, London, SE17 2AW

Tel: 020 7703 9154
Fax: 020 7703 0358
E-mail: iatm@iatm.co.uk
Website: www.iatm.co.uk

Enquiries to: General Manager

Founded: 1962

Organisation type and purpose: Trade association, membership association (membership is by subscription).

Subject coverage: Tour management.

Publications: Printed

Access to staff: Contact by letter, by telephone, by e-mail and via website
Hours: Mon to Fri, 0900 to 1430

Access to building: No access other than to staff

Member organisation of: American Society of Travel Agents (ASTA); website: http://www.asta.org
European Tour Operators Association (ETOA); Weighhouse Street, London; e-mail: http://www.etoa.org; European Travel and Tourism Action Group (ETAG); website: http://www.etag-euro.org

INTERNATIONAL AUTISTIC RESEARCH ORGANISATION – AUTISM RESEARCH LIMITED (IARO)

49 Orchard Avenue, Shirley, Croydon, Surrey, CR0 7NE

Tel: 020 8777 0095
Fax: 020 8776 2362
E-mail: iaro@autismresearch.wanadoo.co.uk
Website: www.iaro.org.uk

Enquiries to: Director
Other contacts: Secretary

Founded: 1981

Organisation type and purpose:
International organisation, membership association (membership is by subscription), present number of members: 300+, voluntary organisation, registered charity (charity number 802391), research organisation.
Information body.
To encourage research into autism and to disseminate the useful results of such research. Information provision and awareness-raising of scientific research into autism.

Subject coverage: Information in autism and the latest research.

Education services: Medical research only.

Publications: Printed

Publications list: Available in print

Access to staff: Contact by letter, by telephone, by fax and by e-mail
Hours: Mon to Fri, 0900 to 1700
Special comments: By appointment only. Charges made to non-members for printed matters.

Access to building: Prior appointment required

Access for disabled people: *Special comments:* No wheelchair access.

Networking: Autism Research Review International; 4182 Adams Avenue, San Diego, CA 92116, USA; tel: (619) 281 7165; fax: (619) 563 6840; website: http://www.AutismResearchInstitute.com
Autism Society of America; 7910 Woodmont Avenue, Suite 300, Bethesda, Maryland 20814–3067, USA; tel: (301) 657 0881; fax: (301) 657 0869; website: http://www.autism-society.org
Autistik (Autism Society of the Czech Republic); Estonia Autistic Society; Tartu EE2400, Estonia; Indiana Research Centre, Indiana University, Indiana Institute on Disability Community, Indiana's Centre for Excellence on Disability; 2853 East Tenth Street, Bloomington, IN 74708–2696, USA; tel: (812) 855 6508; fax: (812) 855 9630; e-mail: cbow-man@indianna.edu

INTERNATIONAL BAR ASSOCIATION (IBA)

10th Floor, 1 Stephen St, London, W1T 1AT

Tel: 020 7691 6868
Fax: 020 7691 6544
E-mail: iba@int-bar.org
Website: www.ibanet.org

Founded: 1947

Organisation type and purpose: A global organisation of international legal practitioners, bar associations and law societies. Membership of more than 40,000 individual lawyers and 197 bar associations and law societies spanning all continents.
To promote an exchange of information between legal associations world-wide; to support the independence of the judiciary and the right of lawyers to practise their profession without interference.
Influences the development of international law reform and shapes the future of the legal profession throughout the world; provides support of human rights for lawyers world-wide through its Human Rights Institute; has considerable expertise in providing assistance to the global legal community.

Subject coverage: International law and the legal profession globally; human rights.

Publications: Printed
Order printed publications from: Online shop (discount for members)

Publications list: Available online

Access to staff: Contact by letter, by telephone, by fax and via website
Hours: Mon to Fri, 0900 to 1730

Also at: Latin America office; Rua Helena, 170–cjs 141–142, 04552–050 Sao Paulo/SP, Brazil; tel: +55 11 3044 1456; fax: +55 11 3044 0803; Middle East office; Dubai International Financial Centre, Office 15, L3, B4 Gate Village Business Centre, PO Box 113355, Sheikh Zayed Road, Dubai, UAE; tel: +971 4 401 9563; fax: +971 4 401 9990

Links with: IBA Human Rights Institute (IBAHRI)

INTERNATIONAL BEE RESEARCH ASSOCIATION (IBRA)

16 North Road, Cardiff, CF10 3DY

Tel: 029 2037 2409
Fax: 056 0113 5640
E-mail: mail@ibra.org.uk
Website: www.ibra.org.uk

Enquiries to: Executive Director
Direct e-mail: jonessl@ibra.org.uk

Founded: 1949

Organisation type and purpose:
International organisation, learned society, membership association (membership is by subscription), present number of members: 395, registered charity (charity number 209222), museum, consultancy, publishing house.
Library; Research Data Collection.
The world information service for bee science and beekeeping.

Subject coverage: Apiculture; bees (all species, but especially honeybees); substances used by bees; plants foraged by bees; bee products and their uses; pollination by bees and other insects; pests and diseases of bees; history of beekeeping; beekeeping development programmes in the Third World.

Collection: Apis Library, Morland, Manley and Essinger Collections
Eva Crane Library (over 40,000 publications)
Historical and Contemporary Beekeeping Material
Picture Collection

Non-library collection catalogue: All or part available in-house and in print

Library catalogue: All or part available in-house

Publications: Printed, and electronic and video, and microform publications
Order printed publications from: IBRA Bookshop, 16 North Road, Cardiff, CF10 3DY; website: http://www.ibra.org.uk/shop
Order electronic and video publications from: IBRA Bookshop, 16 North Road, Cardiff, CF10 3DY; website: http://www.ibra.org.uk/shop

Publications list: Available online and in print

Access to staff: Contact by letter, by telephone, by fax, by e-mail, in person and via website. Appointment necessary. Non-members charged.
Hours: Mon to Fri, 1000 to 1600

Access to building: Contact before visiting
Hours: Mon to Fri, 1000 to 1600

Access for disabled people: Limited access (stairs, no lift, parking difficult), but most information offered online or by telephone

Links with: International Union for Biological Sciences; Bat. 442, Université Paris Sud 11, 91405 Orsay Cedex, France; tel: +33 1 69 15 50 27; e-mail: secretariat@iubs.org; website: http://www.iubs.org
National Library of Wales; Aberystwyth; tel: 01970 632800; fax: 01790 615709; website: http://www.llgc.org.uk

INTERNATIONAL BIBLE STUDENTS ASSOCIATION

Watch Tower House, The Ridgeway, London, NW7 1RN

Tel: 020 8906 2211
Fax: 020 8371 0051
E-mail: ssmith@uk.jw.org
Website: www.watchtower.org
Website: www.jw-media.org

Enquiries to: Public Relations Manager
Direct e-mail: opi@wtbts.org.uk

Founded: 1914

Organisation type and purpose:
International organisation, membership association (membership is by qualification), present number of members: Britain: 133,900, world-wide: 7,313,173, voluntary organisation, registered charity (charity number IBSA: 216647; Watch Tower: 1077961), publishing house.
To promote understanding of the Bible and its message. Bible-based educational work.

Subject coverage: Comprehensive Bible education (free).

Publications: Printed, and electronic and video

Publications list: Available online and in print

Access to staff: Contact by letter and by telephone
Hours: Mon to Fri, 0800 to 1200 and 1300 to 1700

Connections with: Watch Tower Bible and Tract Society of Pennsylvania; 25 Columbia Heights, Brooklyn, NY 11201, USA; tel: +1 718 560 5000

INTERNATIONAL BIOGRAPHICAL CENTRE (IBC)

Melrose Press Limited, St Thomas Place, Ely, Cambridgeshire, CB7 4GG

Tel: 01353 646600
Fax: 01353 646601
E-mail: info@intbiogcentre.com
Website: www.melrosepress.co.uk

Enquiries to: Chief Executive

Organisation type and purpose: Publishing house.

Subject coverage: Publishers of biographical reference books in areas such as music, literature, medicine, the arts in general.

Publications: Printed

Publications list: Available in print

Access to staff: Contact by letter, by telephone, by fax and by e-mail
Hours: Mon to Fri, 0900 to 1700

INTERNATIONAL BOATBUILDING TRAINING COLLEGE (IBTC)

Sea Lake Road, Oulton Broad, Lowestoft, Suffolk, NR32 3LQ

Tel: 01502 569663
Fax: 01502 500661
E-mail: ibtc@globalnet.co.uk
Website: www.htk.co.uk/ibtc

Enquiries to: Managing Director
Other contacts: Course Secretary for general.

Founded: 1974

Organisation type and purpose: Service industry, training organisation.
Provision of practical training in boatbuilding skills.

Subject coverage: Boatbuilding, boatyard and marine management.

Access to staff: Contact by letter, by telephone, by fax, by e-mail and via website. Appointment necessary.
Hours: Mon to Fri, 0830 to 1630

Access for disabled people: Parking provided, ramped entry, toilet facilities

Parent body: Broadblue Limited; at the same address

INTERNATIONAL CAMELLIA SOCIETY (ICS)

UK Region, 41 Galveston Road, London, SW15 2RZ

Tel: 020 8870 6884
Fax: 020 8874 4633
E-mail: patricia_short@btconnect.com
Website: www.camellia-ics.org

Enquiries to: Honorary Secretary

Founded: 1962

Organisation type and purpose:
International organisation, membership association (membership is by subscription).

Subject coverage: History, nomenclature, cultivation, propagation, exhibition and arrangement of camellias; trial grounds (2 in England, 1 in Scotland, 1 in N Ireland).

Publications: Printed

Access to staff: Contact by letter, by telephone, by fax and by e-mail
Hours: Mon to Fri, 0900 to 1700

INTERNATIONAL CENTRE FOR BIRDS OF PREY (ICBP)

Great Boulsdon, Newent, Gloucestershire, GL18 1JJ

Tel: 01531 820285/821581
E-mail: jpj@icbp.org
Website: www.icbp.org

Enquiries to: Director
Direct tel: 01531 820286
Direct e-mail: info@icbp.org

Founded: 1967; formerly called The Falconry Centre, The National Birds of Prey Centre

Organisation type and purpose: Public facility, open seven days a week, ten months of the year. Suitable for ages: all, research and conservation organisation.
Conservation through education, captive breeding and research.

Subject coverage: Information on birds of prey and owls, welfare and management, captive breeding, education on them, research projects, hunting with them.

Information services: Courses on falconry, training birds of prey, demonstration training, PWLO training.

Special visitor services: Three flying demonstrations daily.

Education services: Group education facilities.

Publications: Printed, and electronic and video

Access to staff: Contact by letter, by telephone and by e-mail
Hours: Open to public Feb to Nov, Mon to Sun

Access to building: Ten months of the year
Hours: 1030 to 1730
Special comments: Closed December and January.

Access for disabled people: Parking provided, ramped entry, level entry, access to all public areas, toilet facilities

Links with: 200 international connections

INTERNATIONAL CENTRE FOR CONSERVATION EDUCATION (ICCE)

Brocklebank House, Butts Lane, Woodmancote, Cheltenham, Gloucestershire, GL52 9QH

Tel: 01242 674839
Fax: 01242 674839
E-mail: icce@brocklebank.plus.com
Website: www.icce.org.uk

Enquiries to: Executive Director
Direct e-mail: enquiries@icce.org.uk

Founded: 1984

Organisation type and purpose:
International organisation, registered charity (charity number 289468), consultancy, publishing house.
Environmental education. To promote greater understanding of global environmental issues and sustainable development.

Subject coverage: Environmental education and development of resources for all levels.

Collection: Books, games and packs
Environmental photolibrary

Publications: Printed, and electronic and video, and microform publications

Publications list: Available online and in print

Access to staff: Contact by letter, by telephone and by e-mail
Hours: Mon to Fri, 0900 to 1700

INTERNATIONAL CENTRE FOR DISTANCE LEARNING (ICDL)

Open University, Library and Learning Resources Centre, Walton Hall, Milton Keynes, Buckinghamshire, MK7 6AA

Tel: +44 (0)1908 659001
E-mail: lib-help@open.ac.uk
Website: icdl.open.ac.uk/

Founded: 1983

Organisation type and purpose: University department or institute.
Documentation Centre.
Documentation centre specialising in distance education across the world.

Subject coverage: Distance education encompassing all disciplines and all education levels.

Collection: Approximately 15,000 printed items; books, journals, conference papers, research reports, dissertations and other types of literature, all relating to the theory and practice of distance education
Distance education library

Non-library collection catalogue: All or part available online

Library catalogue: All or part available online and in-house

Access to staff: Contact by letter, by telephone, by fax, by e-mail, in person and via website
Hours: Helpdesk enquiries by e-mail, telephone, webchat, web form, fax, letter – Mon to Thu, 0900 to 2000; Fri, Sat, 0900 to 1700; Sun, 1200 to 1700

Access to building: Staff and students only
Hours: Mon to Thu, 0830 to 1830; Fri 0830 to 1700

Access for disabled people: Parking provided, level entry, toilet facilities

Parent body: Open University

INTERNATIONAL CENTRE FOR PROTECTED LANDSCAPES (ICPL)

8E, Cefn Llan Science Park, Aberystwyth, Ceredigion, SY23 3AH

Tel: 01970 622620
Fax: 01970 622619
Website: www.protected-landscapes.org

Enquiries to: Executive Director

Founded: 1991

continued overleaf

Organisation type and purpose: Training organisation, consultancy, research organisation.
To promote the concept of integrated conservation and development especially in relation to protected areas, through professional training, higher education, research and consultancy.

Subject coverage: Protected areas and landscapes, integrated conservation and development.

Library catalogue: All or part available in-house

Publications list: Available in print

Access to staff: Contact by letter, by telephone, by fax, by e-mail and via website. Appointment necessary.
Hours: Mon to Fri, 0900 to 1700

Access to building: Prior appointment required

Access for disabled people: Parking provided, ramped entry, access to all public areas, toilet facilities

Member of: The World Conservation Union (IUCN)

INTERNATIONAL CENTRE FOR RESEARCH IN ACCOUNTING (ICRA)

The Management School, University of Lancaster, Lancaster, LA1 4YX

Tel: 01524 593632
Fax: 01524 847321
E-mail: p.pope@lancaster.ac.uk

Enquiries to: Director

Founded: 1971

Organisation type and purpose: Registered charity (charity number 501487), research organisation.

Subject coverage: Accountancy, particularly the financial reporting practices of companies and their regulation and standard-setting processes, corporate governance, derivative products.

Publications: Printed, and electronic and video

Access to staff: Contact by letter, by telephone, by fax and by e-mail
Hours: Mon to Fri, 0900 to 1700

Links with: Lancaster University

INTERNATIONAL CENTRE FOR TECHNICAL RESEARCH (ICTR)

Formal name: Centre for Technical Research International

115 Dollis Hill Lane, London, NW2 6HS

Tel: 020 8450 8383
Fax: 020 8452 3366
E-mail: info@ictr.org.uk
Website: www.ictr.org.uk

Enquiries to: Chairman
Other contacts: Director

Founded: 1983

Organisation type and purpose: International organisation, university department or institute, consultancy.

Subject coverage: A non-profit-making organisation aimed at the transfer of technology to third-world countries via consultancy, education and conferences.

Publications: Printed
Order printed publications from: ICTR Office

Access to staff: Contact by letter, by fax and by e-mail
Hours: Mon to Fri, 0900 to 1700

Access for disabled people: Ramped entry, level entry, access to all public areas

INTERNATIONAL CHAMBER OF COMMERCE (UNITED KINGDOM) (ICC UK)

12 Grosvenor Place, London, SW1X 7HH

Tel: 020 7838 9363
Fax: 020 7235 5447
E-mail: richardbate@iccorg.co.uk
Website: www.iccbookshop.com

Enquiries to: Director

Founded: 1920

Organisation type and purpose: International organisation, membership association (membership is by subscription), present number of members: 350.

Publications: Printed

Publications list: Available in print

Access to staff: Contact by letter, by telephone, by fax and by e-mail. Appointment necessary.
Hours: Mon to Fri, 0900 to 1700

INTERNATIONAL CHAMBER OF SHIPPING (ICS)

Carthusian Court, 12 Carthusian Street, London, EC1M 6EZ

Tel: 020 7417 8844
Fax: 020 7417 8877
E-mail: ics@marisec.org
Website: www.marisec.org
Website: www.marisec.org/pubs

Enquiries to: Secretary General

Founded: 1921

Organisation type and purpose: International organisation, trade association, membership association, publishing house.

Subject coverage: International shipping, safe ship operations e.g. tanker safety, helicopter and ship operations, prevention of drugs trafficking.

Publications: Printed
Order printed publications from: Marisec Publications
at the same address, e-mail: publications@marisec.org

Publications list: Available online and in print

Access to staff: Contact by letter, by telephone, by fax and by e-mail
Hours: Mon to Fri, 0900 to 1700

Has consultative status with the: International Maritime Organization; Various inter-governmental organisations

Members are the: General Council of British Shipping; National shipowners' associations in 34 countries

INTERNATIONAL CHILDCARE TRUST (ICT)

Development House, 56–64 Leonard Street, London EC2A 4LT

Tel: 020 7065 0970
Fax: 020 7065 0971
E-mail: info@ict-uk.org
Website: www.ict-uk.org

Enquiries to: CEO

Founded: 1982

Organisation type and purpose: International organisation, registered charity.
Eradicate poverty and protect the basic rights of children and young people anywhere in the world who are in condition of need, hardship or distress, by preventing and relieving sickness and advancing their education.

Subject coverage: The charity develops partnerships with local people and organisations according to their needs and in accordance with their culture. The Trust never funds other projects.

Publications: Electronic and video

Access to staff: Contact by letter, by telephone, by fax, by e-mail and via website
Hours: Mon to Fri, 0900 to 1700

Links with: BOND; CSC

INTERNATIONAL CLEMATIS SOCIETY (ICIS)

3 Cuthberts Close, Waltham Cross, Hertfordshire, EN7 5RB

Tel: 01992 636524
E-mail: clematis@clematisinternational.com
Website: www.clematisinternational.com

Enquiries to: Secretary

Founded: 1984

Organisation type and purpose: International organisation, membership association (membership is by subscription), present number of members: 275.

Subject coverage: Clematis, cultivation and propagation.

Publications: Printed

Access to staff: Contact by letter, by telephone, by e-mail and via website
Hours: Mon to Fri, 0900 to 1700

INTERNATIONAL COCOA ORGANISATION (ICCO)

Commonwealth House, 1–19 New Oxford Street, London, WC1A 1NU

Tel: 020 7400 5050
Fax: 020 7421 5500
E-mail: info@icco.org
Website: www.icco.org

Enquiries to: Information Officer
Direct e-mail: library@icco.org

Founded: 1973

Organisation type and purpose: International organisation.
Intergovernmental organisation.

Subject coverage: Cocoa, economics, production and processing.

Trade and statistical information: Statistics: production and consumption

Publications: Printed

Publications list: Available online and in print

Access to staff: Contact by letter, by telephone, by fax, by e-mail and via website. Appointment necessary.
Hours: Library: 0900 to 1700 by appointment

Affiliated to: UNCTAD

INTERNATIONAL COLLEGES OF ISLAMIC SCIENCES (ICIS)

Unit 1A Crusader House, 249–289 Cricklewood Broadway, London, NW2 6NX

Tel: 020 8450 8383
Fax: 020 8452 3366
E-mail: registrar@kolieh.com

Enquiries to: Chairman
Other contacts: Registrar

Founded: 1990

Organisation type and purpose:
International organisation, registered charity (charity number 802651), university department or institute.
Education.

Subject coverage: Islamic higher education.

Publications: Printed

Publications list: Available in print

Access to staff: Contact by letter, by telephone and by fax
Hours: Mon to Fri, 1000 to 1730

Parent body: International Centre for Technical Research; tel: 020 8450 8383; fax: 020 8452 3366

INTERNATIONAL COMMISSION ON ZOOLOGICAL NOMENCLATURE (ICZN)

The Natural History Museum, Cromwell Road, London, SW7 5BD

Tel: 020 7942 5653
E-mail: iczn@nhm.ac.uk
Website: www.iczn.org

Enquiries to: Scientific Administrator
Other contacts: Executive Secretary

Founded: 1895

Organisation type and purpose:
International organisation (membership is by election or invitation), present number of members: 28.
International Commission for the furtherance of stability and universality in the nomenclature of animals.

Subject coverage: Zoological nomenclature, maintenance and interpretation of the International Code of Zoological Nomenclature, rulings on particular problems.

Publications: Printed

Access to staff: Contact by letter and by e-mail
Hours: Mon to Fri, 0900 to 1700

Links with: International Union of Biological Sciences

INTERNATIONAL COMMITTEE FOR THE CONSERVATION OF THE INDUSTRIAL HERITAGE (TICCIH)

Chygarth, 5 Beacon Terrace, Camborne, Cornwall, TR14 7BU

Tel: 01209 612142
Fax: 01209 612142
E-mail: stuartbsmith@chygarth.co.uk
Website: www.mnactec.com/ticcih
Website: www.ticcih.org

Enquiries to: Secretary

Founded: 1978

Organisation type and purpose:
International organisation, membership association (membership is by subscription), present number of members: 500, registered charity (charity number 1079809).
To promote the preservation and interpretation of industrial sites throughout the world.

Subject coverage: International co-operation in the preservation, conservation, investigation, documentation, research and presentation of industrial heritage, promotion of education in these matters. This includes the physical remains of the industrial past, such as landscapes, sites, structures, plant, equipment, products and other fixtures and fittings, as well as the documentation, consisting of both verbal and graphic material, and memories and opinions of the people involved.

Publications: Printed

Publications list: Available in print

Access to staff: Contact by letter, by telephone, by fax, by e-mail and via website
Hours: Mon to Fri, 0900 to 1700

Links with: ICOMOS; tel: +33 145 67 6770; fax: +33 145 66 0622; e-mail: secretariat@icomos.org; national representatives and correspondents in 49 countries

INTERNATIONAL COMPLIANCE ASSOCIATION (ICA)

Wrens Court, 52–54 Victoria Road, Sutton Coldfield, Birmingham, B72 1SX

Tel: 0121 362 7747
Fax: 0121 240 3002
E-mail: ica@int-comp.org
Website: www.int-comp.org

Organisation type and purpose:
Professional body for compliance practitioners world-wide.
To advance knowledge and learning in the field of anti-money laundering, financial crime prevention and compliance practice; to develop the skills, expertise and standing of anti-money laundering, financial crime prevention and compliance professionals worldwide; to undertake research and to make representation of a technical nature to regulatory and governmental bodies and other agencies in order to promote greater understanding of the benefits of compliance, financial crime prevention and anti-money laundering practice; to develop an effective and coherent approach to the prevention of money laundering, financial crime and the mitigation of regulatory compliance risk; to establish and maintain standards for professionals through education, training and examination programmes; to promote and enhance the ICA Code of Ethics, by encouraging business to be conducted with integrity, diligence and professionalism; to promote courses, conferences and meetings as a mechanism to discuss, exchange information and enhance understanding of international issues in the field; to provide a forum for members to develop professional and working relationships within the industry and with related professions and organisations.

Subject coverage: Anti-money laundering, financial crime prevention and compliance practice.

Access to staff: Contact by letter, by telephone, by fax and by e-mail

Also at: Dubai Office; Dubai International Financial Centre, Centre of Excellence, The Gate Village, Building 2, Level 3, PO Box 506745, Dubai; tel: +971 4 4019310; e-mail: info@ictmiddleeast.com; Singapore Office; 10 Shenton Way, 12–01 MAS Building, Singapore 079117; tel: +65 6500 0010; fax: + 65 6327 9618; e-mail: enquiries@int-comp.org

INTERNATIONAL COUNCIL FOR SELF-ESTEEM (ICSE)

5 Ferry Path, Cambridge, CB4 1HB

Tel: 01223 365351
Fax: 01223 365351
E-mail: esteemhere@aol.com
Website: www.murraywhite-selfesteem.co.uk

Enquiries to: UK Representative

Founded: 1990

Organisation type and purpose:
International organisation, learned society, present number of countries in membership: 70.
To promote concept of self-esteem and its significance; facilitates the co-ordination of self-esteem activities throughout the world.

Subject coverage: Self-esteem in homes, schools and organisations, behaviour issues.

Publications: Printed

Publications list: Available online and in print

Access to staff: Contact by letter, by telephone, by e-mail, in person and via website. Appointment necessary.
Hours: Mon to Fri, 0900 to 1700

INTERNATIONAL COUNCIL OF TANNERS (ICT)

Leather Trade House, Kings Park Road, Moulton Park, Northampton, NN3 6JD

Tel: 01604 679999
Fax: 01604 679998
E-mail: sec@tannerscouncilict.org
Website: www.tannerscouncilict.org

Enquiries to: Secretary
Direct tel: 01604 679917

Founded: 1926

Organisation type and purpose:
International organisation.

Subject coverage: Leather production and related activities.

continued overleaf

Trade and statistical information: Surveys of production and relevant information e.g. environmental regulations, normally restricted to members

Publications: Printed

Access to staff: Contact by letter, by fax and by e-mail
Hours: Mon to Fri, 0900 to 1700

INTERNATIONAL COUNCIL ON MONUMENTS AND SITES UK (ICOMOS-UK)

70 Cowcross Street, London, EC1M 6EJ

Tel: 020 7566 0031
Fax: 020 7566 0045
E-mail: admin@icomos-uk.org
Website: www.icomos.org/uk

Enquiries to: The Secretary

Founded: 1965

Organisation type and purpose:
International organisation, advisory body, membership association (membership is by subscription), present number of members: 250, voluntary organisation, registered charity (charity number 1057254).

Subject coverage: Preservation and management of monuments and historic sites.

Publications: Printed

Publications list: Available online and in print

Access to staff: Contact by letter and by fax
Hours: Irregular, dependent on part-time staff

Links with: ICOMOS International Secretariat; 49–51 rue de la Fédération, 75015 Paris, France

INTERNATIONAL CRAFT AND HOBBY FAIR LIMITED (ICHF Ltd)

Dominic House, Seaton Road, Christchurch, Dorset, BH23 5HW

Tel: 01425 272711
Fax: 01425 279369
E-mail: info@ichf.co.uk
Website: www.ichf.co.uk

Enquiries to: Manager

Founded: 1976

Organisation type and purpose: Service industry.
Exhibition Organisers.

Subject coverage: Crafts and hobbies, design and technology, needlecraft.

Publications: Printed

Access to staff: Contact by letter, by telephone, by fax, by e-mail and via website
Hours: Mon to Fri, 0900 to 1700
Special comments: All listings, addresses and exhibiting companies are held solely for ICHF use only.

INTERNATIONAL CREMATION FEDERATION (ICF)

Van Stolkweg 29A, 2585 JN, The Hague, The Netherlands

Tel: +31 70 351 8836
Fax: +31 70 351 8827
E-mail: keizer@facultatieve.com
Website: www.int-ciem-fed.org

Enquiries to: Secretary-General

Founded: 1937

Organisation type and purpose:
International organisation, advisory body, registered charity.
The provision of a central, international, source of help, advice and information to all those interested or involved in any aspect of cremation.

Subject coverage: All aspects of cremation.

Trade and statistical information:
International cremation statistics, cremation figures and details of cremation societies throughout the world

Publications: Printed

Access to staff: Contact by letter, by telephone, by fax and by e-mail
Hours: Mon to Fri, 0900 to 1700

INTERNATIONAL DANCE TEACHERS' ASSOCIATION (IDTA)

International House, 76 Bennett Road, Brighton, East Sussex, BN2 5JL

Tel: 01273 685652
Fax: 01273 674388
E-mail: info@idta.co.uk
Website: www.idta.co.uk

Enquiries to: General Secretary
Other contacts: Administration Officer

Founded: 1903

Organisation type and purpose:
International organisation, professional body (membership is by qualification), present number of members: 6,000, service industry, suitable for ages: all.
Awarding body.

Subject coverage: Dance (social and theatre); statistics related to dance; amateur tests in dance.

Collection: History of Dance

Publications: Printed, and electronic and video
Order printed publications from: IDTA Sales Ltd – International Sales
at the same address, tel: 01273 608583

Publications list: Available online and in print

Access to staff: Contact by letter, by fax, by e-mail and via website
Hours: Mon to Fri, 0900 to 1700

Access to building: No access other than to staff

Affiliated to: British Council of Ballroom Dancing; Central Council of Physical Recreation

Member of: Council for Dance Education and Training; Stage Dance Council International; 13 Braemar Road, Fallowfield, Manchester, M14 6PQ

INTERNATIONAL FEDERATION OF ACTORS (FIA)

31 rue de l'Hôpital, 1030 Brussels

Tel: 0032 (0)2 235 08 74
Fax: 0032 (0)2 235 08 61
E-mail: office@fia-actors.com
Website: www.fia-actors.com

Enquiries to: General Secretary

Founded: 1952

Organisation type and purpose: Trade union.
Representation of 100 performers' unions in 75 countries.

Subject coverage: FIA provides four main services to member unions: representation at the various international organisations as an accredited non-governmental organisation; defence of the artistic freedom of performers; union development; information exchange.

Access to staff: Contact by letter, by telephone, by fax and by e-mail.
Appointment necessary.
Hours: Mon to Fri, 0900 to 1700

INTERNATIONAL FEDERATION OF AROMATHERAPISTS (IFA)

7B Walpole Court, Ealing Green, Ealing, London W5 5ED

Tel: 020 8567 2243
Fax: 020 8840 9288
Website: www.ifaroma.org/

Enquiries to: Public Relations Manager
Direct e-mail: office@ifarom.org
Other contacts: Chairperson

Founded: 1985

Organisation type and purpose:
International organisation, professional body, registered charity (charity number 327290).
Registration of courses.

Subject coverage: Aromatherapy, aromatherapy training, registered courses.

Collection: Aromatherapy books
Lists of members and courses

Publications: Printed

Access to staff: Contact by letter, by telephone and by fax
Hours: Mon to Fri, 0900 to 1700
Special comments: Charges for some services.

Affiliated to: ICM; Unit 15, Tavern Quay, Commercial Centre, Rope Street, London, SE16 1TX

Member of: Aromatherapy Organisations Council; PO Box 19834, London, SE25 6LB

INTERNATIONAL FEDERATION OF BUSINESS AND PROFESSIONAL WOMEN (IFBPW)

PO Box 568, Horsham, West Sussex, RH13 9ZP

Tel: 01403 739343
Fax: 01403 734432
E-mail: members@bpwintl.com
Website: www.bpwintl.com

Enquiries to: Director
Other contacts: International President

Founded: 1930

Organisation type and purpose: International organisation, membership association (membership is by subscription), present number of members: 38,000, voluntary organisation, registered charity. International non-governmental organisation.
Promote the status of women.

Subject coverage: Business and professional women and all issues relating to achieving equal status for women in political, economic and civil spheres of society.

Publications: Printed

Publications list: Available in print

Access to staff: Contact by letter, by telephone, by fax, by e-mail, in person and via website. Appointment necessary.
Hours: Mon to Fri, 0900 to 1700

Subsidiary regional groups: Africa; Asia and Pacific; Europe; Latin America and Spanish-speaking West Indies; North America and non-Spanish-speaking West Indies

INTERNATIONAL FEDERATION OF GYNAECOLOGY AND OBSTETRICS (FIGO)

70 Wimpole Street, London, W1G 8AX

Tel: 020 7224 3270
Fax: 020 7935 0736
E-mail: figo@figo.org
Website: www.figo.org

Enquiries to: Secretariat
Other contacts: Secretary General

Founded: 1954

Organisation type and purpose: International organisation, membership association (membership is by subscription), present number of members: 103 national societies.
Non-governmental organisation.

Subject coverage: Obstetrics and gynaecology.

Publications: Printed

Publications list: Available online

Access to staff: Contact by letter, by telephone, by fax, by e-mail, in person and via website
Hours: Mon to Fri, 0900 to 1700

Cooperation with: 19 non-governmental organisations involved in women and children's health

Incorporated in Geneva, its title is the: Fédération Internationale de Gynécologie et d'Obstétrique

INTERNATIONAL FEDERATION OF INSPECTION AGENCIES (IFIA)

Formal name: International Federation of Inspection Agencies Limited

22 Great Tower Street, London, EC3R 5HE

Tel: 020 7283 1001/020 7280 3200
Fax: 020 7626 4416

Enquiries to: Director General
Direct e-mail: secretariat@ifia-federation.org

Founded: 1982

Organisation type and purpose: Trade association.

INTERNATIONAL FEDERATION OF PROFESSIONAL AROMATHERAPISTS (IFPA)

82 Ashby Road, Hinckley, Leicestershire, LE10 1SN

Tel: 01455 637987
Fax: 01455 890956
E-mail: admin@ifparoma.org
Website: www.ifparoma.org

Enquiries to: Administrator
Other contacts: Membership Secretary (for membership enquiries)

Founded: 2002

Organisation type and purpose: International organisation, professional body, membership association (membership is by subscription, qualification), present number of members: 1731, registered charity (charity number 1091325).

Subject coverage: Aromatherapy, qualified therapists, educational standards.

Publications: Printed

Access to staff: Contact by letter, by telephone, by fax, by e-mail and via website
Hours: Mon to Fri, 0900 to 1700

Access for disabled people: Parking provided, level entry, toilet facilities

Subsidiary body: 48 accredited schools throughout the UK and overseas

INTERNATIONAL FERTILISER SOCIETY (IFS)

PO Box 4, York, YO32 5YS

Tel: 01904 492700
Fax: 01904 492700
E-mail: secretary@fertiliser-society.org
Website: www.fertiliser-society.org

Enquiries to: Secretary

Founded: 1947

Organisation type and purpose: International organisation, learned society, professional body.

Subject coverage: Scientific, technical, economic and environmental aspects of the production, marketing, distribution, use and application of fertilisers and crop nutrients.

Collection: Complete proceedings of the Society from 1947 (foundation) to date (approx 670)
Complete set of papers written by Dr George Cooke FRS

Library catalogue: All or part available online

Publications: Printed

Publications list: Available online

Access to staff: Contact by letter, by telephone, by fax, by e-mail and via website
Hours: Mon to Fri, 0900 to 1700

INTERNATIONAL FOOD INFORMATION SERVICE (IFIS)

Lane End House, Shinfield Road, Shinfield, Reading, Berkshire, RG2 9BB

Tel: 0118 988 3895
Fax: 0118 988 5065
E-mail: ifis@ifis.org
Website: www.foodsciencecentral.com

Enquiries to: Head of Marketing & Sales

Founded: 1968

Organisation type and purpose: International organisation, service industry, registered charity (charity number 1068176), publishing house.
International co-operative organisation.
Information, products and services to the food science, food technology and human nutrition sectors.

Subject coverage: Food science, food technology and human nutrition – all aspects, including biotechnology, food safety and toxicology, food psychology, sensory analysis, novel foods, pet foods, economics, all commodities (meat, fish, etc.), standards and patents relating to food, legislation, engineering and packaging.

Publications: Printed, and electronic and video

Access to staff: Contact by letter, by telephone, by fax, by e-mail and via website. Appointment necessary.
Hours: Mon to Fri, 0900 to 1700

Sponsored by: CAB International; Deutsche Landwirtschafts-Gesellschaft; Germany; Institute of Food Technologists (IFT); USA

INTERNATIONAL FRIENDSHIP LEAGUE, BRITISH SECTION (IFL)

Head Office, 3 Creswick Road, Acton, London, W3 9HE

Website: www.ifl-peacehaven.co.uk

Enquiries to: Chairman

Founded: 1931

Organisation type and purpose: Membership association (membership is by subscription), voluntary organisation.

Subject coverage: International friendship and understanding by services of home hospitality, pen friends, entertaining and helping overseas visitors.

Publications: Printed

Access to staff: Contact by letter
Hours: Mon to Fri, 0900 to 1700
Special comments: By letter only, except in connection with the Guest House.

Affiliated to: United Nations Association

Includes the: IFL Pen Friend Service (Overseas); 3 Creswick Road, Acton, London, W3 9HE; International Guest House; Peace Haven, 3 Creswick Road, Acton, London, London, W3 9HE; tel: 020 8752 0055; fax: 020 8752 0066; e-mail: ifl -peacehaven@tiscali.co.uk

Parent body: IFL Head Office; 3 Creswick Road, Acton, London, W3 9HE

INTERNATIONAL FUND FOR ANIMAL WELFARE (IFAW)

87–90 Albert Embankment, London, SE1 7UD

Tel: 020 7587 6700
Fax: 020 7587 6720
Website: www.ifaw.org

Enquiries to: Public Relations Manager
Direct tel: 020 7587 6708
Direct fax: 020 7587 6718
Direct e-mail: lkey@ifaw.org

Founded: 1969

Organisation type and purpose:
International organisation, present number of members: 2 million worldwide.
Conservation organisation.

Subject coverage: Animal welfare, conservation.

Collection: Picture and video library
Digital picture library

Publications: Printed, and electronic and video

Access to staff: Contact by letter, by telephone, by fax, by e-mail and via website
Hours: Mon to Fri, 0900 to 1730

Access to building: Prior appointment required

Parent body: IFAW; International headquarters, 411 Main Street, Yarmouth Port, MA 02675, USA; tel: 00 1 508 744 2076; fax: 00 1 508 744 2079

INTERNATIONAL GLACIOLOGICAL SOCIETY (IGS)

Scott Polar Research Institute, Lensfield Road, Cambridge, CB2 1ER

Tel: 01223 355974
Fax: 01223 354931
E-mail: igsoc@igsoc.org
Website: www.igsoc.org

Enquiries to: Secretary-General
Other contacts: Assistant to Secretary-General

Founded: 1936

Organisation type and purpose:
International organisation, learned society (membership is by subscription), present number of members: 700, registered charity (charity number 231043).
To facilitate communication and information exchange between all individuals having a scientific, practical or general interest in any aspect of snow and ice.

Subject coverage: Glaciology, cryosphere, atmospheric ice, avalanches, chemistry of ice and snow, floating ice, glacial geology, glaciers, ground ice, ice, ice and climate, ice cores, icebergs, permafrost, physics of ice and snow, sea ice, snow, Antarctica, Greenland.

Collection: Book, documents and manuscripts on various aspects of glaciology

Publications: Printed

Publications list: Available online and in print

Access to staff: Contact by letter, by telephone, by fax and by e-mail.
Appointment necessary.
Hours: Mon to Fri, 0830 to 1630

INTERNATIONAL GLAUCOMA ASSOCIATION (IGA)

Woodcote House, 15 Highpoint Business Village, Henwood, Ashford, Kent, TN24 8DH

Tel: 01233 648164
Fax: 01233 648179
E-mail: info@iga.org.uk
Website: www.glaucoma-association.com

Enquiries to: Head of Marketing & PR
Direct tel: 01233 648169
Direct e-mail: s.zerbib@iga.org.uk
Other contacts: CEO

Founded: 1974

Organisation type and purpose:
International organisation (membership is by subscription), present number of members: 6,000, charity registered in England and Wales (charity number 274681) and Scotland (charity number SC 041550).
Seeks to raise awareness of glaucoma, to promote research related to early diagnosis and treatment, and to provide support to patients and all those who care for them.

Subject coverage: Glaucoma, its diagnosis, treatment and research.

Information services: Sightline (tel. 01233 648170), Mon to Fri, 0930 to 1700

Trade and statistical information:
Glaucoma prevalence information, high-risk categories and groups

Non-library collection catalogue: All or part available online

Publications: Printed

Publications list: Available online and in print

Access to staff: Contact by letter, by telephone, by fax, by e-mail and via website.
Appointment necessary.
Hours: Mon to Fri, 0930 to 1700

Access to building: Prior appointment required

Links with: International Agency for the Prevention of Blindness

INTERNATIONAL GRAINS COUNCIL (IGC)

One Canada Square, Canary Wharf, London, E14 5AE

Tel: 020 7513 1122
Fax: 020 7513 0630
E-mail: igc-fac@igc.org.uk
Website: www.igc.org.uk

Enquiries to: Executive Director

Founded: 1949

Organisation type and purpose:
International organisation, present number of members: 26 governments including the European Community. Intergovernmental commodity organisation, administers the Grains Trade Convention of the International Grains Agreement 1995 and provides administrative services for the Food Aid Convention of the IGA.
To further international cooperation in trade in grains, to promote the expansion of grains trade, to contribute to the stability of the international grain market, and to enhance food security.

Subject coverage: Statistics and general information on wheat and coarse grains, market developments; long-term and short-term outlook for world grain economy, grain production, use, consumption, stocks, trade and prices; review of national grain policies and their effects; grain handling and transportation, including ocean freight rates; international co-operation and wheat agreements, food aid shipments.

Trade and statistical information: Details of international trade in wheat, wheat flour and coarse grains, excepting Intra-EC

Non-library collection catalogue: All or part available online

Publications: Printed

Publications list: Available online and in print

Access to staff: Contact by letter, by fax and by e-mail. Appointment necessary. Non-members charged.
Hours: Mon to Fri, 0900 to 1730

INTERNATIONAL GRAPHOLOGY ASSOCIATION (IGA)

Stonedge, Dunkerton, Bath, BA2 8AS

Tel: 01761 437809
Fax: 01761 432572
E-mail: ljw@graphology.org.uk
Website: www.graphology.org.uk

Enquiries to: Director

Founded: 1983

Organisation type and purpose:
Professional body, suitable for ages: adults, consultancy, research organisation.
International professional society.
Provision of training and examination in graphology. Undertaking research.

Subject coverage: Graphology; handwriting; analysis for personality assessment.

Collection: Handwriting samples

Publications: Printed

Publications list: Available in print

Access to staff: Contact by letter, by telephone, by fax, by e-mail, in person and via website. Appointment necessary.
Hours: Mon to Fri, 0900 to 1700

INTERNATIONAL GUILD, BUTLER ADMINISTRATORS AND PERSONAL ASSISTANTS

12 Little Bornes, Alleyn Park, Dulwich, London, SE21 8SE

Tel: 020 8670 5585
Fax: 020 8670 8424
Website: www.ivorspencer.com

Enquiries to: Chief Executive

Founded: 1981

Organisation type and purpose:
Professional body.

Subject coverage: Butler administrators and personal assistants.

Access to staff: Contact by letter, by telephone, by fax, by e-mail and via website
Hours: Mon to Fri, 0900 to 1700

INTERNATIONAL HEALTH AND BEAUTY COUNCIL (IHBC)

c/o VTCT, 3rd Floor, Eastleigh House, Market Street, Eastleigh, Hampshire, SO50 9FD

Tel: 023 8068 4500
Fax: 023 8065 1493
E-mail: info@vtct.org.uk
Website: www.vtct.org.uk

Enquiries to: Information Officer
Other contacts: Head of Quality Assurance for training centres as opposed to individual enquiries.

Founded: 1962

Organisation type and purpose:
International organisation.
Awarding body – service sector (beauty therapy).

Subject coverage: All aspects of health and beauty, qualification and training.

Education services: Courses are provided at more than 400 centres in the UK, mostly Colleges of Further Education.

Collection: Photographs of treatments

Publications: Printed

Access to staff: Contact by letter
Hours: Mon to Fri, 0900 to 1700
Special comments: No visitors in person.

Affiliated to: Action for Lifelong Learning Limited; tel: 01243 842064; fax: 01243 842489; e-mail: info@vtct.org.uk; Vocational Awards International Limited; tel: 01243 842064; fax: 01243 842489; e-mail: info@vtct.org.uk

Subsidiary of: Vocational Training Charitable Trust (VTCT); tel: 023 8068 4500; fax: 023 8065 1493; e-mail: info@vtct.org.uk

INTERNATIONAL HOSPITAL FEDERATION (IHF)

46–48 Grosvenor Gardens, London, SW1W 0EB

Tel: 020 7881 9222
Fax: 020 7881 9223
E-mail: 101662.1262@compuserve.com
Website: www.hospitalmanagement.net

Enquiries to: Director General

Organisation type and purpose:
International organisation, voluntary organisation.
Dependent non-governmental association.

Subject coverage: Planning and management of hospitals and health services.

Publications: Printed

Access to staff: Contact by letter, by telephone, by fax, by e-mail and via website
Hours: Mon to Fri, 0900 to 1700

Collaboration with: Kings Fund Library

Official liaison with the: International Council of Nurses; World Health Organization; World Medical Association

INTERNATIONAL HOUSE (IH)

106 Piccadilly, London, W1V 9FL

Tel: 020 7518 6900
Fax: 020 7518 6941
E-mail: info@ihlondon.com
Website: www.international-house.org
Website: www.ihlondon.com

Enquiries to: Director

Founded: 1953

Organisation type and purpose:
Professional body, training organisation.

Access to staff: Contact by letter, by telephone, by fax, by e-mail, in person and via website. Appointment necessary.
Hours: Mon to Fri, 0900 to 1700

INTERNATIONAL IMMIGRATION ADVISORY SERVICES

65 Kingsway, Manchester, M19 2LL

Tel: 0161 224 1973
Fax: 0161 224 4449
E-mail: intias@hotmail.com

Enquiries to: Principal
Direct tel: 07785 541375

Founded: 1991

Organisation type and purpose:
Consultancy.

Subject coverage: International immigration, nationality and law.

Access to staff: Contact by letter, by telephone, by fax and by e-mail. Appointment necessary. All charged.
Hours: Mon to Fri, 0900 to 1730; Sat, 1030 to 1400

Access to building: No prior appointment required

Access for disabled people: Level entry, toilet facilities

INTERNATIONAL INSTITUTE FOR CONSERVATION OF HISTORIC AND ARTISTIC WORKS (IIC)

6 Buckingham Street, London, WC2N 6BA

Tel: 020 7839 5975
Fax: 020 7976 1564
E-mail: iic@iiconservation.org
Website: www.iiconservation.org

Enquiries to: Executive Secretary

Founded: 1950

Organisation type and purpose:
International organisation, membership association, registered charity (charity number 209677).

Subject coverage: Conservation of heritage.

Publications: Printed

Publications list: Available online and in print

Access to staff: Contact by letter, by telephone, by fax, by e-mail and via website. Access for members only.

INTERNATIONAL INSTITUTE FOR ENVIRONMENT AND DEVELOPMENT (IIED)

3 Endsleigh Street, London, WC1H 0DD

Tel: 020 7388 2117
Fax: 020 7388 2826
E-mail: iied@iied.org
Website: www.iied.org

Enquiries to: Information Officer
Direct e-mail: info@iied.org

Founded: 1971

Organisation type and purpose: Registered charity (charity number 800066), research organisation.
Promotion of sustainable patterns of world development.

Subject coverage: Natural resources, human settlements, governance, climate change, sustainable markets.

Non-library collection catalogue: All or part available online

Publications: Printed, and electronic and video

Publications list: Available online and in print

Access to staff: Contact by letter, by telephone, by fax and by e-mail
Hours: Mon to Fri, 0900 to 1700

Also at: International Institute for Environment and Development; 4 Hanover Street, Edinburgh, EH2 2EN; tel: 0131 624 7040

INTERNATIONAL INSTITUTE FOR STRATEGIC STUDIES (IISS)

13–15 Arundel Street, London, WC2R 3DX

Tel: 020 7379 7676
Fax: 020 7836 3108
E-mail: iiss@iiss.org
Website: www.iiss.org

Enquiries to: Librarian
Direct tel: 020 7395 9122
Direct e-mail: library@iiss.org

Founded: 1958

Organisation type and purpose:
International organisation, membership association (membership is by subscription), research organisation.

Subject coverage: Nuclear issues; arms control, agreements, negotiations and possibilities; regional security issues (worldwide); armed forces of the world; current conflict situations; non-military aspects of national security (economic, demography, scarce resources, environment, etc.).

Information services: Library

Collection: Subject files from 1958

Trade and statistical information: Data on holdings of weapons (by system) for all countries of the world

Non-library collection catalogue: All or part available online and in-house

Library catalogue: All or part available online and in-house

Publications: Printed, and electronic and video
Order printed publications from: Journals Customer Services, Taylor and Francis, Cheriton House, North Way, Andover, Hampshire, SP10 5BE; tel: 020 7017 5544; fax: 020 7017 4760; e-mail: or book.orders@routledge.co.ukjournals.orders@tandf.co.uk

Publications list: Available online and in print

continued overleaf

Access to staff: Contact by letter, by telephone, by fax, by e-mail, in person and via website. Non-members charged.

Access to building: No prior appointment required
Hours: Institute: Mon to Fri, 0900 to 1800
Library: Mon to Fri, 1000 to 1700

INTERNATIONAL INSTITUTE OF COMMUNICATIONS (IIC)

2 Printers Yard, 90A The Broadway, London SW19 1RD

Tel: 020 8417 0600
Fax: 020 8417 0800
E-mail: enquiries@iicom.org
Website: www.iicom.org

Enquiries to: Projects Executive

Founded: 1968

Organisation type and purpose:
Membership association.
Global forum for communications.

Subject coverage: Communications; copyright; all aspects of telecommunication; all aspects of broadcasting, radio, television, multimedia; satellite communications; development in its political, social, cultural, economic spheres; regulatory side of above topics/subjects.

Collection: Regulatory and legislative materials, e.g. acts, statutes, bills, etc. on broadcasting and telecommunications, principally in Europe but increasingly outside Europe

Trade and statistical information: Telecom voice traffic flows, television flows

Publications: Printed

Publications list: Available in print

Access to staff: Contact by letter, by telephone, by fax and by e-mail.
Appointment necessary.
Hours: Mon to Fri, 0930 to 1730

INTERNATIONAL INSTITUTE OF HEALTH AND HOLISTIC THERAPIES (IIHHT)

VTCT, 3rd Floor, Eastleigh House, Upper Market Street, Eastleigh, Hampshire, SO50 9FD

Tel: 023 8068 4500
Fax: 023 8065 1493
E-mail: info@vtct.org.uk
Website: www.vtct.org.uk

Enquiries to: Information Officer
Direct e-mail: recordsoffice@vtct.org.uk
Other contacts: Head of Quality Assurance for training centres as opposed to individual enquiries.

Founded: 1962

Organisation type and purpose:
International organisation. International education organisation. Provides qualifications in holistic, health, fitness and complementary therapies.

Subject coverage: Body massage, aromatherapy, reflexology.

Education services: Courses are provided at Centres across the UK, primarily in Colleges of Further Education.

Publications: Printed

Access to staff: Contact by letter
Hours: Mon to Fri, 0900 to 1700
Special comments: No visitors in person.

Affiliated to: Action for Lifelong Learning Limited; tel: 01243 842064; fax: 01243 842489; e-mail: info@vtct.org.uk; Vocational Awards International Limited; tel: 01243 842064; fax: 01243 842489; e-mail: info@vtct.org.uk

Subsidiary of: Vocational Training Charitable Trust (VTCT); tel: 023 8668 4500; fax: 023 8064 1493; e-mail: info@vtct.org.uk

INTERNATIONAL INSTITUTE OF RISK AND SAFETY MANAGEMENT (IIRSM)

70 Chancellors Road, London, W6 9RS

Tel: 020 8600 5536/7/8/9
Fax: 020 8741 1349
E-mail: enquiries@iirsm.org
Website: www.iirsm.org

Enquiries to: Organising Secretary

Founded: 1975

Organisation type and purpose:
International organisation, professional body (membership is by qualification), registered charity (charity number 269326).
The institute's main objective is to advance public education in accident prevention and occupational health in industry.

Subject coverage: General safety; safety management; principles of risk management; international organisations.

Publications: Printed

Access to staff: Contact by letter, by telephone, by fax, by e-mail and via website.
Access for members only.
Hours: Mon to Fri, 0900 to 1700

Affiliated to: British Safety Council; tel: 020 8741 1231; fax: 020 8741 4555

INTERNATIONAL INSTITUTE OF SPORTS THERAPY (IIST)

VTCT, 3rd Floor, Eastleigh House, Upper Market Street, Eastleigh, Hampshire, SO50 9FD

Tel: 023 8068 4500
Fax: 023 8065 1493
E-mail: info@vtct.org.uk
Website: www.vtct.org.uk

Enquiries to: Information Officer
Direct e-mail: recordsoffice@vtct.org.uk
Other contacts: Head of Quality Assurance for training centres as opposed to individual enquiries.

Founded: 1962

Organisation type and purpose:
International organisation.
Provision of qualifications in fitness and sport therapies.

Subject coverage: All aspects of health, fitness and sports therapy and especially centres providing training in these subjects. Largest Awarding Body in this sector, courses are provided across the UK, primarily in Colleges of Further Education.

Collection: Photographs of treatments

Publications: Printed

Access to staff: Contact by letter
Hours: Mon to Fri, 0900 to 1700
Special comments: No visitors in person.

Affiliated to: Action for Lifelong Learning Limited; tel: 01243 842064; fax: 01243 842489; e-mail: info@vtct.org.uk; Vocational Awards International Limited; tel: 01243 842064; fax: 01243 842489; e-mail: info@vtct.org.uk

Susidiary of: Vocational Training Charitable Trust (VTCT); tel: 023 8068 4500; fax: 023 8065 1493; e-mail: info@vtct.org.uk

INTERNATIONAL INTELLIGENCE ON CULTURE (IIC)

4 Baden Place, Crosby Row, London, SE1 1YW

Tel: 020 7403 6454
Fax: 020 7403 2009

Enquiries to: Information Officer
Direct tel: 020 7403 7001

Founded: 1994

Organisation type and purpose:
Independent company specialising in cultural policy analysis and intelligence; consultancy; research; project management; training; and advisory and information services with an international cultural dimension.
To provide a comprehensive range of services and respond to the needs of the international cultural sector.

Subject coverage: Policy intelligence, consultancy, research, project management, training, information and advice services for the international cultural sector.

Publications: Printed
Order printed publications from: Library and Publications, Arts Council of England
4 Great Peter Street, London, SW1P 3NQ, tel: 020 7973 6931, fax: 020 7973 6590, e-mail: enquiries@artscouncil.org.uk

Publications list: Available in print

Access to staff: Contact by letter, by telephone, by fax and by e-mail
Hours: Mon to Fri, 0930 to 1730; please call to check opening times of enquiry service, which are subject to change
Special comments: Offices are not open for drop-in services.

Funded by: Irish Arts Council

Links with: Arts Council of Scotland; Arts Council of Wales; British Film Institute; Crafts Council; Cultural Information and Research Centres Liaison in Europe (CIRCLE); Museum and Galleries Commission

INTERNATIONAL INTERFAITH CENTRE (IIC)

17 Courtiers Green, Clifton Hampden, Abingdon, Oxon, OX14 3EN

E-mail: iic@interfaith-centre.org
Website: www.interfaith-centre.org

Founded: 1993

Organisation type and purpose:
International organisation, registered charity, consultancy, research organisation.

To facilitate interreligious encounter and dialogue.

Subject coverage: Religion, interreligious issues, interfaith issues, projects, conferences, contacts and research, courses, videos.

Collection: Interfaith and religious journals from around the world

Publications: Printed, and electronic and video
Order printed publications from: Main address
Order electronic and video publications from: e-mail: iic@interfaith-centre.org

Publications list: Available online

Access to staff: Contact by letter, by e-mail and via website

INTERNATIONAL LABOUR ORGANISATION (ILO)

International Labour Office, Millbank Tower, 21–24 Millbank, London, SW1P 4QP

Tel: 020 7828 6401
Fax: 020 7233 5925
E-mail: london@ilo.org
Website: www.ilo.org/london

Enquiries to: Manager, Publications/ Information Unit
Direct e-mail: brett@ilo.org

Founded: 1919

Organisation type and purpose: International organisation.
The UN specialised agency concerned with work and employment issues.

Subject coverage: International labour standards; labour statistics; management; workers' education; women and work; industrial relations; migrant labour; labour administration; employment and conditions of work; labour legislation; human rights; freedom of association; training, retraining and rehabilitation; safety and health.

Collection: All ILO publications and documents since its establishment in 1919

Publications: Printed

Publications list: Available online and in print

Access to staff: Contact by letter, by telephone, by fax and by e-mail. Appointment necessary.
Hours: Mon to Fri, 1000 to 1300 and 1400 to 1630

Head Office: International Labour Office; Geneva 22, CH 211, Switzerland; tel: + 41 22 799 6111; fax: + 41 22 799 8577; e-mail: communication@ilo.org; website: http:// www.ilo.org

Works with: International Centre for Occupational Safety and Health (CIS)

INTERNATIONAL LANGUAGE (IDO) SOCIETY OF GREAT BRITAIN (ILSGB)

24 Nunn Street, Leek, Staffordshire, ST13 8EA

Tel: 01538 381491
Website: www.users.aol.com/idolinguo

Enquiries to: Honorary Secretary

Founded: 1913

Organisation type and purpose: Membership association.

Subject coverage: The international language IDO.

Publications: Printed

Publications list: Available in print

Access to staff: Contact by letter and by telephone
Hours: Mon to Fri, 0900 to 1700

Affiliated to: International Uniono por la Lingo Internaciona; at the same address

INTERNATIONAL LASER CLASS ASSOCIATION

PO Box 26, Falmouth, Cornwall, TR11 3TN

Tel: 01326 315064
Fax: 01326 318968
E-mail: office@laserinternational.org
Website: www.laserinternational.org

Enquiries to: Executive Secretary

Organisation type and purpose: International organisation.

Subject coverage: Sailing laser class boats.

Access to staff: Contact by e-mail and via website
Hours: Mon to Fri, 0900 to 1730

INTERNATIONAL LAW ASSOCIATION (ILA)

Charles Clore House, 17 Russell Square, London, WC1B 5DR

Tel: 020 7323 2978
Fax: 020 7323 3580
E-mail: info@ila-hq.org
Website: www.ila-hq.org

Enquiries to: Secretary

Founded: 1873

Organisation type and purpose: International organisation, learned society (membership is by subscription, election or invitation), registered charity (charity number 249637).

Subject coverage: Space law, international monetary law, maritime neutrality, international human rights law and practice, water resources law, coastal state jurisdiction over marine pollution, international commercial arbitration, legal aspects of sustainable development, refugee procedures, legal aspects of inter-country adoption and protection of the family, the formation of customary international law, international securities regulation, cultural heritage law, international law in national courts, regional economic development law, arms control and disarmament law, feminism and international law, extradition and human rights, international civil and commercial litigation, international trade law, Islamic law and international law, internally displaced persons, aspects of the law of state succession, diplomatic protection of persons and property, accountability of international organisations.

Publications list: Available in print

Access to staff: Contact by letter, by telephone, by fax and by e-mail. Appointment necessary.
Hours: Mon to Thu, 0900 to 1700

Has: 50 branches world-wide

INTERNATIONAL LEAD AND ZINC STUDY GROUP (ILZSG)

2 King Street, London, SW1Y 6QL

Tel: 020 7484 3300
Fax: 020 7930 4635
E-mail: root@ilzsg.org
Website: www.ilzsg.org

Enquiries to: Information Officer

Founded: 1959

Organisation type and purpose: International organisation, research organisation.

Subject coverage: Lead and zinc.

Trade and statistical information: International trade and world situation in lead and zinc, including movements of stocks and prices

Publications: Printed

Publications list: Available in print

Access to staff: Contact by letter and via website
Hours: Mon to Fri, 0900 to 1700

Founded in 1959 by the: United Nations

INTERNATIONAL LEAD ASSOCIATION (ILA)

17A Welbeck Way, London, W1G 9YJ

Tel: 020 7499 8422
Fax: 020 7493 1555
E-mail: enq@ila-lead.org
Website: www.ila-lead.org

Enquiries to: Director

Founded: 1946

Organisation type and purpose: Trade association.

Subject coverage: Building, batteries, coatings, environment, health and safety, extraction, refining and production, noise insulation, economics and statistics.

Non-library collection catalogue: All or part available online

Library catalogue: All or part available online

Publications: Printed, and electronic and video

Publications list: Available online

Access to staff: Contact by letter, by telephone, by fax, by e-mail and via website. Appointment necessary.
Hours: Mon to Fri, 0930 to 1715

INTERNATIONAL MARINE CONTRACTORS ASSOCIATION (IMCA)

52 Grosvenor Gardens, London, SW1W 0AU

Tel: 020 7824 5520
Fax: 020 7824 5521
E-mail: imca@imca-int.com

continued overleaf

Website: www.imca-int.com

Enquiries to: Chief Executive

Founded: 1995

Organisation type and purpose: International organisation, trade association (membership is by subscription), present number of members: 530, service industry.

Subject coverage: Offshore, marine and underwater engineering companies.

Publications: Printed, and electronic and video
Order printed publications from: via website

Publications list: Available online and in print

Access to staff: Contact by letter, by telephone, by fax, by e-mail, in person and via website. Appointment necessary.
Hours: Mon to Fri, 0900 to 1700

Access to building: No prior appointment required

INTERNATIONAL MARITIME ORGANIZATION (IMO)

4 Albert Embankment, London, SE1 7SR

Tel: 020 7735 7611
Fax: 020 7587 3210
E-mail: info@imo.org
Website: www.imo.org

Enquiries to: Head, Public Information Services
Direct tel: 020 7587 3153

Founded: 1959

Organisation type and purpose: International organisation.
To promote safety and security at sea and to prevent pollution of the sea from ships.

Subject coverage: Prevention of marine pollution, safety at sea, security, IMO conventions, technical co-operation.

Collection: Maritime Knowledge Centre: houses a complete collection of IMO publications, IMO meetings documents in English, French and Spanish (some reports in Russian, Chinese and Arabic)
UN documents related to the maritime world

Trade and statistical information: Casualty statistics, marine pollution, maritime transport, safety of life at sea

Non-library collection catalogue: All or part available online

Library catalogue: All or part available online

Publications: Printed, and electronic and video
Order printed publications from: Publishing Services
Order electronic and video publications from: Publishing Services

Publications list: Available online and in print

Access to staff: Contact by letter, by telephone, by fax, by e-mail and via website. Appointment necessary.
Hours: Mon to Fri, 0900 to 1700
Special comments: Closed for Christmas.

Access to building: Prior appointment required

Access for disabled people: Toilet facilities

Parent body: United Nations

INTERNATIONAL MOHAIR ASSOCIATION (IMA)

10–12 The Grove, Ilkley, West Yorkshire, LS29 9EG

Tel: 01943 817149
Fax: 01943 817150
E-mail: gerhard.sperling@mohair.de
Website: www.int-mohair.com

Enquiries to: Manager

Founded: 1974

Organisation type and purpose: Trade association.
To promote, advance and protect the interests of its members and their manufactured mohair products.

Subject coverage: Mohair.

Publications: Printed

Access to staff: Contact by letter, by telephone, by fax, by e-mail and via website. Appointment necessary.
Hours: Mon to Thu, 0930 to 1230

INTERNATIONAL NETWORK FOR THE AVAILABILITY OF SCIENTIFIC PUBLICATIONS (INASP)

58 St. Aldates, Oxford, OX1 1ST

Tel: 01865 249909
Fax: 01865 251060
E-mail: inasp@inasp.info
Website: www.inasp.info

Enquiries to: Director

Founded: 1992

Organisation type and purpose: International organisation.
Charity.
INASP is a programme of the International Council for Science (ICSU). It aims to improve worldwide access to information.

Subject coverage: Information about research publication and access, information about library and book development in developing and transitional countries.

Publications: Printed, and electronic and video

Publications list: Available online

Access to staff: Contact by letter, by telephone, by fax, by e-mail and via website. Appointment necessary.
Hours: Mon to Fri, 0900 to 1700

INTERNATIONAL OIL POLLUTION COMPENSATION FUNDS (IOPC Funds)

Portland House, Bressenden Place, London, SW1E 5PN

Tel: 020 7592 7100
Fax: 020 7592 7111
E-mail: info@iopcfund.org
Website: www.iopcfund.org

Enquiries to: Information Officer

Founded: 1978

Organisation type and purpose: International organisation.
The International Oil Pollution Compensation Funds are two intergovernmental organisations which provide compensation for oil pollution damage resulting from spills of persistent oil from tankers.

Subject coverage: Oil pollution compensation.

Publications list: Available online

Access to staff: Contact by letter, by telephone, by fax, by e-mail and via website. Appointment necessary.
Hours: Mon to Fri, 0900 to 1730

Access to building: Prior appointment required

Access for disabled people: Access to all public areas

INTERNATIONAL ORDER OF KABBALISTS (IOK)

6 Oakwood, 62 King Charles Road, Surbiton, Surrey, KT5 8QR

Fax: 020 8390 5604
E-mail: iokoffice@yahoo.com
Website: www.internationalorderofkabbalists.org.uk

Enquiries to: Secretary

Founded: 1969

Organisation type and purpose: Membership association (membership is by subscription).

Subject coverage: The Kabbalah, related occult and esoteric subjects.

Publications: Printed

Publications list: Available online and in print

Access to staff: Contact by letter, by fax, by e-mail and via website
Hours: Mon to Fri, 0900 to 1700

INTERNATIONAL OTTER SURVIVAL FUND (IOSF)

7 Black Park, Broadford, Isle of Skye, IV49 9DE

Tel: 01471 822487
Fax: 01471 822487
E-mail: enquiries@otter.org
Website: www.otter.org

Enquiries to: Director
Direct e-mail: grace@otter.org

Founded: 1993

Organisation type and purpose: Registered charity (charity number SC003875).
Wildlife conservation.

Subject coverage: Otter ecology and conservation, wildlife, wild animal care and treatment.

Education services: Talks and field trips for natural history societies, universities, schools and anyone interested in otters and wildlife. Special Otter Watching Days and training in otter surveying.

Non-library collection catalogue: All or part available in print

Library catalogue: All or part available online and in print

Publications: Printed, and electronic and video
Order printed publications from: www.ottershop.co.uk
Order electronic and video publications from: www.ottershop.co.uk

Publications list: Available online and in print

Access to staff: Contact by letter, by telephone, by fax, by e-mail and via website. Appointment necessary.
Hours: Mon to Fri, 0900 to 1700

Access to building: Prior appointment required
Hours: Mon to Fri, 0900 to 1700

INTERNATIONAL PEN

9–10 Charterhouse Buildings, Goswell Road, London, EC1M 7AT

Tel: 020 7253 4308
Fax: 020 7253 5711
E-mail: intpen@dircon.co.uk
Website: www.oneworld.org/internatpen

Enquiries to: Administrative Secretary
Direct e-mail: frank.geary@internationalpen.org.uk
Other contacts: Administrative Assistant for subscriptions, general information.

Founded: 1921

Organisation type and purpose:
International organisation, professional body, voluntary organisation, registered charity (charity number 1010627).
Non-governmental organisation.
PEN originally stood for Poets, Essayists, Novelists, but now membership is open to all writers.

Subject coverage: Literature as common currency between nations; freedom of expression and free press; origins and history of International PEN; positions of banned, imprisoned or otherwise mistreated writers.

Publications: Printed

Access to staff: Contact by letter, by telephone, by fax and by e-mail
Hours: Mon to Fri, 1030 to 1800

Access to building: No access other than to staff

In consultative relation with: UNESCO

Other addresses: 132 centres in 95 countries throughout the world including:; English Centre; 152–156 Kentish Town Road, London, NW1 9QB; tel: 020 7267 9444; International PEN; International PEN; International PEN; Scottish Centre; c/o Greenleaf Editorial, 126 West Princess Street, Glasgow, G4 9DB; Welsh Centre; 80 Plymouth Road, Gwynneth Street, Penarth, CF64 5DL

INTERNATIONAL PESTICIDE APPLICATION RESEARCH CENTRE (IPARC)

Imperial College at Silwood Park, Sunninghill, Ascot, Berkshire, SL5 7PY

Tel: 020 7594 2234
Fax: 020 7594 2450
E-mail: g.matthews@imperial.ac.uk
Website: www.bio.ic.ac.uk/staff/gamat/matthews.htm

Enquiries to: Information Officer

Founded: 1955; formerly called Overseas Spraying Machinery Centre

Organisation type and purpose: University department or institute, consultancy, research organisation.

Subject coverage: Pest management, particularly equipment needed for effective and safe application of pesticides. This includes vector control as well as agriculture.

Collection: Pesticide application equipment with emphasis on that which is manually carried or operated

Access to staff: Contact by e-mail

INTERNATIONAL PHONETIC ASSOCIATION (IPA)

Centre for Language & Communication Studies, Arts Building, Trinity College, Dublin, Dublin 2, Republic of Ireland

Tel: 00 353 1 608 1348
Fax: 00 353 1 677 2694
E-mail: anichsid@tcd.ie
Website: www.arts.gla.ac.uk/IPA/ipa.html

Enquiries to: Treasurer

Founded: 1886

Organisation type and purpose:
International organisation, learned society (membership is by subscription), present number of members: 900.

Subject coverage: Phonetics and phonology; the International Phonetic Alphabet.

Publications: Printed

Access to staff: Contact by letter, by telephone, by fax, by e-mail and via website
Hours: Mon to Fri, 0900 to 1700

INTERNATIONAL POWERED ACCESS FEDERATION LIMITED (IPAF)

Bridge End Business Park, Milnthorpe, LA7 7RH

Tel: 015395 62444
Fax: 015395 64686
E-mail: info@ipaf.org
Website: www.ipaf.org

Enquiries to: Managing Director

Founded: 1983

Organisation type and purpose:
International organisation, trade association (membership is by subscription), training organisation.
To represent the interests of the mobile elevating work platform industry on an international basis.

Subject coverage: Powered access equipment.

Collection: British, EC, US, Canadian Standards for powered access equipment (on mobile elevated) work platforms

Publications: Printed

Access to staff: Contact by letter, by telephone, by fax, by e-mail and via website. Appointment necessary. Non-members charged.
Hours: Mon to Fri, 0900 to 1700

INTERNATIONAL PRIMATE PROTECTION LEAGUE (UK) (IPPL)

166 Gilmore Road, London, SE13 5AE

Tel: 020 8297 2129
Fax: 020 8297 2099
E-mail: enquiries@ippl-uk.org
Website: www.ippl-uk.org

Enquiries to: Conservation and Welfare Officer

Founded: 1976

Subject coverage: Protection of primates.

Publications: Printed

Access to staff: Contact by letter, by telephone, by e-mail and via website. Appointment necessary. Letter of introduction required.
Hours: Mon to Fri, 0900 to 1700

Access to building: Prior appointment required

INTERNATIONAL PSYCHOANALYTICAL ASSOCIATION (IPA)

Broomhills, Woodside Lane, London, N12 8UD

Tel: 020 8446 8324
Fax: 020 8445 4729
E-mail: ipa@ipa.org.uk
Website: www.ipa.org.uk

Enquiries to: Membership Secretary

Founded: 1908

Organisation type and purpose:
Professional body, membership association (membership is by subscription), present number of members: 12,000.

Subject coverage: Psychoanalysis.

Publications: Printed
Order printed publications from: Karnac Books

Publications list: Available online

Access to staff: Contact by e-mail
Hours: Mon to Fri, 0900 to 1700

INTERNATIONAL RECORDS MANAGEMENT TRUST (IRMT)

Suite 14/15, 88–90 Hatton Garden, London EC1N 8PN

Tel: 020 7831 4101
Fax: 020 7831 6303
E-mail: info@irmt.org
Website: www.irmt.org

Founded: 1989

Organisation type and purpose: To develop new strategies for managing public sector records, through consultancy, education and research.
Registered charity (charity number 3477376).

Subject coverage: Records management, archives, education, consultancy.

continued overleaf

Access to staff: Contact by letter, by telephone, by fax and by e-mail
Hours: 1000 to 1730

INTERNATIONAL SAFETY COUNCIL

21 Tilton Road, Borough Green, Sevenoaks, Kent, TN15 8RS

Tel: 01732 886581
E-mail: smitht@nsc.org
Website: www.nsc.org

Enquiries to: Executive Director

Founded: 1913

Organisation type and purpose:
International organisation.
Non-profitmaking public service organisation holding consulting status with the United Nations.

Subject coverage: Health and Safety: occupational, home and community, public, transportation.

Trade and statistical information:
Worldwide accident statistics

Non-library collection catalogue: All or part available online

Library catalogue: All or part available online and in print

Publications: Printed

Publications list: Available online and in print

Access to staff: Contact by letter, by telephone, by e-mail and via website
Hours: Mon to Fri, 0900 to 1700

Also at: International Safety Council; 1121 Spring Lake Drive, Itasca, Illinois, USA; tel: 00 1 630 285 1121; fax: 00 1 630 285 1613; e-mail: smitht@nsc.org; website: http:.//www .nsc.org

Parent body: National Safety Council (USA); 1121 Spring Lake Drive, Itasca, Illinois, USA; tel: 00 1 708 285 1121; fax: 00 1 708 285 1613

INTERNATIONAL SCHOOL OF LONDON (ISL)

139 Gunnersbury Avenue, London, W3 8LG

Tel: 020 8992 5823
Fax: 020 8993 7012
E-mail: mail@isllondon.org
Website: www.isllondon.org

Enquiries to: Development Officer

Founded: 1972

Organisation type and purpose: Education

Subject coverage: Primary and secondary education; international baccalaureate; ESL, intensive English; mother tongue languages taught.

Access to staff: Contact by letter, by telephone, by fax, by e-mail and via website
Hours: Mon to Fri, 0800 to 1800

Access to building: Prior appointment required
Hours: Mon to Fri, 0800 to 1700

INTERNATIONAL SEISMOLOGICAL CENTRE (ISC)

Pipers Lane, Thatcham, Newbury, Berkshire, RG19 4NS

Tel: 01635 861022
Fax: 01635 872351
E-mail: admin@isc.ac.uk
Website: www.isc.ac.uk

Enquiries to: Director
Other contacts: Administration Officer for publication sales.

Founded: 1964

Organisation type and purpose:
International organisation, consultancy, research organisation.
Collection, collation, analysis and publication of world earthquake data.

Subject coverage: Seismology; world earthquakes.

Collection: Complete sets of seismological journals and other historical published matter

Publications: Printed, and electronic and video

Access to staff: Contact by e-mail
Hours: Mon to Fri, 0900 to 1700

Links with: UNESCO; Paris, France; WMO; Geneva

INTERNATIONAL SHAKESPEARE ASSOCIATION (ISA)

Shakespeare Centre, Henley Street, Stratford-upon-Avon, Warwickshire, CV37 6QW

Tel: 01789 201840
Fax: 01789 294911
E-mail: isa@shakespeare.org.uk
Website: www.shakespeare.org.uk

Enquiries to: Executive Secretary

Founded: 1974

Organisation type and purpose:
International organisation, learned society (membership is by subscription), present number of members: 600.

Subject coverage: Shakespearean research, publication, translation and performance, initiation and planning of international Shakespeare congresses.

Collection: Archive of the International Shakespeare Association and books donated to it are deposited in the Shakespeare Centre Library at the same address

Publications: Printed

Publications list: Available in print

Access to staff: Contact by letter, by telephone, by fax and by e-mail
Hours: Mon to Fri, 0900 to 1700

INTERNATIONAL SHEEP DOG SOCIETY, THE (ISDS)

Clifton House, 4a Goldington Road, Bedford, MK40 3NF

Tel: 01234 352672
Fax: 01234 348214
E-mail: office@isds.org.uk
Website: www.isds.org.uk

Enquiries to: Chief Executive

Founded: 1906

Organisation type and purpose:
Membership association (membership is by subscription), present number of members: 5000, registered charity (charity number 209009).
To maintain a breed register (Stud Book) for working sheepdogs as represented by the Border Collie, organise the major UK National and World Sheepdog trials, and provide a range of member services.

Subject coverage: Sheepdog trialling in the UK.

Collection: Breed records for ISDS registered dogs

Publications: Printed

Access to staff: Contact by letter, by telephone, by fax and by e-mail. Access for members only.
Hours: Mon to Fri, 0900 to 1700

Access to building: No access other than to staff

INTERNATIONAL SOCIETY FOR SOIL MECHANICS AND GEOTECHNICAL ENGINEERING (ISSMGE)

City University London, Northampton Square, London, EC1V 0HB

Tel: 020 7040 8154
Fax: 020 7040 8832
E-mail: secretariat@issmge.org
Website: www.issmge.org

Enquiries to: Secretary General

Organisation type and purpose:
International organisation, professional body.

Subject coverage: Soil mechanics, foundation engineering, geotechnical engineering, environmental geotechnics.

Access to staff: Contact by e-mail and via website

INTERNATIONAL SOCIETY FOR TRENCHLESS TECHNOLOGY (ISTT)

15 Belgrave Square, London, SW1X 8PS

Tel: 020 850 9119
Fax: 020 850 7447
E-mail: info@istt.com
Website: www.istt.com

Enquiries to: Executive Secretary
Other contacts: Membership Secretary for alternative contact.

Founded: 1986

Organisation type and purpose:
International 'not-for-profit' professional organisation, membership is by subscription, present number of members: 3,500, registered charity (charity number 295274).
ISTT aims to promote and increase the use of trenchless technology worldwide. Trenchless technology is for the installation and maintenance of underground utility services with minimum surface excavation.

Trenchless technology has been accepted by the United Nations Environment Programme
(UNEP) as an Environmentally Sound Technology for supporting its sustainability initiatives

Subject coverage: Information on the various types of trenchless technology for the installation, renovation and repair of pipeline systems under ground in order to minimise excavation and environmental damage.

Trade and statistical information: World data on the use of trenchless technology and advice on the latest techniques

Library catalogue: All or part available online

Publications: Printed, and electronic and video

Publications list: Available online

Access to staff: Contact by letter, by fax, by e-mail, in person and via website
Hours: Mon to Fri, 0900 to 1700

Access to building: Belgrave Square is the registered address only. The staff are home based using the internet. For contact use fax or e-mail

INTERNATIONAL STAR REGISTRY (ISR)

23–28 Penn Street, London, N1 5DL

Tel: 020 7684 4444
Fax: 020 7684 4443
E-mail: orion@starregistry.co.uk
Website: www.international-star-registry.org

Enquiries to: Public Relations Manager

Founded: 1991

Organisation type and purpose:
International organisation, service industry.
Name-a-star service. Naming a star in the heavens as a gift idea.

Subject coverage: Astronomy, naming stars in the heavens.

Collection: Your Place in the Cosmos, volumes I to V
Register of International Star Registry star names worldwide, 1979–1999

Publications: Printed

Access to staff: Contact by letter, by telephone, by fax, by e-mail and via website
Hours: Mon to Fri, 0900 to 1700

Access to building: Prior appointment required

Has: 16 offices worldwide

INTERNATIONAL STEEL TRADE ASSOCIATION (ISTA)

Broadway House, Tothill Street, Westminster, London, SW1H 9NQ

Tel: 020 7799 2662
Fax: 020 7799 2468
E-mail: hbailey@steeltrade.co.uk
Website: www.steeltrade.co.uk

Enquiries to: Director

Founded: 1969

Organisation type and purpose: Trade association.

Subject coverage: International iron and steel trade.

Access to staff: Access for members only.
Hours: Mon to Fri, 0930 to 1730

INTERNATIONAL STUDENTS HOUSE (ISH)

1 Park Crescent, London, W1B 1SH

Tel: 020 7631 8300
Fax: 020 7631 8307
E-mail: info@ish.org.uk
Website: www.ish.org.uk

Founded: 1965

Organisation type and purpose: To provide housing and social facilities for overseas students.

Subject coverage: Welfare advice service for overseas students.

Publications: Printed

Access to staff: Contact by letter, by telephone, by fax, by e-mail and via website.
Appointment necessary.
Hours: 24-hour access

Access for disabled people: Parking provided, level entry, toilet facilities

INTERNATIONAL SUGAR ORGANIZATION (ISO)

1 Canada Square, Canary Wharf, Docklands, London, E14 5AA

Tel: 020 7513 1144
Fax: 020 7513 1146
E-mail: exdir@isosugar.org
Website: www.isosugar.org

Enquiries to: Executive Director
Direct e-mail: info@isosugar.org

Founded: 1937

Organisation type and purpose:
International organisation.

Subject coverage: Statistics on production, consumption, exports and imports of sugar in all countries of the world.

Publications: Printed, and electronic and video
Order printed publications from: Publications division, tel: 020 7715 9436; e-mail: publications@isosugar.org; or via website

Publications list: Available online and in print

Access to staff: Contact by letter, by telephone, by fax and by e-mail
Hours: Mon to Fri, 0930 to 1730

Access to building: Prior appointment required

The agreement (ISA) is under the auspices of: UNCTAD; Geneva

INTERNATIONAL SUPPORT VESSEL OWNERS ASSOCIATION (ISOA)

12 Carthusian Street, London, EC1M 6EZ

Tel: 020 7417 8844
Fax: 020 7417 8877
E-mail: isoa@marisec.org

Enquiries to: Assistant Secretary

Founded: 1985

Organisation type and purpose: Shipping association.
Common forum for discussion of issues specific to the offshore industry, in particular international support vessel owners.

Access to staff: Contact by letter, by telephone, by fax and by e-mail
Hours: Mon to Fri, 0900 to 1700

INTERNATIONAL SWAMINARAYAN SATSANG ORGANISATION (ISSO)

ISSO Central Office, 72 Colmer Road, Streatham, London, SW16 5JS

Tel: 020 8830 0771
Fax: 020 8830 0804
E-mail: info@swaminarayan.info
Website: www.isso-europe.org

Enquiries to: General Secretary

Founded: 1990

Organisation type and purpose:
International organisation, learned society, registered charity.
Religious Hindu organisation specialising in the Swaminarayan Faith/Sect.

Subject coverage: Information from authentic sources on the Swaminarayan Sect of Hinduism.

Collection: References available through published and unpublished documents on the way of life in Gujarat, India, about 200 years ago

Publications: Printed, and electronic and video
Order printed publications from: International Swaminarayan Satsang Organisation
e-mail: central@issa.org.uk

Access to staff: Contact by letter, by fax and by e-mail. Appointment necessary.
Hours: Mon to Fri, 0900 to 1700

Associate temple: Swaminarayan Temples; 37 Forradsgatan, Mariestad, S-54235, Sweden; tel: 00 46 501 12473; e-mail: sweden@isso.org.uk

Parent body: Shree Swaminarayan Temple; Kalupur Ahmedabad, Gujarat, 380 001, India; tel: 00 91 79 213 6818; fax: 00 91 79 745 2145; e-mail: info@swaminarayan.info

Swaminarayan Temples in: Leicester; 139–141 Loughborough Road, Leicester, LE4 5LQ; tel: 0116 2666 210; fax: 0116 2666 210; e-mail: leicester@isso.org.uk; London; 72 Colmer Road, London, SW16 5SZ; tel: 020 8679 8050; e-mail: streatham@isso.org.uk

INTERNATIONAL TABLE TENNIS FEDERATION (ITTF)

Chemin de la Roche 11, Renens/Lausanne, 1020, Switzerland

Tel: 00 41 21 340 70 90
Fax: 00 41 21 340 70 99
E-mail: ittf@ittf.com
Website: www.ittf.com

Enquiries to: Executive Director

Founded: 1926

continued overleaf

Organisation type and purpose: International organisation. Governing body of the sport.

Subject coverage: Table tennis.

Publications: Printed

Publications list: Available online and in print

Access to staff: Contact by letter, by telephone, by fax, by e-mail and via website. Appointment necessary.
Hours: Mon to Fri, 0900 to 1700

Access to building: Prior appointment required

Access for disabled people: Access to all public areas

Other offices: ITTF; 1125 Colonel by Drive, Ontario, K1S 5RI, Canada; tel: 00 1 613 7332468; fax: 00 1 613 7334603; e-mail: ittf@ittf.com; Marketing Division & President's Office,

INTERNATIONAL TANKER OWNERS POLLUTION FEDERATION LIMITED (ITOPF)

1 Oliver's Yard, 55 City Road, London, EC1Y 1HQ

Tel: 020 7566 6999
Fax: 020 7566 6950
E-mail: central@itopf.com
Website: www.itopf.com

Enquiries to: Information Officer
Direct e-mail: deborahansell@itopf.com

Founded: 1968

Organisation type and purpose: International organisation, membership association.
ITOPF offers a broad range of technical and information services in the field of spill response, damage assessment, claims analysis and contingency planning to its shipowner members and associates, their pollution insurers and other groups worldwide.

Subject coverage: Regulations and insurance aspects of oil and chemical spills from ships; organisation and contingency planning for spill clean-up; clean-up equipment and techniques; environmental effects of marine pollution; environmental planning.

Collection: Trade literature covering all types of spill clean-up equipment
Books, journal articles, conference papers on oil pollution from tankers and related topics

Library catalogue: All or part available in-house

Publications: Printed

Publications list: Available in print

Access to staff: Contact by letter, by telephone, by fax, by e-mail and via website. Appointment necessary.
Hours: Mon to Fri, 0900 to 1700

INTERNATIONAL TEA COMMITTEE LIMITED (ITC)

1 Carlton House Terrace, London, SW1Y 5DB

Tel: 020 7839 5090
E-mail: info@inttea.com
Website: www.inttea.com/

Enquiries to: Executive Assistant
Direct e-mail: rumi.ali@inteacom.globalnet.co.uk

Organisation type and purpose: Membership association.
Statistical secretariat for tea throughout the world.

Subject coverage: Tea statistics for producing, consuming countries; acreage; world auction prices; imports, exports, consumption, supply and absorption.

Trade and statistical information: Statistics for tea going back over 60 years

Publications: Printed

Access to staff: Contact by letter, by telephone, by fax, by e-mail and via website
Hours: Mon to Fri, 0830 to 1630

INTERNATIONAL THEATRE INSTITUTE LIMITED (ITI)

ITI @ Goldsmiths College, University of London, Lewisham Way, New Cross, London, SE14 6NW

Tel: 020 7919 7276
Fax: 020 7919 7277
E-mail: iti@gold.ac.uk
Website: iti.gold.ac.uk

Enquiries to: Administrator

Founded: 1948

Organisation type and purpose: International organisation, membership association (membership is by subscription), registered charity (charity number 295092). Non-governmental organisation under the auspices of UNESCO. To facilitate networking and exchange of information, produce events and play an active role in promoting cultural exchange.

Subject coverage: Theatre, dance and music theatre. Facilitates international contacts, research and networking in the performing arts. (Members may also approach any of the 95 centres worldwide.)

Collection: Archive containing performing arts books, journals, directories, scripts, reviews and funding information from around the world

Publications: Printed

Publications list: Available in print

Access to staff: Contact by letter, by telephone, by fax and by e-mail. Appointment necessary. Access for members only.
Hours: Mon to Fri, 0930 to 1730
Special comments: Open 2 days per week.

Access to building: No prior appointment required

Has: 95 national centres around the world

Secretariat of the: ITI; Paris

Works in liaison with: AICT (critics); AITA (amateur theatre); ASSITEJ (young people's theatre); FIA (actors' federation); FIRT (arts research); OISTAT (scenographers and technicians); SIBMAS (libraries and museums); UNIMA (puppeteers)

INTERNATIONAL THERAPY EXAMINATION COUNCIL (ITEC)

4 Heathfield Terrace, London, W4 4JE

Tel: 020 8994 4141
Fax: 020 8994 7880
E-mail: info@itecworld.co.uk
Website: www.itecworld.co.uk

Enquiries to: Director

Founded: 1973

Organisation type and purpose: International awarding body for therapy qualifications.
Provides a syllabus and examinations for professional vocational qualifications in beauty, complementary and sports therapies.

Subject coverage: ITEC provide an independent examination system for the beauty, therapy, health, sport and leisure industries, and complementary therapies.

Publications: Printed

Publications list: Available online and in print

Access to staff: Contact by letter, by telephone, by fax and by e-mail. Appointment necessary.
Hours: Mon to Fri, 0900 to 1700

Parent body: ITEC Professionals; at the same address; tel: 020 8994 7856; fax: 020 8994 7880; e-mail: professionals@itecworld.co.uk

INTERNATIONAL TRANSPORT WORKERS' FEDERATION (ITF)

49–60 Borough Road, London, SE1 1DR

Tel: 020 7403 2733
Fax: 020 7357 7871
E-mail: mail@itf.org.uk
Website: www.itfglobal.org

Enquiries to: General Secretary
Direct tel: 020 7940 9257
Direct fax: 020 7407 0319
Direct e-mail: hawke_jenny@itf.org.uk

Founded: 1896

Organisation type and purpose: Trade union.
International trade union federation.
Provides a wide range of support and advice for its affiliated unions.

Subject coverage: Transport industry and trade unionism.

Collection: 19th- and 20th-century trade union history (held by Warwick University)

Library catalogue: All or part available in-house

Publications: Printed, and electronic and video

Publications list: Available in print

Access to staff: Contact by letter and by e-mail. Appointment necessary.
Hours: Mon to Fri, 0900 to 1700

Access to building: Prior appointment required

Access for disabled people: Ramped entry

INTERNATIONAL TREE FOUNDATION (ITF)

Sandy Lane, Crawley Down, Crawley, West Sussex, RH10 4HS

Tel: 01342 717300
Fax: 01342 718282
E-mail: info@internationaltreefoundation.org
Website: www.internationaltreefoundation.org

Enquiries to: Information Officer

Founded: 1924

Organisation type and purpose: Membership and supporter association (membership is by subscription), present number of members: 3000, registered charity (charity number 1106269).
To protect and plant trees worldwide.

Subject coverage: Tree planting, tree care, tree protection, in UK and overseas.

Publications: Printed, and electronic and video

Access to staff: Contact by letter, by telephone, by fax, by e-mail and via website
Hours: Mon to Fri, 0900 to 1630

Access to building: No access other than to staff

INTERNATIONAL UNDERWRITING ASSOCIATION (IUA)

Formal name: International Underwriting Association of London

London Underwriting Centre, 3 Minster Court, Mincing Lane, London, EC3R 7DD

Tel: 020 7617 4444
Fax: 020 7617 4440
E-mail: info@iua.co.uk
Website: www.lirma.co.uk
Website: www.iua.co.uk

Enquiries to: Chief Executive
Direct tel: 020 7617 4446
Direct e-mail: michelle.bolton@iua.co.uk
Other contacts: Press & PR Manager for general enquiries.

Founded: 1998

Organisation type and purpose: Trade association.
For ordinary members, central accounting and processing of insurance and reinsurance contracts, also central settlement of claims. Representation and research provision.

Subject coverage: International insurance, reinsurance; reinsurance statistics; earthquake studies, bodily injury awards trends, regulation, claims, marine insurance and reinsurance, aviation, eRisks and industry clauses.

Collection: Master copy of all publications and information relevant to members held

Trade and statistical information: Reports of information meetings and seminars, annual membership statistics, earthquakes hazard atlas, reports of forum meetings, marine statistics, eLondon company market statistics, UK Bodily Injury Studies

Publications: Printed, and electronic and video
Order printed publications from: Publications Distribution Manager, IUA
3 Minster Court, Mincing Lane, London, EC3R 7DD, tel: 020 7617 5443, fax: 020 7617 9440, e-mail: anthony.dickinson@iua.co.uk

Publications list: Available in print

Access to staff: Contact by letter, by telephone, by fax, by e-mail and via website
Hours: Mon to Fri, 0900 to 1700

Access to building: Prior appointment required

Access for disabled people: Ramped entry, access to all public areas, toilet facilities

INTERNATIONAL VISUAL COMMUNICATION ASSOCIATION (IVCA)

19 Pepper Street, Glengall Bridge, Docklands, London, E14 9RP

Tel: 020 7512 0571
Fax: 020 7512 0591
E-mail: info@ivca.org
Website: www.ivca.org

Enquiries to: Information Officer
Direct e-mail: davecomley@ivca.org

Founded: 1988/89

Organisation type and purpose: International organisation, advisory body, trade association.
Provides collective voice for the business communication industry, and products and services to benefit membership.

Subject coverage: Business communications, industry and products, film and video.

Trade and statistical information: Data on the UK business communications industry

Publications: Printed

Publications list: Available online

Access to staff: Contact by letter, by telephone, by e-mail and via website
Hours: Mon to Fri, 0930 to 1730

Access to building: Prior appointment required

Parent body: Independent Television Association Limited (ITVA)

INTERNATIONAL VOLUNTARY SERVICE (IVS GB)

Thorn House, 5 Rose Street, Edinburgh, EH2 2PR

Tel: 0131 243 2745
Fax: 0131 243 2747
E-mail: info@ivsgb.org
Website: www.ivsgb.org

Enquiries to: Administrator

Founded: 1931

Organisation type and purpose: International organisation (British branch), voluntary organisation, registered charity.

Subject coverage: Opportunities for short-term and long-term voluntary work throughout Britain and the world.

Publications: Printed

Publications list: Available online

Access to staff: Contact by letter, by telephone, by fax, by e-mail, in person and via website
Hours: Mon to Fri, 0900 to 1700

Parent body: Service Civil International (SCI); a worldwide movement

INTERNATIONAL VOLUNTARY SERVICE (NORTH)

Castlehill House, 21 Otley Road, Leeds, West Yorkshire, LS6 3AA

Tel: 0113 230 4600
Fax: 0113 230 4610
E-mail: info@ivsgb.org
Website: www.ivsgbn.demon.co.uk

Enquiries to: Regional Co-ordinator
Direct e-mail: info@ivsgb.org
Other contacts: National Fundraiser

Founded: 1931

Organisation type and purpose: International organisation, national organisation, voluntary organisation, registered charity (charity number 275424).
To promote peace, justice and international understanding through voluntary work.

Subject coverage: Information on over 700 international work camps, on opportunities for short and medium term volunteering for British volunteers in Europe, North America, CIS, North Africa, Japan and Australia.

Publications: Printed

Access to staff: Contact by letter and by e-mail
Hours: Mon to Fri, 0900 to 1700

Other addresses: IVS – Scotland; 7 Upper Bow, Edinburgh, EH1 2JN; tel: 0131 226 6722; fax: 0131 226 6723; e-mail: ivsgbscot@ivsgbscot.demon.co.uk; IVS – South; Old Hall, East Bergholt, Colchester, CO7 6TQ; tel: 01206 298215; fax: 01206 299043; e-mail: ivsgbsouth@ivsgbsouth.demon.co.uk

Parent body: Service Civil International (SCI)

INTERNATIONAL WATER ASSOCIATION (IWA)

12 Alliance House, Caxton Street, London, SW1H 0QS

Tel: 020 7654 5500
Fax: 020 7654 5555
E-mail: water@iwahq.org
Website: www.iwahq.org

Enquiries to: Executive Director

Founded: 1965

Organisation type and purpose: International organisation, professional body, membership association (membership is by subscription), registered charity (charity number 1076690).
Global reference point and network for water professionals.

Subject coverage: Wastewater treatment processes, water reuse, impact of pollutants on water bodies; water suppliers nationally and worldwide.

Non-library collection catalogue: All or part available online

continued overleaf

Publications: Printed
Order printed publications from: website: http://www.iwapublishing.com; Distributor: Portland Customer Services, Commerce Way, Colchester, CO2 8HP, UK; tel: 01206 796351; fax: 01206 799331; e-mail: sales@portland-services.com

Publications list: Available online and in print

Access to staff: Contact by letter and by e-mail
Hours: Mon to Fri, 0900 to 1700

Access to building: Prior appointment required

Affiliated to: World Health Organisation

Non-governmental organisation of: The United Nations

INTERNATIONAL WHALING COMMISSION (IWC)

The Red House, 135 Station Road, Impington, Cambridge, CB24 9NP

Tel: 01223 233971
Fax: 01223 232876
E-mail: secretariat@iwcoffice.org
Website: www.iwcoffice.org

Enquiries to: Editor

Founded: 1946

Organisation type and purpose: International organisation, membership association, present number of members: 89 member nations.
Conservation of whales and regulation of whaling.

Subject coverage: Whales, whaling, population, biology, resource management, ecosystem management, genetics, statistical surveys, whale catch and sightings database.

Non-library collection catalogue: All or part available in print

Publications: Printed, and electronic and video
Order printed publications from: PA to the Secretary, IWC

Publications list: Available online and in print

Access to staff: Contact by letter, by telephone, by fax, by e-mail and via website. Appointment necessary.
Hours: Mon to Fri, 0900 to 1700
Special comments: Dependent upon availability of staff.

Access to building: Prior appointment required
Hours: Mon to Fri, 0900 to 1700

Access for disabled people: Parking provided, ramped entry
Special comments: Level access on ground floor.

INTERNATIONAL WILDLIFE COALITION TRUST (IWCT)

141A High Street, Edenbridge, Kent, TN8 5AX

Tel: 01732 866955
Fax: 01732 966995
E-mail: iwcuk@iwcmail.demon.co.uk
Website: www.iwctk9.co.uk

Enquiries to: Director

Founded: 1987

Organisation type and purpose: International organisation, voluntary organisation, registered charity (charity number 1035381).

Subject coverage: Animal welfare.

Publications list: Available online and in print

Access to staff: Contact by letter, by telephone, by fax, by e-mail, in person and via website. Appointment necessary.
Hours: Mon to Fri, 0900 to 1700

Access to building: Prior appointment required

INTERNATIONAL WINE & FOOD SOCIETY (IWFS)

4 St James's Square, London, SW1Y 4JU

Tel: 020 7827 5732
Fax: 020 7827 5733
E-mail: sec@iwfs.org
Website: www.iwfs.org

Enquiries to: International Secretariat

Founded: 1933

Organisation type and purpose: International organisation, membership association (membership is by subscription), present number of members: 6,200.
Educational and social.

Subject coverage: Every aspect of wine and cookery, gastronomy.

Collection: Library is situated in Guildhall Public Library, City of London

Publications: Printed

Publications list: Available in print

Access to staff: Contact by letter, by telephone, by fax and by e-mail. Appointment necessary. Non-members charged.
Hours: Mon to Fri, 1000 to 1630
Special comments: Membership card required.

Also: 130 local branches worldwide

INTERNATIONAL YOUTH FOUNDATION OF GREAT BRITAIN (IYF)

6a Pont Street, London, SW1X 9EL

Tel: 020 7235 7671
Fax: 020 7235 7370
E-mail: info@euyo.org.uk
Website: www.euyo.org.uk

Enquiries to: Secretary General

Founded: 1978

Organisation type and purpose: International organisation, registered charity (charity number 281420).

Subject coverage: Youth orchestras, choirs, ballet, opera, folk and youth bands, formation and development of national youth orchestras, music and education in the European Union.

Publications: Printed

Access to staff: Contact by letter, by telephone, by fax and by e-mail
Hours: Mon to Fri, 0930 to 1730

Under its auspices is the: European Union Youth Orchestra (EUYO); at the same address; tel: 020 7235 7671; fax: 020 7235 7370; e-mail: info@euyo.org.uk

INTERNATIONAL ZEN ASSOCIATION (UNITED KINGDOM) (IZAUK)

91–93 Gloucester Road, Bristol, BS7 8AT

Tel: 0117 942 4347
Website: www.izauk.org

Enquiries to: Information Officer

Founded: 1986

Organisation type and purpose: Registered charity (charity number 296285).
Spiritual and religious practice.

Subject coverage: Soto Zen Buddhism.

Publications: Printed

Access to staff: Contact by letter, by telephone, by e-mail and in person
Hours: By arrangement

Branches: 10 subsidiary groups in the United Kingdom, in Bristol, Manchester, London, Leeds, Norwich, Oxford, Brighton and Wells-next-the-Sea

Member organisation of: Association Zen Internationale; 175 rue de Tolbiac, Paris, 75013, France

INTERPAVE, THE PRECAST CONCRETE PAVING AND KERB ASSOCIATION

60 Charles Street, Leicester, LE1 1FB

Tel: 0116 253 6161
Fax: 0116 251 4568
E-mail: info@paving.org.uk
Website: www.paving.org.uk

Enquiries to: Secretary

Organisation type and purpose: Trade association.

Subject coverage: Precast concrete paving flags, block paving and kerbs.

Library catalogue: All or part available online

Publications: Printed

Publications list: Available online

Access to staff: Contact by letter, by telephone, by fax and by e-mail. Appointment necessary.
Hours: Mon to Fri, 0900 to 1700

Member organisation of: British Precast Concrete Federation

INVENSYS APV

23 Gatwick Road, Crawley, West Sussex, RH10 9JB

Tel: 01293 527777
Fax: 01293 552640
Website: www.apv.co.uk

Enquiries to: Marketing Manager
Direct tel: 01293 574380

Founded: 1910

Organisation type and purpose: International organisation.
Company.
Provision of components, process engineering, automation and service to the food, drink, pharmaceutical and healthcare industries.

Subject coverage: Design, production, installation and technical know-how of food, liquid food and pharmaceutical engineering processes. Provision of automation solutions to the above industries.

Access to staff: Contact by letter, by telephone and by fax. Appointment necessary.
Hours: Mon to Fri, 0900 to 1700

Access for disabled people: Ramped entry

Parent body: Invensys plc; Invensys House, Carlisle Place, London, SW1P 1BX; tel: 020 7834 3848; fax: 020 7834 3879

INVERCLYDE LIBRARIES

Central Library, Clyde Square, Greenock, Renfrewshire, PA15 1NA

Tel: 01475 712323
Fax: 01475 712339
E-mail: library.central@inverclyde.gov.uk
Website: www.inverclyde.gov.uk/Libraries

Enquiries to: Librarian

Organisation type and purpose: Local government body, public library.

Subject coverage: General, local history.

Collection: Watt Library (local history, 18th- and 19th-century publications)

Library catalogue: All or part available online and in-house

Access to staff: Contact by letter, by telephone, by fax, by e-mail and in person
Hours: Mon, Tue, Thu, 0930 to 1900; Fri, 0930 to 1700; Wed, 0930 to 1300; Sat, 1000 to 1300

INVESTMENT MANAGEMENT ASSOCIATION (IMA)

65 Kingsway, London, WC2B 6TD

Tel: 020 7831 0898
Fax: 020 7831 9975
E-mail: ima@investmentuk.org
Website: www.investmentuk.org

Enquiries to: Head of Communications

Founded: 1959; created by the merger of Association of Unit Trusts and Investment Funds (AUTIF) and Fund Managers Association (FMA) (year of change 2002); formerly called Unit Trust Association

Organisation type and purpose: Trade association (membership is by subscription) for asset management companies. Affiliate membership for service providers to asset management companies.

Subject coverage: Unit trusts, open-ended investment companies (OEICs), ISAs, investment, saving, pensions, markets.

Collection: Historical statistics

Trade and statistical information: UK data on asset management, unit trusts OEIC and ISA sales data

Publications: Printed

Publications list: Available online and in print

Access to staff: Contact by letter, by telephone and by e-mail
Hours: Mon to Fri, 0900 to 1700

Access to building: No access other than to staff

INVESTOR RELATIONS SOCIETY (IRS)

Bedford House, 3 Bedford Street, London, WC2E 9HD

Tel: 020 7379 1763
Fax: 020 7240 1320
E-mail: enquiries@irs.org.uk
Website: www.ir-soc.org.uk

Enquiries to: General Manager

Founded: 1980

Organisation type and purpose: The UK's professional body for investor relations practitioners. Has almost 600 members from corporates and consultancies from across the UK, Europe and beyond and includes the majority of the FTSE 100 and a healthy representation from the FTSE 250.
To promote best practice in investor relations; to support the professional development of its members; to represent their views to regulatory bodies, the investment community and government; and to act as a forum for issuers and the investment community.

Subject coverage: The communication of information and insight between a company and the investment community. This process enables a full appreciation of the company's business activities, strategy and prospects and allows the market to make an informed judgement about the fair value and appropriate ownership of a company.

Publications: Electronic and video
Order electronic and video publications from: Download from website

Publications list: Available online

Access to staff: Contact by letter, by telephone, by fax and by e-mail

Member organisation of: Global Investor Relations Network (GIRN)

IOP: THE PACKAGING SOCIETY (IOP)

Springfield House, Springfield Business Park, Grantham, Lincolnshire, NO31 7BG

Tel: 01476 514590
Fax: 01476 514591
E-mail: gordon.stewart@piabc.org.uk
Website: www.iop.co.uk

Enquiries to: Head of Education, Training & Development
Direct tel: 01664 502150
Direct e-mail: gordon-stewart@iop.co.uk

Founded: 1947

Organisation type and purpose: Professional body, present number of members: 3500, registered charity (charity number 295762), consultancy, publishing house.
Supports courses at Brunel and Loughborough Universities.
To promote packaging and provide education and training in packaging technology.

Subject coverage: Packaging technology, packaging and the environment, legislation, packaging education and qualification, packaging publications, overseas contacts and exhibitions.

Collection: Reference library dedicated to packaging, packaging technology and related topics. Includes British Standards, periodicals and technical conference papers in addition to text books

Trade and statistical information: Details of overseas trade exhibitions related to packaging and grants available to firms

Publications: Printed, and electronic and video

Access to staff: Contact by letter, by telephone, by fax, by e-mail and via website. Appointment necessary.
Hours: Mon to Fri, 0900 to 1700
Special comments: Three steps up to front door.

Secretariat for the: Packaging Federation; at the same address; Pressure Sensitive Manufacturers Association; at the same address

IP FEDERATION (IPF)

Fifth Floor, 63–66 Hatton Garden, London, EC1N 8LE

Tel: 020 7242 3923
Fax: 020 7242 3924
E-mail: admin@ipfederation.com
Website: www.ipfederation.com

Enquiries to: Administrator

Founded: 1920

Organisation type and purpose: Membership association (membership is by subscription, qualification), present number of members: 50, manufacturing industry, service industry.
Spokesman for industry on intellectual property (patents, trade marks, designs and copyright).

Subject coverage: Industry views on trade marks, patents, copyright and industrial designs.

Access to staff: Contact by letter, by telephone and by e-mail
Hours: Mon to Fri, 0900 to 1700

IP3

Formal name: Institute of Paper, Printing and Publishing

Runnymede Malthouse, off Hummer Road, Egham, Surrey, TW20 9BD

Tel: 0870 330 8625
Fax: 0870 330 8615
E-mail: info@ip3.org.uk
Website: www.ip3.org.uk/

Enquiries to: Information Officer

Founded: 2004

Organisation type and purpose: Professional body.

Publications: Printed

continued overleaf

Access to staff: Contact by telephone, by fax and by e-mail
Hours: Mon to Fri, 0900 to 1700

IPSEA (IPSEA)

Formal name: Independent Parental Special Education Advice

Hunters Court, Debden Road, Saffron Walden, Essex, CB11 4AA

Tel: 01799 582030 (admin. only); 0800 018 4016 (main helpline)
Website: www.ipsea.org.uk

Enquiries to: Administrator
Direct tel: 01394 384711
Direct fax: 01394 446577

Organisation type and purpose: Voluntary organisation.

Subject coverage: IPSEA offers free and independent advice and support to parents of children with special educational needs including, free advice on LEAs' legal duties towards children with SEN, free home visits where necessary, free support and possible representation for those parents appealing to the Special Educational Needs Tribunal, and free second opinions on a child's needs and the provision required to meet those needs.

Publications: Printed

Publications list: Available in print

Access to building: No prior appointment required

IPSOS MORI (MORI)

79–81 Borough Road, London, SE1 1FY

Tel: 020 7347 3000
Fax: 020 7347 3800
E-mail: ashish.prashar@ipsos.com
Website: www.mori.com/pubinfo/articles.htm

Enquiries to: Marketing Executive
Direct e-mail: patricia.ifejika@mori.com
Other contacts: Head of Communications Department

Founded: October 2005

Organisation type and purpose:
International organisation, research organisation.
Full market research agency.

Subject coverage: Specialist knowledge of over 40 specialist business areas, including financial, corporate image, employee, leisure and tourism, and social research.

Publications: Printed, and electronic and video
Order printed publications from: Marketing Department

Publications list: Available online

Access to staff: Contact by telephone and by e-mail
Hours: Mon to Fri, 0830 to 1800

Other addresses: Ipsos MORI; Kings House, Kymberley Road, Harrow, HA1 1PT; tel: 020 8861 8000; fax: 020 8861 5515

IPSWICH INSTITUTE

Formal name: Ipswich Institute Reading Room & Library

Reading Room and Library, 15 Tavern Street, Ipswich, Suffolk, IP1 3AA

Tel: 01473 253992
E-mail: library@ipswichinstitute.org.uk
Website: www.ipswichinstitute.org.uk

Enquiries to: General Manager

Founded: 1824

Organisation type and purpose:
Membership association (membership is by subscription), present number of members: 2400, registered charity (charity number 304772).
Independent subscription library with 9,000 stock items, plus reading room and refreshment facilities. To advance the education of the inhabitants of Ipswich and neighbourhood.

Subject coverage: Fiction and non-fiction books, local history, audiobooks, music CDs, newspapers, magazines.

Library catalogue: All or part available online

Access to staff: Contact by letter, by telephone and by e-mail
Hours: Mon to Fri, 0900 to 1700; Sat, 0900 to 1600

Access to building: No prior appointment required
Special comments: Membership organisation – one visit acceptable prior to membership.

Access for disabled people: Library & reading room, cafe and restaurant at ground floor, disabled WC

Also at: Ipswich Institute; Admiral's House, 13 Tower Street, Ipswich, Suffolk, IP1 3BE; tel: 01473 253992

Member organisation of: Association of Independent Libraries; Leeds Library, 18 Commercial Street, Leeds, LS1 6AL; website: www.independentlibraries.co.uk

IQEA LIMITED

Formal name: Improving the Quality of Education for All

Sycamores, Holebottom Road, Todmorden, Lancashire, OL14 8DD

Tel: 01706 839274
Fax: 01706 839274
E-mail: admin@iqea.com
Website: www.iqea.com

Enquiries to: Managing Director
Direct tel: 07920 449247
Other contacts: IQEA Co-ordinator for details about schools involved in the project

Founded: 2002

Organisation type and purpose:
International organisation, advisory body, learned society (membership is by election or invitation), present number of members: 100 schools, university department or institute, suitable for ages: primary and secondary, training organisation, consultancy, research organisation.
School Improvement Network.
To support school improvement efforts locally, nationally and internationally. The key purpose is to enhance the quality of student learning and achievement.

Subject coverage: The quality of education in primary and secondary schools.

Library catalogue: All or part available in-house and in print

Publications: Printed

Access to staff: Contact by letter, by telephone, by fax, by e-mail, in person and via website. Appointment necessary. Non-members charged.
Hours: Mon to Fri, 0900 to 1700

Access to building: No public access

IRAN SOCIETY

2 Belgrave Square, London, SW1X 8PJ

Tel: 020 7235 5122
Fax: 020 7259 6771
E-mail: info@iransociety.org
Website: www.iransociety.org

Enquiries to: Honorary Secretary

Organisation type and purpose:
Membership association (membership is by subscription, election or invitation), present number of members: 350, voluntary organisation (charity number 248678).
Promotes the study of Iran, its peoples and culture and particularly aims to advance education through the study of language, literature, art, history, religion, antiquities, usages, institutions and customs of Iran.

Subject coverage: Iran (excluding contemporary politics).

Access to staff: Contact by letter, by telephone, by fax, by e-mail and via website
Hours: Wed to Fri, 0930 to 1700

IRISH COUNCIL OF CHURCHES & THE IRISH INTER-CHURCH MEETING (ICC & IICM)

48 Elmwood Avenue, Belfast, BT9 6AZ

Tel: 028 9066 3145
Fax: 028 9066 4160
E-mail: info@irishchuches
Website: info@irishchurches.org

Enquiries to: Administrator

Founded: 1922

Organisation type and purpose: National organisation, registered charity (charity number XN 48617).
Church body.

Subject coverage: Information on Irish ecumenism.

Publications list: Available online and in print

Access to staff: Contact by letter, by telephone, by fax, by e-mail and in person
Hours: Mon to Fri, 0900 to 1700

IRISH FOOTBALL ASSOCIATION (IFA)

20 Windsor Ave, Belfast BT9 6EG

Tel: 028 9066 9458
E-mail: info@irishfa.com

Website: www.irishfa.com

Enquiries to: General Secretary
Other contacts: President

Founded: 1880; merged with the Irish Football League (IFL, founded 1890) (year of change 2003)

Organisation type and purpose: Sporting body.

Subject coverage: Soccer in Northern Ireland, Irish league clubs.

Access to staff: Contact by letter, by telephone, by fax and by e-mail
Hours: Mon to Fri, 0900 to 1700

IRISH LINEN GUILD

Formal name: The Irish Linen Guild Ltd.

c/o Riverside Factory, Victoria Street, Lurgan, Craigavon, County Armagh, BT67 9DU

E-mail: info@irishlinen.co.uk
Website: www.irishlinen.co.uk

Enquiries to: Director
Other contacts: Webmaster

Founded: 1928

Organisation type and purpose:
Professional body, membership association (membership is by qualification), present number of members: 5.
Promotion of Irish linen.

Subject coverage: History and production of Irish linen, sourcing Irish linen products including fabric for clothing and household textiles, and made up household textile products. Information about current manufacturers and suppliers.

Collection: http://www.lisburncity.gov.uk/irish-linen-centre-and-lisburn-museum/general-information/

Publications: Electronic and video

Publications list: Available in print

Access to staff: Contact by letter, by e-mail and via website

IRISH SEA FORUM (ISF)

Oceanography Laboratories, The University of Liverpool, Liverpool, L69 3BX

Tel: 0151 794 4089
Fax: 0151 794 4099
E-mail: d.f.shaw@liv.ac.uk
Website: www.liv.ac.uk/

Enquiries to: Director
Other contacts: Administrative Officer for all information about Irish Sea Forum.

Founded: 1992

Organisation type and purpose:
Membership association (membership is by subscription), present number of members: 95, voluntary organisation.
Non-profit making organisation operating within the University of Liverpool; liaison with industry and commerce, voluntary and statutory organisations, and educational establishments on all shores of the Irish Sea, individual membership welcomed from those wishing to support the purpose of the Forum.
To bring together those who are interested in the enhancement of the environmental health of the Irish Sea and its coastal features and estuaries, and the sustainable development of its resources.

Subject coverage: All aspects of environmental management pertaining to the Irish Sea.

Publications: Printed

Publications list: Available in print

Access to staff: Contact by letter, by telephone, by fax, by e-mail and via website. Appointment necessary.
Hours: Mon to Fri, 0900 to 1700

Access to building: No prior appointment required

IRISH TEXTS SOCIETY (ITS)

Royal Bank of Scotland, Drummonds Branch, 49 Charing Cross, Admiralty Arch, London, SW1A 2DX

Website: www.ucc.ie/locus/ITS.html

Enquiries to: Secretary
Direct e-mail: shuttonseanfile@aol.com
Other contacts: Honorary Treasurer; email burnsfarm@iol.ie for book orders, membership queries/applications.

Founded: 1898

Organisation type and purpose: Learned society (membership is by subscription), publishing house.

Subject coverage: Irish language, history; texts and translations; poetry and prose.

Collection: The archives of the Society are in the Library of University College Cork, Ireland

Publications: Printed

Publications list: Available in print

Access to staff: Contact by letter and by e-mail
Hours: Mon to Fri, 0900 to 1700

Connections with: ITS/UCC Seminar (annually); website: www.ucc.ie/locus/its.html

IRM UK STRATEGIC IT TRAINING LIMITED (IRM UK)

Bishops Walk House, 19–23 High Street, Pinner, Middlesex, HA5 5PJ

Tel: 020 8866 8366
Fax: 020 8866 7966
E-mail: customerservice@irmuk.co.uk
Website: www.irmuk.co.uk

Enquiries to: Managing Director
Direct e-mail: jeremy.hall@irmuk.co.uk

Founded: 1999

Organisation type and purpose: Service industry, training organisation.

Subject coverage: Seminars and conferences on business process management, enterprise architecture, data management, software development, value-driven IT, mastering the requirements process, project management, information quality.

Publications: Electronic and video

Access to staff: Contact by letter, by telephone, by fax, by e-mail and via website. Appointment necessary.
Hours: Mon to Fri, 0900 to 1700

Access to building: No access other than to staff

Access for disabled people: Access to all public areas

IRONBRIDGE GORGE MUSEUM TRUST (Ironbridge Gorge Museums)

Coach Road, Coalbrookdale, Telford, Shropshire, TF8 7DQ

Tel: 01952 433522
Fax: 01952 433204
E-mail: info@ironbridge.org.uk
Website: www.ironbridge.org.uk

Enquiries to: Head of Marketing
Direct e-mail: marketing@ironbridge.org.uk

Founded: 1967

Organisation type and purpose: Registered charity (charity number 503717-R), museum, suitable for ages: 5+.

Subject coverage: A series of museums and monuments which capture the stories of Britain's Industrial Revolution. Ten museums covering six square miles of East Shropshire coalfields.

Information services: Library available for reference (for conditions see Access). Educational and school visits, tel: 01952 433970 or e-mail: education@ironbridge.org.uk. Group visits: telephone, or e-mail: visits@ironbridge.org.uk.

Special visitor services: Guided tours, materials and/or activities for children.

Education services: Group education facilities, resources for Key Stages 1, 2, 3 and 4 and Further or Higher Education.

Services for disabled people: For the visually impaired; for the hearing impaired; displays and/or information at wheelchair height.

Collection: Collection on the life and works of Thomas Telford
Elton Collection (paintings, prints, book, pamphlets and memorabilia relating to the history of the Industrial Revolution)

Non-library collection catalogue: All or part available online, in-house and in print

Library catalogue: All or part available online

Publications: Printed, and electronic and video
Order printed publications from: Mail Order Department

Access to staff: Contact by letter, by fax and by e-mail
Hours: Mon to Fri, 0900 to 1700

Access for disabled people: Parking provided, ramped entry, toilet facilities
Special comments: Sites vary, access guides available on request.

Historic Site: Blists Hill Victorian Town; Broseley Pipeworks; Coalport China Museum; Enginuity; Ironbridge Gorge Museum Trust; Jackfield Tile Museum; Museum of Iron; Museum of the Gorge; Tar

continued overleaf

Tunnel; The Darby Houses; The Iron Bridge and Tollhouse; The Merrythought Teddy Bear Shop and Museum

Links with: Association for Industrial Archaeology

Maintains the: Blists Hill Open Air Museum; Broseley Pipeworks Museum; Coalbrookdale Museum of Iron and Furnace; Coalport China Museum; Jackfield Tile Museum; Long Warehouse, which houses the Ironbridge Institute and the Museum library and archives; Museum of the Gorge

Manages: Ironbridge Institute

Secretariat of the: Association for Industrial Archaeology (AIA)

IRONBRIDGE GORGE MUSEUM TRUST – MUSEUM LIBRARY

Coach Road, Coalbrookdale, Telford, Shropshire, TF8 7DQ

Tel: 01952 432141
Fax: 01952 432237
E-mail: library@ironbridge.org.uk
Website: www.ironbridge.org.uk

Enquiries to: Librarian and Information Officer

Founded: 1968

Organisation type and purpose: Registered charity, suitable for ages: 16+.
Private library. Courses at the Library run from Birmingham University.

Subject coverage: Industrial history, particularly East Shropshire Coalfield; history of technology; museology.

Education services: Group education facilities, resources for Further or Higher Education.

Non-library collection catalogue: All or part available in-house

Library catalogue: All or part available in-house

Access to staff: Contact by letter, by telephone, by fax and by e-mail. Appointment necessary.
Hours: Mon to Fri, 0900 to 1700

Access to building: Prior appointment required
Hours: Mon to Fri, 0930 to 1700

Access for disabled people: Toilet facilities
Special comments: Many stairs, access to ground floor only and not to library itself. Staff happy to assist disabled users, please telephone for information.

Links with: Birmingham University

IRONBRIDGE INSTITUTE

Ironbridge Gorge Museum Trust, Coalbrook, Telford, Shropshire, TF8 7DX

Tel: 01952 432751
Fax: 01952 435937
E-mail: j.p.fletcher@bham.ac.uk
Website: www.ironbridge.bham.ac.uk

Enquiries to: Administrator

Founded: 1980

Organisation type and purpose: University department or institute.
Postgraduate training and professional development.

Subject coverage: All aspects of the industrial past, industrial archaeology, management of heritage resources (museums, historic buildings, townscapes and the natural environment).

Collection: Elton Collection
Telford Collection

Access to staff: Contact by letter, by telephone, by fax, by e-mail and in person
Hours: Mon to Fri, 0900 to 1700

Managed jointly by the: Institute of Archaeology and Antiquity; The University of Birmingham; Ironbridge Gorge Museum Trust

ISBA

Formal name: ISBA – The Voice of British Advertisers

Langham House, 1B Portland Place, London, W1B 1PN

Tel: 020 7291 9020
Fax: 020 7291 9030
E-mail: answers@isba.org.uk
Website: www.isba.org.uk

Enquiries to: Director of Marketing Services
Other contacts: Director of Membership Development

Founded: 1900

Organisation type and purpose:
Membership association (membership is by subscription), present number of members: over 310 companies.
Non-profit-making organisation representing advertisers to the Government, media, agencies and other organisations.
ISBA acts as a catalyst encouraging advertisers to join forces, debate and take action on any issue affecting market communications.

Subject coverage: Advertising in the UK and overseas; voluntary controls; legislation: terms and conditions of business in all advertising media; public relations; direct marketing; sales promotion.

Publications: Printed

Publications list: Available in print

Access to staff: Contact by letter, by fax, by e-mail and via website
Hours: Mon to Fri, 0900 to 1730

Associated with: Advertising Association (AA); World Federation of Advertising and the Advertisers (WFA)

ISI (EUROPE, MIDDLE-EAST AND AFRICA) (ISI)

Formal name: Institute for Scientific Information

Thomson Reuters, 77 Hatton Garden, London, EC1N 8JS

Tel: 020 7433 4000
Fax: 020 7433 4001
Website: scientific.thomson.com/isi/
Website: www.isinet.com/emea

Enquiries to: Press Office
Direct tel: 020 7433 4691
Direct e-mail: eoin.bedford@thomsonreuters.com

Founded: 1958 (USA)

Organisation type and purpose: Service industry, research organisation.

Subject coverage: Produces multidisciplinary and scientific information tools for the international research community. ISI's databases link the researcher to the world's scholarly literature through its indexes of bibliographic information and cited references. Areas covered include all areas of pure and applied sciences, social sciences, arts and humanities.

Publications: Printed, and electronic and video, and microform publications

Publications list: Available online and in print

Access to staff: Contact by letter, by telephone, by fax, by e-mail and via website
Hours: Mon to Fri, 0900 to 1730

Access to building: Prior appointment required

Access for disabled people: Toilet facilities

Other addresses for ISI: ISI (Australia & New Zealand) (ISI); 100 Harris Street, Pyrmont, NSW 2009, Australia; tel: +61 (2) 8587 7948; fax: +61 (2) 8587 7848; e-mail: asiainfo@isinet.com; ISI (Japan) (ISI); Thomson Corporation KK, Palaceside Building 5F, 1–1-1 Hitotsubashi, Chiyoda-ku, Tokyo, 100–0003, Japan; tel: +81 3 5218 6530; fax: +81 3 5218 6536; e-mail: jpinfo@isinet.com (inquiries); ISI (North America, Latin America and Caribbean) (ISI); 3501 Market Street, Philadelphia, PA 19104, USA; tel: +1 215 386 0100; fax: +1 215 386 2911; e-mail: sales@isinet.com; ISI (People's Republic of China) (ISI); Room 1291/1292 Pana Tower, #128 Zhi Chun Road, Hai Dan District, Beijing, 100086, PR China; tel: +86 10 8261 1504; fax: +86 10 6257 8045; e-mail: chinainfo@isinet.com; ISI (Republic of Korea) (ISI); 10FL Daenong Building, 33–1 Mapo-dong, Mapo-ku, Seoul, 121–708, Republic of Korea; tel: +82 2 711 3412; fax: + 82 2 711 3520; e-mail: koreainfo@isinet.com; ISI (South/South East Asia, Hong Kong & Taiwan) (ISI); 6 Battery Road #29–03, Standard Chartered Bank Building, Singapore, 049909; tel: +65 6879 4118; fax: + 65 6223 2634; e-mail: asianinfo@isinet.com (inquiries)

Subsidiary of: ISI; 3501 Market Street, Philadelphia, PA 19104, USA; tel: +1 215 386 0100; fax: +1 215 386 2911; e-mail: sales@isinet.com

ISLAMIC CULTURAL CENTRE

London Central Mosque, 146 Park Road, London, NW8 7RG

Tel: 020 7724 3363
Fax: 020 7724 0493
E-mail: islamic200@aol.com
Website: www.islamicculturalcentre.co.uk

Enquiries to: Director-General

Founded: 1977

Organisation type and purpose: Place of worship and for cultural activities.

Information point for the religion of Islam, facility provider for Muslim community and advice to government, local authorities, statutory bodies and voluntary organisations.

Subject coverage: Islam, religion, culture, history (modern and ancient), Arabic language, art and heritage.

Collection: Numerous books, documents in Arabic, Urdu, Farsi, etc on the religion of Islam, history, culture etc

Publications: Printed, and electronic and video

Access to staff: Contact by letter, by telephone, by fax, by e-mail and in person. Appointment necessary.
Hours: Mon to Fri, 0900 to 1700
Special comments: No filming or press interviews without prior arrangement.

Access to building: No prior appointment required
Special comments: Prior appointment required for media.

Access for disabled people: Parking provided, ramped entry, level entry, access to all public areas, toilet facilities

ISLAND HISTORY TRUST

Dockland Settlement, 197 East Ferry Road, London, E14 3BA

Tel: 020 7987 6041
E-mail: eve@islandhistory.org.uk
Website: www.islandhistory.org.uk

Founded: 1980

Organisation type and purpose: A community history project dedicated to recording and preserving the history of London's Isle of Dogs.

Subject coverage: History of the Isle of Dogs.

Information services: Family history on Isle of Dogs.

Special visitor services: Access to photograph collections.

Education services: Resources for schools.

Collection: Local photographs and ephemera

Non-library collection catalogue: All or part available in-house

Library catalogue: All or part available in-house

Publications: Printed
Order printed publications from: above address

Access to staff: Contact by letter, by telephone, by e-mail and in person. Appointment necessary.
Hours: Tue to Thu, 0900 to 1700

Access to building: *Hours:* Tue, Wed and 1st Sun of the month, 1330 to 1630; at other times by appointment

Access for disabled people: Major events only

ISLE OF AXHOLME FAMILY HISTORY SOCIETY (IofAFHS)

117 Fieldside, Epworth, nr Doncaster, DN9 1DR

Tel: 01427 873944
E-mail: secretary@axholme-fhs.org.uk
Website: www.axholme-fhs.org.uk

Enquiries to: Secretary
Other contacts: Chairman (webmaster@axholme-fhs.org.uk)

Founded: 1988

Organisation type and purpose: Membership association (membership is by subscription), present number of members: 180, voluntary organisation, research organisation.
To assist people with an ancestry or an interest in the 12 parishes of the Isle of Axholme.

Subject coverage: Family history in the 12 Lincolnshire parishes west of the River Trent, i.e. the Isle of Axholme.

Collection: Transcriptions of parish registers, census returns
Local historical matters in booklets, CD-ROMs and floppy disks pertaining to the Isle of Axholme

Library catalogue: All or part available in-house

Publications: Printed, and electronic and video
Order printed publications from: J Oliver, 17B West End Road, Epworth, Doncaster, DN9 1LA
Order electronic and video publications from: Isle of Axholme Family History Society, Alberma, Luddington Road, Garthorpe, Isle of Axholme, Lincolnshire, DN17 4RU; e-mail: interests@axholme-fhs.org.uk

Publications list: Available online and in print

Access to staff: Contact by letter, by telephone, by e-mail and via website
Hours: Daily, 1000 to 2200

Access to building: 4th Thu in month, except Aug and Dec
Hours: 0700 to 2100

Access for disabled people: Yes
Hours: 1830 to 2130

ISLE OF MAN CIVIL REGISTRY

The Registries, Deemsters Walk, Bucks Road, Douglas, Isle of Man, IM1 3AR

Tel: 01624 687039
Fax: 01624 685237
E-mail: civil@registry.gov.im

Enquiries to: Registrar

Organisation type and purpose: Manx government body.

Subject coverage: Isle of Man Records of birth, death and marriage registrations, parish records of baptisms, marriages and burials pre-1878 (Church of England).

Publications: Printed

Access to staff: Contact by letter, by telephone, by fax, by e-mail and in person
Hours: Mon to Fri, 0900 to 1300 and 1400 to 1700

Access to building: No prior appointment required

Access for disabled people: Parking provided, level entry, access to all public areas, toilet facilities

ISLE OF MAN DEPARTMENT OF TOURISM AND LEISURE

Sea Terminal Buildings, Douglas, Isle of Man, IM1 2RG

Tel: 01624 686801
Fax: 01624 686800
E-mail: tourism@gov.im
Website: www.visitisleofman.com

Enquiries to: Tourist Information Manager
Direct tel: 01624 686851
Direct fax: 01624 627443
Direct e-mail: steve.dawson@gov.im

Organisation type and purpose: National government body.
Promotion of tourism and leisure.

Subject coverage: Promotion of tourism in the Isle of Man.

Publications: Printed

Publications list: Available online and in print

Access to staff: Contact by letter, by telephone, by fax, by e-mail and in person
Hours: Winter: Mon to Fri, 0915 to 1700
Summer: Daily, 0915 to 1900

Access for disabled people: Parking provided, level entry, toilet facilities

ISLE OF MAN PUBLIC RECORD OFFICE (IOMPRO)

Unit 40A, Spring Valley Industrial Estate, Braddan, Douglas, Isle of Man, IM2 2QS

Tel: 01624 693569
Fax: 01624 613384
E-mail: public.records@registry.gov.im
Website: www.gov.im/registries/publicrecords

Enquiries to: Public Records Officer

Founded: 1992

Organisation type and purpose: National government body, statutory body.
Record office.

Subject coverage: History of public administration in the Isle of Man.

Collection: Records of the Isle of Man Government and other public bodies, particularly 20th century

Access to staff: Contact by letter, by telephone, by fax and by e-mail. Appointment necessary.
Hours: Mon to Thurs, 0900 to 1300 and 1400 to 1730; Fri, 0900 to 1300 and 1400 to 1700

Access to building: If opening hours are difficult, please contact staff to discuss alternative arrangements
Hours: Thu, 0930 to 1300, and 1400 to 1700; Fri, 0930 to 1300 and 1400 to 1630

Parent body: Isle of Man Government; General Registry

ISLE OF MAN TRANSPORT

Banks Circus, Douglas, Isle of Man, IM1 5PT

Tel: 01624 663366

continued overleaf

Fax: 01624 663637
E-mail: info@busandrail.dtl.gov.im

Enquiries to: Director

Founded: 1873

Organisation type and purpose: National government body, service industry.
Government transport undertaking bus and rail, public transport operator.

Subject coverage: Public transport on the Isle of Man: railway, bus, tram network and workshops.

Publications: Printed

Access to staff: Contact by letter, by telephone, by fax and by e-mail
Hours: Mon to Fri, 0900 to 1700

Access to building: No access other than to staff

Access for disabled people: Toilet facilities

Connections with: Isle of Man Government; Department of Tourism & Leisure, Sea Terminal, Douglas, Isle of Man

Constituent bodies: Isle of Man Bus Service; Isle of Man Railway; Manx Electric Railway; Snaefell Mountain Railway

ISLE OF WIGHT ARCHAEOLOGY AND HISTORIC ENVIRONMENT SERVICE

County Archaeological Centre, 61 Clatterford Road, Carisbrooke, Newport, Isle of Wight, PO30 1NZ

Tel: 01983 823810
Website: www.iwight.com/living_here/planning/archaeology

Organisation type and purpose: A local government body which advises individuals, organisations and the local planning authority on managing, preserving and understanding archaeological remains on the Isle of Wight.

Subject coverage: Archaeology and history of the Isle of Wight.

Collection: Sites and Monuments Record (SMR), a computerised database cataloguing archaeological information, complemented by documentary archives and historic maps, aerial photographs and an archaeological library; access is by prior appointment only

ISLE OF WIGHT CHAMBER OF COMMERCE, TOURISM AND INDUSTRY (IWCCTI)

Mill Court, Furrlongs, Newport, Isle of Wight, PO30 2AA

Tel: 01983 520777
Fax: 01983 554555
E-mail: chamber@iwchamber.co.uk
Website: www.iwchamber.co.uk

Enquiries to: Membership Officer
Direct tel: 01983 554541

Founded: 1910

Organisation type and purpose: Membership association.

Subject coverage: A chamber of commerce for Isle of Wight businesses, business advice and support, export documentation service.

Collection: All relevant business support books, Croner, etc.

Publications: Printed

Access to staff: Contact by e-mail
Hours: Mon to Fri, 0900 to 1700

Access to building: Prior appointment required

Access for disabled people: Parking provided

ISLE OF WIGHT COLLEGE

Medina Way, Newport, Isle of Wight, PO30 5TA

Tel: 01983 526631
Fax: 01983 521707
E-mail: library@iwcollege.ac.uk
Website: www.iwcollege.ac.uk

Enquiries to: Learning Resources Centre Manager
Direct tel: 01983 550789
Direct e-mail: bev.vaughan@iwcollege.ac.uk

Founded: 1954

Organisation type and purpose: College of further education, 6th form and higher education.

Subject coverage: Horticulture, health and community studies, crafts, education, computer studies, engineering, construction, business studies, management, office skills, adult education, travel and tourism, local history, composites, marine engineering, fitness, fashion, performing arts, animal care, A-levels.

Library catalogue: All or part available online

Access to staff: Contact by letter, by telephone, by e-mail and via website. Appointment necessary. Access for members only.
Hours: Term-time: Mon to Thu, 0830 to 1930; Fri 0830 to 1700.
Vacations: Mon to Fri, 0900 to 1400.
Special comments: Use of learning resources centre is for registered College students or members of staff; members of the public can use the LRC for reference only. IT facilities available only to College students and staff.

Access for disabled people: Blue Badge - friendly site: park anywhere as long as parked safely and blue badge displayed; lift between floors.

ISLE OF WIGHT LIBRARIES – REFERENCE LIBRARY

Lord Louis Library, Orchard Street, Newport, Isle of Wight, PO30 1LL

Tel: 01983 823800
Fax: 01983 825972
E-mail: reflib@postmaster.co.uk

Enquiries to: Reference Librarian

Organisation type and purpose: Local government body, public library.

Subject coverage: General, Isle of Wight and related areas, local history, maritime history, local geology and archaeology, European Information Relay, family history.

Collection: Isle of Wight local collection
Maritime collection

Library catalogue: All or part available in-house

Publications: Printed

Access to staff: Contact by letter, by telephone, by fax, by e-mail and in person
Hours: Mon to Wed and Fri, 0930 to 1730; Thu, 1000 to 2000; Sat, 0900 to 1700; Sun, 1000 to 1600

Access for disabled people: Ramped entry, level entry, access to all public areas

Links with: County Library Headquarters; Parkhurst Road, Newport, Isle of Wight, PO30 5TX; tel: 01983 825717; fax: 01983 528047

ISLE OF WIGHT LIBRARY SERVICE

Library Headquarters, 5 Mariners Way, Somerton Industrial Estate, Cowes, Isle of Wight, PO31 8PD

Tel: 01983 203880
Website: www.iwight.gov.uk/thelibrary

Enquiries to: Head of Libraries and Information Services

Founded: 1904

Organisation type and purpose: Local government body, public library, suitable for ages: all.

Subject coverage: General, Isle of Wight and related areas.

Collection: Isle of Wight, music scores, maritime history

Non-library collection catalogue: All or part available in-house

Access to staff: Contact by letter, by telephone, by fax, by e-mail and in person
Hours: Mon to Fri, 0900 to 1700

Access to building: Prior appointment required

Access for disabled people: Ramped entry, access to all public areas

ISLE OF WIGHT RECORD OFFICE

26 Hillside, Newport, Isle of Wight, PO30 2EB

Tel: 01983 823820/823821
Fax: 01983 823820
E-mail: record.office@iow.gov.uk
Website: www.iwight.com/library/record_office
Website: www.a2a.pro.gov.uk

Enquiries to: County Archivist

Founded: 1961

Organisation type and purpose: Local government body.
To preserve archives relating to Isle of Wight and make them available to the public for research purposes.

Subject coverage: Local history and genealogy relating to Isle of Wight.

Collection: Numerous including:
Records of parish churches, nonconformist churches, estates, businesses, local government, schools, hospitals
Census returns, newspapers, copy wills, photographs and maps

Non-library collection catalogue: All or part available online and in-house

Access to staff: Contact by letter, by telephone, by fax, by e-mail, in person and via website
Hours: Mon, 0930 to 1225 and 1300 to 1700; Tue to Fri, 0900 to 1225 and 1300 to 1700
Special comments: Appointment necessary to view material held on microfilm/fiche.

Access for disabled people: Parking provided
Special comments: Telephone Record Office to reserve a parking space. Access to building is possible for wheelchairs, but assistance required.

ISLES OF SCILLY WILDLIFE TRUST (IOSWT)

Carn Thomas, St Mary's, Isles of Scilly, TR21 0PT

Tel: 01720 422153
Fax: 01720 422153
E-mail: enquiries@ios-wildlifetrust.org.uk
Website: www.ios-wildlifetrust.org.uk

Founded: 1986; formerly called Isles of Scilly Environmental Trust (year of change 2001)

Organisation type and purpose: Membership association (membership is by subscription), registered charity (charity number 293512), conservation.

Subject coverage: Wildlife habitat management, satellite environmental records centre.

Publications: Printed
Order printed publications from: the office or the website

Publications list: Available online and in print

Access to staff: Contact by letter, by telephone, by fax, by e-mail and in person. Appointment necessary.
Hours: Mon, Tue and Fri, 1000 to 1600; by appointment for other times

Links with: The Wildlife Trust (UK Office); The Kiln, Waterside, Mather Road, Newark, Nottinghamshire, NG24 1WT; tel: 01636 677711; fax: 01636 670001

ISLINGTON ARCHAEOLOGY AND HISTORY SOCIETY

Formal name: Islington Archaeology and History Society

8 Wynyatt Street, EC1V 7HU

Tel: 020 7833 1541
Website: www.iahs.org.uk

Founded: 1975

Organisation type and purpose: Membership association (membership by subscription).
To arrange lectures, visits and courses in relation to the archaeology and history of the London Borough of Islington.
To publish work on the archaeology and history of the Borough.
To cooperate with local government bodies and other agencies in matters of planning and development within the Borough in order to record and protect Islington's sites that are of archaeological and historical importance.

Publications: Printed

Access to staff: Contact by letter and by telephone

ISLINGTON LIBRARY AND HERITAGE SERVICES

Central Library, 2 Fieldway Crescent, Islington, London, N5 1PF

Tel: 020 7527 6900
Fax: 020 7527 6902
E-mail: library.informationunit@islington.gov.uk
Website: www.islington.gov.uk/libraries

Enquiries to: Information Manager
Direct tel: 020 7527 6922
Direct fax: 020 7527 6926
Direct e-mail: john.smith@islington.gov.uk
Other contacts: Central Reference Librarian (tel: 020 7527 6931)

Organisation type and purpose: Local government body, public library service.

Subject coverage: General, local community information, photography and local history of Islington.

Information services: Online local information directory, online resources – general and business, European information, reference and information library.

Services for disabled people: Adaptive hardware and software in all branches, but especially at Central Reference Library.

Collection: Local History Archive
Joe Orton Book Jacket Collection
Local history archives
Sadlers Wells Collection (at Finsbury library)
Sickert Collection

Trade and statistical information: General collection of trade directories and statistical information

Library catalogue: All or part available online

Publications: Printed
Order printed publications from: Central Reference Library, at the same address; tel: 020 7527 6931; fax: 020 7527 6939; e-mail: centralref.library@islington.gov.uk

Publications list: Available in print

Access to staff: Contact by letter, by telephone, by fax, by e-mail, in person and via website. Appointment necessary.

Access for disabled people: All buildings fully accessible

Branch libraries: Archway Library; Hamlyn House, Highgate Hill, London, N19 5PH; tel: 020 7527 7820; e-mail: archway.library@islington.gov.uk; Finsbury Library; 245 St. John Street, London, EC1V 4NB; tel: 020 7527 7960; e-mail: finsbury.library@islington.gov.uk; John Barnes Library; 275 Camden Road, London, N7 0JN; tel: 020 7527 7900; e-mail: johnbarnes.library@islington.gov.uk; Lewis Carroll Children's Library; 180 Copenhagen Street, London, N1 0ST; tel: 020 7527 7936; e-mail: lewiscarroll.library@islington.gov.uk; Mildmay Library; 21–23 Mildmay Park, London, N1 4NA; tel: 020 7527 7880; e-mail: mildmay.library@islington.gov.uk; N4 Library; 26 Blackstock Road, London, N4 2DW; tel: 020 7527 7800; e-mail: n4.library@islington.gov.uk; North Library; Manor Gardens, London, N7 6JX; tel: 020 7527 7840; e-mail: north.library@islington.gov.uk; South Library; 115–117 Essex Road, London, N1 2SL; tel: 020 7527 7860; e-mail: south.library@islington.gov.uk; West Library; Bridgeman Road, London, N1 1BD; tel: 020 7527 7920; e-mail: west.library@islington.gov.uk

Branch museums: Islington Museum; 245 St John Street, London, EC1V 4NB; tel: 020 7527 3235; e-mail: islington.museum@islington.gov.uk

Branches: First Steps Learning Centre; Central Library, 2 Fieldway Crescent, London, N5 1PF; tel: 020 7527 7002; e-mail: sineadgannon@isonline.org; Islington Computer Skills Centre; Finsbury Library, 245 St. John Street, London, EC1V 4NB; tel: 020 7713 6593; e-mail: info@icskills.co.uk; Islington Local History Centre; Finsbury Library, 245 St. John Street, London, EC1V 4NB; tel: 020 7527 7988; e-mail: local.history@islington.gov.uk

ISMITHERS RAPRA

Formal name: Smithers Rapra Technology Limited

Shawbury, Shrewsbury, Shropshire, SY4 4NR

Tel: 01939 250383
Fax: 01939 251118
E-mail: publications@ismithers.net
Website: www.ismithers.net
Website: www.polymer-books.com

Direct e-mail: cparkinson@ismithers.net

Founded: 1920

Organisation type and purpose: Independent plastics and rubber consultancy; technology and information services; membership association (membership is by subscription); research organisation; publishing house.

Subject coverage: Rubber, plastics and allied fields, synthesis and applications design, additives, processing, properties and testing, market information, chemical resistance, industrial hazards, thermal transition, trade names, adhesives, standards and specifications.

Collection: Porritt and Dawson Collection (on rubbers and plastics)

Non-library collection catalogue: All or part available online

Library catalogue: All or part available online

Publications: Printed
Order printed publications from: Publications Sales

Publications list: Available online and in print

Access to staff: Contact by letter, by telephone, by fax, by e-mail and via website. Appointment necessary. Access for members only. All charged.
Hours: Mon to Fri, 0800 to 1645

Access to building: Prior appointment required

ISO/BIZZARRINI CLUB

47 St Margarets Road, Twickenham, Middlesex, TW1 2LL

Tel: 020 8891 6663
E-mail: iso.bizz@tesco.net

Enquiries to: Secretary

Founded: 1988

Organisation type and purpose: Membership association.

Subject coverage: All aspects (spares, technical and encouragement) of owning and maintaining an ISO or Bizzarrini car.

Access to staff: Contact by letter, by telephone and by e-mail
Hours: Mon to Fri, 0900 to 1700

ISRAEL GOVERNMENT TOURIST OFFICE (IGTO)

UK House, 180 Oxford Street, London, W1D 1NN

Tel: 020 7299 1111
Fax: 020 7299 1112
E-mail: info@igto.co.uk
Website: www.thinkisrael.com

Enquiries to: Office Manager and PA
Direct tel: 020 7299 1100

Organisation type and purpose: National government body.
National government tourist office.
To advertise, sell and promote Israel as a destination for winter sun holidays, pilgrimages, vacations, birdwatching, hiking, etc.

Subject coverage: Holidays in Israel, pilgrimages and Holy Land tours, hotel lists, traveller information, trade information and Israel events.

Collection: Feature article library
Photograph and slide library (CD-ROM)
Video library (DVD)

Trade and statistical information: Data on number of visitors to Israel from United Kingdom and world-wide.
Statistics and data on different type of visitors, i.e. how many arrive as pilgrims, birdwatchers, holiday, etc

Publications: Printed

Access to staff: Contact by letter, by telephone, by fax and by e-mail
Special comments: By appointment only

Parent body: Israel Ministry of Tourism; Jerusalem

ISRAELI EMBASSY

2 Palace Green, London, W8 4QB

Tel: 020 7957 9500
Fax: 020 7957 9555
E-mail: info-sec@london.mfa.gov.il
Website: london.mfa.gov.il

Enquiries to: Information Officer

Organisation type and purpose: National government body.

Access to staff: Contact by letter, by telephone, by fax and by e-mail
Hours: Mon to Thu, 0900 to 1800; Fri, 0900 to 1400

Also at: Israeli Embassy; 15A Old Court Place, London, W8 4PL

ISSB LIMITED

Formal name: Iron and Steel Statistics Bureau

1 Carlton House Terrace, London, SW1Y 5DB

Tel: 020 7343 3900
Fax: 020 7343 3901
E-mail: info@issb.co.uk
Website: www.issb.co.uk

Organisation type and purpose: To provide statistical information on the steel industry and trade in steel and related products including raw materials.

Subject coverage: International steel statistics.

Trade and statistical information: World data on steel production

Publications: Printed

Access to staff: Contact by letter, by telephone, by fax, by e-mail and via website. All charged.
Hours: Mon to Fri, 0900 to 1700

Subsidiary company of: UK Steel Association; Broadway House, Tothill Street, London, SW1H 9NQ; tel: 020 7222 7777; fax: 020 7222 3531; e-mail: enquiries@uksteel.org.uk

ITALIAN CULTURAL INSTITUTE

39 Belgrave Square, London, SW1X 8NX

Tel: 020 73964425
E-mail: library.icilondon@esteri.it
Website: www.bibliowin.it/iic/ICLN
Website: www.icilondon.esteri.it

Founded: 1950

Organisation type and purpose: National government body, membership association (membership is by subscription).
The cultural office of the Italian Embassy.
To promote Italian culture in the United Kingdom.

Subject coverage: General and language studies in Italy; education in Italy; bursaries; music and arts; exhibitions; study qualifications; Italy and events of Italian interest.

Collection: Dante Collection
Italian contemporary fiction and poetry
Collection of videos especially Italian Cinema
Collection of books on Italian art and 19th-/20th-century history
Collection of books for students and teachers for whom Italian is a foreign language

Library catalogue: All or part available online

Access to staff: Contact by letter, by telephone, by fax, by e-mail, in person and via website. Appointment necessary.
Hours: By appointment only; flexible times and dates, but normally Mon to Fri, 1030 to 1330 and 1430 to 1800

ITRI INNOVATION LTD

Unit 3, Curo Park, Frogmore, St. Albans, Hertfordshire, AL2 2DD

Tel: 01727 875544
Fax: 01727 871341
E-mail: info@itri.co.uk
Website: www.lead-free.org
Website: www.itri-innovation.com

Enquiries to: Information Officer
Direct e-mail: jeremy.pearce@itri.co.uk; tony.wallace@itri.co.uk

Founded: 1932; formerly called Tin Technology Ltd (year of change 2008)

Organisation type and purpose: Membership association (membership is by subscription), present number of members: 75, research organisation.

Subject coverage: Tin and its alloys and compounds, and their applications, solder and soldering, tin and tin alloy plating, pewter, bearing metals, whitemetals, tin in cast iron, organo-tins and other tin chemicals, fire retardants, non-toxic ammunition, lead-free wheel weights.

Collection: 40,000 published papers on tin from 1932 – on microfiche

Trade and statistical information: Tin – production information and statistics

Non-library collection catalogue: All or part available online and in-house

Publications: Electronic and video

Publications list: Available in print

Access to staff: Contact by letter, by telephone, by fax, by e-mail and via website. Appointment necessary. Non-members charged.
Hours: Mon to Fri, 0900 to 1645

Access to building: Prior appointment required

Access for disabled people: Parking provided, ramped entry, toilet facilities
ITRI Ltd; Unit 3, Curo Park, Frogmore, St Albans, Hertfordshire, AL2 2DD

IWSC: THE WOOD TECHNOLOGY SOCIETY (IWSc)

Formal name: IWSc: The Wood Technology Society, a Division of the Institute of Materials, Minerals and Mining

! Carlton House Terrace, London, SW1Y 5DB

Tel: 0207 451 7415
Fax: 0207 839 1702
E-mail: apitman@trada.co.uk
Website: www.iom3.org/content/wood-technology

Enquiries to: Executive Advisor, Wood Technology
Direct tel: 07795 561057

Founded: 1955

Organisation type and purpose: Professional body (membership is by qualification, election or invitation), present number of members: 1,400, registered charity.

Subject coverage: The study of timber and wood-based materials.

Information services: Enquiries, loan available to members, referral service.

Special visitor services: Please contact the Library prior to a visit to make an appointment.

Collection: Library consists of approximately 300 text books, directories and Journal of the The Institute of Wood Science and Wood Focus

Library catalogue: All or part available in-house

Publications: Printed

Access to staff: Contact by letter, by telephone, by fax, by e-mail and via website. Appointment necessary.
Hours: Mon to Fri, 0900 to 1700

J S PUBLICATIONS

PO Box 505, Newmarket, Suffolk, CB8 7TF

Tel: 01638 561590
Fax: 01638 560924
E-mail: ukrew@jspubs.com
Website: www.jspubs.com

Enquiries to: Customer Services Manager

Founded: 1988

Organisation type and purpose: Publishing house.

Subject coverage: Publishers of the UK Register of Expert Witnesses, the UK's largest and longest established database of vetted expert witnesses. Recognised by the UK legal profession and various Government bodies, the Register provides a listing of individuals who are both expert in their own field and qualified to give expert evidence in court and write expert reports connected with litigation. Also available is a full range of support services for both instructing solicitors (e.g. assistance in locating a specific expert) and experts themselves (newsletters/factsheets/helpline).

Publications: Printed, and electronic and video

Access to staff: Contact by letter, by telephone, by fax, by e-mail and via website
Hours: Mon to Fri, 0900 to 1700

JACOB SHEEP SOCIETY

14 Mortimer Road, Kenilworth, Warwickshire, CV8 1FR

Tel: 01923 855393
Fax: 01923 855393
E-mail: valhunt@jacobsheep.freeserve.co.uk

Enquiries to: Secretary

Founded: 1979

Organisation type and purpose:
Membership association (membership is by subscription), present number of members: 763, registered charity.
Sheep breed society.

Access to staff: Contact by letter, by telephone and by e-mail
Hours: Mon to Fri, 0930 to 1500

Links with: National Sheep Association (NSA); Malvern, Worcestershire

JAGUAR ENTHUSIASTS' CLUB (JEC)

Abbeywood Office Park, Emma Chris Way, Filton, Bristol, BS34 7JU

Tel: 01179 698186
Fax: 01179 791863
E-mail: jechq@btopenworld.com
Website: www.jec.org.uk

Enquiries to: General Manager
Direct e-mail: graham.searle@btinternet.com

Founded: 1984

Organisation type and purpose:
Membership association.
To maintain and promote interest in Jaguar cars.

Subject coverage: History of Jaguar cars, technical information, insurance, specialist tools, parts, rallies and shows, books and accessories, specialist guide.

Publications: Printed

Access to staff: Contact by letter, by telephone, by fax, by e-mail, in person and via website
Hours: Mon to Fri, 0800 to 1700

JAMAICA TRADE COMMISSION (JAMPRO)

Formal name: Jamaica Promotions Corporation

1 Prince Consort Road, London, SW7 2BZ

Tel: 020 7584 8894
Fax: 020 7823 9886
E-mail: jamhigh@jhcuk.com
Website: www.investjamaica.com

Enquiries to: Trade Commissioner

Organisation type and purpose:
International organisation, national government body, manufacturing industry, service industry.
Investment; trade; promotion.

Subject coverage: Trade and investment information in Jamaica.

Access to staff: Contact by letter, by telephone, by fax, by e-mail and via website. Appointment necessary.
Hours: Mon to Fri, 0930 to 1700

JANE AUSTEN SOCIETY

20 Parsonage Rd, Henfield, W. Sussex, BNS 9JG

Tel: 01273 494210
E-mail: hq@jasoc.org.uk
Website: www.janeaustensociety.org.uk

Enquiries to: Honorary Secretary

Founded: 1940

Organisation type and purpose: Learned society (membership is by subscription), present number of members: 1,700 UK, 350 overseas, registered charity (charity number 1040613).

Subject coverage: Life and works of Jane Austen, the Austen family, English literature, Georgian history and female novelists of the 18th and 19th centuries.

Collection: Collection of documents, books and memorabilia held at Jane Austen's house and museum at Chawton, Hampshire; tel or fax: 01420 83626

Publications list: Available online and in print

Access to staff: Contact by letter, by telephone and by e-mail
Hours: Mon to Fri, 0900 to 1700

Branches: 10 branches in the UK and overseas societies in Australia, Canada, the USA, and Japan

JANE'S INFORMATION GROUP (Jane's)

Sentinel House, 163 Brighton Road, Coulsdon, Surrey, CR5 2YH

Tel: 020 8700 3700
Fax: 020 8763 1006
Website: www.janes.com/
Website: catalogue.janes.com

Enquiries to: PR Manager
Direct tel: 020 8700 3745
Direct e-mail: amanda.castle@janes.com

Founded: 1898

Organisation type and purpose:
International organisation, publishing house.
Publishers of defence, transport and law enforcement information to governments, militaries, businesses and universities worldwide.

Subject coverage: Technical specifications, quantities, details of manufacturers and users of defence, aerospace and law enforcement, terrorism and security as well as transportation equipment; geopolitical and strategic information. Also analysis and consulting services are offered in all mentioned areas.

Collection: Back numbers of Jane's Yearbooks

Non-library collection catalogue: All or part available online and in print

Publications: Printed, and electronic and video, and microform publications

Publications list: Available online and in print

Access to staff: Contact by letter, by telephone, by fax, by e-mail and via website. Appointment necessary. All charged.
Hours: Mon to Fri, 0900 to 1700

Access to building: Prior appointment required

Access for disabled people: Parking provided, level entry, access to all public areas, toilet facilities

Parent body: The Woodbridge Company Limited

JANSSEN-CILAG LIMITED

PO Box 79, Saunderton, High Wycombe, Buckinghamshire, HP14 4HJ

Tel: 01494 567444
Fax: 01494 567445
E-mail: medinfo@janssen-cilag.co.uk
Website: www.janssen-cilag.co.uk

continued overleaf

Enquiries to: Information Officer

Organisation type and purpose: Trade association, research organisation.

Subject coverage: Pharmaceutical medicine: gastroenterology, antifungals, anaesthesia, drug safety, psychiatry, pain, neurology.

Part of: Johnson and Johnson

JAPAN FOUNDATION

Formal name: Kokusai Koryu Kikin (in Japanese)

Russell Square House, 10–12 Russell Square, London, WC1B 5EH

Tel: 020 7436 6695
Fax: 020 7323 4888
E-mail: info@jpf.org.uk

Enquiries to: Assistant Programme Officer

Founded: 1972

Organisation type and purpose: Promotion of Japanese culture overseas through various grant programmes.

Subject coverage: Japanese culture, enquiries may be referred to the appropriate organisations.

Collection: Reference books

Publications: Printed

Access to staff: Contact by letter, by telephone, by fax, by e-mail and in person. Appointment necessary.
Hours: Mon to Fri, 0930 to 1730

Parent body: Japan Foundation (Kokusai Koryu Kikin); Ark Mori Building, 1–12–32 Akasaka, Minato-ku, Tokyo, 107, Japan

JAPAN NATIONAL TOURIST ORGANIZATION (JNTO)

Heathcoat House, 20 Savile Row, London, W1S 3PR

Tel: 020 7734 9638
Fax: 020 7734 4290
E-mail: info@jnto.co.uk
Website: www.jnto.go.jp

Enquiries to: Public Relations Manager
Other contacts: Deputy Director

Founded: 1953

Organisation type and purpose: National government body.
Tourist office.
Promoting Japan as a business and leisure travel destination. Offering information and advice to people planning to visit Japan.

Subject coverage: All areas of travel to and within Japan including transport (rail, air, ferry, bus), accommodation, attractions, resorts, places to visit, package holidays and tours, travelling on a budget, food, shopping, climate, etc; festivals, events, conventions, conferences and exhibitions in Japan, conference and convention facilities; other information.

Collection: Films, videos and slides

Trade and statistical information: Statistics on number of visitors to Japan (by country and purpose of visit) and on number of Japanese overseas travellers

Non-library collection catalogue: All or part available in-house

Publications: Printed

Publications list: Available in print

Access to staff: Contact by telephone, by fax, by e-mail and in person
Hours: Mon to Fri, 0930 to 1730
Special comments: Closed on some Japanese National Holidays.

Links with: Asia Travel Marketing Association; Association of National Tourist Office Representatives; Pacific Asia Travel Association

Parent body: Japan National Tourist Organization; 2–10–1 Yuraku-cho, Chiyoda-ku, Tokyo, 100, Japan

JAPAN SOCIETY OF THE UK

Formal name: Japan Society of the UK

Swire House, 59 Buckingham Gate, London, SW1E 1AJ

Tel: 020 7828 6330
Fax: 020 7828 6331
E-mail: info@japansociety.org.uk
Website: www.japansociety.org.uk/

Enquiries to: Office Director
Direct e-mail: john.toppon@japansociety.org.uk

Founded: 1891

Organisation type and purpose:
Membership organisation and information service.
To enhance Anglo-Japanese relations with the aim of providing a better mutual understanding of the cultures, societies and businesses of Japan and the United Kingdom.
Registered charity (charity number 1063952)

Subject coverage: Anglo-Japanese relations

Collection: Library of 6,000 vols

Library catalogue: All or part available online

Access to staff: Contact by letter, by telephone, by fax, by e-mail and via website. Appointment necessary.

Access to building: *Special comments:* Library: Wed, 1400 to 1700; Fri, 1200 to 1500

JAPANESE CHAMBER OF COMMERCE AND INDUSTRY IN THE UNITED KINGDOM (JCCI)

5th Floor, Salisbury House, 29 Finsbury Circus, London, EC2M 5QQ

Tel: 020 7628 0069
Fax: 020 7374 2280
E-mail: chamber@jcci.org.uk
Website: www.jcci.org.uk

Enquiries to: Manager (Research and PR)

Founded: 1959

Organisation type and purpose: Trade association (membership is by subscription). Chamber of Commerce for Japanese companies in the United Kingdom.

Subject coverage: Japanese commercial interests in the United Kingdom; United Kingdom trade with Japan.

Access to staff: Contact by letter, by telephone, by fax and by e-mail. Appointment necessary.
Hours: Mon to Fri, 0930 to 1230 and 1330 to 1730

Access to building: Prior appointment required

JAPANESE CONSULATE-GENERAL

2 Melville Crescent, Edinburgh, EH3 7HW

Tel: 0131 225 4777
Fax: 0131 225 4828
Website: www.edinburgh.uk.emb-japan.go.jp

Enquiries to: Consul-General

Founded: 1991

Organisation type and purpose: Diplomatic mission.

Subject coverage: Information relating to Japan (information section), passports, visas, etc. (consular section).

Publications: Printed

Access to staff: Contact by letter, by telephone and by fax. Appointment necessary.
Hours: Mon to Fri, 0930 to 1300 and 1430 to 1730

Parent body: Ministry for Foreign Affairs; Tokyo, Japan

JAPANESE EMBASSY (JICC)

Japan Information and Cultural Centre, 101–104 Piccadilly, London, W1V 9FN

Tel: 020 7465 6500
Fax: 020 7465 6546
E-mail: info@ld.mofa.go.jp
Website: www.embjapan.org.uk

Enquiries to: Information Officer

Organisation type and purpose: National government body.

Subject coverage: All cultural aspects of Japan, lists of specialised companies or organisations for specific requests.

Collection: Small library (no appointment necessary, open to the public, Mon to Fri, 0930 to 1245 and 1430 to 1700)
Slide, video and artefact collections for schools and organisation (apply in writing, free of charge)

Trade and statistical information: Basic statistics on culture, population and economy

Publications: Printed

Access to staff: Contact by letter, by telephone, by fax, by e-mail and via website. Appointment necessary.
Hours: Mon to Fri, 0930 to 1300 and 1430 to 1700
Special comments: Slides, videos, etc only to organisations not individuals; does not provide tourist information.

JENNIFER TRUST FOR SPINAL MUSCULAR ATROPHY (JTSMA)

40 Cygnet Court, Timothy's Bridge Rd, Stratford-upon-Avon, Warwickshire, CV37 9NW

Tel: 01789 267520
Fax: 01789 268371
E-mail: office@jtsma.org.uk
Website: www.jtsma.org.uk

Enquiries to: Information Officer

Founded: 1985

Organisation type and purpose: Charitable org. (No. 1106815) UK-wide cover. Informs, supports and empowers families and individuals affected by all forms of SMA and raises awareness of the condition. Free services. Small experienced and qualified support services team – contact by phone or email. If newly diagnosed, an Outreach Worker can visit. Has a network of peer support volunteers all with personal experience and understanding of SMA. Also funds and supports the research community addressing the causes, treatment and management of SMA. Free membership upon application but do not have to be a member to use services.

Subject coverage: Information and support re: living with spinal muscular atrophy.

Library catalogue: All or part available in print

Publications: Printed
Order printed publications from: www.jtsma.org.uk

Publications list: Available online and in print

Access to staff: Contact by letter, by telephone, by fax, by e-mail and via website
Hours: Mon to Fri, 09.00 to 16.30

Access to building: Wheelchair accessible

JEROME K JEROME SOCIETY (JKJ Society)

Tony Gray, Fraser Wood, Mayo & Pinson, 15 Lichfield Street, Walsall, West Midlands, WS1 1TS

Tel: 01922 627077
Fax: 01922 721065
E-mail: tonygray@jkj.demon.co.uk
Website: www.jeromekjerome.com

Enquiries to: Honorary Secretary
Direct tel: 07801 788532

Founded: 1984

Organisation type and purpose: Learned society (membership is by subscription), present number of members: 150, registered charity (charity number 517057).
To stimulate interest in Jerome's works; access to the author's birthplace in Belsize House, Bradford St, Walsall.

Subject coverage: Life and works of Jerome Klapka Jerome (1859–1927), novelist and playwright.

Publications: Printed
Order printed publications from: Order the hb book from e-mail: or idlethoughts@jeromekjerome.comjeremy@jeremynicholas.com

Access to staff: Contact by letter, by fax, by e-mail and via website
Hours: Mon to Fri, 0900 to 1700

Access to building: By prior appointment with Yvette Fletcher, tel: 01922 633214
Hours: Mon to Fri, 0900 to 1700, subject to prior appointment

JERSEY ARCHIVE

Clarence Road, St Helier, Jersey, JE2 4JY, Channel Islands

Tel: 01534 833300
Fax: 01534 833101
E-mail: archives@jerseyheritage.org
Website: www.jerseyheritage.org

Founded: 1993

Organisation type and purpose: Archive or Record Office.

Subject coverage: The written history of Jersey.

Collection: The Jersey Archive collects and preserves the records of the States of Jersey, States Committees and Departments, The Royal Court, The Lieutenant Governor, parishes, churches, businesses, societies and individuals relating to the Island.

Non-library collection catalogue: All or part available online and in-house

Publications: Printed

Access to staff: Contact by letter, by telephone, by fax, by e-mail, in person and via website
Hours: Tue to Thu, 0900 to 1700; last Thu of month, 0900 to 1900; 3rd Saturday of month, 0900 to 1300

Access to building: No prior appointment required
Special comments: Passport or driving licence required as ID on first visit

Access for disabled people: Full disabled access, parking provided, level entry, toilet facilities
Special comments: Hearing Loop; lift to Reading Rooms.

Links with: Jersey Heritage Trust; Jersey Museum, The Weighbridge, St Helier, Jersey, JE2 3NF, Channel Islands; tel: 01534 633300; fax: 01534 633301

JERSEY LIBRARY

Halkett Place, St Helier, Jersey, JE2 4WH, Channel Islands

Tel: 01534 448700
Fax: 01534 448730
E-mail: je.library@gov.je
Website: www.gov.je/library

Enquiries to: Chief Librarian

Founded: 1743

Organisation type and purpose: Public library.

Subject coverage: Channel Islands bibliography and history, geography, archaeology, particularly the Bailiwick of Jersey.

Collection: 17th- and 18th-century belles lettres and religion
Falle Collection

Library catalogue: All or part available online and in-house

Access to staff: Contact by letter, by telephone, by fax, by e-mail and in person
Hours: Mon, Wed, Thu, Fri, 0930 to 1730; Tue, 0930 to 1930; Sat, 0930 to 1600

Access for disabled people: Level entry, access to all public areas, toilet facilities

JERSEY TOURISM

Liberation Square, St Helier, Jersey, JE1 1BB, Channel Islands

Tel: 01534 500700
Fax: 01534 500899
E-mail: info@jersey.com

Organisation type and purpose: National government body.

Subject coverage: Jersey.

Publications list: Available online

Access to staff: Contact by e-mail
Hours: Mon to Fri, 0900 to 1700

Access for disabled people: Ramped entry

JESUS COLLEGE OLD LIBRARY

Jesus College, Cambridge, CB5 8BL

Tel: 01223 339405
Fax: 01223 324910
E-mail: access@jesus.cam.ac.uk
Website: www.jesus.cam.ac.uk

Enquiries to: Keeper or Assistant Keeper of the Old Library
Direct tel: 01223 339427
Direct e-mail: sch1000@hermes.cam.ac.uk (Keeper)
Other contacts: archives@jesus.cam.ac.uk; f.willmoth@jesus.cam.ac.uk (Assistant Keeper)

Founded: c.1500; formerly called The Library, Jesus College (year of change 1912)

Organisation type and purpose: Historic library of a college of University of Cambridge.

Subject coverage: Subjects directly related to University studies prior to 1900, especially theology, classics, mathematics and law.

Information services: Queries by post, telephone or e-mail will be answered; e-mailers please give postal address.

Collection: Medieval manuscripts
Military books of the 16th–18th centuries
Malthus Collection, deriving from T. R. Malthus (1766–1834) and his relatives

Non-library collection catalogue: All or part available in print

Library catalogue: All or part available in-house

Access to staff: Contact by letter and by e-mail. Appointment necessary. Letter of introduction required.
Hours: Mon, Tue, Thu, Fri, 1000 to 1300 and 1415 to 1700
Special comments: The Assistant Keeper shares her time between the Old Library and the College Archives (tel: 01223 339439).

Access to building: Prior appointment required

Access for disabled people: Disabled access can be provided, but is slow to operate

JETRO LONDON (JETRO)

Formal name: Japan External Trade Organisation

Japan Trade Centre, MidCity Place, 71 High Holborn, London, WC1V 6AL

Tel: 020 7421 8300

continued overleaf

Fax: 020 7421 0009
E-mail: ldnresearch@jetro.go.jp
Website: www.jetro.go.jp/uk
Website: www.jetro.go.jp

Enquiries to: Information Officer

Founded: 1958

Organisation type and purpose: International organisation.
Japanese government-related trade promotion organisation.

Subject coverage: Promotion of trade between Japan and the UK.

Trade and statistical information: Statistics related to Japan

Library catalogue: All or part available in-house

Publications: Printed, and electronic and video
Order printed publications from: Japan External Trade Organisation, 2–5 Toranomon 2-chome, Minato-ku, Tokyo, 105–8466, Japan; tel: +81 3 3582 5511; fax: +81 3 3587 0219
OCS Tokyo (door-to-door delivery service), 2–9 Shibaura, Minato-ku, Tokyo, 108–8701, Japan; tel: +81 3 5476 8131; fax: +81 3 3453 8091
Public Relations Department (for advice first), JETRO London; tel: 020 7470 4700; fax: 020 7491 7570

Publications list: Available online and in print

Access to staff: Contact by letter and by fax. Appointment necessary.
Hours: Mon to Fri, 0930 to 1230 and 1330 to 1730
Special comments: If contacting by fax, give full address as reply is by letter.

Access to building: Prior appointment required
Hours: Mon to Fri, 0930 to 1230 and 1400 to 1630

Funded by: Ministry of Economy, Trade and Industry, Japan

JEWEL & ESK COLLEGE (JEC)

Edinburgh Campus, 24 Milton Road East, Edinburgh, EH15 2PP

Tel: 0131 344 7000
Fax: 0131 344 7001
E-mail: pmccafferty@jec.ac.uk
Website: www.jec.ac.uk

Enquiries to: Marketing Officer
Direct tel: 0131 344 7199
Direct e-mail: marketing@jec.ac.uk

Founded: 1987; formerly called Jewel & Esk Valley College (year of change 2007)

Organisation type and purpose: Local government body, suitable for ages: 12+, training organisation.
Further education college.

Subject coverage: Business and management studies, office systems and administration, hairdressing and hospitality, caring studies, video production studies, educational support, computing and music, general education, mathematics and science, electronic engineering, electrical engineering, building, manufacturing, plant and instrumentation, sport and leisure, safety and first aid.

Information services: tel: 0131 344 7152

Special visitor services: tel: 0131 344 7405

Education services: tel: 0131 344 7166

Services for disabled people: tel: 0131 344 7405

Non-library collection catalogue: All or part available online, in-house and in print

Library catalogue: All or part available online and in-house

Publications: Printed, and electronic and video

Publications list: Available online and in print

Access to staff: Contact by letter, by telephone, by fax, by e-mail, in person and via website
Hours: Mon to Fri, 0830 to 1630

Access to building: No prior appointment required
Hours: Edinburgh Campus: Mon, Fri, 0845 to 1630, Tue, Wed, Thu, 0845 to 1930
Midlothian Campus: Mon to Fri, 0845 to 1630

Access for disabled people: Parking provided, ramped entry, level entry, access to all public areas, toilet facilities

Also at: Jewel & Esk College; Midlothian Campus, 46 Dalhousie Road, Dalkeith, Midlothian, EH22 3FR; tel: 0131 344 7000; e-mail: info@jevc.ac.uk

Parent body: Lothian Region Department of Education

JEWELLERY DISTRIBUTORS' ASSOCIATION (JDA)

Federation House, 10 Vyse Street, Birmingham, B18 6LT

Tel: 0121 237 1100
Fax: 0121 236 3921
E-mail: secretariat@jda.org.uk
Website: www.jda.org.uk

Enquiries to: Manager

Founded: 1947

Organisation type and purpose: Trade association (membership is by subscription).
The Jewellery Distributors Association is the national trade body for distributors and wholesalers of precious and fashion jewellery.

Subject coverage: Product – fashion and precious jewellery.

Publications list: Available in print

Access to staff: Contact by letter, by telephone, by fax, by e-mail and in person
Hours: Mon to Fri, 0900 to 1700

Access for disabled people: Parking provided, ramped entry, level entry, access to all public areas, toilet facilities
Special comments: Lift.

Parent body: British Jewellery and Giftware Federation Limited; at the same address; tel: 0121 236 2657; fax: 0121 236 3921

JEWISH BLIND AND DISABLED (JBD)

35 Langstone Way, London, NW7 1GT

Tel: 020 8371 6611
Fax: 020 8371 4225
E-mail: info@jbd.org
Website: www.jbd.org

Founded: 1969

Organisation type and purpose: National organisation, voluntary organisation, registered charity (charity number 259480).

Subject coverage: Welfare services, particularly sheltered housing, for Jewish blind or disabled people, couples or families.

Publications: Printed

Access to staff: Contact by letter, by telephone, by fax, by e-mail and via website
Hours: Mon to Thu, 0905 to 1730; Fri, 0905 to 1400

Access for disabled people: Parking provided, ramped entry, level entry, access to all public areas, toilet facilities

JEWISH CARE

Amelie House, Maurice and Vivienne Wohl Campus, 221 Golders Green Road, London, NW11 9DQ

Tel: 020 8922 2222, 020 8922 2233 (minicom)
Fax: 020 8922 1998
E-mail: info@jcare.org
Website: www.jewishcare.org

Enquiries to: Jewish Care Direct
Direct tel: 020 8922 2222
Direct fax: 020 8922 1998
Direct e-mail: info@jcare.org

Founded: 1990

Organisation type and purpose: Voluntary organisation, registered charity (charity number 802559).
Voluntary association.
Provides a wide range of social services for the Jewish Community living in Greater London and the South East.

Subject coverage: Information on all Jewish Care Resource Centres including: residential homes, day centres, social services, home care, specialist services, including services for people who are mentally ill, physically disabled, visually impaired, as well as Holocaust survivors and refugees.

Collection: Archive material on Jewish Welfare Board and Jewish Blind Society dating back to 1819 held at University of Southampton

Publications: Printed

Access to staff: Contact by letter and by e-mail
Hours: Mon to Fri, 0900 to 1730

Access to building: Prior appointment required

Access for disabled people: Level entry, toilet facilities

Affiliated to: Central Council for Jewish Social Service

Trustees for: Relief of the Jewish Poor Registered

JEWISH EAST END CELEBRATION SOCIETY (JEECS)

PO Box 57317, London, E1 3WG

E-mail: enquiries@jeecs.org.uk
Website: www.jeecs.org.uk

Organisation type and purpose: A registered charity (no. 1107714), with membership by subscription, which focuses on Jewish life and culture in the East End of London, documenting past Jewish life and preserving the area's Jewish heritage, and reinvigorating and supporting current Jewish life through education, events, publications and good relations with other cultures represented in the area.

Subject coverage: Jewish life and culture in the East End of London.

Publications: Printed

JEWISH EDUCATION BUREAU (JEB)

8 Westcombe Avenue, Leeds, West Yorkshire, LS8 2BS

Tel: 0345 567 40 70
Fax: 0845 003 5370
E-mail: jeb@jewisheducationbureau.co.uk
Website: www.jewisheducationbureau.co.uk

Enquiries to: Director
Direct e-mail: rabbi@jewisheducationbureau.co.uk

Founded: 1974

Organisation type and purpose: Consultancy.
Promotes the study of Judaism as a world religion in British schools and colleges through religious education, multicultural education and the humanities.

Subject coverage: Judaism; anti-Semitism, especially the Holocaust; Israel.

Education services: Visits to schools and colleges; visits to synagogues arranged.

Collection: Collection of books on the Holocaust, women, stories, inter-faith dialogue, Anglo-Jewry.

Library catalogue: All or part available in print

Access to staff: Contact by telephone and by e-mail. Appointment necessary. All charged.
Hours: Mon to Fri, 0900 to 1700

Links with: Consultation of Northern Religious Education Centres; Professional Council for Religious Education

JEWISH HISTORICAL SOCIETY OF ENGLAND (JHSE)

33 Seymour Place, London, W1H 5AP

Tel: 020 7723 5852
Fax: 020 7723 5852
E-mail: info@jhse.org
Website: www.jhse.org

Enquiries to: Administrator
Other contacts: Board of Deputies of British Jews for general Jewish queries.

Founded: 1893

Organisation type and purpose: International organisation, learned society (membership is by subscription), present number of members: 720, registered charity (charity number 217331).

Subject coverage: Anglo-Jewish history.

Collection: Library is the Mocatta Library which is now the University College London, Jewish Studies Library

Publications: Printed

Access to staff: Contact by letter, by telephone, by fax and by e-mail. Appointment necessary.
Hours: Answerphone service
Special comments: 15 hours weekly, on various days

Links with: Anglo-Jewish Archives

JEWISH MARRIAGE COUNCIL (JMC)

23 Ravenshurst Avenue, London, NW4 4EE

Tel: 020 8203 6311
Fax: 020 8203 8727
E-mail: info@jmc-uk.org

Enquiries to: Director

Founded: 1946

Organisation type and purpose: National organisation, voluntary organisation, registered charity (charity number 1078723). Recognised by the Lord Chancellor's Department, Office of the Chief Rabbi and local authorities.

Subject coverage: Marriage preparation, guidance and counselling; family and individual counselling, divorce counselling, marriage bureau and divorce advisory service, mediation service.

Publications: Printed

Publications list: Available in print

Access to staff: Contact by letter, by telephone, by fax and by e-mail
Hours: Mon to Fri, 0935 to 1730
Special comments: Closes at 1400 on Fridays in winter.

Access for disabled people: Ramped entry

Branch office: Jewish Marriage Council (JMC); Nicky Alliance Centre, 85 Middleton Road, Manchester, M8 4JY; tel: 0161 740 5764

JEWISH MUSIC INSTITUTE (JMI)

Room 536 SOAS, University of London, Thornhaugh Street, Russell Square, London, WC1H OXG

Tel: 0207 898 4307
E-mail: jewishmusic@jmi.org.uk
Website: www.jmi.org.uk

Enquiries to: Administrator
Direct tel: 0207 898 4307
Other contacts: Events Co-ordinator

Founded: 1983; formerly called Jewish Music Heritage Trust

Organisation type and purpose: An independent, non-religious arts organisation with charitable status, based at the University of London's School of Oriental and African Studies (SOAS) and working closely with the School's Department of Music and the SOAS library. The institute documents, preserves and teaches all aspects of the Jewish musical heritage, and presents that heritage to the public, supporting university courses and running workshops, summer schools, regular classes and outreach projects. Aims to provide an international focus for study and musicianship through such initiatives as the International Forum for Suppressed Music, the International Forum for Yiddish Culture and the Forum for the Promotion of Arab-Jewish Dialogue through Music.

Subject coverage: All aspects of the Jewish musical heritage, including liturgical, classical, ethnic and folk music and music suppressed by the Nazi and Soviet regimes.

Education services: Summer schools, regular classes and events.

Collection: Library of recordings, books, manuscripts and scores in all genres of Jewish music, dating from the Middle Ages to the present

Access to staff: Contact by letter, by fax, by e-mail and via website

JOCKEY CLUB

151 Shaftesbury Avenue, London, WC2H 8AL

Tel: 020 7189 3800
Fax: 020 7189 3801
E-mail: info@thejockeyclub.co.uk
Website: www.thejockeyclub.co.uk

Enquiries to: Public Relations Officer

Founded: 1752

Organisation type and purpose: National organisation (membership is by election or invitation).
Regulatory body for horseracing in Great Britain.
To set and maintain standards for racing, to support the British Horseracing Board in administering and developing the best interests of horseracing and breeding.

Subject coverage: Safety and welfare of horse and rider, licensing individuals and racecourses, and compiling and applying rules of racing.

Access to staff: Contact by letter, by telephone, by fax and by e-mail
Hours: Mon to Fri, 0900 to 1700

JODRELL BANK OBSERVATORY

Jodrell Bank, Lower Withington, Macclesfield, Cheshire, SK11 9DL

Tel: 01477 571321
Fax: 01477 571618
Website: www.jb.man.ac.uk

Enquiries to: Public Relations Manager

Founded: 1957

Organisation type and purpose: University department or institute, research organisation.

Subject coverage: Astronomy; radio astronomy techniques, radio telescope design and control, low noise receive-systems, long and short baseline interferometry; signal processing and computing techniques; galactic structure;

continued overleaf

hydrogen line observations; radio sources and source surveys and identifications; pulsars; radio stars; active galactic nuclei; radio galaxies; quasars; cosmic microwave background.

Access to staff: Contact by letter
Hours: Mon to Fri, 0900 to 1700

Part of: Department of Physics and Astronomy, University of Manchester

JOHANN STRAUSS SOCIETY OF GREAT BRITAIN

12 Bishams Court, Church Hill, Caterham, Surrey, CR3 6SE

Tel: 01883 349681
E-mail: strauss.sec@btinternet.com

Enquiries to: Honorary Secretary

Founded: 1964

Organisation type and purpose: Learned society (membership is by subscription), present number of members: 550, voluntary organisation.
Musical appreciation society.

Subject coverage: History of the Strauss family and their music, performance and recording of lesser-known works of the Strauss family and their Viennese contemporaries.

Publications: Printed

Access to staff: Contact by letter and by telephone
Hours: Mon to Fri, 0900 to 1700

Affiliated to other: Johann Strauss Societies in Vienna, France, Germany, Italy, Japan, Poland, Southern Africa, Sweden, Australia, Romania, Czech Republic and Slovakia

JOHN BUCHAN SOCIETY (JBSoc)

The Toft, 37 Waterloo Road, Lanark, ML11 7QH

Tel: 01555 662103
E-mail: glennismac2000@yahoo.co.uk
Website: www.johnbuchansociety.co.uk

Enquiries to: Honorary Secretary

Founded: 1979

Organisation type and purpose: Learned society, voluntary organisation.
To promote a wider understanding and appreciation of the life and works of John Buchan and to support the John Buchan Centre at Broughton, near Peebles.

Non-library collection catalogue: All or part available in-house

Publications: Printed

Access to staff: Contact by letter, by telephone and by e-mail. Access for members only.
Hours: Mon to Fri, 0900 to 1700

JOHN CABOT CITY TECHNOLOGY COLLEGE (John Cabot CTC)

Formal name: John Cabot City Technology College Bristol Trust

Woodside Road, Kingswood, South Gloucestershire, BS15 8BD

Tel: 0117 976 3000
Fax: 0117 976 0630
E-mail: info@cabot.ac.uk
Website: www.cabot.ac.uk

Enquiries to: Principal

Founded: 1993

Organisation type and purpose: Suitable for ages: 11 to 19.
Independent state maintained secondary school.

Subject coverage: Specialist education in maths, science and technology.

Publications: Printed

Access to staff: Contact by letter
Hours: Hire of facilities out of hours

JOHN CLARE SOCIETY

9 The Chase, Ely, Cambridgeshire, CB6 3DR

Tel: 01353 668438 (evenings)
Website: vzone.virgin.net/linda.curry/jclare
Website: human.ntu.ac.uk/clare.html
Website: www.johnclare.org.uk

Enquiries to: Honorary Secretary
Other contacts: Chairman for website, e-mail, linked to university.

Founded: 1981

Organisation type and purpose: International organisation, learned society (membership is by subscription), present number of members: 650, voluntary organisation.

Subject coverage: Promoting the study of the life and works of John Clare, poet (1793–1864).

Collection: None owned by the Society but note:
Manuscripts and books (at Northampton Central Reference Library)
Manuscripts (the largest collection at Peterborough Museum)

Publications: Printed

Publications list: Available online and in print

Access to staff: Contact by letter and by telephone
Hours: Mon to Fri, 0900 to 1700
Special comments: Enquiries by letter enclosing sae please.

Autonomous affiliate: John Clare Society of North America; Executive Director, Department of English, University of Maryland, Baltimore County, Baltimore, MD21250, USA; tel: 00 1 410 455 2164

Member of: The Alliance of Literary Societies; Hon. Secretary, 71 Stepping Stones Road, Coventry, CV5 8JT

JOHN FROST NEWSPAPERS

Formal name: John Frost Newspapers Limited

22B Rosemary Avenue, Enfield, Middlesex, EN2 0SS

Tel: 020 8366 1392/0946
Fax: 020 8366 1379
E-mail: andrew@johnfrostnewspapers.com
Website: www.johnfrostnewspapers.co.uk
Website: www.johnfrostnewspapers.com

Enquiries to: Archivist

Founded: 1965

Organisation type and purpose: Research organisation.
In depth files on crime, royalty, war, politics, pop.

Subject coverage: UK and overseas newspapers reporting outstanding events since 1640 – political, economy, royalty, disasters, crime, sport, war, etc.

Collection: 100,000 press cuttings reporting historic and outstanding events, from 1640 to present day
100,000 newspapers: British and overseas

Publications: Printed

Publications list: Available online and in print

Access to staff: Contact by letter, by telephone and by fax. Appointment necessary.
Hours: Mon to Fri, 0900 to 1700

Access to building: Prior appointment required

Access for disabled people: Toilet facilities

Also at: John Frost Newspapers; 8 Monks Avenue, New Barnet, Hertfordshire, EN5 1DB; tel: 020 8440 3159

JOHN INNES CENTRE AND SAINSBURY LABORATORY (JIC)

Norwich Research Park, Colney, Norwich, Norfolk, NR4 7UH

Tel: 01603 450000
Fax: 01603 450045
Website: www.jic.bbsrc.ac.uk

Enquiries to: Librarian
Direct e-mail: jic.library@bbsrc.ac.uk
Other contacts: Archivist for Historical Collections Librarian.

Founded: 1994

Organisation type and purpose: Registered charity (charity number 223852), research organisation.

Subject coverage: Mostly at postgraduate level and above, currently includes classical botany, horticulture, crop plants, plant breeding, classical and molecular plant genetics, plant genome mapping, plant biochemistry, physiology and cell biology, plant virology and pathology and plant biotechnology. In addition, we hold material on microbial genetics (notably Streptomyces and Rhizobium), nitrogen fixation and enzymology, bioinorganic chemistry, history of genetics, history of plant sciences.

Collection: Cyril Darlington Library
History of Genetics Library
John Innes reprint collection and archives
John Innes Trustees' collection of rare botanical books
William Bateson Library and letters

Non-library collection catalogue: All or part available online and in print

Library catalogue: All or part available in-house

Publications: Printed

Access to staff: Contact by telephone and by e-mail. Appointment necessary. Non-members charged.

Hours: Mon to Fri, 0900 to 1700

Access to building: Prior appointment required

Grant-aided by: Biotechnology and Biological Sciences Research Council (BBSRC)

JOHN INNES MANUFACTURERS ASSOCIATION (JIMA)

Horticulture House, 19 High Street, Theale, Reading, Berkshire, RG7 5AH

E-mail: john.innes@the-hta.org.uk
Website: www.johninnes.info

Enquiries to: Secretary and PR Officer

Founded: 1977

Organisation type and purpose: Trade association.

Subject coverage: Loam-based potting mixes and related growing media for both amateur gardening and professional growers in the United Kingdom.

Publications: Printed

Publications list: Available online and in print

Access to staff: Contact by letter, by telephone, by fax and by e-mail. Appointment necessary.
Hours: Mon to Fri, 0900 to 1800

JOHN LEWIS PARTNERSHIP

171 Victoria Street, London, SW1E 5NN

Tel: 020 7828 1000
Website: www.waitrose.com
Website: www.johnlewis.com
Website: www.johnlewispartnership.co.uk

Enquiries to: Manager, Business Information
Direct tel: 020 7592 6219
Direct fax: 020 7592 6294
Direct e-mail: business_information@johnlewis.co.uk

Organisation type and purpose: Service industry.
Retail business run on co-operative principles.

Subject coverage: Retailing; industrial democracy.

Trade and statistical information: Weekly trading figures for John Lewis plc are published in The Gazette of the John Lewis Partnership and on the corporate website

Library catalogue: All or part available in-house

Access to staff: Appointment necessary.
Hours: Mon to Fri, 0900 to 1700

Access to building: Prior appointment required

JOHN MEADE FALKNER SOCIETY (JMF Soc)

Greenmantle, Main Street, Kings Newton, Melbourne, Derbyshire, DE73 8BX

Tel: 01332 865315
E-mail: nebuly@hotmail.co.uk
Website: www.johnmeadefalknersociety.co.uk

Enquiries to: Honorary Secretary

Founded: 1999

Organisation type and purpose: Learned society (membership is by subscription), present number of members: 56, voluntary organisation.
To promote the appreciation and study of John Meade Falkner's life, times and works.

Library catalogue: All or part available in-house

Publications: Printed
Order printed publications from: Honorary Secretary

Publications list: Available online

Access to staff: Contact by letter, by telephone, by e-mail and via website
Hours: Mon to Fri, 0900 to 1700

JOHNSON MATTHEY TECHNOLOGY CENTRE (JMTC)

Blounts Court, Sonning Common, Reading, Berkshire, RG4 9NH

Tel: 0118 924 2000
Fax: 0118 924 2254
Website: www.matthey.com

Founded: 1817

Organisation type and purpose: Manufacturing industry, research organisation.
Serving the Catalysts and Chemicals, and Precious Metals Divisions of Johnson Matthey plc.

Subject coverage: Platinum group metals; gold; base metals; inorganic chemistry; materials science; catalysis; pollution control; fuel cells; electrochemistry

Collection: London Collection (books c. 1850 to early 1900s on history of London)

Publications: Printed

Access to staff: Contact by telephone and by fax
Hours: Mon to Fri, 0900 to 1700

JOINT ASSOCIATION OF CLASSICAL TEACHERS (JACT)

Senate House, Malet Street, London, WC1E 7HU

Tel: 020 7862 8719
Fax: 020 7255 2297
E-mail: office@jact.org
Website: www.jact.org

Enquiries to: Administrator

Founded: 1961

Organisation type and purpose: Professional body, registered charity (charity number 313165).

Subject coverage: Teaching of Classics (Greek, Latin, classical civilisation and ancient history) at all levels; bibliographic and teaching aids.

Publications: Printed, and microform publications

Access to staff: Contact by letter, by telephone, by fax, by e-mail and in person. Appointment necessary.
Hours: Tues to Fri, 1000 to 1700

JOINT COUNCIL FOR LANDSCAPE INDUSTRIES (JCLI)

c/o The Landscape Institute, 6–8 Barnard Mews, London, SW11 1QU

Tel: 020 7350 5200
Fax: 020 7350 5201

Enquiries to: Secretary
Direct e-mail: paull@landscapeinstitute.org
Other contacts: Committee Services Officer

Organisation type and purpose: National organisation.
Umbrella body for the landscape industry.

Subject coverage: Co-ordinates views of member organisations and represents those members in all matters of common interest and concerns at all levels, including Local and National Government and internationally represents British landscape interests and promotes and encourages greater public interest.
Order printed publications from: The Landscape Institute

Publications list: Available in print

Access to staff: Contact by letter, by telephone, by fax and by e-mail
Hours: Mon to Fri, 0900 to 1700

Connections with: Arboricultural Association (AA); British Association of Landscape Industries (BALI); Horticultural Trades Association (HTA); Institute of Leisure and Amenity Management (ILAM); Landscape Institute (LI); National Farmers Union (NFU)

JOINT COUNCIL FOR QUALIFICATIONS

Sixth Floor, 29 Great Peter Street, London, SW1P 3LW

Tel: 020 7638 4132
Fax: 020 7374 4343
E-mail: info@jcq.org.uk
Website: www.jcq.org.uk

Enquiries to: Office Manager

Founded: 2004

Organisation type and purpose: Membership association (membership is by election or invitation), suitable for ages: 11 to 19.

Library catalogue: All or part available online

Publications: Printed
Order printed publications from: See list of Member Awarding Bodies

Publications list: Available online

Access to staff: Contact by letter, by fax and by e-mail
Hours: Mon to Fri, 0900 to 1700

Member Awarding Body: Assessment and Qualifications Alliance; Stag Hill House, Guildford, Surrey, GU2 7XJ; tel: 01483 506506; Edexcel; One90 High Holborn, London, WC1V 7BH; tel: 0844 576 0025; Northern Ireland Council for the Curriculum Examinations and Assessment; 29 Clarendon Road, Belfast, BT1 3BG; tel: 028 9026 1200; OCR; Syndicate Buildings, 1 Hills Road, Cambridge, CB1 2EU; tel: 01223 553998; Scottish Qualifications Authority; The Optima Building, 58 Robertson Street,

continued overleaf

Glasgow G2 8DQ; The City and Guilds London Institute; 1 Giltspur Street, London, EC1A 9DD; WJEC/CBAC; 245 Western Avenue, Cardiff, CF5 2YX; tel: 02920 265000

JOINT COUNCIL FOR THE WELFARE OF IMMIGRANTS (JCWI)

115 Old Street, London, EC1V 9RT

Tel: 020 7251 8708
Fax: 020 7251 8707
E-mail: info@jcwi.org.uk
Website: www.jcwi.org.uk

Enquiries to: Office Manager
Direct e-mail: info@jcwi.org.uk
Other contacts: Training Officer (for training)

Founded: 1967

Organisation type and purpose:
Membership association (membership is by subscription), present number of members: 1,000, voluntary organisation, training organisation, campaign organisation, publishing house.
1,000 affiliated organisations and individuals; mainly black and ethnic minority organisations, advice agencies, community relations councils, local authorities, solicitors.
Immigration law advice and training agency.

Subject coverage: Immigration, nationality and refugee law and practice.

Information services: Free telephone advice service for the public, Wed 1100 to 1300.

Special visitor services: Two solicitors providing legally-funded help; representation at competitive rates for individuals who do not qualify for public funding.

Publications: Printed

Publications list: Available online and in print

Access to staff: Contact by letter, by telephone, by fax and by e-mail. Appointment necessary.
Hours: Mon to Fri, 0900 to 1700

Access for disabled people: Ramped entry, toilet facilities

JOINT INDUSTRY BOARD FOR THE ELECTRICAL CONTRACTING INDUSTRY (JIB)

Kingswood House, 47–51 Sidcup Hill, Sidcup, Kent, DA14 6HP

Tel: 020 8302 0031
Fax: 020 8309 1103
Website: www.jib.org.uk

Enquiries to: Chief Executive

Founded: 1968

Organisation type and purpose:
Membership association (membership is by qualification), present number of members: 27,000.
Implements national wage agreement and working rules in the electrical contracting industry.

Subject coverage: Wage rates and terms and conditions of employment for hourly paid employees in the electrical contracting industry.

Publications: Printed, and electronic and video

Access to staff: Contact by letter
Hours: Mon to Fri, 0900 to 1700

JOINT LIBRARY OF THE HELLENIC AND ROMAN SOCIETIES

3rd Floor, Senate House, Malet Street, London, WC1E 7HU

Tel: 020 7862 8709
Fax: 020 7862 8735
Website: icls.sas.ac.uk/library/Home.htm

Enquiries to: Librarian
Direct tel: 020 7862 8710
Direct fax: 020 7862 8724
Direct e-mail: colin.annis@sas.ac.uk

Founded: 1950

Organisation type and purpose: Private library combined with Institute of Classical Studies Library.

Subject coverage: All aspects of classical civilisation, including archaeology, art and architecture, language and literature, history, law, politics, religion, philosophy and science relating to the Minoan, Mycenaean, Ancient Greek and early Byzantine World, and also to early Italic and Etruscan civilisations, and to the Roman World from the beginning of the 5th century AD (including Roman Britain).

Collection: 110,000 monographs and pamphlets
20,000 bound volumes of periodicals
6,800 slides
675 current periodicals taken

Library catalogue: All or part available online

Publications: Printed
Order printed publications from: Secretary, Hellenic Society, at the same address, tel: 020 7862 8730; fax: 020 7862 8731; e-mail: office@hellenicsociety.org.uk
Secretary, Roman Society, at the same address, tel: 020 7862 8727; fax: 020 7862 8728; e-mail: office@romansociety.org

Publications list: Available online and in print

Access to staff: Contact by letter, by telephone, by fax, by e-mail and in person. Access for members only.
Hours: Mon to Fri, 0930 to 1800
Term time: Tue, Wed and Thu, 0930 to 2000; Sat, 1000 to 1630; closed Sat during August

Combined with: Institute of Classical Studies Library (ICS)

JOINT NATURE CONSERVATION COMMITTEE (JNCC)

Monkstone House, City Road, Peterborough, Cambridgeshire, PE1 1JY

Tel: 01733 562626
Fax: 01733 555948
E-mail: communications@jncc.gov.uk
Website: www.jncc.gov.uk

Founded: 1991

Organisation type and purpose: Advisory body.
Responsible to the UK Government for research and advice on nature conservation at both UK and international levels, on behalf of the Countryside Council for Wales, Natural England, Scottish Natural Heritage, and the Council for Nature Conservation and the Countryside (Northern Ireland); the Committee also includes independent members.

Subject coverage: Nature conservation

Publications: Printed
Order printed publications from: NHBS, 2–3 Wills Road, Totnes, Devon, TQ9 5XN, tel: 01803 865913, fax: 01803 865280, e-mail: nhbs@nhbs.co.uk

Publications list: Available online and in print

Access to staff: Contact by letter, by telephone, by fax, by e-mail and via website. Appointment necessary.
Hours: Mon to Thu, 0830 to 1700; Fri, 0830 to 1630

Also at: JNCC (Aberdeen Office); Dunnet House, 7 Thistle Place, Aberdeen, AB10 1UZ; tel: 01224 655704; fax: 01224 621488; e-mail: communications@jncc.gov.uk; website: http://www.jncc.gov.uk

JOINT SERVICES COMMAND & STAFF COLLEGE LIBRARY (JSCSC)

Faringdon Road, Watchfield, Shrivenham, Wiltshire, SN6 8TS

Tel: 01793 788236
Fax: 01793 788281
E-mail: infodesk.jscsc@defenceacademy.mod.uk

Enquiries to: Librarian

Founded: 1997

Organisation type and purpose: National government body, central government establishment.
Military staff training college.

Subject coverage: Air power, aviation (military), modern warfare, historical warfare, defence policy and studies, NATO, Warsaw Pact countries, international affairs, communications skills, management techniques, Armed Forces, sea power, Royal Navy, navies, land warfare, British Army, armies and Royal Air Force, leadership, campaign studies.

Collection: Extensive archive of British military documents and books dating back to the 18th century

Library catalogue: All or part available online and in-house

Publications: Printed
Order printed publications from: e-mail: ibrary.jscsc@defenceacademy.mod.uk

Access to staff: Contact by letter, by telephone, by fax and by e-mail. Appointment necessary.
Hours: Mon to Fri, 0800 to 1800

Access to building: Prior appointment required
Hours: Mon to Fri, 0800 to 1800

Access for disabled people: Access to all public areas

Parent body: Ministry of Defence

JONES LANG LASALLE

22 Hanover Square, London, W1A 2BN

Tel: 020 7493 6040
Fax: 020 7399 5818
E-mail: andy.mottram@eu.jll.com
Website: www.joneslanglasalle.co.uk

Enquiries to: Information Manager
Direct e-mail: infodesk@en.jll.com

Founded: 1999

Organisation type and purpose: Consultancy.

Subject coverage: Real estate.

Publications: Printed

Publications list: Available online and in print

Access to staff: Contact by letter and by e-mail
Hours: Mon to Fri, 0900 to 1730

Access to building: No access other than to staff

JORDAN INFORMATION BUREAU (JIB)

6 Upper Phillimore Gardens, London, W8 7HB

Tel: 020 7937 9499
Fax: 020 7937 6741
E-mail: info@jiblondon.com
Website: www.jordanembassyuk.gov.jo

Enquiries to: Director
Other contacts: Information Officer

Founded: 1992

Organisation type and purpose: Part of Diplomatic Mission.
Press, media and information section.

Subject coverage: General information about Jordan, history, politics, economy, culture, social life, and the Middle East Peace process.

Collection: Library containing information on Jordan and the Middle East

Publications: Printed, and electronic and video

Access to staff: Contact by letter, by telephone, by fax, by e-mail and via website
Hours: Mon to Fri, 0900 to 1600

Access to building: No prior appointment required

Connections with: Embassy of The Hashemite Kingdom of Jordan; 6 Upper Phillimore Gardens, London, W8 7HB

JORDANS LIMITED

21 St Thomas Street, Bristol, BS1 6JS

Tel: 0117 923 0600
Fax: 0117 923 0063
E-mail: businessinformation@jordans.co.uk
Website: www.jordans.co.uk

Enquiries to: Customer Service Administrator
Direct tel: 0117 918 1283
Direct e-mail: denise_sebastian@jordans.co.uk
Other contacts: Customer Services Administrator for purchase of data, or for quotations.

Founded: 1898

Organisation type and purpose:
Registration agents, law agents.
Business information provider.
Publishing house, printers and stationers.

Subject coverage: Company financial information including information for marketing, credit checking, performance analysis, status reports, money-laundering report, official filings at Companies House.

Trade and statistical information: Industry sector reports: financial analysis of companies by industry region, size, growth etc

Publications: Printed, and electronic and video

Publications list: Available online and in print

Access to staff: Contact by letter, by telephone, by fax, by e-mail, in person and via website. Appointment necessary.
Hours: Mon to Fri, 0900 to 1700

Other addresses: Jordans Limited; 20–22 Bedford Row, London, WC1R 4JS; tel: 020 7400 3333; fax: 020 7400 3366; Jordans Limited; 44 Whitchurch Road, Cardiff, CF4 3UQ; tel: 029 2037 1901; fax: 029 2038 2342; Oswalds; 24 Great King Street, Edinburgh, EH3 6QN; tel: 0131 557 6966; fax: 0131 556 2917

Parent body: West of England Trust Limited; 21 St Thames Street, Bristol, BS1 6JS

JOSEPH ROWNTREE FOUNDATION (JRF)

The Homestead, 40 Water End, York, YO30 6WP

Tel: 01904 629241
Fax: 01904 620072
E-mail: info@jrf.org.uk
Website: www.jrf.org.uk

Enquiries to: Information Services Officer
Direct tel: extn 243
Direct e-mail: info@jrf.org.uk

Founded: 1904; formerly called Joseph Rowntree Village Trust (year of change 1959); formerly called Joseph Rowntree Memorial Trust (year of change 1990)

Organisation type and purpose: Endowed foundation, funding large, UK-wide research and development programme.
Housing Association.

Subject coverage: Housing research; social policy; social care; poverty; housing associations; New Earswick (model village); Rowntree family history.

Collection: Archive at Borthwick Institute, University of York

Library catalogue: All or part available in-house

Publications: Printed, and electronic and video

Publications list: Available online

Access to staff: Contact by letter, by telephone, by fax and by e-mail.
Appointment necessary.
Hours: Mon to Fri, 0900 to 1230 and 1400 to 1700

Access to building: Prior appointment required

Links with: Joseph Rowntree Housing Trust; The Garth, White Rose Avenue, New Earswick, YO32 4TZ

JOSEPHINE BUTLER SOCIETY (JBS)

4 The Hedges, Maidstone, Kent, ME14 2JW

Tel: 01622 679630
Website: www.jbs.webeden.co.uk

Enquiries to: Honorary Correspondence Secretary

Founded: 1869

Organisation type and purpose:
Membership association (membership is by subscription), present number of members: 90, voluntary organisation.

Subject coverage: Objects: to promote a high and equal standard of morality and sexual responsibility for men and women in public opinion, law and practice. To secure the abolition of state regulation of prostitution internationally and prevent all forms of exploitation of prostitutes by third parties. To examine existing and proposed legislation on all matters connected with prostitution, and to promote social, legal and administrative reform, the law as it affects prostitutes and related subjects, e.g. kerb crawling, sexual offences, etc. Combating the traffic in persons (known in the past as the White Slave Trade).

Collection: Main JBS collection is held at the Women's Library, London; smaller collection at the Durham University Library, Durham

Library catalogue: All or part available online

Publications: Printed

Access to staff: Contact by letter and by telephone
Hours: Mon to Fri, 0900 to 1700

Links with: Anti-Slavery Society; tel: 020 7924 9555; fax: 020 7738 4110; e-mail: antislavery@gn.apc.orb; Church Army; tel: 020 8318 1226; Church of England Board for Social Responsibility; tel: 020 7222 9011; Council for Voluntary Services; Fawcett Society; tel: 020 7628 4441; fax: 020 7628 2865; e-mail: fawcett@gn.apc.org; website: http://www.gn.apc.org/fawcett
Human Rights Network; International Abolitionist Federation; France; e-mail: b .amont@libertysurf.fr; International Alliance of Women; tel: 612 6568 6239 (Australia); International Council of Women; tel: 00 331 47–42–19–40; fax: 00 331 42–66–26–23 (France); e-mail: icw_cif@wanadoo.fr; Minority Rights Group; tel: 020 7978 9498; Mothers Union; tel: 020 7222 5533; National Council of Women of Great Britain; tel: 020 7354 2395; fax: 020 7354 9214; website: http://www/cerbernet.co.uk/ncwgb/
Salvation Army; tel: 020 7332 0022; fax: 020 7236 6272; Wellclose Trust; tel: 01823 325 632

JOSIAH WEDGWOOD & SONS LIMITED

Barlaston, Stoke-on-Trent, Staffordshire, ST12 9ES

Tel: 01782 204141
Fax: 01782 204666
Website: www.wedgwood.co.uk

Enquiries to: Public Relations Manager
Direct tel: 01782 282516
Direct fax: 01782 204433
Direct e-mail: andrew.stanistreet@wedgwood.com

Founded: 1759

Organisation type and purpose: Manufacturing industry, museum.

Subject coverage: Manufacturing processes of fine bone china and earthenware, company history from 1759.

Collection: Museum of ceramics and manuscripts

Access to staff: Contact by letter, by fax and by e-mail
Hours: Mon to Fri, 0900 to 1700

JOZEF PILSUDSKI INSTITUTE OF RESEARCH LIMITED

Historical Institute, 238–240 King Street, London, W6 0RF

Tel: 020 8748 6197
Fax: 020 8748 6197
E-mail: instytut@pilsudski.org.uk

Enquiries to: General Secretary
Direct tel: 020 8579 3823

Founded: 1947

Organisation type and purpose: Learned society (membership is by election or invitation), present number of members: 140, registered charity, museum, research organisation.
Reference library.
Historical research into the recent history of Poland in relation to work and deeds of Jozef Pilsudski.

Subject coverage: The Struggle for Polish independence before and during World War I, political and military events during the years of independence 1918–1939 and organisation of the Polish State.

Collection: Archives of documents, manuscripts and photographs (mostly in Polish)
Militaria Library related to recent history of Poland before 2nd World War
Museum of personal objects of Marshal Pilsudski

Non-library collection catalogue: All or part available in-house

Library catalogue: All or part available in-house

Publications: Printed

Publications list: Available in print

Access to staff: Contact by letter, by telephone, by fax, by e-mail and in person
Hours: Tue and Thu, 1000 to 1700; or by appointment

Access for disabled people: Ramped entry

JUDGE INSTITUTE OF MANAGEMENT

University of Cambridge, Trumpington Street, Cambridge, CB2 1AG

Tel: 01223 339700
Fax: 01223 339701
E-mail: enquiries@jbs.cam.ac.uk
Website: www.jims.cam.ac.uk

Enquiries to: Communications Manager
Direct tel: 01223 388608
Direct fax: 01223 766920
Direct e-mail: press-publicity@jims.cam.ac.uk

Founded: 1990

Organisation type and purpose: University Business School.

Subject coverage: Management studies, business and management.

Trade and statistical information: Market and company information

Non-library collection catalogue: All or part available online

Library catalogue: All or part available online

Publications: Printed, and electronic and video
Order printed publications from: Publications Secretary
As main address

Publications list: Available online and in print

Access to staff: Contact by letter, by telephone, by fax, by e-mail and via website
Hours: Mon to Fri, 0900 to 1700

Access to building: No access other than to staff

Access for disabled people: Parking provided, level entry, access to all public areas, toilet facilities

Links with: Cambridge Business Research Centre (CBRC); Cambridge Entrepreneurship Centre; CMI; Management Studies Group; Department of Engineering, University of Cambridge; Massachusetts Institute of Technology (MIT)

JUNIOR CHAMBER INTERNATIONAL LONDON (JCI)

33 Queen Street, London, EC4R 1AP

Tel: 020 7203 1951
Website: www.jcilondon.org.uk

Enquiries to: President
Direct e-mail: simon.bucknall@jcilondon.org.uk

Founded: 1953; formerly called Junior Chamber of Commerce for London (year of change 2004)

Organisation type and purpose: International organisation (membership is by election or invitation), present number of members: 135, voluntary organisation, suitable for ages: 18 to 40, training organisation.
Part of a worldwide organisation dedicated to developing the business and managerial skills of the future business leaders of our communities.

Subject coverage: Concentrates on 5 areas: international, business networking, community projects, leadership development and management opportunities.

Access to staff: Contact by e-mail
Hours: Mon to Fri, preferably evenings

Affiliated to: British Junior Chamber, which is affiliated to Junior Chamber International

Headquarters address: British Junior Chamber (BJC); 12 Regent Place, Rugby, Warwickshire, CV21 2PM; tel: 01788 572795; fax: 01788 542091; e-mail: 1007633171@compuserve.com

JUPITER OWNERS' AUTO CLUB (JOAC)

Redbrook, 6 Rudhall Meadow, Ross-on-Wye, Herefordshire, HR9 7AW

Tel: 01989 767 815
E-mail: davehkennedy@wyenet.co.uk
Website: www.jowettjupiter.co.uk

Enquiries to: Membership Secretary
Direct tel: 01273 843457
Direct e-mail: ghis@jowettjupiter.co.uk

Founded: 1962

Organisation type and purpose: Membership association (membership is by subscription), present number of members: 220.
Club for owners of Jowett Jupiter Cars 1950–54.

Subject coverage: About 900 Jowett Jupiters were built from 1950 to 1954 – many still survive and we aim to keep these interesting and rare collectible cars on the road and restored.

Access to staff: Contact by letter, by e-mail and via website
Hours: Mon to Fri, 0900 to 1700

JUSTICE

59 Carter Lane, London, EC4V 5AQ

Tel: 020 7329 5100
Fax: 020 7329 5055
E-mail: admin@justice.org.uk
Website: www.justice.org.uk

Enquiries to: Director
Other contacts: Legal Officer

Founded: 1957

Organisation type and purpose: Membership association (membership is by subscription), present number of members: 2,000, voluntary organisation, registered charity (charity number 1058580).
An international non-governmental organisation concerned with promoting observance of the rule of law, law reform and the legal protection of human rights.

Subject coverage: Law reform, rule of law, access to justice, human rights in UK and EU.

Collection: Archive material 1990-.
ICJ reports
Justice reports and memoranda

Publications: Printed

Publications list: Available in print

Access to staff: Contact by letter

Hours: Mon to Fri, 0930 to 1730

British Section of the: International Commission of Jurists; Geneva

JUSTICE FOR ALL VACCINE-DAMAGED CHILDREN (JVDC)

Erin's Cottage, Fussell's Buildings, Whiteway Road, Bristol, BS5 7QY

Tel: 0117 955 7818

Enquiries to: Secretary
Other contacts: Justice and Basic Support for MMR vaccine damage.

Founded: 1981

Organisation type and purpose: Voluntary organisation.
To ensure the safer manufacture of vaccines, that all medical personnel are aware of the Vaccine Damage Payments Act (1979), that all adverse reactions are reported to the Committee on Safety of Medicines.

Subject coverage: Compensation for vaccine-damaged children.

Access to staff: Contact by telephone
Hours: Mon to Sun, 0900 to 2100 telephone only

Also at: Justice for all Vaccine-Damaged Children; 99 Hendris Road, Kirkcaldy, Fife, KY2 5DB

Other vaccine damage groups: Justice, Awareness, Basic Support (JABS); 1 Gawsworth Road, Golbourne, Warrington, Cheshire, WA3 3RF; tel: 01942 713565; The Informed Parent; PO Box 870, Harrow, Middlesex; tel: 020 8861 1022; Victims of Vaccination Support Group; 27 Malcolm Grove, Rednal, Birmingham, BH5 9BS; tel: 0121 2437759

JUVENILE DIABETES RESEARCH FOUNDATION (JDRF)

19 Angel Gate, City Road, London, EC1V 2PT

Tel: 020 7713 2030
Fax: 020 7713 2031
E-mail: info@jdrf.org.uk
Website: www.jdrf.org.uk

Enquiries to: Director of Communications

Founded: 1986

Organisation type and purpose: National organisation, registered charity in England and Wales (No. 295716) and in Scotland (No. SC040123).
To find a cure for diabetes through the support of research. To provide information about the progress of research.

Publications: Printed
Order printed publications from: website: http://www.jdrf.org.uk

Access to staff: Contact by letter, by telephone, by fax, by e-mail and via website
Hours: Mon to Fri, 0900 to 1730
Special comments: 3rd floor – lift access.

Access to building: Prior appointment required

Affiliated to: The Juvenile Diabetes Foundation International; 120 Wall Street, New York, USA; website: http://www.jdrf.org

Also at: JDRF Scotland; JDRF c/o Subsea 7, Greenwell Base, Greenwell Rd, East Tullos Industrial Estate, Aberdeen, AB12 3AX; tel: 0151 709 5533; website: http://www.jdrf.org
JDRF South West; 2 Berkeley Square, Clifton, Bristol; tel: 0117 9452491; JDRF West Midlands; Suite 32, Fifth Floor, Queensgate, 121 Suffolk Street, Queensway, Birmingham, B1 1LX; tel: 0121 685 7102

JVC PROFESSIONAL EUROPE LTD. (JVC)

JVC House, JVC Business Park, 12 Priestley Way, London, NW2 7BA

Tel: 020 8208 6200
Fax: 020 8208 6260
E-mail: sales@jvcpro.co.uk
Website: www.jvcpro.co.uk

Enquiries to: Sales Manager
Direct tel: 020 8208 6204

Founded: 1988

Organisation type and purpose: Manufacturing industry.
UK marketing and distribution of JVC professional broadcast, display and security products.

Subject coverage: Manufacturer of professional video equipment, projection, displays, 3D, CCTV and security.

Publications: Printed
Order printed publications from: e-mail: marketing@jvcpro.co.uk

Publications list: Available online

Access to staff: Contact by letter, by telephone, by e-mail and via website
Hours: Mon to Fri, 0900 to 1730

Access to building: *Hours:* Mon to Fri, 0900 to 1700

Access for disabled people: Ramped entry, toilet facilities

KAPUSTIN SOCIETY, THE

9 Burnside Close, Twickenham, Middlesex, TW1 1ET

Tel: 020 8287 5518
Fax: 020 8287 5518
E-mail: KapustinSoc@blueyonder.co.uk
Website: www.trg.ed.ac.uk

Enquiries to: Secretary

Founded: 2002

Organisation type and purpose: Learned society, membership association (membership is by subscription).

Subject coverage: Music of Nikolai Kapustin (1937-).

Publications: Printed

Access to staff: Contact by letter, by telephone, by fax and by e-mail. Appointment necessary.
Hours: Mon to Fri, 0900 to 1700

Access to building: Prior appointment required

Access for disabled people: Parking provided, level entry, toilet facilities

KARMANN GHIA OWNERS' CLUB (GB)

13 Hilltop Road, Toms Lane, Kings Langley, Hertfordshire, WD4 8NS

Tel: 01923 263658
E-mail: john@jfigg.freeserve.co.uk

Enquiries to: General Secretary

Founded: 1982

Organisation type and purpose: National organisation.

Subject coverage: Karmann Ghia motorcars, sale of cars, insurance benefits, club events, national related events, international events, specialist services.

Collection: History of the manufacture of the car
Service and repair data

Access to staff: Contact by letter, by telephone and by e-mail
Hours: Mon to Fri, 0900 to 1700

KATE SHARPLEY LIBRARY (KSL)

BM Hurricane, London, WC1N 3XX

E-mail: info@katesharpleylibrary.net
Website: www.katesharpleylibrary.net

Enquiries to: Information Officer

Founded: 1979

Organisation type and purpose: Voluntary organisation, research organisation, publishing house.
To research and publish materials on anarchist history especially in areas that have been ignored or misrepresented by academic experts.

Subject coverage: Anarchism; anarcho-syndicalism; council communism; Labour Movement; Libertarian socialism; revolutionary industrial unionism (Industrial Workers of the World); situationism; Spanish Civil War and Resistance; Syndicalism.

Collection: The Library covers Anarchist, Syndicalist, Libertarian Socialist, Situationist and Council Communist books, pamphlets and periodicals in all languages
Various archive collections including Albert Meltzer papers (Anarchism)

Non-library collection catalogue: All or part available in-house

Library catalogue: All or part available in-house

Publications: Printed

Publications list: Available online and in print

Access to staff: Contact by letter, by e-mail and via website. Appointment necessary.

Other address: Kate Sharpley Library (KSL); PMB 820, 2425 Channing Way, Berkeley, California, CA 94704, USA

KAWASAKI TRIPLES CLUB (GB)

PO Box 528, Kings Langley, Herts WD5 5AF

Tel: 020 8737 9755
Fax: 0115 913 4223
E-mail: Roger.ramm@blueyonder.co.uk
Website: www.kawasakitriplesclub.co.uk

continued overleaf

Enquiries to: Membership Secretary
Direct tel: 07779094462
Direct e-mail: downpipe3@ntlworld.com

Founded: 1980; formerly called Classic Kawasaki Club

Organisation type and purpose: International organisation, membership association (membership is by subscription).

Subject coverage: Historical reference for Kawasaki motorcycles; holds two rallies per year.

Access to staff: Contact by letter, by telephone, by fax, by e-mail and via website. Appointment necessary.
Hours: Mon to Fri, 0900 to 1700

Access to building: No prior appointment required
Special comments: Museum visits by appointment only.

Has connections with: Various worldwide clubs

KEELE UNIVERSITY LIBRARY

Keele, Staffordshire, ST5 5BG

Tel: 01782 733535
Fax: 01782 734502
E-mail: libhelp@keele.ac.uk
Website: www.keele.ac.uk/depts/li

Founded: 1949

Organisation type and purpose: University Library.

Subject coverage: American studies; English; history; music; philosophy; economics; history; education; biological sciences; pharmacology; management; chemistry; communication and neuroscience; computer science; geology; mathematics; physics; medicine; geography; international relations; industrial relations; law; politics; criminology; social gerontology; psychology; social policy; social work; physiology; sociology; social anthropology.

Collection: Arnold Bennett Collection
Sneyd Papers (Sneyd family of Keele Hall 1600 onwards)
Spode Papers

Trade and statistical information: European Documentation Centre

Publications: Printed

Access to staff: Contact by letter, by telephone, by fax, by e-mail, in person and via website. Appointment necessary.
Hours: Semester time: from 2012/13 24/7
Vacations: please enquire

Access for disabled people: Accessible, via entrance on ground floor

Member organisation of: SCONUL Access; Society of College, National and University Libraries

KEEP BRITAIN TIDY

Elizabeth House, The Pier, Wigan, Lancashire, WN3 4EX

Tel: 01942 612621
Fax: 01942 824778
E-mail: enquiries@keepbritaintidy.org
Website: www.keepbritaintidy.org

Enquiries to: Reception
Direct tel: 01942 612621
Direct e-mail: enquiries@keepbritaintidy.org

Founded: 1961; formerly called Keep Britain Tidy Group (year of change 1987); formerly called EnCams (year of change 2009)

Organisation type and purpose: Voluntary organisation, registered charity (charity number 1071737), consultancy. Independent national agency for the improvement of the quality of local environments.

Subject coverage: Local Environmental Quality and associated anti-social behaviour, Cleaner Safer Greener Network, Eco-Schools Programme, Green Flag for Parks, Quality Coast Award and Blue Flag Awards.

Collection: Documents, posters, printed materials, leaflets, etc.

Non-library collection catalogue: All or part available online, in-house and in print

Library catalogue: All or part available in-house

Publications: Printed

Publications list: Available online

Access to staff: Contact by letter, by telephone, by fax, by e-mail, in person and via website. Access for members only.
Hours: Mon to Fri, 0700 to 1900

Access to building: Only one Central Services Office
Hours: Mon to Fri, 0845 to 1800

Access for disabled people: Access to all public areas, toilet facilities

KEIGHLEY & DISTRICT FHS

2 The Hallows, Shann Park, Keighley, West Yorkshire, BD20 6HY

Tel: 01535 672144
E-mail: suedaynes@hotmail.co.uk
Website: www.kdfhs.org.uk

Enquiries to: Honorary Secretary
Other contacts: Administration and Programme Secretary

Founded: 1986

Organisation type and purpose:
Membership association (membership is by subscription), present number of members: 300, voluntary organisation.
To exchange information, ideas regarding individual family histories and discuss research problems.

Subject coverage: Family history in the Keighley and District Area, which includes: Bingley to the east, west to Kildwick, Skipton and the Aire Valley, and the villages of the Worth Valley, Haworth, Oakworth, Oxenhope, etc.

Non-library collection catalogue: All or part available in-house

Library catalogue: All or part available in-house

Publications: Printed
Order printed publications from: Publications Secretary, 13 King Edward Street, Sutton in Craven, Keighley, West Yorkshire, BD20 7ET; e-mail: a.thorley171@btinternet.com

Publications list: Available online and in print

Access to staff: Contact by letter, by e-mail and via website. Appointment necessary. Access for members only.
Hours: Mon to Fri, 0900 to 1700

Access to building: at Keighley Public Library, Local Studies Library on 1st floor
Hours: Mon to Fri, 0900 to 1900; Sat, 0900 to 1700
Special comments: Access to Society's reference library for members only on sight of membership card.

Access for disabled people: Use Albert Street entrance and lift to 1st floor
Hours: Mon to Fri, 0900 to 1900; Sat, 0900 to 1700

Links with: Federation of Family History Societies; Artillery House, 15 Byron Street, Manchester, M3 4PF; e-mail: admin@ffhs.org.uk

Membership Secretary: Keighley & District FHS; Mrs B Hetherington, Greengate House, Greengate, Silsden, Keighley, West Yorkshire, BD20 9LA; e-mail: bhetherington@btinternet.com

KELVEDON HATCH SECRET BUNKER

Brentwood, Essex, CM14 5TL

Tel: 01277 364883
Fax: 01277 365260
E-mail: mike@japar.demon.co.uk
Website: www.japar.demon.co.uk

Enquiries to: Managing Director

Founded: 1994

Organisation type and purpose: Nuclear bunker.

Subject coverage: Cold War bunker built in 1952 for government.

Access to staff: Contact by letter, by fax, by e-mail and via website
Hours: Mar to Oct, Mon to Fri, 1000 to 1600; Sat and Sun, 1000 to 1700
Nov to Feb, Thu to Sun, 1000 to 1600
Special comments: Charge for admission.

Access for disabled people: Parking provided, toilet facilities
Special comments: Limited entry.

KENNEL CLUB

1–5 Clarges Street, Piccadilly, London, W1J 8AB

Tel: 0844 770 5235
Fax: 020 7518 1058
Website: www.thekennelclub.org.uk/library
Website: www.dogimages.org.uk
Website: www.thekennelclub.org.uk/gallery

Enquiries to: Library and Collections Manager
Direct tel: 020 7518 1009
Direct fax: 020 7518 1045
Direct e-mail: library@thekennelclub.org.uk

Founded: 1873

Organisation type and purpose:
Membership association (membership is by election or invitation).
To promote in every way the general improvement of dogs.

Subject coverage: Dogs: choice, care, training, breeding, health, welfare, showing, obedience, agility, working and field trials, pedigree dog registration.

Collection: Books, archive, photographs, artwork, ephemera, etc.

Library catalogue: All or part available online

Publications: Printed, and electronic and video

Publications list: Available online

Access to staff: Contact by letter, by telephone, by e-mail, in person and via website
Hours: Mon to Fri, 0930 to 1630

Access to building: Prior appointment required
Hours: Library: Mon to Fri, 0930 to 1630

Access for disabled people: Ground floor, no steps, accessible bathroom

KENSINGTON AND CHELSEA (ROYAL BOROUGH) LIBRARY (RBKC)

Central Library, Phillimore Walk, London, W8 7RX

Tel: 020 7937 3010
Fax: 020 7361 2976
E-mail: libraries@rbkc.gov.uk
Website: www.rbkc.gov.uk/leisureandlibraries/libraries.aspx

Enquiries to: Head of Library Service
Other contacts: Head of Service

Founded: 1965

Organisation type and purpose: Local government body, public library.

Subject coverage: General, biography and genealogy, customs and folklore.

Collection: Kensington and Chelsea local history and current information
Records of the Chelsea Arts Club 1890–1974

Non-library collection catalogue: All or part available in-house

Library catalogue: All or part available online and in-house

Publications list: Available in print

Access to staff: Contact by letter, by telephone, by fax, by e-mail, in person and via website
Hours: Mon, Tue, Thu, Fri, 0930 to 2000; Wed, Sat, 0930 to 1700; Sun 1300 to 1700

KENT AND EAST SUSSEX RAILWAY (K&ESR)

Tenterden Town Station, Tenterden, Kent, TN30 6HE

Tel: 01580 765155
Fax: 01580 765654
E-mail: enquiries@kesr.org.uk
Website: www.kesr.org.uk

Enquiries to: Commercial Manager
Other contacts: Bookings and Administration Secretaries for general information and bookings.

Founded: 1971

Organisation type and purpose: Voluntary organisation, registered charity.
Preserved steam railway operating between Tenterden, Kent and Bodiam, East Sussex.

Access to staff: Contact by letter, by telephone, by fax and by e-mail
Hours: Mon to Fri, 0900 to 1700
Special comments: Trains run approximately 190 days per year – please telephone for timetable details.

Access for disabled people: Parking provided, ramped entry, level entry, toilet facilities

KENT ARCHAEOLOGICAL SOCIETY (KAS)

The Museum, St Faith's Street, Maidstone, Kent, ME14 1LH

E-mail: research@kentarchaeology.org.uk
Website: www.kentarchaeology.org.uk

Enquiries to: Librarian
Direct tel: 01795 472218
Direct fax: 01795 472218
Direct e-mail: dr.fh.panton@grove-end-tunstall.fsnet.co.uk; secretary@kentarchaeol
Other contacts: Hon Gen Sec

Founded: 1857

Organisation type and purpose: Learned society, present number of members: c. 1,300, voluntary organisation, registered charity (charity number 2243382), suitable for ages: all, training organisation, research organisation, publishing house.
To promote the study and publication of archaeology and history in all their branches, especially within the ancient county of Kent. Library open (on request to Hon. Librarian) to bona fide non-members, lectures, training.

Subject coverage: Fieldwork; vernacular architecture, historic buildings and churches; place names; visual records; local history.

Collection: Extensive collections on history, etc., Kent, runs of County, National (UK) and overseas (Western Europe) publications on archaeological, genealogical, numismatic, place names, ecclesiastical records, etc.; manuscript material held by Kent County Council Archives, Centre for Kentish Studies

Non-library collection catalogue: All or part available online

Library catalogue: All or part available online and in-house

Publications: Printed

Publications list: Available in print

Access to staff: Contact by letter, by telephone and by e-mail. Appointment necessary. Letter of introduction required.
Hours: Members: Mon to Sat, 1000 to 1630; Sun, 1100 to 1600 (other times by appointment) on production of membership card and signing of visitors book
Non-members: by appointment with Hon. Librarian

KENT COUNTY COUNCIL LIBRARIES, REGISTRATION AND ARCHIVES (KCC Libraries, Registration and Archive)

Kent History & Library Centre, James Whatman Way, Maidstone, Kent, ME14 1LQ

Tel: 08458 247200
Fax: 01622 696450
E-mail: libraries@kent.gov.uk
Website: www.kent.gov.uk/libraries

Enquiries to: Information Services Team
Direct tel: 01622 696438
Direct fax: 01622 696445
Direct e-mail: libraries.informationservices@kent.gov.uk

Organisation type and purpose: Public library

Collection: Wide range of online databases
Canterbury Cathedral and City, archives
Kent History & Library Centre, archives

Library catalogue: All or part available online and in-house

Publications list: Available online

Access to staff: Contact by letter, by telephone, by fax, by e-mail, in person and via website

Access to building: *Hours:* Mon to Wed & Fri, 0900 to 1800; Thurs, 0900 to 2000; Sat, 0900 to 1700; check branch libraries online

Branch libraries: Ashford Gateway Plus; Church Road, Ashford, TN23 1AS; tel: 08458 247200; fax: 01233 620295; e-mail: ashfordlibrary@kent.gov.uk; Canterbury Library; 18 High Street, Canterbury, CT1 2JF; tel: 08458 247200; fax: 01227 768338; Dartford Library; Market Street, Dartford, DA1 1EU; tel: 08458 247200; fax: 01322 278271; e-mail: dartfordlibrary@kent.gov.uk; Dover Discovery Centre; Market Square, Dover, CT16 1PH; tel: 08458 247200; fax: 01304 225914; e-mail: doverlibrary@kent.gov.uk; Folkestone Library; 2 Grace Hill, Folkestone, CT20 1HD; tel: 08458 247200; fax: 01303 242907; e-mail: folkestonelibrary@kent.gov.uk; Gravesend Library; Windmill Street, Gravesend, DA12 1BE; tel: 08458 247200; fax: 01474 320284; e-mail: gravesendlibrary@kent.gov.uk; Margate Library; Thanet Gateway Plus, Cecil Square, Margate, CT9 1RE; tel: 08458 247200; fax: 01843 293015; e-mail: margatelibrary@kent.gov.uk; Sevenoaks Library; Buckhurst Lane, Sevenoaks, TN13 1LQ; tel: 08458 247200; fax: 01732 742682; e-mail: sevenoakslibrary@kent.gov.uk; Sittingbourne Library; Central Avenue, Sittingbourne, ME10 4AH; tel: 08458 247200; fax: 01795 428376; e-mail: sittingbournelibrary@kent.gov.uk; Tonbridge Library; Avebury Avenue, Tonbridge, TN9 1TG; tel: 08458 247200; fax: 01732 358300; e-mail: tonbridgelibrary@kent.gov.uk; Tunbridge Wells Library; Mount Pleasant Road, Tunbridge Wells, TN1 1NS; tel: 08458 247200; fax: 01892 514657; e-mail: tunbridgewellslibrary@kent.gov.uk

Member organisation of: Association of Local Government Information Services; Chartered Institute of Librarians and Information Professionals (CILIP); European Public Information Centre Network (EPIC); International Association of Music Librarian; Kent Information and Libraries Network

KENT FAMILY HISTORY SOCIETY (KFHS)

Bullockstone Farm, Bullockstone Road, Herne Bay, Kent, CT6 7NL

Tel: 01227 363030

continued overleaf

E-mail: kristn@globalnet.co.uk
Website: www.kfhs.org.uk

Enquiries to: Secretary

Founded: 1974

Organisation type and purpose:
International organisation, membership association (membership is by subscription), present number of members: 3500, voluntary organisation.
To promote interest in family history research in Kent.

Subject coverage: Family history in Kent, including the diocese of Canterbury and part of the Rochester diocese.

Library catalogue: All or part available in-house

Publications: Electronic and video, and microform publications
Order microform publications from: Kent Family History Society
41 The Street, Kennington, Ashford, Kent, TN24 9HD

Publications list: Available in print

Access to staff: Contact by letter, by e-mail and via website. Non-members charged.
Hours: Mon to Fri, 0900 to 1700

KENT INSTITUTE OF ART AND DESIGN AT MAIDSTONE (KIAD)

Oakwood Park, Oakwood Road, Maidstone, Kent, ME16 8AG

Tel: 01622 757286
Fax: 01622 621100
E-mail: admissions@ucreative.ac.uk
Website: www.kiad.ac.uk

Enquiries to: Head of Library and Learning Resources
Direct e-mail: vcrane@kiad.ac.uk

Founded: 1988

Organisation type and purpose: Suitable for ages: 18+.
College of higher and further education.
Art, design and architecture education.

Subject coverage: Fine art, architecture, fashion design, interior design, graphic design, film and video, photography, jewellery and precious metalwork, ceramics, illustration.

Collection: Early printed books and books from private presses
Slide collection

Library catalogue: All or part available online

Access to staff: Contact by letter. Appointment necessary. Letter of introduction required.
Hours: Mon to Fri, 0900 to 1900

Location: Kent Institute of Art and Design; New Dover Road, Canterbury, Kent, CT1 3AN; tel: 01227 769371; fax: 01227 817500; e-mail: librarycant@kiad.ac.uk; Kent Institute of Art and Design; Fort Pitt, Rochester, Kent, ME1 1DZ; tel: 01634 830022; fax: 01634 820300; e-mail: libraryroch@kiad.ac.uk

KENT WILDLIFE TRUST

Tyland Barn, Sandling, Maidstone, Kent, ME14 3BD

Tel: 01622 662012
Fax: 01622 671390
E-mail: kentwildlife@cix.co.uk
Website: www.kentwildlife.org.uk

Enquiries to: Director

Founded: 1958

Organisation type and purpose:
Membership association (membership is by subscription), present number of members: 13,000, registered charity (charity number 239992).
One of 46 county wildlife trusts.
To secure a better future for the native wildlife of Kent.

Subject coverage: Wildlife conservation in Kent.

Publications: Printed

Access to staff: Contact by letter, by telephone, by fax and by e-mail
Hours: Mon to Fri, 0900 to 1700

Parent body: The Wildlife Trust

KERRIER DISTRICT COUNCIL

Dolcoath Avenue, Camborne, Cornwall, TR14 8SX

Tel: 01209 614000
Fax: 01209 614491
E-mail: kerrierdc@kerrier.gov.uk

Enquiries to: Chief Executive
Other contacts: Marketing & Public Relations Officer for press/media enquiries.

Organisation type and purpose: Local government body.

Subject coverage: Local government services.

Publications: Printed
Order printed publications from: Marketing & Public Relations Officer, Kerrier District Council
at the same address, tel: 01209 614000, fax: 01209 614494, e-mail: marketing@ kerrier,gov,uk

Access to staff: Contact by letter, by telephone, by fax and by e-mail
Hours: Mon to Fri, 0900 to 1700

Access to building: Prior appointment required
Hours: 0845 to 1715
Special comments: No prior appointment required for Revenues and Benefits

Access for disabled people: Parking provided, level entry, toilet facilities

KESTON INSTITUTE

PO Box 752, Oxford, OX1 9QF

E-mail: admin@keston.org.uk
Website: www.keston.org.uk

Founded: 1970

Organisation type and purpose: Registered charity (charity number 314103).

Subject coverage: Keston promotes religious freedom and studies religious affairs in the postcommunist and communist world. Its unique archive and library are now housed at Baylor University, Texas, USA.

Access to staff: Contact by letter and by e-mail

KETTERING BOROUGH COUNCIL

Municipal Offices, Bowling Green Road, Kettering, Northamptonshire, NN15 7QX

Tel: 01536 410333
Fax: 01536 532424
E-mail: customerservices@kettering.gov.uk
Website: www.kettering.gov.uk

Direct e-mail: media@craftscouncil.org.uk

Organisation type and purpose: Local government body.

Subject coverage: Information on the Borough of Kettering.

Education services: via Northamptonshire County Council, tel: 01604 236236.

Services for disabled people: via Northamptonshire County Council, tel: 01604 236236.

Publications: Printed

Publications list: Available online and in print

Access to staff: Contact by letter, by telephone, by fax, by e-mail, in person and via website. Appointment necessary.
Hours: Mon to Fri, 0830 to 1730; Sat, 0900 to 1300

Access for disabled people: Parking provided, toilet facilities
Special comments: Access to all public areas

KEYGRAPHICA (Keygraphica)

PO Box 1381, Rugby, Warwickshire, CV21 2ZF

Tel: 01788 536389
Fax: 01788 550152

Enquiries to: Secretary

Organisation type and purpose: Trade association.

Subject coverage: Artwork; photographic facilities; toolmaking; anodising; etching; plating; litho and screen printing; paint spraying; laminating; press work; die cutting; stamping-embossing; casting; machine engraving; injection moulding; standards.

KIDDERMINSTER LIBRARY

Market Street, Kidderminster, Worcestershire, DY10 1AD

Tel: 01562 824500
Fax: 01562 512907
E-mail: kidderminsterlib@worcestershire .gov.uk
Website: www.worcestershire.gov.uk/ homepage.htm

Enquiries to: Information Officer

Founded: 1855

Organisation type and purpose:
International organisation, membership association (membership is by subscription), public library, consultancy, research organisation.

Subject coverage: General, including music; local studies on Kidderminster and nearer parts of Salop in particular, Worcestershire and Shropshire in general; carpets and textiles.

Collection: Carpet and Textile Collection
Local History Collection (Worcestershire and Salop)

Non-library collection catalogue: All or part available online

Publications: Printed

Access to staff: Contact by letter, by telephone, by fax, by e-mail, in person and via website
Hours: Mon, Fri, 0930 to 1730; Tue,Wed, Thu, 0930 to 2000; Sat 0930 to 1730

Access for disabled people: Access to all public areas, toilet facilities

Library of the: Worcestershire County Libraries

KIDS

6 Aztec Row, Berners Road, London, N1 0PW

Tel: 020 7359 3635
Fax: 020 7359 3520
E-mail: enquiries@kids.org.uk
Website: www.kids.org.uk

Enquiries to: Information Officer

Founded: 1970; formerly called Kids Active, HAPA

Organisation type and purpose:
Membership association, registered charity (charity number 275936).
Working with disabled children, young people and their families.

Subject coverage: KIDS is the leading national voice for the policy and practice of inclusive play. This is undertaken by promoting inclusive play nationwide via training, consultancy and publications, and by providing play opportunities on seven adventure playgrounds in London. KIDS works with disabled children and their families. KIDS works in partnership with parents to provide services that aim to meet the full range of children's needs, including educational, social, developmental and emotional. These services include early years education, play and leisure facilities, family support, and advice.

Publications: Printed, and microform publications

Publications list: Available online and in print

KIDSCAPE

2 Grosvenor Gardens, London, SW1W 0DH

Tel: 020 7730 3300
Fax: 020 7730 7081
E-mail: contact@kidscape.org.uk
Website: www.kidscape.org.uk

Enquiries to: Director

Founded: 1984

Organisation type and purpose: Registered charity (charity number 326864), training organisation, research organisation.

Subject coverage: Child protection, anti-bullying.

Information services: Parents' anti-bullying helpline: 08451 205 204 (Mon to Fri, 1000 to 1600)

Publications: Printed, and electronic and video
Order printed publications from: website: http://www.kidscape.org.uk/shop
Order electronic and video publications from: website: http://www.kidscape.org.uk/shop

Publications list: Available online

Access to staff: Contact by letter, by telephone, by fax, by e-mail, in person and via website. Appointment necessary.
Hours: Mon to Fri, 1000 to 1600

KILVERT SOCIETY

30 Bromley Heath Avenue, Downend, Bristol, BS16 6JP

Tel: 0117 957 2030
E-mail: via website
Website: www.communigate.co.uk/here/kilvertsociety

Enquiries to: Honorary Secretary
Other contacts: Membership Secretary (for enquiries from prospective new members)

Founded: 1948

Organisation type and purpose: Learned society (membership is by subscription), present number of members: 646, voluntary organisation.
To foster an interest in the Reverend Francis Kilvert, his work, his diary, and the countryside he loved.

Subject coverage: Rev Francis Kilvert and his Diary.

Collection: At Radnorshire Museum, Llandrindod Wells

Non-library collection catalogue: All or part available in-house

Publications: Printed
Order printed publications from: Publications Officer, Kilvert Society Publications, Tregothnan, Pentrosfa Crescent, Llandrindod Wells, Powys, LD1 5NW; tel: 01597 822062

Publications list: Available in print

Access to staff: Contact by letter, by telephone and via website
Hours: Mon to Fri, 0900 to 2100
Special comments: No personal callers.

Access to building: No prior appointment required

Also at: Membership Secretary, Kilvert Society; Seend Park Farm, Semington,Trowbridge, Wiltshire, BA14 7LH

KING'S COLLEGE LIBRARY

King's College, Cambridge, CB2 1ST

Tel: 01223 331232
Fax: 01223 331891
E-mail: library@kings.cam.ac.uk
Website: library.kings.cam.ac.uk

Enquiries to: Librarian
Direct tel: 01223 331337
Other contacts: Archivist for modern manuscripts and college archives only; Rowe Music Librarian for the music collection.

Organisation type and purpose: University department or institute.

Subject coverage: Academic subjects, incorporating a music library.

Collection: English books printed before 1800
Incunabula
Keynes Library (English literature, including 17th-century plays; manuscripts by and concerning Isaac Newton; works of a number of authors important in the history of thought. The Newton Manuscripts are available on microfilm in the University Library; modern Literary Papers in the fields of 20th-century art, literature and economics including Rupert Brooke, E.M. Forster, T.S. Eliot and members of the Bloomsbury group. Papers of Economists (J.M. Keynes, J.M. Robinson, Richard Kahn, Nicholas Kaldor)
College's own administrative records, 11th-21st centuries.
Rowe Music Library (collected works and scores; strong in 18th-century music, especially Handel)

Non-library collection catalogue: All or part available online, in-house and in print

Library catalogue: All or part available online and in-house

Access to staff: Contact by letter, by telephone, by fax, by e-mail, in person and via website. Appointment necessary. Access for members only. Letter of introduction required.
Hours: Mon to Fri, 0900 to 1730

KING'S COLLEGE LONDON INFORMATION SERVICES CENTRE AT WESTON EDUCATION CENTRE

Cutcombe Road, London, SE5 9RJ

Tel: 020 7848 5541/2
Fax: 020 7848 5550
Website: www.kcl.ac.uk/iss/library/denmark.html

Enquiries to: Information Services Centre Manager
Direct tel: 020 7848 5554
Direct e-mail: david.crossinggum@kcl.ac.uk

Organisation type and purpose: University library, NHS Trust

Subject coverage: Clinical medicine and dentistry, health services, biomedical sciences.

Collection: Historical texts

Library catalogue: All or part available online

Access to staff: Contact by letter, by telephone, by fax and by e-mail. Appointment necessary. Access for members only.
Hours: Mon to Fri, 0830 to 2100; Sat, 0930 to 1730; Sun, 1100 to 1900

Parent body: King's College London; Strand, London, WC2R 2LS

KING'S COLLEGE LONDON – MAUGHAN LIBRARY AND INFORMATION SERVICES CENTRE

Chancery Lane, London, WC2R 1LR

Tel: 020 7848 2424

continued overleaf

Fax: 020 7848 2277
E-mail: issenquiry@kcl.ac.uk
Website: www.kcl.ac.uk/iss

Enquiries to: Site Services Manager
Direct e-mail: vivien.robertson@kcl.ac.uk

Founded: 1829

Organisation type and purpose: University library.

Subject coverage: American studies, Australian studies, Byzantine and modern Greek, classics, cultural and creative industries, digital culture and technology, English, European studies, film studies, French, geography, German, history, linguistics, music, philosophy, Portuguese and Brazilian studies, Spanish and Spanish-American studies, theology and religious studies, war studies, law (including the Institute of Taxation's Tony Arnold Library), medical ethics, computer science, engineering, mathematics and physics

Collection: Adam Collection (20th-century poetry, Romanian and French literature)
Box Collection (Hebrew and Old Testament studies)
Carnegie Collection of British Music (early 20th-century British music)
Cohn Collection (German and Swiss Law)
De Beer Collection (works on or about Charles Darwin)
Early Science Collection (science and technology mainly 1800–1915)
Foreign and Commonwealth Office Historical Collection (European diplomatic history, British colonial history, voyages and travels, international law and relations)
Glaessner Collection (history of the German Democratic Republic)
Guy's Hospital Medical School Historical Collection (medicine pre-1900)
Guy's Hospital Physical Society Collection (science and pre-1900 medicine)
H. G. Adler Collection (history of the Holocaust)
Hamilton Collection (military history and poetry)
Institute for the Study and Treatment of Delinquency Collection (the causes of crime and the punishment, treatment and rehabilitation of offenders)
Institute of Psychiatry Historical Collection (psychology and psychiatry)
Jeremy Adler Collection (poetry and German literature)
Kantorowicz Collection (German literature and Judaica)
King's College School of Medicine and Dentistry (pre-1900 medicine)
Marsden Collection (philology, early Bibles, voyages and travels)
Maurice Collection (19th-century military history)
Mottram Collection (English and American literature)
Rainbow Collection (liturgical music)
Rare Books Collection (mostly pre-1801 items in a wide range of subjects, including, science, classics, travel, theology, Portuguese studies, Greece and the eastern Mediterranean)
Ratcliff Collection (liturgy and church history)
Relton Collection (ecclesiastical history and Christian dogmatic theology)
Ruggles Gates Collection (genetics, eugenics, botany)
Skeat and Furnivall Collection (Old and Middle English, Elizabethan literature, linguistics, philology)
St Thomas's Hospital Historical Medical Collection (medicine)
Stebbing Collection (marine zoology)
Wheatstone Collection (physics, telegraphy)

Non-library collection catalogue: All or part available online and in-house

Library catalogue: All or part available online

Access to staff: Contact by letter, by telephone, by fax and by e-mail. Non-members charged.
Hours: Term time: Mon to Thur, 0830 to 2030; Fri, 0830 to 1730; Sat, 0930 to 1730; Sun, 1100 to 1900; check website for vacation opening hours

Access to building: *Hours:* Term time: Mon to Fri, 0830 to 2200; Sat, 0930 to 1730; Sun, 1100 to 1900; check website for vacation opening hours

Access for disabled people: Ramps to entrance, lifts provide access to most of building, induction loops at service desks

Constituent part of: University of London

KING'S COLLEGE LONDON – NEW HUNT'S HOUSE INFORMATION SERVICES CENTRE

Guy's Campus, London, SE1 1UL

Tel: 020 7848 6740
Fax: 020 7848 6743
E-mail: james.ackroyd@kcl.ac.uk
Website: www.kcl.ac.uk

Enquiries to: Manager

Founded: 1903

Organisation type and purpose: University library.

Subject coverage: Medical and related sciences, medical librarianship and information work, dental science, history of medicine.

Collection: Historical collection of printed books
Books by Guy's Men 19th and 20th centuries

Library catalogue: All or part available online

Publications: Printed

Access to staff: Contact by letter, by telephone, by fax and by e-mail. Appointment necessary.
Hours: Term time: Mon to Fri, 0900 to 2045, Sat, 0900 to 1645
Vacations: Mon to Fri, 0900 to 1900

Member of: South Thames Regional Library and Information Service

Other addresses: King's College London; Warner Dental Library

Parent body: University of London

KING'S COLLEGE LONDON – ST THOMAS' HOUSE INFORMATION SERVICES CENTRE (KCL)

Westminster Bridge Road, London, SE1 7EH

Tel: 020 7188 3740
Fax: 020 7188 8358
E-mail: issenquiry@kcl.ac.uk
Website: www.kcl.ac.uk/iss

Enquiries to: NHS Information Specialist
Direct tel: 020 7188 3744
Direct e-mail: sarah.lawson@kcl.ac.uk

Founded: 1903

Organisation type and purpose: University library, NHS Trust.

Subject coverage: Medicine, health care, history of medicine.

Collection: History of St Thomas' Hospital
Printed books and manuscripts on medicine and related sciences

Library catalogue: All or part available online

Access to staff: Contact by letter, by telephone, by fax, by e-mail, in person and via website. Access for members only.
Hours: Term time: Mon to Fri, 0900 to 1700

Member organisation of: London Health Libraries network; website: http://www.londonlinks.nhs.uk

KING'S COLLEGE LONDON – STAMFORD STREET INFORMATION SERVICES CENTRE

Franklin-Wilkins Building, 150 Stamford Street, London, SE1 8WA

Tel: 020 7848 4498
Fax: 020 7848 4290
E-mail: peter.walsh@kcl.ac.uk
Website: www.kcl.ac.uk

Enquiries to: Manager

Founded: 1829

Organisation type and purpose: University library.

Subject coverage: Education, life sciences, management, nutrition, nursing, pharmacy.

Collection: Listed under the Strand Campus entry

Library catalogue: All or part available online

Access to staff: Contact by letter and by telephone
Hours: Mon to Fri, 0900 to 2100; Sat, 0930 to 1730

Also at: Director of Library Services (no library at this address); King's College London, London, WC2R 2LS; tel: 020 7848 2139; fax: 020 7848 1777; website: http://www.kcl.ac.uk/depsta/iss/servicesindex.html
Information Services Centre; New Hunt's House, Guys Hospital, St Thomas Street, London, SE1 9RT; tel: 020 7848 6600; fax: 020 7848 6743; website: http://www.kcl.ac.uk/depsta/iss/sites/guys/topguys.html
Information Services Centre; Franklin-Wilkins Building, 150 Stamford Street, London, SE1 9NN; tel: 020 7848 4378; website: http://www.kcl.ac.uk/depsta/iss/sites/waterloo/topwaterloo.html
King's College London; Strand, London, WC2R 2LS; Library and Information Services Centre; Chancery Lane, London,

WC2A 1LR; tel: 020 7848 2424; fax: 020 7848 2277; website: http://www.kcl.ac.uk/depsta/iss/sites/chancery/index.html
Medical Library; Weston Education Centre, Cutcombe Road, London, SE5 9JP; tel: 020 7848 5541; fax: 020 7848 5550; website: http://www.kcl.ac.uk/depsta/iss/sites/denmarkhill/topdenmarkhill.ht
Medical Library; St Thomas' Hospital, Lambeth Palace Road, London, SE1 7EH; tel: 020 7928 9292 ext 2367; fax: 020 7401 3932; website: http://www.kcl.ac.uk/depsta/iss/sites/stthomas/topthomas.html

KING'S FUND

11–13 Cavendish Square, London, W1G 0AN

Tel: 020 7307 2400
Fax: 020 7307 2801
Website: www.kingsfund.org.uk

Enquiries to: Chief Executive
Other contacts: Director of Corporate Affairs

Founded: 1897

Organisation type and purpose: Registered charity (charity number 207401), training organisation, research organisation.
To promote good health in London, to reduce inequalities in health, to promote the benefits of diversity, to involve the public in health policymaking and to break down boundaries between organisations working for health.

Subject coverage: Health care (not clinical medicine), grant making, training and education, social care and policy and public health.

Collection: Health Services library; reports and journals in health and social care

Publications: Printed
Order printed publications from: King's Fund Bookshop, at the same address; tel: 020 7307 2591; e-mail: bookshop@kingsfund.org.uk

Publications list: Available online and in print

Access to staff: Contact by letter, by telephone and in person
Hours: Mon to Fri, 0900 to 1700

Access to building: No prior appointment required

Access for disabled people: Parking provided, level entry, access to all public areas, toilet facilities

KING'S FUND INFORMATION AND LIBRARY SERVICE

Formal name: The King's Fund

11–13 Cavendish Square, London, W1G 0AN

Tel: 020 7307 2568
Fax: 020 7307 2805
E-mail: enquiry@kingsfund.org.uk
Website: www.kingsfund.org.uk

Enquiries to: Librarian

Founded: 1897

Organisation type and purpose: Registered charity.
The King's Fund seeks to understand how the health system in England can be improved. Using that insight, we work with individuals and organisations to shape policy, transform services and bring about behaviour change.

Subject coverage: Health care policy, social care policy, planning, organisation and management, leadership; hospital and community-based health services in the UK.

Collection: 150 current serial titles
Over 100,000 items included on the library database
Collection of NHS Policy Reports (earliest 1897)
Department of Health Circulars
King's Fund Publications
WHO – Regional Office for Europe Publications

Non-library collection catalogue: All or part available online and in-house

Library catalogue: All or part available online and in print

Publications: Printed, and electronic and video

Publications list: Available online and in print

Access to staff: Contact by letter, by telephone, by fax, by e-mail, in person and via website
Hours: Weekdays 0930 to 1730

Access for disabled people: Level entry, access to all public areas, toilet facilities

KING'S LYNN LIBRARY

London Road, King's Lynn, Norfolk, PE30 5EZ

Tel: 01553 772568 or 761393
Fax: 01553 769832
E-mail: kings.lynn.lib@norfolk.gov.uk
Website: www.library.norfolk.gov.uk

Enquiries to: Manager
Other contacts: Community Librarian

Founded: 1904

Organisation type and purpose: Local government body, public library.

Subject coverage: General, history of King's Lynn and West Norfolk.

Collection: St Margaret's Library Collection (founded 1631)
St Nicholas' Library Collection (founded 1617)
Stanley Library Collection (founded 1854)
Medical, historical, religious and travel works of 15th to 19th centuries

Non-library collection catalogue: All or part available in-house

Library catalogue: All or part available online

Access to staff: Contact by letter, by telephone, by fax, by e-mail and in person
Hours: Mon to Fri, 0900 to 1700

Access for disabled people: Ramped entry

Parent body: Norfolk County Council Library and Information Service

KINGSTON LIBRARIES

Kingston Library, Fairfield Road, Kingston upon Thames, Surrey, KT1 2PS

Tel: 020 8547 6400
Fax: 020 8547 6401
Website: www.kingston.gov.uk/Enjoying/Libraries/default.htm

Enquiries to: Head of Library Services
Direct tel: 020 8547 6413
Direct fax: 020 8547 6426
Direct e-mail: jo.gloyn@rbk.kingston.gov.uk
Other contacts: Information Librarian

Founded: 1902

Organisation type and purpose: Local government body, public library.

Subject coverage: General, English literature, fine arts, statistics, non-HMSO and HMSO government publications.

Library catalogue: All or part available online

Access to staff: Contact by letter, by telephone, by fax and by e-mail.
Appointment necessary.
Hours: Mon, 0930 to 1900; Tue and Fri, 0930 to 1730; Wed, closed; Thu, 0930 to 2000; Sat, 0900 to 1730

Access for disabled people: Ramped entry, access to all public areas

Parent body: Royal Borough of Kingston upon Thames

KINGSTON UNIVERSITY

Information Services, Penrhyn Road, Kingston upon Thames, Surrey, KT1 2EE

Tel: 020 8547 2000
Fax: 020 8417 2111
E-mail: library@kingston.ac.uk
Website: www.kingston.ac.uk/library

Enquiries to: Director of Information Services

Organisation type and purpose: University library.

Subject coverage: Business, law, chemistry, pharmacy, life sciences, mathematics, computer science, surveying, civil, mechanical, production and aeronautical engineering, geography, geology, art and design, architecture, performing art, social sciences, economics, history, English, education, healthcare studies.

Collection: Iris Murdoch Collections, Vane Ivanovic Library, Sheridan Morley Theatre Collection

Non-library collection catalogue: All or part available online

Library catalogue: All or part available online

Publications: Printed

Access to staff: Contact by letter, by telephone, by e-mail, in person and via website
Hours: Mon to Fri, 0900 to 1700
Special comments: Please see website for full details.

Access to building: *Special comments:* Visitors are advised to carry identification.

KIPLING SOCIETY

6 Clifton Road, London, W9 1SS

Tel: 020 7286 0194
E-mail: jmkeskar@btinternet.com
Website: www.kipling.org.uk

Enquiries to: Honorary Secretary
Direct tel: 020 7286 0194
Direct e-mail: jmkeskar@btinternet.com
Other contacts: Honorary Librarian (for the library)

Founded: 1927

Organisation type and purpose: Learned society (membership is by subscription), registered charity (charity number 278885).

Subject coverage: Life, works and associations of Rudyard Kipling 1865–1936; 5 meetings annually and an annual luncheon in central London with guest speakers.

Collection: Library of books on and by R Kipling

Non-library collection catalogue: All or part available online

Library catalogue: All or part available online and in-house

Publications: Printed

Access to staff: Contact by letter, by telephone, by e-mail and via website
Hours: Mon to Fri, 0900 to 1700
Special comments: Library open to the public, by appointment with the Librarian.

Library housed at: City University; Northampton Square, London; tel: 020 7359 2464

Representative in: USA and Australia

KIRKLEES COLLEGE – HUDDERSFIELD CENTRE (KC)

Library, New North Road, Huddersfield, West Yorkshire, HD1 5NN

Tel: 01484 536521
Fax: 01484 511885
Website: www.huddcoll.ac.uk

Enquiries to: Librarian
Direct e-mail: libraryenquiries@kirkleescollege.ac.uk

History of institution: created by the merger of Huddersfield Technical College and Dewsbury College (year of change 2008)

Subject coverage: Business studies, catering, engineering, science, construction, computing, music, social work, leisure and recreation, motor vehicle technology, education and training, art and design, hairdressing, animal care sciences.

Library catalogue: All or part available online and in-house

Publications: Electronic and video

Access to staff: Contact by letter, by telephone, by fax, by e-mail and in person. Appointment necessary.
Hours: Mon to Thu, 0845 to 2000; Fri, 0845 to 1600

Access for disabled people: Parking provided, level entry, access to all public areas, toilet facilities
Special comments: Lifts for disabled

KIRKLEES METROPOLITAN BOROUGH COUNCIL

Cultural Services Headquarters, Red Doles Lane, Huddersfield, West Yorkshire, HD2 1YF

Tel: 01484 226300
Fax: 01484 226342
Website: www.kirkleesmc.gov.uk

Enquiries to: Head of Service
Other contacts: (1) Assistant Head of Service (2) Assistant Head of Service for (1) libraries and information service (2) community history, arts and town halls.

Organisation type and purpose: Local government body, museum, art gallery, public library.

Subject coverage: Local government services.

Library catalogue: All or part available in-house

Publications: Printed
Order printed publications from: Bibliographical Services, at the same address, tel: 01484 226374, fax: 01484 226342, e-mail: julie.peel@kirkleesmc.gov.uk

Publications list: Available in print

Access to staff: Contact by letter, by telephone, by fax, by e-mail, in person and via website
Hours: Mon to Fri, 0900 to 1700

KITE SOCIETY OF GREAT BRITAIN (KSGB)

PO Box 2274, Great Horkesley, Colchester, Essex, CO6 4AY

Tel: 01206 271489
Fax: 01206 271489
E-mail: info@thekitesociety.org.uk
Website: www.thekitesociety.org.uk

Enquiries to: General Secretary

Founded: 1979

Organisation type and purpose: Membership association.

Subject coverage: Kite design, kite groups, kite events, kite shops, kite-flying.

Publications: Printed

Access to staff: Contact by letter, by telephone, by fax and by e-mail
Hours: Mon to Fri, 0900 to 1700

Has: most local kite groups as affiliates

KNITTING & CROCHET GUILD OF GREAT BRITAIN

PO Box 4421, Kidderminster, Worcestershire, DY11 6YW

E-mail: info@knitting-and-crochet-guild.org.uk
Website: www.knitting-and-crochet-guild.org.uk

Direct e-mail: info@knitting-and-crochet-guild.org.uk

Organisation type and purpose: A registered national educational charity (no. 01113468).

Subject coverage: Knitting and crochet.

Collection: Library of books, periodicals and patterns
Collection of garments, samples, domestic knitting machines, yarns, tools and ephemera from the past two hundred years

KNITTING INDUSTRIES' FEDERATION (KIF)

12 Beaumanor Road, Leicester, LE1 5XY

Tel: 0116 266 3332
Fax: 0116 266 3335
E-mail: directorate@knitfed.co.uk

Enquiries to: Director

Founded: 1942

Organisation type and purpose: Trade association (membership is by subscription), present number of members: 300, manufacturing industry.

Subject coverage: Industrial relations, trade policy, government lobbying, environment, health and safety statistics.

Trade and statistical information: Knitstats – comprehensive summary of knitting industry statistics

Publications: Printed

Access to staff: Contact by letter, by telephone, by fax and by e-mail. Appointment necessary. Non-members charged.
Hours: Mon to Fri, 0900 to 1700

Access to building: No prior appointment required

A sector of the: British Clothing Industry Association Limited

KNOWLEDGE SERVICES, NHS HEALTH SCOTLAND

NHS Health Scotland, The Priory, Canaan Lane, Edinburgh, EH10 4SG

Tel: 0141 800 7227
E-mail: nhs.healthscotland-knowledge@nhs.net
Website: www.healthscotland.com/knowledge

Enquiries to: Knowledge Services Manager
Direct tel: 0131 536 5578
Direct e-mail: juliagreen@nhs.net

History of institution: formerly called Health Promotion Library Scotland (year of change 2003); formerly called Health Scotland Library (year of change 2011)

Organisation type and purpose: Knowledge Services for the public health workforce in Scotland

Subject coverage: Health improvement, health promotion, public health, health inequalities

Library catalogue: All or part available online

Publications: Printed
Order printed publications from: e-mail: nhs.healthscotland-knowledge@nhs.net

Publications list: Available online

Access to staff: Contact by letter, by telephone, by e-mail and via website
Hours: Mon to Thu, 0900 to 1630; Fri, 0900 to 1600

Also at: NHS Health Scotland; Elphinstone House, 65 West Regent Street, Glasgow, G2 2AF; tel: 0141 354 2974; e-mail: charis .miller@nhs.net

KNOWSLEY LIBRARY SERVICE

Huyton Library, Civic Way, Huyton, Knowsley, Merseyside, L36 9GD

Tel: 0151 443 3738
Fax: 0151 443 3739
E-mail: huyton.lending.library@knowsley .gov.uk
Website: history.knowsley.gov.uk
Website: www.knowsley.gov.uk

Enquiries to: Information Services Manager

Organisation type and purpose: Local government body, public library.

Subject coverage: General and local history.

Collection: Local history of Knowsley Metropolitan Borough

Library catalogue: All or part available online

Publications: Printed

Publications list: Available in print

Access to staff: Contact by letter, by telephone, by fax, by e-mail, in person and via website
Hours: Mon to Fri, 0915 to 1900; Sat, 1000 to 1600; Sun, 1200 to 1600

Access for disabled people: Parking provided, ramped entry, level entry, access to all public areas, toilet facilities

KODÁLY INSTITUTE OF BRITAIN (KIB)

Queen's Gate School, 133 Queen's Gate, London, SW7 5LE

Tel: 020 7823 7371 or 020 7589 3056
Fax: 020 7584 7691

Enquiries to: Administrator
Other contacts: Director

Founded: 1994

Organisation type and purpose: International organisation, professional body (membership is by subscription), present number of members: 150, training organisation.
Music education/training for adults using the Kodály concept.

Subject coverage: Principles and practice of the Kodály concept.

Publications: Printed, and electronic and video

Publications list: Available in print

Access to staff: Contact by letter, by telephone and by fax. Appointment necessary.
Hours: Mon to Sun, 0900 to 2200

Parent body: International Kodály Society; Budapest, Hungary

Subsidiary: Liszt Academy of Music; Budapest

KOREA NATIONAL TOURISM ORGANIZATION (KNTO)

3rd Floor, New Zealand House, Haymarket, London, SW1Y 4TE

Tel: 020 7321 2535
Fax: 020 7321 0876
E-mail: london@mail.knto.or.kr
Website: www.tour2korea.com

Enquiries to: Director
Other contacts: Marketing Manager

Founded: 1960

Organisation type and purpose: National government body.
Tourist office.
To promote travel and tourism to South Korea.

Subject coverage: Tourism in Korea.

Publications: Printed

Publications list: Available online

Access to staff: Contact by letter, by telephone, by fax, by e-mail, in person and via website. Appointment necessary. Access for members only.
Hours: Mon to Fri, 0900 to 1700

Access to building: *Hours:* Mon to Fri, 0900 to 1700

Access for disabled people: Access to all public areas

Has: over 50 overseas branches

KPMG

8 Salisbury Square, London, EC4Y 8BB

Tel: 020 7311 1000

Enquiries to: Tax Librarian
Direct e-mail: john.ridgley@kpmg.co.uk

Organisation type and purpose: Accounting and management consultancy.

Subject coverage: Accountancy; auditing; company law; corporate finance; taxation; management in many countries and various industries.

Non-library collection catalogue: All or part available in-house

Access to staff: Contact by telephone and by e-mail. Appointment necessary. Access for members only.
Hours: Mon to Fri, 0930 to 1730

Access to building: No prior appointment required

LA LECHE LEAGUE (GREAT BRITAIN) (LLLGB)

PO Box 29, West Bridgford, Nottingham, NG2 7NP

Tel: 0845 456 1866; 0115 981 5599
E-mail: lllgb@wsds.co.uk
Website: www.laleche.org.uk
Website: www.lllbooks.org.uk

Enquiries to: Administrator

Founded: 1973

Organisation type and purpose: Membership association (membership is by subscription), present number of members: 1,000, registered charity (charity number 283771).
To provide information, help and support to mothers wanting to breastfeed.

Subject coverage: Breastfeeding.

Non-library collection catalogue: All or part available online and in print

Publications: Printed
Order printed publications from: LLL Books Ltd, PO Box 29, West Bridgford, Nottingham, NG2 7NP

Publications list: Available online and in print

Access to staff: Contact by letter and by telephone
Hours: 24-hour helpline
Office admin: Mon to Fri, 0900 to 1800

Access to building: No access other than to staff

Also at: LLLGB; Administrative Office, PO Box 29, West Bridgford, Nottingham, NG2 7NP; tel: 0115 945 5772

LABAN CENTRE LONDON

Formal name: Laban Centre for Movement and Dance Limited

14–18 Creekside, Deptford, London, SE8 3DZ

Tel: 020 8692 4070 ext 120
Fax: 020 8694 8749
E-mail: library@laban.co.uk
Website: www.laban.co.uk

Enquiries to: Librarian

Organisation type and purpose: Registered charity (charity number 801973), suitable for ages: 18+.

Subject coverage: Practical and academic education in dance and movement, all kinds of dance: ballet, contemporary, social, theatre, community, dance therapy and related subjects e.g. anatomy, music, psychology, scenography, dance notation, Rudolf Laban, dance medicine, Pilates, European Tanz theatre.

Collection: Grey Literature
Laban Collection (Laban's work in Germany, 1920–1930s) – microfiche
Other printed and audio visual materials
Peter Williams Collection (books, photographs, manuscripts etc, 1930–1995)
Peter Brinson Collection (sociology, education, working archive of 'Ballet for All')
Shirley Wynn Collection (historical dance, notation)

Non-library collection catalogue: All or part available in-house

Library catalogue: All or part available in-house

Publications: Printed

Publications list: Available online

Access to staff: Contact by letter, by telephone, by fax, by e-mail, in person and via website. Appointment necessary. Non-members charged.
Hours: Term time: Mon, Wed & Thu, 0900 to 2000; Tue, 0900 to 1930; Fri, 0900 to 1700; Sat, 1030 to 1430
Vacations: Mon to Fri, 0900 to 1700

LABAN GUILD FOR MOVEMENT AND DANCE

5/24 Westcote Road, Reading, Berkshire, RG30 2DE

Tel: 0118 961 6903

Enquiries to: Secretary

Founded: 1946

Organisation type and purpose:
International organisation, membership association (membership is by subscription), present number of members: 400, registered charity, voluntary organisation (charity number 266435).
To promote and advance the study of Laban based movement and dance. Provides a resource for its members within which they can experience teaching, development, exchange of information and a sense of identity. Promotes the development of movement as an art form, the study of human movement, particularly recognising the contribution made by the late Rudolf Laban.

Publications: Printed

Access to staff: Contact by letter
Hours: Mon to Fri, 0900 to 1700

LABORATORY ANIMAL SCIENCE ASSOCIATION (LASA)

PO Box 3993, Tamworth, Staffordshire, B78 3QU

Tel: 01827 259130
Fax: 01827 259188
E-mail: info@lasa.co.uk
Website: www.lasa.co.uk

Enquiries to: Secretary

Organisation type and purpose: Learned society (membership is by subscription). Advancement of care, welfare and use of animals and replacement where appropriate.

Subject coverage: Animal welfare, refinement in animal studies, alternatives to animal use, education, training in laboratory animal science, laboratory animal health, regulatory controls over uses of laboratory animals, laboratory animal genetics, laboratory animal nutrition, toxicology tests, management of laboratory animal units.

Publications: Printed

Publications list: Available in print

Access to staff: Contact by letter, by telephone, by fax and by e-mail
Hours: Mon to Fri, 0900 to 1700

Affiliated to: Federation of European Laboratory Animal Science Associations (FELASA)

LABOUR PARTY

Eldon House, Regent Centre, Newcastle Upon Tyne, NE3 3PW

Tel: 08705 900 200
Website: www.labour.org.uk/

Organisation type and purpose: Internal resource centre of a political party.

Subject coverage: Social sciences, especially politics, labour history.

Collection: Archives of the Labour Party held at National Museum of Labour History, 103 Princess Street, Manchester M1 6DD, Tel no: 0161 228 7212

Access to staff: Contact by letter, by telephone, by fax and by e-mail
Hours: No access

LABOUR RELATIONS AGENCY (LRA)

Head Office, 2–16 Gordon Street, Belfast, BT1 2LG

Tel: 028 9032 1442
Fax: 028 9033 0827
E-mail: info@lra.org.uk
Website: www.lra.org.uk

Enquiries to: Director
Other contacts: (1) Director (Corporate Services) (2) Director (Advisory Services) (3) Director (Conciliation and Arbitration)

Founded: 1976

Organisation type and purpose: Statutory body.
Provides mediation, arbitration, conciliation and advisory services to employers, trade unions etc and issues codes of practice on employment relations matters.

Subject coverage: Joint consultative and negotiating machinery, employment relations legislation, internal relations and communications, grievance, disciplinary, dismissal and redundancy procedures, trade union recognition, terms and conditions of employment, recruitment, selection and induction, payment systems and job evaluation, manpower planning, labour turnover and absenteeism, employment relations research, training, maternity provisions and legislation, equality legislation.

Publications: Printed

Publications list: Available online and in print

Access to staff: Contact by letter, by telephone, by fax, by e-mail and in person. Appointment necessary.
Hours: Mon to Fri, 0900 to 1700

Access to building: No prior appointment required

Access for disabled people: Ramped entry, level entry, access to all public areas, toilet facilities
Special comments: Parking provided at head office.

Regional Office: Labour Relations Agency; 1–3 Guildhall Street, Londonderry, BT48 6BB; tel: 028 7126 9639; fax: 028 7126 7729; e-mail: info@lra.org.uk; website: www.lra.org.uk

LACE GUILD

The Hollies, 53 Audnam, Stourbridge, West Midlands, DY8 4AE

Tel: 01384 390739
Fax: 01384 444415
E-mail: hollies@laceguild.org
Website: www.laceguild.demon.co.uk

Enquiries to: Administrative Officer; Accounts Officer
Other contacts: Headquarters staff (for availability on a daily basis)

Founded: 1976

Organisation type and purpose:
International organisation, national organisation, membership association (membership is by subscription), present number of members: 5,000 approx, voluntary organisation, registered charity (charity number 274397), museum, suitable for ages: all.
Accredited museum (number RD 1950).
The role of The Lace Guild is to promote understanding and appreciation of all aspects of lace and lacemaking.

Subject coverage: All aspects of lace including: history (social and technical); making of all English and most European bobbin, needle and craft laces; equipment and materials; publications; exhibitions; courses.

Collection: Collections of lace and lace-related artefacts, including patterns, tools, materials, sample books
Comprehensive library of books, magazines (from around the world), photographs, documents and study folios covering every aspect of lace

Non-library collection catalogue: All or part available in-house

Library catalogue: All or part available online and in print

Publications: Printed

Publications list: Available online and in print

Access to staff: Contact by letter, by telephone, by fax, by e-mail and via website. Appointment necessary.
Hours: Mon to Fri, 0900 to 1600

Access to building: Prior appointment required
Hours: Mon to Fri, 0900 to 1600

LACROSSE SCOTLAND

Tel: 07764 943053
E-mail: president@lacrossescotland.com
Website: www.lacrossescotland.com

Enquiries to: President
Other contacts: Membership Secretary

Organisation type and purpose: Governing body for lacrosse in Scotland.

Subject coverage: All aspects of lacrosse in Scotland from schools to international fixtures.

Access to staff: Contact by telephone and by e-mail

LADIES EUROPEAN TOUR (LET)

The Old Hall, Dorchester Way, Macclesfield, Cheshire, SK10 2LQ

Tel: 01625 611444
Fax: 01625 610406
E-mail: mail@ladieseuropeantour.com
Website: www.ladieseuropeantour.com

Enquiries to: Executive Director

Founded: 1988

Organisation type and purpose: Professional sports body.

Subject coverage: Women's professional golf.

Publications: Printed

Access to staff: Contact by letter, by fax, by e-mail and via website. Appointment necessary.
Hours: Mon to Fri, 0900 to 1700

LADIES' GOLF UNION (LGU)

The Scores, St Andrews, Fife, KY16 9AT

Tel: 01334 475811
Fax: 01334 472818
E-mail: info@lgu.org
Website: www.lgu.org

Enquiries to: CEO

Founded: 1893

Organisation type and purpose: Membership association.

Subject coverage: Ladies' amateur golf from 1893.

Collection: Photograph albums 1893–1929
Records of British ladies' golf since 1893

Publications: Printed

Access to staff: Contact by letter, by telephone, by fax, by e-mail and via website
Hours: Mon to Fri, 0900 to 1700

LAKE DISTRICT NATIONAL PARK AUTHORITY (LDNPA)

Murley Moss Business Park, Oxenholme Road, Kendal, Cumbria, LA9 7RL

Tel: 01539 724555\ Minicom no. 01539 731263
Fax: 01593 740822
E-mail: hq@lake-district.gov.uk
Website: www.lake-district.gov.uk

Enquiries to: Communications Manager
Direct tel: 01539 792683
Direct fax: 01539 740822
Direct e-mail: mick.casey@lake-district.gov .uk

Founded: 1951

Organisation type and purpose: Local government body, membership association (membership is by election or invitation), present number of members: 26, service industry.
To conserve and enhance natural beauty, wildlife and cultural heritage of the National Park, promote opportunities for understanding and enjoyment of its special qualities, seeking to foster economic and social well-being of its local communities.

Subject coverage: Information on the National Park: access, conservation, landscape, historic sites, buildings etc, farming, mining and quarrying, traffic and parking, tourism. Local community, control of development.

Publications: Printed

Publications list: Available online and in print

Access to staff: Contact by letter, by telephone, by fax, by e-mail and via website. Appointment necessary.
Hours: Mon to Thu, 0900 to 1700; Fri, 0900 to 1645

Access for disabled people: Parking provided, level entry, toilet facilities

Member of: Association of National Park Authorities (ANPA); Ponsford House, Moretonhampstead, Newton Abbot, Devon, TQ13 8NL; tel: 01647 440245; Federation of Nature and National Parks of Europe

LAKELAND DIALECT SOCIETY (LDS)

Gale View, Main Street, Shap, Penrith, Cumbria, CA10 3NH

Tel: 01931 716386
E-mail: lakespeak@aol.com
Website: www.lakelanddialectsociety.org

Enquiries to: Honorary Secretary
Other contacts: Vice President and Editor, tel: 01931 715359

Founded: 1939

Organisation type and purpose: Membership association (membership is by subscription), present number of members: 300, voluntary organisation.

Subject coverage: The Cumbrian dialect in general, its origins and its use today.

Collection: Small collection of Cumbrian dialect literature, minute books and papers of the Society (held in Carlisle Library, Globe Lane, Carlisle). May be viewed by arrangement

Publications: Printed, and electronic and video

Access to staff: Contact by letter, by telephone, by e-mail, in person and via website
Hours: Mon to Fri, 0900 to 1800
Special comments: Evenings after 1945 hours.

Access to building: No prior appointment required

Internal links with: Cumberland Women's Institute; Yorkshire Dialect Society; Librarian, School of English, University of Leeds, Leeds, LS2 9JT

LAMBETH ARCHIVES DEPARTMENT

Minet Library, 52 Knatchbull Road, London, SE5 9QY

Tel: 020 7926 6076
Fax: 020 7926 6080

Enquiries to: Archivist

Organisation type and purpose: Local government body, public library.
Record office.
To preserve and make accessible the records of the London Borough of Lambeth, its predecessors, and the records of Lambeth people and places.

Subject coverage: Records of the London Borough of Lambeth and its predecessors; deposited records of local Lambeth organisations; local history and topography of Lambeth and the old county of Surrey; manorial records; estate records; business records.

Collection: Crystal Palace Collection (books, programmes, cuttings)
South London Theatres Collection (playbills and programmes)
Surrey Collection
Vauxhall Gardens Collection (playbills, cuttings, songbooks, manuscripts)
Woolley Collection of Doulton and other stoneware

Publications: Printed

Publications list: Available in print

Access to staff: Contact by letter, by telephone, by fax, by e-mail and in person. Appointment necessary.
Hours: Mon to Fri, 0900 to 1700

Access for disabled people: Ramped entry

Parent body: London Borough of Lambeth

LAMBETH PALACE LIBRARY

London, SE1 7JU

Tel: 020 7898 1400
Fax: 020 7928 7932
E-mail: lpl.staff@lpl.c-of-e.org.uk
Website: www.lambethpalacelibrary.org

Enquiries to: Librarian

Founded: 1610

Organisation type and purpose: Academic Research Library.

Subject coverage: Ecclesiastical history, particularly of the Church of England; general history; palaeography; early printing; art history; American colonial history; bibliography; genealogy; topography.

Collection: Archives of the Province of Canterbury, including marriage allegations, wills, Court of Arches, etc
Incunables (200)
Manuscripts from 9th century to present (4,000)
Papers of the Archbishops of Canterbury from the 16th century
Papers of the Bishops of London, including extensive collections concerning colonial America and the West Indies from the 17th century
Papers of the Commonwealth, Earls of Shrewsbury, Anthony Bacon, George Carew (Earl of Totnes), Commissioners for Building 50 New Churches (Queen Anne Churches)
Papers of societies, etc, within the Church of England, Anglo-Continental Society, Christian Faith Society, Church of England Temperance Society, Church Union, Clergy Orphan Corporation, Confraternity of the Blessed Sacrament, etc
Papers of statesmen and bishops, Gladstone, Selborne, Bishops G K A Bell, A C Headlam, E J Palmer, C Wordsworth, etc
Printed books collection (approximately 200,000 items)
Prints collection (church topography and portraits)
Records of Lambeth Conferences, from 1867
Records of the Incorporated Church Building Society (19th and 20th centuries, 16,000 originals and database)
Registers of foreign churches, Basra, Khartoum, Shanghai, Shantung
Registers of the Archbishops of Canterbury, from 13th century

continued overleaf

Sion College collection (manuscripts and printed books pre-1850)
STC Titles (3,500)

Non-library collection catalogue: All or part available online, in-house and in print

Library catalogue: All or part available in-house

Publications: Printed, and microform publications

Publications list: Available in print

Access to staff: Contact by letter, by telephone, by fax and in person. Letter of introduction required.
Hours: Mon to Fri, 1000 to 1700
Special comments: Closed for 10 days at Christmas and Easter.

Access for disabled people: Parking, bathroom facilities, ramp, hearing induction loop.

Funded by: Church Commissioners for England (Church of England)

LAMBRETTA CLUB GB (LCGB)

8 Trent Close, Rainhill, Prescot, Merseyside, L35 9LD

Tel: 0151 426 9839
Fax: 0151 426 9839
E-mail: lcgb2@blueyonder.co.uk
Website: www.lcgb.co.uk

Enquiries to: General Secretary
Direct tel: 07966 265588 (Mobile)

Founded: 1953

Organisation type and purpose:
International organisation, membership association.
To further the interests of Lambretta enthusiasts worldwide.

Subject coverage: Everything for the Lambretta enthusiast from shows, events, competition, technical information, DVLA approved for registration problems.

Collection: Various books and manuals relevant to Lambretta

Publications: Printed, and electronic and video

Access to staff: Contact by letter, by telephone, by fax and by e-mail
Hours: Mon to Fri, 0930 to 1730
Special comments: Contact by fax, 0930 to 1730, mark for the attention of Kev Walsh.

LANARK LIBRARY

Lindsay Institute, 16 Hope Street, Lanark, ML11 7LZ

Tel: 01555 661144
E-mail: lanark.ref@library.s-lanark.org.uk
Website: www.slleisureandculture.co.uk

Enquiries to: Reference Library Supervisor

Founded: 1914

Organisation type and purpose: Leisure and Culture Trust, public library.

Subject coverage: Reference, local and family history.

Collection: William Smellie Collection (mainly 18th-century midwifery, obstetrics, gynaecology)
Robert Owen Collection (co-operative movement, New Lanark)
Coalburn Collection (330 images of a coal mining village c. 1880–1930)
Poster Collection (200+ posters of local events, including circuses, visiting shows, sports and civic functions)
Image Collection 3,281 items – mainly local views, people and events, but with a proportion of South Seas images (New Zealand, Samoa, etc.), Algiers & environs and a collection of 'Moral Tales'.

Library catalogue: All or part available in-house

Access to staff: Contact by letter, by telephone, by e-mail and in person
Hours: Mon, 0915 to 1930; Tue and Thu, 0915 to 2000; Wed and Sat, 0915 to 1700; Fri, 0930 to 1930
Special comments: Dedicated Reference/Local History staff available Mon, 1230 to 1930; Tue to Thu, 0915 to 1700; Sat, 0930 to 1700. Only available on alternate Wednesdays and Saturdays. It is advisable to contact in advance of any visit to ensure full access.

Access to building: Public access during opening hours

Access for disabled people: To ground and second floors only. Internet access is also available on second floor.

LANCASHIRE AND CHESHIRE ANTIQUARIAN SOCIETY (LCAS)

59 Malmesbury Road, Cheadle Hulme, Cheadle, Cheshire, SK8 7QL

Tel: 0161 439 7202
E-mail: morrisgarratt@sky.com
Website: www.landcas.org.uk

Enquiries to: Honorary Secretary

Founded: 1883

Organisation type and purpose: Learned society (membership is by subscription), present number of members: 320, suitable for all ages

Subject coverage: Interests are broad, encompassing national and local events and all historical aspects of the life and topography of the region. Current fields of study include archaeology, both traditional and industrial; architecture and the arts; social and economic history, particularly religious and educational developments; the history of trade, trades and transport; and the history of institutions and local government.

Collection: Library books, chiefly relating to the north-west of England, (c.1,600 vols)

Library catalogue: All or part available in print

Publications: Printed

Publications list: Available online

Access to staff: Contact by letter, by telephone, by e-mail and via website
Hours: Mon to Fri, 0930 to 1630 (Portico Library)

Access to building: No access other than to staff
Special comments: Library housed in Manchester Central Library. Members may request library tickets.

Also at: c/o Portico Library; 57 Mosley Street, Manchester, M2 3HY; tel: 0161 236 6785; Honorary Membership Secretary (subscriptions); 3 Syddal Crescent, Bramhall, Stockport

LANCASHIRE ARCHIVES

Record Office, Bow Lane, Preston, Lancashire, PR1 2RE

Tel: 01772 533039
Fax: 01772 533050
E-mail: record.office@lancashire.gov.uk
Website: www.a2a.org.uk
Website: www.archives.lancashire.gov.uk

Enquiries to: Archives Service Manager

Founded: 1940

Organisation type and purpose: Local government body.
County record office.
Providing archive services to Lancashire, Blackburn with Darwen, and Blackpool.

Subject coverage: Historical primary source material relating to all aspects of life and society in Lancashire, 12th century to present day.

Special visitor services: Regular sessions for new users – see website for details

Education services: Schools service available from September 2012

Services for disabled people: Building is fully accessible

Collection: More than 8 miles of archives, too extensive to specify
Extensive local history collection
For listings see Guide to Lancashire Record Office and Guide to Lancashire Record Office, a Supplement 1977–1989 and Lancashire Archives website

Non-library collection catalogue: All or part available online and in-house

Library catalogue: All or part available online and in-house

Publications: Printed, and microform publications
Order printed publications from: see above
Order microform publications from: see above

Publications list: Available online and in print

Access to staff: Contact by letter, by telephone, by fax, by e-mail, in person and via website
Hours: Mon, Wed, Fri, 0900 to 1700; Tue, 0900 to 2030; Thu, 1000 to 1700
Open 2nd Sat of each month (except holiday weekends), 1000 to 1600
Special comments: County Archives Research Network (CARN) ticket required (can be issued on production of an acceptable ID).

Access to building: *Hours:* Mon, Wed, Fri, 0900 to 1700; Tue, 0900 to 2030; Thu, 1000 to 1700
Open 2nd Sat of each month (except holiday weekends), 1000 to 1600
Special comments: County Archives Research Network (CARN) ticket required (can be issued on production of an acceptable ID).

Access for disabled people: Parking provided, access to all public areas, toilet facilities
Hours: as above

Special comments: Disabled persons' lift.

Provides archive services for unitary councils under joint agreement: Blackpool Council and Blackburn with Darwen Council

LANCASHIRE COUNTY LIBRARY AND INFORMATION SERVICE

Harris Library, Market Square, Preston, Lancashire, PR1 2PP

Tel: 01772 532676
Fax: 01772 555527
E-mail: harris.enquiries@lancashire.gov.uk
Website: www.lancashire.gov.uk/libraries

Founded: 1879

Organisation type and purpose: Local government body, public library.

Subject coverage: Business information, commerce, standards, general information in social studies and humanities fields, community history, genealogy, market research reports

Collection: Dr. Shepherd Library of mostly 18th- and 19th-century books of medical, general and historical interest
Francis Thompson Collection (poetry)
Local Studies – Lancashire
Spencer Collection of Children's Books
Stocks Massey Music Library (Burnley Central Library)

Non-library collection catalogue: All or part available online

Library catalogue: All or part available online

Publications: Printed

Access to staff: Contact by letter, by telephone, by fax, by e-mail and in person
Hours: Mon, Wed, Fri, 0930 to 1930; Tue, Thu, Sat, 0930 to 1700; Sun, 1100 to 1600

Access for disabled people: Ramped entry, lift

Parent body: Lancashire County Council

LANCASHIRE COUNTY MUSEUM SERVICE

Stanley Street, Preston, Lancashire, PR1 4YP

Tel: 01772 534061
Fax: 01772 534079
E-mail: museums.enquiries@lancashire.gov.uk
Website: www.lancsmuseums.gov.uk

Enquiries to: Marketing Assistant

Founded: 1983

Organisation type and purpose: Local government body, suitable for ages: all. Administrative body for the local government museums.

Subject coverage: The subjects covered by the museums of Lancashire include: military history, local history, social history, maritime history, textile machinery, art, fine art, childhood collections, geology, natural science and conservation.

Access to staff: Contact by letter, by telephone, by fax, by e-mail and via website
Hours: Mon to Fri, 0900 to 1700

Access for disabled people: Ramped entry, access to all public areas, toilet facilities

Museums, Galleries or Historic Sites: Fleetwood Museum; Queens Terrace, Fleetwood, Lancashire, FY7 6BT; tel: 01253 876621; fax: 01253 878088; e-mail: fleetwood.museum@lancashire.gov.uk; Gawthorpe Hall; Padiham, Nr Burnley, BB12 8UA; tel: 01282 771004; fax: 01282 770178; e-mail: gawthorpe.hall@lancashire.gov.uk; Helmshore Mills Textile Museum; Holcombe Road, Helmshore, Rossendale, Lancashire, BB4 4NP; tel: 01706 226459; fax: 01706 218554; e-mail: helmshore.museum@lancashire.gov.uk; Judges' Lodgings; Church Street, Lancaster, LA1 1YS; tel: 01524 32808; e-mail: judges.lodgings@lancashire.gov.uk; Lancaster Castle; Shire Hall, Castle Parade, Lancaster, LA1 1YJ; tel: 01524 64998; fax: 01524 847914; Lancaster City Museum; Market Square, Lancaster, LA1 1HT; tel: 01524 64637; fax: 01524 841692; e-mail: lancaster.citymuseum@lancashire.gov.uk; Lancaster Cottage Museum; 15 Castle Hill, Lancaster, LA1 1HT; tel: 01524 64637; fax: 01524 841692; Lancaster Maritime Museum; Custom House, St. George's Quay, Lancaster, LA1 1RB; tel: 01524 382264; fax: 01524 841692; Museum of Lancashire; Stanley Street, Preston, PR1 4YP; tel: 01772 534075; fax: 01772 534079; Queen Street Mill; Harle Skye, Burnley, Lancashire, BB10 2HX; tel: 01282 412555; fax: 01282 430220; e-mail: queenstreet.mill@lancashire.gov.uk; Rossendale Museum; Whitaker Park, Rawtenstall, Rossendale, BB4 6RE; tel: 01706 244682; fax: 01706 250037; e-mail: rossendalemuseum@lancashire.gov.uk

Parent body: Lancashire County Council; County Hall, Preston, Lancashire

LANCASHIRE TEACHING HOSPITALS NHS FOUNDATION TRUST

Library and Information Service, Royal Preston Hospital, Sharoe Green Lane, Preston, Lancashire, PR2 9HT

Tel: 01772 522763
Fax: 01772 523491
E-mail: mandy.beaumont@lthtr.nhs.uk
Website: www.lancsteachinghospitals.nhs.uk

Enquiries to: Knowledge and Library Services Manager
Direct e-mail: library.RPH@lthtr.nhs.uk

Organisation type and purpose: National government body.
Health library.
Multiprofessional library.

Subject coverage: Medicine, health sciences, NHS management, nursing, general practice.

Library catalogue: All or part available in-house

Publications: Printed

Publications list: Available online

Access to staff: Contact by letter, by telephone, by fax, by e-mail, in person and via website. Appointment necessary. All charged.
Hours: Wed, Fri, 0900 to 1700; Mon, Tue, Thu, 0900 to 1900

Member of: British Medical Association (BMA); Library and Information Health Network Northwest (LIHNN); Royal College of Surgeons

LANCASHIRE TEXTILE MANUFACTURERS' ASSOCIATION (LTMA)

4 St Andrew's Street, Blackburn, Lancashire, BB1 8AE

Tel: 01254 580248
Fax: 01254 580248
E-mail: enquiries@ltma.co.uk
Website: ltma.co.uk

Enquiries to: Secretary
Direct e-mail: s.walsh@ltma.co.uk

Founded: 1850

Organisation type and purpose: A non-profit making trade organisation, the operating costs of which are met by an annual levy on members who are drawn from an area encompassing Cumbria, Lancashire, Greater Manchester and West Yorkshire.
To provide practical and up-to-date help and advice on any problem that its textile industry member companies may face; to act as a first point of contact for sales or supply enquiries from third parties; to promote the benefits to the regional economy of a strong and healthy textile industry.

Subject coverage: Services to member organisations: a comprehensive industrial relations service, including assistance in resolving disputes; advice on employment law, training and health and safety matters; district negotiations on wages, conditions of service and holidays; interpretation and implementation of both local and national agreements; commercial and economic information; seminars on subjects of special interest to members; information on grant aid as and when available from both central and local government and the EU; a bi-annual survey of wage levels within the industry; assistance with legally required employment documentation; representation at employment tribunals if necessary; assistance in drafting company policy documents.

Publications: Printed

Access to staff: Contact by letter, by telephone, by fax, by e-mail and via website

Member organisation of: United Kingdom Fashion and Textiles Association

LANCASTER CENTRAL LIBRARY

Market Street, Lancaster, LA1 1HY

Tel: 01524 580700
Fax: 01524 580709
E-mail: lancaster.library@lancscc.gov.uk
Website: www.lancashire.gov.uk/libraries/librarydetails/libsearch1.asp?name=Lancaster

Enquiries to: Librarian
Other contacts: District Manager; Community History Manager

Founded: 1932

Organisation type and purpose: Public library.

continued overleaf

Subject coverage: General, local history.

Information services: Information Desk, Quick Reference, Online Reference Library.

Education services: Heritage Centre (local, community and family history).

Trade and statistical information: via the Online Reference Library accessible to library members

Non-library collection catalogue: All or part available online

Library catalogue: All or part available online

Access to staff: Contact by letter, by telephone, by fax, by e-mail, in person and via website
Hours: Mon to Wed and Fri, 0930 to 1700; Thu, 0930 to 1900; Sat, 0930 to 1600

LANCASTER CITY COUNCIL

Town Hall, Lancaster, LA1 1PJ

Tel: 01524 582000, 01524 582175 (minicom)
Fax: 01524 582161
E-mail: customerservices@lancaster.gov.uk
Website: www.lancaster.gov.uk

Enquiries to: Chief Executive

Founded: 1974

Organisation type and purpose: Local government body.

Subject coverage: Public and local information about services available within the Lancaster district.

Collection: Various public records relating to the Lancaster district
Publications: Printed

Access to staff: Contact by letter, by telephone, by fax, by e-mail, in person and via website
Hours: Mon to Fri, 0845 to 1715

LANCASTER CITY MUSEUMS

Market Square, Lancaster, LA1 1HT

Tel: 01524 64637
Fax: 01524 841692
E-mail: Museums.Enquiries@lancashire.gov.uk
Website: www.lancsmuseum.gov.uk

Founded: 1923

Organisation type and purpose: Local government body, museum, suitable for ages: 5+.

Subject coverage: King's Own Royal Regiment, maritime history, archaeology, local history, social history, costume, numismatics, fine art, decorative art, transport, military history.

Information services: Guided tours on request.

Special visitor services: Guided tours, materials and/or activities for children.

Education services: Group education facilities, resources for Key Stages 1, 2, 3 and 4 and Further or Higher Education.

Services for disabled people: For the visually impaired; displays and/or information at wheelchair height.

Collection: Archive and library relating to the King's Own Royal Regiment (Lancaster) (inc. important MSS)

Publications: Printed

Access to staff: Contact by letter, by telephone, by fax, by e-mail, in person and via website. Appointment necessary.
Hours: Mon to Sat, 1000 to 1700
Special comments: Prior appointment required.

Access to building: No prior appointment required
Hours: Mon to Sat, 1000 to 1700
Special comments: Closed Christmas and New Year.

Access for disabled people: Ramped entry, access to all public areas

Comprises 3 local government museums and a trustee museum: King's Own Regimental Museum

Museum sites: City Museum; same address; Cottage Museum; 15 Castle Hill, Lancaster; Lancaster Maritime Museum; St George's Quay, Lancaster, LA1 1RB; tel: 01524 64637; fax: 01524 841692; e-mail: awhite@lancaster.gov.uk

Parent body: Lancaster City Council; at the same address

Supported by: Friends of Lancaster City Museum; at the same address

LANCASTER UNIVERSITY LIBRARY

Bailrigg, Lancaster, LA1 4YH

Tel: 01524 592536
Fax: 01524 63806/65719
E-mail: library@lancaster.ac.uk
Website: www.libweb.lancs.ac.uk
Website: cat.lib.lancs.ac.uk
Website: primo-se1.lancs.ac.uk/primo_library/libweb/action/search.do?dscnt=1&dstmp=1338201808951&vid=LUL_VU1&fromLogin=true

Enquiries to: Librarian
Direct e-mail: c.powne@lancaster.ac.uk

Founded: 1963

Organisation type and purpose: University library.

Subject coverage: Usual fields of university study, science and technology, social sciences, business studies, humanities.

Collection: Beetham Vestry Library
Burnley Grammar School Collection (rare books, 17th and 18th centuries)
Business histories
European Documentation Centre
Ford Railway Collection
Headlam-Morley religious pamphlets
Jack Hylton Archive
Legal History Collection
Library of the Fell and Rock Climbing Club of the English Lake District
Patten Second World War Pamphlet Collection
Preston Library (Cartmel Priory)
Quaker Collection
Redlich Collection (music)
Socialist Collection

Trade and statistical information: Numerous holdings, including government publications, to support the teaching and research of the Economics Department and Management School

Library catalogue: All or part available online

Publications: Electronic and video
Order electronic and video publications from: Available through web pages: lancaster.libguides.com

Access to staff: Contact by letter, by telephone, by fax, by e-mail and in person. Non-members charged.
Hours: Term time & Easter Vacation: Mon to Fri 1000 to 2000; Sat to Sun, 1300 to 1800. Summer & Christmas Vacations: Mon to Fri 1000 to 2000; Sat, 1300 to 1700; Sun, closed

Access to building: *Hours:* Term time & Easter Vacation: Mon – Sat 0800–2400; Sun, 1000 – 2100.
Summer & Christmas Vacations: Mon – Fri 0800–2200; Sat, 1000 -1700; Sun, closed

Parent body: Lancaster University; Bailrigg, Lancaster, LA1 4YW; tel: 01524 65201; fax: 01524 846243

LANDCRAB OWNERS CLUB INTERNATIONAL LIMITED (LOCI)

5 Rolston Avenue, Huntington, York, YO31 9JD

Tel: 01904 620125 (evenings only)
Website: www.landcrab.net

Enquiries to: Chairman
Other contacts: Spares Secretary, Historian

Founded: 1988

Organisation type and purpose: Membership association (membership is by subscription), voluntary organisation.

Subject coverage: Austin Morris Wolseley 1800 and 2200s, from 1964 to 1975 (ADO 17): advice; spares; interest and exhibitions of these vehicles.

Non-library collection catalogue: All or part available in-house

Library catalogue: All or part available in-house

Publications: Printed

Access to staff: Contact by letter and by telephone
Hours: Telephone: evenings only

Has: Local groups

Member of: Federation of British Historic Vehicle Clubs (FBHVC); PO Box 2506, Henfield, West Sussex; tel: 01273 495051

LANDLIFE

National Wildflower Centre, Court Hey Park, Liverpool, L16 3NA

Tel: 0151 737 1819
Fax: 0151 737 1820
E-mail: info@landlife.org.uk
Website: www.landlife.org.uk

Enquiries to: Administrator
Other contacts: Chief Executive

Founded: 1975

Organisation type and purpose: National organisation, voluntary organisation, registered charity (charity number 290510). Landlife is a charity taking action for a better environment by creating new opportunities for wildlife and encouraging people to enjoy them.

Subject coverage: Wildflower landscaping and gardening, creative conservation consultancy service, environmental advice for community groups and schools, derelict land reclamation techniques and research, sales of wildflower seed, plants and publications.

Library catalogue: All or part available online and in print

Publications: Printed

Publications list: Available online and in print

Access to staff: Contact by letter, by telephone, by fax and by e-mail. Appointment necessary.
Hours: Mon to Fri, 0900 to 1700

Access for disabled people: Parking provided, ramped entry, toilet facilities

Links with: National Wildflower Centre; (Landlife's Millennium project); tel: 0151 737 1819; fax: 0151 737 1820; e-mail: info@nwc.org.uk; UK MAB Urban Forum; Urban Wildlife Partnership; Wildlife Trusts

Trading subsidiary: Landlife Wildflowers Limited; tel: 0151 737 1819; fax: 0151 737 1820; e-mail: info@wildflower.org.uk

LANDMARK INFORMATION GROUP

7 Abbey Court, Eagle Way, Sowton, Exeter, Devon, EX2 7HY

Tel: 01392 441700
Fax: 01392 441709
Website: www.landmark-information.co.uk
Website: www.promap.co.uk
Website: www.home-envirosearch.com
Website: www.old-maps.co.uk

Enquiries to: Customer Services

Founded: 1995

Organisation type and purpose: Service industry.
Suppliers of environmental risk information, current and historical mapping.

Subject coverage: Environmental risk management, digital mapping, contaminated land, previous land use, current land use.

Collection: Digital historical maps (with OS) Environmental information database

Publications: Printed, and electronic and video

Access to staff: Contact by letter, by telephone, by fax, by e-mail and via website
Hours: Mon to Fri, 0900 to 1700

Access to building: No access other than to staff
Hours: Mon to Fri, 0900 to 1700

Access for disabled people: Level entry, toilet facilities

Other address: Landmark Information Group; 3rd Floor, Challanger House, 42 Adler Street, London, E1 1EE; tel: 020 7958 4999; fax: 020 7958 4981; e-mail: mailbox@landmark-information.co.uk; Prodat Systems plc; Northpoint House, Highlands Lane, Henley on Thames, Oxon, RG9 4PR; tel: 01491 413030; fax: 01491 413031; e-mail: sales@promap.co.uk

Parent body: Daily Mail and General Trust Group (DMGT); Northcliffe House, 2 Derry Street, Kensington, London, W8 5TT

LANDMARK TRUST

Shottesbrooke, Maidenhead, Berkshire, SL6 3SW

Tel: 01628 825920
Fax: 01628 825417
Website: www.landmarktrust.org.uk

Enquiries to: Public Relations Manager

Founded: 1965

Organisation type and purpose: Registered charity in England and Wales (charity number 243312) and Scotland (charity number SC039205).
Building preservation charity.

Subject coverage: Restoration of historic buildings for self-catering holidays all year round.

Collection: A picture library of all Landmarks.

Publications: Printed

Access to staff: Contact by letter
Hours: Mon to Fri, 0900 to 1700

LANDS TRIBUNAL FOR SCOTLAND (LTS)

George House, 126 George Street, Edinburgh, EH2 4HH

Tel: 0131 271 4350
Fax: 0131 271 4399
E-mail: mailbox@lands-tribunal-scotland.org.uk
Website: www.lands-tribunal-scotland.org.uk

Enquiries to: Clerk to the Tribunal
Other contacts: Depute Clerk

Founded: 1971

Organisation type and purpose: Judicial body.
Various jurisdictions relating to valuation of land in Scotland.

Subject coverage: Discharge and variation of title conditions; determination of disputed compensation (e.g. following compulsory purchase); disputed valuations for tax purposes (e.g. assessment for ratings); appeals against Keeper of the Registers of Scotland and disputes arising from Tenants' Rights legislation in relation to tenants' right to buy.

Access to staff: Contact by letter, by telephone, by fax, by e-mail and in person
Hours: Mon to Thu, 0900 to 1700; Fri, 0900 to 1600

Access to building: *Hours:* as above

Access for disabled people: *Hours:* as above

LANDSCAPE INSTITUTE (LI)

Charles Darwin House, 12 Roger Street, London, WC1N 2JU

Tel: 020 7685 2640
Fax: 020 7685 2641
E-mail: lesleym@landscapeinstitute.org
Website: www.landscapeinstitute.org

Founded: 1929

Organisation type and purpose: Professional body.
To promote the highest standard of professional service in the application of the arts and sciences of landscape architecture, management and science.

Subject coverage: Landscape design, management, conservation or restoration.

Publications: Printed

Publications list: Available online

Access to staff: Contact by letter, by telephone, by fax and by e-mail
Hours: Mon to Fri, 0900 to 1700

Access to building: No prior appointment required
Hours: Library: Mon to Fri, 0900 to 1700

Member of: Construction Industry Council; International Federation of Landscape Architects (IFLA); World Conservation Union (IUCN)

LANDSCAPE RESEARCH GROUP LTD (LRG)

PO Box 1482, Oxford, OX4 9DN, UK

E-mail: admin@landscaperesearch.org
Website: www.landscaperesearch.org.uk

Enquiries to: Administrator

Founded: 1967

Organisation type and purpose: International organisation, learned society (membership is by subscription), voluntary organisation, registered charity (charity number 287610).

Subject coverage: Landscape: aesthetics, design, management, conservation, perception, assessment, planning; landscape and the arts; landscape, literature and ecology.

Publications: Printed

Access to staff: Contact by letter and by e-mail
Hours: Mon to Fri, 0900 to 1700

LANGHOLM LIBRARY

The Library Buildings, High Street, Langholm, Dumfries & Galloway, DG13 0DJ

Enquiries to: Chairman

Founded: 1800

Organisation type and purpose: Voluntary organisation, registered charity (charity number SC 011403).

Library catalogue: All or part available in-house

Access to staff: Contact by letter. Appointment necessary.
Hours: Tue, Fri, 1000 to 1200; Thu, 1900 to 2100

LANGTON MATRAVERS LOCAL HISTORY AND PRESERVATION SOCIETY (LMLHPS)

Barton, The Hyde, Langton Matravers, Swanage, Dorset, BH19 3HE

Tel: 01929 423168
Website: www.langtonia.org.uk

Enquiries to: Membership Secretary
Direct tel: 01929 421481
Direct e-mail: localhistory@langtonia.org.uk
Other contacts: Publicity Officer, tel: 01929 422218

Founded: 1971

Organisation type and purpose: Learned society (membership is by subscription), registered charity (charity number 272407), museum.
To research and publish local history.

Subject coverage: Local history, family history, local industries.

Collection: Genealogical charts, transcripts of parish registers, memorial inscriptions, national census returns, etc.
Local history library

Non-library collection catalogue: All or part available in-house

Library catalogue: All or part available in-house

Publications list: Available online and in print

Access to staff: Contact by letter, by telephone, by e-mail, in person and via website
Hours: Mon to Fri, 0900 to 1700

Access to building: No prior appointment required
Hours: Apr 1 to Sept 30: Mon to Sat, 1000 to 1200 and 1400 to 1600
Special comments: Or by appointment.

Access for disabled people: Parking provided, level entry, access to all public areas

Parent body for: Langton Matravers Museum; at the same address

LANTERNHOUSE

Formal name: Lanternhouse International

Lanternhouse, The Ellers, Ulverston, Cumbria, LA12 0AA

Tel: 01229 581127; minicom no. 01229 587146
Fax: 01229 581232
E-mail: welcome@lanternhouse.org
Website: www.lanternhouse.org

Enquiries to: Communications Co-ordinator

Organisation type and purpose: International organisation, registered charity (charity number 265461), art gallery, suitable for ages: all, consultancy, research organisation, publishing house.
Artist-led company pioneering the arts of celebration and ceremony.

Subject coverage: Arts of celebration.

Special visitor services: Guided tours.

Education services: Group education facilities.

Publications: Printed

Access to staff: Contact by letter, by telephone, by fax, by e-mail and via website. Appointment necessary.
Hours: Mon to Fri, 0900 to 1700

Access for disabled people: Parking provided, level entry, access to all public areas, toilet facilities

LARGS AND NORTH AYRSHIRE FAMILY HISTORY SOCIETY

c/o Bogriggs Cottage, Carlung, West Kilbride, Ayrshire, KA23 9PS

Tel: 01294 823690
Website: www.lnafhs.freeyellow.com

Enquiries to: General Secretary

Founded: 1988

Organisation type and purpose: Membership association, present number of members: 140.
Family history society.

Subject coverage: Advice in family history research sources.

Library catalogue: All or part available in-house

Access to staff: Contact by letter and by telephone
Hours: Mon to Fri, 0900 to 1700

LASA

3rd Floor, Universal House, 88 Wentworth Street, London, E1 7SA

Tel: 020 7377 2748
Fax: 020 7247 4725
E-mail: info@lasa.org.uk
Website: www.lasa.org.uk
Website: www.rightsnet.org.uk
Website: www.multikulti.org.uk
Website: ictknowledgebase.org.uk
Website: www.suppliersdirectory.org.uk
Website: ukriders.lasa.org.uk
Website: ictchampion.lasa.org.uk

Founded: 1984; formerly called London Advice Services Alliance (year of change 2010)

Organisation type and purpose: Voluntary organisation, registered charity, training organisation, consultancy, research organisation.

Subject coverage: Research and consultancy into advice service provision and development; training to advice workers on welfare rights; IT consultancy and advice to voluntary sector; website services and case management software.

Publications: Printed, and electronic and video

Publications list: Available online

Access to staff: Contact by letter, by telephone, by fax, by e-mail and via website
Hours: Mon to Fri, 0930 to 1700
Special comments: Charges for major undertakings such as consultancies and research.

Access to building: Mon to Fri, 0900 to 1700

LATIN MASS SOCIETY

11–13 Macklin Street, London, WC2B 5NH

Tel: 020 7404 7284
Fax: 020 7831 5585
E-mail: info@lms.org.uk
Website: www.lms.org.uk

Enquiries to: Secretary

Founded: 1965

Organisation type and purpose: Learned society, registered charity.

Subject coverage: Preservation and restoration of the Tridentine Rite of Mass in the Catholic Church,
restoration of the church's treasury of liturgical music, esp. Gregorian chant.

Publications: Printed, and electronic and video

Publications list: Available online and in print

Access to staff: Contact by letter, by telephone, by fax, by e-mail, in person and via website
Hours: Mon to Fri, 0930 to 1700

Access to building: *Hours:* Mon to Fri, 0930 to 1700
Special comments: Entryphone only.

Access for disabled people: Lift

Affiliated to: Una Voce International; 44 Queensway, Shotley Bridge, Consett, Co. Durham, DH8 0RZ

LAUTERPACHT CENTRE FOR INTERNATIONAL LAW, UNIVERSITY OF CAMBRIDGE (LCIL)

5 Cranmer Road, Cambridge, CB3 9BL

Tel: 01223 335358
Fax: 01223 300406
E-mail: admin@lcil.cam.ac.uk
Website: lcil.law.cam.ac.uk

Enquiries to: Administrator

Founded: 1983

Organisation type and purpose: University department or institute.

Subject coverage: Public international law.

Order printed publications from: Cambridge University Press
Edinburgh Building, Shaftesbury Road, Cambridge, CB2 2RU

Publications list: Available online

Access to staff: Contact by letter, by e-mail and via website. Appointment necessary.
Hours: Mon to Fri, 0900 to 1700

Access to building: By prior appointment.

LAVENDER LINE LIMITED

Isfield Station, Isfield, Uckfield, East Sussex, TN22 5XB

Tel: 01825 750515
Website: www.lavender-line.co.uk

Enquiries to: Secretary

Founded: 1992

Organisation type and purpose: Registered charity (charity number 1010085), museum.

Subject coverage: Preservation and running a railway.

Collection: Steam engines, steam crane, main line and industrial diesel locomotives, some running and some in the course of restoration and repair

Non-library collection catalogue: All or part available online

Access to staff: Contact by letter, by telephone and in person
Hours: Mon to Fri, 0900 to 1700

Access for disabled people: Parking provided, ramped entry
Special comments: Not suitable for the severely disabled

LAW CENTRES FEDERATION (LCF)

PO Box 65836, London, EC4P 4FX

Tel: 020 7842 0720
Fax: 020 7842 0721
E-mail: info@lawcentres.org.uk
Website: www.lawcentres.org.uk

Enquiries to: Office Manager

Founded: 1978

Organisation type and purpose: Voluntary organisation.
Representative body for the national network of Law Centres.

Subject coverage: Information about Law Centres generally, how they originated, what they do, how to set one up, how to develop existing services; their place in the provision of legal services; whereabouts of Law Centres and the areas of legal advice in which they specialise.

Publications: Printed

Access to staff: Contact by letter, by telephone, by fax, by e-mail and via website
Hours: Mon to Fri, 1000 to 1700

Branches: Avon and Bristol Law Centre; 2 Moon Street, Bristol, BS2 8QE; tel: 0117 924 8662; fax: 0117 924 8020; e-mail: mail@ablc.demon.co.uk; website: http://www.avonandbristollawcentre.org.uk
Barnet Law Service (Law Centre); 9 Bell Lane, London, NW4 2BP; tel: 020 8203 4141; fax: 020 8203 8042; e-mail: admin@barnetlaw.org.uk; website: http://www.barnetlaw.co.uk
Battersea Law Centre (part of South-West London Law Centres); 125 Bolingbroke Grove, London, SW11 1DA; tel: 020 7585 0716; fax: 020 7585 0718; e-mail: solicitors@battersealawcentre.fsnet.co.uk; Birmingham Law Centre; Dolphin House, 54 Coventry Road, Birmingham, B10 0RX; tel: 0121 766 7466; fax: 0121 766 8860; e-mail: admin@birminghamlawcentre.org.uk; website: http://www.birminghamlawcentre.org.uk
Bradford Law Centre; 31 Manor Row, Bradford, West Yorkshire, BD1 4PS; tel: 01274 306617; fax: 01274 390939; e-mail: enquiries@bradfordlawcentre.co.uk; Brent Community Law Centre; 389 High Road, Willesden, London, NW10 2JR; tel: 020 8451 1122; fax: 020 8830 2462; e-mail: brentlaw@brentlaw.org.uk; Bury Law Centre; 8 Bank Street, Bury, BL9 0DL; tel: 0161 272 0666; fax: 0161 272 0031; e-mail: info@burylawcentre.co.uk; website: http://www.burylawcentre.co.uk
Cambridge House Law Centre; 131 Camberwell Road, Camberwell, London, SE5 0HF; tel: 020 7358 7000; fax: 0845 305 2160; e-mail: info@ch1889.org; website: http://www.ch1889.org/lawcentre/
Camden Community Law Centre; 2 Prince of Wales Road, London, NW5 3LG; tel: 020 7284 6510; fax: 020 7267 6218; e-mail: admin@cclc.org.uk; website: http://www.cclc.org.uk
Cardiff Law Centre; 41–42 Clifton Street, Cardiff, CF24 1LS; tel: 029 2049 8117; fax: 029 2049 7118; e-mail: cardiff.lawcentre@dial.pipex.com; Central London Law Centre; 14 Irving Street, London, WC2H 7AF; tel: 020 7839 2998; fax: 020 7839 6158; website: http://www.londonlawcentre.org.uk
Chesterfield Law Centre; 44 Park Road, Chesterfield, Derbyshire, S40 1XZ; tel: 01246 550674; fax: 01246 551069; e-mail: clc@chesterfieldlawcentre.org.uk; website: http://www.chesterfieldlawcentre.org.uk
Coventry Law Centre; Oakwood House, St Patricks Road Entrance, Coventry, CV1 2HL; tel: 024 7622 3053; fax: 024 7622 8551; e-mail: enquiries@covlaw.org.uk; website: http://www.covlaw.org.uk
Cross Street Law Centre; 4 Cross Street, Erith, Kent, DA8 1AB; tel: 020 8311 0555; fax: 01322 331 073; website: http://www.tmlc.org.uk
Croydon and Sutton Law Centre (part of South West London Law Centres); 79 Park Lane, London, CRO 1JG; tel: 020 8667 9226; fax: 020 8662 8079; Cumbria Law Centre; 8 Spencer Street, Carlisle, CA1 1BG; tel: 01228 515129; fax: 01228 515819; e-mail: reception@comlaw.co.uk; website: http://www.communitylaw.org.uk
Derby Community Legal Advice Centre; Stuart House, Green Lane, Derby, DE1 1RS; tel: 01332 295711; fax: 01332 228701; e-mail: advice@citizensadviceandlawcentre.org; website: www.derbylawcentre.org
Devon Law Centre; Frobisher House, 64–66 Ebrington Street, Plymouth, Devon, PL4 9AQ; tel: 01752 519794; fax: 01752 519795; e-mail: information@devonlawcentre.org.uk; website: http://www.devonlawcentre.org.uk
Gloucester Law Centre; 75–81 Eastgate Street, Gloucester, GL1 1PN; tel: 01452 423492; fax: 01452 387594; e-mail: admin@gloucesterlawcentre.co.uk; website: http://www.gloucesterlawcentre.co.uk
Greenwich Community Law Centre; 187 Trafalgar Road, London, SE10 9EQ; tel: 020 8853 2550; fax: 020 8858 5253; e-mail: info@gclc.co.uk; Hackney Community Law Centre; 8 Lower Clapton Road, London, E5 0PD; tel: 020 8985 8364; fax: 020 8533 2018; e-mail: info@hclc.org.uk; website: http://www.hclc.org.uk
Hammersmith and Fulham Law Centre; 142–144 King Street, London, W6 0QU; tel: 020 8741 4021; fax: 020 8741 1450; e-mail: hflaw@hflaw.ogr.uk; Harehills and Chapletown Law Centre; 263 Roundhay Road, Leeds, LS8 4HS; tel: 0113 249 1100; fax: 0113 235 1185; e-mail: admin@leedslawcentre.org.uk; Haringey Law Centre; Ground Floor, 7 Holcombe Road, Tottenham, London, N17 9AA; tel: 020 8808 5354; fax: 020 8801 1516; e-mail: tottenhamlawcentre@tiscali.co.uk; Hillingdon Law Centre; 12 Harold Avenue, Hayes, Middlesex, UB3 4QW; tel: 020 8561 9400; fax: 020 8756 0837; e-mail: info@hillingdonlawcentre.co.uk; website: http://www.hillingdonlaw.org.uk
Hounslow Law Centre; 51 Lampton Road, Hounslow, Middlesex, TW3 1JG; tel: 020 8570 9505; fax: 020 8572 0730; e-mail: info@hounslowlawcentre.org.uk; website: http://www.hounslowlawcentre.org.uk
Isle of Wight Law Centre; Exchange House, St Cross Lane, Newport, Isle of Wight, PO30 5BZ; tel: 01983 524715; fax: 01983 522606; e-mail: iowlc@iowlc.org.uk; Islington Law Centre; 161 Hornsey Road, London, N7 6DU; tel: 020 7607 2461; fax: 020 7700 0072; e-mail: info@islingtonlaw.org.uk; website: http://www.islingtonlaw.org.uk
Kingston and Richmond Law Centre (part of South West London Law Centres); Siddeley House, 50 Canbury Park Road, Kingston, KT2 6LX; tel: 020 8547 2882; fax: 020 8547 2350; Kirklees Law Centre; Units 11/12, Empire House, Wakefield Old Road, Dewsbury, West Yorkshire, WF12 8DJ; tel: 01924 439829; fax: 01924 868140; e-mail: manager@kirkleeslc.org.uk; Lambeth Law Centre; Unit 4, The Co-op Centre, 11 Mowll Street, London, SW9 6BG; tel: 020 7840 2000; fax: 020 7820 8303; e-mail: admin@lambethlawcentre.org; Law Centre (Northern Ireland); Western Area Office, 9 Clarendon Street, Londonderry, BT48 7EP; tel: 028 7126 2433; fax: 028 7126 2343; e-mail: admin.derry@lawcentreniwest.org; website: http://www.lawcentreni.org
Law Centre (Northern Ireland); 124 Donegall Street, Belfast, BT1 2GY; tel: 028 9024 4401; fax: 028 9023 6340; e-mail: admin.belfast@lawcentreni.org; website: http://www.lawcentreni.org
Luton Law Centre; 6th Floor, Cresta House, Alma Street, Luton, Bedfordshire, LU1 2PL; tel: 01582 481000; fax: 01582 482581; e-mail: admin@lutonlawcentre.org.uk; Merton Law Centre (part of South West London Law Centres); 112 London Road, Morden, Surrey, SM4 5AX; tel: 020 8543 4069; fax: 020 8542 3814; Newcastle Law Centre; 1st floor, 1 Charlotte Square, Newcastle Upon Tyne, NE1 4XF; tel: 0191 230 4777; fax: 0191 233 0295; e-mail: info@newcastlelawcentre.co.uk; North Kensington Law Centre; 74 Golborne Road, London, W10 5PS; tel: 020 8969 7473; fax: 020 8968 0934; e-mail: info@nklc.co.uk; website: http://www.nklc.co.uk
North Manchester Law Centre; Harpurhey District Centre, off Rochdale Road, Harpurhey, Manchester, M9 4DH; tel: 0161 205 5040; fax: 0161 205 8654; e-mail: info@nmlc.org.uk; website: http://www.nmlc.org.uk
Nottingham Law Centre; 119 Radford Road, Nottingham, NG7 5DU; tel: 0115 978 7813; fax: 0115 979 2969; e-mail: enquiries@nottinghamlawcentre.org.uk; website: http://www.nottinghamlawcentre.org.uk
Oldham Law Centre; First Floor, Archway House, Bridge Street, Oldham, OL1 1ED; tel: 0161 627 0925; fax: 0161 620 3411; e-mail: admin@oldhamlawcentre.org; Paddington Law Centre; 439 Harrow Road, London, W10 4RE; tel: 020 8960 3155; fax: 020 8968 0417; e-mail: paddingtonlaw@btconnect.com; Plumstead Community Law Centre; 105 Plumstead High Street, London, SE18 1SB; tel: 020 8855 9817; fax: 020 8316 7903; Rochdale Law Centre; 15 Drake Street, Rochdale, OL16 1RE; tel: 01706 657766; fax: 01706 346588; e-mail: info@rochdalelawcentre.org.uk; website: http://www.rochdalelawcentre.org.uk

continued overleaf

Saltley and Nechells Law Centre; 2 Alum Rock Road, Saltley, Birmingham, B8 1JB; tel: 0121 328 2307; fax: 0121 327 7486; e-mail: snlc@snlc.co.uk; Sheffield Law Centre; 1st Floor, Waverley House, 10 Joiner Street, Sheffield, S3 8GW; tel: 0114 273 1888; fax: 0114 273 7778; e-mail: post@slc.org.uk; website: http://www.slc.org.uk
South Manchester Law Centre; 584 Stockport Road, Manchester, M13 0RQ; tel: 0161 225 5111; fax: 0161 225 0210; e-mail: admin@smlc.org.uk; website: http://www .smlc.org.uk
South West London Law Centre; 101a Tooting High Street, London, SW17 0SU; tel: 020 8767 2777; fax: 020 8767 2711; website: www.swllc.org.uk
Southwark Law Centre; Hanover Park House, 14–16 Hanover Park, Peckham, London, SE15 5HG; tel: 020 7732 2008; fax: 020 7732 2034; Springfield Law Centre; Springfield Hospital, 61 Glenburnie Road, London, SW17 7DJ; tel: 020 8767 6884; fax: 020 8767 6996; e-mail: info@ springfieldlawcentre.org.uk; Streetwise Community Law Centre; 1–3 Anerley Station Road, Penge, London, SE20 8PY; tel: 020 8778 5854; fax: 020 8776 9392; Surrey Law Centre; 34–36 Chertsey Street, Guildford, Surrey, GU1 4HD; tel: 01483 215000; fax: 01483 750770; e-mail: info@ surreylawcentre.org; website: www .surreycommunity.info/surreylawcentre/
Tower Hamlets Law Centre; 214 Whitechapel Road, London, E1 1BG; tel: 020 7247 8998; fax: 020 7247 9424; e-mail: info@ thlc.co.uk; website: http://www.thlc.co.uk
Trafford Law Centre; 4th Floor, John Darby House, 88–92 Talbot Road, Old Trafford, Manchester, M16 0GS; tel: 0161 872 3669; fax: 0161 872 2208; e-mail: admin@ traffordlawcentre.org.uk; website: www .traffordlawcentre.org.uk
Vauxhall Law and Information Centre; Vauxhall Training and Enterprise Centre, Silvester Street, Liverpool, L5 8SE; tel: 0151 482 2001; fax: 0151 207 4948; Wandsworth and Merton Law Centre (part of the South-West London Law Centres); 101a Tooting High Street, London, SW17 0SU; tel: 020 8767 2777; fax: 020 8767 2711; e-mail: info@ swllc.org.uk; Warrington Law Centre; The Boultings, Winwick Street, Warrington, Cheshire, WA2 7TT; tel: 01925 258360; fax: 01925 637668; e-mail: admin@ warringtonlawcentre.com; website: http:// www.warringtonlawcentre.org
Wiltshire Law Centre; Temple House, 115–118 Commercial Road, Swindon, Wiltshire, SN1 5PL; tel: 01793 486926; fax: 01793 432193; e-mail: info@wiltslawcentre.co.uk; website: http://www.wiltslawcentre.org.uk
Wythenshawe Law Centre; 260 Brownley Road, Wythenshawe, Manchester, M22 5EB; tel: 0161 498 0905/6; fax: 0161 498 0750; e-mail: info@wlawcentre.co.uk

Links with: Scottish Association of Law Centres; c/o Renfrewshire Law Centre, 65–71 George Street, Paisley, PA1 2JY; tel: 0141 561 7266; fax: 0141 944 7605; e-mail: jonsalc@ hotmail.co.uk; website: vwww .scotlawcentres.blogspot.com

Member organisations: AIRE Advice on Individual Rights in Europe; Third Floor, 17 Red Lion Square, London, WC1R 4QH; tel: 020 7831 3850; fax: 020 7404 7760; e-mail: aire@binternet.com; Castlemilk Law and Money Advice Centre; 155 Castlemilk Drive, Castlemilk, Glasgow, G45 9AD; tel: 0141 634 0313; fax: 0141 634 1944; e-mail: mail@ castlemilklawcentre.co.uk; Disability Law Service; Ground Floor, 39–45 Cavell Street, London, E1 2BP; tel: 020 7791 9800 (Minicom 020 7791 9801); fax: 020 7791 9802; e-mail: advice@dls.org.uk; website: www.dls.org.uk
EarthRights solicitors; 36 Town Street, Thaxted, Essex, CM6 2LA; tel: 01371 831936; e-mail: jd1@earthrights.org.uk; website: http://www.earthrights.org.uk
Ethnic Minorities Law Centre; 41 St. Vincent Place, 2nd Floor, Glasgow, G1 2ER; tel: 0141 204 2888; fax: 0141 204 2006; e-mail: admin@ emlc.org.uk; website: www.emlc.org.uk
Free Legal Advice Centre (Ireland); 13 Lower Dorset Street, Dublin 1, Ireland; tel: +353 1874 5690; fax: +353 1874 5320; e-mail: info@flac.ie; website: www.flac.ie
Govan Law Centre (Associate Member); 47 Burleigh Street, Govan, Glasgow, GS1 3LB; tel: 0141 440 2503; fax: 0141 445 3934; e-mail: mail@govanlc.com; Greater Manchester Immigration Aid Unit; 1 Delaunays Road, Crumpsall Green, Manchester, M8 4QS; tel: 0161 740 7722; fax: 0161 740 5172; e-mail: gmaiau@ein.org.uk; Mary Ward Legal Centre; 26–27 Boswell Street, London, WC1N 3JZ; tel: 020 7831 7079; fax: 020 7831 5431; e-mail: enquiries@marywardlegal.org .uk; website: wwww.marywardlegal.org.uk

LAW COMMISSION

Formal name: The Law Commission of England and Wales

Steel House, 11 Tothill Street, London, SW1H 9LJ

Tel: 020 3334 0200
Fax: 020 3334 0201
E-mail: chief.executive@lawcommission.gsi .gov.uk
Website: www.lawcom.gov.uk

Enquiries to: Librarian
Direct tel: 020 3334 0221
Direct fax: 020 3334 0202
Direct e-mail: library@lawcommission.gsi.gov .uk
Other contacts: Chief Executive

Founded: 1965

Organisation type and purpose: Statutory body, law reform body for England & Wales.

Subject coverage: Law, programmes of the Law Commission.

Library catalogue: All or part available in-house

Publications: Printed
Order printed publications from: The Stationery Office

Publications list: Available online

Access to staff: Contact by letter, by telephone and by e-mail
Hours: Open to the staff of the Commission 24 hours a day
Special comments: No public access.

Parent body: Ministry of Justice

LAW SOCIETY LIBRARY

Formal name: Law Society of England and Wales

113 Chancery Lane, London, WC2A 1PL

Tel: 0870 606 2511; 020 7320 5972
Fax: 020 7831 1687
E-mail: library@lawsociety.org.uk
Website: www.lawsociety.org.uk/library

Founded: 1825

Organisation type and purpose: Professional representative body for solicitors in England and Wales.

Subject coverage: Law: UK including England, Scotland, Wales, Northern Ireland; Eire; and European Union; Channel Islands; Isle of Man.

Information services: The library runs a document delivery service and answers legal information enquiries from members of the Law Society.

Collection: Over 43,000 vols of material dating back to the 13th century, comprising practitioner textbooks (current and previous edns), public legislation (up-to-date and historical), private and local legislation, law reports, parliamentary material, journals and legal encyclopaedias (current and previous edns).
Historical collections (trials, legal history, history of solicitors' profession, archives)
Mendham Collection of religious books (on loan to Canterbury Cathedral Library)
Parliamentary papers, 1801 onwards (on microfiche)

Non-library collection catalogue: All or part available in print

Library catalogue: All or part available online

Publications: Printed
Order printed publications from: website: http://www.lawsociety.org.uk/bookshop

Publications list: Available online

Access to staff: Contact by letter, by telephone, by fax, by e-mail, in person and via website. Access for members only. Non-members charged.
Hours: Mon to Fri, 0900 to 1700, telephone enquiries Mon to Fri 0900 to 1300

Access to building: *Hours:* Library open Mon to Fri, 0900 to 1700
Special comments: Non-members can apply for a pass to use the Library for a day at a cost of £16. See website for details.

Access for disabled people: Access to library via lift; equipped for sight-impaired members to use computers.

LAW SOCIETY OF NORTHERN IRELAND (LSNI)

The Law Society House, 96 Victoria Street, Belfast, BT1 3GN

Tel: 028 9023 1614
Fax: 028 9031 1323
E-mail: info@lawsoc-ni.org
Website: www.lawsoc-ni.org

Enquiries to: Head of Library and Information Services
Direct tel: 028 9024 6440
Direct e-mail: heather.semple@lawsoc-ni.org

Organisation type and purpose: Professional body.

Subject coverage: Responsible for the regulation and representation of solicitors in Northern Ireland. Required by statute to regulate the admission, education and ethics of the profession. Provides a range of member services.

Library catalogue: All or part available online

Publications: Printed

Publications list: Available in print

Access to staff: Contact by letter, by telephone, by fax and by e-mail. Access for members only.
Hours: Mon to Fri, 0900 to 1700
Special comments: Members' only library – other users by appointment.

Access for disabled people: Toilet facilities

Affiliated to: CCBE; International Bar Association

LAW SOCIETY OF SCOTLAND

26 Drumsheugh Gardens, Edinburgh, EH3 7YR

Tel: 0131 226 7411
Fax: 0131 225 2934
E-mail: lawscot@lawscot.org.uk
Website: www.lawscot.org.uk

Enquiries to: Director, Corporate Communications (for media enquiries)

Founded: 1949

Organisation type and purpose: Statutory body, professional body (membership is by qualification), present number of members: 8,600, service industry.
The promotion of the interests of the solicitor's profession in Scotland and the interests of the public in relation to that profession.

Subject coverage: Information to solicitors re council and committee work. Information to public re solicitors in Scotland.
Information on international law, law reform, practice management, legal education, seminars, and referral to solicitors in Scotland. Information on Scots Law, legal history and legal topics to the public.

Publications: Printed

Access to staff: Contact by letter, by telephone, by fax, by e-mail and via website
Hours: Fri, 0900 to 1630

Access to building: Prior appointment required

Brussels Office: Law Society of Scotland; 142–144 avenue de Tervuren, 1150 Brussels, Belgium; tel: 00 32 2 743 8585; fax: 00 32 2 743 8586; e-mail: brussels@lawsociety.org.uk

Links with: various Scottish faculties of solicitors and bar associations, new lawyers associations and commercial organisations

LAWN TENNIS ASSOCIATION (LTA)

Queen's Club, West Kensington, London, W14 9EG

Tel: 020 7381 7000
Fax: 020 7381 5965
Website: www.LTA.org.uk

Enquiries to: Information Officer
Direct tel: 020 7381 7111
Direct fax: 020 7381 3773
Other contacts: Chief Executive

Organisation type and purpose: Membership association.
Governing body of the game of lawn tennis in Great Britain.

Subject coverage: Tennis: rules and equipment, coaching, affiliated clubs, championships.

Collection: Tennis magazines and journals

Publications: Printed

Access to staff: Contact by letter, by telephone, by fax, by e-mail and in person
Hours: Mon to Fri, 0915 to 1715

Member of: International Tennis Federation; Lawn Tennis Association

LAWRENCE BATLEY CENTRE FOR THE NATIONAL ARTS EDUCATION ARCHIVE @YSP (NAEA@YSP)

The Lawrence Batley Centre, Bretton Hall West Bretton, Wakefield, West Yorkshire, WF4 4LG

Tel: 01924 830690
E-mail: leonard.bartle@YSP.co.uk
Website: www.artsedarchive.org.uk/collections.aspx.

Enquiries to: Custodian or Centre Administrator
Direct tel: 01924 830690

Founded: 1985

Organisation type and purpose: Museum, art gallery, research organisation.
Education archive.

Subject coverage: Visual and performing arts education.

Collection: More than 100 catalogued collections, and others not yet catalogued, of complex and extensive material tracing the development of art education in the UK, includes papers; letters; paintings; drawings; games; puzzles; video and film; photography, etc including:
A E Halliwell Collection (graphic design)
Franz Cizek Collection (children's art)
Alexander Barclay-Russell Collection (children's art)
Sir Alec Clegg and the West Riding Collections (children's art)
Independent Television Commission Collection (videos of ITV Schools Programmes 1960–1992, ITV and Channel 4 Adult Education Programmes 1962–1992)
Nicolai Legat Collection (ballet)
Richard Hamilton (student artwork)
Victor Pasmore (student artwork)
Tom Hudson (student artwork)
Don Pavey Collection (games and puzzles)
Philip Rawson (sculpture)

Non-library collection catalogue: All or part available online

Library catalogue: All or part available online

Publications: Printed

Access to staff: Contact by letter, by telephone, by e-mail and via website. Appointment necessary.
Hours: Mondays and Tuesdays, 0900 to 1700
Special comments: Closed weekends and Bank Holidays.

Access to building: Prior appointment required
Hours: Prior appointment required for Collections: Mondays and Tuesdays to Thu, 0900 to 1700

Access for disabled people: Level entry, access to all public areas, toilet facilities

LCIA

Formal name: London Court of International Arbitration

70 Fleet Street, London, EC4Y 1EU

Tel: 020 7936 7007
Fax: 020 7936 7008
E-mail: lcia@lcia.org
Website: www.lcia.org

Enquiries to: Registrar
Other contacts: Manager – Membership & Conferences for membership or conference enquiries.

Founded: 1892

Organisation type and purpose: The expert and cost-effective administration of arbitration and ADR worldwide, under LCIA and other rules and procedures.

Subject coverage: International commercial dispute resolution.

Publications: Printed

Access to staff: Contact by letter, by telephone, by fax, by e-mail and via website. Appointment necessary.
Hours: Mon to Fri, 0900 to 1700

Access to building: No access other than to staff
Hours: Mon to Fri, 1000 to 1700
Special comments: No smoking or eating in the library.

LE VELO CLUB LIMITED

74 Warwick Avenue, Quorn, Loughborough, Leicestershire, LE12 8HE

Tel: 01509 554230
E-mail: davidfbod@yahoo.co.uk
Website: www.leveloclub.org.uk

Enquiries to: Honorary Secretary

Founded: 1950

Organisation type and purpose: Membership association (membership is by subscription), present number of members: 1,300.
To promote enjoyment, riding and restoration of LE, Valiant, Vogue and Viceroy motorcycles.

Subject coverage: Technical and historical information on LE Velocette motorcycle and its derivatives.

Collection: Extensive collection of original drawings (now on CD-ROM)

Non-library collection catalogue: All or part available online

Publications: Printed

Access to staff: Contact by letter, by e-mail and via website
Hours: Mon to Fri, 0900 to 1700

LEA-FRANCIS OWNERS' CLUB (LFOC)

Longcroft, Kingswood Road, Hillesley, Wotton-under-Edge, Glos GL12 7RB

Tel: 01453 520092
Website: www.lfoc.org

Enquiries to: General Secretary
Direct e-mail: secretary@lfoc.org

Founded: 1953

Organisation type and purpose:
International organisation, membership association (membership is by subscription), present number of members: 340.
Factory records and histories of individual vehicles, technical details and information on the repair and maintenance of most models.
Preservation and use of Lea-Francis vehicles.

Subject coverage: History of all Lea-Francis products, production history, racing history, as well as history of individual vehicles, technical information on all models.

Information services: Full records of all Lea-Francis products

Collection: Catalogues, information sheets, brochures and other sales literature issued by Lea-Francis Cars
Technical literature and handbooks for most models

Publications: Printed, and electronic and video

Access to staff: Contact by letter, by telephone, by e-mail and via website
Hours: Mon to Sun, 0900 to 2200

Access to building: No access other than to staff

LEAD SHEET ASSOCIATION (LSA)

Unit 10, Archers Park, Branbridges Road, East Peckham, Tonbridge, Kent, TN12 5HP

Tel: 01622 872432
Fax: 01622 871649
E-mail: info@leadsheetassociation.org.uk
Website: www.leadsheetassociation.org.uk

Enquiries to: Administrator
Other contacts: General Manager

Founded: 1926

Organisation type and purpose: Trade association (membership is by subscription, election or invitation), manufacturing industry, training organisation, consultancy.

Subject coverage: Technical advice and training on the specification and use of rolled lead sheet in the construction industry.

Collection: All relevant industry publications

Trade and statistical information:
Confidential industry statistics not for general release

Publications: Printed

Publications list: Available online and in print

Access to staff: Contact by letter, by telephone, by fax, by e-mail and via website. Appointment necessary.
Hours: Mon to Fri, 0900 to 1700

LEAD SMELTERS AND REFINERS ASSOCIATION (LSRA)

c/o 17a Welbeck Way, London, W1G 9YJ

Tel: 020 7499 8422
Fax: 020 7493 1555
E-mail: enq@ila-lead.org

Enquiries to: Dr David Wilson
Direct e-mail: enq@ila-lead.org

Organisation type and purpose: Trade association.

Subject coverage: Smelting and refining of lead.

Trade and statistical information:
Confidential – not generally available

Access to staff: Contact by letter, by telephone and by fax
Hours: Mon to Fri, 0900 to 1700

LEADHILLS AND WANLOCKHEAD RAILWAY

The Station, Leadhills, Lanarkshire, ML12 6XP

Tel: 01555 662963
E-mail: secretary@leadhillsrailway.co.uk
Website: www.leadhillsrailway.co.uk

Enquiries to: Secretary
Other contacts: Publicist (e-mail: davidwinpenny@hotmail.com)

Founded: 1983

Organisation type and purpose:
Membership association (membership is by subscription), voluntary organisation.

Subject coverage: Railway preservation.

Special visitor services: Train service Sat and Sun during May to Sept

Education services: Museum in shop

Non-library collection catalogue: All or part available online

Publications: Printed

Access to staff: Contact by letter, by telephone, by e-mail and via website. Appointment necessary.
Hours: Mon to Fri, 0900 to 1700

Access to building: *Hours:* Sat and Sun, 1000 to 1700

Access for disabled people: Access to building, but restricted access on train

LEAGUE AGAINST CRUEL SPORTS LIMITED (LACS)

83–87 Union Street, London, SE1 1SG

Tel: 020 7403 6155
Fax: 020 7403 4532
Website: www.league.uk.com

Enquiries to: Information Officer
Direct e-mail: press@league.org.uk
Other contacts: PA to Chief Executive

Founded: 1924

Organisation type and purpose: National organisation, membership association (membership is by subscription), voluntary organisation.
Company.
To campaign to end cruel sports and to protect threatened animals.

Subject coverage: Hunting of wild animals with dogs, hare coursing, shooting, wildlife protection and conservation.

Trade and statistical information:
Information on hunted animals and on cruel sports

Publications: Printed

Publications list: Available online and in print

Access to staff: Contact by letter, by telephone, by fax and by e-mail
Hours: Mon to Fri, 0900 to 1700

LEAGUE FOR THE EXCHANGE OF COMMONWEALTH TEACHERS (LECT)

Commonwealth House, 7 Lion Yard, Tremadoc Road, London, SW4 7NQ

Tel: 0870 770 2636
Fax: 0870 770 2637
E-mail: info@lect.org.uk
Website: www.lect.org.uk

Enquiries to: Director
Direct e-mail: anna.tomlinson@lect.org.uk

Founded: 1901

Organisation type and purpose:
International organisation, membership association, present number of members: 2500, registered charity.

Subject coverage: Education in the Commonwealth including information about international professional D+V for teachers.

Publications: Electronic and video

Access to staff: Contact by letter, by telephone, by fax, by e-mail, in person and via website
Hours: Mon to Fri, 0900 to 1700

LEARNING & SKILLS COUNCIL LONDON NORTH (LSC London North)

Dunmayne House, 1 Fox Lane, Palmers Green, London, N13 4AB

Tel: 0845 019 4158
Fax: 020 8882 5931

Enquiries to: Customer Services

Founded: 1991

Organisation type and purpose: Statutory body, training organisation.
Organisation and strategic funding of post-16 education (excluding higher education) in London North area.

Subject coverage: Information available for youth programmes, adult training and initiatives, business services, information for employers/employees. Special projects including equal opportunities policies, special needs provision, childcare, capacity building for voluntary sector, and other ongoing projects.

Publications: Printed

Publications list: Available in print

Access to staff: Contact by letter, by telephone, by fax and in person
Hours: Mon to Fri, 0900 to 1700

Access to building: No access other than to staff

Access for disabled people: Parking provided, level entry, access to all public areas, toilet facilities

LEARNING AND SKILLS COUNCIL SOUTH EAST

Princes House, 53 Queens Road, Brighton, BN1 3XB

Tel: 01273 783555
Fax: 01273 783507
E-mail: info@lsc.gov.uk
Website: www.lsc.gov.uk/regions/SouthEast/

Enquiries to: Marketing and PR Manager
Direct tel: 01329 228502

Founded: 2001

Organisation type and purpose: Local government body, service industry.
Comprises five local Councils.
Post-16 learning and education.

Subject coverage: Support for post-16 and education.

Trade and statistical information: Labour and market economic information for Hampshire

Access to staff: Contact by letter, by telephone and by fax
Hours: Mon to Fri, 0900 to 1700

LEARNING AND SKILLS COUNCIL THAMES VALLEY (LSC)

LSC South East, Pacific House, Imperial Way, Reading, RG2 0FT

Tel: 0845 019 4147
Fax: 0118 908 2109
E-mail: SE-ESFCo-financing@lsc.gov.uk
Website: www.lsc.gov.uk

Enquiries to: Regional ESF Administrator
Direct tel: 01273 783614

Founded: 2001

Organisation type and purpose: National government body, national organisation, service industry, training organisation.
To plan and fund all post-16 training and education, except higher education.
To raise participation and attainment through high quality education and training that puts learners first.

Subject coverage: Investors in people, training, National Vocational Qualification, local labour market,
workforce development, modern apprenticeship, Foundation Apprenticeship, adult learning, schools, college, 6th forms, ESF funding, management development.

Collection: Various business and grants databases

Publications: Printed

Access to staff: Contact by letter, by telephone, by fax, by e-mail and via website
Hours: Mon to Fri, 0900 to 1700

Access to building: No access other than to staff

Access for disabled people: Parking provided, ramped entry, toilet facilities

Funded by: Central Government

National Office: Learning and Skills Council; Cheylesmore House, Quinton Road, Coventry, CV1 2WT; tel: 024 7670 3241; fax: 024 7686 3100; e-mail: nationalinfo@lsc.gov.uk

LEARNING AND SKILLS DEVELOPMENT NETWORK (LSN)

Fifth Floor, Holborn Centre, 120 Holborn, London, EC1N 2AD

Tel: 0845 071 0800
E-mail: enquiries@lsneducation.org.uk
Website: www.lsneducation.org.uk
Website: www.lsda.org.uk

Enquiries to: Information Officer
Other contacts: Communications Manager, tel: 020 7840 5360 for press and PR.

Founded: 1995; formerly a part of the Learning and Skills Development Agency (year of change 2006)

Organisation type and purpose: National development agency, educational organisation.
Research for the further education sector.

Subject coverage: Information for education managers on aspects of post-16 further education which relate to: developing competence, curriculum and staff management, curriculum planning and management, equal opportunities, flexible learning, provision for adults, new technologies, European links, governors, quality issues, key skills, professional development, vocational learning and research for the post-16 sector.

Non-library collection catalogue: All or part available in-house

Publications: Printed

Publications list: Available online and in print

Access to staff: Contact by letter, by telephone, by fax, by e-mail and via website. Appointment necessary.
Hours: Mon to Fri, 0900 to 1700

Access to building: Prior appointment required

LEARNING AND TEACHING SCOTLAND (LTS)

The Optima, 58 Robertson Street, Glasgow, G2 8DU

Tel: 0141 282 5000
Fax: 0141 282 5050
E-mail: enquiries@ltscotland.org.uk
Website: www.ltscotland.org.uk

Enquiries to: Senior Communications and Information Officer
Direct e-mail: t.wallace@ltscotland.org.uk

Founded: 2000

Organisation type and purpose: Executive non-departmental public body sponsored by Scottish Government, Learning and Teaching Scotland is the main organisation for the development and support of the Scottish curriculum, combining expertise in the curriculum 0–18 with advice on the use of ICT in education.

Subject coverage: LTS is responsible for leading and supporting improvement in the delivery of education for children and young people; working closely with a wide range of partner organisations to share interesting innovative practice; providing advice, support, resources and staff development, which can enhance the quality of learning and teaching; playing a key role in all major developments in Scottish education; moving education forward in partnership with key stakeholders.

Library catalogue: All or part available in-house

Publications: Printed
Order printed publications from: Learning and Teaching Scotland, Distribution Centre, 7 Tom Johnston Road, West Pitkerro, Dundee, DD4 8XD

Publications list: Available online

Access to staff: Contact by letter, by telephone, by fax, by e-mail, in person and via website. Appointment necessary.
Hours: Mon to Fri, 0845 to 1645

Funded by: Scottish Government

LEARNING CENTRE LIBRARY

Walsall Hospitals NHS Trust, Manor Hospital, Moat Road, Walsall, West Midlands, WS2 9PS

Tel: 01922 656628
Fax: 01922 656220
E-mail: kaljinder.dhanda@walsallhospitals.nhs.uk

Enquiries to: Librarian
Direct tel: 01922 656920

Founded: 1970

Organisation type and purpose: NHS hospital library.

Subject coverage: Medical information.

Information services: Multi-disciplinary collection of medical and healthcare textbooks covering undergraduate and postgraduate. Split across two sites.

Special visitor services: All staff and students on placement or working for Walsall Healthcare NHS Trust, including members of other Base libraries. Reference only to non-members.

Non-library collection catalogue: All or part available online

Library catalogue: All or part available online

Access to staff: Access for members only. Non-members charged.
Hours: Mon to Fri, 0900 to 1700

Access for disabled people: Ground floor access.

LEARNING ON SCREEN

Enquiries to: Administrator

Founded: 1968

Organisation type and purpose: International organisation, trade association (membership is by subscription), present number of members: 150, registered charity (charity number 325081-R).

continued overleaf

Members are concerned with the production and use of materials for learning and training. They include broadcasters, producers, universities, colleges and schools.

Subject coverage: Uses of screen-based media in education and training, selection of video equipment for education and training, production of material for education and training, research into the effectiveness of screen-based material for learning and training, television in distance learning.

Publications: Printed

Access to staff: Contact by letter, by telephone, by e-mail and via website. Appointment necessary.
Hours: Mon to Fri, 0830 to 1600

Recognised by the: Department for Education and Employment; Scottish Education Department; Welsh Education Office

LEARNING THROUGH LANDSCAPES (LTL)

Third Floor, Southside Offices, The Law Courts, Winchester, Hampshire, SO23 9DL

Tel: 01962 846258
Fax: 01962 869099
E-mail: schoolgrounds-uk@ltl.org.uk
Website: www.ltl.org.uk

Enquiries to: Information Officer

Founded: 1990

Organisation type and purpose: Registered charity.
To improve the quality of school grounds.

Subject coverage: School grounds.

Collection: Around 1000 documents on school grounds projects and associated organisations

Library catalogue: All or part available in-house

Publications: Printed, and electronic and video
Order printed publications from: Southgate Publishers Limited
The Square, Sandford, Crediton, Devon, EX17 4LW, tel: 01363 776888, fax: 01363 776889

Publications list: Available in print

Access to staff: Contact by letter, by telephone, by fax, by e-mail and via website. Appointment necessary.
Hours: Mon to Fri, 0900 to 1700
Special comments: Charges for some services.

LEATHER CONSERVATION CENTRE

University Campus, Boughton Green Road, Moulton Park, Northampton, NN2 7AN

Tel: 01604 719766
E-mail: lcc@northampton.ac.uk
Website: www.leatherconservation.org

Enquiries to: Head of Conservation

Founded: 1978

Organisation type and purpose: Registered charity (charity number 276485).

Subject coverage: Conservation and analysis of historical leather, history of leather manufacture.

Collection: Reference collection of leather types

Publications: Printed
Order printed publications from: Above address

Publications list: Available online and in print

Access to staff: Contact by letter, by telephone and by e-mail. Appointment necessary.
Hours: Mon to Fri, 0900 to 1700

Associate member of: British Leather Confederation

Member organisation of: Historic Houses Association

LEATHERHEAD FOOD INTERNATIONAL (LFI)

Randalls Road, Leatherhead, Surrey, KT22 7RY

Tel: 01372 376761
Fax: 01372 386228
E-mail: help@lfra.co.uk
Website: www.leatherheadfood.com/lfi

Enquiries to: Business Manager, Library and Electronic Information
Direct tel: 01372 822279
Direct fax: 01372 822268
Direct e-mail: library@lfra.co.uk

Organisation type and purpose: Scientific and information services for the international food industry

Subject coverage: Food science and technology, nutrition, sensory analysis, analytical chemistry, food microbiology, food hygiene, food toxicology.

Publications: Printed, and electronic and video
Order printed publications from: http://www.leatherheadfood.com/lfi/submenu.asp?section=11§ionname=Bookshop
Order electronic and video publications from: http://services.leatherheadfood.com/foodline/subscribe.aspx

Publications list: Available online

Access to staff: Contact by letter, by telephone, by fax, by e-mail, in person and via website. Access for members only. Non-members charged.
Hours: Mon to Fri, 0830 to 1730
Special comments: Non-members at the discretion of the Librarian.

LEBANESE EMBASSY

21 Kensington Palace Gardens, London, W8 4QN

Tel: 020 7229 7265
Fax: 020 7243 1699
E-mail: emb.leb@btinternet.com

Enquiries to: Ambassador's Secretary

Organisation type and purpose: National government body.
Embassy.
The issue of visas and passports, and actions as power of attorney (Consular Section).

Subject coverage: Lebanon; its economy and tourism.

Publications: Printed

Access to staff: Contact by letter, by telephone, by fax, by e-mail and in person. Appointment necessary.
Hours: Mon to Fri, 0900 to 1500

Parent body: Ministry for Foreign Affairs; Beirut, Lebanon

LEBRECHT MUSIC AND ARTS PHOTO LIBRARY

3 Bolton Road, London, NW8 0RJ

Tel: 020 7625 5341
Fax: 020 7625 5341
E-mail: pictures@lebrecht.co.uk
Website: www.lebrecht.co.uk
Website: www.authorpictures.co.uk

Enquiries to: Director

Founded: 1992

Organisation type and purpose: Consultancy, research organisation.
Picture library.
Supply of arts and music pictures to commercial clients from the world's largest specialist music archive, with access to over 8m. arts pictures.

Subject coverage: Lebrecht Music & Arts Picture Library consists of three specialist libraries, covering music (classical, rock, pop, jazz, opera, ballet), literature (authors, manuscripts, fictional heroes, theatre, book covers, illustrations, literary arts), and history through fine arts (especially strong on Russian, French, Italian and English art).

Collection: New York Public Library (Performing Arts division)
Alan Bush Foundation
Kurt Weill Foundation
Martinu Archives
Royal Academy of Music Collection of Images
Ben Uri Russian Collection

Non-library collection catalogue: All or part available online, in-house and in print

Library catalogue: All or part available online and in-house

Publications list: Available online

Access to staff: Contact by letter, by telephone, by fax, by e-mail and via website. Appointment necessary.
Hours: Mon to Fri, 0900 to 1730

LEEDS (SOUTH) METHODIST CIRCUIT OFFICE

Trinity House, Lodge Lane, Leeds, West Yorkshire, LS11 6LR

Tel: 0113 271 6641

Enquiries to: Superintendent Minister
Other contacts: Circuit Minister

Founded: 18th century

Organisation type and purpose: Voluntary organisation.
Church organisation.

Subject coverage: Methodist Churches in South Leeds.

Access to staff: Contact by letter, by telephone and by e-mail
Hours: Mon to Fri, 0900 to 1700

LEEDS CITY LIBRARIES – BUSINESS AND PATENT INFORMATION SERVICES (BAPIS)

Central Library, Calverley Street, Leeds, LS1 3AB

Tel: 0113 247 8266
Fax: 0113 247 8268
E-mail: piu@leeds.gov.uk
Website: www.businessandpatents.org
Website: www.bapisleeds.blogspot.com
Website: www.leedsinventorsgroup.blogspot.com

Enquiries to: Manager
Other contacts: Librarian

History of institution: incorporates the former Patent Information Unit and Information for Business (year of change 2004)

Organisation type and purpose: Local government body, public library.

Subject coverage: All aspects of business, commerce, statistics, company information, market research, job-seeking, intellectual property (IP) trademarks, patents registered designs and copyright.

Information services: Tailored marketing lists, enquiry service, patent and trademarks searching and information on IP

Collection: British Standards
Company Information
D & B KBE
MINT, FAME
KeyNote Market Research
Mintel Market Research
Marquesa
DWPI
Derwent Innovations Index
GPI
Trade Marks
Patent information
Leeds Inventors Group

Library catalogue: All or part available online and in-house

Publications: Printed
Order printed publications from: e-mail: piu@leeds.gov.uk

Access to staff: Contact by letter, by telephone, by fax, by e-mail, in person and via website
Hours: Mon to Fri, 0900 to 1700; Sat, 1000 to 1300
Special comments: Phone to make an appointment for a one-to-one consultation on IP.

Access to building: *Hours:* Mon to Wed, 0900 to 2000; Thu and Fri, 0900 to 1700; Sat, 1000 to 1700; Sun, 1300 to 1700

Access for disabled people: Ramped entry, toilet facilities, lift

LEEDS COLLEGE OF TECHNOLOGY (LCOT)

Cookridge Street, Leeds, West Yorkshire, LS2 8BL

Tel: 0113 297 6300\ Minicom no. 0113 297 6470
Fax: 0113 297 6301
E-mail: technologycampus@leedscitycollege.ac.uk

Enquiries to: Librarian
Direct tel: 0113 297 6353
Direct e-mail: library@leeds-lcot.ac.uk

Organisation type and purpose: Suitable for ages: 16+.
Further education college.

Subject coverage: Engineering, manufacturing, computing, business, media studies, health and social care.

Library catalogue: All or part available online

Access to staff: Contact by letter, by telephone, by fax, by e-mail and in person
Hours: Mon to Thu, 0830 to 2030; Fri, 0830 to 1630
Special comments: Letter of introduction required for non LCOT students.

Access for disabled people: Ramped entry, access to all public areas, toilet facilities
Special comments: Above disabled facilities for Central Site only.

Also at: Leeds College of Technology; East Street, Leeds, LS2 8PH; tel: 0113 297 7272; fax: 0113 297 7273; Leeds College of Technology; Westland Road, Leeds, LS11 5SB; tel: 0113 297 9400; fax: 0113 297 9401

LEEDS INDUSTRIAL MUSEUM

Armley Mills, Canal Road, Armley, Leeds, West Yorkshire, LS12 2QF

Tel: 0113 263 7861
Fax: 0113 224 4365
E-mail: neil.dowlan@leeds.gov.uk
Website: www.leeds.gov.uk
Website: www.leeds.gov.uk/tourinfo/attract/museums/armley/index.html
Website: www.leeds.gov.uk/tourinfo/events/lmg_arm.html

Enquiries to: Curator
Direct tel: 0113 224 4372
Direct e-mail: amy.jenkinson@leeds.gov.uk

Founded: 1982

Organisation type and purpose: Local government body, professional body, museum.
Museum holding information on Leeds' industrial history.

Subject coverage: Leeds industrial history, printing, photography, cinematography, engineering, textiles, ready-made clothing, locomotive building, cranes, transport (road rollers, etc.).

Information services: Library available for reference by appointment (for conditions see Access).

Special visitor services: Materials and/or activities for children.

Collection: Working exhibits include:
1904 Spinning Mule
Ploughing engine, mill engine, steam locomotive
1920s cinema
Archives of photographs/documents relating to Leeds industries

Non-library collection catalogue: All or part available in-house

Library catalogue: All or part available in-house

Publications: Printed

Access to staff: Contact by letter, by telephone, by fax, by e-mail, in person and via website. Appointment necessary.
Hours: By appointment only, Tues 1100 to 1630; Wed 0900 to 1630; Thu, 0900 to 1400

Access to building: Museum opening hours
Hours: Tues to Sat, 1000 to 1700; Sun, 1300 to 1400

Access for disabled people: Parking provided, ramped entry, toilet facilities
Special comments: Access to most areas; touch trail; lift to all floors.

Parent body: Director of Museums and Galleries; Leeds City Council, Leisure Services Department, Museums & Galleries Division, Leeds Town Hall, Leeds, West Yorkshire

LEEDS LIBRARY

18 Commercial Street, Leeds, LS1 6AL

Tel: 0113 245 3071
Fax: 0113 245 1191
E-mail: enquiries@theleedslibrary.org.uk
Website: www.theleedslibrary.org.uk

Enquiries to: Librarian

Founded: 1768

Organisation type and purpose: Independent subscription library (company number 5577905; charity number 1114386).

Collection: Library of 135,000 items
Civil War pamphlets
Reformation Tracts

Library catalogue: All or part available online and in print

Publications: Printed

Access to staff: Contact by letter, by telephone, by fax, by e-mail and via website. Appointment necessary. Letter of introduction required.
Hours: Mon to Fri, 0900 to 1700; 1st Sat of the month, 0930 to 1300

LEEDS LIBRARY AND INFORMATION SERVICES

Central Library, Municipal Buildings, Calverley Street, Leeds, West Yorkshire, LS1 3AB

Tel: 0113 247 6016
Fax: 0113 247 4222
E-mail: enquiry.express@leeds.gov.uk
Website: www.leeds.gov.uk/libraries

Enquiries to: Manager

Organisation type and purpose: Local government body, public library.

Subject coverage: Business and company information, patents information, local history (Leeds and Yorkshire) also general information service covering all other subjects; separate Art and Music Libraries; Research Library.

Collection: Art Library:
Gillow Archives (business archives of Gillow Furniture Company)

continued overleaf

Kitson Collection (early English watercolours and Rembrandt etchings)
Leeds pottery (including Pattern Books)
Sanderson Collection (19th-century fashion plates and periodicals)
Music Library:
Scores and cassettes, compact discs
Taphouse Collection (17th- and 18th-century music and books on music)
Business and Research Library:
British Standards
Gascoigne Collection (military and naval history)
Gott Bequest (early gardening books)
HMSO publications
Leeds Philatelic Society Library
Local History Collection (Leeds and Yorkshire)
Extensive archive of Leeds Theatre materials, including posters, indexed by actor, theatre, play, author, etc.
Porton Collection (Judaica)
Private press and early printed books
Yorkshire Ramblers Club Library (mountaineering, speleology)

Non-library collection catalogue: All or part available in-house

Library catalogue: All or part available in-house

Access to staff: Contact by letter, by telephone, by fax and by e-mail
Hours: Mon, Tue, Wed, 0900 to 2000; Thu, Fri, 0900 to 1700; Sat, 1000 to 1700; Sun, 1300 to 1700

Access for disabled people: Level entry, toilet facilities

LEEDS MEDICAL INFORMATION (LMI)

University of Leeds, Leeds, West Yorkshire, LS2 9JT

Tel: 0113 343 5552
Fax: 0113 343 5568
E-mail: lmi@leeds.ac.uk
Website: www.leeds.ac.uk/lmi/
Website: www.leeds.ac.uk/lmi/publications .html

Enquiries to: Manager
Direct tel: 0113 343 4381
Direct e-mail: n.v.king@leeds.ac.uk

Founded: 1974

Organisation type and purpose: University library.
Academic publishing unit and information consultancy; based at the University of Leeds.

Subject coverage: Clinical cancer (oncology), cancer; palliative care

Publications: Printed

Access to staff: Contact by letter, by telephone, by fax and by e-mail
Hours: Mon to Fri, 0900 to 1700

Parent body: University of Leeds

LEEDS METROPOLITAN UNIVERSITY

City Campus Library, Leslie Silver Building, Woodhouse Lane, Leeds, West Yorkshire, LS1 3ES

Tel: 0113 812 5963
E-mail: A.Sargeant@leedsmet.ac.uk
Website: libraryonline.leedsmet.ac.uk

Enquiries to: Secretary
Direct e-mail: infodesk.lc@leedsmet.ac.uk

Organisation type and purpose: University library services.

Subject coverage: Accounting and finance; art, design, film, TV and photography; architecture; landscape design; business studies, management, law; health and science; hospitality management; social sciences; computing and information systems; education; languages; sport science; sport and leisure; tourism; construction; quantity surveying; civil engineering; environmental health; urban development.

Collection: Collection of the West Yorkshire Society of Architects
European Documentation Centre

Non-library collection catalogue: All or part available online

Library catalogue: All or part available online

Access to staff: Contact by letter, by telephone, by e-mail, in person and via website. Non-members charged.
Hours: Term time: Mon to Thu, 0830 to 2000; Fri, 0830 to 1900; Sat, 1000 to 1600; Sun, 1000 to 1800
Special comments: Restrictions on accessing online information services apply. Charges made for borrowing.

Branch libraries: Headingley Library; James Graham Building, Beckett Park, Leeds, LS6 3HF; tel: 0113 812 1000

LEEDS TRINITY UNIVERSITY COLLEGE

Library, Andrew Kean Learning Centre, Brownberrie Lane, Horsforth, Leeds, West Yorkshire, LS18 5HD

Tel: 0113 283 7100
Fax: 0113 283 7200
E-mail: helpdesk@leedstrinity.ac.uk
Website: www.leedstrinity.ac.uk/services/library/Pages/default.aspx

Founded: 1966; formerly called Trinity & All Saints College (year of change 2009)

Organisation type and purpose: University library.

Subject coverage: Education; Business, Marketing and Management; Media, Film and Culture; Journalism; Psychology; Sport, Health and Nutrition; Theology & Religious Studies; English; History.

Collection: Yorkshire Local History Collection

Library catalogue: All or part available online

Access to building: Those living or working locally may apply for Visiting Membership. Proof of identity (e.g. passport), address (e.g. recent utility bill) and passport-sized photograph required. Application in person required at Learning Centre Helpdesk, Ground Floor, Andrew Kean Learning Centre.
Hours: Term time: Mon to Thu, 0830 to 2400; Fri, 0830 to 2000; Sat, 1100 to 1645; Sun, 1100 to 2045
Special comments: Swipe card only access from 1900 Monday to Friday and at weekends. No access to College network or IT facilities provided for Visiting Members.

Affiliated to: University of Leeds

LEEK GROWERS' ASSOCIATION (TLGA)

133 Eastgate, Louth, Lincolnshire, LN11 9QG

Tel: 01507 602427
Fax: 01507 607165
E-mail: crop.association@pvga.co.uk
Website: www.british-leeks.co.uk

Enquiries to: Membership Secretary

Founded: 1980s

Organisation type and purpose: National organisation, trade association.

Subject coverage: Leeks.

Access to staff: Contact by letter, by telephone, by fax and by e-mail
Hours: Mon to Fri, 0900 to 1700

LEGAL ACTION GROUP (LAG)

Formal name: LAG Education and Service Trust Limited

242 Pentonville Road, London, N1 9UN

Tel: 020 7833 2931
Fax: 020 7837 6094
E-mail: lag@lag.org.uk
Website: www.lag.org.uk

Enquiries to: Director

Founded: 1972

Organisation type and purpose: Voluntary organisation, registered charity (charity number 265703).
Solicitors, barristers, advisers, academics, students and others, concerned to improve legal services to the community.

Subject coverage: Legal services, legal profession, social welfare, law, penal affairs and crime.

Publications: Printed

Publications list: Available online and in print

Access to staff: Contact by e-mail and via website. Appointment necessary.
Hours: Mon to Fri, 1000 to 1700

LEGAL SERVICES OMBUDSMAN

3rd Floor, Sunlight House, Quay Street, Manchester, M3 3JZ

Tel: 0161 839 7262/Lo-call 0845 601 0794
Fax: 0161 832 5446
E-mail: lso@olso.gsi.gov.uk
Website: www.olso.org

Enquiries to: Information Officer

Founded: 1990

Subject coverage: Deals with complaints about the behaviour and quality of service of solicitors if the Solicitors Complaints Bureau has failed to provide satisfaction.

Publications: Printed

Access to staff: Contact by letter, by telephone, by fax and by e-mail
Hours: Mon to Fri, 0900 to 1630

Access to building: No prior appointment required

Access for disabled people: Level entry

LEICESTER CENTRAL LEARNING AND INFORMATION LIBRARY

Bishop Street, Leicester, LE1 6AA

Tel: 0116 299 5401
Fax: 0116 299 5444
E-mail: central.reference@leicester.gov.uk
Website: www.leicester.gov.uk/libraries

Enquiries to: Manager
Direct e-mail: michael.lewis@leicester.gov.uk
Other contacts: Duty Officer

Founded: 1905; formerly called Reference and Information Library (year of change 2007)

Organisation type and purpose: Public library.

Subject coverage: General public library subject coverage.

Collection: Stretton Collection of of books and memorabilia relating to British railway development from the late 19th century
Stretton railway collection

Trade and statistical information: Small collection of UK government statistics

Non-library collection catalogue: All or part available in-house

Library catalogue: All or part available online

Access to staff: Contact by letter, by telephone, by fax, by e-mail, in person and via website
Hours: Mon to Thu, 0930 to 1900; Fri, 0900 to 1700; Sat, 0900 to 1600

Access to building: *Hours:* as for access to staff

Access for disabled people: Disabled access door and ramp, lift access to first floor
Hours: as for access to staff

LEICESTER CENTRAL LENDING LIBRARY

54 Belvoir Street, Leicester, LE1 6QG

Tel: 0116 299 5402
Fax: 0116 299 5434
E-mail: artsl203@leicester.gov.uk

Enquiries to: Manager

Organisation type and purpose: Public library.

Access to staff: Contact by letter, by telephone, by fax, by e-mail and in person
Hours: Mon to Thu, 0930 to 1900; Fri, 0930 to 1700; Sat, 0900 to 1600

Access to building: No prior appointment required

Access for disabled people: Ramped entry

LEICESTER CITY COUNCIL

New Walk Centre, Welford Place, Leicester, LE1 6ZG

Tel: 0116 254 9922
Fax: 0116 254 5531
Website: www.demontforthall.co.uk
Website: www.leicester.gov.uk
Website: www.leicestermuseums.ac.uk
Website: www.leicesterspark.co.uk
Website: www.leicester-env-city.org.uk

Enquiries to: Chief Executive

Organisation type and purpose: Local government body.

LEICESTER LONGWOOL SHEEP BREEDERS ASSOCIATION (LLSBA)

Driffield Agricultural Society, The Showground, Kelley Thorpe, Driffield, East Yorkshire, YO25 9DN

Tel: 01377 257494
Fax: 01377 257464
E-mail: office@driffieldshow.co.uk
Website: www.stockmaster.co.uk

Enquiries to: Secretary

Founded: 1883

Organisation type and purpose: Membership association (membership is by subscription), present number of members: 81.
Breed society.

Publications: Printed

Publications list: Available online

Access to staff: Contact by letter, by telephone, by fax, by e-mail and in person
Hours: Mon to Fri, 0900 to 1700

Connected with: National Sheep Association (NSA); Rare Breeds Survival Trust (RBST)

LEICESTER YMCA ADVICE & SUPPORT CENTRE (YASC)

Y Advice and Support Centre, The Dawn Centre, Conduit Street, Leicester, LE2 0JN

Tel: Homeless Support: 0116 221 2787
Fax: 0116 221 2785
E-mail: via website
Website: www.leicesterymca.co.uk/homeless-support.php
Website: www.leicesterymca.co.uk

Organisation type and purpose: Drop-in centre for homeless people, based in Leicester city centre, close to the train station.

Subject coverage: Practical help, such as breakfast, emergency food parcels where possible, access to toilets, showers, washing facilities and toiletries, free laundry facilities for rough sleepers, a change of clothes, access to telephone for non-personal calls. Advice and information: help finding accommodation in emergency or longer term, welfare benefits advice and assistance, advice on managing debt, information and signposting to specialist drugs and alcohol agencies, a year-round health promotion programme, specialist mental health advice, help establishing identification. Education and activities: the day centre delivers a wide range of activities including home economics, IT, arts and diversity, creative writing, photography and jobs club. The sessions identify interests and capabilities, focussing on personal development, building on self-esteem personal achievements. Medical Services: a full range of health services is accessible via YASC, provided by The Homeless Primary Healthcare Service. Psychologists and mental health practitioners are also provided by Leicestershire Partnership NHS Trust.

Access to staff: Contact by letter, by telephone, by fax, in person and via website
Hours: Mon to Fri, 0800 to 1600
Special comments: No appointment is necessary.

Access to building: *Hours:* Mon to Fri, 0800 to 1600

LEICESTERSHIRE ARCHAEOLOGICAL AND HISTORICAL SOCIETY (LAHS)

The Guildhall, Leicester, LE1 5FQ

E-mail: rjb16@le.ac.uk
Website: le.ac.uk/lahs

Enquiries to: Webmaster

Founded: 1855

Organisation type and purpose: International organisation, national organisation, learned society (membership is by subscription), registered charity.

Subject coverage: Archaeology; local history; Leicestershire vernacular architecture; history of Leicester and Leicestershire.

Collection: Local History and Archaeology Library

Library catalogue: All or part available online and in-house

Publications: Printed
Order printed publications from: website: http://www.le.ac.uk/publications/orderform.html

Publications list: Available online

Access to staff: Contact by letter and by e-mail
Hours: Mon to Fri, 0900 to 1700

LEICESTERSHIRE CHAMBER OF COMMERCE (LCCI)

1 Mill Lane, Leicester, LE2 7HU

Tel: 0116 247 1800
Fax: 0116 247 0430
E-mail: leics@chamberofcommerce.co.uk
Website: www.chamberofcommerce.co.uk

Enquiries to: Chief Executive

Founded: 1860

Organisation type and purpose: Membership association (membership is by subscription), present number of members: 1,500, manufacturing industry, service industry.

Subject coverage: International trade services, training, general employment information, business networking events.

Publications: Printed

Access to staff: Contact by letter, by telephone, by e-mail and via website. Appointment necessary. Access for members only.

continued overleaf

Hours: Mon to Fri, 0900 to 1630

Access to building: Prior appointment required

LEICESTERSHIRE COUNTY COUNCIL (LLIS)

Libraries & Information Service, County Hall, Glenfield, Leicester, LE3 8SS

Tel: 0116 265 7372
Fax: 0116 265 7370
Website: www.leics.gov.uk/libraries

Enquiries to: Chief Librarian
Other contacts: Head of Library Services for Education for Library Services for Education/Schools.

Organisation type and purpose: Local government body, statutory body, public library.

Subject coverage: General; Leicestershire.

Collection: Hunting Collection at Melton Mowbray Library

Library catalogue: All or part available online

Publications: Printed
Order printed publications from: Publicity and Promotions Officer, Leicestershire Libraries and Information Service
County Hall, tel: 0116 265 7386, fax: 0116 265 7370

Publications list: Available in print

Access to staff: Contact by letter, by telephone, by fax, by e-mail, in person and via website
Hours: Mon to Fri, 0900 to 1700

Other addresses: Library Services for Education; 929–931 Loughborough Road, Rothley, Leicester, LE7 7NH; tel: 0116 267 8000; fax: 0116 267 8039; e-mail: gwillars@leics.gov.uk

LEICESTERSHIRE LIBRARY SERVICES (LLS)

County Hall, Glenfield, Leicester, LE3 8SS

Tel: 0116 305 7015
Fax: 0116 305 6960
E-mail: libraries@leics.gov.uk
Website: www.leics.gov.uk/libraries

Enquiries to: Head of Library Services
Other contacts: Local Government Information Librarian

Organisation type and purpose: Local government body, statutory body, public library.

Subject coverage: General, Leicestershire.

Collection: Hunting collection at Melton Mowbray library

Library catalogue: All or part available online

Publications: Printed

Publications list: Available in print

Access to staff: Contact by letter, by telephone, by fax, by e-mail, in person and via website
Hours: Mon to Fri, 0900 to 1700

Parent body: Leicestershire County Council

LEICESTERSHIRE MUSEUMS SERVICE

County Hall, Glenfield, Leicester, LE3 8RA

Tel: 0116 265 6781
Fax: 0116 264 5820
E-mail: museums@leics.gov.uk
Website: www.leics.gov.uk/museums

Enquiries to: Director

Organisation type and purpose: Local government body, museum.
Headquarters of Leicestershire Museums.

Subject coverage: Coal mining

Collection: Library of coal-mining at Snibston Museum, Coalville

Non-library collection catalogue: All or part available in-house

Access to staff: Contact by letter, by telephone, by fax, by e-mail, in person and via website. Appointment necessary.
Hours: Mon to Fri, 0900 to 1630

Access to building: Prior appointment required

Access for disabled people: Parking provided, toilet facilities

LEISURE AND OUTDOOR FURNITURE ASSOCIATION (LOFA)

113 Worcester Road, Chichester, PO19 5EE

Tel: 01243 839593
Fax: 01243 839467
E-mail: info@lofa.com
Website: www.lofa.com

Enquiries to: Secretary

Founded: 1967

Organisation type and purpose:
Membership and trade association for companies that manufacture garden furniture, barbecues, hammocks, parasols or soft furnishings in the UK or are an exclusive or non-exclusive distributor, holding stocks in the UK, or a non-UK based company with a subsidiary or an exclusive representative, operating in the UK.

Subject coverage: LOFA members supply an extensive selection of garden and leisure furniture in a range of materials including all types of wood, cane, cast and wrought metal, plastic and resin, and lightweight tubular metal.

Publications: Electronic and video
Order electronic and video publications from: Download from website

Publications list: Available online

Access to staff: Contact by letter, by telephone, by fax and by e-mail

LEISURE DATABASE COMPANY, THE

33 Bedford Street, Covent Garden, London, WC2E 9EJ

Tel: 020 7379 3197
Fax: 020 7379 0898
Website: www.theleisuredatabase.com

Enquiries to: Managing Director
Direct tel: 020 7395 6171
Other contacts: Director, Sales and Subscriptions for sales enquiries.

Founded: 1981

Organisation type and purpose: Research organisation.
Commercial information company.
Providing the country's leading database of sports, health and fitness provision.

Subject coverage: Sports provision, health and fitness.

Trade and statistical information: Sport facilities charges in London.
Data on Leisure Facility Management: UK-wide.
Data on health and fitness clubs: UK-wide.
Data on public sector sports provision: UK-wide

Publications: Printed, and electronic and video

Publications list: Available in print

Access to staff: Contact by letter, by telephone, by fax and by e-mail
Hours: Mon to Fri, 0900 to 1800

LEISURE, CULTURE AND LIFELONG LEARNING

Libraries and Heritage Central Library, Lichfield Street, Walsall, West Midlands, WS1 1TR

Tel: 01922 653110
Fax: 01922 654013
E-mail: librarycentref@walsall.gov.uk
Website: www.walsall.gov.uk/libraries

Enquiries to: Information Officer

Founded: 1906

Organisation type and purpose: Local government body, public library.

Subject coverage: Tourist information, clubs and societies relating to Walsall, business information, council information, European information.

Collection: Guardian 1990– , KBE–Current, Social Trends, Times 1990– (CD-ROMs)

Non-library collection catalogue: All or part available online

Library catalogue: All or part available online

Publications: Printed

Access to staff: Contact by letter, by telephone, by fax, by e-mail and in person
Hours: Mon to Fri, 0900 to 1700

Member organisation of: Black Country Libraries in Partnership

LEO BAECK COLLEGE LIBRARY (LBC)

Sternberg Centre for Judaism, 80 East End Road, London, N3 2SY

Tel: 020 8349 5610
Fax: 020 8349 5619
E-mail: library@lbc.ac.uk
Website: www.lbc.ac.uk

Enquiries to: Librarian
Direct e-mail: annette.boeckler@lbc.ac.uk

Founded: 1956

Organisation type and purpose:
International organisation, registered charity (charity number 209777), suitable for ages: postgraduate.
Academic Judaica Library with 60,000 volumes, 40 periodicals.
Rabbinic training and Jewish college.

Subject coverage: Jewish studies.

Information services: Academic Judaica Library with 60,000 volumes, 40 periodicals.

Education services: Offers Rabbinic studies, Jewish Adult learning, GCSE exams, lectures, Shiurim, MA and Advanced Diploma courses, Early Years courses in Jewish education

Collection: Library: 30,000 books, pamphlets, etc.

Library catalogue: All or part available online

Publications: Printed, and electronic and video

Publications list: Available online and in print

Access to staff: Appointment necessary.
Hours: Mon to Fri, 0900 to 1700

LEONARD CHESHIRE

Head Office, 66 South Lambeth Road, London, SW8 1RL

Tel: 020 3242 0200
Fax: 020 3242 0250
E-mail: info@lcdisability.org
Website: www.leonard-cheshire.org

Enquiries to: Information Resources Officer

Founded: 1948

Organisation type and purpose: Voluntary organisation.
To provide choice and opportunity to people with disabilities, emphasising the right of the individual to decide how he or she wants to live.

Subject coverage: Operating in 55 countries worldwide. It promotes the care, general well-being and rehabilitation of people with physical and learning disabilities. In the UK the Foundation comprises 85 Cheshire Homes offering a range of care services, including full-time residential care, respite and day care and short-stay holiday breaks. Some of these also offer accommodation for full or semi-independent living with all the advantages of separate housing combined with 24-hour help close at hand if needed. In addition, there are a growing number of Care at Home Services (37 in 1993) which provide personal care and undertake day to day tasks for people with disabilities in their own homes.

Collection: Personal Collection of Founder, Group Captain Leonard Cheshire VC, available in hardcopy, microform; also audiovisual and photographs available
Administrative Archive of organisations he founded: Leonard Cheshire, Ryder-Cheshire and World Memorial Fund

Non-library collection catalogue: All or part available in-house

Publications: Printed, and electronic and video

Publications list: Available in print

Access to staff: Contact by letter, by telephone, by fax, by e-mail and via website
Hours: Mon to Fri, 0900 to 1700

Access to building: Prior appointment required

Access for disabled people: Parking provided, level entry, access to all public areas, toilet facilities

LEONARD CHESHIRE DISABILITY ARCHIVE

Head Office, Leonard Cheshire Disability, 66 South Lambeth Road, London, SW8 1RL

Tel: 020 3242 0200
Fax: 020 3242 0250
E-mail: info@LCDisability.org
Website: www.lcdisability.org/
Website: www.leonard-cheshire.org

Enquiries to: Archivist
Direct e-mail: archive@lcdisability.org

Founded: 1948

Organisation type and purpose:
International organisation, voluntary organisation, registered charity (charity number 218186).
The parent body The Leonard Cheshire Foundation offers services to people with disabilities.

Subject coverage: Leonard Cheshire (the man), Group Captain Lord Cheshire of Woodhall, VC OM DSO DFC.
Leonard Cheshire Foundation's work; Ryder-Cheshire Foundation's work; services for people with disabilities provided by these organisations.

Non-library collection catalogue: All or part available in-house

Access to staff: Contact by letter, by telephone and by fax. Appointment necessary.
Hours: Mon to Fri, 0900 to 1700
Special comments: Some material on restricted access.

LEPRA HEALTH IN ACTION (LEPRA)

28 Middleborough, Colchester, Essex, CO1 1TG

Tel: 01206 216700
Fax: 01206 762151
E-mail: lepra@leprahealthinaction.org
Website: www.leprahealthinaction.org

Enquiries to: Information Officer
Direct e-mail: irenea@leprahealthinaction.org
Other contacts: Communications Officer; Direct Marketing Officer

Founded: 1924; formerly called British Leprosy Relief Association (year of change 2008)

Organisation type and purpose: Registered charity (number 213251 in England and Wales and SC039715 in Scotland).
Restoring health, hope and dignity to people affected by leprosy and other diseases of poverty.

Subject coverage: Health education, advocacy, research into treatment of diseases of poverty.

Publications: Printed
Order printed publications from: website: http://www.leprahealthinaction.org/category/information/leprosy-review

Publications list: Available online

Access to staff: Contact by letter, by telephone, by fax, by e-mail, in person and via website
Hours: Mon to Fri, 0900 to 1700

Access for disabled people: Disabled Access

Subsidiary body: LEPRA India; Post Box 1518, Krishnapuri Colony, West Marredpally, Secunderabad, 500 026, India; tel: +91 040 44586060 / 27802139 / 27807314; fax: +91 040 27801391; e-mail: info@leprahealthinaction.in; website: https://leprasociety.org

LESOTHO HIGH COMMISSION

7 Chesham Place, London, SW1X 8HN

Tel: 020 7235 5686
Fax: 020 7235 5023
E-mail: lhc@lesotholondon.org.uk
Website: www.lesotholondon.org.uk

Enquiries to: First Secretary
Other contacts: First Secretary, Information Officer

Founded: 1966

Organisation type and purpose:
International organisation, national government body.
Diplomatic mission.

Subject coverage: Lesotho.

Access to staff: Contact by letter, by telephone, by fax, by e-mail and via website. Appointment necessary.
Hours: Mon to Fri, 0900 to 1245 and 1400 to 1600

Access to building: No access other than to staff

LEUKAEMIA & LYMPHOMA RESEARCH (LLR)

43 Great Ormond Street, London, WC1N 3JJ

Tel: 0207 5040101
E-mail: info@beatingbloodcancers.org.uk
Website: www.beatingbloodcancers.org.uk

Enquiries to: Clinical Information Officer
Direct tel: 0207 504 2260
Direct e-mail: kcampbell@llresearch.org.uk

Founded: 1960; formerly called Leukaemia Research Fund, Leukaemia Research

Organisation type and purpose: National organisation, voluntary organisation, registered charity (charity number 216032), research organisation.
Improving treatment, finding cures and causes of leukaemia, lymphoma, myeloma, myelodysplasia, myeloproliferative disorders and aplastic anaemia.

Subject coverage: Leukaemia, acute leukaemia in children, coping with childhood leukaemia, acute lymphoblastic leukaemia, acute myeloid leukaemia, chronic myeloid leukaemia, bone marrow and stem cell transplantation, the lymphomas, multiple myeloma, myelodysplastic syndromes, aplastic

continued overleaf

anaemia, dictionary of leukaemia and related diseases, chronic lymphocytic leukaemia, less common disorders related to leukaemia, myeloproliferature disorders.

Information services: Information on leukaemia, lymphoma, myeloma and related conditions

Special visitor services: None

Services for disabled people: None

Publications: Printed

Publications list: Available online

Access to staff: Contact by letter, by telephone, by fax, by e-mail and via website
Hours: Mon to Fri, 0930 to 1645

Access to building: No public access

Member organisation of: UK Co-ordinating Committee for Cancer Research, Cancer Campaigning Group

LEUKAEMIA CARE SOCIETY

2 Shrubbery Avenue, Worcester, WR1 1QH

Tel: 01905 330003 or Care Line: 0800 1696680
Fax: 01905 330090
E-mail: info@leukaemiacare.org.uk
Website: www.leukaemiacare.org.uk

Enquiries to: Network Operations Manager
Direct e-mail: Dawn.knott@leukaemiacare .org.uk

Founded: 1967

Organisation type and purpose: Voluntary organisation, registered charity (charity number 259483).

Subject coverage: Information about leukaemia and allied blood disorders, friendship, support and practical help for sufferers and their relatives, caravan holidays, limited financial assistance.

Publications: Printed

Access to staff: Contact by letter, by telephone, by fax, by e-mail and via website. Appointment necessary.
Hours: 0900 to 1630
Special comments: Telephone diversion outside office hours.

LEUKAEMIA RESEARCH UNIT

Centre for Adult Leukaemia, Hammersmith Hospital/Imperial College, Du Cane Road, London, W12 0NN

Tel: 020 8383 3238
Fax: 020 8740 9679

Enquiries to: Chairman

Founded: 1988

Organisation type and purpose:
Professional body, university department or institute.

Subject coverage: Leukaemia.
Order printed publications from: Chairman, Department of Haematology
Imperial College School of Medicine, Hammersmith Hospital, Du Cane Road, London, W12 0NN

LEWIS CARROLL SOCIETY (LCS)

50 Lauderdale Mansions, Lauderdale Road, London, W9 1NE

E-mail: markrichards@aznet.co.uk
Website: lewiscarrollsociety.org.uk

Enquiries to: Chairman

Founded: 1969

Organisation type and purpose:
International organisation, learned society (membership is by subscription), present number of members: 450, registered charity (charity number 266239), suitable for all ages.

Subject coverage: Charles Dodgson: life and works (Lewis Carroll).

Publications: Printed

Publications list: Available online and in print

Access to staff: Contact by letter, by e-mail and via website
Hours: Mon to Fri, 0900 to 1700

LEWISHAM LOCAL HISTORY AND ARCHIVES CENTRE

Lewisham Library, 199–201 Lewisham High Street, London, SE13 6LG

Tel: 020 8314 8509/8501
Fax: 020 8297 1169
E-mail: local.studies@lewisham.gov.uk
Website: www.lewisham.gov.uk

Enquiries to: Archivist

Founded: 1960

Organisation type and purpose: Local government body, public library.
Archives.
Archive and local studies service for the London Borough of Lewisham.

Subject coverage: London Borough of Lewisham; history.

Collection: Archives of the Borough and predecessor authorities, and of organisations within the Borough
Local studies material relating to the Borough
Small museum collection

Non-library collection catalogue: All or part available online and in-house

Library catalogue: All or part available online and in-house

Publications list: Available online and in print

Access to staff: Contact by letter, by telephone, by fax, by e-mail and in person
Hours: Mon, 1000 to 1700; Fri, Sat, 0900 to 1700; Tue and Thu, 0900 to 2000
Special comments: Appointments advised.

Access for disabled people: Access to all public areas

Parent body: London Borough of Lewisham; London, SE6

LEWISHAM REFERENCE LIBRARY

199–201 Lewisham High Street, London, SE13 6LG

Tel: 020 8297 9430
Fax: 020 8314 8556
E-mail: reference.library@lewisham.gov.uk
Website: www.lewisham.gov.uk

Enquiries to: Reference Librarian

Organisation type and purpose: Local government body, public library.

Subject coverage: Arts, humanities and social sciences, specialist holding at Library Service Bookstore, Hither Green Lane, London SE13 6TJ: biology.

Library catalogue: All or part available in-house

Access to staff: Contact by telephone, by e-mail and in person
Hours: Mon, 1000 to 2000; Tue, Thu, 0900 to 2000; Wed, Fri, 0900 to 1800; Sat, 0900 to 1700; Sun, 1300 to 1600

Access for disabled people: Parking provided, level entry, access to all public areas, toilet facilities

Member organisation of: South East Area Libraries Information Service

LGC

Formal name: LGC

Queens Road, Teddington, Middlesex, TW11 0LY

Tel: 020 8943 7000
Fax: 020 8943 2767
E-mail: info@lgc.co.uk
Website: www.lgc.co.uk

Enquiries to: Client Services

Organisation type and purpose:
International organisation, statutory body, service industry, training organisation, consultancy, research organisation.

Subject coverage: Analytical chemistry, methods of analysis: wines, soft drinks, spirits, beer, sugar composites, foods, pesticide formulations and residues, drug analysis, radionuclides in water, water analysis, environmental analysis and advice, contaminated land analysis, background information on a wide variety of products, including plastics, chemicals, hydrocarbon and essential oils, safety and health, analytical quality control and certified reference materials, lifesciences (DNA services) and analytical molecular biology.

Library catalogue: All or part available in-house

Publications: Printed

Publications list: Available in print

Access to staff: Contact by letter, by telephone, by fax and by e-mail
Hours: Mon to Fri, 0900 to 1730

Access to building: No access other than to staff

LIBERAL DEMOCRATS

4 Cowley Street, London, SW1P 3NB

Tel: 020 7222 7999
Fax: 020 7799 2170
E-mail: libdems@cix.co.uk
Website: www.libdems.org.uk

Enquiries to: Information Officer
Direct tel: 020 7227 1385

Organisation type and purpose:
Membership association (membership is by subscription), present number of members: 90,000.
Political party.

Subject coverage: Party policy, party structure and organisation, party history.

Collection: Liberal Party archive held at London School of Economics and Political Science Library, Houghton Street, London, WC2A 2AE
SDP archive held at Albert Sloman Library, University of Essex

Publications: Printed
Order printed publications from: Liberal Democrat Publications
4 Cowley Street, London, SW1P 3NB, tel: 020 7222 7999, fax: 020 7799 2170, e-mail: ld-membservs@cix.co.uk

Publications list: Available in print

Access to staff: Contact by letter, by telephone, by fax, by e-mail and via website
Hours: Mon to Fri, 0930 to 1730

Full member of the: Federation of European Liberal Democrat and Reform Parties (ELDR); Building Leo (D2), 55C rue Wiertz, Brussels, B-1047, Belgium; tel: + 322 284 3169; fax: + 322 231 1907; Liberal International (LI); 1 Whitehall Place, London, SW1A 2HE; tel: 020 7839 5905; fax: 020 7925 2685; e-mail: worldlib@cix.co.uk

Other addresses: Liberal Democrats, Wales; Bay View House, 102 Bute Street, Cardiff, CF1 6AD; tel: 029 2031 3400; fax: 029 2031 3401; e-mail: ldwales@cix.co.uk; Scottish Liberal Democrats; 4 Clifton Terrace, Edinburgh, EH12 5DR; tel: 0131 337 2314; fax: 0131 337 3566; e-mail: scotlibdem@cix.co.uk; website: www.scotlibdems.org.uk

LIBERAL INTERNATIONAL (LI)

1 Whitehall Place, London, SW1A 2HD

Tel: 020 7839 5905
Fax: 020 7925 2685
E-mail: all@liberal-international.org
Website: www.liberal-international.org

Enquiries to: Secretary General
Other contacts: (1) Programme Officer (2) Political Assistant for (1) specific information about member parties (2) specific information about member parties and general information.

Founded: 1947

Organisation type and purpose:
International organisation.
A global network of Liberals as well as the world union of Liberal parties. It acts as a platform and political meeting point and represents its member parties. The main goal of the organisation is the promotion of Liberal values.

Subject coverage: International liberalism, human rights, democratisation, tolerance, freedom and an economy based on market principles.

Collection: Basic documents on liberal ideology

Publications: Printed

Access to staff: Contact by letter, by telephone, by fax, by e-mail and via website. Access for members only.
Hours: Mon to Fri, 0900 to 1700

Access to building: No access other than to staff

LIBERAL JUDAISM

The Montagu Centre, 21 Maple Street, London, W1T 4BE

Tel: 020 7580 1663
Fax: 020 7631 9838
E-mail: montagu@liberaljudaism.org
Website: www.liberaljudaism.org

Enquiries to: Office Manager
Direct tel: 020 7631 9822
Direct e-mail: s.o'dwyer@liberaljudaism.org

Founded: 1902

Organisation type and purpose:
International organisation, membership association (membership is by subscription), present number of members: over 9,000, voluntary organisation, registered charity (charity number 236590), publishing house.
National organisation of synagogues.

Subject coverage: Progressive Judaism in Great Britain, education, Liberal Judaism.

Publications: Printed, and electronic and video
Order printed publications from: Liberal Judaism, at the same address; e-mail: books@liberaljudaism.org

Publications list: Available online and in print

Access to staff: Contact by letter, by fax, by e-mail and in person
Hours: Mon to Thu, 0900 to 1700; Fri, 0900 to 1500

Access to building: No access other than to staff

Affiliated to: World Union for Progressive Judaism

LIBERTARIAN ALLIANCE (LA)

Suite 35, 2 Lansdowne Mews, Mayfair, London, W1J 6HL

Tel: 07956 472199
E-mail: sean@libertarian.co.uk
Website: www.libertarian.co.uk

Enquiries to: Director

Founded: 1965

Organisation type and purpose: Voluntary organisation, publishing house.
Political organisation, radical pro-free market and civil libertarian group.

Subject coverage: Libertarian issues, civil and economic liberties, free market economics, database on scholars, scholarship and organisations in these areas.

Collection: Photographs of leading contemporary and historical Libertarian and Classical Liberal scholars and writers

Publications: Printed

Publications list: Available online and in print

Access to staff: Contact by letter, by telephone and by e-mail. Appointment necessary.
Hours: Mon to Fri, 0900 to 1700

Affiliated to: International Society for Individual Liberty; Libertarian International; Liberty: The National Council for Civil Liberties

Subsidiary body: British Association of Libertarian Feminists

LIBERTY

Formal name: National Council for Civil Liberties

21 Tabard Street, Borough, London, SE1 4LA

Tel: 020 7403 3888
Fax: 020 7407 5354
Website: www.liberty-human-rights.org.uk

Enquiries to: Information Officer

Founded: 1934

Organisation type and purpose: National organisation, membership association (membership is by subscription), present number of members: 7000.
Commissions and publishes research, and runs the Civil Liberties Library.

Subject coverage: Civil liberties, especially administration of justice, children's rights, women's rights and sex discrimination, race discrimination, discrimination against homosexuals, police powers, official secrecy and freedom of information, privacy; Bill of Rights; human rights, prisoners' rights, academic freedom, securing services, Northern Ireland, public order, policing, criminal justice.

Collection: Collection of publications since the foundation in 1934

Library catalogue: All or part available in-house

Publications: Printed

Publications list: Available in print

Access to staff: Contact by letter. Appointment necessary. All charged.
Hours: Mon to Fri, 1000 to 1300 and 1400 to 1730

Affiliated to: International League for Human Rights

Charitable arm is the: Civil Liberties Trust

Established by members of, and shares premises with, the: National Council of Civil Liberties

LIBRARY AND MUSEUM OF FREEMASONRY

Formal name: Library and Museum Charitable Trust of the United Grand Lodge of England

Freemasons' Hall, Great Queen Street, London, WC2B 5AZ

Tel: 020 7395 9251
Fax: 020 7404 7418
E-mail: libmus@freemasonry.london.museum
Website: www.freemasonry.london.museum

Enquiries to: Director

continued overleaf

Other contacts: Librarian (for research queries)

Founded: 1838

Organisation type and purpose: Professional body, registered charity (charity number 1058497), museum.
Research library.

Subject coverage: Freemasonry, fraternal and friendly societies and related subjects.

Collection: Objects and artifacts relating to English and world freemasonry. Archives of the United Grand Lodge of England.

Non-library collection catalogue: All or part available online and in-house

Library catalogue: All or part available online

Access to staff: Contact by letter, by telephone, by fax, by e-mail, in person and via website
Hours: Mon to Fri, 1000 to 1700

LIBRARY CAMPAIGN

22 Upper Woburn Place, London, WC1H 0TB

Tel: 0845 450 5946
Fax: 0845 450 5946
E-mail: librarycam@aol.com
Website: www.librarycampaign.com

Enquiries to: Secretary

Founded: 1984

Organisation type and purpose: Registered Charity (England and Wales no. 1102634), national organisation, advisory body, membership association (membership is by subscription), present number of members: 600, voluntary organisation.
Charitable aims: to advance the lifelong education of the public by the promotion, support, assistance and improvement of libraries, and through the activities of friends and user groups; to be the national voice of users of library services through a network of local groups; to co-ordinate a network of Friends of Library Groups.

Subject coverage: Information on local user groups for libraries, where they are and how to start a group.

Publications: Printed

Access to staff: Contact by letter, by telephone and by e-mail
Special comments: 24-hour answerphone. The Campaign is run by volunteers

Access to building: None – address is accommodation address only

Member organisations: Has approximately 40 local organisations

LIBRARY OF AVALON (LOA)

Rear Courtyard, 'Glastonbury Experience' 2–4 High Street, Glastonbury, Somerset, BA6 9DU

Tel: 01458 832759
E-mail: librarian@libraryofavalon.org.uk
Website: www.libraryofavalon.org.uk

Enquiries to: Honorary Secretary

Founded: 1988

Organisation type and purpose: Membership association (membership is by subscription), present number of members: 109, voluntary organisation, registered charity (charity number 1065014).

Subject coverage: Arthurian and related subjects; earth mysteries; history and archaeology; alternative and complementary medicine; psychology, personal development, social psychology; astrology; occult and esoteric thought and studies, including magical practice and theory; mythology; comparative religion including paganism; eastern religion and philosophy; Glastonbury.

Collection: A selection of magazines on paganism and earth mysteries (reference only)
Book catalogue held on database (title, author and publisher details only, no text)
Wessex research group collection
Willem Koppejan collection
Rilko collection

Non-library collection catalogue: All or part available online and in-house

Library catalogue: All or part available in-house

Publications list: Available online

Access to staff: Contact by letter, by telephone, by e-mail, in person and via website
Hours: Mon, Wed, Thu, 1330 to 1630; Tue, 1100 to 16.30; Fri, 1200 to 1700; Sat, 1200 to 1600; Sun (most; tel. to check), 1200 to 1500
Special comments: Specialist library open to the public with reading room, but only members may take publications out of the building.

Access to building: *Hours:* as above

Access for disabled people: Ramped entry

LIBRARY RESEARCH AGENCY

Burberry, Devon Road, Salcombe, Devon, TQ8 8HJ

Tel: 01548 842769
Fax: 01548 842536

Enquiries to: Managing Director

Founded: 1983

Organisation type and purpose: Public library, university library, university department or institute, research organisation.

Subject coverage: Research in French, German, Russian, Serbo-Croat, Bulgarian languages, from major libraries, cryptology, cryptanalysis.

Access to staff: Contact by letter, by telephone and by fax
Hours: Mon to Fri, 0900 to 1700

LICENSED TAXI DRIVERS ASSOCIATION (LTDA)

LTDA Taxi House, Woodfield Road, London, W9 2BA

Tel: 020 7286 1046
Fax: 020 7286 2494
E-mail: via website
Website: www.ltda.co.uk

Organisation type and purpose: Trade association for licensed taxi drivers.

Subject coverage: Offers legal representation, leisure discounts, tax investigations, insurance.

Access to staff: Contact by letter, by telephone, by fax and via website

LICHFIELD DISTRICT COUNCIL

District Council House, Frog Lane, Lichfield, Staffordshire, WS13 6YU

Tel: 01543 308000; minicom no. 01543 308078
Fax: 01543 309899
E-mail: enquiries@lichfielddc.gov.uk

Enquiries to: Chief Executive

Founded: 1974

Organisation type and purpose: Local government body.

Subject coverage: All functions of the local authority; planning, economic development, leisure and environmental health.

Access to staff: Contact by letter, by telephone and by fax. Appointment necessary.
Hours: Mon to Fri, 0845 to 1715

Access for disabled people: Parking provided, ramped entry, toilet facilities

LICHFIELD RECORD OFFICE (LRO)

The Friary, Lichfield, Staffordshire, WS13 6QG

Tel: 01543 510720
E-mail: lichfield.record.office@staffordshire.gov.uk
Website: www.staffordshire.gov.uk/archives/lich.htm

Enquiries to: Area Archivist

Founded: 1959

Organisation type and purpose: Local government body. To preserve and make available archives of the diocese of Lichfield and archives created in, and/or relating to, the city of Lichfield and the town of Burton upon Trent and their surrounding areas.

Subject coverage: Ecclesiastical, social, economic and political history of the diocese and City of Lichfield and of Burton upon Trent; genealogy.

Non-library collection catalogue: All or part available online, in-house and in print

Publications: Printed

Publications list: Available online and in print

Access to staff: Contact by letter, by telephone, by fax, by e-mail and in person. Appointment necessary.

Access to building: *Hours:* Mon, Tue, Wed, 0930 to 1700; Thu, 1130 to 1900; Fri, closed; 2nd Sat of each month, 0930 to 1230
Special comments: Some records closed for 30 or more years from latest date.

Branches: Staffordshire Record Office; Eastgate Street, Stafford; tel: 01785 278379; e-mail: staffordshire.record.office@

staffordshire.gov.uk; Stoke on Trent Archives; tel: 01782 238420; e-mail: stoke .archives@stoke.gov.uk

Parent body: Staffordshire and Stoke on Trent Archive Service

LIDDELL HART CENTRE FOR MILITARY ARCHIVES (LHCMA)

King's College London, Strand, London, WC2R 2LS

Tel: 020 7848 2015
Fax: 020 7848 2760
E-mail: archives.web@kcl.ac.uk
Website: www.kcl.ac.uk/iss/archives

Enquiries to: Director of Archives and Information Management

Founded: 1964

Subject coverage: Archive repository for the papers of senior defence personnel, authors and commentators on international security and defence policy, with the scope of the holdings ranging from high-level defence policy and strategic planning, to the command of individual units in the field in almost every major campaign in which British troops have fought from 1900 to present day. Additional material on the history of science and journalism, and the study of racial interaction and colonial administration.

Collection: The Centre holds the papers of over 700 senior defence personnel, including:
Sir Basil Liddell Hart (1895–1970)
FM Lord Alanbrooke (1883–1993)
FM Lord Allenby (1861–1936)
ACM Sir Robert Brooke-Popham (1878–1953)
Sir Arthur Bryant (1899–1985)
Sir Frank Cooper (1922–2002)
Maj-Gen. J. F. C. Fuller (1878–1966)
Gen. Sir Ian Hamilton (1853–1947)
Gen. Lord Ismay (1887–1965)
Gen. Sir Richard O'Connor (1889–1981)
FM Lord Milne (1866–1948)
FM Sir Archibald Montgomery-Massingberd (1871–1947)
FM Sir William Robertson (1860–1933)
Gen. Sir Hugh Stockwell (1903–1986)
Television documentary archives include:
The Nuclear Age (1989)
The Death of Yugoslavia (1995)
The Washington Version (1992) (Gulf War)
The Fall of the Wall (1994)

Non-library collection catalogue: All or part available online

Access to staff: Contact by letter, by telephone, by fax, by e-mail and via website. Appointment necessary. Letter of introduction required.
Hours: Mon to Fri, 0930 to 1730

Access for disabled people: Level entry, toilet facilities

LIFE

LIFE House, 1 Mill Street, Leamington Spa, Warwickshire, CV31 1ES

Tel: 01926 421587
Fax: 01926 336497
E-mail: info@lifecharity.org.uk
Website: www.lifecharity.org.uk

Enquiries to: Trustee

Other contacts: Research Officer

Founded: 1970

Organisation type and purpose: Voluntary organisation, registered charity.
Opposed to all direct abortion and offering free practical help to women with unplanned pregnancies. Counselling before and after abortion. Accommodation for homeless pregnant women.

Subject coverage: Abortion, pregnancy, birth, counselling after abortion, housing single mothers, infertility, fertility control, infertility treatment, school talks and study days.

Publications: Printed, and electronic and video

Access to staff: Contact by letter, by telephone, by fax, by e-mail and via website
Hours: Mon to Fri, 0900 to 1700

LIFE EDUCATION CENTRES (LEC)

1st Floor, 53–56 Great Sutton Street, London, EC1V 0DG

Tel: 020 7490 3210
Fax: 020 7490 3610

Enquiries to: Director of Research
Direct e-mail: enquiries@lifeeducation.org.uk

Founded: 1979

Organisation type and purpose: Registered charity (charity number 800727), suitable for ages: 3 to 15, training organisation, publishing house.
Drug prevention charity for children, schools and families.

Subject coverage: Drug prevention (theory, research), drug information (effects etc), evaluation of drug prevention programmes.

Collection: Drug prevention and research: books, reports, journals, newspaper clippings

Trade and statistical information: Statistical information on drug use (especially youth). Data on prevention programme effects (especially LEC)

Publications: Printed, and electronic and video
Order printed publications from: Publications Manager, Life Education Centres at the same address

Publications list: Available in print

Access to staff: Contact by letter, by telephone and by fax
Hours: Mon to Fri, 0900 to 1700

Parent body: Life Education International (LEI)

LIFETIME MANAGEMENT OF MATERIALS ADVISORY SERVICE (LMM)

National Physical Laboratory, Hampton Road, Teddington, Middlesex, TW11 0LW

Tel: 020 8943 6142
E-mail: lmm@npl.co.uk
Website: www.npl.co.uk/npl/lmmt/aqueous/about_ncs.html

Enquiries to: Executive Secretary
Direct tel: 020 8943 6179

Founded: 1975; formerly called National Corrosion Service (year of change 2007)

Organisation type and purpose: Advisory body, consultancy, research organisation.
The United Kingdom's gateway to corrosion, materials expertise and advice.

Subject coverage: Corrosion control and prevention; design and selection of materials; coating systems; cathodic protection; environmental factors; failure analysis and investigations.

Publications: Printed

Publications list: Available online and in print

Access to staff: Contact by letter, by telephone, by fax, by e-mail and via website. Appointment necessary.
Hours: Mon to Fri, 0900 to 1700

Constituent part of: Serco Group plc; Serco House, 16 Bartley Wood Business Park, Hook, Hants, RG27 9UY

LIFT AND ESCALATOR INDUSTRY ASSOCIATION (LEIA)

33–34 Devonshire Street, London, W1G 6PY

Tel: 020 7935 3013
Fax: 020 7935 3321
E-mail: enquiries@leia.co.uk

Enquiries to: Director

Founded: 1997

Organisation type and purpose: Trade association, present number of members: c. 150.

Subject coverage: Lifts, escalators, passenger conveyors, safety, design and standardisation.

Access to staff: Contact by letter, by telephone and by fax
Hours: Mon to Fri, 0900 to 1700

Member of: Specialist Engineering Contractors Group

LIFTING EQUIPMENT ENGINEERS ASSOCIATION (LEEA)

3 Osprey Court, Kingfisher Way, Hinchingbrooke Business Park, Huntingdon, Cambridgeshire, PE29 6FN

Tel: 01480 432801
Fax: 01480 436314
E-mail: mail@leea.co.uk
Website: www.leea.co.uk

Enquiries to: Chief Executive

Founded: 1944

Organisation type and purpose: Trade association.

Subject coverage: Lifting equipment.

Library catalogue: All or part available online and in-house

Publications: Printed

Publications list: Available online and in print

Access to staff: Contact by letter, by telephone, by fax and by e-mail. Appointment necessary. Access for members only.
Hours: Mon to Fri, 0830 to 1700

LIGHTING INDUSTRY ASSOCIATION (LIA)

Formal name: The Lighting Industry Association Ltd

Stafford Park 7, Telford, Shropshire, TF3 3BQ

Tel: 01952 290905
Fax: 01952 290906
E-mail: info@thelia.org.uk
Website: www.thelia.org.uk

Enquiries to: Marketing Communications Manager
Direct e-mail: joj@thelia.org.uk

Founded: 2012

Organisation type and purpose: Trade Association.

Subject coverage: Strengthen the industry and promote the benefits of good quality lighting by representing all aspects of UK, EU and international legislation and standards at the highest level whilst protecting the interests of both the public and members.

Publications: Printed, and electronic and video

Access to staff: Contact by letter, by telephone, by e-mail and via website. Appointment necessary.
Hours: Mon to Fri, 0900 to 1700

LINACRE COLLEGE LIBRARY

St Cross Road, Oxford, OX1 3JA

Tel: 01865 271650
Fax: 01865 271668
E-mail: library@linacre.ox.ac.uk
Website: www.linacre.ox.ac.uk

Enquiries to: Librarian
Direct tel: 01865 271661

Founded: 1962

Organisation type and purpose: University library.

Subject coverage: Small coverage in all disciplines.

Collection: Ryle Collection (early 20th-century philosophy in England)

Library catalogue: All or part available online

Access to staff: Contact by e-mail
Hours: Mon to Fri, 0900 to 1700

Access to building: No prior appointment required
Special comments: Access is restricted to members of Linacre College.

Access for disabled people: Toilet facilities

Constituent part of: University of Oxford

LINCOLN CATHEDRAL LIBRARY

Minster Yard, Lincoln, LN2 1PX

Tel: 01522 561640
E-mail: librarian@lincolncathedral.com
Website: www.lincolncathedral.com

Enquiries to: Librarian

Founded: 1092

Organisation type and purpose: Cathedral library.

Subject coverage: Early printed books (especially 17th century); cathedrals (especially Lincoln); ecclesiastical history and architecture; liturgy.

Collection: 3,000 17th-century pamphlets and Broadsides
E. J. Willson Collection (architectural drawings)
John Wilson Library (17th- and 18th-century theological works)
Medieval manuscripts
19th-century Religious Tracts
Pre-1800 printed books
Post-medieval manuscripts

Non-library collection catalogue: All or part available online

Library catalogue: All or part available online

Publications: Printed

Publications list: Available in print

Access to staff: Contact by letter, by telephone, by e-mail and via website. Appointment necessary. Letter of introduction required.
Hours: Mon, Tue, 1000 to 1230 and 1400 to 1600

Access to building: No access other than to staff
Hours: Exhibition open April to October: Mon to Fri, 1300 to 1500; Sat, 1100 to 1500; closed Sun

Links with: Lincoln Record Society; Lincoln Cathedral Library, Minster Yard, Lincoln, LN2 1PX; e-mail: secretary@lincoln-record-society.org.uk; website: http://www.lincoln-record-society.org.uk

LINCOLN CITY COUNCIL

City Hall, Beaumont Fee, Lincoln, LN1 1DB

Tel: 01522 881188
Fax: 01522 521736
Website: www.lincoln-info.org.uk

Enquiries to: Policy Officer
Direct tel: 01522 873384
Direct e-mail: nicola.desforges@lincoln.gov.uk

Organisation type and purpose: Local government body.

Subject coverage: Local government services.

Access to staff: Contact by letter, by telephone, by fax and by e-mail
Hours: Mon to Fri, 0900 to 1700

LINCOLN COLLEGE LIBRARY

Lincoln College, Turl Street, Oxford, OX1 3DR

Tel: 01865 279831
E-mail: library@lincoln.ox.ac.uk
Website: www.lincoln.ox.ac.uk/index.php?page=welcome+to+the+library

Enquiries to: Librarian

Founded: 1427

Organisation type and purpose: University department or institute.

Subject coverage: General.

Collection: Senior library of rare books

Access to staff: Contact by letter and by e-mail. Access for members only.
Hours: Mon to Fri, 0900 to 1700

Constituent part of: University of Oxford

LINCOLN LONGWOOL SHEEP BREEDERS ASSOCIATION

Lincolnshire Showground, Grange-de-Lings, Lincoln, LN2 2NA

Tel: 01522 511395
Fax: 01552 520345
E-mail: lincolnlongwool@lineone.net

Enquiries to: Secretary
Direct tel: 01522 730033

Organisation type and purpose: Membership association (membership is by subscription), present number of members: 90 approx, registered charity (charity number 215539).

Subject coverage: Lincoln longwool sheep.

Access to staff: Contact by letter, by telephone, by fax and by e-mail
Hours: Mon to Fri, 0900 to 1700

LINCOLN RECORD SOCIETY (LRS)

Lincoln Cathedral Library, Minster Yard, Lincoln, LN2 1PX

E-mail: secretary@lincoln-record-society.org.uk
Website: www.lincoln-record-society.org.uk

Enquiries to: Honorary Secretary

Founded: 1910

Organisation type and purpose: Learned society.

Subject coverage: History of the ancient county and diocese of Lincoln.

Publications: Printed
Order printed publications from: Boydell & Brewer Ltd

Publications list: Available online and in print

Access to staff: Contact by letter and by e-mail

Links with: Society for Lincolnshire History and Archaeology; The Survey of Lincoln

LINCOLN RED CATTLE SOCIETY

Showground, Grange-de-Lings, Lincoln, LN2 2NA

Tel: 01522 511395
E-mail: secretary@lincolnredcattlesociety.co.uk
Website: www.lincolnredcattlesociety.co.uk

Enquiries to: Secretary

Founded: 1896

Organisation type and purpose: Membership association (membership is by subscription), present number of members: 175 approx, registered charity (charity number 215662).

Access to staff: Contact by letter, by telephone and via website
Hours: Mon to Fri, 0800 to 1600

LINCOLN'S INN LIBRARY

The Honourable Society of Lincoln's Inn, The Treasury Office, Lincoln's Inn, London, WC2A 3TL

Tel: 020 7242 4371
Fax: 020 7404 1864
E-mail: library@lincolnsinn.org.uk
Website: www.lincolnsinn.org.uk/lib_gen.asp

Enquiries to: Librarian
Direct tel: 020 7693 5160
Direct e-mail: librarian@lincolnsinn.org.uk

Founded: c. 15th century

Organisation type and purpose: Legal library.

Collection: 150,000 vols of English law, Commonwealth law and Parliamentary papers
Hale Manuscripts
Black Books (Inn records, 1422 to present)

Non-library collection catalogue: All or part available in print

Library catalogue: All or part available online

Access to staff: Contact by letter, by telephone, by fax, by e-mail and via website. Appointment necessary. Access for members only.
Hours: Normal: Mon to Fri, 0900 to 2000; every 4th Sat, by rotation with other Inns of Court libraries, 1000 to 1700
Aug to mid-Sept: Mon to Fri, 0930 to 1800

Access to building: Open to all members of the Inn and all barristers with chambers in the Inn and their pupils. Barristers who are not members and have chambers elsewhere are welcome to use the Library for material not held by their own Inn, but may not borrow. Solicitors may use the library as last resort only. Other researchers by appointment.

LINCOLN-ZEPHYR OWNERS CLUB

22 New North Road, Hainault, Ilford, Essex, IG6 2XG

Tel: 020 8500 4039
Website: www.lzoc.org

Enquiries to: Information Officer

Founded: 1968

Subject coverage: Lincoln-Zephyr cars.

Access to staff: Contact by letter and by telephone
Hours: Mon to Fri, 0900 to 1700

LINCOLNSHIRE ARCHIVES (LA)

St Rumbold Street, Lincoln, LN2 5AB

Tel: 01522 782040 (search room bookings), 526204 (enquiries)
Fax: 01522 530047
E-mail: lincolnshire_archive@lincolnshire.gov.uk
Website: www.lincolnshire.gov.uk/archives

Enquiries to: Site Coordinator

Founded: 1948

Organisation type and purpose: Local government body.
Record office.

Subject coverage: History of the historical County and the ancient Diocese of Lincoln; rights of way; boundary delineation; family history; local and village history; school and university projects; leisure and general interest, research, educational research, official and legal enquiries.

Collection: Business records
Ecclesiastical records
Estate and family records
Foster Library (local history, national, historical and archaeological journals)
Local authority and public records

Non-library collection catalogue: All or part available online and in-house

Library catalogue: All or part available online and in-house

Publications: Microform publications

Publications list: Available online and in print

Access to staff: Contact by letter, by telephone, by fax, by e-mail, in person and via website. Appointment necessary.
Hours: Tue to Sat, 1000 to 1600; Mon, closed
Special comments: Reader Ticket (apply in person).

Access for disabled people: Parking provided, level entry, access to all public areas, toilet facilities

Incorporated within the service is the:
Lincoln Diocesan Record Office

Parent body: Lincolnshire County Council

LINCOLNSHIRE LIBRARY SERVICE

Education and Cultural Services Directorate, County Offices, Newland, Lincoln, LN1 1YL

Tel: 01522 782010
Fax: 01522 516137
E-mail: library.support@lincolnshire.gov.uk
Website: www.lincolnshire.gov.uk

Enquiries to: Customer Services
Direct e-mail: customer_services@lincolnshire.gov.uk

Founded: 1974

Organisation type and purpose: Local government body, public library.

Subject coverage: General, music and drama, education, local government and management, agriculture, foreign languages, medicine, Tennyson, literature, local studies.

Collection: Abell Collection (local studies, 90 scrapbooks) at Central Library, Lincoln
Armitage Collection (drainage of the county) at Central Library, Lincoln
Banks Collection (Sir Joseph Banks collection of letters, manuscripts and drawings on Lincolnshire and Lincolnshire churches) at Central Library, Lincoln
Binnal Collection (Louth and Lincolnshire) at Louth Library
Exley Collection (Lincolnshire) at Central Library, Lincoln
Goulding Collection (Lincolnshire and Louth) at Louth Library
Lincolnshire illustrations index
Medical Library at Lincoln County Hospital
Medical Library at Pilgrim Hospital, Boston
Newcombe Library (17th- and early 18th-century theology, philosophy and history) at Grantham Library
Newton Collection (material by and about Sir Isaac Newton) at Lincoln Central and Grantham Libraries
Pye Collection (Grimsby and Cleethorpes district) at Central Library, Lincoln
Ross Collection (Lord Monson's collection on Lincoln and Lincolnshire villages) at Central Library, Lincoln
Tennyson Research Collection
Wheeler Collection (drainage of the Fens and the building of the port of Boston) at Boston Library
DVDs, music CDs

Non-library collection catalogue: All or part available online

Library catalogue: All or part available online

Publications list: Available in print

Access to staff: Contact by letter, by telephone, by fax, by e-mail and via website. Appointment necessary.
Hours: Mon to Fri, 0900 to 1700

Access for disabled people: Level entry

Constituent bodies: Tennyson Research Centre

Parent body: Lincolnshire County Council; County Offices, Newland, Lincoln

LINCOLNSHIRE TOURIST GUIDES ASSOCIATION

Winterbourne, Church Lane, Tathwell, Louth, Lincolnshire, LN11 9SR

Tel: 01507 604717
E-mail: jrbh@btinternet.com

Enquiries to: Booking Officer

Founded: 1985

Organisation type and purpose: Tourist guides association.

Subject coverage: Guided walks and tours, talks on all aspects of Lincolnshire's heritage.

Access to staff: Contact by letter, by telephone and by e-mail
Hours: Mon to Fri, 0900 to 1700

LINDE MATERIAL HANDLING (UK) LTD

Kingsclere Road, Basingstoke, Hampshire, RG21 6XJ

Tel: 01256 342000
Fax: 01256 342923
E-mail: enquiries@linde-mh.co.uk
Website: www.linde-mh.co.uk/

Enquiries to: Public Relations Officer

Founded: 1943; formerly called Lansing Linde Limited (year of change 2003)

Organisation type and purpose: Manufacturing industry.

Subject coverage: Materials handling using industrial trucks, including freight, warehousing, high density storage; fork truck operation and maintenance; rental and leasing.

Publications: Printed

Access to staff: Contact by letter, by telephone and by fax

continued overleaf

Hours: Mon to Fri, 0900 to 1700

Access to building: No prior appointment required

LINEN HALL LIBRARY

17 Donegall Square North, Belfast, BT1 5GB

Tel: 028 9032 1707
Fax: 028 9043 8586
E-mail: info@linenhall.com
Website: www.linenhall.com

Enquiries to: Librarian

Founded: 1788

Organisation type and purpose: Registered charity.
Independent subscription library.

Subject coverage: Irish (especially Ulster) local history and biography, Irish bibliography, Irish genealogy, Belfast printed books, political literature and general subjects.

Collection: Belfast printed book collection
Genealogical collection
Irish newspaper and periodical collection
Irish postcard collection
Kennedy collection of Ulster poetry
Northern Ireland political collection
Theatre and Performing Arts Archive

Non-library collection catalogue: All or part available online

Library catalogue: All or part available online and in-house

Publications: Printed, and electronic and video, and microform publications

Publications list: Available online and in print

Access to staff: Contact by letter, by telephone, by fax, by e-mail, in person and via website
Hours: Mon to Fri, 0930 to 1730; Sat, 0930 to 1300

Access to building: No prior appointment required

Access for disabled people: Access to all public areas, toilet facilities

LINK CENTRE FOR DEAFENED PEOPLE (LINK)

19 Hartfield Road, Eastbourne, East Sussex, BN21 2AR

Tel: 01323 638230, 01323 739998 (minicom)
Fax: 01323 642968
E-mail: info@linkdp.org
Website: www.linkdp.org

Enquiries to: Helpdesk

Founded: 1972

Organisation type and purpose: Voluntary organisation, registered charity.
Rehabilitation for deafened adults.

Subject coverage: Care and welfare of adults with severe or total irreversible deafness or severe progressive deafness not compensated by hearing aids, sudden deafness, speech conservation, speech-reading, lipreading, counselling, rehabilitation, advice and help to family or companion of the sufferer, self-management of deafness, psychosocial rehabilitation.

Publications list: Available online and in print

Access to staff: Contact by letter, by telephone, by fax and by e-mail.
Appointment necessary.
Hours: Mon to Fri, 0900 to 1700

Access for disabled people: Ramped entry, access to all public areas, toilet facilities
Special comments: Loop available.

LINNEAN SOCIETY OF LONDON

Burlington House, Piccadilly, London, W1J 0BF

Tel: 020 7434 4479
Fax: 020 7287 9364
E-mail: info@linnean.org
Website: www.linnean.org

Enquiries to: Librarian
Other contacts: Deputy Librarian (for IT queries)

Founded: 1788

Organisation type and purpose: Learned society (membership is by election or invitation), present number of members: 3,000, registered charity.
Promote taxonomy in all its branches.

Subject coverage: Anthropology; natural history; evolutionary biology; botany; zoology; taxonomy; history of science.

Collection: Correspondence and manuscripts of 18th- and 19th-century naturalists
J. E. Smith Collection
J. Insch Tea Library
Linnaean Collection

Non-library collection catalogue: All or part available online

Library catalogue: All or part available online

Publications: Printed
Order printed publications from: Office Manager

Publications list: Available online and in print

Access to staff: Contact by letter, by telephone, by fax, by e-mail, in person and via website. Appointment necessary.
Hours: Mon to Fri, 1000 to 1700
Special comments: Letter of introduction required for manuscript access only.

Access to building: No prior appointment required

Links with: Institute of Biology; International Association of Plant Taxonomists

LIST AND INDEX SOCIETY (L&I)

c/o The National Archives, Kew, Richmond-upon-Thames, Surrey, TW9 4DU

Tel: 020 8392 5343
Fax: 020 8487 9210
E-mail: listandindexsociety@nationalarchives.gov.uk

Enquiries to: Secretary

Founded: 1965

Organisation type and purpose: Learned society (membership is by subscription).

Subject coverage: To publish and provide Public Record Office search room lists and indexes, coverage – public records from 13th to 20th centuries.

Publications: Printed

Publications list: Available in print

Access to staff: Contact by letter, by fax and by e-mail
Hours: Mon to Fri, 0900 to 1700

Affiliated to: Public Record Office

LISTENING BOOKS

12 Lant Street, London, SE1 1QH

Tel: 020 7407 9417
Fax: 020 7403 1377
E-mail: info@listening-books.org.uk
Website: www.listening-books.org.uk

Enquiries to: Membership Services Assistant

Founded: 1959; formerly called The National Listening Library

Organisation type and purpose: Charity supplying audiobooks to people who find it diffiuclt to read due to illness or disabilty.

Subject coverage: A postal and digital audiobook library service for people who cannot read or hold a book in the usual way, due to illness, disability or special education needs.

Education services: Audiobooks to support the National Curriculum

Services for disabled people: Yes, the charity operates for people with illnesses and disabilties

Library catalogue: All or part available online and in print

Publications: Printed

Access to staff: Contact by letter, by telephone, by fax, by e-mail and via website
Hours: Mon to Fri, 0900 to 1700

Access to building: Prior appointment required

LISTER INSTITUTE OF PREVENTIVE MEDICINE

PO Box 1083, Bushey, Hertfordshire, WD23 9AG

Tel: 01923 801886
Fax: 01923 801886
E-mail: secretary@lister-institute.org.uk
Website: www.lister-institute.org.uk

Enquiries to: Secretary

Founded: 1891

Organisation type and purpose: Registered charity (charity number 206271).
Promoting biomedical excellence in the UK through the support of research projects with implications for preventive medicine.

Subject coverage: Biomedical research in the UK within research institutions.

Publications: Printed

Access to staff: Contact by letter, by telephone, by fax, by e-mail and via website
Hours: Mon to Fri, 0930 to 1700

Access to building: No access other than to staff

LISU

Loughborough University, Loughborough, Leicestershire, LE11 3TU

Tel: 01509 635680
Fax: 01509 635699
E-mail: lisu@lboro.ac.uk
Website: www.lboro.ac.uk/departments/dis/lisu

Enquiries to: Director

History of institution: formerly called Library and Information Statistics Unit (year of change 2004)

Organisation type and purpose: Research organisation, publishing house, consultancy.

Subject coverage: Analysis, interpretation, and publication of statistical information for and about the library domain in the UK and Europe. Also undertakes research and consultancy projects for a wide range of organisations.

Publications: Printed, and electronic and video

Publications list: Available online and in print

Access to staff: Contact by letter, by telephone, by fax, by e-mail and via website. Appointment necessary.
Hours: Mon to Fri, 0900 to 1700

Constituent part of: Loughborough University; Department of Information Science

LISZT SOCIETY, THE

9 Burnside Close, Twickenham, Middlesex, TW1 1ET

Tel: 020 8287 5518
Fax: 020 8287 5518
E-mail: LisztSoc@blueyonder.co.uk

Enquiries to: Secretary

Founded: 1950

Organisation type and purpose: Learned society.
To encourage, and promote enjoyment in and appreciation of the music of Liszt, to draw attention to live performances or recordings, to encourage research into his compositions and life and the exchange of views and information about them.

Subject coverage: Music of Franz (Ferenc) Liszt, 1811–1886: his life, times, influence and contemporaries.

Publications: Printed
Order printed publications from: Hardie Press (for scores)
details from the Society

Access to staff: Contact by letter, by telephone, by fax and by e-mail. Appointment necessary.
Hours: Mon to Sun, 0800 to 2200

Access to building: Prior appointment required

Access for disabled people: Parking provided, level entry, toilet facilities

Connections with: Liszt Societies Worldwide

LITERARY & PHILOSOPHICAL SOCIETY OF NEWCASTLE UPON TYNE

23 Westgate Road, Newcastle upon Tyne, NE1 1SE

Tel: 0191 232 0192
Fax: 0191 261 4494
E-mail: library@litandphil.org.uk
Website: www.litandphil.org.uk

Enquiries to: Librarian
Founded: 1793

Organisation type and purpose: Learned society (membership is by subscription), present number of members: 1,200, registered charity (charity number 528069). Private subscription library.

Subject coverage: The humanities with older scientific and technological material of particular importance to the region, plus local collections relating to Northumberland and Durham, 19th-century periodicals.

Collection: Joseph Crawhall collection
Douglas W Dickenson collection for the history of the Northern Architectural Association
Manuscripts and other documents recording the history of the Society
Northern Arts manuscript collection
Pamphlets and tracts from 19th-century onwards
Rosner collection of books, periodicals and reports on Town Planning
Wesley Historical Society collection relating to Methodism in the North East
Range of 19th-century periodicals

Publications: Printed

Access to staff: Contact by letter, by telephone, by fax, by e-mail and in person. Appointment necessary.
Hours: Mon to Fri, 0930 to 1900; Tue, 0930 to 2000; Sat, 0930 to 1300

LITTLE ROYALTY

2 Ninehams Gardens, Caterham, Surrey, CR3 5LP

Tel: 020 8660 3738

Enquiries to: Manager

Founded: 1997

Organisation type and purpose: Service industry.

Subject coverage: Restoration of soft toys damaged by owners and time, in as authentic a manner possible. Also completion of unfinished needlework projects including cross stitch kits, tapestries and dress-making projects.

Access to staff: Contact by letter and by telephone
Hours: Mon to Fri, 0900 to 1700
Special comments: Please send an sae for price list.

LIVERPOOL & SW LANCASHIRE FAMILY HISTORY SOCIETY (L&SWLFHS)

6 Kirkmore Road, Liverpool, L18 4QN

E-mail: patchwork34@waitrose.com
Website: www.liverpool-genealogy.org.uk

Enquiries to: General Secretary

Founded: 1976

Organisation type and purpose: Learned society (membership is by subscription), present number of members: 2,050, registered charity (charity number 512908). To provide educational facilities for the study of family history in the area, to transcribe, index, and wherever possible publish relevant material, and to provide links with other similar societies.

Subject coverage: Family history and genealogy in the area of the ancient County of Lancashire known as the Hundred of West Derby.

Publications: Printed, and electronic and video, and microform publications
Order printed publications from: Publications Officer, Liverpool & SW Lancashire Family History Society, 9 Manor Road, Lymm, Cheshire, WA13 0AY; tel: 01925 755469; e-mail: joe.griffiths@lineone.net

Publications list: Available online and in print

Access to staff: Contact by letter
Hours: Mon to Fri, 0900 to 1700

Local groups covering: Liverpool, Leigh & District, Southport; Widnes, Skelmersdale & Upholland, Warrington

LIVERPOOL ASSOCIATION OF DISABLED PEOPLE (LAD)

Lime Court Centre, Upper Baker Street, Liverpool, L6 1NB

Tel: 0151 263 8366, 0151 260 3187 (minicom)
Fax: 0151 263 1855
E-mail: ladisabled@freenetname.co.uk
Website: www.ladisabled.co.uk

Enquiries to: Manager

Founded: 1966

Organisation type and purpose: Advisory body, membership association (membership is by subscription), voluntary organisation.

Subject coverage: Campaigns for civil and welfare rights of disabled people.

Publications: Printed

Access to staff: Contact by letter, by telephone, by fax and by e-mail. Appointment necessary.
Hours: Mon to Thu, 0900 to 1700; Fri, 0900 to 1630

Access for disabled people: Parking provided, level entry, access to all public areas, toilet facilities

Member of: BCODP; FIAC

LIVERPOOL CHAMBER OF COMMERCE AND INDUSTRY

Number One, Old Hall Street, Liverpool, L3 9HG

Tel: 0151 227 1234
Fax: 0151 236 0121
E-mail: chamber@liverpoolchamber.org.uk
Website: www.liverpoolchamber.org.uk

Enquiries to: Infopool Agent
Direct tel: 0845 145 1115
Direct fax: 0845 145 1116

continued overleaf

Direct e-mail: infopool@liverpoolchamber.org.uk

Founded: 1850

Organisation type and purpose: Membership association.
Delivering accredited services for members and other businesses which improve their profit and increase their efficiency. Providing opportunities for contact and trade between members. Representing members' needs and views at local, national and international levels. Work in partnership with other organisations to improve the prosperity of the region.

Subject coverage: Mailing lists, company information, financial information, product sourcing, market research, grant searches, employment law, pay statistics, local economic surveys, international trade, trade missions (inward and outward), international market awareness events, European funding schemes, transnational links, Ordnance Survey (large and small scale mapping), The Stationery Office, British Standards, Health and Safety Agency, original research.

Collection: Reference library, over 700 directories, electronic sources

Publications: Printed

Access to staff: Contact by letter, by telephone, by fax, by e-mail, in person and via website
Hours: Mon to Fri, 0900 to 1700

Access for disabled people: Ramped entry, access to all public areas, toilet facilities

LIVERPOOL CHARITY AND VOLUNTARY SERVICES (LCVS/ United Way)

151 Dale Street, Liverpool, L2 2AH

Tel: 0151 227 5177
Fax: 0151 237 3998
E-mail: info@lcvs.org.uk
Website: www.lcvs.org.uk

Enquiries to: Chief Executive

Founded: 1909

Organisation type and purpose: Professional body, voluntary organisation, registered charity (charity number 223485).

Subject coverage: The information and advisory service is for and about the voluntary sector, and includes charity law, charity registration, sources of funding, management, the workings of government, local, central and European.

Collection: Small library of information relating to voluntary organisations and charities archive material

Publications list: Available in print

Access to staff: Contact by letter, by telephone, by fax, by e-mail and via website
Hours: Mon to Fri, 0900 to 1700

LIVERPOOL HOPE UNIVERSITY

Hope Park, Liverpool, L16 9JD

Tel: 0151 291 2001
Fax: 0151 291 2037
E-mail: murrays@hope.ac.uk
Website: www.hope.ac.uk/library

Enquiries to: Director of Library and Learning Support
Direct tel: 0151 251 3528
Other contacts: Head of Library Service

Founded: 1844; formerly called Liverpool Hope University College; formerly called Liverpool Institue of Higher Education (LIHE)

Organisation type and purpose: Suitable for ages: 18+.

Subject coverage: Information technology; media; creative and performing arts; psychology; theology; sociology; social work; physical education; business and management; law; politics; art; music; literature; geography; tourism; education; history; children's fiction; science; environmental science; sport; drama.

Collection: Gradwell Collection, theology
Picton Collection, theology
National Ex-Church of England Society, religious education
Radcliffe Library from Liverpool Cathedral and St Aidans, theology
Professor Andrew F. Walls African-Asian Christianity Collection
Archbishop Stuart Blanch (1918–94)

Library catalogue: All or part available online

Access to staff: Contact by letter, by telephone, by fax, by e-mail and via website. Appointment necessary.
Hours: Term time: Mon, Thu, 0900 to 1845; Fri, 0900 to 1645; Sun, 1400 to 1645 (see website for details)

Access to building: *Special comments:* University ID card or signing in required.

Access for disabled people: Parking provided, level entry, access to all public areas, toilet facilities, lift

LIVERPOOL INSTITUTE FOR PERFORMING ARTS (LIPA)

Mount Street, Liverpool, L1 9HF

Tel: 0151 330 3000
Fax: 0151 330 3131
E-mail: reception@lipa.ac.uk
Website: www.lipa.ac.uk

Founded: 1990

Organisation type and purpose: Membership association, present number of members: 725, university library, suitable for ages: 18+.
Degree-awarding body, Liverpool John Moores University.

Subject coverage: Performing arts, sound technology, performance design, acting, dance, music, enterprise management, community arts.

Library catalogue: All or part available in-house

Access to staff: Contact by letter, by telephone, by fax, by e-mail and via website. Appointment necessary.
Hours: Mon to Fri, 0900 to 1700

LIVERPOOL JOHN MOORES UNIVERSITY – AVRIL ROBARTS LEARNING RESOURCE CENTRE

79 Tithebarn Street, Liverpool, L2 2ER

Tel: 0151 231 4022
Fax: 0151 231 4479
Website: www.ljmu.ac.uk/lea
Website: www.ljmu.ac.uk/lea/avril

Enquiries to: Principal Information Officer (Operations)
Direct e-mail: c.haddock@ljmu.ac.uk

Organisation type and purpose: University department or institute.
Learning resource centre.

Subject coverage: Sciences, engineering, health and applied social sciences.

Library catalogue: All or part available online

Publications: Printed

Publications list: Available online and in print

Access to staff: Contact by letter, by fax and by e-mail
Hours: Mon to Thu, 0900 to 2100; Fri, 0930 to 1700; Sat, Sun, 1000 to 1600

Access for disabled people: Disabled access available

LIVERPOOL JOHN MOORES UNIVERSITY – LIBRARY AND STUDENT SUPPORT (LJMU)

Aldham Robarts Learning Resource Centre, Mount Pleasant Campus, Maryland Street, Liverpool, L3 5UZ

Tel: 0151 231 3544
Fax: 0151 231 3113
E-mail: m.melling@ljmu.ac.uk
Website: www.ljmu.ac.uk/lea

Enquiries to: Director of Learning and Information Services

Organisation type and purpose: University Library.

Subject coverage: Art and design; fashion; business; management; law; civil, mechanical, electrical and electronic engineering; surveying; architecture; natural sciences; health; humanities; social sciences; sport and recreation; librarianship; computing; home economics; languages; education; social work.

Collection: Everyman Theatre Archive
Frankie Vaughan Collection of Scores and Parts
Jon Savage Punk Collection
Liddle Hart Collection on Fashion
Stafford Beer Collection
Cold War Collection
Barry Miles Archive

Library catalogue: All or part available online

Publications: Printed

Publications list: Available in print

Access to staff: Contact by letter, by telephone, by fax, by e-mail and via website. Appointment necessary. Non-members charged.
Hours: Mon to Fri, 0900 to 1700

LIVERPOOL LIBRARIES AND INFORMATION SERVICES

Formal name: City of Liverpool Libraries and Information Services (Dept)

Central Library, William Brown Street, Liverpool, L3 8EW

Tel: 0151 233 5835/36, 0151 233 5850 (minicom)
Fax: 0151 233 5886
E-mail: refbt.central.library@liverpool.gov.uk
Website: www.liverpool.gov.uk/libraries

Enquiries to: Head of Libraries and Information Services
Direct tel: 0151 233 6346
Direct fax: 0151 233 6399
Other contacts: Team Leader, Services to Business for main contact for business information services.

Founded: 1852

Organisation type and purpose: Local government body, public library.
Reorganised into three departments; information services, lending services, record office and family history services.

Subject coverage: All subject fields are covered, including: arts and recreation; government, law, economics, transport, business information, statistics; librarianship, religion, philosophy, sociology and education; language, literature, history and topography; local studies; science and technology, including computers, health and safety, medicine, engineering, patents and standards, publications of British Government and International organisations.

Collection: British Government publications
Carl Rosa Opera Collection
Earl of Derby Papers
Complete set of BSI
Parish Registers and other church records
European Union documents
H. F. Hornby bequest and other rare book collections consisting of c. 12,000 manuscripts, finely printed and illustrated books and fine bindings; c. 8,000 etchings, engravings and woodcuts; c. 75,000 bookplates
Historical Collection of Childrens' books
Liverpool City Council Archives and a wide range of deposited archives
Merseyside County Council, Merseyside Development Corporation and joint authority archives
Melly Papers
Moore Papers
Norris Papers
Patent specifications, including Patent Co-operation Treaty, European, US and GB (on CD-ROM)
Roscoe Papers
UN and WHO collection
Walter Crane Collection

Trade and statistical information: Wide range of official and commercial statistical publications, including UK government, EU, UN, Mintel and Keynote market research reports

Non-library collection catalogue: All or part available in-house

Library catalogue: All or part available in-house

Publications list: Available in print

Access to staff: Contact by letter, by telephone, by fax, by e-mail and in person
Hours: Mon to Thu, 0900 to 1800; Fri, 0900 to 1800; Sat, 0900 to 1700; Sun, 1200 to 1600

Access for disabled people: Parking provided, ramped entry, toilet facilities
Special comments: IT equipment and software available for disabled customers – Contact services to Disabled People Unit, 0151 233 5865

Parent body of: LADSIRLAC; tel: 0151 233 5825; fax: 0151 233 5886; e-mail: stb.central.library@liverpool.gov.uk; Liverpool Record Office and Family History Service; tel: 0151 233 5817; fax: 0151 233 5886; e-mail: recoffice.central.library@liverpool.gov.uk

LIVERPOOL MEDICAL INSTITUTION (LMI)

114 Mount Pleasant, Liverpool, L3 5SR

Tel: 0151 709 9125
Fax: 0151 707 2810
E-mail: library@lmi.org.uk
Website: www.lmi.org.uk

Enquiries to: Librarian

Founded: 1779

Organisation type and purpose: Learned society (membership is by election or invitation), present number of members: 1200, registered charity (charity number 210112).

Subject coverage: History of medicine.

Collection: Historical Collection of medical books

Non-library collection catalogue: All or part available in-house and in print

Library catalogue: All or part available in-house

Publications: Printed

Access to staff: Contact by letter, by telephone, by fax, by e-mail and via website. Appointment necessary. Access for members only. Letter of introduction required. Non-members charged.
Hours: Mon to Fri, 0930 to 1730

Access to building: Prior appointment required

Access for disabled people: Parking provided, ramped entry, level entry, access to all public areas, toilet facilities

LIVERPOOL RECORD OFFICE AND LOCAL HISTORY SERVICE

Liverpool Libraries Satellite Service, Unit 33, Wellington Employment Park South, Dune's Way, Liverpool, L5 9ZS

Tel: 0151 233 5817
Fax: 0151 233 5824
E-mail: recoffice.central.library@liverpool.gov.uk
Website: www.liverpool.gov.uk
Website: www.liverpool.gov.uk/archives

Enquiries to: Manager

Founded: 1850

Organisation type and purpose: Local government body, public library.

Subject coverage: Local history, family history, primarily City of Liverpool, but some more general material for Merseyside and Lancashire and Cheshire.

Collection: Archives and local studies materials on all aspects of the City's history

Non-library collection catalogue: All or part available online and in-house

Library catalogue: All or part available online and in-house

Publications: Printed, and electronic and video
Order microform publications from: Microform Academic Publishers
Order electronic and video publications from: North West Film Archive

Publications list: Available online and in print

Access to staff: Contact by letter, by telephone, by fax, by e-mail, in person and via website. Appointment necessary.
Hours: Mon to Sat, 0930 to 1700

Access to building: *Hours:* Tue to Sat, 0930 to 1630
Special comments: By appointment only, minimum 24 hours' notice.

Access for disabled people: Ramped entry, toilet facilities

LIVERPOOL SCHOOL OF TROPICAL MEDICINE

Pembroke Place, Liverpool, L3 5QA

Tel: 0151 708 9393
Fax: 0151 708 8733
E-mail: robbinsv@liverpool.ac.uk

Enquiries to: Director
Other contacts: (1) Librarian (2) Secretary LATH for (1) library and publications (2) Liverpool Associates in Tropical Health Limited.

Founded: 1898

Organisation type and purpose: Registered charity (charity number 222655), university department or institute, research organisation.

Subject coverage: Human health in tropical and developing countries; tropical community health; management in primary health care; health information systems, health education and promotion; clinical tropical medicine; tropical paediatrics and child health; maternal health; parasitology, medical entomology; immunology and molecular biology as applied to tropical medicine; veterinary parasitology; epidemiology and statistics.

Collection: Archive collection on all aspects of the School's history
Dawes Parasitology Collection
Library of some 40,000 volumes
Reference collections of trypanosomes of man and animals
Rodent malaria parasites and Leishmania

Publications: Printed

Publications list: Available in print

Access to staff: Contact by letter, by telephone, by fax, by e-mail and via website. Appointment necessary.
Hours: Mon to Fri, 0900 to 1700

continued overleaf

Affiliated to: University of Liverpool

Subsidiary body: Liverpool Associates in Tropical Health (LATH)

LIVING STREETS (PA)

3rd Floor, 31–33 Bondway, London, SW8 1SJ

Tel: 020 7820 1010
Fax: 020 7820 8208
E-mail: info@pedestrians.org.uk
Website: www.pedestrians.org.uk

Enquiries to: Director

Founded: 1929

Organisation type and purpose: National organisation, membership association (membership is by subscription), present number of members: 1400, voluntary organisation, registered charity (charity number 206006), suitable for ages: all. Living Streets is a national charity working to create streets and public spaces that people on foot can use and enjoy.

Subject coverage: Statistical, legal, parliamentary, local government, town planning, highway and traffic engineering, and medical aspects of walking with special regard for its safety and convenience.

Collection: Association archives

Publications: Printed

Publications list: Available online and in print

Access to staff: Contact by letter, by telephone, by fax, by e-mail and via website
Hours: Mon to Fri, 0930 to 1730

Affiliated to: Federation of Europe Pedestrians Associations; International Federation of Pedestrians

Local contacts: Countrywide

LLANELLI LIBRARY

Vaughan Street, Llanelli, Carmarthenshire, SA15 3AS

Tel: 01554 773538
Fax: 01554 750125
E-mail: libraries@carmarthenshire.gov.uk

Enquiries to: Manager

Founded: 1860

Organisation type and purpose: Local government body, public library.

Subject coverage: General.

Collection: 1800 coal mine plans
Collection of manuscripts
Theodore Nichol Collection

Non-library collection catalogue: All or part available in-house

Library catalogue: All or part available online and in-house

Publications: Printed

Publications list: Available online and in print

Access to staff: Contact by letter, by telephone, by fax and in person
Hours: Mon to Fri, 0900 to 1700

Access to building: No access other than to staff

Access for disabled people: Ramped entry, access to all public areas, toilet facilities
Special comments: Lift to first floor.

LLANGEFNI LIBRARY

Lon y Felin, Llangefni, Anglesey, LL77 7RT

Tel: 01248 752908
Fax: 01248 752999
E-mail: jrtlh@ynysmon.gov.uk
Website: www.ynysmon.gov.uk

Enquiries to: Manager

Founded: 1996

Organisation type and purpose: Local government body, public library.

Subject coverage: Local history, the Isle of Anglesey.

Collection: Local studies collection – Isle of Anglesey

Non-library collection catalogue: All or part available in-house

Library catalogue: All or part available online

Access to staff: Contact by letter, by telephone, by fax, by e-mail and in person
Hours: Mon to Fri, 0900 to 1700

Access to building: No prior appointment required

Access for disabled people: Parking provided, level entry, access to all public areas, toilet facilities

Parent body: Isle of Anglesey County Council; Library, Information and Archives Services

LLOYD'S REGISTER OF SHIPPING

71 Fenchurch Street, London, EC3M 4BS

Tel: 020 7709 9166
Fax: 020 7488 4796
Website: www.lr.org

Enquiries to: Information Officer and Archivist
Direct tel: 020 7423 2475
Direct fax: 020 7423 2039
Direct e-mail: histinfo@lr.org

Founded: 1760

Organisation type and purpose: International organisation, advisory body, statutory body, service industry, training organisation, consultancy, research organisation, publishing house.
Classification Society and Independent Inspection Agency.

Subject coverage: Ships: classification, specification and advisory service, international conventions, Register Book (full details of all known merchant ships of the world over 100 tons), statistics, technical records; offshore services: certification and classification in connection with steel and concrete, submersibles and underwater habitats, welding, linepipe etc; land-based industry: rail, nuclear power stations, thermal and hydroelectric power stations, oil refineries and chemical plants, freight containers, and general engineering; other services include yachts, cargo gear, docks etc; instrumentation; refrigeration and cold stores; mass-produced machinery; computer services; offshore rigs.

Collection: Complete set of the Lloyd's Register Statistical Tables from 1878 to date
Complete set of the Lloyd's Register of Ships from 1764 to date
Complete set of the Lloyd's Register of Yachts from 1878 to 1980
Complete set of the Lloyd's Register Casualty Return 1890 to date

Trade and statistical information: Shipping statistics 1878 to date
Casualty (shipping) information from 1890 to date
Shipping Information (Specific Ships) 1764 to date
Shipowners 1876 to date
Yachts 1904 to 1980
Shipbuilders 1886 to date

Non-library collection catalogue: All or part available in-house

Library catalogue: All or part available online and in-house

Publications: Printed, and electronic and video
Order printed publications from: Lloyd's Register
71 Fenchurch Street, London, EC3M 4BS; e-mail rules@lr.org

Publications list: Available online

Access to staff: Contact by letter, by telephone, by fax, by e-mail, in person and via website. Appointment necessary. All charged.
Hours: Mon to Fri, 0930 to 1200 and 1300 to 1630
Special comments: Closed on public holidays and between Christmas and New Year.

Access for disabled people: Access to all public areas, toilet facilities
Special comments: Entry to building by lift; prior notice appreciated but not necessary.

The IMarEST Collection at Lloyd's Register: The Institute of Marine Engineering, Science and Technology; Library collection held at the Information Centre, Lloyd's Register, 71 Fenchurch Street, London, EC3M 4BS; tel: 020 7423 2707; e-mail: library@lr.org; website: http://www.lr.org/about_us/shipping_information/IMarEST_Collection_at_LR.aspx

LOCAL AUTHORITIES COORDINATORS OF REGULATORY SERVICES (LACORS)

Local Government House, Smith Square, London, SW1P 3HZ

Tel: 020 7665 3888
Fax: 020 7665 3887
E-mail: info@lacors.gov.uk
Website: www.lacors.gov.uk

Enquiries to: Executive Director

Founded: 1978

Organisation type and purpose: Local government statutory body.

Subject coverage: Food, trading standards, health and safety, animal health and welfare, environmental protection, private-sector housing, licensing and gambling

Publications list: Available in print

Access to staff: Contact by letter, by telephone, by fax, by e-mail and via website
Hours: Mon to Fri, 0900 to 1700

Access to building: Prior appointment required

Access for disabled people: Ramped entry

LOCAL AUTHORITY ACTION FOR SOUTHERN AFRICA (LAACTSA)

c/o Glasgow City Council, DRS, 229 George Street, Glasgow, G1 1QU

Tel: 0141 287 8665
Fax: 0141 287 9958
E-mail: john.mcfadden@drs.glasgow.gov.uk

Enquiries to: Membership Secretary

Founded: 1995

Organisation type and purpose: Local government body, advisory body, membership association (membership is by subscription), present number of members: 60 UK Councils, training organisation, consultancy, research organisation.
Supporting development and democracy in post-apartheid South Africa.

Subject coverage: Local government in Southern Africa (South Africa and other countries within SADC – Angola, Mozambique, Zambia, Zimbabwe, Tanzania, DRC, Lesotho, Namibia, Swaziland, Botswana, Malawi, Seychelles and Mauritius). British local government links with Southern Africa.

Publications: Printed

Access to staff: Contact by letter, by fax and by e-mail
Hours: Wed to Fri, 1000 to 1800

Sister organisation: Action for Southern Africa (ACTSA); 231 Vauxhall Bridge Road, London, SW1V 1EH; tel: 020 3263 2001; fax: 020 7931 9398; e-mail: info@actsa.org

Special interest group of: Local Government Association LGA (LGIB)

LOCAL AUTHORITY CATERERS ASSOCIATION (LACA)

Bourne House, Horsell Park, Woking, Surrey, GU21 4LY

Tel: 01483 766777
Fax: 01483 751991
E-mail: admin@laca.co.uk
Website: www.laca.co.uk

Enquiries to: Administrator

Founded: 1991

Organisation type and purpose:
Professional body.
Providers of catering services and supplies to education, social services, leisure and civil catering.

Subject coverage: Catering with local authorities, including education, welfare, civic, leisure; development of school meals services.

Trade and statistical information: Data on uptake of school meals.
Data on volume of purchasers in local authority catering

Publications: Printed

Access to staff: Contact by letter, by telephone, by fax and by e-mail
Hours: Mon to Fri, 0900 to 1700

LOCAL GOVERNMENT ASSOCIATION (LGA)

Local Government House, Smith Square, London, SW1P 3HZ

Tel: 020 7664 3000
Fax: 020 7664 3030
E-mail: info@local.gov.uk
Website: www.local.gov.uk/association

Enquiries to: LG Connect

Founded: 1997

Organisation type and purpose: Local government body.
The national voice for local authorities in England and Wales, speaking for 350 local authorities representing 50m. people.

Subject coverage: Local government in England and Wales, policy including finance, education, libraries, economic development, social services, transport, leisure, housing, tourism, contracts, environment, personnel, police, fire, consumer protection, health, etc.

Collection: Policy and structure issues; review team; finance; economic development, tourism and leisure; legal and parliamentary; planning, transport, environment and housing

Publications: Printed
Order printed publications from: LG Connect, Publication Sales, Local Government House, Smith Square, London, SW1P 3HZ; tel: 020 7664 3000

Publications list: Available online

Access to staff: Contact by letter, by telephone, by fax and by e-mail
Hours: Mon to Fri, 0900 to 1700

Autonomous Welsh arm replaces the: Assembly of Welsh Counties; Committee of Welsh Districts

LOCAL GOVERNMENT BOUNDARY COMMISSION FOR SCOTLAND

Thistle House, 91 Haymarket Terrace, Edinburgh, EH12 5HD

Tel: 0131 538 7510
Fax: 0131 538 7511
E-mail: secretariat@scottishboundaries.gov.uk
Website: www.lgbc-scotland.gov.uk

Enquiries to: Secretary

Founded: 1973

Organisation type and purpose: Statutory body. Advisory non-departmental public body, constituted under the Local Government (Scotland) Act 1973, reporting to the Scottish Government.

Subject coverage: Local government boundaries.

Publications: Printed, and electronic and video
Order printed publications from: The Secretary

Publications list: Available online

Access to staff: Contact by letter, by telephone, by fax, by e-mail and via website
Hours: Mon to Fri, 0900 to 1700

LOCAL GOVERNMENT BOUNDARY COMMISSION FOR WALES (LGBCW)

1st Floor, Caradog House, 1–6 St Andrews Place, Cardiff, CF10 3BE

Tel: 029 2039 5031
Fax: 029 2039 5250
E-mail: lgbc.wales@wales.gsi.gov.uk
Website: www.lgbc-wales.gov.uk

Enquiries to: Secretary

Founded: 1972

Organisation type and purpose: National government body.
A statutory body that reviews local government electoral and boundary arrangements in Wales.

Subject coverage: The work of the LGBCW involves local government electoral and boundary reviews in Wales since 1972.

Collection: All reports published and related working files and maps

Publications: Printed

Publications list: Available online and in print

Access to staff: Contact by letter, by telephone, by fax and by e-mail.
Appointment necessary.
Hours: Mon to Fri, 0800 to 1630

Parent body: National Assembly for Wales; Cathays Park, Cardiff, CF10 3NQ

LOCAL GOVERNMENT INTERNATIONAL BUREAU (LGIB)

Local Government House, Smith Square, London, SW1P 3HZ

Tel: 020 7664 3100
Fax: 020 7664 3128
E-mail: info@local.gov.uk
Website: www.lgib.gov.uk

Enquiries to: Public Relations Manager
Direct tel: 020 7664 3112
Other contacts: Twinnings Officer for information about town twinning and local authority international links.

Founded: 1988

Organisation type and purpose:
International organisation, local government body, national organisation, professional body (membership is by qualification), present number of members: 500.
European and International Affairs Unit of the Local Government Association and Welsh Local Government Association. LGIB also represents Northern Ireland Local Government Association. Funded from the local government revenue support grant.

Subject coverage: European policy and legislation as it affects UK local government, European information of interest to local government, details of international

continued overleaf

representation by UK local government, projects and funding, development cooperation, information on international linking (eg town twinning).

Collection: Committee of the Regions papers
EU legislation and policy

Library catalogue: All or part available online

Publications: Printed, and electronic and video

Publications list: Available online and in print

Access to staff: Contact by letter, by telephone, by fax, by e-mail and via website
Hours: Mon to Fri, 0900 to 1700
Special comments: No visitors as no library facilities.

British member of the: Council of European Municipalities and Regions (CEMR); International Union of Local Authorities (IULA)

Other addresses: Brussels Office; Rue d'Arlon 22, 1050 Brussels, Belgium; tel: 00 32 2 502 3680; fax: 00 32 2 502 4035; e-mail: brussels.office@lgib.org

Parent body: Local Government Association

LOCAL GOVERNMENT OMBUDSMAN

Formal name: Commission for Local Adminstration in England

10th Floor, Millbank Tower, Millbank, London, SW1P 4QP

Tel: 020 7217 4620
Fax: 020 7217 4621
E-mail: advice@lgo.org.uk
Website: www.lgo.org.uk

Enquiries to: LGO Advice Team
Direct tel: 0300 061 0614
Direct fax: 024 7682 0001

Founded: 1974

Organisation type and purpose: Statutory body.

Subject coverage: Local Government Ombudsmen investigate complaints of injustice arising from maladministration by local authorities and certain other bodies. They look into complaints about most council services, including social care and privately arranged care. The objective is to secure, where appropriate, satisfactory redress for complainants and better administration for the authorities. The Ombudsmen have the power to examine files of local authorities and to interview officers and members. The authority must consider an Ombudsman's report and recommendations and notify him/her of the action it intends to take.

Collection: All investigation reports

Library catalogue: All or part available in-house

Publications: Printed
Order printed publications from: Communications Assistant, Local Government Ombudsman, at the same address; tel: 020 7217 4683; fax: 020 7217 4621; e-mail: t.davey@lgo.org.uk

Publications list: Available online and in print

Access to staff: Contact by letter, by telephone, by fax and by e-mail. Appointment necessary.
Hours: Mon to Fri, 0900 to 1700
Special comments: Personal callers by appointment only.

Access to building: No prior appointment required
Hours: Mon to Fri, 0900 to 1700

Access for disabled people: Ramped entry, toilet facilities

Also at: Local Government Ombudsman; The Oaks No. 2, Westwood Way, Westwood Business Park, Coventry, CV4 8JB; tel: 024 7682 0000; fax: 024 7682 0001; Local Government Ombudsman; Beverley House, 17 Shipton Road, York, YO30 5FZ; tel: 01904 380200; fax: 01904 380269

LOCAL GOVERNMENT REFORM SOCIETY (LGRS)

14 Princes Avenue, Bognor Regis, West Sussex, PO21 2DY

Tel: 01243 863726

Enquiries to: General Secretary
Other contacts: Information Officer

Founded: 1960

Organisation type and purpose: International organisation, voluntary organisation.
Non-profit-making organisation.
Radical reform of local government to guarantee real democratic and public trustee basis.

Subject coverage: History of local government and its reform, private bills relating to local government, corruption in local government, maladministration, reform of individual authorities, rating reform and use of the local referendum.

Publications: Printed

Access to staff: Contact by letter
Hours: Mon to Fri, 0900 to 1700

LOCAL STUDIES CENTRE

Local Studies Centre, North Shields Library, Howard House, 54a Saville Street, North Shields, Tyne & Wear, NE30 1NT.
(temporary address, see website for updates)

Tel: 0191 643 5270
E-mail: local.studies@northtyneside.gov.uk
Website: www.northtyneside.gov.uk/libraries/index.htm

Enquiries to: Librarian

Founded: 1974

Organisation type and purpose: Local government body.
Archive.

Subject coverage: Contains printed sources dealing with people and organisations in or from the present North Tyneside Borough, past, present and future. There is also a collection of local photographs.

Collection: All photographs and materials on film are available as usual.
We have some of our collection in storage until we move back into the library building but we do not have a date for this yet, rendering some of the materials inaccessible for the foreseeable future – mainly reference book stock and some files.

Non-library collection catalogue: All or part available online and in-house

Library catalogue: All or part available online and in-house

Access to staff: Contact by letter, by telephone, by fax, by e-mail and in person

Access to building: *Special comments:* No public toilet facilities (some accross the street)

Access for disabled people: Lift to the first floor.

Links with: North Tyneside Council

LONDON 21 SUSTAINABILITY NETWORK

Unit LS2, The Kensington Charity Centre, Fourth Floor, Charles House, 375 Kensington High Street, W14 8QH

Tel: 020 7471 6795
Fax: 020 7471 6796
E-mail: office@london21.org
Website: www.london21.org

Enquiries to: Coordinator
Direct e-mail: vinciane.rycroft@london21.org

Founded: 1998

Organisation type and purpose: Voluntary organisation.
Network.
To promote, support and network community-based action for a greener, healthier London; to engage communities and individuals with local sustainability issues.

Subject coverage: Information on organisations and projects regarding sustainability and Agenda 21 in Greater London and community initiatives. Channels for policy formation and information exchange.

Access to staff: Contact by letter, by telephone and by e-mail. Access for members only.
Hours: Monday to Fri, 0930 to 1700

LONDON ACADEMY OF DRESSMAKING AND DESIGN (LADD)

18 Dobree Avenue, Willesden, London, NW10 2AE

Tel: 020 8451 7174
Fax: 020 8459 7927
E-mail: info@londonacademy.com
Website: www.londonacademy.com

Enquiries to: Principal Designer

Founded: 1969

Organisation type and purpose: Dressmaking, design and fashion college.

Subject coverage: Advanced designing in ladies' and children's wear, bridal wear, fashion drawing, draping, bead and silk embroidery, grading, soft furnishing, millinery, swim wear and lace appliqué; senior diploma, basic and advanced diploma, basic foundation diploma.

Publications: Printed

Access to staff: Contact by letter, by telephone, by fax, by e-mail, in person and via website. Appointment necessary.
Hours: Mon to Fri, 0930 to 1730

LONDON AND MIDDLESEX ARCHAEOLOGICAL SOCIETY (LAMAS)

Museum of London, London Wall, London, EC2Y 5HN

Tel: 020 7814 5734
Fax: 020 7600 1058
E-mail: sbrooks@museumoflondon.org.uk
Website: www.lamas.org.uk

Enquiries to: Hon. Secretary
Direct e-mail: kthomas@museumoflondon.org.uk

Founded: 1855

Organisation type and purpose:
Membership association (membership is by subscription), present number of members: 666, voluntary organisation, registered charity (charity number 267552).
To further the study of archaeology, local history and the historic buildings of the London area and to publish the results of such research; to encourage public interest in those areas and so promote preservation of historic buildings, ancient monuments and other remains of historic or archaeological interest.

Subject coverage: History and archaeology of London and the London area; preservation of historic buildings in this area.

Collection: Books and periodicals

Library catalogue: All or part available in-house

Publications: Printed

Publications list: Available online

Access to staff: Contact by letter, by telephone, by fax, by e-mail and via website
Hours: Mon to Fri, 0900 to 1700

Access to building: Prior appointment required
Special comments: Members only

Links with: about 50 local societies in London

Member organisation of: Council for British Archaeology

LONDON ASSOCIATION OF PRIMAL PSYCHOTHERAPISTS (LAPP)

West Hill House, 6 Swains Lane, London, N6 6QU

Tel: 020 7267 9616, 020 7482 4212 (minicom)
Fax: 020 7485 7957
E-mail: info@lapp.org
Website: www.lapp.org

Enquiries to: General Secretary

Founded: 1990

Organisation type and purpose:
Professional body (membership is by qualification, election or invitation), present number of members: 55, voluntary organisation.

Subject coverage: Psychotherapy.

Access to staff: Contact by letter, by telephone, by fax, by e-mail and via website. Appointment necessary. Non-members charged.
Hours: Mon to Fri, 0900 to 1900; Sat

Affiliated to: The United Kingdom Council for Psychotherapy (UKCP); tel: 020 7436 3002

LONDON BAPTIST ASSOCIATION (LBA)

235 Shaftesbury Avenue, London, WC2H 8EP

Tel: 020 7692 5592
Fax: 020 7692 5593
E-mail: lbaoffice@londonbaptist.org.uk
Website: www.londonbaptist.org.uk

Enquiries to: Secretary

Founded: 1865

Organisation type and purpose:
Membership association (membership is by election or invitation), registered charity.

Subject coverage: Baptist churches in Greater London.

Collection: Records of statistics, ministers, locations of Baptist Churches in Greater London, 1865 onwards

Publications: Printed

Access to staff: Contact by letter, by fax and by e-mail
Hours: Mon to Fri, 0900 to 1700

Affiliated to: Baptist Union of Great Britain

LONDON BEREAVEMENT RELIEF SOCIETY

175 Tower Bridge Road, London, SE1 2AH

Tel: 020 7407 7585
Fax: 020 7403 6711

Enquiries to: Information Officer

Founded: 1823

Organisation type and purpose: Registered charity (charity number 208260).

Subject coverage: Financial relief in relation to bereavement.

Publications: Printed

Access to staff: Contact by letter
Hours: Mon to Fri, 0900 to 1700

LONDON BOROUGH OF BARKING AND DAGENHAM

Civic Centre, Dagenham, Essex, RM10 7BN

Tel: 020 8592 4500, 020 8227 2685 (minicom)
Fax: 020 8595 3758
E-mail: jbufton@barking-dagenham.gov.uk
Website: www.barking-dagenham.gov.uk

Enquiries to: Chief Executive

Organisation type and purpose: Local government body.

Subject coverage: Council.

Access to staff: Contact by letter, by telephone, by fax, by e-mail and via website
Hours: Mon to Fri, 0900 to 1700

Access for disabled people: Parking provided, ramped entry

LONDON BOROUGH OF BARNET ARCHIVES AND LOCAL STUDIES CENTRE

80 Daws Lane, Mill Hill, London, NW7 4SL

Tel: 020 8959 6657
E-mail: library.archives@barnet.gov.uk
Website: www.earl.org.uk/familia
Website: www.hmc.gov.uk
Website: www.barnet.gov.uk/localstudies

Enquiries to: Local Studies Manager

Founded: 1965

Organisation type and purpose: Local government body, public library.

Subject coverage: All aspects of local study for the area of the London Borough of Barnet.
Records of predecessor authorities.

Non-library collection catalogue: All or part available online and in-house

Access to staff: Contact by letter, by telephone, by e-mail, in person and via website. Appointment necessary.
Hours: Tue, Wed, Fri, 0930 to 1630; Thu, 1300 to 1900

LONDON BOROUGH OF BEXLEY CENTRAL LIBRARY AND LOCAL STUDIES

Townley Rd, Bexleyheath, DA6 7HJ

Tel: 020 8303 7777
Fax: 020 8304 7058
E-mail: libraries@bexley.gov.uk
Website: elibrary.bexley.gov.uk/rooms

Founded: 1899

Organisation type and purpose: Local government body, public library.

Subject coverage: Public library service. Local collections.

Collection: Local studies collections

Non-library collection catalogue: All or part available online

Library catalogue: All or part available online

Publications: Printed
Order printed publications from: Bexley Local Studies and Archives Centre, Central Library, Townley Road, Bexleyheath, Kent, DA6 7HJ; tel: 020 8303 7777

Publications list: Available online and in print

Access to staff: Contact by letter, by telephone, by fax, by e-mail and in person. Appointment necessary.
Hours: Dependent on service

Access for disabled people: Access to all public areas

continued overleaf

Branches: Bexley Village, Blackfen, Bostall, Crayford, Erith, North Heath, Sidcup, Slade Green, Thamesmead, Upper Belvedere, Welling; See website

Headquarters address: Bexley Libraries, Arts and Archives; Footscray Offices, Maidstone Road, Sidcup, Kent, DA14 5HS.; e-mail: libraries@bexley.gov.uk

LONDON BOROUGH OF CAMDEN

Camden Town Hall, Judd Street, London, WC1H 9JE

Tel: 020 7278 4444
Fax: 020 7974 3210
E-mail: info@camden.gov.uk
Website: cindex.camden.gov.uk
Website: www.camden.gov.uk

Enquiries to: Chief Executive
Direct e-mail: emily.banfield@camden.gov.uk

Organisation type and purpose: Local government body.

Subject coverage: Camden Council services and referral to other local services.

Library catalogue: All or part available online

Publications: Printed

Access to staff: Contact by letter, by telephone, by fax, in person and via website
Hours: Mon to Fri, 0900 to 1700

Other address: Camden Information Services; Crowndale Centre, 218 Eversholt Street, London, NW1 1BD; tel: 020 7974 1656; fax: 020 7974 1566; e-mail: camdeninformationservices@camden.gov.uk

LONDON BOROUGH OF CAMDEN – LEISURE AND COMMUNITY SERVICES DEPARTMENT

Crowndale Centre, 216–218 Eversholt Street, London, NW1 1DE

Tel: 020 7974 4001
Fax: 020 7974 1615

Enquiries to: Librarian
Direct e-mail: mike.clarke@camden.gov.uk

Founded: 1965

Organisation type and purpose: Public library.

Subject coverage: General public library service, philosophy and psychology.

Collection: Kate Greenaway collection of early children's books
Special collections on philosophy and psychology

Non-library collection catalogue: All or part available online and in-house

Library catalogue: All or part available online

Publications list: Available online

Access to staff: Contact by letter, by telephone, by fax, by e-mail, in person and via website
Hours: Mon to Fri, 0900 to 1700

Access to building: No access other than to staff
Hours: Central Reference Library: Mon, Thu, 1000 to 1900; Tue, Wed, Fri, 1000 to 1800; Sat, 1000 to 1700

Access for disabled people: Level entry, toilet facilities

Also at: Central Reference Library; Swiss Cottage, 88 Avenue Road, London, NW3 3HA; tel: 020 7974 6522; fax: 020 7974 6505

LONDON BOROUGH OF ENFIELD – ENFIELD TOWN LIBRARY

66 Church Street, Enfield, Middlesex, EN2 6AX

Tel: 020 8379 8341
Fax: 020 8379 8331
E-mail: central.library@enfieldgov.uk
Website: www.enfield.gov.uk/library
Website: www.enfield.gov.uk/24hourlibrary
Website: www.enfield.gov.uk/localinformation
Website: en-gb.facebook.com/pages/Enfield-Library-and-Museum-Service/125768384131910
Website: https://twitter.com/enfieldlibrary

Enquiries to: Librarian
Direct e-mail: central.reference.library@enfield.gov.uk
Other contacts: Local History Librarian, tel: 020 8379 2724

Founded: 1908

Organisation type and purpose: Local government body, public library.

Non-library collection catalogue: All or part available online

Library catalogue: All or part available online and in-house

Access to staff: Contact by letter, by telephone, by fax, by e-mail, in person and via website
Hours: Enfield Town Library: Mon, Tue, Thu & Sat, 0930 to 2000; Wed & Fri, 0930 to 1730; please check for all other libraries

Branch libraries: Bowes Road Library; Bowes Road, London, N11 1BD; tel: 020 8379 1707; e-mail: bowesroadlibrary@yahoo.co.uk; Bullsmoor Library; Kempe Road, Enfield, Middlesex, EN1 1QS; tel: 020 8379 1723; e-mail: bullsmoor.library@enfield.gov.uk; Enfield Highway Library; 258 Hertford Road, Enfield, Middlesex, EN3 5BN; tel: 020 8379 1710; e-mail: enfield.highway.library@enfield.gov.uk; Fore Street Library; 109–111 Fore Street, Edmonton, N18 2XF; tel: 020 8379 1717; e-mail: weir.hall.library@enfield.gov.uk; John Jackson Library; Agricola Place, Enfield, Middlesex, EN1 1DW; tel: 020 8379 1709; e-mail: bush.hill.library@enfield.gov.uk; Oakwood Library; 185–187 Bramley Road, Enfield, Middlesex, N14 4XA; tel: 020 8379 1711; e-mail: oakwood.library@enfield.gov.uk; Ponders End Library; College Court, High Street, Enfield, Middlesex, EN3 4EY; tel: 020 8379 1712; e-mail: ponders.end.library@enfield.gov.uk; Winchmore Hill Library; Greens Lane, Winchmore Hill, London, N21 3AP; tel: 020 8379 1718; e-mail: winchmore.hill.library@enfield.gov.uk

Main libraries: Edmonton Green Library; 36–44 South Mall, Edmonton, London, N9 0TN; tel: 020 8379 2600; e-mail: edmonton.green.library@gov.uk; Ordnance Road Library; 645 Hertford Road, Enfield, Middlesex, EN3 6ND; tel: 020 8379 1725/6; e-mail: ordnance.road.library@enfield.gov.uk; Palmers Green Library; Broomfield Lane, Palmers Green, London, N13 4EY; tel: 020 8379 2711; e-mail: palmers.green.library@enfield.gov.uk; Ridge Avenue Library; Ridge Avenue, Winchmore Hill, London, N21 2RH; tel: 020 8379 1714/5; e-mail: ridge.avenue.library@enfield.gov.uk; Southgate Circus Library; High Street, Southgate, London, N14 6BP; tel: 020 8350 1124; e-mail: southgate.circus.library@enfield.gov.uk

LONDON BOROUGH OF HAVERING LIBRARY SERVICE

Central Library, St Edwards Way, Romford, Essex, RM1 3AR

Tel: 01708 432393
Fax: 01708 432391
E-mail: informationservices.library@havering.gov.uk
Website: www.havering.gov.uk

Enquiries to: Information Services Manager
Other contacts: Borough Library Manager

Founded: 1965

Organisation type and purpose: Local government body, public library.

Subject coverage: General reference material, central government publications, European information, local history.

Collection: Local studies

Non-library collection catalogue: All or part available online, in-house and in print

Library catalogue: All or part available online and in print

Publications: Printed

Publications list: Available in print

Access to staff: Contact by letter, by telephone, by fax and by e-mail. Appointment necessary.
Hours: Mon, 1000 to 2000; Tue to Fri, 0900 to 2000; Sat, 0900 to 1600

Parent body: London Borough of Havering; (Romford) Town Hall, Romford, Essex, RM1 3BD; tel: 01708 434343

LONDON BOROUGH OF HOUNSLOW (LBH)

The Civic Centre, Lampton Road, Hounslow, Middlesex, TW3 4DN

Tel: 020 8583 2000
Fax: 020 8583 2598
E-mail: information.ced@hounslow.gov.uk
Website: www.lbhounslow.gov.uk

Enquiries to: Customer Services Manager
Direct tel: 020 8583 2590
Direct fax: 020 8583 2592

Founded: 1965

Organisation type and purpose: Local government body.

Subject coverage: Council information, council tax, refuge, planning, environmental education, leisure services, housing, councillors, groups, societies, organisations, charities and advice-givers.

Access to staff: Contact by letter, by telephone, by fax, by e-mail, in person and via website. Appointment necessary.

Hours: Mon to Thu, 0845 to 1700; Fri, 0845 to 1645

Access for disabled people: Parking provided, ramped entry, access to all public areas, toilet facilities

LONDON BOROUGH OF LEWISHAM

Lewisham Town Hall, Catford, London, SE6 4RU

Tel: 020 8695 6000
Fax: 020 8314 5659
Website: www.lewisham.gov.uk

Enquiries to: Chief Executive
Direct e-mail: barry.quirk@lewisham.gov.uk

Organisation type and purpose: Local government body.

Subject coverage: Local government services.

Access to staff: Contact by letter, by telephone, by fax, by e-mail and in person
Hours: Mon to Fri, 0900 to 1700

Access to building: No prior appointment required

Access for disabled people: Parking provided, ramped entry, level entry, access to all public areas, toilet facilities

LONDON BOROUGH OF LEWISHAM – LIBRARY SERVICE

1st Floor, Town Hall Chambers, Rushey Green, Catford, London, SE6 4RU

Tel: 020 8314 8024
Fax: 020 8314 3229

Enquiries to: Librarian

Organisation type and purpose: Local government body, public library.

Subject coverage: General, local studies.

Non-library collection catalogue: All or part available in-house

Access to staff: Contact by letter, by telephone, by fax and in person
Hours: Varies from library to library

Libraries at: Blackheath Village Library; 3–4 Blackheath Grove, London, SE3 0DD; tel: 020 8852 5309; Catford Library; Laurence House, Catford, London, SE6 4RU; tel: 020 8314 6399; fax: 020 8314 1110; Crofton Park Library; Brockley Road, London, SE4 2AF; tel: 020 8692 1683; Downham Library; Moorside Road, Downham, London, BR1 5EP; tel: 020 8698 1475; Forest Hill Library; Dartmouth Road, London, SE23 3HZ; tel: 020 8699 2065; fax: 020 8699 8296; Grove Park Library; Somertrees Avenue, London, SE12 0BX; tel: 020 8857 5794; Lewisham Library; 199–201 Lewisham High Street, London, SE13 6LG; tel: 020 8297 9677, minicom 8369; fax: 020 8297 1169; Lewisham Reference Library; 199–201 Lewisham High Street, London, SE13 6LG; tel: 020 8297 9430; fax: 020 8297 1169; Local Studies Centre; 199–201 Lewisham High Street, London, SE13 6LG; tel: 020 8297 0682; fax: 020 8297 1169; Manor House Library; Old Road, Lee, London, SE13 5SY; tel: 020 8852 0357; New Cross Library; 283/5 New Cross Road, London, SE14 6AS; tel: 020 8694 2534; Sydenham Library; Sydenham Road, London, SE26 5SE; tel: 020 8778 7563; Torridon Road Library; Torridon Road, Catford, London, SE6 1RQ; tel: 020 8698 1590; Wavelengths Library; Griffin Street, Deptford, London, SE8 4RJ; tel: 020 8694 2535; fax: 020 8694 9652

LONDON BOROUGH OF TOWER HAMLETS

Mulberry Place, 5 Clove Crescent, London, E14 2BG

Tel: 020 7364 5000
Fax: 020 7364 4296
Website: www.towerhamlets.gov.uk/

Enquiries to: Press Office

Organisation type and purpose: Local government body.

LONDON BUDDHIST CENTRE (LBC)

51 Roman Road, Bethnal Green, London, E2 0HU

Tel: 0845 458 4716
Fax: 0871 433 5995
E-mail: info@lbc.org.uk
Website: www.lbc.org.uk
Website: www.londonbuddhistcentre.com

Enquiries to: Centre Director
Other contacts: Assistant Centre Director

Founded: 1978

Organisation type and purpose: International organisation, voluntary organisation, registered charity.
Religious centre.

Subject coverage: Buddhism, the Western Buddhist Order; meditation, yoga, Tai Chi, acupuncture, alternative health, Alexander Technique, osteopathy, reflexology, shiatsu, homoeopathy, naturopathy, nutritional therapy, medical herbalism, massage, kinesiology, hypnotheraphy, polarity therapy, reiki, counselling and psychotherapy.

Collection: Book, video and audio-tape library

Publications: Printed, and electronic and video
Order printed publications from: Books, Windhorse Publications, 11 Park Road, Birmingham, B13 8AB, tel: 0121 449 9997, e -mail: shantavira@compuserve.com
Order electronic and video publications from: Audio Artefacts, Dharmachakra, 3 Coral Park, Henley Road, Cambridge, CB1 3EA, tel: 01223 516821, e-mail: orders@ dharmachakra.freeserve.co.uk
Visual Artefacts, Clearvision Trust, 16–20 Turner Street, Northern Quarter, Manchester, M4 1DZ, tel: 0161 839 9579, fax: 0161 839 4815, e-mail: clearvision@clear -vision.org

Publications list: Available in print

Access to staff: Contact by letter, by telephone, by fax, by e-mail, in person and via website. Appointment necessary.
Hours: Mon to Fri, 1000 to 1700

Access to building: No prior appointment required
Hours: Mon to Fri, 1000 to 1700

Centre of the: Friends of the Western Buddhist Order (FWBO); 30 Chantry Road, Birmingham, B13 8AL; tel: 0121 449 3700; fax: 0121 449 3780; e-mail: communications@ fwbo.org; website: http://www.fwbo.org/

Has: 22 public centres in UK and retreat centres and smaller groups, also centres abroad

LONDON BUDDHIST VIHARA

Dharmapala Building, The Avenue, Chiswick, London, W4 1UD

Tel: 020 8995 9493
Fax: 020 8994 8130
E-mail: london.vihara@virgin.net
Website: www.londonbuddhistvihara.org

Enquiries to: Secretary
Other contacts: Head Monk

Founded: 1926

Organisation type and purpose: Voluntary organisation.
Religious institution.
To spread knowledge of Buddhism.

Subject coverage: General Buddhism, specialising in the Theravada tradition; teaching of Pali and Sinhala languages (the latter to GCSE); meditation.

Collection: Buddhist scriptures written in Pali language on Ola leaves (palm leaves) Reference Library (over 3500 titles) of books in English, Pali, Sinhalese, Burmese and many European languages

Library catalogue: All or part available in-house

Publications: Printed

Access to staff: Contact by letter, by telephone, by fax, by e-mail and in person
Hours: 0900 to 2100, seven days a week

Access to building: No access other than to staff

Access for disabled people: Ramped entry, access to all public areas, toilet facilities

Managers: Maha Bodhi Society of Sri Lanka

Owned by: Anagarika Dharmapala Trust (Sri Lanka)

LONDON BUSINESS SCHOOL (LBS)

Sussex Place, Regent's Park, London, NW1 4SA

Tel: 020 7262 5050
Fax: 020 7724 7875
Website: www.london.edu/library/

Enquiries to: Librarian
Other contacts: Information Service Manager for enquiries about fee-based business research.

Organisation type and purpose: University department or institute.

Subject coverage: Management and business management; education; international business; marketing; market data; production; finance; company financial data; accounting; economics and economic forecasting; industries; operational research; statistics; computers and data processing; Europe.

continued overleaf

Collection: Corporate Library: annual reports of about 8,000 British, European, North American, and Asian Pacific companies
Market Research Reports

Library catalogue: All or part available online

Publications: Printed

Access to staff: Non-members charged.
Hours: Mon to Fri, 0900 to 1700

Access for disabled people: Level entry, toilet facilities

Affiliated to: University of London

Other addresses: London Business School Information Service (fee-based); tel: 020 7723 3404; fax: 020 7706 1897; e-mail: infoserve@london.edu

LONDON CENTRE FOR FASHION STUDIES (LCFS)

Bradley Close, 8 White Lion Street, Islington, London, N1 9PF

Tel: 020 7713 1991
Fax: 020 7713 1997
E-mail: design.london@northumbria.ac.uk
Website: www.fashionstudies.co.uk
Website: www.fashion.studies.com

Enquiries to: Director

Founded: 1991

Organisation type and purpose: University department or institute, suitable for ages: 18+, training organisation, consultancy, publishing house.
Independent fashion school.

Subject coverage: Fashion: pattern technology, pattern grading techniques, grading and dress modelling, fashion business, marketing, merchandising, production, teacher training – fashion teachers.

Publications: Printed, and electronic and video

Publications list: Available in print

Access to staff: Contact by letter, by telephone, by fax, by e-mail, in person and via website
Hours: Open some evenings

In partnership with: Middlesex University

LONDON CENTRE FOR PSYCHOTHERAPY (LCP)

32 Leighton Road, London, NW5 2QE

Tel: 020 7482 2002
Fax: 020 7482 4222
Website: www.lcp-psychotherapy.org.uk

Enquiries to: Chairman

Founded: 1973

Organisation type and purpose:
Professional body (membership is by subscription, qualification), present number of members: 200, registered charity (charity number 267244), training organisation.

Subject coverage: Psychotherapy.

Access to staff: Contact by letter, by telephone, by e-mail and via website
Hours: Mon to Fri, 1000 to 1600

Access to building: Prior appointment required

LONDON CHAMBER OF COMMERCE AND INDUSTRY (LCCI)

33 Queen Street, London, EC4R 1AP

Tel: 020 7248 4444
Fax: 020 7489 0391
E-mail: lc@londonchamber.co.uk
Website: www.londonchamber.co.uk

Enquiries to: Information Officer
Direct e-mail: info@londonchamber.co.uk

Founded: 1881

Organisation type and purpose:
Membership association (membership is by subscription), present number of members: 3500.
To help London businesses succeed by promoting their interests and expanding their opportunities as members of a worldwide business network.

Subject coverage: Business information in the broadest sense, company information, market information, economic and financial data, suppliers of goods and services, occupational; Euro Information Centre, European legislation.

Trade and statistical information: Activities on the London Economy. European statistics

Publications: Printed

Access to staff: Contact by letter, by telephone, by fax, by e-mail, in person and via website. Non-members charged.
Hours: Mon to Fri, 0900 to 1730

Access to building: No prior appointment required for members
Hours: Mon to Fri, 0900 to 1730
Special comments: Access free to members only; no access to non-members.

Access for disabled people: Level entry, toilet facilities

LONDON CHAMBER OF COMMERCE AND INDUSTRY EXAMINATIONS BOARD (LCCIEB)

Athena House, 112 Station Road, Sidcup, Kent, DA15 7BJ

Tel: 020 8302 0261
Fax: 020 8302 4169
E-mail: enquiries@ediplc.com
Website: www.lccieb.com

Enquiries to: General Manager – Sales and Marketing

Founded: 1887

Organisation type and purpose:
International organisation, registered charity.
Examinations board and business-related NVQ awarding body.

Subject coverage: LCCIEB offers a wide range of qualifications both timetabled and on demand. English and International Languages, Information Technology, Secretarial and Business Administration, Customer Service and Marketing, Finance, Travel and Tourism and a wide range of business-related NVQs.

Publications list: Available online and in print

Access to staff: Contact by letter, by telephone, by fax, by e-mail and via website
Hours: Mon to Fri, 0900 to 1700

Access to building: No access other than to staff

LONDON CHAMBER PLAYERS (LCP)

PO Box 84, London, NW11 8AL

Tel: 020 8455 6799
Fax: 020 8455 6799
E-mail: london-players@excite.com

Enquiries to: Director
Direct fax: 020 8455 6799

Founded: 1979

Organisation type and purpose: Registered charity, suitable for ages: children, adults
Musical performances.

Subject coverage: Music, music education

Access to staff: Contact by letter, by telephone, by fax and by e-mail.
Appointment necessary.
Hours: Mon to Fri, 0930 to 1730

Access to building: Prior appointment required

LONDON CITY PRESBYTERIAN CHURCH

St Botolph-without-Aldersgate, Aldersgate Street, London, EC1A 4EU

Website: www.londonfreechurch.org.uk

Enquiries to: Information Officer
Direct e-mail: davidtastrain@ntlworld.com

History of institution: formerly called Free Church of Scotland; formerly called Cole Abbey Presbyterian Church (year of change c. 2003)

Organisation type and purpose:
Membership association (membership is by qualification), voluntary organisation, registered charity.

Subject coverage: History and present activities of Reformed and Presbyterian Churches.

Access to staff: Contact by letter, by telephone, by fax and via website
Hours: Mon to Fri, 0900 to 1700

Access to building: Prior appointment required

LONDON CLEARING HOUSE LIMITED, THE (LCH)

Aldgate House, 33 Aldgate High Street, London, EC3N 1EA

Tel: 020 7426 7000
Fax: 020 7426 7001
E-mail: karen.swift@lchclearnet.com
Website: www.lch.com

Enquiries to: Corporate Communications Director
Direct tel: 020 7426 7234

Direct fax: 020 7426 7665
Direct e-mail: matchm@lch.co.uk

Founded: 1888

Organisation type and purpose: International organisation, present number of members: 116, service industry.
To clear contracts traded on London's major exchanges. Clearing house for LCH Repoclear – Interbank trades in European Government Repos; Clearing house for LCH Swapclear – Interbank interest rate swaps. Clearing house for LCH Equity Clear – equities traded on the London Stock Exchange's SETS system.

Subject coverage: Risk management, clearing, settlement.

Publications: Printed
Order printed publications from: Member Liaison Department
at the same address

Publications list: Available in print

Access to staff: Contact by telephone, by fax, by e-mail and via website
Hours: Mon to Fri, 0930 to 1730

LONDON COLLEGE OF COMMUNICATION (LCC)

Information Services: Library, Elephant and Castle, London, SE1 6SB

Tel: 020 7514 8026
Fax: 020 7514 6597
E-mail: libraryenquiries@lcc.arts.ac.uk
Website: www.arts.ac.uk/library

Other contacts: Information Services Librarian (for access to the Library)

Organisation type and purpose: University department or institute.

Subject coverage: Art and design; fine art; graphic design; animation; printing and publishing; film and video; journalism; media; photography.

Collection: Printing Historical Collection – The Art of the Western Book
Zine collection

Library catalogue: All or part available online

Publications: Printed

Access to staff: Contact by letter and by e-mail. Appointment necessary.
Hours: Mon to Thu, 0930 to 2015; Fri, 0930 to 1745; Sat, 1000 to 1545
Vacation opening times: please telephone to confirm

Constituent part of: University of the Arts London

LONDON COLLEGE OF FASHION LIBRARY

20 John Princes Street, London, W1G 0BJ

Tel: 020 7514 7453/7455
Fax: 020 7514 7580
Website: www.linst.ac.uk/library

Enquiries to: Chief Librarian
Direct tel: 020 7514 7518

Subject coverage: Fashion, design, clothing manufacture, embroidery, hairdressing, beauty therapy, costume history, textile history, footwear and accessories.

Collection: Clothing Institute Special Collection on historic tailoring
Fashion Photographs
Hairdressers Journal (bound volumes 1882 to the present; unique in the world)
History of Costume Collection

Access to staff: Appointment necessary.
Hours: Mon to Thu, 0930 to 2015; Fri, 1000 to 1715

Constituent college of the: London Institute

Other address: Cordwainers at The London College of Fashion; 182 Mare Street, London, E8 3RE

LONDON COLLEGE OF MASSAGE (LCM)

16 Bramley Court, Wickham Street, Kent, DA16 3DG

Tel: 020 3259 0000
E-mail: training@londoncollegeofmassage.co.uk
Website: www.massagelondon.com

Enquiries to: Director

Founded: 1987

Organisation type and purpose: Training organisation.
Clinic.

Subject coverage: Massage training and treatments; complementary health; anatomy and physiology; remedial and sports massage and other related postgraduate courses.

Collection: Dissertations relating to massage therapy

Publications: Printed, and electronic and video

Publications list: Available in print

Access to staff: Contact by letter, by telephone, by fax and by e-mail. Appointment necessary.
Hours: Mon to Fri, 1100 to 1900

Affiliated to: British Complementary Medicine Association; 9 Soar Lane, Leicester, LE3 5DE; tel: 0116 242 5406; fax: 0116 242 5496; British Massage Therapy Council; 17 Rymers Lane, Oxford, OX4 3JU; tel: 01865 774123; fax: 01865 774123; Institute of Complementary Medicine; PO Box 194, London, SE16 1QZ; tel: 020 7237 5165; fax: 020 7237 5175

LONDON COLLEGE OF OSTEOPATHIC MEDICINE/ OSTEOPATHIC ASSOCIATION CLINIC (LCOM)

8–10 Boston Place, London, NW1 6QH

Tel: 020 7262 1128
Fax: 020 7723 7492

Enquiries to: Administrator

Founded: 1946

Organisation type and purpose: Registered charity (charity number 209713), suitable for ages: postgraduates, training organisation.
Postgraduate college training (qualified doctors only) in osteopathy, charity clinic for osteopathic patients.

Publications: Printed

Access to staff: Contact by letter, by telephone and by fax. Appointment necessary.
Hours: Mon to Fri, 0930 to 1645

LONDON COLLEGE OF TRADITIONAL ACUPUNCTURE AND ORIENTAL MEDICINE (LCTA)

60 Ballards Lane, Finchley, London, N3 2BU

Tel: 020 8371 0820
Fax: 020 8371 0830
E-mail: college@lcta.com
Website: www.lcta.com

Enquiries to: Course Administrator

Founded: 1992

Organisation type and purpose: Training organisation.

Subject coverage: Professional training in acupuncture, oriental herbal medicine, tui na massage, nutrition and medical qi gong.

Publications: Printed

Access to staff: Contact by letter, by telephone, by fax, by e-mail and via website. Appointment necessary.
Hours: Mon to Sun, 0900 to 1730

LONDON CYCLO-CROSS ASSOCIATION (LCCA)

25 Lenham Road, Platt Heath, Kent, ME17 2NY

Tel: 01622 850533
E-mail: MondSBarry@aol.com
Website: www.britishcycling.org.uk

Enquiries to: General Secretary
Direct tel: 020 8662 3963

Organisation type and purpose: Voluntary organisation.
Cyclo-cross racing.

Subject coverage: Sport, cycling, mountain biking, competition, cyclo-cross.

Access to staff: Contact by letter, by telephone, by e-mail and via website
Hours: Mon to Fri, 0900 to 1700

Parent body: British Cycling; Stuart Street, Manchester, M11 4DQ; tel: 0870 871 2000; fax: 0870 871 2001; e-mail: cyclo-cross@britishcycling.org.uk; website: www.britishcycling.org.uk

LONDON DISTRICT SURVEYORS ASSOCIATION (LDSA)

c/o Building Control Officer, London Borough of Merton, Merton Civic Centre, London Road, Morden, Surrey, SM4 5DX

Tel: 020 8545 3121
Fax: 020 8543 6085
E-mail: trevor.mcintosh@merton.gov.uk
Website: www.londonbuildingcontrol.org

Enquiries to: Honorary Secretary

Founded: 1987

continued overleaf

Organisation type and purpose: Professional body (membership is by election or invitation), present number of members: 33.
An organisation of the Heads of the Building Control service in all the 32 London Boroughs and the City of London.
To further the profession and be a vehicle for achieving uniformity; to collate and disseminate information and to cooperate with similar bodies; to promote training and continuing professional development; to petition, confer with and promote deputations to government and other public or professional bodies; to guide the building control offices in London with up-to-date, expert advice to achieve uniformity of interpretation and operation of the Building Regulations.

Subject coverage: Commitees include those dealing with the following subjects: electrical and mechanical; career development and training; management and legislation; publications and seminars; safety at sports grounds; fire safety and means of escape; licensing; technical and foundations; LANTAC; and marketing. IT working party and benchmark forum.

Collection: Minutes of general meetings, policy decisions, questions and information

Publications: Printed, and electronic and video
Order printed publications from: LDSA Publications
From: LDSA Contact details above

Publications list: Available online and in print

Access to staff: Contact by letter, by e-mail and via website
Hours: Mon to Fri, 0900 to 1700

A region of the: District Surveyors Association (of England & Wales) (DSA); c/o LABC Services, Third floor, 66 South Lambeth Road, London, SW8 1RL; tel: 0844 561 6136; fax: 01625 435076; e-mail: info@labc.uk.com; website: http://www.labc.uk.com

Liaison with bodies such as: London Fire and Emergency Planning Authority (LFEPA); 8 Albert Embankment, London, SE1 7SD; tel: 020 7587 2000; e-mail: info@london-fire.gov.uk

LONDON DOUGLAS MOTOR CYCLE CLUB LIMITED (LDMCC)

48 Standish Avenue, Stoke Lodge, Patchway, Bristol, BS34 6AG

Tel: 01454 898185
E-mail: info@douglasmcc.co.uk
Website: www.douglasmotorcycles.co.uk

Enquiries to: Membership Secretary
Direct e-mail: via website

Founded: 1928

Organisation type and purpose: Membership association (membership is by subscription), present number of members: 1,100.

Subject coverage: Douglas motor cycles manufactured at Kingswood, Bristol 1907–1957; spares service for pre-war and post-war machines; marque specialist providing technical information on most models; a register of all Douglas machines known to the club throughout the world providing a source of information for identification and dating; machine transfers and badges.

Collection: Archive of technical information

Publications: Printed

Access to staff: Contact by letter
Hours: Mon to Fri, 0900 to 1700

Affiliated to: Auto Cycle Union under title of 'LDMCC' as 'Non-Territorial Club'

LONDON ELECTRONICS COLLEGE (LEC)

20 Penywern Road, London, SW5 9SU

Tel: 020 7373 8721
Fax: 020 7244 8733
E-mail: contact@lec.org.uk
Website: www.lec.org.uk

Enquiries to: Principal

Founded: 1892

Organisation type and purpose: Independent further and higher education.

Subject coverage: Electronics, TV and video, telecommunications, microprocessors, software, IT, computer systems, networks.

Access to staff: Appointment necessary.
Hours: Mon to Fri, 0900 to 1700

LONDON FERTILITY CENTRE (LFC)

Formal name: London Fertility Centre Ltd

Cozens House, 112a Harley Street, London, W1G 7JH

Tel: 020 7224 0707
Fax: 020 7224 3102
E-mail: info@lfc.org.uk
Website: www.lfc.org.uk

Enquiries to: Information Officer
Other contacts: General Manager.

Founded: 1990; formerly called London Gynaecology and Fertility Centre Ltd (year of change 2010)

Organisation type and purpose: Assisted conception, IVF and gynaecology

Subject coverage: Gynaecology and fertility.

Publications: Printed

Access to staff: Contact by letter, by telephone, by fax, by e-mail and via website
Hours: Mon to Fri, 0900 to 1730; Sat, Sun, 0900 to 1600

Access for disabled people: Ramped entry, toilet facilities

Parent body: Spire Healthcare; 120 Holborn, London

LONDON FIRE AND EMERGENCY PLANNING AUTHORITY (LFEPA)

169 Union Street, London, SE1 0LL

Tel: 020 8555 1200
E-mail: libraryservices@london-fire.gov.uk
Website: www.london-fire.gov.uk

Enquiries to: Library Information Resources Centre Manager
Direct tel: 020 8555 1200 ext. 30426/7

Founded: 1983

Organisation type and purpose: Local government body.
Responsible for running London Fire Brigade and providing emergency planning in London.

Subject coverage: Fire protection, fire fighting, fire prevention, chemical hazards, history of fire fighting, emergencies.

Library catalogue: All or part available in-house

Access to staff: Contact by letter, by telephone, by e-mail and via website. Appointment necessary.
Hours: Mon to Fri, 0900 to 1700

Also known as: London Fire Brigade

Member organisation of: Fire Information Group (an information exchange co-operative in the fire and loss prevention field)

LONDON GREEN BELT COUNCIL

4A Paddock Way, Fenny Stratford, Milton Keynes, MK2 2NB

Tel: 07794 592924
E-mail: info@londongreenbeltcouncil.org.uk
Website: www.londongreenbeltcouncil.org.uk

Enquiries to: Honorary Secretary

Founded: 1954

Organisation type and purpose: Grouping of organisations with an interest in preserving and promoting the Green Belt. No individual members.

Subject coverage: Green Belts, and particularly the Metropolitan Green Belt.

Member organisations: Campaign to Protect Rural England; Local amenity societies; Open Spaces Society; Parish councils; Ramblers Association

LONDON GYMNASTICS (LG)

E-mail: information@londongym.org.uk
Website: www.londongym.org.uk

Enquiries to: Regional Administrator

Organisation type and purpose: Membership association (membership is by subscription), voluntary organisation. Governing body of the sport for London.

Subject coverage: Gymnastics & trampolining, pre-school, boys, girls, adults, special needs, competitive and recreational, all information regarding gymnastic clubs in the Greater London area, (UKCC) gymnastic coaching courses, GymMark Courses, gymnastic competitions and events.

Access to staff: Contact by e-mail and via website

Parent body: British Gymnastics Association (BG); tel: 01952 820330

LONDON HAZARDS CENTRE (LHC)

Hampstead Town Hall Centre, 213 Haverstock Hill, London, NW3 4QP

Tel: 020 7794 5999

Fax: 020 7794 4702
E-mail: mail@lhc.org.uk
Website: www.lhc.org.uk

Enquiries to: The Advice Worker
Other contacts: Information Officer

Founded: 1984

Organisation type and purpose: Advisory body, membership association (membership is by subscription), voluntary organisation, registered charity (charity number 1981088), training organisation, consultancy, research organisation, publishing house.
Work with tenants associations and workplace safety representatives.

Subject coverage: Work-related ill health, occupational health and safety law, health and safety in the workplace and the community.

Publications: Printed

Publications list: Available online and in print

Access to staff: Contact by letter, by telephone, by fax, by e-mail and via website
Hours: Mon, Tue, Thu, Fri, 1000 to 1200 and 1400 to 1700
Special comments: Charges to professional organisations, solicitors, media, etc. Free service only to Londoners.

Access to building: No prior appointment required

Connections with: London Hazards Centre Trust Ltd; at the same address

LONDON INSTITUTE FOR CONTEMPORARY CHRISTIANITY (LICC)

St Peters Church, Vere Street, London, W1G 0DQ

Tel: 020 7399 9555
Fax: 020 7399 9556
E-mail: mail@licc.org.uk
Website: www.licc.org.uk

Enquiries to: Executive Director

Founded: 1982

Organisation type and purpose: Registered charity (charity number 286102), training organisation. Christian adult education.

Subject coverage: The relevance and application of the Bible and the Christian faith in today's world, application of biblical teaching to contemporary issues and everyday life.

Publications: Printed, and electronic and video

Access to staff: Contact by letter, by telephone, by fax, by e-mail and in person
Hours: Mon to Fri, 0900 to 1700

LONDON INVESTMENT BANKING ASSOCIATION (LIBA)

6 Frederick's Place, London, EC2R 8BT

Tel: 020 7796 3606
Fax: 020 7796 4345
E-mail: liba@liba.org.uk
Website: www.liba.org.uk

Enquiries to: Secretary

Organisation type and purpose: Trade association (membership is by subscription).

Subject coverage: Investment banking and securities industry in the United Kingdom including corporate finance, asset management and securities trading, and the regulation thereof.

Collection: Book of Prospectuses, June 1939 to August 1984
Issuing House Year Book from 1939 to 1987
Prospectuses on UK companies to 6 June 1939
Times (later Extel)

Publications: Printed

Access to staff: Contact by letter and by e-mail
Hours: Mon to Fri, 0930 to 1730

Access to building: No access other than to staff

LONDON IRISH CENTRE

50–52 Camden Square, London, NW1 9XB

Tel: 020 7916 2222
Fax: 020 7916 2638
E-mail: info@londonirishcentre.org
Website: www.londonirishcentre.org

Enquiries to: Director

Founded: 1954

Organisation type and purpose: Advisory body, voluntary organisation, registered charity (charity number 221172), training organisation, research organisation.

Subject coverage: Welfare, culture and social events.

Information services: Advice and support; social and cultural activities.

Education services: Various classes.

Access to staff: Contact by letter, by telephone, by fax, by e-mail, in person and via website
Hours: Mon to Fri, 0900 to 1700

Access to building: *Hours:* 0900 to 2200

Access for disabled people: Lift assistance

LONDON JEWISH CULTURAL CENTRE

Ivy House, 94–96 North End Road, London, NW11 7SX

Tel: 020 8457 5000
E-mail: admin@ljcc.org.uk
Website: www.ljcc.org.uk

Organisation type and purpose: A registered charity (no. 1081014) and company limited by guarantee (charity number 3811133), funded by donors, benefactors and supporters and by income generated from courses and events.

Subject coverage: Jewish history, life and learning, languages, current affairs, music, literature, art and film.

Education services: Day and evening courses in Jewish history, life and learning, languages, current affairs, music, literature, art and film, and outreach courses to the wider community. Holocaust and Anti-racism Education Department.

Collection: Archive of Jewish-related feature and documentary film

LONDON LESBIAN & GAY SWITCHBOARD (LLGS)

PO Box 7324, London, N1 9QS

Tel: 0300 330 0630 (helpline); 020 7837 6768 (office)
Fax: 020 7837 7300
E-mail: admin@llgs.org.uk
Website: www.llgs.org.uk

Enquiries to: Administrator
Direct tel: 020 7837 6768

Founded: 1974

Organisation type and purpose: Voluntary organisation, registered charity (charity number 296193).
To provide information and advice to lesbians, gay men, bisexual and trans people, and to anyone with questions about sexuality.

Subject coverage: Sexual health, legal advice and information, for all callers around lesbian, gay, bisexual and transgender issues (LGBT).

Publications list: Available online and in print

Access to staff: Contact by letter, by telephone, by fax, by e-mail and via website

Access to building: No access other than to staff and volunteers

Links with: Telephone Helplines Association (THA)

LONDON LIBRARY

14 St James's Square, London, SW1Y 4LG

Tel: 020 7930 7705
Fax: 020 7766 4766
E-mail: membership@londonlibrary.co.uk
Website: www.londonlibrary.co.uk

Enquiries to: Librarian

Founded: 1841

Organisation type and purpose: Membership association (membership is by subscription), present number of members: 7,000, registered charity (charity number 312175).
Independent subscription library (lending and reference).

Subject coverage: Extensive collection of books and periodicals in English and all major European languages within the arts and humanities with particular strengths in literature, history and related subjects. Good representation of fine and applied art, architecture, bibliography, philosophy, religion, topography and travel, with some coverage of the social sciences.

Collection: Heron-Allen Collection (on Omar Khayyam)
Higginson Collection (books on hunting and field sports)

Non-library collection catalogue: All or part available online

continued overleaf

Access to staff: Contact by letter, by telephone, by fax, by e-mail and via website. Appointment necessary. Access for members only. Letter of introduction required. All charged.
Hours: Mon to Wed, 0930 to 1930; Thu to Sat, 0930 to 1730

LONDON LIBRARY & INFORMATION DEVELOPMENT UNIT (LLIDU)

20 Guildford Street, London, WC1N 1DZ

Tel: 020 7692 3389
Fax: 020 7692 3393
E-mail: ldnlidu@llidu.ac.uk
Website: www.londonlinks.ac.uk

Enquiries to: Head of Unit
Other contacts: Unit Coordinator

Founded: April 2001

Organisation type and purpose: NHS health care library information network; 50 library service points offering a range of services. The Unit is a strategic and advisory body working closely with Workforce Development Confederations and other stakeholders and professional colleagues to coordinate and develop library and information services for all NHS staff in line with national policy guidance.

Subject coverage: Strategic advice on library and information services to support NHS staff.

Publications: Electronic and video

Publications list: Available online

Access to staff: Contact by telephone, by fax, by e-mail and via website
Hours: Mon to Fri, 0900 to 1700

Access to building: Prior appointment required

Affiliated to: London Department of Postgraduate Medical & Dental Education; NHS London Region

LONDON MARATHON

Formal name: The Flora London Marathon

PO Box 1234, London, SE1 8RZ

Tel: 020 7620 4117
Fax: 020 7620 4208
Website: www.london-marathon.co.uk

Enquiries to: Administrator

Organisation type and purpose: Registered charity (charity number 283813).
Organisation of sporting events.

Access to staff: Contact by letter, by telephone and by fax
Hours: Mon to Fri, 0900 to 1700

Access to building: No access other than to staff

LONDON MATHEMATICAL SOCIETY (LMS)

De Morgan House, 57–58 Russell Square, London, WC1B 4HS

Tel: 020 7637 3686
Fax: 020 7323 3655
E-mail: lms@lms.ac.uk
Website: www.lms.ac.uk

Enquiries to: Executive Secretary

Founded: 1865

Organisation type and purpose: Learned society.

Subject coverage: Mathematics.

Collection: Photographs of academic mathematicians from 1865 onwards to the present

Publications: Printed, and electronic and video
Order printed publications from: Oxford University Press

Publications list: Available online and in print

Access to staff: Contact by letter, by telephone, by fax and by e-mail
Hours: Mon to Fri, 0930 to 1700

Access to building: Prior appointment required

LONDON MEDIEVAL SOCIETY (LMS)

The Colloquia Secretary, 3 Rothwell Street, London, NW1 8YH

Tel: 020 7722 1040
E-mail: thodgsonjones@googlemail.com
Website: www.the-lms.org

Enquiries to: Membership Secretary
Direct e-mail: r.ellis@qmul.ac.uk

Founded: 1946

Organisation type and purpose: Learned society (membership is by subscription), present number of members: 20, voluntary organisation.

Subject coverage: Literature and language relating to the medieval European vernaculars and to medieval Latin; historical and cultural context of medieval Europe.

Access to staff: Contact by letter, by telephone and by e-mail
Hours: Mon to Fri, 0900 to 1700

LONDON MENNONITE CENTRE

Formal name: London Mennonite Centre

14 Shepherds Hill, Highgate, London N6 5AQ

Tel: 020 8340 8775
Fax: 020 8341 6807
E-mail: lmc@menno.org.uk
Website: www.menno.org.uk

Organisation type and purpose: To embody Mennonite and Anabaptist ideas and insights within the wider church and cultivate Christian discipleship as a whole way of life.

Subject coverage: Mennonites, Anabaptism and Christianity.

Collection: Library of Anabaptism, Mennonite history and theology, Radical Reformation, Amish and Hutterites.

Access to staff: Contact by letter, by telephone, by fax, by e-mail, in person and via website
Hours: Mon to Fri, 0900 to 1700

LONDON METROPOLITAN ARCHIVES (LMA)

40 Northampton Road, London, EC1R 0HB

Tel: 020 7332 3820
Fax: 020 7833 9136
E-mail: ask.lma@cityoflondon.gov.uk
Website: www.cityoflondon.gov.uk/archives/lma

Enquiries to: Assistant Director (Heritage)

Founded: 1965

Organisation type and purpose: Local government body.
Record office.

Subject coverage: London County Council, Greater London Council, Metropolitan Board of Works, Middlesex County Council, London local government, education, health, topography, the built environment, philanthropy, transport, parish and diocesan administration, history of medicine, City of London Corporation.

Collection: 100 kilometres of archives including:
Local government
Ecclesiastical
Health
Family
Business
Manorial and other records
Prints and drawings (over 40,000 items) including:
Harben Bequest
John Burns Collection
Hanslip Fletcher Studio Collection
110,000 printed monographs
London Directories (from 1744)
London local government publications and minutes
350,000 photographs forming a visual record of the history and topography of London, from the late 19th century to the 1980s, schools, housing, transport, parks, bridge, public buildings, private and historic buildings and houses, street scenes, including:
Whiffin Collection
Olney Collection
Morris Collection
Over 10,000 maps and plans
Archives of the Family Welfare Association
Books and pamphlets of the Charity Organisation Society to 1946
London Library of John Burns (19th-century LCC Councillor)
London Topographical Library
London Vestry and District Board Reports 1855–1900
Minute books of the Charity Organisation Society to 1946
Microfilmed archives on charities from 1869

Non-library collection catalogue: All or part available online and in-house

Library catalogue: All or part available online and in-house

Publications: Printed

Publications list: Available in print

Access to staff: Contact by letter, by telephone, by fax, by e-mail, in person and via website
Hours: Mon, Wed, Fri, 0930 to 1645; Tue, Thu, 0930 to 1930; selected Sat, please enquire for details

Parent body: City of London; Guildhall, PO Box 270, London, EC2P 2EJ; tel: 020 7606 3030

LONDON METROPOLITAN POLYMER CENTRE (LMPC)

London Metropolitan University, JCAAD, 41–71 Commercial Road, London, E1 1LA

Tel: 020 7320 2807
Fax: 020 7320 1830
E-mail: polymers@londonmet.ac.uk
Website: www.londonmet.ac.uk/polymers

Enquiries to: Senior Lecturer, Polymers
Direct tel: 020 7320 1880
Direct e-mail: e.onyshchenko@londonmet.ac.uk
Other contacts: Elena Onyshchenko

Founded: 1896

Organisation type and purpose: University department or institute, training organisation, consultancy, research organisation.
short courses, distance learning programmes.
To provide education, training, consultancy and research for the UK and International Polymer and allied industries.

Subject coverage: Polymer materials and composites, polymer processing, mould and die design, injection moulding, extrusion, blown film, blow moulding, thermo vacuum forming, materials testing and characterisation, industrial studies, training, education, short courses, distance learning programmes, consultancy, research.

Trade and statistical information: Information on polymer materials and processing

Publications: Printed, and electronic and video

Publications list: Available online and in print

Access to staff: Contact by letter, by telephone, by fax, by e-mail and via website. Appointment necessary.
Hours: Mon to Fri, 0900 to 1700
Special comments: Voicemail active out of hours.

Access for disabled people: Ramped entry, toilet facilities

LONDON METROPOLITAN UNIVERSITY

31 Jewry Street, London, EC3N 2EY

Tel: 020 7423 0000
Website: www.londonmet.ac.uk/library

Enquiries to: Help Desk at any of the sites who will refer on if necessary

Founded: 1896

Organisation type and purpose: Suitable for ages: 18+.

Subject coverage: Business, environment, social studies, science, computing, engineering, humanities, teaching.
Art and design: cabinet making, design studies, design for disability, fine arts, furniture design, production and history, interior design, jewellery, media studies, musical instrument technology, photography, silversmithing.
Management, accountancy, economics, financial services, law, shipping and transport, civil aviation, computing and information systems, psychology.

Collection: European Documentation Centre
TUC Library Collections
Workers Educational Association Archive

Library catalogue: All or part available online

Access to staff: Contact by letter and by telephone
Hours: Mon to Fri, 0900 to 1700

Other addresses: London Metropolitan University; Commercial Road ILRC, 41–71 Commercial Road, London, E1 1LA; tel: 020 7320 1863; fax: 020 7320 1862; London Metropolitan University; Moorgate Library, 84 Moorgate, London, EC2M 6SQ; tel: 020 7320 1561; fax: 020 7320 1565; London Metropolitan University; City Campus, Calcutta House Library, Old Castle Street, London, E1 7NT; tel: 020 7320 1000; fax: 020 7320 1177; London Metropolitan University; Ladbroke House Library, Highbury Grove, London, N5 2AD; tel: 020 7133 5149; fax: 020 7133 5100; London Metropolitan University; Holloway Road Learning Centre, 236–250 Holloway Road, London, N7 6PP; tel: 020 7133 2442; fax: 020 7133 2066

LONDON NARROW BOAT ASSOCIATION (LNBA)

Battlebridge Moorings, Wharfdale Road, London, N1 9UY

Tel: 07970 799032

Enquiries to: Secretary

Founded: 1978

Organisation type and purpose: Membership association (membership is by election or invitation), voluntary organisation.
Waterways campaigning.

Subject coverage: Moorings in London area.

Access to staff: Contact by letter

Members of: Aylesbury Canal Society (ACS); Canal Basin, Walton Street, Aylesbury, HP21 7QG; Inland Waterways Association (IWA); Island House, Moor Road, Chesham, HPS 1WA

LONDON NATURAL HISTORY SOCIETY (LNHS)

21 Green Way, Frinton-on-Sea, Essex, CO13 9AL

Tel: 01255 674678
Fax: 01255 674678
Website: www.users.globalnet.co.uk~lnhsweb

Enquiries to: Secretary

Founded: 1858

Organisation type and purpose: Learned society (membership is by subscription).

Subject coverage: Natural history of the London area, research and identification of species, observation and conservation, botany, ecology, entomology, geology, ornithology.

Collection: Library is housed at Imperial College of Science, Technology and Medicine, Central Libraries

Publications: Printed

Access to staff: Contact by letter
Hours: Mon to Fri, 0900 to 1700

LONDON PLAYING FIELDS FOUNDATION (LPFF)

73 Collier Street, London, N1 9BE

Tel: 0845 026 2292
E-mail: enquiries@lpff.org.uk
Website: www.lpff.org.uk

Enquiries to: Chief Executive
Other contacts: Operations Director

Founded: 1890

Organisation type and purpose: Registered charity, voluntary organisation (charity number 302925).
The main charity for the provision, protection and promotion of playing fields in Greater London.

Subject coverage: Managing sports facilities within the Greater London area, including football, cricket, rugby, hockey and tennis, for the use of local communities, especially the young, the elderly, the disabled and the disadvantaged.

Publications: Printed

Access to staff: Contact by letter, by telephone, by fax, by e-mail and via website. Appointment necessary.
Hours: Mon to Fri, 0900 to 1730

LONDON RECORD SOCIETY

PO Box 691, Exeter, EX1 9PH

E-mail: londonrecordsoc@btinternet.com
Website: www.londonrecordsociety.org.uk

Enquiries to: Honorary Secretary
Other contacts: Honorary Editor (for book proposals)

Founded: 1964

Organisation type and purpose: Learned society, registered charity.
Publishing society.
To publish editions of primary sources for London history.

Subject coverage: Primary sources and archives on the history of London.

Publications: Printed
Order printed publications from: Website: http://www.londonrecordsociety.org.uk

Publications list: Available online and in print

Access to staff: Contact by letter, by e-mail and via website. Appointment necessary.

LONDON RETAIL MEAT TRADERS LIMITED (LRMTA)

Gate 27, Central Markets, Smithfield, London, EC1A 9EB

continued overleaf

Tel: 020 8248 0732
Fax: 020 8329 1463

Enquiries to: Secretary

Founded: 1926

Organisation type and purpose: National organisation, trade association (membership is by election or invitation), present number of members: 350, service industry.

Subject coverage: Meat retailing, small-scale meat processing, training.

Access to staff: Contact by letter, by telephone and by fax
Hours: Mon to Thu, 0800 to 1500

Affiliated to: National Federation of Meat & Food Traders; Tunbridge Wells, Kent, TN1 1YW; tel: 01892 541412; fax: 01892 535462; e-mail: INFO@NFMFT.co.uk

Members include: local butchers associations

LONDON SCHOOL OF HYGIENE AND TROPICAL MEDICINE (LSHTM)

Keppel Street, London, WC1E 7HT

Tel: 020 7927 2276
Fax: 020 7927 2273
E-mail: library@lshtm.ac.uk
Website: www.lshtm.ac.uk/as/library/libintro.htm

Founded: 1899

Organisation type and purpose: University department or institute.
Postgraduate medical school.

Subject coverage: Environmental health, epidemiology, human nutrition, medical microbiology, entomology, parasitology, medical statistics, population studies and demography, tropical medicine, public health, health policy, the health of developing countries and international health.

Collection: Historical collection (books on public health and tropical medicine)
Manson Collection (papers of Sir Patrick Manson)
Reece Collection (on vaccination)
Ross Archives (papers of Sir Ronald Ross)

Non-library collection catalogue: All or part available online

Library catalogue: All or part available online and in print

Publications: Printed

Access to staff: Contact by letter, by telephone, by e-mail and via website
Hours: Mon to Fri, 0930 to 1730

Access for disabled people: Ramped entry, toilet facilities

Parent body: University of London

LONDON SCHOOL OF JOURNALISM LIMITED (LSJ)

126 Shirland Road, London, W9 2BT

Tel: 020 7289 7777
Fax: 020 7432 8141
E-mail: info@lsjournalism.com
Website: www.home-study.com
Website: www.lsj.org

Enquiries to: Administrator
Direct tel: 020 7432 8140
Direct fax: 020 7432 8140
Direct e-mail: enquiries@lsjournalism.com
Other contacts: Director of Studies for tutorial course information.

Founded: 1921

Organisation type and purpose: Training organisation. Training by distance learning. Postgraduate attendance courses.

Subject coverage: Training for news journalism, freelance writing and creative writing, both by distance learning and by attendance classes.

Publications: Printed

Access to staff: Contact by letter, by telephone, by fax, by e-mail and via website. Appointment necessary.
Hours: Mon to Fri, 1000 to 1630
Special comments: Times may vary, telephone in advance.

Member of: (OLF) (ABCC); Association of British Correspondence Colleges; (OLF) (ABCC) (ODLQC); Open and Distance Learning Quality Council

LONDON SCHOOL OF PUBLISHING (LSP)

David Game House, 69 Notting Hill Gate, London, W11 3JS

Tel: 020 7221 3399
Fax: 020 7243 1730
E-mail: lsp@easynet.co.uk
Website: www.publishing-school.co.uk

Enquiries to: Course Director
Other contacts: Courses Coordinator

Founded: 1983

Organisation type and purpose: Training organisation.
Training courses that run in the evening on a part time basis. Courses run in Feb, Oct and May – some day courses available.
To provide training courses and programmes for graduates who wish to enter the publishing industry, as well as for those who are in the early stages of their publishing careers, or those who wish to change career paths.

Subject coverage: Training in: editing (book and magazine), feature writing, picture research, QuarkXpress, Photoshop, HTML, Dreamweaver, magazine subediting, writing for the Web.

Education services: Training in publishing.

Publications: Printed

Publications list: Available online and in print

Access to staff: Contact by telephone and by e-mail
Hours: Mon to Fri, 0930 to 1830
Special comments: No weekend access.

Access to building: *Hours:* Mon to Fri, 0900 to 1830

Access for disabled people: Access to all public areas
Hours: Mon to Fri, 0900 to 1800

Links with: London School of Public Relations; National Union of Journalists (NUJ)

LONDON SCHOOL OF THEOLOGY (LST)

Green Lane, Northwood, Middlesex, HA6 2UW

Tel: 01923 456190
Fax: 01923 456001
E-mail: library@lst.ac.uk
Website: www.lst.ac.uk

Enquiries to: Librarian
Direct tel: 01923 456192
Direct e-mail: library@lst.ac.uk

Founded: 1943; formerly called London Bible College (year of change 2004)

Organisation type and purpose: Suitable for ages: 18+.
To prepare students for Christian ministry and to further the academic study and research of theology.

Subject coverage: Theology, predominant emphasis is on theology, Music/Worship, and counselling, all within a Christian context.

Collection: Papers of Dr Donald Guthrie (not yet catalogued or otherwise organised)

Library catalogue: All or part available online and in-house

Access to staff: Contact by letter, by telephone, by fax, by e-mail, in person and via website. Appointment necessary. Non-members charged.
Hours: Mon to Fri, 0900 to 1700
Special comments: If at all possible visitors are encouraged to visit during vacations as space in the library is in heavy demand during term time

Links with: Middlesex University

Subsidiary body: Centre for Islamic Studies; LST Postgraduate School of Theology

LONDON SOCIETY

Mortimer Wheeler House, 46 Eagle Wharf Road, London, N1 7ED

Tel: 020 7253 9400
E-mail: info@londonsociety.org.uk
Website: www.londonsociety.org.uk

Enquiries to: Administrator

Founded: 1912

Organisation type and purpose: National organisation, membership association (membership is by subscription), registered charity (charity number 206270).
Advancing the practical improvement and artistic development of London.

Subject coverage: Ancient and modern London, history, architecture and planning, improvement and enhancement of London by the efforts of its citizens, the environment, visits to places of interest within Greater London.

Collection: Library; 3,000 books, 100 maps, housed in the Museum of London (Mortimer Wheeler House)

Library catalogue: All or part available online

Publications: Printed

Access to staff: Contact by letter, by telephone and by e-mail. Appointment necessary.

Hours: Wed and Fri, 0900 to 1630

Links with: Europa Nostra; website: http://www.europanostra.org/
Green Belt Council; website: http://www.londongreenbeltcouncil.org.uk/lgbc%20website/index.html

LONDON SOUTH BANK UNIVERSITY – ENGINEERING, SCIENCE AND THE BUILT ENVIRONMENT

103 Borough Road, London, SE1 OAA

Tel: 020 7815 8320
Fax: 020 7815 8366
Website: www.lsbu.ac.uk/esbe/

Enquiries to: Faculty Administrative Officer
Direct e-mail: teidyk@lsbu.ac.uk
Other contacts: Information Advisers

Organisation type and purpose: University library, university department or institute.

Subject coverage: Architecture; town planning; built environment law; land and building economics; estate management; construction; civil engineering.

Collection: Reference collection on architectural theory, history, practice and related crafts and technology, 17th–20th centuries (particularly strong 1717–1759 and 1880–1920)

Library catalogue: All or part available online

Access to staff: Contact by letter, by telephone and by fax
Hours: Term time: Mon, Tue, Thu, 0830 to 2100; Wed, Fri, 0830 to 1900
Vacations: 0900 to 1700
Special comments: Non-members must apply for reference facilities in writing.

Access to building: No prior appointment required
Special comments: In term time, unless a member of the M25 Group. In vacation, any university students may have reference access on production of current ID card.

Access for disabled people: Toilet facilities
Special comments: Main floor of library accessible by lift, gallery level by arrangement.

LONDON SOUTH BANK UNIVERSITY – LIBRARY

103 Borough Road, London, SE1 0AA

Tel: 020 7815 6607
Fax: 020 7261 1865
E-mail: library@lsbu.ac.uk
Website: www.sbu.ac.uk/lioa

Enquiries to: Director of Learning Information Services
Direct tel: 020 7815 6601
Direct fax: 020 7815 6699
Direct e-mail: john.akeroyd@sbu.ac.uk

Organisation type and purpose: University library.

Subject coverage: Business studies; accountancy; management; finance; public sector studies; chemical engineering; electrical engineering; electronics; mathematics and computing; mechanical and production engineering; environmental engineering; bakery; building technology, practice and management; civil and structural engineering; transportation; land economics; multi-environment; architecture; law; humanities; nursing; health services; occupational hygiene; sociology; biotechnology; social policy; education; town planning.

Collection: Architectural books 1717–1740, 1790–1830, 1880–1920
Building manuals, directories and patents 1750 to date

Publications: Printed

Access to staff: Contact by letter. Appointment necessary. Letter of introduction required.
Hours: Mon to Fri, 0900 to 2100

LONDON SOUTH BANK UNIVERSITY – SYSTEMS AND LEARNING TECHNOLOGIES (LSBU – SALT)

103 Borough Road, London, SE1 0AA

Tel: 020 7815 6668
Website: www1.lsbu.ac.uk/clsd/itsupport

Enquiries to: Team Leader

Founded: 1982

Organisation type and purpose: University department or institute, consultancy, research organisation.

Access to staff: Contact by letter, by telephone, by fax, by e-mail, in person and via website. Appointment necessary.
Hours: Mon to Fri, 0900 to 1700

Access to building: Prior appointment required

Access for disabled people: Access to all public areas

Constituent part of: Centre for Learning Support and Development

LONDON SUBTERRANEAN SURVEY ASSOCIATION (LSSA)

98 Cambridge Gardens, London, W10 6HS

Tel: 020 8968 1360
E-mail: wolstan-dixie@hotmail.co.uk

Enquiries to: Secretary

Founded: 1968

Organisation type and purpose: Learned society (membership is by election or invitation).

Subject coverage: Man-made or used underground space or constructions in London and their effect on surface development.

Collection: Books, maps, pamphlets, grey literature, press cuttings, videos, photographs, illustrations

Non-library collection catalogue: All or part available in-house

Library catalogue: All or part available in-house

Access to staff: Contact by letter, by telephone and by e-mail. Non-members charged.
Hours: Mon to Fri, 1000 to 1700

Links with: Subterranea Britannica

LONDON SYMPHONY ORCHESTRA LIMITED (LSO)

Barbican Centre, London, EC2Y 8DS

Tel: 020 7588 1116
Fax: 020 7374 0127
E-mail: admin@lso.co.uk
Website: www.lso.co.uk

Enquiries to: Head of Marketing
Direct fax: 020 7638 4578

Founded: 1904

Organisation type and purpose: International organisation, registered charity (charity number 232391).
Orchestra, arts organisation.

Subject coverage: Orchestra, music, classical music, arts.

Collection: LSO Archives, photographs, publicity material including programmes

Publications: Printed, and electronic and video

Publications list: Available in print

Access to staff: Contact by letter, by telephone, by fax, by e-mail and via website. Appointment necessary.
Hours: Mon to Fri, 0930 to 1800

Other address: LSO St Luke's; UBS & LSO Music Education Centre, 161 Old Street, London, EC1V 9NJ; tel: 020 7588 1116; fax: 020 7384 0127; e-mail: swales@lso.co.uk

LONDON TANKER BROKERS' PANEL LIMITED (LTBP)

Copenhagen House, 5–10 Bury Street, London, EC3A 5AT

Tel: 020 7456 6600
Fax: 020 7456 6601
E-mail: ltbp@worldscale.co.uk
Website: www.ltbp.co.uk

Enquiries to: Managing Director

Founded: 1953

Organisation type and purpose: Consultancy.

Subject coverage: Oil tanker freight rates, AFRA (average freight rate assessment), time charter rates, assessment of freight consideration for tankers.

Collection: Tanker freight rates

Publications: Printed

Publications list: Available in print

Access to staff: Contact by letter, by telephone, by fax and by e-mail. Appointment necessary.
Hours: Mon to Fri, 0900 to 1700

LONDON THAMES GATEWAY FORUM OF VOLUNTARY AND COMMUNITY ORGANISATIONS (LTGF)

The Brady Centre, 192 Hanbury Street, London, E1 5HU

Tel: 020 7377 1822
Fax: 020 7247 5637
E-mail: info@ltgdc.org.uk

continued overleaf

Enquiries to: Information Officer
Other contacts: Director, Regeneration for planning and regeneration.

Founded: 1975

Organisation type and purpose:
Membership association (membership is by qualification), present number of members: 506, voluntary organisation.

Subject coverage: Geography, sociology and politics of urban change in the London Thames Gateway area and the inner city generally, environment, regeneration issues.

Non-library collection catalogue: All or part available in-house

Library catalogue: All or part available in-house

Publications: Printed

Publications list: Available online and in print

Access to staff: Contact by letter, by telephone, by fax and by e-mail.
Appointment necessary.
Hours: Mon to Fri, 1000 to 1800

Access to building: No access other than to staff, prior appointment required
Hours: Mon to Fri, 1000 to 1800

Access for disabled people: Parking provided, ramped entry, toilet facilities
Special comments: Need to pre-check for parking space.

LONDON THEOLOGICAL SEMINARY (LTS)

104 Hendon Lane, London, N3 3SQ

Tel: 020 8346 7587
E-mail: admin@ltslondon.org
Website: www.ltslondon.org

Enquiries to: Administrator

Founded: 1977

Organisation type and purpose: Registered charity. Training for Christian ministry.

Subject coverage: Theology.

Collection: Dr Martyn Lloyd-Jones' Library

Library catalogue: All or part available in-house

Access to staff: Contact by letter and by e-mail
Hours: Mon to Fri, 0900 to 1700

LONDON TOPOGRAPHICAL SOCIETY (LTS)

Southgate, 7 Linden Avenue, Dorchester, Dorset, DT1 1EJ

Tel: 01305 261548
E-mail: patfrazer@yahoo.co.uk
Website: www.topsoc.org

Enquiries to: Honorary Secretary

Founded: 1880

Organisation type and purpose: Learned society (membership is by subscription), present number of members: 1,100.
To publish material relating to the study of London topography.

Subject coverage: London topography, maps, prints and views.

Publications: Printed
Order printed publications from: Honorary Treasurer, Flat 13, 13 Tavistock Place, London, WC1H 9SH

Publications list: Available online and in print

Access to staff: Contact by letter and by e-mail
Hours: No access.

LONDON TRAVELWATCH

Formal name: London Transport Users' Committee

6 Middle Street, London, EC1A 7JA

Tel: 020 7505 9000
Fax: 020 7505 9003
E-mail: info@londontravelwatch.org.uk
Website: www.londontravelwatch.org.uk

Enquiries to: Chief Executive
Direct e-mail: jo.debank@londontravelwatch.org.uk
Other contacts: Casework Team

Founded: 2000

Organisation type and purpose: National government body, advisory body, statutory body, membership association, present number of members: 21.
Statutory consumer watchdog.
Acts as an appeals body considering suggestions and complaints concerning the service.
To represent the interests of transport provided, procured or licensed by Transport for London, Heathrow Express, Eurostar and the national railways in and around London.

Subject coverage: Matters relating to public transport in and around London; problems faced by people using public transport in and around London.

Collection: An extensive library of transport related material
The Cullen inquiry into the Ladbroke Grove Rail crash (transcript)
The Uff inquiry into the Southall Rail crash (transcript)
The Fennell inquiry into the Kings Cross Fire (transcript)
The Hidden inquiry into the Clapham Junction Rail crash (transcript)

Trade and statistical information: Data on users' comments, complaints and suggestions

Publications list: Available online

Access to staff: Contact by letter, by telephone, by fax, by e-mail and in person.
Appointment necessary.
Hours: Mon to Fri, 0900 to 1700

Access for disabled people: Wheelchair access, hearing loop

LONDON UNDERGROUND RAILWAY SOCIETY (LURS)

54 Brinkley Road, Worcester Park, Surrey, KT4 8JF

Tel: 020 8330 1855
Website: www.lurs.org.uk

Enquiries to: Secretary

Founded: 1961

Organisation type and purpose:
Membership association (membership is by subscription), present number of members: 900, voluntary organisation.

Subject coverage: All aspects of London's underground railways, past, present and future.

Collection: Cartographic Collection
Chandos Papers
Photographic Collection
Sound and Vision Collection

Publications: Printed

Access to staff: Contact by letter
Hours: Mon to Fri, any reasonable time

LONDON VIDEO TRADE ASSOCIATION

314 Walworth Road, London, SE17 2NA

Tel: 020 7703 3081
Fax: 020 7703 3081

Enquiries to: Secretary

Founded: 1982

Organisation type and purpose: Trade association (membership is by qualification), present number of members: 44.
Help and advice to video shops.

Subject coverage: Video trade.

Access to staff: Contact by letter, by telephone, by fax and in person
Hours: Mon to Fri, 1030 to 1800

Access for disabled people: Ramped entry

LONDON VOLUNTARY SERVICE COUNCIL (LVSC)

356 Holloway Road, London, N7 6PA

Tel: 020 7700 8107
Fax: 020 7700 8108
E-mail: info@lvsc.org.uk
Website: www.lvsc.org.uk

Enquiries to: Resource Officer
Direct tel: 020 7700 8192

Organisation type and purpose: Voluntary organisation, registered charity (charity number 276886).

Subject coverage: Social policy affecting London's voluntary sector, organisational support for London's voluntary sector, information on London's voluntary sector.

Collection: Over 5000 items related to London's voluntary and community sector including general information and organisational development information.
Access to Funderfinder by appointment.

Library catalogue: All or part available in-house

Publications: Printed

Publications list: Available in print

Access to staff: Contact by letter, by telephone, by fax, by e-mail and in person
Hours: Varies for different services

LONDON WILDLIFE TRUST

Skyline House, 200 Union Street, London, SE1 0LX

Tel: 020 7261 0447
Fax: 020 7261 0538
E-mail: enquiries@wildlondon.org.uk
Website: www.wildlondon.org.uk

Enquiries to: Education Coordinator

Founded: 1981

Organisation type and purpose:
Membership association (membership is by subscription), registered charity (charity number 283895).
The London Wildlife Trust fights to sustain and enhance London's wildlife habitats to create a city richer in wildlife.

Subject coverage: Wildlife, urban wildlife, site protection and management, environmental education and training.

Collection: Environmental education publications

Publications: Printed

Publications list: Available in print

Access to staff: Contact by letter, by telephone, by fax, by e-mail and via website. Appointment necessary.
Hours: Mon to Fri, 0930 to 1730

Access to building: No prior appointment required

Affiliated to: Wildlife Watch

Manages: 57 sites across London

Part of: Wildlife Trusts

LONG DISTANCE WALKERS' ASSOCIATION LIMITED (LDWA)

Bellevue, Princes Street, Ulverston. LA12 7NB

E-mail: chair@ldwa.org.uk
Website: www.ldwa.org.uk

Enquiries to: General Secretary
Other contacts: Long Distance Path Information Officer (for information about long distance paths and routes)

Founded: 1972

Organisation type and purpose:
Membership association (membership is by subscription), present number of members: 6,500, voluntary organisation, recognised governing body.
To further the interests of those who enjoy long distance walking.

Subject coverage: Long distance walking, paths and trails.

Collection: Details of over 600 walks and trails etc. are held

Publications: Printed
Order printed publications from:
Merchandising Officer, Long Distance Walkers' Association
2 Sandy Lane, Beeston, Nottinghamshire, NG9 3GS; tel: 0115 922 1849

Access to staff: Contact by letter, by e-mail and via website

Affiliated to: European Ramblers Association; Ramblers Association; Scottish Rights of Way Society; Sports Council

LOTTERIES COUNCIL

2 Regan Road, Moira, Swadlincote, Derbyshire, DE12 6DS

Tel: 01925 710880
Fax: 01925 710880
E-mail: tina@lotteriescouncil.org.uk
Website: www.lotteriescouncil.co.uk

Enquiries to: Secretary
Other contacts: Executive Officer

Founded: 1979

Organisation type and purpose: Trade association, present number of members: 248.

Subject coverage: Management of lotteries; accounting procedures; requirements under the Gambling Act 2005. History of lotteries in the UK; lottery regulations.

Publications: Printed

Access to staff: Contact by letter, by telephone and by e-mail
Hours: Mon to Thu, 0900 to 1400

Other addresses: Executive Officer – Tina Sandford; 42 Kynaston Road, Shrewsbury, SY1 3JN; tel: 01743 469400; e-mail: tina@lotteriescouncil.org.uk

LOTUS SEVEN CLUB

Formal name: Lotus Seven Club of Great Britain

PO Box 777, Haywards Heath, West Sussex, RH16 2YA

Tel: 07000 572582
Fax: 07000 572582
E-mail: adrian.williams@lotus7club.com
Website: www.lotus7club.co.uk

Enquiries to: Membership Secretary

Founded: 1985

Organisation type and purpose:
International organisation, membership association, present number of members: 3000.

Subject coverage: Lotus Seven from 1957 to 1973 and the Caterham Seven from 1973 to date.

Collection: Video lending library (members only)
Original Lotus Seven Specifications

Publications: Printed

Access to staff: Contact by letter, by telephone, by fax, by e-mail and via website
Hours: Mon to Fri, 0900 to 1700

LOUGHBOROUGH UNIVERSITY – DEPARTMENT OF INFORMATION SCIENCE (DIS)

Epinal Way, Loughborough, Leicestershire, LE11 3TU

Tel: 01509 223051
Fax: 01509 223053
E-mail: dis@lboro.ac.uk
Website: www.lboro.ac.uk/departments/dis

Enquiries to: Head of Department
Direct tel: 01509 223065

Founded: 1972

Organisation type and purpose: University department or institute.

Subject coverage: Exploitation of business information; database design and development; marketing library and information services; development of expert systems for library and information services; archives and records management; conservation of materials; communications and information networks; intellectual property law; distance learning in library and information education; information skills; cataloguing and bibliographic control of materials; library planning, information, dissemination, strategic planning, electronic document delivery, electronic journals/publishing.

Collection: Mary Ward Collection of children's literature
Parish Libraries of Ashby de la Zouch and Loughborough (on deposit)

Trade and statistical information: A range of statistical and related data as accumulated through various research projects and studies (including that of LISU)

Non-library collection catalogue: All or part available in-house

Publications: Printed

Access to staff: Contact by letter, by telephone, by fax and by e-mail.
Appointment necessary.
Hours: Mon to Fri, 0900 to 1700

Access for disabled people: Parking provided, ramped entry, access to all public areas, toilet facilities

Constituent bodies: Higher Education Academy Information and Computer Science Study Centre; tel: 01509 635708; fax: 01509 223053; e-mail: a.s.mcnab@lboro.ac.uk; Library and Information Statistics Unit (LISU); tel: 01509 635680; fax: 01509 635699; e-mail: c.creaser@lboro.ac.uk

LOUGHBOROUGH UNIVERSITY – UNIVERSITY LIBRARY

Loughborough, Leicestershire, LE11 3TU

Tel: 01509 222360
Fax: 01509 223993
E-mail: library@lboro.ac.uk
Website: www.lboro.ac.uk/library

Enquiries to: Head of Planning and Resources
Direct tel: 01509 222355
Direct e-mail: j.g.walton@lboro.ac.uk

Organisation type and purpose: University library.

Subject coverage: Art; business studies; design and technology; economics; English and drama; European studies; geography; human sciences; information studies; management; social sciences; chemical engineering; chemistry; civil engineering; computer studies; electrical and electronic engineering; human biology; ergonomics; materials technology; mathematics; mechanical engineering; physics; transport technology; manufacturing engineering; sports science.

Non-library collection catalogue: All or part available online

Library catalogue: All or part available online

continued overleaf

Access for disabled people: Parking provided, level entry, access to all public areas, toilet facilities

Links with: LISU

LOUTH NATURALISTS' ANTIQUARIAN AND LITERARY SOCIETY (LNALS)

The Museum, 4 Broadbank, Louth, Lincolnshire, LN11 0EQ

Tel: 01507 601211
E-mail: louthmuseum@btconnect.com
Website: www.louth.org.uk

Enquiries to: Manager

Founded: 1884

Organisation type and purpose: Learned society (membership is by subscription), present number of members: 205, registered charity (charity number 504370), museum, publishing house.

Subject coverage: Local history relating to Louth and district.

Collection: Architectural Drawings of James Fowler, FRIBA, 1828–92, architect of Louth
Paintings by Peter DeWint
Works of Thomas Wilkinson Wallis, 1821–1903, internationally known woodcarver
Louth-made flat-weave carpets
Brick making
1920 Louth flood interpretation
Domestic and commercial bygones

Publications: Printed
Order printed publications from: Louth Museum, 4 Broadbank, Louth, LN11 0EQ; tel. 01507 601211

Access to staff: Contact by letter, by telephone, by e-mail and in person. Appointment necessary. Non-members charged.

Access to building: No prior appointment required
Hours: April to October: Tue to Sat, 1000 to 1600

Access for disabled people: Fully accessible

Member organisation of: Lincoln Record Society; Society for Lincolnshire History and Archaeology

LP GAS ASSOCIATION (LPGA)

Unit 14, Bow Court, Fletchworth Gate, Burnsall Road, Coventry, CV5 6SP

Tel: 024 7667 2108
E-mail: mail@lpga.co.uk
Website: www.lpga.co.uk

Enquiries to: Director General

Founded: 1970

Organisation type and purpose: Professional body, trade association (membership is by subscription), present number of members: 180.

Subject coverage: Liquefied petroleum gas, safety, standards, distribution, storage, handling and utilisation, LPG cylinders, hoses, vessels and systems.

Collection: Codes of practice for the LP Gas Industry

Publications: Printed

Publications list: Available online and in print

Access to staff: Contact by letter, by telephone, by fax, by e-mail and via website
Hours: Mon to Thu, 0830 to 1700; Fri, 0830 to 1630

Member of: Association Européen des Gas de Petrole Lingfiés (AEGPL)

LSE LIBRARY

London School of Economics and Political Science (LSE), 10 Portugal Street, London, WC2A 2HD

Tel: 020 7955 7229
Fax: 020 7955 7454
E-mail: library@lse.ac.uk
Website: www.library.lse.ac.uk

Enquiries to: Director of Library Services
Other contacts: Archivist

Founded: 1896

Organisation type and purpose: University library.

Subject coverage: Accounting; anthropology; climate change; economics; geography; government; history; industrial relations; law; philosophy; politics; population studies; psychology; social administration; sociology; statistics.

Collection: Archives and private papers on recent political, social and economic history, social anthropology and the history of the London School of Economics; including papers of the Liberal Party, the Independent Labour Party, John Stuart Mill, Beatrice and Sidney Webb, Fabian Society, William Beveridge, George Lansbury, Hugh Dalton, Walter Citrine, Bronislaw Malinowski, C A R Crosland and the Hall-Carpenter Archives of lesbian and gay activism
Collections of rare books on political, economic and social subjects from the 16th century to the present day
The Library is a depository for the United Nations, the United States Government and is a European Documentation Centre
A large collection of publications from intergovernmental organisations and national governments world-wide, with particular emphasis on statistics

Non-library collection catalogue: All or part available online

Library catalogue: All or part available online

Publications: Printed

Access to staff: Contact by letter, by telephone, by fax, by e-mail, in person and via website. Non-members charged.
Hours: Core hours: Mon to Fri, 0900 to 2000
Hours vary throughout year, full details on website
Special comments: Charges to commercial/business users.
Letter of introduction required in certain circumstances.

Access for disabled people: Level entry, access to all public areas, toilet facilities

Parent body: London School of Economics and Political Science

LUBRICANTS UK LIMITED

Castrol Technology Centre, Whitchurch Hill, Pangbourne, Reading, Berkshire, RG8 7QR

Tel: 0118 984 3311
Fax: 0118 976 5536
E-mail: toomeym@castrol.com
Website: www.castrol.com

Enquiries to: Librarian
Direct tel: 0118 976 5396

Founded: 1899

Organisation type and purpose: Research organisation.
Research and development on lubricants, greases, antifreeze, hydraulic fluids etc.

Subject coverage: Lubrication, tribology, greases, antifreeze, hydraulic fluids.

Library catalogue: All or part available in-house

Access to staff: Contact by letter, by telephone, by fax and by e-mail. Appointment necessary.
Hours: Mon to Fri, 0900 to 1700

Parent body: BP plc; Britannic House, 1 Finsbury Circus, London, EC2M 7BA

LUDLOW MUSEUM RESOURCE CENTRE

Ludlow Museum Resource Centre, 7–9 Parkway, Ludlow, Shropshire, SY8 2PG

Tel: 01584 813665
Fax: 01584 813666
E-mail: llmrc@shropshire.gov.uk
Website: www.shropshire.gov.uk/museums.nsf

Organisation type and purpose: Museum. Formed in 1833 as a museum.

Subject coverage: History of Ludlow including its archaeology and geology.

Collection: Geological, biological, social history collections

Non-library collection catalogue: All or part available in-house

Library catalogue: All or part available in-house

Access to staff: Contact by letter, by telephone, by fax, by e-mail and in person. Appointment necessary.
Hours: Mon to Fri, 0900 to 1700

Access to building: Prior appointment required

Access for disabled people: Parking nearby

Also at: Ludlow Museum; Castle Street, Ludlow. SY8 1AS; tel: 01584 878765; e-mail: ludlow.museum@shropshire.gov.uk

LUPUS UK

St James House, Eastern Road, Romford, Essex, RM1 3NH

Tel: 01708 731251
Fax: 01708 731252
E-mail: headoffice@lupusuk.org.uk
Website: www.lupusuk.org.uk

Enquiries to: Administrator
Other contacts: Director

Founded: 1990

Organisation type and purpose: Registered charity.
Fund-raising for medical research into cure and treatment for lupus; publicity and information.

Subject coverage: Systemic lupus erythematosus, its nature, treatment and research; support for sufferers from the disease.

Publications: Printed

Publications list: Available online and in print

Access to staff: Contact by letter, by telephone, by fax, by e-mail and in person
Hours: Mon to Fri, 0900 to 1700

LUTON CENTRAL LIBRARY

St Georges Square, Luton, Bedfordshire, LU1 2NG

Tel: 01582 547418
Fax: 01582 547461
E-mail: libraryinfo@lutonculture.com
Website: www.lutonlibraries.co.uk

Enquiries to: Director of Libraries
Direct tel: 01582 547422
Direct e-mail: jean.george@lutonculture.com
Other contacts: Central Library Manager (for administration of building and services); Information & E-Delivery Services Manager (for information services, adult/young people services)

Organisation type and purpose: Charitable trust, public library.

Subject coverage: General, and the history of Luton.

Collection: Workshop manual collection
Local studies collection, focusing on Luton

Non-library collection catalogue: All or part available in-house

Library catalogue: All or part available online

Publications: Printed, and electronic and video

Access to staff: Contact by letter, by telephone, by fax, by e-mail, in person and via website
Hours: Mon, 1100 to 1900; Tue to Thu, 0900 to 1900; Fri, 0900 to 1700; Sat, 0930 to 1600; Sun, 1000 to 1600

Branch libraries: Leagrave Library; Marsh Road, Luton, Bedfordshire, LU3 2NL; tel: 01582 556650; Marsh Farm Library Library; Lea Manor High School, Northwell Drive, Luton, Bedfordshire, LU3 2TL; tel: 01582 574803; Wigmore Library; Wigmore Lane, Luton, Bedfordshire, LU2 8DJ; tel: 01582 706340

Parent body: Luton Cultural Services Trust; LCST HQ, 4th floor, Luton Central Library, St Georges Square, Luton, LU1 2NG; tel: 01582 547470; fax: 01582 547461; website: http://www.lutonculture.com

LUTYENS TRUST

Goddards, Abinger Common, Dorking, Surrey, RH5 6JH

Tel: 01306 730487
Website: www.lutyenstrust.org.uk

Enquiries to: Honorary Secretary

Founded: 1984

Organisation type and purpose: Learned society (membership is by subscription), present number of members: 350, registered charity (charity number 326776).
The Lutyens' Trust is an educational charity that acts as a source of information and help on the care and maintenance of the works of Sir Edwin Lutyens.
To protect the spirit and substance of the work of Sir Edwin Lutyens OM.

Subject coverage: Historical and technical information on the buildings designed by Edwin Lutyens in 1889–1944.

Collection: Goddards, a Lutyens house. Though still owned by the Lutyens Trust, it is managed by the Landmark Trust

Publications: Printed

Access to staff: Appointment necessary.
Hours: Mon to Fri, 0900 to 1700
Special comments: Open Wed afternoon between Apr and Sept; appointments to be made with The Landmark Trust.

Access to building: Prior appointment required

Goddards transferred to the: Landmark Trust

LUXEMBOURG EMBASSY

Formal name: Ambassade du Grand-Duché de Luxembourg à Londres

27 Wilton Crescent, London, SW1X 8SD

Tel: 020 7235 6961
Fax: 020 7235 9734

Enquiries to: Counsellor
Direct e-mail: londres.amb@mae.etat.lu

Organisation type and purpose: Embassy/Consulate.

Subject coverage: Luxembourg: its history, political system, geography, economy, taxation, statistics, cultural life, education, commerce.

Collection: Memorials (Journal Officiel du Grand-Duché de Luxembourg), 3 series A, B and C covering laws, regulations and administration, company information

Access to staff: Contact by letter and by e-mail. Appointment necessary.
Hours: Mon to Fri, 0900 to 1700

LUXEMBOURG TOURIST OFFICE

Sicilian House, Sicilian Avenue, London, WC1 1QH

Tel: 020 7434 2800
Fax: 020 7430 1773
E-mail: tourism@luxembourg.co.uk
Website: www.luxembourg.co.uk

Enquiries to: Director

Founded: 1954

Organisation type and purpose: National government body.

Subject coverage: Luxembourg (the country and city).

Trade and statistical information: General statistics on Luxembourg

Publications: Printed, and electronic and video

Access to staff: Contact by letter, by telephone, by fax, by e-mail, in person and via website
Hours: Mon to Fri, 1000 to 1700

Access to building: *Hours:* Mon to Fri, 1000 to 1700

Access for disabled people: Level entry, lift
Special comments: Lift.

LYMPHOMA ASSOCIATION

PO Box 386, Aylesbury, Buckinghamshire, HP20 2GA

Tel: 01296 619400
Fax: 01296 619400
E-mail: information@lymphomas.org.uk
Website: www.lymphomas.org.uk
Website: www.takeapitstop.org.uk

Enquiries to: Lymphoma Association helpline
Direct tel: 0808 808 5555
Direct e-mail: information@lymphomas.org.uk

Founded: 1986

Organisation type and purpose: The Lymphoma Association provides free information and support to anyone affected by lymphoma; whether patient, carer, family member, friend, or health professional.

Subject coverage: The Lymphoma Association helps anyone affected by lymphoma; Hodgkin and non-Hodgkin lymphomas.

Information services: www.lymphomas.org.uk/information-and-support/information-about-lymphoma/frequently-asked-questions/download-or-order

Collection: DVDs, CDs, loan collection

Publications: Printed, and electronic and video
Order printed publications from: https://www.lymphomas.org.uk/information-and-support/information-about-lymphoma/frequently-asked-questions/download-or-order

Publications list: Available online and in print

Access to staff: Contact by letter, by telephone, by fax, by e-mail and via website
Hours: Mon to Thu, 0900 to 1800; Fri, 0900 to 1700

LYMPHOMA RESEARCH TRUST

Trustees Department, 5th Floor East, 250 Euston Road, London, NW1 2PG

Tel: 020 7380 9931
E-mail: hannah.jetuah@uclh.nhs.uk
Website: www.lymphoma-research-trust.org.uk

Founded: 1973

Organisation type and purpose: A registered charity (charity number 263424). Strives to improve the life expectancy and quality of life of patients with Hodgkin's Lymphoma and non-Hodgkin's Lymphoma. Supports research into the treatment of

continued overleaf

lymphoma. Makes grants to medical researchers at the Lymphoma Trials Office who organise clinical trials and operate a database with over 18,000 patients on it.

Subject coverage: The database contains details of patients' treatments and annual follow-ups, and provides a valuable record of the outcome of different treatments for lymphomas. The clinical trials assess whether new treatments work better than existing ones, and test different combinations of treatments to see which are most effective. The information gained from these trials improves knowledge of lymphoma and enables patients to be treated more effectively.

Access to staff: Contact by letter, by telephone and by e-mail

Links with: University College London Hospitals NHS Foundation Trust (UCLH); 250 Euston Road, London, NW1 2PG; tel: 0845 1555 000

MAARA

Formal name: Midlands Asthma and Allergy Research Association

7 Stadium Business Court, Millennium Way, Pride Park, Derby, DE24 8HP

Tel: 01162 479888
Fax: 01162 479888
E-mail: enquiries@maara.org
Website: www.maara.org

Enquiries to: General Manager

Founded: 1968

Organisation type and purpose: Registered charity (charity number 257131).
Concerned with funding research into asthma and other allergies, runs an information service and is renowned for aerobiological research.
Main aim is to fund research into the cause and treatment of asthma and allergy.

Subject coverage: Information on asthma and other allergic conditions, aerobiology, patient education, pollen and spore levels, pollen forecasts, anaphylaxis.

Trade and statistical information: Aerobiological data

Publications: Printed

Publications list: Available online

Access to staff: Contact by letter, by telephone, by fax, by e-mail, in person and via website. Appointment necessary.
Hours: Mon to Fri, 0900 to 1630

Branches: MAARA; PO Box 1057, Leicester, LE2 3GZ; tel: 01162 479888; e-mail: eva .day@virgin.net

MACAULAY LAND USE RESEARCH INSTITUTE (Macaulay Institute)

Craigiebuckler, Aberdeen, AB15 8QH

Tel: 01224 395000
Fax: 01224 395010
E-mail: l.robertson@macaulay.ac.uk
Website: www.macaulay.ac.uk

Enquiries to: Librarian
Direct e-mail: e.mackenzie@macaulay.ac.uk

Founded: 1987

Organisation type and purpose: Research organisation.

Subject coverage: Soil science; crop suitability; land use; hill farming; plant physiology; peat and forest soils; forestry; environmental conservation and pollution; land reclamation; drainage; water research.

Library catalogue: All or part available in-house

Publications: Printed

Publications list: Available in print

Access to staff: Contact by letter, by telephone, by fax, by e-mail and via website. Appointment necessary.
Hours: Mon to Thu, 0900 to 1700; Fri, 0900 to 1600

Access to building: Prior appointment required

Access for disabled people: Parking provided, level entry, access to all public areas, toilet facilities

Grant administered by the: Scottish Government

MACCLESFIELD BOROUGH COUNCIL

Town Hall, Macclesfield, Cheshire, SK10 1AH

Tel: 01625 500500, 01625 500321 (minicom)
Fax: 01625 504203
Website: www.macclesfield.gov.uk

Enquiries to: Public Relations Manager
Direct tel: 01625 504165
Direct fax: 01625 504155

Founded: 1974

Organisation type and purpose: Local government body.

Subject coverage: Services and amenities of the local borough council.

Access to staff: Contact by letter, by telephone, by fax and by e-mail. Appointment necessary.
Hours: Mon to Thu, 0845 to 1700; Fri, 0845 to 1630

Access for disabled people: Parking provided, ramped entry, toilet facilities

MACECORP LIMITED (AIIT)

Somers House, 1 Somers Road, Reigate, Surrey, RH2 9DU

Tel: 01737 224427
Fax: 01737 224428
Website: www.aiit.com/

Enquiries to: Managing Director
Other contacts: Senior Consultant for Research Head.

Founded: 1985

Organisation type and purpose:
International organisation, advisory body, professional body, consultancy, research organisation.
IT and telecommunications management consultancy.

Subject coverage: IT, telecommunications, market research, business strategy, market positioning, IT budgeting, and resourcing, partnership search, product/vendor/ objective analyses, support and training in product launch, information services, temporary experts.

Trade and statistical information: European telecommunications spend statistics, voice resale markets in Europe, key European and International IT activities

Publications: Printed

Publications list: Available in print

Access to staff: Contact by letter, by telephone, by fax, by e-mail and via website. Appointment necessary.
Hours: Mon to Fri, 0900 to 1800

Access to building: Prior appointment required

Associates in: France, Germany, Ireland, Italy, Netherlands, Belgium, Spain, Sweden and USA

MACMILLAN CANCER RELIEF

39 Albert Embankment, London, SE1 7UQ

Tel: 020 7340 7840, 0808 808 0121 (minicom)
Fax: 020 7840 7841
E-mail: via website
Website: www.macmillan.org.uk

Enquiries to: Corporate Communications Assistant
Direct tel: 020 7840 7817
Direct e-mail: oplummer@macmillan.org.uk

Founded: 1911

Organisation type and purpose: Voluntary organisation, registered charity (charity number 261017).
Helps to provide expert care and practical and emotional support for people living with cancer, including families, friends and carers. In order to achieve this it raises funds for specialist Macmillan nurses and doctors, builds vitally needed treatment centres, provides grants for patients with financial difficulties, offers training and resources to cancer self-help and support groups, and provides a range of information locally and nationally.

Subject coverage: General information on help for cancer patients, applications for financial grants accepted from health professionals on behalf of cancer patients, domiciliary nursing care for cancer patients.

Collection: Cancer information

Publications: Printed, and microform publications

Publications list: Available online and in print

Access to staff: Contact by letter, by telephone, by fax, by e-mail and via website
Hours: Mon to Fri, 0930 to 1930

Affiliated to: BACUP; Breast Cancer Care; British Colostomy Association; CancerLink; National Association of Laryngectomee Clubs

MACULAR DISEASE SOCIETY (MDS)

PO Box 1870, Andover, Hampshire, SP10 9AD

Tel: 01264 350551
Fax: 01264 350558
E-mail: info@maculardisease.org
Website: www.maculardisease.org

Enquiries to: Information
Direct tel: helpline: 0845 241 2041

Founded: 1987

Subject coverage: Macular disease, sight impairment, low vision aids, emotional support.

Collection: Information material (booklets, pamphlets, etc., free on request via helpline)

Trade and statistical information: Data on sight impairment

Publications: Printed

Access to staff: Contact by letter, by telephone, by fax and by e-mail
Hours: Mon to Fri, 0900 to 1700

Access to building: No access other than to staff

MADE-UP TEXTILES ASSOCIATION LIMITED (MUTA)

MUTA, c/o Luther Pendragon, Priory Court, Pilgrim Street, London, EC4V 6DR

Tel: 0207 618 9196
Fax: 0207 329 7301
E-mail: info@muta.org.uk
Website: www.performancetextiles.org.uk

Enquiries to: Secretariat

Founded: 1919

Organisation type and purpose: Trade association.

Subject coverage: MUTA is a trading name of the Performance Textiles Association Ltd Registered in England No. 152795.

Publications: Printed

Publications list: Available online

Access to staff: Contact by letter, by telephone, by fax, by e-mail and via website
Hours: Mon to Fri, 0900 to 1700

MAG (UK)

Formal name: Motorcycle Action Group

PO Box 750, Warwick, CV34 9FU.

Tel: 01926 844064
Fax: 01926 844065
E-mail: mag-hq@mag-uk.org
Website: www.mag-uk.org

Enquiries to: General Secretary
Direct e-mail: nich.brown@mag-uk.org

Founded: 1973

Organisation type and purpose: National organisation, membership association (membership is by subscription), present number of members: 10,000 individual, plus 40,000 via club affiliation, lobbying and campaigning organisation on behalf of motorcyclists' rights, voluntary organisation, consultancy, research organisation, publishing house.
Representative lobby group for motorcyclists, i.e. user group, service organisation, multiple member benefits.

Subject coverage: Motorcycle user-related information.

Collection: Motorcycle-related archive, mostly hard copy, PC-indexed

Trade and statistical information: Some statistical source data from outside bodies, government, etc

Non-library collection catalogue: All or part available online and in print

Library catalogue: All or part available online and in print

Publications: Printed

Access to staff: Contact by letter, by telephone, by fax, by e-mail and via website. Access for members only. Non-members charged.
Hours: Mon to Fri, 0900 to 1700

Access to building: Prior appointment required

Affiliated to: Federation of European Motorcyclists Associations (FEMA); Rue Des Champs 62, 1040 Brussels, Belgium; tel: +32 2 736 9407; fax: +32 2 736 9401; e-mail: info@fema-online.eu; website: http://www.fema-online.eu

MAGDALEN COLLEGE

Library and Archives, Oxford, OX1 4AU

Tel: 01865 276045
Fax: 01865 276057
E-mail: library@magd.ox.ac.uk
Website: www.magd.ox.ac.uk/college_life/libraries_and_archives.shtml

Enquiries to: Librarian
Other contacts: Archivist, tel: 01865 276088 for archives queries

Founded: 1458

Organisation type and purpose: College library and archives.

Subject coverage: All taught subjects; college-related archives.

Collection: Gibbard Bequest 1608 (medical books)
Goodyer Bequest 1664 (botanical books)
Throckmorton Bequest 1626 (continental books)

Non-library collection catalogue: All or part available in-house

Library catalogue: All or part available online

Publications: Printed
Order printed publications from: Home Bursar's Office, Magdalen College, Oxford OX1 4AU

Publications list: Available online

Access to staff: Contact by letter, by telephone, by e-mail and via website. Appointment necessary.
Hours: Mon to Fri, 0900 to 1700

Access to building: Members only, or by appointment

MAGIC CIRCLE, THE

Centre for the Magic Arts, 12 Stephenson Way, London, NW1 2HD

Tel: 020 7387 2222
Fax: 020 7387 5114
E-mail: secretary@themagiccircle.co.uk
Website: www.themagiccircle.co.uk

Enquiries to: Secretary
Direct tel: 020 7387 2222

Founded: 1905

Organisation type and purpose: Membership association (membership is by subscription, qualification, election or invitation), present number of members: 1400.

Subject coverage: Art of magic, magical inventions and presentations.

Access to staff: Contact by letter, by telephone and by fax
Hours: Mon to Fri, 0900 to 1700

MAGIC LANTERN SOCIETY (MLS)

South Park, Galphay Road, Kirkby Malzeard, Ripon, North Yorkshire, HG4 3RX

Tel: 01765 658485
Fax: 01765 658485
E-mail: lmh.smith@magiclanternsocy.demon.co.uk
Website: www.magiclantern.org.uk

Enquiries to: Honorary Secretary

Founded: 1976

Organisation type and purpose: Learned society (membership is by subscription), present number of members: 400.

Subject coverage: All aspects of pre-cinema optical entertainment.

Publications: Printed

Publications list: Available in print

Access to staff: Contact by letter, by telephone, by fax, by e-mail and via website
Hours: Mon to Fri, 0900 to 1700

MAGISTRATES' ASSOCIATION (MA)

28 Fitzroy Square, London, W1T 6DD

Tel: 020 7387 2353
Fax: 020 7383 4020
E-mail: communications@magistrates-association.org.uk
Website: www.magistrates-association.org.uk

Enquiries to: Communications Director (for media and public relation enquiries, information enquiries)
Direct e-mail: information@magistrates-association.org.uk

Founded: 1920

Organisation type and purpose: Membership association.
To advise and represent magistrates in England and Wales.

Subject coverage: All matters of relevance to the lay magistracy.

Collection: A small library of law books relating to magistrates' courts and the magistracy

continued overleaf

Library catalogue: All or part available in-house

Publications: Printed

Access to staff: Contact by letter, by telephone, by fax, by e-mail, in person and via website. Appointment necessary. Access for members only.
Hours: Mon to Fri, 0915 to 1700

Access to building: Prior appointment required
Hours: Mon to Fri, 0930 to 1700

Access for disabled people: Very limited – toilets accessible only via stairs

MAHARISHI FOUNDATION

Beacon House, Willow Walk, Woodley Park, Skelmersdale, Lancashire, WN8 6UR

Tel: 01695 728847
E-mail: reception@maharishi-european-sidhaland.org.uk
Website: www.maharishi.co.uk

Enquiries to: Administrator
Direct tel: 020 7937 3353
Direct fax: 020 7376 9625

Founded: 1975

Organisation type and purpose: Registered charity (charity number 270157).
Educational charity.
To advance the education of the public by establishing, conducting and maintaining an institution of higher education; and by offering such courses of instruction to the public as will promote the mental and creative development of the individual.

Subject coverage: Transcendental meditation, Maharishi's Vedic Science, Maharishi's Vedic approach to health, Maharishi's integrated system of education, Maharishi Ayur Veda, Maharishi Jyotish, Maharishi Sthapatya Ved, Maharishi Gandharva Ved.

Order printed publications from: Maharishi Ayur-Veda Products, FREEPOST 5128, Skelmersdale, Lancashire, WN8 6BR, tel: 01695 51015, fax: 01695 50517

Publications list: Available online and in print

Access to staff: Contact by letter, by telephone, by fax, by e-mail and via website
Hours: Mon to Fri, 1000 to 1700

Affiliated to: Maharishi University of Natural Law; at the same address

National Enquiry Office: Beacon House; Woodley Park, Skelmersdale, Lancashire, WN8 6UR; tel: 01695 51213

MAIDENHEAD LIBRARY

St Ives Road, Maidenhead, Berkshire, SL6 1QU

Tel: 01628 796969
Fax: 01628 796971
E-mail: via website
Website: www.rbwm.gov.uk

Enquiries to: Librarian

Organisation type and purpose: Local government body, registered charity, public library.

Library catalogue: All or part available online

Access to staff: Contact by letter, by telephone, by fax, by e-mail, in person and via website
Hours: Mon and Wed, 0930 to 1700; Tue and Thu, 0930 to 2000; Fri, 0930 to 1900; Sat, 0930 to 1600

Access for disabled people: Ramped entry, access to all public areas, toilet facilities
Special comments: Parking opposite in the road, unreserved.

Parent body: Royal Borough of Windsor and Maidenhead

MAIDSTONE & TUNBRIDGE WELLS NHS TRUST (MTW)

The Library, Tunbridge Wells Hospital, Tonbridge Road, Pembury, Kent, TN2 4QJ

Tel: 01892 635884; 635489
Fax: 01892 634841
E-mail: gm.e.mtw-tr.library@nhs.net
Website: www.mtwlibrary.nhs.uk
Website: www.southeastlibrarysearch.nhs.uk

Founded: 1974

Organisation type and purpose: Education (NHS).

Subject coverage: General surgery, otolaryngology, general practice, general medicine, trauma and orthopaedics, maternity.

Non-library collection catalogue: All or part available online

Library catalogue: All or part available online

Access to staff: Contact by telephone, by e-mail and in person. Non-members charged.
Hours: Mon to Thu 0830 to 1930, Fri 0830 to 1700

Access for disabled people: Level entry, access to all public areas, toilet facilities

Member of: Health Libraries Network

MAIDSTONE BOROUGH COUNCIL

Maidstone House, King Street, Maidstone, Kent, ME15 6JQ

Tel: 01622 602000
Fax: 01622 692246
E-mail: customercare@maidstone.gov.uk
Website: www.maidstone.gov.uk

Enquiries to: Chief Executive

Founded: 1974

Organisation type and purpose: Local government body.

Subject coverage: Local government services.

Publications list: Available online and in print

Access to staff: Contact by letter, by telephone, by fax, by e-mail, in person and via website
Hours: Mon to Thu, 0830 to 1700; Fri, 0830 to 1630

Access for disabled people: Parking provided, level entry, toilet facilities

MAKING MUSIC (NFMS)

Formal name: National Federation of Music Societies

2–4 Great Eastern Street, London, EC2A 3NW

Tel: 020 7422 8280
Fax: 020 7422 8299
E-mail: info@makingmusic.org.uk
Website: www.makingmusic.org.uk

Enquiries to: Communications Manager
Direct e-mail: sarah.robinson@makingmusic.org.uk

Founded: 1935

Organisation type and purpose: Membership association (membership is by subscription), present number of members: 2,650, registered charity (charity number 249219), training organisation, research organisation.
Making Music provides members with services and information to aid them in their voluntary activities.

Subject coverage: Forming and running amateur music groups in the voluntary sector e.g. choirs, orchestras, music clubs, steel bands, jazz groups, classical Indian etc.

Non-library collection catalogue: All or part available online and in print

Publications: Printed, and electronic and video

Access to staff: Contact by letter, by telephone, by fax, by e-mail and via website
Hours: Mon to Fri, 1000 to 1800

Affiliated to: Association of British Orchestras; Incorporated Society of Musicians; Music Education Council (MEC); National Campaign for the Arts; National Music Council of Great Britain; Voluntary Arts Network; World Federation of Amateur Orchestras

MALACOLOGICAL SOCIETY OF LONDON (The Malsoc)

Central Science Laboratory, Sand Hutton, York YO10 4JW

Tel: 01904 462349
E-mail: vasiliki@flari.fsnet.co.uk
Website: www.malacsoc.org.uk/index.html

Enquiries to: Honorary Secretary

Founded: 1893

Organisation type and purpose: Learned society.

Subject coverage: Molluscan biology, applied malacology, zoology, marine biology, snail culture, slugs and snails in agriculture, ecology, biochemistry, parasitology.

Publications: Printed
Order printed publications from: Oxford University Press
Great Clarendon Street, Oxford, OX2 6DP, tel: 01865 267907, e-mail: jnlorders@oup.co.uk

Access to staff: Contact by letter, by fax and by e-mail
Hours: Mon to Fri, 0900 to 1700

MALAYSIAN INDUSTRIAL DEVELOPMENT AUTHORITY (MIDA)

17 Curzon Street, London, W1J 5HR

Tel: 020 7493 0616
Fax: 020 7493 8804
E-mail: midalon@btconnect.com
Website: www.mida.gov.my

Enquiries to: Director

Founded: 1967

Organisation type and purpose: National government body.
Malaysian Government body.
Promotes inward investment into Malaysia's manufacturing sector.

Subject coverage: Investment opportunities in Malaysia's manufacturing sector.

Publications: Printed

Publications list: Available in print

Access to staff: Contact by letter, by telephone, by fax, by e-mail and in person
Hours: Mon to Fri, 0900 to 1700

Headquarters: Malaysian Industrial Development Authority (MIDA); Plaza Sentral, Jalan Stesen Sentral 5, KL Sentral, 50470 Kuala Lumpur, Malaysia; tel: +60 3 2267 3633; fax: +60 3 2274 7970; e-mail: promotion@mida.gov.my

MALONE SOCIETY

c/o Dr C. Richardson, School of English, University of Kent, Canterbury, CT2 7NX

Tel: 01227 824656
E-mail: c.t.richardson@kent.ac.uk
Website: ies.sas.ac.uk/malone/index.htm

Enquiries to: Orders Secretary

Founded: 1906

Organisation type and purpose: International organisation, learned society (membership is by subscription), present number of members: 650, registered charity (charity number 1027048).
To make accessible materials for the study of English drama up to 1642 by editing and publishing dramatic texts and related documents.

Subject coverage: English drama up to 1642.

Publications: Printed
Order printed publications from: Orders Secretary, at the same address

Publications list: Available online

Access to staff: Contact by letter, by telephone and by e-mail
Hours: Mon to Fri, 0900 to 1700

Access to building: No access other than to staff

MALTA TOURIST OFFICE

Malta House, 36–38 Piccadilly, London, W1J 0LD

Tel: 020 7292 4900
Fax: 020 7734 1880
E-mail: office.uk@visitmalta.com
Website: www.visitmalta.com

Enquiries to: Director
Direct e-mail: john.montague@visitmalta.com

Organisation type and purpose: National government body.
Tourist office.

Subject coverage: General tourist information.

Trade and statistical information: Number of tourists to Malta.
Percentage of countries visiting Malta

Library catalogue: All or part available in-house

Publications: Printed, and electronic and video

Access to staff: Contact by letter, by telephone, by fax, by e-mail, in person and via website. Appointment necessary.
Hours: Mon to Fri, 0900 to 1700

Access for disabled people: Level entry

Parent body: Malta Tourism Authority; Merchants Str, Valletta, Malta; tel: 00 356 2122 4444; fax: 00 356 2122 0401; e-mail: info@visitmalta.com

MALTSTERS ASSOCIATION OF GREAT BRITAIN (MAGB)

31B Castlegate, Newark, Nottinghamshire, NG24 1AZ

Tel: 01636 700781
Fax: 01636 701836
E-mail: info@magb.org.uk
Website: www.malt.info.com
Website: www.ukmalt.com

Enquiries to: Executive Director

Founded: 1827

Organisation type and purpose: Trade association.

Subject coverage: Malting.

Access to staff: Contact by letter, by telephone and by fax
Hours: Mon to Fri, 0900 to 1700

MALVERN LIBRARY

Graham Road, Malvern, Worcestershire, WR14 2HU

Tel: 01905 822722
Fax: 01684 892999
E-mail: malvernlib@worcestershire.gov.uk
Website: www.worcestershire.gov.uk

Founded: 1905

Organisation type and purpose: Local government body, public library.

Subject coverage: General, local history of Malvern.

Collection: Local Studies Collection, including a substantial collection of illustrations

Non-library collection catalogue: All or part available in-house

Library catalogue: All or part available online

Access to staff: Contact by letter, by telephone, by fax, by e-mail and in person. Appointment necessary.
Hours: Mon, Fri, 0900 to 1730; Tue to Thu, 0900 to 2000; Sat, 0900 to 1730; Sun, closed

Access to building: No prior appointment required
Special comments: Closed on bank holidays, Good Friday and over Christmas.

Access for disabled people: Parking provided, ramped entry

Constituent part of: Worcestershire County Council; County Hall, Spetchley Road, Worcester, WR5 2NP; tel: 01905 763763; fax: 01905 766244; e-mail: kkirk@worcestershire.gov.uk

MAMMAL SOCIETY

3 The Carronades, New Road, Southampton, SO14 0AA

Tel: 023 8023 7874
Fax: 023 8063 4726
E-mail: enquiries@mammal.org.uk
Website: www.mammal.org.uk

Enquiries to: Office Manager

Founded: 1954

Organisation type and purpose: Membership association (membership is by subscription), present number of members: 2,000, voluntary organisation, registered charity (charity number 278918).
To protect British mammals, halt the decline of threatened species and advise on all issues affecting British mammals.

Subject coverage: British mammals, their biology, conservation, ecology, management, distribution and status, and methods of study.

Publications: Printed

Publications list: Available online

Access to staff: Contact by letter, by telephone, by fax, by e-mail and via website
Hours: Mon to Fri, 0900 to 1700

Access to building: No access other than to staff

Member organisation of: IUCN

MAN B&W DIESEL LIMITED, PAXMAN

Paxman Works, PO Box 8, Colchester, Essex, CO1 2HW

Tel: 01206 795151
Fax: 01206 797869
E-mail: info@man-mn.com

Enquiries to: Information Officer
Direct tel: 01206 875508
Direct e-mail: mike.johnson@alstom.ind.com

Founded: 1865

Organisation type and purpose: Trade association.

Subject coverage: General engineering, diesel engines, design and manufacture.

Library catalogue: All or part available in-house

continued overleaf

Access to staff: Contact by letter, by telephone, by fax and by e-mail. Appointment necessary. Letter of introduction required.
Hours: Mon to Thu, 0900 to 1700; Fri, 0900 to 1600

MANAGEMENT CONSULTANCIES ASSOCIATION (MCA)

49 Whitehall, London, SW1A 2BX

Tel: 020 7321 3990
Fax: 020 7321 3991
E-mail: mca@mca.org.uk
Website: www.mca.org.uk

Enquiries to: Deputy Director
Direct tel: 020 7321 3993
Direct e-mail: lydia.waliszak@mca.org.uk

Founded: 1956

Organisation type and purpose: Trade association (membership is by qualification), present number of members: 39.

Subject coverage: Management consulting, selection of management consultants, statistics relating to members' earnings, career guidance, case studies, journal and reports on management issues.

Trade and statistical information: Members' earnings broken down by type or consultancy work performed and industry

Publications: Printed

Access to staff: Contact by letter, by telephone, by fax, by e-mail and via website. Appointment necessary.
Hours: Mon to Fri, 0900 to 1700

Access to building: Prior appointment required

Member of: Federation of European Management Consultancies Associations; 3/4/5 Avenue des Arts, Brussels, B-1210, Belgium; tel: +32 2 250 0650; fax: +32 2 250 0651; e-mail: feaco@feaco.org

MANCHESTER AND LANCASHIRE FAMILY HISTORY SOCIETY (M&LFHS)

Clayton House, 59 Piccadilly, Manchester, M1 2AQ

Tel: 0161 236 9750
Fax: 0161 237 3812
E-mail: office@mlfhs.org.uk
Website: www.mlfhs.org.uk

Enquiries to: General Secretary

Founded: 1964

Organisation type and purpose: Membership association (membership is by subscription), present number of members: 3,200, registered charity (charity number 515599).

Subject coverage: Genealogy, heraldry and local history.

Library catalogue: All or part available in-house

Publications: Printed, and electronic and video, and microform publications

Publications list: Available online and in print

Access to staff: Contact by letter, by telephone, by fax, by e-mail, in person and via website
Hours: Mon, Fri, 1015 to 1300; Tue, Thu, 1015 to 1600

Branches: Anglo Scottish Branch; Bolton & District Branch; Irish Ancestry Branch; Oldham & District Branch

MANCHESTER ARTS LIBRARY

Central Library, St Peter's Square, Manchester, M2 5PD

Tel: 0161 234 1974
Fax: 0161 234 1961
E-mail: arts@libraries.manchester.gov.uk
Website: www.manchester.gov.uk/libraries

Enquiries to: Arts Coordinator

Founded: 1852

Organisation type and purpose: Local government body, public library.

Subject coverage: Art and design in general, costume and fashion, town planning, architecture, decorative arts, antiques, interiors, textiles, ceramics, sculpture, drawing and painting, graphics, photography, cinema, radio and TV, theatre, dance, sport and recreation.

Collection: 18th- and 19th-century sales catalogues
Local Theatre Material Collection (estimated 30,000 items, from mid-18th century to present day)
News Chronicle Photograph Collection (52 boxes, mainly 1940–60 costume accessories)
Many important 19th-century periodicals.
Videos and DVDs of classic films.

Access to staff: Contact by letter, by telephone, by fax, by e-mail, in person and via website
Hours: Mon to Thu, 1000 to 2000; Fri, Sat, 1000 to 1700

Access for disabled people: Ramped entry, lift, toilet facilities
Special comments: Limited parking; access to most areas; staff will assist with access to lifts etc as required.

MANCHESTER BUSINESS SCHOOL (MBS)

Booth Street West, Manchester, M15 6PB

Tel: 0161 275 6507
Fax: 0161 275 6505
E-mail: directorsteam@mbs.ac.uk
Website: www.mbs.ac.uk

Enquiries to: Information and Services Manager
Direct tel: 0161 275 6499
Other contacts: Head of Business Information Service for an information brokerage to companies on a fee-paying basis.

Founded: 1965

Organisation type and purpose: University department or institute.

Subject coverage: Management science and education, marketing, production, finance, personnel management, economics, operations research, accounting, computing, statistics, business and companies information, market data.

Collection: Business and management journals, both printed and electronic
20,000 books

Trade and statistical information: Collection of UK and other official statistics – OECD, European Union, UN, ILO.
Also various trade association statutes

Publications: Printed

Access to staff: Contact by letter, by telephone, by fax and by e-mail. Non-members charged.
Hours: Term time: Mon to Fri, 0830 to 2030; Sat, 0930 to 1700
Vacations: Mon to Fri, 1000 to 1700
Special comments: The library is open to members of MBS and postgraduates and staff of other Manchester Universities. Researchers from other universities may use the library for reference purposes, by arrangement. All other users are charged an access fee.

Faculty of: Business Administration, University of Manchester, but separately funded

Member of: Manchester Federal School of Business and Management

MANCHESTER CENTRAL LIBRARY

St Peter's Square, Manchester, M2 5PD

Tel: 0161 234 1900, 0161 234 1984 (minicom)
Fax: 0161 234 1963

Organisation type and purpose: Public library.

MANCHESTER CENTRAL LIBRARY – SOCIAL SCIENCES LIBRARY

St Peter's Square, Manchester, M2 5PD

Tel: 0161 234 1983, 0161 234 1983/4 (minicom)
Fax: 0161 234 1927
E-mail: socsci@libraries.manchester.gov.uk
Website: www.manchester.gov.uk/libraries

Enquiries to: Librarian

Founded: 1852

Organisation type and purpose: Public library.

Subject coverage: Bibliography, philosophy, religion, social sciences, home economics, archaeology, geography, history, biography within subject areas indicated.

Collection: 18th- and 19th-century pamphlets
National newspapers (on microfilm)
Parish registers and related genealogical material
Parliamentary papers
Private press books

Access to staff: Contact by letter, by telephone, by fax, by e-mail, in person and via website
Hours: Mon to Thu, 1000 to 2000; Fri and Sat, 1000 to 1700

Access for disabled people: Ramped entry

MANCHESTER CENTRE FOR REGIONAL HISTORY (MCRH)

Department of History and Economic History, Manchester Metropolitan University, Room 103, Geoffrey Manton Building, Rosamond Street West, Manchester, M15 6LL

Tel: 0161 247 6491
E-mail: c.horner@mmu.ac.uk
Website: www.mcrh.mmu.ac.uk

Founded: 1998

Organisation type and purpose: Research centre of Manchester Metropolitan University.

Subject coverage: History of Manchester and the northwest of England.

Publications: Printed

MANCHESTER CITY GALLERIES

Mosley Street, Manchester, M2 3JL

Tel: 0161 235 8888, 0161 235 8893 (minicom)
Fax: 0161 235 8899
E-mail: k.cope@manchester.gov.uk
Website: www.cityartgalleries.org.uk

Enquiries to: Administration

Founded: 1882

Organisation type and purpose: Local government body, art gallery, historic building, house or site, suitable for ages: all. Administrative body for the Manchester City Art Galleries and Museums.

Subject coverage: Fine and decorative art from antiquity to present day; costume, picture, decorative art, and costume restoration.

Special visitor services: Guided tours, tape recorded guides, materials and/or activities for children.

Education services: Group education facilities, resources for Key Stages 1, 2, 3 and 4 and Further or Higher Education.

Collection: 20th-century British paintings
Assheton-Bennett Collection of English silver and 17th-century Dutch paintings
Old Masters
Pre-Raphaelites
Thomas Greg Collection of English pottery

Non-library collection catalogue: All or part available online, in-house and in print

Publications: Printed

Access to staff: Contact by letter, by telephone and via website. Appointment necessary.
Hours: Mon to Fri, 0900 to 1700

Galleries and historic houses: Gallery of Costume; Platt Hall, Wilmslow Road, Rusholme, Manchester, M14 5LL; tel: 0161 224 5217; fax: 0161 256 3278; Heaton Hall; Heaton Park, Prestwich, Manchester, M25 5SW; tel: 0161 773 1231; Manchester Art Gallery; Mosley Street, Manchester, M2 3JL; tel: 0161 235 8888; fax: 0161 235 8899; Queen's Park Conservation Studio; Queen's Park, Rochdale Road, Harpurhey, Manchester, M9 5SH; tel: 0161 205 2645; fax: 0161 205 6164; Wythenshawe Hall; Wythenshaw Park, Northenden, Manchester, M23 0AB; tel: 0161 998 2331

Parent body: Manchester City Council; website: www.manchester.gov.uk

MANCHESTER GEOGRAPHICAL SOCIETY (MGS)

Meadowbank, Ringley Road, Radcliffe, Manchester, M26 1FW

Tel: 0161 723 1433
E-mail: paulhindle@talktalk.net
Website: www.mangeogsoc.org.uk

Enquiries to: Honorary Secretary

Founded: 1884

Organisation type and purpose: Learned society, registered charity (charity number 1134626), runs lecture series, research organisation, publishing house.
To encourage the study of geography at all levels.

Subject coverage: Geography.

Collection: Library – held by John Rylands University Library of Manchester

Library catalogue: All or part available online and in print

Publications: Printed, and electronic and video
Order electronic and video publications from: website: http://www.mangeogsoc.org.uk/nwgeog.htm

Publications list: Available online

Access to staff: Contact by letter, by telephone, by e-mail and via website

MANCHESTER LANGUAGE AND LITERATURE LIBRARY

Central Library, St Peter's Square, Manchester, M2 5PD

Tel: 0161 234 1972
Fax: 0161 234 1963
E-mail: lang_lit@libraries.manchester.gov.uk
Website: www.manchester.gov.uk/libraries/central/langlit/index.htm

Enquiries to: Librarian

Founded: 1852

Organisation type and purpose: Local government body, public library.

Subject coverage: Language; literature; folklore.

Collection: Alexander Ireland Collection (works by or relating to Charles and Mary Lamb, William Hazlitt, Leigh Hunt, Thomas and Jane Carlyle, Ralph W Emerson)
Bellot Chinese Collection
Brontë Collection
Coleridge Collection
de Quincey Collection
Elizabeth Gaskell Collection
Foreign library (lending collection of literature in 28 languages)
Index of local translators
James L Hodson Collection
Language courses on tape for loan (72 languages)
Literature and criticism on cassette
Manchester Ballad and Chapbook Collections
Videos of literary interest

Non-library collection catalogue: All or part available in-house

Access to staff: Contact by letter, by telephone, by fax, by e-mail and in person
Hours: Mon to Thu, 0900 to 2000; Fri, 0900 to 1700; Sat, 0900 to 1700

MANCHESTER LAW LIBRARY (MILLS)

Formal name: Manchester Incorporated Law Library Society

14 Kennedy Street, Manchester, M2 4BY

Tel: 0161 236 6312
Fax: 0161 236 6119
E-mail: librarian@manchester-law-library.co.uk
Website: www.manchester-law-library.co.uk

Enquiries to: Librarian

Founded: 1820

Organisation type and purpose: Membership association.
Subscription Library for practising barristers, solicitors and in-house lawyers.

Subject coverage: All aspects of law likely to be of interest to practising lawyers.

Collection: nominate reports and local and personal acts from 1837

Library catalogue: All or part available in-house

Access to staff: Contact by letter, by telephone, by fax, by e-mail and in person. Access for members only. All charged.

Access to building: *Hours:* Mon to Fri, 0900 to 1700
Special comments: members only

MANCHESTER METROPOLITAN UNIVERSITY – DEPARTMENT OF INFORMATION AND COMMUNICATIONS

Geoffrey Manton Building, Rosamond Street West, off Oxford Road, Manchester, M15 6LL

Fax: 0161 247 6351
E-mail: infocomms-hums@mmu.ac.uk
Website: www.hlss.mmu.ac.uk/infocomms/

Enquiries to: Executive assistant, HLSS

Organisation type and purpose: University department or institute.

Subject coverage: Library and information education and research.

Access to staff: Contact by letter, by telephone, by fax, by e-mail and via website. Appointment necessary.
Hours: Mon to Fri, 0900 to 1700

Access for disabled people: Parking provided, level entry, access to all public areas, toilet facilities

MANCHESTER METROPOLITAN UNIVERSITY – UNIVERSITY LIBRARY

All Saints Building, Grosvenor Square, Oxford Road, Manchester, M15 6BH

Tel: 0161 247 3096
Fax: 0161 247 6349
E-mail: lib-website@mmu.ac.uk

continued overleaf

Website: www.mmu.ac.uk/services/library
Enquiries to: Librarian
Direct e-mail: c.harris@mmu.ac.uk

Founded: 1992

Organisation type and purpose: University library.

Subject coverage: Art and design; business studies; clothing technology; education; finance and accounting; health sciences; home economics; hotel and catering studies; humanities; languages; law; librarianship; management; media studies; music; psychology; science; social sciences; speech pathology; sports science and technology.

Collection: Artists Archives, including Barnet Freedman, Rigby Graham, Paul Hogarth
Book Design Collection (12,000 items including 1,000 artists' books)
Children's Book Collection (3,000 items, 19th- and 20th-century books and periodicals)
Cotton Collection (history of 20th-century cotton trade)
Historical collection of books on cookery and household management from the 17th to mid-20th century
Laura Seddon Collection of Victorian and Edwardian greeting cards
Local Studies (3,000 items)
Manchester Society of Architects' Library (books on 18th- and 19th-century architecture)
Morten-Dandy Collection (19th-century children's fiction, textbooks, readers and picture books)
Nonesuch Press (250 items)
Sir Harry Page Collection of Victorian Ephemera

Library catalogue: All or part available online

Publications: Printed

Access to staff: Contact by letter, by e-mail and via website. Appointment necessary.
Hours: Mon to Fri, 0900 to 1630

MANCHESTER ROOM@CITY LIBRARY (MALS)

The Manchester Room@City Library, Elliot House, 151 Deansgate, Manchester, M3 3WD

Tel: 0161 234 1979
E-mail: contact@manchester.gov.uk
Website: www.manchester.gov.uk/libraries/arls
Website: www.images.manchester.gov.uk

Enquiries to: Archives & Local Studies Officer
Direct tel: 0161 234 1960
Direct e-mail: r.bond@manchester.gov.uk

Founded: 1991

Organisation type and purpose: Local government body, public library.
Local studies service for City of Manchester.

Subject coverage: Political, economic, religious, educational and historical development of Manchester and the region.

Collection: Print Collection (approx. 145,000 items, prints, photographs, postcards, etc.) of which 77,000 available in digital form
Microform collections:
Census Returns (Manchester 1841–1901)
Directories of Manchester, 1772–1969
Local Newspapers from early 18th century
Parish Registers (large collection, Manchester, Cheshire and Lancashire)

Non-library collection catalogue: All or part available online, in-house and in print

Library catalogue: All or part available online and in-house

Publications: Printed, and microform publications

Access to staff: Contact by letter, by telephone, by fax, by e-mail, in person and via website
Hours: Mon to Thu, 0900 to 2000; Fri and Sat, 0900 to 1700

Access for disabled people: Disabled entrance on Jacksons Row; lift available.

Parent body: Manchester City Council; Town Hall, Manchester, M60 2LA; tel: 0161 234 5000; website: http://www.manchester.gov.uk

MANIPULATION ASSOCIATION OF CHARTERED PHYSIOTHERAPISTS (MACP)

Chartered Society of Physiotherapy, 14 Bedford Row, London, WC1R 4ED

Tel: 01202 706161
E-mail: admin@macpweb.org
Website: www.macpweb.org

Enquiries to: Administrator

Founded: 1967

Organisation type and purpose: Professional body (membership is by qualification), present number of members: 1,100, training organisation.
To maintain and further develop clinical excellence in neuro-musculoskeletal physiotherapy which will be of benefit to the current and future needs of both the profession and the general public.

Subject coverage: Physiotherapy, manual therapy, manipulation, neuro-musculoskeletal physiotherapy.

Publications: Printed
Order printed publications from: Manual Therapy, Churchill Livingstone Marketing, Robert Stevenson House, 1–3 Baxter's Place, Leith Walk, Edinburgh, EH1 3AF; tel: 0800 801 405

Publications list: Available online

Access to staff: Contact by letter, by telephone, by e-mail and via website
Hours: Mon to Fri, 0900 to 1700

Constituent part of: Chartered Society of Physiotherapy; 14 Bedford Row, London, WC1R 4ED; tel: 020 7366 6666; fax: 020 7306 6611

MANORIAL SOCIETY OF GREAT BRITAIN (MSGB)

104 Kennington Road, London, SE11 6RE

Tel: 020 7735 6633
Fax: 020 7582 7022
E-mail: manorial@msgb.co.uk
Website: www.msgb.co.uk

Enquiries to: Chairman
Direct tel: 020 7582 1588

Founded: 1906

Organisation type and purpose: International organisation, learned society (membership is by election or invitation), research organisation, publishing house.

Subject coverage: Holders and addresses of feudal titles; legal research into titles; holders and addresses of British peerage and baronetage; publishers; conference and exhibitions (all historical) organisers. Sale price of titles sold ranges from £5,000 to £30,000: 80% UK, most of Europe and US.

Collection: Historical, topographical and genealogical library
Paper file on 4,500 manors and feudal baronies. Not available to general public

Publications: Printed, and electronic and video

Publications list: Available in print

Access to staff: Contact by letter, by telephone, by fax and by e-mail. Appointment necessary.
Hours: Mon to Fri, 1000 to 1700
Special comments: No members of the public, except by appointment.

Access to building: Prior appointment required

Access for disabled people: No disabled access

Affiliated to: English Manor Register Ltd; As above; tel: 020 7735 6633; fax: 020 7582 1588; Institute of Constitutional research; As above; tel: 020 7735 6633; fax: 020 7582 1588; Manorial Auctioneers Limited; As above; tel: 020 7582 1588; fax: 020 7582 7022; e-mail: manorial@msgb.co.uk; Smith's Peerage Limited; tel: 020 7735 6633; fax: 020 7582 7022; e-mail: manorial@msgb.co.uk

MANUFACTURING TECHNOLOGIES ASSOCIATION (MTA)

62 Bayswater Road, London, W2 3PS

Tel: 020 7298 6413
E-mail: rorgill@mta.org.uk
Website: www.mta.org.uk

Enquiries to: Marketing Manager
Direct e-mail: bromige@mtta.co.uk

Founded: 1919

Organisation type and purpose: Trade association.
Representing metal-cutting and metal-forming manufacturers.

Subject coverage: Information supplied on: statistics, education and training, technical assistance, i.e. CE marks, standards, public relations, relevant exhibitions in the United Kingdom and abroad, trade missions, distributor and agent information, market sector reports, meetings, presentations, publications, industry representation.

Trade and statistical information: A full range of data on machine tool users and suppliers

Publications: Printed, and electronic and video

Publications list: Available in print

Access to staff: Contact by letter, by telephone, by fax, by e-mail and via website. Non-members charged.
Hours: Mon to Fri, 0900 to 1700

Access to building: No access other than to staff
Special comments: Prior appointment required for access to library

MANX NATIONAL HERITAGE LIBRARY AND ARCHIVE SERVICE

Manx Museum, Douglas, Isle of Man, IM1 3LY

Tel: 01624 648000
Fax: 01624 648001
E-mail: library@mnh.gov.im
Website: www.manxnationalheritage.im/what-we-do/our-collections/library-archives/

Enquiries to: Library & Archive Services Officer
Direct tel: 01624 648040
Direct e-mail: paul.weatherall@gov.im

Founded: 1886

Organisation type and purpose: National Library and Archives of the Isle of Man.

Subject coverage: Isle of Man, Manx Gaelic.

Special visitor services: Film theatre, restaurant, galleries.

Collection: Family papers of the Derby and Atholl families, relating to their Lordship of the Isle of Man
Manx government records, 1417 to the present.

Non-library collection catalogue: All or part available online and in-house

Library catalogue: All or part available online, in-house and in print

Publications: Printed, and electronic and video
Order printed publications from: Website

Publications list: Available online and in print

Access to staff: Contact by letter, by telephone, by fax, by e-mail, in person and via website
Hours: Mon to Sat, 1000 to 1700
Closed last week in January, Christmas day, New Year's Day, Tynwald Day (July 5)

Access to building: *Hours:* Mon to Sat, 1000 to 1700 Closed last week in January, Christmas day, New Year's Day, Tynwald Day (July 5th)

Access for disabled people: Disabled access to all floors
Hours: Mon to Sat, 1000 to 1700 Closed last week in January, Christmas day, New Year's Day, Tynwald Day (July 5)

MAPLE SOCIETY

The Membership Secretary, 12 Rustens Manor Road, Wymondham, Norfolk, NR18 0NH

Enquiries to: Membership Secretary
Other contacts: Chairman for technical information.

Founded: 1991

Organisation type and purpose: International organisation, membership association (membership is by subscription), present number of members: 152.
To dispense information on and facilitate the study of Maples.

Subject coverage: Cultivation and after care, indentification, historical information of Maple species and 'Japanese Maples'.

Publications: Printed

Access to staff: Contact by letter and by telephone

MARENDAZ SPECIAL CAR REGISTER

c/o 107 Old Bath Road, Cheltenham, Gloucestershire, GL53 7DA

Enquiries to: Registrar

Founded: 1971

Organisation type and purpose: Register.

Subject coverage: Marendaz Special cars, technical information, historical data, photographs.

Access to staff: Contact by letter

MARGARINE AND SPREADS ASSOCIATION (MSA)

6 Catherine Street, London, WC2B 5JJ

Tel: 020 7836 2460
Fax: 020 7379 5735
E-mail: jhowarth@fdf.org.uk
Website: www.margarine.org.uk

Enquiries to: Secretary General
Direct tel: 020 7420 7121 (direct)

Founded: 1966

Organisation type and purpose: Trade association (membership is by subscription, qualification, election or invitation), present number of members: nine, manufacturing industry.

Subject coverage: The UK margarine and spread industry, including the history and chemistry of margarine and spreads and how they are manufactured. Nutrition and health information relating to the role played by fats in the diet. Specialist area: all legislation pertaining to food.

Trade and statistical information: Production statistics and value

Publications: Printed

Access to staff: Contact by letter, by telephone, by fax, by e-mail and via website. Appointment necessary.
Hours: Mon to Fri, 0930 to 1730

Links with: International Federation of Margarine Associations (IFMA); International Margarine Association of the countries of Europe (IMACE)

Member of: The Food and Drink Federation

MARGERY KEMPE SOCIETY, THE

1 Auckland Road, London, SW11 1EW

Tel: 020 7924 5868

Enquiries to: Honorary Treasurer

Founded: 1999

Organisation type and purpose: National organisation, learned society (membership is by subscription), present number of members: 15.
To encourage and facilitate study of Margery Kempe, late medieval female piety.

Subject coverage: Margery Kempe.

Publications: Printed

Access to staff: Contact by letter
Hours: Mon to Fri, 0900 to 1700

MARIA MONTESSORI INSITITUTE AMI (MMI)

Formal name: Maria Montessori Training Organisation

26 Lyndhurst Gardens, London, NW3 5NW

Tel: 020 7435 3646
Fax: 020 7431 8096
E-mail: info@mariamontessori.org
Website: www.mariamontessori.org

Founded: 1952

Organisation type and purpose: Registered charity (charity number 313087).
Training adults to work with children using the Montessori approach to education.
Also runs five Montessori schools in London.

Subject coverage: Institute that trains people in the Montessori approach to education, specialising in children under six years old (AMI International Diploma on completion).

Publications: Printed

Access to staff: Contact by letter, by telephone, by fax and by e-mail.
Appointment necessary.
Hours: Mon to Fri, 0900 to 1600

Links with: Association Montessori Internationale (AMI); Koninginneweg 161, 1075 CN Amsterdam, Netherlands; tel: +31 206 798932; fax: +31 206 767341; e-mail: ami@xs4all.nl; website: http://www.montessori-ami.org

MARINE CONSERVATION SOCIETY (MCS)

Unit 3 Wolf Business Park, Alton Road, Ross-on-Wye HR9 5NB

Tel: 01989 566017
Fax: 01989 567815
E-mail: info@mcsuk.org
Website: www.mcsuk.org
Website: www.goodbeachguide.co.uk
Website: www.fishonline.org

Enquiries to: Enquiries Officer

Founded: 1983

Organisation type and purpose: Professional body, membership association (membership is by subscription), registered charity (charity number 1004005).
The UK's national charity for the protection of the marine environment and its wildlife.

Subject coverage: Water quality, coastal zone management, marine debris, fisheries, marine wildlife, toxins in the marine environment, coral reefs.

Collection: Marine environment and marine wildlife photographic library

continued overleaf

Transparencies available for use under licence and fee

Trade and statistical information: Annual Beachwatch Report (sources and quantity of UK beach litter).
Good Beach Guide (recommended UK beaches where bathing water quality is considered safe to use),
Good Fish Guide

Library catalogue: All or part available in-house

Publications: Printed

Publications list: Available online

Access to staff: Contact by letter, by telephone, by fax, by e-mail and via website
Hours: Mon to Fri, 0900 to 1700

Access to building: No prior appointment required
Special comments: Members only

Also at: Marine Conservation Society; 11A Chester Street, Edinburgh, EH3 7RF; tel: 0131 226 6360; fax: 0131 226 2391; e-mail: scotland@mcsuk.org

MARINE ENGINE AND EQUIPMENT MANUFACTURERS ASSOCIATION (MEEMA)

56 Braycourt Avenue, Walton-on-Thames, Surrey, KT12 2BA

Tel: 01932 224910
Fax: 01932 224910
E-mail: bcbaali@aol.com
Website: www.bmif.co.uk

Enquiries to: Secretary

Founded: 1960

Organisation type and purpose: Trade association, present number of members: 75.

Subject coverage: For UK companies within the British Marine Industries Federation who have a common interest in the manufacture or distribution and retail sales of marine engines and related equipment, including personal watercraft.

Access to staff: Contact by letter, by telephone, by fax and by e-mail
Hours: Mon to Fri, 0900 to 1700

Affiliated to: British Marine Industries Federation; tel: 01784 473377; fax: 01784 439678; e-mail: bmif@bmif.co.uk

MARINE LEISURE ASSOCIATION (MLA)

General Secretary, Marine Leisure Association, Burrwood, 24 Peterscroft Avenue, Southampton, SO40 7AB

Tel: 023 8029 3822
Fax: 023 8029 3888
E-mail: info@marineleisure.co.uk
Website: www.marineleisure.co.uk

Enquiries to: General Secretary

Founded: 1964; formerly called Association of Bonded Sailing Companies, National Federation of Sea Schools, Yacht Charter Assocation (year of change 2005)

Organisation type and purpose: Trade association for training, charter and holidays.
Formed to offer the general public better protection, guidance and advice. A Group Association within the BMF (British Marine Federation), representing MLA Members' views within the BMF Council. All members are expected to abide by both the MLA Code of Conduct and the BMF Code of Practice. Has representation on various National Committees to safeguard interests of Members and the general public.

Subject coverage: Marine leisure industry.

Trade and statistical information: Statistics on the marine leisure industry including participation, economic benefits, labour market assessment, tourism and industry assessment

Publications: Printed

Access to staff: Contact by letter, by telephone, by fax, by e-mail and via website. Appointment necessary.
Hours: Mon to Fri, 0900 to 1700

Parent body: British Marine Federation (BMF); tel: 01784 473377; fax: 01784 439678; e-mail: info@britishmarine.co.uk; website: http://www.britishmarine.co.uk

MARINE SOCIETY, THE

202 Lambeth Road, London, SE1 7JW

Tel: 020 7261 9535
Fax: 020 7401 2537
E-mail: enq@marine-society.org
Website: www.marine-society.org

Enquiries to: Director

Founded: 1756

Organisation type and purpose: Voluntary organisation, registered charity (charity number 313013), training organisation. Education, training and welfare of seafarers.

Subject coverage: Merchant Navy, Royal Navy, careers at sea, seafaring.

Collection: All above records held at National Maritime Museum
British Ship Adoption Society (from 1936)
Incorporated Thames Nautical Training College (from 1862)
Marine Society Records (from 1756)
Seafarers Education Service (from 1919)

Publications: Printed

Access to staff: Contact by letter, by telephone, by fax, by e-mail, in person and via website
Hours: Mon to Fri, 0900 to 1700

Access to building: Prior appointment required

Access for disabled people: Parking provided, ramped entry

MARITIME AND COASTGUARD AGENCY (MCA)

Spring Place, 105 Commercial Road, Southampton, SO15 1EG

Tel: 023 8032 9100; 0870 600 6505 (infoline)
Fax: 023 8032 9122
E-mail: infoline@mcga.gov.uk
Website: www.mcga.gov.uk

Enquiries to: Publications Manager
Direct tel: 023 8032 9401
Direct e-mail: mca_mic@mcga.gov.uk

Founded: 1998

Organisation type and purpose: National Government Agency.

Subject coverage: Civil maritime search and rescue, maritime safety, major oil spillages and other hazardous substances at sea from ships, civil maritime emergencies, safety advice and assistance to local authorities, and port and harbour authorities, merchant shipping, carriage by sea of dangerous goods, hovercraft and high-speed craft legislation, safety of navigation and related topics, ownership of items found in or on the shores of the sea or any tidal water.

Trade and statistical information: National and international fleet and accident statistics

Publications: Printed

Access to staff: Contact by letter, by telephone, by fax, by e-mail and via website. Appointment necessary.
Hours: Mon to Fri, 0900 to 1700

Access for disabled people: Level entry, toilet facilities

Executive Agency of: Department of Transport

Other addresses: Branches throughout the UK

MARITIME INFORMATION ASSOCIATION (MIA)

The Marine Society, 202 Lambeth Road, London, SE1 7JW

Website: www.maritime-information.org

Enquiries to: Honorary Secretary

Founded: 1977

Organisation type and purpose: Professional body (membership is by subscription).
Forum for those active in maritime information, with regular visits, an annual conference and opportunities to network.

Subject coverage: Marine technology; shipping; shipbuilding; marine engineering and telecommunications; maritime law and economics; maritime history; ports; cargo handling; fisheries; offshore activities (not marine biology or life sciences).

Publications: Printed

Access to staff: Contact by fax

MARKET RESEARCH SOCIETY (MRS)

15 Northburgh Street, London, EC1V 0JR

Tel: 020 7490 4911
Fax: 020 7490 0608
E-mail: info@mrs.org.uk
Website: www.mrs.org.uk

Founded: 1946

Organisation type and purpose: Professional body.

Subject coverage: Methodology of market research; market research industry.

Non-library collection catalogue: All or part available online and in-house

Library catalogue: All or part available online and in-house

Publications: Printed, and electronic and video
Order electronic and video publications from: http://www.rbg.org.uk

Publications list: Available online

Access to staff: Contact by letter, by telephone, by fax, by e-mail and via website. Access for members only.
Hours: Mon to Fri, 1000 to 1700

MARKETING GUILD, THE

Regency House, Westminster Place, York Business Park, York, YO26 6RW

Tel: 01904 520820
Fax: 01904 520899
E-mail: help@marketing-guild.com
Website: www.marketing-guild.com

Enquiries to: Managing Director

Founded: 1986

Organisation type and purpose: Professional body (membership is by subscription), present number of members: 1400, service industry.
Marketing ideas and support for professional and service businesses.

Subject coverage: Marketing and sales information, ideas and strategies.

Publications: Printed, and electronic and video

Publications list: Available online and in print

Access to staff: Contact by letter, by telephone and by e-mail. Non-members charged.
Hours: Mon to Fri, 0900 to 1700

Connected with and at the same address as the: Internet Marketing Guild

MARKS AND CLERK

Sussex House, 83–85 Mosley Street, Manchester, M2 3LG

Tel: 0161 236 2275
Fax: 0161 236 5846
E-mail: manchester@marks-clerk.com
Website: www.marks-clerk.com

Enquiries to: Information Manager
Direct tel: 0161 233 5803

Founded: 1887

Organisation type and purpose: Service industry.
Professional firm of patent and trade mark agents.

Subject coverage: Patents; trade marks; designs; copyright; licensing; intellectual property; technology licensing, litigation.

Access to staff: Contact by letter, by telephone, by fax and by e-mail. Appointment necessary.
Hours: Mon to Fri, 0900 to 1700

MARLOWE SOCIETY

Chairman, 27 Melbourne Court, Randolph Avenue, London, W9 1BJ

E-mail: valerie.colin-russ@marlowe-society.org
Website: www.marlowe-society.org

Enquiries to: Membership Secretary
Other contacts: See website

Founded: 1955

Organisation type and purpose: International organisation, learned society (membership is by subscription), present number of members: 200, registered charity (charity number 1075418).
To promote interest and research into Christopher Marlowe, Elizabethan poet/ dramatist.

Subject coverage: Christopher Marlowe's life and works; his associates; his contribution to the growth of secular drama; life in the Tudor period; contemporary dramatists, particularly those influenced by Marlowe. A memorial in Poets Corner, Westminster Abbey 2002.

Collection: Library – visit by appointment only

Non-library collection catalogue: All or part available online

Library catalogue: All or part available online

Publications: Printed

Publications list: Available online

Access to staff: Contact by letter, by telephone, by fax, by e-mail and via website. Appointment necessary.
Hours: Mon to Fri, 0900 to 1700

MARTIN CENTRE FOR ARCHITECTURAL AND URBAN STUDIES

University of Cambridge, Department of Architecture, 1–5 Scroope Terrace, Cambridge, CB2 1PX

Tel: 01223 760113
E-mail: mc@arct.cam.ac.uk
Website: www.arct.cam.ac.uk

Enquiries to: Martin Centre Secretary
Direct e-mail: mc@arct.cam.ac.uk

Founded: 1967

Organisation type and purpose: University department or institute, research organisation.

Subject coverage: Environmental design, architectural acoustics, energy conservation, Third World planning and construction technology, building in earthquake areas, computer-aided design.

Collection: British New Towns collection

Publications: Printed

Access to staff: Contact by letter, by telephone, by e-mail and via website
Hours: Mon to Fri, 0900 to 1700

Within the: Cambridge University Department of Architecture

MARX MEMORIAL LIBRARY

37A Clerkenwell Green, London, EC1R 0DU

Tel: 020 7253 1485
Fax: 020 7251 6039
E-mail: info@marx-memorial-library.org
Website: www.marx-memorial-library.org

Enquiries to: Librarian

Founded: 1933

Organisation type and purpose: National organisation, membership association (membership is by subscription), registered charity (charity number 270309), historic building, house or site.
Independent subscription library.
To provide materials for the study of Marxism, socialism and history of working class movements.

Subject coverage: Marxist classics, philosophy, economics, political theory, labour and trade union history, social conditions and movements, early socialist thought (radical, chartist, etc.), international working class movement), socialist countries, Spanish Civil War, US Labor Movement, peace.

Collection: BSP and SDF pamphlets
Daily Worker and Morning Star (bound vols)
General Strike
International Brigade – Spanish Civil War (International Brigade Archive)
J. D. Bernal Peace Movement Library (books and documents from the libraries of Prof. J. D. Bernal and Ivor Montagu)
James Klugman Collection (books, pamphlets and tracts mainly of the Chartist and early British Labour Movement, and ceramics)
John Williamson American Labour History Collection
May Day
Photograph library
Spanish War and International Brigade Collection
US labour and socialist history 1920–70s

Publications: Printed, and electronic and video, and microform publications

Access to staff: Contact by letter, by telephone, by fax, by e-mail and in person. Appointment necessary. Access for members only.
Hours: Mon to Thu, 1300 to 1800 (visitors 1300 to 1400, or by appointment)

Access for disabled people: Ramped entry
Special comments: Access to ground floor. Books brought to desk on ground floor for readers unable to reach first floor reading room.

MARY ROSE TRUST (PORMR)

College Road, HM Naval Base, Portsmouth, Hampshire, PO1 3LX

Tel: 023 9275 0521
Fax: 023 9287 0588
E-mail: mail@maryrose.org
Website: www.maryrose.org

Founded: 1979

Organisation type and purpose: Museum, research organisation, tourist attraction. Registered charity (charity number 277503); Registered company number 1415654 England; VAT registration number GB 339 0628 49.
Designated as an Outstanding Collection and MLA Accredited Museum.
Objectives: to find, record, excavate, raise, bring ashore, preserve, publish, report on and display for all time in Portsmouth the Mary Rose. To establish, equip and maintain a museum or museums in Portsmouth to house the Mary Rose and related or

continued overleaf

associated material. To promote and develop interest, research and knowledge relating to the Mary Rose and all matters relating to the underwater cultural heritage. All for the education and benefit of the nation.

Subject coverage: Henry VIII's warship Mary Rose, launched in 1511, social and maritime history of the Tudor period, evolution of the wooden ship in the late medieval period, conservation and care of material excavated from wet sites, archaeology and underwater technology.

Collection: The Mary Rose (the only recovered 16th-century warship) together with the excavated military, domestic and personal artefacts, ecofacts and human remains
Excavation archive
Photographic library for hire

Non-library collection catalogue: All or part available online

Publications: Printed, and electronic and video

Publications list: Available online

Access to staff: Contact by letter, by telephone, by e-mail and via website. Appointment necessary.
Hours: Mon to Fri, 1000 to 1700
Special comments: The Trust is located in an operational Naval Base. MoD security restrictions may apply.

Constituent bodies: Mary Rose Society and Mary Rose Information Group; c/o The Mary Rose Trust, College Road, HM Naval Base, Portsmouth, Hampshire, PO1 3LX; tel: 023 9275 0521; fax: 023 9287 0588; e-mail: mail@maryrose.org

MASTER CARVERS' ASSOCIATION

Unit 2, 15B Vandyke Road, Leighton Buzzard, Bedfordshire, LU7 3HG

Tel: 01525 851594
Fax: 01525 851594
E-mail: info@mastercarvers.co.uk
Website: www.mastercarvers.co.uk

Enquiries to: Honorary Secretary

Founded: 1897

Organisation type and purpose: Trade association.
Promotion and protection of the interests of stone carving, woodcarving and modelling generally, and of the members of the Association in particular.

Subject coverage: Wood and stone carving; architectural furniture, restoration, ecclesiastical, heraldic, conservation, apprenticeship; rates of wages and conditions of service; modelling.

Publications: Printed

Access to staff: Contact by letter, by telephone, by fax and by e-mail. Appointment necessary.
Hours: Mon to Fri, 0900 to 1700

MASTER LOCKSMITHS ASSOCIATION (MLA)

5D Great Central Way, Woodford Halse, Daventry, Northamptonshire, NN11 3PZ

Tel: 01327 262255
Fax: 01327 262539
E-mail: enquiries@locksmiths.co.uk
Website: www.locksmiths.co.uk/

Enquiries to: Chief Executive Officer

Founded: 1958

Organisation type and purpose: Advisory body, professional body, trade association, training organisation, consultancy.

Subject coverage: Physical security, mechanical security, locks, safes, vehicle security, access systems, training, consultancy, expert witness, product testing, keycutting, bolts.

Collection: Collection of books on locksmithing – reference purposes and for use by members only

Publications: Printed

Access to staff: Contact by letter, by telephone, by fax and by e-mail. Appointment necessary. Letter of introduction required.
Hours: Mon to Fri, 0830 to 1700

Affilated to: Associated Locksmiths of Ireland

Affiliated to: Associated Locksmiths of America; European Locksmiths Federation

Subsidiary body: British Locksmiths Institute; MLA Trade Division

MASTER PHOTOGRAPHERS ASSOCIATION OF GREAT BRITAIN (MPA)

Jubilee House, 1 Chancery Lane, Darlington, Co Durham, DL1 5QP

Tel: 01325 356555
Fax: 01325 357813
E-mail: mpa@mpauk.com
Website: www.mpauk.com

Enquiries to: Chief Executive

Founded: 1952

Organisation type and purpose: Trade association.

Subject coverage: Association for full-time professional photographers.

Access to staff: Contact by letter, by telephone, by fax, by e-mail and via website
Hours: Mon to Fri, 0900 to 1700

MASTERFOODS EDUCATION CENTRE (MEC)

4 Bedford Square, London, WC1B 3RA

Tel: 020 7255 1100
Fax: 020 7631 0602
Website: www.pet-educationresources.co .uk

Enquiries to: Public Relations Manager
Direct e-mail: mec@uk.grayling.com

Founded: 1971

Organisation type and purpose: Suitable for ages: 4 to 11.

Subject coverage: Resource material for schools about pets and responsible pet ownership; putting pets onto the National Curriculum in schools – applicable to Key Stages 1 and 2.

Publications: Printed

Publications list: Available online and in print

Access to staff: Contact by letter, by telephone, by fax and by e-mail
Hours: Mon to Fri, 0900 to 1700

MASTERS OF DEERHOUNDS ASSOCIATION (MDHA)

Bilboa House, Dulverton, Somerset, TA22 9DW

Tel: 01398 323475

Enquiries to: Honorary Secretary

Founded: 1951

Organisation type and purpose: Membership association.
Governing body of packs of hounds hunting wild deer in Great Britain.

Subject coverage: Conservation and control of the last remaining sizeable herd of red deer in England, hunting wild deer with recognised packs of hounds.

Publications: Printed

Access to staff: Contact by letter and by telephone
Hours: Mon to Fri, 0900 to 1700

MASTIC ASPHALT COUNCIL (MAC)

PO Box 77, Hastings, East Sussex, TN35 4WL

Tel: 01424 814400
Fax: 01424 814446
E-mail: masphaltco@aol.com
Website: www.masticasphaltcouncil.co.uk

Enquiries to: Director

Founded: 1948

Organisation type and purpose: Trade association.

Subject coverage: Information on the use of mastic asphalt with member lists and insurance backed guarantees.

Collection: Technical guide on the application of mastic asphalt. Information regarding codes of practice and British Standards

Publications list: Available in print

Access to staff: Contact by letter, by telephone, by fax, by e-mail and via website. Appointment necessary.
Hours: Mon to Fri, 0900 to 1700

Access to building: Prior appointment required

Member of: National Specialist Contractors Council (NSCC)

MATERIALS HANDLING ENGINEERS ASSOCIATION (MHEA)

2B Hills Lane, Ely, Cambridgeshire, CB6 1AY

Tel: 01353 666298
Fax: 01353 666298
E-mail: pw@mhea.co.uk
Website: www.mhea.co.uk

Enquiries to: Secretary

Other contacts: Chairman of Technical Committee for technical or publications

Founded: 1938

Organisation type and purpose: Trade association.

Subject coverage: The UK centre for technical and commercial excellence regarding the manufacture and use of bulk and continuous materials handling equipment

Publications: Printed

Publications list: Available in print

Access to staff: Contact by letter, by telephone, by fax, by e-mail and via website
Special comments: Charges to non-members if justified.

Access to building: No access other than to staff

MATERIALS SCIENCE LIBRARY

Formal name: University of Cambridge Department of Materials Science and Metallurgy Library

New Museums Site, Pembroke Street, Cambridge, CB2 3QZ

Tel: 01223 334300 (dept); 01223 334318 (library)
Fax: 01223 334567 (dept)
E-mail: library@msm.cam.ac.uk
Website: www.msm.cam.ac.uk/library

Enquiries to: Librarian

Organisation type and purpose: University department or institute.

Subject coverage: Materials science, metallurgy, access to external library services.

Collection: Department's PhD and MPhil theses.

Library catalogue: All or part available online

Access to staff: Contact by letter, by telephone, by fax, by e-mail and in person. Appointment necessary.
Hours: During library office hours, Mon to Fri, 0900 to 1500
Special comments: Single member of staff. Please make appointment before any special journey to the library. Library may be unstaffed in particular on Fri in vacations.

Access to building: For members of the department and external visitors.
Hours: 24 hours for members of the department; Mon to Fri, 0900 to 1500 for others
Special comments: Very restricted parking. Parking on site only by special arrangement.

Access for disabled people: Access to library on 4th floor via user-operated lifts

MATHEMATICAL ASSOCIATION (MA)

259 London Road, Leicester, LE2 3BE

Tel: 0116 221 0013
Fax: 0116 212 2835
E-mail: office@m-a.org.uk
Website: www.m-a.org.uk

Enquiries to: Senior Administrator
Direct e-mail: senioradministrator@m-a.org.uk

Founded: 1871

Organisation type and purpose: Membership association (membership is by subscription), registered charity (charity number 313281).
To support and improve the teaching of mathematics.

Subject coverage: Mathematics and the teaching of mathematics.

Collection: Library housed in Leicester University Library

Library catalogue: All or part available in-house

Publications: Printed

Publications list: Available online and in print

Access to staff: Contact by letter, by telephone, by fax, by e-mail, in person and via website
Hours: Mon to Fri, 0900 to 1700

Access to building: No prior appointment required

Affiliated to: JMC

MATHEMATICS RESEARCH CENTRE (MRC)

University of Warwick, Coventry, Warwickshire, CV4 7AL

Tel: 024 7652 8317
Fax: 024 7652 3548
E-mail: mrc@maths.warwick.ac.uk
Website: www.maths.warwick.ac.uk/research

Enquiries to: MRC Coordinator

Founded: 1968

Organisation type and purpose: University department or institute, research organisation.
Symposium and Conference organisation in Mathematics.

Subject coverage: Mathematics.

Access to staff: Contact by e-mail. Appointment necessary.
Hours: Mon to Thu, 0900 to 1700 Fri 0900 to 16.00

Associated with: Mathematics Department, University of Warwick

MATRA ENTHUSIASTS CLUB UK (MEC UK)

4 Maplewood Close, Totton, Southampton, SO40 8WH

Tel: 02380 867804
Fax: 02380 873469
E-mail: clive@automatra.co.uk
Website: www.matra-club.net

Enquiries to: Membership Secretary
Direct tel: 01509 852974
Direct e-mail: philipjowen@yahoo.co.uk

Founded: 1983

Organisation type and purpose: International organisation, membership association (membership is by subscription), present number of members: 100.

Subject coverage: Technical and historical information on Matra cars from 1964 to 2002, including DJet, M530, Bagheera, Rancho, Murena, Espace, Avantime.

Collection: Most books and magazines in English and French about Matra automobiles or containing road tests or reports of related products

Publications: Printed

Access to staff: Contact by letter, by telephone, by fax, by e-mail and via website
Hours: Telephone, daily, 1700 to 2100

Links with: French, Belgian and other European clubs and the North American Matra Register

MCC LIBRARY

Formal name: Marylebone Cricket Club Library

Lord's Cricket Ground, St John's Wood, London, NW8 8QN

Tel: 020 7616 8559
Fax: 020 7616 8659
E-mail: mcclibrary@mcc.org.uk
Website: www.lords.org/history/mcc-library

Enquiries to: Research Officer

Founded: 1787

Organisation type and purpose: Membership association (membership is by election or invitation), historic building, house or site.
Private Cricket Club.

Subject coverage: History of cricket, modern cricket, scores and statistics, real tennis, some other sports, history of Lord's and the MCC.

Collection: Early cricket books and bats
Sir George Allen scrapbooks

Non-library collection catalogue: All or part available in-house

Library catalogue: All or part available in-house

Access to staff: Contact by letter, by telephone, by e-mail and via website. Appointment necessary.
Hours: Mon to Thu, 1000 to 1700; Fri, 1000 to 1600
Special comments: Open Sat and Sun by arrangement on cricket days.

Access to building: Prior appointment required

Access for disabled people: *Special comments:* Library is accessed only by stairs.

MCDOUGALL TRUST

Formal name: Arthur McDougall Fund

6 Chancel Street, London, SE1 0UX

Tel: 020 7620 1080
Fax: 020 7928 1528
E-mail: admin@mcdougall.org.uk
Website: www.mcdougall.org.uk

Enquiries to: Executive Secretary
Other contacts: Chairman (for formal correspondence)

Founded: 1948

continued overleaf

Organisation type and purpose: Voluntary organisation, registered charity (charity number 212151), research organisation, publishing house.
To advance study and knowledge of economic and political science, especially electoral science and methods of election and government of representative organisations of all kinds.

Subject coverage: All aspects of elections including: voting methods whether majority, preferential or proportional representation systems, electoral law and practice, election monitoring, election campaigns, balloting in organisations of all kinds, representation and democracy, political science, suffrage.

Information services: Enquiries in writing preferred.

Special visitor services: Visitors by prior appointment.

Collection: 2,500 books and 2,500 pamphlets
Early pamphlets on PR in Britain, USA, Australia, including Charles Dodgson
Papers of Lord Courtney of Penwith and Dr J. F. S. Ross
Pamphlets donated by H. R. Droop
Extensive press cuttings and other printed material from mid-19th century on electoral reform, proportional representation, suffrage and related issues
Reports on various recent international election observation missions

Trade and statistical information: Electoral statistics relating to elections in the United Kingdom, Ireland and elsewhere

Non-library collection catalogue: All or part available in-house

Library catalogue: All or part available in-house

Publications: Printed
Order printed publications from: Executive Secretary, McDougall Trust

Access to staff: Contact by letter, by telephone, by fax and by e-mail. Appointment necessary. Letter of introduction required.
Hours: Mon to Fri, 1000 to 1700
Special comments: By arrangement only.

Access for disabled people: Toilet facilities
Special comments: Wheelchair stair climber (Victorian building).

Constituent bodies: Lakeman Library for Electoral Studies; 6 Chancel Street, London, SE1 OUX; tel: 020 7620 1080; fax: 020 7928 1528; website: http://www.mcdougall.org.uk

Links with: Electoral Reform Society (Library holding includes ERS archives); tel: 020 7620 1080; fax: 020 7928 1528; e-mail: admin@mcdougall.org.uk; website: http://www.mcdougall.org.uk

MCTIMONEY CHIROPRACTIC ASSOCIATION (MCA)

Crowmarsh Gifford, Wallingford, Oxfordshire, OX10 8DJ

Tel: 01491 829211
Fax: 01491 829492
E-mail: admin@mctimoney-chiropractic.org
Website: www.mctimoneychiropractic.org

Enquiries to: Administrator
Other contacts: Executive Liaison Officer

Founded: 1979

Organisation type and purpose: Professional association, training and research organisation.

Subject coverage: McTimoney Chiropractic, education, training and information.

Trade and statistical information: Membership and subject information data

Publications: Printed

Access to staff: Contact by letter, by telephone, by fax and by e-mail. Appointment necessary. Non-members charged.
Hours: Mon to Fri, 0900 to 1700

MDC EVALUATIONS

Unit 4, Greenways Business Park, Bellinger Close, Chippenham, Wiltshire, SN15 1BN

Tel: 01249 467272
Fax: 01249 467273
Website: www.mdcevaluations.co.uk

Enquiries to: PA to Technical Director

Founded: 2002

Subject coverage: Predicted transmitting abilities for dairy bulls and cows in UK. Genetic trends in UK dairy industry. Industry statistics (UK dairy industry). Technical information on UK evaluation system for dairy bulls and cows.

Trade and statistical information: Statistics on UK dairy industry

Non-library collection catalogue: All or part available online

Publications: Printed

Publications list: Available online

Access to staff: Contact by letter, by telephone, by fax, by e-mail and via website
Hours: Mon to Fri, 0900 to 1700

ME ASSOCIATION (MEA)

Formal name: Myalgic Encephalopathy Association

7 Apollo Office Court, Radclive Road, Gawcott, Buckinghamshire, MK18 4DF

Tel: 01280 818968
E-mail: meconnect@meassociation.org.uk
Website: www.meassociation.org.uk

Enquiries to: Publicity Manager
Direct tel: 01406 370293
Direct e-mail: tbritton02@yahoo.com

Founded: 1976

Organisation type and purpose: A registered charity (charity number 801279).
The MEA is a campaigning national charity that provides information and support to an estimated 240,000 people in the United Kingdom with ME/Chronic Fatigue Syndrome, their families and carers. This is provided through a quarterly magazine, literature, education and training. It also runs ME Connect, the United Kingdom's premier helpline for people with ME/CFS. The charity supports research into the physical nature and cause of ME via The MEA Ramsay Research Fund.

Subject coverage: Myalgic encephalopathy (ME) information, support, education and training.

Information services: Telephone helpline: 0844 576 5326, open daily, 1000 to 1200 and 1400 to 1600 and 1900 to 2100

Non-library collection catalogue: All or part available online and in print

Library catalogue: All or part available online and in print

Publications: Printed
Order printed publications from: Buckinghamshire office; tel. 01280 818968; e-mail meconnect@meassociation.org.uk

Publications list: Available online and in print

Access to staff: Contact by letter, by telephone, by e-mail, in person and via website
Hours: Mon to Fri, 0930 to 1630

Also at: The ME Association, Publicity, Communications and PR; 60 Broadgate, Weston, Spalding, PE12 6HY; tel: 01406 370293; e-mail: tbritton02@yahoo.com

MÉDECINS SANS FRONTIÈRES (MSF)

67–74 Saffron Hill, London, EC1N 8QX

Tel: 020 7404 6600
Fax: 020 7404 4466
E-mail: office@london.msf.org
Website: www.msf.org

Enquiries to: Public Information Administrator
Direct tel: 020 7404 6600
Other contacts: (1) Fundraising Administrator (2) Recruitment Assistant for either donation enquiries or recruitment enquiries

Founded: 1971

Organisation type and purpose: International organisation, voluntary organisation, registered charity (charity number 1026588).
To provide medical emergency relief to victims of disaster worldwide.

Subject coverage: Humanitarian and medical aid, emergency relief.

Publications: Printed
Order printed publications from: Médecins Sans Frontières
8 Rue Saint Sabin, Paris Cedex 11, 75544, France, tel: 00 33 1 40 21 29 29, fax: 00 33 1 48 06 68 68, e-mail: office@paris.msf.org

Access to staff: Contact by letter, by telephone, by fax, by e-mail and via website. Appointment necessary.
Hours: Mon to Fri, 0900 to 1800
Special comments: No wheelchair access

International office: Médecins Sans Frontières; 39 Rue de la Tourelle, Brussels, B-1040, Belgium; tel: 00 32 2 280 18 81; fax: 00 32 2 280 01 73

MEDIATION UK

Alexander House, Telephone Avenue, Bristol, BS1 4BS

Tel: 0117 904 6661
Fax: 0117 904 3331
E-mail: contracts@agreements.co.uk

Website: www.mediation.org.uk

Enquiries to: Director

Founded: 1984

Organisation type and purpose: National organisation, membership association (membership is by subscription), present number of members: 503, registered charity (charity number 1019275).
Network of projects, organisations and individuals interested in mediation and constructive conflict resolution; umbrella organisation for mediation schemes in the UK.
Mediation UK is a national charity which represents and promotes mediation within local communities. It has a membership of 170 registered services throughout the UK which offer mediation to parties in dispute. The majority of these services are free to the user, and a national helpline exists to direct the public to their nearest mediation service. Services specialise in one or more areas including neighbour disputes, school bullying, and victim/offender mediation. Mediation UK also supports mediation within the workplace, and sectors like the health service. Mediation UK is actively involved in encouraging the establishment of new mediation services around the country, as well as ensuring mediation services adhere to quality standards and guidelines.

Subject coverage: Mediation and constructive conflict resolution, including neighbour disputes and community mediation; victim/offender mediation; conflict resolution and mediation in schools; other conflict resolution projects; training in mediation and conflict resolution skills.

Publications: Printed, and electronic and video

Publications list: Available in print

Access to staff: Contact by letter, by telephone, by fax, by e-mail and via website. Appointment necessary.
Hours: Mon to Fri, 0900 to 1700

Also at: Mediation Wales; 1 The Spa Centre, Station Crescent, Llandrindod Wells, Powys, LD1 5BB; tel: 01597 829100

MEDIAWATCH–UK

3 Willow House, Kennington Road, Ashford, Kent, TN24 0NR

Tel: 01233 633936
Fax: 01233 633836
E-mail: info@mediawatchuk.org
Website: www.mediawatchuk.org

Enquiries to: Director

Founded: 1965

Organisation type and purpose: National organisation, membership association (membership is by subscription), voluntary organisation.
Campaigning for good media standards and effective reform of the law on obscenity.

Subject coverage: Mass media, broadcasting, programme standards, online safety, obscene publications.

Publications: Printed
Order printed publications from: Mediawatch–UK

Access to staff: Contact by letter, by telephone, by fax, by e-mail and in person. Appointment necessary.
Hours: Mon to Fri, 0930 to 1730

MEDICAL ADVISORY SERVICE (MAS)

PO Box 3087, London, W4 4ZP

Tel: 020 8994 9874 (general medical)
Website: www.medicaladvisoryservice.org.uk

Enquiries to: Director
Direct tel: 020 8995 8503 (admin. only)
Direct fax: 020 8995 3275 (admin. only)

Founded: 1986

Organisation type and purpose: Registered charity (charity number 295953).

Subject coverage: General medical helpline to the public.

Publications: Printed
Order printed publications from: Medical Advisory Service, PO Box 3087, London, W4 4ZP

Publications list: Available in print

Access to staff: Contact by letter and by telephone
Hours: Mon to Sun, 1800 to 2000

Links with: Sleep Matters; PO Box 3087, London, W4 4ZP; tel: 020 8994 9874

MEDICAL ADVISORY SERVICES FOR TRAVELLERS ABROAD (MASTA)

29 Harley Street, London, W1G 9QR

Tel: 09068 224100 Travellers Healthline
Fax: 020 7323 5843
E-mail: rattewell@masta.org
Website: www.masta.org

Enquiries to: Medical Director

Founded: 1984

Organisation type and purpose: Advisory body, professional body, service industry, training organisation, research organisation.

Subject coverage: Health risks for travellers abroad; information is maintained on 230 countries, and 84 conditions and diseases that affect travellers in varying living conditions. Healthcare items catalogue for travellers.

Publications: Printed
Order printed publications from: Travellers Healthline
tel: 09068 224100

Publications list: Available in print

Access to staff: Contact by telephone, by e-mail and via website
Hours: 24-hour helpline

Associated with: Boots Travel Clinics; MASTA Travel Clinics

Sales and Marketing & Technical: MASTA; Moorfield Road, Yeadon, Leeds, LS19 7BN; tel: 0113 238 7500

MEDICAL COUNCIL ON ALCOHOL, THE (MCA)

4 St Andrew's Place, Regent's Park, London, NW1 4LB

Tel: 020 7487 4445
Fax: 020 7935 4479
E-mail: mca@medicouncilalcol.demon.co.uk
Website: www.medicouncilalcol.demon.co.uk

Enquiries to: Administrative Secretary

Founded: 1967

Organisation type and purpose: Professional body (membership is by subscription), present number of members: 370, voluntary organisation, registered charity (charity number 265242).
Devoted to improving medical understanding of alcohol-related problems, their prevention and treatment.

Subject coverage: Alcohol and alcoholism: medical aspects and facilities for dealing with the problem.

Collection: Information on alcohol in relation to health including education of medical students on alcohol

Trade and statistical information: Morbidity and mortality statistics

Publications: Printed

Publications list: Available in print

Access to staff: Contact by letter, by telephone, by fax and by e-mail. Appointment necessary.
Hours: Mon to Fri, 0930 to 1630

MEDICAL DEFENCE UNION LIMITED (MDU)

230 Blackfriars Road, London, SE1 8PJ

Tel: 020 7202 1500
Fax: 020 7202 1666
Website: www.the-mdu.com

Enquiries to: Librarian
Direct e-mail: media@the-mdu.com

Founded: 1885

Organisation type and purpose: Membership association (membership is by subscription), service industry.

Subject coverage: Medical negligence, litigation, ethics.

Non-library collection catalogue: All or part available online

Access to staff: Access for members only.
Hours: Mon to Wed, 1030 to 1730

Access to building: Prior appointment required

Access for disabled people: Parking provided

MEDICAL FOUNDATION FOR THE CARE OF VICTIMS OF TORTURE

111 Isledon Road, London, N7 7JW

Tel: 020 7697 7777
Fax: 020 7697 7799
E-mail: info@torturecare.org.uk
Website: www.torturecare.org.uk

Enquiries to: Information Officer

continued overleaf

Founded: 1986

Organisation type and purpose: Registered charity (charity number 1000340).
The Medical Foundation aims to provide survivors of torture in the UK with medical treatment, practical assistance and psychotherapeutic support, document evidence of torture, provide training for health professionals working with torture survivors, educate the public and decision-makers about torture and its consequences, ensure that Britain honours its international obligations towards asylum seekers and refugees.

Subject coverage: Medical foundation providing survivors of torture in the UK with medical treatment, social assistance and psychotherapeutic support, documentation of evidence of torture, education of the public and decision-makers about torture and its consequences.

Collection: Library

Non-library collection catalogue: All or part available in-house and in print

Library catalogue: All or part available in-house

Publications: Printed

Publications list: Available online and in print

Access to staff: Contact by letter and by telephone
Hours: Mon to Fri, 0900 to 1830

Access to building: Prior appointment required
Hours: Mon to Fri, 1000 to 1700

Access for disabled people: Ramped entry, lift, toilet facilities

MEDICAL INDEMNITY REGISTER (MIR)

PO Box 44375, London, SW19 8WA

Tel: 020 8540 0677
Fax: 020 8540 5677
E-mail: malpractice@btconnect.com
Website: www.medicalindemnity.com

Enquiries to: Registrar

Founded: 1990

Organisation type and purpose: Advisory body, medical malpractice insurance for individuals and companies, present number of members: 2,000, training organisation.

Subject coverage: Pre-hospital life support (PHLS), medical malpractice and public liability insurance.

Information services: Occasional Newsletter, M.I.R. NEWS.

Education services: First Aid and EMT training.

Non-library collection catalogue: All or part available online

Publications: Printed

Publications list: Available online and in print

Access to staff: Contact by letter, by telephone, by fax, by e-mail and via website. Non-members charged.
Hours: Mon to Fri, 0900 to 1700

Access to building: No access other than to staff

Insurers: Marketform Limited

MEDICAL PRACTITIONERS' UNION (MPU)

128 Theobald's Road, London, WC1X 8TN

Tel: 020 3371 2013
E-mail: carol.english@unitetheunion.org

Founded: 1914

Organisation type and purpose: Trade union.

Subject coverage: Medico-politics; National Health Service, industrial relations, equal opportunities.

Publications: Printed

Publications list: Available in print

Access to staff: Contact by letter and by e-mail

Section of: Unite; tel: 020 7611 2500; website: http://www.unitetheunion.org

MEDICAL PROTECTION SOCIETY (MPS)

Granary Wharf House, Leeds, LS11 5PY

Tel: 0845 605 4000
Fax: 0113 241 0500
E-mail: info@mps.org.uk
Website: www.medicalprotection.org/uk

Enquiries to: Library & Information Manager
Direct tel: 0113 241 0615
Direct e-mail: tony.albrow@mps.org.uk

Founded: 1892

Organisation type and purpose: International organisation, advisory body, professional body (membership is by subscription), service industry.
MPS is the leading provider of comprehensive professional indemnity and expert advice to doctors, dentists and health professionals around the world. It is a mutual, not-for-profit medical defence organisation, offering more than 265,000 members help with legal and ethical problems that arise from their professional practice. This includes clinical negligence claims, complaints, medical council inquiries, legal and ethical dilemmas, disciplinary procedures, inquests and fatal accident inquiries. MPS is not an insurance company. The benefits of membership are discretionary.

Subject coverage: Medico-legal matters.

Publications: Printed
Order printed publications from: Publications free to members and freely available on website

Publications list: Available online

Access to staff: Contact by letter, by telephone, by fax, by e-mail and via website. Appointment necessary. Access for members only.
Hours: Mon to Fri, 0800 to 1630

Access for disabled people: Access to all public areas, toilet facilities

Also at: Medical Protection Society; 33 Cavendish Square, London, W1G 0PS; tel: 0845 605 4000; e-mail: info@mps.org.uk

MEDICAL RESEARCH COUNCIL CANCER DIVISION, MRC CLINICAL TRIALS UNIT (MRC CTU)

222 Euston Road, London, NW1 2DA

Tel: 020 7670 4700
Fax: 020 7670 4818
E-mail: contact@ctu.mrc.ac.uk
Website: www.ctu.mrc.ac.uk

Enquiries to: Information Officer
Direct tel: 020 7670 4737
Direct e-mail: ch@ctu.mrc.ac.uk

Founded: 1977

Organisation type and purpose: Membership association, present number of members: 80, research organisation.
The conduct of multi-centre clinical trials in the treatment of HIV, cancer, and associated research.

Subject coverage: To design, conduct and analyse clinical trials in cancer in most solid tumour sites, mainly on behalf of the MRC. To undertake teaching, supervisory, editorial and refereeing work.
The Cancer Division is a member of the editorial boards of various journals including the British Medical Journal, British Cancer Journal, Clinical Oncology etc.
The Cancer Division is the UK editorial office for the journal Statistics in Medicine.

Publications: Printed

Publications list: Available online and in print

Access to staff: Contact by letter, by fax, by e-mail and via website. Appointment necessary.
Hours: Mon to Fri, 0900 to 1700

Parent body: Medical Research Council; Head Office, 20 Park Crescent, London, W1N 4AL; tel: 020 7636 5422

MEDICAL RESEARCH COUNCIL – COGNITION AND BRAIN SCIENCES UNIT (MRC–CBU)

15 Chaucer Road, Cambridge, CB2 7EF

Tel: 01223 355294
Fax: 01223 359062
Website: www.mrc-cbu.cam.ac.uk

Founded: 1944; formerly called MRC Applied Psychology Unit (year of change 1997)

Organisation type and purpose: Research organisation.

Subject coverage: Fundamental human psychological functions in domains such as attention, memory, language and emotion. Clinical implications for patient therapy and rehabilitation.

Non-library collection catalogue: All or part available online

Library catalogue: All or part available in-house

Publications list: Available online

Access to staff: Contact by letter and by e-mail. Appointment necessary.
Hours: Mon to Fri, 0900 to 1700

Access to building: No access other than to staff

Access for disabled people: Parking provided, ramped entry, toilet facilities

MEDICAL RESEARCH COUNCIL – HARWELL

Harwell, Didcot, Oxfordshire, OX11 0RD

Tel: 01235 841000 extn. 1121
Fax: 01235 841200
E-mail: m.bulman@har.mrc.ac.uk
Website: www.har.mrc.ac.uk/initial.html

Enquiries to: Librarian

Organisation type and purpose: Research organisation.

Subject coverage: Mammalian genetics, particularly mouse genetics.

Library catalogue: All or part available online

Access to staff: Contact by telephone and by e-mail. Appointment necessary.
Hours: Mon to Fri, 0900 to 1700

MEDICAL SOCIETY OF LONDON

11 Chandos Street, London, W1M 0EB

Tel: 020 7580 1043
Fax: 020 7580 5793

Enquiries to: Registrar

Founded: 1773

Organisation type and purpose: Learned society (membership is by election or invitation), registered charity.

Subject coverage: Medicine and the history of medicine.

Publications: Printed

Access to staff: Contact by letter. Appointment necessary.
Hours: Mon to Fri, 0900 to 1700

MEDICAL WOMEN'S FEDERATION (MWF)

Tavistock House North, Tavistock Square, London, WC1H 9HX

Tel: 020 7387 7765
Fax: 020 7388 9216
E-mail: admin.mwf@btconnect.com
Website: www.medicalwomensfederation.org.uk

Enquiries to: Honorary Secretary

Founded: 1917

Organisation type and purpose: Membership association (membership is by subscription), present number of members: c.1,500, voluntary organisation, registered charity (charity number 261820).

Subject coverage: Careers for women doctors working on a full- or part-time basis.

Collection: Archives on history of women in medicine (now on permanent loan to the Wellcome Institute on the History of Medicine)

Publications: Printed

Access to staff: Contact by letter, by telephone, by fax, by e-mail and via website
Hours: Mon to Fri, 0900 to 1700

Access to building: Prior appointment required

Links with: Medical Womens' International Association

MEDICINES AND HEALTHCARE PRODUCTS REGULATORY AGENCY (MHRA)

Information Centre, 10th Floor, Market Towers, 1 Nine Elms Lane, London, SW8 5NQ

Tel: 020 7084 2000
Fax: 020 7084 2353
E-mail: info@mhra.gsi.gov.uk
Website: www.mhra.gov.uk

Enquiries to: Central Enquiry Point, Information Centre
Direct e-mail: florence.palmer@mhra.gsi.gov.uk

Founded: 1989; created by the merger of Medicines Control Agency (MCA) and Medical Devices Agency (MDA) (year of change 2003)

Organisation type and purpose: National government body, statutory body. Executive Agency of the Department of Health. Regulatory body for human medicines and devices in the UK.

Subject coverage: Safeguarding public health by ensuring that medicines and medical devices work, and are acceptably safe.

Collection: British National Formulary 1947 to date
British Pharmaceutical Codex 1923 to date
British Pharmacopoeia 1898 to date
Data Sheet Compendiums 1974 to date

Non-library collection catalogue: All or part available online

Library catalogue: All or part available online

Publications list: Available online

Access to staff: Contact by letter, by telephone, by fax and by e-mail
Hours: Mon to Fri, 0900 to 1700
Special comments: A private information centre serving MHRA staff, only open to researchers as a last resort.

Executive agency of: Department of Health

MEDIEVAL SETTLEMENT RESEARCH GROUP (MSRG)

c/o Dr Neil Christie, School of Archaeology and Ancient History, University of Leicester, Leicester, LE1 7RH

Tel: 0116 252 2617
Fax: 0116 252 5005
E-mail: njc10@leicester.ac.uk
Website: www.britarch.ac.uk/msrg

Enquiries to: Honorary Secretary
Other contacts: Treasurer (for membership); Editor (for publications); President

Founded: 1986; created by the merger of Medieval Village Research Group (MVRG, founded 1952) and the Moated Sites Research Group (founded 1971) (year of change 1986)

Organisation type and purpose: Learned society (membership is by subscription), registered charity (charity number 801634), research organisation.
To advance knowledge of rural settlements of all kinds, particularly those of the 5th to 16th centuries. To publish an annual journal, Medieval Settlement Research, to help disseminate research, finds, and debates.

Subject coverage: Medieval settlements, landscapes and people – with an emphasis on rural sites across time, such as villages, hamlet, manors and farmsteads; British and Irish and some Continental rural settlement studies, especially for the 5th to 16th centuries.

Collection: The Library is held as part of the Marc Fitch Library, The University of Leicester – for information contact the School of English Local History, The University of Leicester
The former MVRG sites archive is held on the MSRG's behalf by the National Monuments Record in Swindon (English Heritage). Archive has a computerised index

Publications: Printed
Order printed publications from: Annual journal

Publications list: Available online and in print

Access to staff: Contact by letter, by telephone, by fax, by e-mail and via website. Appointment necessary.
Hours: Mon to Fri, 0900 to 1700

Affiliated to: Council for British Archaeology (CBA); St Mary's House, 66 Bootham, York, YO30 7BZ; tel: 01904 671417; fax: 01904 671384; e-mail: archaeology@csi.com; website: http://www.britarch.ac.uk
Society for Medieval Archaeology (SMA); website: http://www.socmedarch.org

MEDITERRANEAN ASSOCIATION TO SAVE THE SEA TURTLES (MEDASSET)

c/o 24 Park Towers, 2 Brick Street, London, W1J 7DD

Tel: 020 7629 0654
Fax: 020 7629 0654
E-mail: medasset@medasset.org
Website: www.medasset.org
Website: www.euroturtle.org

Enquiries to: Communications Officer
Direct tel: +30 210 3613572
Direct fax: +30 210 3613572

Founded: 1988

Organisation type and purpose: An international not-for-profit environmental NGO registered as a charity (charity number 1077649) and private company in the UK and as a Non Profit Organisation in Greece. MEDASSET plays an active role in the study and conservation of sea turtles and their habitats throughout the Mediterranean, through scientific research, environmental education, political lobbying and raising public awareness.The organisation has been

continued overleaf

a Partner to the Mediterranean Action Plan (MAP) of UNEP and a Permanent Observer-member of the Bern Convention at the Council of Europe since 1988.

Collection: Videos, CDs, slides, newspaper cuttings
Holds an extensive list of related publications, technical reports, papers, etc.

Non-library collection catalogue: All or part available online and in-house

Library catalogue: All or part available in-house

Publications: Printed, and electronic and video
Order printed publications from: http://www.medasset.org

Publications list: Available online and in print

Access to staff: Contact by letter, by telephone, by fax, by e-mail and via website. Appointment necessary. Letter of introduction required.
Hours: Mon to Fri, 0900 to 1700
Special comments: Telephone first for access hours.

Also at: MEDASSET Greece; 1(c) Licavitou Street, Athens 10672, Greece; tel: +30 210 3613572; +30 210 3640389; fax: +30 210 3613572; e-mail: medasset@medasset.gr; website: http://www.medasset.gr

MEDITERRANEAN GARDEN SOCIETY UK BRANCH (MGS UK)

Baldocks, Chiddingstone Causeway, Tonbridge, TN11 8JX

E-mail: hma@clara.net
Website: www.mediterraneangardensociety.org

Enquiries to: Chairman

Founded: 1995

Organisation type and purpose:
International organisation, membership association (membership is by subscription), present number of members: 1,600, voluntary organisation.
To promote understanding and interest in Mediterranean plants and gardening and water-wise gardening.

Subject coverage: The society provides a forum for members on any related Mediterranean garden/plant topics.

Publications: Printed
Order printed publications from: mgssecretary@gmail.com

Publications list: Available online

Access to staff: Contact by e-mail

Also at: Mediterranean Garden Society; Sparoza, PO Box 14, 190 02 Peania, Greece

MEDWAY ARCHIVES AND LOCAL STUDIES CENTRE (MALSC)

MALSC, Medway Council, Gun Wharf, Dock Road, Chatham, Kent, ME4 4TR

Tel: 01634 332714
E-mail: malsc@medway.gov.uk
Website: www.medway.gov.uk/archives
Website: cityark.medway.gov.uk
Website: libcat.medway.gov.uk/cgi-bin/vps2_viewpoint.sh

Enquiries to: Archivist
Direct tel: 01634 332714
Direct e-mail: malsc@medway.gov.uk
Other contacts: Local Studies Librarians (for local studies stock)

Founded: 1990

Organisation type and purpose: Local government body, local studies library (reference only).
Archives.

Subject coverage: Archives: Rochester City Council, Rochester upon Medway City Council, Hoo Rural District Council, Chatham Borough Council, Rochester City Council, Gillingham Borough Council, Strood Rural District Council, parish councils for northwest Kent, state school and school board records (Medway Council area), Rochester Cathedral, Hawkins' Hospital (Chatham), Rochester Dickens' Fellowship, Watts' Charity (Rochester), St. Bartholomew's Hospital (admin records only) (Rochester/Chatham), Foord Almshouses (Rochester), Earls of Darnley of Cobham Hall, Best family of Boxley and Chatham, Winget Ltd (Strood), Blaw Knox Ltd (Rochester), Phillips and Pett Ltd (Strood and Rochester), Rogers, Stevens and Chance (Chatham), Church of England parishes (Rochester Archdeaconry area), Methodist Church Medway Towns Circuit, Chatham Memorial Synagogue (Rochester), Unitarian Church (Chatham), Congregational Church (Clover Street, Chatham), Medway Conservancy Board, Medway Navigation Company, Port of Rochester shipping registers and crew lists, Medway and Swale Dock Labour Board, Rochester and District Natural History Society, Dickens' Country Protection Society, Old Roffensian Society (Rochester), City of Rochester Society, King's School (Rochester), Sir Joseph Williamson's Mathematical School (Rochester). Please note that not all collections are fully accessible until they are catalogued.
Local studies: Percy Fitzgerald Collection, Dickens' collection, naval collection, local history, Medway Council area and Kent topography, Kent periodicals, census, IGI, GRO Index, public access computers, CD-Roms, OS maps, electoral registers, telephone and street directories, local area newspapers and parish register index fiche.

Education services: Outreach programme and educational local history packs by arrangement.

Services for disabled people: DDA compliant for access

Collection: Naval collection, Percy Fitzgerald collection
Usual local authority archive stock

Trade and statistical information: Historic Census

Non-library collection catalogue: All or part available online and in print

Library catalogue: All or part available online and in-house

Publications: Printed, and electronic and video, and microform publications

Access to staff: Contact by letter, by telephone, by e-mail and in person. Appointment necessary.
Hours: Mon, Tue, Thu, Fri, 0900 to 1700; Sat, 0900 to 1600; Wed, closed
Special comments: CARN reader's ticket for archives.

Access for disabled people: Pay and display car park, level entry, wheelchair access to all public areas, toilet facilities, loop system, screen reader software, evac chair

Parent body: Medway Council; Directorate of Regeneration and Community Services; tel: 01634 306000; fax: 01634 732848; website: http://www.medway.gov.uk

MEDWAY COUNCIL

Medway Libraries, c/o Chatham Library, Gun Wharf, Dock Road, Chatham, Kent, ME4 4TX

Tel: 01634 337799
Fax: 01634 337800
E-mail: chatham.library@medway.gov.uk
Website: www.medway.gov.uk/libraries
Website: https://medway.spydus.co.uk

Enquiries to: Librarian

Founded: 1998

Organisation type and purpose: Local government body, public library.

Subject coverage: Business information, European information, UK Online Centre, archives, local studies

Library catalogue: All or part available online

Access to staff: Contact by letter, by telephone, by fax, by e-mail and in person
Hours: Mon, Wed and Fri, 0900 to 1800; Tue, 1000 to 1900; Thu, 0900 to 1900; Sat, 0900 to 1700

Access to building: No prior appointment required

Also at: Medway Archives and Local Studies Centre; Clocktower Building, Civic Centre, Strood, ME2 4AU; tel: 01634 332714; fax: 01634 297060; e-mail: local.studies@medway.gov.uk; website: http://cityarc.medway.gov.uk

Member organisation of: UK Online Centre

MEDWAY LIBRARIES AND ARCHIVES SERVICE

Strood Library, 32 Bryant Road, Strood, Kent ME2 3EU

Tel: 01634 33836
E-mail: sandra.seamark@medway.gov.uk
Website: www.medway.gov.uk/libraries

Enquiries to: Librarian

Founded: 1998

Organisation type and purpose: Local government body, public library.

Subject coverage: Libraries, archives

Collection: Dickens, Naval

Trade and statistical information: See website

Access to staff: Contact by letter, by telephone, by e-mail, in person and via website

Other address: Medway Archives and Local Studies Centre; Clocktower Building, Civic Centre, Strood, ME2 4AU; tel: 01634 332714

MEET A MUM ASSOCIATION (MAMA)

National MAMA Office, 7 Southcourt Road, Linslade, Leighton Buzzard, Bedfordshire LU7 2QF

Tel: 0845 120 6162
E-mail: Meet-A-Mum.Assoc@cableinet.co.uk
Website: www.mama.co.uk/

Enquiries to: Manager
Direct e-mail: jeanette@mama.co.uk
Other contacts: Helpline Administrator for listing details.

Founded: 1979

Organisation type and purpose: National organisation, membership association (membership is by subscription), registered charity (charity number 283271).
National charity.

Subject coverage: Support for mums or mums-to-be with post-natal depression or a feeling of isolation.

Non-library collection catalogue: All or part available in-house

Publications: Printed

Publications list: Available online and in print

Access to staff: Contact by letter, by telephone, by e-mail and via website
Hours: Mon to Fri, 1000 to 1530

Access to building: No prior appointment required

Has: over 35 local groups throughout the UK

MEETINGS INDUSTRY ASSOCIATION (MIA)

PO Box 515, Kelmarsh, Northampton, NN6 9XW

Tel: 0845 230 5508
Fax: 0845 230 7708
E-mail: info@mia-uk.org
Website: www.mia-uk.org

Enquiries to: Chief Executive
Direct e-mail: janee@mia-uk.org

Founded: 1990

Organisation type and purpose:
Membership and professional association for all organisations involved in the meetings industry for the UK & Ireland. Its own accreditation scheme, AIM, is the only meetings industry standard endorsed by VisitBritain, Visit England, Visit Wales, Meeting Professionals International and the Association of British Professional Conference Organisers.
To encourage improvement of service and facilities offered by the UK meetings industry through the sharing of best practice and the setting of standards.

Subject coverage: The meetings industry.

Education services: Learning and Development Academy training courses (see website).

Publications: Electronic and video
Order electronic and video publications from: tel: 0845 230 5508; e-mail: sarahp@mia-uk.org

Publications list: Available online

Access to staff: Contact by letter, by telephone, by fax and by e-mail

MELTON BOROUGH COUNCIL

Council Offices, Nottingham Road, Melton Mowbray, Leicestershire, LE13 0UL

Tel: 01664 502502
Fax: 01664 410283
Website: www.melton.gov.uk

Enquiries to: Public Relations Manager
Direct tel: 01664 502385

Organisation type and purpose: Local government body.

Access to staff: Contact by letter, by telephone and by fax
Hours: Mon to Fri, 0900 to 1700

MEN OF THE STONES (MOS)

Beech Croft, Weston-under-Lizard, Shifnal, Shropshire, TF11 8JT

Tel: 01952 850269
Fax: 01952 850269
E-mail: mltebbutt@lineone.net

Enquiries to: Chairman
Direct tel: 07980 63118 (mobile)
Other contacts: Honorary Secretary

Founded: 1947

Organisation type and purpose: Learned society, membership association (membership is by subscription), present number of members: 465, registered charity (charity number 229497).
A society advocating the use of stone and other natural and local building materials, for encouraging craftsmanship and preserving good architectural qualities.

Subject coverage: Architecture and good buildings of all periods; conservation, preservation, repair; use and re-use of stone and other natural and local materials; constructional arts and crafts of architecture, including stone masonry, sculpture, carving; gilding; pargetting, wrought iron and cast lead work, stone roof slating.

Publications: Printed

Access to staff: Contact by letter, by telephone and by e-mail
Hours: Mon to Fri, 0900 to 1700

Affiliated to: Ancient Monuments Society; English Heritage (West Midlands Region); tel: 0121 625 6820; Georgian Group; Society for the Protection of Ancient Buildings

Links with: Collyweston Stone Slaters Trust; Orton Trust Stonemasonry Training Centre

MENINGITIS RESEARCH FOUNDATION

Midland Way, Thornbury, Bristol, BS35 2BS

Tel: 01454 281811
Fax: 01454 281094
E-mail: info@meningitis.org
Website: www.meningitis.org

Enquiries to: Head of Communications and Campaigns
Direct e-mail: harpinderc@meningitis.org

Founded: 1989

Organisation type and purpose: Registered charity (charity number 1091105).

Subject coverage: Meningitis Research Foundation funds vital scientific research into the prevention, detection and treatment of meningitis and septicaemia – the blood poisoning form of the disease. Raises awareness of the diseases, and offers support through in-depth information and befriending to those affected.

Collection: General Public – Symptoms Literature
Health Professionals – Diagnosis guidelines and treatment protocols, and photo library

Library catalogue: All or part available online

Publications: Printed, and electronic and video

Publications list: Available online and in print

Access to staff: Contact by letter, by telephone, by fax and by e-mail
Hours: Mon to Fri, 0900 to 1700; 24-hour Helpline: 0808 800 3344

Access for disabled people: Parking provided, toilet facilities

Other addresses: Meningitis Research Foundation; 63 Lower Gardiner Street, Dublin 1, Republic of Ireland; tel: +353 1 819 6931; fax: +353 1 819 6931; e-mail: meningitis@iol.ie; Meningitis Research Foundation; 133 Gilmore Place, Edinburgh, EH3 9PP; tel: 0131 228 3322; fax: 0131 221 0300; e-mail: info@scotland-meningitis.org.uk; Meningitis Research Foundation; 71 Botanic Avenue, Belfast, BT7 1JL; tel: 028 9032 1283; fax: 028 9032 1284; e-mail: info@meningitis-ni.org

MENTAL HEALTH FOUNDATION (MHF)

9th Floor, Sea Containers House, 20 Upper Ground, London, SE1 9QB

Tel: 020 7803 1101
Fax: 020 7803 1111
E-mail: mhf@mhf.org.uk
Website: www.mentalhealth.org.uk

Enquiries to: Head of Information
Direct tel: 020 7802 0315
Direct e-mail: press@mhf.org.uk

Founded: 1949

Organisation type and purpose: Registered charity (charity number 801130).
Mental Health Foundation incorporating the Foundation for People with Learning Disabilities, is the leading UK charity working in mental health and learning disabilities.
With pioneering research and community projects we aim to improve the support available for people with mental health problems and people with learning disabilities.

Subject coverage: Mental health, learning disabilities, mental illness, depression, anxiety, dementia, manic depression,

continued overleaf

schizophrenia, stress therapy, psychiatry, psychology, user movement, attention deficit, conduct disorder, eating disorder.

Publications: Printed, and electronic and video

Publications list: Available online and in print

Access to staff: Contact by letter, by telephone, by fax, by e-mail and via website
Hours: Mon to Fri, 0900 to 1700 plus Dial & Listen Service

Other address: Mental Health Foundation – Scotland Office; 24 St George's Square, Glasgow, G2 1EG; tel: 0141 572 0125; fax: 0141 572 0246; e-mail: scotland@mhf.org .uk

MENTAL HEALTH MEDIA (MHM)

The Resource Centre, 356 Holloway Road, London, N7 6PA

Tel: 020 7700 8171
Fax: 020 7686 0959
Website: www.mhmedia.com

Enquiries to: Director
Direct tel: 020 7700 8131

Founded: 1983

Organisation type and purpose: Voluntary organisation, registered charity (charity number 286467), training organisation, consultancy, research organisation.
A charity working with the media, statutory and voluntary organisations and service users to break down the stigma of mental distress.

Subject coverage: Mental health and distress, well-being, stress and stress management, ability and disability, community care, coping with bereavement, cultural identity and racism, women and well-being, counselling and psychotherapy, learning difficulties, sexuality, child abuse, advocacy, housing, video production and working with the media.

Publications: Electronic and video

Publications list: Available in print

Access to staff: Contact by letter, by telephone, by fax and by e-mail. Appointment necessary.
Hours: Mon to Fri, 0900 to 1800

MENTAL WELFARE COMMISSION FOR SCOTLAND (MWC)

K Floor, Argyle House, 3 Lady Lawson Street, Edinburgh, EH3 9SH

Tel: 0131 222 6111
Fax: 0131 222 6112
E-mail: enquiries@mwcscot.org.uk
Website: www.mwcscot.org.uk

Enquiries to: Communications Manager

Founded: 1960

Organisation type and purpose: Statutory body.

Subject coverage: Mental welfare.

Collection: Mental Health Law
Reports and Grey Literature (relating to Mental Health)
Small collection of reference books and some journal titles

Library catalogue: All or part available in-house

Publications: Printed

Publications list: Available online

Access to staff: Contact by letter, by telephone, by fax, by e-mail and via website
Hours: Mon to Fri, 0900 to 1700

Access to building: Prior appointment required

Access for disabled people: Access to all public areas

MENZIES CENTRE FOR AUSTRALIAN STUDIES (MCAS)

King's College London, The Australia Centre, Strand, London, WC2B 4LG

Tel: 020 7557 7160
Fax: 020 7240 8292
E-mail: menzies.centre@kcl.ac.uk
Website: www.kcl.ac.uk/menzies

Enquiries to: Head

Founded: 1982

Organisation type and purpose: University department or institute.

Subject coverage: Australian tertiary education; Australian literature, poetry and drama; international relations, history, politics, art, film; Australian scholarships and fellowships administered by MCAS.

Collection: Australia House Library (old Australian High Commission Library)
Files of Britain-Australia Bicentennial Committee

Non-library collection catalogue: All or part available online

Publications: Printed

Publications list: Available online and in print

Access to staff: Contact by letter, by telephone, by fax and by e-mail. Appointment necessary.
Hours: Mon to Fri, 1000 to 1700
Special comments: Secretarial staff answer telephone enquiries; academic staff available for comment and research advice on Australian subjects. Access to Australia House library collection with permission from MCAS.

Access to building: Prior appointment required

Constituent part of: King's College London, University of London

Funded by: The Australian Government

Links with: Sir Robert Menzies Memorial Foundation

MERCEDES-BENZ CLUB LIMITED

18 Viga Road, Winchmore Hill, London, N21 1HJ

Tel: 07071 818868
Website: www.mercedes-benzownersclub .co.uk

Enquiries to: Director and Membership Secretary
Direct e-mail: vharris@mercedes -benzownersclub.co.uk

Founded: 1952

Organisation type and purpose: Membership association (membership is by subscription), present number of members: 8,000.

Subject coverage: Mercedes-Benz cars.

Collection: Library of books and documents covering Mercedes-Benz cars from 1884 to the present

Publications: Printed

Access to staff: Contact by e-mail and via website
Hours: Mon to Fri, 0900 to 1700

MERCHANT TAYLORS' COMPANY

Formal name: Guild of Merchant Taylors of the Fraternity of St John Baptist in the City of London

Merchant Taylors' Hall, 30 Threadneedle Street, London, EC2R 8JB

Tel: 020 7450 4440
Fax: 020 7450 4499
E-mail: livery@merchant-taylors.co.uk
Website: www.merchant-taylors.co.uk

Founded: 1327

Organisation type and purpose: Membership association (membership is by election or invitation).
City of London Livery Company.

Access to staff: Contact by letter, by telephone, by fax, by e-mail and via website

MERCK, SHARP AND DOHME RESEARCH LABORATORIES (MSDRL)

Hertford Road, Hoddesdon, Hertfordshire, EN11 9BU

Tel: 01992 467272
Fax: 01992 451075
E-mail: externalaffairs_uk@merck.com
Website: www.msd-uk.com/
Website: www.merck.com

Enquiries to: Literature Resources Associate
Direct tel: 01279 440131
Direct fax: 01279 440667

Founded: 1983

Organisation type and purpose: International organisation.
Research division of multinational pharmaceutical company.

Subject coverage: Medicinal and organic chemistry; diseases of central nervous system; pharmacology; biochemistry.

Non-library collection catalogue: All or part available in-house

Library catalogue: All or part available in-house

Publications: Printed
Order printed publications from: Public Affairs Department, Merck & Co Inc, Whitehouse Station, New Jersey, 08889–0100, USA, tel: 00 1 908 423 1000

Access to staff: Contact by letter and by e-mail
Hours: Mon to Fri, 0900 to 1700
Special comments: Not open to the public.

Links with: Merck & Co Inc; One Merck Drive, PO Box 100, Whitehouse Station, NJ 08889–0100, USA

MERIONETH HISTORICAL AND RECORD SOCIETY (MHRS)

Bryn Bedd, Nantgwynant, Caernarfon, Gwynedd, LL55 4NL

Tel: 01766 890550
E-mail: Merfynwyntomos@gwynedd.gov.uk

Enquiries to: Hon. Membership Secretary

Founded: 1939

Organisation type and purpose: Learned society (membership is by subscription), present number of members: 318, voluntary organisation.

Subject coverage: History, geography and literature of Merioneth.

Publications: Printed

Access to staff: Contact by letter, by telephone and by e-mail

MERRIST WOOD CAMPUS

Worplesdon, Guildford, Surrey, GU3 3PE

Tel: 01483 884000
Fax: 01483 884001
E-mail: mwinfo@guildford.ac.uk
Website: www.guildford.ac.uk

Enquiries to: Learner Services
Direct tel: 01483 884040

Founded: 1945

Organisation type and purpose: Suitable for ages: 16+.
College of the land-based industries.

Subject coverage: Arboriculture, horticulture, countryside, practical habitat management, small-scale farming, plant production, garden design, landscape construction, equine studies, animal care, greenkeeping and sports turf management, professional floristry, golf studies, bespoke training, public services

Publications: Printed

Access to staff: Contact by letter, by telephone, by fax, by e-mail, in person and via website
Hours: Mon to Fri, 0900 to 1700

MERSEYSIDE INDUSTRIAL HERITAGE SOCIETY (MIHS)

Merseyside Maritime Museum, Albert Dock, Liverpool, L3 4AQ

Tel: 0151 478 4402
Fax: 0151 478 4590

Enquiries to: Secretary

Founded: 1964

Organisation type and purpose: Learned society.

Subject coverage: Industrial archaeology and history, particularly of Merseyside; history of public services, docks, railways, canals, manufacturing industries, buildings, trades, chemical industry, transport, power generation, mining and quarrying.

Collection: Site Record Cards (held by Merseyside Archaeological Service, tel: 0151 478 4258)

Publications: Printed

Publications list: Available in print

Works closely with: Merseyside Maritime Museum (part of National Museums and Galleries on Merseyside); Albert Dock, Liverpool, L3 4AQ; tel: 0151 207 0001

MERSEYSIDE RECORD OFFICE

Liverpool Libraries Satellite Service, Unit 33, Wellington Employment Park South, Dunes Way, Liverpool, L5 9ZS

Tel: 0151 233 5817
Fax: 0151 233 5824
E-mail: recoffice.central.library@liverpool.gov.uk

Enquiries to: Archivist

Founded: 1974

Organisation type and purpose: Local government body.
Record office.

Subject coverage: Merseyside County Council, residuary body and joint authority records; Liverpool, Southport and Wirral coroners; some hospital records; some nonconformist church records; some business records; social agencies, e.g. League of Welldoers.

Non-library collection catalogue: All or part available in-house

Publications: Printed

Access to staff: Contact by letter, by telephone, by fax, by e-mail and in person. Appointment necessary.
Hours: Mon to Sat, 0900 to 1700
Special comments: Search fee for written enquiries requiring research.
Proof of identity required, including address.

Access to building: *Hours:* Tue to Sat, 0930 to 1630
Special comments: Appointment only, minimum 24 hours' notice.

Access for disabled people: Ramped entry, toilet facilities

MERTHYR TYDFIL COUNTY BOROUGH COUNCIL (MTCBC)

Civic Centre, Castle Street, Merthyr Tydfil, Mid Glamorgan, CF47 8AN

Tel: 01685 725000
Fax: 01685 722146
E-mail: customer.care@merthyr.gov.uk
Website: www.merthyr.gov.uk

Enquiries to: Public Relations Manager
Direct tel: 01685 725166
Direct fax: 01685 374397
Direct e-mail: public.relations@merthyr.gov.uk

Founded: 1996

Organisation type and purpose: Local government body.

Subject coverage: Local government, education, social services, community services, technical services, local government finance.

Library catalogue: All or part available online, in-house and in print

Publications list: Available online and in print

Access to staff: Contact by letter, by telephone, by fax, by e-mail and via website. Appointment necessary.
Hours: Mon to Thu, 0830 to 1700; Fri, 0830 to 1630

MERTHYR TYDFIL PUBLIC LIBRARIES

Central Library, High Street, Merthyr Tydfil, Mid Glamorgan, CF47 8AF

Tel: 01685 723057
Fax: 01685 370690
E-mail: library.services@merthyr.gov.uk

Enquiries to: Librarian

Founded: 1935

Organisation type and purpose: Local government body, public library.

Subject coverage: Local history collection, the borough of Merthyr Tydfil, 19th-century iron and steel industry, coal mining in South Wales, Quakerism, Aberfan and the 1966 disaster.

Collection: Aberfan Tribunal Report
Photographic collection – Borough of Merthyr Tydfil
Welsh ballads

Non-library collection catalogue: All or part available online and in print

Library catalogue: All or part available online and in-house

Publications: Printed, and electronic and video

Publications list: Available in print

Access to staff: Contact by letter, by telephone, by fax, by e-mail and in person
Hours: Mon, Fri, 0900 to 1800; Tue, 0900 to 1900; Wed, Thurs, 0900 to 1730

Access to building: No access other than to staff

Access for disabled people: Ramped entry

MERTON COLLEGE LIBRARY

Merton College, Oxford, OX1 4JD

Tel: 01865 276380
Fax: 01865 276361
E-mail: library@merton.ox.ac.uk
Website: www.lib.ox.ac.uk/libraries/libcats.html

Enquiries to: Librarian

Founded: 1264

Organisation type and purpose: University department or institute, college library of the University of Oxford

Subject coverage: General, no special fields.

Collection: Max Beerbohm Collection
F H Bradley Collection
Brenchley Collection of printed materials by T S Eliot
Medieval manuscripts
Merton College Archives

continued overleaf

Merton Blackwell Collection of archival material relating to Sir Basil Blackwell and Blackwells booksellers and publishers

Non-library collection catalogue: All or part available online and in-house

Library catalogue: All or part available online and in-house

Access to staff: Contact by letter, by telephone, by fax and by e-mail. Appointment necessary.
Hours: Mon to Fri, 0900 to 1700

Access to building: Prior appointment required

MERTON LIBRARIES AND HERITAGE SERVICES

12th Floor, Merton Civic Centre, London Road, Morden, Surrey, SM4 5DX

Tel: 020 8545 3783
Fax: 020 8545 3237
E-mail: ingrid.lackajis@merton.gov.uk
Website: www.merton.gov.uk
Website: www.merton.gov.uk/libraries

Enquiries to: Head of Library and Heritage Services
Direct tel: 020 8545 3770
Direct e-mail: library.enquiries@merton.gov .uk

Organisation type and purpose: Local government body, museum, public library.

Subject coverage: General and local studies: at Morden Library; William Morris, Horatio Nelson: at Wimbledon Library; business and European information: at Morden Library; Merton Local Studies Centre.

Collection: The following are all in Local Studies Centre:
Carters Tested Seeds Collection at Morden
Simpson Papers at Morden
Tom Francis Picture Collection (transparencies) at Morden

Non-library collection catalogue: All or part available online and in-house

Library catalogue: All or part available online and in-house

Publications: Printed

Access to staff: Contact by letter, by telephone, by fax, by e-mail and in person. Appointment necessary.
Hours: Variable hours – please contact for details

Access to building: Appointment required

Parent body: London Borough of Merton, Community and Housing Department; Merton Civic Centre, London Road, Morden, Surrey, SM4 5DX; website: http://www .merton.gov.uk

MESEMB STUDY GROUP (MSG)

Formal name: Mesembryanthemum Study Group

Brenfield, Bolney Road, Ansty, West Sussex, RH17 5AW

Tel: 01444 459151
Fax: 01444 454061
E-mail: msg@cactus-mall.com
Website: www.mesemb.org/index.html

Enquiries to: Honorary Secretary

Founded: 1985

Organisation type and purpose: International organisation, membership association (membership is by subscription).

Subject coverage: Study of plants of the family mesembryanthemaceae.

Publications: Printed

Publications list: Available in print

Access to staff: Contact by letter, by telephone, by fax, by e-mail and via website. Appointment necessary.
Hours: Mon to Fri, 0900 to 1700

Access to building: Prior appointment required

Access for disabled people: Level entry

MESSERSCHMITT OWNERS CLUB (MOC)

169 Coulsdon Road, Coulsdon, Surrey, CR5 1EG

Tel: 01527 61826
Website: www.messerschmitt.co.uk

Enquiries to: General Secretary

Founded: 1956

Organisation type and purpose: Membership association.

Subject coverage: Preservation of Messerschmitt/Fend vehicles and historic technical data relating to their design, specific vehicle information, given chassis numbers etc.

Collection: Refer to Messerschmitt Foundation of Great Britain, 0121 744 2615

Publications: Printed

Access to staff: Contact by letter and by e-mail
Hours: Mon to Fri, 0900 to 1700

Affiliated to: Messerschmitt Club Deutschland eV

MET OFFICE – EDINBURGH

Saughton House, Broomhouse Drive, Edinburgh, EH11 3XQ

Tel: 0131 528 7319
Fax: 0131 244 8389
E-mail: metlib@metoffice.gov.uk
Website: www.metoffice.gov.uk

Enquiries to: Archive Information Officer

Founded: 1854

Organisation type and purpose: National government body.
Public record office.

Subject coverage: Meteorology, climatology.

Collection: Weather records for Scotland

Non-library collection catalogue: All or part available in-house

Library catalogue: All or part available online

Access to staff: Contact by letter, by telephone, by fax and by e-mail. Appointment necessary.
Hours: Mon to Fri, 0930 to 1600

Access for disabled people: Yes
Hours: Mon to Fri, 0930 to 1600

Branch of: National Meteorological Library; Met Office, FitzRoy Road, Exeter, Devon, EX1 3PB; tel: 0870 900 0100; fax: 0870 900 5050; e-mail: enquiries@metoffice.gov.uk

MET OFFICE – EXETER

FitzRoy Road, Exeter, Devon, EX1 3PB

Tel: 01392 885680
Fax: 01392 885681
E-mail: enquiries@metoffice.gov.uk
Website: www.metoffice.com

Enquiries to: Press Officer
Direct tel: 01392 886655
Direct e-mail: pressoffice@metoffice.gov.uk
Other contacts: Library Information Officer tel: 01344 854841/856694; Archive Manager tel: 01344 855960

Founded: 1854

Organisation type and purpose: National government body.
Government Agency (Trading Fund).
The UK's National Met Service providing advice on the world's weather and natural environment to private and public sector customers.

Subject coverage: Meteorology, climatology and most aspects of atmospheric and related sciences, application and meteorological information to weather-sensitive activities and planning, fundamental research in meteorology and professional training.

Collection: Original weather records (4.5 km of shelves) archived under the terms of the Public Records Act
Rare and historical books and pamphlets on meteorology and climatology held in conjunction with the Royal Meteorological Society

Publications: Printed

Access to staff: Contact by telephone
Hours: By telephone to Customer Centre – 24 hours
Special comments: National Meteorological Library and Archives open to the general public.

Access for disabled people: Parking provided, ramped entry, toilet facilities

Trading arm of the: Ministry of Defence

METAL PACKAGING MANUFACTURERS ASSOCIATION (MPMA)

The Stables, Tintagel Farm, Sandhurst Road, Wokingham, Berkshire, RG40 3JD

Tel: 01189 788433
Fax: 01189 788433
E-mail: enquiries@mpma.org.uk
Website: www.mpma.org.uk

Enquiries to: Director

Founded: 1977

Organisation type and purpose: Trade association.

Subject coverage: Metal packaging; cans, tins, and other containers and closures.

Trade and statistical information: UK statistics

Access to staff: Contact by e-mail

Hours: Mon to Fri, 0900 to 1700

Access to building: No access other than to staff

METALFORMING MACHINERY MAKERS ASSOCIATION LIMITED (MMMA)

The Cottage, Down End, Hook Norton, Oxfordshire, OX15 5LW

Tel: 01608 737129
Fax: 01295 253333
E-mail: enquiries@mmma.org.uk
Website: www.mmma.org.uk

Enquiries to: Secretary

Founded: 1949

Organisation type and purpose: Trade association.

Subject coverage: Metal forming machinery trade.

Publications: Printed

Access to staff: Contact by letter, by telephone, by fax and by e-mail
Hours: Mon to Fri, 0900 to 1700

Member of: METCOM

METALS INDUSTRY SKILLS & PERFORMANCE LIMITED

5–6 Meadowcourt, Amos Road, Sheffield, South Yorkshire, S9 1BX

Tel: 0114 244 6833
Fax: 0114 256 2855
E-mail: enquiries@metskill.co.uk
Website: www.metskill.co.uk

Enquiries to: Director, Marketing and Communications
Direct e-mail: d.vinall@metskill.co.uk

Founded: 1990

Organisation type and purpose: Membership association (membership is by subscription), present number of members: 90 companies, training organisation, consultancy.
To raise the profile, quality and effectiveness of training, to contribute to the competitive success of the UK steel industry, to influence the training field.

Subject coverage: All types of education, training, qualifications and skills for the steel and metals industries.

Trade and statistical information: An analysis of steel industry skills.
Workforce Development Plan

Publications: Electronic and video

Publications list: Available in print

Access to staff: Contact by letter, by telephone, by fax, by e-mail and via website. Appointment necessary.
Hours: Mon to Fri, 0900 to 1700

Access to building: Prior appointment required

Access for disabled people: Parking provided, level entry, toilet facilities

Also at: Metals Industry Skills and Performance Limited; Suite 15, Vision Point, Vaughan Trading Estate, Sedgely Road East, Tipton, West Midlands, DY4 7UJ; tel: 0121 521 5511/5512/5513; fax: 0121 521 5510; e-mail: enquiries@metskill.co.uk

Has a division: Metals Industry Competitive Enterprise (MICE); e-mail: enquiries@metalsindustry.co.uk

Parent body: UK Steel Association

METAMORPHIC ASSOCIATION (MA)

PO Box 32368, London, SW17 8YB

Tel: 0870 770 7984
Fax: 020 8672 5951
E-mail: metamorphicassoc@aol.com
Website: www.metamorphicassociation.org.uk

Enquiries to: Director

Founded: 1979

Organisation type and purpose: Membership association (membership is by qualification), present number of members: 500+, registered charity (charity number 326525), training organisation.

Subject coverage: Teaching and practice of the Metamorphic Technique for self-healing and personal growth.

Publications: Printed, and electronic and video

Publications list: Available online and in print

Access to staff: Contact by letter, by telephone, by fax, by e-mail and in person. Appointment necessary.
Hours: Mon to Fri, 0930 to 1730

METANOIA INSTITUTE

13 North Common Road, Ealing, London, W5 2QB

Tel: 020 8579 2505
Fax: 020 8832 3070
E-mail: info@metanoia.ac.uk
Website: www.metanoia.ac.uk

Enquiries to: General Manager

Founded: 1994

Organisation type and purpose: Membership association (membership is by subscription), present number of members: 1000, registered charity (charity number 1050175), suitable for ages: adults, training organisation.
Training in counselling, psychotherapy and counselling psychology – part-time.

Subject coverage: Training in counselling, psychotherapy and counselling psychology with optional academic awards validated by Middlesex University at BA, MSc, Masters, Doctorate level.

Library catalogue: All or part available in-house

Publications: Printed

Access to staff: Contact by letter, by telephone, by fax, by e-mail, in person and via website
Hours: Mon to Fri, 0900 to 1700
Special comments: Training at weekends 0930 to 1730.

Access to building: No prior appointment required
Hours: Mon to Fri, 0900 to 1700
Special comments: Trainees only at weekends.

Access for disabled people: Ramped entry, toilet facilities

METEOROLOGICAL OFFICE

Weather Centres/Climate Offices: Aberdeen Weather Centre; Lime Street, Aberdeen, AB11 5FJ; tel: 01224 210574; fax: 01224 210575; Belfast Climate Offices; 32 College Street, Belfast, BT1 6BQ; tel: 028 9032 8457; fax: 028 9032 8457; Belfast Weather Centre; Meteorological Office, Belfast International Airport, Belfast, BT29 4AB; tel: 028 9442 2339; fax: 028 9445 4091; Birmingham Weather Centre; 2040 The Crescent, Birmingham Business Park, Birmingham, B37 7YE; tel: 0121 717 0575; fax: 0121 717 0577; Bristol Weather Centre; 8th Floor, The Gaunt's House, Denmark Street, Bristol, BS1 5DH; tel: 0117 927 9298; fax: 0117 927 9060; Cardiff Weather Centre; Southgate House, Wood Street, Cardiff, CF1 1EW; tel: 029 2039 7020; fax: 029 2039 0435; Glasgow Weather Centre; Wallace House, 220 St Vincent Street, Glasgow, G2 5QD; tel: 0141 248 3451; fax: 0141 303 0101; Leeds Weather Centre; Oak House, Park Lane, Leeds, LS3 1EL; tel: 0113 245 1990; fax: 0113 2457760; London Weather Centre; 127 Clerkenwell Road, London, EC1R 5DB; tel: 020 7242 3663; fax: 020 7404 4314; Manchester Weather Centre; Applicon House, Exchange Street, Stockport, Cheshire, SK3 0ER; tel: 0161 477 1060; fax: 0161 476 0714; Newcastle Weather Centre; Portman House, Portland Road, Newcastle upon Tyne, NE2 1AQ; tel: 0191 232 3808; fax: 0191 261 4965; Norwich Weather Centre; Rouen House, Rouen Road, Norwich, Norfolk, NR1 1RB; tel: 01603 660779; fax: 01603 623531; Scottish Climate Office; Wallace House, 220 St Vincent Street, Glasgow, G2 5QD; tel: 0141 303 0110; fax: 0141 303 0101; Southampton Weather Centre; 160 High Street, Southampton, SO14 2BT; tel: 023 8022 8844; fax: 023 8022 8846

METHODIST ARCHIVES AND RESEARCH CENTRE (JRULM)

John Rylands University Library of Manchester, Deansgate, Manchester, M3 3EH

Tel: 0161 834 5343 or 6765
Fax: 0161 834 5574
E-mail: peter.nockles@man.ac.uk
Website: rylibweb.man.ac.uk/data1/dg/text/method.html

Enquiries to: Methodist Librarian

Organisation type and purpose: University library.

Subject coverage: Methodist church archives, Methodist history, women's studies, family history, chapel history, popular religion, social history, Methodist theology, Wesley family.

Collection: Books, letters, diaries, printed works of John Wesley
Collection of Class Tickets and Circuit Plans
Diaries (some 80 volumes, of prominent Methodists)

continued overleaf

General pamphlet literature, 1562–1933 (6000 items)
Letters of Methodist Ministers (50,000 items)
Pamphlet literature of the Methodist Movement (600 items)
Percy Collection (nucleus of a collection of hymn books, some 3000)
Papers of John and Mary Fletcher, 43 boxes of manuscripts

Publications: Printed

Publications list: Available in print

Access to staff: Contact by letter, by telephone, by fax, by e-mail and via website. Appointment necessary.
Hours: Mon to Fri, 1000 to 1730; Sat, 1000 to 1300
Special comments: E-mail or letter are preferred.

METHODIST MISSIONARY SOCIETY (MMS)

Methodist Church House, 25 Marylebone Road, London, NW1 5JR

Tel: 020 7486 5502
Fax: 020 7467 3761
E-mail: helpdesk@methodistchurch.org.uk
Website: www.methodist.org.uk

Founded: 1818

Organisation type and purpose: Registered Charity (charity number 1132208)

Subject coverage: Missionary work overseas since 1786.

Collection: Records of British Methodist Missionary Work (including photographs) from late 18th century to 1945, worldwide cover and on microfiche
Later accessions continue to be made available, 19th-century publications held with archives

Publications: Printed, and microform publications

Access to staff: Contact by letter. Letter of introduction required.
Hours: Mon to Thu, 0900 to 1700

Archives are held at the: Special Collections Reading Room; The Library, School of Oriental and African Studies, Thornhaugh Street, Russell Square, London, WC1H 0XG; tel: 020 7691 3347

METROPOLITAN BOROUGH OF BURY (Bury Metro)

Town Hall, Knowsley Street, Bury, Lancashire, BL9 0SW

Tel: 0161 253 5000
Fax: 0161 253 5079
E-mail: b.hargreaves@bury.gov.uk
Website: www.bury.gov.uk

Enquiries to: Information Officer

Founded: 1974

Organisation type and purpose: Local government body (membership is by election or invitation), present number of members: 51.

Subject coverage: Local government services.

Publications list: Available in print

Access to staff: Contact by letter, by telephone, by fax, by e-mail and via website. Appointment necessary.
Hours: Mon to Fri, 0900 to 1700

Access for disabled people: Parking provided, ramped entry, level entry, access to all public areas, toilet facilities

METROPOLITAN BOROUGH OF DONCASTER (DMBC)

2 Priory Place, Doncaster, South Yorkshire, DN1 1BN

Tel: 01302 734444
Fax: 01302 734040
Website: www.doncaster.gov.uk

Enquiries to: Chief Executive
Other contacts: Press and Public Relations Manager for media, public relations.

Founded: 1974

Organisation type and purpose: Local government body.

Subject coverage: Doncaster Borough, local authority matters.

Access to staff: Contact by letter, by telephone, by fax and by e-mail
Hours: Mon to Fri, 0900 to 1700

Access to building: No prior appointment required

METROPOLITAN BOROUGH OF KNOWSLEY

Municipal Buildings, Archway Road, Huyton, Merseyside, L36 9YU

Tel: 0151 489 6000
Fax: 0151 443 3507
E-mail: knowsley@connect.org.uk
Website: www.knowsley.gov.uk

Enquiries to: Chief Executive
Direct tel: 0151 443 3772
Direct fax: 0151 443 3030
Direct e-mail: steve.gallagher@knowsley.gov.uk

Founded: 1974

Organisation type and purpose: Local government body.

Subject coverage: Local government services.

Publications: Printed, and electronic and video

Access to staff: Contact by letter, by telephone, by fax, by e-mail and via website
Hours: Mon to Fri, 0900 to 1700

Access to building: No access other than to staff

Access for disabled people: Parking provided, level entry, toilet facilities

METROPOLITAN BOROUGH OF WIGAN (Wigan Council)

Town Hall, PO Box 36, Library Street, Wigan, Lancashire, WN1 1NN

Tel: 01942 244991
Fax: 01942 827451
Website: www.wiganmbc.gov.uk

Enquiries to: Chief Executive
Direct tel: 01942 827001

Founded: 1246

Organisation type and purpose: Local government body.

Subject coverage: Local government services, all aspects of the lives of 310,000 citizens from architects to gravediggers.

Trade and statistical information: Census details and demographic analyses, employment figures and resource procurement advice

Non-library collection catalogue: All or part available in-house

Library catalogue: All or part available in-house

Publications: Printed

Publications list: Available in print

Access to staff: Contact by letter, by telephone, by fax, by e-mail and in person
Hours: Mon to Fri, 0900 to 1700

Access to building: No access other than to staff

Access for disabled people: Ramped entry, access to all public areas, toilet facilities

METROPOLITAN POLICE ECONOMIC SPECIALIST CRIME OCU (MPS Specialist Crime OCU)

67–73 Buckingham Gate, London, SW1E 6BE

Tel: 020 7230 1212
Fax: 020 7230 1133

Enquiries to: Grade 9
Direct tel: 020 7230 1220
Direct e-mail: fraud.alert@met.police.uk

Organisation type and purpose: National government body.

Access to staff: Contact by letter
Hours: Mon to Fri, 0900 to 1700

METROPOLITAN SOCIETY FOR THE BLIND (MSB)

Lantern House, 102 Bermondsey Street, London, SE1 3UB

Tel: 020 7403 6184
Fax: 020 7234 0708
E-mail: enquiries@blindaid.org.uk

Enquiries to: Secretary

Founded: 1834

Subject coverage: The MSB assists blind and partially sighted residents of 12 Inner London Boroughs and the City of London.

Access to staff: Contact by letter, by telephone, by fax and by e-mail
Hours: Mon to Fri, 0930 to 1600

Access for disabled people: Level entry, access to all public areas, toilet facilities

MG OCTAGON CAR CLUB

Unit 1–3, Parchfields Farm, Trent Valley, Rugeley, Staffordshire, WS15 3HB

Tel: 01889 574666
Fax: 01889 574555
E-mail: harry@mgoctagoncarclub.com
Website: www.mgoctagoncarclub.com

Enquiries to: Secretary

Founded: 1969

Organisation type and purpose: International organisation, membership association (membership is by subscription). Caters for Pre-1956 MGs only.

Subject coverage: Pre-1956 MG parts, literature and publications, advice and assistance, valuations.

Collection: Chassis files, workshop manuals, parts lists, hand books

Publications: Printed

Publications list: Available online and in print

Access to staff: Contact by letter, by telephone, by fax, by e-mail and via website. Appointment necessary.
Hours: Mon to Fri, 0900 to 2200

MG OWNERS' CLUB

Octagon House, 1 Over Road, Swavesey, Cambridgeshire, CB24 4QZ

Tel: 01954 231125
Fax: 01954 232106
E-mail: mginfo@mgownersclub.co.uk
Website: www.mgownersclub.co.uk
Website: www.mgocspares.co.uk
Website: www.mgocworkshop.co.uk

Enquiries to: Secretary

Founded: 1973

Organisation type and purpose: Membership association (membership is by subscription), present number of members: 30,000.
To assist all owners of MG motor cars to run and maintain their vehicles at reasonable cost.

Subject coverage: MG motor cars from 1920s to present day.

Trade and statistical information: Full technical support service available for members, by telephone, email, written enquiry, fax, for all MG models.
Full range of spares available for visitors and on mail order, competitive specialist insurance scheme

Publications: Printed, and electronic and video

Access to staff: Contact by letter, by telephone, by fax, by e-mail, in person and via website
Hours: Mon to Fri, 0900 to 1730; Sat, 1000 to 1300

Access for disabled people: Parking provided, ramped entry, toilet facilities

MG OWNERS' CLUB (NORTHERN IRELAND) (MGOC (NI))

17 Meadowlands, Newtownabbey, Co Antrim, BT37 0UR

Tel: 028 9086 2807
E-mail: mgocni@btinternet.com
Website: www.mgocni.co.uk

Enquiries to: Secretary

Founded: 1981

Organisation type and purpose: Membership association.

Subject coverage: The MG car in Northern Ireland.

Access to staff: Contact by letter and by e-mail
Hours: Mon to Fri, 0900 to 1700

Affiliated to: MGOC, Swavesey

MI-21 WORLD METAL INDEX (MI-21 WMI)

Sheffield Libraries, Archives and Information, Central Library, Surrey Street, Sheffield, South Yorkshire, S1 1XZ

Tel: 0114 273 4714; 0114 273 4744
Fax: 0114 275 7405
E-mail: wmi@sheffield.gov.uk
Website: www.sheffield.gov.uk/worldmetalindex
Website: www.mi-21.com

Enquiries to: Information LIbrary Officer

Organisation type and purpose: Local government body.
Information service.

Subject coverage: The World Metal Index is the key to a unique collection of standards and specifications, trade literature and technical journals on both ferrous and non-ferrous metals. Over 200,000 individual metal grades are included, both current and historical. Together with Namtec and TWI, MI-21 World Metal Index provides in-depth information and technical support services. 20,000 datasheets currently available online by subscription. Access to remaining 180,000 as well as additonal resources and services of WMI is by telephone, fax and e-mail. 24-hour access to search the database by grade name, trade name, chemical and mechanical properties.
Information on metal properties, heat treatment, working, fabrication, welding, machining, corrosion, fatigue, creep and rupture properties.

Information services: Metals identification service; metals information service.

Collection: National standards and specifications: BS, BSEN, BSENISIO, ASTM, AMS, DIN, AFNOR, UNI; emerging producer nations' standards, e.g. China

Trade and statistical information: Trade literature collection from metal producers and suppliers

Access to staff: Contact by letter, by telephone, by fax, by e-mail and via website. Appointment necessary. All charged.
Hours: Mon to Fri, 0930 to 1630

Links with: National Metals Technology Centre (Namtec); Swinden House, Moorgate Road, Rotherham, South Yorkshire, S60 3AR; tel: 01709 724990; fax: 01709 724999; e-mail: info@namtec.co.uk; website: http://www.namtec.co.uk

MID DEVON DISTRICT COUNCIL

Phoenix House, Phoenix Lane, Tiverton, Devon EX16 6PP

Tel: 01884 255255
Fax: 01884 234318
Website: www.middevon.gov.uk

Enquiries to: Communication and Reputation Manager
Direct e-mail: communications@middevon.gov.uk

Organisation type and purpose: Local government body

Subject coverage: Provision of local services ranging from planning to recycling.

Publications list: Available in print

Access to staff: Contact by letter, by telephone, by fax, by e-mail and in person
Hours: Mon to Thu, 0900 to 1700; Fri, 0900 to 1630

MID SUFFOLK DISTRICT COUNCIL

Council Offices, 131 High Street, Needham Market, Suffolk, IP6 8DL

Tel: 01449 720711, 01140 727120 (minicom)
Fax: 01449 721946
E-mail: customerservice@csduk.com
Website: www.mid-suffolk-dc.gov.uk

Enquiries to: Publicity and Information Officer
Direct tel: 01449 727193
Direct fax: 01449 727187
Direct e-mail: elizabeth.woolnough@midsuffolk.co.uk

Organisation type and purpose: Local government body.

Access to staff: Contact by letter, by telephone and by fax
Hours: Mon to Fri, 0900 to 1700

MIDDLE EAST CENTRE LIBRARY AND ARCHIVES (MEC)

St Antony's College, Woodstock Road, Oxford, OX2 6JF

Tel: 01865 284700
Fax: 01865 311475
E-mail: mastan.ebtehaj@sant.ox.ac.uk
Website: www.sant.ox.ac.uk/areastudies/middle-east.shtml

Enquiries to: Librarian
Direct tel: 01865 284764
Other contacts: Archivist; tel: 01865 284706, e-mail: debbie.usher@sant.ox.ac.uk

Organisation type and purpose: University department or institute.
Regional centre of postgraduate college of Oxford University.

Subject coverage: Modern history, politics, international affairs and economics of the Middle East.

Collection: Papers of many Middle East diplomats

Access to staff: Contact by letter, by fax and by e-mail. Appointment necessary. Access for members only. Letter of introduction required.
Hours: Mon to Fri, 0930 to 1245 and 1345 to 1715

Includes the: Middle East Centre; tel: 01865 284764

MIDDLE EAST LIBRARIES COMMITTEE (UK) (MELCOM (UK))

The Library, School of Oriental and African Studies, University of London, Thornhaugh Street, Russell Square, London, WC1H 0XG

Tel: 020 7898 4152
Fax: 020 7436 3844
E-mail: lis-middleeast@mailbase.ac.uk
Website: www.ex.ac.uk/melcom/

Enquiries to: Secretary
Direct tel: 020 7323 6099
Direct e-mail: pc7@soas.ac.uk

Founded: 1967

Organisation type and purpose: Voluntary organisation, university department or institute.
Libraries having substantial Middle East collections, and of individuals in the UK concerned with collecting, organising and making available materials on the Middle East.

Subject coverage: Middle Eastern studies from the rise of Islam to the present; Islamic studies; Arabic, Persian and Turkish studies.

Collection: Collections are held by most of the member libraries; notable are those of Cambridge University Library; Middle East Centre, St Antony's College Oxford; Durham University Library; British Library Oriental Collections; London University School of Oriental and African Studies Library; John Rylands University Library of Manchester; Exeter University Library and The Bodleian Library, Oxford. Documents are held by the Documentation Unit, Centre for Middle Eastern and Islamic Studies, University of Durham and the Documentation Unit, Centre for Arab Gulf Studies, University of Exeter; Selly Oak Colleges Library, Birmingham; Edinburgh University Library

Publications: Printed
Order printed publications from: Joppa Books Ltd
68 High Road, Byfleet, Surrey, KT14 7QL, tel: 01932 336777, fax: 01932 348881, e-mail: joppa@dial.pipex.com

Publications list: Available online

Access to staff: Contact by e-mail
Hours: Mon to Fri, 0900 to 1700

Affiliated to: British Society for Middle Eastern Studies

MIDDLE TEMPLE LIBRARY

Formal name: The Honourable Society of the Middle Temple Library

Middle Temple Lane, London, EC4Y 9BT

Tel: 020 7427 4830
Fax: 020 7427 4831
E-mail: library@middletemple.org.uk
Website: www.middletemplelibrary.org.uk

Enquiries to: Keeper of the Library

Founded: 1641

Organisation type and purpose: Legal library.

Subject coverage: Law.

Collection: 150,000 vols of mainly English law
Law Reports
Government publications
Ecclesiastical Collection
Rare Books Collection
EU Collection
American Collection
Capital Punishment Collection
Middle Temple Archive (administrative, financial, membership and property records of the Inn since 1501)

Non-library collection catalogue: All or part available in-house

Library catalogue: All or part available online

Access to staff: Contact by letter, by telephone, by fax and by e-mail.
Appointment necessary. Access for members only. Non-members charged.
Hours: Term time: Mon to Thu, 0900 to 2000; Fri, 0900 to 1900; every fourth Sat in rotation with the other Inns of Court Libraries, 1000 to 1700

Access to building: Private library for use by members of the four Inns of Court. Enquiries under special circumstances from non-members, for whom access is strictly by appointment. Visits for research by appointment only.
Hours: Term time: Mon to Thu, 0900 to 2000; Fri, 0900 to 1900. Vacation time: Mon to Fri, 0900 to 1730

Access for disabled people: Wheelchair ramp at library entrance; lift to all floors

MIDDLESBROUGH LIBRARIES AND INFORMATION

Central Library, Victoria Square, Middlesbrough, TS1 2AY

Tel: 01642 729001
Fax: 01642 729954
E-mail: reference_library@middlesbrough.gov.uk
Website: www.middlesbrough.gov.uk

Enquiries to: Reference Librarian

Organisation type and purpose: Local government body, public library.

Subject coverage: All areas covered, local history of Middlesbrough and surrounding area, North Yorkshire and South Durham.

Collection: Dickie Collection (maritime subjects)
William Kelly Collection (mostly theological works and bibles)
All major national newspapers published in England from 1990 to 1996 on CD-ROM
North Eastern Daily Gazette, Middlesbrough, 1869 to present (microfilm); Times, 1785 to present, many other local and national newspapers

Library catalogue: All or part available online

Publications: Printed

Access to staff: Contact by letter, by telephone, by fax, by e-mail and in person. Appointment necessary.
Hours: Mon, Tue, Thu, 0930 to 1900; Wed, Fri, Sat, 0930 to 1700

Comprises: 11 libraries

Links with: other Teesside Archives

MIDDLESEX UNIVERSITY

Learning Resources, The Sheppard Library, The Burroughs, London, NW4 4BT

Tel: 020 8411 5234
Fax: 020 8362 5163
E-mail: via website
Website: www.lr.mdx.ac.uk/

Enquiries to: Director of Learning Resources and University Librarian

Founded: 1973

Organisation type and purpose: University library.

Subject coverage: Accountancy and finance; business; mathematics; business studies; management; marketing; economics; computing science; product design; geography; pollution; art and design; interior design; humanities; law; sociology and social policy; social work; psychology; criminology; architecture and interior design; education; performance arts (music, dance, drama); computer graphics; flood hazard research; hotel catering and tourism management; psychology; robotics; transport planning and management; teacher training; education; nursing; health studies.

Collection: Runnymede Trust Library
Black Theatre Forum Archive
Bernie Grant Archive
Hall-Carpenter Archive (jointly held with BLPES), a national lesbian and gay archive, 40,000 items of press cuttings

Non-library collection catalogue: All or part available online

Library catalogue: All or part available online

Access to staff: Contact by letter, by telephone, by fax, by e-mail and via website. Appointment necessary. Letter of introduction required. Non-members charged.
Hours: Hours vary (term time only) by campus, within: Mon to Thu, 0900 to 2000; Fri, 0900 to 1800; Sat, 1100 to 1700

Access to building: *Hours:* Mon to Thu, 0830 to 2200; Fri, 0830 to 2000; Sat, 1100 to 1700

Access for disabled people: Parking provided
Special comments: Access arrangements vary at each campus.

Campuses at: Archway; 10 Highgate Hill, London, N19 5ND; Cat Hill; Barnet, Hertfordshire, EN4 8HT; tel: 020 8411 5042; Hendon; The Burroughs, London, NW4 4BT; Trent Park; Bramley Road, London, N14 4YZ

MIDLAND RAILWAY CENTRE

Butterley Station, Ripley, Derbyshire, DE5 3QZ

Tel: 01773 747674
Fax: 01773 570721
E-mail: information@midlandrailwaycentre.co.uk

Enquiries to: Manager

Founded: 1969

Organisation type and purpose: Membership association (membership is by subscription), present number of members: 1,200, voluntary organisation, registered charity (charity number 502278), museum, training organisation.

Subject coverage: Railway history, demonstration signal box, Victorian railwayman's church. 3.5-mile heritage railway, Golden Valley Light Railway (2ft gauge), Butterley Park Miniature Railway (3.5in and 5in gauges), model railways.

Collection: Archive of railway books, records and photography
Collection of railway equipment, mainly Midland Railway, its predecessors and successors
Princess Royal Class Locomotive Trust Depot
Midland Diesel Group collection of main line diesel power
Stationary Power Gallery

Publications: Printed

Access to staff: Contact by letter, by telephone and by fax. Appointment necessary.
Hours: Mon to Fri, 0900 to 1700

Access to building: Prior appointment required
Hours: Static display: daily, 1000 to 1615
Closed Christmas Day

Access for disabled people: Parking provided, toilet facilities

Affiliated to: Midland Railway Enterprises plc; Midland Railway Trust

MIDLANDS AGRICULTURAL INFORMATION GROUP (MidAIG)

Warwickshire College, Moreton Morrell Centre, Moreton Morrell, Warwick, CV35 9BL

Tel: 01926 318278
Fax: 01926 318300
E-mail: info@warkscol.ac.uk

Enquiries to: Membership Secretary
Direct e-mail: librarymm@warkscol.ac.uk

Founded: 1982

Organisation type and purpose: Voluntary organisation.
An informal group of information services personnel who meet annually with an informal network to assist each other professionally – inter-library cooperation.

Subject coverage: Generally land-based industries: agriculture, horticulture, conservation of natural resources, food science and applied biology, equine industry, small animal care, arboriculture, construction, greenkeeping.

Access to staff: Contact by letter, by telephone, by fax and by e-mail. Appointment necessary.
Hours: Mon to Thu, 0830 to 2200; Fri, 0830 to 1700; Sat, 1000 to 1600
Vacations: Mon to Fri, 0915 to 1645

Access to building: Prior appointment required

Access for disabled people: Level entry, access to all public areas, toilet facilities

Members are: Librarians and information professionals and other staff in libraries and information services with an agricultural/ land-based industry related subject area or interest

MIDLANDS CLUB CRICKET CONFERENCE (MCCC)

65 Tilesford Close, Monkspath, Solihull, West Midlands, B90 4YF

Tel: 0121 744 6746; 07890 739489
E-mail: murray.ali@gmail.com
Website: www.mccc.co.uk

Enquiries to: Honorary Secretary

Founded: 1947

Organisation type and purpose: Membership association, voluntary organisation.

Subject coverage: All matters relating to cricket.

Publications: Printed

Access to staff: Contact by letter, by telephone, by e-mail and via website
Hours: Mon to Fri, 0900 to 2100

MIDLOTHIAN COUNCIL

Midlothian House, Buccleuch Street, Dalkeith, Midlothian, EH22 1DN

Tel: 0131 270 7500, 0131 271 3610 (minicom)
Fax: 0131 271 3050
Website: www.midlothian.gov.uk
Website: www.earl.org.uk/partners/midlothian/index.html

Enquiries to: Communications Manager
Direct tel: 0131 271 3425
Direct fax: 0131 271 3536
Direct e-mail: Susan.Whiteford@midlothian.gov.uk

Founded: 1996

Organisation type and purpose: Local government body.

Subject coverage: Information about council services available to the people of Midlothian, and how to access them.

Library catalogue: All or part available in-house

Publications: Printed

Publications list: Available online

Access to staff: Contact by letter, by e-mail and via website
Hours: Mon to Fri, 0930 to 1530

Access to building: No prior appointment required

MIDLOTHIAN COUNCIL LIBRARY SERVICES

Library Headquarters, 2 Clerk Street, Loanhead, Midlothian, EH20 9DR

Tel: 0131 271 3980
Fax: 0131 440 4635
E-mail: library.hq@midlothian.gov.uk
Website: www.midlothian.gov.uk/library

Enquiries to: Library Services Manager
Direct tel: 0131 271 3970
Direct e-mail: alan.reid@midlothian.gov.uk

Founded: 1996

Organisation type and purpose: Local government body, public library.

Subject coverage: General, local history of Midlothian.

Collection: Black Collection (Penicuik historical interest)
Midlothian Council Archive

Library catalogue: All or part available online

Publications: Printed, and electronic and video

Publications list: Available online and in print

Access to staff: Contact by letter, by telephone, by fax, by e-mail and via website. Appointment necessary.
Hours: Mon to Thu, 0900 to 1700; Fri, 0900 to 1530
Special comments: Opening hours vary, contact individual branch.

Access for disabled people: Parking provided, ramped entry, toilet facilities

Branch libraries: Bonnyrigg Library; 31 Polton Street, Bonnyrigg, Midlothian, EH19 3HB; tel: 0131 663 6762; fax: 0131 654 9019; e-mail: bonnyrigg.library@midlothian.gov.uk; Dalkeith Library; White Hart Street, Dalkeith, Midlothian, EH22 1AE; tel: 0131 663 2083; fax: 0131 654 9029; e-mail: dalkeith.library@midlothian.gov.uk; Danderhall Library; 1a Campview, Danderhall, Midlothian, EH22 1QD; tel: 0131 663 9293; e-mail: danderhall.library@midlothian.gov.uk; Gorebridge Library; 98 Hunterfield Road, Gorebridge, Midlothian, EH23 4TT; tel: 01875 820630; fax: 01875 823657; e-mail: gorebridge.library@midlothian.gov.uk; Loanhead Library; George Avenue, Loanhead, Midlothian, EH20 9HD; tel: 0131 440 0824; e-mail: loanhead.library@midlothian.gov.uk; Local Studies Library; 2 Clerk Street, Loanhead, Midlothian, EH20 9DR; tel: 0131 271 3976; fax: 0131 440 4635; e-mail: local.studies@midlothian.gov.uk; Mayfield Library; Stone Avenue, Mayfield, Dalkeith, Midlothian, EH22 5PB; tel: 0131 663 2126; e-mail: mayfield.library@midlothian.gov.uk; Newtongrange Library; St David's, Newtongrange, Midlothian, EH22 4LG; tel: 0131 663 1816; fax: 0131 654 1990; e-mail: newtongrange.library@midlothian.gov.uk; Penicuik Library; The Penicuik Centre, Carlops Road, Penicuik EH26 9EP; tel: 01968 664050; fax: 01968 679408; e-mail: penicuik.library@midlothian.gov.uk; Roslin Library; 9 Main Street, Roslin, Midlothian, EH25 9LD; tel: 0131 448 2781; e-mail: roslin.library@midlothian.gov.uk; Woodburn Library; Dalkeith Leisure Centre, 6 Woodburn Road, Dalkeith, Midlothian, EH22 2AR; tel: 0131 654 4323; e-mail: woodburn.library@midlothian.gov.uk

Parent body: Midlothian Council; Midlothian House, Buccleuch Street, Dalkeith, Midlothian, EH22 1DJ; tel: 0131 270 7500; fax: 0131 271 3050; e-mail: enquiries@midlothian.gov.uk

MIGRAINE ACTION (MA)

27 East Street, Leicester, LE1 6NB

continued overleaf

Tel: 0116 275 8317
Fax: 0116 254 2023
E-mail: info@migraine.org.uk
Website: www.migraine.org.uk
Website: www.migraine.org.uk/youngmigraineurs

Founded: 1958

Organisation type and purpose: Migraine Action is the UK's leading charity dedicated to individuals affected by migraine. It is a registered charity that aims to bridge the gap between the migraineur and the medical world by providing information on all aspects of the condition and its management.

Subject coverage: Has a wide range of information booklets available on migraine, including preventative and acute treatments, migraine triggers, stress management, complementary therapies, and migraine in children and young people.

Information services: Dedicated telephone helpline: 0116 275 8317, to give information and advice to migraineurs and those affected by migraine.

Education services: Migraine education days held throughout the UK. These give migraineurs the opportunity to meet with others affected in their area, hear from experts in the field, and learn more about Migraine Action's work on their behalf.

Publications: Printed
Order printed publications from: Visit our online shop for a full list of leaflets: http://www.migraine.org.uk/shop; tel: 0116 275 8317; e-mail: info@migraine.org.uk

Publications list: Available online

Access to staff: Contact by letter, by telephone, by fax, by e-mail and via website. Appointment necessary.
Hours: Mon to Fri, 0930 to 1630

Access to building: *Hours:* Mon to Fri, 0930 to 1630

MIGRAINE TRUST

Formal name: The Migraine Trust

52–53 Russell Square, London, WC1B 4HP

Tel: 020 7631 6975
Fax: 020 7436 2886
E-mail: info@migrainetrust.org
Website: www.migrainetrust.org

Enquiries to: Information and Enquiry Service
Direct tel: 020 7631 6975
Direct fax: N/A
Direct e-mail: info@migrainetrust.org

Founded: 1965

Organisation type and purpose: National organisation, registered charity (charity number 1081300).
The Migraine Trust is the health and medical research charity for migraine in the United Kingdom. It is committed to funding and promoting research, raising awareness and providing information and advocacy.

Subject coverage: An Information and Enquiry Service is available for questions people may have about migraine, other headaches and their management. All information is based on the best available evidence.
The Migraine Trust produces a range of fact sheets and information packs covering such issues as medication, specialist clinics, young migraine sufferers and managing migraine in the workplace.

Information services: Information and Enquiry Service – for questions about migraine, other headaches and their management; tel: 020 7631 6975; e-mail: info@migrainetrust.org.

Publications: Printed
Order printed publications from: info@migrainetrust.org

Publications list: Available in print

Access to staff: Contact by letter, by telephone, by fax, by e-mail and via website
Hours: Answerphone before 0900 and after 1700

MIGRANTS RESOURCE CENTRE

24 Churton Street, London, SW1V 2LP

Tel: 020 7834 2505
Website: www.migrantsresourcecentre.org.uk

Organisation type and purpose: The Centre works with migrants and refugees from all over the world, providing assistance and advice and helping to enable full participation in British society.

Information services: Online Centre.
Legal Advice Team at: Derry House, Penfold Street, London, NW8 8HJ; tel: 0845 241 0961

MILITARY HERALDRY SOCIETY

The Cloth Insignia Research and Collectors Society, Windyridge, 27 Sandbrook, Ketley, Telford, Shropshire, TF1 5BB

Tel: 01952 270221
Website: www.militaryheraldrysociety.co.uk

Enquiries to: Publicity Officer
Direct tel: 01952 270221
Direct e-mail: billbowbagins@hotmail.com

Founded: 1951

Organisation type and purpose:
International organisation, membership association (membership is by subscription), present number of members: 320, research organisation.
Collecting.

Subject coverage: Research and study of military cloth insignia (formation signs, shoulder titles, regimental and unit flashes, skill-at-arms and similar cloth items).

Publications: Printed

Access to staff: Contact by letter, by telephone and by e-mail

MILITARY VEHICLE TRUST (MVT)

General Secretary, Meadowhead Cottage, Beaumaris Avenue, Blackburn, Lancashire, BB2 4TP

Tel: 01254 202253
E-mail: gensec@mvt.org.uk
Website: www.mvt.org.uk

Enquiries to: Membership Secretary
Direct tel: 0845 475 1941
Direct e-mail: membershipsec@mvt.org.uk

Founded: 1968

Organisation type and purpose:
Membership association, registered charity.
Contact with owners of all ex-military vehicles to share information and give advice on preservation, and to provide details of club activities. Vehicle verification service. Shop. Monitoring of new legislation to ensure continuing use of preserved vehicles.

Subject coverage: Preservation and restoration of historic military vehicles.

Collection: Vehicle manual library (for the use of members)

Library catalogue: All or part available online

Publications: Printed

Access to staff: Contact by letter, by telephone, by e-mail and via website
Hours: Evenings and weekends, up to 2100

MILTON KEYNES & NORTH BUCKS CHAMBER OF COMMERCE (MKCOC)

World Trade Center @ The Hub, 9 Rillaton Walk, Central Milton Keynes, MK9 2FZ

Tel: 01908 259000
Fax: 01908 246799
E-mail: enquiry@mk-chamber.co.uk
Website: www.mk-chamber.co.uk

Enquiries to: Information Services Manager
Direct tel: 01908 259433

Founded: 1995

Organisation type and purpose:
Membership association (membership is by subscription), present number of members: over 1400.
Business Link brings together a wide range of support services for growing businesses in Milton Keynes. Part of a national network it is committed to improving the competitiveness of UK Industry and Commerce.

Subject coverage: International trade, Europe desk, business information (local, UK and worldwide).

Collection: Business and trade directories, reference books
CD-ROM and online databases

Trade and statistical information:
International trade department covers export and import worldwide.
Milton Keynes and North Bucks Economic survey

Publications: Printed

Access to staff: Contact by letter, by telephone, by fax and by e-mail.
Appointment necessary. All charged.
Hours: Mon to Fri, 0900 to 1700

Access to building: Prior appointment required

Affiliated to: Association of British Chambers of Commerce; Business Link

Parent body: Milton Keynes and North Buckinghamshire Chamber of Commerce

MILTON KEYNES COLLEGE LEARNING RESOURCES CENTRE

Chaffron Way Campus, Woughton Campus West, Leadenhall West, Milton Keynes, Buckinghamshire, MK6 5LP

Tel: 01908 684444, 01908 684401 (minicom)
Fax: 01908 684399

Enquiries to: Learning Resources Manager
Direct tel: 01908 684429

Organisation type and purpose: Suitable for ages: 16+.

Subject coverage: Business, administrative, secretarial subjects, social care; non-advanced engineering (electrical, electronic, mechanical, motor vehicle), hospitality and catering, beauty therapy, sport and leisure and general education, art and design.

Library catalogue: All or part available in-house

Access to staff: Contact by letter, by telephone, by fax and in person
Hours: Term time: Mon to Thu; 0900 to 2000; Fri, 1000 to 1600
Vacations: hours will differ

Other addresses: Bletchley Centre; Sherwood Drive, Bletchley, Milton Keynes, Buckinghamshire, MK3 6DR; tel: 01908 684444; fax: 01908 684199

MILTON KEYNES COUNCIL (MKC)

Civic Offices, 1 Saxon Gate East, Milton Keynes, Buckinghamshire, MK9 3HG

Tel: 01908 691691, 01908 252727 (minicom)
Fax: 01908 252456

Enquiries to: Public Relations Manager

Founded: 1997

Organisation type and purpose: Local government body.

Subject coverage: Local government services.

MIND (THE MENTAL HEALTH CHARITY)

Formal name: National Association for Mental Health

Granta House, 15–19 Broadway, Stratford, London, E15 4BQ

Tel: 020 8519 2122
Fax: 020 8522 1725
E-mail: contact@mind.org.uk
Website: www.mind.org.uk

Enquiries to: Administrator
Direct tel: 020 8215 2235
Direct fax: 020 8215 2468
Direct e-mail: k.field@mind.org.uk

Founded: 1945

Organisation type and purpose: Membership association (membership is by subscription), voluntary organisation, registered charity (charity number 219830).

Subject coverage: Mental health, mental illness, the mental health services, service provision, especially community care, rights of service recipients, legislation, treatments, sources of therapy, voluntary associations, housing, women; employment.

Non-library collection catalogue: All or part available online, in-house and in print

Library catalogue: All or part available in-house

Publications: Printed

Publications list: Available online and in print

Access to staff: Contact by letter, by telephone, by fax, by e-mail and via website. Appointment necessary.
Hours: Mon to Fri, 0915 to 1715

Access to building: No prior appointment required

Branch at: Mind Cymru; 3rd Floor, Quebec House, Castlebridge Road East, Castlebridge, Cardiff, CF11 9AB; tel: 029 2039 5123

MINERAL INDUSTRY RESEARCH ORGANISATION (MIRO)

Concorde House, Trinity Park, Solihull, Birmingham, West Midlands, B37 7UQ

Tel: 0121 635 5225
Fax: 0121 635 5226
E-mail: mail@miro.co.uk
Website: www.miro.co.uk

Enquiries to: Administrator

Founded: 1972

Organisation type and purpose: Membership association (membership is by subscription), present number of members: 70, consultancy, research organisation.
To organise collaborative research projects.

Subject coverage: Geosciences, mineral exploration; mining, mineral processing, metal refining, recycling and environmental issues.

Collection: The Stan Nelmes Collection – a collection of books, journals and reports of interest to those in the metallurgical industry dating from 1903 to 1990, 66 titles in total

Non-library collection catalogue: All or part available online and in print

Library catalogue: All or part available online and in print

Publications: Printed, and electronic and video
Order printed publications from: Administrator, MIRO

Publications list: Available online and in print

Access to staff: Contact by letter, by telephone, by fax, by e-mail and via website
Hours: Mon to Fri, 0900 to 1700

Access to building: Prior appointment required

Access for disabled people: Ramped entry, access to all public areas, toilet facilities

Member of: Association of Independent Research and Technology Organisations (AIRTO); Mining Association of the United Kingdom

MINERALOGICAL SOCIETY OF GREAT BRITAIN AND IRELAND (MinSoc)

8–12 Baylis Mews, Amyand Park Road, Twickenham TW1 3HQ

Tel: 020 8 891 6600
Fax: 020 8 891 6599
E-mail: info@minersoc.org
Website: www.minersoc.org.uk

Enquiries to: Executive Director
Direct e-mail: kevin@minersoc.org

Founded: 1876

Organisation type and purpose: International organisation, learned society, registered charity (charity number 233706), publishing house.

Subject coverage: Mineralogy, petrology, geochemistry, crystallography and environmental science.

Library catalogue: All or part available online

Publications: Printed, and electronic and video

Publications list: Available online and in print

Access to staff: Contact by letter, by telephone, by fax, by e-mail and via website. Appointment necessary.
Hours: Mon to Fri, 0900 to 1700

Access to building: Prior appointment required
Hours: Mon to Fri 0900 to 1700
Special comments: Library housed at Kingston University.

MINERALS ENGINEERING SOCIETY (MES)

2 Ryton Close, Blyth, Worksop, Nottinghamshire, S81 8DN

Tel: 01909 591940
Fax: 01909 591940
E-mail: hon.sec.mes@lineone.net
Website: www.mineralsengineering.org

Enquiries to: Honorary Secretary

Founded: 1958

Organisation type and purpose: Learned society.

Subject coverage: Minerals engineering; mineral processing; coal preparation.

Publications: Printed

Access to staff: Contact by letter, by telephone, by fax and by e-mail
Hours: Mon to Fri, 0700 to 2200

MINI MARCOS OWNERS CLUB (MMOC)

28 Meadow Road, Claines, Worcester, WR3 7PP

Tel: 01905 458533
E-mail: roger@minimarcos.plus.com
Website: www.minimarcos.org.uk

Enquiries to: Secretary

Founded: 1977

Organisation type and purpose: International organisation, membership association (membership is by subscription).

continued overleaf

Subject coverage: History and development of Mini Marcos and Mini Jem cars, history of Kingfisher Sprint cars.

Publications: Printed
Order printed publications from: Publications Officer, Mini Marcos Owners Club, 16 Townfield, Kidford, Billingshurst, West Sussex, RH14 0LZ

Publications list: Available online

Access to staff: Contact by letter, by telephone, by e-mail, in person and via website
Hours: Evenings and weekends

Links with: RACMSA

MINI OWNERS CLUB

Formal name: National Mini Owners Club

15 Birchwood Road, Boley Park, Lichfield, Staffordshire, WS14 9UN

Tel: 01543 257956
Fax: 01543 257956
E-mail: nmoc@yahoo.com
Website: www.miniownersclub.co.uk

Enquiries to: Secretary

Founded: 1979

Organisation type and purpose: Membership association (membership is by subscription).

Subject coverage: Mini cars, technical advice.

Access to staff: Contact by letter, by telephone, by fax, by e-mail and via website
Hours: Mon to Sun, 0900 to 2100

MINIATURE AFV ASSOCIATION (MAFVA)

Formal name: Miniature Armoured Fighting Vehicles Association

45 Balmoral Drive, Holmes Chapel, Cheshire, CW4 7JQ

Tel: 01477 535373
Fax: 01477 535892
E-mail: mafvahq@aol.com
Website: www.mafva.net

Enquiries to: Honorary Secretary

Founded: 1965

Organisation type and purpose: International organisation, membership association (membership is by subscription), present number of members: 7,500, voluntary organisation.
Collection and dissemination of information on military vehicles and equipment.

Subject coverage: Armoured fighting vehicles and other military equipment, arms, materials and accoutrements from World War I to date; scale models and information, markings, colour schemes, badges and insignia.

Information services: Available to members.

Collection: Collection of military insignia (particularly cloth) of the British Army, British Indian Army and Army Cadet Force, 1914 to date: quantity several thousand
Vehicle markings and colour schemes

Non-library collection catalogue: All or part available in-house

Publications: Printed, and electronic and video
Order printed publications from: Honorary Secretary

Publications list: Available online and in print

Access to staff: Contact by letter, by telephone, by fax, by e-mail, in person and via website. Appointment necessary. Non-members charged.
Hours: Daily

Access to building: Prior appointment required

MINISTRY OF DEFENCE – TECHNICAL INFORMATION CENTRE ROYAL ENGINEERS (TICRE)

Chetwynd Barracks, Chilwell, Nottingham, NG9 5HA

Tel: 0115 957 2310
Fax: 0115 957 2294

Enquiries to: Librarian
Direct tel: 0115 957 2309

Founded: 1979

Organisation type and purpose: National government centre, of the Ministry of Defence.
To provide technical information for the Corps of Royal Engineers.

Subject coverage: Civil, mechanical and electrical engineering, construction, fortifications.

Library catalogue: All or part available in-house

Publications: Printed

Access to staff: Contact by letter, by telephone and by fax. Appointment necessary.
Hours: Mon to Thu, 0800 to 1630; Fri, 0800 to 1330

Access to building: Prior appointment required
Hours: Mon to Thu, 0800 to 1630; Fri, 0800 to 1330

MINISTRY OF DEFENCE INFORMATION AND LIBRARY SERVICE – GLASGOW

Room 1410, Kentigern House, 65 Brown Street, Glasgow, G2 8EX

Tel: 0141 224 2500
Fax: 0141 224 2257

Enquiries to: Librarian
Direct tel: 0141 224 2501

Organisation type and purpose: National government body.
Central government department.

Subject coverage: Defence policy, armed forces, public administration, management, computing and information science, health and safety, standards, military science and engineering.

Collection: Full set of British standards on CD-ROM

Library catalogue: All or part available in-house

Access to staff: Appointment necessary.
Hours: Mon to Fri, 0900 to 1700

Branch of the: Ministry of Defence Information and Library Service, Whitehall Library

MINISTRY OF DEFENCE INFORMATION AND LIBRARY SERVICE – WHITEHALL INFORMATION AND LIBRARY CENTRE (MOD)

Ground Floor, Zone D, Main Building, Whitehall, London, SW1A 2HB

Tel: 020 7218 4445
Fax: 020 7218 5413
E-mail: cio-svcslibrary-office@mod.uk
Website: www.mod.uk

Organisation type and purpose: National government body.

Subject coverage: Defence policy, organisation, strategy and technology; politics, government and international relations; management; computers; public administration.

Library catalogue: All or part available in-house

Access to staff: Contact by letter. Appointment necessary.
Hours: Mon to Fri, 0830 to 1630

MINISTRY OF JUSTICE (MoJ)

1st Floor, Tower, 102 Petty France, London, SW1H 9AJ

Tel: 020 3334 3000
E-mail: moj.library@justice.gsi.gov.uk
Website: www.justice.gov.uk

Founded: 2008; created by the merger of Department of Constitutional Affairs Library and parts of the Home Office Library (year of change 2008); incorporates the former Prison Service HQ Library, which became part of Home Office Library (year of change 2003)

Organisation type and purpose: Government department

Subject coverage: Prisons, probation, criminology, criminal justice, civil justice, courts, human rights, law, constitutional reform

Collection: Publications by MoJ and its agencies and predecessor departments

Trade and statistical information: see MoJ website

Library catalogue: All or part available in-house

Publications: Electronic and video

Access to staff: Access for members only.
Hours: Monday to Friday, 0900 to 1700
Special comments: MoJ Library is a library of last resort for departmental publications only

MINTEL INTERNATIONAL GROUP

18–19 Long Lane, London, EC1A 9PL

Tel: 020 7606 4533
Fax: 020 7606 5932
Website: www.cior.com

Enquiries to: Director

Founded: 1972

Organisation type and purpose: Research organisation.
Global information provider.

Subject coverage: Retailing, retailers, retail trade and retail topics in the UK and Europe, retailers based elsewhere but with a presence in the European market, global cross border activity.

Collection: Specialist retailing library and files (including historical information)
Extensive files on individual retail companies and operations, UK, Europe especially
Retail sector information
Retail statistical data

Trade and statistical information: Retail trade data by country, by sector, data on cross-border retailing and retailers

Publications: Printed, and electronic and video

Publications list: Available in print

Access to staff: Contact by letter, by telephone, by fax and in person
Hours: Mon to Fri, 0900 to 1730

Other locations: Chicago; Frankfurt; Sydney; Belfast; Los Angeles

MINTEL INTERNATIONAL GROUP LIMITED

18–19 Long Lane, London, EC1A 9HE

Tel: 020 7606 4533
Fax: 020 7606 5932
E-mail: enquiries@mintel.com
Website: www.mintel.com

Enquiries to: Head of Marketing
Direct e-mail: stevec@mintel.com

Founded: 1972

Organisation type and purpose: Research organisation.
Consumer research publisher.

Subject coverage: Pan-European studies, FMCG (fast moving consumer goods) markets, food and drink, retail industry, leisure industry, personal finance industry, new products, company profiles, consumer research, lifestyles, business to business, Irish, industrial.

Trade and statistical information: Comprehensive market data on all UK consumer, European and Industrial markets

Publications: Printed

Publications list: Available in print

Access to staff: Contact by telephone, by e-mail and via website
Hours: Mon to Fri, 0900 to 1700

Affiliated to: Chartered Institute of Marketing

MIRA LIMITED

Formal name: Motor Industry Research Association

Watling Street, Nuneaton, Warwickshire, CV10 0TU

Tel: 024 7635 5000
Fax: 024 7635 5355
E-mail: enquiries@mira.co.uk
Website: www.mira.co.uk/aic

Enquiries to: Information Officer
Direct tel: 024 7635 5275
Direct fax: 024 7635 5036

Founded: 1946

Organisation type and purpose: Consultancy, research organisation.

Subject coverage: Automobile engineering; problems applicable to motor vehicles including noise, vibration, comfort, safety and air pollution.

Trade and statistical information: World data on automotive industry

Publications: Printed

Publications list: Available online and in print

Access to staff: Contact by e-mail and via website. Appointment necessary. Non-members charged.
Hours: Mon to Fri, 0900 to 1600

European agent for the: Japan Society of Automotive Engineers Review

MISCARRIAGE ASSOCIATION

17 Wentworth Terrace, Wakefield, WF1 3QW

Tel: 01924 200799
Fax: 01924 298834
E-mail: info@miscarriageassociation.org.uk
Website: www.miscarriageassociation.org.uk

Enquiries to: Administrator

Founded: 1982

Organisation type and purpose: Registered charity (charity number 1076829).
Has a network of over 200 volunteer telephone contacts and 50 support groups in the UK.
To provide support and information for all on the subject of pregnancy loss.

Subject coverage: Management and understanding of miscarriage in hospitals and the community.

Publications: Printed

Publications list: Available online and in print

Access to staff: Contact by letter, by telephone, by fax, by e-mail and via website
Hours: Mon to Fri, 0900 to 1600

MISSING PEOPLE

284 Upper Richmond Road West, London, SW14 7JE

Tel: 020 8392 4545
E-mail: services@missingpeople.org.uk
Website: www.missingpeople.org.uk

Enquiries to: Co-founders (for senior management)

Founded: 1992

Organisation type and purpose: National organisation, registered charity (charity number 1020419).
Offers a lifeline for the 250,000 people who run away and go missing each year. For those left behind, it searches and provides specialised support to end the heartache and confusion.

Subject coverage: Missing persons.

Special visitor services: Helpline: 0500 700 700; Message Home, 0800 700 740: 24-hr freephone service to help missing adults reach advice and support and to reconnect with their family or carers via a message or a 3-way call; Runaway Helpline, 0808 800 7070: national, free and confidential 24-hr service for anyone who has run away from home or care, or been forced to leave home.

Publications: Printed

Access to staff: Contact by letter, by telephone, by e-mail and via website
Hours: 24-hour service

Also at: Message Home; at the same address; tel: 020 8392 4559; e-mail: services @missingpeople.org.uk; Runaway Helpline; at the same address; tel: 020 8392 4559; e-mail: services @missingpeople.org.uk

MISSIO

Formal name: Also known as Pontifical Mission Societies

23 Eccleston Square, London, SW1V 1NU

Tel: 020 7821 9755
Fax: 020 7630 8466
E-mail: director@missio.org.uk
Website: www.missio.org.uk

Enquiries to: Director

Founded: 1833; formerly called Pontifical Mission Societies (year of change 2009)

Organisation type and purpose: Registered charity (charity number 1056651).
Support of the Catholic Church in mission areas.

Publications: Printed

Access to staff: Contact by letter, by e-mail and via website
Hours: Mon to Fri, 0900 to 1700

MISSION AVIATION FELLOWSHIP (UK) (MAF (UK))

Castle House, Castle Hill Avenue, Folkestone, Kent, CT20 2TN

Tel: 0845 8509505
Fax: 01303 852800
E-mail: supporter.relations@maf-uk.org

Enquiries to: Chief Executive

Founded: 1947

Organisation type and purpose: International organisation, registered charity (charity number 1064598).
Providing aviation and technical support to church, mission and relief agencies in the developing world.

Subject coverage: Speakers and presentations of the work on Mission Aviation Fellowship are available on request.

Publications: Printed, and electronic and video

continued overleaf

Access to staff: Contact by letter, by telephone, by fax and by e-mail. Appointment necessary.
Hours: Mon to Fri, 0900 to 1700

Branches: Mission Aviation Fellowship; 29 Canal Street, Glasgow, G4 0AD; tel: 0141 332 5222; fax: 0141 332 5222; e-mail: maf-scot .off@maf-uk.org

Member organisation of: Evangelical Alliance; Global Connections

MISSION TO SEAFARERS, THE

St Michael Paternoster Royal, College Hill, London, EC4R 2RL

Tel: 020 7248 5202
Fax: 020 7248 4761
E-mail: general@missiontoseafarers.org
Website: www.missiontoseafarers.org

Enquiries to: Public Relations Officer

Organisation type and purpose: Voluntary organisation, registered charity (charity number 212432).
The Mission to Seafarers, a world mission agency of the Anglican church, cares for the welfare of seafarers of all nationalities and faiths in ports around the world.

Subject coverage: Seafarers' conditions and welfare.

Collection: Selected archive material of The Mission to Seafarers and activities

Publications: Printed

Access to staff: Contact by letter, by telephone, by fax, by e-mail and via website. Appointment necessary.
Hours: Mon to Fri, 0900 to 1700

Access to building: Prior appointment required

Members of: International Christian Maritime Association (ICMA); Herald House, 15 Lambs Passage, London EC1Y 8TQ, UK; tel: 020 7256 9216; fax: 020 7256 9217; e-mail: icma.secgen@btconnect.com; website: www.icma.as

MISSIONARY INSTITUTE LONDON (MIL)

Holcombe House, The Ridgeway, London, NW7 4HY

Tel: 020 8906 1893
Fax: 020 8906 4937
E-mail: mil@mdx.ac.uk

Enquiries to: Librarian
Other contacts: Secretary for enquiries about courses.

Founded: 1969

Organisation type and purpose: Registered charity (charity number 269713), university department or institute.

Subject coverage: Theology, missiology, church history, social anthropology.

Library catalogue: All or part available in-house

Access to staff: Contact by letter, by fax and by e-mail
Hours: Mon to Fri, 0900 to 1700

Access to building: Prior appointment required
Hours: Mon to Fri, 0900 to 1700
Special comments: No loans to non-registered students.

Access for disabled people: Parking provided, level entry

MK1 CORTINA OWNERS CLUB

The Membership Secretary, 51 Studley Rise, Trowbridge, BA14 0PD

Tel: 01225 763888
E-mail: info@mk1cortina.com
Website: www.mk1cortina.com

Enquiries to: Membership Secretary
Direct e-mail: alison-membership@blueyonder.co.uk

Founded: 1982

Organisation type and purpose:
Membership association (membership is by subscription), present number of members: 1,100, voluntary organisation.
Car club.

Subject coverage: Ford Cortina Mk1 car events, spares sourcing, legislation, insurance.

Publications: Printed

Publications list: Available in print

Access to staff: Contact by letter, by telephone, by fax, by e-mail and via website
Hours: Mon to Fri, 1800 to 2130

MND SCOTLAND

Formal name: Scottish Motor Neurone Disease Association

76 Firhill Road, Glasgow, G20 7BA

Tel: 0141 945 1077
Fax: 0141 945 2578
E-mail: info@mndscotland.org.uk
Website: www.mndscotland.org.uk

Enquiries to: Information Officer – Librarian

Founded: 1981

Organisation type and purpose: Voluntary organisation, registered charity (charity number SCO 02662).
Aims to ensure that people with motor neurone disease secure the care and support they need. Activites: a network of MND Care Team Specialists throughout Scotland; specialist equipment loan service; family information evenings, library and information service; study days for health and social care professionals; small grants to individuals in need; counselling service; holiday caravan; welfare and benefits service.

Subject coverage: Motor neurone disease/amyotrophic lateral sclerosis; palliative care; carers; bereavement; disability issues; carers' issues; community care; complementary medicine; health care; charity management.

Information services: Library and Information Service for patients/families, and health and social care professionals.

Education services: MND Study Days for health professionals.

Library catalogue: All or part available online

Publications: Printed

Publications list: Available online and in print

Access to staff: Contact by letter, by telephone, by fax, by e-mail, in person and via website
Hours: Mon to Fri, 0900 to 1700; out-of-hours answerphone
Special comments: Information Officer works part-time, so appointment necessary.

Access to building: No prior appointment required
Hours: Mon to Fri, 0900 to 1700
Special comments: Library: by appointment only.

Access for disabled people: Parking provided, level entry, toilet facilities, fully accessible

Links with: International Alliance of MND/ALS Associations; Scottish Health Information Network (SHINE); website: http://www.shinelib.org.uk
Scottish Health Libraries Catalogue (SHELCAT); website: http://www.shelcat.org

MOBILITY INFORMATION SERVICE – TELFORD (MIS)

20 Burton Close, Dawley, Telford, TF4 2BX

Tel: 01743 340269
E-mail: mis@nmcuk.freeserve.co.uk
Website: www.mis.org.uk

Enquiries to: Chief Officer
Other contacts: Information Officer (for general information on mobility matters)

Founded: 1979

Organisation type and purpose:
International organisation, voluntary organisation, registered charity (charity number 1085593).
Provides mobility information to disabled people in order to help them attain independence.

Subject coverage: Information on all aspects of mobility.

Collection: Hamilton Index
Handynet database
Rehadat

Non-library collection catalogue: All or part available online and in-house

Publications: Printed

Publications list: Available online and in print

Access to staff: Contact by letter, by telephone, by e-mail and via website
Hours: Tue, Fri, 1030 to 1530

Access to building: No public access

Access for disabled people: No public access

MOD ADMIRALTY LIBRARY

Naval Historical Branch, No. 24 Store, PP 20, Main Road, HM Naval Base, Portsmouth, PO1 3LU

Tel: 023 9272 5297
Fax: 023 9272 4003
E-mail: cnsnhbal@a.dii.mod.uk

Enquiries to: Admiralty Librarian

Founded: 1809

Organisation type and purpose: National government body.
Historical Library.

Subject coverage: History of the Royal Navy, with particular reference to administration, policy, doctrine, operations, strategy, tactics, hydrography, naval aviation, signalling and gunnery.

Collection: Approximately 180,000 vols and 100,000 pamphlets, in the process of being catalogued
Catalogue of manuscripts and some printed charts searchable on the National Museum of the Royal Navy website
Historical collections of the Royal Naval Medical Services held at the Institute of Naval Medicine.

Library catalogue: All or part available online, in-house and in print

Publications: Printed

Access to staff: Contact by letter, by telephone, by fax, by e-mail and in person. Appointment necessary.
Hours: Tue to Thu, 1000 to 1645

Access to building: Appointment necessary
Hours: Tue to Thu, 1000 to 1700

Access for disabled people: Access to all public areas, toilet facilities. Reserved parking space adjacent to building

Branches: Admiralty Library, Portsmouth; No. 12 Store, PP 64, Semaphore Tower Road, HM Naval Base, Portsmouth, PO1 JNH; tel: 023 9272 3795; fax: 023 9272 3942; e-mail: library@nmrn.org.uk; website: http://www.royalnavalmuseum.org
Historical Library; Institute of Naval Medicine, Crescent Road, Alverstoke, Gosport, Hampshire, PO12 2DL; tel: 023 9276 8238; fax: 023 9250 4823; e-mail: inm-cs-infohistlib@mod.uk; website: http://www.royalnavy.mod.uk/training-and-people/rn-life/medical-branch/institute-of-naval-medicine

Constituent part of: Naval Historical Branch (NHB); No. 24 Store, PP 20, Main Road, HM Naval Base, Portsmouth PO1 3LU; tel: 02392 725300; fax: 02392 724003

MODEL YACHTING ASSOCIATION (MYA)

Five Oaks, Church Lane, Oakley, Bedfordshire, MK43 7RU

Tel: 01234 822408
E-mail: m.clifton@easynet.co.uk
Website: www.radiosailing.org.uk

Enquiries to: Information Officer
Direct tel: 01789 751800
Direct e-mail: graham.reeves@virgin.net

Founded: 1911

Organisation type and purpose: Membership association.
National sporting authority.

Subject coverage: Competitive sailing of wind-powered models; design, construction, operation of model yachts; locations of affiliated clubs; history of the sport.

Collection: Comprehensive reference library of printed books and magazines since 1879
Minutes and other administrative records of the MYA since 1931

Publications: Printed

Publications list: Available in print

Access to staff: Contact by letter, by telephone and by e-mail
Hours: Mon to Fri, 0900 to 2100

Associated with: Central Council for Physical Recreation; International Sailing Federation (Radio Sailing Division) (ISAF/RSD); Royal Yachting Association

MODERN CHURCH (MC)

Modern Church Office, 9 Westward View, Liverpool, Merseyside, L17 7EE

Tel: 0845 345 1909
E-mail: office@modernchurch.org.uk
Website: www.modernchurch.org.uk

Enquiries to: Administrator

Founded: 1898

Organisation type and purpose: Learned society (membership is by subscription), present number of members: 700, voluntary organisation, registered charity (charity number 281573).

Subject coverage: Church affairs, especially Church of England; theology; philosophy of religion; ethics.

Publications: Printed
Order printed publications from: www.modernchurch.org.uk

Publications list: Available online

Access to staff: Contact by letter, by telephone, by e-mail and via website. Appointment necessary.
Hours: Mon to Fri, 0900 to 1500

MODERN HUMANITIES RESEARCH ASSOCIATION (MHRA)

1 Carlton House Terrace, London, SW1Y 5AF

E-mail: mail@mhra.org.uk
Website: www.mhra.org.uk

Enquiries to: Honorary Secretary

Founded: 1918

Organisation type and purpose: International organisation, learned society, registered charity.

Subject coverage: Modern and medieval languages and literatures, including English.

Publications: Printed, and electronic and video
Order printed publications from: http://www.mhra.org.uk/Publications/Ordering/index.html
Order electronic and video publications from: http://www.mhra.org.uk/Publications/Ordering/index.html

Publications list: Available online and in print

Access to staff: Contact by letter, by e-mail and via website. Appointment necessary.

MODERN PENTATHLON ASSOCIATION OF GREAT BRITAIN, THE (MPAGB and Pentathlon GB)

Wessex House, University of Bath, Claverton Down, Bath, BA2 7AY

Tel: 01225 386808
Fax: 01225 386995
E-mail: admin@pentathlongb.org
Website: www.pentathlongb.org

Enquiries to: Administration Officer

Founded: 1948

Organisation type and purpose: Membership association (membership is by subscription), present number of members: 10,000, voluntary organisation.
Governing body and co-ordinating authority.

Subject coverage: Modern pentathlon – compilation of five sports: fencing, swimming, shooting, running and riding; biathlon, triathlon, tetrathlon, pentathlon, biathle, coaching and events.

Access to staff: Contact by letter, by telephone, by fax, by e-mail and via website
Hours: Mon to Fri, 0900 to 1700

MOLE VALLEY DISTRICT COUNCIL

Pippbrook, Dorking, Surrey, RH4 1SJ

Tel: 01306 885001, 01372 819094 (minicom)
Fax: 01306 876821
E-mail: information@molevalley.gov.uk
Website: www.molevalley.gov.uk

Enquiries to: Communications Officer
Direct tel: 01306 879113
Other contacts: communications@molevalley.gov.uk

Founded: 1974

Organisation type and purpose: Local government body.

Subject coverage: Local authority services, Mole Valley district including the main towns of Dorking and Leatherhead.

Trade and statistical information: Data on area and population

Publications: Printed

Access to staff: Contact by letter, by telephone, by fax, by e-mail and in person
Hours: Mon to Fri, 0830 to 1700; helpline open same hours

Parent body: Surrey County Council; County Hall, Penrhyn Road, Kingston upon Thames, KT1 2DN; tel: 020 8541 8800; fax: 020 8541 9005

MONEYFACTS PUBLICATIONS

Formal name: Moneyfacts Group plc

Moneyfacts House, 66–70 Thorpe Road, Norwich, Norfolk, NR1 1BJ

Tel: 01603 476476
Fax: 01603 476477
E-mail: enquiries@moneyfacts.co.uk

Enquiries to: Librarian

Founded: 1988

continued overleaf

Organisation type and purpose: Research organisation, publishing house.

Subject coverage: Mortgage, savings, pensions, investments, and business finance information.

Trade and statistical information: UK mortgage, savings and investment rates, offshore mortgage and savings rates, business finance data, data on life, pensions and unit trust products

Publications: Printed

Publications list: Available in print

Access to staff: Contact by letter, by telephone and by fax. All charged.
Hours: Mon to Fri, 0900 to 1700

Access for disabled people: Parking provided, ramped entry

MONMOUTHSHIRE COUNTY COUNCIL

County Hall, Croesyceiliog, Cwmbran, Gwent, NP44 2XH

Tel: 01633 644644
Fax: 01633 644666
Website: www.monmouthshire.gov.uk

Enquiries to: Communication Officer
Direct tel: 01633 644402
Direct e-mail: paulaskyrme@monmouthshire.gov.uk

Founded: 1996

Organisation type and purpose: Local government body.

Subject coverage: Local government services, background to Monmouthshire.

Collection: The former Gwent County Record Office and Archives hold all records and collections

Order printed publications from: Community Spirit (residents' newspaper)

Access to staff: Contact by letter, by telephone, by fax and by e-mail. Appointment necessary.
Hours: Fri, 0900 to 1600

Access to building: By appointment

Access for disabled people: Parking provided, level entry, toilet facilities

MONMOUTHSHIRE LIBRARIES AND INFORMATION SERVICE (MLIS)

Chepstow Library, Manor Way, Chepstow, NP16 5HZ

Tel: 01291 635730
Fax: 01291 635736
E-mail: infocentre@monmouthshire.gov.uk
Website: www.monmouthshire.gov.uk/leisure/libraries
Website: libraries.monmouthshire.gov.uk

Enquiries to: Principal Librarian

Founded: 1996

Organisation type and purpose: Local government body, public library.

Subject coverage: Local studies, historical Monmouthshire, advice and self-help information.

Collection: Chepstow Collection (material pertaining to Chepstow, donated by the Chepstow Society in 1952 and housed in Chepstow Library)

Trade and statistical information: Welsh Assembly Government collection at Chepstow

Non-library collection catalogue: All or part available online

Library catalogue: All or part available online

Publications list: Available in print

Access to staff: Contact by letter, by telephone, by fax, by e-mail, in person and via website

Access to building: *Hours:* Hours vary from site to site

Access for disabled people: Ramped entry

Branch libraries: Abergavenny Library; Baker Street, Abergavenny, NP7 5BD; tel: 01873 735980; fax: 01873 735985; e-mail: abergavennylibrary@monmouthshire.gov.uk; Caldicot Library; Woodstock Way, Caldicot, NP26 4DB; tel: 01291 426425; fax: 01291 426426; e-mail: caldicotlibrary@monmouthshire.gov.uk; Chepstow Library and Information Centre; Manor Way, Chepstow, NP16 5HZ; tel: 01291 635730; fax: 01291 635736; e-mail: chepstowlibrary@monmouthshire.gov.uk; Gilwern Library; Gilwern Community Education Centre and Library, Common Road, Gilwern; tel: 01873 833055; fax: 01873 833055; e-mail: gilwernlibrary@monmouthshire.gov.uk; Monmouth Library; Rolls Hall, Whitecross Street, Monmouth, NP25 3BY; tel: 01600 775215; fax: 01600 775218; e-mail: monmouthlibrary@monmouthshire.gov.uk; Usk Library; 18A Maryport Street, Usk, NP15 1AE; tel: 01291 674925; fax: 01291 674924; e-mail: usklibrary@monmouthshire.gov.uk

Parent body: Monmouthshire County Council; tel: 01633 644644; fax: 01633 644545

MONTESSORI SOCIETY AMI (UK)

26 Lyndhurst Gardens, London, NW3 5NW

Tel: 020 7435 7874
E-mail: info@montessori-uk.org
Website: www.montessorisociety.org.uk

Enquiries to: Honorary Secretary

Founded: 1935

Organisation type and purpose: National organisation, professional body, membership association (membership is by subscription), present number of members: 300, voluntary organisation.
To spread the ideas of child development and philosophy set out by Dr Maria Montessori to parents and others concerned with children.

Subject coverage: Montessori system of education, child development, location of Montessori schools, training, training courses recognised by AMI, apparatus, supply information, Montessori literature.

Publications: Printed, and electronic and video
Order electronic and video publications from: Book order form

Publications list: Available in print

Access to staff: Contact by letter, by telephone and by e-mail. Appointment necessary. Letter of introduction required.
Hours: Mon to Fri, 0900 to 1630
Special comments: Answerphone for other times.

Affiliated to: Association Montessori Internationale (AMI); tel: + 31 20 679 8932; fax: + 31 20 676 7341; e-mail: ami@xs4all.nl; website: http://www.montessori-ami.org

MONUMENTAL BRASS SOCIETY

c/o H. M. Stuchfield, Lowe Hill House, Stratford St Mary, Suffolk, CO7 6JX

Tel: 01206 337239
Fax: 01206 861852
E-mail: martinstuchfield@btconnect.com
Website: www.mbs-brasses.co.uk

Founded: 1887

Organisation type and purpose: Learned society.

Subject coverage: Preservation of monumental brasses, indents of lost brasses and incised slabs.

Publications: Printed

Access to staff: Contact by letter, by fax and by e-mail
Hours: Mon to Fri, 0900 to 1700

MOOR GREEN (Moor Green)

Formal name: Moor Green (Brain Injury Rehabilitation Centre)

Moseley Hall Hospital, Alcester Road, Moseley, Birmingham, B13 8JL

Tel: 0121 442 3400
Fax: 0121 442 3420
E-mail: Liz.wright@sbcht.wmids.nhs.uk

Enquiries to: Clinical Manager

Founded: 1967

Organisation type and purpose: National Health Service.
To provide out-patient rehabilitation following brain injury. Assessment for services and equipment etc. To provide information, advice, counselling, loan equipment and special services.

Subject coverage: Rehabilitation of people who have suffered head injuries (middle to late stage treatment).

Collection: Literature on brain injury

Publications: Printed

Access to staff: Contact by letter, by telephone and by fax. Appointment necessary.
Hours: Mon to Fri, 0900 to 1700

Links with: West Midlands Rehabilitation Centre; Oak Tree Lane, Selly Oak, Birmingham, B29 6JA

MORAVIAN CHURCH IN GREAT BRITAIN

Moravian Church House, 5–7 Muswell Hill, London, N10 3TJ

Tel: 020 8883 3409
Fax: 020 8365 3371

E-mail: moravianchurchhouse@btinternet.com
Website: www.moravian.org.uk

Enquiries to: General Secretary
Other contacts: Archivist for visits to the archives and library.

Founded: 1457

Organisation type and purpose: International organisation, present number of members: 2,000, voluntary organisation, registered charity.
Christian church.
To worship God and spread the gospel.

Subject coverage: History, doctrine and practices of the Moravian Church in the UK and overseas.

Collection: Manuscript diaries and letters from the 18th and 19th centuries relating to the growth and work of the Church, especially in West Indies and Labrador
Numerous letters from John Wesley to Moravian leaders

Publications: Printed

Publications list: Available online and in print

Access to staff: Contact by letter, by telephone and by e-mail. Appointment necessary.
Hours: Mon to Fri, 0930 to 1700

MORAY COUNCIL DEPARTMENT OF EDUCATIONAL SERVICES

Council Offices, High Street, Elgin, Moray, IV30 1BX

Tel: 01343 543451
Fax: 01343 563478
E-mail: campbea@moray.gov.uk
Website: www.moray.gov.uk

Enquiries to: Libraries and Museums Manager
Direct tel: 01343 563398
Other contacts: Principal Librarian

Organisation type and purpose: Local government body, public library.

Subject coverage: General, local history of Moray, Nairn and Banffshire, family history.

Collection: Archives of preceding and current local authorities
Falconer Papers
Local history collection
Local newspapers on microfilm
Microfilm records of births, marriages and deaths and early census returns
Wittet and Doig Collection of 10,000 architectural plans, 1828–1900

Non-library collection catalogue: All or part available online

Library catalogue: All or part available online

Publications: Printed
Order printed publications from: Principal Librarian (Central Services), Elgin Library, Cooper Park, Elgin, Morayshire, IV30 1BX; tel: 01343 562607; fax: 01343 562630; e-mail: elgin.library@moray.gov.uk

Publications list: Available online

Access to staff: Contact by letter, by telephone, by fax, by e-mail and in person
Hours: Mon to Fri, 0845 to 1700

Member organisation of: European Information Relay; Scottish Library and Information Council

MORAY COUNCIL LOCAL HERITAGE SERVICE

Old East End School, Institution Road, Elgin, Moray, IV30 1RP

Tel: 01343 569011
E-mail: heritage@moray.gov.uk
Website: www.moray.org/heritage/roots.html
Website: www.moray.org/heritage/index.html

Enquiries to: Local Heritage Officer

Founded: 1996

Organisation type and purpose: Local government body, research organisation.

Subject coverage: Sources relating to Moray including archives, books, maps, newspapers and genealogical records.

Education services: Resources for Further or Higher Education.

Non-library collection catalogue: All or part available in-house

Library catalogue: All or part available in-house

Access to staff: Contact by letter, by telephone, by e-mail, in person and via website

Access to building: No prior appointment required
Hours: Mon, Wed, Thu, Fri, 1000 to 1700; Tue, 1000 to 2000; Sat, 1000 to 1200

Access for disabled people: Access to all public areas

MORDEN LIBRARY

Merton Civic Centre, London Road, Morden, Surrey, SM4 5DX

Tel: 020 8545 4040, 020 8946 1136 (minicom)
Fax: 020 8545 4037
E-mail: morden.library@merton.gov.uk

Enquiries to: Library and Service Manager
Direct tel: 020 8545 3775
Direct e-mail: di.reynolds@merton.gov.uk

Founded: 1960

Organisation type and purpose: Local government body, public library.

Subject coverage: General, local history covering the area of Merton London Borough and its predecessor authorities.

Collection: Collection of Catalogues etc from Carters Tested Seeds
Lord Nelson
Simpson Papers
Tom Francis Collection of photographic negatives
William Morris, books, pictures and other material

Non-library collection catalogue: All or part available in-house

Library catalogue: All or part available in-house

Publications: Printed

Publications list: Available in print

Access to staff: Contact by letter, by telephone, by fax, by e-mail and in person
Hours: Mon, Tue, Thu, Fri, 0930 to 1900; Wed, 0930 to 1300; Sat, 0930 to 1700

Access to building: No prior appointment required

Access for disabled people: Parking provided, level entry, access to all public areas, toilet facilities

Also at the same address: Merton Local Studies Centre; tel: 020 8545 3239

Parent body and at the same address: London Borough of Merton, Merton Library Service

MOREDUN RESEARCH INSTITUTE

Pentlands Science Park, Bush Loan, Penicuik, Midlothian, EH26 0PZ

Tel: 0131 445 5111
Fax: 0131 445 6235
E-mail: library@mri.sari.ac.uk
Website: www.mri.sari.ac.uk

Enquiries to: Librarian

Founded: 1920

Organisation type and purpose: Research organisation.

Subject coverage: Veterinary aspects of bacteriology, microbiology, pathology, molecular biology, parasitology, immunology, virology, especially relating to ruminants and particularly sheep.

Non-library collection catalogue: All or part available in-house

Library catalogue: All or part available in-house

Publications: Printed

Access to staff: Contact by telephone and by e-mail. Appointment necessary.
Hours: Mon to Fri, 0850 to 1715

Access to building: Prior appointment required

Access for disabled people: Level entry

Funded by: Scottish Executive Environment and Rural Affairs Department

Links with: BBSRC

Parent body: Moredun Foundation

MORLEY COLLEGE

Formal name: Morley College (1993) Limited

61 Westminster Bridge Road, London, SE1 7HT

Tel: 020 7928 8501
Fax: 020 7928 4074
E-mail: enquiries@morleycollege.ac.uk
Website: www.morleycollege.ac.uk

Enquiries to: Library Manager
Direct tel: 020 7450 9229

Organisation type and purpose: Registered charity.
Adult education.

Subject coverage: Music, art, languages (self-tuition courses), social studies, literature, theatre, exercise and health, self-tuition wordprocessing, spreadsheets etc, courses, multimedia.

continued overleaf

Access to staff: Contact by letter, by telephone, by e-mail and in person. Appointment necessary. Access for members only.
Hours: Term time: Mon to Thu, 1100 to 2000; Fri, 1100 to 1900

MOROCCAN NATIONAL TOURIST OFFICE (MNTO)

Formal name: Moroccan National Tourist Office

205 Regent Street, London, W1B 4HB

Tel: 020 7437 0073
Fax: 020 7734 8172
E-mail: mnto@btconnect.com
Website: www.tourism-in-morocco.com

Enquiries to: Director
Other contacts: Information Officer for information relevant to tourism in Morocco.

Founded: 1916

Organisation type and purpose: National government body.
Morocco's official tourist representation, under the jurisdiction of the Moroccan Tourism Ministry.
The main objective of the MNTO is to promote Morocco abroad as a distinctive destination choice for tourism.

Subject coverage: Tourist information and advice for Morocco.

Collection: Maps
Posters
Slides (are kept in our office library)

Trade and statistical information: Information is obtainable from the Moroccan Embassy; tel: 020 7581 5001; contact the Economic Attaché

Publications: Printed, and electronic and video

Publications list: Available in print

Access to staff: Contact by letter, by telephone, by fax, by e-mail and in person. Appointment necessary.
Hours: Mon to Fri, 0900 to 1730

Parent body: Moroccan National Tourist Office, Rabat, Morocco; 31 Angle Rue Oued Fès Avenue, Al Abtal-Agdal-Rabat, Morocco; tel: 00 2123 7 681531/32/33; fax: 00 2123 7 777437 or 681527; e-mail: visitmorocco@onmt.org.ma

MORRAB LIBRARY

Morrab House, Morrab Gardens, Penzance, Cornwall, TR18 4DA

Tel: 01736 364474
Website: www.morrablibrary.co.uk

Enquiries to: Librarian
Other contacts: Chairman (for committee decisions)

Founded: 1818

Organisation type and purpose: Membership association (membership is by subscription).
Independent library.

Subject coverage: General: all subjects, particularly history, English literature, theology, art. Special collections; Cornish collections; archival holdings, mostly Cornish; photographic archive (West Cornwall).

Collection: Stock of 50,000 books
Dawson Collection: Napoleana, Peers of the Realm
Photographic archive
Borlase manuscripts

Non-library collection catalogue: All or part available in-house

Library catalogue: All or part available in-house

Access to staff: Contact by letter, by telephone, by e-mail and in person. Appointment necessary. Non-members charged.
Hours: Tue to Fri, 1000 to 1600; Sat, 1000 to 1300
Special comments: Appointment necessary for archives.

MORRIS COWLEY & OXFORD OWNERS CLUB (MCOC)

202 Chantry Gardens, Southwick, Trowbridge, Wiltshire, BA14 9QX

Tel: 01225 766800

Enquiries to: Secretary

Founded: 1979

Organisation type and purpose: Membership association (membership is by subscription).
To supply parts to classic vehicle owners, clubs etc.

Subject coverage: General information which appertains to the Morris Cowley, Oxford and Isis range of vehicles (built 1954–60); spares availability, costing and cars for sale. Also information/membership for owners of Hindustan Ambassadors.

Publications: Printed

Access to staff: Contact by letter, by telephone and in person
Hours: Mon to Fri, 0900 to 2100, and weekends

MORRIS FEDERATION (MF)

Corner Cottage, 2 Lower Street, Sproughton, Ipswich, IP8 3AA

Tel: 01473 742334
E-mail: archive@morrisfed.org
Website: www.morrisfed.org

Enquiries to: Archive Officer
Direct e-mail: archive@morrisfed.org

Founded: 1975; formerly called Women's Morris Federation

Organisation type and purpose: Membership association (membership is by subscription), present number of members: 420, voluntary organisation.
To promote Morris dancing.

Subject coverage: Morris dancing, sword dancing, mumming.

Collection: Archive of Morris material

Non-library collection catalogue: All or part available in-house and in print

Library catalogue: All or part available in-house

Publications: Printed
Order printed publications from: Jenny Everett, MF Treasurer, Corner Cottage, 2 Lower Street, Sproughton, Ipswich IP8 3AA

Publications list: Available in print

Access to staff: Contact by letter, by telephone and by e-mail. Appointment necessary. Access for members only. All charged.
Hours: Mon to Sun, 1800 to 2000

Access to building: Prior appointment required

Also at: FeeLock (MF Secretary); 28 Fairstone Close, Hastings, Sussex, TN35 5EZ; tel: 01424 436052; e-mail: sec@morrisfed.org

Links with: English Folk Dance & Song Society; tel: 020 7485 2206; fax: 020 7284 0534; Morris Ring; Open Morris; Sword Dance Union

MORRIS MARINA / ITAL DRIVERS' CLUB (MIDC)

12 Nithsdale Road, Liverpool, L15 5AX

Enquiries to: Membership Secretary

Founded: 1984; formerly called Morris Marina Owners' Club (year of change 1986)

Organisation type and purpose: International organisation, membership association (membership is by subscription), present number of members: 5.
To assist owners and enthusiasts of Morris Marina and Ital cars and their derivatives to restore, maintain, preserve and operate the cars.

Subject coverage: Maintenance, preservation and restoration of Morris Marina and Ital cars; historical and production information on Morris Marina and Ital cars.

Collection: Technical reference library; workshop manuals, parts lists, magazine articles, etc., register

Publications: Printed, and electronic and video
Order printed publications from: J G Lawson at above address

Publications list: Available in print

Access to staff: Contact by letter. Appointment necessary. Access for members only.
Hours: Mon to Fri, 0900 to 1700

Links with: Sun-Tor Register; 35 Walkerith Road, Morton, Gainsborough, Lincolnshire, DN21 3DA

MORRIS MARINA OWNERS CLUB AND MORRIS ITAL REGISTER

39 Portley Road, Dawley, Telford, Shropshire, TF4 3JW

Tel: 01952 504900
E-mail: ajmmarina@aol.com

Enquiries to: General Secretary
Other contacts: Life President, Chairman

Founded: 1985

Organisation type and purpose: Membership association (membership is by subscription), present number of members: 450.

Subject coverage: Morris Marina and Morris Ital, saloon, coupe, estate, van, pickup, caravanette and motor caravan versions marketed and produced worldwide.

Collection: Information collected and held by members, brochures, workshop manuals, road test reports, press release information

Publications: Printed

Access to staff: Contact by letter, by telephone and by e-mail
Hours: Mon to Fri, 0900 to 1700

MORRIS MINOR OWNERS CLUB LIMITED

8 Castings Road, Sir Francis Ley Industrial Estate, Derby, DE23 8YL

Tel: 01332 291675
Fax: 01332 290661
E-mail: andrew.booth@morrisminoroc.co.uk
Website: www.morrisminoroc.co.uk

Enquiries to: Membership Administrator
Other contacts: Magazine Editor for magazine entries.

Founded: 1976

Organisation type and purpose: Membership association (membership is by subscription), present number of members: 13,500.

Subject coverage: General information on all Morris Minor cars manufactured between 1948 and 1971.

Publications: Printed

Access to staff: Contact by letter, by telephone, by fax, by e-mail and via website
Hours: Mon to Fri, 0900 to 1700. 24-hour answerphone

MORTAR INDUSTRY ASSOCIATION (MIA)

156 Buckingham Palace Road, London, SW1W 9TR

Tel: 020 7730 8194
Fax: 020 7730 4355
E-mail: james@qpa.org
Website: www.mortar.org.uk

Enquiries to: Secretary

Founded: 1971

Organisation type and purpose: Trade association.
To promote the use of all factory made mortars, to further this it maintains an interest in and actively promotes masonry construction in the wider sense.

Subject coverage: Factory-made mortars for constructing brickwork, blockwork and stonework, external render, internal plaster and paving mortar.

Publications: Printed, and electronic and video

Publications list: Available in print

Access to staff: Contact by letter, by telephone, by fax, by e-mail and via website
Hours: Mon to Fri, 0900 to 1700

Founder member of: Masonry Society

Parent body: Quarry Products Association (QPA); at the same address

MOTABILITY

Warwick House, Roydon Road, Harlow, Essex, CM19 5PX

Tel: 0845 456 4566
Fax: 01279 632000
Website: www.motability.co.uk

Enquiries to: Customer Helpline

Founded: 1977

Organisation type and purpose: Registered charity (charity number 299745).
The Motability Scheme is the UK's leading car scheme for disabled people providing affordable, convenient, trouble-free motoring to 430,000 disabled customers and their families. Powered wheelchairs and scooters can also be financed using the scheme. Motability also provides financial assistance to customers who would otherwise be unable to afford the mobility solution they need.

Subject coverage: Cars and powered wheelchairs, for recipients of the higher rate mobility component of DLA (Disability Living Allowance), or the war pensioners' mobility supplement.

Publications: Printed, and electronic and video

Access to staff: Contact by letter, by telephone and by fax
Hours: Mon to Fri, 0845 to 1715

Access for disabled people: Parking provided, access to all public areas, toilet facilities

MOTHERS' UNION

Mary Sumner House, 24 Tufton Street, London, SW1P 3RB

Tel: 020 7222 5533
Fax: 020 7227 9736
E-mail: marketing@themothersunion.org
Website: www.themothersunion.org

Enquiries to: Head of Marketing
Other contacts: Communications Officer

Founded: 1876

Organisation type and purpose: International organisation, voluntary organisation, registered charity.
To strengthen and preserve marriage and Christian family life.

Subject coverage: Family and marriage-related subjects, role and status of women overseas, law reform, the media, prayer and spirituality.

Collection: Committee and administrative archives, founder's correspondence
Set of MU periodicals

Non-library collection catalogue: All or part available online and in print

Library catalogue: All or part available online

Publications: Printed
Order printed publications from: e-mail: marketing@themothersunion.org

Publications list: Available online and in print

Access to staff: Contact by letter, by telephone, by fax, by e-mail, in person and via website
Hours: Mon to Fri, 0900 to 1800

Links with: 66 dioceses in the British Isles and 27 provinces of the Anglican Communion worldwide

MOTO GUZZI CLUB GB (MGCGB)

Mole Cottage, 26 The Crescent, The Wells, Epsom, Surrey, KT18 7LL

Tel: 01372 724681
Fax: 01372 724681
Website: www.motoguzzigb.com

Enquiries to: General Secretary

Founded: 1976

Organisation type and purpose: Membership association (membership is by subscription), present number of members: 3000.

Subject coverage: All aspects of Moto Guzzi motorcycle ownership; discounts, technical advice, local club branches, social events, continental touring, factory visits, deals on insurance and valuation service, DVLA approved for marque requests.

Publications: Printed

Access to staff: Contact by letter, by telephone and by fax
Hours: Mon to Fri, 1800 to 2000

Parent body: British Motorcycle Federation

MOTOR CARAVANNERS' CLUB

Formal name: The Motor Caravanners' Club Limited

22 Evelyn Close, Twickenham, Middlesex, TW2 7BN

Tel: 020 8893 3883
Fax: 020 8893 8324
E-mail: info@motorcaravanners.eu
Website: www.motorcaravanners.eu

Enquiries to: Executive Secretary

Founded: 1961

Organisation type and purpose: Membership association (membership is by subscription), present number of members: 15,000.

Subject coverage: Leisure and holiday camping activities, motor caravans, motor homes, RVs, DIY conversions, UK touring, European touring, technical information, legislation interpretation.

Library catalogue: All or part available in print

Publications: Printed

Publications list: Available in print

Access to staff: Contact by letter, by telephone, by fax, by e-mail and via website
Hours: Mon to Thu, 0900 to 1700; Fri, 0900 to 1400

Member organisation of: Fédération Internationale de Camping et de Caravanning (FICC)

MOTOR CYCLE INDUSTRY ASSOCIATION LIMITED (MCI)

1 Rye Hill Office Park, Allesley, Coventry, CV5 9AB

Tel: 02476 408000
E-mail: press@mcia.co.uk
Website: www.mcia.co.uk

Direct fax: 02476 408001
Direct e-mail: press@mcia.co.uk

Founded: 1910

Organisation type and purpose: Trade Association.

Subject coverage: Structure of the UK motor cycle industry, manufacture, technical and legislative information, imports, accessories, market statistics, GetOn Campaign, Ride to Work Campaign. Available for media comment on any matters relating to motorcycling.

Trade and statistical information: Data on import and export production, vehicles in use and registrations by type and capacity of mopeds and motorcycles

Publications: Printed

Publications list: Available in print

Access to staff: Contact by letter, by fax and by e-mail
Hours: Mon to Fri, 0900 to 1700

Subsidiary and at the same address is: Motorcycle Industry Exhibitions (MCIE), Electric Motorcycle Industry Association (eMCI), Motorcycle Industry Trainers Association (MCITA)

MOTOR CYCLING CLUB LIMITED (MCC)

20 Old Shipyard Centre, West Bay, Bridport, Dorset, DT6 4HG

Tel: 01308 420706
E-mail: johnaley@portwrinkle.fsnet.co.uk
Website: www.themotorcyclingclub.org.uk

Enquiries to: Secretary General

Founded: 1901

Organisation type and purpose: Membership association (membership is by subscription), present number of members: 1,050.
Motor club.
Organisation of motoring events, particularly classic trials for motorcycles and cars.

Access to staff: Contact by letter, by telephone, by e-mail and via website
Hours: Day or evening
Special comments: No personal callers.

MOTOR INSURANCE REPAIR RESEARCH CENTRE (MIRRC/ Thatcham)

Colthrop Way, Thatcham, Berkshire, RG19 4NR

Tel: 01635 868855
Fax: 01635 871346
E-mail: enquiries@thatcham.org
Website: www.NCSR.co.uk
Website: www.thatcham-orangepages.info
Website: www.ncwr.co.uk
Website: www.thatcham.org

Enquiries to: Public Relations Manager
Direct tel: 01635 294829
Direct fax: 01635 861862
Direct e-mail: lesley@thatcham.org
Other contacts: Research and Operations Director for research or engineering enquiry.

Founded: 1969

Organisation type and purpose: Training organisation, consultancy, research organisation, publishing house.
Sponsored by Motor Insurance Companies and Lloyds Syndicates.

Subject coverage: Vehicle body repair, cost control and standards improvement.

Publications: Printed, and electronic and video, and microform publications
Order printed publications from: Subscriptions Department, MIRRC/Thatcham
Colthrop Way, Thatcham, Berkshire, RG19 4NR

Access to staff: Contact by letter, by telephone, by fax, by e-mail and via website. Appointment necessary.
Hours: Mon to Thu, 0830 to 1630; Fri, 0830 to 1545

Access for disabled people: Parking provided, toilet facilities

Sponsored by: Lloyds Syndicates; Motor insurance companies

MOTOR INSURERS' BUREAU (MIB)

Linford Wood House, 6–12 Capital Drive, Milton Keynes, Buckinghamshire, MK14 6XT

Tel: 01908 830001
Fax: 01908 671660
E-mail: enquiries@mib.org.uk

Enquiries to: Finance Director

Founded: 1946

Organisation type and purpose: International organisation, membership association (membership is by qualification). To compensate victims of uninsured/ untraceable drivers. United Kingdom's green card bureau.

Subject coverage: Green card matters. Compensation from uninsured and untraced accidents.

Access to staff: Contact by letter, by telephone and by fax
Hours: Mon to Fri, 0900 to 1700

MOTOR NEURONE DISEASE ASSOCIATION (MND Association)

PO Box 246, Northampton, NN1 2PR

Tel: 01604 250505
Fax: 01604 624726
E-mail: enquiries@mndassociation.org
Website: www.mndassociation.org

Enquiries to: Information Services Coordinator

Founded: 1979

Organisation type and purpose: Voluntary organisation, registered charity.

Subject coverage: Management, research and symptoms of motor neurone disease; care of patients, including information, compiled by professionals, for medical and paramedical staff; equipment, including loan service.

Collection: Unpublished reports on Motor Neurone Disease

Publications: Printed

Publications list: Available in print

Access to staff: Contact by letter, by telephone, by fax, by e-mail and via website
Hours: Mon to Fri, 0900 to 1700

Member and Secretariat of: International Alliance of ALS/MND Associations

Member of: Association of Medical Research Charities; Neurological Alliance

MOTOR SPORTS ASSOCIATION (MSA)

Formal name: The Royal Automobile Club Motor Sports Association Limited

Motor Sports House, Riverside Park, Colnbrook, Slough, Berkshire, SL3 0HG

Tel: 01753 765000
Fax: 01753 682938
E-mail: msa_mail@compuserve.com
Website: www.msauk.org

Enquiries to: Communications Manager
Other contacts: Corporate Executive (for media, PR, etc.)

Founded: 1979

Organisation type and purpose: Statutory body.
Governing body of motor car sport in Great Britain and Northern Ireland.

Subject coverage: Motor car sport, racing, rallying, autotests and trials, grasstrack, historic cars, karting, technical and medical administration, safety; fire precautions.

Publications: Printed, and electronic and video
Order printed publications from: Data Base Controller

Publications list: Available online and in print

Access to staff: Contact via website. Appointment necessary.
Hours: Mon to Fri, 0900 to 1730

Access for disabled people: Access to all public areas, toilet facilities

Has: 17 regional associations

MOUNT SAINT BERNARD ABBEY LIBRARY

Coalville, Leicestershire, LE67 5UL

Tel: 01530 832298 or 832022
Fax: 01530 814608
E-mail: mountsaintbernard@btinternet.com

Enquiries to: Librarian

Founded: 1835

Organisation type and purpose: Registered charity (charity number 211004).

Subject coverage: All aspects of theology, specialising in monasticism and patrology.

Collection: Recusant literature from the 16th-17th centuries
Two 12th-century manuscripts

Access to staff: Contact by letter, by telephone, by fax and by e-mail
Hours: Mon to Fri, 0900 to 1700

Access to building: No access other than to staff, prior appointment required

MOUNTAIN LEADER TRAINING SCOTLAND (MLTS)

Glenmore, Aviemore, Inverness-shire, PH22 1QU

Tel: 01479 861248
Fax: 01479 861249
E-mail: smltb@aol.com
Website: www.mltscotland.org

Enquiries to: Executive Secretary

Founded: 1964; scottish mountain leader training board formed from Scottish Sports Council

Organisation type and purpose: National government body, training organisation.

Subject coverage: All aspects of training and assessment of those involved in leading groups hill walking, mountaineering and climbing in the United Kingdom.

Access to staff: Contact by letter, by telephone, by fax, by e-mail and in person. Appointment necessary.
Hours: Mon to Fri, 0900 to 1700

MOUNTAIN RESCUE COUNCIL (MRC)

69 Werneth Road, Glossop, Derbyshire, SK13 6NF

Tel: 01457 869506
Fax: 01457 869506

Enquiries to: Honorary Secretary

Founded: 1930

Organisation type and purpose: Voluntary organisation (charity number 222596).
Representative body dealing with mountain rescue in England and Wales.

Subject coverage: Search and rescue of people in mountainous or wild places; assistance to statutory bodies with off-road incidents.

Publications: Printed, and microform publications

Access to staff: Contact by letter and by telephone
Hours: Mon to Fri, 0900 to 1700

Some support from the: Department of Health and Social Security; Home Office

MOVEMENT FOR REFORM JUDAISM

Sternberg Centre for Judaism, 80 East End Road, Finchley, London, N3 2SY

Tel: 020 8349 5640
Fax: 020 8349 5699
E-mail: admin@reformjudaism.org.uk
Website: www.reformjudaism.org.uk

Enquiries to: Public Relations Manager
Direct tel: 020 8349 5689

Organisation type and purpose: Registered charity (charity number 250060).
Religious body.

Subject coverage: All matters relating to the practices of Reform Judaism.

Collection: Leo Baeck College Rabbinical seminary and library

Publications: Printed

Access to staff: Contact by letter, by telephone, by fax, by e-mail and via website. Appointment necessary.
Hours: Mon to Thu, 0930 to 1700; Fri, 0930 to 1500, excluding Jewish Holy Days

Access for disabled people: Parking provided, toilet facilities

Links with: 42 synagogues throughout the United Kingdom

MRC

Formal name: Medical Research Council

Head Office, 20 Park Crescent, London, W1B 1AL

Tel: 020 7636 5422
Fax: 020 7436 6179
E-mail: corporate@headoffice.mrc.ac.uk
Website: www.mrc.ac.uk/

Enquiries to: Information Officer
Direct e-mail: corporate@headoffice.mrc.ac.uk

Founded: 1913

Organisation type and purpose: Research organisation.
To promote the balanced development of medical and related biological research and to advance knowledge that will lead to the maintenance and improvement of human health.

Subject coverage: Medical and scientific research. Cannot give personal medical advice.

Publications: Printed, and electronic and video

Publications list: Available in print

Access to staff: Contact by letter, by telephone, by fax, by e-mail and via website
Hours: Mon to Fri, 0900 to 1700

MRC HUMAN GENETICS UNIT (MRC HGU)

Formal name: Medical Research Council Human Genetics Unit

Crewe Road, Edinburgh, EH4 2XU

Tel: 0131 332 2471
Fax: 0131 467 8456
E-mail: corporate@headoffice.mrc.ac.uk
Website: www.hgu.mrc.ac.uk/

Enquiries to: Librarian
Direct tel: 0131 467 8420

Founded: 1913

Organisation type and purpose: Research Organisation.

Subject coverage: Human genetics; cancer genetics; population genetics; gene therapy; molecular biology, mouse genetics developmental biology; molecular cytogenetics; chromosome structure; yeast molecular genetics; bioinformatics.

Collection: MRC Human Genetics Unit reprints by unit staff, 1948 to the present

Non-library collection catalogue: All or part available in-house

Library catalogue: All or part available in-house

Publications: Printed

Publications list: Available in print

Access to staff: Contact by letter, by telephone, by fax, by e-mail and in person. Appointment necessary.
Hours: Mon to Fri, 0845 to 1645

MRC HUMAN NUTRITION RESEARCH (MRC HNR)

Elsie Widdowson Laboratory, Fulbourn Road, Cambridge, CB1 9NL

Tel: 01223 426356
Fax: 01223 437515
E-mail: susan.jones@mrc-hnr.cam.ac.uk
Website: www.mrc-hnr.cam.ac.uk

Enquiries to: Librarian

Founded: 1998; incorporates the former MRC Dunn Nutrition Unit (year of change 1998)

Organisation type and purpose: Advisory body, research organisation.
Collaborative centre.

Subject coverage: HNR is a Medical Research Council unit which exists to advance knowledge of the relationships between human nutrition and health by providing a national centre of excellence for the measurement and interpretation of biochemical, functional and dietary indications of nutritional status and health.

Collection: Library of nutrition publications
Archival material

Trade and statistical information: Nutrition information

Non-library collection catalogue: All or part available in-house

Library catalogue: All or part available in-house

Publications list: Available online

Access to staff: Contact by telephone, by fax, by e-mail and via website.
Appointment necessary.
Hours: Mon to Fri, 1030 to 1330 and 1400 to 1530

Access to building: *Special comments:* Reference only

Access for disabled people: Parking provided, level entry, access to all public areas, toilet facilities

Links with: Addenbrooke's Hospital; Cambridge; tel: 01223 245151; website: http://www.addenbrookes.org.uk
University of Cambridge; tel: 01223 337733; website: http://www.cam.ac.uk

Parent body: Medical Research Council; 14th Floor, One Kemble Street, London WC2B 4AN; tel: 01793 416200; website: http://www.mrc.ac.uk

MRC INSTITUTE OF HEARING RESEARCH

University Park, University of Nottingham, Nottingham, NG7 2RD

Tel: 0115 922 3431
Fax: 0115 951 8503
E-mail: enquiries@ihr.mrc.ac.uk
Website: www.ihr.mrc.ac.uk

Enquiries to: Information Officer
Other contacts: Unit Manager

Founded: 1977

Organisation type and purpose: Research organisation.

Subject coverage: Auditory Processessing Disorder, hereditary deafness, neural representation of complex sounds, assessment of cochlear function in humans, auditory perception, hearing disability, rehabilitation and benefit from hearing aids, cochlear implants, service delivery and rehabilitation, clinical studies of tinnitus, epidemiological and public health aspects of hearing disorders, causes, consequences and management of middle ear disease.

Publications: Printed, and electronic and video

Publications list: Available online

Access to staff: Contact by letter, by fax, by e-mail and via website
Hours: Mon to Fri, 0900 to 1700

Parent body: Medical Research Council; tel: 020 7636 5422; fax: 020 7436 6179

MS TRUST

Formal name: Multiple Sclerosis Trust

Spirella Building, Bridge Road, Letchworth Garden City, Hertfordshire, SG6 4ET

Tel: 01462 476700
Fax: 01462 476710
E-mail: info@mstrust.org.uk
Website: www.mstrust.org.uk

Founded: 1993; formerly called MS Research Trust (year of change 2001)

Organisation type and purpose: Charity working with and for the 100,000 people in the United Kingdom with multiple sclerosis (MS), to enable them to live their lives to the full. Provides information, education for health professionals, research into better management of MS, support for anyone affected by MS.

Subject coverage: Multiple sclerosis: information on all aspects of the disease, especially the management of symptoms.

Information services: Information for anyone affected by multiple sclerosis, either personally or professionally. Publications, newsletters and personal enquiry service.

Education services: Education courses for health and social care professionals working with people with MS.

Publications: Printed, and electronic and video
Order printed publications from: tel: 01462 476700; e-mail: info@mstrust.org.uk; website: http://www.mstrust.org.uk/publications; or by post
Order electronic and video publications from: tel: 01462 476700; e-mail: info@mstrust.org.uk; website: http://www.mstrust.org.uk/publications; or by post

Publications list: Available online and in print

Access to staff: Contact by letter, by telephone, by fax, by e-mail and via website
Hours: Mon to Fri, 0900 to 1700; answerphone outside office hours

Access to building: No access other than to staff

MSD BIOLOGICS (UK) LTD

PO Box 2, Billingham, Cleveland, TS23 1YN

Tel: 01642 363511
Fax: 01642 364463

Enquiries to: Librarian
Direct tel: 01642 364484

Founded: 1999; formerly called Avecia Biologics, Avecia Biotechnology, Avecia Lifescience Molecules, Zeneca Lifescience Molecules, ICI Bio Products (year of change 2010)

Organisation type and purpose: Research organisation.

Subject coverage: Health care, bioscience.

Access to staff: Contact by letter, by telephone and by fax
Hours: Mon to Fri, 0900 to 1700

Parent body: Merck Sharp & Dohme (Holdings) Ltd; Hertford Road, Hoddesdon, Hertfordshire, EN11 9BU

MSI MARKETING RESEARCH FOR INDUSTRY (MSI)

Viscount House, River Lane, Saltney, Chester, Cheshire, CH4 8RH

Tel: 01244 681186
Fax: 01244 681457
E-mail: enquiries@msi-marketingresearch.co.uk

Enquiries to: Managing Director
Other contacts: Sales and Marketing Co-ordinator for marketing purposes.

Founded: 1980

Organisation type and purpose: Consultancy, research organisation.

Subject coverage: Market research across wide range of sectors; principally covering non-consumer markets such as industrial, engineering and construction markets.

Publications: Printed, and electronic and video

Publications list: Available in print

Access to staff: Contact by letter, by telephone, by fax and by e-mail. Appointment necessary.
Hours: Mon to Fri, 0900 to 1700

MULLARD SPACE SCIENCE LABORATORY (MSSL)

Department of Space and Climate Physics, University College London, Holmbury St Mary, Dorking, Surrey, RH5 6NT

Tel: 01483 274111
Fax: 01483 278312
Website: www.mssl.ucl.ac.uk/

Enquiries to: Director

Organisation type and purpose: University department or institute, research organisation.

Subject coverage: X-ray astronomy; solar X-ray studies; magnetospheric studies; earth remote sensing for climate and geodetic studies.

Publications list: Available online and in print

Also at: Department of Space and Climate Physics; University College London, Gower Street, London, WC1E 6BT; tel: 020 7679 2000

MULTI-FAITH CENTRE (MFC)

Formal name: The Multi-Faith Centre at the University of Derby

University of Derby, Kedleston Road, Derby, DE22 1GB

Tel: 01332 591285
E-mail: mfc@derby.ac.uk
Website: www.multifaithcentre.org

Enquiries to: Centre Director

Founded: 1999

Organisation type and purpose: Registered charity (charity number 1087140), university department or institute, research organisation.
Information on world religious traditions and commitments, and inter-faith and multi-faith initiatives.

Subject coverage: Religious organisations in the United Kingdom, religions, statistics, demographics, inter-faith relations.

Collection: Collection of questionnaires underlying the publication, Religions in the UK: A multi-faith directory
Directories of many UK religious organisations
Ephemera from many religious organisations

Trade and statistical information: Data on religious organisations in the UK, data on religious statistics

Non-library collection catalogue: All or part available in-house

Library catalogue: All or part available in-house

Publications: Printed
Order printed publications from: The Multi-Faith Centre at the University of Derby

Access to staff: Contact by letter, by telephone, by e-mail and via website. Appointment necessary.
Hours: Mon to Fri, 0900 to 1700

Access to building: Prior appointment required

MULTIPLE BIRTHS FOUNDATION (MBF)

Hammersmith House – Level 4, Queen Charlotte's & Chelsea Hospital, Du Cane Road, London, W12 0HS

Tel: 020 8383 3519

Fax: 020 8383 3041
E-mail: mbf@imperial.nhs.uk
Website: www.multiplebirths.org.uk

Enquiries to: Administrator

Founded: 1988

Organisation type and purpose: Registered charity (charity number 1094546).
To offer professional support for families with multiple births as well as advice and training to medical, educational and other professionals involved in their care.

Subject coverage: Multiple births.

Collection: Library and resource centre of books, journals, articles and videos relating to multiple births.

Publications: Printed

Publications list: Available online and in print

Access to staff: Contact by letter, by telephone and by e-mail
Hours: Mon to Fri, 0900 to 1700

MULTIPLE SCLEROSIS INTERNATIONAL FEDERATION (MSIF)

3rd Floor, Skyline House, 200 Union Street, London, SE1 0LX

Tel: 020 7620 1911
Fax: 020 7620 1922
E-mail: info@msif.org
Website: www.msif.org

Enquiries to: Chief Executive

Founded: 1967

Organisation type and purpose: International organisation, membership association (membership is by subscription, qualification, election or invitation), present number of members: 42 autonomous national member societies, voluntary organisation, registered charity.
Coordinating the work of national MS societies worldwide.

Subject coverage: The full integration of people with MS, international development, coordination and furthering of the work of national MS societies worldwide, scientific research and educational information relating to MS; development of existing societies.

Publications: Printed
Order printed publications from: e-mail: info@msif.org

Access to staff: Contact by letter, by telephone, by fax, by e-mail and via website. Appointment necessary.
Hours: Mon to Fri, 0930 to 1730

Access for disabled people: Parking provided, ramped entry, access to all public areas, toilet facilities

Member organisations: 42 national MS societies

MULTIPLE SCLEROSIS NATIONAL THERAPY CENTRES

PO Box 126, Whitchurch,Shropshire, SY14 7WL

Tel: 01296 713901
E-mail: info@msntc.org.uk
Website: www.msntc.org/uk

Enquiries to: Administrator
Other contacts: Chairman

Founded: 1994; formerly called ARMS (Multiple Sclerosis Research) Limited

Organisation type and purpose: Statutory body, voluntary organisation, registered charity.
50 centres provide therapy information and support to Multiple Sclerosis sufferers.

Subject coverage: Multiple sclerosis, self-help disease management, support and information, treatment by professional therapists, support for carers of people with MS, information on MS for the general public.

Publications: Printed

Access to staff: Contact by letter, by telephone, by e-mail and via website

MULTIPLE SCLEROSIS RESOURCE CENTRE (MSRC)

7 Peartree Business Centre, Peartree Road, Stanway, Colchester, Essex, CO3 0JN

Tel: 01206 505444
Fax: 01206 505449
E-mail: themsrc@yahoo.com
Website: www.msrc.co.uk

Enquiries to: Office Manager
Direct tel: 01206 505453
Direct fax: 01206 505449
Direct e-mail: info@msrc.co.uk
Other contacts: Counsellors for counselling – 24-hour telephone counselling 0800 783 0518.

Founded: 1993

Subject coverage: Offers support to those affected by MS, information helpline, support counselling, referal to other agencies, publications.

Publications: Printed

Publications list: Available in print

Access to staff: Contact by letter, by telephone, by fax, by e-mail, in person and via website. Appointment necessary.
Hours: Mon to Fri, 0900 to 1700

Access for disabled people: Parking provided, ramped entry

MULTIPLE SCLEROSIS SOCIETY (MSS)

Formal name: Multiple Sclerosis Society of Great Britain and Northern Ireland

MS National Centre, 372 Edgware Road, Cricklewood, London, NW2 6ND

Tel: 020 8438 0700
Fax: 020 8438 0701
E-mail: info@mssociety.org.uk
Website: www.mssociety.org.uk

Enquiries to: Information Officer
Direct tel: 020 8438 0799
Direct e-mail: infoteam@mssociety.org.uk
Other contacts: Information Officers

Founded: 1953

Organisation type and purpose: The Society is a registered charity (charity number 207495), which offers support to all those affected by MS. To this end it funds MS research, provides information, grants (financial assistance), education and training on MS. It produces numerous publications on MS and runs a freephone specialist Helpline.

Subject coverage: Research into the cause and cure of multiple sclerosis, issues relating to all those affected by multiple sclerosis.

Information services: Enquiry line and library.

Services for disabled people: Services available.

Collection: Oliver Ball Library

Library catalogue: All or part available online

Publications: Printed, and electronic and video
Order printed publications from: website: http://www.mssociety.org.uk/publications

Publications list: Available online and in print

Access to staff: Contact by letter, by telephone, by fax, by e-mail, in person and via website
Hours: Mon to Fri, 0900 to 1700

Access to building: No prior appointment required
Hours: Mon to Fri, 0900 to 1700

Access for disabled people: Parking provided, ramped entry, toilet facilities
Hours: Mon to Fri, 0900 to 1700

Affiliated to: Multiple Sclerosis International Federation (MSIF)

Branches: Multiple Sclerosis Society in Scotland; Ratho Park, 88 Glasgow Road, Ratho Station, Newbridge, EH28 8PP; tel: 0131 335 4050; fax: 0131 335 4051; e-mail: enquiries@mssocietyscotland.org.uk; website: http://www.mssocietyscotland.org.uk
Multiple Sclerosis Society Northern Ireland; 34 Annadale Avenue, Belfast, BT7 3JJ; tel: 028 9080 2802; e-mail: info@mssocietyni.co.uk; website: http://www.mssocietyni.co.uk
Multiple Sclerosis Society Wales/Cymru; Temple Court, Cathedral Road, Cardiff, CF11 9HA; tel: 029 2078 6676; fax: 029 2078 6677; e-mail: mscymruwales@mssociety.org.uk; website: http://www.mssociety.org.uk/wales

MURRAY EDWARDS COLLEGE

Rosemary Murray Library, Murray Edwards College, Huntingdon Road, Cambridge, CB3 0DF

Tel: 01223 762202
Fax: 01223 763110
E-mail: library@murrayedwards.cam.ac.uk
Website: www.murrayedwards.cam.ac.uk/exploring/rosemarymurraylibrary

Enquiries to: Librarian

Founded: 1954; formerly called New Hall (year of change 2008)

Organisation type and purpose: College library

continued overleaf

Subject coverage: All Tripos subjects and those of the special collections

Collection: Bequests of Eleonora Duse, Elizabeth Rawson, classics and ancient history, and Dorothy Gabe, French Women's studies

Library catalogue: All or part available online and in-house

Publications: Printed

Access to staff: Appointment necessary. Access for members only.
Hours: Mon to Fri, 0900 to 1700

Access for disabled people: Level entry, toilet facilities

Parent body: University of Cambridge

MUSCULAR DYSTROPHY CAMPAIGN (MDC)

61 Southwark Street, London, SE1 0HL

Tel: 020 7803 4800; 020 7401 3495
Fax: 020 7401 3495
E-mail: info@muscular-dystrophy.org
Website: www.muscular-dystrophy.org

Enquiries to: Information Officer

Founded: 1959

Organisation type and purpose: Voluntary organisation, registered charity (charity number 205395).
Medical research.
Support and care.

Subject coverage: Neuromuscular conditions, muscular dystrophy, aids and equipment, research.

Publications: Printed

Publications list: Available in print

Access to staff: Contact by letter, by telephone and by fax
Hours: Mon to Fri, 0900 to 1700

Member organisation of: European Alliance of Neuromuscular Disorders Associations (EADMA)

MUSEUM OF ADVERTISING & PACKAGING

Albert Warehouse, The Docks, Gloucester, GL1 2EH

Tel: 01452 302309
Website: www.themuseum.co.uk

Enquiries to: Curator

Founded: 1984

Organisation type and purpose: Museum.

Subject coverage: Advertising, packaging and social history 1850 to present.

Collection: Television commercial programmes
The Robert Opie Collection (300,000 items relating to the history of the consumer society)

MUSEUM OF ENGLISH RURAL LIFE (MERL)

University of Reading, Redlands Road, Reading, RG1 5EX

Tel: 0118 378 8660
Fax: 0118 378 5632
E-mail: merl@reading.ac.uk
Website: www.reading.ac.uk/merl

Enquiries to: Librarian
Other contacts: Archivist for archive and photographic enquiries.

Founded: 1951

Organisation type and purpose: Museum, university department or institute, research organisation.

Subject coverage: Agricultural and rural history including history of agricultural engineering, and food manufacturing and processing industries, agricultural societies, history of environmental organisations, rural industries, farm implements, craft tools, machines, domestic equipment; agricultural museology.

Collection: Book collections:
NIRD and Milk Marketing Board Collection (Dairying); Nuptown House and Fussell Collections (pre-1850 agriculture and agricultural history); Edgar Thomas Collection (agricultural research papers)
Archive collections:
Records of agricultural engineering, processing and seed production firms; records of agricultural cooperatives and organisations; records of countryside and rural affairs organisations; farm records collection; records relating to crafts and rural industries; agricultural research papers
Photographic collections:
Local collections; press collections (including 'Farmers Weekly' and 'Farmer and Stockbreeder' Archives); countryside and environment collections; farm machinery and engineering collections; film and video collections

Trade and statistical information: Agricultural statistics.
Food consumption and expenditure statistics

Non-library collection catalogue: All or part available online and in-house

Library catalogue: All or part available online

Access to staff: Contact by letter, by telephone, by fax, by e-mail, in person and via website. Appointment necessary.
Hours: Mon to Fri, 0900 to 1700

Access to building: *Hours:* Museum: Tue to Fri, 0900 to 1700; Sat and Sun, 1400 to 1630
Reading Room, for access to library and archives: Mon to Fri, 0900 to 1700

Parent body: University of Reading

MUSEUM OF LONDON DOCKLANDS

Library and Archives, Museum of London Docklands, No 1 Warehouse, West India Quay, Hertsmere Road, London, E14 4AL

Tel: 020 7001 9844
Fax: 020 7001 9801
Website: www.museumoflondon.org.uk/docklands

Enquiries to: General Enquiries
Direct e-mail: info.docklands@museumoflondon.org.uk

Founded: 1984

Organisation type and purpose: Museum, historic building, house or site, suitable for ages: 5+.

Subject coverage: The history and development of the Port of London from 1770 to date, including the current regeneration of London's Docklands, the enclosed docks and riverside wharves, the docks and river, cargo handling, dock trades, dock police, dock equipment, labour history of the docks, tools and equipment used in the docks.

Collection: 20,000 photographs of docks and river
British Ports Authority archive covering the port transport industry nationally from 1911–75
Coal Meter's Society archive c. 1750 to c. 1980
Data on the registered dock labour force in London (1950–1988)
Data on the trade of the port of London (1800 to the present)
Docklands Forum archive 1975–1995
Historic films of docks 1921–1970
Port of London Authority records 1909 to date (historic records only, i.e. non-operational)
Records of the Corporation of London River Thames Committee (1770–1857) and the Thames Conservators (1857–1909)
The surviving business records of the private dock companies operating on the Thames (1799–1909)

Trade and statistical information: Data on the trade of the Port of London (1800 to the present).
Data on the registered dock labour force in London 1950–1988

Non-library collection catalogue: All or part available in-house

Library catalogue: All or part available in-house

Publications: Printed, and electronic and video
Order printed publications from: website: http://www.museumoflondonshop.co.uk
Order electronic and video publications from: http://www.museumoflondonshop.co.uk

Access to staff: Contact by letter, by telephone, by fax, by e-mail, in person and via website. Appointment necessary.
Hours: Mon to Fri, 1030 to 1630

Access for disabled people: Parking provided, ramped entry, access to all public areas, toilet facilities, dedicated disabled persons' lift
Special comments: Dedicated disabled persons lift

Branch museums: Museum of London Docklands; at same address

Funded by: Corporation of London (COL) and Department for Culture, Media and Sport (DCMS)

Parent body: Museum of London; 150 London Wall, London, EC2Y 5HN; tel: 020 7001 9844; e-mail: info@museumoflondon.org.uk; website: http://www.museumoflondon.org.uk

MUSEUM OF THE HISTORY OF EDUCATION

Leeds University, Parkinson Court, Leeds, West Yorkshire, LS2 9JT

Tel: 0113 233 4665/4545
Fax: 0113 233 4529
Website: education.leeds.ac.uk/edu/inted/museum.htm

Enquiries to: Curator

Founded: 1951

Organisation type and purpose: Museum. University collection and centre for research and publication.

Subject coverage: History of education and educational administration.

Collection: Board of Education files 1939–1945
Educational artefacts
Library of the history of education
Pupil exercise books
West Riding County Council Education Committee Minutes 1904–1974 and other documents

Publications: Printed

Access to staff: Contact by letter and by telephone. Appointment necessary.
Hours: Mon, Wed, Fri, 1330 to 1630; Thu, 1330 to 1630; Tue closed

Access to building: Prior appointment required
Special comments: The museum is closed for staff and public holidays and when in use by students.
Prior booking of visits advised.

Access for disabled people: Ramped entry

MUSEUMS ASSOCIATION (MA)

24 Calvin Street, London, E1 6NW

Tel: 020 7426 6970
Fax: 020 7426 6961
E-mail: info@museumsassociation.org
Website: www.museumsassociation.org

Enquiries to: Information
Direct tel: 020 7426 6950

Founded: 1889

Organisation type and purpose: Professional body, registered charity (charity number 313024).

Subject coverage: Museums, particularly professional matters and training.

Publications: Printed, and electronic and video

Publications list: Available online and in print

Access to staff: Contact by letter, by telephone, by fax, by e-mail and via website. Appointment necessary.
Hours: Mon to Fri, 0900 to 1700

Access to building: *Hours:* Mon to Fri, 0900 to 1700

MUSEUMS GALLERIES SCOTLAND (MGS)

1 Papermill Wynd, McDonald Road, Edinburgh EH7 4QL

Tel: 0131 550 4100
Fax: 0131 550 4139
E-mail: inform@museumsgalleriesscotland.org.uk
Website: www.museumsgalleriesscotland.org.uk

Enquiries to: Research Manager

Founded: 1964; formerly called Scottish Museums Council

Organisation type and purpose: National organisation, membership association, present number of members: 200+, registered charity (charity number SCO 15593).
MGS is the membership organisation for museums and galleries in Scotland.

Subject coverage: Museums/galleries as applied to Scotland.

Collection: General information on Scottish museums and galleries

Trade and statistical information: Data on the number and nature of museums in Scotland

Library catalogue: All or part available in-house

Access to staff: Contact by letter, by telephone, by fax, by e-mail and via website
Hours: Mon to Fri, 0900 to 1700

MUSEUMS, LIBRARIES AND ARCHIVES COUNCIL (MLA)

Grosvenor House, 14 Bennetts Hill, Birmingham, B2 5RS

Tel: 0121 345 7300
Fax: 0121 345 7303
E-mail: info@mla.gov.uk
Website: www.mla.gov.uk

Direct e-mail: john.harrison@mla.gov.uk

Founded: 2000

Organisation type and purpose: To connect people and change lives through museums, libraries and archives; to increase and sustain participation; to put museums, libraries and archives at the heart of national, regional and local life; to establish a world class and sustainable sector and put it on the best footing for the future; to lead sector strategy and policy development.

Subject coverage: Museums, libraries and archives

Access to staff: Contact by letter, by telephone, by fax, by e-mail and via website

Regional 'Renaissance' programmes: East Midlands, East of England, London, North East, North West, South East, South West, West Midlands, Yorkshire

MUSHROOM GROWERS' ASSOCIATION (MGA)

2 St Paul's Street, Stamford, Lincolnshire, PE9 2BE

Tel: 01780 766888
Fax: 01780 766558
E-mail: carolyn@snowcapmushrooms.co.uk

Enquiries to: Secretary to the Association

Founded: 1945

Organisation type and purpose: Trade association (membership is by subscription).

Subject coverage: Mushroom cultivation.

Publications: Printed

Access to staff: Contact by letter
Hours: Mon to Fri, 0900 to 1700

Specialist branch of the: National Farmers' Union

MUSIC EDUCATION COUNCIL (MEC)

54 Elm Road, Hale, Altrincham, Cheshire, WA15 9QP

Tel: 0161 928 3085
Fax: 0161 929 9648
E-mail: ahassan@easynet.co.uk
Website: www.mec.org.uk

Enquiries to: Professional Officer

Organisation type and purpose: Membership association (membership is by subscription), present number of members: 168 corporate, 70 individual, registered charity (charity number 270004).
Umbrella body for music education and training.

Subject coverage: Music education.

Publications: Printed

Access to staff: Contact by letter, by telephone, by fax and by e-mail
Hours: Mon to Fri, 0900 to 1700

Acts as UK's representative body on: International Society for Music Education

MUSIC IN HOSPITALS (MiH)

Case House, 85–89 High Street, Walton-on-Thames, Surrey, KT12 1DZ

Tel: 01932 260810
Fax: 01932 224123
E-mail: info@musicinhospitals.org.uk
Website: www.musicinhospitals.org.uk

Enquiries to: Chief Executive

Founded: 1948

Organisation type and purpose: Registered charity (charity number 1051659).

Subject coverage: Provides live concerts in hospitals, hospices, nursing homes, day centres throughout the United Kingdom. These are given by carefully selected professional musicians who are chosen not only for their high standard of musicianship, but also for their ability to relate to the most confused, apathetic or ill and to involve them in the performance.

Publications: Printed

Access to staff: Contact by letter, by telephone, by fax and by e-mail
Hours: Mon to Fri, 0830 to 1700

Also at: Music in Hospitals – Northwest; RNCM , 124 Oxford Road, Manchester, M13 9RD; tel: 0161 907 5387; fax: 0161 273 7611; Music in Hospitals Scotland; 10 Forth Street, Edinburgh, EH1 3LD; tel: 0131 556 5848; fax: 0131 556 0225; Welsh Office; 25 Ystrad Drive, Johnstown, Carmarthen, SA31 3PG; tel: 01267 242981; fax: 0167 242981

MUSIC MASTERS' AND MISTRESSES' ASSOCIATION (MMA)

Wayfaring, Smithers Lane, East Peckham, Tonbridge, Kent, TN12 5HT

Tel: 01622 871576
Fax: 01622 871576
E-mail: admin@mma-online.org.uk

Enquiries to: Administrator

Organisation type and purpose: Membership association.

Subject coverage: Teaching of music in schools.

Publications: Printed

Access to staff: Contact by letter, by telephone, by fax and by e-mail
Hours: Mon to Fri, 0900 to 1700

MUSICAL BOX SOCIETY OF GREAT BRITAIN (MBSGB)

PO Box 373, Welwyn, AL6 0WY

E-mail: mail@mbsgb.org.uk
Website: www.mbsgb.org.uk

Enquiries to: Secretary

Founded: 1962

Organisation type and purpose: International organisation, membership association (membership is by subscription), voluntary organisation.
Collectors, museums, restorers.
To promote the preservation, restoration and enjoyment of mechanical music.

Subject coverage: Mechanical music, technical details, history, restoration and repair, dealers and auctioneers, authors.

Collection: Society Archives

Publications: Printed

Publications list: Available in print

Access to staff: Contact by letter, by e-mail and via website
Hours: Mon to Fri, 0900 to 1700

MUSICIANS' UNION (MU)

60–62 Clapham Road, London, SW9 0JJ

Tel: 020 7582 5566
Fax: 020 7582 9805
E-mail: info@musiciansunion.org.uk
Website: www.musiciansunion.org.uk

Enquiries to: Deputy General Secretary

Founded: 1893

Organisation type and purpose: Trade union (membership is by subscription), present number of members: 31,000.

Subject coverage: Music, rates for musicians, contract advice.

Publications: Printed

Access to staff: Contact by letter, by fax and via website
Hours: 1000 to 1730

Access to building: Prior appointment required

Also at: Musicians' Union; 40 Canal Street, Manchester, M1 3WD; tel: 0161 236 1764; fax: 0161 236 0159; Musicians' Union; 11 Sandyford Place, Glasgow, G3 7NB; tel: 0141 248 3723; fax: 0141 204 3510; Musicians' Union; Benson House, Lombard Street, Birmingham, B12 0QN; tel: 0121 622 3870; fax: 0121 622 5361; Musicians' Union; 131 St Georges Road, Bristol, BS1 5UW; tel: 0117 926 5438; fax: 0117 925 3729

MUSLIM EDUCATIONAL TRUST (MET)

130 Stroud Green Road, London, N4 3RZ

Tel: 020 7272 8502
Fax: 020 7281 3457
E-mail: info@muslim-ed-trust.org.uk
Website: www.muslim-ed-trust.org.uk

Enquiries to: Director
Other contacts: Assistant Director and Sales Manager.

Founded: 1966

Organisation type and purpose: Registered charity (charity number 313192), suitable for ages: 4 to 18, publishing house.
Educational charity.

Subject coverage: Muslim, Islamic education in a non-Muslim country; religious education for Muslim children; Islamic studies.

Publications: Printed

Publications list: Available online and in print

Access to staff: Contact by letter, by telephone and by fax. Appointment necessary.
Hours: Mon to Fri, 0900 to 1700

Affiliated to: Religious Education Council of UK and Eire; CEM, Royal Buildings, Victoria Street, Derby, DE1 1GW; tel: 01332 296655; fax: 01332 343253

MUSLIM WOMEN'S WELFARE ASSOCIATION

425 Lea Bridge Road, London, E10 7EA

Tel: 020 8539 7478
Fax: 020 8539 7478

Enquiries to: Co-ordinator

Founded: 1983

Access to staff: Contact by letter, by telephone, by fax and in person
Hours: Mon to Fri, 1000 to 1530

Access to building: No access other than to staff

Access for disabled people: Level entry

MUSLIM WORLD LEAGUE

46 Goodge Street, London, W1T 4LU

Tel: 020 7636 7568
Fax: 020 7637 5034
E-mail: info@mwllo.org.uk

Enquiries to: Deputy Director

Founded: 1982

Organisation type and purpose: International organisation, registered charity (charity number 290098).
To help the community in educational, cultural and religious matters.

Subject coverage: Information about the problems, rights, duties etc concerning the Muslim Community in UK and Eire.

Library catalogue: All or part available in-house

Access to staff: Contact by letter, by telephone, by fax, by e-mail and in person. Appointment necessary. Letter of introduction required.
Hours: Mon to Fri, 1030 to 1600

Access to building: No prior appointment required

Links with: Muslim World League (MWL); PO Box 537, Makkah, Saudi Arabia; tel: 00 9662 560 0919; fax: 00 9662 560 1267/560 1319; e-mail: mul@aol.com; Supreme Council of Mosques; Makkah, Saudi Arabia

MVRA LIMITED

Glenfield Business Park, Philips Road, Blackburn, Lancashire, BB1 5QH

Tel: 0870 458 3051
Fax: 0870 458 3149
E-mail: info@mvra.com
Website: www.mvra.com

Enquiries to: Managing Director
Direct e-mail: enquiry@mvra.com
Other contacts: Membership Services Manager for membership.

Founded: 1988

Subject coverage: Motor industry, accident management, quality repairers, quality body and mechanical garages/repairers.

Trade and statistical information: Data covering all aspects of the motor industry

Access to staff: Contact by letter, by telephone and by e-mail
Hours: Closed Bank Holidays

Access to building: Mon to Fri, 0900 to 1700

Access for disabled people: Parking provided, toilet facilities

MYCOBACTERIUM REFERENCE UNIT (MRU)

Public Health Laboratory, King's College Hospital (Dulwich), East Dulwich Grove, London, SE22 8QF

Tel: 020 8693 1312
Fax: 020 8346 6477
Website: www.phls.co.uk

Enquiries to: Director

Organisation type and purpose: National government body, research organisation.

Subject coverage: Laboratory diagnosis of tuberculosis and other mycobacterial diseases in man and animals; identification and sensitivity testing of mycobacteria; advice on treatment of such diseases. Basic research into host pathogen interactions and the epidemiology of mycobacterial diseases.

Access to staff: Contact by letter and by fax
Hours: Mon to Fri, 0900 to 1715

Links to: Public Health Laboratory Service (PHLS); 61 Colindale Avenue, London, NW9

MYCOLOGY REFERENCE CENTRE

Department of Microbiology, University of Leeds, Leeds, West Yorkshire, LS2 9JT

Tel: 0113 233 5600/1
Fax: 0113 233 5640
Website: www.leeds.ac.uk/mbiology/res/mycol/mrl.htm

Enquiries to: Clinical Scientist

Organisation type and purpose: Diagnostic medical laboratory.

Subject coverage: Diseases of man and animals caused by infection with fungi; allergy to fungi; examination of cultures; tissue section; serological and molecular tests; antifungal assays.

Access to staff: Contact by letter, by telephone and by fax. All charged.
Hours: Mon to Fri, 0900 to 1700
Special comments: Posting of samples subject to Royal Mail regulations.

Parent bodies: Leeds Teaching Hospitals NHS Trust; Leeds, LS1 3EX; University of Leeds; Leeds, LS2 9JT

MYFANWY TOWNSEND MELANOMA RESEARCH FUND

6 Manor Road, East Grinstead, West Sussex, RH19 1LR

Tel: 01342 322508
E-mail: harry@melanoma-fund.co.uk
Website: www.melanoma-fund.co.uk

Founded: c. 2000

Organisation type and purpose: Registered charity (charity number 1085969).
To raise awareness and publicise the deadly nature of malignant melanoma and diagnostic signs and precautions that should be taken, to educate about the disease, to fund research to find a cure, to make diagnosis more readily available (e.g. through free walk-in clinics).
There is an Melanoma Awareness Week annually in June, as well as promotions for Sun Hat Days and awareness days for Primary Schools.

Subject coverage: Melanoma.

Access to staff: Contact by letter, by telephone and by e-mail

NACELL

Formal name: National Advisory Centre on Early Language Learning

c/o CILT, the National Centre for Languages, 20 Bedfordbury, London, WC2N 4LB

Tel: 020 7379 5101
Fax: 020 7379 5082
Website: www.nacell.org.uk

Enquiries to: Information Officer
Direct e-mail: primarylanguages@cilt.org.uk

Organisation type and purpose: NACELL is a Department for Education and Skills Initiative to promote and develop the provision and quality of Modern Foreign Language learning in the Primary sector.
NACELL is coordinated by CILT, the National Centre for Languages. National organisation, registered charity (charity number 313938), public library, university department or institute, suitable for ages: all.

Subject coverage: Early language learning, primary languages, teaching foreign languages to young children (under 11s).

Non-library collection catalogue: All or part available online and in-house

Library catalogue: All or part available online and in-house

Order printed publications from: Central Books Ltd
99 Wallis Road, London, E9 5LN, tel: 0845 4589910, e-mail: mo@centralbooks.com

Publications list: Available online and in print

Access to staff: Contact by letter, by telephone, by fax, by e-mail, in person and via website
Hours: Term time, Mon, Tue, Thu, Fri, 1030 to 1700; Wed, 1030 to 2000; Sat, 1000 to 1300: Vacations, Mon to Fri, 1030 to 1700

Access to building: No prior appointment required
Hours: Term time, Mon, Tue, Thu, Fri, 1030 to 1700; Wed, 1030 to 2000; Sat, 1000 to 1300: Vacations, Mon to Fri, 1030 to 1700

Access for disabled people: Toilet facilities

Parent body: CILT, the National Centre for Languages; at the same address

NACRO, THE CRIME REDUCTION CHARITY

Formal name: Nacro

159 Clapham Road, London, SW9 0PU

Tel: 020 7840 6464
Fax: 020 7840 6420
E-mail: helpline@nacro.org.uk
Website: www.nacro.org.uk

Enquiries to: Resettlement Helpline Officer

Founded: 1966

Organisation type and purpose: To reduce crime by giving disadvantaged people – offenders and those at risk of offending – a positive stake in society. Provides direct services (education and employment, housing, youth projects, advice), and consultancy and training services. Runs a resettlement helpline to give advice and information to ex-offenders, their family and friends and others around issues such as housing and employment.

Subject coverage: Resettlement services for ex-offenders, Rehabilitation of Offenders Act 1974, special needs housing, employment, training, education, youth crime, crime and criminal justice (especially prisons), mentally disordered offenders, community safety, race and criminal justice.

Publications: Printed

Publications list: Available online

Access to staff: Contact by letter, by telephone, by fax and by e-mail
Hours: Mon to Fri, 0900 to 1700

NAFAS

Formal name: National Association of Flower Arrangement Societies

Osborne House, 12 Devonshire Square, London, EC2M 4TE

Tel: 020 7247 5567
Fax: 020 7247 7232
E-mail: flowers@nafas.org.uk
Website: www.nafas.org.uk

Enquiries to: Administrator

Founded: 1959

Organisation type and purpose:
Membership association, present number of members: 100,000, registered charity (charity number 289038), suitable for ages: 8+.
Education charity.
To promote the art and teaching of flower arranging.

Subject coverage: Flower arranging.

Library catalogue: All or part available in-house

Publications: Printed

Publications list: Available in print

Access to staff: Contact by letter, by telephone, by fax, by e-mail and via website. Appointment necessary.
Hours: Mon to Fri, 0900 to 1700

Access to building: Prior appointment required

Affiliated to: Royal Horticultural Society

NAMIBIA HIGH COMMISSION

Formal name: High Commission for the Republic of Namibia

6 Chandos Street, London, W1G 9LU

Tel: 020 7636 6244
Fax: 020 7687 5694
Website: www.namibhc.org.uk

Enquiries to: Information Officer
Direct e-mail: info@namibiahc.org.uk
Other contacts: First Secretary for Political Affairs and Trade; First Secretary for Commonwealth Affairs and Education; First Secretary for Consular Matters

Organisation type and purpose: National government body, national organisation.
Protocol and bilateral relations between Namibia and the UK, consular enquiries (visas, work permits, passports). Tourism departments, political, economic, trade and educational links between Namibia and the UK.

Subject coverage: General enquiries regarding geography, wildlife and environment of Namibia; Namibian cultures and customs; economic and political affairs; education and other matters. Contact names and addresses of individuals and organisations in Namibia can be provided.

Information services: All enquiries regarding Namibia: politics, economy, trade, education, tourism, wildlife and environment.

Education services: The High Commission encourages twinning links between UK and Namibian schools, and will assist with school visits to Namibia.

continued overleaf

Collection: Outside Namibia, the most comprehensive collection of materials relating to Namibian history and culture is held at: Namibia Resource Centre, Basler Afrika Bibliographien, PO Box 2037, 4001, Basel, Switzerland

Trade and statistical information: The Commercial Attaché can answer most enquiries, and help establish commercial relationships with Namibian companies

Publications: Printed

Access to staff: Contact by letter, by telephone, by fax, by e-mail, in person and via website. Appointment necessary.
Hours: Mon to Fri, 0900 to 1300 and 1400 to 1700
Special comments: Excepting Namibian and UK public holidays.

NAPO

4 Chivalry Road, Battersea, London, SW11 1HT

Tel: 020 7223 4887
Fax: 020 7223 3503
E-mail: info@napo.org.uk
Website: www.napo.org.uk

Enquiries to: Information Manager

Founded: 1912

Organisation type and purpose: Professional body, trade union, present number of members: 9,500.
Trade union and professional association for Family Court and probation staff.

Subject coverage: Probation Service, criminal justice system, Family Court Service.

Publications: Printed

Access to staff: Contact by letter, by telephone, by fax, by e-mail and via website. Appointment necessary.
Hours: Mon to Fri, 0900 to 1700

Access to building: Prior appointment required

NAPOLEONIC SOCIETY

Formal name: Napoleonic Society of Great Britain

157 Vicarage Road, Leyton, London, E10 5DU

Tel: 020 8539 3876
Fax: 020 8539 3876
E-mail: keys@fsmail.net

Enquiries to: Secretary

Founded: 1969

Organisation type and purpose: Learned society.

Subject coverage: Napoleon. French and Napoleonic history 1769–1945.

Non-library collection catalogue: All or part available in-house

Library catalogue: All or part available in-house

Publications: Printed

Access to staff: Contact by letter, by telephone, by fax and by e-mail. Appointment necessary.
Hours: Mon to Sat, 1100 to 1900

Access for disabled people: Limited access

NASPCS

Formal name: National Advisory Service for Parents of Children with a Stoma

51 Anderson Drive, Valley View Park, Darvel, Ayrshire, KA17 0DE

Tel: 01560 322024
E-mail: john@stoma.freeserve.co.uk

Enquiries to: Chairman

Founded: 1986

Organisation type and purpose: National organisation, membership association, present number of members: 650 families, voluntary organisation, registered charity (charity number 327922).
National advisory service for parents of incontinent children and children with a stoma. Membership is free.
To provide a contact and information service for parents, on the practical day-to-day management of a child with either a colostomy, ileostomy or urostomy.

Subject coverage: Bladder and bowel incontinence, ileostomy, urostomy, colostomy, Hirschsprung's disease, imperforate anus, cloacal exstrophy, exompholus, prune belly syndrome, Vater syndrome, ectopia vesicae, colonic/intestinal neuronal dysplasia and gastroschisis.

Publications: Printed

Publications list: Available in print

Access to staff: Contact by letter, by telephone and by e-mail
Hours: Mon to Fri, 0900 to 1700

Access to building: No access other than to staff

Members of: International Ostomy Association

Membership Secretary: NASPCS; Maran Bank, Main Street, Glenfarg, Tayside, PH2 9NT; tel: 01577 830661

Northern Ireland Representative: NASPCS; 11 Earlford Heights, Doagh Road, Newtownabbey, Belfast, BT36 8WZ; tel: 01232 837972

NASUWT THE TEACHERS UNION

Hillscourt Eductaion Centre, Rose Hill, Rednal, Birmingham, B45 8RS

Tel: 0121 453 6150
Fax: 0121 457 6208/9
E-mail: nasuwt@mail.nasuwt.org.uk
Website: www.nasuwt.org.uk

Founded: 1919

Organisation type and purpose: Professional body, trade union, present number of members: 280,000.

Subject coverage: Salaries, superannuation and conditions of service of UK teachers; education in the UK; primary and secondary school education; teacher training and education; equality.

Publications: Printed
Order printed publications from: website: http://www.nasuwt.org.uk

Publications list: Available online

Access to staff: Contact by letter, by telephone, by fax, by e-mail and via website. Appointment necessary.
Hours: Mon to Fri, 0830 to 1730

Affiliated to: Education International; European Trade Union Committee for Education; Federation of Professional Workers; Irish Congress of Trade Unions; National Foundation for Educational Research; Scottish Trades Union Congress; Trades Union Congress; Welsh Trades Union Congress

Headquarters address: NASUWT; Hillscourt Education Centre, Rosehill, Rednal, Birmingham, B45 8RS; tel: 0121 453 6150; fax: 0121 457 6208/9; e-mail: nasuwt@mail.nasuwt.org.uk; website: http://www.nasuwt.org.uk

NATIONAL 39/45 MILITARY VEHICLE GROUP

9 Cordelia Way, Rugby, Warwickshire, CV22 6JU

Tel: 01788 812250

Enquiries to: Treasurer

Founded: 1972

Organisation type and purpose: Membership association, voluntary organisation, research organisation.

Subject coverage: Restoration of World War II Allied and Axis military vehicles and equipment, uniforms, memoirs, archives; film advice and vehicle supply; vehicle date verification.

Collection: Archive photographs and drawings of airborne vehicle modifications British and American military vehicle numbers

Publications: Printed

Access to staff: Contact by letter and by telephone
Hours: Telephone after 1800

NATIONAL ACCESS & SCAFFOLDING CONFEDERATION (NASC)

4th Floor, 12 Bridewell Place, London EC4V 6AP

Tel: 020 7822 7400
Fax: 020 7822 7401
E-mail: enquiries@nasc.org.uk
Website: www.nasc.org.uk

Enquiries to: Director

Founded: 1943

Organisation type and purpose: Trade association.

Subject coverage: All aspects of scaffolding; technical information, safety, suppliers and contractors.

Publications: Printed

Publications list: Available in print

Access to staff: Contact by letter, by telephone and by fax
Hours: Mon to Fri, 0900 to 1700

Member of: National Specialist Contractors Council (NSCC)

NATIONAL ACQUISITIONS GROUP (NAG)

12–14 King Street, Wakefield, WF1 2SQ

Tel: 01924 383010
Fax: 01924 383010
E-mail: nag1@btconnect.com
Website: www.nag.org.uk

Enquiries to: Administrator

Founded: 1986

Organisation type and purpose:
Professional body, membership association (membership is by subscription), present number of members: 351.
Bringing together those concerned in library acquisitions, publishers, booksellers, system suppliers and librarians (public, academic, special, etc.).

Subject coverage: Library acquisitions and collections management in the United Kingdom and the Republic of Ireland, technological developments, producers, suppliers and libraries.

Publications: Printed, and electronic and video
Order printed publications from: Available as part of membership benefits
Order electronic and video publications from: As part of membership benefits and/or downloadable

Publications list: Available online

Access to staff: Contact by letter, by telephone, by fax, by e-mail and via website
Hours: Most office hours

Access to building: *Hours:* Most office hours

Access for disabled people: *Special comments:* Steep stairs in old building

Links with: CILIP; 7 Ridgmount Street, London, WC1E 7AE; tel: 020 7255 0500; website: http://www.cilip.org.uk

NATIONAL AEROSPACE LIBRARY (NAL)

The Hub, Fowler Avenue, IQ Farnborough, Hants, GU14 7JP.

Tel: 01252 701038 ; 01252 701060
E-mail: hublibrary@aerosociety.com
Website: www.aerosociety.com

Enquiries to: Librarian

Founded: 2007; incorporates the former Library of the Royal Aeronautical Society

Organisation type and purpose: Learned society, registered charity (charity number 313708).

Subject coverage: Aeronautics, astronautics, aerospace engineering, aerospace history, space, air law, air power, air transport, guided flight, aerospace propulsion, flight testing, avionics, rotorcraft, aviation medicine, piloting, aerodynamics, aircraft maintenance, aircraft structures and materials. An extensive collection of material relating to the development and recent technical advances in aeronautics, aviation and aerospace technology from the earliest times through to current operations and technology.

Collection: 30,000 books, 1,000 periodical titles, 40,000 technical reports, 100,000 photographs, 200 current journal titles
Extensive collection (in excess of 200,000) of aviation photographs, glass lantern slides and lithographs
Books, letters, papers and manuscripts of early pioneers, including:
Major B. F. S. Baden-Powell (1860–1937)
Sir George Cayley (1773–1857)
C. G. Grey (1875–1953)
Lawrence Hargrave (1850–1915)
John Stringfellow (1799–1883)
Katharine Wright (1874–1929)
Orville Wright (1871–1948)
Wilbur Wright (1867–1912)
F. S. Barnwell (1880–1938, Design notebooks)
Various papers relating to the long history of the Society
Cuthbert-Hodgson Collection (ballooning and early aeronautical material)
Maitland Airship Collection
Poynton Collection (early ballooning, etc.)
Air Ministry/Ministry of Aircraft Production Air Publications
Air Accidents Investigations Branch Reports
Advisory Committee for Aeronautics/ Aeronautical Research Council (ARC) technical reports
Society of British Aircraft Constructors/ Aerospace Companies (SBAC) Minutes 1916–2000
The Air Pilot/UK Aeronautical Information Publication (AIP) August 1948–1999

Library catalogue: All or part available online

Publications: Printed

Access to staff: Contact by letter, by telephone, by e-mail, in person and via website
Hours: Tues to Fri, 1000 to 1600

Administered by: Royal Aeronautical Society; 4 Hamilton Place, London, W1J 7BQ; tel: 0207 499 3515; website: www .aerosociety.com

NATIONAL AIDS TRUST (NAT)

New City Cloisters, 196 Old Street, London, EC1V 9FR

Tel: 020 7814 6767
Fax: 020 7216 0111
E-mail: info@nat.org.uk
Website: www.nat.org.uk
Website: www.worldaidsday.org

Founded: 1988

Organisation type and purpose: National organisation, voluntary organisation, registered charity (charity number 297977).
The National Aids Trust's (NAT) vision is a world in which people living with HIV are treated as equal citizens with respect, dignity and justice, are diagnosed early and receive the highest standards of care, and in which everyone knows how and is able to protect themselves and others from HIV infection.
All the Trust's work is focused on achieving four strategic goals:
- Effective HIV prevention in order to halt the spread of HIV
- Early diagnosis of HIV through ethical, accessible and appropriate testing
- Equitable access to treatment, care and support for people living with HIV
- Eradication of HIV-related stigma and discrimination

Subject coverage: Policy; World Aids Day; employers' initiatives; special projects.

Collection: Art of Awareness Collection: 100 framed images created depicting AIDS awareness, various media

Library catalogue: All or part available in-house

Publications: Printed, and electronic and video

Publications list: Available online and in print

Access to staff: Contact by letter, by telephone, by fax, by e-mail and via website. Appointment necessary.
Hours: Mon to Fri, 0900 to 1700

Access to building: No prior appointment required

NATIONAL ANIMAL WELFARE TRUST (NAWT)

Tyler's Way, Watford Bypass, Watford, Hertfordshire, WD25 8WT

Tel: 020 8950 0177
Fax: 020 8420 4454
E-mail: watford@nawt.org.uk
Website: www.nawt.org.uk

Enquiries to: Chief Executive

Founded: 1971

Organisation type and purpose: Registered charity, voluntary organisation (charity number 1090499).
Rescue and rehoming of unwanted animals.

Subject coverage: Animal rescue and rehoming.

Publications: Printed

Access to staff: Contact by letter, by telephone, by fax, by e-mail, in person and via website
Hours: Administration: Mon to Fri, 0900 to 1700; Rescue Centres: Watford, 1100 to 1500; Langport (Somerset), 1100 to 1530; Cornwall, 1300 to 1600; Berkshire, 1100 to 1600

Access for disabled people: Parking provided, ramped entry, access to all public areas, toilet facilities

Other addresses: National Animal Welfare Trust; Heaven's Gate Farm, West Henley, Langport, Somerset, TA10 9BE; tel: 01458 252656; fax: 01458 253806; National Animal Welfare Trust; Trindledown Farm, Wantage Lane, Great Shefford, Newbury, Berkshire, RG17 7DQ; tel: 01488 638584; fax: 01488 638141; National Animal Welfare Trust; Wheal Alfred Farm, Wheal Alfred Road, Hayle, Cornwall, TR27 5JT; tel: 01736 756005

NATIONAL ANKYLOSING SPONDYLITIS SOCIETY (NASS)

Unit 0.2, One Victoria Villas, Richmond upon Thames, Surrey, TW9 2GW

Tel: 020 8948 9117
E-mail: admin@nass.co.uk
Website: www.nass.co.uk

Enquiries to: Administrator

Founded: 1976

continued overleaf

Organisation type and purpose: Registered charity (charity number 272258). NASS is a membership charity which gives information and support to people with ankylosing spondylitis. Has over 80 branches in the United Kingdom.

Subject coverage: Ankylosing spondylitis.

Publications: Printed, and electronic and video
Order electronic and video publications from: www.nass.co.uk

Publications list: Available online and in print

Access to staff: Contact by letter, by telephone, by e-mail and via website
Hours: Mon to Fri 0900 to 1200

Access to building: No public access

Links with: Ankylosing Spondylitis International Federation; at the same address

NATIONAL ANTI-HUNT CAMPAIGN (NAHC)

PO Box 66, Stevenage, SG1 2TR

Tel: 01442 240246
Fax: By arrangement
Website: www.liberation-mag.org.uk/nahc.htm

Enquiries to: Information Officer
Direct e-mail: info@savethepigeons.org

Founded: 1992

Organisation type and purpose: Membership association (membership is by subscription), voluntary organisation. Peaceful legal campaigning against all hunting with dogs.

Subject coverage: All areas relating to hunting with hounds, legal problems with hunt trespass etc.

Publications: Printed

Access to staff: Contact by letter, by telephone, by fax and by e-mail
Hours: Mon to Fri, 0900 to 1700

NATIONAL ARCHIVES (TNA)

Formal name: The National Archives

Kew, Richmond, Surrey, TW9 4DU

Tel: 020 8876 3444; minicom no. 020 8392 9198
E-mail: http://www.nationalarchives.gov.uk/contact/form
Website: www.nationalarchives.gov.uk
Website: www.nationalarchives.gov.uk/catalogue

Founded: 1838; created by the merger of Public Record Office (PRO) and Historical Manuscripts Commission (HMC); (The Office of Public Sector Information was incorporated in 2006) (year of change 2004)

Organisation type and purpose: National government body, government department and executive agency under the Secretary of State for Justice.
National Archive Office.

Subject coverage: As the official archive for England, Wales and the central UK government, The National Archives holds records ranging from parchment and paper scrolls through to digital files and archived websites. Increasingly, these records are being put online, making them universally accessible. The collection covers the British Isles, the territories that formed the British Empire and the countries of the Commonwealth.
The National Archives is at the heart of information policy, setting standards and supporting innovation in information and records management across the UK, providing advice on opening up and encouraging the re-use of public sector information. Through its efforts in promoting best practice in information management, it looks to ensure the survival of today's information for the future.

Education services: See website: http://www.nationalarchives.gov.uk/teachers.

Collection: The collections are too numerous to specify (documents number many millions, and currently cover 100 miles of shelving)
Famous documents include the Domesday Book, Shakespeare's will, the Log of HMS Victory, World Wars documents

Non-library collection catalogue: All or part available online

Library catalogue: All or part available online

Publications: Printed

Publications list: Available online and in print

Access to staff: Contact by letter, by telephone, by fax, by e-mail, in person and via website
Hours: Mon, Fri, 0900 to 1700; Tue, Thu, 0900 to 1900; Wed, 1000 to 1700; Sat, 0930 to 1700

Access to building: Access during open hours. A reader's ticket is required for access to orginal documents. A ticket can be obtained free of charge by bringing proof of identity and proof of address. A list of suitable identification documents is on the website at: http://www.nationalarchives.gov.uk/registration
Hours: Mon, Fri, 0900 to 1700; Tue, Thu, 0900 to 1900; Wed, 1000 to 1700; Sat, 0930 to 1700

Access for disabled people: Parking provided, level entry, access to all public areas, toilet facilities; for more information see website: http://www.nationalarchives.gov.uk/visit/disabled.htm?source=ddmenu_visit7

NATIONAL ARCHIVES OF SCOTLAND (NAS)

HM General Register House, 2 Princes Street, Edinburgh, EH1 3YY

Tel: 0131 535 1314
Fax: 0131 535 1360
E-mail: enquiries@nas.gov.uk
Website: www.nas.gov.uk

Enquiries to: Keeper of the Records of Scotland

Founded: 1789

Organisation type and purpose: National government body, statutory body.
Record office and archive.
Repository for the public and legal records of Scotland, accepts many local and private archives for which it is felt to be the most suitable repository.

Subject coverage: Scottish affairs, history, topography, law, genealogy.

Collection: Administrative records of pre-Union Scotland, registers of central and local courts of law, public registers of property rights and legal documents, local and church records and private archives (computerised database for some)
Records of Scottish parliament and government departments, nationalised industries, maps and plans, and business records

Non-library collection catalogue: All or part available online, in-house and in print

Library catalogue: All or part available online and in-house

Publications: Printed, and electronic and video

Publications list: Available online and in print

Access to staff: Contact by letter, by telephone, by fax, by e-mail and in person
Hours: Mon to Fri, 0900 to 1700

Access for disabled people: For wheelchair users and people with mobility impairments disabled parking is available within the car park off West Register Street. Note that this parking is limited and it is recommended an appointment is made. Access to the building can be made via either a ramp or disabled lift adjacent to the car park. Disabled toilet facilities are available on all floors.

NATIONAL ART LIBRARY (NAL)

Victoria and Albert Museum, Cromwell Road, South Kensington, London, SW7 2RL

Tel: 020 7942 2400
Fax: 020 7942 2394 or 2401
E-mail: nal.enquiries@vam.ac.uk
Website: www.vam.ac.uk/nal

Enquiries to: Deputy Keeper
Direct tel: 020 7942 2562
Direct e-mail: j.meriton@vam.ac.uk
Other contacts: Head of Information Services, e-mail: m.flynn@vam.ac.uk

Founded: 1837

Organisation type and purpose: National organisation, art gallery, historic building, house or site.
National Art Library, open to the public, research library.

Subject coverage: Architecture, fine and applied art and design of all periods and western countries, as well as Indian, Islamic and Far Eastern; prints, drawings, paintings; modern art; design; sculpture; metalwork; book production and the art of the book (bindings, illustration, fine printing); history of art; crafts; history of printing; history of costume; private presses; photography; artists' books; comics; children's books; calligraphy; manuscript illumination; heraldry; interior design; furniture and woodwork; ceramics and glass; textiles and dress; museums and museology; Beatrix Potter; Natalia Goncharova; Mikhail Larionov.

Collection: The General Collection contains: 1,000,000 books, 2,000 current periodical titles, 9,000 closed periodical titles, 60,000 exhibition catalogues, 300 illuminated manuscripts, 50,000 sales catalogues, 20,000 information files, literature from international exhibitions
Archives, artists' books, letters and manifestos, books using innovative technology or structure, books with notable dustjackets, calligraphy, children's books, comics and graphic novels, documentary manuscripts, early printed books, ephemera and jobbing printing, fine and noteworthy bindings and printing, illuminated manuscripts, modern book and magazine design, typography, writing and lettering books
Artists' books
Exhibition catalogues
Sales catalogues
Trade literature
The Special Collections are varied and include:
19th-century Periodicals
Clements Collection of armorial bindings
Cole Collection: diaries, notebooks, correspondence and books of Sir Henry Cole
Forster Collection: English literature and history 16th to 19th centuries (including manuscripts of Charles Dickens)
Dyce Collection: literature and theatre, Britain and Europe 16th to 19th centuries
Harrod Collection: 19th-century illustrated books
Hole Bequest: 17th- and 18th-century literature
Hutton Bequest: works on fencing, swordsmanship, weapons and self-defence
Jobbing Printing Collection: material from the 1920s, 1930s and 1960s
Jones Collection: literature and works relating to art and manufacturing
Osbert Lancaster Collection: comic art, humour
Larionov Collection: work by Larionov and Goncharova, theatre and opera in Europe (especially Russia and France)
Liberty and Company Printed Catalogues Collection
Linder Bequest and Collection: Beatrix Potter drawings, watercolours, manuscripts and letters (held at Blythe House)
Guy Little Bequest: children's books
Mediaeval manuscripts
Osman-Gidal Collection: photojournalism
Pinto Bequest: directories relating to London and the provinces
Piot Collection: fairs and festivals
Queen Mary's Collection of children's books (held at Blythe House)
Rakoff Collection: comics and graphic novels
Renier Collection (held at Blythe House)
Weale Collection: part of the working library of W H James Weale, Keeper of the National Art Library, 1890–1899

Library catalogue: All or part available online

Publications: Printed

Publications list: Available online

Access to staff: Contact by letter, by telephone, by fax, by e-mail, in person and via website
Hours: Tue, Wed, Thu, Sat, 1000 to 1730; Fri, 1000 to 1830
Special comments: Closed Bank Hol weekends, Christmas to New Year (except for 1 day) and two weeks' annual stocktaking in Aug. (check website for full details of closures).
All users must register after showing means of identification, access with readers' tickets only; visitors by prior appointment for reserved materials.

Access to building: No prior appointment required
Hours: Sun to Sat, 1000 to 1745; Fri, 1000 to 2200 (selected galleries remain open after 1800)
Special comments: Closed 24, 25 & 26 Dec.

Access for disabled people: Parking provided, ramped entry, toilet facilities
Special comments: 4 parking bays for vehicles with stickers for disabled people, next to the Exhibition Road entrance.

Parent body: Victoria and Albert Museum

Subsidiary body: Archive of Art and Design; 23 Blythe Road, London, W14 0QF; tel: 020 7603 1514; fax: 020 7602 0980; e-mail: archive@vam.ac.uk; website: http://www.vam.ac.uk/resources/archives

NATIONAL ASSEMBLY FOR WALES

Library, New Crown Building, Cathays Park, Cardiff, CF10 3NQ

Tel: 029 2082 5449 or 823683
Fax: 029 2082 5508
Website: www.wales.gov.uk

Enquiries to: Librarian
Direct tel: 029 2082 3362

Founded: 1999

Organisation type and purpose: National government body.

Subject coverage: Local government; housing; education; health and social services; public finance and administration; law; libraries and museums; agriculture; economic planning; land use; transport and highways; tourism; ancient monuments; national parks; water; environment.

Trade and statistical information: Welsh statistics

Library catalogue: All or part available in-house

Publications: Printed
Order printed publications from: website: http://www.wales.gov.uk

Publications list: Available online

Access to staff: Appointment necessary.
Hours: Mon to Fri, 0900 to 1700

Access to building: By appointment

NATIONAL ASSOCIATION FOR CHILDREN OF ALCOHOLICS (Nacoa)

PO Box 64, Fishponds, Bristol, BS16 2UH

Tel: 0117 924 8005 (admin); 0800 358 3456 (helpline)
E-mail: helpline@nacoa.org.uk
Website: www.nacoa.org.uk

Enquiries to: Administrator
Other contacts: Chief Executive

Founded: 1990

Organisation type and purpose: Advisory body, membership association, registered charity (charity number 1009143), research organisation.
To raise the public consciousness to the needs of children of alcohol-dependent parents, educate professionals as to their specific needs, provide advice, information and fellowship and promote research.

Subject coverage: Information and advice on children of alcohol-dependent parents for professionals and client group; other resources available, suggested reading.

Publications: Printed

Publications list: Available online and in print

Access to staff: Contact by letter, by telephone, by fax and by e-mail
Hours: Administration: Mon to Fri, 1000 to 1600
Helpline: Mon, Fri, 1000 to 1900; Tues, Wed, Thu, 1000 to 2100; Sat, 1000 to 1500

NATIONAL ASSOCIATION FOR COLITIS AND CROHN'S DISEASE (NACC)

4 Beaumont House, Sutton Road, St Albans, Hertfordshire, AL1 5HH

Tel: 01727 830038 (admin); 844296 (information)
Fax: 01727 862550
E-mail: nacc@nacc.org.uk
Website: www.nacc.org.uk

Enquiries to: Director
Direct tel: 01727 734479
Other contacts: PA to Director

Founded: 1979

Organisation type and purpose: Membership association (membership is by subscription), present number of members: 28,000, voluntary organisation (charity number 282732).

Subject coverage: Inflammatory bowel diseases, colitis, Crohn's disease, support of sufferers and their families.

Publications: Printed, and electronic and video

Access to staff: Contact by letter, by telephone, by fax, by e-mail and via website
Hours: Mon to Fri, 0900 to 1700

Has: 65 area groups in the UK

NATIONAL ASSOCIATION FOR ENVIRONMENTAL EDUCATION (UK) (NAEE (UK))

University of Wolverhampton, Walsall Campus, Gorway Road, Walsall, West Midlands, WS1 3BD

Tel: 01922 631200
E-mail: info@naee.org.uk
Website: www.naee.org.uk

Enquiries to: National Coordinator
Other contacts: Co-Chair

Founded: 1968

continued overleaf

Organisation type and purpose:
Membership association (membership is by subscription), registered charity, suitable for ages: all, early years to university.
Offers guidance and assistance in the delivery of environmental education for sustainable development within the formal education sector.

Subject coverage: Environmental education in schools.

Publications: Printed

Publications list: Available in print

Access to staff: Contact by letter, by telephone, by e-mail, in person and via website. Appointment necessary.
Hours: Thu

Access to building: Prior appointment required
Special comments: Please telephone for details.

Access for disabled people: Parking provided

Links with: Environmental Education Advisers Association; Field Studies Council

NATIONAL ASSOCIATION FOR GIFTED CHILDREN (NAGC)

Suite 1.2, Challenger House, Sherwood Drive, Bletchley, Milton Keynes, Buckinghamshire, MK3 6DP

Tel: 01908 646433
Fax: 0870 7703219
E-mail: amazingchildren@nagcbritain.org.uk
Website: www.nagcbritain.org.uk

Enquiries to: Education Consultant

Founded: 1965

Organisation type and purpose: National organisation, membership association (membership is by subscription), present number of members: 2500, voluntary organisation, registered charity (charity number 313182), suitable for ages: 0 to 20, training organisation, consultancy, research organisation, publishing house.
To support children with high learning potential, their families and schools concerned with their education and welfare.

Subject coverage: Identification; support of social, emotional and learning needs of children with high learning potential; partnership work between parents and schools

Information services: Information and Advice Line, Consultancy Service

Services for disabled people: Dual and multiple exceptionality

Collection: Books on gifted children and their needs

Publications: Printed

Publications list: Available in print

Access to staff: Contact by letter, by telephone, by e-mail, in person and via website. Appointment necessary. All charged.
Hours: Information and Advice Line Monday, Wednesday and Thursday 0900 to 1630
Special comments: Free access for website and telephone information. Charges for indepth consultancy, workshops and training.

Access to building: Prior appointment required

Access for disabled people: Access to all public areas

Member of: GT Voice; National Children's Bureau; Telephone Helplines Association

NATIONAL ASSOCIATION FOR LITERATURE DEVELOPMENT (NALD)

PO Box 49657, London, N8 7YZ

E-mail: director@nald.org
Website: www.nald.org

Enquiries to: Co-ordinator
Direct e-mail: steve@inck.fsnet.co.uk

Organisation type and purpose: National organisation, membership association (membership is by subscription), present number of members: 144.

Subject coverage: Networking and professional development information for literature development sector.

Publications: Electronic and video

Publications list: Available online

Access to staff: Contact by letter, by telephone, by e-mail, in person and via website
Hours: Mon to Fri, 0900 to 1700

Access to building: No access other than to staff

NATIONAL ASSOCIATION FOR PASTORAL CARE IN EDUCATION (NAPCE)

c/o Institute of Education, University of Warwick, Coventry, Warwickshire, CV4 7AL

Tel: 024 7652 3810
Fax: 024 7652 4110
E-mail: base@napce.org.uk
Website: www.napce.org.uk

Enquiries to: Base Administrator
Other contacts: Chairman for press contact.

Founded: 1982

Organisation type and purpose:
International organisation, membership association (membership is by subscription), present number of members: 1500, registered charity (charity number 291295), training organisation, research organisation, publishing house.

Subject coverage: Pastoral care in schools and colleges, personal-social education, effective learning.

Collection: Small collection of materials on bullying

Publications: Printed, and electronic and video, and microform publications

Publications list: Available online and in print

Access to staff: Contact by letter, by telephone, by fax, by e-mail and via website. Appointment necessary.
Hours: Mon to Fri, 0900 to 1330

Chairman: National Association for Pastoral Care in Education

NATIONAL ASSOCIATION FOR PATIENT PARTICIPATION (NAPP)

19 Harvey Road, Walton on Thames, Surrey, KT12 2PZ

Tel: 01932 242350
E-mail: enquire@napp.org.uk
Website: www.napp.org.uk

Enquiries to: Hon Secretary
Direct tel: 01932 242350

Founded: 1978

Organisation type and purpose: National organisation, membership association (membership is by subscription), voluntary organisation, registered charity (charity number 292157).
Promotes patient participation in primary health care at local GPs surgeries, health centres.
Promotes and supports patient's participation in their own primary health care with their GPs through a network of regional representatives. N.A.P.P. is the patient's participation voice at meetings and conferences organised by NHS and health organisations.

Subject coverage: Practical advice, guidance and information to affiliated patients groups who are located in local surgeries.
Experienced help provided in setting up patients' groups and network potential via affiliation.

Publications: Printed
Order printed publications from: Numerous

Publications list: Available online and in print

Access to staff: Contact by letter, by telephone, by e-mail and via website. All charged.
Hours: 24 hours (answerphone)
Special comments: Volunteers work from home.

Links with: Proprietary Association of Great Britain; Self Care Forum

Member organisation of: NCVO Affiliation

Regular contact with: Department of Health; Royal College of General Practitioners

NATIONAL ASSOCIATION FOR PREMENSTRUAL SYNDROME (NAPS)

41 Old Road, East Peckham, Kent TN12 5AP

Tel: 0870 777 2178
E-mail: contact@pms.org.uk
Website: www.pms.org.uk

Enquiries to: Chief Executive

Founded: 1984

Organisation type and purpose: Advisory body, membership association (membership is by subscription), voluntary organisation, registered charity (charity number 289901), research organisation.

Subject coverage: Premenstrual syndrome, postnatal depression and tension.

Collection: Bibliographical research database available to professional members

Publications: Printed

Publications list: Available online and in print

Access to staff: Contact by letter, by telephone, by e-mail and via website
Hours: 24-hour information line

NATIONAL ASSOCIATION FOR PRIMARY EDUCATION (NAPE)

Nape National Office, Moulton College, Moulton, Northampton, NN3 7RR

Tel: 01604 647646
Fax: 01604 647660
E-mail: nationaloffice@nape.org.uk
Website: www.nape.org.uk

Enquiries to: Honorary Secretary
Direct tel: 01865 890281
Other contacts: Press & Information Officer (for comments on policy and educational news)

Founded: 1980

Organisation type and purpose: International organisation, national organisation, advisory body, membership association (membership is by subscription, election or invitation), present number of members: 200,000 covered by group membership, voluntary organisation, registered charity (charity number 289645), suitable for ages: birth to 13, training organisation, consultancy, research organisation.
To promote high quality education for every child from birth to 13 years.

Subject coverage: Primary education, funding of schools, class sizes, current issues in education as they arise, e.g. OfSTED inspections, teacher stress/morale, inclusion, home/school partnership, workload, teacher shortage, classroom assistant issues.

Publications: Printed, and electronic and video

Publications list: Available in print

Access to staff: Contact by letter, by telephone, by fax, by e-mail and via website. Appointment necessary.
Hours: Mon to Fri, 0900 to 1330
Special comments: School term time only.

NATIONAL ASSOCIATION FOR SPECIAL EDUCATIONAL NEEDS, THE (NASEN)

NASEN House, 4–5 Amber Business Village, Amber Close, Amington, Tamworth, Staffordshire, B77 4RP

Tel: 01827 311500
Fax: 01827 313005
E-mail: welcome@nasen.org.uk
Website: www.nasen.org.uk

Enquiries to: Honorary General Secretary

Founded: 1992

Organisation type and purpose: National organisation, membership association (membership is by subscription), present number of members: 11,200, service industry, voluntary organisation, registered charity (charity number 1007023), suitable for ages: mainly KS1, KS2 and KS3, training organisation, research organisation, publishing house.
NASEN aims to promote the education, training, advancement and development of all those with special educational needs.

Subject coverage: Development of children and young people with special educational needs, education, welfare, treatment, rehabilitation, equal opportunities.

Publications: Printed, and electronic and video

Publications list: Available online and in print

Access to staff: Contact by letter, by telephone, by fax, by e-mail, in person and via website. Appointment necessary.
Hours: Mon to Fri, 0900 to 1700

Access to building: Prior appointment required

Access for disabled people: Parking provided, ramped entry, toilet facilities

NATIONAL ASSOCIATION FOR THE RELIEF OF PAGET'S DISEASE (NARPD)

323 Manchester Road, Walkden, Worsley, Manchester, M28 3HH

Tel: 0161 799 4646
Fax: 0161 799 6511
E-mail: director@paget.org.uk
Website: www.paget.org.uk

Enquiries to: Director

Founded: 1973

Organisation type and purpose: Membership association (membership is by subscription), present number of members: 2400, registered charity (charity number 266071).
To offer information and support for those suffering from Paget's Disease. To raise awareness of the disease to the medical profession and the public at large. To encourage and assist research.

Subject coverage: Information on research into the cause, prevention, treatment and cure of Paget's Disease of the bone, and support for sufferers and their families.

Publications: Printed

Publications list: Available in print

Access to staff: Contact by letter, by telephone, by fax, by e-mail and via website. Appointment necessary.
Hours: Mon to Fri, 0900 to 1700

Access to building: Prior appointment required

Access for disabled people: Parking provided

Links with: Paget's Disease Foundation of America; Paget's Disease Support Group; New Zealand

NATIONAL ASSOCIATION FOR THE TEACHING OF ENGLISH (NATE)

50 Broadfield Road, Sheffield, South Yorkshire, S8 0XJ

Tel: 0114 255 5419
Fax: 0114 255 5296
E-mail: info@nate.org.uk
Website: www.nate.org.uk

Enquiries to: Director

Founded: 1963

Organisation type and purpose: NATE is the UK's professional body for all those involved in English education from pre-school to university. It is a membership organisation. NATE supports effective teaching and learning, keeps teachers informed about current developments and provides them with a voice at a national level. NATE welcomes as members anyone who works in, or has an interest in, English education at any level.
The association is run on a voluntary basis through elected executive and council committees.
The association has a range of committees and standing working parties that address current concerns, disseminate knowledge and ideas, promote the work of the association and seek to represent the views of the association to national bodies, local education authorities, the DCSF, OFSTED, QCDA and Examination Boards.
The association conducts research into the teaching of English.
NATE is an active member of the International Federation of the Teachers of English where it seeks to share the experience of English teachers in the UK and learn from teachers in diverse parts of the world.

Subject coverage: Teaching of English through all age ranges.

Publications: Printed
Order printed publications from: website: http://www.nate.org.uk

Publications list: Available online and in print

Access to staff: Contact by letter, by telephone, by fax and by e-mail. Appointment necessary.
Hours: Mon to Fri, 0830 to 1700

Is organised into: 14 Regions in the UK

Member organisation of: College of Teachers; International Federation for the Teaching of English

NATIONAL ASSOCIATION FOR VOLUNTARY AND COMMUNITY ACTION (NAVCA)

The Tower, 2 Furnival Square, Sheffield, South Yorkshire, S1 4QL

Tel: 0114 278 6636
Fax: 0114 278 7004
E-mail: navca@navca.org.uk
Website: www.navca.org.uk

Enquiries to: Policy and Communications Officer

Founded: 1991; formerly called National Association of Councils for Voluntary Service

Organisation type and purpose: National organisation, membership association (membership is by qualification). National voice of local third sector infrastructure in England. Members work with 164,000 local

continued overleaf

third sector groups and organisations that provide community services, regenerate neighbourhoods, promote volunteering and tackle discrimination in partnership with local public bodies.

Subject coverage: Information on management of voluntary organisations, contacts in local infrastructure organisations and councils for voluntary service, setting up and managing voluntary organisations.

Publications: Printed

Publications list: Available online and in print

Access to staff: Contact by letter, by telephone, by fax and by e-mail. Appointment necessary.
Hours: Mon to Fri, 0900 to 1700

Access to building: Prior appointment required

Access for disabled people: Access to all public areas, toilet facilities

Member of: National Council for Voluntary Organisations (NCVO); Volunteering England

Subsidiary bodies: 364 local third sector infrastructure organisations in England

NATIONAL ASSOCIATION OF ADULT PLACEMENT SERVICES (NAAPS)

6 The Cotton Exchange, Old Hall Street, Liverpool, L3 9LQ

Tel: 0151 227 3499
Fax: 0151 236 3590
Website: naaps.org.uk

Enquiries to: Co-ordinator
Direct e-mail: jackie@naaps.org.uk

Founded: 1992

Organisation type and purpose: National organisation, membership association (membership is by subscription), present number of members: 1500+, voluntary organisation, registered charity (charity number 1019231).
To promote and develop adult placement services as a resource within the community.

Subject coverage: Adult placement.

Access to staff: Contact by letter, by telephone and by fax
Hours: Mon to Fri, 0900 to 1700

NATIONAL ASSOCIATION OF AGRICULTURAL CONTRACTORS (NAAC)

Samuelson House, 62 Forder Way, Hampton, Peterborough, PE7 8JB

Tel: 0845 644 8750
Fax: 01733 352806
E-mail: jill.hewitt@naac.co.uk
Website: www.naac.co.uk

Enquiries to: Chief Executive

Founded: 1893

Organisation type and purpose: Trade association.

Subject coverage: Contract services to agriculture and allied land-based industries including crop protection and spraying, whole farm and whole crop contracting, vegetation control, mobile seed cleaning and processing, cultivating and harvesting of all UK crops.

Publications: Printed

Access to staff: Contact by letter, by telephone, by fax, by e-mail and via website
Hours: Mon to Fri, 0900 to 1700

NATIONAL ASSOCIATION OF BANK & INSURANCE CUSTOMERS (NABIC)

E-mail: webmaster@lemonaid.net
Website: www.lemonaid.net

Enquiries to: Information Officer
Other contacts: Chief Executive for press comment, member query or complaint.

Founded: 1991

Organisation type and purpose:
International organisation, membership association (membership is by subscription), present number of members: 25,000, training organisation, consultancy, research organisation.
To protect and promote the interests of private and commercial users of bank and insurance services through information, education and mediation processes. To build a detailed database of procedures and abuses.

Subject coverage: Banking, insurance, legal representation, customer complaints, recalculation of bank statements to find errors, business planning services, business planning software and customer service standards.

Collection: Database of queries and complaints and standard responses

Trade and statistical information: Data on the frequency and type of bank and insurance disputes

Publications: Printed, and electronic and video

Access to staff: Contact by letter, by telephone, by fax, by e-mail and via website
Hours: Mon to Fri, 0900 to 1700

NATIONAL ASSOCIATION OF BRITISH MARKET AUTHORITIES (NABMA)

13 Moor Road, Wigan, Lancashire, WN5 8DN

Tel: 01942 203797
Fax: 01942 205885
E-mail: nabma@nabma.com
Website: www.nabma.com

Enquiries to: General Secretary

Founded: 1919

Organisation type and purpose: Local government body, membership association.

Subject coverage: Organisation and operation by local authorities of markets of all kinds including open retail markets, market halls, wholesale fruit, vegetable, flower, fish and meat markets; livestock markets; public abattoirs, and pleasure fairs.

Publications: Printed

Access to staff: Contact by letter, by telephone and by fax
Hours: Mon to Fri, 0900 to 1700

Member of: European Association of Livestock Markets; World Union of Wholesale Markets

NATIONAL ASSOCIATION OF CHILD CONTACT CENTRES (NACCC)

Minerva House, Spaniel Row, Nottingham, NG1 6EP

Tel: 0845 4500280
Fax: 0845 4500420
E-mail: contact@naccc.org.uk
Website: www.naccc.org.uk

Enquiries to: Administrator
Other contacts: Chief Executive for matters of policy as opposed to administration.

Organisation type and purpose: Registered charity (charity number 1003868).
To promote safe child contact within a national framework of 325 Child Contact Centres

Subject coverage: Neutral meeting places where children of separated families can spend time with one or both parents, and sometimes other family members, in a safe and comfortable environment when there is no viable alternative.

Publications: Printed, and electronic and video

Publications list: Available online

NATIONAL ASSOCIATION OF CHIMNEY SWEEPS (NACS)

Unit 15, Emerald Way, Stone Business Park, Stone, Staffordshire, ST15 0SR

Tel: 01785 811732
Fax: 01785 811712
E-mail: nacs@chimneyworks.co.uk
Website: www.nacs.org.uk

Enquiries to: Administrator

Founded: 1982

Organisation type and purpose: Trade association.

Subject coverage: Chimney sweeping and chimneys in general.

Library catalogue: All or part available in-house

Publications: Printed

Access to staff: Contact by letter, by telephone, by fax and by e-mail
Hours: Mon to Fri, 0800 to 1600

Access to building: Prior appointment required

Access for disabled people: Parking provided, level entry

Links with: HETAS; tel: 01242 513747; fax: 01242 513747; e-mail: billk@albionmillshouse.freeserve.co.uk; NACE; tel: 01773 599095; fax: 01773 599195; e-mail: info@nace.org.uk; NFA; tel: 0121 200 2100; fax: 0121 200 1306

Member of: European Federation of Chimney Sweeps (ESCHFO); tel: +49 2241 340713; fax: +49 2241 340710; e-mail: ziv-kelz-quadt@schornsteinfeger.de

NATIONAL ASSOCIATION OF CHOIRS (NAC)

Fig Tree House, 9 The Green, Glinton, Peterborough, Cambridgeshire, PE6 7JN

Tel: 01733 252464
Fax: 01733 252464
E-mail: gensecnac@gensecnac.force9.co.uk
Website: www.ukchoirsassoc.co.uk

Enquiries to: General Secretary

Founded: 1920

Organisation type and purpose: Voluntary organisation.

Subject coverage: Study and performance of choral music, choral societies and choirs.

Publications: Printed

Publications list: Available in print

Access to staff: Contact by letter, by telephone, by fax, by e-mail and via website
Hours: Any day up to 2200

Affiliated to: British Federation of Music Festivals

Member of: British Federation of Youth Choirs; National Choral Advisory Body

NATIONAL ASSOCIATION OF CITIZENS ADVICE BUREAUX (NACAB)

Myddelton House, 115–123 Pentonville Road, London, N1 9LZ

Tel: 020 7833 2181 (Admin only)
Fax: 020 7833 4371 (Admin only)
Website: www.nacab.org.uk
Website: www.adviceguide.org.uk

Enquiries to: Communications Assistant

Founded: 1939

Organisation type and purpose: National organisation, advisory body, voluntary organisation, registered charity.
To provide information and advice on any topic.

Subject coverage: Debt and consumer, social security, employment, housing, property and land, family and personal, administration of justice, taxes and duties, local information, health, national and international travel, transport and holidays, education, immigration and nationality, communication and leisure.

Publications: Printed

Access for disabled people: Parking provided, level entry, access to all public areas, toilet facilities
Special comments: Myddleton House only.

Affiliated to: Advice Services Alliance; National Council for Voluntary Organisations

Has: approximately 1300 CABs throughout the country

Links with: Citizens Advice Scotland

NATIONAL ASSOCIATION OF CLINICAL TUTORS UK (NACT UK)

Norfolk House East, 499 Silbury Boulevard, Milton Keynes, MK2 9AH

Tel: 01908 488033
Fax: 01296 715255
E-mail: office@nact.org.uk
Website: www.nact.org.uk

Enquiries to: Chairman

Founded: 1969

Organisation type and purpose: Professional body.

Subject coverage: Postgraduate medical education; career counselling in medicine; educational techniques related to postgraduate medicine.

Publications: Printed

Access to staff: Contact by letter, by telephone, by fax and by e-mail. Appointment necessary. Access for members only.
Hours: Mon to Fri, 0900 to 1700

NATIONAL ASSOCIATION OF COMMERCIAL FINANCE BROKERS (NACFB)

3 Silverdown Office Park, Fair Oak Close, Exeter, Devon, EX5 2UX

Tel: 01392 440040
Fax: 01392 363931
E-mail: admin@nacfb.org.uk
Website: www.nacfb.org

Founded: 1992

Organisation type and purpose: The UK's trade body for business finance brokers.
To raise standards of proper professional practice in the commercial broker industry.

Subject coverage: Commercial finance, leasing and asset finance, vehicle finance. NACFB has established complaints and disciplinary procedures designed to eliminate unacceptable working practices among its members; it aims to protect its members and their clients against restrictive practices within the industry; in the interests of members and their clients, the NACFB monitors legislation and makes representations to the government and regulators; it furthers the principles of good practice by seeking to work with kindred associations and interest groups, and by providing education and training for its members and their employees.

Publications: Electronic and video
Order electronic and video publications from: Website; accessible only by members

Publications list: Available online

Access to staff: Contact by letter, by telephone, by fax and by e-mail

NATIONAL ASSOCIATION OF CYCLE TRADERS LIMITED (ACT)

31a High Street, Tunbridge Wells, Kent, TN1 1XN

Tel: 01892 526081
Fax: 01892 544278
E-mail: info@actsmart.biz
Website: www.act-bicycles.com

Enquiries to: Information Officer

Founded: 1920

Organisation type and purpose: Trade association.

Subject coverage: Cycle safety and standards, cycle mechanics accreditation scheme, cycle retailing, technical information.

Publications: Printed

Access to staff: Contact by letter, by e-mail and via website
Hours: Mon to Fri, 0900 to 1700

NATIONAL ASSOCIATION OF DEAFENED PEOPLE (NADP)

PO Box 50, Amersham, Buckinghamshire, HP6 6XB

Tel: 0845 055 9663
Fax: 01305 262591
E-mail: enquiries@nadp.org.uk
Website: www.nadp.org.uk

Enquiries to: Honorary Secretary

Founded: 1984

Organisation type and purpose: Membership association (membership is by subscription), present number of members: 300, voluntary organisation, registered charity (charity number 294922).
To provide a network of information and support for deafened people.

Subject coverage: Increasing public awareness of the needs and problems of deafened people; the promotion of an improvement in the rehabilitation, education, training, re-training and employment opportunities available for deafened people.

Publications: Printed
Order printed publications from: Postal or e -mail address shown above

Publications list: Available online and in print

Access to staff: Contact by letter, by fax, by e-mail and via website

Access to building: No access to office

NATIONAL ASSOCIATION OF DECORATIVE & FINE ARTS SOCIETIES (NADFAS)

NADFAS House, 8 Guilford Street, London, WC1N 1DT

Tel: 020 7430 0730
Fax: 020 7242 0686
E-mail: enquiries@nadfas.org.uk
Website: www.nadfas.org.uk

Enquiries to: PA to Chairman & Chief Executive

Founded: May 1968

Organisation type and purpose: International organisation, membership association (membership is by subscription), present number of members: 88,000, registered charity (charity number 263487), art gallery.
Arts educational charity.
Volunteer-led cultivation, appreciation and study of the decorative and fine arts, and giving aid to the preservation of national artistic heritage for the benefit of the general public.

continued overleaf

Subject coverage: Decorative and fine arts. NADFAS is an arts educational organisation based on leisure interests rather than careers. It consists of member societies that meet on a monthly basis for lectures, and organises visits to places of historic interest and museums. In addition members carry out voluntary work in museums, historic houses and churches.

Publications: Printed
Order printed publications from: Manager, NADFAS Enterprises
at the same address

Access to staff: Contact by letter, by telephone and by e-mail
Hours: Mon to Fri, 0930 to 1730

Access to building: No prior appointment required

Has: 320 societies in the UK, 22 in Australia and 9 in Europe

Head Office: National Association of Decorative & Fine Arts Societies (NADFAS); at the same address

NATIONAL ASSOCIATION OF EDUCATIONAL INSPECTORS, ADVISERS AND CONSULTANTS (NAEIAC)

Woolley Hall, Woolley, Wakefield, West Yorkshire, WF4 2JR

Tel: 01226 383428
Fax: 01226 383427
E-mail: naeiac@gemsoft.co.uk
Website: www.naeiac.co.uk

Enquiries to: General Secretary

Founded: 1918

Organisation type and purpose: National organisation, professional body, trade union (membership is by subscription).

Subject coverage: Education from pre-school to higher education: curriculum, management, inspection and advice.

Publications: Printed

Access to staff: Contact by letter, by telephone, by fax, by e-mail and via website
Hours: Mon to Thu, 0830 to 1700; Fri, 0830 to 1630

Representation on: Soulbury Committee

NATIONAL ASSOCIATION OF FARRIERS, BLACKSMITHS AND AGRICULTURAL ENGINEERS (NAFBAE)

Avenue B, 10th Street, National Agricultural Centre, Stoneleigh, Kenilworth, Warwickshire, CV8 2LG

Tel: 02476 696595
Fax: 02476 696708
E-mail: nafbaehq@nafbae.org.uk

Enquiries to: Membership Secretary
Other contacts: National Organiser

Founded: 1904

Organisation type and purpose: National organisation, trade association (membership is by subscription).

Access to staff: Contact by letter, by telephone, by fax and by e-mail. Access for members only.
Hours: Mon to Fri, 0900 to 1700

Access to building: No prior appointment required

NATIONAL ASSOCIATION OF FUNERAL DIRECTORS (NAFD)

618 Warwick Road, Solihull, West Midlands, B91 1AA

Tel: 0845 230 1343
Fax: 0121 711 1351
E-mail: info@nafd.org.uk
Website: nafd.org.uk

Enquiries to: Chief Executive Officer

Founded: 1905

Organisation type and purpose: Trade association, present number of members: 3272.

Subject coverage: All aspects of the funeral profession.

Publications: Printed

Access to staff: Contact by letter, by telephone, by fax, by e-mail, in person and via website
Hours: Mon to Fri, 0900 to 1700

Access to building: No prior appointment required

Access for disabled people: Parking provided

NATIONAL ASSOCIATION OF GOLDSMITHS OF GREAT BRITAIN AND IRELAND (NAG)

78A Luke Street, London, EC2A 4XG

Tel: 020 7613 4445
Fax: 020 7613 4450
E-mail: nag@jewellers-online.org
Website: www.jewellers-online.org

Enquiries to: Information Manager
Direct e-mail: information@jewellers-online.org

Founded: 1894

Organisation type and purpose: Trade association (membership is by subscription, election or invitation), present number of members: 1,000 companies, training organisation, consultancy, publishing house.
To provide services, support, education and information to best encourage professionalism in the retail jewellery industry.

Subject coverage: All aspects of the jewellery industry; history, materials, gems, gold, silver, retail, valuations.

Publications: Printed
Order printed publications from: NAG switchboard

Publications list: Available in print

Access to staff: Contact by letter, by fax, by e-mail and via website. Appointment necessary. Access for members only.
Hours: Mon to Fri, 0900 to 1700

NATIONAL ASSOCIATION OF HEALTH WORKERS FOR TRAVELLERS (NAHWT)

Balsall Heath Health Centre, 43 Edward Road, Balsall Heath, Birmingham, B12 9LB

Tel: 0121 446 2300
Fax: 0121 446 5936
E-mail: joanne.davis@hobtpct.nhs.uk

Enquiries to: Secretary

Founded: 1992

Subject coverage: Health care relating to Travellers and Gypsies in Britain.

Access to staff: Contact by letter, by fax and by e-mail
Hours: Mon to Wed, 0900 to 1700

Access to building: No access other than to staff

Links with: Community Practioners and Health Visitors Association; 40 Bermondsey Street, London, SE1 3UD; tel: 020 7939 7000; fax: 020 7403 2976

NATIONAL ASSOCIATION OF INDEPENDENT TRAVEL AGENTS (NAITA)

79–80 Margaret Street, London, W1W 8TA

Tel: 020 7323 3408
Fax: 020 7323 5189
E-mail: naita@advantage4travel.com
Website: www.advantage4travel.com

Enquiries to: Manager
Direct e-mail: debbiew@advantage4travel.com
Other contacts: Membership Co-ordinator for membership enquiries.

Founded: 1978

Organisation type and purpose: National organisation, trade association (membership is by subscription), present number of members: 904.
Commercial and Marketing Consortia (Travel).
To enhance, from a commercial and marketing viewpoint, the business and professionalism of our members (independent travel agents in the UK) and help maximise their profitability.

Subject coverage: Travel trade consortia for independent travel agents in the UK, offering commercial and marketing support, to include signage, window decals, hanging banners, late availability board, tactical campaigns, monthly magazine and supplier-led promotions, together with a professional sales development team offering expert advice and support to all members.

Access to staff: Contact by letter, by telephone, by fax, by e-mail and via website. Appointment necessary.
Hours: Mon to Fri, 0830 to 1800

Trading as: Advantage Travel Centres; 38 Anderston Quay, Glasgow, G3 8BX; tel: 0141 248 3466; fax: 0141 248 5170; e-mail: glasgow@advantage4travel.com

NATIONAL ASSOCIATION OF KARATE AND MARTIAL ART SCHOOLS NATIONAL GOVERNING BODY (NAKMAS National Governing Body)

PO Box 262, Herne Bay, Kent, CT6 9AW

Tel: 01227 370055
Fax: 01227 370056
E-mail: info@nakmas.org.uk
Website: www.nakmas.org.uk

Enquiries to: Chair
Direct tel: 01227 376180
Direct fax: 01227 370056
Direct e-mail: joe.ellis@nakmas.org.uk

Founded: 1992

Organisation type and purpose: A non-funded national governing body for traditional and modern martial arts with over 73,000 members within the UK. An independent publisher with offices in Kent and Buckinghamshire.

Subject coverage: Traditional and modern martial arts.

Publications: Printed

Access to staff: Contact by letter, by telephone, by fax, by e-mail and via website. Appointment necessary.
Hours: Mon to Thu, 0900 to 1600; Fri, 0900 to 1500

Member organisation of: Sport & Recreation Alliance (formerly known as the CCPR); Anti-Bullying Alliance and the National Autistic Society

NATIONAL ASSOCIATION OF LADIES' CIRCLES (NALC)

Formal name: National Association of Ladies' Circles of Great Britain and Ireland

Marchesi House, 4 Embassy Drive, Edgbaston, Birmingham, B15 1TP

Tel: 0121 456 0304
E-mail: headquarters@ladies-circle.org.uk
Website: www.ladies-circle.org.uk

Enquiries to: Association Secretary

Founded: 1936

Organisation type and purpose: National organisation, membership association (membership is by subscription), present number of members: 6,500, voluntary organisation.

Subject coverage: Charities, fundraising, community service, women's issues, family issues.

Publications: Printed

Access to staff: Contact by letter, by telephone, by fax, by e-mail and via website
Hours: Mon to Fri, 0900 to 1700

Affiliated to: Ladies Circle International; at the same address

NATIONAL ASSOCIATION OF LARYNGECTOMEE CLUBS (NALC)

Lower Ground Floor, 152 Buckingham Palace Road, London, SW1W 9TR

Tel: 020 7730 8585
Fax: 020 7730 8584
E-mail: info@laryngectomy.org.uk
Website: www.laryngectomy.org.uk

Enquiries to: Association Secretary

Founded: 1976

Organisation type and purpose: National organisation, membership association, present number of members: 97 clubs with 5,000 members, voluntary organisation, registered charity (charity number 273635). National Association with clubs situated throughout the UK for those who have undergone a laryngectomy operation, their family and friends.

Subject coverage: Rehabilitation of laryngectomee patients, availability of speech aids and medical supplies.

Publications: Printed, and electronic and video

Publications list: Available in print

Access to staff: Contact by letter, by telephone, by fax, by e-mail and via website. Appointment necessary.
Hours: Mon to Thu, 0900 to 1630; Fri, 0900 to 1600

Links with: Macmillan Cancer Support; National associations in various countries

NATIONAL ASSOCIATION OF LICENSED PARALEGALS (NALP)

3.08 Canterbury Court, 1–3 Brixton Road, London, SW9 6DE

Tel: 020 3176 0900
Fax: N/A
E-mail: info@nationalparalegals.co.uk
Website: www.nationalparalegals.com/nalp.htm

Enquiries to: Chief Executive
Other contacts: Business Development Manager, Membership

Founded: 1987

Organisation type and purpose: Self-regulatory and professional body, suitable for ages: 18+. Educational, training and career development organisation.

Subject coverage: Career guidance for paralegals, qualifications by examination and otherwise for paralegals, training for career progression, seminars, workshops and courses on legal subjects.

Publications: Printed

Access to staff: Contact by letter, by telephone, by e-mail and via website. Appointment necessary.
Hours: Mon to Fri, 0930 to 1730

Access to building: Prior appointment required
Hours: Mon to Fri, 0900 to 1800

Access for disabled people: *Hours:* Mon to Fri, 0930 to 1730

NATIONAL ASSOCIATION OF LOCAL COUNCILS (NALC)

109 Great Russell Street, London, WC1B 3LD

Tel: 020 7637 1865
Fax: 020 7436 7451
E-mail: nalc@nalc.gov.uk
Website: www.nalc.gov.uk

Enquiries to: Deputy Chief Executive

Founded: 1947

Organisation type and purpose: Local government body, membership association.

Subject coverage: Any matter to do with small scale local government, particularly rural, legal and financial.

Collection: A complete law library

Publications: Printed

Access to staff: Contact by letter, by fax and by e-mail. Appointment necessary.
Hours: Mon to Fri, 0900 to 1700

Access to building: No access other than to staff

NATIONAL ASSOCIATION OF MASTER BAKERS (NAMB)

21 Baldock Street, Ware, Hertfordshire, SG12 9DH

Tel: 01920 468061
Fax: 01920 461632
E-mail: namb@masterbakers.co.uk
Website: www.masterbakers.co.uk

Enquiries to: Chief Executive

Founded: 1887

Organisation type and purpose: Trade association.

Subject coverage: Bread, flour and confectionery.

Collection: Copies of Bakers' Review from 1887 to present day

Publications: Printed

NATIONAL ASSOCIATION OF MASTER LETTER CARVERS (NAMLC)

c/o NAMM, 1 Castle Mews, Rugby, CV21 2XL

Tel: 01788 542264
Fax: 01788 542276
E-mail: enquiries@namm.org.uk

Enquiries to: Honorary Secretary

Founded: 1920

Organisation type and purpose: Trade association, present number of members: 50, consultancy.
Publication of list of members. Setting recommended prices.

Subject coverage: Hand-carved lettering in stone and wood, memorials, monuments, etc.

Collection: History of Association Minutes since 1920

Publications: Printed

Access to staff: Contact by letter and by telephone
Hours: Mon to Fri, 0900 to 1700

NATIONAL ASSOCIATION OF MEMORIAL MASONS (NAMM)

1 Castle Mews, Rugby, CU21 2XL

Tel: 01788 542264
Fax: 01788 542276
E-mail: enquiries@namm.org.uk
Website: www.namm.org.uk

continued overleaf

Enquiries to: National Executive Officer

Founded: 1907

Organisation type and purpose: Trade association (membership is by subscription).

Subject coverage: All matters relating to natural stone memorials, standards in the trade, training.

Publications: Printed
Order printed publications from: National Association of Memorial Masons, as above

Access to staff: Contact by letter, by telephone, by fax and by e-mail
Hours: Mon to Fri, 0900 to 1700

Associate member of: Council of British Funeral Services; Institute of Cemetery and Crematorium Management

NATIONAL ASSOCIATION OF MINING HISTORY ORGANISATIONS (NAMHO)

Peak District Mining Museum, The Pavilion, Matlock Bath, Derbyshire, DE4 3NR

Tel: 01629 583834
Website: www.namho.org

Enquiries to: Honorary Secretary

Founded: 1979

Organisation type and purpose: National organisation, learned society (membership is by election or invitation), present number of members: 75, voluntary organisation, registered charity (charity number 297301). Representative body for mining history.

Subject coverage: Mining history; past and present mining in the UK; access policy and legislation thereon; conservation and display of artefacts; production of codes of practice on research techniques.

Publications: Printed

Access to staff: Contact by letter and by telephone
Hours: Mon to Fri, 0900 to 1700
Special comments: SAE required for reply.

Member of: National Caving Association; Momomark House, 27 Old Gloucester Street, London, WC1N 3XX

NATIONAL ASSOCIATION OF MUSIC EDUCATORS (NAME)

Gordon Lodge, Snitterton Road, Matlock, Derbyshire, DE4 2JG

Tel: 01629 760791
E-mail: musiceducation@name.org.uk
Website: www.name.org.uk

Enquiries to: Business Manager

Founded: 1996

Organisation type and purpose: Company limited by guarantee, registered charity.

Subject coverage: Music education.

Publications: Printed
Order printed publications from: NAME Business Manager at same address

Publications list: Available online and in print

Access to staff: Contact by letter, by telephone, by e-mail and via website
Hours: Mon to Fri, 0900 to 1700

NATIONAL ASSOCIATION OF PENSION FUNDS (NAPF)

NIOC House, 4 Victoria Street, London, SW1H 0NX

Tel: 020 7808 1300
Fax: 020 7222 7585
E-mail: jane.dawson@napf.co.uk
Website: www.napf.co.uk

Enquiries to: Public Relations Manager
Other contacts: Press Officer

Founded: 1923

Organisation type and purpose: Trade association.

Subject coverage: All aspects of occupational pensions, both benefits and investments.

Publications: Printed, and electronic and video

Publications list: Available online and in print

Access to staff: Contact by letter, by telephone, by fax, by e-mail and via website. Appointment necessary.
Hours: Mon to Fri, 0915 to 1715

NATIONAL ASSOCIATION OF POULTRY SUPPLIERS

1 Belgrove, Tunbridge Wells, Kent, TN1 1YW

Tel: 01892 541412
Fax: 01892 535462
E-mail: naps@nfmft.co.uk

Enquiries to: Secretary
Direct e-mail: graham@nfmft.co.uk

Organisation type and purpose: National organisation, trade association (membership is by subscription).

Subject coverage: All aspects of wholesale poultry trade.

Access to staff: Contact by letter, by telephone and by fax
Hours: Mon to Fri, 0900 to 1700

NATIONAL ASSOCIATION OF PRISON VISITORS (NAPV)

29 Kimbolton Road, Bedford, MK40 2PB

Tel: 01234 359763
Fax: 01234 359763

Enquiries to: General Secretary

Founded: 1924

Organisation type and purpose: National organisation, membership association (membership is by subscription), present number of members: 1400, voluntary organisation, suitable for ages: 21 to 70.

Subject coverage: Concern and friendship for, and visits to, people in prison.

Publications: Printed

Access to staff: Contact by letter, by telephone and by fax
Hours: Mon to Fri, 0900 to 1700

NATIONAL ASSOCIATION OF PUBLIC GOLF COURSES (NAPGC)

12 Newton Close, Redditch, Worcestershire, B98 7YR

Tel: 01527 542106
Fax: 01527 455320
E-mail: eddiemitchell@blueyonder.co.uk
Website: www.napgc.org.uk

Enquiries to: Secretary

Founded: 1927

Organisation type and purpose: Voluntary organisation.
Specially for the cohesion of golf clubs formed on public golf courses.

Subject coverage: Golf club and course management authority integration, national golf tournaments for public course clubs.

Publications: Printed

Links with: English Golf Union; Royal & Ancient Golf Club of St Andrews

NATIONAL ASSOCIATION OF ROUND TABLES OF GREAT BRITAIN AND IRELAND (RTBI)

Marchesi House, 4 Embassy Drive, Edgbaston, Birmingham, B15 1TP

Tel: 0121 456 4402
Fax: 0121 456 4185
E-mail: hq@roundtable.org.uk
Website: www.roundtable.org.uk

Founded: 1927

Organisation type and purpose:
Membership association (membership is by election or invitation), present number of members: 5,500
Fellowship.

Subject coverage: Community service, normally within local Table area.

Publications: Printed

Access to staff: Contact by letter, by telephone, by fax, by e-mail and via website
Hours: Mon to Fri, 0900 to 1700

Access for disabled people: Access to all public areas

NATIONAL ASSOCIATION OF SCHOOLMASTERS AND UNION OF WOMEN TEACHERS (NASUWT)

Northern Ireland Centre, Ben Madigan House, Edgewater Office Park, Edgewater Road, Belfast, BT3 9JQ

Tel: 028 9078 4480
Fax: 028 9078 4489
E-mail: rc-nireland@mail.nasuwt.org.uk
Website: www.northern-ireland.nasuwt.org.uk

Enquiries to: Regional Organiser (Northern Ireland)

Founded: 1962

Organisation type and purpose: National organisation, trade union (membership is by subscription), present number of members: 11,100 in NI.

Subject coverage: All matters pertaining to school teachers.

Non-library collection catalogue: All or part available online and in print

Library catalogue: All or part available online and in print

Publications: Printed

Access to staff: Contact by letter, by telephone, by fax, by e-mail and via website
Hours: Mon to Fri, 0830 to 1730

Access to building: Prior appointment required
Hours: Mon to Fri, 0830 to 1730

Access for disabled people: Parking provided, access to all public areas, toilet facilities

Parent body: National Association of Schoolmasters and Union of Women Teachers; Rose Hill, Rednal, Birmingham, B45 8RS; tel: 0121 453 6150; fax: 0121 457 6208/9; e-mail: nasuwt@mail.nasuwt.org.uk

NATIONAL ASSOCIATION OF SESSIONAL GPS (NASGP)

PO Box 188, Chichester, West Sussex, PO19 2FP

Fax: 01243 536428
E-mail: info@nasgp.org.uk
Website: www.nasgp.org.uk

Enquiries to: Chief Executive

Founded: 1997

Organisation type and purpose: National organisation, membership association (membership is by subscription), present number of members: 2,500, voluntary organisation.
Independent voluntary organisation of non-principal general practitioners, such as locums and assistants, who work in the NHS, to improve the status and welfare of its members.

Subject coverage: Non-principal general practitioners in the NHS.

Publications list: Available online

Access to staff: Contact by letter, by fax, by e-mail and via website
Hours: Mon to Fri, 0900 to 1700

NATIONAL ASSOCIATION OF SHOPFITTERS (NAS)

NAS House, 411 Limpsfield Road, The Green, Warlingham, Surrey, CR6 9HA

Tel: 01883 624961
Fax: 01883 626841
E-mail: nas@clara.net
Website: www.shopfitters.org

Enquiries to: Director

Founded: 1919

Organisation type and purpose: Trade association.

Subject coverage: Shopfitting.

Publications: Printed

Publications list: Available online and in print

Access to staff: Contact by letter, by telephone, by fax, by e-mail and via website
Hours: Mon to Fri, 0900 to 1700

Affiliated to: International Shopfitters Organisation

Houses the: Automatic Door Suppliers Association

NATIONAL ASSOCIATION OF STEEL STOCKHOLDERS (NASS)

First Floor, The Citadel, 190 Corporation Street, Birmingham, B4 6QD

Tel: 0121 200 2288
Fax: 0121 236 7444
E-mail: info@nass.org.uk
Website: www.nass.org.uk

Enquiries to: Director-General

Founded: 1928

Organisation type and purpose: Trade association.

Subject coverage: United Kingdom steel stockists and suppliers.

Publications: Printed, and electronic and video
Order printed publications from: e-mail: info@nass.org.uk
Order electronic and video publications from: e-mail: info@nass.org.uk

Access to staff: Contact by letter, by telephone, by fax, by e-mail and via website
Hours: Mon to Fri, 0900 to 1700

NATIONAL ASSOCIATION OF SWIMMING CLUBS FOR THE HANDICAPPED (NASCH)

The Willows, Mayles Lane, Wickham, Hampshire, PO17 5ND

Tel: 01329 833689
E-mail: naschswim-willows@yahoo.co.uk
Website: www.nasch.org.uk

Enquiries to: Administrator

Founded: 1965

Organisation type and purpose: Membership association (membership is by subscription), present number of members: 101, registered charity (charity number 247772).

Subject coverage: Swimming for the handicapped, including swimming aids, hoists and other equipment, tuition, formation of clubs, insurance, and the Distance Award (incentive) scheme. Regional and national swimming galas.

Publications: Printed
Order printed publications from: Administrator

NATIONAL ASSOCIATION OF TEACHERS OF DANCING (NATD)

Bateman House, 44–47 The Broadway, Thatcham, Newbury, Berkshire, RG19 3HP

Tel: 01635 868888
Fax: 01635 872301
E-mail: info@natd.org.uk
Website: www.natd.org.uk

Enquiries to: General Secretary

Founded: 1906

Organisation type and purpose: Membership association (membership is by subscription), training organisation.

Subject coverage: Dance teaching.

Access to staff: Contact by letter, by telephone, by fax, by e-mail and via website
Hours: Mon to Fri, 0830 to 1600

Access to building: No access other than to staff

NATIONAL ASSOCIATION OF THE LAUNDERETTE INDUSTRY LIMITED (NALI)

146 Welling Way, Welling, Kent, DA16 2RS

Tel: 020 8856 9798
Fax: 020 8856 9394

Enquiries to: Secretary

Organisation type and purpose: Trade association.

Subject coverage: Launderettes and coin-operated dry cleaners.

Publications: Printed

Access to staff: Contact by letter, by telephone and by fax
Hours: Mon to Fri, 0900 to 1700

NATIONAL ASSOCIATION OF TOOL DEALERS (NATD)

225 Bristol Road, Edgbaston, Birmingham, B5 7UB

Tel: 0121 446 6688
Fax: 0121 446 5215

Enquiries to: Managing Director

Founded: 1899

Organisation type and purpose: Trade association.
Representation of members interests to government and others.

Subject coverage: Hand and power tools.

Publications: Printed

Member of: BHF Group

NATIONAL ASSOCIATION OF TOY AND LEISURE LIBRARIES (NATLL)

1A Harmood Street, London, NW1 8DN

Tel: 020 7428 2281
Fax: 020 7428 2281
E-mail: admin@playmatters.co.uk
Website: www.natll.org.uk

Enquiries to: Helpline
Direct tel: 020 7428 2286
Direct e-mail: helpline@playmatters.co.uk

Founded: 1967

Organisation type and purpose: National organisation, membership association (membership is by subscription), present number of members: 500 toy libraries, 2 leisure libraries, voluntary organisation, registered charity (charity number in England and Wales 270291 and in Scotland SCO39458), suitable for ages: Toy Library – 0 to 12, usually extended for children with special needs; Leisure Libraries – adults with special needs and their families, training organisation.
The national body for toy and leisure libraries throughout the United Kingdom. Toy libraries lend good quality, carefully

continued overleaf

chosen toys to all families with young children, including children with special needs. They offer a befriending, supportive service to parents and carers. NATLL offers help, advice, information support and training for people setting up and running toy and leisure libraries; offers a range of publications on running toy libraries, toys and play; organises training courses for the voluntary and statutory sectors; offers Quality Assurance Scheme 'Quality Play Matters' to member toy libraries; has contracts with: the Department for Education to deliver services under Every Child Matters, the Scottish Executive, the Welsh Assembly and a number of local authorities.

Subject coverage: Toy libraries; leisure libraries; toys and play, particularly for children with special needs; learning through play, recreational activities for adults with additional needs.

Information services: Helpline, website, publications.

Special visitor services: Outreach Workers in selected areas of the UK.

Education services: Training, quality assurance.

Services for disabled people: Toy libraries offer loan of specialist toys and equipment, multi-sensory experiences and support to families of children with special needs.

Collection: Good Toy Guide
Play Matters magazine

Publications: Printed, and electronic and video
Order printed publications from: website; mail order from HQ
Order electronic and video publications from: website; mail order from HQ

Publications list: Available online and in print

Access to staff: Contact by letter, by telephone, by fax, by e-mail and via website. Appointment necessary.
Hours: Mon to Fri, 0900 to 1700
Special comments: Please send A4 sae.

Access to building: Prior appointment required

Access for disabled people: Fully acccessible

Also at: National Association of Toy and Leisure Libraries; Gilmerton Community Centre, 4 Drum Street, Edinburgh, EH17 8QG; tel: 0131 664 2746; fax: 0131 664 2753; e-mail: natll.scotland@playmatters.co.uk; National Association of Toy and Leisure Libraries (in Wales); Suite 11, 65 Penarth Road, Cardiff, CF10 5DL; tel: 029 2023 0047; e-mail: walesadmin@playmatters.co.uk

Member organisation of: International Toy Library Association; website: http://www.itla-toylibraries.org
NCVCCO; NCVO; VOLCUF

NATIONAL ASSOCIATION OF WIDOWS (NAW)

48 Queens Road, Coventry, Warwickshire, CV1 3EH

Tel: 024 7663 4848
Website: www.nawidows.co.uk

Enquiries to: Administrator

Founded: 1971

Organisation type and purpose: National organisation (membership is by subscription), present number of members: 3,000, voluntary organisation, registered charity (charity number 1096896).
Run by widows for widows; providing friendship and support with local branches throughout the country; Headquarters membership is also available for widows who have no local contact.

Publications: Printed

Access to staff: Contact by letter, by telephone and by e-mail
Hours: Mon, Tue, Thu, Fri, 0900 to 1600

Access to building: No prior appointment required

Access for disabled people: Lift

NATIONAL ASSOCIATION OF WOMEN PHARMACISTS (NAWP)

c/o The Royal Pharmaceutical Society of Great Britain, 1 Lambeth High Street, London, SE1 7JN

E-mail: enquiries@nawp.org.uk
Website: www.nawp.org.uk

Enquiries to: Honorary Secretary
Direct tel: 01296 712568
Direct e-mail: renatainglis@hotmail.com

Founded: 1905

Organisation type and purpose: Professional body (membership is by subscription, qualification), present number of members: 300.

Subject coverage: Pharmacy, academic, hospital, community, industrial; returners, continuing education.

Collection: Early records and newsletters held in the Archives of the Royal Pharmaceutical Society of Great Britain

Publications: Printed

Access to staff: Contact by telephone, by e-mail and via website
Hours: 24-hour access

Links with: Royal Pharmaceutical Society of Great Britain; 1 Lambeth High Street, Lambeth, London, SE1 7JN

Member organisation of: Standing Conference of Women Returners Network; Standing Conference of Women's Organisations

NATIONAL ASSOCIATION OF WOMEN'S CLUBS (NAWC)

5 Vernon Rise, King's Cross Road, London, WC1X 9EP

Tel: 020 7837 1434
Fax: 020 7713 0727

Enquiries to: Administrator
Other contacts: National Secretary

Founded: 1935

Organisation type and purpose: Registered charity (charity number 273397), voluntary organisation.
To advance education and recreation or leisure time occupation for women in the interests of social welfare.

Subject coverage: Assistance in running or opening new clubs for women to provide education and recreation.

Collection: Minutes of meetings, photographs

Publications: Printed

Access to staff: Contact by letter, by telephone and by fax
Hours: Mon to Fri, 0930 to 1630

Affiliated to: National Council of Women of Great Britain

Member of: Women's National Commission

NATIONAL ASSOCIATION OF YOUTH ORCHESTRAS (NAYO)

Central Hall, West Tollcross, Edinburgh, EH3 9BP

Tel: 0131 221 1927
Fax: 0131 229 2921
E-mail: admin@nayo.org.uk
Website: www.nayo.org.uk

Enquiries to: General Manager
Other contacts: Administrator

Founded: 1961

Organisation type and purpose: Voluntary organisation, registered charity (charity number 281493).
To represent youth orchestras throughout the UK and to foster their development.

Subject coverage: Youth orchestral work: training, performance repertoire, organisation and maintenance, touring, international exchanges, courses; Edinburgh and Glasgow Festivals of British Youth Orchestras; European Youth Music Week, Allianz Cornhill Musical Insurance Youth Orchestra Awards, Allianz Cornhill Musical Insurance Conducting Prize/Seminar.

Collection: Marion Semple Weir Library of Chamber Music

Library catalogue: All or part available online, in-house and in print

Publications: Printed

Access to staff: Contact by letter, by telephone, by fax, by e-mail and via website. Appointment necessary.
Hours: Mon to Fri, 0900 to 1700

Access to building: Prior appointment required

Affiliated to: Association of British Orchestras; Edinburgh Festival Fringe; European Association of Youth Orchestras; Incorporated Society of Musicians; Music Education Council; Voluntary Arts Network

NATIONAL ASSOCIATION OF YOUTH THEATRES (NAYT)

The Arts Centre, Vane Terrace, Darlington, Co Durham, DL3 7AX

Tel: 01325 363330
Fax: 01325 363313
E-mail: nayt@btconnect.com
Website: www.nayt.org.uk

Enquiries to: Management Assistant

Founded: 1982

Organisation type and purpose: NAYT works with over 1,000 groups and individuals to support the development of youth theatre activity through information and support services, advocacy, training, participation and partnerships. Registration is free and open to any group or individual using theatre techniques in their work with young people, outside of formal education. Registered charity (charity number 1046042).

Subject coverage: Youth theatre provision, practice and location in the United Kingdom, public and national support.

Publications: Printed

Access to staff: Contact by letter, by telephone and by e-mail. Appointment necessary.
Hours: Mon to Fri, 0900 to 1700

Access to building: Prior appointment required

Funded by: Arts Council England; Department for Education; The D'Oyly Carte Charitable Trust

NATIONAL AURICULA & PRIMULA SOCIETY (SOUTHERN)

67 Warnham Court Road, Carshalton Beeches, Surrey, SM5 3ND

E-mail: lawrencew67@googlemail.com
Website: www.southernauriculaprimula.org

Enquiries to: Honorary Secretary

Founded: 1876

Organisation type and purpose: Learned society (membership is by subscription).

Subject coverage: Breeding and cultivation of auriculas, primroses, polyanthus, and all primula species and hybrids, their exhibition and history.

Publications: Printed

Access to staff: Contact by letter and by e-mail
Hours: Mon to Fri, 0900 to 1700

Affiliated to: Royal Horticultural Society

Has a: Midland and West Section; Northern Section

NATIONAL AUTISTIC SOCIETY (NAS)

393 City Road, London, EC1V 1NG

Tel: 020 7833 2299; 0845 070 4004 (Autism Helpline)
Fax: 020 7833 9666
E-mail: nas@nas.org.uk
Website: www.autism.org.uk

Enquiries to: Information Centre
Direct tel: 020 7903 3599
Direct e-mail: info@nas.org.uk

Founded: 1962

Organisation type and purpose: National organisation, membership association (membership is by subscription), present number of members: 19,000, voluntary organisation, registered charity (charity number 269425).

Subject coverage: Autism; the Autism Helpline provides impartial and confidential information, advice and support for people with an autistic spectrum disorder, their families and professionals.

Information services: Enquiry service, document delivery.

Collection: Library of books, journals, videos
Database of 25,000 records online at http://www.autism.org.uk/autismdata

Non-library collection catalogue: All or part available online

Library catalogue: All or part available online

Publications: Printed, and electronic and video
Order printed publications from: Central Books Ltd, 99 Wallis Road, London, E9 5LN; tel: 0845 458 9911; fax: 0845 458 9912; e-mail: nas@centralbooks.com

Publications list: Available online and in print

Access to staff: Contact by letter, by telephone, by fax, by e-mail and via website
Hours: Mon to Fri, 0930 to 1700

Access to building: Prior appointment required
Hours: Mon to Fri, 1000 to 1600

Access for disabled people: Parking provided, ramped entry, toilet facilities

NATIONAL AUTOCYCLE AND CYCLEMOTOR CLUB LTD (NACC)

7 St. Nicholas Road, Copmanthorpe, York, YO23 3UX

Tel: 01904 704373
E-mail: info@thebuzzingclub.co.uk
Website: www.thebuzzingclub.co.uk

Founded: 1981

Organisation type and purpose: International organisation, membership association (membership is by subscription), present number of members: 1,800. Library covering machines for which the club caters. Aims to promote interest, restoration and use of all autocycles, cyclemotors and mopeds under 100cc.

Subject coverage: Restoration and preservation of autocycles, cyclemotors and mopeds under 100cc marque enthusiasts, help and advice, library, transfers, etc. Certified machine dating. Authorised by the DVLA to approve V765 applications for the retention or original registration marks and age-related registration numbers.

Collection: Parts lists, manuals, road tests, sales cats, etc.

Non-library collection catalogue: All or part available in-house

Library catalogue: All or part available in-house

Publications: Printed

Publications list: Available in print

Access to staff: Contact by letter, by telephone, by e-mail and via website
Hours: 0900 to 2100

Special comments: By telephone, e-mail or letter to the Chairman; please enclose sae for reply.

Access to building: No access other than to staff

NATIONAL BED FEDERATION (NBF)

High Corn Mill, Chapel Hill, Skipton, North Yorkshire, BD23 1NL

Tel: 0845 055 6406
Fax: 0845 055 6407
E-mail: info@bedfed.org.uk
Website: www.bedfed.org.uk

Enquiries to: Administrator
Other contacts: PR Consultant for media and consumer enquiries

Founded: 1912

Organisation type and purpose: Trade association (membership is by subscription), present number of members: 72, manufacturing industry.
To represent UK manufacturers of beds and mattresses and their suppliers.

Subject coverage: Beds and mattresses in the UK market.

Publications: Printed

Publications list: Available online

Access to staff: Contact by letter, by telephone, by fax, by e-mail and via website
Hours: Mon to Fri, 0900 to 1700

NATIONAL BEEF ASSOCIATION (NBA)

Mart Centre, Tyne Green, Hexham, NE46 3SG

Tel: 01434 601005
Fax: 01434 601008
E-mail: info@nationalbeefassociation.com
Website: www.nationalbeefassociation.com/

Enquiries to: General Secretary

Founded: 1998

Organisation type and purpose: Trade association (membership is by subscription), present number of members: 3000, voluntary organisation.
Umbrella organisation to help the cattle industry.

Access to staff: Contact by letter, by telephone and by e-mail
Hours: Mon to Fri, 0900 to 1700

NATIONAL BLOOD AUTHORITY (NBA)

Oak House, Reeds Crescent, Watford, Hertfordshire, WD24 4QN

Tel: 01923 486800
Fax: 01923 486801
Website: www.blood.co.uk

Enquiries to: Head of Corporate Communications
Direct tel: 0113 214 8734
Direct fax: 0113 214 8736
Direct e-mail: jim.moir@nbs.nhs.uk

Organisation type and purpose: National government body.

continued overleaf

Part of the National Health Service. Control of collection, processing and distribution of blood and blood products in England.

Subject coverage: Collection, processing, testing and distribution of blood products in England from voluntary unpaid donors.

Access to staff: Contact by letter. Appointment necessary.
Hours: Mon to Fri, 0900 to 1700

Links with: Northern Ireland Blood Transfusion Service; Scottish National Blood Transfusion Service; Welsh Blood Service

National Blood Service Centres: NBS Birmingham Blood; Vincent Drive, Edgbaston, Birmingham, B15 2DG; tel: 0121 253 4000; fax: 0121 253 4005; NBS Brentwood; Crescent Drive, Brentwood, Essex, CM15 8DP; tel: 01277 306000; fax: 01227 306132; NBS Bristol; Southmead Road, Bristol, BS10 5ND; tel: 0117 991 2000; fax: 0117 991 2002; NBS Cambridge; Long Road, Cambridge, CB2 2PT; tel: 01223 548000; fax: 01223 548114; NBS Lancaster; Royal Lancaster Infirmary, Ashton Road, Lancaster, LA1 4GT; tel: 01524 306250; fax: 01524 306273; NBS Leeds; Bridle Path, Leeds, LS15 7TW; tel: 0113 214 8600; fax: 0113 214 8737; NBS Liverpool; West Derby Street, Liverpool, L7 8TW; tel: 0151 551 8800; fax: 0151 551 8896; NBS Manchester; Plymouth Grove, Manchester, M13 9LL; tel: 0161 251 4200; fax: 0161 251 4331; NBS Newcastle; Holland Drive, Newcastle upon Tyne, NE2 4NQ; tel: 0191 219 4400; fax: 0191 219 4505; NBS North London; Colindale Avenue, London, NW9 5BG; tel: 020 8258 2700; fax: 020 8258 2970; NBS Oxford; John Radcliffe Hospital, Headington, Oxford, OX3 9DU; tel: 01865 447900; fax: 01865 447915; NBS Plymouth; Derriford Hospital, Derriford Road, Plymouth, PL6 8DH; tel: 01752 617815; fax: 01752 617806; NBS Sheffield; Longley Lane, Sheffield, S5 7JN; tel: 0114 203 4800; fax: 0114 203 4911; NBS South Thames; 75 Cranmer Terrace, London, SW17 0RB; tel: 020 8258 8300; fax: 020 8258 8453; NBS Southampton; Coxford Road, Southampton, SO16 5AF; tel: 023 8029 6700; fax: 023 8029 6760

Other addresses: Bio Products Laboratory; Dagger Lane, Elstree, Hertfordshire, WD6 3BX; tel: 020 8258 2200; fax: 020 8258 2601

NATIONAL BOTANIC GARDEN OF WALES, THE (NBGW)

Llanarthne, Carmarthenshire, SA32 8HG

Tel: 01558 668768
Fax: 01558 668933
E-mail: reception@gardenofwales.org.uk
Website: www.gardenofwales.org.uk

Enquiries to: Executive Director for Development

Founded: 2000

Organisation type and purpose:
International organisation, registered charity (charity number 1036354), research organisation.

Subject coverage: Botanic garden.

Access to staff: Contact by letter, by telephone, by fax and by e-mail
Hours: Summer, Mon to Sun, 1000 to 1800
Winter, Mon to Sun, 1000 to 1630

Access for disabled people: Parking provided, level entry, access to all public areas, toilet facilities

NATIONAL CAMPAIGN FOR FIREWORK SAFETY (NCFS)

118 Long Acre, London, WC2E 9PA

Tel: 020 7836 6703
Fax: 020 7836 6703
Website: www.cgsystems.co.uk/ncfs
Website: www.firework.co.uk/ncfp

Enquiries to: Director

Founded: 1969

Organisation type and purpose:
International organisation, national organisation, membership association (membership is by subscription), present number of members: 370,000, voluntary organisation, registered charity, research organisation.
To amend the 1875 and 1976 firework laws; to introduce legislation restricting fireworks to holders of licences over the age of 18 for properly organised firework displays and a national training scheme. To promote history and education on the subject.

Subject coverage: International firework legislation, history of fireworks, education and technical training, films and documentaries.

Trade and statistical information: Firework accident statistics

Non-library collection catalogue: All or part available in-house

Library catalogue: All or part available online and in print

Publications: Printed, and microform publications

Access to staff: Contact by letter, by telephone, by fax and by e-mail. Appointment necessary. Non-members charged.
Hours: Mon to Fri, 0900 to 1800
Special comments: Not weekends except 15 October to 10 November.

Access to building: No access other than to staff, prior appointment required

Links with: Age Concern; Cats Protection League; CBI; Fire Brigades Union; Institute of Trading Standards Offices; London Fire & Civil Defence Authority; National Canine Defence League; National Federation of Retirement Pensioners; Royal College of Nursing; RSPCA; TUC; UK Noise Association (UKNA)

Other addresses: NCFS Manchester; 19 Plummer Avenue, Cholton, Manchester, M21 2FU; NCFS Northumberland; 53 Longstone Close, Bradwell, Northumberland, NE67 5BS

NATIONAL CAMPAIGN FOR NURSERY EDUCATION (NCNE)

Formal name: The National Campaign for Real Nursery Education

Membership Secretary, Tachbrook Nursery School, Aylesford Street, London, SW1V 3RT

E-mail: ncrne@yahoo.co.uk
Website: www.ncne.co.uk

Enquiries to: Membership Secretary
Direct e-mail: head@tachbrooknursery.co.uk

Founded: 1965

Organisation type and purpose:
Membership association (membership is by subscription), service industry, suitable for ages: 3 to 5.
Campaign Group.
To campaign for the expansion of state-funded nursery education, and to defend existing provision.

Subject coverage: Necessity of education for two years before statutory school age, extension and protection of the provision of education.

Publications: Printed

Access to staff: Contact by letter
Hours: Mon to Fri, 0900 to 1700

NATIONAL CARAVAN COUNCIL LIMITED (NCC)

Catherine House, Victoria Road, Aldershot, Hampshire, GU11 1SS

Tel: 01252 318251
Fax: 01252 322596
E-mail: info@thencc.org.uk
Website: www.thencc.org.uk

Enquiries to: Director General

Founded: 1939; incorporates the former National Park Home Council

Organisation type and purpose: Trade association (membership is by subscription), present number of members: 800.
Representative body.

Subject coverage: Centre of information on all aspects of the caravan industry providing an advisory service on technical legislation, regulation and commercial matters.

Non-library collection catalogue: All or part available online

Publications: Printed

Access to staff: Contact by letter, by telephone, by fax, by e-mail and via website. Access for members only. Letter of introduction required.
Hours: Mon to Fri, 0900 to 1700

NATIONAL CARE ASSOCIATION (NCHA)

45–49 Leather Lane, London, EC1N 7TJ

Tel: 020 7831 7090
Fax: 020 7831 7040
E-mail: info@nationalcareassociation.org.uk
Website: www.nca.gb.com

Enquiries to: Chief Executive

Founded: 1981

Organisation type and purpose: Trade association.

Subject coverage: Community care, social security, residential care, nursing home care.

Publications list: Available in print

Access to staff: Contact by letter, by telephone, by fax and by e-mail. Appointment necessary.

Hours: Mon to Fri, 0900 to 1700

Access to building: Prior appointment required

Access for disabled people: Access to all public areas

Subsidiary body: National Care Homes Association Commercial Limited

NATIONAL CARPET CLEANERS ASSOCIATION (NCCA)

Formal name: Carpet Cleaners Association Ltd

62C London Road, Oadby, Leicestershire, LE2 5DH

Tel: 0116 271 9550
Fax: 0116 271 9588
E-mail: admin@ncca.co.uk
Website: www.ncca.co.uk

Founded: 1968

Organisation type and purpose: A non-profit-making body, the only nationally recognised trade association dedicated to the cleaning of carpets, hard flooring, upholstery, curtains and other soft furnishings.
The principal objective is the establishment and maintenance of minimum standards within the carpet and upholstery cleaning industry, with the dual aim of safeguarding the reputation of the industry and protecting its customers, whether in the domestic or commercial sphere.

Subject coverage: Cleaning of all types of flooring and soft furnishings; hard floor restoration; rug cleaning and repair; leather furniture cleaning and restoration; carpet and fabric repair; fabric and fibre protection; curtain cleaning; carpet fitting; fire and flood restoration.

Education services: Comprehensive compulsory training programme for members, plus advanced courses, workshops, branch meetings, technical roadshows and other events.

Access to staff: Contact by letter, by telephone, by fax and by e-mail

NATIONAL CATALOGUING UNIT FOR THE ARCHIVES OF CONTEMPORARY SCIENTISTS (NCUACS)

University of Bath, Claverton Down, Bath, BA2 7AY

Tel: 01225 383522
Fax: 01225 386229
E-mail: lispbh@bath.ac.uk
Website: www.bath.ac.uk/ncuacs

Enquiries to: Director

Founded: 1973; carries out the functions of the former Contemporary Scientific Archives Centre (year of change 1987)

Organisation type and purpose: Research organisation.
Locating, cataloguing and finding places of permanent deposit for the manuscript papers of eminent contemporary British scientists and engineers.

Subject coverage: Professional and personal papers and correspondence of distinguished UK scientists and engineers deceased since c. 1950; scientific source material; cataloguing such material.

Publications: Printed

Publications list: Available online

Access to staff: Contact by letter and by e-mail
Hours: Mon to Fri, 0900 to 1700

Access to building: No access other than to staff

NATIONAL CENTRE FOR EARLY MUSIC (NCEM)

St Margaret's Church, Walmgate, York, YO1 9TL

Tel: 01904 658338
Fax: 01904 612631
E-mail: info@ncem.co.uk
Website: www.ncem.co.uk

Organisation type and purpose: Administered by the York Early Music Foundation, registered charity (charity number 1068331), certificate of incorporation 3499629. Offers conference and recording facilities and performances of early music. Hosts the York Early Music Festival and the Beverley and East Riding Early Music Festival.

Education services: Year-round community and education programme.

Access for disabled people: The Centre is flat-floored throughout, making it accessible for wheelchair users. There are two designated disabled parking places in the adjacent car park, an entrance ramp and disabled toilet facilities

NATIONAL CENTRE FOR EATING DISORDERS (NcfeD)

54 New Road, Esher, Surrey, KT10 9NU

Tel: 0845 838 2040
Fax: 01372 469550
E-mail: admin@ncfed.com
Website: www.eating-disorders.org.uk

Enquiries to: Information Officer

Founded: 1984

Organisation type and purpose: Professional body, training organisation, consultancy.
Treatment service for eating disorders and weight problems. Training for counselling skills in eating disorders.

Subject coverage: Compulsive or binge eating, bulimia nervosa, anorexia, obesity, slimming pill abuse, body image problems and therapies for eating problems.

Publications: Printed

Publications list: Available online and in print

Access to staff: Contact by letter, by telephone, by e-mail and via website. Appointment necessary.
Hours: Mon to Fri, 0900 to 1700

Access to building: Prior appointment required

Affiliated to: up to 60 individual therapists nationwide receiving referrals from head office.

NATIONAL CENTRE FOR SOCIAL RESEARCH

35 Northampton Square, London, EC1V 0AX

Tel: 020 7250 1866
Fax: 020 7250 1524
E-mail: info@natcen.ac.uk
Website: www.natcen.ac.uk

Enquiries to: Information Officer
Direct e-mail: linda.maynard@natcen.ac.uk

Founded: 1969

Organisation type and purpose: Registered charity, research organisation.

Subject coverage: Social research, especially social policy surveys and survey methodology.

Publications: Printed

Publications list: Available online

Access to staff: Contact by letter, by telephone, by fax and by e-mail
Hours: Mon to Fri, 0900 to 1700

Access to building: No access other than to staff
Special comments: Only to consult the National Centre Publications.

NATIONAL CENTRE FOR TRAINING AND EDUCATION IN PROSTHETICS AND ORTHOTICS (NCTEPO)

Curran Building, 131 St James' Road, Glasgow, G4 0LS

Tel: 0141 548 3814
Fax: 0141 552 1283
E-mail: h.smart@strath.ac.uk
Website: www.recal.org.uk

Enquiries to: Information Officer
Direct tel: 0141 548 3814
Direct fax: 0141 552 1283
Direct e-mail: h.smart@strath.ac.uk

Founded: 1978

Organisation type and purpose: University department or institute.
University of Strathclyde Centre, having an internationally used library and information service.

Subject coverage: Prosthetics and orthotics, related physical medicine and rehabilitation engineering.

Non-library collection catalogue: All or part available online

Publications: Printed, and electronic and video

Access to staff: Contact by letter, by telephone, by fax and by e-mail. Appointment necessary.
Hours: Mon to Fri, 0900 to 1700

Access to building: No prior appointment required

Parent body: University of Strathclyde; tel: 0141 552 4400

NATIONAL CENTRE FOR YOUNG PEOPLE WITH EPILEPSY (NCYPE)

St Piers Lane, Lingfield, Surrey, RH7 6PW

Tel: 01342 832243
Fax: 01342 834639
E-mail: info@ncype.org.uk
Website: www.ncype.org.uk

Enquiries to: Media and Communications Officer
Direct tel: extn. 310
Direct e-mail: kohaire@ncype.org.uk
Other contacts: Admissions Co-ordinator (for further information about admission to the NCYPE)

Founded: 1897

Organisation type and purpose: National organisation, voluntary organisation, registered charity (charity number 311877), suitable for ages: 5 to 25.
The NCYPE is the major provider of specialised services for young people with epilepsy in the UK. It provides education, treatment, assessment, rehabilitation and care to young people with epilepsy and other complex neurological disorders in partnership with Great Ormond Street Hospital for Children NHS Trust. It provides residential medical care and education for children and young people with epilepsy and other complex special needs.

Subject coverage: Multidisciplinary team-working between many different experts, medical consultants, teachers, nurses, therapists, psychologists, carers and skilled support staff supports the many different needs of students and helps each individual achieve their true potential.

Publications: Printed
Order printed publications from: Marketing Development Officer, NCYPE, tel: 01342 832243

Access to staff: Contact by letter, by telephone, by fax, by e-mail and via website. Appointment necessary. Letter of introduction required.
Hours: Mon to Fri, 0830 to 1700

Access to building: Prior appointment required

Access for disabled people: Parking provided, toilet facilities

Member organisation of: Association of National Specialist Colleges; Joint Epilepsy Council for Great Britain and Ireland; National Association of Independent and Non-maintained Special Schools; National Association of Special Schools

Partnership with: Great Ormond Street Hospital for Children NHS Trust

NATIONAL CHEMICAL EMERGENCY CENTRE (NCEC)

AEA, The Gemini Building, Fermi Avenue, Harwell, Didcot, Oxon OX11 0QR

Tel: 0870 190 6621
Fax: 0870 190 6614
E-mail: ncec@aeat.com
Website: www.the-ncec.com
Website: www.aeat.com

Enquiries to: Manager

Founded: 1973

Organisation type and purpose: The UK's National Chemical Emergency Centre – operating within AEA as a commercial company providing products, services and advice to public and private sector organisations worldwide.

Subject coverage: Safety data sheet management, COSHH, REACH, GHS/CLP, chemical legislation consultancy, chemical emergency response, chemical hazards database, chemical health and safety, chemical risk management, training.

Publications: Printed, and electronic and video

Access to staff: Contact by letter, by telephone, by fax, by e-mail and via website
Hours: Mon to Fri, 0800 to 1630 (for non-emergency calls)
Special comments: 24-hour emergency information service provided to public emergency services and industry.

NATIONAL CHILDREN'S CENTRE

Brian Jackson House, New North Parade, Huddersfield, West Yorkshire, HD1 5JP

Tel: 01484 519988
Fax: 01484 435150
E-mail: nfo@nccuk.org.uk

Enquiries to: Chief Executive

Founded: 1975

Organisation type and purpose: Registered charity.

Subject coverage: Childcare, education, families from overseas, training young people, addressing offending, school truancy, homeless families, family support, parent training.

Collection: Brian Jackson archive, contains manuscripts, printed works on social and political history, childcare issues and educational issues

Publications: Printed

Access to staff: Contact by letter, by telephone and by fax
Hours: Mon to Fri, 0900 to 1700

Access for disabled people: Ramped entry, level entry, access to all public areas, toilet facilities

NATIONAL CHRYSANTHEMUM SOCIETY (NCS)

c/o Mr Peter Fraser, 317 Plessey Road, Blyth, Northumberland, NE24 3LJ

Tel: 01670 353580
E-mail: peter@fpeter.fsnet.co.uk
Website: www.ncsuk.info/index.htm

Enquiries to: Membership Secretary

Founded: 1846

Organisation type and purpose: International organisation, advisory body, membership association (membership is by subscription), present number of members: 4,000, voluntary organisation, registered charity (charity number 248484), suitable for ages: 10+, consultancy.
British registry office for chrysanthemums. To promote the growing of chrysanthemums.

Subject coverage: Chrysanthemum cultivation, pest and disease control, literature.

Publications: Printed, and electronic and video

Publications list: Available in print

Access to staff: Contact by letter, by telephone, by fax and in person
Hours: Mon to Fri, 0900 to 1700

Access to building: Prior appointment required

Access for disabled people: Access to all public areas, toilet facilities

Affiliated to: Royal Horticultural Society

Has: 6 regional groups, South, West, Midland, North, Welsh, Scottish, access via main office

NATIONAL CHURCHES TRUST

31 Newbury Street, London, EC1A 7HU

Tel: 020 7600 6090
Fax: 020 7796 2442
E-mail: info@nationalchurchestrust.org
Website: www.nationalchurchestrust.org

Enquiries to: Office Manager
Other contacts: Grants Manager (for applications for funding)

Founded: 1953; formerly called Historic Churches Preservation Trust (year of change 2007)

Organisation type and purpose: National organisation, registered charity (charity number 1119845).
A charity that offers financial assistance to Christian churches of any recognised denomination for essential fabric repairs and alteration such as entrances/kitchens/toilets to allow community use of the building.

Subject coverage: Churches, chapels and meeting houses in the UK.

Information services: Information for those seeking funding for repair/alteration to church buildings

Publications: Printed
Order printed publications from: Friends (£20 joining fee) receive the above free of charge

Access to staff: Contact by letter, by telephone, by fax, by e-mail and via website
Hours: Mon to Fri, 0930 to 1730

Access to building: No access other than to staff

NATIONAL CO-OPERATIVE ARCHIVE

Co-operative College, Holyoake House, Hanover Street, Manchester, M60 0AS

Tel: 0161 246 2925
Fax: 0161 246 2946
E-mail: archive@co-op.ac.uk
Website: www.archive.coop

Enquiries to: Archivist
Direct e-mail: gillian@co-op.ac.uk

Founded: 1869; formerly called Co-operative Union Archive (year of change 2000); formerly called Co-operative College Archive (year of change 2000)

Organisation type and purpose: National Co-operative Archive is home to a wide array of records relating to the history of the world-wide co-operative movement.

Subject coverage: History of the British co-operative movement; contemporary co-operative developments and issues; overseas co-operative movements; history of the labour movement in Britain; co-operative leaders and social reformers; co-operation; co-operative history nationally and internationally; co-operative society history and histories; co-operative film archive; co-operative archive; international economic development; centre for alternative industrial and technological systems archive; co-operative oral history archive.

Collection: Christian Socialists: books, pamphlets and periodicals
Co-operative Society histories and rule books
Co-operative Society pamphlets, 1830 to date
MS Collection of E O Greening correspondence and documents (11,000 items)
MS Collection of G J Holyoake correspondence and documents, 1835–1903 (4000 items)
MS Collection of Robert Owen correspondence and documents, 1820 onwards (3000 items)
Rare 19th century books, newspapers and periodicals on co-operation and social reform
CAITS Archive
Midlands Co-operative Society Archive
Co-operative Group South East, South Midlands and Northern Region Co-operative Archive
Co-operative Youth Movements
National Co-operative Film Archive
Co-operative Oral History Archive
Periodicals

Non-library collection catalogue: All or part available online, in-house and in print

Publications: Printed
Order printed publications from: Available on request

Access to staff: Contact by letter, by telephone, by fax, by e-mail and via website. Appointment necessary.
Hours: Mon to Fri, 1000 to 1700

Access to building: *Hours:* Mon to Fri, 1000 to 1700
Special comments: By appointment.

Access for disabled people: As above

Governing body: Co-operative Heritage Trust; 5th Floor, New Century House, Corporation Street, Manchester M60 4ES; e-mail: cht@co-op.ac.uk; website: http://www.co-operativeheritage.coop

Member organisation of: Co-operatives UK; Euro-co-op; International Co-operative Alliance

NATIONAL COASTWATCH INSTITUTION

HeadQuarters, Unit 26 Basepoint Business Centre, Exeter, EX2 8LB

Tel: 0300 111 1202; 0845 460 1202
E-mail: info@nci.org.uk
Website: www.nci.org.uk/contact

Founded: 1994

Organisation type and purpose: Registered charity (charity number 1045645), voluntary organisation.
Established to restore a visual watch along UK shores after many small coastguard stations were closed. Each station assists in the protection and preservation of life at sea and around the UK coastline. Currently over 40 NCI stations are fully operational and manned by over 1,700 volunteers keeping watch around the British Isles from Cornwall in the South West to Wearside in the North East.

Subject coverage: While high technology and sophisticated systems are aids to improved safety, a computer cannot spot a distress flare, an overturned boat or a yachtsman or fisherman in trouble. Other vulnerable activities like diving, wind surfing and canoeing are made safer with visual surveillance. NCI watchkeepers provide the eyes and ears along the coast, monitoring radio channels and providing a listening watch in poor visibility. They are trained to deal with emergencies, offering a variety of skills and experience, and full training by the NCI ensures that high standards are met. Over 170,000 hours of organised coastal surveillance are completed each year, all at no cost to the public.

Information services: Printable map of NCI stations; useful information for mariners and walkers; guide for potential new stations.

Publications: Printed

Access to staff: Contact by letter, by telephone, by e-mail and via website

NATIONAL COLLECTION OF TYPE CULTURES (NCTC)

Health Protection Agency Culture Collections, Porton Down, Salisbury, Wiltshire, SP4 0JG

Tel: 01980 612512
Fax: 01980 611315
E-mail: hpacultures@hpa.org.uk
Website: www.hpacultures.org.uk

Founded: 1920

Organisation type and purpose: Research organisation.
Maintaining and supplying cultures of authenticated bacteria of medical/veterinary interest.

Subject coverage: Microbiology, especially medical/veterinary; reference strains of bacteria for particular usage (taxonomic), antibiotic assay, teaching, controls for bacteriological tests; freeze-drying; mycoplasmas; plasmid-bearing strains; availability of cultures in other culture collections (UK and abroad).

Collection: Early works on bacteriology, etc.

Non-library collection catalogue: All or part available online

Access to staff: Contact by letter, by telephone, by fax, by e-mail and via website
Hours: Mon to Fri, 0900 to 1700

Access to building: Prior appointment required

Access for disabled people: Parking provided, ramped entry, level entry, access to all public areas, toilet facilities

European Resource Centre for: Plasmids

Links with: European Culture Collection Organisation; World Federation for Culture Collections

Member organisation of: United Kingdom National Culture Collection (UKNCC)

Parent body: Health Protection Agency; website: www.hpa.org.uk

NATIONAL COLLEGE OF HYPNOSIS AND PSYCHOTHERAPY (NCHP)

PO Box 5779, Loughborough, LE12 5ZF

Tel: 01509 881477
E-mail: enquiries@nchp.org.uk
Website: www.hypnotherapyuk.net

Enquiries to: Administrator

Founded: 1977

Organisation type and purpose: Hypno-psychotherapy training.

Subject coverage: Hypno-psychotherapy.

Access to staff: Contact by letter, by telephone, by fax, by e-mail, in person and via website. Appointment necessary.
Hours: Mon to Fri, 0900 to 1700

Access to building: Prior appointment required

Access for disabled people: Level entry

Links with: UK Council for Psychotherapy (UKCP); 2nd Floor, Edward House, 2 Wakley Street, London, EC1V 7LT; tel: 0870 167 2131; website: http://www.psychotherapy.org.uk

NATIONAL COMPUTING CENTRE LIMITED (NCC)

Formal name: National Computing Centre

Oxford House, Oxford Road, Manchester, M1 7ED

Tel: 0161 228 6333
Fax: 0161 242 2499
E-mail: info@ncc.co.uk
Website: www.ncc.co.uk

Enquiries to: Marketing Manager
Direct tel: 0161 242 2146
Direct e-mail: Michael.Dean@ncc.co.uk
Other contacts: IT Manager/Director

Founded: 1966

Organisation type and purpose: National organisation, membership association (membership is by subscription), present number of members: 1300, research organisation.
Promotes the most effective use of IT.

Subject coverage: IT: all aspects of computing in UK and internationally.

Non-library collection catalogue: All or part available online

Publications: Printed, and electronic and video

Publications list: Available online and in print

continued overleaf

Access to staff: Contact by letter, by telephone, by fax, by e-mail and via website. Appointment necessary. Non-members charged.
Hours: Mon to Fri, 0900 to 1700

Access to building: Prior appointment required

Access for disabled people: Access to all public areas

NATIONAL CONSUMER CREDIT FEDERATION (NCCF)

98–100 Holme Lane, Sheffield, South Yorkshire, S6 4JW

Tel: 0114 234 8101
Fax: 0114 234 5459
E-mail: nccf@talk21.com

Enquiries to: General Secretary

Founded: 1927

Organisation type and purpose: Trade association (membership is by subscription).

Subject coverage: Consumer credit.

Publications: Printed

Access to staff: Contact by letter, by telephone and by fax
Hours: Mon to Fri, 0930 to 1630

NATIONAL CONSUMER FEDERATION (NCF)

24 Hurst House, Penton Rise, London, WC1X 9ED

Tel: 020 7837 8545
Fax: 020 7837 8545
E-mail: secretary@ncf.info
Website: www.ncf.info

Enquiries to: Honorary Secretary

Founded: 2001

Organisation type and purpose: Voluntary organisation.
Co-ordinates the activities of local consumer groups and represents the views of consumers to government and business.

Subject coverage: Consumer affairs, consumer law, food.

Publications: Printed, and electronic and video

Access to staff: Contact by letter, by telephone, by fax, by e-mail and via website. Non-members charged.
Hours: Mon to Fri, 0900 to 1200; outside office hours, by e-mail

NATIONAL CORRESPONDENCE CHESS CLUB

81 Surrey Street, Norwich, NR1 3PG

Tel: 01603 491199
E-mail: simoncarer@aol.com

Enquiries to: Chairman

Founded: 1932

Organisation type and purpose: National organisation (membership is by subscription).
Postal Chess Club.

Subject coverage: Correspondence chess.

Access to staff: Contact by letter and by e-mail
Hours: Any reasonable time.

Affiliated to: British Postal Chess Federation; e-mail: norman.king2@virgin.net

NATIONAL COUNCIL FOR DRAMA TRAINING (NCDT)

5 Tavistock Place, London, WC1H 9SS

Tel: 020 7387 3650
Fax: 020 7681 4733
E-mail: ncdt@lineone.net
Website: www.ncdt.co.uk

Enquiries to: Executive Secretary

Founded: 1976

Organisation type and purpose: National government body, professional body, registered charity.
Accreditation body maintaining standards at professional drama schools.

Subject coverage: List of courses in professional, vocational actor and stage management training accredited by the NCDT.

Non-library collection catalogue: All or part available online

Publications: Printed

Publications list: Available online and in print

Access to staff: Contact by letter, by telephone, by fax, by e-mail and via website
Hours: Mon to Fri, 0930 to 1730

Access to building: No access other than to staff

Members of the organisation are: BBC; British Actors Equity; Channel 4; Conference of Drama Schools; Society of London Theatre; Theatre Management Association

NATIONAL COUNCIL FOR SCHOOL SPORT (NCSS)

c/o RFU National Centre for Schools and Youth, Castlecroft Stadium, Castlecroft Road, Wolverhampton, West Midlands, WV3 8NA

Tel: 01902 380302
Fax: 01902 380311
E-mail: info@ncss.org.uk
Website: www.ncss.org.uk

Enquiries to: Honorary Secretary

Founded: 1948

Organisation type and purpose: Membership association (membership is by subscription, election or invitation), present number of members: 31, voluntary organisation.
To co-ordinate the work of the National School Sports Associations. To represent the views of members to government departments, National Sports Associations, local education authorities and wherever else necessary.

Subject coverage: School sports organisations – governing and regional bodies details of activities staged with participation and spectator figures, general details and participation in sports in schools, coaching development plans for sports. International schools activities.
Sports activities of children (5 to 18 years), administration of school sport at national and local level, formation of new associations in sports where none exists.

Publications: Printed

Access to staff: Contact by letter and by e-mail
Hours: Mon to Fri, 0900 to 1700

Executive Officer: National Council for School Sport; 95 Boxley Drive, West Bridgford, Nottinghamshire, NG2 7GN; tel: 0115 923 1229; e-mail: schoolsport@ntlworld.com

NATIONAL COUNCIL FOR THE DIVORCED AND SEPARATED (NCDS)

National Secretary, c/o 101 Anson Road, Southtown, Great Yarmouth, Norfolk, NR31 0EG

Tel: 07041 478120
E-mail: info@ncds.org.uk

Enquiries to: Honorary Secretary

Organisation type and purpose: Membership association (membership is by qualification), present number of members: 10,000, voluntary organisation.
A means of meeting people in, or who have been in, a situation similar to their own, giving opportunity for a social life again.

Subject coverage: All aspects relating to separation and divorce.

Publications: Printed

Access to staff: Contact by letter, by telephone, by e-mail and via website
Hours: Mon to Sat, 0900 to 2000

Has: 6 Regional Clubs and several non-regional branches

NATIONAL COUNCIL FOR THE TRAINING OF JOURNALISTS (NCTJ)

The New Granary, Station Road, Newport, Saffron Walden, Essex, CB11 3PL

Tel: 01799 544014
Fax: 01799 544015
E-mail: info@nctj.com
Website: www.nctj.com

Founded: 1951

Organisation type and purpose: National organisation, awarding body, learned society, registered charity (charity number 1026685), training organisation.
Training and examining organisation.
To advance the education and training of trainee journalists and press photographers.

Subject coverage: Careers and training in journalism, at college/university, by distance learning.

Trade and statistical information: UK newspaper industry's own training scheme for journalists

Publications: Printed, and electronic and video
Order printed publications from: Online shop

Publications list: Available online

Access to staff: Contact by letter, by telephone, by fax, by e-mail and via website. Appointment necessary.
Hours: Mon to Fri, 0900 to 1700

Access for disabled people: Parking provided, access to all public areas

Wholly-owned trading company: NCTJ Training Ltd; tel: 01799 544014; fax: 01799 544015; e-mail: info@nctj.com

NATIONAL COUNCIL FOR VOLUNTARY ORGANISATIONS (NCVO)

Regent's Wharf, 8 All Saints Street, London, N1 9RL

Tel: 020 7713 6161
Fax: 020 7713 6300
E-mail: ncvo@ncvo-vol.org.uk
Website: www.ncvo-vol.org.uk/publications
Website: www.ncvo-vol.org.uk

Founded: 1919

Organisation type and purpose: Membership association (membership is by subscription, qualification), present number of members: 8,300 voluntary organisations, voluntary organisation, registered charity (charity number 225922).
NCVO champions the cause of voluntary organisations and works to increase their effectiveness.

Subject coverage: Voluntary organisations and their response to current social issues; resources for voluntary organisations; interests and independence of such organisations; current legislation; government funding and its efficient use; trustee and governance issues; relationship of sector with business and public sectors, rural aspects.

Trade and statistical information: Data on voluntary sector issues, e.g.: size of sector, profiling of areas of work

Publications: Printed
Order printed publications from: Website:
http://www.ncvo-vol.org.uk/publications
Tel: 0800 279 8798
In person: at NCVO reception (see address above)

Publications list: Available online

Access to staff: Contact by letter, by telephone, by fax, by e-mail and via website
Hours: Mon to Fri, 0900 to 1700

Access for disabled people: Level entry, toilet facilities

NATIONAL COUNCIL FOR VOLUNTARY YOUTH SERVICES (NCVYS)

3rd Floor, Lancaster House, 33 Islington High Street, London, N1 9LH

Tel: 020 7278 1041
Fax: 020 7833 2491
E-mail: mail@ncvys.org.uk
Website: www.ncvys.org.uk

Founded: 1936

Organisation type and purpose: Established in 1936, the National Council for Voluntary Youth Services is a diverse and growing network of over 280 national organisations and regional and local networks that work with and for young people. Our mission is to work with our members from voluntary and community organisations to build thriving communities and sustainable networks that help all young people achieve their potential. Registered charity (charity number 1093386). Registered company 4385383

Subject coverage: Voluntary youth services and social issues affecting young people; child protection; equal opportunities, diversity, youth participation.

Publications: Printed

Publications list: Available online and in print

Access to staff: Contact by letter, by telephone, by fax, by e-mail and via website. Appointment necessary. Non-members charged.
Hours: Mon to Fri, 0900 to 1700

NATIONAL COUNCIL OF PAKISTANI ORGANISATIONS (UK) (NCOPO)

103 Wexham Close, Luton, Bedfordshire, LU3 3TX

Tel: 01582 598394
Fax: 01582 618335
E-mail: mshafikhan@hotmail.com

Enquiries to: Chairman

Founded: 1982

Organisation type and purpose: National organisation, advisory body, learned society (membership is by qualification), voluntary organisation, consultancy.
To guide and support organisations and individuals as and when needed for their development in the community in every respect of their life. Also to help in social, welfare and cultural development, legal matters, and encourage integration of Pakistani community into the host community.

Subject coverage: All aspects of Pakistan as a country and Pakistani culture in general.

Access to staff: Contact by letter, by telephone and by fax
Hours: Any reasonable time

Access to building: Prior appointment required

NATIONAL COUNCIL OF VOLUNTARY CHILD CARE ORGANISATIONS (NCVCCO)

Unit 25 Angel Gate, City Road, London, EC1V 2PT

Tel: 020 7833 3319
Fax: 020 7833 8637
E-mail: office@ncvcco.org
Website: www.ncvcco.org/

Enquiries to: Information Officer
Direct e-mail: ian@ncvcco.org

Founded: 1942

Organisation type and purpose: Membership association (membership is by subscription), present number of members: 110, voluntary organisation, registered charity (charity number 1044239).
To assist the work of English child care charities.

Subject coverage: Child care particularly in the voluntary sector; residential care of children, day care of children, family support within communities, fostering and adoption, funding for voluntary child care groups, European initiatives including child care and funding.

Collection: Small library on child care and the voluntary sector (for members' use only)

Publications: Printed

Publications list: Available in print

Access to staff: Contact by letter, by telephone, by fax and by e-mail
Hours: Mon to Fri, 0900 to 1700

Access to building: Prior appointment required

Member of: European Forum for Child Welfare; International Forum for Child Welfare

NATIONAL COUNCIL OF WOMEN OF GREAT BRITAIN (NCW)

36 Danbury Street, London, N1 8JU

Tel: 020 7354 2395
Fax: 01325 367378

Enquiries to: President

Founded: 1895

Organisation type and purpose: National organisation, membership association (membership is by subscription), present number of members: 1,000 plus 70 affiliated societies, voluntary organisation, registered charity.
To improve the quality of life for all, and to encourage the effective participation of women in the life of the nation.

Subject coverage: Arts, consumer affairs, education, health, housing, international affairs, mass media, scientific development, social welfare, status and employment of women and transport.

Collection: Minutes of meetings 1890 to date, working papers etc
NCW archives
Publications and reports produced by NCW

Publications: Printed

Publications list: Available online and in print

Access to staff: Contact by letter, by telephone and by e-mail
Hours: Mon to Fri, 0900 to 1700

Access to building: No prior appointment required
Special comments: Pre-1980 archive deposited with London Record Office

Access for disabled people: Level entry

Has: 70 affiliated organisations

Member of: International Council of Women

NATIONAL DAY NURSERIES ASSOCIATION (NDNA)

Oak House, Woodvale Road, Brighouse, West Yorkshire, HD6 4AB

continued overleaf

Tel: 0870 774 4244
Fax: 0870 774 4243
E-mail: info@ndna.org.uk
Website: www.ndna.org.uk
Website: www.ndna.org.uk/publications

Enquiries to: Membership Officer
Direct e-mail: jacqui.smith@ndna.org.uk

Founded: 1991

Organisation type and purpose:
Membership association (membership is by subscription), present number of members: 2300, registered charity (charity number 1078275).
A national childcare charity that is dedicated to the provision, support and promotion of high quality care and education for all children in the early years.

Subject coverage: Advice, support and training to help nurseries deliver quality early years education and care.

Publications: Printed

Publications list: Available online and in print

Access to staff: Contact by letter, by telephone, by fax and by e-mail.
Appointment necessary.
Hours: Mon to Fri, 0900 to 1700

NATIONAL DEAF CHILDREN'S SOCIETY (NDCS)

15 Dufferin Street, London, EC1Y 8UR

Tel: 0808 800 8880 (freephone helpline, voice and text)
Fax: 020 7251 5020
E-mail: helpline@ndcs.org.uk
Website: www.ndcs.org.uk

Founded: 1944

Organisation type and purpose: NDCS is an organisation of families, parents and carers providing emotional and practical support through a freephone helpline, a network of trained support workers, a wide range of other support services and publications, and a website.

Subject coverage: Childhood deafness, audiology, technology for deaf children, benefits for deaf children, education and communication.

Publications: Printed

Publications list: Available in print

Access to staff: Contact by letter, by telephone, by fax and by e-mail.
Appointment necessary.
Hours: Mon to Fri, 0900 to 1700
Special comments: Helpline: Mon to Fri, 0930 to 1700; Sat 0930 to 1200.

Access to building: Prior appointment required

Access for disabled people: Level entry, access to all public areas, toilet facilities, loop system in meeting room

Also at: NDCS Northern Ireland; Wilton House, 5 College Square North, Belfast, BT1 6AR; tel: 028 9031 3170 (voice and text); fax: 028 9031 3170; NDCS Scotland; Second Floor, Empire House, 131 West Nile Street, Glasgow, G1 2RX; tel: 0141 354 7850 (voice and text); fax: 0141 331 2780; e-mail: ndcs .scotland@ndcs.org.uk; NDCS Wales; 4 Cathedral Road, Cardiff, CF11 9LJ; tel: 029 20373474; minicom: 029 20232739; fax: 029 20379800; e-mail: ndcswales@ndcs.org.uk

Branches: 120 local deaf children's societies

Member organisation of: Deaf Accord

NATIONAL DEBTLINE (NDL)

Tricorn House, 51–53 Hagley Road, Edgbaston, Birmingham, B16 8TP

Tel: 0808 808 4000
Fax: 0121 410 6230
E-mail: via website: http://www .nationaldebtline.co.uk
Website: www.nationaldebtline.co.uk

Direct tel: 0121 410 6251/2

Founded: 1987

Organisation type and purpose: Voluntary organisation, registered charity (charity number 1099506).
Telephone helpline for debt.

Subject coverage: National telephone helpline for people with debt problems; covers all aspects of dealing with debt issues, e.g. repossession, magistrates court, county court and high court procedures, negotiations with creditors, bankruptcy, consumer credit, benefits and income maximisation. National Debtline can also assist callers who wish to set up a debt management plan (DMP), a debt relief order (DRO) or an individual voluntary arrangement (IVA) to deal with their debts.

Collection: Library of relevant publications to money advice work including some legislation and case reports, books and periodicals

Library catalogue: All or part available in-house

Publications: Printed
Order printed publications from: National Debtline

Publications list: Available online and in print

Access to staff: Contact by letter, by telephone, by fax, by e-mail and via website
Hours: Mon to Fri, 0900 to 2100; Sat, 0930 to 1300
Special comments: 24-hour voicemail service.

A project of: Money Advice Trust; 21 Garlick Hill, London, EC4V 2AU; website: http://www.moneyadvicetrust.org

NATIONAL DEPOSIT FRIENDLY SOCIETY LIMITED (NDFS)

4–5 Worcester Road, Clifton, Bristol, BS8 3JL

Tel: 0117 973 9003
Fax: 0117 974 1367
E-mail: enquiries@nationalfriendly.co.uk
Website: www.nationaldeposit.co.uk

Enquiries to: Information Officer

Founded: 1868

Organisation type and purpose: National organisation, service industry.
Friendly Society – provision of life assurance, investments, sickness, accident and medical insurance for members.

Access to staff: Contact by letter and by e-mail
Hours: Mon to Fri, 0900 to 1700

Access to building: Prior appointment required

NATIONAL DISABILITY ARTS FORUM (NDAF)

Website: www.ndaf.org

Enquiries to: Director

Founded: 1990

Organisation type and purpose: National organisation, membership association, registered charity.

Subject coverage: Disability arts, arts and disability.

Collection: Disability Arts Database, UK and Europe; UK Arts Access Database

Publications: Printed

Publications list: Available online

Access to staff: Contact by letter, by telephone, by fax, by e-mail and in person.
Appointment necessary.
Hours: Mon to Fri, 0900 to 1700

Access to building: No access other than to staff

Also at: National Disability Arts Forum

NATIONAL DOG TATTOO REGISTER

PO Box 5720, Harwich, Essex, CO12 3SY

Tel: 01255 552455
Fax: 01255 552412

Subject coverage: Identification of individual dogs by marking with tattoo. Register of marked dogs makes tracing of individual dogs possible.

Access to staff: Contact by letter, by telephone and by fax
Hours: Access seven days a week

NATIONAL EARLY MUSIC ASSOCIATION (NEMA)

137 Preston Road, Wembley, HA9 8NW

Tel: 020 8904 1076
Fax: 020 8723 7787
E-mail: richardbethell@btinternet.com
Website: www.nema-uk.org

Enquiries to: Administrator

Founded: 1981

Organisation type and purpose:
International organisation, membership association (membership is by subscription), present number of members: 350, voluntary organisation, registered charity (charity number 297300).

Subject coverage: Mediaeval, renaissance, baroque music; singing; dance; instrument makers; early music in education; amateur and professional music-making; societies concerned with early music and dance; promotion of conferences and workshops.

Publications: Printed

Publications list: Available online

Access to staff: Contact by letter, by

telephone, by fax and by e-mail
Hours: Mon to Fri, 0900 to 1700

NATIONAL ECZEMA SOCIETY (NES)

Hill House, Highgate Hill, London, N19 5NA

Tel: 020 7281 3553 (Business only); 0800 0891122 (Helpline)
Fax: 020 7281 6395
E-mail: helpline@eczema.org
Website: www.eczema.org

Direct tel: 0207 281 3553
Other contacts: Helpline for advice, 0800 to 2000

Founded: 1975

Organisation type and purpose: Registered charity (charity number 1009671).
To help those affected by eczema to make informed choices through information, advice and support. Campaign to raise awareness and understanding of eczema. To run continuous research programme to gather the facts about eczema and its treatment. To provide education and training to spread awareness among the medical profession and general public. Organises fundraising to support the work of the charity.

Subject coverage: Management and care of eczema; details of research into eczema treatments and advice on products suitable for people with eczema, information on complementary therapy treatments.

Publications: Printed

Publications list: Available online and in print

Access to staff: Contact by letter, by telephone, by fax, by e-mail and via website
Hours: Mon to Fri, 0800 to 2000 (helpline staff only)

Access to building: No access other than to staff

NATIONAL EDUCATIONAL VIDEO LIBRARY (NEVL)

Arfon House, Bontnewydd, Caernarfon, Gwynedd, LL54 7UN

Tel: 01286 676001
Fax: 01286 676001
E-mail: tryfannevl@aol.com

Enquiries to: Manager

Founded: 1997

Organisation type and purpose:
International organisation, professional body, suitable for ages: Key Stage 1 to 4 and Further Education.
Sale of films, video and multimedia kits; film to video transfer.

Subject coverage: Educational and training material available on history, geography, business studies, technology, sport science, biology, mathematics, home economics, arts and crafts, social studies and teacher education.

Library catalogue: All or part available in-house

Publications list: Available in print

Access to staff: Contact by letter, by telephone and by fax
Hours: Mon to Fri, 0900 to 1700

Parent body: Tryfan Audio Visual Services (TAVS); tel: 01286 676001; e-mail: tryfanav@aol.com

NATIONAL ELECTRONIC AND VIDEO ARCHIVE OF THE CRAFTS (NEVAC)

University of the West of England – Bristol, School of Creative Arts, Bower Ashton Campus, Kennel Lodge Road, off Clanage Road, Bristol, BS3 2JT

Tel: 0117 328 4746
E-mail: matthew.partington@uwe.ac.uk
Website: www.media.uwe.ac.uk/nevac

Organisation type and purpose: Aims to gather and digitise interviews with people engaged in crafts.

Subject coverage: Crafts and craftsmen.

NATIONAL ENDOMETRIOSIS SOCIETY

Suite 50, Westminster Palace Gardens, 1–7 Artillery Row, London, SW1P 1RR

Tel: 020 7222 2781
Fax: 020 7222 2786
E-mail: nes@endo.org.uk
Website: www.endo.org.uk

Enquiries to: Chief Executive
Other contacts: Office Manager

Founded: 1981

Organisation type and purpose:
Membership association (membership is by subscription), present number of members: 2600, voluntary organisation, registered charity (charity number 1035810).

Subject coverage: Endometriosis, support for sufferers.

Publications: Printed

Publications list: Available in print

Access to staff: Contact by letter, by telephone, by fax and in person
Hours: Mon to Fri, 0900 to 1700
Special comments: Helpline, some mornings, most evenings, some afternoons

NATIONAL ENERGY ACTION (NEA)

St Andrew's House, 90–92 Pilgrim Street, Newcastle upon Tyne, NE1 6SG

Tel: 0191 261 5677
Fax: 0191 261 6496
E-mail: info@nea.org.uk
Website: www.nea.org.uk

Enquiries to: Library Manager

Founded: 1981

Organisation type and purpose: Registered charity (charity number 290511).
To develop policies and practices to tackle the heating and insulation problems of low-income households through improvements in energy efficiency.

Subject coverage: Fuel poverty, energy efficiency.

Publications: Printed

Publications list: Available in print

Access to staff: Contact by letter, by telephone, by fax and by e-mail. Appointment necessary.
Hours: Mon to Thu, 0930 to 1630; Fri, 0930 to 1600

NATIONAL ENERGY FOUNDATION (NEF)

Davy Avenue, Knowlhill, Milton Keynes, Buckinghamshire, MK5 8NG

Tel: 01908 665555
E-mail: nef@natenergy.org.uk
Website: www.natenergy.org.uk
Website: www.greenergy.org.uk
Website: www.powered.org.uk
Website: www.solar-schools.org.uk

Enquiries to: Deputy Director
Other contacts: Manager, NEF Renewables for information about Renewable Energy.

Founded: 1988

Organisation type and purpose: National organisation (membership is by election or invitation), registered charity (charity number 298951).
Encouraging the sustainable use of energy.

Subject coverage: Energy efficiency, renewable energy.

Publications: Printed, and electronic and video

Access to staff: Contact by letter, by telephone, by e-mail and via website. Appointment necessary.
Hours: Mon to Fri, 0900 to 1700

Access to building: Prior appointment required

Access for disabled people: Level entry, access to all public areas, toilet facilities

NATIONAL EQUINE DEFENCE LEAGUE

Oaktree Farm, Wetheral Shields, Wetheral, Carlisle, Cumbria, CA4 8JA

Tel: 01228 560082
Fax: 01228 560985

Enquiries to: Organising Secretary

Founded: 1909

Organisation type and purpose:
Membership association (membership is by subscription), voluntary organisation, registered charity (charity number 280700).

Subject coverage: Animal welfare matters.

Publications: Printed

Publications list: Available in print

Access to staff: Contact by letter, by telephone, by fax and in person
Hours: Mon to Sat, 0930 to 1730

Access for disabled people: Parking provided, ramped entry, toilet facilities

NATIONAL EXAMINATION BOARD IN OCCUPATIONAL SAFETY AND HEALTH (NEBOSH)

Dominus Way, Meridian Business Park, Leicester, LE19 1QW

Tel: 0116 263 4700
Fax: 0116 282 4000
E-mail: info@nebosh.org.uk
Website: www.nebosh.org.uk

Enquiries to: Information Officer

Founded: 1979

Organisation type and purpose:
Examination board.

Subject coverage: The NEBOSH National General Certificate in Occupational Health and Safety.
The NEBOSH National Diploma in Occupational Health and Safety.
The NEBOSH Specialist Diploma in Environmental Management.
The NEBOSH National Certificate in Construction Safety and Health.
The NEBOSH International General Certificate in Occupational Safety and Health.
The NEBOSH Certificate in Fire Safety and Risk Management.

Publications: Printed

Publications list: Available online and in print

Access to staff: Contact by letter, by telephone, by fax, by e-mail and via website
Hours: Mon to Fri, 0900 to 1700

Access for disabled people: Parking provided, level entry, toilet facilities

NATIONAL EXHIBITORS ASSOCIATION (NEA)

29A Market Square, Biggleswade, Bedfordshire, SG18 8AQ

Tel: 01767 312986
E-mail: peter.cotterell@eou.org.uk
Website: www.seoevent.co.uk

Enquiries to: Information Officer

Founded: 1988

Organisation type and purpose: Trade association.

Access to staff: Contact by letter, by telephone and by fax
Hours: Mon to Fri, 0900 to 1700

NATIONAL EXTENSION COLLEGE (NEC)

Formal name: Open Schools Trust t/a National Extension College

The Michael Young Centre, Purbeck Road, Cambridge, CB2 2HN

Tel: 01223 400200
Fax: 01223 400399
E-mail: info@nec.ac.uk
Website: www.nec.ac.uk
Website: www.nec.ac.uk/resources

Enquiries to: Customer Relations Manager
Direct tel: 0800 389 2839
Direct fax: 01223 400321
Other contacts: Customer Relations Adviser

Founded: 1963; began trading as national extension college Open Schools Trust (year of change 2011)

Organisation type and purpose: Registered charity (charity number 1113456), suitable for ages: all.
Providers of open and distance learning materials.

Subject coverage: Open learning resources for the following areas; A level, GCSE, IGCSE, language and communications skills, learning and study skills, numeracy and literacy skills, IT user skills, foreign language skills, NVQs in accounting and administration, marketing, vocational and professional skills, training, IT and office skills, small business development, voluntary work, care and childcare NVQs, caring and health, counselling and guidance, staff development, resource development, leisure and general interest.
Home Study courses in the following areas: GCSE, IGCSE and A level, book-keeping and accounting, management and professional skills, personal development, business skills, office skills, childcare and early years.

Publications: Printed, and electronic and video

Publications list: Available online and in print

Access to staff: Contact by letter, by telephone, by fax, by e-mail, in person and via website. Appointment necessary.
Hours: Mon to Fri, 0900 to 1700

Access to building: No access other than to staff

Access for disabled people: Parking provided, toilet facilities

Trades as part of: Open Schools Trust

NATIONAL EYE RESEARCH CENTRE (NERC)

Bristol Eye Hospital, Lower Maudlin Street, Bristol, BS1 2LX

Tel: 0117 929 0024
Fax: 0117 925 1421
E-mail: nerc-charity@bris.ac.uk
Website: www.nerc.co.uk

Enquiries to: Director

Founded: 1986

Organisation type and purpose: Registered charity (charity number 294087), research organisation.
Research into eye diseases and eye disabilities, and the prevention of blindness.

Subject coverage: Research projects being funded into the causes and treatment of eye disease and disabilities of the eye, and the prevention of blindness.

Publications: Printed

Access to staff: Contact by letter, by telephone, by fax and by e-mail. Appointment necessary.
Hours: Mon to Fri, 0900 to 1700

Other addresses: National Eye Research Centre (Yorkshire) (NERC(Y)); Eye Department, Leeds General Infirmary, Leeds, LS2 9NS; tel: 0113 292 2837; fax: 0113 292 2837; e-mail: nercy.lgi@leedsth.nhs.uk

Subsidiary body: Corneal Support Group; Rotary Eye Bank Campaign

NATIONAL FAMILY MEDIATION (NFM)

4 Barnfield Hill, Exeter, Devon, EX1 1SR

Tel: 01392 271610
Fax: 01392 271945
E-mail: general@nfm.org.uk
Website: www.nfm.org.uk

Enquiries to: Administrator
Direct fax: 020 7838 5994
Other contacts: Communications Manager (for press enquiries)

Founded: 1991

Organisation type and purpose: Registered charity (charity number 1074796).
A service with over 50 branches throughout the United Kingdom.

Subject coverage: Provision of assistance to separating or divorcing parents in making joint decisions regarding children, finance and property, family mediation, separation and divorce.

Publications: Printed

Access to staff: Contact by letter, by telephone, by e-mail and via website
Hours: Mon to Fri, 0900 to 1630

Branches: African-Caribbean Family Mediation Service (Lambeth, Lewisham, Wandsworth, Southwark); 2–4 St John's Crescent, Brixton, London, SW9 7LZ; tel: 020 7737 2366; fax: 020 7733 0637; e-mail: donna@acfms.org; Berkshire FMS (Reading, Newbury and Wokingham); Third Floor, 160–163 Friar Street, Reading, RG1 1HE; tel: 0118 957 1159; fax: 0118 958 4755; e-mail: roger@berksfm.fsnet.co.uk; Birmingham and District FMS (Birmingham, Solihull, Walsall); First Floor, Coleridge Chambers, 177 Corporation Street, Birmingham, B4 6RG; tel: 0121 233 1999; fax: 0121 233 3399; e-mail: bdfm@netcomuk.co.uk; Boys and Girls Welfare Society Mediation Services (Cheshire); Goss Chambers, Goss Street, Chester, CH1 2BG; tel: 01244 400658; fax: 01244 343751; e-mail: cms.bgws@virgin.net; Bristol FMS (Avon and South Gloucestershire); 25 Hobbs Lane, Bristol, BS1 5ED; tel: 0117 929 2002; fax: 0117 929 9312; e-mail: mediation@bfmbristol.co.uk; Cambridge and District FMS (Cambridge, Huntingdon and surrounding areas); Essex House, 71 Regent Street, Cambridge, CB2 1AB; tel: 01223 576308; fax: 01223 576309; e-mail: contact@cfadc.freeserve.co.uk; Central Middlesex Family Mediation (Harrow, Ealing, Hillingdon, Brent); Civic Centre Complex, Station Road, Harrow, London, HA1 2HX; tel: 020 8427 2076; fax: 020 8861 3471; e-mail: familymediation@ukf .net; Chiltern FMS (Amersham, Watford, Aylesbury); 1 King George V Road, Amersham, Buckinghamshire, HP6 5TT; tel: 01494 732782; fax: 01494 732782; Cleveland FMS (Cleveland and neighbouring areas); St Mary's Centre, 82–90 Corporation Road, Middlesbrough, Cleveland, TS1 2RW; tel: 01642 222967; fax: 01642 210782; e-mail: clevelandfms@compuserve.com; Coventry and Warwickshire FMS; Suite 11, Koco Building, The Arches, Spon End, Coventry, CV1 3QJ; tel: 024 7671 7109; fax: 024 7671 7119; e-mail: cw.fms@virgin.net; Cumbria

FMS; Stricklandgate House, 92 Stricklandgate, Kendal, LA9 4PU; tel: 01539 733705; fax: 01539 733705; e-mail: nwcfms@mail.nch.org.uk; Derbyshire FMS; NCH Action for Children, 32a Newbold Road, Chesterfield, North Derbyshire, S41 7PH; tel: 01246 277422; fax: 01246 277363; e-mail: mddfmp@mail.nch.org.uk; Durham and Darlington Family Mediation (County Durham and Darlington); First Floor, 72–76 North Road, Durham City, DH1 4SQ; tel: 0191 386 5418; fax: 0191 386 3057; e-mail: nedadfm@mail.nch.org.uk; Exeter and District FMS (Exeter and East Devon); 49 Polsloe Road, Exeter, EX1 2DT; tel: 01392 410529; e-mail: nfmexeter@eurobell.co.uk; Eye to Eye Mediation (Inner London Probation Area); NCH Action for Children, 231 Camberwell New Road, London, SE5 0TH; tel: 020 7701 1114 or 703 2532; fax: 020 7703 6129; e-mail: inetem@mail.nch.org.uk; Family Mediation (Hull) (Kingston upon Hull, East Yorkshire, North and North-East Lincolnshire); 34 Bishop Lane, Hull, HU1 1PA; tel: 01482 329740; fax: 01482 323991; e-mail: dorothy@familymediation.karoo.uk; Family Mediation (North Wiltshire) (West and North Wiltshire, parts of Berkshire, Gloucestershire, Oxon); 34 Milton Road, Swindon, Wiltshire, SN1 5JA; tel: 01793 527285; fax: 01793 420532; e-mail: admin@familymediation.fsnet.co.uk; Family Mediation Centre (Greater Manchester); 21 Knowsley Street, Bury, Lancashire, BL9 0ST; tel: 0161 797 9910; fax: 0161 763 9311; e-mail: nwfmsgm@mail.nch.org.uk; Family Mediation Service (North West Yorkshire) (Harrogate, Craven and Richmondshire, Hambleton); 13 Dragon Parade, Harrogate, North Yorkshire, HG1 5BZ; tel: 01423 525156; fax: 01423 520983; e-mail: fmsnwy@lineonline.net; Family Mediation Service (Northumberland and Tyneside FMS) (Newcastle, Gateshead, North Tyneside, Northumberland); NCH, MEA House, Ellison Place, Newcastle upon Tyne, NE1 8XS; tel: 0191 261 9212; fax: 0191 233 0634; e-mail: nenatfms@mail.nch.org.uk; Family Mediation Service Cardiff; 42 Cardiff Street, Cardiff, CF10 2GE; tel: 029 2022 9692; fax: 029 2039 9505; Gloucestershire Family Mediation; PO Box 95, Gloucester, GL1 3YG; tel: 01452 411843; fax: 01452 418441; e-mail: gfm@mediation.fsbusiness.co.uk; Gwent Mediation Service; NCH, 66 Lower Dock Street, Newport, NP20 1EF; tel: 01633 263 065; fax: 01633 222743; e-mail: wagms@mail.nch.org.uk; Hampshire FMS (Hampshire and Isle of Wight); 58d High Street, Cosham, Portsmouth, PO6 3AG; tel: 023 9243 3388; fax: 023 9243 3358; e-mail: admin@hantsmed.org.uk; Herefordshire FMS (Herefordshire and surrounding area); Second Floor, Berrows Business Centre, Hereford, HR1 2HE; tel: 01432 264087/277996; fax: 01432 351993; e-mail: herefordshire@familymediation.fslife.co.uk; Hertfordshire and Essex FMS (West Essex and parts of Hertfordshire); Sewell House, 349 The Hides, Harlow, Essex, CM20 3QY; tel: 01279 426749; fax: 01279 426749; e-mail: hefms@dial.pipex.com; Hertfordshire FMS; 62–72 Victoria Street, St Albans, Hertfordshire, AL1 3XH; tel: 01727 839300; fax: 01727 839123; e-mail: admin@hertsfms.fsnet.co.uk; Jersey Family Mediation; 2 Charles House, Charles Street, St Helier, Jersey, JE2 4SF; tel: 01534 734980; fax: 01534 619945; e-mail: relate.jersey@jerseymail.co.uk; Kent FMS; 6 Park Road, Sittingbourne, Kent, ME10 1DR; tel: 01795 429689; fax: 01795 476949; e-mail: familymediation.kent@virgin.net; Lancashire FMS; 19 Ribblesdale Place, Preston, Lancashire, PR1 3NA; tel: 01772 204248; fax: 01772 204246; e-mail: mediation@lfms.net; Lincolnshire FMS; Claxlete House, 62 Clasketgate, Lincoln, LN2 1JZ; tel: 01522 575700; fax: 01522 575700; e-mail: lfms@lincs-ln2.freeserve.co.uk; Mediation in Divorce (South West London); 13 Rosslyn Road, East Twickenham, London, TW1 2AR; tel: 020 8891 6860; fax: 020 8891 3107; e-mail: admin@mediationindivorce.co.uk; Merseyside FMS; 5a Swiss Road, Liverpool, L6 3AT; tel: 0151 260 9155; fax: 0151 260 0548; e-mail: mediation@pss.org.uk; Milton Keynes Family Mediation (Milton Keynes, North Buckinghamshire, North Hertfordshire and Bedfordshire); City Counselling Centre, 320 Saxon Gate West, Central Milton Keynes, Buckinghamshire, MK9 2ES; tel: 01908 231293; fax: 01908 690211; e-mail: familymediationmk@talk21.com; Norfolk FMS; Charing Cross Centre, 17–19 St John Maddermarket, Norwich, Norfolk, NR2 1DL; tel: 01603 620 588; fax: 01603 620 588; e-mail: norfolk.fammed@lineone.net; North Devon FMS; The Castle Centre, Castle Street, Barnstaple, Devon, EX31 1DR; tel: 01270 321888; fax: 01271 321888; e-mail: ndfms@lineone.net; North London FMS (Barnet, Haringey, Hertsmere and Enfield); 267 Ballards Lane, Finchley, London, N12 8NR; tel: 020 8343 9899; fax: 020 8445 6603; e-mail: nlmed@email.com; North Staffordshire FMS (Stafford, Stoke and North Staffordshire); Winton House, Stoke Road, Stoke-on-Trent, Staffordshire, ST4 2RN; tel: 0845 602 0301/01782 416111; fax: 01782 416444; e-mail: nsfms@hotmail.com; Northamptonshire FMS; 49 York Road, First Floor, Northampton, NN1 5QJ; tel: 01604 636651; fax: 01604 637313; e-mail: familymediation@excite.co.uk; Northern Ireland Family Mediation Service; 76 Dublin Road, Belfast, BT2 7HP; tel: 028 9032 2914; fax: 028 9315 298; Nottinghamshire Children and Families Mediation Service (FAME); 3 Pelham Court, Pelham Road, Nottingham, NG5 1AP; tel: 0115 985 8855; fax: 0115 962 3606; e-mail: mj@famenottingham.fsbusiness.co.uk; Oxfordshire FMS; First Floor, 125 London Road, Headington, Oxford, OX3 9HZ; tel: 01865 741781; fax: 01865 744393; e-mail: oxmedserv@aol.com; Peterborough and District FMS; 61 Broadway, Peterborough, Cambridgeshire, PE1 1SY; tel: 01733 347353; fax: 01733 347353; e-mail: pfms@tinyonline.co.uk; Plymouth Mediation (Plymouth and District); St Peter's Centre, 18 Harwell Street, Plymouth, PL1 5BA; tel: 01752 312121; fax: 01752 312123; e-mail: plymed@dial.pipex.com; Salisbury and District FMS (Salisbury, South Wiltshire, North Dorset, North West Hampshire); 24b St Edmund's Church Street, Salisbury, Wiltshire, SP1 1EF; tel: 01722 332936; fax: 01722 332936; e-mail: fms@southwilts.nda.co.uk; Scarborough and District FMS; 1 Westbourne Grove, Scarborough, North Yorkshire, YO11 2DJ; tel: 01723 507775; fax: 01723 507775; e-mail: manager@sdfms.fsnet.co.uk; Shropshire Family Mediation; 65 Withywood Drive, Malinslee, Telford, Shropshire, TF3 2HU; tel: 01952 520091; fax: 01952 520092; e-mail: shropshire.mediation1@virgin.net; Somerset FMS; The Myrtle Tree, 34 Bridge Street, Taunton, Somerset, TA1 1UD; tel: 01823 352013; fax: 01823 352013; e-mail: mary@relate-somerset.org.uk; South Essex FMS; 29 Harcourt Avenue, Southend-on-Sea, Essex, SS2 6HT; tel: 01702 436466; fax: 01702 431173; e-mail: mediation.southessexrelate@virgin.net; South Staffordshire FMS (South Staffordshire, Cannock, Lichfield, Tamworth); 33 Park Road, Cannock, Staffordshire, WS11 1JN; tel: 01543 572600; fax: 01543 579390; e-mail: ssfmscannock@hotmail.com; South Yorkshire FMS; Queen's Building, 55 Queen Street, Sheffield, S1 2DX; tel: 0114 275 2227; fax: 0114 275 3996; e-mail: user@syfm.fsnet.co.uk; South-East London Family Mediation Bureau (Bexley, Bromley, Croydon and surrounding areas); 5 Upper Park Road, Bromley, Kent, BR1 3HN; tel: 020 8460 4606; fax: 020 8466 6572; e-mail: info@familymediationlondon.org.uk; Sunderland and South Tyneside FMS (Sunderland, Washington, Houghton-le-Spring, South Shields, Jarrow); 54 John Street, Sunderland, Tyne and Wear, SR1 1QH; tel: 0191 514 3849; fax: 0191 514 2481; e-mail: sastfms@aol.com; Surrey FMS; 316 High Street, Dorking, Surrey, RH4 1QX; tel: 01306 741777; fax: 01306 741383; e-mail: surreyfms@cs.com; Sussex FMS (East and West Sussex); Garton House, 22 Stanford Avenue, Brighton, East Sussex, BN1 6DD; tel: 01273 550563; fax: 01273 555412; e-mail: sxfms@supanet.com; Thames Valley FMS (South Buckinghamshire, East Berkshire, High Wycombe, Slough, Windsor and Bracknell); Windsor Magistrates Court, Side Entrance, Alma Road, Windsor, Berkshire, SL4 3HD; tel: 01753 830770; fax: 01753 830770; e-mail: thames@valleyfm.fsnet.co.uk; The FMS-Institute of Family Therapy (Central London and North West); 24–32 Stephenson Way, London, NW1 2HX; tel: 020 7391 9150; fax: 020 7391 9169; e-mail: ift@psyc.bbk.ac.uk; West Yorkshire FMS (Bradford, Wakefield, Dewsbury, Halifax, Huddersfield, Leeds); 31 Manor Road, Bradford, West Yorkshire, BD1 4PS; tel: 01274 732768 or 0845 419403; fax: 01274 730115; e-mail: wyfamilymed@netscapeonline.co.uk; Worcestershire FMS; 14 Castle Street Street, Worcester, WR1 3ZB; tel: 01905 610925; fax: 01905 619526; e-mail: worcester@familymediation.fsbusiness.co.uk; York FMS (York, Selby, parts of Ryedale and Hambleton); The Old Coach House, Grange Garth, York, YO10 4BS; tel: 01904 646068; fax: 01904 646068; e-mail: yorkfms@care4free.net

Links with: Dorset Relate; 8 Maumbury Road, Dorchester, Dorset, DT1 1QW; tel: 01305 751781; fax: 01305 751781; e-mail: general@dorsetfamilymediation.co.uk; Leicester Relate; 83 Aylestone Road, Leicester, LE2 7LL; tel: 0116 254 1149; North East London FMS (Ilford, Romford, Barking and Dagenham); Relate Office, Althorne Way, Dagenham, Essex, RM10 7AY; tel: 020 8593 6827; fax: 020 8593 8111; e-mail: nel_mediation@talk21.com; North Wales FMS (Colwyn Bay, Rhyl, Bangor); Eryl Wen, Eryl Place, Llandudno, LL30 2TX; tel: 01492 870876; fax: 01492 870846

NATIONAL FARMERS' UNION (NFU)

Agriculture House, Stoneleigh Park, Stoneleigh, Warwickshire, CV8 2TZ

Tel: 024 7685 8500
Fax: 024 7685 8501
E-mail: nfu@nfu.org.uk
Website: www.nfu.org.uk

Enquiries to: Press Officer
Direct tel: 020 7331 7295
Direct fax: 020 7331 7370
Direct e-mail: sharon.hockley@nfu.org.uk
Other contacts: Director General; President for general management; 'politics'.

Founded: 1908

Organisation type and purpose: Trade association (membership is by subscription), present number of members: 135,000.
Representing farmers and growers in England and Wales.
To provide farmers and growers with professional and technical services.

Subject coverage: Policy, economic, legal and other material relating to agriculture, horticulture, land use, agricultural trade and statistics, livestock and crop production.

Collection: British Farmer, NFU Magazine, NFU Business
NFU yearbooks since 1910

Trade and statistical information: UK Agricultural (June census) statistics from 1866.
Agricultural statistics from 1940.
Household food consumption survey from 1940

Publications: Printed

Publications list: Available online

Access to staff: Contact by letter, by telephone, by fax and by e-mail.
Appointment necessary. Non-members charged.
Hours: Archives held in out-of-town store, 48 hours notice needed for retrieval

Access to building: No access other than to staff

Affiliated to: CBI; European Federation of Farmers' Organisations (COPA); International Chamber of Commerce (ICC); International Federation of Agricultural Producers (IFPA)

Has: 8 regional offices, HQ outstations and approximately 400 local branches

NATIONAL FEDERATION OF 18 PLUS GROUPS OF GB (18 PLUS)

8–10 Church Street Chamber, Church Street, Newent, Gloucestershire, GL18 1PP

Tel: 01531 821210
Fax: 01531 821474
E-mail: office@18plus.org.uk
Website: www.18plus.org.uk

Enquiries to: Administrator
Other contacts: Honorary General Secretary

Founded: 1941

Organisation type and purpose:
Membership association (membership is by subscription), present number of members: 1,200, voluntary organisation, suitable for ages: 18 to 35, training organisation.
A social activities organisation for young adults wishing to make friends and take part in a wide range of activities.

Subject coverage: Social group, personal development training and a variety of activities.

Publications: Printed

Access to staff: Contact by letter, by telephone, by fax, by e-mail and via website
Hours: 24-hour answerphone

NATIONAL FEDERATION OF ANGLERS (NFA)

Halliday House, Egginton Junction, Hilton, Derbyshire, DE65 6GU

Tel: 01283 734735
Fax: 01283 734799
E-mail: office@nfahq.freeserve.co.uk

Enquiries to: Administration Manager

Founded: 1903

Organisation type and purpose: Voluntary organisation.
Governing body of coarse angling.

Subject coverage: Fisheries and fishing; coarse fishing; problems of pollution, water abstraction and land drainage, fishery protection; research; competitions, sponsored events.

Publications: Printed

Access to staff: Contact by letter and by e-mail
Hours: Mon to Fri, 0900 to 1700

Member of: Confédération Internationale de la Pêche Sportive (CIPS)

NATIONAL FEDERATION OF BUILDERS (NFB)

B&CC Building Manor Royal, Crawley, West Sussex, RH10 9QP

Tel: 08450 578160
Fax: 08450 578161
E-mail: marketing@builders.org.uk
Website: builders.org.uk/

Direct e-mail: paul.smith@citypress.co.uk

Organisation type and purpose: Trade association.

Subject coverage: Building companies, SMEs.

NATIONAL FEDERATION OF DEMOLITION CONTRACTORS LIMITED (NFDC LTD)

Resurgam House, 1a New Road, The Causeway, Staines, Middlesex, TW18 3DH

Tel: 01784 456799
Fax: 01784 461118
E-mail: info@demolition-nfdc.com
Website: www.demolition-nfdc.com

Enquiries to: National Secretary
Direct e-mail: howard@demolition-nfdc.com

Founded: 1941

Organisation type and purpose: Trade association.

Subject coverage: General demolition, demolition of mass and reinforced concrete structures, chimney demolition, dangerous structures, machinery dismantling, shoring, site clearance and excavation, demolition by licensed explosives engineers, asbestos stripping and disposal, thermic boring, plant hire, supplies of hardcore, sale of reclaimed building materials.

Publications: Printed, and electronic and video

Access to staff: Contact by letter, by telephone, by fax, by e-mail and via website.
Appointment necessary.
Hours: Mon to Fri, 0900 to 1700

Access for disabled people: Parking provided

Founder member of: European Demolition Association; tel: + 31 30 259 8330; fax: + 31 30 259 8600; e-mail: eda@eda-demolition.com

NATIONAL FEDERATION OF FISH FRIERS LIMITED (NFFF)

New Federation House, 4 Greenwood Mount, Meanwood, Leeds, West Yorkshire, LS6 4LQ

Tel: 0113 230 7044
Fax: 0113 230 7010
E-mail: mail@federationoffishfriers.co.uk
Website: www.federationoffishfriers.co.uk

Enquiries to: General Secretary
Direct tel: 0113 230 7009
Direct e-mail: denise.dodd@federationoffishfriers.co.uk

Founded: 1913

Organisation type and purpose: Trade association, training provider, industry standards scheme provider.
Looks after the interests of fish friers throughout the United Kingdom.

Subject coverage: Covers interests of the members of the fish frying trade; fish, potatoes and other cooking ingredients, frying and refrigeration equipment, health and safety issues.

Publications: Printed

Access to staff: Contact by letter, by telephone, by fax, by e-mail and via website.
Appointment necessary.
Hours: Mon to Fri, 0900 to 1700

NATIONAL FEDERATION OF MEAT AND FOOD TRADERS, THE (NFMFT)

1 Belgrove, Tunbridge Wells, Kent, TN1 1YW

Tel: 01892 541412
Fax: 01892 535462
E-mail: info@nfmft.co.uk

Enquiries to: Chief Executive

Founded: 1888

Organisation type and purpose: Trade association.

Subject coverage: Represents the interests of member independent retail butchers in England and Wales.

Publications: Printed

Access to staff: Contact by letter, by telephone, by fax and by e-mail. Appointment necessary. Access for members only. Letter of introduction required.
Hours: Mon to Fri, 0900 to 1715

NATIONAL FEDERATION OF ROOFING CONTRACTORS LIMITED (NFRC)

24 Weymouth Street, London, W1G 7LX

Tel: 020 7436 0387
Fax: 020 7637 5215
E-mail: info@nfrc.co.uk
Website: www.nfrc.co.uk

Enquiries to: Secretary
Other contacts: (1) Membership Secretary (2) Public Relations Executive for media, publications information.

Founded: 1893

Organisation type and purpose: Trade association.

Subject coverage: Technical roofing information, insurance schemes, education and training in roofing, product and application standards, health and safety.

Publications: Printed, and electronic and video

Publications list: Available online and in print

Access to staff: Contact by letter, by telephone, by fax, by e-mail and via website. Appointment necessary.
Hours: Mon to Fri, 0900 to 1700

Member of: National Specialist Contractors Council (NSCC); Carthusian Court, 12 Carthusian Street, London, EC1M 6EZ; tel: 0870 429 6351; fax: 0870 429 6352

NATIONAL FEDERATION OF SUBPOSTMASTERS (NFSP)

Evelyn House, 22 Windlesham Gardens, Shoreham-by-Sea, West Sussex, BN43 5AZ

Tel: 01273 452324
Fax: 01273 465403
E-mail: admin@nfsp.org.uk
Website: www.subpostmasters.org.uk

Enquiries to: Information Officer

Founded: 1897

Organisation type and purpose: National organisation, trade association, trade union (membership is by subscription), present number of members: 14,000.
Certificated independent trade union recognised by The Post Office to represent subpostmasters.

Subject coverage: Post office management.

Access to staff: Contact by letter and by telephone
Hours: Mon to Fri, 0900 to 1700

Access to building: No access other than to staff

NATIONAL FEDERATION OF TERRAZZO MARBLE & MOSAIC SPECIALISTS (NFTMMS)

PO Box 2843, London, W1A 5PG

Tel: 0845 609 0050
Fax: 0845 607 8610
E-mail: dslade@nftmms.org
Website: www.nftmms.org

Enquiries to: Secretary

Founded: 1933

Organisation type and purpose: Trade association (membership is by election or invitation), present number of members: 40.

Subject coverage: Technical advice on the laying of terrazzo, mosaic and marble; granite; limestone; investigation of complaints; inspection and reports on work, application etc.

Publications: Printed

Access to staff: Contact by letter, by telephone, by fax and by e-mail
Hours: Mon to Fri, 0900 to 1700

NATIONAL FEDERATION OF THE BLIND OF THE UNITED KINGDOM (NFBUK)

Sir John Wilson House, 215 Kirkgate, Wakefield, West Yorkshire, WF1 1JG

Tel: 01924 291313
Fax: 01924 200244
E-mail: nfbuk@nfbuk.org
Website: www.nfbuk.org

Enquiries to: Honorary General Secretary
Other contacts: Public Relations Officer for information.

Founded: 1947

Organisation type and purpose: Membership association (membership is by subscription), present number of members: 2000, registered charity, voluntary organisation (charity number 236629). Campaigning organisation.

Subject coverage: The real needs of the blind and partially-sighted from their perspective e.g. a safer environment, obstructions in pavements, and the particular needs of the deafblind.

Publications: Printed, and electronic and video

Publications list: Available in print

Access to staff: Contact by letter, by telephone, by fax and by e-mail
Hours: Mon, Tue, Thu, Fri, 0900 to 1600; Wed, closed

NATIONAL FEDERATION OF WOMEN'S INSTITUTES (NFWI)

104 New Kings Road, Fulham, London, SW6 4LY

Tel: 020 7371 9300
Fax: 020 7736 3652
E-mail: gensec@nfwi.org.uk
Website: www.thewi.org.uk

Enquiries to: General Secretary

Founded: 1915

Organisation type and purpose: Membership association (membership is by subscription), present number of members: 205,000, voluntary organisation, registered charity.

Subject coverage: Rural affairs, current and public affairs, particularly on environment and issues of concern to women, health, social welfare, employment, standards of life, home economics, music and drama, education, crafts, sport.

Collection: The Women's Library, Old Castle Street, London E1

Publications: Printed

Publications list: Available in print

Access to staff: Contact by letter, by telephone, by fax, by e-mail and via website
Hours: Mon to Fri, 0900 to 1700

Access for disabled people: None

Also at: Denman College; Marcham, Abingdon, Oxfordshire, OX13 6NW; tel: 01865 391991; fax: 01865 391966; e-mail: info@denman.org.uk; NFWI Wales Office (NFWI); 19–21 Cathedral Road, Cardiff, CF1 9LJ; tel: 02920 221712; fax: 02920 387236

NATIONAL FEDERATION OF WOMEN'S INSTITUTES – WALES (NFWI–Wales)

19 Cathedral Road, Cardiff, CF11 9HA

Tel: 029 2022 1712
E-mail: walesoffice@nfwi-wales.org.uk
Website: www.thewi.org.uk

Enquiries to: Head of Wales Office
Other contacts: Administrative/Public Affairs Officer (for preliminary enquiries)

Founded: 1915

Organisation type and purpose: Membership association (membership is by subscription), present number of members: 20,000, voluntary organisation, registered charity (charity number 803793), suitable for ages: 16+.
The National Federation of Women's Institutes offers opportunities for all women to enjoy friendship, to learn, to widen their horizons, and together to influence local, national and international affairs.

Non-library collection catalogue: All or part available online

Publications list: Available in print

Access to staff: Contact by letter, by telephone, by e-mail and via website
Hours: Mon to Fri, 0900 to 1700

Branches: 13 Federation offices throughout Wales

NATIONAL FILM AND TELEVISION SCHOOL (NFTS)

Beaconsfield Studios, Station Road, Beaconsfield, Buckinghamshire, HP9 1LG

Tel: 01494 671234
Fax: 01494 674042
E-mail: info@nfts.co.uk
Website: www.nfts.co.uk

Enquiries to: Registrar
Direct tel: 01494 731425

Founded: 1971; formerly called National Film School (year of change 1982)

Organisation type and purpose: National organisation, suitable for ages: postgraduate, training organisation.

continued overleaf

Subject coverage: Information about MA and Diploma courses in directing (animation, documentary or fiction), cinematography, composing for film and television, digital post-production, editing, producing, producing and directing television entertainment, production design, production management, screenwriting, script development, SFX/VFX, sound design, sound recording

Publications: Electronic and video

Access to staff: Contact by letter, by telephone, by fax, by e-mail, in person and via website. Appointment necessary.
Hours: Mon to Fri, 0930 to 1730

Access for disabled people: Parking provided, level entry, toilet facilities
Hours: During NFTS opening hours
Special comments: Most areas accessible. Special arrangements can be made for individual requirements, preferably give advance notice

Links with: ShortCourses@NFTS; at Beaconsfield Studios; tel: 01494 677903; fax: 01494 678708; e-mail: shortcourses@nfts.co.uk; website: http://www.nfts.co.uk

NATIONAL FILM BOARD OF CANADA (NFB)

Canada House, Trafalgar Square, London, SW1Y 5BJ

Tel: 020 7258 6480
Fax: 020 7258 6532
E-mail: london@nfb.ca
Website: www.nfb.ca

Enquiries to: Sales Representative
Direct tel: 020 7258 6482
Direct e-mail: s.swan@nfb.ca

Founded: 1939

Organisation type and purpose: Film production and distribution.

Subject coverage: Film and video production and distribution.

Collection: Collection of 17,000 titles, mainly documentaries and animation (includes educational programmes)

Publications: Printed, and electronic and video

Access to staff: Contact by letter, by telephone, by fax, by e-mail and via website
Hours: Mon to Fri, 1000 to 1800

NATIONAL FILM THEATRE (NFT)

South Bank Centre, Belvedere Road, Waterloo, London, SE1 8XT

Tel: 020 7928 3535
Fax: 020 7815 1419
E-mail: nft@bfi.org.uk
Website: www.bfi.org.uk/nft50
Website: www.bfi.org.uk/nft

Enquiries to: Press and Marketing Department

Founded: 1952

Organisation type and purpose: Cinema.

Subject coverage: Film and video information related to its own screening.

Publications: Printed, and electronic and video

Access to staff: Contact by letter, by telephone, by fax, by e-mail and via website
Hours: Mon to Fri, 1000 to 1800

Access for disabled people: Parking provided, level entry, toilet facilities

Parent body: British Film Institute; 21 Stephen Street, London, W1P 1PL

NATIONAL FOREST COMPANY

Enterprise Glade, Bath Yard, Bath Lane, Swadlincote, Derbyshire, DE12 6BD

Tel: 01283 551211
Fax: 01283 552844
E-mail: enquiries@nationalforest.org
Website: www.nationalforest.org

Founded: 1995

Organisation type and purpose: Government-funded company.
Creating a new multi-purpose forest in the Midlands (Leicestershire, Derbyshire, Staffordshire).

Subject coverage: Grants for woodland creation, forestry investment and sponsorship opportunities in the National Forest.

Publications: Printed

Publications list: Available online and in print

Access to staff: Contact by letter and by e-mail
Hours: Mon to Fri, 0900 to 1700

NATIONAL FOUNDATION FOR EDUCATIONAL RESEARCH

Chestnut House, Tawe Business Village, Phoenix Way, Enterprise Park, Llansamlet, Swansea, West Glamorgan, SA7 9LA

Tel: 01792 459800
Fax: 01792 797815
E-mail: scya@nfer.ac.uk
Website: www.nfer.ac.uk

Enquiries to: Information Officer
Other contacts: Head of NFER Welsh Unit

Founded: 1946

Organisation type and purpose: Registered charity (charity number 313392), suitable for ages: 3 to 100, research organisation.
Education research – independent charity. NFER conducts independent and objective research through external sponsors and customers. Through its own resources conducts evaluations and surveys and develops tests and assessment materials. NFER Welsh unit at Swansea also specialises in Welsh language research.

Subject coverage: Education and training.

Access to staff: Contact by letter, by telephone and by fax
Hours: Mon to Fri, 0900 to 1700

Access for disabled people: Parking provided

Main office: National Foundation for Educational Research (NFER); The Mere, Upton Park, Slough, SL1 2DQ; tel: 01753 574123

NATIONAL FOX WELFARE SOCIETY (NFWS)

135 Higham Road, Rushden, Northamptonshire, NN10 6DS

Tel: 01933 411996
Fax: 01933 397324
E-mail: natfox@ntlworld.com
Website: www.nfws.org.uk/
Website: www.mange.org.uk

Enquiries to: Any Co-ordinator

Founded: 1993

Organisation type and purpose: National organisation, membership association (membership is by subscription), voluntary organisation.
Animal welfare society providing advice and practical assistance on all fox-related issues.

Subject coverage: All fox-related subjects, behaviour, rescue, advice, help with treatment for injuries and/or mange.

Publications: Printed

Publications list: Available in print

Access to staff: Contact by letter, by telephone, by e-mail and via website
Hours: Mon to Fri, 1000 to 1800
Special comments: 24 hours, 365 days a year for emergencies.

Access to building: No access other than to staff

NATIONAL GALLERIES OF SCOTLAND

Press and Information Department, Dean Gallery Lodge, Belford Road, Edinburgh, EH4 3DS

Tel: 0131 624 6200
Fax: 0131 343 3250
Website: www.nationalgalleries.org

Enquiries to: Press and Information Assistant
Direct tel: 0131 624 6332
Direct e-mail: pressinfo@nationalgalleries.org

Founded: 1859

Organisation type and purpose: Art gallery.

Subject coverage: Provision of information on the National Gallery of Scotland, Scottish National Gallery of Modern Art, Scottish National Portrait Gallery and Dean Gallery.

Order printed publications from: Publications Department, National Galleries of Scotland, Dean Gallery, Belford Road, Edinburgh, EH4 3DS, tel: 0131 624 6256/6259/6261, fax: 0131 315 2963, e-mail: publications@nationalgalleries.org

Publications list: Available online and in print

Access to staff: Contact by letter, by telephone and by e-mail
Hours: Mon to Sun, 1000 to 1700

Access to building: No prior appointment required
Hours: Mon to Sun, 1000 to 1700

Access for disabled people: Access to all public areas, toilet facilities

Also at: Duff House; Banff, Banffshire, AB45 2SX; tel: 01261 818181; fax: 01261 818181; e-mail: duff.house@aberdeenshire.gov.uk; website: http://www.duffhouse.com
National Gallery of Scotland; The Mound, Edinburgh, EH2 2EL; tel: 0131 624 6200; fax: 0131 220 0917; e-mail: nginfo@nationalgalleries.org; website: http://www.nationalgalleries.org
Paxton House; Berwick-upon-Tweed, Berwickshire, TD15 1SZ; tel: 01289 386291; fax: 01289 386660; e-mail: info@paxtonhouse.com; website: http://www.paxtonhouse.co.uk
Scottish National Gallery of Modern Art; 75 Belford Road, Edinburgh, EH4 3DR; tel: 0131 624 6200; fax: 0131 343 2802; e-mail: gmainfo@nationalgalleries.org; website: http://www.nationalgalleries.org
Scottish National Portrait Gallery; 1 Queen Street, Edinburgh, EH2 1JD; tel: 0131 624 6200; fax: 0131 558 3691; e-mail: pginfo@nationalgalleries.org; website: http://www.nationalgalleries.org
The Dean Gallery; 73 Belford Road, Edinburgh, EH4 3DS; tel: 0131 624 6200; fax: 0131 343 2802; e-mail: deaninfo@nationalgalleries.org; website: http://www.nationalgalleries.org

NATIONAL GALLERY

Technical Library, Scientific Department, Trafalgar Square, London, WC2N 5DN

Tel: 020 7747 2400 ext. 2829
Fax: 020 7839 3897
Website: www.nationalgallery.org.uk

Enquiries to: Technical Librarian
Direct tel: 020 7747 2829

Founded: 1950

Organisation type and purpose: National government body, museum, art gallery, research organisation.
Art museum departmental library. Non-Governmental Departmental Body.

Subject coverage: Materials, techniques and history of painting, particularly of European easel painting from c. 1300 to 1900, scientific examination of works of art, climate control for works of art, safe exhibition and storage conditions.

Collection: Eastlake Collection of early books and manuscripts on materials and techniques of painting, and other arts and crafts (part)

Publications: Printed
Order printed publications from: National Gallery Company Limited
St Vincent House, 30 Orange Street, London, WC2H 7HH, tel: 020 7281 9080

Publications list: Available online and in print

Access to staff: Contact by letter, by telephone and by fax
Hours: Mon to Fri, 0930 to 1730
Special comments: No enquiries in person.

Access to building: National Gallery hours, daily, 1000 to 1800 except Wed, 1000 to 2100

Access for disabled people: Lift
Hours: Mon to Fri, 1000 to 1730

NATIONAL GAS ARCHIVE, THE

Unit 1, Europa Court, Europa Boulevard, Warrington, WA5 7TN

Tel: 01925 425740
Fax: 01925 425748
E-mail: archive@uk.ngrid.com
Website: www.gasarchive.org

Enquiries to: Archivist

Founded: 1995

Organisation type and purpose: National organisation.

Subject coverage: Gas history, technical and engineering history, chemical industry.

Non-library collection catalogue: All or part available online, in-house and in print

Library catalogue: All or part available in-house

Access to staff: Contact by letter, by telephone, by fax, by e-mail and via website. Appointment necessary.
Hours: Mon to Fri, 0900 to 1700

Access to building: Prior appointment required

Access for disabled people: Parking provided, level entry, toilet facilities

Connections with: National Grid

NATIONAL GERBIL SOCIETY (NGS)

373 Lynmouth Avenue, Morden, Surrey, SM4 4RY

Tel: 020 8241 8942
Fax: 0870 1600 845
E-mail: jackie@gerbils.co.uk
Website: www.gerbils.co.uk

Enquiries to: Honorary Secretary

Founded: 1970

Organisation type and purpose: National organisation, membership association (membership is by subscription), present number of members: 80, suitable for ages: all.
To promote the keeping of gerbils and jirds as exhibition animals and as pets, and to promote education about gerbils and how to keep them.

Subject coverage: Information on the keeping and healthcare etc of all species of gerbils and jirds.

Publications: Printed

Access to staff: Contact by letter, by telephone and by e-mail
Hours: Telephone only, Mon to Fri, 1800 to 2200

NATIONAL GOVERNORS' ASSOCIATION (NGA)

36 Great Charles Street, Birmingham B3 3JY

Tel: 0121 237 3780
Fax: 0121 233 1323
E-mail: governorhq@nga.org.uk
Website: www.nga.org.uk

Enquiries to: Administrator

Founded: 2006; created by the merger of the National Governors' Council (NGC) and the National Association of School Governors (NASG)

Organisation type and purpose: National organisation, membership association (membership is by qualification), voluntary organisation, registered charity (charity number 1070331), suitable for ages: nursery to 18.
The national voice for school governing bodies, members are local associations of governing bodies.
Promoting the education and welfare of children and the high standards of schools through the effectiveness of governing bodies.

Subject coverage: Matters relating to school governance.

Publications: Printed

Access to staff: Contact by letter, by telephone, by fax, by e-mail and via website
Hours: Mon to Fri, 0900 to 1700

NATIONAL HAIRDRESSERS' FEDERATION (NHF)

One Abbey Court, Fraser Road, Priory Business Park, Bedford, MK44 3WH

Tel: 0845 345 6500
Fax: 01234 838875
E-mail: enquiries@nhf.info

Enquiries to: General Secretary

Founded: 1942

Organisation type and purpose: National organisation, trade association (membership is by subscription), present number of members: 7,500, service industry.
Seeks to advance, defend, promote, protect and represent the interests of hairdressing salon owners in every possible way.

Subject coverage: Matters affecting hairdressers' employment, independent contractors in salons, management of hairdressing business.

Publications: Printed

Access to staff: Contact by letter, by telephone, by fax and by e-mail.
Appointment necessary.
Hours: Mon to Fri, 0900 to 1700

Access to building: No access other than to staff

Affiliated to: Coiffure Europe; Godierserf 400 Huizen, PO Box 212, Huizen, 1270 AE Huizen, The Netherlands; tel: 00 31 35 525 9200; fax: 00 31 35 526 3786; Organisation Mondiale de la Coiffure; 1–3 Place de la Bourse, F75082, Paris, Cedex 02, France; tel: 00 33 1 42 61 59 09; fax: 00 33 1 42 61 66 83; e-mail: omcoif@wanadoo.fr

NATIONAL HAMSTER COUNCIL (NHC)

PO Box 4, Llandovery, SA20 0ZH

Tel: 01550 720127
E-mail: peter@towyvale.com
Website: www.hamsters-uk.org

Enquiries to: Secretary
Direct tel: 01793 764450
Direct e-mail: rosiehams@yahoo.co.uk

continued overleaf

Founded: 1949

Organisation type and purpose: Membership association.
Governing body of the hamster fancy in the UK.
Represents the interests of all concerned with the keeping, exhibiting and/or breeding of all species of hamsters.

Subject coverage: Hamsters.

Access to staff: Contact by letter, by telephone, by e-mail and via website
Hours: Mon to Fri, 0900 to 1700

NATIONAL HEART FORUM (NHF)

Victoria House, 7th Floor, Southampton Row, London, WC1B 4AD

Tel: 020 7831 7420
Fax: 020 3077 5964
E-mail: nhf-post@heartforum.org.uk
Website: www.heartforum.org.uk

Enquiries to: Administrative Co-ordinator
Direct e-mail: dan.french@heartforum.org.uk
Other contacts: Deputy Chief Executive (for press, media, general)

Founded: 1989; formerly called National Forum for the Prevention of Coronary Heart Disease

Organisation type and purpose: Membership association (membership is by election or invitation), present number of members: 50 organisations, registered charity (charity number 803286).

Subject coverage: Influencing the prevention of heart disease and associated chronic diseases

Information services: Free weekly e-news briefing service by subscription; e-mail: briefings@heartforum.org.uk

Publications: Printed
Order printed publications from: Enquire at NHF office for availability

Publications list: Available online and in print

Access to staff: Contact by letter, by telephone, by fax, by e-mail and via website. Appointment necessary.
Hours: Mon to Fri, 0900 to 1730

Access to building: Appointment required

NATIONAL HERITAGE LIBRARY

313–315 Caledonian Road, London, N1 1DR

Tel: 020 7609 9639
E-mail: marg_mcniel@o2.co.uk

Enquiries to: Director

Founded: 1971

Organisation type and purpose: Membership association (membership is by subscription), suitable for ages: all.
A vast, comprehensive educational reference collection covering every aspect of what there is to see throughout the landscape and culture of the British Isles.

Subject coverage: Everything there is to see throughout the landscape and culture of the British Isles: every kind of arts, cultural, environmental, historical and sporting site. Every facet of past and present social history, including: education, social welfare, public buildings, commerce, transport and travel, industry both past and present, alternative technology, religions, farming, historical buildings.

Collection: Books and maps, and extensive fieldwork research and photographic recording by the Founder-Director since the 1960s including over 250,000 photographs in colour, recording a vast range of sites, including many unique photographs of buildings important in their country's social history that have since been demolished

Non-library collection catalogue: All or part available in-house

Library catalogue: All or part available in-house

Publications: Printed

Access to staff: Contact by letter and by e-mail. Appointment necessary.
Hours: Open by prior appointment

Access to building: Prior appointment required

Access for disabled people: Parking provided, level entry

NATIONAL HERITAGE MEMORIAL FUND (NHMF)

7 Holbein Place, London, SW1W 8NR

Tel: 020 7591 6000
Fax: 020 7591 6001
E-mail: enquire@hlf.org.uk
Website: www.hlf.org.uk

Enquiries to: Information Officer
Direct tel: 020 7591 6042/3/5

Founded: 1980

Organisation type and purpose: Non-departmental public body.

Publications: Printed

Publications list: Available online and in print

Access to staff: Contact by letter, by telephone, by fax, by e-mail and via website. Appointment necessary.
Hours: Mon to Fri, 0900 to 1730

Access to building: Prior appointment required
Hours: 0930 to 1730

Access for disabled people: Parking provided, ramped entry, access to all public areas, toilet facilities

NATIONAL HOME IMPROVEMENT COUNCIL (NHIC)

Carlyle House, 235 Vauxhall Bridge Road, London, SW1V 1EJ

Tel: 020 7828 8230
Fax: 020 7828 0667
E-mail: info@nhic.org.uk
Website: www.nhic.org.uk

Enquiries to: Director

Founded: 1975

Organisation type and purpose: Advisory body, trade association, research organisation, consultancy.

Subject coverage: Condition of housing stock, market research on home improvement, attitude research to home improvement.

Library catalogue: All or part available online

Access to staff: Contact by letter, by telephone, by fax and by e-mail
Hours: Mon to Fri, 0900 to 1700

Established the: NHIC Educational Trust in 1980 to further its aims

NATIONAL HOSPITAL DEVELOPMENT FOUNDATION

Formal name: The National Hospital for Neurology and Neurosurgery Development Foundation

National Hospital, PO Box 123, Queen Square, London, WC1N 3BG

Tel: 020 7829 8724
Fax: 020 7676 2068
E-mail: theresa.dauncey@uclh.nhs.uk
Website: www.nationalbrainappeal.org

Enquiries to: Director

Founded: 1984

Organisation type and purpose: Registered charity (charity number 290173).

Subject coverage: Neurology and neurosurgery.

Access to staff: Contact by letter, by telephone, by fax, by e-mail and via website
Hours: Mon to Fri, 0900 to 1700

NATIONAL HOSPITAL FOR NEUROLOGY AND NEUROSURGERY DEVELOPMENT FOUNDATION (NHDF)

Box 123, Queen Square, London, WC1N 3BG

Tel: 020 7829 8724
Fax: 020 7676 2068
Website: www.uclh.nhs.uk/Charities+at+UCLH/National+Hospital+Development+Foundation

Enquiries to: Chief Executive
Direct e-mail: theresa.dauncey@uclh.nhs.uk

Founded: c. 2000

Organisation type and purpose: Registered charity (number 290173).
The charity dedicated to raising funds for cutting edge equipment, buildings and research for The National Hospital for Neurology and Neurosurgery of UCL Hospitals which, together with the Institute of Neurology, is a world-wide leader in the research and treatment of brain disorders.

Subject coverage: Neurological conditions, either from birth, through injury, or a slowly developing illness that occurs later in life., including multiple sclerosis (MS), brain and spinal cancer, epilepsy, Parkinson's disease, stroke, Alzheimer's disease and head injury.

Publications: Electronic and video

Publications list: Available online

Access to staff: Contact by letter, by telephone, by fax and by e-mail

Links with: University College London Hospitals NHS Foundation Trust (UCLH); 250 Euston Road, London, NW1 2PG; tel: 0845 1555 000

NATIONAL HOUSEWIVES ASSOCIATION (NHA)

30 Tollgate, Bretton, Peterborough, Cambridgeshire, PE3 9XA

Tel: 01733 333138

Enquiries to: Chairman

Founded: 1973

Organisation type and purpose: National organisation, voluntary organisation.
Aims to put forward the voice of the housewife on matters that are of concern to them. Campaigning for Elderly Residential Homes not to be closed.

Subject coverage: Consumer affairs.

Publications: Printed

Access to staff: Contact by letter and by telephone
Hours: Mon to Fri, 0900 to 1700

Links with: Consumers in European Community Group (this is being taken over by NCC); London Food Commission; Ministry of Agriculture, Fisheries and Food; National Consumer Council; Potato Marketing Board; Soil Association; Women's Farming Union

NATIONAL HOUSING FEDERATION (NHF)

Lion Court, 25 Procter Street, London WC1V 6NY

Tel: 020 7067 1010
Fax: 020 7067 1011
E-mail: info@housing.org.uk
Website: www.housing.org.uk

Enquiries to: Communications Officer
Direct e-mail: NickF@housing.org.uk

Founded: 1935

Organisation type and purpose: Voluntary organisation.
Central representative body for social housing providers in England.

Subject coverage: Housing associations, research and training.

Publications: Printed

Publications list: Available online and in print

East Midlands, West Midlands and South West Regions: National Housing Federation; 101 Victoria Street, Bristol, BS1 5UY; tel: 0117 929 7388; fax: 0117 930 4423

North East, North West and Yorkshire and Humberside Regions: National Housing Federation; City Point, 701 Chester Road, Stretford, Manchester, M32 0RW; tel: 0161 848 8132; fax: 0161 858 8134

NATIONAL ICE SKATING ASSOCIATION OF THE UNITED KINGDOM (NISA)

Grains Building, High Cross Street, Hockley, Nottingham, NG1 3AX

Tel: 0115 988 8060
Fax: 0115 988 8061
E-mail: via website
Website: www.iceskating.org.uk

Founded: 1879; formerly called National Skating Association (year of change 1990)

Organisation type and purpose: The governing body responsible for figure skating and short track speed in the United Kingdom.
To promote, encourage and to further the growth of skating as a sport and a leisure activity.

Subject coverage: Ice skating.

Publications: Electronic and video

Access to staff: Contact by letter, by telephone, by fax and via website

Affiliates: Northern Ireland Ice Skating Association (NIISA)

NATIONAL INFORMATION FORUM

33 Highshore Road, London, SE15 5AF

Tel: 020 7708 5943
Website: www.nif.org.uk

Enquiries to: Director

Founded: 1981

Organisation type and purpose: Advisory body, membership association (membership is by election or invitation), voluntary organisation, registered charity (charity number 1099335).
Encourages provision of information to disabled people and others seriously disadvantaged by lack of information.

Subject coverage: Provision of information to disabled people and carers and others disadvantaged by lack of information, particularly asylum seekers and refugees.

Information services: Via website

Publications: Printed, and electronic and video
Order printed publications from: Postal address
Order electronic and video publications from: Postal address

Publications list: Available online

Access to staff: Contact by letter and by telephone
Hours: Mon to Fri, 0900 to 1700
Special comments: Staff cannot respond to individual problems.

Access to building: No public access

NATIONAL INSTITUTE FOR BIOLOGICAL STANDARDS AND CONTROL (NIBSC)

Formal name: National Institute for Biological Standards and Control – a Centre of the Health Protection Agency

Blanche Lane, South Mimms, Potters Bar, Hertfordshire, EN6 3QG

Tel: 01707 641000
Fax: 01707 646845
E-mail: library@nibsc.hpa.org.uk
Website: www.nibsc.ac.uk

Enquiries to: Information Services Manager
Direct e-mail: anita.brewer@nibsc.hpa.org.uk

Organisation type and purpose: Research organisation.
National control and standardisation laboratory for biologicals used in medicine; operates as one of eight European control authorities for testing of biologicals.

Subject coverage: Standardisation and control of antisera, bacterial and viral vaccines, blood products, enzymes and hormones, AIDS, biochemistry, chemistry, haematology, endocrinology, microbiology, immunobiology, virology, electronmicroscopy.

Collection: Publications on biological standards

Library catalogue: All or part available online

Publications: Printed

Access to staff: Appointment necessary.
Hours: Mon to Fri, 0900 to 1700

Funded by: Department of Health

NATIONAL INSTITUTE FOR CAREERS EDUCATION AND COUNSELLING (NICEC)

Sheraton House, Castle Park, Cambridge, CB3 0AX

Tel: 01223 460277
Fax: 01223 311708
E-mail: nicec@crac.org.uk
Website: www.crac.org.uk/nicec

Enquiries to: Chair

Founded: 1975

Organisation type and purpose: Registered charity (charity number 313164), consultancy, research organisation.
Careers.
To develop theory, enhance practice and inform policy in the field of careers.

Subject coverage: Theory, policy and practice in careers guidance and career development.

Collection: CRAC/NICEC library is now held at the Library, University of London Institute of Education, 20 Bedford Way, London WC1H 0AL and at the Library, University of Derby, Kedleston Road, Derby DE22 1GB

Library catalogue: All or part available online

Publications: Printed

Publications list: Available online and in print

Access to staff: Contact by letter, by telephone, by fax and by e-mail
Hours: Mon to Fri, 0900 to 1700

Access to building: Prior appointment required

Sponsored by: Careers Research and Advisory Centre (CRAC)

NATIONAL INSTITUTE FOR MEDICAL RESEARCH (NIMR)

Formal name: MRC National Institute for Medical Research

The Ridgeway, Mill Hill, London, NW7 1AA

Tel: 020 8816 2228

continued overleaf

Fax: 020 8816 2230
E-mail: library@nimr.mrc.ac.uk
Website: www.nimr.mrc.ac.uk

Enquiries to: Librarian

Founded: 1913

Organisation type and purpose: Research organisation.
Research Council Institute.
To undertake a broad spectrum of basic medical research.

Subject coverage: Molecular biology, biochemistry, parasitology, virology, neuroscience, embryology, immunology, cell biology, developmental biology, basic biomedical sciences, structural biology, bioinformatics.

Collection: NIMR Archives
MRC Publications

Library catalogue: All or part available online

Publications: Printed

Access to staff: Contact by letter, by telephone and by e-mail. Appointment necessary. Access for members only. Letter of introduction required.
Hours: Mon to Fri, 0900 to 1700

Access to building: Prior appointment required
Special comments: Intending visitors should write, requesting permission from the Institute Director.

Constituent part of: Medical Research Council (MRC); 20 Park Crescent, London, W1B 1AL; tel: 020 7636 5422; fax: 020 7436 6179

NATIONAL INSTITUTE OF ADULT CONTINUING EDUCATION (ENGLAND AND WALES) (NIACE)

21 De Montfort Street, Leicester, LE1 7GE

Tel: 0116 204 4200
Fax: 0116 285 4514
Website: www.niace.org.uk

Organisation type and purpose: National organisation, voluntary organisation, registered charity (charity number 2603322), suitable for ages: 19+, consultancy.

Subject coverage: Adult and continuing education, community education, education for the disadvantaged, the unemployed and the elderly.

Publications list: Available online and in print

Access to staff: Contact by letter, by telephone, by e-mail and via website
Hours: Mon to Fri, 0900 to 1700

Access to building: Prior appointment required
Hours: Mon to Fri, 0900 to 1700

Access for disabled people: Level entry, toilet facilities

Also at: NIACE Dysgu Cymru (Welsh Office); 35 Cathedral Road, Cardiff, CF11 9HB; tel: 029 2037 0900; fax: 029 2037 0909; e-mail: enquiries@niacedc.org.uk

Associated body: Basic Skills Agency

NATIONAL INSTITUTE OF APPLIED POLAROLOGY RESEARCH (NIAPR)

6 Beechvale, Hillview Road, Woking, Surrey, GU22 7NS

Enquiries to: Director of Research

Founded: 1938

Organisation type and purpose: Advisory body, research organisation.

Subject coverage: Applied research in polarology; research into polarological-analytical methodologies for detecting savantism within the dormant 85% of brain tissue; application research for detecting savantism within large groups of individuals in employment, education, hospitals, prisons, sporting and entertainment arenas and by census; research into polarogenesis methodology for creating and developing savantism by mental polarisational-operational research, and by neural and cardiac stimulation from polar-physiotherapy; polar-psychology research to encourage incipient generation of brilliant ideas, inventions, talents and knowledge.

Publications: Printed

Access to staff: Contact by letter
Hours: Mon to Fri, 0900 to 1700

Links with: British Polarographic Research Institute; Institute of Pure Polarology Research; National Centres for Polarological and Polarographic Operational Research; Polarographic Society; UK Polarosciences Research Establishment; Departments of Pure and Applied Polarology

Parent body: British Polarological Research Society (BPRS); 6 Beechvale, Hillview Road, Woking, Surrey, GU22 7NS

NATIONAL INSTITUTE OF CARPET AND FLOORLAYERS (NICF)

4C St Mary's Place, The Lace Market, Nottingham, NG1 1PH

Tel: 0115 958 3077
Fax: 0115 941 2238
E-mail: info@nicfltd.org.uk
Website: www.nicfltd.org.uk

Founded: 1979

Organisation type and purpose: Trade association.

Subject coverage: Carpets of all types, carpet fitting, resilient floorcoverings, wood, laminate.

Collection: Carpet manufacturers, their products and types

Access to staff: Contact by letter, by telephone, by fax, by e-mail and via website
Hours: Mon to Fri, 0900 to 1700

NATIONAL INSTITUTE OF CONDUCTIVE EDUCATION (NICE)

Cannon Hill House, 14 Russell Road, Moseley, Birmingham, B13 8RD

Tel: 0121 449 1569
Fax: 0121 449 1611
E-mail: foundation@conductive-education.org.uk
Website: www.conductive-education.org.uk

Enquiries to: HR Officer
Direct e-mail: mskerrett@conductive-education.org.uk

Founded: 1986

Organisation type and purpose: Membership association (membership is by subscription), registered charity (charity number 295873).

Subject coverage: Conductive education, Hungary, special educational needs, Parkinson's disease, cerebal palsy, stroke, head injury, disability issues.

Collection: Conductive education – all aspects and all media

Non-library collection catalogue: All or part available in-house

Publications: Printed
Order printed publications from: Librarian

Publications list: Available online and in print

Access to staff: Contact by letter, by telephone, by fax, by e-mail, in person and via website. Appointment necessary. Non-members charged.
Hours: Mon to Fri, 0900 to 1700

Access to building: *Hours:* Mon to Fri, 0900 to 1600 during term time only

Access for disabled people: Parking provided, level entry, access to all public areas, toilet facilities

NATIONAL INSTITUTE OF ECONOMIC AND SOCIAL RESEARCH (NIESR)

2 Dean Trench Street, Smith Square, London, SW1P 3HE

Tel: 020 7222 7665
Fax: 020 7654 1900
E-mail: library@niesr.ac.uk
Website: www.niesr.ac.uk

Enquiries to: Librarian
Direct tel: 020 7654 1907
Other contacts: Communications Officer (for press/publication enquiries)

Founded: 1938

Organisation type and purpose: Research organisation.

Subject coverage: Economic conditions in the United Kingdom and the world; economic forecasting; education and training; employment.

Information services: For NIESR research staff only.

Collection: Runs of international and foreign statistics difficult to find elsewhere

Library catalogue: All or part available in-house

Publications: Printed

Publications list: Available online

Access to staff: Contact by e-mail. Appointment necessary. Letter of introduction required.
Hours: Mon to Fri, 0930 to 1730

NATIONAL INSTITUTE OF MEDICAL HERBALISTS LIMITED (NIMH)

Elm House, 54 Mary Arches Street, Exeter, Devon, EX4 3BA

Tel: 01392 426022
Fax: 01392 498963
E-mail: info@nimh.org.uk
Website: www.nimh.org.uk

Enquiries to: Information Officer

Founded: 1864

Organisation type and purpose:
Professional body, training organisation, research organisation.

Subject coverage: Herbs, use of herbs in treatment of disease, how medical herbalists work, training in medical herbalism, pharmacology of plant medicines.

Publications: Printed

Access to staff: Contact by letter, by telephone, by fax and by e-mail
Hours: Mon, Fri, 1000 to 1600; Tue, Wed, Thu, 0930 to 1530

NATIONAL INSULATION ASSOCIATION LIMITED (NIA)

2 Vimy Court, Vimy Road, Leighton Buzzard, Bedfordshire, LU7 1FG

Tel: 08451 636363
Fax: 01525 854918
E-mail: info@nationalinsulationassociation.org.uk
Website: www.nationalinsulationassociation.org.uk/

Enquiries to: Press Officer (Evolution PR Ltd)
Direct e-mail: nia@evolution-pr.co.uk

Founded: 1975

Organisation type and purpose: Trade association (membership is by subscription), present number of members: 130.

Subject coverage: Cavity wall insulation; loft insulation; draught proofing; insulated thermal linings

Trade and statistical information: United Kingdom injected cavity wall insulation market

Publications: Printed

Access to staff: Contact by letter, by telephone, by fax, by e-mail and via website
Hours: Mon to Fri, 0900 to 1700

NATIONAL JOINT COUNCIL FOR THE MOTOR VEHICLE RETAIL AND REPAIR INDUSTRY (NJCMVR&RI)

201 Great Portland Street, London, W1W 5AB

Tel: 01788 538309
Fax: 01788 538335

Enquiries to: Secretary
Direct tel: 01892 664353
Direct e-mail: coryton@supanet.com
Other contacts: Joint Secretary representing the trade unions interests.

Founded: 1943

Organisation type and purpose:
Membership association (membership is by qualification), service industry.
Negotiating and dispute resolving body.

Subject coverage: Terms and conditions of employment in the industry.

Publications: Printed
Order printed publications from: Business Stationery, Retail Motor Industry Federation Unit C, Brewery Industrial Estate, Wenlock Road, London, N1 7TA, tel: 020 7307 3429, fax: 020 7490 4197

Access to staff: Contact by letter, by telephone and by fax
Hours: Mon to Fri, 0900 to 1700

NATIONAL KIDNEY FEDERATION (NKF)

The Point, Coach Road, Shireoaks, Worksop, Nottinghamshire, S81 8BW

Tel: 01909 544999
Fax: 01909 481723
E-mail: nkf@kidney.org.uk
Website: www.kidney.org.uk

Enquiries to: Chairman
Other contacts: Chief Executive

Founded: 1978

Organisation type and purpose: National organisation, membership association (membership is by subscription), present number of members: 25,000, voluntary organisation, registered charity (charity number 1106735).

Subject coverage: Care of persons suffering from kidney failure – medical, social and psychological aspects, treatment options, availability of renal services, issues in transplantation, representation of patients' interests to government.

Library catalogue: All or part available online, in-house and in print

Publications: Printed

Publications list: Available online and in print

Access to staff: Contact by letter, by telephone, by fax, by e-mail, in person and via website
Hours: Mon to Fri, 0900 to 1700

Access to building: *Hours:* Mon to Fri 0900 to 1700

Access for disabled people: Yes
Hours: Mon to Fri, 0900 to 1700

Affiliated to: CEAPIR; European Kidney Federation (CEAPIR)

NATIONAL LANDLORDS' ASSOCIATION (NLA)

22–26 Albert Embankment, London, SE1 7TS

Tel: 020 7840 8900
Fax: 0871 247 7535
E-mail: info@landlords.org.uk
Website: www.landlords.org.uk

Enquiries to: Head of External Relations
Direct tel: 020 7840 8904
Direct e-mail: simon.gordon@landlords.org.uk

Founded: 1973; formerly called Small Landlords Association (year of change 2004)

Organisation type and purpose: Trade association (membership is by subscription), voluntary organisation.
To protect and promote the interests of the individual private landlord of residential property.

Subject coverage: Landlord and tenant matters, residential property, the Housing Acts and 1977 Rent Act.

Publications: Printed

Access to staff: Contact by letter, by telephone, by e-mail and via website.
Access for members only. All charged.
Hours: Mon to Fri, 0900 to 1700

NATIONAL LIBRARY OF SCOTLAND (NLS)

George IV Bridge, Edinburgh, EH1 1EW

Tel: 0131 623 3700
Fax: 0131 623 3701
E-mail: l.tulloch@nls.uk
Website: www.nls.uk
Website: www.nls.ac.uk/catalogues/index.html

Enquiries to: Head of Access and Enquiries
Other contacts: Director of Collections and Research (for access to manuscript, rare book, music and map collections)

Founded: 1682

Organisation type and purpose: Non-departmental public body.
British legal deposit library since 1710.
To acquire, preserve and make available the printed, manuscript and digital record of Scotland's culture.

Subject coverage: The national reference collection in Scotland of printed material in English and for the humanities; all European and Western languages. The foreign scientific periodicals of the Royal Society of Edinburgh were recently taken over to complement British scientific periodicals received by legal deposit. Extensive coverage of printed materials of Scottish relevance.
Manuscript collection relates mainly to Scottish history and literature and activities of Scots, at home and abroad.
Map collection: extensive collection of current and recent atlases and maps of all areas; large historical collection, especially maps of Scotland.
Music collection: classical music of all periods, historical Scottish collection, popular music received by legal deposit.
Scottish Screen Archive.

Information services: Enquire of Head of Information Systems

Special visitor services: Enquire of Head of Access and Enquiries

Education services: Enquire of Head of External Relations

Services for disabled people: Enquire of Head of Access and Enquiries

Collection: Astorga Collection (Hispanic)
Balfour Collection (Handel)
Birkbeck Collection (printing and typography)
Blaikie Collection (Jacobite movement)
Blair Collection (Scottish Gaelic and Celtic)
Blairs Collection (theology)

continued overleaf

British Architectural Library of unpublished manuscripts in microform
Bute Collection (English plays)
Campbell of Islay (Scottish Gaelic and Celtic)
Christie's Pictorial Archive in microform
Combe Collection (phrenology)
Cowan Collection (theology)
Crawford Collection (German theses and programmata)
Early Scottish Book Collections (Rosebery, Lauriston Castle, Ferguson)
Dieterichs Collection (early German theses and programmata)
Dowden Collection (theology)
Early English Newspapers in microform
Ferguson Collection (early Scottish books)
Glen Collection (Scottish music)
Graham Brown Collection (Alps and mountaineering)
Gray Collection (theology)
Haxton Collection (theology)
Hew Morison Collection (Scottish Gaelic and Celtic)
Hopkinson Collections (Berlioz and Verdi)
Incunabula Collection
Ingli's Collection (Scottish music)
John Murray Archive (manuscript archive of John Murray publishing house)
Jolly Collection (theology)
Labour History Collection
Lauriston Castle Collection (early Scottish books)
Lloyd Collection (Alps and mountaineering)
Lyle Collection (ships and shipping)
Macadam Collection (baking and confectionery)
McCurdy Collection (Leonardo da Vinci)
McDonald Collection (colour slides of town planning)
Maclure Collection (French Revolution)
Maitland Thomson (English plays)
Marischal Collection (Scottish maps)
Murdoch Henderson Collection (Scottish music)
Newman Collection (road-books)
Ossian Collection
Protestant Institute Collection (theology)
Rosebery Collection (early Scottish books)
Scottish Screen Archive
Tait Collection (civil engineering)
Thomason Tracts Collection in microform
Thorkelin Collection (Scandinavian and Icelandic)
Townley Collection (7,500 postcards on early 20th-century topography and railways)
Warden Collection (Arctic and Antarctic exploration)

Non-library collection catalogue: All or part available online and in print

Library catalogue: All or part available online

Publications: Printed, and microform publications

Publications list: Available online

Access to staff: Contact by letter, by fax, by e-mail, in person and via website
Hours: Main Reading Room: Mon, Tue, Thu, Fri, 0930 to 2030; Wed, 1000 to 2030; Sat, 0930 to 1300
Map Reading Room: Mon, Tue, Thu, Fri, 0930 to 1700; Wed, 1000 to 1700; Sat, 0930 to 1300

Also at: Map Reading Room; 33 Salisbury Place, Edinburgh, EH9 1SL; tel: 0131 226 4531; Scottish Screen Archive; 39–41Montrose Avenue, Hillington Park, Glasgow G52 4LA; tel: 0845 366 4600; e-mail: ssaenquiries@nls.uk; website: http://ssa.nls.uk

NATIONAL LIBRARY OF WALES

Llyfrgell Genedlaethol Cymru, Aberystwyth, Ceredigion, SY23 3BU

Tel: 01970 632800
Fax: 01970 615709
Website: www.llgc.org.uk

Enquiries to: Librarian
Direct tel: 01970 632805
Direct fax: 01970 632886
Direct e-mail: mdn@llgc.org.uk

Founded: 1907

Organisation type and purpose: National government body.
Entitled to privileges under the Copyright Acts.

Subject coverage: General reference material, specialising in printed, manuscript and graphic material relating to Wales and other Celtic countries.

Collection: Archives of Welsh Churches
Arthuriana
Bourdillon Collection of medieval French romance
Court of Great Sessions records
Egyptology Collection
Estate records
Geoff Charles Photographic Collection
Gregynog and other private presses
H I Bell Collection on papyrology
Howell Lloyd Davies Collection of dictionaries and grammars
Papers of eminent Welsh scholars and literary figures
Political papers of Lloyd George, Clement Davies, Desmond Donnelly, James Griffiths, etc
Pre-1858 Welsh ecclesiastical probate records
Sidney Hartland Collection of ethnology and folklore
Sir John Williams Collection
Thomas Stanford Collections of incunabula including Euclid
Tithe maps relating to Wales

Publications: Printed
Order printed publications from: Marketing Department, The National Library of Wales at the same address; tel: 01970 632858, fax: 01970 615709

Publications list: Available online and in print

Access to staff: Contact by letter, by telephone, by fax, by e-mail and in person
Hours: Mon to Fri, 0930 to 1800; Sat, 0930 to 1700
Special comments: Closed Bank Holidays. Closed first full week in Oct.

NATIONAL LIFE STORIES (NLS)

British Library, 96 Euston Road, London, NW1 2DB

Tel: 020 7412 7404
Fax: 020 7412 7441
E-mail: nls@bl.uk
Website: www.bl.uk/oralhistory
Website: www.bl.uk/nls
Website: www.cadensa.bl.uk

Enquiries to: Archive Assistant
Other contacts: Oral History Curator

Founded: 1987

Organisation type and purpose: Registered charity (charity number 327571), research organisation.
Collecting and archiving oral histories.

Subject coverage: Oral history.

Collection: C409 City Lives
C410 Living Memory of the Jewish Community
C466 Artists' Lives
C467 Architects' Lives
C468 Fawcett Collection
C532 Lives in Steel
C736 Legal Lives
C821 Food: From Source to Salespoint
C872 Book Trade Lives
C960 Crafts Lives
C963 Lives in the Oil Industry
C1007 An Oral History of the Post Office
C1015 Oral History of Wolff Olins
C1029 Down to Earth: An Oral History of British Horticulture
C1173 Oral History of British Theatre Design
C1276 Authors' Lives
C1316 The Legacy of the English Stage Company
C1364 An Oral History of the Water Industry
C1367 An Oral History of Barings
C1379 An Oral History of British Science

Non-library collection catalogue: All or part available online

Library catalogue: All or part available online

Publications: Printed, and electronic and video
Order printed publications from: British Library bookshop; tel: 020 7412 7735

Access to staff: Contact by letter, by telephone, by fax and by e-mail.
Appointment necessary.
Hours: Mon to Fri, 0900 to 1700

Access for disabled people: Ramped entry, access to all public areas, toilet facilities
Special comments: Parking spaces for disabled people are in Midland Road.

NATIONAL LITERACY TRUST (NLT)

68 South Lambeth Road, London, SW8 1RL

Tel: 020 7587 1842
Fax: 020 7587 1411
E-mail: contact@literacytrust.org.uk
Website: www.literacytrust.org.uk

Founded: 1993

Organisation type and purpose: Voluntary organisation, registered charity.
Raise literacy standards and encourage more reading and writing for pleasure.

Subject coverage: Literacy news and initiatives; policy summaries and responses; research summaries

Publications: Printed, and electronic and video
Order printed publications from: via website

Publications list: Available online

Access to staff: Contact by letter, by telephone, by fax, by e-mail and via website
Hours: Mon to Fri, 0900 to 1700

Constituent bodies: Reading Champions; website: http://www.readingchampions.org.uk
Reading Connects; website: http://www.readingconnects.org.uk
Reading is Fundamental, UK; website: http://www.rif.org.uk
Reading the Game; website: http://www.readingthegame.org.uk
Talk To Your Baby; website: http://www.talktoyourbaby.org.uk

NATIONAL LOTTERY COMMISSION (NLC)

101 Wigmore Street, London, W1U 1QU

Tel: 020 7016 3400
Fax: 020 7016 3401
E-mail: publicaffairs@natlotcomm.gov.uk
Website: www.natlotcomm.gov.uk

Enquiries to: Communications Officer
Direct e-mail: c.wotherspoon@natlotcomm.gov.uk

Founded: 1999; formerly called Oflot (year of change 1999)

Organisation type and purpose: National government body.
Non-departmental public body (NDPB).
Regulator of the National Lottery.

Subject coverage: The National Lottery, regulation, gambling.

Trade and statistical information: Quarterly Lottery sales data, and quarterly returns to good causes

Publications: Printed, and electronic and video
Order printed publications from: e-mail: publicaffairs@natlotcomm.gov.uk
Order electronic and video publications from: website: http://www.natlotcomm.gov.uk; publicaffairs@natlotcomm.gov.uk

Access to staff: Contact by letter, by telephone, by fax, by e-mail, in person and via website. Appointment necessary.
Hours: Mon to Fri, 0900 to 1700

Access for disabled people: Access to all public areas, toilet facilities

Parent body: DCMS; 2–4 Cockspur Street, London, SW1Y 5DH; tel: 020 7211 6200; fax: 020 7211 6201; e-mail: enquiries@culture.gov.uk; website: http://www.culture.gov.uk

NATIONAL MARKET TRADERS' FEDERATION (NMTF)

Hampton House, Hawshaw Lane, Hoyland, Barnsley, South Yorkshire, S74 0HA

Tel: 01226 749021
Fax: 01226 740329
E-mail: enquiries@nmtf.co.uk
Website: www.nmtf.co.uk

Enquiries to: Chief Executive Officer

Founded: 1899

Organisation type and purpose: National organisation, trade association (membership is by subscription), present number of members: 34,000.

Subject coverage: Retail markets in the UK; market law.

Collection: Documents of the Royal Commission on Market Rights and Tolls (1891)

Publications: Printed

Access to staff: Contact by letter, by telephone, by fax, by e-mail and via website
Hours: Mon to Fri, 0900 to 1700

Access to building: *Hours:* Mon to Fri, 0900 to 1700

Access for disabled people: Parking provided, ramped entry, toilet facilities
Hours: Mon to Fri, 0900 to 1700

Affiliated to: Retail Markets Alliance (RMA); World Union of Wholesale Markets (WUWM)

NATIONAL MEASUREMENT OFFICE (NMO)

Stanton Avenue, Teddington, Middlesex, TW11 0JZ

Tel: 020 8943 7272
Fax: 020 8943 7270
E-mail: info@nmo.gov.uk
Website: www.bis.gov.uk/nmo

Enquiries to: General Receptionist
Other contacts: Business Team Managers for Certification Services, ACB and Quality Management, Regulation, Enforcement, National Measurement System, Gas and Electricity Meters

Founded: 1987; formerly called National Weights and Measures Laboratory (year of change 2009)

Organisation type and purpose: National government body.
Executive Agency.

Subject coverage: Legal metrology in the United Kingdom; examination and approval of new weighing and measuring equipment to be used for trade, calibration, testing and quality management certification, training. Also provides policy support to Ministers on measurement issues and a measurement infrastructure which enables innovation and growth, promotes trade and facilitates fair competition and the protection of consumers, health and the environment.

Publications: Printed, and electronic and video

Publications list: Available online and in print

Access to staff: Contact by letter, by telephone, by fax, by e-mail and via website. Appointment necessary.
Hours: Mon to Fri, 0900 to 1700

Links with: International Organisation of Legal Metrology; tel: 020 8943 7247; e-mail: info@nmo.gov.uk; website: http://www.oiml.org/
OIML Publications, Bureau International de Métrologie Légale (BIML); 11 rue Turgot, Paris 75009, France; tel: +33 1 48 78 12 82; fax: +33 1 42 82 17 27; e-mail: biml@oiml.org; website: http://www.oiml.org/

Parent body: Department for Business, Innovation and Skills; 1 Victoria Street, London, SW1H 0ET; tel: 020 7215 5000; e-mail: http://www.bis.gov.uk/contact/other-enquiries; website: http://www.bis.gov.uk

NATIONAL MEDIATION CENTRE (NMC)

23 St James Gardens, Swansea, West Glamorgan, SA1 6DY

Tel: 01792 469626
Fax: 01792 650642

Enquiries to: Chief Executive

Founded: 1995

Organisation type and purpose: International organisation, national organisation, professional body, service industry, training organisation.
Provider of mediation service.

Subject coverage: Dispute resolution, mediation.

Access to staff: Contact by letter, by telephone, by fax and by e-mail
Hours: Mon to Fri, 0900 to 1700

NATIONAL MEMORIAL ARBORETUM

Croxall Road, Alrewas, Burton-on-Trent, Staffordshire, DE13 7AR

Tel: 01283 792333
Fax: 01283 792034
E-mail: info@thenma.org.uk
Website: www.thenma.org.uk

Founded: 2001

Organisation type and purpose: National organisation, registered charity (charity number 1043992).

Subject coverage: Tree planting, tree collections, Armed Service contacts, educational visits, conference and events facilities.

Special visitor services: Group visits welcomed by prior arrangement.

Education services: School visits welcomed by prior arrangement.

Collection: FEPOW Memorial Building

Publications: Printed
Order printed publications from: tel: 01283 792333

Access to staff: Contact by letter, by telephone, by fax, by e-mail, in person and via website. Appointment necessary.
Hours: Daily, 0900 to 1700

Access to building: *Hours:* Daily, 0900 to 1700; closed Christmas Day

Access for disabled people: Parking provided, level entry, toilet facilities

Constituent part of: The Royal British Legion; 48 Pall Mall, London, SW1Y 5JY; tel: 020 7973 7207

NATIONAL METEOROLOGICAL LIBRARY AND ARCHIVE (Met Office Library)

Fitzroy Road, Exeter, EX1 3PB

Tel: 01392 884841
Fax: 01392 885681
E-mail: metlib@metoffice.gov.uk
Website: www.metoffice.com/corporate/library/index.html

Enquiries to: Information Officer
Direct tel: 01392 360987 (Archive Manager)

continued overleaf

Other contacts: Archive Manager

Founded: 1870

Organisation type and purpose: National government body, learned society, public library. Specialist meteorological records and publications.
To provide public access to official meteorological records and the comprehensive meteorological library.

Subject coverage: Meteorology, climatology and most aspects of atmospheric and related sciences; original weather reports; summaries and published books, articles and pamphlets; approximately 3m. items, from 16th century to date.

Collection: Library and archive collections of the Meteorological Office; books, documents and photographs
Original weather records archived under the terms of Public Records Act
Rare and historical books and pamphlets on meteorology and climatology held in conjunction with the Royal Meteorological Society

Non-library collection catalogue: All or part available online

Library catalogue: All or part available online and in-house

Publications: Microform publications

Publications list: Available online

Access to staff: Contact by letter, by telephone, by fax and by e-mail. Appointment necessary.

Access to building: *Hours:* Mon to Thu 0830 to 1700, Fri 0830 to 1630 (Archive Tue to Fri, 1000 to 1700); closed bank holidays

Access for disabled people: Ramped entry, toilet facilities

Constituent part of: Met Office; tel: 0870 900 0100; e-mail: enquiries@metoffice.gov.uk; website: http://www.metoffice.gov.uk

NATIONAL MUSEUM OF SCIENCE AND INDUSTRY

Constituent bodies: National Museum of Photography, Film and Television; National Railway Museum; Science Museum; Science Museum Library

NATIONAL MUSEUM WALES (NMGC/NMGW)

Library, Cathays Park, Cardiff, CF10 3NP

Tel: 029 2057 3202
E-mail: library@museumwales.ac.uk
Website: www.nmgw.ac.uk

Enquiries to: Librarian

Founded: 1907

Organisation type and purpose: National government body, museum, art gallery. Established by Royal Charter.

Subject coverage: Archaeology; art; botany; geology; industrial archaeology; zoology; museum science; architecture; private press; in particular, the special interests of Wales in those subjects.

Collection: Library of the Cambrian Archaeological Association
Library of the Cardiff Naturalists Society
Tomlin Collection (conchology)
Vaynor Collection (astronomy, travels)
Willoughby Gardner Collection (early books on natural history)

Non-library collection catalogue: All or part available online, in-house and in print

Library catalogue: All or part available in-house

Publications: Printed

Publications list: Available in print

Access to staff: Contact by letter, by telephone, by e-mail and via website. Appointment necessary.
Hours: Tue to Fri, 1000 to 1700

Access for disabled people: Parking provided, ramped entry, toilet facilities

Funded by: National Assembly for Wales

Parent body: National Museum Wales

NATIONAL MUSEUMS AND GALLERIES OF WALES

Constituent parts: Big Pit National Mining Museum of Wales; Blaenafon, Torfaen, NP4 9XP; tel: 01495 790311; fax: 01495 792618; e-mail: bigpit@nmgw.ac.uk; Museum of the Welsh Woollen Industry; Museum of Welsh Life; St Fagans, Cardiff, CF5 6XB; tel: 029 2057 3500; fax: 029 2057 3490; National Museum & Gallery Cardiff; Cathays Park, Cardiff, CF1 3NP; tel: 029 2039 7951; fax: 029 2037 3219; Roman Legionary Museum; High Street, Caerleon, NP6 1AE; tel: 01633 423134; fax: 01633 422869; Segontium Roman Museum; Beddgelert Road, Caernarfon, Gwynedd, LL55 2LN; tel: 01286 675625; fax: 01286 678416; Turner House Gallery; Plymouth Road, Penarth, South Glamorgan, CF64 3DM; tel: 029 2070 8870; Welsh Industrial and Maritime Museum; Welsh Slate Museum; Gilfach Ddu, Llanberis, Gwynedd, LL55 4TY; tel: 01286 870630; fax: 01286 871906

NATIONAL MUSEUMS OF SCOTLAND (NMS)

Chambers Street, Edinburgh, EH1 1JF

Tel: 0131 247 4137 (library enquiries); 0131 247 4219 (museum enquiries)
Fax: 0131 247 4819 (general); 0131 247 4311 (library)
E-mail: info@nms.ac.uk
Website: www.nms.ac.uk

Enquiries to: Librarian
Direct tel: 0131 247 4042
Direct fax: 0131 220 4819
Other contacts: Librarian (for specific enquiries); PR & Marketing Assistant

Organisation type and purpose: Registered charity (charity number SC 011130), museum.
Non-departmental public body – NDPB.

Subject coverage: Decorative arts; archaeology; ethnography; history, especially Scottish; geology; zoology; history of science and technology; museology and museum conservation; military history, especially of the Scottish regiments.
The Museum of Scotland tells for the first time the history of Scotland – its land, its people, and their achievements – through the incomparable national collections. The collections include that started by the Society of Antiquaries in 1781 and continued in the former Museum of Antiquities.

Information services: Library available for reference (for conditions see Access above), online searching, CD-ROM-based services, bibliography compilation, selective dissemination services.

Special visitor services: Guided tours.

Education services: Group education facilities, resources for Key Stages 1 and 2, 3, 4 and further or higher education.

Services for disabled people: For the visually impaired; for the hearing impaired.

Collection: J A Harvie-Brown manuscripts, library and reprint collections (natural history)
Society of Antiquaries of Scotland manuscripts and archives
The Duke of Cumberland's Papers (microfilm)
W S Bruce manuscripts (natural history)
William Jardine manuscripts (natural history)
Book stock: 80,000 on arts, 30,000 on science, 800 current periodicals

Non-library collection catalogue: All or part available in-house

Library catalogue: All or part available in-house

Publications: Printed, and electronic and video
Order printed publications from: NMS Publishing, Royal Museum, Chambers Street, Edinburgh, EH1 1JF; tel: 0131 247 4026; fax: 0131 247 4012; e-mail: publishing@nms.ac.uk

Publications list: Available online and in print

Access to staff: Contact by letter, by telephone, by fax, by e-mail and via website. Appointment necessary.
Hours: Royal Museum Library: Mon to Fri, 1000 to 1300 and 1400 to 1700
National War Museum of Scotland Library: Tue, 1000 to 1230, or by appointment

Access for disabled people: Access to all public areas, toilet facilities
Special comments: Level entry at the Museum of Scotland.

Also at: National War Museum of Scotland; Edinburgh Castle; Museum of Scotland; Chambers Street

Branch museums: Museum of Flight; East Fortune Airfield, East Lothian; tel: 01620 880308; fax: 01620 880355; e-mail: info@nms.ac.uk; Museum of Scottish Country Life; Wester Kittochside, East Kilbride, G76 9HR; tel: 01355 224181; fax: 01355 571290; e-mail: info@nms.ac.uk; National War Museum of Scotland; Edinburgh Castle, Edinburgh, EH1 2NG; tel: 0131 225 7534; fax: 0131 225 3848; e-mail: library@nms.ac.uk; Royal Museum & Museum of Scotland; Chambers Street, Edinburgh, EH1 1JF; tel: 0131 247 4219/4422; fax: 0131 220 4819; e-mail: info@nms.ac.uk or library@nms.ac.uk; Shambellie

House; New Abbey, Dumfriesshire; tel: 01387 850375; fax: 01387 850461; e-mail: info@nms.ac.uk

The library also includes the collection of the former: Museum of Antiquities Library

NATIONAL MUSIC COUNCIL (NMC)

c/o BASCA, 26 Berners Street, London, W1T 3LR

E-mail: info@nationalmusiccouncil.org.uk
Website: www.nationalmusiccouncil.org.uk

Enquiries to: Administrator
Direct e-mail: info@nationalmusiccouncil.org.uk

Founded: 1953

Organisation type and purpose: Membership association (membership is by subscription), registered charity (charity number 239178).
National forum.

Subject coverage: Music; the encouragement of development of all British musical activities. Issues facing those working in music in the United Kingdom.

Publications: Printed, and electronic and video

Publications list: Available online

Access to staff: Contact by letter and by e-mail. Appointment necessary.

NATIONAL NEIGHBOURHOOD WATCH ASSOCIATION (NNWA)

Schomberg House, 80–82 Pall Mall, London, SW1Y 5HF

Tel: 020 7772 3348
Fax: 020 7662 3513
E-mail: uknwt@neighbourhoodwatch.net
Website: www.neighbourhoodwatch.net

Enquiries to: Director General
Direct e-mail: john.howell@dia.pipex.com

Founded: 1982

Organisation type and purpose: Registered charity (charity number 1049584).

Subject coverage: Establishment and best practice of Neighbourhood Watch, community safety and crime prevention in relation to Neighbourhood Watch activities.

Publications: Printed

Publications list: Available online

Access to staff: Contact by letter, by telephone, by fax, by e-mail and via website. Appointment necessary. Letter of introduction required.
Hours: Mon to Fri, 0900 to 1700

Access to building: Prior appointment required

Access for disabled people: Level entry

NATIONAL NEWPIN

Sutherland House, 35 Sutherland Square, Walworth, London, SE17 3EE

Tel: 020 7358 5900
Fax: 020 7701 2660
E-mail: nationalnewpin@talk21.com
Website: www.newpin.org.uk

Enquiries to: Information Officer

Founded: 1982

Organisation type and purpose: International organisation, voluntary organisation, registered charity (charity number 1022931).
To help parents with children under 6.

Subject coverage: Helps parents under stress break the cyclical effect of destructive family behaviour. Through a network of local centres, expectant mothers, parents, carers and children are offered a unique opportunity to achieve positive changes in their lives and relationships based on respect, support, equality and empathy. The work focuses on alleviating maternal depression and other mental distress.

Access to staff: Contact by letter, by telephone, by fax, by e-mail, in person and via website. Appointment necessary.
Hours: Mon to Fri, 0900 to 1700

Centres at: Chesterfield NEWPIN; 10 & 11 The Villas, Walton Hospital, Chesterfield, Derbyshire, S40 3HN; tel: 01246 552867; fax: 01246 558747; Deptford NEWPIN; Deptford Mission, 1 Creek Road, Deptford, London, SE8 3BT; tel: 020 8694 6052; e-mail: centre@deptfordnewpin.freeserve.co.uk; Feltham NEWPIN; Hunter House, Highfields Road, Highfields Estate, Feltham, Middlesex, TW13 4DL; tel: 020 8893 1716; fax: 020 8893 1377; Foyle NEWPIN; 18–19 Jasmine Court, Waterside, Derry, BT47 2DZ; tel: 0150 434 4477; fax: 0150 434 4477; e-mail: foyle.newpin@virgin.net; Greenwich and Lewisham NEWPIN; 1–4 Bissextile House, Bliss Crescent, Lewisham, London, SE13 7RH; tel: 020 8694 0201; fax: 020 8694 0201; Hoxton NEWPIN; St John's Centre, 85 Pitfield Street, London, N1 6NP; tel: 020 7739 9196; e-mail: centre@hoxtonnewpin.freeserve.co.uk; Newham NEWPIN; Mayflower Centre, Vincent Street, Canning Town, London, E16 1LZ; tel: 020 7473 6688; fax: 020 7473 6688; NEWPIN; 10–12 Rathmullan Drive, Rathcoole, Newtonabbey, BT37 9NF; tel: 028 9086 6622; fax: 028 9086 6722; e-mail: centre@rathcodenewpin.freeserve.co.uk; NEWPIN; 160 Wincobank Avenue, Sheffield, S5 6BB; tel: 0114 256 1533; St Paul's NEWPIN; St Paul's Centre, Rossmore Road, London, NW1 6NJ; tel: 020 7724 6765; Sutton NEWPIN; 204 Thornton Road, St Helier Estate, Carshalton, Surrey, SM5 1NF; tel: 020 8646 8604; Tower Hamlets NEWPIN; Bancroft Green, Hadleigh Close, London, E1 4LH; tel: 020 7423 9656; Walworth NEWPIN; 35 Sutherland Square, London, SE17 3EE; tel: 020 7703 5271; Wandsworth NEWPIN; Patmore Centre, Patmore Street, London, SW8 4JD; tel: 020 7622 2750; fax: 020 7622 7338

NATIONAL NUCLEAR LABORATORY (NNL)

Information Retrieval Service (IRS), B709, Springfields Works, Salwick, Preston, Lancashire, PR4 0XJ

Tel: 01772 764884
Fax: 01772 762385
E-mail: louise.collins@nnl.co.uk
Website: www.nnl.co.uk/

Enquiries to: Information Officer

History of institution: formerly called AEA Technology, Northern Research Laboratories, NSTS, Nexia Solutions

Organisation type and purpose: Research organisation.
Government.

Subject coverage: Nuclear fuel technology; industrial research.

Library catalogue: All or part available online and in-house

Publications list: Available in print

Access to staff: Contact by letter, by telephone and by e-mail
Hours: Mon to Fri, 0900 to 1700

NATIONAL OCEANOGRAPHIC LIBRARY (NOL)

National Oceanography Centre, University of Southampton Waterfront Campus, European Way, Southampton, SO14 3ZH

Tel: 023 8059 6116
Fax: 023 8059 6115
E-mail: nol@noc.soton.ac.uk
Website: www.soton.ac.uk/library/about/nol

Enquiries to: Head of Information Services
Direct e-mail: nol@noc.soton.ac.uk

Founded: 1995

Organisation type and purpose: University academic unit, research council and consultancy.

Subject coverage: Ocean and earth sciences: marine chemistry, biology, geology, geophysics and physics, ocean engineering, associated ocean instrumentation for deep oceans and shallow seas, air-sea interaction, waves, currents, sea levels, coastal oceanography, water mass dynamics, seabed topography, sediment mobility, deep ocean, biological organisms etc., terrestrial geology, palaeontology

Collection: Discovery Investigations Collection, Simonsen Collection, Expedition reports. Archives of the National Oceanography Centre

Non-library collection catalogue: All or part available online

Library catalogue: All or part available online

Access to staff: Contact by letter, by telephone, by e-mail and via website. Appointment necessary.
Hours: Mon to Fri, 0930 to 1730
Special comments: Business and commercial use charged

Access to building: Prior appointment required

Access for disabled people: Access to all public areas

Partnership: Natural Environment Research Council; and University of Southampton

NATIONAL OFFICE ANIMAL HEALTH (NOAH) (NOAH)

3 Crossfield Chambers, Gladbeck Way, Enfield, Middlesex, EN2 7HF

Tel: 020 8367 3131
Fax: 020 8363 1155

continued overleaf

E-mail: noah@noah.co.uk
Website: www.noah.co.uk
Website: www.noahcompendium.co.uk
Website: www.pethealthinfo.org.uk

Enquiries to: Communications Manager

Founded: 1986

Organisation type and purpose: National organisation, trade association (membership is by subscription).
NOAH represents the UK animal medicine industry: its aim is to promote the benefits of safe, effective, quality medicines for the health and welfare of all animals.

Subject coverage: Animal medicines and issues relating to the animal medicine industry. The production of healthy food from healthy animals and the role of animal medicines (including antibiotics, vaccines, antiparasite products). Medicines for companion animals. How animal medicines are approved, and their use controlled. The Code of Practice for the Promotion of Animal Medicines.

Trade and statistical information: Summary data on the animal medicine market in the UK (ex-manufacturers' prices). Summary data available to view at www.noah.co.uk

Publications: Printed, and electronic and video

Publications list: Available online and in print

Access to staff: Contact by letter, by fax, by e-mail and via website
Hours: Mon to Fri, 0900 to 1700
Special comments: Electronic contact preferred.

Access to building: No access other than to staff

Associated body of: Pet Health Council (PHC); website: http://www.pethealthcouncil.co.uk

Member organisation of: Animal Medicines Training Regulatory Authority (AMTRA); website: http://www.amtra.org.uk
IFAH – Europe; website: http://www.ifaheurope.org
IFAH (International Federation for Animal Health); website: http://www.ifahsec.org
Pet Advisory Committee (PAC); website: http://www.petadvisory.org.uk
Responsible Use of Medicines in Agriculture Alliance (RUMA); website: http://www.ruma.org.uk
The Institute of Grocery Distribution (IGD); website: http://www.igd.com

Trustee of: National Pet Month; website: http://www.nationalpetmonth.org.uk

NATIONAL OPERATIC AND DRAMATIC ASSOCIATION (NODA)

58–60 Lincoln Road, Peterborough, PE1 2RZ

Tel: 0870 770 2480
Fax: 0870 770 2490
E-mail: info@noda.org.uk
Website: www.noda.org.uk

Enquiries to: Chief Executive

Founded: 1899

Organisation type and purpose:
Membership association (membership is by subscription), present number of members: 2500 societies, 3000 individuals, registered charity (charity number 254640).
Servicing amateur theatre societies.

Subject coverage: Pantomime agency; sales of sheet music; rehearsal material for plays; musicals, operettas, operas and pantomimes at discounts to members; insurance for amateur theatre, help and advice.

Collection: Collection of vocal scores (some first editions)
Rehearsal material at discounts to members
Sheet music

Publications: Printed

Publications list: Available online

Access to staff: Contact by letter, by telephone, by fax, by e-mail and via website. Appointment necessary.
Hours: Mon to Fri, 0900 to 1700
Special comments: Non-members by special arrangement.

Access to building: Prior appointment required

NATIONAL ORGANISATION OF ASIAN BUSINESSES (NOAB)

East End House, Kenrick Way, West Bromwich, West Midlands, B71 4EA

Tel: 0121 553 1999
Fax: 0121 525 6565
E-mail: tonydeep@eastendfoods.co.uk

Enquiries to: Manager

Founded: 1993

Organisation type and purpose: Voluntary organisation.

Subject coverage: Representation of the interests of Asian businesses at a national level.

Access to staff: Contact by letter, by telephone, by fax and by e-mail
Hours: Mon to Fri, 0900 to 1700

Access for disabled people: Parking provided, ramped entry, toilet facilities

NATIONAL OSTEOPOROSIS SOCIETY

Camerton, Bath, BA2 0PJ

Tel: 01761 471771 (Switchboard); 0845 450 0230 (Helpline)
Fax: 01761 471104
E-mail: info@nos.org.uk
Website: www.nos.org.uk

Enquiries to: Information Centre

Founded: 1986

Organisation type and purpose:
Membership association (membership is by subscription), voluntary organisation, registered charity (charity number 1102712 in England and Wales and SC 039755 in Scotland).

Subject coverage: Information on treatment and prevention of osteoporosis for the general public and the medical professions, hormone replacement therapy (HRT), the menopause.

Information services: Information Centre

Education services: Education Officer

Publications: Printed
Order printed publications from: Information Centre

Publications list: Available online and in print

Access to staff: Contact by letter, by telephone, by fax, by e-mail, in person and via website. Appointment necessary.
Hours: Mon to Fri, 0900 to 1600; Helpline: Mon to Fri, 0900 to 1700

Access to building: Prior appointment required

Access for disabled people: Parking provided, level entry, toilet facilities

Affiliated to: Association of Medical Research Charities; European Foundation for Osteoporosis; Long-term Medical Conditions Alliance; National Council of Women of Great Britain

NATIONAL OUTDOOR EVENTS ASSOCIATION (NOEA)

PO Box 4495, Wells, BA5 9AS

Tel: 01749 674 531
E-mail: secretary@noea.org.uk
Website: www.noea.org.uk

Enquiries to: General Secretary

Founded: 1979

Organisation type and purpose: Trade association.

Subject coverage: General and technical information on the world of outdoor events for clients and suppliers, basic standards and codes of practice, hazards and risk assessment, statutory requirements.

Publications: Printed

Publications list: Available in print

Access to staff: Contact by letter, by telephone and by e-mail
Hours: Mon to Fri, 0900 to 1700

Access to building: No access other than to staff

Access for disabled people: Level entry

NATIONAL PEST TECHNICIANS ASSOCIATION (NPTA)

NPTA House, Hall Lane, Kinoulton, Nottingham, NG12 3EF

Tel: 01949 81133
Fax: 01949 823905
E-mail: officenpta@aol.com
Website: www.npta.org.uk

Enquiries to: Administrator

Founded: 1993

Organisation type and purpose:
Professional body.

Subject coverage: Pest control.

Publications: Printed

Publications list: Available online and in print

Access to staff: Contact by letter, by telephone, by fax, by e-mail and via website. Appointment necessary.
Hours: Mon to Fri, 0900 to 1700

NATIONAL PHARMACY ASSOCIATION (NPA)

Mallinson House, 38–42 St Peter's Street, St Albans, Hertfordshire, AL1 3NP

Tel: 01727 832161
Fax: 01727 840858
E-mail: npa@npa.co.uk
Website: www.npa.co.uk

Enquiries to: Information Operations Manager
Direct tel: 01727 858687 (ext. 3207)
Direct fax: 01727 795902
Direct e-mail: s.garner@npa.co.uk

Founded: 1921

Organisation type and purpose: Trade association.

Subject coverage: Community pharmacy; prescription and other medicines.

Collection: Foreign pharmacopoeias

Publications: Printed

Access to staff: Contact by letter, by telephone, by fax and by e-mail. Access for members only. Non-members charged.
Hours: Mon to Fri, 0900 to 1800; Sat, 0900 to 1300

NATIONAL PHILATELIC SOCIETY (NPS)

c/o The British Postal Museum & Archive, Freeling House, Phoenix Place, London WC1X 0DL

Tel: 020 7239 2571
E-mail: nps@ukphilately.org.uk/nps
Website: ukphilately.org.uk

Enquiries to: General Secretary
Direct e-mail: nps@ukphilately.org.uk

Founded: 1899

Organisation type and purpose: International organisation, membership association (membership is by subscription), present number of members: 4,700, philatelic library, suitable for ages: 14+, publishing house.
Non-profit-making society.

Subject coverage: Philately, postal history, stamp collecting and related hobby material.

Collection: Collection of forged stamps
Library of philatelic and postal history works, philatelic journals
Reference collection of philatelic archive material

Library catalogue: All or part available online and in-house

Publications: Printed

Access to staff: Contact by letter and by telephone
Hours: Tue, Wed, Thu, 1100 to 1615; and 2nd Sat in each month

Access to building: No prior appointment required
Hours: Tue, Wed, Thu, 1100 to 1615; and 2nd Sat in each month

NATIONAL PHYSICAL LABORATORY (NPL)

Queens Road, Teddington, Middlesex, TW11 0LW

Tel: 020 8977 3222
Fax: 020 8943 6458
E-mail: enquiry@npl.co.uk
Website: www.npl.co.uk

Enquiries to: National Physical Laboratory Helpline
Direct tel: 020 8943 6880
Direct e-mail: susan.evans@npl.co.uk

Founded: 1900

Organisation type and purpose: National organisation, consultancy, research organisation.
UK national standards laboratory. Development of highly accurate measurement techniques and their application for industry and government.

Subject coverage: National and international standards, physics and engineering, including electrical and optical standards and standards of radioactivity and measurement of ionizing radiations, physical acoustics and noise, application of computers and information technology, engineering materials, environmental metrology, measurement and calibration, research and development, knowledge transfer.

Publications: Printed

Access to staff: Contact by letter, by telephone, by fax, by e-mail and via website
Hours: Mon to Fri, 0900 to 1700

Operated on behalf of the: Department of Trade and Industry by NPL Management Limited; a wholly owned subsidiary of Serco Group plc

NATIONAL PIERS SOCIETY (NPS)

4 Tyrrell Road, South Benfleet, Essex, SS7 5DH

Tel: 01268 757291
Fax: 020 7483 1902
E-mail: pjredditch@msn.com
Website: www.piers.co.uk

Enquiries to: Honorary Secretary
Other contacts: Chairman

Founded: 1976

Organisation type and purpose: Learned society (membership is by subscription), voluntary organisation, research organisation.

Subject coverage: Piers: construction, history, uses, development, architecture, maintenance, grant aid, assessment and surveying, construction materials, design, engineering, shipping associations, attractions (e.g. theatres); pier tramways and railways.

Collection: Copies of most books covering piers, their construction and history; various documents, information files, photographs, drawings and souvenirs

Publications: Printed
Order printed publications from: Piers Information Bureau
3 Withburn Close, Upton, Wirral, L49 6QH, tel: 0151 606 0595

Publications list: Available in print

Access to staff: Contact by letter, by telephone, by fax and by e-mail
Hours: Mon to Fri, 0900 to 1700

Links with: British Association of Leisure Parks, Piers and Attractions; Paddle Steamer Preservation Society

NATIONAL PIGEON ASSOCIATION (NPA)

Bridge Villa, Main Street, Pollington, Goole, East Yorkshire, DN14 0DW

Tel: 01405 869516
Fax: 01405 869516
E-mail: tracey@edwardspm.fsnet.co.uk
Website: www.zyworld.com/NPA/index.htm

Enquiries to: Secretary

Organisation type and purpose: Membership association (membership is by subscription), present number of members: 856, voluntary organisation.
For breeding and exhibition of fancy pigeons.

Subject coverage: Feeding, rearing, management and exhibition of fancy pigeons in general, with advice on sources of further information. Contacts supplied for specialist breed clubs.

Publications: Printed, and electronic and video

Access to staff: Contact by letter and by telephone
Hours: Mon to Fri, 0900 to 1700

Access to building: No access other than to staff

Rings and lost birds: The Ring Distributor; Bridge Villa, Main Street, Pollington, Goole, DN14 0DW; tel: 01405 869516

NATIONAL POISONS INFORMATION SERVICE (CARDIFF CENTRE) (NPIS)

Gwenwyn Ward, Llandough Hospital, Penarth, Cardiff, CF64 2XX

Tel: 029 2071 5013
Fax: 029 2070 4357
E-mail: poison.information@cardiffandvale.wales.nhs.uk

Enquiries to: Manager

Founded: 1963

Organisation type and purpose: Welsh Office service.
Advice on poisonings by all routes, to medical personnel only.

Subject coverage: Specialist information on all types of poisoning, clinical toxicology; pharmacology.

Publications list: Available in print

Access to staff: Contact by letter, by telephone, by fax and by e-mail
Hours: 24-hour service, 365 days a year
Special comments: Not a public access service.

Part of: National Poisons Information Service

NATIONAL POISONS INFORMATION SERVICE, EDINBURGH CENTRE (NPIS Edinburgh/SPIB)

Scottish Poisons Information Bureau, Royal Infirmary, Edinburgh, EH16 4SA

Tel: 0131 242 1383
Fax: 0131 242 1387
E-mail: spib@luht.scot.nhs.uk
Website: www.toxbase.org
Website: www.show.scot.nhs.uk/spib

Enquiries to: Manager
Other contacts: Information Officer

Founded: 1963

Organisation type and purpose: Advisory body.
Poisons information for medical professionals.

Subject coverage: Toxicology, poisons information, chemicals.

Information services: Clinical toxicology management advice for registered NHS users

Access to staff: Contact by letter, by telephone, by fax, by e-mail and via website
Hours: Mon to Fri, 0900 to 1600
Special comments: Medical profession only

NATIONAL POLICE LIBRARY (NPIA)

Formal name: National Policing Improvement Agency

NPIA Bramshill, Hook, Hampshire, RG27 0JW

Tel: 01256 602650
Fax: 01256 602285
E-mail: library@npia.pnn.police.uk
Website: www.npia.police.uk

Enquiries to: Librarian
Direct tel: 01256 602861

Founded: 1948; formerly called Police College (year of change 1948); formerly called Police Staff College (year of change 1979); formerly called National Police Training (year of change 1993); formerly called Centrex (year of change 2007)

Organisation type and purpose: NPIA provides and supports a range of products and services that underpins its commitment to improving policing priorities in: personal development and HR; systems and IT services; science and forensics; operational policing services; programmes for improvement and research; identification resources and databases

Subject coverage: Police-related subjects, criminal justice, management.

Collection: Annual Report of HM Inspectors of Constabulary, 1858 to date
Police and Constabulary Almanac, 1858 to date
Police Journal, 1928 to date
Police Review, 1893 to date

Library catalogue: All or part available online and in-house

Access to staff: Contact by letter, by telephone, by fax, by e-mail, in person and via website. Appointment necessary. Letter of introduction required. Non-members charged.
Hours: Mon to Thu, 0830 to 1700; Fri, 0830 to 1600

Access for disabled people: Restricted access

Parent body: National Policing Improvement Agency; tel: 01256 602100

NATIONAL PONY SOCIETY (NPS)

Willingdon House, 102 High Street, Alton, Hampshire, GU34 1EN

Tel: 01420 88333
Fax: 01420 80599

Enquiries to: Secretary

Founded: 1893

Organisation type and purpose: Membership association.

Subject coverage: Training for stud assistant's qualification, British Riding Pony Stud Book registration, native breeds, showing competitions, sales, welfare of ponies, training of judges.

Publications: Printed

Representation on: Association of British Equine Societies; British Show Pony Society; Councils of the British Horse Society; Joint Measurement Board; NASTA; National Equine Welfare Council

NATIONAL PORTAGE ASSOCIATION (NPA)

Kings Court, 17 School Road, Hall Green, Birmingham, B28 8JG

Tel: 0121 244 1807
Fax: 0121 244 1801
E-mail: info@portage.org.uk
Website: www.portage.org.uk

Enquiries to: Administrator
Direct e-mail: administrator@portage.org.uk

Founded: 1976

Organisation type and purpose: Voluntary organisation, registered charity (charity number 1087865), company limited by guarantee (company number 4165317). Educational organisation.

Subject coverage: Support for families caring for children with special needs by promoting and supporting portage educational home visiting services.

Publications: Printed

Publications list: Available online and in print

Access to staff: Contact by letter, by telephone, by fax, by e-mail and via website
Hours: Office hours

NATIONAL PORTRAIT GALLERY (NPG)

Heinz Archive and Library, St Martin's Place, London, WC2H 0HE

Tel: 020 7321 6617
Fax: 020 7306 0056
E-mail: arc@npg.org.uk
Website: www.npg.org.uk

Enquiries to: Head of Archive and Library
Direct tel: 020 7321 6617
Direct fax: 020 7306 0056
Direct e-mail: archiveenquiry@npg.org.uk

Founded: 1856

Organisation type and purpose: National body, history and art gallery, suitable for all ages. Heinz Archive and library.
Founded in 1856 to collect portraits of men and women who have made and are continuing to make a significant contribution to the history and culture of Britain. Portraits from the collection are on display in locations around the country.

Subject coverage: British portraits and portrait artists, 1400s to present day.

Information services: Library available for reference by appointment Tue to Fri, 1000 to 1700; consultation service Wed, 1400 to 1700.

Collection: Unparalleled collection of British portraiture, comprising primary collection of portraits in all media and reference collections of portrait photographs and prints and drawings
Collection of approximately 600,000 reproductions and illustrations of portraits held in public and private collections worldwide, arranged in separate 'sitter' and 'artist' files; extensive index to portraits reproduced or cited in publications
Collection of artists' sitter books, account books, correspondence and papers, and research papers relating to portrait artists
Institutional records of the Gallery, including acquisition, conservation, exhibition and administrative records

Non-library collection catalogue: All or part available online, in-house and in print

Library catalogue: All or part available online and in-house

Publications: Printed, and microform publications

Publications list: Available online and in print

Access to staff: Contact by letter, by telephone and by e-mail. Appointment necessary.

Access to building: Access to Heinz Archive and Library by appointment only.
Hours: Reference: Tue to Fri, 1000 to 1700; consultation service: Wed, 1400 to 1700
Special comments: Access to Heinz Archive and Library by appointment only.

Access for disabled people: Ramped entry, toilet facilities

Also at: Beningbrough Hall; Beningbrough, York, North Yorkshire, YO30 1DD; tel: 01904 472027; website: http://www.nationaltrust.org.uk/main/w-beningbroughhallandgardens
Bodelwyddan Castle; Bodelwyddan, Rhyl, Denbighshire, LL18 5YA; tel: 01745 584060; fax: 01745 584563; website: http://www.bodelwyddan-castle.co.uk
Gawthorpe Hall; Padiham, nr Burnley, Lancashire, BB12 8UA; tel: 01282 771004; website: http://www.nationaltrust.org.uk/main/w-gawthorpehall

Montacute House; Montacute, Somerset, TA15 6XP; tel: 01935 823289; website: http://www.nationaltrust.org.uk/main/w-vh/w-visits/w-findaplace/w-montacute

NATIONAL RECORDS OF SCOTLAND (NRS)

New Register House, Edinburgh, EH1 3YT

Tel: 0131 334 0380
Fax: 0131 314 4400
E-mail: records@gro-scotland.gsi.gov.uk
Website: www.gro-scotland.gov.uk
Website: www.scotlandspeople.gov.uk

Enquiries to: Registrar General

Founded: 1855; formerly called General Register Office for Scotland

Organisation type and purpose: National government body.

Subject coverage: Registration of births, deaths, marriages, civil partnerships, divorces, dissolution of civil partnerships, adoptions, stillbirths, gender recognition, change of name in Scotland, census of population of Scotland, vital and population statistics for Scotland, law governing marriage in Scotland, NHS Central Register for Scotland.

Collection: Old parish registers of births, deaths and marriages (1553–1854)
Records of the decennial censuses of the population of Scotland (1841–1911 are open to the public)
Statutory registers of births, deaths, marriages, stillbirths, adoptions, civil partnerships and divorces

Trade and statistical information: Population, census and vital events data for Scotland

Non-library collection catalogue: All or part available online and in-house

Library catalogue: All or part available in-house

Publications: Printed, and electronic and video

Publications list: Available online and in print

Access to staff: Contact by letter, by telephone, by fax, by e-mail and in person. All charged.
Hours: Mon to Fri, 0900 to 1630
Special comments: Disabled persons can be accompanied by a helper.
Orders accepted by post or fax or by credit card on direct tel: 0131 314 4411, but not by e-mail.

Access for disabled people: Ramped entry, toilet facilities

Also at: National Records of Scotland; Ladywell House, Edinburgh, EH12 7TF; tel: 0131 334 0380; fax: 0131 314 4344; e-mail: customer@gro-scotland.gsi.gov.uk

Branches: Census, Population Statistics, Corporate Services, Vital Events and National Health Service Central Register; Ladywell House, Corstorphine, EH12 7TF; tel: 0131 334 0380

Part of the devolved: Scottish Administration under the Scotland Act 1998

Scottish counterpart of the: Identity and Passport Service in England and Wales

NATIONAL REGISTER OF PERSONAL TRAINERS (NRPT)

4 Bradbury Road, Newnham, Northants NN11 3HD

Tel: 0844 8484 644
E-mail: sam@nrpt.co.uk
Website: www.nrpt.co.uk

Enquiries to: Membership Co-ordinator
Direct tel: 0844 8484 644
Direct e-mail: sam@nrpt.co.uk

Founded: 1992

Organisation type and purpose: National organisation, membership association (membership is by subscription), service industry.

Subject coverage: Personal fitness trainers across the UK, information about personal training and personal training companies.

Access to staff: Contact by letter, by telephone, by e-mail and via website
Hours: Mon to Fri, 1000 to 1600

Access to building: None

NATIONAL REGISTER OF WARRANTED BUILDERS (NRWB)

4 Brooklands Avenue, Cambridge, CB2 2BB

Tel: 01223 508407
Fax: 01223 300848
E-mail: registrar@fmb.org.uk
Website: www.fmb.org.uk

Enquiries to: Registrar

Founded: 1980

Organisation type and purpose: Trade association (membership is by subscription, qualification), present number of members: 3000.

Access to staff: Contact by letter and by e-mail
Hours: Mon to Fri, 0900 to 1700

Links to: Federation of Master Builders (FMB); 14–15 Great James Street, London, WC1N 3DP

NATIONAL RIFLE ASSOCIATION/ NATIONAL SHOOTING CENTRE LIMITED (NRA)

Bisley Camp, Brookwood, Woking, Surrey, GU24 0PB

Tel: 01483 797777
Fax: 01483 797285
E-mail: info@nra.org.uk
Website: www.nra.org.uk

Enquiries to: Chief Executive
Direct tel: ext 126
Direct e-mail: elaine.buttle@nra.org.uk
Other contacts: Membership Secretary for membership enquiries.

Founded: 1860

Organisation type and purpose: International organisation, membership association (membership is by subscription), present number of members: 5500, registered charity, suitable for ages: all.
Governing body of full-bore rifle and pistol shooting in the UK. Central body for affiliated schools and 1000 shooting clubs and associations.

Subject coverage: Full-bore rifle and pistol shooting, marksmanship, rules and regulations in competition shooting, construction of new ranges.

Collection: Archives since the Association's foundation in 1860
Museum of historic fire arms and memorabilia

Publications: Printed

Access to staff: Contact by letter, by telephone, by fax and by e-mail
Hours: Mon to Fri, 0900 to 1700

Member of: British Shooting Sports Council; Great Britain Target Shooting Federation

NATIONAL RIVERS AUTHORITY (NRA)

Regional Offices: Anglian Region; Kingfisher Home, Goldhay Way, Orton Goldhay, Peterborough, Cambridgeshire, PE2 0ZE; tel: 01733 371811; fax: 01733 231840; North West Region; PO Box 432, Warrington, WA4 1HH; North West Region; Richard Fairclough House, Knutsford Road, Warrington, WA4 1HG; tel: 01925 53999; fax: 01925 415961; North West Region; Road Three, Winsford Industrial Estate, Winsford, CW7 3SL; North West Region; Abbotsfield Road, Reginald Road Industrial Estate, St Helens, WA9 4HU; North West Region; Chertsey Hill, London Road, Carlisle, CA1 2QX; North West Region; Holme Road, Bamber Hill, Preston, PR5 6BP; Northumbria & Yorkshire Region; Eldon House, Regent Centre, Gosforth, Newcastle upon Tyne, NE3 3UB; tel: 0191 213 0266 or 284 5069; Northumbria & Yorkshire Region; 21 Park Square South, Leeds, LS1 2QG; tel: 0113 244 0191; fax: 0113 246 1889; Severn Trent Region; Sapphire East, 550 Streetsbrook Road, Solihull, Birmingham, B91 9QT; tel: 0121 711 2324; fax: 0121 711 5824; Severn Trent Region; PO Box 299, Shrewsbury, Shropshire, SY3 8WD; Severn Trent Region, Upper Severn Area; Hafren House, Welshpool Road, Shelton, Shrewsbury, Shropshire, SY3 8BB; South Western Region; Manley House, Kestrel Way, Exeter, EX2 7LQ; tel: 01392 444000; fax: 01392 444238; South Western Region, Bridgewater Office; Rivers House, East Quay, Bridgwater, Somerset, TA6 4YS; tel: 01278 457333; fax: 01278 452985; Southern Region; Portfield Depot, Oving Road, Chichester, PO20 6AG; Southern Region; Guildbourne House, Chatsworth Road, Worthing, West Sussex, BN11 1LD; tel: 01903 820692; fax: 01903 821832; Southern Region; Southern Region Laboratory, 4 The Meadows, Waterberry Drive, Waterlooville, PO7 7XX; Southern Region; 20 Manners View, Newport, Isle of Wight, PO30 5FA; Southern Region; Ladymead, Guildford, GU1 1BZ; Thames Region; Isis House, Howbery Park, Wallingford, Oxfordshire, OX10 8BD; Thames Region; 3rd Floor, Kings Meadow House, Kings Meadow Road, Reading, RG1 8DG; tel: 0118 953 5000; fax:

continued overleaf

0118 950 0388; Welsh Region; Rivers House, St Mellons Business Park, St Mellons, Cardiff, CF3 0LT; tel: 029 2077 0088; fax: 029 2079 8555

NATIONAL ROLLER HOCKEY ASSOCIATION OF ENGLAND LTD (NRHA)

82 Greenfield Road, Farnham, Surrey, GU9 8TQ

Tel: 07702 503383
Fax: 01252 723635
E-mail: gail-whattingham@tinyonline.co.uk
Website: www.nrha.co.uk

Enquiries to: Public Relations Manager
Other contacts: General Secretary; Archive Historian

Founded: 1912

Organisation type and purpose: Statutory body, membership association, present number of members: 1,500.
Governing body of the sport.

Subject coverage: Club addresses, organisation of taster courses; help with development and coaching, courses on coaching for all coaches and referees to international standard.

Non-library collection catalogue: All or part available in print

Publications: Printed, and electronic and video

Access to staff: Contact by letter, by telephone, by fax, by e-mail and via website
Hours: Mon to Fri, 0900 to 1700

Links with: British Skater Hockey Association; European Committee of Roller Skating (CERS); International Federation of Roller Skating (FIRS); National Skating Association; Sport England

Member organisation of: Central Council of Physical Recreation

NATIONAL SCHIZOPHRENIA FELLOWSHIP (SCOTLAND) (NSF(S))

6 Newington Business Centre, Dalkeith Road Mews, Edinburgh, EH16 5GA

Tel: 0131 662 4359
Fax: 0131 662 2289
E-mail: info@nsfscot.org.uk
Website: www.nsfscot.org.uk

Enquiries to: Information Officer

Founded: 1984

Organisation type and purpose:
Membership association (membership is by subscription), present number of members: 500, voluntary organisation, registered charity (charity number SCO 13649).

Subject coverage: Mental illness, particularly schizophrenia.

Library catalogue: All or part available in-house

Publications: Printed

Publications list: Available online and in print

Access to staff: Contact by letter, by telephone, by fax, by e-mail and in person
Hours: Mon to Fri, 0900 to 1700

Access for disabled people: Level entry

NATIONAL SCHOOLS SEVENS (NSS)

PO Box 52, East Peckham, Tonbridge, Kent, TN12 5ZP

Tel: 01622 871170
Fax: 01622 873426
E-mail: ns7s@btinternet.com
Website: www.armyns7.co.uk

Enquiries to: Tournament Organisers

Founded: 1939

Organisation type and purpose: National organisation.
Rugby Union Tournament for schoolchildren.
To provide a first class Rugby Union Tournament for Schools aged 13 to 18.

Subject coverage: Seven-a-side rugby union in schools.

Publications: Printed

Access to staff: Contact by letter, by telephone, by fax, by e-mail and via website
Hours: Sun to Sat, 0900 to 1700

Access for disabled people: Toilet facilities

NATIONAL SCREEN AND SOUND ARCHIVE OF WALES (NSSAW)

The National Library of Wales, Aberystwyth, SY23 3BU

Tel: 01970 632828
Fax: 01970 632544
E-mail: agssc@llgc.org.uk
Website: archif.com

Founded: 2001

Organisation type and purpose: National archive.

Subject coverage: Films, television programmes, videos, sound recordings and music relating to Wales and the Welsh.

Special visitor services: Viewing and listening services.

Collection: Incorporates the collections of:
Wales Film and Television Archive
National Library of Wales' Sound and Moving Image collection

Access to building: *Hours:* Mon to Fri, 1000 to 1700

NATIONAL SECULAR SOCIETY (NSS)

25 Red Lion Square, London, WC1R 4RL

Tel: 020 7404 3126
Fax: 0870 762 8971
E-mail: enquiries@secularism.org.uk
Website: www.secularism.org.uk

Enquiries to: Administrator

Founded: 1866

Organisation type and purpose:
Campaigning organisation (membership is by subscription), voluntary organisation.

Subject coverage: Secular humanism; atheism; civil liberties; rational education; freethought history.

Collection: C Bradlaugh MP – papers at Bishopsgate Library, Liverpool Street, London EC2

Library catalogue: All or part available in-house

Publications: Printed

Access to staff: Contact by letter, by telephone, by e-mail and via website. Appointment necessary.
Hours: Mon to Fri, 0900 to 1700

Access to building: Prior appointment required

Affiliates of: Abortion Rights; Amnesty International; European Humanist Federation; International Humanist and Ethical Union; Liberty; Network for Peace.; International Humanist and Ethical Union

NATIONAL SHEEP ASSOCIATION (NSA)

The Sheep Centre, Malvern, Worcestershire, WR13 6PH

Tel: 01684 892661
Fax: 01684 892663
E-mail: enquiries@nationalsheep.org.uk

Enquiries to: Chief Executive

Founded: 1892

Organisation type and purpose:
Membership association (membership is by subscription), present number of members: 12,000, registered charity (charity number 249255).
Agricultural organisation.
Representative body for sheep farmers.

Subject coverage: Sheep and the UK sheep industry.

Publications: Printed

Access to staff: Contact by letter.
Appointment necessary.
Hours: Mon to Fri, 0900 to 1700

NATIONAL SMALL-BORE RIFLE ASSOCIATION (NSRA)

Lord Roberts Centre, Bisley Camp, Brookwood, Woking, Surrey, GU24 0NP

Tel: 01483 485500
Fax: 01483 476392
E-mail: info@nsra.co.uk
Website: www.nsra.co.uk

Enquiries to: Information Officer
Direct tel: 01483 485505
Direct e-mail: jpage@nsra.co.uk

Founded: 1901

Organisation type and purpose:
Membership association (membership is by subscription), present number of members: 15,500, voluntary organisation, registered charity (charity number 215468).
Governing body for small-bore rifle and pistol shooting, and air rifle and air pistol shooting, and match crossbow shooting.

Subject coverage: Rifle, pistol small-bore target shooting; air rifle, air gun (.177 calibre) target shooting; match crossbow shooting;

range construction, firearms legislation, sale of ammunition, guns and equipment to members.

Publications: Printed, and electronic and video

Publications list: Available in print

Access to staff: Contact by letter, by telephone, by fax, by e-mail and in person. Access for members only.
Hours: Mon to Fri, 0900 to 1700

Access to building: No prior appointment required

Member of: British Olympic Association; British Shooting; British Shooting Sports Council; Great Britain Target Shooting Federation; International Shooting Sport Federation

NATIONAL SOCIETY FOR EDUCATION IN ART AND DESIGN (NSEAD)

3 Mason's Wharf, Corsham, Wiltshire, SN13 9FY

Tel: 01225 810134
Fax: 01225 812730
E-mail: lesleybutterworth@nsead.org
Website: www.nsead.org

Enquiries to: Office Manager
Direct e-mail: info@nsead.org

Founded: 1888; formerly called Society of Art Masters, National Society for Art Education

Organisation type and purpose: Learned society, trade union (membership is by subscription), present number of members: 2,000, publishing house.

Subject coverage: Art and design in education across all education sectors; careers in art and design; international and national contacts in field of art and design education.

Information services: Employment, professional development, art and design education.

Special visitor services: Archives by appointment.

Education services: Extensive – see http://www.nsead.org.

Trade and statistical information: Data on art education development throughout the world via the International Society for Education in Art

Publications: Printed

Publications list: Available online and in print

Access to staff: Contact by letter, by telephone, by fax, by e-mail and via website. Appointment necessary.
Hours: Mon to Fri, 0900 to 1700

Access to building: *Hours:* Mon to Fri, 0900 to 1700

Access for disabled people: *Hours:* Mon to Fri, 0900 to 1700

Member organisation of: International Society for Education in Art

NATIONAL SOCIETY FOR EPILEPSY (NSE)

Chesham Lane, Chalfont St Peter, Buckinghamshire, SL9 0RJ

Tel: 01494 601300, 01494 601400 (Helpline)
Fax: 01494 871927
Website: www.epilepsysociety.org.uk/forprofessionals
Website: www.epilepsysociety.org.uk

Enquiries to: Epilepsy Information Services Administrator
Direct tel: 01494 601392
Direct fax: 01494 601337

Founded: 1892

Organisation type and purpose: National organisation (membership is by subscription), voluntary organisation, registered charity (charity number 206186), training organisation, research organisation. To provide long-term and respite residential care for adults with epilepsy, to research into, and provide assessment and treatment services for, adults with epilepsy, to raise public awareness and understanding, to provide information, training and other support to people with epilepsy and their carers.

Subject coverage: Epilepsy; help for people with epilepsy, residential homes, treatment, care and rehabilitation, research, diagnosis, support and management.

Non-library collection catalogue: All or part available online

Publications: Printed, and electronic and video
Order printed publications from: Order online or telephone for an information list

Publications list: Available online and in print

Access to staff: Contact by letter and by telephone
Hours: Mon to Fri, 0900 to 1700
Special comments: Helpline open Mon to Fri, 1000 to 1600.

Access for disabled people: Level entry, access to all public areas, toilet facilities

Affiliated to: National Hospital of Neurology and Neurosurgery

NATIONAL SOCIETY FOR PHENYLKETONURIA (NSPKU)

Formal name: National Society for Phenylketonuria (United Kingdom)

PO Box 26642, London, N14 4ZF

Tel: 020 8364 3010
Fax: 0845 004 8341
E-mail: info@nspku.org
Website: www.nspku.org

Enquiries to: Administrator

Founded: 1973

Organisation type and purpose: Registered charity (charity number 273670).

Subject coverage: Help and advice for people with PKU, their families and carers.

Publications: Printed
Order printed publications from: Administrator, at above address

Publications list: Available online and in print

Access to staff: Contact by letter, by telephone and by e-mail
Hours: 24 hours

NATIONAL SOCIETY FOR RESEARCH INTO ALLERGY (NSRA)

2 Armadale Close, Hollycroft, Hinckley, Leicestershire, LE10 0SZ

Tel: 01455 250715
E-mail: eunicerose@talktalk.net
Website: all-allergy.org

Enquiries to: Honorary Secretary
Other contacts: Honorary Vice-Chairperson; tel: 01455 291294

Founded: 1980

Organisation type and purpose: Advisory body, membership association (membership is by subscription), voluntary organisation, registered charity (charity number 32608). Aims to see allergy and intolerance accepted and for there to be adequate, effective and safe treatment within the NHS. To assist and impart information to GPs, hospital doctors, and members of other caring and teaching professions, as well as sufferers.

Subject coverage: Eczema, asthma, urticaria, hyperactivity, irritable bowel syndrome, Crohn's disease, migraine, arthritis, airborne allergy, ME, post-viral syndrome, PIMS and any other allergy or sensitivity, determination of allergy, medically backed diets, substitute foods, hyperventilation, criminal behaviour, thyroid problems.

Information services: For people suffering or needing to know more about all aspects of allergy/intolerance.

Publications: Printed

Publications list: Available in print

Access to staff: Contact by letter, by telephone, by e-mail and in person. Appointment necessary.
Hours: Mon to Fri, 0900 to 1700

NATIONAL SOCIETY OF ALLIED AND INDEPENDENT FUNERAL DIRECTORS (SAIF)

SAIF Business Centre, 3 Bullfields, Sawbridgeworth, Hertfordshire, CM21 9DB

Tel: 0845 230 6777
Fax: 01279 726300
E-mail: info@saif.org.uk
Website: www.saif.org.uk

Enquiries to: Administration Manager
Direct e-mail: linda@saif.org.uk

Founded: 1989

Organisation type and purpose: Trade association (membership is by subscription), present number of members: over 1,000.

Subject coverage: All aspects of the UK funeral service.

Access to staff: Contact by letter, by telephone, by fax and by e-mail
Hours: Mon to Fri, 0900 to 1700

NATIONAL SOCIETY OF ALLOTMENT AND LEISURE GARDENERS LIMITED (NSALG)

O'Dell House, Hunters Road, Corby, Northamptonshire, NN17 5JE

Tel: 01536 266576
Fax: 01536 264509
E-mail: natsoc@nsalg.org.uk

Enquiries to: General Secretary

Founded: 1930

Organisation type and purpose:
Membership association (membership is by subscription), present number of members: 80,000, voluntary organisation.
National representative body.
Represents the interests of allotment holders.

Subject coverage: Horticulture and gardening; interpretation of allotments legislation; environmental planning and development; preparation of leases and tenancy agreements.

Trade and statistical information: Allotment survey

Publications: Printed

Access to staff: Contact by letter, by telephone and by fax
Hours: Mon to Fri, 0900 to 1700

Affiliated to: International League of Leisure Gardens

NATIONAL SOCIETY OF MASTER THATCHERS (NSMT)

20 The Laurels, Tetsworth, Thame, Oxfordshire, OX9 7BH

Tel: 01844 281568
Fax: 01844 281568
E-mail: nsmt@bigfoot.com
Website: www.nsmt.hypermart.net

Enquiries to: Secretary

Founded: 1963

Organisation type and purpose: Trade association (membership is by qualification), present number of members: 80, voluntary organisation.

Subject coverage: Thatching.

Publications: Printed

Access to staff: Contact by letter and by e-mail
Hours: Evenings and weekends

NATIONAL SOIL RESOURCES INSTITUTE (SSLRC)

Cranfield University, Silsoe, Bedfordshire, MK45 4DT

Tel: 01525 863242
Fax: 01525 863253
Website: www.silsoe.cranfield.ac.uk/nsri

Enquiries to: Development Manager
Direct tel: 01525 863263
Direct e-mail: t.mayr@cranfield.ac.uk

Founded: 2001

Organisation type and purpose:
Consultancy, research organisation.

Subject coverage: Soils and land use, crop suitability, suitability of land for a wide range of uses, chemical and physical properties of soils, environmental risk assessment and pollution control.

Non-library collection catalogue: All or part available in-house and in print

Publications: Printed, and electronic and video
Order printed publications from: Publications Officer, National Soil Resources Institute at the same address, tel: 01525 863242, fax: 01525 863253, e-mail: e.m.paynter@cranfield.ac.uk

Publications list: Available online and in print

Access to staff: Contact by letter, by telephone, by fax, by e-mail and via website. Appointment necessary.
Hours: Mon to Fri, 0900 to 1700

Access to building: Prior appointment required

Access for disabled people: Level entry, toilet facilities

Other addresses: National Soil Resources Institute; NSRI, North Wyke, Okehampton, Devon, EX20 2SB; tel: 01837 89188; fax: 01837 82139; National Soil Resources Institute; NSRI, The Innovation Centre, York Science Park, Heslington, York, YO10 5DG; tel: 01904 435220; fax: 01904 435221; National Soil Resources Institute; NSRI, Cambria House, 29, Newport Road, Cardiff, CF24 0TP; tel: 07775 865701

Parent body: Cranfield University

NATIONAL SPECIALIST CONTRACTORS COUNCIL (NSCC)

6–8 Bonhill Street, London, EC2A 4BX

Tel: 0844 249 5351
Fax: 0844 249 5352
E-mail: enquiries@nscc.org.uk
Website: www.nscc.org.uk

Enquiries to: Director

Founded: 1994

Organisation type and purpose: Trade association.
Umbrella association representing the interests of trade associations in the construction industry.

Subject coverage: Contractors and sub-contractors in the specialist sector and trade sector of construction.

Access to staff: Contact by letter, by telephone, by fax and by e-mail
Hours: Mon to Fri, 0900 to 1700

Has: 32 member organisations

NATIONAL SPIRITUAL ASSEMBLY OF THE BAHA'IS OF THE UNITED KINGDOM (NSA UK)

National Baha'i Centre, 27 Rutland Gate, London, SW7 1PD

Tel: 020 7584 2566
Fax: 020 7584 9402
E-mail: secretariat@bahai.org.uk
Website: bahainews-uk.info
Website: www.bahai.org.uk
Website: www.bahaibooks.org.uk

Enquiries to: Office of Public Information
Direct e-mail: opi@bahai.org.uk

Founded: 1923

Organisation type and purpose: Elected governing council of UK Baha'i community, registered charity (charity number 250851). Religious charity.

Subject coverage: The Baha'i Faith – its history, teachings, national and international standing, including its accreditation with the United Nations.

Collection: Afnan Trust Library (by appointment only)

Publications: Printed, and electronic and video
Order printed publications from: The Coordinator, Baha'i Books UK, 5 Station Approach, Oakham, Rutland, LE15 6QW; tel: 01572 722780; fax: 01572 724280; e-mail: sales@books.bahai.org.uk
Order electronic and video publications from: Baha'i Books UK (as above)

Publications list: Available online and in print

Access to staff: Contact by letter, by telephone, by fax, by e-mail, in person and via website. Appointment necessary.
Hours: Mon to Fri, 0930 to 1700

Access to building: *Hours:* Mon to Fri, 0930 to 1700

Access for disabled people: Lift, toilet facilities
Special comments: Lift does not reach top floor of Baha'i Centre.

NATIONAL STOOLBALL ASSOCIATION (SE)

Formal name: Stoolball England

53 Kings Road, Horsham, West Sussex, RH13 5PP

Tel: 01403 252419
E-mail: kr.price@homecall.co.uk
Website: www.stoolball.org.uk

Enquiries to: Honorary Secretary
Other contacts: Insurance Officer (for personal accident and public liability); tel: 01293 772469; e-mail leddy@tiscali.co.uk; Sales Officer (for stoolball equipment); tel: 01403 252419; e-mail: kr.price@homecall.co.uk

Founded: 1979

Organisation type and purpose: Advisory body, voluntary organisation.
Recognised governing body of stoolball.

Subject coverage: All enquiries about stoolball.

Collection: Archive records from 1880–1950 held at Barbican Museum, Lewes, Sussex; appointment needed for inspection

Publications: Printed, and electronic and video
Order electronic and video publications from: Honorary Secretary

Publications list: Available online and in print

Access to staff: Contact by letter, by telephone, by e-mail and via website

Hours: Any reasonable time, answerphone available

Access to building: Prior appointment required

Access for disabled people: Parking provided

NATIONAL SWEET PEA SOCIETY (NSPS)

8 Wolseley Road, Parkstone, Poole, Dorset, BH12 2DP

Tel: 01202 734088
E-mail: bg.bulstrode@btinternet.com
Website: www.sweetpeas.org.uk

Enquiries to: Secretary

Founded: 1900

Organisation type and purpose:
Membership association, registered charity.

Subject coverage: Breeding, cultivation, development of lathyrus odoratus (sweet pea) and other lathyrus species; exhibiting and garden decoration.

Collection: All publications, since the formation of the Society in 1901

Publications: Printed

Access to staff: Contact by letter and by telephone. Access for members only.
Hours: Mon to Fri, 0900 to 1700

Affiliated to: Royal Horticultural Society

NATIONAL SYMPHONY ORCHESTRA (NSO)

Formal name: National Symphony Orchestra of London

177 John Ruskin Street, London, SE5 0PQ

Tel: 020 7703 3148
Fax: 020 7703 5334
E-mail: enquiries@nso.co.uk
Website: www.nso.co.uk

Enquiries to: Artistic Director

Founded: 1940

Organisation type and purpose: Symphony orchestra.

Subject coverage: Music, arts, entertainment.

Publications: Electronic and video

Access to staff: Contact by letter, by telephone, by e-mail and in person
Hours: Mon to Fri, 0900 to 1700

NATIONAL TAXI ASSOCIATION (NTA)

5 Clifton Hill, Brighton, East Sussex, BN1 3HL

Tel: 01273 729403
Fax: 01273 728122
E-mail: enquiries@brighton-streamline.co.uk
Website: www.brighton-streamline.co.uk

Enquiries to: Administrator

Founded: 1967

Organisation type and purpose: National organisation, trade association (membership is by subscription).

Subject coverage: Taxi cabs.

Access to staff: Contact by letter and by e-mail
Hours: Mon to Fri, 0900 to 1700

NATIONAL THEATRE (NT)

Upper Ground, London, SE1 9PX

Tel: 020 7452 3000 (box office); 020 7452 3333 (stage door/admin); 020 7452 3009 (minicom)
Fax: 020 7452 3030 (box office)
Website: www.nationaltheatre.org.uk

Enquiries to: Information Officer
Direct tel: 020 7452 3400

Founded: 1963

Organisation type and purpose: Registered charity (charity number 224223).
The National Theatre is central to the creative life of the country. In its three theatres on the South Bank in London, it presents an eclectic mix of new plays and classics, with seven or eight productions in repertory at any one time. It aims constantly to re-energise the great traditions of the British stage and to expand the horizons of audiences and artists alike. It aspires to reflect in its repertoire the diversity of the culture. At its Studio, the National offers a space for research and development of the NT's stages and the theatre as a whole. Through the NT Education Department, tomorrow's audiences are addressed. Through an extensive programme of Platform performances, backstage tours, foyer music, exhibitions, and free outdoor entertainment it recognises that the theatre does not begin and end with the rise and fall of the curtain. And by touring, the National shares its work with audiences in the UK and abroad.

Subject coverage: World drama; free exhibitions and live music; platform performances and events; education and community outreach work; theatre backstage tours; bookshop; bars and restaurants.

Non-library collection catalogue: All or part available online

Publications: Printed
Order printed publications from: National Theatre Bookshop at the address above; tel: 020 7452 3456; e-mail: bookshop@nationaltheatre.org.uk

Access to staff: Contact by letter, by telephone and by fax
Hours: Foyers: Mon to Sat, 1000 to 2300; Box Office: Mon to Sat, 1000 to 2000

Access for disabled people: Parking provided, ramped entry, access to all public areas, toilet facilities
Special comments: Audio-described and sign language interpreted performances.

NATIONAL TORTOISE CLUB OF GREAT BRITAIN & TORTOISE HELPLINE

2 Laith Close, Cookridge, Leeds, West Yorkshire, LS16 6LE

Tel: 0113 267 7587

Enquiries to: Chairman/Founder

Founded: 1970

Organisation type and purpose:
International organisation, advisory body, membership association, voluntary organisation, consultancy.
Advisory service UK and Europe; funded entirely by Founders.
Permanent sanctuary to any tortoise, on request, free.

Subject coverage: All aspects of the needs of tortoises and box tortoises (often incorrectly called turtles) throughout the year; health and sickness, diet, hibernation, breeding, care and well-being of all species.

Information services: Free helpline.

Education services: Founder accepts invitations to appear on TV and radio.

Publications: Printed

Access to staff: Contact by letter and by telephone
Hours: Mon to Fri, 0900 to 1700
Special comments: Enclose an sae for reply, donations appreciated. If messages left on answerphone no calls back made without assurance that reversed charges will be accepted.

NATIONAL TRACTION ENGINE TRUST (NTET)

153 Micklefield Road, High Wycombe, Buckinghamshire, HP13 7HA

Tel: 01494 521727
Fax: 01494 521727
E-mail: suejackson@themutual.net

Enquiries to: Secretary General

Founded: 1954

Organisation type and purpose:
Membership association (membership is by subscription), voluntary organisation, registered charity.
Most local steam groups with similar aims are affiliated.

Subject coverage: History of engines and their manufacturers, as well as up-to-date information as to repairs, spares and information about traction engine rallies each year, for organisers and the general public, preservation and operation of steam-powered traction engines.

Publications: Printed

Access to staff: Contact by letter, by telephone, by fax and by e-mail
Hours: Mon to Fri, 0900 to 1700

NATIONAL TROLLEYBUS ASSOCIATION (NTA)

24 Heath Farm Road, Ferndown, Dorset, BH22 8JW

Website: www.trolleybus.co.uk/nta

Enquiries to: Editor
Direct e-mail: cisgar@btinternet.com
Other contacts: editor.tm@btinternet.com

Founded: 1963

Organisation type and purpose:
Membership association.
To produce publications relating to trolleybuses and to preserve trolleybuses (five of which are currently owned).

continued overleaf

Subject coverage: Description of present day trolleybus operation, new vehicle developments, system histories, comprehensive worldwide trolleybus news with maps and illustrations.

Collection: H Brearley, photographic collection
R F Mack, photographic collection

Trade and statistical information: Statistics on all aspects of trolleybuses and trolleybus systems.
Information on new vehicles, technical developments, etc

Publications: Printed

Publications list: Available online

Access to staff: Contact by letter and by e-mail
Hours: Mon to Fri, 0900 to 1700

Affiliated to: NTA (1963) Ltd

Also at: Membership Enquiries, National Trolleybus Association; 2 St John's Close. Claines, Worcester, WR3 7PT

Subsidiary for publication sales: NTA Sales; 164 Kinson Road, Kinson, Bournemouth, BH10 5EN

NATIONAL TRUST (NT)

Formal name: National Trust for Places of Historic Interest or Natural Beauty

36 Queen Anne's Gate, London, SW1H 9AS

Tel: 020 7222 9251
Fax: 020 7222 5097
E-mail: enquiries@thenationaltrust.org.uk
Website: www.nationaltrust.org.uk

Enquiries to: Director General
Other contacts: Customer Care Manager for general enquiries.

Founded: 1895

Organisation type and purpose: National organisation, membership association (membership is by subscription), present number of members: 2.9 million, voluntary organisation, registered charity (charity number 205846), museum, historic building, house or site, suitable for ages: all, research organisation, publishing house.
Membership is the principal means by which the NT is supported, but access to its services is not restricted to members.
The National Trust preserves places of historic interest or natural beauty for all to enjoy, now and forever.

Subject coverage: Conservation of buildings and land of historic interest or natural beauty held in perpetuity for the nation, inalienably. History of the National Trust. Visitor management, sustainability, policy issues etc.

Collection: Details may be found in the Trust's handbook and on the website
Some country houses contain antiquarian libraries for which the central catalogue is still in the development stage. All these collections are managed and accessed by different arrangements, many of which are local to the property itself

Publications: Printed, and electronic and video

Publications list: Available online and in print

Access to staff: Contact by letter, by telephone, by fax, by e-mail, in person and via website
Hours: Mon to Fri, 0900 to 1700

Other addresses: Learning Community and Volunteering Office; Rowan House, Kembrey Park, Swindon, Wiltshire, SN2 6UG; tel: 0870 609 5383; National Trust Conservation Directorate; 33 Sheep Street, Cirencester, Gloucestershire, CL7 1RQ; tel: 0870 609 5382; National Trust Enterprises; The Stable Block, Heywood House, Westbury, Wiltshire, BA13 4NA; tel: 0870 609 5381; National Trust for Scotland; Wemyss House, 28 Charlotte Square, Edinburgh, EH2 4ET; tel: 0131 243 9300; National Trust Office for Northern Ireland; Rowallane House, Saintfield, Ballynahinch, Co Down, BT24 7LH; tel: 028 9751 0721; fax: 028 9751 1242; National Trust Office for Wales; Trinity Square, Llandudno, LL30 2DE; tel: 01492 860123; fax: 01492 860233; National Trust Theatre Projects; The National Trust, Sutton House, 2 & 4 Homerton High Street, Hackney, London, E9 6JQ; tel: 020 8986 0242; The National Trust Membership Department; PO Box 39, Bromley, Kent, BR1 3XL; tel: 020 8466 6824

Regional Offices: National Trust, Devon & Cornwall; Killerton House, Broadclyst, Exeter, Devon, EX5 3LE; tel: 01392 881691; fax: 01392 881954; National Trust, Devon & Cornwall; Lanhydrock, Bodmin, Cornwall, PL30 4DE; tel: 01208 74281; fax: 01208 77887; National Trust, East Anglia (Bedfordshire, Cambridgeshire, Essex, part of Hertfordshire, Norfolk & Suffolk); The Dairy House, Ickworth, Suffolk, IP29 5QE; tel: 0870 609 5388; fax: 01284 736066; National Trust, East Midlands (Derbyshire, Leicestershire, South Lincolnshire, Northamptonshire, Nottinghamshire & Rutland); Clumber Park Stableyard, Worksop, Nottinghamshire, S80 3BE; tel: 01909 486411; fax: 01909 486377; National Trust, North West (Cheshire, Cumbria, Greater Manchester & Lancashire, Merseyside); The Hollens, Grasmere, LA22 9QZ; tel: 0870 609 5391; fax: 015394 35353; National Trust, South East (East Sussex, Kent, Surrey & West Sussex); Polesden Lacey, Dorking, Surrey, RH5 6BD; tel: 01372 453401; fax: 01372 452023; National Trust, Thames & Solent (Berkshire, Buckinghamshire, Hampshire, part of Hertfordshire, Isle of Wight, Greater London & Oxfordshire); Hughenden Manor, High Wycombe, Buckinghamshire, HP14 4LA; tel: 01494 528051; fax: 01494 463310; National Trust, Wessex (Bristol/Bath, Dorset, Gloucestershire, Somerset & Wiltshire); Eastleigh Court, Bishopstrow, Warminster, Wiltshire, BA12 9HW; tel: 01985 843600; fax: 01985 843624; National Trust, West Midlands (Birmingham, Hereford, Shropshire, Staffordshire, Warwickshire & Worcestershire); Attingham Park, Shrewsbury, Shropshire, SY4 4TP; tel: 01743 708100; fax: 01743 708150; National Trust, Yorkshire & North East (Co Durham, Newcastle & Tyneside, Northumberland); Scots' Gap, Morpeth, Northumberland, NE61 4EG; tel: 01670 774691; fax: 01670 774317; National Trust, Yorkshire & North East (Yorkshire, Teesside & N Lincolnshire); Goddards, 27 Tadcaster Road, York, YO24 1GG; tel: 01904 702021; fax: 01904 771970

NATIONAL TRUST (DEVON & CORNWALL REGIONAL OFFICES) – BODMIN

Formal name: National Trust for Places of Historic Interest or Natural Beauty

Lanhydrock, Bodmin, Cornwall, PL30 4DE

Tel: 01208 74281
Fax: 01208 77887
E-mail: enquiries@thenationaltrust.org.uk
Website: www.nationaltrust.org.uk

Enquiries to: Customer Service Manager

Founded: 1895

Organisation type and purpose: National organisation, independently owned, membership association (membership is by subscription), registered charity (charity number 205846), historic building, house or site, suitable for ages: all.

Subject coverage: Administration and management of Trust sites in the region. The preservation and upkeep of places of historic interest and natural beauty in Cornwall.

Publications list: Available online and in print

Links with: Trevithick Trust; Trevithick Road, Pool, Redruth, Cornwall, TR15 3NP; tel: 01209 210900; e-mail: info@ trevithicktrust.com

National Trust Sites: Antony House; Torpoint, Plymouth, PL11 2QA; tel: 01752 812191; Cornish Mines & Engines; Trevithick Road, Pool, Redruth, Cornwall, TR15 3NP; tel: 01209 210900; Cotehele House; St. Dominick, Saltash, Cornwall, PL30 5AD; tel: 01579 351346; e-mail: cctlce@ smtp.ntrust.org.uk; Godolphin Estate; Lizard Countryside Office, Helston, Cornwall; tel: 01326 562882; Lanhydrock House; Cornwall; tel: 01208 73320; e-mail: clhlan@smtp.ntrust.org.uk; Lawrence House Museum; 9 Castle Street, Launceston, Cornwall, PL15 8BA; tel: 01566 773277; Levant Steam Engine; Trewellard, Pendeen, St Just, Cornwall; tel: 01736 786156; St Michael's Mount; Marazion, Penzance, Cornwall, TR17 0EF; tel: 01736 710507/ 710233; e-mail: godolphin@manor-office.co .uk; Tintagel Old Post Office; Fore Street, Tintagel, Cornwall, PL34 0DB; tel: 01840 770024; Trerice Manor House; Kestle Mill, Newquay, Cornwall, TR8 4PG; tel: 01637 875404

NATIONAL TRUST (DEVON & CORNWALL REGIONAL OFFICES) – EXETER

Formal name: National Trust for Places of Historic Interest or Natural Beauty

Killerton House, Broadclyst, Exeter, Devon, EX5 3LE

Tel: 01392 881691
Fax: 01392 881954
E-mail: enquiries@thenationaltrust.org.uk
Website: www.nationaltrust.org.uk

Enquiries to: Service Supporter Manager

Founded: 1895

Organisation type and purpose: National organisation, independently owned, membership association (membership is by subscription), registered charity (charity number 205846), historic building, house or site, suitable for ages: lifelong.
Administration and management of Trust sites in Devon.

Subject coverage: The preservation and upkeep of places of historic interest and natural beauty in Devon.

Non-library collection catalogue: All or part available in-house

Library catalogue: All or part available in-house

Publications list: Available online and in print

Access to staff: Contact by letter, by telephone, by fax, by e-mail, in person and via website
Hours: Sun to Sat, 0900 to 1700

Access to building: *Hours:* Generally 1100 to 1700, but please check before visit

National Trust sites: A La Ronde; Summer Lane, Exmouth, Devon, EX8 5BD; tel: 01395 265514; Arlington Court; Arlington, Barnstaple, Devon, EX31 4LP; tel: 01271 850296; fax: 01271 850711; Bradley House; Totnes Road, Newton Abbot, Devon, TQ12 6BN; tel: 01626 354513; Buckland Abbey; Yelverton, Devon, PL20 6EY; tel: 01822 853607; fax: 01822 855448; Castle Drogo; Drewsteignton, Exeter, Devon, EX6 6PB; tel: 01647 433306; fax: 01647 433186; Clyston Mill; Killerton, Broadclyst, Exeter, Devon, EX5 3EW; tel: 01392 462425; Coleton Fishacre House; Coleton, Brownstone Road, Kingswear, Dartmouth, Devon, TQ6 0EQ; tel: 01803 752466; Compton Castle; Marldon, Paignton, Devon, TQ3 1TA; tel: 01803 875740; Finch Foundary Museum of Rural Industry; Sticklepath, Okehampton, Devon, EX20 2NW; tel: 01837 840046; Killerton House; Broadclyst, Exeter, Devon, EX5 3LE; tel: 01392 881345; Knightshayes Court; Bolham, Tiverton, Devon, EX16 7RQ; tel: 01884 254665; Loughwood Meeting House; Dalwood, Axminster, Devon, EX13 7DU; tel: 01392 881691; fax: 01392 881954; Marker's Cottage; Killerton, Broadclyst, Exeter, Devon, EX5 3HR; tel: 01392 461546; Newhall Equestrian Centre; Killerton, Broadclyst, Exeter, Devon, EX5 3LW; tel: 01392 462453; Old Bakery, Manor Mill and Forge; Branscombe, Seaton, Devon, EX12 3DB; tel: 01297 680333; Overbeck's Museum and Gardens; Sharpitor, Salcombe, Devon, 01548 842893; tel: 01548 842893; Saltram House; Plympton, Plymouth, Devon, PL7 1UH; tel: 01752 333500; fax: 01752 336474; Shute Barton; Shute, Axminster, Devon, EX13 7PT; tel: 01297 34692; Watersmeet House; Watersmeet Road, Lynmouth, Devon, EX35 6NT; tel: 01598 753348

NATIONAL TRUST (EAST MIDLANDS REGIONAL OFFICE)

Formal name: National Trust for Places of Historic Interest or Natural Beauty

Clumber Park Stableyard, Worksop, Nottinghamshire, S80 3BE

Tel: 01909 486411
Fax: 01909 486377
E-mail: enquiries@thenationaltrust.org.uk
Website: www.nationaltrust.org.uk

Enquiries to: Customer Service Manager

Founded: 1895

Organisation type and purpose: National organisation, independently owned, membership association (membership is by subscription), registered charity (charity number 205846), historic building, house or site, suitable for ages: Lifelong.
Administration and management of Trust sites in the East Midlands.

Subject coverage: The preservation and upkeep of places of historic interest and natural beauty in Derbyshire, Leicestershire, South Lincolnshire, Northamptonshire, Nottinghamshire and Rutland.

Publications list: Available online and in print

Access to staff: Contact by letter, by telephone, by fax, by e-mail, in person and via website
Hours: Mon to Fri, 0900 to 1700

National Trust sites: Belton House; Belton, Grantham, Lincolnshire, NG32 2LS; tel: 01476 566116; e-mail: belton@smpt.ntrust.org.uk; Calke Abbey; Ticknall, Derbyshire; tel: 01332 863822; e-mail: ecbxxx@smpt.ntrust.org.uk; Canons Ashby House; Canons Ashby, Daventry, Northamptonshire, NN1 6SD; tel: 01327 860044; fax: 01327 860168; e-mail: canonsashby@ntrust.org.uk; Grantham House; Castle Gate, Grantham, Lincolnshire, NG31 6SS; tel: 01909 486411 (Regional Office); Gunby Hall; Gunby, Spilsby, Lincolnshire, PE23 5SS; tel: 01909 486411 (Regional Office); Hardwick Hall; Doe Lea, Chesterfield, Derbyshire, S44 5QJ; tel: 01246 850430; Kedleston Hall; Kedleston, Derby, DE22 5JH; tel: 01332 842191; fax: 01332 841972; e-mail: kedlestonhall@ntrust.org.uk; Lyveden New Bield; Oundle, Peterborough, Northamptonshire, PE8 5AT; tel: 01832 205358; e-mail: lyvedennewbield@ntrust.org.uk; Mr Straws House; 7 Blyth Grove, Worksop, Nottinghamshire, S81 0JG; tel: 01909 482380; e-mail: estxxx@smtp.ntrust.org.uk; Museum of Childhood; Sudbury Hall, Sudbury, Ashbourne, Derbyshire, DE6 5HT; tel: 01283 585305; Priest's House; 39 Church Street, Easton on the Hill, Stamford, Northamptonshire, PE9 3LL; tel: 01909 486411 (Regional Office); Stainsby Mill; c/o Hardwick Hall, Doe Lea, Chesterfield, Derbyshire, S44 5QJ; tel: 01246 850430; e-mail: ehwxxx@smtr.ntrust.org.uk; Staunton Harold Church; Staunton Harold, Ashby-de-la-Zouch, Leicestershire; tel: 01332 863822; fax: 01332 865272; e-mail: stauntonharold@ntrust.org.uk; Sudbury Hall; Sudbury, Ashbourne, Derbyshire, DE6 5HT; tel: 01283 585305; Tattershall Castle; Tattershall, Lincoln, LN4 4LR; tel: 01526 342543; e-mail: tattershallcastle@ntrust.org.uk; The Workhouse; Upton Road, Southwell, Nottinghamshire, NG25 0PT; tel: 01636 817250; Whitegates Cottage; Gunby Hall Estate, Mill Lane, Bratoft, Spilsby, Lincolnshire; tel: 01909 486411 (Regional Office); Woolsthorpe Manor; 23 Newton Way, Woolsthorp-by-Colsterworth, Grantham, Lincolnshire, NG33 5NR; tel: 01476 860338

NATIONAL TRUST (EAST OF ENGLAND REGIONAL OFFICE)

Formal name: National Trust for Places of Historic Interest or Natural Beauty

Westley Bottom, Bury St Edmunds, Suffolk, IP33 3WD

Tel: 01284 747500
Fax: 01284 747506
E-mail: enquiries@thenationaltrust.org.uk
Website: www.nationaltrust.org.uk

Enquiries to: Customer Service Manager

Founded: 1895

Organisation type and purpose: National organisation, independently owned, membership association (membership is by subscription), registered charity (charity number 205846), historic building, house or site, suitable for ages: lifelong.
Administration and management of Trust sites in East Anglia.

Subject coverage: The preservation and upkeep of places of historic interest and natural beauty in Bedfordshire, Cambridgeshire, Essex, part of Hertfordshire, Norfolk and Suffolk.

Publications list: Available online and in print

Access to staff: Contact by letter, by telephone, by fax, by e-mail, in person and via website
Hours: Mon to Fri, 0900 to 1700

National Trust sites: Anglesey Abbey, Gardens and Lode Mill; Quy Road, Nr Lode, Cambridge, CB5 9EJ; tel: 01223 811200; e-mail: aayusr@ntrust.org.uk; Blickling Hall; Blickling, Norwich, Norfolk, NR11 6NF; tel: 01263 738030; e-mail: blickling@ntrust.org.uk; Bourne Mill; Bourne Road, Colchester, Essex, CO2 8RT; tel: 01206 572422; Coggeshall Grange Barn; Grange Hill, Coggeshall, Colchester, Essex, CO6 1RE; tel: 01376 562226; Elizabethan House Museum; 4 South Quay, Great Yarmouth, Norfolk, NR30 2QH; tel: 01493 855746; fax: 01493 745459; Felbrigg Hall; Felbrigg, Norwich, Norfolk, NR11 8PR; tel: 01263 837444; e-mail: afgusr@smtp.ntrust.org.uk; Guildhall of Corpus Christi; Market Place, Sudbury, Suffolk, CO10 9QZ; tel: 01787 247646; e-mail: almjtg@smtp.ntrust.org.uk; Horsey Windpump; Horsey, Great Yarmouth, Norfolk, NR29 4EF; tel: 01493 393904 (on open days); e-mail: horsey@ntrust.org.uk; Houghton Mill; Houghton, Huntingdon, Cambridgeshire, PE28 2EZ; tel: 01480 301494; Ickworth House, Park & Garden; Horringer, Bury St Edmunds, Suffolk, IP29 5QE; tel: 01284 735270; Melford Hall; Long Melford, Sudbury, Suffolk, CO10 9AA; tel: 01787 880286; e-mail: amdklx@smtp.ntrust.org.uk; Oxburgh Hall; Oxborough, Kings Lynn, Nofolk, PE33 9PS; tel: 01366 328258; fax: 01366 328066; e-mail: aohusr@smtp.ntrust.org.uk; Paycocke's; West Street, Coggeshall, Colchester, Essex, CO6 1NS; tel: 01376 561305; Peckover House; North Brink, Wisbech, Cambridgeshire, PE13 1JR; tel: 01945 583463; e-mail: aprigix@smtp.ntrust.org.uk; Ramsey Abbey Gatehouse; Abbey School, Ramsey, Huntingdon, Cambridgeshire, PE17 1DH; tel: 0870 609 5388; Shaw's Corner; Ayot St Lawrence, Welwyn Garden City, Hertfordshire, AL6 9BX; tel: 01438 820307; e-mail:

continued overleaf

shawscorner@ntrust.org.uk; Suffolk Horse Museum; The Market Hill, Woodbridge, Suffolk, IP12 4LP; tel: 01394 380643; Sutton Hoo; Woodbridge, Suffolk; tel: 01394 389700; Theatre Royal; Westgate Street, Bury St Edmunds, Suffolk, IP33 1QR; tel: 01284 769505; Wimpole Hall; Arrington, Royston, Hertfordshire, SG8 0BW; tel: 01223 207257; fax: 01223 207383; e-mail: aweusr@smtp.org.uk

NATIONAL TRUST (NORTH WEST REGIONAL OFFICE)

Formal name: National Trust for Places of Historic Interest or Natural Beauty

The Hollens, Grasmere, Cumbria, LA22 9QZ

Tel: 015394 35599
Fax: 015394 35353
E-mail: enquiries@thenationaltrust.org.uk
Website: www.nationaltrust.org.uk

Enquiries to: Customer Service Manager

Founded: 1895

Organisation type and purpose: National organisation, independently owned, membership association (membership is by subscription), registered charity (charity number 205846), historic building, house or site, suitable for ages: lifelong.
Administration and management of Trust sites in the North West region.

Subject coverage: The preservation and upkeep of places of historic interest and natural beauty in Cheshire, Cumbria, Greater Manchester and Lancashire, Merseyside.

Publications list: Available online and in print

Access to staff: Contact by letter, by telephone, by fax, by e-mail, in person and via website
Hours: Mon to Fri, 0900 to 1700

National Trust sites: 20 Forthlin Road; Liverpool, L24 1YP; tel: 0151 427 7231 (bookings); e-mail: 20forthlinroad@ntrust.org.uk; Beatrix Potter Gallery; Main Street, Hawkshead, Ambleside, Cumbria, LA22 0NS; tel: 015394 36355; fax: 015394 36187; e-mail: beatrixpottergallery@ntrust.org.uk; Cartmel Gatehouse Heritage Centre; Cavendish Street, Cartmel, Grange-over-Sands, Cumbria, LA11 6QA; tel: 015395 36874; fax: 015395 36636; e-mail: cartmelpriory@ntrust.org.uk; Dunham Massey; Altrincham, Greater Manchester, Cheshire, WA14 4SJ; tel: 0161 941 1025; fax: 0161 929 7508; e-mail: dunhammassey@ntrust.org.uk; Gawthorpe Hall; Padiham, Burnley, Lancashire, BB12 8UA; tel: 01282 771004; fax: 01282 770178; e-mail: gawthorpehall@ntrust.org.uk; Hill Top; Near Sawrey, Ambleside, Cumbria, LA22 0LF; tel: 015394 36269; fax: 015394 36188; e-mail: hilltop@ntrust.ofg.uk; Little Moreton Hall; Congleton, Cheshire, CW12 4SD; tel: 01260 272018; e-mail: littlemoretonhall@ntrust.org.uk; Lyme Park; Disley, Stockport, Cheshire, SK12 2NX; tel: 01663 762023; fax: 01663 765035; e-mail: lymepark@ntrust.org.uk; Nether Alderley Mill; Congleton Road, Nether Alderley, Macclesfield, Cheshire, SK10 4TW; tel: 01625 584412; e-mail: netheralderleymill@ntrust.org.uk; Quarry Bank Mill and Styal Estate; Quarry Bank Road, Styal, Wilmslow, Cheshire, SK9 4LA; tel: 01625 527468; fax: 01625 539267; e-mail: quarrybankmill@ntrust.org.uk; Rufford Old Hall; Rufford, Ormskirk, Lancashire, L40 1SG; tel: 01704 821254; fax: 01704 821254; e-mail: ruffordhall@ntrust.org.uk; Sizergh Castle and Garden; Sizergh, Kendal, Cumbria, LA8 8AE; tel: 01539 560070; fax: 015395 61621; e-mail: ntrust@sizerghcastle.fsnet.co.uk; Speke Hall; The Walk, Liverpool, L24 1XD; tel: 0151 427 7231; fax: 0151 427 9860; e-mail: spekehall@ntrust.org.uk; Tatton Park; Knutsford, Cheshire, WA16 6QN; tel: 01625 534400; fax: 01625 534403; e-mail: tatton@cheshire.gov.uk; Townend; Troutbeck, Windermere, Cumbria, LA23 1LB; tel: 01539 432628; e-mail: townend@ntrust.org.uk; Wordsworth House; Main Street, Cockermouth, Cumbria, CA13 9RX; tel: 01900 824805; fax: 01900 824805; e-mail: wordsworthhouse@ntrust.org.uk

NATIONAL TRUST (SOUTH EAST REGIONAL OFFICE)

Formal name: National Trust for Places of Historic Interest or Natural Beauty

Polesden Lacey, Dorking, Surrey, RH5 6BD

Tel: 01372 453401
Fax: 01372 452023
E-mail: se.enquiries@nationaltrust.org.uk
Website: www.nationaltrust.org.uk

Enquiries to: Reception

Founded: 1895

Organisation type and purpose: National organisation, independently owned, membership association (membership is by subscription), registered charity (charity number 205846), historic building, house or site, suitable for ages: lifelong.
Administration and management of Trust sites in the South East region.

Subject coverage: The preservation and upkeep of Trust properties of historic interest and natural beauty in East Sussex, Kent, Surrey and West Sussex.

Publications list: Available online and in print

Access to staff: Contact by letter, by telephone, by fax, by e-mail, in person and via website
Hours: Mon to Fri, 0900 to 1700

National Trust sites: Alfriston Clergy House; The Tye, Alfriston, Polegate, East Sussex, BN26 5TL; tel: 01323 870001; fax: 01323 871318; e-mail: alfriston@nationaltrust.org.uk; Bateman's; Bateman's Lane, Burwash, Etchingham, East Sussex, TN19 7DS; tel: 01435 882302; fax: 01435 882811; e-mail: batemans@nationaltrust.org.uk; Bodiam Castle; Bodiam, Robertsbridge, East Sussex, TN32 5UA; tel: 01580 830436; fax: 01580 830398; e-mail: bodiamcastle@nationaltrust.org.uk; Chartwell; Mapleton Road, Westerham, Kent, TN16 1PS; tel: 01732 868381; fax: 01732 868193; e-mail: chartwell@nationaltrust.org.uk; Clandon Park; West Clandon, Guildford, Surrey, GU4 7RQ; tel: 01483 222482; fax: 01483 223479; e-mail: clandonpark@nationaltrust.org.uk; Claremont Landscape Garden; Portsmouth Road, Esher, Surrey, KT10 9JG; tel: 01372 467806; e-mail: claremont@nationaltrust.org.uk; Emmetts Garden; Ide Hill, Sevenoaks, Kent, TN14 6AY; tel: 01732 751509; e-mail: emmetts@nationaltrust.org.uk; Hatchlands Park; East Clandon, Guildford, Surrey, GU4 7RT; tel: 01483 222482; fax: 01483 223176; e-mail: hatchlands@nationaltrust.org.uk; Ightham Mote; Ivy Hatch, Sevenoaks, Kent, TN15 0NT; tel: 01732 810378; fax: 01732 811029; e-mail: ighthammote@nationaltrust.org.uk; Knole; Sevenoaks, Kent, TN15 0RP; tel: 01732 462100; fax: 01732 465528; e-mail: knole@nationaltrust.org.uk; Lamb House; West Street, Rye, East Sussex, TN31 7ES; e-mail: lambhouse@nationaltrust.org.uk; Monk's House; Rodmell, Lewes, East Sussex, BN7 3HF; e-mail: monkshouse@nationaltrust.org.uk; Nymans; Handcross, nr Haywards Heath, West Sussex, RH17 6EB; tel: 01444 405250; e-mail: nymans@nationaltrust.org.uk; Oakhurst Cottage; Hambledon, Godalming, Surrey, GU8 4HF; e-mail: oakhurstcottage@nationaltrust.org.uk; Petworth House; Church Street, Petworth, West Sussex, GU28 0AE; tel: 01798 342207; fax: 01798 342963; e-mail: petworth@nationaltrust.org.uk; Polesden Lacey; Great Bookham, Dorking, Surrey, RH5 6BD; tel: 01372 452048; fax: 01372 452023; e-mail: polesdenlacey@nationaltrust.org.uk; Quebec House; Quebec Square, Westerham, Kent, TN16 1TD; River Wey & Godalming Navigations and Dapdune Wharf; Dapdune Wharf, Wharf Road, Guildford, Surrey, GU1 4RR; tel: 01483 561389; fax: 01483 531667; e-mail: riverwey@nationaltrust.org.uk; Scotney Castle Garden and Estate; Lamberhurst, Tunbridge Wells, Kent, TN3 8JN; tel: 01892 893868; fax: 01892 890110; e-mail: scotneycastle@nationaltrust.org.uk; Shalford Mill; Shalford, Guildford, Surrey, GU4 8BS; tel: 01483 561389; e-mail: shalfordmill@nationaltrust.org.uk; Sheffield Park Garden; Sheffield Park, East Sussex, TN22 3QX; tel: 01825 790231; e-mail: sheffieldpark@nationaltrust.org.uk; Sissinghurst Castle Garden; Sissinghurst, Cranbrook, Kent, TN17 2AB; tel: 01580 710700; fax: 01580 710702; e-mail: sissinghurst@nationaltrust.org.uk; Smallhythe Place; Smallhythe, Tenterden, Kent, TN30 7NG; tel: 01580 762334; fax: 01580 762334; e-mail: smallhytheplace@nationaltrust.org.uk; South Foreland Lighthouse; The Front, St Margaret's Bay, Dover, Kent, CT15 6HP; tel: 01304 852463; fax: 01304 215484; e-mail: southforeland@nationaltrust.org.uk; Standen; West Hoathly Road, East Grinstead, West Sussex, RH19 4NE; tel: 01342 323029; fax: 01342 316424; e-mail: standen@nationaltrust.org.uk; Uppark House; South Harting, Petersfield, GU31 5QR; tel: 01730 825415; fax: 01730 825873; e-mail: uppark@nationaltrust.org.uk; Wakehurst Place; Ardingly, Haywards Heath, West Sussex, RH17 6TN; tel: 01444 894066; fax: 01444 894069; e-mail: wakehurst@kew.org; Winkworth Arboretum; Hascombe Road, Godalming, Surrey, GU8 4AD; tel: 01483 208477; e-mail: winkwortharboretum@nationaltrust.org.uk

NATIONAL TRUST (THAMES AND SOLENT REGIONAL OFFICE)

Formal name: National Trust for Places of Historic Interest or Natural Beauty

Hughenden Manor, High Wycombe, Buckinghamshire, HP14 4LA

Tel: 01494 755500
Fax: 01494 463310
E-mail: enquiries@thenationaltrust.org.uk
Website: www.nationaltrust.org.uk

Enquiries to: Marketing and Supporter Development Manager
Direct tel: 01494 755550

Founded: 1895

Organisation type and purpose: National organisation, independently owned, membership association (membership is by subscription), registered charity (charity number 205846), historic building, house or site, suitable for ages: lifelong.
Administration and management of Trust sites in the Thames and Solent region.

Subject coverage: The preservation and upkeep of places of historic interest and natural beauty in Berkshire, Buckinghamshire, Hampshire, part of Hertfordshire, Isle of Wight, Greater London and Oxfordshire.

Publications list: Available online and in print

Access to staff: Contact by letter, by telephone, by fax, by e-mail, in person and via website
Hours: Mon to Fri, 0900 to 1700

National Trust sites: 2 Willow Road; 2 Willow Road, Hampstead, London, NW3 1TH; tel: 020 7435 6166; e-mail: 2willowroad@nationaltrust.org.uk; Basildon Park; Lower Basildon, Reading, Berkshire, RG8 9NR; tel: 0118 984 3040; e-mail: basildonpark@nationaltrust.org.uk; Boarstall Tower; Boarstall, Aylesbury, Buckinghamshire, HP18 9UX; tel: 01844 239339; Buscot Old Parsonage; Buscot, Faringdon, Oxfordshire, SN7 8DQ; tel: 01793 7622209; e-mail: buscot@nationaltrust.org.uk; Buscot Park; Buscot, Faringdon, Oxfordshire, SN7 8BU; tel: 01367 240786; fax: 01367 241794; e-mail: estbuscot@aol.com; Carlyle's House; 24 Cheyne Row, Chelsea, London, SW3 5HL; tel: 020 7352 7087; fax: 020 7352 5108; e-mail: carlyleshouse@nationaltrust.org.uk; Claydon House; Middle Claydon, Near Buckingham, Buckinghamshire, MK18 2EY; tel: 01296 730349; fax: 01296 738511; e-mail: claydon@nationaltrust.org.uk; Cliveden; Taplow, Maidenhead, Buckinghamshire, SL6 0JA; tel: 01628 605069; fax: 01628 669461; e-mail: cliveden@nationaltrust.org.uk; Eastbury Manor House; Eastbury Square, Barking, IG11 9SN; tel: 020 8724 1002; fax: 020 8724 1003; e-mail: eastburyhouse@lbbd.gov.uk; Fenton House; Windmill Hill, Hampstead, London, NW3 6RT; tel: 020 7435 3471; e-mail: fentonhouse@nationaltrust.org.uk; Greys Court; Rotherfield Greys, Henley-on-Thames, Oxfordshire, RG9 4PG; tel: 01491 628529; fax: 01491 628935; e-mail: greyscourt@nationaltrust.org.uk; Hinton Ampner; Bramdean, Arlesford, Hampshire, SO24 0LA; tel: 01962 771305; fax: 01962 793101; e-mail: hintonampner@nationaltrust.org.uk; Hughenden Manor Estate; Hughenden Valley, High Wycombe, Buckinghamshire, HP14 4LA; tel: 01494 755573; fax: 01494 474284; e-mail: hughenden@nationaltrust.org.uk; Long Crendon Court House; Long Crendon, Aylesbury, Buckinghamshire, HP18 9AN; tel: 01494 528051; fax: 01280 822850; Mottisfont Abbey; Mottisfont, Romsey, Hampshire, SO51 0LP; tel: 01794 340757; fax: 01794 341492; e-mail: mottisfontabbey@nationaltrust.org.uk; Needles Old Battery; West Highdown, Totland, Isle of Wight, PO39 0JH; tel: 01983 754772; Old Town Hall, Newtown; Newtown, Newport, Isle of Wight, PO30 4PA; tel: 01983 531785; Rainham Hall; The Broadway, Rainham, Essex, RM13 9YN; tel: 020 7447 6605; Sandham Memorial Chapel; Harts Lane, Burghclere, Newbury, Hampshire, RG20 9JT; tel: 01635 278394; fax: 01635 278394; e-mail: sandham@nationaltrust.org.uk; Sutton House; 2/4 Homerton High Street, Hackney, London, E9 6JQ; tel: 020 8986 2264; e-mail: suttonhouse@nationaltrust.org.uk; The Vyne; Sherborne St John, Basingstoke, Hampshire, RG24 9HL; tel: 01256 883858; fax: 01256 881720; e-mail: thevyne@nationaltrust.org.uk; Waddesdon Manor; Waddesdon, Aylesbury, Buckinghamshire, HP18 0JH; tel: 01296 653226; fax: 01296 653212; e-mail: waddesonmanor@nationaltrust.org.uk; West Wycombe Park; West Wycombe, Buckinghamshire, HP14 3AJ; tel: 01494 513569

NATIONAL TRUST (WESSEX REGIONAL OFFICE)

Formal name: National Trust for Places of Historic Interest or Natural Beauty

Bishopstrow, Warminster, Wiltshire, BA12 9HW

Tel: 01985 843600
Fax: 01985 843624
E-mail: enquiries@thenationaltrust.org.uk
Website: www.nationaltrust.org.uk

Enquiries to: Customer Service Manager

Founded: 1895

Organisation type and purpose: National organisation, independently owned, membership association (membership is by subscription), registered charity (charity number 205846), historic building, house or site, suitable for ages: lifelong.
Administration and management of Trust sites in the Wessex region.

Subject coverage: The preservation and upkeep of places of historic interest and natural beauty in Bristol/Bath, Dorset, Gloucestershire, Somerset and Wiltshire.

Publications list: Available online and in print

Access to staff: Contact by letter, by telephone, by fax, by e-mail, in person and via website
Hours: Mon to Fri, 0900 to 1700

National Trust sites: Avebury; Barn Gallery, High Street, Avebury, Marlborough, Wiltshire, SN8 1RF; tel: 01672 539494; e-mail: avebury@ntrust.org.uk; Barrington Court; Barrington, Ilminster, Somerset, TA19 0NQ; tel: 01460 241938; fax: 01460 241938; e-mail: barringtoncourt@ntrust.org.uk; Bath Assembly Rooms; Bennett Street, Bath, BA1 2QH; tel: 01225 477789; Chedworth Roman Villa; Yanworth, Cheltenham, Gloucestershire, GL54 3LJ; tel: 01242 890256; Clevedon Court; Tickenham Road, Clevedon, Somerset, BS21 6QU; tel: 01275 872257; Coleridge Cottage; 35 Lime Street, Nether Stowey, Bridgwater, Somerset, TA5 1NQ; tel: 01278 732662; Corfe Castle; West Street, Corfe Castle, Wareham, Dorset, BH20 5EZ; tel: 01929 481294; Dunster Castle; Dunster, Minehead, Somerset, TA24 6SL; tel: 01643 821314; fax: 01643 823000; e-mail: wdugen@smtp.ntrust.org.uk; Dyrham Park; Dyrham, Chippenham, SN14 8ER; tel: 01179 372501; e-mail: dyrhampark@ntrust.org.uk; Great Chalfield Manor; Melksham, Wiltshire, SN12 8NJ; tel: 01225 782239; fax: 01225 783379; Hardy's Cottage; Higher Bockhampton, Dorchester, Dorset, DT2 8QL; tel: 01305 262366; Horton Court; Horton, Chipping Sodbury, Bristol, BS17 6QR; tel: 01249 730141; King John's Hunting Lodge; Axbridge, Somerset, BS26 2AP; tel: 01934 732012; Kingston Lacy; Wimbourne, Dorset, BH21 4EA; tel: 01202 883402; Kingston Lacy; Wimbourne, Dorset, BH21 4EA; tel: 01202 883402; fax: 01202 882402; Lacock Abbey and Fox Talbot Museum; Lacock, Chippenham, Wiltshire, SN15 2LG; tel: 01249 730227; Little Clarendon House; Dinton, Salisbury, Wiltshire, SP3 5DZ; tel: 01985 843600 (Regional Office); Lodge Park House; Aldsworth, Cheltenham, Gloucestershire, GL54 3PP; tel: 01450 844130; fax: 01451 844131; e-mail: lodgepark@ntrust.org.uk; Lytes Cary Manor; nr Charlton Mackrell, Somerton, Somerset, TA11 7HU; tel: 01985 224471; e-mail: lytescarymanor@ntrust.org.uk; Max Gate; Alington Avenue, Dorchester, Dorset, DT1 2AA; tel: 01305 262538; fax: 01305 250978; Mompesson House; The Close, Salisbury, Wiltshire, SP1 2EL; tel: 01722 335659; fax: 01722 321559; e-mail: mompessonhouse@ntrust.org.uk; Montacute House; Montacute, Somerset, TA15 6XP; tel: 01935 823289; e-mail: montacute@ntrust.org.uk; Newark Park; Ozleworth, Wotton under Edge, Gloucestershire, GL12 7PZ; tel: 01453 842644; Philipps House and Ditton Park; Ditton, Salisbury, Wiltshire, SP3 5HH; tel: 01985 843600 (Regional Office); Snowshill Manor; Snowshill, Broadway, Gloucestershire, WR12 7JU; tel: 01386 852410; fax: 01386 852410; e-mail: snowshillmanor@ntrust.org.uk; Stonehenge Down; Amesbury, Salisbury, Wiltshire, SP4 7DE; tel: 01980 624715 (Infoline); Stourhead House; Stourton, Warminster, Wiltshire, BA12 6QD; tel: 01747 841152; Westwood Manor; Westwood, Bradford on Avon, Wiltshire, BA15 2AF; tel: 01225 863374; White Mill; Sturminster Marshall, Wimborne, Dorset, BH21 4BX; tel: 01258 858051

NATIONAL TRUST (YORKSHIRE & NORTH EAST REGIONAL OFFICES) – MORPETH

Formal name: National Trust for Places of Historic Interest or Natural Beauty

Scots' Gap, Morpeth, Northumberland, NE61 4EG

Tel: 01670 774691
Fax: 01670 774317
E-mail: enquiries@thenationaltrust.org.uk
Website: www.nationaltrust.org.uk

Enquiries to: Communications Marketing Manager
Direct tel: 07500 993500
Direct e-mail: eve.jackson@nationaltrust.org.uk

continued overleaf

Founded: 1895

Organisation type and purpose: National organisation, independently owned, membership association (membership is by subscription), registered charity (charity number 205846), historic building, house or site, suitable for ages: lifelong.
Administration and management of Trust sites in the North East.

Subject coverage: The preservation and upkeep of Trust properties of historic interest and natural beauty in Co Durham, Newcastle and Tyneside, Northumberland.

Publications list: Available online and in print

Access to staff: Contact by letter, by telephone, by e-mail, in person and via website
Hours: Mon to Fri, 0900 to 1700

Access to building: *Hours:* Mon to Fri, 0900 to 1700

National Trust sites: Cherryburn; Station Bank, Mickley, Stocksfield, Northumberland, NE43 7DD; tel: 01661 843276; e-mail: cherryburn@nationaltrust.org.uk; Cragside House; Rothbury, Morpeth, Northumberland, NE65 7PX; tel: 01669 620333; fax: 01669 620066; e-mail: cragside@nationaltrust.org.uk; Dunstanburgh Castle; Craster, Alnwick, Northumberland; tel: 01665 576231; George Stephenson's Birthplace; Street House, Wylam, Newcastle upon Tyne, Northumberland, NE41 8BP; tel: 01661 853457; fax: 01670 774317; Gibside; nr Rowlands Gill, Burnopfield, Newcastle upon Tyne, Tyne & Wear, NE16 6BG; tel: 01207 542255; fax: 01207 542255; e-mail: gibside@nationaltrust.org.uk; Hadrian's Wall & Housesteads Roman Fort; Bardon Mill, Hexham, Northumberland, NE47 6NN; tel: 01434 344363 (EH Custodian); Lindisfarne Castle; Holy Island, Berwick-upon-Tweed, Northumberland, TD15 2SH; tel: 01289 389244; fax: 01289 389349; e-mail: lindisfarne@nationaltrust.org.uk; Ormesby Hall; Ormesby, Middlesbrough, Cleveland, TS7 9AS; tel: 01642 324188; fax: 01642 300937; e-mail: ormesbyhall@nationaltrust.org.uk; Souter Lighthouse; Coast Road, Whitburn, Sunderland, Tyne and Wear, SR6 7NH; tel: 0191 529 3161; 01670 773966 (Infoline); fax: 0191 529 0902; e-mail: souter@nationaltrust.org.uk; Wallington; Cambo, Morpeth, Northumberland, NE6 4AR; tel: 01670 773967 (Infoline); fax: 01670 774420; e-mail: wallington@nationaltrust.org.uk; Washington Old Hall; The Avenue, District 4, Washington Village, Washington, Tyne and Wear, NE38 7LE; tel: 0191 416 6879; fax: 0191 416 2065; e-mail: washington.oldhall@nationaltrust.org.uk

NATIONAL TRUST (YORKSHIRE & NORTH EAST REGIONAL OFFICES) – YORK

Formal name: National Trust for Places of Historic Interest or Natural Beauty

Goddards, 27 Tadcaster Road, York, YO24 1GG

Tel: 01904 702021
Fax: 01904 771970
E-mail: enquiries@thenationaltrust.org.uk
Website: www.nationaltrust.org.uk

Enquiries to: Marketing & Supporter Development Manager
Direct e-mail: yne.customerservice@nationaltrust.org.uk

Founded: 1895

Organisation type and purpose: National organisation, independently owned, membership association (membership is by subscription), registered charity (charity number 205846), historic building, house or site, suitable for ages: lifelong.
Administration and management of Trust sites in Yorkshire and the North East.

Subject coverage: The preservation and upkeep of Trust properties of historic interest and natural beauty in Yorkshire, Teesside and North Lincolnshire.

Publications list: Available online and in print

Access to staff: Contact by letter, by telephone, by fax, by e-mail, in person and via website
Hours: Mon to Fri, 0900 to 1700

National Trust sites: Beningbrough Hall; Beningbrough, York, YO30 1DD; tel: 01904 472027; fax: 01904 470002; e-mail: beningbrough@nationaltrust.org.uk; East Riddlesden Hall; Bradford Road, Keighley, West Yorkshire, BD20 5EL; tel: 01535 607075; fax: 01535 691462; e-mail: eastriddlesden@nationaltrust.org.uk; Fountains Abbey & Studley Royal; Fountains, Ripon, North Yorkshire, HG4 3DY; tel: 01765 608888; fax: 01765 601002; e-mail: fountainsenquiries@nationaltrust.org.uk; Mount Grace Priory; Osmotherley, Northallerton, North Yorkshire, DL6 3JG; tel: 01609 883494; Nostell Priory; Doncaster Road, Wakefield, West Yorkshire, WF4 1QE; tel: 01924 863892; fax: 01924 866846; e-mail: nostellpriory@nationaltrust.org.uk; Nunnington Hall; Nunnington, York, YO62 5UY; tel: 01439 748283; fax: 01439 748284; e-mail: nunningtonhall@nationaltrust.org.uk; Treasurer's House; Minster Yard, Chapter House Street, York, YO1 7JL; tel: 01904 624247; fax: 01904 647372; e-mail: treasurershouse@nationaltrust.org.uk; Yorkshire Coast; Old Coastguard Station, The Dock, Robin Hood's Bay, Whitby, North Yorkshire, YO22 4SJ; tel: 01947 885900; e-mail: yorkshirecoast@nationaltrust.org.uk

NATIONAL TRUST FOR SCOTLAND (NTS)

28 Charlotte Square, Edinburgh, EH2 4ET

Tel: 0131 243 9300
Fax: 0131 243 9301
E-mail: information@nts.org.uk
Website: www.nts.org.uk

Enquiries to: Archivist
Direct tel: 0131 243 9524
Direct e-mail: swilson@nts.org.uk

Founded: 1931

Organisation type and purpose: Independently owned, membership association (membership is by subscription), registered charity (charity number SCO07410), suitable for ages: all.
Conservation of sites which have significance for the natural or built heritage of Scotland.

Subject coverage: Practical aspects of conserving and making available to the public, with information and visitor services, country houses, small buildings, gardens, battlefields, and countryside and all places of natural beauty or historic or architectural interest in Scotland.

Collection: Archives of the National Trust for Scotland (1931-current) and some collections of family papers associated with some of our properties
A small reference library

Non-library collection catalogue: All or part available in-house

Library catalogue: All or part available in-house

Publications: Printed

Publications list: Available in print

Access to staff: Contact by letter, by telephone, by fax and by e-mail
Hours: Mon to Fri, 0930 to 1630
Special comments: Limited disabled access.

Other locations: National Trust for Scotland (London Office); 19 Cockspur Street, London, SW1Y 5BL; tel: 020 7321 5765; fax: 020 7389 0758; National Trust for Scotland (North America); One Boston Place, Fifth Floor, Boston, MA 02108, USA; tel: 00 1 617 619 3631; e-mail: nationaltrustforscotland@mediaone.net

Regional Offices: Highlands and Islands Regional Office (North); Balnain House, 40 Huntly Street, Inverness, IV3 5HR; tel: 01463 232034; fax: 01463 732620; Highlands and Islands Regional Office (South); Lochvoil House, Dunuraran Road, Oban, PA34 4NE; tel: 01631 570000; fax: 01631 570011; National Trust for Scotland (North-East Region); The Stables, Castle Fraser, Sauchen, Inverurie, Aberdeenshire, AB51 7LD; tel: 01463 232034; fax: 01463 732620; National Trust for Scotland (South Region); Northgate House, 32 Northgate, Peebles, EH45 8RS; tel: 01721 722502; fax: 01721 726000; National Trust for Scotland (West Region); Greenbank House, Flenders Road, Clarkston, Glasgow, G76 8RB; tel: 0141 616 2266; fax: 0141 616 0550

NATIONAL TRUST FOR SCOTLAND (NORTH-EAST REGION)

The Stables, Castle Fraser, Sauchen, Inverurie, Aberdeenshire, AB51 7LD

Tel: 01330 833225
Fax: 01330 833666
Website: www.nts.org.uk

Enquiries to: Public Affairs Manager
Direct tel: 01330 833559
Direct e-mail: glovie@nts.org.uk

Founded: 1931

Organisation type and purpose: National organisation, independently owned, membership association (membership is by subscription), registered charity (charity number SCO 07410), suitable for ages: all.
Administration and management of Trust sites in Perthshire, Angus, Aberdeen and Grampian.

Subject coverage: Heritage, conservation and environmental projects.

Publications list: Available in print

Access to staff: Contact by letter, by telephone and by fax
Hours: Mon to Fri, 0900 to 1700

National Trust for Scotland sites: Angus Folk Museum; Kirkwynd, Glamis, Forfar, Angus, DD8 1RT; tel: 01307 840288; Barry Water Mill; Barry, Carnoustie, Angus, DD7 7RJ; tel: 01241 856761; Castle Fraser; Sauchen, Inverurie, Aberdeenshire, AB51 7LD; tel: 01330 833463; fax: 01330 833819; Craigievar Castle; Alford, Aberdeenshire, AB33 8JF; tel: 013398 83635; fax: 013398 83280; Crathes Castle, Garden & Estate; Banchory, Aberdeenshire, AB31 5QJ; tel: 01330 844525; fax: 01330 844797; e-mail: crathes@nts.org.uk; Drum Castle, Garden & Estate; Drumoak, Banchory, Aberdeenshire, AB31 5EY; tel: 01330 811204; fax: 01330 811962; e-mail: drum-castle@nts.org.uk; Dunkeld; Ell Shop, The Cross, Dunkeld, Perthshire, PH8 0AN; tel: 01350 727460; e-mail: dunkeld@nts.org.uk; Dunkeld and The Hermitage; Dunkeld, Perthshire; tel: 01350 728641 (Ranger Office); fax: tel/fax 01796 473233 (Killiecrankie Visitor Centre); Finavon Doocot; Finavon, Angus; Fyvie Castle; Fyvie, Turriff, Aberdeenshire, AB53 8JS; tel: 01651 891266; fax: 01651 891107; Haddo House; Ellon, Aberdeenshire, AB41 7EQ; tel: 01651 851440; fax: 01651 851888; e-mail: haddo@nts.org.uk; House of Dun; Montrose, Angus, DD10 9LQ; tel: 01674 810264; fax: 01674 810722; e-mail: houseofdun@nts.org.uk; J M Barrie's Birthplace; 9 Brechin Road, Kirriemuir, Angus, DD8 4BX; tel: 01575 572646; Killiecrankie Visitor Centre; Pitlochry, Perth & Kinross, PH16 5LG; tel: 01796 473233; e-mail: killiecrankie@nts.org.uk; Leith Hall, Garden & Estate; Huntly, Aberdeenshire, AB54 4NQ; tel: 01464 831216; fax: 01464 831594; e-mail: leithhall@nts.org.uk; Museum of Farming Life; Pitmedden Garden, Ellon, Aberdeenshire, AB41 0PD; tel: 01651 842352; fax: 01651 843 188; e-mail: sburgess@nts.org.uk; Pitmedden Garden; Ellon, Aberdeenshire, AB41 7PD; tel: 01651 842352; fax: 01651 843188

Parent body: National Trust for Scotland; 28 Charlotte Square, Edinburgh, EH2 4ET; tel: 0131 243 9300; fax: 0131 243 9301; e-mail: information@nts.org.uk

NATIONAL TRUST FOR SCOTLAND (SOUTH REGION)

Northgate House, 32 Northgate, Peebles, Borders, EH45 8RS

Tel: 01721 722502
Fax: 01721 726000
E-mail: information@nts.org.uk
Website: www.nts.org.uk

Enquiries to: Director
Direct e-mail: dmcallister@nts.org.uk

Founded: 1931

Organisation type and purpose: Independently owned, membership association (membership is by subscription), registered charity (charity number SCO 07410), suitable for ages: all.

Subject coverage: Specific information on its own properties and sites also conservation, environmental issues and heritage. Administration and management of Trust sites in Dumfries and Galloway, Scottish Borders, Edinburgh and The Lothians, and Fife.

Trade and statistical information: Tourist, visitor attractions, building conservation

Access to staff: Contact by letter, by telephone, by fax and by e-mail. Appointment necessary.
Hours: Mon to Fri 0900 to 1700

National Trust for Scotland sites: Balmerino Abbey; Balmerino, Fife; Broughton House; 12 High Street, Kirkcudbright, Dumfries & Galloway, DG6 4JX; tel: 01557 330437; e-mail: broughtonhouse@nts.org.uk; Caiy Stane; Caiystane View, Edinburgh; Falkland Palace; Falkland, Cupar, Fife, KY15 7BU; tel: 01337 857397; fax: 01337 857980; e-mail: falklandpalace@nts.org.uk; Georgian House; 7 Charlotte Square, Edinburgh, EH2 4DR; tel: 0131 226 3318; e-mail: thegeorgianhouse@nts.org.uk; Gladstone's Land; 477B Lawnmarket, Edinburgh, EH1 2NT; tel: 0131 226 5856; fax: 0131 226 4851; Hill of Tarvit Mansion House & Gardens; Cupar, Fife, KY15 5PB; tel: 01334 653127; House of the Binns; Linlithgow, West Lothian, EH49 7NA; tel: 01506 834255; e-mail: houseofthebinns@nts.org.uk; Kellie Castle and Garden; Pittenweem, Anstruther, Fife, KY10 2RF; tel: 01333 720271; fax: 01333 720326; Newhailes; Newhailes Road, Musselburgh, East Lothian, EH21 6RY; tel: 0131 665 1546; No 28 Charlotte Square; Edinburgh, EH2 4ET; tel: 0131 243 9300; fax: 0131 243 9339; Preston Mill and Phantassie Doocot; East Linton, East Lothian, EH40 3DS; tel: 01620 860426; Robert Smail's Printing Works; 7–9 High Street, Inverleithen, Borders, EH44 6HA; tel: 01896 830206; e-mail: smails@nts.org.uk; Royal Burgh of Culross; Culross, Fife, KY12 8JH; tel: 01383 880359; fax: 01383 882675; Threave; Castle Douglas, Dumfries & Galloway, DG7 1RX; tel: 01556 502575; fax: 01556 502683; e-mail: threave@nts.org.uk

Parent body: National Trust for Scotland; Wemyss House, 28 Charlotte Square, Edinburgh, EH2 4ET; tel: 0131 243 9300; fax: 0131 243 9301; e-mail: information@nts.org .uk

NATIONAL TRUST FOR SCOTLAND (WEST REGION)

Greenbank House, Flenders Road, Clarkston, Glasgow, G76 8RB

Tel: 0141 616 2266
Fax: 0141 616 0550
E-mail: kcarr@nts.org.uk
Website: www.nts.org.uk

Enquiries to: Public Relations Officer
Other contacts: Regional Director (for policy)

Founded: 1931

Organisation type and purpose: National organisation, membership association, present number of members: 246,000, voluntary organisation, registered charity (charity number SCO 07410), suitable for ages: all.

Subject coverage: Specific information on the properties, also conservation and environmental issues, particularly in this region of Scotland. Administration and management of Trust sites in Ayrshire and Arran, Greater Glasgow and Clyde Valley and Cental Scotland.

Collection: Many collections appropriate to individual properties (details on request)

Trade and statistical information: Tourist, visitor attractions, building conservation

Publications: Printed, and electronic and video

Publications list: Available in print

Access to staff: Contact by letter, by telephone, by fax, by e-mail and via website
Hours: Mon to Fri, 0900 to 1700

National Trust for Scotland sites: Alloa Tower; Alloa Park, Alloa, FK10 1PP; tel: 01259 211701; fax: 01259 218744; Bannockburn Heritage Centre; Glasgow Road, Bannockburn, Stirling, FK7 0LJ; tel: 01786 812664; fax: 01786 810892; Batchelors' Club; Sandgate Street, Tarbolton, South Ayrshire, KA5 5RB; tel: 01292 541940; Black Hill; Lanark, South Lanarkshire; Brodick Castle Garden and Country Park; Brodick, Isle of Arran; tel: 01770 302202; fax: 01770 302312; e-mail: brodick@nts.org.uk; Culzean Castle and Country Park; Maybole, South Ayrshire, KA19 8LE; tel: 01655 884455; fax: 01655 884503; e-mail: culzean@nts.org.uk; David Livingstone Centre; 165 Station Road, Glasgow, South Lanarkshire, G72 9BT; tel: 01698 8231140; fax: 01698 821424; Holmwood House; 61–63 Netherlee Road, Cathcart, Glasgow, G44 3YG; tel: 0141 637 2129; fax: 0141 637 2129; e-mail: holmwood@nts.org.uk; Hutchesons' Hall; 158 Ingram Street, Glasgow, G1 1EJ; tel: 0141 552 8391; fax: 0141552 7031; e-mail: hutchesonshall@nts.org.uk; Menstrie Castle; Castle Street, Menstrie, Clackmannanshire; Moirlanich Longhouse; Near Killin, Stirling; Museum of Scottish Country Life; Wester Kittochside, East Kilbride, G76 9HR; tel: 01355 224181; fax: 01355 571290; Pollok House; Pollok Country Park, 2060 Pollokshaws Road, Glasgow, G43 1AT; tel: 0141 616 6410; fax: 0141 616 6521; e-mail: pollokhouse@nts.org.uk; Souter Johnnie's Cottage; Main Road, Kirkoswald, Ayrshire, KA19 8HY; tel: 01655 760603; Tenement House; 145 Buccleuch Street, Garnethill, Glasgow, G3 6QN; tel: 0141 333 0183; e-mail: tenementhouse@nts.org.uk; The Hill House; Upper Colquhoun Street, Helensburgh, G849AJ; tel: 01436 673900; fax: 01436 674685; The Pineapple; North of Airth, Falkirk; tel: 01324 831137; Weaver's Cottage; Shuttle Street, The Cross, Kilbarchan, Renfrewshire, PA10 2JG; tel: 01505 705588

Parent body: National Trust for Scotland; Wemyss House, 28 Charlotte Square, Edinburgh, EH2 4ET; tel: 0131 243 9300; fax: 0131 243 9301; e-mail: information@nts.org .uk

NATIONAL TRUST FOR SCOTLAND HIGHLANDS AND ISLANDS OFFICE (NORTH)

Balnain House, 40 Huntly Street, Inverness, IV3 5HR

Tel: 01463 232034
E-mail: information@nts.org.uk
Website: www.nts.org.uk

continued overleaf

Enquiries to: Director

Organisation type and purpose: Independently owned, membership association (membership is by subscription), voluntary organisation, registered charity, suitable for ages: all.

Subject coverage: Specific information on its own properties and sites also conservation, environmental issues and heritage.
Administration and management of Trust sites in Ross-shire, Inverness, Nairn, Moray and The Black Isle, and Northern Islands.

National Trust for Scotland sites: Balmacara Estate; Lochalsh House (NTS), Balmacara, Kyle, Ross-shire, IV40 8DN; tel: 01599 566359; e-mail: balmacara@nts.org.uk; Boath Doocot; Auldearn, Nairn, Moray; Brodie Castle; Brodie, Forres, Moray, IV36 2TE; tel: 01309 641371; fax: 01309 641600; e-mail: brodiecastle@nts.org.uk; Culloden Moor Visitors Centre; Culloden Moor, Inverness, Highland, IV2 5EU; tel: 01463 790607; fax: 01463 794294; e-mail: rmackenzie@nts.org.uk; Strome Castle; Ross-shire

Parent body: National Trust for Scotland

NATIONAL TRUST FOR SCOTLAND HIGHLANDS AND ISLANDS OFFICE (SOUTH)

Lochvoil House, Dunuaran Road, Oban, Argyll, PA34 4NE

Tel: 01631 570000
Fax: 01631 570011
E-mail: information@nts.org.uk
Website: www.nts.org.uk

Enquiries to: Director

Organisation type and purpose: Registered charity (charity number SCO 07410), suitable for ages: all.
Administration and management of Trust sites in Argyll & Lochaber and West Coast Islands.

Subject coverage: Heritage, conservation and environmental projects.
Administration and management of Trust sites in Argyll and Lochaber, and West Coast Islands.

Access to staff: Contact by letter, by telephone, by fax and by e-mail. Appointment necessary.
Hours: Mon to Fri, 0900 to 1700

National Trust for Scotland sites: Glencoe and Dalness; The National Trust for Scotland Visitor Centre, Glencoe, Argyll, PH49 4LA; tel: 01855 811729; fax: 01855 811772; e-mail: glencoe@nts.org.uk; Glenfinnan Monument; National Trust for Scotland Information Centre, Glenfinnan, Highland, PH37 4LT; tel: 01397 722250; e-mail: glenfinnan@nts.org.uk

Parent body: National Trust for Scotland; 28 Charlotte Square, Edinburgh, EH2 4ET; tel: 0131 243 9300; fax: 0131 243 9301; e-mail: information@nts.org.uk

NATIONAL TRUST MIDLANDS (WEST)

Formal name: National Trust for Places of Historic Interest or Natural Beauty

Attingham Park, Shrewsbury, Shropshire, SY4 4TP

Tel: 01743 708100
Fax: 01743 708150
E-mail: enquiries@thenationaltrust.org.uk
Website: www.nationaltrust.org.uk

Enquiries to: Customer Service Manager

Founded: 1895

Organisation type and purpose: National organisation, independently owned, membership association (membership is by subscription), registered charity (charity number 205846), historic building, house or site, suitable for ages: all.
Administration and management of Trust sites in the West Midlands.

Subject coverage: The preservation and upkeep of Trust properties of historic interest and natural beauty in Birmingham, Herefordshire, Shropshire, Staffordshire, Warwickshire and Worcestershire.

Publications list: Available online and in print

Access to staff: Contact by letter, by telephone, by e-mail, in person and via website
Hours: Mon to Fri, 0900 to 1700

National Trust sites: Attingham Hall; Attingham Park, Shrewsbury, Shropshire, SY4 4TP; tel: 01743 709203; fax: 01743 708175; e-mail: attingham@nationaltrust.org.uk; Baddesley Clinton Hall; Rising Lane, Baddesley Clinton Village, Knowle, Solihull, West Midlands, B93 0DQ; tel: 01564 783294; fax: 01564 782706; e-mail: baddesleyclinton@nationaltrust.org.uk; Benthall Hall; Broseley, Shropshire, TF12 5RX; tel: 01952 882159; e-mail: benthall@nationaltrust.org.uk; Berrington Hall; Leominster, Herefordshire, HR6 0DW; tel: 01568 615721; fax: 01568 613263; e-mail: berrington@.nationaltrust.org.uk; Brockhampton House and Estate; Bringsty, Worcester, WR6 5TB; tel: 01885 482077; e-mail: brockhampton@nationaltrust.org.uk; Charlecote Park; Warwick, CV35 9ER; tel: 01789 470277; fax: 01789 470544; e-mail: charlecotepark@nationaltrust.org.uk; Croft Castle & Parkland; Leominster, Herefordshire, HR6 9PW; tel: 01568 780246; e-mail: croftcastle@nationaltrust.org.uk; Dudmaston Hall; Quatt, Bridgnorth, Shropshire, WV15 6QN; tel: 01746 780866 (Dudmaston Estate); fax: 01746 780744; e-mail: dudmaston@nationaltrust.org.uk; Farnborough Hall; Banbury, OX17 1DU; tel: 01295 690002; e-mail: farnboroughhall@nationaltrust.org.uk; Greyfriars; Friar Street, Worcester, WR1 2LZ; tel: 01905 23571; e-mail: greyfriars@nationaltrust.org.uk; Hanbury Hall; School Road, Hanbury, Droitwich, Worcestershire, WR9 7EA; tel: 01527 821214; fax: 01527 821251; e-mail: hanburyhall@nationaltrust.org.uk; Morville Hall; Morville, Bridgnorth, Shropshire, WV16 5NB; tel: 01743 708100 (Regional Office); e-mail: morvillehall@nationaltrust.org.uk; Moseley Old Hall; Moseley Old Hall Lane, Fordhouses, Wolverhampton, West Midlands, WV10 7HY; tel: 01902 782808; e-mail: moseleyoldhall@nationaltrust.org.uk; Packwood House; Lapworth, Solihull, West Midlands, B94 6AT; tel: 01564 783294; fax: 01564 782706; e-mail: packwood@nationaltrust.org.uk; Sunnycroft; 200 Holyhead Road, Wellington, Telford, Shropshire, TF1 2DR; tel: 01952 242884; e-mail: sunnycroft@nationaltrust.org.uk; Upton House & Gardens; Near Banbury, Oxfordshire, OX15 6HT; tel: 01295 670266; e-mail: uptonhouse@nationaltrust.org.uk; Wall Roman Site (Letocetum); Wall, Lichfield, Staffordshire, WS14 0AW; tel: 01543 480768; e-mail: letocetum@nationaltrust.org.uk; Wightwick Manor; Wightwick Bank, Wolverhampton, West Midlands, WV6 8EE; tel: 01902 761108 (Infoline); fax: 01902 764663; e-mail: wightwickmanor@nationaltrust.org.uk; Wilderhope Manor; Longville, Much Wenlock, Shropshire, TF13 6EG; tel: 01694 771363; e-mail: wilderhopemanor@nationaltrust.org.uk

NATIONAL TRUST OFFICE FOR NORTHERN IRELAND

Rowallane House, Saintfield, Ballynahinch, Co Down, BT24 7LH

Tel: 020 9751 0721
Fax: 028 9751 1242
Website: www.ntni.org.uk

Enquiries to: Manager

Organisation type and purpose: National organisation, membership association (membership is by subscription), registered charity (charity number 205846), suitable for ages: all.
The preservation and upkeep of places of historic interest or natural beauty.

Subject coverage: The conservation of places of historic interest or natural beauty in Northern Ireland.

Access to staff: Contact by letter, by telephone, by fax and by e-mail
Hours: Mon to Fri, 0900 to 1700

Other Trust sites: Ardress House; 64 Ardress Road, Portadown, Co Armagh, BT62 1SQ; tel: 028 3885 1236; fax: 028 3885 1236; e-mail: ardress@nationaltrust.org.uk; Castle Coole; Enniskillen, Co Fermanagh, BT74 6JY; tel: 028 6632 2690; fax: 028 6632 5665; e-mail: castlecoole@nationaltrust.org.uk; Castle Ward; Strangford, Downpatrick, Co Down, BT30 7LS; tel: 028 4488 1204; fax: 028 4488 1729; e-mail: castleward@nationaltrust.org.uk; Derrymore House; Bessbrook, Newry, Co Armagh, BT35 7EF; tel: 028 3083 8361; e-mail: derrymore@nationaltrust.org.uk; Florence Court; Enniskillen, Co Fermanagh, BT92 1DB; tel: 028 6634 8249; fax: 028 6634 8873; e-mail: florencecourt@nationaltrust.org.uk; Gray's Printing Press; 49 Main Street, Strabane, Co Tyrone, BT82 8AU; tel: 028 7188 0055; fax: 028 7188 0055; Hezlett House; 107 Sea Road, Castlerock, Coleraine, Co Londonderry, BT51 4TW; tel: 028 7084 8567; fax: 028 2073 1582; e-mail: hezletthouse@nationaltrust.org.uk; Mount Stewart House, Garden and Temple of the Winds; Newtownards, Co Down, BT22 2AD; tel: 028 4278 8387; fax: 028 4278 8569; e-mail: mountstewart@nationaltrust.org.uk; Patterson's Spade Mill; Templepatrick, Co Antrim, BT39 0AP; tel: 028 9443 3619; fax: 028 9443 9713; e-mail:

patterson@nationaltrust.org.uk; Rowallane Garden; Saintfield, Ballynahinch, Co Down, BT24 7LH; tel: 028 9751 0131; fax: 028 9751 1242; e-mail: rowallane@nationaltrust.org.uk; Springhill; 20 Springhill Road, Moneymore, Magherafelt, Co Londonderry, BT45 7NQ; tel: 028 8674 8210; fax: 028 8674 8210; e-mail: springhill@nationaltrust.org.uk; The Argory; Moy, Dungannon, Co Tyrone, BT71 6NA; tel: 028 8778 4753; fax: 028 8778 9598; e-mail: argory@nationaltrust.org.uk; Wellbrook Beetling Mill; 20 Wellbrook Street, Corkhill, Cookstown, Co Tyrone, BT80 9RY; tel: 028 8674 8210/8675 1735; fax: 028 8675 1735; e-mail: wellbrook@nationaltrust.org.uk

NATIONAL TRUST OFFICE FOR WALES

Trinity Square, Llandudno, LL30 2DE

Tel: 01492 860123
Fax: 01492 860233
E-mail: ntwales@nt.org.uk
Website: www.nt.org.uk

Enquiries to: Marketing Manager

Organisation type and purpose: National organisation, independently owned, membership association (membership is by subscription), registered charity (charity number 205846), suitable for ages: all.
The preservation and upkeep of places of historic interest or natural beauty.

Access to staff: Contact by letter, by telephone, by fax, by e-mail and via website
Hours: Mon to Fri, 0900 to 1700

Other Trust sites: Aberconwy House; Castle Street, Conwy, Gwynedd, LL32 8AY; tel: 01492 592246; Aberdulais Falls and Turbine House; Aberdulais, Neath, West Glamorgan, SA10 8EU; tel: 01639 636674; e-mail: gaberd@smtp.ntrust.org; Chirk Castle; Chirk, Wrexham, Clwyd, LL14 5AF; tel: 01691 777701; e-mail: gcwmsn@smtp.ntrust.org.uk; Conwy Suspension Bridge; Conwy, Gwynedd, LL32 8LD; tel: 01492 573282; Dinefwr; Llandeilo, SA19 6RT; tel: 01558 825912; e-mail: gdrcsh@smtp.ntrust.org.uk; Dolaucothi Gold Mines; Pumsaint, Llanwrda, Carmarthenshire, SA19 8US; tel: 01558 650177; e-mail: gdoest@smtp.ntrust.org.uk; Erddig Hall; Wrexham, Clwyd, LL13 0YT; tel: 01978 355314 (info 01978 315151); e-mail: geroff@smtp.ntrust.org.uk; Llanerchaeron; Aberaeron, Ceredigion, SA48 8DG; tel: 01545 570200; e-mail: glnest@smtp.ntrust.org.uk; Penrhyn Castle; Bangor, Gwynedd, LL57 4HN; tel: 01248 353084; fax: 01248 371281; Plas Newydd; Llanfairpwll, Anglesey, Gwynedd, LL61 6DQ; tel: 01248 714795; e-mail: ppnmsn@smtp.ntrust.org.uk; Plas Yn Rhiw; Rhiw, Pwllheli, Gwynedd, LL53 8AB; tel: 01758 780219; e-mail: gprmet@smtp.ntrust.org.uk; Powis Castle & Garden; Welshpool, Powys, SY21 8RF; tel: 01938 551920; e-mail: ppcmsn@smtp.ntrust.org.uk; Tudor Merchant's House; Quay Hill, Tenby, Pembrokeshire, SA70 7BX; tel: 01834 842279; Ty Mawr Wybrnant; Penmachno, Betws-y-Coed, Conwy, LL25 0HJ; tel: 01690 760213; Ty'n-Y-Coed Uchaf; Penmachno, Betws-y-Coed, Conwy, LL24 0PS; tel: 01690 760229

NATIONAL TRUST THEATRE

Sutton House, 2–4 Homerton High Street, Hackney, London, E9 6JQ

Tel: 020 8986 0242
Fax: 020 8985 2343
Website: www.nationaltrust.org.uk/learning

Enquiries to: Administrator
Direct e-mail: learning@nationaltrust.org.uk

Founded: 1977

Organisation type and purpose: Registered charity (charity number 205846), suitable for ages: all.

Collection: Stage Costumes – mainly Tudor and Victorian

Publications: Printed

Access to staff: Contact by letter, by telephone, by fax and by e-mail. Appointment necessary.
Hours: Mon to Fri, 0930 to 1730

Access to building: Prior appointment required

Access for disabled people: Toilet facilities
Hours: Mon to Fri, 0930 to 1730
Special comments: No lift to upper floors.

Also at: The National Trust Learning; Rowan, Kembrey Park, Swindon, SN2 6UG

NATIONAL TYRE DISTRIBUTORS ASSOCIATION (NTDA)

8 Temple Square, Aylesbury, Buckinghamshire, HP20 2QH

Tel: 08449 670707
Fax: 01296 488675
E-mail: info@ntda.co.uk
Website: www.ntda.co.uk

Enquiries to: Director

Founded: 1936

Organisation type and purpose: Trade association.

Subject coverage: Tyres, the tyre industry and fast-fit products in the United Kingdom.

Trade and statistical information: Market Monitor (monthly)

Publications: Printed

Access to staff: Contact by letter, by fax and by e-mail
Hours: Mon to Fri, 0900 to 1700

NATIONAL UNION OF KNITWEAR, FOOTWEAR AND APPAREL TRADES (KFAT)

55 New Walk, Leicester, LE1 7EB

Tel: 0116 255 6703
Fax: 0116 254 4406
E-mail: info@community-tu.org
Website: www.kfat.org.uk

Enquiries to: General Secretary
Other contacts: (1) Research and Press Officer (2) Deputy General Secretary for either press enquiries or general enquiries.

Founded: 1991

Organisation type and purpose: Trade union, present number of members: 30,000.

Subject coverage: Industrial relations issues for the knitwear, footwear, leather, hosiery, and apparel industries.

Publications: Printed

Access to staff: Contact by letter and by e-mail
Hours: Mon to Fri, 0900 to 1700

Access to building: No prior appointment required

Affiliated to: General Federation of Trade Unions; International Textile Garment and Leather Workers Federation; Labour Party; Trades Union Congress

NATIONAL UNION OF RESIDENTS ASSOCIATIONS (NURA)

20 Park Drive, Romford, Essex, RM1 4LH

Tel: 01708 749119
Fax: 01708 736213
E-mail: info@ian-henry.com

Enquiries to: Chairman

Founded: 1927

Organisation type and purpose: Voluntary organisation.
Co-ordinating body of ratepayers, residents and kindred.

Subject coverage: Interests of ratepayers; economical local government administration, finance, transport and public utilities; non-party politics in local government.

Publications: Printed

Access to staff: Contact by letter, by telephone, by fax and by e-mail
Hours: Sat, Sun, 0900 to 1900

Access to building: No access other than to staff

NATIONAL UNION OF STUDENTS (NUS)

Formal name: National Union of Students

2nd Floor, Centro 3, Mandela Street, London, NW1 0DY

Tel: 0871 221 8221
Fax: 0871 221 8222
E-mail: nusuk@nus.org.uk
Website: www.nusonline.co.uk

Enquiries to: National Secretary

Founded: 1922

Organisation type and purpose: National organisation, membership association (membership is by subscription, qualification), present number of members: 650, voluntary organisation, training organisation, research organisation, publishing house.
To represent the interests of students' unions and students in the United Kingdom.

Subject coverage: All aspects of student and students' union life.

Publications: Printed

Publications list: Available online and in print

continued overleaf

Access to staff: Contact by letter, by telephone, by fax, by e-mail and via website. Appointment necessary. Non-members charged.
Hours: Mon to Fri, 0900 to 1700
Special comments: Parking by advance notice.

Access for disabled people: Ramped entry, toilet facilities
Special comments: Parking provided by appointment.

NATIONAL UNION OF TEACHERS (NUT)

Hamilton House, Mabledon Place, London, WC1H 9BD

Tel: 020 7388 6191
Fax: 020 7387 8458
Website: www.teachers.org.uk

Enquiries to: Information Officer
Direct tel: 020 7380 4713
Direct e-mail: j.friedlander@nut.org.uk

Founded: 1870

Organisation type and purpose: Trade union (membership is by subscription), present number of members: 314,174.

Subject coverage: Education.

Collection: Archives now at Modern Records Centre, Warwick University, Coventry CV4 7AL, tel: 01203 524219
Government publications since 1816
NUT Annual Reports, 1871 to the present
Schoolmaster (now the Teacher), No. 1 (January 1872-)
Union publications since its inception in 1870

Non-library collection catalogue: All or part available online and in print

Publications: Printed

Access to staff: Contact by letter, by telephone, by fax and by e-mail. Appointment necessary.
Hours: Mon to Fri, 0900 to 1700
Special comments: Quick reference enquiries, and access to NUT documentation only for members and others.

Access to building: No prior appointment required

Affiliated to: Trades Union Congress; tel: 020 7636 4030; fax: 020 7636 0632; e-mail: info@tuc.org.uk

NATIONAL VINTAGE TRACTOR AND ENGINE CLUB (NVTEC)

c/o B. Chester, National Chairman, Low Moor Farm, Marton-le-Moor, Ripon, North Yorkshire, HG4 5AR

Tel: 01765 603418
E-mail: brianchester@tiscali.co.uk
Website: www.nvtec.co.uk

Founded: 1965

Organisation type and purpose: Membership association (membership is by subscription), present number of members: 5800.

Subject coverage: History of agricultural vehicles, machines, hand tools and all associated equipment.

Collection: Workshop manuals and sales literature

Publications: Printed

Access to staff: Contact by letter, by telephone, by fax and by e-mail
Hours: Mon to Fri, 0900 to 2200

Affiliated to: National Traction Engine Trust

Archivist: National Vintage Tractor and Engine Club; Waylode, Tetbury Road, Old Sodbury, Bristol, BS17 6RJ; tel: 01454 313305

Has: 33 groups of NVTEC throughout England and Wales with another 25 separate clubs affiliated

NATIONAL WAITING LIST HELPLINE (NWLH)

St Margaret's House, 21 Old Ford Road, London, E2 9PL

Tel: 020 8983 1133
Fax: 020 8983 1553

Enquiries to: Information Manager
Direct tel: 020 8983 1225
Direct e-mail: info@collegeofhealth.org.uk

Founded: 1991

Organisation type and purpose: Advisory body, registered charity.

Subject coverage: Waiting lists for patients waiting for NHS treatment or surgery.

Trade and statistical information: Data on the length of waiting lists in England by hospital and surgical speciality

Publications: Electronic and video

Access to staff: Contact by telephone
Hours: Mon, Thu, 1100 to 1900; Fri, 1100 to 1700

Access to building: No access other than to staff

Parent body: College of Health

NATIONAL WATER SPORTS TRAINING CENTRE

Isle of Cumbrae, Millport, Ayrshire, KA28 0HQ

Tel: 01475 530757
Fax: 01475 530013
E-mail: cumbraecentre@sportscotland.org.uk
Website: www.nationalcentrecumbrae.org.uk

Enquiries to: Principal

Founded: 1974

Organisation type and purpose: National government body, advisory body, registered charity, training organisation.

Subject coverage: Specialist knowledge of all watersports: all aspects of sailing, kayaking and sub-aqua.

Publications: Printed

Access to staff: Contact by letter, by telephone, by fax and in person. Appointment necessary.
Hours: Any reasonable time

Managed by: SportScotland

NATIONAL WILDFLOWER CENTRE

Court Hey Park, Roby Road, Liverpool, L16 3NA

Tel: 0151 738 1913
E-mail: info@nwc.org.uk
Website: www.wildflower.co.uk

Founded: 2001

Organisation type and purpose: A registered charity (charity number 1078314). Visitor centre set in Victorian Court Hey Park.

Subject coverage: Wild flowers.

Education services: Educational facilities.

NATIONAL WOMEN'S REGISTER (NWR)

23 Vulcan House, Vulcan Road North, Norwich, Norfolk, NR6 6AQ

Tel: 0845 450 0287
Fax: 01603 407003
E-mail: office@nwr.org.uk
Website: www.nwr.org.uk

Enquiries to: Administrator
Direct tel: 0845 450 0287
Direct e-mail: office@nwr.org.uk
Other contacts: Membership Co-ordinator; Communications Co-ordinator (for publicity)

Founded: 1960

Organisation type and purpose: Membership association (membership is by subscription), registered charity (charity number 295198).

Subject coverage: Organisation for women only; discussion groups to expand horizons, make new friends, explore new interests, lively conversation and informal discussion.

Collection: NWR archive held at The Women's Library

Publications: Printed

Access to staff: Contact by letter, by telephone, by fax, by e-mail and via website
Hours: Mon, Tue, Thu, 0930 to 1615; Wed, 0900 to 1430

Branches: National organisations in Australia, Netherlands, South Africa and Zimbabwe; subsidiary groups in Europe

NATIONAL YOUTH AGENCY

Eastgate House, 19–23 Humberstone Road, Leicester, LE5 3GJ

Tel: 0116 242 7350
Fax: 0116 242 7444
E-mail: nya@nya.org.uk
Website: www.nya.org.uk

Enquiries to: Reception
Direct fax: 0116 285 3775
Direct e-mail: info@nya.org.uk

Organisation type and purpose: Registered charity (charity number 1035804).
Specified public body.
A resource agency in informal social education.

Subject coverage: The work of the youth service statutory and voluntary, major issues affecting the lives of young people, the curriculum for informal social and health education, education and training initiatives, community involvement and participation, counselling and information for young people, training in youth work.

Collection: Archive material on intermediate treatment
Archive material on the Youth Service
Educational kits and games
Videos

Non-library collection catalogue: All or part available online

Publications: Printed
Order printed publications from: Sales Department, tel: 0116 285 3709; fax: 0116 285 3777; e-mail: sales@nya.org.uk

Publications list: Available online and in print

Access to staff: Contact by letter, by telephone, by e-mail and via website. Appointment necessary.
Hours: Mon to Thu, 0900 to 1730; Fri, 0900 to 1700

Access for disabled people: Level entry, toilet facilities
Special comments: Disabled lift into NYA library available.

Funded by: in part through the Local Government Association

NATIONAL YOUTH JAZZ ORCHESTRA OF GREAT BRITAIN (NYJO)

11 Victor Road, Harrow, Middlesex, HA2 6PT

Tel: 020 8863 2717
Fax: 020 8863 8685
E-mail: bill.ashton@virgin.net
Website: www.classical-artists.com/nyjo

Enquiries to: Musical Director

Founded: 1965

Organisation type and purpose: National organisation, membership association (membership is by qualification, election or invitation), registered charity (charity number 274578), suitable for ages: up to 25.
Provides an opportunity for gifted young musicians to meet together and play big band jazz to a very high standard. Enables young musicians to gain experience of working to professional standards in major concert venues.

Subject coverage: All aspects of the National Youth Jazz Orchestra of Great Britain. Becoming a participating musician, obtaining recordings, concert dates, becoming a friend.

Publications: Printed

Access to staff: Contact by letter, by telephone, by fax, by e-mail and via website
Hours: Mon to Fri, 0900 to 1700
Special comments: No callers in person.

Access to building: No access other than to staff

NATIONAL YOUTH ORCHESTRAS OF SCOTLAND (NYOS)

13 Somerset Place, Glasgow, G3 7JT

Tel: 0141 332 8311
Fax: 0141 332 3915
E-mail: info@nyos.co.uk
Website: www.nyos.co.uk

Enquiries to: Chief Executive

Founded: 1979

Organisation type and purpose: Membership association (membership is by subscription), present number of members: 360, suitable for ages: 8 to 28.
Classical and Jazz orchestras.
To provide top class education and performance experience.

Subject coverage: Orchestral training, development of youth musicians in Scotland, orchestral music, chamber music, jazz music, professional tuition.

Publications: Electronic and video

Access to staff: Contact by letter, by telephone, by fax and by e-mail
Hours: Mon to Fri, 0930 to 1730

Member of: Association of British Orchestras; European Federation of National Youth Orchestras; National Association of Youth Orchestras; National Federation of Music Societies; World Federation of Amateur Orchestras

Subsidiary body: Camerata Scotland (NYOS Chamber Orchestra); National Children's Orchestra of Scotland; National Youth Jazz Orchestra of Scotland; National Youth Orchestra of Scotland; NYOS Futures; NYOS Strings

NATIONAL YOUTH THEATRE OF GREAT BRITAIN (NYT)

Woolyard, 52 Bermondsey Street, London, SE1 3UD

Tel: 020 7281 3863
E-mail: info@nyt.org.uk
Website: www.nyt.org.uk

Enquiries to: Communications Officer
Other contacts: Development Manager for sponsorship and donations.

Founded: 1956

Organisation type and purpose: Voluntary organisation, registered charity (charity number 306075), suitable for ages: 14 to 21.

Access to staff: Contact by letter, by telephone, by e-mail and via website
Hours: Mon to Fri, 1000 to 1800

Access for disabled people: Level entry, access to all public areas, toilet facilities

NATURAL DEATH CENTRE

In The Hill House, Watley Lane, Twyford, Winchester. SO21 1QX

Tel: 01962712690
E-mail: contact@naturaldeath.org.uk
Website: www.naturaldeath.org.uk

Enquiries to: Manager
Direct e-mail: rosie@naturaldeath.org.uk

Founded: 1991

Organisation type and purpose: Voluntary organisation, registered charity, research organisation, publishing house.

Subject coverage: Death, dying, cardboard coffins, cheap coffins, shrouds, helpful undertakers, crematoria, funeral suppliers, funeral directors, befriending network for those with critical illness, green burial grounds, green, or family-organised funerals.

Publications: Printed, and electronic and video

Publications list: Available online

Access to staff: Contact by letter, by telephone and by e-mail. Appointment necessary.
Hours: Mon to Fri, 1100 to 1400

Also at the same address: Association of Natural Burial Grounds

NATURAL ENGLAND

3rd Floor, Touthill Close, City Road, Peterborough, PE1 1XN

Tel: 0300 060 0910
E-mail: library@naturalengland.org.uk
Website: www.naturalengland.org.uk

Enquiries to: Information and Library Services

Founded: 2006; created by the merger of English Nature, the landscape, access and recreation elements of the Countryside Agency, and the environmental land management functions of the Rural Development Service (year of change 2006)

Organisation type and purpose: Advisory body, statutory body.
Natural England aims to conserve and enhance the natural environment, for its intrinsic value, the wellbeing and enjoyment of people and the economic prosperity that it brings.

Subject coverage: Natural England has been charged with the responsibility to ensure that England's unique natural environment including its land, flora and fauna, freshwater and marine environments, geology and soils are protected and improved. It also has responsibility for helping people enjoy, understand and access the natural environment.

Publications: Printed

Publications list: Available online and in print

Access to staff: Contact by letter, by telephone, by fax, by e-mail and via website
Hours: Mon to Thu, 0900 to 1700; Fri, 0900 to 1630

Access to building: Prior appointment required

Access for disabled people: Ramped entry

Headquarters address: Natural England; 1 East Parade, Sheffield, S1 2ET; tel: 0114 241 8920; fax: 0114 241 8921; e-mail: enquiries@naturalengland.org.uk; website: http://www.naturalengland.org.uk

NATURAL ENVIRONMENT RESEARCH COUNCIL (NERC)

Polaris House, North Star Avenue, Swindon, Wiltshire, SN2 1EU

Tel: 01793 411500

continued overleaf

Fax: 01793 411501
E-mail: requests@nerc.ac.uk
Website: www.nerc.ac.uk

Enquiries to: Information Officer

Founded: 1965

Organisation type and purpose: Research organisation.
The Natural Environment Research Council (NERC) is the leading body in the UK for research, survey, monitoring and training in the environmental sciences. NERC funds research in universities and in its own centres, surveys and units.

Subject coverage: Science policy, science and technology, natural environment.

Publications: Printed

Publications list: Available online

Access to staff: Contact by letter, by telephone, by fax and by e-mail
Hours: Mon to Fri, 0900 to 1700

Centre for Coastal and Marine Science, incorporating the following institutes: Dunstaffnage Marine Laboratory; PO Box 3, Oban, Argyll, PA34 4AD; tel: 01631 562244; fax: 01631 565518; Plymouth Marine Laboratory; Prospect Place, Plymouth, PL1 3DH; tel: 01752 633100; fax: 01752 633101; Proudman Oceanographic Laboratory; Bidston, Birkenhead, L43 7RA; tel: 0151 653 8633; fax: 0151 653 6269

Centre for Ecology & Hydrology, incorporating the following institutes: Institute of Freshwater Ecology; The Ferry House, Far Sawrey, Ambleside, Cumbria, LA22 0LP; tel: 01539 442468; fax: 01539 446914; Institute of Hydrology; Maclean Building, Crowmarsh Gifford, Wallingford, Oxfordshire, OX10 8BB; tel: 01491 838800; fax: 01491 692424; Institute of Terrestrial Ecology; Monks Wood, Abbots Ripton, Huntingdon, PE28 2LS; tel: 01487 773381; fax: 01487 773467; Institute of Virology and Environmental Microbiology; Mansfield Road, Oxford, OX1 3SR; tel: 01865 281630; fax: 01865 281696

NERC Centres and Surveys: British Antarctic Survey; High Cross, Madingley Road, Cambridge, CB3 0ET; tel: 01223 221400; fax: 01223 362616; British Geological Survey; Kingsley Dunham Centre, Keyworth, Nottingham, NG12 5GG; tel: 0115 936 3100; fax: 0115 936 3200; Southampton Oceanography Centre; (a joint venture between NERC and the University of Southampton), Empress Dock, Southampton, SO14 3ZH; tel: 023 8059 6666; fax: 023 8059 6032

NATURAL HISTORY MUSEUM (NHM)

Cromwell Road, London, SW7 5BD

Tel: 020 7942 5000
Fax: 020 7942 5559
E-mail: library@nhm.ac.uk
Website: www.nhm.ac.uk/research-curation/library/index.html
Website: www.nhm.ac.uk

Enquiries to: Librarian
Other contacts: Specialist Library and Information Services, see below.

Founded: 1881

Organisation type and purpose: International organisation, national government body, museum, public library, suitable for ages: all, training organisation, research organisation.

Subject coverage: Botany; biodiversity; entomology; geography, expeditions and travel; mineralogy; museum techniques; oceanography; ornithology; palaeontology; parasitology; physical anthropology; tropical medicine; zoology; environmental studies.

Information services: Library available for reference (for conditions, see Access), online searching, bibliography compilation, selective dissemination services. Helpline available; tel: 020 7942 5460 (information line); field study tours; study days for teachers and museum professionals.

Special visitor services: Guided tours.

Services for disabled people: Hearing loop, displays and/or information at wheelchair height.

Collection: Albert Gunther (zoology)
Day Library (natural history dealers)
John Murray (oceanography)
Joseph Banks (natural history, notebooks, etc. from Cook's first voyage around the world)
Linnaeus Collection (binomial nomenclature system in classification; works on plants and animals)
Richard Owen (anatomy)
Robert Brown (botany, including material from the Australian expedition 1801–1805)
Sloane (natural history and collection of curiosities and artefacts of c. 1753. Sloane's collection was the foundation of the British Museum)
Sowerby (natural history, especially botany; the family were artists and publishers)
Sydney Parkinson (natural history; drawings)
Tweeddale Library (zoology)
Walsingham (entomology)
Walter Rothschild (zoology)

Library catalogue: All or part available online

Publications: Printed

Publications list: Available online and in print

Access to staff: Contact by letter, by telephone, by fax, by e-mail and via website. Appointment necessary.
Hours: Mon to Fri, 1000 to 1630

Access for disabled people: Access to all public areas, toilet facilities

Branch museums: Zoological Museum Library; Tring, Hertfordshire, HP23 6AP; tel: 020 7942 6159

Other libraries: Botany Library; tel: 020 79425685; e-mail: botlib@nhm.ac.uk; Earth Sciences Library; tel: 020 7942 5476; e-mail: earthscilib@nhm.ac.uk; Entomology Library; tel: 020 7942 5751; e-mail: entlib@nhm.ac.uk; General and Zoology Libraries; tel: 020 7942 5460; e-mail: genlib@nhm.ac.uk; Ornithological and Rothschild Libraries; Akeman Street, Tring, Hertfordshire, HP23 6AP; tel: 020 7942 6158; fax: 020 7942 6150; e-mail: ornlib@nhm.ac.uk

NATURAL HISTORY SOCIETY OF NORTHUMBRIA (NHSN)

Great North Museum, Hancock, Barras Bridge, Newcastle upon Tyne, NE2 4PT

Tel: 0191 232 6386
Fax: 0191 232 2177
E-mail: nhsn@ncl.ac.uk
Website: www.nhsn.ncl.ac.uk

Enquiries to: Secretary
Other contacts: Archivist

Founded: 1829

Organisation type and purpose: Learned society (membership is by subscription), advisory body, present number of members: 850, voluntary organisation, registered charity, museum, publishing house.

Subject coverage: Natural history of Northumberland and Durham, with particular reference to geology, ornithology, entomology, mammalia and botany; also Farne Islands ecology.

Information services: Library Information, tel: 0191 222 3555

Collection: The library of the NHSN houses a large natural history archive, which includes the internationally important Thomas Bewick collection of watercolour and pencil drawings
Special collection of early natural history books from late 18th to 19th century

Non-library collection catalogue: All or part available in-house

Library catalogue: All or part available in-house

Publications: Printed

Publications list: Available online and in print

Access to staff: Contact by letter, by telephone, by fax, by e-mail and in person
Hours: Mon to Fri, 1000 to 1300
Special comments: Library: open to the public. Archives and Special Collections: by prior appointment.

Access to building: No prior appointment required
Hours: 1000 to 1700

Access for disabled people: Yes
Hours: 1000 to 1700

NATURAL SCIENCES COLLECTIONS ASSOCIATION (NatSCA)

Paul A. Brown, Department of Entomology, Natural History Museum, Cromwell Road, London, SW7 5BD

Tel: 020 7942 5196
E-mail: p.brown@nhm.ac.uk
Website: natsca.info

Enquiries to: Chair

Founded: 2003; incorporates the former Biology Curators Group (year of change 1975); incorporates the former Natural Sciences Conservation Group (year of change 1995)

Organisation type and purpose: National organisation, advisory body, professional body, membership association (membership is by subscription), voluntary organisation.

To promote: the care, knowledge and use of natural sciences collections and their conservation; and museum-based, natural sciences-related activities.

Subject coverage: The acquisition, long-term care and use of natural sciences collections. The propagation of natural sciences information to a wide range of users, and the promotion of natural sciences.

Trade and statistical information: Nature, content and possible use of museum-based natural sciences collections, as well as many non-museum-based collections

Publications: Printed

Publications list: Available online

Access to staff: Contact by letter, by telephone, by e-mail, in person and via website. Appointment necessary.
Hours: Mon to Fri, 0900 to 1700

NATURE IN ART TRUST

Wallsworth Hall, Main A38, Twigworth, Gloucester, GL2 9PA

Tel: 01452 731422
Fax: 01452 730937
E-mail: ninart@globalnet.co.uk
Website: www.nature-in-art.org.uk

Enquiries to: Director

Founded: 1982

Organisation type and purpose: Registered charity (charity number 1000553), museum, art gallery.
Registered with the Museum and Galleries Commission number 935.

Subject coverage: All aspects of art inspired by nature, through the ages; the use of art in environmental and conservation education, and contacts with contemporary artists from the UK and abroad.

Collection: The Trust owns and manages Nature in Art, the world's first museum dedicated exclusively to art inspired by nature, it includes:
Work of any media of international stature, scope and appeal
Work spanning 1500 years collected from over 60 countries
Small library containing slide collection and reference collection

Publications: Printed

Access to staff: Contact by letter, by telephone, by fax, by e-mail and via website. Appointment necessary.
Hours: Tue to Sun, 1000 to 1700; closed Mon, and December 24/25/26

Access to building: No prior appointment required
Special comments: Appointment required for the library, but not for the gallery etc.

Access for disabled people: Parking provided, ramped entry, access to all public areas, toilet facilities

Affiliated to: Area Museums Council for the South West; Gloucestershire Museums Group; Museums Association; Natur and Kunst (Germany)

NATURIST FOUNDATION

Sheepcote Lane, Orpington, Kent, BR5 4ET

Tel: 01689 871200
E-mail: natfound@hotmail.co.uk
Website: www.naturistfoundation.org

Enquiries to: General Secretary
Other contacts: Trustees

Founded: 1948

Organisation type and purpose: Registered charity (charity number 271420), voluntary organisation

Subject coverage: Naturist recreational facilities locally and throughout the United Kingdom

Access to staff: Contact by letter, by telephone, by e-mail and via website
Hours: Mon, Thu, Fri, Sat and Sun, 0930 to 1700

Links with: Central Council for British Naturism; International Naturist Federation

Member organisation of: ASA; Kent County Playing Fields Association; RLSS

NAUTICAL INSTITUTE

202 Lambeth Road, London, SE1 7LQ

Tel: 020 7928 1351
Fax: 020 7401 2817
E-mail: pubs@nautinst.org
Website: www.nautinst.org

Enquiries to: Chief Executive
Direct e-mail: sec@nautinst.org

Founded: 1972

Organisation type and purpose: Professional body, registered charity (charity number 1002462).
To promote high standards of competence at sea and in the management of maritime operations

Subject coverage: Navigation, seamanship, maritime operations.

Publications: Printed, and electronic and video

Publications list: Available online and in print

Access to staff: Contact by letter, by telephone, by fax, by e-mail and via website. Appointment necessary.
Hours: Mon to Fri, 0900 to 1700

Access to building: No access other than to staff

NAVY RECORDS SOCIETY (NRS)

Pangbourne College, Pangbourne, Berkshire, RG8 8LA

E-mail: honsec@navyrecords.org.uk
Website: navyrecords.org.uk

Enquiries to: Honorary Secretary
Other contacts: Membership Secretary

Founded: 1893

Organisation type and purpose: International organisation, learned society (membership is by subscription), present number of members: 725, registered charity (charity number 210836).
Publication of naval texts.

Subject coverage: Naval history of Britain, as recorded in documents and published in some 150 volumes since 1893; the series includes the papers of famous naval commanders as well as statesmen and administrators of the Royal Navy; virtually every campaign in which the Navy has fought from the 15th century is covered; other subjects are: naval administration, shipbuilding and victualling, manning the fleet, everyday life at sea, naval songs, health of seamen, signals, fighting instructions, maritime law and piracy, naval brigades, Naval Air Service.

Non-library collection catalogue: All or part available online and in print

Publications: Printed

Publications list: Available in print

Access to staff: Contact by letter, by e-mail and via website
Hours: Mon to Fri, 0900 to 1700

NCB

Formal name: National Children's Bureau

8 Wakley Street, Islington, London EC1V 7QE

Tel: 020 7843 6000
Fax: 020 7843 6007
E-mail: library@ncb.org.uk
Website: ncb.org.uk/policy-evidence/information-centre

Direct tel: 020 7843 6008

Founded: 1963

Organisation type and purpose: Registered charity (charity number 2633796).

Subject coverage: Children and young people including children in care, children's services, child protection, adolescence, children's rights and participation, crime and youth justice, disability and special educational needs, PSHE and sex education, HIV/AIDS, family law, family and parenting, child health, child psychology, poverty and social exclusion, early childhood, play.

Collection: Children's Play Information Service (http://ncb.org.uk/cpis)

Library catalogue: All or part available online

Publications: Printed

Publications list: Available online and in print

Access to staff: Contact by telephone, by e-mail, in person and via website. Appointment necessary. All charged.
Hours: Mon to Fri, 1000 to 1700
Special comments: Enquiry line: 1000 to 1200 and 1400 to 1600.

Access for disabled people: Parking provided, level entry, toilet facilities
Special comments: Parking available on request.

Links with: Children in Scotland; tel: 0131 228 8484; Children in Wales; tel: 029 2034 2434

NCDL

Formal name: National Canine Defence League

17 Wakley Street, London, EC1V 7RQ

Tel: 020 7837 0006
Fax: 020 7833 2701
E-mail: info@ncdl.org.uk
Website: www.ncdl.org.uk

Enquiries to: Information Officer
Direct tel: 020 7833 7657
Direct e-mail: victoria.horsley@ncdl.org.uk

Founded: 1891

Organisation type and purpose: Voluntary organisation, registered charity (charity number 227523).
To protect and defend all dogs, rehabilitation and re-homing of stray and abandoned dogs, no healthy dog is ever destroyed.

Subject coverage: Dog legislation, welfare and control, in particular rescue and care of stray dogs.

Collection: Annual Reports from the start of the League in 1897, old photos

Publications: Printed

Publications list: Available in print

Access to staff: Contact by letter, by telephone, by fax, by e-mail and via website. Appointment necessary.
Hours: Mon to Fri, 0900 to 1645

Member of: Association of British Dogs and Cats Homes (ABDCH); The Secretary, ABDCH, Battersea Dogs Home, 4 Battersea Park Road, London, SW8 4AA

Rehoming Centres at: NCDL Ballymena; Fairview, 60 Teeshan Road, Ballymena, Co Antrim, BT43 5PN; tel: 028 2565 2977; fax: 028 2565 8463; NCDL Bridgend; Tondu Road, Bridgend, Mid Glamorgan, CF31 4LH; tel: 01656 652771; fax: 01656 647495; NCDL Canterbury; Radfall Road, Chestfield, Whitstable, Kent, CT5 3ER; tel: 01227 792505; fax: 01227 793988; NCDL Darlington; Hill House Farm, Sadberge, Co Durham, DL2 1SL; tel: 01325 333114; fax: 01325 333048; NCDL Dumfries; Dovecotewell, Glencaple, Dumfriesshire, DG1 4RH; tel: 01387 770346; fax: 01387 770242; NCDL Evesham; 89 Pitcher's Hill, Wickhamford, Evesham, Worcesterhire, WR11 6RT; tel: 01386 830613; fax: 01386 832617; NCDL Ilfracombe; Hazeldene, West Down, Ilfracombe, Devon, EX34 8NU; tel: 01271 812709; fax: 01271 814098; NCDL Kenilworth; Honiley, Kenilworth, Warwickshire, CV8 1NP; tel: 01926 484398; fax: 01926 484196; NCDL Leeds; Eccup Lane, Adel, Leeds, LS16 8AL; tel: 0113 261 3194; fax: 0113 230 0886; NCDL Merseyside; Whiston Lane, Huyton, Liverpool, L36 6HP; tel: 0151 480 0660; fax: 0151 480 6176; NCDL Newbury; Plumb's Farm, Hamstead Marshall, Newbury, Berkshire, RG20 0HR; tel: 01488 658391; fax: 01488 657211; NCDL Roden; Roden Lane Farm, Roden, Telford, Shropshire, TF6 6BP; tel: 01952 770225; fax: 01952 770416; NCDL Salisbury; 45 Amesbury Road, Newton Tony, Wiltshire, SP4 0HW; tel: 01980 629 634; fax: 01980 629 706; NCDL Shoreham; Brighton Road, Shoreham-by-Sea, West Sussex, BN43 5LT; tel: 01273 452576; fax: 01273 440856; NCDL Snetterton; North Farm Kennels (Snetterton), North End Road, Snetterton, Norfolk, NR16 2LD; tel: 01953 498377; fax: 01953 498325; NCDL West Calder; Bentyhead, Hartwood Road, West Calder, West Lothian, EH55 8LE; tel: 01506 873459; fax: 01506 873275

NCS UK LIMITED

71 Ancastle Green, Henley-on-Thames, Oxfordshire, RG9 1TS

Tel: 01491 411717
Fax: 01491 411231
E-mail: info@ncscolour.co.uk
Website: www.ncscolour.co.uk

Enquiries to: Customer Services

Founded: 1997

Organisation type and purpose: Colour services, products and training.

Subject coverage: Use of the NCS – Natural Colour Systemí© in manufacturing, architecture, design, research, education.

Education services: Training courses. Seminars. Teacher's Guide. Range of individual exercises for teaching colour skills. NCS accreditation courses.

Non-library collection catalogue: All or part available online

Library catalogue: All or part available online

Publications: Printed, and electronic and video
Order printed publications from: website: www .ncscolour.co.uk; tel: 01491 411717
Order electronic and video publications from: website: http://www.ncscolour.co.uk; tel: 01491 411717

Publications list: Available online and in print

Access to staff: Contact by letter, by telephone, by fax, by e-mail and via website. Appointment necessary.
Hours: Mon to Fri, 0900 to 1730

Parent body: NCS Colour AB; PO Box 49022, 100 28, Stockholm, Sweden

NCT

Alexandra House, Oldham Terrace, London, W3 6NH

Tel: 0300 330 0770 (enquiry line); 0844 243 6000 extn 2315 (library)
Fax: 0844 243 6001
E-mail: library@nct.org.uk
Website: www.nct.org.uk
Website: www.nctshop.co.uk

Enquiries to: Information Officer and Librarian

Founded: 1956; formerly called National Childbirth Trust (year of change 2008)

Organisation type and purpose: Membership association (membership is by subscription), registered charity (charity number 801395).
To offer information and support in pregnancy, childbirth and early parenthood. We aim to give every parent the chance to make informed choices.

Subject coverage: Pregnancy, childbirth, first two years of parenthood, maternity care, breastfeeding, homebirth, caesarean.

Collection: Archive of NCT materials and other relevant materials – books, videos, films, slides.

Non-library collection catalogue: All or part available in-house

Library catalogue: All or part available online and in-house

Publications: Printed, and electronic and video
Order printed publications from: NCT Shop, 239 Shawbridge Street, Glasgow, G43 1QN; tel: 0845 8100 100; fax: 0845 8100 120; e-mail: contactus@nctshop.co.uk
Order electronic and video publications from: NCT shop

Publications list: Available online and in print

Access to staff: Contact by letter, by telephone, by fax and by e-mail. Appointment necessary. Letter of introduction required. Non-members charged.
Hours: Mon to Fri, 0900 to 1700
Special comments: Library and information service is mainly for use of members.

Access for disabled people: Parking may be provided, if available.
Special comments: Restricted wheelchair access to library.

Branches: across the United Kingdom

NEATH PORT TALBOT COUNTY BOROUGH COUNCIL

Civic Centre, Port Talbot, West Glamorgan, SA13 1PJ

Tel: 01639 686868
Fax: 01639 763444
E-mail: contactus@npt.gov.uk
Website: www.npt.gov.uk

Founded: 1996

Organisation type and purpose: Local government body.

Access to staff: Contact by letter, by telephone, by fax, by e-mail and via website. Appointment necessary.
Hours: Mon to Fri, 0900 to 1700

Also at: Civic Centre Neath; Neath; tel: 01639 686868; fax: 01639 763444

NEIL MUNRO SOCIETY, THE

8 Briar Road, Kirkintilloch, Glasgow, G66 3SA

Tel: 0141 776 4280
Fax: 0141 776 4280
E-mail: brian@bdosborne.fsnet.co.uk
Website: www.neilmunro.co.uk

Enquiries to: Secretary

Founded: 1996

Organisation type and purpose: Learned society (membership is by subscription), present number of members: 180, voluntary organisation.

Subject coverage: Life and work of Neil Munro (1863–1930) Scottish novelist, poet, critic and journalist.

Collection: Archival Collection of books, MSS relating to Neil Munro held by Royal College of Physicians and Surgeons of Glasgow on behalf of Society.

Non-library collection catalogue: All or part available online

Publications: Printed

Access to staff: Contact by letter, by telephone, by e-mail and via website
Hours: Mon to Fri, 0900 to 1700

Access to building: Prior appointment required
Hours: Mon to Fri, 0900 to 1700
Special comments: Archive held by Royal College of Physicians and Surgeons of Glasgow.

NEL

Formal name: National Engineering Laboratory

East Kilbride, Glasgow, G75 0QU

Tel: 01355 220222
Fax: 01355 272999
E-mail: info@tuvnel.com
Website: www.nel.uk

Enquiries to: Information Officer

Founded: 1947

Organisation type and purpose: Service industry, consultancy, research organisation.

Subject coverage: Fluid power engineering, heat exchangers, heat transfer, offshore engineering, physical properties of liquids and gases, pumps, software, structural analysis and testing, turbo machinery, control of noise and vibration in machinery.

Publications: Printed

Access to staff: Contact by letter, by fax, by e-mail and via website
Hours: Mon to Fri, 0900 to 1700

Business of the: TÜV Suddeutschland Group

NERINE AND AMARYLLID SOCIETY (NAAS)

2 The Grove, Ickenham, Uxbridge, Middlesex, UB10 8QH

Tel: 01895 464694
Fax: 0870 0529321
E-mail: roger.beauchamp@btinternet.com
Website: www.nerine.org.uk

Enquiries to: Secretary

Founded: 1997

Organisation type and purpose: National organisation, membership association (membership is by subscription), present number of members: 140.
For the study, dissemination and collection of all information concerning all genera within the family Amaryllidaceae and closely associated families.

Subject coverage: All aspects of all genera in the family Amaryllidaceae.

Publications: Printed

Publications list: Available in print

Access to staff: Contact by letter, by telephone, by fax and by e-mail

NESCOT (NORTH EAST SURREY COLLEGE OF TECHNOLOGY)

Reigate Road, Ewell, Epsom, Surrey, KT17 3DS

Tel: 020 8394 3055
Fax: 020 8394 3030
E-mail: lrc@nescot.ac.uk

Enquiries to: LRC Manager

Founded: 1954

Subject coverage: Biology, building and construction, health and social care, business and computing, art, design, photography, performing arts.

Library catalogue: All or part available online

Access to staff: Contact by letter, by telephone, by fax, by e-mail and in person
Hours: Term time: Mon, Tue, 0830 to 1900; Wed, 0830 to 1700; Thu, 0830 to 1930; Fri, 0830 to 1630
Vacations: Mon to Fri, 0900 to 1630 (unless otherwise stated)

Access to building: No prior appointment required
Hours: Advance notification preferred

Access for disabled people: Parking provided, ramped entry, access to all public areas, toilet facilities

NETHERLANDS – BRITISH CHAMBER OF COMMERCE

307–308 High Holborn, London, WC1V 7LS

Tel: 020 7405 1358
Fax: 020 7405 1689
E-mail: nbcc@btinternet.com
Website: www.nbcc.co.uk

Enquiries to: Manager
Direct fax: 020 7831 4831

Founded: 1891

Organisation type and purpose: International organisation, advisory body, membership association (membership is by subscription), present number of members: 300, consultancy.
Chamber of Commerce.
To provide information on Anglo-Dutch trade.

Subject coverage: Anglo-Dutch trade.

Publications: Printed, and electronic and video

Publications list: Available online and in print

Access to staff: Contact by letter, by telephone, by fax, by e-mail, in person and via website. Appointment necessary. Non-members charged.
Hours: Mon to Fri, 0900 to 1700

Other addresses: Netherlands – British Chamber of Commerce; NZ Voorburgwal 328L, 1012 RW, Amsterdam, The Netherlands; tel: + 31 20 421 7040; fax: + 31 20 421 7003; e-mail: nbccnl@btinternet.com

NETWORK 81

1–7 Woodfield Terrace, Chapel Hill, Stansted, Essex, CM24 8AJ

Tel: 0845 077 4055
Fax: 0845 077 4057
E-mail: network81@btconnect.com
Website: www.network81.org

Enquiries to: Administrator
Other contacts: National Development Manager

Founded: 1986

Organisation type and purpose: Voluntary organisation, registered charity (charity number 1061950).

Subject coverage: Help, support and advice for parents of children with special educational needs through the assessment and statementing process; 1996 Education Act, Part IV, code of practice.

Publications: Printed

Publications list: Available online

Access to staff: Contact by letter, by telephone, by fax, by e-mail and via website
Hours: Mon to Fri, 0900 to 1500
Special comments: Helpline: 1000 to 1300.

NEUROFIBROMATOSIS ASSOCIATION

Quayside House, 38 High Street, Kingston on Thames, KT1 1HL

Tel: 020 8439 1234
Fax: 020 8439 1200
E-mail: nfa@zetnet.co.uk
Website: www.nfauk.org.uk

Enquiries to: General Secretary
Other contacts: Helpline: 0845 602 4173 (Mon, Thu, 0900 to 1600; Tue, 0900 to 1200)

Founded: 1982

Organisation type and purpose: Membership association (membership is by subscription), present number of members: 2300, registered charity (charity number 1078790).
To provide help and support to those affected, their families and friends.

Subject coverage: Information on neurofibromatosis for GPs and health visitors, patients and carers, public; access to consultants via medical advisory board; data for researchers (subject to ethical controls); information on learning difficulties with neurofibromatosis.

Publications: Printed, and electronic and video
Order electronic and video publications from: see website

Publications list: Available online

Access to staff: Contact by letter, by telephone, by fax and by e-mail
Hours: Mon to Fri, 0900 to 1700

Connections with: Genetic Interest Group (GIG); International Neurofibromatosis Association; LMCA Neurological Alliance

NEW ALLIANCE

PO Box 13199, London, SW6 6ZU

Tel: 020 7385 9757
E-mail: info@newalliance.org.uk
Website: www.newalliance.org.uk/contact.htm
Website: www.newalliance.org.uk

Enquiries to: Campaign Manager

continued overleaf

Other contacts: Treasurer for donations, legacies

Founded: 1997

Organisation type and purpose: Learned society, voluntary organisation, consultancy, research organisation, publishing house, campaigning group.
Educating business and the public about the alternatives to European Union membership.

Subject coverage: European Union, defence, policing, criminal justice and legal issues, constitution, taxation, business legislation, employment policy, regional policy, the Euro, economic and monetary union, environment, motoring, agriculture, ID cards, referendum issues, BBC coverage, public consultations, metrication.

Non-library collection catalogue: All or part available online, in-house and in print

Publications: Printed, and electronic and video
Order electronic and video publications from: Can be supplied via electronic and paper media to schools and recognised research institutions

Publications list: Available online

Access to staff: Contact by letter, by telephone, by e-mail and via website
Hours: Mon to Sun, 0900 to 2100

Access to building: No access other than to staff

Affiliated organisation: National Referendum Campaign

Affiliated to: Statewatch

NEW COLLEGE LIBRARY

Holywell Street, Oxford, OX1 3BN

Tel: 01865 279580
Fax: 01865 279590
E-mail: library@new.ox.ac.uk
Website: www.new.ox.ac.uk/The_Library

Enquiries to: Librarian
Direct e-mail: naomi.vanloo@new.ox.ac.uk

Founded: 1379

Organisation type and purpose: University college library.

Subject coverage: Subjects studied by undergraduates in the University of Oxford; the subjects covered by the special collections listed.

Collection: Archives collection since the foundation of the College
Medieval manuscripts
Early printed books
Papers of Lord Milner (Bodley deposit)
Seton-Watson Collection (Eastern Europe)

Library catalogue: All or part available online and in-house

Publications: Printed, and microform publications

Access to staff: Contact by letter, by telephone and by e-mail. Appointment necessary. Access for members only. Letter of introduction required.
Hours: Mon to Fri, 0900 to 1700

Access to building: *Hours:* Mon to Fri, 0930 to 1245 and 1415 to 1645

Constituent part of: University of Oxford

NEW ENGLISH ART CLUB (NEAC)

17 Carlton Terrace, London, SW1Y 5BD

Tel: 020 7930 6844
Fax: 020 7930 7830
E-mail: press@mallgalleries.com
Website: www.mallgalleries.org.uk

Enquiries to: Secretary
Other contacts: Marketing and Communications Officer

Founded: 1885

Organisation type and purpose: Membership association (membership is by election or invitation), present number of members: 84, registered charity (charity number 295780).
To foster and promote the art of draughtsmanship and observation.

Publications: Printed

Access to staff: Contact by letter, by telephone, by fax and by e-mail. Appointment necessary.
Hours: Mon to Fri, 0930 to 1700

Access to building: No access other than to staff

Access for disabled people: Stairlift, toilet facilities
Special comments: Stairlift

Links with: Federation of British Artists; 17 Carlton House Terrace, London, SW17 5BD; tel: 020 7930 6844; fax: 020 7839 7830

NEW FOREST PONY BREEDING AND CATTLE SOCIETY (NFPB & CS)

The Corner House, Ringwood Road, Brausgoe, Hampshire, BH23 8AA

Tel: 01425 672775
Fax: 01425 672775
E-mail: info@newforestpony.com
Website: newforestpony.com

Enquiries to: Curator

Founded: 1938

Organisation type and purpose: Membership association (membership is by subscription), present number of members: 1200, registered charity (charity number 1064746).
Breed society.
Conserve and promote New Forest ponies.

Subject coverage: New Forest ponies.

Collection: Stud book back numbers

Publications: Printed

Access to staff: Contact by letter, by telephone, by fax and by e-mail. Appointment necessary.
Hours: Telephone: 0830 to 0930 and evenings

Chairman: New Forest Pony Breeding and Cattle Society; Randalls Farm, Burley Street, Ringwood, Hampshire; tel: 01425 402459; e-mail: forestpony@enterprise.net

Daughter New Forest Pony Societies in the: Netherlands, France, Belgium, Sweden, Finland, Germany, North America and Australia

Member of: National Pony Society

NEW IMPERIAL OWNERS' ASSOCIATION (NIOA)

Smithy Cottage, Arddleen, Llanymynech, Montgomeryshire. SY22 6RX

Tel: 01938 590744
E-mail: info@newimperial.co.uk
Website: www.newimperial.co.uk

Enquiries to: Honorary Secretary

Founded: 1987

Organisation type and purpose: International organisation, membership association (membership is by subscription), present number of members: 315.
Historic motorcycle club.

Subject coverage: Information about New Imperial motor cycles manufactured in Birmingham between 1901 and 1939.

Publications: Printed

Access to staff: Contact by letter, by telephone and by e-mail. Appointment necessary.
Hours: Daily, 0900 to 2200

Links with: Federation of British Historic Vehicle Clubs; tel: 01865 400845; fax: 01865 400845; e-mail: secretary@fbhvc.co.uk

NEW INTERNATIONALIST (NI)

55 Rectory Road, Oxford, OX4 1BW

Tel: 01865 811400
Fax: 01865 793152
E-mail: ni@newint.org
Website: www.newint.org

Enquiries to: Administrator

Founded: 1972

Organisation type and purpose: Publishing house.

Subject coverage: Global political and social stories.

Publications: Printed

Access to staff: Contact by letter and by e-mail
Hours: Mon to Fri, 0930 to 1730

NEW PRODUCERS ALLIANCE (NPA)

9 Bourlet Close, London, W1W 1PB

Tel: 020 7580 2480
Fax: 020 7580 2484
E-mail: queries@npa.org.uk
Website: www.npa.org.uk

Enquiries to: Administrator

Founded: 1993

Organisation type and purpose: National organisation, membership association (membership is by subscription), present number of members: c. 1000, registered charity (charity number 1059200), training organisation.
Training and information for film makers.

Subject coverage: Film production, development and distribution.

Collection: Reference books and magazines relating to the film industry

Non-library collection catalogue: All or part available online

Publications list: Available online

Access to staff: Contact by letter, by telephone, by fax, by e-mail and via website. Appointment necessary.
Hours: Mon to Fri, 0900 to 1700

NEW ZEALAND HIGH COMMISSION

New Zealand House, 80 Haymarket, London, SW1Y 4TQ

Tel: 020 7930 8422
Fax: 020 7839 4580
E-mail: aboutnz@newzealandhc.org.uk
Website: www.nzembassy.com/uk

Organisation type and purpose: New Zealand Government Representative.

Subject coverage: Limited general information e.g. not on immigration; research and development in government, industry, universities, institutes and associations.

Access to staff: Contact by letter, by telephone, by fax, by e-mail and via website
Hours: Mon to Fri, 0900 to 1700

Access to building: Prior appointment required

Access for disabled people: Ramped entry

Parent body: Ministry of Foreign Affairs and Trade; Private Bag 18–901, Wellington, New Zealand

NEW ZEALAND IMMIGRATION SERVICE

Mezzanine Floor, New Zealand House, 80 Haymarket, London, SW1Y 4TE

Tel: 0906 9100 100
Fax: 020 7973 0370
Website: www.immigration.govt.nz

Organisation type and purpose: International organisation.

Subject coverage: Emigration to New Zealand.

Access to building: No prior appointment required
Hours: Mon to Fri, 1000 to 1545

NEWBURY LIBRARY

The Wharf, Newbury, Berkshire, RG14 5AU

Tel: 01635 519900
Fax: 01635 519906
E-mail: newburylibrary@westberks.gov.uk
Website: www.westberks.gov.uk/libraries

Enquiries to: Librarian

Organisation type and purpose: Local government body, public library.

Subject coverage: General public library material, Newbury and West Berkshire local history.

Collection: West Berkshire local history collection

Library catalogue: All or part available online

Access to staff: Contact by letter, by telephone, by fax, by e-mail, in person and via website
Hours: Mon, Tue, Thu, 0900 to 1900; Wed, Fri, 0900 to 1700; Sat, 0930 to 1600

Access to building: *Hours:* Mon, Tue, Thu, 0900 to 1900; Wed, Fri, 0900 to 1700; Sat, 0930 to 1600

Access for disabled people: Level entry, access to all public areas, toilet facilities

Parent body: West Berkshire District Council; Council Offices, Market Street, Newbury, RG14 5LD; tel: 01635 42400; fax: 01635 519392; website: http://www.westberks.gov.uk

NEWCASTLE COLLEGE LIBRARY SERVICES

Rye Hill Campus, Scotswood Road, Newcastle upon Tyne, NE4 7SA

Tel: 0191 200 4020
Fax: 0191 200 4100
E-mail: thelibrary@ncl-coll.ac.uk
Website: ncl-coll.ac.uk

Enquiries to: Head of Library Services
Direct tel: 0191 200 4017

Subject coverage: Engineering, construction, art and design, food industries, computing, business studies, information technology, music, performing arts, humanities, science, hotel and catering management, leisure, childcare, social welfare, training/education, local studies.

Collection: Local collection

Library catalogue: All or part available online

Publications: Printed

Access to staff: Contact by letter, by telephone, by fax and by e-mail. Appointment necessary.
Hours: Mon to Fri, 0900 to 1700

NEWCASTLE LIBRARIES

City Library, New Bridge Street, Newcastle upon Tyne, NE1 8AX

Tel: 0191 277 4100
Fax: 0191 277 4137
E-mail: tony.durcan@newcastle.gov.uk

Enquiries to: Head of Culture, Libraries and Lifelong Learning
Direct tel: 0191 211 5383
Direct fax: 0191 211 5602
Direct e-mail: tony.durcan@newcastle.gov.uk
Other contacts: City Libraries' Manager

Founded: 1880

Organisation type and purpose: Local government body, public library.

Subject coverage: Local studies for city and region; general reference collections; genealogy, local and national; patents; business information; community information.

Collection: Auty-Hastings Collection of glass plate negatives and prints, 1890–1920 (local scenes)
British Standards, full set (CD-ROM)
British, European, American and PCT Patent specifications
C. P. Taylor Collection (playwrights' manuscripts)
Clark Music Library (concert programmes, theatre playbills, c.1880–1920, with indexes in the care of the Local History Librarian)
Gibsone's Conches (over 20,000 watercolour paintings of conch shells bought for the City in 1889)
Local studies illustrations collection c. 70,000 items
Newspapers 1707 to date
Northern Playwrights Collection
Patents collection (UK, Europe, USA, Japan)
Seymour Bell Collection (plans and charts of the sea)
Thomas Bewick Collection (the 18th-century engraver's books and blocks, Pease Bequest)
Thomlinson Collection (16th- to 18th-century books)
Tyneside Unidentified Flying Objects Society Collection

Non-library collection catalogue: All or part available in-house

Library catalogue: All or part available online

Publications: Printed

Publications list: Available in print

Access to staff: Contact by letter, by telephone, by fax, by e-mail, in person and via website
Hours: Mon, Thu, 0900 to 2000; Tue, Wed, Fri, Sat, 0900 to 1700

Access for disabled people: Ramped entry, automatic doors at main entrance, toilet facilities

Parent body: City of Newcastle upon Tyne, Chief Executive's Office Directorate

NEWCASTLE UNIVERSITY

Robinson Library, Back Jesmond Road West, Newcastle upon Tyne, NE2 4HQ

Tel: 0191 222 7662
Fax: 0191 222 6235
E-mail: lib-readerservices@newcastle.ac.uk
Website: www.ncl.ac.uk/library

Enquiries to: Librarian
Direct tel: 0191 222 7674; 0191 222 7671 (Special Collections Librarian)
Direct e-mail: wayne.connolly@newcastle.ac.uk
Other contacts: Special Collections Librarian

Founded: 1963

Organisation type and purpose: University library.

Subject coverage: Accounting and finance, management, economics, geography, politics, sociology and anthropology, architecture, planning, English (literature and linguistics), fine art, modern languages, music, archaeology, classics, history, religious studies, museum studies, medicine, dentistry, speech, psychology, education, law, agriculture and biological sciences (including marine), chemical engineering, civil engineering, electrical engineering, marine technology, mechanical materials and manufacturing engineering, chemistry, physics, statistics, computing science, geomatics, mathematics (applied, pure and engineering).

Collection: Collections include:
Barry MacSweeney Papers (poetry)
Catherine Cookson Collection

continued overleaf

Chapbooks and Broadsides (many of these chapbooks are available on microfilm)
C. V. Stanford Collection (musical manuscripts)
Gertrude Bell Collection (history and archaeology of the Middle East)
Lady Plowden Papers (education)
Library of Japanese science and technology
Merz Collection (mathematics and philosophy)
Pybus Collection (medical history)
Robert White Collection (English literature, Border history and Antiquities)
Robinson Collection (multilingual rare books covering exploration, literature and music)
Runciman Papers (early 20th-century politics)
Shefton Collection (Greek archaeology)
Sid Chaplin Papers (literature)
Trevelyan Papers (19th- and 20th-century arts, literature and politics)
UK Government publications
Victorian Collection (literature)
Wallis Collection (mathematics)

Non-library collection catalogue: All or part available online

Library catalogue: All or part available online

Access to staff: Contact by letter, by telephone, by fax, by e-mail and in person. Appointment necessary. Non-members charged.
Hours: Term time: Mon to Fri, 0900 to 2100; Sat and Sun 1000 to 1730.
Vacations: variable, see website or telephone

Access for disabled people: Parking provided, level entry, toilet facilities

NEWHAM ASIAN WOMEN'S PROJECT (NAWP)

661 Barking Road, Plaistow, London, E13 9EX

Tel: 020 8472 0528
Fax: 020 8503 5673
E-mail: info@nawp.org
Website: www.nawp.org

Founded: 1987

Organisation type and purpose: Registered charity (charity number 1001834).
Specialist domestic violence service for Asian women. Also provides consultations and research relating to relevant proposed and existing legislation.

Subject coverage: Offers advice service, counselling support, refuge for women and children, a sexual health, exploitation and abuse project, education and training (extended to all black and ethnic minority women), and specialist support services for young Asian women who are vulnerable to self-harm and suicide in the East London area. NAWP does not provide emergency assistance.

Information services: Rights-based advice and information services; free confidential legal advice and assistance.

Education services: English language and other mainstream educational support, and vocational courses.

Library catalogue: All or part available online

Publications: Electronic and video
Order electronic and video publications from: Download from website

Publications list: Available online

Access to staff: Contact by letter, by telephone, by fax, by e-mail and in person

NEWLIFE FOUNDATION FOR DISABLED CHILDREN

Newlife Centre, Hemlock Way, Cannock, Staffordshire, WS11 7GF

Tel: 01543 462777
Fax: 01543 468999
E-mail: info@newlifecharity.co.uk
Website: www.newlifecharity.co.uk

Enquiries to: Chief Executive

Founded: 1991; formerly called Birth Defects Foundation; formerly called Happy Birthday Appeal

Organisation type and purpose: Registered charity (charity number 1001817).

Subject coverage: Birth defects.

Publications: Printed

Publications list: Available online and in print

Access to staff: Contact by letter, by telephone, by fax, by e-mail, in person and via website. Appointment necessary.
Hours: Helpline: Mon to Fri, 0930 to 1900; Sat, 0930 to 1700
Office: Mon to Fri, 0930 to 1700

Access for disabled people: Parking provided, level entry, access to all public areas, toilet facilities

NEWMAN UNIVERSITY COLLEGE

Library, Genners Lane, Bartley Green, Birmingham, B32 3NT

Tel: 0121 476 1181
Fax: 0121 476 1196
E-mail: library@newman.ac.uk
Website: www.newman.ac.uk

Enquiries to: Librarian

Founded: 1968

Organisation type and purpose: University College.

Subject coverage: Counselling, creative arts, drama, early childhood education and care, education in general, English language, English literature, history, IT, initial teacher education, management, media, physical education, psychology, religious education, sports science, theology, West Midlands history.

Collection: West Midlands history – books, pamphlets, photographs

Library catalogue: All or part available online

Access to staff: Contact by letter, by telephone, by fax, by e-mail and via website
Hours: Mon, Tue, Thu, 0845 to 2100; Wed, 0945 to 2100; Fri, 0845 to 1700; Sat, 1000 to 1500

Access to building: *Special comments:* Access to the library is usually available, when both the library and main Newman reception are open. Occasionally, due to unforeseen circumstances, it is necessary to amend these hours at short notice, so it is recommended to call the library prior to a visit.

Research degrees validated by: Leicester University

NEWPORT AND GWENT CHAMBER OF COMMERCE AND INDUSTRY (ngb2b)

Unit 30, The Orion Suite, Enterprise Way, Newport, Gwent, NP20 2AQ

Tel: 01633 222664
Fax: 01633 222301
E-mail: info@ngb2b.org.uk
Website: www.ngb2b.co.uk

Enquiries to: International Trade Manager
Direct e-mail: jennifer@ngb2b.org.uk

Founded: 1867

Organisation type and purpose: Membership association (membership is by election or invitation).

Subject coverage: Material sourcing, financial references, EC legislation, national legislation, export documentation, certificates of origin, VAT legislation, local affairs, available grants via Welsh Office, local developments, infogrants, inforules, training courses. Information and product sourcing, training and seminars, exporting, certificates of origin, networking, commercial services, databases, newsletters, marketing services, credit checks, Chambersign, representation.

Collection: HMSO Customs and Tariffs
Local business directories
Overseas national directories
Parliamentary and EC year books
Croner's Reference Books (various titles)

Publications: Printed

Publications list: Available in print

Access to staff: Contact by letter, by telephone, by fax, by e-mail, in person and via website
Hours: Mon to Fri, 0900 to 1200, 1300 to 1700

Access to building: Prior appointment required

Access for disabled people: Parking provided, toilet facilities

Affiliated organisations: Chepstow Chamber of Commerce & Tourism; Gwent Business Women's Network; Monmouth District Chamber of Commerce; Newport Business Club; Newport Chamber of Trade; Royal Forest of Dean Business and Professional Club

NEWPORT CITY COUNCIL

Civic Centre, Newport, Gwent, NP20 4UR

Tel: 01633 656656
Fax: 01633 232537
Website: www.newport.gov.uk

Enquiries to: Managing Director

Founded: 1996

Organisation type and purpose: Local government body.

Subject coverage: Newport.

Trade and statistical information: Newport inward investment

Publications: Printed

Access to staff: Contact by letter, by telephone and by fax. Appointment necessary.
Hours: Mon to Fri, 0830 to 1630

NEWPORT COMMUNITY LEARNING AND LIBRARIES

Central Library, John Frost Square, Newport, Gwent, NP20 1PA

Tel: 01633 656656
Fax: 01633 414705
E-mail: central.library@newport.gov.uk
Website: www.newport.gov.uk/libraries

Enquiries to: Librarian

Organisation type and purpose: Public library.

Subject coverage: Local history; local Chartism, general reference, family history.

Services for disabled people: Wheelchair available, hearing loops.

Collection: Arthur Machen Collection (local author)
Haines Collection (local history)
Phillips Collection (mainly private press books and the arts)
Mrs Delany's Letters (local history)

Non-library collection catalogue: All or part available online and in-house

Library catalogue: All or part available online

Access to staff: Contact by letter, by telephone, by fax, by e-mail and in person
Hours: Mon to Fri, 0900 to 1800; Sat, 0900 to 1600

Access for disabled people: Level entry, toilet facilities

Parent body: Continuing Learning and Leisure; Newport County City Council

NEWQUEST (HERALD & TIMES) LTD

Formal name: Scottish Media Group Newspapers

200 Renfield Street, Glasgow, G2 3QB

Tel: 0141 302 7000
Fax: 0141 302 7383
E-mail: ian.watson@glasgow.newsquest.co.uk

Enquiries to: Information Officer
Direct e-mail: newslib@glasgow.newsquest.co.uk

Founded: 1783

Organisation type and purpose: Service industry, publishing house.
Newspaper publisher.

Subject coverage: Current affairs, sport, arts.

Collection: Extensive Photo Collection (c. 5 million)

Publications: Printed, and electronic and video, and microform publications

Publications list: Available online

Access to staff: Contact by letter, by fax and by e-mail. Appointment necessary. All charged.
Hours: Mon to Fri, 0900 to 1700

Access to building: Prior appointment required

Access for disabled people: Parking provided, level entry, toilet facilities

NEWS INTERNATIONAL NEWSPAPERS LIMITED

Information Services, 1 Viginia Street, London, E98 1ES

Tel: 020 7782 6000
E-mail: info@newsint.co.uk
Website: www.newsinternational.co.uk/

Enquiries to: Information Services Manager
Direct tel: 020 7782 6398
Direct fax: 020 7782 3650

Organisation type and purpose: Newspaper publishing.

Access to staff: Contact by letter. Appointment necessary. Non-members charged.
Hours: Mon to Fri, 0900 to 1700

Access to building: Prior appointment required

Access for disabled people: Ramped entry, toilet facilities

Subsidiary of: News Corporation; website: www.newscorp.com

NEWSPAPER PUBLISHERS ASSOCIATION LIMITED (NPA)

8th Floor, St Andrew's House, 18–20 St Andrew Street, London, EC4A 3AY

Tel: 020 7636 7014
Fax: 020 7631 5119
E-mail: lynne_anderson@newspapersoc.org.uk

Direct tel: 020 7931 3806
Direct e-mail: Guy.Black@telegraph.co.uk

Founded: 1906

Organisation type and purpose: Trade association.
National newspapers.

Subject coverage: Distribution, advertising, marketing, newsprint.

Access to staff: Appointment necessary.
Hours: Mon to Fri, 0900 to 1700

NEWSPAPER SOCIETY, THE (NS)

Bloomsbury House, 74–77 Great Russell Street, London, WC1B 3DA

Tel: 020 7636 7014
Fax: 020 7631 5119
E-mail: ns@newspapersoc.org.uk
Website: www.newspapersoc.org.uk/new-reports/publications/a-zpublications.html
Website: www.newspapersoc.org.uk.

Enquiries to: Communications Executive
Direct fax: 020 7580 7167
Direct e-mail: lisa_mccarthy@newspapersoc.org.uk

Founded: 1836

Organisation type and purpose: Trade association (membership is by subscription, qualification), present number of members: 327.
Represents the regional and local press in the UK.

Subject coverage: All information relating to Britain's regional press: including training, technical, industrial relations, legal and government matters, advertising sales and distribution, free newspapers, research, editorial readership, newspapers in education, press regulation and promotion.

Publications: Electronic and video

Publications list: Available online

Access to staff: Contact by letter, by fax and by e-mail
Hours: Mon to Fri, 0900 to 1700

Member of: European Newspaper Publishers' Association; International Federation of Newspaper Publishers; Newspaper Conference

NEWSROOM, GUARDIAN AND OBSERVER ARCHIVE AND VISITOR CENTRE

60 Farringdon Road, London, EC1R 3GA

Tel: 020 7886 9898
Fax: 020 7490 8359
E-mail: newsroom@guardian.co.uk
Website: www.guardian.co.uk/newsroom

Enquiries to: Centre Administrator

Organisation type and purpose: To preserve and promote the histories and values of the Guardian, The Observer and Guardian Unlimited through archive, education and exhibitions.

Subject coverage: Newspapers

Collection: Individual collections (correspondence, diaries, notebooks, original sketches and photographs):
Jane Bown (Observer photographer)
WP Crozier (editor of the Guardian 1932–44)
Richard Fry (financial editor of the Guardian 1939–65)
Jean Stead (home news editor 1969–78 and reporter)
Donald Trelford (editor of the Observer 1975–93)
Corporate records:
The Guardian Archive (1968 to present)
The Observer Archive (1917 to present)
Newspaper holdings:
Guardian Weekly (1920–49, 1972-current)
Guardian Commercial (1920–39)
Observer magazine (1964–94)
Bound volumes of the original newspapers are held but for preservation reasons surrogates are used where available.

Order electronic and video publications from:
Guardian (14 July 1984 to present)
Observer (3 January 1993 to present)

Access to staff: Contact by letter, by telephone, by fax, by e-mail, in person and via website
Hours: Mon to Fri, 1000 to 1700

NEXUS INSTITUTE

119 University Street, Belfast, BT7 1HP

Tel: 028 9032 6803

continued overleaf

Fax: 028 9032 5623
E-mail: info@nexusinstitute.org
Website: www.nexusinstitute.org

Enquiries to: Manager

Founded: 1984

Organisation type and purpose: Voluntary organisation, registered charity (charity number XN 46002), training organisation. Counselling.
For adult survivors of sexual abuse.

Subject coverage: Field of sexual abuse, counselling of sexual abuse survivors, counsellor training.

Publications: Printed

Access to staff: Contact by letter, by telephone and by e-mail. Appointment necessary. All charged.
Hours: Mon to Thu, 0900 to 1700; Fri, 0900 to 1600
Special comments: Evening appointments available by arrangement.

Other branches: Nexus Institute; 38 Clarendon Street, Londonderry, BT48 7ET; Nexus Institute; 6 Portmore Street, Portadown, BT62 3NG; Nexus Institute; 104 Irvinestown Road, Enniskillen, BT74 6DN

NFSH THE HEALING TRUST

Formal name: The NFSH Charitable Trust Ltd.

21 York Road, Northampton, NN1 5QG

Tel: 01604 603247
Fax: 01604 603534
E-mail: office@thehealingtrust.org.uk
Website: www.thehealingtrust.org.uk/

Founded: 1954

Organisation type and purpose: A registered charity (number 1094702), membership organisation (membership is by subscription).
Spiritual healing.
To raise the standards and awareness of healing in the UK and overseas.

Subject coverage: National standards of training delivered by accredited trainers; a minimum of two years' training period with national standards of final assessment; professional code of conduct, disciplinary procedures, professional insurance; over 50 Healing Centres throughout the UK, staffed by volunteer members; accreditation of independent voluntary centres that meet Healing Trust standards.

Access to staff: Contact by letter, by telephone, by fax, by e-mail, in person and via website

NFU SCOTLAND (NFUS)

Rural Centre, West Mains, Ingliston, Newbridge, Midlothian, EH28 8LT

Tel: 0131 472 4000
Fax: 0131 472 4010
E-mail: webmaster@nfus.org.uk
Website: www.nfus.org.uk

Enquiries to: Chief Executive

Founded: 1913

Organisation type and purpose: Professional body (membership is by subscription), voluntary organisation. Represents the political interests of the Scottish agricultural, horticultural and crofting industries and acts as a professional association for Scottish farmers, growers and crofters.

Subject coverage: Cereals, fish farming, horticulture, legal, labour and technology matters, livestock, milk, potatoes, poultry, publicity, animal health and welfare, crofting, pigs, environment, landlord/tenant, parliamentary.

Publications: Printed

Access to staff: Contact by letter and by fax
Hours: Mon to Fri, 0900 to 1700

NGS PICTURE LIBRARY

Formal name: National Galleries of Scotland Picture Library

National Galleries of Scotland, Scottish National Gallery of Modern Art, 75 Belford Road, Edinburgh, EH4 3DS

Tel: 0131 624 6258; 0131 624 6260
Fax: 0131 623 7135
E-mail: picture.library@nationalgalleries.org
Website: www.nationalgalleries.org

Organisation type and purpose: National organisation, art gallery, public library.

Subject coverage: Brings together the works in all the collections of the National Galleries of Scotland including photographs and slides; material depicting the work of artists from the Renaissance to the present day, including the major painters, and a wide variety of subjects, media and styles.

Non-library collection catalogue: All or part available online, in-house and in print

Library catalogue: All or part available online, in-house and in print

Publications: Printed
Order printed publications from: website: http://www.nationalgalleries.org/shop/online/8:398/category/575

Publications list: Available online and in print

Access to staff: Contact by letter, by telephone, by fax, by e-mail and via website. Appointment necessary.
Hours: Mon to Fri, 0900 to 1700

Access to building: No prior appointment required
Hours: Daily, 1000 to 1700; Thu to 1900
Special comments: Closed 25, 26 December; open 1 January, 1200 to 1700

Access for disabled people: Access to all public areas, toilet facilities

Parent body: National Galleries of Scotland; Belford Road, Edinburgh, EH4 3DR; tel: 0131 624 6200; fax: 0131 623 7126; e-mail: enquiries@nationalgalleries.org; website: http://www.nationalgalleries.org

NGS: GARDENS OPEN FOR CHARITY (NGS)

Formal name: National Gardens Scheme

Hatchlands Park, East Clandon, Guildford, Surrey, GU4 7RT

Tel: 01483 211535
Fax: 01483 211537
E-mail: ngs@ngs.org.uk
Website: www.ngs.org.uk

Enquiries to: Marketing Communications Manager
Direct tel: 01483 213900
Direct e-mail: cmorley@ngs.org.uk

Founded: 1927

Organisation type and purpose: Voluntary organisation, registered charity (charity number 1112664).

Subject coverage: Approximately 3,700 mainly privately owned gardens in England and Wales are opened to the public on behalf of the NGS each year, in order to raise money for good causes.

Publications: Printed
Order printed publications from: Website

Publications list: Available online

Access to staff: Contact by letter, by telephone, by fax, by e-mail and via website
Hours: Mon to Fri, 0900 to 1700

Fund-raising body for: Arthritis Research UK; Crossroads Care; Gardeners' Royal Benevolent Society; Help the Hospices; Local charities nominated by garden owners; Macmillan Cancer Support; Marie Curie Cancer Care; National Trust Careership Scheme; Perennial (Gardeners' Royal Benevolent Society); Queens Nursing Institute; Royal Gardeners' Orphan Fund

NHBC

Formal name: National House Building Council

Buildmark House, Chiltern Avenue, Amersham, Buckinghamshire, HP6 5AP

Tel: 0870 2414302
Fax: 01494 735201
E-mail: mediaenquiries@nhbc.co.uk
Website: www.nhbc.co.uk

Enquiries to: Head of Corporate Communications
Direct tel: 01494 735262
Other contacts: Media Manager (for company information)

Founded: 1936

Organisation type and purpose: National organisation, professional body, present number of members: 17,000 registered builders, a non-profit-distributing company limited by guarantee.
Independent standard-setting body for the UK house-building industry.
Aims to improve standards of new homes in the UK, benchmark best practice and work with builders to raise standards and protect homeowners.

Subject coverage: NHBC sets standards for the building of new homes in the UK. It raises standards by providing new home warranty and insurance services for home buyers, setting construction standards for new homes and inspecting at key stages, registering builders and being a service provider of health and safety, training and engineering services.

Trade and statistical information: New house-building statistics, e.g. UK new home starts and completions, UK average daily sales, new home prices

Publications: Printed

Publications list: Available in print

Access to staff: Contact by letter, by telephone and by e-mail. Appointment necessary.
Hours: Mon to Fri, 0900 to 1730

Access to building: Prior appointment required
Hours: Mon to Fri, 0900 to 1730

Access for disabled people: Parking provided, level entry

Also at: Belfast, Edinburgh, Droitwich, London, Milton Keynes and York; Addresses available on website pages

NHS BORDERS LIBRARY SERVICE

NHS Borders Library, Education Centre, Borders General Hospital, Melrose, Roxburghshire, TD6 9BD

Tel: 01896 827620; 01896 661630 (minicom)
E-mail: library@borders.scot.nhs.uk

Enquiries to: Librarian
Direct e-mail: moira.mitchell@borders.scot.nhs.uk

Founded: 1974; formerly a part of Edinburgh Napier University Library (year of change 2011)

Organisation type and purpose: NHS Library

Subject coverage: Nursing, primary care, medicine, psychiatry, public health, psychology, complementary therapies, social work, childcare, NHS management.

Non-library collection catalogue: All or part available online

Library catalogue: All or part available online

Access to staff: Contact by letter, by telephone, by fax, by e-mail and in person. Non-members charged.
Hours: Mon to Thu, 0900 to 2100; Fri, 0900 to 1700

Access to building: No prior appointment required

Access for disabled people: Level entry, toilet facilities

NHS EDUCATION FOR SCOTLAND

22 Queen Street, Edinburgh, EH2 1JX

Tel: 0131 226 7371
Fax: 0131 225 9970
E-mail: enquiries@nes.scot.nhs.uk
Website: www.nes.scot.nhs.uk

Direct tel: 0131 220 8603
Other contacts: Corporate Services Manager

Founded: 2002

Organisation type and purpose: National government body, statutory body, training organisation.
Oversight of postgraduate education of doctors, dentists, clinical psychologists, midwives, nurses, and allied health professions.

Subject coverage: Postgraduate medical and dental education in Scotland.

Access to staff: Contact by letter, by telephone and by e-mail
Hours: Mon to Fri, 0900 to 1730

Access for disabled people: Level entry, toilet facilities

Accountable to the: Scottish Executive

NHS ESTATES, INFORMATION CENTRE

Department of Health, 1 Trevelyan Square, Boar Lane, Leeds, West Yorkshire, LS1 6AE

Tel: 0113 254 7070
Fax: 0113 254 7167
E-mail: enquiries@ic.nhs.uk
Website: www.nhsestates.gov.uk/publications_guidance/index.asp

Enquiries to: Information Officer

Organisation type and purpose: National government body.
To enable optimum use of the estates for better healthcare.

Subject coverage: Health estate management, Health buildings and facilities design, Health technical advice on building components, access to Department of Health Library database, fire and safety design – Health buildings, estate policy advice Health estate.

Collection: Archival Health buildings directorate publications
Collection of audiovisual material – slides, photographs of hospital building projects (various stages)
Very old departmental circulars and letters

Non-library collection catalogue: All or part available in-house

Library catalogue: All or part available in-house

Publications: Printed, and electronic and video
Order printed publications from: HMSO, PO Box 276
London, SW8 5DT, tel: 0870 600 5522, fax: 0870 600 5533

Publications list: Available online and in print

Access to staff: Contact by telephone, by e-mail and via website. Appointment necessary.
Hours: Mon to Thu, 0830 to 1730; Fri, 0830 to 1700

Access for disabled people: Ramped entry, access to all public areas, toilet facilities
Special comments: Parking provided upon request.

Parent body: Department of Health

NIAB

Formal name: National Institute of Agricultural Botany

Huntingdon Road, Cambridge, CB3 0LE

Tel: 01223 342200
Fax: 01223 277602
E-mail: info@niab.com
Website: www.niab.com

Founded: 1919

Organisation type and purpose: Membership association (membership is by subscription), present number of members: 2500, registered charity, research organisation.

Subject coverage: Variety testing of most agricultural and horticultural crops (except fruit), choice of variety, seed certification, seed testing procedures, botanical description of varieties, plant pathology, plant science research.

Collection: Seed catalogues (1900-)

Publications: Printed

Publications list: Available online and in print

Access to staff: Contact by letter, by telephone, by e-mail, in person and via website. Appointment necessary. Access for members only. Non-members charged.
Hours: Mon to Thu, 0900 to 1700; Fri, 0900 to 1645
Special comments: Association members only.

Access to building: No prior appointment required

Access for disabled people: Ramped entry, toilet facilities

Includes the: Official Seed Testing Station for England and Wales; at the same address

NICKEL INSTITUTE (NI)

The Holloway, Alvechurch, Birmingham, B48 7QB

Tel: 01527 584777
Fax: 01527 585562
E-mail: birmingham@nickelinstitute.org
Website: www.nickelinstitute.org

Enquiries to: European Director
Other contacts: Technical Director

Founded: 1957

Organisation type and purpose: International organisation, present number of members: 15 industrial members, consultancy.
Market development organisation, offering expert advice in the form of published information and discussion with consultants.
To support, sustain and defend worldwide use of nickel and its alloys.

Subject coverage: Oil and gas industry, marine offshore industry, electroplating and electroforming, welding, casting and foundry, chemical, environmental, all as applied to nickel and its alloys (especially stainless steel).

Collection: Computer databases
Technical publications on nickel and its alloys
Videos

Non-library collection catalogue: All or part available online

Library catalogue: All or part available online

continued overleaf

Publications: Printed, and electronic and video

Publications list: Available online and in print

Access to staff: Contact by letter, by telephone, by fax, by e-mail and in person. Appointment necessary.
Hours: Mon to Fri, 0900 to 1700
Special comments: By prior appointment

Access for disabled people: *Special comments:* By prior appointment

Has: offices in 8 countries

Head office: NI; 55 University Avenue, Suite 1801, Toronto, Ontario, M5T 2H7, canada; tel: +1 416 591 7999; fax: +1 416 591 7987; e-mail: ni_toronto@nickelinstitute.org; website: www.nickelinstitute.org

NIELSEN

3rd Floor, Midas House, 62 Goldsworth Road, Woking, Surrey, GU21 6LQ

Tel: 01483 712200
Fax: 01483 712201
E-mail: libraries.book@nielsen.com
Website: www.nielsenbook.co.uk

Enquiries to: Head of Data Sales – Libraries
Direct e-mail: Paul.Dibble@nielsen.com

Founded: 2002; formerly called Book Data, Whitaker Information Services, First Edition (year of change 2002)

Organisation type and purpose: The leading data supplier for the book industry, playing a pivotal role within the industry and offering a comprehensive source of bibliographic data and associated services worldwide. Working with publishers large and small, data is collected from 60,000 publishers in over 70 countries. Over 18.6m. titles are held and millions of changes are made annually to ensure that the most timely, accurate and comprehensive data is available.

Subject coverage: Bibliographic data (books and multimedia products), acquisitions, search and discovery, cataloguing, ordering and promotion.

Publications: Electronic and video

Publications list: Available online

Access to staff: Contact by letter, by telephone, by fax, by e-mail, in person and via website. Appointment necessary. Access for members only.
Hours: Mon to Fri, 0900 to 1700

Access to building: Prior appointment required

Access for disabled people: Parking provided, disabled lift, toilet facilities

NIGERIAN HIGH COMMISSION

Nigeria House, 9 Northumberland Avenue, London, WC2N 5BX

Tel: 020 7839 1244
Fax: 020 7839 8746
Website: www.nigeriahighcommissionuk.com

Enquiries to: Librarian
Direct tel: ext 279 or 303

Other contacts: Head of Chancery for official government statements.

Founded: 1960

Organisation type and purpose: National government body.

Subject coverage: Federal government of Nigeria matters e.g. history, economics, laws etc.
Tourist information.

Library catalogue: All or part available in-house

Publications: Printed

Access to staff: Contact by letter, by telephone and by fax. Appointment necessary.
Hours: Library: Mon to Fri, 1000 to 1700
Offices: Mon to Fri, 0900 to 1700

Access to building: Prior appointment required

Consular Section: Nigerian High Commission; 56–57 Fleet Street, London, EC4; tel: 020 7353 3776

NISSAN INSTITUTE OF JAPANESE STUDIES

University of Oxford, 27 Winchester Road, Oxford, OX2 6NA

Tel: 01865 274570
Fax: 01865 274574
E-mail: secretary@nissan.ox.ac.uk
Website: www.nissan.ox.ac.uk

Enquiries to: Secretary

Founded: 1981

Organisation type and purpose: University institute.
To promote the study of modern and contemporary Japan within the University of Oxford.

Subject coverage: The modern history, politics, anthropology, economy, international relations, society and education systems of Japan.

Collection: See Bodleian Japanese Library (separate institution from the Nissan Institute)

Publications: Printed

Access to staff: Contact by letter, by fax, by e-mail and via website. Appointment necessary.
Hours: Mon to Fri, 0900 to 1230 and 1400 to 1645
Special comments: Primarily university access.

Access for disabled people: Ramped entry, lift

Parent body: University of Oxford

NO PANIC

Formal name: National Organisation for Phobias, Anxiety Neurosis Information and Care

93 Brands Farm Way, Randlay, Telford, Shropshire, TF3 2JQ

Tel: 01952 590005
Fax: 01952 270962
E-mail: ceo@nopanic.org.uk
Website: www.nopanic.org.uk

Enquiries to: Chief Executive

Founded: 1991

Organisation type and purpose: International organisation, membership association (membership is by subscription), present number of members: 2,500, voluntary organisation, registered charity (charity number 1018184).
The relief and rehabilitation of people suffering from anxiety disorders.

Subject coverage: Sufferers and carers of anxiety disorders caused by panic attacks, phobias, obsessive/compulsive disorders and tranquilliser withdrawal.

Library catalogue: All or part available online and in print

Publications: Printed, and electronic and video

Publications list: Available online and in print

Access to staff: Contact by letter, by telephone and by fax. Appointment necessary.
Hours: Mon to Fri, 0900 to 1700

NOC LIBRARY (GIRDLESTONE MEMORIAL)

Nuffield Orthopaedic Centre, National Health Service Trust, Headington, Oxford, OX3 7LD

Tel: 01865 738147
Fax: 01865 738146
E-mail: library@ouh.nhs.uk
Website: noclibrary.com

Enquiries to: Library and Information Services Manager

Organisation type and purpose: NHS Library.

Subject coverage: Orthopaedics, orthopaedic engineering (bio-mechanics), rehabilitation, rheumatology, metabolic disease of bone, orthopaedic and trauma nursing.

Collection: Small collection of early orthopaedic texts

Non-library collection catalogue: All or part available in-house

Library catalogue: All or part available online

Access to staff: Contact by letter, by telephone, by fax, by e-mail, in person and via website
Hours: 0830 to 1700

Access to building: 24-hour card access for members

Access for disabled people: Level entry, access to all public areas

Links with: South Central Strategic Health Authority; website: http://www.nesc.nhs.uk
University of Oxford; Nuffield Department of Orthopaedic, Rheumatology and Musculoskeletal Sciences

NOISE ABATEMENT SOCIETY (NAS)

44 Grand Parade, Brighton, East Sussex, BN2 9QA

Tel: 01273 682223
Fax: 01273 682223
E-mail: info@noise-abatement.org
Website: www.noiseabatementsociety.com

Enquiries to: Director
Direct e-mail: info@noise-abatement.org

Founded: 1959

Organisation type and purpose: National organisation, membership association (membership is by subscription), voluntary organisation, registered charity (charity number 272040), research organisation.
To reduce noise from all sources.

Subject coverage: Noise abatement in all fields.

Publications: Printed

Access to staff: Contact by letter, by telephone, by fax, by e-mail, in person and via website. Appointment necessary. Access for members only.
Hours: Mon to Fri, 0900 to 1600

Access to building: No access other than to staff

Affiliated to: International Association Against Noise

NORDOFF ROBBINS LONDON CENTRE

2 Lissenden Gardens, London, NW5 1PQ

Tel: 020 7267 4496
Fax: 020 7267 4369
E-mail: admin@nordoff-robbins.org.uk
Website: www.nordoff-robbins.org.uk

Enquiries to: Administrator

Founded: 1980; please select Nordoff-Robbins Music Therapy Centre (year of change 2009)

Organisation type and purpose: National Headquarters of Nordoff Robbins charity (RCN 280960), which provides music therapy services and music and health projects nationally, and education and training in and about music therapy, and undertakes research in music therapy.
Music therapy clinic, music therapy training degree course, research department.

Subject coverage: Music therapy; music and health.

Information services: Comprehensive music therapy library open to the general public by arrangement.

Collection: Comprehensive music therapy library open to the general public by arrangement

Library catalogue: All or part available in-house

Publications: Printed, and electronic and video
Order printed publications from: e-mail: admin@nordoff-robbins.org.uk
Order electronic and video publications from: e-mail: admin@nordoff-robbins.org.uk

Publications list: Available in print

Access to staff: Contact by telephone and via website. Appointment necessary.
Hours: Mon to Fri, 0900 to 1700

Access to building: Prior appointment required

Hours: Mon to Fri, 0900 to 1630; Sat, 0900 to 1500
Special comments: Telephone before coming. Library for reference only.

Access for disabled people: Ramped entry, toilet facilities

Links with: City University London (validating partner for training programmes); Northampton Square, London, EC1V 0HB; tel: 020 7040 5060; e-mail: enquiries@city.ac.uk; website: http://www.city.ac.uk

NORFOLK & NORWICH MILLENNIUM LIBRARY

The Forum, Millennium Plain, Norwich, Norfolk, NR2 1AW

Tel: 01603 774774
Fax: 01603 774705
E-mail: millennium.lib@norfolk.gov.uk
Website: www.library.norfolk.gov.uk

Enquiries to: Central Information Team
Direct tel: 01603 774775
Direct e-mail: info.services.dcs@norfolk.gov.uk

Organisation type and purpose: Local government body, public library.

Subject coverage: History of Norfolk and Norwich; history of 2nd Air Division, 8th US Army Air Force, 1942–1945; USA travel and culture; general subjects.

Collection: American Memorial Library (US life and history)
Bosworth Harcourt and Buck bequests (theatrical, literary and historical)
Colman and Rye Collections of Local History (seriously affected by the fire of 1994)
Norwich City Library, 1608 (incunabula, theology and general literature)
Photographic collections by G C Davies, T D Eaton, P H Emerson, Payne Jennings
Publications of the Public Record Office, Historical Manuscripts Commission
Family history resources on microfilm and microfiche include Indexes to Births, Marriages and Deaths (national), Probate Indexes (national) and Census returns and name indexes (local)
Market research, business information, newspapers, etc. online
Database of local organisations (Icon) available in library and via the internet

Non-library collection catalogue: All or part available online

Library catalogue: All or part available online

Access to staff: Contact by letter, by telephone, by fax, by e-mail, in person and via website
Hours: Mon to Fri, 0900 to 2000, Saturday 0900 to 1700

Access for disabled people: Parking provided, ramped entry, access to all public areas, toilet facilities

Member organisation of: Anglian Libraries Information Exchange Scheme (ANGLES)

Parent body: Norfolk Library and Information Service; County Hall , Martineau Lane, Norwich; tel: 01603 222049; fax: 01603 222422

NORFOLK & NORWICH NOVI SAD ASSOCIATION (NNNSA)

Glebelands, Star Lane, Rockland St Mary, Norwich, Norfolk, NR14 7BX

Tel: 01508 480262
Fax: 01508 480262
E-mail: peter@beckleyp.freeserve.co.uk

Enquiries to: Honorary Secretary

Founded: 1985

Organisation type and purpose: National organisation, membership association (membership is by subscription).

Subject coverage: Promoting informal links between people and organisations in the City of Norwich and the County of Norfolk, and those in the municipality of Novi Sad, Serbia; supports the official twinning between the City of Norwich and the City of Novi Sad.

Collection: Archive material relating to the twinning links between the cities of Norwich and Novi Sad

Publications: Printed

Access to staff: Contact by letter, by telephone, by fax and by e-mail
Hours: Mon to Fri, 0900 to 1700

Links with: City Council Novi Sad; Norfolk County Council; Norwich City Council

NORFOLK AND NORWICH ARCHAEOLOGICAL SOCIETY (NNAS)

64 The Close, Norwich, NR1 4DH

Tel: 01603 891437
Website: www.nnas.info

Enquiries to: Librarian

Founded: 1846

Organisation type and purpose: Learned society (membership is by subscription), present number of members: 400, registered charity (charity number 311116).

Subject coverage: Archaeology, history, architecture and antiquities of the county of Norfolk.

Collection: On loan to Norfolk Record Office, County Hall, Norwich:
King Collection of drawings and watercolours of East Anglian specimens of stained and painted glass
Transcripts of Norfolk Parish Registers

Library catalogue: All or part available online and in-house

Publications: Printed

Access to staff: Contact by letter, by telephone and via website. Appointment necessary. Access for members only.
Hours: Mon to Fri, 0900 to 1700

Access to building: By appointment

NORFOLK ASSOCIATION OF VILLAGE HALLS (NAVH)

20 Market Place, Hingham, Norwich, Norfolk, NR9 4AF

Tel: 01953 851408
Fax: 01953 850695
E-mail: nrcc@norfolkrcc.org.uk

continued overleaf

Enquiries to: Secretary

Founded: 1984

Organisation type and purpose:
Membership association (membership is by subscription), present number of members: 310, voluntary organisation, registered charity (charity number 1053152).

Subject coverage: Management of village halls and community centres, training for committee members, sources of funds and charity law.

Access to staff: Contact by letter, by telephone, by fax and by e-mail. Appointment necessary. Access for members only.
Hours: Mon to Fri, 0900 to 1700

Access to building: Prior appointment required

NORFOLK CHURCH TRUST LIMITED (NCT)

9 The Old Church, St Matthews Road, Norwich, Norfolk, NR1 1SP

Tel: 01603 767576
Fax: 01986 798776
E-mail: secretary@norfolkchurchestrust.co.uk
Website: www.norfolkchurchestrust.co.uk

Enquiries to: Chief Executive/Company Secretary

Founded: 1976

Organisation type and purpose:
Membership association (membership is by subscription, election or invitation), present number of members: 1,300, voluntary organisation, registered charity (charity number 271176), consultancy.
To ensure Christian Churches remain open as places of worship in Norfolk and the Diocese of Norwich.

Subject coverage: General state of repair, restoration and maintenance of the churches in Norfolk.

Information services: Information and guidance on the restoration/conservation/state of the churches in Norfolk.

Publications: Printed
Order printed publications from: 9 The Old Church, St Matthews Road, Norwich, NR1 1SP

Access to staff: Contact by letter, by telephone, by fax and by e-mail
Hours: Mon to Sun, 0800 to 2000

NORFOLK COUNTY ASSOCIATION OF PARISH & TOWN COUNCILS (NCAPTC)

North Wing, County Hall, Norwich, Norfolk, NR1 2UF

Tel: 01603 664869
Fax: 01603 664871
E-mail: enquiries@norfolkalc.gov.uk

Enquiries to: Executive Officer

Founded: 1941

Publications list: Available in print

Access to staff: Contact by letter, by telephone, by fax and by e-mail. Access for members only.
Hours: Mon to Fri, 0900 to 1700

Affiliated to: National Association of Local Councils (NALC)

NORFOLK COUNTY COUNCIL LIBRARY AND INFORMATION SERVICE

County Hall, Martineau Lane, Norwich, Norfolk, NR1 2UA

Tel: 0344 800 8020
Fax: 01603 222422
E-mail: libraries@norfolk.gov.uk
Website: www.norfolk.gov.uk

Enquiries to: Head of Library and Information Service

Founded: 1974

Organisation type and purpose: Local government body, public library.
Headquarters and administration centre, no library at this address.

Subject coverage: General.

Collection: Norwich: Colman and Rye local studies collection
King's Lynn: St Margaret's Parish collection
Thetford: Duleep Singh collection
Thetford: Thomas Paine collection

Non-library collection catalogue: All or part available online and in-house

Library catalogue: All or part available online

Access to staff: Contact by letter, by telephone, by fax and by e-mail. Appointment necessary.
Hours: Mon to Fri, 0900 to 1700

Access to building: No prior appointment required

Main libraries: Great Yarmouth Library; Tollhouse Street, Great Yarmouth, Norfolk, NR30 2SH; tel: 01943 844551; fax: 01943 857628; e-mail: yarmouth.lib@norfolk.gov.uk; King's Lynn Library; London Road, King's Lynn, Norfolk, PE30 5EZ; tel: 01553 772568; fax: 01553 769832; e-mail: kings.lynn.lib@norfolk.gov.uk; Norfolk & Norwich Millennium Library; The Forum, Millennium Plain, Norwich, Norfolk, NR2 1AW; tel: 01603 774774; fax: 01603 774705; e-mail: millennium.lib@norfolk.gov.uk; Thetford Library; Raymond Street, Thetford, Norfolk, IP24 2EA; tel: 01842 752048; fax: 01842 750125; e-mail: thetford.lib@norfolk.gov.uk

NORFOLK COUNTY PETANQUE ASSOCIATION (NCPA)

26 Sun Lane, Norwich, NR3 3NF

Tel: 01603 419897

Enquiries to: Secretary
Direct e-mail: normanguest.petanque@lineone.net

Organisation type and purpose:
Membership association (membership is by subscription), present number of members: 235 (in Norfolk only).
A sporting association.
To promote and foster the game of Pétanque in Norfolk.
To promote and organise Pétanque competitions.

Subject coverage: The rules of Pétanque and method of play; how to construct, and dimensions of, a playing surface.

Access to staff: Contact by letter, by telephone and by e-mail
Hours: Mon to Fri, 0900 to 1700

NORFOLK FAMILY HISTORY SOCIETY

Kirby Hall, 70 St Giles Street, Norwich, Norfolk, NR2 1LS

Tel: 01603 763718
E-mail: nfhs@paston.co.uk
Website: www.norfolkfhs.org.uk

Enquiries to: Company Secretary

Founded: 1968

Organisation type and purpose:
Membership association (membership is by subscription), present number of members: 4000, registered charity (charity number 1055410).

Non-library collection catalogue: All or part available online

Publications list: Available online and in print

Access to staff: Contact by letter and in person
Hours: Tue, Thu, Sun, 1000 to 1300; Wed, 1000 to 1600
Special comments: Donations invited from visiting non-members.

Access to building: No prior appointment required

Access for disabled people: Parking provided, ramped entry, toilet facilities

NORFOLK RECORD OFFICE

The Archive Centre, Martineau Lane, Norwich, Norfolk, NR1 2DQ

Tel: 01603 222599
Fax: 01603 761885
E-mail: norfrec@norfolk.gov.uk
Website: archives.norfolk.gov.uk

Enquiries to: County Archivist

Founded: 1963

Organisation type and purpose: Local government body.
County Record Office.

Subject coverage: Norfolk Record Office holdings.

Collection: Archives for the County of Norfolk and Diocese of Norwich, 11th to 21st centuries

Non-library collection catalogue: All or part available online, in-house and in print

Publications: Printed, and microform publications

Publications list: Available online and in print

Access to staff: Contact by letter, by telephone, by fax, by e-mail, in person and via website. Appointment necessary.

Access to building: *Hours:* Mon, Wed, Thu and Fri, 0900 to 1700; Tue, 0930 to 1700; Sat, 0900 to 1200. Closed bank holidays and Sat

before Easter, and spring and summer bank holidays; closed for two weeks in late Nov and early Dec for stocktaking
Special comments: County Archive Research Network reader's ticket required for access to original manuscripts.

NORFOLK YOUTH MUSIC TRUST

Wahnfried, 4 Church Close, Buxton, Norwich, Norfolk, NR10 5ER

Tel: 01603 279742
E-mail: info@norfolk-youth-music-trust.org.uk
Website: norfolk-youth-music-trust.org.uk

Enquiries to: Chairman/Secretary

Founded: 2001; formerly called Music at Saint George's (year of change 2001)

Organisation type and purpose: Voluntary organisation, registered charity (charity number 1043945).
To promote, encourage, maintain, develop and improve public education in, and appreciation of, the art and science of music in all its aspects within the county of Norfolk. The trust also aims to help the development of highly talented Norfolk-based young musicians to pursue careers as professionals by offering annual grants and occasional public performing opportunities. Successful applicants will already be highly skilled in one or more of the six disciplines (brass, keyboard, percussion, strings, voice and woodwind) and will be either undergoing a period of study at a music college or specialist school, or who have made plans to do so.

Subject coverage: Occasional promotions of young musicians' concerts, plus annual round of grants available to under-30s engaged in studies to become professional musicians.

Collection: Norfolk 'Icon'

Trade and statistical information: Database in Local Studies Library, Norwich

Non-library collection catalogue: All or part available in-house

Library catalogue: All or part available in-house and in print

Publications: Printed, and electronic and video
Order printed publications from: Postal address

Publications list: Available online

Access to staff: Contact by letter, by telephone, by e-mail and via website. Appointment necessary.
Hours: Mon to Fri (except Wed) 0900 to 1400

Access for disabled people: Full access for public concerts
Hours: Concert performance times only

NORSKE VERITAS (DNV)

Palace House, 3 Cathedral Street, London, SE1 9DE

Tel: 020 7357 6080
Fax: 020 7716 6736
Website: www.dnv.com/maritime/publicationlist/index.asp
Website: www.dnv.com

Enquiries to: Information Scientist
Direct tel: 020 7716 6583
Direct fax: 020 7716 6730

Founded: 1864

Organisation type and purpose: Service industry, training organisation, consultancy. Provides consulting, engineering, verification, certification and training services.

Subject coverage: Industrial safety, offshore oil and gas, chemical industries, risk assessment, safety management, environmental management, quality management, marine transport, reliability assessment, loss prevention, environmental assessment, environmental risk, safety assessment.

Collection: Books, reports, documents, periodicals, legislation, standards, codes, guidelines

Non-library collection catalogue: All or part available in-house

Library catalogue: All or part available in-house

Publications: Printed, and electronic and video
Order printed publications from: For international orders, Distribution Department
Det Norske Veritas, Norwegian Office, e-mail: distribution@dnv.com
Information Scientist, Det Norske Veritas Aberdeen Office

Publications list: Available online and in print

Access to staff: Contact by letter, by telephone and by fax
Hours: Mon to Fri, 0900 to 1700

Access to building: No access other than to staff

Access for disabled people: Level entry, access to all public areas

Other offices: Det Norske Veritas (DNV); Cromarty House, 67–72 Regent Quay, Aberdeen, AB11 5AR; tel: 01224 335000; fax: 01244 593311

Parent body: Det Norske Veritas, Norway (DNV); Veritasveien 1, 1322 Høvik, Norway; tel: +47 67 57 99 00; fax: +47 67 57 99 11; website: http://www.dnv.com

NORTH & WESTERN LANCASHIRE CHAMBER OF COMMERCE (NWLCC)

9–10 Eastway Business Village, Oliver's Place, Fulwood, Preston, Lancashire, PR2 9WT

Tel: 01772 653000
Fax: 01772 655544
E-mail: info@lancschamber.co.uk
Website: www.lancschamber.co.uk

Enquiries to: Chief Executive

Founded: 1916

Organisation type and purpose: Membership association, present number of members: 1,400.
To promote, protect and develop the local business community at local, national and international level.

Subject coverage: Export, training, market research, business information, library, databases.

Publications: Printed

Publications list: Available in print

Access to staff: Contact by letter, by telephone, by fax, by e-mail and via website. Non-members charged.
Hours: Mon to Fri, 0900 to 1700

Access to building: Prior appointment required

Access for disabled people: Parking provided, ramped entry, toilet facilities

NORTH AYRSHIRE INFORMATION AND CULTURE

Library Support, Dunlop Centre, Dreghorn

Tel: 01294 215547
Fax: 01294 219605
E-mail: libraryhq@north-ayrshire.gov.uk
Website: www.ers.north-ayrshire.gov.uk

Enquiries to: Systems and Support Officer
Direct e-mail: amcallister@north-ayrshire.gov.uk

Founded: 1996

Organisation type and purpose: Local government body, public library and education resource service.

Subject coverage: Local history and archives relating to Cunninghame, North Ayrshire, Burghs in that area, the islands of Arran and Millport.

Information services: Macmillan Cancer Information Service in Saltcoats library.

Education services: Education Resource Service to support primary, secondary and special schools in North Ayrshire

Collection: North Ayrshire Heritage Centre encompassing the North Ayrshire Museum and Local and Family History Service

Non-library collection catalogue: All or part available in-house

Library catalogue: All or part available online

Publications: Printed
Order printed publications from: North Ayrshire Heritage Centre, Manse Street, Saltcoats, Ayrshire, KA21 5AA; tel: 01294 464174; fax: 01294 464174

Publications list: Available in print

Access to staff: Contact by letter, by telephone, by fax, by e-mail, in person and via website. Appointment necessary.
Hours: Mon to Thu, 0900 to 1645; Fri, 0900 to 1630

Access to building: No prior appointment required
Hours: Mon to Thu, 0900 to 1645; Fri, 0900 to 1630

Access for disabled people: Parking provided, ramped entry, toilet facilities

NORTH CORNWALL DISTRICT COUNCIL (NCDC)

Higher Trenant Road, Wadebridge, Cornwall, PL27 6TW

continued overleaf

Tel: 01208 893333
Fax: 01208 893232
E-mail: public.relations@ncdc.gov.uk
Website: www.ncdc.gov.uk

Enquiries to: Information Officer
Direct tel: 01208 893318

Founded: 1974

Organisation type and purpose: Local government body.

Access to staff: Contact by letter, by fax and via website
Hours: Mon to Thu, 0845 to 1700; Fri, 0845 to 1630

Access for disabled people: Parking provided, ramped entry, toilet facilities

NORTH COUNTRY CHEVIOT SHEEP SOCIETY

Wallacehall West, Waterbeck, Lockerbie, DG11 3HR

Tel: 01461 600646
E-mail: alison.brodie@nc-cheviot.co.uk
Website: www.nc-cheviot.co.uk

Enquiries to: Secretary

Founded: 1945

Organisation type and purpose: Membership association (membership is by subscription), present number of members: 400, registered charity (charity number SCO 12265).
To promote the North Country Cheviot sheep breed.

Subject coverage: Information on the sustainability of North Country Cheviot sheep in different environments and for different breeding/crossing programmes.

Publications: Printed

Publications list: Available in print

Access to staff: Contact by letter, by telephone, by fax, by e-mail, in person and via website. Appointment necessary.
Hours: Mon to Fri, 0900 to 1700

NORTH DEVON BRITISH MOTORCYCLE OWNERS CLUB (NDBMOC)

32 Merrythorn Road, Fremington, Barnstaple, Devon, EX31 3AL

Tel: 01271 379170
E-mail: andylin@andbmocl.freeserve.co.uk
Website: www.ndbmoc.freeserve.co.uk

Enquiries to: Secretary

Founded: 1978

Organisation type and purpose: Membership association (membership is by subscription), present number of members: 120, suitable for ages: 18+.

Subject coverage: Post-war British motorcycles, mechanical and electrical advice for most popular models: AMC, Ariel, BSA Norton, Triumph, Vincent.

Publications: Printed

Access to staff: Contact by letter and by telephone
Hours: Any reasonable time after 1800

Access for disabled people: Ramped entry, access to all public areas, toilet facilities

NORTH DEVON LOCAL STUDIES CENTRE

Library and Record Office, Tuly Street, Barnstaple, Devon, EX31 1EL

Tel: 01271 388607

Enquiries to: Librarian
Other contacts: (1) Archivist (2) Curator for (1) documents (2) photographs.

Founded: 1988

Organisation type and purpose: Local government body, public library, suitable for ages: school and adult.

Subject coverage: Local, house and family history.

Access to staff: Contact by letter and in person
Hours: Mon, Tue, Thu, Fri, 0930 to 1700; Wed, 0930 to 1300; Sat, 0930 to 1400

Other addresses: West Country Studies Library; Castle Street, Exeter; tel: 01392 384216

Parent body: Devon County Council; Topsham Road, Exeter

NORTH DEVON RECORD OFFICE (NDRO)

North Devon Library and Record Office, Tuly Street, Barnstaple, Devon, EX31 1EL

Tel: 01271 388608
Fax: 01271 388608
E-mail: ndevrec@devon.gov.uk
Website: www.devon.gov.uk/record_office.htm

Enquiries to: Archivist

Founded: 1988

Organisation type and purpose: Local government body.

Subject coverage: Archives for North Devon area.

Collection: Records of local authorities, Devon County Council; North Devon and Torridge District Councils and their predecessors, the urban and rural district councils; the borough councils of Barnstaple, Bideford, Great Torrington and South Molton; parish councils
Public records, shipping registers, Quarter sessions, Petty Sessional Division records, local hospitals
Poor Law Union and Public Assistance Institution records
Taw and Torridge Fishery Board records
Education records
Ecclesiastical records for the Archdeaconry of Barnstaple, including parish registers and records
Records of nonconformist denominations (including the Bible Christian branch of the Methodist Church founded in North Devon)
Collections of estate records and private papers
Records of local solicitors; businesses; clubs and societies; charities and trusts
Parish registers, electoral registers, wills and land tax assessments (microfilm or microfiche)

Non-library collection catalogue: All or part available online

Access to staff: Contact by letter, by telephone, by e-mail and in person. Appointment necessary.

Access for disabled people: Level entry, access to all public areas, toilet facilities

NORTH EAST CHAMBER OF COMMERCE, TRADE & INDUSTRY (NECC)

Aykley Heads Business Centre, Aykley Heads, Durham, DH1 5TS

Tel: 0191 386 1133
Fax: 0191 386 1144
E-mail: info@necc.co.uk
Website: www.necc.co.uk

Enquiries to: Information Services Manager

Founded: 1995

Organisation type and purpose: Membership association (membership is by subscription), present number of members: 5,500, service industry, training organisation. Chamber of Commerce.
Business services and representation of members.

Subject coverage: All aspects of business information with specific reference to commerce and industry in the North East.

Publications: Printed, and electronic and video

Access to staff: Contact by letter, by telephone, by fax, by e-mail, in person and via website. Appointment necessary. Access for members only. Non-members charged.
Hours: Mon to Fri, 0900 to 1700

Member organisation of: Association of British Chambers of Commerce

Partner in the five offices of: Business Link (North East)

NORTH EAST DERBYSHIRE DISTRICT COUNCIL (NEDDC)

Council House, Saltergate, Chesterfield, Derbyshire, S40 1LF

Tel: 01246 231111
Fax: 01246 550213
E-mail: connectne@ne-derbyshire.gov.uk
Website: www.ne-derbyshire.gov.uk

Founded: 1974

Organisation type and purpose: Local government body.

Subject coverage: Local government services.

Publications: Printed

Access to staff: Contact by letter, by telephone, by fax, by e-mail and via website
Hours: Mon to Fri, 0900 to 1700

NORTH EAST LINCOLNSHIRE ARCHIVES

Town Hall, Town Hall Square, Grimsby, Lincolnshire, DN31 1HX

Tel: 01472 323585
Fax: 01472 323581
E-mail: archives@nelincs.gov.uk
Website: www.nelincs.gov.uk/art-culture-and-leisure/records-and-archives

Enquiries to: Archivist

Founded: 1951; formerly called Grimsby Borough Archives Office (year of change 1974); formerly called South Humberside Area Archives Office (year of change 1996)

Organisation type and purpose: Local government body.

Subject coverage: Archives for local authorities in North East Lincolnshire and North Lincolnshire including Grimsby Borough (1201–1996), local boards of health, rural sanitary authorities, urban sanitary authorities, burial boards, school boards, education committees (and over 100 schools), rural district councils, urban district councils (1894–1974), borough councils (1974–1996), parish councils, registers of Grimsby ships (1824–1988), register of Grimsby fishing apprentices (1879–1937) Grimsby fishing vessel crew lists (1864–1914), manorial records, public records.
The office is not a Diocesan Record Office. For original church records, etc. see Lincolnshire Archives, Lincoln.

Collection: Archives collected by the North Lincolnshire Museum, Scunthorpe
Local and Personal Acts, Private Acts (of Parliament, 1889–1966)
Parish registers of the eleven northern Deaneries of the Diocese of Lincoln (microfiche, appointment required to consult)

Non-library collection catalogue: All or part available online

Publications: Printed

Publications list: Available in print

Access to staff: Contact by letter, by telephone, by fax and by e-mail. Appointment necessary.
Hours: Mon to Thu, 0930 to 1230 and 1300 to 1600

Access to building: Prior appointment required

Access for disabled people: Ramped entry, access to all public areas, toilet access

NORTH EAST LINCOLNSHIRE LIBRARY SERVICE

Formal name: North East Lincolnshire Council Public Library Service

Central Library, Town Hall Square, Grimsby, Lincolnshire, DN31 1HG

Tel: 01472 323600
Fax: 01472 323634
E-mail: lib@nelincs.gov.uk
Website: www.nelincs.gov.uk/libraries

Enquiries to: Head of Cultural Services
Direct tel: 01472 323611
Direct fax: 01472 323618
Direct e-mail: steve.hipkins@nelincs.gov.uk
Other contacts: Principal Librarian (Strategy and Support, tel. 01472 323612)

Founded: 1996

Organisation type and purpose: Public library.

Subject coverage: General, local history, family history.

Collection: Business and company information
Local history collection (Grimsby, Cleethorpes and surrounding area)
Skelton Collection (posters and handbills of local printers), Ruhleben collection WWI

Trade and statistical information: UK markets

Non-library collection catalogue: All or part available online

Library catalogue: All or part available online and in-house

Access to staff: Contact by letter, by telephone, by fax, by e-mail, in person and via website
Hours: Mon to Fri, 0830 to 1930; Sat, 0900 to 1600; Sun, 1000 to 1600

Branches: One central and 10 branch libraries

Parent body: North East Lincolnshire Council

NORTH EAST OF SCOTLAND DOUBLE BASS SOCIETY

343 Holburn Street, Aberdeen, AB10 7FQ

Tel: 01224 590521

Enquiries to: Honorary Secretary

Founded: 1996

Organisation type and purpose: Voluntary organisation.
To promote the enjoyment of, listening to and playing of the double bass repertoire.

Subject coverage: History of the double bass in North East Scotland.

Access to staff: Contact by letter
Hours: Mon to Fri, 0900 to 1700

NORTH EAST WORCESTERSHIRE COLLEGE (NEW College)

Slideslow Drive, Bromsgrove, Worcestershire, B60 1PQ

Tel: 01527 570020
Fax: 01527 572900

Enquiries to: Assistant Principal, Learner Services
Direct tel: 01527 572517
Direct fax: 01527 572560
Direct e-mail: cduncan@ne-worcs.ac.uk

Founded: 1988

Organisation type and purpose: Suitable for ages: 16+.
College of further education.

Subject coverage: Business, management, law, art and design, media studies, music, hospitality and catering, community care, social work, secretarial studies, travel and tourism, IT, automotive, engineering, hair and beauty, childhood studies, sixth form studies, foundation learning, teacher education, public services, sport

Access to staff: Contact by letter. Appointment necessary. Letter of introduction required.
Hours: Mon to Thu, 0830 to 2000; Fri, 0830 to 1630
Special comments: Access to registered staff and students by arrangement.

Also at: North East Worcestershire College; Peakman Street, Redditch, B98 8DW; tel: 01527 570020

NORTH EASTERN EDUCATION AND LIBRARY BOARD (NEELB/NELS)

Library Headquarters, Demesne Avenue, Ballymena, Co Antrim, BT43 7BG

Tel: 028 2566 4100
Fax: 028 2563 2038
E-mail: info.neelb@ni-libraries.net
Website: www.ni-libraries.net

Enquiries to: Librarian

Organisation type and purpose: Northern Ireland Government body.
Public and schools library.

Subject coverage: North Eastern local studies plus all public and schools library subjects.
Community Services Unit.

Non-library collection catalogue: All or part available online

Library catalogue: All or part available online

Publications: Printed

Access to staff: Contact by letter, by telephone, by fax, by e-mail, in person and via website
Hours: Mon to Fri, 0900 to 1700
Special comments: Branch libraries have late night and Sat opening.

Access to building: No prior appointment required

Access for disabled people: Ramped entry, access to all public areas, toilet facilities

NORTH HAMPSHIRE CHAMBER OF COMMERCE AND INDUSTRY (NHCCI)

Winchester Business Centre, 10 Parchment Street, Winchester, Hampshire, SO23 8AT

Tel: 01962 841000
Fax: 01962 870423
E-mail: winchester@nhcci.co.uk
Website: www.nhcci.co.uk/

Enquiries to: Secretary

Founded: 1918

Subject coverage: Business information and support.

Publications: Printed

Access to staff: Contact by letter, by telephone, by fax and in person
Hours: Mon to Fri, 0900 to 1700

Business Helpline: Hampshire Training and Enterprise Council Limited; 25 Thackeray Mall, Fareham, PO16 0PQ; tel: 0800 373833

Member of: Hampshire Chambers of Commerce

Other addresses: North; Blackwater Valley Enterprise Trust, Princes Gardens, Aldershot, GU11 1BJ; tel: 0800 132301; South East; South East Hampshire Chamber of

continued overleaf

Commerce and Industry, 27 Guildhall Walk, Portsmouth, PO1 2RP; tel: 0800 132302; South West; Southampton Chamber of Commerce and Industry, 53 Bugle Street, Southampton, SO14 2LF; tel: 0800 132303

Other local offices at: Basingstoke Chamber of Commerce (BCC); Business Support Centre, Deanes Building, London Road, Basingstoke, RG21 7YP; tel: 01256 352275; fax: 01256 479391; North East Hampshire; Civic Offices, Harlington Way, Fleet, GU51 4AE; tel: 01252 811470; fax: 01252 812096; Winchester; Abbey Mill, Colebrook Street, Winchester, SO23 9LH; tel: 01962 841000; fax: 01962 870423

NORTH HERTFORDSHIRE DISTRICT COUNCIL (NHDC)

Council Offices, Gernon Road, Letchworth, Hertfordshire, SG6 3JF

Tel: 01462 474000
Fax: 01462 474227
Website: www.north-herts.gov.uk

Organisation type and purpose: Local government body.

Subject coverage: Housing advice, leisure, community development, planning, building control, environmental health, health and safety, community grants, community safety, economic development, noise and environmental pollution, electoral services, council tax/housing benefits, local government finance.

Collection: Hitchin and Letchworth museums

Publications: Printed

Access to staff: Contact by letter, by telephone, by fax, by e-mail and in person
Hours: Mon to Fri, 0900 to 1700

Access to building: *Hours:* Mon to Fri, 0900 to 1700

Access for disabled people: Fully accessible

Also at: Finance and Regulatory Services; Town Lodge, Gernon Road, Letchworth, Hertfordshire, SG6 3HN

NORTH HERTS & DISTRICT CITIZENS ADVICE BUREAU

The Town Hall, Melbourn Street, Royston, Hertfordshire, SG8 7DA

Tel: 01763 238020
Fax: 01763 238017
E-mail: bureau@roystoncab.cabnet.org.uk

Enquiries to: Manager
Direct tel: 01763 238017

Organisation type and purpose: Voluntary organisation, registered charity (charity number 1086489).

Access to staff: Contact by letter, by fax and by e-mail
Hours: Mon to Fri, 1000 to 1300

NORTH KESTEVEN DISTRICT COUNCIL (NKDC)

Council Offices, Kesteven Street, Sleaford, Lincolnshire, NG34 7EF

Tel: 01529 414155
Fax: 01529 413956
E-mail: customer_services@n-kesteven.gov.uk
Website: www.n-kesteven.gov.uk

Enquiries to: Press and Publications Officer
Direct tel: ext 2467
Direct e-mail: julie_wetton@n.kesteven.gov.uk

Organisation type and purpose: Local government body, advisory body, statutory body, service industry, training organisation, consultancy, research organisation.

Subject coverage: Environmental health, planning, council tax, business rates, housing benefits.

Access to staff: Contact by letter, by telephone, by fax, by e-mail and via website
Hours: Mon to Thu, 0830 to 1700; Fri, 0830 to 1630

Access to building: No access other than to staff

Access for disabled people: Parking provided, ramped entry, toilet facilities

NORTH LANARKSHIRE COUNCIL

PO Box 14, Civic Centre, Windmillhill Street, Motherwell, North Lanarkshire, ML1 1AB

Tel: 01698 302222
Fax: 01698 275125
Website: www.northlanarkshire.gov.uk

Enquiries to: Chief Executive

Founded: 1996

Organisation type and purpose: Local government body.

Subject coverage: Local government affairs.

NORTH LANARKSHIRE COUNCIL – EDUCATION RESOURCE SERVICE (ERS)

Department of Education, 8 Kildonan Street, Coatbridge, Lanarkshire, ML5 3LP

Tel: 01236 434377
Fax: 01236 436224
E-mail: ERSMail@northlan.gov.uk
Website: www.northlan.gov.uk

Enquiries to: Principal Librarian

Founded: 1996

Organisation type and purpose: Local government body, suitable for ages: 3 to 18. School library service.
To provide advice, support and resources to all educational establishments in North Lanarkshire.

Subject coverage: Educational resources: nursery, primary, special and secondary schools.

Collection: Artefacts and staff development
Pre 5 years Multimedia collections
5 to 14 years Multimedia collections
Support for Learning

Access to staff: Contact by letter, by telephone, by fax and by e-mail.
Appointment necessary.
Hours: Mon to Thu, 0845 to 1645; Fri, 0845 to 1615
Special comments: Resources available to the general public for reference only.

Affiliated to: Education Department; Municipal Buildings, Kildonan Street, Coatbridge, ML5 3BT; tel: 01236 812222; fax: 01236 812247

NORTH LANARKSHIRE COUNCIL – INFORMATION SECTION

Formal name: North Lanarkshire Libraries and Information Service

Motherwell Library, 35 Hamilton Road, Motherwell, North Lanarkshire, ML1 3BZ

Tel: 01698 332628
Fax: 01698 332625
Website: www.northlan.gov.uk

Enquiries to: Libraries & Information Manager
Direct tel: 0141 304 1843

Founded: 1904

Organisation type and purpose: Local government body, public library.

Subject coverage: General subjects.

Collection: Chinese collection of books and magazines for children and adults
Gaelic collection of books and magazines for children and adults
Urdu collection of books and magazines for children and adults

Publications: Printed
Order printed publications from: North Lanarkshire Libraries and Information Service, Motherwell Library; tel: 01698 332628

Access to staff: Contact by letter, by telephone, by fax and via website
Hours: Mon, Tue, Thu, Fri, 0900 to 1930; Wed, 0900 to 1200, lending library, 0900 to 1730 Information library, Sat, 0900 to 1600

Access to building: No prior appointment required

Access for disabled people: Ramped entry, toilet facilities
Special comments: Ramp/lift to ground floor, lift to first floor

Other locations: 24 branches and 6 mobile vans

Parent body: North Lanarkshire Council

NORTH LANARKSHIRE COUNCIL ARCHIVES

North Lanarkshire Heritage Centre, High Road, Motherwell, ML1 3HU

Tel: 01698 524712; 01698 274597
Fax: 01698 268867
E-mail: museums@northlan.gov.uk
Website: www.northlanarkshire.gov.uk/archives

Enquiries to: Archivist
Direct e-mail: mcgheewi@northlan.gov.uk

Founded: 1996

Organisation type and purpose: Local government body.
Local authority archive.

Subject coverage: Holds archives of: landed estates; local firms and individuals; clubs and societies; historical miscellany; prior local authorities (including cemetery and poor law records).

Education services: Staff available for talks.

Collection: Archive

Non-library collection catalogue: All or part available online, in-house and in print

Library catalogue: All or part available in-house

Access to staff: Contact by letter, by telephone, by fax, by e-mail and in person. Appointment necessary.
Hours: Mon to Fri, 1000 to 1700

Access to building: Prior appointment required

Access for disabled people: Yes

Links with: North Lanarkshire Museums & Heritage; Museums & Heritage Manager, Lower Ground Floor, Municiple Buildings, Kildonan Street, Coatbridge, ML5 3BT; tel: 0141 812 387

NORTH LINCOLNSHIRE COUNCIL

Pittwood House, Ashby Road, Scunthorpe, Lincolnshire, DN16 1AB

Tel: 01724 296296, 01724 296294 (minicom)
Fax: 01724 296079
Website: www.northlincs.gov.uk

Enquiries to: Library and Information Services Manager
Direct tel: 01724 297869
Direct fax: 01724 296343
Direct e-mail: customerservice@northlincs.gov.uk

Founded: 1996

Organisation type and purpose: Local government body.
Created as a unitary council following abolition of the County of Humberside. Unitary council responsible for all local government services, including 82 schools, 25,500 pupils and a gross budget (annual) of £315m.

Subject coverage: Local government.

Library catalogue: All or part available online

Access to staff: Contact by letter, by telephone, by fax, by e-mail and in person
Hours: Mon to Thu, 0830 to 1700; Fri, 0830 to 1630

Access to building: No prior appointment required

Access for disabled people: Parking provided, ramped entry, access to all public areas, toilet facilities

NORTH LINCOLNSHIRE LIBRARY AND INFORMATION SERVICES

North Lincolnshire Central Library, Carlton Street, Scunthorpe, North Lincolnshire, DN15 6TX

Tel: 01724 860161
Fax: 01724 860161
E-mail: library.enquiries@northlincs.gov.uk
Website: www.northlincs.gov.uk/library
Website: www.facebook.com/northlincolnshirelibraries

Enquiries to: Library and Information Services Manager

Founded: 1996

Organisation type and purpose: Local government body, statutory body, service industry, public library.

Subject coverage: General, local and family history (North Lincolnshire), steel industry (Scunthorpe), Wesley family.

Non-library collection catalogue: All or part available online and in-house

Library catalogue: All or part available online

Access to staff: Contact by letter, by telephone, by fax, by e-mail, in person and via website
Hours: Mon 0900 to 1700; Tue 0900 to 1600; Wed 0900 to 1900; Thu 0900 to 1600; Sat 0900 to 1600

Access to building: See website for opening hours and access

Branches: 14 libraries and two mobile libraries; See website for details

Parent body: North Lincolnshire Council; website: http://www.northlincs.gov.uk

NORTH NORFOLK DISTRICT COUNCIL

Holt Road, Cromer, Norfolk, NR27 9EL

Tel: 01263 513811
Fax: 01263 515042
E-mail: districtcouncil@north-norfolk.gov.uk
Website: www.north-norfolk.gov.uk

Enquiries to: Communications Manager
Direct tel: 01263 516344
Direct e-mail: media@north-norfolk.gov.uk

Organisation type and purpose: Local government body.

Subject coverage: Local government.

Collection: Library of photographs of North Norfolk

Publications: Printed

Access to building: No prior appointment required

NORTH OF ENGLAND INSTITUTE OF MINING AND MECHANICAL ENGINEERS

Neville Hall, Westgate Road, Newcastle upon Tyne, NE1 1SE

Tel: 0191 232 2201
Fax: 0191 232 2201
E-mail: office@mininginstitute.org.uk

Enquiries to: Administrator
Other contacts: Honorary Secretary for qualification queries.

Founded: 1852

Organisation type and purpose: Learned society, professional body (membership is by subscription), present number of members: 480, registered charity (charity number 220208).

Subject coverage: Mining and allied subjects: history and technology.

Collection: A large number of MSS and other collections

Non-library collection catalogue: All or part available in-house

Library catalogue: All or part available in-house

Access to staff: Contact by letter and by telephone. Appointment necessary. Non-members charged.
Hours: Library: to be arranged.

NORTH OF ENGLAND MULE SHEEP ASSOCIATION (NEMSA)

Eslaforde, Wear View, Frosterley, Bishop Auckland, Co Durham, DL13 2RB

Tel: 01388 527411
Fax: 01388 526728
Website: www.nemsa.co.uk

Enquiries to: Secretary
Direct e-mail: info@nemsa.co.uk

Founded: 1980

Organisation type and purpose: Membership association (membership is by subscription), present number of members: 1024, registered charity.
Breed society, promotional body.

Subject coverage: The North of England Mule is the top commercial breeding sheep for prime lamb production.

Publications: Printed, and electronic and video
Order printed publications from: http://www.nemsa.co.uk

Publications list: Available online

Access to staff: Contact by letter, by telephone, by fax and by e-mail
Hours: Mon to Fri, 0900 to 1700

NORTH OF ENGLAND ZOOLOGICAL SOCIETY (NEZS)

Formal name: North of England Zoological Society

Chester Zoo, Caughall Road, Upton by Chester, Chester, Cheshire, CH2 1LH

Tel: 01244 380280
Fax: 01244 371273
E-mail: marketing@chesterzoo.co.uk
Website: www.chesterzoo.org

Enquiries to: Director

Founded: 1934

Organisation type and purpose: International organisation, membership association (membership is by subscription), present number of members: 17,000 plus, registered charity (charity number 306077), suitable for ages: all.

Subject coverage: Zoological.

Library catalogue: All or part available in-house

Publications: Printed, and electronic and video

Access to staff: Contact by letter and by e-mail
Hours: Mon to Fri, 0900 to 1200

Access to building: No prior appointment required
Special comments: Access to library, Mon to Fri, 1200 to 1500

Access for disabled people: Parking provided, ramped entry, toilet facilities

continued overleaf

Special comments: Electric scooters and chairs for hire, tactile maps.

Member of: European Association of Zoos and Aquaria (EAZA); Federation of Zoological Gardens of Great Britain and Ireland; World Association of Zoos and Aquariums (WAZA)

NORTH SOMERSET COUNCIL

Town Hall, Weston-Super-Mare, Somerset, BS23 1UJ

Tel: 01934 888888
Fax: 01934 888822
E-mail: customer.services@n-somerset.gov.uk
Website: www.n-somerset.gov.uk

Enquiries to: Marketing and Communications Manager
Direct tel: 01275 888728
Direct e-mail: vanessa.setterington@n-somerset.gov.uk

Founded: 1996

Organisation type and purpose: Local government body.

Subject coverage: Local government services.

NORTH STAFFORDSHIRE CHAMBER OF COMMERCE AND INDUSTRY

Commerce House, Festival Park, Stoke-on-Trent, Staffordshire, ST1 5BE

Tel: 01782 202241
Fax: 01782 274394
E-mail: staffordchamber@nscci.co.uk
Website: www.northstaffs.chamber.co.uk

Enquiries to: Information Services Manager

Founded: 1949

Organisation type and purpose: Membership association (membership is by subscription), present number of members: 1054.
Chamber of Commerce.

Subject coverage: Business information and advice; importing and exporting advice and documentation; training; translations; UK and international credit checking; trade missions; UK and overseas marketing and sourcing information.

Trade and statistical information: Product information on the ceramic industry.
Trade in North Staffordshire

Publications: Printed

Publications list: Available online

Access to staff: Contact by letter, by telephone and by fax. Non-members charged.
Hours: Mon to Fri, 0900 to 1700

Member of: Association of British Chambers of Commerce

Partner in: Business Link Staffordshire

NORTH TRAFFORD COLLEGE LIBRARY

Talbot Road, Stretford, Manchester, M32 0XH

Tel: 0161 886 7012
Fax: 0161 872 7921
E-mail: enquiries@trafford.ac.uk

Enquiries to: Senior Librarian
Direct e-mail: jim.temple@ntc.ac.uk

Organisation type and purpose: College of further education.

Subject coverage: Gas engineering; chemical process engineering; automotive engineering; mechanical, electrical, electronic engineering; computing; business studies; childcare; building services; CAD; health care; music; science; community studies; social care; basic skills; ESOL; business studies; accounting; teacher training; information technology.

Library catalogue: All or part available in-house

Access to staff: Access for members only.
Hours: Mon, Thu, 0845 to 1900; Tue, Wed, Fri, 0845 to 1700

NORTH TYNESIDE LIBRARIES

Central Library, Northumberland Square, North Shields, Tyne and Wear, NE30 1QU

Tel: 0191 200 5424
Fax: 0191 200 6118
E-mail: contact.us@northtyneside.gov.uk
Website: www.northtyneside.gov.uk/libraries

Enquiries to: Libraries and Information Manager

Founded: 1870

Organisation type and purpose: Local government body, public library.

Subject coverage: General and local studies.

Collection: Edington collection of prints and engravings (7000 items, Northumberland and Tyne and Wear)
British Standards in microform

Publications: Printed
Order printed publications from: Publications Department, Wallsend Library
Ferndale Avenue, Wallsend, NE26 7NB, tel: 0191 200 6968, fax: 0191 200 6967

Access to staff: Contact by letter, by telephone, by fax, by e-mail and in person
Hours: Central Library: Mon and Fri, 0930 to 1730; Tue and Thu, 0930 to 1900; Sat, 0930 to 1700, Wed, 0930 to 1230.
Times vary for other libraries

Other addresses: Battle Hill Library; Berwick Drive, Battle Hill, Wallsend, Tyne & Wear, NE28 9EF; tel: 0191 200 6976; Coast Road Library; 25 Coast Road, North Shields, NE29 7PG; tel: 0191 200 5857; Cullercoats Library; St George's Road, Cullercoats, North Shields, NE30 3JY; tel: 0191 200 8537; Fordley Library; Fern Drive, Dudley, Northumberland, NE23 7AG; tel: 0191 200 8014; Forest Hall Library; Whitfield Road, Forest Hall, Newcastle, NE12 0LJ; tel: 0191 200 7839; Howdon Library; Churchill Street, Howdon, Wallsend, Tyne & Wear, NE28 7TG; tel: 0191 200 6979; Killingworth Library; White Swan Centre, Citadel East, Killingworth, Newcastle, NE12 6SS; tel: 0191 200 8266; Longbenton Library; Black Friars Way, Longbenton, Newcastle, NE12 8SY; tel: 0191 200 7865; Monkseaton Library; Woodleigh Avenue, Monkseaton, Whitley Bay, NE25 8ET; tel: 0191 200 8538; Shiremoor Library; Stanton Road, Shiremoor, Newcastle upon Tyne, NE27 0PW; tel: 0191 200 8539; Tynemouth Library; Front Street, Tynemouth, North Shields, NE30 4DZ; tel: 0191 200 5856; Wallsend Library; Ferndale Avenue, Wallsend, Tyne & Wear, NE28 7NB; tel: 0191 200 6968; fax: 0191 200 6967; Whitley Bay Library; Park Road, Whitley Bay, NE26 1EJ; tel: 0191 200 8500; fax: 0191 200 8536; Wideopen Library; Canterbury Way, Wideopen, Newcastle, NE13 6JJ; tel: 0191 200 7900

Parent body: North Tyneside Council

NORTH WALES TOURISM (NWT)

77 Conway Road, Colwyn Bay, Conwy, LL29 7LN

Tel: 01492 531731
Fax: 01492 530059
E-mail: croeso@nwt.co.uk
Website: www.nwt.co.uk

Enquiries to: Manager
Other contacts: Visitor Services Manager for management and operation of tourist information centre.

Founded: 1991

Organisation type and purpose: Advisory body, membership association (membership is by subscription), service industry.
Private company. Affiliated local government body. Part statutory body.
To promote North Wales as a holiday destination and provide aftercare services through Tourist Information Centres.

Subject coverage: North Wales tourist attractions, mountains, Snowdonia National Park, stately homes, castles, Isle of Anglesey, sailing, golf, pony trekking, cycling and walking. All areas of North Wales and its activities.

Publications: Printed

Publications list: Available in print

Access to staff: Contact by letter, by telephone, by fax, by e-mail and via website
Hours: Mon to Fri, 0900 to 1700

Parent body: Wales Tourist Board; Brunel House, 2 Fitzallan Road, Cardiff, C72 1UY; tel: 029 2049 9909; fax: 029 2048 5031

Tourist Information Centres: Bangor; Town Hall, Ffordd Deiniol, Bangor, LL57 7RE; tel: 01248 352786; fax: 01248 362701; e-mail: bangor.tic@gwynedd.gov.uk; Betws-y-Coed; tel: 01690 710426; Caernarfon; Oriel Pendeitsh, Castle Street, Caernarfon, LL55 1SE; tel: 01286 672232; fax: 01285 678209; e-mail: caernarfon.tic@gwynedd.gov.uk; Colwyn Bay; Imperial Building, Princes Drive, Colwyn Bay, LL29 8LF; tel: 01492 530478; fax: 01492 534789; e-mail: colwynbay.tic@virgin.net; Conwy; Conwy Castle Visitor Centre, Conwy, LL32 8LD; tel: 01492 592248; fax: 01492 573545; e-mail: conwy.tic@virgin.net; Holyhead; Stena Line, Terminal 1, Holyhead, LL65 1DQ; tel: 01407 762622; fax: 01407 761462; e-mail: holyhead.tic@virgin.net; Llanberis; 41a High Street, Llanberis, LL55 4EH; tel: 01286 870765; fax: 01286 871924; e-mail: llanberis.tic@gwynedd.gov.uk; Llandudno; 1–2 Chapel Street, Llandudno, LL30 2YU; tel: 01492 876413; fax: 01492 872722; e-mail: llandudno.tic@

virgin.net; Llanfairpwllgwyngyll; Station Site, Llanfairpwllgwyngyll, LL61 5UJ; tel: 01248 713177; fax: 01248 715711; e-mail: llanfairpwll.tic@virgin.net; Llangollen; Town Hall, Castle Street, Llangollen, LL20 5PD; tel: 01978 860828; fax: 01978 861563; e-mail: llangollen.tic@virgin.net; Mold; Library, Museum and Gallery, Earl Road, Mold, CH7 1AP; tel: 01352 759331; fax: 01352 759331; e-mail: mold.tic@virgin.net; Porthmadog; Y Ganolfan, High Street, Porthmadog, LL49 9LP; tel: 01766 512981; fax: 01766 515312; e-mail: porthmadog.tic@gwynedd.gov.uk; Prestatyn; Offa's Dyke Centre, Central Beach, Prestatyn, LL19 7EY; tel: 01745 889092; Pwllheli; Min-y-Don, Station Square, Pwllheli, Gwynedd, LL53 6HE; fax: 01758 701651; e-mail: pwllheli.tic@gwynedd.gov.uk; Rhyl; Children's Village, The Promenade, Rhyl, Denbighshire, LL18 1HZ; tel: 01745 355068; fax: 01745 342255; e-mail: rhyl.tic@denbighshire.gov.uk; Ruthin; Ruthin Craft Centre, Park Road, Ruthin; tel: 01824 703992; fax: 01824 703992; Wrexham; tel: 01978 292015

NORTH WARWICKSHIRE BOROUGH COUNCIL

The Council House, South Street, Atherstone, Warwickshire, CV9 1BD

Tel: 01827 715341
Fax: 01827 719130
E-mail: customerservices@northwarks.gov.uk
Website: www.northwarks.gov.uk

Enquiries to: Chief Executive

Founded: 1974

Organisation type and purpose: Local government body.

Publications: Printed

Access to staff: Contact by letter, by telephone, by fax, by e-mail, in person and via website. Appointment necessary. Access for members only.
Hours: Mon to Fri, 0850 to 1715

NORTH WEST EMPLOYERS (NWEO)

Formal name: North Western Local Authorities' Employers' Organisation

6th Floor, Delphian House, Riverside, New Bailey Street, Manchester, M3 5AP

Tel: 0161 834 9362
Fax: 0161 831 7268
E-mail: mail@nweo.org.uk
Website: www.nweo.org.uk

Enquiries to: Human Resources Adviser
Other contacts: Learning and Development; Member Development; Human Resources; Local Government

Founded: 1920

Organisation type and purpose: Local government body, advisory body, training organisation, consultancy.

Subject coverage: Training, conditions of service, industrial relations, personnel, management.

Publications: Printed

Access to staff: Contact by letter, by telephone and by e-mail. Appointment necessary.
Hours: Mon to Fri, 0845 to 1645

NORTH WEST FILM ARCHIVE (NWFA)

Manchester Metropolitan University, Minshull House, 47–49 Chorlton Street, Manchester, M1 3EU

Tel: 0161 247 3097
Fax: 0161 247 3098
E-mail: n.w.filmarchive@mmu.ac.uk
Website: www.nwfa.mmu.ac.uk

Enquiries to: Collection Assistant

Founded: 1977

Organisation type and purpose: University department / institute.
Public film archive.
Rescuing and ensuring the survival of moving images about the North West of England for the education and enjoyment of the region's people, both today and in the future.

Subject coverage: North West of England (Greater Manchester, Lancashire, Cheshire, Merseyside, Cumbria): mid-1890s to the present; working life and leisure, traditions, industry, two World Wars, healthcare, housing, transport, professional and amateur material on all gauges.

Collection: Collection of over 31,500 items dating from pioneer days of film in mid-1890s to contemporary video productions, all relating to life in the North West of England. It includes cinema newsreels, documentaries, advertising and promotional material, educational and travel films, home movies, corporate videos and regional television programmes
Complementary collections of photographs, taped interviews and original documentation relating to North West's film and cinema industries

Non-library collection catalogue: All or part available online and in-house

Publications: Printed, and electronic and video

Publications list: Available online

Access to staff: Contact by letter, by telephone, by fax, by e-mail and in person. Appointment necessary.
Hours: Mon to Fri, 0900 to 1700

Access for disabled people: Parking provided, ramped entry, access to all public areas, toilet facilities

Parent body: Manchester Metropolitan University Library Service

NORTH WEST KENT FAMILY HISTORY SOCIETY (NWKFHS)

51 Newbury Avenue. Maidstone, ME16 0RG

E-mail: secretary@nwkfhs.org.uk
Website: www.nwkfhs.org.uk

Founded: 1978

Organisation type and purpose: International organisation, membership association (membership is by subscription), present number of members: 2,000, registered charity (charity number 282627R). To further education and research in genealogy and family history.

Subject coverage: Family history in North West Kent and the South East area of London once part of the ancient county of Kent, including Dartford, Sevenoaks, Bromley, Bexley.

Information services: Society Library and Resource Centre, Summerhouse Drive, Joydens Wood Estate, Bexley, DA5 2EE.

Collection: Library of indexes and other references for North West Kent and South East London area, held on CD, microfiche or printed form

Non-library collection catalogue: All or part available in-house

Library catalogue: All or part available online and in-house

Publications: Printed, and electronic and video, and microform publications
Order printed publications from: NWKFHS, 141 Princes Road, Dartford, DA1 3HJ
Order electronic and video publications from: 141 Princes Road, Dartford, DA1 3HJ

Publications list: Available online and in print

Access to staff: Contact by letter, by e-mail and via website
Hours: None

Branches: Bromley, Dartford, Sevenoaks, Society Library and Resource Centre, Summerhouse Drive, Joydens Wood Estate, Bexley, DA5 2EE

Member organisation of: Federation of Family History Societies (FFHS)

Membership Secretary: North West Kent Family History Society; 46 Pollards Oak Crescent. RH8 0JQ; e-mail: membership@nwkfhs.org.uk

NORTH WEST LEICESTERSHIRE DISTRICT COUNCIL (NWLDC)

Council Offices, Coalville, Leicester, LE67 3FJ

Tel: 01530 454545
Fax: 01530 454546
E-mail: info@nwleicestershire.gov.uk
Website: www.nwleics.gov.uk

Enquiries to: Chief Executive

Founded: 1973

Organisation type and purpose: Local government body.

Subject coverage: Local government services.

Publications: Printed

Access to staff: Contact by letter, by telephone, by fax, by e-mail and in person
Hours: Mon to Fri, 0900 to 1700

Access for disabled people: Parking provided, level entry, toilet facilities

NORTH WEST LONDON HOSPITALS NHS TRUST

John Squire Library, Watford Road, Harrow, Middlesex, HA1 3UJ

Tel: 020 8869 3322 (enquiries)
Fax: 020 8869 3332
E-mail: jslib@clara.net
Website: www.jslib.clara.net

Enquiries to: Head Librarian

Organisation type and purpose: Hospital.

Subject coverage: Clinical, medical and complementary basic sciences, nursing and health service management.

Library catalogue: All or part available online

Publications: Printed

Access to staff: Contact in person
Hours: Mon to Fri, 0900 to 1800

Access to building: No prior appointment required
Hours: Mon to Fri, 0900 to 1800
Special comments: Must have bona fide need to access library resources.

Funded by: Central and North West London NHS Foundation Trust; London Deanery; North West London Hospitals NHS Trust

NORTH WEST SOUND ARCHIVE

North West Sound Archive, Clitheroe Museum, Clitheroe Castle, Clitheroe, Lancashire, BB7 1AZ

Tel: 01200 427897
Fax: 01200 427897
E-mail: nwsa@ed.lancscc.gov.uk

Founded: 1979

Organisation type and purpose: Collects, records and preserves sound recordings relevant to the northwest of England.

Subject coverage: Sound recordings relating to all aspects of life in the northwest of England.

Education services: Education packs for schools.

Collection: Collection includes c. 140,000 recordings on all aspects of northwest life

Library catalogue: All or part available in-house

Publications list: Available in print

Access to staff: Contact by letter, by telephone, by fax, by e-mail and in person. Appointment necessary.
Hours: Mon to Fri, 0845 to 1700

Access to building: *Hours:* Mon to Fri, 0845 to 1700

NORTH WILTSHIRE DISTRICT COUNCIL (NWDC)

Monkton Park, Chippenham, Wiltshire, SN15 1ER

Tel: 01249 706111
Fax: 01249 443158
Website: www.northwilts.gov.uk

Enquiries to: Public Relations Manager
Direct tel: 01249 706618
Direct fax: 01249 654999
Direct e-mail: plangcaster@northwilts.gov.uk
Other contacts: Chief Executive

Founded: 1974

Organisation type and purpose: Local government body.

Subject coverage: Services and amenities of the District Council.

Publications: Printed

Access to staff: Contact by letter, by telephone and by fax
Hours: Mon to Thu, 0900 to 1700; Fri, 0900 to 1630

NORTH YORK MOORS NATIONAL PARK AUTHORITY

The Old Vicarage, Bondgate, Helmsley, North Yorkshire, YO62 5BP

Tel: 01439 770657
Fax: 01439 770691
E-mail: info@northyorkmoors-npa.gov.uk
Website: www.northyorkmoors.org.uk

Enquiries to: Information Officer

Founded: 1952

Organisation type and purpose: Local government body.
National Park administration.
To conserve and enhance the natural beauty, wildlife and cultural heritage of the area, and to promote opportunities for the understanding and enjoyment of the special qualities of the area by the public.

Subject coverage: North York Moors: history, geography, archaeology, agriculture, ecology, planning, tourism, travel.

Publications: Printed

Publications list: Available online and in print

Access to staff: Contact by letter, by telephone, by fax and by e-mail. Appointment necessary.
Hours: Mon to Thu, 0830 to 1700; Fri, 0830 to 1630

Access for disabled people: Parking provided, level entry, toilet facilities

Member organisation of: Association of National Park Authorities

NORTH YORKSHIRE COUNTY COUNCIL, LIBRARY AND INFORMATION CENTRE

Victoria Avenue, Harrogate, North Yorkshire, HG1 1EG

Tel: 0845 0349520
Fax: 01423 523158
E-mail: harrogate.library@northyorks.gov.uk
Website: www.northyorks.gov.uk/libraries

Enquiries to: Community and Information Officer

Founded: 1887

Organisation type and purpose: Local government body, public library.

Subject coverage: General, family history.

Collection: Illustrated 19th- and 20th-century English books
Mineral waters: books and pamphlets from 1572, with particular reference to Harrogate from 1626

Parent body: North Yorkshire County Council, Library and Information Centre; 21 Grammar School Lane, Northallerton, DL6 1DF; tel: 01609 767800; fax: 01609 780793

NORTH YORKSHIRE COUNTY COUNCIL, LIBRARY AND INFORMATION SERVICES

21 Grammar School Lane, Northallerton, North Yorkshire, DL6 1DF

Tel: 01609 533800
Fax: 01609 780793
E-mail: libraries@northyorks.gov.uk
Website: www.northyorks.gov.uk/libraries

Enquiries to: General Manager: Libraries

Founded: 1974

Organisation type and purpose: Local government body, public library.

Subject coverage: General.

Collection: Bertram Unne Photograph Collection of Yorkshire landscape, people and buildings 1945–1975, now housed at County Records Office.
Pratt collection and editions of some 210 titles from private presses (at Northallerton).
Mineral waters: books and pamphlets from 1572 with particular reference to Harrogate from 1626 (at Harrogate).
North Yorkshire Census Returns: 1841, 1851, 1861, 1871, 1881 held at local core libraries.
Petyt Collection of material on 17th-century history and theology (at Skipton).

Non-library collection catalogue: All or part available in-house

Library catalogue: All or part available in-house

Department of the: North Yorkshire County Council

Has: 42 libraries and one Supermobile library in the region

NORTH YORKSHIRE COUNTY RECORD OFFICE (NYCRO)

Malpas Road, Northallerton, North Yorkshire, DL7 8TB

Tel: 01609 777585
E-mail: archives@northyorks.gov.uk

Enquiries to: Archives Development Manager

Organisation type and purpose: Local government body.
Record office.

Subject coverage: Manuscript sources relating to North Yorkshire, including historical and geographical subjects.

Publications: Printed

Access for disabled people: Parking provided, level entry, toilet facilities

Parent body: North Yorkshire County Council

NORTH-EAST CLUB FOR PRE-WAR AUSTINS (NECPWA)

6 College View, Monkwray, Whitehaven, Cumbria

Tel: 01946 67640
E-mail: john@johnandcarolyn.freeserve.co.uk
Website: www.necpwa.demon.co.uk

Enquiries to: Honorary Secretary

Founded: 1966

Organisation type and purpose: Membership association.
Restoration and regular use of historic motor vehicles.

Subject coverage: The restoration and usage of historic motor vehicles. Members own many different makes of vehicles both pre- and post-war.

Collection: Club library of obsolete magazines, handbooks, manuals etc

Publications: Printed

Access to staff: Contact by letter
Hours: Mon to Fri, 0900 to 1700

NORTHAMPTON BOROUGH COUNCIL

The Guildhall, St Giles Square, Northampton, NN1 1DE

Tel: 01604 838383; 01604 838970 (minicom)
Fax: 01604 838729
E-mail: enquiries@northampton.gov.uk
Website: www.northampton.gov.uk

Organisation type and purpose: Local government body.

Subject coverage: Normal range of council subjects, housing, environmental health, planning, council tax, cleansing.

Collection: Home of the National Boot and Shoe collection

Publications: Printed

Access to staff: Contact by letter, by telephone, by fax, by e-mail, in person and via website. Appointment necessary.
Hours: Mon to Fri, 0900 to 1700

Access for disabled people: Access to all public areas

Neighbourhood Environmental Services Directorate: Northampton Borough Council; Westbridge Depot, St James Mill Road, Northampton, NN5 5JW; tel: 01604 838281

Planning and Regeneration Directorate: Northampton Borough Council; Cliftonville House, Bedford Road, Northampton, NN4 7NR

NORTHAMPTONSHIRE INSPECTION AND ADVISORY SERVICE (NIAS)

PO Box 216, John Dryden House, 8–10 The Lakes, Northampton, NN4 7DD

Tel: 01604 236242
Fax: 01604 236240
E-mail: nias@northamptonshire.gov.uk

Enquiries to: Chief Education Adviser
Direct e-mail: cpdnias@northamptonshire.gov.uk

Founded: 1995

Organisation type and purpose: Local government body, suitable for ages: nursery and 4 to 18, training organisation, consultancy, publishing house.
To provide educational consultancy and training, school inspection and curriculum resources.

Subject coverage: Specialising in educational consultancy, training, school inspection, curriculum resources.

Publications: Printed, and electronic and video
Order printed publications from: NIAS Products, Training and Sales
Spencer Centre, Lewis Road, Northampton, NN5 7BJ, tel: 01604 587441, fax: 01604 757799

Publications list: Available in print

Access to staff: Contact by letter, by telephone, by fax and by e-mail. Appointment necessary.
Hours: Mon to Fri, 0900 to 1700

Access for disabled people: Parking provided, level entry, toilet facilities

Administrative Centres: NIAS Computer/Audio Visual Centre; Covington Street, Northampton, NN15JU; tel: 01604 24190; NIAS Inspection Services; Cliftonville Middle School, Cliftonville Road, Northampton, NN1 5BW; tel: 01604 259876; e-mail: niasclif@easymail.rmplc.co.uk; NIAS TPS; Spencer Centre, Lewis Road, Northampton, NN5 7BJ; tel: 01604 758758; e-mail: spencer@rtcnias.rmplc.co.uk

Professional development centres: Corby PDC; Firdale, Cottingham Road, Corby, Northamptonshire, NN17 1TD; tel: 01536 266833; e-mail: corby.north@easymail.rmplc.co.uk; Northampton PDC; Barry Road, Northampton, NN1 5JS; tel: 01604 30815; e-mail: northampton.north@easymail.rmplc.co.uk; Wellingborough PDC; 86 Stanley Road, Wellingborough, Northamptonshire, NN8 1DY; tel: 01933 225104; e-mail: welling.north@easymail.rmplc.co.uk

NORTHAMPTONSHIRE LIBRARIES AND INFORMATION SERVICE (NLIS)

PO Box 216, John Dryden House, 8–10 The Lakes, Northampton, NN4 7DD

Tel: 01604 236236
Fax: 01604 237937
E-mail: nlis@northamptonshire.gov.uk
Website: www.northamptonshire.gov.uk

Organisation type and purpose: Local government body, public library.

Collection: Beeby Thompson Collection (geology)
Charles Bradlaugh Collection (local MP, 19th century)
H. E. Bates Collection
John Clare Collection (poems, MSS, etc. of local poet)
Leather and Footwear Collection
Philip Doddridge Collection (collection of a local minister, 18th century; nonconformist church history)
Sir Henry Dryden Collection (architectural drawings)

Non-library collection catalogue: All or part available online

Library catalogue: All or part available online

Publications: Printed

Publications list: Available online and in print

Access to staff: Contact by letter, by telephone, by fax, by e-mail and via website
Hours: Please contact Enquiries

Branches: in Northampton, Weston Favell, Corby, Kettering, Wellingborough, Rushden, Daventry, Towcester, and 28 others

Parent body: Northamptonshire County Council

NORTHAMPTONSHIRE LIBRARIES AND INFORMATION SERVICE – DAVENTRY LIBRARY

North Street, Daventry, Northamptonshire, NN11 4GH

Tel: 01327 703130
Fax: 01327 300501
E-mail: davlib@northamptonshire.gov.uk

Enquiries to: Librarian

Organisation type and purpose: Local government body, public library.

Subject coverage: General; local information and local history.

Non-library collection catalogue: All or part available online, in-house and in print

Library catalogue: All or part available online

Publications list: Available in print

Access to staff: Contact by letter, by telephone, by fax, by e-mail and in person. Appointment necessary.
Hours: Mon, Thu, Fri, 0900 to 1800; Tue, 0900 to 1900; Wed, 0900 to 1230; Sat, 0930 to 1600

Access for disabled people: Parking provided, ramped entry, level entry, access to all public areas, toilet facilities

Parent body: Northamptonshire Libraries & Information Service (NLIS); tel: 01604 236236; fax: 01604 237937; e-mail: nlis@northamptonshire.gov.uk

NORTHAMPTONSHIRE RECORD OFFICE (NRO)

Wootton Hall Park, Northampton, NN4 8BQ

Tel: 01604 762129
E-mail: archivist@northamptonshire.gov.uk
Website: www.northamptonshire.gov.uk/heritage
Website: www.a2a.pr.gov.uk

Enquiries to: County Archivist

Founded: 1920

Organisation type and purpose: Local government body.
Record office and archives repository.

Subject coverage: A great variety of records in different formats are preserved: charters, court rolls, deeds, parish and non-conformist registers, maps, letters, diaries, accounts, minute books, wills, photographs and films. They include the official, judicial and

continued overleaf

administrative records of the county and other local government authorities, records of the diocese of Peterborough covering Northamptonshire, the Soke of Peterborough and Rutland, probate records for the same area as well as records of local families and estates, business and professional firms and societies.

Education services: Contact Heritage Education Officer: heritagelearning@northamptonshire.gov.uk

Collection: Houses the Library of the Northamptonshire Antiquarian Society and other donated specialist libraries
Includes records of the former Soke of Peterborough

Non-library collection catalogue: All or part available online

Publications: Printed, and microform publications

Access to staff: Contact by letter, by telephone, by e-mail and in person
Hours: Tue to Thu, 0900 to 1700; Fri, 0900 to 1600; Sat, 0900 to 1300. Closed Mon.

Access to building: No prior appointment required

Access for disabled people: Parking provided, level entry, toilet facilities

Parent body: Northamptonshire County Council (NCC)

NORTHAMPTONSHIRE RECORD SOCIETY

Wootton Hall Park, Northampton, NN4 8BQ

Tel: 01604 762297
Website: www.northamptonshirerecordsociety.org.uk/

Enquiries to: Secretary

Founded: 1920

Organisation type and purpose: Learned society (membership is by subscription), registered charity (charity number 204597).
Historical research of all aspects of the ancient County of Northamptonshire.

Subject coverage: Local history of Northamptonshire in all its forms.

Collection: Extensive library, members only, others on request, but not for removal from the premises

Library catalogue: All or part available in-house

Publications: Printed
Order printed publications from: Secretary

Publications list: Available in print

Access to staff: Contact by letter, by telephone and in person. Access for members only.
Hours: Wed and Thu only, 1000 to 1200 and 1330 to 1630
Special comments: Access to the library normally Wed and Thu, 1030 to 1630, non-members by prior appointment.

Access to building: No prior appointment required
Hours: Wed and Thu only, 1000 to 1200 and 1330 to 1630

NORTHBROOK COLLEGE, SUSSEX

Littlehampton Road, Worthing, West Sussex, BN12 6NU

Tel: 01903 606060
Fax: 01903 606007

Enquiries to: Head of Library Services

Organisation type and purpose: College of further and higher education.

Subject coverage: Broad range of curriculum topics in further and higher education.

Access to staff: Contact by letter
Hours: Mon to Fri, 0900 to 1700

Liaison with: LASER; West Sussex County Library

Member of: Circle of Sussex College Librarians (COSCOL); Surrey and Sussex Libraries in Cooperation (SASLIC)

NORTHERN ARC LIMITED (NA)

Great Western Business Centre, Emlyn Square, Swindon, Wiltshire, SN1 5BP

Tel: 0845 600 9966
E-mail: info@northernarcltd.co.uk
Website: www.businesslinksw.co.uk

Enquiries to: Information Officer
Direct e-mail: sarah.harris@businesslinksw.co.uk

Founded: 1995; formerly called Business Link Berkshire and Wiltshire (year of change 2007)

Organisation type and purpose: Training organisation, consultancy.
Single point of contact for local businesses to access advice, information, training and finance.

Subject coverage: Business advice, business start-up advice, training for business, property information, innovation advice, information on exporting, market intelligence, economic and demographic information for Wiltshire and Berkshire; local business information including company information, market intelligence and funding searches.

Publications list: Available in print

Access to staff: Contact by letter, by telephone, by fax, by e-mail, in person and via website
Hours: Mon to Fri, 0900 to 1700
Special comments: Charges made for most services.

Access to building: Prior appointment required

Access for disabled people: Parking provided, ramped entry

Parent body: GWEBusiness West Ltd; Great Western Business Centre, Emlyn Square, Swindon, SN1 5BP; tel: 01793 428320; fax: 01793 428345; e-mail: tony.horn@gwebusinesswest.co.uk; website: http://www.gwebusinesswest.co.uk

NORTHERN HAMSTER CLUB (NHC)

Club Secretary, 1 Richard Avenue, Smithies, Barnsley. S71 1UZ

Tel: 01226 218439
E-mail: enquiries@northernhamsterclub.co.uk
Website: www.northernhamsterclub.com/

Enquiries to: Membership Secretary

Founded: 1947

Organisation type and purpose: Membership association (membership is by subscription), present number of members: 90, voluntary organisation, suitable for ages: all.
Promote the keeping, exhibition and breeding of all species of hamster.

Subject coverage: Keeping, breeding and exhibition of all species of hamster.

Publications: Printed

Access to staff: Contact by letter, by telephone, by e-mail and via website
Hours: Mon to Sun, 0900 to 2100

Affiliated to: National Hamster Council; PO Box 154, Rotherham, S66 0FL

NORTHERN IRELAND AGRICULTURAL PRODUCERS' ASSOCIATION

15 Molesworth Street, Cookstown, Co Tyrone, BT80 8NX

Tel: 028 8676 5700
Fax: 028 8675 8598
E-mail: niapa@hotmail.com

Enquiries to: Information Officer

Founded: 1974

Organisation type and purpose: Advisory body, membership association (membership is by subscription).
To assist farmers. Farmers representative group, provide farm insurance.

Access to staff: Contact by letter, by telephone, by fax, by e-mail and in person
Hours: Mon to Fri, 0900 to 1700

NORTHERN IRELAND ARCHERY SOCIETY (NIAS)

43 Greenwell Street, Newtownards, Co. Down, BT23 7LP

Tel: 028 9181 9529
Website: www.ni-archery.co.uk

Enquiries to: President

Founded: 1953; formerly called Ulster Archery Association (year of change late 1970s)

Organisation type and purpose: One of the smallest Regional Societies within Archery GB, which is the governing body of archery within Great Britain.
Currently has 24 active clubs with a total membership of over 300.

Subject coverage: All types of archery: indoor target, outdoor target, field and clout, as well as all styles: barebow, recurve, compound and longbow.

Access to staff: Contact by letter and by telephone

Member organisation of: Archery GB

NORTHERN IRELAND ASSEMBLY LIBRARY

Parliament Buildings, Stormont, Belfast, BT4 3XX

Tel: 028 9052 1250
Fax: 028 9052 1922
E-mail: issuedesk.library@niassembly.gov.uk

Enquiries to: Librarian (Resource Team)
Direct e-mail: george.woodman@niassembly.gov.uk

Founded: 1921

Organisation type and purpose: National government body.
Government library.
To serve staff and members of Northern Ireland Assembly; to act as reference library for Northern Ireland Government Departments.

Subject coverage: Northern Ireland Parliamentary and Assembly papers, debates and legislation, since 1921; Westminster Parliament Sessional and House of Lords papers and debates; Northern Ireland Departmental papers; Northern Ireland history, politics and government; Irish history; statute law and constitutional law.

Collection: 18th- and 19th-century travel books relating to Ireland
Back runs of Belfast newspapers, Irish Times and Times extending back to at least 1921
Complete set of Hansard dating back to the 1830s
Complete sets of Northern Ireland legislation and very large collection of official publications
Statutes, journals and votes of pre-1800 Irish Parliament

Non-library collection catalogue: All or part available in-house

Library catalogue: All or part available in-house

Access to staff: Contact by letter, by telephone, by fax and by e-mail
Hours: Mon to Fri, 0900 to 1700
Special comments: Access normally limited to members and staff of the NI Assembly and staff of the NI Government Departments.

Access to building: Prior appointment required
Hours: Mon to Fri, 0900 to 1700 and when Northern Ireland Assembly is sitting (closes 30 minutes after House rises)

Access for disabled people: Parking provided, ramped entry, toilet facilities

NORTHERN IRELAND ASSOCIATION OF CITIZENS ADVICE BUREAUX (NIACAB)

11 Upper Crescent, Belfast, BT7 1NT

Tel: 028 9023 1120
Fax: 028 9023 6522
Website: www.niacab.org

Enquiries to: Senior Information Officer

Founded: 1974

Organisation type and purpose: Voluntary organisation, registered charity (charity number 85136).
To develop networks with other agencies to ensure that individuals do not suffer through ignorance of either their rights or of the services available to them, or through an inability to explain their needs effectively.

Subject coverage: General information for CAB workers in Northern Ireland; social policy background information based on evidence from CABx.

Collection: Northern Ireland statutes and statutory rules

Publications: Printed

Access to staff: Contact by letter and by telephone
Hours: Mon to Fri, 0900 to 1700

Subsidiary bureaux throughout: Northern Ireland

NORTHERN IRELAND ATHLETIC FEDERATION (NIAF)

Athletics House, Old Coach Road, Belfast, BT9 5PR

Tel: 028 9060 2707
Fax: 028 9030 9939
E-mail: info@niathletics.org

Enquiries to: Administrator

Founded: 1989

Organisation type and purpose: Governing body of athletics in Northern Ireland.

Subject coverage: Amateur athletics.

Access to staff: Contact by letter and by e-mail
Hours: Mon to Fri, 0900 to 1700

Affiliated to: UK Athletics

NORTHERN IRELAND CHILDMINDING ASSOCIATION (NICMA)

16–18 Mill Street, Newtownards, Co Down, BT23 4LU

Tel: 028 9181 1015
Fax: 028 9182 0921
E-mail: bridget.nodder@nicma.org
Website: www.nicma.org

Enquiries to: Director

Founded: 1984

Organisation type and purpose: Membership association (membership is by subscription, election or invitation), present number of members: 2500, voluntary organisation, registered charity (charity number XO 549), training organisation.
Child care organisation.
To promote the development of children by providing quality home-based care within registered settings.

Subject coverage: All aspects of child care provision.

Publications: Printed

Publications list: Available online and in print

Access to staff: Contact by letter, by telephone, by fax, by e-mail, in person and via website. Appointment necessary.
Hours: Mon to Fri, 0900 to 1700

Access for disabled people: Level entry, toilet facilities

NORTHERN IRELAND COMMUNITY RELATIONS COUNCIL (CRC)

6 Murray Street, Belfast, BT1 6DN

Tel: 028 9022 7500
Fax: 028 9022 7551
E-mail: info@nicrc.org.uk
Website: www.nicrc.org.uk

Enquiries to: Information Officer

Founded: 1990

Organisation type and purpose: Advisory body, voluntary organisation, registered charity (charity number XR 16701), consultancy, publishing house.

Subject coverage: Northern Ireland, peace, conflict resolution, community relations and cultural diversity.

Collection: Reference library

Library catalogue: All or part available in-house

Publications: Printed

Publications list: Available online

Access to staff: Contact by letter, by telephone, by fax, by e-mail, in person and via website. Appointment necessary.
Hours: Mon to Fri, 0900 to 1700

Access to building: No prior appointment required

Access for disabled people: Ramped entry, toilet facilities
Special comments: Elevator to 1st floor. Toilet facilities on ground floor.

NORTHERN IRELAND COUNCIL FOR VOLUNTARY ACTION (NICVA)

61 Duncairn Gardens, Belfast, BT15 2GB

Tel: 028 9087 7777, 028 9087 7776 (minicom)
Fax: 028 9087 7799
E-mail: info@nicva.org
Website: www.nicva.org
Website: www.communityni.org
Website: www.grant-tracker.org

Enquiries to: Information Officer

Founded: 1938

Organisation type and purpose: Membership association (membership is by subscription), present number of members: over 1,000, voluntary organisation, registered charity (charity number XN47024), training organisation, research organisation.
Umbrella body for voluntary and community groups.

Subject coverage: Social policy, social action, voluntary action, community development, funding information, research, charity advice.

Collection: Library (books, grey literature) of more than 2,000 items
Journals and periodicals

continued overleaf

Trade and statistical information: Data on the economic contribution and structure of the voluntary and community sector in Northern Ireland

Non-library collection catalogue: All or part available online

Library catalogue: All or part available in-house

Publications: Printed, and electronic and video
Order printed publications from: Information Officer
Order electronic and video publications from: Online subscription at http://www.grant-tracker.org

Publications list: Available online

Access to staff: Contact by letter, by telephone, by fax, by e-mail, in person and via website. Appointment necessary.
Hours: Mon to Thu, 0900 to 1700; Fri, 0900 to 1630
Special comments: Some charges made, e.g. photocopying, consultancy services.

Access to building: Prior appointment required for the library
Special comments: Prior appointment required for the library

Access for disabled people: Parking provided, ramped entry, level entry, access to all public areas, toilet facilities

NORTHERN IRELAND ENVIRONMENT AGENCY (NIEA)

Klondyke Building, Cromac Avenue, Lower Ormeau Road, Belfast, BT7 2JA

Tel: 028 9056 9230
Fax: 028 9056 9264
E-mail: nieainfo@doeni.gov.uk
Website: www.ni-environment.gov.uk

Other contacts: Director of Water Quality, Director of Natural Heritage, Director of Built Heritage (for specific research)

History of institution: formerly called Environment and Heritage Service (year of change 2008)

Organisation type and purpose: National government body.

Subject coverage: Built Heritage, Natural Heritage, Environmental Protection.

Publications: Printed
Order printed publications from: at the same address

Access to staff: Contact by letter, by telephone, by fax and by e-mail. Appointment necessary.

Access to building: *Hours:* Mon to Fri, 0900 to 1700

Also at: Northern Ireland Environment Agency; Water Management Unit, 7 Antrim Road, Lisburn; tel: 028 9262 3100; e-mail: waterinfo@doeni.gov.uk; Northern Ireland Environment Agency; Built Heritage, Waterman House, 5–33 Hill Street, Belfast, BT1 2LA; tel: 028 9023 5000; fax: 028 9054 3111; e-mail: bh@doeni.gov.uk

NORTHERN IRELAND ENVIRONMENT AGENCY – MONUMENTS AND BUILDINGS RECORD (NIEA–MBR)

5–33 Hill Street, Belfast, Town Parks, BT1 2LA

Tel: 028 9054 3159
Fax: 028 9054 3111
E-mail: hmenquiries@doeni.gov.uk
Website: www.doeni.gov.uk/niea

Enquiries to: Secretary
Direct tel: 028 9054 3159
Direct fax: 028 9054 3111

Founded: 1992; formerly called Environment and Heritage Service; formerly called Archaeological Survey

Organisation type and purpose: National government body.

Subject coverage: Archaeological sites, listed buildings, photographic and drawings archive, historic monuments and buildings, historic gardens, industrial archaeology, maritime archaeology, defence heritage sites, library.

Education services: Groups catered for by prior arrangement.

Collection: John McGeagh, Robert McKinstry and Philip Bell architectural collection (Copyright NIEA: Built Heritage)
Clokey stained glass collection
JKS St.Joseph Aerial photos (reference only)
John Seeds architectural photographic collection (Copyright NIEA: Built Heritage)
McCutcheon Industrial Archaeology Archive (Crown Copyright)
Northern Ireland Sites and Monuments Record

Non-library collection catalogue: All or part available online

Library catalogue: All or part available in-house

Publications: Printed
Order printed publications from: Postal address for NIEA, above

Publications list: Available in print

Access to staff: Contact by letter, by telephone, by fax, by e-mail and in person
Hours: 0900 to 1700

Access to building: *Hours:* 0930 to 1300 and 1400 to 1630

Access for disabled people: Ramped entry, toilet facilities
Hours: 0930 to 1300 and 1400 to 1630

Parent body: Department of the Environment; Clarence Court, Belfast, Town Parks, BT2 8GB; tel: 028 9054 0540

NORTHERN IRELAND ENVIRONMENT LINK (NIEL)

89 Loopland Drive, Belfast, BT6 9DW

Tel: 028 9045 5770
Fax: 028 9094 2151
E-mail: info@nienvironmentlink.org
Website: www.nienvironmentlink.org

Enquiries to: Director
Other contacts: Communications and Membership Officer

Founded: 1990

Organisation type and purpose: Membership association (membership is by subscription), present number of members: 109, voluntary organisation, registered charity (charity number XR 19598).
Umbrella and networking body for voluntary environmental groups.

Subject coverage: Environmental issues, conservation, pollution and countryside management, sustainable development, waste management, biodiversity, environmental education. Policy and policy development.

Collection: Library of recent government and NGO publications

Library catalogue: All or part available in-house

Publications: Printed

Publications list: Available online

Access to staff: Contact by letter, by telephone, by fax, by e-mail, in person and via website. Appointment necessary.
Hours: Mon to Fri, 0900 to 1700

NORTHERN IRELAND FEDERATION OF CLUBS

1 Sultan Square, Belfast, BT12 4SU

Tel: 028 9029 5134
Fax: 028 9023 3286
E-mail: info@nifederationofclubs.com
Website: www.nifederationofclubs.com/

Enquiries to: Executive Secretary
Direct e-mail: info@nifederationofclubs.com

Founded: 1983

Organisation type and purpose: Advisory body, trade union (membership is by subscription), present number of members: 301, service industry, voluntary organisation, consultancy, research organisation.

Subject coverage: Information on the N Ireland Registration of Clubs Order and Accounts Regulations 1996. Private member clubs, management, contracts of employment for persons employed in registered clubs, and general advice.

Publications: Printed
Order printed publications from: Media Marketing
B1.01 Portview Trade Centre, Belfast, BT4 1RX, tel: 028 9045 9864, fax: 028 9045 9034

Access to staff: Contact by letter, by telephone, by fax, by e-mail and via website. Appointment necessary.
Hours: Mon to Fri, 0900 to 1700

Access to building: Prior appointment required

Access for disabled people: Access to all public areas, toilet facilities

NORTHERN IRELAND HEALTH AND SOCIAL SERVICES LIBRARY

Queen's University Medical Library, Mulhouse Building, Mulhouse Road, Belfast, BT12 6DP

Tel: 028 9063 2504
Fax: 028 9063 5038
E-mail: med.office@qub.ac.uk

Enquiries to: Information Officer

Founded: 1954

Organisation type and purpose: University department or institute.
University medical and regional health service library.

Subject coverage: Medicine, dentistry, nursing, paramedical subjects, health organisation and social services.

Collection: Samuel Simms Collection on the history of medicine and other historical works
Works by Northern Ireland doctors

Non-library collection catalogue: All or part available online

Library catalogue: All or part available online

Access to building: No access other than to staff

NORTHERN IRELAND LOCAL GOVERNMENT ASSOCIATION (NILGA)

Unit 5B, Castlereagh Business Park, 478 Castlereagh Road, Belfast, BT5 6BQ

Tel: 028 9079 8972
Fax: 028 9079 1248
Website: www.nilga.org

Enquiries to: Chief Executive

Founded: 2001

Organisation type and purpose: Local government body.
An organisation representing the interests of local government in Northern Ireland.

Subject coverage: The functions and responsibilities of District Councils in Northern Ireland.

Publications: Printed

Access to staff: Contact by letter and by fax
Hours: Mon to Fri, 0900 to 1700

Member of: Local Government International Bureau; tel: 020 7664 3100

Representing the British section of: CEMR; IULA

NORTHERN IRELAND MASTER PLUMBERS' ASSOCIATION (NIMPA)

38 Hill Street, Belfast, BT1 2LB

Tel: 028 9032 1731
Fax: 028 9024 7521
E-mail: info@crawfordsedgwick.co.uk

Enquiries to: Secretary

Founded: 1931

Organisation type and purpose: Trade association.

Subject coverage: Plumbing and mechanical services.

Access to staff: Contact by letter, by telephone, by fax and by e-mail
Hours: Mon to Fri, 0900 to 1700

Member organisation of: Scottish & Northern Ireland Plumbing Employers' Federation; 2 Walker Street, Edinburgh, EH3 7LB; tel: 0131 225 2255; fax: 0131 226 7638; e-mail: info@snipef.org; website: http://www.snipef.org

NORTHERN IRELAND OMBUDSMAN

Formal name: Assembly Ombudsman for Northern Ireland/Northern Ireland Commissioner for Complaints

Progressive House, 33 Wellington Place, Belfast, BT1 6HN

Tel: 028 9023 3821; 0800 343424 freephone
Fax: 028 9023 4912
E-mail: ombudsman@ni-ombudsman.org.uk
Website: www.ni-ombudsman.org.uk

Enquiries to: Office Manager

Founded: 1969

Organisation type and purpose: Statutory body.
Ombudsman.

Subject coverage: Complaints from people who claim to have suffered injustice because of maladministration by government departments and public bodies in Northern Ireland.

Publications: Printed

Publications list: Available online

Access to staff: Contact by letter, by telephone, by fax, by e-mail, in person and via website. Appointment necessary.
Hours: Personal callers: Mon to Fri, 0930 to 1600

Access for disabled people: Level entry, access to all public areas, toilet facilities

NORTHERN IRELAND OPTOMETRIC SOCIETY (NIOS)

PO Box 28, Dromore, County Down, BT25 1YH, Northern Ireland

Tel: 028 8224 2137
Fax: 028 8224 9330
E-mail: lizgillespie.nios@btopenworld.com
Website: www.nios.org

Enquiries to: Secretary

Founded: 1952

Organisation type and purpose: Professional body (membership is by subscription).

Subject coverage: The NIOS represents the profession of optometry in Northern Ireland. The core activity of the society is to promote high standards of primary eye care, and to enhance further education and learning.

Trade and statistical information: Data on number of optometrists resident or practising in Northern Ireland

Access to staff: Contact by letter
Hours: Mon to Fri, 0900 to 1700

NORTHERN IRELAND POSTAL CHESS ASSOCIATION

27 Cherry Valley Gardens, Belfast, BT5 6PQ

Tel: 028 9059 1142
E-mail: david.blair4@ntlworld.com
Website: www.chessmail.com

Enquiries to: Honorary Secretary & Treasurer

Founded: 1985

Organisation type and purpose: Membership association (membership is by subscription).
To organise and play correspondence chess nationally and internationally.

Subject coverage: Correspondence chess.

Library catalogue: All or part available online

Publications: Electronic and video
Order electronic and video publications from: Editor, Chessmail; e-mail: editor@chessmail.com

Publications list: Available online and in print

Access to staff: Contact by letter and by e-mail
Hours: Mon to Fri, 1700 to 1900; Sat, Sun, 0900 to 1700
Special comments: No phone Mon to Fri, 0900 to 1700

Affiliated to: British Postal Chess Federation

NORTHERN IRELAND TOURIST BOARD (NITB)

St Anne's Court, 59 North Street, Belfast, BT1 1NB

Tel: 028 9023 1221
Fax: 028 9024 0960
E-mail: info@nitb.com
Website: www.ni-tourism.com
Website: www.nitb.com

Enquiries to: Information Officer
Direct e-mail: lking@nitb.com
Other contacts: (1) Research and Information Librarian (2) Photographic Librarian for (1) reports etc (2) film and transparencies.

Founded: 1948

Organisation type and purpose: Local government body, statutory body.
National tourist board.

Subject coverage: Northern Ireland tourism facts and figures, accommodation, transport and sightseeing information, activities and events.

Collection: Photographic library, 30,000 transparencies for loan and hire, plus videos and slides
Research library (5000 titles) NI and UK tourism statistics, market research, planning, environment, annual reports etc
TIC – booklets, brochures, maps – leaflets on particular places or subjects, some free

Publications: Printed

Access to staff: Contact by letter, by telephone, by fax, by e-mail, in person and via website. Appointment necessary.
Hours: Mon to Fri, 0900 to 1700
Research Library: Tue, Thu, 0900 to 1700; Wed, 0900 to 1500

NORTHERN IRELAND TRANSPLANT ASSOCIATION (NITA)

6 Hillview Road, Carrickfergus BT38 8YW

Tel: 07900980863
E-mail: nitransplant@hotmail.co.uk
Website: www.nitransplant.org

Enquiries to: Chairperson

continued overleaf

Direct tel: 07900980863
Direct e-mail: nitransplant@hotmail.co.uk
Other contacts: Secretary

Founded: October 1991

Organisation type and purpose:
Membership association (membership is by election or invitation), present number of members: approx. 200, registered charity (charity number XO 19630).
To advise and support those involved with organ transplants, including donor families, and to supply relevant information. To encourage registration of donors and the carrying of organ donor cards.

Subject coverage: Organ transplantation and donors.

Publications: Printed
Order printed publications from: email address

Access to staff: Contact by letter, by telephone, by e-mail and via website
Hours: 24-hour telephone answering service

NORTHERN IRELAND, WESTERN EDUCATION AND LIBRARY BOARD

Library Headquarters, 1 Spillars Place, Omagh, Co Tyrone, BT78 1HG

Tel: 028 8224 4821
Fax: 028 8224 6716
Website: www.ni-libraries.net

Enquiries to: Librarian

Organisation type and purpose: Local government body, statutory body (membership is by election or invitation), present number of members: 21, public library.
Public Library Service; District Libraries at Londonderry, Omagh, Co Tyrone and Enniskillen/County Fermanagh, Limavady and Strabane.
Some material for consultation only.

Subject coverage: Humanities, history, local history, education, business, fine arts and bibliographical.

Collection: William Carleton Collection
Nawn Collection (local and Irish history)
Local and Irish history
Material on Ireland; Art; Bibliophily
Irish Joint Fiction Reserve (authors A, F and I)

Trade and statistical information:
Regulatory, economic, financial, technical and marketing material

Non-library collection catalogue: All or part available online and in-house

Library catalogue: All or part available online and in print

Publications: Printed

Access to staff: Contact by letter, by telephone, by fax, by e-mail, in person and via website. Appointment necessary.
Hours: Library HQ and Divisional HQs, Mon to Fri, 0900 to 1715
Branch libraries vary, all are open Tue pm, Fri and Sat 1000 to 1300; telephone for more precise details

North West Divisional Library: Northern Ireland, Western Education and Library Board; 35 Foyle Street, Londonderry, BT48 6AL; tel: 028 7127 2300; fax: 028 7126 9084

Other libraries: Castlederg Library; 1a Hospital Road, Castlederg, BT81 7BU; tel: 028 8167 1419; fax: 028 8167 9048; e-mail: castlederg.library@ni-libraries.net; Central Library; 35 Foyle Street, Londonderry, BT48 6AL; tel: 028 7126 6888; fax: 028 7126 9084; Creggan Library; 59 Central Drive, Creggan Estate, Londonderry, BT48 9QH; tel: 028 7126 6168; fax: 028 7130 8939; e-mail: creggan.library@ni-libraries.net; Dungiven Library; 74 Main Street, Dungiven, Co Londonderry, BT47 4LD; tel: 028 7174 1475; e-mail: dungiven.library@ni-libraries.net; Enniskillen Library; Halls Lane, Enniskillen, BT74 7DR; tel: 028 6632 2886; fax: 028 8632 4685; e-mail: enniskillen.library@ni-libraries .net; Fintona Library; 112–114 Main Street, Fintona, BT78 2BY; tel: 028 8284 1774; fax: 028 8284 1774; e-mail: fintona.library@ni -libraries.net; Irvinestown Library; Main Street, Irvinestown, Co Fermanagh, BT94 1GT; tel: 028 6862 1383; fax: 028 6862 1383; e-mail: irvinestown.library@ni-libraries.net; Limavady Library; 5 Connell Street, Limavady, Co Londonderry, BT49 0EA; tel: 028 7776 2540; fax: 028 7772 2006; e-mail: limavady.library@ni-libraries.net; Lisnaskea Library; Drumhaw, Lisnaskea, Co Fermanagh, BT92 0FC; tel: 028 6772 1222; fax: 028 6772 1222; e-mail: lisnaskea.library@ ni-libraries.net; Newtownstewart Library; Main Street, Newtownstewart, BT87 4AA; tel: 028 8266 1245; fax: 028 8266 1245; e-mail: newtonstewart.library@ni-libraries.net; Omagh Library; 1 Spillars Place, Omagh, BT78 1HL; tel: 028 8224 4821; fax: 028 8224 6722; e-mail: omagh.library@ni-libraries.net; Shantallow Library; 92 Racecourse Road, Shantallow, Co Londonderry, BT4 8DA; tel: 028 7135 4185; fax: 028 7135 4122; e-mail: shantallow.library@ni-libraries.net; Sion Mills Library; Church Square, Sion Mills, BT78 9HA; tel: 028 8265 8513; fax: 028 8265 8513; e-mail: sionmills.library@ni-libraries .net; Strabane Library; 1 Railway Road, Strabane, BT82 8AN; tel: 028 7188 3686; fax: 028 7138 2745; e-mail: strabane.library@ni -libraries.net; Strathfoyle Library; Claragh Crescent, Strathfoyle, Co Londonderry, BT47 7HQ; tel: 028 7186 0385; fax: 028 7186 0385; e-mail: strathfoyle.library@ni-libraries.net; Waterside Library; 23 Glendermott Road, Waterside, Londonderry, BT47 1BG; tel: 028 7134 2963; fax: 028 7131 8283; e-mail: waterside.library@ni-libraries.net

South West Divisional Library: Northern Ireland, Western Education and Library Board; Halls Lane, Enniskillen, BT74 7DR; tel: 028 6632 2886; fax: 028 6632 4685; e-mail: enniskillen.library@ni-libraries.net

NORTHERN MINE RESEARCH SOCIETY (NMRS)

Winshaw Barn, Chapel-le-Dale, Ingleton, Yorkshire, LA6 3AT

Tel: 01524 241851
E-mail: sbassham@nildram.co.uk
Website: www.nmrs.org.uk

Enquiries to: Publication Sales
Direct tel: 01282 614615
Direct e-mail: mansemins@btopenworld.com
Other contacts: Editor (for publishing enquiries); Recorder (for historical requests)

Founded: 1960

Organisation type and purpose: Learned society (membership is by subscription), present number of members: 400, registered charity (charity number 326704), suitable for ages: 18+, research organisation, publishing house.
Researching all aspects of the history of Britain's extractive (mining and quarrying) industries.

Subject coverage: British mining history, mining technology, past and present mining of minerals in UK, some aspects of University field work.

Collection: Documents, maps and plans relating to British mines
Indexes of mining sites
Mining history books

Trade and statistical information: Historical data on the production of materials in Britain

Non-library collection catalogue: All or part available online and in-house

Library catalogue: All or part available in-house

Publications: Printed

Publications list: Available online and in print

Access to staff: Contact by letter and by e-mail
Hours: Recorder only, by appointment.

Access to building: Recorder only, by appointment

Access for disabled people: Recorder only

Member organisation of: Association for Industrial Archaeology; Council for British Archaeology Group 4; National Association of Mining History Organisations

NORTHERN REGION FILM AND TELEVISION ARCHIVE (NRFTA)

School of Arts and Media, Teesside University, Middlesborough, Tees Valley, TS1 3BA

Tel: 01642 384022
Fax: 01642 384099
E-mail: enquiries@nrfta.org.uk
Website: www.nrfta.org.uk

Founded: 1998

Organisation type and purpose: Public sector moving image archive serving County Durham, Northumberland, Tees Valley and Tyne and Wear.

Subject coverage: Film and television in County Durham, Northumberland, Tees Valley, and Tyne and Wear.

Collection: Important collections include:
BBC Look North collection
Tyne Tees Television collection
Border Television collection
Turners' Film Unit collection
Tyne and Wear Archives Service (TWAS) collection

Access to staff: Contact by letter, by telephone, by e-mail and via website. Appointment necessary.
Hours: Mon to Thu, 0900 to 1700; Fri, 0900 to 1630

NORTHMOOR TRUST

Northmoor Trust, Hill Farm, Little Wittenham, Abingdon, Oxon

Tel: 01865 407792
Fax: 01865 407131
E-mail: admin@northmoortrust.co.uk
Website: www.northmoortrust.co.uk

Enquiries to: Chief Executive

Founded: 1967

Organisation type and purpose: A conservation charity (registered charity number 1095057) finding working solutions to the challenges faced by farming, conservation and forestry.
To educate and engage people in their local landscape and inspire them to take action to protect it; to demonstrate sustainability in a way that integrates production from the land, wildlife-rich habitats and natural systems.

Subject coverage: Manages an estate of 300 hectares, including Little Wittenham Nature Reserve and Wittenham Clumps, a conservation farm, a woodland dedicated to forestry research and Project Timescape, the Trust's visitor centre.

Special visitor services: Varied programme of events, including green birthday parties.

Education services: Events for primary and secondary schools; farm visits arranged.

Access to staff: Contact by letter, by telephone, by fax and by e-mail

NORTHUMBERLAND ARCHIVES

Woodhorn Museum and Northumberland Archives

Tel: 01670 528080
Fax: 01670 528083
E-mail: collections@woodhorn.org.uk
Website: www.nationalarchives.gov.uk/a2a
Website: www.experiencewoodhorn.com

Enquiries to: Head of Collections

History of institution: incorporates the former Northumberland Record Office

Organisation type and purpose: Local government body (charitable trust).
Archive service.

Subject coverage: Historic records relating to the County of Northumberland.

Collection: Main map collection for the county including enclosure awards, deposited plans, estate maps, tithe awards, ordnance survey maps
Main photographic collection for the county
Family and estate papers
Manorial
Business
Records of the Society of Antiquaries of Newcastle upon Tyne
Private small collections

Non-library collection catalogue: All or part available online

Library catalogue: All or part available online

Publications: Printed, and microform publications

Publications list: Available in print

Access to staff: Contact by letter, by telephone, by fax, by e-mail, in person and via website
Hours: Wed to Sun, 1000 to 1600; Mon, Tue, closed

Access to building: No prior appointment required

Access for disabled people: Parking provided – charge of £2.50 daily

Branch of: Berwick Record Office; Council Offices, Wallace Green, Berwick upon Tweed, Northumberland, TD15 1ED; tel: 01289 301865; e-mail: lbankier@woodhorn.org.uk

NORTHUMBERLAND COLLECTIONS SERVICE

Woodhorn Experience, Northumberland Museums and Archives, Queen Elizabeth II Country Park, Ashington, Northumberland, NE63 9YF

Tel: 01670 528080
Fax: 01670 514815
E-mail: ask@northumberland.gov.uk
Website: www.northumberland.gov.uk/collections/

Enquiries to: Senior Archivist

Organisation type and purpose: Local government body.
Archive service.

Subject coverage: Historic records relating to the county of Northumberland.
Incorporates Northumberland County Archive Service (formerly Northumberland Record Office), Northumberland County Council's Local Studies Collection, and Northumberland County Council's Modern Records Service

Non-library collection catalogue: All or part available in-house

Publications: Printed

Publications list: Available in print

Access to staff: Contact by letter, by telephone, by fax, by e-mail and in person

Constituent bodies: Berwick Record Office; Council Offices, Wallace Green, Berwick upon Tweed, Northumberland, TD15 1ED; tel: 01259 330044 ext 230

NORTHUMBERLAND COLLEGE

College Road, Ashington, Northumberland, NE63 9RG

Tel: 01670 814200 extn 241
Fax: 01670 841201
E-mail: lrc.admin@northland.ac.uk
Website: www.northland.ac.uk

Enquiries to: Librarian

Organisation type and purpose: Suitable for ages: 16+.
College of further education.

Subject coverage: General fiction and Young Adult Fiction, Agriculture
Animal care
Arboriculture
Art
Business
Carpentry & Joinery
Construction
Early Years Education
Engineering
Environmental science
Equine
Fisheries
Floristry
Gamekeeping
Hairdressing & Beauty Therapy
Health & Social Care
Horticulture
Hospitality & Catering
IT & computing
Outdoor Education
Photography
Plastering
Plumbing
Sport & Leisure
Teaching
Travel & Tourism
Veterinary Nursing

Collection: Friends of Kirkley Hall Archive

Non-library collection catalogue: All or part available in-house

Library catalogue: All or part available online

Publications: Printed
Order printed publications from: Librarian

Publications list: Available online

Access to staff: Contact by letter, by telephone, by fax and by e-mail
Hours: Up to date opening hours available to Guests on the LRC area of Blackboard, via the College website

Access for disabled people: Parking provided, ramped entry, access to all public areas, toilet facilities

Also at: Northumberland College At Kirkley Hall; Kirkley Hall, Ponteland, NE20 0AQ; tel: 01670 814200 extn 519; e-mail: lrc.admin@northland.ac.uk

NORTHUMBERLAND COUNTY LIBRARY – HEXHAM

Queen's Hall, Beaumont Street, Hexham, Northumberland, NE46 3LS

Tel: 01434 652488
Fax: 01434 652490
E-mail: hexhamlibrary@northumberland.gov.uk

Enquiries to: Librarian

Organisation type and purpose: Public library.

Collection: Census returns, parish registers, newspapers all on microfilm
International Genealogical Index (on microfilm)
The Brough Collection: Local History Sources

Non-library collection catalogue: All or part available in print

Library catalogue: All or part available online

Publications: Printed

Access to staff: Contact by letter, by telephone, by fax, by e-mail and in person
Hours: Mon to Wed, 0930 to 1700; Fri, 0930 to 1930; Sat, 0930 to 1230

Access for disabled people: Level entry

NORTHUMBERLAND COUNTY LIBRARY SERVICE

County Hall, Morpeth, Northumberland, NE61 2EF

Tel: 0845 600 6400
E-mail: libraries@northumberland.gov.uk
Website: www.northumberlandlibraries.com

Direct tel: 01670 500391
Direct e-mail: infohelp@northumberland.gov.uk

Founded: 1926

Organisation type and purpose: Public library.

Subject coverage: General, modern poetry, cinema, Northumberland.

Collection: Film and cinema
Modern poetry
Northern Poetry Library
Northumberland

Library catalogue: All or part available online

Access to staff: Contact by letter, by telephone, by e-mail, in person and via website
Hours: Mon to Fri, 0900 to 1930; Sat, 0930 to 1230

Parent body: Northumberland County Council; County Hall, Morpeth, Northumberland, NE61 2EF; tel: 0845 600 6400; website: http://www.northumberland.gov.uk

NORTHUMBRIA UNIVERSITY – EUROPEAN DOCUMENTATION CENTRE

City Campus Library, Ellison Place, Newcastle upon Tyne, NE1 8ST

Tel: 0191 243 7709
Fax: 0191 227 4563
E-mail: maimie.balfour@northumbria.ac.uk
Website: www.northumbria.ac.uk/edc

Enquiries to: Information Specialist
Direct e-mail: ask4help@northumbria.ac.uk

Founded: 1974

Organisation type and purpose: University library.
To provide a service of EU information in the northern region of the United Kingdom to all staff and students internally and in Higher or Further Education institutions, and external clients.

Subject coverage: EU legislation, EU policy, EU statistics, official publications, etc., including information officially published by all the EC institutions.

Collection: EU information deposited by the Commission of the EC

Non-library collection catalogue: All or part available online

Access to staff: Contact by letter, by telephone, by fax and by e-mail. Appointment necessary.
Hours: See website: http://www.northumbria.ac.uk/edc

NORTHUMBRIA UNIVERSITY – UNIVERSITY LIBRARY

Formal name: University of Northumbria at Newcastle

Ellison Place, Newcastle upon Tyne, NE1 8ST

Tel: 0191 227 4125
Fax: 0191 227 4563
E-mail: ask4help@northumbria.ac.uk
Website: www.northumbria.ac.uk/sd/central/library
Website: prism.talis.com/northumbria-ac/

Enquiries to: Director of Academic Services
Direct tel: 0191 227 4126
Direct e-mail: jane.core@northumbria.ac.uk

History of institution: formerly called Newcastle Polytechnic (year of change 1992)

Organisation type and purpose: University Library.

Subject coverage: Art and design, economics, education, English literature, geography, government, history, law, librarianship and information science, modern languages, nursing, midwifery and allied health, philosophy, politics, psychology, religion, social welfare, sociology, accountancy, building, business, chemistry, civil engineering, electrical and electronic engineering, industrial design, management, marketing, materials science, mathematics, mechanical engineering, statistics, surveying, computing, physics.

Collection: Visual Art UK Archives

Library catalogue: All or part available online

Publications: Printed

Access to staff: Contact by letter, by telephone, by e-mail, in person and via website
Hours: Term time: Mon to Thu, 0900 to 2100; Fri, 0900 to 1900; Sat, 0930 to 1700; Sun, 1100 to 1700

Access to building: Visitors welcome; Northumbria members and subscribers, smartcard to enter University
Hours: Term time: 24-hour opening to students and staff; vacations: daily, 0800 to 2400
Special comments: Visitors require proof of identity, incl. photo. No entry without a smartcard outside staff-supervised hours.

Access for disabled people: Ramped entry, access to all public areas, toilet facilities

NORTON OWNERS CLUB (NOC)

Clifton House, 4a Goldington Road, Bedford, MK40 3NF

Tel: 01234 352672
E-mail: secretary@nortonownersclub.org
Website: www.noc.co.uk

Enquiries to: Secretary

Founded: 1959

Organisation type and purpose: International organisation, membership association (membership is by subscription), present number of members: 5,000, voluntary organisation.
To promote an interest in Norton Motorcycles.

Subject coverage: Technical, historical, model, type information on Norton Motorcycles.

Non-library collection catalogue: All or part available in-house

Library catalogue: All or part available in-house

Publications: Printed, and electronic and video

Publications list: Available online and in print

Access to staff: Contact by letter, by telephone and by e-mail
Hours: Mon to Fri, 0900 to 1700

Access to building: No access

NORWEGIAN TRADE COUNCIL

Formal name: Royal Norwegian Embassy, Trade and Technology Office

Charles House, 5–11 Regent Street, London, SW1Y 4LR

Tel: 020 7389 8800
Fax: 020 7973 0189
E-mail: london@ntc.no
Website: www.ntclondon.com

Enquiries to: Information Officer

Organisation type and purpose: National government body.

Subject coverage: Companies in Norway, export products, Norwegian companies in UK and Ireland.

Collection: Norway export brochures

Non-library collection catalogue: All or part available in-house

Library catalogue: All or part available in-house

Publications: Printed

Access to staff: Contact by letter, by telephone, by fax, by e-mail and via website
Hours: Mon to Fri, 0900 to 1700

Access to building: No access other than to staff

Access for disabled people: Level entry

NORWICH CITY COLLEGE OF FURTHER EDUCATION

Library, Ipswich Road, Norwich, Norfolk, NR2 2LJ

Tel: 01603 773224
Fax: 01603 760326
E-mail: tis@ccn.ac.uk
Website: heritage.ccn.ac.uk

Enquiries to: Learning Resources Manager
Direct tel: 01603 773045

Organisation type and purpose: FE and HE College library.

Subject coverage: Business management, hospitality industry, science, construction, electrical and mechanical engineering, hair, beauty, sport and leisure, health, social care and early years education.

Non-library collection catalogue: All or part available in-house

Library catalogue: All or part available online

Publications: Printed
Access for disabled people: Parking provided, access to all public areas, toilet facilities

NORWICH CITY COUNCIL

City Hall, Norwich, Norfolk, NR2 1NH

Tel: 01603 622233\ Minicom no. 01603 212059
Fax: 01603 213000
Website: www.norwich.gov.uk

Enquiries to: Public Relations Manager

Organisation type and purpose: Local government body.

Access to staff: Contact by letter, by telephone, by fax and in person. Appointment necessary.
Hours: Mon to Fri, 0900 to 1700

NORWICH PUPPET THEATRE (NPT)

Formal name: Norwich Puppet Theatre Trust Ltd

St James's, Whitefriars, Norwich, Norfolk, NR3 1TN

Tel: 01603 615564
Fax: 01603 617578
E-mail: info@puppettheatre.co.uk
Website: www.puppettheatre.co.uk

Enquiries to: Manager
Other contacts: Education & Outreach Officer

Founded: 1978

Organisation type and purpose: Registered charity (charity number 271041).
Theatre.
Puppet theatre with 20-year archive of own puppets, access to some written references.

Subject coverage: Puppetry and puppet theatre.

Education services: Gemma Khawaja, Education & Outreach Officer

Collection: Puppets from the last 20 years

Access to staff: Contact by letter, by telephone, by fax, by e-mail and in person. Appointment necessary.
Hours: Mon to Fri, 0930 to 1630

Access to building: Mon to Fri; performance Sat
Hours: Mon to Fri, 0930 to 1630; other times by appointment

Access for disabled people: Level entry, access to all public areas, toilet facilities

NOTTINGHAM BUSINESS CENTRES

Lenton Boulevard, Nottingham, NG7 2BY

Tel: 0115 955 2107/0115 915 9245
Fax: 0115 955 2108
E-mail: info@nottinghambusinesscentres.co.uk
Website: www.nbtg.co.uk

Enquiries to: Service Manager

Organisation type and purpose: Local government body, service industry.
Commercial property provider and business support.
Provide managed workspace (offices and workshops) for start-up and expanding small businesses in Nottingham City area.

Subject coverage: Commercial property, licensed business accommodation, managed workspace, business centres, support for start-up businesses, support for expanding small businesses, availability of business premises in Nottingham.

Trade and statistical information: Data on the cost of business premises.
Data on support available for small businesses in Nottingham

Publications: Printed

Access to staff: Contact by letter, by telephone and by fax. Appointment necessary.
Hours: Mon to Fri, 0830 to 1700

Links with: Nottingham City Council; Design & Property Services, Severns House, Middle Pavement, Nottingham, NG1 7BW; tel: 0115 915 5555; fax: 0115 915 8307

Satellite Offices: Ashforth Business Centre; Ashforth Street, St Ann's, Nottingham, NG3 4BG; tel: 0115 955 2017/0115 915 9245; fax: 0115 955 2108; Bulwell Business Centre; Sellers Wood Drive, Bulwell, Nottingham, NG6 8GN; tel: 0115 955 2107 (main switchboard); fax: 0115 955 2108; Helston Drive Business Centre

NOTTINGHAM CENTRAL LIBRARY

Angel Row, Nottingham, NG1 6HP

Tel: 0115 915 2828; minicom no. 0115 915 2847
Fax: 0115 915 2840
E-mail: enquiryline@nottinghamcity.gov.uk
Website: www.mynottingham.gov.uk/libraries

Enquiries to: Librarian
Direct tel: 0115 915 2842
Direct e-mail: enquiryline@nottinghamcity.gov.uk

Founded: 1868

Organisation type and purpose: Local government body, public library.

Subject coverage: Information service offered across all subject areas, and specialist local studies service.

Collection: Byron Collection
D. H. Lawrence Collection
Local Printing Collection
Robin Hood Collection
UK Ordnance Survey and street maps
Drama sets
Music sets
19th century government publications

Library catalogue: All or part available online and in-house

Access to staff: Contact by letter, by telephone, by fax, by e-mail, in person and via website
Hours: Mon, 0900 to 1900, Tues 0930 to 1900, Weds, Thurs, 0900 to 1900, Fri, 0900 to 1730, Sat, 0900 to 1600

Access for disabled people: Ramped entry, access to all public areas, toilet facilities

Links with: Nottinghamshire County Library; Trent Bridge House, Fox Road, West Bridgford, Nottingham, NG2 6BJ; tel: 0115 982 3823; fax: 0115 977 2428

NOTTINGHAM CITY COUNCIL

Loxley House, Station Street, Nottingham, NG2 3NG

Tel: 0115 915 5555
Website: www.nottinghamcity.gov.uk

Direct fax: 0115 915 4434

Founded: 1996

Organisation type and purpose: Local government body.

Publications: Printed

Publications list: Available in print

Access to staff: Contact by letter, by telephone, by fax, in person and via website
Hours: Mon to Fri, 0900 to 1700

Access for disabled people: Parking provided, ramped entry, level entry, toilet facilities

NOTTINGHAM TRENT UNIVERSITY

Libraries and Learning Resources, Boots Library, Goldsmith Street, Nottingham, NG1 5LS

Tel: 0115 848 6434
Fax: 0115 848 4485
E-mail: libweb@ntu.ac.uk
Website: www.ntu.ac.uk/llr
Website: opac.ntu.ac.uk

Enquiries to: Administrative Services Manager
Direct tel: 0115 8482775
Direct e-mail: helen.bran@ntu.ac.uk

Organisation type and purpose: University library.

Subject coverage: Art and design, humanities, business, law, education, science and technology, social sciences, animal, rural and environmental sciences, architecture, design and the built environment.

Collection: Lace collection

Trade and statistical information: Statistics collection (United Kingdom and EC)

Publications: Printed, and electronic and video

Access to staff: Contact by letter, by telephone, by fax, by e-mail and in person. Non-members charged.

Access to building: *Hours:* Term time: Mon to Fri, 0830 to 2100; Sat, 0900 to 1700; Sun, 1400 to 1900. Vacations: Mon to Fri, 0830 to 1700; Sat, 1000 to 1400 (closed Sat during August). IT resources rooms open 24 hours.

Also at: Brackenhurst Campus Library; Nottingham Trent University, Nottingham Road, Southwell, NG25 0QF; tel: 01636 8175249; Clifton Campus Library; Nottingham Trent University, Clifton Lane, Nottingham, NG11 8NS; tel: 0115 848 6612; fax: 0115 848 6304

NOTTINGHAMSHIRE ARCHIVES

County House, Castle Meadow Road, Nottingham, NG2 1AG

Tel: 0115 958 1634; 0115 950 4524
Fax: 0115 941 3997
E-mail: archives@nottscc.gov.uk
Website: www.nottinghamshire.gov.uk/archives

Enquiries to: Archivist

Founded: 1949

Organisation type and purpose: Local government body.

Subject coverage: Archives of Nottinghamshire County and Nottingham City, also the Southwell and Nottingham Diocesan Record Office.

Collection: Local authority records, including county, district and parish councils
Public records, including courts and hospitals
Ecclesiastical records, including parish and non-conformist
Family and estate
Business
Societies and organisations

Non-library collection catalogue: All or part available online and in-house

Library catalogue: All or part available in-house

Publications: Microform publications

Publications list: Available online and in print

Access to staff: Contact by letter, by telephone, by fax, by e-mail, in person and via website
Hours: Mon, Wed to Fri, 0900 to 1645; Tue, 0900 to 1915; Sat, 0900 to 1245
Special comments: CARN Readers Ticket required to consult original archives (but not books or microfiche).

Access for disabled people: Parking provided, level entry, toilet facilities
Special comments: Please ring to book parking space.

NOTTINGHAMSHIRE FAMILY HISTORY SOCIETY (NFHS)

The Secretary, 8 Westmaner Court, Hall Drive, Chilwell, Nottingham, NG9 5DQ

Tel: 0115 967 7075
Website: www.nottsfhs.org.uk

Enquiries to: Secretary

Founded: 1971

Organisation type and purpose: Membership association (membership is by subscription), present number of members: 1,800, registered charity (charity number 515898), research organisation.

Subject coverage: Family history in Nottinghamshire.

Publications: Printed, and electronic and video, and microform publications
Order printed publications from: Notts FHS, 10 Sherwin Walk, St Anns, Nottingham, NG3 1AH

Publications list: Available online and in print

Access to staff: Contact by letter, by e-mail and via website
Hours: Mon to Fri, 0900 to 2100

NOTTINGHAMSHIRE LIBRARIES, ARCHIVES & INFORMATION

Nottinghamshire County Council, Culture & Community, 4th Floor, County Hall, West Bridgford, Nottingham, NG2 7QP

Tel: 0115 977 4401
Fax: 0115 977 2806
E-mail: cslibraries@nottscc.gov.uk
Website: www.nottscc.gov.uk/libraries

Enquiries to: Librarian
Direct e-mail: contact.libraries@nottscc.gov.uk
Other contacts: Head of Libraries (Libraries, Archives & Information)

Founded: 1998

Organisation type and purpose: Local government body, public library.

Subject coverage: General, local archives.

Non-library collection catalogue: All or part available online

Library catalogue: All or part available online and in-house

Publications: Printed
Order printed publications from: e-mail: carole.tailby@nottscc.gov.uk or contactlibraries@nottscc.gov.uk; 4th Floor County Hall, NG2 7QP

Publications list: Available online and in print

Access to staff: Contact by letter, by telephone, by fax, by e-mail and in person
Hours: Public Libraries (core times): Mon to Fri, 0930 to 1700; Sat, 0900 to 1300
Special comments: County Library Headquarters Sections at 4th Floor, County Hall, West Bridgford, Nottingham, NG2 7QP: Mon to Fri, 0830 to 1630; not available Sat.

Branch libraries: Arnold Library; Front Street, Arnold, Nottingham, NG5 7EE; tel: 0115 920 2247; fax: 0115 967 3378; e-mail: Arnold.library@nottscc.gov.uk; Beeston Library; Foster Avenue, Beeston, Nottingham, NG9 1AE; tel: 0115 925 5168; fax: 0115 922 0841; e-mail: beeston.library@nottscc.gov.uk; Mansfield Library; Four Seasons Centre, Westgate, Mansfield, Nottinghamshire, NG18 1NH; tel: 01623 627591; fax: 01623 629276; e-mail: mansfield.library@nottscc.gov.uk; Newark Library; Beaumond Gardens, Baldertongate, Newark on Trent, Nottinghamshire, NG24 1UW; tel: 01636 703966; fax: 01636 610045; e-mail: newark.library@nottscc.gov.uk; Nottinghamshire Archives; County House, Castle Meadow Road, Nottingham, NG2 1AG; tel: 0115 950 4524; fax: 0115 941 3997; e-mail: archives@nottscc.gov.uk; Retford Library; Churchgate, Retford, Nottinghamshire, DN22 6PE; tel: 01777 708724; fax: 01777 710020; e-mail: retford.library@nottscc.gov.uk

County Library Headquarters – Education Library Service: Nottinghamshire County Council; Glaisdale Parkway, Nottingham, NG8 4GP; tel: 0115 985 4200; fax: 0115 928 6400; e-mail: valerie.sawyer@nottscc.gov.uk

NOTTINGHAMSHIRE LOCAL HISTORY ASSOCIATION (NLHA)

6 Cornwall Road, Retford, DN22 6SH

Tel: 01777 702475
Website: www.nlha.org.uk

Enquiries to: Chairman
Direct tel: 01623 870515
Other contacts: Membership Secretary (for membership)

Founded: 1960

Organisation type and purpose: Membership association (membership is by subscription), present number of members: 250, voluntary organisation.
Support to history societies, educational institutes, individuals.

Subject coverage: Local history of Nottinghamshire.

Publications: Printed
Order printed publications from: The Editor, NLHA The Notts Historian, 30 Repton Road, West Bridgford, Nottinghamshire, NG2 7EJ; tel: 0115 923 3901

Access to staff: Contact by letter and by telephone
Hours: Mon to Fri, 0900 to 1700

NSPCC

Formal name: National Society for the Prevention of Cruelty to Children

Weston House, 42 Curtain Road, London, EC2A 3NH

Tel: 020 7825 2500 (24-hour child protection helpline: 0808 800 5000)
Fax: 020 7825 2525
E-mail: info@nspcc.org.uk
Website: www.nspcc.org.uk/inform
Website: www.nspcc.org.uk

Enquiries to: NSPCC and ChildLine Public Enquiry Point
Direct tel: 020 7825 2775
Direct fax: 020 7825 2763
Direct e-mail: info@nspcc.org.uk
Other contacts: Records Manager

Founded: 1884

Organisation type and purpose: Voluntary organisation, registered charity (charity number 216401).
Child protection agency.

Subject coverage: Child protection; child abuse; neglect; domestic violence; child welfare; family therapy; social work; prevention; statistics; child development; positive parenting.

Collection: Archives and historical material on the NSPCC dating back to 1884

Library catalogue: All or part available online

Publications: Printed
Order printed publications from: NSPCC Publications tel: 020 7825 7422

Publications list: Available online and in print

Access to staff: Contact by letter, by telephone, by e-mail and via website. Appointment necessary.
Hours: Mon to Fri, 0900 to 1700

Special comments: Library suitable for child protection practitioners and researchers by appointment only. Restricted access to some of the archives.

Access for disabled people: Parking provided, level entry, toilet facilities

NSU OWNERS CLUB (NSUOC)

Nutleigh, Rabies Heath Road, Bletchingley, Surrey, RH1 4LX

Tel: 01883 744431
Fax: 01883 742437
E-mail: nsuoc@btinternet.com
Website: www.nsuoc.co.uk

Enquiries to: General Secretary

Founded: 1961

Organisation type and purpose: International organisation, membership association (membership is by subscription), present number of members: 170.

Subject coverage: Technical advice on NSU cars, contact address in UK and overseas, sources of new and used parts.

Collection: Collection of cards, posters, sales brochures, videos, photographs
Repair books, parts books for most models

Trade and statistical information: Product market values

Publications: Printed

Access to staff: Contact by letter, by telephone and by fax. Appointment necessary.
Hours: Up to 2130

Affiliated to: NSU Gmbh; Postfach 1144, 7107 Neckarsulm, Germany

NSU RO80 CLUB GB

Round Barn, Entwistle, Bolton, Lancashire

Tel: 01204 852425

Enquiries to: Membership Secretary

Founded: 1980

Organisation type and purpose: Membership association (membership is by subscription), present number of members: 100.
Club association.

Subject coverage: NSU, Wankel engine motor car.

Publications: Printed

Publications list: Available in print

Access to staff: Contact by letter and by telephone
Hours: Mon to Fri, 0800 to 2130

Access to building: No access other than to staff

NUCLEAR INDUSTRY ASSOCIATION (NIA)

Carlton House, 22a St James's Square, London, SW1Y 4JH

Tel: 020 7766 6640
Fax: 020 7839 1523
E-mail: info@niauk.org
Website: www.niauk.org

Enquiries to: Chief Executive
Direct e-mail: john.mcnamara@niauk.org
Other contacts: Information Officer for information requests on nuclear power.

Organisation type and purpose: NIA was established in the early 1960s; it is the trade association and information and representative body for the British civil nuclear industry; it represents over 80 companies including the operators of the nuclear power stations, those engaged in decommissioning, waste management, nuclear liabilities management and all aspects of the nuclear fuel cycle, nuclear equipment suppliers, engineering and construction firms; nuclear research organisations; and legal, financial and consultancy companies.

Subject coverage: Nuclear power and its connection with: the environment, UK business, energy costs, pollution and waste, energy strategies, nuclear reactors, DTI and parliament, safety.

Publications: Printed

Access to staff: Contact by letter, by telephone, by fax, by e-mail and via website. Appointment necessary.
Hours: Mon to Fri, 0900 to 1700

NUFFIELD COLLEGE LIBRARY

New Road, Oxford, OX1 1NF

Tel: 01865 278550
Fax: 01865 278621
E-mail: library-enquiries@nuffield.ox.ac.uk
Website: www.nuffield.ox.ac.uk/library

Enquiries to: Librarian
Direct e-mail: librarian@nuffield.ox.ac.uk

Founded: 1937

Organisation type and purpose: Library of a college of the University of Oxford.

Subject coverage: Social sciences (economics, politics, sociology).

Collection: G. D. H. Cole Collection
Modern manuscripts (political, social, economic)
William Cobbett Collection
Lord Cherwell Archives

Non-library collection catalogue: All or part available online

Library catalogue: All or part available online

Access to staff: Contact by letter, by telephone, by fax, by e-mail, in person and via website. Appointment necessary.
Hours: Mon to Fri, 0930 to 1730
Special comments: No information service outside the University, except for Archives.

NUFFIELD COUNCIL ON BIOETHICS (NCOB)

28 Bedford Square, London, WC1B 3JS

Tel: 020 7681 9619
Fax: 020 7637 1712
E-mail: bioethics@nuffieldfoundation.org
Website: www.nuffieldfoundation.org/bioethics

Enquiries to: Director

Founded: 1991

Organisation type and purpose: Voluntary organisation.
Voluntary council.

Subject coverage: Ethical questions raised by recent advances in biological and medical research, home and abroad.

Collection: Material on bioethics abroad
Press cuttings on bioethics in the UK

Publications: Printed

Publications list: Available online

Access to staff: Contact by letter, by fax and by e-mail
Hours: Mon to Fri, 0900 to 1700

Appointed by the: Trustees of the Nuffield Foundation

NURSING AND MIDWIFERY COUNCIL (NMC)

23 Portland Place, London, W1B 1PZ

Tel: 020 7637 7181
Fax: 020 7436 2924
E-mail: communications@nmc-uk.org
Website: www.nmc-uk.org

Enquiries to: Communications Manager
Direct e-mail: nina.rossi@nmc-uk.org

Founded: 2002

Organisation type and purpose: Registered charity in England (charity number 1091434) and Scotland (charity number SC038362).
Statutory regulatory body.
To safeguard the health and wellbeing of the public by continually regulating, reviewing and promoting nursing and midwifery standards.
Aims to uphold the reputation of the professions in the eyes of the public, government, other healthcare organisations, and nurses and midwives themselves.

Subject coverage: Issues relating to the Council's statutory responsibilities regarding registration, pre-registration and post-registration education; professional conduct of all nurses and midwives on the Council's register in the United Kingdom.

Publications: Printed
Order printed publications from: http://nmc-uk.linney.com/orderpage1.aspx

Publications list: Available online and in print

Access to staff: Contact by letter, by telephone, by fax, by e-mail, in person and via website
Hours: Mon to Fri, 0800 to 1700

Access to building: Prior appointment usually required

Access for disabled people: Ramped entry, toilet facilities

NUTRICIA LIMITED

New Market Avenue, Whitehorse Business Park, Trowbridge, Wiltshire, BA14 0XQ

Tel: 01225 711677
Fax: 01225 711972

Enquiries to: Librarian
Direct tel: ext 1731
Direct e-mail: bwilliams@nutricia.co.uk

continued overleaf

Organisation type and purpose: Manufacturing industry.

Subject coverage: Infant nutrition, general nutrition, food technology and milk technology.

Collection: Infant feeding bottles dating back to the early 18th century

Library catalogue: All or part available in-house

Publications: Printed

Publications list: Available in print

Access to staff: Contact by letter and by e-mail
Hours: Tue to Thu, 0900 to 1600

Access to building: No access other than to staff

Access for disabled people: Parking provided, toilet facilities

Subsidiary of: Nutricia Limited

NUTRITION SOCIETY (Nut Soc)

Unit 10, Cambridge Court, 210 Shepherds Bush Road, London, W6 7NJ

Tel: 020 7602 0228
Fax: 020 7602 1756
E-mail: info_officer@nutsoc.org.uk
Website: www.nutritionsociety.org

Enquiries to: Chief Executive
Direct e-mail: office@nutsoc.org.uk

Founded: 1941

Organisation type and purpose: Learned society, registered charity (charity number 272071).

Subject coverage: Nutrition.

Publications: Printed

Publications list: Available online and in print

Access to staff: Contact by letter, by telephone, by fax, by e-mail and via website
Hours: Mon to Fri, 0900 to 1700

Headquarters address: Nutrition Society; 10 Cambridge Court, 210 Shepherds Bush Road, London, W6 7NJ; tel: 020 7602 0228; fax: 020 7602 1756

OAKLANDS COLLEGE

Smallford Campus, Hatfield Road, St Albans, Hertfordshire, AL4 0JA

Tel: 01727 737700
Fax: 01727 737752
E-mail: gill.hall@oaklands.ac.uk
Website: colleges.herts.ac.uk
Website: www.oaklands.ac.uk

Enquiries to: Learning Resources Supervisor
Direct tel: 01727 737716/7

Founded: 1921

Organisation type and purpose: College learning resources centre.

Subject coverage: Science and husbandry of British agriculture, horticulture, floristry, equine studies and small animal care.

Non-library collection catalogue: All or part available online

Library catalogue: All or part available online

Access to staff: Contact by letter, by telephone, by fax and by e-mail
Hours: Term time: Mon to Thu, 0900 to 2000; Fri, 0900 to 1600
Vacations: Mon to Thu, 0900 to 1700; Fri, 0900 to 1630

Other sites at: Oakland College; St Albans City Campus; tel: 01727 737000; fax: 01727 737010; Oakland College; Borehamwood Campus; tel: 01727 737400; fax: 01727 737440; Oakland College; Welwyn Garden City Campus, Welwyn Garden City; tel: 01707 737500; fax: 01707 737544

OCCUPATIONAL AND ENVIRONMENTAL DISEASES ASSOCIATION (OEDA)

PO Box 26, Enfield, Middlesex, EN1 2NT

Tel: 020 8360 6413
Website: www.oeda.demon.co.uk

Enquiries to: Director
Direct fax: 020 8360 6413

Founded: 1978

Organisation type and purpose: Voluntary organisation, registered charity (charity number 1031036), consultancy, asbestos research organisation and information resource.
Advice on prevention and information to help those affected by asbestos.

Subject coverage: Asbestos-related illnesses including asbestosis, mesothelioma, pneumoconiosis, pleural plaques, and asbestos-related lung cancer

Collection: Early papers on asbestos

Publications: Printed

Publications list: Available in print

Access to staff: Contact by letter. Appointment necessary.
Hours: Mon to Fri, 0930 to 1700

Access to building: Prior appointment required

Access for disabled people: *Special comments:* All communications by letter or phone

OCKENDEN INTERNATIONAL

PO Box 1275, Woking, Surrey GU22 2FT

Tel: 01483 772012
Fax: 01483 750774
E-mail: enquiries@ockenden.org.uk
Website: www.ockenden.org.uk

Enquiries to: Head of Policy
Direct e-mail: graham.wood@ockenden.org.uk

Founded: 1951

Organisation type and purpose: International organisation, registered charity (charity number 1053720).
Assistance to refugees.

Subject coverage: Support to refugees and displaced people, primarily overseas but also through reception services and residential care in the United Kingdom.

Collection: Annual Reports of Ockenden Venture's work from the early 1960s

Publications: Printed, and electronic and video

Access to staff: Contact by letter, by fax and by e-mail
Hours: Mon to Fri, 0900 to 1730

Access for disabled people: Parking provided, level entry, toilet facilities

Member agency of the: British Aid to Afghanistan Group; British Refugee Council; International Consortium for Refugees in Iran

OFCOM

Riverside House, 2a Southwark Bridge Road, London, SE1 9HA

Tel: 020 7981 3000
Fax: 020 7981 3333
Website: www.ofcom.org.uk
Website: www.ofcom.org.uk/consumer_guides/

Enquiries to: Ofcom Contact Centre
Direct tel: 0845 456 3000; 0845 456 6006 (textphone)
Direct fax: 0845 456 3333
Direct e-mail: contact@ofcom.org.uk

Founded: 2003; combined from Broadcasting Standards Commission, Independent Television Commission, Oftel, Radio Authority, Radiocommunications Agency

Organisation type and purpose: Communications regulator
Responsible for: complaints handling (including telecommunications, broadcasting content and TV/radio interference); general enquiries or queries regarding licensing spectrum (including fees), broadcasting or telecommunications; business radio licensing authorisations; publication requests

Publications: Printed

Publications list: Available online

Access to staff: Contact by telephone, by fax and by e-mail

OFFA'S DYKE ASSOCIATION (ODA)

West Street, Knighton, Powys, LD7 1EN

Tel: 01547 528753
E-mail: oda@offasdyke.demon.co.uk
Website: www.offasdyke.demon.co.uk

Enquiries to: Centre Manager

Founded: 1969

Organisation type and purpose: Membership association, registered charity (charity number 503821).
Official tourist information centre.

Subject coverage: Offa's Dyke as walking route (facilities and accommodation for walkers), history of Offa and the Dyke, history of Knighton as tourist centre, Welsh Border environmental and planning issues.

Collection: Frank Noble library of books etc on Offa's Dyke and Welsh Border History

Publications: Printed, and electronic and video

Publications list: Available online and in print

Access to staff: Contact by letter, by telephone, by fax, by e-mail, in person and via website
Hours: Easter to end October: daily, 1000 to 1700
End of October to Easter: Mon, Wed, Fri, Sat, 1000 to 1600; Tue, Thu, 1000 to 1700

Access for disabled people: Parking provided, level entry, access to all public areas, toilet facilities

Connections with: Countryside Commission; Countryside Council for Wales; Powys County Council; Wales Tourist Board; Youth Hostels Association

OFFENDER'S TAG ASSOCIATION (OTA)

128 Kensington Church Street, London, W8 4BH

Tel: 020 7221 7166
Fax: 020 7792 9288
E-mail: ota@stacey-international.co.uk
Website: www.offenderstag.co.uk

Enquiries to: Director

Founded: 1982

Organisation type and purpose: Independent organisation.
To promote use of electronic tagging to reduce offending.

Subject coverage: Penal affairs, electronic monitoring of offenders.

Publications: Printed

Publications list: Available online and in print

Access to staff: Contact by letter, by fax and by e-mail
Hours: Mon to Fri, 0900 to 1700

Access to building: No prior appointment required

OFFICE FOR NATIONAL STATISTICS (ONS)

Government Buildings, Cardiff Road, Newport, NP10 8XG

Tel: 0845 6013034; minicom no. 01633 812399
Fax: 01633 652747
E-mail: info@statistics.gov.uk
Website: www.ons.gov.uk

Founded: 1996

Organisation type and purpose: Government department and agency for the collection and publication of UK industrial and economic and social statistics, reports to United Kingdom Statistics Authority.

Subject coverage: Statistics on national income, finance, balance of payments, household expenditure; social statistics; regional statistics; employment/unemployment data; census; economy.

Trade and statistical information: Statistics on: manufacturing of specific products, selected service industries, invisible trade, gross national product, balance of payments, price indices, social and regional trends, census and demographic data, social surveys and social historical data

Library catalogue: All or part available online

Publications: Printed, and electronic and video
Order printed publications from: Palgrave Macmillan for all ONS Publications

Publications list: Available online and in print

Access to staff: Contact by letter, by telephone, by fax, by e-mail and in person. Appointment necessary.
Hours: Mon to Fri, 0900 to 1700

Access for disabled people: Ramped entry; toilet facilities

Also at: Office for National Statistics; Segensworth Road, Titchfield, Fareham, Hampshire, PO15 5RR; tel: 0845 601 3034; e-mail: info@ons.gov.uk

OFFICE FOR NATIONAL STATISTICS LIBRARY (LONDON)

1 Drummond Gate, London, SW1V 2QQ

Tel: 0845 6013034\ Minicom no. 01633 812399
Fax: 01633 652747
E-mail: info@statistics.gov.uk
Website: www.statistics.gov.uk

Enquiries to: Librarian

Founded: 1996

Organisation type and purpose: National government body.

Subject coverage: Demography, epidemiology, vital registration e.g. births, deaths and marriages, survey methodology, census, economic and financial data, business data, data from the government's statistical service.

Collection: All published census data from 1801 onwards
Demographic and health statistics 1837 onwards
Government social survey reports 1941 onwards
International statistics, e.g. UN, WHO

Publications list: Available online

Access to staff: Contact by letter, by telephone, by fax, by e-mail and in person
Hours: Mon to Fri, 0900 to 1700

Access to building: No prior appointment required
Hours: Mon to Fri, 0900 to 1700

Access for disabled people: Ramped entry, toilet facilities

Branch library: Segensworth Road; Titchfield, Fareham, Hampshire, PO15 5RR

Other addresses: Office for National Statistics Library (Newport); Government Buildings, Cardiff Road, Newport, Gwent, NP9 1XG; tel: 0845 6013034

OFFICE OF COMMUNICATIONS (OFCOM)

Riverside House, 2a Southwark Bridge Road, London SE1 9HA

Tel: 020 7981 3000
Fax: 020 7981 3333
E-mail: ofcomnews@ofcom.org.uk
Website: www.ofcom.org.uk

Enquiries to: Information Officer
Direct e-mail: ofcomnews@ofcom.org.uk

Founded: 1984; formerly called Office of Telecommunications (OFTEL)

Organisation type and purpose: National government body.
Non-ministerial government department.

Subject coverage: Telecommunications, information technology, consumer affairs and competition policy.

Collection: Public register of licences, approved apparatus and approved maintainers of the apparatus (visitors by prior appointment)

Library catalogue: All or part available in-house

Publications: Printed

Publications list: Available online and in print

Access to staff: Contact by letter, by telephone, by fax, by e-mail and via website. Appointment necessary.
Hours: Mon to Fri, 0930 to 1200 and 1400 to 1600
Special comments: Access only allowed by prior appointment.

Parent body: Department of Trade and Industry – for Library Service

OFFICE OF FAIR TRADING (OFT)

Fleetbank House, 2–6 Salisbury Square, London, EC4Y 8JX

Tel: 020 7211 8000
Fax: 020 7211 8800
E-mail: enquiries@oft.gsi.gov.uk
Website: www.oft.gov.uk

Enquiries to: Publicity Officer
Direct e-mail: laura.osborne@oft.gsi.gov.uk

Founded: 1973

Organisation type and purpose: National government body.

Subject coverage: Consumer affairs, consumer credit (including trader guidance), competition policy, monopolies, mergers, restrictive trade practices, anti-competitive practices, estate agency.

Collection: Consumer Credit Licences public register
Estate Agents Act public register
Restrictive Trading Agreements public register

Non-library collection catalogue: All or part available online

Publications: Printed

Publications list: Available online and in print

Access to staff: Contact by letter, by telephone, by fax, by e-mail and via website
Hours: Mon to Fri, 0900 to 1700

Access to building: Prior appointment required
Special comments: Access only to public registers by appointment.

continued overleaf

Common service ties exist with the: Department of Trade and Industry

Parliamentary responsibility lies with the: Secretary of State for Trade and Industry

OFFICE OF GAS AND ELECTRICITY MARKETS (Ofgem)

9 Millbank, London, SW1P 3GE

Tel: 020 7901 7000
Fax: 020 7901 7066
E-mail: library@ofgem.gov.uk
Website: www.ofgem.gov.uk

Enquiries to: Librarian
Direct tel: 020 7901 7003
Direct e-mail: keith.smith@ofgem.gov.uk

Founded: 1999; created by the merger of OFFER and OFGAS (year of change 1999)

Organisation type and purpose: National government body, advisory body, statutory body, regulatory body.
Independent government watchdog for the gas and electricity industry.

Subject coverage: Regulation of the gas and electricity industry.

Collection: Various journals on the gas, electricity and utility industry

Library catalogue: All or part available in-house

Publications: Printed

Publications list: Available online and in print

Access to staff: Contact by telephone and by e-mail
Hours: Mon to Fri, 800 to 1730

Access to building: Prior appointment required

Access for disabled people: Access to all public areas, toilet facilities

OFFICE OF HEALTH ECONOMICS (OHE)

Southside, 7th Floor, 105 Victoria Street, London, SW1E 6QT

Tel: 020 7747 8850
Fax: 020 7747 8851
Website: www.ohe.org

Enquiries to: Business Executive
Direct e-mail: ksheppard@ohe.org

Founded: 1962

Organisation type and purpose: Consultancy, research organisation, publishing house.

Subject coverage: Economics of the pharmaceutical industry, healthcare, health technology, assessment, biotechnology industry and related public policy issues.

Trade and statistical information: Compendium of Health Statistics, providing statistical data on health and healthcare in the UK and comparative data with economically developed nations.
Health Economics Evaluation Database (HEED) containing approximately 23,500 economic evaluations, carefully selected for use by health economists

Publications: Printed, and electronic and video

Publications list: Available online and in print

Access to staff: Contact by letter, by telephone, by fax, by e-mail and via website
Hours: Mon to Fri, 0900 to 1700

Access to building: Prior appointment required

Funded by: Association of the British Pharmaceutical Industry; 12 Whitehall, London, SW1A 2DY; tel: 020 7930 3477; fax: 020 7747 1411; e-mail: abpi@abpi.org.uk

OFFICE OF MANPOWER ECONOMICS (OME)

6th Floor, Victoria House, Southampton Row, London, WCIB 4AD

Tel: 020 7271 0497
Fax: 020 7271 0499
Website: www.ome.uk.com

Enquiries to: Press Officer
Direct tel: 020 7271 0468

Founded: 1971

Organisation type and purpose: Secretariat to the Independent Pay Review Bodies and Police Boards

Access to staff: Contact by letter and by telephone
Hours: Mon to Fri, 0900 to 1700

Access for disabled people: Toilet facilities

OFFICE OF THE CHIEF RABBI

Formal name: Office of the Chief Rabbi of the United Hebrew Congregations of the Commonwealth

305 Ballards Lane, London, N12 8GB

Tel: 020 8343 6301
Fax: 020 8343 6310
E-mail: info@chiefrabbi.org
Website: www.chiefrabbi.org

Enquiries to: Chief Executive
Other contacts: Director of Communications for media.

Founded: 1700

Organisation type and purpose: Religious institution.

Subject coverage: Judaism.

Collection: Anglo-Jewish historical archives

Publications: Printed

Publications list: Available online and in print

Access to staff: Contact by letter, by telephone, by fax, by e-mail and via website. Appointment necessary.
Hours: Mon to Fri, 0900 to 1700

Access to building: Prior appointment required

Houses the: Chief Rabbinate of the British Commonwealth

Other addresses: Court of The Chief Rabbi

OFFICE OF THE PARLIAMENTARY AND HEALTH SERVICE OMBUDSMAN (PHSO)

Millbank Tower, Millbank, London, SW1P 4QP

Tel: 0845 015 4033
Fax: 0300 061 4000
E-mail: phso.enquiries@ombudsman.org.uk
Website: www.ombudsman.org.uk

Enquiries to: Information Manager
Direct tel: 0300 061 3997
Direct fax: 0300 061 1565
Direct e-mail: lrc@ombudsman.gsi.gov.uk

Founded: 1967

Organisation type and purpose: Statutory body.
Investigation of complaints by members of the public who have suffered injustice through maladministration by government departments or certain public bodies, or the National Health Service.

Subject coverage: Ombudsman schemes.

Publications: Printed

Access to staff: Contact by letter, by telephone, by fax, by e-mail and via website
Hours: Mon to Fri, 0900 to 1700

Access to building: No prior appointment required

OFFICE OF THE REPRESENTATIVE OF NOVI SAD (ORNS)

Glebelands, Star Lane, Rockland St Mary, Norwich, Norfolk, NR14 7BX

Tel: 01508 480262
Fax: 01508 480262
E-mail: orns@lineone.net

Enquiries to: Appointed Representative

Founded: 1999

Organisation type and purpose: To represent the city of Novi Sad in Great Britain and elsewhere.

Subject coverage: Information on Novi Sad and its environs, information for businesses, assistance in making commercial contacts.

Access to staff: Contact by letter, by telephone, by fax and by e-mail
Hours: Mon to Fri, 0900 to 1700

Links with: British Embassy; Belgrade; Serbian Embassy; London

OFFICE OF TIBET

Tibet House, 1 Culworth Street, London, NW8 7AF

Tel: 020 7722 5378
Fax: 020 7722 0362
E-mail: samdup@tibet.ca
Website: www.tibet.com

Enquiries to: Secretary/Press & Information Officer

Founded: 1981

Organisation type and purpose: To represent the Central Tibetan Administration of His Holiness the Dalai Lama based in Dharamsala, India. The Office of Tibet based in London is the official agency of His Holiness the Dalai Lama for the UK, Northern Europe, the Baltic States and Poland.

Subject coverage: Information on Tibet and Tibetan affairs, including the Central Tibetan Administration of His Holiness the Dalai Lama.

Collection: Small information library on Tibet and Tibetan affairs

Publications list: Available in print

Access to staff: Contact by letter, by telephone, by fax, by e-mail and via website. Appointment necessary.
Hours: Mon to Fri, 0900 to 1700

Parent body: Central Tibetan Administration of H H the Dalai Lama; Dharamsala, India; tel: +91 1892 222457; fax: +91 1892 224957; e-mail: diir@gov.tibet.net; website: http://www.tibet.net

OFFICE OF WATER SERVICES (OFWAT)

Centre City Tower, 7 Hill Street, Birmingham, B5 4UA

Tel: 0121 644 7500
Fax: 0121 644 7559
E-mail: mailbox@ofwat.gsi.gov.uk
Website: www.ofwat.gov.uk

Enquiries to: Librarian & Information Services Manager
Direct tel: 0121 625 1361
Direct fax: 0121 625 1362

Founded: 1989

Organisation type and purpose: National government body.
Central government department.
Economic regulator for the water industry.

Subject coverage: Water industry; economic regulation, privatisation, consumer protection.

Collection: Director General's register

Publications: Printed, and electronic and video

Publications list: Available online and in print

Access to staff: Contact by letter, by telephone, by fax, by e-mail and via website. Appointment necessary.
Hours: Mon to Fri, 0930 to 1630

Access to building: Prior appointment required
Hours: Mon to Fri, 0930 to 1630
Regulates 34 privately-owned companies

OFFICE OF WATER SERVICES – COMPANIES REGULATED BY OFWAT

Local Water Companies Regulated by OFWAT: Albion Water Limited; 71 Clarence Road, Teddington, Middlesex, TW11 0BN; tel: 020 8977 3955; fax: 020 8977 3185; website: http://www.albionwater.co.uk
Independent Water Networks Ltd; Driscoll 2, Ellen Street, Cardiff, CF10 4BP; tel: 0845 055 6196; website: www.iwnl.co.uk
Peel Water Networks; Peel Dome, The Trafford Centre, Manchester, M17 8PL; website: www.peel.co.uk
SSE Water Ltd; 55 Vastern Road, Reading, RG1 8BU; tel: 0118 958 0100; fax: 0118 953 4028; website: www.sse.com
Veolia Water Projects; Fifth Floor, Kings Place, 90 York Way, London, N1 9AG; tel: 0207 843 8500; fax: 0207 843 8560; website: www.veoliawater.co.uk

Water and Sewerage Companies Regulated by OFWAT: Anglian Water Services Limited; Anglian House, Ambury Road, Huntingdon, Cambridgeshire, PE29 3NZ; tel: 01480 323000; fax: 01480 323115; website: www.anglianwater.co.uk
Dwr Cymru Cyfyngedig (Welsh Water); Pentwyn Road, Nelson, Treharris, Mid Glamorgan, CF46 6LY; tel: 01443 452300; fax: 01443 452323; website: http://www.dwrcymru.co.uk
Northumbrian Water Limited; Abbey Road, Pity Me, Durham, DH1 5FJ; tel: 0191 383 2222; fax: 0191 384 1920; website: http://www.nwl.co.uk/
Severn Trent Water Limited; Severn Trent Centre, 2 Saint John's Street, Coventry, CV1 2LZ; tel: 024 7771 5000; website: http://www.stwater.co.uk
South West Water Limited; Peninsula House, Rydon Lane, Exeter, EX2 7HR; tel: 01392 446688; fax: 01392 434966; website: http://www.southwestwater.co.uk
Southern Water Services Limited; Southern House, Yeoman Road, Worthing, Sussex, BN13 3NX; tel: 01903 264444; fax: 01903 262185; website: http://www.southernwater.co.uk
Thames Water Utilities Limited; Clearwater Court, Vastern Road, Reading, Berkshire, RG1 8DB; tel: 0845 9200 888; fax: 01793 424291; website: http://www.thameswater.co.uk
United Utilities Water plc; Haweswater House, Lingley Mere Business Park, Lingely Green Avenue, Great Sankey, Warrington, WA5 3LP; tel: 0845 746 2255; fax: 01925 237073; website: http://www.unitedutilities.com/
Wessex Water Services Limited; Claverton Down Road, Claverton Down, Bath, BA2 7WW; tel: 01225 526000; fax: 01225 528000; website: http://www.wessexwater.co.uk
Yorkshire Water Services Limited; Western House, Western Way, Bradford, BD6 2LZ; tel: 01274 691111; fax: 01274 604764; website: http://www.yorkshirewater.com/

Water only Companies Regulated by OFWAT: Bristol Water plc; PO Box 218, Bridgwater Road, Bristol, BS99 7AU; tel: 0117 966 5881; fax: 0117 963 4576; website: www.bristolwater.co.uk
Cambridge Water Company plc; 41 Rustat Road, Cambridge, CB1 3QS; tel: 01223 706050; fax: 01223 214052; website: http://www.cambridge-water.co.uk/
Cholderton and District Water Company Limited; Estate Office, Cholderton, Salisbury, Wiltshire, SP4 0DR; tel: 01980 629203; fax: 01980 629307; website: www.choldertonwater.co.uk
Dee Valley Water plc; Packsaddle, Wrexham Road, Rhostyllen, Wrexham, Clwyd, LL14 7EH; tel: 01978 846946; fax: 01978 846888; website: www.deevalleywater.co.uk
Portsmouth Water plc; PO Box 8, West Street, Havant, Hampshire, PO9 1LG; tel: 023 9249 9888; fax: 023 9245 3632; website: http://www.portsmouthwater.co.uk
Sembcorp Bournemouth Water Ltd; George Jessel House, Francis Avenue, Bournemouth, BH11 8NX; tel: 01202 591111; fax: 01202 597022; website: http://www.sembcorpbw.co.uk
South East Water Ltd; Rocfort Road, Snodland, Kent, ME6 5AH; tel: 033 3000 0002; fax: 01634 242764; website: http://www.southeastwater.co.uk
South Staffordshire Water plc; Green Lane, Walsall, West Midlands, WS2 7PD; tel: 01922 638282; fax: 01922 723631; website: http://www.south-staffs-water.co.uk
Sutton and East Surrey Water plc; London Road, Redhill, Surrey, RH1 1LJ; tel: 01737 772000; fax: 01737 766807; website: http://www.waterplc.com

OFFICERS' ASSOCIATION

1st Floor, Mountbarrow House, 6–20 Elizabeth Street, London, SW1W 9RB

Tel: 020 7808 4160
Fax: 020 7808 4161
E-mail: info@officersassociation.org.uk
Website: www.officersassociation.org.uk

Founded: 1920

Organisation type and purpose: The Officers' Association, which was founded 90 years ago, is the only charity dedicated exclusively to supporting officers and ex-officers from all three services and their dependants.

Subject coverage: Providing employment services for service leavers and ex-serving officers at all stages of their working lives, and benevolence services in the form of financial and welfare support.

Access to staff: Contact by letter, by telephone, by fax and by e-mail
Hours: Mon to Fri, 0900 to 1700

Member organisation of: COBSEO

OFFSHORE ENGINEERING INFORMATION SERVICE

Heriot-Watt University Library, Edinburgh, EH14 4AS

Tel: 0131 451 3579
Fax: 0131 451 3164
E-mail: R.A.MacLeod@hw.ac.uk
Website: www.techextra.ac.uk/offshore

Founded: 1974

Organisation type and purpose: Registered charity, university department or institute, consultancy, research organisation.

Subject coverage: Petroleum and offshore engineering, marine technology, petroleum and marine environmental protection, offshore health and safety.

Publications: Printed, and electronic and video

Access to staff: Contact by letter and by e-mail. Appointment necessary. All charged.
Hours: Mon to Fri, 0900 to 1700

Parent body: Heriot-Watt University Library

OFFSHORE SUPPORT VESSEL ISSUES COMMITTEE

Chamber of Shipping, Carthusian Court, 12 Carthusian Street, London, EC1M 6EZ

Tel: 020 7417 2819
Fax: 020 7600 1534
E-mail: postmaster@british-shipping.org
Website: www.british-shipping.org/

Enquiries to: Secretary

Organisation type and purpose: Trade association.
Represents the owners and operators of UK-based Offshore Support Vessels (OSV's).

Subject coverage: Offshore support vessels serving oil and gas installations.

Access to staff: Contact by letter and by e-mail
Hours: Mon to Fri, 0900 to 1700

One of the Committees of the: Chamber of Shipping

OIL AND COLOUR CHEMISTS ASSOCIATION (OCCA)

Priory House, 967 Harrow Road, Wembley, Middlesex, HA0 2SF

Tel: 020 8908 1086
Fax: 020 8908 1219
E-mail: gensec@occa.org.uk
Website: www.surfex2010.net
Website: surfacecoatingsonline.net

Enquiries to: General Secretary
Direct e-mail: enquiries@occa.org.uk
Other contacts: Assistant General Secretary

Founded: 1917

Organisation type and purpose: Learned society, professional body (membership is by qualification), registered charity, training organisation.

Subject coverage: Raw materials, plant, equipment and services for the paint, ink, resins, varnishes, drying oils, lacquers, adhesives, and treated fabrics industries; organic surface coatings in general.

Library catalogue: All or part available online and in print

Publications: Printed, and electronic and video

Publications list: Available online and in print

Access to staff: Contact by letter, by telephone, by fax, by e-mail and via website
Hours: Mon to Fri, 0900 to 1700

Access to building: No access other than to staff

OLDHAM COLLEGE

Rochdale Road, Oldham, Lancashire, OL9 6AA

Tel: 0161 624 5214
Fax: 0161 785 4234
E-mail: info@oldham.ac.uk
Website: www.oldham.ac.uk/

Enquiries to: Librarian

Organisation type and purpose: Suitable for ages: 16+.

Subject coverage: Mechanical, electrical, electronic and production engineering; building; business studies; mathematics; computing; catering; performing arts.

Access to staff: Contact by telephone, by fax, by e-mail and via website
Hours: Mon to Fri, 0900 to 1700

Access to building: No prior appointment required

Access for disabled people: Level entry

OLDHAM LIBRARIES

Union Street, Oldham, Lancashire, OL1 1DN

Tel: 0161 911 4634/4645 general; 4643 Reference Library
Fax: 0161 911 4630
E-mail: oldham.library@oldham.gov.uk
Website: www.oldham.gov.uk

Enquiries to: Principal Libraries Officer
Direct tel: 0161 911 4632

Organisation type and purpose: Local government body, public library.

Subject coverage: General.

Collection: British Standards on microfiche
Cobbett Collection (books by and about William Cobbett, 1762–1835)

Publications list: Available in print

Access to staff: Contact by letter, by telephone, by fax, by e-mail, in person and via website
Hours: Mon, Wed, Thu, 0930 to 1900; Tue, Fri, 0930 to 1700; Sat, 0930 to 1600

Access for disabled people: Ramped entry, access to all public areas, toilet facilities

OLDHAM LOCAL STUDIES AND ARCHIVES

84 Union Street, Oldham, Lancashire, OL1 1DN

Tel: 0161 770 4654
E-mail: archives@oldham.gov.uk
Website: www.oldham.gov.uk/info/200537/contact/local_studies_and_archives

Enquiries to: Local Studies Officer
Other contacts: Archives Officer (for use of archives)

Founded: 1885

Organisation type and purpose: Local government body, public library.

Subject coverage: History of Oldham, records of predecessor authorities, Oldham County Borough, Urban Districts of Chadderton, Crompton, Failsworth, Lees, Royton, Saddleworth, Springhead and Uppermill.

Collection: Butterworth MSS including press reports 1829 to 1843, notes for Baines History of Lancashire (1836)
Census returns (microfilm)
Extensive record of local Co-operative Society and textile trade unions
Higson antiquarian collection
Newspapers including the Oldham Chronicle 1854 to date, Oldham Standard 1859–1946 (microfilm)
Oldham Walton Archive (collection of material about Sir William Walton)
Oral history
Parish Registers (microfilm)
Personal papers of Dame Sarah and Marjory Lees of Werneth Park including suffragette material
Rowbottom Diaries: daily events in Oldham 1787–1829
Books, pamphlets, maps, press cuttings
20,000 photographs of Oldham's past

Non-library collection catalogue: All or part available in-house

Publications: Printed, and microform publications

Publications list: Available online and in print

Access to staff: Contact by letter, by telephone, by e-mail and in person
Hours: Mon, Thu, 1000 to 1900; Tue, 1000 to 1400; Wed, Fri, 1000 to 1700; Sat, 1000 to 1600

Access for disabled people: Ramped entry, toilet facilities

OMNIBUS SOCIETY (OS)

100 Sandwell Street, Walsall, WS1 3EB

Website: www.omnibussoc.org

Enquiries to: Secretary

Founded: 1929

Organisation type and purpose: Voluntary organisation, registered charity (charity number 1048887).
Independent society.
To study every aspect of the history and development of road passenger transport.

Subject coverage: Public road passenger transport, mainly UK but to a lesser extent abroad, traffic, engineering and methods of operation of buses, coaches, trams and trolleybuses, current and historical.

Collection: The society has a large collection of timetables, fare tables, directories, tickets and other items, many dating back 60 to 70 years

Publications: Printed

Access to staff: Contact by letter and via website. Appointment necessary. Non-members charged.
Hours: Mon to Fri, 0900 to 1700

Access for disabled people: Access available at library

ONE NORTH EAST

Stella House, Goldcrest Way, Newburn Riverside, Newcastle upon Tyne, NE15 8NY

Tel: 0191 229 6200
Fax: 0191 229 6201
E-mail: enquiries@onenortheast.co.uk
Website: www.onenortheast.co.uk

Enquiries to: Corporate Marketing Manager

Founded: 1999

Organisation type and purpose: Regional development agency.

Subject coverage: Economic, business and industrial information on the north of England, environment, investment, technologies, statistical data.

Non-library collection catalogue: All or part available online and in print

Library catalogue: All or part available online

Publications: Printed

Publications list: Available online

Access to staff: Contact by letter, by telephone, by fax, by e-mail and via website. Appointment necessary.
Hours: Mon to Fri, 0900 to 1700

Access for disabled people: Ramped entry, access to all public areas, toilet facilities

ONE PARENT FAMILIES SCOTLAND (OPFS)

13 Gayfield Square, Edinburgh, EH1 3NX

Tel: 0131 556 3899/4563; 0808 801 0323 (Helpline)
Fax: 0131 557 7899
E-mail: info@opfs.org.uk
Website: www.opfs.org.uk

Enquiries to: Information Officer

Founded: 1945

Organisation type and purpose:
Membership organisation (membership is free), present number of members: 400, a charitable company limited by guarantee (company registered at Edinburgh 94860, charity number SCO 06403).
Informing, supporting and inspiring lone parents and services for lone parents and other families.
Advice and support to lone parents in Scotland

Subject coverage: One-parent families, all organisations working for one-parent families, children, divorce and separation, conciliation, health, housing, holidays, childcare, poverty, maintenance, social security/tax, rights issues, statistics, women's issues.

Information services: 29 fact sheets for lone parents, a quarterly e-bulletin and a web site.

Special visitor services: Visits can be arranged for agencies from other countries.

Education services: Training programme for lone parents and agencies working with lone parents.

Services for disabled people: Fact sheets for lone-parent families with disabilities.

Collection: Library of books, leaflets and press cuttings

Publications: Printed, and electronic and video
Order printed publications from: e-mail: info@opfs.org.uk

Publications list: Available online and in print

Access to staff: Contact by letter, by telephone, by fax, by e-mail and via website. Appointment necessary.
Hours: Mon to Fri, 0930 to 1630

Access to building: Headquarters office in first floor flat
Hours: Mon to Fri, 0930 to 1630

Access for disabled people: Limited access

Works in association with: Parenting Across Scotland; 1 Boroughloch Square, Edinburgh, EH8 9NJ; tel: 0131 319 8071; e-mail: pas@children1st.org.uk; website: http://www.parentingacrossscotland.org.

ONE PLUS ONE

Formal name: One Plus One Marriage and Partnership Research

1 Benjamin Street, London, EC1M 5QG

Tel: 020 7553 9530
Fax: 020 7553 9550
E-mail: info@oneplusone.org.uk
Website: www.oneplusone.org.uk

Enquiries to: Information Officer
Other contacts: Communications Co-ordinator for press enquiries.

Founded: 1971

Organisation type and purpose: Registered charity (charity number 1087994), research organisation.
To conduct research into all aspects of marriage and partnership, and to put research findings into use in initiatives such as training programmes.

Subject coverage: All aspects of marriage, divorce and relationships, including both statistics, research reports, international and historical trends.

Information services: Online resources for academics, students, researchers and practitioners involved in the field of family and relationships.

Collection: Marriage manuals of historic interest.
Information on One plus One research and projects

Library catalogue: All or part available in-house

Publications: Printed

Publications list: Available online

Access to staff: Contact by e-mail and via website. Appointment necessary. Non-members charged.
Hours: Mon to Fri, 1000 to 1600

Access to building: Prior appointment required.
Hours: Library; Mon to Fri, 1000 to 1600.
Special comments: Library available by appointment only.

Access for disabled people: Access to all public areas.

ONLINE DATA SERVICES (ODS)

74 Chancery Lane, London, WC2A 1AA

Tel: 020 7404 2100
Fax: 020 7404 8600
E-mail: theapexgroup@netscapeonline.co.uk

Enquiries to: Managing Director

Founded: 1998

Organisation type and purpose:
Consultancy, research organisation.
Business and Information Publisher.

Subject coverage: Market intelligence reports on business, retailing, leisure, consumer and retail markets. Bespoke market and business analysis.

Trade and statistical information: Market intelligence on wide variety of UK markets. Special projects on Europe/World by request

Publications: Printed

Publications list: Available in print

Access to staff: Contact by letter, by telephone and by fax
Hours: Mon to Fri, 0900 to 1700

Access to building: No access other than to staff

Parent body: The Apex Group; at the same address

OPEN AND DISTANCE LEARNING QUALITY COUNCIL (ODLQC)

44 Bedford Row, London, WC1R 4LL

Tel: 020 7447 2543
E-mail: info@odlqc.org.uk
Website: www.odlqc.org.uk

Enquiries to: Chief Executive

Founded: 1969

Organisation type and purpose: Registered charity (charity number 325125).
Independent body, formed with the co-operation of the Secretary of State for Education and Science.
Accrediting body and advisory service for Open and Distance Learning.

Subject coverage: Education, training and tuition, open and distance learning methods and activities, standards and improvement, new techniques, assessment, quality control and accreditation.

Publications: Printed

Access to staff: Contact by letter, by telephone, by fax, by e-mail and via website
Hours: Mon to Fri, 0900 to 1700

OPEN COLLEGE NETWORK LONDON REGION (OCNLR)

Unit 15, Angel Gate, 326 City Road, London, EC1V 2SF

Tel: 020 7278 5511
Fax: 020 7833 8289
E-mail: enquiries@ocnlr.org.uk
Website: www.ocnlr.org.uk

Enquiries to: Chief Executive

Organisation type and purpose: Awarding body.

Access to staff: Contact by letter, by telephone, by fax and by e-mail
Hours: Mon to Fri, 0900 to 1700

OPEN COLLEGE OF THE ARTS (OCA)

Unit 1B, Redbrook Business Park, Wilthorpe Road, Barnsley, South Yorkshire, S75 1JN

Tel: 0800 731 2116
Fax: 01226 730838
E-mail: enquiries@oca-uk.com
Website: www.oca-uk.com
Website: www.weareoca.com
Website: oca-elements.com

Enquiries to: Academic Services
Direct tel: 01226 730495

Founded: 1987

continued overleaf

Organisation type and purpose: Registered charity (charity number 327446), suitable for ages: 16+.
Distance learning.

Subject coverage: Art and design, painting, drawing, textiles, sculpture, garden design, interior design, music, calligraphy, creative writing, water colour, printmaking, art history, photography.

Publications: Printed
Order printed publications from: OCA

Access to staff: Contact by letter, by telephone, by fax, by e-mail and via website
Hours: Office: Mon to Thu, 0900 to 1700; Fri, 0900 to 1600

Links with: Buckinghamshire New University

OPEN SPACES SOCIETY (OSS)

Formal name: Commons, Open Spaces and Footpaths Preservation Society

25A Bell Street, Henley-on-Thames, Oxfordshire, RG9 2BA

Tel: 01491 573535
Fax: 01491 573051
E-mail: hq@oss.org.uk
Website: www.oss.org.uk

Enquiries to: General Secretary

Founded: 1865

Organisation type and purpose: Learned society, professional body (membership is by subscription), present number of members: 2,600, voluntary organisation, registered charity (charity number 214753).

Subject coverage: Public rights of way, protection of common land, village greens, open spaces, public paths, public access to the countryside.

Collection: Reports of the Society's work since 1868

Publications: Printed

Publications list: Available online and in print

Access to staff: Contact by letter, by telephone, by fax and by e-mail. Access for members only.
Hours: Mon to Fri, 0930 to 1730

OPEN UNIVERSITY (OUCEM)

Centre for Education in Medicine, Walton Hall, Crowther 208, Milton Keynes, Buckinghamshire, MK7 6AA

Tel: 01908 653776
Fax: 01908 659374
E-mail: oucem@open.ac.uk
Website: iet.open.ac.uk/oucem/

Enquiries to: Personal Assistant

Organisation type and purpose: University department or institute. Training organisation, consultancy, research organisation, publishing house.
Postgraduate medical education.

Subject coverage: Postgraduate and continuing medical education.

Publications: Printed, and electronic and video

Publications list: Available online and in print

Access to staff: Contact by letter, by telephone, by fax, by e-mail and via website. Appointment necessary.
Hours: Mon to Fri, 0830 to 1700

Access for disabled people: Parking provided, ramped entry, access to all public areas, toilet facilities

Link with: Open University (IET); Institute of Educational Technology, Milton Keynes, MK7 6AA; tel: 01908 274066; fax: 01908 654173; e-mail: iet-queries@open.ac.uk

OPEN UNIVERSITY LIBRARY AND LEARNING RESOURCES CENTRE (OU)

Walton Hall, Milton Keynes, Buckinghamshire, MK7 6AA

Tel: 01908 653138
Fax: 01908 653571
E-mail: lib-help@open.ac.uk
Website: library.open.ac.uk

Enquiries to: Director of Library Services
Direct tel: 01908 653254
Direct e-mail: n.whitsed@open.ac.uk

Founded: 1969

Organisation type and purpose: University library.

Subject coverage: Modern languages, arts, mathematics, computing, science, social sciences, technology, education, environmental sciences, educational research, management, vocational qualifications, health and social welfare, law.

Collection: Open University distance teaching materials, including television and radio programmes, illustrations and photographs relating to OU work; Fauvel history of mathematics collection held for the British Association for the History of Mathematics; Jennie Lee papers (archive); Betty Boothroyd papers (archive); Walter Perry (first OU vice-chancellor) papers (archive)

Non-library collection catalogue: All or part available online

Library catalogue: All or part available online

Access to staff: Contact by letter, by telephone, by fax, by e-mail, in person and via website
Hours: Mon, Wed, 0830 to 1930; Tue, Thu, 0830 to 2100; Fri, 0830 to 1700; Sat 0900 to 1700

Access for disabled people: Parking provided, access to all public areas, toilet facilities

OPEN UNIVERSITY PRESS (Open UP)

McGraw-Hill House, Shoppenhangers Road, Maidenhead, Berkshire, SL6 2QL

Tel: 01628 502500
Fax: 01628 770224
E-mail: enquiries@openup.co.uk
Website: www.openup.co.uk

Enquiries to: Marketing Manager

Organisation type and purpose: Publishing house.

Subject coverage: Education, higher education, health and social welfare, sociology, politics, psychology, counselling, management, criminology, and media, film and cultural studies.

Publications: Printed
Order printed publications from: Open University Press, McGraw-Hill House, Shoppenhangers Road, Maidenhead, SL6 2QL

Publications list: Available in print

Access to staff: Contact by letter, by telephone, by fax, by e-mail and via website. Appointment necessary.
Hours: Mon to Fri, 0900 to 1700

OPTICAL CONSUMER COMPLAINTS SERVICE (OCCS)

PO Box 219, Petersfield, GU32 9BY

Tel: 0844 800 5071
Fax: 01730 265058
E-mail: postbox@opticalcomplaints.co.uk
Website: www.opticalcomplaints.co.uk

Enquiries to: Administrator

Founded: 1992

Organisation type and purpose: Advisory body.
Provides mediation in disputes between patients and registered opticians relating to goods or services supplied by opticians.

Subject coverage: Availability of professional advisers, optical matters, such as eye examination results, prescriptions, dispensing, spectacles, frames, lenses and contact lenses; resolution of complaints by negotiation; communication between practitioners and customers.

Publications: Printed

Access to staff: Contact by letter, by telephone, by fax, by e-mail and via website
Hours: Mon to Fri, 0900 to 1700

Access to building: Not open to visitors

OR SOCIETY (ORS)

Formal name: Operational Research Society

Seymour House, 12 Edward Street, Birmingham, B1 2RX

Tel: 0121 233 9300
Fax: 0121 233 0321
E-mail: email@theorsociety.com
Website: www.theorsociety.com

Enquiries to: General Secretary

Founded: 1954

Organisation type and purpose: Learned society, professional body (membership is by subscription), present number of members: 3,000 (charity number 313713), training organisation, research organisation, publishing house.
Conference organisation. Careers information provider.

Subject coverage: Operational research, management science.

Collection: The Society has a library based at Brunel University Library, Uxbridge

Trade and statistical information: Salaries in operational research

Publications: Printed

Access to staff: Contact by letter, by telephone, by fax, by e-mail and via website. Appointment necessary.
Hours: Mon to Fri, 0830 to 1630

Member organisation of: International Federation of Operational Research Societies (IFORS)

ORAL HISTORY SOCIETY

c/o Department of History, University of Essex, Wivenhoe Park, Colchester, Essex, CO4 3SQ

Tel: 020 7412 7404
Fax: 020 7412 7441
E-mail: rob.perks@bl.uk
Website: www.ohs.org.uk

Enquiries to: Secretary
Direct tel: 020 7412 7405
Other contacts: Editor

Founded: 1969

Organisation type and purpose:
International organisation, national organisation, advisory body, learned society (membership is by subscription), present number of members: c. 1,000, voluntary organisation, registered charity (charity number 288805), training organisation, publishing house.
Regular exchange of information with US oral history organisations and other major fields of oral history activity worldwide.

Subject coverage: Oral history, life story research, reminiscence therapy, local history, sound recording and archiving, interviewing skills, women's history, ethnic community history, sociology and social studies.

Education services: Joint training programme with the British Library

Collection: Central oral history database at the British Library
Informed access to oral history collections throughout Great Britain

Publications: Printed

Publications list: Available in print

Access to staff: Contact by letter, by telephone, by fax and by e-mail
Hours: Mon to Fri, 1000 to 1800

Administers: Oral History Society Regional Network; local membership through local representatives

Links with: British Library Oral History Section; History Workshop movement

ORCHESTRA OF ST JOHN'S (OSJ)

The White House, Eltham College, Grove Park Road, London, SE9 4QF

Tel: 020 8857 8579
Fax: 020 8857 9340
E-mail: info@osj.org.uk

Enquiries to: Assistant to the Chief Executive
Other contacts: (1) Marketing Manager; (2) Concerts Director for (1) Promotional/ Marketing; (2) Concerts, Engagements.

Founded: 1967

Organisation type and purpose: Service industry, registered charity (charity number 289106), suitable for ages: all.
Orchestra (performing arts).
Education, concerts, activities.

Subject coverage: Orchestral music.

Publications: Printed, and electronic and video

Access to staff: Contact by telephone and by e-mail
Hours: Mon to Fri, 0930 to 1730

Connections with: Choir of the Orchestra of St John's (COSJ)

ORCHID SOCIETY OF GREAT BRITAIN (OSGB)

c/o 16 The Rise, Amersham, Buckinghamshire, HP7 9AG

Tel: 01494 434730
E-mail: annerutter@dsl.pipex.com
Website: www.orchid-society-gb.org.uk

Enquiries to: Honorary Secretary

Founded: 1951

Organisation type and purpose:
Membership association (membership is by subscription), present number of members: 1,100, voluntary organisation, registered charity (charity number 261273).

Subject coverage: Growing, conservation and identification of orchids.

Collection: Books, many out of print
Library of 35mm slides of orchids

Publications: Printed

Access to staff: Contact by letter, by telephone and by e-mail
Hours: Mon to Sun, 0900 to 1700
Special comments: sae required for reply.

Affiliated to: American Orchid Society; Royal Horticultural Society

ORDERS AND MEDALS RESEARCH SOCIETY (OMRS)

PO Box 1233, High Wycombe HP11 9BW

Tel: 01494 441207
E-mail: generalsecretary@omrs.org.uk
Website: www.omrs.org.uk

Enquiries to: Membership Secretary
Direct e-mail: membershipsecretary@omrs.org.uk

Founded: 1942

Organisation type and purpose: Learned society (membership is by subscription, election or invitation), present number of members: 2170.

Subject coverage: British Orders, decorations and medals, foreign Orders etc, to a lesser extent, history, provenance and description.

Publications: Printed

Access to staff: Contact by letter
Hours: Mon to Fri, 0900 to 1700

Also at: Orders and Medals Research Society; PO Box 248, Snettisham, Kings Lynn, PE31 7TA

ORDNANCE SURVEY (OS)

Adanac Drive, SOUTHAMPTON, SO16 0AS

Tel: 08456 05 05 05
Fax: 0845 0990 494
E-mail: customerservice@ordnancesurvey.co.uk
Website: www.ordnancesurvey.co.uk
Website: www.shop.ordnancesurveyleisure.co.uk/

Enquiries to: Customer Service Advisor
Direct tel: 08456 050505;

Founded: 1791

Organisation type and purpose: National government body.
Government agency; national mapping organisation.

Subject coverage: Survey and mapping of Great Britain, geodesy, surveying, photogrammetry, remote sensing, cartography, GIS.

Library catalogue: All or part available in-house

Publications: Printed, and electronic and video
Order printed publications from: Sales are through agents – a list is available

Publications list: Available online and in print

Access to staff: Contact by letter, by telephone, by fax, by e-mail and via website
Hours: Mon to Fri, 0830 to 1730
Special comments: Charges made for some services.

Access to building: No prior appointment required
Hours: Exhibition Centre: 0900 to 1700

ORDNANCE SURVEY OF NORTHERN IRELAND (OSNI)

Colby House, Stranmillis Court, Belfast, BT9 5BJ

Tel: 028 9025 5755
Fax: 028 9025 5700
E-mail: customerservices@lpsni.gov.uk
Website: www.osni.gov.uk

Founded: 1791

Organisation type and purpose: National government body.
To supply mapping and geographical information for Northern Ireland.

Collection: Archive of aerial photographs
Archive of large-scale and small-scale maps, street maps and atlases
Digital topographical archive

Publications: Printed, and electronic and video

Publications list: Available online and in print

Access to staff: Contact by letter, by telephone, by fax, by e-mail, in person and via website
Hours: Mon to Fri, 0900 to 1700

Access for disabled people: Parking provided, ramped entry, toilet facilities

ORFF SOCIETY UK

7 Rothesay Avenue, Richmond-upon-Thames, Surrey, TW10 5EB

Tel: 020 8876 1944
Fax: 020 8876 1944
E-mail: orffsocuk@btconnect.com
Website: www.orff.org.uk

Enquiries to: Honorary Secretary

Founded: 1964

Organisation type and purpose:
Professional body (membership is by subscription), present number of members: 127, suitable for all ages, training organisation.
To promote the experience and understanding of Carl Orff's approach to music education; a creative way of teaching music to groups using voices in speech/singing, movement/dance and percussion instruments.

Subject coverage: Information, both specific and related to the Orff approach to music education, as applied to all types of schooling including special education.

Collection: A wide range of books and articles (some in German) on the subject of Orff-Schulwerk (the international name of the Orff approach to music education) by British and American authors

Publications: Printed

Access to staff: Contact by letter, by telephone, by fax, by e-mail and via website
Hours: Mon to Sun, 0900 to 1900

Access to building: Prior appointment required
Hours: By arrangement

ORGANIC FOOD FEDERATION (OFF)

31 Turbine Way, EcoTech Business Park, Swaffham, Norfolk, PE37 7XD

Tel: 01760 720444
Fax: 01760 720790
E-mail: info@orgfoodfed.com

Enquiries to: Executive Secretary

Founded: 1986

Organisation type and purpose:
International organisation, membership association (membership is by qualification), present number of members: 350.
Certification body.
To provide certification to producers, processors, importers and retailers of organic food.

Subject coverage: The Federation provides inspection, certification and registration of organic foods. Represents members' interests in communicating with government and European institutions.

Access to staff: Contact by letter, by telephone, by fax and by e-mail
Hours: Mon to Fri, 0900 to 1700

Connections with: Defra; Nobel House, 17 Smith Square, London, SW1P 3JR; tel: 020 7238 5605

ORGANISATION FOR PROFESSIONALS IN REGULATORY AFFAIRS (TOPRA)

Bellerive House, 3 Muirfield Crescent, London, E14 9SZ

Tel: 020 7510 2560
Fax: 020 7537 2003
E-mail: info@topra.org
Website: www.topra.org
Website: www.topra.org/intouch

Enquiries to: Executive Director

Organisation type and purpose: A non-profit organisation, the global organisation for regulatory affairs professionals and for those who have an interest in regulatory affairs in the healthcare sector. The current membership is drawn from over 40 countries and members are in industry, the regulatory agencies and the consultancy community, and work in all sectors including medical technologies, biotech, borderline products and pharmaceuticals.

Subject coverage: Regulatory affairs in the healthcare sector.

Education services: Offers an MSc in Regulatory Affairs validated by the University of Wales and an MSc in Medical Technology Regulatory Affairs through collaboration with Cranfield Health Partnership.

Publications: Printed, and electronic and video

Publications list: Available online

Access to staff: Contact by letter, by telephone, by fax and by e-mail

Links with: TOPRA North America

ORGANISATION OF BLIND AFRICAN CARIBBEANS (OBAC)

Gloucester House, 8 Camberwell New Road, London, SE5 0TA

Tel: 020 7735 3400
Fax: 020 7582 8334
E-mail: info@obac.org.uk
Website: www.obac.org.uk

Enquiries to: Director

Founded: 1988

Organisation type and purpose: Voluntary organisation, registered charity (charity number 1042756), training organisation.
OBAC provides information, advice and support on a range of issues such as: welfare rights, housing, immigration, training, education, employment issues, counselling, aids and adaptation for visually impaired people.

Subject coverage: Welfare rights, housing, immigration, training, education, employment issues, counselling, aids and adaptation for visually impaired people.

Publications: Printed, and electronic and video

Access to staff: Contact by letter, by telephone, by fax, by e-mail and in person
Hours: Mon to Fri, 0930 to 1730
Special comments: Full disabled access.

Access for disabled people: Ramped entry, toilet facilities
Special comments: Chairlift.

ORGANON LABORATORIES LIMITED

Cambridge Science Park, Milton Road, Cambridge, CB4 0FL

Tel: 01223 432700
Fax: 01223 424368
Website: www.organon.com

Enquiries to: Medical Information Officer
Direct tel: 01223 432756

Founded: 1935

Organisation type and purpose:
Manufacturing industry.
Pharmaceutical manufacturing company.

Subject coverage: Clinical pharmacology; contraception; hormone replacement therapy (HRT), (CNS) depression.

Access to staff: Contact by letter, by telephone and by fax
Hours: Mon to Fri, 0900 to 1700

Access to building: No access other than to staff

Access for disabled people: Parking provided

Parent body: AKZO

ORIEL COLLEGE LIBRARY

Oxford, OX1 4EW

Tel: 01865 276558
E-mail: library@oriel.ox.ac.uk

Enquiries to: Librarian

Founded: 1326

Organisation type and purpose: University department or institute.
Library of a college of University of Oxford.

Subject coverage: General, matters relating to old members of the college, Oxford Movement.

Collection: Orielensia – books by or about old members
Tractarian and Oxford Movement Collection

Access to staff: Appointment necessary.
Hours: Mon to Fri, 0930 to 1700

Access to building: Appointment must be made before entry is allowed

ORKNEY LIBRARY AND ARCHIVE

44 Junction Road, Kirkwall, Orkney, KW15 1AG

Tel: 01856 873166
Fax: 01856 875260
E-mail: general.enquiries@orkneylibrary.org.uk
Website: www.orkneylibrary.org.uk

Enquiries to: Librarian
Other contacts: Archivist

Founded: 1683

Organisation type and purpose: Local government body, public library.

Subject coverage: Orkney.

Collection: Archives, church records, records of local authority of Orkney, Customs and Excise, Sheriff Court, Earldom Estate, private papers, business archive
Orkney Room collection – books, pamphlets
Photographic archive (40,000 negatives)

Sound archive (2,000 tapes)

Library catalogue: All or part available online

Access to staff: Contact by letter, by telephone, by fax, by e-mail and in person
Hours: Library: Mon and Thu, 0915 to 1900; Tue, Wed, Fri and Sat, 0915 to 1700
Archive: Mon, Tue, Fri and Sat, 0915 to 1700; Thu, 0915 to 1900; closed Wed

Access to building: Main entrance on Junction Road
Hours: As opening hours above

Access for disabled people: Ramped entry, toilet facilities, lift

ORKNEY TOURIST BOARD

6 Broad Street, Kirkwall, Orkney, KW15 1NX

Tel: 01856 872856/872001
Fax: 01856 875056
E-mail: info@orkney.com
Website: www.orkney.com

Enquiries to: Chief Executive

Organisation type and purpose: Statutory body (membership is by subscription), present number of members: 320.
Local area Tourist Board.

Subject coverage: Tourism in Orkney.

Trade and statistical information: Tourism in Orkney

Publications: Printed, and electronic and video

Access to staff: Contact by letter, by fax and via website. Appointment necessary.
Hours: Mon to Fri, 0900 to 1700

ORTON TRUST

7 Drake Close, Rothwell, Northamptonshire, NN14 6DJ

Tel: 01536 711600 (Courses Director home telephone)
E-mail: info@ortontrust.org.uk
Website: www.ortontrust.org.uk

Enquiries to: Courses Director

Founded: 1968

Organisation type and purpose: Registered charity (charity number 304232), training organisation.

Subject coverage: Traditional stonemasonry skills, restoration and conservation of historic buildings, stone sculpture and lettering.

Access to staff: Contact by letter, by telephone, by e-mail and via website
Hours: Mon to Fri, 0900 to 1700

OSCAR WILDE SOCIETY

Secretary, 22 Edric Road, London, SE14 5EL

Tel: 07980 221632
E-mail: michael.seeney@btinternet.com
Website: www.oscarwildesociety.co.uk

Founded: 1990

Organisation type and purpose: Membership association (membership is by subscription), literary society.
Devoted to the appreciation of Oscar Wilde, promoting knowledge and study of his life, personality and works.

Subject coverage: Oscar Wilde.

Publications: Printed
Order printed publications from: Donald Mead, 63 Lambton Road, London, SW20 0LW; e-mail: donmead@wildean.demon.co.uk

Access to staff: Contact by letter, by telephone, by e-mail and via website
Hours: No set hours

OUTDOOR INDUSTRIES ASSOCIATION (COLA)

Morritt House, 58 Station Approach, South Ruislip, Middlesex, HA4 6SA

Tel: 020 8842 1111
Fax: 020 8842 0090
E-mail: info@outdoorindustriesassociation.co.uk
Website: www.outdoorindustriesassociation.co.uk

Enquiries to: Administration Officer
Direct e-mail: info@outdoorindustriesassociation.co.uk
Other contacts: Director, Financial Controller; Marketing Director

Founded: 1961

Organisation type and purpose: Trade association.
The Outdoor Industries Association is the UK's leading trade body for manufacturers, suppliers and retailers of outdoor clothing and equipment.

Subject coverage: Clothing, equipment and accessories for camping, outdoor leisure, climbing, mountaineering, walking, hiking and canoeing, manufacturers' trade names and retailers.

Publications: Printed

Access to staff: Contact by letter, by telephone, by fax and by e-mail
Hours: Mon to Fri, 0900 to 1700

OUTSELL, INC

25 Floral Street, London, WC2E 9DS

Tel: 020 8090 6590
E-mail: info@outsellinc.com
Website: www.outsellinc.com

Enquiries to: Research and Consultancy Director

Founded: 1985; incorporates the former Electronic Publishing Services (year of change 2008)

Organisation type and purpose: Consultancy, market research, publishing house.

Subject coverage: All aspects of the publishing industry and electronic publishing, including online.

Collection: Library of documents and publications on electronic information products and services

Trade and statistical information: Data on electronic information services, especially statistics on UK, EU and North American services

Publications: Electronic and video

Publications list: Available online

Access to staff: Contact by letter, by telephone and by e-mail. Appointment necessary. All charged.
Hours: Mon to Fri, 0930 to 1730

Access to building: Prior appointment required

OUTSIDERS

Formal name: The Outsiders Trust

4S Leroy House, 436 Essex Road, London, N1 3QP

Tel: 020 7354 8291
E-mail: office@outsiders.org.uk
Website: www.outsiders.org.uk

Enquiries to: Co-ordinator
Direct e-mail: trust@outsiders.org.uk

Founded: 1972; incorporates the former Sexual Health and Disability Alliance; incorporates the former Association to Aid the Personal and Sexual Relationships of People with a Disability (SPOD) helpline (year of change 2002)

Organisation type and purpose: Registered charity (charity number 290482).
To assist the sexual and personal relationships of people with disabilities.

Information services: Sex and disability helpline.

Services for disabled people: Peer support network for people with physical and social disabilities. Local lunches held around the UK.

Publications: Printed

Publications list: Available online and in print

Access to staff: Contact by letter, by telephone and by e-mail

Access to building: No public access

Access for disabled people: At public lunches

OUTWARD BOUND TRUST

Hackthorpe Hall, Hackthorpe, Penrith, Cumbria, CA10 2HX

Tel: 01931 740000
Fax: 01931 740001
E-mail: enquiries@outwardbound.org.uk
Website: www.theoutwardboundtrust.org.uk

Enquiries to: Administrator

Founded: 1941

Organisation type and purpose: Registered charity (charity number 1128090), training organisation.
Educational charity.

Subject coverage: Outdoor learning, adventure, development training, safety in the outdoors, professional development, personal development.

Publications: Printed, and electronic and video
Order printed publications from: Marketing, The Outward Bound Trust, Hackthorpe Hall, Hackthorpe, Penrith, Cumbria, CA10 2HX; tel: 01931 740000

continued overleaf

Access to staff: Contact by letter, by telephone, by fax, by e-mail and via website
Hours: Mon to Fri, 0900 to 1730

Also at: The Outward Bound Trust – Aberdovey; Aberdovey, Gwynedd, LL35 0RA; tel: 01654 767464; The Outward Bound Trust – Eskdale; Eskdale Green, Holmrook, Cumbria, CA19 1TE; tel: 01946 723281; The Outward Bound Trust – Loch Eil; Loch Eil, Fort William, Inverness-shire, PH33 7NN; tel: 01397 772866; The Outward Bound Trust – Ullswater; Penrith, Cumbria, CA11 0JL; tel: 08705 134227

OVERSEAS ADOPTION HELPLINE

64–66 High Street, Barnet, Hertfordshire, EN5 5SJ

Tel: 0870 516 8742 Helpline
Fax: 0208 440 5675
Website: www.oah.org.uk

Enquiries to: Director
Direct tel: 020 8449 2562

Founded: 1997

Organisation type and purpose: Registered charity (charity number 1067313).
Provides information and advice to inter-country adopters, inter-country adopted people and their families and also for professionals involved in inter-country adoption.

Subject coverage: Inter-country adoption.

Publications: Printed

Publications list: Available online and in print

Access to staff: Contact by telephone and by e-mail
Hours: Mon to Fri, 0900 to 1300 and 1400 to 1700

OVERSEAS DEVELOPMENT INSTITUTE (ODI)

111 Westminster Bridge Road, London, SE1 7JD

Tel: 020 7922 0300
Fax: 020 7922 0399
E-mail: odi@odi.org.uk
Website: www.odi.org.uk

Enquiries to: Publications Officer

Founded: 1960

Organisation type and purpose: Registered charity (charity number 228248), research organisation.
ODI is Britain's leading independent think-tank on international development and humanitarian issues.
ODI's mission is to inspire and inform policy and practice which lead to the reduction of poverty, the alleviation of suffering and the achievement of sustainable livelihood in developing countries.

Subject coverage: Overseas development, aid, development policy, trade adjustment, finance, food aid, food security, disasters, environment, agriculture, extension, pastoralism, irrigation, water resources, rural forestry.

Collection: Grey literature collection of the Rural Resources Management Group

Non-library collection catalogue: All or part available online and in-house

Library catalogue: All or part available in-house

Publications: Printed

Publications list: Available in print

Access to staff: Contact by letter, by telephone, by fax, by e-mail and in person
Hours: Mon to Fri, 0930 to 1700
Special comments: In person, Mon to Thu, 1000 to 1700 only.

Access to building: No prior appointment required

Affiliated to: European Association of Development Institutes (EADI); Information for Development Coordinating Committee (IDCC)

Houses the: Agricultural Administration Unit

Subsidiary body: Agricultural Research and Extension Network; Humanitarian Policy Group; Humanitarian Practice Network; Pastoral Development Network; Rural Development Forestry Network; Water Resources Group

OVERSEAS SERVICE PENSIONERS' ASSOCIATION (OSPA)

138 High Street, Tonbridge, Kent, TN9 1AX

Tel: 01732 363836
Fax: 01732 365070
E-mail: mail@ospa.org.uk
Website: www.ospa.org.uk

Enquiries to: Secretary

Founded: 1960

Organisation type and purpose:
Membership association (membership is by qualification), present number of members: c. 4,200.
To represent, safeguard and promote the interests of members in all matters relating to or affecting Overseas Service pensions, and to promote understanding of all aspects of the former Colonial Service/HMOCS in British colonial rule and development.

Subject coverage: Matters relating directly or indirectly to Service pensions of former members of the Colonial Service and HM Overseas Civil Service; general interest in past British administration and development in former and present colonial territories.

Publications: Printed
Order printed publications from: The Secretary, OSPA, 138 High Street, Tonbridge, Kent TN9 1AX

Access to staff: Contact by letter, by telephone, by fax and by e-mail. Appointment necessary.
Hours: Mon to Thu, 0900 to 1630

OXFORD BROOKES UNIVERSITY – HARCOURT HILL LIBRARY

Harcourt Hill Campus, Oxford, OX2 9AT

Tel: 01865 488222; 488319 (Oxford Centre for Methodism and Church History)
Fax: 01865 488224
E-mail: hhlibenquiries@brookes.ac.uk
Website: www.brookes.ac.uk/library/harcourt.html
Website: prism.talis.com/brookes/

Enquiries to: Library Manager (access) or Subject Librarians (subject-related enquiries)
Other contacts: Senior Subject Librarian, Education; Assistant Subject Librarian, Education; Assistant Subject Librarian, Human Development

Organisation type and purpose: University library.

Subject coverage: Education, theology, human development, communication, sports and coaching.

Collection: Wesley Historical Society library and archives
Westminster College archives
Art collections such as the Methodist Collection of Modern Christian Art and works by James Smetham
Archives of Bletchley Park College and Lady Spencer Churchill College

Library catalogue: All or part available online

Access to staff: Contact by letter, by telephone, by fax, by e-mail and via website
Hours: Term time: Mon to Thu, 0830 to 2100; Fri, 0830 to 1800; Sat, Sun, 1200 to 1800
Vacations: Mon to Fri, 0900 to 1700

Access for disabled people: This Library is approached by a ramp and has automatic doors. A lift provides access to the Lower Ground Floor.

OXFORD BROOKES UNIVERSITY – HEADINGTON LIBRARY

Headington Campus, Gipsy Lane, Headington, Oxford, OX3 0BP

Tel: 01865 483156
Fax: 01865 483998
E-mail: library@brookes.ac.uk
Website: www.brookes.ac.uk/library
Website: prism.talis.com/brookes/

Enquiries to: Director of Learning Resources and University Librarian

Organisation type and purpose: University library.

Subject coverage: Architectural planning and estate management, social sciences, education, management and business studies, humanities, arts, languages, construction, sciences, catering and tourism, publishing, nursing, theology.

Collection: Andre Deutsch Collection (the published output of Andre Deutsch Ltd and Allan Wingate as well as titles from Deutsch's own personal library)
Dorset House Archive (the history of the first School of Occupational Therapy in the United Kingdom, the Casson family and the wider history of Occupational Therapy education in Britain from 1930 to 1980)
Fuller Collection (books, pamphlets, journals and cuttings on catering, cookery and gastronomy)
Harold Fullard Collection of Atlases
Jane Grigson Collection (books and pamphlets on cookery and gastronomy)
Ken Hom Library (books on cookery and gastronomy)
Medical Sciences Video Archive (biographical interviews with leading medical scientists)

National Brewing Library (a unique English-language collection relating to brewing, other alcoholic beverages and dependent trades)
Oxfordshire Society of Architects Collection (books and journals about architecture and construction, on permanent loan from the local branch of the Royal Institute of British Architects)
Publishing in Africa Collection (materials relating to publishing and the book trade in Africa)

Library catalogue: All or part available online

Publications: Printed

Access to staff: Contact by letter, by telephone, by fax, by e-mail and via website
Hours: Term time: Mon to Thu, 0900 to 2200; Fri, 0900 to 2000; Sat and Sun, 1000 to 1600. Vacations: Mon to Fri, 0900 to 1700

OXFORD BROOKES UNIVERSITY – WHEATLEY LIBRARY

Wheatley Campus, Oxford, OX33 1HX

Tel: 01865 485869
E-mail: library@brookes.ac.uk
Website: www.brookes.ac.uk/library
Website: catalogue.brookes.ac.uk

Enquiries to: Head of Learning Resources

Founded: 1948

Organisation type and purpose: University library.

Subject coverage: Business, management, economics, computing, mathematics and engineering

Library catalogue: All or part available online

Access to staff: Contact by letter, by telephone, by e-mail and via website
Hours: Term time: Mon to Fri, 0900 to 1700; open some Sat and Sun, 1000 to 1600; see website for details.

OXFORD BUSINESS COLLEGE (OBC)

65 George St, Oxford, OX1 2BQ

Tel: 01865 791908
Fax: 01865 245059
E-mail: enquiries@oxfordbusinesscollege.co.uk
Website: www.oxfordbusinesscollege.co.uk

Enquiries to: Principal

Founded: 1985

Organisation type and purpose: Suitable for ages: 17+, training organisation.

Subject coverage: Marketing, business, management and law; English language, secretarial studies, computing, cookery.

Publications: Printed

Access to staff: Contact by letter, by telephone and by fax
Hours: Mon to Fri, 0900 to 1730

OXFORD CENTRE FOR HEBREW AND JEWISH STUDIES

Yarnton Manor, Church Lane, Yarnton, Oxford, OX5 1PY

Tel: 01865 377946
Fax: 01865 375079
E-mail: enquiries@ochjs.ac.uk
Website: associnst.ox.ac.uk/ochjs

Enquiries to: Librarian
Direct e-mail: muller.library@ochjs.ac.uk
Other contacts: Manager

Founded: 1972

Organisation type and purpose: Registered charity (charity number 309720), university department or institute, suitable for ages: post-graduate.

Subject coverage: Hebrew and Jewish studies.

Collection: The Centre's Leopold Muller Memorial Library holds a wide range of collections, for more information contact the Librarian.

Non-library collection catalogue: All or part available in-house

Library catalogue: All or part available in-house

Publications: Printed
Order printed publications from: For Israel Studies, Journals Division
Indiana University Press, 601 N Morton Street, Bloomington, IN 47404, USA
Other titles, Oxford Centre for Hebrew and Jewish Studies

Publications list: Available in print

Access to staff: Contact by letter, by telephone, by fax and by e-mail.
Appointment necessary.
Hours: Mon to Fri, 0900 to 1700

Access to building: No prior appointment required

OXFORD CENTRE FOR ISLAMIC STUDIES

George Street, Oxford, OX1 2AR

Tel: 01865 278730
Fax: 01865 248942
E-mail: islamic.studies@oxcis.ac.uk
Website: www.oxcis.ac.uk

Enquiries to: Enquiry Line

Subject coverage: Islam.

Access to staff: Contact by letter, by telephone, by fax, by e-mail and via website
Hours: Mon to Fri, 0900 to 1700

OXFORD CITY COUNCIL

St Aldate's Chambers, St Aldate's, Oxford, OX1 1DS

Tel: 01865 249811
Fax: 01865 252338
Website: www.oxford.gov.uk

Enquiries to: Chief Executive

Organisation type and purpose: Local government body.

Publications: Printed

Access to staff: Contact by letter, by telephone, by fax and in person
Hours: Mon to Fri, 0900 to 1700

OXFORD DOWN SHEEP BREEDERS ASSOCIATION

Hillfields Lodge, Lighthorne, Warwickshire, CU35 0BQ

Tel: 01926 650098
E-mail: cqlfroehlich@hotmail.com

Enquiries to: Secretary

Founded: 1889

Organisation type and purpose: Sheep breed society.

Subject coverage: Oxford Down sheep.

Access to staff: Contact by letter, by telephone and by e-mail
Hours: Mon to Fri, 0900 to 1700

OXFORD EDUCATIONAL RESOURCES LIMITED (OER)

PO Box 106, The Barn, Kidlington, Oxfordshire, OX5 1HY

Tel: 01865 842552
Fax: 01865 842551
E-mail: sales@oer.co.uk
Website: www.oer.co.uk

Enquiries to: Managing Director

Founded: 1978

Organisation type and purpose: Training organisation.
Publishing and distribution of non-book material.

Subject coverage: Training material for medicine, health and biology.

Publications list: Available in print

Access to staff: Contact by fax and by e-mail
Hours: Mon to Fri, 0900 to 1700

OXFORD INFORMATION CENTRE (Oxford TIC)

15–16 Broad Street, Oxford, OX1 3AS

Tel: 01865 252200
Fax: 01865 240261
E-mail: tic@oxford.gov.uk
Website: www.visitoxford.org

Enquiries to: Tourist Information Centre Manager
Direct tel: 01865 252300
Direct e-mail: jbassett@oxford.gov.uk
Other contacts: TIC Team Leader

Founded: 1939

Organisation type and purpose: Local government body.
Tourist Information Centre.
To assist local people and visitors to make the most of the time they spend in Oxford and the surrounding area.

Subject coverage: Tourist information including: guided walking tours, maps, guides and accommodation, reservations (B&B), local information, tickets for attractions.

Services for disabled people: Disabled access, hearing loop

Trade and statistical information: see website: http://www.visitoxford.org

Non-library collection catalogue: All or part available online

continued overleaf

Publications: Printed, and electronic and video
Order electronic and video publications from: Downloadable free

Publications list: Available online and in print

Access to staff: Contact by letter, by telephone, by fax, by e-mail, in person and via website
Hours: Mon to Sat, 0930 to 1700; Sun and Public Holidays, 1000 to 1600

Access to building: As above

Access for disabled people: Level entry
Hours: As above

Parent body: Oxford City Council

OXFORD INSTITUTE OF RETAIL MANAGEMENT (OXIRM)

Said Business School, University of Oxford, Park End Street, Oxford, OX1 1HP

Tel: 01865 288800
Fax: 01865 288801
E-mail: oxirmenquiries@sbs.ox.ac.uk
Website: www.sbs.ox.ac.uk/oxirm

Enquiries to: Centre Administrator
Direct tel: 01865 288720
Direct e-mail: oxirmenquiries@sbs.ox.ac.uk
Other contacts: Research Director

Founded: 1985

Organisation type and purpose: University department or institute, research organisation.

Subject coverage: Retail management.

Information services: The Institute is not generally able to assist with ad hoc information requests.

Special visitor services: Visiting academics and research students can be hosted through established University schemes.

Education services: Provides executive education for retail and related businesses, conducts research commissioned by private and public sector organizations, and contributes retail education to degree programmes in management studies.

Collection: Research papers, reports, directories, etc.

Publications: Printed, and electronic and video
Order printed publications from: e-mail: oxirmenquiries@sbs.ox.ac.uk
Order electronic and video publications from: oxirmenquiries@sbs.ox.ac.uk

Publications list: Available online and in print

Access to staff: Contact by letter, by telephone, by fax and by e-mail. Appointment necessary. Letter of introduction required.
Hours: Mon to Fri, 0900 to 1700

Access to building: By invitation only.
Special comments: Academic status generally required.

OXFORD MISSION

General Secretary, PO Box 86, Romsey, Hampshire, SO51 8YD

Tel: 01794 515004
Fax: 01794 515004
Website: www.oxford-mission.org/home/index.html

Founded: 1879

Organisation type and purpose: Registered charity, mission.
Runs a boys' orphanage, St Joseph's Primary School, an English-medium primary school, hostels, training schemes for less academic boys, and an ENT/eye clinic at Behala, India; boarding schools, Christian students' hostels, St Anne's Medical Centre, an orphanage, a primary school and a Bangladeshi Brotherhood of St Paul at Barisal, Bangladesh; and a Bangladeshi Sisterhood in Jobarpar to supervise boys' and girls' hostels and a play-centre for small children, help in St Gabriel's School and supervise St Mary's Home in Barisal.

Subject coverage: Children's welfare and education.

Publications: Printed, and electronic and video
Order printed publications from: The UK office, except:
Down to the Sea, from The Memoir Club, Stanhope Old Hall, Stanhope, Co. Durham, DL13 2PF
Whether we be many or few, from Christians Aware, Leicester, tel: 0116 254 0770
Order electronic and video publications from: The UK office

Access to staff: Contact by letter, by telephone, by fax, by e-mail and via website
Hours: Mon, Tue, Thu, Fri, 0930 to 1530
Special comments: Not Wed.

Also at: Editor, Oxford Mission News; 6 Lodge Vale, East Wellow, Romsey, Hants, SO51 6AU; tel: 01794 323387; Mother Winifred, All Hallows Convent; Ditchingham, Bungay, Suffolk, NR35 2DT; Oxford Mission; Bogra Road, PO Box 21, Barisal, 8200 Bangladesh; Oxford Mission; Barisha, Kolkata 700 008, India; Oxford Mission, Christa Sevika Sangha; PO Box Jobarpar 8240, Barisal Division, Uz. Agailjhara, Bangladesh

OXFORD PRESERVATION TRUST (OPT)

10 Turn Again Lane, St Ebbes, Oxford, OX1 1QL

Tel: 01865 242918
Fax: 01865 246706
E-mail: info@oxfordpreservation.org.uk
Website: www.oxfordpreservation.org.uk

Enquiries to: Director

Founded: 1927

Organisation type and purpose: Membership association (membership is by subscription), present number of members: 1,000, registered charity (charity number 203043).
Area of concern, Oxford and its Green Belt setting.

Subject coverage: Conservation in Oxford and its Green Belt.

Collection: Archives accessed through Trust Office

Publications: Printed

Access to staff: Contact by letter, by telephone, by fax and by e-mail. Appointment necessary.
Hours: Mon to Fri, 0900 to 1600

Links with: Civic Trust; Europa Nostra; Europa Nostra

OXFORDSHIRE COUNTY COUNCIL (OCC)

Community Services, Central Library, Westgate, Oxford, OX1 1DJ

Tel: 01865 815549
Fax: 01865 721694
E-mail: oxfordcentral.library@oxfordshire.gov.uk
Website: www.oxfordshire.gov.uk
Website: www.libcat.oxfordshire.gov.uk

Organisation type and purpose: Local government body, public library.

Subject coverage: Logic, New Testament, international relations, women, costumes, gypsies, customs and folklore, inland waterways, nuclear physics, hydraulic engineering, woodworking, India, Indian religions (Buddhism, etc.), indoor games and amusements, genealogy, heraldry and family history, local studies in Oxfordshire, internal-combustion engines, motor vehicle engineering, cleaning and dyeing, accountancy, rubber technology, business information.

Non-library collection catalogue: All or part available online

Library catalogue: All or part available online

Access to staff: Contact by letter, by telephone, by e-mail and in person
Hours: Contact for details

OXFORDSHIRE FAMILY HISTORY SOCIETY (OFHS)

19 Mavor Close, Woodstock, Oxford, OX20 1YL

Website: www.ofhs.org.uk

Enquiries to: Honorary Secretary
Direct tel: 01993 812258
Other contacts: Membership Secretary

Founded: 1976

Organisation type and purpose: Membership association (membership is by subscription), present number of members: 1,300, registered charity (charity number 275891).

Subject coverage: Family history.

Collection: Library

Publications: Printed, and microform publications
Order printed publications from: Oxfordshire Family History Society, Windmill Place, Windmill Road, Minchinhampton, Stroud, Gloucestershire, GL6 9EE; tel: 01453 881446; e-mail: HKearsey@aol.com

Publications list: Available in print

Access to staff: Contact by letter
Hours: Mon to Fri, 0900 to 1700
Special comments: No office.

OXFORDSHIRE RECORD OFFICE (ORO)

St Luke's Church, Temple Road, Cowley, Oxford, OX4 2HT
Tel: 01865 398200
Fax: 01865 398201
E-mail: archives@oxfordshire.gov.uk
Website: www.oxfordshire.uk/oro

Enquiries to: Archives Manager

Founded: 1935

Organisation type and purpose: Local government body, professional body.
Record office.

Subject coverage: Records of Oxfordshire.

Collection: Quarter Sessions, local government, diocesan and parish, and private records

Non-library collection catalogue: All or part available online and in-house

Publications list: Available in print

Access to staff: Contact by letter, by telephone, by fax, by e-mail and in person
Hours: Wed to Sat, 0900 to 1700

Access for disabled people: Parking provided, ramped entry, access to all public areas, toilet facilities

OXFORDSHIRE RECORD SOCIETY

Bodleian Library, Oxford, OX1 3BG

Tel: 01865 277164
E-mail: srt@bodley.ox.ac.uk

Enquiries to: Secretary

Founded: 1919

Organisation type and purpose: Learned society.
Exists to publish editions of Oxfordshire local history texts.

Subject coverage: Oxfordshire local history.

Access to staff: Contact by letter and by e-mail
Hours: Mon to Fri, 0900 to 1700

OXFORDSHIRE RURAL COMMUNITY COUNCIL (ORCC)

Jericho Farm, Worton, Near Cassington, Witney, Oxfordshire, OX29 4SZ

Tel: 01865 883488
Fax: 01865 883191
E-mail: oxonrcc@ruralnet.org.uk

Enquiries to: Chief Executive

Founded: 1920

Organisation type and purpose: Voluntary organisation, registered charity (charity number 900560).

Subject coverage: Oxfordshire Rural Community Council (ORCC) supports, promotes and develops local voluntary action and rural services (including shops and rural transport). Offers information on a wide range of local voluntary organisations, community and self-help groups. Provides information and advises village hall management committees and advises on sources of grants for community projects. Also provides parish councils with advice and guidance in partnership with the Oxfordshire Association of Local Councils and the Oxfordshire Playing Fields Association. (All three organisations based at Jericho Farm.)

Publications: Printed

Access to staff: Contact by letter, by telephone, by fax and by e-mail.
Appointment necessary.
Hours: Mon to Fri, 0900 to 1700

Access to building: Prior appointment required

Houses the: Oxfordshire Association of Local Councils; tel: 01865 883488; fax: 01865 883191; e-mail: oalc@ruralnet.org.uk; Oxfordshire Playing Fields Association; tel: 01865 883488; fax: 01865 883191; e-mail: oxonrcc@ruralnet.org.uk

OXFORDSHIRE STUDIES

Central Library, Westgate, Oxford, OX1 1DJ

Tel: 01865 815749
Fax: 01865 810187
E-mail: oxfordshire.studies@oxfordshire.gov.uk
Website: www.oxfordshire.gov.uk/oxfordshirestudies
Website: www.oxfordshire.gov.uk/heritagesearch

Enquiries to: Local Studies Manager

Founded: 1991

Organisation type and purpose: Local government body, museum, public library.
Local studies and family history resource centre for Oxfordshire.

Subject coverage: Oxfordshire local studies, local history and archaeology, family history, maps, photographs and oral history.

Collection: Indexes and databases
Oxfordshire printed materials, microforms, digital resources
Photographs and audiotapes
Catalogues

Non-library collection catalogue: All or part available online and in-house

Library catalogue: All or part available online and in-house

Access to staff: Contact by letter, by telephone, by fax, by e-mail and in person.
Appointment necessary.
Special comments: Booking advisable for access to microfilms and computers, appointments may be necessary for specialist advice.

Access to building: *Hours:* Tue, Thu, Fri, Sat, 0900 to 1700; Mon, Wed, Sun closed.

Access for disabled people: Access to all public areas

Parent body: Oxfordshire County Council

P & O GROUP

Formal name: The Peninsular and Oriental Steam Navigation Company

16 Palace Street, London, SW1E 5JQ

Tel: 020 7901 4000
Fax: 020 7901 4015
E-mail: communications@pogroup.com
Website: www.pogroup.com

Founded: 1837

Organisation type and purpose: Service industry.

Subject coverage: Shipping, present day and historical (since c. 1830), other transport and logistics (present day), constituent companies, history and current operations of P & O constituent companies.

Access to staff: Contact by letter, by telephone, by fax, by e-mail, in person and via website. Appointment necessary.
Hours: Mon to Fri, 0900 to 1700

Access to building: Prior appointment required

Access for disabled people: Ramped entry, access to all public areas, toilet facilities

PACKAGING AND INDUSTRIAL FILMS ASSOCIATION (PIFA)

3rd Floor, Gothic House, Barker Gate, Nottingham, NG7 7GR

Tel: 0115 959 8389
Fax: 0115 959 9326
E-mail: pafa@pafa.org.uk
Website: www.pifa.co.uk

Enquiries to: Chief Executive
Other contacts: PR Principal for exhibitions, press releases, presentations and essential media contacts.

Founded: 1957

Organisation type and purpose: National organisation, trade association (membership is by subscription).
To communicate with Government, Government Agencies, Ministers and MPs on all issues affecting the competitiveness, environmental performance and operation of the industry. To provide factual and scientific information to universities, schools, local authorities and other social groups.

Subject coverage: Production and conversion of plastics films used in healthcare, agriculture, packaging, building construction, commerce and industry. Issues include competitiveness, the environment, safety, trade matters, processes, products and applications, education and public awareness.

Trade and statistical information: Detailed production/consumption, import/export and related statistics maintained

Non-library collection catalogue: All or part available online and in print

Publications: Printed

Publications list: Available online and in print

Access to staff: Contact by letter, by telephone, by fax, by e-mail and via website.
Appointment necessary.
Hours: Mon to Fri, 0900 to 1700

Access to building: No prior appointment required

Access for disabled people: Parking provided, toilet facilities

Affiliated to: British Plastics Federation

Member of: C of C; CBI; Plasteurofilm; Polymer NTO

PADDLE STEAMER PRESERVATION SOCIETY (PSPS)

17 Stockfield Close, Hazlemere, High Wycombe, Buckinghamshire, HP15 7LA

Tel: 01494 812979

Enquiries to: Secretary

Founded: 1959

Organisation type and purpose: Membership association (membership is by subscription), present number of members: 4000, voluntary organisation.
Education of the public in the appreciation of paddle steamers and their preservation.

Subject coverage: Paddle steamers of Britain and Europe.

Collection: Library of Paddle Steamer photographs and books

Publications: Printed

Access to staff: Contact by letter
Hours: Mon to Fri, 0900 to 1700

Affiliated to: Transport Trust

PAGAN FEDERATION (PF)

BM Box 7097, London, WC1N 3XX

Tel: 07986 034387
E-mail: secretary@paganfed.org
Website: www.paganfed.org

Enquiries to: Secretary
Direct e-mail: secretary@paganfed.org

Founded: 1971

Organisation type and purpose: To inform the public about Paganism and to support Pagans in the practice of their religion.

Subject coverage: Nature, spirituality, goddess worship, Wicca (the old religion of witchcraft), Druidism, Shamanism, Pagan folklore and belief, contemporary Pagan ritual practices, religious and legal rights, defamation of Pagans, concerns about ritual child abuse, Pagan ethics, inter-faith dialogue, worship of traditional European deities.

Collection: Cuttings collection – stories on Pagan-related subjects
Extensive collection of Pagan and esoteric magazines, back issues and current issues

Library catalogue: All or part available in-house

Publications: Printed

Publications list: Available in print

Access to staff: Contact by letter and by e-mail
Hours: Mon to Fri, 0900 to 1700

Access to building: No access other than to staff

PAIN RELIEF FOUNDATION (PRF)

Clinical Sciences Centre for Research and Education, University Hospital Aintree, Lower Lane, Liverpool, L9 7AL

Tel: 0151 529 5820
Fax: 0151 529 5821
E-mail: secretary@painrelieffoundation.org.uk
Website: www.painrelieffoundation.org.uk

Enquiries to: Information and Education Services
Direct tel: 0151 529 5838
Direct e-mail: mm27@liv.ac.uk

Founded: 1979

Organisation type and purpose: Registered charity; research & education.

Subject coverage: All chronic pain conditions, causes, treatment.

Information services: Patient/public information leaflets about chronic pain.

Education services: Postgraduate education courses for health professionals.

Publications: Printed
Order printed publications from: Pain Relief Foundation

Publications list: Available online

Access to staff: Contact by letter, by telephone, by fax and by e-mail
Hours: Mon to Fri, 0900 to 1700

Access to building: No access other than to staff

Links with: Pain Research Institute

PAIN SOCIETY

9 Bedford Square, London, WC1B 3RE

Tel: 020 7631 8870
Fax: 020 7323 2015
E-mail: info@britishpainsociety.org
Website: www.painsociety.org

Enquiries to: Honorary Secretary

Founded: 1967

Organisation type and purpose: Professional body.

Subject coverage: Pain research and management, education, organisation of pain clinics.

Publications: Printed

Access to staff: Contact by letter, by telephone, by fax, by e-mail and via website
Hours: Mon to Fri, 0930 to 1730
Special comments: Letters preferred, no personal callers.

Access to building: No access other than to staff

British Chapter of the: International Association for the Study of Pain

PAINT RESEARCH ASSOCIATION (PRA)

PRA Coatings Technology Centre, 14 Castle Mews, High Street, Hampton, Middlesex, TW12 2NP

Tel: 020 8487 0800
Fax: 020 8487 0801
E-mail: library@pra-world.com
Website: www.pra-world.com

Enquiries to: Librarian
Direct e-mail: n.morgan@pra-world.com

Founded: 1926

Organisation type and purpose: Research organisation.

Subject coverage: Paint science and technology; corrosion; deterioration and biodeterioration of materials; pigments; oils; resins; polymers; paint application; health hazards and toxicology; industrial hazards and anti-pollution legislation; organic and inorganic chemistry; analytical chemistry; anti-fouling technology; spectroscopy; rheology; colour science and colourimetry; paint testing; powder coatings; radiation curing; microbiology; building materials; standards, specifications, reports and patents.

Information services: Literature and patent searches.

Trade and statistical information: Available in Coatings COMET

Publications: Printed, and electronic and video

Publications list: Available online and in print

Access to staff: Contact by letter, by telephone, by fax, by e-mail and via website. Non-members charged.
Hours: Mon to Fri, 0900 to 1700

Access to building: Prior appointment required

Access for disabled people: Parking provided, level entry, toilet facilities

Parent body: PERA; Nottingham Road, Melton Mowbray, Leicestershire LE13 0PB, UK; tel: 01664 501501; fax: 01664 501554; e-mail: innovation@pera.com; website: http://www.pera.com

PAINTING AND DECORATING ASSOCIATION (PDA)

32 Coton Road, Nuneaton, Warwickshire, CV11 5TW

Tel: 024 7635 3776
Fax: 024 7635 4513
E-mail: info@paintingdecoratingassociation.co.uk
Website: www.paintingdecoratingassociation.co.uk

Enquiries to: Chief Executive

Founded: 2002; created by the merger of British Decorators Association and Painting and Decorating Federation (year of change 2002)

Organisation type and purpose: Trade association.

Subject coverage: All matters relating to the decorating industry, arbitration, insurance, training and education, employment legislation.

Publications: Printed

Access to staff: Contact by letter, by telephone, by fax, by e-mail and via website. Appointment necessary. Non-members charged.
Hours: Mon to Fri, 0900 to 1700

Access to building: Prior appointment required

Access for disabled people: Parking provided, level entry, access to all public areas

Member of: National Specialist Contractors Council (NSCC); tel: 0870 429 6351

PAINTING AND DECORATING FEDERATION (PDF)

32 Coton Road, Nuneaton, Warwickshire CV11 5TW

Tel: 02476 353776
Fax: 02476 354513
E-mail: info@paintingdecoratingassociation.co.uk
Website: www.paintingdecoratingassociation.co.uk/

Enquiries to: Executive Administrator

Founded: 1942

Organisation type and purpose: Trade association.

Subject coverage: Painting and decorating.

Publications: Printed
Order printed publications from: The Health & Safety in Painting publication is available from Construction Industry Publications (CIP); tel: 0121 722 8200

Access to staff: Contact by letter, by telephone, by fax, by e-mail and via website
Hours: Mon to Fri, 0930 to 1715

Member of: National Specialist Contractors Council (NSCC); tel: 020 7608 5090; fax: 020 7608 5081

PALAEONTOGRAPHICAL SOCIETY

Department of Palaeontology, Natural History Museum, Cromwell Road, London, SW7 5BD

Tel: 020 7942 5712
E-mail: s.long@nhm.ac.uk
Website: www.palaeosoc.org

Enquiries to: Secretary

Founded: 1847

Organisation type and purpose: Learned society.
To figure and describe British fossils by publishing monographs restricted geographically, stratigraphically and palaeontologically.

Subject coverage: British fossils; study of geology in relation to fossils, particularly by publications upon them.

Non-library collection catalogue: All or part available online

Publications: Printed
Order printed publications from: Dr Martin Munt, Marketing Manager, Palaeontographical Society, Natural History Museum, Cromwell Road, London SW7 5BD

Publications list: Available online

Access to staff: Contact by letter, by e-mail and via website
Hours: Mon to Fri, 1000 to 1600

PALAEONTOLOGICAL ASSOCIATION

School of Geography, Earth and Environmental Sciences, Plymouth University, PL4 8AA, UK

Tel: 01752 584775
Fax: 01752 584776
E-mail: secretary@palass.org
Website: www.palass.org

Enquiries to: Secretary
Other contacts: Executive Officer for membership enquiries; publication orders.

Founded: 1957

Organisation type and purpose: Learned society.

Subject coverage: Palaeontology.

Publications: Printed
Order printed publications from: Executive Officer

Publications list: Available online and in print

Access to staff: Contact by letter, by telephone, by fax and by e-mail. Appointment necessary.
Hours: Mon to Fri, 0900 to 1700

Other address: Palaeontological Association; Executive Officer, Institute of Geography and Earth Sciences, University of Wales Aberystwyth, Aberystwyth, Ceredigion, SY23 3BD; tel: 01970 627107; fax: 01970 627107; e-mail: palass@palass.org

PANAMANIAN EMBASSY

40 Hertford Street, London, W1J 7SH

Tel: 020 7493 4646
Fax: 020 7493 4333
E-mail: emb.pan@lineone.net
Website: www.panamainfo.com
Website: www.presidencia.gob.pa/gobierno.html
Website: www.panamatours.com

Enquiries to: Counsellor

Organisation type and purpose: International organisation.

Subject coverage: Education; economy; culture; politics; historical and geographical information about Panama, tourism etc.

Publications: Printed

Access to staff: Contact by letter, by fax and by e-mail
Hours: Mon to Fri, 1030 to 1630

PANHARD ET LEVASSOR CLUB GB

La Dyna, 11 Arterial Avenue, Rainham, Essex, RM13 9PD

Tel: 01708 524425
E-mail: denise.polley@yahoo.co.uk
Website: www.panhardclub.co.uk

Enquiries to: Vice President/Membership Secretary

Organisation type and purpose: Membership association (membership is by subscription), present number of members: 55.

Subject coverage: Deals mainly with the 1950s and 1960s cars, but information can be obtained about any Panhard Levassor cars.

Access to staff: Contact by letter, by telephone and by e-mail
Hours: Mon to Fri, 0900 to 2100

PANOS LONDON

Formal name: Panos Institute London

9 White Lion Street, London, N1 9PD

Tel: 020 7278 1111
Fax: 020 7278 0345
E-mail: info@panos.org.uk
Website: www.panos.org.uk

Enquiries to: External Relations Assistant
Direct tel: 020 7239 7609

Founded: 1986

Organisation type and purpose: Panos works to provide the world's poorest people with access to information on issues that affect them, and to make their voices heard on decisions that relate to their lives.

Subject coverage: Environment, HIV/AIDS, communication for development, technology issues, oral testimony, globalisation and trade, research communication.

Library catalogue: All or part available online

Publications: Printed

Publications list: Available online

Access to staff: Contact by letter, by telephone, by fax, by e-mail and via website. Appointment necessary. All charged.
Hours: Mon to Fri, 0930 to 1730

Parent body to: Panos Picture Library; 1 Chappel Court, Borough High Street, London, SE1 1HH; tel: 020 7234 0010

Sister organisations: Worldwide including Asia, Africa, America and the Caribbean

PANOS PICTURE LIBRARY

1 Honduras Street, London, EC1Y OTH

Tel: 020 7253 1424
Fax: 020 7253 2752
E-mail: pics@panos.co.uk
Website: www.panos.co.uk

Enquiries to: Archive Manager
Direct e-mail: david@panos.co.uk

Subject coverage: Third World issues.

Parent body: Panos Institute; 9 White Lion Street, London, N1 9PD; tel: 020 7278 1111

PANTHER ENTHUSIASTS CLUB UK

91 Fleet Road, Farnborough, Hampshire, GU14 9RE

Tel: 01252 540217
Fax: 01252 540217
E-mail: george@pantherclub.co.uk
Website: www.pantherclub.co.uk

Enquiries to: Secretary

Founded: 1998

Organisation type and purpose: Membership association (membership is by subscription), present number of members: 450.

Subject coverage: Panther cars.

Access to staff: Contact by letter, by telephone and by fax
Hours: Mon to Fri, 0900 to 1700

PAPER AGENTS ASSOCIATION

48, Courtmoor Avenue, Fleet, Hampshire, GU52 7UE

continued overleaf

Tel: 01252 680449
Fax: 07092 386132
E-mail: info@paa.org.uk
Website: www.paa.org.uk

Enquiries to: Director

Founded: 1924

Organisation type and purpose: Trade association for the paper and board industry. To promote a better and closer understanding among accredited agents and mill-owned sales offices in the United Kingdom and Eire representing overseas paper and board makers, and to represent their legitimate overall best interests in the local market. There are 38 members of the Association, ranging from small independently owned businesses to the UK sales subsidiaries of multinational paper-making companies. Between them they account for some 40% of all the paper and board consumed in the UK.

Subject coverage: Members of the Association are divided into four sections representing the various grades of paper and board imported: Publication and Fine Papers; Corrugated Case Materials; Packaging, Industrial and Other Papers; Cartonboards, Industrial and Other Boards.

Publications: Electronic and video
Order electronic and video publications from: Download from website

Access to staff: Contact by letter, by telephone, by fax and by e-mail

Affiliated member of: Confederation of Paper Industries

Affiliates: Paper Agents Golfing Society (PAGS)

PAPER INDUSTRY TECHNICAL ASSOCIATION (PITA)

5 Frecheville Court, Bury, Lancashire, BL9 0UF

Tel: 0161 764 5858
Fax: 0161 764 5353
E-mail: info@pita.co.uk
Website: www.pita.co.uk

Enquiries to: Chief Executive
Other contacts: Operations Executive for membership enquiries.

Founded: 1920

Organisation type and purpose: Professional body (membership is by subscription), present number of members: 1700.

Subject coverage: Papermaking technology, coating technology, finishing, environmental issues.

Collection: Complete set of Paper Technology formerly Paper Technology and Industry
Conference proceedings for all association events and many others

Non-library collection catalogue: All or part available online, in-house and in print

Publications: Printed, and electronic and video

Publications list: Available online and in print

Access to staff: Contact by letter, by telephone, by fax and by e-mail. Appointment necessary.
Hours: Mon to Fri, 0900 to 1730

Access for disabled people: Parking provided

PAPER MAKERS ALLIED TRADES ASSOCIATION (PMATA)

24 Beatrice Road, Worsley, Manchester, M28 2TN

Tel: 0161 794 5734
Fax: 0161 793 0827

Enquiries to: Honorary Secretary

Founded: 1931

Organisation type and purpose: Trade association (membership is by subscription), manufacturing industry.
Fostering good relations between the paper industry and its suppliers.

Subject coverage: Paper industry, chemicals and supplies.

PAPERS PAST

Chapel Row, Truro, Cornwall TR1 2EA

Tel: 01872 261220
Fax: 01872 261220
Website: www.paperspast.co.uk/

Enquiries to: Archivist

Founded: 1981

Organisation type and purpose: Mail order birthday/anniversary newspaper supplier.

Subject coverage: Archive newspapers. Early 19th century to early 21st century.

Collection: Newspapers

Publications: Printed

Access to staff: Contact by letter, by telephone and by fax
Hours: Mon to Sun, 0900 to 1900

Access to building: No access other than to staff

PAPYRUS

Formal name: PAPYRUS prevention of young suicide

Lodge House, Thompson Park, Ormerod Road, Burnley, Lancashire, BB11 2RU

Tel: Helpline – HOPELineUK: 0800 068 4141; Admin: 01282 432555
Fax: 01282 432777
E-mail: admin@papyrus-uk.org
Website: www.papyrus-uk.org

Founded: 1997

Organisation type and purpose: Registered charity (charity number 1070896).
A voluntary organisation committed to the prevention of young suicide and the promotion of mental health and emotional wellbeing.
To promote an understanding of the unique contribution that parents, families and carers can make to suicide prevention and to promote public awareness of the importance of emotional well-being and sound mental health.

Subject coverage: UK resources and support for those dealing with suicide, depression or emotional distress – particularly teenagers and young adults. Providing assistance to parents and others in a caring or professional role, supporting vulnerable young people, being represented in policy-making decisions at all levels and monitoring their implementation, encouraging, initiating and taking part in the development of learning opportunities for all, encouraging, taking part and/or initiating research into suicide prevention, campaigning for adequate mental health services for young people, and an easily accessible route to such help on an informal basis, promoting awareness of the risk of mental or emotional distress during adolescence and throughout life, and helping to remove the stigma of such occurrences, encouraging the promotion of emotional well-being and sound mental health, in all levels of education, co-operating with professional, statutory and voluntary bodies working in the suicide prevention field, encouraging and disseminating examples of good practice in suicide prevention.

Publications: Printed, and electronic and video

Publications list: Available online

Access to staff: Contact by letter, by telephone, by fax, by e-mail and via website
Hours: Helpline: Mon to Fri, 1000 to 1700 and 1900 to 2200; Sat, Sun, 1400 to 1700
Admin tel: Mon to Fri, 0900 to 1700

PARENTS FOR INCLUSION (Pi)

Lambeth Accord, 336 Brixton Road, London SW9 7AA

Tel: 020 7738 3888
E-mail: info@parentsforinclusion.org
Website: www.parentsforinclusion.org

Founded: 1984

Organisation type and purpose: Voluntary organisation, registered charity.
To promote inclusive education of children with SEN or disabilities. Parents helping parents so that their disabled children can learn, make friends and have a voice in ordinary school and throughout life. Aims to help parents whose children are said to have special educational needs to get the support their children need in mainstream schools.

Subject coverage: Disability, inclusive education and training for parents and young people.

Publications list: Available in print

Access to staff: Contact by letter, by telephone and by e-mail. Appointment necessary.
Hours: Mon to Fri, 0900 to 1700
Special comments: Inclusion Helpline: Termtime, Wed, Fri 1000 to 1200

Access for disabled people: Parking provided for blue badge holders, ramped entry, lifts and access to all public areas, accessible toilet facilities

PARKES LIBRARY

The Hartley Library, University of Southampton, Highfield, Southampton, SO17 1BJ

Tel: 023 8059 2721 or 8059 3335
Fax: 023 8059 5451
E-mail: library@soton.ac.uk; archives@soton.ac.uk
Website: www.soton.ac.uk/library/resources/collections/parkes/index.html
Website: www-lib.soton.ac.uk
Website: www.southampton.ac.uk/archives/cataloguedatabases/guideintro.html

Enquiries to: Librarian

Organisation type and purpose: University library.
Library collection within the Southampton University Library; devoted to relations between Jewish and non-Jewish communities.

Subject coverage: History of Jewish communities; Zionism and Palestine; Middle Eastern history and Israel; Jewish society, religion and ethics; Jewish-Christian relations; anti-Semitism.

Collection: Manuscript collections covering all aspects of Anglo-Jewry and its origins, relating to national and international organisations and to individuals within the Jewish community

Library catalogue: All or part available online

Publications: Printed

Access to staff: Contact by letter, by telephone, by fax, by e-mail and in person
Hours: Mon to Fri, 0930 to 1700

PARKINSON'S UK

215 Vauxhall Bridge Road, London, SW1V 1EJ

Tel: Helpline: 0808 800 0303
Fax: 020 7233 9908
E-mail: hello@parkinsons.org.uk
Website: www.parkinsons.org.uk

Enquiries to: Advisory Services Senior Coordinator

Founded: 1969

Organisation type and purpose: We bring people with Parkinson's, their carers and families together via our network of local groups, our website and free confidential helpline. Specialist nurses, our supporters, staff and publications provide information and training on every aspect of Parkinson's. We also fund major research projects and campaign for better services.

Subject coverage: We look at why Parkinson's occurs, the wide variety of symptoms the condition may cause and the range of treatments and support available.

Information services: Information sheets and booklets available to download on all issues relating to Parkinson's.

Publications: Printed, and electronic and video

Publications list: Available in print

Access to staff: Contact by letter, by telephone, by fax, by e-mail and via website. Appointment necessary.
Hours: Helpline: Mon to Fri, 0900 to 2000; Sat 1000 to 1400

Access to building: Prior appointment required

Branches: Scotland; Forsythe House, Lommond Court, Castle Business Park, Stirling, FK9 4TU; tel: 01786 433811; fax: 01786 431811; e-mail: pds.scotland@parkinsons.org.uk; website: http://www.parkinsons.org.uk

Member organisation of: European Parkinson's Disease Association

Member organisations: over 300 branches throughout the UK.

PARLIAMENTARY ADVISORY COUNCIL FOR TRANSPORT SAFETY (PACTS)

St Thomas' Hospital, Governors Hall, Block 5 South Wing, Lambeth Palace Road, London, SE1 7EH

Tel: 020 7922 8112
Fax: 020 7401 8740
E-mail: admin@pacts.org.uk
Website: www.pacts.org.uk

Enquiries to: Administrator

Founded: 1982

Organisation type and purpose: Membership association (membership is by subscription), present number of members: 250, voluntary organisation, registered charity (charity number 1068607), research organisation.
Parliamentary advisory body (transport safety).

Subject coverage: Road, rail and air transport safety. PACTS advises parliamentarians on issues of transport safety based on research solutions.

Publications: Printed

Publications list: Available online

Access to staff: Contact by telephone and by e-mail
Hours: Mon to Fri, 0900 to 1700

Founder member of: European Transport Safety Council (ETSC); Rue du Cornet 34, Brussels, B-1040, Belgium

PARLIAMENTARY AND HEALTH SERVICE OMBUDSMAN

Formal name: Office of the Parliamentary Commissioner for Administration and the Health Service Commissioners

Millbank Tower, Millbank, London, SW1P 4QP

Tel: 0300 061 4104
Fax: 0300 061 1565
E-mail: lrc@ombudsman.org.uk
Website: www.ombudsman.org.uk

Enquiries to: Information Officer

Founded: 1967

Organisation type and purpose: National organisation.

Subject coverage: Ombudsman issues.

Order printed publications from: Stationery Office (for purchase)

Access to staff: Contact by letter, by telephone, by fax and by e-mail
Hours: Mon to Fri, 0900 to 1700

PARLIAMENTARY AND SCIENTIFIC COMMITTEE

48 Westminster Palace Gardens, Artillery Row, London, SW1P 1RR

Tel: 020 7222 7085
Fax: 020 7222 5355

Enquiries to: Secretary

Founded: 1939

Organisation type and purpose: Membership association (membership is by subscription).

Subject coverage: Parliament and science.

Publications: Printed

Access to staff: Contact by letter, by telephone and by fax
Hours: Mon to Fri, 1000 to 1800

PARLIAMENTARY ARCHIVES

Parliamentary Archives, Houses of Parliament, London, SW1A 0PW

Tel: 020 7219 3074
Fax: 020 7219 2570
E-mail: archives@parliament.uk
Website: www.parliament.uk/archives
Website: www.portcullis.parliament.uk

Enquiries to: Clerk of The Records

Founded: 1946

Organisation type and purpose: One of the Offices of Parliament.
To preserve and make available the archives of Parliament.

Subject coverage: History of both Houses of Parliament, history of the Palace of Westminster; the Private Bill Records contain a great deal of information about local history, e.g. local government, railways, roads, canals, electricity, gas and water works; political history from the special collections; legal and contemporary issues. Sources for genealogists include certain legislation, Private Bill evidence, Protestation Returns of 1642 and other Lords papers.

Collection: Records of the House of Lords from 1497 and of the House of Commons from 1547, papers of 1st Viscount Samuel, Lord Beaverbrook, Lloyd George, Bonar Law and others

Trade and statistical information: Published Parliamentary reports.
Evidence given to select committees

Non-library collection catalogue: All or part available online and in-house

Library catalogue: All or part available online and in-house

Publications: Printed, and microform publications

Publications list: Available online and in print

Access to staff: Contact by letter, by telephone, by fax, by e-mail and via website. Appointment necessary.

continued overleaf

Hours: Mon, Wed to Fri, 0930 to 1700; Tue, 0930 to 2000, booking one week in advance only when Parliament is in session

Access for disabled people: Toilet facilities
Special comments: Parking by special arrangement, access by lift.

PARLIAMENTARY MONITORING SERVICES (PMS)

19 Douglas Street, London, SW1P 4PA

Tel: 020 7233 8283
Fax: 020 7821 9352
E-mail: thomas.warren@dods.co.uk
Website: www.politicalwizard.co.uk

Enquiries to: Managing Director

Founded: 1978

Organisation type and purpose: Research organisation, publishing house.
We are an independent commercial political research, news and publishing company.

Subject coverage: Politics: local, national and European Union, legislation, issues and personalities.

Publications: Printed, and electronic and video

Publications list: Available in print

Access to staff: Contact by letter, by telephone, by fax and by e-mail. Appointment necessary.
Hours: Mon to Fri, 0900 to 1730

Access to building: No prior appointment required

Subsidiary body: PMS Publications Limited

PARTIALLY SIGHTED SOCIETY (PSS)

PO Box 322, Doncaster, South Yorkshire, DN1 2XA

Tel: 01302 323132
Fax: 01302 368998
E-mail: info@partsight.org.uk

Enquiries to: Information Officer

Founded: 1973

Organisation type and purpose: Membership association, voluntary organisation, registered charity (charity number 254052).
Helping the visually impaired make best use of their remaining sight.

Subject coverage: Education, employment, mobility, daily living, leisure, aids and adaptations in relation to living with partial sight.

Publications: Printed

Publications list: Available in print

Access to staff: Contact by letter, by telephone, by fax, by e-mail and via website. Appointment necessary.
Hours: Mon to Fri, 0900 to 1700

PARTNERSHIP FOR THEOLOGICAL EDUCATION (PTE)

Formal name: Luther King House Library

Luther King House, Brighton Grove, Rusholme, Manchester, M14 5JP

Tel: 0161 249 2514
Fax: 0161 248 9201
E-mail: library@lkh.co.uk
Website: www.lutherkinghouse.org.uk
Website: www.lkhlibrarycatalogue.org.uk

Enquiries to: Learning Resources Tutor
Other contacts: Learning Resources Assistant

Founded: 1988; formerly called Manchester Christian Institute (year of change 1992); formerly called Northern Federation for Training in Ministry (year of change 2000)

Organisation type and purpose: Registered charity, university department or institute. Theological college.

Subject coverage: Theology; Free Church and general ecclesiastical history; ministry; Bible commentaries; worship; social sciences; biography; history; philosophy; ethics; missiology; spirituality; pastoral theology; ecumenism; comparative religion; community studies.

Collection: Collections housed in the John Rylands Library, Manchester
Hobill Collection and Primitive Methodist Material
Northern (Congregational College) Collection
Rawdon Collection of historical Baptist material, mostly from 18th and 19th centuries (Northern Baptist College Deposit)
Unitarian College Collection (McLachlan Library) Unitarian and Nonconformist history, Socinianism

Non-library collection catalogue: All or part available online

Library catalogue: All or part available online

Access to staff: Contact by letter, by telephone, by fax, by e-mail, in person and via website. Appointment necessary. Non-members charged.
Hours: Mon to Fri, 0900 to 1700

Access for disabled people: Parking provided, ramped entry, toilet facilities

Constituent bodies: Hartley Victoria College; Luther King House Open College; Northern Baptist College; Northern College (United Reformed and Congregational); Unitarian College

Links with: William Temple Foundation; at the same address

Recognised by the: Department of Religions and Theology of the University of Manchester; Department of Theology and Religious Studies of the University of Chester

PASSAGE

Formal name: The Passage

St Vincent's Centre, Carlisle Place, London SW1P 1N

E-mail: info@passage.org.uk
Website: www.passage.org.uk

Founded: 1980

Organisation type and purpose: A Christian charitable organisation.
Runs London's largest voluntary sector day centre for homeless and vulnerable people: each day it helps more than 200 men and women.
To provide resources that encourage, inspire, and challenge homeless people to transform their lives.

Subject coverage: Day cservices offering: basic care, individual assessment and advice, health, housing, pastoral and spiritual care, education, training and employment. Outreach services to contact rough sleepers. Hostel accommodation moving towards resettlement and further steps to independence. Supported semi-independent accommodation moving towards independence and reintegration. Welcomes and treats clients with respect and dignity, finding out what they need and want. Offers professional and appropriate advice and help according to client needs and aspirations. Tries to agree an action plan with clients that is time-limited, with the aim of supporting clients out of homelessness.

Publications: Electronic and video
Order electronic and video publications from: website: http://www.writesofpassage.org.uk

Access to staff: Contact by letter, by telephone and by e-mail

A constitutional partnership between: Daughters of Charity of St Vincent de Paul and Westminster Cathedral

PASSENGER SHIPPING ASSOCIATION (PSA)

1st Floor, 41–42 Eastcastle Street, London, W1W 8DW

Tel: 020 7436 2449
Fax: 020 7636 9206
E-mail: kathryn@psa-ace.org
Website: www.ferryinformationservice.co.uk
Website: www.cruiseinformationservice.co.uk

Enquiries to: Director
Other contacts: Administrator

Organisation type and purpose: Membership association (membership is by subscription).

Subject coverage: Passenger shipping.

Access to staff: Contact by e-mail
Hours: Mon to Fri, 0900 to 1700

Access to building: No access other than to staff, prior appointment required

PASSIVE FIRE PROTECTION FEDERATION (PFPF)

Tournai Hall, Evelyn Woods Road, Aldershot, Hampshire, GU11 2LL

Tel: 01252 357841
Fax: 01252 357831
E-mail: admin@pfpf.org
Website: pfpf.org/

Enquiries to: Secretary
Direct e-mail: membership@pfpf.org

Organisation type and purpose: Trade association, present number of members: 16.
Federation of trade associations, test houses, certification and government bodies involved in passive fire protection.

Subject coverage: Trade associations, test houses, certification and government bodies involved in passive fire protection.

Access to staff: Contact by letter, by telephone, by fax, by e-mail and via website
Hours: Mon to Fri, 0900 to 1700

PASTEL SOCIETY (PS)

17 Carlton House Terrace, London, SW1Y 5BD

Tel: 020 7930 6844
Fax: 020 7839 7830
E-mail: press@mallgalleries.com
Website: www.thepastelsociety.org.uk
Website: www.mallgalleries.org.uk

Enquiries to: Secretary
Other contacts: Marketing and Communications Officer

Founded: 1898

Organisation type and purpose: Membership association (membership is by election or invitation), present number of members: 68, voluntary organisation, registered charity (charity number 200048).
To foster and promote the art of pastel painting.

Subject coverage: Pastel art.

Collection: Examples of pastel artists' work on slides, photos and some original pastel paintings

Publications: Printed

Access to staff: Contact by letter, by telephone, by fax, by e-mail and via website. Appointment necessary.
Hours: Mon to Fri, 0930 to 1700

Access to building: No access other than to staff, prior appointment required
Hours: Mon to Fri, 0930 to 1700

Access for disabled people: Stairlift; toilet facilities
Special comments: Stairlift.

Links with: Federation of British Artists (FBA); at the same address

PATENT OFFICE

Cardiff Road, Newport, South Wales, NP10 8QQ

Tel: 01633 814000, Operator; 0845 9500505, Central Enquiry Unit (local rate); 0645 222 250 (minicom, local rate)
Fax: 01633 814444
E-mail: enquiries@patent.gov.uk
Website: www.patent.gov.uk

Enquiries to: Information Officer
Direct fax: 01633 813600

Founded: 1852

Organisation type and purpose: National government body.
Executive agency of the Department of Trade and Industry.

Subject coverage: All areas of Intellectual Property incorporating: Patents, Designs, Trade marks and Copyright.

Publications: Printed, and electronic and video

Access to staff: Contact by letter, by telephone, by fax, by e-mail, in person and via website
Hours: Mon to Fri, 0900 to 1700

Access to building: No prior appointment required
Special comments: Trade Mark Searches in Newport require an appointment.

Other addresses: The Patent Office; Harmsworth House, 13–15 Bouverie Street, London, EC4Y 8DP; tel: 020 7596 6518; e-mail: enquiries@patent.gov.uk

PATHOLOGICAL SOCIETY OF GREAT BRITAIN AND IRELAND

2 Carlton House Terrace, London, SW1Y 5AF

Tel: 020 7976 1260
Fax: 020 7930 2981
E-mail: admin@pathsoc.org
Website: www.pathsoc.org

Enquiries to: Administrator

Founded: 1906

Organisation type and purpose: Learned society (membership is by election or invitation), present number of members: 1,500 (charity number 214702).
Research communication for the continuing education of pathologists.

Subject coverage: Pathology.

Publications: Printed

Access to staff: Contact by letter, by telephone, by fax and by e-mail
Hours: Mon to Fri, 0900 to 1730

PATTERN, MODEL AND MOULDMAKERS ASSOCIATION (PMMMA)

c/o Eur. Ing. Andrew Turner, National Metalforming Centre, 47 Birmingham Road, West Bromwich, West Midlands, B70 6PY

Tel: 0121 601 6976
Fax: 01544 340332
E-mail: andrew@pmmma.co.uk
Website: www.pmmma.co.uk

Organisation type and purpose: Trade association.

Subject coverage: Pattern-making, industrial patterns and moulds.

Access to staff: Contact by letter, by telephone and by fax

PCET PUBLISHING

27 Kirchen Road, London, W13 0UD

Tel: 020 8567 9206 or 5343
Fax: 020 8566 5120
E-mail: info@pcet.co.uk
Website: www.pcet.co.uk

Enquiries to: Managing Director
Direct e-mail: Director@pcet.co.uk

Founded: 1964

Organisation type and purpose: Publishing house.
Non-profit making publisher of educational visual aids.

Subject coverage: Educational visual aids in all areas of the National Curriculum, except modern languages.

Publications: Printed

Publications list: Available in print

Access to staff: Contact by letter, by telephone, by fax, by e-mail and via website. Appointment necessary.
Hours: Mon to Fri, 0900 to 1700

PDSA

Whitechapel Way, Priorslee, Telford, Shropshire, TF2 9PQ

Tel: 01952 290999
Fax: 01952 291035
E-mail: pr@pdsa.org.uk
Website: www.pdsa.org.uk

Enquiries to: Public Relations Manager

Founded: 1917

Organisation type and purpose: Registered charity (charity number 208217).
The PDSA provides free veterinary treatment to sick and injured pets whose owners qualify for help, by receiving either Housing Benefit or Council Tax Benefit, and live within an area served by a PDSA PetAid hospital or PetAid practice.

Subject coverage: Veterinary and associated social and educational subjects (eg pet care).

Publications: Printed

Publications list: Available in print

Access to staff: Contact by letter, by telephone, by fax, by e-mail and via website
Hours: Mon to Fri, 0900 to 1700

PEAK DISTRICT NATIONAL PARK AUTHORITY (PDNPA)

National Park Office, Aldern House, Baslow Road, Bakewell, Derbyshire, DE45 1AE

Tel: 01629 816200
Fax: 01629 816310
E-mail: customer.service@peakdistrict.gov.uk
Website: www.peakdistrict.gov.uk

Enquiries to: Head of Communications (for media enquiries)
Direct tel: 01629 816356
Direct e-mail: john.fern@peakdistrict.gov.uk

Founded: 1951

Organisation type and purpose: Local government body, advisory body, statutory body, training organisation, publishing house.

Subject coverage: The Peak District National Park, conservation of the National Park environment, integrated rural development, moorland erosion, recreation, and restoration; general information on the history, geology, agriculture, wildlife, and recreation opportunities, rural public transport, environmental education and training.

Publications: Printed

Publications list: Available in print

Access to staff: Contact by letter, by telephone, by e-mail and via website. Appointment necessary.
Hours: Mon to Fri, 0845 to 1700

Access to building: Prior appointment required

Access for disabled people: Parking provided, ramped entry, toilet facilities

PEEBLES AREA LIBRARY

Chambers Institution, High Street, Peebles, Borders, EH45 8AG

Tel: 01721 720123
Fax: 01721 724424
E-mail: libpeebles@scotborders.gov.uk

Enquiries to: Area Librarian
Direct e-mail: ptaylor@scotborders.gov.uk

Founded: 1859

Organisation type and purpose: Local government body, public library.

Subject coverage: General, Peeblesshire local history, John Buchan material.

Library catalogue: All or part available in-house

Access to staff: Contact by letter, by telephone, by fax, by e-mail and in person
Hours: Mon, Wed and Fri, 0930 to 1700; Tue and Thu, 0930 to 1900; Sat, 0900 to 1230

Access for disabled people: Lift to Library area on first floor only

Parent body: Scottish Borders Library Service; St Marys Hill, Selkirk, TD7 5EW; tel: 01750 20842; fax: 01750 22875

PEMBROKE COLLEGE

McGowin Library, Oxford, OX1 1DW

Tel: 01865 276409
Fax: 01865 276418
Website: www.pmb.ox.ac.uk

Enquiries to: Librarian/Archivist
Direct e-mail: library@pmb.ox.ac.uk

Founded: 1624

Organisation type and purpose: College library.

Subject coverage: Aristotle, Samuel Johnson, College history.

Collection: Archive of Pembroke College
Aristotle (Chandler Collection)
Samuel Johnson

Access to staff: Contact by letter, by telephone, by fax and by e-mail. Appointment necessary. Letter of introduction required.
Hours: Mon to Fri, 0900 to 1700

PEMBROKESHIRE COAST NATIONAL PARK AUTHORITY (PCNPA)

Llanion Park, Pembroke Dock, Pembrokeshire, SA72 6DY

Tel: 0845 345 7275
Fax: 01646 689076
E-mail: info@pembrokeshirecoast.org.uk
Website: www.pcnpa.org.uk

Enquiries to: Switchboard

Founded: 1952

Organisation type and purpose: Local government body, advisory body, statutory body, present number of members: 18
National Park Authority and Local Planning Authority.
Conservation of landscape, wildlife and culture of the National Park; promotion of the enjoyment and understanding of the park's special qualities; fostering the social and economic well-being of the local community.

Subject coverage: Conservation, National Parks, recreation, countryside access, interpretation, education, local information, communities, cultural heritage, wildlife, planning.

Collection: Local maps and aerial photographs
Planning Records
Teachers' Resources

Trade and statistical information: Statistics on the National Park (as available)

Publications: Printed, and electronic and video
Order printed publications from: Tenby Information Centre Manager, Pembrokeshire Coast National Park Authority, Ruabon House, South Parade, Tenby, SA70 7DL

Publications list: Available online and in print

Access to staff: Contact by letter, by telephone, by fax, by e-mail, in person and via website
Hours: Headquarters: Mon to Thu, 0900 to 1700; Fri, 0900 to 1630

Access for disabled people: Parking provided, ramped entry, wheelchair lifts and toilet facilities

Branches: Carew Castle and Tidal Mill; Carew, Pembrokeshire, SA70 8SL; tel: 01646 651782; fax: 01646 651782; e-mail: enquiries@carewcastle.com; Castell Henllys Iron Age Fort; Meline, Crymych, Pembrokeshire, SA41 3UT; tel: 01239 891319; fax: 01239 891319; e-mail: enquiries@castellhenllys.com; Cilrhedyn Woodland Centre; Llanychaer, Fishguard, Pembrokeshire, SA65 9TN; tel: 01348 881441; fax: 01348 881713; National Park Information Centre (all year); Ruabon House, South Parade, Tenby, SA70 7DL; tel: 01834 845040; fax: 01834 840871; e-mail: contact.centre@pembrokeshire.gov.uk; National Park Information Centre (seasonal); Bank Cottages, Long Street, Newport, SA42 0TN; tel: 01239 820912; fax: 01239 820912; Oriel Y Parc Landscape Gallery and National Park Information Centre; The Grove, St Davids, Pembrokeshire, SA62 6NW; tel: 01437 725087; fax: 01437 720099; e-mail: enquiries@stdavids.pembrokeshirecoast.org.uk

Links with: Parc Naturel Regional d'Armorique; 15 place aux Foires, BP 27, 29590 Le Faou, France; tel: +33 2 98 81 90 08; fax: +33 2 98 81 90 09

PEMBROKESHIRE COUNTY COUNCIL

County Hall, Haverfordwest, Pembrokeshire, SA61 1TP

Tel: 01437 764551
Fax: 01437 775303
E-mail: enquiries@pembrokeshire.gov.uk
Website: www.pembrokeshire.gov.uk

Enquiries to: Head of Marketing Communications
Direct tel: 01437 775850
Direct e-mail: david.thomas@pembrokeshire.gov.uk

Founded: April 1996

Organisation type and purpose: Local government body.

Subject coverage: All local government services.

Collection: County archives department, county libraries and county museums

Publications: Printed

Access to staff: Contact by letter, by telephone, by fax, by e-mail, in person and via website. Appointment necessary.
Hours: Mon to Fri, 0900 to 1700

Access for disabled people: Parking provided, level entry, toilet facilities

PEMBROKESHIRE RECORD OFFICE

The Castle, Haverfordwest, Pembrokeshire, SA61 2EF

Tel: 01437 763707
Fax: 01437 768539
E-mail: record.office@pembrokeshire.gov.uk
Website: www.pembrokeshire.gov.uk/archives

Enquiries to: Archivist

Founded: 1963

Organisation type and purpose: Local government body.
Local authority record office.

Subject coverage: The history of Pembrokeshire.

Collection: Pembrokeshire historical material, mainly manuscript collections

Non-library collection catalogue: All or part available in-house

Library catalogue: All or part available in-house

Publications list: Available in print

Access to staff: Contact by letter, by telephone, by fax, by e-mail, in person and via website
Hours: Mon to Thu, 0900 to 1645; Fri, 0900 to 1615

Access to building: No access other than to staff and areas available to the public, i.e. search rooms and toilets
Hours: Mon to Thu, 0900 to 1645; Fri, 0900 to 1615
Special comments: First Mon in the month, 1000 to 1645. First Sat in the month, except bank holiday weekends, 0930 to 1230.

Access for disabled people: Parking provided, ramped entry, access to all public areas, toilet facilities

PENGUIN COLLECTORS' SOCIETY (PCS)

c/o 31 Myddelton Square, London, EC1R 1YB

Tel: 020 7278 8064
E-mail: treasurer@penguincollectorssociety.org
Website: www.penguincollectorssociety.com

Enquiries to: Secretary/Treasurer

Founded: 1974

Organisation type and purpose: Charity (membership is by subscription), present number of members: c. 400.
Study, research, and publishing on 20th-century books, especially those published by Penguin Books Limited.

Subject coverage: Penguin Books, their history and publications.

Publications: Printed

Publications list: Available in print

Access to staff: Contact by e-mail and via website
Hours: PCS has no staff – volunteers only

Access to building: PCS has no premises.

PENNINE WAY ASSOCIATION (PWA)

29 Springfield Park Avenue, Chelmsford, Essex, CM2 6EL

Tel: 01245 256772
E-mail: penninewayassociation@hotmail.com
Website: www.penninewayassociation.co.uk

Enquiries to: Chairman
Direct e-mail: penninewayassociation@hotmail.com

Founded: 1971; formerly called Pennine Way Council (year of change 1992)

Organisation type and purpose: Membership association (membership is by subscription), present number of members: 360, voluntary organisation, registered charity (charity number 511519).

Subject coverage: To secure the protection of the Pennine Way, to provide information about the Way to the public, to educate users of the Way and its environs in a proper respect for the countryside, and to provide a forum in which different interests connected with the Way and its use can discuss problems of mutual concern.

Publications: Printed

Access to staff: Contact by letter, by telephone, by e-mail and via website
Hours: Answerphone

PENSIONS ADVISORY SERVICE LTD (TPAS)

11 Belgrave Road, London, SW1V 1RB

Tel: 0845 6012923
Fax: 020 7233 8016
E-mail: enquiries@pensionsadvisoryservice.org.uk
Website: www.pensionsadvisoryservice.org.uk
Direct fax: 020 7592 7000

Founded: 1983

Organisation type and purpose: Advisory body, voluntary organisation.
To provide help and advice on various pension problems, helps to resolve any difficulties encountered with the trustees or administrators of pension schemes.

Subject coverage: Occupational and personal pensions and state pensions.

Publications: Printed

Publications list: Available online and in print

Access to staff: Contact by letter, by telephone, by fax and by e-mail
Hours: Mon to Fri, 0900 to 1700

Access to building: No access other than to staff

PENSIONS MANAGEMENT INSTITUTE (PMI)

PMI House, 4–10 Artillery Lane, London, E1 7LS

Tel: 020 7247 1452
Fax: 020 7365 0603
E-mail: enquiries@pensions-pmi.org.uk
Website: www.pensions-pmi.org.uk

Enquiries to: Head of Qualifications and Student Services

Founded: 1976

Organisation type and purpose: Professional body (membership is by subscription), present number of members: 4,500.
PMI sets and promotes standards of excellence and lifelong learning for pensions professionals, trustees and those working in the employee benefits field, through its qualifications, membership and ongoing support services.

Subject coverage: Pension schemes, administration and management; pensioners.

Publications: Printed

Access to staff: Contact by letter, by telephone, by fax, by e-mail and via website
Hours: Mon to Fri, 0900 to 1700

PENSIONS OMBUDSMAN

6th Floor, 11 Belgrave Road, London, SW1V 1RB

Tel: 020 7834 9144
Fax: 020 7821 0065

Enquiries to: Administrator
Direct e-mail: michael.lydon@pensions-ombudsman.org.uk
Other contacts: Press Officer for press enquiries.

Founded: 1990

Organisation type and purpose: Independent statutory body.

Subject coverage: In cases where a complaint or dispute cannot be resolved, normally after the intervention of OPAS, an application can be made to the Pensions Ombudsman for an adjudication. The Ombudsman can investigate and determine any complaint or dispute of fact or law involving the management of occupational and personal pension schemes. The services of the Ombudsman are available to scheme members, and prospective members of schemes, as well as (in some circumstances) employers, trustees or managers.

Publications: Printed

Access to staff: Contact by letter, by telephone, by fax and by e-mail
Hours: Mon to Fri, 0900 to 1700
Special comments: No personal callers.

PENSIONS REGULATOR

Napier House, Trafalgar Place, Brighton, East Sussex, BN1 4DW

Tel: 0870 606 3636
Fax: 0870 241 1144
E-mail: customersupport@thepensionsregulator.gov.uk
Website: www.thepensionsregulator.gov.uk
Website: www.trusteetoolkit.co.uk

Enquiries to: Customer Support

Founded: 2005

Organisation type and purpose: Statutory body.
UK regulator of work-based pensions schemes.

Subject coverage: Work-based pensions industry.

Publications list: Available online and in print

Access to staff: Contact by letter, by telephone, by fax, by e-mail and via website
Hours: Mon to Fri, 0900 to 1730

PENWITH DISTRICT COUNCIL

Council Offices, St Clare, Penzance, Cornwall, TR18 3QW

Tel: 01736 362341
Fax: 01736 336595
Website: www.penwith.gov.uk

Organisation type and purpose: Local government body.

PEOPLE & PLANET

51 Union Street, Oxford, OX4 1JP

Tel: 01865 245678
Fax: 01865 791927
E-mail: people@peopleandplanet.org
Website: peopleandplanet.org

Enquiries to: Administrator

Founded: 1969

Organisation type and purpose: Student action on world poverty, human rights and the environment.

Subject coverage: Global poverty, human rights and the environment, campaigning and education with UK students.

Publications: Printed

Access to staff: *Hours:* Mon to Fri, 1000 to 1600

PEPYS LIBRARY

Magdalene College, Cambridge, CB3 0AG

Tel: 01223 332125
E-mail: pepyslibrary@magd.cam.ac.uk
Website: www.magd.cam.ac.uk/pepys/index.html

Enquiries to: Pepys Librarian
Direct e-mail: pepyslibrary@magd.cam.ac.uk

Founded: 1703

Organisation type and purpose: Private library with restricted public access.

continued overleaf

Subject coverage: Pre-1703 printed books and manuscripts (nautical, musical, literary, ballads, prints and drawings, calligraphy, medieval manuscripts).

Collection: Personal library of the diarist and Secretary of the Admiralty, Samuel Pepys (1633–1703), bequeathed by him to his old college. Preserved in its original presses as it was at the time of his death.

Library catalogue: All or part available in print

Publications: Printed

Access to staff: Contact by letter and by e-mail. Appointment necessary. Letter of introduction required.
Special comments: Researchers should make requests for appointments in writing, giving details of the nature of research and material required.
General visitors may visit without appointment. Groups must not exceed 10 people.

Access to building: *Hours:* Michaelmas and Lent terms: Mon to Sat, 1400 to 1500
Easter term to end of August: Mon to Fri, 1400 to 1600
Sat, 1200 to 1300 and 1400 to 1500
Refer to website for exact dates
Special comments: Access is via a flight of about 20 stairs; there is no lift

Access for disabled people: Not accessible by wheelchair

PERFECT INFORMATION (PI)

35 Chiswell Street, London, EC1Y 4SE

Tel: 020 7892 4200
Fax: 020 7892 4201
E-mail: research@perfectinfo.com
Website: www.perfectinfo.com

Enquiries to: Director

Founded: 1990

Organisation type and purpose: Service industry.

Subject coverage: All compliance documentation released by UK listed companies including: directors shareholdings, board changes, changes in substantial shareholdings, results, bids, acquisitions, report and accounts, circulars to shareholders, all available online in original form with an archive back to 1982.

Collection: All UK Company Reports and accounts
EDGAR SEC filings and International Bonds
Entire London Stock Exchange microfiche collection back to 1982
European and Asian Company Annual Reports
RNS Announcements
UK Company Circulars

Publications: Electronic and video

Access to staff: Contact by letter, by telephone, by fax, by e-mail and via website. All charged.
Hours: Mon to Fri, 0900 to 1730

Connections with: Centaur Communications; 50 Poland Street, London, W1F 7AX

Other address: Perfect Information Inc (PI); 245 Park Avenue, 39th Floor, New York, NY 10167, USA; tel: 1 212 792 4350; fax: 1 212 792 4307

PERFORMING RIGHT SOCIETY LIMITED (PRS)

29–33 Berners Street, London, W1T 3AB

Tel: 020 7580 5544
Fax: 020 7306 4550
E-mail: press@mcps-prs-alliance.co.uk
Website: www.prs.co.uk

Enquiries to: Chief Executive

Founded: 1914

Organisation type and purpose:
Membership association (membership is by subscription).
To license the public performance, broadcast and cable transmission of its composer and publisher members' copyright.

Subject coverage: Music copyright and royalties; public performance; broadcasting; collection and distribution of performance royalties.

Publications: Printed

Access to staff: Contact by letter, by telephone, by fax, by e-mail and via website. Appointment necessary.
Hours: Mon to Fri, 0900 to 1700

Access for disabled people: Ramped entry

Affiliated to: similar performing right organisations, throughout the world

Links with: British Music Rights; Mechanical Copyright Protection Society Limited

PERMANENT WAY INSTITUTION (PWI)

4 Coombe Road, Folkestone, CT19 4EG

Tel: 01303 275835
E-mail: secretary@permanentwayinstitution.com
Website: www.permanentwayinstitution.com

Enquiries to: Secretary

Founded: 1884

Organisation type and purpose: Learned society (membership is by subscription), present number of members: 2,800 British Isles, 1,500 rest of world.

Subject coverage: Railway permanent way engineering (concerning railway track infrastructure): design, construction and maintenance.

Non-library collection catalogue: All or part available online

Library catalogue: All or part available online and in-house

Publications: Printed
Order printed publications from: Secretary, Permanent Way Institution or online

Publications list: Available online and in print

Access to staff: Contact by letter, by telephone, by e-mail and via website
Hours: Mon to Fri, 0900 to 1630

Has: 19 sections in UK, 1 for all Ireland, 5 overseas

Links with: Union of European Railway Engineer Associations; Verband Deutscher Eisenbahn Ingenieure (VDEI); Germany

Member organisation of: Union of European Railway Engineer Associations (UEEIV)

PERSONAL FINANCE SOCIETY (PFS)

42–48 High Road, South Woodford, London, E18 2JP

Tel: 020 8530 0852
Fax: 020 8530 3052
E-mail: customer.serv@thepfs.org
Website: www.thepfs.org/

Enquiries to: Press and PR Co-ordinator
Direct e-mail: alex.thompson@cii.co.uk

Founded: 2004; created by the merger of The Society of Financial Advisers and the Life Insurance Association (1972)

Organisation type and purpose:
Professional body (membership is by subscription), present number of members: 25,000.

Subject coverage: Life assurance; pensions; unit-linked products; financial services; professional education, ethics and standards.

Publications: Printed

Access to staff: Contact by letter, by telephone, by fax, by e-mail and via website. Appointment necessary.
Hours: Mon to Fri, 0900 to 1700

Associated with: Chartered Insurance Institute (London); LIA Ireland; Dublin; National Association of Life Underwriters; Washington, DC, USA

Network of: 35 regions in UK and Ireland

PERSONAL SAFETY MANUFACTURERS ASSOCIATION (PSMA)

Tamesis House, 35 St Philip's Avenue, Worcester Park, Surrey, KT4 8JS

Tel: 020 8330 6446
Fax: 020 8330 7447
E-mail: psma@tamgroup.co.uk

Enquiries to: General Secretary

Founded: 1998

Organisation type and purpose: Trade association.

Subject coverage: Production and marketing of industrial protective and safety equipment within the PSE Directive of the EC.

Publications: Printed

Access to staff: Contact by e-mail
Hours: Mon to Fri, 0900 to 1700

Access to building: Prior appointment required

Affiliated to: British Safety Industry Federation (BSIF); St Asaph Business Park, St Asaph, Denbighshire, LL17 0LJ; tel: 01745 585600; fax: 01745 585800; e-mail: info@bsif.co.uk; website: www.bsif.co.uk

PERTH AND KINROSS COUNCIL

2 High Street, Perth, Tayside, PH1 5PH

Tel: 01738 475000
Fax: 01738 475710
E-mail: enquiries@pkc.gov.uk
Website: www.pkc.gov.uk

Enquiries to: Research and Consultation Assistant
Direct tel: 01738 475084
Direct fax: 01738 475010
Direct e-mail: tbrunton@pkc.gov.uk

Founded: 1996

Organisation type and purpose: Local government body.

Subject coverage: Information on the council, tourism, socio-economic property, education, roads, planning, leisure and cultural services, social work, law and administration, environmental health, Europe social policy, finance, human resources, housing.

Access to staff: Contact by letter
Hours: Mon to Fri, 0900 to 1700

Access for disabled people: Ramped entry, toilet facilities

PERTH AND KINROSS LIBRARIES

A K Bell Library, York Place, Perth, Perthshire, PH2 8EP

Tel: 01738 444949; 01738 620114 (minicom, textphone)
Fax: 01738 477010
E-mail: library@pkc.gov.uk
Website: www.pkc.gov.uk/library

Enquiries to: Head of Libraries and Archives
Direct e-mail: mmoir@pkc.gov.uk

Founded: 1996

Organisation type and purpose: Local government body, public library.

Subject coverage: General, local history, local archives, Scots language.

Collection: Atholl Collection (17th and 18th century Scottish folk and dance music)
District archives
Local history
McIntosh Collection (17th century ecclesiastical and general works)
William Soutar Collection (poetry and Scottish literature)

Non-library collection catalogue: All or part available in print

Publications: Printed

Publications list: Available online and in print

Access to staff: Contact by letter, by telephone, by fax, by e-mail, in person and via website. Appointment necessary.
Hours: Mon, Wed, 0930 to 1700; Tue, Thu, 0930 to 2000; Fri, 0900 to 1700; Sat, 0930 to 1600

Access for disabled people: Parking provided, level entry, access to all public areas, toilet facilities

Part of: Perth and Kinross Council; 2 High Street, Perth; tel: 01738 475000; fax: 01738 475710; website: pkc.gov.uk

PERTHES ASSOCIATION

PO Box 773, Guildford, GU1 1XN

Tel: 01483 306637
E-mail: info@perthes.org.uk
Website: www.perthes.org.uk

Enquiries to: Administrator
Direct tel: 01483 447122

Founded: 1976

Organisation type and purpose: National organisation, membership association (membership is by subscription), present number of members: 803 full, 2,000 part members, voluntary organisation, registered charity (charity number 326161), suitable for all ages.

Subject coverage: Help, advice and support to sufferers of Perthes Disease of the hip, all forms of osteochondritis and MED (multiple epiphyseal dysplasia), in both children and adults; medical information, financial advice (benefits), housing, education, special equipment and clothing, counselling.

Publications: Printed
Order printed publications from: Secretary, at the same address

Access to staff: Contact by letter, by telephone, by e-mail, in person and via website. Appointment necessary. Access for members only. Non-members charged.
Hours: Mon to Fri, 0900 to 1700, tel and e-mail
Special comments: 0900 to 1300 tel.

Links with: Contact a Family; Long Term Medical Conditions Alliance; NCVO; RADAR

PERTHSHIRE TOURIST BOARD (PTB)

Administrative Headquarters, Lower City Mills, West Mill Street, Perth, Tayside, PH1 5QP

Tel: 01738 627958/9
Fax: 01738 630416
E-mail: info@perthshire.co.uk
Website: www.perthshire.co.uk/

Enquiries to: Chief Executive
Other contacts: Head of Marketing; Head of Visitor Services

Organisation type and purpose: Statutory body, membership association (membership is by subscription), present number of members: 1300.
Non-governmental public body, area tourist board.
To position Perthshire as a world-class destination, where visitor expectations are exceeded through product quality, delivery of service and unique destination characteristics, in such a manner that Perthshire's maximum potential for long-term economic and social prosperity is realised through a sustainable tourism industry.

Subject coverage: Information on all matters pertaining to tourism in Perthshire, 2000 square miles in Central Scotland, accommodation, visitor attractions, sporting and recreational facilities, events and entertainments.

Trade and statistical information: Data on the volume and value of tourism in Perthshire. Research and statistical information.
Marketing advice to Tourist Board members

Publications: Printed, and electronic and video

Publications list: Available online and in print

Access to staff: Contact by letter, by telephone, by fax, by e-mail, in person and via website
Hours: Mon to Fri, 0900 to 1700
Special comments: Administrative Headquarters is open office hours; tourist information centres open longer, particularly during tourist season.

Tourist Information Centres: Aberfeldy (open all year); The Square, Aberfeldy, Perthshire, PH15 2DD; tel: 01887 820276; fax: 01887 829495; e-mail: aberfeldytic@perthshire.co.uk; Auchterarder (open all year); 90 High Street, Auchterarder, Perthshire, PH3 1BJ; tel: 01764 663450; fax: 01764 664235; e-mail: auchterardertic@perthshire.co.uk; Blairgowrie (open all year); 26 Wellmeadow, Blairgowrie, Perthshire, PH10 6AS, Ski-line 875800; tel: 01250 872960; fax: 01250 873701; e-mail: blairgowrietic@perthshire.co.uk; Crieff (open all year); High Street, Crieff, Perthshire, PH7 3HU; tel: 01764 652578; fax: 01764 655422; e-mail: crieffic@perthshire.co.uk; Dunkeld (open all year); The Cross, Dunkeld, Perthshire, PH8 0AN; tel: 01350 727688; fax: 01350 727688; e-mail: dunkeldtic@perthshire.co.uk; Kinross (open all year); Heart of Scotland Visitor Centre, adjacent to service area, Junction 6, M90, Kinross, Perthshire, KY13 7NQ; tel: 01577 863680; Activity line: 01577 861186; fax: 01577 863370; e-mail: kinrosstic@perthshire.co.uk; Perth (open all year); Lower City Mills, West Mill Street, Perth, PH1 5QP; tel: 01738 450600; fax: 01738 444863; e-mail: perthtic@perthshire.co.uk; Pitlochry (open all year); 22 Atholl Road, Pitlochry, Perthshire, PH16 5BX; tel: 01796 472215 or 472751; fax: 01796 474046; e-mail: pitlochrytic@perthshire.co.uk

PET CARE TRUST (PCT)

Bedford Business Centre, 170 Mile Road, Bedford, MK42 9TW

Tel: 01234 273933
Fax: 01234 273550
E-mail: info@petcare.org.uk
Website: www.petcare.org.uk

Enquiries to: Operations Manager
Direct e-mail: rosie.loft@petcare.org.uk

Founded: 1986

Organisation type and purpose: National organisation, professional body, trade association (membership is by subscription), present number of members: 1506, service industry, voluntary organisation, registered charity (charity number 1052488), suitable for ages: all, training organisation.
To promote high standards of training in the industry; to promote responsible pet ownership.

Subject coverage: Training information and information on pet care and related legislation.

continued overleaf

Trade and statistical information: Data on pet care industry, market and population

Publications: Printed

Access to staff: Contact by letter, by telephone, by fax and by e-mail. Appointment necessary.
Hours: Mon to Fri, 0830 to 1700

Access to building: Prior appointment required

Access for disabled people: Parking provided, level entry, toilet facilities

Subsidiary body: British Dog Groomers Association; tel: 01234 273933; fax: 01234 273550; e-mail: pat@petcare.org.uk

PET FOOD MANUFACTURERS' ASSOCIATION LIMITED (PFMA)

20 Bedford Street, Covent Garden, London, WC2E 9HP

Tel: 020 7379 9009
Fax: 020 7379 8008
E-mail: info@pfma.org.uk
Website: www.pfma.com

Enquiries to: Administration Secretary

Founded: 1971

Organisation type and purpose: Trade association.

Subject coverage: General information relating to the UK prepared pet food industry, pet-related issues and interests.

Trade and statistical information: Data on UK prepared pet food market.
Data on UK dog and cat populations

Access to staff: Contact by letter, by telephone, by fax and by e-mail
Hours: Mon to Fri, 0900 to 1700

Access to building: No access other than to staff

Member of: FEDIAF; Avenue Louise 89, Brussels, B-1050, Belgium

PETA FOUNDATION

Formal name: People for the Ethical Treatment of Animals Foundation

PO Box 36678, London, SE1 1YE

Tel: 020 7357 9229
Fax: 020 7357 0901
E-mail: info@peta.org.uk
Website: www.petaf.org.uk

Organisation type and purpose: Registered charity in England & Wales (charity number 1056453) dedicated to establishing and protecting the rights of all animals. Works mainly in the UK, but also responds to requests for information and resources from overseas.

Subject coverage: PETA and its affiliates around the world educate policy-makers and the public about cruelty to animals and promote an understanding of the right of all animals to be treated with respect.
PETA works through public education, research, legislation, special events, celebrity involvement and protest campaigns.

Education services: Education Department: events and free education materials.

Publications: Electronic and video
Order electronic and video publications from: via website

Access to staff: Contact by letter, by telephone, by fax and by e-mail

Links with: PETA charities in USA, France, Germany, Netherlands, India, Asia-Pacific and Spain

PETERBOROUGH CENTRAL LIBRARY AND THEATRE

Broadway, Peterborough, Cambridgeshire, PE1 1RX

Tel: 01733 864270
Fax: 01733 555277
E-mail: centrallibrary@vivacity-peterborough.com
Website: www.peterborough.gov.uk/leisure_and_culture/libraries.aspx

Organisation type and purpose: Local government body, public library.
Central reference library for the Greater Peterborough area.

Subject coverage: General, history and study of Peterborough and its area, business information, environmental information, open learning and training materials and information (the Learning Centre), European Union information (European Public Information Centre).

Collection: John Clare Collection
Local history collection

Non-library collection catalogue: All or part available online and in-house

Access to staff: Contact by letter, by telephone, by fax, by e-mail and in person
Hours: Tue, Wed, Fri, 0900 to 1700; Mon, Thu, 0900 to 1900; Sat 0900 to 1600

Access to building: No prior appointment required

Access for disabled people: Parking provided, level entry, access to all public areas, toilet facilities

Parent body: Peterborough Culture and Leisure Trust

PETERBOROUGH REGIONAL COLLEGE LIBRARY

Park Crescent, Peterborough, Cambridgeshire, PE1 4DZ

Tel: 01733 762137
Fax: 01733 767986
Website: www.peterborough.ac.uk

Enquiries to: Library Manager

Organisation type and purpose: College of further and higher education.

Subject coverage: Accounting; electrical engineering; mechanical engineering; building construction; chemistry; physics; mathematics; biology; psychology; sociology; economics; geography; geology; English literature; management; catering; media; history; sport; computing; hairdressing; beauty therapy; childcare; health & social care; motor vehicles; plumbing; ESOL, foreign languages.

Library catalogue: All or part available in-house

Access to staff: Appointment necessary.
Hours: Term time: Mon to Thu, 0830 to 1945; Fri, 0830 to 1700

Access for disabled people: Parking provided, level entry, toilet facilities

PETERBOROUGH ROYAL FOXHOUND SHOW SOCIETY

East of England Showground, Peterborough, Cambridgeshire, PE2 6XE

Tel: 01733 234451
Fax: 01733 370038
E-mail: andrew@eastofengland.org.uk

Enquiries to: Secretary

Founded: 1878

Organisation type and purpose: Foxhound show society.

Subject coverage: Foxhounds; breeding and showing.

Collection: Handwritten record books listing winners in each of the above classes, over the years

PETROC

Old Sticklepath Hill, Barnstaple, Devon, EX31 2BQ

Tel: 01271 338170 (main library line)
Fax: 01271 388121
E-mail: library@petroc.ac.uk
Website: www.petroc.ac.uk

Enquiries to: Head of Learning Resources and ILT
Other contacts: Learning Resources Team Leader; Learning Resources Co-ordinators

History of institution: created by the merger of East Devon College and North Devon College (year of change 2008)

Organisation type and purpose: Suitable for ages: mainly 16 to 19.
College of further education.

Subject coverage: Academic subjects and some local material.

Non-library collection catalogue: All or part available online

Library catalogue: All or part available online

Access to staff: Contact by letter, by telephone, by fax and by e-mail
Hours: Term time: Mon, 0900 to 1700; Tues and Wed, 0830 to 2000; Thu, 0830 to 1900; Fri, 0830 to 1630
Vacations: Mon to Fri, 0900 to 1300

Access for disabled people: Parking provided, access to all public areas, toilet facilities

PETROL RETAILERS ASSOCIATION (PRA)

201 Great Portland Street, London, W1W 5AB

Tel: 020 7307 3593
Fax: 020 7307 3592
E-mail: feedback@rmif.co.uk
Website: www.rmif.co.uk

Enquiries to: Secretary

Founded: 1913

Subject coverage: Petrol retailing.

Member of the: Retail Motor Industry Federation

Other addresses: Petrol Retailers Association; 107a Shore Road, Belfast, BT15 3BB; tel: 028 9037 0137; fax: 028 9037 0706

PETROLEUM OPEN LEARNING (OPITO)

Minerva House, Bruntland Road, Portlethan, Aberdeen, AB12 4QL

Tel: 01224 787800
Fax: 01224 787830
E-mail: richard.bain@opito.net
Website: www.petroleumopenlearning.com

Enquiries to: Technical Sales Manager
Direct tel: 01224 787813

Founded: 1988

Organisation type and purpose: OPITO – The Oil and Gas Academy is the industry's focal point for skills, training and workforce development. The Academy is a self-sustaining, employer- and trade union-led organisation committed to developing and sustaining a safe, skilled and effective workforce now and in the future. This is achieved by working in collaboration with: industry employers, learning and training providers, education and academia and partnership organisations.

Subject coverage: Oil and gas well technology, petroleum processing technology, health and safety.

Publications: Printed

Publications list: Available online and in print

Access to staff: Contact by letter, by telephone, by fax, by e-mail, in person and via website. Appointment necessary.
Hours: Mon to Fri, 0900 to 1700

Access for disabled people: Parking provided, ramped entry, level entry, access to all public areas, toilet facilities

Parent body: OPITO – The Oil and Gas Academy; Minerva House, Bruntland Road, Portlethen, Aberdeen, AB12 4QL; tel: 01224 787800; fax: 01224 787830; website: http://www.opito.com

PEWTER SOCIETY

37 Hurst Lane, Bollington, Cheshire, SK10 5LT

E-mail: secretary@pewtersociety.org
Website: www.pewtersociety.org

Enquiries to: Secretary

Founded: 1918

Organisation type and purpose: Learned society, present number of members: 250, voluntary organisation.

Subject coverage: Antique pewter – its history, manufacture and social context; identification, conservation and information about specific pewterers.

Collection: The library holds all British and many foreign books published on pewter and many papers on pewter and pewter-related topics

Library catalogue: All or part available online and in-house

Publications: Printed, and electronic and video

Publications list: Available online

Access to staff: Contact by letter, by e-mail and via website
Special comments: No access

Access to building: No access

PHARMACEUTICAL SOCIETY OF NORTHERN IRELAND (PSNI)

73 University Street, Belfast, BT7 1HL

Tel: 028 9023 1163
Fax: 028 9043 9919

Enquiries to: Chief Executive Secretary & Registrar
Direct e-mail: mark.neale@psni.org.uk
Other contacts: Secretary

Founded: 1925

Organisation type and purpose: Statutory body, professional body (membership is by qualification), present number of members: 1700, service industry.
Registration authority for pharmacists and pharmacies in Northern Ireland.

Subject coverage: Pharmaceutical matters.

Access to staff: Contact by letter, by telephone, by fax and by e-mail
Hours: Mon to Fri, 0900 to 1700

PHILADELPHIA ASSOCIATION (PA)

4 Marty's Yard, 17 Hampstead High Street, London, NW3 1QW

Tel: 020 7794 2652
Fax: 020 7794 2652
E-mail: paoffice@globalnet.co.uk

Enquiries to: Administrator

Founded: 1965

Organisation type and purpose: Registered charity.
Charity in the field of mental health.

Subject coverage: Training in phenomenology and psychoanalytic psychotherapy, residential therapeutic communities, psychotherapy referrals.

Library catalogue: All or part available in-house

Publications: Printed

Access to staff: Contact by letter, by telephone and by fax. Appointment necessary.
Hours: Mon, 1330 to 1730; Tue, Thu, Fri, 1630 to 2030

Access to building: No access other than to staff

PHILATELIC TRADERS SOCIETY LIMITED (PTS)

PO Box 371, Fleet, Hampshire, GU52 6ZX

Tel: 01252 628006
Fax: 01252 684674
E-mail: info@philatelic-traders-society.co.uk
Website: www.philatelic-traders-society.co.uk

Enquiries to: General Secretary

Founded: 1949

Organisation type and purpose: Trade association.

Subject coverage: Philatelic trade; support for stamp collecting as a hobby; organisers of the two national stamp exhibitions, Spring Stampex and Autumn Stampex.

Publications: Printed

Access to staff: Contact by letter, by telephone, by fax, by e-mail and in person. Appointment necessary.
Hours: Mon to Thu, 1000 to 1700; Fri, 1000 to 1300

Constituent bodies: Stampex Ltd; tel: 01252 628006; fax: 01252 684674

PHILIPPINE EMBASSY

9a Palace Green, London, W8 4QE

Tel: 020 7937 1600
Fax: 020 7937 2925
E-mail: embassy@philemb.demon.co.uk
Website: www.microtron.net/philemb/index.shtml

Enquiries to: H E The Ambassador
Direct e-mail: embassy@philemb.co.uk
Other contacts: Information Officer

Organisation type and purpose: International organisation.

Subject coverage: The Philippines: Consular matters.

Publications: Printed

Access to staff: Contact by letter, by telephone, by fax, by e-mail, in person and via website. Appointment necessary.
Hours: Mon to Fri, 0900 to 1700
Special comments: Closed during Philippine holidays.

Access to building: No prior appointment required
Hours: Mon to Fri, 0900 to 1700

Other addresses: Office of the Tourism Attaché; 146 Cromwell Road, London, SW7 4EF; tel: 020 7835 1100; fax: 020 7835 1926; e-mail: Tourism@pdot.co.uk; Philippine Department of Trade; 1A Cumberland House, Kensington Court, London, W8; tel: 020 7937 7998 1898; fax: 020 7937 2747; e-mail: dtilondon@aol.com

PHILOLOGICAL SOCIETY

School of Oriental and African Studies, University of London, Thornhaugh Street, Russell Square, London, WC1H 0XG

Tel: 020 7898 4376
E-mail: secretary@philsoc.org.uk
Website: www.philsoc.org.uk

Enquiries to: Honorary Secretary
Founded: 1841

Organisation type and purpose: Learned society, present number of members: 860, registered charity (charity number 1014370).

continued overleaf

To investigate and promote the study and knowledge of the structure, affinities, and history of language.

Subject coverage: Linguistics; philology.

Publications: Printed
Order printed publications from: http://www.wiley.com/bw/journal.asp?ref=0079–1636

Access to staff: Contact by letter and by e-mail
Hours: Mon to Fri, 0900 to 1700

PHONOGRAPHIC PERFORMANCE LIMITED (PPL)

1 Upper James Street, London, W1F 9DE

Tel: 020 7534 1000
Fax: 020 7534 1111

Enquiries to: Public Relations Manager

Founded: 1934

Organisation type and purpose:
Membership association.
Established by the UK record companies as a non-profit company to license the broadcast and public performance of their sound recordings.
Copyright licensing body.

Subject coverage: Copyright relating to public performance and broadcasting of commercial sound recordings, including records, tapes and re-recordings, in the United Kingdom, on behalf of the British record industry.

Publications: Printed

Publications list: Available in print

Access to staff: Contact by letter, by telephone and by fax
Hours: Mon to Fri, 0930 to 1730

Links with: BPI; IFPI

PHOTO MARKETING ASSOCIATION INTERNATIONAL (UK) LIMITED (PMA)

Wisteria House, 28 Fulling Mill Lane, Welwyn, Hertfordshire, AL6 9NS

Tel: 0870 240 4542
Fax: 01438 716572
E-mail: pmauk@pmai.org
Website: www.pmai.org

Enquiries to: Director of UK operations
Other contacts: Administration Manager

Founded: 1923

Organisation type and purpose:
International organisation, trade association (membership is by subscription), consultancy.
To expand the photographic industry and to make its members more profitable.

Subject coverage: Photographic industry trends – worldwide, consumer research, the photo, video and digital industries, retailers, minilabs, wholesale photo finishers, camera repairers, school photographs.

Trade and statistical information: Industry trends report – annual statistics on the photo industry

Publications: Printed, and electronic and video, and microform publications

Access to staff: Contact by letter, by telephone, by fax, by e-mail and via website. Appointment necessary. Non-members charged.
Hours: Mon to Fri, 0930 to 1730

Affiliated to: Photo Marketing Association International; 3000 Picture Place, Jackson, Michigan, 49201, USA

Subsidiary body: APL Services Limited

PHOTOGRAPHIC WASTE MANAGEMENT ASSOCIATION (PWMA)

Ambassador House, Brigstock Road, Thornton Heath, Surrey, CR7 7JG

Tel: 020 8665 5395
Fax: 020 8665 6447
E-mail: pwma@admin.co.uk

Enquiries to: Secretary

Founded: 1993

Organisation type and purpose: Trade association.

Subject coverage: Photographic waste management.

Publications: Printed

Access to staff: Contact by letter
Hours: Mon to Fri, 0900 to 1700

Member of: British Imaging and Photographic Association

PHYSICAL PROPERTIES DATA SERVICE (PPDS)

TUV NEL Ltd, Scottish Enterprise Technology Park, East Kilbride, South Lanarkshire, G75 0QU

Tel: 01355 272527
Fax: 01355 272265
E-mail: ppds@tuvnel.com
Website: www.ppds.co.uk
Website: www.nelfood.com

Enquiries to: Manager
Direct tel: 01355 593775
Direct e-mail: ajohns@tuvnel.com

Organisation type and purpose: Service industry, training organisation, consultancy, research organisation.

Subject coverage: Constant, thermodynamic and transport properties for over 1,500 organic compounds; vapour liquid equilibrium package containing seven different methods and nine different calculations; data for petroleum fractions and steam; liquid properties for 22 aqueous solutions and 97 commercial heat transfer fluids.

Publications: Printed, and electronic and video

Access to staff: Contact by letter, by telephone, by fax, by e-mail and via website
Hours: Mon to Fri, 0900 to 1700

Access to building: No access other than to staff

PHYSIO FIRST

Minerva House, Tithe Barn Way, Swan Valley, Northampton, NN4 9BA

Tel: 01604 684960
E-mail: minerva@physiofirst.org.uk
Website: www.physiofirst.org.uk

Enquiries to: General Secretary

Founded: 1951; formerly called Organisation of Chartered Physiotherapists in Private Practice (year of change 2006)

Organisation type and purpose:
Professional body (membership is by subscription, qualification), present number of members: 3,800.
Represents private practitioners, provides members with education, information and legal advice, to ensure patients of high professional standards.

Subject coverage: Back care, neck care; sports injury treatments, arthritic conditions, neurological stress, chest complaints.

Publications: Printed

Publications list: Available in print

Access to staff: Contact by letter, by telephone, by fax and by e-mail. Appointment necessary.
Hours: Mon to Fri, 0900 to 1700

Access to building: *Hours:* Mon to Fri, 0900 to 1700

Occupational Group of: Chartered Society of Physiotherapy

PHYSIOLOGICAL SOCIETY, THE

PO Box 11319, London, WC1X 8WP

Tel: 020 7269 5710
Fax: 020 7269 5720
E-mail: admin@physoc.org
Website: www.physoc.org

Enquiries to: Chief Executive

Founded: 1876

Organisation type and purpose: Learned society (membership is by election or invitation), registered charity (charity number 211585).

Subject coverage: Physiological and cognate biomedical sciences; special interest groups on autonomic function, blood-brain barrier, cardiovascular control, comparative and invertebrate neuroscience, cellular neurophysiology, comparative physiology, developmental physiology, epithelia and membrane transport, gastrointestinal tract, heart and cardiac muscle, history of physiology, human physiology, higher sensory functions, ionic channels, microvascular and endothelial physiology, muscle contraction, neuroendocrinology, placental and perinatal physiology, renal physiology, respiratory physiology, sensorimotor control, smooth muscle, somatosensory physiology; physiology as a career.

Collection: Archives (held at Wellcome Institute for the History of Medicine)
Video and film collection

Publications: Printed

Access to staff: Contact by letter, by telephone, by fax, by e-mail and via website. Appointment necessary.
Hours: Mon to Fri, 0900 to 1700

Access to building: Prior appointment required

Accredited society of the: Foundation for Science and Technology

Affiliated to: Biosciences Foundation; Institute of Biology

Supports the: International Union of Physiological Sciences (Munich)

PIANOFORTE TUNERS ASSOCIATION (PTA)

10 Reculver Road, Herne Bay, Kent, CT6 6LD

Tel: 01227 368808
Fax: 01227 368808
E-mail: secretary@pianotuner.org.uk
Website: www.pianotuner.org.uk

Enquiries to: Secretary

Founded: 1913

Organisation type and purpose: Professional body, advisory body.

Subject coverage: Pianoforte tuning, training facilities, entry into the industry.

Publications: Printed

Access to staff: Contact by letter, by telephone and by fax
Hours: Including evenings

PILKINGTON GROUP LTD

Pilkington Technology Centre, Hall Lane, Lathom, Ormskirk, Lancashire, L40 5UF

Tel: 01695 50000
Fax: 01695 54366
E-mail: kevin.green@pilkington.com

Enquiries to: Information Manager
Direct tel: 01695 54231

Founded: 1826

Organisation type and purpose: Manufacturing industry.

Subject coverage: Fundamental research in flat glass, applied research leading to improvements in the manufacturing of glass and related materials, development of new processes and products in flat glass, pressed and moulded glass, optical, ophthalmic and other special glasses, surface-treated glass.

Collection: Comprehensive collection of books on glass

Library catalogue: All or part available in-house

Access to staff: Contact by letter, by telephone, by fax and by e-mail. Appointment necessary.
Hours: Mon to Fri, 0900 to 1700
Special comments: By appointment only.

Access to building: By appointment only.

PIRA INTERNATIONAL

Cleeve Road, Leatherhead, Surrey, KT22 7RU

Tel: 01372 802050
Fax: 01372 802239
E-mail: infocentre@pira-international.com
Website: www.pira-international.com

Enquiries to: Information Services Manager

Organisation type and purpose: Consultancy.

Subject coverage: Pulping and pulp evaluation, paper and board making, water and effluent treatment, printing, imaging, inks, packaging, paper and board testing, printing machinery, package development and testing, management, marketing, publishing, nonwovens, statistical and technical information.

Library catalogue: All or part available in-house

Publications: Printed, and electronic and video

Publications list: Available online and in print

Access to staff: Contact by letter, by e-mail and via website. Appointment necessary. Access for members only. Non-members charged.
Hours: Mon to Fri, 0900 to 1700

Access to building: Prior appointment required
Special comments: Members only.

PLACE ARTIST DEVELOPMENT, THE (TPAD)

17 Dukes Road, London, WC1H 9PY

Tel: 020 7121 1040
Fax: 020 7121 1141
E-mail: artistdevelopment@theplace.org.uk
Website: www.theplace.org.uk

Enquiries to: Assistant
Direct tel: 020 7121 1040

Founded: 1990

Organisation type and purpose: Membership association (membership is by subscription), present number of members: 1,400.
Information and advice service for the independent dance profession.

Subject coverage: Contemporary dance, venues, promoters, dance artists in the UK and Europe, rehearsal spaces for dance in Greater London, information for new dance companies. Contacts for choreographers, dancers and dance managers in the United Kingdom and the rest of the world.

Collection: Publicity, annual reports etc from regional arts boards, venues and festivals, funding guides and directories, key reports, periodicals

Publications: Printed

Publications list: Available in print

Access to staff: Contact by letter, by telephone, by fax, by e-mail, in person and via website. Appointment necessary.
Hours: Tue to Fri, 1000 to 1800

Access to building: No prior appointment required

Access for disabled people: Parking provided, level entry, access to all public areas, toilet facilities

Parent body: Contemporary Dance Trust Ltd; The Place, 17 Dukes Road, London, WC1H 9PY; tel: 020 7121 1000; fax: 020 7121 1142

PLAID CYMRU – THE PARTY OF WALES

Tŷ Gwynfor, Marine Chambers, Cwrt Anson Court, Glanfa'r Iwerydd, Caerdydd/Cardiff, CF10 4AL

Tel: 029 20472272
Fax: 029 20491 453
E-mail: post@plaidcymru.org
Website: plaidcymru.org

Enquiries to: Communications Officer
Other contacts: Press Officer (for press enquiries)

Founded: 1925

Organisation type and purpose: Membership association (membership is by subscription), present number of members: 10,800.
Political party.
To achieve full national status for Wales by electoral means.

Subject coverage: Politics in Wales.

Collection: Collections are held on the party's behalf in the National Library of Wales, including the whole party archive extending back to 1925

Publications: Printed, and electronic and video, and microform publications

Publications list: Available in print

Access to staff: Contact by letter, by telephone, by fax and by e-mail. Appointment necessary.
Hours: Mon to Fri, 0830 to 1700

Access to building: No prior appointment required
Special comments: Party Archive kept at the National Library of Wales.

PLAIN LANGUAGE COMMISSION

Formal name: Clearest.co.uk ltd

The Castle, 29 Stoneheads, Whaley Bridge, High Peak, Derbyshire, SK23 7BB

Tel: 01663 733177
Fax: 01663 735135
E-mail: cutts@clearest.co.uk
Website: www.clearest.co.uk

Enquiries to: Director

Founded: 2006

Organisation type and purpose: Consultancy.

Subject coverage: Editorial expertise and training courses on the use of plain language in business, government departments, local authorities and the law.

Publications: Printed
Order printed publications from: Website or postal address above

Publications list: Available online

Access to staff: Contact by letter, by telephone, by fax and by e-mail. Appointment necessary.
Hours: Mon to Fri, 0900 to 1700

Access to building: No access other than to staff

PLANET RETAIL

Greater London House, Hampstead Road, London NW1 7EJ

Tel: 020 7728 5600
Fax: 020 7728 4999
E-mail: info@planetretail.net
Website: www.planetretail.net

Enquiries to: Press
Direct e-mail: michael.berggren@planetretail.net

Founded: 1989; formerly called M+M Planet Retail

Organisation type and purpose: Market research.
Online database on international retailers.

Subject coverage: Retail marketing.

Non-library collection catalogue: All or part available online

Library catalogue: All or part available online

Publications: Printed, and electronic and video

Publications list: Available online

Access to staff: Contact by e-mail
Hours: Mon to Fri, 0900 to 1700

Holding Company: M & M Planet Retail SA; Avenue Louise 113, 1050 Brussels, Belgium

Other addresses: M & M Planet Retail; Dreieichstrasse 59, Frankfurt am Main, D-60594, Germany; tel: + 49 69 96 21 75 0; fax: + 49 69 96 21 75 40

PLANNED ENVIRONMENT THERAPY TRUST ARCHIVE AND STUDY CENTRE (PETT Archive and Study Centre)

Church Lane, Toddington, Cheltenham, Gloucestershire, GL54 5DQ

Tel: 01242 620125
E-mail: archive@pettrust.org.uk
Website: pettrust.org.uk

Enquiries to: Dr. Craig Fees, RMARA

Founded: 1989

Organisation type and purpose: Charitable Trust

Subject coverage: Archive, library and other materials related to planned environment therapy, therapeutic community, milieu therapy, and progressive, alternative and democratic education more generally.

Non-library collection catalogue: All or part available online and in-house

Access to staff: Contact by letter, by telephone, in person and via website

Access to building: *Hours:* Mon to Fri, 0900 to 1500 by appointment; extended or other times by special arrangement.

PLANT HERITAGE (NCCPG)

Formal name: National Council for the Conservation of Plants and Gardens

12 Home Farm, Loseley Park, Guildford, Surrey, GU3 1HS

Tel: 01483 447540
Fax: 01483 458933
E-mail: info@plantheritage.org.uk
Website: www.plantheritage.com

Enquiries to: Plant Conservation Officer
Other contacts: Executive Officer

Founded: 1978

Organisation type and purpose: National organisation overseeing the conservation of plants in cultivation through the National Plant Collections scheme; supported by members and area groups; registered charity (charity number 1004009).

Subject coverage: Matters relating to organisation of Plant Heritage/NCCPG, the National Collection Scheme,
conservation of plants in cultivation and general conservation information.

Collection: Plant Heritage co-ordinates the 650 collections registered under its National Collections Scheme
(50,000 plants held in the collections)

Non-library collection catalogue: All or part available online

Publications: Printed

Publications list: Available online and in print

Access to staff: Contact by letter, by telephone, by fax, by e-mail and via website. Appointment necessary.
Hours: Mon to Fri, 0900 to 1700

Access to building: Ground floor

Access for disabled people: Fully accessible

Links with: all the major horticultural bodies in Great Britain; over 40 county-based groups throughout Great Britain

PLANTLIFE – THE WILD PLANT CONSERVATION CHARITY

21 Elizabeth Street, London, SW1W 9RP

Tel: 020 7808 0100
Fax: 020 7730 8377
E-mail: enquiries@plantlife.org.uk
Website: www.plantlife.org.uk

Enquiries to: Public Relations Manager

Founded: 1989

Organisation type and purpose: International organisation, membership association (membership is by subscription), present number of members: 11,500 individuals, voluntary organisation, registered charity (charity number 1059559). Wild plant conservation charity.

Subject coverage: Conservation of wild plants and their habitats in the British Isles, including lichens, bryophytes, algae, fungi.

Publications: Printed

Access to staff: Contact by letter
Hours: Mon to Fri, 0900 to 1700

Members: Botanical Society of Edinburgh; Botanical Society of The British Isles; British Bryophyte Society; British Ecology Society; British Lichen Society; British Phycological Society; British Pteridological Society; Butterfly Conservation Society; Fauna and Flora International; Friends of the Earth; Royal Society for the Protection of Birds; South London Botanical Institute; Wildflower Society

Other address: Plantlife; Strome House, North Strome, Lochcarron, Ross-shire, IV54 8YJ; tel: 01520 722588; fax: 01520 722660

PLASTICS & BOARD INDUSTRIES FEDERATION (PBIF)

Rock House, Maddacombe Road, Kingskerswell, Newton Abbot, Devon, TQ12 5LF

Tel: 01803 403303
Fax: 01803 873167
E-mail: pbifoffice@aol.com
Website: www.pbif.co.uk

Enquiries to: Chief Executive

Founded: 1987

Organisation type and purpose: International organisation, trade association (membership is by subscription), present number of members: 150.

Subject coverage: High frequency welding of thermoplastics; heat sealing and creasing of polypropylene, converting of board.

Library catalogue: All or part available in-house

Publications: Printed

Access to staff: Contact by letter, by telephone, by fax, by e-mail, in person and via website. Appointment necessary.
Hours: Mon to Fri, 0900 to 1700

PLASTICS HISTORICAL SOCIETY (PHS)

31A Maylands Drive, Sidcup, Kent, DA14 4SB

Tel: 020 8302 0684
E-mail: r_chambers@lineone.net

Enquiries to: Honorary Secretary

Founded: 1986

Organisation type and purpose: International organisation, learned society, membership association (membership is by subscription), present number of members: 250.
Recording the history of plastics and rubber.

Subject coverage: History of plastics and rubber, conservation and preservation of plastics and rubbers.

Collection: Collection of plastics artefacts and historical records

Publications: Printed

Access to staff: Contact by letter
Hours: Mon to Fri, 0900 to 1700

Parent body: Institute of Materials; 1 Carlton House Terrace, London, SW1Y 5DB; tel: 020 7451 7300; fax: 020 7839 1702

PLAY WALES

Formal name: Play Wales/Chwarae Cymru

Baltic House, Mount Stuart Street, Cardiff, CF10 5FH

Tel: 029 2048 6050
Fax: 029 2048 9359
E-mail: mail@playwales.org.uk
Website: www.playwales.org.uk
Website: www.chwaraecymru.org.uk

Enquiries to: Information Officer

Organisation type and purpose: Advisory body, membership association, voluntary organisation, registered charity, consultancy.

Subject coverage: Children's play; to provide or assist in the provision of children's play facilities and services, to offer advice and training.

Collection: Specialist Library containing books on children's play (theory and practical books), child development, social and political issues related to children

Library catalogue: All or part available in-house

Publications: Printed
Order printed publications from: Office Manager

Publications list: Available in print

Access to staff: Contact by letter, by telephone, by fax and by e-mail. Appointment necessary.
Hours: Tue to Thu, 1000 to 1400
Special comments: At other times by prior appointment.

Access to building: Prior appointment required
Hours: Mon to Fri, 0900 to 1700

Access for disabled people: Parking provided, ramped entry, toilet facilities

Also at: Play Wales Chwarae Cymru; Station House, Bastion Road, Prestatyn; Play Wales Chwarae Cymru; Units 8/9 Tai Tywyn Business Centre, Sandy Lane, LL19 7SF

PLAYBACK

Formal name: Playback Recording Service for the Blind

Playback Recording Service, Centre for Sensory Impaired, 17 Gullane Street, Glasgow, G11 6AH

Tel: 0141 334 2983
Fax: 0141 334 2983
Website: www.play-back.com

Enquiries to: Producer
Direct e-mail: peter.fraser@play-back.org.uk
Other contacts: Librarian (for tape library)

Founded: 1987

Organisation type and purpose: Registered charity (charity number SCO 01189), voluntary organisation.
Provides professional-quality recorded material to all over the UK, as well as parts of the USA, Australia, New Zealand and Canada. Set up to provide a free service to blind and visually impaired people, Playback is also available for individual and commercial recording needs at a small charge or donation. It has never refused to record any material requested, the philosophy being that, if it's available in print, it should be available on tape for all audiences to access.

Subject coverage: Tape library and reading service, newspapers, magazines.
Playback Magazine continues to be the flagship recording of the service, providing news, information and entertainment to thousands of people, mainly in the West of Scotland, but also throughout the United Kingdom, USA, Canada, Australia and New Zealand.

Collection: The tape library contains over 1,000 titles spanning a wide range of subjects. Some of the titles, particularly a number of Scottish books, have been recorded by volunteer readers
Audio-described videos

Library catalogue: All or part available online

Publications: Electronic and video

Publications list: Available online

Access to staff: Contact by letter, by telephone, by fax and by e-mail

PLAYBOARD NI

7 Crescent Gardens, Belfast, BT7 1NS

Tel: 028 9080 3380
Fax: 028 9080 3381
E-mail: information@playboard.co.uk
Website: www.playboard.org

Enquiries to: Director of Corporate Services & Finance
Other contacts: Communication/Membership Officer (for general information requests)

Founded: 1985

Organisation type and purpose: Advisory body, membership association (membership is by subscription), present number of members: 170, voluntary organisation, registered charity (charity number XO139/90), training organisation, consultancy, research organisation.
PlayBoard NI is the lead agency for children's play in Northern Ireland. It works to promote the child's right to play by providing quality play opportunities for all children, supported by development, policy, information, training and consultancy services.

Subject coverage: Information relating to children's play and general issues impinging on children's lives, particularly in Northern Ireland.

Collection: Reference library on issues relating to children's play and children's lives

Library catalogue: All or part available in-house

Publications: Printed
Order printed publications from: Communication/Membership Officer

Publications list: Available online and in print

Access to staff: Contact by letter, by telephone, by fax, by e-mail and via website. Appointment necessary.
Hours: Mon to Thu, 0930 to 1630; Fri, 0930 to 1530

Access for disabled people: Level entry, toilet facilities, lift provided

PLAYER PIANO GROUP (PPG)

9 Christy Avenue, Chelmsford, Essex CM1 2BG

Tel: 01245 603201
E-mail: secretary@playerpianogroup.org.uk
Website: www.playerpianogroup.org.uk

Enquiries to: Secretary

Founded: 1959

Organisation type and purpose: Voluntary organisation.

Subject coverage: Mechanical music, player pianos, pianolas, reproducing pianos, piano rolls, performers, catalogues, sales and exchanges, history of the instrument, its mechanisms, repair and restoration.

Publications: Printed

Links with: Sister societies in the UK, Germany, Netherlands, USA, Australia

PLIMSOLL PUBLISHING LIMITED

Scotswood House, Teesdale South, Stockton-on-Tees, Cleveland, TS17 6SB

Tel: 01642 626400
Fax: 01642 626410
E-mail: enquiries@plimsoll.co.uk
Website: www.plimsoll.co.uk

Enquiries to: Marketing Officer

Founded: 1986

Organisation type and purpose: Publishers of financial analysis.

Subject coverage: Financial analysis of various sectors of UK industry by the analysis of individual players.

Publications: Printed, and electronic and video

Publications list: Available online and in print

Access to staff: Contact by letter, by telephone, by fax, by e-mail and via website. Appointment necessary.
Hours: Mon to Fri, 0830 to 1700

Access to building: Prior appointment required

Access for disabled people: Access to all public areas

PLUMPTON COLLEGE

Ditchling Road, Plumpton, Lewes, East Sussex, BN7 3AE

Tel: 01273 890454
Fax: 01273 890071
E-mail: enquiries@plumpton.ac.uk
Website: www.plumpton.ac.uk

Enquiries to: Librarian
Direct tel: 01273 892041
Direct e-mail: anne.boryer@plumpton.ac.uk

Organisation type and purpose: College providing land-based courses in partnership with schools, for those in further education and for those in higher education.

Subject coverage: Agriculture, livestock, equestrian, horticulture, floristry, conservation, wine studies, agricultural mechanics, animal care, forestry.

Library catalogue: All or part available online and in-house

Publications: Printed

Access to staff: Contact by telephone, by fax, by e-mail, in person and via website. Appointment necessary.
Hours: Mon to Fri, 0900 to 2200

continued overleaf

Also at: Ivyland Farm; Netherfield, Battle, East Sussex; tel: 01424 838620

Associate college of: University of Brighton

PLUNKETT FOUNDATION

The Quadrangle, Woodstock, Oxfordshire, OX20 1LH

Tel: 01993 810730
Fax: 01993 810849
E-mail: info@plunkett.co.uk
Website: www.plunkett.co.uk

Enquiries to: Information Officer
Direct e-mail: k.targett@plunkett.co.uk
Other contacts: Financial Administrator for book purchase.

Founded: 1919

Organisation type and purpose:
International organisation, advisory body, membership association (membership is by subscription), present number of members: 150, registered charity (charity number 313743), public library, training organisation, consultancy, research organisation.
Information centre.
To provide information, advice and consultancy about co-operative enterprise and other member-controlled business models.

Subject coverage: Co-operative enterprise (all sectors, especially agriculture), farmer-controlled business, international project management, rural enterprise development, co-operative business training and education, co-operative legislation.

Collection: Co-operative Congress Reports (1869–1931)
Irish Homestead (vol. I to vol. XXX)
Journals
Library of 30,000 books and documents covering all aspects of co-operative enterprise
Research reports
Sir Horace Plunkett's Diaries (1881–1932) and Letters
Yearbook of Co-operative Enterprise 1927–1994 (now retitled World of Co-operative Enterprise 1995–2000)

Trade and statistical information: Detailed data on the trading activity of farmer-controlled businesses (including co-operatives) in the UK, covering farm supplies and the marketing of farm produce

Non-library collection catalogue: All or part available in-house

Library catalogue: All or part available online

Publications: Printed

Access to staff: Contact by letter, by telephone, by fax, by e-mail and via website. Appointment necessary.
Hours: Mon to Fri, 0900 to 1700

Access to building: Prior appointment required

Access for disabled people: Parking provided, level entry, toilet facilities

PLYMOUTH AND WEST DEVON RECORD OFFICE (PWDRO)

Unit 3, Clare Place, Coxside, Plymouth, Devon, PL4 0JW

Tel: 01752 305940
Fax: 01752 222196
E-mail: pwdro@plymouth.gov.uk
Website: www.plymouth.gov.uk/archives
Website: www.plymouth.gov.uk/archivecatalogue
Website: www.a2a.org.uk
Website: www.findmypast.co.uk

Enquiries to: Archivist

Founded: 1952

Organisation type and purpose: Local government body. Archive.

Subject coverage: The records of Plymouth and the West Devon area.

Education services: Learning Officer

Collection: Archive

Non-library collection catalogue: All or part available online and in-house

Access to staff: Contact by letter, by telephone, by e-mail, in person and via website. Appointment necessary.
Hours: Tue to Thu, 0930 to 1700; Fri, 0930 to 1600
Special comments: Identification required for visits.

Access to building: *Hours:* Tue to Thu, 0930 to 1700; Fri, 0930 to 1600

Access for disabled people: By appointment
Hours: Tue to Thu, 0930 to 1700; Fri, 0930 to 1600
Special comments: Disabled access is at the rear. Please call in advance.

PLYMOUTH ATHENAEUM

Derrys Cross, Plymouth, Devon, PL1 2SW

Tel: 01752 266079
E-mail: bussec@plymouthathenaeum.co.uk
Website: www.plymouthathenaeum.co.uk

Founded: 1812

Organisation type and purpose: Cultural society and membership organisation (membership by subscription).

Subject coverage: Arts, literature, science and technology.

Access to staff: Contact by letter, by telephone, by fax, by e-mail and via website
Hours: Mon to Fri, 1000 to 1700

PLYMOUTH CITY COUNCIL

Civic Centre, Armada Way, Plymouth, Devon, PL1 2EW

Tel: 01752 668000
Fax: 01752 264819
E-mail: pccmail@plymouth.gov.uk
Website: www.plymouth.gov.uk

Direct e-mail: communications@plymouth.gov.uk

Organisation type and purpose: Local government body.

Access to staff: Contact by letter, by telephone, by fax, by e-mail and in person
Hours: Mon to Fri, 0900 to 1700

PLYMOUTH COLLEGE OF ART AND DESIGN LEARNING RESOURCE CENTRE (PCAD)

Tavistock Place, Plymouth, Devon, PL4 8AT

Tel: 01752 203412
Fax: 01752 203444
E-mail: enquiries@plymouthart.ac.uk

Enquiries to: Librarian

Organisation type and purpose: Suitable for ages: 16+.
College of further education and higher education.

Subject coverage: Architecture; colour; communications; design crafts; fashion; film and television; fine art; graphic design; industrial design; painting and decorating; photography; printing; textiles.

Library catalogue: All or part available online

Publications: Printed

Access to staff: Contact by telephone and by e-mail. Appointment necessary.
Hours: Term time: Mon to Thu, 0845 to 1930; Fri, 0845 to 1730
Vacation time: Mon to Fri, 1000 to 1600

Access to building: *Hours:* Mon to Thu, 0845 to 1900; Fri, 0845 to 1700

Affiliated to: Open University; University of Plymouth

PLYMOUTH LIBRARY SERVICES

Formal name: City of Plymouth Library and Information Services

Central Library, Drake Circus, Plymouth, Devon, PL4 8AL

Tel: 01752 305923
Fax: 01752 305905
E-mail: library@plymouth.gov.uk
Website: www.plymouth.gov.uk/libraries
Website: www.libcat.info

Founded: 1876

Organisation type and purpose: Local government body, public library.

Subject coverage: General, technical, naval history, local studies, music theory, scores and sets of parts, drama, patents.

Collection: Baring-Gould collection (folksongs, folklore, novels, travel writing)
Eden Phillpotts collection (novels)
Moxon Collection of Ornithology and Travel (mainly 19th century)
Music collection (orchestral parts and scores)
Local, naval and family history
Patent Abridgements from 1855
Special indexes: Broderick – History of Devonport; Honeywill – Submarines; Larn – Shipwrecks of Devon; Akerman – Dictionary of British Fighting Ships

Library catalogue: All or part available online

Publications: Printed

Publications list: Available online

Access to staff: Contact by letter, by telephone, by fax, by e-mail, in person and via website
Hours: Mon to Fri, 0900 to 1900; Sat, 0900 to 1700
Special comments: Patent enquiries, Mon to Fri, 0900 to 1700 only.

Access for disabled people: Parking provided, level entry, access to all public areas
Special comments: Lift to 1st floor.

PLYMOUTH LOCAL AND NAVAL STUDIES LIBRARY

Plymouth Central Library, Drake Circus, Plymouth, PL4 8AL

Tel: 01752 305909
E-mail: library@plymouth.gov.uk
Website: www.plymouth.gov.uk/libraries

Enquiries to: Librarian

Organisation type and purpose: Local government body, public library.

Subject coverage: History of Plymouth, West Devon and South East Cornwall; family history; naval history.

Collection: Books and pamphlets, maps, newspapers, illustrations, family history resources

Library catalogue: All or part available online

Publications: Printed
Order printed publications from: Library or library website

Publications list: Available online

Access to staff: Contact by letter, by telephone, by e-mail, in person and via website
Hours: Mon to Fri, 0900 to 1900; Sat, 0900 to 1700

Access to building: No prior appointment required
Hours: Mon to Fri, 0900 to 1900; Sat 0900 to 1700

Access for disabled people: Lift to first floor

Member organisation of: Naval and Maritime Libraries and Archives Group (NMLAG)

PLYMOUTH PROPRIETARY LIBRARY

Alton Terrace, 111 North Hill, Plymouth, Devon, PL4 8JY

Tel: 01752 660515

Enquiries to: Librarian

Founded: 1810

Organisation type and purpose: Membership association (membership is by subscription), present number of members: 110, registered charity (charity number 1015700).
Private subscription library.

Subject coverage: General recreational library, 19th and 20th century novels, general non-fiction.

Collection: Devon and Cornwall local studies section

Library catalogue: All or part available in-house

Access to staff: Contact by letter and by telephone. Appointment necessary.
Hours: Mon, Tue, Thu, Fri, 0930 to 1700; Wed, 0930 to 1400; Sat, 0930 to 1230

PLYMOUTH UNIVERSITY

Charles Seale-Hayne Library, Drake Circus, Plymouth, Devon, PL4 8AA

Tel: 01752 588588
Fax: 01752 587100
Website: www.plymouth.ac.uk/library

Enquiries to: Library & IT Gateway Manager
Direct tel: 01752 587171
Direct e-mail: libraryservices@plymouth.ac.uk

Organisation type and purpose: University library.

Subject coverage: Agriculture, architecture, art and design, computing, civil engineering, economics, education, electronic engineering, English literature, environmental sciences, geography, geology, health services, history, law, life sciences, management, marine sciences, mathematics, mechanical engineering, medicine, petroleum geology, politics, psychology, shipping, social work, sociology, transport.

Trade and statistical information: UK core statistical data

Library catalogue: All or part available online

Access to staff: Contact by letter, by telephone, by e-mail and via website
Hours: Mon to Fri, 0900 to 1700
Special comments: See website for detailed opening hours.
Reference only, except for Associate Membership scheme.
Limited access to electronic information.

PMS PUBLICATIONS LIMITED (PMS)

Formal name: Parliamentary Monitoring Services

19 Douglas Street, Westminster, London, SW1P 4PA

Tel: 020 7233 8283
Fax: 020 7821 9352

Enquiries to: Managing Director

Founded: 1935

Organisation type and purpose: Research organisation, publishing house.
News agency for politics and government. To inform clients of what is happening in government and throughout the UK and the EU.

Subject coverage: Political, parliamentary, local government, European Union.

Collection: Databases of biographical information on MPs, peers, top civil servants and local authorities

Publications: Printed, and electronic and video

Publications list: Available in print

Access to staff: Contact by letter, by fax and by e-mail. Access for members only.
Hours: Mon to Fri, 0900 to 1700

Also at the same address: Parliamentary Monitoring Services

POETRY BOOK SOCIETY (PBS)

Dutch House, 307–308 High Holborn, London, WC1V 7LL

Tel: 020 7831 7468
Fax: 020 7831 6967
E-mail: info@poetrybooks.co.uk
Website: www.poetrybooks.co.uk

Enquiries to: Director

Founded: 1953

Organisation type and purpose: International organisation, membership association (membership is by subscription), present number of members: c. 2,200, registered charity (charity number 313753), suitable for ages: seven+.
A publicly-funded membership book club promoting contemporary poetry.

Subject coverage: Contemporary poetry published in the UK and Eire since 1953; educational resources for 7- to 18-year-olds.

Publications: Printed, and electronic and video

Access to staff: Contact by letter, by telephone, by fax, by e-mail and via website
Hours: Mon to Fri, 0930 to 1730

POETRY LIBRARY

Formal name: Saison Poetry Library

Royal Festival Hall, Southbank Centre, London, SE1 8XX

Tel: 020 7921 0943; 020 7921 0664
Fax: 020 7921 0939
E-mail: info@poetrylibrary.org.uk
Website: www.poetrylibrary.org.uk

Enquiries to: Poetry Librarian
Direct tel: 020 7921 0940

Founded: 1953

Organisation type and purpose: National organisation, membership association, present number of members: 21,200, public library, research organisation.
Special arts library.

Subject coverage: Modern poetry from all English-speaking countries of the world; modern poetry translated from other languages; pre-20th-century poetry translated by contemporary English language poets; poetry for children, poetry on tape, video, record, CD and CD-ROM.

Collection: Alec Craig Bequest
Howard Sargent collection of press cuttings
Images of poets
Large collection of poetry magazines
Rare modern first editions
SIGNAL collection of children's poetry
Sylvia Townsend Warner Bequest
Tapes, records, videos, CD-ROMs

Non-library collection catalogue: All or part available in-house

Library catalogue: All or part available in-house

Publications: Printed

continued overleaf

Publications list: Available in print

Access to staff: Contact by letter, by telephone, by fax, by e-mail, in person and via website
Hours: Tue to Sun, 1100 to 2000

Access for disabled people: Level entry

Parent body: Arts Council England; South Bank Board

POETRY SOCIETY

22 Betterton Street, London, WC2H 9BX

Tel: 020 7420 9880
Fax: 020 7240 4818
E-mail: info@poetrysociety.org.uk
Website: www.poetrysociety.org.uk

Founded: 1909

Organisation type and purpose:
Membership association, registered charity.
Arts centre for poetry; registered charity supported by the Arts Council.
To promote the study, use and enjoyment of poetry.

Subject coverage: Poetry and poets, information on writing or publishing poetry, contemporary poetry events, competitions, festivals, teachers' poetry resource.

Services for disabled people: Audio tapes of Poetry Review and Poetry News for blind and partially-sighted members.

Publications: Printed

Access to staff: Contact by letter, by telephone, by fax, by e-mail and via website
Hours: Mon to Fri, 1000 to 1800

Access to building: Prior appointment required

Access for disabled people: Lift to basement performance space; toilet facilities; induction loop

POLAR DATA CENTRE (PDC BAS)

British Antarctic Survey, High Cross, Madingley Road, Cambridge, CB3 0ET

Tel: 01223 221400
Fax: 01223 362616
E-mail: pdc@bas.ac.uk
Website: www.antarctica.ac.uk/pdc

History of institution: formerly called Antarctic Environmental Data Centre (year of change 2009)

Organisation type and purpose: Research organisation.
A virtual data centre proving a gateway to the distributed data holdings of the British Antarctic Survey. One of the Designated Centres of the UK Natural Environment Research Council (NERC). The UK National Data Centre within the Antarctic Data Management System (ADMS).
Responsible for ensuring the secure, long-term management of BAS data holdings.

Subject coverage: Information on data sets collected by BAS and other NERC-sponsored organisations in the Antarctic covering the physical, biological and geological sciences.

Trade and statistical information: Under Article III(1)(c) of the Antarctic Treaty, data are to be freely exchanged between Treaty parties. Therefore, within the Antarctic scientific community data are made freely available

Non-library collection catalogue: All or part available online

Publications: Electronic and video

Access to staff: Contact by e-mail and via website
Hours: Mon to Fri, 0900 to 1700
Special comments: E-mail is the preferred form of contact.

Member organisation of: One of the Designated Data Centres of the UK Natural Environment Research Council (NERC); The UK National Antarctic Data Centre within the Antarctic Data Management System

Parent body: British Antarctic Survey; at the same address

POLICE HISTORY SOCIETY

64 Nore Marsh Road, Wootton Bassett, Wiltshire

Website: www.policehistorysociety.co.uk

Enquiries to: Honorary Secretary
Other contacts: Membership Secretary (for membership enquiries)

Founded: 1985

Organisation type and purpose:
Membership association (membership is by subscription), present number of members: 400, registered charity, voluntary organisation (charity number 295540).
To bring together those interested in the history of the police and policing. NB: The PHS is not primarily concerned with family historical research and holds no police personnel records.

Subject coverage: History of policing; history of crime.

Publications: Printed

Access to staff: Contact by letter and by e-mail
Hours: Mon to Fri, 0900 to 1700
Special comments: SAE for reply essential.

Also at: Membership Secretary, Police History Society; Foxtrot Oscar, 37 South Lawne, Bletchley, Milton Keynes, MK3 6BU; tel: 0161 962 3764

POLICE SUPERINTENDENTS' ASSOCIATION OF ENGLAND AND WALES

67A Reading Road, Pangbourne, Berkshire, RG8 7JD

Tel: 0118 984 4005
Fax: 0118 984 5642
E-mail: enquiries@policesupers.com
Website: www.policesupers.com

Founded: 1952

Organisation type and purpose: The professional association that represents the senior police officers in the 43 Home Office Police Forces, British Transport Police, Civil Nuclear Constabulary and Isle of Man Police in the rank of Superintendent and Chief Superintendent.
To lead and develop the police service to improve the standard of policing; to provide support and advice to members regarding conditions of service, health & welfare; to contribute and influence policing policy and practice at the national strategic level.

Subject coverage: Policing and senior police officers.

Publications: Printed, and electronic and video
Order printed publications from: tel: 0118 984 4005
Order electronic and video publications from: Download from website

Access to staff: Contact by letter, by telephone, by fax and by e-mail

POLICY PRESS

University of Bristol, Fourth Floor, Beacon House, Queen's Road, Clifton, Bristol, BS8 1QU

Tel: 0117 331 4054
Fax: 0117 331 4093
E-mail: tpp-info@bristol.ac.uk
Website: www.policypress.org.uk

Enquiries to: Marketing Executive
Direct tel: 0117 331 4096
Other contacts: Director

Founded: 1995

Organisation type and purpose: Publishing house, publishing policy research.

Subject coverage: Community care, environment, family policy and child welfare, criminal justice, ageing, education, governance, health, housing, labour markets, urban policy, gender, voluntary sector, welfare and poverty.

Publications: Printed, and electronic and video
Order printed publications from: Customer Services, Marston Book Services, PO Box 269, Abingdon, Oxfordshire, OX14 4YN; tel: 01235 465500; fax: 01235 465556; e-mail direct.orders@marston.co.uk

Publications list: Available online and in print

Access to staff: Contact by letter, by telephone, by fax, by e-mail and via website
Hours: Mon to Fri, 0900 to 1700

Links with: University of Bristol

POLISH CULTURAL INSTITUTE (PCI)

34 Portland Place, London, W1B 1HQ

Tel: 0870 774 2300/2
Fax: 020 7637 2190
E-mail: pci@polishculture.org.uk
Website: www.polishculture.org.uk

Enquiries to: Director
Direct tel: 0870 774 2300/2

Organisation type and purpose: National government body.
Promotion of Polish culture in the UK.

Subject coverage: Poland and Polish music, film, theatre, literature and art, Polish history, geography.

Collection: Library of reference books, video, slides and music recordings, newspapers both Polish and English

Trade and statistical information: Some economic information on Poland

Non-library collection catalogue: All or part available online

Library catalogue: All or part available in-house

Publications list: Available in print

Access to staff: Contact by letter, by telephone, by fax, by e-mail and via website
Hours: Mon to Fri,1000 to 1600

Access to building: No prior appointment required
Hours: Mon, Tue, Wed, Fri, 1200 to 1600; Thu, 1600 to 2000

Part of: Polish Embassy in London

POLISH EMBASSY

Formal name: Embassy of the Republic of Poland

47 Portland Place, London, W1B 1JH

Tel: 0870 7742 700
Fax: 020 7323 4018
E-mail: polishembassy@polishembassy.org.uk
Website: www.polishembassy.org.uk
Website: www.paiz.gov.pl
Website: www.bmb.pl
Website: www.poland.pl

Enquiries to: Counsellor (Press & Information)

Organisation type and purpose: National government body.
Embassy.

Subject coverage: General enquiries relating to Poland, current political and economic situation, culture and tourism, visas etc.

Trade and statistical information: Trade information from the Commercial Office

Publications: Printed

Access to staff: Contact by letter, by fax, by e-mail and via website
Hours: Mon to Fri, 0830 to 1630
Special comments: Visa enquiries should be made to the Consulate General
Tourism enquiries to the Polish National Tourist Office.

Other addresses: Commercial Counsellors Office to the Embassy of the Republic of Poland; 15 Devonshire Street, London, W1N 2AR; tel: 020 7580 5481; fax: 020 7323 0195;
Consulate General of the Republic of Poland; 73 New Cavendish Street, London, W1N 4HQ; tel: 0870 7742 800; fax: 020 7323 2320; e-mail: consulate@polishconsulate.co.uk; website: www.polishconsulate.co.uk
Consulate General of the Republic of Poland; 2 Kinnear Road, Edinburgh, EH3 5PE; tel: 0131 552 0301; fax: 0131 552 1086; e-mail: edinburgh@polishconsulate.org; website: www.polishconsulate.org
Polish Cultural Institute; 34 Portland Place, London, W1N 4HQ; tel: 0870 7742 900; fax: 020 7637 2190; e-mail: pci@polishculture.org.uk; website: www.polishculture.org

POLISH LIBRARY

238–246 King Street, London, W6 0RF

Tel: 020 8741 0474
Fax: 020 8741 7724
E-mail: polish.library@posk.org

Enquiries to: Librarian

Founded: 1942

Organisation type and purpose: Membership association (membership is by subscription), present number of members: 2000+, voluntary organisation, registered charity (charity number 236745), research organisation, publishing house.
Specialised library. Public library circulating service.
Collecting and the dissemination of information, worldwide, on the subject of Polish emigrés in the UK.

Subject coverage: Polish culture, history, literature, language, geography, economics, politics, sociology, folklore, arts, philosophy, religious life, militaria.

Collection: Anglo-Polish relations
Archives of some Polish organisations
Joseph Retinger private papers
Polish emigré publications
Polish underground opposition and Solidarity publications
Works by and about Joseph Conrad

Non-library collection catalogue: All or part available in-house

Library catalogue: All or part available in-house

Publications: Printed
Order printed publications from: e-mail: Polish.library@mailbox.ac.uk

Access to staff: Contact by letter, by telephone, by fax, by e-mail, in person and via website. Letter of introduction required.
Hours: Mon and Wed, 1000 to 2000; Fri, 1000 to 1700, Sat, 1000 to 1300

Access for disabled people: Ramped entry, access to all public areas, toilet facilities

Houses the: Joseph Conrad Society; tel: 020 8741 0474 (library)

Parent body: Polish Social and Cultural Association Limited (POSK); tel: 020 8741 1940; fax: 020 8746 3796; e-mail: admin@posk.org; website: http://www.posk.org

POLITICAL STUDIES ASSOCIATION (PSA)

National Office, Department of Politics, University of Newcastle, Newcastle-upon-Tyne, NE1 7RU

Tel: 0191 222 8021
Fax: 0191 222 3499
E-mail: psa@ncl.ac.uk
Website: www.psa.ac.uk

Founded: 1950

Organisation type and purpose: A membership association open to everyone interested in the study of politics, current number of members: over 1,700.
Membership spans academics in political science and current affairs, theorists and practitioners, policy-makers, journalists, researchers, politics teachers and students in higher education.
To develop and promote the study of politics.

Subject coverage: Politics and political science.

Publications: Printed

Publications list: Available online

Access to staff: Contact by letter, by telephone, by fax and by e-mail

PONTEFRACT REGISTER OFFICE

Old Town Hall, Bridge Street, Pontefract, West Yorkshire, WF8 1PG

Tel: 01977 722670
Fax: 01977 722676

Enquiries to: Superintendent Registrar

Founded: 1837

Organisation type and purpose: Local government body, statutory body.

Access to staff: Contact by letter, by telephone, by fax and in person.
Appointment necessary.
Hours: Mon to Fri, 0900 to 1630
Special comments: Sat by prior appointment.

Access to building: No prior appointment required

Access for disabled people: Parking provided, ramped entry

PONTELAND LOCAL HISTORY SOCIETY

127 Middle Drive, Darras Hall, Newcastle-upon-Tyne, NE20 9DS

E-mail: jmichaeltaylor@btinternet.com
Website: www.ponthistsoc.freeuk.com

Enquiries to: Secretary
Direct tel: 01661 823880

Founded: 1968

Organisation type and purpose: Membership association (membership by subscription).
To promote interest in local history.

Publications: Printed

Access to staff: Contact by letter, by e-mail and via website

Affiliated to: Association of Northumberland Local History Societies

PONY CLUB OF GREAT BRITAIN

Formal name: The Pony Club

Stoneleigh Park, Kenilworth, Warwickshire, CV8 2RW

Tel: 024 7669 8300
Fax: 024 7669 6836
E-mail: enquiries@pcuk.org
Website: www.pcuk.org

Enquiries to: Chief Executive
Other contacts: PA to the Chief Executive

Founded: 1929

Organisation type and purpose: Membership association (membership is by subscription), registered charity (charity number 1050146), suitable for ages: under 25.
To encourage young people to ride and to learn to enjoy horses and riding: to provide instruction in riding, horsemanship and the proper care of their animals: to promote the highest ideals of sportsmanship, citizenship and loyalty.

continued overleaf

Subject coverage: Running an equestrian-orientated youth organisation; information on all matters relating to equestrianism and horse care for young people.

Publications: Printed

Publications list: Available in print

Access to staff: Contact by letter, by telephone, by fax, by e-mail and via website
Hours: Mon to Fri, 0900 to 1700

Has: 2200 affiliated branches overseas in 17 countries; 347 branches and over 400 centres in the UK

POOLE CENTRAL LIBRARY

Dolphin Centre, Poole, Dorset, BH15 1QE

Tel: 01202 262424
Fax: 01202 262442
E-mail: libraries@poole.gov.uk
Website: www.boroughofpoole.com/libraries

Enquiries to: Information Services Librarian
Direct tel: 01202 262421
Other contacts: Central Library Manager

Founded: 1885

Organisation type and purpose: Local government body, public library.

Subject coverage: General information.

Non-library collection catalogue: All or part available in-house

Library catalogue: All or part available in-house

Access to staff: Contact by letter, by telephone, by fax, by e-mail, in person and via website
Hours: Mon to Fri, 0900 to 1800; Sat, 0900 to 1700

Access for disabled people: Access to all public areas, toilet facilities (radar key)
Hours: As above

Parent body: Borough of Poole, Culture and Community Learning Services; Central Library, Dolphin Centre, Poole, Dorset, BH15 1QE, UK; tel: 01202 262421; fax: 01202 262442; e-mail: libraries@poole.gov.uk; website: http://www.boroughofpoole.com/libraries

POPULATION CONCERN

Studio 325, Highgate Studios, 53–79 Highgate Road, London, NW5 1TL

Tel: 020 7241 8500
Fax: 020 7267 6788
Website: www.populationconcern.org.uk

Enquiries to: Education Officer

Founded: 1974

Organisation type and purpose: Registered charity (charity number 1001698).
Originally set up as the international division of the UK FPA; an independent charitable organisation since April 1991.

Subject coverage: Reproductive and sexual health, gender, poverty alleviation, young people, population and related issues.

Trade and statistical information: Data on world population, youth around the world, young people's sexual and reproductive health, and reproductive risk

Library catalogue: All or part available in-house

Publications: Printed, and electronic and video
Order printed publications from: Education Officer, Population Concern
e-mail: education@populationconcern.org.uk

Access to staff: Contact by letter, by telephone, by fax, by e-mail and via website
Hours: Mon to Fri, 0900 to 1700

Collaborates with: International Planned Parenthood Federation (IPPF); Marie Stopes International (MSI)

Recognised by the: United Nations Population Fund (UNFPA)

POPULATION INVESTIGATION COMMITTEE (PIC)

London School of Economics and Political Science, Houghton Street, London, WC2A 2AE

Tel: 020 7955 7666
Fax: 020 7955 6831
E-mail: pic@lse.ac.uk
Website: www.lse.ac.uk/depts/pic

Enquiries to: General Secretary

Founded: 1936

Organisation type and purpose: Professional body, membership association (membership is by election or invitation), present number of members: 11, registered charity (charity number 263783), research organisation.

Subject coverage: Demography and population studies.

Publications: Printed
Order printed publications from: Population Investigation Committee, Room PS201, Houghton Street, London, WC2A 2AE, tel: 020 7955 7666, fax: 020 7955 6831, e-mail: pic@lse.ac.uk
Order electronic and video publications from: http://www.popstudies.net

Publications list: Available online

Access to staff: Contact by letter, by telephone, by fax, by e-mail and via website. Appointment necessary.
Hours: Mon to Fri, 1000 to 1600

PORSCHE CLUB GREAT BRITAIN (PCGB)

Cornbury House, Cotswold Business Village, London Road, Moreton-in-Marsh, Gloucestershire, GL56 0JQ

Tel: 01608 652911
Fax: 01608 652944
E-mail: cluboffice@porscheclubgb.com
Website: www.porscheclubgb.com

Enquiries to: Club Manager
Other contacts: Publications Manager

Founded: 1961

Organisation type and purpose: Membership association (membership is by subscription), present number of members: c.16,000.

Subject coverage: All information covering Porsche models manufactured from 1948 to the present day; provision of display cars; technical information; Porsche motorsport.

Collection: Archive of information, photographs, objects and memorabilia relating to Porsche

Publications: Printed

Access to staff: Contact by letter, by telephone, by fax, by e-mail and via website. Appointment necessary.
Hours: Mon to Fri, 0900 to 1700

Access to building: Access for members only
Hours: Mon to Fri, 0900 to 1700

Access for disabled people: Ramped entry, toilet facilities

PORTIA CAMPAIGN (PORTIA)

The Croft, West Common, Bowness-on-Solway, Cumbria, CA7 5AG

Tel: 016973 51820
Website: www.portia.org

Enquiries to: Chairman

Founded: 1971

Organisation type and purpose: Membership association (membership is by subscription), present number of members: 470, voluntary organisation.
Counselling.

Subject coverage: Shoplifting allegations, cot-death allegations, risk of baby-snatching, false imprisonment.

Publications: Printed, and electronic and video
Order printed publications from: Infinity Junction
PO Box 64, Neston DO, CH64 0WB, e-mail: http//:www.infinityjunction.com

Access to staff: Contact by letter, by telephone, by fax, by e-mail, in person and via website
Hours: 24 hours

PORTLAND COLLEGE

Nottingham Road, Mansfield, Nottinghamshire, NG18 4TJ

Tel: 01623 499111
Fax: 01623 499133
E-mail: college@portland.ac.uk
Website: www.portland.ac.uk/

Enquiries to: Admissions Officer
Direct fax: 01623 499134
Direct e-mail: marketing@portland.ac.uk

Founded: 1950

Organisation type and purpose: Voluntary organisation, registered charity (charity number 214339).

Subject coverage: Residential courses for all categories of physically disabled persons, except the totally blind, from 16 years of age upwards; vocational courses in business, technical studies and horticulture; foundation and further education; adult basic education; alternative and augmentative communication skills, unit for head injured (SPAN).

Publications: Printed

Access to staff: Contact by letter, by telephone and by fax. Appointment necessary.
Hours: Mon to Fri, 0900 to 1700

Recognised by the: British Accreditation Council

PORTSMOUTH & SOUTH EAST HAMPSHIRE CHAMBER OF COMMERCE AND INDUSTRY

Formal name: Hampshire Chamber of Commerce

Regional Business Centre, Harts Farm Way, Havant, Hampshire, PO9 1HR

Tel: 023 9244 9449
Fax: 023 9244 9444
E-mail: jill.mcdonagh@hampshirechamber.co.uk
Website: www.hampshirechamber.co.uk

Enquiries to: Membership Services Manager
Direct e-mail: nicholas.hoath@hampshirechamber.co.uk

Founded: 1883

Organisation type and purpose: Membership association.
Chamber of Commerce.

Subject coverage: Business information, helpline, export and import advice, documentation, trade missions, training, lobbying and representation.

Information services: Provision of credit checks and database lists.

Trade and statistical information: Economic survey of members for ABCC quarterly survey

Publications: Printed

Access to staff: Contact by telephone and by e-mail
Hours: Mon to Fri, 0900 to 1700

Access to building: No prior appointment required
Hours: Mon to Fri, 0900 to 1700

Access for disabled people: Parking provided, level entry, access to all public areas, toilet facilities

PORTSMOUTH CITY COUNCIL (PCC)

Civic Offices, Guildhall Square, Portsmouth, Hampshire, PO1 2BG

Tel: 023 9282 2251
E-mail: general@portsmouthcc.gov.uk
Website: www.portsmouthcc.gov.uk

Enquiries to: Chief Executive
Direct tel: 023 9283 4009

Organisation type and purpose: Local government body.

Subject coverage: Services and amenities of the city council.

PORTSMOUTH CITY COUNCIL LIBRARY SERVICE

Portsmouth Central Library, Guildhall Square, Portsmouth, Hampshire, PO1 2DX

Tel: 023 9281 9311
Fax: 023 9283 9855
E-mail: reference.library@portsmouthcc.gov.uk

Enquiries to: Library Service Manager
Direct e-mail: chris.goddard@plymouth.gov.uk

Organisation type and purpose: Local government body, public library.

Subject coverage: General reference library, particularly strong in areas of law, patent information, business information, art, local history (Hampshire), naval history, genealogy. European Public Information Centre.

Collection: Art Monographs
British Government Publications
British Standards
Charles Dickens Collection
Conan Doyle Collection
Genealogical Collection
HMSO Collection (selected subjects, 1972-)
Law Library
Local History Collection
Maps Collection
Naval Collection (12,000 vols)
Patent Abridgements, 1607 to 1992
State Papers (Calendars and Rolls)
Statistics Collection
UK Patent bibliographic data and full text 1993 to date on CD-ROM

Trade and statistical information: Extensive collection of UK and foreign trade directories.
UK and European statistical information.
Some market research material

Library catalogue: All or part available online and in-house

Access to staff: Contact by letter, by telephone, by fax, by e-mail and in person
Hours: Mon to Fri, 0900 to 1900; Sat, 0930 to 1600
Special comments: Access to historical collections requires proof of name and address.

Member of: HATRICS Centre; Patent Information Network

PORTSMOUTH MUSEUMS AND RECORDS SERVICE

City Museum and Records Office, Museum Road, Portsmouth, Hampshire, PO1 2LJ

Tel: 02392 827261, 02392 876550 (minicom)
Fax: 02392 875276
E-mail: searchroom@portsmouthcc.gov.uk
Website: www.portsmouthrecordsoffice.co.uk/
Website: www.portsmouthmuseums.co.uk

Enquiries to: Manager
Other contacts: (1) Commercial Manager; (2) Visitor Services Officer for (1) marketing; (2) group bookings.

Founded: 1972

Organisation type and purpose: Local government body, museum, art gallery.

Subject coverage: The Story of Portsmouth; Living in Portsmouth; Fine and Decorative Art Gallery; and The Records Office.

Information services: Special visitor services: Guided tours. Education services: Group education facilities, resources for Key Stages 1, 2 and 3. Services for disabled people: For the hearing impaired.

Collection: 17th-century furniture
Art Deco furniture
Frank Dobson sculptures (terracotta and bronze)
Ceri Richards relief work 'Le Piano'.
Ronal Ossory Dunlop painting 'Still Life with Black Bottle'.
JMW Turner RA watercolour 'Gosport, the Entrance to Portsmouth Harbour' c. 1829
Local History:
Sir Alec Rose (Round the World Yachtsman – artefacts)
Verrecchia ice cream parlour and artefacts
Records Office contains the official records of the City of Portsmouth from the 14th century, church registers and records, some of which begin in the reign of Henry VIII, and large collections of deposited records of private, commercial, families and other organisations

Access to staff: Contact by letter, by telephone, by fax and by e-mail

Access to building: No prior appointment required
Hours: Museum: daily, 1000 to 1700 except 24 to 26 Dec
Records Office: Mon to Fri, 1000 to 1700, closed on Public Holidays and 24 to 26 Dec

Access for disabled people: Parking provided, ramped entry, level entry, access to all public areas, toilet facilities
Special comments: Induction loops.

PORTSMOUTH NHS LIBRARY SERVICE

Library, The Quad, Queen Alexandra Hospital, Portsmouth, Hampshire, PO6 3LY

Tel: 023 9228 6039
Fax: 023 9228 6880
E-mail: library.qah@porthosp.nhs.uk
Website: www.porthosp.nhs.uk/library-services.html

Enquiries to: Library Services Manager

Organisation type and purpose: National Health Service library.

Subject coverage: Multi-disciplinary health care.

Access to staff: Contact by letter, by telephone, by fax, by e-mail and via website. Appointment necessary.
Hours: Mon to Fri, 0830 to 1630

Branch libraries: Education Centre; St Mary's Hospital, Portsmouth, Hampshire, PO6 3AD; tel: 023 9228 6000 extn 4855

Parent body: Portsmouth Hospitals NHS Trust

POST ABORTION COUNSELLING SERVICE (PACS)

340 Westbourne Park Road, London, W11 1EQ

Tel: 020 7221 9631
E-mail: abortion@pacs.org.uk

Enquiries to: Counsellor

Founded: 1986

Organisation type and purpose: Advisory body, professional body, registered charity (charity number 802225), training organisation.

continued overleaf

Counselling service.
To offer pre-abortion counselling and training for other professionals in the field.

Subject coverage: The need for counselling as a result of an abortion.

Publications: Printed

Access to staff: Contact by letter and by telephone. Appointment necessary. All charged.
Hours: Mon to Fri, 0900 to 2000
Special comments: 24-hour answerphone, counselling all hours by appointment.

Member of: British Association of Counselling

POST OFFICE VEHICLE CLUB (POVC)

32 Russell Way, Leighton Buzzard, Bedfordshire, LU7 3NG

Tel: 01525 382129
E-mail: povehclub@aol.com
Website: www.povehclub.org.uk

Enquiries to: Honorary Secretary
Direct e-mail: povcmembership@btinternet.com

Founded: 1962

Organisation type and purpose: Membership association.

Subject coverage: Preservation of Royal Mail and British Telecom vehicles; DVLA appointed for GPO and Post Office vehicles for V765 registration restoration.

Collection: Books
Photographs
Vehicle data and manuals
Vehicle records

Non-library collection catalogue: All or part available in-house and in print

Publications: Printed
Order printed publications from: 124 Shenstone Avenue, Norton, Stourbridge, West Midlands, DY8 3EJ

Publications list: Available in print

Access to staff: Contact by letter, by telephone, by fax, by e-mail and via website. Appointment necessary. Access for members only.
Hours: Mon to Fri, 1900 to 2100; Sat, Sun, 0900 to 1800

POST VINTAGE HUMBER CAR CLUB

Formal name: PVHCC Ltd

1 Hilberry Rise, Berrydale, Northampton, NN3 5ER

Tel: 01604 404363
E-mail: pvhumber.carclub@talk21.com
Website: www.humber.org.uk

Enquiries to: Director
Other contacts: Secretary

Founded: 1974

Organisation type and purpose: Membership association (membership is by subscription), present number of members: 700+.
Preservation and enjoyment derived from the ownership and enthusiasm for Humber cars.

Subject coverage: Humber cars from 1932 to 1976.

Non-library collection catalogue: All or part available online

Publications: Printed

Access to staff: Contact by letter, by telephone, by e-mail and via website. Appointment necessary.
Hours: Mon to Fri, 0800 to 2200; Sat, Sun, 1000 to 2000

Member organisation of: Federation of British Historic Vehicle Clubs (FBHVC)

Member organisations: in more than 20 countries

Parent body: PVHCC Ltd; 1 Hilberry Rise, Northampton, NN3 5ER; tel: 01604 404363

POST-WAR THOROUGHBRED CAR CLUB

Church Villas, 22 Burhill Road, Hersham, Walton on Thames, Surrey, KT12 4JF

Tel: 01932 29101
Fax: 01932 29101

Enquiries to: Membership Secretary

Founded: 1978

Organisation type and purpose: Membership association (membership is by subscription), present number of members: 100.
Historic car club.

Subject coverage: British motor vehicles registered between the years 1945–1974.

Access to staff: Contact by letter
Hours: Mon to Fri, 0900 to 1700

POSTAL HISTORY SOCIETY (PHS)

Tumblins, Winterborne Stickland, Blandford Forum, Dorset DT11 0ED

Tel: 01258 880841
Fax: 01258 880841
E-mail: claire@historystore.ltd.uk
Website: www.postalhistory.org.uk

Founded: 1936

Organisation type and purpose: Learned society (membership is by subscription), present number of members: 318.

Subject coverage: History of communications by post or telegraph.

Information services: Queries on postal history answered, preferably by e-mail.

Special visitor services: Library open to members by appointment

Education services: Speakers provided to other groups.

Collection: Library

Library catalogue: All or part available online and in-house

Publications: Printed
Order printed publications from: Publications Officer, Postal History Society, Oast House West, Golden Hill, Wiveliscombe, Somerset TA4 2NT; tel:01984 624527; e-mail: gmarkb34@btinternet.com

Publications list: Available online and in print

Access to staff: Contact by letter, by telephone, by fax, by e-mail, in person and via website. Appointment necessary. Non-members charged.
Hours: Mon to Fri, 0900 to 1700
Special comments: Please leave message if telephone not manned

Affiliated to: Association of British Philatelic Societies Limited; tel: 020 7490 3112

POTATO COUNCIL

Potato Council, Agriculture and Horticulture Development Board, Stoneleigh Park, Kenilworth, Warwickshire, CV8 2TL

Tel: 0247 669 2051
E-mail: info@ahdb.org.uk
Website: www.potato.org.uk

Enquiries to: Information Resources Manager
Direct tel: 01865 782270
Direct fax: 01865 782283

Founded: 1997; formerly called British Potato Council (year of change 2008)

Organisation type and purpose: Non-departmental Public Body. Levy funded by the British Potato Industry, providing sponsorship of research and development, knowledge transfer, promotion of British ware and seed potatoes, collection and dissemination of market information and statistics – all activities contributing towards increasing the competitiveness of the British potato industry, and increasing the usage of British potatoes.

Subject coverage: Potato storage; varieties; pests; diseases; production; marketing; cookery; all aspects, though mainly of UK interest.

Collection: Some grey literature, collection of published articles going back to 1950s and 1960s on computerised retrieval system

Trade and statistical information: Data on the production of potatoes in Great Britain and volume of trade throughout the world. Producer, wholesale and retail prices. Crop progress reports

Non-library collection catalogue: All or part available in-house

Publications: Printed, and electronic and video
Order printed publications from: Publications, at the same address, tel: 01865 782222, fax: 01865 782283, e-mail: publications@potato.org.uk

Access to staff: Contact by letter, by fax and by e-mail. Appointment necessary.
Hours: Mon to Fri, 0900 to 1700
Special comments: Photocopies cannot be supplied.

Parent body: Agriculture and Horticulture Development Board (AHDB); Area 2B, Nobel House, 17 Smith Square, London, SW1P 3JR; tel: 020 7238 3079; e-mail: info@ahdb.org.uk; website: http://www.ahdb.org.uk

POTATO PROCESSORS ASSOCIATION (PPA)

4a Torphichen Street, Edinburgh, EH3 8JQ

Tel: 0131 229 9415
Fax: 0131 229 9407
E-mail: neil.cuthbert@sfdf.org.uk

Enquiries to: Secretary

Organisation type and purpose: Trade association (membership is by subscription).

Subject coverage: Potato processing.

Access to staff: Contact by letter, by telephone, by fax and by e-mail. Appointment necessary.
Hours: Mon to Fri, 0900 to 1700

Member of: EUITP

POWER GENERATION CONTRACTORS ASSOCIATION (PGCA)

Westminster Tower, 3 Albert Embankment, London, SE1 7SL

Tel: 020 7793 3040
Fax: 020 7793 1576

Enquiries to: Director

Organisation type and purpose: Trade association.

Subject coverage: Project management and engineering services for utility and industrial power stations, water tube and shell boilers; steam, gas, water and wind turbine generators, condensing and feed heating plant, high integrity pipework, auxiliary and ancillary plant, nuclear engineering, environmental systems, retrofit, refurbishment, repair, maintenance and construction services.

Access to staff: Contact by fax
Hours: Mon to Fri, 0900 to 1700

Federated in: BEAMA

POWERFUL INFORMATION

City Discovery Centre, Bradwell Abbey, Milton Keynes, Buckinghamshire, MK13 9AP

Tel: 01908 320033
Fax: 01908 320033
E-mail: info@powerfulinformation.org
Website: www.powerfulinformation.org

Enquiries to: Manager
Direct e-mail: admin@powerfulinformation.org

Founded: 1990

Organisation type and purpose: Registered charity working in grassroots international development.

Subject coverage: Powerful Information is a British charity working to empower communities in low-income countries to tackle the root causes of poverty and injustice and reduce the impact of environmental degradation. It works with and through local partners to provide education and training, and supports practical grassroots initiatives that build social capital, promote social justice and raise public awareness of important social and environmental issues.

Access to staff: Contact by letter, by telephone, by e-mail and via website. Appointment necessary.
Hours: Mon to Fri, 0900 to 1700

Access for disabled people: Parking provided, level entry, access to all public areas, toilet facilities
Hours: As above.

POWERGEN UK PLC

Power Technology, Ratcliffe on Soar, Nottingham, NG11 0EE

Tel: 0115 936 2000
Fax: 0115 936 2711
E-mail: liz.day@powertech.co.uk
Website: www.powertech.co.uk

Enquiries to: Information Officer
Direct tel: 0115 936 2360
Direct fax: 0115 362 647

Founded: 1989

Organisation type and purpose: Service industry.
Electricity and gas utility.

Subject coverage: Environment; wind power; NDT; metallurgy; combustion and fossil fuel; all subjects relating to electricity production, organisation and maintenance; does not include nuclear generation or electricity transmission.

Collection: CEGB and Powergen reports

Non-library collection catalogue: All or part available in-house

Library catalogue: All or part available in-house

Publications: Printed

Access to staff: Contact by letter, by telephone, by fax, by e-mail and via website. Appointment necessary.
Hours: Mon to Fri, 0900 to 1700

Access for disabled people: Parking provided, level entry, toilet facilities

Head Office: Powergen plc; Westwood Way, Westwood Business Park, Coventry, CV4 8LG; tel: 01203 424000; fax: 01203 425432

POWYS COUNTY ARCHIVES OFFICE

County Hall, Llandrindod Wells, Powys, LD1 5LG

Tel: 01597 826088
Fax: 01597 826087
E-mail: archives@powys.gov.uk
Website: archives.powys.gov.uk
Website: www.powys.gov.uk

Enquiries to: Manager
Other contacts: Assistant Archivist

Founded: 1991

Organisation type and purpose: Local government body.
Archives office.

Subject coverage: Local history of former counties of Breconshire, Montgomeryshire and Radnorshire, 15th century to 20th century.

Collection: Public Records, incl. Quarter Sessions records
Official Records
Estate and Solicitors' collections
Records of local historical interest, incl. manuscripts and photographs
Census returns (microfiche)
Parish registers (microfilm)
A growing collection of local history books on Powys

Non-library collection catalogue: All or part available in-house

Library catalogue: All or part available online and in-house

Publications: Printed

Access to staff: Contact by letter, by telephone, by fax and by e-mail. Appointment necessary.
Hours: Tue to Thu, 1000 to 1230 and 1330 to 1700; Fri, 1000 to 1230 and 1330 to 1600; closed at all other times

Part of: Powys County Council; Recreation, Culture and Countryside

POWYS COUNTY COUNCIL

County Hall, Llandrindod Wells, Powys, LD1 5LG

Tel: 01597 826000
Fax: 01597 826230
E-mail: customer@powys.gov.uk
Website: www.powys.gov.uk

Enquiries to: Relevant department

Founded: 1996

Organisation type and purpose: Local government body.

Subject coverage: Community services, children, families and lifelong learning, economy and community regeneration, technical and local services.

Access to staff: Contact by letter, by telephone, by fax, by e-mail and in person
Hours: Mon to Thu, 0900 to 1700; Fri 0900 to 1630

POWYS LIBRARY SERVICE

Library HQ, Cefnllys Lane, Llandrindod Wells, Powys, LD1 5LD

Tel: 01597 826860
Fax: 01597 826872
Website: www.powys.gov.uk/libraries

Enquiries to: County Librarian

Organisation type and purpose: Local government body, public library.

Subject coverage: General.

Collection: Gregynog Press Collection (at Newtown Area Library)
Local history collections (relating to Powys and to the former counties of Breconshire, Montgomeryshire and Radnorshire)

Library catalogue: All or part available online and in-house

Access to staff: Contact by letter, by telephone, by fax, by e-mail, in person and via website
Hours: HQ: Mon to Fri, 0900 to 1700; for branches, see website

Branches: within the Recreation and Culture directorate of Powys County Council

POWYS SOCIETY

Flat D, 87 Ledbury Road, London, W11 2AG

Tel: 020 7238 4456 (office); 020 7243 0168 (evening)
E-mail: postmaster@powys-society.org
Website: www.powys-society.org

Enquiries to: Honorary Secretary
Direct e-mail: chris.thd.thomas@hotmail.co.uk

Founded: 1967

Organisation type and purpose: Learned society (membership is by subscription), present number of members: 298, registered charity (charity number 801332).
Literary society. Aims to publicise the literary and artistic contribution of all members of the Powys Family, in particular John Cowper (1872–1963), Theodore Francis Powys (1875–1953) and Llewelyn Powys (1884–1939), and their wide circle of friends.

Subject coverage: Lives and works of the three writers: John Cowper Powys, Theodore Francis Powys and Llewelyn Powys, other members of the Powys family and their circle of friends.

Collection: Major collections of books, manuscripts and letters, etc. relating to the Powys family, held at the Dorset County Museum, Dorchester, Dorset

Non-library collection catalogue: All or part available in-house

Library catalogue: All or part available in-house

Publications: Printed
Order printed publications from: Publications Manager, The Powys Society, 23 Cleveland Walk, Bath, BA2 6JW, tel: 01225 469004, e-mail: sm@gotadsl.co.uk

Publications list: Available in print

Access to staff: Contact by letter, by telephone, by e-mail and via website
Hours: Mon to Fri, 0900 to 1700

Access to building: By arrangement only

PRACTICAL ACTION PUBLISHING

The Schumacher Centre for Technology and Development, Bourton-on-Dunsmore, Rugby, CV23 9QZ

Tel: 01926 634501
Fax: 01926 634502
E-mail: publishinginfo@practicalaction.org.uk
Website: www.itdgpublishing.org.uk
Website: www.developmentbookshop.com

History of institution: formerly called ITDG Publishing

Organisation type and purpose: Publishing house.

Subject coverage: Development technology for developing world, water and sanitation, development and disaster relief, food security.

Library catalogue: All or part available in-house

Publications list: Available in print

Access to staff: Contact by letter and by fax
Hours: Mon to Fri, 0830 to 1730

Access to building: Prior appointment required

PRADER-WILLI SYNDROME ASSOCIATION (UK) (PWSA (UK))

125A London Road, Derby, DE1 2QQ

Tel: 01332 365676
Fax: 01332 360401
E-mail: admin@pwsa.co.uk
Website: www.pwsa.co.uk

Enquiries to: Administrator
Other contacts: Welfare Services and Regional Groups Coordinator (for welfare queries, new diagnosis)

Founded: 1981

Organisation type and purpose: Voluntary organisation, registered charity (charity number 284583).
Voluntary support group.

Subject coverage: The Prader-Willi Syndrome, support and information for sufferers and carers.

Library catalogue: All or part available in-house

Publications: Printed, and electronic and video
Order printed publications from: above address

Publications list: Available in print

Access to staff: Contact by letter, by telephone, by fax, by e-mail, in person and via website
Hours: Mon to Fri, 0930 to 1530
Special comments: Answerphone available.

Access to building: Prior appointment required

Access for disabled people: Access to first floor offices only

PRE-SCHOOL LEARNING ALLIANCE

National Centre, The Fitzpatrick Building, 188 York Way, London, N7 9AD

Tel: 020 7697 2500
Fax: 020 7700 0319
E-mail: info@pre-school.org.uk
Website: www.pre-school.org.uk

Enquiries to: Information Services
Direct tel: 020 7697 2595

Founded: 1961; formerly called Pre-school Playgroups Association (year of change 1995)

Organisation type and purpose: An educational charity specialising in the early years, and a membership association providing practical support to over 15,000 early years settings and contributing to the care and education of over 800,000 young children and their families each year.

Subject coverage: Products and services include specialist publications, childcare services, quality assurance, campaigning, research, training and family programmes; offers a range of independent professional information, advice, support and guidance tailored especially to meet the needs of young children and their families, students, early years practitioners and professionals.

Publications: Printed
Order printed publications from: www.pre-school.org.uk/shop

Publications list: Available online and in print

Access to staff: Contact by letter, by telephone, by fax and by e-mail
Hours: Mon to Fri, 0900 to 1700

Constituent bodies: 4 divisional offices, 400 county and branch sub-committees

PRECAST FLOORING FEDERATION (PFF)

60 Charles Street, Leicester, LE1 1FB

Tel: 0116 253 6161
Fax: 0116 251 4568
E-mail: info@precastfloors.info
Website: www.precastfloors.info

Enquiries to: Secretary

Organisation type and purpose: Trade association.

Subject coverage: Precast concrete flooring units of all types.

Publications: Printed

Access to staff: Contact by letter, by telephone, by fax and by e-mail
Hours: Mon to Fri, 0900 to 1700

Product association of the: British Precast Concrete Federation

PREHISTORIC SOCIETY

Institute of Archaeology, University College London, 31–34 Gordon Square, London, WC1H 0PY

Website: www.ucl.ac.uk/prehistoric

Enquiries to: Administrative Assistant
Direct e-mail: prehistoric@ucl.ac.uk

Founded: 1935

Organisation type and purpose: Learned society.

Subject coverage: Prehistory.

Publications: Printed

Access to staff: Contact by letter
Hours: Mon to Fri, 0900 to 1700

PREMIER CHRISTIAN RADIO

Formal name: Premier – Christian Radio for London

PO Box 13000, London, SW1E 5PP

Tel: 020 7233 6705
Fax: 020 7233 6706
E-mail: premier@premier.org.uk
Website: www.premier.org.uk
Website: www.radioondemand.net
Website: www.christianityandrenewal.com

Enquiries to: Administrator
Direct e-mail: crystal.callow@premier.org.uk

Founded: 1995

Organisation type and purpose: Registered charity (charity number 287610).
Radio station.

Subject coverage: Christian broadcasting and publishing, telephone helpline, internet services via website, Christian resources.

Publications: Printed

Access to staff: Contact by letter, by telephone, by fax, by e-mail and via website
Hours: Mon to Fri, 0900 to 1700

Access to building: No access other than to staff

Publishing subsidiary: Monarch CCP; PO Box 17911, London, SW1E 5ZR; tel: 020 7316 1450; fax: 020 7316 1453; e-mail: monarchccp@premier.org.uk

Telephone Helpline: Lifeline; at the same address; tel: 020 7316 0808; e-mail: lifeline@premier.org.uk

PRESBYTERIAN CHURCH OF WALES (PCW)

Tabernacle Chapel, 81 Merthyr Road, Whitchurch, Cardiff, CF14 1DD

Tel: 029 2062 7465
Fax: 029 2061 6188
E-mail: swyddfa.office@ebcpcw.org.uk
Website: www.ebcpcw.org.uk

Enquiries to: Manager

Organisation type and purpose: Registered charity.
Christian church, excepted charity.
To propagate the Gospel of Jesus Christ.

Subject coverage: The history, organisation and current position of the Presbyterian Church of Wales.

Collection: The Presbyterian Church of Wales Archive is housed in the National Library, Aberystwyth

Publications: Printed
Order printed publications from: The Manager, Y Bwthyn Press, Lôn Ddewi, Caernarfon, Gwynedd, LL55 1ER, tel: 01286 672018, fax: 01286 677823

Access to staff: Contact by letter, by telephone, by fax, by e-mail and via website. Appointment necessary.
Hours: Mon to Fri, 0900 to 1700

PRESBYTERIAN HISTORICAL SOCIETY OF IRELAND

26 College Green, Belfast, BT71LN

Tel: 028 9072 7330
E-mail: phsilibrarian@pcinet.org
Website: www.presbyterianhistoryireland.com

Enquiries to: Librarian/Assistant Secretary

Founded: 1907

Organisation type and purpose: Learned society (membership is by subscription) but library and archive are open to all, present number of members: 350, registered charity.
Historical society for the Presbyterian Church in Ireland; the Non-Subscribing Presbyterian Church of Ireland and the Reformed Presbyterian Church of Ireland.

Subject coverage: History of Presbyterianism and the Presbyterian Churches in Ireland, with congregational, genealogical and biographical information.

Special visitor services: Microfilm reader; photocopying service; digital book scanning

Collection: Books and pamphlets (c. 550 to pre-1851)
Periodicals
Congregational histories
Biographies of ministers
Photographs of ministers and churches
Collection of Irish Presbyterian communion tokens
Presbyterian artefacts including McCahan bequest collection (historical books and manuscripts)
Microfilms of Presbyterian church records
Some original Presbyterian church records
Personal papers of ministers

Library catalogue: All or part available in-house

Publications: Printed

Publications list: Available online

Access to staff: Contact by letter, by telephone, by e-mail and in person
Hours: Tue, Wed, 0930 to 1630; Thu, 0930 to 1300

Access for disabled people: Ramp access to front of College Green; library facilities are on ground floor with disabled toilet facilities

PRESCRIPTION PRICING AUTHORITY (PPA)

Bridge House, 152 Pilgrim Street, Newcastle upon Tyne, NE1 6SN

Tel: 0191 232 5270
Fax: 0191 232 5250
Website: www.ppa.org.uk

Enquiries to: Director of Information Technology
Direct fax: 0191 203 5270
Direct e-mail: douglas.ball@ppa.nhs.uk

Founded: 1911

Organisation type and purpose: Statutory body.
Information on drugs dispensed and prescribed in England. Details on prescribers and dispensers. Drug coding and descriptive information.
Authorise and make payment to dispensing contractors in England with regard to NHS prescriptions. Provide prescribing information and systems to NHS bodies and prescribers. Detection and prevention of fraud. Management of Low Income Scheme.

Subject coverage: Drug prescribing in England, volume of drugs in the UK, updates on drug prices, standard drug file/drug coding systems and information for research groups. Details on prescribing and dispensing contractors.

Publications: Printed, and electronic and video

Access to staff: Contact by letter and by e-mail. Appointment necessary.
Hours: Mon to Fri, 0900 to 1700
Special comments: Access only by appointment.

PRESS ASSOCIATION (PA)

PA News Library, PA News Centre, Central Park, New Lane, Leeds, West Yorkshire, LS11 5DZ

Tel: 0870 830 6824
Fax: 0870 830 6825
E-mail: newslibrary@pa.press.net
Website: www.palibrary.press.net

Enquiries to: News Librarian
Other contacts: Picture Librarian for photo library.

Founded: 1926 (library)

Organisation type and purpose: National organisation, service industry.
News agency.
Cuttings from all national papers.

Subject coverage: Archive news material from 1926 to date covering a very wide range of subjects in 15 million press cuttings from all British national newspapers, some back to 1928; domestic news photographs from 1910 to present day.

Collection: News library
Photo library

Access to staff: Contact by telephone, by fax, by e-mail and in person. Appointment necessary. All charged.
Hours: Daily, 0700 to 2300

PRESS COMPLAINTS COMMISSION (PCC)

Halton House, 20–23 Holborn, London, EC1N 2JD

Tel: 020 7831 0022
Fax: 020 7831 0025
E-mail: complaints@pcc.org.uk
Website: www.pcc.org.uk

Enquiries to: Information and Events Manager
Direct e-mail: pcc@pcc.org.uk

Founded: 1991

Organisation type and purpose: The PCC is an independent self-regulatory body that deals with complaints about the editorial content of newspapers and magazines (and their websites). It has 17 members drawn from the lay public and the press who form the Commission.

Subject coverage: The PCC investigates complaints raised with it under the Editors' Code by individuals, companies and organisations. It keeps industry standards high by training journalists and editors, and works pro-actively behind the scenes to prevent harassment and media intrusion. It can also provide pre-publication advice to journalists and the public.

Education services: Talks/seminars provided for groups of journalism and media studies students by prior appointment.

Publications: Printed

Access to staff: Contact by letter, by telephone, by fax, by e-mail and via website
Hours: 0900 to 1730
Special comments: 24-hour Advice Line for use in emergencies only: 07659 152656

Access to building: Prior appointment required
Hours: 0930 to 1730

PRESSURE GAUGE AND DIAL THERMOMETER ASSOCIATION (PGDT)

136 Hagley Road, Edgbaston, Birmingham, B16 9PN

Tel: 0121 454 4141
Fax: 0121 454 4949
E-mail: info@pgdt.org
Website: www.pgdt.org

Enquiries to: Secretary

Organisation type and purpose: Trade association.

Subject coverage: Pressure gauges and pressure measurement, temperature gauges and measurement.

Publications: Printed

Access to staff: Contact by e-mail and via website
Hours: Mon to Fri, 0900 to 1700

PRESTON BOROUGH COUNCIL

PO Box 10, Town Hall, Preston, Lancashire, PR1 2RL

Tel: 01772 906000
Fax: 01772 906195
E-mail: info@preston.gov.uk
Website: www.preston.gov.uk

Enquiries to: Public Relations Manager
Direct tel: 01772 906464
Direct e-mail: al.mazzafiore@pbcpr.demon.co.uk

Organisation type and purpose: Local government body.

Subject coverage: Local government services.

Publications: Printed

Access to staff: Contact by letter and by e-mail
Hours: Mon to Fri, 0900 to 1700

PRESTRESSED CONCRETE ASSOCIATION (PCA)

4th Floor, 60 Charles Street, Leicester, LE1 1FB

Tel: 0116 253 6161
Fax: 0116 251 4568

Enquiries to: Secretary

Organisation type and purpose: Trade association.

Subject coverage: Precast pretensioned concrete bridge beams, double tee beams and other precast prestressed units.

Publications: Printed

Access to staff: Contact by letter, by telephone, by fax and by e-mail
Hours: Mon to Fri, 0900 to 1700

Product association of the: British Precast Concrete Federation

PRIMARY IMMUNODEFICIENCY ASSOCIATION (PiA)

Alliance House, 12 Caxton Street, London, SW1H 0QS

Tel: 020 7976 7640
Fax: 020 7976 7641
E-mail: info@pia.org.uk
Website: pia.org.uk

Enquiries to: Chief Executive
Direct e-mail: chris@pia.org.uk

Founded: 1989

Organisation type and purpose: Membership association, present number of members: 2,000, voluntary organisation, registered charity (charity number 1107233).

Subject coverage: All primary immunodeficiencies and how they affect individuals.

Publications list: Available online and in print

Access to staff: Contact by letter, by telephone, by fax, by e-mail and via website. Appointment necessary.
Hours: Mon to Fri, 0900 to 1700

Member of: European Patients Primary Immunodeficiency Collaboration (EPPIC); International Patient of Primary Immunodeficiencies (IPOPI)

PRINCE'S FOUNDATION (PFBE)

Formal name: The Prince's Foundation for the Built Environment

19–22 Charlotte Road, London, EC2A 3SG

Tel: 020 7613 8500
Fax: 020 7613 8599
E-mail: enquiries@princes-foundation.org
Website: www.princes-foundation.org

Enquiries to: Librarian
Direct tel: 020 7613 8507
Direct e-mail: library@princes-foundation.org

Founded: 1998; formerly called The Prince of Wales's Institute of Architecture (year of change 2000)

Organisation type and purpose: Educational charity and architecture and urban design consultancy.

Subject coverage: Traditional and sustainable architecture and urbanism, community planning, traditional art, building crafts, Islamic arts, environmental building techniques, urban design and regeneration.

Information services: Members-only Library.

Special visitor services: By previous arrangement with the librarian.

Collection: Library includes the collections of the late John Julius Stanton and others, and books on Islamic art and architecture, some donated by Issam El Said
Special Collections: His Royal Highness Collection, books on indefinite loan from the private collection of HRH The Prince of Wales

Non-library collection catalogue: All or part available in-house

Library catalogue: All or part available in-house

Publications: Printed, and electronic and video
Order printed publications from: Tradition & Sustainability available in bookshops from September 2010
Senior Fellows Series can be purchased on-line from the INTBAU website: http://www.intbau.org
Limited availability of back catalogue, enquiries e-mail: library@princes-foundation.org

Publications list: Available in print

Access to staff: Contact by letter, by telephone, by fax and by e-mail. Appointment necessary.
Hours: Mon to Fri, 1000 to 1730

Access to building: Prior appointment required
Hours: Mon to Fri, 0900 to 1700

Access for disabled people: Ramped entry, access to all public areas, accessible doors to all areas, lift servicing all floors, accessible toilets (fully DDA-compliant)
Hours: Mon to Fri, 0900 to 1700

Links with: INTBAU, International network for traditonal building, architecture & urbanism; The Prince's Charities; The Prince's Drawing School; The Prince's School of Traditional Art

PRINCE'S TRUST, THE

Head Office, 18 Park Square East, London, NW1 4LH

Tel: 020 7543 1234, 020 7543 1374 (minicom)
Fax: 020 7543 1200
E-mail: info@princes-trust.org.uk
Website: www.princes-trust.org.uk

Enquiries to: Press Office
Direct tel: 020 7543 1382
Other contacts: Information Officer for research enquiries.

Founded: 1973

Organisation type and purpose: Registered charity (charity number 1053579).
The Prince's Trust is the UK's leading youth charity, offering 14–30 year olds the training, funding or support they need to gain confidence, improve life skills or get into work.

Subject coverage: Young people; youth disadvantage; youth unemployment; young people and New Deal; young people and volunteering.

Publications: Printed, and electronic and video
Order printed publications from: Literature Distribution Service
tel: 020 8957 5190

Publications list: Available in print

Access to staff: Contact by letter, by telephone and via website
Hours: Mon to Fri, 0900 to 1700

Access to building: No prior appointment required
Special comments: Research/information needs in writing to the Information Officer.

Other addresses: Various offices across the UK; tel: 0800 842 842 (freephone)

PRINCIPAL REGISTRY OF THE FAMILY DIVISION (PROBATE DEPARTMENT)

First Avenue House, 42–49 High Holborn, London, WC1V 6NP

Tel: 020 7947 7000
Fax: 020 7947 6946
Website: www.courtservice.gov.uk

Enquiries to: Manager Probate Department

Organisation type and purpose: National government body.

Subject coverage: Wills and grants of probate and administration.

Collection: All wills in England and Wales since 1858

Publications: Printed

Access to staff: Contact by telephone and in person
Hours: Mon to Fri, 1000 to 1630
Special comments: General enquiries only by telephone.

Access for disabled people: Access to all public areas, toilet facilities

All requests for copies of wills/grants by post: York Probate Sub-Registry (provide full name of deceased, data of death, locality, where resided, cheque for £5 payable to H.M.P.G.); Duncombe Place, York, YO1 7EA

PRISON ADVICE AND CARE TRUST (PACT)

Family Support Services, 254 Caledonian Road, Islington, London, N1 0NG

Tel: 020 7278 3981
Fax: 020 7278 8765
E-mail: info@prisonadvice.org.uk
Website: www.imprisonment.org.uk

Enquiries to: Family Services Manager

Founded: 1974

Organisation type and purpose: Voluntary organisation, registered charity (charity number 219278).
Gives support advice and help to prisoners' wives, children and any family member or friend who has someone in prison.

Subject coverage: Welfare benefits, penal systems, 'families and friends' finance, visiting prisons, prison regulations, assisted visits, accommodation. Overnight accommodation for families visiting London prisons/attending trials/appeals.

Collection: Leaflets, booklets, books and publications relating to penal establishments, rules etc

Publications: Printed

Access to staff: Contact by letter, by telephone, by fax, by e-mail and via website. Appointment necessary.
Hours: Mon to Fri, 0930 to 1700

Liaison with other groups involved in similar work eg: Federation of Prisoners' Families Support Groups; NACRO; Prison Reform Trust; Various statutory bodies

Other addresses: All Day Children's Visits; HMP Holloway, Parkhurst Road, London, N7 0NU; Holloway Visitors' Centre; HMP Holloway, Parkhurst Road, London, N7 0NU; tel: 020 7700 1567; Pentonville Visitors' Centre; HMP Pentonville, Caledonian Road, London, N7 8TT; tel: 020 7609 3860

Registered Office and Administration: PACT; Lincoln House, 1–3 Brixton Road, London, SW9 6DE

PRISON OFFICERS' ASSOCIATION (POA)

Cronin House, 245 Church Street, Edmonton, London, N9 9HW

Tel: 020 8803 0255
Fax: 020 8803 1761

Enquiries to: General Secretary

Organisation type and purpose: Trade union, present number of members: 34,000.

Subject coverage: Trade union view of issues relating to the working and operational conditions of HM Prisons Service.

Access to staff: Contact by letter. Appointment necessary. Letter of introduction required.
Hours: Mon to Fri, 0900 to 1700

Affiliated to: EUROFEDOP; TUC

PRISON REFORM TRUST (PRT)

15 Northburgh Street, London, EC1V 0JR

Tel: 020 7251 5070
Fax: 020 7251 5076
E-mail: prt@prisonreformtrust.org.uk
Website: www.prisonreformtrust.org.uk

Founded: 1981

Organisation type and purpose: National organisation, voluntary organisation, registered charity (charity number 1035525), research organisation.
The work of the Prison Reform Trust is aimed at creating a just, humane and effective penal system.

Subject coverage: Prison regimes, alternatives to custody and sentencing policy.

Collection: Press cuttings
Official reports
Prison statistics
Wide variety of UK and international reports and papers

Publications: Printed

Publications list: Available online and in print

Access to staff: Contact by letter, by telephone, by e-mail and via website
Hours: Mon to Fri, 0930 to 1730

PRISON SERVICE COLLEGE LIBRARY

Prison Service College, Newbold Revel, Rugby, Warwickshire, CV23 0TH

Tel: 01788 804119
Fax: 01788 804114
E-mail: catherine.fell@noms.gsi.gov.uk

Enquiries to: Librarian

Founded: 1960

Organisation type and purpose: National government body, training organisation. Central government training establishment.

Subject coverage: Penology and criminology; history of the prison service in England and Wales; comparative material on penal establishments in other countries; management and training; forensic psychology and psychiatry.

Collection: Miscellaneous 19th-century reports on prison-related matters
Reports of Directors of Convict Prisons
Reports of HM Inspectors of Prisons from 1835
Reports of the Prison Commission/Prison Department from 1878

Library catalogue: All or part available in-house

Publications: Printed

Access to staff: Contact by letter, by telephone, by fax and by e-mail. Appointment necessary.
Hours: Mon, 1000 to 1730; Tue to Thu, 0830 to 1730; Fri 0830 to 1400

Parent body: HM Prison Service; website: http://www.hmprisonservice.gov.uk

PRISONERS ABROAD (PA)

89–93 Fonthill Road, Finsbury Park, London, N4 3JH

Tel: 020 7561 6820
Fax: 020 7561 6821
E-mail: info@prisonersabroad.org.uk
Website: www.prisonersabroad.org.uk

Founded: 1978; formerly called National Council for the Welfare of Prisoners Abroad (year of change 2003)

Organisation type and purpose: International organisation, registered charity (charity number 1093710).
Providing information, advice and support to British citizens held in prison abroad, to their families, and when they return to the United Kingdom.

Subject coverage: Judicial procedures; prisoners' rights; information services; prisoner transfer treaties; extradition; prison conditions; welfare services; resettlement; family support.

Publications: Printed

Publications list: Available online

Access to staff: Contact by letter, by telephone, by fax, by e-mail, in person and via website. Appointment necessary.
Hours: Mon to Fri, 1000 to 1600

Access to building: *Hours:* Mon to Fri, 1000 to 1600

Access for disabled people: *Hours:* Mon to Fri, 1000 to 1600

PRIVATE LIBRARIES ASSOCIATION (PLA)

Ravelston, South View Road, Pinner, Middlesex, HA5 3YD

E-mail: dchambers@aol.com
Website: www.the-old-school.demon.co.uk/pla.htm

Enquiries to: Chairman

Founded: 1956

Organisation type and purpose: Learned society.
Society of book collectors.

Subject coverage: Book collecting.

Trade and statistical information: Data on privately printed books worldwide in English

continued overleaf

Publications: Printed
Order printed publications from: Publications Secretary, Claude Cox Books
3 Silent Street, Ipswich, IP1 1TF

Publications list: Available online and in print

Access to staff: Contact by letter and by e-mail

In liaison with the: Library Association

Links with: Society of Private Printers

PROBATE OFFICES

Local offices: 1st Floor, Crown Building, Rivergate, Peterborough, PE1 1EJ, tel: 01733 562802; Bangor Probate Sub-Registry; Council Offices, Ffordd Gwynedd, Bangor, Gwynedd, LL57 1DT; tel: 01248 362410; Birmingham District Probate Registry; The Priory Courts, 33 Bull Street, Birmingham, B4 6DU; tel: 0121 681 3400; Bodmin Probate Sub-Registry; Market Street, Bodmin, Cornwall, PL31 2JW; tel: 01208 72279; Brighton District Probate Registry; William Street, Brighton, Sussex, BN2 2LG; tel: 01273 684071; Bristol District Probate Registry; Ground Floor, The Crescent Centre, Temple Back, Bristol, BS1 6EP; tel: 0117 9273915; Carlisle Probate Sub-Registry; Courts of Justice, Earl Street, Carlisle, Cumbria, CA1 1DJ; tel: 01228 521751; Carmarthen Probate Sub-Registry; 14 King Street, Carmarthen, SA31 1BL; tel: 01267 236238; Chester Probate Sub-Registry; 5th Floor, Hamilton House, Hamilton Place, Chester, CH1 2DA; tel: 01244 345082; Exeter Probate Sub-Registry; Finance House, Barnfield Road, Exeter, Devon, EX1 1QR; tel: 01392 274515; Gloucester Probate Sub-Registry; 2nd Floor, Combined Court Building, Kimbrose Way, Gloucester, GL1 2DG; tel: 01452 522585; Ipswich District Probate Registry; Haven House, 17 Lower Brook Street, Ipswich, Suffolk, IP4 1DN; tel: 01473 253724; Lancaster Probate Sub-Registry; Mitre House, Church Street, Lancaster, LA1 1HE; tel: 01524 36625; Leeds District Probate Registry; 3rd Floor, Coronet House, Queen Street, Leeds, LS1 2BA; tel: 0113 243 1505; Leicester Probate Sub-Registry; 5th Floor, Leicester House, Lee Circle, Leicester, LE1 3RE; tel: 0116 2538558; Lincoln Probate Sub-Registry; 360 High Street, Lincoln, LN5 7PS; tel: 01522 523648; Liverpool District Probate Registry; Queen Elizabeth II Law Courts, Derby Square, Liverpool, L2 1XA; tel: 0151 236 8264; Maidstone Probate Sub-Registry; The Law Courts, Barker Road, Maidstone, ME18 8EW; tel: 01622 202048; Manchester District Probate Registry; 9th Floor, Astley House, 23 Quay Street, Manchester, M2 4AT; tel: 0161 834 4319; Middlesbrough Probate Sub-Registry; Teesside Combined Court Centre, Russell Street, Middlesbrough, Cleveland, TS1 2AE; tel: 01642 340001; Newcastle District Probate Registry; 2nd Floor, Plummer House, Croft Street, Newcastle upon Tyne, NE1 6NP; tel: 0191 261 8383; Norwich Probate Sub-Registry; Combined Court Building, Bishopsgate, Norwich, NR3 1UR; tel: 01603 728267; Nottingham Probate Sub-Registry; Butt Dyke House, Park Row, Nottingham, NG1 6GR; tel: 0115 941 4288; Oxford District Probate Registry; Oxford Combined Court Building, St Aldates, Oxford, OX1 1LY; tel: 01865 793 055; Peterborough Probate Sub-Registry; 1st Floor; Principal Registry of the Family Division; Probate Department, First Avenue House, 42–49 High Holborn, London, WC1V 6NP; tel: 020 7947 6983; Probate Registry of Wales; PO Box 474, 2 Park Street, Cardiff, CF10 1TB; tel: 029 2037 6479; Sheffield Probate Sub-Registry; PO Box 832, The Law Courts, 50 West Bar, Sheffield, S3 3YR; tel: 0114 281 2596; Stoke on Trent Probate Sub-Registry; Combined Court Centre, Bethesda Street, Hanley, ST1 3BP; tel: 01782 854065; Winchester District Probate Registry; 4th Floor, Cromwell House, Andover Road, Winchester, Hampshire, SO23 7EW; tel: 01962 863771; York Probate Office; 1st Floor, Castle Chambers, Clifford Street, York, YO1 9RG; tel: 01904 666777

PROCESSORS AND GROWERS RESEARCH ORGANISATION (PGRO)

The Research Station, Great North Road, Thornhaugh, Peterborough, Cambridgeshire, PE8 6HJ

Tel: 01780 782585
Fax: 01780 783993
Website: www.pgro.co.uk

Enquiries to: Director

Founded: 1944

Organisation type and purpose: Research organisation.

Subject coverage: Production and harvesting of vegetables, primarily for processing for human consumption; seeds and seed health, general agronomy, evaluation of crop protection materials and techniques, evaluation of new varieties.

Publications: Printed

PROCTER & GAMBLE TECHNICAL CENTRES LIMITED (P&G)

Newcastle Technical Centre, PO Box Forest Hall No 2, Newcastle upon Tyne, NE12 9TS

Tel: 0191 228 1000
Fax: 0191 228 1021
Website: www.uk.pg.com

Enquiries to: Business Information Services Manager
Direct tel: 0191 228 1728

Founded: 1837

Organisation type and purpose: Manufacturing industry, research organisation.
Company technical centre; formerly known as Procter & Gamble Research and Development Laboratories.

Subject coverage: Soaps and detergents, cleaning products, oils and fats, fatty acids and derivatives, related chemistry and technology.

Non-library collection catalogue: All or part available in-house

Library catalogue: All or part available in-house

Publications list: Available online

Access to staff: Contact by letter and by fax
Hours: Mon to Fri, 0830 to 1630

Access to building: No prior appointment required

PRODUCERS ALLIANCE FOR CINEMA AND TELEVISION (PACT)

Procter House, 1 Procter Street, Holborn, London, WC1V 6DW

Tel: 020 7067 4367
Fax: 020 7067 4377
Website: www.pact.co.uk

Enquiries to: Information Manager
Direct e-mail: anish@pact.co.uk

Founded: 1991

Organisation type and purpose: Trade association.
Represents United Kingdom independent production companies of feature films and broadcast television.

Subject coverage: Industrial relations within the independent broadcast, television and feature film production industry, copyright, commissioning, financing.

Publications: Printed

Publications list: Available in print

Access to staff: Contact by telephone. Access for members only.
Hours: Mon to Fri, 0930 to 1800

PRODUCTION MANAGERS ASSOCIATION

Ealing Studios, Ealing Green, Ealing, London, W5 5EP

Tel: 020 8758 8699
E-mail: pma@pma.org.uk
Website: www.pma.org.uk

Founded: 1991

Organisation type and purpose: A professional body of film, television, corporate and multi-media production managers. All 200 members have a minimum of 3 years' experience as a Production Manager and at least six broadcast credits (or equivalent).
Within the film and television industry the Association provides a unique network for both freelance and permanently employed Production Managers.

Subject coverage: Film and television producing.

Information services: Members can phone for free professional advice on tax, VAT, PAYE, payroll, employment and personnel, health and safety, commercial and legal issues.

Publications: Electronic and video
Order electronic and video publications from: Download from website

Access to staff: Contact by letter, by telephone and by e-mail

PROFESSIONAL ASSOCIATION OF NURSERY NURSES (VOICE)

Formal name: VOICE the Union

2 St James' Court, Friar Gate, Derby, DE1 1BT

Tel: 01332 372337
Fax: 01332 290310
E-mail: enquiries@voicetheunion.org.uk
Website: www.voicetheunion.org.uk

Enquiries to: Senior Professional Officer
Direct e-mail: richardfraser@voicetheunion.org.uk (Communications Officer)
Other contacts: Communications Officer

Founded: 1982; formerly called Professional Association of Nursery Nurses (year of change 2008)

Organisation type and purpose: Professional body, trade union (membership is by subscription), for qualified education professionals, including teachers, support staff, nursery nurses, nannies and other childcarers.

Subject coverage: Terms and conditions of employment within education and childcare, nannies at home and abroad, contracts, etc., the role of the nursery nurse.

Publications: Printed
Order printed publications from: e-mail: publications@voicetheunion.org.uk

Publications list: Available online and in print

Access to staff: Contact by letter, by telephone, by fax, by e-mail and via website. Appointment necessary. Access for members only.
Hours: Mon to Fri, 0900 to 1700

Access to building: Prior appointment required
Hours: Mon to Fri, 0900 to 1700

Access for disabled people: Parking provided, level entry

Headquarters address: Voice; at the same address; tel: 01332 372337; fax: 01332 290310; e-mail: hq@voicetheunion.org.uk; website: http://www.voicetheunion.org.uk

PROFESSIONAL CLASSES AID COUNCIL (PCAC)

10 St Christopher's Place, London, W1U 1HZ

Tel: 020 7935 0641

Enquiries to: Secretary
Other contacts: Deputy Secretary

Founded: 1921

Organisation type and purpose: National organisation, voluntary organisation, registered charity (charity number 207292).

Subject coverage: Sources of charitable help to those with a professional background.

Publications: Printed

Access to staff: Contact by letter and by telephone
Hours: Mon to Fri, 0930 to 1700

Access to building: No access other than to staff

Administers the: Guild of Aid for Gentlepeople; at the same address

PROFESSIONAL GOLFERS ASSOCIATION (PGA)

Centenary House, The Belfry, Sutton Coldfield, West Midlands, B76 9PT

Tel: 01675 470333
Fax: 01675 477888
E-mail: media@pga.org.uk

Enquiries to: Media Department

Founded: 1901

Organisation type and purpose: Membership association.

Subject coverage: The game of golf.

Publications: Printed

Access to staff: Contact by letter
Hours: Mon to Fri, 0900 to 1700

PROFESSIONAL PHOTOGRAPHIC LABORATORIES ASSOCIATION (PPLA)

Wisteria House, 28 Fulling Mill Lane, Welwyn, Hertfordshire AL6 9NS

Tel: 01438 840367
Fax: 01438 716572
E-mail: pmauk@pmai.org
Website: www.pmai.org

Enquiries to: Secretary
Other contacts: Administration Manager for office contact.

Founded: 1984

Organisation type and purpose: Trade association.
To promote and foster excellence in all areas of professional photographic laboratory work.

Subject coverage: Professional photographic processing (silver halide), digital imaging, inkjet and all normal fields of output.

Publications: Printed, and electronic and video

Access to staff: Contact by letter, by telephone, by fax, by e-mail, in person and via website
Hours: Mon to Fri, 0900 to 1700

A section of: Photo Marketing Association International

Connections with: British Photographic Association

PROFESSIONAL PUBLISHERS ASSOCIATION (PPA)

Queens House, 28 Kingsway, Holborn, London, WC2B 6JR

Tel: 020 7404 4166
Fax: 020 7404 4167
E-mail: barry.mcilheney@ppa.co.uk
Website: www.ppa.co.uk

Enquiries to: Communications Manager
Direct tel: 0207 400 7528
Direct fax: 0207 404 4167
Direct e-mail: info@ppa.co.uk

Founded: 1913; formerly called Society of Weekly Newspaper and Periodical Proprietors; formerly called Periodical Publishers Association (year of change 2011)

Organisation type and purpose: To promote and protect the interests of the UK magazine and business media industry.

Subject coverage: The PPA promotes and protects the interests of print and online publishers of consumer and business media in the UK. The PPA has around 200 publishing companies in its membership, which collectively produce more than 2,500 consumer and business magazines and journals as well as digital media, data products and events. For more information visit www.ppa.co.uk.

Publications: Printed, and electronic and video

Access to staff: Contact by letter, by telephone, by fax and via website

Also at: PPA Scotland; 22 Rhodes Park, Tantallon Road, North Berwick, EH39 5NA; tel: 01620 890800; e-mail: kathy.crawford@ppascotland.co.uk; website: http://www.ppa.co.uk/scotland

Links with: at the same address; AOP (Association of Online Publishers); APA (Association of Publishing Agencies)

Member organisation of: EMMA (European Magazine Media Association); FIPP (International Federation of the Periodical Press); the funding body for Advertising Standards Authority; the funding body for Press Complaints Commission

PROFESSIONAL SPEAKERS ASSOCIATION (PSA)

12 Russell Close, Uttoxeter, Staffordshire, ST14 8HZ

Tel: 0845 3700 504
Fax: 0845 3700 503
E-mail: admin@professionalspeaking.biz
Website: www.professionalspeakersassociation.co.uk

Enquiries to: Administration Manager

Founded: 1999

Organisation type and purpose: Professional association.
Represents 'experts who speak' who are based in the UK.

Subject coverage: Public speaking.

Publications: Printed

Access to staff: Contact by letter, by telephone, by fax and via website

Member organisation of: International Federation for Professional Speakers (IFFPS)

PROPERTY CONSULTANTS SOCIETY LIMITED (PCS)

Basement Office, Surrey Court, Surrey Street, Arundel, West Sussex, BN18 9DT

Tel: 01903 889590
Fax: 01903 883787
E-mail: info@propertyconsultantssociety.org
Website: www.propertyconsultantssociety.org

Enquiries to: Secretary
Direct e-mail: may-david@btconnect.com

Founded: 1954

Organisation type and purpose: Professional body (membership is by qualification, election or invitation), present number of members: 600, service industry.

Subject coverage: Property consultancy.

Publications: Printed

Access to staff: Contact by letter, by

continued overleaf

telephone, by fax, by e-mail and via website
Hours: Mon to Fri
Special comments: Part-time staff only.

PROPERTY OMBUDSMAN (TPO)

Beckett House, 4 Bridge Street, Salisbury, Wiltshire, SP1 2LX

Tel: 01722 333306
Fax: 01722 332296
E-mail: admin@tpos.co.uk
Website: www.tpos.co.uk

Enquiries to: Ombudsman (for initial enquiries)

Founded: 1998; formerly called Ombudsman for Estate Agents (year of change 2009)

Organisation type and purpose:
Membership association (membership is by subscription, qualification), present number of members: 583, service industry.

Subject coverage: Disputes between member agencies and actual or potential buyers or sellers, tenants or landlords of property in the UK.

Publications: Printed, and electronic and video

Access to staff: Contact by letter, by telephone, by fax, by e-mail and via website. All charged.
Hours: Mon to Fri, 0900 to 1645

PROPERTY PEOPLE PUBLICATIONS LIMITED

232 Great Guildford Business Square, 30 Great Guildford Street, London, SE1 0HS

Tel: 020 7401 2075
Fax: 020 7928 4887
E-mail: edit@ppmagazine.co.uk
Website: www.hera-group.co.uk

Enquiries to: Managing Director
Other contacts: Editor for editorial enquiries.

Founded: 1997

Organisation type and purpose: Publishing house.

Subject coverage: People working in housing, students on full-time housing courses.

Publications: Printed

Access to staff: Contact by letter, by telephone, by fax, by e-mail and via website
Hours: Mon to Fri, 0900 to 1700

PROQUEST INFORMATION AND LEARNING

The Quorum, Barnwell Road, Cambridge, CB5 8SW

Tel: 01223 215512
Fax: 01223 215513
E-mail: marketing@proquest.co.uk
Website: www.proquest.co.uk/

Enquiries to: Marketing Manager
Direct e-mail: chesterfield@proquest.co.uk

Founded: 1973

Organisation type and purpose: Publishing house.

Subject coverage: Bibliographies, library catalogues, reference works to archives, official publications, literature, literary history, newspapers on CD-ROM and the World Wide Web, performing arts, visual arts and architecture, history, economics and statistics, cartography and climate, natural sciences, medical, education, science and technology reference.

Publications: Electronic and video, and microform publications

Publications list: Available online and in print

Access to staff: Contact by e-mail
Hours: Mon to Fri, 0900 to 1700

PROSPECT

Prospect House, 75–79 York Road, London, SE1 7AQ

Tel: 020 7902 6600
Fax: 020 7902 6667
E-mail: enquiries@prospect.org.uk
Website: www.prospect.org.uk

Enquiries to: Assistant General Secretary
Other contacts: Deputy General Secretary

Founded: 1913

Organisation type and purpose: Trade union (membership is by subscription), present number of members: c. 100,000. Statutory body responsible to the Secretary of State for Industry.

Subject coverage: Pay and conditions, market testing, trade unions, public sector pay, privatisation, GCHQ trade union ban, research, health and safety, equal opportunities, air traffic control, PFI.

Publications: Printed, and electronic and video

Publications list: Available in print

Access to staff: Contact by letter, by telephone, by fax and by e-mail. Appointment necessary.
Hours: Mon to Fri, 0900 to 1700

Access for disabled people: Ramped entry, access to all public areas, toilet facilities
Special comments: Help with parking can be arranged prior to attendance.

Associated with: Council of Civil Service Unions (CCSU); IFATSEA; PSI; TUC

Office at: Prospect Midlands; Unit 4, Midland Court, Central Park, Leicester Road, Lutterworth, LE17 4PN; tel: 01455 555200; fax: 01455 558711; Prospect North West/North Wales; Unit 1F, Ground Floor, Columbus Quay, Riverside Drive, Liverpool, L3 4DB; tel: 0151 728 9028; fax: 0151 728 9072; Prospect Scotland; Suite 4, 1st Floor, Glenarchy House, 20 Union Street, Edinburgh, EH1 3LR; tel: 0131 558 2660; fax: 0131 558 5280; Prospect South East; Flaxman House, Logmore Lane, Chertsey, Surrey, KT16 9JS; tel: 01932 577007; fax: 01932 567707; Prospect South West / Wales; Newminster House, 27–29 Baldwin Street, Bristol, BS1 1LT; tel: 0117 929 4441; fax: 0117 927 6111

PROSTATE CANCER CHARITY (PCC)

1st Floor Cambridge House, 100 Cambridge House, Hammersmith, London W6 0LE

Tel: 020 8222 7622
Fax: 020 8222 7639
E-mail: olivia.burns@prostate-cancer.org.uk
Website: www.prostate-cancer.org.uk

Enquiries to: Communications Manager
Direct e-mail: carla.blatt@prostate-cancer.org.uk

Founded: 1996

Organisation type and purpose: National organisation, voluntary organisation, registered charity, research organisation. Support and information organisation. Research, support and information.

Subject coverage: Prostate cancer support and information; information on treatments and their side-effects; general support from counsellors and other sufferers; help for both patients and their families; research into prostate cancer and its treatment.

Publications: Printed

Publications list: Available in print

Access to staff: Contact by letter, by telephone, by fax, by e-mail, in person and via website
Hours: Mon to Fri, 0900 to 1700
Helpline: Mon to Fri, 1000 to 1600

PROSTATE HELP ASSOCIATION

PHA, Langworth, Lincoln, LN3 5DF

E-mail: philip@bph.org.uk
Website: www.prostatehelp.me.uk

Enquiries to: Secretary

Founded: 1993

Organisation type and purpose: Help and information for prostate problems.

Subject coverage: Prostatitis, BPH and prostatic cancer.

Publications list: Available in print

Access to staff: Contact by letter, by e-mail and via website

PRS FOR MUSIC

Copyright House, 29–33 Berners Street, London, W1T 3AB

Tel: 020 7580 5544
Fax: 020 7306 4455
E-mail: info@mcps.co.uk
Website: www.prsformusic.com

Enquiries to: Corporate Communications

Founded: 1997; created by the merger of Mechanical-Copyright Protection Society Limited (MCPS, founded 1924) and PRS; formerly called MCPS–PRS Alliance (year of change 2009)

Organisation type and purpose:
Membership association (membership is by subscription).
Licenses the recording of its composer and publisher members copyright musical works in many different formats.

Subject coverage: Music copyright and royalties; licensing of music recorded into any format; collection and distribution of mechanical royalties.

Publications: Printed

Access to staff: Contact by letter, by telephone, by fax, by e-mail and via website. Appointment necessary.
Hours: Mon to Fri, 0900 to 1700

Access for disabled people: Ramped entry

PSORIASIS ASSOCIATION

Dick Coles House, 2 Queensbridge, Northampton, NN4 7BF

Tel: 08456 760076
Fax: 01604 251621
E-mail: mail@psoriasis-association.org.uk
Website: www.psoriasis-association.org.uk
Website: www.psoteen.org.uk

Enquiries to: Chief Executive
Other contacts: Information and Communications Manager

Founded: 1968

Organisation type and purpose: Membership organisation providing information and support to people affected by psoriasis; aiming to support people who have psoriasis; to raise awareness of psoriasis; to fund research into causes, treatments and care of psoriasis.

Subject coverage: Psoriasis, psoriatic arthropathy and all aspects relating to them.

Publications: Printed, and electronic and video
Order printed publications from: Psoriasis Association, Dick Coles House, 2 Queensbridge, Northampton, NN4 7BF
Order electronic and video publications from: Psoriasis Association, Dick Coles House, 2 Queensbridge, Northampton, NN4 7BF

Publications list: Available in print

Access to staff: Contact by letter, by telephone, by fax and by e-mail. Appointment necessary.
Hours: Mon to Thurs, 0900 to 1700; Fri, 0900 to 1630

Links with: AMRC; APPGS; LTCA; Skin Care Campaign

PSYCHIATRIC REHABILITATION ASSOCIATION (PRA SERVICES)

Bayford Mews, Bayford Street, Hackney, London, E8 3SF

Tel: 020 8985 3570
Fax: 020 8986 1334
E-mail: admin@centreforbetterhealth.org.uk
Website: www.praservices.org.uk
Website: www.c4bh.org.uk

Enquiries to: Director
Other contacts: Association Secretary

Founded: 1959

Organisation type and purpose: Membership association (membership is by election or invitation), present number of members: 800, voluntary organisation, registered charity (charity number 227891), training organisation, consultancy.
PRA aims to stimulate the individual recovering from mental health problems towards greater initiative and social awareness. It prepares and encourages the individual to play an active part in the community.

Subject coverage: PRA is a partnership of patients, relatives, friends and professional workers, and has developed a wide range of community care facilities for people suffering from mental health problems, study of social problems associated with mental illness, geographical incidence of mental illness, lifestyle analysis, training of professional and voluntary workers, group work.

Information services: E-mail: info@praservices.org.uk

Non-library collection catalogue: All or part available online and in-house

Publications: Printed, and electronic and video, and microform publications

Access to staff: Contact by letter, by telephone, by fax, by e-mail and via website. Appointment necessary.
Hours: Mon to Fri, 0900 to 1700

Administers: Centre for Better Health (C4BH); Bayford Mews, Bayford Street, London, E8 3SF; tel: 020 8985 3570; fax: 020 8986 1334; e-mail: admin@praservices.org.uk; website: http://www.praservices.org.uk
Et Cetera Gallery (Hackney); 1A Darnley Road, London, E9 6QH; tel: 020 8985 7758; website: http://www.praservices.org.uk
Et Cetera Workshop (Haringey); Unit 26G3, N17 Studios, 785/788 High Road, London, N17 0DA; tel: 020 8808 5970; fax: 020 8808 5945; e-mail: etceteraworkshop@praservices.org.uk; website: http://www.praservices.org.uk
Hackney Day Centre; 1A Darnley Road, London, E9 6QH; tel: 020 8985 4617; e-mail: darnleyroad@praservices.org.uk; Mitchley Industrial Education Unit and Day Centre (Haringey); Unit 18G, N17 Studios, 784/788 High Road, London, N17 0DA; tel: 020 8808 2833; fax: 020 8880 9075; website: http://www.praservices.org.uk
Southwood Smith Centre (Islington); Southwood Smith Street, London, N1 0XN; tel: 020 7226 2244; e-mail: swsmithcentre@praservices.org.uk; website: http://www.praservices.org.uk
Stean Street Industrial Education Unit (Hackney); 13 Stean Street, London, N8 4ED; tel: 020 7254 9103; fax: 020 7254 2691; e-mail: pramembers@yahoo.co.uk; website: http://www.praservices.org.uk

Member organisations: Haringey User Network (HUN) (Haringey); Unit 26G3, N17 Studios, 784/788 High Road, London, N17 0DA; tel: 020 8885 1258; e-mail: info@haringeyusernetwork.org.uk; website: http://www.haringeyusernetwork.org.uk

PSYCHIATRY RESEARCH TRUST

Box 87, De Crespigny Park, Denmark Hill, London, SE5 8AF

Tel: 020 7703 6217
Fax: 020 7848 5115
E-mail: l.pease@iop.kcl.ac.uk
Website: www.iop.kcl.ac.uk

Enquiries to: Administrator

Founded: 1982

Organisation type and purpose: Registered charity (number 284286).
Founded with the sole aim of raising funds for research into mental illness and brain disease in support of the vital research work of the Institute of Psychiatry, King's College, University of London.

Subject coverage: Funds research projects covering a wide spectrum of mental health conditions and brain disease, lectures in aspects of mental health, bursaries to enable students to study and also to carry out research projects, prizes to encourage excellence in research by trainee psychiatrists and basic scientists, the purchase of essential research equipment.

Publications: Printed
Order printed publications from: Postal address

Access to staff: Contact by letter, by telephone, by fax and by e-mail

Constituent part of: The Institute of Psychiatry, King's College, University of London

PSYCHOTHERAPY CENTRE

67 Upper Berkeley Street, London, W1H 7QX

Tel: 020 7723 6173
E-mail: psychotherapy@the-wordsmith.co.uk
Website: www.the-psychotherapy-centre.org.uk

Enquiries to: Principal

Founded: 1960

Organisation type and purpose: International organisation, consultancy, research organisation, publishing house. Treatment and referral centre. Training college.

Subject coverage: Psychotherapy, emotional problems, neuroses, compulsions, addictions, relationship problems, psycho-sexual and marital difficulties, phobias, anxiety, alcoholism, insomnia, migraine, parenthood etc.

Publications: Printed

Publications list: Available in print

Access to staff: Contact by letter and by telephone. Appointment necessary.
Hours: Mon to Fri, 0900 to 1700

Access to building: Prior appointment required

PUBLIC AND COMMERCIAL SERVICES UNION (PCS)

160 Falcon Road, London, SW11 2LN

Tel: 020 7924 2727
Fax: 020 7924 1847
Website: www.pcs.org.uk

Enquiries to: Information Officer
Direct tel: 020 7801 2650
Direct e-mail: info@pcs.org.uk
Other contacts: General Secretary

Founded: 1998

Organisation type and purpose: Trade union.
Trade Union with its own library.

continued overleaf

Subject coverage: Employment law, health and safety, industrial relations, civil service, childcare/work life balance, Civil Service, conditions of service, economic issues, employment issues, equal opportunities, Europe, government, health and safety, international affairs (ie non-Europe), legislation, maternity/paternity, organisations, parliament, partnership, pay, PCS, pensions, professional management, politics, privatisation – primarily civil service, private sector, public sector, social welfare, trade unions, unemployment.

Library catalogue: All or part available in-house

Publications: Printed

Access to staff: Contact by letter, by telephone, by fax and by e-mail. Access for members only.
Hours: Mon to Fri, 0830 to 1700

Affiliated to: Council of Civil Service Unions; International Confederation of Free Trade Unions; Public Services International

Member of: Trades Union Congress; Congress House, Great Russell Street, London, WC1B 3LS

PUBLIC HEALTH LABORATORY SERVICE – COMMUNICABLE DISEASE SURVEILLANCE CENTRE (CDSC)

61 Colindale Avenue, London, NW9 5EQ

Tel: 020 8200 6868
Fax: 020 8200 7868
E-mail: ross.mcewan@hpa.org.uk
Website: www.phls.co.uk

Enquiries to: Information Officer
Direct tel: 020 8200 6868 ext 4473
Direct e-mail: eyusuf@phls.org.uk

Organisation type and purpose:
Professional body.
Unit of the Public Health Laboratory Service. Prevention and control of human communicable disease through surveillance, epidemiological investigation, research, teaching and training.

Subject coverage: Human infectious diseases: prevalence in England and Wales, and abroad when it is relevant to England and Wales; control and surveillance of such disease.

Publications: Printed

Access to staff: Contact by letter
Hours: Mon to Fri, 0900 to 1700

Part of: National Health Service

PUBLIC MONUMENTS AND SCULPTURE ASSOCIATION (PMSA)

70 Cowcross Street, London, EC1M 6EJ

Tel: 020 7490 5001
E-mail: pmsa@btconnect.com
Website: www.pmsa.org.uk

Enquiries to: Office Administrator

Founded: 1991

Organisation type and purpose:
Membership association (membership is by subscription), present number of members: 250, voluntary organisation, registered charity, suitable for ages: 18+, consultancy, research organisation.
The promotion, protection and public appreciation of historic and contemporary public sculpture and monuments.
Preserving Britain's sculptures and public art for future generations. Save Our Sculpture project monitors works at risk. Campaigns for improved conservation and maintenance. The Association's National Recording Project, a survey of public works in Britain, is partially complete: it is a central information resource for scholars, conservators and custodians.

Subject coverage: Art history (sculpture); sculpture conservation; topographical spread of public works in Britain, their description, history and condition; British sculptors; the local and social significance of public monuments; owners and custodians of same; the groups involved with public art or similar, either voluntary or commercial (i.e. commissioning agencies); regional arts bodies; amenity societies, e.g. Fountain Society/Twentieth Century Society; listing and planning regulations.

Information services: Via e-mail

Non-library collection catalogue: All or part available online and in print

Publications: Printed, and electronic and video
Order printed publications from: Liverpool University Press

Publications list: Available online and in print

Access to staff: Contact by letter, by telephone, by e-mail and via website

PUBLIC RECORD OFFICE OF NORTHERN IRELAND (PRONI)

Use website: http://www.proni.gov.uk

Tel: 02890534800
E-mail: proni@dcalni.gov.uk
Website: www.proni.gov.uk
Website: www.proni.gov.uk/index/research_and_records_held.htm
Website: www.proni.gov.uk /index/search_the_archives/ecatalogue.htm

Enquiries to: Head of Public Services
Direct e-mail: proni@dcalni.gov.uk

Founded: 1923

Organisation type and purpose: National government body.
Record office.
To identify, preserve and provide access to Northern Ireland's archival heritage.

Subject coverage: Information relating to the political, economic and social history of Northern Ireland as found in both official and private records. Genealogy; local history; government records; non-departmental public bodies records; academic research.

Collection: Archives of the Northern Ireland Departments of government, public bodies and courts of law
Papers of private individuals, estate, school, and business records, wills, and church records

Non-library collection catalogue: All or part available online and in-house

Library catalogue: All or part available online

Publications: Printed

Publications list: Available online and in print

Access to staff: Contact by letter, by telephone, by fax, by e-mail, in person and via website
Hours: Mon, Tue, Wed, Fri, 0900 to 1645; Thu, 1000 to 2045

Access for disabled people: Parking provided, ramped entry, access to all areas; Induction loop for hearing impaired; mono mouse/computer for enlarging text
Special comments: Staff assistance, if required. Please ask in advance if possible.

Parent body: Department of Culture, Arts and Leisure

PUBLIC RELATIONS CONSULTANTS ASSOCIATION LIMITED (PRCA)

Willow House, Willow Place, London, SW1P 1JH

Tel: 020 7233 6026
Fax: 020 7828 4797
E-mail: katie.goodrum@prca.org.uk
Website: www.prca.org.uk

Enquiries to: Office Manager

Founded: 1969

Organisation type and purpose: Trade association (membership is by qualification), present number of members: 150.

Subject coverage: Public relations industry, statistics, membership.

Collection: Archive library

Trade and statistical information: Case histories
Benchmarking study in PR consultancy industry

Publications: Printed
Order printed publications from: Public Relations Consultants Association Limited e-mail: info@prca.org.uk

Publications list: Available online and in print

Access to staff: Contact by letter, by telephone, by fax, by e-mail, in person and via website. Appointment necessary.
Hours: Mon to Fri, 0900 to 1800

Access to building: No prior appointment required

PUBLISHERS ASSOCIATION (PA)

29b Montague Street, London, WC1B 5BW

Tel: 020 7691 9191
Fax: 020 7691 9199
E-mail: mail@publishers.org.uk
Website: www.publishers.org.uk

Direct tel: 020 7691 9191
Direct e-mail: mail@publishers.org.uk

Founded: 1896

Organisation type and purpose: Trade association (membership is by subscription).

Organised into core activity and divisions: International Division, Educational Publishers Council, Academic and Professional Division, Electronic Publishers Forum.
Subject coverage: Matters relating to publishing; not contracts with authors or the placing of manuscripts.

Collection: Books about publishing; list available

Trade and statistical information: Statistical information on publishing

Publications: Printed, and electronic and video

Publications list: Available online and in print
Access to staff: Contact by letter, by telephone, by fax, by e-mail and via website. Access for members only. Non-members charged.
Hours: Mon to Fri, 0930 to 1730

Access to building: Prior appointment required

Affiliated to: Federation of European Publishers; International Publishers Association

PUBLISHERS LICENSING SOCIETY LIMITED (PLS)

5 Dryden Street, London, WC2E 9NB

Tel: 020 7829 8486
Fax: 020 7829 8488
E-mail: pls@pls.org.uk

Enquiries to: Manager

Founded: 1981

Organisation type and purpose: Trade association, present number of members: 1600.

Subject coverage: Photocopying and digital licensing. Copyright information relevant to the publishing industry.

Publications: Printed

Publications list: Available in print

Access to staff: Contact by letter, by telephone, by fax, by e-mail and via website
Hours: Mon to Fri, 0900 to 1700

Links with: Association of Learned and Professional Society Publishers (ALPSP); South House, The Street, Clapham, Worthing, Sussex, BN13 3UU; tel: 01903 871686; fax: 01903 871457; e-mail: sec-gen@alsp.org; Copyright Licensing Agency; 90 Tottenham Court Road, London, W1T 0LP; tel: 020 7631 5500; fax: 020 7631 5555; e-mail: cla@cla.co.uk; Periodical Publishers Association (PPA); Queens House, 28 Kingsway, London, WC2B 6JR; tel: 020 7404 4166; fax: 020 7404 4167; e-mail: info1@ppa.co.uk; Publishers Association (PA); 29B Montague Street, London, WC1B 5BH; tel: 020 7691 9191; fax: 020 7691 9199; e-mail: mail@publishers.org.uk

PUBLISHING SCOTLAND (PS)

Scott House, 10 South St Andrew Street, Edinburgh EH2 2AZ

Tel: 0131 228 6866
Fax: 0131 524 8157
E-mail: enquiries@publishingscotland.org
Website: www.publishingscotland.org
Website: www.booksfromscotland.com

Enquiries to: Training and Information Manager
Direct e-mail: joan@publishingscotland.org

Founded: 1974; formerly called Scottish Publishers Association (year of change 2007)

Organisation type and purpose: Network and development body, incorporating trade association (membership is by subscription).

Subject coverage: Publishing, book fairs, training, publicity and marketing, information provision.

Access to staff: Contact by letter, by telephone, by fax, by e-mail and via website. Appointment necessary.
Hours: Mon to Fri, 0900 to 1700

Access to building: Prior appointment required
Hours: Mon to Fri, 0900 to 1700

Access for disabled people: Ramped entry and lift

Constituent bodies: Booksource; 50 Cambuslang Road, Cambuslang Investment Park, Glasgow, G32 8NB; tel: 0845 370 0063; fax: 0845 370 0064; e-mail: info@booksource.net; website: http://www.booksource.net

PUPPET CENTRE TRUST (PCT)

Battersea Arts Centre, Lavender Hill, London, SW11 5TN

Tel: 020 7228 5335
E-mail: pct@puppetcentre.org.uk
Website: www.puppetcentre.org.uk

Enquiries to: Administrator

Founded: 1974

Organisation type and purpose: A national development agency for the art form of puppetry.

Subject coverage: The overall mission for the Puppet Centre Trust is to develop and promote the art form of puppetry within the context of contemporary performance practice.

Collection: Puppetry Archives and Historical Puppet Collection now housed in Bridgenorth
Puppet Centre Library housed at Central School of Speech and Drama
Both available by appointment

Publications: Printed
Order printed publications from: Administrator

Access to staff: Contact by letter, by telephone and by e-mail. Appointment necessary.

PURBECK DISTRICT COUNCIL (PDC)

Westport House, Worgret Road, Wareham, Dorset, BH20 4PP

Tel: 01929 556561
Fax: 01929 552688
E-mail: performanceunit@purbeck-dc.gov.uk
Website: www.dorsetforyou.com/

Organisation type and purpose: Local government body.

Subject coverage: Services and functions of the district council.

Access to staff: Contact by letter, by telephone, by fax, by e-mail, in person and via website
Hours: Offices: 0845 to 1645; telephone access: 0830 to 1700

PUSEY HOUSE LIBRARY

Formal name: Dr Pusey's Library

Pusey House, 61 St Giles, Oxford, OX1 3LZ

Tel: 01865 278415
E-mail: chapter@puseyhouse.org.uk
Website: http:www.puseyhouse.org.uk

Enquiries to: Custodian
Direct tel: 01865 288024
Other contacts: The Archivist for all enquiries relating to archive holdings

Founded: 1884

Organisation type and purpose: Theological resource centre and chaplaincy.

Subject coverage: Patristics, liturgy, church history (especially Oxford Movement).

Collection: 19th-century pamphlets

Non-library collection catalogue: All or part available in-house

Library catalogue: All or part available in-house

Publications: Microform publications

Access to staff: Contact by letter, by telephone, by e-mail, in person and via website. Appointment necessary. Access for members only. Letter of introduction required. All charged.
Hours: Term time: Mon to Fri, 0900 to 1230 and 1400 to 1630; Sat, by appointment only
Vacation opening: by appointment only

QUALITY ASSURANCE AGENCY FOR HIGHER EDUCATION (QAA)

Southgate House, Southgate Street, Gloucester, GL1 1UB

Tel: 01452 557000
Fax: 01452 557070
E-mail: comms@qaa.ac.uk
Website: www.qaa.ac.uk

Founded: 1997; formerly called Higher Education Quality Council (year of change 1997)

Organisation type and purpose: An independent public body, a company limited by guarantee, a registered charity (charity numbers 1062746 and SC037786), governed by a Board, which has overall responsibility for the conduct and strategic direction of its business.
Principal role is to safeguard and help to improve the academic standards and quality of higher education.

Subject coverage: QAA works with universities and colleges to define standards for higher education, through a framework known as the Academic Infrastructure, which includes the qualifications frameworks for the UK. QAA also carries out reviews of higher education institutions

continued overleaf

against these standards and publishes their outcomes. It advises governments on applications for the grant of degree-awarding powers, university title, or designation as a higher education institution.

Publications: Printed
Order printed publications from: Linney Direct, Adams Way, Mansfield, Nottinghamshire, NG18 4FN; tel: 01623 450788; fax: 01623 450481; e-mail: qaa@linneydirect.com

Publications list: Available online and in print

Access to staff: Contact by letter, by telephone, by fax, by e-mail and via website. Appointment necessary.
Hours: Mon to Fri, 0900 to 1700

Funded by: subscriptions from universities and colleges of higher education, and through contracts with the main higher education funding bodies

QUALITY BRITISH CELERY ASSOCIATION (QBCA)

133 Eastgate, Louth, Lincolnshire, LN11 9QG

Tel: 01507 602427
Fax: 01507 607165
E-mail: crop.association@pvga.co.uk

Enquiries to: Membership Secretary

Founded: 1980s

Organisation type and purpose: National organisation, trade association.

Subject coverage: Celery production.

Access to staff: Contact by letter, by telephone, by fax and by e-mail
Hours: 0900 to 1700

QUALITY GUILD

Westwinds, Lambley Bank, Scotby, Carlisle, Cumbria, CA4 8BX

Tel: 01228 631681
E-mail: info@qgbiz.co.uk
Website: www.qualityguild.co.uk

QUALITY IMPROVEMENT AGENCY FOR LIFELONG LEARNING (QIA)

Friars House, Manor House Drive, Coventry, CV1 2TE

Tel: 0870 162 0632
Fax: 0870 162 0633
Website: www.qia.org.uk/
Website: www.lsrc.org.uk

Enquiries to: Communications Officer
Direct tel: 0870 211 3434
Direct e-mail: gillian.dyer@qia.org.uk

Founded: 2006; formerly a part of the Learning and Skills Development Agency

Organisation type and purpose: Research organisation.
Quango.

Subject coverage: Further education, research, teaching and learning.

Collection: Library catalogue

Non-library collection catalogue: All or part available in-house

Library catalogue: All or part available in-house

Publications: Printed, and electronic and video
Order printed publications from: Learning and Skills Development Agency
Citadel Place, Tinworth Street, London, SE11 5EF, tel: 020 7840 5400, fax: 020 7840 5401, e-mail: p.fielding@lsda.org.uk

Publications list: Available in print

QUARRY PRODUCTS ASSOCIATION (QPA)

156 Buckingham Palace Road, London, SW1W 9TR

Tel: 020 7730 8194
Fax: 020 7730 4355
E-mail: info@qpa.org
Website: www.qpa.org

Enquiries to: Press and Information Officer
Direct e-mail: clements@qpa.org

Founded: 1997

Organisation type and purpose: Trade association.

Subject coverage: Construction aggregates, (ie crushed rock, sand, gravel and slag), asphalt and coated macadam for roads and other surfacing uses, (but not asphalts used in roofing, building and waterproofing), lime for building and industrial uses, agricultural lime (information from ALPC). Ready mixed concrete technology, production, origins, use, specifications and testing, quality assurance.
Sand and gravel industry, planning, technical, environmental, waste management.

Collection: Overseas periodicals on bitumen, asphalt, concrete and quarrying from 1930s

Trade and statistical information: Data on UK and European production of ready mix concrete

Publications: Printed

Access to staff: Contact by letter, by telephone, by fax and by e-mail
Hours: Mon to Fri, 0900 to 1700

Access to building: No access other than to staff

Affiliated to: European Aggregates Association (UEPG); European Asphalt Pavement Association; European Ready Mixed Concrete Association

QUEEN ELIZABETH'S FOUNDATION FOR DISABLED PEOPLE (QEF)

Leatherhead Court, Woodlands Road, Leatherhead, Surrey, KT22 0BN

Tel: 01372 841100
Fax: 01372 844072
E-mail: info@qef.org.uk
Website: www.qef.org.uk

Enquiries to: Chief Executive

Founded: 1934

Organisation type and purpose: Registered charity (charity number 251051).
To provide services for disabled people.

Subject coverage: Brain injury rehabilitation at Banstead; mobility information advice and assessment at Carshalton; residential vocational training at Leatherhead; development of independent living skills at Leatherhead.

Non-library collection catalogue: All or part available online and in print

Publications: Printed

Access to staff: Contact by letter, by telephone and by fax. Appointment necessary.
Hours: Mon to Fri, 0900 to 1700

Also at: Banstead, Carshalton, Leatherhead

QUEEN MARGARET UNIVERSITY (QMU)

Formal name: Queen Margaret University, Edinburgh

Queen Margaret University Drive, Musselburgh, East Lothian, EH21 6UU

Tel: 0131 474 0000
Fax: 0131 474 0001
E-mail: lrchelp@qmu.ac.uk
Website: www.qmu.ac.uk/lb

Founded: 1875; formerly called Queen Margaret University College (year of change 2007)

Organisation type and purpose: University library.

Subject coverage: Arts therapies; business and management; dietetics and nutrition; events management; nursing; physiotherapy; occupational therapy; radiography; speech therapy; communication studies; podiatry; retailing; drama; hospitality studies; tourism.

Information services: Access to books, journals and archive for all users. Network resources subject to user status.

Special visitor services: Member of Sconul Access; member of ELISA scheme.

Education services: Information literacy sessions and workshops; sessions for local schools; regular book swap and reading groups

Services for disabled people: Assistive technology room available.

Collection: University archive, especially relating to domestic science

Non-library collection catalogue: All or part available in-house

Library catalogue: All or part available online

Access to staff: Contact by letter, by telephone, by fax, by e-mail, in person and via website. Appointment necessary.
Hours: Term time: Mon to Fri, 0900 to 2100; Sat and Sun, 0900 to 1700
Vacation: Mon to Fri, 0900 to 1700

Access to building: Via main reception
Hours: The LRC is open 24/7; however non-University members cannot enter after 2100
Special comments: Visitor card mandatory.

Access for disabled people: Access to all public areas
Hours: The LRC is open 24/7; however non-University members cannot enter after 2100
Special comments: Visitor card mandatory.

QUEEN MARY, UNIVERSITY OF LONDON (QMW)

Mile End Road, London, E1 4NS

Tel: 020 7882 3027
Fax: 020 7882 7525
E-mail: j.e.clarke@qmul.ac.uk
Website: www.qmul.ac.uk

Enquiries to: Public Relations Manager
Direct tel: 020 7882 5314
Direct fax: 020 7882 5556
Direct e-mail: n.relph@qmul.ac.uk

Founded: 1887

Organisation type and purpose:
International organisation, university department or institute.
Constituent college of the University of London.
University college providing higher education and offering research opportunities in medicine, science, engineering, arts and law.

Subject coverage: Medicine, dentistry; science – physics, chemistry, biochemistry, mathematics, astronomy, computer; engineering – electronic, mechanical, civil, materials, aeronautical; arts – English, German, French, Russian, Hispanic studies, history; law; social sciences – economics, geography, politics.

Non-library collection catalogue: All or part available online

Access to staff: Contact by letter, by telephone, by fax, by e-mail and via website
Hours: Mon to Fri, 0900 to 1700

QUEEN MARY, UNIVERSITY OF LONDON – MAIN LIBRARY (QMUL)

Mile End Road, London, E1 4NS

Tel: 020 7882 3300
Fax: 020 8981 0028
E-mail: library-enquiries@qmul.ac.uk
Website: www.mds.qmw.ac.uk/
Website: www.qmw.ac.uk

Enquiries to: Director of Academic Information Services
Other contacts: Reference Librarian for telephone enquiries.

Organisation type and purpose: University library, research organisation.
European Documentation Centre.

Subject coverage: Arts: language and literature – English, Classical, French, German, Italian, Romanian, Russian, Spanish; history, history of art, drama and theatre; engineering: electrical, electronic, aeronautical, civil, mechanical, geomaterials, materials; informatics and mathematical sciences: computer science, mathematical sciences, information technology, astronomy; physical, biological and basic medical sciences: aquatic biology, microbiology, genetics, ecology, botany, zoology, biochemistry, plant physiology, animal physiology, environmental biology, molecular biology, chemistry (organic, inorganic, physical, structural), physics (astrophysics, mathematical, nuclear, polymer, theoretical, experimental); laws: English law, international law, comparative law, credit and commercial law, legal theory, socio-legal studies, intellectual property law, banking law, international arbitration, international business taxation; social studies: economics, applied econometrics, geography, social analysis, health care, information and planning, political studies, public policy, statistics, operational research, business studies, East London studies.

Collection: Alumni Collections (St Bartholomew's Hospital, Smithfield)
Alumni Collections (The Royal London Hospital, Whitechapel)
Archives of Westfield College
Camps and Cameron Collection on legal and forensic medicine (written application essential for access)
Constance Maynard Archive
Lyttleton Family Letters and Papers
Manuscripts on the History of Art
People's Palace Archive
Rare book collection (17th- and 18th-century English and European literature)

Access to staff: Contact by letter, by telephone, by fax, by e-mail and via website
Hours: Access other than to University members normally restricted to term time: Mon to Fri, 1700 to 2100; Sat, 1000 to 1600
Vacations: Mon to Fri, 0900 to 1700

A college of the: University of London

Medical Library: Queen Mary, University of London; Royal London Hospital Medical College, Whitechapel, London, E1 2AD; tel: 020 7882 7112; Queen Mary, University of London; Charterhouse Square, London, EC1M 6BG; tel: 020 7882 6019; Queen Mary, University of London; Medical College of St Bartholomew's Hospital, West Smithfield, London, EC1A 7BE; tel: 020 7601 7853

QUEEN MARY, UNIVERSITY OF LONDON – SCHOOL OF ELECTRONIC ENGINEERING AND COMPUTER SCIENCE

Mile End Road, London, E1 4NS

Tel: 020 7882 5217
Fax: 020 7882 7064
E-mail: sue.white@eecs.qmul.ac.uk
Website: www.eecs.qmul.ac.uk

Enquiries to: Research Co-ordinator

History of institution: formerly called Queen Mary, University of London – Department of Computer Science (year of change 2008)

Organisation type and purpose: University department or institute.

Subject coverage: Computer science, electronic engineering.

Publications list: Available online

Access to building: Prior appointment required

QUEEN VICTORIA HOSPITAL NHS FOUNDATION TRUST (QVH)

Library, Holtye Road, East Grinstead, West Sussex, RH19 3DZ

Tel: 01342 414266
Fax: 01342 414005
E-mail: library@qvh.nhs.uk
Website: ksslks.co.uk/sussex/kqv.asp

Enquiries to: Library Services Manager
Other contacts: Library Supervisor

Organisation type and purpose: Staff library.

Subject coverage: Burns, plastic and reconstructive surgery, hand surgery, oral and maxillofacial surgery, ophthalmic and corneoplastic surgery and nursing.

Library catalogue: All or part available online

Access to staff: Contact by letter, by telephone, by fax and by e-mail.
Appointment necessary.
Hours: Mon to Fri, 0930 to 1230

Access to building: Prior appointment required; no access to physical library
Hours: Daily, 24-hour access only for registered members
Special comments: Library is behind several security doors.

Access for disabled people: No access to physical library for disabled people; however, library staff will provide information on request
Special comments: Library is on second floor with no lift.

Constituent part of: Kent, Surrey and Sussex Library and Knowledge Services Health Libraries Network; Calverley House, Tunbridge Wells, Kent, TN1 2TU; tel: 01892 704240; website: http://www.ksslibraries.nhs.uk

QUEEN'S COLLEGE LIBRARY

Oxford, OX1 4AW

Tel: 01865 279130
Fax: 01865 790819
E-mail: library@queens.ox.ac.uk
Website: www.queens.ox.ac.uk

Enquiries to: Librarian
Direct tel: 01865 279213
Direct e-mail: amanda.saville@queens.ox.ac.uk

Founded: 1341

Organisation type and purpose: College library.

Subject coverage: Subject coverage which is likely to be of interest to others lies in those traditional areas, such as theology, philosophy etc., where the library has substantial holdings of older works; theology; philosophy; classics; history, ancient and modern; geography (mainly topography); politics; law; economics; English, French, German, Spanish and Russian languages and literature.

Collection: Incunabula (280 items)
Manuscripts (560 items, 10th to 20th centuries)
Oakes Collection (American history)
Peet Memorial Library (Egyptology)
c. 70,000 books printed before 1800

Non-library collection catalogue: All or part available online and in print

Library catalogue: All or part available online and in-house

continued overleaf

Access to staff: Contact by letter, by telephone, by fax, by e-mail and via website. Appointment necessary.
Hours: Mon to Fri, 0900 to 1700

Access to building: Prior appointment required for non members of the College

Access for disabled people: To ground floor only
Hours: During staffed hours

Constituent part of: The University of Oxford

QUEEN'S NURSING INSTITUTE (QNI)

3 Albemarle Way, Clerkenwell, London, EC1V 4RQ

Tel: 020 7549 1400
Fax: 020 7490 1269
E-mail: mail@qni.org.uk
Website: www.qni.org.uk

Enquiries to: Director

Founded: 1887; formerly called Queen's Institute of District Nursing (year of change 1973)

Organisation type and purpose: National organisation, professional body, registered charity (charity number 213128).

Subject coverage: Community nursing from its foundation in 1887 to the present day.

Collection: Archival material in connection with district (community) nursing

Publications: Printed, and electronic and video, and microform publications

Publications list: Available online and in print

Access to staff: Contact by letter, by telephone, by fax, by e-mail and via website. Appointment necessary.
Hours: Mon to Fri, 0900 to 1730

QUEEN'S UNIVERSITY BELFAST (QUB)

McClay Library, 10 College Park, Belfast BT7 1LP

Tel: 028 9097 6135
E-mail: library@qub.ac.uk
Website: www.qub.ac.uk/lib

Enquiries to: Library Manager
Direct tel: 028 9097 6144

Organisation type and purpose: University library.
The McClay Library covers arts, social sciences, science & engineering; there is also a Medical and Biomedical Library.

Collection: Special Collections of early printed and manuscript materials

Library catalogue: All or part available online

Publications: Printed

Access to staff: Contact by letter, by telephone, by e-mail, in person and via website. Non-members charged.
Hours: See website for details

QUEEN'S UNIVERSITY BELFAST – MCCLAY LIBRARY

Information Services, The McClay Library, 10 College Park, Belfast, BT7 1LP

Tel: 028 9097 6344 (Information Desk)
E-mail: library@qub.ac.uk
Website: www.qub.ac.uk/directorates/InformationServices/TheLibrary

Organisation type and purpose: University library, with computing and media services.

Library catalogue: All or part available online

R J TALBOTT

Springfields, 10 Sandy Lane, Scalford, Leicestershire, LE14 4DS

Tel: 01664 444668
Fax: 01664 444420
E-mail: rjtalbott@rjtalbott.plus.com

Enquiries to: Director

Founded: 1986

Organisation type and purpose: Consultancy.
Specialising in videofilm evidence for courts showing disability related to compensation.

Subject coverage: Medical videofilm maker.

Publications: Printed

Access to staff: Contact by letter and by fax. Appointment necessary.
Hours: Mon to Fri, 0900 to 1700 (but clients are usually visited)

Access to building: No access other than to staff

Access for disabled people: Parking provided

Associated with: International Paraplegic Claims Service

RAC LIVE – 1740 LIVE TRAFFIC AND WEATHER INFORMATION

RAC Motoring Services, Great Park Road, Bradley Stoke, Bristol, BS32 4QN

Tel: 1740 from any mobile (calls cost up to 59p per minute) also on 0906 470 1740 land-line (calls charged at 60p per minute)
Website: www.rac.co.uk/travelservices/traffic by phone
Website: www.rac.co.uk

Organisation type and purpose: Membership association (membership is by subscription).
RAC Live is the brand name operated by RAC Trafficmaster Telematics Limited.

Subject coverage: Live traffic information on your mobile available 24 hours a day: up-to-the-minute traffic information on over 8,000 miles of motorways and major A roads, latest national and local weather forecasts.
After listening to traffic information, talk to an RAC advisor to find an alternative route, plan routes across UK and Europe, provide general UK and European driving information and traffic regulations.

Access to staff: Contact by telephone
Hours: Mon to Fri, 0700 to 2000; Sat, 0900 to 1700; Sun 0900 to 1700

RAC LIVE – RAC ROUTE MINDER

RAC Motoring Services, Great Park Road, Bradley Stoke, Bristol, BS32 4QN

Tel: 0800 096 1740
Website: www.rac.co.uk/travelservices/route_minder/

Organisation type and purpose: Membership association (membership is by subscription).
RAC Live is the brand name operated by RAC Trafficmaster Telematics Limited.

Subject coverage: Web-based personalised and proactive traffic information service: delivers relevant traffic information alerts via email and text messages, provides unlimited access to colour map that displays live traffic information.

Access to staff: Contact by telephone
Hours: Mon to Fri, 0800 to 2000; Sat, 0900 to 1700; Sun, 0900 to 1900

RAC TRAVEL INFORMATION

RAC Live, RAC Motoring Services, Great Park Road, Bradley Stoke, Bristol, BS32 4QN

Tel: 0906 470 1740 (calls charged at 60p per minute)
Website: www.racbusiness.co.uk
Website: www.bsm.co.uk
Website: www.rac.co.uk

Enquiries to: RAC Travel Information Department

Organisation type and purpose: Membership association (membership is by subscription).

Subject coverage: Dynamic traffic updates on the UK motorway and trunk road network: UK and European route information (a charge is made for posted or faxed routes); various UK and European travel-related enquiries.

Access to staff: Contact by telephone
Hours: Advisors available: Mon to Fri, 0700 to 2000; Sat, 0900 to 1700; Sun, 0900 to 2100
Recorded UK road traffic information is 24 hours

RACE WALKING ASSOCIATION (RWA)

Hufflers, Heard's Lane, Shenfield, Brentwood, Essex, CM15 0SF

Tel: 01277 220687
Fax: 01277 212380
E-mail: racewalkingassociation@btinternet.com
Website: www.racewalkingassociation.btinternet.co.uk

Enquiries to: Honorary General Secretary

Founded: 1907; formerly called Southern Counties Road Walking Association (year of change 1910); formerly called Road Walking Association (year of change 1954)

Organisation type and purpose: Voluntary organisation, governing body of race walking.
The development, promotion and control of race walking in England, the Isle of Man and the Channel Islands.

Subject coverage: Policy; organisation and rules; clubs and athletes; coaches, officials and judging, events; history; relations with other sporting organisations.

Information services: Monthly magazine, archive material, general advice.

Collection: List of clubs and officials
Lists of events
Historical material
Minutes

Non-library collection catalogue: All or part available online

Publications: Printed, and electronic and video
Order printed publications from: Honorary General Secretary
Order electronic and video publications from: Honorary General Secretary

Access to staff: Contact by letter, by telephone, by fax, by e-mail and via website
Hours: Mon to Fri, 0800 to 2000

Access to building: No access.

Access for disabled people: No access.

Branches: Midlands Area RWA; 49, Debdale Avenue, Lyppard Woodgreen, Worcester, WR4 0RP; tel: 01905 616718; e-mail: perry.sevenacres@worcester.gov.uk; Northern Area RWA; 14, Watery Lane, Dunholme, Lincoln, LN2 3QW; tel: 01673 861208; e-mail: rjackson43@hotmail.co.uk; Southern Area RWA; Glenthorne, 65, Liverpool Road, Walmer, Deal, CT14 7NN; tel: 01304 368324; e-mail: bettychrisf@hotmail.com

RADCLIFFE SCIENCE LIBRARY

Parks Road, Oxford, OX1 3QP

Tel: 01865 272800
Fax: 01865 272821
E-mail: rsl.enquiries@bodleian.ox.ac.uk
Website: www.bodleian.ox.ac.uk
Website: www.bodleian.ox.ac.uk/science

Enquiries to: Keeper of Scientific Books
Direct tel: 01865 272820
Direct fax: 01865 272832
Direct e-mail: rsl.enquries@bodleian.ox.ac.uk
Other contacts: (1) Subject consultants (2) Administrator (for bibliographical enquiries or admin.)

Founded: 1749

Organisation type and purpose: University library, legal deposit library, the main science lending and reference library of University of Oxford, part of Bodleian Libraries Services.

Subject coverage: All pure sciences, mathematics, engineering and medicine.

Collection: Acland (medical pamphlets and offprints)
Child (pamphlets and offprints on coconuts)
Hardy (mathematical pamphlets and offprints)
Le Gros Clark (anatomical pamphlets and offprints)
Seckerson (pamphlets, offprints and portraits related to eponymous syndromes and diseases)
Tylor (anthropological pamphlets and offprints)
Van Heyningen (pamphlets and offprints in pathology)

Library catalogue: All or part available online

Access to staff: Contact by letter, by telephone, by e-mail, in person and via website
Hours: Term time: 0830 to 2150
Vacation: 0830 to 1850

Access for disabled people: Level entry, toilet facilities, accessible lift, disabled parking bay by appointment

RADIO MANX LIMITED

PO Box 1368, Broadcasting House, Douglas Head, Douglas, Isle of Man, IM99 1SW, Isle of Man

Tel: 01624 682600
Fax: 01624 682604
Website: www.radiott.com
Website: www.manxradio.com

Enquiries to: Managing Director
Direct e-mail: stewartwatterson@manxradio.com
Other contacts: (1) News Editor (2) Sales Director for (1) news releases (2) advertising services.

Founded: 1964

Organisation type and purpose: Service industry, publishing house.
News and current affairs source – Isle of Man.
Public service broadcaster. Provision of radio advertising services.

Subject coverage: News and current affairs; information and views – Isle of Man.
Isle of Man advertising market.

Trade and statistical information: Average listenership base – 80% adult population of Isle of Man. In consequence, very effective, and wide-ranging across all demographics, advertising service

Publications: Printed

Access to staff: Contact by letter, by fax, by e-mail and via website
Hours: Mon to Fri, 0900 to 1700

RADIO, ELECTRICAL AND TELEVISION RETAILERS' ASSOCIATION (RETRA)

Retra House, St John's Terrace, 1 Ampthill Street, Bedford, MK42 9EY

Tel: 01234 269110
Fax: 01234 269609
E-mail: retra@retra.co.uk
Website: www.retra.co.uk

Founded: 1942

Organisation type and purpose: Trade association for independent electrical retailers and servicing organisations.
To foster among the membership a culture of fair dealing with consumers; to encourage the achievement of high standards of retailing and related service activities within the trade; to provide members with a range of benefits, industry information and legal advice; to represent their interests at a national level – maintaining a dialogue with manufacturers, government and other key organisations.

Subject coverage: Represents more than 1,400 members, operating from over 2,300 outlets in the UK; members include electrical retailers, service engineers, custom installers, computer stores and electronic music shops.

Access to staff: Contact by letter, by telephone, by fax and by e-mail

RADISH GROWERS' ASSOCIATION

133 Eastgate, Louth, Lincolnshire, LN11 9QG

Tel: 01507 602427
Fax: 01507 607165
E-mail: crop.association@pvga.co.uk

Enquiries to: Membership Secretary

Founded: c.1980

Organisation type and purpose: National organisation, trade association.

Subject coverage: Radishes.

Access to staff: Contact by letter, by telephone, by fax and by e-mail

RADNORSHIRE SOCIETY

49 Holcombe Drive, Llandrindod Wells, Powys, LD1 6DN

Tel: 01597 823142
E-mail: c.p.f.hughes@btinternet.com
Website: www.radnorshiresociety.org

Enquiries to: Hon. Secretary

Founded: 1930

Organisation type and purpose: Learned society (membership is by subscription), present number of members: 450.

Subject coverage: History, natural history, archaeology of the old county of Radnor.

Publications: Printed

Access to staff: Contact by letter, by telephone and by e-mail. Appointment necessary. Access for members only.
Hours: Mon to Fri, 0900 to 1700

Access to building: No prior appointment required

RADZINOWICZ LIBRARY

Formal name: University of Cambridge, Institute of Criminology, Radzinowicz Library

Sidgwick Avenue, Cambridge, CB3 9DA

Tel: 01223 335386
Fax: 01223 335356
E-mail: crimlib@hermes.cam.ac.uk
Website: www.crim.cam.ac.uk/library

Enquiries to: Librarian

Founded: 1960

Organisation type and purpose: University department or institute. Departmental library. Research library.

Subject coverage: Criminology, penology, forensic psychiatry, forensic psychology, deviance, policing, criminal justice (foreign and historical materials are included), criminal law.

continued overleaf

Library catalogue: All or part available online

Publications: Electronic and video
Order electronic and video publications from: website: http://www.crim.cam.ac.uk/library/pubs.html

Access to staff: Contact by letter, by telephone, by fax and by e-mail. Appointment necessary. Letter of introduction required.
Hours: Mon to Fri, 0900 to 1600

RAF CENTRE OF AVIATION MEDICINE (RAF CAM)

RAF Henlow, Henlow, Bedfordshire, SG16 6DN

Tel: 01462 851515; extn 8045
Fax: 01462 857681
E-mail: rafcamlibrarian@yahoo.co.uk
Website: rafcam.heritage4.com

Enquiries to: Librarian
Direct tel: extn 8048
Direct e-mail: wilkinsonn807@henlow.raf.mod.uk
Other contacts: Officer Commanding Centre of Aviation Medicine (for non-service personnel who wish to visit the collection)

Founded: 2000; created by the merger of Institute of Aviation Medicine, Farnborough and RAF Institute of Health, RAF Halton

Organisation type and purpose: National government body, training organisation, research organisation.

Subject coverage: Medicine, especially those areas most relevant to aviation; physiology; neurology; psychology; occupational health.

Collection: Technical reports of British and overseas government agencies relevant to aviation and aviation medicine

Non-library collection catalogue: All or part available in-house

Library catalogue: All or part available in-house

Access to staff: Contact by letter, by telephone, by fax and by e-mail. Appointment necessary.
Hours: Mon to Thu, 0900 to 1630; Fri, 0900 to 1600
Special comments: All non-service personnel must first seek the permission of the Officer Commanding by letter.

Access for disabled people: Level entry, toilet facilities

RAIL PASSENGERS COUNCIL (RPC)

Freepost WA 1521, Warrington, WA4 6GP

Tel: 08453 022 022
Fax: 0845 850 1392
Website: www.rail-reg.gov.uk

Enquiries to: External Relations and Policy Manager

Founded: 1994

Organisation type and purpose: National government body.
Statutory consumer body of 14 members appointed by the Secretary of State, representing the interests of users of rail services and facilities.
The Rail Passengers Committees and the LTUC represent passenger interests locally, the RPC on a national scale.

Subject coverage: Rail users' consumer matters, monitoring and investigating policies and performance of train and station operators.
For passenger complaints, assessing hardship when stations or lines proposed for closure, see RUCCs and LRPC, which represent passengers' interests locally.

Publications: Printed

Access to staff: Contact by letter, by telephone, by fax and by e-mail. Appointment necessary.
Hours: Mon to Fri, 0900 to 1700

Affiliated to: London Transport Users Committee (LTUC); Rail Passengers Committees (RPC)

Branches at: East RPC Eastern England; 3rd Floor, Stuart House, City Road, Peterborough, Cambridgeshire, PE1 1QF; tel: 01733 312188; fax: 01733 891286; **London area** See the London Transport Users Committee; **Midlands** RPC Midlands; 6th Floor, The McLaren Building, 35 Dale End, Birmingham, B4 7LN; tel: 0121 212 2133; fax: 0121 236 6945; **North East** Also has responsibility for Tyne & Wear Metro services; Hilary House, St Saviour's Place, York, YO1 7PJ; tel: 01904 625615; fax: 01904 643026; **North West** Also has responsibility for Greater Manchester Metrolink services; Third Floor, 82 King Street, Manchester, M2 4WQ; tel: 0161 228 6247; fax: 0161 236 1476; **Scotland** RPC Scotland; also has responsibility for shipping services operated by Caledonian MacBrayne; Room 514, Corunna House, 29 Cadogan Street, Glasgow, G2 7AB; tel: 0141 221 7760; fax: 0141 221 3393; **South** RPC Southern England; 3rd Floor, Centric House, 390–391 Strand, London, WC2R 0LY; tel: 020 7240 5308; fax: 020 7240 8923; **Wales** RPC Wales – Cymru; St David's House, Wood Street, Cardiff, CF10 1ES; tel: 029 2022 7247; fax: 029 2022 3992; **West** RPC Western England; 10th Floor, Tower House, Fairfax Street, Bristol, BS1 3BN; tel: 0117 926 5703; fax: 0117 929 4140

Resourced by: Office of the Rail Regulator

RAILWAY CORRESPONDENCE AND TRAVEL SOCIETY (RCTS)

Littlecote, 365 Old Bath Road, Cheltenham, Gloucestershire, GL53 9AH

Tel: 01242 523917
E-mail: peter@littlecote.freeserve.co.uk
Website: www.rcts.org.uk

Enquiries to: Book Publications Sales Manager

Founded: 1928

Organisation type and purpose: Membership association (membership is by subscription), voluntary organisation.

Collection: Historic working time-tables collection (for members only)
Photographic portfolio (for members only)

Publications: Printed

Publications list: Available online and in print

Access to staff: Contact by letter, by e-mail and via website
Hours: Mon to Fri, 0900 to 1700

Affiliated to: a number of similar organisations in the UK and overseas

Has: 26 branches within the UK

RAILWAY HERITAGE TRUST

40 Melton Street, London, NW1 2EE

Tel: 020 7557 8090
Fax: 020 7557 9700
E-mail: rht@networkrail.co.uk

Enquiries to: Executive Director

Founded: 1985

Organisation type and purpose: Advisory body.
Independent company, sponsored by Network Rail and BRB (Residuary) Ltd, which offers grant aid for the conservation of listed buildings and structures owned by those sponsors.
Heritage funding agency.

Subject coverage: Repair, restoration and conservation of listed and historic railway buildings and structures owned by Network Rail and BRB (Residuary) Ltd, grant aid for this purpose.

Publications: Printed

Access to staff: Contact by letter, by telephone, by fax and by e-mail. Appointment necessary.
Hours: Mon to Fri, 0900 to 1700

RAILWAY INDUSTRY ASSOCIATION (RIA)

22 Headfort Place, London, SW1X 7RY

Tel: 020 7201 0777
Fax: 020 7235 5777
E-mail: ria@riagb.org.uk
Website: www.riagb.org.uk

Enquiries to: Director

Founded: 1875

Organisation type and purpose: Trade association.

Subject coverage: Railway equipment, railway infrastructure, standards and specifications.

Publications: Printed

Publications list: Available in print

Access to staff: Contact by letter, by telephone, by fax and by e-mail
Hours: Mon to Fri, 0900 to 1700

RAILWAY PRESERVATION SOCIETY OF IRELAND (RPSI)

Whitehead Excursion Station, Castleview Road, Whitehead, Carrickfergus, Co Antrim, BT38 9NA

Tel: 028 9337 3968
E-mail: rpsitrains@hotmail.com
Website: www.steamtrainsireland.com

Enquiries to: Honorary Secretary

Other contacts: Chairman

Founded: 1964

Organisation type and purpose:
Membership association (membership is by subscription), present number of members: 1,100, voluntary organisation, registered charity. Aims to restore, maintain and operate preserved steam locomotives and historic carriages on the main line railways of Ireland.

Subject coverage: Irish railway preservation, steam & diesel locomotives, vintage rolling stock.

Collection: Irish steam & diesel locomotives and rolling stock

Non-library collection catalogue: All or part available online

Publications: Printed

Access to staff: Contact by letter, by e-mail and via website. Appointment necessary.

Access to building: On advertised open days, otherwise by prior appointment.

Access for disabled people: Parking provided, ramped entry

Member organisation of: Heritage Railway Association (HRA)

RAJAR

Formal name: Radio Joint Audience Research Limited

6th Floor, 55 New Oxford Street, London WC1A 1BS

Tel: 020 7395 0630
Fax: 020 7395 0631
E-mail: info@rajar.co.uk
Website: www.rajar.co.uk

Enquiries to: Chief Executive

Founded: 1992

Organisation type and purpose: Research organisation.
Joint industry research organisation. Management of UK's agreed system of radio audience measurement.

Subject coverage: National and local estimates of radio listening analysis by time period and with demographic breakdowns.

Publications: Electronic and video

Access to staff: Contact by letter, by e-mail and via website. Appointment necessary.
Hours: Mon to Fri, 0930 to 1730

RALEIGH SAFETY SEVEN AND EARLY RELIANT OWNERS CLUB (Raleigh/Reliant OC)

17 Courtland Avenue, Chingford, London, E4 6DU

Enquiries to: Secretary

Founded: 1967

Organisation type and purpose:
Membership association (membership is by subscription), present number of members: 180–200.

Subject coverage: Technical information and spares for all Raleigh motorised vehicles and Reliant vehicles up to the Regal models.

Collection: Library of Raleigh and Reliant vehicle literature

Publications: Printed

Access to staff: Contact by letter
Hours: Mon to Fri, 0900 to 1700
Special comments: sae with enquiries; library is open to members only.

RAMBLERS' ASSOCIATION (RA)

2nd Floor, Camelford House, 89 Albert Embankment, London, SE1 7TW

Tel: 020 7339 8500
Fax: 020 7339 8501
E-mail: ramblers@ramblers.org.uk
Website: www.ramblers.org.uk

Enquiries to: Information Officer
Direct e-mail: ruths@ramblers.org.uk

Founded: 1935

Organisation type and purpose: National organisation, membership association (membership is by subscription), present number of members: 140,000, voluntary organisation, registered charity (charity number 306089).
Encouraging walking, protecting footpaths, campaigning for responsible freedom to roam, defending the beauty of the countryside.

Subject coverage: Walking; rights of way and footpath law; care of the countryside and preservation of natural beauty; protection of footpaths and provision of access to open country; long-distance footpath information; all matters connected with walking.

Publications: Printed

Publications list: Available online and in print

Access to staff: Contact by letter, by telephone, by fax, by e-mail, in person and via website
Hours: Mon to Fri, 1000 to 1700

Access to building: No prior appointment required

Access for disabled people: Parking provided, ramped entry, access to all public areas, toilet facilities

Other addresses: Ramblers' Association, Scotland (RA Scotland); Kingfisher House, Auld Mart Business Park, Milnathort, Kinross, KY13 9DA; tel: 01577 861222; fax: 01577 861333; e-mail: enquiries@scotland.ramblers.org.uk; Ramblers' Association, Wales; Ty'r Cerddwyr, High Street, Gresford, Wrexham, LL12 8PT; tel: 01978 855148; fax: 01978 854445; e-mail: cerddwyr@wales.ramblers.org.uk

RAMSGATE LIBRARY

Guildford Lawn, Ramsgate, Kent, CT11 9AJ

Tel: 01843 593532
Fax: 01843 852692

Enquiries to: Librarian
Other contacts: Heritage Officer

Founded: 1904

Organisation type and purpose: Local government body, public library.

Subject coverage: Parish records, census returns, photographs, press cuttings, maps and ephemera relating to the history of Ramsgate.

Collection: Ramsgate Archive Collections have been moved to the East Kent Archives Centre, Dover
Collections of books, photographs, maps and postcards relating to the history of Ramsgate

Library catalogue: All or part available in-house

Access to staff: Contact by letter, by telephone and by fax
Hours: Mon to Thu, 0930 to 1800; Fri, 0930 to 1900; Sat, 0930 to 1700
Special comments: Heritage staff are available to assist on Thursdays.

Access to building: No access other than to staff

Parent body: Kent County Council; Sessions House, County Hall, Maidstone, Kent

RAPE AND SEXUAL ABUSE SUPPORT CENTRE (RASASC)

PO Box 383, Croydon, Surrey, CR9 2AW

Tel: 020 8683 3311 (Counselling and Office); 020 82391124 (minicom); 08451 221 331 (helpline)
Fax: 020 8683 3366
E-mail: info@rasasc.org.uk
Website: www.rasasc.org.uk

Enquiries to: CEO

Founded: 1984

Organisation type and purpose: Voluntary organisation, registered charity (charity number 1085104), training organisation, consultancy.

Subject coverage: Support to anyone aged 14 and above who has been raped or sexually abused, however long ago. Support and advice to friends/family/partners, and other agencies working with rape or sexual abuse victims. External training to other organisations. Database of other statutory and otherwise relevant organisations for referral. Helpline support for male victims.

Publications: Printed

Access to staff: Contact by letter, by telephone, by fax, by e-mail and via website. Appointment necessary.
Hours: Mon to Fri, 1000 to 1600
Special comments: Helpline: Mon to Fri, 1200 to 1430 and 1900 to 2130; Sat, Sun and bank holidays, 1430 to 1700
Counselling: Mon to Fri, 1000 to 1600

Access to building: No access other than to staff

Access for disabled people: Parking provided, level entry, toilet facilities
Special comments: Staff only, at present. (December 2001)

RAPIER REGISTER

The Smithy, Tregynon, Newtown, Powys, SY16 3EH

Tel: 01686 650396

Enquiries to: Membership Secretary

continued overleaf

Founded: 1953

Organisation type and purpose:
International organisation, membership association (membership is by subscription), present number of members: 150, voluntary organisation.
Motor club catering for the needs of persons owning and driving Lagonda Rapiers and Rapier cars built between 1934 and 1938.

Subject coverage: General and technical information on Lagonda Rapiers and Rapier cars manufactured between 1934 and 1938. Location of available spare parts for same.

Publications: Printed

Access to staff: Contact by letter and by telephone
Hours: Mon to Fri, 0900 to 2200

RAPTOR FOUNDATION

Formal name: Bird of Prey Rescue Centre

The Heath, St Ives Road, Woodhurst, Cambridgeshire, PE28 3BT

Tel: 01487 741140
Fax: 01487 841140
E-mail: heleowl@aol.com
Website: www.homepages.tesco.net/~raptor.foundation

Enquiries to: Director
Other contacts: Founder

Founded: 1989

Organisation type and purpose:
Membership association (membership is by subscription), present number of members: 210, registered charity (charity number 1042085), research organisation.
Care and rehabilitation of raptors.

Trade and statistical information: Over 350 rescued raptors

Access to staff: Contact in person
Hours: 24 hours a day for rescue daily, 1030 to 1700 for visitors

Access for disabled people: Parking provided, ramped entry, access to all public areas, toilet facilities

RARE BREEDS SURVIVAL TRUST (RBST)

National Agricultural Centre, Stoneleigh Park, Kenilworth, Warwickshire, CV8 2LG

Tel: 024 7669 6551
Fax: 024 7669 6706
E-mail: enquiries@rbst.org.uk
Website: www.rbst.org.uk

Enquiries to: Administrator

Founded: 1973

Organisation type and purpose:
Membership association (membership is by subscription), present number of members: c. 8000, registered charity (charity number 269442).
The conservation of rare breeds of farm livestock.

Subject coverage: Rare breeds of farm livestock.

Non-library collection catalogue: All or part available in-house

Access to staff: Contact by letter, by telephone, by fax, by e-mail and via website. Appointment necessary.
Hours: Mon to Fri, 0900 to 1700

Access to building: No prior appointment required

RATHBONE

4th Floor, Churchgate House, 56 Oxford Street, Manchester, M1 6EU

Tel: 0161 236 5358
Fax: 0161 238 6356
Website: www.rathbonetraining.co.uk

Enquiries to: Helpline Co-ordinator
Direct e-mail: advice@rathbonetraining.co.uk
Other contacts: Marketing and External Affairs Manager for overall responsibility for marketing, public relations and information.

Founded: 1969; formerly called Rathbone Training

Organisation type and purpose: Advisory body, voluntary organisation, registered charity (charity number 287120), training organisation.
Charity is a training provider. Special education advice line to parents and children with special needs.

Subject coverage: Advice for parents and children with special needs on all aspects of education, statementing, exclusion etc.

Collection: Elfrida Rathbone archives

Publications: Printed

Publications list: Available in print

Access to staff: Contact by letter, by telephone, by fax and by e-mail
Hours: Mon to Fri, 1000 to 1600

Development Officer (London & South): Rathbone Training; 260–268 Poplar High Street, London, E14 0BB; tel: 020 7538 2041; fax: 020 7537 9399

Development Officer (Midlands & Wales): Rathbone Training; 1st Floor, Wrekin House, Market Street, Wellington, Telford, Shropshire, TF1 1DT; tel: 01952 245000; fax: 01952 261771

Development Officer (North): Rathbone Training; 165 Cardigan Road, Leeds, LS6 1QL; tel: 0113 278 9333; fax: 0113 278 9870

Director for Scotland: Rathbone Training; C.I. Building, Scott Street, Motherwell, ML1 1PN; tel: 01698 252326; fax: 01698 251400

RAVENSBOURNE COLLEGE OF DESIGN AND COMMUNICATION LRC

Walden Road, Chislehurst, Kent, BR7 5SN

Tel: 020 8289 4900
Fax: 020 8325 8320
E-mail: lrc@rave.ac.uk
Website: intranet.rave.ac.uk/lrc

Enquiries to: Director of Information Services
Direct tel: 020 8289 4919
Direct e-mail: s.bowman@rave.ac.uk

Organisation type and purpose: College of higher education.

Subject coverage: Broadcasting, fashion design, furniture design, graphic design, moving image, product design, television.

Library catalogue: All or part available online

Access to staff: Contact by letter, by telephone, by fax and by e-mail. Appointment necessary.
Hours: Mon to Fri, 0900 to 1700

Funded by: HEFCE

RAY SOCIETY

Department of Zoology, The Natural History Museum, Cromwell Road, South Kensington, London, SW7 5BD

Tel: 020 7942 5276
Fax: 020 7942 5433
E-mail: t.ferrero@nhm.ac.uk
Website: www.scionpublishing.com

Enquiries to: Honorary Secretary

Founded: 1844

Organisation type and purpose: Learned society (membership is by subscription), present number of members: 357, registered charity (charity number 208082).

Subject coverage: Natural history; botany; zoology mainly of Britain and NW Europe but also of wider interest.

Publications: Printed, and electronic and video
Order printed publications from: Scion Publishing Ltd, The Old Hayloft, Vantage Buisness Park, Bloxham Road, Banbury, OX16 9UX; e-mail: info@scionpublishing.com; tel: 01295 258577; fax: 01295 275624
Concessionary sales to members are available through the Honorary Secretary
Order microform publications from: Microform Academic Publishers, Microform (Wakefield) Limited, Main Street, East Andsley, Wakefield, WF3 2AT
For purchase of any Ray Society 'I' publications, see addresses for printed publications
Order electronic and video publications from: Pisces Conservation Ltd, IRC House, The Square, Pennington, Lymington, SO41 8GN; e-mail: pisces@irchouse.demon.co.uk; tel: 01590 676622; fax: 01590 675599

Publications list: Available online and in print

Access to staff: Contact by letter, by telephone, by fax, by e-mail and via website. Appointment necessary.
Hours: Mon to Fri, 0900 to 1700
Special comments: Visitor regulations for the Natural History Museum apply.

Access for disabled people: Parking provided, ramped entry, access to all public areas, toilet facilities

RAYNAUD'S & SCLERODERMA ASSOCIATION

112 Crewe Road, Alsager, Cheshire, ST7 2JA

Tel: 01270 872776
Fax: 01270 883556
E-mail: info@reynauds.org.uk
Website: www.raynauds.org.uk

Enquiries to: Chief Executive

Founded: 1982

Organisation type and purpose:
Membership association (membership is by subscription), voluntary organisation, registered charity (charity number 326306), research organisation.

Subject coverage: Raynaud's, Scleroderma, Vibration White Finger, Sjögren's Syndrome, chilblains, Systemic Lupus Erythematosus, Teenage Raynaud's, Erythromelalgia, advances in research, funding for research.

Publications: Printed, and electronic and video

Publications list: Available in print

Access to staff: Contact by letter, by telephone, by fax, by e-mail, in person and via website
Hours: Mon to Fri, 0900 to 1700
Special comments: Answering machine available.

Access for disabled people: Parking provided, level entry, toilet facilities

RE-SOLV – THE SOCIETY FOR THE PREVENTION OF SOLVENT AND VOLATILE SUBSTANCE ABUSE (Re-Solv)

30a High Street, Stone, Staffordshire, ST15 8AW

Tel: 01785 817885
Fax: 01785 813205
E-mail: information@re-solv.org
Website: www.re-solv.org

Enquiries to: Information Officer

Founded: 1984

Organisation type and purpose: National organisation, membership association (membership is by subscription), registered charity (charity number 326732).
Aims to prevent death, suffering and crime that may result as a consequence of solvent and volatile substance abuse. Provides information and support to anyone concerned about or interested in solvent and volatile substance misuse issues.

Subject coverage: Prevention of solvent and volatile substance abuse.

Trade and statistical information: Solvent and volatile substance abuse statistics, i.e. mortality statistics

Publications: Printed, and electronic and video
Order printed publications from: Website
Order electronic and video publications from: Website

Publications list: Available online and in print

Access to staff: Contact by letter, by telephone, by fax, by e-mail and via website
Hours: Mon to Fri, 0900 to 1700; closed public holidays
Special comments: Answerphone services are in operation outside office hours and provide referral details.

Access to building: No access other than to staff

Branches: Re-Solv North East; 7 Burrow Street, South Shields, Tyne and Wear, NE33 1PP; tel: 0191 497 5522; e-mail: northeast@re-solv.org; Re-Solv Scotland; Suite 6, 53–58 South Avenue, Blantyre Industrial Estate, Blantyre, Lanarkshire, G72 0XB; tel: 07505 000024; e-mail: scotland@re-solv.org; Re-Solv Wales; First Floor, 21A Berriew Street, Welshpool, Powys, SY21 7SQ; tel: 01938 556790; e-mail: wales@re-solv.org

READING BOROUGH COUNCIL

Civic Offices, PO Box 17, The Civic Centre, Reading, Berkshire, RG1 7TD

Tel: 0118 939 0900; 0118 939 0700 (minicom)
Fax: 0118 958 9770
Website: www.reading.gov.uk

Enquiries to: Public Relations Manager
Direct tel: 0118 939 0333
Direct fax: 0118 939 0282
Direct e-mail: carl.welham@reading.gov.uk

Founded: 1998

Organisation type and purpose: Local government body.

Subject coverage: All aspects of local government.

Publications: Printed, and electronic and video

Publications list: Available in print

Access to staff: Contact by letter, by telephone, by fax, by e-mail, in person and via website
Hours: Mon to Fri, 0900 to 1700

Access for disabled people: Parking provided, ramped entry, access to all public areas, toilet facilities

READING CENTRAL LIBRARY

Abbey Square, Reading, Berkshire, RG1 3BQ

Tel: 0118 901 5950
Fax: 0118 901 5954
E-mail: info@readinglibraries.org.uk
Website: www.readinglibraries.org.uk

Enquiries to: Librarian

Founded: 1883

Organisation type and purpose: Local government body, public library.

Subject coverage: General; business information; information on Reading and Berkshire.

Information services: Internet access provided free of charge at all libraries.

Collection: Local Studies Library
Mary Russell Mitford collection
Vocal sets collection

Library catalogue: All or part available online and in-house

Publications list: Available in print

Access to staff: Contact by letter, by telephone, by fax, by e-mail, in person and via website
Hours: Mon, Fri, 0900 to 1730; Tue, Thu, 0900 to 1900; Wed, 0900 to 1700; Sat, 0930 to 1700

Access to building: No access other than to staff
Hours: Mon, Fri, 0900 to 1730; Tue, Thu, 0900 to 1900; Wed, 0900 to 1700; Sat, 0930 to 1700

Access for disabled people: Level entry, access to all public areas, toilet facilities

Branch libraries: Battle Library; tel: 0118 901 5100; fax: 0118 901 5101; Caversham Library; tel: 0118 901 5103; fax: 0118 901 5104; Palmer Park Library; tel: 0118 901 5106; fax: 0118 901 5107; Southcote Library; tel: 0118 901 5109; fax: 0118 901 5110; Tilehurst Library; tel: 0118 901 5112; fax: 0118 901 5113; Whitley Library; tel: 0118 901 5115; fax: 0118 901 5116

Parent body: Reading Borough Council; Civic Offices, Reading, Berkshire, RG1 7TD; tel: 0118 939 0900

RECORD OFFICE FOR LEICESTERSHIRE, LEICESTER AND RUTLAND

Long Street, Wigston Magna, Leicester, LE18 2AH

Tel: 0116 257 1080
Fax: 0116 257 1120
E-mail: recordoffice@leics.gov.uk

Enquiries to: Senior Archivist

Organisation type and purpose: Local government body.
Record Office.

Subject coverage: Local archives and local studies including manuscripts, books, maps, photographs and all other archive material relating to Leicestershire, Leicester and Rutland.

Collection: Collections include:
Books, magazines and pamphlets on Leicestershire and Rutland
Census returns for Leicestershire and Rutland 1841–1901 on microform
Directories and electoral registers
Files of local newspapers
Illustrations of people and places
Oral history tapes and sound recordings
Ordnance Survey maps
Photographs and archive films
Archives of:
Leicestershire and Rutland County Councils
Borough of Leicester (from 1103)
Courts of Quarter Sessions and Petty Sessions
Poor Law Unions
Probate Registry (wills from 1858)
Anglican and nonconformist churches
Archdeaconry of Leicester (including wills and inventories from 1496)
Landed estates and families
Solicitors, commercial firms and manufacturers
Clubs, societies and other organisations
Military, Leicestershire Regiment

Non-library collection catalogue: All or part available online and in-house

Library catalogue: All or part available online and in-house

Publications: Printed

Access to staff: Contact by letter, by telephone, by fax, by e-mail and in person
Hours: Mon, Tue, Thu, 0915 to 1700; Wed, 0915 to 1930; Fri, closed; Sat, 0915 to 1215
Special comments: Readers ticket required (proof of name and address is necessary).

Access for disabled people: Parking provided, ramped entry, access to all public areas, toilet facilities

Constituent part of: Leicestershire County Council's Community Services

continued overleaf

Part funded by: Leicester City Council and Rutland County Council

RECORD SOCIETY OF LANCASHIRE AND CHESHIRE

John Rylands University of Manchester Library, Oxford Road, Manchester, M13 9PP

E-mail: rslc@lineone.net

Enquiries to: Council Secretary

Founded: 1878

Organisation type and purpose:
Membership association, registered charity (charity number 500434).
To transcribe and publish original documents relating to the two palatine counties.

Non-library collection catalogue: All or part available online

Publications: Printed, and microform publications
Order microform publications from: Chadwyck -Healey Limited, The Quorum, Barnwell Road, Cambridge, CB5 8SW, tel: 01223 215512

Publications list: Available online and in print

Access to staff: Contact by letter and by e-mail
Hours: Mon to Fri, 0900 to 1700

RECRUITMENT AND EMPLOYMENT CONFEDERATION (REC)

3rd Floor, Steward House, 16a Commercial Way, Woking, Surrey, GU21 1ET

Tel: 020 7462 3260
Fax: 01483 714979
E-mail: info@rec.uk.com
Website: www.rec.uk.com

Enquiries to: Chief Executive

Founded: 1930

Organisation type and purpose:
Professional body (membership is by qualification), present number of members: 6,000 corporate, 7,000 individual, service industry, registered charity (charity number 803141), university department or institute, suitable for ages: 18+, training organisation.

Subject coverage: Employment consultancy and agency practice; employment legislation relevant to employment agencies; professional qualifications in recruitment and employment agency practice.

Publications: Printed

Access to staff: Contact by letter, by telephone, by fax, by e-mail and via website
Hours: Mon to Fri, 0830 to 1730

Other office: REC; 36–38 Mortimer Street, London, W1W 7RG; tel: 020 7462 3260; fax: 020 7255 2878

REDBRIDGE PUBLIC LIBRARIES

Central Library, Clements Road, Ilford, Essex, IG1 1EA

Tel: 020 8708 2414
Fax: 020 8708 2571
E-mail: central.library@redbridge.gov.uk
Website: www.redbridge.gov.uk

Enquiries to: Chief Librarian
Other contacts: Local Studies Librarian

Organisation type and purpose: Public library.

Subject coverage: General; social problems and services, local history of Redbridge, insurance, youth organisations, public health, family history.

Collection: Local History including part of the Brand Collection (Ilford and Essex history)

Non-library collection catalogue: All or part available online and in-house

Library catalogue: All or part available online

Access to staff: Contact by letter, by telephone, by e-mail and in person
Hours: Mon to Fri, 0930 to 2000; Sat, 0930 to 1600

REDCAR AND CLEVELAND COUNCIL

Town Hall, Fabian Road, South Bank, Middlesbrough, Cleveland, TS6 9AR

Tel: 01642 444000
Fax: 01642 444584

Enquiries to: Chief Executive

Organisation type and purpose: Local government body.
Unitary authority.

Access to staff: Contact by letter, by telephone and by fax. Appointment necessary.
Hours: Mon to Fri, 0900 to 1700

REDCAR LIBRARY & CUSTOMER SERVICES

Redcar Library & Customer Services, Kirkleatham Street, Redcar, Cleveland,

Tel: 01642 444141
E-mail: redcar_library@redcar-cleveland.gov.uk
Website: www.redcar-cleveland.gov.uk/libraries/index2.htm

Enquiries to: Senior Librarian

Organisation type and purpose: Local government body.
Public library.

Subject coverage: Lending library, reference section, and customer services

Collection: Family History Resources: largely in microform, for East Cleveland area, some national coverage
Local history collection: mainly covering the old North Riding of Yorkshire, East Cleveland and the present borough

Non-library collection catalogue: All or part available online and in-house

Library catalogue: All or part available online

Access to staff: Contact by letter, by telephone, by e-mail, in person and via website
Hours: Mon, Tue, Wed, Fri, 0900 to 1800; Thu, 0900to 1700; Sat, 0930 to 1230

Access for disabled people: Level entry, access to all public areas, toilet facilities

Connections with: Redcar and Cleveland Borough Council; Chief Executive's Department, Redcar and Cleveland House, Kirkleatham Street, Redcar, TS10 1XX; Teesside Archives; Exchange House, 6 Marton Road, Middlesbrough, TS1 1DB; tel: 01642 248321; fax: 01642 248391; e-mail: teesside_archives@middlesbrough.gov.uk

REDDITCH LIBRARY

15 Market Place, Redditch, Worcestershire, B98 8AR

Tel: 01527 63291
Fax: 01527 68571
E-mail: redditchlib@worcestershire.gov.uk

Enquiries to: Librarian

Organisation type and purpose: Local government body, public library.

Subject coverage: Local history of the Redditch area, including Bordesley Abbey, the needle industry, and Redditch New Town.

Collection: Needle District Almanacs (annual directories 1873–1936)
Redditch census schedules (1841–91)
Redditch Indicator (from 1859)

Non-library collection catalogue: All or part available online

Library catalogue: All or part available online

Access to staff: Contact by letter
Hours: Mon, Thu, Fri, 0930 to 2000; Tue, Wed, 0930 to 1730; Sat, 0930 to 1730
Special comments: Proof of name and address required.

Parent body: Worcestershire County Council

REFEREES' ASSOCIATION

Unit 12, Ensign Business Centre, Westwood Way, Westwood Business Park, Coventry, CV4 8JA

Tel: 024 7642 0360
Fax: 024 7767 7234
E-mail: ra@footballreferee.org
Website: www.footballreferee.org

Enquiries to: General Secretary
Direct e-mail: arthur@footballreferee.org

Founded: 1908

Organisation type and purpose:
Membership association (membership is by subscription), training organisation.

Subject coverage: Implementation of the laws of association football. Recruitment and training of referees.

Publications: Printed

Access to staff: Contact by letter, by telephone, by fax and by e-mail.
Appointment necessary.
Hours: Mon to Fri, 0830 to 1630

REFINED SUGAR ASSOCIATION (RSA)

154 Bishopsgate, London, EC2M 4LN

Tel: 020 7377 2113
Fax: 020 7247 2481
E-mail: durhamn@sugar-assoc.co.uk

Enquiries to: Secretary

Founded: 1891

Organisation type and purpose: International organisation, trade association (membership is by election or invitation), present number of members: 115.

Subject coverage: Sugar.

REFRACTORY USERS FEDERATION (RUF)

5th Floor, Broadway House, Tothill Street, London, SW1H 9NQ

Tel: 020 7799 2020
Fax: 020 7233 1930

Enquiries to: Executive Secretary

Founded: 1945

Organisation type and purpose: Trade association (membership is by subscription), present number of members: 10.

Subject coverage: Matters relating to refractory contracting, industrial relations, terms and conditions of employment for refractory bricklayers and labourers, and training.

Publications: Printed

Access to staff: Contact by letter, by telephone and by fax
Hours: Mon to Fri, 0900 to 1700

REFUGEE ACTION

The Old Fire Station, 150 Waterloo Road, London, SE1 8SB

Tel: 020 7654 7700
Fax: 020 7654 0696
E-mail: info@refugee-action.org.uk
Website: www.refugee-action.org.uk
Website: www.refugee-action.org.uk/RAP/default.aspx

Founded: 1981

Organisation type and purpose: Registered charity (number 283660), an independent national charity that works with refugees to build new lives in the UK.
Provides advice and support to asylum seekers and refugees in the North West, the Midlands, London, South West and South Central. Exists to enable refugees to build new lives, through advice and information, community development, enhancing opportunity, and campaigning for refugee rights.

Subject coverage: Refugee Action's Asylum Advice teams provide a reception service for newly arrived asylum seekers, as well as advice and advocacy. The Choices service provides independent advice to asylum seekers considering returning voluntarily to their country of origin. Refugee Action's community development workers promote the development of refugee communities. It also runs innovative projects to enhance opportunities for refugees and asylum seekers.

Publications: Printed, and electronic and video
Order printed publications from: Communications office, tel: 020 7654 7705; e-mail: publications@refugee-action.org.uk
Order electronic and video publications from: Download from website

Publications list: Available online

Access to staff: Contact by letter, by telephone, by fax and by e-mail
Special comments: Contact local regional offices for asylum advice, community development or volunteering enquiries.

Branches: Offices across 10 regions of England

REFUGEE COUNCIL (BRC)

240–250 Ferndale Road, Brixton, London, SW9 8BB

Tel: 020 7346 6700
Fax: 020 7346 6701
Website: www.refugeecouncil.org.uk

Enquiries to: Media Officer
Direct tel: 020 7346 1214
Direct e-mail: philippa.mcintyre@refugeecouncil.org.uk

Organisation type and purpose: Voluntary organisation, registered charity (charity number 1014576).

Subject coverage: Asylum and refugee issues in the UK.

Non-library collection catalogue: All or part available in-house

Library catalogue: All or part available in-house

Order printed publications from: e-shop: http://www.refugeecouncil.org.uk

Publications list: Available online

Access to staff: Contact by letter, by telephone, by fax, by e-mail and in person. Appointment necessary.
Hours: Mon to Fri, 1000 to 1700

Access to building: No prior appointment required

Member organisation of: European Council on Refugees and Exiles (ECRE); Human Rights Documentation Systems; International Refugee Documentation Network (IRDN)

REGENT'S COLLEGE LIBRARY

Library, Inner Circle, Regent's Park, London, NW1 4NS

Tel: 020 7487 7448
Website: www.regents.ac.uk/library.htm

Enquiries to: Head Librarian
Direct e-mail: collinsm@regents.ac.uk

Founded: 1985

Organisation type and purpose: College of higher education.

Subject coverage: Business, management, psychotherapy and counselling.

Non-library collection catalogue: All or part available online

Library catalogue: All or part available online

Access to staff: Contact by letter, by telephone and by e-mail. Appointment necessary. Access for members only.
Hours: Mon to Fri, 0900 to 1700

REGENT'S PARK COLLEGE (RPC)

Formal name: Regent's Park College, University of Oxford

Pusey Street, Oxford, OX1 2LB

Tel: 01865 288120
Fax: 01865 288121
E-mail: library@regents.ox.ac.uk
Website: www.rpc.ox.ac.uk
Website: www.lib.ox.ac.uk/libraries/guides/REG.html
Website: solo.bodleian.ox.ac.uk

Enquiries to: College Librarian
Direct e-mail: emma.walsh@regents.ox.ac.uk
Other contacts: Assistant Librarian (Main Library); Archivist and Library Assistant (Angus Library)

Founded: 1810

Organisation type and purpose: Registered charity (charity number 309710).
Permanent Private Hall of the University of Oxford.
The Angus library also houses the library of the Baptist Union of Great Britain and the archives of the Baptist Missionary Society.

Subject coverage: Baptist history.

Collection: Baptist Historical Society, library
Baptist Missionary Society Archives
Baptist Union of Great Britain: minute books, some records, library
David Nicholls Collection: separate location from both libraries
4,000 books on theology, church and state, politics, philosophy, Caribbean studies (especially Haiti)

Non-library collection catalogue: All or part available online and in-house

Library catalogue: All or part available online and in-house

Publications: Printed, and electronic and video, and microform publications

Publications list: Available online

Access to staff: Contact by letter, by telephone, by fax and by e-mail. Appointment necessary. Letter of introduction required.
Hours: Mon to Fri, 0930 to 1600
Special comments: College Library: members only.
Angus Library: by appointment, with references.

Access to building: *Hours:* Mon to Fri, 0900 to 1700

REGIMENTAL OFFICE ROYAL IRISH REGIMENT

5 Waring Street, Belfast, BT1 2EW

Tel: 028 9023 2086
Fax: 028 9023 2086
E-mail: nirmuseum@yahoo.co.uk
Website: rurmuseum.tripod.com/

Enquiries to: Curator

continued overleaf

Organisation type and purpose: Professional body.

Subject coverage: History of the Royal Irish Regiment and the Royal Ulster Rifles.

REGISTER OF APPAREL AND TEXTILE DESIGNERS (RATD)

3 Queen Square, London, WC1N 3AR

Tel: 020 7843 9460
E-mail: laurian.davies@ukft.org

Enquiries to: Manager

Founded: 1986

Organisation type and purpose: Trade association (membership is by subscription), present number of members: over 400, consultancy.

Subject coverage: Design; clothing; textiles; printed textiles; woven textiles; sourcing freelance designers for manufacturers and retailers in the UK and overseas; help and advice to freelance designers who are members of the Register.

Collection: Library of information relevant to freelance designers

Publications: Printed

Publications list: Available in print

Access to staff: Contact by telephone and by e-mail. Appointment necessary. Access for members only. Non-members charged.
Hours: Mon to Fri, 0900 to 1700
Special comments: Access only available to members of the Register of Apparel and Textile Designers.

Access to building: By appointment

Parent bodies: UKFT; tel: 020 7843 9460; e-mail: info@ukft.org; website: www.ukft.org
UKFT (UK Fashion & Textile Association); tel: 020 7843 9460

REGISTER OF UNUSUAL MICRO-CARS (RUM Cars)

School House Farm, Boarden Lane, Hawkenbury, Staplehurst, Kent, TN12 0EB

Tel: 01580 891377
E-mail: jeanrumcars@cs.com

Enquiries to: Secretary
Other contacts: Editor, tel: 01908 321737 for magazine input.

Founded: 1980

Organisation type and purpose: National organisation, membership association (membership is by subscription).

Subject coverage: Three- and four-wheeled post-war (1947 onwards) road going vehicles with engines of 700cc or less, manufactured in small numbers, small electric vehicles and invalid carriages.

Collection: Sales brochure, contemporary road tests etc, originals and photostats of magazine articles on all kinds of micro-cars

Publications: Printed

Access to staff: Contact by letter, by telephone and by e-mail. Appointment necessary.
Hours: any day, before 2030

Access to building: Prior appointment required

REGISTERED NURSING HOME ASSOCIATION (RNHA)

John Hewitt House, Tunnel Lane, Kings Norton, Birmingham, B30 3JN

Tel: 0121 451 1088
Fax: 0121 486 3175
E-mail: info@rnha.co.uk
Website: www.rnha.co.uk

Enquiries to: Chief Executive

Founded: 1968

Organisation type and purpose: Advisory body, trade association (membership is by subscription), present number of members: 1400, service industry.
Independent nursing homes, clinics and hospitals registered under the Care Standards Act 2000.

Subject coverage: Advice and support, including legal advice, to members; assistance to members of the public in looking for a place in a nursing home; lobbying government and other official bodies.

Library catalogue: All or part available in-house

Publications: Printed

Publications list: Available in print

Access to staff: Contact by letter, by telephone, by fax and by e-mail. Appointment necessary.
Hours: Mon to Thur, 0830 to 1630; Fri, 0830 to 1600

Access for disabled people: Parking provided

Founder member of: Independent Care Organisations Network (ICON); Joint Care Council (JCC)

REGISTRAR OF PUBLIC LENDING RIGHT (PLR)

Richard House, Sorbonne Close, Stockton-on-Tees, TS17 6DA

Tel: 01642 604699
Fax: 01642 615641
E-mail: theregistrar@plr.uk.com
Website: www.plr.uk.com

Enquiries to: Registrar's Personal Assistant

Founded: 1979

Organisation type and purpose: National government body.
Makes payments to authors for loans of their books from public libraries.

Subject coverage: Public library book issues and associated statistics.

Publications: Printed

Publications list: Available in print

Access to staff: Contact by letter, by telephone, by fax, by e-mail and via website. Appointment necessary.
Hours: Mon to Thu, 0900 to 1700; Fri, 0900 to 1630

Funded by: Department for Culture, Media and Sport; tel: 020 7211 6000

REGISTRY TRUST LIMITED (RTL)

153–157 Cleveland Street, London, W1T 6QW

Tel: 020 7380 0133
Fax: 020 7388 0672
E-mail: info@registry-trust.org.uk
Website: www.registry-trust.org.uk

Founded: 1986

Organisation type and purpose: Register of Judgments, Orders and Fines (England and Wales).
Register of Decrees (Scotland).
Registers of Judgments (Northern Ireland, Republic of Ireland, Jersey and Isle of Man).

Subject coverage: Court money judgments.

Access to staff: Contact by letter, by telephone, by e-mail and via website. All charged.
Hours: Mon to Fri, 0900 to 1700
Special comments: The staff of Registry Trust Limited do not accept unsolicited sales calls.

Access to building: There is no public access to the building or to Registry Trust Limited

RELATE

Herbert Gray College, Little Church Street, Rugby, Warwickshire, CV21 3AP

Tel: 01788 573241
Fax: 01788 535007
E-mail: enquiries@relate.org.uk
Website: www.relate.org.uk

Enquiries to: Information Officer
Direct e-mail: kim.atkins@relate.org.uk
Other contacts: Communications Assistant

Founded: 1938

Organisation type and purpose: Registered charity, training organisation.
Co-ordinates the activities of local marriage guidance centres.

Subject coverage: Relationship counselling, marriage, family life and personal relationships and educational programmes related to those relationships, sexual problems, divorce, stress and depression.

Publications: Printed

Access to staff: Contact by letter, by telephone, by fax and by e-mail. Appointment necessary.
Hours: Mon to Fri, 0900 to 1700

Access to building: No access other than to staff

Other addresses: Local centres in England, Wales and Northern Ireland (see Yellow Pages)

RELATIVES AND RESIDENTS ASSOCIATION (RRA)

5 Tavistock Place, London, WC1H 9SN

Tel: 020 7692 4302 (admin)
Fax: 020 7916 6093
E-mail: relres@totalise.co.uk

Enquiries to: Administrator

Other contacts: Advice Line Worker/Co-ordinator for advice offered to callers on the advice line.

Founded: 1992

Organisation type and purpose: National organisation, membership association (membership is by subscription), voluntary organisation, registered charity (charity number 1020194).

Subject coverage: Issues relating to long-term care for older people in, or considering admission to, residential or nursing homes. Offers mutual support and advice, facilitates the setting up of groups of relatives in homes. Has a black and ethnic minority involvement and guides for good practice.

Publications: Printed

Publications list: Available in print

Access to staff: Contact by letter, by telephone and by e-mail
Hours: Advice Line: Mon to Fri, 1000 to 1230 and 1330 to 1700
Admin: Mon to Fri, 0900 to 1700

Access to building: No access other than to staff

RELIEF FUND FOR ROMANIA (RFFR)

54–62 Regent Street, London, W1B 5RE

Tel: 020 7733 7018
Fax: 020 7737 4960
E-mail: mail@relieffundforromania.co.uk
Website: www.relieffundforromania.co.uk

Enquiries to: Executive Director
Other contacts: Project Director for grant applications.

Founded: 1989

Organisation type and purpose: International organisation, registered charity (charity number 1046737).

Subject coverage: Aid and development for children and adults in Romania's institutions, focus on medical improvements, mental health, disabled issues and groups, funding emerging Romanian NGO sector.

Collection: Photo library and videos of Romanian institutions 1989 to present day
Press cuttings of socio-political and charity subjects from 1989 to present

Access to staff: Contact by letter, by telephone and by fax
Hours: Mon to Fri, 0930 to 1830

RELIGIOUS EDUCATION

University of Birmingham, Selly Oak Campus, Weoley Park Road, Birmingham, B29 6LL

Tel: 0121 415 8290
Fax: 0121 414 5619
E-mail: g.m.teece@bham.ac.uk

Enquiries to: Head of Centre
Direct e-mail: c.b.oconnor@bham.ac.uk

Founded: 1974; formerly called Regional Religious Education Centre (Midlands) (year of change 1994)

Organisation type and purpose: University department or institute.
To promote good practice in religious education.

Subject coverage: Multi-faith religious education, moral education, personal and social development in education, research and curriculum development.

Collection: Artefacts
Audio cassettes
Posters
Slides
Videos

Publications: Printed

Access to staff: Contact by letter, by telephone, by fax, by e-mail and in person. Appointment necessary.
Hours: Mon to Fri, 0900 to 1700

Connections with: National Association of SACREs (NASACRE)

RELIGIOUS SOCIETY OF FRIENDS (QUAKERS) – BRITAIN YEARLY MEETING

Friends House, 173–177 Euston Road, London, NW1 2BJ

Tel: 020 7663 1135
Fax: 020 7663 1001
E-mail: library@quaker.org.uk
Website: www.quaker.org.uk/library

Enquiries to: Librarian

Founded: c. 1650

Organisation type and purpose: Religious body, present number of members: c. 16,500, voluntary organisation, registered charity (charity number 1127633).
Library for the storage and dissemination of information about Quakers and repository of the central archives of the Religious Society of Friends in Britain and the local archives of London Quaker meetings; point of contact for the Friends Historical Society.

Subject coverage: Quakers, especially Quaker thought, history and Quakerism, peace, anti-slavery, conscription.

Collection: Central archives of the Society in Britain
Digest registers of births, marriages and burials on microfilm (search fee payable)
Local Quaker archives for London and Middlesex area
Manuscripts, tracts and pictures
Printed material on Quakers since the mid-17th century
Records of other bodies with Quaker associations

Non-library collection catalogue: All or part available online and in-house

Library catalogue: All or part available online and in-house

Publications: Printed, and microform publications
Order microform publications from: World Microfilms, London, W9 2HH; website: http://www.microworld.uk.com
Academic Microforms Ltd, Wick, Scotland, KW1 4DD; website: http://www.academicmicroforms.com

Access to staff: Contact by letter, by telephone, by fax, by e-mail, in person and via website
Hours: Tue to Fri, 1000 to 1700
Mon to Fri, 0930 to 1700 for telephone queries
Special comments: Registration, with proof of ID and address, required for admission to the Library. Archives and manuscripts under 50 years old are not normally open. Charge for use of Digest registers of births, marriages and burials microfilms (appointment recommended).

Access to building: Wheelchair accessible

Access for disabled people: Level entry, wheelchair accessible, toilet facilities
Special comments: Access to library reading room; access to basement restaurant by lift only, but level entry to cafe in ground floor Quaker Centre.

Parent body: Britain Yearly Meeting of the Religious Society of Friends (Quakers); Friends House, Euston Road, London NW1 2BJ; tel: 020 7663 1000; website: http://www.quaker.org.uk

REMAP

Formal name: Technical Help for Disabled People

D9, Chaucer Business Park, Kemsing, Sevenoaks, Kent, TN15 6YU

Tel: 0845 130 0456
Fax: 0845 130 0789
E-mail: data@remap.org.uk
Website: www.remap.org.uk

Founded: 1964

Organisation type and purpose: Registered charity (charity number 1000456). Has 107 branches (panels) across UK.

Subject coverage: Design, manufacture and supply or adaptation of equipment to meet the individual needs of a disabled person when there is no suitable equipment on the market; no general information.

Publications: Printed

Publications list: Available in print

Access to staff: Contact by letter, by telephone, by fax and by e-mail
Hours: Mon to Thu, 0930 to 1600; 24-hour answerphone

REMOTE SENSING AND PHOTOGRAMMETRY SOCIETY (RSPSoc)

School of Geography, University of Nottingham, University Park, Nottingham, NG7 2RD

Tel: 0115 951 5435
Fax: 0115 951 5249
E-mail: rspsoc@nottingham.ac.uk
Website: www.rspsoc.org

Enquiries to: Executive Secretary
Direct tel: 0115 951 5435
Direct fax: 0115 951 5249
Direct e-mail: rspsoc@rspsoc.org

Founded: 2001

Organisation type and purpose: Learned society (membership is by subscription), present number of members: 1,000, registered charity (charity number 292647).

continued overleaf

Subject coverage: Remote sensing; sensors; platforms; image processing; interpretation equipment; resource surveys; applications of remote sensing in land use, soil mapping, geology, geomorphology, hydrology, meteorology, oceanography; monitoring of pollution and natural hazards; organisations world-wide, photogrammetry.

Publications: Printed

Access to staff: Contact by letter, by telephone, by fax and by e-mail
Hours: Mon to Fri, 0900 to 1700

Associate member of: International Society for Photogrammetry and Remote Sensing; Joint Branch of International Remote Sensing Activities (JOBRESA)

RENAL ASSOCIATION, THE (RA)

Secretariat, Durford Mill, Petersfield, Hampshire, GU31 5AZ

Tel: 0870 458 4155
Fax: 0870 442 9940
E-mail: renal@mci-group.com
Website: www.renal.org

Enquiries to: General Secretary

Founded: 1950

Organisation type and purpose: Learned society, registered charity (charity number 800733).

Subject coverage: Research into renal disease, treatment of renal disease.

Publications: Printed

Access to staff: Contact by letter, by telephone, by fax and by e-mail
Hours: Mon to Fri, 0900 to 1700

Affiliated to: European Renal Association; International Society of Nephrology

RENAULT CLASSIC CAR CLUB (RCCC)

5 Evesham Walk, Sandhurst, Berkshire, GU47 0YU

Website: www.renaultclassiccarclub.com

Enquiries to: Membership Secretary

Founded: 2001

Organisation type and purpose: International organisation, membership association (membership is by subscription), present number of members: 70.
Restoration and use of rear-engine Renaults, parts supply and advice, general purchase advice, workshop manuals – printed or on CD-ROM.

Subject coverage: Restoration and use of classic rear-engine Renaults, parts availability, technical information, buying and selling of parts and cars. Anything that will assist members keeping rear-engine Renault cars on the road.

Collection: Various technical and workshop manuals

Publications: Printed, and electronic and video

Access to staff: Contact by letter, by e-mail and via website
Hours: Mon to Fri, 0900 to 1700

RENEWABLEUK

Greencoat House, Francis Street, London, SW1P 1DH

Tel: 020 7901 3000
Fax: 020 7901 3001
E-mail: info@renewable-uk.com
Website: www.bwea.com

Founded: 1978; formerly called British Wind Energy Association (BWEA) (year of change 2010)

Organisation type and purpose: The trade and professional body for the UK wind and marine renewables industries, membership organisation (current number of members: 643 corporate members).
Primary purpose is to promote the use of wind, wave and tidal power in and around the UK; acts as a central point for information for members and a lobbying group to promote wind energy and marine renewables to government, industry, the media and the public; researches and finds solutions to current issues and generally acts as the forum for the UK wind, wave and tidal industry.

Subject coverage: Renewable energy in the UK.

Publications: Electronic and video
Order electronic and video publications from: website

Publications list: Available online

Access to staff: Contact by letter, by telephone, by fax and by e-mail

Also at: RenewableUK – Cymru; Temple Court, 13A Cathedral Road, Caerdydd/ Cardiff, CF11 9HA; tel: 029 2022 0700; e-mail: cymru@renewable-uk.com

RENFREWSHIRE COUNCIL

Council Headquarters, North Building, Cotton Street, Paisley, Renfrewshire, PA1 1WB

Tel: 0141 842 5000
Fax: 0141 840 3335
E-mail: chiefexex@renfrewshire.gov.uk
Website: www.renfrewshire.gov.uk

Enquiries to: Chief Executive
Direct tel: 0141 840 3213
Direct fax: 0141 840 3349

Founded: April 1996

Organisation type and purpose: Local government body.

Access to staff: Contact by letter, by telephone, by fax and in person
Hours: Mon to Thu, 0845 to 1645; Fri, 0845 to 1555

RENFREWSHIRE LIBRARY SERVICE

Library Support Services, Gallowhill Community Centre, Netherhill Road, Paisley, PA3 4SF

Tel: 0141 887 2723
Fax: 0141 887 9557
E-mail: libraries.els@renfrewshire.gov.uk
Website: www.renfrewshire.gov.uk

Enquiries to: Libraries Manager

Organisation type and purpose: Local government body, public library.

Subject coverage: General reference; local history; local government; community services; welfare; information for the elderly; library automation.

Collection: Bannatyne Club collection
Gardner collection (books printed in Paisley)
Local newspapers on microfiche
Maitland Club collection
Rowat collection

Library catalogue: All or part available online and in-house

Access to staff: Contact by letter, by telephone, by fax, by e-mail, in person and via website
Hours: Mon to Thu, 0900 to 1700; Fri, 0900 to 1600

Parent body: Renfrewshire Council; Education and Leisure Services

RENOLD PLC

Renold House, Styal Road, Wythenshawe, Manchester, M22 5WL

Tel: 0161 498 4500
Fax: 0161 437 7782
E-mail: enquiry@renold.com
Website: www.renold.com

Enquiries to: Marketing Manager
Direct tel: 0161 498 4531

Organisation type and purpose: International organisation, manufacturing industry.

Subject coverage: All aspects of mechanical power transmission, including: roller chains, wheels and pinions; conveying and elevating chains and wheels; gears; worm gear speed reducers; worm gear sets; spur, helical and spiral bevel gearboxes; shaft mounted gear units; geared motors; variable speed drives, couplings, clutches and brakes; sprag clutches for over-running, indexing and backstopping; vibratory shaker drives; power transmission accessories; machine tools; helical rotors for air compressors.

Collection: Fully classified catalogue collection of archival material relating to the establishment of the power transmission industry in the UK in the late 19th century

Publications list: Available in print

Access to staff: Contact by letter, by telephone, by e-mail and via website
Hours: Mon to Thu, 0900 to 1700; Fri, 0900 to 1600

REPETITIVE STRAIN INJURY AWARENESS (RSI Awareness)

Keytools Ltd, Abacus House, 1 Spring Crescent, Southampton, SO17 2FZ

Tel: 023 8029 4500
Fax: 023 8029 4501
E-mail: rsia@keytools.co.uk
Website: rsi.org.uk

Enquiries to: Director

Founded: 1989; formerly called Repetitive Strain Injury Association

Organisation type and purpose: To provide advice, information and support from those concerned about repetitive strain injury.

Subject coverage: Repetitive strain injuries.

Information services: Information website, events, advice, workshops, support groups.

Non-library collection catalogue: All or part available online

Publications: Printed
Order printed publications from: Website (factsheets available for download)

Publications list: Available online and in print

Access to staff: Contact by letter, by telephone, by fax, by e-mail and via website
Hours: Mon to Fri, 0900 to 1700

Access to building: Prior appointment required

Access for disabled people: Disabled access available
Special comments: By appointment.

RESCUE – THE BRITISH ARCHAEOLOGICAL TRUST (RESCUE)

15A Bull Plain, Hertford, SG14 1DX

Tel: 01992 553377
E-mail: rescue@rescue-archaeology.freeserve.co.uk
Website: www.rescue-archaeology.org.uk

Enquiries to: Membership Secretary

Founded: 1972

Organisation type and purpose: National organisation, membership association (membership is by subscription), registered charity (charity number 1064836).
Independent charitable trust.
To promote and foster the discovery, excavation, preservation, recording and study of archaeology in Great Britain for the public benefit.

Subject coverage: Organisation and funding of archaeology legislation and archaeology, current archaeological projects and news, recording methods, artefact excavation and storage methods.

Publications: Printed

Publications list: Available online and in print

Access to staff: Contact by letter
Hours: Mon, Fri, 0900 to 1700; Wed, morning only; answerphone when office closed

RESEARCH AND DEVELOPMENT SOCIETY (R&D Society)

6–9 Carlton House Terrace, London, SW1Y 5AG

Tel: 020 7451 2513
E-mail: rdsociety@royalsociety.org
Website: www.rdsoc.org

Enquiries to: Administrative Secretary

Founded: 1962; formerly called London Group for the Study of the Administration of Research and Development (LGARD) (year of change 1964)

Organisation type and purpose: Learned society, membership association (membership is by application), present number of members: 360.

Subject coverage: Research and development, largely industrial; R&D management; science policy.

Collection: Symposium Proceedings (9 vols, 1976–87)

Publications: Printed

Publications list: Available online

Access to staff: Contact by letter, by telephone and by e-mail
Hours: Mon to Fri, 0900 to 1700

Access to building: No access other than to staff

RESEARCH DEFENCE SOCIETY (RDS)

25 Shaftesbury Avenue, London, W1D 7EG

Tel: 020 7287 2818
Fax: 020 7287 2627
Website: www.rds-online.org.uk/

Enquiries to: Executive Director

Founded: 1908

Organisation type and purpose: Membership association, present number of members: 9800.

Subject coverage: Experimental research involving the use of animals; regulations and conditions under which such work is conducted in the UK; importance of such experiments to the welfare of mankind and animals; welfare of laboratory animals; proposed legislative changes; development of alternative methods.

Access to staff: Contact by letter, by telephone, by fax, by e-mail and via website
Hours: Mon to Fri, 0900 to 1700

RESEARCH INSTITUTE FOR INDUSTRY (RIfI)

School of Engineering Sciences, University of Southampton, Southampton, SO17 1BJ

Tel: 023 8059 7052
Fax: 023 8059 7051
E-mail: rifi@soton.ac.uk
Website: www.rifi.soton.ac.uk

Founded: 2002

Organisation type and purpose: University department or institute, consultancy.
To offer to industry the facilities and expertise of the School of Engineering Sciences at the University of Southampton on an applied research or consultancy basis.

Subject coverage: Composite fabrication and testing, computational fluid dynamics, cryogenics, refrigeration and engineering for low temperatures, electrochemical engineering, electromechanical systems, energy systems, erosion and corrosion, fuel cells and batteries, engineering design and analysis, engineering materials, experimental mechanics, failure analysis and mechanical property determination, finite element analysis, marine technology and industrial aerodynamics, micro electro-mechanical systems (MEMS), nano-indentation, surface engineering and tribology, software engineering, materials testing, metallographic examination and analysis, fatigue, creep fracture, fracture mechanics, corrosion, wear, surface treatments, heat treatment, welding, significance of defects, plastics, composites, electron microscopy, electron microprobe analysis, failure analysis, machinability and surfacing.

Access to staff: Contact by letter, by telephone, by fax and by e-mail.
Appointment necessary.
Hours: Mon to Fri, 0900 to 1700

RESEARCH INTO AGEING (RiA)

207–221 Pentonville Road, London, N1 9UZ

Tel: 020 7239 1895
E-mail: helen.rippon@ageing.org
Website: www.ageing.org/
Website: research.helptheaged.org.uk/

Enquiries to: Head of Research
Direct tel: 020 7239 1896
Direct e-mail: james.goodwin@helptheaged.org.uk
Other contacts: Information and Projects Manager

Founded: 1976

Organisation type and purpose: Voluntary organisation, registered charity (charity number 277468), suitable for ages: 45+, research organisation.
Raises funds to support medical research to investigate the common diseases and disabilities of later life.

Subject coverage: Research into age-related disease and disability. Makes grants for medical research into diseases of the older generations; osteoporosis, bone disease and loss, visual problems in old age, reaction to drugs, hypothermia, incontinence, loss of smell and taste, exercise and mobility, dementia (including Alzheimer's Disease), nutrition, cellular ageing, urinary incontinence, leg ulcers, breathlessness, nutrition, pressure sores and the ageing process itself.

Trade and statistical information: Ageing epidemiology/demography, health/diseases in later life

Publications: Printed, and electronic and video

Publications list: Available in print

Access to staff: Contact by letter, by telephone, by fax and by e-mail.
Appointment necessary.
Hours: Mon to Fri, 0930 to 1730

Funded by: Help the Aged; as above

RESTAURANT ASSOCIATION (RA)

c/o BHA, Queens House, 55–56 Lincoln's Inn Fields, London, WC2A 3BH

Tel: 0207 404 7744
Fax: 0207 404 7799
E-mail: bha@bha.org.uk
Website: www.ragb.co.uk

Enquiries to: Commercial Manager
Direct e-mail: pauline.jackson@bha.org.uk
Other contacts: Communications and IT Manager for publications and website.

continued overleaf

Founded: 1967; rejoined the british hospitality association (broke away to form the restaurant association of great britain in 1967) (year of change 2003)

Organisation type and purpose: National organisation, advisory body, trade association (membership is by subscription), present number of members: 3000, service industry, research organisation, publishing house.

Subject coverage: Restaurant industry in Britain.

Trade and statistical information: Size, diversity, performance and trends of restaurant industry in Britain

Publications: Printed

Access to staff: Contact by letter, by telephone, by fax and by e-mail
Hours: Mon to Fri, 0900 to 1730

Trading division of: British Hospitality Association

RESTORMEL BOROUGH COUNCIL

Borough Offices, Penwinnick Road, St Austell, Cornwall, PL25 5DR

Tel: 01726 223300
Fax: 01726 223301
E-mail: rbc@restormel.gov.uk
Website: www.restormel.gov.uk

Enquiries to: Chief Executive

Founded: 1974

Organisation type and purpose: Local government body.

Subject coverage: All local government issues.

Publications: Printed
Order printed publications from: Corporate Policy Officer, Restormel Borough Council Penwinnick Road, St Austell, Cornwall, PL25 5DR, tel: 01726 223514, fax: 01726 223526, e-mail: fbowler@restormel.gov.uk

Access to staff: Contact by letter, by telephone, by fax, by e-mail, in person and via website. Appointment necessary.
Hours: Mon to Fri, 0900 to 1700

Access for disabled people: Parking provided, ramped entry, access to all public areas, toilet facilities

Also at: Tourism & Publicity Offices; Marcus Hill, Newquay, Cornwall, TR7 1AF; tel: 01637 854000; fax: 01637 854044; e-mail: holidaytime@newquay.org.uk

RETAIL INTELLIGENCE WORLDWIDE (RIW Research)

Richmond Bridge House, 419 Richmond Road, Twickenham, TW1 2EX

Tel: 020 3005 9862
E-mail: monica.woods@riwresearch.com
Website: www.riwresearch.com

Founded: 1975

Organisation type and purpose: Information broker.
Specialist retail consulting firm.

Subject coverage: European retailing and consumer goods research service; information available on companies, distribution, food and drink, leisure, DIY, mail order, clothing, convenience stores, CTNs, newsagents, department stores, electrical stores, footwear, furniture, health and beauty, jewellery, opticians, variety stores, off-licences.

Information services: Specialist desk research service on retail and consumer markets around the world.

Collection: Photographic collection of retailers around the world, over 300,000 images

Trade and statistical information: Information available for all sectors listed

Library catalogue: All or part available in-house

Publications: Printed

Access to staff: Contact by telephone and by e-mail
Hours: Mon to Fri, 0900 to 1730

RETAIL MOTOR INDUSTRY FEDERATION (RMIF)

201 Great Portland Street, London, W1W 5AB

Tel: 020 7580 9122
Fax: 020 7580 6376
E-mail: firstnamelastname@rmif.co.uk
Website: www.rmif.co.uk

Founded: 1913

Organisation type and purpose: Trade association.

Subject coverage: UK retail motor industry – sales, service and maintenance of new and used cars, trucks and motorcycles, and associated activities.

Trade and statistical information: Data on sales and service in the UK motor industry

Publications: Printed

Access to staff: Contact by letter, by telephone, by fax and by e-mail
Hours: Mon to Fri, 0900 to 1700

Members: Bodyshop Services Division (BSD); Cherished Numbers Dealers Association (CNDA); Independent Garage Division (IGD); Motorcycle Retailers Association (MRA); Motorcycle Rider Training Association (MRTA); National Franchised Dealers Association (NFDA); Petrol Retailers Association (PRA); Society of Motor Auctions (SMA)

RETHINK

Formal name: National Schizophrenia Fellowship

15th Floor, 89 Albert Embankment, London, SE1 7TP

Tel: 0300 5000 927
E-mail: info@rethink.org
Website: www.rethink.org

Founded: 1972

Organisation type and purpose:
Membership association (membership is by subscription), present number of members: 7,500, voluntary organisation, registered charity (charity number 271028).
Organisation for people with a severe mental illness, their families and carers; membership £24 pa To help everyone affected by severe mental illness, including schizophrenia, to recover a better quality of life.

Subject coverage: Schizophrenia and severe mental illness, the effect it has on people with the condition, on relatives and on friends of sufferers; professional workers caring for service users or clients (not aspects involving clinical or medical judgement); community care.

Publications: Printed

Publications list: Available online and in print

Access to staff: Contact by letter, by telephone, by fax, by e-mail and via website. Appointment necessary.
Hours: Mon to Fri, 0900 to 1700

Branches: 120 relative/sufferer local support groups and 380 projects (day care, employment or care homes); Operations London and East; 89 Albert Embankment, London, SE1 7TP; tel: 0300 5000 927; fax: 020 7820 1149; e-mail: info@london.rethink.org; Rethink Information and Advice Service; 89 Albert Embankment, London; tel: 0300 500 927; fax: 020 7820 1149; e-mail: info@nsf.org.uk

Member organisation of: Disability Alliance; EUFAMI; National Council for Voluntary Organisations

RETIRED GREYHOUND TRUST (RGT)

Park House, Park Terrace, Worcester Park, Surrey, KT4 7JZ

Tel: 0844 826 8424
Fax: 0844 826 8425
Website: www.retiredgreyhounds.co.uk

Organisation type and purpose: Registered charity (charity number 269668).

Subject coverage: Welfare of retired greyhounds.

Access to staff: Contact by letter, by telephone, by fax and via website

Branches: Throughout England, Scotland and Wales

RETRAINING OF RACEHORSES (RoR)

75 High Holborn, London, WC1V 6LS

Tel: 01780 740773
E-mail: info@ror.org.uk
Website: www.ror.org.uk

Other contacts: Director of Operations (for applications to enter the RoR Series)

Founded: 2000

Organisation type and purpose: Registered charity (number 1084787).
British Horseracing's official charity for the welfare of horses who have retired from racing.

Subject coverage: Retraining retired racehorses.

Information services: Horse Helpline, by phone (as above) or e-mail: asktheexperts@ror.org.uk.

Access to staff: Contact by letter, by telephone and by e-mail

Also at: Director of Operations, Retraining of Racehorses; Ash Cottage, Back Street, East Garston, Hungerford, Berkshire, RG17 7EX; tel: 01488 648998; 07836 293191; e-mail: darbuthnot@ror.org.uk

RETREAD MANUFACTURERS ASSOCIATION (RMA)

PO Box 320, Crewe, Cheshire, CW2 6WY

Tel: 01270 561014
Fax: 01270 668801
E-mail: rma@greentyres.com
Website: www.retreaders.co.uk
Website: www.retreaders.org.uk

Enquiries to: Director
Other contacts: (1) Secretary; (2) Technical Consultant for (1) In Director's absence; (2) Technical enquiries only, tel 01782 659674.

Founded: 1946

Organisation type and purpose: National organisation, trade association (membership is by subscription), present number of members: 85.

Subject coverage: Tyre retreading; standards and tyre disposal, tyre recycling.

Publications: Printed

Access to staff: Contact by letter, by telephone, by fax and by e-mail. Appointment necessary.
Hours: Mon to Fri, 0930 to 1600

Access for disabled people: Parking provided, access to all public areas, toilet facilities

Founder member of: British Tyre Industry Federation; International Organization of Tyre Retreaders (BIPAVER); Retreading Division; tel: 01782 417777; fax: 01782 417766; e-mail: retreads@ukonline.co.uk; Tyre Industry Council

RETREAT ASSOCIATION (RA)

Kerridge House, 42 Woodside Close, Amersham, Buckinghamshire

Tel: 0149 443 3004
Fax: 0871 715 1917
E-mail: info@retreats.org.uk
Website: www.retreats.org.uk

Enquiries to: Director

Founded: 1989

Organisation type and purpose: Voluntary organisation, registered charity (charity number 328746). A federation of five member groups. Has 230 retreats and retreat houses in Britain and Ireland. Provides information to the public, and support and networking for organisers.

Subject coverage: Christian spirituality, spiritual direction.

Information services: Information and resources in connection with Christian retreats and spiritual direction.

Collection: Small specialised library on Christian spirituality

Publications: Printed
Order printed publications from: Order direct or online

Publications list: Available online and in print

Access to staff: Contact by letter, by telephone, by fax, by e-mail and via website. Appointment necessary.
Hours: 0930 to 1730

Access for disabled people: There is no access for disabled: the offices are at the top of a three-storey building with no lift

Member organisation of: Affiliates of the Retreat Association (non-denominational) (AFF); Association for Promoting Retreats (APR); Baptist Union Retreat Group (BURG); Catholic Network for Retreats & Spirituality (CNRS); Methodist Retreat & Spirituality Network (MRSN); United Reformed Church Retreats Group (URCG)

RETT UK

Langham House West, Mill Street, Luton, Bedfordshire LU1 2NA

Tel: 01582 798911
Fax: 01582 724129
E-mail: info@rettuk.org
Website: www.rettuk.org

Enquiries to: Support Team
Other contacts: Family Support Manager

Founded: 1985

Organisation type and purpose: Membership association (membership is by subscription), voluntary organisation, registered charity (charity number 1137820).

Subject coverage: Rett syndrome, treatment and care, research, social support.

Publications: Printed
Order printed publications from: Enquiries to main office on 01582 798910

Publications list: Available online and in print

Access to staff: Contact by letter, by telephone, by fax, by e-mail and in person. Appointment necessary.
Hours: Mon to Fri, 0900 to 1600

Access to building: *Hours:* Mon to Fri, 0900 to 1600

Access for disabled people: Ground floor office
Hours: Mon to Fri, 0900 to 1600

RETURNED VOLUNTEER ACTION (RVA)

76 Wentworth Street, London, E1 7SA

Tel: 020 7247 6406
E-mail: retvolact@lineone.net

Enquiries to: Membership Officer

Founded: 1963

Organisation type and purpose: Membership association.

Subject coverage: Advice and help for prospective and returned overseas volunteers, understanding of the causes of poverty and inequality, relationship between north and south.

Collection: Newsletters, annual reports, catalogues and other information from development-related UK groups and campaign organisations, as well as NGOs

Publications: Printed

Publications list: Available in print

Access to staff: Contact by letter and by e-mail. Appointment necessary.
Hours: By appointment
Special comments: Please phone first.

Links with: Action Village India; 76 Wentworth Street, London, E1 7SA; tel: 020 7247 6406; e-mail: info@actionvillageindia.org.uk; website: http://www.actionvillageindia.org.uk

REUTERS GROUP PLC

85 Fleet Street, London, EC4P 4AJ

Tel: 020 7250 1122
Fax: 020 7542 4064
Website: www.reuters.com

Enquiries to: Director Corporate Communications
Direct tel: 020 7542 4890
Other contacts: Group Archivist for information on Reuters history.

Founded: 1851

Organisation type and purpose: International organisation, service industry.

Subject coverage: Worldwide news coverage of general, political, cultural, sports, economic, financial and scientific matters and events; information and quotes on and from world's money, fixed-income, equity, commodity and energy markets.

Publications: Printed

Access to staff: Contact by letter, by telephone, by fax and by e-mail
Hours: Mon to Fri, 0900 to 1700

Access to building: No access other than to staff

RFCA GREATER LONDON

Formal name: Reserve Forces & Cadets Association for Greater London

Fulham House, 87 Fulham High Street, London, SW6 3JS

Tel: 0845 130 7888
E-mail: reception@gl.rfca.mod.uk
Website: www.reserve-forces-london.org.uk

Enquiries to: Secretary

Founded: 1908

Organisation type and purpose: National organisation, membership association (membership is by election or invitation), voluntary organisation.
Voluntary association, financed by central government through the Ministry of Defence.
To look after the interests of the Reserve Forces.

Subject coverage: Recruiting and housing of the Reserves Forces and Cadets in Greater London.

Access to staff: Contact by letter, by telephone and via website. Appointment necessary.
Hours: Mon to Thu, 0900 to 1300, 1400 to 1700; Fri, 0900 to 1300, 1400 to 1600

RHM TECHNOLOGY

Formal name: RHM Technology – a trading name of RHM Group Ltd

The Lord Rank Centre, Lincoln Road, High Wycombe, Buckinghamshire, HP12 3QR

Tel: 01494 526191
Fax: 01494 428080
Website: www.rhmtech.co.uk

Enquiries to: Commercial Manager
Direct tel: 01494 428153
Direct e-mail: david.scott@rhm.com

Founded: 1963

Organisation type and purpose: Service industry, consultancy.
Science, engineering and information services for the food industry.

Subject coverage: Food science and technology; cereal chemistry; baking; bread; flour milling, cake, fruit preserves; electron microscopy; microbial biochemistry; food analysis and microbiology; mycotoxin analysis; protein chemistry; process engineering; GM testing and analysis (quantitative).

Library catalogue: All or part available in-house

Access to staff: Appointment necessary.
Hours: Mon to Fri, 0900 to 1700

Research and engineering company within: Rank Hovis McDougall

RHODODENDRON, CAMELLIA AND MAGNOLIA GROUP OF THE RHS (The Rhododendron Group)

Botallick, Lanreath, Looe, PL13 2PF

Tel: 01503 220215
E-mail: patbucknell@btinternet.com
Website: www.rhodogroup.rhs.org

Enquiries to: Honorary Secretary

Organisation type and purpose:
International organisation, membership association (membership is by subscription), present number of members: 800.

Subject coverage: The propagation, preservation and cultivation of rhododendrons, camellias and magnolias. Group branch garden visits and lectures. Holidays and tours for Group members.

Non-library collection catalogue: All or part available online

Publications: Printed

Access to staff: Contact by letter, by telephone and by e-mail
Hours: Mon to Fri, 0900 to 1700

Parent body: Royal Horticultural Society; 80 Vincent Square, London, SW1P 2PE; tel: 020 7834 4333

RHONDDA CYNON TAFF COUNTY BOROUGH LIBRARIES (RCT CBC)

Tel: 01443 773204
Fax: 01443 777047
Website: www.rhondda-cynon-taff.gov.uk/libraries
Website: www.rhondda-cynon-taff.gov.uk/photos

Enquiries to: Principal Librarian
Direct tel: 01685 880060
Direct fax: 01685 881181
Direct e-mail: norma.d.jones@rhondda-cynon-taff.gov.uk

Organisation type and purpose: Local government body, public library.

Subject coverage: Local history of Rhondda-Cynon-Taff, music, general.

Library catalogue: All or part available online

Publications: Printed

Access to staff: Contact by letter, by telephone, by fax and by e-mail
Hours: Mon to Fri, 0900 to 1700

Admin Dept.: Penygraig Library; Tylacelyn Road, Penygraig, Rhondda

Other addresses: Aberdare Library (Principal Librarian); Green Street, Aberdare, CF44 7AG; tel: 01685 880050; fax: 01685 881181; Pontypridd Library (Area Librarian-South); Library Road, Pontypridd; tel: 01443 486850; fax: 01443 493258; The Education Centre (County Borough Librarian); Grawen Street, Porth, Rhondda; tel: 01443 687666; fax: 01443 680286; Treorchy Library; tel: 01443 773204

Parent body: Rhondda Cynon Taff County Borough Council; tel: 01443 687666; fax: 01443 680286

RHONDDA CYNON TAFF COUNTY BOROUGH LIBRARIES – ABERDARE

Central Library, Green Street, Aberdare, Mid Glamorgan, CF44 7AG

Tel: 01685 880050
Fax: 01685 881181
E-mail: aberdare.library@rhondda-cynon-taff.gov.uk
Website: www.rhondda-cynon-taff.gov.uk/libraries/index.htm

Enquiries to: County Borough Librarian

Organisation type and purpose: Local government body, public library.

Subject coverage: General, local history of the Cynon Valley.

Collection: W W Price Collection (local history)

Non-library collection catalogue: All or part available in-house

Library catalogue: All or part available online

Publications: Printed

Access to staff: Contact by letter, by telephone, by fax, by e-mail, in person and via website
Hours: Mon to Fri, 0900 to 1800; Sat, 0900 to 1300

Access for disabled people: Ramped entry; lift to Reference Department.

RHONDDA HERITAGE PARK

Lewis Merthyr Colliery, Coed Cae Road, Trehafod, Pontypridd, Rhondda Cynon Taff, CF37 2NP

Tel: 01443 682036
Fax: 01443 687420
E-mail: reception@rhonddaheritagepark.com
Website: www.rhonddaheritagepark.com

Enquiries to: County Borough Museums Officer, Rhondda Cynon Taff
Other contacts: Marketing Officer for promotion/public relations.

Founded: 1989

Organisation type and purpose: Local government body, museum, art gallery, historic building, house or site, suitable for ages: all. Children's play park, shop, restaurant. Conference facilities available. Tourist attraction.

Subject coverage: Heritage, mining. Black Gold includes three audiovisual shows telling the history of the Rhondda Valleys and mining. A guided tour with an ex-miner includes a visit to the Grade II listed pit head buildings and a trip to 'pit bottom' to experience life as a miner in the 1950s. A reconstructed village street and art gallery at the visitor centre.

Special visitor services: Guided tours, materials and/or activities for children.

Education services: Group education facilities, resources for Key Stages 1, 2, 3 and 4.

Services for disabled people: For hearing impaired.

Collection: Books, photographs, domestic artefacts, shop artefacts
Variety of mining machinery including:
Hand tools, colliers' tools, 1850–1950
Mine rescue, breathing apparatus, smoke helmets
Mining instruments, methonometers, hygrometers, dust sampling equipment, etc.
Large colliery machinery and engines, Lewis Merthyr winding engine, ventilation fans preserved in situ, 1880/1890

Non-library collection catalogue: All or part available in-house

Publications: Electronic and video

Access to staff: Contact by letter and by e-mail. Appointment necessary.
Hours: Mon to Fri, 0900 to 1700

Access to building: No prior appointment required
Hours: Daily 1000 to 1800. Closed 25 Dec to Jan 1 inclusive, and Mondays Oct to Easter

Access for disabled people: Parking provided, ramped entry, level entry, toilet facilities, lift. Access to most areas.

Parent body: Rhondda Cynon Taff County Borough Council; The Pavilions, Clydach Vale, CF40 2XX; tel: 01443 424000

RHS GARDEN HARLOW CARR

Formal name: The Royal Horticultural Society's Garden Harlow Carr

Crag Lane, Harrogate, North Yorkshire, HG3 1QB

Tel: 01423 565418
Fax: 01423 530663
E-mail: admin-harlowcarr@rhs.org.uk

Other contacts: Curatorial department for written enquiries on horticulture.

Founded: 1950

Organisation type and purpose:
Membership association (membership is by subscription), present number of members: 365,000, registered charity (charity number 222879), museum.
Educational charity.
Selects shrubs, trees and plants to discover their suitability for northern conditions.

Subject coverage: Gardening and horticulture, particularly relating to the conditions in the north of England.

Collection: Four important national plant collections – rheum (rhubarb), fuchsia sect. Quelusia (provisional collection), dryopteris and polypodium (ferns)

Publications: Printed

Access to staff: Contact by letter. Access for members only.
Hours: Mon to Fri, 0900 to 1700

Access for disabled people: Parking provided, level entry, toilet facilities

RHS LINDLEY LIBRARY (RHS)

Formal name: Royal Horticultural Society

80 Vincent Square, Westminster, London, SW1P 2PE

Tel: 020 7821 3000
Fax: 020 7630 6060
Website: www.rhs.org.uk/libraries
Website: www.rhs.org.uk

Enquiries to: Head of Library and Archives
Direct tel: 020 7821 3050
Direct fax: 020 7828 3022
Direct e-mail: library.london@rhs.org.uk

Founded: 1804

Organisation type and purpose: Learned society, professional body, registered charity, research organisation.

Subject coverage: Non-commercial horticulture and silviculture, all plants, trees and shrubs, both ornamental and culinary, plant pests and diseases, garden design, history of gardening, floras, botanical art, flower arranging, to a lesser extent books on systematic botany, agriculture and forestry.

Collection: Bunyard Collection of books on fruit (part of the Lindley Library)
Lindley Library (horticultural and botanical books from the 16th century to the present)
Art Collections – 25,000 original botanical drawings
Horticultural Taxonomy Collection (held at Lindley Library, Wisley)

Library catalogue: All or part available in-house

Publications: Printed
Order printed publications from: RHS Enterprises Ltd, RHS Garden, Wisley, nr Woking, Surrey, GU23 6QB; e-mail: mailorder@rhs.org.uk

Publications list: Available online

Access to staff: Contact by letter, by telephone, by fax, by e-mail and in person. Appointment necessary.
Hours: Mon to Fri, 1000 to 1700 excluding Bank Holidays

Access to building: No prior appointment required

Access for disabled people: Ramped entry

Administers: Harlow Carr Garden Library; RHS Garden Harlow Carr, Harrogate, Yorkshire; Hyde Hall Garden Library; RHS Garden Hyde Hall, Rettendon, Essex; Rosemoor Garden Library; RHS Garden Rosemoor, Great Torrington, Devon, EX38 8PH

Also at: RHS Lindley Library, RHS Garden Wisley; Woking, Surrey, GU23 6QB; tel: 01483 212428; e-mail: library.wisley@rhs.org.uk; website: http://www.rhs.org.uk/libraries

RICABILITY (RICA)

Formal name: Research Institute for Consumer Affairs

Unit G03, The Wenlock, 50–52 Wharf Road, London, N1 7EU

Tel: 020 7427 2460; textphone no. 020 7427 2469
Fax: 020 7427 2468
E-mail: mail@ricability.org.uk
Website: www.ricability.org.uk
Website: www.ricability-digitaltv.org.uk
Website: www.product-reviews.org.uk

Enquiries to: Administrator

Founded: 1991

Organisation type and purpose: Voluntary organisation, registered charity (charity number 1007726), research organisation.
Independent charity set up by the Consumers' Association. Ricability is the trading name of the Research Institute for Consumer Affairs.
To carry out research and publish unbiased information on products and services used by consumers who are older or disabled.

Subject coverage: Consumer information, disabled people, older people, carers, disability equipment, disability services, research, information, product testing and assessment, digital television, digital switchover, product reviews, online product reviews, assistive technology, car adaptations.

Publications: Printed, and electronic and video

Publications list: Available online and in print

Access to staff: Contact by letter, by telephone, by fax, by e-mail and via website
Hours: Mon to Fri, 0900 to 1700

Access for disabled people: Access to all public areas, fully adapted toilet
Special comments: Fully accessible and accessible information: tape, braille and large print.

RICARDO UK

Shoreham Technical Centre, Shoreham-by-Sea, West Sussex, BN43 5FG

Tel: 01273 455611
Fax: 01273 464124
E-mail: infoservices@ricardo.com
Website: www.ricardo.com

Enquiries to: Information Manager
Direct tel: 01273 794230
Direct fax: 01273 794555

Founded: 1915

Organisation type and purpose: Consultancy.

Subject coverage: Internal combustion engineering research, diesel engines, petrol engines, automotive engineering, noise reduction, combustion, exhaust emissions, fuel technology, lubrication, transmissions, finite element stress analysis, computational fluid dynamics, design, vehicle systems, control and electronics.

Library catalogue: All or part available online

Publications: Printed, and electronic and video

Publications list: Available online and in print

Access to staff: Contact by letter, by telephone, by fax, by e-mail and via website. All charged.
Hours: Mon to Fri, 0900 to 1700

Access to building: No access other than to staff

Parent body: Ricardo Group plc; Shoreham Technical Centre, Shoreham-by-Sea, West Sussex, BN43 5FG; tel: 01273 455611; fax: 01273 464124

RICHARD III SOCIETY

4 Oakley Street, Chelsea, London, SW3 5NN

Tel: 01689 823569
E-mail: information@richardiii.net
Website: www.richardiii.net
Website: www.r3.org

Enquiries to: Secretary
Other contacts: Research Officer for research-related queries.

Founded: 1924

Organisation type and purpose: Learned society.

Subject coverage: Life and times of King Richard III and the social and political history of late 15th-century England.

Collection: Richard III Society Library

Library catalogue: All or part available in-house

Publications: Printed
Order printed publications from: Membership Dept (also Sales Dept), Time Travellers Limited
Sales Liaison Officer, 42 Pewsey Vale, Forest Park, Bracknell, RG12 9YA

Publications list: Available online and in print

Access to staff: Contact by letter, by telephone and by e-mail
Hours: Mon to Fri, 0900 to 1700

RICHARD JEFFERIES SOCIETY

Pear Tree Cottage, Longcot, Oxfordshire, SN7 7SS

Tel: 01793 783040
E-mail: info@richardjefferiessociety.co.uk
Website: richardjefferiessociety.co.uk

Enquiries to: Honorary Secretary

Founded: 1950

continued overleaf

Organisation type and purpose: Learned society (membership is by subscription), present number of members: 260, registered charity (charity number 1042838).
Literary society. Manages the Richard Jefferies Museum at Coate, near Swindon.

Subject coverage: Life, writings and associations of Richard Jefferies (1848–1887), whose principal subjects are: nature, the Victorian rural scene, agriculture, late Victorian London, gamekeeping and poaching, spiritual philosophy.

Collection: Library of first and early editions of Jefferies' works, studies and biographies, unpublished essays and letters issued posthumously, photographs, paintings, family memorabilia

Non-library collection catalogue: All or part available online, in-house and in print

Library catalogue: All or part available in-house

Publications: Printed, and electronic and video
Order printed publications from: website: http://richardjefferiessociety.co.uk

Publications list: Available online

Access to staff: Contact by letter, by telephone, by e-mail and via website
Hours: Mon to Sun, 0900 to 1600

Access to building: No prior appointment required
Hours: Richard Jefferies Museum at Coate, Swindon: Wed, 2nd of month, 1000 to 1600; Every Sun, May to Sep, 1400 to 1700
Special comments: Other times by appointment.

Access for disabled people: Museum on 3 floors – no access to 1st and 2nd floors for wheelchairs

Affiliated to: Alliance of Literary Societies; website: http://www.allianceofliterarysocieties.org.uk

RICHMOND UPON THAMES COLLEGE (RuTC)

The Library, Egerton Road, Twickenham, Middlesex, TW2 7SJ

Tel: 020 8607 8356
Fax: 020 8607 8360
Website: www.richmond-utcoll.ac.uk

Enquiries to: Learning Resources Manager

Founded: 1977

Subject coverage: Humanities, social sciences, literature, science, technology, education, business studies, art and design.

Non-library collection catalogue: All or part available online

Access to staff: Contact by letter, by telephone and via website. Appointment necessary.
Hours: Mon to Fri, 0900 to 1700

Access to building: Prior appointment required

Access for disabled people: Level entry, toilet facilities

RICHMOND UPON THAMES LIBRARIES AND INFORMATION SERVICES

Education and Childen's Services, Regal House, London Road, Twickenham, Middlesex, TW1 3QB

Tel: 020 8831 6136
Fax: 020 8891 7904
E-mail: libraries@richmond.gov.uk
Website: www.richmond.gov.uk

Enquiries to: Head of Libraries and Culture
Other contacts: Assistant Head of Library and Information Services

Organisation type and purpose: Local government body, public library.

Subject coverage: General.

Collection: Alexander Pope Collection within the Twickenham local collection (Twickenham District Library)
Douglas Sladen Collection of correspondence and printed ephemera relating to his life and interests
George Vancouver Collection
Hansard, House of Commons and House of Lords debates
Other debates and historic journals
Official Journal of the EC
Richmond upon Thames and Barnes local collections
Sir Richard Burton Collection of books and other items
Telephone Directories (microfiche)
Times (microfilm)
Various statistical sources including many OPCS monitors, Annual abstract of Stats, Monthly digest of Stats, Regional Trends, Social Trends, EUROSTAT, United Nations Statistical Year-Book, OECD reports on countries, Europa World Year Book, EC publications, please note most of these would be held at Central Reference Library only

Library catalogue: All or part available online

Publications: Printed, and electronic and video

Access to staff: Contact by letter, by telephone, by fax, by e-mail, in person and via website
Hours: Mon to Fri, 0900 to 1700

District libraries at: East Sheen; Richmond; Teddington; Twickenham

Member of: SHARE

Other addresses: Reference and Information Services; Old Town Hall, Whittaker Avenue, Richmond-upon-Thames, Surrey, TW9 1TP; tel: 020 8940 5529; fax: 020 8940 6899; e-mail: reference.services@richmond.gov.uk

RICHMOND: THE AMERICAN INTERNATIONAL UNIVERSITY IN LONDON

Queen's Road, Richmond-upon-Thames, Surrey, TW10 6JP

Tel: 020 8332 8210
Fax: 020 8332 3050
E-mail: library@richmond.ac.uk
Website: www.richmond.ac.uk

Enquiries to: University librarian
Direct tel: 020 8332 8279
Direct e-mail: trewf@richmond.ac.uk

Founded: 1972

Organisation type and purpose: University library.
Independent American international university, for liberal arts and professional studies.

Subject coverage: Business administration, economics, anthropology and sociology, international business, political science, international relations, psychology, women's studies, art history, studio art, theatre arts, British studies, English literature, history, French, computer science, mathematical sciences, communications, environmental studies, modern languages, philosophy and religion, systems engineering and management.

Collection: N J Cann Bequest (history of art)
Harvard Core Collection (gift of Sir Cyril Taylor and Roger O Walther)
Asa Briggs Collection (gift of Lord Asa Briggs)

Non-library collection catalogue: All or part available online

Library catalogue: All or part available online

Access to staff: Appointment necessary.
Hours: Mon to Fri, 0900 to 1700

Access for disabled people: *Hours:* Mon to Thu, 0900 to 2100; Fri, 0900 to 1700; Sat, closed; Sun, 1300 to 2300

Other addresses: Richmond: the American International University in London; 1 Saint Alban's Grove, Kensington, London, W8 5PN; tel: 020 7368 8510

RIDER HAGGARD SOCIETY (RHS)

27 Deneholm, Whitley Bay, Tyne and Wear, NE25 9AU

Tel: 0191 252 4516
E-mail: rb27allen@blueyonder.co.uk
Website: www.riderhaggardsociety.org.uk

Enquiries to: Honorary Secretary

Founded: 1984

Organisation type and purpose: International organisation, learned society (membership is by subscription), present number of members: 106.

Subject coverage: Works by the author Rider Haggard and about him, his family and any relevant ephemera.

Information services: On request.

Special visitor services: On request.

Education services: Research help.

Non-library collection catalogue: All or part available online and in print

Publications: Printed
Order printed publications from: Postal address

Publications list: Available online and in print

Access to staff: Contact by letter, by telephone, by e-mail, in person and via website. Appointment necessary.
Hours: Any time

Links with: Alliance of Literary Societies (ALS)

RILEY MOTOR CLUB LIMITED

Treelands, 127 Penn Road, Wolverhampton, West Midlands, WV3 0DU

Tel: 01902 773197

Enquiries to: Honorary Secretary

Founded: 1925

Organisation type and purpose: Membership association.

Subject coverage: History of Riley cars, technical information, source of spares, restoration and maintenance.

Access to staff: Contact by letter and by telephone
Hours: Mon to Fri, 0900 to 1700

RILEY REGISTER

56 Cheltenham Road, Bishops Cleeve, Cheltenham, Gloucestershire, GL52 8LY

Tel: 01242 673598
Website: www.rileyregister.com

Enquiries to: Membership Secretary

Founded: 1954

Organisation type and purpose: Membership association (membership is by subscription).

Subject coverage: One make car club for Rileys up to 1940; sources of spares.

Publications: Printed

Access to staff: Contact by letter and by telephone
Hours: Mon to Fri, 0900 to 1700

RILEY RM CLUB

509 Preston New Road, Blackburn, Lancashire, BB2 7AN

Tel: 01254 265789
E-mail: gensec@rileyrmclub.org.uk
Website: www.rileyrmclub.org.uk

Enquiries to: General Secretary

Founded: 1969

Organisation type and purpose: International organisation, membership association (membership is by subscription).

Subject coverage: Preservation of RM Rileys, spares, technical information and social activities.

Collection: Archives covering the majority of cars still in existence
Magazines and technical literature
Spare parts for members' cars

Publications: Printed

Access to staff: Contact by letter, by telephone and by e-mail
Hours: 0900 to 2100

RIPON CATHEDRAL LIBRARY

Ripon Cathedral, Ripon, North Yorkshire, HG4 1QR

Tel: 01765 603462

Enquiries to: Canon Librarian

Subject coverage: Church history; New Testament; personalities and leaders within the church (mainly 20th century); prayer and spirituality.

Collection: Higgins Library
Library of Canon A Stephenson
Most of the Cathedral's special collections are housed in the Brotherton Library, Leeds University

Access to staff: Appointment necessary.
Hours: Mon to Fri, 0900 to 1700

RIPON HISTORICAL SOCIETY

Stone Cottage, Wath-in-Nidderdale, Pateley Bridge, North Yorkshire, HG3 5PL

E-mail: gdl@globalnet.co.uk
Website: www.yorksgen.org.uk

Enquiries to: Honorary Secretary

Founded: 1986

Organisation type and purpose: Membership association (membership is by subscription), present number of members: 343+, voluntary organisation.

Subject coverage: The history of the City of Ripon and the surrounding districts, its heritage and the preservation and protection of items of historic or public interest, family history of the area.

Collection: Microfilms of many of the records of Ripon (held in six Record Offices) are available in the new Ripon County Library

Publications: Printed, and microform publications
Order printed publications from: Publications Officer, Ripon Historical Society
Aldergarth, Galphay, Ripon, North Yorkshire, HG4 3NJ, tel: 01765 658602, e-mail: hebden1name@btopenworld.com

Publications list: Available in print

Access to staff: Contact by letter and by e-mail
Hours: Mon to Fri, 0900 to 1700

Family history group: Ripon, Harrogate & District Family History Group; 18 Aspin Drive, Knaresborough, North Yorkshire, HG5 8HH

Membership Secretary: Ripon Historical Society; Downe, Baldersby, Thirsk, North Yorkshire, YO7 4PP; e-mail: dolonic@cs.com

RNIB NATIONAL LIBRARY SERVICE

Far Cromwell Road, Bredbury, Stockport, Cheshire, SK6 2SG

Tel: 0303 123 9999
Fax: 0161 355 2098
E-mail: library@rnib.org.uk
Website: www.rnib.org.uk/library

Enquiries to: Marketing Communications Officer
Direct tel: 0161 355 2080
Direct e-mail: megan.gilks@nlbuk.org

Founded: 1882; created by the merger of National Library for the Blind and RNIB (year of change 2007); formerly called National Library for the Blind

Organisation type and purpose: National organisation (membership is by subscription), voluntary organisation, registered charity (charity number 226227), consultancy.
A gateway to free comprehensive library services for those who cannot read print and their intermediaries. Its aim is to enable all visually impaired people to have the same access to library services as sighted people.

Subject coverage: Library service to blind and partially sighted readers, including a range of electronic library services via the internet.

Collection: Collection of 40,000 titles in Braille including fiction and non-fiction, books for younger readers (aged eight or over) and Braille sheet music.
Giant Print Library (books in 24pt type) for children, young people and adults.
Small collection of large print books covering classics and standard titles.
Over 17,000 titles in the Talking Book service.

Non-library collection catalogue: All or part available online

Library catalogue: All or part available online and in print

Publications: Printed, and electronic and video
Order printed publications from: Helpline: 0303 123 9999

Publications list: Available online

Access to staff: Contact by letter, by telephone, by fax, by e-mail and via website. Appointment necessary.
Hours: Mon to Fri, 0845 to 1800; Sat, 0900 to 1600

Access to building: Prior appointment required

Access for disabled people: Parking provided, ramped entry, access to all public areas

Links with: IFLA

RNID

19–23 Featherstone Street, London, EC1Y 8SL

Tel: 0808 808 0123 (Textphone 0808 808 9000)
Fax: 020 7296 8199
E-mail: informationline@mid.org.uk
Website: www.rnid.org.uk

Enquiries to: Information Line
Direct tel: 0808 808 0123
Direct e-mail: informationline@rnid.org.uk

Founded: 1911

Organisation type and purpose: Registered charity (charity number 207720), working to change the world for the UK's 9 million deaf and hard of hearing people. Does this with the help of members, by campaigning and lobbying, raising awareness of deafness and hearing loss, providing services and through social, medical and technical research.

Subject coverage: Deafness, hearing loss, hearing, tinnitus, communication support, BSL, sign language, lip-reading, campaigns, information, services, and research into deafness and hearing loss.

continued overleaf

Collection: One of Europe's largest library collections of materials on all aspects of deafness and hearing research
Rare pre-1800 book collection on deafness

Library catalogue: All or part available in-house

Publications: Printed

Publications list: Available online and in print

Access to staff: Contact by letter, by telephone, by fax, by e-mail and via website. Appointment necessary.
Hours: Mon to Fri, 0900 to 1700

Access to building: Unable to provide a drop-in service – please contact the Information Line before visiting
Hours: 0900 to 1700

Access for disabled people: Toilet facilities, lifts and BSL interpreters
Special comments: Lift from pavement level

Other addresses: RNID Products; 1 Haddonbrook Business Centre, Fallodan Road, Orton Southgate, Peterborough, PE2 6YX; tel: 01733 232607 (textphone 01733 238020); fax: 01733 361161; website: www.rnid.org.uk/shop
RNID Typetalk; PO Box 284, Liverpool, L69 3UZ; tel: 18001 0800 500 888 (textphone users), 0800 7311 888 (hearing people); fax: 0151 709 8119; website: http://www.rnid-typetalk.org.uk

RNID SCOTLAND

Formal name: Royal National Institute for Deaf and Hard of Hearing People (Scotland)

Empire House, 131 West Nile Street, Glasgow, G1 2RX

Tel: 0141 341 5330; 0141 341 5347 (minicom)
Fax: 0141 354 0176
E-mail: RNIDScotland@rnid.org.uk
Website: www.rnid.org.uk

Enquiries to: Regional Communications Officer

Founded: 1966

Organisation type and purpose: Membership association (membership is by subscription), registered charity (charity number 207720).

Subject coverage: Information, training, specialist telephone services, assistive devices, communication services unit, employment training and skills service.

Non-library collection catalogue: All or part available online

Publications: Printed

Publications list: Available online and in print

Access to staff: Contact by letter, by telephone, by fax, by e-mail, in person and via website. Appointment necessary.
Hours: Mon to Fri, 0900 to 1700

Access for disabled people: Toilet facilities, lift

Head Office: Royal National Institute for Deaf and Hard of Hearing People; 19–23 Featherstone Street, London, EC1Y 8SL; tel: 020 7296 8000; textphone 0808 808 0123 and 0808 808 9000; fax: 020 7296 8199; e-mail: helpline@rnid.org.uk

ROAD OPERATORS SAFETY COUNCIL (ROSCO)

Osborn House, 20 High Street South, Olney, Bucks, MK46 4AA

Tel: 01234 714420
E-mail: admin@rosco-uk.org
Website: www.rosco.org.uk

Enquiries to: Executive Officer

Founded: 1955

Subject coverage: Road safety in the bus and coach industry, accidents and safe driving.

Publications: Printed

Access to staff: Contact by letter, by telephone and by fax
Hours: Mon to Fri, 0900 to 1700

ROADPEACE

Shakespeare Business Centre, 245A Coldharbour Lane, London, SW9 8RR

Tel: 020 7733 1603 (office); 0845 4500 355 (helpline)
E-mail: info@roadpeace.org
Website: www.roadpeace.org

Enquiries to: Charity Coordinator

Founded: 1992

Organisation type and purpose: Membership association (charity number 1087192).

Subject coverage: People bereaved or injured by road crash.

Information services: Emotional and practical support for those bereaved or injured in a road crash.

Access to staff: Contact by letter, by telephone, by e-mail and via website
Hours: Mon to Fri, 0900 to 1700

ROBENS CENTRE FOR OCCUPATIONAL HEALTH & SAFETY

University of Surrey, 3–4 Huxley Road, Surrey Research Park, Guildford, Surrey, GU2 7RE

Tel: 01483 686690
Fax: 01483 686691
E-mail: cohs@surrey.ac.uk
Website: www.surrey.ac.uk/Robens/rbhome.html

Enquiries to: Administrator

Founded: 1978

Organisation type and purpose: University department or institute, consultancy, research organisation.

Subject coverage: Toxicology, occupational health and hygiene, environmental health, microbiology, analytical chemistry, psychology, ergonomics, human physiology, epidemiology and overseas development.

Publications: Printed

Publications list: Available in print

Access to staff: Contact by letter, by fax and by e-mail
Hours: Mon to Fri, 0900 to 1700

Access for disabled people: Parking provided

ROBERT GORDON UNIVERSITY – GEORGINA SCOTT SUTHERLAND LIBRARY

Garthdee Road, Garthdee, Aberdeen, AB10 7QE

Tel: 01224 263450
Fax: 01224 263460
E-mail: library@rgu.ac.uk
Website: www.rgu.ac.uk/library
Website: www.rgu.ac.uk/library/service/special.htm

Enquiries to: Director of Knowledge and Information Services
Direct tel: 01224 263452
Direct fax: 01224 263455

Organisation type and purpose: University library.

Subject coverage: Applied science, architecture, art, business management, computer science, engineering (mechanical, electrical, offshore), food and nutrition, health, librarianship, information studies, mathematics, nursing, pharmacy, public administration, social studies, surveying, law, physiotherapy, occupational therapy, radiography, European information, tourism.

Collection: Art and architecture antiquarian collection

Library catalogue: All or part available online

Access to staff: Contact by letter, by telephone, by fax, by e-mail, in person and via website
Hours: Details of opening hours during term time and vacations (for the Georgina Scott Sutherland Library and the St Andrew Street Library) are available online

Access for disabled people: Parking provided, ramped entry, level entry, toilet facilities
Special comments: Details of staff contacts and assistance available can be found online.

ROBERT GORDON UNIVERSITY – SCHOOL OF INFORMATION AND MEDIA

Faculty of Management Building, Garthdee Road, Aberdeen, AB10 7QE

Tel: 01224 263900
Fax: 01224 263553
E-mail: sim@rgu.ac.uk
Website: www.rgu.com
Website: www.rgu.ac.uk

Enquiries to: Head of School
Direct tel: 01224 263901

Founded: 1751

Organisation type and purpose: University department or institute, training organisation, consultancy, research organisation.
The School undertakes teaching and research, consultancy and training in the fields of library and information sciences, publishing, corporate and technical communications, and modern languages.

Publications: Printed, and electronic and video

Access to staff: Contact by letter, by telephone, by fax and by e-mail. Appointment necessary. All charged.
Hours: Mon to Fri, 0900 to 1700

Access to building: No access other than to staff
Special comments: See separate entry for the University's library.

ROBINSON COLLEGE LIBRARY

Grange Road, Cambridge, CB3 9AN

Tel: 01223 339100

Enquiries to: Librarian
Direct tel: 01223 339124

Organisation type and purpose: University department or institute.
College Library of the University of Cambridge.

Subject coverage: General, for undergraduate teaching.

Access to staff: Access for members only.
Hours: Mon to Fri, 0900 to 1700

ROCHDALE LIBRARIES

Wheatsheaf Library, Baillie Street, Rochdale, Lancashire, OL16 1JZ

Tel: 01706 924900
Fax: 01706 924992
E-mail: library.service@rochdale.gov.uk
Website: www.rochdale.gov.uk/

Enquiries to: Reference and Information Development Librarian
Direct fax: 01706 924934

Organisation type and purpose: Local government body, public library.

Subject coverage: General, local history, international collection on co-operation.

Collection: Collection of books on the co-operative movement and co-operation (700 items)
Tim Bobbin (John Collier) collection

Non-library collection catalogue: All or part available online and in-house

Library catalogue: All or part available online and in-house

Publications: Printed

Access to staff: Contact by letter, by telephone, by fax, by e-mail and in person
Hours: Mon, 0930 to 1930; Tue to Fri, 0930 to 1730; Sat, 0930 to 1700

Parent body: Rochdale Metropolitan Borough Council

ROCHFORD DISTRICT COUNCIL

Council Offices, South Street, Rochford, Essex, SS4 1BW

Tel: 01702 546366
Fax: 01702 545737
E-mail: information@rochford.gov.uk

Enquiries to: Civic and Public Relations Officer
Direct tel: 01702 318144
Direct fax: 01702 318161
Direct e-mail: helen-collins@rochford.gov.uk

Founded: 1974

Organisation type and purpose: Local government body.

Publications: Printed

Access to staff: Contact by letter, by telephone, by fax, by e-mail and in person
Hours: Mon to Thu, 0830 to 1700; Fri, 0830 to 1630

ROCKEFELLER MEDICAL LIBRARY

UCL Institute of Neurology, The National Hospital, 23 Queen Square, London, WC1N 3BG

Tel: 020 7829 8709
E-mail: library@ion.ucl.ac.uk
Website: www.ion.ucl.ac.uk/library

Enquiries to: Librarian

Founded: 1950

Organisation type and purpose: University department or institute.
Postgraduate medical institute.

Subject coverage: Clinical neurology and allied fields, historical neurology, neurosurgery and neuroscience.

Collection: Historical neurology
Queen Square Collection (of staff publications)
Current Neurology, Neurosurgery and Neuroscience books, journals and multimedia

Non-library collection catalogue: All or part available online

Library catalogue: All or part available online

Access to staff: Contact by letter, by telephone, by e-mail, in person and via website. Appointment necessary.
Hours: Mon to Fri, 0900 to 1700

Access to building: Prior appointment required

Links with: National Hospital for Neurology and Neurosurgery; University of London

Parent body: University College London

RODBASTON COLLEGE

Rodbaston, Penkridge, Stafford, ST19 5PH

Tel: 01785 712209
Fax: 01785 715701
E-mail: enquiries@southstaffs.ac.uk

Enquiries to: Reception

Organisation type and purpose: Suitable for ages: 16+.
College for training and education in the land-based industries.

Subject coverage: Courses available in areas of study for the land-based industries.

Access to staff: Contact by letter
Hours: Mon to Fri, 0900 to 1700

ROFFEY PARK INSTITUTE

Forest Road, Horsham, West Sussex, RH12 4TB

Tel: 01293 851644
Fax: 01293 851565
E-mail: info@roffeypark.com
Website: www.roffeypark.com

Enquiries to: Manager, Learning Resource Centre
Direct tel: 01293 854052
Direct e-mail: lrc@roffeypark.com

Founded: 1946

Organisation type and purpose: Registered charity (charity number 254591), training organisation, consultancy.
Independent management education institute.

Subject coverage: Manager development, interpersonal relationships, developing the developers, personal effectiveness, assessment centres, self-managed learning, teamwork, organisational and leadership development, human resources.

Library catalogue: All or part available online and in print

Publications: Printed, and electronic and video
Order printed publications from: Marketing Department

Publications list: Available online

Access to staff: Contact by letter, by telephone, by e-mail, in person and via website. Appointment necessary. Access for members only. Non-members charged.

Access to building: Only when Roffey Park is open, and only to registered course participants.
Hours: Mon to Fri, 0900 to 1700
Special comments: Roffey Park course participants only

Access for disabled people: Available to course participants

ROLLS-ROYCE ENTHUSIASTS' CLUB (RREC Limited)

The Hunt House, High Street, Paulerspury, Towcester, Northamptonshire, NN12 7NA

Tel: 01327 811788
Fax: 01327 811797
E-mail: admin@rrec.org.uk
Website: www.rrec.org.uk

Enquiries to: General Secretary

Founded: 1957

Organisation type and purpose: International organisation, membership association (membership is by subscription), present number of members: 9,800.

Subject coverage: Rolls-Royce and Bentley archives containing car build records from 1904 onwards.

Publications: Printed

Access to staff: Contact by letter, by telephone, by fax and by e-mail. Appointment necessary.
Hours: Mon to Fri, 0900 to 1700

ROLLS-ROYCE PLC

Library Services, Rolls-Royce plc, PO Box 31, Victory Road, Derby, DE24 8BJ

Tel: 01332 242424
Fax: 01332 247886

Enquiries to: Technical Librarian
Direct tel: 01332 248277

continued overleaf

Organisation type and purpose: Manufacturing industry.

Subject coverage: Gas turbines, aerospace, aerodynamics, mechanical engineering, materials, fluid mechanics, jet propulsion, aero engines.

Publications: Printed

Access to staff: Contact by letter, by telephone and by fax
Hours: Mon to Fri, 0800 to 1600

ROMANIAN CULTURAL CENTRE

8th Floor, 54–62 Regent Street, London, W1B 5RE

Tel: 020 7439 4052
Fax: 020 7437 5908
E-mail: mail@romanianculturalcentre.org.uk
Website: www.romanianculturalcentre.org.uk

Organisation type and purpose: An independent association which promotes Romanian cultural programmes and acts as a focus for the Romanian community in Britain.

Subject coverage: Romanian culture.

ROMANY AND TRAVELLER FAMILY HISTORY SOCIETY (RTFHS)

c/o Ms. Margaret Montgomery (Secretary), 7 Park Rise, Northchurch, Berkhamsted, Hertfordshire, HP4 3RT

Website: www.rtfhs.org.uk

Organisation type and purpose: A non-political non-profit self-help group, with membership by subscription.

Subject coverage: Romany and traveller family history.

Publications: Printed

ROSE BRUFORD COLLEGE

Lamorbey Park, Sidcup, Kent, DA15 9DF

Tel: 020 8308 2600
Fax: 020 8308 0542
E-mail: enquiries@bruford.ac.uk
Website: www.bruford.ac.uk

Enquiries to: Librarian
Direct tel: 020 8308 2626

Founded: 1950

Organisation type and purpose: A university sector institution.

Subject coverage: Theatre, literature, drama, music.

Library catalogue: All or part available in-house

Publications: Printed

Access to staff: Contact by letter, by telephone, by fax, by e-mail and in person. Appointment necessary.
Hours: Mon to Fri, 0900 to 1700

Access to building: By appointment
Hours: Mon to Fri, 0900 to 1700

Access for disabled people: By appointment
Hours: Mon to Fri, 0900 to 1700

ROSKILL INFORMATION SERVICES LIMITED

54 Russell Road, London SW19 1QL

Tel: 020 8417 0087
Fax: 020 8417 1308
E-mail: info@roskill.co.uk
Website: www.roskill.com

Enquiries to: Information Officer
Other contacts: General Manager

Founded: 1930

Organisation type and purpose: Consultancy, publishing house.

Subject coverage: Publishes reports on the markets for metals and minerals, covering production, consumption, prices of, and trade in, the materials covered; end-use materials covered include plastics, paints and pigments, paper and pulp.

Trade and statistical information: Production and consumption information on metals and minerals, e.g. base minerals, precious metals, industrial minerals and ferroalloys.
Statistical information on plastics, paper and pulp, paints and pigments, filler materials, etc

Library catalogue: All or part available in-house

Publications: Printed

Publications list: Available online and in print

Access to staff: Contact by letter, by telephone, by fax, by e-mail and via website. Appointment necessary.
Hours: Mon to Fri, 0800 to 1700

Access to building: No prior appointment required

Affiliated to: Roskill Consulting Group

Parent body: Roskill Information Services Limited

ROSPA ADVANCED DRIVERS AND RIDERS (RoADAR)

Edgbaston Park, 353 Bristol Road, Edgbaston, Birmingham, B5 7ST

Tel: 0121 248 2000
Fax: 0121 248 2001
E-mail: mrae@rospa.com
Website: www.roadar.org

Enquiries to: Administrator
Direct tel: 0121 248 2099

Organisation type and purpose: Membership association (membership is by subscription, qualification), registered charity (charity number 207823).

Subject coverage: Advanced driving; advanced motorcycling; tests and courses; road safety.

Library catalogue: All or part available in-house

Publications: Printed, and electronic and video
Order printed publications from: Customer Support
Order electronic and video publications from: jbartlett@rospa.com

Publications list: Available online and in print

Access to staff: Contact by letter, by telephone, by fax and by e-mail
Hours: Mon to Fri, 0900 to 1700

Access to building: Prior appointment required
Hours: Mon to Fri, 0900 to 1700

Access for disabled people: Toilet facilities

Constituent part of: Royal Society for the Prevention of Accidents; tel: 0121 248 2000; fax: 0121 248 2001; e-mail: help@rospa.co.uk; website: http://www.rospa.com

ROSPA DRIVER AND FLEET SOLUTIONS (RoSPA)

Formal name: Royal Society for the Prevention of Accidents

Edgbaston Park, 353 Bristol Road, Edgbaston, Birmingham, B5 7ST

Tel: 0121 248 2233
Fax: 0121 248 2050
E-mail: sales@rospa.co.uk

Enquiries to: Manager
Direct tel: 0121 248 2037
Direct e-mail: halcock@rospa.co.uk

Organisation type and purpose: National organisation, professional body, registered charity (charity number 207823), training organisation, consultancy, research organisation, publishing house. Providing workplace safety and Driver and Fleet Solutions.
RoSPA's purpose is to enhance the quality of life by exercising a powerful influence for accident prevention.

Subject coverage: Training operation in all aspects of defensive driving for companies.

Collection: General Road Safety/Driving – books, documents and workplace safety.

Non-library collection catalogue: All or part available in-house

Library catalogue: All or part available in-house

Publications list: Available in print

Access to staff: Contact by letter, by telephone, by fax, by e-mail, in person and via website. Appointment necessary. All charged.
Hours: Mon to Fri, 0900 to 1700

Access to building: No prior appointment required
Hours: Mon to Fri, 0900 to 1700
Special comments: Library available for reference for members only.

Also at: RoSPA Northern Ireland; Nella House, 4 Dargan Crescent, Belfast, BT3 9JP; tel: 028 9050 1160/0870 777 2176; fax: 028 9050 1164/0870 777 2186; RoSPA Scotland; Livingstone House, 43 Discovery Terrace, Heriot-Watt University Research Park, Edinburgh, EH14 4AP; tel: 0131 449 9378; fax: 0131 449 9379; RoSPA Wales; 7 Cleeve House, Lambourne Crescent, Cardiff, CF14 5GP; tel: 029 2025 0600/0870 777 2180; fax: 029 2025 0601/0870 777 2181

ROSPA NATIONAL SAFE DRIVING AWARDS (NSDA)

28 Calthorpe Road, Edgbaston, Birmingham B15 1RP

Tel: 0121 248 2000
Fax: 0121 248 2001
E-mail: enquiries@rospa.com
Website: www.rospa.com

Enquiries to: Administrator
Direct tel: 0121 248 2106
Direct e-mail: dgrady@rospa.com

Organisation type and purpose: Voluntary organisation.

Subject coverage: Safe driving.

Publications: Printed

Access to staff: Contact by letter, by telephone and by fax
Hours: Mon to Fri, 0900 to 1700

Constituent part of: Driver and Fleet Solutions – RoSPA

ROTARY INTERNATIONAL IN GREAT BRITAIN AND IRELAND (RIBI)

Kinwarton Road, Alcester, Warwickshire, B49 6BP

Tel: 01789 765411
Fax: 01789 765570
E-mail: secretary@ribi.org
Website: www.rotary-ribi.org

Enquiries to: Secretary; CEO
Other contacts: The President

Founded: 1914

Organisation type and purpose: Membership association.
For charitable, benevolent and philanthropic purposes.

Subject coverage: Service to the local, national and international communities through projects, ideas and physical assistance, leading to greater international understanding; scholarships and youth exchanges in other countries; ethics in business and professions; the ideal of service.

Publications: Printed, and electronic and video

Access to staff: Contact by letter, by fax, by e-mail and via website
Hours: Mon to Fri, 0900 to 1700

Access for disabled people: Parking provided, ramped entry, toilet facilities

Parent body: Rotary International; One Rotary Center, 1560 Sherman Avenue, Evanston, Illinois, 60201, USA; tel: 00 1 847 866 3000; fax: 00 1 847 328 8554

ROTARY OWNERS' CLUB (ROC)

Dunbar, Ingatestone Road, Highwood, Chelmsford, Essex, CM1 3QU

E-mail: rotaryoc@aol.com
Website: www.rotaryownersclub.co.uk

Enquiries to: Secretary

Founded: 1982

Organisation type and purpose: Membership association (membership is by subscription).

Subject coverage: To encourage the ownership, use of and knowledge relating to the Wankel rotary engine, in particular its application in powered two-wheelers. Information is pooled on the maintenance of such motorcycles; a register is being compiled of all existing machines.

Collection: Copies of owners' manuals, handbook and parts lists available to members.
Discounted spares (oil, spark plugs, batteries, etc.) available to members.

Publications: Printed

Access to staff: Contact by letter and by e-mail
Hours: Mon to Fri, 0900 to 1700

ROTHAMSTED RESEARCH

Harpenden, Hertfordshire, AL5 2JQ

Tel: 01582 763133
Fax: 01582 760981
Website: www.rothamsted.ac.uk

Enquiries to: Librarian
Direct e-mail: res.library@bbsrc.ac.uk

Founded: 1843

Organisation type and purpose: Research organisation.

Subject coverage: Agricultural research (excluding animal husbandry, diseases, etc., plant breeding and agricultural economics); pure research on many botanical and biochemical aspects of agriculture; entomology; farms; insecticides and fungicides; nematology; pedology; plant pathology; soil microbiology; agricultural computer work; statistics.

Collection: Agricultural books, 1471–1840 British Farm Livestock, prints and paintings, 1780–1910

Library catalogue: All or part available online

Publications: Printed

Access to staff: Appointment necessary.
Hours: Mon to Fri, 0900 to 1700

Funded by: Biotechnology and Biological Sciences Research Council

Links with: Broom's Barn Experimental Station; Higham, Suffolk, IP28 6NP; North Wyke Research; Okehampton, Devon, EX20 2SB

ROTHER DISTRICT COUNCIL

Town Hall, Bexhill-on-Sea, East Sussex, TN39 3JX

Tel: 01424 787878
Fax: 01424 787879
E-mail: chiefexec@rother.gov.uk
Website: www.rother.gov.uk

Enquiries to: Chief Executive

Founded: 1974

Organisation type and purpose: Local government body.

Subject coverage: Council issues.

Access to staff: Contact by letter, by telephone, by fax, by e-mail, in person and via website. Appointment necessary.
Hours: Mon to Thu, 0830 to 1700; Fri, 0830 to 1630

Access for disabled people: Ramped entry

Other addresses: Community Help Point (Battle); 6 Market Street, Battle, East Sussex, TN33 0XB; tel: 01424 787478; fax: 01424 787479; e-mail: customerservices@rither.gov.uk; Community Help Point (Bexhill); Amherst Road, Bexhill-on-Sea, East Sussex; tel: 01424 787999; fax: 01424 787766; e-mail: customerservices@rither.gov.uk; Community Help Point (Rye); 25 Cinque Ports Street, Rye, East Sussex, TN31 7AD; tel: 01797 222293; fax: 01797 227576; e-mail: customerservices@rither.gov.uk

ROTHERHAM ARCHIVES AND LOCAL STUDIES SERVICE

Formal name: Rotherham Metropolitan Borough Council: Archives and Local Studies Service

Rotherham Metropolitan Borough Council Archives and Local Studies Service, c/o Clifton Park Museum, Clifton Lane, Rotherham, S65 2AA

Tel: 01709 336633
Fax: 01709 823650
E-mail: archives@rotherham.gov.uk
Website: www.rotherham.gov.uk/info/448/records_and_archives-information_and_advice

Founded: 1986

Organisation type and purpose: Local government body, public library and archive repository.

Subject coverage: The local history of the area of Rotherham MBC.

Collection: Archival holdings include records of Rotherham MBC and predecessor local authorities; quarter sessions and magistrates' courts; hospitals; nonconformist archives; businesses (including iron and steel, glass, coal mining, brass founding, pottery); family and estate records; solicitors Local studies holdings include books and pamphlets; directories; census returns; newspapers; journals; digital and paper maps

Non-library collection catalogue: All or part available online and in-house

Library catalogue: All or part available online and in-house

Publications: Printed

Publications list: Available online and in print

Access to staff: Contact by letter, by telephone, by fax, by e-mail and in person
Special comments: Closed owing to relocation to Clifton Park Museum as of June 2012

Access to building: *Special comments:* Closed owing to relocation to Clifton Park Museum as of June 2012

ROUGH FELL SHEEP BREEDERS ASSOCIATION

High Newstead Farm, Jervaulx, Masham, Ripon, North Yorkshire, HG4 4PJ

Tel: 07746 466794
E-mail: roughfell@fsmail.net
Website: www.roughfellsheep.co.uk

Enquiries to: Secretary

Subject coverage: Rough Fell sheep.

continued overleaf

Publications list: Available in print

ROUNDERS ENGLAND (RE)

Formal name: Rounders England Limited

PO Box 4458, Sheffield, S20 9DP

Tel: 0114 248 0357
E-mail: enquiries@roundersengland.co.uk
Website: www.roundersengland.co.uk/

Other contacts: For further contacts, please use the Rounders England website

Founded: 1943; formerly called National Rounders Association (year of change 2009)

Organisation type and purpose: Rounders England is the sport's governing body in England.

Subject coverage: Provides a structure for the sport from the board, county associations and clubs, through to individual members and volunteers. It is responsible for the management and training of the England squads and works alongside the other home national governing bodies to provide competition opportunities.
Rounders England also co-ordinates a development network that provides a pathway for aspiring players to progress from schools and clubs to the national squad. It provides information about the game, runs coaching and umpiring courses, holds tournaments, sells resources and promotes the sport at all levels.

Collection: Past publications

Publications: Printed

Publications list: Available online and in print

Access to staff: Contact by letter, by telephone, by e-mail and via website
Hours: Mon to Thu, 0900 to 1700; Fri, 0900 to 1600
Special comments: Telephone answering service available at other times.

Access to building: No access other than to staff

Links with: Sport & Recreation Alliance; Burwood House, London, SW1H 0QT; tel: 0207 976 3900; fax: 020 7976 3901; e-mail: info@sportandrecreation.org.uk; website: http://www.sportandrecreation.org.uk/
Sport England; 3rd Floor Victoria House, Bloomsbury Square, London, WC1B 4SE; tel: 0845 850 8508; fax: 0207 383 5740; e-mail: info@sportengland.org; website: http://www.sportengland.org/
Sports Coach UK; Chelsea Close Off Amberley Road, Armley, Leeds, LS12 4HP; tel: 0113–274 4802; website: http://www.sportscoachuk.org/
Women's Sport & Fitness Foundation; Victoria House, Bloomsbury Square, London, WC1B 4SE; tel: 020 7273 1740; fax: 020 7273 1981; e-mail: info@wsff.org.uk; website: http://wsff.org.uk/
Youth Sport Trust; SportPark, Loughborough University, 3 Oakwood Drive, Loughborough, Leicestershire, LE11 3QF; tel: 01509 226 600; fax: 01509 210 851; website: http://www.youthsporttrust.org/

ROUTLEDGE REFERENCE – DIRECTORIES

Albert House, 4th Floor, 1–4 Singer Street, London, EC2A 4BQ

Tel: 020 7017 6000
Fax: 020 7017 6720
E-mail: reference@routledge.co.uk
Website: www.worldwhoswho.com
Website: www.routledge.com/reference
Website: www.worldoflearning.com
Website: www.europaworld.com
Website: www.routledgeonline.com

Enquiries to: Marketing Manager
Direct tel: 020 7017 6566

Organisation type and purpose: Publishing house.

Subject coverage: Geographic, economic and political information on every country in the world; current politics; government; political organisations; diplomatic representation; judicial system; religion; the press; publishers; radio and television; finance; trade and industry; transport; tourism; higher education; the environment; biographies; international organisations.

Publications: Printed, and electronic and video

Publications list: Available online and in print

Access to staff: Contact by e-mail
Hours: Mon to Fri, 0900 to 1700

Other office: Taylor & Francis Books (UK); 2 Park Square, Milton Park, Abingdon, Oxfordshire, OX14 4RN; tel: 020 7017 6000; website: http://www.taylorandfrancisgroup.com

Parent body: Informa plc; 4th Floor, 27 Mortimer Street, London, W1; tel: 020 7017 5000; website: http://www.informa.com

ROVER P4 DRIVERS GUILD

32 Arundel Road, Luton, Bedfordshire, LU4 8DY

Tel: 01582 572499
E-mail: colinb@rptdg.freeserve.co.uk

Enquiries to: Secretary

Founded: 1977

Organisation type and purpose: International organisation, membership association, voluntary organisation.

Subject coverage: Historical, technical, spares sourcing and insurance information, advertisements, events related to P4 Rover cars built between 1950 and 1964.

Publications: Printed

Access to staff: Contact by letter and by telephone
Hours: Mon to Fri, 0900 to 1700

ROVER P5 CLUB

13 Glen Avenue, Ashford, Middlesex, TW15 2JE

Tel: 01784 258166
Fax: 01784 258166
E-mail: membership@roverp5club.org.uk
Website: www.roverp5club.org.uk

Enquiries to: Membership Secretary
Other contacts: Cars for sale register (for purchase or sale of Rover P5 car)

Founded: 1985

Organisation type and purpose: Membership association (membership is by subscription), present number of members: 700, voluntary organisation.
To enable members to keep their examples of the Rover P5 marque running and in good order so that they can derive the maximum pleasure from owning and driving them.

Subject coverage: All aspects of Rover P5 cars, buying and selling, technical data, parts supply, maintenance, club regalia.

Collection: Technical manuals (available to members only)

Publications: Printed

Access to staff: Contact by letter, by telephone, by fax and by e-mail
Hours: Mon to Sun, 0900 to 2100

ROWETT RESEARCH INSTITUTE (RRI)

Greenburn Road, Bucksburn, Aberdeen, AB21 9SB

Tel: 01224 712751
Fax: 01224 715349
E-mail: enquiries@rowett.ac.uk
Website: www.rowett.ac.uk

Enquiries to: Public Relations Manager
Direct tel: 01224 716668
Direct e-mail: s.bird@rowett.ac.uk

Founded: 1913

Organisation type and purpose: Registered charity, training organisation, consultancy, research organisation.
State-aided animal and human nutrition research centre.

Subject coverage: Nutrient absorption, nutrient utilisation, trace elements, growth of skeletal and connective tissue, growth and metabolism of skeletal muscle, ruminant science, fermentation biochemistry, lipid metabolism, appetite control, diet related to health and disease states.

Collection: Agriculture in the 18th and 19th centuries

Non-library collection catalogue: All or part available in-house

Library catalogue: All or part available in-house

Publications: Printed

Publications list: Available online

Access to staff: Contact by letter, by telephone, by fax and by e-mail. Appointment necessary.
Hours: Mon to Fri, 0900 to 1700

Access to building: Prior appointment required

Access for disabled people: Parking provided

Links with: BBSRC; SEERAD

Subsidiary body: Rowett Research Services

ROWLANDS LIBRARY

Charles Hastings Education Centre, Worcestershire Royal Hospital, Charles Hastings Way, Worcester, WR5 1DD

Tel: 01905 760601
Fax: 01905 760866
E-mail: rowlands.library@worcsacute.wmids.nhs.uk
Website: www.wkp.nhs.uk

Enquiries to: Librarian

Founded: 1976

Organisation type and purpose: National government body.
NHS Hospital Trust.

Subject coverage: Medicine, nursing, midwifery, mental health, social care, therapies, pathology, public health, health service management.

Collection: History of Medicine, Royal College of Nursing Resource Centre

Non-library collection catalogue: All or part available online

Access to staff: Contact by letter, by telephone, by fax, by e-mail and via website
Hours: Mon to Fri, 0830 to 1700

Access for disabled people: Parking provided, ramped entry, toilet facilities

ROY CASTLE LUNG CANCER FOUNDATION

The Roy Castle Centre, 4–6 Enterprise Way, Wavertree Tech Park, Liverpool, Merseyside, L13 1FB

Tel: 0151 254 7200
E-mail: foundation@roycastle.org
Website: www.roycastle.org

Founded: 1990; formerly called Lung Cancer Fund

Organisation type and purpose: A registered charity (number 1046854 in England & Wales and SCO37596 in Scotland).
To defeat lung cancer.

Subject coverage: Lung cancer.

Information services: Helpline: 0800 358 7200 (UK only); local information and support groups.

Publications: Electronic and video
Order electronic and video publications from: Download from website

Publications list: Available online

Access to staff: Contact by letter, by telephone, by e-mail and via website
Hours: Helpline: Mon to Fri, 0900 to 1700

ROYAL ACADEMY OF ARTS (RA)

Library, Burlington House, Piccadilly, London, W1J 0BD

Tel: 020 7300 5737
Fax: 020 7300 5765
E-mail: library@royalacademy.org.uk
Website: www.racollection.org.uk

Enquiries to: Librarian

Founded: 1768

Organisation type and purpose: Learned society.

Subject coverage: Fine arts, British art since 1750, The Royal Academy.

Non-library collection catalogue: All or part available online and in-house

Library catalogue: All or part available online and in-house

Access to staff: Contact by letter, by telephone, by fax, by e-mail and via website. Appointment necessary.
Hours: Tue to Fri, 1000 to 1300 and 1400 to 1700

Access to building: *Hours:* Tue to Fri, 1000 to 1300 and 1400 to 1700

Access for disabled people: Parking provided, ramped entry, toilet facilities

ROYAL ACADEMY OF DANCE (RAD)

36 Battersea Square, London, SW11 3RA

Tel: 020 7326 8000
Fax: 020 7924 3129
E-mail: info@rad.org.uk
Website: www.rad.org.uk
Website: www.radenterprises.co.uk
Website: www.radacadabra.org

Enquiries to: Acting Communications Manager
Direct tel: 020 7326 8002
Direct e-mail: fcerrone@rad.org.uk
Other contacts: Press and Marketing Manager

Founded: 1920

Organisation type and purpose: The RAD is a training, membership and examination organisation that promotes knowledge, understanding and practice of dance internationally. It is an international teaching and examining body in classical ballet, and a dance teacher-training body through its Faculty of Education; it holds a specialised reference library and archives and is the home of the Benesh Institute; it is a global organisation involving approximately 13,000 members and present in 79 countries; it is a registered charity England and Wales (charity number 312826).

Subject coverage: Dance and related subjects.

Collection: Benesh Movement Notation Scores
Books, journals, photographs, pictures, programmes, videos and CD-ROMs
Phillip Richardson Library

Library catalogue: All or part available online, in-house and in print

Publications: Printed
Order printed publications from: Royal Academy of Dance Enterprises Ltd; tel: 020 7326 8080; fax: 020 7228 6261; e-mail: sales@rad.org.uk

Publications list: Available online

Access to staff: Contact by letter, by telephone, by fax, by e-mail and via website. Appointment necessary.
Hours: Mon to Thu, 1000 to 1800; Fri, 1000 to 1730

Access to building: Prior appointment required

Access for disabled people: Ramped entry, level entry, toilet facilities

Links with: University of Surrey; tel: 01483 300800; fax: 01483 300803; website: http://www.surrey.ac.uk

ROYAL ACADEMY OF DRAMATIC ART (RADA)

18 Chenies Street, London, WC1E 7PA

Tel: 020 7636 7076
Fax: 020 7323 3865
Website: www.rada.org

Enquiries to: Library Manager
Direct tel: 020 7908 4878
Direct e-mail: library@rada.ac.uk

Founded: 1904

Organisation type and purpose: Registered charity (charity number 312819), suitable for ages: 18 to mid-30s, training organisation.
Academy for professional theatre training, acting and stage management, has 172 full-time students.
Provides courses as above and specialist courses in props, electrics, scene painting and wardrobe.

Subject coverage: Plays, acting, voice and speech, poetry, theatre criticism, theory of drama, theatre history, technical theatre arts, stage management, biography, costume, social history, film.

Collection: Ivo Currall Bequest (450 books and 46 albums of press cuttings by and about George Bernard Shaw)

Library catalogue: All or part available in-house

Access to staff: Contact by letter, by telephone and by e-mail. Appointment necessary. Non-members charged.
Hours: Mon to Wed, 0915 to 1945; Thu, Fri, 1000 to 1830

ROYAL ACADEMY OF ENGINEERING (RAEng)

29 Great Peter Street, London, SW1P 3LW

Tel: 020 7222 2688
Fax: 020 7233 0054
Website: www.raeng.org.uk

Enquiries to: Public Relations Manager
Direct tel: 020 7227 0536
Direct fax: 020 7227 7631
Direct e-mail: iffat.memon@raeng.org.uk

Founded: 1976

Organisation type and purpose:
Membership association (membership is by election or invitation), present number of members: 1170, registered charity (charity number 293074).
The pursuit, encouragement and maintenance of excellence in the whole field of engineering in order to promote the advancement of the science, art and practice of engineering for the benefit of the public.

Subject coverage: Engineering.

Library catalogue: All or part available in-house

Publications list: Available online

Access to staff: Contact by letter, by

continued overleaf

telephone, by fax, by e-mail and via website
Hours: Mon to Fri, 0900 to 1700

ROYAL ACADEMY OF MUSIC

Marylebone Road, London, NW1 5HT

Tel: 020 7873 7323
Fax: 020 7873 7322
E-mail: library@ram.ac.uk
Website: www.ram.ac.uk

Enquiries to: Librarian

Founded: 1822

Organisation type and purpose: Registered charity, suitable for ages: 18+.

Subject coverage: Music performance, orchestras, choirs, opera, conducting, history of music.

Collection: Angelina Goetz Library (full scores)
Robert Spencer Collection (lutenist, 1932–1997, early printed music and manuscripts)
Arthur Sullivan archive (research material, books, scores and serials)
David Munrow Library
G. D. Cunningham Collection (organ music)
Otto Klemperer Collection (scores)
R. J. S. Stevens Savage Collection (early printed music and manuscripts)
Sheet music
Sir Henry Wood Library of orchestral material
Foyle Menuhin Archive

Non-library collection catalogue: All or part available online

Library catalogue: All or part available online and in-house

Publications: Printed

Access to staff: Contact by letter, by e-mail and via website
Hours: 0900 to 1800

Access to building: Prior appointment required

ROYAL AFRICAN SOCIETY

36 Gordon Square, London, WC1H 0PD

Tel: 020 3073 8335
Fax: 020 3073 8340
E-mail: ras@soas.ac.uk

Enquiries to: Office Manager

Founded: 1901

Organisation type and purpose: Voluntary organisation, registered charity (charity number 1062764).

Subject coverage: African affairs.

Publications: Printed

Access to staff: Contact by telephone and by e-mail
Hours: Mon to Fri, 0930 to 1630

Affiliated with joint members to the: African Studies Association of the UK; at the same address

ROYAL AGRICULTURAL COLLEGE (RAC)

Library, Stroud Road, Cirencester, Gloucestershire, GL7 6JS

Tel: 01285 652531
Fax: 01285 889844
E-mail: library@rac.ac.uk
Website: rac.ac.uk

Enquiries to: Librarian
Direct tel: 01285 652531 extn 2274

Founded: 1845

Organisation type and purpose: University library, suitable for ages: 18+.
University sector library.
Undergraduate and postgraduate degrees, research and consultancy in land-based industries and development, and related sectors.

Subject coverage: Agriculture, forestry, horticulture, land use and management including land law, valuation, building construction, taxation, economics, ecology and conservation, farm woodlands, rural planning, business and management, environment, tourism, property agency, wine and viticulture, equine studies, agribusiness, international rural development.

Collection: British Deer Society collection
Historical collection of books on agriculture and land management

Library catalogue: All or part available online

Access to staff: Contact by letter, by telephone, by fax, by e-mail and via website.
Appointment necessary.
Hours: Term time: Mon to Thu, 0900 to 2000; Fri, 0900 to 1700; Sat, 1200 to 1700; Sun, 1200 to 1700
Vacations: Mon to Fri, 0900 to 1700
Special comments: External membership by subscription.

Access for disabled people: Parking provided, level entry, access to all public areas, toilet facilities, automatic entrance doors

ROYAL AGRICULTURAL SOCIETY OF ENGLAND (RASE)

National Agricultural Centre, Stoneleigh Park, Kenilworth, Warwickshire, CV8 2LZ

Tel: 024 7669 6969
Fax: 024 7669 6900
E-mail: jaynesp@rase.org.uk
Website: www.rase.org.uk

Enquiries to: Press Officer
Other contacts: Marketing Manager

Founded: 1840

Organisation type and purpose: Learned society, voluntary organisation, registered charity.
Transfer of technology and information related to agriculture and the rural economy.

Subject coverage: Agriculture in general, horticulture, crop husbandry, machinery, livestock husbandry, entomology.

Collection: Reference library available by appointment

Publications: Printed

Access to staff: Contact by letter, by telephone, by fax, by e-mail and via website.
Appointment necessary.
Hours: Mon to Fri, 0900 to 1700

Affiliated with French equivalent: SAF

Affiliated with German equivalent: DLG

ROYAL AGRICULTURAL SOCIETY OF THE COMMONWEALTH (RASC)

2 Grosvenor Gardens, London, SW1W 0DH

Tel: 020 7259 9678
Fax: 020 7259 9675
E-mail: rasc@commagshow.org
Website: www.commagshow.org

Enquiries to: Honorary Secretary

Founded: 1957

Organisation type and purpose: International organisation, learned society, voluntary organisation, registered charity (charity number 211322).
Promotes agricultural co-operation between the developed and developing Commonwealth countries etc.

Subject coverage: Practice and science of agriculture, improvement of methods of crop production and breeding of livestock, improvement of efficiency of agricultural implements and machinery.

Publications: Printed

Access to staff: Contact by letter, by telephone, by fax and by e-mail.
Appointment necessary.
Hours: Mon to Fri, 0930 to 1700

Comprises the: 42 National Agricultural Show Societies in 21 Commonwealth countries

Links with: Commonwealth Foundation; Commonwealth Secretariat; International Association of Fairs and Expositions (IAFE); Royal Commonwealth Society (RCS)

ROYAL AIR FORCE COLLEGE CRANWELL (RAFC Cranwell)

College Library, Cranwell, Sleaford, Lincolnshire, NG34 8HB

Tel: 01400 261201 extn 6329
Fax: 01400 261201 extn 6266
Website: www.cranwell.raf.mod.uk

Enquiries to: Librarian
Direct tel: 01400 266219

Founded: 1920

Organisation type and purpose: Central government establishment.

Subject coverage: Aeronautics, military science and history (especially air power), RAF history, defence studies, current affairs, air warfare, management sciences, computer sciences, engineering (mechanical, electrical, electronic, materials, aeronautical, aerospace), mathematics, logistics, warfare, weapons.

Information services: General enquiry service.

Collection: College Archives
Part of the library of the late Lord Trenchard
T E Lawrence Collection

Non-library collection catalogue: All or part available in-house

Library catalogue: All or part available in-house

Access to staff: Contact by letter, by telephone and by e-mail. Appointment necessary.
Hours: Mon, Tue, Thu, 0815 to 1700; Wed, Fri, 0815 to 1600

Access to building: Access by prior appointment only

Parent body: Ministry of Defence – Royal Air Force

ROYAL AIR FORCES ASSOCIATION (RAFA)

CHQ, 117½ Loughborough Road, Leicester, LE4 5ND

Tel: 0116 266 5224
Fax: 0116 266 5012
Website: www.rafa.org.uk/

Enquiries to: Secretary General

Organisation type and purpose: Voluntary organisation, registered charity (charity number 226686).
Incorporated by Royal Charter.

Subject coverage: Advice and assistance to those who are eligible on all aspects of welfare, pensions, disability awards, civilian employment.

Publications: Printed

Access to staff: Contact by letter and by telephone. Appointment necessary.
Hours: Mon to Fri, 0900 to 1700

Has: 9 area headquarters within the British Isles

ROYAL ALFRED SEAFARERS' SOCIETY (RASS)

SBC House, Restmor Way, Wallington, Surrey, SM6 7AH

Tel: 020 8401 2889
Fax: 020 8401 2592
E-mail: royalalfred@btopenworld.com

Enquiries to: General Secretary

Founded: 1867

Organisation type and purpose: National organisation, registered charity (charity number 209776).
Providing nursing and residential home care, and sheltered housing for retired seafarers, their dependants and persons who have worked in trades or professions allied to the maritime industry.

Subject coverage: Information on the subject of long-term care facilities for retired seafarers.

Publications: Printed

Access to staff: Contact by letter, by telephone, by fax and by e-mail
Hours: Mon to Fri, 0900 to 1700

Access to building: Prior appointment required
Hours: Mon to Fri, 0900 to 1700

Access for disabled people: Parking provided, level entry, access to all public areas, toilet facilities

Other addresses: Royal Alfred Seafarers' Society; Belvedere House, Weston Acres, Woodmansterne Lane, Banstead, Surrey, SM7 3HA; tel: 01737 360106; fax: 01737 353436; e-mail: home.bns@mha.org.uk; Royal Alfred Seafarers' Society; Royal Alfred House, 5–11 Hartington Place, Eastbourne, BN21 3BS; tel: 01323 721828; fax: 01323 431029; e-mail: home.eas@mha.org.uk

ROYAL AND ANCIENT GOLF CLUB OF ST ANDREWS, THE (R&A)

St Andrews, Fife, KY16 9JD

Tel: 01334 460000
Fax: 01334 460001
E-mail: webmaster@randa.org
Website: www.randa.org
Website: www.opengolf.com

Enquiries to: Secretary

Founded: 1754

Organisation type and purpose:
International organisation (membership is by election or invitation), present number of members: 1800.
Governing Body for the Rules of Golf and Rules of Amateur Status throughout the world (except USA and Canada).

Subject coverage: Golf, British championships and international matches, rules of golf, rules of amateur status, golf clubs and balls.

Access to staff: Contact by letter, by telephone, by fax and by e-mail.
Appointment necessary.
Hours: Mon to Fri, 0900 to 1700

ROYAL ANTHROPOLOGICAL INSTITUTE OF GREAT BRITAIN AND IRELAND (RAI)

50 Fitzroy Street, London, W1T 5BT

Tel: 020 7387 0455
Fax: 020 7388 8817
E-mail: admin@therai.org.uk
Website: www.therai.org.uk

Enquiries to: Director

Founded: 1843

Organisation type and purpose:
International organisation, national organisation, learned society (membership is by election or invitation), present number of members: 1,600, voluntary organisation (charity number 246269), suitable for ages: 16+, publishing house.

Subject coverage: Anthropology.

Collection: Photograph collection at the Institute
The Library, gifted to the British Museum and held at the Centre for Anthropology in London – access to Fellows

Non-library collection catalogue: All or part available in-house

Library catalogue: All or part available in-house

Publications: Printed, and electronic and video
Order printed publications from: Wiley -Blackwell, Journals Dept, 9600 Garsington Road, Oxford, OX4 2DQ; tel: 01865 791100; fax: 01865 791347
Order electronic and video publications from: Articles from backnumbers of JRAI and Anthropology Today available electronically (for a fee) from JSTOR and Ingenta respectively

Publications list: Available in print

Access to staff: Contact by letter, by telephone, by fax and by e-mail.
Appointment necessary. Non-members charged.
Hours: Mon to Fri, 0930 to 1730

ROYAL ARCHAEOLOGICAL INSTITUTE (RAI)

Society of Antiquaries, Burlington House, Piccadilly, London, W1J 0BE

E-mail: admin@royalarchaeolinst.org

Enquiries to: Administrator

Founded: 1844

Organisation type and purpose: Learned society (membership is by subscription), present number of members: 1,500, registered charity (charity number 226222 ACL), suitable for ages: 18+.

Subject coverage: Archaeology, art history, architecture.

Library catalogue: All or part available online and in print

Publications: Printed

Publications list: Available in print

Access to staff: Contact by letter and by e-mail
Special comments: Library (Society of Antiquaries).

ROYAL ARMOURIES LIBRARY – LEEDS

Armouries Drive, Leeds, West Yorkshire, LS10 1LT

Tel: 0113 220 1832
Fax: 0113 220 1934
E-mail: enquiries@armouries.org.uk
Website: www.armouries.org.uk

Enquiries to: Librarian

Organisation type and purpose: National government body, museum.
Operates under a Board of Trustees appointed by the Secretary of State for Culture, Media and Sport.

Subject coverage: The Royal Armouries and its collections, the history and development of European and Oriental arms and armour, including firearms, from the middle ages to the present day; the history of the Tower of London and its institutions.

Collection: A small number of important manuscripts including the earliest known (13th-century) fencing manual, which shows the use of sword and buckler; a 15th-century firework book, which illustrates the manufacture and use of gunpowder; and an account of the jousts between Jehan Chalons of England and Loys de Beul of France at Tours in 1446
Early books on fencing and the art of warfare
Handbooks and manuals on military small arms and artillery
Catalogues of arms and armour sales

continued overleaf

Minute books of the Board of Ordnance (microfilm)
Photographs of objects in the Royal Armouries' own collection, of objects in other collections, and of illustrations of arms and armour in art
40,000 books, pamphlets and journals
150,000 black and white photographs
2,000 colour transparencies

Access to staff: Contact by letter, by telephone, by fax and by e-mail
Hours: Library: Mon to Fri, 1030 to 1630; closed bank holidays

Access to building: No access other than to staff

Also at: Royal Armouries; HM Tower of London, London, EC3N 4AB; tel: 020 7480 6358; fax: 020 7481 2922; Royal Armouries; Fort Nelson, Down End Road, Fareham, Hampshire, PO17 6AN; tel: 01329 233734; fax: 01329 822092

ROYAL ARMOURIES LIBRARY – LONDON

HM Tower of London, London, EC3N 4AB

Tel: 020 3166 6669
Fax: 020 3166 6678
E-mail: enquiries@armouries.org.uk
Website: www.armouries.org.uk

Enquiries to: Librarian
Other contacts: Keeper of Collections (South)

Organisation type and purpose: National government body, museum.
Operates under a Board of Trustees appointed by the Secretary of State for the Environment.

Subject coverage: History of the Tower of London and its institutions, including the Board of Ordnance, the Record office, the Menagerie, the Royal Mint at the Tower, history of fortification.

Collection: A small reference collection of books and pamphlets on arms and armour
Collection of Tower-related prints and manuscripts
Photographic reference archive for Tower-related material

Non-library collection catalogue: All or part available in-house and in print

Library catalogue: All or part available in-house

Order printed publications from: Royal Armouries Museum, Armouries Drive, Leeds, LS10 1LT

Publications list: Available online

Access to staff: Contact by letter, by telephone, by fax and by e-mail. Appointment necessary.
Hours: Library: Mon to Fri, 1000 to 1600 by appointment only

Access to building: *Hours:* Library: Mon to Fri, 1000 to 1600 by appointment only

Access for disabled people: Lift

Also at: Royal Armouries Library; Armouries Drive, Leeds, LS10 1LT; tel: 0113 220 1832

Main Library at: Royal Armouries Museum, Leeds

Outstation at: Fort Nelson

ROYAL ARTILLERY HISTORICAL TRUST (RAHT)

Firepower Royal Artillery Museum, Royal Arsenal (West), Warren Lane, Woolwich, London, SE18 6ST

Tel: 020 8855 7755
Fax: 020 8855 7100
E-mail: info@firepower.org.uk
Website: www.firepower.org.uk

Enquiries to: Honorary Secretary
Direct tel: 0208 312 7120

History of institution: formerly a part of the collections of the Royal Artillery Institution

Organisation type and purpose: Advisory body.

Subject coverage: Administration and control of the museum, library, artefacts and archives.

Non-library collection catalogue: All or part available in-house

Library catalogue: All or part available in-house

Access to staff: Contact by letter, by telephone, by fax, by e-mail, in person and via website. Appointment necessary.
Hours: Mon to Fri, 1000 to 1600

Administers: Firepower; James Clavell Library; Firepower, Royal Arsenal (West), Warren Lane, Woolwich, London, SE18 6ST; tel: 020 8855 7755; e-mail: research@firepower.org.uk; website: http://www.firepower.org.uk
Royal Artillery Library and Archives; The Royal Artillery Museum; Royal Arsenal (West), Warren Lane, Woolwich, London, SE18 6ST; tel: 020 8855 7755; fax: 020 8855 7100; e-mail: research@firepower.org.uk; website: http://www.firepower.org.uk

ROYAL ARTILLERY INSTITUTION (RAI)

Artillery House, Royal Artillery Barracks, Larkhill, Salisbury, Wiltshire, SP4 8QT

Tel: 01980 845528
Fax: 01980 845210
E-mail: ac-rhqra-regtsec@mod.uk

Enquiries to: Regimental Secretary

Founded: 1839

Organisation type and purpose: Professional body.
Regimental institution.

Subject coverage: History of the Royal Regiment of Artillery 1716 to date; artillery, development, c.1650 onwards; history of army ordnance, especially post-1715, military and campaign history; British Army.

Collection: Kaye collection of military history
The manuscripts of General Sir Alexander Dickson
Wide range of published and manuscript works on ordnance from 16th century onwards
RA Journals and Minutes of Proceedings of the RAI

Library catalogue: All or part available in-house

Publications: Printed
Order printed publications from: Property Clerk, Royal Artillery Institution

Access to staff: Contact by letter, by fax and by e-mail. Appointment necessary.
Hours: Mon to Fri, 0900 to 1700

Access to building: No prior appointment required

Links with: Firepower, Royal Artillery Museum; Royal Arsenal, Woolwich, London, SE18 6ST; tel: 020 8855 7755; fax: 020 8855 7100; e-mail: info@firepower.org.uk; website: http://www.firepower.org.uk
James Clavell Library; Firepower, The Royal Artillery Museum, Old Laboratory Office, Royal Arsenal (West), Warren Lane, Woolwich, London, SE18 6ST; Royal Artillery Historical Society; Royal Artillery Barracks, Larkhill, Salisbury, Wiltshire, SP4 8QT; tel: 01980 845367; e-mail: rahs@hqdra.army.mod.ac.uk; Royal Artillery Historical Trust; Old Laboratory Office, Royal Arsenal (West), Warren Lane, Woolwich, London, SE18 6ST; tel: 020 8312 7120; fax: 020 8855 7100; e-mail: marks@firepower.org.uk

ROYAL ARTILLERY LIBRARY

Formal name: James Clavell Library, Royal Artillery Museum

James Clavell Library, Royal Arsenal (West), Warren Lane, Woolwich, London, SE18 6ST

Tel: 020 8312 7125
E-mail: research@firepower.org.uk
Website: www.firepower.org.uk

Enquiries to: Librarian
Direct tel: 0208 312 7120 (Curator)
Other contacts: Curator :

Organisation type and purpose: Independently owned, registered charity.
Part of the Firepower Museum Complex.
To record and promote research into the history of the Royal Artillery and related subjects.

Subject coverage: Materials on Royal Artillery Regimental History; artillery equipment, armed forces, warfare, tactics, training, fortification, military history, military geography and biography.

Collection: Books, journals, pamphlets, manuscripts, diaries, maps, plans, drawings, photographs, film and microfiche

Non-library collection catalogue: All or part available in-house

Library catalogue: All or part available in-house

Publications: Printed

Access to staff: Contact by letter, by telephone, by fax, by e-mail, in person and via website. Appointment necessary.
Hours: Mon to Fri, 0900 to 1600

Access to building: Prior appointment required
Hours: David Evans Reading Room, open for readers Mon to Fri, 1000 to 1600

Links with: Firepower! Royal Artillery Museum; Royal Regiment of Artillery

Parent body: Royal Artillery Historical Trust; Royal Artillery Museum, Royal Arsenal (West), Warren Lane, Woolwich, London, SE18 6ST; tel: 020 8312 7120

ROYAL ASIATIC SOCIETY OF GREAT BRITAIN AND IRELAND

14 Stephenson Way, London, NW1 2HD

Tel: 020 7388 4539
E-mail: kl@royalasiaticsociety.org
Website: www.royalasiaticsociety.org

Enquiries to: Executive Officer
Direct e-mail: cl@royalasiaticsociety.org

Founded: 1823

Organisation type and purpose:
Membership organisation (membership by election).
To provide a forum for those who are interested in the history, languages, cultures and religions of Asia to meet and exchange ideas through lectures, seminars, research and publishing.
Registered charity (charity number 209629)

Subject coverage: History, languages, cultures and religions of Asia.

Collection: Library of 80,000 items, including:
Tod Collection (Indian manuscripts and paintings)
Hodgson Collection (Buddhist and Sanskrit manuscripts)
Ram Raz Collection (architectural drawings)
Raffles and Maxwell Collections (Malay manuscripts)
Howell Collection (early photographs of China and Japan)

Non-library collection catalogue: All or part available in-house

Library catalogue: All or part available in-house

Publications: Printed
Order printed publications from: Books published by the Royal Asiatic Society should be ordered from the Society's publishing partner, Routledge Curzon, Taylor & Francis Ltd, 2 Park Square, Milton Park, Abingdon, Oxon, OX14 4RN; tel: 020 7017 6000; fax: 020 7017 6699; internet: www.routledgecurzon.com

Publications list: Available online

Access to staff: Contact by letter, by telephone, by e-mail and via website. Appointment necessary.

ROYAL ASSOCIATION FOR DEAF PEOPLE (RAD)

Centre for Deaf People, Walsingham Road, Colchester, Essex, CO2 7BP

Tel: 01206 509509, 01206 577090 (minicom)
Fax: 01206 769755
E-mail: info@royaldeaf.org.uk
Website: www.royaldeaf.org.uk

Enquiries to: Administrator

Founded: 1841

Organisation type and purpose: Registered charity (charity number 1081949).
To promote the spiritual, social and general welfare of deaf people.

Subject coverage: Profound hearing impairment, blindness and deafness, problems of deaf people in psychiatric and sub-normal hospitals, social casework and welfare service, the Church's ministry to and the spiritual and pastoral care of deaf/blind and deaf people.

Publications list: Available online and in print

Access to staff: Contact by letter, by telephone, by fax, by e-mail, in person and via website. Appointment necessary.
Hours: Mon to Fri, 0900 to 1700
Special comments: Access also by minicom.

ROYAL ASSOCIATION FOR DISABILITY AND REHABILITATION (RADAR)

Formal name: Royal Association for Disability Rights

12 City Forum, 250 City Road, London, EC1V 8AF

Tel: 020 7250 3222; 020 7250 4119 (minicom, for the hearing impaired only)
Fax: 020 7250 0212
E-mail: radar@radar.org.uk
Website: www.radar.org.uk

Founded: 1977

Organisation type and purpose: Voluntary organisation, registered charity (charity number 273150).
A major national cross-disability organisation run by and working for disabled people.
Working to end discrimination and to promote the independence of disabled people. Campaigning and lobbying on: independent living; civil rights; employment; education; housing; mobility; leisure; social security; and access.

Subject coverage: All aspects of physical disability, except the strictly medical (benefits, employment, education, holidays, housing, legislation, civil rights, mobility, social security, social services).

Publications: Printed
Order printed publications from: RADAR, 12 City Forum, 250 City Road, London, EC1V 8AF, or website: http://www.radar-shop.org.uk

Publications list: Available online and in print

Access to staff: Contact by letter, by telephone, by fax, by e-mail and via website
Hours: Information Dept: Mon to Thu, 1000 to 1600
Other depts: 0900 to 1700

Access to building: *Hours:* 0930 to 1700

Access for disabled people: Parking provided, ramped entry, level entry, access to all public areas, toilet facilities

Organisation of: 600 local and national bodies

ROYAL ASSOCIATION OF BRITISH DAIRY FARMERS (RABDF)

Dairy House, Unit 31, Stoneleigh Deer Park, Stareton, Kenilworth, Warwickshire, CV8 2LY

Tel: 0845 458 2711
Fax: 0845 458 2755
E-mail: office@rabdf.co.uk
Website: www.rabdf.co.uk/

Enquiries to: Press Officer
Direct tel: 01743 344986
Direct e-mail: lizsnaith@btopenworld.com

Founded: 1876

Organisation type and purpose:
Membership association (membership is by subscription), present number of members: 2000, registered charity (charity number 213782).
The RABDF organises The European Dairy Farming Event – the United Kingdom's largest specialist event for dairy farmers and the dairy farming industry. The Association also organises conferences, publishes regular newsletters, liaises with Government and is involved in training.

Subject coverage: Dairy farming and other matters related to dairy cattle.

Publications: Printed

Access to staff: Contact by letter, by telephone and by fax
Hours: Mon to Fri, 0900 to 1700

Organisers of the: Dairy Event

ROYAL AUTOMOBILE CLUB LIBRARY

89 Pall Mall, London, SW1Y 5HS

Tel: 020 7930 2345
Website: www.royalautomobileclub.co.uk

Enquiries to: Librarian
Direct tel: 020 7747 3398
Direct fax: 0870 4606285
Direct e-mail: library@royalautomobileclub.co.uk
Other contacts: Archivist

Founded: 1897; formerly called Automobile Club of Great Britain (and later Ireland) (year of change 1907)

Organisation type and purpose: Private members club (membership by election), present membership approximately 17,000

Subject coverage: History of the Royal Autombile Club, history of motoring and motor sport

Collection: Long runs of motoring periodicals including: Autocar, The Motor, Autosport; motoring books including: racing and production marques and models, biographies, motor sport, technical and legal material; RAC archives including: club handbooks and journals, personal correspondence, membership records, pamphlets, photographs, exhibition programmes, route guides

Non-library collection catalogue: All or part available online

Library catalogue: All or part available in-house

Publications: Printed

Access to staff: Contact by letter, by telephone, by fax and by e-mail.
Appointment necessary. Access for members only. Letter of introduction required.
Hours: Mon to Fri, 0900 to 1700

Access to building: *Special comments:* Researchers only by prior appointment

Member organisation of: international motoring bodies: FIA, FISA, AIT, MSA

ROYAL BIRMINGHAM SOCIETY OF ARTISTS (RBSA Gallery)

4 Brook Street, St Paul's, Birmingham, B3 1SA

Tel: 0121 236 4353
Fax: 0121 236 4555
E-mail: secretary@rbsa.org.uk
Website: www.rbsa.org.uk

Enquiries to: Honorary Secretary
Other contacts: Honorary Curator for gallery hire.

Founded: 1814

Organisation type and purpose:
Independently owned, professional body (membership is by subscription, election or invitation), present number of members: 460 friends, 83 associates, 105 members, registered charity (charity number 528894), museum, art gallery, workshop facilities, suitable for all ages.
To actively encourage the learning, practice and appreciation of fine arts and allied crafts. Fulfilment of a vital community purpose by supporting and showcasing the work of local and national professional artists and crafts people and providing opportunities for amateur artists.

Subject coverage: Practical fine art and allied crafts. History of the Royal Birmingham Society of Artists. All media are represented, from contemporary to traditional. Biennial exhibition of RBSA Permanent Collection.

Collection: Bound Exhibition Catalogues continuous from the early years of the Society
Paintings, prints, sculptures etc donated by artists when elected as full members
Documentation, membership register, diploma works and more from the early years onwards

Publications: Printed

Access to staff: Contact by letter, by telephone, by fax, by e-mail and in person. Non-members charged.
Hours: Mon to Fri, 1030 to 1730

Access to building: No prior appointment required
Hours: Mon to Fri, 1030 to 1730; Sat, 1030 to 1700; Sun, 1300 to 1700
Special comments: Archive that houses the RBSA Collection: by prior appointment. For exhibitions see website, or phone gallery.

Access for disabled people: Level entry, access to all public areas, toilet facilities

ROYAL BOTANIC GARDEN EDINBURGH (RBGE)

Library, 20A Inverleith Row, Edinburgh, EH3 5LR

Tel: 0131 552 7171
Fax: 0131 248 2901
E-mail: library@rbge.org.uk
Website: www.rbge.org.uk

Enquiries to: Librarian
Direct tel: 0131 248 2853

Founded: 1670

Organisation type and purpose: Research organisation.
Administered by a Board of Trustees.

Subject coverage: Plant taxonomy; amenity horticulture; history and current practice of gardening; landscaping; conservation; botanical illustration; botanical travels and explorations; plant collecting; floras of the world.

Collection: Archival material, manuscript and printed, relating to the history of plant sciences and particularly to the Garden (from 1670), and to the Botanical Society of Edinburgh (from 1836)
Correspondence, biographies and portraits of early botanists, horticulturists
Early printed works dating from 1486 on botany, medicine, agriculture, horticulture
Minute Books of the Royal Caledonian Horticulture Society from 1810
Pre-Linnaean botanical literature

Non-library collection catalogue: All or part available online

Library catalogue: All or part available online and in-house

Publications: Printed
Order printed publications from: Publications Department

Publications list: Available online and in print

Access to staff: Contact by letter, by telephone, by fax, by e-mail, in person and via website
Hours: Mon to Fri, 1000 to 1600

Access for disabled people: Parking provided, access to all public areas, toilet facilities

Constituent bodies: Botanical Society for Edinburgh (1872) Botanical Library; Cleghorn Memorial (1941) Botanical Library; Plinian Society of Edinburgh (1841) Botanical Library; Wernerian Society (1856) Botanical Library

Funded by: Scottish Government Rural and Environment Science and Analytical Services Division (RESAS)

ROYAL BOTANIC GARDENS, KEW (RBGK)

Library, Art and Archives, Royal Botanic Gardens, Kew, Richmond, Surrey, TW9 3AE

Tel: 020 8332 5414
Fax: 020 8332 5430
E-mail: library@kew.org
Website: www.kew.org

Enquiries to: Archivist (for Archives enquiries)
Direct tel: 020 8332 5476
Direct e-mail: archives@kew.org; illus@kew.org
Other contacts: Illustrations (for illustrations enquiries)

Founded: 1852 (Library)

Organisation type and purpose: Registered charity, research organisation.
RBG Kew has charitable status and is an exempt charity under the Charities Act 1960.

Subject coverage: Botany (plants and fungi of the world), taxonomy, geography, anatomy, biochemistry, cytology, molecular biology, economic botany, horticulture, plant seed physiology, nomenclature, conservation, RBGK reference collections of living and preserved plants.

Collection: 160,000 monographs, 3,800 serials (1,300 current), 150,000 pamphlets, 200,000 prints and drawings, 4,600 archival collections
Adams Collection (diatom books)
Botanists Portraits Collection
Darlington Reprint Collection (genetics)
Kewensia and archives (RBG Kew's public records)
Linnaean Collection
Plant Illustrations, including the Church, Roxburgh and Tankerville Drawings
RGB Kew also has extensive plant and fungi collections: 7m. plant herbarium specimens, 750,000 fungi specimens, 80,000 economic botany specimens, 40,000 living taxa

Non-library collection catalogue: All or part available online and in-house

Library catalogue: All or part available online

Publications: Printed, and electronic and video
Order printed publications from: Orders from booksellers: Publications Sales, RBG Kew, Richmond, Surrey, TW9 3AE; tel: 020 8332 5776; fax: 020 8332 5646; e-mail: kewscbooks@rbgkew.org.uk
UK Retail Sales: KewBooks, Summerfield House, High Street, Brough, Cumbria, CA17 4AX; tel: 01768 341899; fax: 01768 800707; e-mail: kewbooks.com@btinternet.com; website: http://www.kewbooks.com

Publications list: Available online and in print

Access to staff: Contact by letter, by fax, by e-mail and via website. Appointment necessary.
Hours: Mon to Fri, 0900 to 1700

Access to building: Prior appointment required
Special comments: Only bona-fide researchers.

Access for disabled people: Parking provided, ramped entry, toilet facilities

Sponsored by: Department for Environment, Food and Rural Affairs

ROYAL BRITISH LEGION SCOTLAND (RBLS)

New Haig House, Logie Green Road, Edinburgh, EH7 4HR

Tel: 0131 557 2782
Fax: 0131 557 5819
E-mail: rblshq@care4free.com
Website: www.rblscotland.org.uk

Enquiries to: Press Officer
Direct e-mail: ehfs.pub@btconnect.com

Founded: 1921

Organisation type and purpose:
Membership association (membership is by subscription), present number of members: 62,000, voluntary organisation, registered charity (charity number SCO 03323).

Subject coverage: Assistance to ex-service men and women in Scotland, war disability pensions claims, aid during temporary and chronic illness and unemployment, assistance in the provision of surgical appliances, overseas war graves visits for next-of-kin, provision of sheltered accommodation, sports competitions, piping competitions, opportunity to join social club.

Publications: Printed

Access to staff: Contact by letter, by telephone, by fax, by e-mail and in person
Hours: Mon to Fri, 0915 to 1630

Access to building: No access other than to staff

Access for disabled people: Parking provided, level entry, toilet facilities

Includes the: Earl Haig Fund Scotland; Officers Association Scotland

Member of: British Commonwealth Ex-services League

ROYAL BRITISH LEGION, THE

48 Pall Mall, London, SW1Y 5JY

Tel: 0345 725725
Fax: 020 7973 7399
E-mail: info@britishlegion.org.uk
Website: www.britishlegion.org.uk

Enquiries to: Secretary General
Direct e-mail: scottam@britishlegion.org.uk
Other contacts: Legionline Coordinator for general enquiries.

Founded: 1921

Organisation type and purpose:
Membership association (membership is by qualification), present number of members: 620,000, registered charity (charity number 219279).
To care for, and raise funds for, the disabled and needy in the ex-service community.

Subject coverage: War disability pensions and general welfare benefits applicable to ex-servicemen and women and their dependants; overseas war graves visits; the ex-service community generally.

Publications: Printed

Access to staff: Contact by letter, by telephone, by fax, by e-mail and via website
Hours: Mon to Fri, 0900 to 1700

Access for disabled people: Level entry, access to all public areas, toilet facilities

Member of: British Commonwealth Ex-Services League; Council of British Services and Ex-Services Organisations; World Veterans Federation

Supports the: Attendants Company; Disabled Men's Industries Limited; Officers' Association; Royal British Legion Poppy Appeal and Factory; Royal British Legion Women's Section

ROYAL BRITISH SOCIETY OF SCULPTORS (RBS)

108 Old Brompton Road, London, SW7 3RA

Tel: 020 7373 5554
Fax: 020 7370 3721
E-mail: info@rbs.org.uk
Website: www.rbs.org.uk

Enquiries to: Administrator

Founded: 1904

Organisation type and purpose: Advisory body, membership association (membership is by election or invitation), present number of members: over 400, registered charity (charity number 2817292), art gallery.

Subject coverage: Sculpture.

Access to staff: Contact by letter, by telephone, by fax and by e-mail.
Appointment necessary.
Hours: Mon to Fri, 0930 to 1730

Access to building: No prior appointment required
Hours: Mon to Fri, 0930 to 1730

ROYAL CALEDONIAN CURLING CLUB (RCCC)

Cairnie House, Ingliston Showground, Newbridge, Midlothian, EH28 8NB

Tel: 0131 333 3003
Fax: 0131 333 3323
E-mail: office@royalcaledoniancurlingclub.org
Website: www.rccc.org.uk

Enquiries to: Manager, Finance and Administration
Other contacts: Director of Development for development of the sport.

Founded: 1838

Organisation type and purpose:
Membership association (membership is by subscription), present number of members: 15,000, training organisation.
Governing body for sport of curling in Scotland.

Subject coverage: The sport and game of curling.

Collection: Archive films of grand matches
Royal club annuals from 1839 and many rare books on curling
Various curling artefacts and pictures including trophies and old curling stones

Publications: Printed

Access to staff: Contact by letter, by telephone, by fax and by e-mail.
Appointment necessary.
Hours: Mon to Fri, 0900 to 1700

ROYAL CAMBRIAN ACADEMY OF ART (RCA)

Crown Lane, Conwy, LL32 8AN

Tel: 01492 593413
Fax: 01492 593413
E-mail: rca@rcaconwy.org
Website: www.rcaconwy.org

Enquiries to: Curator

Founded: 1882

Organisation type and purpose:
Membership association (membership is by election or invitation), present number of members: 115, registered charity (charity number 219648), art gallery.

Subject coverage: Past and present members of the Academy since 1882, artists working in Wales.

Collection: Catalogues of every RCA exhibition since 1882

Publications: Printed

Access to staff: Contact by letter, by telephone, by fax, by e-mail and via website
Hours: Tue to Sat, 1100 to 1700; Sun, 1300 to 1630
Special comments: No lift to upstairs gallery.

ROYAL CHORAL SOCIETY (RCS)

Studio 9, 92 Lots Road, London, SW10 0QD

Tel: 020 7376 3718
Fax: 020 7376 3719
Website: www.royalchoralsociety.co.uk

Enquiries to: Administrator
Direct e-mail: helenbody@royalchoralsociety.co.uk

Founded: 1871

Organisation type and purpose:
Membership association (membership is by subscription), registered charity.
Choir.

Subject coverage: Choirs and choral music.

Collection: Archive material (loaned to the Greater London Public Record Office)

Publications: Printed

Access to staff: Contact by letter, by telephone, by fax, by e-mail and via website
Hours: Mon to Fri, 0900 to 1700

Links with: NFMS

Subsidiary body: Friends of the Royal Choral Society

ROYAL COLLEGE OF ANAESTHETISTS

Churchill House, 35 Red Lion Square, London, WC1R 4SG

Tel: 020 7092 1500
Fax: 020 7092 1730
E-mail: info@rcoa.ac.uk
Website: www.rcoa.ac.uk

Organisation type and purpose: The professional body responsible for the specialty of anaesthesia throughout the UK. Ensures the quality of patient care through the maintenance of standards in anaesthesia, critical care and pain medicine.

Subject coverage: Anaesthesia is the largest single hospital specialty in the NHS.

Publications: Printed, and electronic and video
Order electronic and video publications from: Download from website

Publications list: Available online

Access to staff: Contact by letter, by telephone, by fax and by e-mail

ROYAL COLLEGE OF ART LIBRARY (RCA)

Kensington Gore, London, SW7 2EU

Tel: 020 7590 4224
Fax: 020 7590 4500
E-mail: library@rca.ac.uk
Website: www.rca.ac.uk/library

Enquiries to: Library Manager
Direct tel: 020 7590 4225
Direct e-mail: darlene.maxwell@rca.ac.uk
Other contacts: Head of Information & Learning Services

Organisation type and purpose:
Postgraduate college of art, Institution of University Library status.

Subject coverage: Art (particularly 20th century), design (industrial, graphic, fashion, textiles, architecture, interior, illustration,

continued overleaf

vehicle), applied arts (ceramics, metalwork, jewellery), moving image (films, television, animation), photography, humanities.

Collection: College Archive
Colour Reference Collection covering many aspects of colour, including theory, psychology, symbolism and colour music
Theses Collection

Library catalogue: All or part available online

Access to staff: Appointment necessary.
Hours: Term time: Mon to Fri, 0900 to 2100; Sat, 1200 to 1700
Vacations: Mon to Fri, 1000 to 1700

ROYAL COLLEGE OF DEFENCE STUDIES (RCDS)

37 Belgrave Square, London, SW1X 8NS

Tel: 020 7915 4813
Fax: 020 7915 4800
Website: www.mod.uk.rcds/index.html

Enquiries to: Librarian

Founded: 1970

Organisation type and purpose: National government body, learned society (membership is by election or invitation), present number of members: 85 current (on site), historic building, house or site. Government department.
The house originally known as Sefton House was built in 1842 by the Marquess of Westminster. It may be visited on an Open Day.

Subject coverage: Defence, international relations, politics, economics, history.

Library catalogue: All or part available in-house

Publications: Printed

Publications list: Available in print

Access to staff: Access for members only.
Hours: Mon to Fri, 0900 to 1700
Special comments: Members and OGDs.

Access to building: No access other than to staff

Connections with: Ministry of Defence, London (MOD)

ROYAL COLLEGE OF GENERAL PRACTITIONERS (RCGP)

30 Euston Square London NW1 2DA

Tel: 020 3188 7400
E-mail: library@rcgp.org.uk
Website: www.rcgp.org.uk

Enquiries to: Information Officers

Founded: 1952

Organisation type and purpose: Learned society (membership is by qualification), present number of members: 44,000, registered charity (charity number 223106), research organisation.
Encouraging, fostering, and maintaining the highest possible standards in general medical practice.

Subject coverage: General practice, primary health care, practice management, family practice.

Collection: The College library stock includes a unique reference collection of MD and PhD theses from general practice, an international selection of primary care journals and a collection of College publications.

Library catalogue: All or part available online

Publications: Printed, and electronic and video

Publications list: Available online and in print

Access to staff: Contact by letter, by telephone, by fax, by e-mail, in person and via website. Appointment necessary. Access for members only.
Hours: Mon to Fri, 0900 to 1700
Special comments: Book loans to members only.

ROYAL COLLEGE OF GENERAL PRACTITIONERS (SCOTLAND) (RCGP SCOTLAND)

25 Queen Street, Edinburgh, EH2 1JX

Tel: 0131 260 6800
Fax: 0131 260 6836
E-mail: scottishc@rcgp.org.uk

Enquiries to: Deputy Chair (Policy)

Organisation type and purpose: Professional body, membership association (membership is by qualification), present number of members: 3,018 (Scotland), registered charity (charity number 223106), research organisation.

Subject coverage: Academic/quality in General Practice.

Access to staff: Contact by letter and by e-mail
Hours: Mon to Fri, 0900 to 1700

Also at: Royal College of General Practitioners; 14 Princes Gate, Hyde Park, London, SW7 1PU; tel: 020 7581 3232

ROYAL COLLEGE OF MIDWIVES – EDINBURGH

37 Frederick Street, Edinburgh, EH2 1EP

Tel: 0131 225 1633

Enquiries to: Director

Organisation type and purpose: Professional organisation.

Subject coverage: Midwifery.

Access to staff: Contact by letter
Hours: Mon to Fri, 0900 to 1700

ROYAL COLLEGE OF MIDWIVES – LONDON (RCM)

27 Sussex Place, Regent's Park, London, NW1 4RG

Tel: 020 7772 6200
E-mail: rcmlibrary@rcog.org.uk
Website: www.rcm.org.uk/library

Enquiries to: Librarian
Direct tel: 020 7772 6291
Direct fax: 020 7262 8331

Founded: 1881

Organisation type and purpose: Professional body, (membership is by qualification)

Subject coverage: Midwifery: education, profession, training and history; obstetrics; neonatal care; ante-natal care; paediatrics; family planning; role of the midwife in the NHS; sociological and psychological aspects of midwifery; further and higher education.

Collection: College Archive

Non-library collection catalogue: All or part available online and in-house

Library catalogue: All or part available online and in-house

Publications list: Available online and in print

Access to staff: Contact by letter, by telephone, by fax, by e-mail, in person and via website. Appointment necessary.
Hours: Mon to Fri, 0900 to 1800

Access to building: Prior appointment required

Access for disabled people: Access to all public areas, toilet facilities

ROYAL COLLEGE OF MUSIC (RCM)

Library, Prince Consort Road, London, SW7 2BS

Tel: 020 7591 4325
Fax: 020 7589 7740
E-mail: pthompson@rcm.ac.uk
Website: www.rcm.ac.uk

Enquiries to: Librarian
Direct tel: 020 7591 4323

Founded: 1883

Organisation type and purpose: Academic institution and music conservatoire.

Subject coverage: Music: books, autograph manuscripts, scores, sheet music, orchestral parts, choral sets, audio-visual materials.

Collection: Collection of manuscripts of British composers
Heron-Allen Collection of books on the violin
Library of the Concerts of Ancient Music
Library of the Sacred Harmonic Society
Maurice Frost collection
Nicanor Zabaleta archive of harp music
Further listings at www.cecilia-uk.org

Non-library collection catalogue: All or part available online, in-house and in print

Library catalogue: All or part available in-house

Publications: Printed, and microform publications

Access to staff: Contact by letter, by telephone, by fax, by e-mail and in person
Hours: Term time: Mon to Thu, 0900 to 1900; Fri, 0900 to 1730
Vacations: hours may vary
Special comments: Loans to members only.

Access to building: No prior appointment required

ROYAL COLLEGE OF MUSIC FRANK BRIDGE BEQUEST

Royal College of Music, Prince Consort Road, London, SW7 2BS

Tel: 020 8749 2268
E-mail: pbanks@rcm.ac.uk
Website: www.cph.rcm.ac.uk/CPHBridge/Pages/Index.htm

Enquiries to: Chairman

Founded: 1965

Organisation type and purpose: Promotion of the performance of music by Frank Bridge.

Subject coverage: Life and music of Frank Bridge (1879–1941).

Collection: Bridge manuscripts (held in the Library of the Royal College of Music, for access see the entry for the RCM Library)

Publications list: Available online

Access to staff: Contact by letter, by telephone, by e-mail and via website
Hours: Mon to Fri, 0900 to 1700

ROYAL COLLEGE OF NURSING OF THE UNITED KINGDOM (RCN)

20 Cavendish Square, London, W1G 0RN

Tel: 020 7409 3333
Fax: 020 7647 3420
E-mail: rcn.library@rcn.org.uk
Website: www.rcn.org.uk

Enquiries to: Library, Archives and Information Services team
Direct tel: 020 7647 3610

Organisation type and purpose: Professional body, trade union.

Subject coverage: Professional aspects of nursing; nursing practice, management and education; labour relations and legal matters; social services; health services; hospital management.

Services for disabled people: Library and toilets wheelchair accessible, request additional assistance.

Collection: Seymer Collection (historical books on nursing)
Steinberg Collection of Nursing Research Theses

Non-library collection catalogue: All or part available online

Library catalogue: All or part available online

Publications: Printed
Order printed publications from: rcn.library@rcn.org.uk

Access to staff: Contact by letter, by telephone, by fax, by e-mail and via website. Non-members charged.
Hours: Mon, Tue, Thu, Fri, 0900 to 1900; Wed, 1000 to 1900; Sat, 0900 to 1700

Access for disabled people: Ramped entry, toilet facilities

Also at: Royal College of Nursing of the United Kingdom; Ty Maeth, King George V Drive East, Cardiff, CF4 4XZ; tel: 029 2075 1373; Royal College of Nursing of the United Kingdom; 42 Scottish Board, South Oswald Road, Edinburgh, EH9 2HH; tel: 0131 662 1010; Royal College of Nursing of the United Kingdom; 17 Windsor Avenue, Belfast, BT9 6EE; tel: 01232 668236

ROYAL COLLEGE OF OBSTETRICIANS AND GYNAECOLOGISTS (RCOG)

27 Sussex Place, Regent's Park, London, NW1 4RG

Tel: 020 7772 6200
Website: www.rcog.org.uk
Website: www.rcog.org.uk/what-we-do/information-services
Website: www.rcog.org.uk/our-profession/research-services

Enquiries to: Librarian
Direct tel: 020 7772 6309
Direct fax: 020 7262 8331
Direct e-mail: library@rcog.org.uk

Founded: 1929

Organisation type and purpose: Professional body (membership is by qualification).

Subject coverage: Obstetrics, gynaecology and closely related subjects (e.g. urogynaecology).

Collection: Large historical collection in subjects as above
Rare books
College archive
Collection of historical instruments including the Chamberlen forceps

Non-library collection catalogue: All or part available in-house

Library catalogue: All or part available online and in-house

Publications: Printed

Publications list: Available online

Access to staff: Contact by letter, by telephone, by fax, by e-mail, in person and via website. Appointment necessary.
Hours: Mon to Fri, 0900 to 1800

Constituent bodies: National Collaborating Centre for Women's and Children's Health

Houses the: Faculty of Sexual and Reproductive Health Care; Wellbeing of Women (formerly Birthright)

ROYAL COLLEGE OF OPHTHALMOLOGISTS

17 Cornwall Terrace, London, NW1 4QW

Tel: 020 7935 0702
Fax: 020 7935 9838
E-mail: kathy.evans@rcophth.ac.uk
Website: www.rcophth.ac.uk

Enquiries to: Chief Executive

Founded: 1988

Organisation type and purpose: Professional body (membership is by subscription, qualification), present number of members: 4,000, registered charity (charity number 299872).

Subject coverage: Ophthalmology.

Publications: Printed

Publications list: Available in print

Access to staff: Contact by letter, by telephone, by fax and by e-mail
Hours: Mon to Fri, 0900 to 1700

Access to building: Prior appointment required

ROYAL COLLEGE OF ORGANISTS (RCO)

The Royal College of Organists Library, Birmingham City University, City North Campus, Franchise Street, Perry Barr, Birmingham, B42 2SU

Tel: 0121 331 7266
E-mail: library@rco.org.uk
Website: www.rco.org.uk

Enquiries to: General Manager
Other contacts: Director of Academic Development, Library Manager

Founded: 1864

Organisation type and purpose: International organisation, advisory body, learned society, professional body, registered charity (charity number 312847).
Academic institution, especially examining body.

Subject coverage: The organ and music for the organ.

Collection: Houses the library of books, music (mainly organ), manuscripts, records, cassettes and CDs
C. H. Trevor Collection
Cruden Collection
Dalton Bequest
Gordon Phillips Collection
John Ella Bequest
Sowerbutts Collection
T. Lea Southgate Bequest
Tickner Collection
Lady Susi Jeans Collection
Peter Williams Collection
Organ Club Library
David Sanger Collection

Non-library collection catalogue: All or part available online

Library catalogue: All or part available online

Publications: Printed

Publications list: Available in print

Access to staff: Contact by letter, by telephone, by e-mail and in person. Appointment necessary. Non-members charged.
Hours: Mon to Fri, 1000 to 1700
Special comments: Prior appointment necessary.

ROYAL COLLEGE OF PAEDIATRICS AND CHILD HEALTH (RCPCH)

50 Hallam Street, London, W1W 6DE

Tel: 020 7307 5600
Fax: 020 7307 5601
E-mail: enquiries@rcpch.ac.uk
Website: www.rcpch.ac.uk

Enquiries to: Secretary

Founded: 1928

continued overleaf

Organisation type and purpose:
Professional body (membership is by qualification, election or invitation), present number of members: 6500, voluntary organisation, registered charity (charity number 1057744).
Members are paediatricians and other professionals active in the field of child health. The RCPCH forms joint standing committees and working parties with several other professional bodies, for example: the Royal College of Physicians, British Association of Paediatric Surgeons, Association of British Paediatric Nurses, National Association for the Welfare of Children in Hospital, Health Visitors Association, Royal College of Midwives, Royal College of Nursing and Royal College of Obstetricians and Gynaecologists. The RCPCH also engages in consultations with a wide range of organisations including voluntary organisations, for example: Foundation for the Study of Infant Deaths.
To advance the art and science of paediatrics; to raise the standard of medical care for children; to educate and examine those concerned with the health of children; to advance the education of the public in child health.

Subject coverage: Paediatrics, child health, medical training and research.

Non-library collection catalogue: All or part available in-house

Publications: Printed, and electronic and video
Order printed publications from: RCPCH Bookclub, Direct Books
FREEPOST (BH1879), Ringwood, Hampshire, BH24 3BR, tel: 01425 471719, e-mail: directbooks@bmbc.com

Publications list: Available online and in print

Access to staff: Contact by letter, by telephone, by fax, by e-mail and via website. Appointment necessary.
Hours: Mon to Fri, 0900 to 1700

Strong connections with the: Confederation of European Specialists in Paediatrics; International Paediatric Association

ROYAL COLLEGE OF PATHOLOGISTS (RCPath)

2 Carlton House Terrace, St James's, London, SW1Y 5AF

Tel: 020 7451 6700
Fax: 020 7451 6701
E-mail: info@rcpath.org
Website: www.rcpath.org

Enquiries to: Chief Executive

Founded: 1962

Organisation type and purpose:
Professional body (membership is by subscription, qualification), present number of members: 7,500, registered charity (charity number 261035).

Subject coverage: History of pathology, pathology as a science, histopathology, cytology, medical microbiology, clinical biochemistry, virology, immunology, genetics, forensic pathology, haematology.

Library catalogue: All or part available in-house

Publications: Printed
Order printed publications from: Managing Editor, Publications; tel: 020 7451 6730; fax: 020 7451 6701; e-mail: publications@rcpath.org

Publications list: Available online

Access to staff: Contact by letter, by telephone, by fax, by e-mail and via website
Hours: Mon to Fri, 0900 to 1700

Access for disabled people: Ramped entry, toilet facilities

ROYAL COLLEGE OF PHYSICIANS (RCP)

Information Centre and Heritage Centre, 11 St Andrews Place, Regent's Park, London, NW1 4LE

Tel: 020 3075 1539
Fax: 020 7486 3729
E-mail: infocentre@rcplondon.ac.uk
Website: www.rcplondon.ac.uk

Founded: 1518

Organisation type and purpose:
International organisation, professional body (membership is by qualification), registered charity (charity number 210508), suitable for ages: postgraduate, training organisation, research organisation, publishing house. To promote the highest standards of medical practice in order to improve health and healthcare.

Subject coverage: The Information Centre Library covers the College's work, UK health policy and public health. The Heritage Centre covers the history of medicine, medical biography and the history of the College.

Collection: Archives of the College
Manuscripts (mainly personal papers of physicians)
Portraits and photographs (mainly of Fellows of the College)
H. M. Barlow Collection of Bookplates
Dorchester Library (2,101 titles left to the College by the Marquis of Dorchester), includes the Wilton Psalter dating from 1250
Evan Bedford Library of Cardiology
Heberden Library of Rheumatology
Willan Library of the British Association of Dermatology

Non-library collection catalogue: All or part available online and in-house

Library catalogue: All or part available online and in-house

Publications: Printed, and microform publications
Order printed publications from: Publications Department, Royal College of Physicians; tel: 020 7935 1174 ext 358; fax: 020 7486 5425; e-mail: publications@rcplondon.ac.uk

Publications list: Available online and in print

Access to staff: Contact by letter, by telephone, by fax, by e-mail, in person and via website. Appointment necessary. Non-members charged.
Hours: Mon to Fri, 0900 to 1700

Access to building: Some areas open to public. Prior appointment required to access historical collections.
Hours: Mon to Fri, 0900 to 1700

Access for disabled people: Parking provided, level entry, access to all public areas, toilet facilities
Hours: Mon to Fri, 0900 to 1700

ROYAL COLLEGE OF PHYSICIANS AND SURGEONS OF GLASGOW (RCPSG)

Library, 232–242 St Vincent Street, Glasgow, G2 5RJ

Tel: 0141 221 6072
Fax: 0141 221 1804
E-mail: library@rcpsg.ac.uk
Website: www.rcpsg.ac.uk

Enquiries to: Librarian

Founded: 1698

Organisation type and purpose: Learned society, professional body (membership is by qualification, election or invitation), present number of members: 8,500.

Subject coverage: Clinical medicine and surgery, history of medicine, history of Glasgow and West of Scotland.

Collection: Macewen Collection (papers of Sir William Macewen, surgery, late 19th century)
Mackenzie Collection (papers of Dr William MacKenzie, ophthalmology)
Ross Collection (50% of the papers of Sir Ronald Ross, tropical medicine, 19th century)
Glasgow Collection (history of Glasgow and South West Scotland)

Non-library collection catalogue: All or part available online and in print

Library catalogue: All or part available online and in-house

Access to staff: Contact by letter, by telephone, by fax, by e-mail, in person and via website. Appointment necessary.
Hours: Mon to Fri, 0900 to 1700

Access for disabled people: Access to all public areas, toilet facilities

ROYAL COLLEGE OF PHYSICIANS OF EDINBURGH (RCPE)

Library, 9 Queen Street, Edinburgh, EH2 1JQ

Tel: 0131 225 7324
Fax: 0131 220 3939
E-mail: library@rcpe.ac.uk
Website: www.rcpe.ac.uk/library/library.html

Enquiries to: Librarian
Other contacts: Information Librarian for literature searches.

Founded: 1681

Organisation type and purpose: Advisory body, learned society, professional body (membership is by qualification, election or invitation), present number of members: 7000, registered charity (charity number SCO 09465), research organisation.

Subject coverage: Medicine, particularly clinical medicine (excluding since 1900, surgery and allied sciences); history of medicine, particularly Scottish medicine.

Collection: J W Ballantyne Pamphlet Collection on foetal pathology

Manuscripts Collection relating to W Cullen and early Edinburgh Medical School
Sir J Y Simpson Collection on gynaecology and obstetrics

Non-library collection catalogue: All or part available online and in-house

Library catalogue: All or part available online and in-house

Publications: Printed

Publications list: Available online and in print

Access to staff: Contact by letter, by telephone, by fax, by e-mail, in person and via website
Hours: Mon to Fri, 0900 to 1700

ROYAL COLLEGE OF PSYCHIATRISTS (RCPsych)

17 Belgrave Square, London, SW1X 8PG

Tel: 020 7235 2351
Fax: 020 7245 1231
E-mail: infoservices@rcpsych.ac.uk
Website: www.rcpsych.ac.uk

Enquiries to: Library and Information Services Manager
Direct tel: 020 7235 2351 ext 6138
Direct fax: 020 7259 6303
Direct e-mail: infoservices@rcpsych.ac.uk

Organisation type and purpose: Professional body (membership is by qualification).

Subject coverage: Psychiatry; mental illness and health, history of psychiatry.

Collection: Antiquarian books on psychiatry

Non-library collection catalogue: All or part available online and in-house

Library catalogue: All or part available in-house

Publications: Printed, and electronic and video

Publications list: Available online and in print

Access to staff: Contact by letter, by telephone, by fax, by e-mail, in person and via website. Appointment necessary. Access for members only. Letter of introduction required. Non-members charged.
Hours: Mon to Fri, 0930 to 1630

ROYAL COLLEGE OF RADIOLOGISTS (RCR)

38 Portland Place, London, W1B 1JQ

Tel: 020 7636 4432
Fax: 020 7323 3100
E-mail: enquiries@rcr.ac.uk
Website: www.rcr.ac.uk

Enquiries to: Chief Executive

Founded: 1975

Organisation type and purpose: Professional body (membership is by qualification), present number of members: 8,000, registered charity (charity number 211540).

Subject coverage: Science and practice of clinical radiology, clinical oncology.

Publications: Printed

Publications list: Available in print

Access to staff: Contact by letter, by telephone, by fax and by e-mail. Appointment necessary.
Hours: Mon to Fri, 0900 to 1700

ROYAL COLLEGE OF SPEECH AND LANGUAGE THERAPISTS (RCSLT)

2–3 White Hart Yard, London, SE1 1NX

Tel: 020 7378 1200
Fax: 020 7403 7254
Website: www.rcslt.org

Enquiries to: Professional Director
Other contacts: Information Officer for general enquiries re: speech and language therapy profession.

Organisation type and purpose: National organisation, professional body, registered charity (charity number 273724). Examining and registering body.

Subject coverage: Disorders of human communication.

Publications: Printed

Access to staff: Contact by letter and by e-mail
Hours: Mon to Fri, 0900 to 1700

Access to building: Prior appointment required

Access for disabled people: Level entry, toilet facilities

Affiliated to: International Association of Logopaedics and Phoniatrics; Permanent Liaison Committee of Speech Therapists and Logopaedists (EEC)

ROYAL COLLEGE OF SURGEONS OF EDINBURGH (RCSEd)

The Library, Nicolson Street, Edinburgh, EH8 9DW

Tel: 0131 527 1630
Fax: 0131 557 6406
E-mail: library@rcsed.ac.uk
Website: www.library.rcsed.ac.uk

Enquiries to: Librarian

Founded: 1505

Organisation type and purpose: Membership association (membership is by qualification), registered charity, training organisation, research organisation.

Subject coverage: Surgery, history of medicine.

Collection: Records of the institution from 1505; collected papers of notable figures in medicine and surgery, e.g. Joseph Lister, James Young Simpson; large museum; large portrait collection; images collection

Non-library collection catalogue: All or part available online, in-house and in print

Library catalogue: All or part available online, in-house and in print

Publications: Printed

Publications list: Available online

Access to staff: Contact by letter, by telephone, by fax, by e-mail, in person and via website
Hours: Mon to Fri, 0900 to 1700
Special comments: Appointment preferred for non-members, but not essential.

Access for disabled people: Ramped entry, toilet facilities

ROYAL COLLEGE OF SURGEONS OF ENGLAND (RCSEng)

35–43 Lincoln's Inn Fields, London, WC2A 3PE

Tel: 020 7869 6555/6556
E-mail: library@rcseng.ac.uk
Website: www.rcseng.ac.uk/library; www.rcseng.ac.uk/museums

Enquiries to: Archivist
Direct e-mail: archives@rcseng.ac.uk

Founded: 1800

Organisation type and purpose: Medical Royal College, professional body (charity number 212808).

Subject coverage: Surgery: dental and oral surgery, maxillo-facial surgery, orthopaedics and trauma, cardiovascular surgery, neurosurgery, general surgery, urological surgery, otorhinolaryngology, paediatric surgery, plastic and reconstructive surgery; anatomy; pathology; physiology; history of medicine with special emphasis on surgery.

Collection: The Museums and Archives Department includes the Hunterian Museum, the Wellcome Museum of Anatomy and Pathology and the College Archive collections. The museums and archive collections cover the history of surgery and anatomy from the 17th century to the present. The Hunterian Museum contains one of Britain's greatest medical collections, including over 3,000 anatomical and pathological preparations collected by the surgeon John Hunter (1728–1793). The Wellcome Museum of Anatomy and Pathology contains the College's modern teaching collections. It contains over 2,000 anatomical and pathological specimens as well as other resources. It is open to all individuals with a surgical, medical or relevant profession. The College's archive collections include institutional records documenting the College's activities throughout its history, and a diverse range of deposited manuscript and archive collections relating to medicine and surgery. The library possesses one of the finest historical medical collections, including many rare and unique items. The collections are particularly strong in anatomy and surgery, though comparative anatomy and natural history are also well represented. Material for the library was initially purchased to support staff working with the Hunterian Collection now housed in the Hunterian Museum. The tracts and pamphlets collection (c. 30,000 items) is one of the largest of its kind in the UK.

Non-library collection catalogue: All or part available online

Library catalogue: All or part available online

Publications: Printed, and electronic and video

Publications list: Available online

continued overleaf

Access to staff: Contact by letter, by telephone, by e-mail, in person and via website. Appointment necessary.
Hours: Please check website for opening hours and variations
Special comments: Charges may apply to non-members; please see website.

Access to building: Please see website

Access for disabled people: Please see website

ROYAL COLLEGE OF VETERINARY SURGEONS TRUST (RCVS)

Library and Information Service, Belgravia House, 62–64 Horseferry Road, London, SW1P 2AF

Tel: 020 7202 0752
Fax: 020 7202 0751
E-mail: library@rcvstrust.org.uk
Website: www.rcvs.org.uk
Website: www.rcvslibrary.org.uk

Enquiries to: Librarian
Founded: 1844

Organisation type and purpose: Professional body.
Registration and disciplinary body.
Subject coverage: Veterinary science and surgery, comparative medicine, animal breeding and management.
Collection: College Archives
Henry Gray Collection (ornithology, late 19th and early 20th centuries)
Historical Collection (books 1514–1850)
J. P. Megnin Collection of drawings, mainly of birds and parasites, and correspondence
Miss Povey Collection of watercolours by Edward Mayhew

Non-library collection catalogue: All or part available online

Library catalogue: All or part available online

Publications list: Available online

Access to staff: Contact by letter, by telephone, by fax, by e-mail and via website. Appointment necessary. All charged.
Hours: Mon to Fri, 0915 to 1700

Access to building: Prior appointment required

ROYAL COMMISSION ON THE ANCIENT AND HISTORICAL MONUMENTS OF SCOTLAND (RCAHMS)

John Sinclair House, 16 Bernard Terrace, Edinburgh, EH8 9NX

Tel: 0131 662 1456
Fax: 0131 662 1477
E-mail: info@rcahms.gov.uk
Website: www.rcahms.gov.uk
Website: canmore.rcahms.gov.uk
Website: aerial.rcahms.gov.uk
Website: www.scran.ac.uk
Website: www.scotlandsplaces.gov.uk
Website: www.pastmap.org.uk
Website: hla.rcahms.gov.uk

Enquiries to: Chief Executive
Direct e-mail: diana.murray@rcahms.gov.uk

Founded: 1908

Organisation type and purpose: National government body, national organisation, advisory body, statutory body, registered charity, public library.
Information relating to the built heritage of Scotland from the earliest times to the present day.
RCAHMS creates and maintains the above record and makes it available to the public online, in the Search Room and through exhibitions and publications.
Subject coverage: Archaeology, architectural history, landscape history, built heritage, ancient monuments, planning, development and urban history, topography, history, industrial archaeology, aerial photography, and the history of Scotland.

Information services: RCAHMS searchable online resources; telephone, email, letter and fax enquiry service; free public Search Room; RCAHMS publications; online ordering and licensing of images.

Special visitor services: Ability to consult Collection items in the Search Room with staff to assist; digital finding aids to research and consult aerial photography; self-service photocopying and lasercopying; four PCs for online research.

Education services: Group visits; induction and training; lectures; online resources; exhibitions and publications.

Services for disabled people: Building fully accessible; lifts and toilets.

Collection: Historic and modern photographs including aerial photographs
Architectural drawings
Books on archaeology, architecture, topography and local history
Manuscripts
National collection of archaeological excavation archives
Papers of many notable Scottish architects
Plans from archaeological excavations and field surveys
The Aerial Reconnaissance Archives (TARA) of international aerial photography

Non-library collection catalogue: All or part available online, in-house and in print

Library catalogue: All or part available online and in-house

Publications: Printed
Order printed publications from: BookSource, tel: 0845 370 0067; e-mail: orders@booksource.net

Publications list: Available online and in print

Access to staff: Contact by letter, by telephone, by fax, by e-mail, in person and via website
Hours: Monday to Friday, 0930 to 1700

Access to building: No prior appointment required
Hours: Mon, Tue, Wed, Fri, 0930 to 1700; Thu, 0930 to 1800
Special comments: Closed on public and local holidays.

Access for disabled people: Parking provided, ramped entry, access to all public areas, lifts, toilet facilities

Parent body: The Scottish Government; website: http://www.scotland.gov.uk

ROYAL COMMONWEALTH SOCIETY (RCS)

18 Northumberland Avenue, London, WC2N 5AP

Tel: 020 7930 6733
Fax: 020 7930 9705
E-mail: info@rcsint.org
Website: www.rcsint.org

Enquiries to: Head of Public Affairs
Direct tel: 020 7766 9205
Direct e-mail: miles.giljam@rcsint.org

Founded: 1868

Organisation type and purpose:
International organisation, learned society, membership association (membership is by subscription, election or invitation), present number of members: 6500 affiliated to headquarters and 10,000 worldwide, voluntary organisation, registered charity (charity number 226748), art gallery, university library.
International organisation, with 69 self-governing branches and commonwealth societies, operates a private members club, non-governmental organisation.
The RCS promotes, in the UK and internationally, an understanding of the nature and working of the Commonwealth and of the factors that shape the lives of its people and the policies of its governments. Underlying the work of the RCS is the belief that an understanding of the Commonwealth is key to creating successful multicultural societies across the world.

Subject coverage: The Commonwealth and its members, past and present (virtually all subjects relevant to those countries except scientific and technical); some material on non-Commonwealth countries and on the colonial history of other European countries.

Collection: Royal Commonwealth Society Collection housed in the Cambridge University Library, West Road, Cambridge, CB3 9DR; includes:
Cobham Collection (on Cyprus)
Photograph Collection

Publications: Printed

Access to staff: Contact by letter, by telephone, by fax, by e-mail and via website. Appointment necessary.
Hours: Mon to Fri, 0915 to 1715

Access for disabled people: Ramped entry, toilet facilities

Library housed at: Cambridge University Library; West Road, Cambridge, CB3 9DR; tel: 01223 333000; fax: 01223 333160

ROYAL CONSERVATOIRE OF SCOTLAND (RCS)

100 Renfrew Street, Glasgow, G2 3DB

Tel: 0141 270 8268
Fax: 0141 270 8353
E-mail: library@rsamd.ac.uk
Website: www.rcs.ac.uk

Enquiries to: Head of Information Services
Direct e-mail: c.cochrane@rcs.ac.uk

Founded: 1847; formerly called Royal Scottish Academy of Music and Drama (year of change 2011)

Organisation type and purpose: HE Academy.

Subject coverage: Music, drama and dance

Library catalogue: All or part available online

Access to staff: Contact by letter, by telephone, by fax, by e-mail, in person and via website
Hours: Mon to Fri, 0900 to 1700

Access to building: No prior appointment required

Access for disabled people: Access to all public areas

ROYAL CORNWALL AGRICULTURAL ASSOCIATION (RCAA)

Royal Cornwall Showground, Wadebridge, Cornwall, PL27 7JE

Tel: 01208 812183
Fax: 01208 812713
E-mail: info@royalcornwall.co.uk
Website: www.royalcornwall.co.uk

Enquiries to: Secretary

Founded: 1793

Organisation type and purpose: Membership association, registered charity (charity number 250312).
Promotion of agriculture, etc.

Subject coverage: History of the RCAA, general agricultural history of Cornwall.

Collection: Archives of the Royal Cornwall Agricultural Association

Publications: Printed

Access to staff: Contact by letter, by telephone, by fax, by e-mail, in person and via website
Hours: Mon to Fri, 0900 to 1700

ROYAL ECONOMIC SOCIETY (RES)

Secretary-General's Office, School of Economics and Finance, University of St Andrews, St Andrews, Fife, KY16 9AL

Tel: 01334 462479
Fax: 01334 462444
E-mail: royaleconsoc@st-andrews.ac.uk
Website: www.res.org.uk

Enquiries to: RES Administrator
Other contacts: Administrator (for general enquiries); Secretary-General; Media Consultant

Founded: 1902

Organisation type and purpose: Learned society (membership is by subscription).
The promotion, encouragement and application of the study of economic science.

Subject coverage: Economics.

Collection: Archive of RES within the British Library of Political & Economic Science, London

Publications: Printed, and electronic and video
Order printed publications from: RES Administrator or Membership Services, Wiley-Blackwell, e-mail: ecove@wiley.com

Publications list: Available online

Access to staff: Contact by letter, by telephone, by fax, by e-mail and via website. Appointment necessary.
Hours: Mon to Fri, 1000 to 1600

ROYAL ENFIELD OWNERS CLUB (REOC)

30–32 Causeway, Burgh-Le-Marsh, Skegness, Lincolnshire, PE24 5LT

Tel: 01754 810119
Website: www.royalenfield.org.uk

Enquiries to: Membership Secretary

Founded: 1978

Organisation type and purpose: Membership association (membership is by subscription), present number of members: 3,028

Subject coverage: Royal Enfield motor cycles.

Publications: Printed

Access to staff: Contact by letter, by telephone, by e-mail and via website
Hours: Mon to Fri, 0900 to 1700

ROYAL ENGINEERS MUSEUM, LIBRARY AND ARCHIVES (REMLA)

Brompton Barracks, Chatham, Kent, ME4 4UX

Tel: 01634 822221
Fax: 01634 822063
E-mail: mail@re-museum.co.uk

Enquiries to: Head Curator
Other contacts: Documentation Officer, Deputy Curator

Founded: 1813; formerly called Royal Engineers Library; merged with Royal Engineers Museum (year of change 1993)

Organisation type and purpose: Military library.

Subject coverage: All aspects of military engineering world-wide with specific reference to the Royal Engineers; many non-military fields of early technology e.g. photography.

Collection: 2nd copies of RE Units' War Diaries, mainly from the First World War, but some also from other conflicts
Correspondence Books from RE stations, 18th–19th century
Collections of papers of significant Sappers – General Gordon, Kitchener and Burgoyne
Some photographs and maps produced by Engineers, diaries and correspondence relating to members of the Corps from the 18th century to the present day, as well as historical notes by researchers, principally John Connolly, into the early origins of the Corps

Non-library collection catalogue: All or part available in-house

Library catalogue: All or part available in-house

Access to staff: Contact by letter, by telephone and by e-mail. Appointment necessary.
Hours: Mon to Fri, 0900 to 1700
Special comments: Copying charges apply.

Access to building: *Hours:* Museum open: Tue to Fri, 0900 to 1700; Sat, Sun, 1130 to 1700 (last entry each day at 1600)
Library open: Tue and Wed, 1000 to 1300 and 1400 to 1630
Special comments: Access to the Library is by appointment only. As it is in an active barracks, visitors must be escorted at all times.

Access for disabled people: Unfortunately the present Library is not accessible for wheelchair users. Please contact staff to make alternative arrangements

Affiliated to: Royal Engineers Institution; at the same address

ROYAL ENTOMOLOGICAL SOCIETY (RES)

The Mansion House, Chiswell Green Lane, St Albans, AL2 3NS

Tel: 01727 899387
Fax: 01727 894797
E-mail: val@royensoc.co.uk
Website: www.royensoc.co.uk

Enquiries to: Librarian

Founded: 1833

Organisation type and purpose: International organisation, learned society (membership is by election or invitation), registered charity (charity number 213620), suitable for ages: postgraduate+, research organisation, publishing house.
The improvement and diffusion of entomological science.

Subject coverage: Entomology: all aspects but in particular taxonomy with reference to the western palaeoarctic region.

Collection: c. 750 journal titles
c. 11,000 books
c. 30,000 reprints, including the Rothschild collection of siphonaptera reprints (flea)
Archival material
Innumerable monographs
Superb collection of 18th-, 19th- and 20th-century works on insects

Library catalogue: All or part available in-house

Publications: Printed

Publications list: Available online and in print

Access to staff: Contact by letter, by telephone, by fax and by e-mail. Appointment necessary. Non-members charged.
Hours: Mon to Thu, 0900 to 1600; Fri, 0900 to 1530

Access to building: Prior appointment required
Special comments: Access limited to Fellows and Members, except by appointment.

ROYAL ENVIRONMENTAL HEALTH INSTITUTE OF SCOTLAND (REHISi)

19 Torphichen Street, Edinburgh EH3 8HX

Tel: 0131 229 2968
Fax: 0131 228 2926
E-mail: contact@rehis.com

continued overleaf

Website: www.rehis.com

Enquiries to: Chief Executive

Founded: 1983

Organisation type and purpose: Membership association (membership is by qualification), present number of members: 1,100, voluntary organisation, registered Scottish charity (charity number SC0 09406). Awarding body for the environmental health profession in Scotland and a UK Competent Authority for the profession. Awarding body for qualifications in food safety, health and safety, food and health, and infection control.

Subject coverage: Environmental health in Scotland, education and training in environmental health subjects.

Library catalogue: All or part available online and in-house

Publications: Printed
Order printed publications from: Office

Access to staff: Contact by letter, by telephone, by e-mail and via website. Appointment necessary.
Hours: Mon to Fri, 0900 to 1700

Access to building: Prior appointment required

ROYAL FORESTRY SOCIETY (RFS)

102 High Street, Tring, Hertfordshire, HP23 4AF

Tel: 01442 822028
Fax: 01442 890395
E-mail: rfshq@rfs.org.uk
Website: www.rfs.org.uk

Enquiries to: Chief Executive

Founded: 1882

Organisation type and purpose: Learned society (membership is by subscription).

Subject coverage: Forestry; arboriculture; careers advice in these fields.

Collection: Rare forestry books

Publications: Printed

Access to staff: Contact by letter
Hours: Mon to Fri, 0900 to 1700

Access to building: No prior appointment required

ROYAL FREE LONDON NHS FOUNDATION TRUST

Formal name: Royal Free Campus, University College London Medical School

Medical Library, Royal Free Hospital, Rowland Hill Street, London, NW3 2PF

Tel: 020 7794 0500 ext 33202
Fax: 020 7794 3534
E-mail: rlibrary@ucl.ac.uk
Website: www.ucl.ac.uk/medicalschool/facilities/rfhmedlib/

Enquiries to: Librarian

History of institution: incorporates the former Royal Free Hospital School of Medicine (year of change 1998)

Organisation type and purpose: Hospital and University library

Subject coverage: Clinical medicine, nursing and allied health

Library catalogue: All or part available online

Access to staff: Contact by letter. Appointment necessary. Letter of introduction required.
Hours: Mon to Fri, 0900 to 1900;
Sat, 0900 to 1300 (excluding Aug)
Special comments: Members primarily

Access for disabled people: Level entry

Administered by: University College London

ROYAL GEOGRAPHICAL SOCIETY WITH THE INSTITUTE OF BRITISH GEOGRAPHERS (RGS-IBG)

1 Kensington Gore, London, SW7 2AR

Tel: 020 7591 3000
Fax: 020 7591 3001
E-mail: enquiries@rgs.org
Website: www.rgs.org

Enquiries to: Principal Librarian
Direct tel: 020 7591 3041
Direct e-mail: e.rae@rgs.org
Other contacts: Deputy Librarian

Founded: 1830

Organisation type and purpose: Learned society, professional body (membership is by qualification, election or invitation), present number of members: 14,000, registered charity.
Study groups in the subjects listed below. Access to the Society's information resources is available in the Foyle Reading Room.

Subject coverage: Geography, including exploration and travel; cartography, geography of rural and urban areas, medical, transport and population geography, geomorphology, historical geography, quantitative methods, women and geography, planning and geography, industrial activity and area development, biogeography, geography in higher education, social and political geography, transport geography, careers guidance for all geographers, field science training, major research projects overseas.

Non-library collection catalogue: All or part available online and in-house

Library catalogue: All or part available online and in-house

Publications: Printed
Order printed publications from: RGS-IBG Book Series

Publications list: Available in print

Access to staff: Contact by letter, by telephone, by fax, by e-mail, in person and via website. Non-members charged.

Access to building: Apart from Foyle Reading Room, members only
Hours: Mon to Fri, 0930 to 1730 (Foyle Reading Room, 1000 to 1700)

Access for disabled people: Fully accessible

ROYAL GLASGOW INSTITUTE OF THE FINE ARTS, THE (RGI)

RGI, 5 Oswald Street, Glasgow, G1 4QR

Tel: 0141 248 7411
Fax: 0141 221 0417
E-mail: art@royalglasgowinstitute.org
Website: www.royalglasgowinstitute.org

Enquiries to: Secretary

Founded: 1861

Organisation type and purpose: Membership association (membership is by subscription), present number of members: 1200. Registered charity (charity number SC014650)

Subject coverage: Promotion of art by means of an open annual exhibition, the third largest in the United Kingdom. The RGI also owns the RGI Kelly Gallery, 118 Douglas Street, Glasgow, G2 4ET for hire for solo or group exhibitions. Tel: 0141 248 6386; e-mail: curator@royalglasgowinstitute.org

Publications: Printed
Order printed publications from: Secretary

Access to staff: Contact by letter, by telephone, by fax and by e-mail
Hours: Mon to Thu, 0900 to 1600

Access to building: *Hours:* Tues to Fri, 1030 to 1700; Sat, 1030 to 1500

Access for disabled people: Yes
Hours: As above

ROYAL HISTORICAL SOCIETY (RHistS)

University College London, Gower Street, London, WC1E 6BT

Tel: 020 7387 7532
Fax: 020 7387 7532
E-mail: royalhistsoc@ucl.ac.uk
Website: www.royalhistoricalsociety.org

Enquiries to: Executive Secretary
Direct e-mail: s.carr@ucl.ac.uk
Other contacts: Administrative Secretary

Founded: 1868

Organisation type and purpose: Learned society, registered charity.

Subject coverage: History.

Information services: see website.

Collection: A private collection of about 1,000 books dating from 1650 to the present day, some of which are part of the bequest of Sir George Prothero (d. 1922), whose papers are also held in the Society's archives
Collection of publications from national and regional records and historical societies housed within UCL History Library
Papers of the Camden Society

Non-library collection catalogue: All or part available in-house

Library catalogue: All or part available online

Publications: Printed
Order printed publications from: Camden University Press
Boydell and Brewer

Publications list: Available online

Access to staff: Contact by letter, by telephone, by e-mail, in person and via website. Appointment necessary.
Hours: Mon to Fri, 0900 to 1700
Special comments: by appointment

Access to building: by appointment

Headquarters address: University College London; Gower Street, London WC1E 6BT

ROYAL HOLLOWAY INSTITUTE FOR ENVIRONMENTAL RESEARCH (RHIER)

Huntersdale, Callow Hill, Virginia Water, Surrey, GU25 4LN

Tel: 01784 477404
Fax: 01784 477427
E-mail: rhier@rhbnc.ac.uk

Enquiries to: Project Development Officer
Direct e-mail: s.kandiah-evans@rhul.ac.uk
Other contacts: Director, e-mail: e.maltby@rhul.ac.uk

Founded: 1994

Organisation type and purpose: University department or institute.

Subject coverage: Wetland management, wetland conservation, wetland ecosystem functioning, hydroacoustic methods for fish survey.
Global Biological Diversity Conservation Policy.

Publications: Printed

Access to staff: Contact by letter and by e-mail
Hours: Mon to Fri, 0900 to 1700

Access to building: Prior appointment required

Access for disabled people: Parking provided

Connections with: IUCN Commission on Ecosystem Management; Wetland Ecosystems Research Group; Fish Hydroacoustics Unit; tel: 01784 477404; fax: 01784 477427

Parent body: Royal Holloway University of London; tel: 01784 434455

ROYAL HOLLOWAY UNIVERSITY OF LONDON – LIBRARY (RHUL)

Formal name: Royal Holloway and Bedford New College University of London

Egham, Surrey, TW20 0EX

Tel: 01784 443823
E-mail: library@rhul.ac.uk
Website: www.rhul.ac.uk/library

Enquiries to: Director of Library Services
Other contacts: Head of Academic Liaison

Founded: 1886; incorporates the former Bedford College London (year of change 1986)

Organisation type and purpose: University library.
College library of the University of London.

Subject coverage: Arts, classics, drama, theatre studies and film, economics, English and American literature, French, German, Italian language and literature, history, linguistics, management, medical sociology, music, sociology, social administration, social anthropology, Hispanic studies, media arts, history of women.
Sciences: biochemistry, biology, botany, chemistry, geography, geology, mathematics, physics, physiology, psychology and zoology.

Collection: A. V. Coton collection on dance
Collection on theatre
College Archives
Dawson collection of New Zealand poetry and prose published since 1900
Dom Anselm Hughes collection on medieval religious music (includes his personal letters and papers)
Early printed books from 16th century onwards in classics; English and French literature; history; some science, especially botany
Robert Simpson Society Archives comprising books, scores, records, MS sketches and miscellanea relating to the composer
Sir Alfred Sherman Papers
Small but significant collection of works by or about T. E. Lawrence

Non-library collection catalogue: All or part available online

Library catalogue: All or part available online

Publications: Printed

Access to staff: Contact by letter, by telephone, by e-mail, in person and via website. Non-members charged.
Special comments: Appointments necessary if specific specialist help required

Access to building: No prior appointment required
Hours: Please see library website for current opening hours

Access for disabled people: Good access to Bedford Library; access to Founder's Library by arrangement

ROYAL HUMANE SOCIETY (RHS)

50/51 Temple Chambers, 3–7 Temple Avenue, London, EC4Y 0HP

Tel: 020 7936 2942
Fax: 020 7936 2942
E-mail: info@royalhumanesociety.org.uk
Website: www.royalhumanesociety.org.uk

Enquiries to: Secretary
Direct e-mail: secretary@royalhumanesociety.org.uk

Founded: 1774

Organisation type and purpose: Charity Society incorporated by Royal Charter.
Encourages the saving of human life by the giving of award.

Subject coverage: Grants non-pecuniary awards for bravery in saving human life and for the restoration of life by resuscitation.

Collection: Annual reports and casebooks from 1774 to present held by London Metropolitan Archives from autumn 2008

Publications: Printed

Access to staff: Contact by letter, by telephone, by fax and by e-mail. Appointment necessary. All charged.
Hours: Mon to Thu, 1030 to 1630

ROYAL INCORPORATION OF ARCHITECTS IN SCOTLAND (RIAS)

15 Rutland Square, Edinburgh, EH1 2BE

Tel: 0131 229 7545
Fax: 0131 228 2188
E-mail: info@rias.org.uk
Website: www.rias.org.uk

Enquiries to: Secretary

Founded: 1916

Organisation type and purpose: Professional body, membership association, consultancy.

Subject coverage: Architecture, architects and services, history of architecture.

Publications: Printed

Access to staff: Contact by letter, by telephone, by fax, by e-mail and via website. Appointment necessary.
Hours: Mon to Fri, 0900 to 1700

Access to building: *Hours:* Mon to Fri, 0900 to 1700

Branches: Aberdeen, Dundee, Edinburgh, Glasgow, Inverness and Stirling

Links with: Royal Institute of British Architects

ROYAL INSTITUTE OF BRITISH ARCHITECTS (RIBA)

West Midlands, Birmingham and Midland Institute, 9 Margaret Street, Birmingham, B3 3SP

Tel: 0121 233 2321
Fax: 0121 233 4946
E-mail: riba.westmidlands@inst.riba.org

Enquiries to: Administrator

Organisation type and purpose: Professional body (membership is by subscription, qualification), present number of members: 1300 in West Midlands, registered charity.

Non-library collection catalogue: All or part available in-house

Library catalogue: All or part available in-house

Access to staff: Contact by letter, by telephone and by fax. Appointment necessary. Non-members charged.
Hours: Mon to Fri, 0900 to 1700
Special comments: Charges to non-members may be appropriate.

Access to building: No prior appointment required
Special comments: Library only open on set days, telephone for details.

ROYAL INSTITUTE OF BRITISH ARCHITECTS (NORTH WEST REGION) (RIBA NW)

Unit 101, The Tea Factory, 82 Wood Street, Liverpool, L1 4DQ

Tel: 0151 703 0107
Fax: 0151 703 0108
E-mail: riba.northwest@inst.riba.org
Website: www.architecture.com

Enquiries to: Regional Director

Organisation type and purpose: Professional body (membership is by subscription).

Subject coverage: Architecture.

continued overleaf

Publications: Printed
Order printed publications from: RIBA Publications, Construction House, 56–64 Leonard Street, London, EC2A 4LT; tel: 020 7251 0791; fax: 020 7608 2375

Publications list: Available online and in print

Access to staff: Contact by letter, by telephone, by fax, by e-mail and in person
Hours: Mon to Fri, 0900 to 1700

Access to building: *Hours:* Mon to Fri, 0900 to 1700

Parent body: Royal Institute of British Architects (RIBA); 66 Portland Place, London, W1N 4AD

ROYAL INSTITUTE OF INTERNATIONAL AFFAIRS (RIIA, Chatham House)

Chatham House, 10 St James's Square, London, SW1Y 4LE

Tel: 020 7957 5723
Fax: 020 7957 5710
Website: www.chathamhouse.org

Enquiries to: Librarian
Direct e-mail: library@chathamhouse.org

Founded: 1920

Organisation type and purpose:
International organisation, learned society (membership is by subscription), registered charity, research organisation.
The Royal Institute of International Affairs at Chatham House, London, is one of the world's leading institutes for the analysis of international issues. The Institute is independent of government.

Subject coverage: International affairs and relations between all states (diplomatic, political, legal, military, economic and financial) since 1918, with special focus on the most recent 30–35 years; international problems and organisations; foreign and defence policies and (on a limited scale) domestic affairs of all countries.

Collection: Royal Institute of International Affairs archives available to post-graduate researchers by prior application.

Library catalogue: All or part available online

Publications: Printed, and electronic and video

Publications list: Available online

Access to staff: Contact by letter, by telephone, by e-mail and via website. Appointment necessary.
Hours: Mon 1000 to 1730, Tues to Fri 0930 to 1730
Special comments: Primarily for members.

ROYAL INSTITUTE OF NAVIGATION (RIN)

1 Kensington Gore, London, SW7 2AT

Tel: 020 7591 3130
Fax: 020 7591 3131
E-mail: info@rin.org.uk
Website: www.rin.org.uk

Enquiries to: Director

Founded: 1947

Organisation type and purpose:
International organisation, advisory body, learned society (membership is by subscription), present number of members: 3500, registered charity (charity number 251512), public library, publishing house.
To unite in one body those interested in navigation and to advance its science and practice, and to promote knowledge in navigation.

Subject coverage: All aspects of air, sea, vehicle and space navigation; navigation technology, satellite navigation, small craft navigation, general and civil aviation navigation, land navigation, traffic routing, animal navigation, personal navigation, history of navigation, astronomy, bridge design, collision avoidance, weather.

Collection: Library covering all aspects of navigation

Publications: Printed

Access to staff: Contact by letter, by telephone, by fax, by e-mail, in person and via website
Hours: Mon to Fri, 0930 to 1630

Access to building: No access other than to staff

Member of: European Group of Institutes of Navigation (EUGIN); tel: + 31 23 540 2485; fax: + 31 23 540 2486; e-mail: navicons@xs4all.nl; International Association of Institutes of Navigation (IAIN); tel: 01444 232405; fax: 01444 232405; e-mail: prentpage@aol.com

ROYAL INSTITUTE OF OIL PAINTERS (ROI)

17 Carlton House Terrace, London, SW1Y 5BD

Tel: 020 7930 6844
Fax: 020 7839 7830
E-mail: press@mallgalleries.com
Website: www.mallgalleries.org.uk

Enquiries to: Secretary
Other contacts: Marketing and Communications Officer

Founded: 1882

Organisation type and purpose:
Membership association (membership is by election or invitation), present number of members: 68, registered charity (charity number 327615).
To foster and promote the art of oil painting.

Subject coverage: Oil paintings and painters, annual open exhibition.

Publications: Printed

Access to staff: Contact by letter, by telephone, by fax, by e-mail and via website. Appointment necessary.
Hours: Mon to Fri, 0930 to 1700

Access to building: No access other than to staff
Hours: Mon to Fri, 0930 to 1700

Access for disabled people: Stairlift, toilet facilities
Special comments: Stairlift.

Links with: Federation of British Artists (FBA); at the same address

ROYAL INSTITUTE OF PAINTERS IN WATERCOLOURS (RI)

17 Carlton House Terrace, London, SW1Y 5BD

Tel: 020 7930 6844
Fax: 020 7839 7830
E-mail: press@mallgalleries.com
Website: www.mallgalleries.org.uk

Enquiries to: Secretary
Other contacts: Marketing and Communications Officer

Founded: 1831

Organisation type and purpose:
Membership association (membership is by election or invitation), present number of members: 78, voluntary organisation, registered charity (charity number 291405).
To foster and promote the art of watercolour painting.

Subject coverage: Watercolour painting, annual open exhibition.

Publications: Printed

Access to staff: Contact by letter, by telephone, by fax, by e-mail and via website. Appointment necessary.
Hours: Mon to Fri, 0930 to 1700

Access to building: No access other than to staff

Access for disabled people: Stairlift, toilet facilities
Special comments: Stairlift.

Links with: Federation of British Artists; at the same address

ROYAL INSTITUTE OF PHILOSOPHY

14 Gordon Square, London, WC1H 0AR

Tel: 020 7387 4130
Fax: 020 7383 4061
E-mail: secretary@royalinstitutephilosophy.org
Website: www.royalinstitutephilosophy.org

Enquiries to: Secretary

Organisation type and purpose: Learned society.
To promote the study and discussion of philosophy, arrange and sponsor lectures and conferences.

Subject coverage: Philosophy: logic, metaphysics, epistemology, ethics, aesthetics, social and political philosophy; the philosophies of science, religion, history, education, mind and language.

Collection: Bosanquet Collection

Publications: Printed

Access to staff: Contact by letter and by e-mail
Hours: Mon to Fri, 0900 to 1700

ROYAL INSTITUTION OF CHARTERED SURVEYORS (RICS)

12 Great George Street, Parliament Square, London, SW1P 3AD

Tel: 0870 333 1600
Fax: 020 7334 3811
E-mail: contactrics@rics.org
Website: www.rics.org

Enquiries to: Librarian
Direct fax: 020 7334 3784
Direct e-mail: library@rics.org

Founded: 1868

Organisation type and purpose: Professional body (membership is by qualification), present number of members: 120,000.

Subject coverage: Commercial property, leisure property, chartered surveying, property, land, construction, valuation, surveying, town and country planning, construction economics, construction law, housing, agricultural holdings, estate agency, property management, land surveying, hydrographic surveying, landlord and tenant, property tax, quantity surveying, rating, estate management, marine resources.

Collection: Board of Agriculture Reports, 19th century
Historical Collection (pre-1875) on land, measurement and building economics and topography
Royal Commission Reports, 19th century
Topographical collections

Trade and statistical information: Construction workload, housing market trend indicator, commercial property market survey, rural market survey and residential lettings

Library catalogue: All or part available online

Publications: Printed, and electronic and video
Order printed publications from: Mail Order Department, RICS Books, Surveyor Court, Westwood Way Business Park, Coventry, West Midlands, CV4 8JE; tel: 0870 333 1600; fax: 020 7334 3851; e-mail: mailorder@rics.org, website: ricsbooks.com

Publications list: Available online and in print

Access to staff: Contact by letter, by telephone, by fax, by e-mail, in person and via website. Non-members charged.
Hours: Mon to Fri, 0930 to 1730
Special comments: Charges made for access to the Library for non-members.

Access for disabled people: Ramped entry, toilet facilities

Other addresses: Royal Institution of Chartered Surveyors; Surveyor Court, Westwood Way Business Park, Coventry, CV4 8JE; tel: 0870 333 1600; fax: 020 7334 3811; Royal Institution of Chartered Surveyors; 9 Manor Place, Edinburgh, EH3 7DN; tel: 0131 225 7078; fax: 0131 240 0830/31

ROYAL INSTITUTION OF CHARTERED SURVEYORS IN SCOTLAND (RICS)

9 Manor Place, Edinburgh, EH3 7DN

Tel: 0131 225 7078
Fax: 0131 240 0830
E-mail: edlib@rics.org
Website: www.rics.org/library

Enquiries to: Library Manager

Founded: 1897

Organisation type and purpose: International organisation, professional body (membership is by qualification).

Subject coverage: Surveying, building construction, property, rural practice.

Library catalogue: All or part available online

Publications list: Available online

Access to staff: Contact by letter, by telephone, by fax, by e-mail, in person and via website. Appointment necessary. Non-members charged.
Hours: Mon to Fri, 0900 to 1700

Also at: The Librarian, Royal Institution of Chartered Surveyors; 12 Great George Street, Parliament Square, London, SW1P 3AD; tel: 020 7334 3714; fax: 020 7334 3784; e-mail: library@rics.org

ROYAL INSTITUTION OF CORNWALL (RIC)

Courtney Library & Cornish History Research Centre, River Street, Truro, Cornwall, TR1 2SJ

Tel: 01872 242786 (direct line) or 272205
Fax: 01872 240514
E-mail: RIC@royalcornwallmuseum.org.uk
Website: www.royalcornwallmuseum.org.uk

Enquiries to: Librarian Archivist

Founded: 1818

Organisation type and purpose: Learned society; registered charity (charity number 221958). The oldest established Cornish history research centre in the County. Private members library. Access to study area by appointment for students/researchers with introductory letter from academic institution.

Subject coverage: Cornwall and its cultural heritage; the social hisotry of modern Cornwall; medieval and early modern Cornwall; place and locality.

Collection: Doble Collection (hagiography)
Henderson Collection (manuscripts on history, antiquities, topography, Cornwall)
Manuscripts 13th-19th centuries (c. 25,000 items, Cornish estates and people)
Directories and newspapers 1798–1951 and 1965–1973 (original files, Cornwall)
Parish registers (microfilms and transcripts)
CALM (database of archives); MODES (database of museum objects)
Shaw Collection (Methodist church history, Cornwall)
Staal Collection (ceramics, glass, clocks)

Non-library collection catalogue: All or part available in-house

Library catalogue: All or part available in-house

Publications: Printed

Access to staff: Contact by letter, by telephone, by fax, by e-mail and via website. Appointment necessary. Access for members only. Letter of introduction required.
Hours: Museum: Mon to Sat, 1000 to 1645 – last admission at 1600.
Courtney Library: Tues, Wed, Fri, 1000 to 1300 and 1400 to 1600; Sat 1000 to 1300. Closed Sun, Mon and Bank Holidays.
Special comments: To enable the computerization of our collections and make them available on the internet, from June 6 2012 the Courtney Library became a members-only library. Students and researchers may continue to access the library with a current student card or letter from their academic institution. Access by appointment.
Research service – 30 minutes free – thereafter £30 per hour (limited to 1 hour per request).
This time limit is necessary as only one member of staff manages the Library and Archive service.
Photographic collection: available on Thursdays only. For enquiries and appointments email: photographs@royalcornwallmuseum.org.uk or tel: 01872 272205 ext. 244 (answerphone).

Access for disabled people: Ramped entry, Lift access to Library and Archive, toilet facilities. Cafe on ground floor.

Links with: Royal Cornwall Museum and Art Gallery

ROYAL INSTITUTION OF GREAT BRITAIN (RI)

21 Albemarle Street, London, W1S 4BS

Tel: 020 7409 2992
Fax: 020 7629 3569
E-mail: ri@ri.ac.uk
Website: www.rigb.org/

Enquiries to: Head of Collections and Heritage
Direct tel: 020 7670 2924
Direct e-mail: fjames@ri.ac.uk

Founded: 1799

Organisation type and purpose: Learned society (membership is by election or invitation), present number of members: c. 3000.
Scientific body.

Subject coverage: Science for the layman, history and philosophy of science, scientific biography, the social relations of science, solid state and surface chemistry and physics, catalysis, computer molecular modelling.

Collection: Historic apparatus
Manuscripts of famous scientists connected with The Royal Institution eg H Davy, M Faraday, J Tyndall, J Dewar, W H and W L Bragg, G Porter
Pre-1900 scientific books and periodicals
The Royal Institution Administrative Archives

Non-library collection catalogue: All or part available in-house

Library catalogue: All or part available in-house

Publications: Printed, and electronic and video, and microform publications

Publications list: Available in print

Access to staff: Appointment necessary.
Hours: Mon to Fri, 0900 to 1700

Access for disabled people: Level entry, toilet facilities

continued overleaf

Includes the: Davy-Faraday Research Laboratory; Library and Archives; Michael Faraday Museum; Royal Institution Centre for the History of Science and Technology

ROYAL INSTITUTION OF NAVAL ARCHITECTS (RINA)

10 Upper Belgrave Street, London, SW1X 8BQ

Tel: 020 7235 4622
Fax: 020 7259 5912
E-mail: hq@rina.org.uk
Website: www.rina.org.uk

Enquiries to: Executive Officer

Founded: 1860

Organisation type and purpose:
International organisation, learned society, professional body (membership is by qualification, election or invitation), registered charity (charity number 211161).

Subject coverage: Naval architecture, shipbuilding, marine engineering and related subjects.

Non-library collection catalogue: All or part available online and in print

Library catalogue: All or part available in-house

Publications: Printed, and electronic and video
Order printed publications from: e-mail: publications@rina.org.uk
Order electronic and video publications from: e-mail: publications@rina.org.uk

Publications list: Available online and in print

Access to staff: Contact by letter, by telephone, by fax, by e-mail and via website. Appointment necessary. Non-members charged.
Hours: Mon to Fri, 0930 to 1700

ROYAL INSTITUTION OF SOUTH WALES (RISW)

c/o Swansea Museum, Victoria Road, Maritime Quarter, Swansea, West Glamorgan, SA1 1SN

Tel: 01792 653763
Fax: 01792 652585
E-mail: swansea.museum@swansea.gov.uk
Website: www.risw.org.uk

Enquiries to: Honorary Secretary
Direct tel: 01792 874143
Other contacts: Curator for museum/local history

Founded: 1835

Organisation type and purpose: Learned society (membership is by subscription), voluntary organisation, registered charity. Friends of Swansea Museum.

Subject coverage: Local history and studies of Swansea and surrounding area, including natural history, biography, culture, early photography, archaeology, ceramics (Swansea and District) and local topography.

Publications: Printed

Publications list: Available in print

Access to staff: Contact by letter, by telephone and by e-mail. Appointment necessary.
Hours: Mon to Fri, 0900 to 1700

Access to building: Prior appointment required

Access for disabled people: Parking provided

ROYAL LANCASHIRE AGRICULTURAL SOCIETY (RLAS)

PO Box 202, Thornton Cleveleys, FY5 9AW

E-mail: info@rlas.co.uk
Website: www.rlas.co.uk

Enquiries to: Secretary

Founded: 1767

Organisation type and purpose:
Membership association (membership is by subscription), present number of members: 750, registered charity (charity number 1008403).
Promotion of agriculture. Organisation of three-day agricultural show.

Subject coverage: Royal Lancashire Show.

Collection: History of Society held in County Records Office
Show Journals over many years

Publications: Printed

Access to staff: Contact by letter, by telephone, by fax, by e-mail, in person and via website
Hours: Mon to Fri, 0900 to 1700

Access for disabled people: Access to all public areas

Links with: Various breed societies

ROYAL LIFE SAVING SOCIETY (UK)

River House, High Street, Broom, Alcester, Warwickshire, B50 4HN

Tel: 01789 773994
Fax: 01789 773995
E-mail: lifesavers@rlss.org.uk
Website: www.lifesavers.org.uk

Founded: 1891

Organisation type and purpose: A registered charity with a vision to safeguard lives in, on and near water.
The society has more than 11,000 members in 50 branches and 3,000 active lifesaving and lifeguarding clubs and approved training centres throughout the UK and Ireland.

Subject coverage: Lifesavers and lifesaving.

Publications: Electronic and video
Order electronic and video publications from: website

Publications list: Available online

Access to staff: Contact by letter, by telephone, by fax and by e-mail

ROYAL LONDON HOSPITAL ARCHIVES AND MUSEUM

The Royal London Hospital, Whitechapel, London, E1 1BB

Tel: 020 7377 7608
E-mail: rlharchives@bartsandthelondon.nhs.uk
Website: www.bartsandthelondon.nhs.uk/museums
Website: www.a2a.org.uk
Website: www.aim25.ac.uk
Website: www.bartshealth.nhs.uk

Enquiries to: Archivist

Organisation type and purpose: National government body, museum, University department or institute, suitable for ages: 12+.
Archive.

Subject coverage: Hospitals, medical and nursing history, dentistry, orthodontics, forensic medicine, health records.

Collection: Archives of the Royal London Hospital
Archives of the London Chest Hospital
Archives of the Queen Elizabeth Hospital for Children
Archives of the Royal Brompton Hospital
Archives of Royal Brompton & Harefield NHS Trust
Archives of the London Hospital Medical College
Archives of other hospitals in Tower Hamlets and Newham
Collections: Edith Cavell Collection: Nursing history, artefacts and archives 1800s-1915
Eva Luckes Collection
London Hospital Surgical Instruments 18th-20th century
Medical and surgical films
Princess Alexandra School of Nursing: Nursing history, uniforms, equipment etc.1880–1993

Non-library collection catalogue: All or part available in-house

Library catalogue: All or part available in-house

Publications: Printed
Order microform publications from: www.proquest.com/

Publications list: Available online and in print

Access to staff: Contact by letter, by telephone, by fax, by e-mail, in person and via website. Appointment necessary.
Hours: Mon to Fri, 1000 to 1630

Access to building: Open to the public
Hours: Archives, by appointment Mon to Fri, 1000 to 1630; Museum Tue to Fri, 1000 to 1630; closed bank holidays and Christmas to New Year

Access for disabled people: Disabled access available

Affiliated to: Queen Mary University of London

Parent body: Barts Health NHS Trust; Trust Headquarters, Aneurin Bevan House, 81 Commercial Road, London E1 1RD

ROYAL LONDON SOCIETY FOR BLIND PEOPLE (RLSB)

Dorton House, Seal, Sevenoaks, Kent, TN15 0ED

Tel: 01732 592500
Fax: 01732 592506
E-mail: enquiries@rlsb.org.uk

Website: www.rlsb.org.uk

Enquiries to: Resource & Volunteer Manager
Direct tel: 01732 592515

Founded: 1838

Organisation type and purpose: Registered charity (charity number 307892).
Established to ensure that people who have lost their sight in youth have the same life chances as their sighted peers.

Subject coverage: Nursery education of blind or partially sighted children, community education services 5–16, further education from 16 upwards, including mature students, training and rehabilitation, Young People & Adult Support Services.

Collection: Minutes and official reports on the Society dating back to its inception in 1838

Publications: Printed, and electronic and video

Access to staff: Contact by letter, by telephone, by fax, by e-mail and via website. Appointment necessary.
Hours: Mon to Fri, 0900 to 1700

Member organisation of: Blindcare; Greater London Fund for the Blind; Opsis

ROYAL MAIL GROUP EDUCATION SERVICE

PO Box 145, Sittingbourne, Kent, ME10 1NH

Tel: 01795 426465
Fax: 01795 437988
E-mail: royalmail@edist.co.uk
Website: www.teacherspost.co.uk

Enquiries to: Director

History of institution: formerly called Post Office Film and Video Library, and Education Service (year of change 2001)

Organisation type and purpose: Royal Mail education initiatives and resources.

Subject coverage: Full range of educational resources – primary, secondary, higher, supported by video programmes and other material on all aspects of Royal Mail, Post Office, Counters and Parcelforce. Library for GPO classic programmes, e.g. 'Night Mail' on video and many other 1930s subjects. In addition more recent releases, including videos on stamps, the Millennium and other subjects.

Collection: Current Post Office video releases
Archive posters
Classic collection of archive subjects from GPO film unit (1930s) (on DVD)
Classic video collection

Library catalogue: All or part available in print

Publications: Printed

Publications list: Available in print

Access to staff: Contact by letter, by telephone, by fax, by e-mail and in person
Hours: Mon to Fri, 0900 to 1700

Access to building: Prior appointment required

ROYAL MARINES ASSOCIATION (RMA)

Central Office, Building 32, Whale Island, Portsmouth, Hants, PO2 8ER

Tel: 023 9265 1519
Fax: 023 9254 7207
E-mail: chiefexec@rma.org.uk

Enquiries to: Chief Executive

Founded: 1946

Organisation type and purpose: National organisation, membership association (membership is by subscription, qualification), present number of members: 10,000, registered charity (charity number 206003).
Service charity.

Access to staff: Contact by letter, by telephone, by fax and by e-mail
Hours: Mon to Fri, 0900 to 1700

ROYAL MEDICAL SOCIETY (RMS)

Student Centre, 5/5 Bristo Square, Edinburgh, EH8 9AL

Tel: 0131 650 2672
E-mail: enquiries@royalmedical.co.uk
Website: www.royalmedical.co.uk

Enquiries to: Secretary

Founded: 1736

Organisation type and purpose: Learned society.
Historical, medical students' organisation and library.

Subject coverage: Edinburgh medical history.

Collection: Collection of dissertations over last 258 years
Current medical library
Historical medical library
Pathological museum

Publications: Printed

Access to staff: Contact by letter and by e-mail. Appointment necessary.
Hours: Mon to Fri, 1200 to 1700

ROYAL MICROSCOPICAL SOCIETY (RMS)

37–38 St Clements, Oxford, OX4 1AJ

Tel: 01865 248768
Fax: 01865 791237
E-mail: info@rms.org.uk
Website: www.rms.org.uk

Enquiries to: Administrator

Founded: 1839

Organisation type and purpose: Learned society, present number of members: 1,500, registered charity (charity number 241990).
To promote the advancement of microscopical science by discussion and publication of research into improvements in the construction and mode of application of microscopes and into those branches of science where microscopy is important.

Subject coverage: Microscopy.

Collection: Collection of 18th- and 19th-century microscopes – housed at the Museum of the History of Science, Broad Street, Oxford

Non-library collection catalogue: All or part available in print

Publications: Printed

Access to staff: Contact by letter, by telephone, by fax and by e-mail
Hours: Mon to Fri, 0900 to 1700

Affiliated to: International Federation of Societies for Histochemistry and Cytochemistry (IFSHC); International Federation of Societies of Electron Microscopy (IFSEM)

ROYAL MILITARY ACADEMY SANDHURST (RMAS)

Central Library, Camberley, Surrey, GU15 4PQ

Tel: 01276 412367
Fax: 01276 412359
E-mail: aaorgill@aol.com

Enquiries to: Librarian

Organisation type and purpose: Training organisation. Central government military academy.

Subject coverage: War studies and military history; international affairs; political and social studies; Commonwealth of Independent States and the former republics of the Soviet Union.

Collection: Le Marchant Collection of manuscripts relating to the foundation of Sandhurst
Letter Books, RMA Woolwich, 1787–1895
Register of Gentlemen Cadets, RMA Woolwich, 1790–1793 and 1799–1939
Registers of Gentlemen Cadets, RMC Sandhurst, 1806–1945
Sandhurst Papers, 1857–1939

Non-library collection catalogue: All or part available in-house

Library catalogue: All or part available in-house

Publications: Printed

Access to staff: Contact by letter, by telephone and by e-mail
Hours: Mon to Thu, 0830 to 1800; Fri, 0830 to 1630
Special comments: Visitors strictly by appointment only.

Part of: Ministry of Defence

ROYAL NATIONAL CHILDREN'S FOUNDATION (RNCF)

Sandy Lane, Cobham, Surrey KT11 2ES

Tel: 01932 868622
Fax: 01932 866420
E-mail: admin@rncf.org.uk
Website: www.rncf.org.uk

Founded: 2010; created by the merger of Joint Educational Trust (founded 1972) and Royal Wanstead Children's Foundation (founded 1827)

Organisation type and purpose: Registered charity (charity number 310916), suitable for ages: 7 to 18.

continued overleaf

Subject coverage: Provides grants and boarding school places to vulnerable children with social need, not educational need.

Access to staff: Contact by letter, by telephone, by fax, by e-mail and via website
Hours: Mon to Fri, 0900 to 1700

Access to building: No access other than to staff

Access for disabled people: Access to all public areas, toilet facilities

ROYAL NATIONAL COLLEGE FOR THE BLIND (RNC)

College Road, Hereford, HR1 1EB

Tel: 01432 265725
Fax: 01432 376628
E-mail: info@rncb.ac.uk
Website: www.rncb.ac.uk

Enquiries to: Marketing Manager
Other contacts: Central Admissions for advice/guidance on enrolment procedures.

Founded: 1872

Organisation type and purpose: Registered charity (charity number 1000388), training organisation.
Further education and training for people who are blind or partially-sighted.

Subject coverage: Education of the blind and partially sighted, especially education in music technology, piano tuning and repairing, business studies, remedial therapy, computing, performing arts, tele-tutoring, sport and recreation.

Collection: Annual Reports dating from foundation of College in 1872
Braille Library

Library catalogue: All or part available online

Publications: Printed, and electronic and video

Access to staff: Contact by letter, by telephone, by fax, by e-mail and via website. Appointment necessary.
Hours: Mon to Fri, 0900 to 1700

Access for disabled people: Parking provided, ramped entry, level entry, toilet facilities

Member of: Natspec; Opsis

ROYAL NATIONAL INSTITUTE OF THE BLIND (RNIB)

105 Judd Street, London, WC1H 9NE

Tel: 020 7388 1266
Fax: 020 7388 2034
E-mail: helpline@rnib.org.uk
Website: www.rnib.org.uk

Enquiries to: Communications Systems Officer
Direct tel: 020 7391 2396
Direct fax: 020 7391 2221
Direct e-mail: julie-crispin@rnib.org.uk

Organisation type and purpose: Registered charity.

Subject coverage: Advice, support and information for blind and partially-sighted people. Benefit rights, advice on wills and legacies; production of Braille books, periodicals and music; Talking Books; equipment and games for blind and partially sighted people and for deaf-blind people; social and employment rehabilitation and training; education including schools and colleges, advisory and training services; residential services; hotels; research into the prevention of blindness; advice on sport, leisure and the arts; health information service, low-vision expertise, consultancy to health authorities on ophthalmic services.

Information services: Helpline for advice, support and information.

Collection: Early embossed literature (some 100 items, Alston, Frere, Lucas, Moon, Braille)

Publications: Printed

Publications list: Available online and in print

Access to staff: Contact by letter, by telephone, by fax, by e-mail and via website
Hours: Mon to Fri, 0900 to 1700

Access for disabled people: Ramped entry, access to all public areas, toilet facilities

ROYAL NATIONAL INSTITUTE OF THE BLIND – TALKING BOOK SERVICE

UK Customer Service Centre, PO Box 173, Peterborough, PE2 6WS

Tel: 01733 375000
Fax: 01733 375001
E-mail: cservices@rnib.org.uk
Website: www.rnib.org.uk

Enquiries to: General Customer Services

Founded: 1935

Organisation type and purpose:
Subscription library, registered charity.
Postal library for blind and partially sighted people, of any age, offering a wide range of professionally recorded books (CD) on special easy to use playback equipment.

Subject coverage: Talking books.

Publications list: Available online and in print

Access to staff: Contact by letter, by e-mail and via website
Hours: Library: Mon to Fri, 0845 to 1800; Sat, 0900 to 1600

Access to building: No access other than to staff, prior appointment required

Access for disabled people: Parking provided, level entry, access to all public areas, toilet facilities

ROYAL NATIONAL LIFEBOAT INSTITUTION (RNLI)

West Quay Road, Poole, Dorset, BH15 1HZ

Tel: 0845 122 6999
Fax: 01202 663366
E-mail: info@rnli.org.uk
Website: www.rnli.org.uk

Enquiries to: Media Relations Manager

Founded: 1824

Organisation type and purpose: Registered charity.

Subject coverage: Search and rescue at sea, its organisation and statistics; design and construction of lifeboats and their electronic and other equipment; medical and survival techniques and equipment, lifeboat history (since 1824).

Special visitor services: Library/archive available by appointment.

Collection: Lifeboat models
Photographic library (lifeboats since c. 1860)
Royal National Lifeboat Collection
Fine art collection
5 museum sites

Publications: Printed, and electronic and video
Order printed publications from: The Publications Dept, at the above address
Order electronic and video publications from: Film and Image Unit, at the above address

Access to staff: Contact by letter, by telephone, by fax, by e-mail and via website
Hours: Mon to Fri, 0900 to 1700

Access to building: By appointment
Hours: Mon to Fri, 0900 to 1700

Access for disabled people: Lifts; access to display area and library
Hours: Mon to Fri, 0900 to 1700

Administers: Chatham Historic Lifeboat Collection; Grace Darling Museum; Henry Blogg Museum; RNLI Whitby Museum; RNLI Zetland Museum

Provides the secretariat for the: International Lifeboat Federation

ROYAL NATIONAL MISSION TO DEEP SEA FISHERMEN

Shore Street, Fraserburgh, Aberdeenshire, AB43 9BP

Tel: 01346 518388
Fax: 01346 517664

Enquiries to: The Superintendent

Founded: 1881

Organisation type and purpose: Registered charity (charity number 24477).

Subject coverage: Christian missionary and welfare work for fishing communities.

Access to staff: Contact by letter
Hours: Mon to Fri, 0900 to 1700

ROYAL NATIONAL MISSION TO DEEP SEA FISHERMEN, SCOTLAND (Fishermen's Mission)

The Fishermen's Mission, Haypark Business Centre, Marchmont Avenue, Polmont, Falkirk, FK2 0NZ

Tel: 01324 716857
Fax: 01324 716423
E-mail: ian.rnmdsf@talk21.com

Enquiries to: Director Scotland

Founded: 1881

Organisation type and purpose: Voluntary organisation, registered charity (charity number 232822).

Subject coverage: The fishing industry; care of fishermen and their families.

Collection: Records of magazine (Toilers of the Deep) from 1881 onwards

Publications: Printed

Access to staff: Contact by telephone
Hours: Mon to Fri, 0900 to 1700

ROYAL NATIONAL ROSE SOCIETY (RNRS)

Chiswell Green Lane, St Albans, Hertfordshire, AL2 3NR

Tel: 01727 850461
Fax: 01727 850360
E-mail: mail@rnrs.org.uk
Website: www.rnrs.org.uk

Enquiries to: Chief Executive

Founded: 1876

Organisation type and purpose: Membership association (membership is by subscription), present number of members: 3,000, registered charity (charity number 1035848).

Subject coverage: Roses, cultivation and history, etc; trials and exhibitions.

Collection: Society library including the Courtney Page Library

Publications: Printed

Access to staff: Contact by letter, by telephone, by fax, by e-mail and via website
Hours: Mon to Fri, 0900 to 1700

Affiliated to: World Federation of Rose Societies

ROYAL NAVAL ASSOCIATION (RNA)

Room 210, Semaphore Tower, PP70, HM Naval Base Portsmouth, PO1 3LT

Tel: 023 9272 3747
E-mail: nigel@royalnavalassoc.com
Website: www.royal-naval-association.co.uk

Enquiries to: General Secretary

Founded: 1954; incorporates the former Royal Naval Old Comrades Assocns (year of change 1953)

Organisation type and purpose: Registered charity (charity number 266982).

Subject coverage: Support to ex- and serving Naval Service personnel.

Services for disabled people: Shared financial support through SSAFA, RNBT.

Access to staff: Contact by letter and by fax. Access for members only.
Hours: Mon to Fri, 0900 to 1700

Access for disabled people: Lift available

Branches: 361 in UK; 30 overseas; see website for details

ROYAL NAVAL VOLUNTEER RESERVE OFFICERS ASSOCIATION

Formal name: Royal Naval Volunteer Reserve Officers' Association and Naval Club

38 Hill Street, London, W1J 5NS

Tel: 020 7493 7672
Fax: 020 7629 7995
E-mail: cdr@navalclub.co.uk
Website: www.navalclub.co.uk

Enquiries to: Chief Executive

Founded: 1946

Organisation type and purpose: Private members' club (membership is by election or invitation), offering full range of London Club facilities in the heart of Mayfair.

Subject coverage: RN, RNR and RNVR officers and those connected with the sea and maritime affairs. Corporate membership available.

Access to staff: Contact by letter, by telephone, by fax, by e-mail and via website. Appointment necessary. Access for members only.
Hours: Mon to Fri, 0900 to 1700

Access to building: *Hours:* 24-hour access

Access for disabled people: *Hours:* 24-hour access

ROYAL NORFOLK AGRICULTURAL ASSOCIATION (RNAA)

The Showground, Dereham Road, New Costessey, Norwich, Norfolk, NR5 0TT

Tel: 01603 748931
Fax: 01603 748729
E-mail: jpurling@norfolkshowground.com

Enquiries to: Chief Executive
Other contacts: Show Manager

Founded: 1847

Organisation type and purpose: Membership association (membership is by subscription), present number of members: 3500, registered charity (charity number 289581). County show organiser. Promotes improvement in breeding of livestock and plants, invention and improvement of agricultural machines and implements, and skills in agriculture, horticulture and allied systems of husbandry.

Subject coverage: Agricultural shows.

Publications: Printed

Access to staff: Contact by letter, by telephone, by fax and by e-mail. Appointment necessary.
Hours: Mon to Fri, 0900 to 1700

Access for disabled people: Parking provided, ramped entry

Affiliated to: Norfolk Showground Ltd

ROYAL NORTHERN AND UNIVERSITY CLUB (RNUC)

9 Albyn Place, Aberdeen, AB10 1YE

Tel: 01224 583292
Fax: 01224 571082
E-mail: secretary@rnuc.org.uk
Website: www.rnuc.org.uk

Enquiries to: Secretary

Founded: 1854

Organisation type and purpose: Membership association (membership is by election or invitation).

Access to staff: Contact by letter, by fax and by e-mail
Hours: Mon to Fri, 0900 to 1700

Access for disabled people: Parking provided, ramped entry

ROYAL NORTHERN COLLEGE OF MUSIC (RNCM)

124 Oxford Road, Manchester, M13 9RD

Tel: 0161 907 5200
Fax: 0161 273 7611
E-mail: library@rncm.ac.uk
Website: www.rncm.ac.uk
Website: www.rncm.ac.uk/component/content/article/79/27.html

Enquiries to: Librarian
Direct tel: 0161 907 5241; 0161 907 5245
Direct e-mail: anna.wright@rncm.ac.uk; geoff.thomason@rncm.ac.uk
Other contacts: Deputy Librarian

Founded: 1973; please select Royal Manchester College of Music; Northern School of Music (year of change 1973)

Organisation type and purpose: Music college.

Subject coverage: Music; recordings; musicology.

Collection: Adolph Brodsky Collection
Arthur Butterworth manuscripts
Dame Eva Turner Collection of songs
Carl Fuchs Collection
Gordon Green Collection
Halifax Collection
Hansen Collection
Horenstein Collection
Ida Carroll Archive
John Golland manuscripts
Philip Newman Collection
John Ogdon manuscripts
Philip Jones Brass Ensemble Archive
Rawsthorne manuscripts
Richard Hall Collection
RNCM Collection of Historic Musical Instruments, includes Henry Watson Instrument Collection
Rothwell Collection of wind music
Sir Charles Grove Library
Thomas Pitfield Archive

Non-library collection catalogue: All or part available online

Library catalogue: All or part available online

Publications: Printed

Access to staff: Contact by letter, by telephone, by fax, by e-mail and via website. Appointment necessary.
Hours: Term time: Mon to Thu, 0900 to 1900; Fri, 0930 to 1700; Sat 0900 to 1300
Vacations: Mon to Fri, 0930 to 1630

Access for disabled people: The RNCM Library is fully accessible to wheelchair users
Hours: As above

Affiliated to: IAML; website: http://www.iaml.info ; http://www.iaml-uk-irl.org

ROYAL NORWEGIAN EMBASSY

25 Belgrave Square, London, SW1X 8QD

Tel: 020 7591 5500
Fax: 020 7245 6993
E-mail: emb.london@mfa.no

Enquiries to: Press and Information Office

continued overleaf

Other contacts: Consular Section (tel: 020 7591 5500 for passports, visas, etc.)

Organisation type and purpose: Embassy.

Subject coverage: Norway.

Publications: Printed

Access to staff: Contact by letter, by telephone, by fax, by e-mail and in person
Hours: Mon to Fri, 0900 to 1600
Special comments: Consular matters: Mon to Fri, telephone enquiries, 1000 to 1100 only; Mon, Tue, Thu, Fri, personal visits (passports), 1330 to 1500.
Appointment necessary for visa applicants.

Parent body: Royal Ministry of Foreign Affairs; Oslo

ROYAL NUMISMATIC SOCIETY (RNS)

Department of Coins & Medals, The British Museum, London, WC1B 3DG

Tel: 020 7323 8228
Fax: 020 7323 8171
E-mail: info@numismatics.org.uk
Website: www.numismatics.org.uk

Enquiries to: Honorary Secretary

Founded: 1836

Organisation type and purpose: Learned society.

Subject coverage: Numismatics.

Collection: Joint library with British Numismatic Society

Publications: Printed

Access to staff: Contact by letter, by telephone, by fax, by e-mail and via website
Hours: Mon to Fri, 0900 to 1700

Affiliated to: International Numismatic Commission

ROYAL OBSERVATORY GREENWICH (ROG)

Park Row, London, SE10 9NF

Tel: 020 8858 4422 or 020 8312 6632
Fax: 020 8312 6734
E-mail: comments@nmm.ac.uk
Website: www.nmm.ac.uk/places/royal-observatory

Founded: 1675

Organisation type and purpose: National government body, museum, suitable for ages: 7 to adult.
Astronomy information.

Subject coverage: Modern astronomy.

Information services: Recorded information, tel: 020 8312 6565.

Services for disabled people: Planetarium shows can be booked in advance for deaf groups and schools using their own sign-interpreter, and Museum runs a programme of signed events. Contact bookings unit, fax: 020 8312 6522; e-mail: bookings@nmm.ac.uk.

Non-library collection catalogue: All or part available online and in-house

Library catalogue: All or part available online and in-house

Publications: Printed
Order printed publications from: Website or direct

Publications list: Available online and in print

Access to staff: Contact by letter, by telephone, by fax, by e-mail and via website.
Appointment necessary.
Hours: Mon to Fri, 0900 to 1700

Access to building: *Hours:* Mon to Fri, 1000 to 1645; last admission 1630
Special comments: Prior appointment required for reserve collections.

Access for disabled people: Level access to courtyard, Meridian Line, display of transit instruments and gift shop, complete wheelchair access to new planetarium and education centre, limited wheelchair access to historical buildings of Royal Observatory, level ground floor access and a lift to basement gallery in Flamsteed House, all assistance dogs welcome in museum.
Special comments: No wheelchair access to Octagon Room, 28' telescope and Time & Society gallery.

Also at: Royal Observatory Greenwich (ROG) (site location); Greenwich Park, London, SE10 8XJ

ROYAL OCEAN RACING CLUB (RORC)

20 St James's Place, London, SW1A 1NN

Tel: 020 7493 2248 (4 lines)
Fax: 020 7493 5252
E-mail: info@rorc.org.uk

Organisation type and purpose: International organisation, membership association.

Subject coverage: Ocean racing in general and British ocean racing in particular, long-distance yacht racing, design, building, navigation and sailing of sailing vessels, navigation and seamanship.

Collection: British ocean racing records since 1925

Publications: Printed

Access to staff: Contact by letter, by fax and by e-mail. Letter of introduction required.
Hours: Mon to Fri, 0900 to 1800

Access to building: Prior appointment required

Affiliated to: Offshore Racing Council; Royal Yachting Association

ROYAL OPERA HOUSE (ROH)

Covent Garden, London, WC2E 9DD

Tel: 020 7304 4000
Fax: 020 7212 9460
Website: www.royaloperahouse.org
Website: www.royalopera.org
Website: www.royalballet.org
Website: www.artsworld.com

Enquiries to: Director of Press and Communications
Direct tel: 020 7212 9540
Direct fax: 020 7212 9525
Other contacts: (1) Archivist (2) Mailing List Officer for (1) historical information (2) performance details.

Founded: 1858

Organisation type and purpose: Registered charity (charity number 211775).
The mission of the Royal Opera House is to attract, excite, uplift and inspire the widest possible audiences by performing opera and ballet to the highest international standards at affordable prices, to develop the art forms and to promote their appreciation by people of all ages and backgrounds.

Subject coverage: The Royal Opera House, The Royal Opera, The Royal Ballet, historical and current; opera and ballet generally.

Collection: Archive of material relating to The Royal Opera House and its performing companies including:
Administration papers, scores and photos
Costumes and set models

Trade and statistical information: Statistical details relating specifically to the Royal Opera House and its performing companies

Publications: Printed, and electronic and video

Access to staff: Contact by letter, by telephone, by fax and by e-mail
Hours: Mon to Fri, 1000 to 1530
Special comments: No access for personal callers, or to Archive, without appointment.

Access for disabled people: Ramped entry, level entry, access to all public areas, toilet facilities

Subsidiary body: The Royal Ballet; at the same address; The Royal Opera; at the same address

ROYAL PAVILION

4–5 Pavilion Buildings, Brighton, East Sussex, BN1 1EE

Tel: 01273 290900
Fax: 01273 292871
E-mail: visitor.services@brighton-hove.gov.uk
Website: www.royalpavilion.org.uk

Enquiries to: Marketing Manager

Founded: 1851

Organisation type and purpose: Local government body, museum, historic building, house or site.

Subject coverage: History and conservation of the Royal Pavilion, including interior decorations and Regency gardens.

Collection: Photographic material
Typescript of the accounts of the Crace Firm of decorators during their time spent in the Pavilion, 1802–1804, 1815–1819, 1820–1823
Inventory of the Royal Pavilion, 1828
Abstract of accounts of the various firms working in the Royal Pavilion
Letters
Quantities of letters from or about George, Prince of Wales, Mrs Fitzherbert, or concerning Brighton and the Royal Pavilion, but also including letters by Byron
Also 'Esher' letters, volume containing 56 letters to or concerning the Prince of Wales and Mrs Fitzherbert
Plan Registry – Approximately 800 plans of the Pavilion and the Pavilion Estate
Proceedings of the Pavilion Committee, 1850–1923

Proceedings of the Pavilion and Library Committee, 1924–1974
Proceedings of the Fine Art Sub-Committee, 1901–1941

Non-library collection catalogue: All or part available in-house

Library catalogue: All or part available in-house

Publications: Printed
Order printed publications from: Commercial Services, Royal Pavilion
at the same address

Access to staff: Contact by letter, by telephone, by fax, by e-mail and via website. Appointment necessary.
Hours: Mon to Fri, 0900 to 1730. Closed Christmas and Boxing Day
Special comments: No office staff at weekends

Access to building: No prior appointment required
Hours: Oct to Mar: daily, 1000 to 1715 (last admission 1630)
Apr to Sep: daily, 0930 to 1745 (last admission 1700)
Special comments: Prior appointment required for guided tours etc.

Access for disabled people: Level entry, toilet facilities ground floor only
Special comments: Wheelchair access to ground floor only. First floor is not wheelchair accessible.

Parent body: Brighton & Hove City Council

ROYAL PHARMACEUTICAL SOCIETY OF GREAT BRITAIN (RPSGB)

1 Lambeth High Street, London, SE1 7JN

Tel: 020 7735 9141
Fax: 020 7735 7629
E-mail: enquiries@rpsgb.org.uk
Website: www.pharmpress.com
Website: www.pharmj.com
Website: www.rpsgb.org.uk

Enquiries to: Information Librarian
Direct tel: 020 7572 2300
Direct fax: 020 7572 2499
Direct e-mail: library@rpsgb.org.uk

Founded: 1841

Organisation type and purpose:
Professional body (membership is by qualification), present number of members: 47,000.

Subject coverage: Pharmacy practice; pharmaceutical science; pharmacology; therapeutics; medicine; toxicology; chemistry and botany.

Collection: Collection on English and foreign proprietary medicines
Hanbury Library of rare, illustrated, botanical works
Historical collection (including many herbals) from 1485
London, Edinburgh and Dublin Pharmacopoeias from 1618
Records relating to pharmacists from 1841 (comprehensive from 1868 when pharmacists were required to register)

Library catalogue: All or part available online and in-house

Publications: Printed, and electronic and video
Order printed publications from: Pharmaceutical Press, c/o Turpin Distribution, Stratton Business Park, Pegasus Drive, Biggleswade, Bedfordshire, SG18 8TQ; tel: 01767 604971; e-mail: custserv@turpin-distribution.com

Publications list: Available online and in print

Access to staff: Contact by letter, by telephone, by fax, by e-mail and via website. Appointment necessary. Non-members charged.
Hours: Mon, Tue, Wed, Fri, 0900 to 1700; Thu, 1000 to 1745

Access to building: By prior appointment for non-members
Hours: Thu, 1000 to 1745; Mon to Wed and Fri, 0900 to 1700

Access for disabled people: Level entry, stairlift

ROYAL PHARMACEUTICAL SOCIETY OF GREAT BRITAIN – SCOTTISH DEPARTMENT

36 York Place, Edinburgh, EH1 3HU

Tel: 0131 556 4386
Fax: 0131 558 8850
E-mail: support@rpharms.com

Enquiries to: Assistant Secretary

Founded: 1852

Organisation type and purpose:
Professional body.

Subject coverage: Pharmacy.

Collection: Collection of rare herbals, pharmacopoeias etc

Access to staff: Appointment necessary.
Hours: Mon to Fri, 0900 to 1300 and 1400 to 1700

ROYAL PHILATELIC SOCIETY

41 Devonshire Place, London, W1G 6JY

Tel: 020 7486 1044
Fax: 020 7486 0803
E-mail: secretary@rpsl.org.uk
Website: www.rpsl.org.uk

Enquiries to: Honorary Secretary

Founded: 1869

Organisation type and purpose: Learned society.

Subject coverage: Philately.

Access to staff: Contact by letter, by telephone, by fax, by e-mail and via website. Appointment necessary. Access for members only.
Hours: Mon to Fri, 0930 to 1700

ROYAL PHILHARMONIC SOCIETY (RPS)

10 Stratford Place, London, W1C 1BA

Tel: 020 7491 8110
Fax: 020 7493 7463
E-mail: admin@royalphilharmonicsociety.org.uk
Website: www.royalphilharmonicsociety.org.uk/lectures.htm
Website: www.royalphilharmonicsociety.org.uk/awards.htm
Website: www.royalphilharmonicsociety.org.uk/calendar.htm

Enquiries to: General Administrator

Founded: 1813

Organisation type and purpose: National organisation, membership association, registered charity (charity number 213693). Administrators of bequests and trusts, and of awards and competitions.

Subject coverage: History and activities of the Royal Philharmonic Society since its founding in 1813.

Collection: Society's Archives (correspondence, scores, manuscripts, programmes etc) held at the British Library, London

Publications: Printed

Access to staff: Contact by letter, by fax and by e-mail. Appointment necessary.
Hours: Mon to Fri, 1000 to 1700
Special comments: Prior appointment only.

ROYAL PHOTOGRAPHIC SOCIETY OF GREAT BRITAIN, THE (RPS)

Fenton House, 122 Wells Road, Bath, BA2 3AH

Tel: 01225 325733
Fax: 01225 448688
E-mail: rps@rps.org
Website: www.rps.org

Enquiries to: President
Direct tel: 01225 325730
Direct e-mail: liz@rps.org

Founded: 1853

Organisation type and purpose:
International organisation, learned society (membership is by subscription, election or invitation), present number of members: 10,000, registered charity (charity number: 212684).
To promote the art and science of photography.

Subject coverage: History and science of photography, specialises in the 19th century.

Education services: Workshops, lectures, Distinctions, exhibitions

Collection: Now housed at the national Media Museum, Bradford

Publications: Printed

Access to staff: Contact by letter, by telephone, by fax, by e-mail and via website. Appointment necessary. Non-members charged.
Hours: Mon to Fri; 0930 to 1730, closed 24 Dec to 2 Jan

Access to building: No access other than to staff

Also at: 16 Regions, and 15 Groups and Chapters abroad.

ROYAL PIGEON RACING ASSOCIATION (RPRA)

The Reddings, Cheltenham, Gloucestershire, GL51 6RN

continued overleaf

Tel: 01452 713529
Fax: 01452 857119
E-mail: gm@rpra.org
Website: www.rpra.org

Enquiries to: General Manager
Direct e-mail: dorothyhadley@rpra.org

Founded: 1897

Organisation type and purpose:
Membership association.
Control and administration organisation for the sport of long-distance pigeon racing.

Subject coverage: Racing and showing of racing pigeons, racing pigeons in general, control and supply of rings, seals, apparatus and appliances.

Collection: Pigeons in War, Bletchley Park

Publications: Printed
Order printed publications from: Severn Farm Industrial Estate, Severn Road, Welshpool, Powys, SY21 7DF

Access to staff: Contact by letter, by telephone, by fax and by e-mail. Appointment necessary.
Hours: Mon to Fri, 0900 to 1700

Affiliated to: Fédération Colombophile Internationale; Brussels

ROYAL PIONEER CORPS ASSOCIATION

c/o 23 Pioneer Regiment Royal Logistic Corps, St David's Barracks, Graven Hill, Bicester, Oxfordshire, OX26 6HF

Tel: 01869 360694
Fax: 01869 360695
E-mail: royalpioneercorps@gmail.com
Website: www.royalpioneercorps.co.uk

Enquiries to: Controller
Direct e-mail: normanbrown@myself.com

Founded: 1942

Organisation type and purpose:
Membership association (membership is by qualification), present number of members: 3000, registered charity (charity number 801733), suitable for ages: 18+.
To relieve needs, stress and hardship of ex-Pioneers, their wives, widows and dependants.
To foster esprit de corps.

Subject coverage: Royal Pioneer Corps history.

Publications: Printed

Access to staff: Contact by letter and by telephone
Hours: Mon to Fri, 0900 to 1700

ROYAL REGIMENT OF FUSILIERS ASSOCIATION LONDON AREA (RRF Museum (London))

H M Tower of London, London, EC3N 4AB

Tel: 020 7488 5611
Fax: 020 7481 1093

Enquiries to: Curator
Direct e-mail: royalfusiliers@fsmail.net
Other contacts: Archivist for research enquiries.

Founded: 1685

Organisation type and purpose:
Membership association (membership is by subscription, qualification), present number of members: 1000, registered charity (charity number 255042), museum.
Regimental Museum.

Subject coverage: Military and social history.

Collection: Regimental Archives 1685 to 1968

Non-library collection catalogue: All or part available in-house

Library catalogue: All or part available in-house

Publications: Printed

Access to staff: Contact by letter. Appointment necessary.
Hours: Archivist only: 0900 to 1500
Special comments: Subject to HM Tower of London.

ROYAL SCHOOL FOR DEAF CHILDREN, MARGATE AND WESTGATE COLLEGE FOR DEAF PEOPLE (RSDC, Margate)

Formal name: The John Townsend Trust Ltd

Victoria Road, Margate, Kent, CT9 1NB

Tel: 01843 227561; 01843 227531 (minicom)
Fax: 01843 227637
E-mail: enquiries@royalschoolfordeaf.kent.sch.uk
Website: www.townsendtrust.org
Website: http;//www.johntownsendtrust.org

Enquiries to: Chief Executive
Other contacts: Finance and Resources Director/Principal

Founded: 1792; incorporates the former Royal School for Deaf Children (year of change 2008)

Organisation type and purpose: National organisation, registered charity (charity number 1127209), suitable for ages: School: 4 to 16, College: 16+, consultancy. Non-maintained special school and specialist college (DfES number 8667017).
Education and training of pupils and students who are deaf.

Subject coverage: Education of severely to profoundly deaf children and students. All learners have a hearing impairment or associated communication difficulty and many have additional educational, emotional behaviour or medical problems. Provides 38 weeks of full-time education for learners on either a day or residential basis. Also offers 52-week placements in College and short break facilities during holiday periods for College and School.
A large dedicated team of experienced and qualified staff are able to meet the complex and diverse needs of the young people. They offer a high level of pastoral care and independence skills in addition to the National Curriculum, the 14–19 Vocational Curriculum and a wide range of accredited courses.

Collection: Minute books and other records from 1792 (not available to the public)

Publications: Printed

Access to staff: Contact by letter, by telephone, by fax, by e-mail, in person and via website. Appointment necessary.
Hours: Mon to Fri, 0900 to 1700

Access for disabled people: Parking provided, ramped entry, toilet facilities, electronic doors

Also at: Westgate College for Deaf People (further education college); Victoria Road, Margate, Kent CT9 1NB; tel: 01843 233550; fax: 01843 233551; e-mail: enquiries@westgate-college.org.uk

Member organisation of: British Association of Teachers of the Deaf (BATOD); NASEN; National Association of Specialist Colleges (FE) (Charities) (NATSPEC); National Association of Voluntary Independent and Non-Maintained Schools (Charities) (NASS)

ROYAL SCHOOL OF CHURCH MUSIC (RSCM)

19 The Close, Salisbury, Wiltshire, SP1 2EB

Tel: 01722 424848
Fax: 01722 424849
E-mail: enquiries@rscm.com
Website: www.rscm.com

Enquiries to: Publications Department
Direct tel: 01722 424855 (Publications Dept); 0845 021 7726 (music sales)

Founded: 1927; formerly called School of English Church Music (year of change 1945)

Organisation type and purpose:
International educational charity, membership association, registered charity, training organisation, publishing house.
Study and promotion of church music.

Subject coverage: Church music, liturgy, hymnody.

Collection: Maurice Frost Collection of hymnology (on permanent loan to the Royal College of Music)
Archives of Basil Harwood, G.R.Woodward, Sydney Nicholson and Henry Walford Davies

Library catalogue: All or part available in-house

Publications: Printed
Order printed publications from: RSCM Music Direct; tel: 0845 021 7726; fax: 0845 021 8826; e-mail: musicdirect@rscm.com

Publications list: Available online

Access to staff: Contact by letter, by telephone, by fax, by e-mail, in person and via website
Hours: Mon to Fri, 0900 to 1700
Special comments: Access to Library by appointment only.

Access to building: Prior appointment required (library only)
Hours: Mon to Fri, 0900 to 1700

Access for disabled people: Parking provided, level entry, toilet facilities

ROYAL SCHOOL OF NEEDLEWORK (RSN)

Apartment 12a, Hampton Court Palace, Surrey, KT8 9AU

Tel: 020 3166 6932
Fax: 020 8943 4910
E-mail: enquiries@royal-needlework.org.uk
Website: www.royal-needlework.org.uk

Enquiries to: PA & Office Manager
Direct tel: 020 3166 6936

Founded: 1872

Organisation type and purpose: Registered charity (charity number 312774).
To teach, practise and promote hand embroidery to the widest audience – leisure and professional classes; new embroidery commissions undertaken; restoration and conservation of antique textiles to keep the art of hand embroidery alive.

Subject coverage: Teaching traditional hand embroidery techniques with technical excellence.

Collection: Design archive and books on embroidery
Textile collection

Non-library collection catalogue: All or part available in-house

Publications: Printed, and electronic and video
Order printed publications from: e-mail: sales@royal-needlework.org.uk

Access to staff: Contact by letter, by telephone, by fax, by e-mail and via website. Appointment necessary.
Hours: Mon to Fri, 0900 to 1700 – by appointment

Access to building: Prior appointment required

Access for disabled people: Parking provided

ROYAL SCOTTISH ACADEMY (RSA)

Formal name: Royal Scottish Academy of Art and Architecture

The Mound, Edinburgh, EH2 2EL

Tel: 0131 225 6671
Fax: 0131 220 6016
Website: www.royalscottishacademy.org

Enquiries to: Programme Director
Direct e-mail: colingreenslade@royalscottishacademy.org

Founded: 1826

Organisation type and purpose: Learned society, professional body (membership is by election or invitation), present number of members: 113, registered charity (charity number SC 004198), art gallery.
Society of elected and nominated Scottish painters, sculptors, architects and printmakers.
The promotion and furtherance of the visual arts in Scotland.

Subject coverage: Promotion and support of contemporary Scottish art and architecture.

Collection: RSA Permanent Collection of paintings, drawings, scultpure and other related materials. RSA's own archives (minute books, letter collection, photograph collection, etc.) from 1825 onwards
W G Gillies, RSA Bequest (estate of this artist including letters, pictures, catalogues, etc.)

Non-library collection catalogue: All or part available in-house

Library catalogue: All or part available in-house

Publications: Printed

Access to staff: Contact by letter, by telephone, by fax, by e-mail and via website. Appointment necessary.
Hours: Mon to Fri, 1000 to 1700

RSA Permanent Collections located at:
Royal Scottish Academy; The Dean Gallery, 73 Bedford Road, Edinburgh, EH4 3DS; tel: 0131 624 6277

ROYAL SCOTTISH CORPORATION (ScotsCare)

Formal name: The Scottish Hospital of the Foundation of Charles II

37 King Street, Covent Garden, London, WC2E 8JS

Tel: 020 7240 3718
Fax: 020 7497 0184
E-mail: info@scotscare.com
Website: www.royalscottishcorporation.org.uk

Enquiries to: Chief Executive
Other contacts: Welfare Manager for welfare matters.

Founded: 1611

Organisation type and purpose: Voluntary organisation, registered charity (charity number 207326).

Subject coverage: Welfare benefits, disability rights, debt advice.

Access to staff: Contact by letter, by telephone, by fax, by e-mail and via website. Appointment necessary.
Hours: Mon to Fri, 0900 to 1700
Special comments: Callers by strict appointment.

ROYAL SCOTTISH COUNTRY DANCE SOCIETY (RSCDS)

12 Coates Crescent, Edinburgh, EH3 7AF

Tel: 0131 225 3854
Fax: 0131 225 7783
E-mail: info@rscds.org
Website: www.rscds.org

Enquiries to: Office Manager

Founded: 1923

Organisation type and purpose:
International organisation, membership association (membership is by subscription), present number of members: 14,000, registered charity (charity number SC016085), suitable for all ages. Aims to promote and develop Scottish country dancing worldwide for the benefit of present and future generations. Publishes instructional dance and music books which, along with recorded music and other items, are available for purchase through online shop on website.

Subject coverage: Scottish country dances, music, practice, teaching, development and preservation (not Highland dancing).

Collection: Library of old music for Scottish country dancing and other related archive material

Publications: Printed, and electronic and video
Order printed publications from: Main office or website, www.rscds.org
Order electronic and video publications from: Main office or website, www.rscds.org, or downloads from iTunes

Publications list: Available online and in print

Access to staff: Contact by letter, by telephone, by fax, by e-mail, in person and via website
Hours: Mon to Fri, 1000 to 1600

Access to building: Prior appointment may be required
Hours: As above.

Has: Local associations known as Branches throughout the world

ROYAL SCOTTISH FORESTRY SOCIETY (RSFS)

Hagg-on-Esk, Canonbie, Dumfries & Galloway, DG14 0XE

Tel: 013873 71518
Fax: 013873 71418
E-mail: administrator@rsfs.org.uk
Website: www.rsfs.org

Enquiries to: Administrative Director
Other contacts: Editor, Scottish Forestry: editor@rsfs.lumison.co.uk

Founded: 1854

Organisation type and purpose: National organisation, learned society (membership is by subscription), present number of members: 950, voluntary organisation, registered charity (charity number SCO 02058), suitable for ages: all, publishing house.
Independent representative organisation.
The advancement of forestry in all its numerous branches.

Subject coverage: Forestry, woodlands, timber, arboriculture, silviculture, trees, agro forestry, coppicing, community forestry, investment forestry, forestry research, nurseries, forest access, urban forests and trees, social forestry.

Collection: Books and Journals
Library housed in the University of Edinburgh, Department of Forestry.

Trade and statistical information: Data on UK forestry

Publications: Printed, and electronic and video

Access to staff: Contact by letter, by telephone, by fax, by e-mail and via website. Appointment necessary.
Hours: Mon to Fri, 0900 to 1700

Links with: CASHEL – A Forest for a Thousand Years; Loch Lomond; tel: Forest Manager 01360 870450; fax: 01668 213555; e-mail: info@cashel.org.uk; website: www.CASHEL.org.uk
RSFS Forest Trust Company

ROYAL SCOTTISH GEOGRAPHICAL SOCIETY (RSGS)

15–19 North Port, Perth, PH1 5LU

Tel: 01738 455050
E-mail: enquiries@rsgs.org
Website: www.geo.ed.ac.uk/rsgs

Enquiries to: Chief Executive

Founded: 1884

Organisation type and purpose: Learned society (charity number SCO15599). To further the science of geography.

Subject coverage: Geography, topography and travel in Scotland.

Collection: Early maps of Scotland
Geographical journals

Non-library collection catalogue: All or part available in-house

Library catalogue: All or part available online

Publications: Printed

Publications list: Available online

Access to staff: Contact by letter, by telephone, by fax, by e-mail and via website. Appointment necessary.
Hours: Mon to Fri, 0900 to 1700

ROYAL SCOTTISH NATIONAL ORCHESTRA (RSNO)

73 Claremont Street, Glasgow, G3 7JB

Tel: 0141 226 3868
Fax: 0141 221 4317
E-mail: admin@rsno.org.uk
Website: www.rsno.org.uk

Enquiries to: Information Officer
Direct tel: 0141 225 3571
Direct e-mail: daniel.pollitt@rsno.org.uk

Founded: 1891

Organisation type and purpose: Registered charity (charity number SCO10702).
To perform symphony concerts throughout Scotland.

Subject coverage: Orchestral music.

Publications list: Available online and in print

Access to staff: Contact by letter, by telephone, by fax, by e-mail and via website
Hours: Mon to Fri, 0900 to 1730

ROYAL SOCIETY

6–9 Carlton House Terrace, London, SW1Y 5AG

Tel: 020 7451 2500
E-mail: via website
Website: royalsociety.org
Website: royalsocietypublishing.org
Website: royalsociety.org/Catalogues

Founded: 1660

Organisation type and purpose: A registered charity (no. 207043), a learned society, a fellowship of the world's most eminent scientists and the oldest scientific academy in continuous existence, the UK's independent national academy of science promoting the natural and applied sciences, and a funding agency.
To expand the frontiers of knowledge by championing the development and use of science, mathematics, engineering and medicine for the benefit of humanity and the good of the planet. Funding schemes are designed to enhance the UK science base and foster collaboration between UK-based and overseas scientists.

Subject coverage: Natural and applied sciences.

Collection: Library and Archive contain over 70,000 books, paintings, manuscripts, busts and artefacts; the main strength of the collections is in the 17th and 18th centuries – from the 1680s to the mid-19th century the policy of the Library was to acquire every important scientific publication; collections are of international importance in the history of science; resources include manuscripts, printed books and paintings amassed to provide a record of scientific achievements over almost 350 years; Image Library houses a multitude of beautiful treasures including over 6,000 photographs, engravings and paintings of past and present Fellows and a large collection of images taken from manuscripts and printed works; Raymond and Beverly Sackler Archive Resource is a database of biographical information on past Fellows of the Royal Society from 1660 onwards

Non-library collection catalogue: All or part available online

Library catalogue: All or part available online

Publications: Printed, and microform publications
Order microform publications from: Website

Publications list: Available online

Access to staff: Contact by letter, by telephone and via website
Special comments: Researchers in the scholarly use of the Royal Society's collections are welcomed.

Also at: Kavli Royal Society International Centre; Chicheley Hall, Buckinghamshire

ROYAL SOCIETY – ICSU INFORMATION SERVICE

Formal name: The Royal Society for Improving Natural Knowledge

6 Carlton House Terrace, London, SW1Y 5AG

Tel: 020 7451 2500
Fax: 020 7451 2692
E-mail: info@royalsoc.ac.uk
Website: www.codata.org/codata
Website: www.icsu.org
Website: www.royalsoc.ac.uk

Enquiries to: ICSU Information Officer
Direct tel: extn 2587
Direct e-mail: ruth.cooper@royalsoc.ac.uk

Founded: 1660

Organisation type and purpose: Learned society (membership is by election or invitation), present number of members: 1,250.
The UK National Academy of Science.

Subject coverage: Information available on all ICSU activities and related journals and publications. Details of union assemblies, conferences and congresses. Advice on travel to ICSU conferences and grants available. Information concerning ICSU projects also available.

Collection: Archival centre for ICSU-related publications such as newsletters, bulletins and journals

Publications: Printed

Publications list: Available online and in print

Access to staff: Contact by letter, by telephone and via website. Appointment necessary.
Hours: Mon to Fri, 0900 to 1700

Access for disabled people: Parking provided, level entry, access to all public areas, toilet facilities

ROYAL SOCIETY – LIBRARY

6–9 Carlton House Terrace, London, SW1Y 5AG

Tel: 020 7451 2500
Fax: 020 7930 2170
E-mail: library@royalsociety.org
Website: royalsociety.org

Enquiries to: Librarian
Direct tel: 020 7451 2606

Founded: 1660

Organisation type and purpose: Learned society, registered charity (charity number 207043).
The Royal Society is an independent academy promoting the natural and applied sciences.

Subject coverage: All sciences, mathematics, statistics, operational research, physics, space research, crystallography, chemistry, engineering, metallurgy, instrumentation, earth sciences, botany, agriculture, zoology, marine biology, physical anthropology, biochemistry, biophysics, physiology, pharmacology, psychology, medicine (non-clinical), molecular biology, genetics, history of science and technology, science education, international scientific relations, science policy.

Collection: Archives relating to all aspects of the Society and its Fellows
Books and papers by or about Fellows of the Society
Books, manuscripts and items relating to Sir Isaac Newton and other early Fellows
Material on the history of science
Science policy publications

Non-library collection catalogue: All or part available online, in-house and in print

Library catalogue: All or part available online

Publications: Printed

Publications list: Available online

Access to staff: Contact by letter, by telephone, by fax, by e-mail, in person and via website
Hours: Mon to Fri, 1000 to 1700

Access for disabled people: Parking provided, disabled lift entry, access to all public areas, toilet facilities

ROYAL SOCIETY FOR ASIAN AFFAIRS (RSAA)

2 Belgrave Square, London, SW1X 8PJ

Tel: 020 7235 5122
Fax: 020 7259 6771
E-mail: info@rsaa.org.uk
Website: www.rsaa.org.uk

Enquiries to: Secretary
Direct e-mail: sec@rsaa.org.uk; editor@rsaa.org.uk
Other contacts: Editor (for Asian affairs)

Founded: 1901

Organisation type and purpose: Learned society (membership is by qualification, election or invitation), present number of members: 1,136 individuals, 13 corporate, registered charity (charity number 212152).
To promote greater knowledge and understanding of Asia from the Near and Middle East to Japan.

Subject coverage: All aspects of Asian affairs.

Collection: Library of approximately 5,100 books, soon to be available electronically

Non-library collection catalogue: All or part available online

Library catalogue: All or part available online

Publications: Printed

Access to staff: Contact by letter, by telephone, by fax, by e-mail and via website. Appointment necessary. Access for members only.
Hours: Mon to Fri, 0930 to 1700
Special comments: One visit to the library is permitted, after which membership is required.

Access to building: No prior appointment required
Hours: Mon to Thu, 1000 to 1300 and 1400 to 1600; Fri, 1000 to 1300
Special comments: Prior appointment required for non-members.

ROYAL SOCIETY FOR MENTALLY HANDICAPPED CHILDREN AND ADULTS (MENCAP)

4 Swan Courtyard, Coventry Road, Birmingham, B26 1BU

Tel: 0121 707 7877
Fax: 0121 707 3019
E-mail: info@mencap.org.uk

Enquiries to: Head of Advice and Information Service

Founded: 1946

Organisation type and purpose: National organisation, membership association (membership is by subscription), voluntary organisation, registered charity (charity number 222377).
Mencap is the leading charity working with children and adults with learning disabilities in England, Wales and Northern Ireland. It campaigns to ensure that people with a learning disability have the best possible opportunities to live as full citizens. It aims to influence new legislation and raise the profile of learning disability issues. It undertakes research into issues affecting people with a learning disability.

Subject coverage: All aspects of learning disabilities, residential, leisure, holiday, welfare, education and training, employment services.

Publications: Printed, and electronic and video
Order printed publications from: Helpline and Information Unit, MENCAP
123 Golden Lane, London, EC1Y 0RT, tel: 020 7696 6900/6979

Publications list: Available in print

Access to staff: Contact by letter, by telephone, by fax, by e-mail and via website
Hours: Mon to Fri, 0900 to 1700

Access for disabled people: Level entry, toilet facilities

ROYAL SOCIETY FOR PUBLIC HEALTH (RSPH)

John Snow House, 59 Mansell Street, London, E1 8AN

Tel: 020 7265 7300
Fax: 020 7265 7301
E-mail: info@rsph.org.uk
Website: www.rsph.org.uk

Enquiries to: Switchboard

Organisation type and purpose: The Royal Society for Public Health is an independent, multidisciplinary charity organisation, dedicated to the promotion and protection of collective human health and well-being. Registered charity (charity number 1125949), registered Scottish charity (charity number SC040750), incorporated by Royal Charter (charity number RC000825).

Access to staff: Contact by letter, by telephone, by fax, by e-mail and via website. Appointment necessary.
Hours: Mon to Fri, 0900 to 1700

ROYAL SOCIETY FOR THE ENCOURAGEMENT OF ARTS, MANUFACTURES AND COMMERCE (RSA)

8 John Adam Street, London, WC2N 6EZ

Tel: 020 7930 5115
Fax: 020 7839 5805
E-mail: library@rsa.org.uk
Website: www.rsa.org.uk
Website: www.rsa.org.uk/fellowship/facilities.html

Enquiries to: Librarian
Direct tel: 020 7451 6874
Direct e-mail: library@rsa.org.uk

Founded: 1754

Organisation type and purpose: International organisation, membership association (membership is by election or invitation), present number of members: 23,000, registered charity (charity number 212424), research organisation.
Runs conferences and lectures, produces reports relating to education, environment, design, the arts, manufacturing, management.

Subject coverage: A modern library providing background on the RSA's core concerns: arts, manufacturers and commerce, education, design, environment and management. Also 250 years of archives plus a small library to support access to, and interpretation of, the Society's Archive.

Collection: Archives of the Society (from 1754 to present). Accessible via AIM25 gateway
Early works (most listed in British Library 18th-century catalogue)

Non-library collection catalogue: All or part available online

Library catalogue: All or part available online

Publications: Printed

Publications list: Available online

Access to staff: Contact by letter, by telephone, by fax, by e-mail and via website. Appointment necessary.
Hours: Mon to Fri, 0900 to 1700

Access to building: Prior appointment required

Access for disabled people: Ramped entry, access to all public areas, toilet facilities
Special comments: Access has been made by modifications to an 18th-century building, so some routes are circuitous.

ROYAL SOCIETY FOR THE PREVENTION OF ACCIDENTS (RoSPA)

Edgbaston Park, 353 Bristol Road, Birmingham, B5 7ST

Tel: 0121 248 2000
Fax: 0121 248 2001
E-mail: help@rospa.com
Website: www.rospa.com

Enquiries to: Information Services Manager
Direct tel: 0121 248 2063/66
Direct e-mail: infocentre@rospa.com

Founded: 1917

Organisation type and purpose: Membership association (membership is by subscription), registered charity, training organisation, consultancy, publishing house.
To save lives and reduce injuries.

Subject coverage: Occupational health and safety, leisure, road, home, play (ground) and water safety, safety education.

Education services: Training courses.

Collection: 20,000 books and documents
250 journals
British Standards
CD-ROM, Croner, Lawtel
Legislation where relevant to health and safety

Trade and statistical information: Statistics available, primarily for members (charges). Technical and advisory service – members only

Library catalogue: All or part available in-house

Publications: Printed, and electronic and video

Publications list: Available online and in print

Access to staff: Contact by letter, by telephone and by e-mail. Appointment necessary.
Hours: Mon to Fri, 0900 to 1600

continued overleaf

Access to building: Prior appointment required

Access for disabled people: Parking provided, level entry, access to all public areas, toilet facilities

Administers the: RoSPA Advanced Drivers and Riders

Links with: RoSPA Training Centre; Unit 75, Gravelly Industrial Park, Erdington, Birmingham, B24 8TL

Offices in: Wales, Scotland and N Ireland

ROYAL SOCIETY FOR THE PREVENTION OF CRUELTY TO ANIMALS (RSPCA)

Wilberforce Way, Horsham, West Sussex, RH13 9RS

Tel: 0300 123 4555
Fax: 0303 123 0100
Website: www.rspca.org.uk

Enquiries to: Information and Records Manager
Direct tel: 0300 123 0188
Direct fax: 0303 123 0188
Direct e-mail: creed@rspca.org.uk

Founded: 1824

Organisation type and purpose: Registered charity (charity number 219099).

Subject coverage: Welfare of animals of all types, all aspects, history of animal welfare in the 19th and 20th centuries, suppression of cruelty to animals, animal hospitals, clinics and homes, philosophy and ethics of animal welfare and animal rights.

Collection: Complete sets of the Society's publications from 1869: Animal Ways, Animal World and Annual Reports
Minute Books of the Society

Non-library collection catalogue: All or part available in-house

Library catalogue: All or part available in-house

Publications: Printed

Publications list: Available online

Access to staff: Contact by letter, by telephone, by fax and by e-mail. Appointment necessary.
Hours: Mon to Fri, 0930 to 1700

Access to building: *Hours:* Mon to Fri, 0930 to 1700

Access for disabled people: Parking provided, level entry

ROYAL SOCIETY FOR THE PROMOTION OF HEALTH

38a St Georges Drive, London, SW1V 4BH

Tel: 020 7630 0121
Fax: 020 7976 6847
Website: www.rsph.org.uk

Enquiries to: Chief Executive
Direct fax: 020 7828 8913
Direct e-mail: jtatman@rsph.org.uk
Other contacts: Managing Editor for journal-related enquiries.

Founded: 1876

Organisation type and purpose: International organisation, learned society, registered charity (charity number 215520). To promote the exchange of knowledge and experience between health-related professions, to influence health-related legislation and planning, to advance the study of health-related subjects.

Subject coverage: All fields related to medicine, nutrition, hygiene, pharmaceuticals, planning, architecture, housing, environment.

Collection: Essential Food Hygiene

Publications: Printed

Access to staff: Contact by letter, by telephone, by fax, by e-mail and in person. Appointment necessary.
Hours: Mon to Fri, 0900 to 1700

Affiliated to: American Public Health Association; World Federation of Public Health Associations

ROYAL SOCIETY FOR THE PROTECTION OF BIRDS (RSPB)

The Lodge, Potton Road, Sandy, Bedfordshire, SG19 2DL

Tel: 01767 680551
Fax: 01767 692365
Website: www.rspb.org.uk

Enquiries to: Librarian
Direct e-mail: ian.dawson@rspb.org.uk

Founded: 1889

Organisation type and purpose: Membership association (membership is by subscription), registered charity (charity number 207076).

Subject coverage: Birds and birdwatching (but not aviculture); especially protection and conservation in Britain.

Collection: W H Hudson Archive

Library catalogue: All or part available in-house

Publications: Printed

Publications list: Available in print

Access to staff: Appointment necessary.
Hours: Mon to Fri, 0900 to 1700

Member of the global partnership: BirdLife International

Owns or administers: over 150 nature reserves in Great Britain and Northern Ireland

ROYAL SOCIETY FOR THE RELIEF OF INDIGENT GENTLEWOMEN OF SCOTLAND

14 Rutland Square, Edinburgh, EH1 2BD

Tel: 0131 229 2308
Fax: 0131 228 3700

Enquiries to: Information Officer
Other contacts: General Secretary

Founded: 1847

Organisation type and purpose: Voluntary organisation, registered charity (charity number SCO 16095).
To assist ladies of Scottish birth or education with professional or business backgrounds who exist on low incomes and have limited savings. Applications from spinsters, widows and divorcees of 50 years or over.

Collection: Records maintained of ladies who made applications to the Fund over many years

Access to staff: Contact by letter, by telephone, by fax and by e-mail
Hours: Mon to Thu, 0900 to 1700; Fri, 0900 to 1600

ROYAL SOCIETY OF BRITISH ARTISTS (RBA)

17 Carlton House Terrace, London, SW1Y 5BD

Tel: 020 7930 6844
Fax: 020 7839 7830
E-mail: press@mallgalleries.com
Website: www.mallgalleries.org.uk
Website: www.the-rba.org.uk

Enquiries to: Secretary
Other contacts: Marketing and Communications Officer

Founded: 1824

Organisation type and purpose: Membership association (membership is by election or invitation), present number of members: 115, registered charity (charity number 294590).

Subject coverage: British art and artists; annual open exhibition of pictures and sculpture.

Publications: Printed

Access to staff: Contact by letter, by telephone, by fax, by e-mail and via website. Appointment necessary.
Hours: Mon to Fri, 0930 to 1700

Access to building: No access other than to staff
Hours: Mon to Fri, 0930 to 1700

Access for disabled people: Stairlift, toilet facilities
Special comments: Stairlift.

Links with: Federation of British Artists (FBA); at the same address

ROYAL SOCIETY OF CHEMISTRY – LIBRARY AND INFORMATION CENTRE (RSC)

Burlington House, Piccadilly, London, W1J 0BA

Tel: 020 7440 8656
Fax: 020 7287 9798
E-mail: library@rsc.org
Website: www.rsc.org

Enquiries to: Librarian

Founded: 1841

Organisation type and purpose: Learned society.

Subject coverage: Alchemy, analytical chemistry, biochemistry, biography, chemical engineering, chemical industry, chemistry, environment, food science and technology, hazards, health and safety at work, inorganic chemistry, organic chemistry, spectrometry and toxicology.

Collection: Alchemy and chemistry to 1850 (3,000 vols)
Prints and photographs of distinguished chemists (8,000)

Trade and statistical information: Chemical business statistics on a wide variety of chemicals

Non-library collection catalogue: All or part available online and in-house

Library catalogue: All or part available online and in-house

Publications: Printed

Publications list: Available online and in print

Access to staff: Contact by letter, by telephone, by fax, by e-mail and via website. Appointment necessary. Non-members charged.
Hours: Mon to Fri, 0930 to 1730

Access for disabled people: Ramped entry

Constituent bodies: Analytical, Faraday, Dalton, Perkin, Education and Industrial Affairs

ROYAL SOCIETY OF CHEMISTRY – SALES AND CUSTOMER CARE DEPARTMENT

Thomas Graham House, Science Park, Milton Road, Cambridge, CB4 4WF

Tel: 01223 420066
Fax: 01223 426017
E-mail: sales@rsc.org
Website: www.rsc.org

Enquiries to: Sales and Customer Care Department
Direct tel: 01223 432360

Founded: 1980

Organisation type and purpose: Learned society, professional body (membership is by qualification), present number of members: 47,000, registered charity (charity number 207890), publishing house.

Subject coverage: Chemistry (all areas, general, organic, analytical); mass spectrometry; biology; biotechnology; biochemistry; food science; nutrition; pesticides; chemical engineering; toxicology; hazards; health and safety; agrochemicals; business information.

Collection: Library located at Burlington House, Piccadilly, London

Library catalogue: All or part available online

Publications: Printed, and electronic and video

Publications list: Available online and in print

Access to staff: Contact by letter, by telephone, by fax, by e-mail and via website
Hours: Mon to Fri, 0900 to 1700

Member of: Association of Learned and Professional Society Publishers (ALPSP)

Other address: Royal Society of Chemistry (RSC); Burlington House, Piccadilly, London, W1J 0BA; tel: 020 7437 8656; fax: 020 7287 9798

ROYAL SOCIETY OF EDINBURGH (RSE)

22–26 George Street, Edinburgh, EH2 2PQ

Tel: 0131 240 5000
Fax: 0131 240 5024
E-mail: rse@royalsoced.org.uk
Website: www.royalsoced.org.uk

Enquiries to: Chief Executive
Direct e-mail: bmuldoon@royalsoced.org.uk
Other contacts: Journals & Archive Officer for publications and archive information.

Founded: 1783

Organisation type and purpose: Learned society.

Subject coverage: Science and literature; arts and humanities; public administration and business.

Collection: Charles Piazzi Smyth Archive (now housed at the Royal Observatory Edinburgh, Blackford Hill, Edinburgh)
David Hume manuscripts (now housed at the National Library of Scotland, George IV Bridge, Edinburgh)
RSE Archive, including Minute Books, Correspondence etc, held at National Library of Scotland, George IV Bridge, Edinburgh

Non-library collection catalogue: All or part available in-house

Library catalogue: All or part available in-house

Publications: Printed
Order printed publications from: Customer Services, CABI Publishing, Wallingford, Oxfordshire, OX10 8DE; tel: 01491 832111; fax: 01491 829292, e-mail: orders@cabi.org

Access to staff: Contact by letter, by telephone, by fax, by e-mail and via website. Appointment necessary.
Hours: Mon to Fri, 0900 to 1700

Access for disabled people: Ramped access, lift access to most rooms, disabled toilet facilities, induction loop

ROYAL SOCIETY OF LITERATURE (RSL)

Somerset House, Strand, London, WC2R 1LA

Tel: 020 7845 4676
Fax: 020 7845 4679
E-mail: info@rslit.org
Website: www.rslit.org

Enquiries to: Secretary

Founded: 1820

Organisation type and purpose: Learned society (membership is by subscription), registered charity.

Subject coverage: The appreciation of literature in English.

Education services: Monthly lectures.

Publications: Printed

Access to staff: Contact by letter, by telephone, by fax, by e-mail and via website. Appointment necessary.
Hours: Mon to Thu, 0930 to 1730

Access to building: Prior appointment required

Access for disabled people: Toilet facilities
Special comments: Wheelchair lift available.

ROYAL SOCIETY OF MARINE ARTISTS (RSMA)

17 Carlton House Terrace, London, SW1Y 5BD

Tel: 020 7930 6844
Fax: 020 7839 7830
E-mail: press@mallgalleries.com
Website: www.mallgalleries.org.uk

Enquiries to: Secretary
Other contacts: Marketing and Communications Officer

Founded: 1945

Organisation type and purpose: Membership association (membership is by election or invitation), present number of members: 41, registered charity (charity number 289944).

Subject coverage: Marine art, annual open exhibition.

Publications: Printed

Access to staff: Contact by letter, by telephone, by fax and by e-mail. Appointment necessary.
Hours: Mon to Fri, 0930 to 1700

Access to building: Prior appointment required
Hours: Mon to Fri, 0930 to 1700

Access for disabled people: Stairlift; toilet facilities

Links with: Federation of British Artists (FBA); at the same address

ROYAL SOCIETY OF MEDICINE (RSM)

1 Wimpole Street, London, W1G 0AE

Tel: 020 7290 2940/1/2
Fax: 020 7290 2939
Website: www.rsm.ac.uk

Enquiries to: Director of Information Services
Direct tel: 020 7290 2931
Direct fax: 020 7290 2976
Direct e-mail: ian.snowley@rsm.ac.uk

Founded: 1805

Organisation type and purpose: Learned society (membership is by subscription, qualification, election or invitation), present number of members: 18,000, registered charity (charity number 206219), publishing house.

Subject coverage: Medicine in general, biomedical sciences, postgraduate biomedical sciences, archives.

Collection: Chalmers Collection of early medicine
Comfort Collection on gerontology
Historical Medical Collection from 1474
Major periodicals of Europe and America, 19th and 20th centuries

Non-library collection catalogue: All or part available online

Library catalogue: All or part available online

continued overleaf

Publications: Printed
Order printed publications from: Book & Sales Enquiries, RSM Press, 1 Wimpole Street, London, W1G 0AE

Publications list: Available in print

Access to staff: Contact by letter, by telephone, by fax, by e-mail, in person and via website. Access for members only. Non-members charged.
Hours: Mon to Thur, 0900 to 2030; Fri 0900 to 17.30

Access for disabled people: Level entry, access to all public areas, toilet facilities

ROYAL SOCIETY OF MINIATURE PAINTERS, SCULPTORS AND GRAVERS (RMS)

3 Briar Walk, London, SW15 6UD

Tel: 020 8785 2338
E-mail: tremrod@aol.com
Website: www.royal-miniature-society.org.uk

Enquiries to: Executive Secretary

Founded: 1896

Organisation type and purpose:
International organisation, professional body (membership is by election or invitation), present number of members: 160, registered charity (charity number 291389).
Publicising and educating the public about miniature painting.

Subject coverage: All forms of miniature art: painting in all media, etching, silver-point, sculpture, ceramics, glass engraving, enamelling, gold and silver work, jewellery.

Collection: Diploma collection

Publications: Printed
Order printed publications from: Royal Miniature Society, at the main address

Access to staff: Contact by letter, by telephone and by e-mail. Appointment necessary.
Hours: Mon to Fri, 0900 to 1700

Access to building: No access other than to staff
Hours: Only during the exhibition.

Access for disabled people: Ramped entry, access to all public areas, toilet facilities

ROYAL SOCIETY OF MUSICIANS OF GREAT BRITAIN

10 Stratford Place, London, W1C 1BA

Tel: 020 7629 6137
Fax: 020 7629 6137

Enquiries to: Secretary

Founded: 1738

Organisation type and purpose:
Membership association (membership is by election or invitation), present number of members: 1367, registered charity (charity number 208879).
The world's oldest charity for musicians. The Society, founded by Handel and over 200 other musicians to support colleagues and their families in distress owing to illness, accident or old age, continues to support professional musicians and their dependants.

Subject coverage: History of music and musicians, from the 18th century, from the records of the Society; personal files of Members; minute books, accounts etc; much material unavailable elsewhere.

Collection: Manuscript scores (including marches composed for the Society by Haydn, Weber, Cipriani Potter, Bishop and von Winter)

Publications: Printed

Access to staff: Contact by letter, by telephone and by fax
Hours: Mon to Fri, 0900 to 1700

Access to building: No prior appointment required

ROYAL SOCIETY OF PORTRAIT PAINTERS (RP)

17 Carlton House Terrace, London, SW1Y 5BD

Tel: 020 7930 6844
Fax: 020 7839 7830
E-mail: press@mallgalleries.com
Website: www.mallgalleries.org.uk
Website: www.therp.co.uk

Enquiries to: Secretary
Other contacts: Marketing and Communications Officer

Founded: 1891

Organisation type and purpose:
Professional body (membership is by election or invitation), present number of members: 53, registered charity (charity number 327460).
To foster and promote the art of portrait painting.

Subject coverage: Portrait painting and painters, annual open exhibition.

Collection: Examples of portrait painters' work on slides, photographs and some original portrait paintings

Publications: Printed

Access to staff: Contact by letter, by telephone, by fax, by e-mail and via website. Appointment necessary.
Hours: Mon to Fri, 0930 to 1730

Access to building: No access other than to staff
Hours: As above.

Access for disabled people: Stairlift, toilet facilities

Links with: Federation of British Artists (FBA); at the same address

ROYAL SOCIETY OF TROPICAL MEDICINE AND HYGIENE (RSTMH)

50 Bedford Square, London, WC1B 3DP

Tel: 020 7580 2127
Fax: 020 7436 1389
E-mail: mail@rstmh.org
Website: www.rstmh.org

Enquiries to: Administrator

Founded: 1907

Organisation type and purpose: Learned society, registered charity (charity number 208204).
To promote and advance the study, control and prevention of disease in man and other animals in warm climates, to facilitate discussion and the exchange of information among those who are interested in tropical diseases.

Subject coverage: International health, tropical medicine and hygiene, tropical veterinary science.

Publications: Printed
Order printed publications from: Elsevier, Customer Service Department, PO Box 211, 1000 AE Amsterdam, The Netherlands; tel: +31 20 485 3757; fax: +31 20 485 3432; e-mail: journalscustomerserviceemea@elsevier.com

Publications list: Available online and in print

Access to staff: Contact by letter and by e-mail
Hours: Mon to Fri, 0900 to 1700

ROYAL SOCIETY OF ULSTER ARCHITECTS (RSUA)

2 Mount Charles, Belfast, BT7 1NZ

Tel: 028 9032 3760
Fax: 028 9023 7313
E-mail: info@rsua.org.uk

Enquiries to: Director

Founded: 1901

Organisation type and purpose:
Professional body (membership is by subscription), registered charity (charity number NI 00069).

Subject coverage: Advice on selecting an architect. Advice on running architectural competitions.

Access to staff: Contact by letter, by telephone and by fax. Appointment necessary.
Hours: Mon to Fri, 0900 to 1700

Access for disabled people: Ramped entry, toilet facilities

ROYAL TOWN PLANNING INSTITUTE (RTPI)

41 Botolph Lane, London, EC3R 8DL

Tel: 020 7929 9494 (switchboard), 020 7929 9452 (library)
Fax: 020 7929 9490
E-mail: library@rtpi.org.uk
Website: www.rtpi.org.uk
Website: www.rtpiconsultants.co.uk
Website: www.planningsummerschool.com
Website: www.planning.haynet.com
Website: www.planningaid.rtpi.org.uk

Enquiries to: Library and Information Manager
Direct tel: 020 7929 9452

Founded: 1914

Organisation type and purpose:
Professional body, present number of members: 17,500.

Subject coverage: Urban, regional and rural planning, housing, transport, conservation, leisure, spatial planning, recreation, employment, local government.

Non-library collection catalogue: All or part available online

Library catalogue: All or part available online

Publications list: Available online and in print

Access to staff: Contact by letter, by telephone, by fax, by e-mail and via website. Appointment necessary.

Access to building: Prior appointment required

Access for disabled people: Access to all public areas (including library), toilet facilities

Founder member of: Commonwealth Association of Planners; now about 20 members, secretariat in Canada

Merged: ROOM (the National Housing & Town Planning Council)

Other office: RTPI in Scotland; 57 Melville Street, Edinburgh, EH3 7HL; tel: 0131 226 1959; fax: 0131 226 1909; e-mail: scotland@rtpi.org.uk

ROYAL TOWN PLANNING INSTITUTE IN SCOTLAND (RTPI)

18 Atholl Crescent, Edinburgh EH3 8HQ

Tel: 0131 229 9628
Fax: 0131 229 9332
E-mail: scotland@rtpi.org.uk
Website: www.rtpi.org.uk

Enquiries to: National Director

Founded: 1914

Organisation type and purpose:
Professional body (membership is by election or invitation), present number of members: 2,100 in Scotland, 23,000 in UK.
The Royal Town Planning Institute is a charity registered in Scotland (SC037841) and in England and Wales (262865).
To act as the chartered professional body for town planners and to advance the art and science of town planning at national, regional and local levels.

Subject coverage: Town planning: services to professional planners; education for planning; policy on national planning systems and practice; assistance to the public through Planning Aid Scotland (the Institute itself cannot provide advice to the public on individual planning cases).

Library catalogue: All or part available in-house

Publications: Printed
Order printed publications from: Royal Town Planning Institute, 41 Botolph Lane, London, EC3R 8DL, tel: 020 7929 9494, fax: 020 7929 9490, e-mail: online@rtpi.org.uk

Publications list: Available in print

Access to staff: Contact by letter, by telephone, by fax, by e-mail and via website. Appointment necessary.
Hours: Mon to Fri, 0900 to 1700

Access to building: Prior appointment required

Parent body: RTPI; 41 Botolph Lane, London, EC3R 8DL; tel: 020 7929 9494; fax: 020 7929 9490; e-mail: online@rtpi.org.uk

ROYAL UNITED SERVICES INSTITUTE FOR DEFENCE AND SECURITY STUDIES (RUSI)

61, Whitehall, London, SW1A 2ET

Tel: 020 7747 2600
E-mail: defence@rusi.org
Website: www.rusi.org

Enquiries to: Membership Secretary
Other contacts: Librarian; PA to Director

Founded: 1831

Organisation type and purpose:
Membership association, registered charity (charity number 210639), consultancy, research organisation.

Subject coverage: Defence and international security.

Collection: RUSI Library of Military History

Publications: Printed
Order printed publications from: e-mail: publications@rusi.org

Publications list: Available online

Access to staff: Contact by letter, by telephone, by e-mail and via website. Appointment necessary. Access for members only.
Hours: Mon to Fri, 0900 to 1700

Access for disabled people: Toilet facilities

ROYAL VETERINARY COLLEGE ANIMAL CARE TRUST (RVC ACT)

The Royal Veterinary College, Hawkshead Lane, Hatfield, Hertfordshire, AL9 7TA

Tel: 01707 666237
Fax: 01707 666382
E-mail: act@rvc.ac.uk
Website: www.rvc.ac.uk/act

Enquiries to: Director of Fund Raising

Founded: 1982

Organisation type and purpose: Registered charity (charity number 281571).
To support the work of the Royal Veterinary College.

Subject coverage: Education of veterinary students and the treatment of animals, veterinary science, veterinary surgery, animal welfare.

Publications: Printed

Access to staff: Contact by letter, by telephone, by fax, by e-mail and via website. Appointment necessary.
Hours: Mon to Fri, 0900 to 1700

Parent body: Royal Veterinary College; University of London, Royal College Street, London, NW1 0TU; tel: 020 7468 5000; fax: 020 7388 2342

ROYAL VETERINARY COLLEGE LIBRARY (RVC)

Royal College Street, Camden, London, NW1 0TU

Tel: 020 7468 5162
Fax: 020 7468 5162
E-mail: sjackson@rvc.ac.uk
Website: www.rvc.ac.uk/aboutus/Services/Libraries/Index.cfm

Enquiries to: Librarian
Direct tel: 01707 666214
Direct fax: 01707 666214
Other contacts: Deputy Librarian

Founded: 1791

Organisation type and purpose: University department or institute.

Subject coverage: Veterinary science and medicine; pre-clinical and historical material at Royal College Street; current veterinary material at Hawkshead.

Collection: Frank Townend Barton Gift
Granville Penn Gift
Historical collection
James Beart Simonds Collection (veterinary advisor to the Privy Council during the curing of the cattle disease Rinderpest in the 19th century) scrapbooks and extensive notes and photographs
Sir Frederick Smith's Napoleonic manuscripts

Library catalogue: All or part available online

Publications: Printed, and microform publications

Access to staff: Appointment necessary.
Hours: Mon to Fri, 0900 to 1700

Also at: Royal Veterinary College Library; Hawkshead House, Hawkshead Lane, North Mymms, Hatfield, Hertfordshire, AL9 7TA; tel: 01707 666 384; e-mail: sjackson@rvc.ac.uk

Parent body: University of London

ROYAL WATERCOLOUR SOCIETY (RWS)

Bankside Gallery, 48 Hopton Street, London, SE1 9JH

Tel: 020 7928 7521
Fax: 020 7928 2820
E-mail: rws@banksidegallery.com
Website: www.banksidegallery.com

Enquiries to: Gallery Director

Founded: 1804

Organisation type and purpose: Learned society (membership is by election or invitation), present number of members: 90, registered charity (charity number 258348), art gallery.

Subject coverage: Watercolour painting and its history, contemporary work by members of the Society, gallery activities.

Collection: The RWS Diploma collection (1 work from each member of the society, RWS Archive since its inception 200 years ago)

Library catalogue: All or part available in print

Publications: Printed

Access to staff: Contact by letter, by telephone, by fax, by e-mail and via website
Hours: Mon to Fri, 1100 to 1800

Access to building: No prior appointment required

Connected with: Bankside Gallery, home of the RWS

ROYAL WELSH AGRICULTURAL SOCIETY LIMITED (RWAS Ltd)

Llanelwedd, Builth Wells, Powys, LD2 3SY

Tel: 01982 553683
Fax: 01982 553563
E-mail: requests@rwas.co.uk
Website: www.rwas.co.uk

Enquiries to: Secretary

Founded: 1904; formerly called Welsh National Agricultural Society (year of change 1922)

Organisation type and purpose: International organisation, membership association (membership is by subscription), present number of members: 14,000, voluntary organisation, registered charity (charity number 251232), suitable for ages: all.
To promote agriculture, horticulture, forestry and conservation in Wales.

Subject coverage: Any matters relating to the Royal Welsh Show, the Royal Welsh Agricultural Winter Fair, and the Royal Welsh Smallholder and Garden Festival.

Publications: Printed

Publications list: Available online and in print

Access to staff: Contact by letter, by telephone, by fax, by e-mail and via website. Appointment necessary.
Hours: Mon to Fri, 0845 to 1230 and 1330 to 1700
Special comments: Closed on statutory holidays.

Access for disabled people: Ramped entry, toilet facilities

ROYAL WELSH COLLEGE OF MUSIC & DRAMA LIBRARY (RWCMD)

Castle Grounds, Cathays Park, Cardiff, CF10 3ER

Tel: 029 2034 2854
Fax: 029 2039 1304
E-mail: library@rwcmd.ac.uk
Website: www.rwcmd.ac.uk

Enquiries to: Librarian
Direct tel: 029 2039 1330

Founded: 1947; formerly called Welsh College of Music & Drama (year of change 2002); merged with University of Glamorgan (year of change 2007)

Organisation type and purpose: Independent higher education college for training in performing arts.

Subject coverage: Music, theatre, stage design, stage management, creative music technology and recording, technical stage management, music therapy, art management, acting.

Library catalogue: All or part available online

Access to staff: Contact by telephone. Appointment necessary.
Hours: Term time: Mon to Thu, 0830 to 2000; Fri, 0830 to 1800; Sat, 1000 to 1400
Vacation: Mon to Thu, 0900 to 1700; Fri, 0900 to 1630; Sat, closed

Links with: Cardiff Arts Marketing – Organisation of Arts Organisations in Wales; Incorporated Society of Musicians

ROYAL YACHTING ASSOCIATION (RYA)

RYA House, Romsey Road, Eastleigh, Hampshire, SO50 9YA

Tel: 023 8062 7400
Fax: 023 8062 9924
E-mail: admin@rya.org.uk
Website: www.rya.org.uk

Enquiries to: Secretary General
Direct tel: 023 8062 7420
Direct e-mail: rod.carr@ry.org.uk
Other contacts: Chief Executive

Founded: 1875; formerly called Yacht Racing Association (YRA)

Organisation type and purpose: National government body, membership association (membership is by subscription), present number of members: 88,000.
National governing body for recreational boating in the UK.
Represents recreational boating in the UK.

Subject coverage: Boating matters relating to sail cruising, sail racing, windsurfing, motor cruising, powerboating, personal watercraft.

Collection: Minute books of the YRA and RYA meetings 1875-present

Library catalogue: All or part available in-house

Publications: Printed, and electronic and video

Publications list: Available in print

Access to staff: Contact by letter, by fax and by e-mail. Appointment necessary.
Hours: Mon to Fri, 0900 to 1700

Access to building: Prior appointment required

Access for disabled people: Ramped entry, access to all public areas

Has: 1,500 affiliated clubs and classes, 1,500 RYA recognised schools

Houses the: RYA Sailability; tel: 02380 647431; fax: 02380 629924; e-mail: info@rya .sailability.org

Links with: European Boating Association (EBA); European Sailing Federation (EUROSAF); International Sailing Federation (ISAF); Union Internationale Motonautique (UIM)

ROYAL YACHTING ASSOCIATION SCOTLAND (RYA Scotland)

Caledonia House, 1 Redheughs Rigg, South Gyle, Edinburgh, EH12 9DQ

Tel: 0131 317 7388
Fax: 0131 317 8566
E-mail: admin@ryascotland.org.uk

Organisation type and purpose: Training organisation.
National governing body for the sports of sailing, windsurfing, powerboating and personal watercrafting in Scotland.

Publications: Printed, and electronic and video
Order printed publications from: Royal Yachting Association, RYA House, Ensign Way, Hamble, Southampton, SO31 4YA; tel: 023 8060 4100; fax: 023 8060 4299

Publications list: Available online and in print

Access to staff: Contact by letter, by telephone, by fax, by e-mail and in person
Hours: Mon to Fri, 0900 to 1230 and 1315 to 1645

ROYAL ZOOLOGICAL SOCIETY OF SCOTLAND (RZSS)

Edinburgh Zoo, 134 Corstorphine Road, Corstorphine, Edinburgh, EH12 6TS

Tel: 0131 334 9171/2/3
Fax: 0131 316 4050
Website: www.edinburghzoo.org

Enquiries to: Visitor Services Manager
Direct e-mail: marketing@rzss.org.uk

Founded: 1909

Organisation type and purpose: Learned society (membership is by subscription), present number of members: 13,000, registered charity (charity number SCO040604).
To promote, through the preservation of the Society's living collections, the conservation of animal species and wild places through captive breeding, environmental education and scientific research.

Subject coverage: Zoo management, animals in captivity, Scottish wildlife, aviculture, conservation education.

Collection: Animal collection held on the International Species Inventory System (ISIS)

Publications: Printed

Access to staff: Appointment necessary.
Hours: Mon to Fri, 0900 to 1700
Special comments: Seasonal opening hours.

Links with: European Association of Zoos and Aquaria; International Union for Conservation of Nature and Natural Resources; National Federation of Zoological Gardens of Great Britain and Ireland; World Zoo Organisation (IUDZG)

Manages: Highland Wildlife Park; Kincraig; tel: 01540 651270; Scottish National Zoological Park; Edinburgh

RSABI

Rural Centre, West Mains of Ingliston, Newbridge, EH28 8LT

Tel: 0131 472 4166
Fax: 0131 472 4156
E-mail: gatepost@rsabi.org.uk
Website: www.rsabi.org.uk

Enquiries to: Chief Executive
Other contacts: Welfare Manager for all beneficiary contact.

Founded: 1897; formerly called Royal Scottish Agricultural Benevolent Institution (year of change 2005)

Organisation type and purpose: Voluntary organisation, registered charity (charity number SC 009828), suitable for all ages.

To assist those in distress who are or have been in farming, forestry, aquaculture, horticulture and rural estate work in Scotland and their dependants, with modest financial grants and in kind, and welfare assistance tailored to circumstance. Confidential listening helpline now also available.

Subject coverage: Relief of hardship among individuals who have depended on the land in Scotland.

Collection: Records of all meetings of subscribers since 1897

Publications: Printed, and electronic and video

Publications list: Available online

Access to staff: Contact by letter, by telephone, by fax, by e-mail, in person and via website. Appointment necessary.
Hours: Mon to Fri, 0900 to 1700

RSAC MOTORSPORT LTD (RSAC MS)

PO Box 3333, Glasgow, G20 2AX

Tel: 0141 946 5045
Fax: 0141 626 1416
E-mail: mail@rsacmotorsport.co.uk
Website: www.rsacmotorsport.co.uk
Website: www.scottishrally.co.uk

Enquiries to: Director
Direct tel: 07774 788844
Direct e-mail: jcll@rsacmotorsport.co.uk

Founded: 1899

Organisation type and purpose:
Membership association.
Organisation and promotion of motor sport events. Agent of the Scottish Government for authorisation of motoring events on the public highway in Scotland.

Subject coverage: Motor sport

Publications: Printed
Order printed publications from: Director

Access to staff: Contact by letter, by telephone, by fax, by e-mail and in person. Appointment necessary.
Hours: By appointment only.

Member of: Motor Sports Association

RSS CENTRE FOR STATISTICAL EDUCATION (RSS)

Formal name: Royal Statistical Society

Nottingham Trent University, Burton Street, Nottingham, NG1 4BU

Tel: 0115 848 4476
Fax: 0115 848 2998
E-mail: rsscse@ntu.ac.uk
Website: science.ntu.ac.uk/rsscse/

Enquiries to: Director
Direct tel: 0115 848 2118
Direct e-mail: Neville.Davies@ntu.ac.uk

Founded: 1995

Organisation type and purpose: Suitable for ages: all, consultancy, research organisation.

Subject coverage: Teaching statistics at all levels and in all contexts.

Library catalogue: All or part available online

Publications: Printed

Publications list: Available online and in print

Access to staff: Contact by letter, by telephone, by fax and by e-mail
Hours: Mon to Fri, 0900 to 1700

RUBBER CONSULTANTS

Tun Abdul Razak Research Centre, Brickendonbury, Hertford, SG13 8NL

Tel: 01992 554657
Fax: 01992 504248
E-mail: rubbercon@tarrc.co.uk
Website: www.rubberconsultants.com

Enquiries to: Manager

Founded: 1984

Organisation type and purpose:
Consultancy, research organisation.

Subject coverage: All aspects of the science and technology of natural and synthetic rubbers and the use of elastomers in manufactured products, tyre testing, rubber analysis, earthquake protection using structural bearings, information on the rubber industry.

Collection: MORPHS main database

Trade and statistical information: Statistical information on the rubber trade and the international trade in rubber products

Non-library collection catalogue: All or part available in-house

Library catalogue: All or part available in-house

Publications: Printed, and electronic and video

Publications list: Available online and in print

Access to staff: Contact by telephone, by fax, by e-mail and via website. Appointment necessary. All charged.
Hours: Mon to Fri, 0900 to 1700

Access to building: *Special comments:* Appointment required

Constituent part of: Tun Abdul Razak Research Centre

RUBBER STAMP MANUFACTURERS GUILD (RSMG)

2nd floor, Farringdon Point, 29–35 Farringdon Road, London, EC1M 3JF

Tel: 0845 450 1565
Fax: 0207 405 7784
E-mail: info@rsmg.org.uk
Website: www.rsmg.org.uk

Organisation type and purpose: The trade association for the rubber stamp and associated marking devices industry.
Promotes the industry and provides a forum for the exchange of ideas, information and education.

Subject coverage: Offers members the opportunity to keep up to date with emerging technologies and the development of new and exciting products that help to make their customers more efficient and more profitable; workshops, seminars and social gatherings offer an excellent opportunity for networking within the industry.

Access to staff: Contact by letter, by telephone, by fax and by e-mail

Links with: ISEE (International Stamp and Engraving Exhibition)

Member organisation of: AEGRAFLEX

RUGBY BOROUGH COUNCIL

Town Hall, Evereux Way, Rugby, Warwickshire, CV21 2LB

Tel: 01788 533533
Fax: 01788 533577
Website: www.warwickshire.gov.uk

Enquiries to: Public Relations Manager

Organisation type and purpose: Local government body.

Subject coverage: Council services and amenities; corporate services, environmental services, finance, housing, legal services, personnel services, planning development, tourism, economic development, technical services, highways, leisure services, council tax and other payments.

RUGBY FIVES ASSOCIATION (RFA)

2 Rose Street, Tonbridge, Kent TN2 2BN

Tel: 01732 773812
E-mail: ianfuller51@gmail.com
Website: www.rfa.org.uk

Enquiries to: General Secretary

Founded: 1927

Organisation type and purpose: Governing body of the sport.
Promotion of the game and organisation of regional and national championships.

Subject coverage: Rules of the game, championship dates and venues, championship records and past winners, clubs and playing facilities, manufacturers and suppliers of gloves and balls.

Publications: Printed

Publications list: Available in print

Access to staff: Contact by letter, by telephone, by e-mail and via website
Hours: No fixed times

RUGBY FOOTBALL UNION (RFU)

Rugby Road, Twickenham, Middlesex, TW1 1DZ

Tel: 020 8892 2000

Enquiries to: Sales and Marketing Manager
Direct tel: 020 8831 6737
Direct fax: 020 8891 3254
Direct e-mail: tomhill@rfu.com

Founded: 1871; formerly called England Rugby

Organisation type and purpose: National organisation, voluntary organisation.
33 constituent unions.
The promotion of rugby union football.

Subject coverage: Rugby union football; rugby records.

continued overleaf

Publications: Printed

Publications list: Available online

Access to staff: Access for members only.
Hours: Mon to Fri, 0900 to 1700

Access to building: Prior appointment required

Access for disabled people: Access to all public areas

Affiliated to: Committee of Home Unions; Committee of Six Nations (England, Scotland, Ireland, Wales, France and Italy); International Rugby Football Board

RUNNYMEDE BOROUGH COUNCIL

Civic Centre, Station Road, Addlestone, Surrey, KT15 2AH

Tel: 01932 838383
Fax: 01932 838384
E-mail: generalenquiries@runnymede.gov.uk
Website: www.runnymede.gov.uk

Enquiries to: General Enquiries

Founded: 1974

Organisation type and purpose: Local government body.

Publications: Printed

Access to staff: Contact by letter, by telephone, by fax, by e-mail and in person
Hours: Mon to Thu, 0830 to 1700; Fri, 0830 to 1630

Access for disabled people: Parking provided, level entry, toilet facilities

Parent body: Surrey County Council

RUNNYMEDE TRUST

7 Plough Yard, Shoreditch, London, EC2A 3LP

Tel: 020 7377 9222
Fax: 020 7377 6622
E-mail: info@runnymedetrust.org
Website: www.runnymedetrust.org

Founded: 1968; formerly called Runnymede Educational Trust, Runnymede Housing Trust

Organisation type and purpose: Voluntary organisation, registered charity (charity number 1063609), research organisation, publishing house.
Educational charity, research body and social policy think-tank.
To promote the development of a successful, equal and culturally diverse society.

Subject coverage: Social policy issues re multi-ethnicity, race etc. in the UK and how EU legislation affects UK policies.

Collection: Runnymede Trust Library has been donated to the Middlesex University, Centre for Racial Equality Studies

Publications: Printed

Publications list: Available online and in print

Access to staff: Contact by letter and by e-mail
Hours: Mon to Fri, 0900 to 1700
Special comments: Closed to the public.

Access to building: Mon to Fri, 0930 to 1730

Access for disabled people: Access to all public areas
Special comments: No public access to office except for scheduled appointments.

Links with: Commission for the Future of Multi-Ethnic Britain

RUPERT BROOKE MUSEUM & SOCIETY

The Orchard, 45–47 Millway, Grantchester, Cambridge, CB3 9ND

Tel: 01223 551118
E-mail: info@rupertbrookemuseum.org.uk
Website: www.rupertbrookemuseum.org.uk
Website: www.rupertbrookemuseum.org.uk/rupert-brooke-society

Enquiries to: Curator
Other contacts: Secretary (for RB Society information)

Founded: 1999

Organisation type and purpose: International organisation, membership association (membership is by subscription), museum, historic building, house or site.
The Museum covers the life history of Rupert Brooke.
Aims to: foster an interest in the work of Rupert Brooke, increase knowledge and appreciation of Rupert Brooke and of the village of Grantchester, help to preserve places associated with Rupert Brooke.

Subject coverage: The life and works of Rupert Brooke.

Collection: Small collection of books

Publications: Printed

Publications list: Available in print

Access to staff: Contact by letter, by telephone, by fax, by e-mail and via website
Hours: Mon to Sun, 1100 to 1600

Access to building: No prior appointment required
Hours: Jul and Aug: Mon to Sun, 1100 to 1700
Rest of year: Mon to Sun, 1100 to 1600

Access for disabled people: Parking provided
Special comments: Ramped entry to tea pavilion, steps into museum.

RURAL & INDUSTRIAL DESIGN & BUILDING ASSOCIATION (RIDBA)

ATSS House, Station Road East, Stowmarket, Suffolk, IP14 1RQ

Tel: 01449 676049
Fax: 01449 770028
E-mail: secretary@ridba.org.uk
Website: www.ridba.org.uk

Enquiries to: National Secretary

Founded: 1956

Organisation type and purpose: National organisation, advisory body, trade association (membership is by subscription), present number of members: 320.

Subject coverage: Members have expertise in all aspects of rural and industrial buildings and cover: planning, design, new construction (steel, timber, concrete and traditional), conversion, fitting out, health and safety, pollution control, education, animal welfare etc. Regular conferences are organised on subjects of interest, plus regular visits to interesting and up-to-date rural and industrial enterprises and an annual study tour usually in Europe.

Collection: A full set of past journals and newsletters is held and members have access to the old Farm Buildings Centre library at Silsoe College

Trade and statistical information: Members hold data on all aspects of rural buildings

Publications: Printed
Order printed publications from: Editor, Ghyll House Publishing Ltd, ATSS House, Station Road East, Stowmarket, IP14 1RQ, tel: 01449 676049; fax: 01449 770028; e-mail: tony@ghyllhouse.co.uk

Access to staff: Contact by letter, by telephone, by fax and by e-mail.
Appointment necessary.
Hours: Mon to Fri, 0900 to 1700

Access to building: No access other than to staff

RURAL CRAFTS ASSOCIATION

Heights Cottage, Brook Road, Wormley, Godalming, Surrey, GU8 5UA

Tel: 01428 682292
Fax: 01428 685969
E-mail: info@ruralcraftsassociation.co.uk
Website: www.ruralcraftsassociation.co.uk

Enquiries to: Director

Founded: 1970

Organisation type and purpose: Membership association (membership is by subscription), present number of members: 600.
To encourage men and women to make and sell their work and skills, to uphold the quality of work in whatever price range the craft falls, to provide a vigorous forum for the sale of members' work, at a cost they can afford.

Subject coverage: British craftworkers; contact for members of the association and for those wishing to exhibit and presently exhibiting in Rural Crafts Association pavilions at agricultural and equestrian shows, and game fairs nationwide.

Publications: Printed

Access to staff: Contact by letter, by telephone, by fax and by e-mail
Hours: Mon to Fri, 0900 to 1700

Access for disabled people: Good access at all events
Hours: At all opening times

RUSHCLIFFE BOROUGH COUNCIL

Civic Centre, Pavilion Road, West Bridgford, Nottinghamshire, NG2 5FE

Tel: 0115 981 9911
Fax: 0115 945 5882
E-mail: customerservices@rushcliffe.gov.uk
Website: www.rushcliffe.gov.uk

Enquiries to: Public Relations Manager
Direct tel: 0115 9148555

Direct e-mail: media@rushcliffe.gov.uk
Other contacts: Customer Services Centre for all enquiries.

Founded: 1974

Organisation type and purpose: Local government body.

Subject coverage: Council services and amenities; corporate services, environmental services, finance, housing, legal services, personnel services, planning development and tourism, property and technical services, roads and transportation, council tax and other payments.

Publications list: Available online and in print

Access to staff: Contact by letter, by telephone, by fax, by e-mail, in person and via website
Hours: Mon to Fri, 0730 to 1700

Access to building: No prior appointment required
Hours: Mon to Fri, 0830 to 1700

Access for disabled people: Parking provided, level entry, access to all public areas, toilet facilities

RUSKIN COLLEGE LIBRARY

Dunstan Road, Old Headington, Oxford, OX3 9BZ

Tel: 01865 759607
Fax: 01865 554372
E-mail: library@ruskin.ac.uk

Enquiries to: Librarian

Founded: 1899

Organisation type and purpose: Residential college for adult education.

Subject coverage: Social sciences, labour studies, social work, community and youth work, women's studies, history, literature.

Collection: Ewan MacColl and Peggy Seeger Archive

Access to staff: Contact by telephone and by e-mail. Appointment necessary.
Hours: Mon to Thu, 0900 to 1800; Fri, 0900 to 1700; Sat, 1300 to 1700. Vacations: Mon to Fri, 0900 to 1700

RUSKIN LIBRARY

Lancaster University, Lancaster, LA1 4YH

Tel: 01524 593587
Fax: 01524 593580
E-mail: ruskin.library@lancaster.ac.uk
Website: www.lancs.ac.uk/users/ruskinlib

Enquiries to: Director
Other contacts: Deputy Curator; Assistant Curator

Founded: 1998

Organisation type and purpose: Art gallery, university library.

Subject coverage: Art and architecture, history and literature.

Collection: Whitehouse Collection of manuscripts, books, photographs and pictures relating to John Ruskin (1819–1900) and his associates

Non-library collection catalogue: All or part available online

Library catalogue: All or part available online

Publications list: Available online

Access to staff: Contact by letter, by telephone, by fax, by e-mail, in person and via website. Appointment necessary.
Hours: Reading Room: Mon to Fri, 1000 to 1630

Access to building: No access other than to staff
Hours: Public Gallery: Mon to Fri 1000 to 1600

Access for disabled people: Ramped entry, access to all public areas, toilet facilities

RUSKIN SOCIETY

1 The Crescent, Witney, Oxfordshire, OX28 2EL

Tel: 01993 201478
E-mail: theruskinsociety@hotmail.co.uk
Website: www.theruskinsociety.com

Founded: 1932

Organisation type and purpose: The Society was founded to promote interest in all aspects of John Ruskin's life and work. These include art, architecture, politics, economics, and social criticism. Membership is by subscription.

Subject coverage: The life and works of John Ruskin.

Access to staff: Contact by letter, by telephone and by e-mail

Member organisation of: Alliance of Literary Societies

RUSSIAN ORTHODOX CHURCH IN GREAT BRITAIN AND IRELAND, DIOCESE OF SOUROZH

Formal name: Russian Orthodox Patriarchal Church in Great Britain and Ireland, Diocese of Sourozh

Cathedral of the Dormition and All Saints, 67 Ennismore Gardens, London, SW7 1NH

Tel: 020 7584 0096
Fax: 020 7584 9864
E-mail: office@sourozh.org
Website: www.sourozh.org

Enquiries to: Diocesan Administration

Founded: 1962

Organisation type and purpose: To administer the Russian Orthodox community in Great Britain and Ireland. Diocese within the Russian Orthodox Patriarchate of Moscow. Registered charity (charity number 254025).

Subject coverage: Russian Orthodoxy in Great Britain and Ireland.

Access to staff: Contact by letter and by e-mail

Parent body: Russian Orthodox Patriarchate of Moscow; website: http://www.mospat.ru

RUSSO-BRITISH CHAMBER OF COMMERCE (RBCC)

42 Southwark Street, London, SE1 1UN

Tel: 020 7403 1706
Fax: 020 7403 1245
E-mail: infolondon@rbcc.com
Website: www.rbcc.co.uk

Enquiries to: Office Manager
Direct e-mail: office.manager@rbcc.co.uk

Founded: 1916

Organisation type and purpose: To facilitate trade between Britain and Russia, through publications, in-depth regional and company profiles, exhibitions, conferences and business advice.

Publications: Printed

Access to staff: Contact by letter, by telephone, by fax, by e-mail and via website

RUTHERFORD APPLETON LABORATORY (STFC)

Harwell Science and Innovation Campus, Didcot, Oxfordshire, OX11 0QX

Tel: 01235 445384
Fax: 01235 446403
E-mail: library@stfc.ac.uk
Website: www.e-science.stfc.ac.uk/services/library

Organisation type and purpose: National government body, research organisation. Formed by Royal Charter in 2007, the Science and Technology Facilities Council is one of Europe's largest multidisciplinary research organisations supporting scientists and engineers worldwide.

Subject coverage: Elementary particles; computers; lasers; neutron studies; astrophysics; space research; advanced engineering; data collection and transmission; satellites; radio communications; information technology.

Collection: ESA reports (UK national repository)

Non-library collection catalogue: All or part available online

Library catalogue: All or part available online

Access to staff: Contact by e-mail. Appointment necessary.
Hours: Mon to Fri, 1000 to 1600

Constituent part of: Science and Technology Facilities Council (STFC); website: http://www.scitech.ac.uk/Home.aspx

RUTLAND COUNTY LIBRARY

Catmos Street, Oakham, Rutland, LE15 6HW

Tel: 01572 722918
Fax: 01572 724906
E-mail: libraries@rutland.gov.uk
Website: www.rutland.gov.uk/libraries

Enquiries to: Librarian

Organisation type and purpose: Public library.

Subject coverage: General.

Non-library collection catalogue: All or part available online

continued overleaf

Library catalogue: All or part available online

Access to staff: Contact by letter, by telephone, by fax, by e-mail, in person and via website. Appointment necessary.
Hours: Mon, Wed, Fri, 0900 to 1900; Tue, 0900 to 1700; Thu, 0900 to 1700; Sat, 0900 to 1600

RUTLAND LOCAL HISTORY & RECORD SOCIETY (RLHRS)

Rutland County Museum, Catmose Street, Oakham, Rutland, LE15 6HW

Tel: 01572 758440
Fax: 01572 758445
E-mail: enquiries@rutlandhistory.org
Website: www.rutlandhistory.org

Enquiries to: Honorary Secretary
Direct e-mail: secretary@rutlandhistory.org
Other contacts: Hon Editor, e-mail: editor@rutlandhistory.org

Founded: 1979; incorporates the former Rutland Local History Society, Rutland Record Society (year of change 1991); incorporates the former Rutland Field Research Group for Archaeology & History (year of change 1993)

Organisation type and purpose:
Membership association (membership is by subscription), registered charity (charity number 700273).
All aspects of the history of the County of Rutland and the immediate area.

Subject coverage: History and archaeology of Rutland.

Publications: Printed
Order printed publications from: website: www.rutlandhistory.org or www.genfair.co.uk; or by post from RLHRS

Publications list: Available online and in print

Access to staff: Contact by letter, by e-mail and via website. Appointment necessary.

Access to building: Library access by arrangement: resources combined with those of Rutland County Museum and available in study area during opening hours
Hours: Mon, Wed, Fri, Sat, 1000 to 1600
Special comments: Closed Sun, Tue, Thu, Bank Holidays

Access for disabled people: Accessible

Links with: Rutland County Museum; at the same address; e-mail: museum@rutland.gov.uk

RWE NPOWER PLC

Windmill Hill Business Park, Whitehill Way, Swindon, Wiltshire, SN5 6PB

Tel: 01793 892565
Fax: 01793 892994
Website: www.rwenpower.com

Enquiries to: Administrator
Direct e-mail: suzanne.botter@rwenpower.com

Founded: 1990

Organisation type and purpose:
Manufacturing industry, research organisation.
Electricity generation.

Subject coverage: Power generation (thermal), electrical engineering, energy, environment, management, fuels.

Collection: Historical publications on the history of electricity supply in UK
Reports of former CERL, MEL and BNL (microform)

Non-library collection catalogue: All or part available in-house

Library catalogue: All or part available in-house

Publications: Printed

Access to staff: Contact by letter, by telephone, by fax and by e-mail. Appointment necessary.
Hours: Tue and Thu, 0900 to 1630
Special comments: Access is discretionary, depending on nature of enquiry and other commitments.

RYEDALE DISTRICT COUNCIL (RDC)

Ryedale House, Malton, North Yorkshire, YO17 7HH

Tel: 01653 600666
Fax: 01653 696801
E-mail: info@ryedale.gov.uk
Website: www.ryedale.gov.uk

Founded: 1974

Organisation type and purpose: Local government body.

Subject coverage: Local government services.

Publications list: Available online

Access to staff: Contact by letter, by telephone, by fax, by e-mail, in person and via website. Appointment necessary.
Hours: Mon to Fri, 0900 to 1600

Access to building: *Hours:* Mon to Fri, 0900 to 1600

Access for disabled people: Level entry, with hearing loop in reception
Hours: Mon to Fri, 0900 to 1600

SACKLER LIBRARY

1 St John Street, Oxford, OX1 2LG

Tel: 01865 278088 (enquiries and administration)
Fax: 01865 278098
E-mail: james.legg@saclib.ox.ac.uk
Website: www.saclib.ox.ac.uk

Enquiries to: Administrator
Direct e-mail: helen.edwards@ouls.ox.ac.uk
Other contacts: Librarian

Founded: 2001; formerly called Ashmolean Museum Library; formerly called Ashmolean Library (year of change 1901–2001)

Organisation type and purpose: University department or institute.

Subject coverage: Egyptology; Assyriological and Hittite studies; Altertumswissenschaft; papyrology; numismatics; dies and medals; Western art and architecture; Near Eastern classical and European archaeology; Greek and Latin literature; Byzantine studies; patristics.

Library catalogue: All or part available online

Access to staff: Contact by letter, by fax and by e-mail. Letter of introduction required.
Hours: Mon to Fri, 0900 to 2200; Sat, 1000 to 1700

Access for disabled people: Level entry, toilet facilities, lift

Includes the: Griffith Institute Library of Egyptology; tel: 01865 288198 or 278089; e-mail: diane.bergman@saclib.ox.co.uk; Heberden Coin Room Library; tel: as main library; e-mail: diane.bergman@saclib.ox.ac.uk; Main Library; tel: 01865 278092; e-mail: jane.bruder@saclib.ox.co.uk; Western Art Library; tel: 01865 278093/4

SACRO

Formal name: Safeguarding Communities – Reducing Offending

1 Broughton Street, Edinburgh, EH3 6NU

Tel: 0131 624 7270
Fax: 0131 624 7269
E-mail: info@national.sacro.org.uk
Website: www.sacro.org.uk

Founded: 1971; formerly called Scottish Association for the Care and Resettlement of Offenders (SACRO) (year of change 1992); formerly called SACRO (year of change 1998)

Organisation type and purpose:
Membership association, present number of members: 50+ full members, 2,204 associate members, voluntary organisation (charity number SCO 16293).
To provide advice, assistance and support to people in conflict, and particularly those in trouble with the law, those at risk of becoming so, and their families, by direct services provided at local level.

Subject coverage: Criminal justice in Scotland, offenders, mediation, supported accommodation for offenders, alcohol education for probationers, intensive probation programmes, families of offenders, volunteer support, dispute resolution, community mediation, restorative justice.

Publications: Printed
Order printed publications from: Communications Officer

Publications list: Available online and in print

Access to staff: Contact by letter, by telephone, by fax, by e-mail and via website. Appointment necessary.
Hours: Mon to Fri, 0900 to 1700

Access to building: No prior appointment required
Special comments: Non-catalogued, varied filing types; reference only

SADS UK

Formal name: The Ashley Jolly SAD Trust

Suite 6, Churchill House, Horndon Ind. Park, Station Road, West Horndon, CM13 3XD

Tel: 01277 811215
E-mail: sadsuk@btconnect.com
Website: www.sadsuk.org

Founded: c. 2000

Organisation type and purpose: Registered charity (charity number 1113681).
SADS UK raises awareness about heart conditions that can cause a sudden arrhythmic death (SAD). It works with government departments to introduce new guidelines to safeguard those who may be at risk from a fatal cardiac arrhythmia. It raises awareness about conditions that may cause SADS and symptoms that need further investigation. It highlights the fact that conditions can be hereditary.

Subject coverage: SADS UK supports research into the causes of cardiac arrhythmias. This research is essential in order to improve methods of detection and provide even more effective treatments in the future.

Special visitor services: Events and conferences; monthly bereavement support meetings.

Publications: Printed
Order printed publications from: SADS UK, by tel. or e-mail; subscribe to newsletter via website

Publications list: Available online

Access to staff: Contact by letter, by telephone and by e-mail

International affiliate of: SADS Foundation; Salt Lake City, Utah

Works with: SADS USA, Canada, Australia and Europe

SAFETY AND RELIABILITY SOCIETY (SaRS)

Clayton House, 59 Piccadilly, Manchester, M1 2AQ

Tel: 0161 228 7824
Fax: 0161 236 6977
E-mail: secretary@sars.u-net.com
Website: www.sars.org.uk

Founded: 1980

Organisation type and purpose:
Professional institution for all industries.
To represent engineers and scientists working in the important fields of safety and reliability; to enhance the professionalism and reputation of all those involved in safety and reliability technology.
Has members in the UK, mainland Europe, the Middle East, USA and the Asia Pacific region; has an affiliate membership scheme for academic institutions, industrial companies, and other organisations with interests in safety and reliability and engineering risk management.

Subject coverage: Encourages the development and use of safety and reliability technology; provides an international forum for the exchange of information on safety and reliability matters; etablishes professional and educational standards for safety and reliability engineers; establishes standard techniques and encourages consistency in their application; encourages organisations and government departments to apply safety and reliability techniques.

Publications: Printed

Publications list: Available online

Access to staff: Contact by letter, by telephone, by fax and by e-mail

Branches: Six in England, one in Scotland and one in Asia

SAFETY ASSESSMENT FEDERATION (SAFed)

Unit 4, First Floor, 70 South Lambeth Road, Vauxhall, London, SW8 1RL

Tel: 020 7582 3208
Fax: 020 7735 0286
E-mail: diane.mckay@safed.co.uk
Website: www.safed.co.uk

Enquiries to: Technical Director
Other contacts: Technical Manager for detailed technical information.

Founded: 1995; formerly called Council of Independent Inspecting Authorities (CIIA), Independent Engineering Insurance Committee (IEIC); formerly called Associated Offices Technical Committee (AOTC) (year of change 1995)

Organisation type and purpose: Trade association, present number of members: eight full, nine associate.
To represent companies engaged in independent safety inspection, testing and certification of engineering plant and equipment of all types.

Subject coverage: Engineering inspection and design assessment for plant such as boilers, pressure vessels, lifts, cranes, electrical equipment etc, including welding; NDT techniques; export of engineering plant.

Publications: Printed

Publications list: Available in print

Access to staff: Contact by letter, by telephone, by fax and by e-mail
Hours: Mon to Fri, 0900 to 1700

UK member of: Confédération Européenne d'Organismes de Prévention et de Contrôle (CEOC)

SAI GLOBAL (SAI)

Index House, Ascot, Berkshire, SL5 7EU

Tel: 01344 636400
Fax: 01344 291194
E-mail: standards@saiglobal.com
Website: www.ili.co.uk; www.saiglobal .com

Enquiries to: Publishing Director
Direct e-mail: richard.boden@saiglobal.com

Founded: 1949; incorporates the former ILI Ltd

Organisation type and purpose: Service industry, publishing house.
Publishing and distributing technical, legal and regulatory databases.

Subject coverage: Technical standards and specifications from world-wide sources with special knowledge of US industrial and military standards, agents and distributors for BSI, IEEE, API, ASME, NFPA, DoD, MoD, ASTM and numerous other standards authorities, European law, metals and materials databases.

Collection: Over 1m. technical specifications and standards, including all British Standards, US Military Standards, MOD Defence Standards, American Standards and others

Non-library collection catalogue: All or part available online

Publications: Electronic and video

Publications list: Available online

Access to staff: Contact by letter, by telephone, by fax, by e-mail and via website. Appointment necessary.
Hours: Mon to Fri, 0830 to 1730

Also at: SAI Global; 610 Winters Avenue, Paramus, New Jersey, 07652, USA; tel: +1 201 986 1131; fax: +1 201 986 7886; e-mail: uspubsales@saiglobal.com; website: http://www.saiglobal.com

SAIL TRAINING INTERNATIONAL (STI)

5 Mumby Road, Gosport, Hampshire, PO12 1AA

Tel: 023 9258 6367
Fax: 023 9258 4661
E-mail: office@sailtraininginternational.org
Website: www.tallshipsraces.com
Website: www.sailtraininginternational.com
Website: www.ista.co.uk

Enquiries to: Media Publications Manager
Direct e-mail: corinne.hitching@sailtraininginternational.org
Other contacts: Business Director

Founded: 1956

Organisation type and purpose:
International organisation.
Operating as a subsidiary of a registered charity, for the development and education of young people through sail training.
Organisers of the Tall Ships Races.

Subject coverage: Ocean sailing, sail training, race planning, race organisation, event management, adventure activities.

Publications: Printed

Access to staff: Contact by letter, by telephone, by fax and by e-mail
Hours: Mon to Fri, 0900 to 1700

Parent body: Sail Training Association; 2A The Hard, Portsmouth, Hampshire, PO1 3PT; tel: 023 9283 2055

SAILORS CHILDRENS SOCIETY (FORMALLY SAILORS FAMILIES SOCIETY)

Francis Reckitt House, Newland, Cottingham Road, Hull, HU6 7RJ

Tel: 01482 342331
Fax: 01482 447868
E-mail: info@sailorschildren.org.uk
Website: www.sailorschildren.org.uk

Enquiries to: Chief Officer

Founded: 1821

continued overleaf

Organisation type and purpose: Voluntary organisation.

Subject coverage: Welfare and care of seafarers and their families. Respite care for disadvantaged children.

SAILORS' SOCIETY

Sailors' Society, 350 Shirley Road, Southampton, Hampshire, SO15 3HY

Tel: 023 8051 5950
Fax: 023 8051 5951
E-mail: admin@sailors-society.org
Website: www.sailors-society.org

Enquiries to: Head of Operations & Administration
Direct tel: 023 8051 5967
Direct fax: 023 8051 5951

Founded: 1818

Organisation type and purpose: Registered charity (charity number 237778).
International Christian charity working amongst merchant seafarers and their dependants.

Subject coverage: Welfare of seafarers.

Collection: Bound copies of past magazines of Society going back to early 19th century when the Society was founded

Publications: Printed

Access to staff: Contact by letter, by telephone, by fax, by e-mail and in person. Appointment necessary.
Hours: Mon to Fri, 0900 to 1730

Links with: Sister societies in Canada, New Zealand, South Africa, Ghana and Belgium

Member organisation of: International Christian Maritime Association; Merchant Navy Welfare Board

SAINT-GOBAIN (GYPSUM ACTIVITY)

Gypsum Technical Building, East Leake, Loughborough, Leicestershire, LE12 6JS

Tel: 0115 945 1652
Fax: 0115 945 1678
E-mail: liz.redfern@saint-gobain.com

Enquiries to: Head of Information

Organisation type and purpose: Manufacturing industry.

Subject coverage: Gypsum and plaster technology.

Non-library collection catalogue: All or part available in-house

Library catalogue: All or part available in-house

Parent body: Compagnie de Saint-Gobain; Les Miroirs, 18 avenue d'Alsace, 92096 La Defense, Paris, France

SAINT-GOBAIN QUARTZ LTD

PO Box 6, Neptune Road, Wallsend, Tyne and Wear, NE28 6DG

Tel: 0191 262 5311
Fax: 0191 263 8040
E-mail: quartz.sales@saint-gobain.com
Website: www.quartz.saint-gobain.com

Enquiries to: Sales Manager
Direct tel: 0191 259 8315

Founded: 1906; formerly called TSL Group PLC; formerly called TSL Thermal Syndicate PLC; formerly called Thermal Syndicate Ltd.

Organisation type and purpose: Manufacturing industry.

Subject coverage: Transparent and opaque fused quartz, synthetic transparent, translucent fused silica, ingot, plate, rod tube and machined components for fibre optics, semiconductors, heating and lighting, optical aerospace, foundry, chemical, laboratory and refractory industries.

Non-library collection catalogue: All or part available online

Publications: Printed

Publications list: Available online

Access to staff: Contact by letter, by telephone, by fax, by e-mail and via website. Appointment necessary.
Hours: Mon to Thu, 0800 to 1615; Fri, 0800 to 1400

Access to building: No access other than to staff

SALFORD CITY LIBRARIES

Minerva House, Pendlebury Road, Swinton, Manchester, M27 4EQ

Tel: 0161 778 0123
Fax: 0161 728 6145
E-mail: robin.culpin@salford.gov.uk

Enquiries to: Librarian

Founded: 1974

Organisation type and purpose: Local government body, public library.

Subject coverage: General, local history, working class movement, labour movement, James Nasmyth (engineer).

Collection: Boothstown Horticultural and Botanical Collection (18th-century material)
Cowan Collection (theology, 17th century)
Davies Collection (theology, history and literature and political pamphlets of 17th–19th centuries)
Photography Collection
Trinity Collection (theology, 17th–19th centuries)
Working Class Movement Library, banners, pottery and medallions
Workshops Manuals Collection

Publications: Printed

Access to staff: Contact by letter, by telephone, by fax, by e-mail, in person and via website. Appointment necessary.
Hours: Mon to Fri, 0900 to 1700

Comprises the: 17 libraries of the City of Salford, Eccles, Irlam, Swinton and Worsley

SALFORD LOCAL HISTORY LIBRARY (SLHL)

Peel Park, The Crescent, Salford, M5 4WU

Tel: 0161 778 0814
Fax: 0161 745 9490
E-mail: local.history@salford.gov.uk
Website: www.lifetimes.org.uk

Enquiries to: Local History Librarian
Direct tel: 0161 778 0814
Direct e-mail: local.history@salford.gov.uk

Organisation type and purpose: Local government body, public library, suitable for ages: 12+.

Subject coverage: Local history including census returns, parish registers, documents, maps, and photographs chronicling the history of Salford City.

Access to staff: Contact by letter, by telephone, by fax, by e-mail and in person
Hours: Tue, Thu and Fri, 1000 to 1645; Wed, 1000 to 2000; Mon, Closed.

Access to building: No prior appointment required
Hours: As above

Parent body: Salford Community Leisure Limited; at same address

SALFORD TOURIST INFORMATION CENTRE (Salford TIC)

1 The Quays, Salford, Greater Manchester, M50 3SQ

Tel: 0161 848 8601
Fax: 0161 872 3848
E-mail: tic@salford.gov.uk
Website: www.visitsalford.info

Enquiries to: Manager

Founded: 2000

Organisation type and purpose: Local government body.

Subject coverage: Tourist information. Local information, leaflets, Greater Manchester, arts, theatre, small souvenir shop, local history books, maps, postcards, videos, souvenirs, accommodation bookings, boat trips.

Special visitor services: Free access to tourism websites.

Services for disabled people: Hearing loop at desk, easy access for wheelchair users, front desk and internet desk correct height for wheelchair users.

Publications: Printed, and electronic and video

Publications list: Available in print

Access to staff: Contact by letter, by telephone, by fax, by e-mail, in person and via website
Hours: Tue to Fri 1000 to 1715; Sat 1000 to 1600; Sun and Bank Holidays 1100 to 1700; closed Mon

Access for disabled people: Parking provided, level entry, access to all public areas
Special comments: No disabled toilet facilities inside TIC but available in The Lowry

Administered by: Salford City Council

SALISBURY & DISTRICT COUNCIL FOR VOLUNTARY SERVICE (Salisbury CVS)

42 Salt Lane, Salisbury, Wiltshire, SP1 1EG

Tel: 01722 421747
Fax: 01722 415544

E-mail: salisbury.cvs@ruralnet.org.uk

Enquiries to: Chief Executive

Founded: 1973

Organisation type and purpose: Registered charity (charity number 1019716).
Local development agency for community and voluntary activity.

Access to staff: Contact by e-mail
Hours: Mon to Fri, 0930 to 1630

Access to building: Prior appointment required

Access for disabled people: Ramped entry, toilet facilities

Connected with: National Association of Councils for Voluntary Service (NACVS)

SALMON & TROUT ASSOCIATION (S&TA)

Fishmongers' Hall, London Bridge, London, EC4R 9EL

Tel: 020 7283 5838
Fax: 020 7626 5137
E-mail: hq@salmon-trout.org
Website: www.salmon-trout.org

Founded: 1903

Organisation type and purpose: Registered charity (charity number 1123285), membership association with a UK-wide membership (100,000 individual and club members) of game anglers, fishery owners/managers, affiliated trades and members of the public with an interest in conserving the aquatic environment and its dependent species.

Subject coverage: Addresses all issues relevant to fisheries legislation and regulation, together with environmental and species management and conservation. Has close working relationships with government departments and agencies, advising them over fisheries and angling matters and influencing their decision-making processes on behalf of all those with an interest in the aquatic environment.

Publications: Electronic and video
Order electronic and video publications from: Download from website

Access to staff: Contact by letter, by telephone, by fax and by e-mail

Administers: Salmon & Trout Association's honorary Scientific Advisory Panel

Branches: in Scotland and Wales and 12 affiliated branches in England

SALMONS TICKFORD REGISTER (STR)

Formal name: The Register of Motor Vehicles with Salmons Tickford Bodywork – 1898–1954

24 Woodland Rise West, Sheringham, Norfolk, NR26 8PF

Tel: 01263 824045
E-mail: mynard.revarg@tiscali.co.uk

Enquiries to: Secretary and Registrar
Direct e-mail: mynard@telinco.co.uk

Founded: 1998

Organisation type and purpose: Membership association (no charge for membership).
To provide information on Salmons and Tickford-bodied motor cars.

Subject coverage: Salmons and Tickford-bodied cars.

Collection: Collection of photographs of Salmons/Tickford cars, printed brochures, original manuscripts, etc

Non-library collection catalogue: All or part available in-house and in print

Publications: Printed
Order printed publications from: e-mail: mynard.revarg@tiscali.co.uk

Publications list: Available in print

Access to staff: Contact by letter, by telephone, by e-mail and in person. Appointment necessary. Letter of introduction required.
Hours: Sun to Sat, 0900 to 2100

SALT ASSOCIATION

Tel: 015395 68005
E-mail: info@saltinfo.com
Website: www.saltsense.co.uk

Organisation type and purpose: Trade association representing UK manufacturers of salt for domestic, catering, water-softening, industrial and de-icing uses.

Subject coverage: The association supports its members by: representing the technical, social and political views and objectives of the salt industry to relevant government and international organisations; providing a forum where members can exchange knowledge and scientific information on research, legislation, diet and nutrition, technical training, and health and safety issues; promoting balanced exposure for scientific research on salt and human health.

Publications: Electronic and video
Order electronic and video publications from: Download from website

Access to staff: Contact by telephone and by e-mail

Member organisation of: European Salt Producers' Association (EuSalt)

SALTERS' CHEMISTRY CLUB, THE

Salters' Hall, 4 Fore Street, London, EC2Y 5DE

Tel: 020 7628 5962
Fax: 020 7638 3679
E-mail: club@salters.co.uk
Website: www.salters.co.uk

Enquiries to: Administrator

Founded: 1991

Organisation type and purpose: Voluntary organisation, registered charity.

Subject coverage: Promotion of chemistry in schools by establishing school-based chemistry clubs.

Publications: Printed

Access to staff: Contact by letter, by telephone, by fax and by e-mail
Hours: Mon to Fri, 0900 to 1700

Parent body: The Salters' Institute; tel: 020 7628 5962; fax: 020 7638 3679; e-mail: institute@salters.co.uk

SALTERS' COMPANY

Formal name: The Worshipful Company of Salters

Salters' Hall, 4 Fore Street, London, EC2Y 5DE

Tel: 020 7588 5216
Fax: 020 7638 3679
E-mail: clerk@salters.co.uk
Website: www.salters.co.uk

Enquiries to: Clerk

Founded: 1394

Organisation type and purpose: Membership association, present number of members: 195. A livery company of the City of London with charitable interests.

Subject coverage: Promoting careers in chemistry and the chemical industries through its flagship charity The Salters' Institute.

Access to staff: Contact by letter, by telephone, by fax and by e-mail. Appointment necessary. Access for members only.
Hours: Mon to Fri, 0900 to 1700

Access for disabled people: Toilet facilities

Also at the same address: Salters' Chemistry Camps; Salters' Chemistry Club; Salters' Institute; The Charities of Nicholas & Beamond; The James' Smiths' Alms House Charity; The Salters' Charities; The Salters' Charity for the Relief of Need

An investment subsidiary at the same address: The Salters' Management Company Limited

SALTERS' INSTITUTE

Salters' Hall, 4 Fore Street, London, EC2Y 5DE

Tel: 020 7628 5962
Fax: 020 7638 3679
E-mail: institute@salters.co.uk
Website: www.salters.co.uk

Enquiries to: Institute Manager

Founded: 1918; formerly called Salters' Institute of Industrial Chemistry

Organisation type and purpose: Membership association, registered charity.

Subject coverage: Award of Salters' Prizes to final year undergraduates in chemistry or chemical engineering; to Salters' A level chemistry candidates; limited information on research subjects undertaken by Salters' Fellows and Scholars; grants for school chemistry libraries and chemistry equipment; no other help given at undergraduate level.

Access to staff: Contact by letter, by telephone, by fax and by e-mail
Hours: Mon to Fri, 0900 to 1700

Parent body: The Salters' Company; tel: 020 7588 5216; fax: 020 7638 3679

SALVATION ARMY

United Kingdom Territory, Territorial Headquarters, 101 Newington Causeway, London, SE1 6BN

Tel: 020 7367 4500
Fax: 020 7367 4728
E-mail: thq@salvationarmy.org.uk
Website: www.salvationarmy.org.uk

Enquiries to: Press Officer
Direct e-mail: sarah.miller@salvationarmy.org.uk
Other contacts: Media contacts, Media and Press Officer tel no: 020 7367 4700

Founded: 1865

Organisation type and purpose: Voluntary organisation.
Part of the worldwide Christian church, providing social welfare in 108 countries.

Subject coverage: Evangelism; health; social welfare; housing; education; prison welfare; agriculture; emergency aid; refugees; child care; handicapped ministries; leprosaria; care of the aged; community aid; agricultural development; family tracing; feeding programmes; educational programmes.

Collection: Historical information and archive material at The Heritage Centre, tel: 0171 387 1656

Publications: Printed, and electronic and video

Access to staff: Contact by letter, by telephone and by fax. Appointment necessary.
Hours: Mon to Fri, 0815 to 1630
Special comments: No personal callers without prior appointment.

SALVATION ARMY FAMILY TRACING SERVICE

101 Newington Causeway, London, SE1 6BN

Tel: 020 7367 4747
E-mail: family.tracing@salvationarmy.org.uk
Website: www.salvationarmy.org.uk/familytracing

Enquiries to: Director

Founded: 1885; formerly called Salvation Army Investigation Department (year of change 1990)

Organisation type and purpose: International organisation, registered charity, voluntary organisation.
A service for endeavouring to trace members of family with whom contact has been lost for some reason, whether recently or in the distant past, for reconciliation purposes only. Adoption searches are not accepted.

Subject coverage: Tracing missing relatives for the purposes of reconciliation only; counselling for this need (enquiries for friends, adoption, estate, divorce, family tree or business reasons are not accepted).

Publications: Printed

Access to staff: Contact by letter and by telephone. All charged.
Hours: Mon to Fri, 0830 to 1545
Special comments: Enclose an sae for a reply.

Parent body: Salvation Army THQ; 101 Newington Causeway, London, SE1 6BN

SAMARITANS

The Upper Mill, Kingston Road, Ewell, Surrey, KT17 2AF

Tel: 020 8394 8300
Fax: 020 8394 8301
E-mail: admin@samaritans.org
Website: www.samaritans.org.uk

Founded: 1953

Organisation type and purpose: Voluntary organisation, registered charity (charity number 219432). Samaritans is available 24 hours a day to provide confidential emotional support for people who are experiencing feelings of distress or despair, including those which may lead to suicide

Subject coverage: Suicide and emotional support

Collection: Books and leaflets on related subjects
Small collection of books on suicide, parasuicide (epidemiology, prevention, intervention)

Trade and statistical information: Suicide statistics – national and international

Publications: Printed

Access to staff: Contact by letter, by telephone, by e-mail, in person and via website
Hours: Mon to Fri, 0900 to 1700 (admin only). 24-hour access to volunteers
Special comments: Confidential emotional support by phone: 08457 908090; by e-mail: jo@samaritans.org; by letter: Chris, PO Box 90 90, Stirling, FK8 2SA

Access to building: For individual branches, see website

Access for disabled people: Please see website

SANDWELL AND WEST BIRMINGHAM HOSPITALS NHS TRUST (SWBH)

Clinical Library, Sandwell General Hospital, Lyndon, West Bromwich, West Midlands, B71 4HJ

Tel: 0121 507 3587 ext. 3587
Fax: 0121 507 3586
E-mail: clinical.library@swbh.nhs.uk

Enquiries to: Librarian

History of institution: formerly called Sandwell General Hospital

Organisation type and purpose: Hospital.

Subject coverage: Medicine.

Library catalogue: All or part available in-house

Access to staff: Contact by letter, by telephone, by fax and by e-mail
Hours: Mon to Fri, 0830 to 1700

Also at: Sandwell and West Birmingham Hospitals NHS Trust; Bevan Library, City Hospital, Dudley Road, Winson Green, Birmingham B18 4HQ; tel: 0121 507 5245; e-mail: bevan.library@swbh.nhs.uk

SANDWELL COLLEGE

Learning Centre, Wednesbury Campus, Woden Road South, Wednesbury, West Midlands, WS10 0PE

Tel: 0121 556 6000, from 0800 to 2000; 505 6000, any other time
Fax: 0121 253 6069
Website: www.sandwell.ac.uk

Enquiries to: Learning Centre Manager (for each campus)
Direct tel: ext 6615

Founded: 1986; formerly called Warley College, West Bromwich College; includes the former Warley College

Organisation type and purpose: College of further and higher education.
Headquarters for the 3 sites of the college: Wednesbury, West Bromwich and Smethwick.

Subject coverage: Foundry technology; metallurgy; welding; marketing; business economics; management; motor vehicle technology; production and mechanical engineering; photography (the College lists over 130 subjects, but excludes agriculture).

Collection: Diecasting Society Library
Library of the National Foundry College

Non-library collection catalogue: All or part available in-house

Access to staff: Contact by letter, by telephone and in person
Hours: Mon to Thu, 0830 to 2000; Fri, 1000 to 1500
Special comments: Reference only, no loans.

Access for disabled people: Ramped entry, access to all public areas, toilet facilities

Also at: Smethwick Campus; Crochelts Lane, Smethwick, West Midlands; West Bromwich Campus; High Street, West Bromwich, West Midlands

SANDWELL COMMUNITY HISTORY AND ARCHIVES SERVICE (CHAS)

Smethwick Library, High Street, Smethwick, West Midlands, B66 1AA

Tel: 0121 558 2561
Fax: 0121 555 6064
E-mail: archives_service@sandwell.gov.uk
Website: www.archives.sandwell.gov.uk

Founded: 1988

Organisation type and purpose: Local government body, record office.

Subject coverage: Local history of area now covered by Metropolitan Borough of Sandwell.

Collection: Records of churches, schools, organisations, businesses, families and individuals within Sandwell Metropolitan Borough. Notable collections include:
Public records, e.g. magistrates' court, quarter sessions court, coroner's court, hospitals and health authority
Business records, including Patent Shaft Steelworks of Wednesbury, T. W. Camm, Stained Glass Manufacturer of Smethwick, Chance Bros Ltd of Smethwick
Records of the Deanery of Warley and its churches

Records of the Boroughs of Oldbury, Rowley Regis, Smethwick, Tipton, Warley, Wednesbury and West Bromwich

Non-library collection catalogue: All or part available online and in-house

Library catalogue: All or part available online

Access to staff: Contact by letter, by telephone, by fax, by e-mail, in person and via website. Appointment necessary.
Hours: Mon, Tue, Fri, 1000 to 1800; Wed, 1030 to 1800; Thu, closed; Sat, 1000 to 1600

Access for disabled people: Level entry, access to all public areas

Parent body: Sandwell Metropolitan Borough Council; Council House, Oldbury, Warley

SANDWELL METROPOLITAN BOROUGH COUNCIL

Sandwell Information Service, Sandwell Central Library, High Street, West Bromwich, West Midlands, B70 8DZ

Tel: 0121 569 4911
Fax: 0121 525 9465
E-mail: information_service@sandwell.gov.uk
Website: www.libraries.sandwell.gov.uk

Enquiries to: Information Librarian

Organisation type and purpose: Local government body, public library.

Subject coverage: General; local history, business, Europe, local council and community.

Non-library collection catalogue: All or part available in-house

Library catalogue: All or part available online and in-house

Access to staff: Contact by letter, by telephone, by fax, by e-mail, in person and via website
Hours: Mon, Fri, 0930 to 1900; Tue, Thu, 0930 to 1800; Wed, 1030 to 1800; Sat, 0900 to 1600

Access for disabled people: Level entry

Administers: Community History and Archive Service; Smethwick Library, 100 High Street, Smethwick, B66 1AA; tel: 0121 558 2561; fax: 0121 555 6064; e-mail: archives_service@sandwell.gov.uk; website: http://www.libraries.sandwell.gov.uk/archives

SANE

Formal name: Schizophrenia – A National Emergency

1st Floor, Cityside House, 40 Adler Street, London, E1 1EE

Tel: 020 7375 1002
Fax: 020 7375 2162
E-mail: info@sane.org.uk
Website: www.sane.org.uk

Enquiries to: Communications Officer
Direct tel: 020 7422 5557
Direct e-mail: info@saneline.org
Other contacts: Press Officer

Founded: 1986

Organisation type and purpose: National organisation, voluntary organisation, registered charity (charity number 296572), training organisation, research organisation.
SANE campaigns to combat the prejudice and intolerance surrounding mental illness, and improve attitudes and services for individuals coping with mental health problems and their families.
SANELINE is a national mental health helpline providing information and support for people with mental health problems and those who support them.

Subject coverage: Greater public awareness of all mental health problems.

Publications: Printed

Publications list: Available online and in print

Access to staff: Contact by letter, by telephone, by fax and by e-mail. Appointment necessary.
Hours: Mon to Fri, 0900 to 1700
Special comments: SANELINE (helpline), 1300 to 2300 every day.

Access to building: Prior appointment required

Access for disabled people: Parking provided

Has one satellite: Prince of Wales Research Centre (POWIC), Oxford

SANGAT ADVICE CENTRE

Sancroft Road, Harrow, HA3 7NS

Tel: 020 8427 0659
Fax: 020 8863 2196
E-mail: info@sangat.org.uk
Website: www.asiansinharrow.org

Founded: 1997

Organisation type and purpose: A not-for-profit company limited by guarantee, providing the local Asian community with advice and advocacy in such matters as legal rights, housing, debt, welfare benefits, immigration and discrimination.

Access to building: *Hours:* Mon to Fri, 0900 to 1700

Access for disabled people: Accessible for people with mobility problems

SARUM COLLEGE LIBRARY

19 The Close, Salisbury, Wiltshire, SP1 2EE

Tel: 01722 424803
Fax: 01722 338508
E-mail: library@sarum.ac.uk
Website: www.sarum.ac.uk/library

Enquiries to: Librarian
Direct tel: 01722 326899 (Bookshop Manager)
Other contacts: Bookshop Manager

Founded: 1860; formerly called Salisbury and Wells Theological College Library (year of change 1995)

Organisation type and purpose: Registered charity (charity number 309501).
Ecumenical centre for theological education, subscription library.

Subject coverage: Theology, church history, spirituality, biblical studies.

Information services: Online catalogue, enquiry service.

Services for disabled people: Lift

Collection: Bishop Hamilton's Library 19th-century theology, including the Markham Bequest of 276 bound vols of pamphlets
Sowter Clerical Library, some 12,000 vols including local history
Some 6,000 books of historical theology (17th–19th centuries)
Christian Socialist Archive supported by the Christian Socialist Movement
Jubilee Trust Archive
Michael Vasey papers
Br Tristam's papers
Tom Baker papers (former Principal)

Library catalogue: All or part available online

Publications: Printed

Access to staff: Contact by letter, by telephone, by fax, by e-mail, in person and via website. Appointment necessary. All charged.
Hours: Mon to Fri, 0900 to 1300 and 1400 to 1700
Special comments: Library unstaffed daily, 1300 to 1400.

Access to building: *Hours:* Mon to Fri, 0900 to 1700
Special comments: Library unstaffed between 1 and 2 pm each day

Access for disabled people: Lift available
Special comments: If wheelchair users phone ahead, staff will open both doors to library.

Member organisation of: ABTAPL (Association of British Theological and Philosophical Libraries); website: http://www.le.ac.uk/abtapl

SAVE BRITAIN'S HERITAGE (SAVE)

70 Cowcross Street, London, EC1M 6EJ

Tel: 020 7253 3500
Fax: 020 7253 3400
E-mail: office@savebritainsheritage.org
Website: www.savebritainsheritage.org

Founded: 1975

Organisation type and purpose: National organisation, membership association, present number of members: 1,500, voluntary organisation, registered charity (charity number 269129), research organisation, publishing house.
Charitable trust supported by Friends.
Campaign group for historic buildings threatened by neglect or demolition.

Subject coverage: Demolished, threatened or neglected historic buildings; new uses for old buildings and conversions.

Publications: Printed
Order printed publications from: website: http://www.savebritainsheritage.org/publications/publications_in_print.php

Publications list: Available online and in print

Access to staff: Contact by letter, by telephone, by fax and by e-mail
Hours: 0930 to 1730

SBA THE SOLICITORS CHARITY (SBA)

Formal name: Solicitors Benevolent Association

1 Jaggard Way, London, SW12 8SG

Tel: 020 8675 6440
Fax: 020 8675 6441
E-mail: sec@sba.org.uk
Website: www.sba.org.uk

Enquiries to: Secretary

Founded: 1858

Organisation type and purpose:
Professional body (membership is by election or invitation), present number of members: 17,000, registered charity (charity number 208878).

Access to staff: Contact by letter, by telephone, by fax, by e-mail and via website
Hours: Mon to Fri, 0930 to 1730

SCARBOROUGH BOROUGH COUNCIL

Town Hall, St Nicholas Street, Scarborough, North Yorkshire, YO11 2HG

Tel: 01723 232323
Fax: 01723 354979
E-mail: customerfirst@scarborough.gov.uk
Website: www.scarborough.gov.uk

Enquiries to: Office Manager
Direct tel: 01723 232570
Direct e-mail: janet.deacon@scarborough.gov.uk

Founded: 1974

Organisation type and purpose: Local government body.

Subject coverage: All local government services.

Access to staff: Contact by letter, by telephone, by fax, by e-mail, in person and via website
Hours: Mon to Fri, 0830 to 1700

SCARBOROUGH LIBRARY

Formal name: Scarborough Library and Customer Services Centre

Vernon Road, Scarborough, North Yorkshire, YO11 2NN

Tel: 0845 034 9516
Fax: 01723 353893
E-mail: scarborough.library@northyorks.gov.uk
Website: htttp://www.northyorks.gov.uk

Enquiries to: Service Development Officer
Direct tel: 0845 034 9517

Founded: 1930

Organisation type and purpose: Local government body, public library.

Subject coverage: General, local studies relating to Scarborough, the Yorkshire coast, North York Moors, Vale of Pickering and Yorkshire Wolds.

Collection: Censuses 1841–1901
Local newspapers 1839–present
GRO indexes 1837–1997

Non-library collection catalogue: All or part available online

Library catalogue: All or part available online

Access to staff: Contact by letter, by telephone, by fax, by e-mail and in person
Hours: Mon, Tue, Fri, 0900 to 1800; Wed, 1000 to 1800; Thu, 0900 to 1900; Sat, 0900 to 1500; Sun, Closed.
Special comments: Closed public holidays.

Access for disabled people: Ramped entry

Parent body: North Yorkshire County Library; Grammar School Lane, Northallerton, North Yorkshire, DL6 1DF; tel: 01609 767829; fax: 01609 780793; website: http://www.northyorks.gov.uk

SCHERING HEALTH CARE LIMITED

The Brow, Burgess Hill, West Sussex, RH15 9NE

Tel: 01444 232323
Fax: 01444 246613
Website: www.schering.co.uk

Enquiries to: Medical Information Department
Direct e-mail: bsp-communications@bayerhealthcare.com

Organisation type and purpose:
Pharmaceuticals manufacturer.

Subject coverage: Medicine, especially endocrinology, diagnostic radiology, cardiovascular medicine and surgery, dermatology, neurophysiology and pharmacology, urology, obstetrics and gynaecology.

Publications: Printed

Access to staff: Contact by letter and by telephone
Hours: Mon to Fri, 0900 to 1700
Special comments: Schering Health Care Limited operates under the association of British Pharmaceutical Industry's code of practice and is unable to enter into correspondence with individual patients concerning their treatment.

SCHOOL LIBRARY ASSOCIATION (SLA)

Unit 2, Lotmead Business Village, Wanborough, Swindon, Wiltshire, SN4 0UY

Tel: 01793 791787
Fax: 01793 791786
E-mail: info@sla.org.uk
Website: www.sla.org.uk

Enquiries to: Chief Executive

Founded: 1937

Organisation type and purpose:
International organisation, advisory body, professional body (membership is by subscription), registered charity (charity numbers 313660 and SC039453), suitable for ages: 5 to 19, training organisation, publishing house, branches throughout the United Kingdom.
To support the development of school libraries, through advocacy, advice, training and publications.

Subject coverage: School librarianship and information literacy, children's literature and literacy.

Publications: Printed
Order printed publications from: website: http://www.sla.org.uk

Publications list: Available online and in print

Access to staff: Contact by letter, by telephone, by fax and by e-mail. Appointment necessary.
Hours: Mon to Fri, 0900 to 1700

Links with: Cilip; IFLA

Member organisation of: IASL

SCHOOL OF MEDITATION

158 Holland Park Avenue, London, W11 4UH

Tel: 020 7603 6116
E-mail: info@schoolofmeditation.org
Website: www.schoolofmeditation.org

Enquiries to: Administrator

Founded: 1961

Organisation type and purpose:
Membership association (membership is by subscription), present number of members: 700, registered charity (charity number 292171), suitable for ages: 18 to 80.

Subject coverage: Technique of meditation as passed down through the Vedantic tradition; philosophical background.

Access to staff: Contact by letter, by telephone and by e-mail. Appointment necessary.
Hours: Mon to Fri, 0930 to 1600

Branches: The School is based in London with groups in Barnstaple, Basingstoke, Boston, Bournemouth, Chelmsford, Leeds, Norwich, Salisbury, Sheffield and Winchester. There are also groups in Holland, including Amsterdam and in Patras, Greece.

Parent body: Society for Spiritual Development

SCHOOL OF ORAL & DENTAL SCIENCES

Formal name: University of Bristol School of Oral & Dental Sciences

University of Bristol School of Oral & Dental Sciences & Hospital, Lower Maudlin Street, Bristol, BS1 2LY

Tel: 0117 3424309
E-mail: ann.e.jones@bristol.ac.uk
Website: www.bris.ac.uk/dental

Enquiries to: Administrator

History of institution: formerly called Department of Oral & Dental Science & Dental School (year of change 2010)

Organisation type and purpose: University School, multiple Research groups, operating within the University of Bristol School of Oral & Dental Sciences with support from Wellcome Trust and Cancer Research Campaign, suitable for ages: 18+.

Subject coverage: Dental research including the structure, composition and histopathology of teeth; dental caries; periodontal disease; salivary gland disease;

oral cancer; viruses and oral disease; lifecourse epidemiology and population oral health, biomaterials.

Access to staff: Contact by letter, by telephone and by e-mail
Hours: Mon to Fri, 0900 to 1630

Access for disabled people: Parking provided, ramped entry, toilet facilities

SCHOOL SCIENCE SERVICE

41 Orchard Bank, Edinburgh, EH4 2DS

Tel: 0131 332 9886
Fax: 0131 332 7447
E-mail: anne@sciencesleuth.co.uk
Website: www.sciencesleuth.co.uk

Enquiries to: Managing Director
Other contacts: Secretary to Bookings Manager.

Founded: 1989; formerly called The Science Sleuth Shop, Science Sleuth

Organisation type and purpose: Service industry, consultancy.
Practical science workshops for schools, museums and festivals.

Subject coverage: Educational equipment and resources packaged together for use in Primary School Science. The Science Sleuth visits schools, museums and science festivals with story-based science investigations, science toys.

Trade and statistical information: World data on science sleuth investigations for primary schools

Publications: Printed

Publications list: Available in print

Access to staff: Contact by letter, by telephone, by fax, by e-mail and via website
Hours: Mon to Fri, 0900 to 1700

Access to building: No access other than to staff

Close links with: Science Sleuth: Colour Chemistry: DC Electricity: Magnetism: Senses Investigations for science festivals or school visits; tel: 0131 332 7447; fax: 0131 332 7447; e-mail: anne@sciencesleuth.co.uk; The Association for Science Education (ASE); College Lane, Hatfield, AL10 9AA

Other address: The Science Sleuth Shop (Science Sleuth); 41 Orchard Bank, Edinburgh, EH4 1HN; tel: 0131 332 7447; fax: 0131 332 7447; e-mail: anne@sciencesleuth.co.uk

SCHUBERT SOCIETY OF BRITAIN

The German YMCA, 35 Craven Terrace, London, W2 3EL

Tel: 020 7723 5684
Fax: 020 7706 2870
E-mail: u.bauer@german-ymca.org.uk
Website: www.german-ymca.org.uk/schubert-society.html

Enquiries to: Programme Secretary
Direct tel: 020 7723 5684
Direct fax: 020 7706 2870
Direct e-mail: u.bauer@german-ymca.org.uk

Founded: 1957

Organisation type and purpose: Music Society.
To help young musicians on threshold of a professional career. Recitals given at 1500, third Sunday of month, from Oct to May (except Dec) at Lancaster Hall, Lancaster Hall Hotel, Craven Terrace, London, W2, to include at least one work by Franz Schubert.

Subject coverage: Chamber Music Recitals.

Publications: Printed, and electronic and video

Publications list: Available online and in print

Access to staff: Contact by letter, by telephone, by fax, by e-mail and via website
Hours: Mon to Fri, 0900 to 1700

Access for disabled people: Level entry
Special comments: Disabled toilet

SCI (SCI)

Formal name: Society of Chemical Industry

International Headquarters, 14–15 Belgrave Square, London, SW1X 8PS

Tel: 020 7598 1500
Fax: 020 7598 1545
E-mail: secretariat@soci.org
Website: www.soci.org
Website: www.soci.org/Chemistry-and-Industry
Website: www.soci.org/Chemistry-and-Industry/Supply-Line/Company-Listing
Website: www.biofpr.com

Enquiries to: Web Team
Direct tel: 020 7598 1576
Direct e-mail: web@soci.org

Founded: 1881

Organisation type and purpose:
International organisation, learned society (membership is by subscription), present number of members: 5,000, registered charity (charity number 206883).

Subject coverage: The science research, investment and industrial interface.
Chemical technology and biotechnology, pest management, materials, agriculture, food, fine and heavy chemicals manufacture, environmental protection, corporate management, whole company direction, discovery, marketing and distribution, natural and economic sciences, engineering, law and medicine.

Collection: The Society's publications (starting 1881)

Non-library collection catalogue: All or part available online, in-house and in print

Library catalogue: All or part available online, in-house and in print

Publications: Printed

Publications list: Available online and in print

Access to staff: Contact by letter, by telephone, by fax, by e-mail, in person and via website. Appointment necessary.
Hours: Mon to Fri, 0900 to 1700

Access to building: *Hours:* Mon to Fri, 0900 to 1700

Access for disabled people: *Hours:* Mon to Fri, 0900 to 1700

SCIENCE & SOCIETY PICTURE LIBRARY

North Entrance, Science Museum, Exhibition Road, South Kensington, London, SW7 2DD

Tel: 020 7942 4400
Fax: 020 7942 4401
E-mail: piclib@nmsi.ac.uk
Website: www.scienceandsociety.co.uk

Organisation type and purpose: Represents the collections of the Science Museum, the National Railway Museum and the National Museum of Photography, Film and Television, and other related collections.

Subject coverage: Science and people's applications of science.

Collection: More than 150 image collections from within and outside the museums' own core collections, including 70,000 online records and 40,000 digital images. Themes: entertainment and media; medicine and health; natural world; personalities; places; science and technology; society and wars; trade and industry; transport

SCIENCE & TECHNOLOGY FACILITIES COUNCIL (STFC)

Polaris House, North Star Avenue, Swindon, Wiltshire, SN2 1SZ

Tel: 01793 442000
Fax: 01793 442002
E-mail: stfc@stfc.co.uk
Website: www.stfc.ac.uk

Enquiries to: Librarian
Other contacts: Press Officer

Founded: 2007; created by the merger of Particle Physics and Astronomy Research Council (PPARC) and Council for the Central Laboratory of the Research Councils (CCLRC) (year of change 2007)

Organisation type and purpose: Research organisation.
State-aided organisation.
One of the seven research councils. STFC directs and co-ordinates the funding of United Kingdom research into the physics of the Universe.

Subject coverage: Astronomy, planetary science, particle physics, science policy.

Publications: Printed
Order printed publications from: Strategic Planning & Communications, Science & Technology Facilities Council, at the same address

Access to staff: Contact by letter, by telephone, by fax, by e-mail and via website
Hours: Mon to Fri, 0900 to 1700

Laboratories: Daresbury Laboratory; Royal Observatory (Edinburgh); Rutherford Appleton Laboratory

SCIENCE AND ADVICE FOR SCOTTISH AGRICULTURE (SASA)

Formal name: Science and Advice for Scottish Agriculture (Scottish Government Agriculture, Food and Rural Communities Directorate)

Roddinglaw Road, Edinburgh, EH12 9FJ

Tel: 0131 244 8873
Fax: 0131 244 8940

continued overleaf

E-mail: library@sasa.gsi.gov.uk
Website: www.sasa.gov.uk

Enquiries to: Librarian
Direct tel: 0131 244 8826

History of institution: formerly called Scottish Agricultural Science Agency (year of change 2008)

Organisation type and purpose: National government body, research organisation. Provides scientific services and advice in support of Scotland's agriculture and wider environment.

Subject coverage: Seed testing, seed potato classification, plant health, nematology, crop entomology, control of pests, pesticide usage, analytical chemistry, plant varieties, diagnostics and molecular biology.

Trade and statistical information: Pesticide usage surveys for Scotland; pesticide poisoning of animals in Scotland

Library catalogue: All or part available in-house

Publications: Printed

Publications list: Available online

Access to staff: Contact by letter, by telephone, by fax, by e-mail and via website. Appointment necessary.
Hours: Mon to Fri, 0900 to 1700

Access to building: Prior appointment required

Access for disabled people: Parking provided, level entry, toilet facilities

Parent body: Scottish Government, Agriculture, Food and Rural Communities Directorate; Broomhouse Drive, Edinburgh, EH11 3XD; website: http://www.scotland.gov.uk

SCIENCE COUNCIL

32–36 Loman Street, London, SE1 0EH

Tel: 020 7922 7888
Fax: 020 7922 7879
Website: www.sciencecouncil.org

Enquiries to: Chief Executive/Registrar
Direct e-mail: d.garnham@sciencecouncil.org

Founded: 2003

Organisation type and purpose: A membership organisation (current number of member organisations: 30) for learned and professional bodies across science and its applications; works with them to represent this sector to government and others. Promotes the profession of scientist through the Chartered Scientist designation and the development of codes of practice; promotes awareness of the contribution of professional scientists to science and society and advances science education and increased understanding of the benefits of science; provides a forum for discussion and exchange of views and works to foster collaboration between member organisations and the wider science, technology, engineering, mathematics and medical communities to enable inter-disciplinary contributions to science policy and the application of science.

Subject coverage: Science and its applications.

Publications: Electronic and video
Order electronic and video publications from: Download from website

Access to staff: Contact by letter, by telephone, by fax and by e-mail

SCIENCE FICTION FOUNDATION COLLECTION (SFF)

Sydney Jones Library, University of Liverpool, PO Box 123, Liverpool, L69 3DA

Tel: 0151 794 2696
Fax: 0151 794 2681
E-mail: asawyer@liverpool.ac.uk
Website: www.sfhub.ac.uk

Enquiries to: Librarian
Direct tel: 0151 794 3142

Founded: 1970

Organisation type and purpose: Learned society, university library, research organisation. Aims to support and encourage research into science fiction.

Subject coverage: Science fiction and related literary genres, their history and criticism.

Library catalogue: All or part available online

Publications: Printed

Access to staff: Contact by letter, by telephone, by e-mail and via website. Appointment necessary.
Hours: Mon to Fri, 0915 to 1645

Funded by: Science Fiction Foundation; website: http://www.sf-foundation.org

Links with: British Science Fiction Association; website: http://www.bsfa.co.uk/bsfa

SCIENCE OXFORD

1–5 London Place, St Clements, Oxford, OX4 1BD

Tel: 01865 728953
E-mail: info@scienceoxford.com
Website: www.scienceoxford.com

Organisation type and purpose: Administered by the Oxford Trust. A registered charity (no. 292664) and a company limited by guarantee (charity number 1898691). Science Oxford offers exhibitions, a hands-on science gallery and conference facilities.

Subject coverage: Science.

Information services: Information Centre.

Access to building: *Hours:* exhibitions open Mon to Fri, 1000 to 1600; science gallery open Sat in termtime and Mon to Sat during local school holidays

SCIENCE PHOTO LIBRARY (SPL)

327–329 Harrow Road, London, W9 3RB

Tel: 020 7432 1100
Fax: 020 7286 8668
E-mail: info@sciencephoto.com
Website: www.sciencephoto.com

Enquiries to: Sales Manager
Direct e-mail: mark@sciencephoto.com

Founded: 1979

Organisation type and purpose: Service industry.
Specialist image and footage library.

Subject coverage: Images and video clips covering healthcare, science & technology, space, history, environment, animals, plants and flowers.

Education services: Offers a schools subscription for educational establishments to make use of in their teaching.

Non-library collection catalogue: All or part available online

Access to staff: Contact by letter, by telephone, by fax, by e-mail and via website. Appointment necessary. All charged.
Hours: Mon to Fri, 0930 to 1800

Member organisation of: British Association of Picture Libraries and Agencies (BAPLA)

SCIENTIFIC AND MEDICAL NETWORK (SMN)

1 Manchester Court, Moreton-in-Marsh, Gloucestershire GL56 0BY

Tel: 01608 652000
Fax: 01608 652001
E-mail: charla@scimednet.org
Website: www.scimednet.org

Enquiries to: Network Manager
Other contacts: Secretary

Founded: 1973

Organisation type and purpose: International organisation, membership association (membership is by subscription, election or invitation), present number of members: 1,500, registered charity (charity number 1101171).

Subject coverage: Science, medicine and spirituality, consciousness studies.

Publications: Printed, and electronic and video

Publications list: Available online

Access to staff: Contact by letter, by telephone, by fax, by e-mail and via website
Hours: Mon to Fri, 0900 to 1700

SCIENTIFIC APPARATUS RECYCLING SCHEME (SARS)

Department of Biochemistry and Molecular Biology, University College London, London, WC1E 6BT

Tel: 020 7679 2169
Fax: 020 7679 7193
E-mail: w.fleming@ucl.ac.uk

Organisation type and purpose: International organisation, voluntary organisation.
The purpose of SARS is to collect and despatch scientific equipment, books and journals surplus to the requirements of Western European countries to biochemists in need in Central and Eastern Europe.

Parent body: Federation of European Biochemical Societies (FEBS)

SCIENTIFIC COMMITTEE ON ANTARCTIC RESEARCH (SCAR)

SCAR Secretariat, Scott Polar Research Institute, Lensfield Road, Cambridge, CB2 1ER

Tel: 01223 336550
Fax: 01223 336549
E-mail: info@scar.org
Website: www.scar.org

Enquiries to: Executive Director

Founded: 1958

Organisation type and purpose:
International organisation (membership is by election or invitation), present number of members: 31 full members, 4 associates, 9 international scientific unions. Members are National Academic Societies, e.g. The Royal Society (UK).
To initiate, promote and co-ordinate scientific research in Antarctica and to provide scientific advice to the Antarctic Treaty System.

Subject coverage: Antarctic biology, geodesy and geographic information, glaciology, human biology and medicine, physics and chemistry of the atmosphere, solar-terrestrial and astrophysical research, geosciences, environment and conservation, global change, astronomy, oceanography.

Publications list: Available online and in print

Access to staff: Contact by e-mail
Hours: Mon to Fri, 0900 to 1700

Member organisations: National Scientific Academies of Argentina, Australia, Belgium, Brazil, Bulgaria, Canada, Chile, People's Republic of China, Denmark (associate mem.), Ecuador, Finland, France, Germany, India, Italy, Japan, Republic of Korea, Malaysia, Netherlands, New Zealand, Norway, Pakistan (associate mem.), Peru, Poland, Portugal (associate mem.), Romania (associate mem.), Russia, South Africa, Spain, Sweden, Switzerland, Ukraine, United Kingdom, Uruguay, USA

Parent body: International Council of Scientific Unions (ICSU); ICSU Secretariat, 5 rue Auguste Vacquerie, 75116 Paris, France; tel: +33 1 45 25 03 29; fax: +33 1 42 88 94 31; e-mail: secretariat@icsu.org; website: http://www.icsu.org

SCOLIOSIS ASSOCIATION UK (SAUK)

4 Ivebury Court, 323–327 Latimer Road, London, W10 6RA

Tel: 020 8964 5343/1166
Fax: 020 8964 5343
E-mail: sauk@sauk.org.uk
Website: www.sauk.org.uk

Enquiries to: Information Officer

Founded: 1981

Organisation type and purpose:
Membership association, present number of members: 3,500, voluntary organisation, registered charity (charity number 285290).
Offers sufferers a chance to share experience of the physical, emotional and social aspects of scoliosis.

Subject coverage: Scoliosis (i.e. lateral spinal curvature); information about all aspects of scoliosis, but not individual medical advice.

Publications: Printed, and electronic and video

Publications list: Available in print

Access to staff: Contact by letter, by telephone, by fax, by e-mail and via website
Hours: Mon to Fri, 1000 to 1730

Links with: International Federation of Scoliosis Associations

SCOOTACAR REGISTER

18 Holman Close, Aylsham, Norwich, Norfolk, NR11 6DD

Tel: 01263 733861
E-mail: scootacar@btinternet.com
Website: www.scootacar.org.uk

Enquiries to: Secretary

Founded: 1980

Organisation type and purpose:
Membership association.
To locate and register all Scootacars.

Subject coverage: Micro cars, bubble cars, location and registration of Scootacars.

Collection: Photographs
Register of all known cars
Service bulletins
Spares and component numbers
Workshop manuals

Trade and statistical information:
Production figures.
Chassis numbers.
Engine numbers.
Number of cars located

Publications: Printed

Access to staff: Contact by letter, by telephone, by e-mail and via website
Hours: Mon to Sun, 0900 to 2100

SCOPE

6 Market Road, London, N7 9PW

Tel: 020 7619 7100
Fax: 020 7619 7360
Website: www.scope.org.uk

Enquiries to: Library & Information Officer
Direct tel: 020 7619 7340
Direct e-mail: information@scope.org.uk

Founded: 1952; formerly called Spastics Society

Organisation type and purpose: Voluntary organisation, registered charity (charity number 208231).
To ensure that all people with cerebral palsy and related disabilities, their families and carers have access to properly resourced services that meet their needs and full rights to control their own lives.

Subject coverage: Cerebral palsy; attitudes to disability; discrimination against disabled people; education and employment of disabled people.
Equipment, legislation related to disability; statistics on disability.

Collection: Complete run of Developmental Medicine & Child Neurology
Full set of Classics in Developmental Medicine
Full set of Clinics in Developmental Medicine

Trade and statistical information: Disability related statistics eg numbers of disabled people and their income/expenditure, equipment needs etc

Non-library collection catalogue: All or part available in-house

Library catalogue: All or part available in-house

Publications: Printed, and electronic and video
Order printed publications from: Library and Information Unit, SCOPE; at the same address, tel: 020 7619 7342, fax: 020 7619 7360, e-mail: information@scope.org.uk
Order electronic and video publications from: Education Distribution Service (AV material), SCOPE; Unit 2, Drywall Estate, Castle Road, Marston, Sittingbourne, Kent, ME10 3RL, tel: 01795 427614, fax: 01795 474871

Publications list: Available online and in print

Access to staff: Contact by letter, by telephone, by fax, by e-mail, in person and via website
Hours: Helpline (0808 8003333): Mon to Fri, 0900 to 2100; Sat to Sun, 1400 to 1800

Access to building: Prior appointment required
Hours: Mon to Fri, 0900 to 1700
Special comments: Prior appointment required for access to library.

Access for disabled people: Access to all public areas

Has: a network of local offices around England and Wales providing support; over 200 local groups around England and Wales

Helpline: Cerebral Palsy Helpline; PO Box 833, Milton Keynes, Buckinghamshire, MK12 5NY; tel: 0808 800 3333; fax: 01908 321051; e-mail: cphelpline@scope.org.uk

SCOPE – RESPONSE

PO Box 833, Milton Keynes, Buckinghamshire, MK12 5NY

Tel: 0808 800 3333; text SCOPE plus message to 80039
Fax: 01908 321051
E-mail: response@scope.org.uk
Website: www.scope.org.uk

History of institution: formerly called The Spastics Society

Organisation type and purpose: National disability organisation in respect of cerebral palsy, registered charity (charity number 208231).
For disabled people achieving equality; helpline provides free and confidential information, advice and support about cerebral palsy, disability issues and Scope services.

Subject coverage: Cerebral palsy and associated disabilities.

continued overleaf

Publications: Printed, and electronic and video
Order printed publications from: Scope, CP Helpline, PO Box 833, Milton Keynes, MK12 5NY; tel: 01908 321049 (Publications Line)

Publications list: Available online and in print

Access to staff: Contact by letter, by telephone, by fax, by e-mail and via website
Hours: Mon to Fri, 0900 to 1700; closed weekends and bank holidays

SCOTCH WHISKY ASSOCIATION (SWA)

20 Atholl Crescent, Edinburgh, EH3 8HF

Tel: 0131 222 9200
Fax: 0131 222 9237
E-mail: contact@swa.org.uk
Website: www.scotch-whisky.org.uk

Enquiries to: Director of Government and Consumer Affairs
Other contacts: Press & Media Relations Manager for press enquiries

Founded: 1943

Organisation type and purpose: Trade association.
Promotion and protection of Scotch Whisky.

Subject coverage: Scotch whisky trade worldwide; statistical and industry information.

Publications: Printed

Access to staff: Contact by letter, by telephone, by fax, by e-mail and via website

Also at: Scotch Whisky Association; 14 Cork Street, London, W1S 3NS; tel: 020 7629 4384; fax: 020 7493 1398

SCOTLAND IS

Suite 41, Geddes House, Kirkton North, Livingston, EH54 6GU

Tel: 01506 472200
Fax: 01506 460615
E-mail: info@scotlandis.com
Website: www.scotlandis.com

Enquiries to: Membership Liaison Manager
Direct e-mail: karen.meechan@scotlandis.com
Other contacts: General Manager

Founded: 2000; formerly called IMAS, Internet Society (ISOC), Scottish Software Federation (SSF) (year of change 2000)

Organisation type and purpose: Trade association (membership is by subscription), present number of members: 300 companies.
Representative trade organisation for the ICT industry in Scotland. Members encompass a wide cross-section of companies covering the users, academia, developers, applications providers and service providers.
To make the software industry in Scotland collectively successful.

Subject coverage: Computer software.

Publications: Printed, and electronic and video

Publications list: Available online and in print

Access to staff: Contact by letter, by telephone, by fax, by e-mail and via website
Hours: Mon to Fri, 0900 to 1700

Access to building: Prior appointment required

Access for disabled people: Parking provided, ramped entry

Grampian Office: Scotland IS; The Software Centre, Aberdeen Science and Technology Park, Campus 2, Balgowie Drive, Bridge of Don, Aberdeen, AB22 8GU; tel: 01224 332182; fax: 01224 332082; e-mail: info@scotlandis.com

SCOTLAND'S GARDENS (SG)

42A North Castle Street, Edinburgh, EH2 3BN

Tel: 0131 226 3714
E-mail: info@scotlandsgardens.org
Website: www.scotlandsgardens.org

Enquiries to: Director

Founded: 1931

Organisation type and purpose: Registered charity (charity number SCO 11337).
Opening gardens to the public for a range of charities.

Subject coverage: Facilitating the opening of gardens of horticultural interest to the public as a means of raising funds for other worthy charities

Publications: Printed

Access to staff: Contact by letter, by telephone and by e-mail
Hours: Mon to Fri, 0900 to 1700

Access to building: No access other than to staff

SCOTT BADER COMPANY LIMITED

Wollaston, Wellingborough, Northamptonshire, NN29 7RL

Tel: 01933 663100
Fax: 01933 666608
E-mail: enquiries@scottbader.com

Enquiries to: Information Officer

Founded: 1920

Organisation type and purpose: Manufacturing industry.

Subject coverage: Plastics, synthetic resins, their manufacture and technical applications (specifically unsaturated polyester resins, emulsion and solution polymers), polyesters, reinforced plastics, surface coatings for paper, textiles and other materials, adhesives and thickeners.

Collection: Ernest Bader's Archives, founder of the company and pioneer in common ownership of companies

Publications: Printed

Access to staff: Appointment necessary.
Hours: Mon to Fri, 0830 to 1700

SCOTT OWNERS' CLUB (SOC)

Walnut Cottage, Abbey Lane, Aslockton, Nottinghamshire, NG13 9AE

Tel: 01949 851027
Fax: 01949 851027
Website: www.scottownersclub.org

Enquiries to: Public Relations Officer
Other contacts: (1) Membership Secretary; (2) Machine Registrar; (3) Archivist

Founded: 1958

Organisation type and purpose: Membership association (membership is by subscription), present number of members: 650.
To promote interest in Scott and Silk motorcycles and to provide a spares scheme, library, photographic archives, technical information, a machine register, badges, transfers (decals), and mutual support to members.

Subject coverage: Scott motorcycles made 1908–1951, Birmingham Scott 1957–1972, Silk Scott 1970s–1980s and the Silk motorcycle which followed.

Collection: Collections of period photographs, some factory records, engineering drawings, technical information and machine register

Publications: Printed, and electronic and video

Access to staff: Contact by letter, by telephone and by fax
Hours: Mon to Fri, 0900 to 1700
Special comments: Enclose SAE if written reply is required.
No access to facilities without membership.

SCOTT POLAR RESEARCH INSTITUTE (SPRI)

Lensfield Road, Cambridge, CB2 1ER

Tel: 01223 336552
Fax: 01223 336549
E-mail: enquiries@spri.cam.ac.uk
Website: www.spri.cam.ac.uk

Enquiries to: Librarian and Keeper
Direct e-mail: library@spri.cam.ac.uk
Other contacts: Information Assistant (for general library enquiries)

Founded: 1920

Organisation type and purpose: Museum, university department or institute.

Subject coverage: Polar regions; Arctic regions; Antarctic regions including the Falkland Islands; Russian North; snow and ice studies; glaciology; cold regions in general; whaling; sealing; exploration.

Education services: Polar Museum Education and Outreach Service.

Services for disabled people: Induction loop.

Collection: Polar Archives

Non-library collection catalogue: All or part available online, in-house and in print

Library catalogue: All or part available online

Publications: Printed

Publications list: Available in print

Access to staff: Contact by letter, by telephone, by fax, by e-mail, in person and via website. Appointment necessary.
Hours: Mon to Fri, 0900 to 1300 and 1400 to 1730

Access to building: *Hours:* Mon to Fri, 0900 to 1700; Sat, 1000 to 1600

Access for disabled people: Lifts to main entrances; internal lifts to all floors

Constituent part of: University of Cambridge

Houses the: International Glaciological Society; tel: 01223 355974; e-mail: igsoc@igsoc.org; Scientific Committee on Antarctic Research (SCAR); tel: 01223 336550; fax: 01223 336549; e-mail: info@scar.org; World Data Centre for Glaciology, Cambridge; tel: 01223 336565; fax: 01223 336549; website: http://wdcgc.spri.cam.ac.uk

SCOTTISH ACCIDENT PREVENTION COUNCIL (SAPC)

Arcadia Business Centre, Miller Lane, Clydebank, Scotland, G81 1UJ

Tel: 0141 280 0122
Fax: 0141 941 0887
E-mail: secretary@sapc.org.uk
Website: www.sapc.org.uk

Enquiries to: Secretary

Founded: 1930

Organisation type and purpose: Membership association, voluntary organisation, Scottish registered charity.

Subject coverage: Home, road, water and leisure safety.

Access to staff: Contact by letter, by telephone, by fax, by e-mail and via website. Appointment necessary.
Hours: Mon to Fri, 0900 to 1700

Administered by: West Dunbartonshire Community & Volunteering Services; Arcadia Business Centre, Miller Lane, Clydebank, Scotland, G81 1UJ; tel: 0141 941 0886; fax: 0141 941 0887; e-mail: info@wdcvs.com; website: http://www.wdcvs.com

Links with: local authorities, devolved government, national bodies, other voluntary and charitable organisations

SCOTTISH AGRICULTURAL COLLEGE – EDINBURGH (SAC)

West Mains Road, Edinburgh, EH9 3JG

Tel: 0131 535 4000
Fax: 0131 535 4246
Website: www.sac.ac.uk/

Enquiries to: Librarian
Direct tel: 0131 535 4116
Direct e-mail: m.mullay@ed.sac.ac.uk

Founded: 1990; formed from East of Scotland College of Agriculture, Scottish Agricultural Colleges; formerly called Edinburgh School of Agriculture

Organisation type and purpose: consultancy, research organisation.

Subject coverage: All aspects of agriculture excluding fisheries; agricultural economics, farming and engineering; animal nutrition and production; applied plant science; crop production and protection; pests; microbiology; organic and soil science; veterinary medicine; environment; rural affairs.

Collection: Early agricultural texts

Library catalogue: All or part available online

Publications: Printed, and electronic and video

Publications list: Available in print

Access to staff: Contact by letter and by e-mail. Appointment necessary.
Hours: Term time: Mon to Thu, 0845 to 2100; Fri, 0845 to 1700; Sat, Sun, 1000 to 1700
Vacations: Mon to Fri, 0845 to 1700

Combines the: Institute of Ecology and Resource Management, University of Edinburgh; Scottish Agricultural College

Other addresses: Scottish Agricultural College; Craibstone Estate, Auchincruive, Ayrshire

SCOTTISH AGRICULTURAL COLLEGE, AYR (SAC)

Riverside Campus, University Avenue Ayr KA8 0SX

Tel: 01292 886413
E-mail: libraryau@sac.ac.uk
Website: www.sac.ac.uk/library

Enquiries to: Librarian
Direct tel: 01292 886413
Direct e-mail: Libraryau@sac.ac.uk

Founded: 1896; formerly called West of Scotland College of Agriculture (year of change 1990)

Organisation type and purpose: Research organisation, consultancy, independent body funded by the Scottish Office.
Higher education.

Subject coverage: Science and economics of agriculture, horticulture, biotechnology, dairying, milk and milk products, poultry husbandry, agricultural engineering, food sciences, water pollution, conservation, environmental science, countryside recreation, tourism and leisure.

Services for disabled people: Fully accessible. Reader for visually impaired and dyslexic clients, adjustable tables for wheelchairs

Collection: Historical collection on agriculture and horticulture

Library catalogue: All or part available online

Publications: Printed, and electronic and video
Order printed publications from: Publications Unit, SAC, Kings Buildings, West Mains Road, Edinburgh, EH9 3JG; tel: 0131 535 4000
Order electronic and video publications from: http://www.sac.ac.uk/publications/?ff=y

Publications list: Available online

Access to staff: Contact by letter, by telephone, by e-mail, in person and via website. Appointment necessary. Non-members charged.
Hours: Term time: Mon to Fri, 0845 to 2045; Sat,1000 to 1700
Vacations: Mon to Thu, 0845 to 1700; Fri, 0845 to 1645; Sat, 1000–1700
Special comments: Via instant messaging from website

Access to building: No prior appointment required
Hours: Mon to Fri, 0900 to 1630 only

Access for disabled people: Fully wheelchair accessible
Hours: As above.

Links with: University of Glasgow

SCOTTISH AMATEUR MUSIC ASSOCIATION (SAMA)

18 Craigton Crescent, Alva, Clackmannanshire, FK12 5DS

Tel: 01259 760249
E-mail: secretary@sama.org.uk
Website: www.sama.org.uk

Enquiries to: Honorary Secretary

Founded: 1956

Organisation type and purpose: Membership association (membership is by election or invitation), registered charity (charity number SCO 14503).

Subject coverage: The encouragement and stimulation of amateur music-making in Scotland, mainly through summer courses.

Publications: Printed

Publications list: Available in print

Access to staff: Contact by letter, by telephone and by e-mail
Hours: Not always available

SCOTTISH AMATEUR SWIMMING ASSOCIATION (SASA)

National Swimming Academy, University of Stirling, Stirling, FK9 4LA

Tel: 01786 466520
Fax: 01786 466521
E-mail: info@scottishswimming.com
Website: www.scottishswimming.com

Enquiries to: Director of Administration
Direct e-mail: e.mackenzie@scottishswimming.com

Founded: 1888

Organisation type and purpose: Membership association (membership is by subscription), voluntary organisation. National governing body of the sport.

Subject coverage: Speed swimming, masters' swimming, synchronised swimming, long distance swimming, water polo.

Publications: Printed

Access to staff: Contact by letter, by telephone and by e-mail
Hours: Mon to Thu, 0830 to 1700; Fri, 0830 to 1600

Access to building: No prior appointment required

Access for disabled people: Parking provided, level entry, access to all public areas, toilet facilities

Links with: Fédération Internationale de Natation Amateur (FINA); Avenue de Beaumont 9, Lausanne, CH-1012, Switzerland

SCOTTISH AND NORTHERN IRELAND PLUMBING EMPLOYERS' FEDERATION (SNIPEF)

2 Walker Street, Edinburgh, EH3 7LB

Tel: 0131 225 2255
Fax: 0131 226 7638
E-mail: info@snipef.org
Website: www.snipef.org

Enquiries to: Information Officer

Founded: 1923

Organisation type and purpose: Trade association (membership is by subscription, qualification), present number of members: 950, service industry.
The national association for all types of firms involved in the plumbing and domestic heating industry in Scotland and Northern Ireland.

Subject coverage: Customers using SNIPEF members can contact the Federation for advice relating to any plumbing and heating work undertaken by a member firm. In the event that a dispute arises, the customer can contact the Federation, who will advise them on the operation of their complaints procedure through their Code of Fair Trading, which is recognised by the Office of Fair Trading.

Publications: Printed

Access to staff: Contact by letter, by telephone, by fax, by e-mail, in person and via website
Hours: Mon to Thu, 0900 to 1700; Fri, 0900 to 1630

SCOTTISH ANGLERS NATIONAL ASSOCIATION LTD (SANA)

The National Game Angling Centre, The Pier, Loch Leven, Kinross, Scotland, KY13 8UF

Tel: 01577 861116
Fax: 01577 864769
E-mail: admin@sana.org.uk
Website: www.sana.org.uk

Enquiries to: Administrator
Other contacts: Secretary

Founded: 1880

Organisation type and purpose: National organisation, advisory body, membership association (membership is by subscription), service industry, voluntary organisation.
Governing body for the sport of game fishing in Scotland.

Subject coverage: Game fishing, especially in Scotland.

Education services: Angling coaching and instruction

Services for disabled people: via Disabled Committee

Publications: Printed

Access to staff: Contact by letter, by telephone, by fax, by e-mail and via website
Hours: 0930 to 1300 and 1400 to 1630
Special comments: Answering machine available.

Access for disabled people: Good disabled access

SCOTTISH ARCHERY ASSOCIATION (SAA)

E-mail: via website
Website: www.scottisharchery.org.uk

Enquiries to: President
Other contacts: Regional Administrator

Founded: 1949

Organisation type and purpose: Voluntary association, national body for the development of archery in Scotland, affiliated to the national governing body, ArcheryGB.

Subject coverage: There are about 70 senior clubs and 36 junior clubs throughout the whole of Scotland, serving the most densely populated areas.

Access to staff: Contact via website

Affiliated to: ArcheryGB

Links with: Scottish Sports Association; SportScotland

SCOTTISH ASIAN ACTION COMMITTEE (SAAC)

39 Napiershall Street, Glasgow, G20 6EZ

Tel: 0141 341 0025
Fax: 0141 341 0020
E-mail: secretary@saac.freeserve.co.uk

Enquiries to: Secretary
Other contacts: Development Officer

Founded: 1981

Organisation type and purpose: Voluntary organisation.
To provide information and advice to black and ethnic minority communities in Scotland. To combat racism and discrimination through campaigning.

Subject coverage: Black and Asian communities in Scotland, racism, work and equal opportunities, community groups, racial equality standards.

Publications: Printed

Access to staff: Contact by telephone, by fax, by e-mail and in person
Hours: Mon to Fri, 1000 to 1600

SCOTTISH ASSOCIATION FOR MARINE SCIENCE (SAMS)

Scottish Marine Institute, Oban, Argyll, PA37 1QA

Tel: 01631 559000
Fax: 01631 559001
E-mail: info@sams.ac.uk
Website: www.sams.ac.uk

Enquiries to: Communications officer
Direct e-mail: laila.sadler@sams.ac.uk
Other contacts: Head of Communications

Founded: 1884; carries out the functions of the former Dunstaffnage Marine Laboratory (year of change 2000); formerly called Scottish Marine Biological Association (year of change 1992)

Organisation type and purpose: Research and higher education provision in marine science for sustainable seas; learned society; own research vessels, research aquaria, laboratories and advanced sampling and analytical equipment.

Subject coverage: Marine science; Arctic research; marine renewable energy; marine processes and climate; industrial impacts on oceans; prosperity from marine ecosystems; aquaculture; marine spatial planning; marine biotechnology; fisheries; marine technology; scientific diving;

Collection: Research library with historic collection; culture collection of algae and protozoa; Scottish Ocean Explorer Centre (under development)

Non-library collection catalogue: All or part available online and in-house

Library catalogue: All or part available in-house

Publications: Printed, and electronic and video

Publications list: Available online and in print

Access to staff: Contact by letter, by telephone, by fax, by e-mail and via website. Appointment necessary.
Hours: Mon to Fri, 0900 to 1700

Access to building: Prior appointment required

Access for disabled people: Ramped entry, toilet facilities; lift to upper floors

Links with: Natural Environment Research Council; Polaris House, North Star Avenue, Swindon, SN2 1EU; tel: 01793 411500; fax: 01793 411501; website: http://www.nerc.ac.uk

Member organisation of: UHI Millennium Institute; Executive Office, Ness Walk, Inverness, IV3 5SQ; tel: 01463 279000; website: http://www.uhi.ac.uk

SCOTTISH ASSOCIATION FOR PUBLIC TRANSPORT (SAPT)

11 Queen's Crescent, Glasgow, G4 9BL

Tel: 07760 381729
E-mail: sapt@btinternet.com
Website: www.sapt.org.uk

Enquiries to: Secretary

Founded: 1962; formerly called Scottish Railway Development Association (SRDA) (year of change 1972)

Organisation type and purpose: National organisation, membership association (membership is by subscription), present number of members: 150, voluntary organisation.
National organisation (Scotland).
Supporting public transport and environmental improvement.

Subject coverage: All modes of public transport in Scotland; policy and finance; transport-related environmental issues.

Publications: Printed

Access to staff: Contact by letter, by telephone and by e-mail
Hours: Mon to Fri, 0900 to 1700

Member organisation of: Campaign for Better Transport; Environmental Transport Association; TRANSform Scotland; tel: 0131 467 7714; fax: 0131 554 8656; e-mail: campaigns@transformscotland.org.uk

SCOTTISH ATHLETICS LIMITED

Caledonia House, Redheughs Rigg, South Gyle, Edinburgh, EH12 9DQ

Tel: 0131 317 7320
Fax: 0131 317 7321
E-mail: admin@scottishathletics.org.uk
Website: www.scottishathletics.org.uk

Enquiries to: General Manager
Other contacts: Press Officer for media relations

Founded: 1992; formerly called Scottish Athletics Federation (SAF) (year of change 2000); incorporates the former Scottish Amateur Athletics Federation (SAAF), Scottish Womens Amateur Athletics Federation (SWAAF)

Organisation type and purpose: Membership association (membership is by subscription), present number of members: 6,500, voluntary organisation, national sports governing body.
Management, promotion and development of athletics in Scotland.

Subject coverage: Track and field athletics, hill, road and cross-country running, Scottish heavy events, athletics development packages and support from 5 years upwards, coaching courses and examinations.

Collection: Athletics memorabilia

Publications: Printed

Access to staff: Contact by letter, by telephone, by fax, by e-mail and via website. Appointment necessary.
Hours: Mon to Fri, 0900 to 1700

Affiliated to: Commonwealth Games Council for Scotland; tel: 0131 336 1924; UK Athletics; tel: 0121 456 5098; fax: 0121 456 4998

SCOTTISH BAKERS

Formal name: SAMB

4 Torphichen Street, Edinburgh, EH3 8JQ

Tel: 0131 229 1401
Fax: 0131 229 8239
E-mail: alan@scottishbakers.org

Enquiries to: Chief Executive

Founded: 1891

Organisation type and purpose: Trade association (membership is by subscription).

Subject coverage: The baking industry.

Publications: Printed

Access to staff: Contact by letter, by telephone, by fax and by e-mail
Hours: Mon to Fri, 0900 to 1700

SCOTTISH BIBLE SOCIETY

7 Hampton Terrace, Edinburgh, EH12 5XU

Tel: 0131 337 9701
Fax: 0131 337 0641
E-mail: info@scottishbiblesociety.org
Website: www.scottishbiblesociety.org

Founded: 1809; formerly called National Bible Society of Scotland (year of change 2000)

Organisation type and purpose: Registered charity (charity number SCO10767)

Non-library collection catalogue: All or part available online and in print

Publications: Printed

Publications list: Available in print

Access to staff: Contact by letter, by telephone, by fax and by e-mail
Hours: Mon to Fri, 0900 to 1700

SCOTTISH BILLIARDS &SNOOKER ASSOCIATION (SB&SA)

59 Locher Avenue, Houston, Renfrewshire, PA6 7NX

Tel: 07814–150064
E-mail: scottishsnooker147@yahoo.co.uk
Website: www.sbandsa.co.uk

Enquiries to: Secretary

Founded: 2001; carries out the functions of the former Scottish Billiards & Snooker Association (SBSA), and Scottish Snooker Association (SSA) (year of change 2001)

Organisation type and purpose: National government body, national organisation, advisory body, statutory body, membership association (membership is by subscription), present number of members: 200, voluntary organisation, training organisation, consultancy.

Subject coverage: Snooker.

Access to staff: Contact by letter, by telephone and by e-mail
Hours: Mon to Fri, 0900 to 1700

SCOTTISH BORDERS COUNCIL (SBC)

Council Headquarters, Newtown St Boswells, Melrose, Roxburghshire, TD6 0SA

Tel: 01835 824000
Fax: 01835 825001
E-mail: enquiries@scotborders.gov.uk
Website: www.scotborders.org.uk.
Website: www.scotborders.gov.uk

Enquiries to: Head of Communications
Direct tel: 01835 825008
Direct fax: 01825 825059

Founded: 1996; formed from reorganisation of Berwickshire District Council, Borders Regional Council, Ettrick and Lauderdale District Council, Roxburgh District Council, Tweeddale District Council (year of change 1996)

Organisation type and purpose: Local government body.

Subject coverage: Services and amenities; corporate services, education, environmental services, finance, housing, legal services, personnel services, planning development and tourism, property and technical services, roads and transportation, social services, council tax and other payments, registration of births, death and marriages, leisure and recreation, cleansing, environmental health and trading standards.

Access to staff: Contact by letter, by telephone, by fax, by e-mail, in person and via website
Hours: Mon to Thu, 0845 to 1700; Fri, 0845 to 1545

Access for disabled people: Parking provided, ramped entry, access to all public areas

SCOTTISH BOWLING ASSOCIATION (SBA)

National Centre for Bowling, Northfield, Hunters Avenue, Ayr, KA8 9BL

Tel: 01292 294623
Fax: 01292 294623

Enquiries to: Secretary

Founded: 1892

Organisation type and purpose: Membership association.
National Association controlling the level green game of lawn bowls.

Subject coverage: All matters relative to level green lawn bowls.

Publications: Printed

Access to staff: Contact by letter, by telephone, by fax and in person
Hours: Mon to Fri, 0900 to 1630

Associated to: British Isles Bowls Council (BIBC); World Bowls Board (WBB)

SCOTTISH BRAILLE PRESS

Craigmillar Park, Edinburgh, EH16 5NB

Tel: 0131 662 4445
Fax: 0131 662 1968
E-mail: info.sbp@royalblind.org
Website: www.royalblind.org

Enquiries to: Customer Service

Founded: 1881

Organisation type and purpose: Voluntary organisation, registered charity (charity number SC 017167), publishing house.
Printers and publishers of Braille, and suppliers of audio, large-print material, tactile diagrams and material on disk.

Subject coverage: Publishing literature and educational textbooks in Braille, audio and large print.

Non-library collection catalogue: All or part available online and in print

Publications: Printed, and electronic and video

Publications list: Available online and in print

Access to staff: Contact by letter, by telephone, by fax, by e-mail, in person and via website
Hours: Mon to Thu, 0830 to 1630; Fri, 0830 to 1300

Access to building: No prior appointment required

Access for disabled people: Parking provided, ramped entry, access to all public areas, toilet facilities

Associated with: Royal Blind Asylum and School

SCOTTISH BREAST CANCER CAMPAIGN (SBCC)

PO Box 26191, Dunfermline, Fife, KY11 3YG

Tel: 0131 623 0037
Fax: 0131 623 0037
E-mail: enquiries@scottishbreastcancercampaign.org
Website: www.scottishbreastcancercampaign.org

Enquiries to: Convener
Direct tel: 07955 170284
Direct e-mail: info@scottishbreastcancercampaign.org
Other contacts: Board member (for general enquiries)

Founded: 1993

Organisation type and purpose:
Membership association (membership is by subscription), present number of members: 100.
Pressure group and support group.

Subject coverage: Breast cancer services in Scotland.
Campaign for increased state resources for treatment and care for patients and their families and partners, research into the causes (including environmental factors), development and treatment, counselling, and the promotion of local self-help groups.

Publications: Printed

Access to staff: Contact by letter, by fax, by e-mail and via website
Hours: No office, contact should be made as indicated

SCOTTISH BUILDING FEDERATION (SBF)

Crichton House, 4 Crichton's Close, Holyrood, Edinburgh, EH8 8DT

Tel: 0131 556 8866
E-mail: info@scottish-building.co.uk
Website: www.scottish-building.co.uk

Enquiries to: Communications and Marketing Manager
Direct tel: 0131 558 5240
Direct e-mail: lynsey@scottish-building.co.uk

Founded: 1895; formerly called Scottish Building Employers' Federation (SBEF) (year of change 2000)

Organisation type and purpose: Trade Body for the Construction Industry in Scotland.

Subject coverage: Building construction industry, legislation and contracts, education and training, single market, health and safety, industrial relations, technical, environmental.

Publications: Printed

Publications list: Available online and in print

Access to staff: Contact by letter, by e-mail and via website
Hours: Mon to Thu, 0900 to 1700; Fri, 0900 to 1500

Access to building: Prior appointment required

SCOTTISH BUSINESS INFORMATION SERVICE (SCOTBIS)

National Library of Scotland, George IV Bridge, Edinburgh, EH1 1EW

Tel: 0131 623 3818
Fax: 0131 623 3809
E-mail: enquiries@scotbis.com
Website: www.scotbis.com

Enquiries to: Senior Assistant Librarian, Business Information

Founded: 1989

Organisation type and purpose: National organisation.
National business information service.

Subject coverage: Business information, company information, market research, statistics, news information, business journals, remote access to business databases for Scottish residents.

Trade and statistical information: Extensive industry and trade data held

Non-library collection catalogue: All or part available online and in-house

Library catalogue: All or part available online and in-house

Access to staff: Contact by letter, by telephone, by fax, by e-mail, in person and via website
Hours: Mon, Tue, Thu, Fri, 0930 to 1700; Wed, 1000 to 1700.
Special comments: Access to business resources in person available via the General Reading Room of the National Library of Scotland.

Also at: National Library of Scotland; George IV Bridge, Edinburgh, EH1 1EW

SCOTTISH CANOE ASSOCIATION (SCA)

Caledonia House, South Gyle, Edinburgh, EH12 9DQ

Tel: 0131 317 7314
Fax: 0131 317 7319
E-mail: general.office@canoescotland.com
Website: www.scot-canoe.org

Enquiries to: Administrator

Founded: 1939

Organisation type and purpose:
Membership association (membership is by subscription), voluntary organisation.
Governing body of the sport.

Subject coverage: Canoeing.

Non-library collection catalogue: All or part available online

Publications: Printed

Access to staff: Contact by letter, by fax, by e-mail and via website
Hours: Mon to Fri, 0830 to 1330

Federal agreement with: British Canoe Union; tel: 0115 982 1100; Canoe Association for Northern Ireland; Welsh Canoeing Association

SCOTTISH CENTRE FOR CHILDREN WITH MOTOR IMPAIRMENTS (SCCMI)

Craighalbert Centre, 1 Craighalbert Way, Cumbernauld, Strathclyde, G68 0LS

Tel: 01236 456100
Fax: 01236 736889
E-mail: sccmi@craighalbert.org.uk
Website: www.craighalbert.org.uk

Enquiries to: Director
Other contacts: Administrative Officer

Founded: 1991

Organisation type and purpose: Registered charity (charity number SC 008428), suitable for ages: birth–8.
Special needs school.

Subject coverage: Children with motor impairments.

Access to staff: Contact by letter, by telephone, by fax and by e-mail.
Appointment necessary.
Hours: Mon to Thu, 0830 to 1700; Fri, 0830 to 1600

Access for disabled people: Fully accessible

SCOTTISH CHAMBER ORCHESTRA LIMITED (SCO)

4 Royal Terrace, Edinburgh, EH7 5AB

Tel: 0131 557 6800
Fax: 0131 557 6933
E-mail: info@sco.org.uk
Website: www.sco.org.uk

Enquiries to: Finance Director
Direct tel: 0131 478 8345
Direct e-mail: les@sco.org.uk

Founded: 1974; created by the merger of Scottish Baroque Ensemble, Scottish Philharmonia Society (year of change 1981)

Organisation type and purpose:
Professional body (membership is by election or invitation), registered charity (charity number SCO 15039), company limited by guarantee.
To promote interest in and appreciation of classical music throughout Scotland.

Subject coverage: Orchestral music.

Publications: Printed, and electronic and video

Publications list: Available online

Access to staff: Contact by letter, by e-mail and via website
Hours: Mon to Fri, 0930 to 1730

SCOTTISH CHILD LAW CENTRE (SCLC)

54 East Cross Causeway, Edinburgh, EH8 9HD

Tel: 0131 667 6333
Fax: 0131 662 1713
E-mail: enquiries@sclc.org.uk

Enquiries to: Administrator
Other contacts: Director

Founded: 1988

Organisation type and purpose: National organisation, membership association (membership is by subscription), present number of members: 350, registered charity, training organisation. Advice service, provides training and publications.

Subject coverage: All aspects of law relating to children and young people in Scotland up to age 18; family, childcare, abduction and education law, divorce, residence, contact, children's rights, youth offenders and access to files.

Publications: Printed

Publications list: Available in print

Access to staff: Contact by letter, by telephone, by fax and by e-mail
Hours: Mon to Fri, 0930 to 1600

Access to building: No access other than to staff

SCOTTISH CHRISTIAN ALLIANCE LTD

3 Nethercairn Place, Newton Mearns, Glasgow, G77 5SZ

Tel: 0141 571 3804
E-mail: info@thegilvenproject.co.uk

Enquiries to: Director

Founded: 1993; formerly called Christian Alliance (Scotland) Ltd; incorporates the former YWCA of Scotland; incorporates the former Keychange Scotland Ltd (year of change 1997)

Organisation type and purpose: Voluntary organisation, Scottish charity registered with OSCR and relevant local projects, registered with Care Commission.

Subject coverage: Provision of housing support services.

Publications: Printed

Access to staff: Contact by letter, by telephone and by e-mail
Hours: Mon to Fri, 0900 to 1700

SCOTTISH CHURCH HISTORY SOCIETY (SCHS)

16 Murrayburn Park, Edingburgh, EH14 2PX

Tel: 0131 442 3772
E-mail: enquiries@schs.org.uk
Website: www.schs.org.uk

Enquiries to: Honorary Secretary

Founded: 1922

Organisation type and purpose: Learned society.

Subject coverage: History of the Church in Scotland.

Publications: Printed

Access to staff: Contact by letter and by e-mail
Hours: Mon to Fri, 0900 to 1700

SCOTTISH COMMUNITY DRAMA ASSOCIATION (SCDA)

5 York Place, Edinburgh, EH1 3EB

Tel: 0131 557 5552
Fax: 0131 557 5552
E-mail: headquarters@scda.org.uk
Website: www.scda.org.uk

Enquiries to: Administrative Assistant
Other contacts: Chairman for information on website.

Founded: 1926

Organisation type and purpose: Membership association, registered charity (charity number SC021397), training organisation.
Promotes all aspects of amateur/community theatre in Scotland. Open to all amateur clubs and interested individuals.

Subject coverage: Information on all theatre arts, related subjects, details of theatre libraries for hire of scripts, theatre arts for the amateur in Scotland. Professional assistance with amateur productions, workshops etc.

Collection: Five libraries of play scripts situated in major cities in Scotland

Non-library collection catalogue: All or part available in-house

Publications: Printed

Access to staff: Contact by letter, by telephone, by fax, by e-mail, in person and via website
Hours: Mon, 0900 to 1700; Tue, Fri, 1300 to 1700; Wed, 1000 to 1200 and 1300 to 1700; Thu, 1000 to 1200

Affiliated to: Central Council for Amateur Theatre; International Amateur Theatre Association

SCOTTISH CONSERVATIVE PARTY (SCUP)

83 Princes Street, Edinburgh, EH2 2ER

Tel: 0131 247 6890
Fax: 0131 247 6891
E-mail: info@scottishconservatives.com

Enquiries to: Chairman

Organisation type and purpose: Advisory body, membership association (membership is by subscription).
Political organisation.

Subject coverage: Scottish Conservative Party: history, organisation, membership, statements, policies.

Access to staff: Contact by letter, by telephone, by fax and by e-mail.
Appointment necessary.
Hours: Mon to Fri, 0900 to 1700

SCOTTISH COT DEATH TRUST (SCDT)

Royal Hospital for Sick Children, Yorkhill, Glasgow, G3 8SJ

Tel: 0141 357 3946
Fax: 0141 334 1376
E-mail: contact@sidscotland.org.uk
Website: www.sidscotland.org.uk

Enquiries to: Executive Director

Founded: 1985

Organisation type and purpose: Registered charity (charity number SCO 03458).

Subject coverage: Bereavement after cot death, advice on reducing the risks of cot death, information on cot death research.

Education services: Training for health professionals

Publications: Printed

Access to staff: Contact by letter, by telephone, by fax and by e-mail
Hours: Mon to Thu, 0900 to 1700; Fri, 0900 to 1600

Access for disabled people: Parking provided, ramped entry

Links with: SIDS International

SCOTTISH COUNCIL FOR SINGLE HOMELESS (SCSH)

Wellgate House, 200 Cowgate, Edinburgh, EH1 1NQ

Tel: 0131 226 4382
Fax: 0131 225 4382
E-mail: admin@scsh.org.uk
Website: www.scsh.co.uk

Enquiries to: Director
Direct e-mail: robert@scsh.org.uk

Founded: 1974

Organisation type and purpose: Voluntary organisation.
To highlight needs of homeless people, including young people, and offer practical ideas and information to tackle homelessness.

Subject coverage: Homelessness, benefits, community care, housing, education.

Publications: Printed

Publications list: Available online and in print

Access to staff: Contact by letter, by telephone, by fax, by e-mail and via website.
Appointment necessary.
Hours: Mon to Fri, 0900 to 1700
Special comments: Top floor office, lift available.

SCOTTISH COUNCIL FOR VOLUNTARY ORGANISATIONS (SCVO)

Mansfield Traquair Centre, 15 Mansfield Place, Edinburgh, EH3 6BB

Tel: 0131 556 3882
Fax: 0131 556 0279
E-mail: enquiries@scvo.org.uk
Website: www.scvo.org.uk

Enquiries to: Information Service
Direct tel: 0800 169 0022

Founded: 1943

Organisation type and purpose: Voluntary organisation, recognised Scottish charity (charity number SC003558).

Subject coverage: Weekly news and current affairs, policy and lobbying, conferences and seminars, training courses, information and publications, computer software, office supplies, payroll bureau, pensions, insurance for the sector, project development, and direct links with national third sector networks.

Publications: Printed

Publications list: Available online and in print

Access to staff: Contact by letter, by telephone, by fax, by e-mail, in person and via website. Appointment necessary.

continued overleaf

Hours: Mon to Fri, 1000 to 1600

Access for disabled people: Fully accessible

SCOTTISH COUNCIL OF INDEPENDENT SCHOOLS (SCIS)

21 Melville Street, Edinburgh, EH3 7PE

Tel: 0131 220 2106
Fax: 0131 225 8594
E-mail: information@scis.org.uk
Website: www.scis.org.uk

Enquiries to: Director

Founded: 1990

Organisation type and purpose: Advisory body, membership association (membership is by qualification), present number of members: 80 schools, registered charity (charity number SC 018033), suitable for ages: 2 to 18, consultancy.
Key aims are to: provide information, advice and guidance to parents; advance education via curriculum development and the training of teachers; advise member schools and their governing bodies about educational developments and legislation affecting independent schools (e.g. education, taxation, welfare, health and safety); and to communicate and negotiate with the Scottish Parliament, the Government, public and private bodies on behalf of the independent sector.

Trade and statistical information: Information and data on independent schools in Scotland

Library catalogue: All or part available in-house

Publications: Printed

Publications list: Available online and in print

Access to staff: Contact by letter, by telephone, by fax, by e-mail, in person and via website. Appointment necessary.
Hours: Mon to Fri, 0900 to 1700

SCOTTISH COUNCIL ON DEAFNESS (SCoD)

Suite 62, 1st Floor, Central Chambers, 93 Hope Street, Glasgow, G2 6LD

Tel: 0141 248 2474; 0141 248 2477 (textphone)
Fax: 0141 248 2479
E-mail: admin@scod.org.uk
Website: www.scod.org.uk

Enquiries to: Information Officer

Founded: 1927

Organisation type and purpose: Registered charity (charity number SC016957), organisation for deaf issues in Scotland, represents 90 organisations working with and on behalf of deaf sign language users, deafened, deafblind and hard of hearing people. The membership provides an effective working partnership between the voluntary sector, social work and education departments, NHS Trusts, health boards and the Government.

Subject coverage: All aspects of deafness, e.g. deaf sign language users, hard of hearing, deafened, deafblind, agencies for deaf people, employment, voluntary help, advice and information.

Publications: Printed

Publications list: Available online and in print

Access to staff: Contact by letter, by telephone, by fax, by e-mail, in person and via website. Appointment necessary.
Hours: Mon to Fri, 0900 to 1600

Links with: organisations working with deaf, hard of hearing and deafblind people.

SCOTTISH CRICKET UNION (SCU)

National Cricket Academy, MES Sports Centre, Ravelston, Edinburgh, EH4 3NT

Tel: 0131 313 7420
Fax: 0131 313 7430
E-mail: admin.scu@btinternet.com
Website: www.scu.org.uk
Website: www.btinternet.com/~sncl

Enquiries to: Chief Executive

Founded: 1909

Organisation type and purpose: National government body, advisory body (membership is by subscription), present number of members: 800 members, 168 clubs, training organisation, consultancy. Governing body of cricket in Scotland.

Subject coverage: Scottish cricket at domestic and international level.

Publications: Printed

Access to staff: Contact by letter, by telephone, by fax, by e-mail and in person
Hours: Mon to Fri, 0900 to 1700

Affiliated to: International Cricket Council

SCOTTISH CULTURAL PRESS & SCOTTISH CHILDREN'S PRESS (SCP)

Unit 6, Newbattle Abbey Business Park, Newbattle Road, Dalkeith, Midlothian, EH22 3LJ

Tel: 0131 660 6366
Fax: 0870 285 4846
E-mail: info@scottishbooks.com
Website: www.scottishbooks.com

Direct tel: 0131 660 4666

Founded: 1992

Organisation type and purpose: Publisher.

Subject coverage: Children's Scottish fiction and non-fiction including history, literature, poetry, environmental history, biography, Scottish language and folk tradition.

Publications: Printed
Order printed publications from: tel: 0131 660 4666; fax: 0870 285 4846

Publications list: Available online

Access to staff: Contact by letter, by telephone, by fax, by e-mail and via website. Appointment necessary.
Hours: No fixed hours – by appointment only

Access to building: No access other than to staff

SCOTTISH CYCLING (SC)

The Velodrome, London Road, Edinburgh, EH7 6AD

Tel: 0131 652 0187
E-mail: info@scottishcycling.com
Website: www.scottishcycling.com

Enquiries to: Administrator
Direct e-mail: jackie.davidson@scottishcycling.com

Founded: 1889

Organisation type and purpose: Membership association (membership is by subscription), present number of members: 2000.
Governing body for cycle sport in Scotland.

Subject coverage: Cycle sport, road racing, mountain biking, track racing, time trialing, cyclo cross, coaching.

Publications: Printed

Publications list: Available in print

Access to staff: Contact by letter, by telephone, by e-mail, in person and via website. Appointment necessary.
Hours: Mon to Fri, 0900 to 1700

Member of: British Cycling (BC); National Cycling Centre, Stuart Street, Manchester, M11 4DQ; tel: 0870 871 2000; e-mail: info@britishcycling.org

SCOTTISH DANCE TEACHERS' ALLIANCE (SDTA)

101 Park Road, Glasgow, G4 9JE

Tel: 0141 339 8944
Fax: 0141 357 4994
E-mail: sdta@btconnect.com

Enquiries to: Executive Secretary

Founded: 1934

Organisation type and purpose: International organisation, professional body (membership is by qualification).

Subject coverage: Highland, ballet, theatre, ballroom, Latin American Baton, rock 'n roll, disco dancing, line dancing and cheer dance.

Publications: Printed, and electronic and video

Access to staff: Contact by letter, by telephone, by fax and by e-mail
Hours: Mon to Fri, 0900 to 1700

Access to building: No access other than to staff, no prior appointment required

Access for disabled people: Parking provided, ramped entry, level entry, toilet facilities

Links with: SOBHD and BCD/WD&DSC

SCOTTISH DECORATORS FEDERATION (SDF)

Castlecraig Business Park, Players Road, Stirling, FK7 7SH

Tel: 01786 448838
Fax: 01786 450541
E-mail: info@scottishdecorators.co.uk
Website: www.scottishdecorators.co.uk

Enquiries to: Chief Executive

Founded: 1878

Organisation type and purpose: Trade association (membership is by qualification), service industry.

Subject coverage: Painting and decorating.

Publications: Printed
Order printed publications from: Decorating Matters

Access to staff: Contact by letter, by telephone, by fax and by e-mail. Appointment necessary.
Hours: Mon to Fri, 0900 to 16.30

Access for disabled people: no access for disabled

Member of: National Specialist Contractors Council (NSCC)

SCOTTISH DEVELOPMENT INTERNATIONAL (SDI)

150 Broomielaw, Glasgow, G2 8LU

Tel: 0141 228 2828
E-mail: michelle.cowan@scotent.co.uk
Website: www.sdi.co.uk

Enquiries to: Enquiry Fulfillment and Research Service
Direct e-mail: investment@scotent.co.uk

Founded: 2001; formerly called Locate in Scotland (LIS), Scottish Trade International (STI) (year of change 2001)

Organisation type and purpose: International organisation.

Subject coverage: SDI offers help and advice to companies looking for the ideal investment location for their business and provides a range of services for businesses thinking about entering the overseas market.

Access to staff: Contact by letter, by telephone, by e-mail and via website
Hours: Mon to Fri, 0900 to 1700

International Offices: Offices in Brussels, Düsseldorf, Italy, Paris, USA, Tokyo, Seoul, Taipei, Singapore, China, India, Russia, & UAE; SDI; Dover House, Whitehall, London, SW1A 2AU; tel: 020 7839 2117; fax: 020 7839 2975

SCOTTISH DISABILITY SPORT (SDS)

Fife Sports Institute, Viewfield Road, Glenrothes, Fife, KY6 2RB

Tel: 01592 415700
Fax: 01592 415710
E-mail: ssadsds@aol.com
Website: www.scottishdisabilitysport.com

Enquiries to: Administrator

Founded: 1962; formerly called Scottish Sports Association for Disabled People (SSAD)

Organisation type and purpose: Voluntary organisation.

Subject coverage: Sport and recreation for people with disabilities.

Transitional office: Scottish Disability Sport; Caledonian House, South Gyle, Edinburgh, EH12 9DQ; tel: 0131 317 1130; fax: 0131 317 1075; e-mail: ssadsds2@aol.com

SCOTTISH DRUGS FORUM (SDF)

91 Mitchell Street, Glasgow, G1 3LN

Tel: 0141 221 1175
Fax: 0141 248 6414
E-mail: enquiries@sdf.org.uk
Website: www.sdf.org.uk

Enquiries to: Information Officer
Other contacts: Regional Manager (for specific drugs issues)

Founded: 1986

Organisation type and purpose: Membership association (membership is by subscription), voluntary organisation, registered charity (charity number 106295). National policy and information agency working in partnership with others to co-ordinate effective responses to drug use in Scotland.

Subject coverage: Information on drugs issues, information about all (national) drugs projects and groups in Scotland, leaflets and brochures for anyone interested in drugs issues.

Information services: Library of material relevant to drug use in Scotland.

Special visitor services: Visits by appointment.

Publications: Printed, and electronic and video
Order printed publications from: website publications order form

Publications list: Available online and in print

Access to staff: Contact by letter, by telephone, by fax, by e-mail, in person and via website. Appointment necessary.

Access to building: *Hours:* Mon to Fri, 0900 to 1700

Access for disabled people: Lift is wheelchair accessible
Special comments: No disabled toilet.

Also at: Scottish Drugs Forum; 139 Morrison Street, Edinburgh, EH3 8AJ; tel: 0131 221 9300; fax: 0131 221 1556

SCOTTISH ENGINEERING

105 West George Street, Glasgow, G2 1QL

Tel: 0141 221 3181
Fax: 0141 204 1202
E-mail: consult@ScottishEngineering.org.uk
Website: www.ScottishEngineering.org.uk

Enquiries to: Secretary

Founded: 1865; formerly called Scottish Engineering Employers' Association

Organisation type and purpose: Advisory body, professional body (membership is by subscription), present number of members: 400, manufacturing industry, consultancy.

Subject coverage: Employee relations; terms and conditions of employment; employment law and industrial tribunals; health and safety; training and development.

Trade and statistical information: Wage and salary surveys

Publications: Printed

Access to staff: Contact by letter, by telephone and by fax. Appointment necessary. Non-members charged.
Hours: Mon to Fri, 0900 to 1700

Links with: Engineering Employers' Federation

SCOTTISH ENTERPRISE (SE)

Atrium Court, 50 Waterloo St, Glasgow G2 6HQ

Tel: 0141 248 2700
Fax: 0141 221 3217
E-mail: network.helpline@scotent.co.uk
Website: www.scottish-enterprise.com

Enquiries to: Manager, Economic Research
Direct tel: 0141 228 2268
Direct e-mail: gail.rogers@scotent.co.uk

Founded: 1991; formerly called Scottish Development Agency (SDA) (year of change 1991); incorporates the former Scottish Development Agency, Training Agency

Organisation type and purpose: National government body.
Economic development of Scotland.

Subject coverage: Company data, market data, sectoral data, economic data, county data, government publications, in-house reports, strategic research, economic research.

Collection: Internally generated research

Library catalogue: All or part available in-house

Access to staff: *Hours:* Mon to Fri, 0900 to 1700

Access to building: No access other than to staff

SCOTTISH ENVIRONMENT LINK (LINK)

2 Grosvenor House, Shore Road, Perth, PH2 8BD

Tel: 01738 630804
Fax: 01738 643290
E-mail: enquiries@scotlink.org
Website: www.scotlink.org
Website: www.scotlink.org/public/publications/reports.php

Enquiries to: Information Officer

Founded: 1987; formerly called Scottish Wildlife and Countryside Link (SWCL); still known as Scottish LINK

Organisation type and purpose: Membership association, Scottish company limited by guarantee and without a share capital, and a Scottish charity (charity number SC000296).
Voluntary organisations working together to care for and improve Scotland's environment for people and nature. Liaison body for 30 of the main voluntary environmental organisations in Scotland.

Subject coverage: Environmental sustainability in Scotland.

Non-library collection catalogue: All or part available online

Publications: Printed

Publications list: Available online and in print

continued overleaf

Access to staff: Contact by letter, by telephone, by fax, by e-mail and via website
Hours: Mon to Fri, 0900 to 1600

SCOTTISH ENVIRONMENT PROTECTION AGENCY (SEPA)

Erskine Court, The Castle Business Park, Stirling, FK9 4TR

Tel: 01786 457700
Fax: 01786 446885
E-mail: enquiries@sepa.org.uk
Website: www.sepa.org.uk

Enquiries to: Information Scientist
Direct e-mail: alison.mackinnon@sepa.org
Other contacts: Press Officer for press enquiries.

Founded: 1996; formed from Her Majesty's Industrial Pollution Inspectorate (HMIPI), The River Protection Boards (RPB) for Forth, Highland, North East, Solway, Tay, Tweed; formerly called Clyde River Purification Board (RPB) (year of change 1996)

Organisation type and purpose: Statutory body.

Subject coverage: Environmental regulation, air quality, radioactive substances, water quality, pollution, sustainable development, compliance with EU environmental directives.

Collection: Environment
Scotland & Northern Ireland Forum on Environmental Research – library of publications: guidance document, statistics, air quality, water quality, radioactive substances
Organisation/Government reports
Legal information – environment

Trade and statistical information: Statistics: bathing waters; water quality

Non-library collection catalogue: All or part available in-house

Library catalogue: All or part available in-house

Publications: Printed
Order printed publications from: Publications Officer

Publications list: Available online

Access to staff: Contact by telephone, by e-mail and via website. Appointment necessary.
Hours: Mon to Fri, 0900 to 1700

Access to building: Prior appointment required

Access for disabled people: Level entry

Other offices: SEPA North Region HQ; Graesser House, Fodderty Way, Dingwall, IV15 9XB; tel: 01349 862021; SEPA South East Region HQ; Clearwater House, Heriot Watt Research Park, Avenue North, Riccarton, Edinburgh, EH14 4AP; tel: 0131 449 7296; SEPA South West Region HQ; 5 Redwood Crescent, Peel Park, East Kilbride, G74 5PP; tel: 01355 574200

SCOTTISH EXECUTIVE

Information Management Unit, Y Spur, Saughton House, Edinburgh, EH11 3XD

Tel: 0131 244 4556
Fax: 0131 244 4545
E-mail: selibrary@scotland.gsi.gov.uk
Website: www.scotland.gov.uk

Enquiries to: Information Officer
Direct e-mail: selibrary@scotland.gsi.gov.uk

History of institution: formerly called Scottish Office (year of change 1999)

Organisation type and purpose: National government body.
Library and information service, serving the Scottish Executive.

Subject coverage: Scottish administration, education, health, crime, police, prisons, social work, transport.

Non-library collection catalogue: All or part available in-house

Library catalogue: All or part available in-house

Publications: Printed
Order printed publications from: Astron or Blackwells Bookshop, Edinburgh

Publications list: Available online and in print

Access to staff: Appointment necessary.
Hours: Mon to Fri, 0900 to 1700

Access for disabled people: Access to all public areas

SCOTTISH FEDERATION OF HOUSING ASSOCIATIONS LIMITED (SFHA)

38 York Place, Edinburgh, EH1 3HU

Tel: 0131 556 5777
Fax: 0131 557 6028
E-mail: sfha@sfha.co.uk
Website: www.sfha.co.uk

Enquiries to: Administrator
Direct tel: 0131 473 6224
Direct e-mail: smorton@sfha.co.uk

Founded: 1976

Organisation type and purpose: Trade association (membership is by subscription).
Representative body for Registered Social Landlords in Scotland.

Subject coverage: Information on Scottish Registered Social Landlords, housing policy and practice.

Publications: Printed

Access to staff: Contact by letter, by telephone, by fax, by e-mail and via website. Appointment necessary.
Hours: Mon to Fri, 0900 to 1700

Access to building: No access other than to staff

Access for disabled people: Ramped entry
Special comments: Wheelchair lift (external).

Other addresses: Scottish Federation of Housing Associations; 24 Mauchline Place West, Dundee, DD4 8HS; tel: 01382 510656; fax: 01382 510990; Scottish Federation of Housing Associations; 4th Floor, Pegasus House, 375 West George Street, Glasgow, G2 4LW; tel: 0141 332 8113; fax: 0141 332 9684

SCOTTISH FEDERATION OF SEA ANGLERS (SFSA)

Unit 6, Evans Business Centre, Mitchelston Drive, Mitchelston Industrial Estate, Kirkaldy, Fife, KY1 3NB

Tel: 01592 657520
Fax: 01592 657520
Website: www.sfsa.freeserve.co.uk

Founded: 1961

Organisation type and purpose: Membership association (membership is by subscription).
Recognised by Sportscotland as the governing body for the sport of sea fishing in Scotland.

Subject coverage: Sea fishing.

Publications: Printed

Access to staff: Contact by letter, by telephone, by fax and in person. Appointment necessary.
Hours: Mon, Tue, Thu, Fri, 0930 to 1300

Links with: Sea Angling Liaison Committee of Great Britain and Ireland (SALC); tel: 0626 331 330

SCOTTISH FOOD AND DRINK FEDERATION (SFDF)

4A Torphichen Street, Edinburgh, EH3 8JQ

Tel: 0131 229 9415
Fax: 0131 229 9407
E-mail: flora.mclean@sfdf.org.uk
Website: www.sfdf.org.uk

Enquiries to: Director

Founded: 1999

Organisation type and purpose: Trade association (membership is by subscription).

Subject coverage: Primarily policy and regulation relating to food and drink manufacturing industry.

Publications: Printed, and electronic and video

Access to staff: Contact by letter, by telephone, by fax, by e-mail and via website. Appointment necessary.
Hours: Mon to Fri, 0900 to 1700

Constituent part of: Food and Drink Federation; Federation House, 6 Catherine Street, London WC2B 5JJ; tel: 0207 836 2460; fax: 0207 836 0580; website: http://www.fdf.org.uk

SCOTTISH FOOTBALL ASSOCIATION LIMITED (SFA)

Hampden Park, Glasgow, G42 9AY

Tel: 0141 616 6000
Fax: 0141 616 6001
E-mail: info@scottishfa.co.uk
Website: www.scottishfa.co.uk

Enquiries to: Chief Executive

Founded: 1873

Organisation type and purpose: Governing body for football in Scotland.

Subject coverage: Player registrations, the laws of the game, coaching, refereeing, general and specific football matters of public interest.

Collection: Old documents, minute books, etc. are now housed in the Scottish Football Museum at Hampden Park
Various football trophies and mementos

Publications: Printed, and electronic and video

Access to staff: Contact by letter, by telephone, by fax and by e-mail
Hours: Mon to Fri, 0900 to 1700

Member organisation of: Fédération Internationale de Football Association (FIFA); Union Des Associations Européennes de Football (UEFA)

SCOTTISH FOOTBALL LEAGUE, THE (SFL)

Hampden Park, Glasgow, G42 9EB

Tel: 0141 620 4160
Fax: 0141 620 4161
E-mail: info@scottishfootballleague.com

Enquiries to: Secretary

Founded: 1890

Subject coverage: Administration, marketing, promotion, fostering and development of association football, especially via the SFL championship, league cup, and league challenge cup competitions.

Collection: Minute Books 1890–2006
Registration Books 1898–2006
SFL results, appearances, attendances, etc
Various historical documents pertaining to association football

Publications: Printed

Access to staff: Contact by letter, by telephone and by fax
Hours: Mon to Fri, 0900 to 1700; Sat, 0930 to 1200

SCOTTISH FUNDING COUNCIL (SFC)

Formal name: Scottish Further and Higher Education Funding Council

Donaldson House, 97 Haymarket Terrace, Edinburgh, EH12 5HD

Tel: 0131 313 6500
Fax: 0131 313 6501
E-mail: info@sfc.ac.uk
Website: www.sfc.ac.uk

Enquiries to: Assistant Director of Communications
Direct tel: 0131 313 6612
Direct e-mail: communications@sfc.ac.uk

Founded: 2005; replaced Scottish Further Education Funding Council and Scottish Higher Education Funding Council (year of change 2005)

Organisation type and purpose: National government body, advisory body, funding body supporting universities and colleges in the provison of high quality learning and internationally competitive research.

Subject coverage: Funding policies, guidance on the provision of learning and teaching, further and higher education in Scotland.

Trade and statistical information: Data on numbers of students and staff at further and higher education institutions in Scotland; data on income and expenditure of further and higher education institutions in Scotland

Publications: Printed

Publications list: Available online

Access to staff: Contact by letter, by telephone, by e-mail and via website
Hours: Mon to Thurs, 0900 to 1700, and Fri 0900 to 1630

Access to building: Mon to Thurs 0900 to 1700, and Fri 0900 to 1630

SCOTTISH GAELIC TEXTS SOCIETY (SGTS)

c/o McLeish Carswell, 29 St Vincent Place, Glasgow, G1 2DT

Tel: 0141 248 4134
Fax: 0141 226 3118

Enquiries to: Honorary Secretary

Founded: 1934

Organisation type and purpose: Learned society (membership is by subscription), registered charity.

Subject coverage: Scottish Gaelic literature generally, but especially learned texts hitherto unpublished or requiring revision.

Publications: Printed

Publications list: Available in print

Access to staff: Contact by letter
Hours: Mon to Fri, 0900 to 1700

Grant-aided by: three universities

SCOTTISH GAMES ASSOCIATION (SGA)

24 Florence Place, Perth, Tayside, PH1 5BH

Tel: 01738 627782
Fax: 01738 639622
E-mail: andrew@highlandgames.org.uk
Website: www.highlandgames-sga.com

Enquiries to: Honorary Secretary

Founded: 1946

Organisation type and purpose:
Professional body.
National Governing body.

Subject coverage: Professional activities and participation in most games and sports in Scotland.

Publications: Printed
Order printed publications from: The Secretary, Scottish Games Association

SCOTTISH GENEALOGY SOCIETY

15 Victoria Terrace, Edinburgh, EH1 2JL

Tel: 0131 220 3677
Fax: 0131 220 3677
E-mail: enquiries@scotsgenealogy.com
Website: www.scotsgenealogy.com

Enquiries to: Librarian

Founded: 1953

Organisation type and purpose: Learned society.
Genealogy and Family History Library.

Subject coverage: Scottish family history and genealogy.

Collection: Card indexes relating to several families including Stirling and Mackay
Largest Scottish collection of unpublished lists of monumental (graveyard) inscriptions

Library catalogue: All or part available in-house

Publications: Printed, and electronic and video
Order printed publications from: Above address or via website
Order electronic and video publications from: Above address or via website

Publications list: Available online and in print

Access to staff: Contact by letter, by fax, by e-mail, in person and via website
Hours: Mon, Tue, Thu, 1030 to 1730; Wed, 1030 to 1930; Sat, 1000 to 1700
Special comments: Free advice. Non-members charged a daily fee.

Access for disabled people: Limited. Please contact for information.

Member of: Scottish Association of Family History Societies

SCOTTISH GLADIOLUS SOCIETY (SGS)

Ardshiel, Bruce Terrace, Kinghorn, Burntisland, Fife, KY3 9TH

Tel: 01592 892559

Enquiries to: Secretary

Founded: 1972

Organisation type and purpose: National organisation, membership association (membership is by subscription), present number of members: 40, voluntary organisation, research organisation.

Subject coverage: To promote the cultivation, exhibition, research and hybridisation of gladioli. To contribute towards gladioli interest in both Britain and overseas and generally support Scottish flower shows and Scottish horticulture with exhibits, expert show judges and lecturers.

Other address: British Gladiolus Society (BGS); Honorary Correspondence Secretary, 197 Aston Clinton Road, Aylesbury, Buckinghamshire, HP22 5AD

SCOTTISH GROCERS' FEDERATION

222–224 Queensferry Road, Edinburgh, EH4 2BN

Tel: 0131 343 3300
Fax: 0131 343 6147

Enquiries to: Chief Executive

Founded: 1918

Organisation type and purpose: Trade association (membership is by subscription).

Publications: Printed

Access to staff: Contact by letter, by telephone, by fax and in person. Access for members only.
Hours: Mon to Fri, 0900 to 1700

SCOTTISH GROCERY TRADE EMPLOYERS' ASSOCIATION

222–224 Queensferry Road, Edinburgh, EH4 2BN

Tel: 0131 343 3300
Fax: 0131 343 6147

Enquiries to: Chief Executive

Organisation type and purpose: Membership association (membership is by subscription), present number of members: c. 700.

Access to staff: Contact by letter, by telephone and by fax. Appointment necessary. Access for members only.
Hours: Mon to Fri, 0900 to 1700

Parent body: Scottish Grocers' Federation

SCOTTISH HISTORIC BUILDINGS TRUST (SHBT)

42 North Castle Street, Edinburgh, EH2 3BN

Tel: 0131 220 5990
Fax: 0131 220 5991
E-mail: info@shbt.org.uk
Website: www.shbt.org.uk

Enquiries to: Director

Founded: 2003; created by the merger of Scottish Historic Buildings Trust and Cockburn Conservation Trust (year of change 2010); formerly called Alba Conservation Trust (year of change 2010)

Organisation type and purpose: Registered charity.
Building preservation trust.
Acquisition, repair and reuse of buildings of architectural or historic importance throughout Scotland.

Subject coverage: Management and techniques of building conservation.

Collection: Books, journals, reports, slides, etc. on building conservation

Publications: Printed

Access to staff: Contact by letter, by telephone and by e-mail. Appointment necessary.
Hours: Mon to Fri, 0900 to 1700
Special comments: Information only available to registered charities and other non-profit making organisations.

Member organisation of: UK Association of Preservation Trusts; Alhambra House, 27–31 Charing Cross Road, London, WC24 OAU; tel: 0207 925 0199

SCOTTISH HISTORY SOCIETY (SHS)

Dr Katie Stevenson, School of History, University of St Andrews, St Katharine's Lodge, The Scores, St Andrews, KY16 9AL

Tel: 01337 831996
E-mail: kcs7@st-andrews.ac.uk
Website: www.scottishhistorysociety.org

Enquiries to: Honorary Secretary

Organisation type and purpose: Learned society. Publication of documents relevant to Scottish history.

Subject coverage: Scottish history.

Publications list: Available online and in print

SCOTTISH HOCKEY

589 Lanark Road, Edinburgh, EH14 5DA

Tel: 0131 453 9070
Fax: 0131 453 9079
E-mail: via website
Website: www.scottish-hockey.org.uk

Organisation type and purpose: The recognised governing body for the sport of hockey in Scotland, providing for the development, management and promotion of the sport across all ages and abilities.

Subject coverage: Scottish hockey at all levels.

Publications: Electronic and video
Order electronic and video publications from: Download from website

Publications list: Available online

Access to staff: Contact by letter, by telephone, by fax and via website

SCOTTISH HUNTINGTON'S ASSOCIATION

Thistle House, 61 Main Road, Elderslie, Johnstone, Renfrewshire, PA5 9BA

Tel: 01505 322245
Fax: 01505 382980
E-mail: sha-admin@hdscotland.org

Enquiries to: Administrator

Founded: 1989

Organisation type and purpose: Voluntary organisation, registered charity.

Subject coverage: Huntington's Disease.

Publications list: Available in print

Access to staff: Contact by telephone
Hours: Mon to Fri, 0900 to 1700

SCOTTISH JEWISH ARCHIVES CENTRE

Garnethill Synagogue, 129 Hill Street, Glasgow, G3 6UB

Tel: 0141 332 4911
Fax: 0131 332 4911
E-mail: info@sjac.org.uk
Website: www.sjac.org.uk

Enquiries to: Director
Direct e-mail: rvlkaplan@googlemail.com

Founded: 1987

Organisation type and purpose: Registered charity, museum, research organisation.

Subject coverage: History of Jews in Scotland.

Non-library collection catalogue: All or part available in-house

Library catalogue: All or part available in-house

Publications list: Available online

Access to staff: Contact by letter, by e-mail and in person. Appointment necessary.
Hours: Monthly, Sun, 1400 to 1600; Fri morning, by appointment

SCOTTISH JU-JITSU ASSOCIATION (SJJA)

House of Samurai, 93 Douglas Street, Dundee, DD1 5AZ

Tel: 01382 201601
E-mail: scottishjujitsu@aol.com
Website: www.scottishjujitsu.com

Enquiries to: Executive Administrator
Other contacts: Technical Director; Events Director; Communications Director; Operations Director; Projects Director; Director of Junior Training

Founded: 1979

Organisation type and purpose: National organisation, membership association (membership is by subscription), governing body of sport.
To regulate, control and educate in the sport and art of ju-jitsu.

Subject coverage: Information on ju-jitsu clubs throughout Scotland, international ju-jitsu organisations and ko ryu (traditional systems) organisations.

Collection: Coaching videos (only available to members), 'The Essentials' (Robert G. Ross)

Non-library collection catalogue: All or part available in-house

Library catalogue: All or part available in-house

Publications: Printed, and electronic and video

Access to staff: Contact by letter, by telephone, by e-mail and via website. Appointment necessary. Access for members only.
Hours: Mon, Wed and Fri, 1100 to 2200; Tue and Thu, 1100 to 1500; Sat, 1100 to 1300

Access to building: No prior appointment required
Hours: Mon to Fri, 1830 to 2200
Special comments: Main entrance security controlled.

Member organisation of: British Association of Sport and Exercise Sciences; tel: 0113 8126162; fax: 0113 8126163; website: http://www.bases.org.uk
Scottish Schools Sports Association; tel: 0141 353 3215; fax: 0141 353 3815

SCOTTISH LANGUAGE DICTIONARIES LIMITED (SLD)

25 Buccleuch Place, Edinburgh, EH8 9LN

Tel: 0131 650 4149
E-mail: mail@scotsdictionaries.org.uk
Website: www.scotsdictionaries.org.uk

Enquiries to: Director

Founded: 2002; formerly called Scottish National Dictionary Association Ltd, A Dictionary of the Older Scottish Tongue (year of change 2002)

Organisation type and purpose: Membership association, present number of members: 100, registered charity (charity number SC 032910), research organisation, lexicography.

Subject coverage: The multi-volume dictionaries of Scots language, which include historical and regional principles, 12th century to 2005; study of Scottish language; information on Scots language to the present day; smaller, related publications.

Education services: Outreach, teaching packs, schools website: http://www.scuilwab.org.uk

Collection: Word collection in electronic database, in addition to published dictionaries

Publications: Printed, and electronic and video
Order printed publications from: Amazon via website: http://www.scotsdictionaries.org.uk

Publications list: Available in print

Access to staff: Contact by letter, by telephone, by e-mail, in person and via website. Appointment necessary.
Hours: Mon to Fri, 0900 to 1700
Special comments: Visits by prior appointment only. Mornings fully covered. Hours in the office are variable in the afternoon. Please leave message on answerphone.

SCOTTISH LAW COMMISSION (SLC)

140 Causewayside, Edinburgh, EH9 1PR

Tel: 0131 668 2131
Fax: 0131 662 4900
E-mail: info@scotlawcom.gsi.gov.uk
Website: www.scotlawcom.gov.uk

Enquiries to: Librarian

Founded: 1965

Organisation type and purpose: National government body, statutory body.
Law Reform Agency. A statutory body set up under the Law Commissions Act 1965.

Subject coverage: Responsible for keeping under review the law of Scotland and making recommendations for reform.

Collection: Law reform publications from throughout the world

Non-library collection catalogue: All or part available in-house

Library catalogue: All or part available in-house

Publications: Printed
Order printed publications from: Stationery Office

Publications list: Available online

Access to staff: Contact by letter, by telephone and by e-mail. Appointment necessary.
Hours: Mon to Fri, 0900 to 1700

Access to building: Prior appointment required

SCOTTISH LEGAL ACTION GROUP (SCOLAG)

52 Crossgate, Cupar, Fife, KY15 5JX

Tel: 01334 655150
Fax: 01334 654911
E-mail: company.secretary@scolag.org
Website: www.scolag.org

Enquiries to: Administrator
Direct tel: 05600 727138
Direct fax: 05600 727138; 0131 476 5698 (SCOLAG Legal Journal editor)
Direct e-mail: admin@scolag.org; editor@scolag.org
Other contacts: Editor, SCOLAG Legal Journal

Founded: 1975

Organisation type and purpose: Membership association (membership is by subscription).

Subject coverage: Scots law and socio-legal justice in Scotland.

Non-library collection catalogue: All or part available online

Library catalogue: All or part available in print

Publications: Printed
Order printed publications from: Administrator

Access to staff: Contact by letter, by telephone, by fax, by e-mail and via website
Hours: Mon to Fri, 0900 to 1700

SCOTTISH LEGAL AID BOARD

44 Drumsheugh Gardens, Edinburgh, EH3 7SW

Tel: 0131 226 7061; 0845 122 8686 (helpline)
Fax: 0131 220 4878
E-mail: general@slab.org.uk
Website: www.slab.org.uk

Enquiries to: Senior Communications Officer

Founded: 1986; formerly called Legal Aid Assessment Office of the Scottish Home and Health Department, The Legal Aid Central Committee of the Law Society of Scotland (year of change 1987)

Organisation type and purpose: Public body that manages legal aid in Scotland.

Subject coverage: Expenditure on legal aid in Scotland; volumes of legal aid applications and grants in Scotland.

Non-library collection catalogue: All or part available online and in print

Publications: Printed

Publications list: Available online

Access to staff: Contact by letter, by telephone, by fax, by e-mail and via website. Appointment necessary.
Hours: Mon to Fri, 0900 to 1700

Sponsor body: Scottish Executive Justice Department; St Andrews House, Regents Road, Edinburgh; tel: 0131 244 2200

SCOTTISH LIBERAL DEMOCRATS (SLD)

4 Clifton Terrace, Edinburgh, EH12 5DR

Tel: 0131 337 2314
Fax: 0131 337 3566
E-mail: scotlibdem@cix.co.uk
Website: www.scotlibdems.org.uk

Enquiries to: Administrator

Founded: 1989; formerly called Scottish Liberal Party, Scottish Social and Liberal Democrats, SDP (Scotland)

Organisation type and purpose: Membership association (membership is by subscription).
Party political organisation.

Subject coverage: Local government elections, national elections, Scottish Liberal Democrat policies.

Collection: Gladstone's Midlothian speeches Liberal Democrat policy papers

Trade and statistical information: Election statistics

Affiliated to: Liberal Democrats

SCOTTISH LIBRARY AND INFORMATION COUNCIL (SLIC)

151 West George Street, Glasgow, G2 2JJ

Tel: 0141 228 4790
E-mail: slic@slainte.org.uk
Website: www.slainte.org.uk/slic/slicindex.htm

Enquiries to: Director

Founded: 1991

Organisation type and purpose: Advisory body, registered charity.

Subject coverage: All library and information service issues; networking, internet, social inclusion, open learning, further education, college libraries, higher education, school libraries, public libraries, special libraries, performance indicators.

Publications: Printed

Publications list: Available online

Access to staff: Contact by letter, by telephone and by e-mail. Appointment necessary.
Hours: Mon to Fri, 0900 to 1700

SCOTTISH MASK AND PUPPET CENTRE (SMPC)

Formal name: Scottish Mask and Puppet Centre (The Garret Mask & Puppet Centre Trust Ltd)

8–10 Balcarres Avenue, Glasgow, G12 0QF

Tel: 0141 339 6185
Fax: 0141 339 8021
E-mail: info@scottishmaskandpuppetcentre.co.uk
Website: www.scottishmaskandpuppetcentre.co.uk
Website: www.maskandpuppetbooks.co.uk

Enquiries to: Administrator
Other contacts: Exhibitions Curator: malcolm.knight@scottishmaskandpuppetcentre.co.uk

Founded: 1981

Organisation type and purpose: International organisation, advisory body, professional body, membership association (membership is by subscription), voluntary organisation, registered charity (charity number SCO 14379), training organisation, consultancy, research organisation.
To promote, maintain and develop the ancient art of puppets, masks and performing objects; to seek recognition for the medium as an art form in its own right; to dignify the profession; to network internationally.

continued overleaf

Subject coverage: Masks, puppets, performing objects, exhibitions, workshops, performances, networking, commissions, (no loan or hire), collections, publications.

Collection: Malcolm Knight Collection of Puppets and Masks
James Arnott Library
Claude Schumacher Library
The Miles Lee Collection of Puppets
The Caricature Theatre Collection
Harry Vernon Punch and Judy Set
Wayang Golek ASEP Collection

Non-library collection catalogue: All or part available in-house

Library catalogue: All or part available in-house

Publications: Printed
Order electronic and video publications from: website: http://www.maskandpuppetbooks.co.uk

Publications list: Available online and in print

Access to staff: Contact by letter, by telephone, by fax, by e-mail and via website. Appointment necessary.
Hours: Mon to Fri, 1000 to 1600; Sat, 1300 to 1700

Access to building: Prior appointment required
Hours: Mon to Wed, 1300 to 1600; Sat, 1330 to 1600

Access for disabled people: Parking provided, ramped entry, toilet facilities
Special comments: Induction loop provided for theatre.

SCOTTISH MASSAGE THERAPISTS ORGANISATION LIMITED (SMTO)

24 Ellon Road, Bridge of Don, Aberdeen, AB23 8BX

Tel: 01224 822956
Fax: 01224 822960
E-mail: smto@scotmass.co.uk

Enquiries to: Chairman
Other contacts: General Secretary

Founded: 1992

Organisation type and purpose: Professional body.

Subject coverage: Massage, clinical aromatherapy, remedial and sports massage, manipulative therapy, reflexology, on-site seated massage, advanced remedial massage therapy.

Publications: Printed

Access to staff: Contact by letter, by telephone, by fax, by e-mail, in person and via website. Appointment necessary.
Hours: Mon to Fri, 0900 to 1700

SCOTTISH MOTOR MUSEUM TRUST

Motoring Heritage Centre, Loch Lomond Outlets, Main Street, Alexandria, Dumbartonshire, G83 0UG

Tel: 01389 607 862
Fax: 01389 607 862
E-mail: info@motoringheritage.co.uk
Website: www.motoringheritage.co.uk
Website: www.visitlochlomond.org

Enquiries to: Honorary Secretary

Founded: 1995; formerly called Argyll Motor Museum

Organisation type and purpose: Voluntary organisation, registered charity (charity number SCO 28515), museum, historic building, house or site, suitable for ages: 5+.

Subject coverage: Scottish motoring industry.

Information services: Library available for reference.

Special visitor services: Guided tours, materials and/or activities for children.

Collection: Collection of cine-film on Scottish motoring
Film archive of Scottish motoring
Motor cars of Scottish origin
Photographic archive of Scottish transport 1890 to present day

Non-library collection catalogue: All or part available in print

Library catalogue: All or part available in print

Publications: Electronic and video

Access to staff: Contact by letter, by telephone, by fax, by e-mail, in person and via website
Hours: Mon to Fri, 0930 to 1730

Access to building: No prior appointment required
Hours: Daily, 0930 to 1730

Access for disabled people: Parking provided, ramped entry, access to all public areas, toilet facilities

Museum: Motoring Heritage Centre; at same address

SCOTTISH MOTOR TRADE ASSOCIATION LIMITED (SMTA)

Palmerston House, 10 The Loan, South Queensfield, EH30 9NS

Tel: 0131 331 5510
Fax: 0131 331 4296
E-mail: info@smta.co.uk
Website: www.smta.co.uk

Enquiries to: Membership Secretary
Direct e-mail: bill.dunn@smta.co.uk

Founded: 1903

Organisation type and purpose: Advisory body, trade association (membership is by subscription), present number of members: 1000, training organisation, research organisation.

Subject coverage: Employment and personnel issues, health and safety, taxation and VAT, legal information, technical information, Scotsure Insurance Co., SMTA (Trading Partners) Ltd.

Collection: Scottish Motor Show Brochures (1905 to date)
Members Bulletin (monthly)

Trade and statistical information: New vehicle sales – Scotland

Access to staff: Contact by letter, by telephone, by fax, by e-mail, in person and via website. Appointment necessary. Access for members only.
Hours: Mon to Fri, 0900 to 1700

Access to building: No access other than to staff
Hours: Mon to Fri, 0900 to 1700

SCOTTISH NATIONAL INSTITUTION FOR THE WAR BLINDED (SNIWB, LINBURN)

PO Box 500, Gillespie Crescent, Edinburgh, EH10 4HZ

Tel: 0131 229 1456
Fax: 0131 229 4060
E-mail: enquiries@scottishwarblinded.org

Enquiries to: Secretary and Treasurer

Founded: 1915

Organisation type and purpose: Voluntary organisation, registered charity (charity number SC002652).
Training, employment and aftercare for visually impaired Scottish ex-services.

Subject coverage: Care and welfare of blind and visually impaired ex-servicemen and women, setting up of specialised workshops, grants.

Publications: Printed

Publications list: Available in print

Access to staff: Contact by letter, by telephone, by fax and by e-mail. Appointment necessary.
Hours: Mon to Fri, 0900 to 1300 and 1400 to 1700

Access to building: No access other than to staff

Access for disabled people: Parking provided, level entry

Links with: Royal Blind Asylum and School; at the same address

SCOTTISH NATIONAL PARTY (SNP)

107 McDonald Road, Edinburgh, EH7 4NW

Tel: 0131 525 8900
Fax: 0131 525 8901
E-mail: snp.hq@snp.org.uk
Website: www.snp.org

Enquiries to: Policy and information officer
Direct tel: 0131 525 8908

Founded: 1934

Organisation type and purpose: Membership association (membership is by subscription). Political party.

Subject coverage: Party policy and information on Scottish independence in Europe.

Publications: Printed

Access to staff: Contact by letter, by telephone, by fax, by e-mail, in person and via website. Appointment necessary.
Hours: Mon to Fri, 0900 to 1700

SCOTTISH NATIONAL SWEET PEA, ROSE & CARNATION SOCIETY (SNSPRCS)

Mr Iain Silver, Inglewood, Bogsbank Road
West Linton, EH46 7EN

E-mail: society@snsprcs.org.uk
Website: www.snsprcs.org.uk

Enquiries to: General Secretary

Founded: 1919

Organisation type and purpose: National organisation (membership is by subscription), present number of members: 110, voluntary organisation, registered charity (charity number SC009709).

Subject coverage: Information on cultivating and exhibiting sweet peas, roses and carnations.

Access to staff: Contact by letter and by e-mail
Hours: Mon to Fri, 0900 to 1700

SCOTTISH NATURAL HERITAGE, INVERNESS

Great Glen House, Leachkin Road, Inverness, IV3 8NW

Tel: 01463 725290
E-mail: library@snh.gov.uk
Website: www.snh.gov.uk

Enquiries to: Librarian

Founded: 1992; formerly called Countryside Commission for Scotland, Nature Conservancy Council

Organisation type and purpose: National government body.
Library.

Subject coverage: All aspects of nature and landscape conservation, land use and recreation especially in relation to Scotland's natural heritage.

Library catalogue: All or part available in-house

Publications: Printed
Order printed publications from: The Publications Unit can be contacted by phone tel: 01738 458530; e-mail: pubs@snh.gov.uk or via a website publications search: http://www.snh.gov.uk

Publications list: Available online

Access to staff: Contact by letter, by telephone, by e-mail and in person
Hours: Mon to Thu, 0900 to 1700; Fri, 0900 to 1630. If travelling from outside the area, please phone in advance to ensure that staff are available.

Access for disabled people: Library area has wide aisles suitable for wheelchairs.

SCOTTISH NATURAL HISTORY LIBRARY (SNHL)

Foremount House, Kilbarchan, Renfrewshire, PA10 2EZ

Tel: 01505 702419

Enquiries to: Chairman
Other contacts: Honorary Librarian

Founded: 1972

Organisation type and purpose: Learned society, registered charity (charity number SCO 42142), research organisation.
Specialist library.

Subject coverage: All aspects of Scottish natural history.

Collection: The largest separate collection of Scottish natural history books and journals anywhere in the world; some 150,000 items, including some 400 periodicals; several specialised Scottish collections which have been presented to the library

Non-library collection catalogue: All or part available in-house

Library catalogue: All or part available in-house

Publications: Printed

Access to staff: Contact by letter and by telephone
Hours: Mon to Fri, 0900 to 1700

Access to building: Prior appointment required

Works in co-operation with the: British Library; National Library of Scotland; Natural History Museum; Royal Museum of Scotland; Society for the History of Natural History

SCOTTISH OFFICIAL BOARD OF HIGHLAND DANCING (SOBHD)

Heritage House, 32 Grange Loan, Edinburgh, EH9 2NR

Tel: 0131 668 3965
Fax: 0131 662 0404
E-mail: admin@sobhd.net
Website: www.sobhd.net

Enquiries to: Director of Administration

Founded: 1950

Organisation type and purpose: International organisation, professional body (membership is by election or invitation).
Governing body.

Subject coverage: Highland dancing world governing body.

Collection: Collection of books on the subject

Non-library collection catalogue: All or part available in-house

Publications: Printed

Publications list: Available in print

Access to staff: Contact by letter, by telephone, by fax, by e-mail, in person and via website
Hours: Mon to Fri, 0900 to 1700

SCOTTISH OPERA

39 Elmbank Crescent, Glasgow, G2 4PT

Tel: 0141 248 4567
Fax: 0141 221 8812
Website: www.scottishopera.org.uk

Direct tel: 0141 248 4567

Founded: 1962

Organisation type and purpose: National organisation, registered charity (charity number 37531).

Access to staff: Contact by letter, by telephone, by fax, by e-mail and in person. Appointment necessary.
Hours: Mon to Fri, 0930 to 1730

Access to building: No access other than to staff

SCOTTISH ORNITHOLOGISTS' CLUB (SOC)

Waterston House, Aberlady, East Lothian, EH32 0PY

Tel: 01875 871330
Fax: 01875 871035
E-mail: mail@the-soc.org.uk
Website: www.the-soc.org.uk

Enquiries to: Office Manager
Other contacts: Administrative Assistant

Founded: 1936

Organisation type and purpose: Membership association (membership is by subscription), present number of members: 2500, voluntary organisation, registered charity (charity number SC009859), publishing house.
To encourage ornithology in Scotland.

Subject coverage: Conservation and research into birds in Scotland, ornithology in general.

Collection: Extensive ornithological reference library (The George Waterston Library) and archive.
Wildlife art gallery

Library catalogue: All or part available online and in print

Publications: Printed, and electronic and video

Publications list: Available online

Access to staff: Contact by letter, by telephone, by e-mail and in person
Hours: Mon to Fri, 0900 to 1700
Special comments: Please phone beforehand.

Access to building: *Hours:* Mon to Fri, 1000 to 1600; Sat and Sun, 1000 to 1600 (summer, 1200 to 1800)

Access for disabled people: Wheelchair accessible

Has: 14 branches throughout Scotland

SCOTTISH PARACHUTE CLUB

Strathallan Airfield, Auchterarder, Perthshire, PH3 1LA

Tel: 01764 662 572
E-mail: andy@afrew.fsnet.co.uk
Website: www.skydivestrathallan.co.uk

Enquiries to: General Secretary

Founded: 1960

Organisation type and purpose: National organisation, membership association (membership is by subscription), present number of members: 70, voluntary organisation, training organisation.

Subject coverage: Parachute training courses for beginners to experienced jumpers.

Access to staff: Contact by letter, by telephone, by e-mail, in person and via website. All charged.

continued overleaf

Hours: Fri, 1700 to 2100; Sat, Sun, 0900 to 2100

Access to building: No prior appointment required

Access for disabled people: Parking provided, level entry

Connections with: British Parachute Association (BPA); Wharf Way, Glenparva, Leicester, LE2 9TF; tel: 0116 278 5271; fax: 0116 247 7662; Scottish Sport Parachute Association (SSPA); Strathallan Airfield, Auchterarder, Perthshire, PH3 1BE; tel: 01698 812 443

SCOTTISH PARENT TEACHER COUNCIL (SPTC)

Mansfield Traquair Centre, 15 Mansfield Place, Edinburgh EH3 6BB

Tel: 0131 474 6199
E-mail: sptc@sptc.info
Website: www.sptc.info

Enquiries to: Executive Director
Other contacts: Information Officer

Founded: 1948

Organisation type and purpose: Membership association, registered charity. Educational organisation, open to PCs, PTAs and others with an interest in education in Scotland.

Subject coverage: Information about PCs, PTAs in Scotland, Parent/teacher relationships and general information about Scottish education.

Publications: Printed

Access to staff: Contact by letter, by telephone, by fax, by e-mail and via website
Hours: Mon to Fri, 0930 to 1700

SCOTTISH PARTNERSHIP FOR PALLIATIVE CARE (SPPC)

1a Cambridge Street, Edinburgh, EH1 2DY

Tel: 0131 229 0538
Fax: 0131 228 2967
E-mail: office@palliativecarescotland.org.uk
Website: www.palliativecarescotland.org.uk

Enquiries to: Director

Founded: 1991; formerly called Scottish Partnership Agency for Palliative and Cancer Care (SPAPCC) (year of change 2001)

Organisation type and purpose: Registered charity (charity number SC017979).

Subject coverage: Palliative care, specialist palliative care, hospices.

Publications: Printed

Access to staff: Contact by letter, by telephone, by fax and by e-mail
Hours: Mon to Fri, 0900 to 1700

Access to building: No public access to building

Member organisations: more than 50 voluntary and statutory bodies.

SCOTTISH PHARMACEUTICAL FEDERATION (SPF)

135 Wellington Street, Glasgow, G2 2XD

Tel: 0141 221 1235
Fax: 0141 248 5892
E-mail: spf@npanet.co.uk
Website: www.npa.co.uk

Enquiries to: Secretary

Founded: 1919

Organisation type and purpose: Trade association (membership is by subscription), present number of members: 1040.
Trade association for owners of community pharmacies in Scotland.

Access to staff: Contact by letter, by telephone, by fax and by e-mail
Hours: Mon to Fri, 0900 to 1700

Affiliated to: The National Pharmaceutical Association; Mallinson House, 38–42 St Peters Street, St Albans, Hertfordshire, AL1 3NP; tel: 01727 832161; fax: 01727 840858; e-mail: npa@npa.co.uk

SCOTTISH POETRY LIBRARY (SPL)

5 Crichton's Close, Edinburgh, EH8 8DT

Tel: 0131 557 2876
Fax: 0131 557 8393
E-mail: reception@spl.org.uk
Website: www.scottishpoetrylibrary.org.uk

Enquiries to: Librarian
Direct e-mail: julie.johnstone@spl.org.uk

Founded: 1984

Organisation type and purpose: Friends association, present number of members: 750, registered charity (charity number SCO 23311), public library.
Borrowing is free to the general public.

Subject coverage: 20th-century Scottish poetry written in English, Scots and Gaelic; older Scottish poetry; substantial international collection of poetry from Britain, Europe and the rest of the world.

Collection: Edwin Morgan Archive

Non-library collection catalogue: All or part available online

Library catalogue: All or part available online

Publications: Printed, and electronic and video

Access to staff: Contact by letter, by telephone, by fax, by e-mail, in person and via website
Hours: Tue, Wed, Fri, 1000 to 1700; Thu, 1000 to 2000; Sat, 1000 to 1600

Access to building: *Hours:* Tue, Wed, Fri, 1000 to 1700; Thu, 1000 to 2000; Sat, 1000 to 1600

Access for disabled people: Level entry, access to all public areas, toilet facilities

Supported by: Creative Scotland and others

SCOTTISH PRE-SCHOOL PLAY ASSOCIATION (SPPA)

21–23 Granville Street, Glasgow, G3 7EE

Tel: 0141 221 4148
Fax: 0141 221 6043
E-mail: info@sppa.org.uk
Website: www.sppa.org.uk

Enquiries to: Information Officer

Founded: 1966; formerly called Scottish Pre-School Playgroups Association

Organisation type and purpose: Membership association (membership is by subscription), present number of members: 1,100, voluntary organisation, registered charity (charity number SC003725).
SPPA supports community-based early years education and childcare services for children and families.

Subject coverage: The Scottish Pre-school Play Association (SPPA) delivers essential support and guidance to providers of pre-school education and childcare services, including all-day care groups, playgroups, toddler groups and under-fives groups. As a member of SPPA, groups can access a variety of services including an insurance package, a range of early years publications, an information helpline and a quarterly magazine, First Five. SPPA also organises a National Conference which was located in the Glasgow Royal Concert Hall on 4 October 2012.

Trade and statistical information: Annual facts and figures relating to the Association and to member groups

Non-library collection catalogue: All or part available online

Publications: Printed, and electronic and video
Order printed publications from: website: http://www.sppa.org.uk

Publications list: Available online and in print

Access to staff: Contact by letter, by telephone, by fax, by e-mail and in person
Hours: Mon to Fri, 0900 to 1630

Links with: Association of Shetland Playgroups; CALA (Highland); Irish PPA; Northern Ireland PPA; Orkney Pre-School Play Association; PLA (England); Wales PPA

SCOTTISH PUBLIC SERVICES OMBUDSMAN (SPSO)

4 Melville Street, Edinburgh, EH3 7NS

Tel: 0800 377 7330
Fax: 0800 377 7331
E-mail: ask@spso.org.uk
Website: www.spso.org.uk

Enquiries to: SPSO
Direct e-mail: gbyrne@spso.org.uk

Founded: 2002

Organisation type and purpose: Statutory body, appointed by the Crown on the recommendation of the Scottish Parliament.

Subject coverage: The SPSO has two statutory functions. The first is to look at unresolved complaints about public services after they have completed the organisation's complaints procedure. The second is to
improve complaints handling in public services. The SPSO's service is free, independent and
impartial.

Access to staff: Contact by letter, by e-mail and in person
Hours: Mon, Wed to Fri, 0900 to 1700; Tue, 1000 to 1700

SCOTTISH QUALIFICATIONS AUTHORITY (SQA)

The Optima Building, 58 Robertson Street, Glasgow, G2 8DQ

Tel: 0845 279 1000
Fax: 0845 213 5000
E-mail: customer@sqa.org.uk
Website: www.sqa.org.uk

Enquiries to: Customer Contact Centre
Direct tel: 0141 242 2291
Direct fax: 0141 242 2219
Direct e-mail: mike.haggerty@sqa.org.uk

Founded: 1 April 1997; formed from Scottish Examination Board (SEB), Scottish Vocational Educational Council (SCOTVEC)

Organisation type and purpose: Suitable for ages: all.

Subject coverage: Education qualifications in Scotland.

Publications list: Available online and in print

Access to staff: Contact by letter, by telephone, by fax, by e-mail and via website
Hours: Mon to Fri, 0900 to 1700

Other addresses: Scottish Qualifications Authority; Ironmills Road, Dalkeith, Midlothian, EH22 1LE; tel: 0131 663 6601

SCOTTISH RAILWAY PRESERVATION SOCIETY (SRPS)

SRPS Office 17–19 North Street, Bo'ness, West Lothian EH51 0AQ

Tel: 01506 825855
E-mail: office@srps.org.uk
Website: www.srps.org.uk
Website: www.srpsrailtours.com

Enquiries to: SRPS Administrator

Founded: 1961

Organisation type and purpose: The Scottish Railway Preservation Society is a Charitable Company limited by guarantee Scottish Charity No. SCO 02375

Collection: Plates for study
Railway artefacts ranging from railway buildings to locomotives (etc)
Small collection of books on practical aspects of railways and rolling stock, also photographs

Publications: Printed

Access to staff: Contact by letter, by telephone, by fax and by e-mail.
Appointment necessary.
Hours: Mon to Fri, 1000 to 1600

Access for disabled people: Parking provided, ramped entry, toilet facilities

Links with: Heritage Railway Association (HRA); tel: 01707 643568; fax: 01707 643568

SCOTTISH REFUGEE COUNCIL (SRC)

Wellgate House, 200 Cowgate, Edinburgh, EH1 1NQ

Tel: 0131 225 9994
Fax: 0131 225 9997
E-mail: info@scottishrefugeecouncil.org.uk
Website: www.scottishrefugeecouncil.org.uk

Enquiries to: Information Officer
Direct e-mail: media@scottishrefugeecouncil.org.uk
Other contacts: Manager/Policy Development Officer for local services referrals.

Founded: 1985

Organisation type and purpose: Advisory body, voluntary sector organisation, registered charity (charity number SC008639). To assist and advise local authorities and other agencies on all refugee and related issues by providing training, seminars and briefings and assisting with policy development.
To provide advice, information and assistance to asylum seekers and refugees in Scotland. To promote a strategic response to refugee needs. To campaign to ensure Scotland plays a role in meeting the UK's legal and humanitarian obligations under the 1951 UN Convention on Refugees.

Subject coverage: Provides advice, information and legal representation to asylum seekers and refugees in Scotland including information on asylum law and procedures, employment, housing, education, health and welfare.

Publications: Printed

Publications list: Available in print

Access to staff: Contact by letter, by telephone, by fax, by e-mail and via website.
Appointment necessary.
Hours: Mon to Fri, 0900 to 1700

Access for disabled people: Ramped entry, access to all public areas, toilet facilities

Head Office: Scottish Refugee Council; 94 Hope Street, Glasgow, G2 6QA; tel: 0141 248 9799; fax: 0141 243 2499

SCOTTISH RIGHTS OF WAY AND ACCESS SOCIETY (ScotWays)

24 Annandale Street, Edinburgh, EH7 4AN

Tel: 0131 558 1222
Fax: 0131 558 1222
E-mail: info@scotways.com
Website: www.scotways.com

Enquiries to: Access Enquiries Officer
Other contacts: National Secretary; Treasurer; Access Enquiries Assistant; Heritage Paths Project Officer

Founded: 1845; formerly called Scottish Rights of Way Society (year of change 1999)

Organisation type and purpose: National, voluntary organisation.
Registered charity (SC015460)
Membership organisation.
The preservation, defence, restoration and acquisition for the public benefit of rights of access over land in Scotland, including public rights of way and their amenity.

Subject coverage: Public access to the outdoors in Scotland, National Catalogue of Rights of Way, signposting routes, advice on access rights under the Land Reform (Scotland) Act 2003 and public rights of way, publication of maps and guides, Heritage Paths Project.

Collection: Maps and other records of rights of way in Scotland held in 37 volumes and on 122 special 150,000 scale maps; copies available, ask for a quotation of individual routes/maps

Trade and statistical information: Data on access routes, especially rights of way, for every local authority area in Scotland

Publications: Printed

Publications list: Available online and in print

Access to staff: Contact by letter, by telephone, by fax, by e-mail and via website.
Appointment necessary. Non-members charged.
Hours: Mon to Fri, 0900 to 1300

Access for disabled people: Level entry, access to all public areas
Special comments: No disabled toilet facilities.

SCOTTISH RUGBY (SRU)

Formal name: Scottish Rugby Union
Murrayfield, Edinburgh, EH12 5PJ

Tel: 0131 346 5000
Fax: 0131 346 5001
E-mail: feedback@sru.org.uk
Website: www.sru.org.uk

Enquiries to: Human Resources

Founded: 1873

Organisation type and purpose:
International organisation, advisory body, statutory body, membership association.
Governing body of rugby in Scotland.

Subject coverage: Promotion and development of rugby union football in Scotland.

Services for disabled people: Yes – access, toilets and seating. Parking by prior arrangement for Blue Badge holders with Ticket Centre

Collection: Library and museum (undergoing redevelopment)

Publications: Printed

Access to staff: Contact by letter, by telephone, by fax, by e-mail and via website
Hours: Mon to Fri, 0900 to 1700

Member of: International Rugby Board

SCOTTISH RURAL PROPERTY AND BUSINESS ASSOCIATION (SRPBA)

Stuart House, Eskmills Business Park, Musselburgh, Midlothian, EH21 7PB

Tel: 0131 653 5400
Fax: 0131 653 5401
E-mail: info@srpba.com
Website: www.srpba.com

Enquiries to: Chief Executive

Founded: 1906; formerly called Scottish Landowners' Federation (year of change 2004)

Organisation type and purpose:
Membership association (membership is by subscription), present number of members: 3500.

continued overleaf

Subject coverage: Land use advice, legal advice on land management to members only.

Publications: Printed

Access to staff: Contact by letter, by telephone, by fax, by e-mail and via website
Hours: Mon to Thu, 0800 to 1700; Fri, 0800 to 1630

SCOTTISH SALMON PRODUCERS ORGANISATION (SSPO)

Durn, Isla Road, Perth, Tayside, PH2 7HG

Tel: 01738 587000
Fax: 01738 621454
E-mail: enquiries@scottishsalmon.co.uk
Website: www.scottishsalmon.co.uk

Enquiries to: Chief Executive
Direct e-mail: spatten@scottishsalmon.co.uk
Other contacts: Communications Director for all PR and marketing issues.

Founded: 2006

Organisation type and purpose: Trade association (membership is by qualification), present number of members: 50 companies. To promote production of farmed Scottish salmon.

Subject coverage: Farming and production of Scottish salmon.

Trade and statistical information: Salmon production data, import and export data

Publications: Printed

Publications list: Available in print

Access to staff: Contact by letter
Hours: Mon to Fri, 0900 to 1700

SCOTTISH SCHOOL OF REFLEXOLOGY, THE (SSR)

11 Stonefield Park, Ayr, KA7 4HS

Tel: 01292 440730
Fax: 01292 440750
Website: www.reflexscott.co.uk

Enquiries to: Principal

Founded: 1985

Organisation type and purpose: Suitable for ages: 18+, training organisation.
To provide training in knowledge and physical skills to professional level.

Subject coverage: Reflexology and anatomy, physiology, pathology. Magnets and their therapeutic uses, nutritional herbology.

Publications: Printed, and electronic and video

Publications list: Available in print

Access to staff: Contact by letter, by telephone and by fax
Hours: Mon to Thu, 0930 to 1300 and 1415 to 1700; Fri, 0930 to 1300; Sat and Sun, closed

SCOTTISH SCHOOLS EDUCATION RESEARCH CENTRE (SSERC)

Formal name: Scottish Schools Education Research Centre Limited

2 Pitreavie Court, South Pitreavie Business Park, Dunfermline. KY11 8UB

Tel: 01383 626070
Fax: 01383 842793
E-mail: sts@sserc.org.uk
Website: www.sserc.org.uk
Website: www.science3–18.org/sserc

Enquiries to: Chief Executive Officer
Direct e-mail: fred.young@sserc.org.uk

Founded: 1965

Organisation type and purpose: SSERC is a Local Authority shared-service providing support across all 32 Scottish Education Authorities. Our services are available to elected members and officers of Local Authorities, teachers, student teachers and technicians. In addition, the majority of FE colleges and independent schools within Scotland are members of our organisation.

We offer a broad portfolio of services, principally in support of the science and technology areas of the curriculum, including:

health and safety advice for schools and Local Authorities,
professional development programmes for managers, teachers and technicians,
guidance on experiments and practical work,
recommendations on equipment & design of specialist accommodation,
consultancy and technical information,
apparatus testing for safety, performance & conformance with standards,
radiation protection advisory services,
publications including quarterly Bulletins (Primary and Secondary), specialist health and safety guidance, and web-based materials (www.sserc.org.uk).

Subject coverage: It is important that risks are managed responsibly and sensibly. We believe that health and safety legislation should not be a barrier to the provision of valuable learning experiences for young people and we offer a range of training courses and guidance materials which discourage bureaucratic and over-complex methods of risk management.

In addition to our work on management of health and safety, we provide a national programme of
professional development in support of science and technology education. In the period April 2009–March 2012 over 90% of Scottish schools and colleges were represented at one or more of our professional development courses. Such work could not be achieved without the support of a range of partners most notably the Scottish Government and the National Science Learning Centre. In addition, we work closely with the Scottish Technicians Advisory Group to develop a range of specialist courses (levelled and credit-rated by the Scottish Qualifications Authority within the Scottish Curriculum and Qualifications Framework) that will, in time, lead to a Diploma in School Technical Support.

Collection: Selected British and EN standards
Specialised science and technology education journals

Library catalogue: All or part available online and in print

Publications: Printed

Publications list: Available online

Access to staff: Contact by letter, by telephone, by fax, by e-mail, in person and via website. Appointment necessary. Access for members only. Non-members charged.
Hours: Mon to Fri, 0900 to 1700
Special comments: Usually only available to members.

Access to building: Business hours
Hours: Business hours

Access for disabled people: Yes
Hours: Business hours

Funded by: Scottish Local Authorities

SCOTTISH SCREEN ARCHIVE (SSA)

39–41 Montrose Avenue, Hillington Park, Glasgow, G52 4LA

Tel: 0845 366 4600
Fax: 0845 366 4601
E-mail: archive@scottishscreen.com
Website: www.scottishscreen.com
Website: www.pads.ahds.ac.uk:81/SFTACatalogue.html

Enquiries to: Librarian
Direct tel: 0141 337 7407
Direct e-mail: ann.beaton@scottishscreen.com
Other contacts: (1) Access and Admin. Assistant; (2) Production Library Administrator; (3) Curator for (1) Enquiries Broadcasters/general; (2) Public/academic research; (3) Educational.

Founded: 1976; formed from Scottish Screen; formed from Scottish Film and Television Archive (SFTA) (year of change 2001); formerly called Scottish Film Archive (year of change 1997)

Organisation type and purpose: National government body.
Archive.
To locate and preserve moving images made in or about Scotland.

Subject coverage: Non-fiction film material relating to Scotland including documentaries, newsreels, educational, advertising and promotional, industrial, broadcasts and amateur film.

Collection: Film and documentation on the films of Scotland Committee 1938 to 1982
Upper Clyde Shipbuilders 1926 to 1971

Non-library collection catalogue: All or part available online, in-house and in print

Library catalogue: All or part available in-house

Publications: Printed, and electronic and video

Access to staff: Contact by letter, by telephone, by fax and by e-mail. Appointment necessary.
Hours: Mon to Fri, 0900 to 1700

Parent body: Scottish Screen; 249 West George Street, Glasgow, G2 4QE; tel: 0141 302 1700; fax: 0141 302 1711; e-mail: info@scottishscreen.com

SCOTTISH SECONDARY TEACHERS' ASSOCIATION (SSTA)

14 West End Place, Edinburgh, EH11 2ED

Tel: 0131 313 7300
Fax: 0131 346 8057
E-mail: info@ssta.org.uk

Enquiries to: General Secretary

Founded: 1945

Organisation type and purpose: Trade union (membership is by qualification), present number of members: 8000.

Subject coverage: Education in secondary schools in Scotland; general education in Scotland.

Access to staff: Contact by letter, by telephone, by fax and by e-mail. Appointment necessary.
Hours: Mon to Thu, 0900 to 1645; Fri, 0900 to 1615

SCOTTISH SENSORY CENTRE (SSC)

Moray House School of Education, Holyrood Road, Edinburgh, EH8 8AQ

Tel: 0131 651 6501; minicom no. 0131 651 6067
Fax: 0131 651 6502
E-mail: sscmail@ed.ac.uk
Website: www.ssc.education.ed.ac.uk
Website: www.ssc.education.ed.ac.uk/library/list.html

Enquiries to: Resource Library Manager
Direct tel: 0131 651 6069
Other contacts: Administrator

Founded: 1991; created by the merger of Scottish Centre for Education of the Deaf (SCED), Visual Impairment Centre (VIC) (year of change 1991)

Organisation type and purpose: Advisory body, public library, training organisation, educational organisation.
To promote and disseminate effective practices and innovation in the education of children and young people with sensory impairments.

Subject coverage: All aspects of sensory impairment including visual impairment, deaf education, dual sensory impairment and special educational needs.

Information services: Postal Lending Library for members; information enquiries from the public; primary documents available online.

Collection: Resource library contains over 3,000 books, video material, audio cassettes and teaching packs (available for loan to library members)

Library catalogue: All or part available online, in-house and in print

Publications: Printed, and electronic and video
Order printed publications from: Resource Library Manager, Scottish Sensory Centre; tel. 0131 651 6069; e-mail sscmail@ed.ac.uk

Publications list: Available online and in print

Access to staff: Contact by letter, by telephone, by fax, by e-mail and in person. Appointment necessary.
Hours: Mon to Fri, 0930 to 1300 and 1400 to 1630

Access for disabled people: Parking provided, ramped entry and lifts, toilet facilities

Links with: Moray House School of Education; University of Edinburgh; website: http://www.education.ed.ac.uk

SCOTTISH SOCIETY FOR AUTISM (SSA)

Hilton House, Alloa Business Park, Whins Road, Alloa, Clackmannanshire, FK10 3SA

Tel: 01259 720044
Fax: 01259 720051
E-mail: autism@autism-in-scotland.org.uk
Website: www.autism-in-scotland.org.uk

Enquiries to: HR Director

Founded: 1968; formerly called Scottish Society for Autistic Children (SSAC) (year of change 1999)

Organisation type and purpose: Voluntary organisation, registered charity (charity number SC009068).
To ensure the provision of the best possible education, care, support and opportunities for those of all ages with autism, to support families, improve understanding, and develop best practice among carers, professionals and society at large.

Subject coverage: Autism and Aspergers Syndrome.

Information services: Training, advice and support for families and carers of those living with ASD.

Education services: Day and residential school for pupils with ASD.

Publications: Printed

Publications list: Available in print

Access to staff: Contact by letter, by telephone, by fax, by e-mail and via website. Appointment necessary.
Hours: Mon to Thu, 0900 to 1700; Fri, 0900 to 1630

Access for disabled people: Level entry, access to all public areas, toilet facilities

SCOTTISH SOCIETY FOR PSYCHICAL RESEARCH (SSPR)

5 Church Wynd, Kingskettle, By Cupar, Fife, KY15 7PS

Tel: 01337 830387
Fax: 01337 830387
E-mail: archie.lawrie@ukgateway.net

Enquiries to: Honorary Secretary

Founded: 1987

Organisation type and purpose: Learned society, registered charity (charity number SCO 20421), research organisation.

Subject coverage: All types of phenomena known as paranormal or parapsychological, ghosts, poltergeists.

Collection: CD and tape library (members only)

Publications: Printed, and electronic and video

Access to staff: Contact by letter, by telephone, by fax and by e-mail
Hours: 0900 to 2100, later in an emergency

SCOTTISH SOCIETY FOR THE PREVENTION OF CRUELTY TO ANIMALS (Scottish SPCA)

Braehead Mains, 603 Queensferry Road, Edinburgh, EH4 6EA

Tel: 0131 339 0222
Fax: 0131 339 4777
E-mail: enquiries@scottishspca.org
Website: www.scottishspca.org

Enquiries to: Public Relations Director
Other contacts: Press Officer

Founded: 1839; formerly called Aberdeen APCA, Glasgow Dog and Cat Home

Organisation type and purpose: National organisation, advisory body, membership association (membership is by subscription), voluntary organisation, registered charity (charity number SC 006467), suitable for ages: nursery to adult.
Main aim is to prevent animal cruelty and to encourage kindness and humanity in their treatment.

Subject coverage: Prevention of cruelty to animals, animal care, the law regarding animals, education in kind and humane treatment.

Publications: Printed

Access to staff: Contact by letter, by telephone, by fax and by e-mail. Appointment necessary.
Hours: Mon to Fri, 0900 to 1700

Member of: Eurogroup and World Society for the Protection of Animals (WSPA)

SCOTTISH SOCIETY OF THE HISTORY OF MEDICINE (SSHM)

c/o Dr Nigel Malcolm-Smith, 13 Craiglea Drive, Edinburgh, EH10 5PB

Tel: 0131 447 2572
E-mail: nigel@malcolm-smith43.wanadoo.co.uk
Website: www.st-andrews.ac.uk/~sshm

Enquiries to: Honorary Secretary

Founded: 1948

Organisation type and purpose: Learned society (membership is by subscription), present number of members: 200.

Subject coverage: History of medicine.

Collection: Dr Haldane P Tait's book collection is held in the Royal College of Physicians Library, Queen Street, Edinburgh. (subject Paediatrics and Public Health)

Publications: Printed

Access to staff: Contact by letter, by telephone and by e-mail
Hours: Mon to Fri, 0900 to 1700

Affiliated to: British Society for the History of Medicine

SCOTTISH SPINA BIFIDA ASSOCIATION (SSBA)

The Dan Young Building, 6 Craighalbert Way, Cumbernauld, G68 0LS

continued overleaf

Tel: 01236 794500
Fax: 01236 736435
E-mail: mail@ssba.org.uk
Website: ourworld.compuserve.com/homepages/ssbahq
Website: www.ssba.org.uk

Enquiries to: Family Support Service
Direct tel: 01236 794516
Direct e-mail: familysupport@ssba.org.uk

Founded: 1965

Organisation type and purpose:
Membership association, present number of members: 3,500, registered charity (charity number SCO 13328).
To increase public awareness and understanding of spina bifida and/or hydrocephalus. Aims to secure provision for the needs of those with spina bifida and/or hydrocephalus and those of their families.

Subject coverage: Spina bifida, hydrocephalus and allied disorders.

Publications: Printed

Publications list: Available online and in print

Access to staff: Contact by letter, by telephone, by fax, by e-mail, in person and via website
Hours: Mon to Fri, 0900 to 1700

Also at: Fundraising Office, Scottish Spina Bifida Association; The Dan Young Building, 6 Craighalbert Way, Cumbernauld, G68 0LS; tel: 01236 794500; fax: 01236 736435; e-mail: fundraising@ssba.org.uk; website: http://www.ssba.org.uk
Scottish Spina Bifida Association – Family Support Department; The Dan Young Building, 6 Craighalbert Way, Cumbernauld, G68 0LS; tel: 0645 11 11 12 (lo-call routes); fax: 01236 736435; e-mail: familysupport@ssba.org.uk; website: http://www.ssba.org.uk

SCOTTISH SPORTS ASSOCIATION (SSA)

Caledonia House, South Gyle, Edinburgh, EH12 9DQ

Tel: 0131 339 8785
Fax: 0131 339 5168
E-mail: david@info-ssa.org.uk

Enquiries to: Executive Administrator
Other contacts: Chairman

Founded: 1992; formerly called Confederation of National Governing Bodies of Scottish Sport (year of change 1992)

Organisation type and purpose:
Membership association (membership is by election or invitation), present number of members: 78.
To represent the interests of Scottish Sports Governing Bodies.

Subject coverage: Governing Bodies of sport in Scotland.

Publications: Printed

Access to staff: Contact by letter, by telephone, by fax and by e-mail
Hours: Mon to Thu, 0900 to 1700

Access for disabled people: Parking provided, level entry, access to all public areas, toilet facilities

SCOTTISH SQUASH LIMITED

Caledonia House, 1 Redheughs Rigg, South Gyle, Edinburgh, EH12 9DQ

Tel: 0131 317 7343
Fax: 0131 317 7734
E-mail: scottishsquash@aol.com

Enquiries to: Administration Manager

History of institution: formerly called Scottish Squash Rackets Association (SSRA)

Organisation type and purpose:
Membership association.

Subject coverage: Player rankings, events, sources of finance, advice on construction and maintenance, equipment, rules, coaching, training courses, refereeing, history of squash, playing records, fitness.

Publications: Electronic and video

Affiliated to: European Squash Rackets Federation (ESRF); World Squash Federation (WSF)

SCOTTISH SUB-AQUA CLUB (ScotSAC)

Caledonia House, 1 Redheughs Rigg, South Gyle, Edinburgh, EH12 9DQ

Tel: 0131 625 4404
Fax: 0131 317 7202
E-mail: hq@scotsac.com
Website: www.scotsac.com

Enquiries to: Administrator

Founded: 1953

Organisation type and purpose:
Membership association (membership is by subscription), present number of members: 1,900.
National governing body of the sport.

Subject coverage: Information on history of diving, dive training methods, diving equipment, salvage methods, underwater medicine, dive sites, construction of ships, underwater life, marine archaeology, video on diving, underwater sport.

Collection: Library of 760 books on diving, etc.

Publications: Printed

Publications list: Available in print

Access to staff: Contact by letter, by telephone, by fax, by e-mail and via website
Hours: Mon to Thu, 0900 to 1700; Fri, 0900 to 1630

Access for disabled people: Level entry, toilet facilities

SCOTTISH TEXT SOCIETY (STS)

25 Buccleuch Place, Edinburgh EH8 9LN

Tel: 0115 951 5922
Fax: 0115 951 5924
E-mail: editorialsecretary@scottishtextsociety.org
Website: www.scottishtextsociety.org

Enquiries to: Editorial Secretary

Founded: 1882

Organisation type and purpose: Learned society, publishing house.
To further the study and teaching of Scottish literature, its language and history, in particular by publishing editions of original texts.

Subject coverage: Scottish literature especially, although not exclusively, of the medieval and early modern period.

Non-library collection catalogue: All or part available online

Library catalogue: All or part available in-house

Publications: Printed
Order printed publications from: Boydell and Brewer Ltd, PO Box 9, Woodbridge, Suffolk, IP12 3DF; tel. 01394 610600; fax 01394 610316; e-mail trading@boydell.co.uk

Publications list: Available online and in print

Access to staff: Contact by letter, by e-mail and via website. Appointment necessary.
Hours: Mon to Fri, 0900 to 1700

Also at: Scottish Text Society; c/o Editorial Secretary, 25 Buccleuch Place, Edinburgh EH8 9LN

SCOTTISH TOURIST GUIDES ASSOCIATION (STGA)

Norrie's House, 18b Broad Street, Stirling, FK8 1EF

Tel: 01786 447784
Fax: 01786 447784
E-mail: info@stga.co.uk
Website: www.stga.co.uk

Enquiries to: Administrator
Other contacts: Booking Secretary for booking guides.

Founded: 1959

Organisation type and purpose:
Professional body (membership is by subscription, qualification), present number of members: 320, service industry, suitable for ages: 25 to 75.

Subject coverage: Specialised knowledge of Scotland past and present.
Guides are available to conduct tours throughout Scotland.

Publications: Printed

Publications list: Available in print

Access to staff: Contact by letter, by telephone, by fax, by e-mail and via website. Appointment necessary.
Hours: Mon to Fri, 0900 to 1700
Special comments: Please provide sae for reply.

Centralised booking service: STGA booking service; tel: 01786 451953; fax: 01786 451953; e-mail: bookings@stga.co.uk

SCOTTISH TRAMWAY AND TRANSPORT SOCIETY (STTS)

PO Box 7342, Glasgow, G51 4YQ

E-mail: stts.glasgow@virgin.net
Website: www.scottishtransport.org

Enquiries to: General Secretary
Direct tel: 0141 445 3883

Founded: 1951

Organisation type and purpose: Voluntary organisation.

Subject coverage: Scottish tramways, trolleybuses and omnibuses. Glasgow Underground Railway, Strathclyde and Lothian Electric Trains.

Collection: R B Parr photographic collection Scottish Road Public Transport photographic collection

Publications: Printed, and electronic and video

Publications list: Available online and in print

Access to staff: Contact by letter, by telephone, by fax and by e-mail
Hours: Mon to Fri, 0900 to 1700

Affiliated to: AMTUIR (France); Tramway Museum Society; Transport Trust

SCOTTISH TRANSPORT STUDIES GROUP (STSG)

2 Dean Path, Edinburgh, EH4 3BA

E-mail: admin@stsg.org
Website: www.stsg.org

Enquiries to: Secretary
Direct e-mail: admin@stsg.org
Other contacts: Chair

Founded: 1984

Organisation type and purpose:
Membership association (membership is by subscription), present number of members: 130, registered charity.
To stimulate interest in, and awareness of, the transport function and its importance for the Scottish economy; to encourage contacts between operators, public bodies, users, academia and other organisations and individuals with interests in transport in a Scottish context; to issue publications and organise conferences and seminars related to transport policy and research.

Subject coverage: Transport policy in Scotland.

Non-library collection catalogue: All or part available online and in print

Library catalogue: All or part available online and in print

Publications: Printed, and electronic and video
Order electronic and video publications from: www.stsg.org

Publications list: Available online

Access to staff: Contact by letter, by e-mail and via website. Appointment necessary.
Hours: Mon to Fri, 0900 to 1700

SCOTTISH UNIVERSITIES ENVIRONMENTAL RESEARCH CENTRE (SUERC)

Scottish Enterprise Technology Park, Rankine Avenue, East Kilbride, South Lanarkshire, G75 0QF

Tel: 01355 270139; 01355 270102
Fax: 01355 229898
E-mail: director@suerc.gla.ac.uk
Website: www.gla.ac.uk/suerc

Enquiries to: Director
Direct tel: 01355 223332

Founded: 2002; formerly called Scottish Universities Research and Reactor Centre (year of change 2002)

Organisation type and purpose: A collaborative facility operated jointly under a consortium agreement between the University of Glasgow and University of Edinburgh. It hosts five Natural Environment Research Council (NERC) Facilities that are available to UK scientists through competitive application to the relevant Steering Committees. The SUERC Accelerator Mass Spectrometer Laboratory is recognised by NERC as a suitable facility to undertake NERC-funded science.

Subject coverage: Environmental research.

Access to staff: Contact by letter, by telephone, by fax, by e-mail, in person and via website

SCOTTISH URBAN ARCHAEOLOGICAL TRUST (SUAT)

55 South Methven Street, Perth, Tayside, PH1 5NX

Tel: 01738 622393
Fax: 01738 631626
Website: www.suat.demon.co.uk

Enquiries to: Director

Founded: 1982

Organisation type and purpose: Registered charity, research organisation, consultancy. Archaeological research.

Subject coverage: Urban archaeology in Scotland, general archaeology in Scotland.

Access to staff: Contact by letter, by telephone and by fax. Appointment necessary.
Hours: Mon to Fri, 0830 to 1630

Member of: Council for British Archaeology; Council for Scottish Archaeology; Tayside and Fife Archaeological Committee

SCOTTISH WATER

Castle House, 6 Castle Drive, Carnegie Campus, Dunfermline, Fife, KY11 8GG

Tel: 0845 601 8855
E-mail: customer.service@scottishwater.co.uk
Website: www.scottishwater.co.uk

Enquiries to: Customer Services

History of institution: formed from East of Scotland Water (ESW), North of Scotland Water (NoSWA), West of Scotland Water (W'SWA), date of change, 1 April 2002

Subject coverage: Land analysis, environment management, risk analysis, engineering consultancy, water and waste water analysis, waste management, pipeline installation, water charges, recreation, site surveys and site investigation, education.

Library catalogue: All or part available in-house

Publications: Printed

Access to staff: Contact by letter, by telephone, by e-mail and via website
Hours: Mon to Fri, 0900 to 1700

Access to building: No access other than to staff

Access for disabled people: Parking provided, level entry, toilet facilities

SCOTTISH WATER – EDINBURGH (SW)

55 Buckstone Terrace, Fairmilehead, Edinburgh, EH10 6XH

Tel: 0845 601 8855
Fax: 0131 445 5040
E-mail: customer.services@scottishwater.co.uk
Website: www.scottishwater.co.uk

Enquiries to: Customer Service Adviser
Direct tel: 0845 601 8855
Direct e-mail: customer.services@scottishwater.co.uk
Other contacts: Corporate Communications for press enquiries.

Founded: 2002

Organisation type and purpose: Statutory body.

Subject coverage: Supply of water and waste water services to the whole of Scotland

Collection: Small library of books and reports relating to water and waste water services and the water industry. For internal use only.

Library catalogue: All or part available in-house

Publications: Printed

Publications list: Available online

Access to staff: Contact by letter, by telephone, by fax, by e-mail, in person and via website. Appointment necessary.
Hours: Mon to Fri, 0900 to 1700

Access for disabled people: *Hours:* Mon to Fri, 0900 to 1700

Area Offices: Inverness Area Office and Stores; 31 Henderson Drive, Longman North, Inverness, IV1 1TR; tel: 0845 601 8855; e-mail: customer.services@scottishwater.co.uk; Scottish Water; Bullion House, Invergowrie, Dundee, DD2 5BB; tel: 0845 601 8855; e-mail: customer.services@scottishwater.co.uk; Scottish Water; Kingshill House, Arnhall Business Park, Westhill, Aberdeen, AB32 6UF; tel: 0845 601 8855; e-mail: customer.services@scottishwater.co.uk; Scottish Water; 419 Balmore Road, Glasgow, G22 6NU; tel: 0845 601 8855; e-mail: customer.services@scottishwater.co.uk

Head Office: Scottish Water; Castle House, 6 Castle Drive, Carnegie Campus, Dunfermline, KY11 8GG; tel: 0845 601 8855; e-mail: customer.services@scottishwater.co.uk

Subsidiary body: Scottish Water Scientific; Heriot-Watt Research Park, Avenue North, Edinburgh, EH14 4AP; tel: 0845 601 8855; e-mail: customer.services@scottishwater.co.uk

SCOTTISH WATER SKI ASSOCIATION (SWSA)

Townhill Country Park, Townhill, Dunfermline, Fife, KY12 0HT

continued overleaf

Tel: 01383 620123
Fax: 01383 620122
E-mail: info@swsc.fsbusiness.co.uk
Website: www.waterskiscotland.co.uk

Enquiries to: Administrator
Other contacts: National Co-ordinator for first point of contact.

Founded: 1960; formerly called (SWSA) (year of change 1998)

Organisation type and purpose:
Membership association (membership is by subscription), present number of members: 250, voluntary organisation.
To teach and instruct water skiing and wakeboarding including good driving practice.

Subject coverage: All aspects relating to the sports of water skiing and waterboarding.

Non-library collection catalogue: All or part available online

Library catalogue: All or part available online

Access to staff: Contact by letter, by fax and by e-mail
Hours: Tue to Fri, 1300 till dusk; Sat, Sun, 1000 till dusk
Special comments: Closed Monday.

Access to building: No prior appointment required

Access for disabled people: Parking provided, ramped entry, level entry, access to all public areas, toilet facilities

SCOTTISH WIDER ACCESS PROGRAMME (SWAPWest)

300 Cathedral Street, Glasgow, G1 2TG

Tel: 0141 553 2471
Fax: 0141 552 6090
E-mail: swapwest@btconnect.com
Website: www.swap2highereducation.com

Enquiries to: Director

Founded: 1987

Organisation type and purpose:
Membership association (membership is by subscription), present number of members: 30, registered charity (charity number SCO 25833), suitable for adults.

Subject coverage: All aspects of education for adults with few or no formal qualifications.

Access to staff: Contact by letter, by telephone, by fax, by e-mail and via website
Hours: Mon to Fri, 0900 to 1700

SCOTTISH WILDLIFE TRUST (SWT)

Cramond House, 3 Kirk Cramond, off Cramond Glebe Road, Edinburgh, EH4 6HZ

Tel: 0131 312 7765
Fax: 0131 312 8705
E-mail: enquiries@swt.org.uk
Website: www.swt.org.uk

Enquiries to: Receptionist
Other contacts: Communications Manager (for press and media)

Founded: 1964

Organisation type and purpose: Advisory body, membership association (membership is by subscription), present number of members: 31,000, voluntary organisation, registered charity (charity number SC005792), training organisation, consultancy, publishing house.
Campaigning environment body, land managers.
The protection of all forms of Scottish wildlife and the Scottish environment.

Subject coverage: Conservation of all forms of wildlife in Scotland, land use for wildlife interest, biological surveying, environmental education, reserves management, practical land management.

Non-library collection catalogue: All or part available in-house

Library catalogue: All or part available in-house

Publications: Printed

Access to staff: Contact by letter, by telephone, by fax, by e-mail and via website. Appointment necessary.
Hours: Mon to Fri, 0900 to 1700

Administers: 123 reserves, including three visitor centres

Links with: People's Postcode Lottery; Scottish Environment Link; Scottish National Heritage; The Scottish Executive; Wildlife Trusts Partnership

SCOTTISH WOMEN'S AID

2nd Floor, 132 Rose Street, Edinburgh, EH2 3JD

Tel: 0131 226 6606
Fax: 0131 226 2996
E-mail: contact@scottishwomensaid.org.uk
Website: www.scottishwomensaid.org.uk

Organisation type and purpose:
Membership association, voluntary organisation, registered charity (charity number SC001099), training organisation.

Subject coverage: Information, support and refuge for women, children and young people who have been affected by domestic abuse.

Publications: Printed

Publications list: Available online and in print

Access to staff: Contact by letter, by telephone, by fax, by e-mail and via website. Appointment necessary.
Hours: Mon to Fri, 1000 to 1600; except Tue, 1300 to 1600

Access for disabled people: Parking provided, ramped entry, level entry, access to all public areas, toilet facilities

Has: network of 39 local groups throughout Scotland

SCOTTISH WOMEN'S FOOTBALL (SWF)

Hampden Park, Glasgow, G42 9DF

Tel: 0141 620 4580
Fax: 0141 620 4581
E-mail: swf@scottish-football.com
Website: www.scottishwomensfootball.com

Enquiries to: Executive Administrator

Founded: 1972; formerly called Scottish Women's Football Association

Organisation type and purpose:
Membership association (membership is by subscription), present number of members: 3,000.

Subject coverage: Women's and girls' football.

Access to staff: Contact by letter, by telephone, by fax and by e-mail. Appointment necessary.
Hours: Mon to Fri, 0900 to 1700

SCOTTISH WOMEN'S RURAL INSTITUTES (SWRI)

42 Heriot Row, Edinburgh, EH3 6ES

Tel: 0131 225 1724
Fax: 0131 225 8129
E-mail: swri@swri.demon.co.uk
Website: www.swri.org.uk

Enquiries to: General Secretary

Founded: 1917

Organisation type and purpose:
Membership association (membership is by subscription), present number of members: 26,000, voluntary organisation, registered charity (charity number SCO 11901), suitable for ages: 12+, training organisation, consultancy.

Subject coverage: Cookery, crafts, village history.

Collection: Village Histories Collection (histories of many villages in Scotland)

Publications: Printed

Access to staff: Contact by letter, by telephone, by fax, by e-mail and in person
Hours: Mon to Thu, 0900 to 1700; Fri, 0900 to 1530

Access to building: No access other than to staff, prior appointment required

Member organisation of: Associated Country Women of the World

SCOTTISH YOUTH HOSTELS ASSOCIATION (SYHA)

7 Glebe Crescent, Stirling, FK8 2JA

Tel: 01786 891400
Fax: 01786 891333
E-mail: syha@syha.org.uk
Website: www.syha.org.uk

Enquiries to: Public Relations Manager
Direct e-mail: marketing@syha.org.uk

Founded: 1931

Organisation type and purpose: Voluntary organisation, registered charity (charity number SCO 13138).

Subject coverage: Low cost holiday accommodation for all ages; recreational and activity holidays for young people; holiday itineraries using youth hostels.

Publications: Printed

Access to staff: Contact by letter, by telephone, by fax, by e-mail, in person and via website
Hours: Mon to Fri, 0900 to 1700

Access to building: No prior appointment required

Affiliated to: International Youth Hostels Federation

SCOTTISH YOUTH THEATRE (SYT)

105 Brunswick Street, Glasgow, G1 1TF

Tel: 0141 552 3988
Fax: 0141 552 7615
E-mail: info@scottishyouththeatre.org
Website: www.scottishyouththeatre.org

Enquiries to: Marketing Officer
Direct e-mail: emma@scottishyouththeatre.org

Founded: 1976

Organisation type and purpose: Registered charity (charity number SCO 14283), suitable for ages: 3 to 25.
National arts organisation.
Giving children and young people in Scotland the opportunity to reach their creative potential through a quality theatre arts experience.

Subject coverage: Theatre, arts, drama, theatrical training, directing, acting, movement, choreography, technical theatre/stage management, musical theatre.

Education services: Contact: karenm@scottishyouththeatre.org

Publications: Electronic and video

Access to staff: Contact by letter, by telephone, by e-mail, in person and via website
Hours: Mon to Fri, 1000 to 1730

Funded by: Glasgow City Council (GCC); Scottish Arts Council (SAC)

Member organisation of: Federation of Scottish Theatres (FST); Independent Theatre Council (ITC)

SCOUT ASSOCIATION

Gilwell Park, Bury Road, Chingford, London, E4 7QW

Tel: 0845 300 1818
Fax: 020 8433 7103
E-mail: scoutbase@scoutbase.org.uk
Website: www.scoutbase.org.uk

Enquiries to: Public Relations Officer

Founded: 1907

Organisation type and purpose: International organisation, membership association, present number of members: 554,440 members in the UK, registered charity.

Subject coverage: Scout training; outdoor pursuits, skills training and service to the community; needs of the physically handicapped and slow learners; youth education.

Collection: Archives of 90 years of scouting

Publications: Printed, and electronic and video

Publications list: Available online

Access to staff: Contact by letter, by telephone, by fax, by e-mail and via website. Appointment necessary.
Hours: Mon to Fri, 0800 to 2000; Sat 0900 to 1200

Close association with the: Guides Association

Member of: National Council for Voluntary Youth Services; World Scout Bureau in Geneva

SCOUTS SCOTLAND

Formal name: The Scottish Council The Scout Association

Fordell Firs, Hillend, near Dunfermline, Fife, KY11 7HQ

Tel: 01383 419073
Fax: 01383 414892
E-mail: shq@scouts-scotland.org.uk
Website: www.scouts-scotland.org.uk

Enquiries to: Chief Executive

Organisation type and purpose: Membership association (membership is by subscription), present number of members: 41,261, registered charity (Scottish charity number SC017511), training organisation.
The physical, intellectual, social and spiritual development of young people.

Subject coverage: Development programmes and outdoor activities for young people; training of voluntary adult leaders.

Publications: Printed

Access to staff: Contact by letter, by telephone, by fax, by e-mail and via website
Hours: Mon to Fri, 0900 to 1700
Special comments: Prior appointment recommended.

Affiliated to: Scout Association UK; Gilwell Park, Chingford, London, E4 7QW; tel: 020 8433 7100; fax: 020 8433 7103; e-mail: scout.association@scout.org.uk

SCREENWRITERS' WORKSHOP (SW)

Euroscript Ltd, 64 Hemingford Road, London, N1 1DB

Tel: 07958 244 656
E-mail: ask@euroscript.co.uk
Website: www.lsw.org.uk/

Enquiries to: Administrator
Direct e-mail: screenoffice@tiscali.co.uk

Founded: 1983; formerly called London Screenwriters Workshop (LSW) (year of change 1998)

Organisation type and purpose: National organisation, membership association (membership is by subscription), present number of members: 800 approx, training organisation.
To train writers of cinema and TV scripts and offer industry information and networking opportunities.

Subject coverage: Screenwriting for cinema and TV.
Information on writing and marketing scripts.

Access to staff: Contact by letter, by telephone, by e-mail and via website. Appointment necessary.
Hours: Mon to Fri, 0900 to 1700
Special comments: By arrangement or at times of advertised meetings, workshops and seminars.

SCRIPTURE UNION (SU)

207–209 Queensway, Bletchley, Milton Keynes, Buckinghamshire, MK2 2EB

Tel: 01908 856000
Fax: 01908 856111
E-mail: info@scriptureunion.org.uk
Website: www.scriptureunion.org.uk

Enquiries to: Managing Director

Founded: 1867

Organisation type and purpose: International organisation, voluntary organisation, registered charity (charity number 213422), training organisation.
Christian missionary society, member of the Evangelical Alliance.
Evangelising and discipling children, young people and families through school work, missions, holidays, bible ministries, training and resources.

Subject coverage: Christian outreach to children, young people and families through schools, churches, holidays and missions.
Development for church members through training, publications and other resources.

Publications: Printed, and electronic and video
Order printed publications from: Scripture Union Mail Order, PO Box 5148, MLO, Milton Keynes, MK2 2YX; tel: 01980 856006; fax: 01980 856020; e-mail: subs@scriptureunion.org.uk

Publications list: Available online and in print

Access to staff: Contact by letter, by telephone, by fax, by e-mail and via website
Hours: Mon to Fri, 0900 to 1700

Access to building: No prior appointment required

SEA FISH INDUSTRY AUTHORITY (SEAFISH)

18 Logie Mill, Logie Green Road, Edinburgh, EH7 4HS

Tel: 0131 558 3331
Fax: 0131 558 1442
E-mail: seafish@seafish.co.uk
Website: www.seafish.co.uk
Website: www.seafish.co.uk/education

Founded: 1981; formed from Herring Industry Board (HIB) and White Fish Authority (WFA)

Organisation type and purpose: Advisory body, statutory body, training organisation, consultancy, research organisation.
Statutory body; accountable to the Department for Environment, Food and Rural Affairs for broad activities, but funded largely by the fish industry.
The Authority works with the fish industry to meet the demands of consumers, to raise standards throughout the industry, to improve the efficiency and unity of the industry, and to secure a prosperous future for all fish industry sectors. The Authority is

continued overleaf

the Industry Designated Body for training within all sectors of the fish industry, and provides a forum for discussion between sectors.

Subject coverage: Fishery economics; fish industry statistics (trade, landings, consumption, employment etc), infrastructure economics; fishery management; fish stocks and their assessment; marketing of fish within the UK and abroad; quality assurance throughout the fish industry; technology of fish processing; safety and legal compliance surveys of fishing vessels; grants and loans to the fish industry; EU legislation, and perspective on the UK fish industry; training of workers in all industry sectors; studies of fishing gear behaviour; mariculture.

Collection: Collection of fisheries statistical publications from Europe, North America, and also international in scope

Trade and statistical information: Data on UK imports and exports of fish and fish products, data on fish landings into the UK, data on household consumption of fish and fish products in the UK, data on fish landings and trade of European and North American countries (variable information in this case)

Non-library collection catalogue: All or part available in-house

Library catalogue: All or part available in-house

Publications: Printed, and electronic and video

Publications list: Available online and in print

Access to staff: Contact by letter, by telephone, by fax, by e-mail and via website. Appointment necessary.
Hours: Mon to Fri, 0900 to 1700

Access to building: No prior appointment required

Access for disabled people: Ramped entry, toilet facilities

Branches at: Sea Fish Industry Authority; Humber Seafood Institute, Origin Way, Europarc, Grimsby, DN37 9TU; tel: 01472 252300; fax: 01472 268792; e-mail: seafish@seafish.co.uk

SEAFACS INFORMATION AND RESEARCH (SIR)

PO Box 317, Welwyn Garden City, Hertfordshire, AL8 6DP

Tel: 01707 334192
E-mail: seafacs@sir.co.uk
Website: www.sir.co.uk

Enquiries to: Manager

Founded: 1985

Organisation type and purpose: Information Broker, consultancy.

Subject coverage: Shipping, marine insurance, commodities.

Publications: Electronic and video

Access to staff: Contact by letter, by telephone, by e-mail and via website. All charged.
Hours: Mon to Fri, 0930 to 1730

Access to building: No access other than to staff

SEASHELL TRUST

Stanley Road, Cheadle Hulme, Cheshire, SK8 6RQ

Tel: 0161 610 0100
Fax: 0161 610 0101
E-mail: info@seashelltrust.org.uk
Website: www.seashelltrust.org.uk

Enquiries to: School/College Secretary
Other contacts: Principal & Chief Executive

Founded: 1825; formerly called Royal School for the Deaf

Organisation type and purpose: Registered charity (charity number 1092655), school, college and care home provider.
To provide a happy and secure environment for pupils and students in school, college and residence and for the service users at Griffin Lodge; to provide alternative and augmentative communication systems to ensure learners and service users are able to access a communication system appropriate to their needs; to provide an extended curriculum and activities that meet the functional and developmental needs of individuals and promote their independence; to encourage their participation in the local and wider community; to realise individual potential by providing challenges and experiences to develop self-esteem and confidence.

Subject coverage: Operates Royal School Manchester, a day and residential, co-educational, non-maintained special school; Royal College Manchester, an independent specialist college on the same campus that caters for learners of over 19 years; and Griffin Lodge, a residential care home in the community for 12 young adults with complex learning and social communication needs, most of whom are also deaf.

Publications: Electronic and video
Order electronic and video publications from: Downloadable from website

Publications list: Available online

Access to staff: Contact by letter, by telephone, by fax, by e-mail and via website

SEASONAL AFFECTIVE DISORDER ASSOCIATION (SADA)

PO Box 989, Steyning, West Sussex, BN44 3HG

Tel: 01903 814942 (recorded message)
Fax: 01903 879939
Website: www.sada.org.uk

Enquiries to: Administrator

Founded: 1987

Organisation type and purpose: Membership association (membership is by subscription), present number of members: c. 1800, voluntary organisation, registered charity (charity number 800917).

Subject coverage: Depression related to lack of sunlight.

Publications: Printed

Publications list: Available in print

Access to staff: Contact by letter and by fax
Hours: Mon to Fri, 0900 to 1700

SEDGEMOOR DISTRICT COUNCIL

Bridgwater House, King Square, Bridgwater, Somerset, TA6 3AR

Tel: 01278 435435
Fax: 01278 446412

Enquiries to: Media Relations Officer

Organisation type and purpose: Local government.

SEFTON LIBRARY AND INFORMATION SERVICES

Pavilion Buildings, 99–105 Lord Street, Southport, Merseyside, PR8 1RJ

Tel: 01704 533133
Fax: 0151 934 2370
E-mail: library.service@leisure.sefton.gov.uk
Website: www.sefton.gov.uk

Enquiries to: Head of Library and Information Services

Founded: 1974

Organisation type and purpose: Local government body, public library.

Library catalogue: All or part available online

Access to staff: Contact by letter, by telephone, by fax, by e-mail, in person and via website. Appointment necessary.

Access for disabled people: Ramped entry

Parent body: Sefton Metropolitan Borough Council

SELDEN SOCIETY

School of Law, Queen Mary University of London, Mile End Road, London, E1 4NS

Tel: 020 7882 3968
Fax: 020 7882 7042
E-mail: selden-society@qmul.ac.uk
Website: www.selden-society.qmul.ac.uk

Enquiries to: Secretary

Founded: 1887

Organisation type and purpose: Learned society (membership is by subscription), present number of members: 1,700, registered charity (charity number 211536), research organisation, publishing house.
Promotion of research into history of English law, and of legal profession, institutions, etc.

Subject coverage: History of English law and legal institutions, legal literature and records, palaeography, bibliography, history of the legal profession, legal biography; translation, transcription and evaluation of legal manuscripts.

Collection: Own publications 1887–2010

Publications: Printed

Publications list: Available online and in print

Access to staff: Contact by letter, by telephone, by fax, by e-mail and via website.

Appointment necessary.
Hours: Mon, Tue, Thu, 0900 to 1700

SELECT (ECAofS)

Formal name: The Electrical Contractors' Association of Scotland

The Walled Garden, Bush Estate, Midlothian, EH26 0SB

Tel: 0131 445 5577
Fax: 0131 445 5548
E-mail: admin@select.org.uk
Website: www.select.org.uk

Enquiries to: Head of External Affairs

Founded: 1900

Organisation type and purpose: Trade association (membership is by qualification). To represent the electrical, electronic and communications systems industry. To advance and promote members interests. To respond to the key strategic issues facing the industry and the Association.

Subject coverage: Electrical installation, safety and security systems, information technology, telecommunications, electronics, industrial relations and employment law matters; commercial and contractual matters; education, training and health and safety matters; management; marketing, technical advice and on-site inspections.

Publications: Printed

Publications list: Available in print

Access to staff: Contact by letter, by telephone, by fax, by e-mail and in person
Hours: Mon to Fri, 0900 to 1700
Special comments: Charges to non-members under certain circumstances.

Access for disabled people: Parking provided, level entry, access to all public areas, toilet facilities

Member of: International Association of Electrical Contractors (AIE); Specialist Engineering Contractors Group

Subsidiary body: Scottish Electrical Contractors Insurance Company

SELEX GALILEO LTD

300 Capability Green, Luton, LU1 3PG

Tel: 01582 886135
Fax: 01582 795861
E-mail: dawn.couzens@selexgalileo.com
Website: www.selexgalileo.com

Other contacts: Information Resources Officers (for departmental staff)

History of institution: formerly called SELEX Sensors and Airborne Systems Ltd; formerly called BAE Systems Avionics Ltd; formerly called GEC Marconi Ltd (year of change 1998); formerly called Marconi Electronic Systems (year of change 1999)

Organisation type and purpose: International organisation, manufacturing industry.

Subject coverage: Defence electronics, aerospace engineering and technology.

Non-library collection catalogue: All or part available in-house

Library catalogue: All or part available in-house

Access to staff: Contact by letter, by telephone, by fax and by e-mail
Hours: Mon to Thu, 0845 to 1715; Fri, 0845 to 1645
Special comments: No personal visitors. Most information restricted to employees only.

Part of: Finmeccanica

SENSE

101 Pentonville Road, London, N1 9LG

Tel: 0845 127 0060; 0845 127 0062 (textphone)
Fax: 0845 127 0061
E-mail: info@sense.org.uk
Website: www.sense.org.uk

Enquiries to: Information and Advice Service
Direct tel: 0845 127 0066
Direct e-mail: info@sense.org.uk

Founded: 1955

Organisation type and purpose: National organisation, membership organisation, voluntary organisation, registered charity (charity number 289868).
Leading national charity that supports and campaigns for children and adults who are deafblind.

Subject coverage: Provides expert advice and information as well as specialist services to deafblind people, their families, carers and the professionals who work with them; supports people who have sensory impairments with additional disabilities.

Publications: Printed
Order printed publications from: website: http://www.sense.org.uk

Access to staff: Contact by letter, by telephone, by fax, by e-mail and via website
Hours: Mon to Thu, 0900 to 1730; Fri, 0900 to 1700

Access to building: *Hours:* Mon to Fri, 0900 to 1700

Access for disabled people: Wheelchair access, entry ramp, lift to first floor

SEQUAL TRUST

3 Ploughman's Corner, Wharf Road, Ellesmere, Shropshire, SY12 0EJ

Tel: 01691 624222
Fax: 01691 624222
E-mail: info@thesequaltrust.org.uk
Website: www.thesequaltrust.org.uk

Enquiries to: Charity Manager
Direct e-mail: liz@thesequaltrust.org.uk

Founded: 1969

Organisation type and purpose: Membership association (membership is by subscription), registered charity (charity number 260119).
To raise funds to provide communication aids to disabled children and adults on a permanent free loan basis.

Subject coverage: Communication aids for those with speech, movement or learning difficulties.

Services for disabled people: Provision of communication aids for those with speech, movement or learning disabilities.

Publications: Printed

Publications list: Available in print

Access to staff: Contact by letter, by telephone, by fax and by e-mail
Hours: Mon to Fri, 0900 to 1630

Access to building: No visits necessary

SERA

Formal name: Socialist Environment and Resources Association

1 London Bridge, Downstream Building, London SE1 9BG

Tel: 020 7022 1985
E-mail: enquiries@sera.org.uk
Website: www.serauk.org.uk

Enquiries to: National Co-ordinator

Founded: 1973

Organisation type and purpose: National organisation, membership association (membership is by subscription), present number of members: 1,500, voluntary organisation.

Subject coverage: Environmental issues, politics (Labour party), pollution, green economics, trade union issues.

Publications: Printed

Access to staff: Contact by letter, by telephone and by e-mail
Hours: Mon to Fri, 1000 to 1800

Affiliated to: Labour Party

SERIES 2 CLUB LTD

PO Box 61, Aberdare, CF44 4AJ

E-mail: info@series2club.co.uk
Website: www.series2club.co.uk

Enquiries to: Membership Secretary

Founded: 1985

Organisation type and purpose: Membership association (membership is by subscription), present number of members: 800.

Subject coverage: Land Rover Series II 1958–1971, restoration, operation, history, registration enquiries (DVLA Registered Club).

Collection: Technical manuals

Publications: Printed

Access to staff: Contact by letter. Non-members charged.
Hours: Mon to Fri, 1700 to 2000

Member of: Association of Rover Clubs; Federation of British Historic Vehicle Clubs

SERVICES CENTRAL LIBRARY (SCL)

The ACC Memorial Hall, Thornhill Road, Aldershot, Hampshire, GU11 2BG

Tel: 01252 349839
Fax: 01252 349836
E-mail: ets.scl@gtnet.gov.uk

Enquiries to: Librarian

continued overleaf

Direct e-mail: ets.scl@gtnet.gov.uk

Organisation type and purpose: National government body.

Subject coverage: General, particularly computing, law and management, no military stock.

Library catalogue: All or part available in-house

Publications: Printed

Access to staff: Contact by letter. Appointment necessary. Access for members only.
Hours: Mon to Fri, 0900 to 1630

Links with: Army Library Service; Upavon, Pewsey, Wiltshire

SESAME INSTITUTE UK (Sesame)

Christchurch, 27 Blackfriars Road, London, SE1 8NY

Tel: 020 7633 9690
E-mail: sesameinstituteuk@btinternet.com

Enquiries to: Director

Founded: 1964

Organisation type and purpose: Advisory body, professional body (membership is by subscription), registered charity (charity number 263155), suitable for ages: 22+, training organisation.
Recognised by the National Health Service, Department for Education and the British Association for Drama Therapists.
Promotes drama and movement in therapy.

Subject coverage: Drama and movement as therapy in work with the mentally and physically sick and the physically handicapped, training in such special skills, direct patient services.

Publications: Printed, and microform publications

Publications list: Available in print

Access to staff: Contact by letter, by telephone and by e-mail. Appointment necessary.
Hours: Tue, 1000 to 1700; Thu, Fri, 1000 to 1700
Special comments: No disabled access.

Affiliated to: MENCAP; MIND

Member of: European Consortium for Arts Therapies Education

SEVENOAKS DISTRICT COUNCIL

Council Offices, Argyle Road, Sevenoaks, Kent, TN13 1HG

Tel: 01732 227000
Fax: 01732 740693
E-mail: information@sevenoaks.gov.uk
Website: www.sevenoaks.gov.uk

Organisation type and purpose: Local government body.

Subject coverage: Planning and building control, car parking, council tax collection, environmental health, housing benefits, recycling, refuse collection, community and environmental services.

Publications list: Available in print

Access to staff: Contact by letter, by telephone, by fax, by e-mail, in person and via website
Hours: Mon to Thu, 0845 to 1700; Fri, 0845 to 1645

Access for disabled people: Parking provided, level entry, toilet facilities

Local Sub-offices at: Edenbridge Local Office and Tourist Information Centre; Stangrove Park, Edenbridge, Kent; tel: 01732 868110; fax: 01732 868114; e-mail: edenbridgetic@sevenoaks.gov.uk; Swanley Library and Contact Centre; London Road, Swanley, Kent; tel: 01322 614660; fax: 01322 665082; e-mail: information@sevenoaks.gov.uk

SEWELLS INFORMATION & RESEARCH

Media House, Lynchwood, Peterborough Business Park, Peterborough, Cambridgeshire, PE2 6EA

Tel: 01733 468000
Fax: 01733 468349
E-mail: sewells@emap.com
Website: www.sewells.co.uk

Enquiries to: Information Manager
Direct tel: 01733 468290
Direct fax: 01773 468349
Direct e-mail: eric.carnell@emap.com
Other contacts: Production Manager for subscriptions and publishing enquiries.

Founded: 1962

Organisation type and purpose: Advisory body, membership association (membership is by subscription), service industry, training organisation, research organisation, publishing house.
Automotive research information and publications.

Subject coverage: Motor trade management, motor industry in the UK and overseas, statistics, vehicle retailing companies and manufacturers.

Trade and statistical information: UK and European motor industry information and Best Practice publications

Publications: Printed

Publications list: Available online and in print

Access to staff: Contact by letter, by telephone, by fax and by e-mail. Non-members charged.
Hours: Mon to Fri, 0900 to 1730

SEWING MACHINE TRADE ASSOCIATION (SMTA)

70 Walmington Fold, Woodside Park, London N12 7LL

Tel: 020 3302 2934
E-mail: info@smta.org.uk
Website: www.sewingmachine.org.uk

Founded: 1934

Organisation type and purpose: A broad-based organisation representing the interest of high street retailers of household sewing machines and haberdashery, suppliers of machinery to the clothing manufacturing industry and trade distributors. Recognised by local and national government organisations, educational institutions and other trade associations as authoritative voice of the industry.
To offer a courteous and helpful service to the public and to co-operate nationally with each other to assist clients who may have made purchases from other members of the Association.

Subject coverage: Domestic and industrial sewing machines. haberdashery and various other garment making machines

Access to staff: Contact by letter, by telephone and by e-mail
Hours: Office hours

SEXUAL HEALTH AND REPRODUCTIVE CARE (SHARC)

25 Warwick Road, Coventry, CV1 2EZ

Tel: 024 7696 1300
Fax: 024 7696 1339

Enquiries to: Information Officer
Other contacts: Manager, Clinical Medical Officer, Senior Nurse

Founded: 1990; formerly called Well Woman Clinic, Well Women's Services, Women's Health and Information Centre

Organisation type and purpose: Local government body.
Medical services, information service, support groups.

Subject coverage: Women's health, contraception, family planning, health information, pregnancy.
Specialist genetic, sickle cell and thalassaemia services, chlamydia screening for ages 16–24.

Access to staff: Contact by letter, by telephone, by fax and in person. Appointment necessary.
Hours: Mon to Thu, 0830 to 1900; Fri, 0830 to 1630; Sat 1300 to 1630
Special comments: Appointments for clinical services.

Access for disabled people: Parking provided, ramped entry, access to all public areas, toilet facilities
Special comments: Hearing loop, magnifier.

Parent body: Coventry Primary Care Trust; Parkside House, Quinton Road, Coventry, West Midlands, CV1 2NJ; tel: 024 7655 3344

SHAFTESBURY & DISTRICT HISTORICAL SOCIETY

Gold Hill Museum, Shaftesbury, Dorset, SP7 8JW

Tel: 01747 852157
E-mail: enquiries@goldhillmuseum.org.uk
Website: www.shaftesburyheritage.org.uk

Enquiries to: Honorary Secretary

Founded: 1946

Organisation type and purpose: Membership association, voluntary organisation, registered charity (charity number 229883). Local history society and museum.

Subject coverage: Local history of Shaftesbury and district.

Collection: With the support of a Heritage Lottery Grant, Gold Hill Musuem will re-open in 2011 with a new exhibition on the social history of the town and 24 villages that surround the town.
Significant objects from the museum collection include:
Dorset buttons
Maps
Shaftesbury Byzant
Lace-making
Victorian social history
World Wars I and II personal mementoes
Photographs and postcards (incl. 700 slides)
John Rutter's scrap album (19th century)
Medieval alabaster panel, a 1744 fire engine, 2 church bells (16th- and 17th-century), a church font, 1919 Sale of Shaftesbury catalogue
The new Learning Centre will house the Library of local reference books and archival material

Non-library collection catalogue: All or part available in-house

Library catalogue: All or part available in-house

Publications: Printed

Access to staff: Contact by letter, by telephone, by e-mail, in person and via website. Appointment necessary.

Access to building: In 2011 Gold Hill Museum will re-open in Jul and close in Oct; the usal season runs from Apr to Oct; library by appointment only
Hours: 1030 to 1630 during the season
Special comments: By appointment only.

Access for disabled people: Good disabled access; with the refurbishemnt of the museum, access is currently being improved
Hours: 1030 to 1630 during the season
Special comments: By appointment only.

Links with: Shaftesbury Abbey Museum & Garden

Member organisation of: Dorset Museums Association

SHAKESPEARE CENTRE LIBRARY & ARCHIVE

Henley Street, Stratford-upon-Avon, Warwickshire, CV37 6QW

Tel: 01789 204016
Fax: 01789 296083
E-mail: scla@shakespeare.org.uk
Website: www.shakespeare.org.uk/main/3/339

Enquiries to: Head of Collections

Founded: 1847

Organisation type and purpose: Registered charity (charity number 209302).

Subject coverage: Contains combined resources of the Shakespeare Birthplace Trust's Shakespeare Collections, Local Collections and the RSC Archive.
Shakespeare Collections cover all aspects of Shakespeare's life, work and time; editions from the 17th century to present; commentary on the works, translations; theatrical history of the Shakespeare canon; pictorial material including theatrical portraits and illustrations of plays; CDs, films and sound recordings. RSC Archive covers production and administrative archive of the Royal Shakespeare Company and its predecessors from 1879 held on deposit: prompt books; reviews, programmes, photos, and archive video recordings made since 1982. Charges are made for video viewing facilities. Local Collections cover history of Stratford and surrounding area; includes thousands of documents, photos, maps and books, and important documents relating to Shakespeare.

Collection: Archives of the Shakespeare Memorial Theatre 1879–1960 and of the Royal Shakespeare Company 1961 to date
Joe Cocks Studio Collection (photographs of RSC productions 1969–1991)
Bram Stoker Collection (material relating to Henry Irving at the Lyceum Theatre)
Holte Photographic Collections (photographs of RSC productions 1950s–1981)
Reg Wilson Collection (photographs of RSC productions 1961–1997)
Records of the Stratford-upon-Avon Corporation
Records of leading Warwickshire families
Parish and nonconformist registers for Stratford-upon-Avon
Local newspapers

Non-library collection catalogue: All or part available online and in-house

Library catalogue: All or part available online and in-house

Publications: Microform publications

Access to staff: Contact by letter, by telephone, by fax, by e-mail, in person and via website
Hours: Wed to Fri, 1000 to 1630; Sat, 0930 to 1230; Closed Mon, Tue, all Bank Holidays and the preceding Saturdays, Saturday of Shakespeare's Birthday Weekend. It is sometimes possible to arrange access to the collections outside normal opening hours. Please contact us to discuss your needs or any special requirements for access and we will do our utmost to facilitate your visit.
Special comments: ID with address for general use. Letter of introduction required for access to special collections not available in surrogate form.

Access to building: No prior appointment required, except for video viewing, but booking in advance is advisable.
Special comments: Letter of introduction required for the use of some materials.

Access for disabled people: Access to all public areas, toilet facilities
Special comments: Advance notice for wheelchair users advisable. Parking 50 metres.

Constituent bodies: Royal Shakespeare Company Archive and Library

SHAKESPEARE INSTITUTE LIBRARY

Library Services, University of Birmingham, Mason Croft, Church Street, Stratford-upon-Avon, Warwickshire, CV37 6HP

Tel: 0121 414 9525
Fax: 01789 292021
E-mail: silib@bham.ac.uk
Website: www.library.bham.ac.uk/using/libraries/shakespeare.shtml

Enquiries to: Librarian
Other contacts: Information Assistant

Founded: 1951

Organisation type and purpose: University library, university department or institute, postgraduate research institute.

Subject coverage: Shakespeare; English literature 1475–1640; theatre history.

Collection: Archive of New Shakespeare Theatre Company
Archive of the Renaissance Theatre Company
E. K. Chambers Papers
Trevor Howard-Hill Archive
Brian Vickers Archive
Unpublished Shakespeare film script collection
Shakespeare press cuttings collection 1902–
Early English books 1475–1640 (microform)
Three centuries of English and American plays (microform)

Library catalogue: All or part available online

Access to staff: Contact by letter, by telephone, by fax, by e-mail and in person. Appointment necessary.
Hours: Mon to Thu, 0900 to 2000; Fri and Sat, 0900 to 1700; Sun, 1000 to 1700
Special comments: Only members and visitors with valid library cards may be admitted after 1700 and on Sat and Sun. Non-members of the University must bring along at least two different forms of ID in order to obtain a library pass.

Parent body: Library Services (Academic Services); The University of Birmingham, Edgbaston, Birmingham, B15 2TT; tel: 0121 414 5828; e-mail: library@bham.ac.uk; website: http://www.library.bham.ac.uk

SHAP WORKING PARTY ON WORLD RELIGIONS IN EDUCATION (SHAP)

National Society's RE Centre, Church House, Great Smith Street, London, SW1P 3NZ

Tel: 020 7898 1495
Fax: 020 7898 1493
E-mail: mike.berry@natsoc.org.uk
Website: dspace.dial.pipex.com/nsrec

Enquiries to: Secretary

Founded: 1969

Organisation type and purpose: Advisory body, professional body (membership is by election or invitation), training organisation, consultancy.
Concerned with providing accurate information about world religions for schools and institutions of higher education, police, hospitals, prisons, etc.

Subject coverage: Religious education and teaching, the world's major religions.

Publications: Printed

Publications list: Available in print

Access to building: Prior appointment required
Hours: Mon to Fri, 0900 to 1630

continued overleaf

Access for disabled people: Ramped entry, access to all public areas, toilet facilities

Associated with: European Association of World Religions in Education (EAWRE)

SHAPE

Deane House Studios, 27 Greenwood Place, London, NW5 1LB

Tel: 0845 521 3457; 020 7424 7368 (minicom)
Fax: 0845 521 3458
E-mail: info@shape-uk.co.uk
Website: www.shapearts.org.uk

Enquiries to: Chief Executive
Direct e-mail: mhairi@shapearts.org.uk

Founded: 1976

Organisation type and purpose: Advisory body, membership association, voluntary organisation, registered charity (charity number 279184), training organisation.
Ticket Scheme: reduced price tickets and volunteer escorts/drivers for London arts and entertainment events for disabled people or those over 70 years of age. Shape in Education: training for deaf and disabled artists to work in education settings. Shape Training: accredited training courses and placement in all aspects of arts management and practice. Training Support Network for young disabled and deaf people wishing to enter arts industries. Advice and information on training and employment. Local Arts Development: workshops, projects and events for disabled people, people with learning difficulties, mental health system survivors and older people. Deaf Arts Programme: national programme of projects and events promoting deaf arts and equal access to the arts for deaf and hard of hearing people. Advice, Information and Consultancy on all aspects of arts and disability.
Shape opens up access to the arts, enabling greater participation by disabled and older people.

Subject coverage: Disability arts, deaf arts, training courses, ticket scheme with reduced price tickets and volunteer drivers, training placements and accredited courses in arts management.

Collection: Arts-related archives specific to Shape, disability arts

Publications: Printed

Access to staff: Contact by letter, by telephone, by fax and by e-mail
Hours: Mon to Fri, 1000 to 1800

Affiliated to: Shape network, a federation of independent disability arts organisations

Other addresses: Shape in Hammersmith and Fulham; Polish Arts and Cultural Centre, 238–246 Kings Street, Hammersmith, London, W6 0RF; tel: 020 8741 7548 (answer machine) 020 8563 2894 (minicom); fax: 020 8741 6375; Shape in Islington; Room G15, c/o LBI, Arts and Heritage Department, Islington Town Hall, Upper Street, London, N1 1UD; tel: 020 7527 3850; fax: 020 7477 3856; Shape in Wandsworth; BAC, Lavender Hill, London, SW11 5TS; tel: 020 7924 5287; fax: 020 7978 2507

SHARK ANGLING CLUB OF GREAT BRITAIN (SACGB)

The Quay, Looe, Cornwall, PL13 1DX

Tel: 01503 262642
Fax: 01503 262642
E-mail: enquiries@sharkanglingclubofgreatbritain.org.uk

Enquiries to: Secretary

Organisation type and purpose: National organisation, membership association (membership is by subscription), present number of members: 400.

Subject coverage: Shark fishing.

Access to staff: Contact by letter, by telephone, by fax, by e-mail and in person
Hours: 7 days a week.

Access to building: No prior appointment required

SHAW SOCIETY

c/o Alan Knight, 10 Compston Road, London, N1 2PA

Tel: 020 7226 4266
Website: www.shawsociety.org.uk

Enquiries to: Honorary Secretary
Direct e-mail: anthnyellis@aol.com

Founded: 1941

Organisation type and purpose: Membership association (membership is by subscription), present number of members: c. 300, voluntary organisation.

Subject coverage: Life and works of Bernard Shaw.

Other addresses: Membership Secretary; 1 Buckland Court, 37 Belsize Park, London, NW3 4EB; tel: 020 7794 7014; fax: 020 7431 0816; e-mail: shawsociety@blueyonder.co.uk; Newsletter Editor; c/o Philip Riley, 11 Founders House, Aylesford Street, London, SW1V 3QE; tel: 020 7630 1675; e-mail: commonroom04@yahoo.com

SHEFFIELD AND DISTRICT FAMILY HISTORY SOCIETY

12 Birchitt Road, Bradway, Sheffield, S17 4QP

E-mail: secretary@sheffieldfhs.org.uk
Website: www.sheffieldfhs.org.uk

Enquiries to: Honorary Secretary

Founded: 1977

Organisation type and purpose: Membership association (membership is by subscription), present number of members: 1050, voluntary organisation, suitable for ages: all.
To promote, for the benefit and education of the public, the study of genealogy, family history and local history in the County of South Yorkshire.

Subject coverage: Family history, local (Sheffield and District) history, census records, parish records.

Library catalogue: All or part available in print

Publications: Printed, and electronic and video
Order printed publications from: Sheffield and District Family History Society
17 Firshill Road, Sheffield, S4 7BB

Publications list: Available online and in print

Access to staff: Contact by letter, by e-mail and via website
Hours: Library: Mon to Thu, 0930 to 1730; Fri, closed; Sat, 0900 to 1300 and 1400 to 1630

Library facility held at: Sheffield Archives; 52 Shoreham Street, Sheffield, S1 4SP; tel: 0114 203 9395

Member of: Federation of Family History Societies (FFHS)

SHEFFIELD ARCHIVES

52 Shoreham Street, Sheffield, South Yorkshire, S1 4SP

Tel: 0114 203 9395
Fax: 0114 203 9398
E-mail: archives@sheffield.gov.uk
Website: www.sheffield.gov.uk/archives

Enquiries to: Duty Archivist

Organisation type and purpose: Local government body.

Subject coverage: Family and estate records, church records (Church of England, Roman Catholic and Nonconformist), business archives, local authority and public records, trade union archives, antiquarian collections, political party records, societies and institutional records.

Collection: Collections include:
Arundel Castle Manuscripts (Sheffield, Derbyshire, and Nottinghamshire estates of the Dukes of Norfolk)
Business records of industrial history of the area, coal mining, iron and steel, cutlery, silver plate, professional firms, institutions and clubs
Correspondence and papers of Edward Carpenter (1844–1929)
Diocesan records for the Archdeaconry of Sheffield
Papers of the Earls of Wharncliffe
Papers of the Spencer Stanhope and Vernon Wentworth families and estates
Records of the Roman Catholic Diocese of Hallam
Wentworth Woodhouse Muniments (includes the papers of Thomas Wentworth, Earl of Strafford, 2nd Marquis of Rockingham and Edmund Burke)

Non-library collection catalogue: All or part available online and in print

Publications: Printed

Publications list: Available online

Access to staff: Contact by letter, by telephone, by fax, by e-mail and in person
Hours: Mon, 1000 to 1730; Tue to Thu, 0930 to 1730; Fri, closed; Sat, 0900 to 1300 and 1400 to 1700
Special comments: Users of the searchroom must obtain a reader's ticket, two official proofs of identity required on first visit.
Access is suitable for disabled persons and wheelchairs.

Access for disabled people: Level entry, access to all public areas, toilet facilities

SHEFFIELD ASSAY OFFICE (SAO)

Guardians Hall, Beulah Road, Hillsborough, Sheffield, South Yorkshire, S6 2AN

Tel: 0114 231 2121
Fax: 0114 233 9079
E-mail: paragreene@assayoffice.co.uk
Website: www.assayoffice.co.uk/resource.htm
Website: www.assayoffice.co.uk
Website: www.assayoffice.co.uk/info.htm

Enquiries to: Librarian and Curator
Other contacts: Laboratory Manager

Founded: 1773

Organisation type and purpose: Statutory, non-profit making body, UKAS accredited laboratory.

Subject coverage: Jewellery design, silverware design, principally European but worldwide coverage; precious metal assaying including historical material; some information on non-ferrous mining and metallurgy; hallmarking records for Sheffield.

Collection: Catalogues and records from various silversmithing firms no longer in existence (mainly local)
Daybooks from 1773 to 1830 and 1932 to the present
Office records from 1773 (some stored at Sheffield Archives)

Trade and statistical information: Hallmarking figures for UK, produced by British Hallmarking Council

Non-library collection catalogue: All or part available in-house

Library catalogue: All or part available in-house

Publications: Printed

Access to staff: Contact by letter, by telephone, by fax, by e-mail and via website. Appointment necessary. Non-members charged.
Hours: Library and collection: Thu and Fri, 0900 to 1600
Archives at Sheffield Archives: Mon to Sat

Access to building: No prior appointment required
Hours: Mon to Fri, 0900 to 1600

Access for disabled people: Parking provided, ramped entry, access to all public areas

SHEFFIELD CITY COUNCIL (SCC)

Formal name: City of Sheffield Metropolitan District Council

Howden House, 1 Union Street, Sheffield, S1 2HH

Tel: 0114 273 4567
E-mail: firstpoint@sheffield.gov.uk
Website: www.sheffield.gov.uk/

Enquiries to: Media Relations Manager

Founded: 1897

Organisation type and purpose: Local government body.

Subject coverage: Information about Sheffield, trade, tourism, entertainment, sport, education, social services, housing, parks, environmental health, highways, markets, planning, transport and all other local government services in Sheffield.

Access to staff: Contact by letter, by telephone, by e-mail and in person
Hours: Mon to Fri, 0900 to 1700

SHEFFIELD GALLERIES & MUSEUMS TRUST

Leader House, Surrey Street, Sheffield, South Yorkshire, S1 2LH

Tel: 0114 278 2600
Fax: 0114 278 2604
E-mail: info@sheffieldgalleries.org.uk
Website: www.sheffieldgalleries.org.uk

Founded: 1998

Organisation type and purpose: Local government body, registered charity (charity number 1068850).
Administrative body.

Subject coverage: Galleries and Museums Trust has management responsibility for five musems and galleries in Sheffield, including responsibility for policies, forward planning and performance.

Access to staff: Contact by letter, by telephone, by fax, by e-mail and via website. Appointment necessary.
Hours: Mon to Fri, 0900 to 1730

Access for disabled people: Toilet facilities
Special comments: Parking in Surrey Street, one step at door, phone prior to visit if assistance required.

Jointly funded by: Sheffield City Council and the Arts Council of England

Trust sites: Bishops' House; Meersbrook Park, Norton Lees Lane, Sheffield, South Yorkshire, S8 9BE; tel: 0114 278 2600; fax: 0114 278 2604; Graves Art Gallery; Surrey Street, Sheffield, South Yorkshire, S1 1XZ; tel: 0114 273 5158; fax: 0114 273 4705; Mappin Art Gallery; Weston Park, Sheffield, South Yorkshire, S10 2TP; tel: 0114 278 2600; fax: 0114 275 0957; Millennium Galleries; Arundel Gate, Sheffield, South Yorkshire, S1 2PP; tel: 0114 278 2600; fax: 0114 278 2604; Sheffield City Museum; Weston Park, Sheffield, South Yorkshire, S10 2TP; tel: 0114 278 2600; fax: 0114 275 0957

SHEFFIELD HALLAM UNIVERSITY (SHU)

City Campus, Pond Street, Sheffield, South Yorkshire, S1 1WB

Tel: 0114 225 3581
Fax: 0114 225 4985
Website: www.shu.ac.uk

Direct e-mail: pressoffice@shu.ac.uk

Founded: 1843

Organisation type and purpose: University department or institute.

Publications: Printed, and electronic and video

Publications list: Available online and in print

Access to staff: Contact by letter
Hours: Mon to Fri, 0900 to 1700

Access for disabled people: Access to all public areas

SHEFFIELD HALLAM UNIVERSITY – LEARNING CENTRES, LIBRARY RESOURCES AND IT

Howard Street, Sheffield, South Yorkshire, S1 1WB

Tel: 0114 225 3333
Fax: 0114 225 3859
E-mail: learning.centre@shu.ac.uk
Website: www.shu.ac.uk/services/sls/learning/index.html

Organisation type and purpose: University library.

Subject coverage: Adsetts Centre, City Campus: computing, sciences, engineering, built environment, business, management, tourism, hospitality, food, social sciences, history, English, languages, TESOL (Teaching English to Speakers of Other Languages), education, performing arts, communication studies, art, design, fashion, photography, film and media studies, metalwork and jewellery.
Collegiate Learning Centre: health, nursing, midwifery, occupational and physical therapies, paramedicine, radiotherapy and oncology, radiography, operating department practice, sports studies, psychology, social work, social sciences, law and criminology.

Collection: Adsetts Centre:
Corvey collection (18th- and 19th-century books in English)
18th- and 19th-century books on art and design
Archives of Sheffield School of Art 1843–1969
David Morgan Rees collection (photographs of Yorkshire crafts)
Festival of Britain collection
George Fullard drawings
Photographs of the miners' strike 1984–85
Public art research archive
Collegiate Learning Centre:
European Documentation Centre

Library catalogue: All or part available online

Access to staff: Contact by letter, by telephone, by fax, by e-mail, in person and via website. Appointment necessary.

Access to building: *Hours:* Term time: Mon to Thu, 0845 to 2100; Fri, 0845 to 1800; Sat, Sun, 1000 to 1700
Special comments: 24-hour opening for Sheffield Hallam University students operates during term time.

Access for disabled people: Ramped entry, access to all public areas, toilet facilities

Also at: Collegiate Learning Centre; Sheffield, S10 2BP; tel: 0114 225 3333; fax: 0114 225 2476

SHEFFIELD LIBRARIES, ARCHIVES AND INFORMATION – REFERENCE & INFORMATION

Central Library, Surrey Street, Sheffield, South Yorkshire, S1 1XZ

continued overleaf

Tel: 0114 273 4736/7
Fax: 0114 273 5009
E-mail: information.library@sheffield.gov.uk
Website: www.sheffield.gov.uk/informationlibrary
Website: library.sheffield.gov.uk
Website: www.sheffield.gov.uk/libraries

Enquiries to: Information Library Officer

Founded: 1934

Organisation type and purpose: Local government body, public library.

Subject coverage: Business and commercial information on companies, products, suppliers, importers, exporters, trade names. Company information (general and financial information on local, UK and foreign companies); UK telephone directories. All aspects of art, social sciences, science and technology, industry related matters, innovation, trade and technical journals and reports. Official publications, official and non-official national, European and international statistics. Historic and current collection of patents. Current and historic collection of British and world-wide standards and specifications. Metallic materials identification service provided via the World Metal Index (WMI), part of a collection of standards and specifications; trade literature and technical journals on both ferrous and non-ferrous metal. Over 200,000 individual grades are included, both current and historical. MI-21 (Metals Information for the 21st century), a collaboration between the WMI and the Welding Institute (TWI), providing an information resource on metallic materials and welding consumables.

Information services: 24-hour access to search the currently available 20,000 MI-21 World Metal Index datasheets online, by subscription at: http://www.mi-21.com.

Collection: British directories
MINT company database
Company annual reports
Kompass Worldwide (online)
British Standards (online and paper collection of withdrawn and superseded British Standards)
Foreign and international standards
Company financial data, patents, standards, trademarks (online)
Local company and local economic data
Motor vehicle workshop manuals
Market research databases (online)
Radio and TV servicing data
UK patents 1617 to present
Intellectual property information

Library catalogue: All or part available online and in-house

Access to staff: Contact by letter, by telephone, by fax, by e-mail, in person and via website

Access to building: *Hours:* Mon, 1000 to 2000; Tue, Thu, Fri, Sat, 0930 to 1730; Wed, 0930 to 2000
Special comments: Charges may apply for certain services, e.g. photocopying and printing.

Includes the: World Metal Index

Member organisation of: BSI; European Public Information Centre; PatLib UK

Parent body: Sheffield City Council

SHEFFIELD LIBRARIES, ARCHIVES AND INFORMATION SERVICES – ARTS AND SOCIAL SCIENCES AND SPORTS SECTION

Central Library, Surrey Street, Sheffield, South Yorkshire, S1 1XZ

Tel: 0114 273 4747
Fax: 0114 273 5009
E-mail: artsandsport.library@sheffield.gov.uk
Website: www.sheffield.gov.uk/in-your-area/libraries

Enquiries to: Librarian

Organisation type and purpose: Local government body, public library.

Subject coverage: Social sciences including sociology, politics, education and careers, parliamentary and local government information, social welfare, charities and voluntary sector; the arts, leisure including travel and maps, sport and mountaineering, history, language and literature, census, statistics, government publications, abstracts and indexes.

Collection: Physical Education Association's sport collection
Climbing and Mountaineering
Funder Finder: charitable trusts database
International Genealogy Index Great Britain and Ireland
Sheffield Philatelic Society Library (on deposit)

Non-library collection catalogue: All or part available online and in-house

Library catalogue: All or part available online and in-house

Publications: Microform publications

Access to staff: Contact by letter, by telephone, by fax, by e-mail and in person
Hours: Mon, 1000 to 2000; Tue, Thu, Fri, 0930 to 1730; Wed, 0930 to 2000; Sat, 0930 to 1730

Parent body: Sheffield City Council

SHEFFIELD LIBRARIES, ARCHIVES AND INFORMATION SERVICES – CENTRAL MUSIC AND FILM LIBRARY

Formal name: Sheffield Libraries, Archives and Information Services – Music and Film Collection

Music and Film Collection, Central Library, Surrey Street, Sheffield, South Yorkshire, S1 1XZ

Tel: 0114 273 4727/9
Fax: 0114 273 5009
E-mail: musicandav.library@sheffield.gov.uk
Website: www.sheffield.gov.uk/musicandfilm

Organisation type and purpose: Local government body, public library.

Subject coverage: Music (books, scores, sets of orchestral parts and vocal scores, sound recordings), music reference services; DVD and Blu-ray lending collection.

Collection: Bayreuth Collection (Wagner)
Whitworth Collection (organs and organ building)
Both collections now incorporated into the total stock

Library catalogue: All or part available online and in-house

Publications: Printed

Access to staff: Contact by letter, by telephone, by fax, by e-mail and in person
Hours: Mon, 1000 to 2000; Tue, Thu, Fri, Sat, 0930 to 1730; Wed, 0930 to 2000

Access to building: *Hours:* Same as above.

Links with: Yorkshire Libraries and Information

SHEFFIELD LIBRARIES, ARCHIVES AND INFORMATION SERVICES – LOCAL STUDIES LIBRARY

Central Library, Surrey Street, Sheffield, South Yorkshire, S1 1XZ

Tel: 0114 273 4753
Fax: 0114 273 5009
E-mail: local.studies@sheffield.gov.uk
Website: www.picturesheffield.com
Website: www.sheffield.gov.uk/archives

Enquiries to: Local Studies Officer
Direct e-mail: local.studies.library@sheffield.gov.uk

Organisation type and purpose: Public library.

Subject coverage: History, geography, etc. of Sheffield Metropolitan District and surrounding area, articles of local interest in newspapers and periodicals, 19th-century ED returns, 1971, 1981, 1991 Small Area Statistics (local census data), trade directories, newspapers, electoral registers.

Collection: Census records 1841, 1851, 1861, 1871, 1881 for Sheffield and parts of South Yorkshire and North Derbyshire on microfilm; 1891 and 1901 on microfiche (name indexes for Sheffield 1841–81)
Ephemera such as playbills, notices, leaflets
Film and video of scenes of life in Sheffield (some access restrictions for preservation reasons)
Map collection (historic and modern)
Newspapers (files of local papers on microfilm)
Oral history recordings
Photographic collection of 60,000 local images
Sheffield street and trade directories from 1774 to 1974

Library catalogue: All or part available online and in-house

Publications: Electronic and video
Order electronic and video publications from: see website: http://www.sheffield.gov.uk/archives

Publications list: Available online and in print

Access to staff: Contact by letter, by telephone, by fax, by e-mail and in person
Hours: Mon, 1000 to 2000; Tue, Thu, Fri, Sat, 0930 to 1730; Wed, 0930 to 2000

SHELL SERVICES INTERNATIONAL

Business Information Centre, Shell Centre, London, SE1 7NA

Tel: 020 7934 1234
Fax: 020 7934 7679

Enquiries to: Archivist
Direct tel: 020 7934 2328
Other contacts: Head of Business Information Centre

Organisation type and purpose: Industrial company.

Subject coverage: Business aspects of the energy and petrochemical industries worldwide.

Trade and statistical information: Extensive statistical collection

SHELL UK LTD

1 Altens Farm Road, Nigg, Aberdeen, AB12 3FY

Tel: 01224 882000
E-mail: tullosic-enquiries@shell.com
Enquiries to: Information Adviser
Direct tel: 01224 882032

Organisation type and purpose:
International organisation.
Oil and gas company.

Subject coverage: Oil, gas, exploration, production and operation procedures, offshore safety, offshore engineering.

Access to staff: Contact by telephone and by e-mail
Hours: Mon to Fri, 0830 to 1630

Access to building: Not open to the public.

SHELLFISH ASSOCIATION OF GREAT BRITAIN (SAGB)

Fishmongers' Hall, London Bridge, London, EC4R 9EL

Tel: 020 7283 8305
Fax: 020 7929 1389
E-mail: SAGB@shellfish.org.uk
Website: www.shellfish.org.uk

Enquiries to: Secretary
Other contacts: Director

Founded: 1903

Organisation type and purpose: Trade association.
Represents the UK Shellfish industry.

Subject coverage: Shellfish stocks, biology, markets, storage, handling and quality.

Publications: Printed

Access to staff: Contact by letter, by telephone, by fax, by e-mail and via website. Non-members charged.
Hours: Mon to Fri, 0900 to 1700

Links with: Association of Scottish Shellfish Growers

SHELTER

88 Old Street, London, EC1V 9HU

Tel: 0844 515 2000
E-mail: info@shelter.org.uk
Website: england.shelter.org.uk/get_advice
Website: england.shelter.org.uk

Founded: 1966

Organisation type and purpose: A registered charity (charity number 263710 in England and Wales and SC002327 in Scotland).
Works to alleviate the distress caused by homelessness and bad housing.
To make sure that people in housing need can access and keep a home; to drive up the supply of affordable homes in places where people can thrive.

Subject coverage: Gives advice, information and advocacy to people in housing need, and campaigns for lasting political change to end the housing crisis for good.

Information services: Free housing advice helpline: 0808 800 4444; supporter helpdesk (no housing advice): 0300 330 1234; online housing advice (see website); Children's Service gives children's sector professionals who are working with families and young people affected by housing problems direct access to Shelter's specialist advice and advocacy services.

Education services: Online teachers' centre (see website); more than 130 housing and personal development courses to suit all levels (see website).

Collection: Online policy library (see website)

Publications: Printed
Order printed publications from: Shelter

Publications list: Available online and in print

Access to staff: Contact by letter, by telephone, by fax and by e-mail
Hours: Reception: Mon to Fri, 0900 to 1730
Supporter Helpdesk: Mon to Fri, 0900 to 2000; Sat, 0900 to 1300

Also at: Shelter Scotland; 4th floor, Scotiabank House, 6 South Charlotte Street, Edinburgh, EH2 4AW; website: http://scotland.shelter.org.uk

SHERLOCK HOLMES SOCIETY OF LONDON

15 Copperfield Court, 146 Worple Road, Wimbledon, London, SW20 8QA

Tel: 020 8879 0332
E-mail: c.cooke@dsl.pipex.com
Website: www.sherlock-holmes.org.uk

Enquiries to: Secretary

Founded: 1951

Organisation type and purpose:
Membership association.

Subject coverage: Study of the life, work and times of Sherlock Holmes and Dr Watson, with more than a passing interest in the same of Sir Arthur Conan Doyle.

Publications: Printed

Access to staff: Contact by letter, by telephone and by e-mail
Hours: Mon to Fri, 0900 to 1700

SHETLAND ARCHIVES

Formal name: Shetland Museum and Archives

Hay's Dock, Lerwick, Shetland, ZE1 0WP

Tel: 01595 695057 and 01595 741554
Fax: 01595 696729
E-mail: info@shetlandmuseumandarchives.org.uk

Enquiries to: Archivist

Founded: 1976

Organisation type and purpose: Trust administering Museum and Archives for local authority Archives office.

Subject coverage: Shetland.

Collection: Archival and some printed historical matter all concerning Shetland; microfilm copies of demographic records concerning Shetland, and of virtually all newspapers with Shetland news, 1830s onwards

Non-library collection catalogue: All or part available in-house

Publications: Printed
Order printed publications from: Shetland Museum and Archives

Access to staff: Contact by letter, by telephone, by fax, by e-mail and in person
Hours: Mon to Fri, 1000 to 1630; Sat, 1000 to 1300

Access for disabled people: Parking provided, ramped entry, access to all public areas, toilet facilities

Administered by: Shetland Amenity Trust; Garthspool, Lerwick, Shetland; tel: 01595 694688

SHETLAND FAMILY HISTORY SOCIETY (SFHS)

6 Hillhead, Lerwick, Shetland, ZE1 0EJ

E-mail: secretary@shetland-fhs.org.uk
Website: www.shetland-fhs.org.uk

Enquiries to: General Secretary
Other contacts: Membership Secretary (for joining information and application)

Founded: 1991

Organisation type and purpose:
Membership association (membership is by subscription), present number of members: 900, registered charity (charity number SCO 20018).
A focus to share, collate and disseminate genealogical data of Shetland Island families.

Subject coverage: Genealogy of Shetland families, emigration worldwide, family trees, monumental inscriptions, research sources available locally.

Non-library collection catalogue: All or part available in-house

Library catalogue: All or part available in-house

Publications: Printed, and electronic and video

Publications list: Available online and in print

Access to staff: Contact by letter, by e-mail, in person and via website. Appointment necessary.
Hours: Mon to Sat, 1400 to 1600; Mon and Thu, 1900 to 2100

Access for disabled people: Level entry

Links with: Scottish Association of Family History Societies

SHETLAND ISLANDS COUNCIL (SIC)

Town Hall, Hillhead, Lerwick, Shetland, ZE1 0HB

Tel: 01595 693535
Fax: 01595 744509
E-mail: sic@sic.shetland.gov.uk
Website: www.shetland.gov.uk

Enquiries to: Chief Executive

Founded: 1974

Organisation type and purpose: Local government body.

Subject coverage: Local government services.

Access to staff: Contact by letter, by telephone, by fax, by e-mail and in person
Hours: Mon to Fri, 0900 to 1700

SHETLAND LIBRARY

Lower Hillhead, Lerwick, Shetland, ZE1 0EL

Tel: 01595 743868
Fax: 01595 694430
E-mail: shetlandlibrary@sic.shetland.gov.uk
Website: www.shetland-library.gov.uk

Founded: 1950

Organisation type and purpose: Local government body, public library.

Subject coverage: All aspects of Shetland, including its geography, agriculture and local history.

Collection: Local newspapers (on microfilm)

Non-library collection catalogue: All or part available online

Library catalogue: All or part available online

Publications: Printed

Access to staff: Contact by letter, by telephone, by fax, by e-mail and via website. Appointment necessary.
Hours: Mon, Thu, 0930 to 2000; Tue, Wed, Fri, Sat, 0930 to 1700

Access for disabled people: Ramped entry, access to all public areas, toilet facilities

SHETLAND PONY STUD-BOOK SOCIETY (SPSBS)

22 York Place, Perth, Tayside, PH2 8EH

Tel: 01738 623471
Fax: 01738 442274
E-mail: elaineward@shetlandponystudbooksociety.co.uk
Website: www.shetlandponystudbooksociety.co.uk

Enquiries to: Breed Secretary

Founded: 1891

Organisation type and purpose: Membership association (membership is by subscription), present number of members: 2000, registered charity (charity number 38044). Breed society. Maintains records and gives advice on registered Shetland Ponies.

Subject coverage: All subjects concerning Shetland ponies including registrations, pedigrees, performance, exports, welfare, society sales, showing, publications.

Collection: The Shetland Pony Stud-Book (101 volumes)

Publications: Printed

Publications list: Available online and in print

Access to staff: Contact by letter, by telephone, by fax and by e-mail. Appointment necessary.
Hours: Mon to Fri, 0900 to 1700
Special comments: Telephone answered 1100 to 1500 daily.

SHINGLES SUPPORT SOCIETY (SSS)

41 North Road, London, N7 9DP

Tel: 020 7607 9661
E-mail: info@herpes.org.uk
Website: www.shinglessupport.org

Enquiries to: Director

Founded: 1985

Organisation type and purpose: Patient support group.

Subject coverage: Information on drug treatments that a GP can prescribe and self-help therapies.

Publications: Printed

Publications list: Available online and in print

Access to staff: Contact by letter, by telephone and by e-mail. Appointment necessary.
Hours: Mon to Fri, 1000 to 1800

Access to building: Prior appointment required

Access for disabled people: Level entry by circuitous route
Special comments: Disabled access can be arranged if requested in advance.

Parent body: Herpes Viruses Association (HVA); same address

SHIPPING GUIDES LIMITED

Reigate Hill House, 28 Reigate Hill, Reigate, Surrey, RH2 9NG

Tel: 01737 242255
Fax: 01737 222449
E-mail: info@portinfo.co.uk
Website: www.portinfo.co.uk

Enquiries to: Managing Director
Direct e-mail: info@portinfo.co.uk
Other contacts: Sales Co-ordinator

Founded: 1970

Organisation type and purpose: Advisory body, publishing house.
Nautical Advisers.

Subject coverage: Marine publishers, port information, marine manuals, nautical information, nautical advisers, atlases, maps, books and CDs.

Publications: Printed

Publications list: Available online and in print

Access to staff: Contact by letter, by telephone, by fax, by e-mail and in person
Hours: Mon to Fri, 0900 to 1700

Access for disabled people: Yes

SHOOTERS' RIGHTS ASSOCIATION (SRA)

PO Box 3, Cardigan, Ceredigion, SA43 1BN

Tel: 01239 698607
Fax: 01239 698614
E-mail: richard.law@btinternet.com

Enquiries to: Secretary

Founded: 1984

Organisation type and purpose: International organisation, membership association (membership is by subscription), present number of members: 4500, voluntary organisation, training organisation.
For persons who hold firearm or shotgun certificates, are registered dealers, or who are interested in taking up shooting as a pastime.

Subject coverage: Firearms licensing; legal problems arising from the possession and use of firearms.

Collection: Reports about firearms legislation in the UK, including the unpublished Blackwell & McKay Reports

Publications: Printed

Access to staff: Contact by letter, by telephone, by fax and by e-mail. Appointment necessary.
Hours: Mon to Fri, 0900 to 1700

Access to building: Prior appointment required

SHOP AND DISPLAY EQUIPMENT ASSOCIATION (sdea)

24 Croydon Road, Caterham, Surrey, CR3 6YR

Tel: 01883 348911
Fax: 01883 343435
E-mail: enquiries@sdea.co.uk
Website: www.shopdisplay.org

Enquiries to: Administration Manager

Founded: 1947

Organisation type and purpose: Trade association.

Subject coverage: Sourcing manufacturers and suppliers of shopfittings and retail display equipment.

Information services: Information regarding suppliers of shopfittings and retail display equipment

Publications: Printed

Access to staff: Contact by letter, by telephone, by fax, by e-mail and via website
Hours: Mon to Fri, 0900 to 1700

Access to building: No access other than to staff

SHORTHORN CATTLE SOCIETY

National Agricultural Centre, Stoneleigh Park, Kenilworth, Warwickshire, CV8 2LG

Tel: 024 7669 6549
Fax: 024 7669 6729
E-mail: shorthorn@shorthorn.co.uk

Website: www.shorthorn.co.uk

Enquiries to: General Secretary
Other contacts: Secretary

Founded: 1822

Organisation type and purpose:
Membership association (membership is by subscription), present number of members: 1,100, registered charity (charity number 213216).
To keep up a herd book and breed standard, to provide and promote information and advice, genetics and general support for members and supporters of the breed.

Subject coverage: Shorthorn cattle including membership, registration, classification, semen, breed publicity and general information.

Collection: Coates' Herd Books
Year Book and Journals
Photographs

Trade and statistical information:
Wordwide Trade for livestock, semen and embryos

Publications: Printed, and electronic and video

Access to staff: Contact by letter, by telephone, by fax, by e-mail and in person
Hours: Mon to Fri, 0900 to 1600

Access for disabled people: Parking provided

SHREWSBURY COLLEGE OF ARTS & TECHNOLOGY

Learning Resource Centre, London Road, Shrewsbury, Shropshire, SY2 6PR

Tel: 01743 342342
Fax: 01743 342343
E-mail: carolinet@shrewsbury.ac.uk
Website: www.shrewsbury.ac.uk

Enquiries to: Team Leader – Learning Resources
Direct tel: 01743 342354
Direct e-mail: lrlrc@shrewsbury.ac.uk

Organisation type and purpose: Suitable for ages: 16+.
College of further education with some HE provision.

Subject coverage: All areas of further education including accounting, administration, art and design, beauty and holistic therapies, business, care, childcare, computing and IT, construction, engineering, fashion, hairdressing, hospitality and catering, law, media, motor vehicle, music and performing arts, public services, sports and recreation, travel and tourism.

Non-library collection catalogue: All or part available in-house

Library catalogue: All or part available in-house

Access to staff: Contact by letter, by telephone, by fax, by e-mail, in person and via website. Appointment necessary.
Hours: Mon to Fri, 0900 to 1630

Access for disabled people: Parking provided, ramped entry, access to all public areas, toilet facilities

Constituent bodies: Radbrook College Campus; Radbrook Road, Shrewsbury, Shropshire, SY3 9BL; tel: 01743 342642; e-mail: rblrc@shrewsbury.ac.uk

SHREWSBURY SCHOOL LIBRARY

The Schools, Shrewsbury, Shropshire, SY3 7BA

Tel: 01743 280595
Fax: 01743 243107
E-mail: archivist@shrewsbury.org.uk
Website: www.shrewsbury.org.uk

Enquiries to: Taylor Librarian and Archivist

Founded: 1606

Organisation type and purpose:
Independent school library.

Subject coverage: General, for a school library.

Collection: Collection of bookbindings, 12th to 20th centuries, and private press books
Collection on early science, natural history and medicine, documented from 1607
Grammar School Library dating from 1606, 7,500 vols including medieval manuscripts, incunabula, and books of the 16th and 17th centuries
Letters of Charles Darwin
Manuscripts and watercolours relating to Samuel (Erewhon) Butler
Moser collection of 19th-century watercolours
Photographic archive c. 1860 to the present
School and Governing Body Archives, 1552 to the present

Library catalogue: All or part available in-house

Access to staff: Contact by letter, by fax and by e-mail. Appointment necessary. Letter of introduction required.
Hours: Mon to Fri, 0900 to 1700

SHROPSHIRE LIBRARIES

Castle Gates, Shrewsbury, Shropshire, SY1 2AS

Tel: 01743 255308
Fax: 01743 255309
E-mail: libraries@shropshire.gov.uk
Website: www.shropshire.gov.uk/library.nsf

Enquiries to: Librarian

Organisation type and purpose: Local government body, public library.

Subject coverage: General public library

Library catalogue: All or part available online

Publications: Printed

Publications list: Available online

Access to staff: Contact by letter, by telephone, by fax, by e-mail, in person and via website
Hours: Mon, Wed, Fri, 0930 to 1700; Tue and Thu, 0930 to 2000; Sat, 0900 to 1700; Sun, 1300 to 1600

Parent body: Shropshire Council

SHROPSHIRE ARCHAEOLOGICAL AND HISTORICAL SOCIETY (SAHS)

Glebe House, Vicarage Road, Meole Brace, Shrewsbury, SY3 9EZ

Tel: 01743 236914
E-mail: s.baugh@virgin.net
Website: www.shropshirearchaeology.org.uk

Enquiries to: Honorary Secretary
Other contacts: Hon. Editor of 'Transactions'; Hon. Membership Secretary

Founded: 1877

Organisation type and purpose: Learned society (membership is by subscription), present number of members: 329 individual and 40 institutional members.

Subject coverage: Local history and archaeology of Shropshire, parish registers.

Education services: Summer field trips; winter lecture series; occasional day schools.

Collection: J H Smith watercolours of Shropshire churches c. 1840

Non-library collection catalogue: All or part available in-house

Library catalogue: All or part available in-house

Publications: Printed, and electronic and video
Order printed publications from: Hon. Publications Secretary

Access to staff: Contact by letter, by telephone, by e-mail, in person and via website

Access to building: No prior appointment required

Access for disabled people: Parking provided, level entry, access to all public areas, toilet facilities

Incorporating the: Shropshire Parish Register Society

Member of: Council for British Archaeology

The Society's Library is housed at the: Shropshire Archives; Castle Gates, Shrewsbury, SY1 2AQ; tel: 01743 255350; fax: 01743 255355; e-mail: archives@shropshire.gov.uk

SHROPSHIRE ARCHIVES

Castle Gates, Shrewsbury, Shropshire, SY1 2AQ

Tel: 01743 255350
Fax: 01743 255355
E-mail: archives@shropshire.gov.uk
Website: www.shropshirearchives.org.uk

Founded: 1885

Organisation type and purpose: Local government body, public library.
Record office.

Subject coverage: Records and printed works relating to the County of Shropshire; local history, archaeology, genealogy, etc.

Collection: Archives of Anglican Parishes, Nonconformist Churches, Poor Law Unions, Schools, Quarter Sessions, etc.
Estate Records

continued overleaf

J. H. Smith watercolours of Shropshire churches c. 1840
Lily F. Chitty Collection (archaeology)
Local Authority Records
Photographic Archive (from 1842)
Prints, drawings and watercolours
Shrewsbury newspapers from 1772
Shropshire censuses 1841–91
Solicitors' Archives

Non-library collection catalogue: All or part available online and in-house

Library catalogue: All or part available online and in-house

Publications: Printed, and microform publications
Order printed publications from: Shropshire Archives
Order microform publications from: Shropshire Archives

Publications list: Available online

Access to staff: Contact by letter, by telephone, by fax, by e-mail, in person and via website
Hours: Wed, Fri, 1000 to 1700; Thu, 1000 to 2000; Sat, 1000 to 1600
Special comments: Shropshire Archives Reader's Ticket needed for access to originals and some printed material. Some material needs to be requested in advance.

Access for disabled people: Parking provided – please book

Houses the library of the: Shropshire Archaeological and Historical Society

Parent body: Shropshire Council

SHROPSHIRE CHAMBER OF COMMERCE & ENTERPRISE LTD (SCCE)

Trevithick House, Stafford Park 4, Telford, Shropshire, TF3 3BA

Tel: 01952 208200
Fax: 01952 208208
E-mail: enquiries@shropshire-chamber.co.uk
Website: www.shropshire-chamber.co.uk

Enquiries to: Membership/Policy Executive

Organisation type and purpose: Membership association, training organisation.
To offer complete business solutions, to members and non-members.

Subject coverage: Business services, advice, information.

Library catalogue: All or part available in-house

Publications: Printed

Access to staff: Contact by letter, by telephone, by fax, by e-mail, in person and via website. Appointment necessary.
Hours: Mon to Fri, 0900 to 1700
Special comments: Shropshire businesses and members only.

Access to building: No access other than to staff, prior appointment required

Access for disabled people: Parking provided, ramped entry, toilet facilities

Links with: British Chambers of Commerce; Confederation of West Midlands' Chambers of Commerce; Small Business Service

SHROPSHIRE FAMILY HISTORY SOCIETY (SFHS)

16 Glentworth Avenue, Oswestry, Shropshire, SY10 9PZ

E-mail: secretary@sfhs.org.uk
Website: www.sfhs.org.uk/

Enquiries to: Chairman
Direct e-mail: chairman@sfhs.org.uk
Other contacts: Membership Secretary

Founded: 1979

Organisation type and purpose: Membership association (membership is by subscription), present number of members: 2,000, voluntary organisation, registered charity (charity number 514014).

Subject coverage: Family history, research, transcription and indexing of historical records such as parish registers, census returns and monumental inscriptions in the county of Shropshire.

Education services: Talks/courses on family history topics. Voluntary presence in Shropshire Archives to assist the public.

Collection: 1881 Census transcript and index for England and Wales (microfiche)
British Section of the IGI (microfiche)
Early trade directories (microfiche)
Members' Interests (database)
Original Parish Registers Shropshire (microfiche)
Parish Registers of Shropshire (almost complete set of the printed vols)
Quarter Sessions (database)
Shrewsbury Wills from 1858 (database)
Shropshire Monumental Inscriptions (database)
Shropshire Strays (online)

Publications: Printed, and electronic and video
Order printed publications from: Shropshire Family History Society, 68 Oakley Street, Belle Vue, Shrewsbury, Shropshire, SY3 7JZ
Order electronic and video publications from: Shropshire Family History Society, 19 Upper Bar, Newport, Shropshire, TF10 7EH

Publications list: Available online and in print

Access to staff: Contact by letter, by e-mail and via website
Hours: Mon to Fri, 0900 to 1700
Special comments: Please enclose an sae for reply to letters.

Access to building: Library access for members only

Also at: Membership Secretary; Shropshire Family History Society, 18 Gorse Lane, Bayston Hill, Shrewsbury, SY3 0JL

SHROPSHIRE LIBRARIES

Shirehall, Abbey Foregate, Shrewsbury, Shropshire, SY2 6ND

Tel: 01743 255000
Fax: 01743 255050
E-mail: libraries@shropshire.gov.uk
Website: www.shropshire.gov.uk/library.nsf
Website: www.literaryheritage.org.uk
Website: www.shropshireroots.org.uk

Enquiries to: Librarian

Organisation type and purpose: Local government body, public library.

Subject coverage: Music, recorded sound and drama collections, (Library, Castle Gates, Shrewsbury); local government and government publications (Reference Library, Castle Gates, Shrewsbury); European (EC) Information (Reference Library, Castle Gates, Shrewsbury); Shropshire local studies, extensive coverage of Shropshire and the Welsh Marches (Shropshire Archives, Castle Gates, Shrewsbury).

Collection: Shropshire Parochial Libraries (10,000 early printed and rare volumes; Shropshire Archives)
West Midlands creative literature collection (Shrewsbury Library)

Library catalogue: All or part available online

Publications: Printed

Publications list: Available in print

Access to staff: Contact by letter, by telephone, by fax and by e-mail. Appointment necessary.
Hours: Mon to Thu, 0900 to 1700; Fri, 0900 to 1600

Area libraries at: Bridgnorth, Oswestry, Shrewsbury

Constituent part of: Shropshire Council, Community Services Directorate

SIBTHORP LIBRARY

Bishop Grosseteste University College, Lincoln, LN1 3DY

Tel: 01522 583790
Fax: 01522 530243
E-mail: library-enquiries@bishopg.ac.uk
Website: www.bishopg.ac.uk/library

Founded: 1862

Organisation type and purpose: Library of an Anglican university college, principally training teachers but also offering a range of other degrees.

Subject coverage: Education studies; history/heritage studies; geography; English literature; drama; theology; music; art; children's literature.

Collection: Teaching Resources Collection – children's literature and resources to support teachers
Tom Baker, John Tomlinson and Local Studies Collections – local historical interest

Library catalogue: All or part available online

Access to staff: Contact by letter, by telephone, by fax, by e-mail and in person
Hours: Term time: Mon to Thu, 0800 to 2100; Fri, 0030 to 1900; Sat, 1100 to 1800; Sun, 1100 to 1800. Vacation time: Mon to Fri, 0900 to 1700

Member organisation of: Lincolnshire Information Services Network (LISN); SCONUL Access

SICKLE CELL AND THALASSAEMIA FOUNDATION (SSCATF)

A. C. E. Business Centre, 110–120 Wicker, Sheffield, South Yorkshire, S3 8JD

Tel: 0114 275 3209

Fax: 0114 279 6870
E-mail: sscatf1@btconnect.com
Website: www.sscatf-8m.com

Enquiries to: Chairman
Other contacts: Health Officer for health issues specific to the services offered.

Founded: 1997

Subject coverage: Information and advice about Sickle Cell and Thalassaemia. Where to get treatment, to be screened, symptoms of the disorder, applying for financial or other support, respite care, genetic counselling, etc.

Publications: Printed

Access to staff: Contact by letter, by telephone, by fax, by e-mail, in person and via website. Appointment necessary.
Hours: Mon to Fri, 0900 to 1700

Access to building: No prior appointment required
Hours: Mon to Fri, 0700 to 1700; Sat, 0900 to 1700

Access for disabled people: Parking provided, level entry, access to all public areas, toilet facilities

SICKLE CELL SOCIETY

54 Station Road, London, NW10 4UA

Tel: 020 8961 7795
Fax: 020 8961 8346
E-mail: sicklecellsoc@btinternet.com
Website: www.sicklecellsociety.org

Enquiries to: Director
Direct e-mail: sickleinfo.line@btinternet.com
Other contacts: Finance Manager; Fundraising Manager

Founded: 1979

Organisation type and purpose: Voluntary organisation, registered charity (charity number 1046631), suitable for ages: all.

Subject coverage: Information on sickle cell disorders, financial assistance, educational grants, holiday and recreational opportunities.

Publications: Printed

Publications list: Available online and in print

Access to staff: Contact by letter, by telephone, by fax, by e-mail, in person and via website
Hours: Mon to Fri, 0900 to 1700

Access to building: No prior appointment required
Hours: Mon to Fri, 0900 to 1700

Other address: Brent Sickle Link; 25 High Street, Harlesden, NW10; tel: 020 8961 6090

SIGHT SAVERS INTERNATIONAL (SSI)

Grosvenor Hall, Bolnore Road, Haywards Heath, West Sussex, RH16 4BX

Tel: 01444 446600
Fax: 01444 446688
E-mail: info@sightsavers.org
Website: www.sightsavers.org

Enquiries to: Internal Communications Manager
Direct tel: 01444 446661
Direct e-mail: kbirrell@sightsaversint.org

Founded: 1950

Organisation type and purpose:
International organisation, registered charity (charity number 207544).
To prevent and cure blindness in the developing world, to provide training for incurably blind children and adults, and to train local staff.

Subject coverage: Ophthalmology, community ophthalmology education, prevention and cure of blindness in developing countries, training of ophthalmic personnel, training of personnel working with visually handicapped people, education of blind children and rehabilitation for blind adults.

Collection: Small resource centre of books, articles, journals, slides and photos primarily for internal use but available for reference by the public by appointment

Non-library collection catalogue: All or part available in-house

Publications: Printed, and electronic and video

Publications list: Available in print

Access to staff: Contact by letter, by telephone, by fax, by e-mail and via website. Appointment necessary.
Hours: Mon to Fri, 0900 to 1700

Access to building: Prior appointment required
Hours: Mon to Fri, 0900 to 1630

Has consultative status with the: United Nations

In collaboration with the: World Health Organisation

Links with: International Agency for the Prevention of Blindness; International Council for the Education of the Visually Handicapped; World Blind Union

SIGNATURE

Mersey House, Mandale Business Park, Belmont, Durham, DH1 1TH

Tel: 0191 383 1155; minicom no. 0191 383 7915
Fax: 0191 383 7914
E-mail: durham@signature.org.uk
Website: www.signature.org.uk

Enquiries to: Communications Team Support
Direct tel: 0191 383 7922
Direct e-mail: clare.towns@signature.org.uk

Founded: 1982

Organisation type and purpose: Registered charity. A UK awarding body accredited by Ofqual offering a wide range of high quality qualifications in British Sign Language and other forms of communication used by deaf and deafblind people. Also conducts the selection, training and monitoring of assessors. Promotes the importance of professional standards and working practices among those offering linguistic access services. Administers the National Registers for Communication Professionals working with deaf and deafblind people.
To provide knowledge and recognise skills in the languages and communication methods used by deaf people.

Subject coverage: Communicating with deaf and deafblind people, British Sign Language, Lipspeaking, communicating and guiding skills with deafblind people, BSL/English Interpreting, deaf awareness, deafblind awareness.

Education services: Awarding Body for British Sign Language (BSL) and other Deaf-related qualifications.

Publications list: Available online and in print

Access to staff: Contact by letter, by telephone, by fax, by e-mail and via website
Hours: Mon to Thu, 0900 to 1700; Fri, 0900 to 1630
Special comments: All enquiries to Durham office.

Also at: Signature – Northern Ireland Office; Wilton House, 5 College Square North, Belfast, BT1 6AR; tel: 028 9043 8161 (voice and text); fax: 028 9043 8161; website: http://www.signature.org.uk
Signature – Scotland Office; Touchbase Community Suite, 43 Middlesex Street, Glasgow, G41 1EE; tel: 0141 4187191; fax: 0141 4187192; website: http://www.signature.org.uk

SIGNET LIBRARY

Society of Writers to HM Signet, Parliament Square, Edinburgh, EH1 1RF

Tel: 0131 220 3249
Fax: 0131 220 4016
E-mail: library@wssociety.co.uk
Website: www.wssociety.co.uk
Website: signet.nls.uk/webvoy2.htm

Enquiries to: Librarian

Founded: 1594

Organisation type and purpose:
Professional body (membership is by qualification), present number of members: 1,000.

Subject coverage: Law, particularly Scots law; Scottish history.

Collection: Court of Session Papers (2,500 vols); William Roughead Collection (Trials and criminology) (750 vols); Mary, Queen of Scots Collection (250 vols)

Non-library collection catalogue: All or part available online and in-house

Library catalogue: All or part available online and in-house

Access to staff: Contact by letter and by e-mail. Appointment necessary. Access for members only. Non-members charged.
Hours: Mon to Fri, 0930 to 1630

Access for disabled people: Level entry

SIKH EDUCATIONAL ADVISORY SERVICES

Guru Guru House, 42 Park Avenue, Leeds, West Yorkshire, LS15 8EW

Tel: 0113 260 2484

Enquiries to: Director General
Direct tel: 07973 286585

continued overleaf

Founded: 1984

Organisation type and purpose: Advisory body, professional body, suitable for ages: all, training organisation, consultancy. Spiritual counselling.

Subject coverage: Religion, culture, Sikh education, stories, drama, dance, music, language, exhibitions, training.

Publications: Electronic and video

Publications list: Available in print

Access to staff: Contact by letter and by telephone
Hours: Sun to Sat, 0700 to 2100

Access to building: Prior appointment required

Access for disabled people: Parking provided, level entry, toilet facilities

SILK ASSOCIATION OF GREAT BRITAIN (SAGB)

5 Portland Place, London, W1B 1PW

Tel: 020 7636 7788
Fax: 020 7636 7515
E-mail: sagb@dial.pipex.com
Website: www.silk.org.uk

Enquiries to: Secretary

Organisation type and purpose: Trade association.

Subject coverage: All aspects of silk, silk trade and promotion.

Collection: Samples and literature about silk for teachers, graduates and school children

Trade and statistical information: Silk in UK

Publications: Printed, and electronic and video

Access to staff: Contact by letter, by fax and by e-mail
Hours: Mon to Fri, 0900 to 1700

Incorporated when the: Silk and Man-made Fibre Users Association was liquidated

Member of: British Apparel & Textile Confederation; International Silk Association

SILVER SOCIETY

Box 246, 2 Lansdowne Row, London, W1J 6HL

E-mail: secretary@thesilversociety.org
Website: www.thesilversociety.org

Enquiries to: Secretary
Direct e-mail: editor@thesilversociety.org
Other contacts: Editor

Founded: 1958

Organisation type and purpose: Learned society (membership is by election or invitation), present number of members: 415, registered charity (charity number 279352).
To encourage an interest in the craft of the goldsmith and silversmith, past and present.

Subject coverage: Silver; silversmiths; silver workers; gold; goldsmiths; goldworking; plate; plate working/workers; plated wares (Sheffield plate and electroplate); design and designers; social history (with regard to the use of gold, silver and plated wares); biographical information on the above.

Library catalogue: All or part available online

Publications: Printed
Order printed publications from: website: http://www.thesilversociety.org

Publications list: Available online

Access to staff: Contact by letter, by fax, by e-mail and via website

SIMPLIFIED SPELLING SOCIETY (SSS)

23 Albion Street, New Brighton, Wirral, Merseyside, CH45 9LE

Tel: 0151 327 5837
E-mail: bjhughes71@hotmail.com
Website: www.spellingsociety.org

Enquiries to: Secretary

Founded: 1908

Organisation type and purpose: Learned society (membership is by subscription), voluntary organisation, research organisation.
Working for planned change in English spelling for the benefit of learners and users everywhere.

Subject coverage: Modernisation and simplification of English spelling, English spelling systems, literacy, English language teaching, linguistics, psychology of writing systems, lexicography, typography.

Collection: Historical collection of Society material (Mont Follick Collection) in Library of Manchester University, Department of General Linguistics

Publications: Printed

Access to staff: Contact by letter, by telephone, by e-mail and via website. Appointment necessary.
Hours: Any day, 0900 to 2200

Links with: British Dyslexia Association; Initial Teaching Alphabet Federation; UK Reading Association

SINGAPORE HIGH COMMISSION

9 Wilton Crescent, London, SW1X 8SP

Tel: 020 7235 8315
Fax: 020 7245 6583
E-mail: singhc_lon@sgmfa.gov.sg
Website: www.singstat.gov.sg
Website: www.sgnews.info
Website: www.gov.sg
Website: www.mfa.gov.sg/london

Enquiries to: Information Officer
Direct e-mail: Consular enquiries to singhc_con_lon@sgmfa.gov.sg

Organisation type and purpose: National government body.

Subject coverage: Singapore in general.

Publications: Printed

Access to staff: Contact by letter, by telephone and by e-mail
Special comments: Consular hours Mon to Fri, 0930 to 1230

Links with: Contact Singapore; 5 Regent Street, Lower Ground Floor, London, SW1 4LR; tel: 020 7321 5600; website: http://www.contactsingapore.org.sg

Trade Development Board; 53 Monument Street, London, EC3R 8BU; tel: 020 7626 1717; fax: 020 7626 1711

SINGER OWNERS CLUB (SOC)

11 Ermine Rise, Great Casterton, Stamford, Lincolnshire, PE9 4AJ

Tel: 01780 762740
E-mail: martyn@singeroc.idps.co.uk
Website: www.singerownersclub.co.uk

Enquiries to: Secretary

Founded: 1951

Organisation type and purpose: Membership association (membership is by subscription), present number of members: 800.

Subject coverage: Singer motor cars and motor cycles 1876–1970, history of George Singer and the Singer motor companies and Rootes group.

Collection: Photographs and documentation on all Singer models

Publications: Printed

Access to staff: Contact by letter, by telephone, by e-mail and via website
Hours: Mon to Fri, 1900 to 2200

SINO-HIMALAYAN PLANT ASSOCIATION

81 Parlaunt Road, Slough, Berkshire, SL3 8BE

Tel: 01753 542823
Fax: 01753 543823

Enquiries to: Secretary

Founded: 1991

Organisation type and purpose: Membership association (membership is by subscription).

Subject coverage: Sino-Himalayan, i.e. Himalayan and Chinese, mountain plants.

Collection: P N Kohli Memorial Herbarium of Himalayan plant pressed specimens and Memorial Himalayan Garden

Publications: Printed

Access to staff: Contact by letter

SINTO – THE INFORMATION PARTNERSHIP

Formal name: SINTO – the information partnership for South Yorkshire and North Derbyshire

c/o Learning Centre, Sheffield Hallam University, Collegiate Crescent, Sheffield, South Yorkshire, S10 2BP

Tel: 0114 225 5739; 0114 225 5740
Fax: 0114 225 2476
E-mail: sintoenquiry@shu.ac.uk
Website: www.sinto.org.uk

Enquiries to: Director
Direct e-mail: slsdam@exchange.shu.ac.uk

Founded: 1933; created by the merger of Board for Library and Information Services in Sheffield and SINTO (year of change 1991); formerly called Scheme for the Interchange of Technical Publications;

formerly called Sheffield Interchange Organisation; formerly called Sheffield Information Organisation

Organisation type and purpose:
Membership association (membership is by subscription).
To promote and develop library and information services through co-operation, planning and partnership. Provides training and CPD events. SINTO is the Library and Information Plan (LIP) for South Yorkshire and North Derbyshire.

Subject coverage: Access to resources of member libraries with emphasis on business, science and technology.

Publications: Printed, and electronic and video

Access to staff: Contact by letter, by telephone, by fax, by e-mail and via website. Appointment necessary.
Hours: Mon to Fri, 0900 to 1700

SIR ARTHUR SULLIVAN SOCIETY (SASS)

Great Tregue Farmhouse, Lansallos, Looe PL13 2PT

E-mail: secretary@sullivansociety.org.uk
Website: www.sullivansociety.org.uk

Enquiries to: Secretary
Other contacts: Membership Secretary

Founded: 1977

Organisation type and purpose:
International organisation, learned society, membership association (membership is by subscription), present number of members: 400+, voluntary organisation, registered charity (charity number 274022), suitable for ages: all, research organisation, publishing house.
Promotion of the music of Arthur Sullivan.

Subject coverage: All aspects of the life, career and work of Sir Arthur Sullivan (1842–1900), performances and recordings of his music, musical criticism.

Collection: Library of performing material for music by Sullivan, including the only extant orchestral parts for a number of major orchestral works (notably Victoria and Merrie England; L'Ile Enchantée; Thespis; The Merry Wives of Windsor); full choral and orchestral material for Kenilworth (masque); On Shore and Sea (cantata); also vocal, choral scores for operas Haddon Hall and The Chieftain.

Publications: Printed, and electronic and video
Order printed publications from: The Sales Officer, Sir Arthur Sullivan Society, Fuchsia Cottage, Main Road, Colwich, ST17 0XE; e -mail: elaineatsass@aol.com

Publications list: Available online and in print

Access to staff: Contact by letter, by telephone, by e-mail and via website. Appointment necessary.
Hours: Preferred hours for telephone calls 1000 to 2000.

Access to building: By appointment

Also at: Membership Secretary; 71 The Heights, Foxgrove Road, Beckenham, BR3 5BZ

SIR ERNEST CASSEL EDUCATIONAL TRUST

5 Grimston Park Mews, Grimston Park, Tadcaster, North Yorkshire, LS24 9DB

Tel: 01937 834730
E-mail: casseltrust@btinternet.com

Enquiries to: Secretary

Founded: 1919

Organisation type and purpose: Registered charity.
Educational grant-awarding body.

Subject coverage: Overseas research grants in the humanities (administered by the British Academy) for more junior teaching members of faculties; Mountbatten Memorial grants to Commonwealth students taking higher education courses in the UK who run into unforeseen financial difficulties in their final year; grants to organisations in the field of adult and higher education.

Access to staff: Contact by letter, by telephone and by e-mail
Hours: Mon to Fri, 0900 to 1700

SIR NORMAN CHESTER CENTRE FOR FOOTBALL RESEARCH (SNCCFR)

Department of Sociology, University of Leicester, Leicester, LE1 7RH

Tel: 0116 252 2741
Fax: 0116 252 2746
E-mail: footballresearch@le.ac.uk

Enquiries to: Administrator

Founded: 1987

Organisation type and purpose: University department or institute, research organisation.

Subject coverage: Football.

Publications list: Available in print

Access to staff: Contact by letter and by e-mail. Appointment necessary.
Hours: Mon to Fri, 0900 to 1700

Access to building: No prior appointment required
Hours: Mon to Fri, 0930 to 1700

SIRSIDYNIX

Formal name: Sirsi Limited

The Chequers, St Mary's Way, Chesham, Buckinghamshire, HP5 1LL

Tel: 01494 777666
Fax: 01494 777555
E-mail: sales-uk@sirsidynix.co.uk
Website: www.sirsidynix.com

Enquiries to: Sales Director
Direct e-mail: david.green@sirsidynix.co.uk

Founded: 1990

Organisation type and purpose:
Consultancy.
European sales and support office for the Symphony/Unicorn/Horizon/Dynix integrated library management systems.

Subject coverage: Software for libraries and information handlers.

Access to staff: Contact by letter, by telephone, by fax, by e-mail and via website
Hours: Mon to Fri, 0830 to 1730

SKI CLUB OF GREAT BRITAIN

The White House, 57–63 Church Road, Wimbledon, London, SW19 5SB

Tel: 020 8410 2000
Fax: 020 8410 2001
E-mail: skiers@skiclub.co.uk
Website: www.skiclub.co.uk

Enquiries to: Information Officer

Founded: 1903

Organisation type and purpose:
Membership association.
Promoting skiing and snowboarding.

Subject coverage: Recreational skiing, ski mountaineering, ski touring, resorts and holidays, snow conditions, history of skiing, statistics.

Publications: Printed

Access to staff: Contact by letter, by telephone, by fax, by e-mail, in person and via website. Appointment necessary. Access for members only.
Hours: Mon to Fri, 0900 to 1730 (summer); 0900 to 1800 (winter)

Access to building: Prior appointment required
Hours: Mon to Fri, 0900 to 1730
Special comments: Other events held in the library.

Access for disabled people: Ramped entry, level entry, access to all public areas, toilet facilities

SKILL: NATIONAL BUREAU FOR STUDENTS WITH DISABILITIES (Skill)

Unit 3, Floor 3, Radisson Court, 219 Long Lane, London, SE1 4PR

Tel: 020 7450 0620; 0800 328 5050 (information); 0800 068 2422 (textphone)
Fax: 020 7450 0650
E-mail: skill@skill.org.uk
Website: www.skill.org.uk

Enquiries to: Information and Services Manager

Founded: 1974

Organisation type and purpose: Advisory body, membership association (membership is by subscription), present number of members: 1,000, voluntary organisation, registered charity (charity number 801971, also registered in Scotland, number SC039212), suitable for ages: 16+.
Aims to promote opportunities for people with any kind of impairment in 16+ education, training, transition to employment and volunteering.

continued overleaf

Subject coverage: Information and advice for people with disabilities or learning difficulties, their families, friends and people working with them, regarding post-16 education and training.

Publications: Printed, and electronic and video
Order printed publications from: http://www.skill.org.uk/shop/shop.asp
Order electronic and video publications from: e-mail: info@skill.org.uk

Publications list: Available online and in print

Access to staff: Contact by letter, by telephone, by fax, by e-mail and via website
Hours: Information Service helpline: Tue, 1130 to 1330; Thu, 1330 to 1530

Access to building: No access other than to staff

Access for disabled people: Parking provided, ramped entry, level entry, access to all public areas, toilet facilities

Branches: Skill Northern Ireland; Unit 2, Jennymount Court, North Derby Street, Belfast, BT15 3HN; tel: 028 9028 7000; fax: 028 9028 7002; e-mail: info@skillni.org.uk; website: http://www.skillni.org.uk
Skill Scotland; Norton Park, 57 Albion Road, Edinburgh, EH7 5QY; tel: 0131 475 2348; fax: 0131 475 2397; e-mail: admin@skillscotland.org.uk; website: http://www.skill.org.uk/scotland
Skill Wales; Skill Wales, Suite 14, 2nd Floor, The Executive Centre, Temple Court, Cathedral Road, Cardiff, CF11 9HA; tel: 029 2078 6506; e-mail: admin@skillwales.org.uk; website: http://www.skill.org.uk/wales

SKILLS FUNDING AGENCY

26 Kings Hill Avenue, Kings Hill, West Malling, Kent, ME19 4AE

Tel: 0845 377 5000
Fax: 01732 876917
E-mail: info@skillsfundingagency.bis.gov.uk
Website: www.skillsfundingagency.bis.gov.uk

Enquiries to: Information Officer

Founded: 2010; carries out the functions of the former Learning & Skills Council (year of change 2010)

Organisation type and purpose: Service industry, training organisation.
Learning and Business Link.

Subject coverage: Education and training funding, private training companies, FE colleges, adult and community education initiatives, workforce development, investors in people, business and education partnerships.

Publications: Printed, and electronic and video

Access to staff: Contact by letter, by telephone, by fax, by e-mail and via website
Hours: Mon to Fri, 0830 to 1730

Access for disabled people: Parking provided, level entry, access to all public areas, toilet facilities

SKIN, HIDE AND LEATHER TRADERS ASSOCIATION (SHALTA)

Douglas House, Douglas Road, Melrose, Roxburghshire, TD6 9QT

Tel: 01896 822233
Fax: 01896 823344
E-mail: offices@andaco.com

Enquiries to: Secretary General

Founded: 1916

Organisation type and purpose: Trade association.

Subject coverage: Trade in hides, skins and leather both nationally and internationally, contractual information, overseas trade missions.

Access to staff: Contact by letter, by telephone and by fax
Hours: Mon to Fri, 0900 to 1700

Member of: International Council of Hides, Skins and Leather Traders Associations; Union Européenne des Négociants en Cuir et Peaux Brutes

SKIPTON LIBRARY

High Street, Skipton, North Yorkshire, BD23 1JX

Tel: 0845 034 9538
Fax: 01756 798056
E-mail: skipton.library@northyorks.gov.uk

Enquiries to: Librarian
Other contacts: Information Librarian for reference, local and family history.

Founded: 1909

Organisation type and purpose: Public library.

Subject coverage: General reference and information sources, including business information and local history material for the Craven area.

Collection: Petyt Collection of material on 17th century history and theology

Non-library collection catalogue: All or part available in-house

Library catalogue: All or part available in-house

Access to staff: Contact by letter, by telephone, by fax, by e-mail and in person
Hours: Mon, Wed and Thu, 0930 to 1900; Fri, 0930 to 1700; Sat, 0930 to 1600; Tue, closed

Parent body: North Yorkshire County Library; 21 Grammar School Lane, Northallerton, North Yorkshire, DL6 1DF; tel: 01609 780780; fax: 01609 780793

SLOUGH BOROUGH COUNCIL (SBC)

Town Hall, Bath Road, Slough, Berkshire, SL1 3UQ

Tel: 01753 552288; 01753 875030 (minicom)
Fax: 01753 692499
Website: www.slough.gov.uk

Enquiries to: Chief Executive

Organisation type and purpose: Local government body.

Access to staff: Contact by telephone
Hours: Mon to Fri, 0900 to 1645

Other addresses: Wellington House

SLOUGH LIBRARIES

85 High Street, Slough, SL1 1EA

Tel: 01753 535166
Fax: 01753 825050
E-mail: library@slough.gov.uk
Website: www.slough.gov.uk/libraries

Enquiries to: Information Services Librarian
Direct tel: 01753 787511

Organisation type and purpose: Local government body, public library.

Subject coverage: Slough local studies collection; general information; business information; EU information; careers and education.

Library catalogue: All or part available online and in-house

Access to staff: Contact by letter, by telephone, by fax, by e-mail, in person and via website
Hours: Mon, Thu, 0900 to 1700; Tue, Fri, 0900 to 1900; Wed, 0930 to 1900; Sat, 0900 to 1600

Access for disabled people: Ramped entry

SMALL BUSINESS BUREAU LIMITED (SBB)

Curzon House, Church Road, Windlesham, Surrey, GU20 6BH

Tel: 01276 452010
Fax: 01276 451602
E-mail: info@sbb.org.uk
Website: www.smallbusinessbureau.org.uk

Enquiries to: Managing Director

Founded: 1976

Organisation type and purpose: Membership association (membership is by subscription).
Lobbying organisation.

Subject coverage: Small and medium-sized businesses.

Publications: Printed

Access to staff: Contact by letter, by telephone, by fax and by e-mail
Hours: Mon to Fri, 0900 to 1700

SMALL ENTERPRISE RESEARCH TEAM (SERTeam)

Open University Business School, Open University, Walton Hall, Milton Keynes, Buckinghamshire, MK7 6AA

Tel: 01908 655831 / 020 8560 3004
Fax: 01908 655898 / 020 8560 3004
E-mail: oubs-sbrt@open.ac.uk
Website: www.serteam.co.uk

Enquiries to: Secretary

Founded: 1984

Organisation type and purpose: Registered charity (charity number 1100928), university department or institute, research organisation.
Educational research charity.

Subject coverage: Management issues, exporting, regional differences, business services, BS5750, small business policy, small business economy. Further education and colleges report, computers in rural small firms across Europe.

Non-library collection catalogue: All or part available in print

Library catalogue: All or part available in print

Publications: Printed

Publications list: Available online and in print

Access to staff: Contact by telephone, by fax and by e-mail
Hours: Mon to Fri, 0900 to 1700

Access to building: No prior appointment required

Other addresses: Small Enterprise Research Team; 45 Clydesdale Close, Isleworth, London, TW7 6ST; tel: 020 8568 3004; fax: 020 8568 3004; e-mail: b.porter-blake@open.ac.uk

SMALLPEICE ENTERPRISES LIMITED

27 Newbold Terrace East, Leamington Spa, Warwickshire, CV32 4ES

Tel: 01926 336423
Fax: 01926 450679
E-mail: train@smallpeice.co.uk
Website: www.smallpeice.co.uk

Enquiries to: Marketing Assistant

Founded: 1966

Organisation type and purpose:
Professional body, registered charity, training organisation, consultancy.
Training Centre.
Smallpeice combines over 30 years' training experience and specialist industry focus to provide a total training service for engineering and manufacturing companies nationwide.

Subject coverage: Design engineering, Six Sigma; Lean Manufacturing; Autocad; project management; management skills; public courses nationwide; in-company bespoke training; corporate development partnership; strategic conferences; facilitation and consultancy; one-to-one training; ICT-based training partnerships.

Non-library collection catalogue: All or part available online

Publications list: Available in print

Access to staff: Contact by letter, by telephone, by fax, by e-mail and via website
Hours: Mon to Fri, 0830 to 1730

Parent body: The Smallpeice Trust; tel: 01926 333200; fax: 01926 333202

SNACK, NUT AND CRISP MANUFACTURERS ASSOCIATION LIMITED (SNACMA)

37–41 Bedford Row, London, WC1R 4JH

Tel: 020 7611 4660
Fax: 020 7611 4661
E-mail: esa@esa.org.uk
Website: www.esa.org.uk

Enquiries to: Director General

Founded: 1983

Organisation type and purpose: Trade association.

Subject coverage: Snack industry and products; nutritional data; statistics.

Publications: Printed

Access to staff: Contact by letter, by telephone, by fax, by e-mail and via website. Appointment necessary.
Hours: Mon to Fri, 0900 to 1700

Member of: Food and Drink Federation; tel: 020 7836 2460; Potato Processors Association

SNOWDONIA SOCIETY (CESS)

Formal name: Cymdeithas Eryri – Snowdonia Society

Snowdonia Society, Caban, Brynrefail, Gwynedd, LL55 3NR

Tel: 01286685498
E-mail: info@snowdonia-society.org.uk
Website: www.snowdonia-society.org.uk

Enquiries to: Director
Other contacts: Office Administrator

Founded: 1967

Organisation type and purpose:
Membership association (membership is by subscription), with approximately 1600 members, voluntary organisation, registered charity (charity number 253231).
Conservation charity for Snowdonia, aiming to protect the landscape and heritage of Snowdonia.

Subject coverage: Planning, administration and conservation of the Snowdonia National Park and district, transport, wildlife, flora.

Information services: Information about Snowdonia and planning and access issues in the Park.

Special visitor services: The Snowdonia Society's property at Ty Hyll (the Ugly House) is surrounded by a wildlife garden and woodland managed for biodiversity and to preserve native species and encourage natural regeneration.

Education services: Works with school and college groups organising conservation workdays, and several schools are affiliate members of the Society.

Services for disabled people: The property owned by the Snowdonia Society at Ty Hyll (the Ugly House) is accessible to wheelchairs and people with limited mobility, although there is some rough and sloping ground.

Collection: Files on past issues within Snowdonia

Publications: Printed

Access to staff: Contact by letter, by telephone, by e-mail, in person and via website. Appointment necessary.
Hours: Mon to Fri, 0900 to 1700
Special comments: The office may be unstaffed at times if staff at meetings, etc. Call in advance

Access to building: No prior appointment required for Ty Hyll
Hours: Tearoom open Tue to Sun, 1030 to 1600

Affiliated to: Campaign for National Parks; 6–7 Barnard Mews, London, SW11 1QU; tel: 020 792 44077; website: http://www.cnp.org.uk

SNOWSPORT ENGLAND (SSE)

Area Library Building, Queensway Mall, The Cornbow, Halesowen, West Midlands, B63 4AJ

Tel: 0121 501 2314
Fax: 0121 585 6448
E-mail: info@snowsportengland.org.uk
Website: www.snowsportengland.org.uk

Enquiries to: Chief Executive

Founded: 1978; formerly called English Ski Council (year of change 2004)

Organisation type and purpose: Governing body for skiing in England.

Subject coverage: English skiers and skiing, membership scheme, coaching awards scheme, promotion of events, design and development of ski slopes.

Publications: Printed

Publications list: Available in print

Access to staff: Contact by letter and by e-mail
Hours: Mon to Fri, 0900 to 1700

Access to building: Prior appointment required

Access for disabled people: Parking provided, ramped entry, access to all public areas

Grant-aided by: Sport England

SOAS

Formal name: School of Oriental and African Studies

Thornhaugh Street, Russell Square, London, WC1H 0XG

Tel: 020 7898 4163
Fax: 020 7898 4159
E-mail: libenquiry@soas.ac.uk
Website: www.soas.ac.uk/library
Website: www.soas.ac.uk/archives/home.html
Website: lib.soas.ac.uk

Founded: 1916

Organisation type and purpose: University library.

Subject coverage: Asian and African studies in the humanities and social sciences, with special emphasis on anthropology, ethnography, history, language, literature, economics, law, politics, sociology, philosophy, religion and art (particularly Chinese); covers the following areas and regions: Africa, Near and Middle East and Israel, Central Asia, South Asia, South East Asia, East Asia, Oceania.

Collection: Major collections of missionary and business archives relating to Asia and Africa

Library catalogue: All or part available online, in-house and in print

Publications: Printed, and microform publications

continued overleaf

Publications list: Available in print

Access to staff: Contact by fax, by e-mail, in person and via website
Hours: Term time and Christmas and Easter vacations:
Mon to Thu, 0900 to 2330 (issue desk closes at 2000, membership at 1855); Fri, 0900 to 2330 (issue desk and membership close at 1855);
Sat, 1030 to 1800 (staffed: issue and membership desks close at 1745);
Sun, 1030 to 1800 (unstaffed: self-service only)
Summer vacation:
Mon to Fri, 0900 to 2100 (unstaffed after 1700);
Sat, 1030 to 1800 (staffed);
Sun, 1030 to 1800 (unstaffed)
Special comments: Occasional visits allowed for consultation. Non-members of the school may apply for library membership, but a charge may be made and a letter of introduction is required.

Parent body: University of London

SOCIAL CARE ASSOCIATION (SCA)

350 West Barnes Lane, Motspur Park, New Malden, KT3 6NB

Tel: 020 8949 5837
Fax: 020 8949 4384
E-mail: via website
Website: www.socialcareassociation.co.uk

Founded: 1949; formerly called Residential Child Care Association (RCCA) (year of change 1972); formerly called Residential Care Association (RCA) (year of change 1985)

Organisation type and purpose: A professional membership association for anyone who works in social care at any level, in any role and in any area; a UK-wide organisation that believes in and promotes good practice.

Subject coverage: Social care practice.

Publications: Printed, and electronic and video
Order electronic and video publications from: Download from members' section of website

Publications list: Available online

Access to staff: Contact by letter, by telephone, by fax and via website

Also at: Scotland Office; 6 School Wynd, Paisley, Renfrewshire, PA1 2DB; tel: 0141 889 6667; fax: 0141 889 4035

Links with: SCA (Education), a registered charity

SOCIAL CARE INSTITUTE FOR EXCELLENCE (SCIE)

1st Floor, Goldings House, Hay's Lane, London, SE1 2HB

Tel: 020 7089 6840
Fax: 020 7089 6841
E-mail: info@scie.org.uk
Website: www.scie.org.uk
Website: www.scie-socialcareonline.org.uk
Website: www.researchweb.org.uk
Website: www.scie-peoplemanagement.org.uk
Website: www.researchregister.org.uk

Enquiries to: Director of Knowledge Management

Founded: 2001; formerly called National Institute for Social Work (year of change 2001)

Organisation type and purpose: Voluntary organisation; research commissioning body

Subject coverage: Social welfare policy; personal social services; social care.

Non-library collection catalogue: All or part available online

Publications: Printed, and electronic and video
Order printed publications from: http://www.scie.org.uk/publications/ordering/index.asp

Publications list: Available online and in print

Access to staff: Contact by e-mail and via website
Hours: Mon to Fri, 1000 to 1700

Access to building: No prior appointment required
Hours: Mon to Fri, 1000 to 1700

Access for disabled people: Parking provided, access to all public areas, toilet facilities

SOCIAL HISTORY SOCIETY (SHS)

Furness College, Bailrigg, Lancaster, LA1 4YG

Tel: 01524 592547
Fax: 01524 846102
E-mail: l.persson@lancaster.ac.uk
Website: socialhistory.org.uk

Enquiries to: Administrative Secretary

Founded: 1976

Organisation type and purpose: Learned society.

Subject coverage: The history of society in all times and places.

Publications: Printed

Access to staff: Contact by letter, by telephone, by fax, by e-mail and via website. Appointment necessary.
Hours: Tue, 0930 to 1630; Wed, 1330 to 1630; Fri, 0930 to 1700

Access for disabled people: Parking provided, level entry, access to all public areas, toilet facilities

Affiliated to: Association of Learned Societies in the Social Sciences

SOCIAL RESEARCH ASSOCIATION (SRA)

24–32 Stephenson Way, London NW1 2HX

Tel: 0207 388 2391
E-mail: admin@the-sra.org.uk
Website: www.the-sra.org.uk

Enquiries to: Administrator

Founded: 1978

Organisation type and purpose: Membership association.

Subject coverage: Application and development of social research, methodology, funding, training and policy.

Publications: Printed

Access to staff: Contact by letter, by telephone, by e-mail and via website. Appointment necessary.
Hours: Mon to Fri, 0900 to 1700

Affiliated to: ALSISS; ARCISS; SCASS

SOCIAL, EMOTIONAL AND BEHAVIOURAL DIFFICULTIES ASSOCIATION (SEBDA)

Room 211, The Triangle, Exchange Square, Manchester, M4 3TR

Tel: 0161 240 2418
Fax: 0161 838 5601
E-mail: admin@sebda.org
Website: www.sebda.org

Enquiries to: Office Services Manager

History of institution: formerly called Association of Workers for Children with Emotional and Behavioural Difficulties (AWCEBD); formerly called Association of Workers for Maladjusted Children

Organisation type and purpose: Membership association (membership is by subscription), registered charity (charity number 258730), training organisation, consultancy.

Subject coverage: Educational and therapeutic care of disturbed children, staff training and support, emotional and behavioural difficulties, policy development.

Publications: Printed, and electronic and video

Publications list: Available in print

Access to staff: Contact by letter, by telephone, by fax, by e-mail and via website
Hours: Response to telephone enquiries 1000 to 1600

Access to building: Prior appointment required

Access for disabled people: Parking provided, level entry, toilet facilities

Member of: National Children's Bureau; Special Educational Needs National Advisory Council; Young Minds (successor to Child Guidance Trust)

SOCIALIST HEALTH ASSOCIATION (SHA)

22 Blair Road, Manchester, M16 8NS

Tel: 01612861926
E-mail: admin@sochealth.co.uk
Website: www.sochealth.co.uk

Enquiries to: Director

Founded: 1930; formerly called Socialist Medical Association (year of change 1980)

Organisation type and purpose: Membership association (membership is by subscription), present number of members: 800, voluntary organisation.
Political campaigning.

Subject coverage: Structure and accountability of the National Health Service, community care, local authority health responsibilities, health promotion, politics of health, mental health services, primary health care, health inequalities, public health, inequality.

Collection: Archives (held at Hull History Centre)

Publications: Printed

Publications list: Available in print

Access to staff: Contact by letter, by telephone, by e-mail and via website
Hours: Any reasonable hour

Access to building: Prior appointment required

Access for disabled people: Ramped entry

Affiliated to: Labour Party

SOCIALIST INTERNATIONAL WOMEN (SIW)

Maritime House, Old Town, Clapham, London, SW4 0JW

Tel: 020 7627 4449
Fax: 020 7720 4448
E-mail: socintwomen@gn.apc.org
Website: www.socintwomen.org

Enquiries to: General Secretary
Direct fax: 020 7498 1293

Founded: 1907

Organisation type and purpose: International organisation.

Subject coverage: Women; human rights; development; disarmament.

Has: 145 member organisations in different countries; 7 fraternal and associated organisations world-wide

SOCIÉTÉ JERSIAISE

7 Pier Road, St Helier, Jersey, JE2 4XW, Channel Islands

Tel: 01534 758314 (office); 730538 (library); 633398 (photo archive)
Fax: 01534 888262
E-mail: library@societe-jersiaise.org
Website: www.societe-jersiaise.org

Enquiries to: Librarian
Other contacts: Photographic Administrator (for photographic archive)

Founded: 1873

Organisation type and purpose: Learned society.

Subject coverage: Local history, natural history with sections on zoology, ornithology, botany, garden history, entomology, marine biology, archaeology, geology, numismatics, bibliography, mycology, environment, the ancient language.

Collection: Manuscripts, archival documents, correspondence, family papers, ephemera, newspapers, photographs, periodicals and rare books related to Jersey

Non-library collection catalogue: All or part available online and in-house

Library catalogue: All or part available online and in-house

Publications: Printed

Publications list: Available online and in print

Access to staff: Contact by letter, by telephone, by fax, by e-mail, in person and via website
Hours: Mon to Fri, 0900 to 1700

Links with: Jersey Archives Service; tel: 01534 633303; fax: 01534 633301; Jersey Museums Service; The Weighbridge, St Helier, Jersey, JE2 3NF; tel: 01534 633330; fax: 01534 633301

SOCIETY AND COLLEGE OF RADIOGRAPHERS (SCOR)

Quartz House, 207 Providence Square, London, SE1 2EW

Tel: 020 7740 7200
Fax: 020 7740 7204
E-mail: info@sor.org
Website: www.sor.org

Enquiries to: Admin Assistants
Other contacts: Director of Professional Development for professional matters

Organisation type and purpose: Trade union, present number of members: 18,000.

Subject coverage: Radiography and related careers.

Education services: Education for radiographers and related careers.

Publications: Printed

Publications list: Available online and in print

Access to staff: Contact by letter, by telephone, by fax, by e-mail, in person and via website. Appointment necessary.
Hours: Mon to Fri, 0900 to 1700

Access for disabled people: Parking provided, access to all public areas, toilet facilities

SOCIETY FOR ADVANCED LEGAL STUDIES (SALS)

17 Russell Square, London, WC1B 5DR

Tel: 020 7862 5865
Fax: 020 7862 5855
E-mail: sals@sas.ac.uk
Website: www.iats.sas.ac.uk/SALS/society.htm

Enquiries to: Secretary

Founded: 1997

Organisation type and purpose: Learned society (membership is by subscription, qualification).

Access to staff: Contact by e-mail
Hours: Mon to Fri, 0900 to 1700

SOCIETY FOR ANGLO-CHINESE UNDERSTANDING (SACU)

2 Lawnswood Avenue, Poulton-le-Fylde, Lancashire, FY6 7ED

Tel: 01253 894582
Website: www.sacu.org

Enquiries to: Information Officer

Founded: 1965

Organisation type and purpose: Membership association, registered charity. To promote Anglo-Chinese understanding and friendship.

Subject coverage: China and Chinese culture; current events; calligraphy and brush painting (not specialised business or academic information).

Publications: Printed

Access to staff: Contact by letter and by telephone
Hours: Mon to Fri, 0900 to 1700

SOCIETY FOR APPLIED MICROBIOLOGY (SfAM)

Bedford Heights, Brickhill Drive, Bedford, MK41 7PH

Tel: 01234 326661
Fax: 01234 326678
E-mail: communications@sfam.org.uk
Website: www.sfam.org.uk

Enquiries to: Chief Executive Officer
Direct e-mail: pfwheat@sfam.org.uk

Founded: 1931

Organisation type and purpose: International organisation, learned society (membership is by subscription), registered charity (charity number 1123044), company limited by guarantee (registered in England and Wales 6462427).

Subject coverage: All aspects of applied bacteriology and microbiology.

Publications: Printed, and electronic and video
Order printed publications from: Wiley-Blackwell

Publications list: Available online and in print

Access to staff: Contact by letter, by telephone, by fax, by e-mail and via website
Hours: Mon to Fri, 0900 to 1700

Member of: Federation of European Microbiological Societies; International Union of Microbiological Societies; Society of Biology

SOCIETY FOR ARMY HISTORICAL RESEARCH (SAHR)

c/o National Army Museum, Royal Hospital Road, London, SW3 4HT

Enquiries to: Honorary Treasurer
Direct tel: 020 3227 0156
Direct fax: 020 3227 0156
Direct e-mail: guysayle@hotmail.com

Founded: 1921

Organisation type and purpose: Learned society (membership is by subscription), present number of members: 1,000. Military historical research.

Subject coverage: History of British and Commonwealth armies and their ancillary formations. Members' articles/research published in quarterly journal.

Publications: Printed

Access to staff: Contact by letter and by telephone. Access for members only.
Hours: Mon to Fri, 0900 to 1700

SOCIETY FOR CARDIOTHORACIC SURGERY IN GREAT BRITAIN AND IRELAND (SCTS)

35–43 Lincoln's Inn Fields, London, WC2A 3PE

Tel: 020 7869 6893
Fax: 020 7869 6890
E-mail: sctsadmin@scts.org
Website: www.scts.org

Enquiries to: Society Administrator

Organisation type and purpose: Professional body.

Subject coverage: Thoracic and cardiac surgery.

Access to staff: Contact by e-mail
Hours: Mon to Wed, 0800 to 1400; Thur, 0930 to 1430

SOCIETY FOR CO-OPERATION IN RUSSIAN AND SOVIET STUDIES (SCRSS)

320 Brixton Road, London, SW9 6AB

Tel: 020 7274 2282
Fax: 020 7274 3230
E-mail: ruslibrary@scrss.org.uk
Website: www.scrss.org.uk

Enquiries to: Librarian

Founded: 1924; formerly called Society for Cultural Relations with the USSR (year of change 1992)

Organisation type and purpose: Membership association (membership is by subscription), present number of members: 500 and 25 affiliated universities/organisations, voluntary organisation, research organisation.
To facilitate contacts and understanding between the peoples of the UK and the former Soviet Union through language courses, information, library etc.

Subject coverage: Russian history including pre-revolutionary and Soviet history, geography, literature, art, theatre, film, ballet, music, education, sport, social sciences (including ethnography), economics, law.

Collection: Andrew Rothstein Collection (early Soviet documents and pamphlets)
Archive material of the SCR (founded 1924)
Huntly Carter Bequest (early Soviet theatre and architecture photographs)
Children's library
Newspaper cuttings files on all subjects plus many others maintained, mainly Russian press in translation

Trade and statistical information: Statistics, in cuttings files.
Texts in Russian and English of some laws.
Statistical, economic and political data available in variety of subjects

Non-library collection catalogue: All or part available in-house

Library catalogue: All or part available in-house

Publications: Printed

Access to staff: Contact by letter, by telephone, by fax, by e-mail and in person. Appointment necessary. Non-members charged.
Hours: Mon to Fri, 1000 to 1300 and 1400 to 1800

Access to building: *Hours:* Mon to Fri, 1000 to 1800
Special comments: Access is by appointment only.

Access for disabled people: Parking provided, level entry, toilet facilities
Special comments: Prior notice required for parking.

SOCIETY FOR COMPANION ANIMAL STUDIES (SCAS)

10B Leny Road, Callander, Perthshire, FK17 8BA

Tel: 01877 330996
Fax: 01877 330996
Website: www.scas.org.uk

Enquiries to: Executive Director

Founded: 1979

Organisation type and purpose: Membership association (membership is by subscription), present number of members: 400, voluntary organisation, registered charity (charity number 1070938), suitable for ages: 18+.

Subject coverage: Relationship between people and their companion animals; potential therapeutic value in treating psychological problems, mental illness, impaired health, promotion of responsible pet ownership to ensure quality of life of a pet and owner. Training in providing support for bereaved pet owners.

Collection: Library for reference in research at general and academic level
Requests by phone and letter only

Non-library collection catalogue: All or part available in print

Library catalogue: All or part available in-house

Publications: Printed, and electronic and video

Publications list: Available online and in print

Access to staff: Contact by letter, by telephone, by fax and by e-mail. Non-members charged.
Hours: Mon to Fri, 0900 to 1700

Founder member in 1992 of: International Association of Human/Animal Interaction Organisations (IAHAIO)

Informal links with: AFIRAC; France; and other members of IAHAIO; DELTA Society; USA; Organisations having similar interests and concerns in the UK and abroad; Pet Fostering Service; Scotland; tel: 01877 331496; The Blue Cross; (Pet Bereavement Support Service 0800 096 6606); tel: 01993 822651; fax: 01993 823083

SOCIETY FOR COMPUTERS AND LAW (SCL)

10 Hurle Crescent, Clifton, Bristol, BS8 2TA

Tel: 0117 923 7393
Fax: 0117 923 9305
E-mail: ruth.baker@scl.org
Website: www.scl.org

Enquiries to: General Manager

Founded: 1973

Organisation type and purpose: National organisation, professional body, membership association (membership is by subscription), present number of members: 2,500, registered charity (charity number 266331).

Subject coverage: Information technology law, information technology for lawyers.

Information services: News and articles on IT Law

Education services: CPD Courses

Publications: Printed

Access to staff: Contact by letter, by telephone, by fax, by e-mail and via website. Appointment necessary.
Hours: Mon to Fri, 0900 to 1700

Access to building: Prior appointment required
Hours: Mon to Fri, 0900 to 1700

Access for disabled people: Level entry

Links with: British and Irish Legal Information Institute (BAILII); Institute of Advanced Legal Studies, Charles Clore House

Member organisation of: International Federation of Computer Law Associations; website: http://www.ifcla.com

SOCIETY FOR DANCE RESEARCH

Laban Centre London, Laurie Grove, New Cross, London, SE14 6NH

Tel: 020 8692 4070 ext 120
Fax: 020 8694 8749 or 8691 3792
E-mail: sdr1@tinyworld.co.uk

Enquiries to: Administrative Secretary
Direct tel: 01903 742019

Founded: 1982

Organisation type and purpose: Learned society (membership is by subscription), present number of members: 170, voluntary organisation, registered charity, research organisation.
British-based organisation, which promotes and fosters the quality and scope of scholarship and research in all forms of dance.

Subject coverage: Dance.

Publications: Printed

Access to staff: Contact by letter, by telephone and by e-mail
Hours: Mon to Fri, 0900 to 1700
Special comments: Please contact by telephone or fax and leave message.

SOCIETY FOR EARTHQUAKE AND CIVIL ENGINEERING DYNAMICS (SECED)

Institution of Civil Engineers, One Great George Street, London, SW1P 3AA

Tel: 020 7222 7722
Fax: 020 7222 7500

Enquiries to: Secretary
Direct tel: 020 7655 2238
Direct fax: 020 7799 1325
Direct e-mail: caroline.howe@ice.org.uk

Organisation type and purpose: Learned society.

Subject coverage: Earthquakes and engineering; seismology; blast, vibration and impact; soil dynamics and foundation engineering.

Publications: Printed

National section of the: International Association for Earthquake Engineering

SOCIETY FOR EDITORS AND PROOFREADERS (SfEP)

Erico House, 93–99 Upper Richmond Road, London, SW15 2TG

Tel: 020 8785 5617
Fax: 020 8785 5618
E-mail: administration@sfep.org.uk
Website: www.sfep.org.uk

Enquiries to: Administrator
Direct e-mail: executive@sfep.org.uk

Founded: 1988

Organisation type and purpose:
Professional body (membership is by subscription), present number of members: c.1,400, training organisation.
Upholding editorial excellence.

Subject coverage: Copy-editing and proofreading, editorial project management, editorial training, editorial standards. The profession is involved in a wide range of subject areas including: modern languages, business, finance and economics, medicine, music, reference, technical writing, science and computing.

Publications: Printed, and electronic and video

Access to staff: Contact by letter, by telephone, by fax, by e-mail and via website
Hours: 0930 to 1600
Special comments: Personal attendance not encouraged.

SOCIETY FOR ENDOCRINOLOGY

22 Apex Court, Woodlands, Bradley Stoke, Bristol, BS32 4JT

Tel: 01454 642200
Fax: 01454 642222
E-mail: info@endocrinology.org
Website: www.endocrinology.org

Enquiries to: Society Services Manager

Founded: 1946

Organisation type and purpose: Learned society, registered charity (charity number 266813), publishing house.
To promote the advancement of public education in endocrinology.

Subject coverage: Endocrinology; hormones.

Publications: Printed, and electronic and video
Order printed publications from: Portland Press Ltd, Commerce Way, Colchester, Essex, CO2 8HP; tel: 01206 796351; fax: 01206 799331; e-mail: sales@portlandpress.co.uk

Publications list: Available online

Access to staff: Contact by letter
Hours: Mon to Fri, 0900 to 1700

Subsidiary body: BioScientifica Ltd; 22 Apex Court, Woodlands, Bradley Stoke, Bristol, BS32 4JT; tel: 01454 642200; fax: 01454 642222; e-mail: info@endocrinology.org

SOCIETY FOR FOLK LIFE STUDIES

Snibston Discovery Park, Ashby Discovery Park, Ashby Road, Coalville, Leicestershire, LE67 2LN

Tel: 01530 278468
Fax: 01530 813301
Website: www.folklife.org.uk

Enquiries to: Secretary
Direct e-mail: seblittlewood@beamish.org.uk

Founded: 1961

Organisation type and purpose: Learned society (membership is by subscription), present number of members: c. 500, voluntary organisation.

Subject coverage: Traditional ways of life in Great Britain and Ireland, folk life, popular culture, ethnology.

Publications: Printed
Order printed publications from: Society for Folk Life Studies, Welsh Folk Museum St Fagan's, Cardiff, CF5 6XB, tel: 029 2056 9441, fax: 029 2057 8413

Access to staff: Contact by letter, by telephone, by fax, by e-mail and via website
Hours: Mon to Fri, 0900 to 1700

SOCIETY FOR GENERAL MICROBIOLOGY (SGM)

Marlborough House, Basingstoke Road, Spencers Wood, Reading, Berkshire, RG7 1AG

Tel: 0118 988 1800
Fax: 0118 988 5656
E-mail: admin@sgm.ac.uk
Website: www.sgm.ac.uk
Website: www.sgmjournals.org

Enquiries to: Chief Executive
Direct tel: 0118 988 1812
Direct e-mail: r.fraser@sgm.ac.uk

Founded: 1945

Organisation type and purpose:
International organization, learned society (membership is by subscription), present number of members: 5,500, registered charity (charity number 264017), publishing house.
Represents the interests of microbiologists world-wide, particularly in the United Kingdom.

Subject coverage: Microbiology, virology, biotechnology in response to requests from the general public, academia, industry, government and all levels of education. Careers and training in microbiology.

Publications: Printed, and electronic and video
Order printed publications from: website: http://www.sgmjournals.org/subscriptions/pricing
Order electronic and video publications from: website: http://www.sgmjournals.org/subscriptions/pricing

Publications list: Available online and in print

Access to staff: Contact by letter, by telephone, by fax, by e-mail and via website. Appointment necessary.
Hours: Mon to Fri, 0900 to 1700

Links with: Federation of European Microbiology Societies; International Union of Microbiology Societies

SOCIETY FOR INDIVIDUAL FREEDOM (SIF)

PO Box 744, Bromley, Kent, BR1 4WG

Tel: 01424 713737
Fax: 01424 713737
E-mail: chairman@individualist.org.uk
Website: www.individualist.org.uk

Enquiries to: Chairman
Other contacts: President

Founded: 1940

Organisation type and purpose:
Membership association, voluntary organisation.
Lobbying group.
Campaigning for personal freedom.

Subject coverage: Personal freedom, reducing state control and taxation, fostering free enterprise.

Publications: Printed

Publications list: Available in print

Access to staff: Contact by letter, by telephone, by e-mail and via website
Hours: Also evenings

SOCIETY FOR INTERNATIONAL FOLK DANCING (SIFD)

5 South Rise, Carshalton, SM5 4PD

Tel: 020 8395 1400
E-mail: mail@sifd.org
Website: www.sifd.org

Enquiries to: Publicity Officer

Founded: 1946

Organisation type and purpose:
Membership association (membership is by subscription), present number of members: 400, voluntary organisation, registered charity (charity number 284509), suitable for all ages.
Voluntary society.
Support and co-ordination of work of local bodies.

Subject coverage: Traditional folk dances of many countries, especially European; costume and music of those countries.

Publications: Printed, and electronic and video
Order printed publications from: Publications Secretary, Society for International Folk Dancing, 5 South Rise, Carshalton, Surrey, SM5 4PD, tel: 020 8395 1400

Publications list: Available online

Access to staff: Contact by letter, by telephone, by e-mail and via website
Hours: Variable

continued overleaf

Also at: 63 affiliated and associated UK groups; Society for International Folk Dancing; 6 Leveson Crescent, Balsall Common, Coventry, CV7 7DR; tel: 01676 534112; West Midlands Branch

Links with: Central Council for Physical Recreation (CCPR); Francis House, Francis Street, London, SW1P 1DE; tel: 020 8828 3163; fax: 020 8630 8820

SOCIETY FOR ITALIC HANDWRITING (SIH)

203 Dyas Avenue, Great Barr, Birmingham, B42 1HN

Tel: 0121 244 8006
Fax: 0121 244 8006
E-mail: secretary@italic-handwriting.org
Website: www.italic-handwriting.org.uk

Enquiries to: Secretary

Founded: 1952

Organisation type and purpose: Learned society (membership is by subscription), present number of members: 500, registered charity (charity number 287889R).
To sustain the interest in italic handwriting and to secure the advancement of education in relation to handwriting.

Subject coverage: Italic handwriting and Renaissance calligraphy.

Publications: Printed, and electronic and video

Access to staff: Contact by letter, by e-mail and via website
Hours: Mon to Fri, 0900 to 1700

Connections with: Society of Scribes and Illuminators

SOCIETY FOR LIBYAN STUDIES

Institute of Archaeology, 31–34 Gordon Square, London, WC1H 0PY

E-mail: shinleystrong@btconnect.com
Website: www.britac.ac.uk/institutes/libya

Enquiries to: General Secretary

Founded: 1969

Organisation type and purpose: Learned society.

Subject coverage: Libyan life and culture, particularly archaeology, history, Islamic law, geography and geomorphology.

Collection: Specialist works on Libya, including the Goodchild Library

Publications: Printed
Order printed publications from: Website

Publications list: Available online and in print

Access to staff: Contact by letter and by e-mail
Hours: Mon to Fri, 0900 to 1700

SOCIETY FOR LINCOLNSHIRE HISTORY AND ARCHAEOLOGY (SLHA)

Jews' Court, 2 & 3 Steep Hill, Lincoln, LN2 1LS

Tel: 01522 521337
E-mail: info@slha.org.uk
Website: www.slha.org.uk

Enquiries to: Administrator

Founded: 1974

Organisation type and purpose: Learned society, membership association (membership is by subscription), present number of members: 600, voluntary organisation, registered charity (charity number 504766), suitable for ages: all.
To promote interest in and the study of all aspects of Lincolnshire history.

Subject coverage: Lincolnshire history, archaeology, industrial archaeology, topography, architecture, dialect, etc.

Collection: Library for members (at Jews' Court)
Periodicals and valuable material on deposit at the Lincolnshire Archives Office

Library catalogue: All or part available online

Publications: Printed

Publications list: Available online and in print

Access to staff: Contact by letter, by telephone, by e-mail and in person. Appointment necessary. Access for members only.
Hours: Mon to Thu, 1000 to 1300
Special comments: Library open to members and non-members.

Access for disabled people: Very difficult

Trading company is: Lincolnshire Heritage Limited; at the main address; tel: 01522 532280

SOCIETY FOR LOW TEMPERATURE BIOLOGY (SLTB)

The General Secretary, c/o Jon Green, Genómica Funcional, CIC-Biogune, Parque Tecnológico de Vizcaya, Edificio 801A, 1pl., 48160-Derio, Spain

Tel: +34 944 061 326
Fax: +34 944 061 301
E-mail: jgreen@cicbiogune.es
Website: www.sltb.info

Enquiries to: Treasurer
Direct e-mail: mcurry@lincoln.ac.uk

Founded: 1964

Organisation type and purpose: International organisation, learned society.

Subject coverage: Biological effects of low temperature; preservation of cells, tissues, organs, in both plant and animal kingdoms; preservation of genetic stock (plants); adaptation to cold; cryosurgery.

Publications: Printed

Access to staff: Contact by letter, by fax, by e-mail and via website
Hours: Mon to Fri, 0900 to 1700

SOCIETY FOR MUCOPOLYSACCHARIDE DISEASES (MPS)

MPS House, Repton Place, White Lion Road, Amersham, Buckinghamshire, HP7 9LP

Tel: 0845 389 9901
Fax: 0845 389 9902
E-mail: mps@mpssociety.co.uk
Website: www.mpssociety.co.uk

Enquiries to: Chief Executive

Founded: 1982

Organisation type and purpose: International organisation, membership association (membership is by qualification), present number of members: 1500, voluntary organisation, registered charity (charity number 287034).
Members who qualify are: those having MPS, parent or carer.
Provides support and advocacy to individuals and their families affected by MPS diseases, brings about public awareness and raises funds for furthering research.

Subject coverage: Mucopolysaccharide and related diseases; clinical management, gene research, education, home adaptations, welfare benefits, specialist clinics, social events.

Publications: Printed
Order printed publications from: http://www.mpssociety.co.uk

Publications list: Available online and in print

Access to staff: Contact by letter, by telephone, by fax, by e-mail and via website. Appointment necessary.
Hours: Mon to Fri, 0900 to 1700
Out-of-hours helpline: Mon to Fri, 1700 to 2200; Sat, Sun, 0700 to 2200

Access to building: Prior appointment preferred.
Hours: Mon to Fri, 0900 to 1700
Special comments: Subject to adequate staffing.

Access for disabled people: Level entry
Special comments: Limited access to ground floor only.

SOCIETY FOR POPULAR ASTRONOMY (SPA)

Dept DIS, 36 Fairway, Keyworth, Nottingham, NG12 5DU

E-mail: info@popastro.com
Website: www.popastro.com

Enquiries to: Honorary Secretary
Other contacts: Editor Popular Astronomy Magazine (for material for review)

Founded: 1953; formerly called Junior Astronomical Society (year of change 1994)

Organisation type and purpose: Membership association (membership is by subscription), present number of members: 3,000.
To encourage the study and understanding of astronomy, particularly for beginners of all ages and those who prefer a less technical approach.

Subject coverage: Astronomy.

Publications: Printed, and electronic and video

Access to staff: Contact by letter, by e-mail and via website
Hours: Mon to Fri, 0900 to 1700
Special comments: Please send sae with postal enquiries.

Also at: Editor, Popular Astronomy Magazine; 7 Parc-An-Bre Drive, St Dennis, St Austell, PL26 8AS

SOCIETY FOR POST-MEDIEVAL ARCHAEOLOGY, THE (SPMA)

Department of Medieval and Later Antiquities, British Museum, London, WC1B 3DG

Tel: 0191 482 1037
E-mail: cranstone@btinternet.com
Website: www.spma.org.uk/

Enquiries to: Honorary Secretary
Direct fax: 0191 487 2343

Founded: 1966

Organisation type and purpose: Learned society, registered charity (charity number 281651).

Subject coverage: Archaeology in the period of European and Colonial history ranging from the close of the Middle Ages up to the twentieth century.

Publications: Printed

Access to staff: Contact by letter, by fax and by e-mail
Hours: Mon to Fri, 0900 to 1700

Links with: Society for Historical Archaeology; USA

Other address: Secretary; 267 Kells Lane, Low Fell, Gateshead, NG9 5HU

SOCIETY FOR PROMOTING CHRISTIAN KNOWLEDGE (SPCK)

36 Causton Street, London, SW1P 4ST

Tel: 020 7592 3900
Fax: 020 7592 3939
E-mail: spck@spck.org.uk
Website: www.spck.org.uk

Founded: 1698

Organisation type and purpose: Membership association (membership is by election or invitation), present number of members: 300, registered charity (charity number 231144), publishing house.
To promote Christian knowledge.

Collection: Archives of SPCK publications from 1698 (held at Cambridge University Library)

Publications: Printed
Order printed publications from: Trade: MacMillan Distribution, Brunel Road, Houndmills, Basingstoke, RG21 6XS. Tel: 0845 0705656, Email: orders@macmillan.co .uk

Publications list: Available in print

Access to staff: Contact by letter, by telephone and by e-mail
Hours: Mon to Fri, 0900 to 1700

Subsidiary bodies: Sheldon Press; at the same address

SOCIETY FOR PSYCHICAL RESEARCH (SPR)

49 Marloes Road, Kensington, London, W8 6LA

Tel: 020 7937 8984
Fax: 020 7937 8984
Website: www.spr.ac.uk

Enquiries to: Secretary

Founded: 1882

Organisation type and purpose: International organisation, learned society (membership is by election or invitation), present number of members: 1,000, voluntary organisation, registered charity (charity number 207325), suitable for ages: 16+, research organisation.
To advance the understanding of events and abilities commonly described as psychic or paranormal, without prejudice and in a scientific manner. Houses one of the largest libraries in Europe of psychic material.

Subject coverage: Inquiry into the reality and nature of paranormal cognition by means of experiments, and by collecting and analysing accounts of spontaneously occurring incidents that appear to be of this nature. The Society operates without prejudice and can offer no corporate view or opinion.

Collection: Archival material and rare books

Non-library collection catalogue: All or part available in-house

Library catalogue: All or part available in-house

Publications: Printed

Publications list: Available online and in print

Access to staff: Contact by letter, by telephone, by fax and in person. Access for members only. Non-members charged.
Hours: Tue, Wed, Thu, 1300 to 1700 for personal callers

Access to building: No prior appointment required
Hours: Library: Tue, Wed, Thu, 1300 to 1700
Special comments: Free to members, no appointment required for access to library.

SOCIETY FOR RENAISSANCE STUDIES

Dr Gabriele Neher, Department of Art History, Lakeside Arts Centre, The University of Nottingham, NG7 2RD

Tel: 01159 513184
E-mail: gabriele.neher@nottingham.ac.uk
Website: www.rensoc.org.uk

Enquiries to: Honorary Secretary

Founded: 1967

Organisation type and purpose: International organisation, learned society (membership is by subscription), present number of members: 400, registered charity (charity number 1025890).
Promotion of Renaissance studies.

Subject coverage: Art, history, literature and philosophy of the Renaissance.

Publications: Printed
Order printed publications from: Journals Marketing, Wiley-Blackwell Publishing, 9600 Garsington Road, Oxford, OX4 2DQ

Access to staff: Contact by letter, by telephone, by e-mail and via website
Hours: Mon to Fri, 0900 to 1700

Affiliated to: Institutes for the Study of the Renaissance; International Federation of Societies

SOCIETY FOR REPRODUCTION & FERTILITY (SSF)

SRF Business Office, Procon Conferences Ltd, Tattersall House, East Parade, Harrogate, North Yorkshire, HG1 5LT

Tel: 01423 564488
Fax: 01423 701433
Website: www.srf-reproduction.org/

Enquiries to: Secretary
Direct e-mail: SRF@portland-services.com

Founded: 1950

Organisation type and purpose: Learned society.

Subject coverage: Reproductive biology, fertility and infertility in animals and man.

Publications: Printed

Access to staff: Contact by letter, by e-mail and via website
Hours: Mon to Fri, 0900 to 1700

SOCIETY FOR RESEARCH IN THE PSYCHOLOGY OF MUSIC AND MUSIC EDUCATION (SEMPRE)

Institute of Education, 20 Bedford Way, London, WC1H 0AL

Tel: 020 7612 6740
Fax: 020 7612 6741
E-mail: membership@sempre.org.uk
Website: www.srpmme.u-net.com/subs .html

Enquiries to: Membership Secretary

Founded: 1973

Organisation type and purpose: Learned society.

Subject coverage: Psychology of music; music education; music education research; music psychology research; music perception psychology; child development (music); music therapy; social psychology of music.

Publications: Printed

Access to staff: Contact by letter
Hours: Mon to Fri, 0900 to 1700

Affiliated to: International Society for Music Education; UK Council for Music Education and Training

SOCIETY FOR THE HISTORY OF ALCHEMY AND CHEMISTRY (SHAC)

E-mail: Chairman@ambix.org
Website: www.ambix.org

Enquiries to: Honorary Secretary
Direct e-mail: Secretary@ambix.org

Founded: 1935

Organisation type and purpose: Learned society.

Subject coverage: History of alchemy and chemistry.

Publications: Printed

continued overleaf

Access to staff: Contact by letter, by telephone and by e-mail
Hours: Mon to Fri, 0900 to 1700

SOCIETY FOR THE HISTORY OF NATURAL HISTORY (SHNH)

c/o Natural History Museum, Cromwell Road, London, SW7 5BD

Tel: 020 7887 5261
Fax: 020 7887 5391
E-mail: secretary@shnh.org.uk
Website: www.shnh.org.uk

Enquiries to: Honorary Secretary
Other contacts: Treasurer (for sale of publications)

Founded: 1936

Organisation type and purpose: Learned society, professional body (membership is by subscription), present number of members: 650, registered charity (charity number 210355). Promotes the study of all branches of the history of natural history including biographical and bibliographical studies.

Subject coverage: History of botany, geology, zoology and other subjects included in the broad term 'natural history'.

Publications: Printed
Order printed publications from: Society for the History of Natural History, c/o Natural History Museum, Cromwell Road, London, SW7 5BD

Publications list: Available online

Access to staff: Contact by letter, by e-mail and via website. Non-members charged.
Hours: Mon to Fri, 0900 to 1600

Close links with: The Natural History Museum

SOCIETY FOR THE PROMOTION OF HELLENIC STUDIES (SPHS)

Senate House, Malet Street, London, WC1E 7HU

Tel: 020 7862 8730
Fax: 020 7862 8731
E-mail: office@hellenicsociety.org.uk
Website: www.hellenicsociety.org.uk

Enquiries to: Executive Secretary

Founded: 1879

Organisation type and purpose: Learned society.

Subject coverage: Greek art, archaeology, architecture, history, literature, law, politics, religion, philosophy, language, and science of the Minoan, Mycenaean and Hellenic world and the Byzantine Empire, and modern periods.

Collection: Library which (together with the Institute of Classical Studies library) contains some 78,867 monographs and pamphlets and some 15,592 bound vols of periodicals.
526 current periodicals taken
Slides collection of some 6,500 images
Wood donation of the Diaries of Robert Wood and his companions with the sketch books of G. B. Borra

Publications: Printed

Publications list: Available online and in print

Access to staff: Contact by letter, by telephone and by e-mail. Access for members only.
Hours: Mon to Fri, 0900 to 1700

Constituent part of: Hellenic and Roman Societies

Links with: Institute of Classical Studies Library

SOCIETY FOR THE PROMOTION OF ROMAN STUDIES (SPRS)

Senate House, Malet Street, London, WC1E 7HU

Tel: 020 7862 8727
Fax: 020 7862 8728
E-mail: office@romansociety.org
Website: icls.sas.ac.uk/library/home.htm
Website: www.romansociety.org

Enquiries to: Secretary

Founded: 1910

Organisation type and purpose: Learned society (membership is by subscription), present number of members: 2,200, registered charity (charity number 210644).

Subject coverage: Archaeology, architecture, art, history, language, religion, philosophy, law, politics, science and literature of Rome and the Roman Empire to about AD 700; Roman Britain.

Collection: Library, which (together with the Institute of Classical Studies Library) contains some 128,000 monographs and pamphlets and some 16,000 bound vols of periodicals
660 current periodicals taken
Slides collection of some 6,700
Wood donation of the diaries of Robert Wood and his companions with the sketch-books of G. B. Borra

Library catalogue: All or part available online

Publications: Printed, and electronic and video

Publications list: Available online and in print

Access to staff: Contact by letter, by telephone, by fax, by e-mail and in person. Access for members only.
Hours: Mon to Fri, 0930 to 1730

Links with: Co-ordinating Committee for Classics; Fédération Internationale des Études Classiques

SOCIETY FOR THE PROTECTION OF ANCIENT BUILDINGS (SPAB)

37 Spital Square, London, E1 6DY

Tel: 020 7377 1644
Fax: 020 7247 5296
E-mail: info@spab.org.uk
Website: www.spab.org.uk

Enquiries to: Archivist
Other contacts: Promotions Officer for media enquiries

Founded: 1877

Organisation type and purpose: Advisory body, learned society, membership association (membership is by subscription), charitable company (company number 5743962, charity number 111 3753, Scottish charity number SC 039244), suitable for ages: adults, training organisation, publishing house.

Subject coverage: Repair and protection of historic buildings, building conservation in general.

Collection: Manuscript archive of society's work since 1877, about 15,000 files available to researchers by appointment, mills cases held by Mills Archive Trust, Reading

Library catalogue: All or part available in-house

Publications: Printed

Publications list: Available online and in print

Access to staff: Contact by letter, by telephone, by e-mail and via website. Appointment necessary.
Hours: Technical Helpline: Mon to Fri, 0930 to 1230
Special comments: Archivist is part-time.

Access to building: No prior appointment required
Hours: 0930 to 1730

SOCIETY FOR THE PROTECTION OF ANIMALS ABROAD (SPANA)

14 John Street, London, WC1N 2EB

Tel: 020 7831 3999
Fax: 020 7831 5999
E-mail: enquiries@spana.org
Website: www.spana.org

Enquiries to: Chief Executive

Founded: 1923

Organisation type and purpose: International organisation, advisory body, professional body (membership is by election or invitation), present number of members: 192, voluntary organisation, registered charity (charity number 209015). Aims to improve standards of animal care wherever the need arises.

Access to staff: Contact by letter, by telephone, by fax, by e-mail and via website
Hours: Mon to Fri, 0900 to 1700

Member organisation of: IUCN

SOCIETY FOR THE PROTECTION OF UNBORN CHILDREN (SPUC)

3 Whitacre Mews, Stannary Street, London, SE11 4AB

Tel: 020 7091 7091
Fax: 020 7820 3131
E-mail: information@spuc.org.uk
Website: www.spuc.org.uk

Enquiries to: General Secretary
Direct e-mail: paultully@spuc.org.uk
Other contacts: Regional development officers (for provision of educational services to schools, voluntary groups, etc.)

Founded: 1966

Organisation type and purpose: National organisation, membership association (membership is by subscription), present number of members: 46,000, voluntary organisation, suitable for ages: 12+, research organisation.

Parliamentary lobby group.
To affirm, defend and promote the existence and value of human life from the moment of conception, and to defend and protect human life especially in the areas of abortion, handicap, euthanasia, embryo experiments and population control. To examine existing or proposed laws, legislation or regulations relating to abortion and to support or oppose such as appropriate.

Subject coverage: Abortion, human pre-natal development, abortion side-effects, social effects of abortion legislation, handicap, eugenics, euthanasia, infertility treatment and research, human embryo experimentation and population control, cloning, abortifacients (morning-after pill, RU486, 'emergency contraception'), mental incapacity legislation, post-abortion syndrome.

Information services: e-mail: information@spuc.org.uk

Collection: Press cuttings and parliamentary debates, questions, speeches, etc. relating to abortion, euthanasia, embryo research

Publications: Printed, and electronic and video

Publications list: Available in print

Access to staff: Contact by letter, by telephone, by fax, by e-mail and via website. Appointment necessary.
Hours: Mon to Fri, 0900 to 1730

Access to building: Prior appointment required

Access for disabled people: Level entry, access to all public areas, toilet facilities

Affiliated to: International Right to Life Federation; Via Niccolò V 44, 00165 Rome, Italy

Links with: SPUC Educational Research Trust; address as the SPUC

Subsidiary body: ARCH – Abortion Recovery Care and Helpline; 75 Bothwell Street, Glasgow, G2 6TS; tel: 0141 226 5407; 0845 603 8501 (helpline); website: http://www.archtrust.org.uk

SOCIETY FOR THE PROTECTION OF UNBORN CHILDREN – SCOTLAND (SPUC Scotland)

75 Bothwell Street, Glasgow, G2 6TS

Tel: 0141 221 2094
Fax: 0141 225 3696
E-mail: info@spucscotland.org
Website: spucscotland.org/

Enquiries to: Director
Other contacts: Development Officer for matters to do with branches.

Organisation type and purpose: Membership association (membership is by subscription), present number of members: 4500, voluntary organisation.
The protection of all human life from conception to natural death.

Subject coverage: Abortion, cloning, euthanasia.

Publications: Printed, and electronic and video

Access to staff: Contact by letter, by telephone, by fax, by e-mail and in person. Appointment necessary.
Hours: Mon to Fri, 0900 to 1700

Access to building: No prior appointment required

SOCIETY FOR THE SOCIAL HISTORY OF MEDICINE (SSHM)

Department of History, University of Aberdeen, Aberdeen, AB24 3FX

Tel: 01224 272456
Fax: 01224 272203
E-mail: o.walsh@abdn.ac.uk
Website: www.sshm.org

Enquiries to: Honorary Secretary
Direct tel: 01224 273884

Founded: 1970

Organisation type and purpose: Learned society (membership is by subscription), registered charity (charity number 278414).

Subject coverage: Social history of medicine; history of health care and policy.

Publications: Printed

Access to staff: Contact by letter, by telephone, by fax, by e-mail and via website
Hours: Mon to Fri, 0900 to 1700

SOCIETY FOR THEATRE RESEARCH (STR)

The Theatre Museum, 1E Tavistock Street, London, WC2E 7PR

E-mail: e.cottis@btinternet.com
Website: www.str.org.uk

Enquiries to: Honorary Secretary

Founded: 1948

Organisation type and purpose: Learned society (membership is by subscription), present number of members: 750, registered charity (charity number 266186), publishing house.

Subject coverage: History and technique of the British theatre, and allied entertainments.

Collection: The Society's library was amalgamated with that of the Theatre Museum in 1987

Publications: Printed

Publications list: Available online and in print

Access to staff: Contact by letter, by e-mail and via website
Hours: Not applicable

Also at: Society for Theatre Research; PO Box 3214, Brighton, BN2 1LU

Institutional Friends member of: Theatres Advisory Council (TAC); Theatres Trust

SOCIETY FOR UNDERWATER TECHNOLOGY (SUT)

80 Coleman Street, London, EC2R 5BJ

Tel: 020 7382 2601
Fax: 020 7382 2684
E-mail: info@sut.org
Website: www.sut.org.uk

Enquiries to: Executive Secretary
Other contacts: Press and Publications Officer for media or publications enquiries.

Founded: 1966

Organisation type and purpose: International organisation, learned society (membership is by subscription), present number of members: 1,600, registered charity (charity number 256659).
Multidisciplinary learned society bringing together individuals and organisations from industry, government and academia with a common interest in underwater technology, marine science and engineering.

Subject coverage: Marine science and technology applied to: submersible robotic design and operation, diving technology and physiology, scientific diving, underwater acoustics, subsea engineering systems and operations, naval architecture and offshore structures, environmental forces, offshore site investigation, ocean resources, marine pollution and environment, marine biology and archaeology, oceanography, instrumentation, education and training.

Collection: SUT reference material lodged in the IMarE Marine Information centre

Publications: Printed, and electronic and video

Access to staff: Contact by letter, by fax, by e-mail and via website
Hours: Mon to Fri, 0900 to 1700

Other addresses: Aberdeen Office; Innovation Centre, Exploration Drive, Offshore Technology Park, Bridge of Don, Aberdeen, AB23 8GX; tel: 01224 823637; fax: 01224 820236; Southampton branch; Southampton Oceanography Centre, Empress Dock, Southampton

Parent body for: Underwater Science Group

SOCIETY OF ACADEMIC & RESEARCH SURGERY (SARS)

The Royal College of Surgeons of England, 35–43 Lincoln's Inn Fields, London, WC2A 3PE

Tel: 020 7869 6640
Fax: 020 7869 6644
E-mail: sking@rcseng.ac.uk
Website: surgicalresearch.org.uk

Founded: c. 1960

Organisation type and purpose: Professional association for surgeons.
Fosters and enhances research in various disciplines of surgery under its auspices; provides a platform to aspiring surgical trainees to present their laboratory as well as clinical research.

Subject coverage: Surgery; medical research.

Publications: Electronic and video
Order electronic and video publications from: Download from website

Publications list: Available online

Access to staff: Contact by letter, by telephone, by fax and by e-mail

Links with: other important surgical research forums in USA, Europe and South Africa

SOCIETY OF AFGHAN RESIDENTS IN THE UK (SAR)

West Acton Community Centre, Churchill Gardens, Acton, London, W3 0JN

Tel: 020 8993 2129
Fax: 020 8993 8168
E-mail: saruk@btconnect.com

Enquiries to: Chairman
Direct tel: 07947 777705

Founded: 1982

Organisation type and purpose: National organisation, advisory body, membership association (membership is by subscription, qualification, election or invitation), present number of members: 700, voluntary organisation, registered charity (charity number 800460), public library.
Refugee community organisation.

Subject coverage: Housing, health, law, welfare benefits, immigration, education, employment.

Collection: Press cuttings relevant to Afghanistan

Publications: Printed

Access to staff: Contact by letter, by telephone, by fax, by e-mail and in person
Hours: Mon to Fri, 0900 to 1600

Access to building: *Hours:* Mon to Fri, 0900 to 1600

Access for disabled people: *Hours:* Mon to Fri, 0900 to 1600

Also at: Offices in Birmingham, Harrow and Northampton

SOCIETY OF ANTIQUARIES OF LONDON

Burlington House, Piccadilly, London, W1J 0BE

Tel: 020 7734 0193
Fax: 020 7287 6967
E-mail: library@sal.org.uk
Website: www.sal.org.uk

Enquiries to: Librarian
Direct tel: 020 7479 7084

Founded: 1707

Organisation type and purpose: Learned society.

Subject coverage: Archaeology; architectural history; British topography; art history mostly of decorative arts; heraldry; history (mainly British).

Collection: Broadsides, proclamations, Civil War tracts
Incunabula
Jackson Collection (Wiltshire)
Manuscripts, photographs and portraits
Prattinton Collection (Worcestershire)
Prints and drawings (18th and 19th centuries)
Rubbings of all the pre-1700 monumental brasses in Britain
Willson Collection (Lincolnshire)

Library catalogue: All or part available online

Publications: Printed, and microform publications

Access to staff: Contact by letter, by telephone, by fax and by e-mail. Appointment necessary.
Hours: Mon to Fri, 1000 to 1700
Special comments: Closed August.

SOCIETY OF ANTIQUARIES OF NEWCASTLE UPON TYNE

Great North Museum, Hancock, Barras Bridge, Newcastle upon Tyne, NE2 4PT

Tel: 0191 230 2700
E-mail: admin@newcastle-antiquaries.org.uk
Website: www.newcastle-antiquaries.org.uk

Enquiries to: Membership Secretary
Other contacts: Honorary Secretary

Founded: 1813

Organisation type and purpose: Learned society (membership is by subscription), present number of members: 750, registered charity (charity number 230888).

Subject coverage: History and archaeology of Durham, Northumberland and Newcastle upon Tyne.

Collection: Library of 30,000 volumes

Non-library collection catalogue: All or part available in-house

Library catalogue: All or part available in-house

Publications: Printed

Publications list: Available online and in print

Access to staff: Contact by letter, by telephone and by e-mail. Appointment necessary.
Hours: Library: term-time, 1000 to 1600; vacation hours, to be announced

Links with: The Literary and Philosophical Society of Newcastle upon Tyne; 23 Westgate Road, Newcastle upon Tyne, NE1 1SE; tel: 0191 232 0192

SOCIETY OF ANTIQUARIES OF SCOTLAND

Royal Museum, Chambers Street, Edinburgh, EH1 1JF

Tel: 0131 247 4115
Fax: 0131 247 4163
E-mail: f.ashmore@nms.ac.uk
Website: www.socantscot.org

Enquiries to: Director
Other contacts: Publications Assistant for monograph sales and publicity.

Founded: 1780

Organisation type and purpose: Learned society (membership is by election or invitation), present number of members: 3,500, registered charity (charity number SC010240).

Subject coverage: History and archaeology of Scotland.

Collection: Archaeologia Scotica (irregularly from the Society's foundation until 1851)

Library catalogue: All or part available in-house

Publications: Printed
Order printed publications from: Publications Administrator, Society of Antiquaries of Scotland
at the same address, tel: 0131 247 4145, e-mail: r.lancaster@nms.ac.uk

Publications list: Available online and in print

Access to staff: Contact by letter and by telephone. Appointment necessary.
Hours: Mon to Fri, 0900 to 1700
Special comments: Staff work part time – office may be unsupervised at certain times.

SOCIETY OF ARCHER-ANTIQUARIES (SAA)

29 Batley Court, Oldland, South Gloucestershire, BS30 8YZ

Tel: 0117 932 3276
Fax: 0117 932 3276
E-mail: bogaman@btinternet.com
Website: www.societyofarcher-antiquaries.org

Enquiries to: Honorary Secretary

Founded: 1956

Organisation type and purpose: International organisation, learned society (membership is by subscription), present number of members: 250, registered charity, consultancy, research organisation.

Subject coverage: General and specialised information on the history of archery, Asiatic archery, English archery, crossbows, Middle Eastern archery, ethnographical archery, literature and constructional information, bowery, fletchery, legends and practices.

Information services: Information provided to members upon application

Collection: Library and display room

Non-library collection catalogue: All or part available in-house

Library catalogue: All or part available in-house

Publications: Printed

Access to staff: Contact by letter, by telephone, by e-mail and via website. Appointment necessary. Access for members only.
Hours: Mon to Fri, 1800 to 2000; Sat, Sun, 1000 to 1800

Access to building: Prior appointment required. Members only or visitor with Member
Hours: Two Suns a year

Access for disabled people: *Special comments:* Limited disabled access.

Associated with: Royal Toxophilite Society; Simon Foundation at Manchester University

SOCIETY OF AUTHORS (SOA)

84 Drayton Gardens, London, SW10 9SB

Tel: 020 7373 6642
Fax: 020 7373 5768
E-mail: info@societyofauthors.org
Website: www.societyofauthors.org

Enquiries to: General Secretary

Founded: 1884

Organisation type and purpose: Trade union.

Subject coverage: Specialist groups within the Society serve the needs of broadcasters, literary translators, educational writers, medical writers, children's writers, information also on literary agents, publishers, royalties, contracts, authors' rights, public lending right.

Publications: Printed

Publications list: Available online and in print

Access to staff: Contact by e-mail and via website. Appointment necessary. Access for members only. Letter of introduction required.
Hours: Mon to Thu, 0930 to 1730; Fri, 0930 to 1700

Member of: British Copyright Council; European Writers Congress; International Confederation of Societies of Authors and Composers; National Book Committee

SOCIETY OF BIOLOGY

9 Red Lion Court, London, EC4A 3EF

Tel: 020 7936 5900
Fax: 020 7936 5901
E-mail: info@societyofbiology.org
Website: www.societyofbiology.org

Founded: 2009; created by the merger of Institute of Biology and Biosciences Federation (year of change 2009)

Organisation type and purpose: Professional body

Subject coverage: A single unified voice for biology: advising Government and influencing policy; advancing education and professional development; supporting members, and engaging and encouraging public interest in the life sciences.

Publications: Printed

Publications list: Available online and in print

Access to staff: Contact by letter, by telephone, by fax, by e-mail and via website
Hours: Mon to Fri, 0900 to 1700

SOCIETY OF BOOKBINDERS (SOB)

6 Hillside Road, West Kirby, Wirral, CH48 8BB

Tel: 0151 625 2413
E-mail: nat.secretary@societyofbookbinders.com
Website: www.societyofbookbinders.com

Enquiries to: Honorary Secretary
Other contacts: Membership Secretary (for membership enquiries)

Founded: 1974

Organisation type and purpose: Professional body, trade association, membership association (membership is by subscription), present number of members: 650, registered charity (charity number 1032108), training organisation.

Subject coverage: All information appertaining to bookbinding.

Publications: Printed
Order printed publications from: Society of Bookbinders, Little Broxham, Four Elms Road, Four Elms, Kent, TN8 6LR; e-mail: publications@societyofbookbinders.com

Publications list: Available online

Access to staff: Contact by letter, by telephone, by e-mail and via website
Hours: Mon to Fri, 1000 to 1600

Access to building: No access other than to staff

Membership Secretary: Society of Bookbinders; 102 Hetherington Road, Shepperton, Middlesex, TW17 0SW; tel: 01746 763896; e-mail: membership@societyofbookbinders.com

SOCIETY OF BORDER LEICESTER SHEEP BREEDERS

Greenend, St Boswells, Melrose, Roxburghshire, TD6 9ES

Tel: 01835 824207
Fax: 01835 824207
E-mail: info@borderleicesters.co.uk
Website: www.borderleicesters.co.uk

Enquiries to: Membership Secretary

Founded: 1900

Organisation type and purpose: Membership association (membership is by subscription), present number of members: 250, registered charity (charity number SCO 00011). Pedigree sheep breeding.

Subject coverage: Border Leicester Sheep Society, pedigree information and records.

Publications: Printed

Publications list: Available in print

Access to staff: Contact by letter, by telephone, by fax and in person
Hours: Mon to Fri, 0800 to 2100

Access to building: No access other than to staff

SOCIETY OF BOTANICAL ARTISTS (SBA)

1 Knapp Cottages, Wyke, Gillingham, Dorset, SP8 4NQ

Tel: 01747 825718
Fax: 01747 826835
Website: www.society-botanical-artists.org

Enquiries to: Executive Secretary
Direct tel: 01747 852718
Direct e-mail: pam@soc-botanical-artists.org

Founded: 1985

Organisation type and purpose: International organisation, professional body (membership is by election or invitation), present number of members: 190, registered charity (charity number 1047162). Publicising and educating the public about botanical painting.

Subject coverage: Botanical painting.

Publications: Printed

Access to staff: Contact by letter, by telephone, by fax and by e-mail. Appointment necessary.
Hours: Mon to Fri, 0900 to 1700

Access for disabled people: Ramped entry, access to all public areas, toilet facilities

SOCIETY OF BRITISH GAS INDUSTRIES (SBGI)

36 Holly Walk, Leamington Spa, Warwickshire, CV32 4LY

Tel: 01926 334357
Fax: 01926 450459
E-mail: mail@sbgi.org.uk
Website: www.gasjobs.org.uk
Website: www.sbgi.org.uk

Enquiries to: Director
Direct e-mail: claire@sbgi.org.uk

Founded: 1905

Organisation type and purpose: Trade association (membership is by subscription), present number of members: 170 companies.

Subject coverage: Gas industry, products and services providers, manufacturers and contractors, gas suppliers/shippers and transporters.

Publications: Printed

Access to staff: Contact by letter, by telephone, by fax, by e-mail and via website
Hours: Mon to Fri, 0900 to 1700

SOCIETY OF BRITISH WATER & WASTEWATER INDUSTRIES (SBWWI)

38 Holly Walk, Leamington Spa, Warwickshire, CV32 4HY

Tel: 01926 831530
Fax: 01926 831931
E-mail: hq@sbwwi.co.uk
Website: www.sbwwi.co.uk

Enquiries to: Executive Director

Founded: 1986

Organisation type and purpose: Trade association (membership is by subscription, election or invitation), present number of members: 100 companies.
A forum for UK manufacturers and contractors who supply the water industry. Water industry specific, disseminates information, liaises with water companies and other bodies to help members serve the industry better.

Subject coverage: Product standards and approval, regulations, training, product suppliers, contractor services providers.

Collection: OFWAT Reports
Water industry standards

Access to staff: Contact by letter, by telephone, by fax, by e-mail and via website
Hours: Mon to Fri, 0900 to 1700

SOCIETY OF CABLE TELECOMMUNICATION ENGINEERS (SCTE)

Fulton House Business Centre, Fulton Road, Wembley Park, Middlesex, HA9 0TF

Tel: 020 8902 8998
Fax: 020 8903 8719
E-mail: office@scte.org.uk
Website: www.scte.org.uk

continued overleaf

Enquiries to: Secretary
Direct e-mail: sara.waddington@scte.org.uk

Founded: 1945

Organisation type and purpose: Learned society.

Subject coverage: Cable telecommunications.

Publications: Printed

Access to staff: Appointment necessary.
Hours: Mon to Fri, 0900 to 1700

SOCIETY OF COLLEGE, NATIONAL AND UNIVERSITY LIBRARIES (SCONUL)

102 Euston Street, London, NW1 2HA

Tel: 020 7387 0317
Fax: 020 7383 3197
E-mail: info@sconul.ac.uk
Website: www.sconul.ac.uk

Enquiries to: Secretary

Founded: 1950

Organisation type and purpose: International organisation, professional body.

Subject coverage: British academic libraries; advisory committees on: buildings, copyright, health services, information systems and services, performance indicators, publications, scholarly communication, staffing.

Trade and statistical information: Data on funding and activities of university libraries

Publications: Printed

Publications list: Available online and in print

Access to staff: Contact by letter, by telephone, by fax, by e-mail and via website. Appointment necessary.
Hours: Mon to Fri, 0900 to 1700

SOCIETY OF CONSTRUCTION LAW

The Cottage, Bullfurlong Lane, Burbage, Hinckley, LE10 2HQ

Tel: 01455 233253
Fax: 01455 233253
Website: www.scl.org.uk

Founded: 1983

Organisation type and purpose: A membership association, (membership is by subscription), present number of members: 2,149. Members come from all sectors of the construction industry, for example, architects, engineers, surveyors, contractors, developers, solicitors, barristers, arbitrators and experts.
Holds meetings, lectures and social events; publishes papers given to the Society; supports educational bodies, in particular by funding the purchase of books; sponsors an annual prize paper; generally promotes interest in construction law.

Subject coverage: Construction law.

Collection: Construction Law library that used to be housed at the Old Watch House at King's College, London has now been merged with the Maughan library in Chancery Lane; any SCL member who wishes to use the Maughan library should complete the online application form

Publications: Printed, and electronic and video
Order electronic and video publications from: Download from website

Publications list: Available online

Access to staff: Contact by letter, by telephone, by fax and via website

SOCIETY OF CONSULTING MARINE ENGINEERS AND SHIP SURVEYORS (SCMS)

202 Lambeth Road, London, SE1 7JW

Tel: 020 7261 0869
Fax: 020 7261 0871
E-mail: sec@scmshq.org
Website: www.scmshq.org

Enquiries to: Secretary

Founded: 1920

Organisation type and purpose: Learned society.
An MCA appointed certifying authority.

Subject coverage: The interests of consulting engineers, naval architects and ship surveyors; shipbuilding, maritime authorities' activities.

Publications: Printed

Access to staff: Contact by letter, by telephone, by fax and by e-mail
Hours: Mon to Fri, 0900 to 1700

Access to building: Prior appointment required

SOCIETY OF COSMETIC SCIENTISTS (SCS)

GT House, 24–26 Rothesay Road, Luton, Bedfordshire, LU1 1QX

Tel: 01582 726661
Fax: 01582 405217
E-mail: ifscc.scs@btconnect.com
Website: www.scs.org.uk

Enquiries to: Secretary-General

Founded: 1948

Organisation type and purpose: Learned society.

Subject coverage: Cosmetic science.

Publications: Printed

Access to staff: Contact by letter, by telephone, by fax and by e-mail
Hours: Mon to Fri, 0900 to 1700

Affiliated to, and providing the secretariat for, the: International Federation of Societies of Cosmetic Chemists; tel: 01582 726661; fax: 01582 405217; e-mail: ifscc.scs@btconnect.com

SOCIETY OF DAIRY TECHNOLOGY (SDT)

PO Box 12, Appleby in Westmorland, CA16 6HH

Tel: 01768 354034
Fax: 01768 352546
E-mail: execdirector@sdt.org
Website: www.sdt.org

Enquiries to: Executive Director

Founded: 1943

Organisation type and purpose: Learned society (membership is by election or invitation), present number of members: 400, registered charity (charity number 1081615). Education, training and information transfer in dairy sciences and technology.

Subject coverage: Dairy science, dairy technology and dairy research, including husbandry, engineering and education.

Publications: Printed
Order printed publications from: Wiley Blackwell

Publications list: Available online and in print

Access to staff: Contact by letter, by telephone, by fax, by e-mail and via website
Hours: Mon to Fri, 0900 to 1700

Access to building: No access other than to staff

SOCIETY OF DESIGNER CRAFTSMEN (SDC)

24 Rivington Street, London, EC2A 3DU

Tel: 020 7739 3663
Fax: 020 7739 3663
E-mail: info@societyofdesignercraftsmen.org.uk
Website: www.societyofdesignercraftsmen.org.uk

Enquiries to: Hon. Secretary
Other contacts: Chairman

Founded: 1888

Organisation type and purpose: National organisation, advisory body, membership association (membership is by election or invitation), present number of members: 750, registered charity (charity number 328202), training organisation, consultancy. Founded by William Morris and Walter Crane.

Subject coverage: Information on contemporary practitioners in the following crafts: basketry, calligraphy, ceramics, furniture-making, glass-engraving, jewellery, lettering, metalwork, printmaking, sculpture, silversmithing, stained glass making, textiles, toymaking, woodworking.

Collection: Archives of the Arts and Crafts Exhibition Society and the Society of Designer Craftsmen, housed at the Victoria and Albert Museum

Publications: Printed, and electronic and video

Access to staff: Contact by letter, by telephone and by e-mail. Appointment necessary. Access for members only.
Hours: Mon, Wed, Fri, 1400 to 1700

Access to building: Prior appointment required

Access for disabled people: Level entry

SOCIETY OF DYERS AND COLOURISTS (SDC)

Perkin House, 82 Grattan Road, Bradford, West Yorkshire, BD1 2LU

Tel: 01274 725138
Fax: 01274 392888
E-mail: info@sdc.org.uk
Website: www.sdc.org.uk

Founded: 1884; grant of royal charter (year of change 1963)

Organisation type and purpose: A registered charity, a trade association for the dyeing and colouring industry representing members' interests at national and international level, the only international professional society specialising in colour in all its manifestations.
To advance the science of colour by disseminating information through the coloration industry and beyond. Has over 2,000 members in almost 50 countries worldwide, from textile artists to designers and colour technologists to educators.
Performs standardisation work in relation to colour fastness and colour measurement of textiles.

Subject coverage: The science of colour.

Special visitor services: Events and special interest groups for members.

Education services: Light and Colour Experience for schools, a science-based workshop, allows the delivery of the whole of the Key Stage 2 unit on Light in one entertaining session (tel: 01274 725138; e-mail colour-experience@sdc.org.uk); access to qualifications, training and continuing professional development for members.

Collection: Online archive of over 2,500 technical articles from SDC's extensive library on colour and coloration

Publications: Printed, and electronic and video
Order electronic and video publications from: Website

Publications list: Available online

Access to staff: Contact by letter, by telephone, by fax, by e-mail and via website

Has reciprocal affiliate status with: SADFA (South Africa); SDC (Hong Kong) Ltd; SDCANZ (Australia and New Zealand)

Regional officers across the UK and in China, India, Pakistan, Bangladesh and Sri Lanka:

SOCIETY OF EDITORS

University Centre, Granta Place, Mill Lane, Cambridge, CB2 1RU

Tel: 01223 304080
Fax: 01223 304090
E-mail: info@societyofeditors.org
Website: www.societyofeditors.org

Enquiries to: Executive Director
Other contacts: Administrator for administrative matters

Founded: 1946

Organisation type and purpose:
Professional body, over 400 members.
The Society has members in local, regional and national newspapers, magazines, broadcasting, new media, journalism education and media law.
The Society provides collective consultation and representation.

Subject coverage: Collective consultation and representation on all matters of editorial concern including editorial freedom, independence, standards and training, legislation concerning the media. Provision of contacts for media consultancy.

Access to staff: Contact by letter, by telephone, by fax, by e-mail and via website
Hours: Office hours and 24-hour contact

Access to building: No access other than to staff

SOCIETY OF ENGINEERS (INCORPORATED) (SOE)

Guinea Wiggs, Nayland, Colchester, Essex, CO6 4NF

Tel: 01206 263332
Fax: 01206 262624
E-mail: postmaster@theiet.org
Website: www.society-of-engineers.org.uk

Enquiries to: Chief Executive

Founded: 1854

Organisation type and purpose:
International organisation, professional body (membership is by qualification and experience).
To promote the interests of multi-disciplinary engineers worldwide and to provide a forum for discussion; to examine engineers in art and science to ensure that they can apply their theoretical knowledge to practical situations.

Subject coverage: All branches of civil, electrical and mechanical engineering.

Publications: Printed

Access to staff: Contact by letter, by telephone, by fax and by e-mail
Hours: Mon to Thu, 0900 to 1730

SOCIETY OF ENVIRONMENTAL ENGINEERS (SEE)

The Manor House, High Street, Buntingford, Hertfordshire, SG9 9AB

Tel: 01763 271209
Fax: 01763 273255
E-mail: office@environmental.org.uk
Website: www.environmental.org.uk

Enquiries to: Chief Executive

Founded: 1959

Organisation type and purpose: Learned society.
Licensed Member of the Engineering Council (UK) and the Society for the Environment.

Subject coverage: Climatic contamination control, packaging, vibration shock and noise product assurance and reliability, electromagnetic compatibility.

Publications: Printed

Access to staff: Contact by e-mail
Hours: Mon to Fri, 0900 to 1700

Access to building: No access other than to staff

Access for disabled people: Ramped entry, toilet facilities

SOCIETY OF EVENT ORGANISERS (SEO)

29A Market Square, Biggleswade, Bedfordshire, SG18 8AQ

Tel: 01767 316255
Fax: 01767 316255
E-mail: info@seoevent.co.uk
Website: www.seoevent.co.uk

Enquiries to: Manager

Founded: 1996

Organisation type and purpose: Trade association.

Subject coverage: The running of events.

Publications: Printed

SOCIETY OF FLORISTRY LIMITED (SOF)

Meadowside, Hall Road, West Bergholt, Colchester, Essex, CO6 3DU

Tel: 0870 241 0432
Fax: 0870 241 0432
E-mail: info@britishfloristassociation.org

Enquiries to: Secretary
Direct e-mail: secretariat@britishfloristassociation.org

Founded: 1951

Organisation type and purpose:
Professional body (membership is by subscription, qualification), present number of members: 1,164.
A non-profit making organisation, founded with the sole purpose of raising the standards of floristry worldwide.

Subject coverage: Professional floristry, careers information.

Publications: Printed

Publications list: Available in print

Access to staff: Contact by letter, by telephone and by fax
Hours: Mon to Fri, 0900 to 1300

SOCIETY OF FOOD HYGIENE TECHNOLOGY, THE (SOFHT)

The Granary, Middleton House Farm, Tamworth Road, Middleton, Staffs, B78 2BD

Tel: 01827 872500
Fax: 01827 875800
E-mail: admin@sofht.co.uk
Website: www.sofht.co.uk

Enquiries to: Administrator
Direct e-mail: claudetteschlitter@sofht.co.uk

Founded: 1979

Organisation type and purpose: Learned society (membership is by subscription), present number of members: 750.
Dedicated to improving food hygiene and safety within the food industry.

Subject coverage: Food hygiene, hygiene technology, hygiene training, food technology, food science, food safety.

Publications: Printed

Publications list: Available online and in print

Access to staff: Contact by letter, by telephone, by fax, by e-mail and via website

continued overleaf

Hours: Mon to Fri, 0900 to 1700

Access to building: No access other than to staff

SOCIETY OF GARDEN DESIGNERS (SGD)

Katepwa House, Ashfield Park Avenue, Ross-on-Wye, Herefordshire, HR9 5AX

Tel: 01989 566695
Fax: 01989 567676
E-mail: info@sgd.org.uk
Website: www.sgd.org.uk

Enquiries to: Administrator

Founded: 1981

Organisation type and purpose:
Professional body.
Promotion of professional standards in garden design.

Subject coverage: Garden design, accreditation of garden designers, information about journal, visits, events organised by society (some open to public).

Publications: Printed

Publications list: Available online

Access to staff: Contact by letter, by telephone, by fax, by e-mail and via website

Access to building: Prior appointment required
Hours: Mon to Fri, 0900 to 1700 (closed bank holidays)

Links with: Royal Horticultural Society

SOCIETY OF GENEALOGISTS (SoG)

14 Charterhouse Buildings, Goswell Road, London, EC1M 7BA

Tel: 020 7251 8799
Fax: 020 7250 1800
E-mail: info@sog.org.uk
Website: www.sog.org.uk
Website: www.findmypast.com/home.jsp

Enquiries to: Librarian
Direct tel: 020 7702 5485
Direct e-mail: library@sog.org.uk
Other contacts: Genealogist

Founded: 1911

Organisation type and purpose: Learned society, present number of members: c.11,000, registered charity (charity number 233701), training organisation, publishing house.
Educational Charity.
To promote and encourage the study of genealogy and heraldry.

Subject coverage: Genealogy, biography, family history, heraldry, history and topography world-wide, but with emphasis on Great Britain, Ireland, former British Colonies, America and Europe.

Education services: Advice sessions in person or by telephone; lectures, courses and visits; publications.

Services for disabled people: Portable hearing loop.

Collection: Australasian Civil Registration indexes to c.1900
Bank of England Wills 1717–1845 (online)
Bernau index to pre-1800 Chancery records, etc. (microfilm)
Boyd's Inhabitants of London 16th–18th centuries primarily (online)
Boyd's London Burials (adult males, 1538–1853) (online)
Boyd's Marriage Index (c.12% of pre-1837 English marriages) (online)
Civil Service Irreplaceable Evidences of Age c.1855–c.1939 (online)
Estate Duty will indexes 1796–1857 (microfilm)
Family Histories c.15,000
General Register Office, Birth, Marriage and Death Indexes (England and Wales 1837–1925, Scotland 1855–1920) (microfiche and microfilm)
Great Western Railway Probate (Stock Transfer) Registers 1835–1932 (online)
Indexes to Scottish Baptisms and Marriages 1558–1854 (microfiche)
Monumental inscriptions (c.7,000)
Pallot Marriage Index 1780–1837 (online)
Parish Register transcripts (c.10,000)
Teachers' Registration Council Registers 1902–48 (online)
Times births, marriages and deaths announcements 1816–1920 and indexes 1785–1920 (microfilm)
Palmer's index to The Times 1790–1905 (CD-ROM)
Trinity House Petitions 1780–1890 (microfilm) (index online)
Vital Records Indexes for British Isles, Western Europe, Scandinavia, North America, Middle America covering millions of baptisms and marriages between 1538 and 1905 (CD-ROM)
Principal Probate Registry will indexes 1858–1930 (microfilm)
Vicar General Marriage Allegations 1660–1851 (microfilm) (indexed online)
Faculty Office Marriage Allegations 1715–1851 (microfilm) (indexed online)
Marriage licence and will indexes
1841–1901 census indexes for England, Wales and Scotland and some overseas
Unpublished manuscript genealogy research notes and documents (surnames listed on website)
350 Special Collections of extensive genalogical research
c. 7000 unpublished manscript roll pedigrees (surnames listed on website)

Non-library collection catalogue: All or part available online, in-house and in print

Library catalogue: All or part available online and in-house

Publications: Printed
Order printed publications from: Bookshop Manager, Society of Genealogists Enterprises; tel. 020 7702 5480; e-mail sales@sog.org.uk

Publications list: Available online and in print

Access to staff: Contact by letter, by telephone, by fax, by e-mail, in person and via website. Non-members charged.
Hours: Tue, Wed, Sat, 1000 to 1800; Thu, 1000 to 2000
Special comments: Individual staff work a shift system and may not be available during all opening hours.

Access to building: *Hours:* Tue, Wed, Sat, 1000 to 1800; Thu, 1000 to 2000
Special comments: No pens, bags, coats, mobile phones or pagers allowed in the library.

Access for disabled people: Level entry, access to all public areas, toilet facilities
Special comments: Lift will not take larger wheelchairs.

Member organisation of: British Genealogical Record Users Committee

SOCIETY OF GLASS TECHNOLOGY (SGT)

9 Churchill Way, Chapeltown, Sheffield, S35 2PY

Tel: 0114 263 4455
Fax: 0114 263 4411
E-mail: david@glass.demon.co.uk
Website: www.sgt.org

Enquiries to: Librarian
Direct tel: 0114 222 7307
Direct e-mail: lisa@glass.demon.co.uk
Other contacts: Managing Editor (for information)

Founded: 1916

Organisation type and purpose:
International organisation, learned society, membership association (membership is by subscription), present number of members: 900, registered charity (charity number 237438), publishing house.
Education charity promoting the use of glass of any and every kind by holding conferences, promoting exchange, publishing books and journals.
Supports student exchanges around the world.

Subject coverage: Glass science and manufacture, history, art, design and use of glass.

Non-library collection catalogue: All or part available online

Library catalogue: All or part available online

Publications: Printed, and electronic and video

Publications list: Available online and in print

Access to staff: Contact by letter, by telephone, by fax, by e-mail and via website. Appointment necessary. Access for members only. Letter of introduction required.
Hours: Mon, 0900 to 1700

Links with: University of Sheffield; St George's Library, Mappin Street, Sheffield

Member organisation of: International Commission on Glass; website: http://www.icglass.org

SOCIETY OF HOMEOPATHS

11 Brookfield, Duncan Close, Moulton Park, Northampton, NN3 6WL

Tel: 0845 450 6611
Fax: 0845 450 6622
E-mail: info@homeopathy-soh.org
Website: www.homeopathy-soh.org

Founded: 1978

Organisation type and purpose:
Professional body.

Subject coverage: Homeopathy.

Publications: Printed

Publications list: Available online

Access to staff: Contact by letter, by telephone, by fax, by e-mail and via website
Hours: Mon to Fri, 0800 to 1630

Member organisation of: European Council for Classical Homoeopathy (ECCH); International Council for Classical Homoeopathy (ICCH)

SOCIETY OF INDEXERS (SI)

Woodbourn Business Centre, 10 Jessell Street, Sheffield, S9 3HY

Tel: 0114 2449561
E-mail: admin@indexers.org.uk
Website: www.indexers.org.uk

Enquiries to: Administrator

Founded: 1957

Organisation type and purpose: Professional body (membership is by subscription).

Subject coverage: Guidance and support on professional and technical indexing matters for members, publishers and authors; indexing of books, periodicals and other publications; information storage and retrieval, manual, computer-assisted or fully automated; the foregoing techniques in virtually all fields of academic subject specialisation; improvement of standards; training course for indexing.

Publications: Printed

Publications list: Available online and in print

Access to staff: Contact by letter, by telephone, by e-mail and via website
Hours: Mon to Fri, 0930 to 1600

Affiliated bodies: American Society of Indexers; Association of Southern African Bibliographers and Indexers; Australian & New Zealand Society of Indexers; China Society of Indexers; Indexing & Abstracting Society of Canada

SOCIETY OF JEWELLERY HISTORIANS (SJH)

Scientific Research, The British Museum, London, WC1B 3DG

Fax: 01588 620558
E-mail: info@societyofjewelleryhistorians.ac.uk
Website: www.societyofjewelleryhistorians.ac.uk

Enquiries to: Membership Secretary
Direct e-mail: info@societyofjewelleryhistorians.ac.uk

Founded: 1977

Organisation type and purpose: Learned society (membership is by subscription), present number of members: 500, registered charity (charity number 282160), suitable for ages: all.

Subject coverage: History and development of the craft and craftspeople connected with the manufacture, design and processes concerning jewellery.

Publications: Printed

Publications list: Available online and in print

Access to staff: Contact by letter, by fax, by e-mail and via website

SOCIETY OF LEATHER TECHNOLOGISTS AND CHEMISTS LIMITED (SLTC)

8 Copper Leaf Close, Moulton, Northampton, NN3 7HS

E-mail: office@sltc.org
Website: www.sltc.org

Enquiries to: Membership Secretary

Founded: 1897

Organisation type and purpose: Learned society.

Subject coverage: Leather manufacture, science, technology and testing.

Publications: Printed

Access to staff: Contact by e-mail and via website

Founder member of: International Union of Leather Technologists & Chemists Societies (IULTCS)

SOCIETY OF LEY HUNTERS (SOL)

7 Mildmay Road, Romford, Havering, Essex, RM7 7DA

Tel: 01708 732362
E-mail: leyhunter@googlemail.com
Website: www.leyhunter.com

Enquiries to: Secretary
Direct tel: 01425 273517 (Chairman)
Other contacts: Chairman (for media)

Founded: 2000

Organisation type and purpose: International organisation, membership association (membership is by subscription), voluntary organisation, research organisation.

Subject coverage: Ley lines, Neolithic archaeology, alignments, landscape, folklore, pre-Christian religious sites, pre-literacy farming calendars and energy line nodes.

Collection: Archive of researched alignments

Publications: Printed
Order printed publications from: Mr G. Frawley, 17 Victoria Street, Cheltenham, Gloucestershire, GL50 4HU

Access to staff: Contact by letter and by telephone
Hours: Mon to Fri, 0900 to 1700
Special comments: Letter preferred, voluntary staff availability varies.

Access to building: No access other than to staff

Member of: Stone Circle Webring

SOCIETY OF LICENSED CONVEYANCERS, THE

Chancery House, 110 High Street, Croydon, Surrey, CR9 1PF

Tel: 020 8681 1001
Fax: 020 8681 6001

Enquiries to: Chief Executive

Founded: 1988

Organisation type and purpose: Professional body (membership is by qualification), present number of members: 350, service industry.

Subject coverage: Licensed conveyancing, residential conveyancing and related matters.

Trade and statistical information: Licensed conveyancers' fees and market share in England and Wales

Publications: Printed

Access to staff: Contact by letter, by telephone and by fax
Hours: Mon to Fri, 1000 to 1800

Access to building: No access other than to staff

Subsidiary: SLC Lawyer's Services (Provision of seminars, stationery, books etc to non-members); At the same address; tel: 020 8603 5560; fax: 020 8681 6001; e-mail: slccroydon@netscapeonline.co.uk

SOCIETY OF LOCAL COUNCIL CLERKS

No.8 The Crescent, Taunton, Somerset, TA1 4EA

Tel: 01823 253646
Fax: 01823 253681
E-mail: admin@slcc.co.uk
Website: www.slcc.co.uk/

Enquiries to: External Affairs Officer
Direct tel: 01603 871153
Direct fax: 01603 871153
Direct e-mail: alanfairchild@cawston-pc.gov.uk

Organisation type and purpose: Local government body.

Access to staff: Contact by letter, by telephone, by fax and by e-mail
Hours: Mon to Fri, 0900 to 1700

SOCIETY OF LONDON ART DEALERS (SLAD)

Ormond House, 3 Duke of York Street, London, SW1Y 6JP

Tel: 020 7930 6137
Fax: 020 7321 0685
E-mail: sladoffice@aol.com
Website: www.slad.org

Enquiries to: Director General

Founded: 1932

Organisation type and purpose: Trade association.
To promote and protect the good name and the interests of the art trade.

Subject coverage: Advice on areas of specialisation of London's art dealers.

Publications: Printed

Access to staff: Contact by letter, by telephone, by fax and by e-mail
Hours: Mon to Thu, 1000 to 1730

Members: British Art Market Federation

SOCIETY OF LONDON THEATRE (SOLT)

32 Rose Street, London, WC2E 9ET

Tel: 020 7557 6700
Fax: 020 7557 6799
E-mail: enquiries@solttma.co.uk
Website: www.OfficialLondonTheatre.co.uk

Enquiries to: Development Manager (Press/ Statistics)
Other contacts: Head of Publications for show information.

Founded: 1908

Organisation type and purpose: Trade association.
Representing theatre managers, owners and producers in the major West End London Theatres.

Subject coverage: Industrial relations and legal advice, publications, audience research, promotions, theatre tokens, the Laurence Olivier Awards and the Leicester Square half-price ticket booth.

Collection: London Theatre guides since 1921
Audience data since 1981
Production information

Trade and statistical information: Trade news for the media and travel trade (by subscription).
Annual box office data report, audience research

Publications: Printed

Access to staff: Contact by letter, by telephone, by fax, by e-mail and via website. Appointment necessary.
Hours: Mon to Fri, 1000 to 1800

Access to building: No access other than to staff

SOCIETY OF LONDON TOASTMASTERS (SOLT)

148 Park Crescent, Erith, Kent, DA8 3DY

Tel: 01322 341465
Fax: 01322 402619
E-mail: toastmaster_barnes@btinternet.com
Website: www.societyoflondontoastmasters .co.uk

Enquiries to: Honorary Secretary

Founded: 1953

Organisation type and purpose:
Membership association (membership is by qualification, election or invitation), present number of members: 25, service industry, training organisation.
To provide toastmasters, announcers for formal functions, conferences, exhibitions, etc.

Subject coverage: Art of the professional toastmaster, and master of ceremonies, the organisation and running of banquets, conferences, receptions, wedding receptions, etc.

Collection: Large collection of banquet invitations, photographs and menus; books and manuscripts on banqueting protocol held by individual members

Access to staff: Contact by letter, by telephone, by fax, by e-mail, in person and via website
Hours: Any reasonable time

Access to building: No access other than to staff

SOCIETY OF MARITIME INDUSTRIES LIMITED (SMI)

28–29 Threadneedle Street, London EC2R 8AY

Tel: 020 7628 2555
E-mail: info@maritimeindustries.org
Website: www.maritimeindustries.org

Enquiries to: Chief Executive
Direct e-mail: ce@maritimeindustries.org

Founded: 1966

Organisation type and purpose: Trade association.

Subject coverage: Marine equipment for both merchant and naval ships ranging from main engines, auxiliaries, bridge, radar, galley and deck fittings. Also covers the offshore industry and pollution control equipment. Facilitation of overseas port development investment opportunities. Marine science and technology. Oceanology.

Publications: Printed

Access to staff: Contact by letter, by telephone and by e-mail
Hours: Mon to Fri, 0900 to 1700

Subsidiaries: Association of British Offshore Industries; e-mail: aboi@maritimeindustries .org; Association of Marine Scientific Industries; e-mail: amsi@maritimeindustries .org; British Marine Equipment Association; e-mail: bmea@maritimeindustries.org; British Naval Equipment Association; e-mail: bnea@maritimeindustries.org; British Oil Spill Control Association; e-mail: bosca@ maritimeindustries.org; Ports and Terminals Group; e-mail: ptga@maritimeindustries.org

SOCIETY OF MARTIAL ARTS (SMA)

PO Box 34, Manchester, M9 8DN

Tel: 0161 702 1660
Fax: 0161 702 1660
E-mail: registrar@societyofmartialarts.org
Website: www.societyofmartialarts.co.uk

Enquiries to: Registrar
Other contacts: President for founder of the society.

Founded: 1994

Organisation type and purpose:
International organisation, professional body (membership is by qualification), present number of members: 50, research organisation.

Subject coverage: Martial arts education.

Publications: Printed

Access to staff: Contact by letter, by telephone, by fax and by e-mail
Hours: Mon to Fri, 0900 to 1700

Access to building: No access other than to staff, prior appointment required

Connections with: College of Higher Education of Martial Arts (CHEMA); e-mail: principal@chema.co.uk

SOCIETY OF MASTER SADDLERS (SMS)

Green Lane Farm, Stonham, Stowmarket, Suffolk, IP14 5DS

Tel: 01449 711642
Fax: 01449 711642
E-mail: enquiries@mastersaddlers.co.uk
Website: www.mastersaddlers.co.uk

Founded: 1966

Organisation type and purpose: Formed to serve as a trade association for the craft retail saddler, but has since embraced all aspects of the trade.
To safeguard the quality of work, services, training and qualifications of all those who work in the saddlery trade, from manufacturers and retailers through individual craftspeople and saddle fitters.

Subject coverage: Saddlery.

Access to staff: Contact by letter, by telephone, by fax and by e-mail

SOCIETY OF METAPHYSICIANS LIMITED (SofM)

Archers Court, Stonestile Lane, The Ridge, Hastings, East Sussex, TN35 4PG

Tel: 01424 751577
Fax: 01424 751577
E-mail: newmeta@btinternet.com
Website: www.metaphysicians.org.uk
Website: www.btinternet.com/~newmeta/ index/home.html

Enquiries to: Managing Director
Other contacts: Founder President

Founded: 1944

Organisation type and purpose:
International organisation, advisory body, professional body (membership is by qualification, election or invitation), present number of members: 298, voluntary organisation, suitable for ages: all, training organisation, consultancy, research organisation, publishing house.

Subject coverage: Neometaphysics (study and application of fundamental laws), includes all physical and non-physical sciences, parapsychology, paraphysics, esoterics, psychic science, biofeedback systems, bioenergics, psycho-kinetics, neopsychological studies, healing, energy and mind-based, human aura, development of infinitely based administrative systems, alternative medicine.

Collection: Full research data, photographs, etc. on Aura Viewing, including complementary colour method, electro-deposition and corona discharge
Bibliography and equipment
Paraphysics, Psychic Science

Trade and statistical information: World manufactures of aura imaging and radiesthetic equipment

Non-library collection catalogue: All or part available online

Library catalogue: All or part available online, in-house and in print

Publications: Printed

Publications list: Available in print

Access to staff: Contact by letter, by telephone, by fax, by e-mail and via website. Appointment necessary.
Hours: Mon to Fri, 1000 to 1400

Access for disabled people: Parking provided, access to all public areas, toilet facilities

Also at: Istituto Italiano di Ricerche Metafisiche; via Ritmeyer 6-I34/32, Trieste, Italy; fax: 0039 40 224206; e-mail: istmeta@tin.it

Links with: Metaphysical Research Group; tel: 01424 751577; fax: 01424 751577; e-mail: newmeta@btinternet.com

SOCIETY OF MODEL SHIPWRIGHTS (SMS)

5 Lodge Crescent, Orpington, Kent, BR6 0QE

Tel: 01689 827213

Enquiries to: Honorary Secretary

Founded: 1974

Organisation type and purpose: Membership association (membership is by election or invitation), present number of members: 85, suitable for ages: all.
The society is devoted to the research into and the construction of accurate scale models of vessels.

Subject coverage: All matters relating to the construction of scale models of sailing and powered vessels of any period.

Access to staff: Contact by letter and by telephone
Hours: Sun to Sat, 0900 to 2200

SOCIETY OF NURSERY NURSING PRACTITIONERS, THE (SNNP)

40 Archdale Road, East Dulwich, London, SE22 9HJ

Tel: 0845 260 2900
Fax: 0208 693 0555
E-mail: info@snnp.org.uk
Website: www.snnp.org.uk

Enquiries to: Chief Executive

Founded: 1991

Organisation type and purpose: Professional awarding body for all those who work with children from birth to the age of 5. These include childminders, nannies, nursery nurses, workplace nursery nurses, early years practitioners, supervisors, managers, lecturers and hospital baby care unit nursery nurses.

Subject coverage: Child care education, development and training 4.

Publications: Printed

Access to staff: Contact by letter, by telephone, by fax, by e-mail and in person. Appointment necessary.
Hours: Mon to Fri, 0900 to 1700

SOCIETY OF OCCUPATIONAL MEDICINE (SOM)

6 St Andrews Place, Regents Park, London, NW1 4LB

Tel: 020 7486 2641
Fax: 020 7486 0028
E-mail: admin@som.org.uk
Website: https://www.som.org.uk

Founded: 1935; formerly called Association of Industrial Medical Officers (year of change 1965)

Organisation type and purpose: A registered charity (number 268555), a learned body for registered medical practitioners with an involvement or interest in the practice of occupational medicine.

Subject coverage: Protection of the health of people at work, including environmental issues associated with work products and processes. Although the Society does not provide a clinical occupational health service, it seeks to prevent the occurrence of occupational disease and injury across the whole of industry. It also stimulates research and education in occupational medicine and maintains a close relationship with government departments and other agencies in the health and safety field.

Publications: Electronic and video
Order electronic and video publications from: Website

Access to staff: Contact by letter, by telephone, by fax, by e-mail and via website

Links with: British Medical Association; Health & Safety Executive

Regional groups in Central Southern England, London, South Wales and the West of England, West Midlands, East Midlands, Yorkshire, North West, North East, Scotland and Northern Ireland:

SOCIETY OF OPERATIONS ENGINEERS (SOE)

22 Greencoat Place, London, SW1P 1PR

Tel: 020 7630 1111
Fax: 020 7630 6677
E-mail: soe@soe.org.uk
Website: www.iplante.org.uk
Website: www.irte.org.uk
Website: www.soe.org.uk

Enquiries to: Chief Executive

Founded: 2000

Organisation type and purpose: International organisation, learned society, professional body (membership is by election or invitation), present number of members: 18,500, registered charity (charity number 1081753).

Subject coverage: Plant engineering, maintenance, engineering surveying, and inspection, road transport engineering.

Publications: Printed

Publications list: Available online

Access to staff: Contact by letter and by e-mail. Appointment necessary. Access for members only.
Hours: Mon to Fri, 0900 to 1700

SOCIETY OF ORTHOPAEDIC MEDICINE (SOM)

4th Floor, Stanley House, 151 Dale Street, Liverpool, L2 2AH.

Tel: 0151 2373970
Fax: 0151 2373971
E-mail: admin@somed.org
Website: www.somed.org

Founded: 1979

Organisation type and purpose: International organisation, learned society (membership is by qualification), present number of members: 1,400, registered charity, training organisation.

Subject coverage: Orthopaedic medicine, musculoskeletal medicine.

Publications: Printed

Access to staff: Contact by letter, by telephone, by fax, by e-mail and via website
Hours: Mon to Fri, 0900 to 1700

Access to building: No access other than to staff

Links with: British Institute of Musculoskeletal Medicine; Chartered Society of Physiotherapy; Middlesex University; Society of Apothecaries

SOCIETY OF PENSION CONSULTANTS (SPC)

St Bartholomew House, 92 Fleet Street, London, EC4Y 1DG

Tel: 020 7353 1688
Fax: 020 7353 9296
E-mail: john.mortimer@spc.uk.com
Website: www.spc.uk.com

Enquiries to: Secretary

Founded: 1958

Organisation type and purpose: Membership association (membership is by subscription, qualification and election), present number of members: 103 organisations.
Representative body for the providers of the advice and services needed to provide pensions (occupational and personal) and other benefits. Members include pension and actuarial consultants, legal and accounting firms, insurance companies, investment houses and third-party administrators.

Subject coverage: Occupational pension schemes, personal pension schemes and other employee benefit schemes, interests of organisations involved in providing advice and/or services in connection with the setting up or running of pension schemes.

Information services: Only available to members.

Collection: Some records are available through the Pensions Archive Trust

Publications: Printed

Access to staff: Contact by letter, by e-mail and via website. Appointment necessary.
Hours: Mon to Fri, 0900 to 1700

Member organisation of: Occupational Pension Schemes Joint Working Group

SOCIETY OF PLOUGHMEN LIMITED

Quarry Farm, Loversall, Doncaster, South Yorkshire, DN11 9DH

Tel: 01302 852469
Fax: 01302 859880
E-mail: info@ploughmen.co.uk
Website: www.ploughmen.co.uk

continued overleaf

Enquiries to: Secretary

Founded: 1972

Organisation type and purpose: Membership association (membership is by subscription), registered charity (charity number 1062780).
To promote and encourage the art, skill and science of ploughing the land.

Subject coverage: Ploughing.

Publications: Printed

Access to staff: Contact by letter, by telephone, by fax, by e-mail and via website
Hours: Mon to Fri, 0930 to 1630

Links with: World Ploughing Organisation

SOCIETY OF PROFESSIONAL ENGINEERS (SPE)

St Mary House, 15 St Mary Street, Chippenham, Wiltshire, SN15 3WD

Tel: 01249 655398
Fax: 01249 443602
E-mail: spe@abe.org.uk

Enquiries to: Office Co-ordinator

Founded: 1969

Organisation type and purpose: Professional body.

Subject coverage: Maintains a register of well-qualified professional engineers of whatever discipline. Protects, enhances and promotes the status of the professional engineer and promotes the concept of this title throughout the world. Acts as the secretariat and provider of licences and registration cards to suitably qualified professional engineers on behalf of the UIDIP for the English-speaking countries of the world.
UIDIP is currently on hold until further notice.

Publications: Printed

Access to staff: Contact by letter, by telephone, by fax and by e-mail
Hours: Mon to Fri, 0900 to 1700

Member of: Union Internationale des Ingenieurs Professionnels (UIDIP) – Currently on hold until further notice; 66 rue de la Rochefoucauld, Paris, F-75009, France

Twinned with the: Bundesverband der Berufsingenieure Deutschlands (BDI); Germany; tel: 01249 655398; Société Nationale des Ingénieurs Professionnels France (IPF); tel: 01249 655398; South African Society for Professional Engineers (SASPE)

SOCIETY OF RECORDER PLAYERS (SRP)

Linkside, 21 Bereweeke Avenue, Winchester, SO22 6BH

E-mail: secretary@srp.org.uk
Website: www.srp.org.uk

Enquiries to: Secretary

Founded: 1937

Organisation type and purpose: Membership association (membership is by subscription), present number of members: 1,400, voluntary organisation, registered charity (charity number 282751/SC038422), suitable for all ages.

Subject coverage: Recorder playing.

Publications: Printed

Access to staff: Contact by letter, by telephone, by e-mail and via website

Also at: 51 regional branches

SOCIETY OF SALES & MARKETING (SSM)

40 Archdale Road, East Dulwich, London, SE22 9HJ

Tel: 0845 260 2900
Fax: 0208 693 0555
E-mail: info@ssm.org.uk
Website: www.ssm.org.uk

Enquiries to: Chief Executive

Founded: 1980

Organisation type and purpose: International organisation, advisory body, professional body (membership is by subscription, qualification, election or invitation).

Subject coverage: Professional body for those interested in selling and sales management, marketing, retailing and international trade.

Publications: Printed

Access to staff: Contact by letter, by telephone, by fax, by e-mail and in person. Appointment necessary.
Hours: Mon to Fri, 0900 to 1700

SOCIETY OF SCRIBES AND ILLUMINATORS (SSI)

The Art Workers Guild, 6 Queen's Square, London, WC1N 3AT

Tel: 015242 51534
E-mail: scribe@calligraphyonline.org
Website: www.calligraphyonline.org

Enquiries to: Honorary Secretary
Direct e-mail: honsec@calligraphyonline.org

Founded: 1921

Organisation type and purpose: International organisation, professional body (Fellowship by election, Lay Membership by subscription); present number of members: 550, suitable for ages: 16+.
To perpetuate a tradition of craftsmanship in the production of manuscript books and documents; to encourage and influence calligraphy and fine lettering.

Subject coverage: Crafts of writing and lettering, production of manuscript books and documents, fine lettering and calligraphy, lists of calligraphy courses, exhibitions, materials and availability, advice on all aspects of calligraphy and lettering.

Collection: Rare calligraphy books
Reference library
Small permanent exhibition, with historical and modern pieces

Publications: Printed
Order printed publications from: via website

Access to staff: Contact by letter, by telephone, by e-mail and via website
Hours: Mon to Fri, 0900 to 1700

Access to building: No access to building

SOCIETY OF SOLICITORS IN THE SUPREME COURTS OF SCOTLAND (SSC Society)

SSC Library, Parliament House, 11 Parliament Square, Edinburgh, EH1 1RF

Tel: 0131 225 6268
Fax: 0131 225 2270
E-mail: enquiries@ssclibrary.co.uk
Website: www.ssclibrary.co.uk

Enquiries to: Librarian

Founded: 1784

Organisation type and purpose: Learned society (membership is by subscription), present number of members: 300.

Subject coverage: Scottish legal material, statutes, law reports, SIs, textbooks (comprehensive); English legal material, statutes, law reports, SIs, limited selection of textbooks; Scots law in all its branches; UK law where it is common to Scotland and England.

Collection: Court of Session and High Court of Justiciary Opinions from 1982 to date (open, unreported and indexed on database from 1991)
Session papers 1750–1954

Library catalogue: All or part available in-house

Access to staff: Contact by letter, by telephone and by e-mail. Appointment necessary. Access for members only. Non-members charged.
Hours: Mon to Fri, 0930 to 1600

SOCIETY OF SPORTS THERAPISTS (SST)

16 Royal Terrace, Glasgow, G3 7NY

Tel: 0845 6002613
Fax: 0141 3325335
E-mail: admin@society-of-sports-therapists.org
Website: www.society-of-sports-therapists.org

Enquiries to: Chairman
Direct e-mail: webmaster@society-of-sports-therapists.org
Other contacts: Secretary

Founded: 1989

Organisation type and purpose: National government body, advisory body, professional body (membership is by subscription, qualification), present number of members: 1500+, training organisation, consultancy.
To provide a professional and educational identity for sports therapists.

Subject coverage: Sports injury management, treatment and rehabilitation.

Collection: Fact sheets, newsletters, book lists and course and conference details

Access to staff: Contact by letter, by telephone, by fax, by e-mail and via website. Appointment necessary.

Hours: Mon to Fri, 1000 to 1500

Subsidiary body: Sports Rehab & Education; tel: 0141 221 1494; fax: 0141 221 1525

SOCIETY OF ST GREGORY (SSG)

76 Great Bushey Drive, London, N20 8QL

Tel: 020 8445 5724
E-mail: chairman@ssg.org.uk
Website: www.ssg.org.uk

Enquiries to: Chairman

Founded: 1929

Organisation type and purpose: Membership association (membership is by subscription), voluntary organisation, training organisation.

Subject coverage: Roman Catholic worship and church music.

Collection: Church Music
Church Music Association Music Library, 1955–1972
Complete sets, 1929 to date:
Life and Worship
Liturgy
Music and Liturgy

Publications: Printed

Access to staff: Contact by letter, by telephone, by e-mail and via website
Hours: Any reasonable time

SOCIETY OF TELEVISION LIGHTING AND DESIGN (STLD)

E-mail: via website
Website: www.stld.org.uk

History of institution: incorporates the former Society of Television Lighting Directors (year of change 2009)

Organisation type and purpose: A membership association (membership is by subscription) for the television lighting profession.

Subject coverage: Provides a forum that stimulates a free exchange of ideas in all aspects of the television lighting profession.

Publications: Printed

Access to staff: Contact via website

SOCIETY OF TRUST AND ESTATE PRACTITIONERS (STEP)

Artillery House (South), 11–19 Artillery Row, London, SW1P 1RT

Tel: 020 7340 0500
E-mail: step@step.org
Website: www.step.org

Founded: 1991

Organisation type and purpose: A professional body providing members with a local, national and international learning and business network focusing on the responsible stewardship of assets today and across the generations. Full members of STEP are the most experienced and senior practitioners in the field of trusts and estates; has over 14,000 members spread throughout the world's major trust and estate jurisdictions. Members advise clients on the broad business of the management of personal finance.
Provides education, training, representation and networking for its members.

Subject coverage: STEP members help families plan their long-term financial future, facilitating good stewardship and financial planning across future generations. STEP members also help families comply with the often complex tax rules surrounding trusts, estates and inheritance.

Special visitor services: STEP TV

Publications: Printed, and electronic and video
Order printed publications from: e-mail: orders@step.org
Order electronic and video publications from: Website

Publications list: Available online

Access to staff: Contact by letter, by telephone and by e-mail
Hours: Mon to Fri, 0900 to 1730 except bank hols

Branches: Throughout the world

SOCIETY OF VOLUNTARY ASSOCIATES (SOVA)

1st Floor, Chichester House, 37 Brixton Road, London, SW9 6DZ

Tel: 020 7793 0404
Fax: 020 7735 4410
E-mail: london@sova.org.uk
Website: www.sova.org.uk/

Enquiries to: Manager
Direct tel: 0114 282 3187
Direct fax: 0114 282 3292
Direct e-mail: mail@sova.org.uk

Founded: 1975

Organisation type and purpose: National organisation, voluntary organisation, registered charity (charity number 1073877), training organisation, consultancy.
To involve local communities in community safety, crime reduction and offenders' rehabilitation.

Subject coverage: Volunteers within the criminal justice system, partnerships between statutory and voluntary agencies, community action, community safety and community support for ex-offenders.

Collection: Reports on SOVA projects

Publications: Printed

Access to staff: Contact by telephone and by e-mail
Hours: Mon to Fri, 0900 to 1700

Affiliated to: National Council for Voluntary Organizations

SOCIETY OF WEDDING AND PORTRAIT PHOTOGRAPHERS LIMITED (SWPP)

Colomendy House, Ivale Road, Denbigh, Clwyd, LL16 3DF

Tel: 01745 815030
E-mail: info@swpp.co.uk

Enquiries to: Chief Executive

Founded: 1988

Organisation type and purpose: Trade association.

Subject coverage: Training and support in wedding portrait photography and videoing.

Publications: Printed, and electronic and video

Publications list: Available in print

Access to staff: Contact by letter, by telephone and by fax. Appointment necessary.
Hours: Mon to Fri, 0900 to 1700

SOCIETY OF WILDLIFE ARTISTS (SWLA)

17 Carlton House Terrace, London, SW1Y 5BD

Tel: 020 7930 6844
Fax: 020 7839 7830
E-mail: press@mallgalleries.com
Website: www.mallgalleries.org.uk

Enquiries to: Secretary
Other contacts: Marketing and Communications Officer

Founded: 1964

Organisation type and purpose: Membership association (membership is by election or invitation), registered charity (charity number 328717).

Subject coverage: Wildlife art as painting, drawings and sculpture, its exhibition and promotion.

Publications: Printed

Access to staff: Contact by letter, by telephone, by fax, by e-mail and via website. Appointment necessary.
Hours: Mon to Fri, 0930 to 1700

Access to building: No access other than to staff
Hours: Mon to Fri, 0930 to 1700

Access for disabled people: Stairlift, toilet facilities

Links with: Federation of British Artists; at the same address

SOCIETY OF WOMEN ARTISTS, THE (SWA)

1 Knapp Cottages, Wyke, Gillingham, Dorset, SP8 4NQ

Tel: 01747 825718
Fax: 01747 826835
E-mail: pamhenderson@dial.pipex.com
Website: www.society-women-artists.org.uk

Enquiries to: Executive Secretary

Founded: 1855

Organisation type and purpose: International organisation, membership association (membership is by election or invitation), present number of members: 150, registered charity (charity number 298241).

Subject coverage: Art and women artists; annual exhibition of paintings, drawings, prints and sculpture.

Collection: Archive of Art and Design, Victoria and Albert Museum, Blythe House, 23 Blythe Road, London W14 0QF

continued overleaf

Access to staff: Contact by letter, by telephone, by fax and by e-mail
Hours: Mon to Fri, 0900 to 1700

Access to building: No prior appointment required
Special comments: Archives are kept by the Victoria and Albert Museum's Archive of Art and Design.

SOCIETY OF WOOD ENGRAVERS (SWE)

51 Sunningdale, Orton Waterville, Peterborough PE2 5UB

Tel: 01733 391433
Fax: 01733 391433
E-mail: swesec@geriwaddington.com
Website: www.woodengravers.co.uk

Enquiries to: General Secretary
Direct e-mail: swesec@geriwaddington.com

Founded: 1920

Organisation type and purpose:
International organisation, membership association.
Artists' exhibiting society and international contact organisation.

Subject coverage: Printmaking, relief printmaking, wood engraving, its practice, current practitioners and its history.

Collection: Society archives at Manchester Metropolitan University and collection at the Ashmolean Museum Oxford.

Publications: Printed

Access to staff: Contact by letter, by telephone, by fax, by e-mail and via website
Hours: Mon to Fri, 1000 to 1700

SOG LIMITED

PO Box 13, The Heath, Runcorn, Cheshire, WA7 4QF

Tel: 01928 511888
Fax: 01928 567979
E-mail: heath_library@sog.ltd.uk
Website: www.sog.ltd.uk

Enquiries to: Librarian
Direct tel: 01928 513438
Direct fax: 01928 513334

Organisation type and purpose: Service industry.
Facilities management & specialist services.

Subject coverage: Chlor-alkali; chlorine and inorganic derivatives; caustic soda; electrochemistry and electrochemical technology, water, sewage and effluent treatment chemicals. Processes; chlorinated hydrocarbons and derivatives; cleaning and degreasing solvents; refrigerants; CFC alternatives, fluorinated hydrocarbons and derivatives, chlorine containing monomers and polymers; PVC; fluorine containing monomers and polymers; PTFE.

Non-library collection catalogue: All or part available in-house

Library catalogue: All or part available in-house

Publications list: Available in print

Access to staff: Contact by letter, by telephone, by fax, by e-mail and via website. Appointment necessary. Access for members only. All charged.
Hours: Mon to Fri, 0830 to 1200 and 1230 to 1630

Access to building: Prior appointment required

SOIL ASSOCIATION, THE (SA)

Bristol House, 40–56 Victoria Street, Bristol, BS1 6BY

Tel: 0117 929 0661
Fax: 0117 314 5000
Website: www.soilassociation.org

Enquiries to: Information Officer
Direct tel: 0117 914 2444

Founded: 1946

Organisation type and purpose:
Membership association (membership is by subscription), registered charity.

Subject coverage: Organic food and farming, responsible forestry, agriculture.

Publications: Printed

Publications list: Available online and in print

Access to staff: Contact by letter, by telephone, by fax and in person.
Appointment necessary.
Hours: Mon to Fri, 0900 to 1730

Wholly owned subsidiary of: Soil Association Certification Limited; at the same address; tel: 0117 914 2405; fax: 0117 925 2504; e-mail: cert@soilassociation.org

SOIL MECHANICS (SML)

Glossop House, Hogwood Lane, Finchampstead, Wokingham, Berkshire, RG40 4QW

Tel: 0118 932 8888
Fax: 0118 932 8383
E-mail: library@esg.co.uk
Website: www.esg.co.uk

Enquiries to: Librarian
Direct tel: 0118 932 4459
Direct e-mail: peter.eldred@esg.co.uk

Founded: 1943

Organisation type and purpose: Service industry, consultancy.

Subject coverage: Soil mechanics, rock mechanics, geology, geotechnical engineering, site investigation, vibration and dynamics, earthquake engineering, seismicity.

Collection: Results of site investigations throughout the United Kingdom and some overseas localities (microform and scans)

Non-library collection catalogue: All or part available in-house

Library catalogue: All or part available in-house

Access to staff: Contact by telephone, by fax, by e-mail and in person. Appointment necessary. Non-members charged.
Hours: Mon to Fri, 0900 to 1700

Access to building: Prior appointment required
Hours: Mon to Fri, 0900 to 1700

Access for disabled people: Parking provided, level entry, access to all public areas, toilet facilities

Constituent bodies: CL Voelcker (CLV); at the same address; Exploration Associates (EA); at the same address; TES Bretby; at the same address

Parent body: Environmental Scientifics Group Limited (ESGL); at the same address

SOLAR ENERGY SOCIETY (UK-ISES)

School of Technology, Oxford Brookes University, Headington Campus, Gipsy Lane, Oxford, OX3 0BP

Tel: 01865 484367
Fax: 01865 484263
E-mail: ukises@brookes.ac.uk
Website: www.thesolarline.com

Enquiries to: Administrator

Founded: 1974

Organisation type and purpose: Learned society.

Subject coverage: Solar energy.

Publications: Printed

Publications list: Available online and in print

Access to staff: Contact by e-mail
Hours: Mon to Fri, 0900 to 1700

Access to building: No prior appointment required

Section of: International Solar Energy Society; Freiburg, Germany; tel: + 49 761 4590652; fax: + 49 761 4590699; e-mail: info@ises.org

SOLAR TRADE ASSOCIATION (STA)

National Energy Centre, Davy Avenue, Knowlhill, Milton Keynes, Buckinghamshire, MK5 8NG

Tel: 01908 442290
Fax: 01908 665577
E-mail: enquiries@solar-trade.org.uk
Website: www.solar-trade.org.uk

Enquiries to: Chief Executive

Founded: 1974

Organisation type and purpose: Trade association (membership is by election or invitation), present number of members: 170, manufacturing industry, service industry, training organisation, consultancy.
National enquiry centre.

Subject coverage: Solar industry and solar energy utilisation from the commercial point of view, commercial and domestic water heating, swimming pool heating, passive solar design, solar controllers.

Trade and statistical information: National sales of solar systems.
International sales of solar systems

Publications: Printed

Access to staff: Contact by letter, by telephone, by fax and by e-mail
Hours: Mon to Fri, 0900 to 1700

Member of: European Solar Thermal Industries Federation (ESTIF); The Micropower Council

SOLDIER MAGAZINE

Parsons House, Ordnance Road, Aldershot, Hampshire, GU11 2DU

Tel: 01252 347353
Fax: 01252 347358
E-mail: mail@soldiermagazine.co.uk
Website: www.soldiermagazine.co.uk

Enquiries to: Archive/Information Manager
Direct tel: 01252 355056
Direct e-mail: rkusionowicz@soldiermagazine.co.uk

Founded: 1945

Organisation type and purpose: National government body, publishing house.

Subject coverage: The British Army, especially post-1945.

Collection: Magazine archive of every issue printed since 19th March 1945
Photo archive of photographs used in issues of British Army subjects, in colour, and black and white
Crown copyright of photographs taken by Soldier Magazine staff

Library catalogue: All or part available in-house

Publications: Printed

Access to staff: Contact by letter, by telephone, by fax, by e-mail and in person. Appointment necessary.
Hours: Mon to Fri, 0900 to 1600

Access to building: Prior appointment required

Access for disabled people: Parking provided

SOLDIERS, SAILORS, AIRMEN AND FAMILIES ASSOCIATION – FORCES HELP (SSAFA Forceshelp)

19 Queen Elizabeth Street, London, SE1 2LP

Tel: 020 7403 8783
Fax: 020 7403 8815
E-mail: management@ssafa.org.uk
Website: www.ssafa.org.uk

Enquiries to: Welfare Advisors
Other contacts: Director of Welfare & Housing

Founded: 1885

Organisation type and purpose: Voluntary organisation, registered charity (charity number 210760).
Armed Forces National Charity.
Support for serving and ex-service men, women and their families in need.

Subject coverage: Welfare of Armed Service and ex-Service families and dependants.

Collection: Small resource library containing up-to-date benefit, housing and welfare advice leaflets and literature

Non-library collection catalogue: All or part available in-house

Library catalogue: All or part available in-house

Publications: Printed

Access to staff: Contact by letter, by telephone, by fax, by e-mail and via website. Appointment necessary.
Hours: Mon to Fri, 0915 to 1700

Has: 102 Branches throughout the UK and Ireland. Can also be contacted through Citizens Advice Bureaux

SOLICITORS FAMILY LAW ASSOCIATION (SFLA)

PO Box 302, Orpington, Kent, BR6 8QX

Tel: 01689 850227
Fax: 01689 855833
Website: www.sfla.co.uk
Website: www.sfla.org.uk

Enquiries to: Administrative Director

Founded: 1982

Organisation type and purpose: Membership association (membership is by subscription, qualification, election or invitation), present number of members: 5,000, voluntary organisation.

Subject coverage: All solicitor members deal with family law in a constructive rather than aggressive approach to resolving problems flowing from relationship breakdown. The public can contact the Association to receive a list of local members.

Publications: Printed, and electronic and video

Publications list: Available in print

Access to staff: Contact by letter, by telephone, by fax and by e-mail
Hours: Mon to Fri, 0900 to 1700

SOLID FUEL ASSOCIATION (SFA)

7 Swanwick Court, Alfreton, Derbyshire, DE55 7AS

Tel: 01773 835400
Fax: 01773 834351
E-mail: sfa@solidfuel.co.uk
Website: www.solidfuel.co.uk

Enquiries to: General Secretary

Founded: 1994

Organisation type and purpose: National organisation, advisory body, trade association (membership is by subscription), present number of members: 38.

Subject coverage: Utilisation of natural and manufactured solid fuels in domestic heating. Installation and maintenance of solid fuel domestic heating appliances.

Publications list: Available online

Access to staff: Contact by letter, by telephone, by fax, by e-mail and via website
Hours: Mon to Fri, 0900 to 1700

Access to building: No access other than to staff

SOLIHULL CENTRAL LIBRARY

Homer Road, Solihull, West Midlands, B91 3RG

Tel: 0121 704 6965
Fax: 0121 704 6991
E-mail: libraryarts@solihull.gov.uk
Website: www.solihull.gov.uk/libraries

Enquiries to: Head of Libraries
Direct tel: 0121 704 6945
Direct e-mail: tcox@solihull.gov.uk
Other contacts: Head of Information & Local Studies Manager; email: dgill@solihull.gov.uk; tel: 0121 704 6808

Organisation type and purpose: Public library.

Non-library collection catalogue: All or part available online and in-house

Library catalogue: All or part available online and in-house

Access to staff: Contact by letter, by telephone, by fax and by e-mail
Hours: Mon, Thu, 0900 to 2000; Tue, Fri, 0900 to 1800; Wed, 1000 to 1800; Sat, 0900 to 1700

Access to building: No prior appointment required

Access for disabled people: Level entry, access to all public areas, toilet facilities

Branch libraries: Balsall Common; 283 Kenilworth Road, Balsall Common, CV7 7EL; tel: 01676 532590; fax: 01676 530119; Castle Bromwich; Hurst Lane North, Castle Bromwich, B36 0EY; tel: 0121 747 3708; fax: 0121 748 5919; Chelmsley Wood; 10 West Mall, Chelmsley Wood Shopping Centre, Chelmsley Wood, Birmingham B37 5TN; tel: 0121 788 4380; fax: 0121 788 4391; Hampton in Arden; 39 Fentham Road, Hampton in Arden, B92 0AY; tel: 01675 442629; fax: 01675 443608; Hobs Moat; Ulleries Road, Solihull, West Midlands, B92 8EE; tel: 0121 743 4592; fax: 0121 743 2473; Kingshurst; Marston Drive, Kingshurst, B37 6BD; tel: 0121 770 3451; fax: 0121 770 9388; Knowle; Chester House, High Street, Knowle, B93 0LL; tel: 01564 775840; fax: 01564 770953; Marston Green; Land Lane, Marston Green, B37 7DQ; tel: 0121 779 2131; fax: 0121 770 1565; Meriden; The Green, Meriden, CV7 7LN; tel: 01676 522717; fax: 01676 521146; Olton; 169a Warwick Road, Olton, B92 7AW; tel: 0121 706 3038; fax: 0121 708 0549; Shirley; Church Road, Shirley, B90 2AY; tel: 0121 744 1076; fax: 0121 744 5047

SOLIHULL CHAMBER OF INDUSTRY AND COMMERCE

Wellington House, Starley Way, Solihull B37 7HE

Tel: 0121 781 7384
Fax: 0121 781 7395
E-mail: info@solihull-chamber.com
Website: www.solihull-chamber.com

Enquiries to: Director

Founded: 1990

Organisation type and purpose: Membership association (membership is by subscription).

Subject coverage: Business services.

Access to staff: Contact by letter, by telephone and by fax. Appointment necessary.
Hours: Mon to Fri, 0900 to 1700

Associate of: Birmingham Chamber of Commerce (BCI); 75 Harborne Road, Birmingham, B15 3DH; tel: 0121 454 6171

SOLIHULL COLLEGE

Blossomfield Road, Solihull, West Midlands, B91 1SB

Tel: 0121 678 7000
Fax: 0121 678 7200
E-mail: library@solihull.ac.uk
Website: www.solihull.ac.uk

Enquiries to: Library and Learning Centre Manager
Direct tel: 0121 678 7205

Organisation type and purpose: College of further and higher education.

Subject coverage: Education; business studies; art and design; leisure; travel and tourism; hotel and catering studies; teacher training (further education); counselling; humanities; social sciences.

Library catalogue: All or part available online

Access to staff: Contact by letter, by telephone and by e-mail. Appointment necessary.
Hours: Term time: Mon to Thu, 0830 to 2030; Fri, 0830 to 1630; Sat, 0930 to 1300
Vacations: Mon to Fri, 0900 to 1700

SOLIHULL LIBRARY SERVICE

Central Library, Homer Road, Solihull, West Midlands, B91 3RG

Tel: 0121 704 6977
Fax: 0121 704 6212
E-mail: libraryarts@solihull.gov.uk
Website: www.solihull.gov.uk/libraries

Enquiries to: Information and Heritage Services Manager
Direct tel: 0121 704 6808
Direct e-mail: dgill@solihull.gov.uk

Organisation type and purpose: Local government body, public library.

Subject coverage: General library, information and reference service; local and family history resources relating to the area covered by the present Metropolitan Borough of Solihull.

Information services: Business information service, heritage and local studies service.

Education services: Skills for Life Service (courses via Learndirect); Connexions and NextSteps services hosted.

Collection: Records relating to Solihull MBC and its predecessor authorities
Birmingham Small Arms (BSA) company archive collection (motorcycles and small arms)
Photographic archive of Cliff Joiner (Solihull press photographer)
Solihull Bowling Club
Archive of Doris Hamilton Smith (artist and pupil of Edith Holden)

Library catalogue: All or part available online

Access to staff: Contact by letter, by telephone, by fax, by e-mail, in person and via website
Hours: Mon, Thu, 0900 to 2000; Tue, Fri, 0900 to 1800; Wed, 1000 to 1800; Sat, 0900 to 1700

Access to building: Via Library Square, through Touchwood Shopping Centre
Hours: During opening hours

Access for disabled people: Level entry, access to all public areas, public lift, toilet facilities
Hours: During opening hours
Special comments: Disabled parking in Church Hill car park, special needs parking bays in adjacent Touchwood underground car park, with lifts to Library level.

Parent body: Solihull Metropolitan Borough Council; website: http://www.solihull.gov.uk

SOMERSET AND WESSEX EATING DISORDERS ASSOCIATION (SWEDA)

Strode House, 10 Leigh Road, Street, Somerset, BA16 0HA

Tel: 01458 448611
E-mail: admin@swedauk.org
Website: www.swedauk.org

Enquiries to: Manager
Direct e-mail: paula@swedauk.org
Other contacts: Administrator

Founded: 1997

Organisation type and purpose:
Membership association, voluntary organisation, registered charity (charity number 1056441), training organisation.
A charity based on the ethos of being user-led and encouraging self-help and improvement, SWEDA aims to reach out to all affected by eating disorders, sufferers, carers and professionals.

Subject coverage: Eating disorders, helpline and website for sufferers and carers, training and consultation on eating disorders, awareness raising.

Access to staff: Contact by letter, by telephone, by e-mail, in person and via website. Appointment necessary.
Hours: Administrator: Mon to Fri, 0900 to 1300
Special comments: Answerphone at all other times.

Access to building: Prior appointment required
Hours: Wed, 1000 to 1300

SOMERSET ARCHAEOLOGICAL AND NATURAL HISTORY SOCIETY (SANHS)

Somerset Heritage Centre, Brunel Way, Norton Fitzwarren, Taunton, Somerset TA2 6SF

Tel: 01823 272429
Fax: 01823 272429
E-mail: office@sanhs.org
Website: www.sanhs.org

Enquiries to: Office Manager
Other contacts: somstud@somerset.gov.uk

Founded: 1849

Organisation type and purpose: Learned society, registered charity (charity number 201929).

Subject coverage: History, archaeology and natural history of the pre-1974 county of Somerset.

Collection: Pigott and Braikenridge Collections (Somerset drawings)
Tite Collection (Somerset books)

Non-library collection catalogue: All or part available online, in-house and in print

Library catalogue: All or part available in-house

Publications: Printed

Access to staff: Contact by letter, by telephone, by fax, by e-mail and in person
Hours: Tue, Wed, Thu, 0900 to 1700

SOMERSET COLLEGE

Wellington Road, Taunton, Somerset, TA1 5AX

Tel: 01823 366331
Fax: 01823 366418
E-mail: enquiries@somerset.ac.uk
Website: www.somerset.ac.uk

Enquiries to: Information Officer

Founded: 1974

Organisation type and purpose: Suitable for ages: further and higher education.

Subject coverage: Art and design, performing arts, business and management studies, information technology, catering and hospitality, hairdressing and beauty therapy, community and caring services, construction, automotive engineering, engineering technology, humanities, science, access studies, A levels, health studies, leisure and tourism, sports-related courses, courses for students with learning difficulties/disabilities, adult education classes, commercial courses.

Library catalogue: All or part available in-house

Publications: Printed

Publications list: Available online and in print

Access to staff: Contact by letter, by telephone, by fax, by e-mail, in person and via website
Hours: Mon to Fri, 0900 to 1700

Access for disabled people: Parking provided, toilet facilities

SOMERSET COUNSELLING CENTRE (SCC)

38 Belvedere Road, Taunton, Somerset, TA1 1HD

Tel: 01823 337049
E-mail: info@scctaunton.org.uk
Website: www.wpf.org.uk
Website: www.scctaunton.org.uk

Enquiries to: Centre Manager
Other contacts: Counselling Service Manager for referral for counselling.

Founded: 1990

Organisation type and purpose: Voluntary organisation, registered charity (charity number 1038975), training organisation.
Counselling service and training courses.

Subject coverage: Counselling Service.
Assessment and weekly open-ended therapeutic counselling, sliding scale of fees.
Training Workshops

Publications: Printed

Access to staff: Contact by letter, by telephone, by e-mail and via website
Hours: Mon, Wed, Fri, Receptionist usually available 1000 to 1500
Special comments: 24 hours answerphone, calls returned within one working day.

Access for disabled people: Toilet facilities

Affiliated to: Westminster Pastoral Foundation (WPF); 23 Kensington Square, London, W8 5HN; tel: 020 7361 4864; fax: 020 7361 4860; e-mail: counselling@wpf.org.uk

SOMERSET COUNTY FEDERATION OF WOMEN'S INSTITUTES

11 Trull Road, Taunton, Somerset, TA1 4PT

Tel: 01823 284261
Fax: 01823 322545
Website: www.somersetwi.fsbusiness.co.uk

Enquiries to: County Secretary

Founded: 1918

Organisation type and purpose: National organisation, membership association (membership is by subscription), present number of members: 5,500, voluntary organisation, registered charity (charity number 1022578), training organisation.

Access to staff: Contact by letter, by telephone, by fax and by e-mail
Hours: Mon, Tue, Wed, 0930 to 1245 and 1315 to 1530

Access for disabled people: Parking provided, level entry

SOMERSET ENVIRONMENTAL RECORDS CENTRE (SERC)

Tonedale Mill, Wellington, Somerset, TA20 0AW

Tel: 01823 664450
Fax: 01823 652411
E-mail: info@somerc.com
Website: www.somerc.com

Founded: 1989

Organisation type and purpose: Advisory body, training organisation, consultancy.

Subject coverage: Environmental topics specific to Somerset; wildlife, biodiversity, flora, fauna, geological, protected species, habitats, wildlife sites.

Collection: Site specific and location records of more than 4,000 sites

Publications: Printed, and electronic and video

Access to staff: Contact by telephone and by e-mail
Hours: Mon to Fri, 0900 to 1700
Special comments: Charges made for some services.

Affiliated to: National Federation of Biological Recording

Parent body: Somerset Wildlife Trust

SOMERSET FEDERATION OF YOUNG FARMERS CLUB (Somerset YFC)

The Old School, School Road, Weston Zoyland, Bridgwater, Somerset, TA7 0LN

Tel: 01278 681711
Fax: 01278 691912
E-mail: admin@somersetyfc.org.uk
Website: www.somersetyfc.org.uk

Enquiries to: Federation Co-ordinator

Founded: 1934

Organisation type and purpose: Membership association (membership is by subscription), present number of members: 800, registered charity (charity number 273051).

Subject coverage: Agriculture, rural youth work, social education.

Publications list: Available in print

Access to staff: Contact by letter, by telephone, by fax, by e-mail, in person and via website. Non-members charged.
Hours: Mon to Fri, 0900 to 1700

Access for disabled people: Parking provided, level entry, access to all public areas, toilet facilities

Affiliated to: National Federation of Young Farmers Clubs (NFYFC); Stoneleigh Park, Stoneleigh, Warwickshire, CV8 2LG; tel: 024 7685 7200; fax: 024 7685 7229; e-mail: post@nfyfc.org.uk; website: www.nfyfc.org.uk

SOMERSET LIBRARIES

Enquiry Centre, Paul Street, Taunton, Somerset, TA1 3XZ

Tel: 01823 336370
Fax: 01823 272178
E-mail: enquiry@somerset.gov.uk
Website: www.librarieswest.org.uk

Enquiries to: Senior Librarian: Information

Organisation type and purpose: Public library.

Library catalogue: All or part available online

Access to staff: Contact by letter, by telephone, by fax, by e-mail and via website
Hours: Mon, Tue, Thu, 0830 to 1800; Wed, Fri, 0830 to 1900; Sat, 0830 to 1630

Parent body: Library Administration Centre; Mount Street, Bridgwater, Somerset, TA6 3ES; tel: 01278 451201; fax: 01278 452787; website: http://www.somerset.gov.uk

SOMERSET RECORD OFFICE

Formal name: Somerset Heritage and Libraries Service

Brunel Way, Norton Fitzwarren, Taunton, TA2 6SF

Tel: 01823 278805
Fax: 01823 325402
E-mail: archives@somerset.gov.uk
Website: www.somerset.gov.uk

Enquiries to: Archivist

Founded: 1929

Organisation type and purpose: Local government body.
Archive service.

Subject coverage: Historic records of the county of Somerset, churches, societies, businesses and individuals.

Non-library collection catalogue: All or part available online

Library catalogue: All or part available online

Publications: Printed, and electronic and video, and microform publications

Publications list: Available online

Access to staff: Contact by letter, by telephone, by fax and by e-mail.
Appointment necessary.
Hours: Mon, 1400 to 1650; Tue to Thu, 0900 to 1650; Fri, 0900 to 1620; Sat, 0915 to 1215
Special comments: Not open every Saturday.

Access to building: Prior appointment required

Access for disabled people: Ramped entry, access to all public areas, toilet facilities

Parent body: Somerset County Council

SOMERSET STUDIES LIBRARY

Somerset Heritage Centre, Brunel Way, Norton Fitzwarren, Taunton, Somerset, TA2 6SF

Tel: 01823 278805
Fax: 01823 347459
E-mail: somstud@somerset.gov.uk
Website: www.librarieswest.org.uk

Enquiries to: Librarian

Founded: 1973

Organisation type and purpose: County council archives and local studies service.

Subject coverage: History, archaeology, genealogy and natural history of historic county of Somerset.

Library catalogue: All or part available online

Access to staff: Contact by letter, by telephone, by fax, by e-mail and in person
Hours: Mon, 1300 to 1700; Tue to Fri, 0900 to 1700
Special comments: Contact for Saturday openings.

Access to building: *Hours:* Mon, 1300 to 1700; Tue to Fri, 0900 to 1700; contact for Saturday openings

SOMERVILLE COLLEGE LIBRARY

Oxford, OX2 6HD

Tel: 01865 270694
Fax: 01865 270620
E-mail: library@some.ox.ac.uk

Enquiries to: Librarian

Founded: 1879

Organisation type and purpose: University department or institute.
College of University of Oxford.

Subject coverage: Main subjects read in the university.

continued overleaf

Collection: Amelia B Edwards Library and Manuscript Collection
John Stuart Mill Library
Margaret Kennedy correspondence
Percy Withers Library and family correspondence
Vernon Lee (Violet Paget) correspondence

Non-library collection catalogue: All or part available in-house

Library catalogue: All or part available online

Access to staff: Contact by letter, by telephone, by fax and by e-mail. Appointment necessary. Letter of introduction required.
Hours: Mon to Fri, 0900 to 1700

SONS OF DIVINE PROVIDENCE (SDP)

13 Lower Teddington Road, Hampton Wick, Kingston Upon Thames, Surrey, KT1 4EU

Tel: 020 8977 5130
Fax: 020 8977 0105
Website: www.sonsofdivineprovidence.org/literature

Enquiries to: Senior Administrator

Founded: 1952

Organisation type and purpose: Registered charity (charity number 1088675).

Subject coverage: Charitable company running two care homes for the elderly, three residential care homes for people with learning disabilities, a horticultural training centre and units of independent accommodation.

Publications list: Available online

Access to staff: Contact by letter, by telephone and via website. Appointment necessary.
Hours: Mon to Fri, 0900 to 1700

SORIS

PO Box 502, Welwyn Garden City, Hertfordshire, AL7 9HG

Tel: 01707 321680
Fax: 0870 7059037
E-mail: cdrew@soris.org
Website: www.soris.org

Enquiries to: Principal Consultant

Founded: 1980; formerly a part of Chemical Industries' Association (year of change 2001); formerly a part of Chemical Industry Regional Centre of Excellence (CIRCE Ltd) (year of change 2005); formerly called SORIS Ltd (year of change 1992)

Organisation type and purpose:
International organisation, trade association (membership is by subscription), service industry, research organisation.
Provides chemical market intelligence, soft information and tailored introductions.

Subject coverage: Chemical intelligence and information broking for chemistry-using industries.

Collection: Special Chemical Return to 1993

Access to staff: Contact by letter, by telephone, by fax, by e-mail and via website. Appointment necessary. Non-members charged.
Hours: Mon to Fri, 0900 to 1700

Links with: Chemical Business Network Group; Chemical Industries Association; Chemical Industry Consultants Association; Chemical Innovation Knowledge Transfer Network; Chemicals North West; Royal Society of Chemistry; Society of Chemical Industry; Yorkshire Chemical Focus

SOS CHILDREN

Formal name: SOS Children's Villages

Terrington House, 13–15 Hills Road, Cambridge, CB2 1NL

Tel: 01223 365589
E-mail: info@soschildrensvillages.org.uk
Website: www.soschildrensvillages.org.uk

Enquiries to: Chief Executive
Direct e-mail: andrew@soschildrensvillages.org.uk

Founded: 1950s

Organisation type and purpose: Registered charity (charity number 1069204).
The world's largest orphan and abandoned children's charity.

Subject coverage: Provides a new family and home for more than 78,000 children in 500 unique Children's Villages in 124 countries. Also helps a million children and their families through SOS community outreach programmes, playing an important role in supporting the development and sustainability of their local communities, e.g. building and running 231 SOS nurseries and 185 schools, which are open to children in its care and to those from the wider community, and 61 vocational training centres, which equip more than 174,000 children, teenagers and young adults with the practical skills they need to earn a living and lead independent lives. In areas where medical support is scarce or non-existent, it builds SOS medical centres, which provide communities with immediate medical treatment and preventative and palliative care. It also offers skills, training, education, counselling, micro-loans and improved nutrition to vulnerable families, so they are able to provide for their children and stay together through difficult times. In times of conflict, famine or disaster, it provides emergency assistance.

Access to staff: Contact by letter, by telephone and by e-mail

SOUND AND MUSIC

3rd Floor, South Wing, Somerset House, London, WC2R 1LA

Tel: 020 7759 1800
E-mail: info@soundandmusic.org
Website: www.soundandmusic.org

Founded: 2010; created by the merger of British Music Information Centre, Contemporary Music Network, Society for the Promotion of New Music, and Sonic Arts Network (year of change 2010)

Organisation type and purpose: Contemporary arts organisation. A Regularly Funded Organisation of Arts Council England. Registered charity (charity number 1124609).

Subject coverage: Music and sound.

SOUND RESEARCH LABORATORIES LIMITED (SRL)

Head Office & Laboratory, Holbrook Hall, Little Waldingfield, Sudbury, Suffolk, CO10 0TH

Tel: 01787 247595
Fax: 01787 248420
E-mail: srl@soundresearch.co.uk
Website: www.soundresearch.co.uk

Enquiries to: Managing Director

Founded: 1967

Organisation type and purpose: Consultancy.

Subject coverage: Acoustics, noise and vibration control, traffic noise, vehicle noise, auditoria acoustics, industrial noise control, laboratory testing, product development.

Publications: Printed

Access to staff: Contact by letter, by telephone, by fax and by e-mail
Hours: Mon to Fri, 0900 to 1700

Access to building: No access other than to staff

Access for disabled people: Parking provided, level entry, toilet facilities

SOUND SENSE

Riverside House, Rattlesden, Bury St Edmunds, IP30 0SF

E-mail: info@soundsense.org
Website: www.soundsense.org

Organisation type and purpose: Company limited by guarantee registered in England and Wales no 3933421. Registered charity 1080918

Subject coverage: UK professional association promoting community music and supporting community musicians

Access to staff: Contact by letter, by telephone, by fax, by e-mail and via website

SOUTH AFRICA HOUSE LIBRARY

South African High Commission, Trafalgar Square, London, WC2N 5DP

Tel: 020 7451 7299
Fax: 020 7451 7289
E-mail: london.general@foreign.gov.za
Website: www.gov.za
Website: www.safrica.info
Website: www.artslink.co.za
Website: www.southafricahouse.com

Enquiries to: Librarian

Organisation type and purpose: Government (South Africa).

Subject coverage: South Africa.

Publications: Printed, and electronic and video
Order electronic and video publications from:

http://www.info.gov.za/aboutsa/index.htm as text version or http://www.gcis.gov.za/docs/publications/yearbook/index.html for pdf format

Access to staff: Contact by letter and by fax
Hours: Mon to Fri, 0900 to 1300 and 1345 to 1700
Special comments: Fax should be marked Attention Reference Library.

Access to building: No access other than to staff
Special comments: Library not on open access, written enquiries only.

SOUTH AFRICAN TOURISM

5–6 Alt Grove, Wimbledon, London, SW19 4DZ

Tel: 020 8971 9351
Fax: 020 8944 6705
E-mail: info@south-african-tourism.org
Website: www.south-african-tourism.org
Website: www.southafrica.net

Enquiries to: Information Officer

Organisation type and purpose: National government body.

Subject coverage: South African tourism, business travel, special interest tours, conferences and exhibitions, incentives.

Collection: Film and photographs (colour and black-and-white) libraries

Trade and statistical information: Tourist data on South Africa

Publications: Printed, and electronic and video

Access to staff: Contact by letter, by telephone, by fax, by e-mail, in person and via website
Hours: Mon to Fri, 0900 to 1700
Special comments: Appointments by prior arrangement.

Access for disabled people: Level entry, toilet facilities

SOUTH AYRSHIRE LIBRARIES

Formal name: South Ayrshire Library and Information Service

Library Headquarters, John Pollock Centre, Mainholm Road, Ayr

Tel: 01292 294320
Fax: 01292 611593
E-mail: carnegie.library@south-ayrshire.gov.uk
Website: www.south-ayrshire.gov.uk/libraries

Enquiries to: Libraries Manager
Direct tel: 01292 294320
Direct fax: 01292 619019
Direct e-mail: jean.inness@south-ayrshire.gov.uk

Organisation type and purpose: Local government body, public library.

Subject coverage: General, local history of Kyle and Carrick, and South Ayrshire, Robert Burns.

Collection: Ayrshire (Kyle and Carrick from 1975)
Robert Burns Collection

Non-library collection catalogue: All or part available in-house

Library catalogue: All or part available online

Publications: Printed
Order printed publications from: South Ayrshire Book Shop, South Ayrshire Council Library HQ, 26 Green Street, Ayr, KA8 8ED; tel: 01292 288820; fax: 01292 619019; e-mail: jean.inness@south-ayrshire.gov.uk

Publications list: Available in print

Access to staff: Contact by letter, by telephone, by fax, by e-mail and in person. Appointment necessary.
Hours: Mon, Tue, Thu, Fri, 0900 to 1930; Wed, Sat, 0900 to 1700

Access for disabled people: Ramped entry, access to all public areas, toilet facilities

SOUTH BEDFORDSHIRE DISTRICT COUNCIL

The District Offices, High Street North, Dunstable, Bedfordshire, LU6 1LF

Tel: 01582 472222
Fax: 01782 474009 or 01582 474058
Website: www.southbeds.gov.uk

Enquiries to: Chief Executive
Direct tel: 01582 474047
Direct e-mail: communications@centralbedfordshire.gov.uk

Organisation type and purpose: Local government body.

Subject coverage: Local government services: administrative, technical, financial, planning and estates, environmental health and housing.

Publications: Printed

Access to staff: Contact by letter, by telephone, by fax, by e-mail and in person
Hours: Mon to Thu, 0900 to 1700; Fri, 0900 to 1645

Access to building: Mon to Thu, 0900 to 1700; Fri, 0900 to 1645

Access for disabled people: *Hours:* Mon to Thu, 0900 to 1700; Fri, 0900 to 1645

SOUTH BUCKS DISTRICT COUNCIL

Council Offices, Windsor Road, Slough, Berkshire, SL1 2HN

Tel: 01753 533333\ Minicom no. 01753 676251
Fax: 01753 731803
E-mail: sbdc@southbucks.gov.uk
Website: www.southbucks.gov.uk

Enquiries to: Chief Executive

Organisation type and purpose: Local government body.

Subject coverage: All usual local government subjects.

Access to staff: Contact by letter, by telephone, by fax, by e-mail and in person
Hours: Mon to Wed, 0900 to 1730; Thu to Fri, 0900 to 1700

SOUTH DERBYSHIRE DISTRICT COUNCIL (SDDC)

Civic Offices, Civic Way, Swadlincote, Derbyshire, DE11 0AH

Tel: 01283 221000\ Minicom no. 01283 595849
Fax: 01283 595964
E-mail: civic.offices@south-derbys.gov.uk
Website: www.south-derbys.gov.uk

Enquiries to: Customer Services
Direct fax: 01283 595854
Direct e-mail: customer.services@south-derbys.gov.uk

Organisation type and purpose: Local government body.

Subject coverage: All aspects of local government.

Access to staff: Contact by letter, by telephone, by fax, by e-mail and via website
Hours: Mon to Fri, 0900 to 1700

Access for disabled people: Parking provided, ramped entry, level entry, access to all public areas, toilet facilities

SOUTH EAST AREA LIBRARIES INFORMATION CO-OPERATIVE (SEAL)

Peckham Library, 122 Peckham Hill Street, London, SE15 5JR

Tel: 020 7525 0230
E-mail: southwark.libraries@southwark.gov.uk

Enquiries to: Secretary

Founded: 1969

Organisation type and purpose: Local information co-operative.

Subject coverage: The organisation promotes co-operation between all types of libraries located in the London Boroughs of Bexley, Bromley, Greenwich, Lewisham and Southwark, the Medway Council area and the County of Kent. It is not a direct information provider.

Publications: Printed

Access to staff: Contact by letter, by telephone and by e-mail. Appointment necessary.

SOUTH EAST ENGLAND TOURIST BOARD (SEETB)

40 Chamberlayne Road, Eastleigh, Hampshire, SO50 5JH

Tel: 023 8062 5400
E-mail: customerservices@tourismse.com
Website: www.southeastengland.uk.com
Website: www.tourismsoutheast.com
Website: www.southeastwalks.com
Website: www.southeastgardens.co.uk

Enquiries to: Company Secretary

Founded: 1973

Organisation type and purpose: Advisory body, membership association (membership is by subscription), service industry.

continued overleaf

Subject coverage: Tourist information on accommodation, visitor attractions, events of special interest and conference venues in South East England i.e. Kent, Surrey, East and West Sussex.

Trade and statistical information: Tourism volumes and values, hotel occupancies and tourism investments in the area

Publications: Printed

Access to staff: Contact by letter, by telephone, by fax and by e-mail
Hours: Mon to Fri, 0900 to 1700

SOUTH EAST LONDON ARMY CADET FORCE (ACF)

Formal name: Army Cadet Force

Hollyhedge House, Wat Tyler Road, Blackheath, London, SE3 0QZ

Tel: 020 8692 4066
Fax: 020 8694 0566
E-mail: ceoseacf@reserve-forces-london.mod.uk

Enquiries to: Executive Officer

Organisation type and purpose: National organisation, voluntary organisation, suitable for ages: 12 to 18.
The Army Cadet Force is a National Voluntary Youth Organisation. It is sponsored by the Army and provides challenging military, adventurous, and community activities. Its aim is to inspire young people to achieve success in life with a spirit of service to the Queen, their country and their local community, and to develop in them the qualities of a good citizen.

Subject coverage: Adventurous and challenging activities, leadership, character training, work for the community, understanding of the Army and its place in national life.

Publications: Printed
Order printed publications from: ACFA, Holderners House, 51–61 Clifton Street, London, EC2A 4DW
South East London ACF
Hollyhedge House, Wat Tyler Road, Blackheath, SE3 0QZ

Publications list: Available online

Access to staff: Contact by letter, by telephone, by fax and by e-mail
Hours: Mon to Fri, 0900 to 1700

Links with: Department for Education and Employment; National Council for Voluntary Youth Services; Territorial Army Volunteer Reserve

Supports the: Cadet Force, which is sponsored by the Army

SOUTH GLOUCESTERSHIRE COUNCIL (SGC)

Council Offices, Castle Street, Thornbury, Gloucestershire, BS35 1HF

Tel: 01454 868009; 01454 868010 (minicom)
Fax: 01454 863886
E-mail: mailbox@southglos.gov.uk
Website: www.southglos.gov.uk

Founded: 1996

Organisation type and purpose: Local government body.

Subject coverage: Local government services.

Publications: Printed

Publications list: Available online

Access to staff: Contact by letter, by telephone, by fax, by e-mail and via website
Hours: Mon to Thu, 0845 to 1700; Fri, 0845 to 1630

Access to building: No prior appointment required
Hours: Mon to Thu, 0845 to 1700; Fri, 0845 to 1630

Access for disabled people: Parking provided, ramped entry, level entry, access to all public areas, toilet facilities

SOUTH KENT COLLEGE

Shorncliffe Road, Folkestone, Kent, CT20 2TZ

Tel: 01303 858340
Fax: 01303 858400
E-mail: webmaster@southkent.ac.uk
Website: www.southkent.ac.uk

Enquiries to: Head of Learning Centre
Direct e-mail: pennie.newman@southkent.ac.uk

Organisation type and purpose: College of further education.

Subject coverage: Business studies, management, mechanical engineering, electrical and electronic engineering, building, education, social sciences, humanities, sciences, information technology, media studies, catering, health and social care, hairdressing and beauty.

Library catalogue: All or part available online

Access to staff: Contact in person
Hours: Mon, Wed, 0845 to 1700; Tue, Thu, 0845 to 1930; Fri, 0845 to 1615
Special comments: May be closed during vacations, so enquire first.

Access for disabled people: Parking provided, level entry, toilet facilities

Also at: South Kent College; Jemmett Road, Ashford, Kent, TN23 4RJ; tel: 01233 655573; fax: 01233 655501; South Kent College; Maison Dieu Road, Dover, CT16 1DH; tel: 01304 244344; fax: 01304 244301

SOUTH KESTEVEN DISTRICT COUNCIL (SKDC)

Council Offices, St Peters Hill, Grantham, Lincolnshire, NG31 6PZ

Tel: 01476 406080
Fax: 01476 406000
E-mail: d.nicholls@skdc.com
Website: www.skdc.com

Enquiries to: Public Relations Manager
Direct tel: 01476 406128
Direct e-mail: pr@southkesteven.gov.uk
Other contacts: Customer Services Manager

Founded: 1974

Organisation type and purpose: Local government body.

Subject coverage: All aspects of local government.

Publications: Printed

Publications list: Available in print

Access to staff: Contact by letter, by telephone, by fax, by e-mail and via website. Appointment necessary.
Hours: Mon to Thu, 0845 to 1715; Fri, 0845 to 1645

Access for disabled people: Ramped entry, toilet facilities

Connections with: East Midlands Regional Local Government Association (EMRLGA); The Belvoir Suite, Council Offices, Nottingham Road, Melton Mowbray, Leicestershire, LE13 0UL

Member of: East Midlands Regional Assembly; Federation of Economic Development Authorities; FEDA Administrator, 36 Sheep Street, Shipston-on-Stour, Warwickshire, CU36 4AE; Lincolnshire Development Partnership; The Chief Executive, Central Support Team, Lincolnshire County Council, Lincoln; Lincolnshire Local Government Association; The Chief Executive, Lincolnshire County Council, Lincoln; Local Government Association; Local Government House, Smith Square, London, SW1P 3HZ

Other addresses: Bourne Area Office; Town Hall, North Street, Bourne, PE10 9EA; tel: 01476 406071; Market Deeping Area Office; 89 High Street, Market Deeping, PE6 8ED; tel: 01476 406070; Stamford Area Office; 1 Maiden Lane, Stamford, PE9 2AZ; tel: 01476 406072

SOUTH LANARKSHIRE COUNCIL

Council Building, Almada Street, Hamilton, South Lanarkshire, ML3 0AA

Tel: 01698 454444
Fax: 01698 454275

Enquiries to: Chief Executive
Other contacts: Public Relations Manager

Founded: 1996

Organisation type and purpose: Local government body.
Councillors by election 67. Staff 15,000 by appointment.
Unitary Council.

Subject coverage: Local government.

Trade and statistical information: South Lanarkshire statistical information; South Lanarkshire statistical profile contains information on area's characteristics: physical, population, housing, economy and education

Access to staff: Contact by letter, by telephone and by fax. Appointment necessary.
Hours: Mon to Thu, 0845 to 1645; Fri, 0845 to 1615

Member of: Convention of Scottish Local Authorities (COSLA); Edinburgh

Principal Offices: Atholl House; Churchill Avenue, East Kilbride, G74 1LU; tel: 01355 806000; Civic Centre; Andrew Street, East Kilbride, G74 1AB; tel: 01355 806000; Royal

Burgh House; 380 King Street, Rutherglen, G73 1DB; tel: 0141 613 5000; South Vennel; Lanark, ML11 7JT; tel: 01555 673000

SOUTH LANARKSHIRE COUNCIL ARCHIVES AND INFORMATION MANAGEMENT SERVICE

30 Hawbank Road, College Milton, East Kilbride, South Lanarkshire, G74 5EX

Tel: 01355 239193
Fax: 01355 242365
E-mail: archives@southlanarkshire.gov.uk
Website: www.southlanarkshire.gov.uk/gateway
Website: www.scan.org.uk

Enquiries to: Archivist

Founded: 1997

Organisation type and purpose: Local government archive.

Subject coverage: Local, family, social, economic and administrative history of South Lanarkshire.

Collection: Archives of South Lanarkshire Council and predecessor local authorities and public corporations
Deposited archives of business, voluntary organisations and associations in South Lanarkshire

Non-library collection catalogue: All or part available online

Access to staff: Contact by letter, by telephone, by fax and by e-mail. Appointment necessary.
Hours: Mon to Fri, 0930 to 1630; other times by arrangement
Special comments: All visits by appointment only.

SOUTH LANARKSHIRE LIBRARY SERVICE

Formal name: South Lanarkshire Leisure and Culture Ltd

North Stand, Cadzow Ave, Hamilton, ML3 0LX

Tel: 01698 476262
Fax: 01698 476198
E-mail: customer.services@southlanarkshireleisure.co.uk
Website: www.slleisureandculture.co.uk

Enquiries to: Libraries and Museums Manager
Direct tel: 01698 476145
Direct fax: 01698 476198
Direct e-mail: diana.barr@southlanarkshireleisure.co.uk

Organisation type and purpose: public library service

Collection: Collection on Robert Owen and New Lanark (Lanark Library)
William Smellie Collection (obstetrics, midwifery)
Collection on the estates of the Dukes of Hamilton (Hamilton Library)
Lace making (Hamilton Library)

Non-library collection catalogue: All or part available online and in-house

Library catalogue: All or part available online

Access to staff: Contact by letter, by telephone, by fax, by e-mail, in person and via website

SOUTH LONDON BOTANICAL INSTITUTE (SLBI)

323 Norwood Road, London, SE24 9AQ

Tel: 020 8674 5787
Fax: 020 8674 5787
E-mail: info@slbi.org.uk
Website: www.slbi.org.uk

Enquiries to: Chairman

Founded: 1910

Organisation type and purpose: Learned society (membership is by subscription), present number of members: 169, registered charity (charity number 214251).
Education in botany. Small botanic garden, library and herbarium.

Subject coverage: General botany, seed plants, pteridophytes, bryophytes, lichens.

Education services: Adult education classes and school groups (pre-book with Education Officer).

Collection: Extensive herbarium, British and European, including the Beeby and Palmer Collection from the Orkneys and Shetlands, seed collection, pteridophytes, bryophytes, lichen and marine algae
Historic floras; 35mm slide collection
Taxonomic library: British and European floras, British county floras, world floras

Non-library collection catalogue: All or part available online

Library catalogue: All or part available in-house

Publications: Printed
Order printed publications from: Administrator

Access to staff: Contact by letter, by telephone, by fax, by e-mail and via website. Appointment necessary.
Hours: Thu, 1000 to 1600, or by appointment

Access to building: Prior appointment required, except on Thu 1000 to 1600

Access for disabled people: Garden accessible for wheelchairs

SOUTH NORFOLK DISTRICT COUNCIL

South Norfolk House, Swan Lane, Long Stratton, Norwich, Norfolk, NR15 2XE

Tel: 01508 533633
Fax: 01508 533695
Website: www.south-norfolk.gov.uk

Organisation type and purpose: Local government body.

Subject coverage: District Council Services.

Publications: Printed

Access to staff: Contact by letter, by telephone, by fax, by e-mail, in person and via website
Hours: Mon to Thu, 0845 to 1700; Fri, 0845 to 1615

Access for disabled people: Parking provided, level entry, access to all public areas, toilet facilities

SOUTH NORTHAMPTONSHIRE DISTRICT COUNCIL (SNC)

Council Offices, Springfields, Towcester, Northamptonshire, NN12 6AE

Tel: 01327 350211
Fax: 01327 359219
Website: www.southnorthants.gov.uk

Enquiries to: Head of Community and Leisure Development
Direct tel: 01327 322340
Direct fax: 01327 322332
Other contacts: Chief Executive

Founded: 1974

Organisation type and purpose: Local government body.

Subject coverage: Council services and amenities; corporate services, education, environmental services, finance, housing, legal services, personnel services, planning development, property and technical services, roads and transportation, social work, council tax and other payments, leisure and tourism.

Publications: Printed

Access to staff: Contact by letter, by telephone, by fax and in person
Hours: Mon to Fri, 0900 to 1700

SOUTH NOTTINGHAM COLLEGE

Greythorn Drive, West Bridgford, Nottingham, NG2 5GA

Tel: 0115 914 6400
Fax: 0115 914 6444
E-mail: enquiries@snc.ac.uk

Enquiries to: Curriculum Support Manager
Direct tel: 0115 914 6418

Founded: 1971

Organisation type and purpose: Suitable for ages: 16+.
College of further education.

Subject coverage: Printing.

Non-library collection catalogue: All or part available online and in-house

Library catalogue: All or part available online and in-house

Access to staff: Contact by letter, by telephone, by fax and by e-mail. Appointment necessary.
Hours: Mon to Thu, 0830 to 1930; Fri, 0830 to 1600
Special comments: Academic term time only.

Access for disabled people: Parking provided, ramped entry, access to all public areas, toilet facilities

Associate college of: Nottingham Trent University

Other addresses: Charnwood site; tel: 0115 914 6300; fax: 0115 914 6333

SOUTH OXFORDSHIRE DISTRICT COUNCIL (SODC)

Benson Lane, Crowmarsh Gifford, Wallingford, Oxfordshire, OX10 8HQ

Tel: 01491 823000
Fax: 01491 823104
Website: www.southoxon.gov.uk

continued overleaf

Enquiries to: Public Relations Officer
Direct tel: 01491 823748
Direct fax: 01491 823420

Founded: 1974

Organisation type and purpose: Local government body.

Subject coverage: Information relating to council issues can be obtained from the multitude of sources available.

Collection: Documentation, in general, may be viewed but not taken

Publications: Printed

Access to staff: Contact by letter, by telephone, by fax, by e-mail and in person. Appointment necessary.
Hours: Mon to Thu, 0830 to 1700; Fri, 0830 to 1630

Access for disabled people: Parking provided, level entry, toilet facilities

SOUTH RIBBLE BOROUGH COUNCIL

Civic Centre, West Paddock, Leyland, Lancashire, PR25 1DH

Tel: 01772 421491
Fax: 01772 622287
E-mail: info@southribble.gov.uk
Website: www.south-ribblebc.gov.uk

Enquiries to: Public Relations Officer
Direct tel: 01772 625312
Direct e-mail: communications@southribble.gov.uk

Founded: 1974

Organisation type and purpose: Local government body.

Subject coverage: Council services and amenities; corporate services, environmental services, finance, housing, legal services, personnel services, planning development and tourism, property and technical services, roads and transportation, council tax and other payments.

Publications: Printed

Access to staff: Contact by letter, by telephone, by fax and by e-mail
Hours: Mon to Thu, 0830 to 1715; Fri, 0830 to 1645

Access for disabled people: Parking provided, level entry, access to all public areas, toilet facilities

SOUTH SHROPSHIRE DISTRICT COUNCIL (SSDC)

Stone House, Corve Street, Ludlow, Shropshire, SY8 1DG

Tel: 01584 813000
Fax: 01584 813127
E-mail: reception@southshropshire.gov.uk
Website: www.southshropshire.gov.uk/

Enquiries to: Chief Executive
Direct tel: 01584 813201
Direct fax: 01584 813120
Direct e-mail: gcbiggs_ssdc@btconnect.com

Founded: 1974

Organisation type and purpose: Local government body.

Access to staff: Contact by letter, by telephone, by fax, by e-mail, in person and via website
Hours: Mon to Thu, 0840 to 1715; Fri, 0840 to 1630

Access for disabled people: Parking provided, toilet facilities

SOUTH SOMERSET DISTRICT COUNCIL

Council Offices, Brympton Way, Yeovil, Somerset, BA20 2HT

Tel: 01935 462462
Fax: 01935 462503
E-mail: info@southsomerset.gov.uk
Website: www.southsomerset.gov.uk

Enquiries to: Communications Manager
Direct tel: 01935 462122

Founded: 1974

Organisation type and purpose: Local government body.

Subject coverage: Long distance walking routes in South Somerset, circular walks, cycle routes, horse trails in South Somerset, business premises and opportunities available in South Somerset.

Trade and statistical information: Statistical information about South Somerset

Publications: Printed

Access to staff: Contact by letter, by telephone, by fax, by e-mail and in person. Appointment necessary.
Hours: Mon to Fri, 0900 to 1700

SOUTH TYNESIDE COLLEGE – HEBBURN (STC)

Mill Lane, Hebburn, Tyne and Wear, NE31 2ER

Tel: 0191 427 3614
Fax: 0191 427 3555
Website: www.stc.ac.uk

Enquiries to: Assistant Librarian

Founded: 1984

Subject coverage: Mechanical engineering, health studies, performing arts, welding, automobile engineering, social work, child care, health and safety, management, sports, leisure and tourism.

Collection: British Standards on CD-ROM
Bound Copies of Hansard 1988–1999

Library catalogue: All or part available in-house

Access to staff: Contact by letter, by telephone and by fax
Hours: Mon, Wed, 0900 to 2000; Tue, Thu, 0900 to 1700; Fri, 0900 to 1630

Access for disabled people: Parking provided, ramped entry

Other Campus at: South Tyneside College; St Georges Avenue, South Shields, Tyne & Wear, NE34 6ET; tel: 0191 427 3606; fax: 0191 427 3643

SOUTH TYNESIDE COLLEGE – SOUTH SHIELDS

St Georges Avenue, South Shields, Tyne and Wear, NE34 6ET

Tel: 0191 427 3500
Fax: 0191 427 3535
E-mail: margaret.haram@stc.ac.uk

Enquiries to: Librarian
Direct tel: 0191 427 3605

Organisation type and purpose: Post-compulsory education, 14–16 provision College of further and higher education.

Subject coverage: Sixth form, teacher education, business and professional studies, hairdressing and beauty therapies, health care and early years, nautical studies, marine engineering, general engineering

Library catalogue: All or part available in-house

Access to staff: Contact by letter, by telephone and by e-mail
Hours: Term time: Mon to Fri, 0830 to 2000
Vacations: Mon to Fri, 0900 to 1700

Access for disabled people: Parking provided, ramped entry, level entry, access to all public areas, toilet facilities

SOUTH TYNESIDE LIBRARY

Central Library, Prince George Square, South Shields, Tyne and Wear, NE33 2PE

Tel: 0191 427 1818
Fax: 0191 427 8085
E-mail: reference.library@southtyneside.gov.uk
Website: www.southtyneside.info/learningandleisure/libraries.asp

Enquiries to: Libraries Manager
Direct tel: 0191 424 7880
Direct e-mail: mark.freeman@southtyneside.gov.uk

History of institution: created by the merger of Jarrow, Hebburn, Whitburn, South Shields and Boldon Libraries

Organisation type and purpose: Local government body, public library.

Subject coverage: General public library information service, local history of South Tyneside, the Jarrow March, slum clearance, sailing ships, shipbuilding.

Collection: Jarrow March Collection
Kelly Collection; posters from a South Shields jobbing printer c.1790 to c.1880
Manuscripts and local history: Fox, Wallis and Flagg collections
Photograph collections of South Shields: Willetts, Flagg, Parry, Grimes, Cleet, Peterson and Shields Gazette

Library catalogue: All or part available online

Publications: Printed
Order printed publications from: Information and Education Co-ordinator, at the same address; tel. 0191 424 7865; fax 0191 455 8085; e-mail hildred.whale@s-tyneside-mbc.gov.uk

Publications list: Available in print

Access to staff: Contact by letter, by telephone, by fax, by e-mail, in person and via website

Hours: Mon to Thu, 0900 to 1900; Fri, 0900 to 1700; Sat, 0900 to 1600

Member organisation of: MLA (NE)

SOUTH WEST COAST PATH ASSOCIATION (SWCPA)

Bowker House, Lee Mill Bridge, Ivybridge, Devon, PL21 9EF

Tel: 01752 896237
Fax: 01752 893654
E-mail: info@swcp.org.uk
Website: www.swcp.org.uk

Enquiries to: Honorary Secretary

Founded: 1973

Organisation type and purpose: Advisory body, membership association (membership is by subscription), present number of members: 5,000, voluntary organisation, registered charity (charity number 266754). To promote interest in, and the use of, the coast path. To improve standards of waymaking and maintenance.

Subject coverage: The 630 miles of the South West Coast Path, from Minehead to Poole Harbour via Land's End.

Collection: 8,000 colour slides of coastal scenery along 630 miles of coast path
Digital archive of 4,000 images of the South West Coast Path

Publications: Printed

Publications list: Available online and in print

Access to staff: Contact by letter, by telephone, by fax, by e-mail, in person and via website. Appointment necessary.
Hours: Any reasonable time

Access to building: No prior appointment required
Hours: Mon to Fri, 0900 to 1300

Access for disabled people: Yes

SOUTH WESTERN REGIONAL LIBRARY SERVICE (SWRLS)

c/o Library Headquarters, Ridgewood Centre, 244 Station Road, Yate, South Gloucestershire, BS37 4AF

Tel: 01454 865782
Fax: 01454 863309
E-mail: martin.burton@southglos.gov.uk
Website: www.swrls.org.uk

Enquiries to: Director
Direct tel: 07504 047625
Direct e-mail: desk2@csndesk.eclipse.co.uk

Founded: 1937

Organisation type and purpose: Charity aimed at developing library co-operation across the South West of England
Regional library system.

Subject coverage: General; co-operative library service providing access to material held by members.

Publications: Printed

Access to staff: Contact by e-mail

SOUTHAMPTON AND FAREHAM CHAMBER OF COMMERCE AND INDUSTRY

Bugle House, 53 Bugle Street, Southampton, SO14 2LF

Tel: 023 8022 3541
Fax: 023 8022 7426
E-mail: info@soton-chamber.co.uk
Website: www.soton-chamber.co.uk

Enquiries to: Information Officer

Founded: 1851

Organisation type and purpose:
Membership association (membership is by subscription), present number of members: 1,500.
Chamber of Commerce.

Subject coverage: Business enquiries, business training, events and seminars, export documentation and advice, French desk, China desk, lobbying/representation.

Collection: Business directories
Reference books

Publications: Printed

Access to staff: Contact by letter, by telephone, by fax, by e-mail, in person and via website. Appointment necessary. Access for members only. Non-members charged.
Hours: Mon to Fri, 0900 to 1700

Access to building: No prior appointment required

SOUTHAMPTON ARCHIVES

Civic Centre, Southampton, SO14 7LY

Tel: 023 8083 2251
E-mail: city.archives@southampton.gov.uk
Website: www.southampton.gov.uk/archives

Enquiries to: Archivist

Founded: 1953

Organisation type and purpose: Local government body

Subject coverage: Southampton records date from 1199: family, local and maritime history.

Collection: Maritime records: crew lists, 1863–1913; Central Index of Merchant Seamen, 1918–1941; ship registration records 1855–1994
Business records: many local firms' records are held
Parish records: Southampton parishes, 1552 to date
Local government: records of the Council, its departments and absorbed authorities
Public records: coroner's inquests, court records, hospital records
Records of individuals, organisations and institutions

Non-library collection catalogue: All or part available online and in-house

Publications: Printed

Publications list: Available in print

Access to staff: Contact by letter, by telephone, by e-mail, in person and via website
Hours: Tue to Thurs, 10–4

Special comments: Member of CARN system

Access for disabled people: Parking provided, level entry, toilet facilities

SOUTHAMPTON CITY COUNCIL

Civic Centre, Southampton, SO14 7LY

Tel: 023 8022 3855; 023 8083 2798 (minicom)
Fax: 023 8023 4537
E-mail: webmaster@southampton.gov.uk
Website: www.southampton.gov.uk

Direct fax: 023 8023 4527
Other contacts: Head of Marketing and Information Division for head of information services.

Organisation type and purpose: Local government body.

Subject coverage: All information about Southampton, its services and amenities, history, heritage, highways, leisure, events, local housing, social services, education, libraries etc.

Collection: Art gallery
Large variety of accessible information (on request)
Library service including reference

Trade and statistical information: Electoral register, grant schemes in the local area, local business, tourism and historic information, general city information

Publications: Printed, and electronic and video

Access to staff: Contact by letter, by telephone, by fax, by e-mail and via website
Hours: Mon to Fri, 0900 to 1700
Special comments: 24-hour emergency hotline 01703 233344.

Also: Education Services; 4th Floor, Frobisher House, Commercial Road, Southampton; tel: 023 8083 2771; Valuation and Estates Services; Marlands House, Civic Centre Road, Southampton, SO14 7PR; tel: 023 8083 2879

SOUTHAMPTON CITY COUNCIL – CULTURAL SERVICES

Civic Centre, Southampton, SO14 7LP

Tel: 023 8022 3855
Fax: 023 8033 7593
E-mail: s.dawtry@southampton.gov.uk
Website: www.southampton.gov.uk/leisure
Website: www.southampton.gov.uk

Enquiries to: Manager
Direct tel: 023 8083 2768
Direct e-mail: s.harrington@southampton.gov.uk

Founded: 1912

Organisation type and purpose: Local government body.

Subject coverage: Archaeology, particularly British and North European; fine art, particularly 20th century; maritime history; Southampton local history.

Collection: Buchanan Collection (needlework tools and accessories)
Chipperfield Bequest
Hull-Grundy Gift (jewellery)
Jeffress Bequest
Sandell Collection (miscellaneous)

continued overleaf

Smith Bequest
Various local history collections

Non-library collection catalogue: All or part available in-house

Publications: Printed

Publications list: Available in print

Access to staff: Contact by letter, by telephone, by fax, by e-mail and via website. Appointment necessary.
Hours: Mon to Fri, 0900 to 1700

SOUTHAMPTON CITY COUNCIL – HERITAGE ARTS AND ENTERTAINMENT MANAGEMENT

Civic Centre, Southampton, SO14 7LP

Museums and Galleries: God's House Tower Archaeology Museum; Hawthorns Urban Wildlife Centre; John Hamsard Gallery; The University, Southampton, SO9 5NH; Southampton City Art Gallery; Southampton Hall of Aviation; Southampton Maritime Museum; Tudor House Museum

SOUTHAMPTON CITY COUNCIL – LIBRARIES

Southampton Central Library, Civic Centre, Southampton, SO14 7LW

Tel: 023 8083 3777
Fax: 023 8033 6305
E-mail: reference.library@southampton.gov.uk
Website: www.southampton.gov.uk/libraries

Enquiries to: Libraries Manager
Direct tel: 023 8083 2219
Direct e-mail: david.baldwin@southampton.gov.uk

Founded: 1889

Organisation type and purpose: Local government body, public library.

Subject coverage: Large public library. Specialisations are: shipping (especially ocean liners) and marine transport, nautical almanacs and chronology, standards and specifications, genealogy, Hampshire studies, business and commercial information, art monographs, law, careers and education, community information.

Collection: Bowen collection (maritime)
British Standards
Hampshire Collection (particularly Southampton)
Maritime Collection (including a collection on the Titanic disaster and ocean-going liners)

Library catalogue: All or part available online

Publications: Printed, and electronic and video

Publications list: Available in print

Access to staff: Contact by letter, by telephone, by fax, by e-mail, in person and via website
Hours: Mon to Fri, 0930 to 1900; Sat, 0930 to 1600

Access for disabled people: Accessible. Lift available

Parent body: Southampton City Council

SOUTHAMPTON SOLENT UNIVERSITY (SSU)

East Park Terrace, Southampton, SO14 0RJ

Tel: 023 8031 9000
Fax: 023 8022 2259
Website: www.solent.ac.uk/library
Website: www.solent.ac.uk

Enquiries to: Deputy University Librarian
Direct tel: 023 8031 9248
Direct e-mail: enquiries@solent.ac.uk

Founded: 1964; formerly called Southampton Institute

Organisation type and purpose: University department.

Subject coverage: Accountancy, business studies, e-commerce, law, management, computing, information systems, CAD/CAM, naval architecture, yacht and boat design, condition monitoring, electronics, construction, graphic design, fashion, maritime studies, leisure management, fine art, media communications, film studies.

Collection: Multimedia collection (video cassettes/DVDs, audio tapes)
Godden collection (antiques and fine art periodicals and sale catalogues)
Ken Russell Collection (film)
Maritime History collection, including Captain Cooper's Letters and Reports, 1922–56
Slide collection (Art & Design)

Library catalogue: All or part available online

Publications: Printed

Access to staff: Contact by letter, by telephone, by fax, by e-mail, in person and via website
Hours: Term time: Mon to Thu, 0830 to 2100; Fri, 0830 to 1900; Sat, Sun, 1000 to 1700

Access to building: Mountbatten Library, East Park Terrace
Hours: Term time: Mon to Thu, 0830 to 2345; Fri, 0830 to 1900; Sat, Sun, 1000 to 1700

Access for disabled people: Level entry, access to all public areas, toilet facilities

Branch libraries: Warsash Library; Newtown Road, Warsash, Southampton, SO31 9ZL; tel: 01489 576161; fax: 01489 573988

Member organisation of: Hatrics Southern Information Network; 81 North Walls, Winchester, SO23 8BY; tel: 01962 826650; fax: 01962 826615; e-mail: hatricshq@hants.gov.uk; website: www.hants.gov.uk?hatrics/index.html

SOUTHBROOK COMMUNITY MENTAL HEALTH TEAM (SCMHT)

1 Southbrook Road, London, SE12 8LH

Tel: 020 8318 1330
Fax: 020 8297 1448

Enquiries to: Manager

Founded: 1978

Organisation type and purpose: Community Mental Health Team. Provides support and advice for clients with mental health problems who live within the catchment area of Central and East Lewisham.

Subject coverage: Mental health.

Access to staff: Contact by letter, by telephone and in person
Hours: Mon to Fri, 0900 to 1700
Special comments: Residents of Central and East Lewisham only.

Access for disabled people: Ramped entry, level entry, toilet facilities

Parent body: Lewisham Social Care and Health; South London and Maudsley NHS/MH Trust

SOUTHEND-ON-SEA BOROUGH LIBRARIES

Southend Library, Victoria Avenue, Southend-on-Sea, Essex, SS2 6EX

Tel: 01702 215011
Fax: 01702 469241
E-mail: library@southend.gov.uk
Website: www.southend.gov.uk/libraries

Enquiries to: Libraries Services Manager

Organisation type and purpose: Local government body, public library.

Subject coverage: Large general library.

Services for disabled people: Induction loops, magnifying aids, home library service & RNIB talking books.

Collection: Focal point photographic gallery
Specialist collections for local history

Library catalogue: All or part available online

Access for disabled people: Parking provided, level entry, access to all public areas, toilet facilities

Links with: Essex County Libraries; Thurrock Borough Council library services

SOUTHERN AFRICA BUSINESS ASSOCIATION (SABA)

Queensland House, 393 Strand, London, WC2R 0JQ

Tel: 020 7836 9980
Fax: 020 7836 6001
E-mail: info@waba.co.uk
Website: www.saba.co.uk

Enquiries to: Membership Secretary

Founded: 1995

Organisation type and purpose: Trade association (membership is by subscription), present number of members: over 130.
To promote investment into the Southern African region and trade within the region.

Subject coverage: Information on investment effectiveness in the countries of the region: South Africa, Zimbabwe, Mozambique, Zambia, Botswana, Namibia, Malawi, Swaziland, Angola, Lesotho.
General information about the political and economic situation and prospects in each country, investment required, trade agreements.

Publications: Printed

Publications list: Available in print

Access to staff: Contact by letter, by telephone, by fax, by e-mail and via website. Appointment necessary. Non-members charged.
Hours: Mon to Fri, 1000 to 1600

Access to building: Prior appointment required

Access for disabled people: Level entry

SOUTHERN AND SOUTH EAST ENGLAND TOURIST BOARD (STB)

40 Chamberlayne Road, Eastleigh, Hampshire, SO50 5JH

Tel: 023 8062 5400
Fax: 023 8062 0010
E-mail: info@tourismse.com
Website: www.tourismsoutheast.com

Enquiries to: Managing Director

Founded: 1977

Organisation type and purpose: Membership association (membership is by subscription), present number of members: 1,600, service industry.
Promotion and development of tourism.

Subject coverage: Tourism.

Publications: Printed

Access to staff: Contact by letter, by telephone, by fax and by e-mail
Hours: Mon to Thu, 0830 to 1700; Fri, 0830 to 1630

SOUTHERN AREA HOSPICE SERVICES

St John's House, Courtenay Hill, Newry, Co. Down, BT34 2EB

Tel: 028 3026 7711
Fax: 028 3026 8492
E-mail: info@southernareahospiceservices.org
Website: www.southernareahospiceservices.org

Founded: 1989

Organisation type and purpose: Registered charity (charity number XN47329/2).
Provides specialist care for patients affected by cancer, multiple sclerosis, motor neurone disease and other terminal illnesses. Care is provided, without cost, to patients and their families from across the Southern Health Board Area (Northern Ireland). The Hospice provides a holistic approach to care, responding to the physical, psychological and spiritual needs of patients, their relatives and carers. Care is provided by a team of highly trained medics and professionals both at the Hospice and in the community through a wide range of services.

Subject coverage: Services include: 12-bedded in-patient unit; out-patients clinics; home-care visits; day-hospice unit providing respite for families and carers as well as providing complementary therapies and important social interaction for patients; complementary therapies including physiotherapy, reflexology, hand massage and relaxation techniques for both inpatients and day-care patients; emotional and practical support from social workers for the patient and families, providing advice on benefit entitlements, securing care packages for patients after discharge, and offering patient and family counselling; bereavement counselling to families and carers; chaplaincy service providing spiritual support and counselling to the patient and families; patient helpline; (Donaldson Centre) advice and support to patients and their families at early stages of diagnosis of a terminal illness.

Information services: Patient helpline, tel: 028 3026 7711 – a patient or relative can phone the Hospice at any time to speak with the nurse in charge, regarding any queries they may have.

Publications: Electronic and video
Order electronic and video publications from: Download from website

Access to staff: Contact by letter, by telephone and by e-mail
Hours: Helpline: any time
Social Work Dept: Mon to Fri, 0830 to 1630
Donaldson Centre: appointments, Mon to Fri, 1000 to 1500; drop-ins, Tue, 2000 to 2100; Wed, 1100 to 1200; Thu, 1500 to 1600

SOUTHERN BRICK FEDERATION LIMITED

Brick Development Association, 26 Store Street, London, WC1E 7BT

Tel: 020 7323 7030
Fax: 020 7580 3795
E-mail: brick@brick.org.uk

Enquiries to: Secretary

Founded: 1970

Organisation type and purpose: Trade association.

Subject coverage: Clay brickmakers in the South of England.

Access to staff: Contact by letter, by telephone, by fax and by e-mail
Hours: Mon to Fri, 0900 to 1700

Links with: Brick Development Association; tel: 020 7323 7030; fax: 020 7580 3795; e-mail: brick@brick.org.uk; British Ceramic Confederation; tel: 01782 744631; fax: 01782 744102; e-mail: bcc@ceramfed.co.uk; British Ceramic Research Limited; tel: 01782 746476; fax: 01782 412331; e-mail: info@ceram.co.uk

SOUTHERN EDUCATION AND LIBRARY BOARD (SELB)

Library Headquarters, 1 Markethill Road, Armagh, BT60 1NR

Tel: 028 3752 5353
Fax: 028 3752 6879
Website: www.selb.org

Enquiries to: Chief Librarian
Direct tel: 028 3752 0702

Founded: 1974

Organisation type and purpose: Local government body, public library.
Schools library service.

Subject coverage: General, local history, Irish studies.

Collection: Crosslé Collection of manuscripts of local Newry families
Irish and local studies collection
Irish folk music record collection

Publications: Printed

Access to staff: Contact by letter, by telephone, by fax and in person
Hours: Mon to Fri, 0900 to 1700

Access for disabled people: Parking provided, level entry, access to all public areas, toilet facilities

SOUTHERN WATER

Southern House, Yeoman Road, Worthing, West Sussex, BN13 3NX

Tel: 01903 264444
Fax: 01903 691435
Website: www.southernwater.co.uk

Enquiries to: Head of Communications

Organisation type and purpose: Service industry.

Subject coverage: Water supply, sewerage services.

Access to staff: Contact by letter and by fax
Hours: Mon to Fri, 0900 to 1700

Has links with: Scottish Power

SOUTHGATE COLLEGE

Library and Learning Resources Service, High Street, Southgate, London, N14 6BS

Tel: 020 8982 5123
Fax: 020 8982 5118
Website: www.southgate.ac.uk

Enquiries to: Library & Learning Resources Manager
Other contacts: Learning Resources Co-ordinators

Founded: 1963

Organisation type and purpose: Suitable for ages: 16+.
General further education.

Subject coverage: General and vocational, including: business, catering, clothing, design, engineering, health and social care, leisure.

Library catalogue: All or part available in-house

Access to staff: Contact by letter, by telephone and by e-mail
Hours: Term time only, Mon to Thu, 0900 to 2000; Fri, 0900 to 1630
Special comments: Reference use, for print materials only.

Access to building: Prior appointment required

Access for disabled people: Parking provided, level entry

SOUTHWARK LIBRARY AND INFORMATION SERVICES

15 Spa Road, Bermondsey, London, SE16 3QW

Tel: 020 7525 3920 or 3716/7
Fax: 020 7525 1505
E-mail: adrian.olsen@southwark.gov.uk

continued overleaf

Enquiries to: Librarian
Direct tel: 020 7525 1577
Other contacts: Libraries Development Manager

Founded: 1800s

Organisation type and purpose: Local government body, public library.

Subject coverage: General, modern fiction in Swedish, Norwegian and Finnish; local studies; computers and data processing.

Collection: Greater London Audio Specialisation Scheme (mainly black disc): composers, Berlioz and Messaien; jazz artists, JOO-LED; music minus 1; folk music of SE Asia (at Spa Road)
Joint fiction reserves (English, including play sets by authors whose surnames come within the ranges BAJ-BEL (BOS-CAP and RDA-SHV up to and including 1987 only)) (at Spa Road)
Local history and archives collection relating to the London Borough of Southwark (including civil but not parish records)
Local Studies Library (at John Harvard Library, Borough High Street)
London Special Collection Dewey Nos. 000–009 (at Newington Library)
Mother tongue collection – Bengali, Hindi, Punjabi, Gujerati, Urdu, Chinese, Turkish, Greek, Vietnamese (based at various libraries)
Swedish, Norwegian and Finnish fiction (at Rotherhithe Library)

Library catalogue: All or part available online and in-house

Publications: Printed
Order printed publications from: Local Studies Librarian, London Borough of Southwark Local Studies Library, 211 Borough High Street, London, SE1 1JA, tel: 020 7403 3507, fax: 020 7403 8633

Access to staff: Contact by letter, by telephone, by fax and by e-mail. Appointment necessary.
Hours: Mon to Fri, 0900 to 1700

Parent body: Southwark Environment and Leisure Department; Chatelaine House, 186 Walworth Road, London SE17 1JJ; tel: 020 7525 5000

SOUTHWARK LOCAL HISTORY LIBRARY

211 Borough High Street, London, SE1 1JA

Tel: 020 7525 0232
E-mail: local.history.library@southwark.gov.uk
Website: www.southwark.gov.uk/info/200161/local_history_library

Organisation type and purpose: Local government body, public library.
Local history library and archive for London Borough of Southwark area.

Subject coverage: Local history and current affairs of London Borough of Southwark area. Includes extensive sources of interest to family historians with ancestors from the area and the archives of local authorities previous to the present London Borough of Southwark and of other organisations, institutions and individuals.

Collection: The Library Collection includes: printed published books, periodicals, illustrations, maps, cuttings and ephemera, sound recordings, videos
The Archives comprise: the official records of the London Borough of Southwark and its predecessors, the metropolitan boroughs and vestries, and unofficial deposited records of local organisations, institutions, businesses and individuals

Library catalogue: All or part available online and in print

Publications: Printed

Publications list: Available online and in print

Access to staff: Contact by letter, by telephone, by e-mail and in person
Hours: Mon and Thu, 10:00 to 19:00; Tue and Fri, 10:00 to 17:00; Sat, 10:00 to 15:00; Wed and Sun, closed

Access to building: No prior appointment required

Access for disabled people: Level entry, access to all public areas, toilet facilities

SOUTHWELL MINSTER LIBRARY

Formal name: Southwell Minster Historic Chapter Library and Theological Library

The Minster Office, Church Street, Southwell, Nottinghamshire, NG25 0HD

Tel: 01636 812649
E-mail: library@southwellminster.org.uk; christine@whitehouse26.plus.com
Website: www.southwellminster.org.uk

Enquiries to: Honorary Librarians (Historic or Theological Library)

Founded: 1690

Organisation type and purpose: Cathedral libraries.

Subject coverage: Theological Library: Theology

Services for disabled people: No disabled access

Collection: Historic Chapter Library: Old and rare books on theology, history, music, biblical studies, science, geography, classics, law, etc. Local history collection.

Library catalogue: All or part available online

Access to staff: Contact by letter and by e-mail. Appointment necessary.
Hours: Mon to Fri, 1000 to 1700

Access to building: *Hours:* Variable

SPA BUSINESS ASSOCIATION (SpaBA)

The Office Manager, Spa Business Association Ltd, Suite 5–6, Philpot House, Station Road, Rayleigh, Essex, SS6 7HH

Tel: 08707 800 787
Fax: 08707 804 477
E-mail: info@spabusinessassociation.co.uk
Website: www.spabusinessassociation.co.uk

Enquiries to: General Secretary
Other contacts: Chair, Medical Advisory Committee

Founded: 2004

Organisation type and purpose: Advisory body, trade association (membership is by subscription), present number of members: 120, training organisation, consultancy, research organisation.
Promotion of businesses in the spa sector, and of the benefits of using spas for health and wellbeing.

Subject coverage: Spas in the UK and Ireland. Spa Heritage and Tourism. Networking meetings for members and non-members. Quality Standards in spas and promotional campaigns for members.

Publications: Printed

Access to staff: Contact by letter, by telephone, by fax, by e-mail and via website
Hours: Mon to Fri, 0900 to 1700

Affiliated to: European Spas Association; 1, Avenue de la Renaissance, 1000 Bruxelles, Belgium; tel: +32 2733 2661

SPANISH EMBASSY COMMERCIAL OFFICE

66 Chiltern Street, London, W1M 1PR

Tel: 020 7467 2330
Fax: 020 7487 5586
E-mail: buzon.oficial@londres.ofcomes.mcx.es
Website: www.mcx.es/londres

Enquiries to: Information Officer

Organisation type and purpose: National government body.
Embassy department.

Subject coverage: General information on Spain: commercial or investment, specific department promoting export into Spain, foods and wines from Spain, consumer goods, industrial products and services.

Trade and statistical information: General statistical information on trade and investment to and from Spain

Publications: Printed

Access to staff: Contact by letter, by telephone, by fax, by e-mail and via website
Hours: Mon to Thu, 0900 to 1700; Fri, 0900 to 1500
Special comments: Requests in writing.

Access to building: No access other than to staff

Access for disabled people: Access to all public areas

Connections with: ICEX; PO Castellana 14–16, 28046 Madrid; tel: 00 34 91 349 3500; fax: 00 34 91 431 6128; website: http://www.icex.es

Parent body: Spanish Embassy; 39 Chesham Place, London, SW1X 8SB; tel: 020 7235 5555; fax: 020 7259 5392; e-mail: embespuk@mail.mae.es

SPANISH TOURIST OFFICE (STO)

64 North Row

E-mail: londres@tourspain.es
Website: www.spain.info

Direct e-mail: info.londres@tourspain.es

Organisation type and purpose: National government body.
Tourist information office.

Subject coverage: Tourist information about Spain.

Publications: Printed, and electronic and video

Access to staff: Contact by letter, by e-mail, in person and via website
Hours: Mon to Fri, 0915 to 1615
Special comments: By previous appointment only

Parent body: Turespaña; José Lazaro Galdiano 6, 28036 Madrid, Spain; tel: 00 34 91 343 3500

SPARTAN OWNERS' CLUB (SOC)

28 Ashford Drive, Ravenshead, Nottingham, NG15 9DE

Tel: 01623 409351
Fax: 01623 409352
Website: www.spartan-oc.demon.co.uk

Enquiries to: Secretary

Founded: 1978

Organisation type and purpose: Membership association (membership is by subscription), present number of members: 350–400, suitable for ages: 17+.
To bring together owners, builders and enthusiasts of the Spartan car.

Subject coverage: All aspects of the Spartan kit car.

Publications: Printed

Access to staff: Contact by letter, by telephone, by fax and via website
Special comments: Telephone between 1800 and 2000 only.

SPEAKABILITY

Formal name: Action for Dysphasic Adults

1 Royal Street, London, SE1 7LL

Tel: 020 7261 9572 (Administration)
Fax: 020 7928 9542
E-mail: speakability@speakability.org.uk
Website: www.speakability.org.uk

Enquiries to: Chief Executive

Founded: 1979

Organisation type and purpose: National organisation, voluntary organisation, registered charity (charity number 295094).
Supporting people with aphasia/dysphasia and their carers and friends, through its information service and national network of groups; influencing individuals and organisations in order to improve services for people with aphasia.

Subject coverage: Dysphasia/Aphasia, speech and language problems after stroke, head injury or neurological condition.

Collection: Database of information for people with Aphasia, carers and professionals

Publications: Printed, and electronic and video

Publications list: Available in print

Access to staff: Contact by letter, by telephone, by fax, by e-mail and via website
Hours: Free Helpline: 080 8808 9572 Mon to Fri, 1000 to 1600
24-hour answerphone

Has: national network of support groups

Links with: Association of Speech & Language Therapists; British Aphasiology Society (BAS)

SPECIAL EDUCATION CONSORTIUM

8 Wakely Street, London, EC1V 7QE

Tel: 020 7843 6334; 020 7843 6060
Fax: 020 7843 6313
E-mail: cdc@ncb.org.uk

Enquiries to: SEC Co-ordinator

Organisation type and purpose: Advisory body, voluntary organisation, registered charity (charity number 258825).
To protect and promote the interests of disabled children and children with special educational needs during the passage of legislation that may affect them.

Subject coverage: Special educational needs and disability – policy, practice and legislation in this field.

Access to staff: Contact by letter, by telephone, by fax and by e-mail
Hours: Mon to Fri, 0900 to 1700

Access to building: Prior appointment required

Access for disabled people: Ramped entry, level entry, toilet facilities

Registered under the auspices of: The Council for Disabled Children; at The National Children's Bureau

SPECIAL EDUCATIONAL NEEDS TRIBUNAL (SENT)

50 Victoria Street, London, SW1H 0NW

Tel: 020 7925 6902
Fax: 020 7926 6926
E-mail: sendistqueries@hmcts.gsi.gov.uk
Website: www.sentribunal.gov.uk

Enquiries to: Secretary

Founded: 1994

Organisation type and purpose: Statutory body.

Subject coverage: Appeals by parents against local decisions about children's special educational needs.

Trade and statistical information: Volume of SEN appeals by type, nature of SEN and local authority area

Publications: Printed, and electronic and video
Order printed publications from: DfES Publications Centre, Special Educational Needs Tribunal
PO Box 5050, Sherwood Park, Annersley, Nottingham, NG15 0DJ, tel: 0845 602 2260, fax: 0845 603 3360, e-mail: dfes@prolog.uk.com
Order electronic and video publications from: SENT
As main address

Access to staff: Contact by letter, by telephone, by fax, by e-mail and via website
Hours: Mon to Fri, 0900 to 1700

Access to building: Prior appointment required

SPECIAL OLYMPICS GREAT BRITAIN (SOGB)

6–8 Great Eastern Street, London, EC2A 3NT

Tel: 020 7247 8891
Fax: 020 7247 2393
E-mail: karen.wallin@sogb.org.uk
Website: www.sogb.org.uk

Enquiries to: Administrator
Direct e-mail: peju.oriunuta@sogb.org.uk
Other contacts: Chief Executive Officer

Founded: 1978

Organisation type and purpose: International organisation, national government body, membership association, present number of members: 30,000, registered charity (charity number 800329), suitable for all ages, training organisation.
To provide year-round training and competition in Olympic sports for all with a mental handicap.

Subject coverage: Sport for people with learning disabilities.

Publications: Printed, and electronic and video

Publications list: Available in print

Access to staff: Contact by letter, by telephone, by fax, by e-mail and in person. Appointment necessary. Letter of introduction required.
Hours: Mon to Fri, 0900 to 1700

Access to building: Prior appointment required

Parent body: Special Olympics International; 1133 19th Street NW, Washington, DC 20036–3604, USA

SPECIALIST CHEESEMAKERS ASSOCIATION (SCA)

17 Clerkenwell Green, London, EC1R 0DP

Tel: 020 7253 2114
Fax: 020 7608 1645
E-mail: info@specialistcheesemakers.co.uk
Website: www.specialistcheesemakers.co.uk

Enquiries to: Secretary

Founded: 1989

Organisation type and purpose: Membership association (membership is by subscription), present number of members: Over 400.

Subject coverage: Representation of the interests of specialist cheesemakers, providing a link between cheesemakers, retailers and wholesalers, providing promotional opportunities and own hygiene scheme.

Publications: Printed

Publications list: Available online

Access to staff: Contact by letter, by telephone, by fax, by e-mail and via website
Hours: Mon to Fri, 0900 to 1700

Access to building: No access other than to staff

SPELTHORNE BOROUGH COUNCIL

Council Offices, Knowle Green, Staines, TW18 1XB

continued overleaf

Tel: 01784 451499
E-mail: customer.services@spelthorne.gov.uk
Website: www.spelthorne.gov.uk

Enquiries to: Communications Manager
Direct tel: 01784 446297
Direct e-mail: news@spelthorne.gov.uk
Other contacts: PR and Communications Officer

Organisation type and purpose: Local government body.

Subject coverage: Local government services.

Publications: Printed
Order printed publications from: Louise King, tel: 01784 444260

Publications list: Available online and in print

Access to staff: Contact by letter, by telephone, by e-mail, in person and via website
Hours: Mon to Fri, 0900 to 1700

Access for disabled people: Parking provided, ramped entry, toilet facilities

Parent body: Surrey County Council

SPINAL INJURIES ASSOCIATION (SIA)

SIA House, 2 Trueman Place, Oldbrook, Milton Keynes, MK6 2HH

Tel: 0845 678 6633
Fax: 0845 070 6911
E-mail: sia@spinal.co.uk
Website: www.spinal.co.uk

Founded: 1974

Organisation type and purpose: National organisation, advisory body, membership association (membership is by subscription), present number of members: 5,500, voluntary organisation, registered charity (charity number 1054097), consultancy, publishing house.
Self-help group.

Subject coverage: Paraplegia, tetraplegia, the spinal-cord injured, wheelchair living, self-help aids, personal care, mobility, employment, integration, welfare benefits, sexuality, continence, parenthood, aids and equipment, pain, and an online message board and chat room.

Information services: Advice line and website with chatroom and message board, as well as access to a range of publications about spinal cord injury.

Library catalogue: All or part available online and in print

Publications: Printed, and electronic and video

Publications list: Available online and in print

Access to staff: Contact by letter, by telephone, by fax, by e-mail and via website. Appointment necessary.
Hours: Mon to Fri, 0930 to 1630

Access to building: *Hours:* Mon to Fri, 0900 to 1700

Access for disabled people: Parking provided, level entry, access to all public areas, toilet facilities

Links with: Scottish Spinal Cord Injuries Association; some 136 other bodies

SPINAL INJURIES SCOTLAND (SIS)

Festival Business Centre, 150 Brand Street, Glasgow, G51 1DH

Tel: 0141 427 7686
Fax: 0141 427 9258
E-mail: info@sisonline.org
Website: www.sisonline.org

Enquiries to: Office Manager

Founded: 1960

Organisation type and purpose: National organisation, membership association, present number of members: c. 1200, voluntary organisation, registered charity (charity number SC 015405).
Specifically for spinally injured people, their families, friends and carers.

Subject coverage: Advice, support, access, accessible holiday information, manufacturers and suppliers of equipment etc.

Publications: Printed

Access to staff: Contact by letter, by telephone, by fax, by e-mail and in person
Hours: Mon to Fri, 0900 to 1700

Access to building: No prior appointment required

Access for disabled people: Parking provided, level entry, access to all public areas, toilet facilities
Special comments: None

Acts in association with the: Spinal Injuries Association

SPINAL RESEARCH

Formal name: International Spinal Research Trust

Unit 8A, Bramley Business Centre, Station Road, Bramley, Guildford, Surrey, GU5 0AZ

Tel: 01483 898786
Fax: 01483 898763
E-mail: info@spinal-research.org
Website: www.spinal-research.org

Enquiries to: Chief Executive
Other contacts: Head of Fundraising

Founded: 1981

Organisation type and purpose: International organisation, registered charity (charity number 281325), research organisation.
Spinal Research exists to fund research with the sole aim of finding a treatment for paralysis caused by spinal cord injury.

Subject coverage: Research into ending the permanence of paralysis caused by spinal cord injury.

Publications: Printed, and electronic and video

Access to staff: Contact by letter, by telephone, by fax, by e-mail, in person and via website
Hours: Mon to Fri, 0900 to 1730

Access to building: No prior appointment required

Access for disabled people: Parking provided, level entry, access to all public areas, toilet facilities

SPLIT SCREEN VAN CLUB (SSVC)

Old Mills Cottage, Old Mills Road, Elgin, Moray, IV30 1YH

Tel: 01343 550639
E-mail: cjtasker@hotmail.com
Website: www.ssvc.org.uk

Enquiries to: Information Officer
Other contacts: President/Membership Secretary; email: president@ssvc.org.uk for membership.

Founded: 1983

Organisation type and purpose: National organisation, membership association (membership is by subscription), present number of members: 1100.
To preserve and celebrate these unique vintage Volkswagen vans and also the expertise needed to maintain and restore them.

Subject coverage: Split screen Volkswagen vans, their history, restoration and maintenance.

Collection: Details of over 500 vans and their histories are collated on the van register.

Publications: Printed
Order printed publications from: Membership Secretary or via website
e-mail: membership@ssvc.org.uk

Access to staff: Contact by letter, by telephone, by e-mail and via website
Hours: Mon to Fri, 0900 to 1700

SPORT ENGLAND

3rd Floor Victoria House, Bloomsbury Square, London, WC1B 4SE

Tel: 020 7273 1551
Fax: 020 7383 5740
Website: www.sportengland.org

Enquiries to: Information Centre
Direct e-mail: jordan.russell@sportengland.org

Founded: 1997

Organisation type and purpose: National government body. Receives an annual grant-in-aid from the Department for Culture, Media and Sport and in turn distributes grants; 9 regional offices and 5 national sports centres.

Subject coverage: Sport and physical recreation: administration; grants; design, planning and provision of facilities; technical and architectural factors; development of sport in general; sport for specific groups e.g. unemployed, children etc; governing bodies; sports science and medicine; sports sociology; legislation; sports psychology; individual sports; sporting events.

Collection: 700 Journals
30,000 books and journal articles
Small video collection

Library catalogue: All or part available in-house

Publications: Printed
Order printed publications from: Sport England, PO Box 255, Wetherby, West Yorkshire, LS23 7LZ, tel: 0870 521 0255, fax: 0870 521 0266

Publications list: Available online and in print

Access to staff: Contact by letter, by telephone, by e-mail, in person and via website. Appointment necessary.
Hours: Mon to Fri, 1330 to 1600
Special comments: Postgraduate students only.

Access for disabled people: Toilet facilities

Regional Sports Councils are: East Midlands Region; Grove House, Bridgford Road, West Bridgford, Nottinghamshire, NG2 6AP; tel: 0115 982 1887; fax: 0115 945 5236; East Region; Crescent House, 19 The Crescent, Bedford, MK40 2QP; tel: 01234 345222; fax: 01234 359046; London Region; PO Box 480, Crystal Palace National Sports Centre, Ledrington Road, London, SE19 2BQ; tel: 020 8778 8600; fax: 020 8676 9812; North East Region; Aykley Heads, Durham, DH1 5UU; tel: 0191 384 9595; fax: 0191 384 5807; North West Region; Astley House, Quay Street, Manchester, M3 4AE; tel: 0161 834 0388; fax: 0161 835 3678; South East Region; 51A Church Street, Caversham, Reading, Berkshire, RG4 8AX; tel: 0118 948 3311; fax: 0118 947 5935; South West Region; Ashlands House, Ashlands, Crewkerne, Somerset, TA18 7LQ; tel: 01460 73491; fax: 01460 77263; West Midlands Region; 1 Hagley Road, Five Ways, Edgbaston, Birmingham, B16 8TT; tel: 0121 456 3444; fax: 0121 456 1583; Yorkshire Region; 4th Floor, Minerva House, East Parade, Leeds, LS1 5PS; tel: 0113 243 6443; fax: 0113 242 2189

SPORT HORSE BREEDING OF GREAT BRITAIN (SHB(GB))

96 High Street, Edenbridge, Kent, TN8 5AR

Tel: 01732 866277
Fax: 01732 867464
E-mail: office@sporthorsegb.co.uk
Website: www.sporthorsegb.co.uk

Enquiries to: General Secretary

Founded: 1884

Organisation type and purpose: Advisory body, membership association (membership is by subscription), present number of members: c. 4000, registered charity.
To develop and improve the breeding of the British sport horse.

Subject coverage: Horse breeding, registration and shows.

Collection: Stud Books

Library catalogue: All or part available in-house

Access to staff: Contact by letter, by telephone, by fax and by e-mail
Hours: Mon to Fri, 0900 to 1700

SPORTING FIATS CLUB (SFC)

Elms Farm, Long Clawson, Melton Mowbray, Leicestershire, LE14 4NG

Tel: 01664 822395
E-mail: webmaster@sportingfiatsclub.com
Website: www.sportingfiatsclub.com

Enquiries to: Membership Secretary
Other contacts: Chairman for organisational, alliance or regulatory enquiries.

Founded: 1978

Organisation type and purpose: Membership association (membership is by subscription), present number of members: 500.
To further interest in and enjoyment of Fiat motor cars, worldwide, centred in the UK.

Subject coverage: Fiat cars.

Publications: Printed, and electronic and video

Access to staff: Contact by letter, by telephone, by e-mail and via website
Hours: Mon to Fri, 1000 to 2200

Affiliated to: Group B Car Club; Motor Sport Association; XI/9 Owners Club

SPORTS INDUSTRIES FEDERATION, THE (TSIF)

Federation House, National Agricultural Centre, Stoneleigh Park, Kenilworth, Warwickshire, CV8 2RF

Tel: 024 7641 4999
Fax: 024 7641 4990
Website: www.sports-life.com

Enquiries to: Head of Membership & Development
Other contacts: Chief Executive

Founded: 1920

Organisation type and purpose: Trade association, membership association (membership is by subscription).

Subject coverage: Lists of suppliers of sports equipment and capital goods equipment. Playground safety guidelines, information on British and European standards relevant to sports industry.

Trade and statistical information: Data on imports and exports of sports equipment between the United Kingdom and the European Union and non-European Union Countries.
Quarterly United Kingdom sports trends and surveys.
Statistics relating to tennis court construction, sports surfaces, angling trade and play equipment

Publications list: Available online

Access to staff: Contact by letter, by telephone, by fax, by e-mail and via website
Hours: Mon to Fri, 0900 to 1700

Access to building: Prior appointment required

Access for disabled people: Parking provided, toilet facilities

Houses the: Angling Trade Association; Golf Ball Manufacturers Conference

SPORTS TURF RESEARCH INSTITUTE, THE (STRI)

St Ives Estate, Bingley, West Yorkshire, BD16 1AU

Tel: 01274 565131
Fax: 01274 561891
E-mail: info@stri.co.uk
Website: www.stri.co.uk

Enquiries to: External Affairs Manager
Other contacts: Chief Executive

Founded: 1929

Organisation type and purpose: International organisation, advisory body, professional body (membership is by subscription), training organisation, consultancy, research organisation, publishing house.
The STRI is the leading independent organisation in turf grass research and agronomy. Our aims are to carry out research and promote innovation; provide advisory and consultancy services; educate and inform through training and publications.

Subject coverage: Drainage of sports fields and golf courses, design and construction of golf courses and sports fields, specifications for drainage and construction, irrigation, advisory work including maintenance and management programmes on any sports surface, artificial surfaces, research into turf problems, training courses, publications and books.

Collection: Library on turf-related publications including rare publications and journals

Library catalogue: All or part available in-house

Publications: Printed, and electronic and video

Publications list: Available online and in print

Access to staff: Contact by letter, by telephone, by fax, by e-mail and via website. Appointment necessary.
Hours: Mon to Fri, 0900 to 1700

Access to building: Prior appointment required

Access for disabled people: Parking provided, level entry

Links with: All Sports Governing Bodies including:; Association of Independent Research & Technology Organisations (AIRTO); Football Association; Royal & Ancient Golf Club of St Andrews; Sport England; Sports Council

SPORTSCOTLAND

Caledonia House, South Gyle, Edinburgh, EH12 9DQ

Tel: 0131 317 7200
Fax: 0131 317 7202
E-mail: library@sportscotland.org.uk
Website: www.sportscotland.org.uk

Enquiries to: Information Officer

Founded: 1972

Organisation type and purpose: Non-departmental public body.
The national agency for sport in Scotland.

continued overleaf

Subject coverage: Sport in Scotland, physical recreation, facilities, coaching, sports and associated organisations contacts, participation statistics, sports sponsorship, drugs in sport.

Collection: 10,000 books and 120 current journals

Trade and statistical information: Data on sports facilities located in Scotland, data on countryside recreation sites located in Scotland, National Lottery-funded projects for sport in Scotland

Library catalogue: All or part available online and in-house

Publications: Printed

Publications list: Available online

Access to staff: Contact by letter, by telephone, by fax, by e-mail and via website. Appointment necessary.
Hours: Mon to Fri, 0900 to 1700

Access to building: Prior appointment required
Hours: Mon to Fri, 0900 to 1700

Access for disabled people: Parking provided, level entry

Funded by: Central Government under Royal Charter

SPORTSCOTLAND NATIONAL CENTRE CUMBRAE

Sportscotland National centre Cumbrae, Isle of Cumbrae, Ayrshire, KA28 OHQ

Tel: 01475 530 757
Fax: 01475 530 013
E-mail: cumbraecentre@sportscotland.org.uk
Website: www.nationalcentrecumbrae.org.uk

Enquiries to: Principal

Founded: 1974

Organisation type and purpose: National government body, advisory body, registered charity, training organisation.
To train instructors in watersports, to train the national sailing squads, to offer high-level instruction in watersports to all. Scotland's premier watersports training facility.

Subject coverage: All aspects of watersport; yacht cruising, dinghy sailing and racing, catamaran sailing, windsurfing, sailing, canoeing, powerboating and powerboat racing, sub aqua.

Publications: Printed

Publications list: Available in print

Access to staff: Contact by letter, by telephone, by fax, by e-mail, in person and via website
Hours: Mon to Fri, 0900 to 1700

Access for disabled people: Parking provided, ramped entry, toilet facilities
Hours: Mon to Fri, 0900 to 1700

Constituent part of: Scottish Sports Council Trust Company; Doges, Templeton on the Green, 62 Templeton Street, Glasgow, G40 1DA; tel: 0141 534 6500; fax: 0141 534 6501; website: http://www.sportscotland.org.uk

SPORTSCOTLAND NATIONAL CENTRE INVERCLYDE

Burnside Road, Largs, Ayrshire, KA30 8RW

Tel: 01475 674666
Fax: 01475 674720
E-mail: john.kent@sportscotland.org.uk
Website: www.sportscotland.org.uk

Enquiries to: Manager
Other contacts: Office Manager for bookings.

Founded: 1970

Organisation type and purpose: National government body, registered charity. Residential Sports Centre.
Provision of sport facilities for National Teams, clubs, society of coaches, education groups, schools, colleges, sportspeople, conference and commercial seminars.

Subject coverage: Sports coaching and awards, educational field work, fitness testing, sports science and medicine, residential sports coaching. Corporate team building, sports days and events.

Trade and statistical information: United Kingdom market for residential sports training for elite athletes, clubs, sports groups and corporate activities

Publications: Printed, and electronic and video

Publications list: Available online and in print

Access to staff: Contact by letter, by telephone, by fax, by e-mail and via website. Appointment necessary. All charged.
Hours: Mon to Sun, 0800 to 2300

Access to building: Prior appointment required

Access for disabled people: Parking provided, ramped entry

Parent body: SportScotland; tel: 0131 317 7200; fax: 0131 317 7202

SPRAYED CONCRETE ASSOCIATION (SCA)

Tournai Hall, Evelyn Woods Road, Aldershot, Hampshire, GU11 2LL

Tel: 01252 357842
Fax: 01252 357831
E-mail: admin@sca.org.uk
Website: www.sca.org.uk

Enquiries to: Secretary

Founded: 1976

Organisation type and purpose: Trade association, present number of members: 41. Contractors, manufacturers and others involved in sprayed concrete. Operates, through CITB, a certificate scheme for operatives.

Subject coverage: Sprayed concrete, gunite, shotcrete.

Publications: Printed

Publications list: Available online and in print

Access to staff: Contact by letter, by telephone, by fax, by e-mail and via website
Hours: Mon to Fri, 0900 to 1700

SPRU (SCIENCE AND TECHNOLOGY POLICY RESEARCH)

The Freeman Centre, University of Sussex, Falmer, Brighton, East Sussex, BN1 9QE

Tel: 01273 686758
Fax: 01273 685865
E-mail: b.a.merchant@sussex.ac.uk
Website: www.sussex.ac.uk/spru/library
Website: www.sussex.ac.uk/spru
Website: sprulib.central.sussex.ac.uk

Enquiries to: Information Officer
Direct tel: 01273 678178
Direct e-mail: m.e.winder@sussex.ac.uk
Other contacts: Information Services Manager

Founded: 1966

Organisation type and purpose: University department or institute, research organisation.

Subject coverage: Economics of technical change, technology and innovation management, science and technology indicators, research evaluation, technology transfer, technology in developing countries, energy policy, national science and technology policies, environmental and social implications of technical change, chemical, biological and nuclear arms control. Sectors studied include: energy, electronics, information and communications technologies, weapons, building, automobiles, mining, food, chemicals, pharmaceuticals, biotechnology, complex systems.

Collection: Specialist science and technology policy collection, including a large holding of grey literature, and a core science and technology policy journals collection

Trade and statistical information: Statistics, particularly on R & D expenditure and funding, and science and technology

Publications: Printed
Order printed publications from: e-mail: spru_library@sussex.ac.uk

Access to staff: *Hours:* Mon to Fri, 0900 to 1300 and 1400 to 1700
Special comments: Charges to non-academic non-members.

Houses the former: Armaments and Disarmaments Information Unit

SSCCI LTD

Ridings House, Ridings Park, Eastern Way, Cannock, Staffordshire, WS11 2FJ

Tel: 01543 460050
Fax: 01543 462822

Enquiries to: Chief Executive

Founded: 1994; formerly called East Mercia Chamber of Commerce and Industry (EMCCI)

Organisation type and purpose: Service industry, training organisation, consultancy.

Subject coverage: Business information, international trade and documentation, training, health and safety consultancy, quality consultancy, environmental consultancy, late payment of debt and financial business reports.

Collection: Comprehensive library of UK and international business directories

Access to staff: Contact by letter
Hours: Mon to Fri, 0830 to 1730

ST ALBANS CITY AND DISTRICT COUNCIL

District Council Offices, Civic Centre, St Peter's Street, St Albans, Hertfordshire, AL1 3JE

Tel: 01727 8662100
Fax: 01727 8662100
Website: www.stalbans.gov.uk

Enquiries to: Public Relations Officer

Organisation type and purpose: Local government body.

Subject coverage: Local government services.

ST ANDREWS COMMUNITY LIBRARY

Church Square, St Andrews, Fife, KY16 9NN

Tel: 01334 659378
E-mail: standrews.library@fife.gov.uk

Enquiries to: Library Supervisor

History of institution: formerly called Hay Fleming Library

Organisation type and purpose: Local government body, public library.

Non-library collection catalogue: All or part available online and in-house

Library catalogue: All or part available online and in-house

Access to staff: Contact by letter, by telephone and by e-mail

Access for disabled people: Ramped entry, lift to first floor

Branch library of: Fife Council Library

ST ANNE'S COLLEGE

Library, Woodstock Road, Oxford, OX2 6HS

Tel: 01865 274810
Fax: 01865 274899
E-mail: library@st-annes.ox.ac.uk
Website: www.lib.ox.ac.uk/libraries/guides/ann.html

Enquiries to: Librarian

Founded: 1879

Organisation type and purpose: University department or institute.
College library.

Subject coverage: Most undergraduate subjects in arts, social sciences and sciences, education and anthropology.

Collection: Handover Bequest (typography and history of printing)

Library catalogue: All or part available online

Access to staff: Contact by letter.
Appointment necessary.
Hours: Mon to Fri, 0900 to 1700

Access to building: Only by appointment after prior application to Librarian

Parent body: University of Oxford

ST BRIDE LIBRARY

Bride Lane, Fleet Street, London, EC4Y 8EE

Tel: 020 7353 4660
Fax: 020 7583 7073
E-mail: library@stbridefoundation.org

Enquiries to: Librarian

Founded: 1891

Organisation type and purpose: Public reference library.

Subject coverage: Printing (history and technology) and related subjects (paper, binding, graphic design, typography, typefaces, calligraphy, illustration, printmaking, publishing, bookselling, social and economic aspects of printing and book trades). The collection comprises books, printing types, antique presses, photographs, etc.

Collection: Historical collection dealing with printing, publishing, graphic design and related subjects, early technical manuals, trade literature, manufacturers' prospectuses, type specimens, trade serials, directories, prints, drawings and artefacts
Archives and Collections
Broadside Collection (18th century songsheets, 19th century broadsides, chapbooks)
Eric Gill Collection (drawings for printing types and stone cut inscriptions)
Leaflets, broadsides, union reports on printing trade relations from 1785
Manuals and periodicals on shorthand (about 3,000 items)
Printing tools and equipment
Prints, drawings and manuscripts

Trade and statistical information: Data on the printing trade, and also on paper and publishing

Library catalogue: All or part available online and in-house

Access to staff: Contact by letter, by telephone, by fax, by e-mail and in person
Hours: Tue, 1200 to 1730; Wed, 1200 to 1900; Thu, 1200 to 1730
Special comments: Reference library.

Parent body: St Bride Foundation; St Bride Library, Bride Lane, Fleet Street, London, EC4Y 8EE; tel: 020 7353 4660; fax: 020 7583 7073; e-mail: library@stbrideinstitute.org; website: www.stbride.org

ST CHRISTOPHER'S FELLOWSHIP

1 Putney High Street, London, SW15 1SZ

Tel: 020 8780 7800
Fax: 020 8780 7801
E-mail: info@stchris.org.uk
Website: www.stchris.org.uk

Organisation type and purpose: Registered charity (number 207782), the only children's charity that is also a housing association.
A leading voluntary provider of services for children, young people and vulnerable adults, providing care, accommodation, advice, education and continuing support, helping to really make a difference, whether this may be a safe, comfortable and caring place to stay, help with homework, or support and advice about education, health, housing and jobs. Provides a continuum of care to service users, offering them as much help as they need to adapt to independent life. Increasingly reaches out to children who are at risk of being placed in care or returning there. Also provides supported housing services, including hostels, flats and shared houses, and a full range of support in areas such as further education, training, employment, and legal issues for young people who need help to make that vital step towards fully independent living.

Subject coverage: Current focus is on adapting therapeutic models of working to meet the needs of all the people who require support. By using established academic theories, the work can be more informed and staff better able to meet the complex needs of service users.

Access to staff: Contact by letter, by telephone, by fax and by e-mail

ST CHRISTOPHER'S HOSPICE

Halley Stewart Library, 51–59 Lawrie Park Road, Sydenham, London, SE26 6DZ

Tel: 020 8768 4660
Fax: 020 8776 9345
Website: www.stchristophers.org.uk

Enquiries to: Librarian
Direct e-mail: n.rattray@stchristophers.org.uk

Founded: 1980 (Library)

Organisation type and purpose: Voluntary organisation, registered charity (charity number 210667).
Hospice library (includes information and education facilities).
Hospice for people with advanced disease.

Subject coverage: All aspects of hospice and palliative care; death and dying, ethical issues, bereavement, children's books on these topics.

Collection: In-house database on the subject (c.10,000 items – mainly books, articles and grey literature)

Library catalogue: All or part available in-house

Publications: Printed

Publications list: Available in print

Access to staff: Contact by letter, by telephone, by fax and by e-mail.
Appointment necessary.
Hours: Mon to Fri, 0900 to 1700

Access for disabled people: Parking provided, ramped entry, toilet facilities

Links with: Hospice Information

ST EDMUNDSBURY BOROUGH COUNCIL

Borough Offices, Angel Hill, Bury St Edmunds, Suffolk, IP33 1XB

Tel: 01284 763233\ Minicom no. 01284 757023
Fax: 01284 757124
E-mail: stedmundsbury@stedsbc.gov.uk
Website: www.stedmundsbury.gov.uk
Website: www.stedmundsbury.gov.uk/moyses.htm

continued overleaf

Enquiries to: Chief Executive

Founded: 1974

Organisation type and purpose: Local government body.

Subject coverage: Local government within St Edmundsbury Borough. Council services, tourist information, economic development.

Publications: Printed

Access to staff: Contact by letter, by telephone, by fax, by e-mail and via website
Hours: Mon to Thu, 0900 to 1700; Fri, 0900 to 1600

Access for disabled people: Parking provided, ramped entry, level entry, toilet facilities

Other offices: St Edmundsbury Borough Council; St Edmundsbury House, Western Way, Bury St Edmunds, Suffolk, IP33 3YS; tel: 01284 763233; fax: 01284 757378; St Edmundsbury Borough Council; Council Offices, Lower Downs Slade, Haverhill, Suffolk, CB9 9EE; tel: 01440 702271; fax: 01440 702397

ST FRANCIS LEPROSY GUILD (SFLG)

73 St Charles Square, London, W10 6EJ

Tel: 020 8969 1345
Fax: 020 8969 3272
E-mail: enquiries@stfrancisleprosy.org

Enquiries to: General Secretary

Founded: 1895

Organisation type and purpose:
Membership association (membership is by subscription), registered charity (charity number 208741), voluntary organisation.
Raising funds for the assistance of Catholic priests, brothers and sisters working among leprosy sufferers whatever their nationality or creed.

Subject coverage: Care for leprosy patients; assistance in the provision of food, drugs, wheelchairs, artificial limbs, hospital equipment and surgical instruments, etc.; information on the leprosy projects and centres assisted.

Publications: Printed

Access to staff: Contact by letter and by e-mail
Hours: Mon to Fri, 1000 to 1700

ST HELENS COLLEGE LIBRARY

Water Street, St Helens, Merseyside, WA10 1PP

Tel: 01744 733766
E-mail: library@sthelens.ac.uk
Website: www.sthelens.ac.uk

Enquiries to: Head of Information and Library Services
Direct tel: 01744 623256

History of institution: formerly called St Helens Community College

Organisation type and purpose: College of further education.

Subject coverage: Business studies; office technology; management; computer-aided design and manufacture; art and design, health and social care.

Non-library collection catalogue: All or part available online

Library catalogue: All or part available online

Publications: Printed
Order printed publications from: Student Services, St Helens College, at the same address

Access to staff: Contact by letter, by telephone, by e-mail and in person. Appointment necessary.
Hours: Term time: Mon to Thu, 0845 to 2000; Fri, 0845 to 1600; Vacations: Mon to Thu, 0900 to 1700; Fri, 0900 to 1600

Access for disabled people: Access to all public areas

The College houses the: St Helens School of Management Studies, a constituent of the North West Regional Management Centre

ST HELENS LIBRARIES

Central Library, Gamble Institute, Victoria Square, St Helens, Merseyside, WA10 1DY

Tel: 01744 456989
Fax: 01744 20836
E-mail: criu@sthelens.gov.uk

Enquiries to: Librarian

Organisation type and purpose: Local government body, public library.

Subject coverage: Local history, glass.

Collection: Sir Thomas Beecham Archive Collection, not the original library of the conductor

Access to staff: Contact by telephone
Hours: Mon, Wed, 0900 to 2000; Tue, Thu, Fri, 0900 to 1700; Sat, 0900 to 1600

Access for disabled people: Access to all public areas

ST HILDA'S COLLEGE LIBRARY

Cowley Place, Oxford, OX4 1DY

Tel: 01865 276884
Fax: 01865 276816
Website: www.sthildas.ox.ac.uk/information/history/archive.htm
Website: www.sthildas.ox.ac.uk/information/library/index.htm

Enquiries to: Librarian
Direct tel: 01865 276848
Direct e-mail: maria.croghan@st-hildas.ox.ac.uk
Other contacts: Archivist for access to the archives and related queries.

Founded: 1893

Organisation type and purpose: University department or institute.
College library.

Subject coverage: General undergraduate collection, languages, literature, history, philosophy, theology, geography, politics, economics, biology, physiology, medicine, physics, chemistry, engineering, fine art, music.

Collection: College archive
History of Women's University Education
Maconchy manuscripts, original music manuscripts of Dame Elizabeth Maconchy (20th century composer)

Non-library collection catalogue: All or part available in-house

Library catalogue: All or part available online

Access to staff: Appointment necessary.
Hours: Mon to Fri, 0900 to 1700

Access for disabled people: *Hours:* Mon to Fri, 0900 to 1700

Parent body: University of Oxford

ST JAMES'S UNIVERSITY HOSPITAL

Medical Library, Level 3, Clinical Sciences Building, Beckett Street, Leeds, West Yorkshire, LS9 7TF

Tel: 0113 2065638
Fax: 0113 2064682
Website: www.leeds.ac.uk/library

Enquiries to: Librarian

History of institution: formerly called St James's and Seacroft University Hospital

Organisation type and purpose: University library.

Subject coverage: Medicine; health care management.

Non-library collection catalogue: All or part available online

Library catalogue: All or part available online

Access to staff: Contact by letter, by telephone and in person. Access for members only.
Hours: Mon to Thu, 0830 to 1800; Fri, 1000 to 1700

Parent body: University of Leeds

ST JOHN – THE PRIORY OF SCOTLAND

The Chancery of the Priory of Scotland, St John's House, 21 St John Street, Edinburgh, EH8 8DG

Tel: 0131 556 8711
Fax: 0131 558 3250
E-mail: info@stjohnscotland.org.uk
Website: www.stjohnscotland.org.uk
Website: www.orderofstjohn.org

Founded: 1947

Organisation type and purpose: Registered Scottish charity (number SC000262).
To improve the safety, health and quality of life of people in need.

Subject coverage: National rescue support: mountain rescue bases and vehicles, St John rescue boat, Loch Lomond; area initiatives: financial support to a wide range of local schemes, including Maggie's Highland Cancer Caring Centre, Disability Sport Fife and Shopmobility; patient care: St John Patient Transport, Dumfries and Galloway, St John Palliative Care Project, Stranraer; accommodation: Strathtyre Holiday Home, Stirlingshire, Archibald Russell Court, Retirement Complex, Polmont; support for other charities: St John transport for charities, St John Crusader canal cruises, St John's Court, Glasgow; overseas projects: St John Eye Hospital, Jerusalem, St John Malawi Primary Healthcare Project.

Publications: Printed
Order printed publications from: The Chancery of the Priory of Scotland in Edinburgh

Access to staff: Contact by letter, by telephone, by fax and by e-mail
Hours: Charity Book Shop open: Tue to Sun

Also at: St John Book Shop; 20 Deanhaugh Street, Stockbridge, Edinburgh

ST JOHN'S COLLEGE LIBRARY

3 South Bailey, Durham, DH1 3RJ

Tel: 0191 334 3500
E-mail: johns.library@durham.ac.uk
Website: www.dur.ac.uk/st-johns.college

Enquiries to: Librarian
Direct tel: 0191 334 3891
Direct e-mail: richard.briggs@durham.ac.uk
Other contacts: Assistant Librarian

Founded: 1909

Organisation type and purpose: College library.

Subject coverage: Mostly theology, some other subject areas.

Library catalogue: All or part available online

Access to staff: Contact by letter and by e-mail. Appointment necessary. Non-members charged.
Hours: Mon to Fri, 0900 to 1400
Special comments: Telephone calls morning only.

Access to building: Prior appointment required

Parent body: University of Durham

ST JOHN'S INSTITUTE OF DERMATOLOGY

Education Centre, St Thomas' Hospital, Lambeth Palace Road, London, SE1 7EH

Tel: 020 7188 6255
Fax: 020 7928 1428
E-mail: derm-courses@kcl.ac.uk

Founded: 1947; formerly called Institute of Dermatology

Organisation type and purpose: University department or institute.
Postgraduate medical school library.

Subject coverage: Dermatology, dermatopathology, some pathology.

Collection: As well as the latest books and journals, there is a small collection of historic books over 100 years old on skin and its diseases, including atlases. There is also a collection of moulages on display

Library catalogue: All or part available in-house

Access to staff: Contact by e-mail. Appointment necessary.
Hours: Mon to Fri, 0930 to 1730

Parent body: Guy's, King's and St Thomas' Schools of Medicine, Dentistry and Biomedical Sciences

ST KITTS TOURISM AUTHORITY

10 Kensington Court, London, W8 5DL

Tel: 020 7376 0881
Fax: 020 7937 6742
Website: www.stkitts-tourism.com

Enquiries to: Manager
Other contacts: Sales Representative

Founded: 1989; formerly called St Kitts and Nevis Department of Tourism

Organisation type and purpose: National government body.
Tourism promotion.

Subject coverage: Travel and tourism information for St Kitts and Nevis, also basic investment information.

Trade and statistical information: Statistical information on tourism arrivals to St Kitts and Nevis.
Relevant cost of a holiday (accommodation, meals and activities)

Publications: Printed

Publications list: Available in print

Access to staff: Contact by telephone
Hours: Mon to Fri, 0930 to 1730

Access to building: No prior appointment required

Parent body: St Kitts and Nevis Department of Tourism; PO Box 132, Basseterre, St Kitts, West Indies

ST LOYE'S FOUNDATION

Brittany House, New North Road, Exeter, Devon, EX4 4EP

Tel: 01392 255428
Fax: 01392 420889
E-mail: info@stloyes.ac.uk
Website: www.stloyesfoundation.org.uk

Founded: 1937

Organisation type and purpose: Registered charity (number 235434).
Training men and women with disabilities for employment and an independent future with hope and dignity.
To be the preferred choice for people seeking help to realise their potential for financial independence through work.

Subject coverage: Individually tailored training and personal development programmes to meet clients' needs and support for the whole person on their journey to sustainable, independent working and social inclusion. Includes a range of training programmes, personal development, support services, employability programmes, work experience, work placement, sustainable employment through 'in work' support.

Publications: Electronic and video
Order electronic and video publications from: website

Access to staff: Contact by letter, by telephone, by fax and by e-mail

Also at: Sefydliad St Loyes (Cardiff Office); 9 Coopers Yard, Curran Road, Cardiff, CF10 5NB; tel: 02920 003777; St Loye's Enterprises; Unit 64 Basepoint, Yeoford Way, Marsh Barton, Trading Estate, Exeter, EX2 8LB; tel: 01392 826120; St Loye's Foundation (Horticulture Dept); Westhill Garden Centre, Exmouth Road, Westhill, Ottery St Mary, EX11 1JS; tel: 01404 823684; St Loye's Foundation (Residential Accommodation); Hope Court, Prince of Wales Road, Exeter, EX4 4PN; tel: 01392 439769; St Loye's Foundation Personal Development Centre; No. 3 The Court Yard, New North Road, Exeter, EX4 4EP; tel: 01392 214955 / 274684

ST LUCIA TOURIST BOARD

Lower Ground Floor, 1 Collingham Gardens, London, SW5 OHW

Tel: 0870 900 7697
Fax: 0207 341 7001
Website: www.bandweb.co.uk/dolphin
Website: www.stlucia.org
Website: www.interknowledge.com/st-lucia
Website: www.stluciajazz.com
Website: www.ansechastanet.com

Enquiries to: Information Officer
Direct tel: 020 7431 3675
Direct e-mail: sonia.joseph@axissm.com
Other contacts: Sales Executive

Founded: 1986

Organisation type and purpose: National Tourist Office.

Subject coverage: General information on the island, hotels, dining out and places to visit. Incentive groups welcome.

Collection: Slide library, brochures, posters

Access to staff: Contact by letter, by telephone, by fax, by e-mail, in person and via website
Hours: Mon to Fri, 0930 to 1730

ST MARY'S UNIVERSITY COLLEGE (SMUC)

Learning Resources Centre, Waldegrave Road, Strawberry Hill, Twickenham, Middlesex, TW1 4SX

Tel: 020 8240 4097

Enquiries to: Customer Services Manager
Direct e-mail: enquiry@smuc.ac.uk

Founded: 1850

Organisation type and purpose: University library, university department or institute.

Subject coverage: Drama, education, English language and literature, film and television, geography, history, Irish studies, management and business studies, media arts, physical theatre, sociology, sport sciences and theology.

Library catalogue: All or part available online

Access to staff: Contact by letter, by telephone, by fax, by e-mail, in person and via website
Hours: 0815 to 2100, term time only

Funded by: HEFC

ST MARY'S UNIVERSITY COLLEGE LIBRARY (BELFAST)

191 Falls Road, Belfast, BT12 6FE

Tel: 028 9026 8237
Fax: 028 9033 3719
E-mail: library@smucb.ac.uk
Website: www.stmarys-belfast.ac.uk

continued overleaf

Enquiries to: Librarian
Direct e-mail: f.jones@smucb.ac.uk

Founded: 1900; formerly called St Mary's College Library (Belfast); incorporates the former St Joseph's College of Education

Organisation type and purpose: University library, university department or institute. University College of The Queen's University Belfast.
Education of teachers for the Catholic education system in Northern Ireland, postgraduate diploma for teachers for Irish medium education, masters degree in education, BA degree in liberal arts.

Subject coverage: Education; religious education; art; physical education; English; drama; history; geography; Celtic; music; mathematics; ICT; science; business studies; European studies; Irish medium; technology and design.

Library catalogue: All or part available online

Access to staff: Contact by letter, by telephone, by e-mail, in person and via website
Hours: Mon to Thu, 0830 to 2100; Fri, 0830 to 1700 (term time)
Special comments: Students from other universities may use the library for study purposes if there is sufficient space. They must show a current students union card and sign the visitors book.

Access to building: Through front entrance on the Falls Road, or the back entrance on Beechmount Avenue
Hours: Open 0830 to 2100 term time only

Access for disabled people: Lifts at front and rear of building

Constituent bodies: Queen's University; Queen's University Belfast, University Road, Belfast, BT7 1NN; tel: 028 9097 3760; e-mail: advisory@qub.ac.uk; website: http://www.qub.ac.uk

ST MUNGO'S COMMUNITY HOUSING ASSOCIATION (St Mungo's)

Formal name: St Mungo Community Housing Association Limited

Griffin House, 2nd Floor, 161 Hammersmith Road, London, W6 8BS

Tel: 020 8762 5500
Fax: 020 8762 5501
E-mail: info@mungos.org
Website: www.mungos.org

Founded: 1969

Organisation type and purpose: Housing association (number LH0279), industrial and provident society (number 20598R).
Providing hostels and care homes; offering long-term and intensive support for the single homeless.

Subject coverage: Rough sleeping, sub-groups of single homeless people (mental health problems, substance misuse, the elderly, women, multiple/complex needs), employment and training for single homeless people, services and facilities for homeless people in London.

Non-library collection catalogue: All or part available in-house

Publications: Printed
Order printed publications from: Marketing and Communications Department

Access to staff: Contact by letter, by telephone, by fax and by e-mail
Hours: Mon to Fri, 0900 to 1700

Access to building: No access other than to staff

ST PAUL'S CATHEDRAL LIBRARY

The Chapter House, St Paul's Churchyard, London, EC4M 8AE

Tel: 020 7246 8342
E-mail: library@stpaulscathedral.org.uk
Website: www.stpauls.co.uk

Enquiries to: Librarian

Organisation type and purpose: Private Cathedral library.

Subject coverage: 17th-century theology.

Collection: Bishop Sumner Collection of 19th-century tracts and pamphlets (6,348 items)
Sacheverell Controversy (233 items)

Access to staff: Contact by letter, by telephone and by e-mail. Appointment necessary.
Hours: Mon, Tue, 0900 to 1700; Fri, 1330 to 1700

The archive of Dean and Chapter is currently deposited at: Guildhall Library; Aldermanbury, London, EC2V 7HH; tel: 020 7332 1868; 020 7332 1870; e-mail: ask.lma@cityoflondon.gov.uk

ST PAUL'S SCHOOL

Formal name: Walker Library

Lonsdale Road, Barnes, London, SW13 9JT

Tel: 020 8746 5413
Fax: 020 8746 5353
E-mail: ama@stpaulsschool.org.uk

Enquiries to: Librarian
Direct tel: 020 8746 5433

Founded: 1509

Organisation type and purpose: School library.

Subject coverage: General subjects, particularly the history of the school and Old Paulines.

Collection: Rare Books Collection (in particular material on John Colet, William Lily, John Milton, G K Chesterton, Laurence Binyon and Edward Thomas)

Library catalogue: All or part available in-house

Publications: Printed

Access to staff: Contact by letter, by telephone, by fax and by e-mail. Appointment necessary. Letter of introduction required.
Hours: Mon to Fri, 0800 to 1600
Special comments: Limited access during school holidays.

ST VINCENT AND THE GRENADINES TOURIST OFFICE (SVGTO)

10 Kensington Court, London, W8 5DL

Tel: 020 7937 6570
Fax: 020 7937 3611
E-mail: svgtourismeurope@aol.com
Website: www.svgtourism.com

Enquiries to: Manager

Organisation type and purpose: National Tourist Office.

Subject coverage: General information on St. Vincent and the Grenadines, including various types of accommodation, places to go, things to see, sports activities available, climate and all the relevant information required when travelling to the islands.

Publications: Printed

Access to staff: Contact by letter, by telephone, by fax, by e-mail and in person. Appointment necessary.
Hours: Mon to Fri, 0930 to 1700

Access to building: No prior appointment required
Hours: Mon to Fri, 0900 to 1630

STAFF AND EDUCATIONAL DEVELOPMENT ASSOCIATION (SEDA)

Woburn House, 20–24 Tavistock Square, London, WC1H 9HF

Tel: 020 7380 6767
Fax: 020 7387 2655
E-mail: office@seda.ac.uk
Website: www.seda.ac.uk

Enquiries to: Administrator

Founded: 1993

Organisation type and purpose: Professional body (membership is by subscription).

Subject coverage: Staff and educational development.

Publications: Printed

Publications list: Available online and in print

Access to staff: Contact by letter, by telephone, by fax, by e-mail and via website
Hours: Mon to Fri, 0900 to 1700

Access to building: Prior appointment required

STAFFORD BOROUGH COUNCIL (SBC)

Civic Centre, Riverside, Stafford, ST16 3AQ

Tel: 01785 619000
Fax: 01785 619119
Website: www.staffordbc.gov.uk

Enquiries to: Chief Executive
Direct e-mail: chiefexecutive@staffordbc.gov.uk

Founded: 1974

Organisation type and purpose: Local government body.

Subject coverage: Local government services.

Access to staff: Contact by letter, by fax and by e-mail. Appointment necessary.
Hours: Mon to Fri, 0900 to 1700

Access to building: No prior appointment required

STAFFORDSHIRE ARCHAEOLOGICAL AND HISTORICAL SOCIETY (SAHS)

6 Lawson Close, Aldridge, Walsall, West Midlands, WS9 0RX

Tel: 01922 452230
E-mail: sahs@sahs.uk.net
Website: www.sahs.uk.net

Enquiries to: Membership Secretary
Direct e-mail: bettysemail@taltalk.net

Founded: 1959; formerly called Lichfield Archaeological and Historical Society (year of change 1961); formerly called Lichfield and South Staffordshire Archaeological and Historical Society (year of change 1995)

Organisation type and purpose: Learned society (membership is by subscription), present number of members: 203, registered charity (charity number 500586), suitable for ages: 16+, publishing house.
Published landscape survey of Shenstone Parish.

Subject coverage: Local history of Staffordshire, in particular South Staffordshire, archaeology of Staffordshire, concentrating on Lichfield and Tamworth areas.

Collection: Transactions of 17 similar societies in UK and abroad held at Lichfield Joint Record Office

Library catalogue: All or part available online, in-house and in print

Publications: Printed, and electronic and video
Order printed publications from: Membership Secretary
Order electronic and video publications from: Membership Secretary

Publications list: Available online and in print

Access to staff: Contact by letter, by telephone, by e-mail and via website
Hours: Any time up to 2200

Links with: Birmingham and District Local History Association; Council for British Archaeology; Friends of Staffordshire and Stoke-on-Trent Archives (FoSSA)

STAFFORDSHIRE LIBRARY AND INFORMATION SERVICES DEPARTMENT

Information Services, Shire Hall Library, Market Street, Stafford, ST16 2LQ

Tel: 01785 278585
Fax: 01785 278599
E-mail: stafford.library@staffordshire.gov.uk
Website: www.staffordshire.gov.uk

Enquiries to: Service Adviser: Knowledge Management, IT & Funding
Direct e-mail: lynne.stanley@staffordshire.gov.uk

Organisation type and purpose: Local government body, public library.

Subject coverage: Staffordshire, music, coal mining, brewing, industry, playsets.

Collection: British Standards
Government publications
National Joint Fiction Reserve KB-KEL, KIN-KZ, LAR-LED, LIA-LOD, MAM-MARN, MAY-MAZ

Library catalogue: All or part available online

Publications: Printed

Access to staff: Contact by letter, by telephone, by fax, by e-mail and via website
Hours: Mon to Fri, 0900 to 1700

Member of: European Information Association; Midlands On-line User Group; The Library Partnership West Midlands (TLPWM)

Parent body: Staffordshire County Council

STAFFORDSHIRE MOORLANDS DISTRICT COUNCIL (SMDC)

Moorlands House, Stockwell Street, Leek, Staffordshire, ST13 6HQ

Tel: 01538 483483
Fax: 01538 483474
Website: www.staffsmoorlands.gov.uk

Enquiries to: Chief Executive
Direct tel: 01538 483400
Direct fax: 01538 483423
Direct e-mail: simon.baker@staffsmoorlands.gov.uk
Other contacts: PR & Media Communications Officer for press contact.

Founded: 1974

Organisation type and purpose: Local government body.

Subject coverage: Local government services: council tax, national non-domestic rates, benefits, housing strategy, tourism, regeneration, industrial and commercial property management, markets, waste collection, street cleaning and public conveniences, waste minimisation and recycling, environmental health, local agenda 21, development control, building conservation, building control, engineering services, car parks, CCTV, leisure services, countryside management.

Collection: Permanent collection of artistic and historical artefacts from across Staffordshire Moorlands

Non-library collection catalogue: All or part available online and in print

Library catalogue: All or part available in print

Publications: Printed, and electronic and video
Order printed publications from: Public Relations & Media Communications Officer tel: 01538 483538, fax: 01538 483423, e-mail: charles.malkin@staffsmoorlands.gov.uk

Publications list: Available in print

Access to staff: Contact by letter, by telephone, by fax, by e-mail, in person and via website. Appointment necessary.
Hours: Mon to Thu, 0900 to 1715; Fri, 0900 to 1645

Access for disabled people: Parking provided, level entry, toilet facilities

Other addresses: Biddulph Councils Connect; Biddulph Town Hall, Biddulph, Stoke-on-Trent, Staffordshire, ST8 6AR; tel: 01782 297837; fax: 01782 297846; e-mail: biddulph.connect@staffsmoorlands.gov.uk; Cheadle Councils Connect; 15–17A High Street, Cheadle, Stoke-on-Trent, Staffordshire, ST10 1AA; tel: 01538 483860; fax: 01538 757495; e-mail: cheadle.connect@staffsmoorlands.gov.uk

STAFFORDSHIRE PARISH REGISTERS SOCIETY (SPRS)

82 Hilport Avenue, Newcastle under Lyme, Staffordshire, ST5 8QT

Tel: 01782 859078
E-mail: secretary@sprs.org.uk
Website: www.staffs.prs.freeserve.co.uk

Enquiries to: Honorary Secretary

Founded: 16 January 1900

Organisation type and purpose: Learned society (membership is by subscription), present number of members: over 150, registered charity (charity number 517646), suitable for ages: all, publishing house.

Subject coverage: The Society was formed to preserve the contents of the parochial registers in Staffordshire by transcribing and printing them. The long-term aim is to publish all the registers down to 1837 for the county of Staffordshire.

Publications: Printed, and microform publications
Order printed publications from: Honorary Secretary
Order microform publications from:
Birmingham & Midland Society for Genealogy & Heraldry
121 Rowood Drive, Damson Wood, Solihull, West Midlands, B92 9LJ, e-mail: mhbmsgh@aol.com

Publications list: Available online and in print

Access to staff: Contact by letter and by e-mail

STAFFORDSHIRE RECORD OFFICE

Eastgate Street, Stafford, ST16 2LZ

Tel: 01785 278379; minicom no. 01785 278376
Fax: 01785 278384
E-mail: staffordshire.record.office@staffordshire.gov.uk
Website: www.staffordshire.gov.uk/archives

Enquiries to: Head of Archive Services

Founded: 1947

Organisation type and purpose: Local government body.
To locate, collect and preserve archive collections relating to past life and activity in the county of Staffordshire and to make these collections available to the public.

Subject coverage: Archives, local history.

Collection: Major archive collections relating to the History of Staffordshire

Non-library collection catalogue: All or part available online

continued overleaf

Publications: Printed, and microform publications

Publications list: Available online and in print

Access to staff: Contact by letter, by telephone, by fax, by e-mail and in person
Hours: Mon, Tue, Thu, 0900 to 1700; Wed, 0900 to 2000; Fri, 0930 to 1630; Sat, 0900 to 1300

Access to building: Prior appointment required
Special comments: Reader's ticket required.

Access for disabled people: Parking provided, ramped entry, access to all public areas, toilet facilities

Also at: Lichfield Record Office; The Friary, Lichfield, WS13 6QG; tel: 01543 510720; e-mail: lichfield.record.office@staffordshire.gov.uk; Stoke on Trent City Archives; City Central Library, Bethesda Street, Hanley, Stoke-on-Trent, Staffordshire; tel: 01782 238420; e-mail: stoke.archives@stoke.gov.uk

STAFFORDSHIRE RECORD SOCIETY

William Salt Library, Eastgate Street, Stafford, ST16 2LZ

E-mail: matthew.blake@btinternet.com

Enquiries to: Honorary Secretary

Founded: 1879

Organisation type and purpose: Learned society (membership is by subscription), present number of members: 300, registered charity.
Publication of historical records relating to the county of Staffordshire.

Subject coverage: Archives, records and history of Staffordshire.

Publications: Printed, and microform publications
Order microform publications from: Chadwyck-Healey, The Quorum, Barnwell Road, Cambridge, CB5 8SW

Access to staff: Contact by letter and by e-mail

STAFFORDSHIRE UNIVERSITY – THOMPSON LIBRARY

Information Services, Thompson Library, College Road, Stoke-on-Trent, Staffordshire, ST4 2XS

Tel: 01782 294369
Fax: 01782 295799
E-mail: d.j.parkes@staffs.ac.uk
Website: www.staffs.ac.uk

Organisation type and purpose: University library, university department or institute.

Subject coverage: Art, law, sciences, social sciences, business, humanities, design, ceramics, engineering, electrical engineering, computing, health

Collection: Arts Archive
Badminton Collection (Badminton Library of Sports and Pastimes)
Dorothy Thompson Collection (Chartism 1800-)
Eysenck Collection (H J Eysenck)
Iris Strange Collection (Campaign for pensions for British war widows, mainly WWII)
Mining Archive (worldwide)
ROAPE (Review of African Studies) Collection
Solon Collection (literature on ceramics)
Staffordshire Film Archive (history of the county and key events)
Victoria Theatre Archive

Non-library collection catalogue: All or part available online

Library catalogue: All or part available online

Access to staff: Contact by letter, by telephone, by e-mail, in person and via website. Non-members charged.
Hours: Mon to Fri, 0900 to 1700

Access to building: Open
Special comments: For 24/7 From 1700 and at weekends ID required

Access for disabled people: yes
Hours: as above

STAG OWNERS CLUB (SOC)

c/o The Membership Secretary, The Old Rectory, Aslacton, Norfolk, NR15 2JN

Tel: 01379 677735
Fax: 01379 677363
E-mail: membership@stag.org.uk
Website: www.stag.org.uk

Enquiries to: Membership Secretary

Founded: 1979

Organisation type and purpose: Membership association (membership is by subscription), present number of members: 5,000, voluntary organisation.
To further interest in the Triumph Stag motor car.

Subject coverage: The Triumph Stag.

Publications: Printed

Access to staff: Contact by letter, by telephone, by e-mail and via website
Hours: Mon to Fri, 0900 to 1700

STAGE MANAGEMENT ASSOCIATION (SMA)

89 Borough High Street, London, SE1 1NL

Tel: 020 7403 7999
E-mail: admin@stagemanagementassociation.co.uk
Website: www.stagemanagementassociation.co.uk

Enquiries to: Administrator

Founded: 1954

Organisation type and purpose: National organisation, professional body (membership is by application), present number of members: 740, representative trade association.
Theatre and television stage management.

Subject coverage: Supporting, representing and promoting stage management in the UK.

Information services: Bi-monthly magazine for members, publications, website members' area resources.

Education services: Short training courses open to members and non-members.

Publications: Printed
Order printed publications from: website: http://www.stagemanagementassociation.co.uk

Publications list: Available online and in print

Access to staff: Contact by letter, by telephone, by e-mail and via website. Appointment necessary.
Hours: Mon to Fri, 1000 to 1600

Access to building: No access other than to staff

In constant correspondence with the: Stage Managers' Association; USA; Theatrical Management Association (TMA)

Links with: Association of British Theatre Technicians (ABTT); British Actors Equity Association; Most theatre organisations; Theatres Trust

Member organisation of: Independent Theatre Council (ITC)

STAINED GLASS GUILD LTD

4 Grosvenor Gardens, Kingston-Upon-Thames, KT2 5BE

Tel: 020 8274 1562
E-mail: info@stainedglassguild.co.uk
Website: www.stainedglassguild.co.uk

Founded: 1977

Organisation type and purpose: The role of the 'guild' is advisory; no charge is made for information on all technical or artistic problems relating to domestic glass from the Victorian/Edwardian period right through to the thirties and Art Deco.

Subject coverage: Stained glass work for private householders, architects, builders, London boroughs and the church.

Access to staff: Contact by letter, by telephone, by e-mail and in person. Appointment necessary.
Special comments: Visitors by appointment only.

Links with: Stained Glass House (working studio); at the same address; e-mail: stainedglass@mail.com

STANDARD VANGUARD OWNERS CLUB

7 Priory Close, Wilton, Salisbury, Wiltshire, SP2 0LD

Tel: 01722 503101

Enquiries to: Secretary

Founded: 1989

Organisation type and purpose: Membership association (membership is by subscription).

Subject coverage: Standard Vanguard cars, preservation and restoration.

Access to staff: Contact by letter and by telephone. Appointment necessary.
Hours: 1000 to 2200, any day

STANDARDS AND TESTING AGENCY (STA)

53–55 Butts Road, Earlsdon Park, Coventry, CV1 3BH

Tel: 0370 000 2288
E-mail: assessments@education.gov.uk
Website: www.education.gov.uk/aboutdfe/armslengthbodies/b00198511/sta

Founded: 2011

Organisation type and purpose: Executive agency of the Department for Education.

Subject coverage: Responsible for the development and delivery of all statutory educational assessments from early years to the end of Key Stage 3 (usually age 14).

Information services: National curriculum assessments helpline: 0300 303 3013 (Mon to Fri, 0800 to 1800)

Order printed publications from: National curriculum assessments orderline: 0300 303 3015

Access to staff: Contact by letter, by telephone, by e-mail and via website

Parent body: Department for Education; Sanctuary Buildings, Great Smith Street, London, SW1P 3BT; tel: 020 7925 5000

Regulated by: Office of Qualifications and Examinations Regulation (Ofqual)

STANDING COMMITTEE ON OFFICIAL PUBLICATIONS (SCOOP)

ISG SCOOP, c/o CILIP, 7 Ridgmount Street, London, WC1E 7AE

Tel: 020 7255 0500
Fax: 020 7255 0501
E-mail: scoop@pjdchapman.co.uk
Website: www.cilip.org.uk/get-involved/special-interest-groups/information-services/scoop/pages/default.aspx
Website: https://sites.google.com/site/referplus/Home/scoop

Enquiries to: Secretary
Direct tel: 0121 507 1857
Direct e-mail: scoop@pjdchapman.co.uk
Other contacts: Chair

Founded: 1971

Organisation type and purpose:
Professional body.
To improve access to UK official information.

Subject coverage: Official publications and information in the UK.

Publications: Printed
Order printed publications from: Secretary, SCOOP, c/o 4 Nursery Drive, Handsworth, Birmingham, B20 2SW; e-mail: scoop@pjdchapman.co.uk

Publications list: Available in print

Access to staff: Contact by letter, by telephone and by e-mail
Hours: Mon to Fri, 0900 to 1700

Parent body: CILIP Information Services Group; 7 Ridgmount Street, London, WC1E 7AE; tel: 020 7255 0500; fax: 020 7255 0501; e-mail: ISGHonSecretary@cilip.org.uk; website: http://www.cilip.org.uk/get-involved/special-interest-groups/information-services/pages/default.aspx

STANDING CONFERENCE ON LIBRARY MATERIALS ON AFRICA (SCOLMA)

c/o Commonwealth Secretariat, Marlborough House, Pall Mall, London, SW1Y 5HX

Tel: 020 7747 6253
Fax: 020 7747 6168
E-mail: scolma@hotmail.com
Website: www.lse.ac.uk/library/scolma

Enquiries to: Chairman

Founded: 1962

Organisation type and purpose: Learned society, registered charity (charity number 325086).
African studies.

Subject coverage: Location of materials relating to African studies, for the following countries and areas: Algeria, Angola, Ascension Island, Benin, Botswana, Burkina Faso, Burundi, Cameroon, Canary Islands, Cape Verde Islands, Central Africa, Chad, Congo (Brazzaville), Democratic Republic of Congo, Djibouti, Ethiopia, Gabon, Gambia, Ghana, Guinea, Guinea-Bissau, Ivory Coast, Kenya, Lesotho, Liberia, Libya, Madagascar, Madeira, Malawi, Mali, Mauritania, Mauritius, Morocco, Mozambique, Namibia, Niger, Nigeria, Principe, Rwanda, St Helena, St Tomé, Senegal, Seychelles, Sierra Leone, Somalia, South Africa, Sudan, Swaziland, Tanzania, Togo, Tristan da Cunha, Tunisia, Uganda, Western Sahara, Zimbabwe.

Publications list: Available online and in print

Access to staff: Contact by letter, by telephone, by e-mail and in person
Hours: Mon to Fri, 0900 to 1700

STAR PUBLISHERS DISTRIBUTORS

112 Whitfield Street, London, W1T 5EE

Tel: 020 7380 0622
Fax: 020 7419 9169
E-mail: indbooks@aol.com

Organisation type and purpose: Bookshop.

Subject coverage: A bookshop exclusively devoted to Indian books. Latest Indian publications (in English, Hindi, Urdu and Punjabi) on art, architecture, fine arts (music, dance, films etc), travel, history, politics, social sciences, business and economics, women's studies, religion and philosophy, reference and encyclopaedias, language and literature, general subjects, and books for children.

Publications: Printed

Parent body: Star Publications; New Delhi, India

STAR, STARLING, STUART & BRITON REGISTER

New Wood Lodge, 2A Hyperion Road, Stourton, Stourbridge, West Midlands, DY7 6SB

Tel: 01384 374329
Website: www.localhistory.scit.wlv.ac.uk/Museum/Transport/Cars/staregister/starreg01.htm

Enquiries to: Registrar

Founded: 1964

Organisation type and purpose:
Membership association (membership is by election or invitation), present number of members: 200.
To promote the restoration and preservation of vehicles manufactured by the Star and Briton Companies of Wolverhampton, England.

Subject coverage: Historical and technical information service on Star, Starling, Stuart and Briton cars and commercial vehicles of Wolverhampton.

Collection: Catalogues, drawings, instructional handbooks and original order specifications on vehicles
Magazine and book references to companies and products, 1869 to 1932

Trade and statistical information: Order books and statistical data on production between 1927 and 1932.
Data prior to 1927 being compiled

Publications: Printed

Access to staff: Contact by letter, by telephone and in person
Hours: Mon to Fri, 0900 to 1700

STATE OF SOUTH AUSTRALIA

The Australia Centre, Strand, London, WC2B 4LG

Tel: 020 7836 3455
Fax: 020 7887 5332
E-mail: enquiries@australianbusiness.co.uk

Enquiries to: Agent General
Direct tel: 020 7887 5124

Founded: 1858

Organisation type and purpose:
Government trade and investment office.

Publications list: Available in print

Access to staff: Contact by letter, by telephone, by fax and by e-mail
Hours: Mon to Fri, 0900 to 1700

Access for disabled people: Level entry, toilet facilities

STATIONERS' AND NEWSPAPER MAKERS' COMPANY

Stationers' Hall, Ave Maria Lane, London, EC4M 7DD

Tel: 020 7248 2934
Fax: 020 7489 1975
E-mail: admin@stationers.org
Website: www.stationers.org

Enquiries to: The Clerk

Founded: 1403

Organisation type and purpose:
Membership association (membership is by election or invitation).
City of London Livery Company.

Collection: Company Archives (1554 to present)

Access to staff: Contact by letter, by telephone, by fax and by e-mail

STATIONERY OFFICE, THE (TSO)

St Crispins, Duke Street, Norwich, NR3 1PD

Tel: 01603 622211
E-mail: customer.services@tso.co.uk
Website: www.clicktso.com
Website: www.thestationeryoffice.com

Enquiries to: Press Officer
Direct tel: 01603 622211
Other contacts: Deputy Manager

Founded: privatised 1996

Organisation type and purpose: National organisation, publishing house.
Retail bookshops, information provider.

Subject coverage: Official and regulatory information.

Collection: The Stationery Office publications
Ordnance Survey
HSE publications
British Standards Distributor including Print on Demand Service

Publications: Printed

Publications list: Available online

Access to staff: Contact by letter, by telephone, by fax, by e-mail, in person and via website
Hours: Mon, Wed, Thu, Fri, 0900 to 1730; Tue, 0930 to 1730; Sat, 1000 to 1500

Access to building: No prior appointment required

Access for disabled people: Level entry

Other addresses: TSO Bookshop; 9–21 Princess Street, Manchester, M60 8AS; tel: 0161 834 7201; TSO Bookshop; 18–19 High Street, Cardiff, CF10 1PT; tel: 029 2039 5548

Other offices: TSO Birmingham; 68–69 Bull Street, Birmingham, B4 6AD; tel: 0121 236 9696; TSO Head Office; St Crispins, Duke Street, Norwich; tel: 0870 600 5522; TSO Head Office; 51 Nine Elms Lane, London, SW8 5DR; tel: 0870 600 5522; TSO Northern Ireland; 16 Arthur Street, Belfast, BT1 4GD; tel: 028 9023 8451; TSO Scotland; 71 Lothian Road, Edinburgh, EH3 9AZ; tel: 0870 606 5566

STATISTICAL SERVICES CENTRE (SSC)

University of Reading, Harry Pitt Building, PO Box 240, Reading, Berkshire, RG6 6FN

Tel: 0118 378 8025
Fax: 0118 975 3169
E-mail: l.e.turner@reading.ac.uk
Website: www.reading.ac.uk/ssc/

Enquiries to: Executive Assistant

Founded: 1982

Organisation type and purpose: Training organisation, consultancy.

Subject coverage: Statistical consultancy, statistical training/courses, statistical computing, database management systems.

Publications: Electronic and video

Publications list: Available online

Access to staff: Contact by letter, by telephone, by fax, by e-mail and via website. Appointment necessary. All charged.
Hours: Mon to Fri, 0900 to 1700

Access for disabled people: Access to all public areas, toilet facilities
Special comments: Lift

Parent body: University of Reading

STATUTE LAW SOCIETY (SLS)

21 Goodwyns Vale, London, N10 2HA

Tel: 020 8883 1700
Fax: 020 8883 7976
E-mail: statutelaw@aol.com
Website: www.statutelawsociety.org

Enquiries to: Administrator

Founded: 1968

Organisation type and purpose: Learned society, registered charity (charity number 261226).

Subject coverage: Statute law and legislation.

Publications: Printed

Access to staff: Contact by letter, by telephone, by e-mail and via website
Hours: Mon to Fri, 0900 to 1700

STAUNTON SOCIETY, THE

98 Cole Park, Twickenham, Middlesex, TW1 1JA

Tel: 020 8744 2868
Fax: 020 8742 2311

Enquiries to: General Secretary

Founded: 1993

Organisation type and purpose: Learned society, membership association (membership is by election or invitation), present number of members: 80.
To further the importance of chess as an educational sport; to provide support and illumination to young players; to make public the achievements of past national figures such as Howard Staunton.

Subject coverage: The life and works of Howard Staunton (1810–1874), chess player, editor of Shakespeare. Editor of The Great Schools of England, education in the endowed schools. Chess play, historical and contemporary. British chess players 19th and 20th century and foreign nationals who have played here over time.

Collection: Limited number of Staunton books. Memorabilia

Publications: Printed

Access to staff: Contact by letter, by telephone and by fax
Hours: Sat & Sun inclusive

STEAM BOAT ASSOCIATION OF GREAT BRITAIN (SBA)

Avoca Cottage, School Lane, Niton, Isle of Wight, PO38 2BP

Tel: 01983 730664
Website: www.steamboat.org.uk

Enquiries to: Honorary Secretary

Founded: 1972

Organisation type and purpose: Membership association (membership is by subscription), present number of members: over 1,000.
A society to foster and encourage steamboating and building, development, preservation and restoration of steam boats and steam machinery.

Subject coverage: Small steam boats and steam launches; other steam machinery.

Collection: Archive collection

Publications: Printed

Access to staff: Contact by letter, by telephone and by e-mail
Hours: Any reasonable time.
Special comments: Staff are volunteers, so not always available.

STEEL CONSTRUCTION INSTITUTE (SCI)

Silwood Park, Buckhurst Road, Ascot, Berkshire, SL5 7QN

Tel: 01344 636525
Fax: 01344 636570
E-mail: library@steel-sci.com
Website: www.steel-sci.com

Enquiries to: Librarian

Founded: 1986

Organisation type and purpose: Research organisation.

Subject coverage: Use of steel in construction onshore and offshore; steel properties, related standards and codes of practice (UK, European and American); steel buildings, bridges, tunnels, offshore platforms.

Publications: Printed

Publications list: Available online

Access to staff: Contact by letter, by telephone, by fax, by e-mail and via website. Appointment necessary. Access for members only. Non-members charged.
Hours: Mon to Fri, 0900 to 1600

STEEL WINDOW ASSOCIATION (SWA)

The Building Centre, 26 Store Street, London, WC1E 7BT

Tel: 020 7637 3571
Fax: 020 7637 3572
E-mail: info@steel-window-association.co.uk
Website: www.steel-window-association.co.uk

Enquiries to: Director
Direct e-mail: dns@windows.fsworld.co.uk

Founded: 1967

Organisation type and purpose: Trade association (membership is by subscription), present number of members: 25.

Subject coverage: Steel window manufacture, supply and installation, technical advice and information.

Publications: Printed

Access to staff: Contact by letter, by telephone, by fax, by e-mail, in person and

via website. Appointment necessary.
Hours: Mon to Fri, 0900 to 1700

STEPHENSON COLLEGE, COALVILLE

Thornborough Road, Coalville, Leicestershire, LE67 3TN

Tel: 01530 836136
Fax: 01530 814253
E-mail: deniser@stephensoncoll.ac.uk
Website: www.stephensoncoll.ac.uk

Enquiries to: Library and Learning Resources Manager
Direct tel: 01530 836136 ext. 181

History of institution: formerly called Coalville Technical College (year of change 1997)

Organisation type and purpose: Suitable for ages: 16+, training organisation.
Further education establishment.

Subject coverage: Business and management; motor vehicle technology; engineering; access to higher education; construction; information technology; health and social care; hair and beauty; early years; uniform services; travel and tourism; teacher training.

Non-library collection catalogue: All or part available in-house

Library catalogue: All or part available in-house

Publications: Printed

Access to staff: Contact by letter, by telephone, by fax, by e-mail and via website. Appointment necessary. Access for members only. Letter of introduction required.
Hours: Mon to Thu, 0830 to 2100; Fri, 0830 to 1630

Access for disabled people: Parking provided, access to all public areas

STERILISED SUTURE MANUFACTURERS ASSOCIATION (SSMA)

Ethicon Limited, PO Box 408, Bankhead Avenue, Edinburgh, EH11 4HE

Tel: 0131 453 5555
Fax: 0131 453 6011

Enquiries to: Honorary Secretary
Other contacts: Chairman of the Technical Committee for matters of a technical nature or if the Hon Secretary is unavailable.

Organisation type and purpose: Trade association (membership is by qualification, election or invitation), present number of members: 3, voluntary organisation.

Subject coverage: Production and supply of surgical sutures.

Access to staff: Contact by letter, by telephone and by fax
Hours: Mon to Fri, 0900 to 1700

Affiliated to: European Association of the Surgical Suture Industry (EASSI); tel: 49 69 2556 1338; fax: 49 69 2556 1471

STEVENAGE BOROUGH COUNCIL (SBC)

Daneshill House, Danestrete, Stevenage, Hertfordshire, SG1 1HN

Tel: 01438 242242
Fax: 01438 242566
Website: www.stevenage.gov.uk

Enquiries to: Public Relations Manager

Organisation type and purpose: Local government body.

Subject coverage: Local government services.

STEVENAGE BUSINESS INITIATIVE (SBI)

Business & Technology Centre, Bessemer Drive, Stevenage, Hertfordshire, SG1 2DX

Tel: 0845 078 0600
Fax: 01438 310001
E-mail: admin@sbi-herts.co.uk
Website: www.sbi-herts.co.uk

Enquiries to: Information Officer

Founded: 1983

Organisation type and purpose: Service industry.
Enterprise agency, free start-up business advice service.

Subject coverage: Business advice.

Access to staff: Contact by letter, by telephone, by fax, by e-mail, in person and via website. Appointment necessary.
Hours: Mon to Thu, 0830 to 1730; Fri, 0830 to 1700

STEWART SOCIETY

53 George Street, Edinburgh, EH2 2HT

Tel: 0131 220 4512
Fax: 0131 220 4512
E-mail: info@stewartsociety.org
Website: www.stewartsociety.org

Enquiries to: Secretary

Founded: 1899

Organisation type and purpose: International organisation, learned society (membership is by subscription), present number of members: 614, voluntary organisation, registered charity (charity number SC 000692), museum, research organisation.

Subject coverage: Stewart and general Scottish history, Stewart genealogy.

Collection: Family papers, old books and family trees pertaining to the Stewarts and Stuarts, members' library

Non-library collection catalogue: All or part available in-house

Library catalogue: All or part available in-house

Publications: Printed

Publications list: Available in print

Access to staff: Contact by letter, by telephone, by fax, by e-mail, in person and via website. Appointment necessary.
Hours: Mon to Fri, 1000 to 1230

STFC DARESBURY LABORATORY (STFC)

Formal name: Science and Technology Facilities Council

Daresbury Science and Innovation Campus, Keckwick Lane, Daresbury, Warrington, Cheshire, WA4 4AD

Tel: 01925 603397
Fax: 01925 603779
E-mail: librarydl@stfc.ac.uk
Website: www.stfc.ac.uk/e-Science/services/22463.aspx

Enquiries to: Library Services Development Manager

Organisation type and purpose: UK Research Council

Subject coverage: Atomic, molecular and condensed matter physics, synchrotron radiation, nuclear structure, accelerator physics, computing and computational science, biological sciences, materials science, engineering.

Library catalogue: All or part available online

Publications: Printed

Access to staff: Contact by letter, by telephone, by fax, by e-mail and in person. Appointment necessary.
Hours: Mon to Fri, 0900 to 1700

Access to building: By appointment only

STILLBIRTH AND NEONATAL DEATH CHARITY (SANDS)

28 Portland Place, London, W1B 1LY

Tel: 020 7436 7940
Fax: 020 7436 3715
E-mail: support@uk-sands.org
Website: www.uk-sands.org

Enquiries to: Administrator
Direct e-mail: katie.duff@uk-sands.org

Founded: 1981

Organisation type and purpose: Membership association (membership is by subscription), present number of members: 970, voluntary organisation, registered charity (charity number 299679).
To support parents when their baby dies at or soon after birth. Training for professionals.

Subject coverage: Death of a baby at or soon after birth (stillbirth, neonatal death), pregnancy losses. Incidence of stillbirth and neonatal death in the UK. Causes of stillbirth and neonatal death. Support and care of families affected, funerals for infants.

Collection: Wide collection on stillbirth, neonatal loss and pregnancy losses

Trade and statistical information: UK stillbirth and neonatal mortality statistics

Publications: Printed

Publications list: Available online and in print

Access to staff: Contact by letter, by telephone, by fax, by e-mail and via website
Hours: Mon to Fri, 0930 to 1700
Special comments: No disabled access.

Access to building: Prior appointment required

STILTON CHEESE MAKERS' ASSOCIATION (SCMA)

PO Box 384A, Surbiton, Surrey, KT5 9YL

Tel: 020 8255 1334
Fax: 020 8255 1335
E-mail: stilton@stiltoncheese.com
Website: www.stiltoncheese.com

Enquiries to: Stilton Information Bureau
Direct tel: 0161 923 4994
Direct fax: 0161 923 4760
Direct e-mail: enquiries@stiltoncheese.com

Founded: 1936

Organisation type and purpose: Trade association (membership is by qualification), present number of members: 5, manufacturing industry.
Promotion of Stilton cheese, protection of Stilton certification trade marks.

Subject coverage: Stilton cheese: all matters including trade mark, manufacture, methods of storing and serving, sources of supply.

Publications: Printed
Order printed publications from: Stilton Information Bureau, c/o BRAZEN, Brazen House, Great Ancoats Street, Manchester, M4 5AJ

Access to staff: Contact by letter, by telephone and by e-mail
Hours: Mon to Fri, 0900 to 1700

Links with: Dairy UK; 93 Baker Street, London, W1U 6RL; tel: 020 7486 7244; fax: 020 7487 4734

STIRLING CENTRE FOR INTERNATIONAL PUBLISHING AND COMMUNICATION

University of Stirling, Stirling, FK9 4LA

Tel: 01786 467510
Fax: 01786 466210
E-mail: publishing@stir.ac.uk
Website: www.publishing.stir.ac.uk
Website: www.stir.ac.uk
Website: www.stir.ac.uk/schools/arts-and-humanities/

Enquiries to: Director and Professor in Publishing Studies
Other contacts: Postgraduate Secretary (for general course enquiries)

Founded: 1982; formerly called Centre for Publishing Studies

Organisation type and purpose: University department or institute, training organisation, consultancy, research organisation, publishing house.
Research and teaching in publishing studies (mainly contemporary) on an international basis.

Subject coverage: Publishing industry, digital publishing, books and magazines, Scottish publishing industry, textual and scholarly editing, authorship and reading, publishing in Africa, China, Europe, Malaysia, developmental issues.

Library catalogue: All or part available online

Publications: Printed

Access to staff: Contact by letter, by telephone, by fax, by e-mail and via website
Hours: Mon to Fri, 0900 to 1700

Co-operative links with similar bodies in: North America, Far East, Australia, Europe

Member organisation of: Association for Publishing Education; website: http://www.publishingeducation.org/
International Association for Publishing Education; Publishing Scotland; website: http://www.publishingscotland.co.uk/

STIRLING COUNCIL ARCHIVE SERVICE (SCAS)

5 Borrowmeadow Road, Springkerse Industrial Estate, Stirling, FK7 7UW

Tel: 01786 450745
E-mail: archive@stirling.gov.uk
Website: www.stirling.gov.uk/services/community-life-and-leisure/libraries-and-archives/archives/archives-general-information

Enquiries to: Council Archivist

Founded: 1996

Organisation type and purpose: Local government body.
Archive.

Subject coverage: Primary sources relating to the area administered by Stirling Council.

Non-library collection catalogue: All or part available in-house and in print

Access to staff: Contact by letter, by telephone, by e-mail, in person and via website
Hours: Mon to Thu, 0900 to 1630

Access for disabled people: Level entry

STIRLING COUNCIL LIBRARIES

Administrative Headquarters, Borrowmeadow Road, Springkerse Industrial Estate, Stirling, FK7 7TN

Tel: 01786 432383
Fax: 01786 432395
E-mail: libraryheadquarters@stirling.gov.uk
Website: www.stirling.gov.uk

Enquiries to: Libraries and Archives Manager
Direct tel: 01786 443398

Founded: 1975

Organisation type and purpose: Local government body, public library.

Subject coverage: Local history of the Stirling District (Stirling County to 1975); general.

Collection: Local and Scottish History Collections
Stirling Journal and Advertiser, local newspaper from 1820–1970
Stirling Observer local newspaper from June 1970
Thomson Collection (theology)

Library catalogue: All or part available online and in-house

Publications list: Available online and in print

Access to staff: Contact by letter, by telephone and by e-mail
Hours: Mon to Fri, 0900 to 1700

Access to building: No prior appointment required

Access for disabled people: Parking provided, ramped entry, access to all public areas

STOCKPORT COLLEGE

Wellington Road South, Stockport, Cheshire, SK1 3UQ

Tel: 0161 958 3471
Fax: 0161 958 3469
E-mail: enquiries@stockport.ac.uk
Website: www.stockport.ac.uk

Enquiries to: Learning Centre Circulation and Operations Manager

Organisation type and purpose: College of further and higher education. Takes students aged 14–16 and 16+.

Subject coverage: Art and design; applied social sciences; building and civil engineering; electrical, mechanical and production engineering; general education; management and business studies; science; computing; nursing; travel and tourism; catering.

Collection: College archives
Video recordings (2500) and DVDs

Non-library collection catalogue: All or part available online

Library catalogue: All or part available online

Access to staff: Contact in person
Hours: Term time: Mon to Thu, 0830 to 2000; Fri, 0830 to 1700
Vacations: Mon to Fri, 0900 to 1700
Special comments: Reference only for non-members (printed materials only).

Access to building: *Special comments:* Please report to main reception as a visitor

Access for disabled people: Access to all public areas

STOCKPORT LOCAL HERITAGE LIBRARY

Central Library, Wellington Road South, Stockport, Cheshire, SK1 3RS

Tel: 0161 474 4530; 0161 474 4541 (minicom)
Fax: 0161 474 4486
E-mail: localheritagelibrary@stockport.gov.uk

Enquiries to: Senior Librarian; Heritage & Archives

Organisation type and purpose: Local government body, public library.

Subject coverage: Stockport archives, family history, local history.

Collection: Christy & Co (hat manufacturers) records
Stockport Sunday School records

Non-library collection catalogue: All or part available in-house and in print

Library catalogue: All or part available online and in-house

Access to staff: Contact by letter, by telephone, by fax, by e-mail and in person. Appointment necessary.

Hours: Mon, 1000 to 2000; Tue, 0900 to 2000; Wed, Thu, 0900 to 1700; Fri, 0900 to 2000; Sat, 0900 to 1600
Special comments: Records held in outstore require advance notice.

Access for disabled people: Lift

STOCKSCOTLAND

The Croft Studio, Croft Roy, Crammon Brae, Tain, Ross-shire, IV19 1JG

Tel: 01862 892298
Fax: 01862 892298
E-mail: info@stockscotland.com
Website: www.stockscotland.com

Enquiries to: Proprietor

Founded: 1992

Organisation type and purpose: Photographic Library.

Subject coverage: Contemporary images of the highlands and islands of Scotland. Photographs available for landscape, tourism, industry, agriculture, transport, fisheries etc.

Library catalogue: All or part available online

Publications: Printed, and electronic and video

Access to staff: Contact by letter, by telephone, by fax, by e-mail and via website. Appointment necessary. All charged.
Hours: Mon to Fri, 0900 to 1700

STOCKTON-ON-TEES BOROUGH COUNCIL

PO Box 11, Municipal Buildings, Church Road, Stockton-on-Tees, Cleveland, TS18 1LD

Tel: 01642 393939
Fax: 01642 393092
Website: www.stockton.gov.uk

Enquiries to: Personnel and Communications Officer

Organisation type and purpose: Local government body.

Subject coverage: Stockton-on-Tees borough services and amenities.

Access to staff: Contact by letter, by telephone, by fax, by e-mail and in person
Hours: Mon to Fri, 0900 to 1700

STOKE-ON-TRENT CLASSIC CAR CLUB

19 Nashe Drive, Blurton, Stoke-on-Trent, Staffordshire, ST3 2HD

Tel: 01782 323167
E-mail: malcolm@classiccarclub.freeserve.co.uk

Enquiries to: Secretary
Other contacts: Chairman

Founded: 2000

Access to staff: Contact by letter and by telephone
Hours: Mon to Fri, 0900 to 1700

STOKE-ON-TRENT COLLEGE

Cauldon Campus, Stoke Road, Shelton, Stoke-on-Trent, Staffordshire, ST4 2DG

Tel: 01782 208208
Fax: 01782 603504
Website: www.stokecoll.ac.uk

Enquiries to: Learning Resources Manager
Other contacts: Cataloguer

Founded: 1947

Organisation type and purpose: Suitable for ages: 16+.
College of further and higher education.

Subject coverage: Building construction, management, office skills, social sciences, science, catering, hairdressing, beauty, computer-aided engineering.

Collection: Construction and Property Information Centre

Library catalogue: All or part available online

Publications: Printed

Access to staff: Contact by letter, by telephone, by fax, by e-mail and in person
Hours: Term time: Mon to Thu, 0830 to 2100; Fri, 0830 to 1800; Sat, 0900 to 1300

Access to building: No access other than to staff

Access for disabled people: Parking provided, ramped entry, level entry, access to all public areas, toilet facilities

Associated with: Forum for Information Resources in Staffordshire (FIRST)

Includes the: Construction and Property Information Centre

STOKE-ON-TRENT LIBRARIES AND ARCHIVES

City Central Library, Bethesda Street, Hanley, Stoke-on-Trent, Staffordshire, ST1 3RS

Tel: 01782 238432
Fax: 01782 238434
E-mail: central.library@stoke.gov.uk
Website: stoke.gov.uk

Enquiries to: Librarian

Organisation type and purpose: Public library.

Subject coverage: General information; ceramics; local history and archives, especially Stoke-on-Trent and Staffordshire.

Collection: Ceramics
Local history collection and archives

Non-library collection catalogue: All or part available online

Library catalogue: All or part available online

Access to staff: Contact by letter, by telephone, by fax, by e-mail and in person
Hours: Mon to Thu, 0900 to 1800; Fri, 0900 to 1700; Sat, 1000 to 1400
Special comments: Archives – closed Mon and Tue; Wed open 1000 to 1800; Thur, Fri, Sat open 1000 to 1400

Parent body: Stoke-on-Trent Libraries and Archives; City Central Library, Bethesda Street, Hanley, Stoke-on-Trent, ST1 3RS; tel: 01782 238455; fax: 01782 238499; e-mail: central.library@.stoke.gov.uk

STOKE-ON-TRENT TOURISM

Hanley Town Hall, Albion Street, Stoke-on-Trent City Centre, ST1 1XP

Tel: 01782 232817
Fax: 01782 237717
E-mail: tourism@stoke.gov.uk
Website: www.visitstoke.co.uk

Enquiries to: Visitor Economy Manager

Organisation type and purpose: Local government body.

Subject coverage: Tourism in the Stoke-on-Trent area and The Potteries.

Access to staff: Contact by letter
Hours: Mon to Fri, 0900 to 1700

STORAGE AND HANDLING EQUIPMENT DISTRIBUTORS' ASSOCIATION (SHEDA)

Heathcote House, 136 Hagley Road, Edgbaston, Birmingham, B16 9PN

Tel: 0121 454 4141
Fax: 0121 454 4949
E-mail: info@sheda.org.uk
Website: sheda.org.uk

Enquiries to: General Secretary

Founded: 1978

Organisation type and purpose: National organisation, trade association (membership is by qualification), present number of members: 60.

Subject coverage: Sources of supply of storage equipment and distributors.

Publications: Printed

Access to staff: Contact by letter, by telephone, by fax, by e-mail and via website
Hours: Mon to Fri, 0900 to 1700

Links with: Storage Equipment Manufacturers Association (SEMA)

STORAGE EQUIPMENT MANUFACTURERS ASSOCIATION (SEMA)

The National Metalforming Centre, 47 Birmingham Road, West Bromwich B70 6PY

Tel: 0121 601 6350
Fax: 0121 601 6387
E-mail: enquiry@sema.org.uk
Website: www.sema.org.uk

Enquiries to: Information Officer

Founded: 1970

Organisation type and purpose: Trade association.

Subject coverage: Storage equipment, racking, shelving etc.

Publications: Printed, and electronic and video

Access to staff: Contact by letter, by telephone, by fax and by e-mail
Hours: Mon to Fri, 0900 to 1700

continued overleaf

Member of: British Materials Handling Federation; tel: 0121 200 2100; fax: 0121 200 1306; e-mail: enquiry@bmhf.org.uk

STOURBRIDGE LIBRARY

Crown Centre, Stourbridge, West Midlands, DY8 1YE

Tel: 01384 812945
Fax: 01384 812946
E-mail: stourbridge.library@dudley.gov.uk
Website: www.dudley.gov.uk/libraries

Enquiries to: Locality Manager
Direct tel: 01384 812951

Organisation type and purpose: Local government body, public library.

Subject coverage: Local history of Stourbridge and the surrounding area, tourist information.

Collection: County Express (local newspaper) 1856 to present, almost all on rollfilm
Stourbridge Census Returns 1841–1901
Stourbridge local history: books, maps, photographs, pamphlets, manuscripts, posters, newspapers

Library catalogue: All or part available online

Access to staff: Contact by letter, by telephone, by fax, by e-mail, in person and via website

Access to building: *Hours:* Mon, 0930 to 1900; Tue to Fri, 0900 to 1900; Sat, 0900 to 1700; Sun 1000 to 1400

Access for disabled people: Level entry

Parent body: Dudley Libraries; St James's Road, Dudley

STOURPORT LIBRARY

County Buildings, Worcester Street, Stourport-on-Severn, Worcestershire, DY13 8EH

Tel: 01905 822722
Fax: 01299 827464
E-mail: stourportlib@worcestershire.gov.uk
Website: www.worcestershire.gov.uk

Enquiries to: Library Manager

Founded: 1969

Organisation type and purpose: Public library.

Subject coverage: General public stock, local history of Stourport, small canal collection.

Collection: Local information about Stourport

Library catalogue: All or part available online

Access to staff: Contact by letter, by telephone, by e-mail and in person
Hours: Mon, Tue, Thu, Fri 0900 to 1730; Sat, 0900 to 1600; Wed, closed

Access to building: No prior appointment required

Access for disabled people: Parking provided, ramped entry, level entry, access to all public areas

STOVE AND FIREPLACE ADVICE (S&FA)

PO Box 583, High Wycombe, HP15 6XT

Tel: 0845 643 1901
Fax: 0870 130 6747
E-mail: advice@stoveandfireplaceadvice.org.uk
Website: www.stoveandfireplaceadvice.org.uk

Enquiries to: Director

Founded: 2010

Organisation type and purpose: Advice source. Advice on stoves, fires & fireplaces – their specification, installation & maintenance.

Subject coverage: Fireplaces, open fires, stoves, roomheaters and fuels (solid fuel, gas, natural and LPG).

Publications list: Available online and in print

Access to staff: Contact by telephone, by fax, by e-mail and via website
Hours: Mon to Fri, 0900 to 1700

Also at: Fireplace PR; PO Box 583, Holmer Green, High Wycombe, Buckinghamshire, HP15 6XT; tel: 01494 411242; fax: 0870 130 6747; e-mail: peterhealy@fireplacepr.co.uk

STRATEGIC PLANNING SOCIETY (SPS)

17 Portland Place, London, W1N 3AF

Tel: 020 7636 7737
Fax: 020 7323 1692
E-mail: enquiries@sps.org.uk
Website: www.sps.org.uk

Enquiries to: Administration Manager
Direct fax: 020 7636 7737
Direct e-mail: a.claase@sps.org.uk
Other contacts: Marketing Manager email: h.stones@sps.org.uk

Founded: 1967

Organisation type and purpose: Learned society, professional body (membership is by subscription), present number of members: 4,000, registered charity (charity number 253879), training organisation.
The Society aims to foster and promote research and best practice in strategic thought and action for the success of individual members and organisations.

Subject coverage: Strategic management and planning knowledge, applications, techniques and a specialist membership advisory network; conferences and workshops; specialist discussion groups.

Trade and statistical information: Index of published material relating to strategic management

Publications: Printed

Access to staff: Contact by letter, by telephone, by fax, by e-mail and via website. Appointment necessary.
Hours: Mon to Fri, 0900 to 1700

STRATFORD LIBRARY

12 Henley Street, Stratford-upon-Avon, Warwickshire, CV37 6PZ

Tel: 01789 292209
Fax: 01926 476763
E-mail: stratfordlibrary@warwickshire.gov.uk
Website: www.warwickshire.gov.uk/libraries

Enquiries to: Information Officer

Organisation type and purpose: Local government body, public library.

Subject coverage: General collection ranging from material for young children to studies at undergraduate level; no special subject areas.

Collection: South Warwickshire census returns 1841–1891 held on microfilm
Stratford Herald on microfilm

Library catalogue: All or part available online

Access to staff: Contact by letter, by telephone, by fax, by e-mail, in person and via website
Hours: Mon, Wed, Thu, Fri, 0900 to 1730; Tue, 1000 to 1730; Sat, 0930 to 1700; Sun, 1200 to 1600

Parent body: Warwickshire County Council

STREETBIKE DRAG CLUB

17 Southampton Road, London, NW5 4JS

Tel: 020 7485 0473
Fax: 020 7813 0198

Enquiries to: Chairman

Founded: 1989

Organisation type and purpose: Membership association (membership is by subscription).
To promote street bike drag races.

STRODE COLLEGE

Church Road, Street, Somerset, BA16 0AB

Tel: 01458 844410
Fax: 01458 844415
Website: www.strode-college.ac.uk

Enquiries to: Head of Learning Resources
Direct tel: 01458 844564
Direct e-mail: cbull@strode-college.ac.uk
Other contacts: Learning Centre Manager for catalogue enquiries, membership.

Founded: 1973

Organisation type and purpose: Suitable for ages: 16+.
Further education college.

Subject coverage: A levels, business studies, engineering, beauty therapy, hairdressing, drama, languages, broadcast media, art and design, sport, social care, childcare, information technology, performing arts, complementary therapies, public services, foundation degrees etc.

Library catalogue: All or part available online and in-house

Access to staff: Contact by letter, by telephone and by fax. Appointment necessary. Access for members only.
Hours: Term time: Monday and Friday 0835 to 1645, Tuesday – Thursday 0835 to 1900, Saturday and Sunday closed.

Special comments: In student vacations call 01458 8444410 to check opening hours

Access for disabled people: Parking provided, level entry, access to all public areas, toilet facilities

STROKE ASSOCIATION (TSA)

Stroke House, 240 City Road, London, EC1V 2PR

Tel: 020 7566 0300; helpline: 0303 303 3100; textphone 020 7251 9096
Fax: 020 7490 2686
E-mail: info@stroke.org.uk
Website: www.stroke.org.uk

Enquiries to: Stroke Information Services

Founded: 1899

Organisation type and purpose: Registered charity (charity number 211015). Concerned with combating stroke in people of all ages; funds research into prevention, treatment and better methods of rehabilitation; helps stroke patients and their families directly through its Rehabilitation and Support Services, including communication support, family and carer support, information services and welfare grants; campaigns, educates and informs to increase knowledge of stroke.

Subject coverage: Stroke research, conditions and welfare of sufferers.

Publications: Printed, and electronic and video
Order printed publications from: The Stroke Association, Publications Department, 1 Sterling Business Park, Salthouse Road, Northampton, NN4 7EX; tel: 01604 687724
Order electronic and video publications from: website: http://www.stroke.org.uk/information/our_publications/index.html

Publications list: Available online and in print

Access to staff: Contact by letter, by telephone, by e-mail and via website
Hours: Telephone helpline: Mon to Fri, 0900 to 1700

STROUD DISTRICT COUNCIL

Ebley Mill, Stroud, Gloucestershire, GL5 4UB

Tel: 01453 766321; minicom no. 01453 754949
Fax: 01453 750932
E-mail: customer.services@stroud.gov.uk
Website: www.stroud.gov.uk

Enquiries to: Principal Marketing Officer
Direct tel: 01453 754385
Direct fax: 01453 754942
Direct e-mail: press@stroud.gov.uk

Founded: 1974

Organisation type and purpose: Local government body.

Subject coverage: Stroud district, services and amenities.

Access to staff: Contact by letter, by telephone, by fax, by e-mail, in person and via website. Appointment necessary.
Hours: Mon to Thu, 0845 to 1700; Fri, 0845 to 1630

Access for disabled people: Parking provided, level entry, access to all public areas, toilet facilities

STRUCTURAL PRECAST ASSOCIATION (SPA)

60 Charles Street, Leicester, LE1 1FB

Tel: 0116 253 6161
Fax: 0116 251 4568
E-mail: spa@britishprecast.org
Website: www.structural-precast-association.org.uk

Enquiries to: Secretary

Founded: 1995

Organisation type and purpose: Trade association.

Subject coverage: Precast concrete structural components for building.

Publications: Printed

Access to staff: Contact by letter, by telephone, by fax, by e-mail and via website
Hours: Mon to Fri, 0900 to 1700

Parent body: British Precast Concrete Federation

STUDENT CHRISTIAN MOVEMENT OF GREAT BRITAIN (SCM)

Unit 504F, The Big Peg, 120 Vyse Street, The Jewellery Quarter, Birmingham, B18 6NE

Tel: 0121 200 3355
E-mail: scm@movement.org.uk
Website: www.movement.org.uk

Enquiries to: Administrator
Other contacts: National Co-ordinator, Groups Worker, Project Worker

Founded: 1889

Organisation type and purpose: National organisation, membership association, registered charity (charity number 1125640). SCM endeavours to present students in further and higher education with an understanding of the Christian faith that is enquiring, ecumenical and related to all aspects of life. SCM currently supports a network of student groups and individual members across Britain.

Subject coverage: Introductions to theology, liberation theology, prophecy, feminist theology, Bible studies, sexuality, spirituality, ecumenism, social action, responsibility, politics.

Non-library collection catalogue: All or part available online

Publications: Printed

Publications list: Available online and in print

Access to staff: Contact by letter, by telephone, by e-mail and via website. Appointment necessary.
Hours: Mon to Fri, 0930 to 1700

Access to building: No prior appointment required

Access for disabled people: Level entry

Affiliated to: Church Together in Britain and Ireland; tel: 020 7523 2139; Churches Together in England; tel: 020 7332 8230; World Student Christian Federation; tel: + 31 20 6754921; e-mail: europe@wscf.xs4all.nl

Has: Local groups

STUDENTS PARTNERSHIP WORLDWIDE (SPW)

Faith House, 2nd Floor, 7 Tufton Street, London, SW1P 3QB

Tel: 020 7222 0138
Fax: 020 7233 0008
E-mail: info@spw.org
Website: www.spw.org

Enquiries to: Operations Manager

Founded: 1985

Subject coverage: Volunteering; development; education; environment; health; youth development in rural Africa and Asia; community development; non-governmental organisation, focus on HIV/AIDS awareness, nutrition, sanitation; method is youth-to-youth approach through informal activities.

Non-library collection catalogue: All or part available online and in-house

Library catalogue: All or part available online and in-house

Publications: Printed, and electronic and video

Access to staff: Contact by letter, by telephone, by fax, by e-mail and via website. Appointment necessary.
Hours: Mon to Fri, 0900 to 1800

Access to building: No access other than to staff

Links with: Duke of Edinburgh; HELP; SAFE

SUBTERRANEA BRITANNICA (SB)

c/o CNHSS Ltd, 96A Brighton Road, South Croydon, Surrey, CR2 6AD

Tel: 020 8688 3593
Website: www.subbrit.org.uk

Enquiries to: Membership Secretary

Founded: 1974

Organisation type and purpose: Learned society (membership is by subscription), voluntary organisation.
Researches concerning the archaeology and history of man-made and man-used underground space. Mainly (but not exclusively) United Kingdom and Europe.

Subject coverage: Man-made and man-used underground space of all kinds and all periods – especially miscellaneous (non coal/non metal) mines, tunnels, ice houses, souterrains, deneholes, rockcut cellars, shelters, underground military structures, etc.

Collection: Correspondence concerning underground sites of all kinds and periods
County files including notes, surveys, newscuttings, offprints, pamphlets
Printed books relating to this subject

Library catalogue: All or part available in-house

continued overleaf

Publications: Printed

Publications list: Available in print

Access to staff: Contact by letter, by telephone and by e-mail. Appointment necessary.
Hours: Sun to Sat, at any reasonable hour
Special comments: Specific research enquiries only.

Access to building: *Special comments:* The past chairman's personal files/library can be accessed by prior arrangement only.

Links with: Association for Industrial Archaeology; Council for British Archaeology; National Association of Mining History Organisations

Secretary/Enquiries: Subterranea Britannica; 14 Maple Close, Sandford, Wareham, Dorset, BH20 7QD; tel: 01929 553872; e-mail: rogerstarling593@btinternet.com

Secretary/Membership: Subterranea Britannica; 13 Highcroft Cottages, London Road, Swanley, Kent, BR8 8DB; tel: 01322 408081; e-mail: nick@catford.fsbusiness.co.uk

SUE RYDER CARE

114–118 Southampton Row, London, WC1B 5AA

Tel: 0845 050 1953
E-mail: info@suerydercare.org
Website: www.suerydercare.org

Organisation type and purpose: A charity registered in England and Wales (number 1052076) and in Scotland (number SC039578).
A leading provider of palliative and end-of-life care research and education. Through its research the centre seeks to make a valuable contribution to policy and practice in previously under-researched areas of palliative and end-of-life care.

Subject coverage: Provides health and social care services in local communities; is one of the largest providers of specialist palliative care in the UK; provides indivualised, compassionate care services to people with end-of-life and long-term needs; supports families, friends and carers. Works through innovation and research to improve standards in long-term and end-of-life care; a research partnership with the University of Nottingham is extending skills and knowledge across the sector; has piloted leading hospice-at-home services and holistic care-management programmes for people with complex physical and psychological needs. Its work goes beyond the UK; with fifty projects across 12 countries in Europe and southern Africa, it is positioned at the centre of an international health and social care partnership.

Publications: Electronic and video
Order electronic and video publications from: Download from website

Publications list: Available online

Access to staff: Contact by letter, by telephone and by e-mail

Also at: Doncaster Office; 2 Carr Square, Sidings Court, Doncaster, DN4 5NU; tel: 01302 380080; fax: 01302 380075; Sudbury Office; First Floor, Kings House, King Street, Sudbury, CO10 2ED; tel: 01787 314200; fax: 01787 319516

Works collaboratively with: Sue Ryder Care Centre for Palliative and End of Life Studies; University of Nottingham

SUFFOLK ACRE (ACRE)

Formal name: Suffolk ACRE (Action with Communities in Rural England)

Brightspace, 160 Hadleigh Road, Ipswich, Suffolk IP2 0HH

Tel: 01473 345300
Fax: 01473 345330
E-mail: info@suffolkacre.org.uk
Website: www.suffolkacre.org.uk
Website: www.suffolkonline.net
Website: www.brightspace.org
Website: www.suffolkcarshare.com

Enquiries to: Chief Executive

Founded: 1937

Organisation type and purpose: Membership association, present number of members: 2,000, voluntary organisation, registered charity (charity number 1062038).
Representative and advisory body for the voluntary social services sector in Suffolk; with a membership of a very large number of voluntary and statutory bodies and individuals.
Community development in rural areas of Suffolk.

Subject coverage: Welfare and quality of life in Suffolk; local communities; village hall regulations; playing fields; job creation programmes; crafts; horticulture; charities; social enterprise; IT; village hall and parish council insurance; transport;

Publications: Printed

Publications list: Available in print

Access to staff: Contact by letter, by telephone, by fax and by e-mail
Hours: Mon to Fri, 0900 to 1700

Access for disabled people: Parking provided, ramped entry, access to all public areas, toilet facilities

Affiliated to: ACRE

SUFFOLK CHAMBER OF COMMERCE, INDUSTRY AND SHIPPING INCORPORATED

Felaw Maltings, South Kiln, 42 Felaw Street, Ipswich, Suffolk, IP2 8SQ

Tel: 01473 680600
Fax: 01473 603888
E-mail: info@suffolkchamber.co.uk
Website: www.suffolkchamber.co.uk

Enquiries to: Business Information Co-ordinator
Direct tel: 01473 694800
Direct e-mail: wendy@suffolkchamber.co.uk

Founded: 1884

Organisation type and purpose: Membership association (membership is by subscription), present number of members: 1,400, service industry.
Chamber of commerce.

Subject coverage: International trade, exporting, business information, business credit checking, personnel assistance.

Collection: Extensive business library

Publications: Printed

Access to staff: Contact by letter, by telephone, by fax, by e-mail, in person and via website
Hours: Mon to Fri, 0900 to 1700

Affiliated to: Association of British Chambers of Commerce

SUFFOLK COASTAL DISTRICT COUNCIL

Melton Hill, Woodbridge, Suffolk, IP12 1AU

Tel: 01394 383789; 01394 444211 (minicom)
Fax: 01394 385100
E-mail: scdc@suffolkcoastal.gov.uk
Website: www.suffolkcoastal.gov.uk

Enquiries to: Communications Manager
Direct tel: 01394 444361
Direct fax: 01394 444690
Direct e-mail: viv.hotten@suffolkcoastal.gov.uk

Founded: 1974

Organisation type and purpose: Local government body.

Subject coverage: Local government services, including local planning, environmental protection, housing enabling, recreation and leisure, recycling and waste management, food safety and tourism.

Special visitor services: Tourist Information Centres at Felixstowe, Woodbridge and Aldeburgh

Publications: Electronic and video
Order electronic and video publications from: news@suffolkcoastal.gov.uk

Publications list: Available online and in print

Access to staff: Contact by letter, by telephone, by fax, by e-mail, in person and via website
Hours: Mon, Tue and Thu, 0845 to 1715; Wed, 0930 to 1715; Fri, 0845 to 1645

Access to building: Melton Hill offices
Hours: Mon, Tue and Thu, 0845 to 1715; Wed, 0930 to 1715; Fri, 0845 to 1645

Access for disabled people: Parking provided, level entry, toilet facilities
Hours: Mon, Tue and Thu, 0845 to 1715; Wed, 0930 to 1715; Fri, 0845 to 1645

Also at: Suffolk Coastal District Council (local area office); 91 Undercliff Road, Felixstowe; tel: 01394 276766

SUFFOLK COLLEGE

Formal name: Suffolk New College

Learning Curve, Rope Walk, Ipswich, Suffolk, IP4 1LT

Tel: 01473 382836
Fax: 01473 230054
Website: www.suffolk.ac.uk

Enquiries to: Learning Curve Co-ordinator

Founded: 1961

Organisation type and purpose: College of higher and further education.

Subject coverage: Computing; engineering; management; construction; social work; nursing; sociology; catering; graphic design; biology; education; midwifery; chemistry; CAD/CAM; personnel management; psychology; business studies; art.

Non-library collection catalogue: All or part available online

Library catalogue: All or part available online

Publications: Printed

Access to staff: Contact by letter. Appointment necessary.
Hours: Mon to Fri, 0900 to 1700

Associate college of: University Campus Suffolk; Waterfront Building, Neptune Quay, Ipswich, IP4 1QJ; tel: 01473 83700; website: http://www.ucs.ac.uk

SUFFOLK HORSE SOCIETY

The Market Hill, Woodbridge, Suffolk, IP12 4LP

Tel: 01394 380643
E-mail: sec@suffolkhorsesociety.org.uk
Website: www.suffolkhorsesociety.org.uk

Enquiries to: Administrator

Founded: 1877

Organisation type and purpose: Registered charity (charity number 220756).

Subject coverage: Breed society for the Suffolk Punch heavy horse.

Collection: Collections held in the Suffolk Horse Museum

Publications: Printed

Access to staff: Contact by letter, by telephone and by e-mail. Appointment necessary.
Hours: Mon to Fri, 0930 to 1730

Access for disabled people: Steps; not suitable for wheelchair access

SUFFOLK LIBRARIES (ACS LAI)

Formal name: Adult and Community Services Libraries Archives and Information

Endeavour House, 8 Russell Road, Ipswich, Suffolk, IP1 2BX

Tel: 01473 265086
Fax: 01473 216843
E-mail: help@suffolklibraries.co.uk
Website: www.suffolk.gov.uk/LeisureAndCulture/Libraries/SuffolkLibrariesDirect
Website: www.suffolk.gov.uk/leisureandculture/libraries

Enquiries to: Information Librarian
Direct tel: 01473 583727
Direct e-mail: roger.mcmaster@suffolk.gov.uk
Other contacts: Head of Service

Founded: 1974

Organisation type and purpose: Local government body, public library.

Subject coverage: General; local studies; local government; business information.

Collection: Benjamin Britten Collection (all published works up to 1973); at Lowestoft Central Library
Cullum Collection (family library of a 19th century gentleman, George Milner-Gibson-Cullum) at Bury St Edmunds Record Office
Fitzgerald Collection at Woodbridge Library
Horse Racing Collection (mainly flat racing; sporting reminiscences; history and anatomy of the horse; steeplechasing; includes the Racing Calendar from 1774 and the Bloodstock Breeders Review from 1912) at Newmarket Branch Library, 1A, The Rookery, Newmarket
Ipswich Old Town Library, including incunabula and manuscripts and rare works from the 16th and 17th centuries at Ipswich School by appointment only
Local Studies Collections at: Suffolk Record Office, 77 Raingate Street, Bury St Edmunds; Central Library, Lowestoft; Woodbridge Branch, New Street, Woodbridge (collection on Sutton Hoo); Suffolk Record Office, Gatacre Road, Ipswich
Seckford Collection (local history of East Anglia, with emphasis on a Woodbridge locality; includes the manuscript of a multi-volume work, Suffolk Moated Houses) at Woodbridge Branch Library

Non-library collection catalogue: All or part available online

Library catalogue: All or part available online

Access to staff: Contact by letter, by telephone, by fax, by e-mail, in person and via website
Hours: Mon to Fri, 0900 to 1700

SUFFOLK LOCAL HISTORY COUNCIL

c/o The Vice Chairman, The Cottage, Little London, Combs, Stowmarket, Suffolk. IP14 2ES

Tel: 01449 674552
E-mail: admin@slhc.org.uk
Website: www.slhc.org.uk

Founded: 1953

Organisation type and purpose: A registered charity (number is 294270) and voluntary organisation, financed by members and governed by an elected executive committee, all of whom are trustees as well as volunteers; membership is by subscription.
To encourage and support the study of local history and to act as an umbrella organisation for groups and individuals with similar interests in the county of Suffolk.

Subject coverage: As well as running various events for the membership, organises the Recorders' Scheme to ensure that changes taking place at local level are adequately recorded for future historians.

Non-library collection catalogue: All or part available online

Publications: Printed

Publications list: Available online

Access to staff: Contact by letter, by telephone, by e-mail and via website
Special comments: Variable, not daily.

SUFFOLK RECORD OFFICE

77 Raingate Street, Bury St Edmunds, Suffolk, IP33 2AR

Tel: 01284 352352
E-mail: bury.ro@libher.suffolkcc.gov.uk
Website: www.suffolk.gov.uk/sro

Enquiries to: Public Service Manager
Direct tel: 01284 352355

Founded: 1974

Organisation type and purpose: Local government body.

Subject coverage: Local history, local studies, family history.

Collection: Records of local authorities, ecclesiastical bodies, families, societies, organisations, businesses and estates relating primarily to Suffolk, 12th to 20th centuries

Non-library collection catalogue: All or part available online and in-house

Library catalogue: All or part available online

Publications: Printed, and microform publications
Order printed publications from: Suffolk Record Office, Gatacre Road, Ipswich, Suffolk, IP1 2LQ, tel: 01473 584542, fax: 01473 584533, e-mail: ipswich.ro@libher.suffolkcc.gov.uk
Order microform publications from: Suffolk Record Office, Gatacre Road, Ipswich, Suffolk, IP1 2LQ, tel: 01473 584542, fax: 01473 584533, e-mail: ipswich.ro@libher.suffolkcc.gov.uk

Access to staff: Contact by letter, by telephone, by fax, by e-mail and in person
Hours: Bury St Edmunds and Ipswich: Mon to Sat, 0900 to 1700
Lowestoft: Mon, Wed, Thu, Fri, 0915 to 1730; Tue, 0900 to 1900; Sat, 0900 to 1700; Sun 1000 to 1600 (no original documents produced on Sunday)
Special comments: CARN ticket required for access to original material.

Also at: Suffolk Record Office; Gatacre Road, Ipswich, Suffolk, IP1 2LQ; tel: 01473 584541; fax: 01473 584533; e-mail: ipswich.ro@libher.suffolkcc.gov.uk; Suffolk Record Office; Central Library, Clapham Road, Lowestoft, Suffolk, NR32 1DR; tel: 01502 405357; fax: 01502 405350; e-mail: lowestoft.ro@libher.suffolkcc.gov.uk

Parent body: Suffolk County Council; Endeavour House, Russell Road, Ipswich, IP1 2BX; tel: 01473 583000

SUGAR ASSOCIATION OF LONDON (SAL)

154 Bishopsgate, London, EC2M 4LN

Tel: 020 7377 2113
Fax: 020 7247 2481
E-mail: durhamn@sugar-assoc.co.uk

Enquiries to: Secretary

Founded: 1882

Organisation type and purpose: International organisation, trade association (membership is by election or invitation), present number of members: 130.

Publications: Printed

continued overleaf

Access to staff: Contact by letter, by telephone and by fax. All charged.
Hours: Mon to Fri, 0900 to 1700

SUGAR NUTRITION UK (SNUK)

25 Floral Street, Covent Garden, London, WC2E 9DS

Tel: 020 7189 8301
Fax: 020 7189 8101
E-mail: info@sugar-bureau.co.uk
Website: www.sugarnutrition.org.uk

Enquiries to: Information Manager

Founded: 1964; formerly called The Sugar Bureau (year of change 2012)

Organisation type and purpose: Trade association and scientific research funder.

Subject coverage: Information on sugar (the generic product), diet and health, consumers and the media.

Publications: Printed
Order printed publications from: See website (resources now mainly online)

Publications list: Available online

Access to staff: Contact by letter, by telephone, by e-mail and via website. Appointment necessary.
Hours: Mon to Fri, 0900 to 1700

Access to building: No access

Member of: European Sugar Manufacturers Committee (CEFS); Food and Drink Federation; World Sugar Research Organisation

SUGAR TRADERS ASSOCIATION OF THE UNITED KINGDOM (STAUK)

Czarnikow Group Limited, 24 Chiswell Street, London, EC1Y 4SG

Tel: 020 7972 6631
Fax: 020 7972 6699
E-mail: dclark@czarnikow.com
Website: www.sugartraders.co.uk

Enquiries to: Honorary Secretary

Founded: 1952

Organisation type and purpose: Trade association (membership is by subscription, election or invitation), present number of members: 12.
To promote, develop and protect the international trade in sugar.

Subject coverage: Raw cane sugar; beet white sugar.

Access to staff: Contact by telephone and by e-mail. Access for members only.
Hours: Mon to Fri, 0900 to 1700

Member organisation of: ASSUC aisbl, European Association of Sugar Traders; Boite 24, Square Ambiorix 32, 1000 Brussels, Belgium; tel: +32 2 7366873; fax: +32 2 7326766; e-mail: assuc@assuc.eu

SUN CHEMICAL LIMITED

Cray Avenue, St Mary Cray, Orpington, Kent, BR5 3PP

Tel: 01689 894000
Website: www.sunchemical.com

Enquiries to: Manager, Information Department
Direct tel: 01689 894208
Direct fax: 01689 894128
Direct e-mail: barry.hermiston@sunchemical.com

Founded: 1877; formerly called Coates Brothers plc (year of change 2000)

Organisation type and purpose: Manufacturing industry.

Subject coverage: Printing inks and printing processes.

Access to staff: Appointment necessary.
Hours: Mon to Fri, 0900 to 1700

SUNBEAM RAPIER OWNERS CLUB (SROC)

7 Barnfield, Tattenhall, Chester, CH3 9HE

Tel: 01829 770762
E-mail: sroc.membership@btinternet.com
Website: www.sunbeamrapier.com

Enquiries to: Membership Secretary
Other contacts: The Editor, e-mail: sunbeams92@tiscali.co.uk (for magazine advertising)

Founded: 1979

Organisation type and purpose: Membership association (membership is by subscription), present number of members: 300–350.

Subject coverage: Sunbeam Rapier cars, details of spare parts availability, technical advice, details and dates of club events, details of cars for sale, objectives of the club.

Collection: Rootes Archive Centre, Cherwell Business Village, Southam Road, Banbury, Oxon, OX16 2SP

Publications: Printed
Order printed publications from: Short Cuts newsletter (occasional issues)

Access to staff: Contact by letter, by telephone, by e-mail and via website
Hours: Mon to Fri, 1800 to 2200; Sat and Sun, 0900 to 1700

Member organisation of: Association of Rootes Car Clubs (ARCC); tel: 01993 878471

SUNBEAM TIGER OWNERS CLUB

8 Villa Real Estate, Consett, Co Durham, DH8 6BJ

Tel: 01207 508296
Fax: 01207 582297

Enquiries to: Membership Secretary

Founded: 1976

Organisation type and purpose: International organisation, membership association (membership is by subscription).

Subject coverage: Sunbeam Tiger cars.

Access to staff: Contact by letter and by telephone
Hours: Mon to Fri, 0900 to 1700

SUNBEAM VENEZIA TOURING MILANO

Briarstone House, 51 Cheadle Road, Uttoxeter, Staffordshire, ST14 7BX

Tel: 01889 568346
Fax: 01889 568346

Enquiries to: General Secretary
Direct tel: 00 1 603 675 6622
Direct e-mail: jaars@emailmv.comt

Founded: 1969

Organisation type and purpose: Membership association (membership is by subscription), present number of members: 10, voluntary organisation, training organisation, consultancy, research organisation.

Subject coverage: Full and general information club for Rootes, full history of car manufacturers Touring Milano; special mark Sunbeam Venezia, diesel powered cars and transport; technical advice and spares manufacturing.

Collection: Lord Rootes collection, some paperwork, touring, liquidator, body-builders 1963–5
Photographs, handbooks, spares

Publications: Printed

Access to staff: Contact by letter and by e-mail. Appointment necessary. Non-members charged.
Hours: Mon to Fri, 0900 to 1700

Archives and technical details: Sunbeam Venezia Touring Milano; 362 Dingleton Hill Road, RR 3 Box 33, Cornish, New Hampshire, NH 03745, USA; tel: +1 603 675 6622; e-mail: jaars@emailmv.com

SUNBED ASSOCIATION (TSA)

Chess House, 105 High Street, Chesham, Buckinghamshire, HP5 1DE

Tel: 01494 785941
Fax: 01494 786791
E-mail: info@sunbedassociation.org.uk
Website: www.sunbedassociation.org.uk

Enquiries to: Chief Executive

Founded: 1995

Organisation type and purpose: Trade association (membership is by subscription), present number of members: 25 manufacturing industry and 1,500 service industry.

Subject coverage: Manufacture and use of sunbeds.

Collection: Standards for the manufacture and use of sunbeds

Trade and statistical information: Comprehensive industry statistics, training programme

Publications: Printed

Access to staff: Contact by letter, by telephone, by fax and by e-mail
Hours: Mon to Fri, 0900 to 1700

SUNDERLAND CITY COUNCIL, CITY SERVICES DIRECTORATE

City Library and Arts Centre, Fawcett Street, Sunderland, Tyne and Wear, SR1 1RE

Tel: 0191 561 1235
Fax: 0191 565 0506
E-mail: libraries@sunderland.gov.uk
Website: www.sunderland.gov.uk/libraries

Organisation type and purpose: Local government body, art gallery, public library.

Subject coverage: General, local studies, commercial and technical fields, and art.

Collection: Bob Mason Collection (Maritime history)
Local collection on Sunderland and County Durham (8,000 volumes, 12,000 illustrations, 2,000 maps)

Non-library collection catalogue: All or part available online, in-house and in print

Library catalogue: All or part available online

Publications list: Available in print

Access to staff: Contact by letter, by telephone, by fax and by e-mail
Hours: Mon to Fri, 0900 to 1700

Access for disabled people: Access to all public areas

Constituent part of: NETWORK

SUNDERLAND VOLUNTEER LIFE BRIGADE (SVLB)

The Watch House, Pier View, Roker, Sunderland, Tyne and Wear, SR6 0PR

Tel: 0191 5672579
E-mail: sunderland.vlb@aol.com
Website: www.communigate.co.uk/ne/svlb/index.phtml

Enquiries to: Company Secretary
Direct tel: 07847 004983
Direct e-mail: rroberts61@btinternet.com

Founded: 1877

Organisation type and purpose: Professional body, present number of members: 65 active members, voluntary organisation, registered charity (number 1105980) and company limited by guarantee (number 4978640).
Coastal search, cliff rescue, coastwatch and museum, Duke of Edinburgh Award; headquartered at The Watch House, a historic building.

Subject coverage: Volunteer life brigade, search, rescue, coastwatch and museum; SVLB history – 130 years of life saving on the coast of Sunderland. Volunteers are needed for all teams. Members must be over 18. Duke of Edinburgh Award training is available to 14 to 18 year olds.

Collection: Model ships, historical photographs and life-saving equipment.

Publications: Printed
Order printed publications from: Secretary Rose Roberts telephone 0191 5292651 or e-mail rroberts61@btinternet.com

Publications list: Available online and in print

Access to staff: Contact by letter, by telephone, by e-mail and in person
Hours: Sunday, bank hols & first Saturday of each month, 1200 to 1600 or by appointment

Access to building: *Hours:* Sunday, bank hols, first Saturday of each month and special events, 1200 to 1600

Links with: Coastguard, National Coastwatch Institute, RNLI

SUPPLY CHAIN KNOWLEDGE CENTRE (SCKC)

Cranfield Centre for Logistics & Supply Chain, Cranfield School of Management, Cranfield, Bedfordshire, MK43 0AL

Tel: 01234 754931
Fax: 01234 754930
E-mail: sckc@cranfield.ac.uk
Website: www.sckc.info
Website: www.logisticsweb.co.uk
Website: www.ila.co.uk

Enquiries to: Knowledge Manager

Founded: 1970

Organisation type and purpose: University department or institute.
Information centre (logistics).

Subject coverage: Logistics, supply chain management, materials handling, warehouse design including cold stores, physical distribution, pallet testing, freight transport, ergonomics.

Collection: Extensive collection of 35mm slides of materials handling equipment

Publications: Printed, and electronic and video

Publications list: Available online and in print

Access to staff: Contact by e-mail and via website. Appointment necessary. Access for members only. Non-members charged.
Hours: Mon to Fri, 0900 to 1730

Division of: Cranfield Centre for Logistics & Supply Chain

SUPREME COURT LIBRARY

Queen's Building, Royal Courts of Justice, Strand, London, WC2A 2LL

Tel: 020 7947 6587
Fax: 020 7947 6661

Enquiries to: Librarian
Direct tel: 020 7947 7198

Founded: 1972

Organisation type and purpose: National government body.
Department for Constitutional Affairs Library and Information Services.
Primarily for the use of the Judiciary and Officials of the Royal Courts of Justice.

Subject coverage: English law; some coverage of the Commonwealth and EC law.

Collection: Old editions of legal textbooks
Transcripts of the Determinations of the Immigration Appeal Tribunal
Transcripts of the judgements of the Court of Appeal (Civil Division, 1951 to date)

Library catalogue: All or part available in-house

Access to staff: Contact by letter and by fax. Appointment necessary.
Hours: Mon to Fri, 1000 to 1630; during legal vacations 0930 to 1630

Access for disabled people: *Special comments:* Access provided throughout the library and court buildings

SURF LIFE SAVING GB (SLSGB)

Formal name: Surf Life Saving Great Britain

19 Southernhay West, Exeter, EX1 1PJ

Tel: 01392 218007
Fax: 01392 217808
E-mail: mail@slsgb.org.uk
Website: www.slsgb.org.uk

Enquiries to: Executive Officer

Founded: 1955

Organisation type and purpose: Membership association, voluntary organisation, registered charity (charity number 1015668), training organisation.

Subject coverage: Life-saving on beaches with surf, training, awards, youth development.

Publications: Printed

Access to staff: Contact by letter, by telephone and by fax. Appointment necessary.
Hours: Mon to Fri, 0900 to 1700

SURFACE ENGINEERING ASSOCIATION (SEA)

Federation House, 10 Vyse Street, Birmingham, B18 6LT

Tel: 0121 237 1123
Fax: 0121 237 1124
E-mail: info@sea.org.uk
Website: www.sea.org.uk
Website: www.bstsa.org.uk

Enquiries to: Chief Executive
Other contacts: Member Services Manager

Founded: 1887

Organisation type and purpose: Trade association (membership is by subscription), present number of members: 500, manufacturing industry, consultancy.
To promote the interests of the UK surface engineering activity.

Subject coverage: Metal finishing, coating metal, putting metal coatings on other products, supply of materials or services to companies, sub-contractors for finishing, surface engineering, surface coating materials, economics, health and safety, environmental issues.

Collection: Standards for surface engineering

Trade and statistical information: Some data on value of the surface engineering industry

Publications: Printed

Publications list: Available online

Access to staff: Contact by letter, by telephone, by fax, by e-mail and via website. Appointment necessary.
Hours: Mon to Fri, 0900 to 1700
Special comments: Some services are for members only.

Access for disabled people: Level entry, access to all public areas, toilet facilities

Affiliated to: CBI; CETS

Member of: The British Jewellery and Giftware Federation (BJGF)

SURREY ARCHAEOLOGICAL SOCIETY

Castle Arch, Guildford, Surrey, GU1 3SX

Tel: 01483 532454
Fax: 01483 532454
E-mail: info@surreyarchaeology.org.uk
Website: www.surreyarchaeology.org.uk

Enquiries to: Honorary Secretary

Founded: 1854

Organisation type and purpose: Learned society.
To promote the study of archaeology and antiquities within the historic county of Surrey.

Subject coverage: Archaeological, antiquarian or historical material relating to historic county of Surrey including building records, records and manuscripts, cartographic and pictorial material, ceramics, ecclesiastical history and industrial history.

Collection: The Society's collections, research material and library are housed at Castle Arch

Non-library collection catalogue: All or part available online and in-house

Library catalogue: All or part available online and in-house

Publications: Printed

Publications list: Available online and in print

Access to staff: Contact by letter, by telephone, by fax, by e-mail, in person and via website. Appointment necessary. Non-members charged.
Hours: Mon to Fri, 1030 to 1630
Special comments: Non-members, first visit free, subsequent visits £8.00 each

Access to building: Prior appointment required

SURREY COMMUNITY ACTION (SCA)

Astolat, Coniers Way, New Inn Lane, Burpham, Guildford, Surrey, GU4 7HL

Tel: 01483 566072
Fax: 01483 440508 or 0870 0566147
E-mail: info@surreyca.org.uk
Website: www.surreyca.org.uk

Enquiries to: Information Officer

Founded: 1950

Organisation type and purpose:
Membership association (membership is by subscription), present number of members: 600, voluntary organisation, registered charity (charity number 1056527).
Independent registered charity working with communities to strengthen voluntary action.
To enhance the quality of life for people in Surrey by promoting, supporting and strengthening voluntary action.

Subject coverage: Local charities and voluntary groups, including village halls and good neighbour car schemes; volunteering and voluntary transport schemes; local training; rural communities in Surrey; local grant schemes and funding sources.

Publications: Printed

Access to staff: Contact by letter, by telephone, by fax, by e-mail, in person and via website. Appointment necessary.
Hours: Mon to Fri, 0900 to 1700

Access for disabled people: Parking provided, level entry, access to all public areas, toilet facilities

SURREY COUNTY ARCHAEOLOGICAL UNIT (SCAU)

Surrey History Centre, Goldsworth Road, Woking, Surrey, GU21 6ND

Tel: 01483 518777
Fax: 01483 518780
E-mail: archaeology.scau@surreycc.gov.uk
Website: www.surreycc.gov.uk/archaeology

Enquiries to: Unit Manager
Direct tel: 01483 518777
Other contacts: Archaeological Project Officer

Founded: 1991

Organisation type and purpose: Local government body, professional body.

Subject coverage: Archaeological information for Surrey.

Collection: Archive of archaeological material from a number of sites in Surrey

Publications: Printed

Access to staff: Contact by letter, by telephone and by e-mail. Appointment necessary.
Hours: Mon to Fri, 0800 to 1600

Access to building: Prior appointment required

Access for disabled people: Parking provided, level entry, access to all public areas, toilet facilities

Parent body: Surrey County Council; County Hall, Kingston upon Thames; tel: 020 8541 8800; fax: 020 8541 9004

SURREY COUNTY COUNCIL LIBRARIES

Surrey County Council, Room 356, County Hall, Kingston upon Thames, Surrey, KT1 2DY

Tel: 01483 543599
Fax: 01483 543597
Website: www.surreycc.gov.uk/libraries

Organisation type and purpose: County council libraries service.

Subject coverage: Council's 54 libraries.

Library catalogue: All or part available online

Access to staff: Contact by letter, by telephone, by fax, by e-mail, in person and via website

SURREY GUILD OF CRAFTSMEN (SGC)

Surrey Guild Craft Gallery, 1 Moushill Lane, Milford, Godalming, Surrey, GU8 5BH

Tel: 01483 424769

Enquiries to: Administrator

Organisation type and purpose: Membership association.

Subject coverage: Craftworkers in the county; craft activities and techniques; professional craftsmen in Surrey.

Publications: Printed

Access to staff: Contact by e-mail. Appointment necessary. Access for members only. Letter of introduction required.

Access to building: *Hours:* Mon to Sun, 1030 to 1700

Access for disabled people: *Special comments:* Assistance provided, please telephone before visiting

Member of: South East Arts Association

SURREY HEATH ARCHAEOLOGICAL & HERITAGE TRUST (SHAHT)

Archaeology Centre, 4–10 London Road, Bagshot, Surrey, GU19 5HN

Tel: 01276 451181

Founded: 1988

Organisation type and purpose: Learned society (membership is by subscription), present number of members: 200, voluntary organisation, registered charity (charity number 299409), museum, suitable for ages: 9 to 75, training organisation, research organisation.

Subject coverage: Archaeology of Borough of Surrey Heath; mesolithic to post-industrial revolution.

Non-library collection catalogue: All or part available in-house

Library catalogue: All or part available in-house

Access to staff: Contact by letter and by telephone
Hours: By appointment

Access to building: No prior appointment required

SURREY HEATH BOROUGH COUNCIL (SHBC)

Surrey Heath House, Knoll Road, Camberley, Surrey, GU15 3HD

Tel: 01276 707100
Fax: 01276 707177
E-mail: enquiries@surreyheath.gov.uk
Website: www.surreyheath.gov.uk

Enquiries to: Chief Executive

Founded: 1974

Organisation type and purpose: Local government body.

Subject coverage: Local authority, housing, planning, environmental health, recreation, council tax, benefits.

Publications: Printed

Access to staff: Contact by letter, by telephone, by fax, by e-mail, in person and via website
Hours: Mon to Thu, 0830 to 1730; Fri, 0900 to 1700

Access for disabled people: Parking provided, ramped entry, level entry, toilet facilities

Link with: Surrey County Council

SURREY HERITAGE

Surrey History Centre, 130 Goldsworth Road, Woking, Surrey, GU21 6ND

Tel: 01483 518737
Fax: 01483 518738
E-mail: shs@surreycc.gov.uk
Website: www.surreycc.gov.uk/surreyhistoryservice

Enquiries to: Surrey History Centre Helpdesk
Other contacts: Head of Heritage (for matters of overall policy and complaints)

Founded: 1998; created by the merger of Surrey Record Office, Surrey Local Studies Library, Guildford Muniment Room (year of change 1998)

Organisation type and purpose: Local government body.
County archives and local studies library.

Subject coverage: Surrey records and history, including material on churches, houses, schools, businesses, charitable institutions (reformatories, asylums, etc.), local government and local legal institutions (i.e. quarter sessions and petty sessions), urban growth and housing development, railways and other public undertakings, family and estate papers; not matters dealt with by central government or heavy industries.

Collection: John Broadwood and Sons Ltd, piano manufacturers: records
Barclay collection of watercolours by John Hassell (1767–1825)
Dennis Specialist Vehicles Ltd, makers of fire engines, buses and other specialist vehicles: records
Photographs of Surrey by Francis Frith
Papers relating to C. L. Dodgson (Lewis Carroll) and of Dodgson family
Goulburn family of Betchworth: papers, including Henry Goulburn (1784–1856), politician
Gertrude Jekyll (1843–1932), garden designer of Munstead: papers including garden designs
More and More-Molyneux family of Loseley House: papers, particularly relating to Tudor and Stuart Surrey
Queen's Royal Surrey Regiment and predecessors, including Queen's Royal Regiment (West Surrey) and East Surrey Regiment: records
IGI complete

Non-library collection catalogue: All or part available online and in-house

Library catalogue: All or part available online

Publications: Printed, and microform publications

Publications list: Available online

Access to staff: Contact by letter, by telephone, by fax, by e-mail and via website. Appointment necessary.

Access to building: *Hours:* Tue, Wed, Fri, 0930 to 1700; Thu, 0930 to 1930; Sat, 0930 to 1600
Special comments: CARN tickets, Surrey Library cards or ID required

Access for disabled people: Parking provided, ramped entry, access to all public areas, toilet facilities

SURREY PERFORMING ARTS LIBRARY

Denbies Wine Estate, London Road, Dorking, Surrey, RH5 6AA

Tel: 01306 887509
Fax: 01306 875074
E-mail: performing.arts@surreycc.gov.uk
Website: www.surreycc.gov.uk/libraries

Enquiries to: Senior Librarian
Direct tel: 01306 875453

Founded: 1981

Organisation type and purpose: Local government body, public library.

Subject coverage: Performing arts, including music, drama, theatre, arts, dance and cinema.

Collection: CD and DVD collections within the subject areas
Performance materials; sets of plays, vocal scores, orchestral parts, chamber music parts

Non-library collection catalogue: All or part available online

Library catalogue: All or part available online

Access to staff: Contact by letter, by telephone, by fax, by e-mail and in person
Hours: Tue and Fri, 1000 to 1700; Thu, 1000 to 2000; Sat, 0930 to 1300; Mon and Wed, closed

Access to building: *Hours:* Tue and Fri, 1000 to 1700; Thu, 1000 to 2000; Sat, 0930 to 1300; Mon and Wed, closed

Access for disabled people: Level entry, access to all public areas
Hours: As above

Parent body: Surrey County Council

SURREY RECORD SOCIETY

c/o Surrey History Centre, 130 Goldsworth Road, Woking, Surrey, GU21 6ND

Tel: 01483 518754
Fax: 01483 518738

Enquiries to: Honorary Secretary

Founded: 1913

Organisation type and purpose: Learned society (membership is by subscription).
The Society exists to publish records relating to the historic county of Surrey, which includes the parishes of South London as far east as Rotherhithe.

Subject coverage: Surrey history and genealogy. No research undertaken.

Publications: Printed

Access to staff: Contact by letter
Hours: Mon to Fri, 0900 to 1700

SURVEY FORCE LIMITED

Algarve House, 140 Borden Lane, Sittingbourne, Kent, ME9 8HW

Tel: 01795 423778
Fax: 01795 423778
E-mail: surveyforce@yahoo.com

Enquiries to: Director
Other contacts: Sales Managers

Founded: 1974

Organisation type and purpose: International organisation, service industry, consultancy, research organisation.

Subject coverage: Market research in chemical, pharmaceutical, health care, electronics, computer, IT, optical, elastomers, rubbers, plastics, food and drink, diagnostics (instrumentation and reagents).

Collection: Market research studies (over 500) covering world, EU, USA, Japan etc, regularly updated

Trade and statistical information:
Computers – World.
Health care – World and USA.
Pharmaceutical – USA, Japan, World.
Electronics – EU, UK, USA, Japan.
Optical – Italy, France, UK, USA.
Elastomers – Europe, USA.
Chemical – World.
IT – World

Non-library collection catalogue: All or part available in print

Publications: Printed, and electronic and video

Publications list: Available in print

Access to staff: Contact by letter, by telephone, by fax and by e-mail. Appointment necessary.
Hours: Mon to Fri, 0900 to 1700

Access to building: Prior appointment required

SUSSEX COUNTY CRICKET CLUB

Eaton Road, Hove, East Sussex, BN3 3AN

Tel: 01273 827100
Fax: 01273 771549
Website: www.sussexcricket.co.uk

Enquiries to: Business Manager
Direct tel: 01273 827102
Direct e-mail: Russell@sussexcricket.co.uk

Founded: 1839

Organisation type and purpose: Membership association (membership is by subscription), present number of members: c. 5,000.
Sporting organisation.

Subject coverage: History of the clubs and its players.

Access to staff: Contact by letter, by telephone, by fax and via website
Hours: Mon to Fri, 0900 to 1700

SUSSEX INDUSTRIAL ARCHAEOLOGY SOCIETY (SIAS)

42 Falmer Avenue, Saltdean, Brighton, East Sussex, BN2 8FG

Tel: 01273 271330
E-mail: ronald@martin42.fsnet.co.uk

continued overleaf

Website: www.sussexias.co.uk

Enquiries to: General Secretary
Other contacts: Treasurer for financial matters.

Founded: 1968

Organisation type and purpose: Membership association (membership is by subscription), present number of members: 350, voluntary organisation, registered charity (charity number 267159), research organisation.

Subject coverage: Sussex industrial archaeology, mills, brickmaking, railways, ice houses, breweries.

Collection: Records of industrial archaeology sites in Sussex

Publications: Printed

Publications list: Available in print

Access to staff: Contact by letter, by telephone and by e-mail
Hours: 0800 to 2300

SUSSEX PAST

Formal name: Sussex Archaeological Society

Bull House, 92 High Street, Lewes, East Sussex, BN7 1XH

Tel: 01273 486260
Fax: 01273 486990
E-mail: admin@sussexpast.co.uk
Website: www.sussexpast.co.uk

Enquiries to: Public Relations Manager
Direct tel: 01273 487188
Direct e-mail: pro@sussexpast.co.uk

Founded: 1846

Organisation type and purpose: Learned society, registered charity, museum.

Subject coverage: Sussex archaeology, local history and historic properties.

Special visitor services: Guided tours.

Education services: Group education facilities.

Collection: Artefacts relating to archaeology and history
Collection of prints, pictures, books related to Sussex
Manuscripts

Publications: Printed

Access to building: Prior appointment required
Hours: Mon to Sat, 1000 to 1700; Sun, 1100 to 1700
Special comments: Library: 01273 405738
Museum: 01273 405739

Affiliated to: Council for British Archaeology

Sussex Past sites: Anne of Cleves House Museum; 52 Southover High Street, Lewes, East Sussex, BN7 1JA; tel: 01273 474610; Fishbourne Roman Palace and Museum; Salthill Road, Fishbourne, Chichester, West Sussex, PO19 3QR; tel: 01243 785859; fax: 01243 539266; e-mail: adminfish@sussexpast.co.uk; Lewes Castle & Museums; 169 High Street, Lewes, East Sussex, BN7 1YE; tel: 01273 486290; e-mail: castle@sussexpast.co.uk; Marlipins Museum; High Street, Shoreham-by-Sea, West Sussex, BN43 5NN; tel: 01273 462994; Michelham Priory; Upper Dicker, Hailsham, East Sussex, BN27 3QS; tel: 01323 844224; The Priest House; North Lane, West Hoathly, East Grinstead, West Sussex, RH19 4PP; tel: 01342 810479; e-mail: priest@sussexpast.co.uk

SUSSEX RECORD SOCIETY

Barbican House, High Street, Lewes, East Sussex, BN7 1YE

Website: www.sussexrecordsociety.org.

Enquiries to: Hon. Secretary
Direct e-mail: richard.martin2083@ntlworld.com

Founded: 1901

Organisation type and purpose: Learned society.

Subject coverage: Publication of texts relating to the history and topography of Sussex.

Publications: Printed, and electronic and video, and microform publications

Publications list: Available online

Access to staff: Contact by letter, by e-mail and via website

SUSTAIN: THE ALLIANCE FOR BETTER FOOD FARMING (Sustain)

94 White Lion Street, London, N1 9PF

Tel: 020 7837 1228
E-mail: sustain@sustainweb.org
Website: www.sustainweb.org

Enquiries to: Co-ordinator

Founded: 1985; created by the merger of National Food Alliance, and Sustainable Agriculture Food and Environment Alliance (year of change 1999)

Organisation type and purpose: Membership association (membership is by application or invitation), present number of members: c. 100, voluntary organisation, registered charity (charity number 1018643). Umbrella group.

Subject coverage: All aspects of food along the length of the food chain, including environment, nutrition, farming, fair trade, animal welfare.

Publications: Printed
Order printed publications from: website: http://www.sustainweb.org/publications

Publications list: Available online

Access to staff: Contact by letter, by telephone, by e-mail and via website. Appointment necessary.
Hours: Mon to Fri, 0900 to 1800

Access to building: Prior appointment required

Access for disabled people: The building is wheelchair accessible

Member organisations: around 100 member organisations

SUSTRANS

Formal name: Sustainable Transport

2 Cathedral Square, College Green, Bristol, BS1 5DD

Tel: 0117 926 8893
Fax: 0117 929 4173
E-mail: info@sustrans.org.uk
Website: www.sustrans.org.uk

Enquiries to: Information Officer
Direct e-mail: press@sustrans.org.uk

Founded: 1978

Organisation type and purpose: Registered charity (charity number 326550). Campaigns for and builds cycle and pedestrian routes.

Subject coverage: The designing and building of traffic-free routes for cyclists, pedestrians and wheelchair users, the National Cycle Network, the need for a new sustainable transport policy which lessens dependence on the motor car.

Collection: About 400 design and policy studies on walking and particularly cycling facilities

Publications: Printed
Order printed publications from: Sustrans Information Service
PO Box 21, Bristol, BS99 2HA, e-mail: info@sustrans.org.uk

Publications list: Available online and in print

Access to staff: Contact by letter, by telephone, by fax, by e-mail and via website. Appointment necessary.
Hours: Mon to Fri, 0900 to 1700

Head Office: Head Office; 35 King Street, Bristol, BS1 4DZ; tel: 0117 926 8893; fax: 0117 929 4173

Regions: North East; Rockwood House, Barn Hill, Stanley, Co Durham, DH9 8AN; tel: 01207 281259; fax: 01207 28113; Northern Ireland; McAvoy House, 17A Ormeau Avenue, Belfast, BT2 8HD; tel: 028 9043 4569; fax: 028 9043 4556; Scotland; 162 Fountainbridge, Edinburgh, EH3 9RX; tel: 0131 624 7660; fax: 0131 624 7764

SUTTON AND EAST SURREY WATER PLC (SESW)

London Road, Redhill, Surrey, RH1 1JJ

Tel: 01737 772000
Fax: 01737 766807
E-mail: customer_services@waterplc.com
Website: www.waterplc.com

Enquiries to: Press Officer
Direct tel: 01372 460111
Direct fax: 01372 470955
Direct e-mail: stuart.hyslop@surreyhouseuk.com

Founded: 1860

Organisation type and purpose: Utility. Water supply company.

Subject coverage: Supplies water only to East Surrey and parts of South London, Sussex and West Kent.

Publications: Printed, and electronic and video

Publications list: Available online and in print

Access to staff: Contact by letter, by telephone, by fax, by e-mail, in person and via website
Hours: Mon to Fri, 0830 to 1700

Access to building: *Hours:* Mon to Fri, 0830 to 1700

Access for disabled people: Level entry

SUTTON COLDFIELD LIBRARY

45 Lower Parade, Sutton Coldfield, West Midlands, B72 1XX

Tel: 0121 464 2274
Fax: 0121 464 0173
E-mail: sutton.coldfield.lending.library@birmingham.gov.uk

Enquiries to: Librarian
Direct tel: 0121 464 0164

Organisation type and purpose: Public library.

Subject coverage: Separate reference library, children's library and music library and a substantial local history section.

Non-library collection catalogue: All or part available online

Library catalogue: All or part available online

Publications: Printed

Access to staff: Contact by letter, by telephone, by fax, by e-mail, in person and via website
Hours: Mon, Wed, Fri, 0900 to 1800; Tue, Thu, 0900 to 2000; Sat, 0900 to 1700

Access for disabled people: Toilet facilities

SUTTON LIBRARY AND HERITAGE SERVICES

Central Library, St Nicholas Way, Sutton, Surrey, SM1 1EA

Tel: 020 8770 4740; 020 8770 4779 (minicom)
Fax: 020 8770 4777
E-mail: sutton.information@sutton.gov.uk
Website: www.sutton-libraries.gov.uk/uhtbin/webcat

Enquiries to: Librarian

Organisation type and purpose: Local government body, public library.

Subject coverage: General, including genealogy and heraldry, local studies.

Collection: Croydon Airport Collection
River Wandle Collection

Library catalogue: All or part available online

Publications: Printed

Publications list: Available in print

Access to staff: Contact by letter, by telephone, by fax, by e-mail and in person
Hours: Mon, 0930 to 2000 (ground floor only); Tue to Thurs, 0930 to 2000; Fri, 0930 to 1800; Sat, 0930 to 1700; Sun, 1300 to 1630

Access for disabled people: Ramped entry, access to all public areas, toilet facilities

SUZY LAMPLUGH TRUST

National Centre for Personal Safety, Hampton House, 20 Albert Embankment, London, SE1 7TJ

Tel: 020 7091 0014
Fax: 020 7091 0015
E-mail: info@suzylamplugh.org
Website: www.suzylamplugh.org

Direct e-mail: press@suzylamplugh.org

Founded: 1986

Organisation type and purpose: Advisory body, voluntary organisation, registered charity (charity number 802567), suitable for ages: all, training organisation, consultancy, research organisation.
The leading authority on personal safety. To reduce violence and aggression in society and help everyone – men, women and children – to gain the knowledge and confidence they need to live safer lives.

Subject coverage: Personal safety, indoors, outdoors, and in the workplace.

Non-library collection catalogue: All or part available online

Library catalogue: All or part available in-house

Publications: Printed, and electronic and video

Publications list: Available online and in print

Access to staff: Contact by letter, by telephone and by fax. Appointment necessary.
Hours: Mon to Fri, 0900 to 1700

SWALE BOROUGH COUNCIL (SBC)

Swale House, East Street, Sittingbourne, Kent, ME10 3HT

Tel: 01795 424341
Fax: 01795 417217
Website: www.swale.gov.uk

Enquiries to: Public Relations Manager
Direct tel: 01795 417400
Direct fax: 01795 417382
Direct e-mail: kimevans@swale.gov.uk

Founded: 1974

Organisation type and purpose: Local government body.

Subject coverage: Local government.

Access to staff: Contact by letter, by telephone, by fax and by e-mail
Hours: Mon to Fri, 0900 to 1700

SWALEDALE SHEEP BREEDERS ASSOCIATION

The Shooting Lodge, High Shipley, Eggleston, Barnard Castle, Co Durham, DL12 0DP

Tel: 01833 650516
Fax: 01833 650516
E-mail: jstephenson@swaledale-sheep.com

Subject coverage: Breeders and breeding of Swaledale Sheep.

SWANSEA CITY AND COUNTY COUNCIL

County Hall, Swansea, West Glamorgan, SA1 3SN

Tel: 01792 636000
Fax: 01792 637206
E-mail: bob.cuthill@swansea.gov.uk
Website: www.swansea.gov.uk

Enquiries to: Information Officer
Direct tel: 01792 636737

Founded: 1996

Organisation type and purpose: Local government body.

Subject coverage: Policy issues, demography including census of the population, local statistics and modernising local government agenda.

Access to staff: Contact by letter, by telephone, by fax, by e-mail and via website. Appointment necessary.
Hours: Mon to Fri, 0830 to 1700

Access for disabled people: Parking provided, ramped entry, level entry, toilet facilities

SWANSEA INSTITUTE OF HIGHER EDUCATION (SIHE)

Townhill Road, Swansea, West Glamorgan, SA2 0UT

Tel: 01792 481000
Fax: 01792 208683
E-mail: enquiry@sihe.ac.uk
Website: www.sihe.ac.uk

Enquiries to: Head of Library and Learning Support Services
Direct tel: 01792 481240
Direct fax: 01792 298017
Direct e-mail: t.lamb@sihe.ac.uk

Organisation type and purpose: Library.

Subject coverage: Art, stained glass, education – primary teacher training, humanities, construction, business, management, law, tourism, leisure, health care, transport, engineering, manufacturing design, optoelectronics computing, safety in leisure pursuits, motor sport, applied design.

Access to staff: Non-members charged.
Hours: Mon to Thu, 0845 to 2100; Fri, 0845 to 1630; Sat, 1000 to 1600

Associated college of: University of Wales

Other addresses: Swansea Institute of Higher Education; Mount Pleasant, Swansea, SA1 6ED; tel: 01792 481000

SWANSEA TRIBOLOGY SERVICES LIMITED (STS Ltd)

5 Penrice Court, Fenrod Business Park, Enterprise Park, Swansea, West Glamorgan, SA6 8QW

Tel: 01792 799036
Fax: 01792 799034
E-mail: oiltest@trib.co.uk
Website: www.trib.co.uk

Enquiries to: Laboratory Director

Founded: 1996

Organisation type and purpose: International organisation, manufacturing industry, service industry, training organisation, consultancy, research organisation, laboratory.

Subject coverage: Tribology, condition monitoring, wear debris monitors, oil analysis, maintenance.

Publications list: Available in print

continued overleaf

Access to staff: Contact by letter, by telephone, by fax, by e-mail, in person and via website. Appointment necessary.
Hours: Mon to Fri, 0900 to 1630

SWANSEA UNIVERSITY – INFORMATION SERVICES AND SYSTEMS

Singleton Park, Swansea, SA2 8PP

Tel: 01792 295175
Fax: 01792 295851
E-mail: library@swansea.ac.uk
Website: www.swan.ac.uk/lis

Enquiries to: Director of Library and Information Services

Founded: 1920

Organisation type and purpose: University Library, IT & Media, Careers and MIS services.

Subject coverage: Humanities, economic and social sciences, physical, natural and engineering sciences, education, business studies, law, history of South Wales coalfield.

Collection: Archives of the South Wales coalfield and other local archives
British Standards
Strong collections in history, mathematics, Celtic studies, Welsh writers in English

Non-library collection catalogue: All or part available online and in-house

Library catalogue: All or part available online

Publications: Printed, and microform publications

Access to staff: Contact by letter, by telephone, by fax, by e-mail and in person. Appointment necessary.
Hours: Term time: Sun to Thu, 0800 to 0200; Fri, Sat, 0800 to 2000
Vacations: Mon to Thu, 0800 to 2000; Fri, Sat, 0800 to 1700; Sun, closed
Special comments: Different hours apply in branch libraries.

Access to building: No prior appointment required

Access for disabled people: Ramped entry, access to all public areas, toilet facilities
Special comments: Special facilities for users with visual impairment.

SWEDENBORG SOCIETY

Swedenborg House, 20–21 Bloomsbury Way, London, WC1A 2TH

Tel: 020 7405 7986
E-mail: james@swedenborg.org.uk
Website: www.swedenborg.org.uk

Enquiries to: Librarian
Other contacts: Secretary

Founded: 1810

Organisation type and purpose: Learned society (membership is by subscription, election or invitation), present number of members: 850, registered charity (charity number 209172), publishing house.
The Swedenborg Society was established for the purpose of printing and publishing the works of Emanuel Swedenborg.

Subject coverage: Life and works of Emanuel Swedenborg and related material.

Collection: Complete works of Swedenborg; all languages and all editions; original archival items re society, Swedenborg, the New Church; collateral works
Completely catalogued reference library
Separate lending library

Non-library collection catalogue: All or part available online

Library catalogue: All or part available online and in-house

Publications: Printed
Order printed publications from: http://www.swedenborg.org.uk

Publications list: Available online and in print

Access to staff: Contact by letter, by telephone, by e-mail and via website. Appointment necessary.
Hours: Mon to Fri, 0930 to 1700

Access to building: Prior appointment required for use of library; please bring ID and proof of address

Links with: similar bodies world-wide; The Library and Archives of The General Conference of the New Church; at the same address

SWEDISH CHAMBER OF COMMERCE FOR THE UNITED KINGDOM

Sweden House, 5 Upper Montagu Street, London, W1H 2AG

Tel: 020 7224 8001
Fax: 020 7224 8884
E-mail: info@scc.org.uk
Website: www.scc.org.uk

Enquiries to: Managing Director

Founded: 1906

Organisation type and purpose: Membership association (membership is by subscription), present number of members: 400.

Subject coverage: General information dealing with Anglo-Swedish trade.

Trade and statistical information: Data on Anglo-Swedish trade

Publications: Printed

Access to staff: Contact by letter, by fax, by e-mail, in person and via website. Non-members charged.
Hours: Mon to Fri, 0900 to 1730

SWIFT CLUB

The Croft, Ash Green, Surrey, GU12 6HD

Tel: 01252 344402
Fax: 01252 311187

Enquiries to: Honorary Secretary

Founded: 1985

Organisation type and purpose: Membership association (membership is by subscription), present number of members: 67, voluntary organisation.

Subject coverage: Technical advice on Swift cars produced by the Swift Motor Co. of Coventry between 1901 and 1931.

Publications: Printed

Access to staff: Contact by letter, by telephone, by fax and by e-mail. Appointment necessary.
Hours: Mon to Sun, 0900 to 2200

SWIM WALES

Wales National Pool, Sketty Lane, Swansea, SA2 8QG

Tel: 01792 513636
Fax: 01792 513637
E-mail: secretary@welshasa.co.uk
Website: www.welshasa.co.uk

Enquiries to: Head of Administration

Founded: 1897; formerly called Welsh Amateur Swimming Association (WASA)

Organisation type and purpose: Membership association (membership is by subscription), present number of members: 9,500, voluntary organisation.
Recognised as the governing body for swimming in Wales; promotes the sport throughout Wales and develops members' potential to represent Wales and Great Britain at European and World levels in swimming, diving and water polo.

Subject coverage: Amateur swimming, diving and water polo.

Access to staff: Contact by letter, by telephone, by fax and by e-mail
Hours: Mon to Fri, 0900 to 1600

SWIMMING POOL AND ALLIED TRADES ASSOCIATION (SPATA)

4 Eastgate House, East Street, Andover, Hampshire, SP10 1EP

Tel: 01264 356210
E-mail: admin@spata.co.uk
Website: www.spata.co.uk

Organisation type and purpose: A membership association for the swimming pools and allied trades.
Sets standards governing the construction and operation of pools, spas, saunas and steam rooms, which members have to follow. Inspects pool contractor members' work before they can join, and periodically reinspects afterwards. Membership includes approx. 200 swimming pool companies in the UK, Ireland and overseas, including contractors, designers, service engineers, trade suppliers, and retailers of pool equipment and ancillaries.

Subject coverage: Swimming pools, spas, saunas, steam rooms.

Publications: Printed
Order printed publications from: Website

Publications list: Available online

Access to staff: Contact by letter, by telephone and by e-mail

Member organisation of: British Swimming Pool Federation; European Union of Swimming Pool and Spa Associations (EUSA)

SWINDON BOROUGH COUNCIL

Civic Offices, Euclid Street, Swindon, Wiltshire, SN1 2JH

Tel: 01793 463000; minicom no. 01793 436659
Fax: 01793 463930
Website: www.swindon.gov.uk

Enquiries to: Chief Executive
Direct tel: 01793 463010
Direct e-mail: gjones@swindon.gov.uk

Organisation type and purpose: Local government body.

Subject coverage: Local government.

Access to staff: Contact by letter, by telephone and by fax
Hours: Mon to Fri, 0900 to 1630

SWINDON BOROUGH COUNCIL LIBRARIES

Central Library, Regent Circus, Swindon, SN1 1QG

Tel: 01793 466035
Fax: 01793 529572
E-mail: ajordan@swindon.gov.uk
Website: www.swindon.gov.uk/libraries

Enquiries to: Central Library
Direct tel: 01793 463238
Direct e-mail: libraries@swindon.gov.uk

Organisation type and purpose: Local government body, public library.

Subject coverage: General, railways.

Collection: Great Western Railway collection
Richard Jefferies manuscript collection
Swindon and Wiltshire local studies

Non-library collection catalogue: All or part available online

Library catalogue: All or part available online

Access to staff: Contact by letter, by telephone, by fax, by e-mail and in person. Appointment necessary. Access for members only.
Hours: Mon to Fri, 0900 to 1700; Sat, 0930 to 1600

Access to building: No prior appointment required

Access for disabled people: Ramped entry, level entry

Parent body: Swindon Borough Council; Civic Offices, Euclid Street, Swindon, SN1 2JH; tel: 01793 445000; e-mail: customerservices@swindon.gov.uk; website: http://www.swindon.gov.uk

Sponsor for: WILCO; Central Library, Regent Circus, Swindon, SN1 1QG; tel: 01793 463797; fax: 01793 529572; e-mail: rtrayhurn@swindon.gov.uk; website: http://www.wilco.org.uk

SWISS COTTAGE CENTRAL LIBRARY

88 Avenue Road, London, NW3 3HA

Tel: 020 7974 4001
Fax: 020 7974 6532
E-mail: swisscottagelibrary@camden.gov.uk
Website: www.camden.gov.uk/ccm/navigation/leisure/libraries-and-online-learning-centres/swiss-cottage-library/

Enquiries to: Customer Services Manager
Direct tel: 020 7974 6531 (not a public number)
Other contacts: Service Delivery Manager

Founded: 1964

Organisation type and purpose: Local government body, public library.

Subject coverage: General library, reference materials, specialist collection of philosophy and psychology; selected official publications.

Collection: Maps
Selected official publications of United Kingdom (some EU)
See website: http://www.camden.gov.uk/ccm/content/leisure/libraries-and-online-learning-centres/twocolumn/reference-information.en for current subscription databases

Trade and statistical information: Selected British official statistics, some EU statistics

Library catalogue: All or part available online

Access to staff: Contact by letter, by telephone, by e-mail and in person
Hours: Mon to Fri, 1000 to 2000; Sat, 1000 to 1700; Sun, 1100 to 1600

Access to building: *Hours:* Mon to Fri, 1000 to 2000; Sat, 1000 to 1700; Sun, 1100 to 1600

Access for disabled people: Level entry, access to all public areas, toilet facilities

Parent body: London Borough of Camden, Culture and Environment; Camden Town Hall Extension, Argyle Street, London WC1H 8EQ; tel: 020 7974 5613; website: https://www.camden.gov.uk/ccm/content/contacts/council-contacts/environment/contact-the-environment-department.en

SWISS EMBASSY

Formal name: Embassy of Switzerland

16–18 Montagu Place, London, W1H 2BQ

Tel: 020 7616 6000
Fax: 020 7724 7001
E-mail: swissembassy@lon.rep.admin.ch
Website: www.swissembassy.org.uk

Organisation type and purpose: National embassy.

Subject coverage: Switzerland: general, commercial, cultural and educational matters.

SWITZERLAND TOURISM

30 Bedford Street, London, WC2E 9ED

Tel: 020 7420 4900
Fax: 00800 100 200 31
E-mail: info.uk@myswitzerland.com
Website: www.myswitzerland.com

Enquiries to: Marketing Services

Founded: 1875

Organisation type and purpose: International organisation.

Access to staff: Contact by letter, by telephone, by fax and by e-mail
Hours: Mon to Fri, 0900 to 1700

Access to building: No access other than to staff, prior appointment required

Access for disabled people: Ramped entry, toilet facilities

SYBIL CAMPBELL COLLECTION

c/o Mr David Farley, University of Winchester, Winchester, Hampshire, SO22 4NR

Fax: 01962 827479
E-mail: libenquiries@winchester.ac.uk
Website: winchester.ac.uk/library

Enquiries to: Librarian
Direct tel: 01962 827306

Founded: 1927; Crosby Hall Library

Organisation type and purpose: Library reference collection reflecting the entrance of women into higher education and into academic and professional life in the late 19th and early 20th century.

Subject coverage: Women's writing and history in the 19th and 20th centuries, women's education and their personal libraries, (auto)biography, women in wartime (including refugees), early 20th century philosophy, literary criticism, poetry and travel.

Collection: Library of 8,000 items

Non-library collection catalogue: All or part available online and in-house

Library catalogue: All or part available online and in-house

Order electronic and video publications from: Seminar Monographs (online)

Access to staff: Contact by letter, by telephone and by e-mail. Appointment necessary.

Administered by: University of Winchester

Parent body: University of Winchester

TACT (TACT)

Formal name: The Adolescent and Children's Trust

The Courtyard, 303 Hither Green Lane, Hither Green, London SE13 6TJ

Tel: 020 8695 8142
E-mail: corporateadmin@tactcare.org.uk
Website: www.tactcare.org.uk

Founded: 1993

Organisation type and purpose: Charity prodiving fostering and adoption services across the UK.

Subject coverage: Adoption and fostering services.

Access to staff: Contact by telephone and by e-mail
Hours: Mon to Fri, 0900 to 1700

TALIS INFORMATION LIMITED

Knights Court, Solihull Parkway, Birmingham Business Park, B37 7YB

Tel: 0870 400 5000
Fax: 0870 400 5001
E-mail: info@talis.com
Website: www.talis.com

continued overleaf

Direct e-mail: sarah.foster@talis.com

Founded: 1969

Organisation type and purpose: UK's leading provider of library management systems and also provides solutions to manage academic course resources, digitised image collections, and maintain a unique database containing over 19 million bibliographical records.

Subject coverage: Library automation, library services, unity web, network services, information delivery services, Talislist – guided learning environment, training and consultancy, Invisage – digital content management, OPAC.

Collection: BLCMP Database of 17 million bibliographic records
Unityweb

Publications: Printed, and electronic and video

Access to staff: Contact by letter, by telephone, by fax, by e-mail and via website. Appointment necessary.
Hours: Mon to Fri, 0900 to 1700

TALKING NEWSPAPER ASSOCIATION OF THE UNITED KINGDOM (TNAUK)

National Recording Centre, 10 Browning Road, Heathfield, East Sussex, TN21 8DB

Tel: 01435 866102
Fax: 01435 865422
E-mail: info@tnauk.org.uk
Website: www.tnauk.org.uk

Enquiries to: Director

Founded: 1974

Organisation type and purpose: Membership association, registered charity (charity number 293656).

Subject coverage: Recording of over 200 national newspapers and magazines on audio tape, audio CD, Daisy CDs and download with full text versions of many publications on CD-ROM, website download and e-mail for visually impaired and disabled people.

Publications: Printed, and electronic and video

Publications list: Available online and in print

Access to staff: Contact by letter, by telephone, by fax, by e-mail and in person
Hours: Mon to Fri, 0900 to 1700

Links with: RNIB; tel: 01435 866102; fax: 01435 865422; e-mail: info@tnauk.org.uk

TALL SHIPS YOUTH TRUST (STA)

2A The Hard, Portsmouth, Hampshire, PO1 3PT

Tel: 023 9283 2055
Fax: 023 9281 5769
E-mail: info@tallships.org
Website: www.tallships.org

Enquiries to: PR & Events Manager
Other contacts: Reservations Supervisor for voyage enquiry.

Founded: 1956; formerly called STA Schooners (year of change 1995); formerly called International STA (year of change 1999); formerly called Sail Training Association (year of change 2004)

Organisation type and purpose: Voluntary organisation, registered charity (charity number 314229), training organisation.
The Tall Ships Youth Trust is dedicated to the personal development of young people, aged 16–25, through the experience of tall ship sailing, aboard one of our Brigs, 'Stavros S Niarchos' and 'Prince William'. Similar opportunities are available on adult voyages (18–75). Voyages are available in the UK, Europe, Caribbean, Mediterranean and transatlantic

Subject coverage: Tall Ships' Voyages and Cutty Sark Tall Ships' Races, personal development of 16 to 25 year olds.
Adult Voyages for 18–75 year olds.
Day Sails for 18–75 year olds.

Trade and statistical information: World's largest and leading sail training organisation

Publications: Printed, and electronic and video

Access to staff: Contact by letter, by telephone, by fax, by e-mail, in person and via website
Hours: Mon to Fri, 0900 to 1700

Member of: Association of Sea Training Organisations; Duke of Edinburgh's Award; tel: 01753 727400; fax: 01753 810666; e-mail: info@theaward.org; Royal Yachting Association; tel: 023 8062 7400; website: www.rya.org

TALYLLYN RAILWAY

Wharf Station, Tywyn, Gwynedd, LL36 9EY

Tel: 01654 710472
Fax: 01654 711755
E-mail: enquiries@talyllyn.co.uk
Website: www.talyllyn.co.uk

Enquiries to: Secretary
Direct e-mail: secretary@talyllyn.co.uk
Other contacts: Chief Executive

Founded: 1865

Organisation type and purpose: Voluntary organisation, museum.
Preservation society. The Talyllyn Railway runs from Tywyn Wharf to Nant Gwernol and was opened in 1866. The Narrow Gauge Railway Museum is at Tywyn.

Subject coverage: Narrow gauge railways; Welsh slate industry history; narrow gauge railway modelling; maintenance of narrow gauge railways, steam and diesel; volunteering.

Special visitor services: Opportunities to drive your own steam train; see Driver Experience on website or telephone for details.

Education services: Narrow Gauge Railway Museum at Tywyn Wharf; facilities for school parties.

Services for disabled people: All advertised trains except the Victorian Train have accommodation for wheelchairs; accessible lavatories are available at Tywyn Wharf and Abergynolwyn.

Collection: The Railway operates 6 historic steam locomotives and a number of historic carriages
The Museum houses several locomotives and a large collection of other items from British and Irish narrow gauge lines
Archives are kept in Dolgellau in conjunction with Gwynedd Council

Non-library collection catalogue: All or part available online

Publications: Printed, and electronic and video, and microform publications
Order printed publications from: Talyllyn Railway Shop, address as above; tel: 01654 711012
Order microform publications from: Films Officer, address as above
Order electronic and video publications from: Talyllyn Railway Shop, address as above; tel: 01654 711012

Publications list: Available online

Access to staff: Contact by letter, by telephone, by fax, by e-mail, in person and via website
Hours: Whenever trains are running; at other times of year Mon to Fri, 0900 to 1700
See website: http://ngrm.org.uk/ for museum opening hours
Special comments: Archives only accessible with introduction; please contact Archives Officer for details.

Access to building: *Hours:* Stations are open whenever trains are running, but shops and refreshment rooms may close earlier. At other times of year at Tywyn Wharf the shop, refreshment room and museum are open on certain days; see website or telephone for details.
See website: http://ngrm.org.uk/ for museum opening hours.

Access for disabled people: Tywyn Wharf and Abergynolwyn: all public areas wheelchair accessible; other stations: please enquire

TAMBA

Formal name: Twins and Multiple Births Association

2 The Willows, Gardner Road, Guildford, Surrey, GU1 4PG

Tel: 01483 304442
Fax: 01483 302483
E-mail: enquiries@tamba.org.uk
Website: www.tamba.org.uk

Enquiries to: Administrator

Founded: 1978; formerly called Twins Clubs Association

Organisation type and purpose: Membership association (membership is by subscription), present number of members: 6000, registered charity (charity number 1076478).

Subject coverage: Multiple births (two three, four or more) families; professional support for parents and carers; ante-natal and post-natal aspects of management; network of local twin clubs for parents; fertility treatment, bereavements; one parent families; special needs groups; education of twins and higher multiples. Super Twins (for families of triplets or more).

Collection: Educational references
Medical references to twins and higher multiples

Publications: Printed, and electronic and video

Publications list: Available in print

Access to staff: Contact by letter, by telephone and by fax
Hours: Mon to Fri, 0930 to 1600
Special comments: Out of hours answerphone.

TAMESIDE ARCHIVES SERVICE

Formal name: Tameside Local Studies and Archives

Tameside Local Studies and Archives Centre, Central Library, Old Street, Ashton-under-Lyne, OL6 7SG

Tel: 0161 342 4242
Fax: 0161 342 4245
E-mail: archives@tameside.gov.uk
Website: www.tameside.gov.uk/history

Enquiries to: Archivist
Other contacts: Local Studies Librarian

Founded: 1976

Organisation type and purpose: Local government body.

Subject coverage: Local public, business, religions, family and regimental records.

Collection: Manchester Regiment Archives

Non-library collection catalogue: All or part available online and in-house

Library catalogue: All or part available in-house

Publications: Printed

Access to staff: Contact by letter, by telephone, by fax, by e-mail, in person and via website
Hours: Mon, Tue, Thu, 0900 to 2000; Wed, Fri, 0900 to 1700; Sat, 0900 to 1600

Access for disabled people: Disabled access available
Hours: As above

Parent body: Tameside Borough Council; Wellington Road, Ashton-under-Lyne

TAMESIDE LIBRARIES INFORMATION SERVICE

Tameside Central Library, Old Street, Ashton-under-Lyne, Lancashire, OL6 7SG

Tel: 0161 342 2031
Fax: 0161 330 4762
E-mail: information.direct@tameside.gov.uk
Website: www.tameside.gov.uk/libraries

Enquiries to: Librarian

Organisation type and purpose: Local government body, public library.

Subject coverage: General.

Collection: HMSO publications

Non-library collection catalogue: All or part available online

Library catalogue: All or part available online

Access to staff: Contact by letter, by telephone, by fax, by e-mail, in person and via website
Hours: Mon, Tue, Thu, 0900 to 2000; Wed, Fri, 0900 to 1700; Sat, 0900 to 1600

Access for disabled people: Ramp access

Parent body: Tameside Metropolitan Borough Council, Community Services

TAMESIDE LOCAL GOVERNMENT INFORMATION SERVICE AND MEMBERS SERVICES

Level B, Council Offices, Wellington Road, Ashton-under-Lyne, Lancashire, OL6 6DL

Tel: 0161 342 8355
Fax: 0161 342 2102
E-mail: tameside-reflib@mcr1.poptel.org.uk

Enquiries to: Democratic Services Officer
Direct tel: 0161 342 3020

Founded: 1982

Organisation type and purpose: Local government body.

Subject coverage: Local government.

Library catalogue: All or part available in-house

Parent body: Tameside Metropolitan Borough Council; Borough Solicitor

TAMESIDE LOCAL STUDIES ARCHIVES CENTRE

Central Library, Old Street, Ashton-under-Lyne, OL6 7SP

Tel: 0161 342 4242
Fax: 0161 342 4245
E-mail: archives@tameside.gov.uk
Website: www.tameside.gov.uk

Enquiries to: Local Studies Librarian
Other contacts: Archivist

Founded: 1976

Organisation type and purpose: Local government body, public library.

Subject coverage: Local history and topography of Tameside area, and background material on Lancashire and Cheshire.

Collection: Manchester Regiment archive collection
Manchester Studies tape collection (oral history interviews recorded c. 1974–1984)

Non-library collection catalogue: All or part available online

Library catalogue: All or part available online

Publications: Printed

Publications list: Available online

Access to staff: Contact by letter, by telephone, by fax, by e-mail, in person and via website
Hours: Mon, Tue, Thu, 0900 to 2000; Wed, Fri, 0900 to 1700; Sat 0900 to 1600

Constituent part of: Sustainable Communities; Community and IT Services, Council Offices, Wellington Road, Ashton-under-Lyne, OL6 6DL

TAMWORTH BOROUGH COUNCIL

Marmion House, Lichfield Street, Tamworth, Staffordshire, B79 7BZ

Tel: 01827 709709
Fax: 01827 709271
E-mail: enquiries@tamworth.gov.uk
Website: www.tamworth.gov.uk

Enquiries to: Public Relations Officer

Organisation type and purpose: Local government body.

TANDRIDGE DISTRICT COUNCIL

Station Road East, Oxted, Surrey, RH8 0BT

Tel: 01883 722000
Fax: 01883 722015
E-mail: the.council@tandridge.gov.uk
Website: www.tandridgedc.gov.uk
Website: www.tandridge.gov.uk

Enquiries to: Information Officer

Organisation type and purpose: Local government body.

Access to staff: Contact by letter, by telephone, by fax, by e-mail and via website. Appointment necessary.
Hours: Mon to Thu, 0900 to 1700; Fri, 0900 to 1630

Access for disabled people: Level entry

Parent body: Surrey County Council

TAUNTON DEANE BOROUGH COUNCIL

The Deane House, Belvedere Road, Taunton, Somerset, TA1 1HE

Tel: 01823 356356\ Minicom no. 01823 356356
Fax: 01823 356329
E-mail: public.relations@tauntondeane.gov.uk
Website: www.tauntondeane.gov.uk/tourism

Enquiries to: Public Relations Manager
Direct tel: 01823 356407

Organisation type and purpose: Local government body.

Subject coverage: Local agenda 21 and domestic energy efficiency information for residents of Taunton Deane in addition to normal local authority functions.

Access to staff: Contact by letter, by telephone, by fax, by e-mail, in person and via website
Hours: Mon to Thu, 0830 to 1730; Fri, 0830 to 1700

Access for disabled people: Parking provided, level entry, toilet facilities

TAUNTON TOURIST INFORMATION CENTRE

Library, Paul Street, Taunton, Somerset, TA1 3XZ

Tel: 01823 336344
Fax: 01823 340308
E-mail: tauntontic@tauntondeane.gov.uk
Website: www.somerset.gov.uk/libraries

Enquiries to: Manager
Founded: 1974

Organisation type and purpose: Local government body.

continued overleaf

To provide a wide range of information on the local area and the UK.

Subject coverage: Tourist information on Taunton and Somerset, holiday information on the whole of the UK, local walks and cycle rides, theatre, gallery and cinema information, local bus and train information. Bookings can be made for National Express coaches, Berrys Coaches, local theatres, local concerts and events, Ticketmaster and YHA membership.

Collection: Reference books for visitors: hotel and other accommodation, various guides and travel information

Publications: Printed, and electronic and video

Access to staff: Contact by letter, by telephone, by fax, by e-mail, in person and via website
Hours: Mon to Sat, 0930 to 1700; Sun (July and Aug), 1100 to 1500

Access for disabled people: Access to all public areas

Parent body: Somerset County Council; Library Headquarters, Mount Street, Bridgewater, Somerset, TA6 3LF; tel: 01278 451201; fax: 01278 452787

TAVISTOCK AND PORTMAN NHS FOUNDATION TRUST LIBRARY

Tavistock Centre, 120 Belsize Lane, London, NW3 5BA

Tel: 020 8938 2520
E-mail: angeladouglas@tavi-port.ac.uk
Website: www.tavistockandportman.ac.uk/library

Enquiries to: Head of Library and Learning Resources

Founded: 1947

Organisation type and purpose: Training organisation and outpatient clinic committed to improving mental health and emotional wellbeing. The Trust believes that high quality mental health services should be available for all who need them.

Subject coverage: Psychoanalysis, psychotherapy, psychology, psychiatry, human relations, social work and social welfare.

Information services: See website: http://www.tavistockandportman.ac.uk/library/e-library.

Special visitor services: See website: http://www.tavistockandportman.ac.uk/library/external-members-and-visitors.

Education services: See website: http://tapthelibrarians.blogspot.co.uk/
http://keepuptodatewithtapsnaps.blogspot.co.uk/

Services for disabled people: See website: http://www.tavistockandportman.ac.uk/library/in-london/accessibility.

Collection: http://repository.tavistockandportman.ac.uk/

Non-library collection catalogue: All or part available online

Library catalogue: All or part available online

Access to staff: Contact by telephone, by e-mail and via website. Non-members charged.
Hours: Mon to Thu, 1000 to 2000; Fri, 1000 to 1800
Special comments: Limited access for non-members in term time.

Access for disabled people: Parking provided, level entry, access to all public areas, toilet facilities

Parent body: Tavistock and Portman NHS Foundation Trust; tel: 020 8940 2520; website: http://www.tavistockandportman.ac.uk

TAVISTOCK INSTITUTE OF HUMAN RELATIONS (TTI)

30 Tabernacle Street, London, EC2A 4UE

Tel: 020 7417 0407
Fax: 020 7417 0566
E-mail: central.admin@tavinstitute.org
Website: www.tavinstitute.org

Enquiries to: Operations Manager

Founded: 1947

Organisation type and purpose: Advisory body, registered charity (charity number 209706), training organisation, research organisation.
Independent social science research.

Subject coverage: Human relations, community care, community organisations, voluntary action, social welfare, employment, vocational training, telematics, action research, group relations training, organisational change and development, evaluation and review.

Publications: Printed

Publications list: Available in print

Access to staff: Contact by letter. Appointment necessary.
Hours: Mon to Fri, 0930 to 1730

Access to building: Prior appointment required

Access for disabled people: Access to all public areas, toilet facilities

TAVISTOCK SUBSCRIPTION LIBRARY

Court Gate, Guildhall Square, Tavistock, Devon, PL19 0AE

Tel: 01822 612352
E-mail: jackwalkerstar@aol.com

Enquiries to: Honorary Secretary

Founded: 1799

Organisation type and purpose: Membership association (membership is by subscription, election or invitation), historic building, house or site.
Independent library.

Subject coverage: Tavistock (Devon) local books and information.

Collection: Tavistock and District

Library catalogue: All or part available in-house and in print

Publications: Printed

Publications list: Available in print

Access to staff: Contact by letter, by telephone and by e-mail. Appointment necessary.
Hours: Mon to Fri, 0900 to 1700

Access to building: Prior appointment required

Access for disabled people: Level entry

Also at: Honorary Secretary, Tavistock Subscription Library; 9 Manor Road, Tavistock, Devon, PL19 0PL; tel: 01822 612352; e-mail: jackwalkerstar@aol.com

Member organisation of: Independent Library Association

TAXBRIEFS LIMITED

2–5 Benjamin Street, London, EC1M 5QL

Tel: 020 7250 0967
Fax: 020 7251 8867
E-mail: info@taxbriefs.co.uk
Website: www.taxbriefs.co.uk

Enquiries to: Director

Founded: 1975

Organisation type and purpose: Publishing house.

Subject coverage: Finance information on pensions, life assurance, taxation.

Library catalogue: All or part available online and in print

Publications: Printed, and electronic and video

Publications list: Available online and in print

Access to staff: Contact by letter, by telephone, by fax, by e-mail and via website
Hours: Mon to Fri, 0900 to 1730

Access to building: Prior appointment required

TAY VALLEY FAMILY HISTORY SOCIETY (TVFHS)

Family History Research Centre, 179–181 Princes Street, Dundee, DD4 6DQ

Tel: 01382 461845
Fax: 01382 461845
E-mail: tvfhs@tayvalleyfhs.org.uk
Website: www.tayvalleyfhs.org.uk

Enquiries to: Honorary Secretary

Organisation type and purpose: Membership association (membership is by subscription), present number of members: 1,500, registered charity.

Subject coverage: Family histories, pedigrees, research interests of members, unpublished birth, marriage and death information, census information 1841–91 and collection of monumental inscriptions, all in the counties of Angus, Fife, Kinross and Perth.

Collection: Extensive collection of family history materials for the counties of Angus, Fife, Kinross and Perth

Library catalogue: All or part available online

Publications: Printed, and microform publications

Publications list: Available in print

Access to staff: Contact by letter, by telephone, by e-mail, in person and via website. Non-members charged.

Access to building: *Hours:* Mon, Tue, Wed, Fri, 1000 to 1600; Sat, 1000 to 1300; Thu, 1000 to 1600 and 1900 to 2100
Special comments: Charge £2 per hour for non-members.

Access for disabled people: Level entry, toilet facilities

TAYLOR INSTITUTION LIBRARY

Formal name: Taylor Institution Library, One of the Bodleian Libraries of the University of Oxford

St Giles', Oxford, OX1 3NA

Tel: 01865 278158
Fax: 01865 278165
E-mail: tay-enquiries@bodleian.ox.ac.uk
Website: www.bodleian.ox.ac.uk/taylor

Enquiries to: Reader Services Coordinator
Direct tel: 01865 278155
Direct e-mail: frank.egerton@bodleian.ox.ac.uk

Founded: 1848

Organisation type and purpose: University department or institute. The Taylor Institution is Oxford University's centre for the study of modern European languages. The building houses two collections: the Taylor Institution (Main) Library, used mainly by postgraduate/academic researchers; and the Teaching Collection, used mainly by undergraduates and taught postgraduates. The Taylor Bodleian Slavonic and Modern Greek Library is housed nearby (47 Wellington Square).

Subject coverage: Medieval and modern continental European (and related) languages and literature, predominantly Spanish and Portuguese, German, French, and Italian; included are those of modern Latin America, the literature of Canada, and North and sub-Saharan Africa; also Linguistics; film studies; women's studies; Celtic; and Dutch, Yiddish, and Afrikaans. Also, at 47 Wellington Square, Russian and other Slavonic (and related) languages, and modern Greek, languages and literature.

Collection: Butler Clarke Collection (Spanish books)
Dante Collection (Italian)
Dawkins Collection (Byzantine and modern Greek books)
Fiedler Collection of German literary, philological and historical works
Finch Collection of literary and linguistic works printed in the 16th, 17th and 18th centuries (Italian and other)
Martin Collection (Spanish and Portuguese books)
Nevill Forbes and W R Morfill Collections of Slavonic books
Rudler Collection of French books (particularly Benjamin Constant items and early 20th-century French writers)
Besterman Voltaire Bequest: collection of works relating to Voltaire and the French Enlightenment with a world locational index of 18th-century editions of Voltaire
Whitechapel and Schweizer Collections of Yiddish Literature
Collection of European writers' letters and manuscripts
Strachan Collection of French 19th-century 'livres d'artiste'

Non-library collection catalogue: All or part available online and in print

Library catalogue: All or part available online

Publications: Printed

Access to staff: Contact by letter, by fax, by e-mail and via website. Appointment necessary. Letter of introduction required.
Hours: See website for details: http://www.bodleian.ox.ac.uk/taylor

Access to building: Visitors are advised to check the library's website beforehand for times of access

Dependent library: Taylor Bodleian Slavonic and Modern Greek Library, University of Oxford; 47 Wellington Square, Oxford, OX1 2JF; tel: 01865 270464; fax: 01865 270469; e-mail: tabs-enquiries@bodleian.ox.ac.uk

Parent body: University of Oxford

TAYLOR NELSON SOFRES PLC

Westgate, London, W5 1UA

Tel: 020 8967 0007
E-mail: enquiries@tnsofres.com
Website: www.tnsofres.com

Enquiries to: Director of Social and Political Research
Direct tel: 020 8332 8551
Direct fax: 020 8332 1090

Organisation type and purpose: Service industry, research organisation.
Engaged in all forms of social and commercial survey research.

Subject coverage: Marketing information – continuous and custom research in over 80 countries. Specialist expertise in IT, telecoms, healthcare, automotive, TV, media, internet, consumer.

Access to staff: Contact by letter, by telephone, by e-mail and via website
Hours: Mon to Fri, 0900 to 1730

Access to building: No access other than to staff

Member of: BMRA; Gallup International Association; MRS

Parent body: SOFRES

TEACHER SCIENTIST NETWORK (TSN)

John Innes Centre, Norwich Research Park, Colney, Norwich, Norfolk, NR4 7UH

Tel: 01603 450000
Fax: 01603 450045
E-mail: ts.network@bbsrc.ac.uk
Website: www.tsn.org.uk

Enquiries to: Co-ordinator

Founded: 1994

Organisation type and purpose:
Membership association (membership is by qualification and is open to all teachers and scientists), present number of members: 350.
Collaboration between teachers of science and professional scientists in the Norfolk area, to enhance science in schools.

Subject coverage: Science education (from 5 to 18 years), networking teachers of science and professional scientists, free resources available.

Publications: Printed

Publications list: Available online

Access to staff: Contact by letter, by telephone, by fax, by e-mail and via website. Appointment necessary.
Hours: Mon to Fri, 0900 to 1700

TEACHING AGENCY

53–55 Butts Road, Earlsdon Park, Coventry, CV1 3BH

Tel: 0800 389 2500
E-mail: gts.enquiries@education.gsi.gov.uk
Website: www.education.gov.uk/aboutdfe/armslengthbodies/b0077806/the-teaching-agency

Founded: 2012

Organisation type and purpose: Executive agency of the Department of Education

Information services: Teaching Information Line advises on recruitment opportunities and handles queries about becoming a teacher, initial teacher training and provision of relevant training; tel: 0800 389 2500
Exams Delivery Support Unit (EDSU) Helpline supports exams office staff, helping them to manage and administer exams; tel: 0300 100 0100
Teacher Enquiry Line handles queries about teacher induction, qualified teacher status and teacher regulation; tel: 0300 790 0225

TEARFUND

100 Church Road, Teddington, Middlesex, TW11 8QE

Tel: 020 8977 9144
Fax: 020 8943 3594
E-mail: enquiry@tearfund.org
Website: www.tearfund.org

Enquiries to: Supporter Enquiries Team

Founded: 1968

Organisation type and purpose:
International organisation, registered charity (charity number 265464).
Relief and development charity.

Subject coverage: Development, overseas aid, evangelical church.

Library catalogue: All or part available in-house

Publications: Printed, and electronic and video

Publications list: Available in print

Access to staff: Contact by letter, by telephone, by e-mail and via website
Hours: Mon to Fri, 0900 to 1700

Other addresses: Tearfund Ireland; 23 University Street, Belfast, BT7 1FY; tel: 028 9032 4940; fax: 028 9023 6930; Tearfund Scotland; Challenge House, 29 Canal Street, Glasgow, G4 0AD; tel: 0141 332 3621; fax: 0141 400 2980

TECHGNOSIS

PO Box 154, Manchester, M20 3AL

Tel: 0161 445 9757
Fax: 0161 434 2913
Website: www.techgnosis-uk.com

Enquiries to: Director

Founded: 1988

Organisation type and purpose: Publishing house, research organisation.
IT information provider.

Subject coverage: Information technology; computing; computer security; software development; telecommunications; office automation, IT end-user profiles; e-commerce.

Publications: Electronic and video

Publications list: Available in print

Access to staff: Contact by letter, by telephone and by fax. Appointment necessary. All charged.
Hours: Mon to Fri, 0900 to 1700

TECHNICAL HELP TO EXPORTERS (THE)

British Standards Institution, 389 Chiswick High Road, London, W4 4AL

Tel: 020 8996 7474
Fax: 020 8996 7048
E-mail: the@bsi-global.com
Website: www.bsi.org.uk

Enquiries to: Business Development Manager

Organisation type and purpose: Training organisation, consultancy, research organisation, publishing house.

Subject coverage: Overseas technical laws, regulations, standards and certification requirements; interpretation and translation of overseas technical requirements; assistance with technical problems and research projects; assistance in obtaining test certificates or approval for products in overseas markets; UK testing and inspection of goods for export.

Collection: Library of over 500,000 foreign laws, regulations, national and non-national standards (BSI library)

Publications: Printed, and electronic and video

Access to staff: Contact by letter, by telephone, by fax and by e-mail. All charged.
Hours: Mon to Fri 0900 to 1700

TEESSIDE ARCHIVES

Exchange House, 6 Marton Road, Middlesbrough, Cleveland, TS1 1DB

Tel: 01642 248321
Fax: 01642 248391
E-mail: teesside_archives@middlesbrough .gov.uk
Website: www.middlesbrough.gov.uk/ teessidearchives

Enquiries to: Archivist

Founded: 1974

Organisation type and purpose: Local government body.

Subject coverage: Archives relating to Middlesbrough, Hartlepool, Stockton on Tees and Redcar and Cleveland Boroughs (formerly Cleveland County).

Education services: An outreach service is available for schools and groups; group visits can be arranged.

Access to staff: Contact by letter, by telephone, by fax and by e-mail. Appointment necessary.
Hours: Mon, Wed, Thu, 0900 to 1700; Tue, 0900 to 2100; Fri, 0900 to 1630

Access for disabled people: Access to all public areas, toilet facilities

TEESWATER SHEEP BREEDERS ASSOCIATION

Wodencroft, Cotherstone, Barnard Castle, Co Durham, DL12 9UQ

Tel: 01833 650032
Fax: 01833 650909
E-mail: wodencroft@freenet.co.uk

Enquiries to: Secretary

Founded: 1949

Organisation type and purpose: Membership association (membership is by subscription).

Subject coverage: Teeswater sheep.

TELECOMMUNICATIONS USERS' ASSOCIATION (TUA)

Woodgate Studios, 2–8 Games Road, Barnet, Hertfordshire, EN4 9HN

Tel: 020 8449 8844
Fax: 020 8447 4901
E-mail: cma@thecma.com
Website: www.tua.co.uk

Enquiries to: Chairman

Founded: 1964

Organisation type and purpose: Independent membership association (membership is by subscription), service industry, training organisation, consultancy, research organisation. Provides information and services to members whilst promoting open competition worldwide.

Subject coverage: Telecommunications and related industries; open telecommunications environment; to lobby and monitor quality of service; consultancy service to members.

Publications: Printed, and electronic and video

Access to staff: Contact by letter, by telephone, by fax, by e-mail and via website. Access for members only.
Hours: Mon to Fri, 0900 to 1700

TELEPHONE PREFERENCE SERVICE (TPS)

DMA House, 70 Margaret Street, London, W1W 8SS

Tel: 020 7291 3320
Fax: 020 7323 4226
E-mail: tps@dma.org.uk
Website: www.tpsonline.org.uk
Website: www.dma.org.uk

Enquiries to: Administrator

Founded: 1995

Organisation type and purpose: Self-regulatory body.
Provide individuals with the opportunity to register not to receive direct marketing telephone calls.

Subject coverage: Restriction on unsolicited sales and marketing telephone calls to individuals.

Publications: Printed, and electronic and video

Access to staff: Contact by letter, by telephone, by fax, by e-mail and via website. Appointment necessary.
Hours: Mon to Fri, 0900 to 1700
Special comments: Charges made to all subscribers (companies making telephone calls).

Affiliated to: Direct Marketing Association (DMA); tel: 020 7291 3300; fax: 020 7523 4226; e-mail: dma@dma.org.uk; OFTEL; tel: 020 7434 8700; fax: 020 7434 8893

TELEPHONES FOR THE BLIND FUND

7 Huntersfield Close, Reigate, Surrey, RH2 0DX

Tel: 01737 248032
Fax: 01737 248032
Website: www.tftb.org.uk

Enquiries to: Hon Secretary

Founded: 1967

Organisation type and purpose: Voluntary organisation (charity number 255155).

Subject coverage: Grants towards the provision of telephones for registered blind people. Referrals must be made through Social Services.

Access to staff: Contact by letter, by telephone and by fax
Hours: Mon to Fri, 1000 to 1600
Special comments: No access to premises allowed.

TELEVISION TRUST FOR THE ENVIRONMENT (TVE)

21 Elizabeth Street, London, SW1W 9RP

Tel: 020 7901 8855
Fax: 020 7901 8856
E-mail: tve@tve.org.uk
Website: www.tve.org

Enquiries to: Distribution Manager
Direct tel: 020 7901 8834
Direct e-mail: distribution@tve.org.uk

Founded: 1984

Organisation type and purpose: International organisation, registered charity.
Film, video and television producer and distributor.
To inform and educate on environmental, health, human rights and developmental issues.

Subject coverage: Environment, health, development, human rights, women's issues.

Collection: Library of over 500 documentaries; substantial archive of environment and development film footage

Non-library collection catalogue: All or part available online

Publications: Electronic and video
Order electronic and video publications from: Distribution Manager

Publications list: Available online

Access to staff: Contact by letter, by telephone, by fax, by e-mail and via website. Appointment necessary.
Hours: Mon to Fri, 0930 to 1800

Access to building: No access other than to staff

Access for disabled people: No wheelchair access – premises on first floor with narrow stairs.

Affiliated to: United Nations Environment Programme; WWF UK

Links with: 57 other organisations throughout the world

TELFORD LIBRARY

St Quentin Gate, Telford, Shropshire, TF3 4JG

Tel: 01952 382918
Fax: 01952 382937
E-mail: telford.library@telford.gov.uk
Website: www.telford.gov.uk/libraries

Enquiries to: Librarian

Organisation type and purpose: Public library.

Library catalogue: All or part available online and in-house

Access to staff: Contact by letter, by telephone, by fax, by e-mail, in person and via website
Hours: Mon, 1000 to 1800; Tue, Wed, Fri, 0930 to 1800; Thu 0930 to 2000; Sat 0930 to 1700

Access for disabled people: Level entry, access to all public areas, toilet facilities

Parent body: Telford & Wrekin Council

TENANT FARMERS ASSOCIATION (TFA)

5 Brewery Court, Theale, Reading, Berkshire, RG7 5AJ

Tel: 0118 930 6130
Fax: 0118 930 3424
E-mail: tfa@tfa.org.uk
Website: www.tfa.org.uk

Enquiries to: Events and Communications Co-ordinator
Other contacts: Membership Co-ordinator

Founded: 1981

Organisation type and purpose: Trade association (membership is by subscription), present number of members: 4,000.
Provides advice, information and a strong lobby for British tenant farmers.

Subject coverage: Agricultural tenancies, agricultural policy, tenant farming, landlord/tenant affairs in rural areas.

Trade and statistical information: Agricultural rent databank (available to tenants only)

Publications: Printed

Access to staff: Contact by letter, by telephone, by fax, by e-mail and via website. Appointment necessary.
Hours: Mon to Fri, 0900 to 1700
Special comments: Full benefits only available to members.

Access to building: No prior appointment required

TENDRING DISTRICT COUNCIL

Town Hall, Station Road, Clacton-on-Sea, Essex, CO15 1SE

Tel: 01255 425501
Fax: 01255 253139
E-mail: Email form on website
Website: www.tendringdc.gov.uk

Enquiries to: Chief Executive

Organisation type and purpose: Local government body.

Publications: Printed

Access to staff: Contact by letter, by telephone, by fax, by e-mail, in person and via website
Hours: Mon to Fri, 0900 to 1700

Access for disabled people: Ramped entry, toilet facilities

TENNIS AND RACKETS ASSOCIATION (The T&RA)

c/o The Queens Club, Palliser Road, West Kensington, London, W14 9EQ

Tel: 020 7386 3447/8
Fax: 020 7385 7424
E-mail: office@tennisandrackets.com
Website: www.real-tennis.com

Enquiries to: Chief Executive

Founded: 1907

Organisation type and purpose:
Membership association (membership is by subscription), present number of members: 2,450, suitable for ages: all.
Governing body of the sports of real tennis and rackets.
To administer and control the games of Tennis (Real Tennis) and Rackets.

Subject coverage: Real tennis and Rackets (not to be confused with lawn tennis and squash rackets); rules; location of courts; history of the games, championships, sponsorship, development, membership, publicity, fixtures, international liaison.

Publications: Printed

Access to staff: Contact by letter, by fax and by e-mail. Appointment necessary.
Hours: Mon to Fri, 0900 to 1700

Member of: CCPR; Sport England

TENNYSON RESEARCH CENTRE

Formal name: Lincolnshire County Council

Central Library, Free School Lane, Lincoln, LN2 1EZ

Tel: 01522 782040
Fax: 01522 575011
E-mail: grace.timmins@lincolnshire.gov.uk
Website: www.lincolnshire.gov.uk/tennyson

Enquiries to: Collections Officer
Direct fax: 01522 545011
Direct e-mail: tennyson@lincolnshire.gov.uk

Founded: 1964

Organisation type and purpose: Research organisation.
Research unit.

Subject coverage: Alfred, Lord Tennyson: life, works, papers.

Information services: Please contact the collections officer for information about services.

Collection: Tennyson Collection includes family libraries, 9,000 letters, manuscripts of the poet's work, family papers, illustrations, proofs, biographical and critical material, including:
Family Libraries: some 350 volumes from the library of Tennyson's father, George Clayton Tennyson, giving an indication of the books Tennyson would have used as a child, when taught by his father. Approximately 2,000 books from Tennyson's own library, reflecting his many interests and often annotated by the poet
Family Papers: family diaries and notebooks including a journal kept by Tennyson's wife, Emily; household books and publishers' accounts
Illustrations: portraits and other illustrative material on Tennyson, his family, contemporaries and places associated with them, including a number of photographs by Julia Margaret Cameron
Letters to and from Tennyson and other members of the family: several thousand letters from eminent Victorians including Browning, Gladstone, Lear and Fitzgerald
Manuscripts: the most complete autograph manuscript of In Memoriam
Plays: Queen Mary, Harold, Becket, The Foresters and an acting copy of The Cup
Proofs: approximately 200 proofs of Tennyson's poetry, a number being significantly corrected in the poet's hand
Biography and Criticism: a comprehensive collection of books and articles, both contemporary and modern, dealing with his life and works
Tennyson's works: an almost complete set of first and other important editions of poetry
'Personalia' includes Tennyson's coat and hat, pipes, spectacles, writing equipment.

Non-library collection catalogue: All or part available in-house and in print

Library catalogue: All or part available online, in-house and in print

Publications: Printed
Order printed publications from: The Tennyson Society, c/o Lincoln Central Library, Free School Lane, Lincoln. LN2 1EZ

Access to staff: Contact by letter, by telephone, by fax, by e-mail and via website. Appointment necessary.
Hours: Mon to Fri, 0930 to 1700

Access for disabled people: Ramped entry, toilet facilities

Parent body: Lincolnshire County Council; County Offices, Newland, Lincoln, LN1 1YL; tel: 01522 553207; fax: 01522 552811

TENOVUS, THE CANCER CHARITY

43 The Parade, Cardiff, CF24 3AB

Tel: 029 2048 2000
Fax: 029 2048 4199
E-mail: post@tenovus.com
Website: www.tenovus.com

Enquiries to: Public Relations Manager
Direct e-mail: natalie.owen@tenovus.org.uk

Founded: 1943

Organisation type and purpose: Registered charity (charity number 1054015).

Subject coverage: Cancer research and patient care.

Collection: Library holds information on over 200 cancers and support organisations

Trade and statistical information: Data on cancer in the UK and in Europe

Publications: Printed

Publications list: Available online and in print

Access to staff: Contact by letter, by telephone, by fax and by e-mail
Hours: Mon to Fri, 0900 to 1700

Access for disabled people: Parking provided, level entry, toilet facilities

TERRENCE HIGGINS TRUST (THT)

314–320 Gray's Inn Road, London, WC1X 8DP

Tel: 020 7812 1600; helpline: 0845 122 1200
Fax: 020 7812 1601
E-mail: info@tht.org.uk
Website: www.tht.org.uk

Enquiries to: Information Officer

Founded: 1982

Organisation type and purpose: Registered charity (charity number 288527), voluntary organisation.

Subject coverage: HIV and AIDS, sexual health.

Publications: Printed
Order printed publications from: Information Department (single copies are free, bulk copies for purchase)

Publications list: Available online and in print

Access to staff: Contact by letter, by telephone, by fax, by e-mail, in person and via website
Hours: Mon to Fri, 0930 to 1730

TETRONICS LIMITED

A2 Marston Gate, Stirling Road, South Marston Business Park, Swindon, Wiltshire, SN3 4DE

Tel: 01793 238 500
Fax: 01793 832 533
E-mail: info@tetronics.com
Website: www.tetronics.com

Enquiries to: Marketing Manager

Founded: 1964

Organisation type and purpose: Manufacturing industry.
Research and development organisation.

Subject coverage: Plasma equipment and furnaces, nanopowders, metal melting and heating, new waste treatment processes, melting of incineration ashes, treatment of steel works dusts and hazardous wastes, refractory metal melting.

Access to staff: Contact by letter, by telephone, by fax and by e-mail
Hours: Mon to Fri, 0900 to 1700

TEXTILE COLLECTION & CONSTANCE HOWARD GALLERY

Goldsmiths, University of London, Deptford Town Hall Building, New Cross Road, London, SE14 6AF

Tel: 020 7717 2210
E-mail: textiles@gold.ac.uk
Website: www.goldsmiths.ac.uk/textile-collection

Organisation type and purpose: Part of Special Collections and Archives, the Library.

Subject coverage: The history of textiles at Goldsmiths from the 1940s to the present day, including works by Goldsmiths alumni and other textile artists, as well as ethnographic and historical textiles and dress.

Collection: A textile reference library, including many books from Eastern Europe.

TEXTILE INDUSTRY CHILDREN'S TRUST (TICT)

Winchester House, 259–269 Old Marylebone Road, London, NW1 5RA

Tel: 020 7170 4117
E-mail: info@tict.org.uk
Website: www.tict.org.uk

Founded: 1968; formerly called Purley Children's Trust (year of change 1999)

Organisation type and purpose: Registered charity (number 257136).
Established to support the education and welfare of children whose parents have worked in fashion, textile retail and manufacturing (UK only). Its mission is to help children achieve their full potential.

Subject coverage: TICT helps children if they suffer financial hardship as a result of divorce, bereavement or other significant circumstances and, as a result, are unable to make the most of their education. It funds places at specialist schools for children with special educational needs such as dyslexia, autism, ADHD, emotional needs and physical disabilities. It pays for boarding at schools that offer vital pastoral care to children who may have been orphaned or who are living in a desperate home situation. It awards hardship grants to cover the cost of uniforms, specialist equipment such as a home computer or funding towards transport to a school. It helps to nurture the talents of gifted children who would benefit from attendance at a school with a focus on music, sport or artistic performance. It also helps with existing school fees where there has been a dramatic change in family circumstances such as death or debilitating illness.

Access to staff: Contact by letter, by telephone and by e-mail

TEXTILE INSTITUTE (TI)

Formal name: The Textile Institute

International Headquarters, 1st Floor, St James's Building, 79 Oxford Street, Manchester, M1 6FQ

Tel: 0161 237 1188
Fax: 0161 236 1991
E-mail: tiihq@textileinst.org.uk
Website: www.textileinstitute.org

Enquiries to: Professional Affairs Manager
Direct e-mail: escott@textileinst.org.uk
Other contacts: Director of Professional Affairs

Founded: 1910

Organisation type and purpose: Professional body.

Subject coverage: Textiles worldwide; textile technology; floorcovering; clothing; industrial textiles; knitting; weaving; design and marketing; finishing; fibre science; footwear.

Non-library collection catalogue: All or part available in-house

Library catalogue: All or part available in-house

Publications: Printed

Publications list: Available in print

Access to staff: Contact by letter, by telephone, by fax, by e-mail and via website. Appointment necessary. All charged.
Hours: Mon to Fri, 0900 to 1700

Access to building: Prior appointment required

TEXTILE SERVICES ASSOCIATION (TSA)

Unit 7, Churchill Court, 58 Station Road, North Harrow, Middlesex, HA2 7SA

Tel: 020 8863 7755
Fax: 020 8861 2115
E-mail: tsa@tsa-uk.org

Enquiries to: Chief Executive

Founded: 1886

Organisation type and purpose: Trade association (membership is by subscription), present number of members: 600.

Subject coverage: Developments within the dry-cleaning, laundry and textile rental industry, national and EU legislation affecting the industry e.g. health and safety, workwear etc. NVQs in the textile rental industry.

Publications: Printed

Publications list: Available in print

Access to staff: Contact by letter, by telephone, by fax, by e-mail and via website. Non-members charged.
Hours: Mon to Fri, 0900 to 1800

Affiliated to: International Committee for Textile Care (CINET)

Works closely with: Guild of Cleaners and Launderers; Cheshire; tel: 0161 483 4655; SATRA; Kettering, Northamptonshire; tel: 01536 410000

TFPL LIMITED

Chancery Exchange, 2nd Floor, 10 Furnival Street, London, EC4A 1AB

Tel: 020 7332 6000
Fax: 0870 333 7131
E-mail: info@tfpl.com
Website: www.tfpl.com

Enquiries to: Managing Director
Direct e-mail: marketing@tfpl.com

Founded: 1987

Organisation type and purpose: Solutions provider delivering training, consultancy and recruitment.

Subject coverage: Working with organisations looking to delivery effective knowledge, information, data and content to organisations across the public, private and third-sector.

Publications list: Available in print

Access to staff: Contact by letter, by telephone, by fax, by e-mail, in person and via website
Hours: Mon to Fri, 0900 to 1800

Owned by: IDOX Plc; 2nd Floor, Chancery Exchange, 10 Furnival Street, London, EC4A 1AB; tel: 0207 332 6000; fax: 0870 333 7131; e-mail: info@tfpl.com; website: http://www.idoxgroup.com/

THAI EMBASSY

Formal name: Royal Thai Embassy

29–30 Queen's Gate, London, SW7 5JB

Tel: 020 7589 2944
Fax: 020 7823 9695
E-mail: thaiduto@btinternet.com
Website: www.thaiembassyuk.org.uk

Enquiries to: Information Officer
Direct tel: 020 7225 5520
Direct e-mail: thaiembassy.pr@btconnect.com

Organisation type and purpose: Embassy.

Subject coverage: Thailand: government, history, culture, society, economy, arts, language, religion, travel.

Collection: The Embassy's collection is small and mostly in Thai language, though there are a few useful reference books in English

Trade and statistical information: Contact the Office of Commercial Affairs

Access to staff: Contact by letter, by telephone, by fax and by e-mail.
Appointment necessary.
Hours: Mon to Fri, 0930 to 1230 and 1400 to 1700
Special comments: Closed on Thai holidays and UK public holidays.

Access to building: No prior appointment required

Access for disabled people: Toilet facilities

Also at: Office of Commercial Affairs; 11 Hertford Street, Mayfair, London, W1Y 7DX; tel: 020 7493 5749; fax: 020 7493 7416; e-mail: thaicomuk@dial.pipex.com; website: http://www.thaitrade.com
Office of Economics and Financial Affairs; 3rd Floor, 29–30 Queen's Gate, London, SW7 5JB; tel: 020 7589 7266; fax: 020 7589 2624;
Office of Educational Affairs; 28 Prince's Gate, London, SW7 1QF; tel: 020 7584 4538; fax: 020 7823 9896; e-mail: info@oealondon.com

THAMES ROWING COUNCIL – LOWER RIVER (TRC)

45 Sterne Street, London, W12 8AB

Tel: 020 8743 8596

Enquiries to: Honorary Secretary

Organisation type and purpose: Membership association (membership is by qualification), voluntary organisation.
Co-ordinating sports body.
To encourage participation in the sport of rowing.

Subject coverage: Rowing river users, the river Thames.

Access to staff: Contact by letter
Hours: Mon to Fri, 0900 to 1700

Parent body: Amateur Rowing Association

THAMES VALLEY CHAMBER OF COMMERCE AND INDUSTRY

Commerce House, 2–6 Bath Road, Slough, Berkshire, SL1 3SB

Tel: 01753 870518
Fax: 01753 524644
E-mail: enquiries@thamesvalleychamber.co.uk
Website: www.thamesvalleychamber.co.uk
Website: www.euro-info.org.uk

Enquiries to: Information Officer
Direct tel: 01753 870530

Founded: 1927

Organisation type and purpose: Membership association.
Chamber of Commerce.

Subject coverage: Business, local and European Information Centre.

Publications: Printed

Access to staff: Contact by letter, by telephone, by fax, by e-mail and via website.
Appointment necessary.
Hours: Mon to Thu, 0900 to 1700; Fri, 0900 to 1500
Special comments: Charges for some services.

Hosts: Thames Valley European Information Centre; at the same address

THAMES VALLEY UNIVERSITY (TVU)

St Mary's Road, London, W5 5RF

Tel: 020 8579 5000
Website: www.tvu.ac.uk

Enquiries to: Head of Learning and Research Support
Direct tel: 020 8231 2678
Direct fax: 020 8231 2402
Direct e-mail: press@tvu.ac.uk
Other contacts: SMR, LRC Manager for Learning Resource Provision.

Founded: 1993

Organisation type and purpose: University library, university department or institute.

Subject coverage: Business, management, accountancy, law, health sciences, humanities, languages, hospitality, music, information studies, technology, art and design, built environment, sports science.

Non-library collection catalogue: All or part available online

Library catalogue: All or part available online

Publications: Printed

Publications list: Available online

Access to staff: Contact by letter, by telephone, by fax and by e-mail.
Appointment necessary. Access for members only.
Hours: St Mary's Road; term-time: Mon to Thu, 0830 to 2200; Fri to Sun, 0830 to 1800
Special comments: Reciprocal arrangements with similar institutions. Members only primarily, visitors by prior appointment.

Access to building: Prior appointment required
Special comments: 24-hour access to IT facilities during term time – Ealing only

Access for disabled people: Parking provided, ramped entry, level entry, access to all public areas, toilet facilities

Member of: M25 Group; SCONUL

Other departments at: Faculty of Health and Human Sciences; Westel House, 32 Uxbridge Road, London, W5 2BZ; tel: 020 8280 5043; fax: 020 8280 5045; Paul Hamlyn Learning Resource Centre; Wellington Street, Slough, Berkshire, SL1 1YG; tel: 01753 697536; fax: 01753 574264; Wolfson School of Health, Sciences Learning Resource Centre; Royal Berkshire Hospital, Reading, RG1 5AN; tel: 0118 322 7661; fax: 0118 322 8675

THAMES VALLEY UNIVERSITY – LEARNING RESOURCE CENTRE

St Mary's Road, Ealing, London, W5 5RF

Tel: 020 8231 2248
Fax: 020 8231 2631
E-mail: learning.advice@tvu.ac.uk
Website: www.tvu.ac.uk

Enquiries to: Head of Learning Resources
Direct tel: 020 8231 2678
Direct e-mail: press@tvu.ac.uk
Other contacts: Director of Information Services for all ICT within the University.

Founded: 1992

Organisation type and purpose: Learned society, professional body (membership is by qualification), university library, training organisation, research organisation.
Learning Resource Service.

Subject coverage: Management, including marketing, purchasing, business, accounting, languages, hospitality management, law, music, media, health sciences.

continued overleaf

Library catalogue: All or part available online

Publications list: Available online

Access to staff: Contact by letter, by telephone, by fax, by e-mail and via website. Appointment necessary. Access for members only.
Hours: TVU Ealing and PH: Mon to Thu, 0830 to 2200; Fri, Sat, Sun, 0830 to 1800
WIHS Ealing: Mon to Thu, 0830 to 1900; Fri, 1000 to 1700; Sat, 1100 to 1600
Reading: Mon, 1000 to 1930; Tue to Fri, 0830 to 1930; Sat, 0900 to 1300
Special comments: TVU Ealing and PH: Computer access only 2200 to 0600
UK+, SCONUL and M25 Schemes, Shorter hours in vacations, please telephone first.

Access to building: Prior appointment required

Access for disabled people: Parking provided, level entry, access to all public areas, toilet facilities

Location: Paul Hamlyn Learning Resource Centre; Wellington Street, Slough, Berkshire, SL1 1YG; tel: 01753 697536; fax: 01753 697538; Wolfson Institute of Health Sciences Learning Resource Centre; Wexham Park Hospital, Slough, Berkshire, SL2 4HL; tel: 01753 634343; fax: 01753 634344; Wolfson Institute of Health Sciences Learning Resource Centre; Royal Berkshire Hospital, Reading, RG1 5AN; tel: 0118 987 7661; fax: 0118 986 8675; Wolfson Institute of Health Sciences Learning Resource Centre; Westel House, 32 Uxbridge Road, Ealing, London, W5 2BS; tel: 020 8280 5043; fax: 020 8280 5045

THE CAMBRIDGE UNION SOCIETY (CUS)

Keynes Library, 9a Bridge Street, Cambridge, CB2 1UB

Tel: 01223 568445
Fax: 01223 566444
E-mail: librarian@cus.org
Website: www.cus.org

Enquiries to: Librarian
Direct tel: 01223 568445
Direct fax: 01223 566444
Direct e-mail: librarian@cus.org

Founded: 1815

Organisation type and purpose:
Membership association (membership is by subscription), registered charity, historic building, house or site.
To provide services for members, including debates, bar, meeting rooms and library.

Subject coverage: Strong subjects: biography, fiction, local history, leisure interests.
General subjects: history, geography; English, French, German and Italian literature; art, architecture, politics, sociology, anthropology, theology, philosophy, travel, humour

Collection: Fairfax Rhodes Collection (mainly art and literature)
Extensive collection of biographies and memoirs

Non-library collection catalogue: All or part available online

Library catalogue: All or part available in-house

Access to staff: Contact by letter, by telephone, by e-mail and in person. Appointment necessary. Access for members only. Letter of introduction required.
Hours: Term time: Mon to Fri, 0900 to 1730
Special comments: Open to non-members by prior appointment only.

Access to building: Prior appointment required

Access for disabled people: Library is located on first floor with access only by stairs

THE CHARTERED INSTITUTE OF PAYROLL PROFESSIONALS (CIPP)

Shelly House, Farmhouse Way, Monkspath, Solihull, West Midlands, B90 4EH

Tel: 0121 712 1000
Fax: 0121 712 1001
E-mail: info@cipp.org.uk
Website: www.cipp.org.uk

Enquiries to: Marketing Co-ordinator
Direct tel: 0121 712 1019
Direct e-mail: dawn.baxter@cipp.org.uk

Founded: 1985; formerly called Institute of Payroll and Pensions Management (IPPM) (year of change 2006); formerly called Institute of Payroll Professionals (year of change 2011)

Organisation type and purpose: The Chartered Institute of Payroll Professionals (CIPP) is the only membership association for individuals working in payroll and pensions in the UK and has in excess of 5,000 professionals enjoying membership benefits. In addition, the CIPP is the UK's leading provider of education for payroll, and has a Pensions Faculty responsible for delivering qualifications and membership services to those responsible for public sector pensions.

Subject coverage: Membership, training, qualifications, consultancy, specialist interest groups, Payroll Quality Partnership and events for payroll and pensions professionals.

Publications: Printed
Order printed publications from: e-mail: info@cipp.org.uk

Publications list: Available in print

Access to staff: Contact by letter, by telephone, by fax, by e-mail and via website
Hours: Mon to Thu, 0900 to 1700; Fri, 0900 to 1630

Access to building: No access other than to staff

THE CONSERVATION VOLUNTEERS SCOTLAND (TCV Scotland)

Balallan House, 24 Allan Park, Stirling, FK8 2QG

Tel: 01786 479697
Fax: 01786 465359
E-mail: scotland@tcv.org.uk
Website: www.tcv.org.uk/scotland

Enquiries to: Administrator

Founded: 1984

Organisation type and purpose: National organisation, membership association (membership is by subscription), present number of members: 5,000, voluntary organisation, registered charity (charity number 261009), training organisation. Environmental organisation.
To involve people in improving the quality of Scotland's environment through practical conservation.

Subject coverage: Information provided on all aspects of practical conservation and community regeneration work.

Publications: Printed, and electronic and video

Access to staff: Contact by letter, by telephone, by fax, by e-mail, in person and via website
Hours: Mon to Fri, 0900 to 1700
Access to building: No prior appointment required

Access for disabled people: Parking provided, toilet facilities

Also at: Edinburgh, Glasgow, Aberdeen, Inverness, Fife

Constituent bodies: 285 affiliated local conservation groups, collectively known as Community Local Action Network (CLAN)

Constituent part of: The Conservation Volunteers (TCV)

THE DESIGN AND TECHNOLOGY ASSOCIATION (D&TA)

16 Wellesbourne House, Walton Road, Wellesbourne, Warwickshire, CV35 9JB

Tel: 01789 470007
Fax: 01789 841955
E-mail: info@data.org.uk
Website: www.data.org.uk

Founded: 1989; incorporates the former National Association for Teachers of Home Economics (NATHE), date of change, 1 April 2000

Organisation type and purpose:
Professional body (membership is by subscription), number of members: nearly 6,000 registered charity (charity number 1062270), suitable for ages: preschool to post 18, training organisation, consultancy, research organisation. Provides support, advice and subject leadership for all those involved in D&T education
To support, develop and enhance design and technology in all sectors of education and society.

Subject coverage: Design and technology education.
Home economics; nutrition; childcare and development; food and textiles; technology.

Collection: Books and Resources
All issues of the ATDS journal Housecraft from 1928 to 1982 and NATHE journal MODUS, 1928 to present held at Hamilton House
Computerised database
Domestic science archives held at University of Warwick
Design and Technology Library

Publications: Printed, and electronic and video

Publications list: Available online and in print

Access to staff: Contact by letter, by telephone, by fax, by e-mail, in person and via website
Hours: Mon to Fri, 0900 to 1700
Special comments: Library access available for members only.

THE GLASGOW SCHOOL OF ART (GSA)

Library, 167 Renfrew Street, Glasgow, G3 6RQ

Tel: 0141 353 4500
Fax: 0141 353 4670
E-mail: c.nicholson@gsa.ac.uk
Website: www2.gsa.ac.uk/library

Enquiries to: Head of Learning Resources
Direct tel: 0141 353 4550
Other contacts: Archivist for extensive archives of GSA and deposited collections; Curator for Mackintosh and other GSA collections

Founded: 1845

Organisation type and purpose: University library.
Art college library.

Subject coverage: Fine art and design, architecture, art history.

Collection: Books, exhibition catalogues and other documents relating to the history of the School, its staff and students
Glasgow School of Art Archives & Collections
Hill and Adamson Collection of photographic calotypes and carbon prints

Library catalogue: All or part available online

Access to staff: Contact by letter, by telephone and by e-mail. Non-members charged.
Hours: Term Time: Mon to Thu, 0900 to 1945; Fri, 0900 to 1645; Sat, 1200 to 1600
Vacations: Mon to Fri, 0900 to 1645

Access for disabled people: Ramped entry, toilet facilities, lift

THE JAMES HUTTON INSTITUTE (JHI)

Aberdeen: The James Hutton Institute, Craigiebuckler, Aberdeen, AB15 8QH; Dundee: Invergowrie, Dundee, DD2 5DA

Tel: 0844 928 5428
Fax: 0844 928 5429
E-mail: info@hutton.ac.uk
Website: www.hutton.ac.uk

Enquiries to: Librarian
Direct e-mail: library.dundee@hutton.ac.uk

Founded: 2011

Organisation type and purpose: Research organisation.

Subject coverage: All facets of crop research in the northern hemisphere, plant genetics and breeding, plant biotechnology and agronomy, plant pathology and crop protection, biochemistry and plant analyses, biomathematics, potatoes, barley and soft fruit, biodiversity and sustainability, crop suitability, hill farming, climate change, soil science, land use, plant physiology, peat and forest soils, forestry, environmental conservation and pollution, land reclamation, drainage, water research.

Collection: Pethybridge Collection on potato pathology, 1870–1930
Special collections of research literature on raspberries and potatoes now closed

Library catalogue: All or part available in-house

Publications: Printed

Publications list: Available in print

Access to staff: Contact by letter, by telephone, by fax, by e-mail and via website. Appointment necessary.
Hours: Mon to Thu, 0900 to 1700; Fri, 0900 to 1600

Constituent part of: Scottish Research Institutes; BBSRC

Grant administered by the: Scottish Government

THE LEPROSY MISSION INTERNATIONAL (TLMI)

80 Windmill Road, Brentford, Middlesex, TW8 0QH

Tel: 020 8326 6767
Fax: 020 8326 6777
E-mail: friends@tlmint.org
Website: www.leprosymission.org

Enquiries to: Communications Manager

Founded: 1874

Organisation type and purpose: International organisation, voluntary organisation, registered charity.
To minister in the name of Jesus Christ to people affected by leprosy.

Subject coverage: Leprosy (Hansen's disease), historical, medical, current field work.

Collection: Library of leprosy-related books and archive of organisation
Archive photographs dating from 1890s to present
TLM's annual reports (dating back to early 1900s)

Publications: Printed

Publications list: Available in print

Access to staff: Contact via website. Appointment necessary.
Hours: Mon to Fri, 0900 to 1700

Access for disabled people: Parking provided, ramped entry, level entry, access to all public areas, toilet facilities

Also at: Leprosy Mission England and Wales (includes The Channel Islands and The Isle of Man); Goldhay Way, Orton Goldhay, Peterborough, Cambridgeshire, PE2 5GZ; tel: 01733 370505; fax: 01733 404880; e-mail: post@tlmew.org.uk; website: http://www.leprosymission.org.uk
Leprosy Mission Northern Ireland; Lagan House, 2A Queens Road, Lisburn, BT27 4TZ; tel: 028 9038 1842; e-mail: info@tlm-ni.org; website: http://www.tlm-ni.org
Leprosy Mission Scotland; Suite 2, Earlsgate Lodge, Livilands Lane, Stirling, FK8 2BG; tel: 01786 449266; e-mail: office@tlmscotland.org.uk; website: http://www.tlmscotland.org.uk

Member organisation of: Global Connections; Whitefield House, 186 Kennington Park Road, London, SE11 4BT; tel: 020 7207 2157; 020 8133 2958; website: http://www.globalconnections.co.uk
International Federation of Anti-Leprosy Associations (ILEP); 234 Blythe Road, London, W14 0HJ

THE LIBRARY @ RIVERSIDE

Riverside House, Main Street, Rotherham, S60 1AE

Tel: 01709 823611
Fax: 01709 823606
E-mail: central.library@rotherham.gov.uk
Website: www.rotherham.gov.uk

Enquiries to: Librarian

Organisation type and purpose: Local government body, public library.

Subject coverage: General; local history and study of the Rotherham Metropolitan Borough area; South Yorkshire potteries.

Library catalogue: All or part available online and in-house

Publications: Printed

Access to staff: Contact by letter, by telephone, by e-mail, in person and via website
Hours: Mon and Thu, 0900 to 1900; Tue, Wed and Fri, 0900 to 1730; Sat, 0900 to 1600

THE MULTISERVICE ASSOCIATION LTD INCORPORATING THE SOCIETY OF MASTER SHOE REPAIRERS (MSA/SOMSR)

Formal name: The MultiService Association Ltd

PO Box 9378, Newark, NG24 9FE

Tel: 01400 281298
Fax: 01400 282326
E-mail: info@msauk.biz
Website: www.msauk.biz

Enquiries to: Chief Executive

Founded: 1963

Organisation type and purpose: Trade association.

Subject coverage: Shoe repair, shoe care, independent shoe repairers in the UK, training.

Information services: Lastest News, Free Magazine and e-news bulletins. Free MSA Energy cost saving advice. Free MSA Commercial Insurance quotations. Free quotations for MSA Hospital and Medical Care Plans, Travel, Income Protection, Term Life Plan, Personal Accident Plan and Breakdown Recovery Club.

For Members only, Free Health and Safety, Employment Law and COSHH Regulations templates and advice line.

continued overleaf

Education services: Training courses offered and government-sponsored apprentice courses

Publications: Printed, and electronic and video
Order printed publications from: The Editor, MSA Ltd, PO Box 9378, Newark, NG24 9FE
Order electronic and video publications from: Available to download via website www .msauk.biz

Publications list: Available online

Access to staff: Contact by letter, by telephone, by fax, by e-mail and via website. Appointment necessary.
Hours: Tuesday to Thursday , 0900 to 1700

Access to building: By appointment only

Access for disabled people: Yes

THE NATIONAL BENEVOLENT CHARITY

Peter Hervé House, Eccles Court, Tetbury, Gloucestershire, GL8 8EH

Tel: 01666 505500
Fax: 01666 503111
E-mail: office@TheNBC.org.uk
Website: www.TheNBC.org.uk

Founded: 1812

Organisation type and purpose: Registered charity (number 212450).
Financial assistance for the people in need. Residential nursing home in Tetbury, Gloucestershire. Self-contained flats in Old Windsor & Tetbury.

Subject coverage: People in financial distress because of age, illness, disability of some other extenuating circumstance.

Access to staff: Contact by letter, by telephone, by fax, by e-mail and in person. Appointment necessary.
Hours: Mon to Fri, 1000 to 1600

THE NORTHUMBRIAN PIPERS' SOCIETY (NPS)

Park House, Lynemouth, Morpeth, Northumberland, NE61 5XQ

Tel: 01670 860215
E-mail: secretary@northumbrianpipers.org .uk
Website: www.northumbrianpipers.org.uk

Enquiries to: Honorary Secretary

Founded: 1928

Organisation type and purpose: The Northumbrian Pipers' Society is a company limited by guarantee, registered in England and Wales with number 7471625. Charity registration number 1142471.
To support the playing, making and music of the Northumbrian pipes.

Subject coverage: Making of the Northumbrian smallpipes and related technical matters; pipe makers, pipe players and availability of music and recordings, materials, etc.; meetings of pipers within and outside Northumberland.

Collection: W. A. Cocks Collection of Pipes and Manuscripts, held in the Morpeth Chantry Bagpipe Museum

Publications: Printed
Order printed publications from: e-mail: booksales@northumbrianpipers.org.uk

Publications list: Available in print

Access to staff: Contact by letter, by telephone, by e-mail, in person and via website
Hours: By e-mail or phone, any reasonable time; in person by appointment

Also at: Morpeth Chantry Bagpipe Museum; tel: 01670 500717; e-mail: anne.moore@ woodhorn.org.uk

THE PORTICO LIBRARY

57 Mosley Street, Manchester, M2 3HY

Tel: 0161 236 6785
E-mail: librarian@theportico.org.uk
Website: www.theportico.org.uk

Enquiries to: Librarian
Direct e-mail: librarian@theportico.org.uk
Other contacts: Head Cataloguer

Founded: 1806

Organisation type and purpose: Independent members' library (membership is by subscription).

Subject coverage: Travel, biography, topography, novels, poetry, drama, natural philosophy.

Special visitor services: Group visits by arrangement.

Collection: Mainly 19th-century collection, archives of the Insitution since 1806.

Library catalogue: All or part available online, in-house and in print

Publications: Printed
Order printed publications from: Librarian

Publications list: Available online and in print

Access to staff: Contact by letter, by telephone, by e-mail, in person and via website
Hours: 0930 to 1630

Access to building: Via entryphone at Charlotte Street entrance
Hours: Mon to Fri, 0930 to 1630; Thu, 0930 to 1930 (or as advertised)
Special comments: Subscription only, open to researchers, Gallery, Exhibition access freely to all. Access to most events open to all but charges generally apply.

Access for disabled people: No wheelchair access
Special comments: Located on first floor up a few short flights of stairs separated by landings with 'rest chairs'.

Member organisation of: Association of Independent Libraries; website: http://www .independentlibraries.co.uk

THE QUEKETT MICROSCOPICAL CLUB (QMC)

c/o Natural History Museum, Cromwell Road, London, SW7 5BD

Website: www.quekett.org.uk

Enquiries to: Honorary Secretary
Direct e-mail: secretary@quekett.org

Founded: 1865

Organisation type and purpose: Learned society

Subject coverage: Microscopy

Collection: Microscope slides; microscopes; specialist library

Non-library collection catalogue: All or part available in-house

Library catalogue: All or part available in-house

Publications: Printed
Order printed publications from: See Quekett website at http://www.quekett.org.uk/files/ publications/publications.html

Access to staff: Contact by letter, by e-mail and via website. Appointment necessary.
Hours: Mon to Fri, 0900 to 1700

THE QUILTERS' GUILD OF THE BRITISH ISLES (QGBI)

St Anthony's Hall, Peasholme Green, York, YO1 7PW

Tel: 01904 613242
Fax: 01904 632394
E-mail: admin@quiltersguild.org.uk
Website: www.quiltersguild.org.uk

Enquiries to: Guild Administrator

Founded: 1979

Organisation type and purpose: International organisation, national organisation, membership association (membership is by subscription), present number of members: 7,000, voluntary organisation, registered charity (charity number 1067361), museum, suitable for all ages, research organisation.
To promote and maintain the crafts of quilting, patchwork and appliqué from an educational base and historical perspective.

Subject coverage: History of quilting, how to quilt, contemporary quilting, patchwork and appliqué.

Collection: Book library, slide library, study packs, videos
Heritage Quilt Collection
Quilt collection, historical and contemporary

Library catalogue: All or part available in-house

Publications: Printed

Access to staff: Contact by letter, by telephone, by fax, by e-mail and via website. Appointment necessary. Non-members charged.
Hours: Mon to Thu, 0900 to 1700; Fri, 0900 to 1700

Access to building: *Hours:* Please contact for current opening hours

Access for disabled people: Access to all public areas, toilet facilities

THE ROYAL SOCIETY OF ST GEORGE (RSStG)

Enterprise House, 10 Church Hill, Loughton, Essex IG10 1LA

Tel: 020 3225 5011
Fax: 020 8508 4356
E-mail: info@royalsocietyofstgeorge.com
Website: www.royalsocietyofstgeorge.com

Enquiries to: Chairman or Head Office Secretary

Founded: 1894

Organisation type and purpose: Statutory body (membership is by subscription, election or invitation), voluntary organisation, registered charity (charity number 263076).

Subject coverage: Love of England.

Collection: Small archive of memorabilia and books

Publications: Printed
Order printed publications from: Elizabeth Lloyd, Head Office Secretary, contact as above.

Access to staff: Contact by letter, by telephone, by fax, by e-mail and via website. Appointment necessary.
Hours: Mon to Thurs, 1030 to 1530

Access to building: *Hours:* Same as staff hours.

Has: some 100 branches, half of which are overseas

THE SCOTTISH COUNCIL ON VISUAL IMPAIRMENT (SCOVI)

Richard Mazur, Secretary and Treasurer, 8 Netherlea, Scone, Perthshire PH2 6QA

Tel: 01738 551351
E-mail: richard.mazur@scovi.org.uk
Website: www.scovi.org.uk

Enquiries to: Secretary and Treasurer

Founded: 1917; formerly called The Scottish National Federation for the Welfare of the Blind (year of change 2011)

Organisation type and purpose: Voluntary organisation, registered charity (charity number SC 002185).
Parent body for numerous organisations, including local authorities in Scotland, concerned with the welfare of blind and partially sighted people.

Subject coverage: Social work, education and employment services for the blind and partially sighted.

Publications: Printed

Access to staff: Contact by letter, by telephone and by e-mail
Hours: Mon to Fri, 0900 to 1700

THE UNIVERSITY OF MANCHESTER LIBRARY

Oxford Road, Manchester, M13 9PP

Tel: 0161 275 3751
Fax: 0161 273 7488
Website: www.manchester.ac.uk/library

Enquiries to: Administrator
Direct tel: 0161 306 1938
Direct e-mail: lisa.donnelly@manchester.ac.uk
Other contacts: Customer Services and Information (tel: 0161 275 3751)

Founded: 1851; created by the merger of Manchester University Library and the John Rylands Library and UMIST Library

Organisation type and purpose: University library.

Subject coverage: American studies, ancient history, archaeology, architecture, astronomy, audiology, biological sciences, Celtic studies, chemistry, classical studies, computer science, dentistry, drama, earth sciences, education, engineering, English, European studies, French, geography, German, health services administration, history, history of art, history of science and medicine, Italian, law, linguistics, materials science, mathematics, medicine, metallurgy, Middle Eastern studies, military studies, music, nursing, palaeontology, pharmacy, philosophy, physics, planning and landscape, polymer science, Portuguese, psychotherapy, radio astronomy, religious studies, Russian, Spanish, theology.

Collection: Anti-Slavery (Raymond English Collection; H G Wilson Pamphlet Collection)
Architecture (Archives of the Manchester Society of Architects; Archives of the Society of Architectural Historians of GB)
British Standards
Celtic Studies (Strachan Celtic Books; Katharine Tynan Collection)
Childrens' Literature (Alison Uttley Books and Papers; Vera Southgate Booth Collection; Marmion Collection)
Church and Society (Audenshaw Collection; William Temple Collection)
Dante Collection
Drama: see Theatre and Drama
Early Printed Books (Spencer, Aldine, Christie and Bullock Collections)
Education for Special Needs (Deaf Education Collection; Hester Adrian Collection; Hilliard Collection)
English Historians (Papers of E A Freeman, James Tait and T F Tout)
English Literature (George Bellairs, Elizabeth Gaskell, L P Hartley, Howard Spring and Thrale-Piozzi MSS)
Esperanto Collection
European Communities Collection (European Documentation Centre)
Family Muniments (Bagshawe, Bromley-Davenport, Cornwall-Legh, Ducie, Dunham Massey, Legh of Lyme, Tabley and Warburton)
French Studies (Victor Hugo Correspondence; Mazarinades Pamphlets; French Revolution Collection; Alexandre Dumas, père, collection)
Geography (Manchester Geographical Society Collection; Map Collection)
German Studies (Peter Huchel Collection)
Health and Safety Collection
History of Astronomy (Archives of Zdenek Kopal, Bernard Lovell; Jodrell Bank Collection)
History of Chemistry (Papers of John Dalton and H E Roscoe; Partington Collection)
History of Medicine (Manchester Medical Society Collection)
Industrial and Commercial History (Archives of Bolton Cotton Spinners, Thomas Botfield and Co., McConnel and Kennedy, Oldham Textile Employers and Owen Owens)
Journalism (Guardian Archives; Papers of W P Crozier, Alastair Hetherington, P J Monkhouse and C P Scott; Newspaper Collection)
Judaica (Moses Gaster Collection including Genizah Fragments; Haskalah and Marmorstein Collections)
Local History (Cheshire, Lancashire and Derbyshire Family Muniment Collections)
Manchester Museum Collection
Manchester University Archives
Military Studies (Clinton, Auchinleck and Dorman O'Gowan Papers; World War I Collection)
NASA and NIST Deposit Library
Near Eastern Book and MSS Collections (especially Arabic and Persian)
Nonconformity (Methodist Archives; Congregational College, Northern Baptist College and Unitarian College Collections; Papers of T W Manson and Thomas Raffles)
Official Publications (British and International Organisations)
Oriental Book and MSS Collections
Papyri (Arabic, Coptic, Greek, Hieratic and Hieroglyphic)
Philosophy (Papers of Samuel Alexander and Robert Adamson)
Political Economy (W S Jevons Papers)
Political Parties (Labour Party Newscuttings and Pamphlets)
Pre-Raphaelites (Papers of Holman Hunt and John Ruskin)
Private Press Books (eg Kelmscott)
Russian History (eg Alexis Aladin Papers)
Spectral and Technical Data Collection
Sport (Brockbank Cricket Collection)
Suffragette Collections
Theatre and Drama (Papers of Basil Dean, Stephen Joseph, C E Montague and A N Monkhouse; G L Brook, Annie Horniman and Allardyce Nicoll Collections)
Transport (e.g. Kenneth Brown and T J Edmondson Railway Collections)
United Nations Deposit Library
Western Medieval MSS (especially Latin, English and French)

Publications: Printed

Provides headquarters for the: John Rylands Research Institute; Manchester Bibliographical Society; Manchester Medical Society

THE WORSHIPFUL COMPANY OF LIGHTMONGERS

5 Rokefield House, Westcott Street, Westcott, Dorking, Surrey, RH4 3NZ

Tel: 01306 742566
E-mail: clerk@lightmongers.co.uk
Website: www.lightmongers.co.uk

Enquiries to: The Clerk

Founded: 1967

Organisation type and purpose:
Membership association (membership is by election or invitation).
City of London Livery Company.

Access to staff: Contact via website

THE-SRDA

Formal name: The Systems Reliability Data Association

Thomson House, Risley, Warrington, Cheshire, WA3 6AT

Tel: 01925 254249
Fax: 01925 254569
E-mail: the-srda@sercoassurance.com
Website: www.the-srda.net

Enquiries to: Manager

Founded: 2001

continued overleaf

Organisation type and purpose: Membership association, consultancy. Providing services to members for annual subscription.

Subject coverage: Risk assessment, consequence analysis and safety management, reliability analysis and availability management (cross-industry).

Trade and statistical information: Component reliability data bank online at www.the-srda.net (is available to members only)

Publications: Printed

Publications list: Available online

Part of: Serco Ltd

THEATRES TRUST

22 Charing Cross Road, London, WC2H 0QL

Tel: 020 7836 8591
Fax: 020 7836 3302
E-mail: info@theatrestrust.org.uk
Website: www.theatrestrust.org.uk

Enquiries to: Resources Officer
Other contacts: Planning and Heritage Adviser (for planning/architectural advice)

Founded: 1976

Organisation type and purpose: Non-departmental public body, statutory body. To promote the better protection of theatres.

Subject coverage: History and design of theatre buildings, their planning and architecture.

Collection: Planning applications relating to theatres in England, Wales and Scotland since 1976, photos

Non-library collection catalogue: All or part available in-house

Library catalogue: All or part available in-house

Publications: Printed

Publications list: Available online and in print

Access to staff: Contact by letter, by telephone, by fax, by e-mail and via website. Appointment necessary.
Hours: Mon to Fri, 0900 to 1700

Access to building: Prior appointment required
Hours: Mon to Fri, 0900 to 1700

Access for disabled people: No disabled access
Special comments: Steps and narrow lift.

Links with: Theatres Trust Charitable Fund; at the same address

THEATRO TECHNIS

26 Crowndale Road, London, NW1 1TT

Tel: 020 7387 6617
Fax: 020 7383 2545
E-mail: info@theatrotechnis.com
Website: www.theatrotechnis.com

Enquiries to: Co-ordinator

Founded: 1967

Organisation type and purpose: Advisory body, registered charity (charity number 2808859).
Target/client group: the Greek Cypriot community and other English-speaking communities.

Subject coverage: Centre for the Cypriot community offering a range of cultural and social activities including multilingual and multicultural theatre. Advice service covering housing, welfare rights, law, language, family life, advocacy, interpreting and translation services.

Access to staff: Contact by letter, by telephone, by fax and by e-mail. Appointment necessary.
Hours: Mon to Fri, 1000 to 1700

Access to building: No access other than to staff

Access for disabled people: Ramped entry, toilet facilities

THEOSOPHICAL SOCIETY IN ENGLAND (TSIE)

50 Gloucester Place, London, W1U 8EA

Tel: 020 7563 9817
Fax: 020 7935 9543

Enquiries to: National President
Other contacts: Office Administrator

Founded: 1888

Organisation type and purpose: International organisation, membership association, universal brotherhood.

Subject coverage: Theosophy, religion, meditation, philosophy, occultism, mysticism.

Collection: Library of 10,000 vols, bound theosophical magazines.

Publications: Printed, and electronic and video

Publications list: Available in print

Access to staff: Contact by letter, by telephone, by fax and by e-mail. Appointment necessary.

Access to building: No prior appointment required
Hours: general office open Tue to Fri, 1400 to 1830. closed last week of December and first week of January and all of August plus bank holiday Mondays
Special comments: Members and library subscribers; some meetings members only. Library open Mon to Thu 1400 to 1830 for use of members and library subscribers. Open to general public on Sundays (when lectures) from 1600 to 2030. Bookshop open Mon to Thu 1400 to 2030 and on Sundays when public lectures from 1600 to 2030.

Access for disabled people: Portable ramp for access to ground floor and lift from ground floor to library and bookshop on the first floor
Hours: Call ahead on 020 7563 9817/9818 if you wish to visit

Also at: sections and lodges in over 60 countries

Parent body: Theosophical Society; Adyar, Madras, 600020, India

THERAPY TRAINING COLLEGE (LCH)

PO Box 10500, Birmingham, B14 4WB

Tel: 0121 430 3336
E-mail: courses@lesserian.co.uk
Website: www.lesserian.co.uk
Website: www.lesserian.co.uk/courses.htm
Website: www.lesserian.co.uk/recommen .htm
Website: www.lesserian.co.uk/syllabus.htm

Enquiries to: Director

Founded: 1979

Organisation type and purpose: Training organisation.
Training in the curative use of hypnosis.

Subject coverage: The curative use of hypnosis, hypnotherapy and licensed to use 'Lesserian' trademark.

Publications: Printed, and electronic and video

Publications list: Available online and in print

Access to staff: Contact by letter, by telephone, by e-mail and via website. Appointment necessary.
Hours: Mon to Thu, 0900 to 1800

THERMAL ENGINEERING INTERNATIONAL LIMITED (Tei)

PO Box 80, Calder Vale Road, Wakefield, West Yorkshire, WF1 5YS

Tel: 01924 780000
Fax: 01924 201901
E-mail: enquiries@tei.co.uk
Website: www.tei.co.uk

Enquiries to: Director
Direct e-mail: maddisond@tei.co.uk
Other contacts: Technical Director for Ruislip office.

Founded: 1997

Organisation type and purpose: International organisation, manufacturing industry, service industry, consultancy. Design, engineering and commissioning services for utility, industrial and marine boiler plants.

Subject coverage: Steam boiler plant design and engineering and commissioning for utility, industrial and marine industries.

Collection: British, European and USA Standards

Publications: Printed

Access to staff: Contact by letter, by telephone, by fax and by e-mail. Appointment necessary.
Hours: Mon to Fri, 0730 to 1230 and 1400 to 1700

Head office: Thermal Engineering International Limited; Mechanical Services Division, PO Box 80, Calder Vale Road, Wakefield, West Yorkshire, WF1 5PF; tel: 01924 780000; fax: 01924 201901

THERMAL INSULATION CONTRACTORS ASSOCIATION (TICA)

TICA House, Arlington Way, Yarm Road Business Park, Darlington, Co Durham, DL1 4QB

Tel: 01325 466704
Fax: 01325 487691
E-mail: enquiries@tica-acad.co.uk
Website: www.tica-acad.co.uk

Enquiries to: Chief Executive

Founded: 1959

Organisation type and purpose: Trade association, present number of members: 90. Advisory services for members and representation of their interests.

Subject coverage: Thermal insulation contracting, hot and cold insulation in power stations, oil refineries, chemical plant and marine projects, including pipework, plant, ductwork, storage tanks, etc., the insulation of heating and ventilation in schools, hospitals, offices and other buildings, asbestos control and removal, firms undertaking such work, technical information, health, safety and training.

Publications list: Available online and in print

Access to staff: Contact by letter, by telephone, by fax, by e-mail, in person and via website. Non-members charged.
Hours: Mon to Thu, 0830 to 1700; Fri, 0830 to 1530

Access for disabled people: Parking provided

Affiliated to: Fédération Européenne des Syndicats d'Enterprises d'Isolation (FESI); TICA House, Allington Way, Darlington, Co. Durham; tel: 0325 466704; fax: 01325 487691; e-mail: ralphbradley@tica-acad.co.uk; website: http://www.fesi.eu
World Insulation and Acoustics Congress Organisation (WIACO)

Subsidiary bodies: Asbestos Control and Abatement Division (ACAD); tel: 01325 466704; fax: 01325 487691; e-mail: enquiries@tica-acad.co.uk; Insulation and Environmental Training Agency; tel: 01325 466704; fax: 01325 487691; e-mail: ieta@tica-acad.co.uk

THERMAL INSULATION MANUFACTURERS AND SUPPLIERS ASSOCIATION (TIMSA)

Tournai Hall, Evelyn Woods Road, Aldershot, Hampshire, GU11 2LL

Tel: 01252 357844
Fax: 01252 357831
E-mail: timsa@associationhouse.org.uk
Website: www.timsa.org.uk

Enquiries to: Secretary

Founded: 1978

Organisation type and purpose: Trade association, present number of members: 36. Represents major manufacturers, specialist suppliers and distributors and consultants in the UK thermal insulation industry.

Subject coverage: Promotes the correct use and application of thermal insulation and ancillary materials.

Publications: Printed

Publications list: Available in print

Access to staff: Contact by letter, by telephone, by fax, by e-mail and via website
Hours: Mon to Fri, 0900 to 1700

THERMAL SPRAYING AND SURFACE ENGINEERING ASSOCIATION, THE (TSSEA)

18 Hammeton Way, Wellesbourne, Warwick, CV35 9NT

Tel: 01789 842822
Fax: 01789 842229
E-mail: thermal.sprayers@btinternet.com

Enquiries to: General Secretary

Founded: 1934

Organisation type and purpose: International organisation, advisory body, trade association (membership is by subscription), service industry, consultancy.

Subject coverage: Surface coatings on metals or other substrates of other metals, ceramics and cermets.

Publications: Printed

Access to staff: Contact by letter, by telephone, by fax and by e-mail. Appointment necessary.
Hours: Mon to Fri, 0900 to 1700

Affiliated to: The Institute of Materials (IOM); 1 Carlton House Terrace, London, SW1Y 5DB

THIRD AGE TRUST

The Old Municipal Buildings, 19 East Street, Bromley, Kent, BR1 1QE,

Tel: 020 8466 6139
E-mail: via website
Website: www.u3a.org.uk

Organisation type and purpose: A limited company and a registered charity (number 288007).
The national representative body for Universities of the Third Age (U3As) in the UK.
Underpins the work of local U3As by providing educational and administrative support to their management committees and to individual members and assists in the development of new U3As across the UK.

Subject coverage: U3As are self-help, self-managed lifelong learning co-operatives for older people no longer in full-time work, providing opportunities for their members to share learning experiences in a wide range of interest groups and to pursue learning not for qualifications, but for fun.

Access to staff: Contact by letter, by telephone and via website
Hours: Tel. lines open: Mon to Thu, 0900 to 1700; Fri, 0900 to 1300

THISTLE FOUNDATION

Niddrie Mains Road, Edinburgh, EH16 4EA

Tel: 0131 661 3366
Fax: 0131 661 4879
E-mail: via website
Website: www.thistle.org.uk

Founded: 1944

Organisation type and purpose: A registered Scottish charity (number is SC016816).
Supports people with disabilities and long-term health conditions.
Aims to give people independence in their own homes and help bring about a society where everyone has the right to feel involved and empowered to live the life they choose, regardless of their disabilities or health condition.

Subject coverage: Provides a range of supported living and health and well-being services for people with disabilities and health conditions, plus training and consultancy and conference facilities.

Publications: Electronic and video
Order electronic and video publications from: Download from website

Publications list: Available online

Access to staff: Contact by letter, by telephone, by fax and via website

Also at: 25 High Mair, Renfrew, PA4 OSD; tel: 0141 886 3375; fax: 0141 885 1484; Wighton House, East Ct, Edinburgh, EH16 4ED; tel: 0131 661 1543

THOMAS HARDY SOCIETY

PO Box 1438, Dorchester, Dorset, DT1 1YH

Tel: 01305 251501
Fax: 01305 251501
E-mail: info@hardysociety.org
Website: www.hardysociety.org

Enquiries to: Honorary Secretary

Founded: 1968

Organisation type and purpose: Membership association (membership is by subscription), present number of members: 1,500.
Literary society.

Subject coverage: Life and work of Thomas Hardy; country associated with Hardy's writing.

Collection: Comprehensive collection of books by Hardy and all literary criticism held at Dorset County Library, Dorchester Important Hardy collections at Dorset County Museum, Dorchester

Publications: Printed

Publications list: Available in print

Access to staff: Contact by letter, by telephone, by fax, by e-mail, in person and via website. Appointment necessary.
Hours: Mon to Thu, 1400 to 1600

THOMAS LOVELL BEDDOES SOCIETY

9 Amber Court, Belper, Derbyshire, DE56 1HG

Tel: 01773 828066
Fax: 01773 828066
E-mail: dragoman@talktalk.net
Website: www.phantomwooer.org

continued overleaf

Enquiries to: Chair

Founded: 1994

Organisation type and purpose: International organisation, learned society (membership is by subscription, election or invitation), present number of members: 100, registered charity (charity number 1041402), research organisation, publishing house.
To research Beddoes' life, times and work and encourage relevant publications; to further the reading and appreciation of his works by a wider public; to liaise with other groups and organisations; to plan events to further the aims.

Subject coverage: Life and works of Thomas Lovell Beddoes (1803–1849).

Collection: Works of Thomas Lovell Beddoes

Non-library collection catalogue: All or part available online, in-house and in print

Publications: Printed, and electronic and video

Publications list: Available online and in print

Access to staff: Contact by letter, by telephone, by fax, by e-mail and in person
Hours: Mon to Fri, 0900 to 1700

Access to building: Prior appointment required

Links with: Alliance of Literary Societies (ALS); Secretary, 22 Belmont Grove, Havant, Hampshire, PO9 3PU; tel: 01926 337874

THOMAS PAINE SOCIETY

c/o Stuart Hill, 14 Park Drive, Forest Hall, Newcastle, NE12 9JP

E-mail: stuart.hill23@ntlworld.com
Website: www.thomaspainesocietyuk.org.uk

Organisation type and purpose: Membership association (membership is by subscription). Promotes the recognition of Thomas Paine's contribution to the cause of freedom and seeks to spread a knowledge of his work and activities with a view to encouraging the growth of a similar spirit of constructive criticism in every aspect of public life.

Subject coverage: The work and activities of Thomas Paine.

Publications: Printed

THOMAS PLUME'S LIBRARY

Market Hill, Maldon, Essex, CM9 4PZ

Tel: 01621 854850
Fax: 01621 854850
E-mail: info@thomasplumeslibrary.co.uk
Website: htpp://www.thomasplumeslibrary.co.uk

Enquiries to: Librarian

Founded: 1704

Subject coverage: C17th theology, natural philosophy, chemistry, medicine, physics, mathematics, and astronomy.

Collection: Thomas Plume Collection of 8,200 vols, post-Plume collection approx. 1,800, Plume's manuscripts and papers.

Library catalogue: All or part available online and in print

Publications: Printed

Publications list: Available online

Access to staff: Contact by letter, by telephone, by fax, by e-mail, in person and via website
Hours: Tue to Thu, 1400 to 1600; Sat, 1000 to 1200; Mon, Fri, closed

Access to building: *Hours:* Tue to Thu, 1400 to 1600; Sat, 1000 to 1200; Mon, Fri, closed
Special comments: Spiral staircase to 1st floor.

Access for disabled people: No disabled access

THOMAS TALLIS SOCIETY (TTS)

13 Albury Street, London, SE8 3PT

Tel: 020 8691 8337
Fax: 020 8691 8337
Website: www.thomas-tallis-society.org.uk/
Website: www.classical-artists.com/tcc

Enquiries to: Administrator

Founded: 1965

Organisation type and purpose: Choral society.

Subject coverage: The music of Thomas Tallis. The choir performs mainly classical music of all periods. Specialising in programmes to suit different venues, themes.

Publications: Printed

Access to staff: Contact by letter, by telephone and by fax
Hours: Mon to Fri, 0900 to 1700

Connections with: Tallis Chamber Choir (TCC); 13 Albury Street, London, SE8 3PT; tel: 020 8691 8337

THOMPSON HENRY LIMITED

London Road, Sunningdale, Berkshire, SL5 0EP

Tel: 01344 624615
E-mail: thl@thompsonhenry.co.uk

Enquiries to: Managing Director
Direct e-mail: j.dodd@thompsonhenry.co.uk

Founded: 1972

Organisation type and purpose: Service industry.

Subject coverage: Publications and services of the academic publishers represented.

Access to staff: Contact by letter and by e-mail
Hours: Mon to Fri, 0900 to 1700

European agent for: ACLS Humanities E-book; BIOSIS; CAIRN; Global Science Press; NewsBank; Philosophy Documentation Center; RMIT Publishing; STAT!Ref

UK agent for: Readex

THOMSON REUTERS

Enterprise House, Innovation Way, Heslington, York, YO10 5NQ

Tel: 020 7433 4590
Fax: 020 7433 4589
Website: www.thomsonreuters.com
Website: www.organismnames.com
Website: www.biologybrowser.com

Enquiries to: Director, York Operations
Direct e-mail: nigel.robinson@thomsonreuters.com

Founded: 1864; formerly called BIOSIS UK (year of change 2004); formerly called Thomson Reuters Zoological Ltd (year of change 2011)

Organisation type and purpose: Provider of information services and solutions for professionals in life sciences.

Subject coverage: Life sciences – bibliographic data, zoology.

Publications: Printed, and electronic and video
Order electronic and video publications from: Thomson Reuters sales office

Publications list: Available online

Access to staff: Contact by letter, by telephone, by fax, by e-mail and via website
Hours: Mon to Fri, 0900 to 1700

Access to building: No access other than to staff

Parent body: Thomson Reuters; 77 Hatton Garden, London, EC1N 8JS; website: http://www.thomsonreuters.com

THORESBY SOCIETY

Formal name: The Thoresby Society – The Leeds Historical Society

Claremont, 23 Clarendon Road, Leeds, West Yorkshire, LS2 9NZ

Tel: 0113 247 0704
E-mail: secretary@thoresby.org.uk
Website: www.thoresby.org.uk

Enquiries to: Honorary Secretary (for general enquiries)
Direct e-mail: library@thoresby.org.uk
Other contacts: Librarian (for research enquiries)

Founded: 1889

Organisation type and purpose: Historical society (membership is by subscription), present number of members: c. 350, registered charity (charity number 1126086) and company limited by guarantee (company number 6649783).

Subject coverage: Local history of Leeds and surrounding areas.

Collection: Books, pictures, maps and plans, archives

Non-library collection catalogue: All or part available online and in-house

Library catalogue: All or part available in-house

Publications: Printed
Order printed publications from: The Society, by post (address above) or by e-mail: distribution@thoresby.org.uk

Publications list: Available online and in print

Access to staff: Contact by letter, by telephone, by e-mail and via website. Appointment necessary.
Hours: Tue and Thu, 1000 to 1400; phone messages can be left at other times

Access to building: *Hours:* Tue and Thu, 1000 to 1400

Access for disabled people: Parking provided; toilet facilities
Special comments: Library is on first floor; there is no lift.

THREE RIVERS DISTRICT COUNCIL (TRDC)

Three Rivers House, Northway, Rickmansworth, Hertfordshire, WD3 1RL

Tel: 01923 776611
Fax: 01923 896119
E-mail: stuart.marlton@threerivers.gov.uk
Website: www.3rivers.gov.uk

Enquiries to: Public Relations Manager
Direct tel: 01923 727255
Direct fax: 01923 727258

Founded: 1974

Organisation type and purpose: Local government body.

Subject coverage: All local services and amenities covering the Rickmansworth, South Oxhey, Carpenders Park, Chorleywood, Sarratt, Abbots Langley, Moor Park and Maple Cross area, allotments, cemeteries, electoral registration, environmental health, parking, concessionary public transport fares, housing, museums and arts, local planning, building control and development control, council tax and business rates collection, sports and recreation.

Publications: Printed

Access to staff: Contact by letter, by telephone, by fax, by e-mail, in person and via website. Appointment necessary.
Hours: Mon to Thu, 0830 to 1730; Fri, 0830 to 1700

Access for disabled people: Parking provided, level entry, access to all public areas, toilet facilities

THRIVE

The Geoffrey Udall Centre, Beech Hill, Reading, Berkshire, RG7 2AT

Tel: 0118 988 5688
Fax: 0118 988 5677
E-mail: info@thrive.org.uk
Website: www.thrive.org.uk
Website: www.carryongardening.org

Enquiries to: Information Officer
Direct e-mail: gill.bailey@thrive.org.uk

Founded: 1978

Organisation type and purpose: Membership association (membership is by subscription), present number of members: 730, voluntary organisation, registered charity (charity number 277570), suitable for all ages; training organisation, consultancy.
To research, educate and promote the use and advantages of gardening for people with a disability.

Subject coverage: Disability and gardening. Activities focus on promoting the benefits of gardening to individuals and organisations, as well as teaching techniques and practical applications so that anyone with a disability can take part in and benefit from gardening.

Special visitor services: Two gardens (call office for details)

Collection: Library containing comprehensive collection on therapeutic horticulture

Publications: Printed

Publications list: Available online and in print

Access to staff: Contact by letter, by telephone, by fax, by e-mail and via website. Appointment necessary.
Hours: Mon to Fri, 0900 to 1700

Links with: Coventry University; numerous professional and voluntary bodies; Royal Horticultural Society

THROMBOSIS RESEARCH INSTITUTE

Emmanuel Kaye Building, Manresa Road, Chelsea, London, SW3 6LR

Tel: 020 7351 8300
Fax: 020 7351 8317
E-mail: info@tri-london.ac.uk
Website: www.tri-london.ac.uk

Founded: 1989

Organisation type and purpose: Registered charity (charity number 800365). Research institute.
Internationally renowned for pioneering, multi-disciplinary research, the Thrombosis Research Institute was established to conduct research into cardiovascular disease, a major cause of death and disability throughout the world. It comprises two independent charitable foundations based in London, United Kingdom and Bangalore, India (founded 2006). This second facility was set up to study the genetics of heart disease particularly among the South Asian population, who seem to have specific predisposing genetic characteristics, and to develop novel and affordable therapies for disease prevention and treatment.

Subject coverage: Holds an annual international symposium of clinicians. The two partner institutions contribute to a joint, independent research programme.

Publications: Electronic and video

Access to staff: Contact by letter, by telephone, by fax and by e-mail

Also at: Thrombosis Research Institute; 258A, Bommasandra Industrial Area, Anekal Taluk, Bangalore 560 099, India; tel: +91 80 2783 5303; fax: +91 80 2783 5443

THURROCK AND BASILDON COLLEGE

Woodview Campus, Grays, Essex, RM16 2YR

Tel: 01375 362691
Fax: 01375 373356
E-mail: learning@southessex.ac.uk

Enquiries to: Librarian

Founded: 1959

Organisation type and purpose: College of further education.

Subject coverage: Management and business studies, office and information technology, hotels and catering, tourism and leisure, language, hair and beauty technology, motor vehicle studies, art and design, caring, pre-school education, vocational.

Library catalogue: All or part available in-house

Access to staff: Contact by telephone and in person
Hours: Mon, 0845 to 2130; Tue to Thu, 0845 to 1800; Fri, 0845 to 1645

Access for disabled people: Parking provided, level entry, toilet facilities

Other address: Thurrock and Basildon College; Nethermayne Campus, Basildon, Essex, SS16 5NN; tel: 01268 461614

THURROCK UNITARY COUNCIL

Civic Offices, New Road, Grays, Essex, RM17 6SL

Tel: 01375 652652
Fax: 01375 652785
E-mail: general.enquiries@thurrock.gov.uk

Enquiries to: Head of Corporate Communications
Direct tel: 01375 652016
Direct fax: 01375 652874

Organisation type and purpose: Local government body.

Subject coverage: Local government, residential services, regeneration, environmental conservation.

Publications: Printed

Access to staff: Contact by letter, by telephone and by fax
Hours: Mon to Fri, 0900 to 1700

Access to building: *Hours:* Mon to Fri, 0830 to 1700

Access for disabled people: *Hours:* Mon to Fri, 0830 to 1700

TILE ASSOCIATION (TTA)

Forum Court, 83 Copers Cope Road, Beckenham, Kent, BR3 1NR

Tel: 020 8663 0946
Fax: 020 8663 0949
E-mail: info@tiles.org.uk
Website: www.tiles.org.uk

Enquiries to: Executive Officer

Founded: 2000

Organisation type and purpose: Trade association.

Subject coverage: Generic information on wall and floor tiling.

Publications: Printed

Access to staff: Contact by letter, by telephone, by fax, by e-mail and via website. Appointment necessary.
Hours: Mon to Fri, 0900 to 1700

Member organisation of: European Ceramic Tile Manufacturers Association (CET); European Union of Tile Fixers' Associations (EUF); National Specialist Contractors Council (NSCC)

TILES AND ARCHITECTURAL CERAMICS SOCIETY (TACS)

'Oakhurst', Cocknage Road, Rough Close, Stoke on Trent, ST3 7NN

Tel: 0151 207 0001
E-mail: kathbertadams@hotmail.com
Website: www.tilesoc.org.uk

Enquiries to: Secretary

Founded: 1981

Organisation type and purpose: Advisory body, learned society (membership is by subscription), present number of members: 367, registered charity (charity number 289090), research organisation, publishing house.
The study and protection of tiles and architectural ceramics.

Subject coverage: All areas of historical and contemporary tile production and functional applications, as well as tile collecting and tile conservation, architectural ceramics.

Publications: Printed

Publications list: Available online and in print

Access to staff: Contact by letter and by e-mail
Hours: Mon to Fri, 0900 to 1700

TILLENDOVE PICTURE LIBRARY

Bowood, Ewell House Grove, Epsom, Surrey, KT17 1NT

Tel: 07831 598018
Fax: 020 8394 2247
E-mail: tillendove@mailbox.co.uk
Website: www.tillendove.co.uk

Enquiries to: Partner

Founded: 1993

Organisation type and purpose: Service industry.
Press photography library.

Subject coverage: Press photography.

Collection: Photographs of celebrities, film, TV and music
Photographs of public figures

Non-library collection catalogue: All or part available online and in-house

Publications list: Available in print

Access to staff: Contact by letter, by telephone, by fax and by e-mail. All charged.
Hours: Mon to Fri, 0900 to 1700

Access to building: No access other than to staff

TIMBER PACKAGING AND PALLET CONFEDERATION (TIMCON)

840 Melton Road, Thurmaston, Leicester, LE4 8BN

Tel: 0116 264 0579
Fax: 0116 264 0141
E-mail: timcon@associationhq.org.uk
Website: www.timcon.org

Enquiries to: Executive Secretary

Organisation type and purpose: Trade association.

Subject coverage: Wooden cases and pallets; export packing; technical, legislative, environmental and industrial relations matters in the industry.

Publications: Printed

Access to staff: Contact by letter, by telephone, by fax, by e-mail and via website
Hours: Mon to Fri, 0900 to 1700

Access to building: Prior appointment required

Access for disabled people: Access to all public areas

TIMBER TRADE FEDERATION (TTF)

The Building Centre, 26 Store Street, London, WC1E 7BT

Tel: 020 3205 0067
E-mail: via website
Website: www.ttf.co.uk/

Enquiries to: Director General

Founded: 1892

Organisation type and purpose: Trade association.

Access to staff: Contact by letter, by telephone and by e-mail. Appointment necessary. Non-members charged.
Hours: Mon to Fri, 0900 to 1700

Access to building: No prior appointment required

TNS MEDIA INTELLIGENCE LIMITED

Formal name: The Media Monitoring Service

6th Floor, 292 Vauxhall Bridge Road, London, SW1V 1AE

Tel: 0870 202 0100
Fax: 0870 202 0110
E-mail: tnsmi_sales@tnsofres.com
Website: www.tellex.press.net

Enquiries to: Marketing & Communications Manager
Direct tel: 020 7963 7638
Direct fax: 020 7963 7609

Founded: 1954; formerly called Parker Bishop Limited, TNS Tellex Limited (year of change 2002)

Organisation type and purpose: Service industry.
Broadcast reporting service monitoring over 350 television and radio stations throughout the UK; a service providing selective broadcast information to the communications industry including: PR agencies, advertising and design agencies, manufacturing and marketing companies, service companies, government organisations, financial PR agencies and companies.

Subject coverage: Mainly news and current affairs, although any item or station can be monitored with a detailed brief supplied by the client with reasonable notice.

Publications: Printed
Order printed publications from: Publications Department
at the same address, tel: 020 7566 3108

Access to staff: Contact by letter, by telephone, by fax, by e-mail and via website. Appointment necessary.
Hours: Sales office: Mon to Fri, 0700 to 1900

Other addresses: TNS Media Intelligence; Manchester; tel: 0161 228 6922; TNS Media Intelligence; Durham; tel: 0191 386 6767; TNS Media Intelligence; Leeds; tel: 0113 243 4233; TNS Media Intelligence; Peterborough, Cambridgeshire; tel: 01733 896776; TNS Media Intelligence; Cardiff; tel: 029 2039 5313; TNS Media Intelligence; Worthing, West Sussex; tel: 01903 212731; TNS Media Intelligence; Edinburgh; tel: 0131 226 2612

Subsidiary of: Taylor Nelson Sofres plc

TOASTMASTERS FOR ROYAL OCCASIONS

12 Little Bornes, Alleyn Park, Dulwich, London, SE21 8SE

Tel: 020 8670 5585/ 8424
Fax: 020 8670 0055

Enquiries to: President

Founded: 1980

Organisation type and purpose: Professional body, training organisation.

Subject coverage: Royal visits, state banquets etc, in Britain and overseas; all aspects of the preparation and organisation of these events.

Access to staff: Contact by letter, by telephone, by fax and by e-mail
Hours: Mon to Fri, 0900 to 1700

Member of: Guild of International Professional Toastmasters; at the same address

TOASTMASTERS OF GREAT BRITAIN

12 Little Bornes, Alleyn Park, Dulwich, London, SE21 8SE

Tel: 020 8670 5585
Fax: 020 8670 0055
Website: www.ivorspencer.com

Enquiries to: Chief Executive

Founded: 1980

Organisation type and purpose: Advisory body, professional body.

Subject coverage: Organisation of royal events, banquets, conferences, and other ceremonies for firms and public bodies.

Access to staff: Contact by letter, by telephone, by fax and by e-mail. Access for members only.
Hours: Mon to Fri, 0900 to 1700

Member of: Guild of Professional Toastmasters

TOBACCO MANUFACTURERS' ASSOCIATION (TMA)

5th Floor, Burwood House, 14/16 Caxton Street, London, SW1H 0ZB

Tel: 020 7544 0100
Fax: 020 7544 0117
E-mail: information@the-tma.org.uk

Website: www.the-tma.org.uk

Enquiries to: Information and Media Manager
Direct tel: 020 7544 0108

Founded: 1940

Organisation type and purpose: Trade association.

Subject coverage: Tobacco industry; smoking issues.

Non-library collection catalogue: All or part available online, in-house and in print

Access to staff: Contact by letter, by telephone, by fax and by e-mail
Hours: Mon to Fri, 0900 to 1700

Access to building: No access other than to staff

TOC H

3rd Floor, Wing House, Britannia Street, Aylesbury, Buckinghamshire, HP20 1QS

Tel: 01296 331099
Fax: 01296 331135
E-mail: info@toch.org.uk
Website: www.toch.org.uk

Enquiries to: Director

Founded: 1915

Organisation type and purpose:
Membership association, present number of members: 3,061, voluntary organisation, registered charity (charity number 211042). Christian-based, but open to people of all walks of life and faith.
To break down social, racial and cultural barriers by challenging individuals' perceptions of others and the divisions which exist in society.

Subject coverage: Voluntary work, personal and community service.

Collection: Archive of Toc H books and photographs

Publications: Printed

Publications list: Available in print

Access to staff: Contact by letter, by telephone and by fax
Hours: Mon to Fri, 0900 to 1700

TOGETHER (MACA) (MACA)

Formal name: Together (The Mental After Care Association)

12 Old Street, London, EC1V 9BE

Tel: 020 7780 7300
Fax: 020 7780 7301
E-mail: contactus@together-uk.org
Website: www.together-uk.org/

Enquiries to: Press and Publications Officer
Direct e-mail: amanda-williamson@together-uk.org

Founded: 1879

Organisation type and purpose: National organisation, voluntary organisation, registered charity (charity number 211091). Probably the earliest organisation of its kind, established from 1879.
To provide high quality services for people with mental health needs and their carers and to influence policy and practice in relation to mental health.

Subject coverage: Services in the community, hospitals and prisons for people with mental health needs and their carers.

Collection: Archives of the Association dating back to 1879, now held at the Wellcome Trust, London

Library catalogue: All or part available in-house

Publications: Printed

Access to staff: Contact by letter, by telephone, by fax, by e-mail and via website. Appointment necessary.
Hours: Mon to Fri, 0900 to 1730
Special comments: For staff, council members and service users only. No wheelchair access. No public access to library.

Regional Offices: MACA Development Areas (North, Midlands and Scotland); 3 Fieldhouse Road, Rochdale, Lancashire, OL12 0AD; tel: 01706 640 027; fax: 01706 640 027; e-mail: maca-midlandsandnorth@maca.org.uk; MACA London and East; 89 Turners Hill, Cheshunt, Hertfordshire, EN8 9BN; tel: 01992 622 000; fax: 01992 622 621; e-mail: maca-londonandeast@maca.org.uk; MACA South; 94b High Street, Epsom, Surrey, KT19 8BJ; tel: 01372 722 970; fax: 01372 722 980; e-mail: maca.south@maca.org.uk

TOLKIEN SOCIETY

8 Queens Lane, Eynsham, Witney, OX2 4HL

E-mail: tolksoc@tolkiensociety.org
Website: www.tolkiensociety.org

Enquiries to: Membership Secretary
Direct e-mail: membership@tolkiensociety.org
Other contacts: Archivist – archives@tolkiensociety.org for access to the Society's archives.

Founded: 1969

Organisation type and purpose:
International organisation, learned society (membership is by subscription), present number of members: 1,245, voluntary organisation, registered charity (charity number 273809).

Subject coverage: J R R Tolkien, life and works, associated authors, the Inklings etc.

Collection: Archives of Tolkien-related material including newspaper cuttings, fanzines, merchandise and foreign editions

Non-library collection catalogue: All or part available in-house

Publications: Printed
Order printed publications from: Tolkien Society Trading Ltd
8 Chantry Lane, Westbury, Wiltshire, BA13 3BS, tel: 01373 822884, fax: 01373 865001, e-mail: sales@tolkiensociety.org

Access to staff: Contact by letter and by e-mail. Appointment necessary.
Hours: Mon to Fri, 0900 to 1700
Special comments: By special appointment and not usually made on weekends.

Access to building: Prior appointment required

Affiliated to: The Alliance of Literary Societies

Has: 23 affiliated local groups (Smials)

TONBRIDGE & MALLING BOROUGH COUNCIL (TMBC)

Gibson Building, Gibson Drive, Kings Hill, West Malling, Kent, ME19 4LZ

Tel: 01732 844522
Fax: 01732 842170
E-mail: customer.services@tmbc.gov.uk
Website: www.tmbc.gov.uk

Enquiries to: Media and Communications Manager
Direct tel: 01732 876009
Direct e-mail: corporate.communications@tmbc.gov.uk

Organisation type and purpose: Local government body.

Publications: Printed

Access to staff: Contact by letter, by telephone, by fax, by e-mail and in person
Hours: Mon to Fri, 0830 to 1700

Access for disabled people: Parking provided, level entry, toilet facilities

TONSIL

Formal name: The Ongoing Singing Liaison Group

35 Old Lynn Road, Wisbech, Cambridgeshire, PE14 7AJ

E-mail: enquiries@tonsil.org.uk
Website: www.tonsil.org.uk/

Enquiries to: Secretary
Direct e-mail: philliptolley@colcanto.co.uk

Founded: 1988

Organisation type and purpose: Registered charity. Represents 14 organisations promoting choral singing, supporting over 25,000 member choirs and over 500,000 singers

Subject coverage: Singing Days, Singing Projects and Animation Schemes, Training for Animateurs and Singing Leaders.

Access to staff: Contact by letter, by telephone, by fax, by e-mail and via website. Appointment necessary.
Hours: Mon to Fri, 0930 to 1500

Member of: European Federation of Young Choirs

TOOL AND TRADES HISTORY SOCIETY (TATHS)

Southay, Honiton Road, Trull, Taunton, Somerset, TA 3 7EX

Tel: 01823 259770
E-mail: membership@taths.org.uk
Website: www.taths.org.uk

Enquiries to: membership@taths.org.uk

Founded: 1983

continued overleaf

Organisation type and purpose: International organisation, learned society (membership is by subscription), present number of members: 500, registered charity (charity number 290474).
To advance the education of the general public in the history and development of hand tools and their use, and of the people and trades that used them.

Subject coverage: Hand tools; traditional trades using hand tools, e.g. blacksmiths, thatchers, coopers, all woodworking trades, furniture-making, clockmaking, jewellery-making, some building trades, medical and scientific instruments.

Collection: Societies library held a Museum of English Rural Life

Trade and statistical information: Various books & trade catalogues

Non-library collection catalogue: All or part available online and in print

Library catalogue: All or part available online and in print

Publications: Printed, and microform publications

Publications list: Available in print

Access to staff: Contact by letter, by e-mail and via website
Hours: Any evening

Access to building: N/A

Links with: Early American Industries Association (same field in USA) and numerous museums and like-minded organisations

TORBAY COUNCIL

Town Hall, Castle Circus, Torquay, Devon, TQ1 3DR

Tel: 01803 201201
Fax: 01803 292677
E-mail: connections@torbay.gov.uk
Website: www.torbay.gov.uk

Founded: 1998; formerly called Torbay Borough Council (year of change 1998)

Organisation type and purpose: Local government body.

Subject coverage: Local government services.

Publications: Printed

Access to staff: Contact by letter, by telephone, by fax, by e-mail and via website
Hours: Mon to Thu, 0840 to 1715; Fri, 0840 to 1615

Access to building: No access other than to staff

TORBAY LIBRARIES

Torquay Library, Lymington Road, Torquay, Devon, TQ1 3DT

Tel: 01803 208305
Fax: 01803 208307
E-mail: tqreflib@torbay.gov.uk
Website: www.torbay.gov.uk/libraries

Enquiries to: Head of Library Services

Organisation type and purpose: Local government body, public library.

Subject coverage: Devon local studies collection, particularly information on Torbay.

Collection: Devon local studies collection
Census returns on microfilm (local area only)
Cuttings file
Maps
Newspapers (microfilm)

Non-library collection catalogue: All or part available online

Library catalogue: All or part available online

Access to staff: Contact by letter, by telephone, by fax, by e-mail and in person
Hours: Main Library and Local Studies Library: Mon, Wed, Fri, 0930 to 1900; Tue, 0930 to 1700; Thu, 0930 to 1300; Sat, 0930 to 1600

Access for disabled people: Ramped entry, lift to first floor.

Parent body: Torbay Council; e-mail: tqreflib@torbay.gov.uk; website: http://www.torbay.gov.uk/libraries

TORCH TRUST

Formal name: Torch Trust for the Blind

Torch House, Torch Way, Northampton Road, Market Harborough, Leics, LE16 9H

Tel: 01858 438260
Fax: 01858 438275
E-mail: info@torchtrust.org
Website: www.torchtrust.org

Organisation type and purpose: A registered charity (number 1095094) and voluntary organisation, suitable for children and adults.
Its vision is that blind and partially sighted people should be able to read what they want to read, when they want to read it and in a media that they prefer.

Subject coverage: Provides a free postal Christian library service for blind and partially sighted people, and a holiday retreat.

Collection: The Torch Library is the largest collection of Christian books in the English language accessible for those with sight loss – over 2,000 titles covering theological, devotional, missionary, biographical and Christian leisure reading

Library catalogue: All or part available online

Publications: Printed, and electronic and video

Access to staff: Contact by letter, by telephone, by fax and by e-mail

Also at: Torch Holiday and Retreat Centre; 4 Hassocks Road, Hurstpierpoint, West Sussex, BN6 9QN; tel: 01273 832282; e-mail: torchhrc@torchtrust.org

Non-denominational Torch Fellowship Groups meet regularly at 110 locations across the UK:

TORFAEN COUNTY BOROUGH COUNCIL

Civic Centre, Pontypool, Gwent, NP4 6YB

Tel: 01495 762200
Fax: 01495 755513
Website: www.torfaen.gov.uk

Enquiries to: Chief Executive
Direct tel: 01495 766069
Direct fax: 01495 766059

Founded: 1 April 1996

Organisation type and purpose: Local government body.

Publications: Printed

Access to staff: Contact by letter
Hours: Mon to Fri, 0900 to 1700

Other office at: Torfaen County Borough Council; County Hall, Croesyceiliog, Cwmbran

TORFAEN LIBRARY AND INFORMATION SERVICE

Ty Blaen torfaen, Panteg Way, New Inn, Pontypool, NP4 0LS

Tel: 01495 628943
Fax: 01495 628935
E-mail: Cwmbran.library@torfaen.gov.uk
Website: www.torfaen.gov.uk/en/leisure/property.php/mid=42

Enquiries to: Cultural Services Manager
Direct e-mail: Christine.george@torfaen.gov.uk

Founded: 1996

Organisation type and purpose: Local government body, public library.

Subject coverage: General, local studies, advice and self help, bibliotherapy, Macmillan Cancer Information and support Service.

Non-library collection catalogue: All or part available online

Library catalogue: All or part available online

Publications list: Available in print

Access to staff: Contact by letter, by telephone, by fax, by e-mail, in person and via website
Hours: Mon to Fri, 0900 to 1700

Access for disabled people: Toilet facilities

Parent body: Torfaen County Borough Council

TORIT DCE, DONALDSON DUST COLLECTION GROUP

Humberstone Lane, Thurmaston, Leicester, LE4 8HP

Tel: 0116 269 6161
Fax: 0116 269 3028
E-mail: CAP-uk@donaldson.com
Website: www.btrenvironmental.co.uk

Enquiries to: UK Sales Manger
Other contacts: Marketing Officer for publications.

Founded: 1919; formerly called BTR Environmental Limited; formerly called Dust Control Equipment Limited (DCE) (year of change 1998)

Organisation type and purpose: Manufacturing industry.

Subject coverage: Design, manufacture, installation and commissioning of industrial dust control equipment; unit collectors; insertable filters; automatic reverse jet filters; tubular bag filters; complete plant installations; compact venting filters; centralised vacuum cleaning systems.

Collection: Complete Product Literature

Publications: Printed, and electronic and video

Publications list: Available online

Access to staff: Contact by letter, by telephone, by fax, by e-mail and via website. Appointment necessary.
Hours: Mon to Thu, 0830 to 1700; Fri, 0830 to 1545

Access to building: Prior appointment required

TORNADO AND STORM RESEARCH ORGANIZATION (TORRO)

TCO (Thunderstorm) Division, PO Box 84, Oxford, OX1 4NP

Tel: 01865 483761
Fax: 01865 483937
Website: www.torro.org.uk

Enquiries to: Director
Direct e-mail: sam.hall@torro.org.uk
Other contacts: Director, Geography Unit, Oxford Brookes University, Gipsy Lane, Oxford

Founded: 1924; formerly called Thunderstorm Census Organisation (year of change 1982)

Organisation type and purpose: Research organisation.
Organisation for data collection, consultancy and research.

Subject coverage: Thunderstorm frequency in Great Britain, geographical distribution in Great Britain, research into damaging lightning incidents, historical data collection, thunderstorm climatology, rainfall and temperature extremes, damaging hailstones and point rainfalls.

Collection: Database for tornadoes, damaging hailstorms, thunderstorms (UK)
Information on temperature and rainfall extremes
Thunderstorm reports and relevant press cuttings 1925 to date

Publications: Printed

Publications list: Available in print

Access to staff: Contact by letter, by e-mail and via website
Hours: Mon to Fri, 0900 to 1700

Parent body: Tornado and Storm Research Organisation (TORRO); Geography Unit, Oxford Brookes University, Gipsy Lane, Oxford

TORRIDGE DISTRICT COUNCIL (TDC)

Riverbank House, Bideford, Devon, EX39 2QG

Tel: 01237 428700
Fax: 01237 478849
E-mail: customer.services@torridge.gov.uk
Website: www.torridge.gov.uk

Enquiries to: Chief Executive
Direct tel: 01237 428705

Founded: 1974

Organisation type and purpose: Local government body.

TOTAL FINA ELF EXPLORATION UK PLC (TFEEUK)

Crawpeel Road, Altens Industrial Estate, Aberdeen, AB12 3FG

Tel: 01224 297000
Fax: 01224 298000

Enquiries to: Librarian

History of institution: formerly called Elf Exploration UK plc (EEUK), Total Oil Marine (TOM) (year of change 2000)

Organisation type and purpose: Commercial company.

Subject coverage: Oil, gas, exploration and production.

Library catalogue: All or part available in-house

TOURETTES ACTION

Formal name: Tourette Syndrome (UK) Association (Tourettes Action)

Kings Court, 91–93 High Street, Camberley, Surrey GU16 9LQ

Tel: 0300 777 8427 (helpline)
E-mail: admin@tourettes-action.org.uk
Website: www.tourettes-action.org.uk

Enquiries to: Chief Executive
Direct tel: 01276 482901
Direct e-mail: suzanne.dobson@tourettes-action.org.uk
Other contacts: TS Support Manager

Founded: 1980

Organisation type and purpose: National organisation, advisory body, membership association (membership is by subscription, qualification, election or invitation), present number of members: 650, voluntary organisation, registered charity (charity number 1003317).
The object of the Association is the relief of persons who have the neurological movement disorder Gilles de la Tourette Syndrome.

Subject coverage: Tourette Syndrome, a neurological disorder causing motor and vocal tics

Information services: Helpline; information pack available on request.

Publications: Printed, and electronic and video
Order printed publications from: From helpline

Publications list: Available online and in print

Access to staff: Contact by letter, by telephone, by e-mail and via website
Hours: Mon to Fri, 0900 to 1700

Access to building: No access other than to staff

TOURISM AUSTRALIA (TA)

Australia Centre, Australia House, 6th Floor, Melbourne Place/Strand, London, WC2B 4LG

Tel: 020 7438 4601
Fax: 020 7240 6690
Website: www.australia.com
Website: www.tourism.australia.com

Enquiries to: Marketing
Direct e-mail: lcorgan@tourism.australia.com
Other contacts: PR Manager, Advertising Manager

History of institution: formerly called Australian Tourist Commission (year of change 2004)

Organisation type and purpose: National government body.
To promote tourism to Australia.

Subject coverage: Australian travel trade contacts and Australian tourism in general.

Collection: Image library
Tourism Research
Video footage library

Trade and statistical information: Statistical details on Australian tourism, arrival statistics

Publications: Printed, and electronic and video

Access to staff: Contact by letter, by telephone, by fax, by e-mail and via website
Hours: Mon to Fri, 0900 to 1700

Access to building: No prior appointment required

Other addresses: Main office London, representative offices throughout Europe

TOURISM FOR ALL

7A Pixel Mill, 44 Appleby Road, Kendal, Cumbria, LA9 6ES

Tel: 0845 124 9971
Fax: 01539 735567
E-mail: carrie-ann@tourismforall.org.uk
Website: www.tourismforall.org.uk

Enquiries to: Manager
Other contacts: Head of Consultancy Services (for consultancy service of the charity)

Founded: 1981; created by the merger of Holiday Care, the Tourism for All Consortium and IndividuALL; formerly called Holiday Care Service (HCS)

Organisation type and purpose: Voluntary organisation, registered charity (charity number 279169), consultancy, research organisation.

Subject coverage: The UK's central source of information for disabled people and carers wishing to take a holiday break.

Publications list: Available in print

Access to staff: Contact by letter, by telephone, by fax, by e-mail and in person
Hours: Mon to Fri, 0900 to 1700

Access for disabled people: Access to all public areas, toilet facilities

TOURISM NEW ZEALAND (TNZ)

New Zealand House, 80 Haymarket, London, SW1Y 4TQ

continued overleaf

Tel: 020 7930 1662
Fax: 020 7839 8929
Website: www.newzealand.com

Enquiries to: Office Manager
Direct e-mail: alisac@tnz.govt.nz

Organisation type and purpose: National government body.
Government department of New Zealand.

Subject coverage: Accommodation, transport, sights, vehicle hire, special events, outdoor activities, general tourism information, coach tours re New Zealand.

Publications: Printed

Access to staff: Contact by letter, by fax and via website

Member of: Association of National Tourist Office Representatives; UK Chapter of the Pacific Asia Travel Association

TOURISM SOCIETY

Queens House, 55–56 Lincoln's Inn Fields, London WC2A 3BH

Tel: 0207 269 9693
Fax: 0207 404 2465
E-mail: admin@tourismsociety.org
Website: www.tourismsociety.org

Enquiries to: Executive Director
Other contacts: Conference Co-ordinator for forthcoming events.

Founded: 1977

Organisation type and purpose:
Professional body (membership is by subscription), present number of members: 1,300, service industry, suitable for ages: 15+.
Links tourism sectors, enhances members' professionalism and is the leading tourism network.

Subject coverage: Education and training in tourism; tourism management, current issues, news.

Publications: Printed

Publications list: Available in print

Access to staff: Contact by letter, by telephone, by fax and by e-mail. Access for members only.
Hours: Mon to Fri, 0900 to 1700

Sub-groups are: Tourism Management Institute; Tourism Society Consultants Group; Tourism Society Scotland

TOWER HAMLETS LIBRARIES

Bancroft Library, 227 Bancroft Road, London, E1 4DQ

Tel: 020 8980 4366
Fax: 020 8983 4510
Website: www.towerhamlets.gov.uk

Enquiries to: Head of Libraries

Organisation type and purpose: Local government body, public library.

Subject coverage: General, local history, art, music, languages, general and American literature.

Collection: Art Library (Whitechapel Library)
Chinese and Vietnamese literature (4,200 volumes Limehouse Library)
Collection of books in Asian languages (Indian, 12,500 volumes Whitechapel Library)
Inner London Special Collection: General and American literature (Limehouse Library)(closed)
Inner London Special Collections: French, German and Portuguese literature (Limehouse Library)
Joint Fiction Reserve: authors OP-PIC (closed), ST-SZ (current, 7000 volumes, Limehouse Library)
Local History Library, including the Bolt Collection on sailing and early steamships (Bancroft Library)
Music and foreign language records (Whitechapel Library)
Play-Reading sets (Whitechapel Library)
Sound recordings (all main libraries, totalling 55,000)

Library catalogue: All or part available in-house

Publications: Printed

Publications list: Available in print

Access to staff: Contact by letter, by telephone, by fax, by e-mail and in person
Hours: Mon, Tue, Thu, 0900 to 2000; Wed, closed; Fri, 0900 to 1800; Sat, 0900 to 1700

Has: 11 branch libraries

Reference & Information Service: Tower Hamlets Libraries; Bethnal Green Library, Cambridge Heath Road, London, E2 0HL; tel: 020 8980 3902 or 6274; fax: 020 8981 6129; e-mail: 100633.624@compuserve.com

TOWNSWOMEN (TG)

Formal name: Townswomen's Guilds

Tomlinson House, 1st Floor, 329 Tyburn Road, Erdington, Birmingham, B24 8HJ

Tel: 0121 326 0400
Fax: 0121 326 1976
E-mail: tghq@townswomen.org.uk
Website: www.townswomen.org.uk

Enquiries to: National Secretary
Direct e-mail: joanne@townswomen.org.uk
Other contacts: Public Affairs Officer, Press Officer

Founded: 1928; formerly called National Union of Townswomen's Guilds

Organisation type and purpose:
Membership association (membership is by subscription), registered charity (charity number 306072R).
75,000 members in nearly 1,500 Guilds grouped in 114 Federations campaign on national and regional issues.
Organise national and regional events and conferences, national sport and leisure events and competitions.

Subject coverage: Education in citizenship for women, current affairs, leadership, sports, environment, consumer affairs, women's health, Europe; current campaigns include the National Lottery, genetically modified food, transport, long-term care, energy conservation, carers, part-time workers.

Collection: Archives of the Townswomen's Guilds

Publications: Printed

Access to staff: Contact by letter, by telephone, by fax, by e-mail and via website. Appointment necessary.
Hours: Mon to Fri, 0900 to 1700

Member of: Associated Countrywomen of the World; Women's National Commission

TOYHORSE SOCIETY (THI)

Howick Farm, The Haven, Billingshurst, West Sussex, RH14 9BQ

Tel: 01403 822639
Fax: 01403 822014

Enquiries to: President/Director
Direct e-mail: tikadorian@yahoo.co.uk

Founded: 1992; formerly called British Miniature Horse Society (BMHS)

Organisation type and purpose:
International organisation, membership association (membership is by subscription), present number of members: 100, suitable for ages: 5+, training organisation.
To register the stock of miniature horses; foreign bloodline department formed in 1995. To advise on the welfare of miniature horses and arrange seminars for instruction on training, welfare, showing and exhibiting of miniature horses.

Subject coverage: Welfare of miniature horses, training for driving etc.

Collection: AMHA Stud Books
BMHS newsletters, books
BMHS Register
MAFF newsletters
SPSBS Stud Books

Publications: Printed

Access to staff: Contact by letter, by telephone and by fax. Appointment necessary.
Hours: Mon to Fri, 0900 to 1700
Special comments: Charges to non-members for more than basic information.

TOYOTA ENTHUSIASTS' CLUB (TEC)

11 St Georges Crescent, Gravesend, Kent, DA12 4AR

Tel: 01474 746911

Enquiries to: Membership Secretary
Other contacts: Newsletter Editor for information.

Founded: 1991

Organisation type and purpose:
Membership association (membership is by subscription).

Subject coverage: Information on spares and services for all UK import Toyota Models, technical information and vehicle valuation.

Collection: Comprehensive range of motoring literature on all models of Toyota, both domestic and overseas, road tests, sales brochures and historical references

Publications: Printed
Order printed publications from: Newsletter Editor, Toyota Enthusiasts Club
71 Park Road, Chorley, Lancashire, PR7 1QZ, tel: 01257 415795

Access to staff: Contact by letter and by telephone
Hours: 1900 to 2200, everyday

TR REGISTER

Formal name: TR Owners Club Ltd

1B Hawksworth, Southmead Industrial Park, Didcot, Oxfordshire, OX11 7HR

Tel: 01235 818866
Fax: 01235 818867
E-mail: office@tr-register.co.uk
Website: www.tr-register.co.uk

Enquiries to: General Manager

Founded: 1970

Organisation type and purpose: Membership association.
Car enthusiast's club.

Subject coverage: Triumph TR series cars, car register, build records, technical data.

Collection: Books and archives
Material on TR sports cars

Publications: Printed

Access to staff: Contact by letter, by telephone, by fax and by e-mail. Access for members only.
Hours: Mon to Fri, 0900 to 1700

TRADA TECHNOLOGY LIMITED (TTL)

Stocking Lane, Hughenden Valley, High Wycombe, Buckinghamshire, HP14 4ND

Tel: 01494 569600
Fax: 01494 565487
E-mail: information@trada.co.uk
Website: www.trada.co.uk

Enquiries to: Manager, TRADA Information Centre
Other contacts: Special technical enquiry line (for enquiries of a technical nature)

History of institution: formerly called Timber Research and Development Association (TRADA)

Organisation type and purpose: International organisation (membership is by subscription), training organisation, consultancy, research organisation.
Contracted by TRADA to provide research and information services.

Subject coverage: Timber research and most aspects of timber utilisation (excluding paper and furniture), with particular reference to timber in construction, fire, finishes, timber engineering, design; testing of structures and components; timber buildings; training; wood-based sheet materials; pallets and packaging; preservation; timber drying. Product conformity services; quality assurance; health and safety; environmental services to a wide range of industries as well as information services and training courses.

Collection: Compliance with health and safety and environmental legislation
Construction industry information
Construction products directive-related European directives
Information on timber and wood-based products
Standards

Publications: Printed, and electronic and video
Order printed publications from: e-mail: publications@trada.co.uk
Order electronic and video publications from: e -mail: publications@trada.co.uk

Publications list: Available online and in print

Access to staff: Contact by letter, by telephone, by fax, by e-mail and in person
Hours: Mon to Fri, 0900 to 1700

Also at: TRADA Technology Limited; Stirling; tel: 01786 462122; fax: 01786 474412

Sister company: BMTRADA Certification Limited; tel: 01494 569700; fax: 01494 565487; Chiltern International Fire; tel: 01494 569800; fax: 01494 564895; FIRA International Ltd; tel: 01438 777700; fax: 01438 777800

TRADES UNION CONGRESS (TUC)

Congress House, 23–28 Great Russell Street, London, WC1B 3LS

Tel: 020 7636 4030
Fax: 020 7636 0632
E-mail: info@tuc.org.uk
Website: www.tuc.org.uk

Enquiries to: Information Manager
Direct fax: 020 7467 1273

Founded: 1868

Organisation type and purpose: Trade union.

Subject coverage: Trade unions, TUC policy, international and overseas trade unions.

Library catalogue: All or part available in-house

Publications: Printed, and electronic and video
Order printed publications from: Publications Department, Trades Union Congress at the same address, tel: 020 7467 1294, fax: 020 7636 0632, e-mail: smills@tuc.org.uk

Publications list: Available online and in print

Access to staff: Contact by letter, by telephone, by fax, by e-mail and via website
Hours: Mon to Fri, 0915 to 1700
Special comments: Not open to the public. TUC Archive Library at London Metropolitan University accessible by appointment.

Member of: European Trade Union Confederation; International Confederation of Free Trade Unions

TUC Library Collection: London Metropolitan University Learning Centre; 236–250 Holloway Road, London, N7 6PP; tel: 020 7753 3184; fax: 020 7753 3191; e-mail: c.coates@londonmet.ac.uk

TRADES UNION CONGRESS LIBRARY COLLECTIONS (TUC Library Collections)

London Metropolitan University, Learning Centre, 236–250 Holloway Road, London, N7 6PP

Tel: 020 7133 3726
Fax: 020 7133 2529
E-mail: tuclib@londonmet.ac.uk
Website: www.londonmet.ac.uk/tuc
Website: catalogue.londonmet.ac.uk/search~S7
Website: www.unionhistory.info
Website: www.tuc.org.uk

Enquiries to: Librarian
Direct e-mail: c.coates@londonmet.ac.uk

Founded: 1922

Organisation type and purpose: Trade union, university library.
Research collection.

Subject coverage: Trade unions, economic, political and social history, industrial relations, collective bargaining, international affairs, industrial history, education, women's history, colonial policy.

Collection: General Strike Collection
Gertrude Tuckwell Collection (women's trade unionism and welfare, 1890–1921)
London Trades Council Records
Marjorie Nicholson Papers (colonial affairs)
Workers' Educational Association Library and Archive
Labour Research Department Archive

Non-library collection catalogue: All or part available online

Library catalogue: All or part available online and in-house

Publications: Printed, and microform publications
Order microform publications from: Contact TUC Library Collections for distributors' contact details

Access to staff: Contact by letter, by telephone, by fax, by e-mail and via website. Appointment necessary.
Hours: Mon to Fri, 0900 to 1700

Access to building: Prior appointment required

Access for disabled people: Toilet facilities, ramped entry to main building, level entry to collections

Member organisation of: International Association of Labour History Institutions (IALHI)

Parent body: Trades Union Congress; Congress House, Great Russell Street, London, WC1B 3LS; tel: 020 7636 4030

TRADING STANDARDS INSTITUTE (TSI)

1 Sylvan Court, Sylvan Way, Southfields Business Park, Basildon, Essex, SS15 6TH

Tel: 0845 608 9400
Fax: 0845 608 9425
E-mail: institute@tsi.org.uk
Website: www.tradingstandards.gov.uk

Enquiries to: Chief Executive

Founded: 1881; formerly called Institute of Weights and Measures Administration; formerly called Institute of Trading Standards Administration (ITSA) (year of change 2000)

Organisation type and purpose: Professional body (membership is by qualification).
Society for local government officers in trading standards departments.

continued overleaf

Subject coverage: Consumer and trade protection legislation, description of legal requirements, consumer trends, enforcement interests.

Publications: Printed

Access to staff: Contact by letter, by telephone, by fax and by e-mail. Appointment necessary. Access for members only.
Hours: Mon to Fri, 0900 to 1700

Access for disabled people: Access to all public areas

TRAFFIC INTERNATIONAL (TRAFFIC)

219A Huntingdon Road, Cambridge, CB3 0DL

Tel: 01223 277427
Fax: 01223 277237
E-mail: traffic@traffic.org
Website: www.traffic.org

Enquiries to: Information & Publication Officer
Direct e-mail: susan.vivian@traffic.org

Founded: 1976

Organisation type and purpose: International non-governmental organisation (NGO), registered charity (charity number 1076722).

Subject coverage: The wildlife trade-monitoring network, works to ensure that trade in wild plants and animals is not a threat to the conservation of nature.

Trade and statistical information: Available on request

Non-library collection catalogue: All or part available online

Library catalogue: All or part available online, in-house and in print

Publications: Printed
Order printed publications from: Information & Publication Officer, TRAFFIC International; tel: 01223 277427; e-mail: susan.vivian@traffic.org

Publications list: Available online and in print

Access to staff: Contact by letter, by telephone, by fax, by e-mail and via website. Appointment necessary.
Hours: Mon to Fri, 0900 to 1730

Access to building: Prior appointment required

Supported by: IUCN – The World Conservation Union; WWF – World Wide Fund for Nature

TRAFFIC RESEARCH CENTRE (TRC CENTELUP)

Formal name: Centre for Transport Engineering and Land Use Planning

12 Flamsteed Road, Cambridge, CB1 3QU

Tel: 01223 248444 (answer after 7 rings)

Enquiries to: Director

Founded: 1982; formed from Arthur Henderson Consultants (year of change 1982); formerly called Centre for Transport Engineering and Land Use Planning

Organisation type and purpose: Advisory body, learned society, registered charity (charity number 284449), university library, research organisation.
Charitable research trust.
To research and improve safety standards for pedestrians and all road users, improve the efficiency and convenience of all forms of transport for the movement of passengers and freight with particular reference to rail, air and sea terminals.

Subject coverage: Traffic engineering, transport planning, highway layout, highway and traffic safety, education, law enforcement, urban junction design, transport systems appraisal, transport economics.

Collection: Denys Mumby Collection in Transport Economics
London Airport Rapid Transit; Guided Bus concept established 1964

Publications: Printed

Access to staff: Contact by letter and by telephone. Appointment necessary.
Hours: Mon to Fri, 0900 to 1700
Special comments: Reference only.

TRAFFORD MBC (Trafford Libraries)

Waterside House, Sale Waterside, Sale, M33 7ZF

Tel: 0161 912
Fax: 0161 912 2895
E-mail: libraries@trafford.gov.uk
Website: www.trafford.gov.uk

Enquiries to: Librarian

Founded: 1974; formerly called Trafford MBC Education, Arts and Leisure Department, Recreation and Culture Division

Organisation type and purpose: Local government body, public library.

Subject coverage: Local government information, business information and European information at Altrincham library, local studies centre at Sale Library. General public library stock at Altrincham, Urmston, Sale and Stretford libraries. Community and leisure information database and bibliographical services.

Collection: Photo database (digitised photos)
Cruikshank Collection (some 50 examples of the illustrator's work, housed at Altrincham, access strictly by prior appointment)

Non-library collection catalogue: All or part available in-house

Publications: Printed, and electronic and video
Order printed publications from: Bibliographical Services
As main address

Access to staff: Contact by letter, by telephone, by fax, by e-mail and in person
Hours: Mon to Fri, 0830 to 1630

Access to building: Prior appointment required

Access for disabled people: Parking provided, ramped entry

TRANSLATORS ASSOCIATION (TA)

84 Drayton Gardens, London, SW10 9SB

Tel: 020 7373 6642
Fax: 020 7373 5768
E-mail: info@societyofauthors.org
Website: www.societyofauthors.org

Enquiries to: Secretary

Founded: 1958

Organisation type and purpose: Trade association, trade union (membership is by subscription, election or invitation), present number of members: 507.
Specialist section of the Society of Authors, its members are literary translators whose translations of full-length foreign works have already been published in the UK.

Subject coverage: Interests and problems of translators whose work has been published or produced commercially in the UK, general and legal advice on marketing of work, rates of remuneration, contractual arrangements.

Publications: Printed

Access to staff: Contact by letter, by telephone, by fax and by e-mail. Access for members only.
Hours: Mon to Thu, 0930 to 1730; Fri, 0930 to 1300 and 1400 to 1700

Affiliated to: Conseil Européen des Associations de Traducteurs Littéraires; Fédération Internationale de Traducteurs

Parent body: The Society of Authors; at the same address

TRANSPORT & GENERAL WORKERS UNION (TGWU (NCTS))

Northern Carpet Trades' Section, 22 Clare Road, Halifax, West Yorkshire, HX1 2HX

Tel: 01422 360492
Fax: 01422 321146

Enquiries to: Regional Industrial Organiser
Direct e-mail: nhalton@tgwu.org.uk

Founded: 1892

Organisation type and purpose: Trade union, present number of members: 2,000.

Subject coverage: Organisation in the carpet industry, staff and shop floor; history; industrial relations.

Collection: Archives held in Calderdale Central Library (Archives Department)

Publications: Printed

Access to staff: Contact by letter, by telephone, by fax and by e-mail. Appointment necessary. Access for members only.
Hours: Mon to Thu, 0845 to 1645; Fri 0445 to 1545

Access to building: No prior appointment required

Affiliated to: General Federation of Trade Unions (GFTU); National Affiliation of Carpet Trade Unions (NACTU); Trades Union Congress

TRANSPORT ASSOCIATION

Peter Acton Associates, 185 Great Tattenhams, Epsom Downs, Surrey, KT18 5RA

Tel: 01737 362232
Fax: 01737 352323
E-mail: secretary@trans-assoc.co.uk
Website: www.trans-assoc.co.uk

Enquiries to: Secretary

Founded: 1953

Organisation type and purpose: Trade association (membership is by election or invitation), present number of members: 50+ companies.

Subject coverage: Road transport.

Access to staff: Contact by letter, by e-mail and via website
Hours: Mon to Fri, 0900 to 1700

TRANSPORT FOR LONDON (TfL)

Windsor House, 42–50 Victoria Street, London, SW1H 0TL

Tel: 020 7941 4500
Fax: 020 7941 4572
E-mail: enquire@tfl.gov.uk
Website: www.transportforlondon.gov.uk

Enquiries to: Head of Customer Services
Direct tel: 020 7918 4040 Underground; 020 7918 4300 Buses
Direct fax: 020 7918 4093 Underground; 020 7918 3999 Buses
Direct e-mail: Underground: customerservices@email.lul.co.uk;
Other contacts: Buses: customerservices@tfl-buses.co.uk

Founded: 3 July 2000; formerly (as a holding company) London Transport (LRT) (LT), date of change, 3 July 2000; formerly called London Underground Limited (LUL), date of change, 3 July 2000

Organisation type and purpose: Local government body.
TfL is London's integrated transport body. Its role is to implement the Mayor's transport strategy for London and manage the transport services for which the Mayor is responsible.

Subject coverage: Public transport in London and its operation today.

Collection: Historic records held by London's Transport Museum

Publications: Printed

Publications list: Available online

Access to staff: Contact by letter, by telephone, by fax, by e-mail and via website
Hours: Mon to Fri, 0900 to 1700
Special comments: 24 Hours London Travel Information 020 7222 1234.

Access to building: No access other than to staff

Historic records: London's Transport Museum; Covent Garden, London, WC2E 7BB; tel: 020 7379 6344; fax: 020 7836 4118; e-mail: resourcec@ltmuseum.co.uk

Link: London Underground Limited; 55 Broadway, London, SW1H 0BD; tel: 020 7222 5600; fax: 020 7918 3134; e-mail: customerservices@email.lul.co.uk

Responsible to the: Mayor of London; Romney House, 43 Marsham Street, London, SW1P 3PY; tel: 020 7983 4100; e-mail: enquire@london.gov.uk

Subsidiary bodies: Docklands Light Railway; Castor Lane, London, E14 0DS; tel: 020 7363 9700; London Buses; 172 Buckingham Palace Road, London, SW1W 9TN; tel: 020 7222 5600; fax: 020 7918 3999; e-mail: customerservices@TfL-buses.co.uk; London River Services; Tower Pier, Lower Thames Street, London, EC3N 4DT; tel: 020 7941 2400; Street Management; Windsor House, 42–50 Victoria Street, London, SW1H 0TL; tel: 020 7343 5000; website: www.streetmanagement.org.uk
Victoria Coach Station Limited; 164 Buckingham Place, London, SW1W 9TP; tel: 020 7730 3466; website: www.transportforlondon.gov.uk/vcs

TRANSPORT PLANNING SOCIETY (TPS)

One Great George Street, Westminster, London, SW1P 3AA

Tel: 020 7665 2238
Fax: 020 7799 1325
E-mail: tps@ice.org.uk
Website: www.tps.org.uk

Founded: 1997

Organisation type and purpose: Membership association, with over 900 members, a society to facilitate, develop and promote best practice in transport planning and provide a focus for dialogue between all those engaged in it, whatever their background or other professional affiliation.

Subject coverage: Transport planning.

Publications: Electronic and video
Order electronic and video publications from: Download from website

Access to staff: Contact by letter, by telephone, by fax, by e-mail and via website

Links with: Chartered Institute of Logistics and Transport (UK); Chartered Institution of Highways and Transportation; Institution of Civil Engineers; Royal Town Planning Institute

TRANSPORT TRUST

202 Lambeth Road, London, SE1 7JW

Tel: 020 7928 6464
Fax: 020 7928 6565
E-mail: info@transporttrust.com
Website: www.thetransporttrust.org.uk

Enquiries to: Director General
Other contacts: Chairman

Founded: 1965

Organisation type and purpose: National organisation, membership association (membership is by subscription), present number of members: 1500, voluntary organisation, registered charity (charity number 280943).
To promote and encourage the permanent preservation and where necessary the restoration of transport items of historical or technical interest for the benefit of the nation.

Subject coverage: Preservation and restoration of all forms of transport: veteran and vintage cars, aircraft, locomotives, all old ships and canal craft plus inland waterway boats etc, cycles, mail and public coaches, buses, trams, trolley buses, military vehicles.

Collection: An extensive library and archives relating to Britain's transport heritage. Library and archives held at Ironbridge Museum, Shropshire (Tel: 01952 432141)

Library catalogue: All or part available in-house

Publications: Printed

Access to staff: Contact by letter, by telephone, by fax, by e-mail and via website
Hours: Mon to Fri, 0900 to 1700
Special comments: 24-hour answerphone.

Access to building: Prior appointment required
Hours: Mon to Fri, 0900 to 1700

Access for disabled people: Parking provided, ramped entry, access to all public areas, toilet facilities

TRAVEL TRUST ASSOCIATION (TTA)

Albion House, 3rd Floor, High Street, Woking, Surrey, GU21 6BD

Tel: 01483 545787
Fax: 01483 730746
E-mail: info@traveltrust.co.uk
Website: www.traveltrust.co.uk

Direct tel: 01483 545784 (for membership)
Direct e-mail: enquiries@traveltrust.co.uk
Other contacts: george@traveltrust.co.uk (for membership)

Founded: c. 1995

Organisation type and purpose: A travel trade membership association for travel agents, tour operators and travel organisers. Exists in order to protect the customer, with 100% financial protection.

Subject coverage: Should a member for any reason financially fail or cease trading, the Travel Trust Association will liaise with the suppliers and tour operators to ensure that the customer's holiday goes ahead unaffected. If for any reason this is not possible, it will administer a claim for a refund of money that the customer has paid to a member for the holiday.

Access to staff: Contact by letter, by telephone, by fax, by e-mail and via website
Hours: Mon to Fri, 0900 to 1730

Member organisation of: Travel Partnership Corporation (TTPC)

TREE COUNCIL

71 Newcomen Street, London, SE1 1YT

Tel: 020 7407 9992
Fax: 020 7407 9908
E-mail: info@treecouncil.org.uk
Website: www.treecouncil.org.uk

Enquiries to: Director General

Founded: 1974

continued overleaf

Organisation type and purpose: Registered charity.
Company limited by guarantee; promotional, educational and information body.

Subject coverage: Trees in the United Kingdom.

Publications: Printed, and electronic and video
Order printed publications from: via website.

Access to staff: Contact by telephone, by e-mail and via website
Hours: Mon to Fri, 0930 to 1730

TREVITHICK SOCIETY

PO Box 62, Camborne, TR14 7ZN

Tel: 01209 716811
E-mail: k.rickard@talktalk.net
Website: http;//www.trevithick-society.org.uk

Enquiries to: Honorary Secretary
Direct tel: 01872 553488
Direct e-mail: roger.g3tdm@virgin.net

Founded: 1935

Organisation type and purpose: Membership association (membership is by subscription), present number of members: 450.

Subject coverage: Industrial archaeology in Cornwall, mines and mining, Cornish engines and engine houses and other restorations, explosives, transport.

Collection: Collection of artefacts at Geevor Mining Museum, Pendeen, Penzance, and at King Edward Mine, Camborne School of Mines, Cornish mines and engines, Pool, Redruth
Drawings and plans relating to Cornish engines and mines lodged with the County Record Office, Truro

Publications: Printed

Publications list: Available in print

Access to staff: Contact by letter and by e-mail
Hours: Mon to Fri, 0900 to 1700

TRIDENT CAR CLUB

23 Matlock Crescent, Cheam, Sutton, Surrey, SM3 9SS

Tel: 020 8644 9029
E-mail: trident.carclub@virgin.net
Website: www.tridentcarclub.fsnet.co.uk

Enquiries to: Chairman

Founded: 1980

Organisation type and purpose: International organisation, membership association (membership is by subscription), present number of members: 36.
Membership open to owners and those interested in Trident cars.

Subject coverage: Trident cars, technical knowledge, information and experience. Social gatherings.

Publications: Printed

Access to staff: Contact by e-mail and via website

TRIDENT & ROCKET THREE OWNERS CLUB (TR3OC)

6 Beechnut Drive, Darby Green, Camberley, Surrey, GU17 0DJ

Tel: 01252 861259
E-mail: graham.r@talktalk.net
Website: www.tr3oc.org

Enquiries to: Secretary

Founded: 1979

Organisation type and purpose: International organisation, membership association (membership is by subscription), present number of members: 1,100, voluntary organisation, suitable for ages: all.

Subject coverage: 3-cylinder pushrod-engined machines manufactured by Triumph and BSA between 1968 and 1976 and other machines fitted with these engines; technical information and other areas of interest.

Collection: Technical data of original machines and developments, including factory records
All published material concerning the 3-cylinder machines

Trade and statistical information: Machine dating available

Publications: Printed

Access to staff: Contact by letter, by telephone and by e-mail
Hours: Mon to Fri, 0830 to 2200
Special comments: No visits to Committee Members addresses.

TRINIDAD AND TOBAGO HIGH COMMISSION

Formal name: High Commission for the Republic of Trinidad and Tobago, London, United Kingdom

42 Belgrave Square, London, SW1X 8NT

Tel: 020 7245 9351
Fax: 020 7823 1065
E-mail: tthc@btconnect.com
Website: www.tthighcommission.co.uk
Website: www.discovertnt.com
Website: www.gotrinidadandtobago.com

Enquiries to: Information Officer

Organisation type and purpose: Diplomatic Mission.

Subject coverage: Development of bilateral and multilateral relations with the United Kingdom and other accredited countries and international organisations; and provision of consular and immigration services to nationals and non-nationals/visitors to Trinidad and Tobago.

Publications: Printed

Access to staff: Contact by letter, by telephone, by fax and by e-mail. Appointment necessary.
Hours: Monday to Friday, 0900 to 1700

TRINITY COLLEGE LIBRARY

Cambridge, CB2 1TQ

Tel: 01223 338488
Fax: 01223 338532
E-mail: college.library@trin.cam.ac.uk
Website: www.trin.cam.ac.uk

Enquiries to: Librarian

Founded: 1546

Organisation type and purpose: College library in the University of Cambridge.

Subject coverage: Subjects covered by the special collections.

Collection: Papers include: R A Butler, J G Frazer, Otto Frisch, Lord Macaulay, R M Milnes, Lord Houghton, D H Robertson, Henry Sidgwick, Piero Sraffa, Alfred, Lord Tennyson, G P Thomson, William Whewell, Ludwig Wittgenstein
Some catalogues available online
Capell Collection of Shakespeareana*
Incunabula (c. 750 items)
Medieval manuscripts (c. 1,500 items)*
Newton Library
Oriental manuscripts*
Rothschild Collection of 18th-century literature*
* indicates that a printed catalogue exists

Access to staff: Contact by letter, by e-mail and via website. Appointment necessary. Letter of introduction required.
Hours: Mon to Fri, 0900 to 1700

TRINITY COLLEGE LIBRARY (BRISTOL)

Stoke Hill, Bristol, BS9 1JP

Tel: 0117 968 2803
Fax: 0117 968 7470
Website: www.trinity-bris.ac.uk

Enquiries to: Librarian

Founded: 1971; formed by the amalgamation of Clifton Theological, Dalton House Colleges; formed by the amalgamation of Tyndale Hall (year of change 1971)

Organisation type and purpose: Theological College.

Subject coverage: Theology; religion; ecclesiastical history; the Church of England; history; philosophy; ethics; comparative religion.

Library catalogue: All or part available in-house

Access to staff: Contact by letter, by telephone, by fax and by e-mail. Non-members charged.
Hours: Mon to Fri, 0900 to 1700
Special comments: Closed Sat and Sun.

Affiliated to: University of Bristol, which validates the College's degrees

Links with: Church of England

TRINITY COLLEGE OF MUSIC (TCM)

Jerwood Library of the Performing Arts, King Charles Court, Old Royal Naval College, Greenwich, London, SE10 9JF

Tel: 020 8305 3950
Fax: 020 8305 9444
E-mail: a.bowne@trinitylaban.ac.uk
Website: www.tcm.ac.uk
Website: sirsi3.tcm.ac.uk/uhtbin/webcat

Enquiries to: Head Librarian

Founded: 1872

Organisation type and purpose: Suitable for ages: 18+.
Specialist college library for students of music and the performing arts.

Subject coverage: Music.

Collection: Music Preserved (historic recordings of live performances)
Antonio de Almeida Collection
Barbirolli Collection
Sir Frederick Bridge Library
Centre for Young Musicians Library
Christopher Wood Collection
Frank Cordell Collection
Filmharmonic Archive
Lionel Tertis Collection
Mander & Mitchenson Theatre Collection
Shura Cherkassky Collection
William Lovelock Collection

Non-library collection catalogue: All or part available in-house

Library catalogue: All or part available online

Publications: Printed

Access to staff: Contact by letter, by telephone and by e-mail. Appointment necessary.
Hours: Term time: Mon to Thu, 0900 to 1900; Fri, 0900 to 1700
Special comments: Out of term, please telephone.

Access to building: Prior appointment required

Access for disabled people: Parking provided, ramped entry, access to all public areas, toilet facilities

TRIRATNA BUDDHIST ORDER (Triratna)

London Buddhist Centre, 51 Roman Road, Bethnal Green, London, E2 0HU

Tel: 020 8981 1225; minicom no. 0845 458 4716
E-mail: info@lbc.org.uk
Website: www.lbc.org.uk

Enquiries to: Communications Office Director

Founded: 1967

Organisation type and purpose: International organisation (membership is by election or invitation), present number of members: 3,000, registered charity.
Network of affiliated charities.
Religious, Buddhist, teaching Buddhism and meditation.

Subject coverage: Buddhism, Buddhist meditation, health and well-being

Non-library collection catalogue: All or part available online

Library catalogue: All or part available online

Publications: Printed
Order printed publications from: Numerous titles on Buddhism, Meditation and Triratna from Windhorse Publications Ltd, 169 Mill Road, Cambridge, CB1 3AN UK; tel: (1000 to 1700) 01223 911997; e-mail: info@windhorsepublications.com
Order electronic and video publications from: Educational resources from The Clear Vision Trust, 16–20 Turner Street, Manchester, M4 1DZ; tel: 0161 839 9579; e-mail: clearvision@clear-vision.org

Publications list: Available online and in print

Access to staff: Contact by letter, by telephone, by e-mail, in person and via website
Hours: Mon to Fri, 1000 to 1700

Access for disabled people: Access to all public areas

Links with: 30 to 40 other Triratna charities in the United Kingdom and many overseas

Online resource for many audio and transcribed texts important to the Triratna Buddhist Community: Free Buddhist Audio; website: http://www.freebuddhistaudio.com

TRIUMPH 2000/2500/2.5 REGISTER

10 Gables Close, Chalfont St Peter, Gerrards Cross, Buckinghamshire, SL9 0PR

Tel: 01494 582673
E-mail: t2000register@compuserve.com
Website: www.t2000register.org.uk

Enquiries to: Secretary

Founded: 1981

Organisation type and purpose: International organisation, membership association (membership is by subscription), present number of members: 900.

Subject coverage: Triumph 2000, 2500 and 2.5 cars manufactured between 1963 and 1977.

Publications: Printed

Access to staff: Contact by letter, by telephone, by fax and by e-mail
Hours: Evenings and weekends

TRIUMPH MAYFLOWER CLUB

19 Broadway North, Walsall, West Midlands, WS1 2QG

Tel: 01922 633042
E-mail: johnchoaker@btinternet.com
Website: www.triumphmayflowerclub.com

Enquiries to: Membership Secretary

Founded: 1975

Organisation type and purpose: Membership association (membership is by subscription), present number of members: 152.

Subject coverage: Workings, both mechanical and non-mechanical, of the Triumph Mayflower; history of Triumph Mayflower; general information and statistics regarding cars still in existence; technical information, sources of spares.

Collection: Archive of material on the Triumph Mayflower

Publications: Printed

Publications list: Available in print

Access to staff: Contact by letter and by telephone
Hours: Mon to Fri, 1700 to 1930

TRIUMPH RAZOREDGE OWNERS CLUB

62 Seaward Avenue, Barton-on-Sea, Hampshire, BH25 7HP

Tel: 01425 618074
E-mail: davidwickens@clara.net

Enquiries to: Secretary General

Founded: 1975

Organisation type and purpose: Membership association (membership is by subscription), present number of members: 220.

Subject coverage: Triumph Razoredge saloons manufactured between 1946 and 1954, spare parts, technical information.

Publications: Printed

Access to staff: Contact by letter, by telephone and by e-mail
Hours: Mon to Fri, 0900 to 1700

Member of: Historic Vehicle Clubs Committee

TRIUMPH ROADSTER CLUB (TRC)

15 Lower Hill Road, Epsom, Surrey, KT19 8LS

Tel: 01372 812141
Fax: 01372 812141
E-mail: webmaster@triumphroadster.org.uk
Website: www.triumphroadster.org.uk

Enquiries to: Secretary

Founded: 1960

Organisation type and purpose: International organisation, membership association (membership is by subscription), present number of members: 500.
Club for the preservation of Triumph Roadster motor cars (1946–49 18TR and 20TR only).

Subject coverage: Technical information related to the preservation and restoration of 1946–49 Triumph Roadster models 18TR and 20TR, including sources of replacement components, advice on purchase and registration mark authentication.

Publications: Printed

Publications list: Available online

Access to staff: Contact by letter, by telephone, by fax, by e-mail and via website. Appointment necessary.
Hours: Mon to Fri, 0900 to 1700

Affiliated to: Federation of British Historic Vehicle Clubs (FBHVC); Elton House, Church Lane, Tydd St Giles, Wisbech, Cambridgeshire, PE13 5LA; tel: 01945 871295; fax: 01945 870528; e-mail: admin@fbhvc.co.uk; website: www.fbhvc.co.uk

TRIUMPH SPORTS SIX CLUB (TSSC LTD)

Freepost, Lubenham, Market Harborough, Leicestershire, LE16 9TF

Tel: 01858 434424
Fax: 01858 431936
E-mail: tssc@tssc.org.uk
Website: www.tssc.org.uk

Enquiries to: Executive Director
Direct e-mail: trudi@tssc.org.uk

continued overleaf

Founded: 1977

Organisation type and purpose: Membership association (membership is by subscription), present number of members: 9,000.
Classic car club.

Non-library collection catalogue: All or part available in-house

Library catalogue: All or part available in-house

Publications: Printed

Publications list: Available in print

Access to staff: Contact by letter, by telephone, by fax, by e-mail, in person and via website
Hours: Mon to Fri, 0900 to 1700

Access to building: No access other than to staff
Hours: Mon to Fri, 0900 to 1700

Access for disabled people: Ramped entry, access to all public areas, toilet facilities

TRL LTD

Formal name: Transport Research Laboratory

TRL Library and Information Centre, Crowthorne House, Nine Mile Ride, Wokingham, Berks, RG40 3GA

Tel: 01344 770203
Fax: 01344 770193
E-mail: info@trl.co.uk
Website: www.trl.co.uk

Enquiries to: Information Specialist

Founded: 1933; formerly called Road Research Laboratory (year of change 1972); formerly called Transport and Road Research Laboratory (TRRL) (year of change 1992); formerly called Transport Research Laboratory (TRL) (year of change 1992)

Organisation type and purpose: Consultancy. Provides consultancy on transport, civil engineering, vehicle safety, vehicles and environment both in the UK and overseas.

Subject coverage: Planning, design, construction and maintenance of roads and highway structures, particularly bridges and tunnels; safe and convenient movement of people and goods, including the layout of roads and traffic networks, control of traffic flow, study of road accidents and methods of reducing their frequency and severity; transport-planning and land-use strategies; existing and projected passenger and freight transport systems; environmental effects; new transport technology, intelligent transport, crash testing, traffic software, vehicle safety.

Non-library collection catalogue: All or part available in-house

Library catalogue: All or part available in-house

Publications: Printed, and electronic and video, and microform publications
Order printed publications from: via website, or from IHS; tel: 01344 328039; e-mail: trl@ihs.com

Publications list: Available online and in print

Access to staff: Contact by letter, by telephone, by fax, by e-mail and via website. Appointment necessary. All charged.

Access to building: Prior appointment required
Hours: Mon to Fri, 0900 to 1700
Special comments: Discounts to academic and non-commercial organisations; one-day visit charge £30.

Access for disabled people: Access to all public areas, toilet facilities

Links with: Transport Research Foundation; Crowthorne House, Nine Mile Ride, Wokingham, Berkshire RG40 3GA; tel: 01344 773131; fax: 01344 770356; e-mail: enquiries@trl.co.uk; website: http://www.trl.co.uk

TROON @ AYRSHIRE FAMILY HISTORY SOCIETY

c/o MERC, Troon Public Library, South Beach, Troon, Ayrshire, KA10 6EF

E-mail: info@troonayrshirefhs.org.uk
Website: www.troonayrshirefhs.org.uk

Enquiries to: Secretary

Founded: 1989; formerly called Troon and District Family History Society

Organisation type and purpose: Membership association, voluntary organisation.
Family History research.

Subject coverage: Family history in the Troon and surrounding area of Ayrshire.

Publications: Printed, and electronic and video, and microform publications
Order printed publications from: Publications Officer at above address or online (payment by PayPal)

Publications list: Available online and in print

Access to staff: Contact by letter and by e-mail

TROPICAL HEALTH AND EDUCATION TRUST (THET)

5th Floor, 1 Wimpole Street, London, W1G 0AE

Tel: 020 7290 3892
Fax: 020 7290 3890
E-mail: info@thet.org
Website: www.thet.org.uk

Enquiries to: Project Coordinator

Founded: 1988

Organisation type and purpose: Registered charity (charity number 800567).
To develop capacity for healthcare in Africa through collaboration with training institutions in Africa and the UK.

Subject coverage: Training for healthcare in Africa.

Non-library collection catalogue: All or part available online and in-house

Publications: Printed

Access to staff: Contact by letter, by fax and by e-mail. Appointment necessary.
Hours: Mon to Fri, 0900 to 1700

Access to building: Prior appointment required

TT SUPPORTERS CLUB

50 Lyndhurst Road, Birmingham, B24 8QS

Tel: 0121 686 3799
Fax: 0121 686 8700
Website: www.ttsupportersclub.com

Enquiries to: Information Officer

Subject coverage: The Manx motor cycle TT races.

TUBEROUS SCLEROSIS ASSOCIATION (TSA)

PO Box 12979, Barnt Green, Birmingham, B45 5AN

Tel: 0121 445 6970
Fax: 0121 445 6970
E-mail: diane.sanson@tuberous-sclerosis.org
Website: www.tuberous-sclerosis.org

Enquiries to: Support Services Co Ordinator
Other contacts: TS Specialist Advisers; Appeals and Publicity Officer (for advice regarding support and publicity)

Founded: 1977

Organisation type and purpose: Membership association (membership is by subscription), present number of members: 1,500, voluntary organisation, registered charity (charity number 1039549).

Subject coverage: Tuberous sclerosis, epilepsy, autism, behaviour generally, renal problems, symptoms, genetic counselling.

Publications: Printed, and electronic and video

Publications list: Available online and in print

Access to staff: Contact by letter, by telephone, by fax, by e-mail and via website
Hours: Mon to Fri, 0900 to 1700

Links with: Disability Alliance; 1st Floor, Universal House, 88–94 Wentworth Street, London, E1 7SA; tel: 020 7247 8776; Genetics Interest Group; Unity 4D, Leroy House, 436 Essex Road, London, N1 3QP; tel: 020 7704 3141; fax: 020 7359 1447; Neurological Alliance; PO Box 31287, London, NW2 6NL; tel: 020 7831 7522; fax: 020 7831 7522; Tuberous Sclerosis International; Prins Bernhardlaan 36, 3722 AG Bilthoven, The Netherlands

TUG OF WAR ASSOCIATION (ToWA)

Tel: 01452 532788
E-mail: tonymartin@blueyonder.co.uk
Website: www.tugofwar.co.uk

Enquiries to: Area Representatives (see website for contact details)

Founded: 1958

Organisation type and purpose: The governing body for tug of war in England. To develop tug of war.

Subject coverage: Organises men's, women's and youth competitions.

Access to staff: Contact by telephone and by e-mail

Member organisation of: Tug of War International Federation (TWIF)

TUN ABDUL RAZAK RESEARCH CENTRE (TARRC)

Brickendonbury, Hertford, SG13 8NL

Tel: 01992 584966
Fax: 01992 554837
E-mail: general@tarrc.co.uk
Website: www.tarrc.co.uk

Enquiries to: Head of Information

Founded: 1938; formerly called Malaysian Rubber Producers' Research Association (MRPRA)

Organisation type and purpose: Trade association, research organisation.

Subject coverage: Rubber, especially natural rubber, rubber products.

Collection: History of Rubber
MORPHS main database 100,000 documents (mainly on microfilm)
Photographs

Trade and statistical information: SMR Monthly Statistical Bulletin.
Quarterly Statistical Bulletin

Library catalogue: All or part available in-house

Publications: Printed, and electronic and video
Order printed publications from: email: general@tarrc.co.uk

Publications list: Available in print

Access to staff: Contact by letter, by telephone, by fax, by e-mail and via website. Appointment necessary.
Hours: Mon to Fri, 0900 to 1700
Special comments: Charges made to some users.

Parent body: Malaysian Rubber Research and Development Board; PO Box 10508, Kuala Lumpur, 50716, Malaysia

TUNBRIDGE WELLS FAMILY HISTORY SOCIETY

Yew Tree Byre, Yew Tree Lane, Rotherfield, East Sussex, TN6 3QP

Tel: 01892 852334
E-mail: veronicasiddall@hotmail.co.uk
Website: www.tunwells-fhs.co.uk

Enquiries to: Secretary

Founded: 1991

Organisation type and purpose:
Membership association (membership is by subscription), present number of members: 250.
To promote genealogical studies and family history, particularly in the Tunbridge Wells area.

Subject coverage: Family history research in Tunbridge Wells area for members.

Publications: Printed, and electronic and video
Order printed publications from: Tunbridge Wells Family History Society, 16 Hydehurst Close, Crowborough, East Sussex, TN6 1EN

Publications list: Available in print

Access to staff: Contact by letter, by e-mail and via website
Hours: Mon to Fri, 0900 to 1700
Special comments: Evenings (private residence)

TUNNEL LINING MANUFACTURERS ASSOCIATION (TLMA)

60 Charles Street, Leicester, LE1 1FB

Tel: 0116 253 6161
Fax: 0116 251 4568
E-mail: info@britishprecast.org

Enquiries to: Secretary

Organisation type and purpose: Trade association.

Subject coverage: Tunnel linings.

Parent body: British Precast Concrete Federation

TURKISH CYPRIOT CULTURAL ASSOCIATION

14a Graham Road, Hackney, London, E8 1BZ

Tel: 020 7249 7410
Fax: 020 7241 5643

Enquiries to: Chairman
Other contacts: Co-ordinator

Founded: 1977

Organisation type and purpose:
Membership association (membership is by subscription), present number of members: About 400, voluntary organisation, registered charity (charity number 285799).

Subject coverage: Social and cultural problems of the Turkish community and the Turkish Cypriot community in particular.

Access to staff: Contact by letter and by telephone
Hours: Tue to Fri, 1000 to 1700

Access to building: No access other than to staff
Hours: Mon to Fri, 1000 to 1700

TURKISH EMBASSY

Education Counsellor's Office, Tigris House, 256 Edgware Road, London, W2 1DS

Tel: 020 7724 1511
Fax: 020 7724 9989

Enquiries to: Education Counsellor

Organisation type and purpose: National government body.
Education for Turkish students.

Subject coverage: Advice and guidance to Turkish students in UK; Turkish education system and scholarships offered by the Turkish government.

Access to staff: Contact by letter, by telephone and by fax
Hours: Mon to Fri, 0930 to 1630, by telephone; Mon to Fri, 0930 to 1330, in person

Unit of the: Turkish Ministry of National Education in Turkey

TURKISH TOURIST OFFICE (TTO)

4th Floor, 29–30 St James's Street, London, SW1A 1HB

Tel: 020 78397778
Fax: 020 7925 1388
E-mail: info@gototurkey.co.uk
Website: www.gototurkey.co.uk

Enquiries to: Public Relations Officer
Direct e-mail: tourismturkey.mediauk@fd .com

History of institution: formerly called Turkish Information Office

Organisation type and purpose: National government body.
Section of the Turkish Embassy.

Subject coverage: Tourist information on Turkey.

Publications: Printed

Access to staff: Contact by letter, by telephone, by fax, by e-mail, in person and via website
Hours: Mon to Fri, 0930 to 1730

Affiliated to: Ministry of Tourism in Turkey; tel: +312 212 8300; fax: +312 212 8391; e-mail: tanitma@turizm.gov.tr

TURNER LIBRARY

Whitefield Schools and Centre, Macdonald Road, Walthamstow, London, E17 4AZ

Tel: 020 8531 8703
Fax: 020 8527 0907
E-mail: lib@whitefield.org.uk
Website: www.whitefield.org.uk

Enquiries to: Librarian

Organisation type and purpose:
Membership association (membership is by subscription), service industry.
Professional library, with national and international membership, for all who have an interest in special educational needs; based at Whitefield Special School, the largest special school in the United Kingdom.
Current awareness service by post.

Subject coverage: All aspects of special educational needs: curriculum; management; policy; legislation; syndromes and disorders; integration; support teaching.

Collection: Large periodical collection of national and international journals relating to special education, early years education and curriculum

Publications: Printed

Access to staff: Contact by letter, by telephone, by fax, by e-mail and in person. Non-members charged.
Hours: Mon, Thu, 0900 to 1830; Tue, Wed, 0900 to 1700; Fri, 0900 to 1630
Aug, half-terms, Easter: Tue, Wed, Thu, 0900 to 1600
Please check opening hours before visiting during holiday periods
Special comments: Closed all other days and for two weeks at Christmas and New Year.

Access for disabled people: Wheelchair access, disabled lift, lift to seminar rooms

TURNER REGISTER

21 Ellsworth Road, High Wycombe, Buckinghamshire, HP11 2TU

Tel: 01494 445636

Enquiries to: Registrar

Founded: 1960

Organisation type and purpose: Membership association.

Subject coverage: Information relating to design, manufacture, restoration and maintenance of Turner sports and racing cars manufactured by Mr J H Turner in Wolverhampton 1949–1966.

Collection: Copies of original works publications
Manufacturing records of vehicles built
Road Tests from motoring journals

Publications: Printed

Access to staff: Contact by letter
Hours: Mon to Fri, 0900 to 1700

Parent body: Fairthorpe Sports Car Club (Turner Register); 9 Lynhurst Crescent, Hillingdon, Middlesex, UB10 9EF

TURNER SOCIETY

BCM Box Turner, London, WC1N 3XX

Website: www.turnersociety.org.uk

Enquiries to: Chairman

Founded: 1975

Organisation type and purpose: Learned society (membership is by subscription), present number of members: c. 400, registered charity (charity number 269832). To further interest in the life and work of J M W Turner RA.

Subject coverage: The life, work and influence of J M W Turner, RA.

Publications: Printed

Access to staff: Contact by letter

TWI LTD

Granta Park, Great Abington, Cambridgeshire, CB21 6AL

Tel: 01223 899000
Fax: 01223 894342
E-mail: library@twi.co.uk
Website: www.twi.co.uk

Enquiries to: Manager, Information Services
Direct e-mail: linda.dumper@twi.co.uk; weldasearch@twi.co.uk

Founded: 1968; formerly called British Welding Research Association, Institute of Welding (year of change 1968); formerly called The Welding Institute (year of change 1991)

Organisation type and purpose: International organisation, professional body, training organisation, consultancy, research organisation.

Subject coverage: Technology and practice of welding; brazing; soldering; thermal cutting; weld surfacing; metal spraying; inspection and non-destructive testing; QA systems; welding design; welding and joining metallurgy and materials science; performance of welded assemblies (failure, fatigue, brittle fracture, corrosion); fabrication and construction; quality control; joining of plastics and ceramics; adhesives.

Collection: Materials identification
Trade literature on welding equipment and consumables

Library catalogue: All or part available online and in-house

Publications: Printed, and electronic and video

Access to staff: Contact by letter, by telephone, by fax, by e-mail and via website. Appointment necessary. Access for members only.
Hours: Mon to Thu, 0830 to 1630; Fri, 0830 to 1615

Access to building: *Special comments:* By application only

Constituent bodies: Certification Scheme for Welding and Inspection Personnel (CSWIP); Institute of Rail Welding (IORW); School of Welding Technology; Welding and Joining Society (WJS)

TYNDALE HOUSE BIBLICAL STUDIES RESEARCH CENTRE

Tyndale House, 36 Selwyn Gardens, Cambridge, CB3 9BA

Tel: 01223 566601
Fax: 01223 566608
E-mail: librarian@tyndale.cam.ac.uk
Website: www.tyndale.cam.ac.uk

Enquiries to: Librarian
Direct tel: 01223 566604

Founded: c.1940

Organisation type and purpose: Registered charity, university department or institute, research organisation, publishing house.

Subject coverage: Biblical studies and research; theology.

Information services: Photocopy and scanning service accessed from web site.

Collection: Maps of Palestine
The library is said to contain one of the best collections of books and electronic resources on biblical studies in the world

Library catalogue: All or part available online

Publications: Printed

Access to staff: Contact via website. Appointment necessary. Letter of introduction required.
Hours: Mon to Fri, 0900 to 1730

Parent body: Universities and Colleges Christian Fellowship

TYNE & WEAR ARCHIVES (TWAM)

Formal name: Tyne & Wear Archives & Museums

Discovery Museum, Blandford Square, Newcastle upon Tyne, NE1 4JA

Tel: 0191 277 2248
Fax: 0191 230 2614
E-mail: archives@twmuseums.org.uk
Website: www.twmuseums.org.uk/archives

Founded: 1974; created by the merger of Tyne & Wear Archives Service and Tyne & Wear Museums (year of change 2009); formerly called Tyne & Wear Archives Service (year of change 2009)

Organisation type and purpose: Local government body.
Archives service.

Subject coverage: Tyne and Wear, shipbuilding, family history, other aspects of the North-East.

Collection: Records of many organisations, industries and individuals relating to Tyne and Wear

Non-library collection catalogue: All or part available online and in-house

Library catalogue: All or part available online and in-house

Publications: Printed

Access to staff: Contact by letter, by telephone, by fax, by e-mail, in person and via website
Hours: Mon, Tues, Wed, Thu, Fri, 1000 to 1700
Special comments: Closed weekends and all public holidays

Access for disabled people: Parking provided, ramped entry, level entry, access to all areas, toilet facilities

TYNE METROPOLITAN COLLEGE

The Library, Embleton Avenue, Wallsend, Tyne and Wear, NE28 9NJ

Tel: 0191 229 5301
Fax: 0191 229 5243
E-mail: enquiries@tynemet.ac.uk
Website: www.tynemet.ac.uk

Enquiries to: Head of Library Resources

Organisation type and purpose: Suitable for ages: 14+
College of further education.

Subject coverage: All areas covered particularly international baccalaureate, A-levels, art and design, media, engineering, hairdressing

Trade and statistical information: FEFC documents

Non-library collection catalogue: All or part available online

Library catalogue: All or part available online and in-house

Publications: Printed

Access to staff: Contact by letter, by telephone, by fax and by e-mail. Appointment necessary. Access for members only.
Hours: Mon to Thu, 0900 to 2000; Fri, 0900 to 1600; Sat, 1000 to 1300
Vacations: 0900 to 1600

TYNEDALE COUNCIL

Hexham House, Hexham, Northumberland, NE46 3NH

Tel: 01434 652200\ Minicom no. 01434 652323
Fax: 01434 652420
E-mail: ask@northumberland.gov.uk

Website: www.tynedale.gov.uk

Enquiries to: Chief Executive
Other contacts: Public Relations and Marketing Officer for sources of information about the council.

Founded: 1974

Organisation type and purpose: Local government body.
District Council.

Subject coverage: Public information about the work of the Tynedale Council.

Publications: Printed

Access to staff: Contact by letter, by telephone, by fax, by e-mail, in person and via website
Hours: Mon to Thu, 0830 to 1700; Fri, 0830 to 1630

TYNWALD LIBRARY

Legislative Buildings, Finch Road, Douglas, Isle of Man, IM1 3PW

Tel: 01624 685520
Fax: 01624 685522
E-mail: library@tynwald.org.im
Website: www.tynwald.org.im

Founded: 1975; formerly called Central Reference Library (year of change 1987)

Organisation type and purpose: National government body.
Parliamentary library.
To provide a comprehensive source of information and documentation relevant to the work of the Legislature of the Isle of Man.

Subject coverage: General reference collection, especially social sciences, Manx affairs, law, parliament, executive government, official documents.

Information services: Public access to library collections. Research services for Members, Clerks and Officers of Tynwald. One-stop shop for official and parliamentary papers, Manx Statutes and subordinate legislation.

Special visitor services: Regular tours of the legislative chambers and a gift shop.

Education services: School tours, Junior Tynwald for Sixth form students.

Services for disabled people: Library is disabled-friendly, other disabled facilities available.

Collection: Documents produced by the Isle of Man Government (Civil Service)
Laws of the Isle of Man
Parliamentary and any other papers considered by the Legislature of the Isle of Man
Report of the Official Proceedings: Isle of Man (Hansard)

Trade and statistical information: Isle of Man Digest of Economic and Social Statistics (annual)
Isle of Man Government Policy Review (annual).
Census reports
(also on www.gov.im)

Non-library collection catalogue: All or part available in-house

Library catalogue: All or part available online

Publications: Printed
Order printed publications from: Tynwald Library

Access to staff: Contact by letter, by telephone, by fax, by e-mail, in person and via website
Hours: Mon to Fri, 0900 to 1700
Special comments: Research staff unable to undertake research for members of the public.

Access to building: Ground floor public access
Hours: Mon to Fri, 0900 to 1700; evening tours by arrangement

Access for disabled people: Parking provided, toilet facilities, lifts
Hours: Mon to Fri, 0900 to 1700
Special comments: Public tours available, prior notification of attendance of disabled persons appreciated as alternate route is necessary.

Parent body: Clerk of Tynwald's Office; at the same address; tel: 01624 685000; fax: 01624 685004; e-mail: enquiries@tynwald.org.im

UACE

Formal name: Universities Association for Continuing Education

University of Cambridge, Board of Continuing Education, Madingley Hall, Madingley, Cambridge, CB3 8AQ

Tel: 01954 280279
Fax: 01954 280200
E-mail: mer1000@cam.ac.uk
Website: www.uace.org.uk

Enquiries to: Secretary
Direct e-mail: sm120@cam.ac.uk

History of institution: formerly called Polytechnic Association for Continuing Education (PACE), Universities Council for Adult and Continuing Education

Organisation type and purpose: Professional body.
Consultative body for universities and university colleges; information centre for continuing and adult education; liaison and collaborative body with, for example, the Department for Education and Skills.
Co-ordinating policy development for the whole field of continuing education at university level in the UK; acting as a source of information and, where appropriate, pressure on Universities UK, Department for Education and Skills.

Subject coverage: Continuing education, continuing vocational education, part-time student and non-standard student matters in HE, FE/HE links, access and other flexible entry routes, flexible study patterns in higher education, research in continuing education, European and international links in CE development and research, CE provision to counter educational disadvantage (including targeted work with specific groups such as minority ethnic communities, disabled people, unwaged people, socio-economically disadvantaged groups, universities in their relations with the community, workers' education).

Trade and statistical information: Statistical information available on all aspects of CE provision in the higher education sector in the UK

Publications: Printed

Publications list: Available online and in print

Access to staff: Contact by e-mail
Hours: Mon to Fri, 0900 to 1700

Access to building: No access other than to staff

UCL EASTMAN DENTAL INSTITUTE

Formal name: Eastman Dental Institute for Oral Health Care Sciences

Eastman Dental Hospital, 256 Gray's Inn Road, London, WC1X 8LD

Tel: 020 7915 1092
Fax: 020 7915 1274
E-mail: academic@eastman.ucl.ac.uk
Website: www.eastman.ucl.ac.uk

Enquiries to: Admissions Officer

History of institution: formerly called Institute of Dental Surgery

Organisation type and purpose: University department or institute, research organisation.
Postgraduate teaching and research.

Subject coverage: Dentistry, dental research, dental education.

Publications list: Available online

Access to staff: Contact by telephone, by e-mail and via website
Hours: Mon to Fri, 0900 to 1700

Postgraduate institute affiliated to: University College London

UCL INSTITUTE OF CHILD HEALTH LIBRARY (ICH)

30 Guilford Street, London, WC1N 1EH

Tel: 020 7242 9789 extn 2424
Fax: 020 7831 0488
E-mail: library@ich.ucl.ac.uk
Website: www.ich.ucl.ac.uk/library

Enquiries to: Librarian or Deputy Librarian
Other contacts: Assistant Librarian (for SOURCE collection)

Founded: 1945

Organisation type and purpose: University department or institute.

Subject coverage: Paediatrics, diseases of children, SOURCE collection covers disability, mother and child health, HIV/AIDS, poverty and health in less developed countries.

Collection: SOURCE collection: an international information support centre designed to strengthen the management, use and impact of information in health and disability; jointly owned by ICH, Healthlink Worldwide and Handicap International.

Non-library collection catalogue: All or part available online

Library catalogue: All or part available online

continued overleaf

Access to staff: Contact by letter, by telephone, by fax, by e-mail, in person and via website. Appointment necessary.
Hours: Mon to Fri, 0900 to 1800

Access for disabled people: Ramped entry, access to all public areas, chairlifts, toilet facilities

Constituent part of: University College London; Gower Street, London; tel: 020 7679 7700; fax: 020 7679 7373; e-mail: library@ucl.ac.uk; website: http://www.ucl.ac.uk

Links with: Hospital for Sick Children; Great Ormond Street, London; tel: 020 7405 9200; fax: 020 7829 8643; e-mail: info@gosh.nhs.uk

UCL LANGUAGE & SPEECH SCIENCE LIBRARY (NICeST: National Information Centre for Speech-Language Therapy)

UCL Language & Speech Science Library, Chandler House, 2 Wakefield Street, London, WC1N 1PF

Tel: 020 7679 4207
Fax: 020 7679 4238
E-mail: library@langsci.ucl.ac.uk
Website: www.langsci.ucl.ac.uk/library/index.php
Website: www.ucl.ac.uk/Library/hcslib.shtml
Website: www.ucl.ac.uk/Library/blog/hcs/

Enquiries to: Librarian

Founded: 1987; formerly called National Hospital's College of Speech Science (NHCSS) (year of change 1995); formerly called UCL Human Communication Science Library (HCS) (year of change 2008)

Organisation type and purpose: University department or institute.

Subject coverage: Speech, language, and communication disorders; speech and language therapy; linguistics; phonetics.

Collection: Tests and assessments used in clinics and placements; historical collection of books and pamphlets (held in offsite storage).

Non-library collection catalogue: All or part available online

Library catalogue: All or part available online

Access to staff: Contact by telephone, by e-mail and via website. Appointment necessary. Access for members only. Non-members charged.
Hours: Mon to Thu, 0915 to 1900; Fri, 1000 to 1900; Sat in UCL term and Easter vacation, 1100 to 1800.
Special comments: Vacations, please telephone.

Access to building: *Hours:* As library opening hours

Access for disabled people: Ramp, and automatic doors at building entrance; lift, accessible toilets on each floor
Hours: As library opening hours
Special comments: Lift cannot be used for emergency evacuation; library is on 2nd floor.

Branch of: UCL Library Services; Gower St, London WC1

UCLH CHARITABLE FOUNDATION

3rd Floor East, 250 Euston Road, London, NW1 2PG

Tel: 020 7380 9558
Website: www.uclh.nhs.uk/Charities+at+UCLH/UCL+Hospitals+Charitable+Foundation

Organisation type and purpose: A registered charity (number 1077638).
The main fundraising charity for key research, building and equipment projects across all University College London Hospitals.

Subject coverage: With support from the general public, has helped to fund an ultrasound scanner for the Fetal Medicine Unit, research into the treatment and detection of early lung cancer, and the building of a new Cellular Therapy Unit for cancer patients receiving high dose chemo and radiotherapy.

Access to staff: Contact by letter and by telephone
Hours: Mon to Fri, 0800 to 1600

Links with: University College London Hospitals NHS Foundation Trust (UCLH); 250 Euston Road, London, NW1 2PG; tel: 0845 1555 000

UCLH CHARITY

Trustees Department, 250 Euston Road, 5th Floor East, London, NW1 2PG

Tel: 020 344 79605
Fax: 020 344 79544
E-mail: trustees@uclh.nhs.uk
Website: www.uclhcharity.org.uk

Organisation type and purpose: A registered charity (number 229771).
The main charity associated with the 7 general and specialist hospitals of the University College London Hospitals NHS Foundation Trust.

Subject coverage: Provides support for patients (equipment, services), staff (health and welfare) and research.

Publications: Electronic and video
Order electronic and video publications from: Download from website

Publications list: Available online

Access to staff: Contact by letter, by telephone, by fax and by e-mail

Links with: University College London Hospitals NHS Foundation Trust (UCLH); 250 Euston Road, London, NW1 2PG; tel: 0845 1555 000

UFO MONITORS EAST KENT (UFOMEK)

23 Brabner Close, Folkestone, Kent, CT19 6LW

Tel: 07968 583435 / 07091 020078
E-mail: astratech@supanet.com
Website: www.homestead.com/kentufowatch/homepage.html
Website: www.homestead.com/kentufowatch/ufomek.html

Enquiries to: Director of Research and Investigations

Founded: Dec 1995; formerly called National UFO Research Centre

Organisation type and purpose: National organisation, voluntary organisation, research organisation.
Investigation and research into aerial phenomena.

Subject coverage: Information on investigations and research into aerial phenomena in the county of Kent, first and foremost, and nationally in the regions of the UK.

Access to staff: Contact by letter, by telephone, by e-mail and via website
Hours: Sun to Sat, 0900 to 2100

Access to building: No access other than to staff

Connections with: UFO-Trek Information Service; UFO-Trek, c/o 23 Brabner Close, Folkestone, Kent, CT19 6LW; tel: 07091 020078

UK ASSOCIATION OF PRESERVATION TRUSTS (APT)

9th Floor, Alhambra House, 27–31 Charing Cross Road, London, WC2H 0AU

Tel: 0207 930 1629
Fax: 0207 930 0295
E-mail: apt@ahfund.org.uk
Website: www.ukapt.org.uk

Enquiries to: Administrator
Other contacts: Director

Founded: 1989

Organisation type and purpose: Advisory body, membership association (membership is by subscription), present number of members: 235, registered charity (charity number 1027919).
Membership open to building preservation trusts.
To improve effectiveness of building preservation trusts through advice and information. To represent their views and to provide the public with information about them.

Subject coverage: Guidance on setting up a preservation trust, information about building preservation trusts and their projects. Advice on rescuing buildings at risk through partnering building preservation trusts.

Trade and statistical information: Various research data compiled ad hoc. Please ask for further information

Publications: Printed
Order printed publications from: APT

Publications list: Available in print

Access to staff: Contact by letter, by telephone, by fax, by e-mail and via website
Hours: Mon to Fri, 0930 to 1730

Has: 9 Area Committees contactable through the London office

UK CLEANING PRODUCTS INDUSTRY ASSOCIATION (UKCPI)

1st Floor, Century House, High Street, Tattenhall, Cheshire, CH3 9RJ

Tel: 01829 770055

Fax: 01829 770101
E-mail: ukcpi@ukcpi.org
Website: www.ukcpi.org

Enquiries to: Secretary

Founded: 1939

Organisation type and purpose: Trade association.

Subject coverage: Effect of detergents on the environment, human health and safety; regulations affecting the cleaning products industry; history of the UK soap industry.

Trade and statistical information: Basic consumption statistics

Publications: Printed

Access to staff: Contact by letter, by telephone, by fax and by e-mail
Hours: Mon to Fri, 0900 to 1215

Links with: Chemical Industries Association

Member organisation of: Association Internationale de la Savonnerie et de la Détergence (AISE)

UK COLLEGE FOR COMPLEMENTARY HEALTHCARE STUDIES (UK College)

St Charles Hospital, Exmoor Street, London, W10 6DZ

Tel: 020 8964 1206
Fax: 020 8964 1207
E-mail: info@ukcollege.com
Website: www.ukcollege.com

Enquiries to: Administrator
Other contacts: Principal or Director for areas of expertise.

Founded: 1985; formerly called UK Training College for Hypnotherapy and Counselling

Organisation type and purpose: Suitable for ages: Mature students 19+, training organisation.
For complementary healthcare.

Subject coverage: Accredited courses for complementary therapies; BTEC, City and Guilds and VTCT, massage, hypnotherapy, reflexology, counselling, first aid, and aromatherapy, NLP one- and two-day introductory courses.

Collection: Register of Practitioners in United Kingdom (telephone only for nearest one in location)

Library catalogue: All or part available in-house

Publications: Printed

Access to staff: Contact by letter, by telephone, by fax, by e-mail and via website. Appointment necessary.
Hours: Mon to Fri, 0900 to 1700

Access to building: Prior appointment required

Access for disabled people: Parking provided, access to all public areas, toilet facilities

UK CONTRACTORS GROUP (UKCG)

Centrepoint, 103 New Oxford Street, London, WC1A 1DU

Tel: 020 78366636
E-mail: enquiries@ukcg.org.uk
Website: www.ukcg.org.uk/

Enquiries to: Director

Founded: December 2008

Organisation type and purpose: Trade association, present number of members: 35.

Subject coverage: Construction industry.

Access to staff: Contact by letter and by e-mail
Hours: Mon to Fri, 0900 to 1700

Member of: CBI

UK DATA ARCHIVE (UKDA)

University of Essex, Wivenhoe Park, Colchester, Essex, CO4 3SQ

Tel: 01206 872001
Fax: 01206 872003
E-mail: info@data-archive.ac.uk
Website: www.data-archive.ac.uk

Enquiries to: Helpdesk

Founded: 1967; formerly called ESRC Data Bank, ESRC Survey Archive; formerly called ESRC Data Archive (year of change 1996); formerly called The Data Archive (year of change 2000)

Organisation type and purpose: University department or institute.
To preserve, maintain and disseminate research data.

Subject coverage: The UK Data Archive (UKDA) acquires, preserves, disseminates and promotes data, including digital data in the social sciences and humanities.
The UKDA provides resource discovery and support for secondary use of quantitative and qualitative data in research, teaching and learning as a lead partner of the Economic and Social Data Service (ESDS).
The UKDA provides preservation services for other data organisations, facilitates international data exchange, carries out research in digital preservation and provides advice in data management.

Collection: The UKDA houses over 6,000 datasets of interest to researchers, students and teachers in the HE/FE sectors and from many disciplines; datasets cover the full range of the social sciences and most aspects of social and economic study

Non-library collection catalogue: All or part available online and in-house

Publications: Printed

Publications list: Available online

Access to staff: Contact by letter, by telephone, by fax, by e-mail, in person and via website. Appointment necessary.
Hours: Mon to Fri, 0900 to 1700

Funded by: Economic and Social Research Council (ESRC); Joint Information Systems Committee (JISC); University of Essex

UK FASHION EXPORTS (UKFE)

5 Portland Place, London, W1B 1PW

Tel: 020 7636 5577
Fax: 020 7636 7848
E-mail: info@ukfashionexports.com
Website: www.ukfashionexports.com

Enquiries to: Executive Director

Founded: 1940; formed by the amalgamation of British Knitting Export Council (BKEC), Clothing Export Council of Great Britain (CECGB) (year of change 1984); formerly called British Knitting and Clothing Export Council (BKCEC) (year of change 2000)

Organisation type and purpose: Trade association (membership is by subscription).
To promote the export from UK of all clothing and fashion-related accessories.

Subject coverage: Export markets and marketing, export statistics, export procedures and tariffs, information on overseas markets for clothing (members only), general information, to potential buyers of British clothing etc, all relevant details of appropriate UK suppliers.

Collection: Library of commercial information available to member companies (directories, export regulations, buyer information, trade journals (UK and foreign) etc)

Trade and statistical information: Via associated organisations in the British Apparel and Textile Confederation, details of production in UK, numbers employed etc

Library catalogue: All or part available in-house

Publications: Printed

Access to staff: Contact by letter, by telephone, by fax, by e-mail and via website. Appointment necessary.
Hours: Mon to Fri, 0900 to 1800

Affiliated to: British Apparel and Textile Confederation; at the same address; British Clothing Industry Association; at the same address

Subsidiary body: Apparel Marketing Services (Export) Ltd; at the same address

UK HYDROGRAPHIC OFFICE (UKHO)

Admiralty Way, Taunton, Somerset, TA1 2DN

Tel: 01823 337900
Fax: 01823 284077
E-mail: via website www.ukho.gov.uk
Website: www.ukho.gov.uk

Enquiries to: Archives Research Manager
Direct tel: 01823 337900 ext 3409
Direct e-mail: research@ukho.gov.uk

Founded: 1795

Organisation type and purpose: National government body, research organisation.
Producer of navigational charts and related publications.
An appointed place of deposit for its own records under the Public Records Act 1958.

Subject coverage: Navigation; hydrographic surveying; geodesy; photogrammetry; cartography; geophysics; oceanography; meteorology; shipping and ports.

Collection: Archives of hydrographic surveys, Admiralty Charts, navigational information, books, letters

Non-library collection catalogue: All or part available in-house

continued overleaf

Library catalogue: All or part available in-house

Publications: Printed, and electronic and video, and microform publications
Order printed publications from: List of agents for UKHO publications available on website

Access to staff: Contact by letter, by telephone, by fax and by e-mail. Appointment necessary.
Hours: Mon to Fri, 0930 to 1630

Access to building: Prior appointment required

Access for disabled people: Parking provided, toilet facilities, level access, lift to Research Room

A Trading Fund Agency within the: Ministry of Defence

UK INDUSTRIAL VISION ASSOCIATION (UKIVA)

PO Box 25, Royston, Herts, SG8 6TL

Tel: 01763 220981
E-mail: info@ukiva.org
Website: www.ukiva.org

Organisation type and purpose: To promote the use of vision and imaging technology by industry and science in the UK.

Subject coverage: Provides information about image processing and machine vision systems.

Publications: Electronic and video
Order electronic and video publications from: Available to download from free resources section of website by registered visitors

Publications list: Available online

Access to staff: Contact by letter, by telephone, by e-mail and via website

UK INNOVATION RELAY CENTRES

Avon: Bristol; tel: 0117 221 016

Cambridgeshire: Cambridge; tel: 01954 261199

Hampshire: Farnborough; tel: 01252 394607

Kent: Canterbury; tel: 01227 763414

Merseyside: St Helens; tel: 01744 453366

Northern Ireland: Belfast; tel: 028 9052 9475; Belfast; tel: 028 9049 1031

Oxfordshire: Oxford; tel: 01865 784888

Scotland: Aberdeen; tel: 01224 211500; Glasgow; tel: 0141 946 0500; Glasgow; tel: 0141 221 0999; Inverness; tel: 01463 715400; Sterling; tel: 01786 448333

South Yorkshire: Barnsley; tel: 01226 249590

Tyne & Wear: Sunderland; tel: 0191 383 3336

Wales: Cardiff; tel: 029 2082 8739

West Midlands: Coventry; tel: 024 7683 8140

UK JEEP CLUB

Jeep Books Ltd/Jeep Promotions Ltd, 5 Chestnut Avenue, Wheatley Hills, Doncaster, South Yorkshire, DN2 5SW

Tel: 01302 739000
Fax: 01302 739001
E-mail: info@jeepworld.co.uk
Website: www.jeepworld.co.uk

Enquiries to: Editor

Founded: 1990; formerly called C J Jeep Club UK, Jeep Club UK

Organisation type and purpose: Membership association (membership is by subscription), voluntary organisation.

Subject coverage: Jeeps for sale, jeep parts new and used, suppliers, insurance, technical advice, information, events, everything for real jeeps from 1941 Willys to new CJs, Wranglers and Cherokees.

Collection: Many books, magazines, manuals for helping club members, but not for loan

Non-library collection catalogue: All or part available online, in-house and in print

Library catalogue: All or part available in-house and in print

Publications: Printed

Publications list: Available online

Access to staff: Contact by letter, by telephone, by e-mail and via website
Hours: Mon to Fri, 0900 to 1700

UK LUBRICANTS ASSOCIATION LTD (UKLA)

Berkhamsted House, 121 High Street, Berkhamsted, Hertfordshire, HP4 2DJ

Tel: 01442 230589
Fax: 01442 259232
E-mail: enquiries@ukla.org.uk
Website: www.ukla.org.uk

Enquiries to: Executive Director

Founded: 1921; created by the merger of BLF and UEIL (year of change 2005)

Organisation type and purpose: Trade association.

Subject coverage: Lubrication and additives, all aspects of manufacture, distribution and marketing of lubricants.

Publications: Printed

Access to staff: Contact by letter, by fax, by e-mail and via website
Hours: Mon to Fri, 0900 to 1700

UK MAJOR PORTS GROUP (UKMPG)

4th floor, Carthusian Court, 12 Carthusian Street, London, EC1M 6EZ

Tel: 020 7260 1785
Fax: 020 7260 1785
E-mail: richardbird@ukmajorports.org.uk
Website: www.ukmajorports.org.uk

Enquiries to: Executive Director

Founded: 1993; formerly called British Ports Federation (year of change 1992)

Organisation type and purpose: Trade association.

Subject coverage: Policy issues affecting the major ports arising from UK Government, European Commission or other action.

Publications: Printed

Access to staff: Contact by letter, by telephone, by fax and by e-mail
Hours: Mon to Fri, 0900 to 1700

UK NATIONAL COMMITTEE FOR THE PREVENTION OF ALCOHOL AND DRUG DEPENDENCY (NCPA)

BUC Office, Stanborough Park, Watford, Hertfordshire, WD25 9JZ

Tel: 01923 665553
Fax: 01923 893212

Enquiries to: Executive Director

Organisation type and purpose: Membership association (membership is by election or invitation), registered charity (charity number 1008129).

Publications: Printed

Access to staff: Contact by letter, by telephone and by fax
Hours: Fri, 0900 to 1200

Affiliated to: International Commission for the Prevention of Alcoholism and Drug Dependency (an NGO of the WHO and UN); 12501 Old Columbia Pike, Silver Spring, MD 20904, USA

UK PAYMENTS

Formal name: UK Payments Administration Ltd

2 Thomas More Square, London, E1W 1YN

Tel: 020 3217 8200
Fax: 020 7488 6959
E-mail: enquiries@ukpayments.org.uk
Website: www.ukpayments.org.uk

Enquiries to: Director of Communications
Direct tel: 020 3217 8234

Founded: 1985; formerly called APACS Administration Ltd (year of change 2009)

Organisation type and purpose: A service company for the UK payments industry, providing people, facilities and expertise. The payments industry has different players and separate industry groups with UK Payments supplying different services to a wide range of companies with separate external identities.

Subject coverage: UK payments issues including plastic cards, card fraud, cheques, electronic payments and cash.

Publications: Printed

Publications list: Available online

Access to staff: Contact by letter and by e-mail
Hours: Mon to Fri, 0900 to 1700

Links with: Payments Council; 2 Thomas More Square, London, E1W 1YN; tel: 020 3217 8200; e-mail: enquiries@ukpayments.org.uk; website: http://www.paymentscouncil.org.uk
The UK Cards Association; 2 Thomas More Square, London, E1W 1YN; tel: 020 3217 8200; e-mail: support@ukcards.org.uk; website: http://www.theukcardsassociation.org.uk

UK SOCIETY OF INVESTMENT PROFESSIONALS (UKSIP)

21 Ironmonger Lane, London, EC2V 8EY

Tel: 020 7796 3000
Fax: 020 7796 3333
E-mail: uksipstaff@uksip.org
Website: www.uksip.org

Enquiries to: Chief Executive
Other contacts: (1) Director of Finance; (2) Director of Education and IT

Founded: 2000; formerly called Institute of Investment Management and Research (IIMR) (year of change 2000)

Organisation type and purpose: National organisation, professional body (membership is by qualification), present number of members: 4400.
To set standards in profession of fund management and investment research.

Subject coverage: Techniques of investment; stocks and shares and other securities; investment analysis; portfolio management. Careers in investment analysis and fund management.

Publications: Printed

Publications list: Available in print

Access to staff: Contact by letter, by telephone, by fax, by e-mail and via website
Hours: Mon to Fri, 0930 to 1730

Member society of the: Association for Investment Management & Research (AIMR); tel: 00 1 434 951 5489

UK SPRING MANUFACTURERS' ASSOCIATION (UKSMA)

Tel: 0114 252 7997
E-mail: uksma@uksma.org.uk
Website: www.uksma.org.uk

Organisation type and purpose: Trade association providing business support for UK spring makers.

Subject coverage: Actively promotes the UK spring industry, encourages business development, provides information, networking and support.

Access to staff: Contact by telephone and by e-mail

Administered by: Institute of Spring Technology; Henry Street, Sheffield, S3 7EQ; tel: 0114 276 0771; fax: 0114 252 7997; e-mail: ist@ist.org; website: http://www.ist.org.uk

UK STEEL

Broadway House, Tothill Street, London, SW1H 9NQ

Tel: 020 7222 7777
Fax: 020 7222 2782
E-mail: steel@eef.org.uk
Website: www.eef.org.uk/uksteel

Enquiries to: Director
Direct tel: 020 7654 1519
Direct e-mail: irodgers@eef.org.uk

Founded: 1967

Organisation type and purpose: Trade association for the UK steel industry, representing the industry to policy and opinion formers, promoting the industry and the importance of steel to the public, and providing information and services to its members.

Subject coverage: UK steel industry, including its structure, performance (nationally and internationally) and its contribution to the UK economy and everyday life. Specialist knowledge of steel production, processing and steel products; steel standards and steel sourcing; environmental issues relating to the production, processing and recyclability of steel; legislation and representation to government in the United Kingdom, Europe and elsewhere; international trade in steel; other issues affecting steel companies such as transport and haulage, careers in the UK steel industry, and health and safety.

Trade and statistical information: Key statistics for the United Kingdom steel industry available free; other statistics (United Kingdom, Europe, worldwide) available on request and online

Publications: Printed, and electronic and video

Publications list: Available online

Access to staff: Contact by letter, by telephone, by fax and by e-mail
Hours: Mon to Fri, 0900 to 1700

Also at: UK Steel; Swinden House, Rotherham, S60 3AR; tel: 01709 362288; fax: 01709 724999; e-mail: rruddlestone@eef.org.uk

Constituent bodies: ISSB Limited; 1 Carlton House Terrace, London, SW1Y 5DB; tel: 020 7343 3900; fax: 020 7343 3902; e-mail: enquiries@issb.co.uk

Member organisation of: Energy Intensive Users Group (EIUG); Broadway House, Tothill Street, London, SW1H 9NQ; tel: 020 7654 1536; fax: 020 7222 2782

Sponsor of: Challenge of Materials Gallery; Science Museum, Exhibition Road, London, SW7 2DD; tel: 020 7938 8000

UK STEM CELL FOUNDATION (UKSCF)

20 Park Crescent, London, W1B 1AL

Tel: 020 7670 5370
E-mail: info@ukscf.org
Website: www.ukscf.org/foundation

Founded: 2005

Organisation type and purpose: A registered charity (number 1110009).
To support the advance of pioneering stem cell research into medical practice.
Directly funds innovative UK clinical projects with the greatest potential for saving and improving people's lives.

We are determined to fill the critical gap between currently available UK funding and the many promising research projects in need of financial assistance.

Subject coverage: Leading biomedical scientists the world over believe that stem cell research holds the key to curing society's most intractable diseases including Parkinson's, Alzheimer's, multiple sclerosis and heart attack. The scientific and therapeutic benefits to be gained are potentially enormous.

Publications: Electronic and video
Order electronic and video publications from: Download from website

Access to staff: Contact by letter, by telephone and by e-mail

Also at: UK Stem Cell Foundation; Abbey House, 83 Princes Street, Edinburgh EH2 2ER; tel: 0131 718 0684; e-mail: info@ukscf.org

UK THALASSAEMIA SOCIETY (UKTS)

19 The Broadway, Southgate Circus, London, N14 6PH

Tel: 020 882 0011
Fax: 020 8882 8618
E-mail: office@ukts.org
Website: www.ukts.org

Enquiries to: Honorary Secretary

Founded: 1976

Organisation type and purpose: Registered charity (number 275107).

Subject coverage: Information on thalassaemia.

Publications: Printed

Access to staff: Contact by letter, by telephone, by fax, by e-mail, in person and via website
Hours: Mon to Fri, 0900 to 1700

Access for disabled people: Level entry

UK TRADE & INVESTMENT (UKTI)

Kingsgate House, 66–74 Victoria Street, London, SW1E 6SW

Tel: 020 7215 8000
Fax: 020 7828 1281
Website: www.ukinvest.gov.uk/
Enquiries to: Information Officer

Founded: 1977; formerly called Invest-UK, Trade Partners UK, Invest in Britain Bureau (year of change 2003)

Organisation type and purpose: National government body.
Unit of the Department of Trade and Industry and Foreign and Commonwealth Office.
The major role of UKTI is to assist and encourage overseas companies with internationally mobile manufacturing and service sector projects to locate their activities in this country. Particularly interested in securing those projects which bring long-term jobs or which introduce new technologies or management techniques and which improve the UK's competitive manufacturing position. UKTI works in partnership with national development agencies in Scotland, Wales and Northern Ireland and the English regional development agencies.

Subject coverage: The Government's main inward investment agency in the United Kingdom, assisting firms with all aspects of locating or relocating a business or

continued overleaf

expanding existing facilities. UKTI offers a one-stop advisory service in drawing together information from government and public agencies, and can put together a complete package of locations, financial incentives, employment, taxation, entry clearance and immigration, company formation, training, research assistance and product sector advice. The service is both free and confidential.

Trade and statistical information: Comparison statistics for above subjects between UK and EU countries

Publications: Printed, and microform publications
Order printed publications from: DTI Publications
tel: 0870 150 2500, fax: 0870 150 2333, e-mail: publications@dti.gsi.gov.uk

Publications list: Available online and in print

Access to staff: Contact by letter, by telephone, by fax, by e-mail and via website
Hours: Mon to Fri, 0900 to 1700

Parent body: Department of Trade and Industry

UK TRADE AND INVESTMENT, HONG KONG AND MACAO DESK

Bay 960, Kingsgate House, 66–74 Victoria Street, London, SW1E 6SW

Tel: 020 7215 8095
Fax: 020 7215 4074
E-mail: michael.opoku@ukti.gsi.gov.uk
Website: www.uktradeinvest.gov.uk

Enquiries to: Country Manager

History of institution: formerly a part of Department of Trade and Industry (DTI) (year of change 2007)

Organisation type and purpose: National government body.
Trade promotion.

Subject coverage: Exporting to Hong Kong, prospects for investment and other forms of commercial co-operation.

Publications list: Available in print

Access to staff: Contact by letter, by telephone, by fax and by e-mail
Hours: Mon to Fri, 0900 to 1700

Access for disabled people: Access to all public areas

Constituent part of: BERR

UK YOUTH

3rd Floor, Lancaster House, 33 Islington High Street, London, N1 9LH

Tel: 0845 862 0155
Fax: 0845 862 0155
E-mail: info@ukyouth.org
Website: www.ukyouth.org

Enquiries to: Chief Executive
Direct tel: 0845 862 0157
Direct e-mail: jo@ukyouth.org

Founded: 1911; formerly called National Association of Youth Clubs; formerly called Youth Clubs UK (YCUK) (year of change 1999)

Organisation type and purpose: Voluntary organisation, registered charity (charity number 306066).

Subject coverage: Youth, youth work and services.

Non-library collection catalogue: All or part available online and in print

Library catalogue: All or part available online and in print

Publications: Printed, and electronic and video

Publications list: Available online and in print

Access to staff: Contact by letter, by telephone, by fax, by e-mail and via website. Appointment necessary.
Hours: Mon to Fri, 0900 to 1700

Access to building: Prior appointment required

Access for disabled people: Level entry

Affiliated to: European Confederation of Youth Club Organisations (ECYC); Ornevej 45, Copenhagen NV, DK-2400, Denmark; tel: 00 45 38 10 80 38; National Council for Voluntary Organisations; National Council for Voluntary Youth Services

Has: 3 divisions (Scotland, Wales and Northern Ireland); 43 local associations of youth clubs

UK-IDF

c/o Dairy UK, 93 Baker Street, London W1U 6QQ

Tel: 0207 467 2621
Fax: 0207 487 4734
E-mail: iwakeling@dairyuk.org
Website: www.ukidf.org/

Enquiries to: Secretary

Founded: 1950; formerly called United Kingdom Dairy Association

Organisation type and purpose: Membership association (membership is by subscription).
UK National Committee of the International Dairy Federation.

Subject coverage: Hygiene, dairy technology, economics, analytical techniques, nutrition and education.

Publications: Printed

Access to staff: Contact by letter, by telephone, by fax and by e-mail
Hours: Mon to Fri, 0900 to 1700

UKCISA: THE COUNCIL FOR INTERNATIONAL STUDENT AFFAIRS

9–17 St Albans Place, London, N1 0NX

Tel: 020 7107 9922
Fax: 020 7288 4360
Website: www.ukcisa.org.uk

Enquiries to: Membership Secretary

Founded: 1968; formerly called UKCOSA: The Council for International Education

Organisation type and purpose: Advisory body, membership association (membership is by subscription), voluntary organisation, registered charity (charity number 1095294), training organisation, consultancy, research organisation.
To promote the interests of international students.

Subject coverage: All matters affecting international students in the UK.

Trade and statistical information: Comparative statistics on international students

Publications: Printed, and electronic and video
Order printed publications from: Publications Officer, UKCOSA
e-mail: publications@ukcosa.org.uk

Publications list: Available online and in print

Access to staff: Contact by letter, by telephone, by fax, by e-mail and via website
Hours: Telephone: 020 7354 5210: Mon to Fri, 1300 to 1600

UKERNA

Formal name: United Kingdom Education and Research Networking Association

Atlas Centre, Chilton, Didcot, Oxfordshire, OX11 0QS

Tel: 01235 822212
Fax: 01235 822397
E-mail: service@ukerna.ac.uk
Website: www.ja.net
Website: www.ukerna.ac.uk

Enquiries to: Customer Service Director

Founded: 1993

Organisation type and purpose: Statutory body.
UKERNA is responsible for the co-ordination and management of the networking programme of the UK education and research community known as JANET.

Subject coverage: Internetworking for the UK academic and research community, multiservice networking, information superhighway for education, managing the JANET network.

Publications: Printed

Access to staff: Contact by letter, by telephone, by fax and by e-mail. Appointment necessary.
Hours: Mon to Fri, 0800 to 1800

Affiliated to: JISC, HEFCE; Northavon House, Coldharbour Lane, Bristol, BS16 1QD

UKOLN

Library and Learning Centre, University of Bath, Claverton Down, Bath, BA2 7AY

Tel: 01225 386580
Fax: 01225 386838
E-mail: ukoln@ukoln.ac.uk
Website: www.ukoln.ac.uk

Enquiries to: Resource Co-ordinator
Direct tel: 01225 386250
Direct e-mail: b.r.robinson@ukoln.ac.uk
Other contacts: Events Manager (for conference organisation)

Founded: 1977

Organisation type and purpose: Advisory body, research organization.

Subject coverage: UKOLN is a research organisation that aims to inform practice and influence policy in the areas of: digital libraries, information systems, bibliographic management, and web technologies. It provides network information services, including the Ariadne magazine, and runs workshops and conferences.

Publications: Printed, and electronic and video

Access to staff: Contact by letter, by telephone, by e-mail and via website
Hours: Mon to Fri, 0900 to 1700

Funded by: European Union Project Funding; Joint Information Systems Committee of the Higher and Further Education Funding Councils; Museums, Libraries and Archives Council (MLA)

Supported by: University of Bath

UKSPACE (SBAC)

Salamanca Square, 9 Albert Embankment, London, SE1 7SP

Tel: 020 7091 4500
Fax: 020 7091 4545
Website: www.sbac.co.uk

Enquiries to: Policy and Communications
Direct e-mail: mark.watson@sbac.co.uk

Founded: 1975; formerly called United Kingdom Industrial Space Committee (UKISC)

Organisation type and purpose: National organisation, trade association, present number of members: 40. Represents the collective interests of its member companies in increasing space and space-related business, and their share of the home and export markets.

Subject coverage: UK Space Industry – policy and capability. Links to specialist sources.

Access to staff: Contact by letter
Hours: Mon to Fri, 0900 to 1700

Access to building: No access other than to staff

Connections with: Federation of the Electronics Industry; Russell Square House, London, WC1B 5EE; tel: 020 7331 2000; Society of British Aerospace Companies (SBAC); 60 Petty France, London, SW1H 9EU; tel: 020 7227 1000

UKSPILL ASSOCIATION

UK Spill Association, Unit 1, Riverside Business Park, Buxton, Bakewell, Derbyshire DE45 1GS

Tel: +44 (0) 845 6259890
Fax: +44 (0) 845 6259891
E-mail: info@ukspill.org
Website: www.ukspill.org

Enquiries to: Director

Founded: 1981

Organisation type and purpose: Trade association.

Subject coverage: All aspects of the prevention, control and clean-up of marine, inland and industrial pollution, both in the UK and overseas.

Access to staff: Contact by letter
Hours: Mon to Fri, 0900 to 1700

ULSTER COLLEGE OF MUSIC

13 Windsor Avenue, Belfast, BT9 6EE

Tel: 028 9038 1314
E-mail: info@ulstercollegeofmusic.co.uk
Website: www.ulstercollegeofmusic.co.uk/home.cfm

Enquiries to: Administrator
Direct e-mail: annestafford@btinternet.com
Other contacts: Chairman

Founded: 1966

Organisation type and purpose: College of Music.
The training of musicians on all instruments and voice, or vocal and instrumental tuition.

Subject coverage: All aspects of the profession of music.

Library catalogue: All or part available in-house

Access to staff: Contact by letter, by telephone, by e-mail, in person and via website
Hours: Mon to Fri, 1400 to 2030; Sat, 0900 to 1700

Access for disabled people: Toilet facilities
Special comments: Disabled access to ground and first floor only.

ULSTER HISTORICAL FOUNDATION (UHF)

49 Malone Road, Belfast, Co. Antrim, BT9 6RY

Tel: 028 9066 1988
Fax: 028 90661977
E-mail: enquiry@uhf.org.uk
Website: www.ancestryireland.com
Website: www.booksireland.org.uk

Enquiries to: Executive Director
Direct e-mail: fintan@uhf.org.uk

Founded: 1956

Organisation type and purpose: Voluntary organisation, registered charity (charity number XN48460), research organisation, publishing house.
Genealogical research, computerisation of historical records, publications.

Subject coverage: Genealogical research for all of Ireland, history of Ulster, particularly migration to and from, Irish Genealogical Project (for the computerisation of all pre-1900 church and civil records in Ireland), designated centre for Co. Antrim and Co. Down (including Belfast).

Collection: Completed searches regarding Ulster families (approx. 13,000)

Library catalogue: All or part available online and in-house

Publications: Printed, and electronic and video
Order electronic and video publications from: www.booksireland.org.uk or amazon.co.uk or epubdirect.com

Publications list: Available online and in print

Access to staff: Contact by letter, by telephone, by fax, by e-mail, in person and via website
Hours: Mon to Fri, 0930 to 1630

Access to building: No prior appointment required
Hours: Mon to Fri, 0930 to 1630

Access for disabled people: Disabled access available
Hours: Mon to Fri, 0930 to 1630

Links with: Federation of Family History Societies; Irish Family History Foundation; Irish Genealogical Project; Ulster Genealogical and Historical Guild

ULSTER UNIONIST PARTY (UUP)

Strandtown Hall, 2–4 Belmont Road, Belfast, BT4 2AN

Tel: 028 9047 4630
Fax: 028 9065 2149
E-mail: uup@uup.org
Website: www.uup.org

Enquiries to: Party Admin Manager
Direct tel: 028 9046 3201
Direct e-mail: hazel.legge@uup.org
Other contacts: General Secretary

Founded: 1905

Organisation type and purpose: Membership association (membership is by subscription).
Political party.

Access to staff: Contact by letter, by telephone, by fax, by e-mail, in person and via website
Hours: Mon to Fri, 0900 to 1700

Access to building: *Hours:* Mon to Fri, 0900 to 1700

Access for disabled people: Ramp at entrance, disabled toilet facilities, disabled/wheelchair lift
Hours: Mon to Fri, 0900 to 1700

ULSTER WILDLIFE TRUST (UWT)

Ulster Wildlife Trust, 3 New Line, Crossgar, Downpatrick, Co. Down, BT30 9EP

Tel: 028 4483 0282
Fax: 028 4483 0888
E-mail: info@ulsterwildlifetrust.org
Website: www.ulsterwildlifetrust.org

Enquiries to: Marketing Manager
Other contacts: Membership Officer (for membership issues)

Founded: 1978

Organisation type and purpose: Registered charity.

Subject coverage: Nature conservation, biodiversity, marine, planning, environmental education.

Publications: Printed

Publications list: Available online

Access to staff: Contact by letter, by telephone and by e-mail. Appointment necessary.
Hours: Mon to Fri, 0900 to 1700

Member organisation of: The Wildlife Trust; The Kiln, Waterside, Mather Road, Newark, Nottinghamshire, NG24 1WT; tel:

continued overleaf

01636 677711; fax: 01636 670001; e-mail: enquiry@wildlifetrusts.org; website: http://www.wildlifetrusts.org

UNICEF UK (UNICEF)

Formal name: United Nations Children's Fund

Africa House, 64–78 Kingsway, London, WC2B 6NB

Tel: 020 7405 5592
Fax: 020 7405 2332
E-mail: helpdesk@unicef.org.uk
Website: www.unicef.org.uk

Enquiries to: Information Department

Founded: 1947

Organisation type and purpose:
International organisation, registered charity (charity number 1072612).
Fund raising and advocacy organisation, supporting the work of UNICEF in over 160 countries. Helping to provide basic services for children and promoting children's rights.

Subject coverage: Health, children's rights, child labour, nutrition, water and sanitation, children in conflict, education, aid and development work for the improvement of conditions for mothers and children in developing countries; children's issues and rights in the industrialised world.

Collection: Photographs (black and white) and colour transparencies
UNICEF international publications, board papers, speeches

Trade and statistical information: Statistics on child births, deaths, performance, malnutrition, immunisation, primary education, maternal deaths

Publications: Printed
Order printed publications from: UNICEF Unit 1, Rignals Lane, Chelmsford, Essex, CM2 8TU, tel: 01245 476315, fax: 01245 477394

Publications list: Available in print

Access to staff: Contact by letter, by telephone, by fax, by e-mail and via website
Hours: Mon to Fri, 0930 to 1730

Access to building: No access other than to staff

Parent body: United Nations

UNION OF MUSLIM ORGANISATIONS OF UK AND EIRE (UMO)

109 Campden Hill Road, London, W8 7TL

Tel: 020 7221 6608 or 7229 0538
Fax: 020 7792 2130 (on request)

Enquiries to: Secretary-General
Other contacts: Assistant Secretary.

Founded: 1970

Organisation type and purpose: National organisation, membership association (membership is by subscription), present number of members: 214, voluntary organisation.
Voluntary religious organisation, representative body of the Muslim community in UK and Eire.
To co-ordinate the activities of Muslim organisations in the UK and Eire, to negotiate with government departments and serve the religious rights of the British Muslim community.

Subject coverage: Islam; Islamic education; social and cultural aspects of British Muslim activities, including youth activities in the UK; current Mosque projects dealing with any problems faced by Muslim students or workers in the observance of their religions duties.

Publications: Printed

Publications list: Available in print

Access to staff: Contact by letter, by telephone and by fax. Appointment necessary.
Hours: Mon to Fri, 0900 to 1700

Has as members: Local Muslim organisations in UK and Eire

Houses the: National Muslim Education Council and the UMO Youth Council of UK and Eire; tel: 020 7221 6608; fax: 020 7792 2130 (on request); UMO Board of Ulama, UK; UMO Trust

UNION OF SHOP, DISTRIBUTIVE AND ALLIED WORKERS (USDAW)

188 Wilmslow Road, Fallowfield, Manchester, M14 6LJ

Tel: 0161 224 2804
Fax: 0161 257 2566
E-mail: enquiries@usdaw.org.uk
Website: www.usdaw.org.uk

Enquiries to: Head of Media and Communications (applications to use library and archive facilities need to be in writing)

Organisation type and purpose: Trade union, present number of members: 340,000.
The Supervisory, Administrative and Technical Association (SATA) is the white collar section.

Subject coverage: Trade union activity and industrial relations matters in retail and wholesale distribution and associated sectors of food and chemical processing and the catering and hairdressing trades; wages councils; shopping hours and Sunday trading; history of USDAW and earlier shopworker unions.

Collection: Copies of Union journals: New Dawn, The Shop Assistant, Dawn and Usdaw Today, Agenda, Arena, Network Union's Official Records since the 1880s

Publications: Printed

Access to staff: Contact by letter, by telephone, by fax, by e-mail and via website. Appointment necessary.
Hours: Mon to Fri, 0900 to 1700

UNISON

1 Mabledon Place, London, WC1H 9AJ

Tel: 0845 355 0845
Website: www.unison.org.uk

Founded: 1993

Organisation type and purpose: Trade union.

Subject coverage: Trade unions and industrial relations, pay and conditions, public services.

Publications: Printed
Order printed publications from: UNISON Communications, tel: 020 7551 1115

Publications list: Available online and in print

Access to staff: Contact by letter, by telephone, by fax and by e-mail. Appointment necessary.
Hours: Mon to Fri, 0900 to 1700

Affiliated to: Labour Party; Public Services International; Trades Union Congress; website: http://www.tuc.org.uk

UNIT FOR RESEARCH INTO CHANGING INSTITUTIONS (URCHIN)

115 Poplar High Street, London, E14 0AE

Tel: 020 7987 3600
Fax: 020 7515 8627
E-mail: info@meridian.org.uk
Website: www.meridian.org.uk

Enquiries to: Executive Director

Founded: 1981

Organisation type and purpose: Registered charity (charity number 284542), research organisation.
To carry out research into ways to implement and advance the capacity of society and its associated institutions to adapt to change in a functional and realistic manner.

Subject coverage: Management of change, organisational learning, psychoanalysis, social dynamics, pre- and perinatal psychology, primal integration.

Non-library collection catalogue: All or part available online

Library catalogue: All or part available online

Publications: Printed

Publications list: Available online and in print

Access to staff: Contact by letter
Hours: Mon to Fri, 0900 to 1700

UNITARIAN GENERAL ASSEMBLY (GAUFCC)

Formal name: General Assembly of Unitarian and Free Christian Churches

Essex Hall, 1–6 Essex Street, London, WC2R 3HY

Tel: 020 7240 2384
Fax: 020 7240 3089
E-mail: info@unitarian.org.uk
Website: www.unitarian.org.uk

Enquiries to: Information Officer

Founded: 1928

Organisation type and purpose:
Membership association, registered charity (charity number 250788).
Religious, Unitarianism.
Spreads information about liberal religion and provides support services for member groups.

Subject coverage: Current British Unitarian beliefs and practices; liberal religious ideas and principles; personalised weddings, baptisms, child namings and funerals; liberal religious movements abroad, blessings of same-sex relationships.

Collection: Year Books, 1870 to date

Publications: Printed

Publications list: Available in print

Access to staff: Contact by letter, by telephone, by fax, by e-mail and via website. Appointment necessary. Access for members only.
Hours: Mon to Fri, 0900 to 1700
Special comments: Please telephone first.

UNITARIAN HISTORICAL SOCIETY (UHS)

223 Upper Lisburn Road, Belfast, BT10 0LL

E-mail: nspresb@hotmail.com
Website: www.unitarianhistory.org.uk

Enquiries to: Honorary Secretary

Founded: 1916

Organisation type and purpose: Learned society (membership is by subscription), present number of members: 350.

Subject coverage: Unitarian history.

Collection: For library, see Dr Williams's Library

Publications: Printed

Access to staff: Contact by letter and by e-mail
Hours: Mon to Fri, 0900 to 1700

Associated with: General Assembly of Unitarian and Free Christian Churches

UNITED KINGDOM ACCREDITATION SERVICE (UKAS)

21–47 High Street, Feltham, Middlesex, TW13 4UN

Tel: 020 8917 8400
Fax: 020 8917 8500
E-mail: info@ukas.com
Website: www.ukas.com

Enquiries to: Head of Corporate Communications
Direct tel: 020 8917 8554
Direct fax: 020 8917 8754
Direct e-mail: ukas@clear-group.co.uk

Founded: 1995

Organisation type and purpose: Statutory body, service industry.
Accreditation of conformity assessment bodies.

Subject coverage: Interpretation and clarification of conformity assessment standards; calibration: electrical (dc, lf, rf and microwave), mechanical, fluids, thermal, radiological, thermal conductivity, acoustics, humidity, force, mass, accelerometry, magnetic, pressure, hardness, optical, fibre; testing: acoustical, ballistic, biological, chemical, corrosion, dimensional, electrical, EMC, environmental, fire, geological, health and hygiene, information technology, mechanical, metallurgical, NDDT, performance, physical, safety.

Publications: Printed

Access to staff: Contact by letter, by telephone, by fax, by e-mail and via website
Hours: Mon to Fri, 0900 to 1700

UNITED KINGDOM ALLIANCE (UKA)

176 Blackfriars Road, London, SE1 8ET

Tel: 07985 011029

Enquiries to: General Secretary

Founded: 1853

Organisation type and purpose: Membership association (membership is by subscription), present number of members: 500, voluntary organisation, registered charity (charity number 293067).
Education in respect of alcohol and drug abuse.

Subject coverage: Advising on the dangers of alcohol and drug abuse.

Access to staff: Contact by letter
Hours: Mon to Fri, 0900 to 1700

Access to building: No access other than to staff

UNITED KINGDOM ASSOCIATION OF MANUFACTURERS OF BAKERS' YEAST (UKAMBY)

6 Catherine Street, London, WC2B 5JJ

Tel: 020 7420 7109
Fax: 020 7836 0580
E-mail: tom.hollis@fdf.org.uk

Enquiries to: Executive Secretary

Organisation type and purpose: Trade association (membership is by subscription), manufacturing industry.

Subject coverage: Bakers' yeast, legislative developments.

Publications: Printed

Access to staff: Contact by letter, by fax and by e-mail
Hours: Mon to Fri, 0900 to 1700

Member of: Food & Drink Federation

UNITED KINGDOM ASTRONOMY TECHNOLOGY CENTRE (UK ATC)

The Library, Royal Observatory, Blackford Hill, Edinburgh, EH9 3HJ

Tel: Switchboard 0131 668 8100 \ Library 0131 668 8395
Fax: 0131 668 8264
E-mail: user@roe.ac.uk
Website: www.roe.ac.uk/atc/library

Enquiries to: Librarian
Direct tel: 0131 668 8395
Direct e-mail: library@roe.ac.uk

Founded: 1896

Organisation type and purpose: Research organisation.

Subject coverage: National centre for the design and production of state-of-the-art astronomical instrumentation and associated technology, in collaboration with UK organisations and/or overseas partners.

Collection: Crawford Collection of historical books and manuscripts on astronomy, and related subjects from 13th to late 19th century, c. 15,000 items

Non-library collection catalogue: All or part available online

Library catalogue: All or part available online

Publications: Printed

Publications list: Available in print

Access to staff: Contact by letter, by telephone, by fax, by e-mail, in person and via website. Appointment necessary.
Hours: Mon to Fri, 0900 to 1730
Special comments: Not open to the public

Funded by: Science & Technology Facilities Council; Polaris House, North Star Avenue, Swindon, SN2 1SZ; website: http://www.scitech.ac.uk

UNITED KINGDOM ATOMIC ENERGY AUTHORITY

Formal name: United Kingdom Atomic Energy Authority, Culham Centre for Fusion Energy

Fusion Library, Culham Science Centre, Abingdon, Oxfordshire, OX14 3DB

Tel: 01235 466347
Fax: 01235 466887
E-mail: helen.bloxham@ccfe.ac.uk
Website: www.ccfe.ac.uk

Enquiries to: Library Manager

Founded: 1961

Organisation type and purpose: National government body, research organisation.
Fusion research and development.

Subject coverage: Nuclear fusion, plasma physics.

Collection: UKAEA Fusion Reports
JET Reports

Library catalogue: All or part available in-house

Order electronic and video publications from: via website

Publications list: Available online

Access to staff: Contact by letter, by telephone, by fax and by e-mail. Appointment necessary. Access for members only. Non-members charged.
Hours: Mon to Fri, 0815 to 1630

Access to building: Prior appointment required

UNITED KINGDOM CENTRE FOR ECONOMIC AND ENVIRONMENTAL DEVELOPMENT (UK CEED)

Suite 1, Priestgate House, 3–7 Priestgate, Peterborough, Cambridgeshire, PE1 1JN

Tel: 01733 311644
Fax: 01733 312782
E-mail: info@ukceed.org
Website: www.ukceed.org

Enquiries to: Information Officer

Founded: 1984

continued overleaf

Organisation type and purpose: National organisation, registered charity (charity number 289469), research organisation.

Subject coverage: All aspects of environmental economics including energy, coastal, marine, leisure, packaging, sustainable development, land use planning, nuclear, business ethics and corporate environmental reporting, and information and communication technologies; public participation; tourism.

Non-library collection catalogue: All or part available online and in print

Publications: Printed

Access to staff: Contact by letter, by telephone, by fax, by e-mail and via website
Hours: Mon to Fri, 0900 to 1700

UNITED KINGDOM CERTIFICATION AUTHORITY FOR REINFORCING STEELS (UK CARES)

Pembroke House, 21 Pembroke Road, Sevenoaks, Kent, TN13 1XR

Tel: 01732 450000
Fax: 01732 455917
E-mail: general@ukcares.com
Website: www.ukcares.com

Enquiries to: Company Secretary

Founded: 1983

Organisation type and purpose: Third party certification body.

Subject coverage: Reinforcing steels.

Publications: Printed

Publications list: Available online and in print

Access to staff: Contact by letter, by telephone, by fax and by e-mail
Hours: Mon to Fri, 0900 to 1700

UNITED KINGDOM CLINICAL PHARMACY ASSOCIATION (UKCPA)

1st Floor, Publicity House, 59 Long Street, Wigston, Leicester, LE18 2AJ

Tel: 0116 277 6999
Fax: 0116 277 6272
E-mail: admin@ukcpa.com
Website: www.ukcpa.org

Enquiries to: General Manager
Direct e-mail: mmatthews@ukcpa.com

Founded: 1981

Organisation type and purpose: Advisory body, professional body (membership is by subscription), present number of members: 2,000+, training organisation.
Promotes pharmaceutical care for the benefit of patients.

Subject coverage: Clinical pharmacy, education and training, safety and quality of medicines, critical care, care of the elderly, surgery, infection management, respiratory, cardiac, diabetes, emergency care, IT, leadership development, pain management, community, gastroenterology/hepatology and haemostasis, anticoagulation and thrombosis.

Information services: Resource centre, online discussion forums.

Education services: Study days, symposia.

Publications: Printed

Publications list: Available in print

Access to staff: Contact by letter, by telephone, by fax, by e-mail and via website
Hours: Mon to Fri, 0900 to 1700

UNITED KINGDOM FLIGHT SAFETY COMMITTEE (UKFSC)

Graham Suite, Fairoaks Airport, Chobham, Woking, Surrey, GU24 8HX

Tel: 01276 855193
Fax: 01276 855195
E-mail: admin@ukfsc.co.uk
Website: www.ukfsc.co.uk

Enquiries to: Chief Executive

Founded: 1959

Organisation type and purpose: Advisory body, professional body (membership is by subscription, election or invitation), present number of members: 85, voluntary organisation.
To improve aviation safety.

Subject coverage: Aviation safety.

Information services: Website and magazine

Education services: Flight Safety Familiarisation Course

Trade and statistical information: Aviation safety articles and statistics

Library catalogue: All or part available in-house

Publications: Printed

Publications list: Available online

Access to staff: Contact by letter, by telephone, by fax and by e-mail
Hours: Mon to Fri, 0900 to 1630

UNITED KINGDOM FORTIFICATIONS CLUB (UKFC)

4 Mablethorpe Road, Wymering, Portsmouth, Hampshire, PO6 3LJ

Tel: 023 9238 7794
Website: www.mysite.freeserve.com/ukfc

Enquiries to: Chairman
Direct tel: 023 9238 7794 (24 hours)
Other contacts: Webmaster for Internet enquiries email
Peter.Cobb@btopenworld.com.

Founded: 1972

Organisation type and purpose: International organisation, membership association (membership is by subscription), voluntary organisation, research organisation.

Subject coverage: All types of fortification within UK and certain other nations overseas from 2,500 BC to the present day; specifically Iron Age hill and promontory forts, Romano-British camps, forts and towers etc; castle construction; Tudor fortifications: Martello towers and 18th and 19th century fortifications; Georgian and Victorian defences and armoured works; coast artillery, anti-aircraft artillery and field fortifications from both World Wars; Northern Ireland defences; airfield layouts and offshore fortified structures (any period); 130 different subject groupings.

Collection: Cobb Family Archive
Rare books on fortifications, military archaeology and nautical matters
Slide and photographic archives
UKFC Central Archive (over 115 subjects in many volumes)
W E J Parker Archive (Gosport)

Non-library collection catalogue: All or part available in print

Library catalogue: All or part available in-house

Publications: Printed

Publications list: Available online and in print

Access to staff: Contact by letter, by telephone, by e-mail and in person. Appointment necessary.
Hours: Mon to Sat, 0800 to 1130 and 2100 to 2230; Sun and bank holidays, 0830 to 2100

Access to building: Prior appointment required

Connections with: Airfield Research Group; CAMP; USA; CDSG; USA; Coast Defence Study Group; Kent Defence Research Group; tel: 01304 205885; Palmerston Forts Society; tel: 023 9258 6575; Pill Box Study Group; tel: 01502 710149; e-mail: gkdesignresearch@tiscali.co.uk; Society for Army Historical Research

UNITED KINGDOM HOME CARE ASSOCIATION (UKHCA)

Group House, 52 Sutton Court Road, Sutton, SM1 4SL

Tel: 020 8288 1551
Fax: 020 8288 1550
E-mail: enquiries@ukhca.co.uk
Website: www.ukhca.co.uk

Enquiries to: Information Officer

Founded: 1988

Organisation type and purpose: National professional and representative association for the independent, voluntary, and statutory homecare sector, representing 1,600 organisations.

Subject coverage: Domiciliary care, community care, social services, health and safety, contracting services and training, welfare of clients and welfare of care workers.

Publications: Printed

Publications list: Available in print

Access to staff: Contact by letter, by telephone, by fax and by e-mail
Hours: Mon to Fri, 0900 to 1700

Access to building: No access other than to staff

Affiliated to: Care Forum Wales; CCC; NCVO

UNITED KINGDOM ISLAMIC MISSION

Al Furqan School, 27 Arlington Street, Glasgow, G3 6DT

Tel: 0141 331 1119
Fax: 0141 332 2811
E-mail: ukimgla@yahoo.co.uk
Website: www.ukim.org

Enquiries to: Information Officer
Other contacts: President

Founded: 1920

Organisation type and purpose:
Membership association (membership is by subscription), present number of members: 45, voluntary organisation.
Provides information, training and resources on Islam/Muslims.

Subject coverage: Islam/Muslim religion and culture.

Publications: Printed

Publications list: Available in print

Access to staff: Contact by letter, by telephone, by fax, by e-mail and in person. Appointment necessary.
Hours: 1230 to 1630

Also at: United Kingdom Islamic Mission; 19 Carrington Street, Glasgow, G4 6AJ

UNITED KINGDOM PASSPORT SERVICE (UKPS)

Globe House, 89 Eccleston Square, London, SW1V 1PX

Tel: 0870 521 0410
Website: www.passport/gov.uk

Enquiries to: Private Office of Headquarters of UKPS
Direct tel: 020 7901 2428

Organisation type and purpose: National government body.
Executive agency of the Home Office; 7 regional offices.

Subject coverage: Issue of UK passports to British citizens, British Dependent Territories citizens, British Nationals (Overseas); British Overseas citizens, British Subjects and British Protected Persons.

Collection: Records of all UK passport issues including those issued at British Consular posts abroad (at Hayes)

Publications: Printed

Access to staff: Contact by letter and by telephone. Appointment necessary.
Hours: Mon to Fri, 0830 to 1800; Sat, 0900 to 1500
Special comments: Prior appointment is required – 0870 521 0410.

Regional Offices: Belfast Passport Office; tel: 0870 521 0410; Durham Passport Office; tel: 0870 521 0410; Glasgow Passport Office; tel: 0870 521 0410; Liverpool Passport Office; tel: 0870 521 0410; London Passport Office; tel: 0870 521 0410; Newport Passport Office; tel: 0870 521 0410; Peterborough Passport Office; tel: 0870 521 0410

UNITED KINGDOM PETROLEUM INDUSTRY ASSOCIATION LIMITED (UKPIA)

Quality House, Quality Court, Chancery Lane, London, WC2A 1HP

Tel: 020 7269 7600
Fax: 020 7269 7608
E-mail: info@ukpia.com
Website: www.ukpia.com

Enquiries to: Director General

Founded: 1978

Organisation type and purpose: Trade association.

Subject coverage: The downstream oil industry (supply, refining and distribution of petroleum products in the UK and Northern Ireland).

Publications list: Available online

Access to staff: Contact by telephone and via website

Close liaison with: Europia; Institute of Petroleum; Oil & Gas UK; other organisations serving the petroleum field

UNITED KINGDOM SCIENCE PARK ASSOCIATION, THE (UKSPA)

Chesterford Research Park, Little Chesterford, Saffron Walden, Essex, CB10 1XL

Tel: 01779 532050
Fax: 01779 532049
E-mail: info@ukspa.org.uk
Website: www.ukspa.org.uk

Enquiries to: UKSPA Administrator
Other contacts: Business Development Manager

Founded: 1984

Organisation type and purpose:
Membership Association.

Subject coverage: UK science parks; tenant companies of UK science parks; science parks finance, premises, types of business.

Publications: Printed

Publications list: Available online and in print

Access to staff: Contact by letter, by telephone, by fax and by e-mail. Appointment necessary.
Hours: Mon to Fri, 0900 to 1700

Affiliated to: AURIL (Association for University Research and Industry Links); Queens University Belfast, Lanyon North, University Road, Belfast, BT7 1NN; tel: 028 9027 2588; fax: 028 9027 2570; website: www.auril.org.uk
International Association of Science Parks (IASP)

UNITED KINGDOM TRANSPLANT CO-ORDINATORS ASSOCIATION (UKTCA)

PO Box 6300, Birmingham, B15 2RN

Tel: 07071 223171
Fax: 07071 223171
E-mail: secretariat@etco.org

Enquiries to: The Secretariat

Founded: 1983

Organisation type and purpose:
Professional body (membership is by subscription), registered charity (charity number 1065609).
To increase transplantation and organ donation within the UK and Eire.

Subject coverage: Transplantation and organ donation.

Access to staff: Contact by letter, by telephone, by fax and by e-mail
Hours: Mon to Fri, 0900 to 1700

UNITED KINGDOM VINEYARDS ASSOCIATION (UKVA)

PO Box 985, Bottisham, Cambridge, CB5 9WW

Tel: 01223 813812
E-mail: info@ukva.org.uk

Enquiries to: General Secretary

Founded: 1996

Organisation type and purpose: Trade association.
Central body for the affiliated regional associations.

Subject coverage: The growth of the wine trade and the cultivation of vines and making of wine in the United Kingdom; negotiation with central and local government in matters such as planning, rating and taxation, and EC and its wine regulations; the interchange of technical and other information concerning wine or the vine; Quality wine scheme for English and Welsh Wine; and the annual competition and awards for the English and Welsh Wine of the Year.

Publications: Printed

Access to staff: Contact by letter, by telephone, by fax and by e-mail. Appointment necessary.
Hours: Mon to Fri, 0900 to 1700

Affiliated to the: National Farmers Union; Wine and Spirit Association of Great Britain

UNITED KINGDOM WAREHOUSING ASSOCIATION (UKWA)

Walter House, 418–422 Strand, London, WC2R 0PT

Tel: 020 7836 5522
Fax: 020 7438 9379
E-mail: dg@ukwa.org.uk
Website: www.ukwa.org.uk

Founded: 1944

Organisation type and purpose: Trade association.

Subject coverage: Public warehousing information in the UK, warehousing standards, European legislation.

Publications: Printed

Access to staff: Contact by letter, by telephone, by fax, by e-mail and in person. Appointment necessary.
Hours: Mon to Fri, 0900 to 1700

continued overleaf

Member organisation of: European Warehousing and Logistics Confederation; International Federation of Warehousing Logistics Associations

UNITED LODGE OF THEOSOPHISTS (ULT)

62 Queens Gardens, London, W2 3AL

Tel: 020 7723 0688
Fax: 020 7262 8639
E-mail: ult@ultlon.freeserve.co.uk
Website: www.ultlon.freeserve.co.uk

Enquiries to: Information Officer

Founded: 1925

Organisation type and purpose: International organisation, voluntary organisation.

Subject coverage: Theosophy, which is about ethics and comparative religions, the psychic powers in man and the philosophy and exploration of consciousness.

Collection: 19th-century magazines on theosophy: 'Lucifer', 'The Path', 'Theosophy', 'The Theosophical Movement', 'Vidya' and other publications.

Non-library collection catalogue: All or part available online, in-house and in print

Library catalogue: All or part available in-house and in print

Publications: Printed, and electronic and video

Publications list: Available online and in print

Access to staff: Contact by letter, by telephone, by fax, by e-mail, in person and via website. Appointment necessary.
Hours: Mon to Fri, 1000 to 1400; at other times by appointment

Access to building: Prior appointment required
Hours: Mon to Fri, 10:00 to 14:00 or by appointment on Sundays after 18:30

UNITED NATIONS ASSOCIATION OF GREAT BRITAIN AND NORTHERN IRELAND (UNA-UK)

3 Whitehall Court, London, SW1A 2EL

Tel: 020 7766 3444
Fax: 020 7930 5893
E-mail: info@una-uk.org
Website: www.una.org.uk

Enquiries to: Deputy Director
Direct tel: 020 7766 3469
Direct e-mail: southgate@una.org.uk
Other contacts: Head of Advocacy, Executive Director

Founded: 1945

Organisation type and purpose: Voluntary organisation.
Educational and lobbying body.

Subject coverage: United Nations activities and international affairs, especially United Nations and conflict, human rights, environment and development.

Collection: Current UN documents and material relating to 1996

Publications: Printed

Publications list: Available online and in print

Access to staff: Contact by letter, by telephone and by e-mail. Appointment necessary.
Hours: Mon to Fri, 1000 to 1600

Links with: UNA Trust

Member of: World Federation of UNAs; Has consultative status grade 1 with United Nations Economic and Social Council

UNITED NATIONS HIGH COMMISSIONER FOR REFUGEES (UNHCR)

Strand Bridge House, 138–142 Strand, London, WC2R 1HH

Tel: 020 7759 8090
E-mail: gbrloea@unhcr.org
Website: www.unhcr.org.uk/
Website: www.unhcr.org/cgi-bin/texis/vtx/home

Enquiries to: Information Assistant

Founded: 1951

Organisation type and purpose: International organisation.
To assist and protect asylum seekers and refugees.

Subject coverage: Information on refugee situations worldwide, refugee statistics, work of UNHCR and type of assistance provided to refugees.

Collection: Photographs

Trade and statistical information: Statistics on refugees

Publications: Printed, and electronic and video

Access to staff: Contact by letter, by telephone, by fax and by e-mail.
Appointment necessary.
Hours: Mon to Thu, 0900 to 1730; Fri, 0900 to 1500

Parent body: United Nations

UNITED REFORMED CHURCH (URC)

86 Tavistock Place, London, WC1H 9RT

Tel: 020 7916 2020
Fax: 020 7916 2121
E-mail: urc@urc.org.uk
Website: www.urc.org.uk

Enquiries to: General Secretary

Founded: 1972

Organisation type and purpose: Membership association.
Christian Church.

Subject coverage: United Reformed Church affairs and history.

Collection: United Reformed Church Historical Society Library (now at Westminster College, Madingley Road, Cambridge CB3 0AA)

Publications: Printed

Publications list: Available in print

Access to staff: Contact by e-mail.
Appointment necessary.
Hours: Mon to Fri, 0900 to 1630

Member of: Churches Together in Britain and Ireland; Churches Together in England; World Alliance of Reformed Churches; World Council of Churches

Partner in: Council for World Mission

UNITED REFORMED CHURCH HISTORY SOCIETY (URC History Society)

Westminster College, Madingley Road, Cambridge, CB3 0AA

Tel: 01223 741300
Fax: 01223 300765
E-mail: hw374@cam.ac.uk

Enquiries to: Archivist

Founded: 1972; incorporates the former Congregational Historical Society, Presbyterian Historical Society of England and Churches of Christ Historical Society

Organisation type and purpose: Learned society (membership is by subscription), present number of members: 250.

Subject coverage: Denominational church history, in particular that of the United Reformed Church in England and Wales, the Congregational Church of England and Wales and the Presbyterian Church of England.

Collection: Library of Presbyterian Church of England and central/organisational archives of that church
Carruthers Collection of 17th-century dissenting pamphlets

Non-library collection catalogue: All or part available in-house

Library catalogue: All or part available online and in-house

Publications: Printed
Order printed publications from: Address above

Access to staff: Contact by letter, by telephone, by fax and by e-mail.
Appointment necessary. Non-members charged.
Hours: Mon, Wed, Thurs, 0900 to 1600

Access to building: Mon, Wed, Thu, 0900 to 1600

Access for disabled people: *Hours:* Mon, Wed, Thu, 0900 to 1600

UNITED SOCIETY FOR CHRISTIAN LITERATURE (USCL)

Park Place, 12 Lawn Lane, London SW8 1UD

Tel: 020 7582 3535
Fax: 020 7735 7617
E-mail: info@feedtheminds.org

Enquiries to: Information Officer

Founded: 1799

Organisation type and purpose: Registered charity (charity number 226512).

Subject coverage: Christian literature in developing countries, including development of publishing houses through training, etc., training of pastors and ministers.

Collection: Lutterworth Press archive, held at SOAS, London

Publications: Printed

Access to staff: Contact by letter, by telephone, by fax and by e-mail. Appointment necessary.
Hours: Mon to Fri, 0900 to 1700

Links with: Feed the Minds; at the same address

UNITED SOCIETY FOR THE PROPAGATION OF THE GOSPEL (USPG)

Formal name: United Society for the Propagation of the Gospel

Harling House (4th floor), 47–51 Great Suffolk Street, London, SE1 0BS

Tel: 020 7921 2200 or 0845 273 1701
Fax: 020 7921 2222
E-mail: enquiries@uspg.org.uk
Website: www.uspg.org.uk
Website: shop.uspg.org.uk/acatalog

Enquiries to: Supporter Care Coordinator
Other contacts: Archivist (for archival and historical enquiries)

Founded: 1701; created by the merger of Society for the Propagation of the Gospel in Foreign Parts
Universities' Mission to Central Africa
Cambridge Mission to Delhi (joined USPG in 1968) (year of change 1965)

Organisation type and purpose: Voluntary organisation, registered charity (charity number 234518).
USPG is an Anglican mission agency, which works in direct partnership with Anglican Churches in over 50 countries, helping to support vital church work, including healthcare, education, leadership training and action for social justice.

Subject coverage: Anglican church life and mission in many areas of the world, predominantly but not exclusively in the Commonwealth.
The Archive contains the records of USPG and its predecessor Societies from 1701 onwards, including information about former missionaries of the Societies.

Collection: Photograph library (current collection of prints, slides and digital images).
The Society's archives from approximately 1965, plus all files on individual missionaries from the mid-19th century onwards.
Most of the archives to 1965 are at the Rhodes House Library, South Parks Road, Oxford, OX1 3RG and these include:
The historic library collection
Photographs to the 1950s
Records of the Society for the Propagation of the Gospel, 1701–1965
Records of the Universities' Mission to Central Africa, 1858–1965
Records of the Cambridge Mission to Delhi, 1877–1968.

Non-library collection catalogue: All or part available in-house

Publications: Printed, and electronic and video, and microform publications
Order printed publications from: USPG
Order microform publications from: Microform Academic Publishers, Main Street, East Ardsley, Wakefield, WF3 2AT; tel: 01924 825700; website: http//www.microform.co .uk
Order electronic and video publications from: USPG

Publications list: Available online

Access to staff: Contact by letter, by telephone, by fax, by e-mail and via website. Appointment necessary.
Hours: Mon to Fri, 0900 to 1700
Special comments: The Archivist's post is part time.

Member organisation of: Churches Network for Mission; tel: 020 7901 4090; fax: 020 7901 4894; e-mail: info@ctbi.org.uk; Partnership for World Mission (PWM); tel: 020 7898 1328; e-mail: pwm@c-of-e.org.uk

UNITED SYNAGOGUE AGENCY FOR JEWISH EDUCATION (AJE)

Bet Meir Building, 44b Albert Road, Hendon, London, NW4 2SG

Tel: 020 8457 9700
Fax: 020 8457 9707
E-mail: info@aje.org.uk
Website: www.aje.org.uk

Enquiries to: Resource Centre Manager
Direct tel: 020 8457 9717
Direct e-mail: resources@aje.org.uk

Founded: 1995; formed from United Synagogue Board of Religious Education; formed from Institute of Jewish Education (year of change 1995); formerly called Agency for Jewish Education (year of change 2004)

Organisation type and purpose: Membership association, registered charity, training organisation, publishing house. Education resource centre.

Subject coverage: All aspects of Jewish Studies teaching, training and information.

Collection: Education Library containing books on Jewish Studies and teaching methodology

Publications: Printed

Publications list: Available online

Access to staff: Contact by letter, by telephone, by fax, by e-mail, in person and via website. Appointment necessary. Non-members charged.
Hours: Mon to Thu, 0900 to 1700; Fri, 0900 to 1300

UNITED WORLD COLLEGE OF THE ATLANTIC LIMITED (UWC AC)

St Donat's Castle, Llantwit Major, Vale of Glamorgan, CF61 1WF

Tel: 01446 799000
Fax: 01446 799013
E-mail: principal@atlanticcollege.org
Website: www.atlanticcollege.org

Enquiries to: Principal
Other contacts: Director of College Operations

Founded: 1962

Organisation type and purpose: International organisation, registered charity.
International residential 6th form college. International understanding through education and service.

Subject coverage: International baccalaureate, international education, emergency sea rescue services, community service, environmental monitoring (marine).

Publications: Printed

Access to staff: Contact by letter, by telephone, by fax, by e-mail and via website. Appointment necessary.
Hours: Mon to Fri, 0830 to 1630

Access to building: Only by prior appointment

UNITED WORLD COLLEGES (INTERNATIONAL) (UWC)

Formal name: The United World Colleges (International) Ltd

Second floor, 17–21 Emerald Street, London, WC1N 3QN

Tel: 020 7269 7800
Fax: 020 7405 4374
E-mail: uwcio@uwc.org
Website: www.uwc.org

Enquiries to: Executive Director
Other contacts: Communications Co-ordinator

Founded: 1962

Organisation type and purpose: International organisation, membership association (membership is by qualification), present number of members: 33,000, voluntary organisation, registered charity (charity number 313690), suitable for ages: 16 to 19.
The UWC International Office is a co-ordinating office for an international educational movement. The aims of the movement are international education for responsible citizenship with emphasis on service, peace, justice, international understanding and environmental concern.

Publications: Printed, and electronic and video

Access to staff: Contact by letter, by telephone, by fax and by e-mail
Hours: Mon to Fri, 0900 to 1730
Special comments: Closed weekends and holidays.

A member college is: United World College of the Atlantic; St. Donat's Castle, Llantwit Major, Vale of Glamorgan, CF61 1WF; tel: 01446 799000; fax: 01446 799013; e-mail: principal@uwcac.uwc.org

Has: 12 Member Colleges; 132 National Committees

UNIVERSITIES AND COLLEGES ADMISSIONS SERVICE (UCAS)

Rosehill, New Barn Lane, Cheltenham, Gloucestershire, GL52 3LZ

Tel: 01242 544879; minicom no. 01242 544942
Fax: 01242 544954
Website: www.ucas.com

continued overleaf

Enquiries to: Director of Outreach Department
Direct tel: 0870 1122211 (for information and advice on application to higher education)
Direct e-mail: g.jordan@ucas.ac.uk

Founded: 1993

Organisation type and purpose: Higher education admissions service. Managed by representatives of universities and schools.

Subject coverage: Applications for admission to full-time and sandwich first degree, diploma HND, HNC, and Certificate of Higher Education courses at United Kingdom universities (not Open University) and in most colleges of higher education; also manages separate systems for diplomas in social work, nursing and midwifery, and for postgraduate teacher training; promotion of opportunities available in higher education.

Trade and statistical information: Application statistics and related information on access to higher education

Publications: Printed, and electronic and video
Order printed publications from: tel: 01242 544610; e-mail: distribution@ucas.ac.uk

Access to staff: Contact by letter, by telephone, by fax, by e-mail and via website
Hours: Mon to Fri, 0900 to 1700

Access for disabled people: Parking provided, level entry

UNIVERSITIES FEDERATION FOR ANIMAL WELFARE (UFAW)

The Old School, Brewhouse Hill, Wheathampstead, Hertfordshire, AL4 8AN

Tel: 01582 831818
Fax: 01582 831414
E-mail: ufaw@ufaw.org.uk
Website: www.ufaw.org.uk

Enquiries to: Secretary
Other contacts: Scientific Officer (for grants); Editorial Assistant (for Animal Welfare journal); Development Officer (for general scientific information)

Founded: 1926

Organisation type and purpose:
Membership association (membership is by subscription), present number of members: 900, registered charity (charity number 207996), research organisation.
Extensive publications and educational aids on animal welfare.
Promotion of humane behaviour towards wild and domestic animals in the UK and abroad.

Subject coverage: Care and management of laboratory, farm, wild, zoo and companion animals, humane killing, pest control, welfare of animals in the wild.

Publications: Printed, and electronic and video

Publications list: Available in print

Access to staff: Contact by letter, by telephone, by fax and by e-mail.
Appointment necessary.
Hours: Mon to Fri, 0900 to 1600

Access to building: Prior appointment required

UNIVERSITY AND COLLEGE UNION (SCOTLAND) (UCU (Scotland))

6 Castle Street, Edinburgh, EH2 3AT

Tel: 0131 226 6694
Fax: 0131 226 2066
E-mail: edinburgh@ucu.org.uk
Website: www.ucu.org.uk

Other contacts: Research Officer

History of institution: Association of University Teachers (Scotland)

Organisation type and purpose: Trade union.

Subject coverage: Professional and trade union interests of academic and academically-related staff in Scottish Universities; University teaching, quality assurance and research in Scotland.

Access to staff: Contact by letter, by telephone, by fax and by e-mail.
Appointment necessary.
Hours: Mon to Fri, 0900 to 1645

Affiliated to: Scottish Trades Union Congress

UNIVERSITY ASSOCIATION FOR CONTEMPORARY EUROPEAN STUDIES (UACES)

UACES Secretariat, King's College London, Strand, London, WC2R 2LS

Tel: 020 7240 0206
Fax: 020 7240 0206
E-mail: admin@uaces.org
Website: www.uaces.org

Enquiries to: Executive Director

Founded: 1970

Organisation type and purpose:
International organisation, professional body (membership is by subscription), present number of members: 800, registered charity (charity number 274470).

Subject coverage: Contemporary European studies, European integration, European Union.

Publications: Printed, and electronic and video
Order printed publications from:
Contemporary European Studies Series, Sheffield Academic Press, c/o Orca Book Services, Stanley House, 3 Fleets Lane, Poole, Dorset, BH15 3AJ, tel: 01202 665 432, fax: 01202 666 219
For Journal of Common Market Studies/The EU: Annual Review, Contemporary European Studies Series, Blackwell Publishers, PO Box 805, 108 Cowley Road, Oxford, OX4 1FH, tel: 01865 244083, fax: 01865 381381, e-mail: jnlinfo@blackwellpublishers.co.uk

Publications list: Available online and in print

Access to staff: Contact by letter, by fax, by e-mail and via website
Hours: Mon to Fri, 0900 to 1700

UNIVERSITY COLLEGE FALMOUTH LIBRARY

Woodlane, Falmouth, Cornwall, TR11 4RH

Tel: 01326 213815
Fax: 01326 213827
E-mail: library@falmouth.ac.uk
Website: www.falmouth.ac.uk

Enquiries to: Head of Library and Information Services
Direct tel: extn 3815
Direct e-mail: dawn.lawrence@falmouth.ac.uk

History of institution: formerly called Falmouth School of Art and Design

Organisation type and purpose: University department or institute.

Subject coverage: Undergraduate and postgraduate courses in art, design, media and performance. See website for full details.

Collection: 35,000 books/exhibition catalogues
230 current journal subjects in art, design and media studies
Journals Collection – extensive range of contemporary international art and design titles
Broadcasting; journalism, media collection
Illustrated books and graphic novels special collection
Contemporary artists catalogues
Video library (art, film, general)
Cornwall artists

Publications: Printed, and electronic and video

Access to staff: Contact by letter, by telephone, by e-mail and via website.
Appointment necessary.
Hours: Term time: Mon to Thu, 0900 to 2000; Fri, 0900 to 1700; Sat, 1000 to 1800; Sun 1300 to 1800
Vacations: Mon to Fri, 0900 to 1700

Access for disabled people: Level entry, access to all public areas, toilet facilities

UNIVERSITY COLLEGE LONDON – BARTLETT LIBRARY

Formal name: UCL Bartlett Built Environment Library

5th Floor, Wates House, 22 Gordon Street, London, WC1H 0QB

Tel: 020 7679 4900
Fax: 020 7679 7373
E-mail: library@ucl.ac.uk
Website: www.ucl.ac.uk/library

Enquiries to: Librarian

Organisation type and purpose: University library.

Subject coverage: Architecture, town planning, construction management, development planning.

Library catalogue: All or part available online

Access to staff: Contact by e-mail.
Appointment necessary.
Hours: Term time: Mon – Fri, 0900 to 2000; Sat, 0930 to 1630
Vacation: Mon to Fri, 0930 to 1900

Constituent part of: University College London Library; tel: 020 7679 4900; fax: 020 7679 7373; e-mail: library@ucl.ac.uk

UNIVERSITY COLLEGE LONDON – CRUCIFORM LIBRARY

Cruciform Building, Gower Street, London, WC1E 6BT

Tel: 020 7679 6079
Fax: 020 7679 6981
E-mail: clinscilib@ucl.ac.uk
Website: www.ucl.ac.uk/library/crucilib .shtml

Enquiries to: Librarian

Founded: 1907

Organisation type and purpose: University department or institute.

Subject coverage: Clinical medicine, urology

Library catalogue: All or part available online

Access to staff: Contact by letter, by telephone, by e-mail, in person and via website. Appointment necessary. Non-members charged.
Hours: Mon to Fri, 0900 to 1700

Access for disabled people: Ramped entry, toilet facilities
Special comments: Internal lift.

Part of: Royal Free and University College Medical School; UCL Library Services

UNIVERSITY COLLEGE LONDON – JEWISH STUDIES COLLECTION

Gower Street, London, WC1E 6BT

Tel: 020 7679 7793
Fax: 020 7679 7373
E-mail: library@ucl.ac.uk
Website: www.ucl.ac.uk/library

Enquiries to: Jewish Studies Librarian
Direct tel: 020 7679 2598
Direct e-mail: v.freedman@ucl.ac.uk

Founded: 1826

Organisation type and purpose: University library.
Library of the Jewish Historical Society of England.
Incorporates the former Mocatta Library.

Subject coverage: Jewish history, Hebrew and Semitic languages, Bible, Rabbinic literature, mysticism, Jewish philosophy, Hebrew literature and Yiddish language and literature.

Services for disabled people: Alternative-format leaflets, catalogue terminal with large-format keyboard and screen, book fetching service, induction loop, visual magnifiers.

Collection: Abramsky Collection
Albert Hyamson Collection
Altmann Collection
Asher Myers Collection
F. D. Mocatta Collection
Lucien Wolf Genealogical Papers
Moses Gaster Papers
Schachar Collection (of Hassidism)
William Margulies Yiddish Library

Non-library collection catalogue: All or part available online

Library catalogue: All or part available online

Publications: Printed
Order printed publications from: e-mail: library@ucl.ac.uk

Access to staff: Contact by letter, by telephone, by fax, by e-mail and in person
Hours: Mon to Fri, 0900 to 1700

Access to building: Membership required for access to main collection; appointment required for access to special collections. See website for details.
Hours: See website

Access for disabled people: Building accessible (entrance, lift); some items inaccessible, but can be fetched by staff; toilet facilities

Constituent part of: University College London

UNIVERSITY COLLEGE LONDON – JOINT LIBRARY OF OPHTHALMOLOGY

Formal name: Joint Library of Ophthalmology, Moorfields Eye Hospital and UCL Institute of Ophthalmology

11–43, Bath Street, London, EC1V 9EL

Tel: 020 7608 6814
E-mail: ophthlib@ucl.ac.uk
Website: www.ucl.ac.uk/library/iophth .shtml

Enquiries to: Librarian
Direct tel: 020 7608 6815
Direct e-mail: d.heatlie@ucl.ac.uk

Founded: 1947

Organisation type and purpose: University department or institute.
Post-graduate and medical research.

Subject coverage: Ophthalmology and visual sciences, clinical optics (postgraduate only).

Collection: Moorfields Museum, displaying ophthalmic instruments
Long runs of journals in European languages
Collection of Historical Works on ophthalmology, optics and visual science, including
Sir Edward Nettleship Papers and watercolour paintings of the eye.

Library catalogue: All or part available online

Access to staff: Contact by letter, by telephone and by e-mail. Appointment necessary. Non-members charged.
Hours: Mon to Fri, 0900 to 1700

The Joint Library of Ophthalmology serves the employees of: Moorfields Eye Hospital NHS Foundation Trust and UCL Institute of Ophthalmology

UNIVERSITY COLLEGE LONDON – LIBRARY OF THE INSTITUTE OF ARCHAEOLOGY

31–34 Gordon Square, London, WC1H 0PY

Tel: 020 7679 7485
Fax: 020 7383 2572
E-mail: library@ucl.ac.uk
Website: library.ucl.ac.uk/

Enquiries to: Institute Librarian
Direct e-mail: r.kirby@ucl.ac.uk

Other contacts: Library Admission Officer for requests for use of library, cost and access.

Organisation type and purpose: University library, university department or institute.

Subject coverage: Archaeology, particularly general prehistoric, pre-Columbian Latin American, Roman Provinces, Egyptology, pre-Islamic Western Asiatic, Medieval European; environmental archaeology, scientific basis of archaeology; technology and conservation of archaeological material; museology, museum studies and cultural heritage studies.

Collection: Tylecote Collection (archaeometallurgy)
The following have been relocated to The Special Collection Library services at University College:
The Edwards Collection of Egyptology
Air survey photographs of Near Eastern sites
De Navarro Collection (books and journals dealing with La Tène period)
Margaret Wood Collection (English architectural history)
Records of Near Eastern excavations

Library catalogue: All or part available online

Publications: Printed

Access to staff: Contact by letter, by telephone and by e-mail. Appointment necessary. Non-members charged.
Hours: Mon to Fri, 0900 to 1700

Houses the: Institute for Archaeometallurgical Studies

Part of: University College London Library

UNIVERSITY COLLEGE LONDON – LIBRARY OF THE INSTITUTE OF ORTHOPAEDICS

Royal National Orthopaedic Hospital, Brockley Hill, Stanmore, Middlesex, HA7 4LP

Tel: 020 8909 5351
Fax: 020 8909 5390
E-mail: orthlib@ucl.ac.uk
Website: www.ucl.ac.uk/library/iorthlib .shtml

Enquiries to: Institute Librarian

Founded: 1946

Organisation type and purpose: University department or institute.
To form a special collection on orthopaedics.

Subject coverage: Orthopaedics.

Collection: Historical orthopaedic books

Non-library collection catalogue: All or part available online

Library catalogue: All or part available online

Access to staff: Contact by letter, by telephone, by fax, by e-mail and in person. Appointment necessary.
Hours: Mon, Thu, 0830 to 1830; Wed, 0830 to 20.00; Tue, Fri, 0830 to 1700

Access to building: Mon, Thu, 0830 to 1830; Wed, 0830 to 2000; Tue, Fri, 0830 to 1700

Constituent part of: University College London Library; University College London Medical School

UNIVERSITY COLLEGE LONDON – LIBRARY SERVICES

Gower Street, London, WC1E 6BT

Tel: 020 7387 7793
Fax: 020 7380 7373
E-mail: library@ucl.ac.uk
Website: www.ucl.ac.uk/library

Enquiries to: Director of Library Services
Direct tel: 020 7380 7834
Direct e-mail: p.ayris@ucl.ac.uk

Founded: 1826

Organisation type and purpose: University Library.

Subject coverage: UCL Main Library:
Arts, Humanities, Languages and Social Sciences.
UCL Science Library:
Engineering, Life Sciences, Mathematical and Physical Sciences.
Archway Healthcare Library:
Medicine, Nursing and Allied Health.
UCL Bartlett Library:
Architecture, Town Planning.
UCL Cruciform Library:
General Clinical and Medical Sciences.
UCL Ear Institute and RNID Libraries at the Royal National Throat, Nose and Ear Hospital:
Otorhinolaryngology, Audiology, Deaf Studies.
UCL Eastman Dental Institute Library:
Oral Health Sciences.
UCL Institute of Archaeology Library:
Archaeology, Egyptology.
UCL Institute of Child Health Library:
Paediatrics, International Child Health, Paediatric Nursing, Allied Health.
UCL Institute of Neurology, Queen Square Library:
Neurosurgery, Neuroscience.
Joint Moorfields Eye Hospital & the Institute of Ophthalmology Library:
Ophthalmology, Visual Science, Biomedicine, Medicine, Nursing.
UCL Institute of Orthopaedics Library:
Musculoskeletal Sciences, Orthopaedics.
UCL Language & Speech Science Library:
(NICeST: National Information Centre for Speech/Language Therapy), Speech & Language Therapy, Communication Disorders, Linguistics & Phonetics, Special Education, Audiology, Voice.
Royal Free Medical Library, UCL Library Services:
General Clinical and Medical Sciences.
UCL School of Pharmacy Library:
Pharmaceutical Sciences, Pharmacognosy, Pharmacology & Biomedicine.
UCL School of Slavonic & East European Studies Library and Information Services:
Languages, Literature, History, Politics, Economics, Geography and Bibliography of Eastern Europe.
UCL Special Collections:
Medieval period to present day, wide range of subject areas.

Collection: For Special Collections see http://www.ucl.ac.uk/library/special-coll/subject

Libraries of Learned Societies housed at UCL:

Folklore Society Library
Gaelic Society of London
Geologists' Association
Hertfordshire Natural History Society
Huguenot Society
Jewish Historical Society of England
London Mathematical Society
Malacological Society
Museums Association
Philological Society
Royal Historical Society
Viking Society for Northern Research Main Library

See http://www.ucl.ac.uk/library/learnsoc for more information.

Non-library collection catalogue: All or part available in-house

Library catalogue: All or part available online

Access to staff: Contact by letter, by telephone, by fax, by e-mail and in person
Hours: Various: see website

Constituent part of: University of London

Houses the: RNID Library for deaf and hard-of-hearing people

UNIVERSITY COLLEGE LONDON – SPECIAL COLLECTIONS (UCL)

Library Services, Gower Sreet, London, WC1E 6BT

Tel: 020 7679 5197
Fax: 020 7679 5157
E-mail: spec.coll@ucl.ac.uk
Website: www.ucl.ac.uk/Library/special-coll/index.shtml

Enquiries to: Archivist

Organisation type and purpose: University library.

Subject coverage: Special collections from the medieval to the present day covering a wide range of subjects. Highlights include the C K Ogden and Graves Libraries of rare books, incunabula and medieval manuscripts, rich in the fields of science, language and literature; 19th-century collections, notably Jeremy Bentham's manuscripts and the papers of Lord Brougham, renowned in the field of social, political, legal and educational reform, as well as particular strengths in medical and scientific innovation; and 20th-century professorial manuscripts, literary collections and papers, notably the Orwell Archive and the Little Magazines collection.

Collection: Some of the more important special collections are:
G C Allen Papers
Bagehot Notebooks
Bank of London and South America archives
Arnold Bennett Papers
Bentham Collection and Manuscripts (Jeremy Bentham 1748–1832)
Joseph Black lecture notes (chemistry)
John Bright letters (1811–1889)
Brougham Papers (Lord Brougham, 1778–1868)
Carswell Drawings
Chadwick
Dante Collection
De Morgan Papers (mathematics)
Early Renaissance Manuscripts
Flaxman Collection (drawings)
Folklore Society Collection and Archives
Sir Ambrose Fleming Papers
Gaelic Society Collection
Hugh Gaitskell Papers
Graves Library
Haldane Papers
Hertfordshire Natural History Society
Laurence Housman Collection (1865–1959)
Hume Tracts
Incunabula
Jewish Studies
Johnston Lavis Collection
Josephus Collection
James Joyce Collection
Learned Society Libraries
London History Collection
London Mathematical Society Archive
Kathleen Lonsdale Papers
Malacological Society
Medieval Manuscripts
Moses Montefiore Collection and family papers
Charles Kay Ogden Library and Papers (including Basic English)
George Orwell Archive
Mervyn Peake Manuscripts
L. S. Penrose Papers
Piranesi Collection (Books)
William Ramsey Papers
Rossetti Letters
Routledge & Kegan Paul Archives
John Russell Papers
Lord Odo Russell Collection
Julia Strachey Papers
Thane Papers
Underground Presses
David M S Watson Papers (palaeontology, zoology, geology)
Sir Arthur Smith Woodward Papers (palaeontology)
J Z Young Papers
Zola Letters

Non-library collection catalogue: All or part available online, in-house and in print

Library catalogue: All or part available online and in-house

Access to staff: Contact by letter, by telephone, by fax, by e-mail, in person and via website. Appointment necessary.
Hours: Mon to Thu, 0930 to 1700; Fri, 0930 to 1645
Closed Sat and Sun

Access to building: Prior appointment required
Hours: Mon to Thu, 0930 to 1700, Fri 0930 to 1645
Closed Sat and Sun
Special comments: Admission is by UCL ID and/or by completing a reader application form for consultation for manuscripts and archives.

UNIVERSITY COLLEGE PLYMOUTH ST MARK AND ST JOHN (UCP Marjon Library)

Derriford Road, Plymouth, Devon, PL6 8BH

Tel: 01752 636700
Fax: 01752 636820
E-mail: wevans@marjon.ac.uk
Website: www.marjon.ac.uk
Website: www.marjon.ac.uk/facilities/library

Enquiries to: Head of Library
Direct tel: 01752 636700 ext.n 4206
Direct e-mail: libraryenquiries@marjon.ac.uk
Other contacts: Senior Assistant Librarian; Assistant Librarian

Founded: 1840

Organisation type and purpose: Registered charity (charity number 312929).
Higher education.

Subject coverage: Education and teacher training, children, youth and community, English language, literature and writing, speech and language therapy, sport, health, coaching and physical education, drama, live music, media, outdoor adventure, English language teaching

Collection: College archive material 1840 to the present

Library catalogue: All or part available online

Access to staff: Contact by letter, by telephone, by fax, by e-mail and via website. Appointment necessary. Non-members charged.
Hours: Term time: Mon to Fri, 0830 to 2000; Sat and Sun, 1000 to 1645
Summer holidays: Mon to Fri, 0900 to 1700

Access for disabled people: Parking provided, ramped entry, toilet facilities, lifts

UNIVERSITY HOSPITAL LEWISHAM

The Robin Stott Library, Education Centre, Lewisham High Street, London, SE13 6LH

Tel: 020 8333 3030 ext 6454
Fax: 020 8333 3247
E-mail: library@uhl.nhs.uk

Enquiries to: Library Manager
Direct tel: 020 8333 3439
Direct e-mail: jane.coyte@uhl.nhs.uk

Founded: 1969

Organisation type and purpose: Trust hospital, multidisciplinary library.
To provide all Trust staff with the evidence base of health care.

Subject coverage: Medicine and subjects allied to medicine, the National Health Service and health services in general.

Library catalogue: All or part available in-house

Publications: Electronic and video

Access to staff: Contact by letter, by telephone, by fax, by e-mail and in person. Appointment necessary.
Hours: Term time: Mon to Thu, 0900 to 1900; Fri, 0900 to 1700
Vacations: Mon to Fri, 0900 to 1700

UNIVERSITY HOSPITALS BRISTOL NHS FOUNDATION TRUST (UHBristol)

University Hospitals, Bristol Learning Resource Centre, Education Centre, Upper Maudlin Street, Bristol, BS2 8AE

Tel: 0117 342 0105
Fax: 0117 917 0161
E-mail: library@uhbristsol.nhs.uk
Website: www.uhbristol.nhs.uk/library

Enquiries to: Librarian
Direct tel: 0117 342 0105
Direct e-mail: library@uhbristol.nhs.uk

Founded: 1957

Organisation type and purpose: Libraries of a teaching hospital.

Subject coverage: All health-related information.

Collection: Richard Smith Bibliographical Collection of Manuscripts (medicine in Bristol in the 18th and 19th centuries; housed in the Bristol City Archives)

Non-library collection catalogue: All or part available online

Library catalogue: All or part available online

Publications: Printed

Access to staff: Appointment necessary.
Hours: Mon to Fri, 0830 to 1630

Access to building: Prior appointment required

Access for disabled people: Access to all public areas

Also at: Bristol Eye Hospital; Bristol General Hospital; Bristol Haematology and Oncology Centre; St Michael's Hospital

UNIVERSITY OF ABERDEEN – DIRECTORATE OF INFORMATION SYSTEMS AND SERVICES: HISTORIC COLLECTIONS, SPECIAL LIBRARIES AND ARCHIVES

Special Collections Centre, University Library, Bedford Road, Aberdeen, AB24 3AA

Tel: 01224 272598
Fax: 01224 273891
E-mail: speclib@abdn.ac.uk
Website: www.abdn.ac.uk/historic

Enquiries to: Reading Room Manager
Direct tel: 01224 273046
Direct e-mail: m.gait@abdn.ac.uk

Founded: 1495; formerly called Aberdeen University Library, Department of Special Collections and Archives (year of change 1997)

Organisation type and purpose: University library.

Subject coverage: Humanism, renaissance science and medicine, maps, Jacobitism, travel and transport, North-East Scotland.

Collection: Gregory Collection (early science and medicine)
Local Collection (NE Scotland)
Local estate papers
Macbean Jacobite Collection
O'Dell Railway Collection
Taylor Psalmody Collection
Theological Library
Bernard C. Lloyd Walter Scott Collection

Non-library collection catalogue: All or part available online and in print

Library catalogue: All or part available online

Access to staff: Contact by letter, by telephone, by fax, by e-mail, in person and via website
Hours: Mon, Tues, Thur, Fri, 0900 to 1630; Wed 1000 to 1630

Access for disabled people: Ramped entry and a lift inside the building

UNIVERSITY OF ABERDEEN – UNIVERSITY LIBRARY

University of Aberdeen, Bedford Road, Aberdeen, AB24 3AA

Tel: +44 (0)1224 273330
Fax: +44 (0)1224 273956
E-mail: library@abdn.ac.uk
Website: www.abdn.ac.uk

Enquiries to: PA to the Librarian
Direct tel: +44 (0)1224 273385
Direct e-mail: e.fowlie@abdn.ac.uk

Founded: 1495; incorporates the former Northern College of Education, Aberdeen Campus Library (year of change 2001); incorporates the former MacRobert Library (year of change 2001); incorporates the former Reid Library, Rowett Research Institute (year of change 2007)

Organisation type and purpose: University library.

Subject coverage: All subjects covered by the Colleges of Arts and Social Sciences (divinity, history and philosophy; education; language and literature; law; social sciences; business school),
Life Sciences and Medicine (biological sciences, medical sciences, medicine, psychology),
Physical Sciences (engineering and physical sciences, geosciences)

Collection: Aberdeen Harbour Board Archives and Local Collection (history of the University and of the North East of Scotland)
Biesenthal Collection (Hebraica)
Celtic literature
European Documentation Centre
George Washington Wilson (Victorian and Edwardian Photographic Archive)
Gregory Collection (history of science and medicine)
Macbean Collection (Jacobites)
Melvin Collection (classics)
Music Scores
O'Dell Collection (railways)
Taylor Collection (psalmody)
Victorian Literature Collection

Non-library collection catalogue: All or part available online

Library catalogue: All or part available online

Access to staff: Contact by letter, by telephone, by fax, by e-mail and in person. Appointment necessary.
Hours: Term time: Mon to Fri, 0800 to 2200; Sat 0900 to 2200; Sun 1100 to 2200
Vacations: Mon to Fri, 0830 to 1700

Constituent bodies: King's Museum; King's Museum, University of Aberdeen, 17 High Street, Old Aberdeen, AB24 3EE.; tel: +44 (0)1224 274330; e-mail: museum@abdn.ac.uk; website: http://www.abdn.ac.uk/library/about/kings-museum/
Medical Library; Medical Library, University of Aberdeen, Polwarth Building, Foresterhill, Aberdeen, AB25 2ZD.; tel: +44 (0)1224 437870; fax: +44 (0)1224 662454; e-mail: medlib@abdn.ac.uk; website: http://www.abdn.ac.uk/library/about/med/
Reid Library; The Rowett Institute of Nutrition and Health, University of Aberdeen, Greenburn Road, Bucksburn, Aberdeen, AB21 9SB; tel: +44 (0)1224 438703; e-mail: library@rowett.ac.uk; website: http://www.abdn.ac.uk/library/about/reid-library/

continued overleaf

Special Collections Centre; University Library, University of Aberdeen, Bedford Road, Aberdeen, AB24 3AA; tel: +44 (0)1224 272598; fax: +44 (0)1224 273891; e-mail: speclib@abdn.ac.uk; website: http://www.abdn.ac.uk/library/about/special/
Taylor Library; Taylor Library, University of Aberdeen, Taylor Building, Old Aberdeen, AB24 3UB; tel: +44 (0)1224 272601; fax: +44 (0)1224 273893; e-mail: lawlib@abdn.ac.uk; website: http://www.abdn.ac.uk/library/about/taylor/
University Library; University Library, University of Aberdeen, Bedford Road, Aberdeen, AB24 3AA; tel: +44 (0)1224 273600; fax: +44 (0)1224 273956; e-mail: library@abdn.ac.uk; website: http://www.abdn.ac.uk/library/

UNIVERSITY OF ABERTAY DUNDEE (UAD)

Kydd Building, 40 Bell Street, Dundee, DD1 1HG

Tel: 01382 308000
Fax: 01382 308877
E-mail: infodesk@abertay.ac.uk
Website: www.abertay.ac.uk

Enquiries to: Student Recruitment Office
Direct tel: 01382 308080
Direct fax: 01382 308081
Direct e-mail: sro@abertay.ac.uk

Founded: 1888

Organisation type and purpose: International organisation, advisory body, membership association, university library, university department or institute, suitable for ages: all, training organisation, consultancy, research organisation. To provide a high quality learning and scholarly environment for students and staff and to contribute to the development of local companies and the regional economy.

Subject coverage: Undergraduate – accounting, behavioural science, biomedical science, biotechnology, business studies, civil engineering, computer games technology, computer arts, computing, creative sound production, criminological studies, digital forensics, ethical hacking and countermeasures, finance, food and consumer sciences, forensic sciences, game design, golf management, human resource management, law and European business law, management, marketing, media culture and society, mental health nursing, nursing, psychology, sociology, sport and exercise, visual communication, web design.
Postgraduate – bioinformatics, biotechnology, computer games technology, counselling, digital forensics, energy and environment, finance, industrial environmental management, international nursing, management, MBA, oil and gas accounting and finance, psychology.

Non-library collection catalogue: All or part available online

Library catalogue: All or part available online

Publications: Printed, and electronic and video

Publications list: Available online and in print

Access to staff: Contact by letter, by telephone, by fax, by e-mail and via website. Appointment necessary.
Hours: Mon to Fri, 0845 to 1700

Access to building: No access other than to staff
Hours: Term time: Mon to Thu, 0830 to 2200; Fri, 0830 to 2100; Sat, 1000 to 1700; Sun, 1200 to 1700. Vacations: Mon to Fri, 0845 to 1700
Special comments: External membership required for non-members

Access for disabled people: Parking provided, ramped entry, level entry, toilet facilities

UNIVERSITY OF BATH

The Library, Claverton Down, Bath, BA2 7AY

Tel: 01225 385000
Fax: 01225 386229
E-mail: library@bath.ac.uk
Website: www.bath.ac.uk/library

Enquiries to: Office of the University Librarian
Direct tel: 01225 826084

Founded: 1966

Organisation type and purpose: University library.

Subject coverage: Architecture; biological sciences; chemical engineering; chemistry; economics; education; electrical and electronic engineering; management; materials science; mathematics; mechanical engineering; French, German, Italian, Russian and Spanish, modern European studies; modern languages; pharmacy and pharmacology; physics; psychology; social and policy studies; statistics; sports science; medical sciences; computer science.

Collection: The Holburne Museum of Art Library
Pitman Collection (shorthand and phonographic systems, initial teaching alphabet)
Royal Bath & West & Southern Counties Society Library
Watkins/Hudson Industrial Archaeology Collection

Trade and statistical information: European Documentation Centre and other statistical compilations

Non-library collection catalogue: All or part available online

Library catalogue: All or part available online

Access to staff: Contact by letter, by telephone, by fax, by e-mail and via website. Appointment necessary.
Hours: Term time: Mon to Fri, 0900 to 1900
Special comments: See website: http://www.bath.ac.uk/library

Access for disabled people: Level entry, access to all public areas, toilet facilities

UNIVERSITY OF BEDFORDSHIRE

Park Square, Luton, Bedfordshire, LU1 3JU

Tel: 01582 734111
Fax: 01582 489325
E-mail: admission@beds.ac.uk
Website: www.beds.ac.uk
Website: www.lrweb.beds.ac.uk

Enquiries to: Librarian
Direct tel: 01582 489312
Direct e-mail: tim.stone@luton.ac.uk

Founded: 2006

Organisation type and purpose: University library.

Subject coverage: Business; health care and social studies; management; media studies, nursing, psychology, biology and geology.

Non-library collection catalogue: All or part available online

Library catalogue: All or part available online

Access to staff: Contact by letter
Hours: Mon to Thu, 0830 to 2200

Access to building: Prior appointment required

Access for disabled people: Level entry, access to all public areas, toilet facilities

UNIVERSITY OF BIRMINGHAM – EDUCATION LIBRARY

Edgbaston, Birmingham, B15 2TT

Tel: 0121 414 5828
Fax: 0121 471 4691
E-mail: library@bham.ac.uk
Website: www.is.bham.ac.uk/education/

Enquiries to: Librarian

Organisation type and purpose: University library.

Subject coverage: Education, special education, education management, educational psychology, curriculum subjects particularly: religious education, English, maths, geography, history, modern languages, science, physical education.

Collection: Archives of the British Association of Teachers of the Deaf (BATOD)

Access to staff: Contact by letter, by telephone, by fax and by e-mail. Appointment necessary.
Hours: Mon to Fri, 0900 to 1700

UNIVERSITY OF BIRMINGHAM – LIBRARY SERVICES

Edgbaston, Birmingham, B15 2TT

Tel: 0121 414 5828
Fax: 0121 471 4691
E-mail: library@bham.ac.uk
Website: www.library.bham.ac.uk/
Website: www.birmingham.ac.uk/libraries/index.aspx

Enquiries to: Director of Library Services
Direct tel: 0121 414 4740

Founded: 1880; formerly called Information Services (year of change 1997)

Organisation type and purpose: University library.

Subject coverage: All subjects taught and researched at the University of Birmingham. Arts: American studies; ancient history and archaeology; Canadian studies; classical studies (Latin, classical and modern Greek, Byzantine and Ottoman studies); drama and theatre arts; Dutch; English; film studies; fine art; French studies; German studies; history; Italian; linguistics; Middle and Near Eastern ancient history; music; philosophy; Romanian; Russian and other Slavonic languages (e.g. Czech, Polish, Serbo-Croat); Scandinavian (Danish, Icelandic, Norwegian, Swedish); Spanish and Portuguese (including Latin America); theology; cultural studies; West African studies; commerce and social sciences: accounting and finance; business; development administration; economic and social history; economics; education; international studies; local government studies; management; political science; Russian and East European studies; social administration; social policy; social work; sociology; urban and regional studies; law (all in the Harding Law Library); medicine (all in the Barnes Medical Library): anaesthetics; anatomy; cancer studies; general practice; geriatric medicine; haematology; immunology; intensive care; medical microbiology; medicine; neurology; neurosurgery; nursing studies; obstetrics and gynaecology; occupational health; paediatrics and child health; pathology; pharmacology; physiology; psychiatry; rheumatology; public health and epidemiology; social medicine; surgery; dentistry (all in the Ronald Cohen Dental Library, in the Birmingham Dental Hospital); physical education and recreation; sports science; science and engineering as follows: biochemistry; computer science; earth sciences; mathematics and statistics; physics; space research; chemistry; biological sciences (including botany, environmental health, genetics, microbiology, zoology and comparative physiology); psychology; geography; manufacturing and mechanical engineering; civil engineering; electronic and electrical engineering; chemical engineering; metallurgy and materials; minerals engineering.

Collection: Cadbury Research Library
Alma Tadema Collection
Birmingham and West Midlands general local history (including Canal Collection, Cannock Chase Colliery Collection, Priestley Collection, Seward Letters, Slade-Baker Correspondence, West Midland Group on Post-War Planning and Reconstruction Papers)
British business and economic history of the eighteenth to twentieth centuries (including British Cotton Growing Association Papers, Cadbury Papers, Canal Collection, Cannock Chase Colliery Collection, Nineteenth Century Industry Collection)
British Nonconformist history (including Catholic Apostolic Church Collection, Dale Papers, Martineau Collection, Weatherhead Archive)
British Recusant history (including Jerningham Letters, Little Malvern Court Collection)
Church of England history in the nineteenth and twentieth centuries (including Dr Ernest William Barnes, Bishop of Birmingham 1924–1953 Papers, Church Missionary Society Papers, Church Pastoral Aid Society Papers, Stafford Letters)
English literature and drama (including Edgeworth Letters, Marsh Letters, Harriet Martineau Collection, Mill Collection, Modern Poetry Collection, Nicoll Collection, Reed Collection, Seward Letters, Theatre Collection, Wedgwood Collection (philology), Francis Brett Young Collection, David Lodge papers, Noel Coward collection)
English political and related archives of the nineteenth and twentieth centuries (including Lord Avon Papers, Chamberlain Papers (Arthur Neville, Joseph and Sir Joseph Austen), Dale Papers, Dawson Papers, Dixon Letters, Masterman Papers)
General theology and Church history (including Bengeworth Library, Hetherington Collection, St Mary's Warwick Parish Library, Thomas Wigan Library of 17th and 18th century literature and theology)
History of The University of Birmingham
History of science (including Priestley Collection)
Printing history (including Baskerville Collection, Birmingham School of Printing Collection, Bodoni Collection of Early Italian Books, English Special Period 1660–69, Foulis Collection, Kelmscott Press Collection, Mandeville Press Collection, Sceptre Press Collection, Shakespeare Head Press Collection)
Russian history of the late nineteenth and early twentieth centuries (including Dolgorukov Papers, Pashkov Papers, Shishkin Papers)
West Africana (including Bradbury Papers, British Cotton Growing Association Papers, Cadbury Papers (mainly photographs of archaeological interest), Church Missionary Society Papers, Matacong Island Papers)
Archives of special educational associations (National Special Schools Union, National Association of Teachers of the Deaf)
Other English general local and family history (including Jerningham Letters, Mingana collection of Middle Eastern historical manuscripts, Mytton Papers, Shaw Letters, Stafford Letters)
Barber Fine Art Library
Art and architecture topography
Items related to specific works of art in the Barber Collection
Sale catalogues and the history of collecting
Barber Music Library
Barber Opera Archive
Early 20th century classical recordings
English and European instrumental music (including Feeney Collection, Shaw-Hellier Collection)
English and European musical treatises and libretti of the seventeenth and eighteenth centuries
English and European vocal music of the seventeenth and eighteenth centuries (including Shaw-Hellier Collection)
Granville Bantock Collection
Barnes Library
History of medicine (including Birmingham Medical Institute Historical Collection, William Withering Collection)
Baykov Library (European Resource Centre)
History and social sciences of pre- and, especially, post-Revolutionary Russia and of Ukraine, Poland, Hungary and most of the republics of the former Soviet Union (including Pares Collection)
Sports history (especially Olympic Games and athletics, including Abrahams Collection)
Sports science
The Ronald Cohen Dental Library
History of dentistry
Education Library
Children's books, c. 1790–1970
History of education
Mathematics textbooks
Harding Law Library
History of English law
Shakespeare Institute Library
Corelli Collection
18th to 20th century editions of Shakespeare
English Renaissance literature
History of drama and the theatre (including Press Cuttings Collection)
Sources and analogues for Shakespeare's plays

Non-library collection catalogue: All or part available online and in print

Library catalogue: All or part available online

Publications list: Available online

Access to staff: Contact by letter, by telephone, by fax, by e-mail, in person and via website. Appointment necessary. All charged.
Hours: Mon to Fri, 0900 to 1700

Access to building: Full information regarding building access at http://www.birmingham.ac.uk/libraries/info/index.aspx
Special comments: ID required for non-members; limited number of visits per year

Access for disabled people: Parking provided, level entry, access to all public areas, toilet facilities

UNIVERSITY OF BIRMINGHAM – ORCHARD LEARNING RESOURCES CENTRE (OLRC)

Hamilton Drive, Weoley Park Road, Selly Oak, Birmingham, B29 6QW

Tel: 0121 415 8454
Fax: 0121 415 8476
E-mail: olrc@bham.ac.uk
Website: www.olrc.bham.ac.uk

Enquiries to: Library Services Manager
Direct tel: 0121 414 8598
Direct e-mail: d.n.vuong@bham.ac.uk

Founded: 1997; formerly called Selly Oak Colleges Central Library, Westhill College of Higher Education

Organisation type and purpose: University department or institute.

Subject coverage: Art in general, dance and movement, English literature, history, Islamics, leisure, physical education, religious education, Christian ministry, missiology, theology.
Christian theology; Bible; Islam and Christian-Muslim relations; Judaism; world religions; community welfare; social work; overseas development studies; church overseas; church history; mission studies; English as a foreign language; peace studies; Syriac studies; education; Quaker studies (in Woodbrooke College).

Publications: Printed, and microform publications

Access to staff: Contact by letter, by fax, by e-mail and via website. Appointment necessary.
Hours: Mon to Fri, 0900 to 1700

Access to building: Prior appointment required

continued overleaf

Hours: Mon to Fri, 0900 to 1700

Access for disabled people: Parking provided, toilet facilities

Parent body: University of Birmingham; Library Services, Main Library, Edgbaston, Birmingham, B15 2TT; tel: 0121 414 5805; fax: 0121 471 4691; e-mail: library@bham.ac.uk

UNIVERSITY OF BOLTON

Deane Road, Bolton, Lancashire, BL3 5AB

Tel: 01204 903090
Fax: 01204 903166
E-mail: christine.smith@bolton.ac.uk
Website: www.bolton.ac.uk

Enquiries to: Collection Development Manager
Direct tel: 01204 903563
Other contacts: Library Administrator

Founded: 1982; formerly called Bolton Art College, Bolton College of Education (Technical), Bolton Institute of Technology, Bolton Institute of Higher Education (year of change 2005)

Organisation type and purpose: Educational institution.

Subject coverage: Textiles, business studies, psychology, electrical, mechanical and civil engineering, teacher education (FE/HE), art and design.

Library catalogue: All or part available online

Publications list: Available online

Access to staff: Contact via website. Non-members charged.
Hours: Mon to Fri, 0845 to 2100; Sat, 0930 to 1230

Access for disabled people: Access to all public areas, toilet facilities

Member organisation of: SCONUL NoWAL

UNIVERSITY OF BRADFORD – LEARNING SUPPORT SERVICES

Richmond Road, Bradford, West Yorkshire, BD7 1DP

Tel: 01274 233301\ Minicom no. 01274 233687
Fax: 01274 233398
E-mail: Library@bradford.ac.uk
Website: www.brad.ac.uk/lss/library

Enquiries to: Librarian
Direct e-mail: p.m.ketley@bradford.ac.uk

Founded: 1966

Organisation type and purpose: University Library.

Collection: Arthur Raistrick Map Collection
Calvin Wells Collection (archaeological sciences)
Commonweal Collection – non-violence and peace
History of Dyeing Collection
History of Pharmacy Collection
Mitrinovic Library
WR Mitchell Collection (the 'Dalesman' archive)
The Joel M Halpern Balkan Collection
The Waddington – Feather Collection (Yorkshire dialect and poetry)
JB Priestley Collection

Library catalogue: All or part available online

Access to staff: Contact by letter
Hours: Mon to Fri, 0845 to 1730

Access for disabled people: Level entry, access to all public areas, toilet facilities

Includes the: Health Studies Library; tel: 01274 236375; fax: 01274 236470; J B Priestley Library; Yvette Jacobson Library (Management Library); tel: 01274 234401; fax: 01274 234398

UNIVERSITY OF BRIGHTON – EASTBOURNE SITE

The Queenwood Library, Darley Road, Eastbourne, East Sussex, BN20 7UN

Tel: 01273 643822
Fax: 01273 643825
E-mail: askqueenwood@brighton.ac.uk
Website: library.brighton.ac.uk

Enquiries to: Information Services Manager
Direct tel: 01273 643820
Other contacts: User Services Librarian (for most appropriate opening hours, membership queries)

Founded: 1992; created by the merger of Queenwood Library with the Welkin Library and the Podiatry Library (Leaf Hospital) (year of change 2000)

Organisation type and purpose: University library.

Subject coverage: Queenwood Library: physical education, dance, sports and exercise science, leisure and sports studies/ management; physiotherapy, occupational therapy, nursing, podiatry; service management, tourism, hospitality, culinary arts and event management; retail marketing; policing studies
Health Sciences Library, Eastbourne District General Hospital: nursing, midwifery, medicine.

Access to staff: Contact by letter and by telephone. Appointment necessary.
Hours: Mon to Fri, 0900 to 1730

Access for disabled people: Parking provided, ramped entry, access to all public areas, toilet facilities

Also at: Eastbourne District General Hospital Health Sciences Library; King's Drive, Eastbourne, East Sussex, BN21 2UD; tel: 01323 417400 ext n 4048

UNIVERSITY OF BRIGHTON – GRAND PARADE SITE

St Peter's House Library, 16–18 Richmond Place, Brighton, BN2 9NA

Tel: 01273 643221
Fax: 01273 607532
E-mail: asksph@brighton.ac.uk
Website: library.brighton.ac.uk
Website: www.brighton.ac.uk

Enquiries to: Enquiry Desk Team

Founded: 1992

Organisation type and purpose: University library.

Subject coverage: Art and design history, fine arts, graphic design, photography, fashion and textiles, crafts, performing arts, humanities.

Library catalogue: All or part available online

Publications: Printed

Access to staff: Contact by letter, by telephone, by fax, by e-mail, in person and via website

Access to building: *Hours:* Term time: Mon to Thu, 0900 to 2000; Fri, 0900 to 1800; Sat, Sun, 1300 to 1700
Vacations: Mon to Fri, 0900 to 1700

Access for disabled people: Ground floor only

UNIVERSITY OF BRISTOL – LIBRARY

Tyndall Avenue, Bristol, BS8 1TJ

Tel: 0117 928 8000
Fax: 0117 925 5334
E-mail: library-enquiries@bristol.ac.uk
Website: www.bristol.ac.uk/library

Enquiries to: Librarian
Other contacts: Special Collections Librarian

Founded: 1876

Organisation type and purpose: University library, with 10 branch libraries.

Subject coverage: Arts, law, social sciences, science, medicine, engineering and education.

Collection: British philosophers
Business histories
Courtesy books
Early English novels
Early mathematics
Early medical works (including some on spas and mineral waters)
Eyles Collection of early geology
Family papers (Dorset and West Indies, 1650–1948)
General election addresses (acquired with the purchase of the National Liberal Club Library)
Historical chemistry
I K Brunel's papers
Landscape gardening
Penguin Publishing Archives
Sir Allen Lane Collection of Penguin Books, most of them signed by their authors
Somerset Miners Association papers
West Indies papers
Wiglesworth Ornithological Library

Non-library collection catalogue: All or part available online and in-house

Library catalogue: All or part available online and in-house

Access to staff: Contact by letter, by telephone, by fax and by e-mail. Appointment necessary.
Hours: Special Collections: Mon to Wed, 0915 to 1845; Thu, 0945 to 1845; Fri, 0915 to 1645

UNIVERSITY OF BUCKINGHAM LIBRARY

Hunter Street, Buckingham, MK18 1EG

Tel: 01280 814080
Fax: 01280 820312

E-mail: library@buckingham.ac.uk
Website: www.buckingham.ac.uk/library

Enquiries to: Assistant Librarian
Direct tel: 01280 820218

Founded: 1976

Organisation type and purpose: University library.

Subject coverage: Law, politics, economics, accounting and finance, management, history, English and modern languages, information systems, psychology.

Collection: Denning Law Library

Library catalogue: All or part available online

Publications: Printed

Access to staff: Contact by letter, by telephone, by fax, by e-mail and in person
Hours: Mon to Fri, 0900 to 1700

UNIVERSITY OF CAMBRIDGE – BALFOUR AND NEWTON LIBRARIES OF THE DEPARTMENT OF ZOOLOGY

Downing Street, Cambridge, CB2 3EJ

Tel: 01223 336600
Fax: 01223 336676
E-mail: library@zoo.cam.ac.uk
Website: www.zoo.cam.ac.uk/library/index.html

Enquiries to: Librarian
Direct tel: 01223 336648
Direct e-mail: library@zoo.cam.ac.uk
Other contacts: Academic Librarian for letter of application to use library.

Organisation type and purpose: University department or institute.
Departmental library. Balfour Library founded 1883, Newton Library founded 1907.

Subject coverage: Zoology and ecology.

Collection: Newton Collection (ornithology and natural history)
Strickland Collection (ornithology)

Non-library collection catalogue: All or part available online

Library catalogue: All or part available online and in-house

Access to staff: Contact by letter, by telephone, by fax, by e-mail and via website. Appointment necessary. Letter of introduction required.
Hours: Mon to Fri, 0830 to 1700
Special comments: Membership is restricted to members of Cambridge University. Application for access by others by letter to the Academic Librarian.

Access to building: Please telephone in advance of your visit
Hours: Mon to Fri, 0830 to 1700

Access for disabled people: Lift, wheelchair accessible, disabled parking, toilet facilities available
Hours: Mon to Fri, 0830 to 1700
Special comments: Please telephone in advance of your visit

UNIVERSITY OF CAMBRIDGE – BETTY AND GORDON MOORE LIBRARY

Wilberforce Road, Cambridge, CB3 0WD

Tel: 01223 765670
Fax: 01223 765678
E-mail: moore-library@lib.cam.ac.uk
Website: www.lib.cam.ac.uk/BGML

Enquiries to: Librarian

Founded: 2001; incorporates the former Department of Applied Mathematics and Theoretical Physics Library, Department of Pure Mathematics and Mathematical Statistics Library, Wishart Library

Organisation type and purpose: University library.

Subject coverage: Mathematics, physics, astronomy, computer science, materials science and engineering.

Collection: University library collections for mathematics, physics, astronomy, computer science, materials science and engineering.

Library catalogue: All or part available online

Access to staff: Contact by letter, by telephone, by e-mail, in person and via website. Appointment necessary.
Hours: Mon to Fri, 0900 to 1700; Sat, 0900 to 1300

Parent body: Cambridge University Library; West Road, Cambridge, CB3 9DR; tel: 01223 333000; fax: 01223 333160; e-mail: library@lib.cam.ac.uk; website: http://www.lib.cam.ac.uk

UNIVERSITY OF CAMBRIDGE – BOTANIC GARDEN

University Botanic Garden, 1 Brookside, Cambridge, CB2 1JE

Tel: 01223 336265
Fax: 01223 336278
E-mail: enquiries@botanic.cam.ac.uk
Website: www.botanic.cam.ac.uk

Enquiries to: Information Officer
Direct tel: 01223 336265
Direct e-mail: enquiries@botanic.cam.ac.uk

Founded: 1762

Organisation type and purpose: University department or institute.
Sub-department library, of the Department of Plant Sciences.

Subject coverage: Taxonomy of vascular plants; horticulture; the history of botany and horticulture; information on plants within the Garden.

Collection: Indexed collection of living plants
Library of books on horticulture and botany
Nurserymen's catalogues
Slide collection of plants

Publications list: Available in print

Access to staff: Contact by letter and by telephone. Appointment necessary.
Hours: Mon to Fri, 0900 to 1700

Houses the: Cory Library

UNIVERSITY OF CAMBRIDGE – CENTRAL SCIENCE LIBRARY

Arts School, Bene't Street, Cambridge, CB2 3PY

Tel: 01223 334742
Fax: 01223 334748
E-mail: lib-csl-inquiries@lists.cam.ac.uk
Website: www.lib.cam.ac.uk/CSL/

Enquiries to: Librarian
Direct tel: 01223 334744
Direct e-mail: mlw1003@cam.ac.uk

Founded: 1820

Organisation type and purpose: University library.

Subject coverage: Biological, chemical, earth and environmental sciences.

Collection: 19th century scientific books
Biffen Collection on plant breeding (reprints)
Buttress Collection (books and journals on agriculture, formerly the library of the Department of Applied Biology)
Marshall Collection on animal reproduction (reprints)

Non-library collection catalogue: All or part available online

Library catalogue: All or part available online

Access to staff: Contact by letter, by e-mail and via website. Appointment necessary.
Hours: Mon to Fri, 0900 to 1700

Originally the library, but still houses the offices, of the: Cambridge Philosophical Society

Parent body: Cambridge University Library

UNIVERSITY OF CAMBRIDGE – CENTRE OF ISLAMIC STUDIES (CIS)

Faculty of Asian and Middle Eastern Studies, Sidgwick Avenue, Cambridge, CB3 9DA

Tel: 01223 335103
Fax: 01223 335110
E-mail: cis@cis.cam.ac.uk
Website: www.cis.cam.ac.uk

Founded: 1960; formerly called Centre of Middle Eastern and Islamic Studies (CMEIS) (year of change 1999)

Organisation type and purpose: University department or institute, consultancy.
Development of a constructive and critical awareness of the role of Islam in wider society, initially through research programmes about Islam in the United Kingdom and Europe.

Subject coverage: Modern history, culture, politics and economics of the Middle East through research and outreach programmes to interact with policy makers and wider society.

Publications: Electronic and video
Order electronic and video publications from: PDF files available online: http://www.cis.cam.ac.uk/Reports.htm

Publications list: Available online

Access to staff: Contact by letter, by telephone, by fax, by e-mail, in person and via website. Appointment necessary.
Hours: Mon to Fri, 0900 to 1700

continued overleaf

Special comments: Questions and queries can usually be answered by mail; of potential use to traders, politicians and academics.

Links with: Faculty of Asian and Middle Eastern Studies; Sidgwick Avenue, Cambridge CB3 9DA; tel: 01223 335106; fax: 01223 335110; e-mail: enquiries@ames.cam .ac.uk; website: http://www.ames.cam.ac.uk

UNIVERSITY OF CAMBRIDGE – COLMAN LIBRARY OF THE DEPARTMENT OF BIOCHEMISTRY

Tennis Court Road, Cambridge, CB2 1QW

Tel: 01223 333600
Fax: 01223 333345
E-mail: librarian@bioc.cam.ac.uk
Website: www.bio.cam.ac.uk/dept/biochem/ColmanLibrary/index.html

Enquiries to: Librarian
Direct tel: 01223 333613

Founded: 1924

Organisation type and purpose: University department or institute.

Subject coverage: Biochemistry.

Collection: Departmental papers
Departmental archives

Non-library collection catalogue: All or part available online

Library catalogue: All or part available online

Publications: Printed

Access to staff: Contact by telephone, by fax, by e-mail and in person. Appointment necessary. Access for members only.
Hours: Mon to Thu, 0830 to 1700; Fri, 0830 to 1600
Special comments: Non-members by arrangement.

Access to building: Card needed
Hours: Mon to Thu, 0830 to 1700; Fri, 0830 to 1600

Access for disabled people: *Hours:* Mon to Thu, 0830 to 1700; Fri, 0830 to 1600

UNIVERSITY OF CAMBRIDGE – FACULTY OF EDUCATION LIBRARY AND INFORMATION SERVICE

184 Hills Road, Cambridge, CB2 8PQ

Tel: 01223 767700
E-mail: library@educ.cam.ac.uk
Website: www.educ.cam.ac.uk/library

Enquiries to: Faculty Librarian

Founded: 2001; formerly called Department of Education, Institute of Education (year of change 1997); formerly called School of Education (year of change 2001)

Organisation type and purpose: University department or institute.

Subject coverage: Education, including educational research, children with special needs, in-service training of teachers and related subjects, e.g. psychology, philosophy, sociology.

Collection: Collections of school textbooks and books on teaching method in the fields of English, classics, modern languages, science (general), physics, chemistry, biology, mathematics, history, geography
Source material on history of education now transferred to University of Cambridge Library.

Library catalogue: All or part available online

Publications: Printed

Access to staff: Contact by letter, by telephone, by e-mail, in person and via website
Hours: Mon to Fri, 0930 to 1700

Parent body: University of Cambridge; website: http://www.cam.ac.uk

UNIVERSITY OF CAMBRIDGE – GEOGRAPHY DEPARTMENT LIBRARY

Department of Geography, Downing Place, Cambridge, CB2 3EN

Tel: 01223 333391
Fax: 01223 333392
E-mail: library@geog.cam.ac.uk
Website: www.lib.cam.ac.uk

Enquiries to: Librarian
Direct e-mail: rcc23@hermes.cam.ac.uk

Organisation type and purpose: University department or institute.

Subject coverage: Geography and its related subjects: ecology, sociology, cultural studies, economics, politics, history and historical geography, cartography, statistics, research techniques, glaciology, some geology, geomorphology, hydrology, climatology, environmental science, environmental policy etc; remote sensing, geographical information systems, urban planning, substantial regional collections covering India, Africa, North and South America, Soviet and post-Soviet Russia.

Collection: Clark Collection (primarily 18th- and 19th-century books on travel and exploration)

Non-library collection catalogue: All or part available online and in-house

Library catalogue: All or part available online

Access to staff: Contact by letter, by telephone, by e-mail and in person
Hours: Term time: Mon to Fri, 0845 to 1800; Sat, 0845 to 1245
Vacations: Mon to Thu, 0900 to 1300 and 1400 to 1630; Fri, 0900 to 1300 and 1400 to 1530; Sat, closed
Special comments: Visitors by prior appointment during term time. Vacation hours may vary, phone in advance.

UNIVERSITY OF CAMBRIDGE – HADDON LIBRARY OF THE FACULTY OF ARCHAEOLOGY AND ANTHROPOLOGY

Downing Street, Cambridge, CB2 3DZ

Tel: 01223 333505/6
Fax: 01223 333503
E-mail: haddon-library@lists.cam.ac.uk
Website: haddon.archanth.cam.ac.uk

Enquiries to: Librarian

Founded: 1920

Organisation type and purpose: University department or institute.

Subject coverage: Archaeology; biological anthropology; social anthropology.

Collection: Burkitt Collection: archaeology (Europe)
Bushnell Collection: archaeology (Americas)
Clarke bequest (archaeology)
De Navarro Collection: archaeology (Europe)
Frazer bequest (anthropology)
McBurney bequest (archaeology)
McBurney Collection: archaeology and anthropology (world-wide)
Offprints
Pitt-Rivers Collection: archaeology and anthropology (19th century)
Rare books collection: c.600 vols, archaeology and anthropology (17th to 19th centuries)

Library catalogue: All or part available online

Access to staff: Contact by letter, by telephone, by fax, by e-mail and in person. Appointment necessary. Letter of introduction required.
Hours: Mon to Fri, 0900 to 1700

Constituent bodies: Cambridge Antiquarian Society Library

UNIVERSITY OF CAMBRIDGE – INSTITUTE OF ASTRONOMY LIBRARY (IoA)

The Observatories, Madingley Road, Cambridge, CB3 0HA

Tel: 01223 337548
Fax: 01223 337523
E-mail: ioalib@ast.cam.ac.uk
Website: www.ast.cam.ac.uk/library

Enquiries to: Departmental Librarian
Direct tel: 01223 337537

Founded: 1823; formerly called Institute of Theoretical Astronomy, Library of the Observatories, Cambridge Observatory Library (year of change 1972)

Organisation type and purpose: University department or institute.
Departmental library.

Subject coverage: Astronomy and astrophysics.

Collection: John Couch Adams Collection of astronomy books, mostly pre-1850

Library catalogue: All or part available online

Access to staff: Contact by letter, by telephone and by e-mail. Appointment necessary.
Hours: Mon to Fri, 0900 to 1700

UNIVERSITY OF CAMBRIDGE – JOINT LIBRARY OF THE FACULTY OF CLASSICS AND MUSEUM OF CLASSICAL ARCHAEOLOGY

Sidgwick Avenue, Cambridge, CB3 9DA

Tel: 01223 335151
Fax: 01223 335409

E-mail: library@classics.cam.ac.uk
Website: www.classics.cam.ac.uk/library

Enquiries to: Librarian

Founded: 1982; created by the merger of Faculty of Classics Library and Museum of Classical Archaeology Library (year of change 1982)

Organisation type and purpose: University department or institute.
Teaching and research needs of the Faculty of Classics.

Subject coverage: Classics, Greek and Latin literature, ancient history, ancient philosophy, classical philology, classical archaeology, classical art, palaeography, epigraphy and modern Greek.

Collection: J. E. Sandys Collection (classical books)
Owen Collection (ancient philosophy books)
Sir Ellis Minns Collection (palaeography)
Sir Stephen Gaselee Collection (palaeography)
William Martin Leake Collection (classical books and notebooks)

Non-library collection catalogue: All or part available online

Library catalogue: All or part available online

Publications: Printed

Access to staff: Contact by letter, by telephone and by e-mail. Appointment necessary. Letter of introduction required.
Hours: Mon to Fri, 0900 to 1700; Sat (term time) 0900 to 1300

Access for disabled people: Level entry, access to all public areas, toilet facilities

UNIVERSITY OF CAMBRIDGE – KANTHACK & NUTTALL LIBRARY OF THE DEPARTMENT OF PATHOLOGY

Tennis Court Road, Cambridge, CB2 1QP

Tel: 01223 333690
Fax: 01223 333346
E-mail: librarian@path.cam.ac.uk
Website: www.path.cam.ac.uk/~library

Enquiries to: Librarian
Direct tel: 01223 333698
Direct fax: 01223 333698
Other contacts: Library Administrator

History of institution: formerly called Nuttall Library; incorporates the former Molteno Institute, Parasitology Library

Organisation type and purpose: University department or institute.

Subject coverage: Pathology; microbiology; virology; immunology; parasitology; oncology.

Non-library collection catalogue: All or part available online and in-house

Access to staff: Contact by letter and by telephone. Appointment necessary. Access for members only.
Hours: Mon to Fri, 0900 to 1600
Special comments: Non-members by prior arrangement.

Access for disabled people: Ramped entry, toilet facilities

UNIVERSITY OF CAMBRIDGE – LIBRARY OF THE ASIAN AND MIDDLE EASTERN STUDIES (FAMES)

Formal name: University of Cambridge – Faculty of Asian and Middle Eastern Studies Library

Sidgwick Avenue, Cambridge, CB3 9DA

Tel: 01223 335111/2
Fax: 01223 335110
E-mail: library@ames.cam.ac.uk
Website: www.ames.cam.ac.uk/faclib/index.html
Website: www.ames.cam.ac.uk

Enquiries to: Head of Library

Founded: 1935

Organisation type and purpose: University department or institute.
Faculty library; the collection of the Middle East Centre.

Subject coverage: Chinese, Japanese, Sanskrit, modern Indian languages, Persian, Turkish, Arabic, Hebrew, Indian history and archaeology, coverage of the language, literature, history, religion and general culture of all countries of the Middle and Far East Indian sub-continent and Central Asia (but excluding south-east Asia).

Collection: I. B. Horner Collection (paper and letters, etc.)
Israel Abrahams Collection (Rabbinics)
Lattimore Collection on Central Asia and Mongolia
Marshall Collection of Indian photographs (5,000 items on Indian monuments and antiquities)
Middle East Centre Library (modern Middle East – especially the Arabian peninsula and Yemen)
Queens' College Oriental Collection
W. Lockhart Collection (Persian)
Wheeler Collection (700 photographs of Indian archaeology)

Non-library collection catalogue: All or part available online

Library catalogue: All or part available online

Access to staff: Contact by letter, by telephone, by e-mail, in person and via website. Appointment necessary. Letter of introduction required.
Hours: Mon to Fri, 0900 to 1730

Access for disabled people: *Special comments:* Appointment needed.

UNIVERSITY OF CAMBRIDGE – LIBRARY OF THE DEPARTMENT OF CHEMISTRY

Lensfield Road, Cambridge, CB2 1EW

Tel: 01223 336300
Fax: 01223 336362
E-mail: library@ch.cam.ac.uk
Website: www-library.ch.cam.ac.uk

Enquiries to: Librarian
Direct tel: 01223 336329
Other contacts: Deputy Librarian

Organisation type and purpose: University department or institute.

Subject coverage: Inorganic, organic, physical and theoretical chemistry.

Library catalogue: All or part available online

Access to staff: Contact by letter, by telephone, by fax, by e-mail, in person and via website. Appointment necessary. Letter of introduction required.
Hours: Mon to Fri, 0800 to 1630

Access for disabled people: By arrangement

UNIVERSITY OF CAMBRIDGE – LIBRARY OF THE DEPARTMENT OF EARTH SCIENCES

Downing Street, Cambridge, CB2 3EQ

Tel: 01223 333400
Fax: 01223 333450
E-mail: libraryhelp@esc.cam.ac.uk
Website: www.esc.cam.ac.uk

Enquiries to: Librarian

Founded: 1980; created by the merger of Departments of Geology, Mineralogy & Petrology and Geodesy & Geophysics (year of change 1980)

Organisation type and purpose: University department or institute.

Subject coverage: Earth sciences, palaeontology, mineralogy, geophysics, mineral physics, climate change.

Collection: Black Collection
Collection of geological reprints
Collection of mineralogical reprints
Godwin Collection
Extensive geological map collection
W A Dear Collection
Bullard Collection
R G West Collection
Sedgwick Collection
Bulman Collection
Harker Collection
N F Hughes Collection
Macfadyen Collection
Tilley Collection
Whittington Collection
Collection of geophysics offprints

Non-library collection catalogue: All or part available online and in-house

Library catalogue: All or part available online

Publications: Printed

Publications list: Available online

Access to staff: Contact by letter, by telephone, by fax, by e-mail, in person and via website. Letter of introduction required.
Hours: Term time: Mon to Fri, 0900 to 1800; Sat, 1000 to 1300
Vacations: Mon to Fri, 0900 to 1700; Sat, closed
Bullard Laboratory Library is staffed for a couple of hours on Mon, Wed and Fri

Access to building: Access to Bullard is only ever by prior arrangement

Also at: Bullard Laboratory Library; Madingley Road, Cambridge; e-mail: libraryhelp@esc.cam.ac.uk

UNIVERSITY OF CAMBRIDGE – LIBRARY OF THE DEPARTMENT OF GENETICS

Downing Street, Cambridge, CB2 3EH

continued overleaf

Tel: 01223 333999
Fax: 01223 333992
E-mail: info@gen.cam.ac.uk
Website: www.gen.cam.ac.uk/department/library/index.html

Enquiries to: Librarian

Organisation type and purpose: University department or institute.

Subject coverage: Genetics; cytology; parts of biochemistry, cell biology.

Collection: Offprints of papers by past department members and eminent geneticists

Non-library collection catalogue: All or part available in-house

Library catalogue: All or part available online

Access to staff: Contact by letter, by telephone, by fax and by e-mail. Appointment necessary.
Hours: Mon to Fri, 0900 to 1700

Access to building: Must be let in by receptionist
Hours: Mon to Fri, 0900 to 1700, excluding lunchtimes

Access for disabled people: Wheelchair lift and push-button for doors
Hours: as above
Special comments: Some parts of library inaccessible.

UNIVERSITY OF CAMBRIDGE – LIBRARY OF THE DEPARTMENT OF PHYSIOLOGY, DEVELOPMENT AND NEUROSCIENCE (PDN Library)

Downing Street, Cambridge, CB2 3EG

Tel: 01223 333899
Fax: 01223 333840
E-mail: library@pdn.cam.ac.uk
Website: www.pdn.cam.ac.uk/library

Enquiries to: Librarian
Direct tel: 01223 333821

History of institution: created by the merger of School of Anatomy Library and Department of Physiology Library (year of change 2006)

Organisation type and purpose: University department or institute.

Subject coverage: Physiology, human and veterinary anatomy, embryology, developmental biology, neurobiology, neuroscience.

Collection: Boyd histological collection (slides), embryological collection, compiled by Professor J. D. Boyd.
History of physiology.

Non-library collection catalogue: All or part available in-house

Library catalogue: All or part available online, in-house and in print

Access to staff: Contact by letter, by telephone, by fax and by e-mail. Appointment necessary. Letter of introduction required.
Hours: Mon to Fri, 0900 to 1230 and 1400 to 1700
Special comments: Advanced notice required for consultations.

Access to building: Prior appointment required
Hours: Mon to Fri, 0900 to 1230 and 1330 to 1700
Special comments: Prior appointment required for Library and Collections.

Access for disabled people: Fully accessible

UNIVERSITY OF CAMBRIDGE – LIBRARY OF THE DEPARTMENT OF PLANT SCIENCES

Downing Street, Cambridge, CB2 3EA

Tel: 01223 333930
Fax: 01223 333953
E-mail: library@plantsci.cam.ac.uk

Enquiries to: Librarian
Direct tel: 01223 333930

History of institution: formerly called Botany School, University of Cambridge

Organisation type and purpose: University department or institute.

Subject coverage: All aspects of plant sciences: genetics, biochemistry, physiology, ecology and taxonomy, excluding agriculture and forestry, but including quaternary vegetation.

Collection: Early herbals
Simpson Collection of local floras

Access to staff: Contact by letter, by telephone, by fax and by e-mail. Appointment necessary.
Hours: Mon to Fri, 0900 to 1700

UNIVERSITY OF CAMBRIDGE – LIBRARY OF THE DEPARTMENT OF VETERINARY MEDICINE

Madingley Road, Cambridge, CB3 0ES

Tel: 01223 337600
Fax: 01223 337610
Website: www.vet.cam.ac.uk

Enquiries to: Librarian
Direct tel: 01223 337633
Direct e-mail: lel1000@hermes.cam.ac.uk

Founded: 1955

Organisation type and purpose: University department or institute.

Subject coverage: Veterinary medicine.

Collection: Small rare book collection on veterinary medicine.

Library catalogue: All or part available online

Access to staff: Contact by letter, by telephone, by fax and by e-mail. Appointment necessary.
Hours: Mon to Fri, 0900 to 0430

Access to building: *Special comments:* Card access only.

UNIVERSITY OF CAMBRIDGE – LIBRARY OF THE EXPERIMENTAL PSYCHOLOGY LABORATORY

Downing Street, Cambridge, CB2 3EB

Tel: 01223 333554
Fax: 01223 333564
E-mail: library@psychol.cam.ac.uk

Enquiries to: Librarian

Organisation type and purpose: University department or institute.
Teaching and research unit of the University of Cambridge.

Subject coverage: Experimental psychology and psychopathology.

Collection: McCurdy Psychopathology Library (1900-, about 1000 books)
Oldfield Collection (material on vision, 1900–1940, about 100 books)

Access to staff: Appointment necessary.
Hours: Mon to Fri, 0930 to 1700 during full term
Special comments: Please telephone for an appointment outside full term.

UNIVERSITY OF CAMBRIDGE – LIBRARY OF THE FACULTY OF ARCHITECTURE AND HISTORY OF ART

1 Scroope Terrace, Trumpington Street, Cambridge, CB2 1PX

Tel: 01223 332953
Fax: 01223 332960
E-mail: mb151@cam.ac.uk
Website: www.arct.cam.ac.uk/library.html

Enquiries to: Librarian

Organisation type and purpose: University department or institute.

Subject coverage: Architecture; history of art; architecture and design.

Collection: 16th–19th-century architectural special collection
19th- and 20th-century architectural periodicals, mainly European

Library catalogue: All or part available online

Access to staff: Contact by letter
Hours: Term time: 0915 to 1730
Vacation: opening hours vary, but usually 0930 to 1230 and 1430 to 1730

UNIVERSITY OF CAMBRIDGE – LIBRARY OF THE FACULTY OF DIVINITY

West Road, Cambridge, CB3 9BS

Tel: 01223 763040
Fax: 01223 763003
E-mail: library@divinity.cam.ac.uk
Website: www.divinity.cam.ac.uk/library

Enquiries to: Librarian

Founded: 1879

Organisation type and purpose: University department or institute.

Subject coverage: Theology, ecclesiastical history, biblical studies, Judaism, Islam, Hinduism, Buddhism, ethics, philosophy of religion, psychology of religion, sociology of religion, science and religion, patristics, liturgy.

Collection: Feltoe Bequest (liturgy)
Lightfoot Bequest (library of Bishop J. B. Lightfoot 1828–89)

Non-library collection catalogue: All or part available online

Library catalogue: All or part available online

Access to staff: Contact by letter and by e-mail. Appointment necessary. Access for members only.
Hours: Term time: Mon to Fri, 0900 to 1700
Vacations: Mon to Fri, 0900 to 1255 and 1400 to 1630

Access to building: Prior appointment required

Access for disabled people: Access to all public areas

UNIVERSITY OF CAMBRIDGE – MILL LANE LIBRARY OF THE DEPARTMENT OF LAND ECONOMY (DLE)

8 Mill Lane, Cambridge, CB2 1RX

Tel: 01223 337110
Fax: 01223 337130
E-mail: landecon-library@lists.cam.ac.uk
Website: www.landecon.cam.ac.uk/library/library.htm
Website: www.landecon.cam.ac.uk
Website: www.lib.cam.ac.uk/catalogues/opac/union.shtml

Enquiries to: Librarian
Direct e-mail: wt10000@cam.ac.uk

Founded: 1950

Organisation type and purpose: University department or institute.

Subject coverage: Agriculture economics, architecture, environmental policy and law, forestry, housing, land economics, land law, land tenure, land values, regional economics, rural development, town and country planning.

Non-library collection catalogue: All or part available online

Library catalogue: All or part available online

Publications: Printed

Publications list: Available in print

Access to staff: Contact by letter, by telephone, by e-mail, in person and via website
Hours: Mon to Fri, 0900 to 1700
Special comments: No disabled access.

UNIVERSITY OF CAMBRIDGE – MODERN AND MEDIEVAL LANGUAGES LIBRARY (MML Library)

Sidgwick Avenue, Cambridge, CB3 9DA

Tel: 01223 335041
Fax: 01223 335062
E-mail: mmllib@hermes.cam.ac.uk
Website: www.mml.cam.ac.uk/library

Enquiries to: Librarian
Direct tel: 01223 335047
Direct e-mail: aec25@cam.ac.uk

Organisation type and purpose: University department or institute.

Subject coverage: Most Continental European languages and literatures (no Greek); Germanic, Romance and Slavonic groups; linguistics, cinema, literary theory; DVDs and videos.

Collection: Beit Library (German research material)

Library catalogue: All or part available online

Publications: Printed

Access to staff: Contact by letter, by telephone, by fax, by e-mail and in person
Hours: Term time: Mon to Fri, 0900 to 1900; Sat, 1000 to 1600
Vacations: Mon to Fri, 0900 to 1700

Access to building: *Hours:* Term time: Mon to Fri, 0900 to 1900; Sat, 1000 to 1600
Vacations: Mon to Fri, 0900 to 1700

UNIVERSITY OF CAMBRIDGE – RAYLEIGH LIBRARY OF THE DEPARTMENT OF PHYSICS

J.J. Thomson Avenue, Cambridge, CB3 0HE

Tel: 01223 337414
E-mail: librarian@phy.cam.ac.uk
Website: www.phy.cam.ac.uk/library

Enquiries to: Librarian

Organisation type and purpose: University department or institute.
Departmental library.

Subject coverage: Physics, meteorology.

Collection: Maxwell Collection
Napier Shaw Meteorology Library (books and periodicals)
Rayleigh Library (books and periodicals)
History of science

Non-library collection catalogue: All or part available in-house

Library catalogue: All or part available online

Access to staff: Contact by letter, by telephone, by e-mail, in person and via website. Appointment necessary.
Hours: Mon to Fri, 0900 to 1700

Access for disabled people: Parking provided

UNIVERSITY OF CAMBRIDGE – SQUIRE LAW LIBRARY

10 West Road, Cambridge, CB3 9DZ

Tel: 01223 330077
Fax: 01223 330057
E-mail: library@lib.cam.ac.uk
Website: www.lib.cam.ac.uk

Enquiries to: Librarian
Other contacts: Deputy Librarian

Founded: 1904

Organisation type and purpose: University library.

Subject coverage: English, Scottish and Irish law; legal history; Roman law; US law; comparative law; international law; Commonwealth law.

Collection: Commonwealth Law Reform Commissions
International Law Treaty Series
Nominate Reports, pre-1800 Law Books and Manuscripts

Library catalogue: All or part available online

Publications: Printed

Access to staff: Contact by letter, by telephone, by e-mail and via website. Letter of introduction required.
Hours: Mon to Fri, 0900 to 1700

Access for disabled people: Toilet facilities

Part of: Cambridge University Library

UNIVERSITY OF CAMBRIDGE – THE MARSHALL LIBRARY OF ECONOMICS

Sidgwick Avenue, Cambridge, CB3 9DB

Tel: 01223 335217
Fax: 01223 335475
E-mail: marshlib@econ.cam.ac.uk
Website: www.econ.cam.ac.uk/marshlib

Enquiries to: Librarian
Direct tel: 01223 335215

Organisation type and purpose: University department or institute, research organisation.
Research library.

Subject coverage: Economics, statistics.

Non-library collection catalogue: All or part available online and in-house

Publications: Printed

Access to staff: Contact by letter, by telephone, by fax, by e-mail and in person
Hours: Mon to Fri, 0900 to 1700

Access for disabled people: Access to all public areas, toilet facilities

UNIVERSITY OF CAMBRIDGE – WHIPPLE LIBRARY OF THE DEPARTMENT OF HISTORY AND PHILOSOPHY OF SCIENCE

Free School Lane, Cambridge, CB2 3RH

Tel: 01223 334547
Fax: 01223 334554
E-mail: hpslib@hermes.cam.ac.uk
Website: www.hps.cam.ac.uk/library/

Enquiries to: Librarian

Founded: 1944

Organisation type and purpose: University department or institute.
Departmental library attached to the Department of History and Philosophy of Science.

Subject coverage: History and philosophy of science and of medicine, scientific instruments and instrument makers.

Collection: Phrenology Collection
Scientific works of 16th–19th centuries
Works of Robert Boyle
Foster Pamphlet Collection (physiology)

Library catalogue: All or part available online

Access to staff: Appointment necessary.
Hours: Term time: 0930 to 1730
Vacations: 0930 to 1700

Access for disabled people: Lift, Library on 1st floor, please telephone or e-mail in advance of visit.

UNIVERSITY OF CENTRAL LANCASHIRE (LIS)

Learning and Information Services, Preston. Lancashire, PR1 2HE

Tel: 01772 892261
Fax: 01772 892937
E-mail: mahern@uclan.ac.uk
Website: www.uclan.ac.uk/information/services/lis/index.php

Enquiries to: Director of Learning and Information Services
Other contacts: Head of Library Services

Organisation type and purpose: University library, suitable for ages: 18+.

Subject coverage: Social sciences; nursing and midwifery; education; humanities; accountancy; business; management; astronomy; biology; chemistry; mathematics; physics; computing science; electrical and electronic engineering; mechanical engineering; production engineering; construction and urban studies.

Collection: Illustrated Books Collection
Joseph Livesey Collection (temperance)
Local history collections
Preston Incorporated Law Society Library

Non-library collection catalogue: All or part available online

Library catalogue: All or part available online

Publications: Printed

Access to staff: Contact by letter, by telephone, by fax, by e-mail and via website. Appointment necessary. Non-members charged.
Hours: Term time: Mon to Thu, 0830 to 2300; Fri, 0830 to 2000; Sat, Sun, 1000 to 1800
Vacations: Mon, Wed, Fri, 0845 to 1700; Tue, Thu, 0845 to 2000; Sat, 1200 to 1800

Access to building: Prior appointment required
Special comments: Access to non-members by prior arrangement in writing and to Lancashire County Library members via library card.

Access for disabled people: Ramped entry, access to all public areas

UNIVERSITY OF CHESTER

Parkgate Road, Chester, Cheshire, CH1 4BJ

Tel: 01244 511000 (University); 511234 (Learning and information services)
Fax: 01244 511300 (University); 511325 (Learning and information service
E-mail: lis.helpdesk@chester.ac.uk
Website: www.chester.ac.uk/lr

Enquiries to: Customer Services Manager

Founded: 1839; formerly called Chester College of Higher Education (year of change 2003); formerly called University College Chester (year of change 2005)

Organisation type and purpose: University library.

Subject coverage: Art, education, biological science, business and management, computing, criminology, drama, English literature, history, geography, languages, mathematics, nursing and midwifery, social work, sports science, religious studies, psychology, journalism, media and communications, law, graphic design, nutrition and dietetics.

Information services: Helpdesk and reference services.

Services for disabled people: Adjustable tables, specialist software.

Collection: 310,000-vol. academic library

Non-library collection catalogue: All or part available online

Library catalogue: All or part available online and in-house

Publications: Electronic and video

Access to staff: Contact by letter, by telephone, by e-mail and in person
Hours: Term time: Mon to Thu, 0830 to 2100; Fri, 0830 to 2000; Sat, Sun, 1200 to 1800
Vacations: Mon, Tue, Thu, Fri, 0900 to 1730; Wed, 0900 to 2000

Access for disabled people: Ramped entry, toilet facilities, lift

UNIVERSITY OF CHICHESTER LIBRARY (UoC)

Bishop Otter Campus, College Lane, Chichester, West Sussex, PO19 6PE

Tel: 01243 816089
Fax: 01243 816096
Website: www.chi.ac.uk/info/lrc.cfm

Enquiries to: Head of Library Services
Direct tel: 01243 816090
Direct e-mail: s.robertson@chi.ac.uk

Founded: 1977; created by the merger of Bishop Otter College and Bognor Regis College (year of change 1977); formerly called West Sussex Institute of Higher Education (year of change 1995); formerly called Chichester Institute of Higher Education (year of change 1999); formerly called University College Chichester (year of change 2005)

Organisation type and purpose: University library.

Subject coverage: History, English, theology, media studies, fine art, music, dance, performing arts, childhood and youth studies, counselling, social work, sport studies, sport science, sport therapy, physical education, adventure education, management, education, business studies, applied language studies.

Collection: Otter Gallery
Bishop Otter art collection
Chichester Theological Collection
Professor J Dunn collection
Ted Walker Archive
Dance Videos
Children's Resources (Bognor)
Gerard Young Collection (Bognor local history) (Bognor)
Bishop Kemp Collection (Bognor)
John Fines Collection (Bognor)

Trade and statistical information: Social and health statistics

Library catalogue: All or part available online

Access to staff: Contact by letter, by telephone, by fax, by e-mail, in person and via website. Appointment necessary.
Hours: Term time: Mon to Thu, 0845 to 2145; Fri, 0845 to 1700; Sat, Sun, 1000 to 1700
Vacation: Mon to Fri, 0900 to 1700

Access to building: No prior appointment required
Hours: Term time: Mon to Thu, 0845 to 2145; Fri, 0845 to 1700; Sat, Sun, 1000 to 1700
Vacation: Mon to Fri, 0900 to 1700
Special comments: Half-hour only parking, 0800 to 1700

Access for disabled people: Parking provided, ramped entry, level entry, lift, access to all public areas, toilet facilities

Branch libraries: Bognor Regis Campus Library; Upper Bognor Road, Bognor Regis, West Sussex, PO21 1HR; tel: 01243 812099; fax: 01243 812081

UNIVERSITY OF CUMBRIA

Learning and Information Services, Harold Bridges Library, University of Cumbria, Bowerham Road, Lancaster, LA1 3JD

Tel: 01524 384243
Fax: 01524 384588
Website: www.cumbria.ac.uk/services/lis/home.aspx

Enquiries to: Head of Learning and Information Services
Direct tel: 01524 384238
Other contacts: Site Library Managers for Ambleside, Carlisle Fusehill Street, Lancaster; Campus Library Managers for Carlisle Brampton Road, Newton Rigg Libraries

Founded: 1964; created by the merger of St Martin's College, Cumbria Institute of the Arts, Cumbria campuses of University of Central Lancashire (year of change 2007); formerly called University College of St Martin, Lancaster (year of change 1998); incorporates the former Charlotte Mason College, Ambleside (year of change 1996)

Organisation type and purpose: Multi-site university library.

Subject coverage: Education, humanities, health studies, management, nursing, radiography, occupational therapy and midwifery, social studies, outdoor studies

Collection: Large collection of children's books, and teaching and learning materials
Local studies collection (Lancashire, Cumbria and Yorkshire)
Religious and moral studies collection.

Non-library collection catalogue: All or part available online

Library catalogue: All or part available online

Access to staff: Contact by telephone, by fax, by e-mail and in person
Hours: Mon to Fri, 0900 to 1700

Access to building: No prior appointment required

Access for disabled people: Parking provided, ramped entry, access to all public areas, toilet facilities

Also at: The Library, University of Cumbria; Fusehill Street, Carlisle, CA1 2HH; tel: 01228 616218; fax: 01228 616263; e-mail: libcarfs@cumbria.ac.uk; The Library, University of Cumbria; Rydal Road, Ambleside, Cumbria,

LA22 9BB; tel: 015314 30274; fax: 015394 30371; e-mail: libamb@cumbria.ac.uk; The Library, University of Cumbria; Newton Rigg, Penrith, Cumbria, CA11 0AH; tel: 01768 893503; fax: 01768 893506; e-mail: libpen@cumbria.ac.uk; The Library, University of Cumbria; Brampton Road, Carlisle, Cumbria, CA3 9AY; tel: 01228 400312; fax: 01228 514491; e-mail: libcarbr@cumbria.ac.uk

Associated health-related libraries in: Westmoreland and Cumbria

Funded by: Health Authorities; HEFCE; TTA

UNIVERSITY OF DUNDEE – LIBRARY

Small's Wynd, Dundee, DD1 4HN

Tel: 01382 344087
Fax: 01382 229190
E-mail: library@dundee.ac.uk
Website: www.dundee.ac.uk/library/
Enquiries to: Librarian
Direct tel: 01382 344082
Direct e-mail: j.m.bagnall@dundee.ac.uk

Organisation type and purpose: University library.

Subject coverage: Arts, art and design, social sciences, education, environmental studies, law, medicine, dentistry, nursing, science, engineering and applied science including architecture.

Collection: Brechin Diocesan Library
Joan Auld Memorial Collection
Kinnear Allan Ramsay Collection
Kinnear Local Collection
Leng Collection (Scottish philosophical writers)
Nicoll Collection (books on the fine arts)
Thoms mineralogical collection
William Lyon Mackenzie Collection (Canadiana)

Publications: Printed, and microform publications

Access to staff: Contact by letter, by telephone, by fax and by e-mail
Hours: Mon to Fri, 0900 to 1700

UNIVERSITY OF DUNDEE – NINEWELLS LIBRARY

Ninewells Hospital and Medical School, Dundee, DD1 9SY

Tel: 01382 632519
Fax: 01382 566179
E-mail: ninewells-library@dundee.ac.uk
Website: www.dundee.ac.uk/library

Organisation type and purpose: University library.

Subject coverage: Medicine and nursing.

Library catalogue: All or part available online

Access to staff: Contact by letter, by telephone, by e-mail, in person and via website
Hours: Mon to Thu, 0845 to 2200; Fri, 0845 to 1700; Sat, 1200 to 1700.
Closed over Christmas vacation.

Access to building: No prior appointment required

UNIVERSITY OF EAST ANGLIA (DEV)

Formal name: School of International Development

University of East Anglia, Norwich, Norfolk, NR4 7TJ

Tel: 01603 591472
Fax: 01603 451999
E-mail: dev.general@uea.ac.uk
Website: www.uea.ac.uk/dev/co
Website: www.uea.ac.uk/dev/publications
Website: www.uea.ac.uk/dev

Enquiries to: Local Office Administrator
Other contacts: PA to Head of School

Founded: 1973; formerly called School of Development Studies (year of change 2009)

Organisation type and purpose: University department affiliated to the School of International Development, consultancy and research organisation.
Teaching, research and consultancy in international development.

Subject coverage: Research addresses contemporary challenges in developing and transition economies via disciplinary and multi/interdisciplinary approaches in the following groups: Ageing and development; Behavioural and experimental development economics; Business, accountability, regulation and development; Climate change and development; Educational diversity, literacy & development; Global environmental justice; Health policy and practice; Land resources; Social identities, institutions and justice; Social protection and mobile livelihoods.
Consultancy services in: Gender and social development; Literacy and development; Globalisation and transition; Livelihoods and well-being; Natural resources and environment and climate change; Health and HIV and AIDS.
Training courses include: Climate change and development; Gender and development; Gender and internal organisational change; Management information systems for monitoring and evaluation; Monitoring and evaluation for development activities; Water security for policy makers and practitioners.

Publications: Printed

Publications list: Available online

Access to staff: Contact by letter, by telephone, by fax, by e-mail and via website. Appointment necessary.
Hours: Mon to Fri, 0900 to 1700

Access to building: *Hours:* As above.

Access for disabled people: Ramped entry
Hours: As above.

Attached consultancy group: International Development, University of East Anglia; University of East Anglia, Norwich, Norfolk, NR4 7TJ UK; tel: 0603 592813; fax: 01603 591170; e-mail: devco.gen@uea.ac.uk

UNIVERSITY OF EAST ANGLIA – LIBRARY (UEA Library)

University of East Anglia, Norwich, Norfolk, NR4 7TJ

Tel: 01603 592993
Fax: 01603 591010
E-mail: lib.helpdesk@uea.ac.uk
Website: www.uea.ac.uk/is/lib
Enquiries to: Head of User Services
Direct tel: 01603 593440
Direct e-mail: heather.wells@uea.ac.uk

Founded: 1963

Organisation type and purpose: University library.

Subject coverage: Social sciences and the humanities; history; law; education; development studies; biological, chemical, environmental, mathematical, physical and computing sciences; accounting; management; information systems; health sciences; film studies; medicine; pharmacy.

Special visitor services: See: http://www.uea.ac.uk/is/borrowing/externalusers.

Collection: Abbott Collection (English literature)
Anthony Grey Archive
Archives of Modern Writing and Literary Translation
Broke Collection (Military science)
Charles Pick Archive
Doris Lessing Archive
European Documentation Centre (Selective)
Everest Collection
Fisher Theatre, Bungay
G.S. Callendar Archive
H.H. Lamb Archive
Hill Papers
Holloway Collection of Contemporary Culture Records
Illustrated Books
JD Salinger – Hartog Letters
Kenney Papers
Ketton-Cremer Collection (local history)
Lorna Sage Archive
Peterborough Literary Society
Pevsner Art Catalogue Collection
Pritchard Archive
Robert Edric Archive
Roger Deakin Archive
Theatre Quarterly Archive
Tinkler and Williams' Theatre Collection
WG Sebald Audiovisual Archive
Zuckerman Archive

Non-library collection catalogue: All or part available online

Library catalogue: All or part available online

Access to staff: Contact by letter, by telephone, by fax, by e-mail, in person and via website
Hours: Core staff hours Mon to Fri, 0900 to 1700
Special comments: Reference-only to non-registered borrowers.

Access to building: Open 24/7
Hours: Security staff only from midnight to 8am Mon – Fri, 7pm – 11am weekends
Special comments: Valid card holders only outside Library staffed hours

Access for disabled people: Level entry, access to all public areas, toilet facilities. See www.disabledgo.com for full details

Links with: City College Norwich; East Anglian Film Archive; Easton College; Institute of Food Research; Institute of Health & Social Care Studies; Guernsey; INTO University Partnerships; John Innes Centre; Norfolk and Norwich University Hospital; University Campus Suffolk

Member organisation of: SCONUL

UNIVERSITY OF EAST ANGLIA – SCHOOL OF ENVIRONMENTAL SCIENCES (ENV, UEA)

University Plain, Norwich, Norfolk, NR4 7TJ

Tel: 01603 592994
Fax: 01603 593035
E-mail: j.darch@uea.ac.uk
Website: www.uea.ac.uk/env/

Enquiries to: Research Administrator

Organisation type and purpose: University department or institute.

Subject coverage: Environmental sciences, atmospheric chemistry, climatic change, climatic modelling, wind energy, ecology, geophysics, oceanography, health, planning, risk assessment, cost-benefit analysis, environmental assessment and appraisal, geology, geomorphology, quaternary period, global environmental change, air-sea interactions, GIS, waste management, hydrology and hydrogeology, estuaries, soils and land use planning.

Publications: Printed, and electronic and video

Publications list: Available online and in print

Access to staff: Contact by letter, by fax, by e-mail and via website. Appointment necessary.
Hours: Mon to Fri, 0900 to 1700

Includes the: Centre for Environmental Risk; tel: 01603 593129; fax: 01603 507719; e-mail: n.pidgeon@uea.ac.uk; Centre for Social and Economic Research on the Global Environment (CSERGE); tel: 01603 592551; fax: 01603 250588; e-mail: n.k.turner@uea.ac.uk; Climatic Research Unit; tel: 01603 593647; fax: 01603 507784; e-mail: j.palativiof@uea.ac.uk; Tyndall Centre for Climate Change

UNIVERSITY OF EAST LONDON – DOCKLANDS LIBRARY AND LEARNING CENTRE

University Way, London, E16 2RD

Tel: 020 8223 3434
Fax: 020 8223 7497
E-mail: j.a.preece@uel.ac.uk
Website: www.uel.ac.uk

Enquiries to: Manager

Founded: 1999

Organisation type and purpose: University library.

Subject coverage: Art and architecture, social sciences, cultural studies, business studies, computing and engineering.

Collection: Refugee Archive
British Olympic Archive
Diversity Art Forum

Library catalogue: All or part available online

Access to staff: Contact by telephone, by e-mail and via website
Hours: Mon to Fri, 0900 to 1700

Access to building: Prior appointment required

Special comments: No prior appointment required for students and staff of UEL and SCONUL Access scheme card holders.
All other visitors must make advance application.

Access for disabled people: Parking provided, ramped entry, level entry, access to all public areas, toilet facilities

UNIVERSITY OF EAST LONDON – STRATFORD LEARNING RESOURCE CENTRE (UEL)

Holbrook Annexe, Holbrook Road, Stratford, London, E15 3EA

Tel: 020 8223 3251
Fax: 020 8223 3296
Website: www.uel.ac.uk/library

Enquiries to: Manager
Direct e-mail: s.p.lyes@uel.ac.uk

Organisation type and purpose: University library.

Subject coverage: Architecture, building, planning.

Collection: Collection of architectural slides
Collection on architecture (RIBA trade literature)

Library catalogue: All or part available online

Access to staff: Contact by letter, by telephone, by e-mail and via website. Appointment necessary.
Hours: Mon to Thu, 0900 to 1900; Fri, 0900 to 1700
Vacations have varying opening hours

Access to building: Prior appointment required

Access for disabled people: Level entry

UNIVERSITY OF EDINBURGH – CENTRE FOR EDUCATIONAL SOCIOLOGY (CES)

St John's Land, Holyrood Road, Edinburgh, EH8 8AQ

Tel: 0131 651 6238
Fax: 0131 651 6239
E-mail: ces@ed.ac.uk
Website: www.ces.ed.ac.uk

Enquiries to: Administrator
Direct tel: 0131 651 6238
Direct e-mail: ces@ed.ac.uk

Founded: 1972

Organisation type and purpose: University department or institute, research organisation.

Subject coverage: Education, training, youth labour market, transitions to adulthood, information systems.

Library catalogue: All or part available in-house

Publications list: Available online and in print

Access to staff: Contact by letter, by telephone, by fax, by e-mail, in person and via website. Appointment necessary.
Hours: Mon to Fri, 0900 to 1700

Access for disabled people: Access to all public areas, toilet facilities

UNIVERSITY OF EDINBURGH – UNIVERSITY LIBRARY (EUL)

Main Library, George Square, Edinburgh, EH8 9LJ

Tel: 0131 650 3409
Fax: 0131 651 5041
E-mail: is.helpdesk@ed.ac.uk
Website: www.ed.ac.uk/is/library-museum-gallery
Website: www.ed.ac.uk/is

Enquiries to: Director of Library & Collections
Direct tel: 0131 650 3381 (administration); 0131 650 8379 (Centre for Research Collections – CRC)
Direct fax: 0131 650 4978, administration (0131 650 2922 – CRC)
Other contacts: Director of University Collections, e-mail: john.scally@ed.ac.uk; Director of User Services, e-mail bryan.macgregor@ed.ac.uk

Founded: 1580

Organisation type and purpose: University library.
The books acquired by the Library between its foundation in 1580 and the publication of its 3-volume printed catalogue in 1918–23, especially during the period 1710–1837 when it was a library of copyright deposit, now represent a significant historical research resource in most branches of the humanities, especially on the history of Scotland and the United Kingdom, European history and literature, and the Commonwealth and British expansion overseas. The Library also has significant collections of early printed books, and mediaeval and modern Western and Oriental manuscripts. It is a European Documentation Centre, and this facility is focused on the Law and Europa Library.

Subject coverage: The Library serves the needs of the 3 University Colleges and Schools within them: College of Humanities and Social Science; College of Medicine and Veterinary Medicine; College of Science and Engineering. It holds general academic collections in all these fields as well as in-depth collections in many of them.
Astronomy (Royal Observatory), botany (Darwin Library), chemistry (Darwin Library), engineering and geology (Robertson Engineering and Science Library), forestry (Darwin Library), genetics (Darwin Library), mathematics, computer science and physics (James Clerk Maxwell Library), zoology (Darwin Library).
Medicine and medical sciences, dentistry, psychiatry, community medicine (Main Library).
European Union, German public law and political organisation (Law and Europa Library).
Scottish ethnology, folklore, folk tales, oral traditions, customs and belief, literature, dialectology, material culture, ethnomusicology, song, place-names, social history and organisation, urban ethnology, ethnology of religion, emigrant traditions (Scottish Studies Library).
Christianity and Church history, biblical studies, theology, patristics, Church missions, non-Christian religions in relation to Christianity (New College Library), education, psychology, English language teaching, physical education, movement,

leisure studies, sports science and recreational management (Moray House Library), veterinary anatomy, biochemistry, medicine, parasitology, pathology, pharmacology, physiology, animal health and reproduction (Royal (Dick) School of Veterinary Studies Library).

Collection: Size of collections: the Library holds over 3,400,000 printed volumes and pamphlets, as well as many manuscripts and archives of international importance; largest university library in Scotland; its electronic data, including full-text journals and other resources which are now core to its collections, are accessible across the University network and increasingly off-campus
Named special collections, with year of acquisition, include:
Lord Abercromby, 1924 (archaeology, ethnology, linguistics)
Auden, 1982 (W H Auden and associated writers of the 1930s)
John Stuart Blackie, 1895 (Greek)
Blondal, 1950 (Icelandic studies)
Bruce, 1921 (oceanography and Polar studies)
Cameron, 1889 (Celtic studies and theology)
Hugh Cleghorn, 1895 (Indian forestry, land use and botany)
Compton, 1997 (American history)
Corson, 1989 (Sir Walter Scott)
Cumming, 1939 (Italian studies)
William Drummond of Hawthornden, 1620–30 (English, Latin, Italian, French and Spanish literature)
East Asian Studies
Will Foret Archive (Scottish studies)
Geikie, 1915 (geology)
Halliwell-Phillipps, 1866, 1872 (Shakespeare, 17th- and 18th-century English drama)
W B Hodgson, 1880 (economics)
Jameson Collection (mineralogy)
Berriedale Keith, 1944 (Indian literature, history and politics and the constitutional history of the British Commonwealth)
Kennedy-Fraser, c. 1950 (Scottish music, dance, history and literature)
Arthur Koestler, 1985 (literature)
David Laing, 1878 (3,000 Scottish charters, mediaeval and modern manuscripts on Scottish history and literature, early Scottish music texts, and letters of artists)
Kenneth Leighton Manuscripts (music)
John Levy archive (oriental music) (Scottish Studies)
Clement Littill, 1580 (theology)
Lyell Collection (geology)
Mackinnon, 1924 (Celtic studies and theology)
Sir John Murray, 1921 (zoology, geography, geology)
James Nairn, 1678 (theology, philosophy, history and literature)
Penguin Books 1935–1985
Adam Smith, 18th century (literature, classics, political economy, science)
Serjeant, 1996 (Middle East)
Dugald Stewart, 18th–19th centuries (political economy, moral philosophy, mathematics)
James Thin, 1880 (hymnology)
Sir Donald F Tovey, 1940 (music scores and books)
Watt, 1997 (Arabic)
Weiss, 1948 (books on Beethoven)
Un-named special collections:
18th- and 19th-century books on agriculture
Audio-visual Archive (Scottish Studies)
Bundesgesetzblatt
Cases of the European Court of Human Rights
Collection of early printed books on music theory
Debates of the European Parliament
Ecumenical Collection (includes all World Council of Churches and British Council of Churches publications)
European Courts Reports (English, French, German and Dutch language)
Historical collections of Scottish churchmen (books, pamphlets and portraits)
Historical collection of veterinary science, nucleus of which belonged to the school's founder, William Dick
Manuscript collections (mainly Scottish church history, including Thomas Chalmers, 1780–1847, archive of c. 20,000 letters)
Official Journal of the European Union (Communities) (C and L series)
Photographic Archive (Scottish studies)
Sound Archive (10,000 tapes, Scottish studies)
Verhandlungen des Deutschen Bundestages
Libraries of the:
Dumfries Presbytery
Edinburgh Geological Society
Edinburgh Mathematical Society
Lothian Health Services Archives
Royal Physical Society
Royal Scottish Forestry Society
University of Edinburgh Archives
Manuscripts of various scientific societies
Subject specialisations:
African studies
Canadian studies
History of medicine and science
Landscape architecture
New Zealand studies
Scandinavian studies
Modern Scottish and English literature
Scottish studies
South Asian studies
The Church of Scotland
The Scottish Enlightenment
The University of Edinburgh
Poets and writers:
W H Auden
George Mackay Brown
Thomas and Jane Welsh Carlyle
Thomas Chalmers
Helen B Cruikshank
Christopher Murray Grieve ('Hugh MacDairmid')
Norman McCaig
James Leslie Mitchell ('Lewis Grassic Gibbon')
John Middleton Murry
Poets of Scottish Literary Renaissance
Sydney Goodsir Smith
Sir Walter Scott
John Wain

Non-library collection catalogue: All or part available online

Library catalogue: All or part available online

Publications: Printed, and electronic and video
Order printed publications from: Publications, Edinburgh University Library, George Square, Edinburgh, EH8 9LJ, tel: 0131 650 3409, fax: 0131 651 5041, e-mail: IS .Helpdesk@ed.ac.uk

Access to staff: Contact by letter, by telephone, by fax, by e-mail and via website. Appointment necessary. Letter of introduction required. Non-members charged.
Hours: For opening hours information please check website: http://www.ed.ac.uk/is/library-opening
Semester time: Main Library, Mon to Thu, 0900 to 2200; Fri, 0900 to 1900; Sat, 0900 to 1700; Sun, 1200 to 1900; most other major College and School Libraries, Mon to Thu, 0900 to 2200; Fri, Sat 0900 to 1700; Sun, 1200 to 1700;
Vacations: Main Library, Mon to Thurs, 0900 to 2000; Fri, 0900 to 1700; Sat, 1000 to 1300; other libraries vary
Special comments: Members of the University of Edinburgh have full access as of right. They may borrow free of charge and are charged for photocopying, photography and inter-library loans.
External users may be charged for access (consultation and/or borrowing), photocopying, photography and inter-library loans.
Undergraduate students from other European Union HEIs during EUL vacations may have access for reference purposes free of charge on production of their own current ID cards. They may have borrowing facilities on payment of the current external fee.
During term-time they are admitted only by prior arrangement with their own institutions' librarians. Postgraduate students are admitted at all times.
Staff, postgraduate students and undergraduate students from overseas HEIs, including members of Universitas 21, Coimbra, and other groups, will be charged external fees for borrowing unless they are official academic visitors to the University.
Advanced Higher Students, School students and equivalent project-based course students may have access to the Library for consultation purposes free of charge, provided that prior arrangements have been made between each School and the University Library. Other school students are not normally admitted to the Library.
Corporate membership is available on application and by subscription.
Prices, which may be adjusted at any time, are available on request or online: http://www.ed.ac.uk/is/library-museum-gallery.

Access for disabled people: Parking provided, ramped entry, level entry, access to all public areas, toilet facilities
Special comments: These facilities apply to the Main Library. On other sites the provision will vary.

College of Medicine and Veterinary Medicine: Easter Bush Veterinary Centre Library; Royal (Dick) School of Veterinary Studies, Easter Bush, Roslin, Midlothian, EH25 9RG; tel: 0131 650 6405; e-mail: ebvc .library@ed.ac.uk; Roslin Institute Library; Roslin Institute, Roslin Biocentre, Roslin, Midlothian, EH25 9RG; tel: 0131 527 4200; fax: 0131 440 0434; e-mail: roslin.library@ roslin.ed.ac.uk; Royal (Dick) School of Veterinary Studies Library; Royal (Dick) School of Veterinary Studies, Summerhall, Edinburgh, EH9 1QH; tel: 0131 650 6175; fax: 0131 650 6593; e-mail: dick.vetlib@ed.ac .uk; Royal Infirmary Library; Chancellor's Building, 49 Little France Crescent, Edinburgh, EH16 4SB; tel: 0131 242 6340;

continued overleaf

fax: 0131 242 6338; e-mail: royal.infirmary .library@ed.ac.uk; Western General Hospital Library; Western General Hospital, Crewe Road South, Edinburgh, EH4 2XU; tel: 0131 537 2299; e-mail: western.general.library@ed .ac.uk

College of Science and Engineering: Darwin Library; Darwin Building, The King's Buildings, West Mains Road, Edinburgh, EH9 3JU; tel: 0131 650 5784; fax: 0131 650 6702; e-mail: darwin.library@ed.ac .uk; James Clerk Maxwell Library; James Clerk Maxwell Building, The King's Buildings, West Mains Road, Edinburgh, EH9 3JZ; tel: 0131 650 5784; Robertson Engineering and Science Library; James Clerk Maxwell Building,The King's Buildings, West Mains Road, Edinburgh, EH9 3JF; tel: 0131 650 5666; fax: 0131 650 6702; e-mail: robertson.library@ed.ac.uk

Moray House School of Education: Moray House Library; Dalhousie Land, St John Street, Edinburgh, EH8 8AQ; tel: 0131 651 6193; e-mail: morayhse@staffmail.ed.ac.uk

School of Divinity: New College Library; School of Divinity, Mound Place, Edinburgh, EH1 2LU; tel: 0131 650 8957; fax: 0131 650 7952; e-mail: new.college.library@ed.ac.uk

School of Law: Law and Europa Library (European Documentation Centre); Old College, South Bridge, Edinburgh, EH8 9YL; tel: 0131 650 2044; e-mail: law.europa .library@ed.ac.uk

School of Literatures, Languages and Cultures: Scottish Studies Library; School of Scottish Studies, 27– 29 George Square, Edinburgh, EH8 9LD; tel: 0131 650 3060; e-mail: scottish.studies@ed.ac.uk

UNIVERSITY OF ESSEX LIBRARY

Formal name: The Albert Sloman Library, University of Essex

Wivenhoe Park, Colchester, Essex, CO4 3SQ

Tel: 01206 873333
Fax: 01206 872289
E-mail: librarian@essex.ac.uk
Website: libwww.essex.ac.uk

Enquiries to: Librarian

Founded: 1963

Organisation type and purpose: University library.

Subject coverage: Biology, computing science, electronics, health sciences, mathematics, psychology; art, history, language and linguistics, literature and philosophy; accounting and financial management, business studies, economics, government, law, psychoanalysis, sociology. Special emphasis on Latin America, USA and the former Soviet Union.

Collection: Archives of Mrs Mary Whitehouse, CBE
Archives of SCOPE-ENUWAR (Scientific Committee on Problems of the Environmental Consequences of Nuclear War)
Archives of the National Viewers' and Listeners' Association
Archives of the Rowhedge Ironworks Company (1904–1964)
Archives of the Social Democratic Party (SDP)
Lord Rogers of Quarrybank (SDP papers)
Baron Newby of Rothwell (SDP papers)
Archives of the Tawney Society (the SDP 'Think Tank')
Bassingbourn Parish Library
Bean Collection on William Blake
Donald Davie Archive
Edgell Rickword Collection
European Documentation, from 1977
S E Finer Papers (UK transport policy)
George Goddeck Archive (psychoanalysis)
Hervey Benham Sound Archive (local history)
Historical Collection of the Royal Statistical Society
David Kerr Papers (UK health policy)
Letters of T E Lawrence
Levene/Sky Television Political interviews Video Archive
Nolan Committee Papers (Committee of Standards of Conduct in Public Life) 1995–1997
Letters, papers and diaries of Henri and Sophie Gaudier Brzeska
Letters, papers and diaries of John Hassall
National Social Policy and Social Change Archive (QUALIDATA)
Library of the Essex Society for Archaeology and History
Papers and printed books of the Colchester and Coggeshall Meetings of the Society of Friends
Papers of Enid Balint (psychoanalysis)
Papers (1992–93) of the Boundary Commission for England
Papers and Diaries of S L Bensusan
Papers of Lord Alport (Rhodesia, House of Lords, Colchester and Essex)
Papers of Lord Brimelow (Yalta Repatriation Agreement)
Papers on the Third London Airport controversy
Paul Sieghart Human Rights Archive
Russell Collection Family Archive
Sigmund Freud Collection (psychoanalysis)
Sir Vincent Evans Collection (European Court of Human Rights)
Watergate Collection
Windscale Inquiry Papers, 1977 (Nuclear reactor fuel reprocessing)
Margery Allingham / Philip Youngman Carter literary archives
Charter88 Archives (civil, political and human rights)
Bernie Hamilton Archive (human rights)
Colchester Medical Society Library (historical books)

Library catalogue: All or part available online

Publications: Printed

Publications list: Available online and in print

Access to staff: Contact by letter and by fax. Appointment necessary. Letter of introduction required.
Hours: Term time: Mon to Fri, 0800 to 2200; Sat, 0900 to 1800; Sun, 1400 to 1900
Vacations: Mon to Fri, 0900 to 1730

Access for disabled people: Level entry, access to all public areas, toilet facilities

UNIVERSITY OF EXETER – CAMBORNE SCHOOL OF MINES (CSM)

Pool, Redruth, Cornwall, TR15 3SE

Tel: 01209 714866
Fax: 01209 719677
E-mail: libcsm@csm.ex.ac.uk

Enquiries to: Librarian
Direct e-mail: jfoote@csm.ex.ac.uk

History of institution: formerly called Camborne School of Mines

Organisation type and purpose: University department or institute.
Education and research in mining engineering, extractive metallurgy, industrial geology, surveying and minerals resource management, environmental management.

Subject coverage: Metalliferous mining, mineral processing, extractive metallurgy, industrial geology, surveying, minerals resource management, environmental and waste management, mined land reclamation.

UNIVERSITY OF EXETER – ST LUKE'S CAMPUS LIBRARY

Heavitree Road, Exeter, Devon, EX1 2LU

Tel: 01392 264785
E-mail: stllmail@exeter.ac.uk
Website: as.exeter.ac.uk/library/about/exeter/stlukes/

Enquiries to: Librarian
Direct tel: 01392 264785

Founded: 1837; created by the merger of The Institute of Education and St Luke's College of Education (year of change 1978)

Organisation type and purpose: University library, university department or institute. Library of university faculty.

Subject coverage: Education, exercise and sport science.

Collection: National curriculum archive

Non-library collection catalogue: All or part available online

Library catalogue: All or part available online

Access to staff: Contact by letter, by telephone, by e-mail, in person and via website
Hours: The Library is open on weekdays and weekends but times vary during the year, so please check the current opening hours on the website or telephone for up to date information.

Access for disabled people: Parking provided, level entry, toilet facilities, lift, stair-lift.

Parent body: University of Exeter Library

UNIVERSITY OF EXETER – UNIVERSITY LIBRARY

Forum Library, University of Exeter, Stocker Road, Exeter, Devon, EX4 4PT

Tel: 01392 723867
Fax: 01392 263871
E-mail: library@exeter.ac.uk
Website: www.as.exeter.ac.uk/library

Enquiries to: Assistant Director, Collections and Research Support

Founded: 1855

Organisation type and purpose: University library. Serving the community as well as the university staff and students.

Subject coverage: Arts, law, social studies, science and technology.

Collection: Arabic and Gulf Studies
Audio-visual resources
Books and recordings related to American music, especially popular music
Dan Davin book collection of New Zealand literature
European Documentation Centre: European Commision Publications
Imperial Institute collection of photographs
Bill Douglas Centre for Film Studies
Crediton, Ottery St Mary and Totnes Parish Libraries
Dodderidge Collection
Ghana Collection (Scolma Area Specialization Plan)
MSS Collections (West Country authors)
Syon Abbey Collection

Trade and statistical information: EU Statistics

Non-library collection catalogue: All or part available online

Library catalogue: All or part available online

Access to staff: Contact by letter, by telephone, by fax and by e-mail. Appointment necessary.
Hours: Mon to Fri, 0900 to 1700

Includes the: Devon and Exeter Institution Library; Exeter University (St Luke's) Library

Member of: European Information Association

UNIVERSITY OF GLAMORGAN

Learning Resources Centre, Pontypridd, Rhondda Cynon Taff, CF37 1DL

Tel: 01443 482625\ Minicom no. 01443 482322
Fax: 01443 482629
E-mail: smorgan1@glam.ac.uk
Website: www.glam.ac.uk/lrc/home.htm

Enquiries to: Librarian
Direct e-mail: press@glam.ac.uk
Other contacts: Head of Learning Resources Centre

Organisation type and purpose: University library.

Subject coverage: Mathematics; computer science; physics; chemistry; life sciences; geology; chemical, civil, mechanical, manufacturing, electrical and electronic engineering; information technology; building; quantity surveying; estate management; law; politics; public administration; behavioural and communication studies; accountancy; business studies and management; arts and humanities; statistics; safety; languages; nursing and midwifery.

Collection: Centre for the Study of Welsh Writing in English Collection

Publications: Printed

Access to staff: Contact by letter, by telephone, by fax and by e-mail
Hours: Mon to Fri, 0900 to 1700

UNIVERSITY OF GLASGOW – ARCHIVE SERVICES

13 Thurso St, Glasgow, G11 6PE

Tel: 0141 330 5515
Fax: 0141 330 2640
E-mail: enquiries@archives.gla.ac.uk
Website: www.gla.ac.uk/archives
Website: universitystory.gla.ac.uk

Enquiries to: Duty Archivist

History of institution: formerly called Glasgow University Archives & Business Records Centre (year of change 2000)

Organisation type and purpose: University department or institute.
Archive repository.

Subject coverage: Higher education archives and history, business archives, retail, shipbuilding, engineering and textiles archives, Scottish culture, Scottish history.

Information services: Research service available.

Services for disabled people: Wheelchair-accessible, ground-level searchroom available by appointment.

Collection: Glasgow University Archives from 1451
Scottish Business Archives

Non-library collection catalogue: All or part available online and in-house

Library catalogue: All or part available online and in-house

Publications: Printed, and electronic and video

Access to staff: Contact by letter, by telephone, by fax, by e-mail, in person and via website. Appointment necessary.
Hours: Mon to Fri, 0930 to 1700

Access to building: *Hours:* Mon to Fri, 0930 to 1700
Special comments: 4 flights of stairs

Access for disabled people: Parking provided, toilet facilities, ground-level searchroom (appointment required)

Parent body: University of Glasgow Library; Glasgow, G12 8QE; tel: 0141 330 6704; e-mail: library@lib.gla.ac.uk; website: http://www.gla.ac.uk/library

UNIVERSITY OF GLASGOW – DIVISION OF VIROLOGY

Institute of Virology, Church Street, Glasgow, G11 5JR

Tel: 0141 330 4017 or 4029
Fax: 0141 337 2236
Website: www.vir.gla.ac.uk/staff.shtml

Enquiries to: Joint Heads of Division
Direct tel: 0141 330 4029

Founded: 1958; formerly called Institute of Virology (year of change 1994)

Organisation type and purpose: University department or institute.

Subject coverage: Herpes virus genomic and evolutionary biology; herpes virus gene control and latency; herpes virus genome replication; viral structure and assembly; antivirals, vaccines and immunological reagents; eukaryotic mRNA processing in virus infected cells; genomic and functional analysis of bunyavirus; molecular biology of hepatitis B virus; molecular biology of hepatitis C virus; molecular biology of RSV; molecular biology of picorna viruses.

Publications: Printed

Access to staff: Contact by letter, by telephone, by fax and by e-mail
Hours: Mon to Fri, 0900 to 1700
Special comments: Books and journals not available for outside loan.

Access to building: Prior appointment required

Access for disabled people: Ramped entry

Parent body: Medical Research Council; University of Glasgow

UNIVERSITY OF GLASGOW – LANGUAGE CENTRE LIBRARY (UGLC)

Hetherington Building, Bute Gardens, Glasgow, G12 8RS

Tel: 0141 330 4117
Fax: 0141 330 4114
E-mail: lc-librarian@arts.glasgow.ac.uk
Website: www.glasgow.ac.uk/langcent/library

Enquiries to: Librarian

Founded: 1985

Organisation type and purpose: University department or institute.

Subject coverage: Language learning – holdings in Catalan, Czech, French, German, Italian, Polish, Portuguese, Spanish, Russian and 35 other languages.

Non-library collection catalogue: All or part available online

Library catalogue: All or part available online

Publications: Printed

Access to staff: Contact by letter, by telephone, by fax, by e-mail and in person
Hours: Term time: Mon to Thu, 0930 to 2000; Fri, 0900 to 1645
Vacation: Mon to Fri, 0930 to 1645
Special comments: Please phone as opening times vary.

Access for disabled people: Ramped entry, toilet facilities, lift

UNIVERSITY OF GLASGOW – UNIVERSITY LIBRARY

Hillhead Street, Glasgow, G12 8QE

Tel: 0141 330 6704/5
Fax: 0141 330 4952
E-mail: library@lib.gla.ac.uk
Website: www.lib.gla.ac.uk/index.html

Enquiries to: Head of Enquiry Service
Direct e-mail: enquiries@lib.gla.ac.uk
Other contacts: Keeper of Special Collections

Founded: 1451

Organisation type and purpose: University library.

Subject coverage: Social sciences, humanities and medicine; administrative medicine; adult and continuing education; anaesthesia; ancient Near Eastern history; Arabic and Islamic studies; archaeology;

continued overleaf

architecture; art history; bibliography; cardiac surgery; cartography; Celtic; child and adolescent psychiatry; child health; clinical medicine; clinical physics; clinical surgery; community medicine; constitutional law and history; Czech; dental medicine; dermatology; drama; ecclesiastical history; economic history; economics; education; emblem studies; English language and literature; European Community; financial studies; fine art; forensic medicine; French; general practice (medicine); geography; geriatric medicine; German; Greek; haematology; Hebrew and Semitic languages; Hispanic studies; history; immunology; industrial relations; infectious diseases; international economic studies; Italian; Latin; Latin American studies; law; linguistics and phonetics; logic; media studies; medical genetics; medicine; music; neurology; neuropathology; neurosurgery; nursing studies; obstetrics and gynaecology; oncology; ophthalmology; orthopaedics; otolaryngology; pathology; pharmacology; philosophy; plastic surgery; Polish; politics; psychological medicine; psychology; religious studies; Russian; Scottish history; Scottish literature; social and economic research; social administration and social work; sociology; Soviet and East European studies; surgery; theology; veterinary medicine; science and technology; aeronautics and fluid mechanics; agriculture; anatomy; animal developmental biology; animal nutrition; astronomy; bacteriology and immunology; biochemistry; biology; botany; cell biology; chemical physics; chemistry; civil engineering; computing science; conveyancing; economics; electronics and electrical engineering; genetics; geology; history of science; management studies; mathematics; mechanical engineering; mercantile law; microbiology; naval architecture; ocean engineering; parasitology; pathology; physics; physiology; statistics; taxation; topographic science; virology; zoology.

Collection: Blau (200 vols, 16th-century Hebrew books)
Bourgeois (2,000 vols on philology)
Broady and Bisset (2,000 left-wing pamphlets)
Caricatures (3,000 French political caricatures of the Commune and Franco-Prussian war)
Eadie (8,000 vols of biblical studies and early printing)
Euing (15,000 vols including 400 black-letter ballads, 15th- and 16th-century books)
Euing Music (5,300 vols of scores, early printed music, history of music)
Farmer (the library of Henry George Farmer comprising 1,600 printed vols and 600 MSS with special emphasis on oriental and military music)
Ferguson (8,000 vols on alchemy, chemistry, witchcraft, gypsies and secret societies)
Gemmell (90 vols on the Dance of Death)
Geological Society of Glasgow: foreign periodicals
Hamilton (8,000 vols on philosophy)
Hepburn (300 vols mainly of 19th-century English literature)
Hunterian (10,000 vols including 534 incunabula, 649 MSS, especially strong in history of medicine and anatomy)
Institution of Engineers and Shipbuilders in Scotland: Library
Kelvin (papers relating to Lord Kelvin, William Thomson)
MacColl (6,000 letters to and from the art critic and poet, D. S. MacColl)
McGrigor (650 vols and 1,000 pamphlets on Palestine)
Mearns (3,000 vols on hymnology)
Morgan (papers of the poet, Edwin Morgan)
Munro (300 vols of editions of Sir Thomas Browne)
Murray (15,000 vols on bibliography and history of the West of Scotland)
Ogilvie (1,700 vols of 17th-century material and civil war pamphlets)
Robertson (1,000 vols on oriental languages)
Scottish Theatre Archive (playscripts, programmes, press cuttings, financial records, photographs, plans, taped interviews and correspondence)
Simson, Robert, mathematical library (850 vols of early mathematics and astronomy)
Smith (350 vols mostly of rare Glasgow pamphlets)
Spencer (111 vols of books and MSs relating to the Darien Scheme)
Stevenson (900 vols on Semitic languages, literature and archaeology)
Stirling Maxwell (2,000 vols of emblem and fête books)
Tischendorf (2,500 vols on biblical studies, codicology and topography from the library of Konstantin von Tischendorf)
Veitch (600 vols of medieval philosophy)
Walker-Arnott Botanical Collection
Whistler (3,300 vols of letters, MSs and papers of James McNeill Whistler)
Wright (the papers of Harold Wright, mainly concerning late 19th- and early 20th-century British artists and print-makers)
Wylie (1,000 vols on the history and antiquities of Glasgow)

Non-library collection catalogue: All or part available online

Library catalogue: All or part available online

Publications: Printed, and microform publications

Publications list: Available in print

Access to staff: Contact by letter, by telephone, by fax, by e-mail, in person and via website. Appointment necessary.
Hours: Mon to Fri, 0900 to 1955; Sat, 1300 to 1655

Access to building: *Hours:* Mon to Sun, 0715 to 2000
Special comments: Special Collections: Mon to Fri, 0900 to 1700; Sat, 0900 to 1230

Access for disabled people: Level entry, access to all public areas, toilet facilities
Special comments: Emergency egress when lifts not in use by protected stairwells only. Refuge areas available on levels 4 to 11.

UNIVERSITY OF GLOUCESTERSHIRE (UoG)

The Park Campus, Cheltenham, Gloucestershire, GL50 2RH

Tel: 01242 715442
Website: https://infonet.glos.ac.uk/student/Pages/default.aspx
Website: aleph.glos.ac.uk/F?RN=368518371

Enquiries to: LIS Administrator
Direct e-mail: rbashford@glos.ac.uk

Other contacts: Archivist (Archives) (for access to archive collections)

Founded: 1834; Cheltenham Mechanical Institute (year of change 1834); incorporates the former Gloucester Mechanical Institute (year of change 1840); incorporates the former Church Training College, Cheltenham (year of change 1847); incorporates the former St Paul's College of Education (year of change 1920); incorporates the former St Mary's College of Education (year of change 1920); incorporates the former Gloucestershire College of Education (year of change 1967); incorporates the former College of St Paul and St Mary (year of change 1979); incorporates the former Higher Education Section, Gloucestershire College of Arts and Technology (year of change 1980); incorporates the former Cheltenham and Gloucester College of Higher Education (year of change 1990)

Organisation type and purpose: University library.

University, providing foundation degrees, undergraduate and taught postgraduate degrees, research programmes.

Subject coverage: Advertising; animal biology; animation and interactive media; biology; business and management; creative writing; criminology; digital film; education; English language; English literature; environmental policy and management; film and media; fine art – painting and drawing; geography; graphic design; health studies; history; illustration; IT and computing; journalism; landscape architecture; law; leisure, tourism, hospitality and events management; photography; playwork; popular music; psychology; public relations; publishing; religion, philosophy, ethics; social work; sociology; sports and exercise science; sports development and coaching; teacher training; television and radio production.

Collection: Museum or gallery collection, archive, or library special collection: University Archive; Bristol and Gloucestershire Archaeological Society Library; Gloucestershire Poets, Writers and Artists collection: Dymock Poets Archive and Study Centre, Whittington Press Collection, U.A. Fanthorpe Collection, David Elyan Collection, James Elroy Flecker Collection; Paul Oliver Collection of African-American Music; Local Heritage Initiative; Forest of Dean Sculpture Trail Archive.

Non-library collection catalogue: All or part available online and in-house

Library catalogue: All or part available online

Access to staff: Contact by letter, by telephone, by e-mail, in person and via website. Appointment necessary. Non-members charged.
Hours: Mon to Fri, 0900 to 1700

Access to building: *Hours:* Mon to Fri, 0900 to 1700

Access for disabled people: Parking provided, ramped entry, toilet facilities

UNIVERSITY OF GREENWICH – INFORMATION SERVICES AND LIBRARY, AVERY HILL CAMPUS/ GREENWICH CAMPUS

Queen Mary Court, Old Royal Naval College, Park Row, Greenwich, London, SE10 9LS

Tel: 020 8331 8000 (switchboard)
E-mail: a.e.murphy@gre.ac.uk
Website: www.gre.ac.uk/offices/ils/ls

Enquiries to: Head of Learning Services
Direct tel: 020 8331 8196

Founded: 1891; incorporates the former Dartford College of Education (year of change 1972); incorporates the former Avery Hill College (year of change 1985); incorporates the former Garnett College (year of change 1989); incorporates the former Thames College of Health Care Studies, Thames Polytechnic (year of change 1993); incorporates the former Natural Resources Institute (year of change 1996)

Organisation type and purpose: University library.

Subject coverage: Architecture and landscape architecture, built environment, civil engineering, surveying, construction management, biology, chemistry, pharmaceutical science, pharmacy, business and management, computing, IT, earth sciences, engineering, environmental sciences, natural resources, humanities, law, mathematics, statistics, education, social sciences, health, sport science, maritime studies.

Collection: Sidney Keyes Archive
Institutional archives of Woolwich Polytechnic, Thames Polytechnic, Dartford College of Education, Avery Hill College of Education, Garnett College

Library catalogue: All or part available online

Publications list: Available online

Access to staff: Contact by e-mail and via website. Appointment necessary. Non-members charged.

Access to building: *Hours:* Term time: hours vary across campuses, usually: Mon to Fri, 0830 to 2100; Sat and Sun, 1100 to 1900; vacation: Mon to Fri, 0900 to 1900; (see website for details)

Access for disabled people: Ramped entry, level entry, toilet facilities

Branch libraries: University of Greenwich; Drill Hall Library, North Road, Chatham Maritime, Kent, ME4 4TB; tel: 01634 883278; e-mail: E.P.Cooper@greenwich.ac.uk; website: http://campus.medway.ac.uk/library/
University of Greenwich; Dreadnought Library, Maritime Greenwich Campus, 30 Park Row, Greenwich, London, SE10 9LS; tel: 020 8331 7788; e-mail: v.g.malone@gre.ac.uk; website: http://www.gre.ac.uk/offices/ils/ls/services/lib
University of Greenwich; Avery Hill Campus Library, Bexley Road, London, SE9 2PQ; tel: 020 8331 9656; e-mail: v.g.malone@gre.ac.uk; website: http://www.gre.ac.uk/offices/ils/ls/services/lib

UNIVERSITY OF HERTFORDSHIRE

Information Hertfordshire, College Lane, Hatfield, Hertfordshire, AL10 9AB

Tel: 01707 284653
Fax: 01707 284666
E-mail: lihsbuoffice@herts.ac.uk
Website: www.herts.ac.uk/lis
Website: www.voyager.herts.ac.uk
Website: www.herts.ac.uk/uhpress

Enquiries to: Dean / CIO

Founded: 1952; formerly called Hatfield Polytechnic

Organisation type and purpose: University library.

Subject coverage: Accounting, art, biosciences, careers and employment information, computing, design, economics, education, engineering, film and theatre, health, history, law, linguistics, literature, management, marketing, mathematics, midwifery, music, nursing, paramedic sciences, pharmacy, philosophy, physical sciences, physiotherapy, psychology, radiography, social care, social sciences, sports science, technology, tourism.

Non-library collection catalogue: All or part available online

Library catalogue: All or part available online

Order printed publications from: UH Press, tel: 01707 284681

Publications list: Available online and in print

Access to building: No prior appointment required
Hours: Mon to Fri, 0830 to 2200; Sat, Sun, 1100 to 1800
Special comments: Visual ID required for issue of Visitors Day Pass.

Access for disabled people: Parking provided, level entry, toilet facilities

UNIVERSITY OF HUDDERSFIELD – LIBRARY AND COMPUTING CENTRE

Queensgate, Huddersfield, West Yorkshire, HD1 3DH

Tel: 01484 422288
Fax: 01484 517897
E-mail: s.a.white@hud.ac.uk
Website: www.hud.ac.uk/cls

Enquiries to: Director of Computing and Library Services
Direct tel: 01484 472039

Founded: 1841

Organisation type and purpose: University library.

Subject coverage: Architecture, art and design, drama, English, history, hospitality and logistics, chemistry, computing, education, engineering, law, management, marketing, media, music, paramedical subjects including podiatry, social sciences, social work, teacher training, textiles.

Collection: British Music Collection (contemporary music); Rugby League Archive; Huddersfield Mechanics Institute archives; Colne Valley Constituency Labour Party archives
G. H. Wood Collection (free trade, women's employment, co-operative movement)
Huddersfield Labour Party archives
Wesley Historical Society (Yorkshire)
Engineering Industry archives

Non-library collection catalogue: All or part available in-house

Library catalogue: All or part available online

Access to staff: Contact by letter, by telephone, by fax, by e-mail, in person and via website
Hours: Term time: Mon to Fri, 0800 to 1900 hours; Sat and Sun afternoons

Access to building: Access via Student Centre, 4th Floor, Central Services Building
Hours: Term time: Mon to Thu, 0800 to 2400; Fri, 0800 to 2100; Sat, 0930 to 2100; Sun, 1300 to 2100
Vacations: Mon to Thu, 0845 to 2000; Fri, 0845 to 1700
Special comments: Personal reference use only.

Access for disabled people: Level entry, toilet facilities

UNIVERSITY OF HULL – ACADEMIC SERVICES LIBRARIES

Brynmor Jones Library, Cottingham Road, Hull, East Yorkshire, HU6 7RX

Tel: 01482 466581
Fax: 01482 466205
E-mail: libhelp@hull.ac.uk
Website: www.hull.ac.uk/lib

Enquiries to: Director of Academic Services and Librarian
Direct tel: 01482 465436
Direct e-mail: r.g.heseltine@hull.ac.uk

Founded: 1927

Organisation type and purpose: University library.

Subject coverage: Arts, humanities, social sciences, law, pure sciences, applied physics, electronic engineering, education, health sciences.

Collection: South-East Asia Collection
Labour history
Contemporary papers of political and social interest
Local archives

Non-library collection catalogue: All or part available in-house

Library catalogue: All or part available online

Access to staff: Contact by letter, by telephone, by fax, by e-mail and via website. Appointment necessary.
Hours: Mon to Fri, 0900 to 1700

Access to building: *Hours:* Mon to Thu, 0830 to 2200; Fri, 0830 to 2100; Sat, 0900 to 2100; Sun, 1300 to 2100 (term-time hours)

Access for disabled people: Ramped entry, toilet facilities

UNIVERSITY OF KENT – TEMPLEMAN LIBRARY

Canterbury, Kent, CT2 7NU

Tel: 01227 764000
Fax: 01227 823984

continued overleaf

E-mail: library-enquiry@ukc.ac.uk
Website: www.library.ukc.ac.uk/library
Website: www.library.ukc.ac.uk/librarycollections.htm
Website: www.library.ukc.ac.uk/cartoons
Website: www.library.ukc.ac.uk/library/bysubject.htm
Website: www.library.ukc.ac.uk/special

Enquiries to: Director of Information Services and Librarian
Direct tel: 01227 823565
Direct e-mail: m.m.coutts@ukc.ac.uk
Other contacts: Deputy Librarian

Founded: 1963

Organisation type and purpose: University library.
Subject coverage: Humanities: drama and theatre studies; English and American literature; history; classical and archaeological studies, comparative literature; Colonial and Post-Colonial studies, Medieval and Tudor studies; American studies; French, German, Italian, Spanish, linguistics and English language; philosophy, theology and religious studies; applied ethics; propaganda; history of science; modern cultural studies; European culture and languages, cartoons and caricature.
Sciences: chemistry; physics; biosciences; biotechnology; space sciences and astrophysics; materials research; medicine and health sciences; psychotherapy; computing; electronics; mathematics and statistics.
Social Sciences: accounting; anthropology; business; economics; law; politics and international relations; psychology; social and public policy; social work; sociology; conservation and ecology; social anthropology and computing; European regional and transport economics; health behaviour; group processes; health services; urban and regional studies; women's studies; geography; European studies.
Collection: British Chess Federation Library
Cartoons: 20th century cartoons and caricatures
Drama and Theatre:
Frank Pettingell Collection (19th century, texts, mss, playbills)
Melville Collection (1870–1930: typescripts, playbills, theatre records, memorabilia)
Reading-Raynor Collection (texts: biographical, critical, historical)
Richard Fawkes Collection (material on Dion Boucicault)
English Literature:
John Crow Collection
Bonamy Dobree Collection
T S Eliot Collection
Modern Poetry Collection
History of Science:
Maddison Collection of the History of Science
Miscellaneous:
Weatherill Collection (papers of the Speaker of the House of Commons)
C P Davies Wind- and Water-mill Collection
Muggeridge Collection of Windmill Photographs
Lloyd George Collection (signed copies from his library)
European Documentation Centre
Madagascar (formerly SCOLMA SPECIALISATION)
Slide Collection (135,000 slides, chiefly fine arts)
Microfilm Collection:
British Sessional Papers 1801–1969 (microcard)
Landmarks of Science (microcard)
Three Centuries of Drama (microcard)

Non-library collection catalogue: All or part available online

Library catalogue: All or part available online

Publications: Printed, and electronic and video, and microform publications

Publications list: Available online and in print

Access to staff: Contact by letter, by telephone, by fax, by e-mail, in person and via website. Appointment necessary. Non-members charged.
Hours: Mon to Fri, 0900 to 1700
Special comments: Limited availability in evenings and at weekends.

Access to building: No access other than to staff
Hours: Term time: Mon to Fri, 0845 to 2200; Sat, Sun, 1000 to 2200
Vacations: Mon to Fri, 0900 to 1900; Sat, 1100 to 1900; Sun, closed

Access for disabled people: Level entry, access to all public areas, toilet facilities

UNIVERSITY OF LEEDS – DEPARTMENT OF ARABIC AND MIDDLE EASTERN STUDIES

Leeds, West Yorkshire, LS2 9JT

Tel: 0113 343 3421
Fax: 0113 343 3517
E-mail: c.e.honess@leeds.ac.uk

Enquiries to: Secretary

Organisation type and purpose: University department.

Subject coverage: Arabic language; Islamic religion and culture; Mediterranean studies and culture.

Publications: Printed

Access to staff: Contact by letter, by telephone, by fax and by e-mail
Hours: Mon to Fri, 0900 to 1700

UNIVERSITY OF LEEDS – EDUCATION COLLECTION

University Library, Leeds, West Yorkshire, LS2 9JT

Tel: 0113 233 5517
Fax: 0113 233 5539
E-mail: libjms@library.novell.leeds.ac.uk
Website: www.leeds.ac.uk/library/library.html

Enquiries to: Assistant Librarian

Organisation type and purpose: University library.

Subject coverage: Education, psychology, teaching methods of curricular subjects.

Collection: W B Thompson Collection of Greek and Latin school textbooks
Historical collection of biology school textbooks
19th century educational sources and texts

Publications: Printed, and electronic and video

Access to staff: Contact by letter and by e-mail. Appointment necessary.
Hours: Mon to Fri, 0900 to 1700

UNIVERSITY OF LEEDS – UNIVERSITY LIBRARY

Leeds, West Yorkshire, LS2 9JT

Tel: 0113 343 5501
Fax: 0113 343 3556
E-mail: library@library.novell.leeds.ac.uk
Website: www.leeds.ac.uk/library/spcoll/
Website: www.leeds.ac.uk/library/library.html

Enquiries to: Librarian
Direct tel: 0113 343 5663

Founded: 1874

Organisation type and purpose: University library.

Subject coverage: Agriculture; Arabic; architecture; astronomy; bibliography; biology; biophysics; botany; ceramics; chemical engineering and technology; chemistry; China and Chinese studies; civil engineering; classical studies; dentistry; dyes and dyeing; economics; education; electrical engineering; engineering in general; English; food science and technology; French; fuels and fuel technology; geography and topography; geology; German; history; Italian; law; leather and leatherwork; linguistics; mathematics; mechanical engineering; medicine; metallurgy; meteorology; mines and mining; music; numismatics; palaeontology; philosophy; physics; politics; Portuguese; psychology; Russian; science; seismology; Semitics; Slavonic studies; social sciences; Spanish; technology in general; textiles; theology; translations; transport; Yorkshire; zoology.
Law Library: English, European, Commonwealth and American Law, criminology, police studies.

Collection: All Souls' College and Chaston Chapman Collections of early science
Anglo-French Collection (French books reflecting the influence of Great Britain on France to 1850)
Blanche Leigh, J F Preston and Camden Collections (historical books on cookery and domestic management)
Brotherton Collection (rare books and MSS, especially on English literature of the 17th, 18th and 19th centuries and on Romany literature)
Business archives of the West Yorkshire wool textile industry (18th to 20th centuries)
European Documentation Centre
Icelandic Collection
Leeds and West Riding Medico-Chirurgical Society Collection
Leeds Philosophical and Literary Society Library
Leeds Russian Archive (literary and historical MSS)
Liddle Collection of First World War archive materials
Medical classics, originally of the library of the old Infirmary
19th and 20th century educational sources, texts and archives

Quaker literature
Ripon Cathedral Library, and archives of the Dean and Chapter
Roth Collection of Judaica
W B Thompson Collection of Greek and Latin school textbooks
Wentworth-Woolley Hall estate papers (16th to 20th centuries)
Whitaker Collection of Atlases (mainly of the British Isles)
Yorkshire Geological Society Library
Yorkshire Quaker Archives (17th to 20th centuries)

Non-library collection catalogue: All or part available online and in print

Library catalogue: All or part available online

Publications: Printed, and electronic and video

Publications list: Available in print

Access to staff: Contact by letter. Non-members charged.
Hours: Mon to Fri, 0900 to 1700

Access for disabled people: Access to all public areas

UNIVERSITY OF LEICESTER – CLINICAL SCIENCES LIBRARY

Robert Kilpatrick Clinical Sciences Building, PO Box 65, Leicester Royal Infirmary, Leicester, LE2 7LX

Tel: 0116 252 3104
Fax: 0116 252 3107
E-mail: clinlib@leicester.ac.uk
Website: www.le.ac.uk/library/clinical/clinlib.htm

Founded: 1978

Organisation type and purpose: University library.
Hospital library of the Medical School of the University of Leicester.

Subject coverage: Medicine, health, nursing, midwifery and professions allied to medicine and social care.

Non-library collection catalogue: All or part available online

Library catalogue: All or part available online

Access to staff: Contact by letter, by telephone, by fax, by e-mail, in person and via website. Appointment necessary.
Hours: Mon to Fri, 0900 to 2100; Sat, 0900 to 1800; Sun, 1400 to 1800

Access to building: No prior appointment required
Hours: 24-hour access
Special comments: Outside staffed hours, access for University of Leicester staff and students, and NHS staff only.

Access for disabled people: Level entry, access to all public areas, toilet facilities

Links with: Other hospital libraries in the region

UNIVERSITY OF LEICESTER – DAVID WILSON LIBRARY

Box 248, University Road, Leicester, LE1 9QD

Tel: 0116 252 2043
Fax: 0116 252 2066
E-mail: libdesk@le.ac.uk
Website: www.le.ac.uk/library

Enquiries to: Enquiry service

Organisation type and purpose: University library.

Subject coverage: Archaeology; art history; astronomy; biological sciences; chemistry; computing; economic and social history; economics; engineering; English; French; genetics; geography; geology; German; history; Italian; law; local history; management; mass communications; mathematics; microbiology; museum studies; physics; politics; pre-clinical medicine; psychology; social work; sociology; zoology.

Collection: Burrows Collection (20th-century music)
English local history
European documentation
Fairclough Collection (17th century)
Leicester Medical Society
Mathematical Association Library
Orton Papers
Sue Townsend collection

Non-library collection catalogue: All or part available online

Library catalogue: All or part available online

Access to staff: Contact by letter, by telephone, by fax, by e-mail, in person and via website. Appointment necessary. Letter of introduction required. Non-members charged.
Hours: Sep to Jun: Mon to Fri, 0900 to 2100; Sat, 0900 to 1700; Sun, 1200 to 1800
Jul and Aug: Mon to Sat, 0900 to 1700

Access to building: *Hours:* Sep to Jun: Mon to Fri, 0800 to 0000; Sat, Sun, 0900 to 0000
Jul and Aug: Mon to Fri, 0900 to 1730; Sat 0900 to 1800

Branch libraries: Clinical Sciences Library

UNIVERSITY OF LINCOLN – UNIVERSITY LIBRARY

Brayford Pool, Lincoln, LN6 7TS

Tel: 01522 886664
Fax: 01522 886311
E-mail: acquisitions@lincoln.ac.uk
Website: www.lincoln.ac.uk

Enquiries to: University Librarian
Direct tel: 01522 886310
Direct e-mail: isnowley@lincoln.ac.uk

History of institution: formerly called University of Lincolnshire and Humberside

Organisation type and purpose: University library.

Subject coverage: Accountancy, architecture, art and design, building, business, communications, criminology, design, economics, English, environment, film, finance, food management, history, housing, humanities, languages, law, literature, management, marketing, media studies, photography, politics, printing, printmaking, psychology, radio, social policy, social science, social work, sociology, statistics and tourism.

Access to staff: Contact via website

UNIVERSITY OF LIVERPOOL – UNIVERSITY LIBRARY

PO Box 123, Liverpool, L69 3DA

Tel: 0151 794 2674
Fax: 0151 794 2681
Website: www.liv.ac.uk/library

Enquiries to: Librarian
Direct tel: 0151 794 2673
Other contacts: Head of Special Collections and Archives

Organisation type and purpose: University library.

Subject coverage: The main holdings in humanities, social sciences and special collections are housed in the Sydney Jones Library; those in science, medicine, engineering, veterinary and dental science and archives are in the Harold Cohen Library; there are departmental libraries in education, law, archaeology, chemistry, civic design, continuing education, geology, music, oceanography, physics, marine biology (Port Erin, Isle of Man), veterinary science (Leahurst, Wirral).

Collection: Blake Collection (items by and about William Blake)
Brunner Papers (letter-books, accounts, diaries, etc. of Sir John Brunner, 1842–1919, including material on chemical industry)
Campbell Brown Collection (414 books of the 16th-19th centuries, on alchemy and chemistry)
Comte Collection (Positivism)
Fraser Collection (includes about 900 items on tobacco art, English literature, Scottish books, positivism, phrenology, some manuscript material)
Grace Collection (158 books on mathematics, printed 17th-19th centuries)
Manuscript collections of Joseph Blanco White, Charles Booth, John and Katharine Bruce Glasier, Josephine Butler
Noble Collection (fine printed and limited editions of English books of the late 19th and early 20th centuries and many examples of the private presses)
Peers Collection (Spanish Civil War)
Rathbone Papers (family and business papers of the Rathbones, Greenbank, Liverpool, 18th-20th centuries)
Rendall Collection (a. Marcus Aurelius; b. Shakespeare controversy)
Robert Graves Collection
Salisbury Collection (340 scientific books of the 19th century, mostly English)
Science Fiction Foundation Collection (books and magazines of science fiction and fantasy, including critical works and journals. Much foreign-language material, including the Myers Collection of Russian SF; manuscript and archive material of a number of SF writers; pseudo-science material including the Flat Earth Society Papers. c. 25,000 items)
Scott-MacFie Collection (works on Romany and Gypsy lore, books, manuscripts, broadsides, prints, photographs, sheet music, records and tape)
Simey Collection (women in society)
Stapledon Collection (philosophy and science fiction)
Merseyside Poets Collection (manuscripts, first drafts)

continued overleaf

Thomson Collection (114 bound volumes of c. 1200 English pamphlets, 1689–1789)
Un-named collections on the history of medicine, 19th century documents of the US Congress, Latin American topography, selected modern poets
Whale Collection (309 books and pamphlets of the 19th-20th centuries on finance and banking)

Library catalogue: All or part available online

Publications: Printed

Access to staff: Contact by letter, by telephone, by e-mail and in person
Hours: Special collections and archives, Mon to Fri, 0930 to 1645
Special comments: Visitors by appointment for special collections and archives.

Access for disabled people: Ramped entry, access to all public areas, toilet facilities

UNIVERSITY OF LONDON – GERMANIC STUDIES LIBRARY

29 Russell Square, London, WC1B 5DP

Tel: 020 7862 8967
Fax: 020 7862 8970
E-mail: igslib@sas.ac.uk

Enquiries to: Librarian

Founded: 1950

Organisation type and purpose: University library.

Subject coverage: German language and literature of all periods (including Austria and Switzerland).

Collection: Friedrich Gundolf Archive
Lexicography, dialect dictionaries and grammars
Priebsch-Closs Collection (first and early edns of 18th- and early 19th-century authors)
Reference library of some 100,000 vols and 300 current periodicals

Library catalogue: All or part available online

Access to staff: Contact by letter, by telephone, by fax, by e-mail and in person
Hours: Mon to Fri, 0945 to 1730

Access to building: *Hours:* Mon to Fri, 0945 to 1745

Constituent part of: University of London Research Library Services

UNIVERSITY OF LONDON – INTERNATIONAL SCHOOL EFFECTIVENESS AND IMPROVEMENT CENTRE (ISEIC)

Institute of Education, 20 Bedford Way, London, WC1H 0AL

Tel: 020 7612 6347/6323/6409
Fax: 020 7612 6344
E-mail: iseic.admin@ioe.ac.uk
Website: www.ioe.ac.uk/iseic

Enquiries to: Administrator

Founded: 1994

Organisation type and purpose: Membership association (membership is by subscription), present number of members: 1100, university department or institute, research organisation.
Research and consultancy.

Subject coverage: ISEIC brings together academics and professionals involved in research and development work in the fields of school effectiveness and improvement. It engages in consultancy work for LEAs and schools, and runs NSIN, the National School Improvement Network.

Publications: Printed

Publications list: Available online and in print

Access to staff: Contact by letter, by telephone, by fax and by e-mail. Non-members charged.
Hours: Mon to Fri, 0900 to 1700

Subsidiary body: National School Improvement Network (NSIN); at the same address

UNIVERSITY OF NORTHAMPTON

Park Campus, Boughton Green Road, Northampton, NN2 7AL

Tel: 01604 735500
Fax: 01604 718819
Website: library.northampton.ac.uk

Enquiries to: Director of Information Services
Direct tel: 01604 892045
Direct e-mail: Hilary.Johnson@northampton.ac.uk

Organisation type and purpose: University.

Subject coverage: Whole range of social sciences and humanities, education, history of Northamptonshire, American studies, health studies, nursing, leather technology, waste management.

Collection: Collection of the National Leathersellers Centre
Osborne Robinson Collection of posters (1890 onwards) (School of Art and Design)
AEA Technology Wastes Management Collection

Library catalogue: All or part available online

Access to staff: Contact by letter, by telephone, by fax and by e-mail. Appointment necessary.
Hours: Term time: Mon to Fri, 0830 to 2200; Sat, 1000 to 1700; Sun, 1300 to 1700

Access for disabled people: Access to all public areas, toilet facilities

Other address: Avenue Campus; St George's Avenue, Northampton, NN2 6JD

UNIVERSITY OF NOTTINGHAM – DJANOGLY LEARNING RESOURCE CENTRE (DLRC)

Jubilee Campus, Nottingham, NG8 1BB

Website: www.nottingham.ac.uk/is

Organisation type and purpose: University library.

Subject coverage: Education and computer science.

Library catalogue: All or part available online

UNIVERSITY OF NOTTINGHAM – GEORGE GREEN LIBRARY OF SCIENCE AND ENGINEERING

University Park, Nottingham, NG7 2RD

Tel: 0115 951 4570
Fax: 0115 951 4578
Website: www.nottingham.ac.uk/is

Enquiries to: Librarian
Direct tel: 0115 846 7463

Organisation type and purpose: Constituent part of the University library.

Subject coverage: Botany; chemical engineering; chemistry; civil engineering; computer science; electrical and electronic engineering; geology; manufacturing engineering; materials science; mathematics; mechanical engineering; metallurgy; mineral resources engineering; pharmacy; physics; psychology; remote sensing; theoretical mechanics; zoology.

Collection: British Standards
Porter Collection (on ornithology)

Trade and statistical information: International metal statistics

UNIVERSITY OF NOTTINGHAM – GREENFIELD MEDICAL LIBRARY

Queen's Medical Centre, Nottingham, NG7 2UH

Tel: 0115 970 9441
Fax: 0115 970 9449
E-mail: library-medical-enquiries@nottingham.ac.uk
Website: www.nottingham.ac.uk/is/locations/library/greenfield

Enquiries to: Medical Librarian
Direct e-mail: wendy.stanton@nottingham.ac.uk

Founded: 1968

Organisation type and purpose: University library.

Subject coverage: Biochemistry; child health; community health; human anatomy; genetics; medicine; obstetrics and gynaecology; nursing; midwifery; pathology; physiology; pharmacology; psychiatry; surgery; therapeutics; anaesthetics; chemical pathology; chest medicine; dermatology; geriatrics; haematology; histopathology; learning disabilities; neurology; ophthalmology; paediatrics; radiology; rheumatology.

Collection: F H Jacob History of Medicine Collection

Library catalogue: All or part available online

Access to staff: Contact by letter, by telephone, by fax, by e-mail, in person and via website. Non-members charged.
Hours: Mon to Fri, 0800 to 2300

Access for disabled people: Ramped entry, toilet facilities

Other affiliated libraries: School of Nursing Library; Mansfield; School of Nursing Library; Derby

Serves the: Nottingham University; Faculty of Medicine and Health Sciences; University Hospital NHS Trust; Queens Medical Centre

UNIVERSITY OF NOTTINGHAM – HALLWARD LIBRARY

University Park, Nottingham, NG7 2RD

Tel: 0115 951 4557
Fax: 0115 951 4558
Website: www.nottingham.ac.uk/library

Enquiries to: Librarian

Organisation type and purpose: University library.

Subject coverage: American studies (literature and history), archaeology, architecture, art history, child development, classics, economic, industrial and social history, economics, education, including adult education, educational psychology, English language and literature, film and cinema, French language and literature, geography, German language and literature, Hispanic studies (Spanish, Catalan, Portuguese), history, insurance, local government and administration, management, money and banking, music, philosophy, planning and development, politics, Slavonic studies, including Russian, Yugoslav, Serbian, Croatian and Slovene, social administration, social work, sociology, textile history, theology, trade unions and Viking studies.

Collection: Archive of newspaper cuttings (approximately 750,000 cuttings) relating to the politics, social, economic and cultural conditions in Germany (especially East Germany) 1946–1981
Holdings from former East German library (Diesdorf, Magdeburg)
Mellish Collection (meteorology)
Waldheim: A Commission of Enquiry – documentary research material collected by Thames Television for a television programme June 1988
Large collection of microforms, mainly in the arts and humanities
Large collection of CD-ROMs

Trade and statistical information: Large collection of UK government and international statistics

Library catalogue: All or part available online

Publications: Printed, and electronic and video, and microform publications

Branch library of: Nottingham University; Music Library

UNIVERSITY OF NOTTINGHAM – JAMES CAMERON GIFFORD LIBRARY

Sutton Bonington Campus, Loughborough, Leicestershire, LE12 5RD

Tel: 0115 951 6390
Fax: 0115 951 6389
E-mail: suzanna.rogers@nottingham.ac.uk
Website: www.nottingham.ac.uk/is

Enquiries to: Librarian
Direct e-mail: library-biosciences-enquiries@nottingham.ac.uk

Organisation type and purpose: University library.

Subject coverage: Agriculture, horticulture, farm management, food science and microbiology, animal and plant biochemistry and physiology, environmental biology, soil science, applied biology, animal production, nutrition and dietetics, veterinary medicine and science.

Library catalogue: All or part available online

Publications list: Available online

Access to staff: Contact by letter and by e-mail
Hours: Mon to Fri, 0900 to 1700

Constituent part of: University of Nottingham Information Services

UNIVERSITY OF NOTTINGHAM – MANUSCRIPTS AND SPECIAL COLLECTIONS

King's Meadow Campus, Lenton Lane, Nottingham, NG7 2NR

Tel: 0115 951 4565
Fax: 0115 846 8651
E-mail: mss-library@nottingham.ac.uk
Website: www.nottingham.ac.uk/mss

Enquiries to: Manuscripts and Special Collections

Organisation type and purpose: University library.

Collection: Manuscript and Archive Collections:
Includes local ecclesiastical, industrial and trade union collections, substantial collections of local family and estate papers; records of the Severn-Trent Water Authority and its forerunners from the 17th century; records of the General Hospital and other Nottingham hospitals
Manuscript collections in Restoration verse, William of Orange and the 1688 Revolution, the Jacobite Rising of 1745, the American War of Independence, the Peninsular War, the Crimean War, 18th- and 19th-century British and Irish politics and foreign affairs, India of the early 19th century, British colonies of the mid-19th century, history of nonconformity, draining of the Fens, the 17th-century naturalists John Ray and Francis Willoughby
D. H. Lawrence Collection (literary papers, books)
Germany 1946–1981: Archive of Newspaper Cuttings (in German)
Mellish Collection (meteorological papers)
Printed Books Collections:
Benedikz Collection (Icelandic literature, mainly in Icelandic)
Briggs Collection (educational books before 1851)
Cambridge Drama Collection (English plays 1750–1850)
Cambridge Shakespeare Collection (edns of Shakespeare's plays)
East Midlands Collection (Derbyshire, Leicestershire, Lincolnshire, Nottinghamshire, Rutland)
Medical Rare Books Collection
French Revolution Collection
Nottingham Medico-Chirurgical Society Collection
Oakham and Elston Parochial Libraries (17th century)
Coleorton Parish Library Collection
Parker Woodward Collection (on the Bacon-Shakespeare controversy)
Porter Ornithological Collection

Non-library collection catalogue: All or part available online

Library catalogue: All or part available online

Publications: Printed, and electronic and video, and microform publications

Publications list: Available online

Access to staff: Contact by letter, by telephone, by fax, by e-mail and via website. Appointment necessary.
Hours: Mon to Fri, 0900 to 1700
Special comments: ID required for reader ticket.

UNIVERSITY OF OXFORD – BALFOUR LIBRARY (PITT RIVERS MUSEUM)

School of Anthropology and Museum Ethnography, South Parks Road, Oxford, OX1 3PP

Tel: 01865 270928
Fax: 01865 270943
E-mail: librarian@prm.ox.ac.uk
Website: www.lib.ox.ac.uk/olis
Website: www.prm.ox.ac.uk

Enquiries to: Librarian
Direct tel: 01865 270939
Direct e-mail: library@prm.ox.ac.uk
Other contacts: Director of the Museum

Founded: 1884

Organisation type and purpose: Museum, university library, suitable for ages: 18+.

Subject coverage: Anthropology, ethnology, prehistoric archaeology, material culture, museum studies, ethnomusicology, visual anthropology (including ethnographic film and photography), ethnographic art.

Collection: Books owned by Henry Balfour, first curator of the Museum
Collection of over 100,000 anthropological photographs from c.1850 onwards
Collections of papers of Henry Balfour, E. B. Tyler, W. Baldwin Spencer and others who have made important contributions to the history of anthropology and archaeology (separate Manuscript and Photographic Archive, see website)
Ellen Ettlinger Bequest of books on folklore
June Bedford collection of books on ethnographic art

Non-library collection catalogue: All or part available online

Library catalogue: All or part available online and in-house

Publications: Printed

Publications list: Available online and in print

Access to staff: Contact by letter, by telephone, by fax and by e-mail. Appointment necessary.
Hours: Term time: Mon to Fri, 0900 to 1700
Vacations: 0900 to 1230 and 1400 to 1600; closed August
For Christmas and Easter hours, please phone or e-mail
Special comments: Reference only for non-members of the University.

Access for disabled people: Parking provided

continued overleaf

Links with: Institute of Social and Cultural Anthropology; Tylor Library, University of Oxford

UNIVERSITY OF OXFORD – BODLEIAN EDUCATION LIBRARY (EDU)

15 Norham Gardens, Oxford, OX2 6PY

Tel: 01865 274028
Fax: 01865 274027
E-mail: education.library@bodleian.ox.ac.uk
Website: www.education.ox.ac.uk/library

History of institution: formerly called Department of Educational Studies Library (year of change 2007); formerly called Education Library (year of change 2010)

Organisation type and purpose: University department or institute.

Subject coverage: Education; educational psychology; sociology of education; applied social sciences; methodology of teaching of subjects in the secondary school curriculum.

Services for disabled people: Equipment available: magnifier, hearing loop, variable height chairs, lift to library level.
Services available: extended loan periods, book fetching.
Please let staff know if there is anything else they can do to improve your library experience.

Collection: Histories of individual schools and universities
Pre-1918 government publications on education

Library catalogue: All or part available online

Access to staff: Contact by letter, by telephone, by fax, by e-mail and in person
Hours: Term time: Mon to Thu, 0830 to 2030; Fri, 0830 to 1900; Sat, 1300 to 1700; Sun, 1200 to 1600
Vacation: Mon to Fri, 0900 to 1730

Access to building: *Hours:* Term time: Mon to Thu, 0830 to 2030; Fri, 0830 to 1900; Sat, 1300 to 1700; Sun, 1200 to 1600
Vacation: Mon to Fri, 0900 to 1730
Special comments: Visitors should have a Bodleian Reader's Card, available from http://www.bodleian.ox.ac.uk/services/admissions.

Access for disabled people: Parking and lift available
Hours: Office hours (other times by appointment)
Special comments: There is a lift to the library; one reading room is reached by stairs only. Staff will happily fetch any books that are out of reach.

Constituent part of: Bodleian Libraries; Bodleian Library, Broad Street, Oxford, OX1 3BG; tel: 01865 277162; fax: 01865 277182; e-mail: reader.services@bodleian.ox.ac.uk; website: http://www.bodleian.ox.ac.uk

UNIVERSITY OF OXFORD – BODLEIAN SOCIAL SCIENCE LIBRARY

Manor Road Building, Manor Road, Oxford, OX1 3UL

Tel: 01865 271093
Fax: 01865 271072
E-mail: library@ssl.ox.ac.uk
Website: www.ssl.ox.ac.uk

Founded: 2004

Organisation type and purpose: University library.

Subject coverage: Criminology, economics, international development, politics and international relations, refugee studies, Russian and East European studies, social policy and social work, socio-legal studies, sociology.

Collection: 150,000 vols, 1,000 journal and serial subscriptions
Economics and international development working papers from 200 institutions
African and Latin American collections

Trade and statistical information: Data on all international trade

Library catalogue: All or part available online

Access to staff: Contact by letter, by telephone, by fax, by e-mail and via website. Appointment necessary. Access for members only.
Hours: Mon to Fri, 0900 to 1730

Access to building: Term time: Mon to Fri, 0900 to 2200; Sat, 1000 to 1800; Sun, 1200 to 1800
Vacation: Mon to Fri, 0900 to 1900; Sat, 1000 to 1600; Sun, closed

Access for disabled people: Ramped entry, wide doorway, toilet facilities

UNIVERSITY OF OXFORD – COMPUTING LABORATORY

The Library, Wolfson Building, Parks Road, Oxford, OX1 3QD

Tel: 01865 273838
Fax: 01865 273839
E-mail: library@comlab.ox.ac.uk
Website: www.comlab.ox.ac.uk/

Enquiries to: Librarian
Direct tel: 01865 273837
Direct e-mail: Gordon.Riddell@comlab.ox.ac.uk

Organisation type and purpose: University department or institute, research organisation.

Subject coverage: Scientific computation including formal methods, numerical analysis and computational fluid dynamics, and general computing science.

Library catalogue: All or part available online

Publications: Printed

Access to staff: Appointment necessary.
Hours: Mon to Fri, 0900 to 1700

Subsidiary body: Centre for Requirements and Foundations; Numerical Analysis Group (NAGp); Programming Research Group (PRG)

UNIVERSITY OF OXFORD – DEPARTMENT OF EARTH SCIENCES

Parks Road, Oxford, OX1 3PR

Tel: 01865 272000
Fax: 01865 272072
E-mail: jennyc@earth.ox.ac.uk

Enquiries to: Librarian
Direct tel: 01865 272050

Organisation type and purpose: University department or institute.

Subject coverage: Earth sciences; geology; geodesy; mineralogy; geochemistry; geophysics; oceanography; stratigraphy; tectonics; crystallography; petrology; sedimentology.

Collection: Collection of reprints
Wager, Lawrence Rickard (1904–1965) collection

Access to staff: Contact by letter, by telephone, by fax and by e-mail. Appointment necessary. Letter of introduction required.
Hours: Term time; Mon to Thu, 0900 to 1730; Fri, 0900 to 1630
Vacations; Mon to Thu, 0900 to 1730

Access to building: No prior appointment required
Special comments: Bodleian Readers Card required

Access for disabled people: Toilet facilities
Special comments: One step at entrance

UNIVERSITY OF OXFORD – DEPARTMENT OF PHYSICS

Denys Wilkinson Building, Keble Road, Oxford, OX1 3RH

Tel: 01865 273333
Fax: 01865 273418
Website: www2.physics.ox.ac.uk/library/default.asp

Enquiries to: Librarian
Direct tel: 01865 273421
Direct e-mail: library@physics.ox.ac.uk

Organisation type and purpose: University department or institute.

Subject coverage: Theoretical and observational cosmology, galactic astronomy, stellar and interstellar physics, telescopes and instrumentation, nuclear physics, particle physics.

Collection: Astronomical library (not open to the public)

Library catalogue: All or part available in-house

Publications list: Available in print

Access to staff: Access for members only.
Hours: Mon to Fri, 1400 to 1700

Access to building: No access other than to staff

Access for disabled people: Level entry, access to all public areas, toilet facilities

UNIVERSITY OF OXFORD – ENGINEERING SCIENCE LIBRARY

Department of Engineering Science, Parks Road, Oxford, OX1 3PJ

Tel: 01865 273193
Fax: 01865 273010
E-mail: library@eng.ox.ac.uk
Website: www.eng.ox.ac.uk/home.html

Enquiries to: Librarian
Direct e-mail: anne.greig@eng.ox.ac.uk

Organisation type and purpose: University department or institute.

Subject coverage: Engineering.

Publications: Printed

Access to staff: Contact by letter, by telephone and by e-mail. Appointment necessary.
Hours: Mon to Fri, 0900 to 1700

Parent body: Oxford University

UNIVERSITY OF OXFORD – ENGLISH FACULTY LIBRARY

St Cross Building, Manor Road, Oxford, OX1 3UQ

Tel: 01865 271050
Fax: 01865 271054
Website: www.lib.ox.ac.uk
Website: users.ox.ac.uk/~enginfo/

Enquiries to: Librarian
Direct tel: 01865 271051
Direct e-mail: susan.usher@efl.ox.ac.uk

Founded: 1914

Organisation type and purpose: University library.

Subject coverage: English language and literature; Old Norse language and literature.

Collection: E H W Meyerstein's published books and manuscripts
Old Norse: working libraries of E O G Turville-Petre, W P Ker, G Vigfússon, and F York Powell (the last two on loan from Christ Church)
Wilfred Owen Collection (his library, some manuscripts and memorabilia)

Access to staff: Contact by letter, by telephone, by fax and by e-mail. Appointment necessary.
Hours: Termtime: Mon to Fri, 0930 to 1900, Sat 0930 to 1230
Vacations: Mon to Fri, 0930 to 1700
Special comments: Visitors from other academic institutions may normally use the library for reference purposes in the vacations only.

Access for disabled people: Parking provided, ramped entry, level entry, access to all public areas, toilet facilities

UNIVERSITY OF OXFORD – MODERN LANGUAGES FACULTY LIBRARY

Taylor Institution, St Giles, Oxford, OX1 3NA

Tel: 01865 278152
E-mail: graduate.studies@mod-langs.ox.ac.uk
Website: www.ox.ac.uk
Website: users.ox.ac.uk/~mlflinfo/index.html
Website: www.lib.ox.ac.uk

Enquiries to: Librarian
Direct tel: 01865 278155
Direct e-mail: gordon.robson@mlfl.ox.ac.uk
Other contacts: Deputy Librarian for Spanish and Portuguese.

Founded: 1960

Organisation type and purpose: University department or institute.

Subject coverage: Modern European languages and literature; general linguistics, German, French, Italian, Spanish, Portuguese, Latin American, Catalan, Occitan; European cinema.

Collection: Collection of European Newspapers (in original form). This collection is to be disposed of owing to lack of space. Any request from libraries for any part of it will be welcome.
Recordings on audio and video cassette of European literary, historical and cultural works, and cinema

Non-library collection catalogue: All or part available online

Library catalogue: All or part available online

Publications: Printed

Access to staff: Contact by letter, by telephone, by e-mail and in person. Letter of introduction required.
Hours: Term time: Mon to Fri, 0900 to 1800
Vacations: 0900 to 1300 and 1400 to 1730
Summer: 0900 to 1300 and 1400 to 1700

UNIVERSITY OF OXFORD – MUSIC FACULTY LIBRARY

Formal name: Bodleian Music Faculty Library

St Aldate's, Oxford, OX1 1DB

Tel: 01865 276148
E-mail: music.library@bodleian.ox.ac.uk
Website: www.bodleian.ox.ac.uk/music
Website: www.solo.bodleian.ox.ac.uk

Enquiries to: Librarian
Other contacts: Deputy Librarian

Founded: c.1950

Organisation type and purpose: University library.

Subject coverage: Music (western classical tradition).

Collection: Byzantine music
Howes folk music collection
Music from the Oxford University Music Society Library

Library catalogue: All or part available online and in-house

Publications: Printed

Access to staff: Contact by telephone, by e-mail and in person
Hours: Term time: Mon to Fri, 0900 to 1800; Sat, 1000 to 1300
Vacations: shorter hours
Special comments: Non-university members have reference-only access at the discretion of library staff.

UNIVERSITY OF OXFORD – PHYSICAL AND THEORETICAL CHEMISTRY LABORATORY

South Parks Road, Oxford, OX1 3QZ

Tel: 01865 275400
Fax: 01865 275410
E-mail: jacob.klein@chem.ox.ac.uk
Website: physchem.ox.ac.uk

Enquiries to: Head of Department
Direct tel: 01865 275402

Organisation type and purpose: University department or institute.

Subject coverage: Physical, theoretical and computational chemistry.

Access to staff: Contact by letter, by telephone, by fax, by e-mail and via website
Hours: Mon to Fri, 0900 to 1700

UNIVERSITY OF OXFORD – SCHOOL OF GEOGRAPHY AND THE ENVIRONMENT LIBRARY

Parks Road, Oxford, OX1 3QP

Website: www.bodleian.ox.ac.uk/science

Enquiries to: Reader Services Librarian Geography
Direct tel: 01865 272800
Direct e-mail: enquiries.rsl@bodleian.ox.ac.uk

Founded: 1887; housed in the Radcliffe Science Library (year of change 2007)

Organisation type and purpose: University library.

Subject coverage: Geography, environmental sciences and allied subjects, mountaineering.

Collection: Oxford Mountaineering Library
Radcliffe Meteorological Collection held within School of Geography; access for visitors is via the Library

Non-library collection catalogue: All or part available online

Library catalogue: All or part available online

Access to staff: Contact by letter, by telephone, by fax, by e-mail and in person. Appointment necessary.
Hours: Term time: Mon to Fri, 0830 to 2200; Sat, 1000 to 1600; Sun, 1100 to 1700
Vacations: Mon to Fri, 0830 to 1900; Sat, 1000 to 1400

Access for disabled people: Ramped entry, toilet facilities

UNIVERSITY OF OXFORD – SHERARDIAN LIBRARY OF PLANT TAXONOMY

Department of Plant Sciences, South Parks Road, Oxford, OX1 3RB

Tel: 01865 275025
E-mail: enquiries.plant@bodleian.ox.ac.uk
Website: www.bodleian.ox.ac.uk/science

Enquiries to: Sherardian Librarian
Direct tel: 01865 275025
Direct e-mail: anne.townsend@bodleian.ox.ac.uk

Founded: 1621; previously part of Plant Sciences Library, which merged with Radcliffe Science Library (year of change 2010)

Organisation type and purpose: University library.

Subject coverage: Plant taxonomy.

Collection: Sibthorpian and Sherard Collections (historic botanical works)

Non-library collection catalogue: All or part available online and in-house

Library catalogue: All or part available online

continued overleaf

Publications: Printed

Access to staff: Contact by letter, by telephone, by fax, by e-mail, in person and via website. Appointment necessary.
Hours: Mon to Fri, 0900 to 1730

Access for disabled people: Access to all public areas, toilet facilities

Parent body: University of Oxford, Bodleian Libraries

UNIVERSITY OF PORTSMOUTH

University Library, Cambridge Road, Portsmouth, Hampshire, PO1 2ST

Tel: 023 9284 3228
Fax: 023 9284 3233
E-mail: library@port.ac.uk
Website: www.port.ac.uk

Enquiries to: Librarian

Organisation type and purpose: University library.

Subject coverage: Business studies; economics; management; law and criminology; engineering and technology; computing; environmental studies; social sciences; physical and life sciences; health studies; psychology; marine resources; languages and area studies; literature; history; art and design; European studies; media studies.

Collection: Bolton collection (history of architecture)
European Documentation Centre

Library catalogue: All or part available online

Access to staff: Contact by letter, by telephone, by fax, by e-mail, in person and via website. Non-members charged.
Hours: Mon to Fri, 0900 to 2045; Sat, Sun, 1000 to 1600
See website for holiday and vacation hours

Access to building: No prior appointment required

Access for disabled people: Level entry, access to all public areas, toilet facilities

UNIVERSITY OF READING – DEPARTMENT OF FOOD AND NUTRITIONAL SCIENCES

PO Box 226, Whiteknights, Reading, Berkshire, RG6 6AP

Tel: 0118 378 8722
Fax: 0118 931 0080
E-mail: r.a.wilbey@reading.ac.uk
Website: www.rdg.ac.uk

Enquiries to: Librarian

Founded: 1892; formerly called Department of Food Biosciences (year of change 2009)

Organisation type and purpose: University department or institute.

Subject coverage: Food, science and technology, nutrition, biotechnology, industrial microbiology and fermentation technology.

Collection: McLachlan Library (food science and technology)

Library catalogue: All or part available in-house

Access to staff: Contact by e-mail
Hours: Mon to Fri, 0900 to 1700

UNIVERSITY OF READING – EUROPEAN DOCUMENTATION CENTRE

Main Library, Whiteknights, PO Box 223, Reading, Berkshire, RG6 6AE

Tel: 0118 378 8782
Fax: 0118 378 6636
E-mail: library-edc@reading.ac.uk
Website: www.reading.ac.uk/library

Enquiries to: EDC Librarian

Founded: 1967

Organisation type and purpose: University library.

Subject coverage: European Communities, European Union.

Collection: Collection of European Communities and European Union published material, donated for the use of the University and local community

Library catalogue: All or part available online

Access to staff: Contact by letter, telephone, by fax, by e-mail and in person. Appointment necessary.
Hours: Mon to Fri, 0900 to 1700; evenings and weekends during term time

Access to building: No prior appointment required

Access for disabled people: Parking provided, access to all public areas

UNIVERSITY OF READING LIBRARY

Whiteknights, PO Box 223, Reading, Berkshire, RG6 6AE

Tel: 0118 378 8770
Fax: 0118 378 6636
E-mail: library@reading.ac.uk
Website: www.reading.ac.uk/library

Enquiries to: Library User Services Manager

Founded: 1926

Organisation type and purpose: University library

Subject coverage: Agriculture (including history), archaeology, classics, community studies, contemporary European studies, economics, education, English, fine art, French, physical sciences, earth sciences, biological sciences, geography, German history, history of art, Italian, land management, law, linguistics, medieval studies, music, philosophy, politics, psychology, sociology, typography and graphic communication.

Collection: Agricultural history
Farm Records
Publishers' and Printers' Archives
Children's Collection (and H. M. Brock)
Cole Library (history of zoology, comparative anatomy and early medicine)
Finzi Collections of English Literature and Music
Henley Parish Library (history, philosophy and literature)
Isotype Collection (statistical information in graphic form)
Music (printed by lithography) and Victorian music covers
Overstone Library (economics, literature, history and travel)
Papers of Lord and Lady Astor
Printed ephemera
Printing history (including Robert Gibbings)
Samuel Beckett Archive
Stenton Library (medieval history)
Turner Collection (French Revolution)

Non-library collection catalogue: All or part available in-house

Library catalogue: All or part available online

Publications: Printed

Publications list: Available online

Access to staff: Contact by letter, by telephone and by e-mail

Access to building: No prior appointment required at University Library
Hours: Hours online at www.reading.ac.uk/library
Special comments: Prior appointment advisable to visit University archives and special collections at Special Collections Services, Redlands Road.

Access for disabled people: Parking provided, ramped entry, level entry, access to all public areas, toilet facilities

Links with: Special Collections Services; University of Reading, Redlands Road, Reading, RG1 5EX; tel: 0118 378 6660; fax: 0118 378 5632; e-mail: specialcollections@reading.ac.uk; website: http://www.reading.ac.uk/special-collections

UNIVERSITY OF ROEHAMPTON

University Library, Roehampton Lane, London, SW15 5SZ

Tel: 020 8392 3770
Fax: 020 8392 3259
E-mail: Library@roehampton.ac.uk
Website: www.roehampton.ac.uk/Library/

Enquiries to: University Librarian
Direct tel: 020 8392 3058
Direct fax: 020 8392 3026
Direct e-mail: susan.scorey@roehampton.ac.uk

Founded: 2000; formerly called Roehampton University (year of change 2011)

Organisation type and purpose: University library.

Subject coverage: English language and literature, modern languages, drama, dance studies, theology and religious studies, history, mathematics education, music, film and TV studies, children's literature, education, sociology, social policy and administration, business studies, applied computing, applied consumer studies, retail and product management, anthropology, biological sciences, health studies, human and social biology, natural resource studies, psychology, counselling, arts therapies, sport studies.

Collection: Children's Literature Collection
Early Childhood Archive
Froebel Archive

Jewish Resources Centre
Ann Hutchinson Guest Collection
Richmal Crompton Collection
Centre for Marian studies

Library catalogue: All or part available online

Access to staff: Contact by letter, by telephone, by fax, by e-mail and via website
Hours: Term time: Mon to Fri, 0800 to 2100; Sat, 1100 to 1800; Sun, 1100 to 1800
Vacations: usually Mon to Fri, 0900 to 1900, Sat, 1100 to 1800; Sun, 1100 to 1800 but phone to confirm.

Affiliated to: M25 Consortium of HE Libraries; SCONUL

Also at: University of Roehampton; Froebel College; University of Roehampton; Southlands College; University of Roehampton; Whitelands College; University of Roehampton; Digby Stuart College

UNIVERSITY OF SALFORD, THE LIBRARY (The Library)

The Crescent, Salford, Manchester, M5 4WT

Tel: 0161 295 2444
Fax: 0161 295 6624
E-mail: its-servicedesk@salford.ac.uk
Website: www.library.salford.ac.uk
Website: www.salford.ac.uk

Founded: 1967; formerly called Information Services Division (ISD) (year of change 2008); formerly called Information & Learning Services (year of change 2010)

Organisation type and purpose: University library, information and learning services.

Subject coverage: Art and design; built environment; business; computing, science and engineering; English, sociology, politics and contemporary history; environment and life sciences; health and social care; law; media, music and performance.

Collection: Arthur Hopcraft Archive
Badnall Papers
Bartington Hall Papers
Bridgewater Estates Archive
British Election Campaign Material
Changing Face of Salford Collection
Dockray Collection
Duke of Bridgewater Archive
English Velvet and Cord Dyers' Association Archive
Lancashire and Yorkshire Railway Drawings
Phil May and Leo Cheney Cartoons
Mather Papers
Oldham and Son Ltd Archive
Revans Collection
Salford Technical and Engineering Association Archive
Stanley Houghton Collection
University of Salford Local Collection
Walter Greenwood Collection
Willink Archive

Trade and statistical information: General statistics issued by UK government departments

Non-library collection catalogue: All or part available online

Library catalogue: All or part available online

Publications: Electronic and video

Publications list: Available online

Access to staff: Contact by letter, by telephone, by fax, by e-mail and via website. Appointment necessary.

Access to building: *Hours:* Term time, main library: Mon to Fri, 0800 to 0000; Sat, 1200 to 1800; Sun, 1200 to 1800
Visit website for other library opening times

Access for disabled people: All libraries have ramp access, toilet facilities, lift

UNIVERSITY OF SHEFFIELD (iSchool @ Sheffield)

Formal name: Information School, The University of Sheffield

Information School, Regent Court, 211 Portobello Street, Sheffield, South Yorkshire, S1 4DP

Tel: 0114 222 2630
Fax: 0114 278 0300
E-mail: is@sheffield.ac.uk
Website: www.shef.ac.uk/is
Website: www.shef.ac.uk/is/publications

Enquiries to: Head of School
Direct tel: 0114 222 2638
Direct e-mail: p.levy@sheffield.ac.uk
Other contacts: Teaching and Learning Manager

Founded: 1963; formerly called Department of Information Studies (year of change 2010)

Organisation type and purpose: University department or institute.

Subject coverage: The iSchool offers a number of taught degree programmes both at graduate (PGCert, PGDip, MA, MSc, MRes, MPhil, PhD) and undergraduate (BA and BSc) level, in the areas of librarianship, digital library management, information literacy, information management, multilingual information management, information systems, chemoinformatics and health informatics. In addition the iSchool has an international research profile within which two main research groups operate: Computational Informatics; and Library and Information Management. The research areas of study undertaken by these groups include: chemoinformatics; information retrieval; information systems; information literacy; reader development; social inclusion; library management; knowledge and information management; health informatics; and educational informatics.

Information services: Consultancy in all aspects of library and information management and information systems.

Education services: Training in all aspects of library and information management and information systems. Occasional short courses. Bespoke training by arrangement.

Publications: Printed, and electronic and video

Publications list: Available online

Access to staff: Contact by letter, by telephone, by fax, by e-mail and via website
Hours: Mon to Fri, 0900 to 1700

Access to building: *Hours:* Mon to Fri, 0900 to 1700
Special comments: Access only from Portobello Street entrance.

Access for disabled people: Ramped entry, toilet facilities
Hours: Mon to Fri, 0900 to 1700

UNIVERSITY OF SHEFFIELD – METALS ADVISORY CENTRE (SUMAC)

Department of Engineering Materials, Sir Robert Hadfield Building, Mappin Street, Sheffield, South Yorkshire, S1 3JD

Tel: 0114 222 5497
Fax: 0114 222 5493
E-mail: sumac@sheffield.ac.uk
Website: www.sumac.group.shef.ac.uk

Enquiries to: Senior Consultant

Founded: 1981

Organisation type and purpose: Advisory body, professional body, university department or institute, consultancy, research organisation.

Subject coverage: Metal component failures, materials selection, mechanical testing, chemical analysis, electron microscopy, materials consultancy service.
Machinery, vehicle and structural malfunction.
Engineering Measurements on operating machinery and plant.

Access to staff: Contact by letter, by telephone, by fax and by e-mail. Appointment necessary.
Hours: Mon to Fri, 0900 to 1700

Access to building: Prior appointment required

Access for disabled people: Parking provided, level entry, access to all public areas, toilet facilities

UNIVERSITY OF SHEFFIELD – THE INSTITUTE FOR LIFELONG LEARNING (TILL)

196–198 West Street, Sheffield, South Yorkshire, S1 4ET

Tel: 0114 222 7000
Fax: 0114 222 7001
E-mail: till@sheffield.ac.uk
Website: www.shef.ac.uk/till

Enquiries to: Publicity Officer
Direct tel: 0114 222 7009
Direct e-mail: k.wainwright@sheffield.ac.uk

Organisation type and purpose: University library, university department or institute, research organisation.
To make the resources of the university available to the public, with a focus on continuing, part-time and flexible education for adults.

Subject coverage: Archaeology, arts, computing and information technology, creative writing, earth sciences, education, film, health, humanities, history, language (French and Spanish), literature, music, natural science, religious studies, theatre studies, social and political studies, botanical illustration, local studies; also part-time degree and certificate courses.

Publications: Printed
Order printed publications from: via http://coursesforeverone.co.uk

continued overleaf

Access to staff: Contact by letter, by telephone, by fax, by e-mail and in person. Appointment necessary.
Hours: Mon to Fri, 0930 to 1640

Access to building: Customers via West Street Reception area
Hours: Mon to Fri, 0930 to 1630

UNIVERSITY OF SHEFFIELD, THE UNIVERSITY LIBRARY

Western Bank Library, University of Sheffield, Sheffield, South Yorkshire, S10 2TN

Tel: 0114 222 7200
Fax: 0114 222 7290
E-mail: library@sheffield.ac.uk
Website: www.shef.ac.uk/library

Enquiries to: Director of Library Services

Founded: 1905

Organisation type and purpose: University library.

Subject coverage: All major subjects except fine art, agriculture.

Collection: Special Collections: http://www.shef.ac.uk/library/special
National Fairground Archive: http://www.nfa.dept.shef.ac.uk/

Library catalogue: All or part available online

Access to staff: Contact by letter, by telephone, by e-mail, in person and via website
Hours: Mon to Thu, 0900 to 1900; Fri, 1000 to 1900; Sat and Sun, 1200 to 1800 (WBL)

Access to building: *Special comments:* Information Commons not open to external users

Access for disabled people: Parking provided, ramped entry, toilet facilities

Constituent bodies: Health Sciences Library; tel: 0114 271 2030; fax: 0114 278 0923; e-mail: library@sheffield.ac.uk; St George's Library; tel: 0114 222 7301; fax: 0114 222 7290; e-mail: library@sheffield.ac.uk; Western Bank Library; tel: 0114 222 7296; fax: 0114 222 7290; e-mail: library@sheffield.ac.uk
Information Commons; tel: 0114 222 9999; e-mail: library@sheffield.ac.uk

UNIVERSITY OF SOUTHAMPTON LIBRARY

University Road, Highfield, Southampton, SO17 1BJ

Tel: 023 8059 2180
Fax: 023 8059 3007
E-mail: libenqs@soton.ac.uk
Website: www.soton.ac.uk/library

Enquiries to: Librarian

Organisation type and purpose: University library.

Subject coverage: All subjects covered by the faculties and departments of the university.

Collection: Cope Collection on Hampshire and the Isle of Wight (Hartley)
European Documentation Centre (Hartley)
Ford Collection of British Official Publications (Hartley)
Parkes Library on relations between the Jewish and non-Jewish peoples (Hartley)
Perkins Agricultural Library (British and Irish writers on agriculture published before 1901; Hartley)
Manuscript collections, principally of 19th and 20th centuries (Hartley) including:
Papers of the first Duke of Wellington
The Palmerston papers
The Mountbatten papers
The Broadlands collections

Non-library collection catalogue: All or part available online

Library catalogue: All or part available online

Publications: Printed

Publications list: Available online

Access to staff: Contact by letter, by telephone, by fax, by e-mail, in person and via website
Hours: Mon to Fri, 0900 to 1700
Special comments: Library collections available for reference only.
Evening and weekend opening at selected sites.
Visitors by prior appointment at the National Oceanographic Library and the Winchester School of Art.

Branch libraries: Avenue Library; Avenue Campus, University of Southampton, Highfield Road, Southampton, SO17 1BF; tel: 023 8059 5432; e-mail: alengs@soton.ac.uk; Hartley Library; University of Southampton, Highfield, Southampton, SO17 1BJ; tel: 023 8059 2180; fax: 023 8059 3007; e-mail: libenqs@soton.ac.uk; Health Services Library; MP883, Level A, South Academic Block, Southampton General Hospital, Tremona Road, Southampton, SO16 6YD; tel: 023 8079 6547; e-mail: hslib@soton.ac.uk; National Oceanographic Library; National Oceanography Centre, Southampton, University of Southampton, Waterfront Campus, European Way, Southampton, SO14 3ZH; tel: 023 8059 6116; fax: 023 8059 6115; e-mail: nol@soc.soton.ac.uk; Parkes Library; Hartley Library, University of Southampton, Highfield, Southampton, SO17 1BJ; tel: 023 8059 3335; fax: 023 8059 3007; e-mail: libenqs@soton.ac.uk; Winchester School of Art Library; Park Avenue, Winchester, Hampshire, SO23 8DL; tel: 023 8059 6982; e-mail: wsa@soton.ac.uk

UNIVERSITY OF ST ANDREWS LIBRARY

Formal name: University Library, University of St Andrews

North Street, St Andrews, Fife, KY16 9TR

Tel: 01334 462281
Fax: 01334 462282
E-mail: library@st-andrews.ac.uk
Website: www.st-andrews.ac.uk/library

Founded: 1411

Organisation type and purpose: University library.

Subject coverage: Subjects of the Faculties of Arts, Divinity, Science and Medicine.

Collection: Large collection of United Kingdom and European community statistical publications
16th-century books (c. 3,500 items)
Andrew Lang Collection
Beveridge Collection (includes bee culture)
Bible Collection
Buchanan Collection (George Buchanan's works)
Copyright deposit collection, 1710–1837
Donaldson Collection (classics)
Finzi Collection (18th-century music scores)
Forbes Collection (early and rare science works)
Incunabula (150 items)
MacGillivray Collection (Celtic history and literature)
Mackay Collection (mathematics)
Manuscripts (over 100,000)
Photographs and prints (c. 300,000)
Runciman Collection
Simson and Wedderburn Collection (early medical books)
STC items (over 1,000 titles)
Valentine Collection (photographs and postcards)
Von Hugel Collection (theology and philosophy)

Non-library collection catalogue: All or part available online

Library catalogue: All or part available online

Publications: Printed
Order printed publications from: http://onlineshop.st-andrews.ac.uk/browse/product.asp?catid=164&modid=1&compid=

Publications list: Available online and in print

Access to staff: Contact by letter, by telephone, by fax, by e-mail and via website. Appointment necessary.
Hours: Mon to Fri, 0845 to 0000; Sat, 0900 to 2100; Sun, 1300 to 0000
Vacations: Mon to Fri, 0900 to 2000

Access to building: University ID required or sign in at Security Desk

Access for disabled people: Level entry, access to all public areas, lift, toilet facilities

Member organisation of: Consortium of European Research Libraries; Research Libraries UK; Scottish Confederation of University and Research Libraries; Tayside and Fife Library Information Network

UNIVERSITY OF STIRLING LIBRARY

Library, Andrew Miller Building, University of Stirling, Stirling, FK9 4LA

Tel: 01786 467235
Fax: 01786 466866
E-mail: library@stir.ac.uk
Website: www.stir.ac.uk
Website: www.is.stir.ac.uk

Enquiries to: Director of Information Services
Other contacts: University Librarian

Founded: 1967

Organisation type and purpose: University library.

Subject coverage: General academic subjects (no engineering).

Collection: Lindsay Anderson Archive
Drummond Collection (religious tracts)
Howietoun Fish Farm Archive
John Grierson Archive (papers relating to the documentary film movement)
Leighton Library (personal collection of Archbishop Leighton 1611–84, 4,000 vols, 16th to 19th centuries)
MacLeod Collection (Scottish theatrical history)
Sir Walter Scott and Scottish authors contemporary with Scott
Tait Collection (left-wing political pamphlets)
Watson Collection (labour history)

Trade and statistical information: General statistical reference section

Non-library collection catalogue: All or part available online

Library catalogue: All or part available online

Publications: Printed
Order printed publications from: Library Office, University of Stirling Library, Andrew Miller Building, University of Stirling, Stirling, FK9 4LA

Publications list: Available online

Access to staff: Contact by letter, by telephone, by fax, by e-mail, in person and via website. Appointment necessary. Non-members charged.
Hours: Mon to Fri, 0900 to 1700

Access to building: *Hours:* Please check website for current opening hours

Access for disabled people: Lift access to all floors

Also at: Highland Health Sciences Library; University of Stirling – Highland Campus, Centre for Health Science, Old Perth Road, Inverness, IV2 3JH; tel: 01463 255600 (extn 7600); fax: 01463 255605; e-mail: hhsl-inverness@stir.ac.uk

UNIVERSITY OF STRATHCLYDE – ANDERSONIAN LIBRARY

Curran Building, 101 St James Road, Glasgow, G4 0NS

Tel: 0141 548 4620
Fax: 0141 552 3304
E-mail: library@strath.ac.uk
Website: www.lib.strath.ac.uk

Enquiries to: Assistant Director: Information Services Directorate (Library & Information Resources)
Direct tel: 0141 548 4602
Direct e-mail: m.roberts@strath.ac.uk

Founded: 1964

Organisation type and purpose: University library.

Subject coverage: All subjects studied in the Faculties of Science, Engineering, Humanities and Social Sciences (including Education) and in the Strathclyde Business School.

Special visitor services: http://www.lib.strath.ac.uk/visitors.htm

Services for disabled people: http://www.lib.strath.ac.uk/libdis.htm

Collection: Aldred Collection (pamphlets on anarchism)
Anderson Collection (founder's library, 1726–1796)
British Standards on microfiche
Jordanhill Archive (Scottish education)
Laing Collection (mathematics, 17th–19th centuries)
British Company Annual Reports Collection
Robertson Collection (West of Scotland)
Royal Scottish Geographical Society Library
Strathclyde Collection (publications by University staff or departments)
Young Collection (alchemy, chemistry, pharmacy, 16th–19th centuries)

Non-library collection catalogue: All or part available online

Library catalogue: All or part available online

Publications: Printed

Access to staff: Contact by e-mail
Hours: Mon to Fri, 0900 to 1700

Access to building: *Hours:* see website: http://www.lib.strath.ac.uk/hours.htm

Access for disabled people: Access to all public areas
Special comments: Lift access to all floors of Andersonian Library.

UNIVERSITY OF STRATHCLYDE – GRADUATE SCHOOL OF ENVIRONMENTAL STUDIES (GSES)

Graham Hills Building, 50 Richmond Street, Glasgow, G1 1XN

Tel: 0141 548 4078
Fax: 0141 548 3489
E-mail: g.s.e.s@strath.ac.uk
Website: www.strath.ac.uk/Departments/GSES/

Enquiries to: Director
Direct e-mail: p.h.booth@strath.ac.uk

Founded: 1992

Organisation type and purpose: University department or institute.

Subject coverage: Environmental issues.

Publications: Printed

Publications list: Available online and in print

Access to staff: Contact by letter, by telephone, by fax and by e-mail. Appointment necessary.
Hours: Mon to Fri, 0900 to 1700

UNIVERSITY OF SUNDERLAND – ASHBURNE LIBRARY

Ashburne House, Backhouse Park, Ryhope Road, Sunderland, Tyne and Wear, SR2 7EF

Tel: 0191 515 2119
Fax: 0191 515 3166
E-mail: jan.dodshon@sunderland.ac.uk
Website: www.library.sunderland.ac.uk/

Enquiries to: Librarian

Organisation type and purpose: University library.

Subject coverage: Art history, design history, sculpture, ceramics, illustration, design, glass, painting, printmaking, photography, model making.

Collection: 40,000 books
Slide collection of 60,000 slides

Non-library collection catalogue: All or part available online

Library catalogue: All or part available online

Access to staff: Contact by letter, by telephone and by e-mail. Appointment necessary. Non-members charged.
Hours: Term Time: Mon, Tue, 0900 to 2100; Wed, Thu, 0900 to 2000; Fri, 0900 to 1700; Sat, 1000 to 1300
Vacation: Mon to Fri, 0900 to 1700
Special comments: Charges to non-members for borrowing; open to general public for reference.

Access to building: No prior appointment required
Hours: As before

Access for disabled people: Parking provided
Special comments: Library on 1st floor – no lift.

UNIVERSITY OF SUNDERLAND – MURRAY LIBRARY

Information Services, The Murray Library, Chester Road, Sunderland, Tyne and Wear, SR1 3SD

Tel: 0191 515 2900
Fax: 0191 515 2904
E-mail: andrew.mcdonald@sunderland.ac.uk
Website: www.library.sunderland.ac.uk

Enquiries to: Director
Direct tel: 0191 515 2905
Direct fax: 0191 515 3914
Other contacts: Assistant Director Information Services

Organisation type and purpose: University library.

Subject coverage: Art and design, education, business management, law, humanities, social studies, computing, mathematics, science, engineering, technology, pharmacy, health studies, environmental studies.

Publications: Printed

Access to staff: Contact by letter, by fax and by e-mail
Hours: Term time: Mon to Thu, 0830 to 2200; Fri, 0830 to 2100; Sat 0945 to 1800; Sun 0945 to 1800
Vacations: Mon to Fri, 0900 to 1700

UNIVERSITY OF SURREY – UNIVERSITY LIBRARY (UniS)

Guildford, Surrey, GU2 7XH

Tel: 01483 683325
Fax: 01483 689500
E-mail: library-enquiries@surrey.ac.uk
Website: talis-prism.lib.surrey.ac.uk/TalisPrism/
Website: portal.surrey.ac.uk:7778/portal/page?_pageid=734,1&_dad=portal&_schema=PORTAL

continued overleaf

Enquiries to: The Librarian

Organisation type and purpose: University library.

Subject coverage: Biomedical sciences, biochemistry, toxicology, nutrition, chemical engineering, environmental strategy, civil engineering, electronic engineering (including satellite research), computing science, mechanical engineering, physics, chemistry, microbiology, economics, sociology, law, dance studies, statistics, politics, psychology, hotel, catering and tourism management, linguistics, music, mathematics, materials science, industrial and environmental health, nursing and midwifery, occupational health and safety, biomedical engineering, translation, sound recording.

Collection: European Documentation Centre (catalogue online)
National Resource Centre for Dance
E H Shepard Archive, original drawings and manuscripts

Non-library collection catalogue: All or part available online

Library catalogue: All or part available online

Access to staff: Contact by telephone, by e-mail and via website
Hours: During semester: Mon to Fri, 0830 to 2100; Sat, 1400 to 1800; Sun, 1400 to 1800
Special comments: Hours alter during vacations – see library website.

Access for disabled people: Parking provided, toilet facilities

Connections with: M25 Consortium of Higher Education Libraries; Surrey and Sussex Libraries in Co-operation (SASLIC); UK Libraries Plus Scheme

UNIVERSITY OF SUSSEX

The Library, Falmer, Brighton, East Sussex, BN1 9QL

Tel: 01273 678163
Fax: 01273 678441
E-mail: library@sussex.ac.uk
Website: www.sussex.ac.uk/library

Enquiries to: Librarian
Direct tel: 01273 678158; 01273 678157 (Special Collections)
Direct e-mail: library.specialcoll@sussex.ac.uk (Special Collections)
Other contacts: Head of Special Collections (for access to special collections, MSS and rare books)

Founded: 1962; incorporates the former Education Library

Organisation type and purpose: University library.

Subject coverage: All arts and social sciences, applied science and technology, biological sciences, mathematics, physical sciences, molecular science, economics (including commerce).

Collection: Special Collections: manuscripts, archives and rare books
Allsop Collection (correspondence, notes and drafts of Kenneth Allsop)
Baker Collection of Fine Books (mainly 19th century, some 180 titles)
Caffyn Books (first and other editions of works by Shelley, and some critical and biographical studies, some 28 items, together with copies of 22 letters from Shelley and other non-printed material)
Carrington Collection (papers of C. E. Carrington and others c.1935–79 on Rudyard Kipling)
Charleston Collection (personal correspondence of members of the Bloomsbury Group)
Common Wealth Collection (papers of the British political organisation 1940 onwards)
Crowther Collection (on scientific journalism and politics, 1920–74)
Benn W. Levy Collection (collection of Benn Wolfe Levy on politics and the theatre, c.1930–70)
Eugene Shulkind Commune collection (periodicals, newspapers, monographs, posters and cartoons from and about the Paris Commune, 1871, some 2,500 items)
Gorer Collection (papers, correspondence, photographs, notebooks, c.1930–80, of Geoffrey Gorer, social anthropologist)
Gregory Collection (papers of Sir Richard Gregory, astronomer and editor of 'Nature' on scientific affairs and journalism, c.1880–1952)
Hogarth Press Collection (items from Leonard Woolf's file collection of Hogarth Press books, augmented by purchases and gifts)
James Stevenson Collection (Baron Stevenson of Holmbury, 1873–1926)
John Hilton Bureau Collection (papers, press-cuttings, written evidence for official enquiries, etc., of the John Hilton Bureau, News of the World Ltd, 1945–68)
Kingsley Martin Collection (correspondence, diaries, notes, pamphlets and press cuttings 1910–69)
Kipling Collection (correspondence, literary manuscripts, press cuttings, drawings, photographs, India and England 1870–1940 of Rudyard Kipling and John Lockwood Kipling, on deposit from the National Trust)
Leonard Woolf Collection (papers of Leonard Woolf on literary, political, domestic and personal affairs c.1890–1969)
Leys Collection (papers of Professor C. T. Leys on the politics and administration of Uganda, 1962–66)
Madge Papers (early poetry, notebooks and correspondence of Charles Madge, 1920–96)
Mass-Observation Archive (see separate entry)
Matusow Collection I (correspondence, press cuttings, court reports, diaries, photographs, tape recordings and films particularly on the politics of the McCarthy period 1950–55)
Matusow Collection II (USA underground ephemera, alternative society material, and Harvey Matusow personalia 1960s–80s)
Monks House Collection (literary papers and correspondence 1900–42 of Virginia Woolf and associated collection of Virginia Woolf books)
Muir/Norden archive (radio comedy scripts and notes 1948–70)
New Statesman Collection (editorial correspondence, drafts, business papers, etc., from the files of The New Statesman 1943–88)
Pledge Collection (papers on the history of science and knowledge, 1919–60, of Humphrey Thomas Pledge, Assistant Keeper and then Keeper of the Science Museum Library)
Reckitt Collection (papers, correspondence and press cuttings of Maurice Benington Reckitt on religion in politics and social questions, and Christian socialism 1915–70)
Rolph Collection (papers of C. H. Rolph including correspondence, news cuttings, etc., relating to Kingsley Martin and The New Statesman)
Rosey Pool Collection (papers, correspondence, photographs, music, etc., on black American literature 1945–70)
Stamp Collection (papers on geographical subjects, especially land use, 1910–65, of Sir Laurence Dudley Stamp, Director of the Land-Use Survey (International Geographical Union))
Travers Collection (mainly 15th- and 16th-century printed books, some 350 titles)
Wartime Social Survey Collection (papers, principally interviews and survey reports, on economic and social conditions in Britain, 1940–41)
World Parliament Association Collection (papers, photographs, minutes, reports, correspondence and programmes, mostly on federalism and world government)

Non-library collection catalogue: All or part available online

Library catalogue: All or part available online

Publications: Printed

Publications list: Available online

Access to staff: Contact by letter, by telephone, by fax, by e-mail, in person and via website
Hours: Term time: 24-hour access from Mon, 0845 to Sat, 1930; Sun, 1230 to 1930
Vacations: Mon, Wed, Thu, Fri, 0900 to 1730; Tue, 0900 to 2000; Sat, closed; Sun, 1300 to 1800

UNIVERSITY OF SUSSEX SPECIAL COLLECTIONS

The Library, University of Sussex, Brighton, East Sussex, BN1 9QL

Tel: 01273 678157
Fax: 01273 678441
E-mail: library.specialcoll@sussex.ac.uk
Website: www.sussex.ac.uk/library/speccoll

Enquiries to: Special Collections Manager

Founded: 1964

Organisation type and purpose: To provide public access to and care for the archives, manuscripts, rare books and art works of the University of Sussex, including the Mass-Observation Archive which is a registered charity. The Mass-Observation Archive continues to operate as a research unit specialising in the collection of autobiographical accounts of everyday life in Britain.

Subject coverage: The University of Sussex holds a number of internationally acclaimed archival, manuscript and rare book collections, mostly relating to 20th-century literary, political and social history.

Collection: Over 100 collections, including:
Several Rare Book collections including Travis and Baker collections
Bloomsbury related collections, including the Monks House Papers (Virginia Woolf)
Archive of Rudyard Kipling

Eugene Schulkind Paris Commune Collection
New Statesman and Kingsley Martin Archives
Mass-Observation Archive: 1937 to mid-1950s
Mass-Observation Archive (phase 2) from 1981 to the present
Related collections of diaries, letters, personal collections and photographs

Non-library collection catalogue: All or part available online

Publications: Printed, and electronic and video
Order printed publications from: All original Mass-Observation book publications and selected collections 1937–55 by theme available from Adam Matthew Publications.

Publications list: Available online and in print

Access to staff: Contact by letter, by telephone, by fax, by e-mail and in person. Appointment necessary.

Access to building: ID required (including photograph); visits to Special Collections by appointment only
Hours: Mon to Thu, 0915 to 1700

Access for disabled people: Level entry, toilet facilities. Assistive technology available in reading room.

Links with: University of Sussex Library; tel: 01273 678163; fax: 01273 678441; website: http://www.sussex.ac.uk/library

UNIVERSITY OF THE ARTS LONDON – CHELSEA COLLEGE OF ART AND DESIGN

Millbank, London, SW1P 4JU

Tel: 020 7514 7773
Fax: 020 7514 7785
E-mail: enquiries@chelsea.arts.ac.uk
Website: www.arts.ac.uk/library

Enquiries to: Assistant Learning Resources Manager
Other contacts: Reader and Information Services Librarian

Founded: 1890; formerly called Chelsea School of Art

Organisation type and purpose: University department or institute. Partnered with Camberwell College of Arts, Central Saint Martins College of Art and Design, London College of Communication, London College of Fashion and Wimbledon College of Art.

Subject coverage: Fine art; modern art history; applied arts; design and design history; women's art.

Collection: Archives of the College
African-Caribbean, Asian and African Art in Britain Archive
Artists' books
Artists' Multiples
European and American Art and Design History from 1850
Exhibition catalogues
Jean Spencer Archive
Kurt Schwitters Archive
Modern Art Periodicals
Women's International Art Club Archive

Non-library collection catalogue: All or part available online

Library catalogue: All or part available online

Publications: Microform publications

Access to staff: Appointment necessary.
Hours: Mon to Fri, 0900 to 1700

Access to building: By appointment only
Hours: Mon to Fri, 0900 to 1700

Access for disabled people: Lift access available
Hours: Mon to Fri, 0900 to 1700

Part of: University of the Arts London

UNIVERSITY OF THE WEST OF ENGLAND – FRENCHAY CAMPUS (BOLLAND) LIBRARY (UWE)

Coldharbour Lane, Bristol, BS16 1QY

Tel: 0117 328 2404
Fax: 0117 328 2407
E-mail: library.admin@uwe.ac.uk
Website: www.uwe.ac.uk/library

Enquiries to: Head of Library Services
Direct tel: 0117 328 2406
Direct e-mail: catherine.rex@uwe.ac.uk

History of institution: formerly called Bristol Polytechnic (year of change 1992)

Organisation type and purpose: University library.

Subject coverage: Nursing and allied health professions (Glenside, Alexandra Warehouse).
Architecture, languages, law, management, social sciences, built environment, business, mathematics, computing, education, engineering, applied science, psychology, environmental health, geography, information science (Frenchay Campus (Bolland) Library).
History, literature, cultural studies, drama, music therapy (St Matthias).
Art, media and design (Bower Ashton).

Library catalogue: All or part available online

Access to staff: Contact by letter, by telephone, by fax, by e-mail, in person and via website. Non-members charged.
Hours: Varies by campus, please see website for details.
Special comments: No charges for use of the library for reference.

Branch libraries: Alexandra Warehouse Library; UWE Library Services, West Quay, Gloucester Docks, Gloucester, GL1 2LG; tel: 0117 3285612; Bower Ashton; UWE Library Services, Kennel Lodge Road, Bristol, BS3 2JT; tel: 0117 328 4750; fax: 0117 328 4745; Glenside; UWE Library Services, Blackberry Hill, Stapleton, Bristol, BS16 1DD; tel: 0117 328 8404; fax: 0117 328 8402; St Matthias; UWE Library Services, Oldbury Court Road, Fishponds, Bristol, BS16 2JP; tel: 0117 328 4472

UNIVERSITY OF THE WEST OF SCOTLAND (UWS)

Paisley, Renfrewshire, PA1 2BE

Tel: 0141 848 3758
Fax: 0141 848 3761
E-mail: library@uws.ac.uk
Website: www.uws.ac.uk

Founded: 2007; created by the merger of University of Paisley and Bell College Hamilton (year of change 2007)

Organisation type and purpose: University library.

Collection: Aviation history collection
Norman Buchan parliamentary papers
Collection of material on Scottish railways including maps
Hugh MacDiarmid collection
L. F. Richardson archive
IUP 19th-century government papers
SLGIU Scottish Poll Tax Archive
Hugh McMahon EU Papers
West of Scotland Community Relations Council Archive
Scottish Milk Marketing Board Archive
20th-century American literature archive and collection
Stuart Harvey Papers

Non-library collection catalogue: All or part available online

Library catalogue: All or part available online

Publications: Printed

Access to staff: Contact by letter, by telephone and by e-mail. Appointment necessary.

Access for disabled people: Level entry, access to all public areas, toilet facilities

Also at: Ayr Campus; University Avenue, Ayr KA8 0SX; tel: 01292 886345; fax: 01292 886288; e-mail: neal.buchanan@uws.ac.uk; Dumfries Campus; The Crichton Library, Dumfries and Galloway College Building, Bankend Road, Dumfries, DG1 4FD; tel: 01387 734275; e-mail: avril.goodwin@uws.ac.uk; Hamilton Campus; Almada Street, Hamilton, ML3 0JB; tel: 01698 283100; e-mail: john.burke@uws.ac.uk

UNIVERSITY OF THE WEST OF SCOTLAND – AYR CAMPUS (UWS Ayr)

University Avenue, Ayr, KA8 0SX

Tel: 01292 886000
Website: www.uws.ac.uk/library

Enquiries to: Librarian
Direct tel: 01292 886345
Direct e-mail: libraryayr@uws.ac.uk

Founded: 1965; created by the merger of University of Paisley and Bell College (year of change 2007); formerly called Craigie College of Education (year of change 1993)

Organisation type and purpose: University library.

Subject coverage: Education, educational psychology, children's books, nursing, health care studies, management and business studies, media studies, film studies, commercial music, digital art.

Non-library collection catalogue: All or part available online

Library catalogue: All or part available online

Access to staff: Contact by letter, by telephone, by e-mail, in person and via website

continued overleaf

Hours: Term time: Mon to Thu, 0900 to 2050; Fri, Sat, 0900 to 1650
Vacations: Mon to Sat, 0900 to 1650

Also at: University of the West of Scotland; Robertson Trust Library and Learning Resources, High Street, Paisley, PA1 2BE; tel: 0141 848 3000; e-mail: library@uws.ac.uk; University of the West of Scotland; Library, Almada Street, Hamilton, ML3 0JB; tel: 01698 894424; e-mail: libraryhamilton@uws.ac.uk; University of the West of Scotland; Crichton Library, Dumfries & Galloway College Building, Bankend Road, Dumfries, DG1 4FD; tel: 01387 734323; e-mail: librarydumfries@uws.ac.uk

UNIVERSITY OF ULSTER (UU)

Information Services Department, Cromore Road, Coleraine, Co Londonderry, BT52 1SA

Tel: 08700 400 700
Website: www.ulster.ac.uk/
Website: www.ulster.ac.uk/library/
Enquiries to: Director of Information Services
Founded: 1984; formed by the merger of New University of Ulster, Ulster Polytechnic (year of change 1984)

Organisation type and purpose: University library.

Subject coverage: Economics, social administration, social organisation, social anthropology, conflict studies, media studies, education, English, Irish, French, German and Spanish languages and literature, linguistics, classics, history, business studies, nursing, psychology, geography, environmental studies, communication studies, biological and biomedical sciences and surface science.

Collection: Denis Johnston Manuscripts
E N Carrothers Collection of Bookplates
English linguistics collection, microfiche
European Documentation Centre
Francis Stewart Archive of literary manuscripts
Headlam-Morley Collection, library of books, pamphlets and manuscripts relating to World War I and the Peace Treaty
Henry Davis gift of incunabula, fine bindings etc
Henry Morris Irish Collection
Irish Travelling People: Resource Collection
John Hewitt Library
Paul Ricard Library relating to World War II
Shiels plays
Stelfox Natural History Collection

Non-library collection catalogue: All or part available in-house

Library catalogue: All or part available online

Publications: Printed

Access to staff: Contact by letter, by telephone, by fax, by e-mail and via website. Appointment necessary. Letter of introduction required.
Hours: Term time: Mon to Fri, 0845 to 2200; Sat, 0100 to 1700
Vacations: Mon to Fri, 0900 to 1700; Sat, closed

Access for disabled people: Parking provided, ramped entry, level entry, toilet facilities

Other campuses at: Belfast campus; York Street, Belfast, BT15 1ED; tel: 08700 400 700; Jordanstown campus; Shore Road, Newtownabbey, Co Antrim, BT37 0BQ; tel: 08700 400 700; Magee campus; Northland Road, Londonderry, BT48 7JL; tel: 08700 400 700

UNIVERSITY OF WALES CENTRE FOR ADVANCED WELSH AND CELTIC STUDIES (CAWCS)

National Library of Wales, Aberystwyth, Ceredigion, SY23 3HH

Tel: 01970 636543
Fax: 01970 639090
E-mail: cawcs@wales.ac.uk
Website: www.wales.ac.uk/cawcs
Enquiries to: Director
Direct e-mail: d.r.johnston@wales.ac.uk
Other contacts: Administrative Officer (for publications)

Organisation type and purpose: Research organisation.
Research, Welsh and Celtic study.

Subject coverage: Language, literature, history and culture of Wales and the other Celtic countries.

Collection: Library books and periodicals – mainly Celtic- and Welsh-language material

Library catalogue: All or part available in-house

Publications: Printed

Publications list: Available online and in print

Access to staff: Contact by letter, by telephone, by fax and by e-mail. Appointment necessary.
Hours: Mon to Fri, 0900 to 1700

Access for disabled people: Level entry, toilet facilities

Constituent part of: University of Wales

UNIVERSITY OF WALES, LAMPETER

Lampeter, Ceredigion, SA48 7ED

Tel: 01570 424997
E-mail: library@lamp.ac.uk
Website: www.lamp.ac.uk/founders_library
Website: www.lamp.ac.uk/library/

Enquiries to: Library Administrator
Direct e-mail: j.bracher@lamp.ac.uk

Founded: 1822; formerly called St David's University College Library

Organisation type and purpose: University library.

Subject coverage: Anthropology, archaeology, classics, film and media, German, history, informatics, philosophy, theology and religious studies, Welsh.

Collection: Early Welsh periodicals
MSS collection includes 15th century Books of Hours and other service books
Pre-1850 material (over 20,000 volumes) includes Tract Collection (printed catalogue published 1975), Incunabula (ca. 60 items representing most early centres of printing)
Welsh Bibles, prayerbooks etc

Library catalogue: All or part available online

Publications: Printed

Access to staff: Contact by letter, by telephone, by fax, by e-mail, in person and via website
Hours: Term time: Mon to Thu, 0900 to 2145; Fri, 0900 to 1945; Sat, 1300 to 1645; Sun, 1300 to 1645
Vacations: Mon to Fri, 0900 to 1645

Access for disabled people: Parking provided, level entry, toilet facilities
Special comments: Ask at counter for access to lift between floors.

Constituent Institution of the: University of Wales

UNIVERSITY OF WALES, NEWPORT

Library and Information Services, Caerleon Campus, PO Box 179, Newport, Gwent, NP18 3YG

Tel: 01633 432101
Fax: 01633 432105
E-mail: lis@newport.ac.uk
Website: www.lis.newport.ac.uk

Enquiries to: Librarian
Direct tel: 01633 432103
Direct fax: 01633 432920
Direct e-mail: lesley.may@newport.ac.uk

Founded: 1974; formerly called Gwent College of Higher Education Library (year of change 1995); formerly called University of Wales College, Newport (year of change 2004)

Organisation type and purpose: University library.

Subject coverage: Art and design, interactive arts, documentary photography, archaeology, education, humanities, environmental science, business, accountancy, human resource management, counselling, technology, computing, electrical and electronic engineering, mechatronics, sports studies, psychology, social sciences.

Collection: David Hurn collection of documentary photography materials
Newport Survey Collection of photographic images

Trade and statistical information: General statistics for Wales.
Education statistics

Non-library collection catalogue: All or part available online

Library catalogue: All or part available online

Publications: Printed

Access to staff: Contact by letter, by telephone, by fax, by e-mail and via website. Appointment necessary.
Hours: Term time: Mon to Thu, 0830 to 2000; Fri, 0930 to 1700; Sat, Sun, 1300 to 1700
Special comments: Access to electronic databases may be restricted.

Access to building: *Hours:* Term time: Mon to Thu, 0830 to 2000; Fri, 0930 to 1700; Sat, Sun, 1300 to 1700
Special comments: Vacation opening hours available on the website.

Access for disabled people: Wheelchair access and lift to upper floor, automatic doors

Also at: Library and Information Services; Allt yr yn Campus, PO Box 180, Newport, NP20 5XR; tel: 01633 432310; fax: 01633 432343; e-mail: dawne.leatherdale@newport.ac.uk

UNIVERSITY OF WARWICK – MAIN LIBRARY

Coventry, Warwickshire, CV4 7AL

Tel: 024 7652 2026
Fax: 024 7652 4211
E-mail: library@warwick.ac.uk
Website: www.warwick.ac.uk/services/library
Website: www.warwick.ac.uk/services/library/mrc/mrc.html
Website: www2.warwick.ac.uk/services/library/researchexchange
Website: www2.warwick.ac.uk/services/library/teachinggrid
Website: www2.warwick.ac.uk/services/library/grid
Website: www2.warwick.ac.uk/services/library/pghub/

Founded: 1965

Organisation type and purpose: University library.

Subject coverage: Social sciences including law; humanities (Western languages only); trade unions, pressure groups and radical political movements; statistics; biological sciences; chemistry; molecular sciences; computer science; engineering; economics; environmental studies; mathematics; physics; business studies; United Kingdom official publications; European Documentation Centre; statistical series.

Services for disabled people: Fetch-and-carry service.

Collection: Economics and Management Working Papers
Employers' Records collections
French Theatre 18th–19th centuries
Modern Records Centre tel no: 024 7652 4219 (collection of British trade union (eg NUR), and employers' records, and records relating to pressure groups and political movements; they include the CBI and TUC archives and the private papers of Sir Victor Gollancz)
Statistics Collection (current and historical)

Non-library collection catalogue: All or part available online

Publications: Printed

Access to staff: Contact by letter, by telephone, by fax, by e-mail, in person and via website
Hours: Term time: Mon to Sun, 0830 to 2130
Opening times may vary during vacations and the summer term
Special comments: Members of the public may access the Library for reference provided they show photographic proof of ID and proof of address.

Access to building: *Hours:* Term time: Mon to Sun, 0830 to 0000
Opening times may vary during vacations and the summer term
Special comments: Visitor access during staff access hours.

Access for disabled people: Parking provided, lift, toilet facilities
Hours: As above

UNIVERSITY OF WESTMINSTER

Headquarter Building, 309 Regent Street, London, W1B 2UW

Tel: 020 7911 5000
Fax: 020 7911 5858
E-mail: course-enquiries@westminster.ac.uk
Website: www.westminster.ac.uk

Founded: 1838; formerly called Royal Polytechnic Institution (year of change 1882); formerly called Regent Street Polytechnic (year of change 1970); formerly called Polytechnic of Central London (PCL) (year of change 1992)

Organisation type and purpose: University department or institute, suitable for ages: 18+, teaching and research organisation.

Subject coverage: Business, management, psychology and social sciences, biosciences, computer sciences, integrated health and complementary therapies, English and linguistics, architecture and the built environment, communications, languages, law, media, arts and design, electronics.

Information services: See: http://www.westminster.ac.uk/study/library-and-it-services.

Collection: University of Westminster Archive Services holds mainly the records of the University and its predecessor bodies, going back to the Royal Polytechnic Institution founded in 1838, and including Regent Street Polytechnic and the Polytechnic of Central London; it also holds records of the Polytechnic Sports and Social Clubs; in addition there are a number of collections deposited or donated to support research, notably in the areas of architecture and town planning
For full details of holdings please see website: http://www.westminster.ac.uk/about/archive-services

Library catalogue: All or part available online and in-house

Publications: Printed
Order printed publications from: Marketing, Communications and Development Department (for list), Cavendish House, 101 New Cavendish St, London, W1W 6XH

Publications list: Available online

Access to staff: Contact by letter, by telephone, by fax, by e-mail and via website
Hours: Mon to Fri, 0900 to 1700
24-hour telephone enquiry service

Access to building: Hours differ at each campus; please contact for details

Access for disabled people: Facilities differ at each site; please contact for details
Special comments: Contact Disabilities Officer for further details: see http://www.westminster.ac.uk/study/disability-services

Also at: 115 New Cavendish Street, London, W1W 6UW; Watford Road, Northwich Park, Harrow, London, HA1 3TP; 35 Marylebone Road, London, NW1 5LS; 4–12 Little Titchfield Street, London, W1W 7UW

UNIVERSITY OF WESTMINSTER – INFORMATION SYSTEMS & LIBRARY SERVICES

115 New Cavendish Street, London, W1W 6UW

Tel: 020 7911 5095
Fax: 020 7911 5093
Website: www.westminster.ac.uk/library

Enquiries to: Director, Information Systems & Library Services
Other contacts: Library Managers for campus-related enquiries.

Founded: 1839; formed by the merger of Holborn College of Law, Languages and Commerce, Regent Street Polytechnic; formerly called Polytechnic of Central London (PCL) (year of change 1992)

Organisation type and purpose: University library, on 4 campuses.

Subject coverage: Planning, architecture, construction, tourism, transport, business management and economics, at 35 Marylebone Road, NW1 5LS (tel. no. for this site and the following sites 020 7911 5000 ext 3047)
Women's studies, economics, economic history, law, politics, psychology, sociology, and languages, civil rights, criminology, EC and Commonwealth law, English law, international law, sociology of law at 4 -12 Little Titchfield Street, London, W1P 7FW, ext 2516
Art and design, communications, film, radio and television, journalism, mass media, computing, photography, business management, engineering, at Harrow Learning Resources Centre, ext 5954
Technical and scientific subjects including mathematics, computing, chemistry, biological sciences, electronic engineering, systems engineering at 115 New Cavendish Street, W1M 8JS ext 3628.

Collection: University Archive: record of predecessor institutions including Royal Polytechnic Institution (1838 – 1881), Regent Street Polytechnic (1881 – 1970), the Polytechnic of Central London (1970 – 1992). Access by appointment

Non-library collection catalogue: All or part available in-house

Library catalogue: All or part available online

Access to staff: Appointment necessary. Access for members only. Non-members charged.
Hours: Term time: Mon to Fri, 0915 to 2100; Sat, Sun, 1100 to 1700
Vacations: Mon to Fri, 0915 to 1700
Special comments: Members only: plus M25, Access schemes members and UK Libraries Plus members.

Access for disabled people: Ramped entry
Special comments: Otherwise varies from campus to campus.

UNIVERSITY OF WINCHESTER LIBRARY

Formal name: Martial Rose Library

Sparkford Road, Winchester, Hampshire, SO22 4NR

Tel: 01962 827306

continued overleaf

Fax: 01962 827443
E-mail: libenquiries@winchester.ac.uk
Website: www.winchester.ac.uk/library

Enquiries to: Librarian

Founded: 1840; formerly called King Alfred's College (year of change 2005)

Organisation type and purpose: University library.

Subject coverage: Art, biology, design and technology, drama, education, English, environmental studies, geography, history, human movement studies, mathematics, music, religious studies, psychology, television studies, archaeology, learning difficulties, American studies, Japanese studies, business studies, sports studies, leisure management, tourism.

Collection: Sybil Campbell Collection; Thorold & Lyttelton Collection

Library catalogue: All or part available online

Publications: Printed

Access to staff: Contact by letter, by telephone, by e-mail and via website
Hours: Mon to Fri, 0900 to 1700

Access for disabled people: Access to all public areas

UNIVERSITY OF WOLVERHAMPTON – LEARNING CENTRE

Telford Campus, Priorslee, Telford, Shropshire, TF2 9NT

Tel: 01902 323983
Fax: 01902 323985
Website: www.wlv.ac.uk/lib

Enquiries to: Librarian
Direct tel: 01902 312672

Founded: 1992; formerly called Wolverhampton Polytechnic

Organisation type and purpose: University library.

Subject coverage: Business and management, social work, engineering design.

Trade and statistical information: United Kingdom statistics

Library catalogue: All or part available online

Access to staff: Contact in person
Hours: Term time: Mon to Fri, 0900 to 2200; Sat & Sun, 1330 to 1730. Vacations: Mon to Fri, 1000 to 1700
Special comments: No staff or counter access until 1100.
Visitors must check in at Reception for Identity Day Pass.

Access for disabled people: Parking provided, level entry, access to all public areas, toilet facilities

UNIVERSITY OF WORCESTER

Peirson Building, Henwick Grove, Worcester, WR2 6AJ

Tel: 01905 855341
Fax: 01905 855197
E-mail: a.hannaford@worc.ac.uk
Website: www.worc.ac.uk/ils

Enquiries to: Director of Information and Learning Services
Other contacts: Customer Services Manager (for use of library)

Subject coverage: Education, humanities, social sciences, environmental science, health, nursing, midwifery, sport studies, business, IT, digital media.

Library catalogue: All or part available online

Publications list: Available online

Access to staff: Contact by telephone, by e-mail and via website. Appointment necessary.
Hours: Mon to Fri, 0900 to 1700
Special comments: Longer opening hours during semester, check with library.

Access to building: No prior appointment required

Access for disabled people: Level entry, access to all public areas, toilet facilities

UNIVERSITY OF YORK

J B Morrell and Raymond Burton Libraries, Heslington, York, YO10 5DD

Tel: 01904 323873
Fax: 01904 323866
E-mail: lib-enquiry@york.ac.uk
Website: www.york.ac.uk/library

Enquiries to: Director of Information

Founded: 1962

Organisation type and purpose: University library and archives.

Subject coverage: Economics; politics; psychology; sociology; social administration; social work; archaeology; education; English and related literature; history; language and linguistics; music; philosophy; biochemistry; biology; chemistry; computer science; electronics; mathematics; physics; architecture; history of art; health sciences; medicine; environment; law; theatre; film; television (J B Morrell and Raymond Burton Libraries). Architecture in general; architectural history and conservation in particular; conservation of historic parks and gardens; continuing education for architectural and related professions (King's Manor Library).

Collection: Copland Collection (scores composed by Aaron Copland)
Cooper Abbs Collection (library of an 18th-century clergyman)
Dyson Collection (English literature of the 17th, 18th and early 19th centuries)
Eliot Collection (20th-century English literature first editions)
Halifax Parish Library (17th-century parish library)
Milner-White Collection (English detective stories)
Milnes-Walker Collection (medicine)
Mirfield Collection (theology pre-1800)
Raymond Burton Yorkshire Collection (books on Yorkshire)
Smith Collection (British engraving and painting in 18th and 19th century)
Slaithwaite Collection (18th-century theology)
York Medical Society Library (medicine)

Non-library collection catalogue: All or part available online

Library catalogue: All or part available online

Publications: Printed

Access to staff: Contact by letter, by telephone, by fax, by e-mail, in person and via website
Hours: Term time opening: Mon to Fri, 0800 to 0000; Sat and Sun, 1000 to 0000 (includes the weekends immediately before and after term)
Special comments: Vacation opening hours vary: see website.

Subsidiary library: King's Manor Library (formerly, up to 1996, the library of the Institute of Advanced Architectural Studies); Exhibition Square, York, YO1 7EP; tel: 01904 323969; fax: 01904 323949

UPKEEP

22–25 Finsbury Square, London, EC2A 1DX

Tel: 020 7256 7646
Fax: 020 7022 1575
E-mail: info@upkeep.org.uk
Website: www.upkeep.org.uk

Enquiries to: Director

Founded: 1983; formerly called The Building Conservation Trust

Organisation type and purpose: Registered charity (charity number 277351), educational charity.
Promotes good practice in building care; provides training courses and education relating to the care, maintenance and refurbishment of buildings of all ages; also operates the Charities Facilities Management Group, a national network for people who look after property in the voluntary sector.

Subject coverage: Building care, repairs, maintenance, facilities management.

Collection: Upkeep Exhibition

Publications: Printed

Access to staff: Contact by letter, by telephone, by fax, by e-mail and via website. Appointment necessary.
Hours: Mon to Fri, 0900 to 1700

UPPER NORWOOD JOINT LIBRARY (UNJL)

Westow Hill, Upper Norwood, London, SE19 1TJ

Tel: 020 8670 2551
Fax: 020 8670 5468
E-mail: info@uppernorwoodlibrary.org
Website: www.uppernorwoodlibrary.org

Enquiries to: Chief Librarian

Founded: 1898

Organisation type and purpose: Local government body, public library.

Subject coverage: History of both Crystal Palaces (Hyde Park and Norwood); the Great Exhibition 1851, the history of Norwood (especially Upper Norwood). Gerald Massey, 1828–1907 (Victorian Chartist, poet, Spiritualist and Egyptologist), Chartist Movement.

Collection: Material relating to Gerald Massey (1828–1907), Victorian Chartist, poet, spiritualist and Egyptologist
Gerald Massey collection
Oral history collection of taped interviews (c. 60) with people who remember Crystal Palace, collected by the Crystal Palace Foundation
The J B Wilson Collection: materials and photographs of the Norwood Area, particularly West Norwood, collected by J B Wilson (d. 1949)

Non-library collection catalogue: All or part available in-house

Library catalogue: All or part available in-house

Access to staff: Contact by letter, by telephone, by fax, by e-mail and in person
Hours: Mon, 1000 to 1900; Tue, Thu, Fri, 0900 to 1900; Sat, 0900 to 1700; Wed and Sun, closed

Access to building: *Hours:* Mon, 1000 to 1900; Tue, Thu, Fri, 0900 to 1900; Sat, 0900 to 1700; Wed and Sun, closed

Access for disabled people: Disabled access available

Funded by: London Boroughs of Croydon and Lambeth

URBAN AND ECONOMICAL DEVELOPMENT GROUP (URBED)

41 Old Birley Street, Manchester, M16 5RF

Tel: 0161 226 5078
Fax: 0161 226 7307
E-mail: urbed@urbed.co.uk
Website: www.urbed.co.uk

Enquiries to: Director

Founded: 1976

Organisation type and purpose: National organisation, consultancy, research organisation.
Urban Regeneration Consultants.

Subject coverage: Town centres, housing, sustainable development and urban regeneration.

Collection: Library of 4000 journals, books and publications of sustainable urban development

Library catalogue: All or part available in-house

Publications: Printed

Publications list: Available in print

Access to staff: Contact by letter, by telephone, by fax and by e-mail. Appointment necessary.
Hours: Mon to Fri, 0900 to 1700

Other addresses: Urban and Economical Development Group; 19 Store Street, London, WC1E 7DH; tel: 020 7436 8050; fax: 020 7436 8083; e-mail: n.falk@urbed.co.uk

UROSTOMY ASSOCIATION (UA)

4 Demontfort Way, Uttoxeter, Staffordshire, ST14 8XY

Tel: 01889 563191
E-mail: secretary.ua@classmail.co.uk
Website: www.urostomyassociation.org.uk

Enquiries to: National Secretary

Founded: 1971

Organisation type and purpose: Voluntary organisation, registered charity (charity number 1131072).

Subject coverage: The Urostomy Association aims to assist all who are about to undergo, or have undergone surgery resulting in the diversion or removal of the bladder with such information, help and support as may be necessary to assist them to resume as full a life as possible with every confidence.

Information services: Magazine; leaflets; DVD; telephone helpline

Special visitor services: Trained visitors available.

Publications: Printed, and electronic and video
Order printed publications from: The National Secretary, Urostomy Association, 4 Demontfort Way, Uttoxeter, Staffordshire, ST14 8XY; tel. 01889 563191; e-mail secretary .ua@classmail.co.uk
Order electronic and video publications from: The National Secretary, 4 Demontfort Way, Uttoxeter, Staffordshire, ST14 8XY; tel. 01889 563191; e-mail secretary.ua@classmail.co.uk

Publications list: Available online and in print

Access to staff: Contact by letter, by telephone, by e-mail, in person and via website. Appointment necessary.
Hours: Mon to Fri, 0900 to 1700

Access to building: By appointment only

Links with: International Ostomy Association

US-UK FULBRIGHT COMMISSION

Fulbright House, 62 Doughty Street, London, WC1N 2JZ

Tel: 020 7404 6994
Fax: 020 7404 6874
E-mail: education@fulbright.co.uk
Website: www.fulbright.co.uk

Enquiries to: Educational Adviser

Founded: 1948; also US-UK Educational Commission

Organisation type and purpose: Anglo-American scholarship organisation (Fulbright grants). Specialised US education library and resource centre.
To promote educational and cultural exchanges between the United States and the United Kingdom. Advisory service on all aspects of education in the USA.

Subject coverage: Education in the US at all levels and for most disciplines; exchanges for British students.

Collection: Application forms for US admissions tests (SAT, GRE, GMAT, TOEFL, USMLE, LSAT, MCAT, ACT) and test preparation books
Reference collection of US education directories

Publications: Printed, and electronic and video

Publications list: Available online and in print

Access to staff: Contact by letter and via website
Hours: Mon, 1330 to 1900; Wed and Fri, 1330 to 1700

USHAW COLLEGE LIBRARY

Formal name: St Cuthbert's College, Durham

Ushaw College, Durham, DH7 9RH

Tel: 0191 373 8516
E-mail: matthew.watson@ushaw.ac.uk
Website: www.ushaw.ac.uk

Enquiries to: Librarian

Founded: 1808

Organisation type and purpose: Library of a Roman Catholic seminary.

Subject coverage: Recusant history, church councils, medieval church history, English civil law to 1840, liturgy.

Collection: 18th century lectures from English College, Douai
John Lingard's Correspondence with Newsham and Wiseman
Lisbon Collection (Archives of English College, Lisbon, 1628–1971)
Printed books from Durham Priory
Weld Bank Parish Library

Non-library collection catalogue: All or part available in-house

Library catalogue: All or part available in-house

Publications: Printed

Access to staff: Contact by letter, by telephone and by e-mail. Appointment necessary.
Hours: No regular hours – e-mail contact preferred
Special comments: Visits by appointment only.

Access to building: Visits by appointment only

Access for disabled people: Parking provided, toilet facilities
Hours: As above, appointment only

Links with: University of Durham

UTTLESFORD DISTRICT COUNCIL

London Road, Saffron Walden, Essex, CB11 4ER

Tel: 01799 510510\Textphone Users 18001
Fax: 01799 510550
E-mail: uconnect@uttlesford.gov.uk
Website: www.uttlesford.gov.uk

Founded: 1974

Organisation type and purpose: Local government body

Subject coverage: Local government services

Access to staff: Contact by letter, by telephone, by fax, by e-mail, in person and via website
Hours: Mon to Thu, 0830 to 1700; Fri, 0830 to 1630

VALE OF GLAMORGAN COUNCIL

Civic Offices, Holton Road, Barry, Vale of Glamorgan, CF63 4RU

continued overleaf

Tel: 01446 700111
Fax: 01446 421479
E-mail: civ@valeofglamorgan.gov.uk
Website: www.valeofglamorgan.gov.uk

Organisation type and purpose: Local government body.

VALE OF GLAMORGAN RAILWAY COMPANY LIMITED (VOGR)

Barry Island Station, Romanwell Road, Barry Island, Vale of Glamorgan, CF62 5TH

Tel: 01446 748816
Fax: 01446 749018
E-mail: valeofglamrail@hotmail.com
Website: www.valeglamrail.co.uk

Enquiries to: Librarian and Archivist

Founded: 1994

Organisation type and purpose: Museum, historic building, house or site, suitable for ages: all.
Steam Heritage Centre for pleasure and educational purposes.

Subject coverage: General railway history (especially South Wales railways), history and information on the Woodham Locomotive Scrapyard.

Information services: Library available for reference

Special visitor services: Guided tours, materials and/or activities for children.

Education services: Group education facilities, resources for Key Stages 1 and 2.

Services for disabled people: Displays and/or information at wheelchair height.

Collection: Reference library
Railwayiana
Victorian Station Building
Steam and diesel locomotives
Coaches, including a Taff Vale Railway one of 1874 being restored
Cranes, steam and hand operated
Woodham collection (photos and scrapbooks)

Library catalogue: All or part available in-house

Publications: Printed

Access to staff: Contact by letter, by telephone, by fax, by e-mail, in person and via website

Access for disabled people: Parking provided, level entry, access to all public areas, toilet facilities
Special comments: Ramped entry to coaches

Affiliated to the: Council for Museums in Wales

VALE OF WHITE HORSE DISTRICT COUNCIL

The Abbey House, Abbey Close, Abingdon, Oxfordshire, OX14 3JE

Tel: 01235 520202
Fax: 01235 554960
Website: www.oxfordshire.gov.ukio.idc-ioid=6.htm/

Organisation type and purpose: Local government body.
District council.

Subject coverage: Waste collection and recycling, housing register, homelessness, planning, building control, leisure facilities, housing benefit, council tax collection, non-domestic rates, car parks, electoral registration.

Access to staff: Contact by letter, by telephone, by fax, by e-mail and in person
Hours: Mon to Fri, 0845 to 1700

Access for disabled people: Ramped entry, access to all public areas, toilet facilities

VALUES INTO ACTION (VIA)

Oxford House, Derbyshire Street, London, E2 6HG

Tel: 020 7729 5436
Fax: 020 7729 7797
E-mail: general@viauk.org
Website: www.viauk.org

Enquiries to: Manager
Other contacts: Administrator

Founded: 1971; formerly called Campaign for People with Mental Handicaps (CPMH) (year of change 1989)

Organisation type and purpose:
Membership association (membership is by subscription), voluntary organisation, registered charity (charity number 1057249), training organisation, research organisation.
VIA is committed to achieving laws, services and public attitudes which will allow people with learning difficulties to become valued citizens.

Subject coverage: Learning difficulties, research training.

Publications: Printed, and electronic and video

Publications list: Available online and in print

Access to staff: Contact by letter, by telephone, by fax and by e-mail.
Appointment necessary.
Hours: Mon to Fri, 0930 to 1630

VANGUARD 3 OWNERS CLUB

14 Kennet Rise, Axford, Marlborough, Wiltshire, SN8 2EZ

Tel: 01672 520154

Enquiries to: General Secretary

Founded: 1990

Organisation type and purpose:
Membership association (membership is by subscription).

Subject coverage: Technical information and sources of spares for Vanguard 3 cars.

Collection: Factory workshop manuals
Technical Bulletins

Publications: Printed

Access to staff: Contact by letter and by telephone
Hours: Mon to Fri, 0900 to 1700, also evenings and weekends

VARIETY CLUB OF GREAT BRITAIN

93 Bayham Street, London, NW1 0AG

Tel: 020 7428 8100
E-mail: info@varietyclub.org.uk
Website: www.varietyclub.org.uk

Enquiries to: Chief Executive

Founded: October 1949

Organisation type and purpose: Registered charity (charity number 209259).
Has 53 chapters in 14 countries and ten regional offices in the UK.
To give financial help to projects and individual disadvantaged children.
Recipients include hospitals, schools, youth groups and individuals. The club helps to provide equipment such as Sunshine Coaches (minibuses), mobility equipment or other specialised equipment for disabled or disadvantaged children.

Subject coverage: Support for disabled and disadvantaged children.

Parent body: Variety Clubs International; 350 Fifth Avenue, Suite 1119, New York, 10118, USA; tel: 00 1 212 695 3818; fax: 00 1 212 695 3857; e-mail: vci@interport.net

VAUGHAN LIBRARY

Harrow School, High Street, Harrow on the Hill, Middlesex, HA1 3HT

Tel: 020 8872 8278
Fax: 020 8872 8013
E-mail: mek@harrowschool.org.uk
Website: www.harrowschool.org.uk

Enquiries to: Librarian
Other contacts: Archivist (for school history)

Founded: 1863

Organisation type and purpose: Suitable for ages: 13 to 18.
Independent school library.

Subject coverage: General.

Collection: Aldine Collection
Byron Collection
Churchill Collection
Harrow School Archive
Sheridan Collection

Non-library collection catalogue: All or part available online

Library catalogue: All or part available online

Access to staff: Contact by letter and by e-mail. Appointment necessary.
Hours: Mon to Fri, 0830 to 1830

VAUXHALL CONVERTIBLE CAR CLUB (VCCC)

47 Brooklands Close, Luton, Bedfordshire, LU4 9EH

Tel: 01582 573269
E-mail: ronnie.goddard@ntlworld.com
Website: www.vccc.org.uk

Enquiries to: Membership Secretary

Founded: 1990; formerly called Vauxhall Cavalier Convertible Club

Organisation type and purpose:
Membership association, voluntary organisation.
Independent organisation to promote the use of Vauxhall convertible cars.

Subject coverage: All aspects of Vauxhall convertible cars; conversion of Cavalier, Astra and Nova cars; agreed value insurance.

Publications: Printed
Order printed publications from: Regalia Officer, Vauxhall Convertible Car Club, 28 Deans Meadow, Dagnall, Berkhamsted, Hertfordshire, HP4 1RW, e-mail: tonycoates@btinternet.com

Access to staff: Contact by letter and by telephone
Hours: Mon to Fri, 0900 to 1700

VAUXHALL DROOP SNOOT GROUP (DSG)

17 Priors Road, Tadley, Hampshire, RG26 4QJ

Tel: 0118 981 5238
Website: come.to/droop.snoot.group

Enquiries to: Information Officer
Other contacts: Public Relations Manager

Founded: 1981

Organisation type and purpose: International organisation, membership association (membership is by subscription), present number of members: 350–400, voluntary organisation. Performance/classic car owners.

Subject coverage: Vauxhall Firenza, Magnum, HP Firenza, Sportshatch, and HS/HSR Chevette vehicle data and specification; production history; competition history; original vehicle data and authentication data; modification/technical material; spares schedules and information; vehicle insurance validations.

Trade and statistical information: Vauxhall performance, race and rally cars 1970–1985

Non-library collection catalogue: All or part available in-house

Publications: Printed, and microform publications

Publications list: Available in print

Access to staff: Contact by letter and by telephone
Hours: Mon to Fri, 1930 to 2230

Links with: Vauxhall Bedford Opel Association (VBOA)

Publicity Office: Vauxhall Droop Snoot Group; 11 New Road, Sands, High Wycombe, Bucks, HP12 4LH; tel: 01494 525948

VAUXHALL OWNERS CLUB (1903–1957) (VOC)

1 Horseshoe Drive, Red Lodge, Bury St Edmunds, Suffolk, IP28 8ER

Tel: 01638 751275
E-mail: barrymharvey@tiscali.co.uk
Website: www.vauxhallownersclub-1903-1957.co.uk

Enquiries to: Membership Secretary

Founded: 1976

Organisation type and purpose: Membership association (membership is by subscription), present number of members: 400.

Subject coverage: Details of 1903–1957 Vauxhall cars, advice on restoration and use, spares scheme.

Collection: Some sales brochures, technical data and house magazines

Publications: Printed

Access to staff: Contact by letter and by telephone
Hours: Evenings and weekends

VAUXHALL VIVA OWNERS CLUB

The Thatches, Snetterton North End, Snetterton, Norwich, Norfolk, NR16 2LD

Tel: 01953 498818
E-mail: adrian@vivaclub.freeserve.co.uk
Website: www.vivaclub.freeserve.co.uk

Enquiries to: Membership Secretary

Founded: 1982

Organisation type and purpose: Membership association (membership is by subscription), present number of members: 1000, voluntary organisation.

Subject coverage: Vauxhall Viva motorcars.

Publications: Printed

Access to staff: Contact by letter, by telephone, by fax and by e-mail. Appointment necessary. Access for members only.
Hours: Mon to Fri, 0900 to 1730 only

Member of: Vauxhall/Bedford/Opel Association (VBOA)

VEGAN SOCIETY

Donald Watson House, 21 Hylton Street, Hockley, Birmingham, B18 6HJ

Tel: 0121 523 1730 .
Fax: 0121 523 1730
E-mail: info@vegansociety.com
Website: www.vegansociety.com

Enquiries to: PR Officer
Direct e-mail: media@vegansociety.com

Founded: 1944

Organisation type and purpose: Membership organisation, Registered Charity (charity number 279228). Provides information on all aspects of veganism – including nutrition and health – to the public, schools, media, healthcare professionals, caterers, food manufacturers etc.

Subject coverage: Vegan diets, animal welfare, land use, nutrition, environment, health.

Information services: All aspects of plant-based living, including vegan nutrition & stock-free farming

Education services: Free visitor service, teaching materials, support for teachers

Services for disabled people: Advocacy for vegans in vulnerable situations

Non-library collection catalogue: All or part available online

Publications: Printed, and electronic and video
Order printed publications from: trademark@vegansociety.com

Publications list: Available online and in print

Access to staff: Contact by letter, by telephone, by fax, by e-mail and via website. Appointment necessary.
Hours: Mon to Fri, 0900 to 1700

Access to building: Prior appointment required

VEGETARIAN SOCIETY OF THE UNITED KINGDOM (VSUK)

Parkdale, Dunham Road, Altrincham, Cheshire, WA14 4QG

Tel: 0161 925 2000
Fax: 0161 926 9182
E-mail: info@vegsoc.org
Website: www.vegsoc.org

Enquiries to: Information Officer

Founded: 1847; formed by the amalgamation of London Vegetarian Society, Vegetarian Society

Organisation type and purpose: Membership association (membership is by subscription), present number of members: 11,500, registered charity (charity number 259358).

Subject coverage: Vegetarianism.

Collection: Collection of books on vegetarianism and Society Journals dating back to 1848

Publications: Printed, and electronic and video

Access to staff: Contact by letter, by telephone, by fax, by e-mail and via website. Appointment necessary.
Hours: Mon to Fri, 0900 to 1700

Access to building: Prior appointment required

Access for disabled people: Ramped entry, toilet facilities

Affiliated to: International Vegetarian Union (IVU)

VEHICLE AND OPERATOR SERVICES AGENCY (VOSA)

Berkeley House, Croydon Street, Bristol, BS5 0DA

Tel: 0117 954 3200
Fax: 0117 954 3212
E-mail: enquiries@vosa.gov.uk
Website: www.vosa.gov.uk/

Enquiries to: Agency Secretariat

Founded: 2003; created by the merger of the Vehicle Inspectorate and the Traffic Area Network Division of the Department for Transport

Organisation type and purpose: National government body.

Subject coverage: Conducting statutory testing of lorries, coaches and buses; supervising the MOT scheme; carrying out roadside checks and other spot checks to ensure vehicles comply with legal standards and regulations; undertaking specialised vehicle inspections; investigating accidents and defects, and overseeing vehicle recall campaigns.

continued overleaf

Publications: Printed, and electronic and video
Order printed publications from: Vehicle Inspectorate, PO Box 12, Swansea, SA1 1BP, tel: 01792 454320

Publications list: Available online and in print

Access to staff: Contact by letter, by telephone, by fax, by e-mail, in person and via website
Hours: Mon to Fri, 0900 to 1700

VEHICLE BUILDERS AND REPAIRERS ASSOCIATION LIMITED (VBRA)

Belmont House, Finkle Lane, Gildersome, Leeds, West Yorkshire, LS27 7TW

Tel: 0113 253 8333
Fax: 0113 238 0496
E-mail: vbra@vbra.co.uk
Website: www.vbra.co.uk

Enquiries to: Director General

Founded: 1914

Organisation type and purpose: Trade association.
1,300 members engaged in vehicle building and repairing industry. To ensure VBRA membership is recognised as a sign of the professional builder and repairer. To develop membership criteria, profitability and relationships with key industry players. To improve communications within the industry. To provide membership benefits and assistance.

Subject coverage: Working conditions and wages in the vehicle body building industry, material and data relating to commercial vehicle body building and body repair, car body repair, market research.

Publications: Printed, and electronic and video

Access to staff: Contact by letter, by telephone, by fax, by e-mail and via website. Appointment necessary. Non-members charged.
Hours: Mon to Fri, 0830 to 1630

Access for disabled people: Ramped entry

Affiliated to: International Association of Vehicle Body Builders and Repairers (AIRC)

VEHICLE CERTIFICATION AGENCY (VCA)

1, The Eastgate Office Centre, Eastgate Road, Bristol, BS5 6XX

Tel: 0117 952 4119
Fax: 0117 952 4103
Website: www.vca.gov.uk

Enquiries to: Librarian

Founded: 1989

Organisation type and purpose: National government body.

Subject coverage: National testing and certification service for new models of road and agricultural vehicles and vehicle parts, administers the compulsory national vehicle type approval schemes and the European whole vehicle approval schemes.

Access to staff: Contact by letter and by e-mail
Hours: Mon to Fri, 0830 to 1700

Access to building: No access other than to staff

Executive Agency of: Department of Transport; e-mail: enquiries@vca.gov.uk

VELOCETTE OWNERS CLUB

12A Hampton Close, Newport, Shropshire, TF10 7RB

Website: www.velocetteowners.com

Enquiries to: Public Relations Officer

Founded: 1957

Organisation type and purpose: Membership association (membership is by subscription), present number of members: 1,700.

Subject coverage: Velocette motorcycles.

Access to staff: Contact by letter
Hours: Mon to Fri, 0900 to 1700

VERE HARMSWORTH LIBRARY (VHL)

Rothermere American Institute, 1a South Parks Road, Oxford, OX1 3UB

Tel: 01865 282700
Fax: 01865 282709
E-mail: vhl@bodleian.ox.ac.uk
Website: www.bodleian.ox.ac.uk/vhl

Enquiries to: Librarian

Founded: 2001

Organisation type and purpose: University library, university department or institute.

Subject coverage: History of the USA, political, economic and social.

Library catalogue: All or part available online

Access to staff: Contact by letter, by telephone, by fax, by e-mail, in person and via website
Hours: Term time: Mon to Fri, 0900 to 1900; Sat' 1000 to 1400
Vacation (Christmas and Easter): Mon to Fri, 0900 to 1900
Vacation (Summer – July to September): Mon to Fri, 0900 to 1700

Access to building: Term time: Mon to Fri, 0900 to 1900; Sat, 1000 to 1400
Vacation (Christmas and Easter): Mon to Fri, 0900 to 1900
Vacation (Summer – July to September): Mon to Fri, 0900 to 1700

Access for disabled people: Level entry, access to all public areas, toilet facilities, lift to upper floors (ask staff to use)

Parent body: Bodleian Libraries, Oxford University

VERIFICATION RESEARCH, TRAINING AND INFORMATION CENTRE (VERTIC)

Development House, 56–64 Leonard Street, London EC2A 4LT,

Tel: 020 7065 0880
Fax: 020 7065 0890
E-mail: info@vertic.org
Website: www.vertic.org/

Enquiries to: Information Officer
Direct e-mail: rocio.escauriaza@vertic.org

Founded: 1986; formerly called Verification Technology Information Centre (VERTIC) (year of change 1998)

Organisation type and purpose: International organisation, registered charity (charity number 1073051), consultancy, research organisation.
Non-Governmental Organisation.

Subject coverage: Research on verification and confidence-building measures in international treaties and agreements, spanning arms control and disarmament, conflict resolution and the environment; nuclear testing; greenhouse gas emissions, climate change.

Collection: Library containing books, journals, news clippings, documents, papers and Hansard on all research areas dating from 1985

Publications: Printed, and electronic and video, and microform publications

Publications list: Available online and in print

Access to staff: Contact by letter, by telephone, by fax, by e-mail and via website. Appointment necessary.
Hours: Mon to Fri, 1000 to 1730
Special comments: Charges for photocopies, free access to the library.

Access to building: No prior appointment required

VERNACULAR ARCHITECTURE GROUP (VAG)

Ashley, Willows Green, Chelmsford, Essex, CM3 1QD

Tel: 01245 361408
Website: www.vag.org.uk

Enquiries to: Honorary Secretary

Founded: 1952

Organisation type and purpose: Learned society, registered charity (charity number 279839).

Subject coverage: Vernacular (smaller traditional) architecture, particularly in the UK.

Publications: Printed

VETERAN CAR CLUB OF GREAT BRITAIN (VCC)

Jessamine Court, 15 High Street, Ashwell, Hertfordshire, SG7 5NL

Tel: 01462 742818
Fax: 01462 742997
E-mail: hq@vccofgb.co.uk
Website: www.vccofgb.co.uk

Enquiries to: Secretary

Founded: 1930

Organisation type and purpose: International organisation, membership association (membership is by subscription, election or invitation), present number of members: 1600.

Subject coverage: Preservation and use of Veteran and Edwardian cars manufactured before 1919.

Collection: Early motoring period literature

Library catalogue: All or part available in-house

Publications: Printed

Access to staff: Contact by letter and by fax. Appointment necessary. Access for members only. Letter of introduction required.
Hours: Mon to Fri, 0930 to 1700

VETERANS AID (VA)

40 Buckingham Palace Road, London, SW1W 0RE

Tel: 020 7828 2468
Fax: 020 7630 6780
E-mail: info@veterans-aid.net
Website: www.veterans-aid.net

Enquiries to: Administrator

Founded: 1932; formerly called Ex-Services Fellowship Centre (year of change 2007)

Organisation type and purpose: Registered charity (charity number 209667).
To relieve distress among ex-service, including merchant service, men and women.

Subject coverage: Assistance to ex-service persons in need.

Access to staff: Contact by letter, by telephone, by fax, by e-mail, in person and via website
Hours: Mon to Thurs, 0900 to 1530; Fri, 0900 to 1330

Also at: New Belvedere House (Hostel for the Homeless); Whitehorse Road, London, E1 0ND; tel: 020 7790 1474; fax: 020 7253 4997

VETERINARY LABORATORIES AGENCY (VLA)

Woodham Lane, New Haw, Addlestone, Surrey, KT15 3NB

Tel: 01932 341111
Fax: 01932 347046
E-mail: enquiries@vla.defra.gsi.gov.uk
Website: www.defra.gov.uk/vla

Enquiries to: Librarian
Direct tel: 01932 357314
Direct fax: 01932 357608
Direct e-mail: library@defra.vla.gov.uk
Other contacts: Library Services Manager

Founded: 1995

Organisation type and purpose: National government body, consultancy, research organisation.
To provide consultancy, surveillance, research, laboratory services and products to promote animal health and welfare and to minimise hazards associated with animals that are important to public health and the environment.

Subject coverage: Investigation and control of diseases of commercial farm animals, animal husbandry, biochemistry, veterinary science and medicine, life sciences as related to animals.

Information services: Library, Information and Records Management.

Collection: 10,000 books, 40,000 bound periodicals, 300 current subscriptions, 10,000 pamphlets, 300 annual reports, collection of staff papers and posters, 3,000 slides

Trade and statistical information: Statistics on outbreaks of animal diseases in the United Kingdom

Library catalogue: All or part available in-house

Publications: Printed, and electronic and video

Publications list: Available in print

Access to staff: Contact by letter, by telephone, by fax, by e-mail and via website. Appointment necessary. Non-members charged.
Hours: Mon to Fri, 0900 to 1645

Access to building: Limited access, appointment necessary

Also at: Central research facility at Weybridge

Constituent bodies: Network of 15 regional laboratories across the UK

Constituent part of: Department for Environment, Food and Rural Affairs (DEFRA)

VICTIM SUPPORT

National Centre, Hallam House, 56–60 Hallam Street, London, W1W 6JL

Tel: 020 7268 0200
Fax: 020 7268 0210
E-mail: contact@victimsupport.org.uk
Website: www.victimsupport.org.uk

Enquiries to: Information Officer
Direct tel: 020 7268 0281
Direct e-mail: info@victimsupport.org.uk
Other contacts: Library/Information Officer for arrangements to use library resources

Founded: 1974

Organisation type and purpose: Voluntary organisation, registered charity (charity number 298028).
Provides emotional support, information and practical help to victims and witnesses of crime and their families. Raises awareness of victims' rights and the effects of crime.

Subject coverage: Services for victims of crime, effects of crime, victims' rights, victims in the criminal justice system, victim policy.

Trade and statistical information: Statistics of referrals to Victim Support by crime. Statistics on use of the Witness Service and Victim Supportline

Non-library collection catalogue: All or part available in-house

Library catalogue: All or part available in-house

Publications: Printed

Access to staff: Contact by letter, by telephone, by fax, by e-mail and via website. Appointment necessary.
Hours: Mon to Fri, 0900 to 1730

Special comments: Access to the collection for reference by postgraduates and professional users only, and by prior appointment with the Library/Information Officer.

Access to building: Prior appointment required

Affiliated to: European Forum for Victim Services; National Council for Voluntary Organisations; Volunteering England; World Society of Victimology

Victim Support has: a Witness Service in every Crown Court and magistrate's court in England and Wales; about 400 local Victim Support services throughout England, Wales and N Ireland

VICTIM SUPPORT SCOTLAND (VSS)

15–23 Hardwell Close, Edinburgh, EH8 9RX

Tel: 0131 668 4486
Fax: 0131 662 5400
E-mail: info@victimsupportsco.org.co.uk
Website: www.victimsupport.sco.org.uk

Enquiries to: Head of Communications and Fundraising
Direct tel: 0131 662 5409
Direct fax: 0131 662 8209
Direct e-mail: david.sinclair@victimsupportsco.org.uk
Other contacts: Communications Officer

Founded: 1985

Organisation type and purpose: Registered charity (charity number SC002138).
Helping the victims and witnesses of crime.

Subject coverage: Information on help available to victims of crime; practical and emotional support and essential information.

Publications: Printed

Publications list: Available online and in print

Access to staff: Contact by letter, by telephone, by fax, by e-mail and via website. Appointment necessary.
Hours: Mon to Fri, 0900 to 1700
24-hour helpline 08456 039213; 24-hour media line 07803 970320

Also at: 32 local victim support branches and witness service offices

VICTORIA COLLEGE EXAMINATIONS (VCM)

52 Bedford Row, London, WC1R 4LR

Tel: 020 7405 6483
E-mail: vcmexams@aol.com
Website: www.vcmexams.com

Enquiries to: Chief Executive

Founded: 1890; incorporates the former Victoria College of Music, London (year of change 2000); incorporates the former College of Violinists (year of change 2000)

Organisation type and purpose: Examining body in music, speech and drama.

Subject coverage: Examinations in performing arts.

Publications: Printed
Order printed publications from: website: http://www.whitepublishing.co.uk

continued overleaf

Publications list: Available online and in print

Access to staff: Contact by letter, by telephone, by e-mail and via website
Hours: All times

Access to building: No access other than to staff

Constituent bodies: College of Violinists; London Music Press (publications department of Victoria College)

Member organisation of: Association of British Choral Directors (ABCD); European Piano Teachers Association (EPTA); European Recorder Teachers Association (ERTA); European String Teachers Association (ESTA); Music Education Council (MEC); Society of Teachers of Recorder Players (STRP); Society of Teachers of Speech and Drama (STSD); Worshipful Company of Musicians

VICTORIA COUNTY HISTORY

Formal name: Victoria History of the Counties of England

Institute of Historical Research, University of London, Senate House, Malet Street, London, WC1E 7HU

Tel: 020 7862 8770
Fax: 020 7862 8749
E-mail: vchevents@sas.ac.uk
Website: www.victoriacountyhistory.ac.uk

Enquiries to: Publications Manager
Direct e-mail: jessica.davies@sas.ac.uk

Founded: 1899

Organisation type and purpose: An encyclopaedic record of England's places and people from earliest times to the present day, written by historians working in counties across England.
To produce an encyclopaedic national history in a series of volumes that cover, county by county, and parish by parish, the general and detailed history of England from earliest times to the present.

Publications: Printed
Order printed publications from: Boydell & Brewer
Order electronic and video publications from: Text of some vols available online at: http://www.british-history.ac.uk

Publications list: Available online

Access to staff: Contact by letter, by telephone and by e-mail

VICTORIA INSTITUTE OR PHILOSOPHICAL SOCIETY OF GREAT BRITAIN (VI)

c/o The Secretary to the Trustees, 41 Marne Avenue, Welling, Kent, DA16 2EY

Tel: 020 8303 0465
Fax: 020 8303 0465
Website: www.faithandthought.org.uk

Enquiries to: Honorary Treasurer
Direct tel: 01279 422661
Direct e-mail: johnbuxton@tesco.net
Other contacts: Editor for publication and material reviews: 110 Flemming Avenue, Leigh-on-Sea, Essex, SS9 3AX, tel: 01702 475110

Founded: 1865; operating as Faith and Thought

Organisation type and purpose: Learned society (membership is by subscription), registered charity (charity number 285871). Faith and thought.

Subject coverage: The interface between science (increasing knowledge) and the Christian revelation contained in the Holy Bible, investigating apparent contradictions and seeking reconciliation.

Collection: Back numbers of Faith and Thought, its predecessor the Journal of the Transactions of the Victoria Institute 1867 to 1989 and its successor Science and Christian Belief from 1989

Publications: Printed

Access to staff: Contact by letter and by telephone
Hours: Mon to Fri, 0900 to 1700
Special comments: The society does not have regular opening times.

Editor (also for book reviews): Faith & Thought; 110 Flemming Avenue, Leigh-on-Sea, Essex, SS9 3AX; tel: 01702 475110; e-mail: reg@luhman.freeserve.co.uk

Editorial Consultant: Victoria Institute or Philosophical Society of Great Britain; 185 Wickham Road, Croydon, Surrey, CR0 8TF; tel: 020 8654 4887

In association with: Christians in Science; The Secretary, 4 Sackville Close, Sevenoaks, Kent, TN13 3QD; tel: 01732 451907; fax: 01732 464253; e-mail: cberry@centrenet.co.uk

VICTORIAN SOCIETY

1 Priory Gardens, Bedford Park, London, W4 1TT

Tel: 020 8994 1019
Fax: 020 8747 5899
E-mail: library@victoriansociety.org.uk
Website: www.victoriansociety.org.uk

Enquiries to: Administrator

Founded: 1958

Organisation type and purpose: Statutory body, learned society, registered charity (charity number 1081435).
Pressure group.
Campaigns for the Victorian and Edwardian historic environment and promotes public understanding of the architecture and decorative arts of the period.

Subject coverage: 19th- and early 20th-century architectural history, conservation legislation and protection of historic buildings, conservation and refurbishment advice, care for Victorian houses.

Collection: Case files relating to individual buildings that have been the subject of listed building consent applications

Non-library collection catalogue: All or part available in-house

Library catalogue: All or part available in-house

Publications: Printed

Publications list: Available online and in print

Access to staff: Contact by letter, by telephone and by e-mail. Appointment necessary.

Access to building: Prior appointment required

VIDEO PERFORMANCE LIMITED (VPL)

1 Upper James Street, London, W1F 9DE

Tel: 020 7534 1400
Fax: 020 7534 1414

Founded: 1984

Organisation type and purpose: Trade association, present number of members: 800.
Music video licensing.

Subject coverage: Music videos.

Access to staff: Contact by letter, by telephone, by fax and by e-mail
Hours: Mon to Fri, 0900 to 1700

Trading division: Music Mall; at the same address; tel: 020 7534 1444; fax: 020 7534 1440; e-mail: info@musicmall.co.uk

VIKING SOCIETY FOR NORTHERN RESEARCH

Department of Scandinavian Studies, University College London, Gower Street, London, WC1E 6BT

Tel: 020 7679 7176
Fax: 020 7679 7750
E-mail: vsnr@ucl.ac.uk
Website: www.nolt.ac.uk/~aezjj/homepage.html

Enquiries to: Honorary Secretary

Founded: 1892

Organisation type and purpose: Learned society.

Subject coverage: Old Norse literature; medieval Scandinavian literature, languages and history; the history and culture of The North (the Viking Age, Viking settlements in British Isles, runes etc).

Collection: Viking Society Library (now housed as part of the University College Collection)

Publications: Printed

Publications list: Available in print

Access to staff: Contact by letter, by telephone, by fax, by e-mail and in person
Hours: Mon to Fri, 1100 to 1700

Links with: Scottish Society for Northern Studies

VINTAGE AUSTIN REGISTER LTD

The Briars, Four Lane Ends, Oakerthorpe, Alfreton, Derbyshire, DE55 7LH

Tel: 01773 831646
E-mail: frank.smith7@tesco.net

Enquiries to: Honorary Secretary

Founded: 1958

Organisation type and purpose: Membership association, voluntary organisation.

Subject coverage: Information on all Austin motor cars produced between 1906 and 1930.

Collection: Handbooks, spares lists, sales brochures for most Austin motor cars 1906–1930

Publications: Printed

Access to staff: Contact by letter, by telephone and by e-mail
Hours: Mon to Fri, 0900 to 1700

VINTAGE GLIDER CLUB (VGC)

Arewa, Shootersway Lane, Berkhamsted, Hertfordshire, HP4 3NP

Tel: 01442 873258
Fax: 01442 873258
E-mail: geoffmoore@madasafish.com
Website: www.vintagegliderclub.org.uk

Enquiries to: Membership Secretary

Founded: 1972

Organisation type and purpose: International organisation, membership association (membership is by subscription), present number of members: 800 internationally, museum.
Museum – flying, restoration.

Subject coverage: History of gliding since the early 1920s, plans of vintage gliders, whereabouts of vintage gliders, gliding museums, dates of rallies and similar events.

Collection: Collection of photographs
Construction plans of gliders especially Slingsby drawings held at Lasham Airfield and microfilm covering a wider range including Slingsby

Publications: Printed

Access to staff: Contact by letter, by fax, by e-mail and via website
Hours: 24-hour answerphone and fax

Associated with: British Gliding Association

VINTAGE MOTOR CYCLE CLUB LIMITED (VMCC)

Allen House, Wetmore Road, Burton on Trent, Staffordshire, DE14 1TR

Tel: 01283 495102
Fax: 01283 510547
E-mail: library@vmcc.net
Website: www.vmcc.net

Enquiries to: Librarian

Founded: 1946

Organisation type and purpose: International organisation, membership association (membership is by subscription), present number of members: 15,573, suitable for ages: all, research organisation.

Subject coverage: Information on motorcycling and motorcycles with related accessories from 1890s to the present. Preservation and use of motorcycles over 25 years old.

Collection: Complete sets of Motorcycle, Motorcycling etc.; Ariel, BSA, Norton, Royal Enfield (early), Scott, Triumph, Velocette (early) and late Zenith works records; other collections held; handbooks, technical information etc.
Photograph collection

Non-library collection catalogue: All or part available online and in-house

Library catalogue: All or part available online and in-house

Publications: Printed

Publications list: Available online and in print

Access to staff: Contact by letter, by telephone, by fax, by e-mail, in person and via website
Hours: Mon to Thu, 0900 to 1730; Fri 0900 to 1600

Access to building: *Hours:* Mon to Thu, 0900 to 1730; Fri, 0900 to 1600
Special comments: Library and archives situated on first floor, no lift access.

Access for disabled people: Access to ground floor; no lift access to first floor.

Affiliated Member of: Auto Cycle Union; tel: 01788 566400; fax: 01788 573585; e-mail: admin@acu.org.uk; Federation of British Historic Vehicle Clubs

Associated Member of: Royal Automobile Club

VINTAGE SPORTS-CAR CLUB LIMITED (VSCC)

The Old Post Office, West Street, Chipping Norton, Oxfordshire, OX7 5EL

Tel: 01608 644777
Fax: 01608 644888
E-mail: info@vscc.co.uk

Enquiries to: Secretary

Founded: 1934

Organisation type and purpose: Membership association.

Subject coverage: General and specialised information on pre-war cars and historic racing cars; mechanical data, history and whereabouts of existing cars; specialist firms; racing and competitions up to the last war; addresses of one-make and other clubs specialising in old cars in the UK and abroad; emphasis on vintage cars made 1919–1930.

Collection: Book library
Film library

Publications: Printed

Access to staff: Contact by letter, by fax and by e-mail
Hours: Mon to Fri, 0900 to 1700

Access to building: No prior appointment required
Hours: Mon to Fri, 0900 to 1700
Special comments: Wednesday preferred.

Member of: Fédération Internationale des Voitures Anciennes; Federation of British Historic Vehicle Clubs

VINTNERS' COMPANY

Vintners' Hall, Upper Thames Street, London, EC4V 3BG

Tel: 020 7236 1863
E-mail: info@vintnershall.co.uk
Website: www.vintnershall.co.uk

Enquiries to: The Clerk

Founded: 1363

Organisation type and purpose: Membership association (membership is by election or invitation).
City of London Livery Company.

Access to staff: Contact by letter, by telephone, by e-mail and via website

VIOLA DA GAMBA SOCIETY (VdGS)

28 Freelands Road, Oxford, OX4 4BT

Tel: 01865 723778
E-mail: admin@vdgs.org.uk
Website: www.vdgs.org.uk

Enquiries to: Administrator

Founded: 1948

Organisation type and purpose: International organisation, learned society (membership is by subscription), present number of members: 530, voluntary organisation, registered charity (charity number 258544), publishing house, research organisation.

Subject coverage: Printed and manuscript sources of music for viols, particularly English sources; limited information on instruments and on original treatises on playing technique.

Publications: Printed, and electronic and video

Access to staff: Contact by letter, by telephone, by fax, by e-mail, in person and via website
Hours: Afternoons and weekends

Links with: Lute Society; Viola da Gamba Society of America

VIRGINIA WOOLF SOCIETY OF GREAT BRITAIN (VWSGB)

Fairhaven, Charnleys Lane, Banks, Southport, Merseyside, PR9 8HJ

Tel: 01704 225232
E-mail: stuart.n.clarke@btinternet.com
Website: www.virginiawoolfsociety.org.uk

Enquiries to: Membership Secretary

Founded: 1998

Organisation type and purpose: Learned society (membership is by subscription), number of members: 400, literary society.

Subject coverage: Virginia Woolf and the Bloomsbury Group.

Publications: Printed

Publications list: Available online

Access to staff: Contact by e-mail
Hours: Mon to Fri, 0900 to 1700

VISIBILITY

2 Queen's Crescent, St George's Cross, Glasgow, G4 9BW

Tel: 0141 332 4632
Fax: 0141 353 2981
E-mail: info@visibility.org.uk
Website: www.visibility.org.uk

Enquiries to: Operational Director

continued overleaf

Direct tel: 0141 572 0744
Direct e-mail: val@visibility.org.uk
Other contacts: Chief Executive Officer for organisational issues, funding, promotion and advertising.

Founded: 1859; formerly called Glasgow & West of Scotland Society for the Blind; formerly called Mission To The Outdoor Blind

Organisation type and purpose: Voluntary organisation, registered charity (charity number SCO 009738).
To support the independence of people with a visual impairment by providing information, welfare rights, home support, social and recreational opportunities, and volunteer support.
To raise awareness of the issues of people who are visually impaired. Research.

Subject coverage: Visual impairment and issues of concern to those working with people with sight impairment.
Awareness of visual impairment/access issues for employers/service providers.

Trade and statistical information: Data on registration in West of Scotland

Publications: Printed, and electronic and video

Access to staff: Contact by letter, by telephone, by fax and by e-mail.
Appointment necessary.
Hours: Mon to Thu, 0900 to 1700; Fri, 0900 to 1630

Access to building: No prior appointment required

Access for disabled people: Ramped entry, access to all public areas, toilet facilities

Members of: National Association of Local Societies for the Visually Impaired (NALSVI); tel: 01582 391848; SCVO

VISIT CORNWALL (VC)

Formal name: Cornwall Development Company

Pydar House, Pydar Street, Truro, Cornwall, TR1 1EA

Tel: 01872 322900
Fax: 01872 322919
E-mail: enquiries@visitcornwall.com
Website: www.visitcornwall.com

Enquiries to: Administrator
Other contacts: Head of Marketing

History of institution: formerly called Cornwall Tourist Board

Organisation type and purpose: Tourism.

Subject coverage: Marketing and promotion of Cornwall as a tourism destination.

Trade and statistical information: Various surveys giving statistical information on aspects of tourism in Cornwall

Publications: Printed

Access to staff: Contact by letter, by telephone, by fax, by e-mail and via website. Appointment necessary. Access for members only.
Hours: Answerphone out of office hours

Parent body: Cornwall Development Company; Pydar House, Pydar Street, Truro, Cornwall, TR1 1EA; tel: 01872 322800; e-mail: mail@cornwalldevelopmentcompany.co.uk; website: http://www.cornwalldevelopmentcompany.co.uk

VISIT FINLAND

Formal name: Visit Finland, Finland Trade Centre UK

177–179 Hammersmith Road, London, W6 8BS

Tel: 020 8600 7260 (trade and press only)
Website: www.visitfinland.com/uk

Organisation type and purpose: National government body, professional body.
National tourist board, promoting Finland in the UK and Ireland.
Working closely with local travel trade and press.

Subject coverage: Travelling to and in Finland; tourism facilities in Finland; addresses and contacts within the travel trade in Finland; timetables; packages available; statistics; tourist attractions.

Collection: Brochures, posters
Photographic library
Video films available on loan

Trade and statistical information: Statistics on tourism to and in Finland

Non-library collection catalogue: All or part available online

Library catalogue: All or part available online

Publications: Printed, and electronic and video
Order printed publications from: Website

Access to staff: Contact via website.
Appointment necessary.
Special comments: Not open to public. Visitors by prior appointment only.

Access to building: Prior appointment required
Hours: Mon to Fri, 0900 to 1700

Parent body: Finnish Tourist Board; PO Box 625, Helsinki, 00101, Finland; tel: + 358 9 4176911; fax: + 358 9 41769399; e-mail: mek@mek.fi

VISIT LONDON

5th Floor, 1 Warwick Row, London, SW1E 5ER

Tel: 020 7234 5800
Fax: 020 7234 5751
Website: www.visitlondon.com

Enquiries to: Information Officer
Direct e-mail: kkelling@visitlondon.com

Organisation type and purpose: Tourist Board.

Subject coverage: What to see, and where to go and stay in London.

Publications: Printed

Publications list: Available online and in print

Access to staff: Contact by letter, by telephone, by fax, by e-mail and via website

VISIT SWEDEN

Sweden House, 5 Upper Montagu Street, London, W1H 2AG

Tel: 020 7108 6168
Fax: 020 7724 5872
E-mail: uk@visitsweden.com
Website: www.visitsweden.com

Enquiries to: Director
Direct tel: 020 7870 5601
Direct e-mail: semmy.rulf@visitsweden.com

Organisation type and purpose: National government body.
Tourist office.

Subject coverage: All aspects of travel to and in Sweden, including ferry routes, airlines, suggested holiday areas.

Access to staff: Contact by letter, by telephone, by fax, by e-mail and via website
Hours: Mon to Fri, 0900 to 1700

VISITDENMARK

55 Sloane Street, London, SW1X 9SY

Fax: 020 7259 5955
E-mail: london@visitdenmark.com
Website: www.visitdenmark.com

Founded: 1948

Organisation type and purpose: National tourist board.

Subject coverage: Travel and tourism to and in Denmark.

Collection: Tourist information, brochures, images, posters

Trade and statistical information: Information for educational purposes is obtainable from the Press and Cultural Department of the Royal Danish Embassy

Publications: Printed

Access to staff: Contact by letter, by fax, by e-mail and via website

Links with: VisitDenmark; Islands Brygge 43–3, 2300 Copenhagen S, Denmark

VISITGUERNSEY

PO Box 23, St Peter Port, Guernsey, GY1 3AN, Channel Islands

Tel: 01481 725552
E-mail: enquiries@visitguernsey.com
Website: www.visitguernsey.com

Founded: 1946

Organisation type and purpose: Local government body.
Tourist office.

Subject coverage: All aspects of the tourism and conference business of the Bailiwick of Guernsey.

Trade and statistical information: Data on the number of visitors to the Island each year

Publications: Electronic and video

Access to staff: Contact by letter, by telephone, by e-mail and via website
Hours: Mon to Fri, 0900 to 1700

Access for disabled people: Ramped entry, toilet facilities

Parent body: States of Guernsey; Sir Charles Frossard House, La Charroterie, St Peter Port, GY1 1FH, Guernsey; tel: 01481 717000; website: www.gov.gg

VISITSCOTLAND

Fairways Business Park, Deer Park Avenue, Livingston, EH54 8AF

Tel: 01506 832213
Website: www.visitscotland.com

Enquiries to: Information Services Manager
Direct e-mail: tom.maxwell@visitscotland.com

History of institution: formerly called Scottish Tourist Board (STB)

Organisation type and purpose: National government body.

Subject coverage: Tourism: development, marketing, research, tourist information.

Publications: Printed

Access to staff: Contact by letter, by telephone, by fax, by e-mail and via website
Hours: Mon to Fri, 0900 to 1700

VISITSCOTLAND (HIGHLANDS)

Peffery House, Strathpeffer, Ross-shire, IV14 9HA

Tel: 01997 421160
Fax: 01997 421168
E-mail: info@visitscotland.com
Website: www.visithighlands.com

Enquiries to: Chief Executive
Direct e-mail: lorna.maclennan@visitscotland.com

Founded: 1996; created by the merger of Aviemore and Spey Tourist Board, Caithness Tourist Board, Fort William and Lochaber Tourist Board, Inverness, Loch Ness and Nairn Tourist Board, Isle of Skye Tourist Board, Ross and Cromarty Tourist Board, Sutherland Tourist Board (year of change 1996)

Organisation type and purpose: Statutory body.
Tourism marketing.

Subject coverage: Tourism in the Highlands of Scotland.

Trade and statistical information: Data on volume and value of tourism in the Highlands

Publications: Printed, and electronic and video

Access to staff: Contact by letter, by telephone, by fax and by e-mail
Hours: Mon to Fri, 0900 to 1700

Access for disabled people: Level entry, toilet facilities

VISITSCOTTISHBORDERS

VisitScotland, Ocean Point One, 94 Ocean Drive, Edinburgh, EH6 6JH

Tel: 01750 20555
Fax: 01750 21886
E-mail: sbtb@scot-borders.co.uk
Website: www.visitscottishborders.com
Website: www.scot-borders.co.uk

Enquiries to: Chief Executive
Direct tel: 01750 23800
Direct e-mail: rgraham@scot-borders.co.uk
Other contacts: Director of Customer Marketing; Director of Development

Founded: 1982; formed from Borders Regional Council (Tourism Division), Borders Tourist Association (year of change 1983); formerly called Scottish Borders Tourist Board (year of change 2006)

Organisation type and purpose: Statutory body, membership association (membership is by subscription), present number of members: 994.
Area Tourist Board.

Subject coverage: Tourism in the Scottish Borders, the attractions, activities, accommodation, business advice, marketing, statistics and research.

Collection: Collection includes 10,000 slide transparencies of the Scottish Borders

Trade and statistical information: Data on visitor statistics, market research, and tourism revenue, wide range of local statistical data on local and national tourism

Library catalogue: All or part available in-house

Publications: Printed

Publications list: Available online and in print

Access to staff: Contact by letter, by telephone, by fax, by e-mail, in person and via website. Appointment necessary.
Hours: Mon to Thu, 0900 to 1700; Fri, 0900 to 1630
Special comments: Tourist information centre opening times vary according to the time of the year.

Access to building: No prior appointment required

Access for disabled people: Parking provided, ramped entry, access to all public areas

Tourist Information Centres: Coldstream; Town Hall, 76 High Street, Coldstream, TD12 4DH; tel: 01890 882607; e-mail: coldstream@scot-borders.co.uk; Eyemouth; Auld Kirk, Market Square, Eyemouth, TD14 5HE; tel: 01890 750678; e-mail: eyemouth@scot-borders.co.uk; Hawick; Drumlanrig's Tower, Tower Knowe, Hawick, TD9 9EN; tel: 01450 327457; fax: 01450 373993; e-mail: hawick@scot-borders.co.uk; Jedburgh; Murrays Green, Jedburgh, TD8 6BE; tel: 01835 863688 or 863435; fax: 01835 864099; e-mail: info@scot-borders.co.uk; Kelso; Town House, The Square, Kelso, TD5 7HF; tel: 01573 223464; e-mail: kelso@scot-borders.co.uk; Melrose; Abbey House, Abbey Street, Melrose, Roxburghshire, TD6 LG; tel: 01896 822555; e-mail: melrose@scot-borders.co.uk; Peebles; High Street, Peebles, EH45 8AG; tel: 01721 720138; fax: 01721 724401; e-mail: peebles@scot-borders.co.uk; Selkirk; Halliwells House, Selkirk, TD7 4BL; tel: 01750 20054; e-mail: selkirk@scot-borders.co.uk

VITAL INFORMATION LIMITED

Stowe Castle Business Park, Buckingham, MK18 5AB

Tel: 01280 827078
Fax: 01280 827077
E-mail: maggie@vitalinformation.co.uk
Website: www.vitalinformation.co.uk

Enquiries to: Director

Founded: 1984

Organisation type and purpose: Information business.

Subject coverage: Life sciences; biology; medicine; veterinary medicine; agriculture; food science; environmental sciences; biotechnology; pharmaceuticals; toxicology; diagnostics; health care; general news services.

Information services: Literature searching, abstracting, indexing, desk research, thesaurus/taxonomy construction.

Access to staff: Contact by letter, by telephone, by fax, by e-mail and via website. Appointment necessary. All charged.
Hours: Mon to Fri, 0900 to 1730

VOCATIONAL AWARDS INTERNATIONAL LIMITED (VAI)

3rd Floor, Eastleigh House, Market Street, Eastleigh, Hampshire, SO50 9FD

Tel: 01243 842064
Fax: 01243 842489
E-mail: info@vtct.org.uk
Website: www.vtct.org.uk

Enquiries to: Information Officer
Other contacts: Head of Quality Assurance, telephone: 023 8068 4500 for training centres as opposed to individual enquiries.

Founded: 1986; formerly a division of International Health and Beauty Council (year of change 1986)

Organisation type and purpose: International organisation.
Promotes qualifications of Vocational Training Charitable Trust (VTCT) internationally.

Subject coverage: Availability of qualifications for beauty, hairdressing, health and fitness and complementary therapies. Also centres providing training.

Publications: Printed

Access to staff: Contact by letter
Hours: Mon to Fri, 0900 to 1700

Parent body: Vocational Training Charitable Trust; at the same address; tel: 023 8068 4500; fax: 023 8065 1493

VOICE OF THE LISTENER AND VIEWER (VLV)

PO Box 401, Gravesend, Kent, DA12 9FY

Tel: 01474 338711; 01474 338716
Fax: 01474 425440
E-mail: info@vlv.org.uk
Website: www.vlv.org.uk

Enquiries to: Chairman

Founded: 1983; incorporates the former Broadcasting Research Unit (Archive) (BRU) (year of change 1990); incorporates the former Voice of the Listener (VOL) (year of change 1991); incorporates the former British Action for Children's Television (Archive) (BACTV) (year of change 1995)

continued overleaf

Organisation type and purpose:
Membership association (membership is by subscription), present number of members: 2,000, voluntary organisation, registered charity (charity number 296207), research organisation, publishing house.
To support high quality, independence and diversity in broadcasting; to maintain the principle of public service in broadcasting; and to represent the interests of listeners and viewers, citizens and consumers in broadcasting.

Subject coverage: Radio and television, broadcasting policy, children's radio and television educational broadcasting, public service broadcasting in the UK, Europe and world-wide.

Collection: British Action for Children's Television (BACTV) Archive, 1988–1995
Broadcasting Research Unit (BRU) Archive, 1980–1991
Voice of the Listener and Viewer Archive, 1984–

Non-library collection catalogue: All or part available online and in print

Library catalogue: All or part available in-house

Publications: Printed, and electronic and video
Order printed publications from: Publications Secretary

Publications list: Available online and in print

Access to staff: Contact by letter, by telephone, by fax and by e-mail
Hours: Mon to Thu, 0900 to 1700

Access to building: Prior appointment required

VOICE: THE UNION FOR EDUCATION PROFESSIONALS

2 St James' Court, Friar Gate, Derby, DE1 1BT

Tel: 01332 372337
Fax: 01332 290310
E-mail: enquiries@voicetheunion.org.uk
Website: www.voicetheunion.org.uk

Enquiries to: General Secretary
Direct e-mail: pressoffice@voicetheunion.org.uk (for media)
Other contacts: Communications Officer (for media).

Founded: 1970; formerly called Professional Association of Teachers (PAT) (year of change 2008); incorporates the former Professional Association of Nursery Nurses (PANN) (year of change 2008)

Organisation type and purpose:
Professional body, trade union (membership is by subscription), present number of members: 38,000.
Teachers, lecturers, education support staff and childcarers.

Subject coverage: Matters of interest to the teaching and child care professions at all levels and in all sectors.

Publications: Printed
Order printed publications from: e-mail: publications@voicetheunion.org.uk

Publications list: Available online and in print

Access to staff: Contact by letter, by telephone, by fax, by e-mail and via website. Appointment necessary. Access for members only.
Hours: Mon to Fri, 0900 to 1700

Access to building: Prior appointment required
Hours: Mon to Fri, 0900 to 1700

Access for disabled people: Parking provided, level entry

Also at: Voice (Scotland); 4–6 Oak Lane, Edinburgh, EH12 6XH; tel: 0131 220 8241; fax: 0131 220 8350; e-mail: scotland@voicetheunion.org.uk

VOLKSWAGEN TYPE 2 OWNERS' CLUB (VWT20C)

57 Humphrey Avenue, Charford, Bromsgrove, Worcestershire, B60 3JD

Tel: 01527 872194
Fax: 01527 872194
E-mail: philshawvw@cs.com
Website: www.vwt2oc.org.uk
Website: www.vanfest.org

Enquiries to: Honorary Club Secretary

Founded: 1991

Organisation type and purpose:
International organisation, advisory body, membership association (membership is by subscription), present number of members: 2500, voluntary organisation.

Subject coverage: Volkswagen Type 2 vehicles, advice and help given to members with any related problem.

Collection: Wide range of printed information concerning Volkswagen Type 2 vehicles

Library catalogue: All or part available in-house

Publications: Printed

Access to staff: Contact by letter, by telephone, by fax, by e-mail, in person and via website. Appointment necessary.
Hours: 7 days, 1000 to 2200

VOLUNTARY SERVICE OVERSEAS (VSO)

317 Putney Bridge Road, London, SW15 2PN

Tel: 020 8780 7200\ Minicom no. 020 8780 7440
Fax: 020 8780 7300
E-mail: enquiry@vso.org.uk
Website: www.vso.org.uk

Enquiries to: Enquiries Unit
Direct tel: 020 8780 7500
Direct fax: 020 8780 7207
Direct e-mail: press@vso.org.uk

Founded: 1958

Organisation type and purpose:
International organisation, present number of members: 1939, voluntary organisation, registered charity (charity number 313757).
Development agency that works through volunteers to tackle disadvantage in developing communities worldwide.

Subject coverage: Advice on volunteering opportunities with VSO.

Publications list: Available online and in print

Access to staff: Contact by letter, by telephone, by fax, by e-mail and via website
Hours: Enquiries unit: Mon to Fri, 0900 to 1700

Access to building: No prior appointment required
Hours: Library: Mon to Fri, 0900 to 1700; Sat, 1000 to 1630

Access for disabled people: Ramped entry, toilet facilities

VOLUNTEER CENTRE (VC)

Formal name: Centre for Community Action, Volunteering & Employment Initiatives

4th Floor, 84 Miller Street, Glasgow, G1 1DT

Tel: 0141 226 3431
Fax: 0141 221 0716
E-mail: info@volunteerglasgow.org
Website: www.volunteerglasgow.org

Enquiries to: Information Officer

Founded: 1970

Organisation type and purpose:
Membership association (membership is by election or invitation), present number of members: 99, registered charity (charity number SCO 05462).
A catalogue of volunteering opportunities available in Glasgow. A resource library of publications relating to volunteering and issues affecting the voluntary sector.
The Centre aims to improve the quality of life for the people of Glasgow by offering opportunities to use and develop their skills in volunteering, training and personal development. In addition, the Centre works in neighbourhoods to develop informal care and support services with vulnerable families and individuals; and in partnership with charitable trusts, local authorities and other organisations to deliver community care services.

Subject coverage: Volunteering, good practice in working with volunteers, befriending, carers, employment issues for voluntary and community organisations, community care, employment training for physically disabled people, health and wellbeing.

Collection: Resource library of books and documents relating to volunteering, the voluntary sector, health and social care, community care, disability, health and safety, employment, education etc
Catalogue of voluntary opportunities for potential volunteers

Non-library collection catalogue: All or part available online

Publications: Printed

Access to staff: Contact by letter, by telephone, by fax, by e-mail, in person and via website
Hours: Mon to Thu, 0900 to 1700; Fri, 0900 to 1600

Access to building: No access other than to staff

VOLUNTEER NOW

34 Shaftesbury Square, Belfast, BT2 7DB

Tel: 028 9020 0850
Fax: 028 9020 0860
E-mail: reception@volunteernow.co.uk
Website: www.volunteernow.co.uk

Enquiries to: Co-ordinator

Founded: 2010; formerly called VSB (year of change 2010)

Organisation type and purpose: Volunteer Now is a regional to local organisation that works to promote, develop and support volunteering across Northern Ireland. The organisation enhances recognition for the contribution volunteers make, provides access to opportunities and encourages people to volunteer. Volunteer Now also provides training, information, guidance and support to volunteer-involving organisations on issues of good practice and policy regarding volunteering, volunteer management, child protection and governance.

Subject coverage: Information on volunteer opportunities throughout Northern Ireland.

Publications list: Available online

Access to staff: Contact by letter, by telephone, by fax, by e-mail, in person and via website. All charged.
Hours: Mon to Fri, 0900 to 1700

Branches: Antrim, Armagh, Bangor, Downpatrick, Dungannon, Enniskillen, Larne, Lisburn, Newry

VOLUNTEERING ENGLAND (VE)

Regents Wharf, 8 All Saints Street, London, N1 9RL

Tel: 0845 305 6979
Fax: 020 7520 8910
E-mail: volunteering@volunteeringengland.org
Website: www.volunteering.org.uk/

Enquiries to: Head of Information

Founded: 2004; created by the merger of the Consortium on Opportunities for Volunteering, the National Centre for Volunteering and Volunteer Development England. Subsequently merged with Student Volunteering England (in 2007).

Organisation type and purpose: Voluntary organisation, registered charity (charity number 1102770).
National development agency for volunteering.

Subject coverage: Information, training and support to organisations who work with volunteers, campaign on public policy.

Collection: Largest library on volunteering in the UK

Library catalogue: All or part available in-house

Publications: Printed
Order printed publications from: MJF Data Management, River House, Riverside Way, Uxbridge, UB8 2YF, tel: 01895 909050, fax: 01895 909060

Publications list: Available in print

Access to staff: Contact by letter, by telephone, by fax and by e-mail. Appointment necessary.
Hours: Mon to Fri, 1000 to 1700

Access to building: Prior appointment required

Access for disabled people: Access to all public areas, toilet facilities

VOLVO ENTHUSIASTS CLUB (VEC)

127 Kidderminster Road, Wribbenhall, Bewdley, Worcestershire, DY12 1JE

Tel: 01872 553740 or 01425 476425
Fax: 01872 553740 (phone first)
Website: www.volvo1800.co.uk
Website: www.volvoenthusiastsclub.co.uk

Enquiries to: Chairman/Founder

Founded: 1989

Organisation type and purpose: International organisation, membership association (membership is by subscription), present number of members: 1500, voluntary organisation.
To encourage ownership, interest, preservation and correct maintenance of all Volvos over 15 years old or out of production, and to serve as a source of technical information and parts through a friendly family-style club.

Subject coverage: Historic and technical information on all Volvo cars, buses and trucks over 15 years old, spares location and availability, restoration advice, guide to purchase, classic Volvo historical data P1800 (Saint Volvo), 120 (Amazon) etc, international register, historic rally-race preparation-information and data-race/rally register.

Collection: Complete Volvo production data for P1800 1961–63 – first 6000 vehicles built by Jensen
Sales brochures – P1800, 120 etc
Technical library – Volvo workshop manuals, parts lists etc
Homologation papers 120, 1800-PV-140 etc
Volvo special tuning data B18/B20 engines and vehicles fitted with these units
Volvo special tools

Trade and statistical information: Production data pre 1990 – rolling over 15 years, all models.
Production data from original records of P1800 1961–1963.
Current vehicle values and trends

Publications: Printed

Access to staff: Contact by letter and by telephone. Non-members charged.
Hours: Mon to Fri, 0900 to 1700

VOLVO OWNERS CLUB

18 Macaulay Avenue, Portsmouth, Hampshire, PO6 4NY

Tel: 023 9238 1494
Fax: 023 9238 1494
E-mail: membership@volvoclub.org.uk
Website: www.Volvoclub.org.uk

Enquiries to: Membership Secretary

Organisation type and purpose: Membership association (membership is by subscription), present number of members: 5000.
Club for owners and enthusiasts of Volvo cars.

Subject coverage: All aspects of the ownership and maintenance of Volvo cars.

Access to staff: Contact by letter, by telephone, by fax, by e-mail and via website
Hours: Mon to Sun

VTCT

Third Floor, Eastleigh House, Market Street, Eastleigh, Hampshire, SO50 9FD

Tel: 023 8068 4500
Fax: 023 8065 1493
E-mail: info@vtct.org.uk
Website: www.vtct.org.uk

Enquiries to: Customer Service Department
Direct e-mail: customerservice@vtct.org.uk
Other contacts: Head of Quality Assurance for potential training centres.

Founded: 1986; formed from International Health and Beauty Council (IHBC) (year of change 1986)

Organisation type and purpose: International organisation, registered charity (charity number 295192). Awarding body (service sector). National and international qualifications in hairdressing, beauty, fitness, sport, holistic and complementary therapies. Supportive qualifications in business organisation, customer service and keyskills.

Subject coverage: Availability of National and Scottish vocational qualifications (NVQs and S/NVQs) and international qualifications in beauty, hairdressing, holistic and complementary, fitness and sports therapies. Courses are provided across the British Isles, primarily in Colleges of Further Education.

Access to staff: Contact by letter, by telephone and by e-mail
Hours: Mon to Fri, 0900 to 1700
Special comments: No visitors in person.

VW OWNERS' CLUB GB (VWOC (GB))

PO Box 7, Burntwood, Walsall, West Midlands, WS7 2SB

E-mail: info@vwocgb.com
Website: www.vwocgb.com

Founded: 1953

Organisation type and purpose: Membership association (membership is by subscription), present number of members: 1,000, voluntary organisation.
To provide a focal group for all enthusiasts of Volkswagen Group vehicles both old and modern. Also, to obtain from associated trades any financial benefits possible for members.

Subject coverage: VW cars including all Volkswagen Group Companies.

Publications: Printed

Access to staff: Contact by letter, by e-mail and via website
Hours: Mon to Fri, 0900 to 1700

WADE SPRING LIMITED

Highfield Street, Long Eaton, Nottingham, NG10 4GY

Tel: 0115 946 3000
Fax: 0115 946 1361
E-mail: sales@wade-spring.co.uk
Website: www.wade-spring.co.uk

Enquiries to: Technical Director

Founded: 1926; incorporates the former Elson & Robbins Limited

Organisation type and purpose: Manufacturing industry.

Subject coverage: Spring cases and assemblies for upholstery and bedding trades.

Access to staff: Contact by letter, by telephone, by fax and by e-mail
Hours: Mon to Fri, 0900 to 1700

WADHAM COLLEGE

The Library, Oxford, OX1 3PN

Tel: 01865 277914
E-mail: library@wadh.ox.ac.uk
Website: www.wadham.ox.ac.uk

Enquiries to: Librarian

Founded: 1610

Organisation type and purpose: University department or institute.
College library.

Subject coverage: General undergraduate material; Spanish (16th and 17th centuries); Persian.

Collection: 16th-century theology (2,000 vols)
16th- and 17th-century Spanish books (1,000 vols)
Persian and Arabic manuscripts (800 items)
Persian lithographs (200 items)
Printed books in Persian, Arabic and European languages on Persian classical literature and history, up to the end of the Constitutional Persian Revolution in 1911

Non-library collection catalogue: All or part available online and in-house

Library catalogue: All or part available online and in-house

Access to staff: Contact by letter, by telephone and by e-mail. Appointment necessary.
Hours: Mon to Fri, 0900 to 1700

Parent body: University of Oxford

WAKEFIELD COLLEGE

Margaret Street, Wakefield, West Yorkshire, WF1 2DH

Tel: 01924 789789\ Minicom no. 01924 789270
Fax: 01924 789340
E-mail: staffmember@wakcoll.ac.uk
Website: www.wakcoll.ac.uk

Enquiries to: Marketing Manager
Direct tel: 01924 789162
Direct fax: 01924 789362

History of institution: formerly called Wakefield District College

Organisation type and purpose: Suitable for ages: 16+.
Further Education College.

Subject coverage: GCSEs, 'A' levels, GNVQs, HNDs, HNCs, NVQs, computer studies, languages, health, child and social care, hospitality, leisure and tourism, business and secretarial, building, technology, CAD/CAM, art, drama, media, graphics, adult education, engineering, hair and beauty, sport studies, public services, horticulture.

Publications: Printed, and electronic and video

Publications list: Available in print

Access to staff: Contact by letter
Hours: Mon to Fri, 0900 to 1700

Access to building: No prior appointment required
Special comments: Report to main reception.

Access for disabled people: Parking provided, ramped entry, access to all public areas, toilet facilities

Connections with: Learndirect Learning Centre; tel: 01924 789333; e-mail: c .furbisher@wakcoll.ac.uk

Other Campuses: Hemsworth SkillsBank; Bank Street, Hemsworth, West Yorkshire, WF9 4JX; tel: 01924 789789 Minicom: 01977 619784; fax: 01977 619480; Thornes Park Campus; Thornes Park, Horbury Road, Wakefield, West Yorkshire, WF2 8QZ; tel: 01924 789789 Minicom: 01924 789800; fax: 01924 789821; Whitwood Campus; Four Lane Ends, Castleford, West Yorkshire, WF10 5NF; tel: 01924 789789 Minicom: 01924 789431; fax: 01924 789478

WAKEFIELD HISTORICAL SOCIETY

18 St Johns Square, Wakefield, West Yorks, WF1 2RA

E-mail: pamjudkins@btinternet.com
Website: www.wakefieldhistoricalsoc.org .uk

Enquiries to: President

Founded: 1924

Organisation type and purpose: Historical Society.
To bring together those with an interest in local or national history.

Access to staff: Contact by letter, by e-mail and via website

WAKEFIELD LIBRARIES AND INFORMATION SERVICE

Library Headquarters, Balne Lane, Wakefield, West Yorkshire, WF2 0DQ

Tel: 01924 302210; typetalk no. 01924 302210
Fax: 01924 302245
E-mail: lib.admin@wakefield.gov.uk
Website: www.wakefield.gov.uk/libraries

Enquiries to: Libraries & Information Services Manager

Founded: 1974

Organisation type and purpose: Local government body, public library.

Subject coverage: General, local and family history.

Collection: British Official Publications, 1974 onwards, all parliamentary and selected non-parliamentary
British Standards
Cryer Collection
J S Fletcher Collection
George Gissing Collection
Henry Moore Collection
Local and Family History (District and Yorkshire) Collection
School Library Service including:
books, posters, audio cassettes, videos
Yorkshire Libraries & Information collections:
Music and drama services (single copies and sets of plays and music)
Provincial Fiction Reserve (N-S section)

Non-library collection catalogue: All or part available in-house

Library catalogue: All or part available in-house

Access to staff: Contact by letter, by telephone, by fax, by e-mail and via website
Hours: Mon to Fri, 0900 to 1700

Access for disabled people: Parking provided, level entry, toilet facilities

Administers: Yorkshire Libraries & Information (YLI); tel: 01924 302214; fax: 01924 302245; e-mail: kholliday@wakefield .gov.uk

WALES COUNCIL FOR VOLUNTARY ACTION (WCVA)

Cyngor Gweithredu Gwirfoddol Cymru, Baltic House, Mount Stuart Square, Cardiff, CF10 5FH

Tel: 0800 2888 329; minicom no. 0808 1 804080
Fax: 029 2043 1701
E-mail: help@wcva.org.uk
Website: www.wcva.org.uk

Enquiries to: WCVA Helpdesk

Founded: 1934

Organisation type and purpose: Trade union (membership is by subscription), present number of members: 3,000 approx, service industry, voluntary organisation, registered charity (charity number 218093).
Promotes and supports voluntary action and community development in Wales.

Subject coverage: Information relating to the voluntary sector in Wales; legal matters, funding advice, Europe and European funding, training, community care, contracting, volunteering matters, community development, voluntary sector liaison with the National Assembly for Wales.

Collection: Comprehensive collection of material relating to the voluntary sector, with particular emphasis on Wales

Trade and statistical information: Database of voluntary organisations in Wales

Library catalogue: All or part available in-house

Publications: Printed, and electronic and video
Order printed publications from: WCVA

Publications, WCVA, at the same address; tel: 029 2043 1723; fax: 029 2043 1701; e-mail: publications@wcva.org.uk

Publications list: Available in print

Access to staff: Contact by letter, by telephone, by fax, by e-mail and via website. Appointment necessary. Non-members charged.
Hours: Mon to Fri, 0900 to 1700

Access for disabled people: Parking provided, ramped entry, access to all public areas, toilet facilities

Also at: WCVA – Mid Wales; Unit 2, Science Park, Cefn Llan, Aberystwyth, Ceredigion, SY23 3AH; tel: 0800 2888 329; e-mail: help@wcva.org.uk; WCVA – North Wales Office; Morfa Hall, Bath Street, Rhyl, Denbighshire, LL18 3EB; tel: 0800 2888 329; e-mail: help@wcva.org.uk

WALES TOURIST BOARD (WTB)

Brunel House, 2 Fitzalan Road, Cardiff, CF24 0UY

Tel: 029 2049 9909
Fax: 029 2048 5031
Website: www.visitwales.com

Enquiries to: Information Development Officer
Direct tel: 029 2047 5277
Direct e-mail: kathryn.newton@wales.gsi.gov.uk

Organisation type and purpose: National government body.
Statutory body.

Subject coverage: Development, marketing and advisory functions relating to tourism in Wales, events, attractions, activities, holidays and accommodation.

Trade and statistical information: Data on the number of overseas visitors, domestic visitors, visitors to attractions in Wales

Publications: Printed, and electronic and video

Publications list: Available in print

Access to staff: Contact by letter, by telephone, by fax and by e-mail
Hours: Mon to Fri, 0900 to 1700

Associated with: British Tourist Authority

WALLCOVERINGS SECTOR COUNCIL (WSC)

British Coatings Federation, The Stables, Thorncroft Manor, Leatherhead, Surrey, KT22 8JB

Tel: 01372 700848
Fax: 01372 700851
E-mail: alison.brown@bcf.co.uk

Enquiries to: Administrator

Founded: 2005; created by the merger of Wallcovering Manufacturers' Association of Great Britain Limited (f. 1970) and British Coatings Federation (year of change 2005)

Organisation type and purpose: Trade association, membership association (membership is by subscription, election or invitation), present number of members: 15.

Subject coverage: Wallcovering manufacture, product standards, pattern book names.

Trade and statistical information: Statistics (very selective distribution)

Access to staff: Contact by letter, by fax and by e-mail
Hours: Mon to Fri, 0900 to 1700

WALLPAPER HISTORY SOCIETY (WHS)

c/o Victoria and Albert Museum, South Kensington, London, SW7 2RL

Tel: 020 7942 2560

Enquiries to: Secretary
Direct tel: 020 8977 4978

Founded: 1986

Organisation type and purpose: Research organisation.

Subject coverage: History of wallpaper, bibliography, specialist conservation sources, manufacturers specialising in the production of reproduction historic papers, details of museums and archives holding wallpapers.

Collection: Please note that the Society itself holds no collections, though it has members and contacts in institutions which do have collections of wallpaper

Publications: Printed

Access to staff: Contact by letter and by telephone
Hours: Mon to Fri, 0900 to 1700

WALMSLEY SOCIETY

April Cottage, 1 Brand Road, Hampden Park, Eastbourne, East Sussex, BN2 9PX

Tel: 01323 506447
Website: www.walmsleysoc.org

Enquiries to: Honorary Secretary
Other contacts: Membership Secretary (for membership enquiries only)

Founded: 1985

Organisation type and purpose: International organisation (membership is by subscription). Literary society. To promote and encourage an appreciation of the literary and artistic heritage left by Leo and J Ulric Walmsley.

Subject coverage: Appreciation of the work of Leo Walmsley (author) and the work of James Ulric Walmsley (artist).

Collection: Various items and information applicable to the aims of the society

Publications: Printed, and electronic and video
Order printed publications from: via website

Publications list: Available online and in print

Access to staff: Contact by letter, by telephone and via website
Hours: Anytime within reason

Also at: Membership Secretary (letter only); 21 The Crescent, Hipperholme, Halifax, Yorkshire, HX3 8NQ

Member organisation of: The Alliance of Literary Societies

WALSALL HOSPITAL NHS TRUST

Manor Hospital Postgraduate Medical Centre, Medical Library, Moat Road, Walsall, West Midlands, WS2 9PS

Tel: 01922 721172

Enquiries to: Librarian

WALSALL LOCAL HISTORY CENTRE

Essex Street, Walsall, West Midlands, WS2 7AS

Tel: 01922 721305
Fax: 01922 634954
E-mail: localhistorycentre@walsall.gov.uk
Website: www.walsall.gov.uk/localhistorycentre

Enquiries to: Archivist/Local Studies Officer

Founded: 1986; formerly called Walsall Archives Service

Organisation type and purpose: Local government body, public library.
Record office, archive and local studies library.

Subject coverage: All aspects of the history of Walsall Metropolitan Borough and its constituent towns: Aldridge, Bloxwich, Brownhills, Darlaston, Willenhall and Walsall. Photographic, map, oral history, ephemera, newspapers, printed materials, archives and family history.

Non-library collection catalogue: All or part available online and in-house

Library catalogue: All or part available online and in-house

Publications: Printed

Publications list: Available online and in print

Access to staff: Contact by letter, by telephone, by fax, by e-mail, in person and via website
Hours: Mon and Fri, closed; Tue and Thu, 0930 to 1730; Wed, 0930 to 1900; Sat, 0930 to 1300

Access for disabled people: Ramped entry, access to all public areas, toilet facilities

WALTHAM FOREST ARCHIVES AND LOCAL STUDIES LIBRARY

Waltham Forest Archives and Local Studies Library, Vestry House Museum, Vestry Road, Walthamstow, London, E17 9NH

Tel: 020 8496 4381
E-mail: vhm.enquiries@walthamforest.gov.uk
Website: www.walthamforest.gov.uk/index/leisure/museums-galleries/archives-local-studies.htm

Enquiries to: Archivist
Other contacts: Local Studies Librarian

Founded: Late 1970s

Organisation type and purpose: Local government body, public library.

Subject coverage: History and development of the area covered by the London Borough of Waltham Forest (comprising the former boroughs of Chingford, Leyton and Walthamstow).

continued overleaf

Collection: Records of Waltham Forest Deanery (including parish records)

Non-library collection catalogue: All or part available in-house

Library catalogue: All or part available in-house

Publications: Printed
Order printed publications from: Linda Weston at Vestry House Museum, Vestry Road, Walthamstow, London, E17 9NH; tel: 020 8496 4391

Publications list: Available in print

Access to staff: Contact by letter, by telephone, by e-mail and in person. Appointment necessary.
Hours: By prior appointment; Thu, Fri and Sat, 1000 to 1300 and 1400 to 1700

Access for disabled people: Stairs to Searchroom (located in a listed building), but appointments can take place in an accessible ground floor room by prior arrangement.

WALTHAM FOREST COLLEGE

Library, Forest Road, Walthamstow, London, E17 4JB

Tel: 020 8501 8501
Fax: 020 8501 8302
E-mail: 2learn@waltham.ac.uk
Website: www.waltham.ac.uk

Enquiries to: Learning Resources Manager
Direct tel: 020 8501 8026
Direct e-mail: pauline.nash@waltham.ac.uk

Founded: 1938

Organisation type and purpose: College of higher education.

Subject coverage: Business studies, management, office technology, computing, electrical and electronic engineering, manufacturing, automobile engineering, art and design, fashion technology, caring, health studies, counselling, ESOL, EFL, catering, meat technology, travel and tourism, hotel management, performing arts, media studies, general education, science, beauty therapy, hairdressing, built environment.

Library catalogue: All or part available in-house

Access to staff: Contact by letter, by telephone, by fax and by e-mail. Appointment necessary.
Hours: Mon to Thu, 0845 to 1900; Fri, 0845 to 1600

WALTHAM FOREST HEALTHCARE LIBRARY (WXUHT)

Whipps Cross Hospital, Leytonstone, London, E11 1NR

Tel: 020 8535 6860
Fax: 020 8535 6973
E-mail: library@whippsx.nhs.uk
Website: www.libnel.nhs.uk

Enquiries to: Librarian
Direct e-mail: angela.head@whippsx.nhs.uk

Organisation type and purpose: NHS Trust Library supporting library and information needs of health and social care staff based in the local health economy.

Subject coverage: Clinical medicine and health and social care.

Library catalogue: All or part available online and in-house

Access to staff: Contact by letter, by telephone, by fax, by e-mail, in person and via website. Non-members charged.
Hours: Mon, Tue, Wed, Fri, 0830 to 1700; Thu, 0830 to 1900

Access for disabled people: Lift access, toilet facilities

WALTHAM FOREST LIBRARIES, MUSEUM & GALLERY SERVICES

Silver Birch House, Uplands Business Park, Black Horse Lane, Walthamstow, London E17 5SD

Tel: 020 8496 3652
E-mail: wf.libs@walthamforest.gov.uk
Website: www.walthamforest.gov.uk/libraries

Enquiries to: Head of Libraries, Museum & Gallery Services
Direct tel: 020 8496 3203; 020 8496 3643 (Libraries Development Manager)
Direct e-mail: lorna.lee@walthamforest.gov.uk
Other contacts: Libraries Development Manager

History of institution: formerly called Waltham Forest Libraries & Cultural Services

Organisation type and purpose: Local government body, public library.

Subject coverage: General; domestic arts and sciences.

Collection: Laser subject specialisation, Dewey 640–649, 663–664, 338.47663–338.47664
William Morris Collection

Access to staff: Contact by letter, by telephone, by e-mail, in person and via website
Hours: Mon to Fri, 0900 to 1700

WALTHAMSTOW HISTORICAL SOCIETY

Vestry House Museum, Vestry Road, London, E17 9NH

Tel: 020 8509 1917
E-mail: ellingham@clara.co.uk
Website: www.walthamstowhistoricalsociety.org

Enquiries to: Publications Secretary

Founded: 1914; formerly called Walthamstow Antiquarian Society (year of change 1986)

Organisation type and purpose: Membership association, registered charity (charity number 277823).
Local history society.

Subject coverage: Local history of Walthamstow and Waltham Forest.

Publications list: Available in print

WANDSWORTH HERITAGE SERVICE

Battersea Library, 265 Lavender Hill, London, SW11 1JB

Tel: 020 8871 7753
Fax: 020 7978 4376
E-mail: heritage@wandsworth.gov.uk
Website: www.wandsworth.gov.uk

Enquiries to: Heritage Officer
Other contacts: Assistant Heritage Officer

Organisation type and purpose: Public library

Subject coverage: Local history library for Wandsworth area

Collection: Photograph collection
Archives of London Borough of Wandsworth and predecessor authorities, local institutions and societies including WWII records, electoral registers
Microfilm resources: Census returns 1841 to 1901 (local area); IGI (1992 edition) for England; local newspapers c.1853 to 1990s (some gaps); maps of local area mid-17th century to present day
Cuttings collections of Mayors of Wandsworth circa 1950s to 1960s
Cuttings collections of Alfred Hurley, proprietor of Tooting and Balham Gazette 1900 to 1947
Wandsworth Scrapbooks circa 1880 to 1939
Battersea Scrapbooks 1901–1939

Non-library collection catalogue: All or part available online and in-house

Library catalogue: All or part available online

Publications: Printed

Access to staff: Contact by letter, by telephone, by fax, by e-mail, in person and via website
Hours: Mon, Wed, Sat: 9am-5pm. Tue, Wed: 9am-8pm. Thu, Sun: Closed.
Special comments: Qualified staff only available Tuesday, Friday and Saturday until 2pm.

Access for disabled people: Located on the first floor, please call and arrangements will be made to bring material downstairs

WANDSWORTH LIBRARIES

Formal name: Wandsworth Library and Heritage Service

Department of Leisure & Amenity Services, Wandsworth Town Hall, Wandsworth High Street, London, SW18 2PU

Tel: 020 8871 6369
Fax: 020 8871 7630
E-mail: libraries@wandsworth.gov.uk
Website: www.wandsworth.gov.uk/libraries

Enquiries to: Librarian

Organisation type and purpose: Local government body, public library.
11 libraries, reference and local archives service.

Collection: Early children's books (tel: 020 8871 7090)
Edward Thomas Collection
G A Henty Collection
William Blake Collection
World War One and Two

Library catalogue: All or part available online

Access to staff: Contact by letter, by telephone, by fax, by e-mail and in person
Hours: Mon to Fri, 0900 to 1700

WAR WIDOWS' ASSOCIATION OF GREAT BRITAIN

c/o 199 Borough High Street, London, SE1 1AA

Tel: 0845 241 2189
E-mail: info@warwidowsassociation.org.uk
Website: www.warwidowsassociation.org.uk

Enquiries to: Secretary

Founded: 1971

Organisation type and purpose: Membership association (membership is by subscription), present number of members: 4,000. Voluntary organisation, registered charity (charity number 1002656).
The improvement of War Widows' Pensions and the regulations pertaining to them; support for War Widows; not grant-making.

Subject coverage: War Widows' pensions; associated DSS benefits.

Publications: Printed

Publications list: Available in print

Access to staff: Contact by letter, by telephone, by e-mail and via website
Hours: Mon to Fri, 0900 to 1700

WARBURG INSTITUTE

Woburn Square, London, WC1H 0AB

Tel: 020 7862 8949
Fax: 020 7862 8955
E-mail: warburg@sas.ac.uk
Website: www.warburg.sas.ac.uk

Enquiries to: Secretary

Founded: 1921

Organisation type and purpose: University department or institute.
Postgraduate research institute.

Subject coverage: History of the classical tradition: those elements of European thought, literature, art and institutions that derive from the ancient world.

Education services: Postgraduate degrees.

Collection: Library (305,000 vols) on the classical tradition
Collection of photographs, primarily designed for the study of iconography
Archive

Non-library collection catalogue: All or part available online and in-house

Library catalogue: All or part available online

Publications: Printed
Order printed publications from: e-mail: warburg.books@sas.ac.uk

Publications list: Available online and in print

Access to staff: Contact by letter, by telephone, by fax, by e-mail, in person and via website. Letter of introduction required.
Hours: Mon to Fri, 1000 to 1800

Access to building: Access to library by library ticket
Hours: Mon to Fri, 1000 to 1800; Sat opening varies

Access for disabled people: Ramped entry front and rear, access to all public areas, toilet facilities
Special comments: Lift access to floors other than ground floor and basement.

Houses the library of: British Numismatic Society; tel: 020 7862 8951 (part time); Folklore Society; tel: 020 7862 8564 (part time); Royal Numismatic Society

Parent body: University of London, School of Advanced Study; tel: 020 7862 8659; fax: 020 7862 8657

WARRINGTON BOROUGH COUNCIL

Town Hall, Warrington, Cheshire, WA1 1UH

Tel: 01925 444400
Fax: 01925 442138
Website: www.warrington.gov.uk

Enquiries to: Head of Communications
Direct tel: 01925 442042
Direct fax: 01925 442024
Direct e-mail: bwilliams@warrington.gov.uk

Organisation type and purpose: Local government body.

Subject coverage: Council services and amenities; corporate services, education, environmental services, finance, housing, legal services, personnel services, planning development and tourism, property and technical services, roads and transportation, social work, council tax and other payments.

Publications: Printed

Access to staff: Contact by letter, by telephone and by fax. Appointment necessary.
Hours: Mon to Fri, 0900 to 1700

WARRINGTON CHAMBER OF COMMERCE AND INDUSTRY

International Business Centre, Delta Crescent, Westbrook, Warrington, Cheshire, WA5 7WQ

Tel: 01925 715150
Fax: 01925 715159
E-mail: info@warrington-chamber.co.uk
Website: www.warrington-chamber.co.uk

Enquiries to: Chief Executive

Founded: 1876

Organisation type and purpose: Trade association. Provides advice and guidance on matters of commercial and industrial concern.

Subject coverage: Export documentation and advice; seminars and training; language provision; general information in fields of industrial and commercial interest.

Publications: Printed

Access to staff: Contact by letter, by telephone, by fax, by e-mail and via website. Appointment necessary.
Hours: Mon to Thu, 0900 to 1700; Fri, 0900 to 1630

Member organisation of: Chambers of Commerce North West; North Cheshire & Wirral Consortium of Chambers of Commerce

WARRINGTON COLLEGIATE

Winwick Road Campus, Winwick Road, Warrington, Cheshire, WA2 8QA

Tel: 01925 494422
Fax: 01925 494422
E-mail: swatkiss@warrington.ac.uk
Website: www.warrington.ac.uk

Founded: 1979; formerly called North Cheshire College

Organisation type and purpose: Further and higher education.

Subject coverage: Construction, engineering, business studies, leisure, media, performing arts and sports studies, travel and tourism, creative arts, health and social care, hairdressing, beauty therapy, holistics.

Collection: Lewis Carroll

Library catalogue: All or part available online and in-house

Access to staff: Contact by letter and by telephone
Hours: Mon to Thu, 0845 to 2000; Fri, 0845 to 1630
Winwick Campus: Sat, 0900 to 1300

Access for disabled people: Parking provided, ramped entry, access to all public areas, toilet facilities

WARRINGTON LIBRARY

Museum Street, Warrington, Cheshire, WA1 1JB

Tel: 01925 442889
Fax: 01925 443257
E-mail: library@warrington.gov.uk
Website: www.warrington.gov.uk/libraries

Enquiries to: Information Services Manager

Founded: 1848

Organisation type and purpose: Local government body, public library.

Subject coverage: Soap industry and manufacture, wire manufacture, welding, general.

Collection: Substantial body of material held on local area in terms of local and family history including: a large collection of manuscripts and archives; local studies books and pamphlets; photographs and other images; voters' lists; maps; ephemera; microform copies of censuses, newspapers, and parish and other church records

Library catalogue: All or part available online

Access to staff: Contact by letter, by telephone, by fax, by e-mail, in person and via website
Hours: Mon to Wed, 0900 to 1800; Thu, 0900 to 1900, Fri, 0900 to 1700; Sat, 0900 to 1600

Access to building: No prior appointment required

Access for disabled people: Disabled access to main entrance, access to all public areas

continued overleaf

Parent body: Warrington Borough Council Culture, Libraries and Heritage Service; website: http://www.warrington.gov.uk

WARWICKSHIRE COLLEGE

Warwick New Road, Leamington Spa, Warwickshire, CV35 5JE

Tel: 01926 318000
Fax: 01926 318111
E-mail: info@warkscol.ac.uk
Website: www.warkscol.ac.uk

Enquiries to: Admission
Direct tel: 0800 783 6767
Other contacts: The Principal

Founded: 1949

Organisation type and purpose: Training and education. Further and higher education.

Subject coverage: Art and design, building and construction, business, accounting and management studies, caring, nursing and social welfare, computing and administration, engineering technology, agriculture, horticulture, machinery, equine studies, animal care, business studies, education, training, media, music, performing arts, veterinary nursing, arboriculture, spa management, English as a foreign language, English as a second language, GCE A levels, GCSEs, hairdressing and beauty therapy, hospitality and catering, languages, motor vehicle technology, sports studies, leisure and tourism, return to learn courses, adult basic education and programmes for students with learning difficulties and disabilities.

Publications: Printed

Publications list: Available online and in print

Access to staff: Contact by letter, by telephone, by fax, by e-mail, in person and via website
Hours: Mon to Fri, 0900 to 1700

WARWICKSHIRE COLLEGE – MORETON MORRELL CENTRE

Formal name: Warwickshire College Royal Leamington Spa and Moreton Morrell

Moreton Morrell, Warwick, CV35 9BL

Tel: 01926 318278
Fax: 01926 318300
E-mail: librarymm@warkscol.ac.uk
Website: www.warkscol.ac.uk

Enquiries to: Librarian

Founded: 1949; formerly called Warwickshire College of Agriculture (year of change 1996)

Organisation type and purpose: Suitable for ages: Further and Higher Education. College for land-based industries.

Subject coverage: Agriculture; agricultural engineering; amenity and commercial horticulture; business studies; equine studies; horse management and horse business management; small animal care; green-keeping; landscaping; woodland and estate maintenance; animal care; pre-veterinary nursing; arboriculture; countryside and rural affairs; human sports science.

Collection: LOOI Horticultural Library
British Horse Society Library

Non-library collection catalogue: All or part available in-house

Library catalogue: All or part available in-house

Publications: Printed, and electronic and video
Order printed publications from: Equi Study at the same address, tel: 01926 318340

Access to staff: Contact by letter, by telephone, by fax, by e-mail and via website. Appointment necessary. Non-members charged.
Hours: Term time: Mon to Thu, 0830 to 2200; Fri, 0830 to 1700; Sat, 1000 to 1600
Vacations: Mon to Fri, 0915 to 1645
Special comments: One free visit, then have to become members; charges to non-members.

Access for disabled people: Level entry, access to all public areas, toilet facilities

Other site at: Warwickshire College; Leamington Centre, Warwick New Road, Leamington Spa, Warwickshire, CV32 5JE; tel: 01926 318000; fax: 01926 318111

WARWICKSHIRE COUNTY RECORD OFFICE

Priory Park, Cape Road, Warwick, CV34 4JS

Tel: 01926 738959
Fax: 01926 738969
E-mail: recordoffice@warwickshire.gov.uk
Website: www.warwickshire.gov.uk/countyrecordoffice
Website: www.a2a.org.uk

Enquiries to: Head of Archive Service

Founded: 1933

Organisation type and purpose: Local government body.
Record office.
To collect, preserve and make accessible the historic records of the County.

Subject coverage: Warwickshire historical records (largely excluding Birmingham and Coventry).

Collection: Warwickshire Historical Manuscripts
Warwickshire Local History Library (printed works)
Warwickshire Map Collection
Warwickshire Photograph Collection
Small reference library of books on Warwickshire

Non-library collection catalogue: All or part available online and in-house

Library catalogue: All or part available in-house

Publications: Printed

Access to staff: Contact by letter, by telephone, by fax, by e-mail, in person and via website
Hours: Tue, Wed, Thu, 0900 to 1730; Fri, 0900 to 1700; Sat, 0900 to 1230
Closed to the public for the first full week of each calendar month.
Special comments: Identification required.

Access to building: *Special comments:* Members and public must be in possession of a CARN reader's ticket or bring proof of ID including name, address and signature to obtain a ticket

Access for disabled people: Limited parking provided (please phone to reserve a space), access to all public areas, readers' tea room, toilet facilities

Parent body: Warwickshire County Council; Shire Hall, Warwick, CV34 4SA; tel: 01926 410410; website: http://www.warwickshire.gov.uk

WARWICKSHIRE FAMILY HISTORY SOCIETY

7 Mersey Road, Bulkington, Nuneaton, Warwickshire, CV12 9QB

E-mail: chairman@wfhs.org.uk
Website: www.wfhs.org.uk

Enquiries to: Chairman
Direct e-mail: secretary@wfhs.org.uk

Founded: 1986

Organisation type and purpose: Membership association (membership is by subscription).

Subject coverage: Family history and genealogy, in particular of Warwickshire.

Collection: IGI
Census 1881

Publications: Printed
Order printed publications from: Publications, Warwickshire Family History Society
26 Flude Road, Binley Woods, Coventry, CV7 9AQ

Publications list: Available online and in print

Access to staff: Contact by letter and by e-mail
Hours: Mon to Fri, 0900 to 1700

Access for disabled people: Parking provided

WARWICKSHIRE LIBRARY AND INFORMATION SERVICE

Barrack Street, Warwick, CV34 4TH

Tel: 01926 412164
Fax: 01926 412165
E-mail: librarieslearningandculture@warwickshire.gov.uk
Website: www.warwickshire.gov.uk/libraries

Enquiries to: Head of Libraries, Learning and Culture

Founded: 1920; formerly called Warwickshire County Library

Organisation type and purpose: Local government body, public library.

Subject coverage: General information service, tourist information, local history.

Collection: George Eliot Collection at Nuneaton Library
Local History collections at Warwick, Leamington, Nuneaton and Rugby Libraries
Michael Drayton Collection at Nuneaton Library
Warwickshire collection at Warwick Library

Music and Drama Collection at Warwick Library

Non-library collection catalogue: All or part available in-house

Library catalogue: All or part available online and in-house

Publications: Printed

Access to staff: Contact by letter, by telephone, by fax, by e-mail, in person and via website
Hours: Mon to Fri, 0900 to 1700

Access to building: No access other than to staff

Branch libraries: in 34 locations

Parent body: Warwickshire County Council

WARWICKSHIRE LOCAL HISTORY SOCIETY (WLHS)

c/o Jackie Bland, Hon. Secretary, 607 Kenilworth Road, Balsall Common, West Midlands, CV7 7DT

Tel: 01676 532349
E-mail: info@warwickshirehistory.org.uk
Website: www.warwickshirehistory.org.uk

Enquiries to: Honorary Secretary

Founded: 1965

Organisation type and purpose: Learned society (membership is by subscription), present number of members: 222, voluntary organisation.

Subject coverage: Warwickshire history.

Publications: Printed
Order printed publications from: Warwickshire Local History Society
28 Lillington Road, Leamington Spa, Warwickshire, CV32 5YY, tel: 01926 422628

Publications list: Available in print

Access to staff: Contact by letter and by e-mail

Member of: British Association for Local History

WASTE WATCH

96 Tooley Street, London, SE1 2TH

Tel: 020 7089 2100
Fax: 020 7403 4802
E-mail: info@wastewatch.org.uk
Website: www.wastewatch.org.uk
Website: www.nrf.org.uk

Enquiries to: Waste Watch Wasteline
Direct tel: 0870 243 0136
Direct e-mail: sam.jarvis@wastewatch.org.uk

Founded: 1991

Organisation type and purpose: Voluntary organisation, registered charity (charity number 1005417).
To promote and support action on waste reduction and recycling.

Subject coverage: Recycling, waste management, waste reduction, recycled products.

Publications: Printed

Publications list: Available online and in print

Access to staff: Contact by letter, by telephone, by fax and via website.
Appointment necessary.
Hours: Mon to Fri, 1000 to 1700

Access to building: No prior appointment required

Part funded by: Department of the Environment's Environmental Action Fund

WATER MANAGEMENT SOCIETY (WMSoc)

6 Sir Robert Peel Mill, Tolson's Enterprise Park, Fazeley, Tamworth, B78 3QD

Tel: 01827 289558
Fax: 01827 250408
E-mail: wmsoc@btconnect.com
Website: www.wmsoc.org.uk

Enquiries to: Information Officer

Founded: 1975

Organisation type and purpose: Professional body, membership association (membership is by qualification), present number of members: 565.

Subject coverage: Specification, selection and operating of equipment and systems applied to the use and re-use of water; cooling systems; cooling towers; air conditioning plants; heat exchangers; de-aeration; boiler and condensate systems; hot water systems; effluents and wastes from water preparation processes; recovery systems; environmental aspects and optimisation of available supplies of water; water audits; risk assessment of water services; in-house treatment for reducing effluent costs; current legislation.

Publications: Printed

Publications list: Available in print

Access to staff: Contact by letter, by telephone, by fax, by e-mail and via website
Hours: Mon to Fri, 0900 to 1600

Access to building: No access other than to staff

WATER UK

1 Queen Anne's Gate, London, SW1H 9BT

Tel: 020 7344 1844
Fax: 020 7344 1866
E-mail: info@water.org.uk
Website: www.water.org.uk

Enquiries to: Chief Executive

Founded: 1998; formerly called Water Companies Association (WCA), Water Services Association (WSA) (year of change 1998)

Organisation type and purpose: Trade association.
Water UK is the industry association that represents water and waste water service suppliers at national and European level.

Subject coverage: Water and wastewater services.

Publications: Printed

Publications list: Available online and in print

Access to staff: Contact by letter, by e-mail and via website
Hours: Mon to Fri, 0900 to 1700

Members of the Association are: 24 water and wastewater companies in England and Wales; Northern Ireland Water Service; website: www.water.org.uk
Scottish Water; website: see water uk website

WAVENEY DISTRICT COUNCIL

Town Hall, High Street, Lowestoft, Suffolk, NR32 1HS

Tel: 01502 562111
Fax: 01502 589327
E-mail: webmaster@waveney.gov.uk
Website: www.waveney.gov.uk

Enquiries to: Chief Executive
Direct tel: 01502 523210

Organisation type and purpose: Local government body.

Publications: Printed

Access to staff: Contact by letter, by telephone, by fax, by e-mail, in person and via website
Hours: Mon to Thu, 0900 to 1700; Fri, 0900 to 1630

Local Offices at: Beccles District Office; 6 Market Street, Beccles, Suffolk, NR34 9QD; tel: 01502 713113; fax: 01502 713113; Bungay District Office; Broad Street, Bungay, Suffolk, NR35 1EE; tel: 01986 892176; Halesworth District Office; London Road, Halesworth, Suffolk, IP9 8LW; tel: 01986 873162; fax: 01986 874516; Tourist Information; Town Hall, Southwold, Suffolk, IP18 6EF; tel: 01502 722366

WAVERLEY CARE HIV AND HEPATITIS C INFORMATION SERVICE

Waverley Care, 2–4 Abbeymount, Edinburgh, EH8 8EJ

Tel: 0131 661 0982
Fax: 0131 652 1780
E-mail: info@waverleycare.org
Website: www.waverleycare.org

Enquiries to: Information Worker
Other contacts: Manager, Waverley Care SOLAS

Founded: 1991

Organisation type and purpose: Voluntary organisation, registered charity (charity number SCO 036500).
HIV and Hepatitis C information and support.

Subject coverage: Supporting the HIV and Hepatitis C community in Scotland

Publications: Electronic and video

Access to staff: Contact by letter, by telephone, by fax, by e-mail, in person and via website
Hours: Mon to Fri, 0900 to 1700

Access to building: No prior appointment required
Hours: Mon to Fri, 0830 to 1530

Access for disabled people: Ramped entry
Special comments: Wheelchair access to ground floor only

continued overleaf

Constituent bodies: Waverley Care Milestone Respite Unit; 113 Oxgangs Road North, Edinburgh, EH14 1EB; tel: 0131 441 6989

Parent body: Waverley Care; Old Coates House, 32 Manor Place, Edinburgh, EH3 7EB; tel: 0131 226 2206; fax: 0131 226 2209

WAX CHANDLERS' COMPANY

Formal name: Worshipful Company of Wax Chandlers

Wax Chandlers' Hall, Gresham Street, London, EC2V 7AD

Tel: 020 7606 3591/2
Fax: 020 7600 5462
E-mail: info@waxchandlershall.co.uk
Website: www.waxchandlershall.co.uk

Enquiries to: Clerk
Other contacts: Beadle for bookings for meetings and banquets.

Founded: Before 1371

Organisation type and purpose: Membership association, service industry. City of London livery company, provider of banqueting and meeting facilities.

Collection: The Company's archive is lodged at Guildhall Library, London, EC2 and is open for public inspection

Publications: Printed

Access to staff: Contact by letter, by telephone, by fax, by e-mail and in person
Hours: Mon to Fri, 0900 to 1700

WEALDEN IRON RESEARCH GROUP

2 West Street Farm Cottages, Maynards Green, Heathfield, Sussex, TN21 0DG

Tel: 01435 812506
E-mail: wirghonsec@hotmail.com
Website: www.wealdeniron.org.uk

Founded: 1968

Organisation type and purpose: A charity whose objects are to advance the education of the public in historical and archaeological study and, in particular, to promote investigation and collate information concerning the Wealden iron industry and related activities for the benefit of the public. In furtherance of this objective:
(1) to publish such information both in regular bulletins and by any other means which the Trustees shall think fit;
(2) to co-operate with and affiliate to other organizations with allied aims as may seem desirable.

Subject coverage: The extinct iron industry of the Weald of Sussex, Kent and Surrey.

Publications: Printed
Order printed publications from: The Publications Officer, 1 Stirling Way, East Grinstead RH19 3HG

Publications list: Available online

Access to staff: Contact by letter, by telephone, by e-mail, in person and via website

WELL DRILLERS ASSOCIATION (WDA)

Unit 22/23, Brindley Road, Dodwells Bridge, Hinckley, Leics, LE10 3BY

Tel: 07736364259
E-mail: david.s.duke@gmail.com
Website: www.welldrillers.org

Enquiries to: Secretary
Other contacts: Chairman and Treasurer

Founded: pre-1940

Organisation type and purpose: Trade association.
Association of water well drillers in the United Kingdom.

Subject coverage: Water-well drilling, pump installation and maintenance.

Publications: Printed

Access to staff: Contact by letter, by telephone and by e-mail
Hours: Mon to Fri, 0900 to 1800

WELLCHILD

16 Royal Crescent, Cheltenham, Gloucestershire, GL50 3DA

Tel: 0845 458 8171
Fax: 01242 530008
E-mail: info@wellchild.org.uk
Website: www.wellchild.org.uk

Enquiries to: Chief Executive

Founded: 1977

Organisation type and purpose: Registered charity (charity no. 289600).
WellChild is the national charity for sick children. It helps children and young people who are seriously ill or have complex conditions and their families throughout the UK by focusing on three key areas – care, support and research.

Subject coverage: Children's health.

Publications: Printed

Access to staff: Contact by letter, by telephone, by fax, by e-mail and via website. Appointment necessary.
Hours: Mon to Fri, 0900 to 1700

WELLCOME LIBRARY

183 Euston Road, London, NW1 2BE

Tel: 020 7611 8722
Fax: 020 7611 8369
E-mail: library@wellcome.ac.uk
Website: library.wellcome.ac.uk

Enquiries to: User Services Manager
Other contacts: Librarian

Founded: 1949

Organisation type and purpose: Registered charity (charity number 210183), research organisation.

Subject coverage: Medicine and its role in society, past and present, including popular science, biomedical ethics and the public understanding of science.

Collection: Over 600,000 books and journals
13,000 original letters and facsimiles of letters by Florence Nightingale, Lord Lister and Melanie Klein
Records of numerous organisations and bodies involved in medical science and health care
Autograph Letters (100,000)
Books from the library of William Morris (including 67 incunabula)
Ethnology and travel c.1800 to c.1940; thereafter medically oriented ethnology and anthropology
Incunabula (over 600 items); early printed books (over 7,000 pre-1641; over 66,000 1641–1850), including about 11,000 items from the Library of the Medical Society of London
Library of the Royal Society of Health
Library of the Society for the Study of Addiction
Microforms (1,600)
Asian collection of 12,000 MSS in 43 eastern languages including Sanskrit, Arabic, Persian, Hebrew, Chinese, Japanese, (c.70 microfilm rolls in oriental languages); 3,000 items printed in Oriental scripts and topographical and other works relevant to oriental studies in Western languages
American Collection including medical imprints from the Hispanic and Portuguese American Empires 1557–1833 and from the British Colonies in America 1720–1820; also material on Amerindian medicine, manuscripts and much reference material, especially bibliographies
200,000 prints, drawings; paintings and photographs, from the Orient to the Americas, (middle ages to present)
Western Manuscripts (9,000)

Non-library collection catalogue: All or part available online, in-house and in print

Library catalogue: All or part available online

Publications: Printed
Order printed publications from: Mrs Tracy Tillotson, tel. 020 7611 8486; fax 020 7611 8369; e-mail t.tillotson@wellcome.ac.uk

Access to staff: Contact by letter, by telephone, by fax, by e-mail, in person and via website
Hours: Mon, Tue, Wed, Fri, 1000 to 1800; Thu, 1000 to 2000; Sat, 1000 to 1600

Funded by: Wellcome Trust

Links with: University College London

WELLCOME LIBRARY – MOVING IMAGE AND SOUND COLLECTION

183 Euston Road, London, NW1 2BE

Tel: 020 7611 8722
Fax: 020 7611 8369
E-mail: library@wellcome.ac.uk
Website: library.wellcome.ac.uk

Enquiries to: Archivist
Direct e-mail: arch+mss@wellcome.ac.uk

History of institution: formerly called Wellcome Trust Medical Film and Video Library

Organisation type and purpose: Research organisation.

Subject coverage: Moving image and sound materials illustrating the evolution of medicine and health over the last 100 years.

A primary source in the study of the use of media as a communication tool in medical science and practice.

Collection: Approx 3,000 film items, 3,000 video items and 2,000 sound items. Mostly available for reference only with a limited number of titles for loan and/or licensing

Non-library collection catalogue: All or part available online and in-house

Library catalogue: All or part available online

Publications: Electronic and video

Publications list: Available online

Access to staff: Contact by letter, by telephone, by fax, by e-mail, in person and via website. Appointment necessary.
Hours: Mon to Fri, 1000 to 1700

Access for disabled people: Fully accessible

WELLCOME TRUST MEDICAL PHOTOGRAPHIC LIBRARY

210 Euston Road, London, NW1 2BE

Tel: 020 7611 8348
Fax: 020 7611 8577
E-mail: photolib@wellcome.ac.uk
Website: www.wellcome.ac.uk/mpl

History of institution: formerly called Wellcome Library for the History and Understanding of Medicine

Organisation type and purpose: Research organisation.

Subject coverage: Images of medical and social history, photographs of clinical medicine and biomedical sciences.

Collection: Over 160,000 images of medical and social history; 17,000 photos of modern clinical medicine and biomedical sciences

Non-library collection catalogue: All or part available online and in-house

Library catalogue: All or part available online

Publications list: Available online and in print

Access to staff: Contact by letter, by telephone, by fax, by e-mail and via website. Appointment necessary.
Hours: Mon to Fri, 0930 to 1730

Access to building: Prior appointment required
Hours: Mon to Fri, 0930 to 1730

WELLCOME-BEIT PRIZE FELLOWSHIPS

Wellcome Trust, Gibbs Building, 215 Euston Road, London NW1 2BE

Tel: +44 (0)20 7611 8888
Fax: +44 (0)20 7611 8545
E-mail: contact@wellcome.ac.uk

Enquiries to: Secretary

Founded: 1909

Organisation type and purpose: Registered charity, research organisation.

Subject coverage: Advancement by research of medicine and of the allied sciences in their relation to medicine.

WELLINGBOROUGH BOROUGH COUNCIL

Council Offices, Swanspool House, Wellingborough, Northamptonshire, NN8 1BP

Tel: 01933 229777
Fax: 01933 231629
E-mail: customerservices@wellingborough.gov.uk
Website: www.wellingborough.gov.uk/

Organisation type and purpose: Local government body.

WELLS AND WALSINGHAM LIGHT RAILWAY (WWLR)

Wells-Next-the-Sea, Norfolk, NR23 1QB

Tel: 01328 710631

Enquiries to: Owner
Direct tel: 01328 711630

Founded: 1982

Organisation type and purpose: Membership association (membership is by subscription), present number of members: 120.

Subject coverage: Steam railway preservation.

Publications: Printed

Access to staff: Contact by letter, by telephone and in person
Hours: Mon to Fri, 0900 to 1700

WELSH ASSOCIATION OF MOTOR CLUBS (WAMC)

General Secretary, 63 Maes y Sarn, Pentyrch, Cardiff, CF15 9QR

Tel: 029 2089 1314
E-mail: secretary@wamcweb.com
Website: www.wamcweb.com/

Enquiries to: Press Officer
Direct e-mail: wamc.pressoffice@wamcweb.com

Founded: 1957

Organisation type and purpose: National government body, membership association (membership is by qualification), present number of members: 100.

Subject coverage: Motor sport in Wales.

Publications: Printed

Access to staff: Contact by letter, by telephone and by fax
Hours: Mon to Fri, 1800 to 2100; Sat, Sun, 1000 to 1800

Associated with: MSA; Motorsport House, Colnbrook, Slough, Berkshire, SL3 0HG

WELSH BLACK CATTLE SOCIETY

13 Bangor Street, Caernarfon, Gwynedd, LL55 1AP

Tel: 01286 672391
Fax: 01286 672022
E-mail: welshblack@btclick.com
Website: www.welshblackcattlesociety.com

Enquiries to: Chief Executive

Founded: 1904

Organisation type and purpose: International organisation (membership is by subscription, qualification, election or invitation), present number of members: 960, registered charity (charity number 244415/acl).

Subject coverage: Breeding of Welsh Black cattle.

Publications: Printed

Access to staff: Contact by letter, by telephone, by fax, by e-mail and in person
Hours: Mon to Fri, 0900 to 1700

Also at: Welsh Black Cattle Society; Royal Welsh Showground, Llanelwedd, Builth Wells, Powys, LD2 3NJ; tel: 01982 551111; fax: 01982 551333

WELSH CENTRE FOR INTERNATIONAL AFFAIRS / CANOLFAN MATERION RHYNGWLADOL CYMRU (WCIA)

Temple of Peace, Cathays Park, Cardiff, CF10 3AP, Cymru/Wales

Tel: 029 2022 8549
Fax: 029 2064 0333
E-mail: centre@wcia.org.uk
Website: www.wcia.org.uk

Enquiries to: Administrative Officer
Direct e-mail: suecoles@wcia.org.uk
Other contacts: Programme Co-ordinator

Founded: 1973; incorporates the former Welsh League of Nations Union, Welsh National Council of the United Nations Association (UNA Wales), Council for Education in World Citizenship-Cymru (CEWC-Cymru) (year of change Various amalgamations)

Organisation type and purpose: International organisation, membership association (membership is by subscription), present number of members: 500. voluntary organisation, suitable for ages 15+.
To promote public awareness of international affairs.

Subject coverage: International political, economic and social affairs; international affairs generally including the UN and its agencies, EU and European affairs, disarmament, development and humanitarian issues.

Information services: Public interpretation displays and interactive sites on the building's history and the work that the institution does.

Special visitor services: Viewing of the First World War National Book of Remembrance for Wales in the building's crypt.

Education services: Global citizenship, sustainable development, human rights and international affairs education – for young people in particular.

Services for disabled people: The Temple of Peace is a fully accessible building for disabled people.

Collection: A library with a good collection on international politics between the two world wars (1918–1939)

continued overleaf

Publications: Printed, and electronic and video
Order printed publications from: Sue Coles, at the above address/contact details
Order electronic and video publications from: Sue Coles, at the above address/contact details

Publications list: Available in print

Access to staff: Contact by letter, by telephone, by fax, by e-mail, in person and via website
Hours: Mon to Fri, 0900 to 1700

Access to building: No prior appointment required
Hours: Mon to Fri, 0900 to 1700

Access for disabled people: All areas of the building are fully accessible to disabled people
Hours: as above

WELSH COLLEGE OF HORTICULTURE

Holywell Road, Northop, Mold, Flintshire, CH7 6AA

Tel: 01352 841000
Fax: 01352 841031
E-mail: info@wcoh.ac.uk
Website: www.wcoh.ac.uk

Enquiries to: Information Centre

Founded: 1953

Organisation type and purpose: Suitable for ages: 16+, training organisation.
College offering courses in land-based subjects for students aged 16+.

Subject coverage: Floristry, landscape design and construction, turf management, market gardening, biological control, equine studies, environmental studies, small animal care, IT, garden centre practices, crop production, nursery stock production, machinery.

Collection: Distance learning courses in floristry and management

Publications: Printed

Access to staff: Contact by letter, by telephone and by fax. Appointment necessary.
Hours: Mon to Fri, 0900 to 1700

Access to building: Prior appointment required

Access for disabled people: Parking provided, ramped entry, level entry, access to all public areas, toilet facilities

WELSH GOVERNMENT – CENTRAL REGISTER OF AERIAL PHOTOGRAPHY FOR WALES

Cartographics, Room G-073a, Crown Offices, Cathays Park, Cardiff, CF10 3NQ

Tel: 029 2082 3819
Fax: 029 2082 3080
E-mail: aerialphotoofficer@wales.gsi.gov.uk

Enquiries to: Aerial Photographs Officer

Organisation type and purpose: National government body, central government department.

Subject coverage: The Central Register aims to index all vertical air survey coverage of Wales flown by the Royal Air Force, Ordnance Survey, commercial air survey companies and other air survey organisations. The Register is a comprehensive source of information about the aerial photography of Wales and advises all interested users. Customers need to supply a map or OS National Grid Reference of their area of interest to perform a cover search.

Collection: The Aerial Photographs Library holds an extensive collection of photographs covering Wales at various dates and scales. The base of the collection is the national 1:10,000 aerial survey flown 1945–52 by the RAF. To this has been added other RAF photographs including the 1969 and 1981 small-scale national surveys; Ordnance Survey 1958–2002; Medmenham 1940–45; and Meridian 1952–83. The Welsh Government has continued to update the collection, which now includes extensive coverage in colour 1983–97. Some oblique and infrared photos are held of the Welsh coastline and also MAFF/ADAS (black and white and colour) from the 1970s–80s.
Full cover of Wales by Getmapping (2000 & 2009), COWI (2006) is available to view in colour on screen.

Publications: Printed

Access to staff: Contact by letter, by telephone and by e-mail. Appointment necessary.
Hours: Mon to Fri, 0900 to 1630

Access to building: Prior appointment required
Special comments: Hand luggage will be liable to search and x-ray to meet security requirements.

Access for disabled people: Parking provided, level entry, toilet facilities

WELSH JUDO ASSOCIATION (WJA)

Welsh Institute of Sport, Sophia Gardens, Cardiff, CF11 9SW

Tel: 029 2033 4945
E-mail: office@welshjudo.com
Website: www.welshjudo.com

Organisation type and purpose: Governing body for the sport of judo in Wales, with various services devolved to it by the British governing body, the British Judo Association; has over 60 member clubs.

Subject coverage: Judo in Wales at all levels.

Publications: Electronic and video
Order electronic and video publications from: Download from website

Publications list: Available online

Access to staff: Contact by letter, by telephone and by e-mail
Hours: Office hours: Mon to Fri, 1000 to 1400

WELSH LANGUAGE SOCIETY

Pen Roc, Rhodfa'r Môr, Aberystwyth, Ceredigion, SY23 2AZ

Tel: 01970 624501
Fax: 01970 627122
E-mail: swyddfa@cymdeithas.com
Website: www.cymdeithas.com

Enquiries to: Administrative Officer
Direct e-mail: dafydd@cymdeithas.org
Other contacts: Assembly Campaigns Officer

Founded: 1962

Organisation type and purpose: Voluntary organisation.
Political pressure group.
To campaign for the Welsh language and Welsh communities.

Subject coverage: Welsh language: its future and campaigns to secure its future; socio-linguistic planning and education; official status of the Welsh language.

Publications: Printed

Access to staff: Contact by letter, by fax, by e-mail and via website. Appointment necessary.
Hours: Mon to Fri, 0930 to 1730

WELSH NATIONAL FOLK DANCE SOCIETY (WNFDS/CGDWC)

Formal name: Cymdeithas Genedlaethol Dawns Werin Cymru

Cymdeithas Genedlaethol Dawns Werin Cymru, Ffynnonlwyd, Trelech, Carmarthen, SA33 6QZ

Tel: 01994 484496
E-mail: secretary@dawnsio.com
Website: www.dawnsio.com

Enquiries to: Honorary Secretary

Founded: 1949; formerly called Welsh Folk Dance Society/Cymdeithas Ddawns Werin Cymru (year of change 2010)

Organisation type and purpose: Membership association (membership is by subscription), present number of members: 264 individuals, 22 groups, voluntary organisation, registered charity (charity number 1023817).
To promote traditional dance and music.

Subject coverage: Welsh folk dancing and music.

Collection: Library at (& courtesy of) the Welsh Folk Museum, St Fagans, Cardiff of early dance manuals and notations

Publications: Printed, and electronic and video
Order printed publications from: Sales Point, Cymdeithas Genedlaethol Dawns Werin Cymru/Welsh National Folk Dance Society, c/o Palas Print, 10 Stryd y Plas, Caernarfon, Gwynedd, LL55 1RR; tel. 01286 674631; e-mail siop@palasprint.com

Publications list: Available online and in print

Access to staff: Contact by letter, by telephone, by e-mail and via website
Hours: Mon to Fri, 0900 to 1700
Special comments: evenings: 1700 to 2200

Affiliated to: Ty Cerdd (Formerly Welsh Amateur Music Federation); Welsh Arts Council

Librarian: Welsh National Folk Dance Society; 8 St Cyre's Road, Penarth, South Glamorgan

WELSH TEACHERS' UNION (UCAC)

Prif Swyddfa UCAC, Ffordd Penglais, Aberystwyth, Ceredigion, SY23 2EU

Tel: 01970 639950
Fax: 01970 626765
E-mail: ucac@athrawon.com
Website: www.athrawon.com

Enquiries to: General Secretary

Founded: 1940

Organisation type and purpose: Trade union (membership is by subscription), present number of members: c.4,800.
As well as safeguarding the rights of teachers and lecturers and ensuring fair salaries, pensions and conditions of employment, UCAC has always campaigned for an independent education system for Wales.

Collection: Archive, Cardiff University

Publications list: Available online

Access to staff: Contact by letter, by telephone, by fax and by e-mail. Appointment necessary. Non-members charged.
Hours: Mon to Thu, 0900 to 1700; Fri, 0900 to 1600
Special comments: Office is closed for a fortnight over Christmas, on St David's Day and during the first week in August; emergency tel. number on office answerphone.

Access for disabled people: yes

WELWYN HATFIELD BOROUGH COUNCIL

Council Offices, Welwyn Garden City, Hertfordshire, AL8 6AE

Tel: 01707 357000
Fax: 01707 357257
E-mail: contact-whc@welhat.gov.uk
Website: www.welhat.gov.uk

Enquiries to: Customer Services Officer

Founded: 1974

Organisation type and purpose: Local government body.

Publications: Printed

Publications list: Available online and in print

Access to staff: Contact by letter, by telephone, by e-mail and via website. Appointment necessary.
Hours: Mon to Thu, 0845 to 1715; Fri, 0845 to 1645

Access to building: *Hours:* Mon to Thu, 0845 to 1715; Fri, 0845 to 1645

Access for disabled people: Parking provided, level entry

WENDY WARR & ASSOCIATES

6 Berwick Court, Holmes Chapel, Cheshire, CW4 7HZ

Tel: 01477 533837
Fax: 01477 533837
E-mail: wendy@warr.com
Website: www.warr.com

Enquiries to: Principal Consultant

Founded: 1992

Organisation type and purpose: Consultancy.

Subject coverage: Cheminformatics, chemical information, scientific, technical and medical information systems, electronic publishing, computational chemistry, drug discovery.

Publications: Printed

Publications list: Available online and in print

Access to staff: Contact by letter, by telephone, by fax, by e-mail, in person and via website
Hours: Mon to Fri, 0900 to 1700

WENSLEYDALE LONGWOOL SHEEP BREEDERS' ASSOCIATION (WLSBA)

Breed Secretary, Coffin Walk, Sheep Dip Lane, Princethorpe, Rugby, Warwickshire, CV23 9SP

Tel: 01926 633439
Website: www.wensleydale-sheep.com

Enquiries to: Membership Secretary
Direct tel: 01388 777852

Founded: 1890

Organisation type and purpose: Membership association (membership is by subscription), present number of members: 210.
Breeding and promotion of Wensleydale sheep.

Subject coverage: Breed characteristics and sales of Wensleydale sheep.

Publications: Printed

Access to staff: Contact by letter and by telephone
Hours: Mon to Fri, 0900 to 1700

WESLEY HISTORICAL SOCIETY (WHS)

7 Haugh Shaw Road, Halifax, HX1 3AH

Tel: 01422 250780
E-mail: johnahargreaves@blueyonder.co.uk
Website: www.wesleyhistoricalsociety.org.uk

Enquiries to: General Secretary
Direct e-mail: jandclenton@blueyonder.co.uk
Other contacts: Registrar (for membership); Librarian (for access to collections); Editor (for offer of articles, advertising rates)

Founded: 1893

Organisation type and purpose: Learned society (membership is by subscription), present number of members: 850, registered charity (charity number 283012).
To promote the study of the history and literature of all branches of Methodism, to accumulate exact knowledge, and to provide a medium of intercourse on all related subjects.

Subject coverage: Methodist history, literature, Methodism, Methodist portraits. No genealogical Methodist records held.

Collection: Bretherton Collection, Guyler Collection. Some archive material, images and cuttings (not on online catalogue). Reference library housed at Oxford Brookes University. Contact library before visiting

Non-library collection catalogue: All or part available online and in-house

Library catalogue: All or part available online and in-house

Publications: Printed
Order printed publications from: c/o The Registrar, Wesley Historical Society, 15 Foxlands Drive, Lloyd Hill, Penn, Wolverhampton, WV4 5NB

Publications list: Available in print

Access to staff: Contact by letter, by telephone and by e-mail. Appointment necessary. Non-members charged.
Hours: Mon to Fri, 0900 to 1700
Special comments: Check library opening times with WHS Library; tel: 01865 488319.

Access to building: Prior appointment required

Access for disabled people: Please telephone in advance to make arrangements

Branch libraries: Wesley Historical Society Library; Harcourt Hill Campus, Oxford Brookes University, Oxford, OX2 9AT; e-mail: pforsaith@brookes.ac.uk; website: http://catalogue.brookes.ac.uk/TalisPrism/?interface=Wesley&newsession=true

Branches: Network of 17 Methodist regional historical societies; c/o Regional Historical Societies Liaison Officer, Wesley Historical Society, 50 Well Oak Park, Dryden Road, Exeter, Devon, EX2 5BB; e-mail: rthorne@fish.co.uk

WEST DUNBARTONSHIRE COUNCIL

Garshake Road, Dumbarton, Strathclyde, G82 3PU

Tel: 01389 737000
Fax: 01389 737070
E-mail: wdcmgr@post.allmac.co.uk
Website: www.west-dunbarton.gov.uk

Enquiries to: Public Relations Manager
Direct tel: 01389 737296
Direct fax: 01389 737578
Direct e-mail: joe.cox@west-dunbarton.gov.uk

Founded: April 1996

Organisation type and purpose: Local government body.

Subject coverage: All local government services.

Non-library collection catalogue: All or part available online

Publications: Printed

Publications list: Available in print

Access to staff: Contact by letter, by telephone, by e-mail and via website
Hours: Mon to Fri, 0900 to 1700

Access for disabled people: Parking provided, ramped entry, toilet facilities

WEST DUNBARTONSHIRE LIBRARIES

Headquarters, Levenford House, Helenslee Road, Dumbarton, Strathclyde, G82 4AH

Tel: 01389 608041
Fax: 01389 608044

Enquiries to: Service Manager
Direct e-mail: dumbarton.library@west-dunbarton.gov.uk

Founded: 1996

Organisation type and purpose: Local government body, public library.

Subject coverage: General and local history of Dunbartonshire, Clyde shipbuilding, sewing machine manufacture, textile industry

Collection: West-Dunbartonshire Archives Singer sewing machines, Dennystown Forge, Dumbarton Burgh Council minutes, 1599–1975
Thompson Collection (local history)
Watchmeal Collection (local history)

Non-library collection catalogue: All or part available online and in-house

Library catalogue: All or part available online and in-house

Publications: Printed, and electronic and video

Access to staff: Contact by letter, by telephone, by fax, by e-mail, in person and via website. Appointment necessary.
Hours: Mon to Fri, 0830 to 1615
Special comments: Telephone switchboard operates from Mon to Fri, 0830 to 1615.

Affiliated to: Glasgow & West of Scotland Family History Society; Library Association; Scottish Genealogy Society; Scottish History Society; Scottish Library and Information Council; Scottish Local Government Information Unit; Scottish Museum Council; Scottish Poetry Library; Scottish Records Association

WEST GLAMORGAN ARCHIVE SERVICE (WGAS)

Civic Centre, Oystermouth Road, Swansea, SA1 3SN

Tel: 01792 636589
Fax: 01792 637130
E-mail: westglam.archives@swansea.gov.uk
Website: www.swansea.gov.uk/westglamorganarchives

Enquiries to: Archivist

Organisation type and purpose: Local government body.
Archive service.

Subject coverage: Local and family history in West Glamorgan.

Collection: Usual local authority holdings

Non-library collection catalogue: All or part available online, in-house and in print

Publications: Printed

Publications list: Available online and in print

Access to staff: Contact by letter, by telephone, by fax, by e-mail and in person
Hours: Tue, 0900 to 1900; Wed to Fri, 0900 to 1700; Sat, 1000 to 1600 (Family History Centre only)

Access for disabled people: Parking provided, ramped entry, level entry, access to all public areas, toilet facilities

Also at: Neath Antiquarian Society Archives; The Mechanics Institute, 4 Church Place, Neath, SA11 3LL; tel: 01639 620139; Port Talbot Family and Local History Centre; Aberafan Library, Port Talbot, SA13 1PB; tel: 01639 763430

WEST HERTS COLLEGE

Hempstead Road, Watford, WD3 5QQ

Tel: 01923 812000
E-mail: anne.harris@westherts.ac.uk
Website: www.westherts.ac.uk

Enquiries to: Head of Learning Resources
Direct tel: 01923 812551

History of institution: created by the merger of Cassio College, Dacorum College and Watford College of Technology (year of change 1991)

Organisation type and purpose: Suitable for ages: 16+.
College of Further and Higher education.

Subject coverage: Catering, Travel and Tourism, Business, IT, Health & Social Care, Hairdressing, Beauty Therapy, Sport, Public Services, Art & Design, Performance, Music, Media, Access to HE, Foundation Degrees

Library catalogue: All or part available online

Publications list: Available online

Access to staff: Contact by telephone. Appointment necessary.
Hours: Mon, 0845 to 1700; Tue to Thu, 0845 to 1900; Fri, 0845 to 1600
College holidays: Mon to Thu, 0900 to 1600
Special comments: Phone to make prior appointment, required because of security checks.

Access for disabled people: Parking provided

WEST KENT COLLEGE (WKC)

Brook Street, Tonbridge, Kent, TN9 2PW

Tel: 01732 358101\ Minicom no. 01732 350763
Fax: 01732 771415
E-mail: marketing@wkc.ac.uk
Enquiries to: Admissions Officer
Direct tel: 01732 358101
Direct fax: 01732 771415

Organisation type and purpose: Training organisation.

Subject coverage: Further and higher education, training courses for business and commerce, professional development courses.

Order printed publications from: Student Services
at the same address, tel: 01732 358101, fax: 01732 771415, e-mail: enquiries@wkc.ac.uk

Access to staff: Contact by letter, by telephone, by fax, by e-mail, in person and via website
Hours: Mon to Fri, 0900 to 1730

In association with: University of Greenwich

WEST LANCASHIRE DISTRICT COUNCIL

52 Derby Street, Ormskirk, Lancashire, L39 2DF

Tel: 01695 577177
Fax: 01695 585082
Website: www.westlancsdc.gov.uk

Enquiries to: Public Relations Manager
Direct tel: 01695 585011
Direct fax: 01695 585220
Direct e-mail: public.relations@westlancsdc.gov.uk

Founded: 1974

Organisation type and purpose: Local government body.

Subject coverage: Policy issues, public relations, leisure, planning, housing, economic development, finance and council tax, civic administration, building control, contract services, environmental health, refuse collection.

Publications: Printed

Access to staff: Contact by letter, by telephone, by fax, by e-mail, in person and via website
Hours: Mon to Fri, 0900 to 1700

Access for disabled people: Parking provided

WEST LOTHIAN COUNCIL

Libraries Department, Bathgate Partnership Centre, South Bridge Street, Bathgate, West Lothian, EH48 1TS

Tel: 01506 281273
E-mail: library.info@westlothian.gov.uk
Website: www.westlothian.gov.uk/libraries

Enquiries to: Support Services Co-Ordinator

Founded: 1996

Organisation type and purpose: Local government body, public library

Subject coverage: General, local studies

Collection: Local history, archives

Non-library collection catalogue: All or part available online

Library catalogue: All or part available online

Access to staff: Contact by letter, by telephone, by e-mail and in person
Hours: Mon to Thu, 0900 to 1700; Fri, 0900 to 1600

WEST LOTHIAN COUNCIL ARCHIVES AND RECORDS CENTRE (WLC ARC)

9 Dunlop Square, Deans Industrial Estate, Livingston, EH54 8SB

Tel: 01506 773770
Fax: 01506 773775
E-mail: archive@westlothian.gov.uk
Website: www.westlothian.gov.uk/tourism/libservices/ves

Enquiries to: Archivist
Other contacts: Local History Librarian (for genealogy enquiries, secondary (published) sources)

Founded: 1995; formerly called Lothian Regional Council (West Lothian Area), West Lothian District Council (year of change 1996); formerly called Livingston Development Corporation (year of change 1997)

Organisation type and purpose: Local government body.
Archive Office.

Subject coverage: New town development (Livingston) in West Lothian.
Archives of local government, private depository.

Education services: Education packs and source boxes available for loan to local schools.

Collection: Livingston Development Corporation Collection (computerised finding aid)

Access to staff: Contact by letter, by telephone and by fax. Appointment necessary.
Hours: Mon to Thu, 0900 to 1700; Fri, 0900 to 1600

Access to building: Prior appointment required

Access for disabled people: Search room is fully accessible
Hours: As above; please phone first

WEST OF SCOTLAND VW CLUB

Formal name: West of Scotland Volkswagen Club

20 Greenlaw Avenue, Paisley, Renfrewshire, PA1 3RD

Tel: 0141 889 6914

Enquiries to: Chairman
Other contacts: Membership Secretary for Club information.

Founded: 1963

Organisation type and purpose: Advisory body, membership association (membership is by subscription), present number of members: 200, consultancy.
Social gatherings, motoring events, helping members with technical and mechanical problems regarding their vehicles.

Subject coverage: General or technical information regarding Volkswagen vehicles, and other relevant makes of vehicles in the V.A.G. group, e.g. Audi.

Publications: Printed

Access to staff: Contact by letter and by telephone
Hours: Mon to Fri, 0900 to 2300
Special comments: All services and information for members only.

Memberships: Harold Cameron; 8 Allander Drive, Torrance, Glasgow, G64 4LG; tel: 01360 622766

WEST OXFORDSHIRE DISTRICT COUNCIL

Council Offices, Woodgreen, Witney, Oxfordshire, OX28 1NB

Tel: 01993 861000
Fax: 01993 861050
E-mail: enquiries@westoxon.gov.uk

Enquiries to: Chief Executive
Other contacts: Visitor and Information Centre Manager for publications.

Organisation type and purpose: Local government body.

Subject coverage: Information for visitors to the district of West Oxfordshire.

Publications: Printed

Access to staff: Contact by letter, by telephone, by fax, by e-mail, in person and via website
Hours: Mon to Fri, 0900 to 1700

Access to building: *Hours:* 09:00 to 5pm

Access for disabled people: Parking provided, ramped entry, level entry, toilet facilities

Other offices: West Oxfordshire District Council; The Town Centre Shop, 3 Welch Way, Witney, Oxon, OX28 1PB; tel: 01993 861000; e-mail: enquiries@westoxon.gov.uk; website: www.westoxon.gov.uk

WEST RIDING TRADE PROTECTION ASSOCIATION (WRTPA)

Protection House, 16–17 East Parade, Leeds, West Yorkshire, LS1 2BS

Tel: 0113 243 2561
Fax: 0113 244 3901
Website: www.wrtpa.com

Enquiries to: General Manager
Other contacts: Company Secretary

Founded: 1848

Organisation type and purpose: Membership association (membership is by subscription), present number of members: 4500.
Credit information and debt recovery agency.

Subject coverage: Debt recovery specialists in both UK and overseas, company monitoring, tracing agents, business and credit information specialists.

Publications: Printed

Publications list: Available in print

Access to staff: Contact by letter, by telephone, by fax, by e-mail, in person and via website. Appointment necessary. Access for members only.
Hours: Mon to Fri, 0900 to 1700

WEST SURREY FAMILY HISTORY SOCIETY (WSFHS)

21 Sheppard Road, Basingstoke, Hampshire, RG21 3HT

Tel: 01256 358454
E-mail: secretary@wsfhs.org
Website: www.wsfhs.org
Website: www.wsfhs.org

Enquiries to: Secretary

Founded: 1974

Organisation type and purpose: Membership society (membership is by subscription), present number of members: about 1,200, voluntary organisation, registered charity (charity number 278091), research and guidance organisation.
To collect, index, co-ordinate, publish and make accessible, in the interests of genealogy, any documents or records relating to the ancient County of Surrey; to promote their preservation; to encourage the study of genealogy.

Subject coverage: Genealogy and family history.

Special visitor services: Regular meetings are held most months of the year at venues in West Surrey: Camberley, Farnham, Guildford, Walton on Thames and Woking. Additionally a computer group meets at Woking.

Non-library collection catalogue: All or part available online, in-house and in print

Publications: Printed, and electronic and video, and microform publications
Order printed publications from: Publications Officer, West Surrey Family History Society, 17 Lane End Drive, Knaphill, Woking, Surrey, GU21 2QQ

Publications list: Available online and in print

Access to staff: Contact by letter, by e-mail and via website
Hours: Mon to Fri, 0900 to 1700

Access for disabled people: Check in advance

WEST SUSSEX COUNTY COUNCIL

County Hall, West Street, Chichester, West Sussex, PO19 1RQ

Tel: 01243 777100
Fax: 01243 777950
E-mail: webmaster@westsussex.gov.uk
Website: www.westsussex.gov.uk

Enquiries to: News Manager
Direct tel: 01243 777117
Direct fax: 01243 777266
Direct e-mail: nigel.galloway@westsussex.gov.uk

Founded: 1889

Organisation type and purpose: Local government body.

Access to staff: Contact by letter, by telephone, by fax, by e-mail, in person and via website
Hours: Mon to Fri, 0900 to 1700

Access for disabled people: Parking provided, toilet facilities
Special comments: Lift into the building

WEST SUSSEX LIBRARY SERVICE

Worthing Reference Library, Richmond Road, Worthing, BN11 1HD

Tel: 01903 704824
Fax: 01903 821902
E-mail: worthing.reference.library@westsussex.gov.uk
Website: www.westsussex.gov.uk

continued overleaf

Enquiries to: Information Librarian

Organisation type and purpose: Local government body, public library.

Subject coverage: Local history; art; folklore; ornithology; zoology; business information sources; law; government publications; European information; family history.

Non-library collection catalogue: All or part available online

Library catalogue: All or part available online

Access to staff: Contact by letter, by telephone, by fax, by e-mail and in person
Hours: Mon to Fri, 0900 to 1900; Sat, 0900 to 1700

Access for disabled people: Ramped entry

WEST SUSSEX RECORD OFFICE (WSRO)

County Hall, Chichester, West Sussex, PO19 1RN

Tel: 01243 753600
Fax: 01243 533959
E-mail: records.office@westsussex.gov.uk
Website: www.westsussex.gov.uk/ccm/navigation/libraries-and-archives/record-office/

Enquiries to: Archivist

Founded: 1946

Organisation type and purpose: Local government body, research organisation.

Subject coverage: 1200 years of the County's history, including the Diocese of Chichester, and the county's landed estates (especially Goodwood, Petworth, Cowdray and Wiston), family papers including Richard Cobden, WS Blunt, and the Wilberforce and Maxse families, and the Royal Sussex Regiment.

Collection: Garland Photographic Collection (70,000 photographs)
Screen Archive South East Film & Video Archive
William Blake (Crookshank Collection)

Non-library collection catalogue: All or part available online, in-house and in print

Library catalogue: All or part available in-house

Publications: Printed, and electronic and video, and microform publications

Access to staff: Contact by letter, by telephone, by fax, by e-mail, in person and via website
Hours: Mon to Fri, 0915 to 1645; Sat, 0915 to 1230 and 1330 to 1630
Special comments: A valid County Archives Research Network Ticket is required to use the search room. This is available free of charge on proof of identity on arrival.

Access for disabled people: Ramped entry, access to all public areas, toilet facilities

Parent body: West Sussex County Council; County Hall, Chichester, PO19 1RG; tel: 01243 777100; fax: 01243 777952

WEST THAMES COLLEGE

London Road, Isleworth, Middlesex, TW7 4HS

Tel: 020 8326 2308
Fax: 020 8569 7787
E-mail: library.services@west-thames.ac.uk
Website: www.west-thames.ac.uk

Enquiries to: Library Services Manager
Direct tel: 020 8326 2310
Direct e-mail: karen.kelly@west-thames.ac.uk

History of institution: formerly called Hounslow Borough College

Organisation type and purpose: Further education.

Subject coverage: Psychology; social sciences; education; computing; language; art; literature; history; biography; art history; graphic design; architecture; physics; chemistry; catering; hairdressing and beauty; health and care; ESOL (English for Speakers of Other Languages); business studies; engineering; construction trade skills; biology.

Collection: Collection relating to Joseph Banks

Library catalogue: All or part available in-house

Publications: Printed

Publications list: Available in print

Access to staff: Contact by letter, by telephone, by fax and by e-mail
Hours: Mon, Fri, 0845 to 1600; Tue, Wed, Thu, 0845 to 2000

Access to building: Prior appointment required

Access for disabled people: Parking provided, ramped entry, toilet facilities
Special comments: Lifts

WEST YORKSHIRE ARCHAEOLOGY ADVISORY SERVICE (WYAAS)

Registry of Deeds, Newstead Road, Wakefield, West Yorkshire, WF1 2DE

Tel: 01924 306797
Fax: 01924 306810
E-mail: wysmr@wyjs.org.uk
Website: www.archaeology.wyjs.org.uk

Enquiries to: Historic Environment Record (HER) Officer (for information on archaeological sites and findspots and some historic buildings)

Organisation type and purpose: Local government body, advisory body, suitable for ages: all.
Provision of advice to local authorities on archaeological matters.

Subject coverage: The area served by the Metropolitan Districts of Bradford, Calderdale, Kirklees, Leeds and Wakefield. All aspects of the archaeology of the area, for all periods up to and including the 'Cold War'. The HER is interested in all new discoveries of sites, artefacts, cartographic, photographic and documentary sources. Planning and research enquiries, site management and heritage issues. The service includes a Historic Buildings Officer and an outreach Education Officer. The HER includes a reference library, the principal oblique aerial photographic collection for West Yorkshire, a number of significant archaeological surveys, as well as details of all known sites, find spots and archaeological monuments within the five Metropolitan Districts.
The HER is interested in liaising with other local and national groups and with individuals who possess information on archaeological sites and historic buildings within West Yorkshire.

Publications: Printed, and electronic and video
Order printed publications from: Resources, West Yorkshire Archaeology Service, PO Box 30, Nepshaw Lane South, Morley, Leeds, LS27 0UG; tel: 0113 383 6404

Publications list: Available in print

Access to staff: Contact by letter, by telephone, by fax and by e-mail. Appointment necessary.
Hours: Mon to Fri, 1000 to 1700

WEST YORKSHIRE ARCHIVE SERVICE – BRADFORD

Bradford Central Library, Prince's Way, Bradford, BD1 1NN,

Tel: 01274 435099
E-mail: bradford@wyjs.org.uk
Website: www.archives.wyjs.org.uk

Enquiries to: Archivist

Founded: 1982

Organisation type and purpose: Local government body.
Record office.

Subject coverage: Primary source material for historical and other purposes.

Collection: Local authority records, parish and nonconformist records, family and estate records, business records, political and trade union records, etc.

Non-library collection catalogue: All or part available online, in-house and in print

Publications: Printed

Publications list: Available online

Access to staff: Contact by letter, by telephone, by fax, by e-mail and in person. Appointment necessary.
Hours: Tue, Thu, Fri 0930 to 1700; Mon and Wed, closed

Constituent part of: West Yorkshire Archive Service; West Yorkshire Joint Services; tel: 0113 289 8214; e-mail: info@wyjs.org.uk; website: http://www.wyjs.org.uk

Supported by: Metropolitan District Councils of Bradford, Calderdale, Kirklees, Leeds and Wakefield

WEST YORKSHIRE ARCHIVE SERVICE – CALDERDALE

Central Library, Northgate, Halifax, West Yorkshire, HX1 1UN

Tel: 01422 392636
E-mail: calderdale@wyjs.org.uk
Website: www.archives.wyjs.org.uk

Enquiries to: Administrator
Direct e-mail: archives@wyjs.org.uk

Founded: 1964; formerly called Calderdale District Archive Service (year of change 1983)

Organisation type and purpose: Local government body.
A county-wide archive service.

Subject coverage: Primary source material for historical and other purposes.

Collection: Local authority records, nonconformist records, family and estate records, business records, charities and societies records, political and trade union records, etc.

Non-library collection catalogue: All or part available online, in-house and in print

Publications: Printed

Publications list: Available online and in print

Access to staff: Contact by letter, by telephone, by e-mail, in person and via website. Appointment necessary.
Hours: Tue, Thu, Fri, 0930 to 1700; Mon, Wed, closed

Access for disabled people: Parking provided, level entry, access to all public areas

Constituent part of: West Yorkshire Archive Service

Supported by: Metropolitan District Councils of Bradford, Calderdale, Kirklees, Leeds and Wakefield

WEST YORKSHIRE ARCHIVE SERVICE – KIRKLEES

Central Library, Princess Alexandra Walk, Huddersfield, West Yorkshire, HD1 2SU

Tel: 01484 221966
E-mail: kirklees@wyjs.org.uk
Website: www.archives.wyjs.org.uk

Enquiries to: Archivist

Founded: 1982

Organisation type and purpose: Local government body.

Subject coverage: Primary source material for historical and other purposes relating to the Kirklees District.

Collection: Local authority records, nonconformist records, family and estate records, business records (especially textile industry), society records, etc.

Non-library collection catalogue: All or part available online, in-house and in print

Publications: Printed, and electronic and video, and microform publications
Order printed publications from: Publication Sales Office, West Yorkshire Archive Service HQ
Registry of Deeds, Newstead Road, Wakefield, WF1 2DE; tel: 01924 305982; e-mail: wakefield@wyjs.org.uk or via e-shop at https://eshop.wyjs.org.uk

Publications list: Available online and in print

Access to staff: Contact by letter, by telephone, by e-mail, in person and via website. Appointment necessary.
Hours: Mon, Tue, Thu, 0930 to 1700; Wed and Fri, closed; 3rd Sat of month, 0900 to 1300

Access for disabled people: There is disabled access

Constituent part of: West Yorkshire Archive Service

Parent body: West Yorkshire Joint Services; PO Box 5, Nepshaw Lane South, Morley, Leeds, LS27 0QP; tel: 0113 2530241; fax: 0113 2530311; e-mail: info@wyjs.org.uk; website: http://www.wyjs.org.uk

Supported by: Metropolitan District Councils of Bradford, Calderdale, Kirklees, Leeds and Wakefield

WEST YORKSHIRE ARCHIVE SERVICE – LEEDS (WYAS)

2 Chapeltown Road, Sheepscar, Leeds, West Yorkshire, LS7 3AP

Tel: 0113 214 5814
E-mail: leeds@wyjs.org.uk
Website: www.archives.wyjs.org.uk

Founded: 1938

Organisation type and purpose: Local government body.
Archive service.

Subject coverage: Primary source material for historical and other purposes.

Collection: Local authority records
Parish and nonconformist records; family and estate records; business records; voluntary bodies, charities and societies records, political and trade union records, manorial records, tithe records, solicitors and estate agents papers
Major deposited collections:
Family and estate archives including:
Baines family of Leeds
Gascoigne family of Parlington
Earl of Mexborough
Earl of Harewood
Ingilby family of Ripley Castle
Lane Fox family of Bramham Park
Newby Hall Estate
Nostell Priory
Ramsden family of Byram
Samuel Smiles papers
Studley Royal Estate including Fountains Abbey
Temple Newsam
Business records, including:
T and M Bairstow
British Coal
Burton Group
Joshua Tetley
John Wilson
Yorkshire Patent Steam Waggon Co

Non-library collection catalogue: All or part available online, in-house and in print

Publications: Printed, and microform publications
Order printed publications from: Sue Pad, WYAS, Wakefield, Newstead Road, Wakefield, WF1 2DE
Order microform publications from: Sue Pad, WYAS, Wakefield, Newstead Road, Wakefield, WF1 2DE

Publications list: Available online and in print

Access to staff: Contact by letter, by telephone, by e-mail, in person and via website. Appointment necessary.
Hours: Mon, Tue, Thur 0900 to 1700; Wed, Fri, closed

Constituent part of: West Yorkshire Archive Service

Supported by: Metropolitan District Councils of Bradford, Calderdale, Kirklees, Leeds and Wakefield

WEST YORKSHIRE ARCHIVE SERVICE – WAKEFIELD

Registry of Deeds Building, Newstead Road, Wakefield, West Yorkshire, WF1 2DE

Tel: 01924 305980
Fax: 01924 305983
E-mail: wakefield@wyjs.org.uk
Website: www.archives.wyjs.org.uk

Enquiries to: Archivist

Organisation type and purpose: Local government body. Archive service.

Subject coverage: Primary source material for historical and other purposes, including administration at county, district and parish levels, religion, law and order, education, health, historical geography, transport, property rights, rights of way, industry.

Collection: Manuscript documentation on the West Riding and on Wakefield District from the Middle Ages to the present day; West Riding Quarter Sessions records; local authority records including former West Riding County Council and West Yorkshire Metropolitan County Council; West Riding Registry of Deeds records; records of public bodies and utilities; county-wide records; Wakefield Diocesan parish records and records of public bodies; nonconformist records; family and estate records; business records; charities and societies records; courts, coroners, estates, schools, probate registry, hospitals, political and trade union records, etc.

Trade and statistical information: 1971 Census of distribution maps. 1960 Land utilisation maps. 19th- and 20th-century records of businesses.

Non-library collection catalogue: All or part available online and in print

Library catalogue: All or part available online and in print

Publications: Printed, and microform publications
Order printed publications from: Administration Officer, West Yorkshire Archive Service, at the same address; tel: 01924 305982; e-mail: spad@wyjs.org.uk
Order microform publications from: Administration Officer, as above

Publications list: Available online and in print

Access to staff: Contact by letter, by telephone, by fax, by e-mail, in person and via website. Appointment necessary.
Hours: Mon, Tue, Thu, 0930 to 1700; 2nd & 4th Mon, 0930 to 2000; 2nd Sat in month, 0930 to 1300; closed Wed, Fri, Sun
Special comments: CARN tickets required. Appointment recommended as the searchrooms can get very busy.

Access for disabled people: Parking provided
Special comments: Disabled access not available; wheelchair users have to be lifted into building or, if able to walk a little, use handrails by steps.

continued overleaf

Constituent part of: West Yorkshire Joint Service; PO Box 5, Nepshaw Lane South, Morley, Leeds, LS27 0PQ; tel: 0113 289 8214; e-mail: info@wyjs.org.uk; website: http://www.wyjs.org.uk

Supported by: Metropolitan District Councils of Bradford, Calderdale, Kirklees, Leeds and Wakefield

Works under the guidance of the: Lord Chancellor's Department with regard to public records; Master of the Rolls with regard to tithe and manorial records

WESTCOUNTRY STUDIES LIBRARY (WSL)

Exeter Central Library, Castle Street, Exeter, Devon, EX4 3PQ

Tel: 01392 384216
Fax: 01392 384228
E-mail: westcountry.library@devon.gov.uk
Website: www.devon.gov.uk/localstudies

Enquiries to: Westcountry Studies Librarian

Founded: 1870; formerly called Royal Albert Memorial; formerly called Exeter City Library (year of change 1974)

Organisation type and purpose: Local government body, public library. Main local studies collection for Devon Library and Information Services. Reference library.

Subject coverage: All aspects of Devon and the adjoining counties, past and present.

Collection: Brooking Rowe collection (local history, brass rubbings, bookplates)
Burnet Morris index on Devon history
Devon and Cornwall Record Society (collections and unpublished transcripts, available to members; membership can be taken out in the library)
Devon Folk Life Register
Heber Mardon Collection of Napoleonic illustrations
Pike Ward collection (Iceland)
Pocknell collection of shorthand books

Non-library collection catalogue: All or part available online

Library catalogue: All or part available in-house

Publications: Printed, and electronic and video, and microform publications

Publications list: Available online

Access to staff: Contact by letter, by telephone, by e-mail, in person and via website
Hours: Mon and Fri, 0930 to 1800; Tue and Thu, 0930 to 1900; Wed, 1000 to 1700; Sat, 0930 to 1600

Branch library: North Devon Local Studies Centre; Tuly Street, Barnstaple, Devon, EX32 7EJ; tel: 01271 388607

Parent body: Devon Library and Information Services; Devon County Council; tel: 01392 384315

WESTERKIRK PARISH LIBRARY

Bentpath, Langholm, Dumfriesshire, DB13 0PB

Enquiries to: Chairman of the Trustees
Direct tel: 013873 70201
Other contacts: Mrs M. Sanderson, Chairman of the Trustees: Westerkirk Schoolhouse, Langholm DG13 0PB, tel: 013873 70201

Founded: 1793

Organisation type and purpose: Library. Registered Scottish charity (charity number SCO20308)

Subject coverage: Parish records

Collection: 8,000 books (mid-18th century to the present)

Access to staff: Contact by letter and by telephone. Appointment necessary.

Access to building: *Hours:* 1st Mon of month, 1900 to 2000 (by appointment with staff)

WESTERN ISLES LIBRARIES

19 Cromwell Street, Stornoway, Isle of Lewis, HS1 2DA

Tel: 01851 708631
Fax: 01851 708676
Website: www.cne-siar.gov.uk

Enquiries to: Chief Librarian
Direct tel: 01851 708641
Other contacts: Senior Librarian Adult Services, Senior Librarian Youth Services

Organisation type and purpose: Local government body, public library.

Subject coverage: General, local history, Gaelic.

Collection: An Comunn Gaidhealach collection of Gaelic and Highland language and history
Donald MacDonald Papers
Gaelic Collection including recorded sound, language, learning, books and periodicals
Local history of the Western Isles
Morrison Manuscripts
School Board minute books
School log books
T B Macaulay photographs collection

Library catalogue: All or part available online

Access to staff: Contact by letter, by telephone, by fax and in person
Hours: Mon to Wed, 1000 to 1700; Thu and Fri, 1000 to 1800; Sat, 1000 to 1700

Access for disabled people: Access to all public areas, toilet facilities

Parent body: Comhairle Nan Eilean Siar (formerly Western Isles Islands Council)

WESTERN KURDISTAN ASSOCIATION

Palingswick House, 241 King Street, London, W6 9LP

Tel: 020 8748 7874
Fax: 020 8741 6436
E-mail: info@westernkurdistan.org.uk
Website: www.westernkurdistan.org.uk

Organisation type and purpose: Community centre for Kurdish refugees, offering help in matters such as immigration, welfare, housing and health, and courses in English language and other subjects. Administers a Kurdish museum, library and archive.

Information services: Newsletter, websites radio and TV broadcasting in Kurdish, English and other languages.

Special visitor services: Kurdish Museum, Library and Archive.

Education services: Courses in English language, computers, internet, media and film-making.

Collection: Historical and cultural archive of the Kurdish community

Access to building: *Hours:* Mon to Fri, 1000 to 1700
Special comments: Access to archive is by appointment only.

WESTMINSTER (ROMAN CATHOLIC) DIOCESAN ARCHIVES

16a Abingdon Road, Kensington, London, W8 6AF

Tel: 020 7938 3580

Enquiries to: Administrator

Organisation type and purpose: Diocesan archive.

Subject coverage: History of England's post-reformation Roman Catholic community.

Non-library collection catalogue: All or part available in-house

Library catalogue: All or part available in-house

Access to staff: Contact by letter and by telephone. Appointment necessary.
Hours: Tue, Wed, Thu, 1000 to 1600

Access to building: Prior appointment required
Hours: Tue, Wed, Thu, 1000 to 1600
Special comments: The Archive is private. Letter of introduction required.

WESTMINSTER ABBEY

Library and Muniment Room, London, SW1P 3PA

Tel: 020 7654 4830
Fax: 020 7654 4827
E-mail: library@westminster-abbey.org
Website: www.westminster-abbey.org/library

Enquiries to: Librarian
Direct tel: 020 7654 4826
Other contacts: Keeper of the Muniments (for archives)

Founded: 1623

Organisation type and purpose: Abbey church library and archives collection.

Subject coverage: History of Westminster Abbey and its precincts, coronations, St Margaret's Westminster.

Collection: c. 14,000 early printed books
c. 70,000 documents relating to the Abbey since 1066
Collection of books on the history of Westminster Abbey
Collection of illuminated and other medieval manuscripts
Collection of Pamphlets belonging to William Camden (1551–1623)
K H Oldaker Collection of English Bookbindings, 1655–1920

Langley collection of prints and drawings
Large photographic collection
Music Collection (mainly late 16th and 17th centuries)

Non-library collection catalogue: All or part available in print

Library catalogue: All or part available in-house

Publications: Printed, and microform publications

Access to staff: Contact by letter, by telephone, by fax, by e-mail and via website. Appointment necessary.
Hours: Mon to Fri, 1000 to 1300 and 1400 to 1645

Access for disabled people: Medieval building with staircases. Please consult staff about alternative arrangements for access to library materials

WESTMINSTER COLLEGE LIBRARY (CAMBRIDGE)

Madingley Road, Cambridge, CB3 0AA

Tel: 01223 741084
Fax: 01223 300765
Website: www.westminster.cam.ac.uk

Enquiries to: Librarian
Direct tel: 01223 741043
Direct e-mail: cr248@cam.ac.uk

Founded: 1844; created by the merger of Presbyterian theological college and a Congregational College; formerly called Cheshunt College, Westminster College

Organisation type and purpose: Suitable for ages: 18+.
Preparation of men and women for the Christian ministry.

Subject coverage: Theological and Biblical studies, particularly Reformed theology and church history, philosophy of religion, Christian ethics and pastoral studies.

Collection: Archives of the Countess of Huntingdon's colleges and chapels
Archive material of the Ecclesiastical History Society of the United Reformed Church
Elias Library of Hymnology
Lewis and Gibson Collection of manuscripts from the Cairo Synagogue Genizah (complements the University Library's Taylor-Schechter Collection)
Library of the Ecclesiastical History Society of the United Reformed Church
Todd Collection of liturgical works

Non-library collection catalogue: All or part available online and in-house

Library catalogue: All or part available online

Access to staff: Contact by letter and by e-mail. Appointment necessary. Letter of introduction required. Non-members charged.
Hours: Mon to Fri, 0900 to 1600
Special comments: Open to members of the Cambridge Theological Federation, ministers of the United Reformed Church and approved external members only.

Parent body: United Reformed Church

WESTMINSTER LIBRARIES AND ARCHIVES

Charing Cross Library, 4 Charing Cross Road, London, WC2H 0HF

Tel: 020 7641 6573
Fax: 020 7641 6551
Website: www.westminster.gov.uk/index/libraries.cfm

Enquiries to: Westminster Libraries Manager
Direct e-mail: a.stevens@dial.pipex.com
Other contacts: Archives Centre for full list of current publications tel no: 020 7641 5180.

History of institution: formerly called Westminster City Archives and Libraries

Organisation type and purpose: Local government body.
Public library and archive.

Subject coverage: Local studies and archives at City of Westminster Archives; music at Westminster Music Library; art and design, official publications, EU at Westminster Reference Library.

Collection: Archive and local history collections (City of Westminster Archives)
Ashbridge Collection (City of Westminster Archives)
Gillow Archives (furniture design history, Victoria Library)
Sherlock Holmes Collection (Marylebone Library)

Non-library collection catalogue: All or part available online

Library catalogue: All or part available online

Publications: Printed

Publications list: Available in print

Access to staff: Contact by letter, by telephone and by e-mail
Hours: Mon to Fri, 0900 to 1700
Special comments: Please telephone individual sites for opening hours and to establish restrictions on access.

Headquarters: Westminster Libraries and Archives Headquarters; Westminster City Hall, Victoria Street, London, SW1E 6QP; tel: 020 7641 2496

Other addresses: Charing Cross Library; Charing Cross Road, London, WC2H 0HG; tel: 020 7641 4628; Church Street Library; Church Street, London, NW8 8EU; tel: 020 7641 5479; City of Westminster Archives Centre; 10 St Ann's Street, London, SW1T 2XR; tel: 020 7641 5180; Maida Vale Library; Sutherland Avenue, London, W9 2QT; tel: 020 7641 3659; Marylebone Library; Marylebone Road, London, NW1 5PS; tel: 020 7641 1037; Mayfair Library; 25 South Audley Street, London, W1Y 5DJ; tel: 020 7641 4903; Paddington Library; Porchester Road, London, W2 5DU; tel: 020 7641 4475; Pimlico Library; Rampayne Street, London, SW1V 2PU; tel: 020 7641 2983; Queen's Park Library; 666 Harrow Road, London, W10 4NE; tel: 020 7641 4575; St James's Library; 62 Victoria Street, London, SW1E 6QP; tel: 020 7641 2989; St John's Wood Library; 20 Circus Road, London, NW8 6PD; tel: 020 7641 5087; Victoria Library; 160 Buckingham Palace Road, London, SW1W 9UD; tel: 020 7641 4287; Westminster Music Library; Victoria Library, 160 Buckingham Palace Road, London, SW1W 9UD; tel: 020 7641 4292; Westminster Reference Library; St Martin's Street, London, WC2H 7HP; tel: 020 7641 4636

Parent body: Westminster City Council

WESTMINSTER REFERENCE LIBRARY

35 St Martins Street, London, WC2H 7HP

Tel: 020 7641 4634/4636/4638
Fax: 020 7641 4606
E-mail: westreflib@dial.pipex.com
Website: www.westminster.gov.uk/libraries/search
Website: www.westminster.gov.uk/libraries/libraries/westref

Enquiries to: Manager
Direct tel: 020 7641 5260
Direct e-mail: tarathoon@dial.pipex.com

History of institution: formerly called Westminster Central Reference Library

Organisation type and purpose: Local government body, public library.

Subject coverage: A general public reference library specialising in the following key areas:
Business: market research, business directories and international telephone directories, company information.
Official Publications: HMSO publications since 1947, Parliamentary papers since 1906, Hansard since 1803, EU Official Publications.
Arts: covering art, fine arts, painting, drawing, sculpture, ceramics, glassware, coins, tapestry, carpets, furniture, jewellery, interior design, costume, goldsmiths' work, silverware, arms and armour, architecture, antiques, collecting, cinema, film, theatre, radio and television and dance.

Collection: EU Depository Library

Trade and statistical information: Wide range of UK, EU and International statistics

Non-library collection catalogue: All or part available online

Library catalogue: All or part available online

Access to staff: Contact by letter, by telephone, by fax, by e-mail, in person and via website
Hours: Mon to Fri, 1000 to 2000; Sat, 1000 to 1700
Special comments: Reference library.

Also at: Marylebone Information Service (MIS); 109–117 Marylebone Road, London, NW1 5PS; tel: 020 7641 1031; fax: 020 7641 1028; e-mail: m.i.s@dial.pipex.com

Parent body: Westminster City Council

WESTON COLLEGE

Learning Resources Centre, Knightstone Road, Weston-super-Mare, Somerset, BS23 2AL

Tel: 01934 411411
Fax: 01934 411410
E-mail: college@weston.ac.uk
Website: www.weston.ac.uk

Enquiries to: Librarian
Direct tel: 01934 411409
Direct e-mail: lrc@weston.ac.uk

continued overleaf

History of institution: formerly called Weston-Super-Mare College of Further Education

Organisation type and purpose: Further Education.

Subject coverage: General, psychology, sociology, social sciences, catering, hairdressing, electronics, engineering, business, care, art, leisure, drugs information base, computer studies, information technology, music technology, sciences, languages, EFL, humanities, education, sign language.

Collection: Drugs information base

Publications: Printed

Access to staff: Contact by letter, by telephone, by fax, by e-mail, in person and via website
Hours: Term time: Mon to Thu, 0845 to 2100, Fri, 0845 to 1700
Vacations: Mon to Fri, 0900 to 1700

Access for disabled people: Parking provided, ramped entry, toilet facilities

Also at: Weston College 6th Form Library; Loxton Road, Weston-super-Mare, Somerset; tel: 01934 411615

WESTONBIRT, THE NATIONAL ARBORETUM

Forestry Commission England, Tetbury, Gloucestershire, GL8 8QS

Tel: 01666 880220
Fax: 01666 880559
E-mail: westonbirt@forestry.gsi.gov.uk
Website: www.forestry.gov.uk/westonbirt
Website: www.fowa.org.uk

Enquiries to: Reception
Direct tel: 01666 880220
Direct fax: 01666 880559
Direct e-mail: westonbirt@forestry.gsi.gov.uk

Founded: 1829

Organisation type and purpose: Government Department

Subject coverage: Arboriculture, forestry, trees and shrubs in general.

Services for disabled people: All main paths and facilities are accessible for less able visitors. Electric scooters and wheelchairs are also available to hire, pre-book on: 01666 881218.

Collection: 600 acres of picturesque, historic landscape, covered by 17 miles of paths; a collection of 16,000 trees, some of the oldest, rarest and largest of their kind in the UK; tree and shrub collection on computer database, over 18,000 records.

Non-library collection catalogue: All or part available in-house

Access to staff: Contact by letter, by telephone, by fax, by e-mail and via website. Appointment necessary.

Access to building: *Hours:* The grounds are open every day of the year; please check website for current times and prices

Access for disabled people: Parking provided, ramped entry, toilet facilities, mobility scooters can be booked

Constituent part of: Forestry Commission

WEYMOUTH COLLEGE

Library, Cranford Avenue, Weymouth, Dorset, DT4 7LQ

Tel: 01305 208820
E-mail: library@weymouth.ac.uk
Website: www.weymouth.ac.uk

Enquiries to: Librarian

Founded: 1985; formerly called South Dorset Technical College (year of change 1985)

Organisation type and purpose: Further education college with some HE courses.

Subject coverage: Art, biology, business studies, careers, catering, chemistry, computer studies, conservation, construction, engineering, geography, hairdressing, history, maths, physics, physical education, sociology, tourism, education, stone carving, beauty, dance, drama, music, management, public services

Collection: Fleet Study archive

Library catalogue: All or part available online and in-house

Publications: Printed

Access to staff: Contact by letter, by telephone, by e-mail and in person
Hours: Term time: Mon, 0830 to 1700; Tue to Thu, 0830 to 2000; Fri, 0830 to 1700; Sat, Sun, closed
Vacations: daily, 0830 to 1700

Access for disabled people: Level entry, access to all public areas, toilet facilities

WHALE AND DOLPHIN CONSERVATION SOCIETY (WDCS)

Brookfield House, 38 St Paul Street, Chippenham, Wiltshire, SN15 1LY

Tel: 01249 449500
Fax: 01249 449501
E-mail: info@wdcs.org
Website: www.bluetravel.co.uk
Website: www.wdcs.org

Founded: 1987

Organisation type and purpose: Registered charity (charity number 1014705).
The global voice for the protection of whales, dolphins and their environment.

Subject coverage: Conservation of all species of whale, dolphin and porpoise.

Publications: Printed

Access to staff: Contact by letter, by telephone, by fax, by e-mail and via website
Hours: Mon to Fri, 0900 to 1700

WHEELYBOAT TRUST, THE

North Lodge, Burton Park, Petworth, West Sussex, GU28 0JT

Tel: 01798 342222
Fax: 01798 342222
E-mail: wheelyboats@tiscali.co.uk
Website: www.wheelyboats.org

Enquiries to: Director

Founded: 1984; formerly called Handicapped Anglers Trust – Boating for the Disabled

Organisation type and purpose: Registered charity (charity number 292216).
Promoting solutions for access by disabled people to fisheries, waterways and other bodies of water.

Subject coverage: Access by disabled people to fisheries and other waterways. Disability Discrimination Act 1995 – advice on implications of the act on fisheries and other waterways.

Access to staff: Contact by letter, by telephone, by fax and by e-mail
Hours: Mon to Fri, 0900 to 1700

Access to building: No access other than to staff

WHERNSIDE MANOR

Formal name: Whernside Manor Bunkhouses

Cave and Fell Centre, Dent, Sedburgh, Cumbria, LA10 5RE

Tel: 01539 625213
E-mail: whernsidemanor@aol.com
Website: www.whernsidemanor.com

Enquiries to: Manager

Founded: 2000; Changed ownership (year of change 2000)

Organisation type and purpose: Historic building, house or site.

Subject coverage: Caving, walking.

Publications: Printed

Access to staff: Contact by letter. Appointment necessary.
Hours: Mon to Fri, 0900 to 1700

Access to building: Prior appointment required

WHICHINTRO.COM

18 Thayer Street, London, W1U 3JY

Tel: 020 7935 6408
Fax: 020 7486 3817
Website: www.whichintro.com

Enquiries to: Information Officer

Founded: 1970; formerly called Society of Marriage Bureaux (SMB) (year of change 1999)

Organisation type and purpose: National organisation (membership is by subscription), service industry, research organisation.
Searchable database on all organisations in UK offering introduction services; plus advice and guidance on selecting and using such agencies.

Subject coverage: Joining a marriage bureau or introductory agency, things to be aware of and alert to, general information about the industry, objective comment on proposed legislation and news items. Comprehensive information on fees, methodology, specialisms and location of introduction agencies.

Collection: Many brochures from introduction agencies
Various books on marriage and finding partners

Trade and statistical information: Number of active agencies; membership numbers; agencies ceasing to trade; new agencies

Publications: Printed, and electronic and video

Access to staff: Contact by letter, by telephone, by e-mail and via website
Hours: Mon to Fri, 0900 to 1700 by telephone.

WHITAKER

Woolmead House West, Bear Lane, Farnham, Surrey, GU9 7LG

Tel: 01252 742500
Fax: 01252 742501

Enquiries to: Sales Manager

Organisation type and purpose: Publishing house.

Subject coverage: Bibliographic files of English language books published in the UK and over 70 other countries which are or were in print and those which are forthcoming.

Trade and statistical information: Data on the publication of English language titles published in the UK or with a stock holding distributor in the UK

Publications: Printed, and electronic and video, and microform publications

Access to staff: Contact by letter, by telephone, by fax and by e-mail
Hours: Mon to Fri, 0900 to 1700

Associated with: BookTrack Limited; tel: 01252 542555; e-mail: booktrack.info@booktrack.co.uk; Teleordering Limited

Connections with: Standard Book Numbering Agency Limited; 12 Dyott Street, London, WC1A 1DF

WHITWELL LOCAL HISTORY GROUP

10 Jubilee Road, Whitwell, Nottinghamshire, S80 4PL

Tel: 01909 723230
E-mail: wlhg@hopkins-uk.co.uk
Website: www.wlhg.co.uk

Enquiries to: Secretary

Founded: 1986

Organisation type and purpose: Local history group.

Subject coverage: Local and national history, allied topics on a variety of subjects.

Education services: Contact with local school.

Publications: Printed

Access to staff: Contact by letter, by telephone, by e-mail and via website

WIENER LIBRARY

Formal name: The Wiener Library for the Study of the Holocaust and Genocide

29 Russell Square, London, WC1B 5DP

Tel: 020 7636 7247
Fax: 020 7436 6428
E-mail: info@wienerlibrary.co.uk
Website: www.wienerlibrary.co.uk

Enquiries to: Librarian
Direct e-mail: library@wienerlibrary.co.uk
Other contacts: Senior Librarian

Founded: 1933; formerly called Institute of Contemporary History and Wiener Library; formerly called Jewish Central Information Office; formerly called The Wiener Library Institute of Contemporary History (year of change 2011)

Organisation type and purpose: Registered charity (number 313015), research library, open to the public.
Extensive archive on the Holocaust and Nazi era, with a collection of over 1m. items.

Subject coverage: Holocaust, Third Reich, fascism, neo-fascism, German-Jewish history, exile and refugee studies, anti-Semitism.

Collection: Books and pamphlets (c. 60,000)
Periodicals (c. 3,000 titles and 140 current subscriptions)
Document collections (c. 1,300)
Eyewitness accounts (of survivors of the Holocaust)
Photo Archive (over 10,000)
Press Archive

Non-library collection catalogue: All or part available online

Library catalogue: All or part available online

Publications: Printed, and electronic and video

Access to staff: Contact by letter, by telephone, by fax, by e-mail, in person and via website. Letter of introduction required.
Hours: Mon to Fri, 10.00 to 17.00; Tue 10.00 to 19.30

Access to building: 5 steps from the street.
Hours: Mon to Fri, 10.00 to 17.00; Tue 10.00 to 19.30

Access for disabled people: Visitors with mobility impairments or conditions which preclude them from using the evacuation chairs in an emergency are advised to inform the Library prior to their visit. The Library will then provide access by these visitors to its materials in an accessible reading room at Birkbeck College.

Links with: Institute of Contemporary History

WIGAN ARCHIVES SERVICE

Leigh Town Hall, Leigh, Lancashire, WN7 1DY

Tel: 01942 404430
Fax: 01942 827645
E-mail: heritage@wlct.org
Website: www.wlct.org/heritage-services/wigan-archives-service.htm

Enquiries to: Archivist

Founded: 1968; formerly called Wigan Record Office

Organisation type and purpose: Local government body.

Collection: Archive

Non-library collection catalogue: All or part available online, in-house and in print

Publications: Printed

Access to staff: Contact by letter, by telephone, by fax, by e-mail and in person. Appointment necessary.
Hours: Tue to Thu, 1000 to 1630

Access to building: Prior appointment required
Hours: To view documents: Tue to Thu, 1000 to 1630

Access for disabled people: Access to all public areas

Parent body: Wigan Leisure and Culture Trust; Robin Park Headquarters, Loire Drive, Robin Park, Wigan. WN5 0UL; tel: 01942 828508; e-mail: leisureenquiries@wlct.org; website: http://www.wlct.org/

WIGAN HERITAGE SERVICE

The Museum of Wigan Life, Library Street, Wigan, Lancashire, WN1 1NU

Tel: 01942 828128
Fax: 01942 827645
E-mail: heritage@wlct.org
Website: www.wlct.org/heritage

Enquiries to: Operations Services Manager
Other contacts: Collection Department Manager for collections.

Founded: 1992

Organisation type and purpose: Local government body, museum, suitable for ages: 12+.

Subject coverage: Local history – all types, genealogy.

Services for disabled people: Displays and/or information at wheelchair height.

Collection: Social and industrial history
Family history, parish records, census material

Access to staff: Contact by letter, by telephone, by fax, by e-mail and in person
Hours: Mon, Tue, Wed, Fri, 1000 to 1700; Thu, 1000 to 2000; Sat, 1100 to 1500

Access to building: No prior appointment required
Hours: Mon,Tue, Fri, 1000 to 1700; Thurs 10.00–20.00 Sat, 1100 to 1500
Special comments: Closed Wednesdays and Sundays

Access for disabled people: Ramped entry, toilet facilities, lift to 1st Floor
Hours: As above

WIGAN LIBRARY

Wigan Life Centre North, The Wiend, Wigan, Lancs, WN1 1NH

Tel: 01942 827621
Fax: 01942 827640
E-mail: wigan.library@wlct.org
Website: www.wlct.org

Enquiries to: Information and Learning Officer
Direct tel: 01942 489772

Organisation type and purpose: Public library.

Subject coverage: General subjects.

Collection: Dootson Collection (Lancashire and local history at Leigh Library)

continued overleaf

Non-library collection catalogue: All or part available online

Library catalogue: All or part available online

Access to staff: Contact by letter, by telephone, by fax, by e-mail, in person and via website
Hours: Mon, Wed, Fri, 0900 to 1700; Tue, Thu, 0900 to 2000; Sat, 0900 to 1700
Special comments: Prior arrangement required to consult the Dootson Collection

Access for disabled people: Ramped entry, toilet facilities

Parent body: Wigan Leisure & Culture Trust; Loire Drive, Robin Park, Wigan, WN5 0UL; tel: 01942 828508; fax: 01942 828540; website: http://www.wlct.org

WILCO

Central Library, Regent Circus, Swindon, Wiltshire, SN1 1QG

Tel: 01793 463796/7
Fax: 01793 541319
E-mail: rtrayhurn@swindon.gov.uk
Website: www.wilco.org.uk

Enquiries to: Secretary
Other contacts: Treasurer

Founded: 1974; formerly called Wiltshire Libraries in Co-operation

Organisation type and purpose: Local government body, membership association (membership is by election or invitation), present number of members: 20 Full, 10 Associate.
Library co-operative scheme between public, government, academic, research and industrial libraries.

Subject coverage: Business, commercial and industrial information, standards, journals, reports, serials, monographs, in a wide range of business topics.

Non-library collection catalogue: All or part available online

Access to staff: Contact by telephone, by fax and by e-mail. Access for members only.
Hours: Mon to Fri, 0930 to 1900; Sat, 0930 to 1600

WILDFOWL & WETLANDS TRUST (WWT)

Slimbridge, Gloucestershire, GL2 7BT

Tel: 01453 891900
Fax: 01453 890827
E-mail: information@wwt.org.uk
Website: www.wwt.org.uk

Enquiries to: Managing Director
Direct e-mail: marketing@wwt.org.uk

Founded: 1946; formerly called Wildfowl Trust

Organisation type and purpose: Registered charity (charity number 1030884).
Trust for conservation, education, and research; 8 visitors centres throughout the UK.

Subject coverage: Conservation of: wildfowl and their habitat, mainly geese, ducks and swans but also considerable data on other waterfowl; wildfowl populations, behaviour, migration, nutrition and disease; breeding of wildfowl; wetlands; ponds, streams, lakes, rivers, marshes, bogs, wet meadows, ecology, management, conservation, aviculture.

Collection: Library of books and documents on wildfowl and wetlands

Publications: Printed

Publications list: Available in print

Access to staff: Contact by letter, by telephone and by fax
Hours: Mon to Fri, 0900 to 1700

Also at: London Wetland Centre; Queen Elizabeth's Walk, Barnes, London, SW13 9WT; tel: 020 8409 4400; e-mail: info.london@wwt.org.uk; National Wetlands Centre Wales; Llanelli Centre, Penclawydd, Llwynhendy, Llanelli, SA14 9SH; tel: 01554 741087; fax: 01554 744101; e-mail: info.llanelli@wwt.org.uk; Wildfowl & Wetlands Trust; Castle Espie, Ballydrain Road, Comber, Co Down, BT23 6EA; tel: 028 9187 4146; fax: 028 9187 3857; e-mail: info.castleespie@wwt.org.uk; Wildfowl & Wetlands Trust; Pintail House, Hundred Foot Bank, Welney, Wisbech, Cambridgeshire, PE14 9TN; tel: 01353 860711; fax: 01353 860711; e-mail: info.welney@wwt.org.uk; Wildfowl & Wetlands Trust; Martin Mere, Burscough, Ormskirk, Lancashire, L40 0TA; tel: 01704 895181; fax: 01704 892343; e-mail: info.martinmere@wwt.org.uk; Wildfowl & Wetlands Trust; District 15, Washington, Tyne & Wear, NE38 8LE; tel: 0191 416 5454; fax: 0191 416 5801; e-mail: info.washington@wwt.org.uk; Wildfowl & Wetlands Trust; Mill Road, Arundel, West Sussex, BN18 9PB; tel: 01903 883355; fax: 01903 884834; e-mail: info.arundel@wwt.org.uk; Wildfowl & Wetlands Trust; Eastpark Farm, Caerlaverock, Dumfriesshire, DG1 4RS; tel: 01387 770200; fax: 01387 770539; e-mail: info.caerlaverock@wwt.org.uk

Constituent bodies: Wildfowl & Wetlands Trust (Consulting) Ltd; Slimbridge, Gloucestershire, GL2 7BT; tel: 01453 891905; fax: 01453 890827; e-mail: consulting@wwt.org.uk; website: http://www.wwtconsulting.co.uk
Wildfowl & Wetlands Trust (Property) Ltd

WILDLIFE TRUSTS

The Kiln, Mather Road, Waterside, Newark, Nottinghamshire, NG24 1WT

Tel: 01636 677711
Fax: 01636 670001
E-mail: info@wildlife-trusts.cix.co.uk
Website: www.wildlifetrust.org

Enquiries to: Information Officer

Founded: 1912; formerly called Royal Society for Nature Conservation

Organisation type and purpose: Voluntary organisation, registered charity (charity number 207238).
The protection of local countryside and wildlife inhabitants.

Subject coverage: Nature conservation, protection and enhancement of species and habitats in the UK; wildlife legislation; history of nature conservation; environmental education; membership and work of Wildlife Trusts.

Publications: Printed

Publications list: Available in print

Access to staff: Contact by letter, by e-mail and via website
Hours: Mon to Fri, 0900 to 1700

Member of: European Environment Bureau; International Union for the Conservation of Nature; Wildlife Link

Regional Offices: Avon Wildlife Trust; Wildlife Centre, 32 Jacob's Wells Road, Bristol, BS8 1DR; tel: 0117 926 8018; fax: 0117 929 7273; e-mail: avonwt@cix.compulink.co.uk; Berkshire, Buckinghamshire & Oxfordshire Wildlife Trust; The Lodge, 1 Armstrong Road, Littlemore, Oxford, OX4 4XT; tel: 01865 775476; fax: 01865 711301; e-mail: bbowt@cix.co.uk; Brecknock Wildlife Trust; Lion House, Bethel Square, Brecon, Powys, LD3 7AY; tel: 01874 625708; fax: 01874 625708; e-mail: brecknockwt@cix.co.uk; Cheshire Wildlife Trust; Grebe House, Reaseheath, Nantwich, Cheshire, CW5 6DG; tel: 01270 610180; fax: 01270 610430; e-mail: cheshirewt@cix.co.uk; Cornwall Wildlife Trust; Five Acres, Aller, Truro, Cornwall, TR4 9DJ; tel: 01872 273939; fax: 01872 225476; e-mail: cornwt@cix.co.uk; Cumbria Wildlife Trust; Brockhole, Windermere, Cumbria, LA23 1LJ; tel: 015394 48280; fax: 015394 48281; e-mail: cumbriawt@cix.co.uk; Derbyshire Wildlife Trust; East Mill, Bridgefoot, Belper, Derby, DE56 1XH; tel: 01773 881188; fax: 01773 821826; e-mail: derbywt@cix.co.uk; Devon Wildlife Trust; Shirehampton House, 35–37 St David's Hill, Exeter, Devon, EX4 4DA; tel: 01392 279244; fax: 01392 433221; e-mail: devonwt@cix.co.uk; Dorset Wildlife Trust; Brooklands Farm, Forston, Dorchester, DT2 7AA; tel: 01305 264620; fax: 01305 251120; e-mail: dorsetwt@cix.co.uk; Durham Wildlife Trust; Rainton Meadows, Chilton Moor, Houghton-le-Spring, Tyne & Wear, DH4 6PU; tel: 0191 584 3112; fax: 0191 584 3934; e-mail: durhamwt@cix.co.uk; Essex Wildlife Trust; Abbotts Hall Farm, Great Wigborough, Colchester, Essex, CO5 7RZ; tel: 01621 862960; fax: 01621 862990; e-mail: admin@essexwt.org.uk; Glamorgan Wildlife Trust; Nature Centre, Fountain Road, Tondu, Bridgend, Mid Glamorgan, CF32 0EH; tel: 01656 724100; fax: 01656 729880; e-mail: glamorganwt@cix.co.uk; Gloucestershire Wildlife Trust; Dulverton Building, Robinswood Hill Country Park, Reservoir Road, Gloucester, GL4 6SX; tel: 01452 383333; fax: 01452 383334; e-mail: gmcg@cix.co.uk; Gwent Wildlife Trust; 16 White Swan Court, Church Street, Monmouth, Gwent, NP25 3NY; tel: 01600 715501; fax: 01600 715832; e-mail: gwentwildlife@cix.co.uk; Hampshire & Isle of Wight Wildlife Trust; Woodside House, Woodside Road, Eastleigh, Hampshire, SO50 4ET; tel: 023 8061 3636; fax: 023 8068 8900; e-mail: hampswt@cix.co.uk; Herefordshire Nature Trust; Lower House Farm, Ledbury Road, Tupsley, Hereford, HR1 1UT; tel: 01432 356872; fax: 01432 275489; e-mail: herefordwt@cix.co.uk; Hertfordshire & Middlesex Wildlife Trust; Grebe House, St Michael's Street, St Albans, Hertfordshire, AL3 4SN; tel: 01727 858901; fax: 01727 854542; e-mail: hertswt@cix.co.uk; Kent Wildlife Trust; Tyland Barn, Sandling, Maidstone, Kent, ME14 3BD; tel: 01622

662012; fax: 01622 671390; e-mail: kentwildlife@cix.co.uk; Lancashire Wildlife Trust; Cuerdon Park Wildlife Centre, Shady Lane, Bamber Bridge, Preston, PR5 6AU; tel: 01772 324129; fax: 01772 628849; Leicestershire & Rutland Wildlife Trust; Longfellow Road, Knighton Fields, Leicester, LE2 6BT; tel: 01162 702999; fax: 01162 709555; e-mail: leicswt@cix.compulink.co.uk; Lincolnshire Wildlife Trust; Banovallum House, Manor House Street, Horncastle, Lincolnshire, LN9 5HF; tel: 01507 526667; fax: 01507 525732; e-mail: lincstrust@cix.compulink.co.uk; London Wildlife Trust; Harling House, 47–51 Great Suffolk Street, London, SE1 0BS; tel: 020 7261 0447; fax: 020 7261 0538; e-mail: londonwt@cix.compulink.co.uk; Manx Wildlife Trust; Conservation Centre, The Courtyard, Tynwald Mills, St Johns, Isle of Man; tel: 01624 801985; fax: 01624 801022; e-mail: manxwt@cix.co.uk; Montgomeryshire Wildlife Trust; Collott House, 20 Severn Street, Welshpool, Powys, SY21 7AD; tel: 01938 555654; fax: 01938 556161; e-mail: montwt@cix.compulink.co.uk; Norfolk Wildlife Trust; 72 Cathedral Close, Norwich, Norfolk, NR1 4DF; tel: 01603 625540; fax: 01603 630593; e-mail: nwt@cix.compulink.co.uk; North Wales Wildlife Trust; 376 High Street, Bangor, Gwynedd, LL57 1YE; tel: 01248 351541; fax: 01248 353192; e-mail: nwwt@cix.compulink.co.uk; Northumberland Wildlife Trust; The Garden House, St Nicholas Park, Jubilee Road, Newcastle upon Tyne, NE3 3XT; tel: 0191 284 6884; fax: 0191 284 6794; e-mail: northwdlife@cix.compulink.co.uk; Nottinghamshire Wildlife Trust; The Old Ragged School, Brook Street, Nottingham, NG1 1EA; tel: 0115 958 8242; fax: 0115 924 3175; e-mail: nottswt@cix.compulink.co.uk; Radnorshire Wildlife Trust; Warwick House, High Street, Llandrindod Wells, Powys, LD1 6AG; tel: 01597 823298; fax: 01597 823274; e-mail: radnorshirewt@cix.compulink.co.uk; Scottish Wildlife Trust; Crammond House, Kirk Crammond, Crammond Glebe Road, Edinburgh, EH4 6NS; tel: 0131 312 7765; fax: 0131 312 8705; e-mail: scottishwt@cix.compulink.co.uk; Sheffield Wildlife Trust; 37 Stafford Road, Sheffield, S2 2FS; tel: 0114 263 4335; fax: 0114 263 4345; e-mail: sheffieldwt@cix.co.uk; Shropshire Wildlife Trust; 193 Abbey Foregate, Shrewsbury, Shropshire; tel: 01743 284280; fax: 01743 284281; e-mail: shropshirewt@cix.co.uk; Somerset Wildlife Trust; Fyne Court, Broomfield, Bridgwater, Somerset, TA5 2EQ; tel: 01823 451587; fax: 01823 451671; e-mail: somwt@cix.co.uk; Staffordshire Wildlife Trust; Coutts House, Sandon, Staffordshire, ST18 0DN; tel: 01889 508534; fax: 01889 508422; e-mail: staffswt@cix.co.uk; Suffolk Wildlife Trust; Brooke House, The Green, Ashbocking, Ipswich, Suffolk, IP6 9JY; tel: 01473 890089; fax: 01473 890165; e-mail: suffolkwt@cix.co.uk; Surrey Wildlife Trust; School Lane, Pirbright, Woking, Surrey, GU24 0JN; tel: 01483 488055; fax: 01483 486505; e-mail: surreywt@cix.co.uk; Sussex Wildlife Trust; Woods Mill, Shoreham Road, Henfield, West Sussex, BN5 9SD; tel: 01273 492630; fax: 01273 494500; e-mail: sussexwt@cix.co.uk; Tees Valley Wildlife Trust; Bellamy Pavilion, Kirkleatham Old Hall, Kirkleatham, Redcar, Cleveland, TS10 5NW; tel: 01642 759900; fax: 01642 480401; e-mail: clevelandwt@cix.co.uk; Ulster Wildlife Trust; 3 New Line, Crossgar, Co Down, BT30 9EP; tel: 028 9083 0282; fax: 028 9083 0888; e-mail: ulsterwt@cix.co.uk; Warwickshire Wildlife Trust; Brandon Marsh Nature Centre, Brandon Lane, Coventry, CV3 3GW; tel: 01203 302912; fax: 01203 639556; e-mail: warkswt@cix.co.uk; Wildlife Trust for Bedfordshire, Cambridgeshire, Northamptonshire and Peterborough; 3B Langford Arch, London Road, Sawston, Cambridge, CB2 4EE; tel: 01223 712400; fax: 01223 712412; e-mail: cambswt@cix.co.uk; Wildlife Trust for Birmingham & Black Country; Unit 310, Jubilee Trade Centre, 130 Pershore Street, Birmingham, B5 6ND; tel: 0121 666 7474; fax: 0121 622 4443; e-mail: urbanwt@cix.co.uk; Wildlife Trust: West Wales; 7 Market Street, Haverfordwest, Dyfed, SA61 1NF; tel: 01437 765462; fax: 01437 767163; e-mail: wildlife@wildlife-wales.org.uk; Wiltshire Wildlife Trust; Elm Tree Court, Long Street, Devizes, Wiltshire, SN10 1NH; tel: 01380 725670; fax: 01380 729017; e-mail: wiltswt@cix.co.uk; Worcestershire Wildlife Trust; Lower Smite Farm, Smite Hill, Hindlip, Worcester, WR3 8SZ; tel: 01905 754919; fax: 01905 755868; e-mail: worcswt@cix.co.uk; Yorkshire Wildlife Trust; 10 Toft Green, York, YO1 6JT; tel: 01904 659570; fax: 01904 613467; e-mail: yorkshirewt@cix.co.uk

The national association of UK's: Urban Wildlife Groups; Wildlife Trusts; Wildlife Watch (the junior branch)

WILDLIFE WATCH

The Kiln, Waterside, Mather Road, Newark, Nottinghamshire, NG24 1WT

Tel: 0870 036 7711
Fax: 0870 036 0101
E-mail: watch@wildlife-trusts.cix.co.uk
Website: www.wildlifetrusts.org/watch

Enquiries to: Development Officer
Direct e-mail: arawson@wildlife-trusts.cix.co.uk
Other contacts: Membership Officer

Founded: 1971; formerly called Watch Trust for Environmental Education, Wildlife WATCH

Organisation type and purpose:
Membership association (membership is by subscription), present number of members: 20,000, voluntary organisation, registered charity (charity number 207238), suitable for ages: 7 to 14.
Junior Branch of The Wildlife Trust.
To encourage young people to investigate and help solve environmental problems.

Subject coverage: Nature conservation, environmental education, activities and projects, advice to teachers and educationalists, site interpretation via local Wildlife Trusts.

Publications: Printed

Publications list: Available in print

Access to staff: Contact by letter, by telephone, by fax, by e-mail and via website. Appointment necessary.
Hours: Mon to Fri, 0900 to 1700

WILKIE COLLINS SOCIETY (WCS)

21 Huson Close, London, NW3 3JW

E-mail: apogee@apgee.co.uk
Website: www.wilkie-collins.info/wilkie_collins_society.htm

Enquiries to: Chairman
Other contacts: Membership Secretary (paul@paullewis.co.uk)

Founded: 1980

Organisation type and purpose:
International organisation, membership association (membership is by subscription), present number of members: 145.
To foster interest in the life and works of Wilkie Collins.

Subject coverage: Wilkie Collins: biographical, literary works.

Publications: Printed
Order printed publications from: Membership Secretary, Wilkie Collins Society, 4 Ernest Gardens, London, W4 3QU; e-mail paul@paullewis.co.uk

Publications list: Available in print

Access to staff: Contact by letter and by e-mail
Hours: Mon to Fri, 0900 to 1700

Links with: Alliance of Literary Societies

WILLIAM COBBETT SOCIETY

c/o Charles Stuart, 6 Lynch Road, Farnham, Surrey, GU9 8BZ

Website: www.williamcobbett.org.uk

Enquiries to: Chairman
Direct tel: 01252 722947
Direct e-mail: charles-stuart3@talktalk.net
Other contacts: Honorary Membership Secretary (for details of membership)

Founded: 1976

Organisation type and purpose: Learned society.

Subject coverage: Life, times and writings of William Cobbett, 1763–1835.

Collection: Complete set of Cobbett's State Trials
Complete set of political registers 1802–31
Large collection of books by and about Cobbett

Publications: Printed

Publications list: Available online and in print

Access to staff: Contact by letter, by telephone and by e-mail
Hours: Mon to Fri, 0900 to 1700

Also at: Honorary Membership Secretary; 1 Meadow View, Spring Grove, Burlesdon, SO31 8BB; tel: 023 8045 5848

WILLIAM HARVEY LIBRARY

GETEC, George Eliot Hospital NHS Trust, College Street, Nuneaton, Warwickshire, CV10 7DJ

Tel: 024 7686 5464
E-mail: library@geh.nhs.uk

Enquiries to: Library Services Manager
Other contacts: Clinical Librarian

History of institution: formerly called George Eliot Postgraduate Education Centre Library (year of change 2006)

continued overleaf

Organisation type and purpose: National Health Service.

Subject coverage: Medicine, nursing, allied health, mental health, health management.

Library catalogue: All or part available online

Access to staff: Contact by letter, by telephone and by e-mail. Access for members only. Non-members charged.
Hours: Mon to Thu, 0830 to 1700; Fri, 0830 to 1630

Access to building: *Hours:* Mon to Fri, 0800 to 1700
Special comments: Outside normal opening hours access is by staff swipe card.

Access for disabled people: Toilet facilities

WILLIAM MORRIS SOCIETY

Kelmscott House, 26 Upper Mall, Hammersmith, London, W6 9TA

Tel: 020 8741 3735
Fax: 020 8748 5207
E-mail: william.morris@care4free.net
Website: www.morrissociety.org

Enquiries to: Curator

Founded: 1956; formerly called Kelmscott Fellowship, William Morris Society

Organisation type and purpose: Learned society (membership is by subscription), present number of members: 1,500, voluntary organisation, registered charity (charity number 261437), museum.

Subject coverage: The life and works of William Morris, his associates and successors in art, craft, design, literature and politics.

Collection: Library of work by and about William Morris, his associates and followers

Non-library collection catalogue: All or part available in-house

Library catalogue: All or part available in-house

Publications: Printed

Publications list: Available in print

Access to staff: Contact by letter, by telephone, by fax, by e-mail, in person and via website
Hours: Thu and Sat, 1400 to 1700

Access to building: No access other than to staff
Hours: Thu & Sat, 1400 to 1700

Access for disabled people: Level entry, toilet facilities

WILLIAM REED PUBLISHING LIMITED

Broadfield Park, Crawley, West Sussex, RH11 9RT

Tel: 01293 613400
Fax: 01293 610322
Website: www.products-online.co.uk
Website: www.william-reed.co.uk

Enquiries to: Information Officer

Founded: 1862

Organisation type and purpose: Publishing house.

Subject coverage: Food and drink manufacturing, retailing, distribution, food and drink industry, petrol forecourt shops, shopping centres; some European coverage.

Collection: Complete runs of journals published eg The Grocer 1865 to date, Off Licence News, Convenience Store, Forecourt Trader, Shopping Centre

Trade and statistical information: Food Marketing Database

Publications: Printed
Order printed publications from: website http://www.products-online.co.uk

Publications list: Available online and in print

Access to staff: Contact by telephone and by e-mail. Appointment necessary. All charged.
Hours: Mon to Fri, 1100 to 1600

WILLIAM SALT LIBRARY

19 Eastgate Street, Stafford, ST16 2LZ

Tel: 01785 278372
Fax: 01785 278414
E-mail: william.salt.library@staffordshire.gov.uk
Website: www.staffordshire.gov.uk/salt.htm

Enquiries to: Librarian

Founded: 1872

Organisation type and purpose: Registered charity (charity number 528570).
The library aims to preserve printed books, manuscripts, pamphlets and illustrative material relating to Staffordshire for future generations.

Subject coverage: Staffordshire local history.

Collection: Collections relating to Staffordshire history, including parish and family histories, topographical histories, pictorial collections, pamphlets, newspapers, periodicals, manuscripts and notes

Non-library collection catalogue: All or part available online and in-house

Library catalogue: All or part available online and in-house

Access to staff: Contact by letter, by telephone, by fax, by e-mail, in person and via website

Access to building: No prior appointment required
Hours: Tue to Thu, 1000 to 1300 and 1400 to 1600; closed Mon & Fri
Special comments: Reader's ticket is required. Reader registration system is in operation. No children under age of 11 unless accompanied by an adult.

Links with: Staffordshire Record Office; Eastgate Street, Stafford, ST16 2LZ; tel: 01785 278379; fax: 01785 278384

WILLIAM SNYDER PUBLISHING ASSOCIATES

5 Five Mile Drive, Oxford, OX2 8HT

Tel: 01865 513186
Fax: 01865 513186
E-mail: snyderpub@aol.com
Website: www.hoovers-europe.com

Enquiries to: Managing Director

Founded: 1992

Organisation type and purpose: Publishing house.

Subject coverage: Distributer of business, health and general reference publications

Library catalogue: All or part available online and in print

Publications: Printed, and electronic and video

Publications list: Available online and in print

Access to staff: Contact by letter, by telephone, by fax, by e-mail and via website

WILTSHIRE & SWINDON USERS NETWORK (WCCUIN)

Formal name: Wiltshire Community Care User Involvement Network

The Independent Living Centre, St George's Road, Semington, BA14 6JQ

Tel: 01380 871800
Fax: 01380 871507
E-mail: adminwsun@btconnect.com
Website: www.wsun.co.uk

Founded: 1993

Organisation type and purpose: Voluntary organisation.
Service-user controlled organisation.

Subject coverage: User involvement in all aspects of community care.

Publications: Printed

Publications list: Available in print

Access to staff: Contact by letter
Hours: Mon to Fri, 0900 to 1700

WILTSHIRE AND SWINDON RECORD OFFICE (WSA)

Formal name: Wiltshire and Swindon Archives

Wiltshire and Swindon History Centre, Cocklebury Road, Chippenham SN15 3QN

Tel: 01249 705500
Fax: 01249 705527
E-mail: archives@wiltshire.gov.uk
Website: www.wshc.eu

Enquiries to: Archivist

Founded: 1947

Organisation type and purpose: Local authority-funded archive service.

Non-library collection catalogue: All or part available online and in-house

Access to staff: Contact by letter, by telephone, by fax, by e-mail and in person
Hours: Tue to Sat, 0930 to 1730

Access for disabled people: Good disabled access

WILTSHIRE ARCHAEOLOGICAL AND NATURAL HISTORY SOCIETY (WANHS)

Wiltshire Heritage Museum, 41 Long Street, Devizes, Wiltshire, SN10 1NS

Tel: 01380 727369
Fax: 01380 722150

E-mail: wanhs@wiltshireheritage.org.uk
Website: www.wiltshireheritage.org.uk

Enquiries to: Director
Direct e-mail: david.dawson@wiltshireheritage.org.uk

Founded: 1853

Organisation type and purpose: Learned society (membership is by subscription), present number of members: c. 1,000, registered charity (charity number 1080096), museum.

Subject coverage: Archaeology, natural history and local history of the county of Wiltshire; prehistoric, Roman and medieval antiquities; family history, biological records, etc.

Information services: Research archive and library, with extensive collections about the archaeology, history and natural history of Wiltshire.

Services for disabled people: The Archive and Library is on the first floor, so it is not easily accessible to those with mobility impairments, but there is a dedicated research area on the ground floor available on request.

Collection: Designated as being of national significance, with important archaeological collections from the Stonehenge and Avebury World Heritage Site, as well as natural history and art collections.

Non-library collection catalogue: All or part available online, in-house and in print

Library catalogue: All or part available in-house

Publications: Printed
Order printed publications from: Website and direct from the Museum

Publications list: Available online

Access to staff: Contact by letter, by telephone, by e-mail and via website
Hours: Mon to Fri, 0900 to 1700

Access to building: *Hours:* Mon to Sat, 1000 to 1700; Sun, 1200 to 1600
Special comments: Library open Tue to Fri, 1000 to 1700; Sat, 1000 to 1700; closed 1st Sat of every month

WILTSHIRE ASSOCIATION OF LOCAL COUNCILS (WALC)

Wyndhams, St Josephs Place, Devizes, Wiltshire, SN10 1DD

Tel: 01380 729549
Fax: 01380 728476
E-mail: office@wiltshire-alc.org.uk
Website: www.wiltshire-alc.org.uk/

Enquiries to: County Secretary
Direct tel: 01380 729549
Other contacts: Local Councils' Adviser

Organisation type and purpose: Advisory body, membership association (membership is by subscription), present number of members: 220.

Access to staff: Contact by letter and by e-mail
Hours: Mon to Fri, 0930 to 1530

WILTSHIRE COLLEGE

The Learning Resources Centre, Southampton Road, Salisbury, Wiltshire, SP1 2LW

Tel: 01722 344325; minicom no. 01722 344307
Fax: 01722 344345
E-mail: lrc_sa@wiltshire.ac.uk
Website: www.wiltshire.ac.uk

Enquiries to: Senior LRC Team Leader
Direct e-mail: sandy.black@wiltshire.ac.uk
Other contacts: Library Learning Assistants (for general enquiries regarding bookstock and loans)

History of institution: created by the merger of Salisbury College and Wiltshire College (year of change 2008)

Organisation type and purpose: Suitable for ages: 16+.
College Learning Resources Centre.

Subject coverage: Computing and administration, management studies, basic and key skills, built environment, foundation studies, technology and science, information technology, performing arts, humanities, social sciences, fashion, art and design, graphics, film, TV and media, health and social care, food and hospitality, tourism, leisure and recreation, construction crafts, hairdressing, beauty therapy, business studies, teacher education.

Non-library collection catalogue: All or part available online and in-house

Library catalogue: All or part available online and in-house

Access to staff: Contact by letter, by telephone, by fax, by e-mail, in person and via website. Appointment necessary. Non-members charged.
Hours: Mon, 0845 to 1700; Tue and Wed, 0845 to 2000; Thu, 0845 to 1830; Fri, 1000 to 1615

Access for disabled people: Parking provided, access to all public areas, toilet facilities

WILTSHIRE COLLEGE LACKHAM

Library & Learning Resources, Lacock, Chippenham, Wiltshire, SN15 2NY

Tel: 01249 466800
Fax: 01249 444474
E-mail: lackham@wiltscoll.ac.uk
Website: www.wiltscoll.ac.uk

Enquiries to: Manager Library and Learning Resources
Direct tel: 01249 466814
Direct e-mail: obrihn@wiltscoll.ac.uk

Founded: 1946; formed by the merger of Lackham College of Agriculture Library; formed by the merger of Lackham College Library (year of change 2001)

Organisation type and purpose: College of further education.

Subject coverage: Agriculture, agricultural economics, horticulture, small animal care, land-based industries, equine studies.

Non-library collection catalogue: All or part available online

Library catalogue: All or part available online

Access to staff: Contact by telephone and by e-mail
Hours: Mon, to Thu, 0845 to 1700; Fri, 1000 to 1700

Access to building: Prior appointment required

Access for disabled people: Lift, toilet facilities

Other addresses: Wiltshire College Chippenham; Cocklebury Road, Chippenham, Wiltshire, SN15 3QD; tel: 01249 464644; e-mail: chippenham@wiltscoll.ac.uk; Wiltshire College Trowbridge; College Road, Trowbridge, Wiltshire, BA14 0ES; tel: 01225 766241; e-mail: trowbridge@wiltscoll.ac.uk

WILTSHIRE COUNTY COUNCIL LIBRARIES AND HERITAGE

Library Headquarters, Community Services Department, Bythesea Road, Trowbridge, Wiltshire, BA14 8BS

Tel: 01225 713701
Fax: 01225 713993
E-mail: libraryenquiries@wiltshire.gov.uk
Website: www.wiltshire.gov.uk

Enquiries to: Information Manager

Organisation type and purpose: Local government body, public library.

Subject coverage: Archaeology of Wiltshire; Christology; conservation of moveable objects of archaeological and historical significance; museums and museology; Wiltshire local studies; European information.

Collection: David Long Collection
Early English Children's Books
Tatham Collection of Girls' School Stories
Wiltshire Collection

Library catalogue: All or part available online

Publications: Electronic and video

Access to staff: Contact by letter, by telephone, by fax, by e-mail, in person and via website
Hours: Admin: Mon to Fri, 0900 to 1700

Access to building: No prior appointment required

Branch libraries: Chippenham Public Library; tel: 01249 650536; fax: 01249 443793; Devizes Public Library; tel: 01380 726878; fax: 01380 722161; Salisbury Public Library; tel: 01722 324145; fax: 01722 413214

Parent body: Wiltshire County Council

WILTSHIRE EDUCATION & LIBRARIES

Salisbury Library and Galleries, Market Place, Salisbury, Wiltshire, SP1 1BL

Tel: 01722 324145
Fax: 01722 413214
Website: www.wiltshire.gov.uk
Website: www.wiltshire.gov.uk/library

Enquiries to: District Librarian
Direct tel: 01722 330606
Direct e-mail: chrisharling@wiltshire.gov.uk
Other contacts: Art Curator, tel: 01722 410614; Reference and Local Studies Library, tel: 01722 411098

continued overleaf

History of institution: formerly called Wiltshire Library and Museum Service

Organisation type and purpose: Local government body, art gallery, public library.

Subject coverage: History of Salisbury and Wiltshire; arts; general subjects.

Collection: Edwin Young Watercolour collection – Victorian watercolours of Salisbury
Creasey Collection of contemporary art
Robin Tonner Collection – 1930s Children's Art
Edgar Barclay Collection – Victorian paintings of Stonehenge
Jerram Collection of Bellringing Books (Guild of Campanologists Collection of books and documents, many hand-annotated, formerly in the Sowter Clerical Library)
John Creasey Literary Museum

Library catalogue: All or part available online

Publications: Printed

Access to staff: Contact by letter, by telephone, by fax, in person and via website
Hours: Mon to Fri, 0900 to 1700

Access for disabled people: Level entry
Special comments: Level entry via side entrance.

Member of: WILCO

Parent body: Wiltshire County Council

WILTSHIRE FAMILY HISTORY SOCIETY

10 Castle Lane, Devizes, Wiltshire, SN10 1HJ

E-mail: society@wiltshirefhs.co.uk
Website: www.wiltshire.fhs.co.uk
Website: www.genfair.com

Other contacts: Membership Secretary; Research Co-ordinator

Founded: 1981

Organisation type and purpose: Membership association (membership is by subscription), present number of members: 2600, voluntary organisation, registered charity (charity number 290284), suitable for ages: adults, research organisation.

Subject coverage: Family and local history in Wiltshire.

Non-library collection catalogue: All or part available online and in-house

Library catalogue: All or part available in-house

Publications: Printed, and microform publications

Publications list: Available online and in print

Access to staff: Contact by letter and by e-mail. Appointment necessary. All charged.
Hours: Variable

Access to building: Prior appointment required
Hours: By arrangement

Access for disabled people: *Special comments:* By arrangement.

WILTSHIRE LIBRARIES AND HERITAGE

Libraries and Heritage Branch, Corporate & Library Services Department, Bythesea Road, Trowbridge, Wiltshire, BA14 8BS

Tel: 01225 713700
Fax: 01225 713993
E-mail: libraryenquiries@wiltshire.gov.uk

Enquiries to: Head of Libraries and Heritage Branch

Organisation type and purpose: Local government body.
Museums Service.

Subject coverage: Wiltshire County Historic Photograph Collection.

Collection: Wiltshire County Historic Photograph Collection, 35,000 records
Museum Objects Database, 155,000 records

Non-library collection catalogue: All or part available in-house

Library catalogue: All or part available online and in-house

Publications: Electronic and video

Access to staff: Contact by letter, by telephone, by fax and by e-mail
Hours: Mon to Fri, 0900 to 1700

Access to building: No prior appointment required
Hours: Mon, Thu, Fri, 0900 to 1900; Tue, 0900 to 1700; Wed, 1000 to 1700; Sat, 0900 to 1600

Access for disabled people: Parking provided, level entry, access to all public areas, toilet facilities

Parent body: Wiltshire County Council

WILTSHIRE MUSIC CENTRE

Formal name: Wiltshire Music Centre Trust Limited

Ashley Road, Bradford-on-Avon, Wiltshire, BA15 1DZ

Tel: 01225 860110; Box Office: 01225 860100
Fax: 01225 860111
E-mail: enquiries@wiltsmusiccentre.fsnet.co.uk
Website: www.wiltshiremusic.org.uk

Enquiries to: Operations Manager
Direct e-mail: info@wiltshiremusic.org.uk

Organisation type and purpose: Registered charity (charity number 1026160).
Purpose-built concert hall and music centre.
Music education, performance, recording and creation.

Subject coverage: The Wiltshire Music Centre Trust has three closely related objectives: the advancement of music education for all ages and levels of ability, in and around the county of Wiltshire, placing the work of young musicians at the heart of this programme; the development of a high-quality, varied and stimulating programme in terms of the scope of activity, breadth of musical cultures and range of people involved; to work with artists, other arts organisations and arts development agencies to achieve sustainable growth in participation, the development of audiences and of the art form.

Publications: Printed

Publications list: Available in print

Access to staff: Contact by letter, by telephone, by fax, by e-mail and in person
Hours: Mon to Fri, 0900 to 1800

Access for disabled people: Parking provided, ramped entry, level entry, toilet facilities
Special comments: Infrared sound relay system; access to all areas on ground floor.

WILTSHIRE RECORD SOCIETY (WRS)

Wiltshire and Swindon History Centre, Cocklebury Road, Chippenham, SN15 3QN

Tel: 01249 705500
Fax: 01249 705527
E-mail: stevenhobbs@wiltshire.gov.uk

Enquiries to: Secretary
Direct e-mail: james5.lee@uwe.ac.uk

Founded: 1936

Organisation type and purpose: Learned society.
Originated as a branch of the Wiltshire Archaeological and Natural History Society but autonomous since 1964.

Subject coverage: The publication of Wiltshire's historical archives.

Publications: Printed

Publications list: Available in print

WIMBLEDON COLLEGE OF ART

Main Building, Merton Hall Road, London, SW19 3QA

Tel: 020 7514 9641
Fax: 020 7514 9642
Website: www.wimbledon.arts.ac.uk

Enquiries to: Head of Learning and Information Resources
Direct tel: 020 8408 5039
Direct e-mail: pjennett@wimbledon.ac.uk

Founded: 1963; formerly called Wimbledon School of Art (year of change 2006)

Organisation type and purpose: Independent art school.

Subject coverage: Fine art, art history, scenography, costume history, dramatic literature.

Collection: Books, journals, video tapes, slides, CD-ROM databases

Library catalogue: All or part available online

Access to staff: Contact by letter, by telephone, by fax and by e-mail.
Appointment necessary.
Hours: Mon to Thu, 1000 to 2030; Fri, 1000 to 1930

Access to building: Prior appointment required
Hours: Mon to Thu, 1000 to 2030; Fri, 1000 to 1930

Access for disabled people: Parking provided

Parent body: University of the Arts London

WIMBLEDON LIBRARY

Wimbledon Hill Road, London, SW19 7NB

Tel: 020 8274 5757
Fax: 020 8944 6804
E-mail: wimbledon.library@merton.gov.uk
Website: https://arena.yourlondonlibrary.net/web/merton/wimbledon-library;jsessionid=5AA7A5520B1407C1E1AC45D6E25448A2

Enquiries to: Library Manager

Organisation type and purpose: Public library.

Subject coverage: General.

Collection: Local studies – materials for the study of Wimbledon, Mitcham, Morden and Merton at Local Studies Centre, Morden Library

Non-library collection catalogue: All or part available online and in-house

Library catalogue: All or part available in-house

Order printed publications from: Local Studies Centre, Morden Library, London Road, Morden, Surrey, SM4 5DX; tel: 020 8545 3239; fax: 020 8545 4037

Access to staff: Contact by letter, by telephone, by fax, by e-mail and in person
Hours: Mon to Fri, 0930 to 1900; Sat, 0930 to 1700

Access to building: No prior appointment required

Access for disabled people: Level entry, toilet facilities

Central reference library for: Merton Library Service

Local studies centre at: Morden Library; Merton Civic Centre, London Road, Morden, Surrey, SM4 5DX; tel: 020 8545 3239; fax: 020 8545 4037

WINCHESTER CITY COUNCIL

City Offices, Colebrook Street, Winchester, Hampshire, SO23 9LJ

Tel: 01962 840222
Fax: 01962 841365
E-mail: info@winchester.gov.uk
Website: www.winchester.gov.uk

Enquiries to: Information Officer

Organisation type and purpose: Local government body.
Provision of local government services to 110,000 residents in the City Council district, which covers 250 sq miles.

Access to staff: Contact by letter, by telephone, by fax, by e-mail, in person and via website
Hours: Mon to Fri, 0900 to 1700

WINCHESTER MUSEUMS

Winchester City Council, City Offices, Colebrook Street, Winchester SO23 9LJ

Tel: 01962 840222
E-mail: museums@winchester.gov.uk
Website: www.winchester.gov.uk

Enquiries to: Head of Museums
Direct tel: 01962 848396
Direct e-mail: gdenford@winchester.gov.uk
Other contacts: Education Officer

Founded: 1847

Organisation type and purpose: Local government body, museum, art gallery, historic building, house or site, suitable for ages: all.

Subject coverage: Winchester Museums is responsible for public galleries at the City Museum, Westgate Museum and City Space. Visitors and researchers wishing to consult the collections should make an appointment with staff.

Special visitor services: Materials and/or activities for children.

Education services: Group education facilities, resources for Key Stages 1 and 2 and Further or Higher Education.

Collection: Archaeology and local history of Winchester and district including topographical prints, photographs and numismatics
Books relating to the history of Winchester and its district

Non-library collection catalogue: All or part available online and in-house

Library catalogue: All or part available in-house

Publications: Printed

Publications list: Available online and in print

Access to staff: Contact by letter, by telephone, by e-mail, in person and via website. Appointment necessary.
Hours: Mon to Fri, 0900 to 1700

Branch museums: City Museum; The Square, Winchester; City Space; Winchester Discovery Centre, Jewry Street, Winchester; Westgate Museum; High Street, Winchester

WINE AND SPIRIT TRADE ASSOCIATION (WSTA)

International Wine and Spirit Centre, 39–45 Bermondsey Street, London SE1 3XF

Tel: 020 7089 3877
Fax: 020 7089 3870
E-mail: info@wsta.co.uk
Website: www.wsta.co.uk

Enquiries to: Press Officer
Direct e-mail: gavin@wsta.co.uk

Founded: 1824; formerly called Wine and Spirit Association of Great Britain and Northern Ireland (year of change 1999)

Organisation type and purpose: Trade association (membership is by subscription).
The WSTA is the UK organisation for the wine and spirit industry representing over 310 companies producing, importing, transporting and selling wines and spirits. It campaigns to promote the industry's interests with governments at home and abroad and works with its members to promote the responsible production, marketing and sale of alcohol.

Subject coverage: Wine and spirit trade.

Publications: Printed
Order printed publications from: tel: 020 7089 3877

Publications list: Available online and in print

Access to staff: Contact by letter, by telephone, by fax, by e-mail and via website. Appointment necessary. Access for members only.
Hours: Mon to Fri, 0915 to 1715

Access to building: Prior appointment required

Affiliated to: Comité Européen de Vins; Brussels, Belgium; tel: 00 32 2 2309970; European Federation of Wine & Spirit Importers and Distributors, London (EFWSID); London; tel: 020 7248 5377; fax: 020 7489 0322; e-mail: efwsid@wsa.org.uk; FIVS; Paris, France; tel: 00 33 1 42 68 82 48

WINE AUSTRALIA

Australia Centre, Strand, London, WC2B 4LG

Tel: 020 7887 5259
Fax: 020 7240 9429
E-mail: uk@wineaustralia.com
Website: www.wineaustralia.com/uk

Founded: 1987

Organisation type and purpose: Generic marketing organisation.

Subject coverage: Australian wine.

Trade and statistical information: World data on export/import of Australian wines – value and volume

Publications: Printed

Access to staff: Contact by letter, by telephone, by fax, by e-mail and via website
Hours: Mon to Fri, 0900 to 1700

Access to building: Prior appointment required

Parent body: Australian Wine & Brandy Corporation; tel: +61 8 8228 2000; fax: +61 8 8228 2022; e-mail: awbc@awbc.com.au

WINSTON CHURCHILL MEMORIAL TRUST

29 Great Smith Street, London, SW1P 3AZ

Tel: 020 7799 1660
Fax: 020 7799 1667
E-mail: office@wcmt.org.uk
Website: www.wcmt.org.uk

Founded: 1965

Organisation type and purpose: Registered charity (charity number 313952).
To provide Travelling Fellowships overseas for British citizens resident in the United Kingdom.

Access to staff: Contact by letter, by telephone, by fax, by e-mail and via website
Hours: Mon to Thu, 0930 to 1700; Fri, 0930 to 1600

WIRELESS FOR THE BEDRIDDEN

159a High Street, Hornchurch, Essex, RM11 3YD

Tel: 01708 621101 or Freephone: 0800 182137
Fax: 01708 620816
E-mail: info@w4b.org.uk
Enquiries to: Chief Executive

continued overleaf

Founded: 1939

Organisation type and purpose: Registered charity (charity number 207400).
To provide radio and television sets to the housebound, disabled and elderly who cannot afford to buy or rent for themselves.

Subject coverage: Provision of radio and television facilities for the needy, elderly, disabled, handicapped or housebound.

Access to staff: Contact by letter, by telephone, by fax and by e-mail
Hours: Mon to Fri, 0830 to 1630

WIRRAL ARCHIVES SERVICE

Wirral Museum, Hamilton Square, Birkenhead, Wirral, CH41 5BR

Tel: 0151 666 3903
E-mail: archives@wirral-libraries.net

Enquiries to: Archivist
Other contacts: Information Services Librarian

Founded: 1974

Organisation type and purpose: Public library.

Subject coverage: Deposit for public records: schools, hospitals, local government and Poor Law. Business and private records. Antiquarian collections.

Collection: Archives of local hospitals
Cammell Laird Shipbuilders archive
Local government records
Macclesfield Collection
Poor Law Records
School records
Unichema Chemicals Limited (Price's Patent Candle Company)

Non-library collection catalogue: All or part available in-house

Library catalogue: All or part available in-house

Access to staff: Contact by letter, by telephone, by fax, by e-mail and in person
Hours: Thu, Fri, 1000 to 1700; Sat, 1000 to 1300

Access for disabled people: Ramped entry, access to all public areas

WIRRAL LIBRARIES (WIZ)

Central Library, Borough Road, Birkenhead, Merseyside, CH41 2XB

Tel: 0151 652 6106/7/8 ext 7
Fax: 0151 653 7320
E-mail: birkenhead.ref@wirral-library.net
Website: www.wirral-libraries.net

Enquiries to: Librarian
Other contacts: Information Services Librarian.

Founded: 1856; created by the merger of Birkenhead, Bebington, Wallasey and Cheshire County Library Services, Wirral (year of change 1974)

Organisation type and purpose: Local government body, public library.

Subject coverage: General public library stock range.

Collection: Birkenhead Photographic Survey 1900–1920 and 1971–1974
Hopps Paintings of Wallasey 1910–1950
Macclesfield Collection
Price Collection (Price's Patent Candle Company and Model Village records 1840–1960)
Priestley Collection of Photographs 1890–1930
Wirral and Cheshire Photographic Survey 1900–1910
Wirral Borough Council Public Records 1833 to date
Wirral Photographic Survey, 1974-to date

Non-library collection catalogue: All or part available in-house

Library catalogue: All or part available online

Access to staff: Contact by letter, by telephone, by fax, by e-mail and in person. Appointment necessary.
Hours: Mon, Tue, Thu, 0900 to 2000; Fri and Sat, 0900 to 1700; closed Wed and Sun

Access to building: Mon, Tue, Thu, 0900 to 2000; Fri and Sat, 0900 to 1700; closed Wed and Sun

Access for disabled people: Ramped entry only; limited disabled access to Reference Department; no ground floor toilets

WIRRAL METROPOLITAN COLLEGE (WMC)

Conway Park Campus

Tel: 0151 551 7621
Website: www.wmc.ac.uk

Enquiries to: Learning Resources Officer
Direct tel: 0151 551 7476
Direct e-mail: shirley.jones@wmc.ac.uk

Organisation type and purpose: Suitable for ages: 16+.
College of further education.

Subject coverage: Business, social sciences, health, hair and beauty, catering

Library catalogue: All or part available online

Access to staff: Contact by letter, by telephone, by e-mail, in person and via website
Hours: Mon to Fri, 0900 to 1800
Wirral Metropolitan College

WIRRAL METROPOLITAN COLLEGE – TWELVE QUAYS CAMPUS (Wirral Met)

Shore Road, Birkenhead, Merseyside, CH41 1AG

Tel: 0151 551 7476
Fax: 0151 551 7476
E-mail: steve.cropper@wmc.ac.uk
Website: www.wmc.ac.uk

Enquiries to: Senior Librarian

Founded: 2003

Organisation type and purpose: Further Education College

Subject coverage: Construction, engineering, caring professions, leisure, tourism and catering, humanities, sciences

Non-library collection catalogue: All or part available in-house

Library catalogue: All or part available online, in-house and in print

Access to staff: Contact by letter, by telephone, by fax and by e-mail. Appointment necessary.
Hours: Mon to Thu, 0845 to 2000; Fri, 0845 to 1600
Special comments: Reference use of collections only.

Access for disabled people: Electric doors, lifts

Other addresses: Wirral Metropolitan College Library; Carlett Park Campus, Eastham, Wirral, CH62 OAY; tel: 0151 551 7866

WISE VEHICLE PROGRAMME (WISE)

Formal name: Women into Science and Engineering

Nottingham Trent University, Burton Street, Nottingham, NG1 4BU

Tel: 0115 848 2101
Fax: 0115 947 2780
E-mail: joyce.bullimore@ntu.ac.uk

Enquiries to: Operational Manager

Founded: 1992

Organisation type and purpose: Suitable for ages: 13 to 14 (girls).

Subject coverage: Women's education.

Access to staff: Contact by letter, by fax and by e-mail
Hours: Mon to Fri, 0900 to 1600

WJEC

245 Western Avenue, Cardiff, CF5 2YX

Tel: 029 2026 5000
E-mail: info@wjec.co.uk
Website: www.wjec.co.uk/

Enquiries to: Chief Executive

Founded: 1948

Organisation type and purpose: Registered charity (charity number 3150875).
Until local government reorganisation in 1996, it was a body established under a statutory order following the 1944 Education Act. Now established as a company limited by guarantee and a charity.

Subject coverage: Examinations at GCE, AEA, GCSE and Entry level, Key Skills, Welsh Baccalaureate, INSET, National Language Unit teaching resources, Welsh for Adults, Welsh Language INSET scheme, Expressive Arts support of National Youth Orchestra of Wales (NYOW), and National Youth Theatre of Wales (NYTW).

Publications: Printed, and electronic and video
Order printed publications from: WJEC Bookshop
tel: 029 2026 5112

Access to staff: Contact by letter, by telephone, by e-mail, in person and via website. Appointment necessary.
Hours: Mon to Fri, 0900 to 1700

Access for disabled people: Parking provided, ramped entry

WM ENTERPRISE

Formal name: West Midlands Enterprise Ltd

Wellington House, 31–34 Waterloo Street, Birmingham, B2 5TJ

Tel: 0121 236 8855
Fax: 0121 233 3942
E-mail: mail@wm-enterprise.co.uk

Enquiries to: Marketing Manager

Founded: 1981; formerly called West Midlands Enterprise Board (WMEB)

Organisation type and purpose: Consultancy, socio-economic research organisation.
Venture capital provider.

Subject coverage: All aspects of the management of local and regional economic development within the UK, Europe and Asia, development of small and medium sized enterprises, business start-up and marketing support.

Access to staff: Contact by letter, by telephone, by fax and by e-mail
Hours: Mon to Fri, 0900 to 1700

WOKING BOROUGH COUNCIL

Civic Offices, Gloucester Square, Woking, Surrey, GU21 1YL

Tel: 01483 755855
Fax: 01483 768746
Website: www.woking.gov.uk

Enquiries to: Public Relations Manager
Direct tel: 01483 743022
Direct fax: 01483 743055
Other contacts: Business Liaison Officer for business enquiries.

Founded: 1895

Organisation type and purpose: Local government body.

Subject coverage: Economic information, population characteristics, vacant sites and business in the area, and tourist information.

Collection: Photographic library of Woking

Publications: Printed, and electronic and video

Publications list: Available in print

Access to staff: Contact by letter, by telephone and by fax. Appointment necessary.
Hours: Mon to Fri, 0900 to 1700 (telephone enquiries)
Mon to Fri, 0900 to 1645 (personal enquiries)

Twin town with: Amstelveen; The Netherlands; Le Plessis Robinson; France

WOKINGHAM LIBRARIES AND INFORMATION SERVICE

Shute End, Wokingham, Berkshire, RG40 1WN

Tel: 0118 974 6000
E-mail: libraries@wokingham.gov.uk
Website: www.wokingham.gov.uk/libraries

Founded: 1998; formerly a part of Berkshire County Council (year of change 1998)

Organisation type and purpose: Public library.

Subject coverage: General (public library network).

Library catalogue: All or part available online

Access to staff: Contact by letter, by telephone, by fax, by e-mail, in person and via website
Hours: Library opening hours vary

Branch libraries: Aborfield Container Library; Parish Council Car Park, Swallowfield Road, Arborfield Cross; tel: 07801 664520; Lower Earley Library; Chalfont Close, Chalfont Way, Lower Earley; tel: 0118 931 2150; fax: 0118 975 0162; Maiden Erlegh Library; Maiden Erlegh Drive, Earley; tel: 0118 966 6630; fax: 0118 966 6630; Spencers Wood Library; Basingstoke Road, Spencers Wood; tel: 0118 988 4771; fax: 0118 988 4771; Twyford Library; Polehampton Close, Twyford; tel: 0118 934 0800; fax: 0118 934 5399; Wargrave Library; Woodclyffe Hostel, Church Street, Wargrave; tel: 0118 940 4656; fax: 0118 940 4656; Winnersh Library; Robin Hood Lane, Winnersh; tel: 0118 974 7979; fax: 0118 974 7989; Woodley Library; Headley Road, Woodley; tel: 0118 940 0304; fax: 0118 969 9807

Headquarters address: Wokingham Library; Denmark Street, Wokingham; tel: 0118 978 1368; fax: 0118 989 1214

WOLFSON CENTRE FOR MAGNETICS TECHNOLOGY

Cardiff School of Engineering, Cardiff University, PO Box 925, Newport Road, Cardiff, CF24 0YF

Tel: 029 2087 6729
Fax: 029 2087 6729
E-mail: wolfson@cf.ac.uk
Website: www.cf.ac.uk/engin/research/wolfson

Enquiries to: Director

Founded: 1969

Organisation type and purpose: University department or institute.
University research centre; formerly Wolfson Centre for the Technology of Soft Magnetic Materials.

Subject coverage: Applications and performance of magnetic materials.

Publications: Printed

Publications list: Available online and in print

Access to staff: Contact by letter, by telephone, by fax, by e-mail and via website.
Appointment necessary.
Hours: Mon to Fri, 0900 to 1700

Access to building: Prior appointment required

Access for disabled people: Parking provided, ramped entry, level entry, toilet facilities

WOLFSON ELECTROSTATICS, UNIVERSITY OF SOUTHAMPTON

Department of Electronics and Computer Science, University of Southampton, Southampton, SO17 1BJ

Tel: 023 8055 2266
Fax: 023 8059 3015
E-mail: wolfson@soton.ac.uk
Website: www.soton.ac.uk/~wolfson

Enquiries to: Technical Director

Founded: 1971; formerly called Wolfson Electrical Engineering Consultancy Service (year of change 1987); formerly called Wolfson Electrostatics Advisory Unit (year of change 1990)

Organisation type and purpose: University department or institute, consultancy, research organisation.

Subject coverage: Electrostatic hazard analysis, explosion prevention and protection, loss prevention, classification of flammable materials, safety audits, electrostatic applications including: liquid and dry powder coatings, precipitation and electrostatic separation, high voltage testing.

Access to staff: Contact by letter, by telephone, by fax and by e-mail.
Appointment necessary.
Hours: Mon to Fri, 0900 to 1700

Access for disabled people: Level entry, toilet facilities, lifts

WOLFSON FOUNDATION

8 Queen Anne Street, London, W1G 9LD

Tel: 020 7323 5730
Fax: 020 7323 3241
Website: www.wolfson.org.uk

Enquiries to: Chief Executive

Founded: 1955

Organisation type and purpose: Registered charity (charity number 206495).

Subject coverage: Funding of charities or exempt charities such as universities in areas such as medicine and health care, research, science, technology and education, arts and the humanities.

Publications: Printed

Access to staff: Contact by letter
Hours: Mon to Fri, 0900 to 1700

Sister trust: Wolfson Family Charitable Trust; tel: 020 7323 5730; fax: 020 7323 3241

WOLFSON HEAT TREATMENT CENTRE (WHTC)

Federation House, 10 Vyse Street, Birmingham, B18 6LT

Tel: 0121 237 1122
Fax: 0121 237 1124
E-mail: derek.close@sea.org.uk
Website: www.sea.org.uk/whtc

Enquiries to: Information Officer
Direct tel: 0121 237 1122

Founded: 1973

Organisation type and purpose: Subscription service for information, advice centre on heat treatment of metals, consultancy, courses.

Subject coverage: Heat treatment of metals, metallurgy, materials standards and specifications, consultancy, failure investigations and reports, heat treatment courses, conferences, safety in heat

continued overleaf

treatment, heat treatment processes and equipment, location of contract heat treatment facilities for engineering companies.

Collection: Library of heat treatment books
Trade literature, equipment suppliers

Trade and statistical information: Data on heat treatment equipment suppliers and suppliers of consumables to the trade

Publications: Printed

Publications list: Available in print

Access to staff: Contact by letter, by telephone and by e-mail. Appointment necessary. Access for members only. Non-members charged.
Hours: Mon to Fri, 0800 to 1600
Special comments: Free to subscribers, consultancy fee for non-subscribers

Associated with: Surface Engineering Association

WOLFSON MICROELECTRONICS LIMITED

Westfield House, 26 Westfield Road, Edinburgh, EH11 2QB

Tel: 0131 272 7000
Fax: 0131 272 7001
E-mail: europe@wolfsonmicro.com
Website: www.wolfsonmicro.com

Enquiries to: Product Marketing Engineer

Founded: 1985

Organisation type and purpose: Manufacturing industry.
Design and manufacture of semiconductor devices.

Subject coverage: Integrated circuit design and manufacture for consumer, PC, audio and imaging applications.

Non-library collection catalogue: All or part available online

Publications: Printed

Access to staff: Contact by letter, by telephone, by fax, by e-mail and via website
Hours: Mon to Fri, 0900 to 1700

Access for disabled people: Access to all public areas
Special comments: Level entrance at back of building

Associated with: Edinburgh University

WOLFSON UNIT FOR MARINE TECHNOLOGY AND INDUSTRIAL AERODYNAMICS (WUMTIA)

University of Southampton, Southampton, SO17 1BJ

Tel: 023 8058 5044
Fax: 023 8059 7594
E-mail: wumtia@soton.ac.uk
Website: www.wolfsonunit.com

Enquiries to: Secretary

Founded: 1968

Organisation type and purpose: Commercial consultancy and research organisation, using skills, knowledge and facilities of university; feedback of commercial problems to academics.

Subject coverage: Towing tank testing of ship models; wind tunnel testing of sailing vessel rigs, keels, superstructures, buildings, road vehicles; computer program bureau service in hydrostatics and stability, ship motions and propulsion, model testing; trials data acquisition; computer modelling; material testing/failure analysis; feasibility studies; expert witnesses.

Publications: Electronic and video

Access to staff: Contact by letter, by telephone, by fax, by e-mail, in person and via website
Hours: Mon to Fri, 0900 to 1700

Parent body: University of Southampton, Department of Ship Science

WOLSELEY 6/80 & MORRIS OXFORD CLUB

21 Bates Lane, Weston Turville, Aylesbury, Bucks, HP22 5SL

Tel: 01296 614065
E-mail: brianspost1@myway.com

Enquiries to: Membership Secretary

Founded: 1977

Organisation type and purpose: Membership association (membership is by subscription).

Subject coverage: Technical information and sources of spares for Wolseley 6/80 and Morris Oxford cars.

Collection: A small collection of workshop manuals and technical data

Publications: Printed

Access to staff: Contact by letter, by telephone, by e-mail and in person
Hours: Sun to Sat, 0900 to 2200
Special comments: Enclose an sae for reply.

WOLVERHAMPTON ARCHIVES AND LOCAL STUDIES (WALS)

Molineux Hotel Building, Whitmore Hill, Wolverhampton WV1 1SF

Tel: 01902 552480; minicom no. 01902 552479
Fax: 01902 552481
E-mail: archives@wolverhampton.gov.uk
Website: www.wolverhampton.gov.uk/archives
Website: www.wolverhampton.gov.uk/library/archives.htm

Enquiries to: City Archivist

Founded: 1978

Organisation type and purpose: Local government body, suitable for ages: 8+.
Archive repository.
To ensure the long-term preservation of the City's documentary heritage and to encourage and develop the use of these materials by the general public and within the council itself.

Subject coverage: Archive and local studies material, local history, genealogy.

Non-library collection catalogue: All or part available in-house

Library catalogue: All or part available in-house

Publications: Printed, and electronic and video

Publications list: Available online and in print

Access to staff: Contact by letter, by telephone, by fax, by e-mail, in person and via website
Hours: Sun & Mon closed; Tue, Thu and Fri, 1000 to 1700; Wed, 1000 to 1900; Sat 1000 to 1300

Access for disabled people: Ramped entry, access to all research facilities, toilet facilities
Hours: Normal opening hours

WOLVERHAMPTON LIBRARIES AND INFORMATION SERVICES

Central Library, Snow Hill, Wolverhampton, West Midlands, WV1 3AX

Tel: 01902 552025; minicom no. 01902 552020
Fax: 01902 552024
E-mail: libraries@wolverhampton.gov.uk
Website: www.wolverhampton.gov.uk/libraries

Enquiries to: Information Officer (Reference)

Organisation type and purpose: Local government body, public library.

Subject coverage: General information in all fields, materials in Asian languages, materials of African-Caribbean interest. On-line resources: business information, newspapers, European information, Wolverhampton local history; popular and classical music on CD; educational and instructional DVDs; music scores.

Special visitor services: Public internet access at all service points.

Library catalogue: All or part available online and in-house

Publications: Printed

Access to staff: Contact by letter, by telephone, by fax, by e-mail, in person and via website
Hours: Mon to Thu, 0900 to 1900; Fri and Sat, 0900 to 1700 at Central Library. Other libraries' opening hours vary – please check for details.

Access to building: No prior appointment required

Access for disabled people: Ramped entry, toilet facilities, adaptive technologies on PCs

Has: 15 service points throughout the City

Links with: MLA, BCLiP, CIlip and SCL

WOLVERHAMPTON MEDICAL INSTITUTE

Bell Library, New Cross Hospital, Wolverhampton, West Midlands, WV10 0QP

Tel: 01902 695322
Fax: 01902 723037
E-mail: jean.paterson@rwh-tr.nhs.uk

Enquiries to: Medical Librarian

Founded: 1971; formerly called South Staffordshire Medical Centre Library

Organisation type and purpose: A group of medical libraries in the NHS including the Eye Infirmary Library, Wolverhampton.

Subject coverage: Medicine, dentistry, veterinary surgery, pharmacy, ophthalmology, physiotherapy, nursing.

Access to staff: Contact by letter, by telephone, by fax and by e-mail
Hours: Mon to Wed, 0830 to 1700; Thu, 0830 to 1830; Fri, 0830 to 1630

WOMEN AGAINST RAPE (WAR)

Crossroads Women's Centre, 25 Wolsey Mews, London, NW5 2DX

Tel: 020 7482 2496, 020 7482 2496 (minicom)
Fax: 020 7267 7297
E-mail: war@womenagainstrape.net
Website: www.womenagainstrape.net

Enquiries to: Secretary

Founded: 1976

Organisation type and purpose: Voluntary organisation.
Pressure group.
To campaign for reform of the law and legal system with respect to violence against women and children.

Subject coverage: Legal advocacy and support for women and girls who have been raped or sexually assaulted. Help with reporting attacks, testifying in court, compensation and other resources for recovery and the prevention of violence against women and children, including for immigrant wives facing domestic violence and rape survivors seeking asylum.

Publications: Printed

Publications list: Available in print

Access to staff: Contact by letter, by telephone, by fax and by e-mail
Hours: Telephone open, Mon to Fri, 1330 to 1600
Centre opening hours, Tue and Wed, 1200 to 1600 and other times by appointment
Special comments: Letters should be addressed to PO Box 287, London, NW6 5QU.

WOMEN IN FILM AND TELEVISION (WFTV)

4th Floor, Unit 2 Wedgwood Mews, 12–13 Greek Street, London, W1D 4BB

Tel: 020 7287 1400
Fax: 020 7287 1500
E-mail: info@wftv.org.uk
Website: www.wftv.org.uk

Enquiries to: Administrator
Direct e-mail: administrator@wftv.org.uk

Founded: 1990

Organisation type and purpose: Trade association (membership is by qualification), present number of members: 1,000.

Access to staff: Contact by letter, by telephone and by e-mail
Hours: Mon to Fri, 1000 to 1800

WOMEN'S AID FEDERATION OF ENGLAND (Women's Aid)

PO Box 391, Bristol, BS99 7WS

Tel: 0117 944 4411
Fax: 0117 924 1703
E-mail: info@womensaid.org.uk
Website: www.womensaid.org.uk

Enquiries to: Information Officer

Founded: 1974

Organisation type and purpose: Membership association (membership is by subscription), present number of members: 120 full, 280 associate, voluntary organisation, registered charity (charity number 1054154).
Co-ordinate work of refuges in England, campaigning and lobbying on behalf of women and children. Provides Freephone 24 hour national domestic violence helpline: 0808 2000 247. Run in partnership between Women's Aid and Refuge.

Subject coverage: Domestic violence in the form of physical violence, sexual abuse and psychological abuse, and related issues: housing, social security, legal rights, women's rights, children.

Library catalogue: All or part available in-house

Publications: Printed

Publications list: Available online and in print

Access to staff: Contact by letter, by telephone, by fax, by e-mail and via website
Hours: Office: 1000 to 1600 only by telephone
Helpline: 24 hours

Access to building: No access other than to staff

Access for disabled people: Ramped entry

Has: over 160 member Refuge Groups in England

WOMEN'S EMPLOYMENT ENTERPRISE & TRAINING UNIT (WEETU)

The Royal Business Centre, 25 Bank Plain, Norwich, NR2 4SF

Tel: 01603 283490
Fax: 01603 283682
E-mail: admin@weetu.org
Website: www.weetu.org

Enquiries to: Chief Executive

Founded: 1988

Organisation type and purpose: Voluntary organisation, training organisation.
To help women deal with economic change, and to improve access to and experience of employment and training, as well as providing information and advice on these issues.

Subject coverage: Adult guidance: women (all ages); women returners; women's self-employment; existing network for women who run their own businesses.

Access to staff: Contact by letter, by telephone, by fax, by e-mail and via website
Hours: Mon to Fri, 0900 to 1700

WOMEN'S ENGINEERING SOCIETY (WES)

c/o The IET, Michael Faraday House, Six Hills Way, Stevenage, Herts, SG1 2AY

Tel: 01438 765506
E-mail: info@wes.org.uk
Website: www.wes.org.uk

Enquiries to: Secretary
Other contacts: President

Founded: 1919

Organisation type and purpose: Professional body, registered charity (charity number 1008913).
To promote the study and practice of engineering among women.

Subject coverage: Engineering, all levels, all fields, particularly relating to women's careers, bursaries, career breaks, equal opportunities, continuing professional development.

Trade and statistical information: Data on women in engineering

Publications: Printed

Access to staff: Contact by letter, by telephone, by fax, by e-mail and via website
Hours: Not Friday

Affiliated to: International Conference of Women Engineers & Scientists (ICWES); Verena Holmes Lecture Fund

WOMEN'S ENVIRONMENTAL NETWORK (WEN)

Real Nappy Project, PO Box 30626, London, E1 1TZ

Tel: 020 7481 9004
Fax: 020 7481 9144
E-mail: info@wen.org.uk
Website: www.wen.org.uk

Enquiries to: Project Worker
Direct e-mail: comms@wen.org.uk
Other contacts: Project Assistant for second-hand nappy exchange.

Founded: 2000

Subject coverage: Information on the environmental impact and the economic, social and health aspects of disposable nappies. Life cycle analyses and other studies on environmental impacts of real versus disposable nappies.

Trade and statistical information: Nappy waste statistics in the UK, and other information relating to the environment, health and economics. List of retailers and businesses (including non-profit) who provide washable cotton nappies for home washing or via nappy laundry delivery service

Library catalogue: All or part available online

Publications: Printed
Order printed publications from: Real Nappy Association
PO Box 3704, London, SE26 4RX

Publications list: Available online and in print

Access to staff: Contact by letter, by telephone, by fax, by e-mail and via website. Appointment necessary.
Hours: Mon to Fri, 1000 to 1800

Access to building: Prior appointment required

Access for disabled people: Level entry

WOMEN'S FARM AND GARDEN ASSOCIATION (WFGA)

175 Gloucester Street, Cirencester, Gloucestershire, GL7 2DP

Tel: 01285 658339
E-mail: admin@wfga.org.uk
Website: www.wfga.org

Enquiries to: Director

Founded: 1899

Organisation type and purpose:
Membership association (membership is by subscription), present number of members: 1,000, registered charity (charity number 212527), training organisation.
Association for professional women in all aspects of agriculture and horticulture. To provide advice and practical training in horticulture through the Women Returners to Amenity Gardening Scheme; to represent women in agriculture and horticulture.

Subject coverage: Programme of specialist workshops, garden tours and visits. Practical horticultural training provided by the Women Returners to Amenity Gardening Scheme; funding for projects in horticulture through the Christine Ladley Fund.

Collection: Archives covering 100 years

Non-library collection catalogue: All or part available in-house

Publications: Printed
Order printed publications from: Available from the office in Cirencester

Access to staff: Contact by letter, by telephone, by e-mail and via website
Hours: Mon to Fri, 0900 to 1700

WOMEN'S FOOD AND FARMING UNION (WFU)

WFU c/o Cargill plc, Witham St Hughs, Lincoln, LN6 9TN

Tel: 0844 335 0342
Fax: 0844 335 0342
E-mail: secretary@wfu.org.uk
Website: www.wfu.org.uk

Enquiries to: President
Direct tel: 07800 664701
Direct e-mail: president@wfu.org.uk
Other contacts: Administrator (for policy administration)

Founded: 1979; formerly called Women's Farming Union (year of change 1997)

Organisation type and purpose:
Membership association (membership is by subscription), voluntary organisation, suitable for ages: 18+, training organisation, research organisation.
To link consumer and producer.

Subject coverage: All aspects of food production, the concerns of consumers, the co-operation between industries related to food and farming; monitors production methods, scientific developments, retail products and the presentation of food in the market place.

Publications: Electronic and video
Order electronic and video publications from: free on application to Secretary

Access to staff: Contact by letter, by telephone, by e-mail and via website
Hours: Mon to Fri, 0900 to 1700
Special comments: Not weekends.

WOMEN'S HEALTH

52 Featherstone Street, London, EC1Y 8RT

Tel: 020 7251 6333, 020 7490 5489 (minicom)
Fax: 020 7608 0928
E-mail: womenshealth@pop3.poptel.org.uk
Website: www.womenshealthlondon.org.uk

Enquiries to: Information Officer

Founded: 1982; formerly called Women's Health and Reproductive Rights Information Centre

Organisation type and purpose: National organisation, membership association (membership is by subscription), voluntary organisation, registered charity (charity number 296002), research organisation. Health information organisation.
To provide health information that enables women to make informed decisions about their health.

Subject coverage: Women's health: menstruation, menopause, gynaecology, abortion, hysterectomy, fibroids, polycystic ovaries, pelvic inflammatory disease.

Collection: Over 5700 books, cuttings, reports on women's health issues

Publications: Printed, and electronic and video

Publications list: Available online and in print

Access to staff: Contact by letter, by telephone, by fax and by e-mail. Appointment necessary.
Hours: Office: Mon to Fri, 0900 to 1700
Helpline enquiries: Mon to Fri, 0930 to 1330

Access for disabled people: Parking provided, ramped entry, toilet facilities

WOMEN'S HEALTH CONCERN (WHC)

4–6 Eton Place, Marlow, Buckinghamshire, SL7 2QA

Tel: 01628 478473
Fax: 01628 482743
E-mail: advice@womens-health-concern.org
Website: www.womens-health-concern.org

Enquiries to: Chief Executive
Direct e-mail: info@womens-health-concern.org

Founded: 1979

Organisation type and purpose: Registered charity (charity number 279651). Provides advice and counselling about the menopause, and information about, and treatment for, sexual health and gynaecological conditions.

Subject coverage: Women's sexual and gynaecological problems and other health matters.

Education services: Professional development seminars (see website)

Publications: Electronic and video

Publications list: Available online

Access to staff: Contact by letter, by telephone, by e-mail and via website
Hours: Mon to Fri, 0900 to 1700

Access to building: No access other than to staff

WOMEN'S INTERNATIONAL LEAGUE FOR PEACE AND FREEDOM UK SECTION (WILPF)

WILPF UK Section, Tindlemanor, 52–54 Featherstone Street, London, EC1Y 8RT

Tel: 020 7250 1968
E-mail: office@ukwilpf.org.uk
Website: www.ukwilpf.org.uk

Founded: 1915

Organisation type and purpose: The WILPF is an international non-government organisation with national sections in 35 countries.
To lobby the UN and its agencies formally on issues related to peace, disarmament and economic justice.

Subject coverage: National and international lobbying, campaigning and networking on all issues affecting peace, civil liberties and human rights, status of all women and disarmament.

Collection: The archives of WILPF and the Women's Peace Movement are held in the LSE library, London

Publications: Printed
Order printed publications from: See contact details above

Publications list: Available in print

Access to staff: Contact by letter, by telephone, by e-mail and via website
Hours: Mon to Fri, 1100 to 1600

Access to building: By prior arrangement

Access for disabled people: Fully accessible

Parent body: WILPF; 1, rue de Varembé, Case Postale 28, 1121 Geneva 20, Switzerland; tel: +41 22919 7080; fax: +41 22919 7081; e-mail: inforequest@wilpf.ch; website: http://www.wilpfinternational.org

WOMEN'S INTERNATIONAL SQUASH PLAYERS ASSOCIATION (WISPA)

27 Westminster Palace Gardens, Artillery Row, London, SW1P 1RR

Tel: 020 7222 1667
Fax: 020 7976 8778
E-mail: wispahq@aol.com
Website: www.wispa.net

Enquiries to: Administrator

Founded: 1983

Organisation type and purpose:
International organisation, professional body (membership is by subscription), present number of members: 300.

Subject coverage: To promote and administer professional squash for women; to promote squash as a game; to advise and assist squash promoters / media / players / officials on all aspects of the game.

Access to staff: Contact by letter, by

telephone, by fax, by e-mail and via website
Hours: Mon to Fri, 0900 to 1700

WOMEN'S LEAGUE OF HEALTH AND BEAUTY (WLHB)

6 Station Parade, Sunningdale, Berkshire, SL5 0EP

Tel: 01344 874787
Fax: 01344 873887
E-mail: tfi@thefitnessleague.com
Website: www.thefitnessleague.com

Enquiries to: Administrator

Founded: 1930; formerly called The Fitness League (year of change 1999); trading as Health and Beauty Exercise

Organisation type and purpose:
Membership association (membership is by subscription), present number of members: 14,000, registered charity (charity number 226127).
To promote health through exercise.

Publications: Printed, and electronic and video

Access to staff: Contact by letter, by telephone, by e-mail and via website
Hours: Mon to Fri, 1000 to 1600

WOMEN'S LIBRARY

London Metropolitan University, Old Castle Street, London, E1 7NT

Tel: 020 7320 2222
Fax: 020 7320 2333
E-mail: twlinfodesk@londonmet.ac.uk
Website: www.thewomenslibrary.ac.uk

Enquiries to: Librarian
Direct tel: 020 7320 3515
Direct e-mail: enquirydesk@thewomenslibrary.ac.uk
Other contacts: Archivist (for non-published material, manuscripts, etc); Curator (for pictorial material)

Founded: 1926; formerly called The Women's Service Library (year of change 1955); formerly called The Fawcett Society (year of change 2001); incorporates the former Fawcett Library, London Guildhall University (year of change 2001)

Organisation type and purpose:
Membership association, university library.

Subject coverage: Women's studies and women's history, particularly in Britain and the Commonwealth.

Collection: Archives of many feminist organisations and of some individual women
Cavendish Bentinck Library. Many thousands of objects in the museum collection.
Josephine Butler Society Library
Sadd Brown Library

Non-library collection catalogue: All or part available online

Library catalogue: All or part available online

Publications: Printed

Access to staff: Contact by letter, by telephone, by fax, by e-mail, in person and via website
Hours: Mon, closed; Tue, Wed and Fri, 0930 to 1730; Thu, 0930 to 2000, Sat, 1000 to 1600.

Access to building: No prior appointment required
Hours: Mon, closed; Tue, Wed and Fri, 0930 to 1700; Thu, 0930 to 2000; Sat, 1000 to 1600

Access for disabled people: Access to all public areas, toilet facilities

WOMEN'S SPORT AND FITNESS FOUNDATION (WSFF)

3rd Floor, Victoria House, Bloomsbury Square, London, WC1B 4SE

Tel: 020 7273 1740
Fax: 020 7273 1981
E-mail: info@wsff.org.uk
Website: www.wsf.org.uk

Enquiries to: Office Manager
Direct tel: 020 7273 1740
Direct e-mail: info@wsff.org.uk

Founded: 1984; formerly called Women's Sports Foundation (year of change 1997)

Organisation type and purpose: Advisory body and charity.
To develop and promote women's sport.

Subject coverage: Women's sport, participation, careers, coaching, media contacts, funding and sponsorship, resources (factsheets and publications).

Collection: Range of resources and publications on women's sport

Trade and statistical information: Data on women's involvement in sport

Publications: Printed, and electronic and video

Publications list: Available online and in print

Access to staff: Contact by letter and by e-mail
Hours: Mon to Fri, 0900 to 1700

Access to building: Appointment required to arrange access through building security
Hours: Mon to Fri, 0930 to 1630

Access for disabled people: Available
Hours: Mon to Fri, 0930 to 1630

WOOD BUREAU

PO Box 9, Farnborough, Hampshire, GU14 6WE

Tel: 01252 522545
Fax: 01252 522546
Website: www.woodbureau.co.uk

Organisation type and purpose: Voluntary organisation.
Wood awareness campaign.

Subject coverage: The promotion of a better understanding of wood, as a basic fibre, common and vital to many and varied industries, to encourage a rational approach to the utilisation of both wood fibre and the forest resource.

WOOD GREEN ANIMAL SHELTERS (WGAS)

King's Bush Farm, London Road, Godmanchester, Cambridgeshire, PE29 2NH

Tel: 0844 248 8181
Fax: 01480 832815
E-mail: info@woodgreen.org.uk
Website: www.woodgreen.org.uk

Enquiries to: Fundraising Department
Direct e-mail: rhiannon.swannell@woodgreen.org.uk
Other contacts: Press and PR officer

Founded: 1924

Organisation type and purpose: Registered charity (charity number 298348).
Animal Welfare organisation.

Subject coverage: Animal rehoming charity, animal welfare, protection, surgery and veterinary services.

Publications: Printed

Publications list: Available online

Access to staff: Contact by letter, by telephone, by fax, by e-mail, in person and via website
Hours: 24-hour service, 365 days a year; open to visitors, 1000 to 1600

Access for disabled people: Parking provided, ramped entry, toilet facilities

Affiliated to: Wood Green Enterprises Ltd; King's Bush Farm, London Road, Godmanchester, Cambridgeshire, PE29 2NH; tel: 08701 904090; e-mail: tina.jeffery@woodgreen.org.uk; website: http://www.woodgreen.org.uk

Also at: Wood Green Animal Shelter; 601 Lordship Lane, Wood Green, London, N22 5LG; tel: 08701 904440; fax: 020 8889 0245; e-mail: info@woodgreen.org.uk; website: http://www.woodgreen.org.uk
Wood Green Animal Shelter; Chishill Road, Heydon, Royston, Hertfordshire, SG8 8PN; tel: 08701 909099; fax: 01763 838824; e-mail: info@woodgreen.org.uk; website: http://www.woodgreen.org.uk

WOOD PANEL INDUSTRIES FEDERATION (WPIF)

28 Market Place, Grantham, Lincolnshire, NG31 6LR

Tel: 01476 563707
Fax: 01476 579314
E-mail: enquiries@wpif.org.uk
Website: www.wpif.org.uk

Enquiries to: Director General

Founded: 1995

Organisation type and purpose: Trade association (membership is by subscription), present number of members: 25.

Subject coverage: Industrial, professional or DIY use of particle boards, chipboard, oriented strand board and medium density fibreboard (MDF); fire and building regulations; design and application data; fixing methods; finishing techniques.

Trade and statistical information: Data on the imports of particle boards and fibreboards into the UK; UK production

Publications list: Available in print

Access to staff: Contact by letter, by telephone, by fax, by e-mail, in person and via website. Appointment necessary.
Hours: Mon to Fri, 0900 to 1700

continued overleaf

Member organisation of: BWF; CEI-BOIS; CPA; EPF; FIRA; TRADA; TTF; WPA

WOODBROOKE QUAKER STUDY CENTRE

1046 Bristol Road, Selly Oak, Birmingham, B29 6LJ

Tel: 0121 472 5171
Fax: 0121 472 5173
E-mail: library@woodbrooke.org.uk
Website: www.woodbrooke.org.uk/woodbrooke

Enquiries to: Librarian
Other contacts: Director

Founded: 1903

Organisation type and purpose: Registered charity (charity number 313816).
Adult religious educational college for Quakers and others.

Subject coverage: Quaker studies, theology.

Collection: Bevan Naish Library of 17th and 18th century Quaker books and pamphlets
Powicke Collection of Richard Baxter books

Non-library collection catalogue: All or part available in-house

Library catalogue: All or part available in-house

Publications: Printed

Access to staff: Contact by letter, by telephone, by fax and by e-mail. Appointment necessary.
Hours: Variable, please enquire

WOODLAND HERITAGE CENTRE

Brokerswood Country Park, Westbury, Wiltshire, BA13 4EH

Tel: 01373 822238
Fax: 01373 858474

Enquiries to: Education Officer
Direct e-mail: woodland.park@virgin.net

Founded: 1971; formerly called Phillip's Countryside Museum; formerly called Woodland Heritage Museum (year of change 1997)

Organisation type and purpose: Registered charity (charity number L246167), museum, suitable for ages: all, but primarily 5 to 11.

Subject coverage: Forestry and forest management, forests for leisure and recreation, public participation in forestry, natural history, botany, flora, fauna, ornithology, ecology and conservation of woodland.

Collection: Barber Collection of Birds' Eggs of the World (approximately 2000 species)

Publications: Printed

Access to staff: Contact by letter, by fax and by e-mail
Hours: Mon to Fri, 0900 to 1700
Special comments: Opening dependent on season, please phone in advance.

Access to building: Prior appointment required
Hours: Mon to Fri, 1000 to 1600; Sat, Sun, 1100 to 1600
Winter: Mon to Fri, 1000 to 1600; Sat, Sun, 1200 to 1600

WOODLAND TRUST

Autumn Park, Dysart Road, Grantham, Lincolnshire, NG31 6LL

Tel: 01476 581111
Fax: 01476 590808
E-mail: enquiries@woodlandtrust.org.uk
Website: www.woodlandtrust.org.uk

Enquiries to: Public Enquiries Officer
Direct tel: 01476 581135

Founded: 1972

Organisation type and purpose: Membership association (membership is by subscription), present number of members: just under 200,000, voluntary organisation, registered charity (charity number 294344). Woodland conservation and creation.

Subject coverage: Conservation and planting of native broadleaved woodland.

Collection: Photographic collection relating to Trust properties

Publications: Printed
Order printed publications from: website: http://www.woodlandtrust.org.uk/publications

Publications list: Available online

Access to staff: Contact by letter, by telephone, by fax, by e-mail and via website
Hours: Mon to Fri, 0830 to 1700

WORCESTER COLLEGE OF TECHNOLOGY (WCT)

Deansway, Worcester, WR1 2JF

Tel: 01905 725555
Fax: 01905 725600
E-mail: studycentres@wortech.ac.uk
Website: www.wortech.ac.uk/campus/study-centres.html
Website: library.wortech.ac.uk/heritage/

Enquiries to: Senior College Librarian
Direct tel: 01905 725576
Direct e-mail: wparry@wortech.ac.uk

Organisation type and purpose: Further and Higher Education College.

Subject coverage: A levels, construction, business studies, hospitality, engineering, electronics, science, mathematics, health and caring, art and design, hair and beauty, local government, HR, law, accountancy, travel and tourism, sports, management, marketing, IT, teacher training, public services, music and performing arts.

Services for disabled people: See: http://www.wortech.ac.uk/campus/campusbuildings/Pages/buildingaccessibility.aspx.

Library catalogue: All or part available online

Access to staff: Contact by letter, by telephone, by e-mail, in person and via website. Appointment necessary.
Hours: Term time: Tue to Thu, 0830 to 1930; Mon, 0830 to 1700; Fri, 0830 to 1630
Vacations: 0900 to 1600

Access for disabled people: Ramped entry, access to all public areas

WORCESTERSHIRE ARCHAEOLOGICAL SOCIETY

E-mail: secretary@worcestershirearchaeologicalsociety.org.uk
Website: worcestershirearchaeologicalsociety.org.uk

Enquiries to: Secretary

Founded: 1854

Organisation type and purpose: Learned society (membership is by subscription).

Subject coverage: Archaeology, architecture, history.

Collection: links with University of Worcester (researchcollections@worc.ac.uk)

Non-library collection catalogue: All or part available online and in-house

Library catalogue: All or part available online and in-house

Publications: Printed
Order printed publications from: Honorary Editor, Worcestershire Archaeological Society, 14 Scobell Close, Pershore, Worcestershire, WR10 1QJ; tel: 01385 554886

Access to staff: Contact by letter and by e-mail. Appointment necessary.
Hours: by letter or email to Hon. Secretary

Access to building: Prior appointment required
Hours: by arrangement

Access for disabled people: Parking provided, level entry, toilet facilities
Special comments: change in the location in progress – please contact in advance

WORCESTERSHIRE HISTORIC ENVIRONMENT AND ARCHAEOLOGY SERVICE (WHEAS)

Formal name: Historic Environment and Archaeology Service, Worcestershire County Council

Woodbury, University of Worcester, Henwick Grove, Worcester, WR2 9AJ

Tel: 01905 855455
Fax: 01905 855035
E-mail: archaeology@worcestershire.gov.uk
Website: www.worcestershire.gov.uk/archaeology

Founded: 1974; formerly a part of Hereford and Worcester County Council (year of change 1998)

Organisation type and purpose: Local government, public library (non-issue), commercial project contracts.

Subject coverage: Archaeology in general and of Worcestershire in particular, historic buildings, aerial photographs, industrial archaeology, archaeological projects.

Non-library collection catalogue: All or part available online and in-house

Library catalogue: All or part available online

Publications: Printed

Publications list: Available online

Access to staff: Contact by letter, by telephone, by fax, by e-mail, in person and via website. Appointment necessary.

Hours: Mon to Fri, 1000 to 1630
Special comments: closed bank holidays.

Parent body: Worcestershire County Council

WORCESTERSHIRE LIBRARIES AND LEARNING SERVICE

Libraries and Learning, County Hall, Spetchley Road, Worcester, WR5 2NP

Tel: 01905 822819
Fax: 01905 766930
E-mail: librarieshq@worcestershire.gov.uk
Website: www.worcestershire.gov.uk/libraries

Enquiries to: Strategic Libraries and Learning Manager
Direct tel: 01905 766946
Other contacts: Personal Assistant/Admin

Founded: 1920

Organisation type and purpose: Local government body, public library.
21 branch libraries, 4 mobile libraries, 1 Library Service at Home vehicle

Subject coverage: General, local history (all libraries), carpet and textile industry (at Kidderminster), needle industry (at Redditch), business information (particularly at Worcester, Kidderminster and Redditch).

Collection: Carpets and Textile Collection (Kidderminster)
A. E. Housman and L. Housman Collection (Bromsgrove)
Needle Industry (Redditch)
Stuart Period Collection (Worcester)
Willis Bund Collection (local studies material, Worcester)

Library catalogue: All or part available online

Access to staff: Contact by letter, by telephone, by fax, by e-mail, in person and via website. Appointment necessary.
Hours: Please see opening times at: http://www.worcestershire.gov.uk/libraries

Access to building: Prior appointment required
Hours: Headquarters: office hours
Branch libraries have various opening hours including some evenings and some Sat; please see: http://www.worcestershire.gov.uk/libraries

Access for disabled people: Avaiable at most libraries; please see: http://www.worcestershire.gov.uk/libraries

Member organisation of: SCL West Midlands; TLP West Midlands

Parent body: Worcestershire County Council

WORCESTERSHIRE RECORD OFFICE

County Hall, Spetchley Road, Worcester, WR5 2NP

Tel: 01905 766351; minicom no. 01905 766399
Fax: 01905 766363
E-mail: recordoffice@worcestershire.gov.uk
Website: www.worcestershire.gov.uk/records

Enquiries to: Archivist

Founded: 1947

Organisation type and purpose: Local government body.

Subject coverage: Local authority, quarter sessions, petty sessions, hospital, coroners, schools, parish, diocesan and privately deposited records relating to Worcestershire.

Collection: Worcestershire photographic survey

Non-library collection catalogue: All or part available in-house

Library catalogue: All or part available online

Publications: Printed

Publications list: Available in print

Access to staff: Contact by letter, by telephone, by fax, by e-mail, in person and via website
Hours: Mon, Fri, 0930 to 1900; Tue to Thu, 0930 to 1730; Sat 0930 to 1600

Access to building: No prior appointment required
Special comments: Reader's ticket required for consultation of original documents.

Access for disabled people: Parking provided, ramped entry

Branches: Worcestershire Library and History Centre (WLHC); Trinity Street, Worcester, WR1 2PW; tel: 01905 765922; fax: 01905 765925; e-mail: wlhc@worcestershire.gov.uk

WORK FOUNDATION, THE

Peter Runge House, 3 Carlton House, London SW1Y 5DG

Tel: 0870 165 6700
Fax: 0870 165 6701
E-mail: enquiries@theworkfoundation.com
Website: www.theworkfoundation.com

Enquiries to: Information Officer

Organisation type and purpose: Membership association, registered charity, training organisation, consultancy, research organisation.
Promoting best practice at work.

Subject coverage: Conditions of employment, health and safety, training, leadership, equal opportunities, employment law, communication at work, total quality.

Publications: Printed, and electronic and video

Publications list: Available in print

Access to staff: Appointment necessary. Non-members charged.
Hours: Mon to Fri, 0900 to 1700

WORKERS' EDUCATIONAL ASSOCIATION (WEA)

Third Floor, 70 Clifton Street, London, EC2A 4HB

Tel: 020 7426 3450
Fax: 020 7426 3451
E-mail: national@wea.org.uk
Website: www.wea.org.uk

Founded: 1903

Organisation type and purpose: The WEA is the largest voluntary sector adult education provider in Britain, reaching over 80,000 people each year. Courses respond to local need, often in partnership with community groups and local charities. Registered charity (number 111275).

Subject coverage: Adult education, day, evening, weekend courses in a wide range of subjects, in liberal academic studies, workplace learning, partnership work, community adult education. See website: http://www.wea.org.uk for full details.

Education services: Runs short (typically ten-week) community adult education courses across England and Scotland.

Collection: The WEA Archive is held at London Metropolitan University, see website: http://www.wea.org.uk/weaarchive/index.htm

Non-library collection catalogue: All or part available in print

Library catalogue: All or part available in print

Publications: Printed

Publications list: Available in print

Access to staff: Contact by letter, by telephone, by e-mail, in person and via website. Appointment necessary.
Hours: Mon to Fri, 0900 to 1700

Also at: WEA East Midlands; 39 Mapperley Road, Mapperley Park, Nottingham, NG3 5AQ; tel: 0115 962 8400; fax: 0115 962 8401; e-mail: eastmidland@wea.org.uk; WEA Eastern Region; Cintra House, 12 Hills Road, Cambridge, CB2 1JP; tel: 01223 350978; fax: 01223 300911; e-mail: eastern@wea.org.uk; WEA London Region; 4 Luke Street, London, EC2A 4XW; tel: 020 7426 1950; fax: 020 7729 9821; e-mail: london@wea.org.uk; WEA National Archive; London Metropolitan University, Learning Centre, 236 Holloway Road, London, N7 6PP; tel: 020 7753 3184; fax: 020 7753 3191; e-mail: c.coates@unl.ac.uk; WEA North East; 21 Portland Terrace, Jesmond, Newcastle upon Tyne, NE2 1QQ; tel: 0191 212 6100; fax: 0191 212 6101; e-mail: northeast@wea.org.uk; WEA North West; Suite 405, The Cotton Exchange Building, Old Hall Street, Liverpool, L3 9JR; tel: 0151 243 5340; fax: 0151 243 5359; e-mail: northwest@wea.org.uk; WEA Scottish Association; Riddle's Court, 322 Lawnmarket, Edinburgh, EH1 2PG; tel: 0131 226 3456; fax: 0131 220 0306; e-mail: scotland@wea.org.uk; WEA South West; Bradninch Court, Castle Street, Exeter, EX4 3PL; tel: 01392 457300; e-mail: southwest@wea.org.uk; WEA Southern Region; 57 Riverside, 2 Sir Thomas Longley Road, Rochester, Kent, ME2 4DP; tel: 01634 298600; fax: 01634 298601; e-mail: southern@wea.org.uk; WEA West Midlands; Fourth Floor, Lancaster House, 67 Newhall Street, Birmingham, B3 1NQ; tel: 0121 237 8120; fax: 0121 237 8121; e-mail: westmidlands@wea.org.uk; WEA Yorkshire and Humber; 6 Woodhouse Square, Leeds, LS3 1AD; tel: 01132 453304; fax: 01132 450883; website: http://yorkshumberwea.org.uk

Member organisation of: National Council for Voluntary Organisations; National Institute of Adult Continuing Education

WORKING CLASS MOVEMENT LIBRARY (WCML)

Jubilee House, 51 The Crescent, Salford, M5 4WX

Tel: 0161 736 3601
Fax: 0161 737 4115
E-mail: enquiries@wcml.org.uk
Website: www.wcml.org.uk

Enquiries to: Library Manager

Founded: c.1950

Organisation type and purpose: Registered charity (charity number 1115731), public library, historic building, house or site, suitable for ages: adults/students.
To assist in the study and research of labour history, the working class and political struggles from 1770 to the present day.

Subject coverage: Trade unions, campaigns for change from Chartism to the present day, poverty and social conditions, politics, economics, working class education, Co-operative Movement.

Collection: Records from brushmakers, shipwrights, boilermakers and many other unions
Papers from playwright Jim Allen, activists such as Benny Rothman and Angela Tuckett, and the Library's founders Eddie and Ruth Frow
Papers relating to the International Brigade in the Spanish Civil War, with a specific focus on volunteers from the North West of England
Banners, photographs, poetry, songs, posters, badges, cartoons etc.

Non-library collection catalogue: All or part available online and in-house

Library catalogue: All or part available online and in-house

Publications: Printed, and microform publications
Order printed publications from: WCML
Order microform publications from: Microform Academic Publishers, Main Street, East Ardsley, Wakefield, WF3 2AP

Publications list: Available online

Access to staff: Contact by letter, by telephone, by fax, by e-mail and via website. Appointment necessary.
Hours: Tue to Fri, 1000 to 1700; third Sat of the month, 1000 to 1600

Access to building: Prior appointment required
Hours: Tue to Fri, 1000 to 1700; third Sat of the month, 1000 to 1600

Access for disabled people: Parking provided, ramped entry, toilet facilities

Administered by: Board of Trustees; at the same address

WORLD AHLUL BAYT ISLAMIC LEAGUE (WABIL)

19 Chelmsford Square, London, NW10 3AP

Tel: 020 8459 8475
Fax: 020 8451 7059
E-mail: wabil@wabil.com
Website: www.wabil.info/

Enquiries to: Secretary General
Direct tel: 020 8459 6051
Direct e-mail: mmusawi@gmail.com
Other contacts: Public Relations Officer

Founded: 1983

Organisation type and purpose: International organisation, voluntary organisation, registered charity (charity number 291922).

Subject coverage: Islam, Shiaism, jurisprudence, scholars' welfare in poor countries, books, charity.

Publications: Printed, and electronic and video

Publications list: Available in print

Access to staff: Contact by letter, by fax and by e-mail
Hours: Mon to Fri, 0900 to 1700

WORLD ARABIAN HORSE ORGANIZATION (WAHO)

Newbarn Farmhouse, Forthampton, Gloucestershire, GL19 4QD

Tel: 01684 274455
Fax: 01684 274422
E-mail: waho@compuserve.com
Website: www.waho.org

Enquiries to: Executive Secretary

Founded: 1972

Organisation type and purpose: International organisation, membership association, present number of members: 54 member countries, 1000 individual associate members, registered charity.

Subject coverage: Arabian horses.

Publications: Printed

Access to staff: Contact by letter, by telephone, by fax, by e-mail and via website. Appointment necessary.
Hours: Mon to Fri, 0900 to 1700

WORLD BOWLS LIMITED

SportScotland, Caledonia House, 1 Redheughs Rigg, South Gyle, Edinburgh, EH12 9DQ

Tel: 0131 317 9764
Fax: 0131 317 9765
E-mail: worldbows@btconnect.com
Website: www.worldbowlsltd.co.uk

Enquiries to: Chief Executive Officer

Founded: 1907; formed by the amalgamation of International Womens Bowling Board (IWBB), World Bowls Board (year of change 2001); formerly called International Bowling Board (IBB) (year of change 1992)

Organisation type and purpose: International organisation, advisory body, membership association (membership is by subscription), present number of members: 53 National Authorities.
Governing body of the sport.

Subject coverage: International competition, laws of game, manufacture and testing of bowls, standards for bowling green surfaces.

Publications: Printed, and electronic and video

Access to staff: Contact by letter, by telephone, by fax and by e-mail
Hours: Mon to Fri, 0900 to 1700

Access for disabled people: Parking provided, level entry, access to all public areas, toilet facilities

WORLD CANCER RESEARCH FUND (WCRF UK) (WCRF UK)

22 Bedford Square, London WC1B 3HH

Tel: 020 7343 4200
Fax: 020 7343 4201
E-mail: wcrf@wcrf.org
Website: www.wcrf-uk.org

Enquiries to: Supporter Services Department
Direct tel: 020 7343 4205

Founded: 1990

Organisation type and purpose: Registered charity (charity number 1000739), suitable for ages: all, research organisation.
To raise awareness of cancer as a preventable disease; to provide advice for healthy living; to translate scientific research findings into accessible form; to motivate individuals to change to healthier diets and lifestyles; to provide supporter services.

Subject coverage: Diet, nutrition, physical activity, weight management and cancer prevention.

Information services: Education department; tel: 020 7343 4200

Education services: Education department; tel: 020 7343 4200

Publications: Printed, and electronic and video
Order printed publications from: website: http://www.wcrf-uk.org/publications or telephone 020 7343 4205
Order electronic and video publications from: website: http://www.wcrf-uk.org/publications

Publications list: Available online and in print

Access to staff: Contact by letter, by telephone, by fax, by e-mail and via website. Appointment necessary.
Hours: Mon to Fri, 0900 to 1730

Access to building: No access other than to staff

Affiliated to: American Institute for Cancer Research; website: http://www.aicr.org
World Cancer Research Fund Hong Kong; website: http://www.wcrf-hk.org
World Cancer Research Fund Netherlands; Netherlands; website: http://www.wcrf-nl.org

WORLD CONFEDERATION FOR PHYSICAL THERAPY (WCPT)

Victoria Charity Centre, 11 Belgrave Road, London, SW1V 1RB

Tel: 020 7931 6465
Fax: 020 7931 6494
E-mail: info@wcpt.org
Website: www.wcpt.org

Enquiries to: Secretary-General

Founded: 1951

Organisation type and purpose: International organisation, professional body (membership is by qualification), present number of members: 106, registered charity (charity number 234307).
WCPT is a confederation of 106 national professional associates around the world. It aims to improve global health care by representing physical therapists (physiotherapists) internationally, enabling information exchange and co-operation among physical therapists across the world, and encouraging high standards of research, education and practice in physical therapy.

Publications: Printed

Publications list: Available online and in print

Access to staff: Contact by letter and by e-mail. Appointment necessary.
Hours: Mon to Fri, 0900 to 1700

Access to building: No prior appointment required

WORLD CURLING FEDERATION (WCF)

74 Tay Street, Perth, Tayside, PH2 8NP

Tel: 01738 451630
Fax: 01738 451641
E-mail: info@worldcurling.org
Website: www.worldcurling.org

Enquiries to: Secretary-General
Other contacts: Media Relations Officer

Founded: 1966; formerly called International Curling Federation (ICF) (year of change 1991)

Organisation type and purpose: International organisation, membership association.
Represents 49 member associations and promotes the sport of curling world-wide.

Subject coverage: The sport of curling world-wide, details of participants and performance, venues of World and World Junior Curling Championships since 1959, organisation of all World and World Wheelchair Curling Championships.

Publications: Printed
Order printed publications from: World Curling Federation, 74 Tay Street, Perth, PH2 8NP

Publications list: Available in print

Access to staff: Contact by letter, by telephone, by fax and by e-mail. Appointment necessary.
Hours: Mon to Fri, 0900 to 1700

Access for disabled people: Ramped entry

WORLD EDUCATION DEVELOPMENT GROUP (WEDG)

98A Broad Street, Canterbury, Kent, CT1 2LU

Tel: 01227 766552
Fax: 01227 766552
E-mail: info@wedg.org.uk
Website: www.wedg.org.uk

Enquiries to: Projects Leader
Other contacts: Development Education Co-ordinator

Founded: 1987

Organisation type and purpose: Development Education Centre

Subject coverage: TWEDG engages with schools, universities, community groups and other educators in East Kent to promote global education and make issues such as sustainable development, social justice and human rights accessible to all. Provides training, a resources centre, workshops, assemblies, support and advice through projects.

Collection: A variety of material for educational use in geography, RE, English, science, etc.
Reference information on Peace, Human Rights, Environment and Development including teachers' packs

Non-library collection catalogue: All or part available online

Publications: Printed, and electronic and video
Order printed publications from: WEDG

Access to staff: Contact by letter, by telephone, by fax, by e-mail and via website. Appointment necessary. Non-members charged.
Hours: Wed, 1400 to 1800; first Sat of month, 1100 to 1300; by appointment at other times

Access to building: No access other than to staff, no prior appointment required
Hours: Wed, 1400 to 1800; first Sat of month, 1100 to 1300

Access for disabled people: Ramped entry

Links with: Kent and the Wider World; website: http://www.commonwork.org/kww/default.htm
PIDEC; website: http://www.pestalozzi.org.uk

Member organisation of: DEA; CAN Mezzanine, 32–36 Loman Street, London, SE1 0EH; website: http://www.dea.org.uk
Local4Global; website: http://www.local4global.org.uk

WORLD EMERGENCY RELIEF (WER)

20 York Buildings, London, WC2N 6JU

Tel: 020 7839 3854
Fax: 020 7839 8202
E-mail: info@wer-uk.org
Website: www.wer-uk.org

Enquiries to: Executive Director
Direct e-mail: alex@wer-uk.org

Founded: 1994

Organisation type and purpose: Registered charity (charity number 1045672).

Access to staff: Contact by letter and by e-mail
Hours: Mon to Fri, 0900 to 1700

Access for disabled people: Access to all public areas

WORLD ENERGY COUNCIL (WEC)

5th Floor, Regency House, 1–4 Warwick Street, London, W1B 5LT

Tel: 020 7734 5996
Fax: 020 7734 5926
Website: www.worldenergy.org

Enquiries to: Information Officer

Founded: 1924; formerly called World Energy Congress

Organisation type and purpose: International organisation, membership association, registered charity (charity number 1086559).
To promote the sustainable supply and use of energy for the greatest benefit of all.

Subject coverage: Energy (all forms, fossil, renewables, nuclear), provision and use thereof, energy-related issues including environmental, efficiency and conservation, economic and social development, financing, technology, policy.

Collection: Small energy library

Trade and statistical information: Triennial surveys of energy resources and national energy databases
Special publications, e.g. WEC Commission report, renewable energy resources, combined heat and power schemes

Publications: Printed, and electronic and video
Order printed publications from: London Office, WEC; e-mail: info@worldenergy.org

Publications list: Available online and in print

Access to staff: Contact by letter, by telephone, by fax and by e-mail. Appointment necessary.
Hours: Mon to Fri, 1000 to 1600

Has: 96 affiliated national energy associations worldwide

WORLD HERITAGE

Heritage House, 25 High West Street, Dorchester, Dorset, DT1 1UW

Tel: 01305 269741
Fax: 01305 268885
E-mail: info@world-heritage.org.uk
Website: www.thedinosaurmuseum.com
Website: www.world-heritage.org.uk
Website: www.tutankhamun-exhibition.co.uk
Website: www.teddybearmuseum.co.uk
Website: www.terracottawarriors.co.uk

Enquiries to: Manager

Founded: 1984

Organisation type and purpose: Museum.
A consortium of independent museums and exhibitions; also operates literature distribution and tourism services.

Subject coverage: Egyptology, dinosaurs, fossils, geology, teddy bears, tourism, museum management, terracotta warriors, photography.

Publications: Printed

Access to staff: Contact by letter, by telephone, by fax, by e-mail and via website. Appointment necessary.
Hours: Mon to Fri, 1000 to 1700

Access to building: All the museums are open daily, except 13 to 26 December
Hours: Times vary for different museums but they are all open through the core times of 1000 to 1600
Special comments: Entrance to the museums is charged for.

continued overleaf

Branch museums: Dinosaur Museum; Icen Way, Dorchester, DT1 1EW; tel: 01305 269880; fax: 01305 268885; e-mail: info@thedinosaurmuseum.com; website: http://www.thedinosaurmuseum.com
Teddy Bear Museum; corner of High East Street and Salisbury Street, Dorchester, DT1 1JU; tel: 01305 266040; fax: 01305 268885; e-mail: info@teddybearmuseum.co.uk; website: http://www.teddybearmuseum.co.uk
Terracotta Warriors Museum; Salisbury Street, Dorchester, Dorset, DT1 1JU; tel: 01305 266040; fax: 01305 268885; e-mail: info@terracottawarriors.co.uk; website: http://www.terracottawarriors.co.uk
Tutankhamun Exhibition; High West Street, Dorchester, DT1 1UW; tel: 01305 269571; fax: 01305 268885; e-mail: info@tutankhamun-exhibition.co.uk; website: http://www.tutankhamun-exhibition.co.uk

WORLD HORSE WELFARE

Anne Colvin House, Snetterton, Norfolk, NR16 2LR

Tel: 01953 498682
Fax: 01953 498373
E-mail: info@worldhorsewelfare.org
Website: www.worldhorsewelfare.org

Founded: 1927; formerly called International League for the Protection of Horses

Organisation type and purpose: International organisation, registered charity (charity number 206658).
Equine welfare organisation.
Working for a world where the horse is used but never abused.

Subject coverage: Equine care and management; transportation of equines for slaughter – overseas; recovery and rehabilitation of equines – UK; NGO training on saddlery, farriery, horse management and nutrition in developing countries.

Publications: Printed
Order printed publications from: Communications Manager

Access to staff: Contact by letter, by telephone, by fax, by e-mail, in person and via website. Appointment necessary.
Hours: Mon to Fri, 0900 to 1700

Collaboration with other major equine organisations eg: Animal Health Trust; Newmarket, Suffolk; International Equestrian Federation, Lausanne, Switzerland (FEI); Liverpool University; Department of Veterinary Clinical Science and Animal Husbandry; Royal (Dick) School of Veterinary Studies, University of Edinburgh

WORLD LAND TRUST

Blyth House, Bridge Street, Halesworth, Suffolk, IP19 8AB

Tel: 0845 054 4422 (local rate, UK only); 01986 874422
Fax: 01986 874425
E-mail: info@worldlandtrust.org
Website: www.worldlandtrust.org
Website: www.carbonbalanced.org
Website: www.focusonforests.org
Website: www.wildlifefocus.org

Other contacts: Education, Training & Outreach Officer

Founded: 1989; formerly called World Wide Land Conservation Trust

Organisation type and purpose: An international conservation charity (registered charity number 1001291).
Takes direct action to save rainforest and other wildlife habitats by providing funds for partner organisations, so that they can purchase land and establish permanent wildlife reserves; works to preserve the world's most biologically important and threatened lands, and has helped purchase and protect over 400,000 acres of habitats rich in wildlife, in Asia, Central and South America and the UK.

Subject coverage: Has a policy of working with local partner organisations, and the Trust does not normally play a direct role in the ownership or the management of the land it conserves.

Education services: Resource packs for schools; internships; Graduate Diploma in Conservation and Project Administration in conjunction with the University of East Anglia.

Publications: Electronic and video
Order electronic and video publications from: Download from website

Publications list: Available online

Access to staff: Contact by letter, by telephone, by fax, by e-mail and via website

Links with: World Land Trust-US; 2806 P Street NW, Washington, DC 20007, USA; fax: +1 603 284 7134; e-mail: info@worldlandtrust-us.org; website: http://www.worldlandtrust-us.org

WORLD NUCLEAR ASSOCIATION (WNA)

Carlton House, 22a St James's Square, London, SW1Y 4JH

Tel: 020 7451 1520
Fax: 020 7839 1501
E-mail: wna@world-nuclear.org
Website: www.world-nuclear.org

Founded: 1975

Organisation type and purpose: International organisation, trade association (membership is by subscription), present number of members: 200, research organisation.

Subject coverage: Uranium: supply and demand, geology, mining, processing, laws and regulations, trade, safety, environmental issues; nuclear power: status world-wide, technology.

Trade and statistical information: Uranium production statistics, international by country; nuclear energy statistics, international by country

Non-library collection catalogue: All or part available online

Publications: Printed, and electronic and video
Order printed publications from: website

Publications list: Available online

Access to staff: Contact by letter, by telephone, by fax and by e-mail. Appointment necessary.
Hours: Mon to Fri, 1000 to 1600

WORLD OWL TRUST

The World Owl Centre, Muncaster Castle, Ravenglass, Cumbria, CA18 1RQ

Tel: 01229 717393
Fax: 01229 717107
E-mail: via website
Website: www.owls.org

Organisation type and purpose: Registered charity (number 1107529).
Exists to advance wildlife conservation by primarily focusing on all owl species and their ecology. Through the promotion of habitat management and restoration, research, captive breeding programmes, and its own education policy, the Trust intends to bring an awareness of conservation and environmental sustainability to all levels of society. On-site facilities are maintained to provide treatment and rehabilitation for sick and injured owls and other wildlife.

Subject coverage: Conservation programmes protect populations of endangered owls until their habitat has been restored and birds held at the Owl Centre can be reintroduced back into the wild.

Special visitor services: Owl Centre, Muncaster Castle; tel: 01229 717614

Publications: Electronic and video
Order electronic and video publications from: Download from website

Publications list: Available online

Access to staff: Contact by letter, by telephone, by fax, in person and via website

Access to building: Free coach and car parking opposite the main gate, with disabled parking
Hours: The Gardens, Owl Centre and MeadowVole Maze open Mon to Sun all year (except Jan), 1030 to 1800 (or dusk if earlier)

Access for disabled people: The main areas of the Gardens and Owl Centre and MeadowVole Maze allow wheelchair access; the ground floor of the Castle (where the majority of the audio tour takes place) is also accessible by wheelchair; accessible toilets are available in the Stable Yard and the Coach Park; dogs are welcome in the Gardens and the Owl Centre if kept on a lead and under control; guide dogs, only, in the Castle, MeadowVole Maze and Café.

Member organisation of: British and Irish Association of Zoos and Aquariums (BIAZA); European Association of Zoos and Aquariums (EAZA)

WORLD PARROT TRUST (WPT)

Glanmor House, Hayle, Cornwall, TR27 4HB

Tel: 01736 751026
Fax: 01736 751028
E-mail: uk@worldparrottrust.org
Website: www.parrots.org

Enquiries to: Administrator
Other contacts: Chairman

Founded: 1989

Organisation type and purpose: International organisation, membership association (membership is by subscription), present number of members: 2,116, registered charity (charity number 800944). Conservation and welfare of parrots.

Subject coverage: Parrot conservation projects, the welfare of pet parrots and aviculture.

Publications: Printed, and electronic and video
Order printed publications from: uk@worldparrottrust.org
Order electronic and video publications from: www.parrots.org

Access to staff: Contact by letter, by telephone, by fax, by e-mail and via website
Hours: Mon to Fri, 0930 to 1730

Links with: Paradise Park (wildlife sanctuary); tel: 01736 753365; fax: 01736 751028

WORLD PHEASANT ASSOCIATION (WPA)

Biology Field Station, Newcastle University, Close House Estate, Heddon-on-the-Wall, Newcastle-upon-Tyne, NE15 0HT

Tel: 01661 853397
Fax: 01661 853397
E-mail: office@pheasant.org.uk
Website: www.pheasant.org.uk

Enquiries to: Administrator
Direct e-mail: Barbara.Ingman@pheasant.org.uk
Other contacts: Director

Founded: 1975; formerly called WPA International (WPA)

Organisation type and purpose: International organisation, membership association, voluntary organisation, registered charity (charity number 271203).

Subject coverage: Conservation, breeding and management of galliformes (pheasants, grouse, quail etc) field studies.

Trade and statistical information: Data on the status and distribution of galliformes worldwide

Publications: Printed, and electronic and video

Publications list: Available online and in print

Access to staff: Contact by letter, by telephone, by fax and by e-mail. Appointment necessary.
Hours: Mon to Fri, 0900 to 1700

Access for disabled people: Parking provided, level entry, access to all public areas, toilet facilities

Specialist group for: Birdlife International

WORLD PLOUGHING ORGANIZATION (WPO)

26 Gable Avenue, Cockermouth, Cumbria, CA13 9BU

Tel: 01900 825686
Fax: 01900 68736
Website: www.worldploughing.org

Enquiries to: Treasurer

Founded: 1952

Organisation type and purpose: Voluntary organisation.

Subject coverage: Standards of ploughmanship, the rules for ploughing, competition ploughing as an incentive to good husbandry of the soil, soil tillage demonstrations and machinery exhibition.

Publications: Printed

Access to staff: Contact by letter
Hours: Mon to Fri, 0900 to 1700

WORLD PROFESSIONAL BILLIARDS AND SNOOKER ASSOCIATION LIMITED (WPBSA)

Suite 2/1, Albert House, 111–117 Victoria Street, Bristol, BS1 6AX

Tel: 0117 317 8200
Fax: 0117 317 8300
E-mail: enq@worldsnooker.com
Website: www.worldsnooker.com

Enquiries to: Company Secretary

Organisation type and purpose: Membership association.
Governing body of the games.

Subject coverage: Details of the professional and amateur games of billiards and snooker.

Collection: Books and records of snooker and billiards from the commencement of the games in 1887 and founding of a formal Snooker and Billiards Association in that year

Access to staff: Contact by letter
Hours: Mon to Fri, 0900 to 1700

WORLD SIKH FOUNDATION

33 Wargrave Road, South Harrow, Middlesex, HA2 8LL

Tel: 020 8864 9228
E-mail: bablibharara@hotmail.com

Enquiries to: Secretary
Direct e-mail: worldsikhfoundation@hotmail.com

Founded: 1960; formerly called Sikh Cultural Society of Great Britain (year of change 1993)

Organisation type and purpose: International organisation, learned society (membership is by subscription), present number of members: 850, voluntary organisation, registered charity (charity number 1054913), publishing house.
Religious society.
To spread message of Sikhism worldwide.

Subject coverage: The Sikh religion.

Publications: Printed

Access to staff: Contact by letter and by telephone
Hours: Mon to Fri, 0900 to 1700

Also at the same address: Guru Nanak Foundation UK

WORLD SOCIETY FOR THE PROTECTION OF ANIMALS (WSPA)

89 Albert Embankment, London, SE1 7TP

Tel: 020 7587 5000
Fax: 020 7793 0208
E-mail: wspa@wspa.org.uk
Website: www.wspa.org.uk

Enquiries to: Supporter Services

Founded: 1980; formerly called ISPA; formerly called WFPA (year of change 1980)

Organisation type and purpose: Membership association, present number of members: 953 member societies in 154 countries, registered charity (charity number 1081849).
Animal welfare charity.

Subject coverage: Wildlife, companion animals, farm animals, animal welfare legislation, disaster relief, humane education, animal protection.

Publications: Printed, and electronic and video

Publications list: Available in print

Access to staff: Contact by letter, by telephone, by fax and by e-mail. Appointment necessary.
Hours: Mon to Fri, 0900 to 1700

Access for disabled people: Parking provided, ramped entry, toilet facilities

Also at: World Society for the Protection of Animals; 90 Eglington Avenue East, Suite 960, Toronto, Ontario, M4P 2Y3, Canada; tel: +1 416 369 0044; fax: +1 416 369 0147; e-mail: wspa@wspa.ca; website: http://www.wspa.ca
World Society for the Protection of Animals; Mall Paseo las Flores Business Center, 5th floor, Apdo Postal 516–3000, Heredia, Costa Rica; tel: +506 2562 1200; fax: +506 2562 1225; e-mail: info@wspala.org; website: http://wspa.or.cr
World Society for the Protection of Animals; PO Box 105476, Dar es Salaam, Tanzania; tel: +255 22 270 1032; fax: +255 22 270 1033; e-mail: enquiries@wspaafrica.org; website: http://www.wspa-international.org
World Society for the Protection of Animals; Lincoln Plaza, Suite 201, 89 South Street, Boston 02111, USA; tel: +1 617 896 9214; fax: +1 617 737 4404; e-mail: wspa@wspausa.org; website: http://www.wspa-usa.org
World Society for the Protection of Animals; 19th Floor, Olympia Thai Tower, 444 Ratchadaphisek Road, Huay Kwang, Bangkok 10310, Thailand; tel: +66 2 513 0475; fax: +66 2 513 0477; e-mail: thailand.enquiries@wspa-asia.org; website: http://www.wspa-international.org
World Society for the Protection of Animals; GPO Box 3294, Sydney, NSW 2001, Australia; tel: +61 2 9902 8000; fax: +61 2 9906 1166; e-mail: wspa@wspa.org.au; website: http://www.wspa.org.au
World Society for the Protection of Animals; Av. Princesa Isabel, 323 – 8 andar, Copacabana, 22011–901, Rio de Janeiro, Brazil; tel: +55 21 3820 8200; fax: +55 21 3820 8229; e-mail: wspabrasil@wspabr.org; website: http://www.wspabrasil.org
World Society for the Protection of Animals; 501B, Dong Wai Diplomatic Building, No. 23, Dongzhimen Wai Avenue, Beijing 100600, People's Republic of China; tel: +86 10 85325211 – 8008; fax: +86 10 85324211; e-mail: alyceyu@wspa-asia.org; website: http://www.wspa-international.org

continued overleaf

World Society for the Protection of Animals; Carrera 13 #29–21 Of. 234, Manzana 1, Parque Central Bavaria, Bogotá, Colombia; tel: +571 288 8829; fax: +571 232 1361; e-mail: wspa@wspa.org.co; website: http://www.wspa-international.org
World Society for the Protection of Animals; Kaiserstrasse 22, 53113, Bonn, Germany; tel: +49 228 956 3455; fax: +49 228 956 3454; e-mail: info@wspa.de; website: http://www.wspa.de
World Society for the Protection of Animals; Benoordenhoutseweg 23, 2596 BA Den Haag, The Netherlands; tel: +31 70 314 2800; fax: +31 70 314 2809; e-mail: info@wspa.nl; website: http://www.wspa.nl
World Society for the Protection of Animals; Private Bag 93220, Parnell 1151, Auckland, New Zealand; tel: +64 9 309 3901; fax: +64 9 336 1947; e-mail: wspa@wspa.org.nz; website: http://www.wspa.org.nz
World Society for the Protection of Animals; Vesterbrogade 34, 1, 1620 Copenhagen V, Denmark; tel: +45 33 93 7212; fax: +45 33 93 7210; e-mail: info@wspa.dk; website: http://www.wspa.dk

Links with: United Nations (consultative status)

Member organisation of: Eurogroup for Animal Welfare

WORLD SQUASH FEDERATION LIMITED (WSF)

6 Havelock Road, Hastings, East Sussex, TN34 1BP

Tel: 01424 429245
Fax: 01424 429250
E-mail: squash@worldsquash.org
Website: www.squash.org

Enquiries to: Chief Executive
Other contacts: Executive Assistant

Founded: 1967; formerly called International Squash Rackets Federation (ISRF) (year of change 1992)

Organisation type and purpose: International organisation.

Subject coverage: The sport of squash, court, clothing, ball, racket specifications; rules, refereeing, coaching, world championships.

Access to staff: Contact by letter, by telephone, by fax, by e-mail and via website. Appointment necessary.
Hours: Mon to Fri, 0900 to 1700

WORLD UNION FOR PROGRESSIVE JUDAISM EUROPEAN BOARD (WUPJ)

Sternberg Centre for Judaism, 80 East End Road, London, N3 2SY

Tel: 020 8349 3779
Fax: 020 8343 5699
E-mail: europeanjudaism@directmail.org

Enquiries to: Administrator

Founded: 1926

Organisation type and purpose: International organisation (membership is by election or invitation), registered charity (charity number 253000).
Nurture and develop progressive Jewish communities in Europe.

Publications: Printed

Access to staff: Contact by letter, by fax and by e-mail
Hours: Mon to Thu, 1030 to 1600

Parent body: World Union for Progressive Judaism; 13 King David Street, Jerusalem 94101, Israel; tel: 00 972 2 6203447; fax: 00 972 2 6203525; e-mail: wupjis@wupj.org.il; website: http://www.wupj.org

WORLD WAR TWO RAILWAY STUDY GROUP

17 Balmoral Crescent, West Molesey, Surrey, KT8 1QA

Tel: 020 8783 1024
E-mail: tcane@ww2rsg.u-net.com
Website: www.2rsg.org

Organisation type and purpose: Membership association.
Research into the use of railways in World War II.

Subject coverage: Use of railways in World War Two, mainly UK railways and the overseas use of railways by British forces. Topics include civil engineering, ambulance trains, rail guns etc.

Publications: Printed

WORLD'S POULTRY SCIENCE ASSOCIATION UK BRANCH (WPSA)

Woodlands, Bradfield St Clare, Bury St Edmunds, Suffolk, IP30 0EQ

Tel: 01284 386520
Fax: 01284 386520
E-mail: wpsa@hotmail.co.uk
Website: www.wpsa-uk.com

Enquiries to: Honorary Secretary

Founded: 1946

Organisation type and purpose: Membership association (membership is by subscription), present number of members: 280, voluntary organisation, registered charity (charity number 803616).
To promote the spread and exchange of information on poultry science and the poultry industry.

Subject coverage: Poultry science and technology, poultry industry.

Publications: Printed

Publications list: Available online

Access to staff: Contact by letter, by telephone, by fax, by e-mail and via website. Access for members only.
Hours: variable part time

Access to building: No

Parent body: World's Poultry Science Association (WPSA); tel: + 31 55 506 6534; fax: + 31 55 506 4858; e-mail: wpsa@xs4all.nl; website: www.wpsa.com

WORLDSCALE ASSOCIATION (LONDON) LIMITED (Worldscale)

Copenhagen House, 5–10 Bury Street, London, EC3A 5AT

Tel: 020 7456 6600
Fax: 020 7456 6601
E-mail: wscale@worldscale.co.uk
Website: www.worldscale.co.uk

Enquiries to: Managing Director

Founded: 1962

Organisation type and purpose: Consultancy.

Subject coverage: Standard of reference for nominal freight scale to the oil tanker industry.

Trade and statistical information: Nominal oil tanker freight rates for worldwide trade

Publications: Printed

Publications list: Available in print

Access to staff: Contact by letter, by telephone, by fax and by e-mail. Appointment necessary.
Hours: Mon to Fri, 0930 to 1730
Special comments: Services offered on an annual subscription basis.

Joint publishers: Worldscale Association (NYC) Inc; 116 John Street, Suite 620, New York, NY 10038, USA; tel: + 1 212 422 2786; fax: +1 212 344 4169; e-mail: worldscale@worldscale-usa.com; website: http://www.worldscale-usa.com

WORSHIPFUL COMPANY OF ACTUARIES

3rd Floor, Cheapside House, 138 Cheapside, London, EC2V 6BW

Tel: 020 7776 3880
E-mail: clerk@actuariescompany.co.uk
Website: www.actuariescompany.co.uk

Enquiries to: The Clerk

Founded: 1979

Organisation type and purpose: Membership association (membership is by election or invitation).
City of London Livery Company.
To extend recognition and understanding of the work of actuaries within the City and beyond through educational and charitable works.

Access to staff: Contact by letter, by telephone, by e-mail and via website

WORSHIPFUL COMPANY OF ARBITRATORS

13 Hall Gardens, Colney Heath, St Albans, Hertfordshire, AL4 0QF

Tel: 01727 826578
Fax: 01727 822652
E-mail: clerk@arbitratorscompany.org
Website: www.arbitratorscompany.org

Enquiries to: The Clerk
Direct tel: 01727 826578
Direct e-mail: clerk@arbitratorscompany.org

Founded: 1981

Organisation type and purpose: Membership association (membership is by election or invitation).
City of London Livery Company. Promotes arbitration and interest in arbitration of the City of London, and supports education in the field of arbitration through charitable works.

Access to staff: Contact by letter, by telephone, by fax, by e-mail and via website. Non-members charged.

WORSHIPFUL COMPANY OF ARMOURERS & BRASIERS

Armourers' Hall, 81 Coleman Street, London, EC2R 5BJ

Tel: 020 7374 4000
Fax: 020 7606 7481

Enquiries to: The Clerk

Founded: 1322

Organisation type and purpose: Livery company.

Access to staff: Contact by letter
Hours: Mon to Fri, 0900 to 1700

Access to building: No access other than to staff

WORSHIPFUL COMPANY OF BAKERS

Bakers' Hall, Harp Lane, London, EC3R 6DP

Tel: 020 7623 2223
Fax: 020 7621 1924
E-mail: clerk@bakers.co.uk
Website: www.bakers.co.uk

Founded: c. 12th century

Organisation type and purpose: Membership association (membership is by election or invitation).
City of London Livery Company.

Access to staff: Contact by letter, by telephone, by fax, by e-mail and via website

WORSHIPFUL COMPANY OF BARBERS, THE (The Barbers' Company)

Barber-Surgeons' Hall, Monkwell Square, Wood Street, London, EC2Y 5BL

Tel: 020 7606 0741
Fax: 020 7606 3857
Website: www.barberscompany.org

Enquiries to: The Clerk

Founded: 1308

Organisation type and purpose: Learned society (membership is by election or invitation).
City of London Livery Company.

Subject coverage: Surgery (up to 1745) and barbery.

Publications: Printed

Access to staff: Contact by letter
Hours: Mon to Fri, 0930 to 1700

Access to building: No access other than to staff

WORSHIPFUL COMPANY OF BASKETMAKERS

Doric House, 108 Garstang Road West, Poulton le Fylde, Lancs, FY6 7SN

Tel: 01253 885776
Fax: 01253 886533
E-mail: clerk@basketmakersco.org
Website: www.basketmakersco.org

Enquiries to: The Clerk

Founded: 1569

Organisation type and purpose: Membership association (membership is by election or invitation).
City of London Livery Company.

Access to staff: Contact by letter, by telephone, by fax, by e-mail and via website

WORSHIPFUL COMPANY OF BLACKSMITHS

48 Upwood Road, Lee, London, SE12 8AN

Tel: 020 8318 9684
Fax: 020 8318 9687
E-mail: hammerandhand@supanet.com
Website: www.blacksmithscompany.org.uk

Enquiries to: Clerk

Founded: 1325

Organisation type and purpose: Membership association.
City of London Livery Company.

Subject coverage: The blacksmith craft.

Publications: Printed

Access to staff: Contact by letter
Hours: Mon to Fri, 0900 to 1700

WORSHIPFUL COMPANY OF BOWYERS

46 The Haydens, Tonbridge, Kent, TN9 1NS

Tel: 07766–023081
E-mail: clerk@bowyers.com
Website: www.bowyers.com/public

Enquiries to: The Clerk
Direct e-mail: clerk@bowyers.com

Founded: 1363

Organisation type and purpose: Membership association (membership is by election or invitation).
City of London Livery Company.
Registered charity (charity number 270702).

Access to staff: Contact by letter and by e-mail

WORSHIPFUL COMPANY OF BRODERERS

Ember House, 35–37 Creek Road, East Molesey, Surrey, KT8 9BE

Tel: 020 8941 3116
Fax: 020 8979 5934
E-mail: clerk@broderers.co.uk
Website: www.broderers.co.uk

Enquiries to: Clerk
Direct e-mail: office@newbycrouch.co.uk

Founded: 1400

Organisation type and purpose: City of London Livery Company.

Subject coverage: The Worshipful Company of Broderers.

Publications: Printed

Access to staff: Contact by letter, by telephone, by fax, by e-mail and via website
Hours: Mon to Fri, 0900 to 1730

WORSHIPFUL COMPANY OF BUILDERS' MERCHANTS

4 College Hill, London, EC4R 2RB

Tel: 020 7329 2189
E-mail: info@wcobm.co.uk

Enquiries to: The Clerk
Direct e-mail: wcobm@aol.com

Organisation type and purpose: Membership association (membership is by election or invitation).
City of London Livery Company.

Access to staff: Contact by letter, by telephone and by e-mail

WORSHIPFUL COMPANY OF BUTCHERS (Butchers' Company)

Butchers' Hall, 87 Bartholomew Close, London, EC1A 7EB

Tel: 020 7606 4106
Fax: 020 7606 4108

Enquiries to: Clerk to the Company

Founded: 1198

Organisation type and purpose: Learned society (membership is by election or invitation), present number of members: 690.

Subject coverage: City Livery Companies, City of London.

Library catalogue: All or part available in-house

Publications: Printed

Access to staff: Contact by letter, by telephone, by fax and by e-mail. Appointment necessary.
Hours: Mon to Fri, 0900 to 1700

Access to building: Prior appointment required
Hours: Mon to Fri, 0900 to 1700

Access for disabled people: Ramped entry, access to all public areas, toilet facilities

WORSHIPFUL COMPANY OF CARMEN

Five Kings House, 1 Queen Street Place, London EC4R 1QS

Tel: 020 7489 8289
Fax: 020 7236 3313
E-mail: enquiries@thecarmen.co.uk
Website: thecarmen.co.uk

Enquiries to: Clerk
Direct e-mail: theclerk@thecarmen.co.uk

Founded: 1517

Organisation type and purpose: Membership association (membership is by election or invitation), present number of members: 550, voluntary organisation.
City of London Livery Company.

Publications: Printed

Access to staff: Contact by letter, by telephone, by fax, by e-mail, in person and via website. Appointment necessary. Letter of introduction required. All charged.
Hours: Mon to Fri, 0900 to 1700

WORSHIPFUL COMPANY OF CHARTERED ACCOUNTANTS IN ENGLAND AND WALES

Larksfield, Kent Hatch Road, Crockham Hill, Edenbridge, Kent, TN8 6SX

Tel: 01732 866423
E-mail: clerk@wccaew.org.uk
Website: www.wccaew.org.uk

Enquiries to: The Clerk

Founded: 1977

Organisation type and purpose:
Membership association (membership is by election or invitation).
City of London Livery Company.
To foster the profession of accountancy and to provide social intercourse and mutual information between members of the Institute of Chartered Accountants in England and Wales.

Access to staff: Contact by letter, by telephone, by e-mail and via website

WORSHIPFUL COMPANY OF CHARTERED ARCHITECTS

82A Muswell Hill Road, London, N10 3JR

Tel: 020 8292 4893
Fax: 020 8292 4893
E-mail: coleadams@architects-livery-company.org
Website: www.architects-livery-company.org

Enquiries to: The Clerk
Direct tel: 020 8292 4893
Direct fax: 020 8292 4893
Direct e-mail: coleadams@architects-livery-company.org

Founded: 1988

Organisation type and purpose:
Membership association (membership is by election or invitation). City of London Livery Company. To advance the profession of architecture, to act as an independent forum for fellowship and exchange of ideas between members.

Access to staff: Contact by letter, by telephone, by fax, by e-mail and via website

WORSHIPFUL COMPANY OF CHARTERED SECRETARIES AND ADMINISTRATORS

Saddlers' House, 3rd Floor, 40 Gutter Lane, London, EC2V 6BR

Tel: 020 7726 2955
E-mail: clerk@wccsa.org.uk
Website: www.wccsa.org.uk

Enquiries to: Clerk

Organisation type and purpose:
Membership association (membership is by election or invitation).
City of London Livery Company.

Access to staff: Contact by letter, by telephone and by e-mail

WORSHIPFUL COMPANY OF CLOCKMAKERS

The Salters' Hall, Fore Street, London EC2Y 5DE

Tel: 020 7638 5500
Fax: 020 7638 5522
E-mail: clerk@clockmakers.org
Website: www.clockmakers.org

Enquiries to: Clerk

Founded: 1631

Organisation type and purpose:
Membership association (membership is by election or invitation), present number of members: 500, registered charity (charity number 275380), museum.

Subject coverage: Antiquarian horology – in particular clockmaking in London.

Collection: Horological library (founded 1813) consisting of books and manuscripts, together with a collection of clocks and watches, which were also originally (1817) intended for reference purposes

Non-library collection catalogue: All or part available in print

Publications: Printed

Access to staff: Contact by letter, by telephone, by fax, by e-mail and via website. Appointment necessary.
Hours: Mon, Wed, Fri, 1000 to 1600

Clockmakers' Museum is at the: Guildhall Library; Aldermanbury, London, EC2P 2EJ; tel: 020 7332 1865

WORSHIPFUL COMPANY OF COACHMAKERS AND COACH HARNESS MAKERS OF LONDON

48 Alderney Street, London, SW1V 4EX

Tel: 07505 089841
E-mail: clerk@coachmakers.co.uk
Website: www.coachmakers.co.uk

Enquiries to: The Clerk

Founded: 1677

Organisation type and purpose:
Membership association (membership is by election or invitation).
City of London Livery Company.

Access to staff: Contact by letter, by telephone, by e-mail and via website

WORSHIPFUL COMPANY OF CONSTRUCTORS

Ragby House, 157 Sidney Road, Walton on Thames, Surrey, KT12 3SA

Tel: 01932 253212
E-mail: m.kearsley1@ntworld.com
Website: www.constructorscompany.co.uk

Enquiries to: The Clerk

Founded: 1990

Organisation type and purpose:
Membership association (membership is by election or invitation).
City of London Livery Company.
To bring together those professionally qualified individuals concerned with all aspects of building design, execution, management, vision and economic appraisal within the framework of Guildery and Livery in the City of London.

Access to staff: Contact by letter, by telephone and by e-mail

WORSHIPFUL COMPANY OF COOKS

18 Solent Drive, Warsash, Southampton, Hants, SO31 9HB

Tel: 01489 579511
E-mail: clerk@cookslivery.org.uk
Website: www.cookslivery.org.uk

Enquiries to: The Clerk

Founded: 1482

Organisation type and purpose:
Membership association (membership is by election or invitation).
City of London Livery Company.
To support the City, the modern catering trade and charitable activities.

Access to staff: Contact by letter and by e-mail

WORSHIPFUL COMPANY OF COOPERS

Coopers' Hall, 13 Devonshire Square, London, EC2M 4TH

Tel: 020 7247 9577
Fax: 020 7377 8061
E-mail: clerk@coopers-hall.co.uk
Website: www.coopers-hall.co.uk

Enquiries to: The Clerk

Founded: 1501

Organisation type and purpose:
Membership association (membership is by election or invitation).
City of London Livery Company.

Access to staff: Contact by letter, by telephone, by fax, by e-mail and via website

WORSHIPFUL COMPANY OF CORDWAINERS (Cordwainers Company)

Clothworkers' Hall, Dunster Court, Mincing Lane, London, EC3R 7AH

Tel: 020 7929 1121
Fax: 020 7929 1124

Enquiries to: The Clerk (Chief Executive)
Direct e-mail: office@cordwainers.org

Founded: 1272

Organisation type and purpose:
Membership association (membership is by election or invitation), present number of members: 248.
City Livery Company.

Collection: Archives and records are held in The Guildhall Library

Access to staff: Contact by letter and by e-mail
Hours: Mon to Fri, 0900 to 1700

Access to building: Prior appointment required

WORSHIPFUL COMPANY OF CURRIERS

4 Little Orchard Place, Esher, Surrey, KT10 9PP

Tel: 01372 462462
E-mail: clerk@curriers.co.uk
Website: www.curriers.co.uk

Enquiries to: The Clerk

Founded: 1367; granted royal charter of incorporation (year of change 1605)

Organisation type and purpose: City of London Livery Company.
Membership association (membership is by election or invitation).
Historical, charitable, social

Subject coverage: Original trade – preparers and finishers of heavy hides for the leather industry.

Access to staff: Contact by letter, by telephone, by e-mail and via website

WORSHIPFUL COMPANY OF CUTLERS

Cutlers' Hall, Warwick Lane, London, EC4M 7BR

Tel: 020 7248 1866
E-mail: clerk@cutlerslondon.co.uk
Website: www.cutlerslondon.co.uk

Enquiries to: The Clerk

Founded: 1416

Organisation type and purpose:
Membership association (membership is by election or invitation).
City of London Livery Company.

Collection: Cutlery
Medals

Access to staff: Contact by letter, by telephone, by e-mail and via website

WORSHIPFUL COMPANY OF DISTILLERS

71 Lincoln's Inn Fields, London, WC2A 3JF

Tel: 020 7405 7091
E-mail: chughes@bcmw.co.uk

Enquiries to: The Clerk

Organisation type and purpose:
Membership association (membership is by election or invitation).
City of London Livery Company.

Access to staff: Contact by letter, by telephone and by e-mail

WORSHIPFUL COMPANY OF DYERS

Dyers Hall, 11–13 Dowgate Hill, London, EC4R 2ST

Tel: 020 7236 7197
Fax: 020 7248 0774
E-mail: clerk@dyerscompany.com
Website: www.dyerscompany.co.uk

Organisation type and purpose: City of London Livery Company.

WORSHIPFUL COMPANY OF ENGINEERS

Wax Chandlers' Hall, 6 Gresham Street, London, EC2V 7AD

Tel: 020 7726 4830
Fax: 020 7726 4820
E-mail: clerk@engineerscompany.org.uk
Website: www.engineerscompany.org.uk

Enquiries to: The Clerk

Organisation type and purpose:
Membership association (membership is by election or invitation).
City of London Livery Company.
To promote the development and advancement of the science, art and practice of engineering through a series of lectures, events and visits.

Access to staff: Contact by letter, by telephone, by fax, by e-mail and via website

WORSHIPFUL COMPANY OF ENVIRONMENTAL CLEANERS (WCEC)

121 Hacton Lane, Upminster, RM14 2NL

Tel: 01708 505548
E-mail: neil.morley@environmental-cleaners.com
Website: www.environmental-cleaners.com

Enquiries to: Clerk of the Company

Founded: 1986

Organisation type and purpose:
Membership association (membership is by election or invitation).
City of London Livery Company.
To encourage and maintain high standards of practice and integrity through social and professional exchange, while supporting and promoting education, training and research projects within the industry.

Access to staff: Contact by letter, by telephone, by e-mail and via website

WORSHIPFUL COMPANY OF FAN MAKERS

Skinners' Hall, 8 Dowgate Hill, London, EC4R 2SP

Tel: 020 7329 4633
Fax: 020 7329 4633
E-mail: clerk@fanmakers.com
Website: www.fanmakers.com

Enquiries to: The Clerk

Founded: 1709

Organisation type and purpose:
Membership association (membership is by election or invitation).
City of London Livery Company.

Collection: Collection of 250 fans

Access to staff: Contact by letter, by telephone, by fax, by e-mail and via website

WORSHIPFUL COMPANY OF FARMERS

Red Copse End, Red Copse Lane, Boars Hill, Oxford, OX1 5ER

Tel: 01865 321580
E-mail: clerk@farmerslivery.org.uk

Enquiries to: The Clerk

Founded: 1952

Organisation type and purpose:
Membership association (membership is by election or invitation).
City of London Livery Company.

Access to staff: Contact by letter, by telephone and by e-mail

WORSHIPFUL COMPANY OF FARRIERS

19 Queen Street, Chipperfield, Kings Langley, Hertfordshire, WD4 9BT

Tel: 01923 260747
Fax: 01923 261677
E-mail: theclerk@wcf.org.uk
Website: www.wcf.org.uk

Enquiries to: Clerk

Founded: 1356

Organisation type and purpose:
Membership association.
City of London Livery Company.

Subject coverage: The welfare of the horse through farriery.

Access to staff: Contact by letter, by telephone, by fax and by e-mail
Hours: Mon to Fri, 0900 to 1700

WORSHIPFUL COMPANY OF FELTMAKERS

Formal name: The Worshipful Company of Feltmakers of London

Clerk to the Trustees, Post Cottage, Greywell, Hook, Hampshire, RG29 1DA

Website: www.feltmakers.co.uk

Enquiries to: The Clerk

Founded: 1604

Organisation type and purpose:
Membership association (membership is by election or invitation).
City of London Livery Company.

Access to staff: Contact by letter, by telephone and by e-mail

Administers: The Feltmakers Charitable Foundation (Charity No. 259906)

WORSHIPFUL COMPANY OF FIREFIGHTERS

20 Aldermanbury, London, EC2V 7GF

Tel: 020 7600 1666
Fax: 020 7600 1666
E-mail: clerk@firefighterscompany.org
Website: www.firefighterscompany.org

Enquiries to: The Clerk

Founded: 1988; formerly called The Company of Firefighters, The Guild of Firefighters

Organisation type and purpose:
Membership association (membership is by subscription, election or invitation), present number of members: 170, registered charity.
Livery company.

Subject coverage: Firefighting and associated products, industry and activities.

Trade and statistical information: Fire fighting and protection

Access to staff: Contact by letter
Hours: Mon to Thu, 0900 to 1700

WORSHIPFUL COMPANY OF FISHMONGERS (The Fishmongers' Company)

Fishmongers' Hall, London Bridge, London, EC4R 9EL

continued overleaf

Tel: 020 7626 3531
Fax: 020 7929 1389
E-mail: enquiries@FishHall.org.uk
Website: www.fishhall.org.uk

Enquiries to: The Clerk
Other contacts: Chief Fisheries Inspector (for Billingsgate Market or other trade enquiries)

Founded: 1272

Organisation type and purpose:
Membership association (membership is by election or invitation), present number of members: 800.
Quality control, health and hygiene inspection service at Billingsgate Market.
Promotion of a healthy, prosperous and sustainable fish and fisheries sector for the long-term benefit of the United Kingdom.

Library catalogue: All or part available in-house

Publications: Printed
Order printed publications from: Fishmongers' Hall

Publications list: Available in print

Access to staff: Contact by letter, by telephone, by fax and by e-mail. Appointment necessary.
Hours: Mon to Fri, 0900 to 1700

Access to building: Prior appointment required.

Links with: Gresham's School; Cromer Road, Holt, Norfolk, NR25 6EA; tel: 01263 714500

WORSHIPFUL COMPANY OF FLETCHERS

Farmers' and Fletchers' Hall, 3 Cloth Street, EC1A 7LD

Tel: 020 7600 2204
Fax: 020 7606 4971
E-mail: ff@chesterboyd.co.uk
Website: www.fletchers.org.uk

Enquiries to: The Clerk
Direct e-mail: fletchersclerk@aol.com

Founded: 1371

Organisation type and purpose:
Membership association (membership is by election or invitation).
City of London Livery Company.

Access to staff: Contact by letter, by telephone, by fax and by e-mail

WORSHIPFUL COMPANY OF FOUNDERS

Founders' Hall, Number One, Cloth Fair, London, EC1A 7JQ

E-mail: founderscompany@aol.com
Website: www.foundersco.org.uk

Enquiries to: The Clerk
Direct tel: 01273 858700
Direct fax: 01273 858900

Organisation type and purpose:
Membership association (membership is by election or invitation).
City of London Livery Company.
To promote technical education and research in founding.

Access to staff: Contact by letter, by telephone, by fax and by e-mail

WORSHIPFUL COMPANY OF FRAMEWORK KNITTERS, THE

86 Park Drive, Upminster, Essex, RM14 3AS

Tel: 01708 510439
Fax: 01708 510439
E-mail: clerk@frameworkknitters.co.uk
Website: www.frameworkknitters.co.uk

Enquiries to: Clerk to the Company

Founded: 1713

Organisation type and purpose:
Membership association (membership is by election or invitation), present number of members: 215.
A City of London livery company.

Publications: Printed

Access to staff: Contact by letter, by telephone, by fax, by e-mail, in person and via website. Appointment necessary.
Hours: Upminster: Mon to Fri, 0900 to 1700
Oadby: Mon to Fri, 0930 to 1330

Access to building: Prior appointment required
Special comments: Archives are deposited at the Guildhall Library.

Subsidiary: Framework Knitters Homes; Corah House, Framework Knitters Cottages, Stoughton Road, Oadby, Leicestershire, LE2 4FQ; tel: 01162 712171; fax: 01162 713894; e-mail: AssistClerk@frameworkknitters.co.uk

WORSHIPFUL COMPANY OF FRUITERERS

Chapelstones, 84 High Street, Codford St Mary, Warminster, Wiltshire, BA12 0ND

Tel: 01985 850682
E-mail: clerk@fruiterers.org.uk
Website: www.fruit-baskets.co.uk/asp/default.asp

Enquiries to: The Clerk

Founded: 1463

Organisation type and purpose:
Membership association (membership is by election or invitation).
City of London Livery Company.
To promote excellence across all sectors of the fruit industry and to support education and research within it.

Access to staff: Contact by letter, by telephone, by fax and by e-mail

WORSHIPFUL COMPANY OF FUELLERS

26 Merrick Square, London, SE1 4JB

E-mail: clerk@fuellers.co.uk
Website: www.fuellers.co.uk

Enquiries to: The Clerk

Organisation type and purpose:
Membership association (membership is by election or invitation).
City of London Livery Company.
To foster the business of persons involved in providing energy for the home, industry, commerce and export.

Access to staff: Contact by letter, by telephone, by e-mail and via website

WORSHIPFUL COMPANY OF FURNITURE MAKERS

Furniture Makers' Hall, 12 Austin Friars, London, EC2N 2HE

Tel: 020 7256 5558
Fax: 020 7256 5155
E-mail: clerk@furnituremakers.org.uk
Website: www.furnituremakers.org.uk

Enquiries to: The Clerk

Founded: 1951

Organisation type and purpose:
Membership association (membership is by election or invitation).
City of London Livery Company.
To foster both the craft and the industry of furniture-making, marketing and retailing in the United Kingdom.

Access to staff: Contact by letter, by fax, by e-mail and via website

WORSHIPFUL COMPANY OF GARDENERS OF LONDON

25 Luke Street, London, EC2A 4AR

Tel: 020 7953 2321
E-mail: clerk@gardenerscompany.org.uk
Website: www.gardenerscompany.org.uk

Enquiries to: The Clerk
Direct tel: 020 7149 6696

Organisation type and purpose:
Membership association (membership is by election or invitation).
City of London Livery Company.
To promote the art and practice of good gardening throughout the country and especially in the London area, to support charitable activities connected with horticulture or the City of London, and to beautify the City of London by encouraging the display of flowers and foliage.

Access to staff: Contact by letter, by telephone, by e-mail and via website

WORSHIPFUL COMPANY OF GIRDLERS

Girdlers' Hall, Basinghall Avenue, London, EC2V 5DD

Tel: 020 7638 0488
E-mail: clerk@girdlers.co.uk

Enquiries to: The Clerk

Founded: 1327

Organisation type and purpose:
Membership association (membership is by election or invitation).
City of London Livery Company.

Access to staff: Contact by letter, by telephone, by e-mail and via website

WORSHIPFUL COMPANY OF GLASS SELLERS OF LONDON

North Farm House, High Road, Loughton, IG10 4JJ

Tel: 0208 502 1958
E-mail: info@glass-sellers.co.uk
Website: www.glass-sellers.co.uk

Enquiries to: The Clerk, Vincent Emms

Founded: 1664

Organisation type and purpose: City of London Livery Company, which received its Charter in 1664.
Stimulates interest in glass in all its aspects and carries out charitable works, with special emphasis on educational projects.

Access to staff: Contact by letter, by telephone, by e-mail and via website
Hours: Mon, to Thu, 1000 to 1600

WORSHIPFUL COMPANY OF GLAZIERS AND PAINTERS OF GLASS (Glaziers Company)

Glaziers' Hall, 9 Montague Close, London Bridge, London, SE1 9DD

Tel: 020 7403 6652
Fax: 020 7403 6652
E-mail: info@worshipfulglaziers.com
Website: www.worshipfulglaziers.com

Enquiries to: Clerk
Direct e-mail: clerk@worshipfulglaziers.com

Founded: 1638

Organisation type and purpose: City of London Livery Company.
Membership association (membership is by election or invitation), present number of members: 300.

Subject coverage: Advice on stained glass, particularly on conservation of historic glass.

Collection: Library on stained glass

Library catalogue: All or part available in-house

Access to staff: Contact by letter, by telephone, by fax and by e-mail.
Appointment necessary.
Hours: Mon to Fri, 1000 to 1600

Access for disabled people: Ramped entry, access to all public areas, toilet facilities

WORSHIPFUL COMPANY OF GLOVERS

Oscar Court, 17 Tite Street, London, SW3 4JR

Tel: 020 7376 3043
E-mail: clerk@theglovercompany.org
Website: www.theglovercompany.org

Enquiries to: The Clerk

Founded: 1349

Organisation type and purpose: Membership association (membership is by election or invitation).
City of London Livery Company.

Publications: Printed

Access to staff: Contact by letter, by e-mail and via website

WORSHIPFUL COMPANY OF GOLD AND SILVER WYRE DRAWERS

Bee Cottage, North Heath, Chieveley, Berkshire, RG20 8UA

Tel: 01635 247014
Fax: 01635 247014
E-mail: clerk@gswd.co.uk
Website: www.gswd.co.uk

Enquiries to: The Clerk

Founded: 1423

Organisation type and purpose: Membership association (membership is by election or invitation).
City of London Livery Company.

Access to staff: Contact by letter, by telephone, by fax, by e-mail and via website

WORSHIPFUL COMPANY OF GOLDSMITHS

Goldsmiths' Hall, Foster Lane, London, EC2V 6BN

Tel: 020 7606 7010
Fax: 020 7606 1511
E-mail: library@thegoldsmiths.co.uk
Website: www.thegoldsmiths.co.uk

Enquiries to: Librarian
Direct e-mail: david.beasley@thegoldsmiths.co.uk
Other contacts: Assistant Librarian (with special responsibility for A-V material)

Founded: 1327

Organisation type and purpose: Membership association (membership is by qualification), present number of members: 1,800.
The Goldsmiths' Company is one of the Twelve Great Livery Companies of the City of London with its roots in the trade guilds of the Middle Ages.
It is responsible for: operating the Goldsmiths' Company Assay Office, which hallmarks precious metal articles of gold, silver, platinum and palladium; promoting excellence in design and craftmanship of silver and jewellery, through exhibitions and other projects; administering charitable trusts to help the disadvantaged; and specific areas of education.

Subject coverage: Assaying and hallmarking of precious metals, gold plate, silver and jewellery, antique and modern, regalia.

Collection: Archives of the Company from 1334
Photographic collection
Slide collection
Twining Collection (books on regalia)
Collection of antique and modern silver, modern jewellery and modern art medals

Non-library collection catalogue: All or part available in-house

Library catalogue: All or part available in-house

Publications: Printed, and electronic and video, and microform publications

Publications list: Available online and in print

Access to staff: Contact by letter, by telephone, by fax and by e-mail.
Appointment necessary.
Hours: Mon to Fri, 1000 to 1645

Access to building: Prior appointment required

Access for disabled people: Disabled entrance, bathroom facilities, street parking
Special comments: Parking subject to availability; entry assisted by a device and staff.

Subsidiary body: Assay Office London

WORSHIPFUL COMPANY OF GROCERS

Grocers' Hall, Princes Street, London, EC2R 8AD

Tel: 020 7606 3113
Fax: 020 7600 3082
E-mail: clerk@grocershall.co.uk
Website: www.grocershall.co.uk

Enquiries to: The Clerk

Founded: c. 12th century

Organisation type and purpose: Membership association (membership is by election or invitation).
City of London Livery Company.

Access to staff: Contact by letter, by telephone, by fax, by e-mail and via website

WORSHIPFUL COMPANY OF GUNMAKERS

Proof House, 48–50 Commercial Road, London, E1 1LP

Tel: 020 7481 2695
E-mail: clerk@gunmakers.org.uk

Enquiries to: The Clerk

Founded: 1637

Organisation type and purpose: Membership assocation (membership is by election or invitation).
City of London Livery Company.

Access to staff: Contact by letter, by telephone, by e-mail and via website

WORSHIPFUL COMPANY OF HACKNEY CARRIAGE DRIVERS

25 The Grove, Parkfield Latimer, Buckinghamshire, HP5 1VE

Website: www.wchcd.com

Enquiries to: The Clerk

Founded: 2004

Organisation type and purpose: Membership association (membership is by election or invitation).
City of London Livery Company.
To raise public awareness of the extremely high standards of the London Hackney Carriage trade and industry.

Access to staff: Contact by letter

WORSHIPFUL COMPANY OF HORNERS

Box 145, Hill House, 148 Upper Richmond Road, London SW15 6NP

Tel: 020 8878 4212
E-mail: horners.clerk@btinternet.com
Website: www.horners.org.uk

Enquiries to: The Clerk

Founded: Royal Charter 1638

Organisation type and purpose: Membership association (membership is by election).
City of London Livery Company.

Collection: Collection of horn artefacts housed in the Museum of Design in Plastics, part of the Arts University College, Bournemouth

continued overleaf

Access to staff: Contact by letter, by telephone and by e-mail

WORSHIPFUL COMPANY OF INFORMATION TECHNOLOGISTS

39A Bartholomew Close, London, EC1A 7JN

Tel: 020 7600 1992
Fax: 020 7600 1991
E-mail: info@wcit.org.uk
Website: www.wcit.org.uk

Enquiries to: The Clerk
Direct e-mail: michael@wcit.org.uk

Founded: 1992

Organisation type and purpose:
Membership association (membership is by election or invitation).
City of London Livery Company.

Access to staff: Contact by letter, by telephone, by fax, by e-mail and via website

WORSHIPFUL COMPANY OF INNHOLDERS

Innholders' Hall, 29–30 College Street, London, EC4R 2RH

Tel: 020 7236 6703
Fax: 020 7236 0059
E-mail: mail@innholders.co.uk

Enquiries to: The Clerk

Founded: 1514

Organisation type and purpose: Voluntary organisation.

Access to staff: Contact by letter, by telephone, by fax and by e-mail
Hours: Mon to Fri, 0900 to 1700

Access to building: No access other than to staff

Access for disabled people: Limited – please enquire prior to visit

WORSHIPFUL COMPANY OF INSURERS

The Insurance Hall, 20 Aldermanbury, London, EC2V 7HY

Tel: 020 7600 4006
Fax: 020 7972 0153
E-mail: enquiries@wci.org.uk
Website: www.wci.org.uk

Enquiries to: The Clerk

Founded: 1970

Organisation type and purpose:
Membership association (membership is by election or invitation).
City of London Livery Company.
To foster the business of Insurers and to provide social intercourse and mutual information between members of that business

Access to staff: Contact by letter, by telephone, by fax, by e-mail and via website

WORSHIPFUL COMPANY OF INTERNATIONAL BANKERS

12 Austin Friars, London, EC2N 2HE

Tel: 020 7374 0212
Fax: 020 7374 0207
E-mail: tim.woods@internationalbankers.co.uk
Website: www.internationalbankers.co.uk

Enquiries to: The Clerk

Organisation type and purpose:
Membership association (membership is by election or invitation).
City of London Livery Company.

Access to staff: Contact by letter, by telephone, by fax, by e-mail and via website

WORSHIPFUL COMPANY OF IRONMONGERS, THE

Ironmongers' Hall, Shaftesbury Place, Barbican, London, EC2Y 8AA

Tel: 020 7606 2726
Fax: 020 7600 3519
E-mail: beadle@ironhall.co.uk

Enquiries to: The Clerk
Other contacts: Hall Manager for conferences and facilities hire.

Founded: 1463

Organisation type and purpose:
Membership association (membership is by election or invitation), voluntary organisation.

Access to staff: Contact by letter, by telephone and by e-mail
Hours: Mon to Fri, 0900 to 1700

Access to building: Prior appointment required

Access for disabled people: Ramped entry, access to all public areas, toilet facilities

WORSHIPFUL COMPANY OF JOINERS AND CEILERS

75 Meadway Drive, Horsell, Woking, Surrey, GU21 4TF

Fax: 01483 720098
E-mail: info@joinersandceilers.co.uk
Website: www.joinersandceilers.co.uk

Enquiries to: The Clerk

Organisation type and purpose:
Membership association (membership is by election or invitation).
City of London Livery Company.

Access to staff: Contact by letter, by telephone, by e-mail and via website

WORSHIPFUL COMPANY OF LAUNDERERS

Launderers' Hall, 9 Montague Close, London, SE1 9DD

Enquiries to: The Clerk
Direct tel: 020 7378 1430

Organisation type and purpose:
Membership association (membership is by election or invitation).
City of London Livery Company.

Access to staff: Contact by letter

WORSHIPFUL COMPANY OF LEATHERSELLERS (Leathersellers)

Leathersellers Hall, St Helen's Place, London, EC3A 6DQ

Tel: 020 7330 1444
Fax: 020 7330 1445
E-mail: enquiries@leathersellers.co.uk
Website: www.leathersellers.co.uk

Enquiries to: Chief Executive

Founded: 1444

Organisation type and purpose: National organisation, membership association (membership is by election or invitation), present number of members: 150, voluntary organisation, registered charity (charity number 278072).
Investment company and grant-giving foundation.

Subject coverage: History of leather trade, history of livery companies.

Library catalogue: All or part available in-house

Access to staff: Contact by letter, by telephone and by e-mail
Hours: Mon to Fri, 0900 to 1700

Access to building: Prior appointment required
Hours: Mon to Fri, 1000 to 1600
Special comments: Bona fide researchers only.

WORSHIPFUL COMPANY OF LORINERS

8 Portland Square, Wapping, London, E1W 2QR

Tel: 020 7709 0222
E-mail: clerk@loriner.co.uk
Website: www.loriner.co.uk

Enquiries to: The Clerk

Founded: 1261

Organisation type and purpose:
Membership association (membership is by election or invitation).
City of London Livery Company.
To maintain manufacturing standards in the trade and the encouragement of the proper use of bits, spurs, stirrups, buckles, bridles, saddle trees and other metal parts of horse tack, together with support for the Mayoralty of the City of London and good fellowship amongst the Livery.

Access to staff: Contact by letter, by telephone and by e-mail

WORSHIPFUL COMPANY OF MAKERS OF PLAYING CARDS (WCMPC)

Flat 5, 15 Greycoat Place, London, SW1P 1SB

Tel: 020 7799 3556
Fax: 020 7799 3557

Enquiries to: Archivist
Other contacts: Clerk

Founded: 1628

Organisation type and purpose:
Membership association (membership is by election or invitation).
City of London Livery Company, with its own, separate Charitable Trust.

Subject coverage: Origins of playing cards worldwide, their manufacture, history, use and games, also ancillary items such as card games, tarot cards etc.

Collection: Famous and large collection of playing cards, kept (on permanent loan) at the Guildhall Library. Prior notice is required for an examination of most exhibits

Publications: Printed

Access to staff: Contact by letter, by telephone, by fax and by e-mail
Hours: Mon to Fri, 0900 to 1700

WORSHIPFUL COMPANY OF MANAGEMENT CONSULTANTS

Copperfield, The Ridgeway, Cranleigh, Surrey, GU6 7HR

Tel: 01483 271459
E-mail: clerk@wcomc.org
Website: www.comc.org.uk

Enquiries to: The Clerk
Direct tel: 01483 271459
Direct e-mail: clerk@wcomc.org.uk

Founded: 1993

Organisation type and purpose: Membership association (membership is by election or invitation).
City of London Livery Company.

Access to staff: Contact by letter, by telephone and by e-mail

WORSHIPFUL COMPANY OF MARKETORS

Plaisterers' Hall, One London Wall, London, EC2Y 5JU

Tel: 0207 796 2045
E-mail: clerk@marketors.org
Website: www.marketors.org

Enquiries to: The Clerk

Founded: 1978

Organisation type and purpose: Membership association (membership is by election or invitation).
City of London Livery Company.
To promote excellence in marketing practice and education, support for the interests of the City of London as well as fellowship amongst its members.

Access to staff: Contact by letter, by telephone, by e-mail and via website

WORSHIPFUL COMPANY OF MASONS

22 Cannon Hill, Southgate, London, N14 6LG

Tel: 020 8882 9520
Fax: 020 8882 9520
E-mail: thecompanyclerk@masonslivery.org
Website: www.masonslivery.org

Enquiries to: Clerk

Founded: 1472

Organisation type and purpose: City of London Livery Company.

Subject coverage: City of London, stonemasonry.

Access to staff: Contact by letter, by telephone, by fax and by e-mail
Hours: Mon to Fri, 0900 to 1700; leave a message if call not answered

WORSHIPFUL COMPANY OF MERCERS (Mercers' Company)

Mercers' Hall, Ironmonger Lane, London, EC2V 8HE

Tel: 020 7726 4991
Fax: 020 7600 1158
E-mail: mail@mercers.co.uk
Website: www.mercers.co.uk

Enquiries to: Archivist and Curator
Direct e-mail: archives@mercers.co.uk

Founded: 1394

Organisation type and purpose: Membership association (membership is by election or invitation), present number of members: 300+.
City of London Livery Company.
Fraternity, corporate body and charitable foundation.

Subject coverage: History of the Mercers' Company and its associated trusts and charities.

Collection: Mercers' Company archives and art collection, 1347 to present

Non-library collection catalogue: All or part available in-house

Library catalogue: All or part available in-house

Publications: Printed

Access to staff: Contact by letter and by e-mail. Appointment necessary.

Access to building: By prior appointment only
Special comments: Access to external researchers will be severely limited from 2010 due to reorganisation.

Access for disabled people: Level entry, toilet facilities

WORSHIPFUL COMPANY OF MUSICIANS

6th Floor, 2 London Wall Buildings, London, EC2M 5PP

Tel: 020 7496 8980
Fax: 020 7588 3633
Website: www.wcom.org.uk

Enquiries to: Clerk
Other contacts: Deputy Clerk; email: deputyclerk@wcom.org.uk

Founded: 1500

Organisation type and purpose: Membership association (membership is by election or invitation), registered charity.

Subject coverage: Grants.

Collection: Archives deposited at the Guildhall Library

Access to staff: Contact by letter and by e-mail
Hours: Mon to Fri, 0900 to 1700

WORSHIPFUL COMPANY OF NEEDLEMAKERS

5 Staple Inn, London, WC1V 7QH

Tel: 020 7242 5031

Enquiries to: The Clerk
Direct e-mail: michael@hobsonarditti.com

Founded: 1656

Organisation type and purpose: Membership association (membership is by election or invitation).
City of London Livery Company.

Access to staff: Contact by letter, by telephone and by e-mail

WORSHIPFUL COMPANY OF PAINTER-STAINERS (Painters' Company)

Painters' Hall, 9 Little Trinity Lane, London, EC4V 2AD

Tel: 020 7236 6258
Fax: 020 7236 0500
E-mail: beadle@painters-hall.co.uk
Website: www.painters-hall.co.uk

Enquiries to: Clerk
Direct tel: 020 7236 7070
Direct fax: 020 7236 7074
Direct e-mail: clerk@painters-hall.co.uk

Founded: 1268/1283; created by the merger of Worshipful Company of Painters and Worshipful Company of Stainers (year of change 1502)

Organisation type and purpose: Membership association (membership is by election or invitation), present number of members: 520, registered charity (charity number 200001), historic building, house or site, suitable for ages: 16+.
City of London Livery Company.

Subject coverage: Historical details of the Company and its membership.

Collection: Assorted paintings and silver of varying degrees of interest
Charters and other documents of historical interest

Non-library collection catalogue: All or part available in-house

Access to staff: Contact by letter, by telephone, by fax and by e-mail. Appointment necessary.
Hours: Mon to Fri, 0900 to 1700

Access to building: Prior appointment required

Access for disabled people: Access to all public areas, toilet facilities

WORSHIPFUL COMPANY OF PATTENMAKERS

3 The High Street, Sutton Valence, Kent, ME17 3AG

Tel: 01622 842440
Fax: 01622 844266
E-mail: clerk@pattenmakers.co.uk
Website: www.pattenmakers.co.uk

Enquiries to: The Clerk

Founded: c. 14th century

continued overleaf

Organisation type and purpose: Membership association (membership is by election or invitation).
City of London Livery Company.

Access to staff: Contact by letter, by telephone, by e-mail and via website

WORSHIPFUL COMPANY OF PAVIORS

3 Ridgemount Gardens, Enfield, Middlesex, EN2 8QL

Tel: 020 8366 1566
E-mail: clerk@paviorscompany.org.uk
Website: www.paviors.org.uk

Enquiries to: The Clerk

Founded: 1479

Organisation type and purpose: Membership association (membership is by election or invitation).
City of London Livery Company.

Access to staff: Contact by letter, by telephone and by e-mail

WORSHIPFUL COMPANY OF PEWTERERS (The Pewterers' Company)

Pewterers' Hall, Oat Lane, London, EC2V 7DE

Tel: 020 7397 8190
Fax: 020 7600 3896
E-mail: clerk@pewterers.org.uk
Website: www.pewterers.org.uk

Enquiries to: Clerk (Chief Executive)

Founded: 1474

Organisation type and purpose: Membership association (membership is by election or invitation), present number of members: 230, voluntary organisation.
City of London Livery Company.
Custodians of the history of pewter and the pewter trade. Promote pewter and the trade, particularly through youth education.

Subject coverage: All aspects of antique and modern pewter.

Collection: Collection of antique pewterware
Comprehensive records of pewter and pewterers since the company's first charter in 1474

Publications: Printed

Access to staff: Contact by letter, by telephone and by fax. Appointment necessary.
Hours: Mon to Fri, 0900 to 1700

Headquarters of the: Association of British Pewter Craftsmen; tel: 0114 266 3084; fax: 0114 267 0910; European Pewter Union; tel: 020 7606 9363; fax: 020 7600 3896; e-mail: epu@pewterers.org.uk

WORSHIPFUL COMPANY OF PLAISTERERS

1 London Wall, London, EC2Y 5JU

Tel: 020 7796 4333
Fax: 020 7796 4334
E-mail: clerk@plaistererslivery.co.uk
Website: www.plaistererslivery.co.uk

Enquiries to: The Clerk

Founded: 1501

Organisation type and purpose: Membership association (membership is by election or invitation).
City of London Livery Company.

Access to staff: Contact by letter, by telephone, by fax and by e-mail

WORSHIPFUL COMPANY OF PLUMBERS (WCP)

Wax Chandlers' Hall, 6 Gresham Street, London, EC2V 7AD

Tel: 020 7796 2468
Fax: 020 7796 2468
E-mail: clerk@plumberscompany.org.uk
Website: www.plumberscompany.org

Enquiries to: Clerk

Founded: 1365

Organisation type and purpose: Membership association.
City of London Livery Company.

Subject coverage: Plumbing.

Collection: Records back to 1365 deposited in the Guildhall Museum

Publications: Printed

Access to staff: Contact by letter
Hours: Mon to Thu, 0900 to 1700

Connections with: Chartered Institute of Plumbing and Heating Engineering (for registered plumbers); CORGI (for registered gas fitters)

WORSHIPFUL COMPANY OF SADDLERS

40 Gutter Lane, Cheapside, London, EC2V 6BR

Tel: 020 7726 8661
Fax: 020 7600 0386
E-mail: clerk@saddlersco.co.uk

Enquiries to: Clerk

Founded: early 12th century

Organisation type and purpose: City of London Livery Company.
Support of trade of saddlery, support of education and charity.

Non-library collection catalogue: All or part available in-house

Library catalogue: All or part available in-house

Access to staff: Contact by letter, by telephone, by fax and by e-mail. Appointment necessary.
Hours: Mon to Fri, 0900 to 1700

WORSHIPFUL COMPANY OF SCIENTIFIC INSTRUMENT MAKERS

Glaziers Hall, 9 Montague Close, London, SE1 9DD

Tel: 020 7407 4832
Fax: 020 7407 1565
E-mail: theclerk@wcsim.co.uk
Website: www.wcsim.co.uk

Enquiries to: The Clerk

Founded: 1956

Organisation type and purpose: Membership association (membership is by election or invitation).
City of London Livery Company.

Access to staff: Contact by letter, by telephone, by fax, by e-mail and via website

WORSHIPFUL COMPANY OF SCRIVENERS

HQS Wellington, Temple Stairs, Victoria Embankment, London, WC2R 2PN

Tel: 020 7240 0529
E-mail: clerk@scriveners.org.uk
Website: www.scriveners.org.uk

Enquiries to: The Clerk

Founded: 1373; formerly called Mysterie of the Writers of the Court Letter

Organisation type and purpose: Membership association (membership is by election or invitation), present number of members: 200, registered charity.
Livery Company of the City of London.
Regulating the standards of Scrivener Notaries

Subject coverage: The profession of public notary principally within the City of London, its history and regulation.

Collection: History and former membership of the company, for which all records are deposited in the City of London Guildhall Library, Aldermanbury, London, EC2P 2EJ

Publications: Printed
Order printed publications from: The Clerk

Access to staff: Contact by letter, by telephone and by e-mail
Hours: Mon, Wed and Thu, 1000 to 1730

WORSHIPFUL COMPANY OF SHIPWRIGHTS

Ironmongers' Hall, Shaftesbury Place, London, EC2Y 8AA

Tel: 020 7606 2376
Fax: 020 7600 8117
Website: www.shipwrights.co.uk

Enquiries to: Clerk
Direct e-mail: clerk@shipwrights.co.uk

Founded: pre 1199

Organisation type and purpose: Membership association (membership is by election or invitation), present number of members: 460, registered charity (charity number 262043 313249).
City of London Livery Company.

Subject coverage: History of the company.

Access to staff: Contact by letter, by telephone, by fax and by e-mail. Appointment necessary.
Hours: Mon to Fri, 0900 to 1700

WORSHIPFUL COMPANY OF SKINNERS

Skinners' Hall, 8 Dowgate Hill, EC4R 2SP

Tel: 020 7236 5629
E-mail: beadle@skinners.org.uk
Website: www.skinnershall.co.uk

Enquiries to: The Clerk

Organisation type and purpose:
Membership association (membership is by election or invitation).
City of London Livery Company.
To increase the prosperity of the Company and to support Skinners' schools.

Access to staff: Contact by letter, by telephone and by e-mail

WORSHIPFUL COMPANY OF SPECTACLE MAKERS (SMC)

Formal name: The Spectacle Makers Company

Apothecaries' Hall, Black Friars Lane, London, EC4V 6EL

Tel: 020 7236 2932
Fax: 020 7329 3249
E-mail: clerk@spectaclemakers.com
Website: www.spectaclemakers.com

Enquiries to: Clerk

Founded: 1629

Organisation type and purpose:
Professional body.
City of London Livery Company.

Subject coverage: Livery company, optical technicians, optics, history of the company.

Collection: Company Records
Library, city history, histories of livery companies

Publications: Printed

Access to staff: Contact by letter
Hours: Mon to Fri, 0900 to 1700

WORSHIPFUL COMPANY OF TALLOW CHANDLERS

4 Dowgate Hill, London, EC4R 2SH

Tel: 020 7248 4726
Fax: 020 7236 0844
E-mail: clerk@tallowchandlers.org
Website: www.tallowchandlers.org

Enquiries to: Clerk

Founded: 1462

Organisation type and purpose:
Membership association.
City of London Livery Company.

Subject coverage: Tallow and candles, tallow trade, oils and fats

Collection: Company documents from 1456

Access to staff: Contact by letter and by e-mail
Hours: Mon to Fri, 0900 to 1700

WORSHIPFUL COMPANY OF TAX ADVISERS

191 West End Road, Ruislip, HA4 6LD

Tel: 01895 625817
E-mail: clerk@taxadvisers.org.uk
Website: www.taxadvisers.org.uk

Enquiries to: The Clerk

Founded: 1995

Organisation type and purpose:
Membership association (membership is by election or invitation).
City of London Livery Company.

Access to staff: Contact by letter, by telephone and by e-mail

WORSHIPFUL COMPANY OF TIN PLATE WORKERS ALIAS WIRE WORKERS (Tin Plate Workers' Company)

Highbanks, Ferry Road, Surlingham, Norfolk, NR14 7AR

Tel: 08456 439967
E-mail: clerk@tinplateworkers.co.uk
Website: www.tinplateworkers.co.uk

Enquiries to: The Clerk

Founded: 1670

Organisation type and purpose:
Membership association (membership is by election or invitation).
City of London Livery Company.

Publications: Printed

Access to staff: Contact by letter, by telephone, by e-mail and via website

WORSHIPFUL COMPANY OF TOBACCO PIPE MAKERS AND TOBACCO BLENDERS

108 Dorset Road, Bexhill on Sea, East Sussex, TN40 2HT

E-mail: tobaccoclerk@btconnect.com
Website: www.tobaccolivery.co.uk/

Enquiries to: Clerk

Founded: 1619/1954

Organisation type and purpose:
Membership association (membership is by election or invitation), present number of members: 160.
City of London Livery Company.
Charitable.

Subject coverage: Benevolence, tobacco products, pipes.

Collection: Some items displayed in Brosely Pipe Museum, Ironbridge

Access to staff: Contact by e-mail

WORSHIPFUL COMPANY OF TURNERS OF LONDON

Skinners' Hall, 8 Dowgate Hill, London, EC4R 2SP

Tel: 020 7236 3605
E-mail: clerk@turnersco.com
Website: www.turnersco.com

Enquiries to: The Clerk

Founded: 1604

Organisation type and purpose:
Membership association (membership is by election or invitation).
City of London Livery Company.
To promote the craft of turning, to participate in the life of the City of London and to support related charities.

Access to staff: Contact by letter, by telephone, by e-mail and via website

WORSHIPFUL COMPANY OF TYLERS AND BRICKLAYERS

30 Shelley Avenue, Tiptree, Essex, CO5 0SF

Tel: 01621 816592
E-mail: tandbclerk@aol.com
Website: www.tylersandbricklayers.co.uk

Enquiries to: The Clerk

Founded: 1568

Organisation type and purpose:
Membership association (membership is by election or invitation).
City of London Livery Company.

Access to staff: Contact by letter, by telephone and by e-mail

WORSHIPFUL COMPANY OF UPHOLDERS

Pembroke Lodge, 162 Tonbridge Road, Hildenborough, Kent TN11 9HP

Tel: 01732 833315
E-mail: clerk@upholders.co.uk
Website: www.upholders.co.uk

Enquiries to: The Clerk

Founded: 1626

Organisation type and purpose:
Membership association (membership is by election or invitation).
City of London Livery Company.

Access to staff: Contact by letter, by telephone and by e-mail

WORSHIPFUL COMPANY OF WATER CONSERVATORS

The Lark, 2 Bell Lane, Worlington, Bury St Edmunds, Suffolk, IP28 8SE

Tel: 01638 510626
Fax: 01638 510626
E-mail: clerk@waterconservators.org
Website: www.waterconservators.org

Enquiries to: The Clerk
Direct tel: 020 8421 0305

Founded: 1994

Organisation type and purpose:
Membership association (membership is by election or invitation).
City of London Livery Company.
To promote the development and advancement of the science, art and practice of water and environmental management and the various scientific subjects related thereto.

Access to staff: Contact by letter, by telephone, by fax and by e-mail

WORSHIPFUL COMPANY OF WAX CHANDLERS

Wax Chandlers Hall, 6 Gresham Street, London, EC2V 7AD

Tel: 020 7726 0710
Fax: 020 7600 5462
E-mail: enquiries@waxchandlershall.co.uk
Website: www.waxchandlershall.co.uk

Enquiries to: The Clerk

continued overleaf

Organisation type and purpose: Membership association (membership is by election or invitation).
City of London Livery Company.

Collection: Archive held by Guildhall Library (open access)

Access to staff: Contact by letter, by telephone, by fax and by e-mail

WORSHIPFUL COMPANY OF WEAVERS

Saddlers' House, Gutter Lane, London, EC2V 6BS

Tel: 020 7606 1155
Fax: 020 7606 1119
E-mail: weavers@weavers.org.uk
Website: www.weavers.org.uk

Enquiries to: Clerk

Founded: 1130

Organisation type and purpose: Membership association (membership is by election or invitation), present number of members: 150.
City of London Livery Company.

Subject coverage: History of the company.

Collection: The company's historical records and admission records are deposited at Guildhall Library

Publications: Printed, and microform publications

Publications list: Available in print

Access to staff: Contact by letter
Hours: Mon to Fri, 0900 to 1700

WORSHIPFUL COMPANY OF WHEELWRIGHTS

7 Glengall Road, Bexleyheath, Kent, DA7 4AL

Tel: 020 8306 5119
Fax: 020 8979 5934
E-mail: enquiries@wheelwrights.org
Website: www.wheelwrights.org

Enquiries to: Clerk

Founded: 1670

Organisation type and purpose: Membership association (membership is by election or invitation), present number of members: 220.

Subject coverage: The craft of wheelwrighting. List of working wheelwrights in the United Kingdom.

Publications: Printed

Access to staff: Contact by letter, by e-mail and via website
Hours: Mon to Fri, 0900 to 1700

WORSHIPFUL COMPANY OF WOOLMEN

56 Lower Way, Great Brickhill, Bucks, MK17 9AG

Tel: 01525 261541
E-mail: clerk@woolmen.com
Website: www.woolmen.com

Enquiries to: The Clerk

Founded: c. 12th century

Organisation type and purpose: Membership association (membership is by election or invitation).
City of London Livery Company.

Access to staff: Contact by letter, by telephone and by e-mail

WORSHIPFUL COMPANY OF WORLD TRADERS (World Traders)

13 Hall Gardens, Colney Heath, St Albans, Herts, AL4 0QF

Tel: 01727 822181
E-mail: clerk@world-traders.org
Website: www.world-traders.org

Enquiries to: Clerk

Founded: 2000

Organisation type and purpose: Membership association (membership is by election or invitation).
City of London Livery Company.

Access to staff: Contact by telephone and by e-mail

Access to building: No access

WORSHIPFUL SOCIETY OF APOTHECARIES OF LONDON

Apothecaries' Hall, Black Friars Lane, London, EC4V 6EJ

Tel: 020 7236 1189
Fax: 020 7329 3177
E-mail: clerk@apothecaries.org
Website: www.apothecaries.org

Enquiries to: The Clerk

Founded: 1617

Organisation type and purpose: Learned society.
City of London Livery Company.

Subject coverage: History of the Society, membership lists since 1617, medical historical matters, non-university medical examination and licensing matters, the following examinations: Licentiate in Medicine and Surgery of the Society of Apothecaries, Diploma in the History of Medicine, Mastership in Medical Jurisprudence, Diploma in Medical Jurisprudence, Diploma in Genito-Urinary Medicine, Diploma in the Philosophy of Medicine, Diploma in Sports Medicine, Diploma in Musculo-Skeletal Medicine, Diploma in Medical Care of Catastrophes, Diploma in Regulatory Toxicology.

Collection: Medical examination matters from 1815
Some records from 1617 to date

Access to staff: Contact by letter, by telephone, by fax and by e-mail. Appointment necessary.
Hours: Mon to Fri, 0900 to 1700

Access to building: Prior appointment required

Access for disabled people: Ramped entry, access to all public areas

Links with: Faculty of the History and Philosophy of Medicine and Pharmacy

WORTHING BOROUGH COUNCIL

Town Hall, Chapel Road, Worthing, West Sussex, BN11 1HA

Tel: 01903 239999, 01903 204500 (minicom)
Fax: 01903 236552
E-mail: enquiries@worthing.gov.uk
Website: www.worthing.gov.uk

Enquiries to: Public Relations Manager

Founded: 1890

Organisation type and purpose: Local government body.

Subject coverage: Two-tier authority. Provider of public services within Worthing Borough.

Access to staff: Contact by letter, by telephone, by fax, by e-mail and via website
Hours: Mon to Fri, 0900 to 1700

Access for disabled people: Parking provided, ramped entry, toilet facilities

WOTTON-UNDER-EDGE HISTORICAL SOCIETY

Wotton-under-Edge Heritage Centre, The Chipping, Wotton-under-Edge, Gloucestershire, GL12 7AD

Tel: 01453 521541
E-mail: info@wottonheritage.com
Website: www.wottonheritage.com

Enquiries to: Honorary Administrator
Other contacts: Society Chairman

Founded: 1945

Organisation type and purpose: Membership association, present number of members: 70, voluntary organisation, registered charity (charity number 291936), museum, suitable for ages: all.

Subject coverage: Local history of Wotton-under-Edge and adjoining parishes, local family history, Wotton-under-Edge and adjoining parishes, tourist information point.

Information services: Tourist Information Point.

Special visitor services: Facilities for local and family history research.

Education services: Education packs available for loan to local schools.

Services for disabled people: Displays and/or information at wheelchair height.

Collection: Books, documents, manuscripts, pictures, photographs and artefacts, all in computerised database
Parish registers and 1891 census on microfiche and 1881 census on CD-ROM

Non-library collection catalogue: All or part available in-house

Publications: Printed, and electronic and video, and microform publications
Order printed publications from: Wotton Heritage Centre

Publications list: Available online

Access to staff: Contact by letter, by telephone, by e-mail and in person
Hours: As for access to building

Access to building: No prior appointment required

Hours: Tue to Fri, 1000 to 1300 and 1400 to 1700 (1600 in winter); Sat, 1000 to 1300; some Sun in summer, 1430 to 1700
Special comments: Charges made for the use of research facilities only.

Access for disabled people: Parking provided, level entry, access to all public areas, toilet facilities
Hours: As above

WOUND CARE SOCIETY (WCS)

PO Box 170, Huntingdon, Cambridgeshire, PE29 1PL

Tel: 01480 434401
Fax: 01480 434401
E-mail: wound.care.society@talk21.com

Enquiries to: Administrator

Founded: 1987

Subject coverage: WCS is a charitable organisation concerned with all aspects of wound care. It is a registered charity which provides educational material to nursing professionals.

Publications: Printed

Access to staff: Contact by letter, by telephone, by fax, by e-mail and via website
Hours: 24 hours Answer Machine

Access to building: No access other than to staff

WPF COUNSELLING AND PSYCHOTHERAPY (WPF)

Formal name: Westminster Pastoral Foundation Counselling and Psychotherapy

23 Magdalen Street, London, SE1 2EN

Tel: 020 7378 2000
Fax: 020 7378 2010
E-mail: reception@wpf.org.uk
Website: www.wpf.org.uk

Enquiries to: Secretary
Other contacts: Appointments Office tel no: 020 7361 4803

Founded: 1970

Organisation type and purpose: Registered charity (charity number 273434), training organisation, consultancy.
Counselling service.
To provide affordable counselling and psychotherapy, to train counsellors and psychotherapists.

Subject coverage: Counselling and psychotherapy.

Access to staff: Contact by telephone
Hours: Mon to Fri, 0900 to 1700

Access for disabled people: Parking provided, ramped entry, toilet facilities

Affiliated Counselling Centres: WPF Counselling and Psychotherapy; 23 Kensington Square, London, W8 5HN; tel: 020 7361 4864

WRC PLC

Frankland Road, Blagrove, Swindon, Wiltshire, SN5 8YF

Tel: 01793 865000
Fax: 01793 865001
E-mail: solutions@wrcplc.co.uk
Website: www.wrcplc.co.uk

Enquiries to: Librarian
Direct tel: 01793 865056
Direct e-mail: martine.gibbons@wrcplc.co.uk

Founded: 1927; formerly called Water Research Centre (WRc)

Organisation type and purpose: Consultancy, research organisation.

Subject coverage: Water supply; drinking water analysis; environmental chemistry; microbiology; quality and health matters; legislation; water pollution; solid wastes and sewage sludge disposal; ecotoxicology; water and waste water treatment; sewage treatment and disposal; sludge treatment; processes automation and control; sewers and sewerage; water mains; marine and freshwater studies including modelling; computing; Water Byelaws Advisory Service.

Publications: Printed
Order printed publications from: Publications Department, WRc Information Resources, Frankland Road, Blagrove, Swindon, Wiltshire, SN5 8YF; tel: 01793 865138; fax: 01793 514562; e-mail: sales@webookshop .com; website: http://www.webookshop.com

Access to staff: Contact by letter, by telephone, by fax, by e-mail and via website
Hours: Mon to Fri, 0930 to 1630

Access to building: No access other than to staff

Also at: WRc-NSF; Unit 30, Fern Close, Pen-y-Fan Industrial Estate, Oakdale, Gwent, NP11 3EH; tel: 01495 236260; fax: 01495 249234; e-mail: info@wrcnsf.com; website: http://www.wrcnsf.com

WREXHAM COUNTY BOROUGH COUNCIL (WCBC)

Guildhall, Wrexham, Clwyd, LL11 1AY

Tel: 01978 292000
Fax: 01978 292106
Website: www.wrexham.gov.uk

Enquiries to: Public Relations Manager
Direct tel: 01978 292275
Direct fax: 01978 292252
Direct e-mail: sue.wynjones@wrexham.gov .uk

Founded: 1996

Organisation type and purpose: Local government body.

Publications: Printed, and electronic and video
Order printed publications from: Publicity Officer, tel: 01978 292274; fax: 01978 297448; e-mail: kesah.trowell@wrexham.gov.uk

Access to staff: Contact by letter, by telephone, by fax, by e-mail, in person and via website. Appointment necessary.
Hours: Mon to Thu, 0845 to 1715; Fri, 0845 to 1645

Access to building: No prior appointment required
Hours: Hours vary

Access for disabled people: Parking provided

WRITERS GUILD OF GREAT BRITAIN (WGGB)

430 Edgware Road, London, W2 1EH

Tel: 020 7723 8074
Fax: 020 7706 2413
E-mail: admin@writersguild.org.uk
Website: www.writersguild.org.uk

Enquiries to: General Secretary

Founded: 1957

Organisation type and purpose: Professional body, trade union, present number of members: 2,000.

Subject coverage: Professional writing in TV, radio, films, theatre, books and multimedia.

Publications: Printed

Access to staff: Contact by letter, by telephone, by fax, by e-mail and via website. Appointment necessary.
Hours: Mon to Fri, 0930 to 1730

Incorporates the: Theatre Writers Union

WRITTLE COLLEGE

Chelmsford, Essex, CM1 3RR

Tel: 01245 424200
Fax: 01245 420456
E-mail: info@writtle.ac.uk
Website: www.writtle.ac.uk

Enquiries to: Librarian

Founded: 1893; formerly called Writtle Agriculture College (year of change 1993)

Organisation type and purpose: Local government body, university library.
Higher Education College.

Subject coverage: Agriculture; agricultural engineering; horticulture (amenity and commercial); agricultural diversification; plant and animal science; soil science; farm and horticultural enterprise management; equine science.

Collection: Collection of 18th- and 19th-century books on agriculture and horticulture

Library catalogue: All or part available online

WWF-UK (WWF)

Panda House, Weyside Park, Godalming, Surrey, GU7 1XR

Tel: 01483 426444
Fax: 01483 426409
Website: www.wwf.org.uk
Website: www.wwflearning.org.uk

Enquiries to: Supporter Relations

Founded: 1961; formerly called World Wildlife Fund (WWF) (year of change 1986); formerly called Worldwide Fund for Nature (WWF) (year of change 2001)

Organisation type and purpose: International organisation, registered charity (charity number 201707).
To conserve species of animals and plants and their habitats, and to reconcile the needs of people with the conservation of the natural environment upon which they depend.

continued overleaf

Subject coverage: Climate change, forests, freshwater, marine and coasts, rare species, toxics, agriculture, plants, tourism, economics, trade and investment, international development, oil, gas and mining, UK social change.

Library catalogue: All or part available in-house

Publications: Printed, and electronic and video
Order printed publications from: Education resources only, WWF-UK
Education Distribution, PO Box 963, Slough, SL2 3RS, tel: 01753 643104, fax: 01753 646553

Publications list: Available online and in print

Access to staff: Contact by letter, by telephone, by fax and by e-mail. Appointment necessary.
Hours: Mon to Fri, 0900 to 1700
Special comments: Library use by appointment.

Access to building: Prior appointment required

Access for disabled people: Parking provided

Affiliated to: International Union for Conservation of Nature and Natural Resources (IUCN)

Other addresses: WWF Cymru; Room 313, Baltic House, Mount Stuart Square, Cardiff, CF10 5FH; tel: 029 2045 4970; fax: 029 2045 1306; e-mail: wwf-uk-wales@wwf.org.uk; WWF Northern Ireland; 13 West Street, Carrickfergus, Co Antrim, BT38 7AR; tel: 028 9335 5166; fax: 028 9336 4448; e-mail: wwf-uk-ni@wwf.org.uk; WWF Scotland; Little Dunkeld, Dunkeld, Perthshire, PH8 0AD; tel: 01887 820449

Parent body: WWF International; Avenue du Mont Blanc, Gland, CH-1196, Switzerland

WYRE BOROUGH COUNCIL

Civic Centre, Breck Road, Poulton-le-Fylde, Lancashire, FY6 7PU

Tel: 01253 891000
Fax: 01253 899000
E-mail: mailroom@wyrebc.gov.uk
Website: www.wyre.gov.uk

Founded: 1974

Organisation type and purpose: Local government body.

Subject coverage: Provision of local government services by a district council, council tax, environmental health, health and safety, housing, transport, sport, leisure and recreation, planning, personnel and management services, tourism.

Publications: Printed

Publications list: Available in print

Access to staff: Contact by letter, by telephone, by e-mail, in person and via website
Hours: Mon to Fri, 0900 to 1700

Access to building: Mon to Fri
Hours: 0830 to 1700

Access for disabled people: Parking provided, ramped entry, level entry, access to all public areas, toilet facilities

XENOPHON

98 Cambridge Gardens, London, W10 6HS

Tel: 020 8968 1360
E-mail: wolstan-dixie@hotmail.co.uk

Enquiries to: Information Officer

Founded: 1979

Organisation type and purpose: Learned society (membership is by election or invitation).

Subject coverage: Recreational and historical cryptography, i.e. codes, ciphers, cryptanalysis, signs, signals, steganography, secret and hidden artificial languages and their recovery.

Collection: Books
Pamphlets
Magazines
Grey literature
Press clippings

Non-library collection catalogue: All or part available in-house

Library catalogue: All or part available in-house

Publications: Printed, and electronic and video

Access to staff: Contact by letter, by telephone and by e-mail. Non-members charged.
Hours: Mon to Fri, 1000 to 1700

XR OWNERS CLUB (XROC)

9 Cope Place, Earls Court Road, Kensington, London, W8 6AA

Tel: 020 7937 7595
E-mail: info@xroc.co.uk
Website: www.xroc.co.uk
Website: www.xrstyle.co.uk/forums

Enquiries to: Club Chairman
Direct tel: see contact information on website
Direct e-mail: john@xroc.co.uk, jaffaxroc@hotmail.co.uk
Other contacts: Vice Chairman, Local Branch Secretaries

Founded: 1983; may be looked for as Ford XR Owners Club

Organisation type and purpose: Car Club.

Subject coverage: Ford XR2, XR3, XR4, XR6 and XR8 information, Supersport Register, classic car insurance (members only), technical information/assistance (members only). Valuations (members only).

Publications: Printed

Access to staff: Contact by letter, by telephone, by e-mail and via website
Special comments: Contact by phone within reason and no later than 9pm

Access to building: No office

YACHT DESIGNERS AND SURVEYORS ASSOCIATION (YDSA)

The Glass Works, Penns Road, Petersfield, Hampshire, GU32 2EW

Tel: 01730 710425/710490
Fax: 01730 710423
E-mail: info@ybdsa.co.uk
Website: www.ydsa.co.uk

Enquiries to: Chief Executive
Direct e-mail: jane@ybdsa.co.uk
Other contacts: Certifying Authority (for MCA Code vessel work)

Founded: 1912

Organisation type and purpose: Professional body (membership is by election or invitation), present number of members: 150.
Training and maintaining of standards.

Subject coverage: Surveyors and designers of small craft, marine surveyors, training, tonnage measurement for registration, certification under the MCA Small Commercial Vessel Code.

Collection: Wide selection of books relating to small craft, dating back to early 20th century

Library catalogue: All or part available in-house

Publications: Printed

Access to staff: Contact by letter, by telephone, by fax, by e-mail, in person and via website. Appointment necessary.
Hours: Mon to Fri, 0900 to 1700

Access to building: Prior appointment required
Hours: Mon to Fri, 0900 to 1700

Access for disabled people: Some parking

Links with: Association of Brokers & Yacht Agents (ABYA); Professional Charter Association (PCA); Yacht Brokers Designers & Surveyors Association (YBDSA)

YACHT HARBOUR ASSOCIATION

Marine House, Thorpe Lea Road, Egham, Surrey, TW20 8BF

Tel: 01784 223817
Fax: 01784 475870
E-mail: lgordon@britishmarine.co.uk
Website: www.yachtharbourassociation.com
Website: www.berthsearch.com

Enquiries to: Administrator
Other contacts: General Manager; Chairman

Organisation type and purpose: Marina trade association.
To develop the marine industry by specifically supporting marina members of the British Marine Federation.
Helps boat users find good quality marinas and helps marina businesses improve their services and operate to high, modern standards. Offers advice in a range of issues, marketing and promotional tools, specific training for marina management and the opportunity to work with other businesses to find the best way to address problems.

Subject coverage: Marina and mooring operators; boatyards; consultants; suppliers of equipment and services to the marina industry, both in the UK and overseas.

Publications: Printed

Access to staff: Contact by letter, by telephone, by fax, by e-mail and via website

Links with: British Marine Federation (BMF)

YEHUDI MENUHIN SCHOOL

Stoke d'Abernon, Cobham, Surrey KT11 3QQ

Tel: 01932 864739
E-mail: reception@yehudimenuhinschool.co.uk
Website: www.yehudimenuhinschool.co.uk

Enquiries to: Headmaster and PA
Direct tel: 01932 584795
Direct fax: 01932 864633
Direct e-mail: nicolaschisholm@yehudimenuhinschool.co.uk
Other contacts: Friends Secretary

Founded: 1963

Organisation type and purpose: Registered charity. Has special status as a Centre of Excellence for the Performing Arts.
Aims to develop the musical potential of gifted young people regardless of race, creed or financial background, both for their own fulfilment and for the benefit and enrichment of others, within an academic environment that supports and develops their social, emotional, aesthetic and physical needs.

Subject coverage: Educates more than 60 talented boys and girls between the ages of 8 and 18. The range of instruments is limited to violin, viola, cello, double bass, guitar and piano. All pupils sing in one of two choirs and all string players also play the piano.

Education services: Partnerships with Surrey County Arts and local maintained schools; works with many Surrey primary and secondary schools to share resources and expertise, supplementing existing music education provision.

Publications: Electronic and video
Order electronic and video publications from: Download from website

Access to staff: Contact by letter, by telephone, by fax and by e-mail

YEMEN EMBASSY

57 Cromwell Road, London, SW7 2ED

Tel: 020 7584 6607
Fax: 020 7584 3759

Enquiries to: Information Officer

Organisation type and purpose: National government body.

Subject coverage: Yemen.

Access to staff: Contact by letter, by telephone and by fax
Hours: Mon to Fri, 0900 to 1700

YEOVIL NIGHT SHELTER PROJECT

13 Wyndham Street, Yeovil, Somerset, BA20 1JH

Tel: 01935 412052
E-mail: support@yeovilnightshelter.com
Website: www.yeovilnightshelter.com

Enquiries to: Manager
Direct tel: 07814 235855
Direct e-mail: chris@yeovilnightshelter.com

Organisation type and purpose: Operation of a night shelter for about 12, where all are welcome, no-one is refused and everyone is fed.

Subject coverage: Clients pay 50p a night to contribute towards a hot nutritious meal, a bed for the night and toast in the morning. Clients while at the shelter have access to shower and laundry facilities. There is a store of clothing for those in need of renewing clothes, and also items in store for those living on the street so that when clients get settled with accommodation they have belongings to take with them. The shelter offers advice on addiction, puts people in touch with services (hospital, doctors, dentists, etc.) and provides support with everyday issues on housing and work information.

Education services: In-house training for volunteers; plans to welcome Year 1 social work students to the project as a first placement and to invite police trainees from Portishead training facility, so that new police can have a better understanding of homeless issues.

Access to staff: Contact by letter, by telephone, by e-mail and via website

Access to building: Shelter open: Sun/Mon night to Thu/Fri night, 2030 to 0830

YHA (ENGLAND AND WALES) (YHA)

Formal name: YHA (England and Wales) Ltd

Trevelyan House, Dimple Road, Matlock, Derbyshire, DE4 3YH

Tel: 01629 592600
Fax: 01629 592702
Website: www.yha.org.uk

Enquiries to: PR assistant
Direct tel: 01629 592779
Direct e-mail: hannahcurzon@yha.org.uk

Founded: 1930; formerly called Youth Hostels Association (England and Wales)

Organisation type and purpose: Registered charity (charity number 301657). To help all, especially young people of limited means, to a greater knowledge, love and care of the countryside, and appreciation of the cultural values of towns and cities, particularly by providing Youth Hostels or other accommodation for them in their travels, and thus to promote their health, recreation and education.

Subject coverage: Young people, education, travel.

Publications: Printed

Access to staff: Contact by telephone and by e-mail
Hours: Mon to Fri, 0900 to 1700

Access for disabled people: Parking provided, ramped entry, toilet facilities at National Office

YMCA ENGLAND (YMCA)

Formal name: Young Men's Christian Associations of England

National Council of YMCAs, 640 Forest Road, London, E17 3DZ

Tel: 020 8520 5599
Fax: 020 8509 3190
E-mail: info@england.ymca.org.uk
Website: www.ymca.org.uk

Enquiries to: Senior Media Officer
Direct tel: 020 7061 3324
Direct fax: 0845 873 6644
Direct e-mail: press@england.ymca.org.uk

Founded: 1844

Organisation type and purpose: International organisation, membership association, voluntary organisation, registered charity (charity number 212810), training organisation.

Subject coverage: Youth and community work; mentoring for young people; rehabilitation of young offenders; sport, health, exercise and fitness; education and training for young people; youth homelessness; residential facilities for young people; adult education; outdoor education; drugs education; extended schools.

Collection: Archive material, photographs and memorabilia relating to the history of the YMCA

Publications: Printed, and electronic and video

Publications list: Available in print

Access to staff: Contact by letter, by telephone, by fax and by e-mail. Appointment necessary.
Hours: Mon to Fri, 0900 to 1730

Access to building: *Hours:* Mon to Fri, 0900 to 1700

Branch office: YMCA Metropolitan Region; 53 Parker Street, London, WC2B 5PT

Has: 160 local YMCA Associations

Member of: National Council for Voluntary Youth Services

YORK ARCHAEOLOGICAL TRUST (YAT)

Formal name: York Archaeological Trust for Excavation and Research Limited

Cromwell House, 13 Ogleforth, York, YO1 7FG

Tel: 01904 663000
Fax: 01904 640024
E-mail: postmaster@yorkarchaeology.co.uk
Website: www.yorkarchaeology.co.uk
Website: www.vikingjorvik.com

Enquiries to: Director
Direct tel: 01904 663001
Direct fax: 01904 663024
Direct e-mail: pvaddyman@yorkarchaeology.co.uk
Other contacts: Head of Finance and Administration for administrative matters.

continued overleaf

Founded: 1972

Organisation type and purpose:
Membership association (membership is by election or invitation), present number of members: c. 100, registered charity (charity number 509060), museum, suitable for ages: all, research organisation, publishing house.

Subject coverage: Archaeology of York and its region; Roman, Anglo Saxon, Viking and medieval archaeology, Jorvik Viking Centre, Archaeological Resource Centre, Barley Hall Medieval Centre, archaeological techniques, visitors' centre and attraction development and management; collections management, maintenance and archaeological artefact conservation, waterlogged archaeological materials.

Collection: Air photographic collections for Yorkshire
Archaeological picture library, with worldwide coverage but specialisation in York, Britain and Viking topics
Artefacts and excavation records relating to the archaeology of York 1972 onwards
CD-ROM on Viking and other subjects
Exhibited collections in Jorvik Viking Centre (Viking age) and of replicas in Barley Hall (medieval)

Publications: Printed, and electronic and video, and microform publications

Publications list: Available online and in print

Access to staff: Contact by letter, by telephone, by fax, by e-mail, in person and via website. Appointment necessary.
Hours: Mon to Fri, 0900 to 1700

Access for disabled people: Level entry, access to all public areas, toilet facilities
Special comments: Visitor Centres: Disabled access available to most areas.
Other Offices: Conditions vary.

Connections with: Archaeological Resource Centre (ARC); St Saviour's Church, St Saviour Gate, York, YO1 8NN; tel: 01904 643211; JORVIK; Coppergate, York, YO1 9WT; tel: 01904 543400; fax: 01904 627097; e-mail: enquiries@vikingjorvik.com

YORK COLLEGE (YC)

Tadcaster Road, Dringhouses, York, YO24 1UA

Tel: 01904 770400
Fax: 01904 770499
Website: www.yorkcollege.ac.uk

Enquiries to: Customer Services
Direct e-mail: customer-services@yorkcollege.ac.uk
Other contacts: Marketing Manager, 01904 770543

Founded: 1827; formed by the merger of York College of Further and Higher Education (YCFHE), York Sixth Form College (YSFC) (year of change 1999)

Organisation type and purpose: Suitable for ages: 16+, training organisation, consultancy.

Subject coverage: Art and design, business, catering, computing, construction, engineering, hair and beauty, health and social care, sport and leisure, fashion, performing arts and A-Levels, etc.

Non-library collection catalogue: All or part available in-house

Library catalogue: All or part available in-house

Publications: Printed

Access to staff: Contact by letter, by telephone, by fax, by e-mail and via website. Appointment necessary.
Hours: Mon to Thu, 0830 to 1930; Fri, 0830 to 1800

Access for disabled people: Parking provided, ramped entry, level entry, toilet facilities

Sixth Form Site: York College; Sim Balk Lane, York; tel: 01904 704141

YORK COUNCIL FOR VOLUNTARY SERVICE (York CVS)

Priory Street Centre, 15 Priory Street, York, YO1 6ET

Tel: 01904 621133
Fax: 01904 630361
E-mail: yorkcvs@yorkcvs.org.uk
Website: www.yorkcvs.org.uk

Enquiries to: Information & Development Manager

Founded: 1939

Organisation type and purpose: Registered charity (charity number 225087).
York CVS provides information and advice on issues which are common to all charities and voluntary groups – fundraising, legal constitutions, volunteering, accounts, etc.

Subject coverage: How to set up and run a voluntary group or charity.

Collection: Books and pamphlets relating to issues concerning the voluntary sector

Publications: Printed

Access to staff: Contact by letter, by telephone, by fax, by e-mail and in person. Appointment necessary.
Hours: Mon to Fri, 0900 to 1630

Access for disabled people: Parking provided, ramped entry, level entry, access to all public areas, toilet facilities
Special comments: Hearing loops in meeting rooms

YORK MINSTER LIBRARY AND ARCHIVES

Dean's Park, York, YO1 7JQ

Tel: 01904 625308 (library); 01904 611118 (archives)
Fax: 01904 611119
E-mail: info@yorkminster.org
Website: www.yorkminster.org/learning/library-archives-conservation

Enquiries to: Librarian
Direct e-mail: archivist@yorkminsterlibrary.org.uk
Other contacts: Archivist

Founded: 627; formerly called York Minster Library

Organisation type and purpose: Registered charity.
Cathedral library and archives.

Subject coverage: Church history, history of York Minster and its attendant bodies (but not the archdiocese), medieval manuscripts, illuminated manuscripts, literature, theology, religious art and architecture, religious literature (poetry, drama), York and Yorkshire local history, historical bibliography, music (religious and secular).

Collection: Library: General Collection; Old Library collections, including items from the collections of Revd Dr Marmaduke Fothergill (d. 1731) and Canon T. F. Simmons (d. 1884); Yorkshire collections, including the Hailstone Collection (printed matter; Edward Hailstone (d. 1890)) and the Foot-Walker Collection; and Yorkshire Parish Library collections.
Archives: Minster archives, from c.1148, including the archives of the Vicars Choral (1252–1936) and the Minster School; small archives of other organisations; personal papers; manuscript collections (MSS XVI and MSS Add.), from late-10th century; music manuscripts, 16th–20th centuries; Hailstone Collection (chiefly documents and manuscript material, 12th–19th centuries); modern media, including photographs, and video and sound recordings.

Non-library collection catalogue: All or part available in-house

Library catalogue: All or part available online

Publications: Printed

Access to staff: Contact by letter, by telephone, by fax, by e-mail and via website. Appointment necessary. Letter of introduction required.
Hours: Mon to Fri, 0900 to 1700

Access for disabled people: One parking space, by appointment; lift to first floor reading room; ground floor toilet facilities

Administered by: Dean and Chapter of York; tel: 01904 557200; website: http://yorkminster.org

Links with: University of York

YORK ST JOHN UNIVERSITY (YSJ)

Lord Mayors' Walk, York, YO31 7EX

Tel: 01904 876700
Fax: 01904 876342
E-mail: library@yorksj.ac.uk
Website: library.yorksj.ac.uk/

Enquiries to: Librarian

Founded: 1841; created by the merger of Ripon College and St John's College, York (year of change 1975); formerly called College of Ripon and York St John; York St John College (year of change 2008)

Organisation type and purpose: University department or institute, suitable for ages: 18+.

Subject coverage: Art, design and technology, English literature, history, business studies, linguistics, psychology, theology and religious studies, counselling, film, TV, performance studies, occupational therapy, physiotherapy, sports and exercise science, teaching studies.

Postgraduate courses in humanities, teaching studies, professional and management studies, health and life sciences, international education.

Collection: University Archive
Language Resources Centre (language teaching materials)
Rees-Williams Collection of 19th-century Children's Literature
York Theatre Royal Contemporary Archive
Religious Education Centre
School library resource collections
Yorkshire Film Archive

Non-library collection catalogue: All or part available online

Library catalogue: All or part available online

Publications: Printed

Publications list: Available online

Access to staff: Contact by letter, by telephone, by fax, by e-mail, in person and via website. Non-members charged.
Hours: Term time: Mon to Thu, 0800 to 2130; Fri, 0800 to 1900; Sat, 0930 to 1700; Sun, 1400 to 1900
Vacations: Mon to Fri, 0900 to 1700

Access for disabled people: Level entry

Constituent bodies: David Hope Religious Education Centre

Links with: Yorkshire Film Archive

YORK TEACHING HOSPITAL NHS FOUNDATION TRUST

York Teaching Hospital Library, 1st Floor, Fountains Learning Centre, York St John University, Lord Mayors Walk, York, YO31 7EX

Tel: 01904 726712
E-mail: library@york.nhs.uk
Website: www.york.nhs.uk

Enquiries to: Senior Librarian

Founded: 1971

Organisation type and purpose: Health library.

Subject coverage: Medicine, nursing, management and all health-related subjects.

Library catalogue: All or part available online

Publications list: Available online

Access to staff: Contact by letter, by telephone, by e-mail and in person. Non-members charged.
Hours: Mon to Fri, 0900 to 1700

Access to building: *Hours:* Users may be able to access the Library outside these hours when the York St John University Library is open

Branch libraries: Scarborough Hospital Library, Woodlands Drive, Scarborough, YO12 6QL; tel: 01723 342184; e-mail: library@acute.sney.nhs.uk

Parent bodies: York Teaching Hospitals NHS FoundationTrust

YORKSHIRE ARCHAEOLOGICAL SOCIETY (YAS)

Claremont, 23 Clarendon Road, Leeds, West Yorkshire, LS2 9NZ

Tel: 0113 245 7910
Fax: 0113 245 7992
E-mail: yas.library@gmail.com
Website: www.users.globalnet.co.uk/~gdl/yasfhs.htm
Website: www.yas.org.uk

Enquiries to: Librarian
Other contacts: Assistant Librarian

Founded: 1863

Organisation type and purpose: Learned society (membership is by subscription), registered charity (charity number 224083).

Subject coverage: Historical sciences, including archaeology, local history, genealogy, with particular emphasis on Yorkshire, but some material on the North of England and England in general.

Collection: Archival material on Yorkshire, 12th to 20th century, including the Wakefield Court Rolls and parish register transcripts
Large collection of national and international journals
Extensive collection of books, maps, photographs, etc. on Yorkshire

Non-library collection catalogue: All or part available online and in-house

Library catalogue: All or part available in-house

Publications: Printed, and microform publications

Publications list: Available online

Access to staff: Contact by letter, by telephone, by fax, by e-mail, in person and via website
Hours: Tue, Wed, Thu, 1000 to 1730; Fri, 1000 to 1300; Sat, 0930 to 1700
Special comments: Appointment necessary for visit to archives.

Access for disabled people: Parking provided
Special comments: Limited access for disabled.

Separate subscription sections at the same address: Family History and Population Studies Section; Industrial History Section; Medieval Section; Parish Register Section; Prehistory Research Section; Roman Antiquities Section

YORKSHIRE DIALECT SOCIETY (YDS)

19 Prospect Close, Swinefleet, East Yorkshire, DN14 8FB

Website: www.yorkshiredialectsociety.org.uk

Enquiries to: Hon Publicity & Information Officer

Founded: 1897

Organisation type and purpose: International organisation, membership association (membership is by subscription), present number of members: 500.
The study, publication, recording and research of dialects, mainly Yorkshire.

Subject coverage: Yorkshire dialects.

Publications: Printed, and electronic and video

Publications list: Available in print

Access to staff: Contact by letter
Hours: Mon to Fri, 0900 to 1700

YORKSHIRE GEOLOGICAL SOCIETY (YGS)

19 Thorngate, Barnard Castle, Co Durham, DL12 8QB

Tel: 01833 638893
E-mail: tjm4@tutor.open.ac.uk
Website: www.yorkgeolsoc.org.uk

Enquiries to: General Secretary

Founded: 1837

Organisation type and purpose: Learned society (membership is by subscription), present number of members: 794 all sections, voluntary organisation, registered charity.

Subject coverage: Geology.

Publications: Printed

Access to staff: Contact by letter, by telephone, by e-mail and via website
Hours: Mon to Fri, 0900 to 1800

Affiliated to: Geologists' Association

YORKSHIRE PHILOSOPHICAL SOCIETY (YPS)

The Lodge, Museum Gardens, York, YO1 7DR

Tel: 01904 656713
Fax: 01904 656713
E-mail: info@yorksphilsoc.org.uk
Website: www.yorksphilsoc.org.uk

Enquiries to: Honorary Archivist
Other contacts: Clerk to the Society (for general information and membership)

Founded: 1822

Organisation type and purpose: Learned society (membership is by subscription, election or invitation), present number of members: 500, registered charity (charity number 529709).

Subject coverage: Natural history, science, archaeology and history of York, Yorkshire and elsewhere.

Collection: Records and publications of the Society from 1822

Publications: Printed

Publications list: Available in print

Access to staff: Contact by letter, by telephone, by fax, by e-mail, in person and via website
Hours: Mon and Wed, 1000 to 1600; Fri, 1000 to 1200

YORKSHIRE TOURIST BOARD (YTB)

312 Tadcaster Road, York, YO24 1GS

Tel: 01904 707961
Fax: 01904 701414
E-mail: info@ytb.org.uk
Website: www.yorkshirevisitor.com
Website: www.yorkshiretouristboard.net
Website: www.venueyorkshire.com

continued overleaf

Website: www.grouptravelyorkshire.com

Enquiries to: Marketing Assistant

History of institution: formerly called Yorkshire and Humberside Tourist Board

Organisation type and purpose: Regional tourist board.

Subject coverage: General tourist information for Yorkshire.

Publications: Printed

Publications list: Available online

Access to staff: Contact by letter, by telephone, by fax and by e-mail
Hours: Mon to Fri, 0900 to 1730

Access for disabled people: Parking provided, ramped entry, level entry, access to all public areas, toilet facilities

YOUNG CLASSICAL ARTISTS TRUST (YCAT)

23 Garrick Street, London, WC2E 9BN

Tel: 020 7379 8477
Fax: 020 7379 8467
E-mail: info@ycat.co.uk
Website: www.ycat.co.uk

Founded: 1984

Organisation type and purpose: Registered charity (number 326490).
Identifying, nurturing, promoting and supporting exceptional UK-based classical artists and ensembles.

Subject coverage: As a classical musicians agency, YCAT liaises with event promoters in the UK and abroad providing performance opportunities and engagements for its artists. As a classical event promoter, it presents concerts to showcase its artists, including concerts in London as part of the YCAT Wigmore Lunchtime Series, Southbank Purcell Room Presentation Concerts and performances in Manchester at the Bridgewater Hall.

Special visitor services: Annual auditions to identify exciting new talent who could benefit from the charity's work, culminating in a public final at Wigmore Hall.

Publications: Electronic and video
Order electronic and video publications from: The Trust, or online stores

Access to staff: Contact by letter, by telephone, by fax and by e-mail
Hours: Mon to Fri, 1000 to 1800

YOUNG LANCASHIRE

10 Fishergate Hill, Preston, Lancashire, PR1 8JB

Tel: 01772 556127
Fax: 01772 251334
E-mail: mail@younglancashire.org.uk
Website: www.younglancashire.org.uk

Enquiries to: Director

Founded: 1923; formerly called Lancashire Youth Clubs Association (year of change 2000); formerly called Lancashire Youth Association (year of change 2009)

Organisation type and purpose: Membership association, present number of members: 107 youth groups and clubs, voluntary organisation, registered charity (charity number 518147), suitable for ages: year 12 students, training organisation. Youth service.

Subject coverage: Personal and social development of young people including those who have disabilities, support and advice to youth groups/clubs, links with other voluntary youth organisations, links with local government youth and community services.

Publications: Printed

Access to staff: Contact by letter, by telephone, by fax, by e-mail and via website. Appointment necessary.
Hours: Mon to Fri, 0930 to 1630

Affiliated to: British Confederation of Youth Clubs; European Federation of Youth Clubs; Irish Confederation of Youth Clubs; UK Youth; 11 Bride Street, London, EC4A 4AS

YOUNG WRITER CHARITABLE TRUST

Secretary, The Glebe House, Church Road, Weobley, Herefordshire, HR4 8SD

Tel: 01544 318901
Fax: 01544 318901
E-mail: info@youngwritertrust.org
Website: www.youngwritertrust.org

Organisation type and purpose: Registered charity (number 1095083).
To support young people through their writing.

Education services: Online games for young writers.

Access to staff: Contact by letter, by telephone, by fax and by e-mail

YOUNGMINDS

48–50 St John Street, London, EC1M 4DG

Tel: 020 7336 8445
Fax: 020 7336 8446
E-mail: enquiries@youngminds.org.uk
Website: www.youngminds.org.uk

Founded: 1992

Organisation type and purpose: Voluntary organisation, registered charity (charity number 1016968).
A voice for young people's mental health and well-being.

Subject coverage: UK charity committed to improving the emotional well-being and mental health of children and young people and empowering their parents or carers.

Trade and statistical information: See website: http://www.youngminds.org.uk/ym-newsroom

Publications: Printed
Order printed publications from: website: http://www.youngminds.org.uk

Publications list: Available online and in print

Access to staff: Contact by letter, by telephone, by fax, by e-mail and via website
Hours: Mon to Fri, 0930 to 1730

Access to building: Prior appointment required

YOUTH CYMRU

Unit D, Upper Boat Business Centre, Pontypridd, Rhondda Cynon Taff, CF37 5BP

Tel: 01443827840
E-mail: mailbox@youthcymru.org.uk
Website: www.youthcymru.org.uk

Enquiries to: Chief Executive

Founded: 1934; formerly called Welsh Association of Youth Clubs (WAYC) (year of change 2003)

Organisation type and purpose: National organisation, membership association (membership is by subscription, qualification), present number of members: 200+ youth groups, voluntary organisation, registered charity (charity number 524480).

Subject coverage: All aspects of youth and community work.

Publications: Printed

Access to staff: Contact by letter, by telephone, by fax and by e-mail. Appointment necessary.
Hours: Mon to Fri, 0845 to 1615

Access to building: Prior appointment required

Access for disabled people: Parking provided, level entry, access to ground floor only, toilet facilities

YOUTH LINK SCOTLAND

Central Hall, West Tollcross, Edinburgh, EH3 9BP

Tel: 0131 229 0339
Fax: 0131 229 0339
E-mail: info@youthlink.co.uk
Website: www.youthlink.co.uk

Enquiries to: Administrator
Direct e-mail: rdambrosio@youthlink.co.uk

Founded: 1942; formerly called Scottish Standing Conference of Voluntary Youth Organisations (SSCVYO) (year of change 1996)

Organisation type and purpose: Voluntary organisation.
Umbrella/intermediary organisation supporting voluntary youth organisations.

Subject coverage: Range of youth issues and related topics such as funding, charity law, peer education, youth work and sustainable development, sport and the arts.

Collection: Catalogue currently being developed

Publications: Printed

Publications list: Available in print

Access to staff: Contact by letter, by telephone, by fax, by e-mail and via website. Appointment necessary. Non-members charged.
Hours: Mon to Fri, 0900 to 1700

Members include: 51 youth organisations

ZEPHYR & ZODIAC MKIV OWNERS CLUB

94 Claremont Road, Rugby, Warwickshire, CV21 3LU

Tel: 01788 574884

Enquiries to: Treasurer

Founded: 1983

Organisation type and purpose: Membership association (membership is by subscription), present number of members: 110, voluntary organisation.

Subject coverage: All aspects of Zephyr and Zodiac MkIV cars.

Publications: Printed

Publications list: Available in print

Access to staff: Contact by letter and by telephone
Hours: Evenings and weekends
Special comments: Not after 2100.

ZINC INFORMATION CENTRE (ZINC)

Wrens Court, 56 Victoria Road, Sutton Coldfield, West Midlands, B72 1SY

Tel: 0121 362 1201
Fax: 0121 355 8727
E-mail: zincinfocentre@hdg.org.uk

Enquiries to: Director

Founded: 2001; formerly called Zinc Development Association (ceased trading) (year of change 2000)

Organisation type and purpose: Trade association.

Subject coverage: A source of information on zinc and its uses.

Publications: Printed

Access to staff: Contact by letter, by telephone, by fax and by e-mail
Hours: Mon to Fri, 0900 to 1700

Operated in conjunction with the: Galvanizers Association

ZOOLOGICAL SOCIETY OF GLASGOW AND WEST OF SCOTLAND

Secretary: George W.H. Thomson, Morrisbank, Bathgate, EH48 1JU

Tel: 0845 108 1426
Fax: 0845 108 1426
Website: www.glasgowzoopark.org.uk

Enquiries to: Secretary
Direct e-mail: registrar@rzss.org.uk

Founded: 1936

Organisation type and purpose: Membership association (membership is by election or invitation), present number of members: 200, registered charity (charity number SCO 02651).

Subject coverage: Zoo biology, biodiversity, environment.

Collection: Books and photographs

Publications: Printed

Access to staff: *Special comments:* Volunteer staff only

Access to building: Prior appointment required

ZOOLOGICAL SOCIETY OF LONDON (ZSL)

Library, Regent's Park, London, NW1 4RY

Tel: 020 7449 6293
Fax: 020 7586 5743
E-mail: library@zsl.org
Website: www.zsl.org

Enquiries to: Librarian

Founded: 1826

Organisation type and purpose: Learned society (membership is by subscription), present number of members: 25,000, registered charity (charity number 208728), research organisation.
ZSL aims to achieve and promote the worldwide conservation of animals and their habitats.

Subject coverage: Zoology, animal conservation, zoo management.

Collection: Archives of ZSL
Current journals on all aspects of zoology, animal conservation and zoos
An extensive photographic collection covering the diversity of nature with special emphasis on endangered and extinct animals
Library specialising in historical taxonomy (200,000 vols)
Collection of works of Gould, Wolf, Tickell, Reeves, Lear and Elliott

Non-library collection catalogue: All or part available online and in-house

Library catalogue: All or part available online and in-house

Publications: Printed

Access to staff: Appointment necessary.
Hours: Mon to Fri, 0930 to 1730

Access to building: Photographic ID and proof of address required

Access for disabled people: *Special comments:* Reading Room accessed via steps or small lift. Facilities are available to use the online catalogue and consult material elsewhere if the Reading Room cannot be accessed.

Parent body: Institute of Zoology; ZSL London Zoo; ZSL Whipsnade Wild Animal Park

ZURICH RISK ENGINEERING UK

Zurich Risk Engineering UK, Park House, Bristol Road South, Rubery, Birmingham, B45 9AH

Tel: 0121 698 5810
E-mail: riskengineering@zurich.co.uk

Enquiries to: Librarian

History of institution: formerly called Zurich Risk Services; formerly called Eagle Star Insurance Company

Organisation type and purpose: Service industry.

Access to staff: Contact by letter
Hours: Mon to Fri, 0900 to 1700

Access to building: No access other than to staff

Index of Abbreviations and Acronyms

The abbreviations and acronyms listed here are cross-referenced by page number to their respective organisations in the Main Directory.

Subject Index

Entries in the Subject Index refer the reader to the page numbers of full entries in the Main Directory.